Ranking the Rock Writers

Rev 6/18/2018

Ranking the Rock Writers

A complete catalog of all the writers appearing on the major pop singles charts, 1955-1991

From "Rock Around The Clock" to "Smells Like Teen Spirit"

Bill Carroll

Cover Art by Lighthouse 24

Ranking the Rock Writers

Published by Carroll Applied Science, LLC
Dallas, TX

Please visit the website at **http://ranking.rocks** for more information or to contact the author.

Ranking the Rock Writers
Bill Carroll

1. Title 2. Author 3. Popular Music/History

Library of Congress Control Number: 2018944237

ISBN-10: 0-692-12217-6

ISBN-13: 978-0-692-12217-4

Praise for **Ranking the Rock Writers:**

"Before there is a record....there is a song. The writers finally have their day in the sun, thanks to Bill Carroll. His love for music is matched only by his tenacity and we get to reap the benefit of that union. This book is a most unique compendium and Bill is the only guy on Earth who would undertake such a project. This one is a keeper on my bookshelf."

Lou Simon
SiriusXM Radio

"A must-have for music lovers, proving what I've always said: The pen is mightier than the chord!"

Rich Appel
Host/Producer/Writer of radio's *that thing with Rich Appel*

"Pop songsters, step out of your cubicles and into the spotlight! *Ranking the Rock Writers* is a remarkable achievement given the size of the task and the tangle of information."

Dann Isbell
Author of *Ranking the '60s* and *Ranking the '70s*

"Here at last is the go-to book for anyone wondering just who it was who wrote the words and music of their favorite hits: the unforgettable songs which speak to and for their heart."

Gary Theroux
Producer/Writer/Host of *The History of Rock 'n' Roll*

To Dann Isbell and Lou Simon
Mentors, friends and fellow chart-hounds.

"And I wrote some rock and roll so you can move..."
--Bruce Johnston
"I Write The Songs"

CONTENTS

FOREWORD

Sometimes Song Lyrics Write Themselves

Michael Sigman

My father, songwriter Carl Sigman (1909-2000), viewed lyric writing as a craft. But once in a while -- as with his best songs, "It's All In The Game" and "Ebb Tide," and a lesser-known gem, "Buona Sera" -- he'd observe that a lyric "wrote itself."

"Buona Sera" would never have come into being had Carl not been stranded in Sicily during World War II. After enlisting in the 82nd Airborne Division, he wrote that outfit's theme song ("All American Soldier" remains the theme to this day) and received a $25 bond from General Matthew Ridgway. Then he went off to Africa to fly gliders. Somehow, a mishap left him in Sicily, alone and away from his unit, for several weeks. During that time, he fell in love with the Italian language and stored away phrases like "Arrivederci, Roma" and "Buona Sera, Signorina" for future use.

After the war, Carl resumed his songwriting career in earnest, haunting the iconic Brill Building to hustle music publishers and singers to record his material. In 1950, Carl's good friend and collaborator Peter DeRose -- they'd co-written the novelty hit "Hop Scotch Polka" and the holiday favorite, "It's A Marshmallow World" -- presented Carl with a melody whose opening notes formed what he called a perfect wedding with the words, "Buona Sera, Signorina." The rest of the lyric, yes, pretty much wrote itself.

On the fifth floor of the Brill, the inimitable Louis Prima -- who happened to be of Sicilian descent – maintained a suite of offices. (Louis' "Gal Friday," Terry Berkowitz, would soon become Carl's wife and my mom!) Carl auditioned the song for Louis, and he recorded it, as did Dean Martin and a bunch of other crooners. "Buona Sera" probably would have gone through life as a sweet love song had Louis not rerecorded it eight years later in a tour de force performance that featured dramatic tempo shifts, scat singing and a swingin' sax break. The record was a hit in the U.S. and Europe and inspired countless rock 'n' rollers -- including Van Morrison, Dick Brave and the Backbeats, and a slew of Eastern European outfits -- to record covers, many of them note-for-note recapitulations of Louis' rockin' interpretation.

(continued)

Carl could hardly believe that his and DeRose's ballad could be so dramatically transformed. But perhaps he shouldn't have been surprised, as this was just another example of the power and versatility of a standard. Carl's own catalogue has featured, among many genre-jumping recordings, Sonny & Cher's jangly folk-rock rendition of "What Now, My Love," Phil Spector's wall-of-sound production of "Ebb Tide" by the Righteous Brothers, and Merle Haggard's No. 1 country recording of "It's All In The Game."

"Buona Sera" became a staple in movie soundtracks like *Big Night* and *Middle Men*. But by far the best usage of the song was in David Simon's brilliant HBO series *Treme*, which paid homage to New Orleans and its rich musical tradition by opening its first episode with a hip DJ playing Louis' swingin' version to a montage of moments from the series that captured the spirit of the city. That Louis, who came of age in New Orleans, had Sicilian heritage -- and that the lyric was written by a Jew from Brooklyn and conceived in Sicily -- was icing on the multi-cultural songwriting cake.

Michael Sigman is a writer/editor, media consultant and the president of Major Songs, a music publishing company. Sigman was the president and publisher of *LA Weekly,* and served as a reporter, then managing editor, then editor-in-chief of *Record World.*

How To Use This Book/FAQs

There are four main reference sections in this book: Writers in alphabetical order (and in rank order to 1000); Songs in alphabetical order; Top 2000 writer teams in rank order (with alphabetical index of writers) and Top 750 acts in rank order (with alphabetical index of acts). These four sections comprise all the individual writers, all the songs and about half the cuts for both writer teams and acts. Decisions on truncating the last two indices were dictated by space considerations.

The song index contains the most complete information. Other indexes have limited information due to space constraints. Using these four indices can answer almost any question asked; some require a little more effort. Here are some sample questions and ways to get at the answers. *You can also go to* ***http://ranking.rocks*** *where there are electronic resources to look up the acts below 750, the writer teams below 2000 and the numerical ranking of writers below 1000.*

Q. How many charted songs did Sting write, and what were they?
A. Start with the writer index for "Sting." Incidentally, if you started with Gordon Sumner and didn't find him, a look to the Alias index would show his name of record. He wrote 23 charted songs.

Q. Who wrote "Young Girl" by The Union Gap Featuring Gary Puckett? Did it chart more than once?
A. Go to the song index, which is in alphabetical order. You will find "Young Girl" was written by Jerry Fuller; it's not in italics, so it only charted once, but it appeared in all three magazines, entering in March 1968, and it peaked at #1.

Q. Did The Mamas and The Papas ever chart a Cynthia Weil song?
A. Go to the Act alphabetical index. The Mamas and The Papas are #114. In the Act numerical index you see that Cynthia Weil is not a supporting writer. They did not.

Q. What about Mama Cass?
A. From the Act alphabetical index you see that Mama Cass is not listed, meaning she was below Act #750. This is a little harder. The best bet is to go to Cynthia Weil's listing in the writer index to scan for songs recorded by Mama Cass. The answer is two: "It's Getting Better" and "Make Your Own Kind Of Music" both in 1969. A list of the acts from 751 to 6057 can be found at the website.

Q. How many songs written by the team of Carole King, Gerry Goffin and Phil Spector charted?
A. Looking in the alphabetical index for writers in the Writer Teams, we see that Carole King had six collaborations in the top 2000, Gerry Goffin had 7 and Phil Spector had 5. The rank they had in common is 1948. Finding that in the numerical order of Writer Teams, the answer is three: "Just Once In My Life" and "Hung On You" by The Righteous Brothers, and "Is This What I Get For Loving You?" by The Ronettes.

Q. What if I didn't find a number in common?
A. That either means they didn't collaborate or they were lower than #2000 as a team. Check the list and index of writer teams from 2001 to the end at the website.

Q. Who wrote "A Taste Of Honey?"
A. Did you mean the vocal or instrumental version? In the song index, we find that it charted five times: four as an instrumental. We see that words and music are credited separately in the copyright [IM]; all the instrumentals are credited to Bobby Scott. Tony Bennett has the sole vocal, credited to Ric Marlow and Bobby Scott.

Q. I know "Roses of Rio" started as a song in another language, but are the English lyrics a translation?
A. "Roses of Rio" is credited to Heino Gaze and Carl Sigman. It is noted [FDE] which means that new English lyrics were written to replace the originals, and are new lyrics, not a translation. The original lyricist is not credited.

Q. Who were the top five writer teams?
A. Easy to find in the numerical ranked Writer Team Index. Lennon-McCartney, Holland-Dozier-Holland, Bacharach-David, Jagger-Richards and Gibb-Gibb-Gibb. Also, check the "Top 30 Writer Teams in Words, Charts and Graphs" section for more analytics and stories.

Q. I don't really understand the scoring. Can you help me be more intuitive about it?
A. Sure. All the details are in the appendix, but it's basically this. Songs are scored by totaling their week-to-week performance, then comparing them to the performance of contemporaneous songs. The average score at any time is 1000; thus, a song that scores 7500 is 7.5 times as popular as the average, which is pretty good. Incidentally, that score puts it in the top 1% for the era 1955-1991.

Q. I found songs and writers with scores of 0.0. How could they have charted?
A. Three ways. Tagalongs (see appendix) with no independent chart life and lesser lifecycles than the master version were given 0 points, but their chart presence was noted. Also, for TSWs, when only one side had an independent chart life, all credit was awarded to that side, but their chart presence was noted. Finally, some songs from 1954 had no chart life in 1955 but were captured for the sake of completeness.

Q. Did B.B. King really write with a guy named Jules Taub?
A. B.B. says no.... The Alias index notes that Jules Taub was also known as Julius Bihari, and the writing credit in the song index has a double-dagger (‡) next to Taub's name. The Bihari brothers were record label executives. The double-dagger indicates that in the opinion of the researcher he was credited but probably not involved in the writing of the song.

Q. Bobby Whitlock is co-credited for writing "Bell Bottom Blues." I thought that was all Clapton.
A. Note that Whitlock's name has an asterisk (*). This means that the primary sources do not agree. In fact, BMI credits him, but the label and copyright do not. The methodology of this book is to be inclusive when there is a credible question, but to note the disagreement.

Q. I found some stuff that I think is wrong.
A. Possible. In a work this size, you can't rule out mistakes; however, in some cases, when you see all the information it changes your mind about what you think you know about a song. Checking the publicly-available resources—copyrights, labels and royalty rights—can sometimes shed new light on old information.

Q. What was the #1 song of the era?
A. With a little digging, you can figure that out from scores, but I have to save something for "Ranking The Rock Era" don't I?

The Writers

Index of all Writers
1955-1991

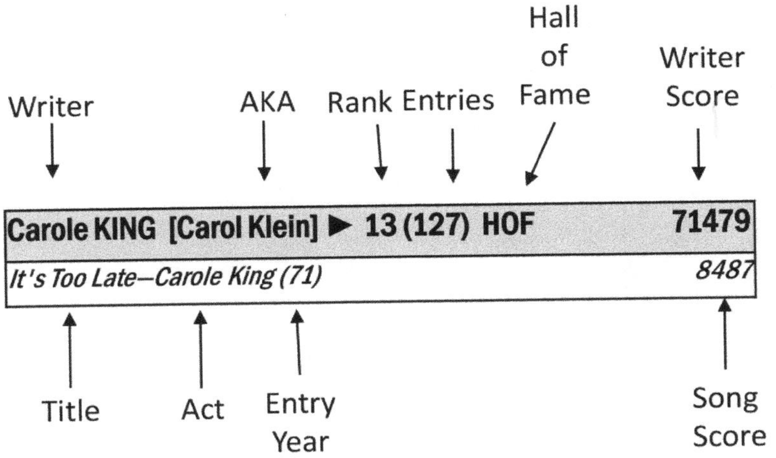

Italics: Multiple Recordings

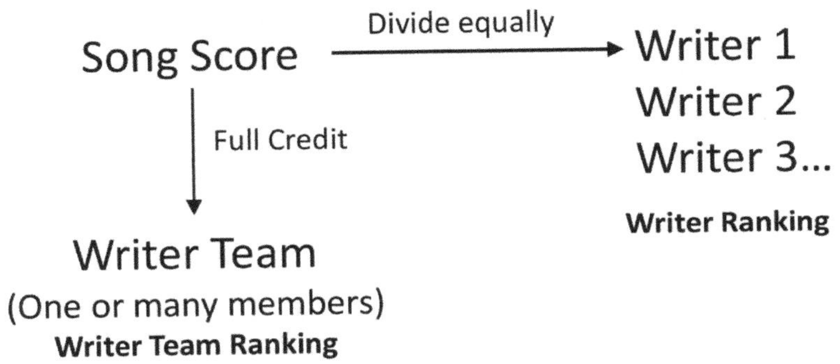

The goal of this database is to assign one name to each writer and one writer to each name in a process called disambiguation. Alternate names were found for about 20% of the 11,834 writers, and there may be more that were not found in this research.

The name chosen for a writer is not necessarily that writer's "real" name, which is sometimes difficult to determine. Alternate names are listed in brackets following the chosen writer name. Scores as shown are rounded to one decimal place below a total score of 10. Because of the calculation there are relatively few writer score ties, which are broken by number of entries then alphabetical order. A full explanation of the scoring methodology can be found in the appendix.

This section is dedicated to ranking individual writers. Writer credit for each song is that song score divided by the number of attributed writers, which can be found in the song index. Individual writer score and rank is based on the total of all such writer credits. Each writer's attributed songs are shown in order of chart strength, beginning with the strongest. Song scores themselves are the full song score; thus song scores are generally not additive to give writer scores.

HOF designates inductee of the Songwriters Hall Of Fame: https://www.songhall.org/.

A

Phil AABERG ▶ 9499 (1)	**23**
Struttin' My Stuff—Elvin Bishop (76)	45
Olivier ABBELOOS ▶ 9740 (1)	**18**
Crazy—Daisy Dee (91)	90
Gregory ABBOTT ▶ 934 (2)	**4752**
Shake You Down—Gregory Abbott (86)	4509
I Got The Feelin' (It's Over)—Gregory Abbott (87)	243
—Lee Abbott see: Jack LEE	
Robert ABDINOOR ▶ 11078 (2)	**3.4**
Nite Rock (Lonely Train)—Nite Rockers (58)	4.3
Oh Baby—Nite Rockers (58)	1.9
Paula ABDUL ▶ 3433 (1)	**850**
The Promise Of A New Day—Paula Abdul (91)	3398
Sigidi ABDULLAH [Sigidi] ▶ 1938 (1)	**2083**
Take Your Time (Do It Right) (Part 1)—S.O.S. Band (80)	4167
Hakeem ABDULSAMAD ▶ 6555 (1)	**157**
Crazy—Boys (90)	472
Khiry ABDULSAMAD ▶ 6556 (1)	**157**
Crazy—Boys (90)	472
Tajh ABDULSAMAD ▶ 6557 (1)	**157**
Crazy—Boys (90)	472
—Joseph Abend see: Hank BEDUCCI	
Georges ABER ▶ 8655 (2)	**44**
Down By The Riverside—Les Compagnons De La Chanson (60)	*175*
Down By The Riverside (Qu'l Fait Bon Vivre)—Les Barclay (60)	*0.0*
Lee Roy ABERNATHY ▶ 2223 (1)	**1725**
Wonderful Time Up There—Pat Boone (58)	1725
Raul ABEYTA ▶ 8370 (1)	**53**
Coming On Too Strong—Wayne Newton (65)	106
Buford ABNER ▶ 3996 (2)	**628**
Daddy-O—Fontane Sisters with Billy Vaughn's Orchestra (55)	*1345*
Daddy-O—Bonnie Lou (55)	*539*
Ewart ABNER ▶ 2364 (8)	**1557**
At My Front Door (Crazy Little Mama)—Pat Boone (55)	*1950*
At My Front Door (Crazy Little Mama)—El Dorados And Magnificents (55)	*653*
At My Front Door—Dee Clark (60)	*260*
Honest I Do—Jimmy Reed (57)	207
The Sun Is Shining—Jimmy Reed (57)	45
Up On The Mountain—Magnificents (56)	11
Down In Virginia—Jimmy Reed (58)	4.6
(Crazy Little Mama Song) At My Front Door—Modernaires (55)	*0.0*
Ronald ABNER ▶ 11483 (1)	**1.5**
I'm A Practical Guy—Lee Rogers (66)	9.1
Maurice ABRAHAMS ▶ 5416 (2)	**291**
Ragtime Cowboy Joe—David Seville And The Chipmunks (59)	852
Take Everything But You—Kitty Kallen (54)	23
Al ABRAMS [Mikaljon] ▶ 4579 (1)	**462**
I Love The Way You Love—Marv Johnson (60)	1848
Bryan ABRAMS ▶ 1748 (3)	**2368**
All 4 Love—Color Me Badd (91)	5388
I Wanna Sex You Up—Color Me Badd (91)	4560
I Adore Mi Amor—Color Me Badd (91)	4094
Lester ABRAMS ▶ 4213 (1)	**562**
Minute By Minute—Doobie Brothers (79)	1123
Rita ABRAMS ▶ 9404 (1)	**24**
Mill Valley—Miss Abrams And The Strawberry Point School Third Grade Class (70)	24
Victor ABRAMS ▶ 8599 (5)	**45**
Tonight My Heart Will Be Crying—Eddie Fisher (57)	*105*
Johnny Be Smart—Sarah Vaughan (55)	19
Love Me My Love—Dean Martin (60)	7.7
Tonight My Heart She Is Crying—El Boy with The Ralph Sayho Calypso Singers (57)	*0.0*
Tonight My Heart She Is Crying—Shirley Bassey (57)	*0.0*
Herb ABRAMSON ▶ 10722 (1)	**5.9**
Long Tall Shorty—Tommy Tucker (64)	12
Jimmie ABSTON ▶ 11510 (1)	**1.4**
No Rebate On Love—Dramatics (75)	2.8
Jack ACKERMAN ▶ 6341 (2)	**181**
Lasting Love—Sal Mineo (57)	*362*
Lasting Love—Kitty Kallen (57)	*0.0*
Andy ACKERS [Andrew A. Acuarulo] ▶ 9787 (1)	**17**
Don't Let The Kiddy Geddin—Kitty Kallen (54)	51
Barbara ACKLIN ▶ 919 (11)	**4811**
Have You Seen Her—Chi-Lites (71)	*5172*
Have You Seen Her—M.C. Hammer (90)	*2337*
Whispers (Gettin' Louder)—Jackie Wilson (66)	1480
Two Little Kids—Peaches & Herb (67)	574
Stoned Out Of My Mind—Chi-Lites (73)	514
From The Teacher To The Preacher—Gene Chandler And Barbara Acklin (68)	379
I Love You—Otis Leavill (69)	154
There Will Never Be Any Peace (Until God Is Seated At The Conference Table)—Chi-Lites (74)	94
Toby—Chi-Lites (75)	48
Have You Seen Her—Band Of Gold (84)	*12*
Let Me Be The Man My Daddy Was—Chi-Lites (69)	7.6
Nick ACQUAVIVA ▶ 2186 (10)	**1766**
In The Middle Of An Island—Tony Bennett with Ray Ellis and His Orchestra (57)	*1952*
Ghost Town—Don Cherry (56)	585
Is This The End Of The Line—Joni James (55)	397
In The Middle Of An Island—"Tennessee" Ernie Ford (57)	*301*
When We Come Of Age—Joni James (54)	291
Never Leave Me—Gale Storm (56)	*1.9*
Never Leave Me—Bob Presto (56)	*1.9*
We Know—Joni James (60)	1.5
In The Middle Of An Island—Anita Kerr Quartet (57)	*0.0*
In The Middle Of An Island—Stan Wilson (57)	*0.0*
—Andrew A. Acuarulo see: Andy ACKERS	
—Frances Adair see: Frances JEFFORDS	
Thomas ADAIR ▶ 7152 (3) HOF	**113**
Julie—Doris Day (56)	172
How Will I Know My Love—Annette (58)	*82*
How Will I Know My Love?—Lennon Sisters (58)	*0.0*
A. Emmett ADAMS ▶ 9807 (3)	**17**
Bells Of St Mary's—Terry & The Mellos featuring Terry Corin (60)	*33*
The Bells Of St. Mary's—Lynn Taylor & The Peachettes (60)	*0.0*
The Bells Of St. Mary's—Baysiders (60)	*0.0*
Ace ADAMS ▶ 10693 (1)	**6.0**
Everybody's Somebody's Fool—Heartbeats (57)	18
Billy ADAMS [Vassilis Dertilis] ▶ 9957 (1)	**15**
Holding My Heart—Bang (2) (90)	44
—Billy Adams see: Kevin ADAMS	
Bobby ADAMS ▶ 4935 (3)	**378**
Shake! Shake! Shake!—Jackie Wilson (63)	477
Years From Now—Jackie Wilson (61)	299
There'll Be No Next Time—Jackie Wilson (62)	80
Bryan ADAMS ▶ 255 (26)	**13436**
(Everything I Do) I Do It For You—Bryan Adams (91)	6505
Heaven—Bryan Adams (85)	3748
Can't Stop This Thing We Started—Bryan Adams (91)	3455
Run To You—Bryan Adams (84)	2374
Summer Of '69—Bryan Adams (85)	1803
Heat Of The Night—Bryan Adams (87)	1717
Straight From The Heart—Bryan Adams (83)	1225
Somebody—Bryan Adams (85)	1191
When The Night Comes—Joe Cocker (89)	1185
It's Only Love—Bryan Adams/Tina Turner (85)	1006
One Night Love Affair—Bryan Adams (85)	925
There Will Never Be Another Tonight—Bryan Adams (91)	822
Cuts Like A Knife—Bryan Adams (83)	762
This Time—Bryan Adams (83)	569
Hearts On Fire—Bryan Adams (87)	514
Teacher, Teacher—38 Special (84)	493
Victim Of Love—Bryan Adams (87)	410
Back To Paradise—38 Special (87)	305
Don't Let Him Know—Prism (82)	259
Another Heartache—Rod Stewart (86)	259
Dangerous—Loverboy (85)	173
Edge Of A Dream—Joe Cocker (84)	113
Can't Wait All Night—Juice Newton (84)	92
Jump—Loverboy (82)	67
Lonely Nights—Bryan Adams (82)	24
Let Me Down Easy—Roger Daltrey (85)	17
Charles ADAMS ▶ 11752 (1)	**0.2**
One Wonderful Love—Ray Smith (60)	1.2
Cliff ADAMS ▶ 8768 (2)	**40**
Ten Lonely Guys—Pat Boone (62)	*317*
Ten Lonely Guys—Ten Broken Hearts (62)	*81*
Clifford ADAMS ▶ 3626 (5)	**761**
Joanna—Kool & The Gang (83)	3511
Tonight—Kool & The Gang (84)	1136
Emergency—Kool & The Gang (85)	915
Let's Go Dancin' (Ooh La, La, La)—Kool & The Gang (82)	654
Big Fun—Kool & The Gang (82)	532
Frank ADAMS ▶ 9156 (1)	**30**
I Wonder Who's Kissing Her Now—Bobby Darin (64)	90
George ADAMS ▶ 10559 (1)	**7.2**
I Wouldn't Lie—Yarbrough & Peoples (86)	29
J.T. ADAMS ▶ 8341 (1)	**54**
The Lost Penny—Brook Benton (62)	54
Kevin ADAMS [Billy Adams] ▶ 2207 (1)	**1742**
Come On Eileen—Dexys Midnight Runners (83)	5225
—Kurt Adams see: Jimmy VAN HEUSEN	
Lee ADAMS ▶ 3379 (8) HOF	**874**
I Want To Be With You—Dee Dee Warwick (66)	*479*
We Love You Beatles—Carefrees (64)	385
Those Were The Days—Carroll O'Connor And Jean Stapleton (As The Bunkers) (71)	313
One Boy—Joanie Sommers (60)	293
I Wanna Be With You—Nancy Wilson (64)	*248*
Superman—Dino, Desi & Billy (66)	15
Kids—Kirby Stone Four (60)	6.7
One Last Kiss—Bobby Vee (60)	6.5
Mark ADAMS ▶ 7227 (4)	**109**
Slide—Slave (77)	640
Watching You—Slave (80)	129
Snap Shot—Slave (81)	53
Just A Touch Of Love—Slave (80)	10
Michael ADAMS ▶ 8473 (1)	**49**
Got To Have Your Lovin'—King Floyd (71)	98
Patrick ADAMS ▶ 2837 (5)	**1162**
Touch Me (All Night Long)—Cathy Dennis (91)	2867
In The Bush—Musique (78)	318
Dance And Shake Your Tambourine—Universal Robot Band (77)	34
When You Wake Up Tomorrow—Candi Staton (79)	16
Love Bug—Bumblebee Unlimited (76)	9.4
Regina ADAMS ▶ 10694 (1)	**6.0**
Everybody's Somebody's Fool—Heartbeats (57)	18
Ritchie ADAMS [Rick Chambers, Richard Adam Ziegler] ▶ 560 (17)	**7717**
Tossin' And Turnin'—Bobby Lewis (61)	*12039*
After The Lovin'—Engelbert Humperdinck (76)	2368
Happy Summer Days—Ronnie Dove (66)	651
The Next Hundred Years—Al Martino (77)	283
Fly By Night—Andy Williams (61)	101
What A Walk—Bobby Lewis (61)	73
This Moment In Time—Engelbert Humperdinck (78)	59
It's Not The Same—Anthony And The Imperials (66)	36
Should Anybody Ask—Garry Bonner (74)	15
Don't Take It Out On Me—Bobbi Martin (66)	13
No One Knows—Every Mother's Son (68)	12
One Life To Live—Wayne Massey (80)	10
Goodbye My Friend—Engelbert Humperdinck (77)	3.4
Don't Tie Me Down—Anthony & The Imperials (67)	3.3
Kentucky Mornin'—Al Martino (77)	2.4
The Tra La La Song (One Banana, Two Banana)—Banana Splits (69)	2.2
Tossin' And Turnin'—Bunny Sigler (73)	*2.2*
—Skipper Adams see: David SEVILLE	
Stanley ADAMS ▶ 1600 (5)	**2644**
What A Diff'rence A Day Makes—Dinah Washington (59)	*4151*
What A Diff'rence A Day Makes—Esther Phillips (75)	*1007*
What A Diff'rence A Day Made—Jerry Martin (55)	*128*
There Are Such Things—Modernaires (57)	1.9
What A Diff'rence A Day Made—Vaughn Monroe & His Orchestra (55)	*0.0*
Terry ADAMS ▶ 7720 (1)	**79**
Get That Gasoline Blues—NRBQ (74)	158

Harold ADAMSON ► 2455 (27) HOF	**1468**
Where Are You—Dinah Washington (62)	*816*
An Affair To Remember (Our Love Affair)—Vic Damone (57)	*779*
Too Young To Go Steady—Nat "King" Cole (56)	*779*
Around The World—Bing Crosby (57)	*591*
Honestly—Kitty Kallen (55)	175
Too Young To Go Steady—Connie Stevens (60)	*53*
Around The World In Eighty Days—McGuire Sisters (57)	*45*
Too Young To Go Steady—Patti Page (56)	*41*
The Woodpecker Song—Bobby Rydell (63)	32
You're A Sweetheart—Little Willie John (58)	*24*
Louella—Pat Boone (57)	20
Separate Tables—Vic Damone (59)	*18*
An Affair To Remember (Our Love Affair)—Nat "King" Cole (57)	*15*
Around The World—Nat "King" Cole (57)	*15*
Where Are You—Duprees featuring Joey Vann (64)	*11*
Daybreak—Al Hibbler (55)	7.4
Everything I Have Is Yours—Dorothy Collins (59)	5.4
You're A Sweetheart—Dinah Washington (62)	*2.7*
Love Me As Though There Were No Tomorrow—Sonny Knight (65)	0.5
An Affair To Remember—Pete King & His Orchestra (57)	*0.0*
An Affair To Remember (Our Love Affair)—Carmen Cavallaro (57)	*0.0*
An Affair To Remember (Our Love Affair)—Angela Drake (57)	*0.0*
Around The World—Don Costa & His Orchestra (57)	*0.0*
Around The World—Jane Morgan (57)	*0.0*
Around The World—Eddie Fisher (57)	*0.0*
Separate Tables—Eydie Gorme (58)	*0.0*
An Affair To Remember—ViVienne (57)	*0.0*
William Stuart ADAMSON ► 5003 (4)	**360**
In A Big Country—Big Country (83)	1155
Fields Of Fire—Big Country (84)	159
Look Away—Big Country (86)	28
Wonderland—Big Country (84)	12
Marvin Lee ADAY [Michael Lee Aday, Meat Loaf] ► 8744 (1)	**41**
Magical—John Parr (85)	81
—Michael Lee Aday see: Marvin Lee ADAY	
Julian ADDERLEY ► 11734 (1)	**0.4**
Sermonette—Della Reese (59)	0.8
Nat ADDERLEY ► 2784 (2)	**1198**
The Work Song—Herb Alpert & The Tijuana Brass (66)	1047
The Jive Samba—Cannonball Adderley Sextet (63)	151
Nat ADDERLEY Jr. ► 3841 (2)	**682**
Stop To Love—Luther Vandross (86)	1129
Give Me The Reason—Luther Vandross (86)	236
Milton ADDINGTON ► 2354 (2)	**1567**
Laurie (Strange Things Happen)—Dickey Lee (65)	1541
The Dodo—Jumpin' Gene Simmons (64)	77
Richard ADDINSELL ► 3789 (3)	**699**
World Outside—Four Coins (58)	*883*
World Outside—Four Aces (58)	*327*
World Outside—Roger Williams (58)	*187*
Barbara ADDOMS ► 11135 (1)	**3.1**
Can't Hold Back (Your Loving)—Kano (81)	12
Dick ADDRISI ► 627 (15)	**6902**
Never My Love—Association (67)	*6833*
Never My Love—5th Dimension (71)	*1564*
Never My Love—Blue Swede (74)	*1499*
We've Got To Get It On Again—Addrisi Brothers (72)	1040
Slow Dancin' Don't Turn Me On—Addrisi Brothers (77)	881
Time For Livin'—Association (68)	639
I Believe You—Dorothy Moore (77)	*596*
Little Miss Sad—Five Emprees (65)	187
Ghost Dancer—Addrisi Brothers (79)	162
Cherrystone—Addrisi Brothers (59)	110
I Believe You—Carpenters (78)	*99*
One Last Time—Glen Campbell (72)	98
Never My Love—Addrisi Brothers (77)	*82*
I Can Feel You—Addrisi Brothers (72)	7.9
Never My Love—Sandpebbles (68)	*3.2*
Don ADDRISI ► 628 (15)	**6902**
Never My Love—Association (67)	*6833*
Never My Love—5th Dimension (71)	*1564*
Never My Love—Blue Swede (74)	*1499*
We've Got To Get It On Again—Addrisi Brothers (72)	1040
Slow Dancin' Don't Turn Me On—Addrisi Brothers (77)	881
Time For Livin'—Association (68)	639
I Believe You—Dorothy Moore (77)	*596*
Little Miss Sad—Five Emprees (65)	187
Ghost Dancer—Addrisi Brothers (79)	162
Cherrystone—Addrisi Brothers (59)	110
I Believe You—Carpenters (78)	*99*
One Last Time—Glen Campbell (72)	98
Never My Love—Addrisi Brothers (77)	*82*
I Can Feel You—Addrisi Brothers (72)	7.9
Never My Love—Sandpebbles (68)	*3.2*
Mickey ADDY ► 5293 (1)	**312**
Remember When—Platters (59)	624
—Joel Adelberg see: Jeff BARRY	
Howard ADELMAN ► 11650 (1)	**0.8**
Piltdown Rides Again—Piltdown Men (60)	2.5
Kay ADELMAN ► 6592 (1)	**154**
I Gotta Go Get My Baby—Teresa Brewer (55)	308
—Keith Adelsohn see: Keith HERMAN	
Lenny ADELSON ► 6779 (4)	**138**
Dancing With My Shadow—Four Voices (58)	256
Calla Calla—Paulette Sisters (58)	12
Away All Boats—Al Hibbler (56)	8.5
Rebel In Town—Crew-Cuts (56)	6.1
David ADELSTEIN ► 5522 (2)	**275**
Don't Give It Up—Robbie Patton (81)	508
Smiling Islands—Robbie Patton (83)	295
Leslie ADEY ► 7845 (1)	**72**
Walking In My Sleep—Roger Daltrey (84)	145
Kayode ADEYEMO ► 3038 (2)	**1048**
Girl You Know It's True—Milli Vanilli (88)	3721
Object Of My Desire—Starpoint (85)	913
John ADKINS ► 6655 (2)	**147**
Georgia Pines—Candymen (67)	277
Deep In The Night—Candymen (68)	26
Gene ADKINSON ► 1700 (8)	**2464**
It's Almost Tomorrow—Dream Weavers (55)	*2855*
It's Almost Tomorrow—Jo Stafford (55)	*1089*
It's Almost Tomorrow—Snooky Lanson (55)	*494*
It's Almost Tomorrow—David Carroll And His Orchestra (55)	*371*
It's Almost Tomorrow—Jimmy Velvet (65)	*117*
You're Mine—Dream Weavers (56)	0.3
It's Almost Tomorrow—Lawrence Welk & His Champagne Music (55)	*0.0*
It's Almost Tomorrow—Ray Anthony & His Orchestra with Don Durant (56)	*0.0*
Lou ADLER ► 803 (10)	**5521**
Poor Side Of Town—Johnny Rivers (66)	*5962*
Wonderful World—Herman's Hermits (65)	*3144*
Wonderful World—Sam Cooke (60)	*1801*
Honolulu Lulu—Jan & Dean (63)	1484
(What A) Wonderful World—Art Garfunkel With James Taylor & Paul Simon (78)	*839*
Poor Side Of Town—Al Wilson (68)	*132*
All Of My Life—Sam Cooke (58)	49
Wonderful World—Ovations (73)	*34*
There's A Girl—Jan & Dean (59)	21
(What A) Wonderful World—Johnny Nash (76)	*17*
Richard ADLER ► 321 (28) HOF	**11427**
Hey There—Rosemary Clooney (54)	*11126*
Everybody Loves A Lover—Doris Day (58)	*2433*
Whatever Lola Wants (Lola Gets)—Sarah Vaughan (55)	*2027*
Hernando's Hideaway—Archie Bleyer (54)	*1629*
Heart—Eddie Fisher (55)	*1418*
Everybody Loves A Lover—Shirelles (62)	*1101*
Hey There—Sammy Davis Jr. (54)	*680*
Girl On Page 44—Four Lads (59)	489
Two Lost Souls—Perry Como & Jaye P. Morgan (55)	411
Rags To Riches—Sunny & The Sunliners (63)	*343*
Heart—Four Aces (55)	*311*
Rags To Riches—Elvis Presley (71)	*223*
Whatever Lola Wants (Lola Gets)—Dinah Shore (55)	*181*
Near To You—Patti Page (55)	*149*
True Love Goes On And On—Burl Ives (63)	121
Old Shoes—Frankie Laine (54)	118
Heart—Peggy Lee (60)	*33*
Rags To Riches—Lenny Welch (66)	*29*
Steam Heat—Pointer Sisters (74)	*15*
Everybody Loves A Lover—Angels (62)	*9.1*
Rags To Riches—Rays Featuring Hal Miller (58)	*6.6*
Hernando's Hideaway—Guy Lombardo & His Royal Canadians (54)	*0.0*
Heart—Norman Brooks (55)	*0.0*
Whatever Lola Wants (Lola Gets)—Ginny Gibson (55)	*0.0*
Whatever Lola Wants—Carmen McRae (55)	*0.0*
Near To You—Eddie Fisher (55)	*0.0*
Hernando's Hideaway—Johnnie Ray (54)	*0.0*
Steam Heat—Patti Page (54)	*0.0*
Steven ADLER ► 1971 (5)	**2043**
Sweet Child O' Mine—Guns N' Roses (88)	4596
Patience—Guns N' Roses (89)	2050
Paradise City—Guns N' Roses (89)	1901
Welcome To The Jungle—Guns N' Roses (88)	1661
Nightrain—Guns N' Roses (89)	9.3
Billy Joe ADMIRE ► 3385 (2)	**872**
The River Is Wide—Grassroots (69)	*1304*
The River Is Wide—Forum (67)	*441*
Antonio ADOLFO [Antonio Adolfo Maurity Sabóia] ► 8258 (1)	**57**
Pretty World—Sergio Mendes & Brasil '66 (69)	226
Bill ADOR [Willy Noël De Moor, Willy de Moor] ► 1678 (2)	**2506**
Jungle Fever—Chakachas (71)	2503
Stories??—Chakachas (72)	7.0
Ernest ADRIAN ► 7522 (1)	**91**
Deeper Shade Of Soul—Urban Dance Squad (90)	545
—Evelyne Adrians see: Lana SEBASTIAN	
Helen ADU [Helen Folasade Adu, Sade] ► 1603 (5)	**2640**
Smooth Operator—Sade (85)	2158
The Sweetest Taboo—Sade (85)	1904
Paradise—Sade (88)	717
Never As Good As The First Time—Sade (86)	603
Your Love Is King—Sade (85)	257
Walter AFANASIEFF [Vladimir Nikitich Afanasieff] ► 1571 (4)	**2694**
Can't Let Go—Mariah Carey (91)	4348
Don't Make Me Wait For Love—Kenny G (87)	854
Can You Stop The Rain—Peabo Bryson (91)	281
Going Home—Kenny G (89)	189
Tawatha AGEE ► 6951 (1)	**126**
Two Hearts—Stephanie Mills featuring Teddy Pendergrass (81)	378
Milton AGER ► 2541 (10) HOF	**1403**
Ain't She Sweet—Beatles (64)	*1085*
Trust In Me—Etta James (61)	*849*
Trust In Me—Patti Page (59)	*544*
Glad Rag Doll—Crazy Otto (55)	428
Hardhearted Hannah—Ray Charles Orchestra & Chorus (60)	179
Forgive Me—Al Martino (65)	177
Are You Sorry—Joni James (59)	78
Ain't She Sweet—Johnston Brothers (55)	*13*
Ain't She Sweet—Modernaires (56)	*4.4*
Trust In Me—Chris Connor (57)	*1.8*
Marcel AGERON [Jacques Larue] ► 4388 (4)	**507**
Padre—Toni Arden (58)	*1727*
Cherry Pink And Apple Blossom White—Alan Dale (55)	*226*
Padre—Valerie Carr (58)	*0.0*
Padre—Sarah Vaughan (58)	*0.0*
Alfie AGIUS ► 3200 (4)	**955**
One Thing Leads To Another—Fixx (83)	2676
Saved By Zero—Fixx (83)	900
Are We Ourselves?—Fixx (84)	811
The Sign Of Fire—Fixx (83)	523
Pete AGNEW ► 10280 (1)	**10**
Holiday—Nazareth (80)	63
Lena AGREE ► 2504 (2)	**1433**
Doggin' Around—Jackie Wilson (60)	*1183*
Stop Doggin' Me Around—Klique (83)	*250*
—Don Louis Agreti see: Don GRADY	
Eden AHBEZ ► 3201 (3)	**955**
Nature Boy—Bobby Darin (61)	*569*
Lonely Island—Sam Cooke (58)	377
Nature Boy—Shields (58)	*8.0*
Fred AHLERT ► 1387 (10) HOF	**3197**
I'm Gonna Sit Right Down And Write Myself A Letter—Billy Williams (57)	*4377*

Fred AHLERT ▶ 1387 (10) HOF *Continued*	**3197**
I Don't Know Why—Linda Scott (61)	1607
I'll Get By (As Long As I Have You)— Billy Williams (58)	239
Where The Blue Of The Night—Tommy Mara (58)	193
The Moon Was Yellow—Frank Sinatra (62)	26
I'm Gonna Sit Right Down And Write Myself A Letter— Fabian (60)	*12*
Love You Funny Thing—Tony Martin (56)	3.7
I'm Gonna Sit Right Down And Write Myself A Letter— Larry Storch (57)	*0.0*
I'm Gonna Sit Right Down And Write Myself A Letter— Harry The Hipster (57)	*0.0*
I'm Gonna Sit Right Down And Write Myself A Letter— Hop A Long Wong (57)	*0.0*
Richard AHLERT ▶ 3796 (5)	**696**
Rusty Bells—Brenda Lee (65)	713
Runnin' Out Of Fools—Aretha Franklin (64)	336
Listen Lonely Girl—Johnny Mathis (64)	323
You Don't Need Me For Anything Anymore— Brenda Lee (69)	117
I'd Do It All Again—Vikki Carr (72)	12
Mustafa AHMED ▶ 11369 (1)	**2.0**
Ya Mama—Wuf Ticket (83)	8.1
—Zyah Ahmonue see: Malcolm ANTHONY	
Ralph AIKENS ▶ 11654 (1)	**0.8**
Riding High—Faze-O (78)	4.8
—Jimmie Ainsworth see: Jimmie O. ROGERS	
Matt AITKEN ▶ 1062 (15)	**4156**
Never Gonna Give You Up—Rick Astley (87)	4405
Together Forever (Remix)—Rick Astley (88)	3168
I Heard A Rumour—Bananarama (87)	2288
This Time I Know It's For Real— Donna Summer (89)	1582
It Would Take A Strong Strong Man—Rick Astley (88)	1136
I Should Be So Lucky—Kylie Minogue (88)	512
It's No Secret—Kylie Minogue (88)	419
I Can't Help It—Bananarama (87)	331
Love In The First Degree—Bananarama (88)	262
More Than Physical—Bananarama (86)	74
Love, Truth And Honesty—Bananarama (88)	64
Showing Out (Get Fresh At The Weekend)— Mel & Kim (87)	51
Nothing's Gonna Stop Me Now—Samantha Fox (87)	50
Wouldn't Change A Thing—Kylie Minogue (90)	19
Love's About To Change My Heart— Donna Summer (89)	12
—Mike Akapoff see: Ernie FREEMAN	
Jerry AKINES ▶ 4548 (6)	**466**
Don't Let The Green Grass Fool You— Wilson Pickett (71)	1388
At The Top Of The Stairs—Formations (68)	132
I'm Gonna Love You—Intrigues (69)	115
One For The Money (Part 1)—Whispers (76)	40
Just A Little Bit More—Intrigues (70)	14
Don't Get Close— Little Anthony & The Imperials (70)	2.7
Jan AKKERMAN ▶ 2960 (1)	**1097**
Hocus Pocus—Focus (73)	2194
Mike AKOPOFF ▶ 11396 (1)	**1.9**
Make A Little Love—Lowell Fulsom (67)	3.8
Harry AKST ▶ 3184 (7) HOF	**961**
Baby Face— Wing And A Prayer Fife And Drum Corps. (75)	*1324*
Baby Face—Bobby Darin (62)	*375*
Baby Face—Little Richard (58)	*195*
Am I Blue—Cher (73)	*17*
Guilty—Crests (62)	9.8
Am I Blue—Ray Charles (61)	*2.8*
Baby Face—Bobby Vee (61)	*2.0*
—Louis Al see: Louis MATHIS	
Jimmy ALAIMO ▶ 7667 (1)	**82**
Dance With Me—Mojo Men (65)	164
Steve ALAIMO ▶ 11702 (1)	**0.6**
Keep The Home Fire Burnin'—Latimore (75)	1.2
Fernando ALBANO ▶ 8051 (4)	**64**
Infatuation (Scapricciatiello)— Renato Carosone (56)	*120*
Do You Love Me Like You Kiss Me (Scapricciatiello)— McGuire Sisters (58)	12
Infatuation (Scapricciatiello)— Paul Weston & His Music From Hollywood (56)	*0.0*
Infatuation—Dick Contino (56)	*0.0*
Damon ALBARN ▶ 9674 (1)	**19**
There's No Other Way—Blur (91)	77
Charles ALBERT ▶ 8466 (1)	**49**
Give Me Your Love—Don Cornell (55)	148
Morris ALBERT [Mauricio Alberto Kaiserman] ▶ 2092 (4)	**1888**
Feelings—Morris Albert (75)	*3636*
Gonna Love You More—George Benson (77)	40
Sweet Loving Man—Morris Albert (75)	25
Feelings—Walter Jackson (76)	*9.1*
Luigi ALBERTELLI ▶ 10228 (1)	**11**
Vado Via—Drupi (73)	*22*
Charles ALBERTINE ▶ 10824 (1)	**5.1**
The Sound Of Surf— Percy Faith And His Orchestra (63)	5.1
Al ALBERTS ▶ 3737 (1)	**715**
Tell Me Why—Bobby Vinton (64)	1431
ALBIN ▶ 10312 (1)	**10**
Low Rider (On The Boulevard)—Latin Alliance (91)	121
Peter ALBIN ▶ 9480 (1)	**23**
Coo Coo— Big Brother And The Holding Company (68)	23
Roye ALBRIGHTON ▶ 11232 (1)	**2.6**
Astral Man—Nektar (75)	11
—Ramon Arcusa Alcón see: Ramon ARCUSA	
Mike ALDAY ▶ 9056 (1)	**32**
Your Graduation Means Goodbye—Cardigans (58)	64
Chuck ALDER ▶ 7651 (2)	**83**
Together—Illusion (69)	240
Let's Make Each Other Happy—Illusion (70)	6.0
John ALDER ▶ 9408 (1)	**24**
Back Of My Hand (I've Got Your Number)— Jags (80)	48
Ava ALDRIDGE ▶ 2085 (4)	**1894**
Sharing The Night Together—Dr. Hook (78)	*3646*
Somebody Send My Baby Home—Lenny LeBlanc (81)	136
Sharing The Night Together—Arthur Alexander (76)	*4.4*
Sharing The Night Together—Lenny LeBlanc (76)	*0.9*
Simon ALDRIDGE ▶ 11587 (1)	**1.1**
Certain Things Are Likely— K.T.P./Kissing The Pink (87)	4.3
Walt ALDRIDGE ▶ 2768 (1)	**1208**
(There's) No Gettin' Over Me—Ronnie Milsap (81)	2415
Dick ALEN ▶ 6506 (1)	**161**
Here Comes The Judge—Pigmeat Markham (68)	646
Aki ALEONG ▶ 11402 (1)	**1.9**
Trade Winds, Trade Winds—Aki Aleong (61)	5.6
Barney ALES ▶ 4427 (3)	**496**
What's The Matter With You Baby— Marvin Gaye & Mary Wells (64)	929
Once Upon A Time—Marvin Gaye & Mary Wells (64)	797
Love Me All The Way—Kim Weston (63)	130
Billy ALESSI ▶ 8619 (3)	**45**
Put Away Your Love—Alessi (82)	61
Oh Lori—Alessi (77)	18
Loverboy—Karen Kamon (84)	10
Bobby ALESSI ▶ 8620 (3)	**45**
Put Away Your Love—Alessi (82)	61
Oh Lori—Alessi (77)	18
Loverboy—Karen Kamon (84)	10
Arthur ALEXANDER ▶ 2127 (5)	**1841**
You Better Move On—Arthur Alexander (62)	838
Every Day I Have To Cry—Steve Alaimo (63)	*472*
Every Day I Have To Cry Some—Arthur Alexander (75)	*304*
Anna (Go To Him)—Arthur Alexander (62)	190
Everyday I Have To Cry—Gentrys (66)	*38*
Dan ALEXANDER ▶ 8952 (1)	**35**
Can't Keep A Good Man Down—Eddie Money (79)	106
—Fitzroy Alexander see: Lord MELODY	
Fred ALEXANDER ▶ 8978 (2)	**34**
Fantastic Voyage—Lakeside (80)	296
Your Love Is On The One—Lakeside (81)	2.8
—Gary Alexander see: Jules ALEXANDER	
George ALEXANDER [Alexander Young] ▶ 11406 (1)	**1.8**
Dear Delilah—Grapefruit (68)	1.8
George Stanley ALEXANDER ▶ 10011 (1)	**14**
What's She Got—Liquid Gold (83)	28
James Edward ALEXANDER ▶ 4834 (11)	**402**
Soul Finger—Bar-Kays (67)	1546
Shake Your Rump To The Funk—Bar-Kays (76)	593
Move Your Boogie Body—Bar-Kays (79)	270
Today Is The Day—Bar-Kays (80)	150
Give Everybody Some—Bar-Kays (67)	97
Freakshow On The Dance Floor—Bar-Kays (84)	79
Too Hot To Stop—Bar-Kays (77)	36
Hit And Run—Bar-Kays (81)	23
Boogie Body Land—Bar-Kays (81)	23
Let's Have Some Fun—Bar-Kays (78)	8.9
Shine—Bar-Kays (79)	7.7
James W. ALEXANDER ▶ 2107 (9)	**1867**
Lookin' For A Love—Bobby Womack (74)	*1838*
Together Let's Find Love—5th Dimension (71)	691
Looking For A Love—J. Geils Band (71)	*652*
Lookin' For A Love—Valentinos (62)	*169*
That's Where It's At—Sam Cooke (64)	137
Keep A Light In The Window Till I Come Home— Solomon Burke (67)	111
Little Things You Do—Sam Cooke (59)	9.7
Let's Go Steady Again—Sam Cooke (66)	1.9
Coming Back To You—Maxine Brown (64)	1.9
John ALEXANDER ▶ 7698 (1)	**80**
My Song—Aretha Franklin (68)	160
Jules ALEXANDER [Jules Gary Alexander, Gary Alexander] ▶ 3744 (2)	**713**
Pandora's Golden Heebie Jeebies— Association (66)	677
Dubuque Blues—Association (69)	37
—Keith Vincent Constantine Alexander see: Keith DIAMOND	
M. ALEXANDER ▶ 9297 (1)	**27**
Mr. President—Dickie Goodman (74)	54
Tracy Lee ALEXANDER [Richard Maes] ▶ 11632 (1)	**0.9**
Willyam, Willyam—Dee Dee Sharp (64)	1.8
Fabian ALFARO ▶ 9443 (1)	**23**
Latin Active—A Lighter Shade Of Brown (91)	164
Barry ALFONSO ▶ 5899 (2)	**231**
Livin' In Desperate Times—Olivia Newton-John (84)	440
All The Right Moves— Jennifer Warnes/Chris Thompson (83)	22
—John Alford see: John ALLISON	
Kenneth J. ALFORD [Kenneth Alford, Frederic Joseph Ricketts] ▶ 3502 (5)	**813**
Colonel Bogey—Mitch Miller And His Orchestra (57)	*631*
Colonel Bogey—Edmundo Ros And His Orchestra (58)	*173*
Colonel Bogey—Art Mooney And His Orchestra (57)	*8.7*
Colonel Bogey—Carlson's Raiders (57)	*0.0*
Colonel Bogey—David Terry & His Orchestra (58)	*0.0*
Roy ALFRED [Fred Royal, Dick Ware] ▶ 542 (22)	**7903**
Rock And Roll Waltz—Kay Starr (55)	7669
Let's Lock The Door (And Throw Away The Key)— Jay & The Americans (64)	1513
The Hucklebuck—Chubby Checker (60)	*1494*
She Can't Find Her Keys—Paul Petersen (62)	821
That's It-I Quit-I'm Movin' On—Sam Cooke (61)	756
Now And For Always—George Hamilton IV (58)	465
My Love Song To You—Bob Manning (54)	464
Wisdom Of A Fool—Five Keys (56)	453
Think Of The Good Times—Jay & The Americans (65)	280
When Rock And Roll Come To Trinidad— Nat "King" Cole (57)	260
Italian Huckle Buck—Lou Monte (54)	*227*
Open Up The Doghouse (Two Cats Are Comin' In)— Dean Martin And Nat "King" Cole (54)	195
Young Abe Lincoln—Don Cornell (55)	*184*
I've Got News For You—Ray Charles (61)	158
My First Formal Gown—Patti Page (56)	126
Promise Her Anything—Dean Martin (57)	34
Young Abe Lincoln—Hugo & Luigi (55)	*16*
Rock Roll Boogie—"Tennessee" Ernie Ford (56)	16
Who's Gonna Take You To The Prom—Gaylords (56)	6.6
Blue Bolero—Richard Hayes (56)	6.4
Who Can Explain— Frankie Lymon and the Teenagers (56)	5.8
The Huckle-Buck (Italian Style)—Lou Monte (60)	*0.0*
Patrick ALGER ▶ 6328 (1)	**182**
First Time Love—Livingston Taylor (80)	364

Augusto ALGUERO ▶ 6451 (3) 168

La Montana (If She Should Come To You)—Frank Devol And His Rainbow Strings (60) 123
If She Should Come To You (La Montana)—Anthony Newley (60) 120
La Montana (If She Should Come To You)—Roger Williams (60) 4.2

Joey ALKES ▶ 10807 (1) 5.2

A Million Miles Away—Plimsouls (83) 16

Davie ALLAN ▶ 4460 (1) 490

Blue's Theme—Arrows Featuring Davie Allen (67) 981

Gene ALLAN [Gene Allan Schachter] ▶ 784 (8) 5653

Mr. Lonely—Bobby Vinton (64) 8492
Coming Home Soldier—Bobby Vinton (66) 2331
Mr. Lonely—Buddy Greco (62) 274
(He's) Raining In My Sunshine—Jay & The Americans (66) 145
Red Roses For Mom—Bobby Vinton (67) 31
Midnight Show—Bobby Vinton (75) 22
It's The Same Old Love—Courtship (72) 7.3
Midnight Show—Ron Dante (75) 3.3

Thomas ALLBERT ▶ 10765 (1) 5.5

A Broken Man—Malibu's (69) 16

Dub ALLBRITTEN ▶ 661 (7) 6612

I'm Sorry—Brenda Lee (60) 9449
Everybody Loves Me But You—Brenda Lee (62) 2490
Anybody But Me—Brenda Lee (61) 806
Eventually—Brenda Lee (61) 281
Sweet Impossible You—Brenda Lee (63) 131
I'm Sorry—Joey Heatherton (72) 61
It Takes One To Know One—Brenda Lee (66) 4.7

Dave ALLDRED ▶ 1550 (14) 2740

Party Doll—Buddy Knox with The Rhythm Orchids (57) 4735
Party Doll—Steve Lawrence (57) 1892
Hula Love—Buddy Knox with The Rhythm Orchids (57) 1598
I'm Stickin' With You—Jimmy Bowen With The Rhythm Orchids (57) 1396
Rock Your Little Baby To Sleep—Buddy Knox with The Rhythm Orchids (57) 698
Click Clack—Dicky Doo And The Don'ts (58) 536
Party Doll—Cat Mother And The All Night News Boys (69) 164
Party Doll—Wingy Manone And His Orchestra (57) 133
I Trusted You—Jimmy Bowen With The Rhythm Orchids (57) 76
Ever Lovin' Fingers—Jimmy Bowen With The Rhythm Orchids (57) 44
I'm Stickin' With You—Fontane Sisters (57) 36
Party Doll—Roy Brown (57) 7.0
I'm Stickin' With You—Roy Brown (57) 0.0
Click Clack—Boyd Bennett & His Rockets (58) 0.0

Al ALLEN ▶ 6081 (1) 208

Just Married—Marty Robbins (58) 416

Brian ALLEN ▶ 4800 (1) 411

What About Love?—Heart (85) 1233

Charles ALLEN ▶ 6279 (1) 186

Lumberjack—Brook Benton (64) 372

Charles Edward ALLEN ▶ 3628 (2) 760

Are You Ready?—Pacific Gas & Electric With The Blackberries (70) 1471
Thank God For You Baby—PG&E (72) 50

Charles Leonard ALLEN ▶ 7014 (8) 122

Shake Your Rump To The Funk—Bar-Kays (76) 593
Move Your Boogie Body—Bar-Kays (79) 270
Today Is The Day—Bar-Kays (80) 150
Too Hot To Stop—Bar-Kays (77) 36
Hit And Run—Bar-Kays (81) 23
Boogie Body Land—Bar-Kays (81) 23
Let's Have Some Fun—Bar-Kays (78) 8.9
Shine—Bar-Kays (79) 7.7

Chris ALLEN ▶ 7645 (2) 83

The World Through A Tear—Neil Sedaka (65) 165
The Answer To My Prayer—Neil Sedaka (66) 84

—Christopher Thomas Allen see: Chris CROSS

Deborah ALLEN ▶ 5463 (1) 284

Baby I Lied—Deborah Allen (83) 851

Diana ALLEN ▶ 11431 (1) 1.7

So True—Peaches & Herb (69) 3.4

Donna ALLEN ▶ 6721 (1) 142

Serious—Donna Allen (87) 852

Fred ALLEN ▶ 10705 (1) 6.0

Free—Fresh Start (74) 18

—George Allen see: Georgio ALLENTINI

Ira ALLEN ▶ 4667 (1) 443

(You Keep Me) Hangin' On—Joe Simon (68) 885

Janna ALLEN ▶ 833 (4) 5294

Private Eyes—Daryl Hall & John Oates (81) 6308
Kiss On My List—Daryl Hall & John Oates (81) 4868
Method Of Modern Love—Daryl Hall & John Oates (84) 1622
Did It In A Minute—Daryl Hall & John Oates (82) 1415

Jeanie ALLEN ▶ 7233 (1) 108

I Found A Love Oh What A Love—Jo Ann & Troy (64) 108

—Joey Allen see: Joseph CAGLE

Laurie ALLEN [Jean Ann Del Grosso] ▶ 6792 (1) 136

Hold On—Sons Of Champlin (76) 273

Lee ALLEN ▶ 5109 (2) 341

Walkin' With Mr. Lee—Lee Allen And His Band (57) 330
Tic Toc—Lee Allen And His Band (58) 11

Leonard ALLEN ▶ 6834 (1) 134

Teenager's Prayer—Joe Simon (66) 134

Linda ALLEN ▶ 4116 (1) 588

Shoeshine Boy—Eddie Kendricks (75) 1176

Lorene ALLEN ▶ 8205 (1) 58

The Pill—Loretta Lynn (75) 175

Marilyn Weiss ALLEN [Cinthy Churchill, Marilyn Weiss] ▶ 9691 (2) 19

You Can't Lie To a Liar—Ketty Lester (62) 38
You Can't Lie To A Liar—Barry Gordon (62) 0.0

Murray ALLEN ▶ 11661 (1) 0.8

Mama's Place—Bing Day (59) 2.3

Na ALLEN [Nathaniel A. Allen Jr.] ▶ 10461 (1) 8.2

Bring It Home (And Give It To Me)—Hot Sauce (72) 8.2

Peter ALLEN ▶ 723 (11) 6063

Arthur's Theme (Best That You Can Do)—Christopher Cross (81) 6911
I Honestly Love You—Olivia Newton-John (74) 5140
Don't Cry Out Loud—Melissa Manchester (78) 1951
I'd Rather Leave While I'm In Love—Rita Coolidge (79) 461
Jennifer—Bobby Sherman (71) 386
I Go To Rio—Pablo Cruise (79) 242
I Honestly Love You—Olivia Newton-John (77) 223
The World Through A Tear—Neil Sedaka (65) 165
Fly Away—Peter Allen (81) 131
The Answer To My Prayer—Neil Sedaka (66) 84
Fly Away—Stevie Woods (82) 19

Ray ALLEN ▶ 2652 (8) 1292

Pepino The Italian Mouse—Lou Monte (62) 2271
Pepino's Friend Pasqual (The Italian Pussy-cat)—Lou Monte (63) 202
That's How It Goes—George Maharis (63) 48
Hey, Stella! (Who Zat Down Your Cellar?)—Crew-Cuts (58) 29
Spanish Nights And You—Connie Francis (66) 28
Dominick The Donkey—Lou Monte with Joe Reisman's Orch. & Chorus (60) 14
First Love—Playmates (59) 12
Mala Femmena—Connie Francis (63) 5.7

Ray (2) ALLEN ▶ 6990 (5) 124

The Lord Is A Busy Man—Merry Macs (55) 247
The Lord Is A Busy Man—Steve Lawrence (55) 0.0
The Lord Is A Busy Man—Nan Wynn (55) 0.0
The Lord Is A Busy Man—Mahalia Jackson (55) 0.0
The Lord Is A Busy Man—Ralph Young (55) 0.0

Rick ALLEN ▶ 1596 (11) 2649

Pour Some Sugar On Me—Def Leppard (88) 3871
Love Bites—Def Leppard (88) 3277
Armageddon It—Def Leppard (88) 2857
Photograph—Def Leppard (83) 1231
Hysteria—Def Leppard (88) 1083
Rocket—Def Leppard (89) 1017
Rock Of Ages—Def Leppard (83) 1009
Animal—Def Leppard (87) 796
Foolin'—Def Leppard (83) 557
Bringin' On The Heartbreak—Def Leppard (84) 157
Rock Brigade—Def Leppard (80) 9.8

Robert ALLEN ▶ 107 (52) 23012

Moments To Remember—Four Lads (55) 7587
Chances Are—Johnny Mathis (57) 5455
No Not Much—Four Lads (56) 4830
It's Not For Me To Say—Johnny Mathis (57) 4673
Everybody Loves A Lover—Doris Day (58) 2433
Theme Song From Song For A Summer Night (Pts. 1 & 2)—Mitch Miller with His Orch. & Chorus (56) 1716
Can You Find It In Your Heart—Tony Bennett with Percy Faith and His Orchestra (56) 1683
Who Needs You—Four Lads (57) 1611
If Dreams Came True—Pat Boone (58) 1550
Enchanted Island—Four Lads (58) 1229
Everybody Loves A Lover—Shirelles (62) 1101
There's Only One Of You—Four Lads (58) 957
A Very Special Love—Johnny Nash (57) 660
I've Been There—Tommy Edwards (59) 630
I Just Don't Know—Four Lads (57) 559
Come To Me—Johnny Mathis (58) 531
Every Step Of The Way—Johnny Mathis (63) 509
Girl On Page 44—Four Lads (59) 489
Teacher Teacher—Johnny Mathis (58) 461
(There's No Place Like) Home For The Holidays—Perry Como (54) 414
Happy Anniversary—Jane Morgan (59) 388
Door Of Dreams—Perry Como (55) 376
No, Not Much—Vogues (69) 361
Moments To Remember—Vogues (69) 335
Al's Place—Al (He's The King) Hirt Trumpet with Chorus and Orchestra (65) 308
I Never Felt More Like Falling In Love—Tony Bennett with Ray Ellis and His Orchestra (57) 304
Sing Along—Jimmy Dean (59) 247
No Not Much—Smoke Ring (69) 215
Eyes Of God—Four Lads (57) 179
Happy Anniversary—Four Lads (59) 171
Baby Has Gone Bye Bye—George Maharis (62) 151
Scene Of The Crime—Dinah Shore (58) 132
The Waiting Game—Harry Belafonte (58) 124
Love Me In The Daytime—Doris Day (59) 115
It Could've Been Worse—Jesse Belvin (59) 89
Being True To One Another—Tony Bennett (59) 89
Pamela Throws A Party—Joe Reisman and His Orchestra And Chorus (57) 60
A Very Special Love—Debbie Reynolds (57) 59
Take The Time—Johnny Mathis (65) 33
Show Folk—Paul Evans (61) 26
Play For Keeps—Jaye P. Morgan (56) 21
I Saw Mommy Do The Mambo (With You Know Who)—Jimmy Boyd (54) 15
Book Of Love—Richard Maltby And His Orchestra (55) 14
Love Me Good—Jo Stafford (56) 14
Everybody Loves A Lover—Angels (62) 9.1
You Know How It Is—Frankie Laine (57) 5.1
A Very Special Love (Song For The Ninth Day)—Mitch Miller & His Orchestra (57) 2.2
It's Not For Me To Say—Cyril Stapleton & His Orchestra (57) 0.0
A Very Special Love (Song For The Ninth Day)—Hi-Lo's (57) 0.0
Enchanted Island—Jane Morgan & The Troubadors (58) 0.0
It's Not For Me To Say—Jane Morgan (57) 0.0
Come To Me—Julie Wilson (58) 0.0

Robert (2) ALLEN ▶ 11432 (1) 1.7

So True—Peaches & Herb (69) 3.4

Robert I. ALLEN ▶ 5444 (6) 288

Tonight I'll Say A Prayer—Eydie Gorme (69) 420
There Should Be Rules (Protecting Fools Who Fall In Love)—Betty Madigan (55) 132
Son Of A Travelin' Man—Ed Ames (69) 22
Little Sister—Connie Stevens (60) 11
Little Sister—Cathy Carr (60) 11
On The Way Out—Walter Scott (58) 1.6

Sara ALLEN ▶ 461 (11) 9051

Maneater—Daryl Hall & John Oates (82) 7727
I Can't Go For That (No Can Do)—Daryl Hall & John Oates (81) 7283
Private Eyes—Daryl Hall & John Oates (81) 6308
You Make My Dreams—Daryl Hall & John Oates (81) 2226
Adult Education—Daryl Hall & John Oates (84) 1464
Did It In A Minute—Daryl Hall & John Oates (82) 1415
Swept Away—Diana Ross (84) 735

Sara ALLEN ▶ 461 (11) *Continued*	**9051**
Possession Obsession—Daryl Hall & John Oates (85)	431
Missed Opportunity—Daryl Hall & John Oates (88)	421
Downtown Life—Daryl Hall & John Oates (88)	326
Why Do Lovers (Break Each Other's Heart?)—Daryl Hall & John Oates (77)	74
Shorty ALLEN ▶ 1157 (2)	**3838**
Rock And Roll Waltz—Kay Starr (55)	7669
Blue Bolero—Richard Hayes (56)	6.4
Steve ALLEN ▶ 2813 (7)	**1178**
Picnic—McGuire Sisters (56)	*1270*
Pretend You Don't See Her—Jerry Vale (57)	*490*
Pretend You Don't See Her—Bobby Vee (64)	*35*
The Rockin' Ghost—Archie Bleyer (56)	22
The Shovel (La Shabla)—Gaylords (59)	*15*
Pretend You Don't See Her—Steve Allen (57)	*0.0*
On The Beach—Playmates (59)	*0.0*
Thomas ALLEN ▶ 1235 (21)	**3621**
Spill The Wine—Eric Burdon And War (70)	*5207*
The Cisco Kid—War (73)	4378
Why Can't We Be Friends?—War (75)	3006
Low Rider—War (75)	2369
Slippin' Into Darkness—War (71)	*2076*
The World Is A Ghetto—War (72)	1817
Gypsy Man—War (73)	1659
Summer—War (76)	1559
Me And Baby Brother—War (73)	1513
All Day Music—War (71)	704
Ballero—War (74)	472
They Can't Take Away Our Music—Eric Burdon And War Featuring Sharon Scott And The Beautiful New Born Children Of Southern California (70)	418
Spill The Wine—Isley Brothers (71)	*409*
Galaxy—War (77)	325
L.A. Sunshine—War (77)	291
Low Rider (On The Boulevard)—Latin Alliance (91)	121
Lonely Feelin'—War (71)	74
You Got The Power—War (82)	35
Slipping Into Darkness—Ramsey Lewis (72)	*35*
Good, Good Feelin'—War (79)	12
Outlaw—War (82)	10
Timmy ALLEN ▶ 7760 (2)	**76**
We've Only Just Begun (The Romance Is Not Over)—Glenn Jones (87)	143
(You're Puttin') A Rush On Me—Stephanie Mills (87)	9.7
Georgio ALLENTINI [George Allen, Giorgio] ▶ 5081 (3)	**346**
Lover's Lane—Georgio (87)	182
Sexappeal—Georgio (87)	161
Tina Cherry—Georgio (87)	2.2
Michele ALLER [Mavis Vegas Davis] ▶ 3052 (3)	**1034**
Take Me Home—Cher (79)	1769
Wasn't It Good—Cher (79)	162
Hell On Wheels—Cher (79)	137
Audrey ALLISON ▶ 544 (6)	**7886**
He'll Have To Go—Jim Reeves (59)	*10202*
Teen Age Crush—Tommy Sands (57)	3179
He'll Have To Stay—Jeanne Black (60)	*3119*
He'll Have To Go—Solomon Burke (64)	*308*
He'll Have To Go—Homer & Jethro (60)	*9.0*
He'll Have To Stay—Corina Minette (60)	*0.0*
Bob ALLISON [Bernard Colin Day] ▶ 8848 (1)	**38**
Are You Sure—Allisons (61)	76
Jerry ALLISON ▶ 701 (12)	**6211**
More Than I Can Say—Leo Sayer (80)	*5089*
Peggy Sue—Buddy Holly / The Crickets (57)	*4478*
That'll Be The Day—Buddy Holly / The Crickets (57)	*4320*
That'll Be The Day—Linda Ronstadt (76)	*1413*
Think It Over—Buddy Holly / The Crickets (58)	325
More Than I Can Say—Bobby Vee (61)	*183*
Peggy Sue—Beach Boys (78)	*133*
Well All Right—Santana (78)	67
That'll Be The Day—Everly Brothers (65)	*5.0*
That'll Be The Day—Buddy Holly & The Three Tunes (57)	*0.0*
That'll Be The Day—Jeff Allen (57)	*0.0*
Peggy Sue—Jackie Walker (57)	*0.0*
Joe ALLISON ▶ 545 (6)	**7886**
He'll Have To Go—Jim Reeves (59)	*10202*
Teen Age Crush—Tommy Sands (57)	3179
He'll Have To Stay—Jeanne Black (60)	*3119*

He'll Have To Go—Solomon Burke (64)	*308*
He'll Have To Go—Homer & Jethro (60)	*9.0*
He'll Have To Stay—Corina Minette (60)	*0.0*
John ALLISON [John Alford] ▶ 8849 (1)	**38**
Are You Sure—Allisons (61)	76
Michael ALLISON ▶ 8579 (1)	**46**
Every Face Tells A Story—Olivia Newton-John (76)	137
Gregg ALLMAN ▶ 2428 (6)	**1495**
Midnight Rider—Gregg Allman (73)	*848*
Midnight Rider—Joe Cocker And The Chris Stainton Band (72)	*542*
Ain't Wastin' Time No More—Allman Brothers Band (72)	67
Dreams—Buddy Miles (70)	29
Melissa—Allman Brothers Band (72)	9.7
Nevertheless—Allman Brothers Band (75)	0.0
—Margarite Almeda see: Sunny SKYLAR	
Tandyn ALMER ▶ 2173 (4)	**1790**
Along Comes Mary—Association (66)	*1719*
Sail On Sailor—Beach Boys (75)	*268*
Sail On Sailor—Beach Boys (73)	*49*
Along Comes Mary—Baja Marimba Band (67)	*7.6*
—Almo see: Alan GORDON	
Marc ALMOND ▶ 7208 (1)	**110**
Tears Run Rings—Marc Almond (88)	110
Carlos ALOMAR ▶ 1789 (3)	**2322**
Fame—David Bowie (75)	5730
Never Let Me Down—David Bowie (87)	447
Lucky In Love—Mick Jagger (85)	377
Peter ALONZO ▶ 6659 (1)	**146**
Coney Island Baby—Excellents (62)	292
James ALPERN ▶ 4802 (1)	**410**
Turtle Power!—Partners In Kryme (90)	820
Edward ALPERSON ▶ 7953 (1)	**67**
Dreamer—Four Aces (56)	135
Herb ALPERT ▶ 1889 (10)	**2153**
Wonderful World—Herman's Hermits (65)	*3144*
Wonderful World—Sam Cooke (60)	*1801*
(What A) Wonderful World—Art Garfunkel With James Taylor & Paul Simon (78)	*839*
Jerusalem—Herb Alpert & The Tijuana Brass (70)	103
Fox Hunt—Herb Alpert And The T.J.B. (74)	63
All Of My Life—Sam Cooke (58)	49
Wonderful World—Ovations (73)	*34*
Magic Man—Herb Alpert (81)	22
There's A Girl—Jan & Dean (59)	21
(What A) Wonderful World—Johnny Nash (76)	*17*
—Randy Alpert see: Randy BADAZZ	
Russell ALQUIST ▶ 6778 (1)	**138**
Sleepy Joe—Herman's Hermits (68)	276
Gerald ALSTON ▶ 9789 (1)	**17**
We Never Danced To A Love Song—Manhattans (77)	34
Alex ALSTONE [Siegfried Alex Stein] ▶ 2826 (4)	**1168**
More—Perry Como (56)	2307
Symphony—Sammy Turner (59)	16
My Arms Are A House—Hank Snow (57)	11
Write To Me From Naples—Dean Martin (57)	10
Ron ALTBACH ▶ 9514 (1)	**22**
A Little Bit Like Magic—King Harvest (73)	67
Don ALTFELD ▶ 2567 (7)	**1374**
The Little Old Lady (From Pasadena)—Jan & Dean (64)	3373
Bucket "T"—Ronny & The Daytonas (64)	293
Batman—Jan & Dean (66)	206
The Anaheim, Azusa & Cucamonga Sewing Circle, Book Review And Timing Association—Jan & Dean (64)	194
Gas Money—Jan & Arnie (58)	118
Judy Loves Me—Johnny Crawford (64)	7.8
One Piece Topless Bathing Suit—Rip Chords (64)	2.4
Emery ALTIMUS ▶ 10927 (1)	**4.3**
Paper Roses—Lola Dee (55)	13
Arthur ALTMAN ▶ 871 (6)	**5099**
I Will Follow Him—Little Peggy March (63)	8660
All Alone Am I—Brenda Lee (62)	5503
Truly, Truly, True—Brenda Lee (65)	274
Am I A Toy Or A Treasure—Kay Starr (54)	233
It's Yours—DeCastro Sisters (56)	27
The Green Years—Eddie Fisher (54)	0.0
Sheron ALTON ▶ 4801 (1)	**411**
What About Love?—Heart (85)	1233

—Gerhard Altstedt see: Otto KOLLMAN	
—Jack Altwerger see: John ALTWERGER	
John ALTWERGER [Jack Altwerger, Georgie Auld] ▶ 9281 (1)	**27**
Bikini—Bikinis (58)	54
Tony ALVAREZ ▶ 8829 (1)	**38**
I'm Not Your Puppet—Hi-C (91)	115
Joey ALVES ▶ 8201 (1)	**58**
Summertime Girls—Y&T (85)	234
Alan ALY [Brandon Aly] ▶ 4891 (2)	**387**
What I Am—Edie Brickell & The New Bohemians (88)	1562
Circle—Edie Brickell & The New Bohemians (89)	371
—Brandon Aly see: Alan ALY	
Louis AMADE ▶ 11037 (1)	**3.7**
If Only I Could Live My Life Again—Jane Morgan (59)	15
Tommy AMATO ▶ 10766 (1)	**5.5**
A Broken Man—Malibu's (69)	16
—Opal Jean Amburgey see: Jean CHAPEL	
Nick AMENO ▶ 8371 (2)	**53**
Hot Shot—Buena Vistas (66)	80
Here Come Da Judge—Buena Vistas (68)	52
Morgan AMES ▶ 4238 (2)	**550**
Baretta's Theme ("Keep Your Eye On The Sparrow")—Rhythm Heritage (76)	*820*
Keep Your Eye On The Sparrow—Merry Clayton (75)	*280*
Nancy AMES ▶ 7928 (1)	**69**
Cinderella Rockafella—Esther & Abi Ofarim (68)	138
—Stuart Ames see: Stuart AVIG	
—Barbara Amesbury see: Bill AMESBURY	
Bill AMESBURY [Barbara Amesbury] ▶ 4924 (1)	**380**
Virginia (Touch Me Like You Do)—Bill Amesbury (74)	380
Tracey AMOS [Tracey Elizondo] ▶ 9221 (1)	**28**
Another Sleepless Night—Shawn Christopher (91)	57
Christina AMPHLETT ▶ 4344 (2)	**516**
I Touch Myself—Divinyls (91)	2042
Make Out Alright—Divinyls (91)	16
Antonio AMURRI ▶ 8424 (1)	**51**
Little Serenade—Teddy Randazzo (58)	*203*
—David Amy see: Bruce BROMBERG	
Bob ANCELL ▶ 10513 (1)	**7.7**
The Creature (From A Science Fiction Movie)—Buchanan & Ancell (57)	15
John ANDALORO ▶ 11586 (1)	**1.1**
Calico—Tommy James (73)	4.3
—Peter Anders see: Pete ANDREOLI	
Beth ANDERSEN ▶ 9410 (1)	**24**
Hold Me—Laura Branigan (85)	48
Tobias ANDERSEN [Tobias William Andersen, Toby Anderson] ▶ 7962 (1)	**67**
Misfit—Curiosity Killed The Cat (87)	336
Adrienne ANDERSON ▶ 1508 (7)	**2847**
Could It Be Magic—Barry Manilow (75)	*2240*
Deja Vu—Dionne Warwick (79)	1382
Some Kind Of Friend—Barry Manilow (83)	602
Daybreak—Barry Manilow (77)	595
Street Singin'—Lady Flash (76)	532
I Go To Rio—Pablo Cruise (79)	242
Could It Be Magic—Donna Summer (76)	*102*
Al ANDERSON ▶ 6407 (4)	**174**
And When She Smiles—Wildweeds (71)	63
No Good To Cry—Poppy Family (71)	*58*
No Good To Cry—Wildweeds (67)	*48*
Mare, Take Me Home—Matthews' Southern Comfort (71)	4.0
—André Cymone/Simon Anderson see: André CYMONE	
Bill ANDERSON ▶ 594 (28) HOF	**7335**
Still—Bill Anderson (63)	*2366*
Think I'll Go Somewhere And Cry Myself To Sleep—Al Martino (66)	683
My Whole World Is Falling Down—Brenda Lee (63)	623
Mama Sang A Song—Stan Kenton (62)	*600*
The Tips Of My Fingers—Roy Clark (63)	*568*
I Love You Drops—Vic Dana (66)	563
The Tip Of My Fingers—Eddy Arnold (66)	*476*
Mama Sang A Song—Walter Brennan (62)	*467*
Sometimes—Facts Of Life (77)	325

Bill ANDERSON ▶ 594 (28) HOF *Continued*	**7335**
I Missed Me—Jim Reeves (60)	253
8 x 10—Bill Anderson (63)	245
City Lights—Debbie Reynolds (60)	*143*
The Lord Knows I'm Drinking—Cal Smith (73)	90
Tip Of My Fingers—Nick Noble (60)	*90*
Losing Your Love—Jim Reeves (61)	60
Saginaw, Michigan—Lefty Frizzell (64)	53
Mama Sang A Song—Bill Anderson (62)	*37*
Still No. 2—Ben Colder (63)	*36*
Still—Sunrays (66)	*36*
City Lights—Ray Price (58)	*32*
City Lights—Don Rondo (58)	*23*
Slippin' Away—Jean Shepard (73)	19
Riverboat—Faron Young (60)	18
It's Not The End Of Everything—Tommy Edwards (60)	17
I Can't Wait Any Longer—Bill Anderson (78)	16
Where Have All Our Heroes Gone—Bill Anderson (70)	6.7
Once A Day—Connie Smith (64)	5.0
City Lights—Ivory Joe Hunter (59)	*4.6*
—E. Anderson see: Chuck BERRY	
Ed ANDERSON ▶ 7328 (1)	**102**
Flamingo L'Amore—Gaylords (58)	*204*
Gary ANDERSON [Gary "U. S." Bonds] ▶ 823 (9)	**5342**
Quarter To Three—U.S. Bonds (61)	8470
School Is Out—Gary (U.S.) Bonds (61)	3371
Not Me—Orlons (63)	1322
She's All I Got—Freddie North (71)	*694*
School Is In—Gary (U.S.) Bonds (61)	434
To The Other Woman (I'm The Other Woman)—Doris Duke (70)	369
She Didn't Know (She Kept On Talking)—Dee Dee Warwick (70)	308
Feet Start Walking—Doris Duke (70)	45
She's All I Got—Johnny Paycheck (71)	*8.0*
Ian ANDERSON ▶ 1283 (8)	**3457**
Bungle In The Jungle—Jethro Tull (74)	1537
Living In The Past—Jethro Tull (72)	1365
The Whistler—Jethro Tull (77)	179
A Passion Play (Edit #8)—Jethro Tull (73)	149
Locomotive Breath—Jethro Tull (76)	145
Hymn 43—Jethro Tull (71)	43
Minstrel In The Gallery—Jethro Tull (75)	28
Skating Away On The Thin Ice Of The New Day—Jethro Tull (75)	24
Jesse ANDERSON ▶ 7874 (4)	**71**
Sweetest One—Metros (67)	63
Come On Sock It To Me—Syl Johnson (67)	14
I Got A Problem—Jesse Anderson (70)	5.1
Believe In Me Baby - Part 1—Jesse James (67)	4.3
John David ANDERSON ▶ 5558 (1)	**271**
Swingin'—John Anderson (83)	543
John Vernon ANDERSON ▶ 6101 (3)	**206**
There's Nothing Better Than Love—Luther Vandross (Duet With Gregory Hines) (87)	326
Crazy—Manhattans (83)	76
Kid Stuff—Lenny White (80)	21
John W. ANDERSON [John William Anderson, John Kasandra] ▶ 9199 (2)	**29**
Trouble Down Here Below—Lou Rawls (67)	23
Don't Pat Me On The Back And Call Me Brother—John W. Anderson Presents KaSandra (68)	5.9
—John Roy Anderson see: Jon ANDERSON	
—John William Anderson see: John W. ANDERSON	
Jon ANDERSON [John Roy Anderson] ▶ 1248 (9)	**3587**
Owner Of A Lonely Heart—Yes (83)	6336
Roundabout—Yes (72)	1487
Your Move—Yes (71)	666
And You And I (Part I)—Yes (72)	447
State Of Independence—Donna Summer (82)	320
Rhythm Of Love—Yes (87)	310
I'll Find My Way Home—Jon & Vangelis (82)	250
It Can Happen—Yes (84)	168
I Hear You Now—Jon And Vangelis (80)	157
—Katherine Anderson see: Katherine SCHAFFNER	
Keith ANDERSON [Bob Andy] ▶ 9223 (1)	**28**
Too Experienced—Eddie Lovette (69)	57
Leroy ANDERSON ▶ 2722 (5) HOF	**1242**
Blue Tango—Bill Black's Combo (60)	1058

Serenata—Sarah Vaughan (60)	112
Forgotten Dreams—Leroy Anderson And His "Pops" Concert Orchestra (57)	*64*
Forgotten Dreams—Cyril Stapleton And His Orchestra (57)	*64*
Forgotten Dreams—Frederick Fennell (57)	*0.0*
Lewis J. ANDERSON ▶ 10854 (1)	**4.9**
Whatever Happened To Old Fashioned Love—B.J. Thomas (83)	4.9
Liz ANDERSON [Elizabeth Jane Haaby] ▶ 4624 (1)	**449**
Ride, Ride, Ride—Brenda Lee (67)	449
Maxi ANDERSON ▶ 8704 (1)	**42**
99 1/2—Carol Lynn Townes (84)	85
Maxwell ANDERSON ▶ 6023 (2)	**215**
September Song—Jimmy Durante (63)	*333*
September Song—Roy Clark (69)	*98*
Melvin ANDERSON [Ade Olayinka] ▶ 4836 (1)	**401**
I Wonder Why—Dion and The Belmonts (58)	802
Rick ANDERSON ▶ 8492 (2)	**48**
Don't Want To Wait Anymore—Tubes (81)	377
Piece By Piece—Tubes (85)	10
Sonny ANDERSON [Walter B. Anderson] ▶ 11784 (1)	**0.0**
Surfer's Stomp—Kay Bell and The Tuffs (62)	0.0
Stig ANDERSON ▶ 965 (10)	**4640**
Dancing Queen—Abba (76)	4560
Waterloo—Abba (Björn, Benny, Anna & Frida) (74)	1880
SOS—Abba (75)	1587
Fernando—Abba (76)	1489
Knowing Me, Knowing You—Abba (77)	1220
I Do, I Do, I Do, I Do, I Do—Abba (76)	1023
The Name Of The Game—Abba (77)	988
Mamma Mia—Abba (76)	636
Honey, Honey—Abba (74)	*432*
Honey Honey—Sweet Dreams (74)	*108*
Terry ANDERSON ▶ 9752 (1)	**18**
Battleship Chains—Georgia Satellites (87)	18
—Toby Anderson see: Tobias ANDERSEN	
—Walter B. Anderson see: Sonny ANDERSON	
William ANDERSON ▶ 6391 (1)	**176**
Dancin'—Crown Heights Affair (77)	176
Benny ANDERSSON ▶ 448 (24)	**9257**
Dancing Queen—Abba (76)	4560
Take A Chance On Me—ABBA (78)	2866
One Night In Bangkok—Murray Head (85)	*2683*
Waterloo—Abba (Björn, Benny, Anna & Frida) (74)	1880
The Winner Takes It All—ABBA (80)	1780
SOS—Abba (75)	1587
Fernando—Abba (76)	1489
Knowing Me, Knowing You—Abba (77)	1220
Does Your Mother Know—ABBA (79)	1098
I Do, I Do, I Do, I Do, I Do—Abba (76)	1023
The Name Of The Game—Abba (77)	988
Mamma Mia—Abba (76)	636
Chiquitita—ABBA (79)	490
When All Is Said And Done—ABBA (82)	452
Honey, Honey—Abba (74)	*432*
Super Trouper—ABBA (81)	194
Money, Money, Money—ABBA (77)	193
Honey Honey—Sweet Dreams (74)	*108*
Lay All Your Love On Me—Information Society (89)	105
The Visitors—ABBA (82)	95
Angeleyes—ABBA (79)	95
One Night In Bangkok—Robey (85)	*55*
Voulez-Vous—ABBA (79)	29
On And On And On—ABBA (81)	12
Mark ANDES ▶ 8484 (2)	**48**
How Can I Refuse—Heart (83)	279
Mechanical World—Spirit (68)	4.1
Matt ANDES ▶ 5172 (1)	**332**
Run Run Run—Jo Jo Gunne (72)	663
—Bonita Ann Andre see: Bonita DONATO	
Fabian ANDRE ▶ 3945 (1)	**645**
Dream A Little Dream Of Me—Mama Cass With The Mamas & The Papas (68)	1936
Mike ANDRE [Michael Joseph Apruzzese] ▶ 11768 (1)	**0.1**
Tic-A-Tee, Tik-A-Tay—Dean Martin (62)	0.4

Ronald ANDRE [Ronald Lawrence Andre, Ronald Lawrence] ▶ 9334 (1)	**26**
Oowee, Oowee—Perry Como (65)	104
Pete ANDREOLI [Peter Anders] ▶ 3123 (8)	**997**
New York's A Lonely Town—Trade Winds (65)	551
Do I Love You?—Ronettes (64)	*462*
(The Best Part Of) Breakin' Up—Ronettes (64)	369
Mind Excursion—Trade Winds (66)	367
Bad Misunderstanding—Critters (66)	321
Mister Lonely—Videls (60)	152
Do I Love You?—Magic Ring (68)	*56*
Now That Summer Is Here—Videls (60)	13
Phillip ANDREULA ▶ 4897 (2)	**386**
Bad Of The Heart—George LaMond (90)	592
Look Into My Eyes—George LaMond (90)	179
Chris Frederick ANDREWS ▶ 2762 (6)	**1213**
It's Alright—Adam Faith With The Roulettes (65)	594
Girl Don't Come—Sandie Shaw (65)	522
Yesterday Man—Chris Andrews (65)	51
Free—Pearly Gate (69)	24
Long Live Love—Sandie Shaw (65)	14
Talk About Love—Adam Faith (65)	8.4
Jack ANDREWS ▶ 4395 (1)	**506**
Underwater—Frogmen (61)	506
Lee ANDREWS [Arthur Lee Andrew Thompson] ▶ 4243 (7)	**547**
Long Lonely Nights—Bobby Vinton (65)	*1021*
Long Lonely Nights—Clyde McPhatter (57)	*517*
Long Lonely Nights—Lee Andrews And The Hearts (57)	*429*
Long Lonely Nights—Dells (70)	*187*
Long Lonely Nights—4 Seasons (64)	*34*
Long, Lonely Nights—Kings (2) (57)	*0.0*
Long Lonely Nights—Kitty Kallen (57)	*0.0*
Maggie ANDREWS [Bud Birmingham, Carson J. Robison, Harry "Rocky" Wilson] ▶ 8531 (1)	**47**
New River Train—Bobby Helms (59)	47
Melanie ANDREWS ▶ 3347 (2)	**887**
Let's Wait Awhile—Janet Jackson (87)	2779
Just Want To Hold You—Jasmine Guy (91)	578
Reggie ANDREWS ▶ 2998 (1)	**1073**
Let It Whip—Dazz Band (82)	2147
Tony ANDREWS ▶ 6214 (1)	**193**
Just Want To Hold You—Jasmine Guy (91)	578
—Andre Andrians see: Paul SEBASTIAN	
—Lina Andrians see: Lana SEBASTIAN	
Alma Bazel ANDROZZO ▶ 6563 (1)	**156**
If I Can Help Somebody—Billy Eckstine (57)	156
—Patricia Andrzejewski see: Pat BENATAR	
—Bob Andy see: Keith ANDERSON	
—Ish Angel see: Ish LEDESMA	
Judy Hart ANGELO ▶ 9651 (1)	**20**
Theme from the TV Show Cheers (Where Everybody Knows Your Name)—Gary Portnoy (83)	39
Bill ANGELOS ▶ 5068 (1)	**350**
One More Time—Ray Charles Singers (64)	701
Maya ANGELOU [Dr. Marguerite Ann Johnson] ▶ 7481 (2)	**93**
You Put It On Me—B.B. King (68)	159
The B.B. Jones—B.B. King (68)	26
Jim ANGLIN ▶ 9260 (1)	**28**
Jealousy—Kitty Wells (58)	28
Héctor ANGULO ▶ 5020 (1)	**358**
Guantanamera—Sandpipers (66)	2149
Luis ANGULO ▶ 8708 (1)	**42**
Oh Lord, Why Lord—Los Pop Tops (68)	125
Victor ANGULO ▶ 10370 (1)	**9.4**
Because Of You—Kracker (72)	47
Colin ANGUS ▶ 6594 (1)	**153**
Move Any Mountain—Shamen (91)	459
Ron ANIELLO [Raun] ▶ 10675 (1)	**6.2**
Am I Forgiven—Isle Of Man (86)	12
Fred ANISFIELD ▶ 4926 (2)	**380**
Backstage—Gene Pitney (66)	697
Does He Really Care For Me—Ruby And The Romantics (65)	62
Paul ANKA [Dee Marak] ▶ 16 (72) HOF	**67142**
Lonely Boy—Paul Anka (59)	*9133*
Put Your Head On My Shoulder—Paul Anka (59)	*7103*

Paul ANKA [Dee Marak] ► 16 (72) HOF	
Continued	**67142**
Diana—Paul Anka (57)	*6742*
She's A Lady—Tom Jones (71)	6556
(You're) Having My Baby—Paul Anka (74)	5226
Puppy Love—Paul Anka (60)	*4237*
Puppy Love—Donny Osmond (72)	*3699*
It's Time To Cry—Paul Anka (59)	3156
My Home Town—Paul Anka (60)	2141
One Man Woman/One Woman Man—Paul Anka with Odia Coates (74)	2087
I Don't Like To Sleep Alone—Paul Anka (75)	2035
Love Me Warm And Tender—Paul Anka (62)	1750
Tonight My Love, Tonight—Paul Anka (61)	1650
You Are My Destiny—Paul Anka (57)	1535
(I Believe) There's Nothing Stronger Than Our Love—Paul Anka With Odia Coates (75)	1370
Dance On Little Girl—Paul Anka (61)	1368
Summer's Gone—Paul Anka (60)	1119
It Doesn't Matter Anymore—Buddy Holly / The Crickets (59)	*1028*
A Steel Guitar And A Glass Of Wine—Paul Anka (62)	1001
The Story Of My Love—Paul Anka (61)	878
Let The Bells Keep Ringing—Paul Anka (58)	792
My Way—Frank Sinatra (69)	*701*
Teddy—Connie Francis (60)	701
Love (Makes The World Go 'round)—Paul Anka (63)	630
Put Your Head On My Shoulder—Lettermen (68)	*571*
Crazy Love—Paul Anka (58)	553
My Way—Elvis Presley (77)	*551*
Hold Me 'til The Morning Comes—Paul Anka (83)	477
Do I Love You—Paul Anka (71)	*446*
Remember Diana—Paul Anka (63)	417
Train Of Love—Annette With The Afterbeats (60)	416
I Love You In The Same Old Way—Paul Anka (60)	330
Anytime (I'll Be There)—Paul Anka (76)	*295*
Every Night (Without You)—Paul Anka (62)	278
My Way—Brook Benton (70)	*250*
Jubilation—Paul Anka (72)	247
Let Me Get To Know You—Paul Anka (73)	204
Midnight—Paul Anka (58)	195
I Love You Baby—Paul Anka (57)	188
Everything's Been Changed—5th Dimension (73)	178
Let Me Try Again (Laisse Moi Le Temps)—Frank Sinatra (73)	148
Cinderella—Paul Anka (61)	143
Put Your Head On My Shoulder—Leif Garrett (78)	*137*
Happier—Paul Anka (76)	102
Tell Me That You Love Me—Paul Anka (57)	91
This Is Your Song—Don Goodwin (73)	89
Don't Ever Leave Me—Paul Anka (59)	87
Hello Jim—Paul Anka (63)	74
Broken Heart And A Pillow Filled With Tears—Patti Page (61)	52
Talk To Me Baby—Annette With The Afterbeats (60)	52
Anytime (I'll Be There)—Frank Sinatra (75)	*48*
Everybody Ought To Be In Love—Paul Anka (77)	42
My Best Friend's Wife—Paul Anka (77)	41
Did You Have A Happy Birthday?—Paul Anka (63)	39
Don't Leave Me In The Morning—Odia Coates (75)	35
(I'm Watching) Every Little Move You Make—Little Peggy March (64)	33
Loveland—Paul Anka (61)	33
Kiss Tomorrow Goodbye—Lainie Kazan (67)	31
It Doesn't Matter Anymore—Linda Ronstadt (75)	*25*
I Don't Need You Anymore—Together? With Jackie DeShannon (80)	25
Your Love—Paul Anka (59)	11
Fools Hall Of Fame—Paul Anka (62)	10
Adam And Eve—Paul Anka (60)	8.5
The Longest Day—Mitch Miller With His Orchestra and Chorus (62)	5.8
Brought Up In New York (Brought Down In L.A.)—Paul Anka (78)	5.4
Don't Say You're Sorry—Paul Anka (61)	4.2
I'm Coming Home—Paul Anka (62)	3.1
Far From The Lights Of Town—Paul Anka (62)	2.7
Do I Love You (Yes In Every Way)—Donna Fargo (78)	*2.7*
Diana—Bobby Rydell (65)	*1.9*
The Bells At My Wedding—Paul Anka (61)	1.2
Lonely Boy—Donny Osmond (72)	*0.0*
Tex ANN [Judy Hayden] ► 9400 (1)	**24**
Muskrat—Everly Brothers (61)	98

John ANNARINO ► 9775 (1)	**17**
Take Life A Little Easier—Rodney Allen Rippy (73)	34
Bill ANSON [Gerry Manners] ► 11785 (1)	**0.0**
The Man Upstairs—Kay Starr (54)	0.0
—Robert Anson see: Philamore LINCOLN	
Adam ANT [Stuart Leslie Goddard] ► 2592 (4)	**1345**
Goody Two Shoes—Adam Ant (82)	1666
Room At The Top—Adam Ant (90)	808
Strip—Adam Ant (84)	350
Desperate But Not Serious—Adam Ant (83)	135
Pete ANTEL [Pete Antell, Peter Blaise Antonio] ► 6085 (3)	**208**
What Are Boys Made Of—Percells (63)	319
Night Time—Pete Antell (62)	93
Yo Me Pregunto—Valrays (64)	4.5
—Pete Antell see: Pete ANTEL	
C. Mark ANTHONY ► 7781 (2)	**75**
Down To The Line—Bachman-Turner Overdrive (75)	290
All The Kids On The Street—Hollywood Stars (77)	5.5
John David ANTHONY ► 5433 (1)	**290**
Keep On Smilin'—Wet Willie (74)	1449
John M. ANTHONY ► 11055 (2)	**3.5**
Where Can You Be—Don Cherry (54)	*11*
Where Can You Be—Jerry Martin (54)	*0.0*
Malcolm ANTHONY [Zyah Ahmonue] ► 7899 (2)	**70**
I Gotta Keep Dancin'—Carrie (77)	62
Olivia (Lost And Turned Out)—Whispers (78)	8.5
—Marc/Mark Anthony see: Mark MUNIZ	
—Mark Anthony see: Tony HATCH	
Michael ANTHONY [Michael Anthony Sobolewski] ► 930 (17)	**4760**
Jump—Van Halen (84)	6595
Why Can't This Be Love—Van Halen (86)	3498
When It's Love—Van Halen (88)	1533
Finish What Ya Started—Van Halen (88)	1115
Panama—Van Halen (84)	1026
I'll Wait—Van Halen (84)	975
Dance The Night Away—Van Halen (79)	922
Top Of The World—Van Halen (91)	819
Love Walks In—Van Halen (86)	778
Dreams—Van Halen (86)	588
Feels So Good—Van Halen (89)	435
Black And Blue—Van Halen (88)	288
And The Cradle Will Rock...—Van Halen (80)	183
Hot For Teacher—Van Halen (84)	182
Beautiful Girls—Van Halen (79)	61
Best Of Both Worlds—Van Halen (86)	29
Runnin' With The Devil—Van Halen (78)	12
Mike ANTHONY [Michael Logiudice] ► 956 (6)	**4671**
Poetry In Motion—Johnny Tillotson (60)	5448
She Say (Oom Dooby Doom)—Diamonds (59)	1292
I'll Never Dance Again—Bobby Rydell (62)	1211
The Grass Is Greener—Brenda Lee (63)	899
Every Little Thing I Do—Dion and The Belmonts (59)	373
Ronnie, Call Me When You Get A Chance—Shelley Fabares (63)	119
Ray ANTHONY [Raymond Antonini] ► 8904 (1)	**36**
Bunny Hop—Applejacks (S) (59)	73
Emil ANTON ► 3078 (2)	**1024**
Dear Lonely Hearts—Nat King Cole (62)	1571
Going Going Gone—Brook Benton (64)	477
Otis ANTONELLI ► 10702 (1)	**6.0**
Jupiter-C—Pat and the Satellites (59)	18
—Raymond Antonini see: Ray ANTHONY	
—Peter Blaise Antonio see: Pete ANTEL	
Anthony ANTONUCCI ► 4391 (3)	**507**
Philadelphia USA—Nu Tornados (58)	*981*
Philadelphia USA—Art Lund (58)	*32*
Philadelphia U.S.A.—Milton DeLugg & His Orchestra (58)	*0.0*
—Benjamin Anzelevitz see: Ben BERNIE	
—Luca Anzilotti see: John Virgo GARRETT III	
Biddu APPAIAH ► 6795 (4)	**136**
Dance The Kung Fu—Carl Douglas (75)	246
Jump For Joy—Biddu Orchestra (76)	15
I Am Somebody—Jimmy James & The Vagabonds (76)	5.6

Dance Little Lady Dance—Danny White (77)	0.6
Mike APPEL ► 2287 (2)	**1651**
Doesn't Somebody Want To Be Wanted—Partridge Family Starring Shirley Jones & Featuring David Cassidy (71)	4568
A Question Of Temperature—Balloon Farm (68)	385
Dave APPELL [David Leon Appell, Dave Leon] ► 86 (50)	**26665**
Bristol Stomp—Dovells (61)	6389
The Wah-Watusi—Orlons (62)	5536
Wild One—Bobby Rydell (60)	4945
Let's Twist Again—Chubby Checker (61)	*3771*
South Street—Orlons (63)	3753
Don't Hang Up—Orlons (62)	3423
Swingin' School—Bobby Rydell (60)	2224
Ride!—Dee Dee Sharp (62)	2161
Popeye The Hitchhiker—Chubby Checker (62)	1843
Good Time Baby—Bobby Rydell (61)	1828
Gravy (For My Mashed Potatoes)—Dee Dee Sharp (62)	1715
Loddy Lo—Chubby Checker (63)	1447
Do The Bird—Dee Dee Sharp (63)	1407
The Cha-Cha-Cha—Bobby Rydell (62)	1405
Dancin' Party—Chubby Checker (62)	1242
Let's Limbo Some More—Chubby Checker (63)	1110
Ding A Ling—Bobby Rydell (60)	936
Dance The Mess Around—Chubby Checker (61)	912
Mornin' Beautiful—Tony Orlando & Dawn (75)	898
Hey, Bobba Needle—Chubby Checker (64)	888
Hully Gully Baby—Dovells (62)	838
Crossfire!—Orlons (63)	821
The Fish—Bobby Rydell (61)	799
I Wanna Thank You—Bobby Rydell (61)	781
Butterfly Baby—Bobby Rydell (63)	757
Wildwood Days—Bobby Rydell (63)	674
Twist It Up—Chubby Checker (63)	596
Wild!—Dee Dee Sharp (63)	555
Do The New Continental—Dovells (62)	542
Let's Do The Freddie—Chubby Checker (65)	474
Rocka Conga—Applejacks (S) (58)	423
Rock Me In The Cradle Of Love—Dee Dee Sharp (63)	350
Betty In Bermudas—Dovells (63)	345
Bon-Doo-Wah—Orlons (63)	289
Surf Party—Chubby Checker (63)	241
She Wants T' Swim—Chubby Checker (64)	241
The Popeye Waddle—Don Covay (62)	223
Lose Her—Bobby Rydell (62)	140
Rules Of Love—Orlons (64)	97
Cherié—Bobby Rydell (61)	89
Teach Me To Twist—Bobby Rydell - Chubby Checker (62)	84
Let's Twist Again—Jive Bunny And The Mastermixers (89)	*80*
Where Did I Go Wrong—Dee Dee Sharp (64)	39
Mother, Please!—Jo Ann Campbell (63)	20
House Of Strangers—Jim Gilstrap (75)	12
Lets Twist Again—Jive Bunny & The Mastermixers (90)	*6.7*
Stop Monkeyin' Aroun'—Dovells (63)	6.3
Jingle Bells Imitations—Bobby Rydell - Chubby Checker (61)	*3.3*
Mexican Hat Twist—Applejacks (S) (61)	2.8
Gee, It's Wonderful—Bobby Rydell (62)	2.2
Carmine APPICE ► 1217 (5)	**3663**
Da Ya Think I'm Sexy?—Rod Stewart (78)	*8390*
Young Turks—Rod Stewart (81)	3203
Do You Think I'm Disco?—Steve Dahl And Teenage Radiation (79)	*131*
Where Is My Mind—Vanilla Fudge (68)	71
Need Love—Vanilla Fudge (69)	16
Harris APPLE ► 11509 (1)	**1.4**
What Do You Know About Love—Apple & Appleberry (74)	2.8
Stanley APPLEBAUM ► 6395 (2)	**175**
Passing Strangers—Sarah Vaughan & Billy Eckstine (57)	328
Wrong Again—Ames Brothers (55)	22
Bobby Ray APPLEBERRY ► 11405 (2)	**1.9**
What Do You Know About Love—Apple & Appleberry (74)	2.8
Air Travel—Ray And Bob (62)	0.9

Mary APPLEGATE [Mary Susan Applegate, Mary Klopprogge] ▶ 5787 (3) 241
Power Of Love—Laura Branigan (87) 653
The Power Of Love—Jennifer Rush (86) 248
The Power Of Love (You Are My Lady)—Air Supply (85) 65

—Michael Joseph Apruzzese see: Mike ANDRE

William AQUART ▶ 9430 (1) 24
My Fantasy—Teddy Riley featuring Guy (89) 71

Fernando ARBEX ▶ 2990 (2) 1078
Hijack—Herbie Mann (75) 825
Louisianna—Mike Kennedy (72) 253

Judith ARBUCKLE ▶ 8227 (1) 58
Anyone Who Knows What Love Is (Will Understand)—Irma Thomas (64) 231

Steve ARCAND ▶ 10738 (1) 5.6
Biscuit's In The House—Biscuit (90) 34

Ramon ARCUSA [Ramon Arcusa Alcón, Ray Blum, Sirarcusa] ▶ 10980 (1) 4.0
He Gives Me Love (La La La)—Lesley Gore (68) 12

Neal ARDEN ▶ 8590 (1) 45
Forgive Me—Kitty Kallen (55) 91

—Rodd Arden see: Dave SILVER

Nicolas ARDITI ▶ 10113 (1) 13
Golly—Four Lads (57) 50

Gianni ARGENIO ▶ 6712 (1) 142
The Way It Used To Be—Engelbert Humperdinck (69) 711

Rod ARGENT ▶ 205 (10) 15435
She's Not There—Zombies (64) 5974
Time Of The Season—Zombies (69) 4521
Hold Your Head Up—Argent (72) 2531
Tell Her No—Zombies (65) 2187
She's Not There—Santana (77) 677
Tell Her No—Juice Newton (83) 483
She's Coming Home—Zombies (65) 256
Imagine The Swan—Zombies (69) 45
She's Not There—Road (69) 35
I Want You Back Again—Zombies (65) 15

Michael ARGUE ▶ 11760 (1) 0.2
Make My Life A Little Bit Brighter—Chester (73) 0.4

Alan ARKIN ▶ 1712 (4) 2448
Banana Boat Song—Tarriers (56) 4406
Banana Boat Song—Fontane Sisters (56) 1239
Banana Boat Song—Steve Lawrence (56) 939
Banana Boat Song—Sarah Vaughan (56) 758

David ARKIN ▶ 1831 (1) 2241
Black And White—Three Dog Night (72) 4482

Robert ARKIN ▶ 5457 (3) 284
The Touchables—Dickie Goodman (61) 620
The Touchables In Brooklyn—Dickie Goodman (61) 231
Santa & The Touchables—Dickie Goodman (61) 0.9

Harold ARLEN [Hyman Arluck] ▶ 1112 (18) HOF 3994
That Old Black Magic—Louis Prima And Keely Smith (58) 1560
Ding Dong! The Witch Is Dead—Fifth Estate (67) 1521
Over The Rainbow—Demensions (60) 1404
That Old Black Magic—Bobby Rydell (61) 886
Let's Fall In Love—Peaches & Herb (66) 707
That Old Black Magic—Sammy Davis Jr. (55) 614
Themes From The Wizard Of Oz—Meco (78) 477
One For My Baby (And One More For The Road)—Tony Bennett with Ray Conniff (57) 254
Come Rain Or Come Shine—Ray Charles (60) 160
Come Rain Or Come Shine—Rosemary Clooney (56) 124
Come Rain Or Come Shine—Jerry Lewis (56) 124
Over The Rainbow—Gary Tanner (78) 109
The Gal That Got Away—Frank Sinatra (54) 37
Old Black Magic—Clovers (59) 4.4
Come Rain Or Come Shine—Ray Charles (68) 1.8
Let's Fall In Love—Linda Scott (63) 1.8
Over The Rainbow—Baysiders (60) 0.0
The Man That Got Away—Jeri Southern (54) 0.0

George ARLOTTA ▶ 11388 (1) 1.9
Gift Of Love—Van Dykes (1) (61) 5.8

—Hyman Arluck see: Harold ARLEN

—George Armand see: Joe REISMAN

Renée ARMAND ▶ 7293 (2) 105
One Day In Your Life—Michael Jackson (81) 181
I'll Have To Go Away—Skylark (73) 29

Antonina ARMATO ▶ 1414 (6) 3139
She Ain't Worth It—Glenn Medeiros featuring Bobby Brown (90) 3857
I'll Get By—Eddie Money (91) 1367
I Still Believe—Brenda K. Starr (88) 1275
What Comes Naturally—Sheena Easton (91) 804
All I'm Missing Is You—Glenn Medeiros (90) 439
I've Been Waiting For You—Guys Next Door (90) 277

Joan ARMATRADING ▶ 8018 (1) 65
Drop The Pilot—Joan Armatrading (83) 65

Andy ARMER ▶ 1477 (2) 2943
Rise—Herb Alpert (79) 5495
Rotation—Herb Alpert (79) 391

—Reginald Moxon Armitage see: Noel GAY

Jo ARMSTEAD ▶ 3004 (12) 1072
Let's Go Get Stoned—Ray Charles Band With The Raelets (66) 900
Jealous Kind Of Fella—Garland Green (69) 810
Casonova (Your Playing Days Are Over)—Ruby Andrews (67) 506
One Step At A Time—Maxine Brown (65) 417
Silly Wasn't I—Valerie Simpson (72) 184
Drop By My Place—Little Carl Carlton (70) 140
I Don't Need No Doctor—Humble Pie (71) 120
I Don't Need No Doctor—New Riders Of The Purple Sage (72) 50
I Don't Need No Doctor—Ray Charles And His Orchestra (66) 48
The Real Thing—Tina Britt (65) 27
Come On Sock It To Me—Syl Johnson (67) 14
Never Had It So Good—Ronnie Milsap (65) 6.7

Charles ARMSTRONG ▶ 8924 (1) 36
What You Got—Duke & The Drivers (75) 36

—Chris Armstrong see: Lester POWELL

Herbie ARMSTRONG ▶ 10717 (1) 5.9
Bad Little Woman—Shadows Of Knight (66) 30

Lillian Hardin ARMSTRONG [Lillian Hardin] ▶ 4158 (3) 577
Bad Boy—Jive Bombers (57) 568
Sweet Lips—Jaye P. Morgan (56) 13
Struttin' With Some Barbecue—Louis Armstrong and Gary Crosby (55) 7.0

Tyrone ARMSTRONG ▶ 11307 (1) 2.3
Freedom—Grandmaster Flash And The Furious 5 (80) 21

William ARMSTRONG ▶ 3610 (1) 768
Slip Away—Clarence Carter (68) 2304

Felix ARNDT ▶ 4932 (2) 379
Nola—Billy Williams (59) 777
Nola—Morgan Brothers (59) 360

Nola ARNDT ▶ 4933 (2) 379
Nola—Billy Williams (59) 777
Nola—Morgan Brothers (59) 360

Gus ARNHEIM ▶ 9829 (1) 16
Sweet And Lovely—April Stevens & Nino Tempo (62) 49

Bruce ARNOLD ▶ 4405 (3) 504
Can't Find The Time—Rose Colored Glass (71) 376
Can't Find The Time—Orpheus (69) 112
Can't Find The Time—Orpheus (68) 16

Calvin ARNOLD ▶ 7441 (1) 96
Funky Way—Calvin Arnold (68) 96

Chris ARNOLD ▶ 1927 (4) 2096
Can't Smile Without You—Barry Manilow (78) 5240
Annabella—Hamilton, Joe Frank & Reynolds (71) 460
Can't You Hear The Song?—Wayne Newton (72) 435
It's Up To You Petula—Edison Lighthouse (71) 153

Eddy ARNOLD ▶ 1323 (9) 3356
You Don't Know Me—Ray Charles (62) 3379
You Don't Know Me—Jerry Vale (56) 2007
You Don't Know Me—Lenny Welch (60) 401
You Don't Know Me—Elvis Presley With The Jordanaires (67) 383
That's How Much I Love You—Pat Boone (58) 361
You Don't Know Me—Mickey Gilley (81) 297
That Do Make It Nice—Eddy Arnold (55) 6.5
You Don't Know Me—Carmen McRae (56) 0.0
You Don't Know Me—Eddy Arnold (56) 0.0

—James Arnold see: Kokomo ARNOLD

Jerry ARNOLD ▶ 9187 (2) 29
Percolatin'—Willie Mitchell (64) 23
Little Boy Blue—Huelyn Duvall (59) 12

Kokomo ARNOLD [James Arnold] ▶ 9273 (1) 27
Milk Cow Blues—Ricky Nelson (60) 27

Malcolm ARNOLD ▶ 3522 (8) 801
March From The River Kwai—Mitch Miller And His Orchestra (57) 631
Lisa—Ferrante & Teicher (62) 100
Lola's Theme—Muir Mathieson (56) 40
Lola's Theme—Steve Allen (56) 21
The River Kwai March—Art Mooney And His Orchestra (57) 8.7
March From The River Kwai—David Terry & His Orchestra (58) 0.0
Lola's Theme—Ralph Marterie & His Orchestra (56) 0.0
River Kwai March—Carlson's Raiders (57) 0.0

Sidney ARODIN [Sidney Arnondin] ▶ 3268 (4) 920
Lazy River—Bobby Darin (61) 1246
Up A Lazy River—Si Zentner And His Orchestra (61) 547
Lazy River—Roberta Sherwood (56) 46
Lazy River—Cathy Ryan (56) 0.0

—Victor Aronson see: Ted KELLEM

—Peter Arpadys see: Pierre-Alain DAHAN

Charles ARRINGTON ▶ 6280 (1) 186
Lumberjack—Brook Benton (64) 372

India ARRINGTON ▶ 8760 (1) 40
Dancin' In The Key Of Life—Steve Arrington (85) 80

—Joseph Arrington Jr. see: Joe TEX

Marshall ARRINGTON ▶ 8606 (1) 45
You Got To Be The One—Chi-Lites (74) 90

Steve ARRINGTON ▶ 7726 (4) 78
Watching You—Slave (80) 129
Dancin' In The Key Of Life—Steve Arrington (85) 80
Snap Shot—Slave (81) 53
Just A Touch Of Love—Slave (80) 10

Brooks ARTHUR [Arnold Brodsky] ▶ 8988 (1) 34
That's How Much—Brian Hyland (60) 102

Jacky ARTHUR ▶ 7930 (1) 69
(I Remember) Summer Morning—Vanity Fare (70) 138

Jeff ARTHUR ▶ 10400 (1) 8.9
Sunshine Ship—Arthur, Hurley & Gottlieb (73) 8.9

Wayne ARTHUR ▶ 11578 (1) 1.1
Boys Do Cry—Joe Bennett And The Sparkletones (59) 2.3

Andy ARTHURS ▶ 7858 (1) 72
Goin' Down (On The Road To L.A.)—Terry Black And Laurel Ward (72) 216

Bobby ARVON [Robert Anthony Arvonio] ▶ 6315 (1) 182
Until Now—Bobby Arvon (77) 182

—Robert Anthony Arvonio see: Bobby ARVON

Ken ASCHER ▶ 2654 (5) 1291
You And Me Against The World—Helen Reddy (74) 1819
Rainbow Connection—Kermit (Jim Henson) (79) 539
Watch Closely Now—Kris Kristofferson (77) 164
Inspiration—Paul Williams (73) 56
With You—Moments (2) (76) 4.5

Robert ASCHER ▶ 2424 (1) 1499
Tracy's Theme—Spencer Ross (59) 1499

Daniel ASH ▶ 3615 (2) 765
So Alive—Love and Rockets (89) 2251
No Big Deal—Love and Rockets (89) 44

Irving ASHBY ▶ 8507 (2) 48
Loco-Motion—Joe "Fingers" Carr (57) 48
Loco Motion—Irving Ashby (57) 48

Reginald ASHBY ▶ 11475 (1) 1.5
Boogie Woogie Country Girl—Southwind (70) 3.1

Clarence ASHE ▶ 9610 (1) 20
Trouble I've Had—Clarence Ashe (64) 20

Peter ASHER ▶ 9347 (1) 26
Don't Pity Me—Peter And Gordon (65) 51

Tony ASHER ▶ 2676 (6) 1279
Wouldn't It Be Nice—Beach Boys (66) 2149
Caroline, No—Brian Wilson (66) 518
God Only Knows—Beach Boys (66) 484
God Only Knows—Marilyn Scott (77) 97
God Only Knows—Vogues (70) 26
Wouldn't It Be Nice—Cantina Band (81) 1.5

Nick ASHFORD ▶ 220 (50) HOF	**15121**
Ain't No Mountain High Enough—Diana Ross (70)	*6311*
Your Precious Love— Marvin Gaye & Tammi Terrell (67)	2938
Ain't Nothing Like The Real Thing— Marvin Gaye & Tammi Terrell (68)	*2127*
You're All I Need To Get By— Marvin Gaye & Tammi Terrell (68)	*2011*
Remember Me—Diana Ross (70)	1429
Solid—Ashford & Simpson (84)	1266
Ain't No Mountain High Enough— Marvin Gaye & Tammi Terrell (67)	*1259*
Reach Out And Touch (Somebody's Hand)— Diana Ross (70)	1230
I'm Every Woman—Chaka Khan (78)	989
The Boss—Diana Ross (79)	954
Let's Go Get Stoned— Ray Charles Band With The Raelets (66)	900
You're All I Need To Get By—Aretha Franklin (71)	*837*
Stuff Like That—Quincy Jones (78)	787
Ain't Nothing Like The Real Thing— Donny & Marie (76)	*755*
California Soul—5th Dimension (68)	*740*
Some Things You Never Get Used To— Diana Ross And The Supremes (68)	717
Keep On Lovin' Me Honey— Marvin Gaye & Tammi Terrell (68)	677
Found A Cure—Ashford & Simpson (79)	550
Good Lovin' Ain't Easy To Come By— Marvin Gaye & Tammi Terrell (69)	443
One Step At A Time—Maxine Brown (65)	417
Surrender—Diana Ross (71)	414
What You Gave Me— Marvin Gaye & Tammi Terrell (69)	406
Who's Gonna Take The Blame— Smokey Robinson & The Miracles (70)	316
Landlord—Gladys Knight & The Pips (80)	315
You're All I Need To Get By— Tony Orlando & Dawn (75)	*303*
Ain't Nothing Like The Real Thing— Aretha Franklin (74)	*267*
You're All I Need To Get By— Johnny Mathis/Deniece Williams (78)	*206*
Didn't You Know (You'd Have To Cry Sometime)— Gladys Knight & The Pips (69)	206
Destination: Anywhere—Marvelettes (68)	203
Don't Cost You Nothing—Ashford & Simpson (78)	201
Silly Wasn't I—Valerie Simpson (72)	184
Street Corner—Ashford & Simpson (82)	163
Onion Song—Marvin Gaye & Tammi Terrell (70)	137
I Don't Need No Doctor—Humble Pie (71)	*120*
California Soul—Marvin Gaye & Tammi Terrell (70)	*116*
Shoe Shoe Shine—Dynamic Superiors (74)	112
Don't Send Nobody Else—Ace Spectrum (74)	73
I Am Your Man—Bobby Taylor & The Vancouvers (68)	68
I Don't Need No Doctor— New Riders Of The Purple Sage (72)	*50*
I Don't Need No Doctor— Ray Charles And His Orchestra (66)	*48*
The Real Thing—Tina Britt (65)	27
Send It—Ashford & Simpson (77)	25
Love Don't Make It Right—Ashford & Simpson (80)	23
Count Your Blessings—Ashford and Simpson (86)	17
It Seems To Hang On—Ashford & Simpson (78)	14
(I'd Know You) Anywhere—Ashford & Simpson (74)	9.9
Ain't Nothing Like The Real Thing— Chris Christian (82)	*8.1*
You're All I Need To Get By—Chris Christian (82)	*8.1*
Never Had It So Good—Ronnie Milsap (65)	6.7
Clouds—Chaka Khan (80)	3.6
Hugh ASHLEY ▶ 5140 (1)	**335**
One Step At A Time—Brenda Lee (57)	335
Leon ASHLEY [Leon S. Walton] ▶ 6503 (2)	**162**
Laura, What's He Got That I Ain't Got— Frankie Laine (67)	*268*
Laura (Tell Me What He's Got That I Ain't Got)— Brook Benton (67)	*55*
Matthew ASHMAN ▶ 9838 (1)	**16**
Do You Wanna Hold Me?—Bow Wow Wow (83)	81
Jan ASHTON [Janet Ann Errico] ▶ 9226 (1)	**28**
I Still Love You—Vejtables (65)	28
John ASHTON ▶ 5221 (3)	**323**
Heartbreak Beat—Psychedelic Furs (87)	523

Love My Way—Psychedelic Furs (83)	375
Pretty In Pink—Psychedelic Furs (86)	330
Tony ASHTON ▶ 3539 (2)	**793**
Resurrection Shuffle—Ashton, Gardner & Dyke (71)	*591*
Resurrection Shuffle—Tom Jones (71)	*202*
—Charles William Ashworth see: Charlie PEACOCK	
Gary ASKENAS ▶ 10062 (1)	**13**
Let's Rock—Ellison Chase (76)	27
Steven ASKEW ▶ 4610 (2)	**451**
Too Shy—Kajagoogoo (83)	2226
Hang On Now—Kajagoogoo (83)	28
Gilbert ASKEY ▶ 6767 (1)	**139**
Runaway Love—Linda Clifford (78)	139
Svend ASMUSSEN ▶ 9907 (1)	**15**
Scandinavian Shuffle—Swe-Danes (60)	15
—David Asner see: Pepper DAVIS	
—Bambaataa Khayan Assim see: Afrika BAMBAATAA	
Ian ASTBURY ▶ 6375 (2)	**177**
Fire Woman—Cult (89)	345
Edie (Ciao Baby)—Cult (89)	9.4
Jon ASTLEY ▶ 6871 (2)	**131**
Put This Love To The Test—Jon Astley (88)	111
Jane's Getting Serious—Jon Astley (87)	76
Rick ASTLEY ▶ 1557 (4)	**2726**
Cry For Help—Rick Astley (91)	1691
She Wants To Dance With Me—Rick Astley (88)	1526
Giving Up On Love—Rick Astley (89)	317
Move Right Out—Rick Astley (91)	74
Jay ASTON ▶ 8652 (2)	**44**
Jealous—Gene Loves Jezebel (90)	164
The Motion Of Love—Gene Loves Jezebel (88)	11
Michael ASTON ▶ 11184 (1)	**2.8**
The Motion Of Love—Gene Loves Jezebel (88)	11
—Bob Astor see: Robert DADE	
June ASTOR ▶ 9592 (1)	**21**
Preacherman—Charlie Russo (63)	41
Jon ASTROP ▶ 3763 (1)	**706**
Touch Me (I Want Your Body)—Samantha Fox (86)	2117
Dadgel ATABAY ▶ 2969 (4)	**1090**
I'll Be By Your Side—Stevie B (91)	907
I Wanna Be The One—Stevie B (89)	535
Love Me For Life—Stevie B (90)	463
If You Leave Me Now—Jaya (89)	414
Tex ATCHISON ▶ 5377 (1)	**298**
Sleepy-Eyed John—Johnny Horton (61)	298
James ATKIN ▶ 3101 (2)	**1010**
Unbelievable—EMF (91)	4783
Lies—EMF (91)	266
George ATKINS ▶ 11758 (1)	**0.2**
Mr. Grillon—Archibald Players (58)	0.4
Jim ATKINS ▶ 11336 (1)	**2.2**
You're The Nearest Thing To Heaven— Johnny Cash And The Tennessee Two (58)	6.6
Roger ATKINS ▶ 1815 (7)	**2274**
Make Me Your Baby—Barbara Lewis (65)	1276
It's My Life—Animals (65)	1231
Workin' On A Groovy Thing—5th Dimension (69)	*962*
Princess In Rags—Gene Pitney (65)	570
Workin' On A Groovy Thing—Patti Drew (68)	*364*
Love Takes A Long Time Growing—Deon Jackson (66)	111
Can't Let You Out Of My Sight— Chuck Jackson & Maxine Brown (65)	32
Craig ATKINSON ▶ 4291 (1)	**530**
Psychotic Reaction—Count Five (66)	2651
—Bob Attlesey see: Bob SHELTON	
—Joe Attlesey see: Joe SHELTON	
Bernard AUBIN ▶ 7929 (1)	**69**
The Kid Is Hot Tonite—Loverboy (81)	138
Brian AUGER ▶ 4252 (1)	**545**
Happiness Is Just Around The Bend— Main Ingredient (74)	545
Roy AUGUST ▶ 11391 (1)	**1.9**
Fancy Free—Oak Ridge Boys (81)	3.8
Frank AUGUSTUS ▶ 4621 (3)	**449**
How About That—Dee Clark (59)	668
Come Tomorrow—Manfred Mann (65)	340
Only A Girl Like You—Brook Benton (66)	3.7

—Georgie Auld see: John ALTWERGER	
Leonard AULETTI ▶ 8905 (1)	**36**
Bunny Hop—Applejacks (S) (59)	73
Georges AURIC ▶ 8996 (1)	**34**
Goodbye Again—Ferrante & Teicher (61)	34
—Timothy James Auringer see: Tim JAMES	
—Rosemary Timotea Aurro see: Timi YURO	
Billy AUSTIN ▶ 9714 (1)	**18**
Is You Is Or Is You Ain't My Baby— Buster Brown (60)	37
Bobby AUSTIN [Fern Foley] ▶ 4265 (1)	**540**
Try A Little Kindness—Glen Campbell (69)	1079
Dallas AUSTIN ▶ 2409 (3)	**1510**
Motownphilly—Boyz II Men (91)	2776
Iesha—Another Bad Creation (91)	1229
Playground—Another Bad Creation (91)	604
David AUSTIN [David Michael Mortimer, David Mortimer] ▶ 8401 (1)	**52**
Shake— Andrew Ridgeley (90)	103
Donald AUSTIN ▶ 10122 (1)	**12**
Crazy Legs—Donald Austin (73)	25
Gene AUSTIN [Lemeul Eugene Lucas] ▶ 7875 (2)	**71**
Lonesome Road—Wonder Who ? (67)	98
Too Late—Gene Austin (57)	22
Sil AUSTIN ▶ 3208 (5)	**951**
Slow Walk—Sil Austin (56)	*1070*
Slow Walk—Bill Doggett (56)	*727*
Birthday Party—Sil Austin (57)	34
Last Time—Sil Austin (57)	19
Slow Walk—Ocie Smith (57)	*0.0*
Tom AUSTIN ▶ 3087 (5)	**1016**
Short Shorts—Royal Teens (58)	*2815*
Believe Me—Royal Teens (59)	925
Harvey's Got A Girlfriend—Royal Teens (58)	14
Short Shorts—Four Winds (58)	*0.0*
Short Shorts—Tiny Bradshaw & His Orchestra (58)	*0.0*
Luis Eduardo AUTE GUTIÉRREZ ▶ 4497 (1)	**477**
Who Will Answer?—Ed Ames (67)	954
—Christine Authors see: Christine HODGSON	
Gene AUTRY ▶ 6307 (4)	**183**
Tears On My Pillow—McGuire Sisters (61)	310
You're The Only Star (In My Blue Heaven)— Billy Vaughn And His Orchestra (60)	23
Goodby Little Darlin'—Johnny Cash (59)	8.0
Here Comes Santa Claus (Right Down Santa Claus Lane)—Elvis Presley (57)	2.1
Tom AUTRY ▶ 7065 (1)	**118**
A Mama And A Papa—Ray Stevens (71)	118
Frankie AVALON [Francis Thomas Avallone] ▶ 7906 (2)	**70**
What Little Girl—Frankie Avalon (58)	134
True, True Love—Frankie Avalon (61)	9.1
Johnny AVERAGE [Michael Hodgkinson] ▶ 7888 (1)	**71**
Ch Ch Cherie—Johnny Average Band (81)	142
Berton AVERRE ▶ 904 (4)	**4906**
My Sharona—Knack (79)	9055
Baby Talks Dirty—Knack (80)	422
Can't Put A Price On Love—Knack (80)	160
Pay The Devil (Ooo, Baby, Ooo)—Knack (81)	87
Jackie AVERY ▶ 7384 (4)	**99**
Aunt Dora's Love Soul Shack—Arthur Conley (68)	65
Shackin' Up—Barbara Mason (75)	53
I Wish It Was Me You Loved—Dells (74)	27
Disco 9000—Johnnie Taylor (77)	6.5
—Shirley Enid Avery see: Teri THORNTON	
Stuart AVIG [Stuart Ames] ▶ 11343 (2)	**2.1**
Greetings (This Is Uncle Sam)—Valadiers (61)	*9.2*
Greetings (This Is Uncle Sam)—Monitors (66)	*5.8*
—Valerie Avon see: Valerie MURTAGH	
Mark AVSEC ▶ 2710 (10)	**1257**
Ah! Leah!—Donnie Iris (80)	767
My Girl—Donnie Iris (82)	523
Love Is Like A Rock—Donnie Iris (81)	454
She Don't Know Me—Bon Jovi (84)	288
Tough World—Donnie Iris (82)	138
Do You Compute?—Donnie Iris (83)	99

Mark AVSEC ► 2710 (10) ***Continued***	**1257**
Samantha (What You Gonna Do?)—Cellarful Of Noise (88)	90
Sweet Merilee—Donnie Iris (81)	79
Injured In The Game Of Love—Donnie Iris (85)	7.2
Only The Lonely (Have A Reason To Be Sad)—La Flavour (80)	5.3
David AXELROD ► 6267 (1)	**188**
Dead End Street—Lou Rawls (67)	375
Charles AXTON ► 3151 (2)	**983**
Last Night—Mar-Keys (61)	4476
Boot-Leg—Booker T. & The MG's (65)	349
Estelle Stewart AXTON ► 7896 (1)	**70**
I Want Someone—Mad Lads (66)	141
Hoyt AXTON ► 184 (8)	**16700**
Joy To The World—Three Dog Night (71)	10869
No No Song—Ringo Starr (75)	3406
Never Been To Spain—Three Dog Night (71)	3156
Greenback Dollar—Kingston Trio (63)	*1014*
Snow Blind Friend—Steppenwolf (71)	326
When The Morning Comes—Hoyt Axton (74)	132
Willie Jean—Sunshine Company (69)	5.8
Greenback Dollar—Virginians (63)	*0.0*
Mae Boren AXTON ► 1335 (4)	**3322**
Heartbreak Hotel—Elvis Presley (56)	*9660*
Heartbreak Hotel—Frijid Pink (70)	*236*
Heartbreak Hotel—Roger Miller (66)	*53*
Heartbreak Hotel—Stan Freberg (56)	*17*
Corina AYALA [Aida Ayala, Corina] ► 4901 (1)	**385**
Temptation—Corina (91)	1924
—Marco Rizo Ayala see: Marco RIZO	
Frances AYCOCK ► 3657 (4)	**747**
Sha La La—Manfred Mann (64)	*1755*
Goodbye My Lover Goodbye—Searchers (65)	344
Sha-La-La—Shirelles (64)	*143*
Hand It Over—Chuck Jackson (64)	56
—Myint Myint Aye see: Annabella LWIN	
John AYLESWORTH ► 6515 (1)	**161**
The Ballad Of Irving—Frank Gallop (66)	483
Jimmy AYRE ► 5272 (2)	**314**
Mambo Rock—Bill Haley And His Comets (55)	*943*
Mambo Rock—Mike Pedicin Quintette (55)	*0.0*
—Muhammad Abdul Aziz see: Jermaine JACKSON	
—Charles Aznaourian see: Charles AZNAVOUR	
Charles AZNAVOUR [Charles Aznaourian, Shanour Varenagh Aznavurjian] ► 3015 (9) HOF	**1066**
Yesterday, When I Was Young—Roy Clark (69)	1095
A Young Girl—Noel Harrison (65)	535
For Mama (La Mamma)—Connie Francis (65)	*438*
For Mama—Jerry Vale (65)	*400*
Yet...I Know (Et Pourtant)—Steve Lawrence (64)	163
I Look At You—Lassies (56)	12
Venice Blue (Que C'Est Triste Venise)—Bobby Darin (65)	7.3
For Mama—Matt Monro (65)	*0.0*
For Mama (La Mamma)—Vic Damone (65)	*0.0*
—Shanour Varenagh Aznavurjian see: Charles AZNAVOUR	
Hurby AZOR ► 1859 (4)	**2193**
Push It—Salt-N-Pepa (87)	1049
Let's Talk About Sex—Salt-N-Pepa (91)	1042
Do You Want Me—Salt-N-Pepa (91)	612
Pump It (Nice An' Hard)—Icy Blu (91)	29

B

Morgan BABB ► 8823 (1)	**38**
Miss You So—Lillian Offitt (57)	38
Mary Jane BABBITT ► 11786 (1)	**0.0**
In A Garden Of Roses—Joni James (54)	0.0
—Edward Chester Babcock see: Jimmy VAN HEUSEN	
Joe BABCOCK ► 3150 (2)	**983**
(I Washed My Hands In) Muddy Water—Johnny Rivers (66)	982
Ghost Train—Marty Robbins (61)	0.4
—Babyface see: Kenneth EDMONDS	
Guy BABYLON ► 11671 (1)	**0.8**
K.I.S.S.I.N.G.—Siedah Garrett (88)	1.5
Steve BACA ► 10474 (1)	**8.0**
Give Me Your Heart—Vanity Kills (91)	16
Johann Sebastian BACH ► 1020 (6)	**4347**
A Lover's Concerto—Toys (65)	*6662*
Joy—Apollo 100 (71)	2041
A Lover's Concerto—Sarah Vaughan (66)	*208*
A Lover's Concerto—Stars On 45 (81)	*12*
Toccata—Sky (81)	9.2
A Lover's Concerto—Mrs. Miller (66)	*9.1*
Burt BACHARACH ► 11 (139) HOF	**72248**
Raindrops Keep Fallin' On My Head—B.J. Thomas (69)	10203
This Guy's In Love With You—Herb Alpert (68)	*9073*
(They Long To Be) Close To You—Carpenters (70)	*7620*
One Less Bell To Answer—5th Dimension (70)	7509
Arthur's Theme (Best That You Can Do)—Christopher Cross (81)	6911
That's What Friends Are For—Dionne & Friends (85)	5417
On My Own—Patti LaBelle & Michael McDonald (86)	5145
What's New Pussycat?—Tom Jones (65)	4965
Blue On Blue—Bobby Vinton (63)	4326
Baby It's You—Smith (69)	*4062*
Only Love Can Break A Heart—Gene Pitney (62)	*3874*
Wishin' And Hopin'—Dusty Springfield (64)	3504
I Say A Little Prayer—Dionne Warwick (67)	*3302*
The Look Of Love—Sergio Mendes & Brasil '66 (68)	*3151*
Walk On By—Dionne Warwick (64)	*2790*
What The World Needs Now Is Love—Jackie deShannon (65)	*2689*
(The Man Who Shot) Liberty Valance—Gene Pitney (62)	2442
Baby It's You—Shirelles (61)	*2409*
Tower Of Strength—Gene McDaniels (61)	2388
I'll Never Fall In Love Again—Dionne Warwick (69)	*2372*
Heartlight—Neil Diamond (82)	2132
Anyone Who Had A Heart—Dionne Warwick (63)	2092
This Girl's In Love With You—Dionne Warwick (69)	*2079*
Message To Michael—Dionne Warwick (66)	2078
Always Something There To Remind Me—Naked Eyes (83)	*1983*
Do You Know The Way To San José—Dionne Warwick (68)	1893
Alfie—Dionne Warwick (67)	*1730*
Wives And Lovers—Jack Jones (63)	1677
I Say A Little Prayer—Aretha Franklin (68)	*1449*
Any Day Now (My Wild Beautiful Bird)—Chuck Jackson (62)	*1371*
Making Love—Roberta Flack (82)	1327
Please Stay—Drifters (61)	*1293*
Don't Make Me Over—Dionne Warwick (62)	*1150*
Promises, Promises—Dionne Warwick (68)	1078
Any Day Now—Ronnie Milsap (82)	*1068*
Love Power—Dionne Warwick & Jeffrey Osborne (87)	1032
Twenty Four Hours From Tulsa—Gene Pitney (63)	977
Casino Royale—Herb Alpert & The Tijuana Brass (67)	880
You'll Never Get To Heaven (If You Break My Heart)—Stylistics (73)	*836*
What The World Needs Now Is Love—Tom Clay (71)	*836*
Don't Make Me Over—Sybil (89)	*835*
Magic Moments—Perry Como (57)	834
I Just Don't Know What To Do With Myself—Dionne Warwick (66)	*827*
Everybody's Out Of Town—B.J. Thomas (70)	796
Reach Out For Me—Dionne Warwick (64)	*794*
Always Something There To Remind Me—R.B. Greaves (70)	*784*
Make It Easy On Yourself—Walker Bros. (65)	*781*
True Love Never Runs Smooth—Gene Pitney (63)	775
The Look Of Love—Dusty Springfield (67)	*749*
Make It Easy On Yourself—Jerry Butler (62)	*738*
Who Is Gonna Love Me?—Dionne Warwick (68)	727
Story Of My Life—Marty Robbins (57)	692
Are You There (With Another Girl)—Dionne Warwick (65)	683
Trains And Boats And Planes—Dionne Warwick (66)	*662*
You'll Never Get To Heaven (If You Break My Heart)—Dionne Warwick (64)	*651*
Living Together, Growing Together—5th Dimension (73)	623
Make It Easy On Yourself—Dionne Warwick (70)	*617*
Alfie—Cher (66)	*533*
I'm A Better Man—Engelbert Humperdinck (69)	523
Windows Of The World—Dionne Warwick (67)	510
Let Me Go To Him—Dionne Warwick (70)	506
Stronger Than Before—Carole Bayer Sager (81)	502
The Green Grass Starts To Grow—Dionne Warwick (70)	502
Don't You Believe It—Andy Williams (62)	496
Paper Mache—Dionne Warwick (70)	479
The April Fools—Dionne Warwick (69)	474
Be True To Yourself—Bobby Vee (63)	466
The Love Of A Boy—Timi Yuro (62)	465
My Little Red Book—Love (66)	458
Odds And Ends—Dionne Warwick (69)	427
I Wake Up Crying—Chuck Jackson (61)	415
Blue Guitar—Richard Chamberlain (63)	413
Another Night—Dionne Warwick (66)	396
Walk On By—Isaac Hayes (69)	*367*
To Wait For Love—Herb Alpert (68)	365
(There's) Always Something There To Remind Me—Lou Johnson (64)	*363*
Trains And Boats And Planes—Billy J. Kramer & The Dakotas (65)	*357*
(There's) Always Something There To Remind Me—Sandie Shaw (64)	*337*
The Blob—Five Blobs (58)	*331*
Love Always—El DeBarge (86)	328
With Open Arms—Jane Morgan (59)	319
I Just Don't Know What To Do With Myself—Gary Puckett (70)	*315*
A House Is Not A Home—Dionne Warwick (64)	*286*
A House Is Not A Home—Brook Benton (64)	*260*
Reach Out For Me—Lou Johnson (63)	*247*
Long Ago Tomorrow—B.J. Thomas (71)	224
Keep Me In Mind—Patti Page (55)	213
Here I Am—Dionne Warwick (65)	188
Night Shift—Quarterflash (82)	178
Lost Horizon—Shawn Phillips (73)	159
A Lifetime Of Loneliness—Jackie De Shannon (65)	158
Who Gets The Guy—Dionne Warwick (71)	147
Front Page Story—Neil Diamond (83)	147
(There's) Always Something There To Remind Me—Dionne Warwick (68)	*141*
Looking With My Eyes—Dionne Warwick (65)	139
Alfie—Eivets Rednow (68)	*134*
(They Long To Be) Close To You—Jerry Butler Featuring Brenda Lee Eager (72)	*133*
Promise Her Anything—Tom Jones (66)	131
Don't Make Me Over—Jennifer Warnes (79)	*131*
Let Me Be Lonely—Dionne Warwick (68)	112
Turn Around—Neil Diamond (84)	110
Me Japanese Boy I Love You—Bobby Goldsboro (64)	104
Walk On By—Sybil (90)	*95*
Don't Make Me Over—Brenda & The Tabulations (70)	*95*
The Look Of Love—Isaac Hayes (71)	*94*
Any Day Now—Percy Sledge (69)	*91*
You're Following Me—Perry Como (61)	83
A Chance For Heaven—Christopher Cross (84)	64
The Breaking Point—Chuck Jackson (61)	46
You Don't Have To Be A Tower Of Strength—Gloria Lynne (61)	44
I Say A Little Prayer—Glen Campbell (71)	*38*
This Empty Place—Dionne Warwick (63)	38
Come And Get Me—Jackie deShannon (66)	34
Close To You—B.T. Express (76)	*31*
The Beginning Of Loneliness—Dionne Warwick (67)	30
Wendy Wendy—Four Coins (58)	26
I Don't Need You Anymore—Together? With Jackie DeShannon (80)	25
Make The Music Play—Dionne Warwick (63)	22
Easy To Love Again—Carole Bayer Sager (81)	22
Close—Keely Smith (60)	22
Please Stay—Dave Clark Five (68)	*19*
Saturday Sunshine—Burt Bacharach (63)	19
I Just Don't Know What To Do With Myself—Tommy Hunt (62)	*13*
Only Love Can Break A Heart—Margaret Whiting (67)	*13*
From Rocking Horse To Rocking Chair—Paul Anka (64)	11
Waiting For Charlie—Etta James (62)	*10*
Walk On By—AWB (79)	*7.4*
Alfie—Cilla Black (66)	*6.1*
I'll Never Fall In Love Again—Burt Bacharach (69)	*4.9*

Burt BACHARACH ▶ 11 (139) HOF *Cont'd*	**72248**
Forgive Me (For Giving You Such A Bad Time)—Babs Tino (62)	3.5
Waiting For Charlie To Come Home—Marlena Shaw (67)	*3.3*
Somebody Else's Sweetheart—Wanderers (61)	1.8
It's The Love That Really Counts (In The Long Run)—Shirelles (62)	1.8
Who's Been Sleeping In My Bed?—Linda Scott (64)	1.3
Walk On By—Gloria Gaynor (75)	*1.1*
Rome Will Never Leave You—Richard Chamberlain (64)	1.0
Only Love Can Break A Heart—Bobby Vinton (77)	*0.9*
Mexican Divorce—Drifters (62)	0.5
The Blob—Zanies (58)	*0.0*
—Carole Bayer Bacharach see: Carole Bayer SAGER	
Randy BACHMAN [Randolph Charles Bachman, R.B. Charles, Charles Spencer] ▶ 198 (17)	**15848**
American Woman—Guess Who (70)	7040
You Ain't Seen Nothing Yet—Bachman-Turner Overdrive (74)	*4251*
These Eyes—Guess Who (69)	*3940*
No Time—Guess Who (69)	3320
Laughing—Guess Who (69)	2066
Takin' Care Of Business—Bachman-Turner Overdrive (74)	1724
These Eyes—Jr. Walker & The All Stars (69)	*1159*
Let It Ride—Bachman-Turner Overdrive (74)	1140
Hey You—Bachman-Turner Overdrive (75)	915
Undun—Guess Who (69)	628
Sweet Lui-Louise—Ironhorse (79)	306
Down To The Line—Bachman-Turner Overdrive (75)	290
No Sugar Tonight—Guess Who (70)	163
You Ain't Seen Nothing Yet—Figures On A Beach (89)	*113*
Lookin' Out For #1—Bachman-Turner Overdrive (76)	76
My Wheels Won't Turn—Bachman-Turner Overdrive (77)	21
What's Your Hurry Darlin'—Ironhorse (80)	15
Robbie BACHMAN ▶ 4225 (2)	**556**
Roll On Down The Highway—Bachman-Turner Overdrive (75)	1108
Down The Road—B.T.O. (78)	6.3
—Johnny Backbeat see: John BADANJEK	
Bill BACKER ▶ 3497 (2)	**816**
I'd Like To Teach The World To Sing (In Perfect Harmony)—New Seekers (71)	*1791*
I'd Like To Teach The World To Sing (In Perfect Harmony)—Hillside Singers (71)	*1474*
Don BACKY [Aldo Caponi] ▶ 9144 (1)	**30**
In Time—Engelbert Humperdinck (72)	121
—Angelo Badalamenti see: Andy BADALE	
Andy BADALE [Angelo Badalamenti, Angelo Badale] ▶ 3954 (4)	**642**
Face It Girl, It's Over—Nancy Wilson (68)	833
I Want To Love You For What You Are—Ronnie Dove (67)	296
Dancin' Out Of My Heart—Ronnie Dove (67)	145
Passport To The Future—Jean Jacques Perrey (70)	20
John BADANJEK [Johnny Backbeat] ▶ 5516 (2)	**275**
Can't Sleep—Rockets (79)	233
Desire—Rockets (80)	85
Wally BADAROU [Wallou Jacques Daniel Badarou] ▶ 3674 (4)	**740**
Something About You—Level 42 (86)	1857
Lessons In Love—Level 42 (87)	1029
Hot Water—Level 42 (86)	48
Running In The Family—Level 42 (87)	42
Randy BADAZZ [Randy Alpert] ▶ 1478 (2)	**2943**
Rise—Herb Alpert (79)	5495
Rotation—Herb Alpert (79)	391
Ronald BADGER ▶ 9612 (2)	**20**
I Want To Know—Sugar Pie DeSanto (60)	48
Paper Roses—Lola Dee (55)	13
Abel BAER ▶ 5400 (3)	**294**
June Night—Jimmy Dorsey Orchestra and Chorus (57)	581
My Mother's Eyes—Russ Hamilton (58)	5.5
There Are Such Things—Modernaires (57)	1.9
Barbara BAER ▶ 4438 (4)	**494**
Sweet Talkin' Guy—Chiffons (66)	1814
Out Of This World—Chiffons (66)	110
Moulty—Barbarians (66)	41
Stop, Look And Listen—Chiffons (66)	9.3
David BAERWALD ▶ 5054 (2)	**353**
Welcome To The Boomtown—David & David (86)	487
Ain't So Easy—David & David (87)	219
Joan BÁEZ ▶ 4871 (1)	**394**
Diamonds And Rust—Joan Baez (75)	394
—Margarita Mimi Baez see: Mimi FARINA	
Harry BAGBY ▶ 6576 (4)	**154**
Rock The Joint—Bill Haley With Haley's Comets (55)	*146*
Dumplin's—Doc Bagby (57)	*116*
Dumplin's—Ernie Freeman (57)	*91*
Rock The Joint—Bill Haley & His Comets (57)	*6.6*
—Ross Bagdasarian see: David SEVILLE	
Sal BAGLIO ▶ 9904 (1)	**15**
Never Tell An Angel (When Your Heart's On Fire)—Stompers (83)	15
Gordon BAHARY ▶ 9781 (1)	**17**
Electric Kingdom—Twilight 22 (83)	51
Tom BAHLER ▶ 634 (6)	**6825**
Julie, Do Ya Love Me—Bobby Sherman (70)	4270
She's Out Of My Life—Michael Jackson (80)	1740
Living In A House Divided—Cher (72)	704
Groovy Summertime—Love Generation (67)	163
The Other Woman—Vicki Lawrence (75)	86
Goin' Home (Sing A Song Of Christmas Cheer)—Bobby Sherman (70)	13
—Harald Baierl see: P.G. WYLDER	
Barry BAILEY ▶ 6866 (2)	**132**
Doraville—Atlanta Rhythm Section (74)	329
Angel (What In The World's Come Over Us)—Atlanta Rhythm Section (75)	66
Guy BAILEY ▶ 8397 (1)	**52**
I Don't Love You Anymore—London Quireboys (90)	104
—J. R. Bailey see: Ralph BAILEY	
Morris BAILEY ▶ 4037 (3)	**618**
Cry Baby Cry—Angels (62)	591
Tear After Tear—Patty LaBelle & Her Blue Belles (62)	50
Take All Of My Life—Carrie Grant And The Grandeurs (62)	5.8
Philip BAILEY ▶ 1164 (7) HOF	**3826**
Shining Star—Earth, Wind & Fire (75)	4991
Easy Lover—Philip Bailey (84)	4579
Saturday Nite—Earth, Wind & Fire (76)	856
Evil—Earth, Wind & Fire (73)	340
Let Me Talk—Earth, Wind & Fire (80)	319
Devotion—Earth, Wind & Fire (74)	186
I Wanna Get Back With You—Louie Louie (90)	136
—Raisie Michael Bailey see: Razzy BAILEY	
Ralph BAILEY [J. R. Bailey, James Ralph Bailey] ▶ 1790 (9)	**2322**
Everybody Plays The Fool—Main Ingredient (72)	*4562*
Everybody Plays The Fool—Aaron Neville (91)	*1326*
Love, Love, Love—Donny Hathaway (73)	309
One Hurt Deserves Another—Raeletts (67)	223
Sweet, Sweet Lovin'—Platters (67)	159
Seven Lonely Nights—Four Tops (75)	54
Put On Your Shoes And Walk—Clarence Carter (73)	45
You Can Call Me Rover—Main Ingredient (73)	28
Three Steps From True Love—Reflections (75)	15
Razzy BAILEY [Raisie Michael Bailey] ▶ 4570 (2)	**464**
9,999,999 Tears—Dickey Lee (76)	264
I Hate Hate—Razzy (74)	200
—Steven John Bailey see: Steven SEVERIN	
Tom BAILEY ▶ 1186 (11)	**3747**
Hold Me Now—Thompson Twins (84)	3557
Lay Your Hands On Me—Thompson Twins (85)	1742
King For A Day—Thompson Twins (86)	1479
Doctor! Doctor!—Thompson Twins (84)	1247
Lies—Thompson Twins (83)	612
Sugar Daddy—Thompson Twins (89)	527
Get That Love—Thompson Twins (87)	480
You Take Me Up—Thompson Twins (84)	304
Love On Your Side—Thompson Twins (83)	286
Nothing In Common—Thompson Twins (86)	272
The Gap—Thompson Twins (84)	95
Sal BAIONNO ▶ 6689 (3)	**144**
Little Pixie—Moe Koffman Quartette (58)	*144*
Little Pixie—Johnnie Pate (58)	*0.0*
Little Pixie—Frank D'Rone (58)	*0.0*
Dan BAIRD ▶ 1661 (1)	**2532**
Keep Your Hands To Yourself—Georgia Satellites (86)	2532
—J. Baird see: Bernard SOLOMON	
Tom BAIRD ▶ 2250 (4)	**1705**
Born To Wander—Rare Earth (70)	1218
Does Your Mama Know About Me—Bobby Taylor & The Vancouvers (68)	703
Good Time Sally—Rare Earth (72)	134
We're Gonna Have A Good Time—Rare Earth (73)	4.3
Adrian BAKER ▶ 7620 (2)	**85**
My Baby's Baby—Liquid Gold (79)	162
The Joy And The Tears—Gidea Park (81)	3.7
Anita BAKER ▶ 2278 (3)	**1661**
Giving You The Best That I Got—Anita Baker (88)	3327
Sweet Love—Anita Baker (86)	1336
Talk To Me—Anita Baker (90)	321
Arthur BAKER ▶ 3218 (4)	**945**
With Every Beat Of My Heart—Taylor Dayne (89)	2568
Planet Rock—Afrika Bambaataa And The Soul Sonic Force (82)	175
Michael chee	81
No Frills Love—Jennifer Holliday (86)	12
Drew BAKER ▶ 10190 (1)	**11**
Pouring Water On A Drowning Man—James Carr (66)	23
George BAKER [Hans Bouwens, Johannes Bowens] ▶ 2399 (3)	**1524**
Little Green Bag—George Baker Selection (70)	1325
Paloma Blanca—George Baker Selection (75)	818
Dear Ann—George Baker Selection (70)	44
—Gloria Shayne Baker see: Gloria SHAYNE	
Hillman BAKER ▶ 10546 (1)	**7.4**
Yea, Yea—Kendall Sisters (58)	15
Jack BAKER ▶ 11567 (1)	**1.2**
I Hear A Rhapsody—Knightsbridge Strings (60)	3.5
James BAKER ▶ 7383 (3)	**99**
It's Been A Long Time—New Birth (74)	176
Granddaddy (Part 1)—New Birth (75)	17
I Wash My Hands Of The Whole Damn Deal (Part 1)—New Birth (74)	11
Jarvis BAKER ▶ 3081 (1)	**1022**
I Love Your Smile—Shanice (91)	4090
—John/Jonathan Baker see: Jon DAY	
LaVern BAKER [Delores Williams] ▶ 5517 (7)	**275**
So High So Low—LaVern Baker (59)	234
I Can't Love You Enough—LaVern Baker (56)	202
That's All I Need—Dorothy Collins (55)	*120*
Tiny Tim—LaVern Baker (59)	102
That's All I Need—LaVern Baker & The Gliders (55)	*0.0*
That's All I Need—Rusty Draper (55)	*0.0*
That's All I Need—Jill Corey (55)	*0.0*
Lefty BAKER [Eustace Britchforth] ▶ 6963 (1)	**125**
Yesterday's Rain—Spanky And Our Gang (68)	125
—Linda Baker see: Linda LAFLAMME	
—McHouston Baker see: Mickey BAKER	
Mickey BAKER [McHouston Baker, S. Gibson] ▶ 2389 (14)	**1533**
Love Is Strange—Mickey & Sylvia (56)	*2019*
Love Is Strange—Peaches & Herb (67)	*1374*
There Oughta Be A Law—Mickey & Sylvia (57)	405
What Would I Do—Mickey And Sylvia (60)	336
Dearest—Mickey & Sylvia (57)	135
Baby You're So Fine—Mickey And Sylvia (61)	*100*
Love Is Strange—Buddy Holly / The Crickets (69)	*11*
Lullabye—Chevrons (60)	8.9
There'll Be No Backin' Out—Mickey And Sylvia (57)	7.1
Starlight—Lee Greenlee (59)	3.9
Love Is Strange—Everly Brothers (65)	*3.4*
Two Shadows On Your Window—Jim Reeves (57)	*3.0*
Two Shadows On Your Window—Mickey & Sylvia (57)	*3.0*
Lovedrops—Mickey And Sylvia (61)	1.8
Mike BAKER ▶ 8627 (1)	**45**
Let Me Go—Rings (81)	45
Pug BAKER ▶ 6262 (1)	**188**
Holdin' On—Tané Cain (82)	376

Ron BAKER ► 3880 (6)	**669**
That's Where The Happy People Go—Trammps (76)	529
Hold Back The Night—Trammps (76)	*426*
Hold Back The Night— Graham Parker And The Rumour (77)	*83*
A Mother For My Children—Whispers (74)	16
This Will Be A Night To Remember— Eddie Holman (77)	6.9
My Mind Keeps Telling Me (That I Really Love You, Girl)—Eddie Holman (72)	5.5
Teddy BAKER ► 9654 (1)	**19**
It's Over—Teddy Baker (81)	19
Tina BAKER ► 10963 (1)	**4.1**
No Frills Love—Jennifer Holliday (86)	12
Walter BAKER ► 11139 (2)	**3.1**
Patty Baby—Terry Noland (58)	*3.1*
Patty Baby—Rick Tucker & The Picks (58)	*3.1*
Yvonne BAKER [Yvonne Martin, Yvonne Mills] ► 2485 (1)	**1445**
Let Me In—Sensations (62)	4334
Jim BALCOM ► 8265 (2)	**56**
Corrido Rock (Pt. 1)—"Handsome" Jim Balcom (58)	*113*
Corrido Rock—Jimmy Church's Magicians (58)	*0.0*
Bobby BALDERAMA ► 6308 (1)	**183**
I Need Somebody—? & The Mysterians (66)	913
Donald BALDWIN ► 6965 (1)	**125**
Happy People—Temptations (74)	375
—John Baldwin see: John Paul JONES	
—David William Balfe see: Rod McQUEEN	
Marty BALIN [Martyn Jeryl Buchwald] ► 991 (4)	**4526**
Miracles—Jefferson Starship (75)	3853
With Your Love—Jefferson Starship (76)	1472
Volunteers—Jefferson Airplane (69)	345
St. Charles—Jefferson Starship (76)	52
—Umpeylia Marema Balinton see: Sugar Pie DeSANTO	
—Harry Balk see: Tom KING	
Ernest R. BALL ► 10871 (1) HOF	**4.7**
When Irish Eyes Are Smiling— Bruce Hayes with Mary Mayo (60)	14
Noel BALL ► 2367 (4)	**1555**
Oh Julie—Crescendos (57)	*2335*
Letter From Sherry—Dale Ward (63)	749
Oh Julie—Sammy Salvo (57)	*27*
Oh Julie—Otis Williams & His Charms (58)	*0.0*
—Reginald Maurice Ball see: Reg PRESLEY	
Roger BALL ► 2778 (3)	**1199**
Pick Up The Pieces—AWB (74)	5059
Cut The Cake—AWB (75)	1651
School Boy Crush—AWB (75)	485
—Timothy Wayne Ball see: Dig WAYNE	
Yvette BALL ► 7665 (2)	**82**
Tears And Laughter—Dinah Washington (62)	241
A City Girl Stole My Country Boy—Patti Page (61)	5.0
Clint BALLARD Jr. ► 225 (23)	**15025**
Game Of Love— Wayne Fontana & The Mindbenders (65)	5647
Good Timin'—Jimmy Jones (60)	4490
You're No Good—Linda Ronstadt (74)	*4190*
Ginger Bread—Frankie Avalon (58)	1599
Little Bitty Girl—Bobby Rydell (60)	741
One Of Us (Will Weep Tonight)—Patti Page (60)	740
You're No Good—Betty Everett (63)	*506*
It's Just A Little Bit Too Late— Wayne Fontana & The Mind-Benders (65)	381
The Ladder Of Love—Flamingos (57)	*228*
I'm Alive—Gamma (79)	*182*
Brigade Of Broken Hearts—Paul Evans (60)	145
Jumpin' Jack—Kalin Twins (58)	105
Banned In Boston—Merv Griffin (61)	67
Fiddle Around—Jan & Dean (66)	59
Speak Her Name—Walter Jackson (67)	46
Preview Of Paradise—Adam Wade (61)	41
I'm Alive—Hollies (65)	*24*
I'll Think Of You—McGuire Sisters (58)	19
Where Did I Make My Mistake—Clyde McPhatter (59)	4.8
Two Long Years—Dick Caruso (60)	3.8
You're No Good—Swinging Blue Jeans (64)	*2.4*
You're No Good—Dee Dee Warwick (63)	*0.0*
The Ladder Of Love—Johnny Nash (57)	*0.0*

—Francis Drake Ballard see: Pat BALLARD	
Glen BALLARD ► 686 (8)	**6338**
Hold On—Wilson Phillips (90)	4433
Man In The Mirror—Michael Jackson (88)	4127
You're In Love—Wilson Phillips (91)	3185
All I Need—Jack Wagner (84)	3171
I Wonder Why—Curtis Stigers (91)	1308
The Dream Is Still Alive—Wilson Phillips (91)	1006
Lady Of My Heart—Jack Wagner (85)	77
It's Gonna Be Special—Patti Austin (84)	25
Hank BALLARD [John Henry Kendricks] ► 67 (20)	**32756**
The Twist—Chubby Checker (61)	*12943*
Twist—Chubby Checker (60)	*9977*
Dance With Me Henry (Wallflower)— Georgia Gibbs (55)	*5087*
Finger Poppin' Time— Hank Ballard And The Midnighters (60)	3101
Let's Go Let's Go Let's Go— Hank Ballard And The Midnighters (60)	2265
Twist—Hank Ballard And The Midnighters (60)	*983*
Hoochi Coochi Coo— Hank Ballard And The Midnighters (60)	741
The Twist (Yo, Twist)—Fat Boys (88)	*725*
The Switch-A-Roo— Hank Ballard And The Midnighters (61)	436
Let's Go Again (Where We Went Last Night)— Hank Ballard And The Midnighters (61)	315
Keep On Dancing— Hank Ballard And The Midnighters (61)	70
Nothing But Good— Hank Ballard And The Midnighters (61)	49
Do You Know How To Twist—Hank Ballard (62)	23
The Twist—Jive Bunny & The Mastermixers (90)	*6.7*
The Twist—Ernie Freeman (62)	*3.6*
Dance With Me Georgie—Bobbettes (60)	*2.5*
The Wallflower (Dance With Me Henry)— Lee Winters (55)	*0.0*
The Italian Wallflower (I'll Dance With Her Henry)— Lou Monte (55)	*0.0*
The Wallflower—Three Rays (55)	*0.0*
The Wallflower—Etta James & The Peaches (55)	*0.0*
Pat BALLARD [Francis Drake Ballard] ► 435 (9)	**9410**
Mr. Sandman—Chordettes (54)	*7421*
Mister Sandman—Four Aces (54)	*1496*
Mister Sandman—Emmylou Harris (81)	*421*
Mr. Santa—Dorothy Collins (55)	*37*
Twelve O'Clock Tonight—Doris Day (57)	34
I Get So Lonely (When I Dream About You)— Four Knights (54)	0.0
Mister Sandman—Lancers (54)	*0.0*
Mister Sandman— Vaughn Monroe & His Orchestra (54)	*0.0*
Mr. Sandman—Buddy Morrow & His Orchestra (54)	0.0
Russ BALLARD ► 318 (17)	**11495**
You Can Do Magic—America (82)	2426
Liar—Three Dog Night (71)	2036
I Know There's Something Going On—Frida (82)	1775
New York Groove—Ace Frehley (78)	1446
Winning—Santana (81)	1205
Can't Shake Loose—Agnetha Faltskog (83)	582
The Border—America (83)	458
So You Win Again—Hot Chocolate (77)	454
Since You Been Gone—Rainbow (2) (79)	*297*
Free Me—Roger Daltrey (80)	279
Since You Been Gone—Head East (78)	*199*
Come And Get Your Love—Roger Daltrey (75)	173
Nowhere To Run—Santana (82)	156
On The Rebound—Russ Ballard (80)	132
I Did It For Love—Night Ranger (88)	63
Since You've Been Gone— Cherie & Marie Currie (79)	*24*
Tragedy—Argent (72)	17
Hubert BALLAY ► 7376 (1)	**99**
Now That You've Gone—Connie Stevens (65)	298
Riccardo BALLERINI ► 7755 (1)	**76**
Boom Boom (Let's Go Back To My Room)— Paul Lekakis (87)	381
Susan BALLION [Siouxsie Sioux] ► 6006 (2)	**217**
Kiss Them For Me—Siouxsie And The Banshees (91)	481
Peek-A-Boo—Siouxsie & The Banshees (88)	289

Michael BALZARY [Flea] ► 10602 (1)	**6.9**
Give It Away—Red Hot Chili Peppers (91)	28
Afrika BAMBAATAA [Bambaataa Khayan Assim] ► 8213 (1)	**58**
Planet Rock— Afrika Bambaataa And The Soul Sonic Force (82)	175
Frankie BANALI ► 6983 (1)	**124**
Bang Your Head (Metal Health)—Quiet Riot (84)	495
Al BANDINI ► 11787 (1)	**0.0**
A Girl, A Girl (Zoom-Ba Di Alli Nella)— Eddie Fisher (54)	0.0
Jon BANFIELD [John Andrew Banfield] ► 8429 (1)	**51**
Tribute (Right On)—Pasadenas (89)	304
—Daniel Bangalter see: Daniel VANGARDE	
—Darrell Banks see: Darrell EUBANKS	
Homer BANKS ► 744 (25)	**5897**
(If Loving You Is Wrong) I Don't Want To Be Right— Luther Ingram (72)	*5399*
Who's Making Love—Johnnie Taylor (68)	*3954*
If You're Ready (Come Go With Me)— Staple Singers (73)	1796
Take Care Of Your Homework—Johnnie Taylor (69)	958
(If Loving You Is Wrong) I Don't Want To Be Right— Barbara Mandrell (79)	*775*
Touch A Hand, Make A Friend—Staple Singers (74)	770
I'll Be Your Shelter (In Time Of Storm)— Luther Ingram (72)	584
I've Got A Feeling (We'll Be Seeing Each Other Again)—Al Wilson (76)	445
Ain't That Loving You (For More Reasons Than One)— Luther Ingram (70)	*442*
I Like What You're Doing (To Me)—Carla Thomas (69)	399
I'll Be The Other Woman—Soul Children (74)	371
Son Of Shaft—Bar-Kays (71)	349
I Could Never Be President—Johnnie Taylor (69)	345
Who's Making Love—Blues Brothers (80)	*342*
Can't You Find Another Way (Of Doing It)— Sam & Dave (68)	318
Who's Making Love—Young-Holt Unlimited (69)	*241*
If Loving You Is Wrong I Don't Want To Be Right— Millie Jackson (75)	*204*
Be What You Are—Staple Singers (73)	122
Ain't That Loving You (For More Reasons Than One)— Isaac Hayes & David Porter (72)	*110*
You Says It All—Randy Brown (79)	77
Slum Baby—Booker T. & The M.G.'s (69)	74
Sugar Bee—Mitch Ryder (69)	30
I Could Never Be Happy—Emotions (72)	21
Too Many Lovers—Shack (71)	20
Taxi—J. Blackfoot (84)	17
James BANKS ► 5560 (3)	**271**
Woman To Woman—Shirley Brown (74)	*767*
Don't Take My Kindness For Weakness— Soul Children (72)	46
Woman To Woman—Barbara Mandrell (78)	*12*
Larry BANKS ► 2962 (1)	**1094**
Go Now!—Moody Blues (65)	2189
Marian BANKS ► 11741 (1)	**0.3**
Heartless—Tommy Leonetti (55)	0.6
—Peter Banks see: Peter W. BANKS	
Peter Douglas Cameron BANKS [Peter Memory Banks] ► 10414 (1)	**8.7**
Dancing In The Shadows—After The Fire (83)	17
Peter W. BANKS [Peter Banks, Peter William Bockbanks] ► 5056 (1)	**353**
Small Beginnings—Flash (72)	706
—Peter Memory Banks see: Peter Douglas Cameron BANKS	
Ron BANKS ► 8999 (1)	**34**
Why Leave Us Alone—Five Special (79)	101
Sidney BANKS [Birdlegs] ► 9923 (1)	**15**
Spring— Birdlegs & Pauline And Their Versatility Birds (63)	15
Tony BANKS ► 654 (15)	**6700**
Invisible Touch—Genesis (86)	3735
In Too Deep—Genesis (87)	2454
Tonight, Tonight, Tonight—Genesis (87)	2246
Throwing It All Away—Genesis (86)	2205
Land Of Confusion—Genesis (86)	2182
No Son Of Mine—Genesis (91)	1981

Tony BANKS ▶ 654 (15) ***Continued***	**6700**
That's All—Genesis (83)	1827
Follow You Follow Me—Genesis (78)	761
No Reply At All—Genesis (81)	731
Paperlate—Genesis (82)	533
Abacab—Genesis (81)	451
Taking It All Too Hard—Genesis (84)	331
Illegal Alien—Genesis (84)	277
Turn It On Again—Genesis (80)	248
Mama—Genesis (83)	137
Royal C. BANNON [R.C. Bannon, Dannie Shipley] ▶ 9007 (1)	**33**
Only One Love In My Life—Ronnie Milsap (78)	67
Phil BAPTISTE [Philip Baptiste, Phil Phillips] ▶ 981 (4)	**4567**
Sea Of Love—Phil Phillips with The Twilights (59)	*5548*
Sea Of Love—Honeydrippers (84)	*3169*
Sea Of Love—Del Shannon (81)	*406*
Verdie Mae—Phil Phillips (59)	11
Bob BARASH ▶ 7015 (1)	**122**
Swingin' Tight—Bill Deal & The Rhondels (69)	243
Dave BARBAROSSA [David Barbe] ▶ 9839 (1)	**16**
Do You Wanna Hold Me?—Bow Wow Wow (83)	81
Richard BARBARY ▶ 8306 (1)	**55**
Ooh Baby—Deon Jackson (67)	110
John BARBATA ▶ 4026 (2)	**621**
Elenore—Turtles (68)	2721
Sound Asleep—Turtles (68)	382
—David Barbe see: Dave BARBAROSSA	
Glen BARBEE ▶ 7855 (1)	**72**
Come Give Your Love To Me—Janet Jackson (83)	144
Billy BARBERIS ▶ 4118 (8)	**587**
Have You Looked Into Your Heart—Jerry Vale (64)	860
Big Wide World—Teddy Randazzo (63)	423
Sinner Man—Trini Lopez (65)	335
In Time—Steve Lawrence (61)	214
A Miracle—Frankie Avalon (62)	65
Around The Corner—Duprees (65)	56
Dear Heart—Teddy Randazzo (63)	13
Lies—Teddy Randazzo (59)	4.2
Gato BARBIERI ▶ 7154 (1)	**113**
Last Tango In Paris—Herb Alpert & The TJB (73)	113
Jose BARBOSA DA SILVA [Sinhô] ▶ 6769 (1)	**138**
Jura (I Swear I Love You)—Les Paul and Mary Ford (61)	277
Chris BARBOSA ▶ 2611 (3)	**1325**
Let The Music Play—Shannon (83)	1909
Give Me Tonight—Shannon (84)	413
Do You Wanna Get Away—Shannon (85)	328
David M. BARBOUR ▶ 10941 (1)	**4.2**
I Don't Know Enough About You—Peggy Lee (56)	8.4
—Mary Ann Barcaro see: Dux DeJOHN	
Lorenzo BARCELATA ▶ 1581 (2)	**2672**
Maria Elena—Los Indios Tabajaras (63)	*2672*
Maria Elena—Billy Mure (63)	*0.0*
Lillian BARCO ▶ 8701 (1)	**42**
(Baby, Baby) Be Good To Me—McGuire Sisters (56)	85
—Annette Bard see: Toni CHILDS	
Bobby BARE ▶ 2415 (5)	**1508**
All American Boy—Bill Parsons And His Orchestra (58)	2944
500 Miles Away From Home—Bobby Bare (63)	*1427*
Five Hundred Miles—Heaven Bound With Tony Scotti (71)	*109*
Application For Love—Roy Clark (63)	24
500 Miles—Hooters (89)	*6.5*
Carl BAREFOOT ▶ 4122 (4)	**586**
Danger! Heartbreak Ahead—Jaye P. Morgan (55)	932
Goodnight Sweet Dreams—Gordon Jenkins And His Orchestra (55)	211
Will You Willyum—Janis Martin (56)	*100*
Will You, Willyum?—Joan Hager (56)	*0.0*
Marshall BARER ▶ 7514 (2)	**91**
I'm Just A Country Boy—George McCurn (63)	*177*
I'm Just A Country Boy—Harry Belafonte (57)	*5.3*
Gene BARGE [Raven Wildroot, Daddy G] ▶ 841 (11)	**5253**
Quarter To Three—U.S. Bonds (61)	8470
School Is Out—Gary (U.S.) Bonds (61)	3371

Twist, Twist Senora—Gary (U.S.) Bonds (62)	1458
We're Gonna Make It—Little Milton (65)	983
School Is In—Gary (U.S.) Bonds (61)	434
That's Enough—Rosco Robinson (66)	369
Love Is A 5-Letter Word—James Phelps (65)	214
You'll Miss Me (When I'm Gone)—Fontella Bass & Bobby McClure (65)	42
As Long As I Got You—Laura Lee (68)	26
Copy Cat—Gary (U.S.) Bonds (62)	9.2
I Got A Problem—Jesse Anderson (70)	5.1
Maurice BARGE ▶ 4447 (1)	**493**
Leaving Me—Independents (73)	986
Lee BARGERON ▶ 7497 (2)	**92**
You've Got Another Thing Coming—Hotel (79)	151
Half Moon Silver—Hotel (80)	51
Camillo BARGONI ▶ 2770 (10)	**1206**
And That Reminds Me—Della Reese (57)	*1323*
And That Reminds Me (My Heart Reminds Me)—4 Seasons (69)	*593*
My Heart Reminds Me—Kay Starr (57)	*496*
Autumn Concerto—Richard Hayman His Harmonica and Orchestra (56)	*0.0*
Autumn Concerto—Carmen Cavallaro And His Orchestra (56)	*0.0*
Autumn Concerto—Billy Vaughn & His Orchestra (56)	*0.0*
Autumn Concerto—Nick Noble (56)	*0.0*
My Heart Reminds Me—Ambrose & His Orchestra (57)	*0.0*
My Heart Reminds Me—Richard Hayman (57)	*0.0*
My Heart Reminds Me—Carmen Cavallaro (57)	*0.0*
Jesse BARISH ▶ 1113 (5)	**3990**
Hearts—Marty Balin (81)	1683
Count On Me—Jefferson Starship (78)	1591
Atlanta Lady (Something About Your Love)—Marty Balin (81)	575
Crazy Feelin'—Jefferson Starship (78)	131
St. Charles—Jefferson Starship (76)	52
Mark BARKAN ▶ 757 (20)	**5792**
She's A Fool—Lesley Gore (63)	3745
The Writing On The Wall—Adam Wade (61)	2168
That's The Way Boys Are—Lesley Gore (64)	1325
I'm Gonna' Be Warm This Winter—Connie Francis (62)	987
Pretty Flamingo—Manfred Mann (66)	644
I'll Try Anything—Dusty Springfield (67)	508
Peace Pipe—B.T. Express (75)	445
If I Didn't Love You—Chuck Jackson (65)	381
I Don't Wanna Be A Loser—Lesley Gore (64)	327
Swingin' Tight—Bill Deal & The Rhondels (69)	243
Good Combination—Sonny & Cher (67)	241
Bring A Little Sunshine (To My Heart)—Vic Dana (65)	185
Let True Love Begin—Nat King Cole (61)	104
Mr. Happiness—Johnny Maestro With The Coeds (61)	61
I'm Indestructible—Jack Jones (67)	61
Help Yourself (To All Of My Lovin')—James & Bobby Purify (68)	28
S.T.O.P. (Stop)—Lorelei (72)	26
Flying Blue Angels—George, Johnny And The Pilots (62)	3.6
Just Let Me Cry—Lesley Gore (63)	3.2
The Tra La La Song (One Banana, Two Banana)—Banana Splits (69)	2.2
—Dave Barker see: David CROOKS	
Kent BARKER ▶ 5047 (3)	**354**
Jody's Got Your Girl And Gone—Johnnie Taylor (71)	731
Pick Up The Pieces—Carla Thomas (67)	176
Standing In For Jody—Johnnie Taylor (72)	103
Stella BARKER ▶ 10577 (1)	**7.1**
Sign Of The Times—Belle Stars (83)	49
Andrew BARKSDALE ▶ 1714 (3)	**2447**
Handy Man—Jimmy Jones (59)	*5670*
Handy Man—James Taylor (77)	*3089*
Handy Man—Del Shannon (64)	*1029*
Chuck BARKSDALE ▶ 6749 (1)	**141**
Use Your Head—Mary Wells (65)	422
Harold BARLOW ▶ 4018 (5)	**622**
Mama—Connie Francis (60)	2155
Ma Ma Ma Marie—Gaylords (58)	*240*
Things I Love—Fidelity's (58)	47
Why Should I Love You—Harptones with The Shytans (54)	*0.0*

Why Should I Love You?—Four Lads (54)	*0.0*
John Perry BARLOW ▶ 7968 (2)	**67**
Bombs Away—Bob Weir (78)	85
The Music Never Stopped—Grateful Dead (75)	49
—Lawrence Barnard see: Larson PAINE	
—Robert Barnard see: Bobby PAINE	
—Bettye Jean Crutcher Barnes see: Bettye CRUTCHER	
David BARNES ▶ 8291 (1)	**55**
Buffalo Soldier—Flamingos (70)	165
Don BARNES ▶ 2816 (6)	**1176**
Caught Up In You—38 Special (82)	1470
Like No Other Night—38 Special (86)	857
If I'd Been The One—38 Special (83)	839
Hold On Loosely—.38 Special (81)	550
You Keep Runnin' Away—38 Special (82)	410
Somebody Like You—38 Special (86)	322
Howard Ellington Riddiford BARNES [Milton Carson, John Jerome] ▶ 2453 (7)	**1469**
A Blossom Fell—Nat "King" Cole (55)	*4027*
Chincherinchee—Perry Como (56)	282
Butterfly—Danyel Gérard (72)	103
How Many—Bill Haley & His Comets (57)	25
A Blossom Fell—Dickie Valentine (55)	*0.0*
A Blossom Fell—Vic Barrett (55)	0.0
Someone Else's Roses—Doris Day (54)	*0.0*
Howard Lee BARNES ▶ 2591 (6)	**1345**
I Really Don't Want To Know—Tommy Edwards (60)	*1085*
I Really Don't Want To Know—Ronnie Dove (66)	*753*
I Really Don't Want To Know—Elvis Presley (70)	*704*
I Really Don't Want To Know—"Little Esther" Phillips (63)	*134*
I Really Don't Want To Know—Solomon Burke (62)	*15*
I Really Don't Want To Know—Les Paul and Mary Ford (54)	*0.0*
Jerry BARNES ▶ 9516 (1)	**22**
Happy Hour—Deodato (82)	44
Jimmy BARNES [James Dixon Swan] ▶ 11581 (1)	**1.1**
Too Much Ain't Enough Love—Jimmy Barnes (88)	5.6
J.J. BARNES ▶ 6405 (2)	**174**
Baby Please Come Back Home—J.J. Barnes (67)	321
I Have Learned To Do Without You—Mavis Staples (70)	41
John BARNES ▶ 10892 (1)	**4.5**
Bullish—Herb Alpert/Tijuana Brass (84)	9.1
Katreese BARNES ▶ 9517 (1)	**22**
Happy Hour—Deodato (82)	44
—Martin Barnes see: Martin LEE	
Sharon BARNES ▶ 11094 (1)	**3.3**
Feels Like Another One—Patti LaBelle (91)	13
Sid BARNES ▶ 4990 (5)	**364**
A Love So Fine—Chiffons (63)	466
Long Live Our Love—Shangri-Las (66)	433
I'll Bet You—Funkadelic (69)	116
Love And Desire (Part I)—Arpeggio (79)	69
Me Without You—Mary Wells (65)	16
—Charlie Barnet see: Dale BENNETT	
Peter BARNETT ▶ 11189 (1)	**2.8**
Maybe This Day—Kissing The Pink (83)	20
—Robin Barnetti see: Robin FOX	
Peter BARNFATHER ▶ 7856 (1)	**72**
Cowboy Convention—Ohio Express (69)	144
Billie BARNUM ▶ 11399 (1)	**1.9**
Communication—David McCallum (66)	3.8
H.B. BARNUM ▶ 2097 (6)	**1882**
Peanut Butter—Marathons (61)	1099
Your Love—Marilyn McCoo And Billy Davis Jr. (77)	879
I Don't Love You No More (I Don't Care About You)—Jimmy Norman (62)	499
You Can Bring Me All Your Heartaches—Lou Rawls (66)	397
Don't Blame The Children—Sammy Davis Jr. (67)	367
Lost Love—H.B. Barnum (61)	287
Addy BARON [Addy Fleger] ▶ 6714 (2)	**142**
I Kneel At Your Throne—Joe Medlin (59)	270
Sad Eyes (Don't You Cry)—Echoes (61)	14

Sandy BARON [Sanford Irving Bereofsky] ▶ 2266 (8)	**1676**
The Writing On The Wall—Adam Wade (61)	2168
A Natural Man—Lou Rawls (71)	1273
That Stranger Used To Be My Girl—Trade Martin (62)	503
Let True Love Begin—Nat King Cole (61)	104
Mr. Happiness—Johnny Maestro With The Coeds (61)	61
Presidential Press Conference—Sickniks (61)	22
His Song Shall Be Sung—Lou Rawls (72)	5.3
Flying Blue Angels—George, Johnny And The Pilots (62)	3.6
Pierre BAROUH ▶ 10891 (2)	**4.6**
A Man And A Woman—Tamiko Jones With Herbie Mann (66)	12
Live For Life—Jack Jones (67)	1.4
Chick BARR ▶ 7678 (1)	**81**
Lonely Saturday Night—Don French (59)	163
Philip BARR ▶ 9806 (1)	**17**
Dear Mrs. Applebee—Flip Cartridge (66)	33
Geoff BARRADALE ▶ 8732 (1)	**41**
Burning Flame—Vitamin Z (85)	122
—Michael Barratt see: Shakin' STEVENS	
Martin BARRE ▶ 10027 (1)	**14**
Minstrel In The Gallery—Jethro Tull (75)	28
Charles BARRETT ▶ 10201 (1)	**11**
Stand Or Fall—Fixx (82)	67
Pat BARRETT ▶ 11788 (1)	**0.0**
Crazy 'Bout Ya Baby—Crew-Cuts (54)	0.0
Richard BARRETT [B. Junior] ▶ 1353 (18)	**3277**
I Want You To Be My Girl—Frankie Lymon and the Teenagers (56)	1339
Look In My Eyes—Chantels (61)	*1253*
Maybe—Three Degrees (70)	*895*
Maybe—Chantels (58)	*847*
Well, I Told You—Chantels (61)	593
Every Night (I Pray)—Chantels (58)	330
ABC's Of Love—Frankie Lymon and the Teenagers (56)	186
Gee Baby (I'm Sorry)—3° Degrees (65)	92
So Much—Little Anthony And The Imperials (58)	42
He's Gone—Chantels (57)	30
I Want You To Be My Boy—Exciters (65)	20
Girl's Work Is Never Done—Chordettes (59)	14
The Plea—Jesters (58)	14
Maybe—Shangri-Las (64)	*8.7*
Look In My Eyes—3° Degrees (66)	*5.3*
If You Try—Chantels (58)	5.1
Summer's Love—Richard Barrett with the Chantels (59)	3.3
I Know I Know—"Pookie" Hudson (63)	2.3
Vinnie BARRETT [Gwendolyn Hines Woolfolk] ▶ 1067 (6)	**4135**
Love Won't Let Me Wait—Major Harris (75)	3713
Sideshow—Blue Magic (74)	*2571*
Just Don't Want To Be Lonely—Main Ingredient (74)	*2140*
Three Ring Circus—Blue Magic (74)	407
Just Don't Want To Be Lonely—Ronnie Dyson (73)	*210*
Sideshow—Band Of Gold (84)	*12*
Ray BARRETTO ▶ 2812 (2)	**1179**
El Watusi—Ray Barretto y su Charanga Moderna (63)	1089
Deeper Shade Of Soul—Urban Dance Squad (90)	545
Steve BARRI [Steven Barry Lipkin] ▶ 440 (26)	**9313**
Eve Of Destruction—Barry McGuire (65)	*6384*
Secret Agent Man—Johnny Rivers (66)	*3877*
A Must To Avoid—Herman's Hermits (65)	2112
You Baby—Turtles (66)	1351
Bella Linda—Grassroots (68)	894
Glory Bound—Grass Roots (72)	745
Things I Should Have Said—Grass Roots (67)	624
Where Were You When I Needed You—Grass Roots (66)	623
I Found A Girl—Jan & Dean (65)	524
Love Pains—Yvonne Elliman (79)	404
Wake Up, Wake Up—Grass Roots (67)	328
(Here They Come) From All Over The World—Jan & Dean (65)	275
Another Day, Another Heartache—5th Dimension (67)	263
Kick That Little Foot Sally Ann—Round Robin (64)	254
Secret Agent Man—Ventures (66)	*212*
Take Me For What I'm Worth—Searchers (66)	212
The Morning Of Our Lives—Arkade (71)	185
Summer Means Fun—Bruce And Terry (64)	77
Can I Get To Know You Better—Turtles (66)	60
I Wouldn't Treat A Dog (The Way You Treated Me)—Bobby Bland (74)	39
This Precious Time—Terry Knight And The Pack (67)	36
Only When You're Lonely—Grass Roots (66)	31
Unless You Care—Terry Black (64)	30
One Piece Topless Bathing Suit—Rip Chords (64)	2.4
Tell 'Em I'm Surfin—Fantastic Baggys (64)	0.9
Eve Of Destruction—Turtles (70)	*0.8*
Eric BARRIER [Eric B.] ▶ 5145 (1)	**334**
Friends—Jody Watley (89)	1337
Chuck BARRIS ▶ 909 (1)	**4864**
Palisades Park—Freddy Cannon (62)	4864
Harry BARRIS ▶ 9105 (1)	**31**
I Surrender, Dear—Aretha Franklin (62)	62
Bob BARRON ▶ 1946 (2)	**2069**
Cindy Oh Cindy—Eddie Fisher (56)	*2225*
Cindy Oh Cindy—Vince Martin with The Tarriers (56)	*1914*
Ary BARROSO ▶ 2492 (2)	**1438**
Brazil—Ritchie Family (75)	*1346*
Brazil—Ritchie Family (76)	*92*
David BARROW ▶ 10752 (1)	**5.5**
Gypsy Spirit—Pendulum (80)	17
Claudja BARRY ▶ 8235 (2)	**57**
Boogie Woogie Dancin' Shoes—Claudja Barry (79)	216
Dancin' Fever—Claudja Barry (78)	43
Jeff BARRY [Joel Adelberg] ▶ 33 (95) HOF	**47971**
Sugar, Sugar—Archies (69)	*12247*
Chapel Of Love—Dixie Cups (64)	*8316*
Do Wah Diddy Diddy—Manfred Mann (64)	*8308*
Hanky Panky—Tommy James And The Shondells (66)	6771
Leader Of The Pack—Shangri-Las (64)	*6265*
Be My Baby—Ronettes (63)	*6059*
I Honestly Love You—Olivia Newton-John (74)	*5140*
Da Doo Ron Ron—Shaun Cassidy (77)	*4512*
Da Doo Ron Ron (When He Walked Me Home)—Crystals (63)	*3838*
Baby, I Love You—Andy Kim (69)	*2808*
Then He Kissed Me—Crystals (63)	2734
Jingle Jangle—Archies (69)	2684
Tell Laura I Love Her—Ray Peterson (60)	*2552*
Bang-Shang-A-Lang—Archies (68)	2330
Take Me Home Tonight—Eddie Money (86)	2098
Lay A Little Lovin' On Me—Robin McNamara (70)	2016
Montego Bay—Bobby Bloom (70)	*1958*
I Wanna Love Him So Bad—Jelly Beans (64)	1628
People Say—Dixie Cups (64)	1548
Maybe I Know—Lesley Gore (64)	1454
River Deep-Mountain High—Supremes & Four Tops (70)	*1281*
Chip Chip—Gene McDaniels (62)	1262
Be My Baby—Andy Kim (70)	*1212*
How'd We Ever Get This Way—Andy Kim (68)	1172
The Kind Of Boy You Can't Forget—Raindrops (63)	1132
Sugar Sugar—Wilson Pickett (70)	*1116*
I Can Hear Music—Beach Boys (69)	*916*
Look Of Love—Lesley Gore (64)	848
Did You See Her Eyes—Illusion (69)	814
So Good Together—Andy Kim (69)	785
Heavy Makes You Happy (Sha-Na-Boom Boom)—Staple Singers (71)	*754*
Baby, I Love You—Ronettes (63)	*719*
Wait 'til My Bobby Gets Home—Darlene Love (63)	657
I Have A Boyfriend—Chiffons (63)	647
Shoot 'em Up, Baby—Andy Kim (68)	590
Sunshine—Archies (70)	589
Give Us Your Blessings—Shangri-Las (65)	*554*
Feelin' So Good (S.k.o.o.b.y.-D.o.o.)—Archies (68)	552
What A Guy—Raindrops (63)	549
Who's Your Baby?—Archies (70)	546
Sugar Sugar—Stars On 45 (81)	*442*
Don't Ever Leave Me—Connie Francis (64)	442
The Last Time I Made Love—Joyce Kennedy & Jeffrey Osborne (84)	369
Sister James—Nino Tempo And 5th Ave. Sax (73)	369
River Deep-Mountain High—Deep Purple (69)	*351*
Rainbow Ride—Andy Kim (68)	351
Good Night Baby—Butterflys (64)	321
Baby Be Mine—Jelly Beans (64)	308
Teenage Sonata—Sam Cooke (60)	307
Leader Of The Pack—Twisted Sister (85)	*289*
Little Bell—Dixie Cups (64)	276
You Should Have Seen The Way He Looked At Me—Dixie Cups (64)	270
That Boy John—Raindrops (63)	228
I Honestly Love You—Olivia Newton-John (77)	*223*
I Wish I Were—Andy Kim (71)	219
A Fine Fine Boy—Darlene Love (63)	184
Out In The Streets—Shangri-Las (65)	175
Not Too Young To Get Married—Bob B. Soxx And The Blue Jeans (63)	171
Give Us Your Blessing—Ray Peterson (63)	*149*
Am I Grooving You—Freddie Scott (67)	148
I'll Take You Where The Music's Playing—Drifters (65)	146
Make Me Happy—Bobby Bloom (71)	141
A Friend In The City—Andy Kim (70)	140
I Left My Heart In The Balcony—Linda Scott (62)	134
I Got To Go Back (And Watch That Little Girl Dance)—McCoys (66)	122
It's Your Life—Andy Kim (70)	116
You Got Style—Jon & Robin (68)	92
Do-Wah-Diddy—Exciters (64)	*55*
Honey Do—Strangeloves (68)	51
Tricia Tell Your Daddy—Andy Kim (69)	44
Wake Up And Love Me—April (74)	34
I Been Moved—Andy Kim (71)	32
How Does It Feel—Illusion (69)	31
Tell Laura I Love Her—Johnny T. Angel (74)	*27*
Be My Baby—Cissy Houston (71)	*24*
River Deep-Mountain High—Ike & Tina Turner (66)	*23*
Montego Bay—Amazulu (87)	*22*
Little Boy—Crystals (64)	22
All Grown Up—Crystals (64)	14
Do Wah Diddy Diddy—Stars On 45 (81)	*12*
We're All Goin' Home—Bobby Bloom (71)	9.2
Da Doo Ron Ron (When He Walked Me Home)—Ian Matthews (72)	*7.8*
Oh My My—Monkees (70)	7.4
I Wonder—Butterflys (65)	7.3
I Can Hear Music—Ronettes Featuring Veronica (66)	*5.6*
Hickory Dickery Dock—Baby Jane And The Rock-A-Byes (63)	3.2
River Deep-Mountain High—Ike & Tina Turner (69)	*3.1*
When The Boy's Happy (The Girl's Happy Too)—Four Pennies (63)	2.7
One More Tear—Raindrops (64)	1.9
We Can't Dance To Your Music—Grass Roots (73)	1.4
Doo Wah Diddy Diddy—Tight Fit (81)	*0.9*
Tell Me What She Said—Playmates (61)	0.5
He Ain't No Angel—Ad Libs (65)	0.5
Sha La Boom Boom—Bobby Bloom (73)	*0.4*
Chapel Of Love—Bette Midler (73)	*0.0*
John BARRY [John Barry Prendergast] ▶ 585 (16) HOF	**7417**
A View To A Kill—Duran Duran (85)	4032
Born Free—Roger Williams (66)	*3587*
Goldfinger—Shirley Bassey (65)	*2651*
Midnight Cowboy—Ferrante & Teicher (69)	1987
Thunderball—Tom Jones (65)	923
Born Free—Hesitations (68)	*597*
All Time High—Rita Coolidge (83)	493
Goldfinger—Billy Strange (65)	*445*
You Only Live Twice—Nancy Sinatra (67)	334
The Best Man In The World—Ann Wilson (86)	298
Diamonds Are Forever—Shirley Bassey (72)	284
Goldfinger—John Barry And His Orchestra (65)	*114*
Theme From King Kong (Pt. 1)—Love Unlimited Orchestra (77)	59
Goldfinger—Meco (82)	*47*
Goldfinger—Jack La Forge, His Piano And Orchestra (65)	*27*
Goldfinger—Jimmy Smith (65)	*0.0*
Len BARRY [Leonard W. Borisoff] ▶ 2459 (10)	**1466**
1-2-3—Len Barry (65)	*5700*
Like A Baby—Len Barry (65)	1065
Hey You! Little Boo-Ga-Loo—Chubby Checker (66)	187
One, Two, Three—Ramsey Lewis (67)	*131*
The Jitterbug—Dovells (62)	85
It's That Time Of The Year—Len Barry (66)	64
Lip Sync (To The Tongue Twisters)—Len Barry (65)	36
Motown Review—Philly Cream (79)	35
Laid Back Love—Major Harris (76)	9.1
I Struck It Rich—Len Barry (66)	1.9

Lloyd BARRY ▶ 8752 (1)	**40**
Super Bowl Shuffle—Chicago Bears Shufflin' Crew (86)	161
Peggy BARSELLA ▶ 10792 (1)	**5.3**
He Wore The Green Beret—Nancy Ames (66)	11
Michael BARSON ▶ 5086 (2)	**345**
Our House—Madness (83)	2122
The Sun And The Rain—Madness (84)	42
Lionel BART [Lionel Begleiter] ▶ 2503 (7)	**1434**
Living Doll—Cliff Richard and The Drifters (59)	*673*
As Long As She Needs Me—Sammy Davis Jr. (63)	306
Do You Mind—Andy Williams (60)	*262*
From Russia With Love—Village Stompers (64)	*141*
Do You Mind—Anthony Newley (60)	*35*
Living Doll—David Hill (59)	*17*
From Russia With Love—Al Caiola (64)	*0.0*
Teddy BART ▶ 10681 (1)	**6.1**
Taste Of Tears—Johnny Mathis (64)	12
Lou BARTEL ▶ 9713 (1)	**18**
Big Brown Eyes—Redjacks (58)	18
—Jonny Bartels see: Kurt FELTZ	
Bobby BARTH ▶ 6746 (2)	**141**
Now Or Never—Axe (82)	139
I Think You'll Remember Tonight—Axe (83)	4.5
—Curt Bartholomew see: Barry CURTIS	
Dave BARTHOLOMEW [Dave Barton] ▶ 116 (60) HOF	**21978**
Ain't That A Shame—Pat Boone (55)	*6966*
I Hear You Knocking—Gale Storm (55)	*5135*
One Night—Elvis Presley (58)	4905
I'm In Love Again—Fats Domino (56)	*3481*
I Hear You Knocking—Dave Edmunds (70)	*3442*
I'm Walkin'—Fats Domino (57)	*2846*
Whole Lotta Loving—Fats Domino (58)	2302
Blue Monday—Fats Domino (56)	2195
Walking To New Orleans—Fats Domino (60)	2113
My Girl Josephine—Fats Domino (60)	*1293*
Let The Four Winds Blow—Fats Domino (61)	*1081*
Valley Of Tears—Fats Domino (57)	1025
I'm Walkin'—Ricky Nelson (57)	*939*
Bo Weevil—Teresa Brewer (56)	*908*
I'm Gonna Be A Wheel Some Day—Fats Domino (59)	900
Ain't That A Shame!—4 Seasons Featuring Frankie Valli (63)	*760*
It Keeps Rainin'—Fats Domino (61)	735
My Girl Josephine—Jerry Jaye (67)	*721*
Ain't It A Shame—Fats Domino (55)	*665*
Country Boy—Fats Domino (60)	600
What A Party—Fats Domino (61)	553
Shu Rah—Fats Domino (61)	516
Witchcraft—Elvis Presley With The Jordanaires (63)	500
It's You I Love—Fats Domino (57)	423
Ain't That A Shame—Cheap Trick (79)	*411*
Wait And See—Fats Domino (57)	406
Natural Born Lover—Fats Domino (60)	381
I'm In Love Again—Fontane Sisters (56)	*355*
When I See You—Fats Domino (57)	328
I Want You To Know—Fats Domino (57)	295
Let The Four Winds Blow—Roy Brown (57)	*280*
Tell Me That You Love Me—Fats Domino (60)	274
Big Beat—Fats Domino (57)	269
Sick And Tired—Fats Domino (58)	248
So Long—Fats Domino (56)	245
Bo Weevil—Fats Domino (56)	*220*
I'm In Love Again—Rick Nelson (63)	*189*
Poor Me—Fats Domino (55)	*184*
Yes My Darling—Fats Domino (58)	141
Honey Chile—Fats Domino (56)	105
Before I Grow Too Old—Fats Domino (60)	92
Little Mary—Fats Domino (58)	72
No, No—Fats Domino (58)	60
I Still Love You—Fats Domino (57)	57
Nothing New (Same Old Thing)—Fats Domino (62)	52
I Hear You Knocking—Fats Domino (61)	*29*
The Rooster Song—Fats Domino (57)	19
Hey La Bas—Fats Domino (57)	19
Don't You Know I Love You—Fats Domino (58)	18
Don't Blame It On Me—Fats Domino (56)	10
I Just Cry—Fats Domino (61)	7.0
Young School Girl—Fats Domino (58)	3.3
My Heart Is Bleeding—Fats Domino (62)	1.6
Dance With Mr. Domino—Fats Domino (62)	1.3
If You Need Me—Fats Domino (60)	1.1
I Hear You Knocking—Smiley Lewis (55)	*0.0*
Ain't That A Shame—Ronnie Gaylord (55)	*0.0*
Bo Weevil—Bonnie Lou (56)	*0.0*
I'm Walkin'—Larry Storch (57)	*0.0*
Poor Me—Bill Carey (55)	*0.0*
Simon BARTHOLOMEW ▶ 9457 (1)	**23**
Never Stop—Brand New Heavies (91)	93
David BARTLETT ▶ 8188 (1)	**59**
This Time It's Real—Tower Of Power (73)	177
Dallas BARTLEY ▶ 10544 (1)	**7.5**
Early In The Mornin'—Ray Charles (61)	22
—Betty Barton see: Bettye SWANN	
Billy BARTON ▶ 6902 (1)	**130**
Dear John—Pat Boone (60)	389
—Dave Barton see: Dave BARTHOLOMEW	
Geri BARTON ▶ 9626 (1)	**20**
Joanie—Frankie Calen (61)	40
Marge BARTON ▶ 4577 (1)	**462**
What Color (Is A Man)—Bobby Vinton (65)	462
Stuart BASCOMBE ▶ 11353 (1)	**2.1**
You And I—Black Ivory (72)	4.3
—Rob Base see: Robert GINYARD	
Joss BASELLI [Joseph Octave Basile, Giuseppe Ottavia Basile] ▶ 7173 (2)	**112**
Time, Time—Ed Ames (67)	216
Free Again—Barbra Streisand (66)	119
Vicki BASEMORE ▶ 6961 (2)	**125**
With A Child's Heart—Michael Jackson (73)	*371*
With A Child's Heart—Stevie Wonder (66)	*4.4*
Count BASIE ▶ 9524 (2)	**22**
Party Blues—Count Basie Small Band with Ella Fitzgerald and Joe Williams (57)	66
Going To Chicago Blues—Count Basie (58)	0.4
Toni BASIL [Antonia Basilotta] ▶ 9726 (1)	**18**
Shoppin' From A To Z—Toni Basil (83)	55
—Giuseppe/Joseph Basile see: Joss BASELLI	
—Antonia Basilotta see: Toni BASIL	
Charles BASKERVILLE ▶ 2000 (5)	**2014**
Daddy's Home—Shep And The Limelites (61)	*4846*
Daddy's Home—Jermaine Jackson (72)	*2516*
Daddy's Home—Cliff Richard (82)	*659*
Daddy's Home—Chuck Jackson & Maxine Brown (67)	*29*
Remember Baby—Shep And The Limelites (63)	4.5
Fritz BASKETT ▶ 7104 (1)	**116**
Silly—Deniece Williams (81)	347
Don BASKIN ▶ 3202 (1)	**955**
Little Girl—Syndicate Of Sound (66)	1909
Richard BASKIN ▶ 3216 (1)	**947**
Will You Still Love Me?—Chicago (86)	2842
Dalibor BASLER ▶ 7507 (1)	**91**
Truly, Truly, True—Brenda Lee (65)	274
Ralph BASS [Ralph Basso Jr.] ▶ 854 (7)	**5200**
Dedicated To The One I Love—Mamas & The Papas (67)	*5052*
Dedicated To The One I Love—Shirelles (61)	*5044*
Dedicated To The One I Love—Shirelles (59)	*96*
Dedicated To The One I Love—Bernadette Peters (81)	*90*
Dedicated To The One I Love—Temprees (72)	*59*
Dedicated To The One I Love—"5" Royales (61)	*58*
Just A Little Bit—Little Milton (69)	3.1
Sid BASS ▶ 7487 (2)	**93**
The Greatest Feeling In The World—Four Tunes (54)	184
My Time For Cryin'—Maxine Brown (62)	1.4
—Thomas Lee Bass see: Tommy LEE	
Clarence BASSETT ▶ 1923 (7)	**2106**
Daddy's Home—Shep And The Limelites (61)	*4846*
Daddy's Home—Jermaine Jackson (72)	*2516*
Daddy's Home—Cliff Richard (82)	*659*
Trickle Trickle—Manhattan Transfer (80)	*88*
Daddy's Home—Chuck Jackson & Maxine Brown (67)	*29*
Remember Baby—Shep And The Limelites (63)	4.5
Trickle, Trickle—Videos (58)	*3.8*
Maurizio BASSI ▶ 4053 (2)	**611**
Tarzan Boy—Baltimora (85)	1208
Living In The Background—Baltimora (86)	15
George BASSMAN ▶ 10310 (2)	**10**
I'm Gettin' Sentimental Over You—Nelson Riddle and His Orchestra (58)	*18*
I'm Gettin' Sentimental Over You—Modernaires (57)	*1.9*
—Ralph Basso Jr. see: Ralph BASS	
Charles BASSOLINE ▶ 7862 (1)	**72**
If This Is Love (I'd Rather Be Lonely)—Precisions (67)	215
Ruth BATCHELOR ▶ 7058 (2)	**118**
King Of The Whole Wide World—Elvis Presley with the Jordanaires (62)	236
Where Do You Come From—Elvis Presley With The Jordanaires (62)	0.9
Robert BATEMAN [Brianbert] ▶ 863 (15)	**5152**
Mashed Potato Time—Dee Dee Sharp (62)	8768
Please Mr. Postman—Marvelettes (61)	*7831*
Please Mr. Postman—Carpenters (74)	*4500*
Playboy—Marvelettes (62)	2321
If You Need Me—Solomon Burke (63)	*786*
Twistin' Postman—Marvelettes (62)	539
If You Need Me—Wilson Pickett (63)	*279*
Skate Now—Lou Courtney (67)	219
Please Mr. Postman—Gentle Persuasion (83)	*45*
Greetings (This Is Uncle Sam)—Valadiers (61)	*9.2*
Please Mr. Postman—Beatles (64)	*6.4*
Greetings (This Is Uncle Sam)—Monitors (66)	*5.8*
I've Got A Notion—Marv Johnson (61)	3.2
Hey Joyce—Lou Courtney (68)	2.4
Right Now And Not Later—Shangri-Las (65)	1.9
Bill BATES ▶ 7157 (1)	**113**
Scotch On The Rocks—Band Of The Black Watch (76)	113
Charles BATES ▶ 8613 (1)	**45**
Hardhearted Hannah—Ray Charles Orch. & Chor. (60)	179
—Elias Otha Bates see: Elias McDANIEL	
Katharine Lee BATES ▶ 10918 (1) HOF	**4.4**
America, The Beautiful—Charlie Rich (76)	18
Leroy R. BATES ▶ 4031 (2)	**620**
There's No Other (Like My Baby)—Crystals (61)	1172
Starlight—Preludes Five (61)	34
—Nicholas James Bates see: Nick RHODES	
Cortez BATEZA ▶ 10493 (1)	**7.9**
Lost—Jery Butler with Riley Hampton's Orchestra (59)	24
Billy BATSTONE ▶ 4732 (1)	**429**
I Still Have Dreams—Richie Furay (79)	429
Michael Philip BATT ▶ 6620 (1)	**150**
Wombling Summer Party—Wombles (74)	150
—Margaret Battavio see: Peggy MARCH	
Tracy BATTEAST ▶ 10785 (1)	**5.3**
A 'Soalin'—Peter, Paul & Mary (63)	16
David BATTEAU ▶ 2467 (6)	**1454**
You're The Love—Seals & Crofts (78)	888
Tell Her She's Lovely—El Chicano (73)	527
Don't Stop—Jeffrey Osborne (84)	436
Automatic Man—Michael Sembello (83)	371
Rainbow's End—Sergio Mendes (83)	227
Discipline Of Love (Why Did You Do It)—Robert Palmer (85)	54
Clyde BATTIN [Skip] ▶ 9300 (1)	**27**
Fancy Nancy—Skip & Flip (59)	54
Lucio BATTISTI ▶ 5376 (1)	**298**
Bella Linda—Grassroots (68)	894
Edgar BATTLE ▶ 1395 (2)	**3185**
Topsy II—Cozy Cole (58)	6164
Topsy I—Cozy Cole (58)	205
Edward BATTS ▶ 7175 (1)	**112**
What Can I Do For You?—Labelle (75)	223
—Victor William Batty see: Steve WOLFE	
Brad BAUDER ▶ 11289 (1)	**2.4**
Cookin'—Al Casey Combo (62)	7.2
Ray BAUDUC ▶ 11177 (1)	**2.9**
Big Noise From Winnetka—Spaghetti Head (75)	11
Bernie BAUM [Bernard Weisbaum] ▶ 1637 (11)	**2561**
(You're the) Devil In Disguise—Elvis Presley With The Jordanaires (63)	3964
Ask Me—Elvis Presley With The Jordanaires (64)	1582
That's Old Fashioned (That's The Way Love Should Be)—Everly Brothers (62)	1204
Young And In Love—Chris Crosby (64)	357
A Time To Love-A Time To Cry (Petite Fleur)—Lou Johnson (65)	*356*
Held For Questioning—Rusty Draper (56)	244
Music, Music, Music—Sensations Featuring Yvonne Baker (61)	*138*

Bernie BAUM [Bernard Weisbaum] ▶ 1637 (11) *Continued*	**2561**
Music, Music, Music—Crazy Otto (55)	*49*
Music Music Music—Happenings (68)	*30*
Music, Music, Music—Teresa Brewer (73)	*9.4*
Today, Tomorrow And Forever—Elvis Presley (64)	1.1
Claude BAUM [Katherine Harrison] ▶ 4857 (1)	**398**
On My Word Of Honor—Platters (56)	795
Duke BAXTER ▶ 5723 (1)	**251**
Everybody Knows Matilda—Duke Baxter (69)	251
Jeff BAXTER ▶ 10079 (2)	**13**
Holiday—Nazareth (80)	63
Wheels Of Fortune—Doobie Brothers (76)	7.7
Les BAXTER ▶ 1161 (4)	**3831**
Quiet Village—Exotic Sounds Of Martin Denny (59)	3813
Sinner Man—Les Baxter, His Chorus and Orchestra (56)	19
The Left Arm Of Buddha—Les Baxter's Orchestra (56)	6.3
Rebel In Town—Crew-Cuts (56)	6.1
Lou BAXTER ▶ 10095 (1)	**13**
Merry Christmas Baby—Chuck Berry (58)	26
Phil BAXTER ▶ 7049 (1)	**119**
Faded Summer Love—Georgie Shaw (56)	119
—Carole Jean Bayer see: Carole Bayer SAGER	
Lee BAYER ▶ 5963 (1)	**222**
I Can't Stop Thinking Of You—Bobbi Martin (65)	444
Nora BAYES [Eleanor Goldberg] ▶ 5995 (2)	**218**
Shine On Harvest Moon—Four Aces (55)	*424*
Shine On Harvest Moon—Google René And His Band (58)	*13*
—Bayété see: Todd COCHRAN	
T.D. BAYLESS [Theodore Debs Bayless] ▶ 8206 (1)	**58**
The Pill—Loretta Lynn (75)	175
Bobby BAYLOR ▶ 7168 (2)	**112**
Walking Along—Diamonds (58)	*783*
Walking Along—Solitaires (58)	*0.0*
Johnny BAYLOR ▶ 7573 (5)	**88**
Always—Luther Ingram (73)	120
More Power To You—Tommy Tate (72)	20
Be Good To Me Baby—Luther Ingram (71)	15
Do You Love Somebody—Luther Ingram (78)	2.7
To The Other Man—Luther Ingram (70)	1.7
Amir BAYYAN [Kevin Bell] ▶ 6728 (3)	**142**
Let's Go Dancin' (Ooh La, La, La)—Kool & The Gang (82)	654
Heart Don't Lie—La Toya Jackson (84)	224
You Got To Keep On Bumpin'—Kay-Gees (74)	61
—Khalis Bayyan see: Ronald BELL	
Eric BAZILIAN ▶ 2886 (8)	**1131**
And We Danced—Hooters (85)	804
Day By Day—Hooters (85)	759
Where Do The Children Go—Hooters (86)	387
All You Zombies—Hooters (85)	225
Never Enough—Patty Smyth (87)	206
Johnny B—Hooters (87)	201
Satellite—Hooters (87)	169
Brother, Don't You Walk Away—Hooters (90)	17
Albert BEACH [Lee Wilson] ▶ 3438 (3)	**849**
I Wish You Love—Gloria Lynne (64)	856
Wedding—June Valli (58)	829
Hey Naughty Papa—Sarah Vaughan (55)	6.3
Jerry BEACH ▶ 8990 (1)	**34**
I'll Play The Blues For You—Albert King (72)	34
Reb BEACH [Richard Earl Beach Jr.] ▶ 4592 (4)	**459**
Seventeen—Winger (89)	595
Can't Get Enuff—Winger (90)	464
Hungry—Winger (89)	31
Madalaine—Winger (88)	27
—Trevor Beacham see: Chris EVANS	
Len BEADLE [Leonard Stanley Beadle, Frank Weston] ▶ 10137 (2)	**12**
She's My Girl—Bobby Shafto (64)	22
Who Needs It—Gene Pitney (64)	2.7
Earl BEAL ▶ 2606 (3)	**1328**
Get A Job—Silhouettes (58)	*5224*
Get A Job—Nino & the Ebb Tides (61)	*88*
Get A Job—Mills Brothers (58)	*0.0*

Joe BEAL ▶ 3046 (12)	**1037**
Jingle Bell Rock—Bobby Helms (57)	*684*
Unsuspecting Heart—Terri Stevens (54)	*610*
Jingle Bell Rock—Bobby Rydell Chubby Checker (61)	*402*
Jingle Bell Rock—Bobby Helms (61)	*209*
Jingle Bell Rock—Bobby Helms (58)	*159*
Unsuspecting Heart—Sunny Gale (54)	*120*
Jingle Bell Rock—Bobby Helms (60)	*119*
Jingle Bell Rock—Bobby Helms (62)	*114*
Jingle Bell Rock—Bobby Rydell Chubby Checker (62)	*14*
Jingle Bell Rock—Bobby Helms (60)	*7.6*
Jingle Bell Rock—Teresa Brewer (58)	*0.0*
Unsuspecting Heart—Georgie Shaw (54)	*0.0*
Eric BEAM ▶ 9900 (1)	**15**
Shoes—Reparata (75)	15
Richard BEAN ▶ 4785 (1)	**416**
Suavecito—Malo (72)	1249
—Teddy Bear see: Ted McRAE	
Frank BEARD ▶ 1608 (16)	**2631**
Legs—ZZ Top (84)	1701
Sleeping Bag—ZZ Top (85)	1591
Tush—ZZ Top (75)	835
La Grange—ZZ Top (74)	740
Stages—ZZ Top (86)	629
Rough Boy—ZZ Top (86)	621
Velcro Fly—ZZ Top (86)	451
Gimme All Your Lovin'—ZZ Top (83)	417
It's Only Love—ZZ Top (76)	308
Doubleback—ZZ Top (90)	295
Sharp Dressed Man—ZZ Top (83)	150
Leila—ZZ Top (81)	45
Arrested For Driving While Blind—ZZ Top (77)	43
Cheap Sunglasses—ZZ Top (80)	32
Give It Up—ZZ Top (91)	23
Enjoy And Get It On—ZZ Top (77)	14
Michael BEARD ▶ 6884 (9)	**131**
Shake Your Rump To The Funk—Bar-Kays (76)	593
Move Your Boogie Body—Bar-Kays (79)	270
Today Is The Day—Bar-Kays (80)	150
Freakshow On The Dance Floor—Bar-Kays (84)	79
Too Hot To Stop—Bar-Kays (77)	36
Hit And Run—Bar-Kays (81)	23
Boogie Body Land—Bar-Kays (81)	23
Let's Have Some Fun—Bar-Kays (78)	8.9
Shine—Bar-Kays (79)	7.7
Nidra BEARD [Nidra Sylvers] ▶ 7596 (1)	**87**
A Night To Remember—Shalamar (82)	260
William Ray BEARD ▶ 8667 (1)	**43**
Remote Control—Reddings (80)	130
Bill BEASLEY ▶ 3016 (1)	**1063**
Too Much—Elvis Presley (57)	4251
Richard BEASLEY ▶ 9818 (1)	**16**
We All Gotta Stick Together—Four Tops (75)	66
Doran BEATTIE ▶ 7672 (1)	**82**
West Coast Woman—Painter (73)	163
E.C. BEATTY ▶ 5234 (1)	**321**
Ski King—E. C. Beatty (59)	321
Harold BEATTY ▶ 6811 (3)	**135**
I'm Gonna Let My Heart Do The Walking—Supremes (76)	385
You're My Driving Wheel—Supremes (76)	21
(Call Me Your) Anything Man—Bobby Moore (75)	1.5
Eleanora BEAUCHAMP ▶ 10543 (1)	**7.5**
Brush Creek Rag—Johnny Maddox And The Rhythmasters (55)	7.5
Tom BEAUDRY ▶ 6693 (1)	**143**
Sing A Song For Freedom—Frijid Pink (70)	430
James BEAUMONT ▶ 3883 (9)	**667**
Since I Don't Have You—Skyliners (59)	*2364*
This I Swear—Skyliners (59)	743
Since I Don't Have You—Don McLean (81)	*545*
Since I Don't Have You—Chuck Jackson (64)	*403*
It Happened Today—Skyliners (59)	229
Since I Don't Have You—Art Garfunkel (79)	*180*
Since I Don't Have You—Eddie Holman (70)	*160*
Since I Don't Have You—Fred Parris & The Five Satins (82)	*4.8*
How Much—Skyliners (60)	1.5
Jean BEAUVOIR ▶ 7056 (1)	**119**
Feel The Heat—Jean Beauvoir (86)	119

Jackey BEAVERS [Robert L. Beavers] ▶ 1518 (3)	**2812**
Someday We'll Be Together—Diana Ross And The Supremes (69)	7492
Do You See My Love (For You Growing)—Jr. Walker & The All Stars (70)	617
That's The Way I Want Our Love—Joe Simon (70)	13
Norman BEAVERS ▶ 9015 (1)	**33**
Fantastic Voyage—Lakeside (80)	296
—Robert L. Beavers see: Jackey BEAVERS	
Gilbert BÉCAUD [François Gilbert Silly] ▶ 515 (16)	**8290**
Love On The Rocks—Neil Diamond (80)	4576
It Must Be Him—Vikki Carr (67)	3693
Let It Be Me—Betty Everett & Jerry Butler (64)	*2995*
Let It Be Me—Everly Brothers (60)	*2197*
The Day The Rains Came—Jane Morgan (58)	*1490*
September Morn'—Neil Diamond (79)	1451
What Now My Love—Sonny & Cher (66)	*986*
What Now My Love—Herb Alpert & The Tijuana Brass (66)	*706*
The Day The Rains Came—Raymond Lefevre and His Orchestra (58)	*623*
What Now My Love—Mitch Ryder (67)	*593*
Let It Be Me—Willie Nelson (82)	*368*
Let It Be Me—Glen Campbell And Bobbie Gentry (69)	*224*
Let It Be Me—Jill Corey (57)	*87*
If Only I Could Live My Life Again—Jane Morgan (59)	15
Let It Be Me—Sweet Inspirations (67)	*6.2*
What Now My Love—"Groove" Holmes (66)	*5.1*
Sidney BECHET ▶ 1325 (5)	**3354**
Petite Fleur (Little Flower)—Chris Barber's Jazz Band (59)	*3264*
A Time To Love-A Time To Cry (Petite Fleur)—Lou Johnson (65)	*356*
Our First Dance (Premier Bal)—Gerard Calvi (60)	1.5
Petite Fleur (Little Flower)—Bob Wilber's Jazz Quartet (59)	*0.0*
Petite Fleur—Bob Crosby & The Bob Cats (59)	*0.0*
Jeff BECK ▶ 4491 (2)	**480**
Over Under Sideways Down—Yardbirds (66)	1583
Happenings Ten Years Time Ago—Yardbirds (66)	652
William BECK ▶ 2039 (9)	**1970**
Love Rollercoaster—Ohio Players (75)	5251
Fire—Ohio Players (74)	4114
Who'd She Coo?—Ohio Players (76)	885
As We Lay—Shirley Murdock (87)	632
Sweet Sticky Thing—Ohio Players (75)	411
Fopp—Ohio Players (76)	398
I Want To Be Free—Ohio Players (75)	335
O-H-I-O—Ohio Players (77)	144
Feel The Beat (Everybody Disco)—Ohio Players (77)	42
Jay BECKENSTEIN ▶ 3467 (3)	**834**
Morning Dance—Spyro Gyra (79)	731
Catching The Sun—Spyro Gyra (80)	88
Shaker Song—Spyro Gyra (78)	14
Nancy BECKER ▶ 4591 (1)	**460**
Teen Commandments—Paul Anka-George Hamilton IV-Johnny Nash (58)	460
Walter BECKER ▶ 607 (18)	**7101**
Rikki Don't Lose That Number—Steely Dan (74)	2950
Do It Again—Steely Dan (72)	*2218*
Reeling In The Years—Steely Dan (73)	2111
Hey Nineteen—Steely Dan (80)	1601
Peg—Steely Dan (77)	1459
Deacon Blues—Steely Dan (78)	825
Josie—Steely Dan (78)	619
FM (No Static At All)—Steely Dan (78)	561
Time Out Of Mind—Steely Dan (81)	531
Black Friday—Steely Dan (75)	400
Show Biz Kids—Steely Dan (73)	342
My Old School—Steely Dan (73)	211
Pretzel Logic—Steely Dan (74)	153
The Fez—Steely Dan (76)	109
Don't Let Me In—Sneaker (82)	80
Do It Again—Club House (83)	*40*
Kid Charlemagne—Steely Dan (76)	16
Bad Sneakers—Steely Dan (75)	13
Dave BECKETT ▶ 9814 (1)	**16**
Could You Ever Love Me Again—Gary & Dave (73)	33

Peter BECKETT ▶ 805 (9)	**5501**
Baby Come Back—Player (77)	6598
Twist Of Fate—Olivia Newton-John (83)	2773
Dare To Fall In Love—Brent Bourgeois (90)	505
Prisoner Of Your Love—Player (78)	430
If Looks Could Kill—Player (82)	197
It's For You—Player (80)	193
The Moment Of Truth—Survivor (84)	138
Silver Lining—Player (78)	87
Love On My Mind Tonight—Temptations (83)	13
Wilson BECKETT ▶ 10522 (1)	**7.6**
You Got To Keep On Bumpin'—Kay-Gees (74)	61
Bob BECKHAM ▶ 9245 (1)	**28**
Danger—Vic Dana (63)	56
Linton BECKLES ▶ 9809 (1)	**17**
Walking Into Sunshine—Central Line (81)	50
Gerry BECKLEY ▶ 623 (5)	**6954**
Sister Golden Hair—America (75)	4201
I Need You—America (72)	1726
Daisy Jane—America (75)	829
Only In Your Heart—America (73)	196
All Around—America (80)	4.7
Fred BECKMEIER ▶ 7682 (1)	**81**
Rock And Roll Dancin'—Beckmeier Brothers (79)	162
Steve BECKMEIER ▶ 7683 (1)	**81**
Rock And Roll Dancin'—Beckmeier Brothers (79)	162
Curtis BEDEAU ▶ 1648 (14)	**2544**
Head To Toe—Lisa Lisa And Cult Jam (87)	4435
Lost In Emotion—Lisa Lisa And Cult Jam (87)	3486
Naughty Girls (Need Love Too)—Samantha Fox (88)	2531
All Cried Out—Lisa Lisa And Cult Jam With Full Force Featuring Paul Anthony And Bow Legged Lou (86)	1667
I Wanna Have Some Fun—Samantha Fox (88)	1135
I Wonder If I Take You Home—Lisa Lisa and Cult Jam with Full Force (85)	656
Thanks For My Child—Cheryl "Pepsii" Riley (88)	509
Little Jackie Wants To Be A Star—Lisa Lisa And Cult Jam (89)	441
Can You Feel The Beat—Lisa Lisa And Cult Jam (85)	231
Basketball—Kurtis Blow (85)	77
Someone To Love Me For Me—Lisa Lisa & Cult Jam (87)	52
Why Can't You Come Home—Ex-Girlfriend (91)	48
Roxanne, Roxanne—UTFO (85)	28
Go For Yours—Lisa Lisa & Cult Jam with Full Force (88)	22
—Lew Bedell see: Lou BIDEU	
Mark BEDFORD ▶ 5330 (1)	**303**
Our House—Madness (83)	2122
—Lewis Joseph Bedinsky see: Lou BIDEU	
Hank BEDUCCI [Joseph Abend] ▶ 7598 (2)	**87**
Harem Dance—Armenian Jazz Sextet (57)	*173*
Harem Dance—Roger King Mozian (57)	*0.0*
Bernice BEDWELL [Tommy Bedwell] ▶ 2388 (1)	**1533**
Lotta Lovin'—Gene Vincent and His Blue Caps (57)	1533
—Tommy Bedwell see: Bernice BEDWELL	
Harold BEEBE ▶ 10877 (1)	**4.7**
Bring Us Together—Patti Page (58)	4.7
John BEEBY ▶ 3181 (1)	**964**
Dreamtime—Daryl Hall (86)	1928
Franny BEECHER ▶ 8490 (2)	**48**
Week End—Kingsmen (58)	102
Blue Comet Blues—Bill Haley And His Comets (56)	29
Michael BEEN ▶ 6136 (2)	**201**
Let The Day Begin—Call (89)	122
The Walls Came Down—Call (83)	80
Garry BEERS ▶ 7575 (2)	**88**
Listen Like Thieves—INXS (86)	251
Don't Change—INXS (83)	23
Nick BEGGS ▶ 4611 (2)	**451**
Too Shy—Kajagoogoo (83)	2226
Hang On Now—Kajagoogoo (83)	28
—Lionel Begleiter see: Lionel BART	
Dominic BEHAN ▶ 8313 (1)	**54**
Off To Dublin In The Green—Abbey Tavern Singers (66)	109
—Israel Isidore Beilin see: Irving BERLIN	

Michael BEINHORN ▶ 8299 (1)	**55**
Rockit—Herbie Hancock (83)	165
Gary BEISBIER ▶ 1413 (5)	**3141**
Don't You Care—Buckinghams (67)	2879
Susan—Buckinghams (67)	2292
Hey Baby (They're Playing Our Song)—Buckinghams (67)	1754
Give It To Me—Mob (71)	71
I Dig Everything About You—Mob (70)	50
Harry BELAFONTE [Raymond Bell, Harry Thomas] ▶ 3570 (5)	**783**
Turn Around—Dick And Deedee (63)	714
Island In The Sun—Harry Belafonte (57)	418
Cocoanut Woman—Harry Belafonte (57)	328
Hold 'Em Joe—Harry Belafonte (57)	139
Don't Ever Love Me—Harry Belafonte (57)	65
—Peter Jan Cor Belenky see: Peter COR	
Adrian BELEW [Robert Steven Belew] ▶ 5662 (2)	**258**
Genius Of Love—Tom Tom Club (82)	529
Oh Daddy—Adrian Belew (89)	126
Carl BELEW ▶ 2120 (7)	**1846**
Lonely Street—Andy Williams (59)	3082
Am I That Easy To Forget—Debbie Reynolds (60)	*1149*
Am I That Easy To Forget—Engelbert Humperdinck (67)	*1119*
What's He Doing In My World—Eddy Arnold (65)	172
Even The Bad Times Are Good—Jerry Wallace (64)	7.3
Am I That Easy To Forget—"Little Esther" Phillips (63)	*5.3*
Am I That Easy To Forget—Skeeter Davis (60)	*0.0*
—Robert Steven Belew see: Adrian BELEW	
Dennis BELFIELD ▶ 10250 (1)	**11**
Smokin' Room—Carl Carlton (75)	11
Gary BELKIN ▶ 11247 (1)	**2.6**
Tower Trot (And Then You Do That Step)—Dick Jacobs And His Chorus And Orchestra (57)	23
Andy BELL [Andrew Ivan Bell] ▶ 3036 (4)	**1049**
Chains Of Love—Erasure (88)	1086
A Little Respect—Erasure (88)	957
Chorus—Erasure (91)	53
Stop!—Erasure (89)	2.3
—Anthony Bell see: Tony BELL	
Archie BELL ▶ 1121 (2)	**3952**
Tighten Up—Archie Bell & The Drells (68)	7682
Girl You're Too Young—Archie Bell & The Drells (69)	332
Benny BELL [Benjamn Zamberg] ▶ 4477 (1)	**485**
Shaving Cream—Benny Bell (75)	485
Cara BELL [Clara Bell Williams] ▶ 9936 (2)	**15**
I Want You To Have Everything—Lee Rogers (64)	27
Boss Love—Lee Rogers (65)	4.2
Christopher BELL ▶ 8729 (1)	**41**
Jealous—Gene Loves Jezebel (90)	164
—Cynthia Bell see: Cynthia STROTHER	
David BELL ▶ 8692 (1)	**42**
Black Hands White Cotton—Caboose (70)	127
Frank BELL ▶ 7606 (3)	**86**
I'm Sincere—Alan Dale (55)	*257*
I'm Sincere—Joe Barrett (55)	*0.0*
I'm Sincere—Shannon Sisters (55)	*0.0*
Jerome BELL ▶ 10158 (1)	**12**
Bounce, Rock, Skate, Roll (Part 1)—Vaughan Mason And Crew (80)	35
Kenneth Edward BELL ▶ 2863 (4)	**1147**
Even The Nights Are Better—Air Supply (82)	2400
Touch Me When We're Dancing—Carpenters (81)	*893*
Black Hands White Cotton—Caboose (70)	127
Touch Me When We're Dancing—Bama (79)	*21*
—Kevin Bell see: Amir BAYYAN	
Larry BELL [Larry Vernard Bell] ▶ 5088 (2)	**344**
If U Were Mine—U-Krew (90)	663
Let Me Be Your Lover—U-Krew (90)	123
Leroy BELL ▶ 2245 (5)	**1708**
Mama Can't Buy You Love—Elton John (79)	2115
Livin' It Up (Friday Night)—Bell & James (79)	1206
If You Wanna Do A Dance—Spinners (78)	168
Easy Come, Easy Go—Spinners (78)	8.8
This Time Baby—Jackie Moore (79)	6.1

Louise BELL [Mary L. Belline] ▶ 5897 (2)	**232**
This Is Real (This Is Love)—Malcolm Dodds (58)	*232*
This Is Real (This Is Love)—Billy Dawn (58)	*0.0*
Marcus BELL [Mark Thomas Bell] ▶ 6648 (1)	**148**
Are You Sure—So (88)	295
Randy BELL ▶ 10490 (1)	**7.9**
Don't Do Me—Randy Bell (84)	7.9
—Raymond Bell see: Harry BELAFONTE	
Richard BELL ▶ 11491 (1)	**1.5**
Diane—Golden Gate (70)	4.4
Ricky BELL ▶ 3691 (1)	**733**
Do Me!—Bell Biv DeVoe (90)	2931
Robert BELL ▶ 947 (33) HOF	**4704**
Celebration—Kool & The Gang (80)	6016
Cherish—Kool & The Gang (85)	3699
Joanna—Kool & The Gang (83)	3511
Ladies Night—Kool & The Gang (79)	3414
Jungle Boogie—Kool & The Gang (73)	2506
Hollywood Swinging—Kool & The Gang (74)	2079
Summertime—DJ Jazzy Jeff & The Fresh Prince (91)	1783
Misled—Kool & The Gang (84)	1436
Get Down On It—Kool & The Gang (82)	1373
Fresh—Kool & The Gang (85)	1367
Victory—Kool & The Gang (86)	1269
Tonight—Kool & The Gang (84)	1136
Take My Heart (You Can Have It If You Want It)—Kool & The Gang (81)	1077
Stone Love—Kool & The Gang (87)	994
Emergency—Kool & The Gang (85)	915
Spirit Of The Boogie—Kool & The Gang (75)	825
Let's Go Dancin' (Ooh La, La, La)—Kool & The Gang (82)	654
Big Fun—Kool & The Gang (82)	532
Funky Stuff—Kool & The Gang (73)	473
Higher Plane—Kool & The Gang (74)	446
Kool And The Gang—Kool & The Gang (69)	329
Jones Vs. Jones—Kool & The Gang (81)	316
Caribbean Festival—Kool & The Gang (75)	268
Open Sesame - Part I—Kool & The Gang (76)	252
Rhyme Tyme People—Kool & The Gang (75)	182
Holiday—Kool & The Gang (87)	126
Let The Music Take Your Mind—Kool & The Gang (70)	85
Love And Understanding (Come Together)—Kool & The Gang (76)	48
Funky Man—Kool & The Gang (70)	41
The Gangs Back Again—Kool & The Gang (69)	37
Steppin' Out—Kool & The Gang (82)	6.6
Who's Gonna Take The Weight (Part One)—Kool & The Gang (71)	4.1
Summer Madness—Kool & The Gang (75)	0.0
Ronald BELL [Khalis Bayyan, Ronald Nathan Bell] ▶ 937 (35) HOF	**4736**
Celebration—Kool & The Gang (80)	6016
Cherish—Kool & The Gang (85)	3699
Joanna—Kool & The Gang (83)	3511
Ladies Night—Kool & The Gang (79)	3414
Jungle Boogie—Kool & The Gang (73)	2506
Hollywood Swinging—Kool & The Gang (74)	2079
Summertime—DJ Jazzy Jeff & The Fresh Prince (91)	1783
Misled—Kool & The Gang (84)	1436
Get Down On It—Kool & The Gang (82)	1373
Fresh—Kool & The Gang (85)	1367
Victory—Kool & The Gang (86)	1269
Tonight—Kool & The Gang (84)	1136
Take My Heart (You Can Have It If You Want It)—Kool & The Gang (81)	1077
Stone Love—Kool & The Gang (87)	994
Emergency—Kool & The Gang (85)	915
Spirit Of The Boogie—Kool & The Gang (75)	825
Let's Go Dancin' (Ooh La, La, La)—Kool & The Gang (82)	654
Big Fun—Kool & The Gang (82)	532
Funky Stuff—Kool & The Gang (73)	473
Higher Plane—Kool & The Gang (74)	446
Kool And The Gang—Kool & The Gang (69)	329
Jones Vs. Jones—Kool & The Gang (81)	316
Caribbean Festival—Kool & The Gang (75)	268
Open Sesame - Part I—Kool & The Gang (76)	252
Rhyme Tyme People—Kool & The Gang (75)	182
Holiday—Kool & The Gang (87)	126
Special Way—Kool & The Gang (87)	122
Let The Music Take Your Mind—Kool & The Gang (70)	85

Ronald BELL [Khalis Bayyan, Ronald Nathan Bell] ▶ 937 (35) HOF *Cont'd*	**4736**
You Got To Keep On Bumpin'—Kay-Gees (74)	61
Love And Understanding (Come Together)—Kool & The Gang (76)	48
Funky Man—Kool & The Gang (70)	41
The Gangs Back Again—Kool & The Gang (69)	37
Steppin' Out—Kool & The Gang (82)	6.6
Who's Gonna Take The Weight (Part One)—Kool & The Gang (71)	4.1
Summer Madness—Kool & The Gang (75)	0.0
Samuel BELL ▶ 5724 (5)	**251**
I Dig You Baby—Jerry Butler (67)	*266*
A Quiet Place—Garnet Mimms & The Enchanters (64)	166
Stay Together Young Lovers—Brenda & The Tabulations (67)	118
I Dig You Baby—Lorraine Ellison (66)	*46*
I Wanna Thank You—Enchanters (2) (64)	10
—Theresa Bell see: Leon HUFF	
Thom BELL ▶ 132 (42) HOF	**20460**
You Make Me Feel Brand New—Stylistics Featuring Airrion Love & Russell Thompkins, Jr. (74)	*5023*
The Rubberband Man—Spinners (76)	4975
I'll Be Around—Spinners (72)	*4157*
Betcha By Golly, Wow—Stylistics Featuring Airrion Love & Russell Thompkins, Jr. (72)	*3608*
La - La - Means I Love You—Delfonics (68)	*3448*
You Are Everything—Stylistics (71)	2438
Break Up To Make Up—Stylistics (73)	*1985*
Didn't I (Blow Your Mind This Time)—Delfonics (70)	*1925*
I'm Doin' Fine Now—New York City (73)	1697
I'm Stone In Love With You—Stylistics (72)	1537
Rockin' Roll Baby—Stylistics (73)	1272
Didn't I (Blow Your Mind)—New Kids On The Block (89)	*1171*
People Make The World Go Round—Stylistics (72)	969
I'm Coming Home—Spinners (74)	*864*
Stop, Look, Listen (To Your Heart)—Stylistics (71)	803
One Man Band (Plays All Alone)—Ronnie Dyson (73)	768
Ready Or Not Here I Come (Can't Hide From Love)—Delfonics (68)	642
You Got Yours And I'll Get Mine—Delfonics (69)	584
Break Your Promise—Delfonics (68)	575
Ghetto Child—Spinners (73)	517
Trying To Make A Fool Of Me—Delfonics (70)	497
I'm Sorry—Delfonics (68)	413
Girl You're Too Young—Archie Bell & The Drells (69)	332
Over And Over—Delfonics (71)	325
Living A Little, Laughing A Little—Spinners (75)	291
Life Is A Song Worth Singing—Johnny Mathis (73)	226
I'm Coming Home—Johnny Mathis (73)	*198*
Let's Make A Promise—Peaches & Herb (68)	188
If You Wanna Do A Dance—Spinners (78)	168
La La Means I Love You—Tierra (81)	*142*
I'll Be Around—What Is This (85)	*124*
Help Me Find A Way (To Say I Love You)—Little Anthony And The Imperials (70)	106
Wake Up Susan—Spinners (76)	104
Somebody Loves You—Delfonics (69)	83
Quick, Fast, In A Hurry—New York City (74)	75
Break Up To Make Up—Cynthia (91)	*49*
I Wanna Be A Free Girl—Dusty Springfield (70)	38
He Don't Really Love You—Delfonics (68)	30
Funny Feeling—Delfonics (69)	24
Betcha By Golly Wow—Band Of Gold (84)	*12*
You Make Me Feel Brand New—Band Of Gold (84)	*12*
Easy Come, Easy Go—Spinners (78)	8.8
Tony BELL [Anthony Salvatore Bell, Anthony Bell] ▶ 4223 (3)	**556**
I'm Stone In Love With You—Stylistics (72)	1537
If You Wanna Do A Dance—Spinners (78)	168
You Call Me Back—Clyde Brown (74)	3.2
Vincent BELL ▶ 2655 (1)	**1291**
The Rain—Oran "Juice" Jones (86)	1291
William BELL [William Yarborough] ▶ 1844 (13)	**2207**
To Be A Lover—Billy Idol (86)	1625
Tryin' To Love Two—William Bell (77)	1573
I Forgot To Be Your Lover—William Bell (69)	558
Any Other Way—Chuck Jackson (63)	175
I Got A Sure Thing—Ollie & The Nightingales (68)	110
Private Number—Judy Clay & William Bell (68)	99
A Tribute To A King—William Bell (68)	66
Everybody Loves A Winner—William Bell (67)	39
Every Man Oughta Have A Woman—William Bell (68)	20
All God's Children Got Soul—Dorothy Morrison (69)	8.0
What A Fool I've Been—Carla Thomas (63)	4.0
You Don't Miss Your Water—William Bell (62)	2.6
Born Under A Bad Sign—William Bell (69)	0.5
—Sammy Bella see: Wilbur MESHEL	
—Daniel Edward Bellack see: Dan BELLOC	
Marc BELLACK ▶ 7835 (3)	**73**
Try It—Ohio Express (68)	125
Bye Bye Baby—U.S. 1 (75)	17
They Don't Make 'Em Like That Any More—Reunion (75)	3.7
David BELLAMY ▶ 1779 (5)	**2337**
Spiders And Snakes—Jim Stafford (73)	3645
Your Bulldog Drinks Champagne—Jim Stafford (74)	437
If I Said You Had A Beautiful Body Would You Hold It Against Me—Bellamy Brothers (79)	232
Nothin' Heavy—David Bellamy (75)	34
Hell Cat—Bellamy Brothers (76)	30
—Emerson Lee Bellamy see: Lee EMERSON	
George BELLAMY ▶ 5952 (1)	**224**
Ridin' The Wind—Tornadoes (63)	224
Roberta BELLAMY ▶ 3466 (1)	**834**
Ruby Ann—Marty Robbins (62)	834
Bruce BELLAND ▶ 1092 (10)	**4038**
26 Miles (Santa Catalina)—Four Preps (58)	2990
Big Man—Four Preps (58)	2564
Down By The Station—Four Preps (59)	1665
Got A Girl—Four Preps (60)	514
More Money For You And Me—Four Preps (61)	130
Cinderella—Four Preps (58)	64
A Letter To The Beatles—Four Preps (64)	55
Sparkle And Shine—Four Coquettes (61)	40
The Big Draft—Four Preps (62)	24
Trouble Maker—Lee Hazlewood (69)	8.9
—Tracey Bryn Belland see: Tracey BRYN	
Barbara BELLE ▶ 10317 (4)	**10**
A Sunday Kind Of Love—Lenny Welch (72)	*26*
A Sunday Kind Of Love—Jan & Dean (62)	*7.3*
Sunday Kind Of Love—Etta James (61)	*5.7*
Sunday Kind Of Love—Fran Warren (58)	*0.8*
Bernard BELLE ▶ 3035 (2)	**1049**
I Like The Way (The Kissing Game)—Hi-Five (91)	2919
Let's Chill—Guy (91)	228
—Jenny Bellestar see: Theresa MATTHIAS	
—Mary L. Belline see: Louise BELL	
Henry BELLINGER ▶ 3535 (1)	**795**
Stick Shift—Duals (61)	795
Sanford BELLINI ▶ 6250 (1)	**189**
Tell Him I'm Not Home—Chuck Jackson (63)	568
Johnnie BELLMON ▶ 4993 (4)	**362**
Don't Let The Green Grass Fool You—Wilson Pickett (71)	1388
One For The Money (Part 1)—Whispers (76)	40
Just A Little Bit More—Intrigues (70)	14
Don't Get Close—Little Anthony & The Imperials (70)	2.7
Isaac BELLO ▶ 9405 (1)	**24**
What Time Is Love?—KLF (91)	73
Lisa Dal BELLO ▶ 5002 (1)	**360**
Pretty Girls—Melissa Manchester (79)	360
Dan BELLOC [Daniel Edward Bellack] ▶ 8038 (2)	**64**
Pretend—Carl Mann (59)	*253*
Mama's Place—Bing Day (59)	2.3
Pete BELLOTTE ▶ 583 (21)	**7434**
Hot Stuff—Donna Summer (79)	8596
Love To Love You Baby—Donna Summer (75)	*4573*
Heaven Knows—Donna Summer With Brooklyn Dreams (79)	3027
I Feel Love—Donna Summer (77)	2815
The Dream (Hold On To Your Dream)—Irene Cara (83)	489
Son Of My Father—Giorgio (72)	*486*
I Love You—Donna Summer (77)	469
Victim Of Love—Elton John (79)	357
Cold Love—Donna Summer (80)	353
Walk Away—Donna Summer (80)	352
Who Do You Think You're Foolin'—Donna Summer (81)	312
Winter Melody—Donna Summer (77)	276
Rumour Has It—Donna Summer (78)	113
Love To Love You Baby—Ritchie Family (76)	*92*
Spring Affair—Donna Summer (76)	*84*
Here She Comes—Bonnie Tyler (84)	61
You Can—Madleen Kane (81)	45
Try Me, I Know We Can Make It—Donna Summer (76)	34
Son Of My Father—Chicory (72)	*31*
Giving Up, Giving In—3° Degrees (79)	4.6
Spring Affair—Donna Summer (77)	*0.0*
Tony BELLUS [Anthony Bellusci] ▶ 3077 (1)	**1024**
Robbin' The Cradle—Tony Bellus (59)	1024
Martin BELMONT ▶ 6543 (1)	**159**
I Need You—Paul Carrack (82)	476
Phil BELMONTE [Ivan Mogull] ▶ 2557 (6)	**1387**
My True Story—Jive Five (61)	2624
After The Lights Go Down Low—Al Hibbler (56)	*1362*
Watch Your Step—Bobby Parker (61)	90
Step Right Up (And Say You Love Me)—Nat King Cole (62)	*36*
After The Lights Go Down Low—George Maharis (62)	*3.1*
Step Right Up (And Say You Love Me)—Teresa Brewer (62)	*0.0*
Henri BELOLO ▶ 1098 (9)	**4023**
Y.M.C.A.—Village People (78)	7239
In The Navy—Village People (79)	3766
Macho Man—Village People (78)	679
Go West—Village People (79)	259
Ready For The '80s—Village People (79)	147
The Best Disco In Town—Ritchie Family (76)	*92*
The Best Disco In Town—Ritchie Family (76)	*92*
I Want To Dance With You (Dance With Me)—Ritchie Family (75)	45
Discomania—Lovers (77)	0.6
Alexei BELOV ▶ 10361 (1)	**9.5**
Try To Find Me—Gorky Park (90)	28
Jesse BELVIN ▶ 1727 (13)	**2413**
Earth Angel (Will You Be Mine)—Penguins (54)	*2284*
Earth Angel (Will You Be Mine)—Crew-Cuts (55)	*1777*
Guess Who—Jesse Belvin (59)	*908*
Earth Angel—New Edition (86)	*545*
Earth Angel (Will You Be Mine)—Vogues (69)	*486*
Earth Angel—Johnny Tillotson (60)	*230*
Guess Who—B.B. King (72)	*229*
Guess Who—Ruby Winters (69)	*84*
Earth Angel (Will You Be Mine)—Gloria Mann (55)	*74*
Earth Angel—Fred Parris & The Five Satins (82)	*4.8*
Old MacDonald—Chargers (58)	*3.9*
Earth Angel—Cleftones (61)	*2.3*
Earth Angel—Les Baxter & The Bombers (54)	*0.0*
JoAnn BELVIN ▶ 4050 (4)	**612**
Guess Who—Jesse Belvin (59)	*908*
Guess Who—B.B. King (72)	*229*
Guess Who—Ruby Winters (69)	*84*
Old MacDonald—Chargers (58)	*3.9*
Jorge BEN [Jorge Lima Menezes] ▶ 4556 (3)	**465**
Mas Que Nada—Sergio Mendes & Brasil '66 (66)	280
Zazueira (Za-zoo-wher'-a)—Herb Alpert & The Tijuana Brass (69)	146
Constant Rain (Chove Chuva)—Sergio Mendes & Brasil '66 (66)	78
Pat BENATAR [Patricia Andrzejewski, Pat Giraldo] ▶ 2249 (6)	**1706**
Treat Me Right—Pat Benatar (81)	1304
Fire And Ice—Pat Benatar (81)	1023
All Fired Up—Pat Benatar (88)	720
Promises In The Dark—Pat Benatar (81)	407
Ooh Ooh Song—Pat Benatar (85)	335
Back To Paradise—38 Special (87)	305
—Jean-Paul Benchetrit see: Jean-Paul DREAU	
—Norma Bender see: Norma MENDOZA	
—Frank Bendinelli see: Ralston McGRIFF	
Joe BENEDETTI ▶ 10728 (1)	**5.7**
When School Starts Again—Tony Perkins (57)	11
Ray BENICH ▶ 10697 (1)	**6.0**
Back To The River—Damnation Of Adam Blessing (70)	30
Benito BENITES [Michael Münzing] ▶ 3072 (2)	**1025**
The Power—Snap! (90)	2984
Ooops Up—Snap! (90)	273

Bennie BENJAMIN [Claude A. Benjamin] ▶ 1513 (23) HOF	**2834**
How Important Can It Be—Joni James (55)	*2495*
Don't Let Me Be Misunderstood— Santa Esmeralda Starring Larry Gomez (77)	*1226*
Don't Let Me Be Misunderstood—Animals (65)	*1016*
How Important Can It Be—Sarah Vaughan (55)	*429*
Fabulous Character—Sarah Vaughan (56)	386
I Don't See Me In Your Eyes Anymore— Charlie Rich (74)	298
Lonely Man—Elvis Presley With The Jordanaires (61)	232
I Don't Want To Set The World On Fire— Somethin' Smith & The Redheads (58)	149
I'll Never Be Free—Kay Starr (61)	118
You're All I Want For Christmas—Brook Benton (63)	41
Of This I'm Sure—Four Aces (55)	37
I'll Step Aside—Georgie Shaw (55)	22
Wheel Of Fortune—LaVern Baker (60)	*15*
Wheel Of Fortune—Knightsbridge Strings (59)	*10*
Thanks To The Fool—Brook Benton (62)	9.6
Oh! What It Seemed To Be—Castells (62)	7.9
These Things I Offer You (For A Lifetime)— Playmates (60)	5.7
A Girl, A Girl (Zoom-Ba Di Alli Nella)— Eddie Fisher (54)	0.0
Don't Let Me Be Misunderstood—Nina Simone (65)	*0.0*
How Important Can It Be—Lou Monte (55)	*0.0*
How Important Can It Be?—Teresa Brewer (55)	*0.0*
How Important Can It Be?—Connee Boswell (55)	*0.0*
Cross Over The Bridge—Patti Page (54)	0.0
—Claude A. Benjamin see: Bennie BENJAMIN	
Dave BENJAMIN ▶ 3786 (1)	**700**
Bust Out—Busters (63)	700
—Tim Benjamin see: Helmut MEYERS	
Boyd BENNETT ▶ 1189 (8)	**3729**
Seventeen—Boyd Bennett And His Rockets (55)	*4540*
Seventeen— Fontane Sisters with Billy Vaughn's Orchestra (55)	*3907*
My Boy Flat Top—Dorothy Collins (55)	*859*
Seventeen—Rusty Draper (55)	*534*
My Boy Flat Top—Boyd Bennett And His Rockets (55)	*350*
Boogie Bear—Boyd Bennett (59)	119
Seventeen—Frankie Ford (61)	*37*
Seventeen—Ella Mae Morse (55)	*0.0*
Dale BENNETT [Charlie Barnet] ▶ 11172 (1)	**2.9**
Skyliner—Carmen McRae (57)	2.9
Dave BENNETT ▶ 7042 (1)	**120**
Bye Bye Blues— Bert Kaempfert And His Orchestra (66)	479
Don BENNETT ▶ 9086 (1)	**32**
Can't Help But Love You—Standells (67)	63
Headley BENNETT [Headley George Bennett, Deadly Headley Bennett, Felix Headley Bennett] ▶ 6316 (1)	**182**
Pass The Dutchie—Musical Youth (82)	1276
James BENNETT ▶ 11652 (1)	**0.8**
My Man--He's A Lovin' Man—Betty LaVett (63)	1.6
—Jane Sperry Bennett see: Jane CONNELL	
Joe BENNETT ▶ 3636 (4)	**756**
Black Slacks—Joe Bennett And The Sparkletones (57)	998
Penny Loafers And Bobby Socks— Joe Bennett And The Sparkletones (57)	241
Rocket—Joe Bennett And The Sparkletones (57)	14
Boys Do Cry—Joe Bennett And The Sparkletones (59)	2.3
Joyce BENNETT ▶ 6079 (3)	**208**
There Oughta Be A Law—Mickey & Sylvia (57)	405
Give A Little Time—Ella Mae Morse (54)	7.1
I Can't Help It—Moments (71)	6.5
Michael BENNETT ▶ 8302 (1)	**55**
Housecall—Shabba Ranks (91)	329
Milton BENNETT ▶ 2963 (1)	**1094**
Go Now!—Moody Blues (65)	2189
Richard Rodney BENNETT ▶ 8689 (1)	**43**
Too Beautiful To Last—Engelbert Humperdinck (72)	85
Richard Winchell BENNETT ▶ 4588 (1)	**460**
Forever In Blue Jeans—Neil Diamond (79)	920
Roy C. BENNETT [Israel Brodsky, Roy Brodsky] ▶ 396 (34)	**9973**
Naughty Lady Of Shady Lane—Ames Brothers (54)	*4011*
Red Roses For A Blue Lady— Bert Kaempfert And His Orchestra (65)	*2472*

When The Boy In Your Arms (Is The Boy In Your Heart)—Connie Francis (61)	2133
Red Roses For A Blue Lady—Vic Dana (65)	*1799*
Kewpie Doll—Perry Como (58)	1744
My Bonnie Lassie—Ames Brothers (55)	1315
Puppet On A String— Elvis Presley With The Jordanaires (65)	1211
If I Had A Girl—Rod Lauren (59)	752
Red Roses For A Blue Lady—Wayne Newton (65)	*706*
Nuttin' For Christmas—Art Mooney And His Orchestra, Vocal By Barry Gordon (55)	*641*
All That I Am— Elvis Presley With The Jordanaires (66)	425
Summer Sounds—Robert Goulet (65)	403
On London Bridge—Jo Stafford (56)	310
Naughty Lady Of Shady Lane—Archie Bleyer (54)	*293*
Nuttin' For Christmas—Joe Ward (55)	*261*
Cap And Gown—Marty Robbins (59)	235
Comin' Down With Love—Mel Gadson (60)	206
New Orleans— Elvis Presley with the Jordanaires (58)	192
Stay Away—Elvis Presley With The Jordanaires (68)	182
Stairway Of Love—Marty Robbins (58)	162
Nuttin' For Christmas— Ricky Zahnd And The Blue Jeaners (55)	*157*
Don't Come Running Back To Me—Nancy Wilson (65)	137
Forty Nine Shades Of Green—Ames Brothers (56)	111
Nuttin' For Christmas—Fontane Sisters (55)	*102*
You're Next—Jimmy Witherspoon (65)	98
Rock Around Mother Goose—Barry Gordon (56)	89
(It Took) One Kiss—Jaye P. Morgan (59)	75
Nuttin' For Christmas—Stan Freberg (55)	*65*
Stop! And Think It Over—Perry Como (67)	48
In Love—Ames Brothers (58)	45
Stay—Ames Brothers (58)	4.0
The Wonderful World Of The Young— Andy Williams (62)	0.9
Nuttin' For Christmas—Kenny & Corky (59)	*0.8*
Nothin' For Christmas—Eartha Kitt (55)	*0.0*
Marc BENNO ▶ 11566 (1)	**1.2**
Tryin' To Stay 'Live—Asylum Choir (72)	2.4
Gary BENSON [Harry Hyams] ▶ 1194 (6)	**3715**
Close To You—Maxi Priest (90)	3399
Let Her In—John Travolta (76)	1980
Miracles—Stacy Lattisaw (83)	523
(I Will Be Your) Shadow In The Street— Allan Clarke (78)	391
Whenever I'm Away From You—John Travolta (76)	222
Slipstream—Allan Clarke (80)	68
Renaldo BENSON ▶ 1829 (5)	**2243**
What's Going On—Marvin Gaye (71)	*5213*
What's Going On—Cyndi Lauper (87)	*885*
Sweet Understanding Love—Four Tops (73)	476
Wholy Holy—Aretha Franklin (72)	151
What's Going On—Quincy Jones (71)	*4.6*
Val BENSON ▶ 6544 (1)	**159**
Sweet Understanding Love—Four Tops (73)	476
Clark BENTLEY ▶ 11489 (1)	**1.5**
Continuing Story Of Harper Valley P.T.A.— Dee Mullins (68)	*4.4*
David Keith BENTLEY ▶ 6427 (1)	**171**
In A Broken Dream—Python Lee Jackson (72)	171
Brook BENTON [Jesse Hollis, Benjamin Franklin Peay] ▶ 236 (42)	**14439**
The Boll Weevil Song—Brook Benton (61)	7091
It's Just A Matter Of Time—Brook Benton (59)	*5155*
Kiddio—Brook Benton (60)	3969
A Lover's Question—Clyde McPhatter (58)	*2994*
A Rockin' Good Way (To Mess Around And Fall In Love)—Dinah Washington & Brook Benton (60)	2398
Looking Back—Nat "King" Cole (58)	*2318*
Thank You Pretty Baby—Brook Benton (59)	1669
Endlessly—Brook Benton (59)	*1535*
Lie To Me—Brook Benton (62)	1517
Same One—Brook Benton (60)	1295
Revenge—Brook Benton (61)	1071
Two Tickets To Paradise—Brook Benton (63)	686
I Got What I Wanted—Brook Benton (63)	672
For My Baby—Brook Benton (61)	549
A Lover's Question—Otis Redding (69)	*429*
Mother Nature, Father Time—Brook Benton (65)	375
So Close—Brook Benton (59)	192

This Time Of The Year—Brook Benton (59)	*185*
I Don't Know—Ruth Brown (59)	179
It's Just A House Without You—Brook Benton (61)	174
Doncha' Think It's Time—Elvis Presley (58)	159
I Want You Forever—Brook Benton (59)	106
With All Of My Heart—Brook Benton (59)	98
Looking Back—Joe Simon (68)	*62*
Stop Foolin'—Brook Benton & Damita Jo (63)	49
A Lover's Question—Jacky Ward (78)	*49*
You Went Back On Your Word—Clyde McPhatter (59)	43
Happy Years—Diamonds (58)	35
A Lover's Question—Ernestine Anderson (61)	*34*
Hurtin' Inside—Brook Benton (59)	33
Nothing In The World—Nat "King" Cole (58)	31
It's Just A Matter Of Time— Sonny James, The Southern Gentleman (70)	*31*
I'll Take Care Of You—Bobby Bland (59)	27
This Time Of The Year—Brook Benton (60)	*22*
Endlessly—Mavis Staples (72)	*14*
I Ain't Giving Up Nothing—Ben Hewitt (59)	13
A Lover's Question—Loggins & Messina (75)	*12*
Love Me Now—Brook Benton (65)	9.3
Looking Back—Dinah Washington (60)	*5.1*
Endlessly—Sonny James (70)	*5.1*
I Just Want To Love You—Clyde McPhatter (60)	5.0
We Can't Believe You're Gone—Bobby Harris (65)	2.3
Michael BERARDI ▶ 11678 (1)	**0.7**
Come Into My Life—Al Martino (71)	2.9
Richard BERARDI ▶ 11679 (1)	**0.7**
Come Into My Life—Al Martino (71)	2.9
—Sanford Irving Bereofsky see: Sandy BARON	
Luciano BERETTA ▶ 7316 (3)	**103**
Tar And Cement—Verdelle Smith (66)	359
Kiss Me And Kiss Me And Kiss Me (Tre Volte Baciami)—Perry Como (59)	111
Nessuno Mi Puo' Giudcare—Gene Pitney (66)	13
Deborah BERG ▶ 5764 (2)	**244**
Nice Girls—Eye To Eye (82)	477
Lucky—Eye To Eye (83)	11
Tony BERG ▶ 7742 (1)	**77**
Straight From The Heart (Into Your Life)— Coyote Sisters (84)	153
Borney BERGANTINE [Biagio Bergantino] ▶ 1457 (2)	**2990**
My Happiness—Connie Francis (58)	*5960*
My Happiness—Fats Domino (57)	*19*
Edith BERGDAHL ▶ 9495 (1)	**23**
Try Again—Dean Martin (54)	68
Norman BERGEN ▶ 11745 (1)	**0.2**
Only A Fool Breaks His Own Heart— Arthur Prysock (65)	0.5
Irral BERGER ▶ 4776 (2)	**418**
Warm And Tender Love—Percy Sledge (66)	*1225*
My Adorable One—Joe Simon (64)	*20*
Irving BERGER ▶ 6465 (2)	**166**
Never Turn Back—Al Hibbler (56)	292
Young Love—Rover Boys (56)	40
Alan BERGMAN ▶ 673 (17) HOF	**6431**
The Way We Were—Barbra Streisand (73)	*6902*
You Don't Bring Me Flowers—Barbra & Neil (78)	6538
It Might Be You—Stephen Bishop (83)	1012
The Way We Were—Gladys Knight & The Pips (75)	*957*
The Windmills Of Your Mind—Dusty Springfield (69)	646
How Do You Keep The Music Playing— James Ingram And Patti Austin (83)	610
Ol' Mac Donald—Frank Sinatra (60)	*604*
The Way He Makes Me Feel—Barbra Streisand (83)	554
In The Heat Of The Night—Ray Charles (67)	495
Nice 'N' Easy—Frank Sinatra (60)	399
I Believe In Love—Kenny Loggins (77)	268
Pretty World—Sergio Mendes & Brasil '66 (69)	226
Sentimental Baby—Frank Sinatra (61)	119
Yellow Bird—Mills Brothers (58)	*107*
Never Be Afraid— Bing Crosby with The Arthur Norman Choir (57)	50
All His Children—Charley Pride/Henry Mancini (72)	9.5
I Believed It All—Pozo Seco Singers (67)	2.4
Marilyn BERGMAN [Marilyn Keith] ▶ 674 (17) HOF	**6431**
The Way We Were—Barbra Streisand (73)	*6902*
You Don't Bring Me Flowers—Barbra & Neil (78)	6538

Marilyn BERGMAN [Marilyn Keith] ▶ 674 (17) HOF *Continued*	**6431**
It Might Be You—Stephen Bishop (83)	1012
The Way We Were—Gladys Knight & The Pips (75)	*957*
The Windmills Of Your Mind—Dusty Springfield (69)	646
How Do You Keep The Music Playing— James Ingram And Patti Austin (83)	610
Ol' Mac Donald—Frank Sinatra (60)	*604*
The Way He Makes Me Feel—Barbra Streisand (83)	554
In The Heat Of The Night—Ray Charles (67)	495
Nice 'N' Easy—Frank Sinatra (60)	399
I Believe In Love—Kenny Loggins (77)	268
Pretty World—Sergio Mendes & Brasil '66 (69)	226
Sentimental Baby—Frank Sinatra (61)	119
Yellow Bird—Mills Brothers (58)	*107*
Never Be Afraid— Bing Crosby with The Arthur Norman Choir (57)	50
All His Children—Charley Pride/Henry Mancini (72)	9.5
I Believed It All—Pozo Seco Singers (67)	2.4
Lee BERKE ▶ 7091 (1)	**116**
Valley Valparaiso— Percy Faith And His Orchestra and Chorus (56)	349
Milton BERLE [Mendel Berlinger] ▶ 6134 (6)	**201**
Not Yet—Susan Hunter (55)	289
I'd Give A Million Tomorrows (For Just One Yesterday)—Billy Vaughn and His Orchestra (55)	*153*
Foolishly—Vic Damone (55)	47
Sam, You Made The Pants Too Long— Barbra Streisand (66)	21
I'd Give A Million Tomorrows (For Just One Yesterday)—Frank Verna (55)	*0.0*
I'd Give A Million Tomorrows (For Just One Yesterday)—Arthur Godfrey (56)	*0.0*
Irving BERLIN [Israel Isidore Beilin] ▶ 281 (54) HOF	**12480**
Puttin' On The Ritz—Taco (83)	3796
Count Your Blessings (Instead Of Sheep)— Eddie Fisher (54)	*2049*
Marie—Bachelors (65)	*1269*
Play a Simple Melody (Spiel mir eine alte Melodie Es Spielt)—Johnny Maddox And The Rhythmasters (55)	*1115*
Always—Sammy Turner (59)	930
God Bless America—Connie Francis (59)	617
You'd Be Surprised—Kathy Linden (58)	369
A Man Chases A Girl (Until She Catches Him)— Eddie Fisher (55)	348
White Christmas—Bing Crosby (61)	*257*
White Christmas—Bing Crosby (54)	*244*
Sisters—Rosemary Clooney & Betty Clooney with Paul Weston & His Orch. (54)	*198*
White Christmas—Bing Crosby (60)	*188*
White Christmas—Bing Crosby (57)	*166*
White Christmas—Bing Crosby (62)	*166*
White Christmas—Bing Crosby (55)	*137*
White Christmas—Bing Crosby (58)	*129*
All Alone—Terri Stevens (58)	98
White Christmas—Bing Crosby (56)	*79*
Alexander's Ragtime Band—Crazy Otto (55)	49
Maybe It's Because (I Love You Too Much)— Sarah Vaughan (59)	42
If You Believe—Johnnie Ray (54)	40
Sayonara—Eddie Fisher (57)	*35*
Let Me Sing And I'm Happy—Jerry Lewis (57)	30
The Call Of The South—Bing & Gary Crosby (54)	22
Love You Didn't Do Right By Me— Rosemary Clooney (54)	*18*
White Christmas—Bing Crosby (59)	*16*
How About Me—Kitty Kallen (56)	15
How Deep Is The Ocean—Miss Toni Fisher (60)	11
White Christmas—Andy Williams (63)	*10*
Marie—Four Tunes (59)	*8.0*
White Christmas—Drifters (55)	*6.0*
White Christmas—Drifters Featuring Clyde McPhatter And Bill Pinckney (62)	*5.8*
Love, You Didn't Do Right By Me—Peggy Lee (54)	*2.7*
White Christmas—Drifters Featuring Clyde McPhatter And Bill Pinckney (60)	*2.2*
White Christmas—Elvis Presley (57)	*2.1*
Easter Parade— Guy Lombardo And His Royal Canadians (55)	*1.9*
Easter Parade—Harry James & His Orchestra (55)	*1.9*
Easter Parade—Rosemary Clooney (55)	*1.9*
Easter Parade—Bing Crosby (55)	*1.9*
Marie—Modernaires (57)	*1.9*
Say It Isn't So—Teddi King (57)	0.9
White Christmas (Finale)—Bing Crosby, Danny Kaye, Peggy Lee & Trudy Stevens (54)	*0.0*
Count Your Blessings Instead Of Sheep— Arthur Godfrey (54)	*0.0*
Count Your Blessings Instead Of Sheep— Rosemary Clooney (54)	*0.0*
Count Your Blessings (Instead Of Sheep)— Bing Crosby (54)	*0.0*
Play a Simple Melody (Spiel mir eine alte Melodie Es Spielt)—Crazy Otto (55)	*0.0*
White Christmas—Mulcays (54)	*0.0*
White Christmas—Rosemary Clooney (54)	*0.0*
White Christmas—Les Paul & Mary Ford (55)	*0.0*
White Christmas—Al Hibbler (56)	*0.0*
White Christmas—Joni James (56)	*0.0*
Sayonara—Gordon MacRae (57)	*0.0*
Sayonara—Pat Kirby (57)	*0.0*
Sisters—Peggy Lee (54)	*0.0*
—Max Berlin see: Marc CERRONE	
—Mendel Berlinger see: Milton BERLE	
—Friedel Berlipp see: Peter POLL	
Arthur BERMAN ▶ 8976 (2)	**35**
Take Me Back Again—Tony Bennett (54)	92
You'll Always Be The One (For Me)—Four Aces (55)	11
Irving BERMAN ▶ 10005 (2)	**14**
Time Out For Tears—Four Tunes (55)	*23*
Time Out For Tears—Chris Connor (57)	*4.7*
Roy BERMINGHAM [Roy Be] ▶ 11595 (1)	**1.0**
Boy Toy—Tia (87)	3.1
Andrew BERNARD ▶ 1034 (2)	**4261**
Judy In Disguise (With Glasses)— John Fred & His Playboy Band (67)	8168
Hey Hey Bunny—John Fred & His Playboy Band (68)	355
Felix BERNARD ▶ 9072 (3)	**32**
Winter Wonderland— Richard Hayman & His Orchestra (54)	*16*
Winter Wonderland—Andrews Sisters (54)	*16*
Winter Wonderland—Ames Brothers (55)	*16*
—Henry Bernard see: Henry GLOVER	
—Lisa Bernard see: Lisa KEITH	
Rod BERNARD ▶ 9375 (1)	**25**
Colinda—Rod Bernard (62)	50
Ralph BERNET ▶ 9598 (1)	**21**
Butterfly—Danyel Gérard (72)	103
Ben BERNIE [Benjamin Anzelevitz] ▶ 10428 (2)	**8.6**
Sweet Georgia Brown—Carroll Bros. (62)	*19*
Sweet Georgie Brown Sweet Georgia Brown— Mindy Carson (57)	*6.8*
Saul BERNIE ▶ 7185 (3)	**111**
Don't Cry, Baby—Etta James (61)	*323*
Bring Back Those Rockabye Baby Days—Tiny Tim (68)	5.9
Don't Cry, Baby—Aretha Franklin (62)	*4.0*
Bert BERNS [Bertrand Russell Berns, Bert Russell] ▶ 98 (59)	**24981**
Hang On Sloopy—McCoys (65)	*6827*
Twist And Shout—Beatles (64)	*6394*
Tell Him—Exciters (62)	*3482*
Cry Baby—Garnet Mimms & The Enchanters (63)	*3220*
Twenty-Five Miles—Edwin Starr (69)	*2304*
Twist And Shout—Isley Brothers (62)	*2072*
I Want Candy—Strangeloves (65)	*1629*
Piece Of My Heart— Big Brother And The Holding Company (68)	*1544*
Hang On Sloopy—Ramsey Lewis Trio (65)	*1400*
Killer Joe—Rocky Fellers (63)	*1215*
A Little Bit Of Soap—Jarmels (61)	*1157*
Here Comes The Night—Them (65)	968
Cry To Me—Betty Harris (63)	*872*
Are You Lonely For Me—Freddie Scott (66)	817
Cry Baby—Janis Joplin (71)	*651*
My Girl Sloopy—Vibrations (64)	*637*
I'll Take Good Care Of You—Garnet Mimms (66)	619
Goodbye Baby (Baby Goodbye)—Solomon Burke (64)	588
Cry To Me—Solomon Burke (62)	*574*
Baby Don't You Weep— Garnet Mimms & The Enchanters (63)	567
Twist And Shout—Beatles (86)	*529*
Everybody Needs Somebody To Love—Wilson Pickett (67)	*511*
Little Bit Of Soap—Nigel Olsson (79)	*508*
A Little Bit Of Soap—Paul Davis (70)	*475*
(My Girl) Sloopy—Little Caesar And The Consuls (65)	*340*
Everybody Needs Somebody To Love— Solomon Burke (64)	*302*
A Little Bit Of Soap—Exciters (66)	*287*
If I Didn't Have A Dime (To Play The Jukebox)— Gene Pitney (62)	279
That's When It Hurts—Ben E. King (64)	261
Piece Of My Heart—Erma Franklin (67)	*223*
Down In The Valley—Solomon Burke (62)	*194*
Cry To Me—Freddie Scott (67)	*178*
I Want Candy—Bow Wow Wow (82)	*177*
One Way Love—Drifters (64)	169
Everybody Do The Sloopy—Johnny Thunder (65)	163
Am I Grooving You—Freddie Scott (67)	148
My Block—Four Pennies (63)	130
Look Away—Garnet Mimms (64)	127
I Got To Go Back (And Watch That Little Girl Dance)— McCoys (66)	122
One Girl—Garnet Mimms (64)	120
Down In The Alley—Ronnie Hawkins (70)	*110*
It's All Over—Ben E. King (64)	100
Hang On Sloopy—Rick Derringer (75)	*96*
Killer Joe—Kingsmen (66)	*94*
Tell Her—Kenny Loggins (89)	*92*
You'd Better Come Home—Russell Byrd (61)	75
His Kiss—Betty Harris (64)	72
Baby Come On Home—Solomon Burke (66)	45
Hang On Sloopy—Lettermen (70)	*42*
Piece Of My Heart—Sammy Hagar (82)	*31*
Get Him—Exciters (63)	26
Yes I Do—Solomon Burke (64)	18
Chick-A-Boom—Van Morrison (67)	12
Heart Be Still—Lorraine Ellison (67)	11
Push Push—Austin Taylor (60)	9.6
Tell Her—Dean Parrish (66)	*9.2*
A Little Bit Of Soap—Garnet Mimms (65)	*5.6*
Sticky, Sticky—Bobby Harris (66)	1.0
Twenty-Five Miles—Mongo Santamaria (69)	*0.9*
Alan BERNSTEIN [Alan Kenneth Bernstein, Alan Kenneth] ▶ 1479 (8)	**2936**
This Girl Is A Woman Now— Gary Puckett And The Union Gap (69)	3064
After The Lovin'—Engelbert Humperdinck (76)	2368
The Next Hundred Years—Al Martino (77)	283
Like A Sunday Morning—Lana Cantrell (75)	69
This Moment In Time—Engelbert Humperdinck (78)	59
A Hurricane Is Coming Tonite—Carol Douglas (75)	24
Goodbye My Friend—Engelbert Humperdinck (77)	3.4
Kentucky Mornin'—Al Martino (77)	2.4
Elmer BERNSTEIN ▶ 791 (21)	**5599**
Baby The Rain Must Fall—Glenn Yarbrough (65)	1545
Themes From The Man With The Golden Arm— Richard Maltby And His Orchestra (56)	*1358*
Walk On The Wild Side - Part 1— Jimmy Smith And The Big Band (62)	*1099*
Main Title And Molly O From The Man With The Golden Arm—Dick Jacobs, His Chorus And Orchestra (56)	*962*
Main Title From The Man With The Golden Arm— Elmer Bernstein And Orchestra (56)	*817*
The Magnificent Seven—Al Caiola And His Orchestra (60)	*595*
Themes From The Man With The Golden Arm— Billy May And His Orchestra (56)	*547*
True Grit—Glen Campbell (69)	516
Walk On The Wild Side—Brook Benton (62)	*459*
Good Friend—Mary MacGregor (79)	419
Love With The Proper Stranger—Jack Jones (64)	341
Delilah Jones—McGuire Sisters (56)	*191*
Main Title Golden Arm— Les Elgart and His Orchestra (56)	*187*
The Song From "Kings Go Forth" (Monique)— Frank Sinatra (58)	170
The Bird Man—Highwaymen (62)	144
The Magnificent Seven—Meco (82)	*47*
(Main Title Theme From) "The Rat Race"— Richard Maltby And His Orchestra (60)	22
Main Title From "The Man With The Golden Arm"— Buddy Morrow And His Orchestra (56)	*18*
Walk On The Wild Side (Part 1)— Elmer Bernstein and Orchestra (62)	*0.0*
Molly-O—Ralph Young (56)	*0.0*
Delilah Jones—Danny Kaye (56)	*0.0*

Herbert BERNSTEIN ▶ 7669 (1)	**82**
Break Out—Mitch Ryder And The Detroit Wheels (66)	164
Leonard BERNSTEIN [Louis Bernstein] ▶ 1692 (10) HOF	**2480**
Tonight—Ferrante & Teicher (61)	*2067*
Somewhere—Len Barry (66)	*857*
Maria—Roger Williams (61)	*513*
Somewhere (From West Side Story)—Barbra Streisand (85)	*378*
Tonight—Eddie Fisher (61)	*339*
Maria—Johnny Mathis (60)	*170*
Somewhere—P.J. Proby (65)	*94*
Maria—Johnny Mathis (61)	*30*
Maria—Clebanoff Strings (61)	*0.0*
Tonight—Jay & The Americans (61)	*0.0*
—Louis Bernstein see: Leonard BERNSTEIN	
—Neil Bernstein see: Neil NEPHEW	
Roger BERNSTEIN ▶ 10993 (1)	**3.9**
Symphony—Sammy Turner (59)	16
Michael BERRIN ▶ 8510 (1)	**48**
Pop Goes The Weasel—3rd Bass (91)	333
Carlos BERRIOS ▶ 4156 (4)	**579**
Temptation—Corina (91)	1924
Together Forever—Lisette Melendez (91)	295
A Day In My Life (Without You)—Lisette Melendez (91)	230
Within My Heart—Voyce (91)	75
Alan BERRY ▶ 11603 (1)	**1.0**
Granny's Pad—Viceroys (63)	5.1
Bill BERRY ▶ 2216 (10)	**1729**
Losing My Religion—R.E.M. (91)	2447
Stand—R.E.M. (89)	1642
Shiny Happy People—R.E.M. (91)	1294
The One I Love—R.E.M. (87)	1261
It's The End Of The World As We Know It (And I Feel Fine)—R.E.M. (88)	87
So. Central Rain (I'm Sorry)—R.E.M. (84)	50
Pop Song 89—R.E.M. (89)	43
Radio Song—R.E.M. (91)	42
Radio Free Europe—R.E.M. (83)	34
Fall On Me—R.E.M. (86)	16
Bob BERRY ▶ 10097 (1)	**13**
Tears From My Heart—Thurston Harris (58)	26
Chuck BERRY [E. Anderson, Charles Edward Anderson Berry] ▶ 46 (59) HOF	**42354**
My Ding-A-Ling—Chuck Berry (72)	5504
Memphis—Johnny Rivers (64)	*5249*
Surfin' U.S.A.—Beach Boys (63)	*4923*
Sweet Little Sixteen—Chuck Berry (58)	*3486*
School Day—Chuck Berry (57)	*3251*
Memphis—Lonnie Mack (63)	*2755*
Maybellene—Chuck Berry (55)	*2343*
Rock And Roll Music—Beach Boys (76)	*2213*
No Particular Place To Go—Chuck Berry (64)	1794
Johnny B Goode—Chuck Berry (58)	*1522*
Rock And Roll Music—Chuck Berry (57)	*1473*
Maybelline—Johnny Rivers (64)	*1388*
Back In The U.S.A.—Linda Ronstadt (78)	*1061*
You Never Can Tell—Chuck Berry (64)	1043
Reelin' And Rockin'—Dave Clark Five (65)	*935*
Promised Land—Elvis Presley (74)	*900*
Nadine (Is It You?)—Chuck Berry (64)	832
Reelin' & Rockin'—Chuck Berry (72)	*791*
Carol—Chuck Berry (58)	*621*
Almost Grown—Chuck Berry (59)	604
Roll Over Beethoven—Electric Light Orchestra (73)	*593*
Surfin' USA—Leif Garrett (77)	*569*
Promised Land—Chuck Berry (64)	*474*
Roll Over Beethoven—Beatles (64)	*308*
Little Marie—Chuck Berry (64)	283
Forty Days—Ronnie Hawkins (59)	276
Sweet Little Rock And Roller—Chuck Berry (58)	268
Back In The USA—Chuck Berry (59)	*253*
Surfin' USA—Beach Boys (81)	*240*
Surfin' U.S.A.—Beach Boys (74)	*230*
Carol—Tommy Roe (64)	*218*
Roll Over Beethoven—Velaires (61)	*171*
Sweet Little Sixteen—Cat Mother And The All Night News Boys (69)	*164*
Oh Baby Doll—Chuck Berry (57)	162
Johnny B. Goode—Dion Di Muci (64)	*147*
Roll Over Beethoven—Chuck Berry (56)	*129*

Let It Rock—Chuck Berry (60)	126
Anthony Boy—Chuck Berry (59)	93
Jo Jo Gun—Chuck Berry (58)	69
Thirty Days (To Come Back Home)—Chuck Berry (55)	*50*
Jaguar And Thunderbird—Chuck Berry (60)	49
Johnny B. Goode—Peter Tosh (83)	*43*
Little Queenie—Bill Black's Combo (64)	*42*
Bye Bye Johnny—Chuck Berry (60)	42
Dear Dad—Chuck Berry (65)	29
Little Queenie—Chuck Berry (59)	*27*
Johnny B. Goode—Coronados (67)	*17*
Memphis, Tennessee—Chuck Berry (59)	*16*
Beautiful Delilah—Chuck Berry (58)	14
Johnny B. Goode—Johnny Winter (70)	*11*
Sweet Little Sixteen—Jerry Lee Lewis (62)	*7.2*
Johnny B Goode—Jive Bunny & The Mastermixers (90)	*6.7*
Roll Over Beethoven—Beatles (64)	*6.4*
School Day (Ring! Ring! Goes The Bell)—"Big" Tiny Little (57)	*0.0*
Roll Over Beethoven—Helene Dixon (56)	*0.0*
Maybellene—Johnny Long & His Orchestra (55)	*0.0*
Maybellene—Jim Lowe (55)	*0.0*
Maybellene—Ralph Marterie & His Orchestra (55)	*0.0*
Thirty Days (To Come Back Home)—Ernest Tubb (56)	*0.0*
Jan BERRY ▶ 476 (18)	**8740**
Surf City—Jan & Dean (63)	6644
The Little Old Lady (From Pasadena)—Jan & Dean (64)	3373
Jennie Lee—Jan & Arnie (58)	*2196*
Dead Man's Curve—Jan & Dean (64)	2112
Drag City—Jan & Dean (63)	1652
Honolulu Lulu—Jan & Dean (63)	1484
Ride The Wild Surf—Jan & Dean (64)	823
I Adore Him—Angels (63)	742
Three Window Coupe—Rip Chords (64)	620
The New Girl In School—Jan & Dean (64)	600
You Really Know How To Hurt A Guy—Jan & Dean (65)	519
Bucket "T"—Ronny & The Daytonas (64)	293
Batman—Jan & Dean (66)	206
The Anaheim, Azusa & Cucamonga Sewing Circle, Book Review And Timing Association—Jan & Dean (64)	194
Jennie Lee—Billy Ward And His Dominoes (58)	*187*
Gas Money—Jan & Arnie (58)	118
Judy Loves Me—Johnny Crawford (64)	7.8
A Beginning From An End—Jan & Dean (66)	5.2
John Bobby BERRY [John Berry] ▶ 928 (10)	**4772**
Pony Time—Chubby Checker (61)	*8332*
The Continental Walk—Hank Ballard And The Midnighters (61)	*672*
Pony Time—Don Covay and The Goodtimers (61)	*281*
The Continental Walk—Rollers (61)	*81*
Gilee—Sonny Spencer (59)	64
Hey Lover—Debbie Dovale (63)	61
(Boo Hoo) I'm Gonna Cry—Lloyd Price (61)	51
Elizabeth—Dave Ford And The Hollywood Flames (62)	14
I'm Hanging Up My Heart For You—Solomon Burke (62)	8.1
Your Memory—Five Satins (60)	3.0
Richard BERRY ▶ 404 (10)	**9772**
Louie Louie—Kingsmen (63)	*9145*
Louie, Louie—Sandpipers (66)	*595*
Moments—Jennell Hawkins (62)	*278*
Louie Louie—Kingsmen (66)	*95*
Louie, Louie—John Belushi (78)	*31*
Louie Louie—Travis Wammack (66)	*12*
Truly—Dinning Sisters Featuring Jean Dinning (55)	9.6
Louie, Louie—Fat Boys (88)	*9.6*
Louie Louie—Paul Revere And The Raiders (63)	*0.0*
Moments To Remember—Joyce Davis (62)	*0.0*
Ruby BERRY ▶ 5475 (1)	**281**
Doll House—Donnie Brooks (60)	563
Bob BERRYHILL ▶ 2016 (7)	**2000**
Wipe Out—Surfaris (63)	*4648*
Wipe Out—Surfaris (66)	*1843*
Wipeout—Fat Boys (87)	*961*
Point Panic—Surfaris (63)	378
Surfer Joe—Surfaris (63)	236
Wipe Out—Jive Bunny & The Mastermixers (90)	*6.7*
Wipe Out—Surfaris (70)	*4.6*
Adele BERTEI ▶ 5535 (1)	**274**
Do It For Love—Sheena Easton (85)	547
—Gerard Bertelkamp see: Beeb BIRTLES	

—Bernd Bertie see: Bert KAEMPFERT	
Umberto BERTINI ▶ 5837 (1)	**238**
On An Evening In Roma—Dean Martin (59)	715
Bob BERTRAM ▶ 11496 (1)	**1.4**
My Girl—Robin Luke (58)	1.4
Bernd BERWANGER ▶ 3530 (1)	**797**
Baby Don't Forget My Number—Milli Vanilli (89)	3187
Janine BEST ▶ 7029 (1)	**121**
Cover Of Love—Michael Damian (89)	482
Pat BEST ▶ 1449 (8)	**3014**
I Understand (Just How You Feel)—G-Clefs (61)	*1958*
I Understand (Just How You Feel)—Freddie And The Dreamers (65)	*489*
(I Love You) For Sentimental Reasons—Sam Cooke (57)	*396*
I Understand Just How You Feel—June Valli (54)	*264*
For Sentimental Reasons—Cleftones (61)	*165*
Lonesome—Four Tunes (54)	22
I Understand Just How You Feel—Four Tunes (54)	*0.0*
For Sentimental Reasons—Spaniels (61)	*0.0*
Harmon BETHEA [Maskman] ▶ 8997 (2)	**34**
One Eye Open—Maskman & The Agents (69)	31
My Wife, My Dog, My Cat—Maskman & The Agents (69)	18
Nuno BETTENCOURT [Billy Vegas] ▶ 1257 (2)	**3558**
More Than Words—Extreme (91)	4589
Hole Hearted—Extreme (91)	2526
Harold BETTERS ▶ 9263 (1)	**28**
Do Anything You Wanna (Part 1)—Harold Betters (64)	110
—Ange Eugene Betti see: Henri BETTI	
Henri BETTI [Ange Eugene Betti] ▶ 4565 (1)	**465**
C'est Si Bon (It's So Good)—Conway Twitty (60)	929
John BETTIS ▶ 218 (20) HOF	**15159**
Crazy For You—Madonna (85)	5216
Top Of The World—Carpenters (73)	*5097*
Slow Hand—Pointer Sisters (81)	4979
Yesterday Once More—Carpenters (73)	*4231*
Only Yesterday—Carpenters (75)	2333
Goodbye To Love—Carpenters (72)	1867
One Moment In Time—Whitney Houston (88)	1663
Human Nature—Michael Jackson (83)	1523
Like No Other Night—38 Special (86)	857
Heart Of The Night—Juice Newton (82)	780
The Woman In Me—Donna Summer (82)	667
I Need To Be In Love—Carpenters (76)	634
Body Rock—Maria Vidal (84)	320
Can You Stop The Rain—Peabo Bryson (91)	281
Wild Again—Starship (88)	102
Those Good Old Dreams—Carpenters (81)	93
So Hard Livin' Without You—Airwaves (78)	89
Yesterday Once More—Spinners (81)	*84*
Top Of The World—Lynn Anderson (73)	*74*
Only One Love In My Life—Ronnie Milsap (78)	67
Dickey BETTS [Forrest Richard Betts] ▶ 891 (8)	**4976**
Ramblin' Man—Allman Brothers Band (73)	3928
Straight From The Heart—Allman Brothers Band (81)	368
Crazy Love—Allman Brothers Band (79)	348
Jessica—Allman Brothers Band (73)	291
Angeline—Allman Brothers Band (80)	161
Blue Sky—Joan Baez (75)	112
Louisiana Lou And Three Card Monty John—Allman Brothers Band (75)	48
Revival (Love Is Everywhere)—Allman Brothers Band (71)	12
—Forrest Richard Betts see: Dickey BETTS	
Paul BETTS ▶ 7884 (1)	**71**
All I Need Is You—Blue Train (91)	284
Craig BEVAN ▶ 7926 (1)	**69**
Counting The Days—Joey Kid (90)	69
Frankie BEVERLY [Howard Beverly] ▶ 5423 (7)	**291**
While I'm Alone—Maze Featuring Frankie Beverly (77)	89
Feel That You're Feelin'—Maze Featuring Frankie Beverly (79)	82
Back In Stride—Maze Featuring Frankie Beverly (85)	42
Love Is The Key—Maze (83)	34
Running Away—Maze Featuring Frankie Beverly (81)	20
Southern Girl—Maze (80)	18
Lady Of Magic—Maze Featuring Frankie Beverly (77)	5.8

—Howard Beverly see: Frankie BEVERLY	
—B. Fresh see: Brenard STALLWORTH	
—Eithne Ni Bhraonain see: ENYA	
Gary BIAS ▶ 4651 (1)	**445**
Sweet Love—Anita Baker (86)	1336
Wayne BICKERTON [Arthur Ronald Bickerton] ▶ 2939 (5)	**1109**
Nothing But A Heartache—Flirtations (69)	822
Can't Stop Loving You—Tom Jones (70)	*812*
Sugar Baby Love—Rubettes (74)	*569*
Sugar Baby Love—Stars On 45 (81)	*12*
Can't Stop Lovin' You—Flirtations (70)	*2.2*
Craig BICKHARDT ▶ 4212 (1)	**562**
Never Been In Love—Randy Meisner (82)	562
Lou BIDEU [Lew Bedell, Lewis Joseph Bedinsky, Billy Joe Hunter] ▶ 4059 (2)	**609**
Percolator (Twist)—Billy Joe & The Checkmates (62)	*1188*
Percolator—Hot Butter (73)	*29*
—Jan Bidewell see: Jan BUCKINGHAM	
Klaus BIEDERMANN ▶ 7191 (1)	**111**
How To Dance—Bingoboys (91)	554
Barney BIGARD ▶ 6501 (3)	**162**
Mood Indigo—Norman Petty Trio (54)	*481*
Mood Indigo Mambo—Perez Prado And His Orchestra (55)	*5.9*
Mood Indigo—Modernaires & George Auld (54)	*0.0*
Giancarlo BIGAZZI ▶ 1580 (3)	**2674**
Gloria—Laura Branigan (82)	4941
Self Control—Laura Branigan (84)	2784
Ti Amo—Laura Branigan (84)	296
Bob BIGELOW ▶ 8614 (1)	**45**
Hardhearted Hannah—Ray Charles Orchestra & Chorus (60)	179
Andrew Martyn BIGGS ▶ 4141 (1)	**582**
Pump Up The Volume—M/A/R/R/S (87)	1163
Cynthia BIGGS ▶ 7101 (1)	**116**
If Only You Knew—Patti LaBelle (84)	347
Howard BIGGS ▶ 8471 (5)	**49**
That's All I Need—Dorothy Collins (55)	*120*
Got You On My Mind—Cookie & His Cupcakes (63)	18
That's All I Need—LaVern Baker & The Gliders (55)	*0.0*
That's All I Need—Rusty Draper (55)	*0.0*
That's All I Need—Jill Corey (55)	*0.0*
Steven Anthony BIGGS ▶ 4142 (1)	**582**
Pump Up The Volume—M/A/R/R/S (87)	1163
—Joe Bihari see: Joe JOSEA	
—Julius Bihari see: Jules TAUB	
—Saul Samuel Bihari see: Sam LING	
Acker BILK [Bernard Stanley Bilk] ▶ 332 (6)	**11094**
Stranger On The Shore—Mr. Acker Bilk (62)	*10177*
Stranger On The Shore—Andy Williams (62)	*1127*
Summer Set—Monty Kelly & His Orchestra (60)	*619*
Stranger On The Shore—Drifters (62)	*88*
Summer Set—Mr. Acker Bilk (60)	*0.0*
Summer Set—Ronnie Chamberlain (60)	*0.0*
—Bernard Stanley Bilk see: Acker BILK	
Micky BILLINGHAM ▶ 5757 (2)	**245**
Tenderness—General Public (84)	715
The Celtic Soul Brothers—Dexys Midnight Runners (83)	19
Bob BILYK [Jerry Renewych] ▶ 8467 (1)	**49**
Fly Little White Dove Fly—Bells (70)	98
Umberto BINDI ▶ 3894 (6)	**665**
You're My World—Helen Reddy (77)	*1277*
You're My World—Cilla Black (64)	*591*
Our Song—Jack Jones (67)	59
Our Concerto—Steve Lawrence (62)	*25*
Our Concerto—Umberto Bindi (60)	*13*
Our Concerto (Il Nostro Concerto)—Al Martino (60)	*0.0*
J.B. BINGHAM ▶ 4094 (1)	**595**
Do What You Wanna Do—Five Flights Up (70)	595
Bernard BINNICK ▶ 3972 (1)	**634**
Keem-O-Sabe—Electric Indian (69)	1268
Dick BIONDI ▶ 10703 (1)	**6.0**
Jupiter-C—Pat and the Satellites (59)	18
Robert BIRCH ▶ 7294 (1)	**105**
Elevate My Mind—Stereo MC's (91)	209

Will BIRCH ▶ 8172 (1)	**60**
Starry Eyes—Records (79)	119
—Birdlegs see: Sidney BANKS	
Edwin BIRDSONG ▶ 8640 (1)	**44**
Me Myself And I—De La Soul (89)	353
—Biri see: Ornella Ferrari COLOMBI	
Dania BIRKS ▶ 7229 (1)	**108**
Supersonic—J.J. Fad (88)	542
—Bud Birmingham see: Maggie ANDREWS	
Beeb BIRTLES [Gerard Bertelkamp] ▶ 3851 (3)	**677**
Happy Anniversary—Little River Band (77)	814
You're Driving Me Out Of My Mind—Little River Band (83)	393
I'll Always Call Your Name—Little River Band (77)	74
Peter BISCHOF-FALLENSTEIN ▶ 2966 (1)	**1092**
Girl I'm Gonna Miss You—Milli Vanilli (89)	3277
—Biscuit see: Steven WALKER	
Barbarella BISHOP ▶ 9370 (1)	**25**
Hey Ladies—Beastie Boys (89)	302
Elvin BISHOP ▶ 1128 (5)	**3934**
Fooled Around And Fell In Love—Elvin Bishop (76)	3573
Travelin' Shoes—Elvin Bishop (74)	259
Sure Feels Good—Elvin Bishop (75)	68
Struttin' My Stuff—Elvin Bishop (76)	45
Spend Some Time—Elvin Bishop Featuring Mickey Thomas (76)	11
James A. BISHOP ▶ 7484 (3)	**93**
I Really Love You—Dee Dee Sharp (65)	171
Chains Of Love—Drifters (65)	12
I Need Love—Barbara Mason (66)	2.9
Joe BISHOP ▶ 6621 (3)	**150**
Woodchopper's Ball—Hutch Davie And His Honky Tonkers (58)	*280*
Blue Flame—Billy Vaughn And His Orchestra (62)	21
Woodchopper's Ball—Winifred Atwell (58)	*0.0*
Randy BISHOP ▶ 8946 (1)	**36**
Day And Night—Wackers (72)	107
Ruth BISHOP ▶ 7934 (1)	**69**
Let's Try Again—Al Hibbler (56)	69
Stephen BISHOP ▶ 491 (6)	**8509**
Separate Lives—Phil Collins and Marilyn Martin (85)	4812
On And On—Stephen Bishop (77)	2162
Save It For A Rainy Day—Stephen Bishop (76)	810
Everybody Needs Love—Stephen Bishop (78)	562
Animal House—Stephen Bishop (78)	152
Unfaithfully Yours (One Love)—Stephen Bishop (84)	11
Joe BISKO ▶ 5655 (1)	**259**
Lonely Street—Clarence Henry (61)	259
Michael BISSELL ▶ 9613 (1)	**20**
Do Ya Do Ya (Wanna Please Me)—Samantha Fox (87)	40
Whelock BISSON ▶ 10969 (1)	**4.0**
What's Happening—Wade Flemons (60)	4.0
George BITZER ▶ 7156 (1)	**113**
Shine Shine—Barry Gibb (84)	339
Burke BIVENS ▶ 3387 (1)	**872**
Josephine—Bill Black's Combo (60)	1744
Edward BIVINS ▶ 3599 (5)	**772**
There's No Me Without You—Manhattans (73)	660
Follow Your Heart—Manhattans (65)	80
We Never Danced To A Love Song—Manhattans (77)	34
I Call It Love—Manhattans (67)	13
Baby I Need You—Manhattans (66)	4.2
Michael BIVINS ▶ 1721 (5)	**2433**
Do Me!—Bell Biv DeVoe (90)	2931
Motownphilly—Boyz II Men (91)	2776
Iesha—Another Bad Creation (91)	1229
Playground—Another Bad Creation (91)	604
Uhh Ahh—Boyz II Men (91)	572
Cesare BIXIO ▶ 4269 (1)	**539**
Mama—Connie Francis (60)	2155
Georges BIZET ▶ 4310 (3)	**526**
Carmen—Herb Alpert & The Tijuana Brass (68)	355
Madrid—Nat "King" Cole (59)	198
March Of The Toreadors—Royal Philharmonic Orchestra (81)	131
Matz BJÖRKLUND ▶ 8663 (1)	**43**
Boogie Woogie Dancin' Shoes—Claudja Barry (79)	216

—Frank Bjorn see: Bent FABRICIUS-BJERRE	
—B. Junior see: Richard BARRETT	
Ben BLACK ▶ 5448 (2)	**287**
Moonlight And Roses (Bring Mem'ries Of You)—Three Suns (54)	*522*
Moonlight And Roses (Bring Mem'ries Of You)—Vic Dana (65)	*340*
Bill BLACK [William Patton Black Jr.] ▶ 1540 (8)	**2773**
Smokie Part Two—Bill Black's Combo (59)	*1354*
Twist-Her—Bill Black's Combo (61)	672
Movin'—Bill Black's Combo (61)	516
So What—Bill Black's Combo (62)	*199*
Willie—Bill Black's Combo (60)	14
So What—Bill Black's Combo (65)	*9.4*
Honky Train—Bill Black's Combo (61)	5.9
Smokie-Part 2—Bill Doggett (60)	*3.0*
Buddy BLACK ▶ 5082 (2)	**345**
Auctioneer—Leroy Van Dyke (56)	*579*
Auctioneer—Chuck Miller (56)	*112*
Carlton BLACK ▶ 6938 (2)	**127**
Tell Him—Patti Drew (67)	*85*
Tell Him—Drew-Vels (64)	*42*
Charlie BLACK ▶ 2974 (6)	**1089**
I Know A Heartache When I See One—Jennifer Warnes (79)	894
Shadows In The Moonlight—Anne Murray (79)	702
Blessed Are The Believers—Anne Murray (81)	389
Lucky Me—Anne Murray (80)	283
Another Sleepless Night—Anne Murray (82)	277
A Little Good News—Anne Murray (83)	89
Cody BLACK ▶ 11484 (1)	**1.5**
I'm A Practical Guy—Lee Rogers (66)	9.1
Don BLACK [Donald Blackstone] ▶ 310 (16) HOF	**11712**
To Sir With Love—Lulu (67)	*10546*
Ben—Michael Jackson (72)	4231
Born Free—Roger Williams (66)	*3587*
Thunderball—Tom Jones (65)	923
Walk Away—Matt Monro (64)	794
Sam—Olivia Newton-John (77)	638
Born Free—Hesitations (68)	*597*
Best Of Both Worlds—Lulu (67)	579
True Grit—Glen Campbell (69)	516
For Mama (La Mamma)—Connie Francis (65)	*438*
Downtown—One 2 Many (89)	438
For Mama—Jerry Vale (65)	*400*
Diamonds Are Forever—Shirley Bassey (72)	284
Every Face Tells A Story—Olivia Newton-John (76)	137
For Mama—Matt Monro (65)	*0.0*
For Mama (La Mamma)—Vic Damone (65)	*0.0*
Edward C. BLACK [Ed Brown] ▶ 7980 (1)	**66**
Evil Boll-Weevil—Grand Canyon (74)	133
Gene BLACK [Walter Eugene Bloch, Gene Bloch, Walter Bloch] ▶ 2801 (2)	**1188**
Never—Heart (85)	2388
Love Touch—Rod Stewart (86)	1772
Jay BLACK [David Blatt] ▶ 8827 (1)	**38**
Livin' Above Your Head—Jay & The Americans (66)	115
John Alden BLACK ▶ 6982 (1)	**124**
I Need You—Pointer Sisters (83)	372
—Lawrence Ernest Black see: Larry BLACKMON	
Marion BLACK ▶ 10369 (1)	**9.4**
Go On Fool—Marion Black (71)	9.4
—William Patton Black Jr. see: Bill BLACK	
Bryan BLACKBURN ▶ 5520 (2)	**275**
Love Is Blue—Dells (69)	*524*
Love Is Blue (L'Amour Est Bleu)—Al Martino (68)	*302*
Tom BLACKBURN ▶ 752 (9)	**5836**
The Ballad Of Davy Crockett—Bill Hayes (55)	*6567*
Ballad Of Davy Crockett—Fess Parker (55)	*2764*
Ballad Of Davy Crockett—"Tennessee" Ernie Ford (55)	*2107*
Pancho Lopez (Davy Crockett)—Lalo Guerrero (55)	*238*
The Ballad Of Davy Crockett—Walter Schumann (55)	*45*
Duvid Crockett (The Ballad Of Davy Crockett)—Mickey Katz And His Orchestra (55)	36
Johnny Tremain—Billy Vaughn and His Orchestra (57)	6.0
The Ballad Of Davy Crockett—Rusty Draper (55)	*0.0*
The Ballad Of Davy Crockett—Steve Allen (55)	*0.0*

Bruce BLACKMAN ► 900 (7)	**4915**
Moonlight Feels Right—Starbuck (76)	3493
I Got To Know—Starbuck (76)	358
Let Me Be—Korona (80)	307
Mrs. Bluebird—Eternity's Children (68)	291
Everybody Be Dancin'—Starbuck (77)	270
Searching For A Thrill—Starbuck (78)	229
Lucky Man—Starbuck (76)	229
Donald BLACKMAN [Donald Triggs] ► 8595 (1)	**45**
Peanut Butter—Twennynine Featuring Lenny White (79)	91
Larry BLACKMON [Lawrence Ernest Black, Larry Ernest Blackmon] ► 2397 (12)	**1527**
Word Up—Cameo (86)	1982
Candy—Cameo (86)	604
She's Strange—Cameo (84)	325
Back And Forth—Cameo (87)	195
Freaky Dancin'—Cameo (81)	40
You Make Me Work—Cameo (88)	37
I Just Want To Be—Cameo (79)	31
Sparkle—Cameo (79)	17
Shake Your Pants—Cameo (80)	13
We're Goin' Out Tonight—Cameo (80)	13
Keep It Hot—Cameo (81)	9.7
It's Serious—Cameo (78)	1.8
Ritchie BLACKMORE ► 3099 (10)	**1010**
Smoke On The Water—Deep Purple (73)	3242
Stone Cold—Rainbow (82)	407
Woman From Tokyo—Deep Purple (73)	226
Street Of Dreams—Rainbow (83)	180
Knocking At Your Back Door—Deep Purple (84)	150
Black Night—Deep Purple (70)	148
Might Just Take Your Life—Deep Purple (74)	27
Emmaretta—Deep Purple (69)	8.7
You Can't Do It Right (With The One You Love)—Deep Purple (74)	4.3
The Bird Has Flown—Deep Purple (69)	0.9
—Donald Blackstone see: Don BLACK	
Christopher BLACKWELL ► 8460 (1)	**50**
Hurting Kind (I've Got My Eyes On You)—Robert Plant (90)	248
Dewayne BLACKWELL ► 383 (10)	**10285**
Mr Blue—Fleetwoods (59)	*9403*
Oh That's Good, No That's Bad—Sam The Sham And The Pharaohs (67)	338
Hickory, Dick And Doc—Bobby Vee (64)	159
Make My Day—T.G. Sheppard w/ Clint Eastwood (84)	132
Mr. Blue—Four Preps (61)	*130*
The Ferris Wheel—Everly Brothers (64)	112
I'm Gonna Hire A Wino To Decorate Our Home—David Frizzell (82)	22
The Last One To Know—Fleetwoods (60)	21
Love Or Money—Blackwells (61)	17
Dick And Jane—Bobby Vinton (75)	8.3
Otis BLACKWELL [John Davenport] ► 73 (46) HOF	**29549**
Don't Be Cruel—Elvis Presley (56)	*10167*
Return To Sender—Elvis Presley With The Jordanaires (62)	9296
All Shook Up—Elvis Presley (57)	*9084*
Handy Man—Jimmy Jones (59)	*5670*
Great Balls Of Fire—Jerry Lee Lewis (57)	*4298*
Handy Man—James Taylor (77)	*3089*
Fever—Peggy Lee (58)	*2762*
Don't Be Cruel—Bill Black's Combo (60)	*2335*
Fever—McCoys (65)	*2289*
Don't Be Cruel—Cheap Trick (88)	*2074*
One Broken Heart For Sale—Elvis Presley With The Mello Men (63)	1777
Just Keep It Up—Dee Clark (59)	1277
(Such An) Easy Question—Elvis Presley With The Jordanaires (65)	1251
Hey Little Girl—Dee Clark (59)	*1126*
Breathless—Jerry Lee Lewis (58)	1107
Handy Man—Del Shannon (64)	*1029*
Fever—Little Willie John (56)	*793*
For My Good Fortune—Pat Boone (58)	*608*
I Told Myself A Lie—Clyde McPhatter (59)	285
Shape I'm In—Johnny Restivo (59)	223
All Shook Up—Suzi Quatro (74)	*154*
Great Balls Of Fire—Tiny Tim (69)	*83*
All Shook Up—Jive Bunny And The Mastermixers (89)	*80*
Don't Be Cruel—Barbara Lynn (63)	*74*

Fever—Rita Coolidge (73)	*72*
I Sit In My Window—Russ Miller (57)	*67*
Paralyzed—Elvis Presley (56)	62
You're The Apple Of My Eye—Four Lovers (56)	41
Fever—Earl Grant (57)	*38*
Sweet Water—Stereos (61)	36
Hey, Little Girl—Foster Sylvers (73)	*24*
Don't Be Cruel (To A Heart That's True)—Elvis Presley (82)	*23*
Shadows Of Love—LaVern Baker (60)	20
Pardon Me—Billy Bland (60)	18
Up Until Now—Johnnie Ray (58)	16
Nothing Will Ever Change—Joni James (58)	14
Let's Talk About Us—Jerry Lee Lewis (59)	9.8
No Regrets—Jimmy Barnes (59)	7.8
Fever—Pete Bennett & The Embers (61)	*7.2*
Great Balls Of Fire—Jive Bunny & The Mastermixers (90)	*6.7*
Slow Motion—Wade Flemons (59)	6.6
Fever—Ray Peterson (57)	*0.0*
Fever—Little Willie John (58)	*0.0*
Great Balls Of Fire—Georgia Gibbs (57)	*0.0*
For My Good Fortune—Mahalia Jackson (58)	*0.0*
I Sit In My Window—Crew-Cuts (57)	*0.0*
Robert BLACKWELL ► 1077 (11)	**4096**
Good Golly Miss Molly—Mitch Ryder And The Detroit Wheels (66)	*2815*
Long Tall Sally—Little Richard (56)	*1982*
Long Tall Sally—Pat Boone (56)	*1222*
Rip It Up—Little Richard (56)	*1068*
Good Golly Miss Molly—Little Richard (58)	*791*
Rip It Up—Bill Haley And His Comets (56)	*751*
Good Golly Miss Molly—Swinging Blue Jeans (64)	*269*
Ready Teddy—Little Richard (56)	244
Long Tall Sally—Cat Mother And The All Night News Boys (69)	*164*
Good Golly Miss Molly—Jive Bunny & The Mastermixers (90)	*6.7*
Good Golly Miss Molly—Valiants (58)	*0.0*
Ronald BLACKWELL ► 488 (4)	**8552**
Lil' Red Riding Hood—Sam The Sham And The Pharaohs (66)	6949
The Hair On My Chinny Chin Chin—Sam The Sham And The Pharaohs (66)	919
How Do You Catch A Girl—Sam The Sham And The Pharaohs (66)	628
The Ferris Wheel—Everly Brothers (64)	112
Jack BLADES ► 1096 (12)	**4028**
High Enough—Damn Yankees (90)	3426
Sentimental Street—Night Ranger (85)	1309
When You Close Your Eyes—Night Ranger (84)	998
Goodbye—Night Ranger (85)	815
Four In The Morning (I Can't Take Any More)—Night Ranger (85)	631
Don't Tell Me You Love Me—Night Ranger (83)	339
(You Can Still) Rock In America—Night Ranger (83)	339
Come Again—Damn Yankees (91)	327
Coming Of Age—Damn Yankees (90)	237
Sing Me Away—Night Ranger (83)	221
The Secret Of My Success—Night Ranger (87)	179
Hearts Away—Night Ranger (87)	8.9
Norm BLAGMAN ► 7869 (3)	**71**
(What A Sad Way) To Love Somebody—Ral Donner (62)	88
It'll Never Be Over For Me—Baby Washington (64)	39
Put The Blame On Me—Elvis Presley (65)	23
Vaclav BLAHA ► 10476 (1)	**8.0**
Blue Skirt Waltz—Luther Brandon And His All American Boys (59)	16
Alan BLAIKLEY [Howard Blaikley] ► 1795 (6)	**2308**
Have I The Right?—Honeycombs (64)	3306
I've Lost You—Elvis Presley (70)	400
I Can't Stop—Honeycombs (64)	362
Zabadak—Dave Dee, Dozy, Beaky, Mick And Tich (67)	272
Boy—Lulu (68)	3.3
Bend It—Dave Dee, Dozy, Beaky, Mick And Tich (67)	0.5
—Howard Blaikley see: Alan BLAIKLEY	
—Howard Blaikley see: Ken HOWARD	
Dennis BLAIR ► 9628 (1)	**20**
Rappin' Rodney—Rodney Dangerfield (83)	140
Frank BLAIR ► 11492 (1)	**1.5**
Sweet Lies—Robert Palmer (88)	4.4

Hal BLAIR ► 633 (10)	**6830**
Ringo—Lorne Greene (64)	5527
Please Help Me I'm Falling—Hank Locklin (60)	*3409*
I'm Yours—Elvis Presley (65)	1788
One Has My Name (The Other Has My Heart)—Barry Young (65)	1343
Not One Minute More—Della Reese (59)	1216
I Was The One—Elvis Presley (56)	930
(I Can't Help You) I'm Falling Too—Skeeter Davis (60)	*543*
Please Help Me I'm Falling—Rusty Draper (60)	*195*
How Many—Bill Haley & His Comets (57)	25
I'm Glad That Your Falling—Betty Madigan (60)	*2.0*
—John Hendry Blair see: Johnny CYMBAL	
Lois Ann BLAISCH ► 987 (1)	**4537**
Could've Been—Tiffany (87)	4537
Bebe BLAKE ► 9132 (1)	**31**
Dreamy Eyes—Four Preps (56)	61
David Marvin BLAKE [D J Quik] ► 7172 (1)	**112**
Tonite—DJ Quik (91)	112
Eubie BLAKE [James Hubert Blake] ► 3975 (7)	**633**
Memories Of You—Four Coins (55)	*1002*
Memories Of You—Benny Goodman Trio with Rosemary Clooney (55)	*204*
Memories Of You—Hugo Winterhalter's Orchestra And Chorus (56)	*31*
Memories Of You—Joe Carr (55)	*0.0*
Memories Of You—Paul Weston & His Orchestra (55)	*0.0*
Memories Of You—Ink Spots (55)	*0.0*
Memories Of You—Glen Gray & His Orchestra (56)	*0.0*
—James Hubert Blake see: Eubie BLAKE	
Lyndell BLAKE ► 9392 (1)	**25**
This Time Make It Funky—Tracie Spencer (91)	123
—Brian Douglas Blanchard see: Brian SOARES	
Jack BLANCHARD ► 2737 (2)	**1231**
Tennessee Bird Walk—Jack Blanchard & Misty Morgan (70)	1149
Humphrey The Camel—Jack Blanchard & Misty Morgan (70)	82
Ollie BLANCHARD ► 1560 (3)	**2717**
Please Love Me Forever—Bobby Vinton (67)	*3277*
Please Love Me Forever—Cathy Jean And The Roommates (61)	*2128*
Please Love Me Forever—Tommy Edwards (58)	*29*
—Carte Blanche see: Bernie TAUPIN	
John BLANCO ► 9945 (1)	**15**
Don't Run My Life—Spys (82)	73
Billy BLAND ► 10235 (1)	**11**
My Heart's On Fire—Billy Bland (61)	11
—Milton Bland see: Monk HIGGINS	
Virginia BLAND [Virginia P. Bland, Vee Pea] ► 8442 (1)	**50**
Good Thing Man—Frank Lucas (77)	101
—Virginia P. Bland see: Virginia BLAND	
Richard BLANDON ► 5413 (2)	**292**
Could This Be Magic—Dubs (57)	551
Don't Ask Me (To Be Lonely)—Dubs (57)	32
Ralph BLANE [Ralph Uriah Hunsecker] ► 10180 (2) HOF	**12**
An Occasional Man—Jeri Southern (55)	*23*
An Occasional Man—Billy May & His Orchestra with Ella Mae Morse (55)	*0.0*
Jock BLANEY ► 7786 (1)	**75**
This Is Ponderous—2NU (90)	300
Boris BLANK ► 5679 (1)	**256**
Oh Yeah—Yello (87)	256
—Peter Blankfield see: Peter WOLF	
Clinton BLANSON ► 7882 (1)	**71**
She's On The Left—Jeffrey Osborne (88)	284
—Betty Blasco see: Betty PETERSON	
Lee BLASTIC ► 8818 (1)	**39**
There's A New Moon Over My Shoulder—Bonnie Guitar (57)	116
—David Blatt see: Jay BLACK	
Marc BLATTE ► 3408 (4)	**859**
When She Was My Girl—Four Tops (81)	1578
Hands Across America—Voices Of America (86)	108
Voo Doo—Rachel Sweet (83)	43
Sad Hearts—Four Tops (82)	38

Eric BLAU ▶ 9180 (1)	**29**
If We Only Have Love—Dionne Warwicke (72)	88
Arthur BLEA ▶ 8195 (1)	**59**
The Fanatic—Felony (83)	294
Victor BLECMAN [Uncle Vic] ▶ 10278 (1)	**11**
Space Invaders—Uncle Vic (80)	11
Adam BLESSING ▶ 10698 (1)	**6.0**
Back To The River—Damnation Of Adam Blessing (70)	30
Archie BLEYER ▶ 9247 (5)	**28**
Eh! Cumpari—Gaylord & Holiday (76)	71
The Dudelsack Song (Play To Me My Darling)—Chordettes (55)	8.4
The White Rose Of Athens—Nana Mouskouri (62)	*0.0*
The White Rose Of Athens—Chordettes (62)	*0.0*
Whistlin' Willie (Our Melody)—Chordettes (56)	*0.0*
Paul Steven BLISS ▶ 1370 (4)	**3248**
Heart Attack—Olivia Newton-John (82)	3891
How Do I Survive—Amy Holland (80)	779
(If There Was) Any Other Way—Celine Dion (91)	479
Innocent Eyes—Graham Nash (86)	45
Peter S. BLISS ▶ 5962 (2)	**223**
I Need You Tonight—Peter Wolf (84)	363
Emotion—Barbra Streisand (85)	41
—Blitz see: Emridge JONES	
—Blitz see: Gary KING	
—Blitz see: Harry J. KING	
—Blitz see: Reggie WHITE	
Marc BLITZSTEIN ▶ 824 (3)	**5333**
Mack The Knife—Bobby Darin (59)	*14687*
Mack The Knife—Ella Fitzgerald (60)	*743*
A Theme From Threepenny Opera (Mack The Knife)—Louis Armstrong And His All-Stars (56)	*570*
—Gene Bloch see: Gene BLACK	
Philippe Gerard BLOCH [Philippe Gerard] ▶ 7289 (1)	**105**
The Magic Tango—Hugo Winterhalter & Orchestra (54)	210
—Walter Bloch see: Gene BLACK	
Alan BLOCK ▶ 3926 (2)	**654**
Walkin' After Midnight—Patsy Cline (57)	*1307*
Walkin' After Midnight—Otis Williams & His Charms (57)	*0.0*
—Ulf Conny Blomquest see: Conny BLOMQVIST	
Conny BLOMQVIST [Ulf Conny Blomquest, Conny Bloom] ▶ 8890 (1)	**37**
All Lips N' Hips—Electric Boys (90)	37
—Philip Wallach Blondheim see: Scott McKENZIE	
Raymond BLOODWORTH ▶ 1854 (10)	**2196**
C'mon Marianne—4 Seasons Featuring The "Sound" Of Frankie Valli (67)	*1901*
Watch The Flowers Grow—4 Seasons Featuring The "Sound" Of Frankie Valli (67)	765
The Girl I'll Never Know (Angels Never Fly This Low)—Frankie Valli (69)	525
C'mon Marianne—Donny Osmond (76)	*435*
Joy—Mitch Ryder (67)	378
Nothing Succeeds Like Success—Bill Deal & The Rhondels (70)	277
Summer And Sandy—Lesley Gore (67)	257
Open Up Your Door—Richard and The Young Lions (66)	71
She Ain't Lovin' You—Distant Cousins (66)	20
Singles Game—Jay And The Techniques (68)	4.6
Bobby BLOOM ▶ 810 (14)	**5431**
Mony Mony—Tommy James And The Shondells (68)	*4671*
Mony Mony "Live"—Billy Idol (87)	*3728*
Indian Giver—1910 Fruitgum Co. (69)	3435
Montego Bay—Bobby Bloom (70)	*1958*
Heavy Makes You Happy (Sha-Na-Boom Boom)—Staple Singers (71)	*754*
Special Delivery—1910 Fruitgum Co. (69)	640
Sunshine—Archies (70)	589
Do It In The Name Of Love—Candi Staton (73)	250
Make Me Happy—Bobby Bloom (71)	141
Mony Mony—Billy Idol (81)	*23*
Montego Bay—Amazulu (87)	*22*
We're All Goin' Home—Bobby Bloom (71)	9.2
Mony Mony—Tight Fit (81)	*0.9*
Sha La Boom Boom—Bobby Bloom (73)	*0.4*
—Conny Bloom see: Conny BLOMQVIST	
Marty BLOOM ▶ 3453 (1)	**841**
Does Your Chewing Gum Lose Its Flavor (On The Bedpost Over Night)—Lonnie Donegan And His Skiffle Group (61)	2524
Rube BLOOM ▶ 2355 (7) HOF	**1566**
Fools Rush In—Rick Nelson (63)	*1909*
Fools Rush In (Where Angels Fear To Tread)—Brook Benton (60)	*1092*
Ev'rybody's Twistin'—Frank Sinatra (62)	90
Don't Worry 'Bout Me—Vincent Edwards (62)	18
Fools Rush In—Etta James (62)	*14*
Maybe You'll Be There—Billy And The Essentials (62)	8.8
Don't Worry About Me—Frank Sinatra (54)	0.0
Vera BLOOM ▶ 7509 (1)	**91**
Jalousie—Caterina Valente (55)	183
William A. BLOOM ▶ 4762 (1)	**422**
Double Dutch Bus—Frankie Smith (81)	843
Ron BLOOMBERG ▶ 7679 (1)	**81**
Lonely Saturday Night—Don French (59)	163
—Kurtis Blow see: Kurt WALKER	
Amanda BLUE [Amanda Blue Leigh] ▶ 7308 (1)	**103**
Little Darlin'—Sheila (81)	206
Barry BLUE [Barry Ian Blue, Barry Ian Green] ▶ 4810 (5)	**409**
Devil's Gun—C.J. & Co. (77)	540
One More Minute—Saint Tropez (79)	182
All Fall Down—Five Star (85)	146
I Eat Cannibals—Total Coelo (83)	141
Dancin' (On A Saturday Night)—Flash Cadillac & The Continental Kids (74)	37
David BLUE [Stuart David Cohen] ▶ 5013 (2)	**359**
Outlaw Man—Eagles (73)	*273*
Outlaw Man—David Blue (73)	*86*
Brian BLUGERMAN ▶ 6606 (1)	**152**
When She Dances—Joey Scarbury (81)	152
—Ray Blum see: Ramon ARCUSA	
—Elisa Blumberg see: Lisa RATNER	
David BLUME ▶ 4316 (1)	**524**
Turn-Down Day—Cyrkle (66)	1047
Martin BLUNT ▶ 10623 (1)	**6.7**
The Only One I Know—Charlatans UK (90)	33
Robbie BLUNT [Philip Donnely] ▶ 4464 (4)	**488**
Big Log—Robert Plant (83)	830
In The Mood—Robert Plant (83)	463
Burning Down One Side—Robert Plant (82)	89
Pledge Pin—Robert Plant (82)	54
Allan BLYE ▶ 9541 (1)	**22**
Baroque-A-Nova—Mason Williams (68)	44
—Dede Blythe see: Dede FAIRBANKS	
—Eddie Bo see: Edwin BOCAGE	
Charles BOBBIT ▶ 1842 (10)	**2209**
Give It Up Or Turnit A Loose—James Brown (69)	1033
Make It Funky (Part 1)—James Brown (71)	869
I'm A Greedy Man - Part 1—James Brown (71)	557
King Heroin—James Brown (72)	531
Papa Don't Take No Mess - Part I—James Brown (74)	475
Gimme Some More—J.B.'s (72)	231
My Part—James Brown (71)	76
Make It Funky (Part 3)—James Brown (71)	76
Pass The Peas—J.B.'s (72)	48
Me And My Baby Got A Good Thing Going—Lyn Collins (72)	17
Dale BOBBITT ▶ 10881 (1)	**4.7**
Free To Carry On—Sandpipers (70)	9.4
—Bobby Z. see: Robert RIVKIN	
Sam BOBRICK ▶ 4290 (3)	**531**
Girl Of My Best Friend—Ral Donner & The Starfires (61)	934
(What A Sad Way) To Love Somebody—Ral Donner (62)	88
It'll Never Be Over For Me—Baby Washington (64)	39
Edwin BOCAGE [Eddie Bo, Eddie Bocage] ▶ 4096 (5)	**594**
My Dearest Darling—Etta James (60)	941
Slippin' And Slidin' (Peepin' And Hidin')—Little Richard (56)	*180*
Hook And Sling-Part 1—Eddie Bo (69)	154
Slipin' And Slidin'—Sing Along With Jim And Monica (64)	*4.1*
Slippin' & Slidin'—Willie Mitchell (67)	*3.3*
—Joseph R. Bochenek see: Joe RAYE	
Jerry BOCK ▶ 2314 (17) HOF	**1607**
Artificial Flowers—Bobby Darin (60)	*1153*
Mr. Wonderful—Peggy Lee (56)	*899*
Mr. Wonderful—Sarah Vaughan (56)	*674*
Mr. Wonderful—Teddi King (56)	*459*
Too Close For Comfort—Eydie Gorme (56)	*381*
Sunrise, Sunset—Roger Williams (67)	144
Fiddler On The Roof—Village Stompers (64)	81
Jacques D'Iraque—Sammy Davis Jr. (56)	80
Uh-Huh Oh Yeah—Steve Lawrence (58)	*75*
Til Tomorrow—Janice Harper (60)	18
Artificial Flowers—Phil Napoleon (60)	*0.0*
Mr. Wonderful—Bette Anne Steele (56)	*0.0*
Mr. Wonderful—Mello-Larks (56)	*0.0*
Too Close For Comfort—Sammy Davis Jr. (56)	*0.0*
Too Close For Comfort—Lillian Briggs (56)	*0.0*
Uh-Huh, Oh Yeah—Jill Corey (58)	*0.0*
Uh Yuh Oh Yeah—Bill Hayes (58)	*0.0*
—Peter William Bockbanks see: Peter W. BANKS	
—Udo Jürgen Bockelman see: Udo JÜRGENS	
Walfried BÖCKER [MC Bones] ▶ 9741 (1)	**18**
Crazy—Daisy Dee (91)	90
Bill BODINE ▶ 9411 (1)	**24**
Hold Me—Laura Branigan (85)	48
Jo BOGAERT [Thomas DeQuincey] ▶ 1879 (3)	**2170**
Pump Up The Jam—Technotronic (89)	3746
Get Up! (Before The Night Is Over)—Technotronic (90)	1473
Rockin' Over The Beat—Technotronic (90)	5.2
Lana BOGAN ▶ 7317 (2)	**102**
Unborn Child—Seals & Crofts (74)	140
Baby, I'll Give It To You—Seals & Crofts (76)	65
Steve BOGARD ▶ 11663 (1)	**0.8**
Freedom Train—James Carr (69)	2.3
Winston BOGART ▶ 8163 (1)	**60**
Goodbye Dad—Castle Sisters (62)	119
Thomas BOGDANY ▶ 2537 (2)	**1406**
Shout! Shout! (Knock Yourself Out)—Ernie Maresca (62)	1995
Come On Little Angel—Belmonts (62)	817
Tim BOGERT ▶ 9536 (2)	**22**
Where Is My Mind—Vanilla Fudge (68)	71
Need Love—Vanilla Fudge (69)	16
Howard BOGGESS ▶ 7126 (1)	**115**
Memory Lane—Hippies (Formerly The Tams) (63)	229
Hamilton BOHANNON ▶ 9092 (2)	**31**
Let's Start The Dance—Hamilton Bohannon (78)	30
Foot Stompin Music—Hamilton Bohannon (75)	1.5
Marc BOLAN [Marc Feld] ▶ 1202 (6)	**3701**
Bang A Gong (Get It On)—T. Rex (71)	*1711*
Get It On—Power Station (85)	*1319*
Hot Love—T. Rex (71)	255
Telegram Sam—T. Rex (72)	197
Ride A White Swan—Tyrannosaurus Rex (71)	185
Bang A Gong—Witch Queen (79)	*34*
Rachel BOLAN [Rachel Southworth] ▶ 2200 (3)	**1751**
18 And Life—Skid Row (89)	1922
I Remember You—Skid Row (89)	1578
Youth Gone Wild—Skid Row (89)	1.6
James BOLDEN [Jacques Pépino] ▶ 11681 (1)	**0.7**
(If You Want It) Do It Yourself—Gloria Gaynor (75)	1.5
Nick BOLDI ▶ 8535 (1)	**47**
I'm In Love With You—Pat Boone (56)	94
Patrick BOLEN ▶ 11146 (1)	**3.0**
Night Pulse—Double Image (83)	9.0
Jesse BOLIAN ▶ 6530 (1)	**160**
I'm Gonna Miss You—Artistics (66)	479
Tommy BOLIN ▶ 5916 (2)	**229**
Must Be Love—James Gang (74)	371
Standing In The Rain—James Gang (74)	43
—Chet Bolins see: Chris DARWAY	
Ferdi BOLLAND ▶ 2281 (2)	**1658**
Rock Me Amadeus—Falco (86)	4222
Vienna Calling—Falco (86)	751
Rob BOLLAND ▶ 2282 (2)	**1658**
Rock Me Amadeus—Falco (86)	4222
Vienna Calling—Falco (86)	751

Jay BOLOTIN ▶ 9703 (1)	**19**
Go Down Easy—Dan Fogelberg (85)	19
—Michael Bolotin see: Michael BOLTON	
Andre BOLTON [L. A. Dre] ▶ 7103 (1)	**116**
Something In My Heart—Michel'le (91)	347
Michael BOLTON [Michael Bolotin] ▶ 596 (14)	**7324**
How Am I Supposed To Live Without You—Michael Bolton (89)	*4042*
Love Is A Wonderful Thing—Michael Bolton (91)	2873
How Can We Be Lovers—Michael Bolton (90)	2141
I Found Someone—Cher (87)	*1409*
How Am I Supposed To Live Without You—Laura Branigan (83)	*1366*
Forever—Kiss (90)	1355
That's What Love Is All About—Michael Bolton (87)	1008
Soul Provider—Michael Bolton (89)	784
Till Somebody Loves You—Henry Lee Summer (91)	275
Love Me Tonight—Blackjack (79)	113
Wait On Love—Michael Bolton (88)	58
I Found Someone—Laura Branigan (86)	*43*
Fool's Game—Michael Bolton (83)	20
Whenever You Close Your Eyes—Tommy Page (91)	11
Jon BON JOVI [John F. Bongiovi] ▶ 173 (18) HOF	**17418**
Livin' On A Prayer—Bon Jovi (86)	5011
Blaze Of Glory—Jon Bon Jovi (90)	4356
You Give Love A Bad Name—Bon Jovi (86)	4318
I'll Be There For You—Bon Jovi (89)	4005
Bad Medicine—Bon Jovi (88)	3448
Born To Be My Baby—Bon Jovi (88)	3071
Wanted Dead Or Alive—Bon Jovi (87)	1804
Lay Your Hands On Me—Bon Jovi (89)	1766
Living In Sin—Bon Jovi (89)	1563
Miracle—Jon Bon Jovi (90)	1209
So Close—Daryl Hall & John Oates (90)	999
We All Sleep Alone—Cher (88)	926
Runaway—Bon Jovi (84)	454
Does Anybody Really Fall In Love Anymore?—Kane Roberts (91)	452
Notorious—Loverboy (87)	386
Sometimes (It's A Bitch)—Stevie Nicks (91)	217
Only Lonely—Bon Jovi (85)	164
In And Out Of Love—Bon Jovi (85)	103
Frank BONARRIGO ▶ 11121 (1)	**3.1**
Nobody But You—Lafayettes (62)	6.3
Angelo BOND ▶ 1141 (17)	**3892**
Somebody's Been Sleeping—100 Proof Aged In Soul (70)	2587
Bring The Boys Home—Freda Payne (71)	2168
Stick-Up—Honey Cone (71)	2010
Pay To The Piper—Chairmen Of The Board (70)	1695
You've Got To Crawl (Before You Walk)—8th Day (71)	724
Women's Love Rights—Laura Lee (71)	705
Cherish What Is Dear To You (While It's Near To You)—Freda Payne (71)	473
Everything Good Is Bad—100 Proof Aged In Soul (72)	364
Rip Off—Laura Lee (72)	327
Power—Temptations (80)	231
Sail Away—Temptations (84)	152
Free Me From My Freedom/Tie Me To A Tree (Handcuff Me)—Bonnie Pointer (78)	106
One Man's Leftovers (Is Another Man's Feast)—100 Proof Aged In Soul (71)	54
90 Day Freeze (On Her Love)—100 Proof Aged In Soul (71)	21
Too Many Cooks (Spoil The Soup)—100 Proof Aged In Soul (69)	3.9
Love And Liberty—Laura Lee (72)	2.7
Stop The World And Let Me Off—Flaming Ember (71)	1.2
Chris BOND ▶ 7628 (1)	**84**
Help Wanted—Hudson Brothers (76)	84
Johnny BOND [Cyrus Whitfield Bond] ▶ 2821 (5)	**1170**
Cimarron (Roll On)—Billy Vaughn And His Orchestra (58)	*540*
10 Little Bottles—Johnny Bond (65)	521
Cimarron (Roll On)—Les Paul and Mary Ford (56)	*70*
Tomorrow Never Comes—B.J. Thomas (66)	51
Glad Rags—Tennessee Ernie Ford (59)	13
—Gary "U. S." Bonds see: Gary ANDERSON	
Leon BONDS ▶ 7001 (1)	**123**

Losers Weepers - Part I—Etta James (70)	123
—Mark Bones see: Bert KAEMPFERT	
Luiz BONFÁ ▶ 6504 (2)	**162**
A Day In The Life Of A Fool—Jack Jones (66)	312
Almost In Love—Elvis Presley With The Jordanaires (68)	11
Mars BONFIRE [Dennis Edmonton, Dennis McCrohan] ▶ 626 (3)	**6904**
Born To Be Wild—Steppenwolf (68)	*6256*
Ride With Me—Steppenwolf (71)	429
Born To Be Wild—Wilson Pickett (69)	*218*
Joann BONGIORNO ▶ 10639 (1)	**6.5**
I'll Release You—Joann Bon And The Coquettes (67)	*33*
—John F. Bongiovi see: Jon BON JOVI	
Jason BONHAM ▶ 8635 (1)	**44**
Wait For You—Bonham (89)	221
John BONHAM ▶ 2194 (7)	**1755**
Whole Lotta Love—Led Zeppelin (69)	*4704*
D'yer Mak'er—Led Zeppelin (73)	1260
Rock And Roll—Led Zeppelin (72)	411
Whole Lotta Love—C.C.S. (71)	*247*
Whole Lotta Love—King Curtis & The Kingpins (71)	*230*
Good Times Bad Times—Led Zeppelin (69)	160
Whole Lotta Love—Wonder Band (79)	*8.7*
Brian BONHOMME ▶ 7276 (1)	**106**
Don't Try To Stop It—Roman Holliday (83)	106
James BONNEFORD ▶ 2373 (6)	**1553**
Cherish—Kool & The Gang (85)	3699
Joanna—Kool & The Gang (83)	3511
Misled—Kool & The Gang (84)	1436
Fresh—Kool & The Gang (85)	1367
Tonight—Kool & The Gang (84)	1136
Emergency—Kool & The Gang (85)	915
Ed BONNER ▶ 11267 (1)	**2.5**
Little Boy Blue—Billy Vaughn and His Orchestra (56)	7.6
Garry BONNER [Elmo] ▶ 379 (20)	**10323**
Happy Together—Turtles (67)	*9222*
She'd Rather Be With Me—Turtles (67)	4329
You Know What I Mean—Turtles (67)	1570
Celebrate—Three Dog Night (70)	1496
She's My Girl—Turtles (67)	1458
The Cat In The Window (The Bird In The Sky)—Petula Clark (67)	667
Jill—Gary Lewis And The Playboys (67)	512
Girls In Love—Gary Lewis And The Playboys (67)	472
Melancholy Music Man—Righteous Brothers (67)	338
As Long As You're Here—Zalman Yanovsky (67)	137
Happy Together (A Fantasy)—Captain & Tennille (80)	*131*
Happy Together—Dawn Featuring Tony Orlando (72)	*124*
Happy Together—Nylons (87)	*56*
Me About You—Lovin' Spoonful (69)	*53*
Me About You—Mojo Men (67)	*43*
The Dance At St. Francis—Barracuda (68)	26
Me About You—Turtles (70)	*3.8*
When The Good Sun Shines—Elmo & Almo (67)	1.9
Kitty Doyle—Dino, Desi & Billy (67)	1.9
Two In The Afternoon—Dino, Desi & Billy (67)	1.4
Lee BONNER ▶ 8943 (2)	**36**
Life's Too Short—Lafayettes (62)	65
Nobody But You—Lafayettes (62)	6.3
Leroy BONNER ▶ 1872 (15)	**2174**
Love Rollercoaster—Ohio Players (75)	5251
Fire—Ohio Players (74)	4114
Funky Worm—Ohio Players (73)	1438
Skin Tight—Ohio Players (74)	1151
Who'd She Coo?—Ohio Players (76)	885
Ecstasy—Ohio Players (73)	621
Sweet Sticky Thing—Ohio Players (75)	411
Fopp—Ohio Players (76)	398
I Want To Be Free—Ohio Players (75)	335
Jive Turkey (Part 1)—Ohio Players (74)	245
Pain (Part 1)—Ohio Players (71)	208
O-H-I-O—Ohio Players (77)	144
Feel The Beat (Everybody Disco)—Ohio Players (77)	42
Got Pleasure—Ohio Players (72)	14
Rattlesnake—Ohio Players (76)	12
Georges BONNET ▶ 11549 (1)	**1.2**
Majorca (Isle Of Love)—Bob Manning (55)	*3.7*
Sean BONNIWELL ▶ 2536 (3)	**1408**
Talk Talk—Music Machine (66)	1229
The People In Me—Music Machine (67)	178
Double Yellow Line—Music Machine (67)	0.5

—Bono see: Paul HEWSON	
Sonny BONO [Salvatore Phillip Bono] ▶ 75 (27)	**29202**
I Got You Babe—Sonny & Cher (65)	*7646*
Bang Bang (My Baby Shot Me Down)—Cher (66)	4642
The Beat Goes On—Sonny & Cher (67)	*2569*
A Cowboy's Work Is Never Done—Sonny & Cher (72)	2314
You Better Sit Down Kids—Cher (67)	2181
Baby Don't Go—Sonny & Cher (65)	1981
Laugh At Me—Sonny (65)	1817
Needles And Pins—Searchers (64)	*1639*
But You're Mine—Sonny & Cher (65)	873
Little Man—Sonny & Cher (66)	785
Just You—Sonny & Cher (65)	645
Where Do You Go—Cher (65)	496
I Got You Babe—UB40 With Chrissie Hynde (85)	*480*
Have I Stayed Too Long—Sonny & Cher (66)	333
You Bug Me Baby—Larry Williams (57)	322
Needles And Pins—Tom Petty and The Heartbreakers (86)	*317*
It's The Little Things—Sonny & Cher (67)	276
I Got You Babe—Etta James (68)	*239*
A Beautiful Story—Sonny & Cher (67)	225
The Revolution Kind—Sonny (65)	160
Needles And Pins—Jackie de Shannon (63)	*136*
Mama Was A Rock And Roll Singer, Papa Used To Write All Her Songs—Sonny & Cher (73)	124
Plastic Man—Sonny & Cher (67)	113
Needles And Pins—Smokie (77)	*47*
Mama (When My Dollies Have Babies)—Cher (66)	43
The Beat Goes On—Lawrence Welk And His Orchestra (67)	*16*
Living For You—Sonny & Cher (66)	13
Karla BONOFF ▶ 2331 (8)	**1585**
All My Life—Linda Ronstadt (featuring Aaron Neville) (90)	933
Someone To Lay Down Beside Me—Linda Ronstadt (76)	*319*
Please Be The One—Karla Bonoff (82)	132
Baby Don't Go—Karla Bonoff (80)	128
I Can't Hold On—Karla Bonoff (78)	77
Lose Again—Linda Ronstadt (77)	32
Someone To Lay Down Beside Me—Karla Bonoff (78)	*15*
Isn't It Always Love—Karla Bonoff (78)	14
Carl BONURA ▶ 2688 (2)	**1272**
I've Had It—Bell Notes (59)	*2423*
I've Had It—Fanny (74)	*121*
Betty BOO [Alison Clarkson] ▶ 10554 (1)	**7.3**
Doin' The Do—Betty Boo (90)	29
Bradford BOOBIS ▶ 8844 (1)	**38**
Eighteen—Connie Francis (57)	76
Chuckii BOOKER [Eugene Booker] ▶ 6484 (1)	**164**
Turned Away—Chuckii Booker (89)	329
—Eugene Booker see: Chuckii BOOKER	
Harry BOOKER ▶ 4117 (1)	**588**
Shoeshine Boy—Eddie Kendricks (75)	1176
—Jessie Mae Booker see: Jessie Mae ROBINSON	
—Robert Nesta Marley Booker see: Bob MARLEY	
—Linda Bookout see: Linda WILLIAMS	
Mark BOON ▶ 5048 (1)	**354**
Sausalito Summernight—Diesel (81)	708
Daniel BOONE [Peter Charles Green] ▶ 3358 (3)	**882**
Beautiful Sunday—Daniel Boone (72)	1614
Annabelle—Daniel Boone (72)	146
Run Tell The People—Daniel Boone (75)	4.6
Len BOONE ▶ 2213 (1)	**1735**
You Made Me Believe In Magic—Bay City Rollers (77)	1735
Pat BOONE [Charles E. Boone] ▶ 4540 (3)	**468**
Wish You Were Here, Buddy—Pat Boone (66)	372
The Exodus Song (This Land Is Mine)—Pat Boone (61)	*190*
Quando, Quando, Quando (Tell Me When)—Pat Boone (62)	2.6
Richard BOONE ▶ 6424 (1)	**171**
The Ballad Of Paladin—Duane Eddy (62)	514
Steve BOONE ▶ 1379 (4)	**3229**
Summer In The City—Lovin' Spoonful (66)	*7015*
You Didn't Have To Be So Nice—Lovin' Spoonful (65)	1761
Full Measure—Lovin' Spoonful (67)	15
Summer In The City—Quincy Jones (73)	*8.5*

Harry BOOROS ▶ 8045 (1)	**64**
Zip Zip—Diamonds (57)	255
Ann BOOTH ▶ 11276 (1)	**2.5**
Run, Woman, Run—Tammy Wynette (70)	7.5
Jim BOOTHE ▶ 3422 (9)	**855**
Jingle Bell Rock—Bobby Helms (57)	*684*
Jingle Bell Rock—Bobby Rydell Chubby Checker (61)	*402*
Jingle Bell Rock—Bobby Helms (61)	*209*
Jingle Bell Rock—Bobby Helms (58)	*159*
Jingle Bell Rock—Bobby Helms (60)	*119*
Jingle Bell Rock—Bobby Helms (62)	*114*
Jingle Bell Rock—Bobby Rydell Chubby Checker (62)	*14*
Jingle Bell Rock—Bobby Helms (60)	*7.6*
Jingle Bell Rock—Teresa Brewer (58)	*0.0*
—Bootsy see: Andy CONNELL	
Rupert BOPAPE ▶ 9588 (3)	**21**
Windy—Paul Gayten (58)	12
Tom Hark—Elias & His Zig Zag Jive Flutes (58)	*4.6*
Tom Hark—Ted Heath and His Orchestra (58)	*4.6*
Michael BORCH ▶ 6744 (1)	**141**
You Wouldn't Listen—I'des Of March (66)	423
Mike BORCHETTA ▶ 6545 (1)	**158**
Rambling—Ramblers (1) (60)	317
Mike BORDIN ▶ 5306 (2)	**309**
Epic—Faith No More (90)	1519
Falling To Pieces—Faith No More (90)	27
Renée BOREK ▶ 7248 (1)	**108**
Solitaire—Embers (61)	323
Bernice BORISOFF ▶ 3973 (1)	**634**
Keem-O-Sabe—Electric Indian (69)	1268
—Leonard W. Borisoff see: Len BARRY	
Aleksandr BORODIN ▶ 6848 (2)	**133**
Baubles Bangles And Beads—Kirby Stone Four (58)	*398*
Baubles Bangles And Beads—Jonah Jones Quartet (58)	*0.0*
Bill BORRELLI ▶ 4314 (6)	**524**
Philadelphia USA—Nu Tornados (58)	*981*
Philadelphia USA—Art Lund (58)	*32*
Here In My Heart—Al Martino (61)	25
Ole Mummer's Strut—Nu Tornados (59)	13
Till You're Back In My Arms—Vince Carson (56)	6.1
Philadelphia U.S.A.—Milton DeLugg & His Orchestra (58)	*0.0*
Thomas BORSDORF ▶ 5740 (1)	**247**
Find Your Way Back—Jefferson Starship (81)	493
—William Paul Borsey Jr. see: Willy DeVILLE	
Gianfranco BORTOLOTTI ▶ 9218 (1)	**28**
Don't You Love Me—49ers (90)	85
Kurt BORUSIEWICZ ▶ 7387 (1)	**99**
Hot Shot—Karen Young (78)	198
Blas BOSHELL ▶ 2513 (2)	**1427**
I've Got The Music In Me—Kiki Dee Band (74)	1416
Step By Step—Kiki Dee Band (75)	11
William BOSKENT ▶ 11362 (1)	**2.1**
Lonely Chair—Lloyd Price (57)	4.2
Jane BOSSUNG ▶ 10320 (1)	**10**
I'm Jealous—Ike & Tina Turner (61)	20
Chris BOSTOCK [Chris D. James] ▶ 5879 (1)	**233**
Just Got Lucky—JoBoxers (83)	467
Perry BOTKIN Jr. ▶ 2053 (6)	**1943**
Nadia's Theme (The Young And The Restless)—Barry De Vorzon and Perry Botkin, Jr. (76)	2470
Wonderful Summer—Robin Ward (63)	1300
I Want My Baby Back—Jimmy Cross (65)	56
Bless The Beasts And Children—Carpenters (71)	*39*
Bless The Beasts And Children—Barry De Vorzon & Perry Botkin, Jr. (77)	*20*
Passion Flower—Caterina Valente (59)	2.0
—Ted Ellis Botkin see: Ted ELLIS	
—Martin Böttcher see: Michael THOMAS	
Gilbert BOTTIGLIER ▶ 10990 (1)	**3.9**
Sweet Summer Music—Attitudes (76)	12
Mitch BOTTLER ▶ 1916 (6)	**2114**
I'd Wait A Million Years—Grass Roots (69)	2231
Sooner Or Later—Grass Roots (71)	1771
Hallelujah—Sweathog (71)	635
Saturday Night, Sunday Morning—Thelma Houston (79)	468
Breakaway—Big Pig (88)	207
The Grooviest Girl In The World—Fun And Games (69)	190

Roddy BOTTUM [Roswell Christopher Bottum] ▶ 5307 (2)	**309**
Epic—Faith No More (90)	1519
Falling To Pieces—Faith No More (90)	27
—Roswell Christopher Bottum see: Roddy BOTTUM	
Nathaniel BOUKNIGHT ▶ 6345 (1)	**181**
Baby Oh Baby—Shells (60)	542
—Bob Boulanger see: Robert BOULANGER	
Georges BOULANGER [George Pantazi] ▶ 1038 (4)	**4251**
My Prayer—Platters (56)	*8202*
My Prayer—Ray, Goodman & Brown (80)	*266*
My Prayer—Johnny Thunder (66)	*34*
My Prayer—Ink Spots (56)	*0.0*
Robert BOULANGER [Bob Boulanger, Van Trevor] ▶ 4617 (2)	**450**
Abigail Beecher—Freddy Cannon (64)	849
That's The Only Way—4 Seasons (63)	51
Carl BOURELLY ▶ 3692 (1)	**733**
Do Me!—Bell Biv DeVoe (90)	2931
Brent BOURGEOIS ▶ 4685 (2)	**438**
I Don't Mind At All—Bourgeois Tagg (87)	540
Dare To Fall In Love—Brent Bourgeois (90)	505
Gene BOURGEOIS [Jivin' Gene] ▶ 6260 (2)	**188**
Breaking Up Is Hard To Do—Jivin' Gene And The Jokers (59)	371
Going Out With The Tide—Jivin' Gene (60)	5.2
Rory BOURKE ▶ 1334 (10)	**3323**
The Most Beautiful Girl—Charlie Rich (73)	5675
I Know A Heartache When I See One—Jennifer Warnes (79)	894
Baby I Lied—Deborah Allen (83)	851
Shadows In The Moonlight—Anne Murray (79)	702
Blessed Are The Believers—Anne Murray (81)	389
Lucky Me—Anne Murray (80)	283
Another Sleepless Night—Anne Murray (82)	277
Easy As Pie—Billy "Crash" Craddock (75)	179
A Little Good News—Anne Murray (83)	89
Patch It Up—Elvis Presley (70)	0.0
Jean-Pierre BOURTAYRE ▶ 5595 (2)	**267**
My Boy—Elvis Presley (75)	*838*
My Boy—Richard Harris (71)	*497*
Ronald BOUTWELL ▶ 6588 (1)	**154**
Waiting At The Bus Stop—Bobby Sherman (71)	308
—Hans Bouwens see: George BAKER	
Jeff BOVA ▶ 9648 (1)	**20**
Boy Blue—Cyndi Lauper (87)	59
Carolyn BOWDEN ▶ 5117 (1)	**340**
Heart Of Stone—Taylor Dayne (90)	1021
Steve BOWDEN [Joseph Steven Bowden] ▶ 8349 (3)	**54**
I'll Say Forever My Love—Jimmy Ruffin (68)	136
I Am The Man For You Baby—Edwin Starr (68)	13
Got To Have You Back—Isley Brothers (67)	11
Cecil BOWEN ▶ 9567 (1)	**21**
I Love You Baby—Dottie And Ray (65)	21
Harold BOWEN ▶ 11130 (1)	**3.1**
Rosanna—Capreez (66)	6.2
Jeff BOWEN ▶ 3914 (7)	**658**
Shakey Ground—Temptations (75)	*796*
You—Marvin Gaye (68)	545
Happy People—Temptations (74)	375
Finder's Keepers—Chairmen Of The Board (73)	201
I Feel Sanctified—Commodores (74)	83
Shakey Ground—Phoebe Snow (77)	*32*
Up The Creek (Without A Paddle)—Temptations (76)	27
Jimmy BOWEN ▶ 1616 (13)	**2619**
Party Doll—Buddy Knox with The Rhythm Orchids (57)	*4735*
Party Doll—Steve Lawrence (57)	*1892*
Hula Love—Buddy Knox with The Rhythm Orchids (57)	1598
I'm Stickin' With You—Jimmy Bowen With The Rhythm Orchids (57)	*1396*
Rock Your Little Baby To Sleep—Buddy Knox with The Rhythm Orchids (57)	698
Swingin' Daddy—Buddy Knox with The Rhythm Orchids (58)	174
Party Doll—Cat Mother And The All Night News Boys (69)	*164*
Party Doll—Wingy Manone And His Orchestra (57)	*133*

I Trusted You—Jimmy Bowen With The Rhythm Orchids (57)	76
Ever Lovin' Fingers—Jimmy Bowen With The Rhythm Orchids (57)	44
I'm Stickin' With You—Fontane Sisters (57)	*36*
Party Doll—Roy Brown (57)	*7.0*
I'm Stickin' With You—Roy Brown (57)	*0.0*
John G. BOWEN ▶ 10858 (1)	**4.9**
I Know What God Is—Perry Como (60)	15
—Johannes Bowens see: George BAKER	
Bugs BOWER ▶ 4277 (5)	**536**
Caterina—Perry Como (62)	1019
My Boyfriend Got A Beatle Haircut—Donna Lynn (64)	62
Java Jones—Donna Lynn (64)	*5.7*
Dream Talk—Herb & Betty Warner (60)	5.2
(These Are) The Closing Credits—Robert Goulet (63)	2.7
Bob BOWERS ▶ 11646 (1)	**0.9**
Down Where The Winds Blow (Chilly Winds)—Serendipity Singers (64)	2.6
Jane BOWERS ▶ 5781 (1)	**242**
El Matador—Kingston Trio (60)	484
Bill BOWERSOCK ▶ 5382 (2)	**298**
Steal The Night—Stevie Woods (81)	687
Just Can't Win 'Em All—Stevie Woods (82)	274
David BOWIE [David Robert Jones] ▶ 135 (28) HOF	**20183**
Let's Dance—David Bowie (83)	6586
Fame—David Bowie (75)	5730
Ice Ice Baby—Vanilla Ice (90)	3735
Golden Years—David Bowie (75)	2034
Blue Jean—David Bowie (84)	1713
China Girl—David Bowie (83)	1598
Space Oddity—David Bowie (73)	1405
Modern Love—David Bowie (83)	935
Under Pressure—Queen & David Bowie (81)	689
Young Americans—David Bowie (75)	599
Day-In Day-Out—David Bowie (87)	582
All The Young Dudes—Mott The Hoople (72)	566
This Is Not America—David Bowie/Pat Metheny Group (85)	554
Changes—David Bowie (74)	*553*
Never Let Me Down—David Bowie (87)	447
Tonight—David Bowie (84)	269
Starman—David Bowie (72)	244
Rebel Rebel—David Bowie (74)	206
Absolute Beginners—David Bowie (86)	201
Changes—David Bowie (72)	*172*
Cat People (Putting Out Fire)—David Bowie (82)	154
Fashion—David Bowie (80)	124
The Jean Genie—David Bowie (72)	102
Sound And Vision—David Bowie (77)	54
TVC 15—David Bowie (76)	45
Without You—David Bowie (84)	39
Ashes To Ashes—David Bowie (80)	20
1984—David Bowie (74)	2.0
David BOWLER ▶ 5639 (1)	**262**
Sayin' Sorry (Don't Make It Right)—Denise Lopez (88)	523
Rick BOWLES ▶ 9181 (1)	**29**
Too Good To Turn Back Now—Rick Bowles (82)	59
Jim BOWLING ▶ 11105 (1)	**3.2**
Bad, Bad Billy—Snuff (83)	9.5
Roger BOWLING ▶ 1160 (3)	**3833**
Coward Of The County—Kenny Rogers (79)	5361
Lucille—Kenny Rogers (77)	2138
Blanket On The Ground—Billie Jo Spears (75)	84
Don BOWMAN ▶ 2943 (2)	**1107**
Wildwood Weed—Jim Stafford (74)	2073
Just To Satisfy You—Waylon & Willie (82)	141
Euday L. BOWMAN ▶ 7566 (3)	**88**
Twelfth Street Rag—Crazy Otto (55)	*49*
Twelfth Street Rag—Mulcays (56)	*33*
Twelfth Street Rag—Crazy Otto (55)	*6.5*
Priscilla BOWMAN ▶ 6610 (5)	**151**
Keep Your Hands Off Of Him—Damita Jo (61)	*114*
Hands Off—Johnny Maddox Orchestra (55)	*95*
Hands Off—Jay McShann's Orchestra (55)	*95*
Hands Off—Frankie Castro (55)	*0.0*
Hands Off—Nan Wynn (55)	*0.0*
—Doc Box see: Jon GORDON	
Mick BOX ▶ 10507 (1)	**7.8**
Sweet Lorraine—Uriah Heep (73)	23

—James H. Boxley see: Hank SHOCKLEE	
—Keith Boxley see: Keith SHOCKLEE	
Marshall BOXLEY ▶ 9470 (1)	**23**
This Thing Called Love—Webs (67)	46
Donald BOYCE ▶ 4822 (2)	**405**
Jungle Boogie—Kool & The Gang (73)	2506
Spirit Of The Boogie—Kool & The Gang (75)	825
Jesse BOYCE ▶ 9884 (1)	**16**
We Fell In Love While Dancing—Bill Brandon (78)	31
Tommy BOYCE [Sidney Thomas Boyce, Christopher Cloud] ▶ 232 (20)	**14711**
Last Train To Clarksville—Monkees (66)	8046
Valleri—Monkees (68)	5053
Come A Little Bit Closer—Jay & The Americans (64)	4277
I Wonder What She's Doing Tonite—Tommy Boyce & Bobby Hart (67)	2377
Pretty Little Angel Eyes—Curtis Lee (61)	2252
Be My Guest—Fats Domino (59)	1844
Words—Monkees (67)	1659
Action—Freddy Cannon (65)	1365
Alice Long (You're Still My Favorite Girlfriend)—Tommy Boyce & Bobby Hart (68)	1025
(I'm Not Your) Steppin' Stone—Monkees (66)	668
Out And About—Tommy Boyce & Bobby Hart (67)	489
Peaches 'N' Cream—Ikettes (65)	487
Tear Drop City—Monkees (69)	461
Lazy Elsie Molly—Chubby Checker (64)	411
Goodbye Baby (I Don't Want To See You Cry)—Tommy Boyce & Bobby Hart (68)	373
Under The Moon Of Love—Curtis Lee (61)	323
Hello Pretty Girl—Ronnie Dove (65)	302
I'll Remember Carol—Tommy Boyce (62)	59
Sometimes She's A Little Girl—Tommy Boyce & Bobby Hart (67)	44
Sweet Little Kathy—Ray Peterson (61)	24
Alphonso BOYD ▶ 5508 (2)	**276**
Shakey Ground—Temptations (75)	*796*
Shakey Ground—Phoebe Snow (77)	*32*
Tony BOYD ▶ 3047 (2)	**1037**
5-10-15-20 (25-30 Years Of Love)—Presidents (70)	2074
That's How Long—Chi-Lites (75)	0.0
Henry BOYE ▶ 6647 (3)	**148**
Echo—Emotions (1) (62)	278
Humpty Dumpty Heart—LaVern Baker (57)	*101*
Humpty Dumpty Heart—Kay Cee Jones (57)	*0.0*
John BOYLAN ▶ 7004 (1)	**123**
Look, Here Comes The Sun—Sunshine Company (68)	245
Terence BOYLAN ▶ 2149 (2)	**1814**
Shake It—Ian Matthews (78)	1691
Look, Here Comes The Sun—Sunshine Company (68)	245
Doug BOYLE ▶ 8461 (1)	**50**
Hurting Kind (I've Got My Eyes On You)—Robert Plant (90)	248
George BOYTER ▶ 10379 (1)	**9.2**
Shape Of Things To Come—Headboys (79)	37
Clement A. BOZEWSKI [Clem Burke] ▶ 558 (8)	**7729**
Call Me—Blondie (80)	10151
Heart Of Glass—Blondie (79)	5717
Rapture—Blondie (81)	5100
One Way Or Another—Blondie (79)	792
Dreaming—Blondie (79)	716
Island Of Lost Souls—Blondie (82)	344
Atomic—Blondie (80)	298
The Hardest Part—Blondie (80)	69
Dale BOZZIO [Dale Frances Consalvi] ▶ 5785 (3)	**242**
Destination Unknown—Missing Persons (82)	419
Windows—Missing Persons (83)	161
Give—Missing Persons (84)	85
Terry BOZZIO ▶ 4283 (5)	**533**
Destination Unknown—Missing Persons (82)	419
Words—Missing Persons (82)	351
Windows—Missing Persons (83)	161
Walking In L.A.—Missing Persons (83)	115
Give—Missing Persons (84)	85
Alan BRACKETT ▶ 10225 (1)	**11**
It's A Happening Thing—Peanut Butter Conspiracy (67)	11
Jacob BRACKMAN ▶ 1984 (6)	**2034**
That's The Way I've Always Heard It Should Be—Carly Simon (71)	2005

Haven't Got Time For The Pain—Carly Simon (74)	1266
Attitude Dancing—Carly Simon (75)	564
If You Only Believe (Jesus For Tonite)—Michel Polnareff (76)	175
All I Want Is You—Carly Simon (88)	154
You Know What To Do—Carly Simon (83)	25
Bobby BRADDOCK ▶ 6609 (2) HOF	**152**
Ballad Of Two Brothers—Autry Inman (68)	334
D-I-V-O-R-C-E—Tammy Wynette (68)	81
Alex BRADFORD ▶ 8420 (1)	**51**
Tiny Tim—LaVern Baker (59)	102
Barker BRADFORD ▶ 5426 (2)	**290**
Clementine—Bobby Darin (60)	*1036*
Clementine—Jan & Dean (60)	*125*
Janie BRADFORD ▶ 1378 (9)	**3234**
Too Busy Thinking About My Baby—Marvin Gaye (69)	3171
Money (That's what I want)—Barrett Strong (60)	*1212*
Money—Kingsmen (64)	*1174*
Hip City - Pt. 2—Jr. Walker & The All Stars (68)	689
Your Old Stand By—Mary Wells (63)	445
Money (That's What I Want) Part 1—Jr. Walker & The All Stars (66)	*391*
Money—Flying Lizards (79)	*317*
All The Love I've Got—Marv Johnson (60)	192
Tie A String Around Your Finger—Marvelettes (63)	0.5
Sylvester BRADFORD ▶ 1918 (7)	**2112**
Tears On My Pillow—Little Anthony And The Imperials (58)	*3214*
I'm Ready—Fats Domino (59)	1028
Wishful Thinking—Little Anthony And The Imperials (59)	138
Uh Huh Mm—Sonny James (57)	100
Walkin' Home From School—Gene Vincent and His Blue Caps (58)	73
Tears On My Pillow—Johnny Tillotson (69)	*7.6*
Tears On My Pillow—Fred Parris & The Five Satins (82)	*4.8*
Carter BRADLEY ▶ 7877 (1)	**71**
Slide—Slave (77)	640
Harold BRADLEY ▶ 8784 (1)	**39**
Hey, Mr. Sax Man—Boots Randolph (64)	118
Jan BRADLEY ▶ 8054 (1)	**64**
I'm Over You—Jan Bradley (65)	127
Michael BRADLEY ▶ 7642 (1)	**83**
When The Rain Begins To Fall—Jermaine Jackson And Pia Zadora (85)	250
Owen BRADLEY ▶ 11397 (1)	**1.9**
Licorice Stick—Pete Fountain (64)	5.7
Tiny BRADSHAW ▶ 6673 (1)	**145**
Soft—Bill Doggett (57)	145
Hans BRADTKE ▶ 5406 (8)	**293**
Summer Wind—Frank Sinatra (66)	*685*
Lovely Ladies Of Milano—Dick Jacobs And His Chorus And Orchestra (57)	100
Summer Wind—Wayne Newton (65)	*84*
Theme From "A Summer Place"—Lolita (61)	*5.4*
Summer Wind—Roger Williams & The Harry Simeone Chorale (65)	*4.2*
The White Rose Of Athens—Nana Mouskouri (62)	*0.0*
The White Rose Of Athens—Chordettes (62)	0.0
The Man With The Banjo—Ames Brothers (54)	*0.0*
Jim BRADY ▶ 10882 (1)	**4.7**
Free To Carry On—Sandpipers (70)	9.4
Billy BRAGG ▶ 8931 (1)	**36**
Won't Talk About It—Beats International (90)	72
Johnny BRAGG ▶ 1606 (1)	**2636**
Just Walking In The Rain—Johnnie Ray (56)	7908
Al BRAGGS ▶ 2326 (4)	**1589**
Share Your Love With Me—Aretha Franklin (69)	*1587*
Share Your Love With Me—Kenny Rogers (81)	*993*
Share Your Love With Me—Bobby Bland (64)	*534*
To Share Your Love—Fantastic Four (67)	*63*
Johannes BRAHMS ▶ 10226 (1)	**11**
Young In Years—Diamonds (59)	33
Jerome BRAILEY ▶ 4065 (3)	**606**
Tear The Roof Off The Sucker (Give Up The Funk)—Parliament (76)	*1416*
We Want The Funk—Gerardo (91)	*667*
Funk'N' Roll (Dancin' In The Funkshine)—Quazar (78)	2.1

Daryl BRAITHWAITE ▶ 6510 (2)	**161**
Higher Than Hope—Daryl Braithwaite (91)	286
I Have The Skill—Sherbs (81)	55
Dave BRAITHWAITE ▶ 9738 (2)	**18**
Teacher—Falcons (60)	25
You're Mine—Falcons (59)	11
James BRALOWER ▶ 10592 (1)	**7.0**
Basketball—Kurtis Blow (85)	77
Derek BRAMBLE ▶ 5346 (2)	**302**
Spice Of Life—Manhattan Transfer (83)	403
Communication—Power Station (85)	401
Randall BRAMBLETT ▶ 6755 (1)	**140**
That's Your Secret—Sea Level (78)	280
Bonnie BRAMLETT [Bonnie Lynn O'Farrell, Bonnie Sheridan] ▶ 1429 (6)	**3077**
Superstar—Carpenters (71)	*6023*
Never Ending Song Of Love—Delaney & Bonnie & Friends (71)	1817
Let It Rain—Eric Clapton (72)	390
Comin' Home—Delaney & Bonnie And Friends Featuring Eric Clapton (70)	84
Superstar—Luther Vandross (84)	*7.6*
Where There's A Will There's A Way—Delaney & Bonnie (72)	1.1
Delaney BRAMLETT [Delaine Alvin Bramlett] ▶ 1424 (8)	**3089**
Superstar—Carpenters (71)	*6023*
Never Ending Song Of Love—Delaney & Bonnie & Friends (71)	1817
Let It Rain—Eric Clapton (72)	390
Comin' Home—Delaney & Bonnie And Friends Featuring Eric Clapton (70)	84
Who Do You Think You Are—Shindogs (66)	19
Superstar—Luther Vandross (84)	*7.6*
God Knows I Love You—Nancy Sinatra (69)	4.6
Where There's A Will There's A Way—Delaney & Bonnie (72)	1.1
Martin BRAMMER ▶ 6351 (1)	**180**
Motortown—Kane Gang (87)	540
—Pierre Brancourt see: Yves-Jacques LAVOT	
Rose BRANDEL ▶ 11133 (1)	**3.1**
Down The Aisle—Ike Clanton (60)	6.1
Dorothy BRANDES ▶ 9877 (1)	**16**
Yes Sir Ee—Dodie Stevens (59)	47
Johnny BRANDON ▶ 10155 (1)	**12**
Nothing Is Too Good For You—Harvey Boys (57)	12
Alan BRANDT ▶ 7419 (2)	**97**
That's All—Rick Nelson (63)	193
I'll Teach You How To Cry—Kitty Kallen (63)	1.4
Eddie BRANDT ▶ 8558 (4)	**46**
Rock And Roll Wedding—Sunny Gale (56)	*53*
I'm Drowning My Sorrows—Teresa Brewer (57)	40
Rock And Roll Wedding—Ella Mae Morse (56)	*0.0*
Rock And Roll Wedding—Helen Grayco (56)	*0.0*
Steve BRANDT ▶ 4744 (1)	**425**
Sandy—Dion (63)	851
Erik BRANN [Erik Braun, Rick Davis] ▶ 8603 (1)	**45**
Soul Experience—Iron Butterfly (69)	180
Richard BRANNAN [Richard Martin Brannan, Spady Brannan] ▶ 10855 (2)	**4.9**
Easy Way Out—Roy Orbison (79)	7.9
Real Love—Dolly Parton (Duet With Kenny Rogers) (85)	6.7
—Spady Brannan see: Richard BRANNAN	
—Boris Peter Bransby-Williams see: Boris WILLIAMS	
Jon BRANT ▶ 7283 (1)	**105**
Tonight It's You—Cheap Trick (85)	422
Vincent BRANTLEY ▶ 2094 (2)	**1887**
Cool It Now—New Edition (84)	3404
Count Me Out—New Edition (85)	371
Harald BRASCHOSS ▶ 8765 (1)	**40**
Silly Milly—Blue Swede (74)	120
Tom BRASFIELD ▶ 1798 (5)	**2295**
Angel In Your Arms—Hot (77)	2701
(There's) No Gettin' Over Me—Ronnie Milsap (81)	2415
Get It Up—Ronnie Milsap (79)	310
That Didn't Hurt Too Bad—Dr. Hook (81)	59
Baby Fat—Robert Byrne (79)	5.8

Bob BRASS ▶ 1316 (5) **3367**
- This Diamond Ring—Gary Lewis And The Playboys (65) 7757
- A Thing Of The Past—Shirelles (61) 654
- I Must Be Seeing Things—Gene Pitney (65) 593
- Little Lonely One—Tom Jones (65) 381
- You're Gonna Need Magic—Roy Hamilton (61) 131

Wayne BRATHWAITE ▶ 1393 (5) **3190**
- There'll Be Sad Songs (To Make You Cry)—Billy Ocean (86) 4280
- When The Going Gets Tough, The Tough Get Going—Billy Ocean (85) 3161
- Love Zone—Billy Ocean (86) 1312
- Love Is Forever—Billy Ocean (86) 997
- The Colour Of Love—Billy Ocean (88) 815

Vito BRATTA ▶ 2083 (4) **1900**
- When The Children Cry—White Lion (88) 2108
- Wait—White Lion (88) 1236
- Tell Me—White Lion (88) 237
- Little Fighter—White Lion (89) 218

Joanne BRATTON [Joanne Jackson Bratton, Joanne Jackson] ▶ 5782 (3) **242**
- Hungry For Love—San Remo Golden Strings (65) 680
- Poor Man's Son—Reflections (65) 257
- Like Columbus Did—Reflections (64) 30

—Erik Braun see: Erik BRANN

Rick BRAUN ▶ 4885 (1) **388**
- Here With Me—REO Speedwagon (88) 776

Cory BRAVERMAN ▶ 9639 (1) **20**
- Fire Sign—Cory (77) 40

Don BRAY ▶ 11298 (1) **2.4**
- I'm Spinning—Kripp Johnson (57) 4.7

Stephen BRAY ▶ 534 (11) **8028**
- Express Yourself—Madonna (89) 3109
- True Blue—Madonna (86) 2906
- Causing A Commotion—Madonna (87) 2831
- Angel—Madonna (85) 1848
- Cross My Broken Heart—Jets (87) 1505
- Baby Love—Regina (86) 1461
- Right On Track—Breakfast Club (87) 1369
- Keep It Together—Madonna (90) 1095
- That's Why—Party (91) 288
- Say It, Say It—E.G. Daily (86) 120
- Sendin' All My Love—Jets (88) 52

Berthold BRECHT ▶ 785 (4) **5646**
- *Mack The Knife—Bobby Darin (59) 14687*
- The Bilbao Song—Andy Williams (61) 936
- *Mack The Knife—Ella Fitzgerald (60) 743*
- *A Theme From Threepenny Opera (Mack The Knife)—Louis Armstrong And His All-Stars (56) 570*

Michael BRECKER ▶ 8357 (1) **53**
- Sneakin' Up Behind You—Brecker Brothers (75) 265

Randy BRECKER ▶ 8358 (1) **53**
- Sneakin' Up Behind You—Brecker Brothers (75) 265

Eric BREED [Eric T. Breed, MC Breed] ▶ 8144 (1) **60**
- Ain't No Future In Yo' Frontin'—M.C. Breed (91) 180

—Eric T. Breed see: Eric BREED

Jim BREEDLOVE ▶ 7060 (4) **118**
- Like A Child—Julie Rogers (65) 179
- Free Me—Johnny Preston (61) 39
- *Get Up! Get Up! (You Sleepyhead)—Jaye P. Morgan (56) 18*
- *Get Up Get Up (You Sleepy Head)—LaVern Baker with The Gliders (56) 0.0*

Lynn BREEDLOVE ▶ 7222 (2) **109**
- Like A Child—Julie Rogers (65) 179
- Free Me—Johnny Preston (61) 39

Walter BREELAND ▶ 7518 (1) **91**
- Night Life—Rusty Draper (63) 273

—Lionel Breeze see: Lyn MURRAY

Alexandre BREFFORT ▶ 11633 (1) **0.9**
- *Irma La Douce—Karen Chandler (60) 4.6*

Peter BREGANTE [Merel Peter Bregante] ▶ 9504 (1) **22**
- Friends—Feather (70) 112

Buddy BREGMAN ▶ 7221 (3) **109**
- When The Tide Is High—Gogi Grant (56) 137
- You're In Love—Gogi Grant (56) 65
- Soon I'll Wed My Love—John Gary (64) 17

—Paul Emil Breitenfield see: Paul DESMOND

Jacques BREL ▶ 1290 (4) **3448**
- Seasons In The Sun—Terry Jacks (74) 6335
- *If You Go Away—Damita Jo (66) 275*
- *If You Go Away—Terry Jacks (74) 227*
- If We Only Have Love—Dionne Warwicke (72) 88

Beverly BREMERS [Beverly Bremers Lipton] ▶ 11162 (1) **2.9**
- Once A Night—Jackie English (80) 5.9

Stan BRENDERS ▶ 10398 (1) **8.9**
- I Envy—Nat "King" Cole (54) 27

Paul BRENNER ▶ 9097 (1) **31**
- I'm New At The Game Of Romance—Jane Morgan with the Troubadors (57) 62

Vance BRESCIA ▶ 4056 (1) **609**
- That Was Then, This Is Now—Micky Dolenz And Peter Tork (Of The Monkees) (86) 609

Jerry BRESLER ▶ 11322 (1) **2.2**
- Keep Your Cotton Pickin' Paddies Offa My Heart—Teresa Brewer (56) 6.7

Ernest BREUER ▶ 3454 (1) **841**
- Does Your Chewing Gum Lose Its Flavor (On The Bedpost Over Night)—Lonnie Donegan And His Skiffle Group (61) 2524

Don BREWER ▶ 773 (4) **5700**
- We're An American Band—Grand Funk (73) 4703
- Shinin' On—Grand Funk (74) 947
- Walk Like A Man—Grand Funk (73) 906
- Take Me—Grand Funk Railroad (76) 141

Michael BREWER ▶ 2956 (3) **1098**
- One Toke Over The Line—Brewer & Shipley (71) 1791
- Tarkio Road—Brewer And Shipley (71) 404
- Shake Off The Demon—Brewer And Shipley (72) 1.9

—Richard Charles Swinn Brewer see: Rik SWINN

Teresa BREWER [Theresa Veronica Breuer] ▶ 10473 (1) **8.0**
- I Love Mickey—Mickey Mantle And Teresa Brewer (56) 24

David BREWIS ▶ 6352 (1) **180**
- Motortown—Kane Gang (87) 540

Dan BREWSTER ▶ 11213 (1) **2.7**
- Let's Dance (Make Your Body Move)—West Street Mob (81) 30

—Jimmy Brewster see: Milt GABLER

Guglielmo BREZZA ▶ 9777 (2) **17**
- *Il Silenzio—Nini Rosso (65) 29*
- *The Silence (Il Silenzio)—Al Hirt (65) 4.5*

—Brianbert see: Brian HOLLAND

—Brianbert see: Robert BATEMAN

Robin BRIANS ▶ 9063 (1) **32**
- 7:30 Guided Tour—Five Americans (68) 32

Edie BRICKELL ▶ 4892 (2) **387**
- What I Am—Edie Brickell & The New Bohemians (88) 1562
- Circle—Edie Brickell & The New Bohemians (89) 371

Leslie BRICUSSE ▶ 625 (19) HOF **6921**
- The Candy Man—Sammy Davis, Jr. With The Mike Curb Congregation (72) 5982
- *Goldfinger—Shirley Bassey (65) 2651*
- *What Kind Of Fool Am I—Sammy Davis Jr. (62) 1653*
- My Kind Of Girl—Matt Monro (61) 1193
- *Who Can I Turn To (When Nobody Needs Me)—Tony Bennett (64) 814*
- If I Ruled The World—Tony Bennett (65) 478
- You Only Live Twice—Nancy Sinatra (67) 334
- Can You Read My Mind—Maureen McGovern (79) 157
- *Who Can I Turn To—Dionne Warwick (65) 151*
- *What Kind Of Fool Am I—Anthony Newley (62) 57*
- The People Tree—Sammy Davis, Jr. With The Mike Curb Congregation (72) 32
- *What Kind Of Fool Am I—Robert Goulet (62) 31*
- *What Kind Of Fool Am I—Mantovani And His Orchestra (62) 0.0*
- *What Kind Of Fool Am I—Billy Eckstine (62) 0.0*
- *What Kind Of Fool Am I—Burt Farber (62) 0.0*
- *What Kind Of Fool Am I—Vic Damone (62) 0.0*
- *What Kind Of Fool Am I—Cordials (62) 0.0*
- *What Kind Of Fool Am I—Billy Daniels (62) 0.0*
- *What Kind Of Fool Am I—Ronnie Aldrich (62) 0.0*

Ambric BRIDGEFORTH ▶ 11101 (1) **3.2**
- Sweat (Til You Get Wet)—Brick (81) 16

Alicia BRIDGES ▶ 2236 (2) **1713**
- I Love The Nightlife (Disco 'round)—Alicia Bridges (78) 3417
- Body Heat—Alicia Bridges (79) 9.2

—Claude Russell Bridges see: Leon RUSSELL

Fred BRIDGES ▶ 7597 (5) **87**
- Drop By My Place—Little Carl Carlton (70) 140
- Catfish—Four Tops (76) 96
- We All Gotta Stick Together—Four Tops (75) 66
- You Made A Believer (Out Of Me)—Ruby Andrews (69) 22
- Hey Boy Take A Chance On Love—Ruby Andrews (67) 8.4

Gil BRIDGES ▶ 11685 (1) **0.7**
- We're Gonna Have A Good Time—Rare Earth (73) 4.3

Jo BRIDGES ▶ 8043 (1) **64**
- Do The Funky Penguin Part 1—Rufus Thomas (71) 256

Eddie BRIGATI ▶ 158 (14) HOF **18671**
- *Groovin'—Young Rascals (67) 9580*
- *People Got To Be Free—Rascals (68) 9189*
- A Beautiful Morning—Young Rascals (68) 5558
- *How Can I Be Sure—Young Rascals (67) 4109*
- A Girl Like You—Young Rascals (67) 2139
- I've Been Lonely Too Long—Young Rascals (67) 1562
- It's Wonderful—Young Rascals (67) 1044
- A Ray Of Hope—Rascals (68) 981
- *Groovin'—Booker T. & The M.G.'s (67) 957*
- *How Can I Be Sure—David Cassidy (72) 939*
- *You Better Run—Young Rascals (66) 833*
- *You Better Run—Pat Benatar (80) 350*
- On A Sunday Afternoon—A Lighter Shade Of Brown (91) 320
- *People Gotta Be Free—5th Dimension (70) 11*

David John BRIGGS ▶ 1352 (2) **3281**
- Lonesome Loser—Little River Band (79) 2874
- Happy Anniversary—Little River Band (77) 814

David Paul BRIGGS ▶ 9173 (1) **29**
- My Dreams—Brenda Lee (64) 59

Fred BRIGGS ▶ 5358 (2) **300**
- Condition Red—Goodees (68) 482
- Pick Up The Pieces—Carla Thomas (67) 176

Vic BRIGGS ▶ 2913 (5) **1119**
- San Franciscan Nights—Eric Burdon And The Animals (67) 1697
- Sky Pilot (Part One)—Eric Burdon & The Animals (68) 1609
- When I Was Young—Eric Burdon & The Animals (67) 1085
- Monterey—Eric Burdon & The Animals (67) 1017
- Anything—Eric Burdon & The Animals (68) 187

—Julian Ferebree Bright see: Larry BRIGHT

Larry BRIGHT [Julian Ferebree Bright] ▶ 11085 (1) **3.3**
- Mojo Workout (Dance)—Larry Bright (60) 13

Plummer Guillermo BRIGHT ▶ 8231 (1) **58**
- Sitting In Limbo—Don Brown (78) 115

Martin BRILEY ▶ 4500 (1) **476**
- The Salt In My Tears—Martin Briley (83) 476

Dmitry BRILL ▶ 4101 (2) **593**
- Groove Is In The Heart—Deee-Lite (90) 2521
- Power Of Love—Deee-Lite (90) 266

Rob BRILL ▶ 8682 (1) **43**
- Like Flames—Berlin (86) 43

Tim BRINKHURST [Timothy London] ▶ 4849 (1) **399**
- Hippychick—Soho (90) 797

Monty BRINKLEY ▶ 8813 (1) **39**
- Can I Call You My Girl—PC Quest (91) 155

John BRINSON ▶ 10937 (1) **4.2**
- I Can't Get Over You—Dramatics (77) 13

Darnell BRISTOL [Dee Bristol] ▶ 2522 (2) **1420**
- Roni—Bobby Brown (88) 1988
- Two Occasions—Deele (88) 1277

—Iris Bristol see: Iris GORDY

Johnny BRISTOL [John William Bristol] ▶ 317 (31) **11525**
- Someday We'll Be Together—Diana Ross And The Supremes (69) 7492
- What Does It Take (To Win Your Love)—Jr. Walker & The All Stars (69) 3648
- *Twenty-Five Miles—Edwin Starr (69) 2304*
- Hang On In There Baby—Johnny Bristol (74) 2126

Johnny BRISTOL [John William Bristol] ▶ 317 (31) *Continued*	**11525**
My Whole World Ended (The Moment You Left Me)—David Ruffin (69)	1875
I Don't Want To Do Wrong—Gladys Knight & The Pips (71)	1596
If I Could Build My Whole World Around You—Marvin Gaye & Tammi Terrell (67)	1524
Love Me For A Reason—Osmonds (74)	1275
Gotta Hold On To This Feeling—Jr. Walker & The All Stars (70)	1160
Daddy Could Swear, I Declare—Gladys Knight & The Pips (73)	1036
Pucker Up Buttercup—Jr. Walker & The All Stars (67)	629
Do You See My Love (For You Growing)—Jr. Walker & The All Stars (70)	617
That's How Love Goes—Jermaine Jackson (72)	467
We've Come Too Far To End It Now—Smokey Robinson & The Miracles (72)	421
Do It To My Mind—Johnny Bristol (76)	404
Take Me Girl, I'm Ready—Jr. Walker & The All Stars (71)	403
Walk In The Night—Jr. Walker & The All Stars (72)	398
La La Peace Song—Al Wilson (74)	*389*
I Can't Stand To See You Cry—Smokey Robinson & The Miracles (72)	290
What Is A Man—Four Tops (69)	266
I'm Still A Struggling Man—Edwin Starr (69)	243
I've Lost Everything I've Ever Loved—David Ruffin (69)	242
Touch Me Baby (Reaching Out For Your Love)—Tamiko Jones (75)	214
You And I—Johnny Bristol (74)	166
Way Back Home—Jr. Walker & The All Stars (71)	*144*
La La Peace Song—O.C. Smith (74)	*80*
That's The Sound That Lonely Makes—Tavares (74)	79
I Can't Believe You Love Me—Tammi Terrell (66)	70
Come On And See Me—Tammi Terrell (66)	32
These Things Will Keep Me Loving You—Velvelettes (66)	17
Twenty-Five Miles—Mongo Santamaria (69)	*0.9*
—Eustace Britchforth see: Lefty BAKER	
Phil BRITO ▶ 4270 (1)	**539**
Mama—Connie Francis (60)	2155
Terry BRITTEN ▶ 444 (15)	**9273**
What's Love Got To Do With It—Tina Turner (84)	6553
We Don't Need Another Hero (Thunderdome)—Tina Turner (85)	3300
Typical Male—Tina Turner (86)	3200
Devil Woman—Cliff Richard (76)	2996
What You Get Is What You See—Tina Turner (87)	776
Two People—Tina Turner (86)	493
Carrie—Cliff Richard (80)	407
Show Some Respect—Tina Turner (85)	346
She's Trouble—Musical Youth (83)	177
Soul Inspiration—Anita Baker (90)	129
How Can I Live Without Her—Christopher Atkins (82)	93
Never Say Die (Give A Little Bit More)—Cliff Richard (83)	83
No One Can Love You More Than Me—Melissa Manchester (83)	32
Don't Talk—Larry Lee (82)	16
Everybody Move—Cathy Dennis (91)	7.4
Britt BRITTON ▶ 4853 (3)	**398**
Dreaming A Dream—Crown Heights Affair (75)	514
Foxy Lady—Crown Heights Affair (76)	250
Every Beat Of My Heart—Crown Heights Affair (75)	32
—William M. A. Broad see: Billy IDOL	
Morris BROADNAX ▶ 2970 (4)	**1090**
Until You Come Back To Me (That's What I'm Gonna Do)—Aretha Franklin (73)	*3181*
Hey Love—Stevie Wonder (67)	53
Just A Little Misunderstanding—Contours (66)	26
Until You Come Back To Me (That's What I'm Gonna Do) (Medley)—Luther Vandross (84)	*7.6*
Bruce BROADUS [Damian Dane] ▶ 8155 (1)	**60**
Exclusivity—Damian Dame (91)	180
Eleanor BROADWATER ▶ 4183 (5)	**571**
Suzie Q (Part One)—Creedence Clearwater Revival (68)	*1687*
Susie Q—Dale Hawkins (57)	*544*
Do You Believe In Shame?—Duran Duran (89)	93
Susie-Q—Crew-Cuts (57)	*0.0*
Susie-Q—José Feliciano (70)	*0.0*
Bill BROCK ▶ 7830 (2)	**73**
I'll Just Have A Cup Of Coffee (Then I'll Go)—Claude Gray (61)	60
Black Cloud—Chubby Checker (63)	13
Blanche BROCK ▶ 6957 (1)	**126**
Beyond The Sunset—Pat Boone (59)	251
Tony BROCK ▶ 5411 (5)	**292**
What Am I Gonna Do (I'm So In Love With You)—Rod Stewart (83)	446
Silver Dreams—Babys (78)	246
Head First—Babys (79)	44
If You've Got The Time—Babys (77)	18
Too Much Ain't Enough Love—Jimmy Barnes (88)	5.6
Virgil BROCK ▶ 6958 (1)	**126**
Beyond The Sunset—Pat Boone (59)	251
—Mary Christine Brockert see: Teena MARIE	
—James Brockman see: James KENDIS	
Marvin Lee BRODIE ▶ 9915 (1)	**15**
Run, Rudolph, Run—Chuck Berry (58)	30
—Arnold Brodsky see: Brooks ARTHUR	
Diane BRODSKY ▶ 8617 (1)	**45**
My Merry-Go-Round—Johnny Nash (73)	134
—Israel/Roy Brodsky see: Roy C. BENNETT	
Nicholas BRODSZKY ▶ 3033 (17)	**1050**
I'll Never Stop Loving You—Doris Day (55)	*1346*
If You Can Dream—Four Aces (56)	*256*
Gal With The Yaller Shoes—Four Aces (56)	209
The Peddler Man (Ten I Loved)—Dean Martin (54)	123
Only Trust Your Heart—Dick Roman (57)	*48*
Only Trust Your Heart—Joni James (57)	*48*
Serenade—Slim Whitman (56)	*32*
No One But You—Charlie Applewhite (54)	22
Be My Love—Joni James (60)	*17*
Serenade—Ray Heindorf & His Orchestra with The Mellomen (56)	*0.0*
I'll Never Stop Loving You—Les Baxter & His Orchestra (55)	*0.0*
I'll Never Stop Loving You—David Whitfield with The Roland Shaw Orchestra (55)	*0.0*
Be My Love—Joanie Sommers (60)	*0.0*
If You Can Dream—Lena Horne (56)	*0.0*
Only Trust Your Heart—Dean Martin (57)	*0.0*
Only Trust Your Heart—Bob Winn (57)	*0.0*
Serenade—Dick Lee (56)	*0.0*
Bruce BRODY ▶ 8572 (1)	**46**
Stop—Sam Brown (89)	138
Bruce BROMBERG [David Amy] ▶ 6488 (1)	**164**
Smoking Gun—Robert Cray Band (87)	491
John BROMLEY ▶ 11737 (1)	**0.3**
Come On Down (From The Top Of That Hill)—Jackie deShannon (67)	0.9
Edgar BRONFMAN [Junior Miles, Sam Roman] ▶ 8419 (1)	**51**
Whisper In The Dark—Dionne Warwick (86)	102
Steve BRONSKI [Steven William Forrest] ▶ 6511 (1)	**161**
Smalltown Boy—Bronski Beat (84)	484
Stan BRONSTEIN ▶ 5728 (2)	**250**
Mongoose—Elephant's Memory (70)	737
Skyscraper Commando—Elephant's Memory (71)	13
Herman BROOD ▶ 6160 (1)	**199**
Saturdaynight—Herman Brood (79)	397
Gary BROOKER ▶ 2043 (8)	**1963**
A Whiter Shade Of Pale—Procol Harum (67)	*3537*
Conquistador—Procol Harum (72)	1102
Homburg—Procol Harum (67)	393
A Whiter Shade Of Pale—R.B. Greaves (70)	*62*
A Whiter Shade Of Pale—Hesitations (68)	*29*
A Whiter Shade Of Pale—Procol Harum (72)	*14*
Whiter Shade Of Pale—Hagar, Schon, Aaronson, Shrieve (84)	*5.6*
A Whiter Shade Of Pale—Shorty Long (69)	*0.4*
Jon BROOKES ▶ 10624 (1)	**6.7**
The Only One I Know—Charlatans UK (90)	33
Julian BROOKHOUSE ▶ 7963 (1)	**67**
Misfit—Curiosity Killed The Cat (87)	336
Robert BROOKINS ▶ 6677 (2)	**145**
She's On The Left—Jeffrey Osborne (88)	284
Innocent—Whispers (90)	221
—Craig Brooks see: Craig SPROVACH	
Arthur BROOKS ▶ 3135 (6)	**991**
For Your Precious Love—Jerry Butler & The Impressions (58)	*1045*
For Your Precious Love—Oscar Toney, Jr. (67)	*778*
For Your Precious Love—Garnet Mimms & The Enchanters (63)	*662*
For Your Precious Love—Jackie Wilson And Count Basie (68)	*411*
Your Precious Love—Linda Jones (72)	*74*
For Your Precious Love—Jerry Butler (66)	*1.4*
—Charles Brooks see: Chuck BROOKS	
—Charles Lee Brooks see: Chuck BROOKS	
Chuck BROOKS [Charles Lee Brooks, Charles Brooks] ▶ 8526 (2)	**47**
You Says It All—Randy Brown (79)	77
Taxi—J. Blackfoot (84)	17
Dianne BROOKS [Gwendolyn Dianne Brooks] ▶ 10071 (2)	**13**
Memories Of A Broken Promise—Motherlode (69)	11
Sugah Wooga—Three Playmates (58)	3.9
—Elmore Brooks see: Elmore JAMES	
—Fred Brooks see: Fred HELLERMAN	
Harry BROOKS ▶ 11476 (1)	**1.5**
Ain't Misbehavin'—Johnnie Ray (56)	4.6
Harvey BROOKS [Harvey Goldstein Brooks, Harvey Goldstein] ▶ 8113 (1)	**61**
What A Wonderful Thing We Have—Fabulous Rhinestones (72)	122
Jack BROOKS ▶ 2810 (7)	**1183**
Ole Buttermilk Sky—Bill Black's Combo (61)	701
Innamorata (Sweetheart)—Dean Martin (56)	*695*
Innamorata (Sweetheart)—Jerry Vale (56)	*652*
The Rose Tattoo—Perry Como (55)	*286*
I Belong To You—Ralph Flanagan and his Orchestra (55)	33
Innamorata—Frank Verna (56)	*0.0*
The Rose Tattoo—Percy Faith & His Orchestra (55)	*0.0*
Joe BROOKS ▶ 277 (5)	**12564**
You Light Up My Life—Debby Boone (77)	*11933*
If Ever I See You Again—Roberta Flack (78)	447
California—Debby Boone (78)	148
Come Share The Good Times With Me—Julie Monday (66)	26
You Light Up My Life—Original Cast (Kacey Cisyk) (77)	*23*
Joe (2) BROOKS ▶ 9483 (1)	**23**
It's Time To Say Goodbye—Third Rail (68)	46
Joey BROOKS ▶ 4490 (2)	**481**
Seein' The Right Love Go Wrong—Jack Jones (65)	553
My Ship Is Comin' In—Walker Bros. (66)	204
John Benson BROOKS ▶ 4994 (2)	**362**
Ninety Nine Years (Dead Or Alive)—Guy Mitchell (56)	635
There Should Be Rules (Protecting Fools Who Fall In Love)—Betty Madigan (55)	132
Mel BROOKS [Melvin Kaminsky] ▶ 11248 (1)	**2.6**
Tower Trot (And Then You Do That Step)—Dick Jacobs And His Chorus And Orchestra (57)	23
Phillips BROOKS ▶ 11588 (1)	**1.1**
Oh Little Town Of Bethlehem—Elvis Presley (57)	2.1
Richard BROOKS ▶ 3136 (6)	**991**
For Your Precious Love—Jerry Butler & The Impressions (58)	*1045*
For Your Precious Love—Oscar Toney, Jr. (67)	*778*
For Your Precious Love—Garnet Mimms & The Enchanters (63)	*662*
For Your Precious Love—Jackie Wilson And Count Basie (68)	*411*
Your Precious Love—Linda Jones (72)	*74*
For Your Precious Love—Jerry Butler (66)	*1.4*
Ron BROOKS ▶ 7687 (1)	**80**
Kiss You Back—Digital Underground (91)	322
Warren BROOKS ▶ 732 (3)	**6000**
Because I Love You (The Postman Song)—Stevie B (90)	5126
Love And Emotion—Stevie B (90)	869
Forever More—Stevie B (91)	4.1

Wayne BROOKS ▶ 10144 (1)	**12**
Bullwhip Rock—Cyclones (58)	12
Bernard BROOMER ▶ 6430 (2)	**170**
Oh, How It Hurts—Barbara Mason (67)	335
International Playboy—Wilson Pickett (73)	10
Ronnie E. BROOMFIELD [Ronald Broomfield, Eugene Wilde] ▶ 8137 (2)	**60**
Don't Say No Tonight—Eugene Wilde (85)	84
Gotta Get You Home Tonight—Eugene Wilde (85)	37
—Raymond Brost see: Ray HENDERSON	
Ian BROUDIE ▶ 4343 (1)	**516**
Pure—Lightning Seeds (90)	516
—Steve Broughton see: Stephen LUNT	
Joe BROUSSARD ▶ 1931 (3)	**2093**
Mr. Big Stuff—Jean Knight (71)	5978
You Think You're Hot Stuff—Jean Knight (71)	154
Got To Have Your Lovin'—King Floyd (71)	98
Stony BROWDER ▶ 5791 (2)	**241**
Cherchez La Femme/Se Si Bon—Dr. Buzzard's Original "Savannah" Band (76)	448
I'll Play The Fool—Dr. Buzzard's Original "Savannah" Band (76)	35
—Thomas August Darnell Browder see: August DARNELL	
—William Neal Browder see: T.G. SHEPPARD	
Al BROWN ▶ 2806 (1)	**1185**
Madison—Al Brown's Tunetoppers Featuring Cookie Brown (60)	1185
Albert Joseph BROWN [Al B. Sure!] ▶ 2662 (5)	**1287**
Nite And Day—Al B. Sure! (88)	1529
Forever My Lady—Jodeci (91)	519
Missunderstanding—Al B. Sure! (90)	313
Off On Your Own (Girl)—Al B. Sure! (88)	288
Just Ask Me To—Tevin Campbell (91)	29
Alex BROWN [Alexandra Louise Brown] ▶ 5269 (2)	**315**
Just Because—Anita Baker (89)	913
Gotta Be Funky—Monk Higgins & The Specialties (72)	20
—Alexandra Louise Brown see: Alex BROWN	
Alfred BROWN ▶ 6082 (1)	**208**
In A Moment—Intrigues (69)	832
Annette E. BROWN ▶ 9161 (1)	**30**
Somebody Else's Guy—Jocelyn Brown (84)	60
Arthur Wilton BROWN ▶ 2371 (2)	**1554**
Fire—Crazy World Of Arthur Brown (68)	6038
Nightmare—Crazy World Of Arthur Brown (68)	45
Billie Jean BROWN ▶ 3752 (2)	**710**
Here Comes The Judge—Shorty Long (68)	1872
I Promise To Wait My Love—Martha Reeves & The Vandellas (68)	345
Bobby BROWN [Robert Barrisford Brown] ▶ 1322 (2)	**3357**
My Prerogative—Bobby Brown (88)	4142
She Ain't Worth It—Glenn Medeiros featuring Bobby Brown (90)	3857
Boots BROWN [Milton Rajonsky, Milton Shorty Rogers] ▶ 4595 (2)	**458**
Cerveza—Boots Brown & His Blockbusters (58)	*269*
Cerveza—Bert Kaempfert And His Orchestra (61)	*188*
Buster BROWN ▶ 5813 (2)	**239**
Fannie Mae—Buster Brown (60)	*717*
Fannie Mae—Mighty Sam (66)	*1.9*
Buster (2) BROWN [Tim Eaton] ▶ 11061 (1)	**3.5**
Falling Out Of Love—Buster Brown (74)	3.5
Charles L. BROWN ▶ 4155 (1)	**579**
Bustin' Loose (Part 1)—Chuck Brown & The Soul Searchers (79)	579
Charles Mose BROWN ▶ 5760 (4)	**245**
Please Come Home For Christmas—Eagles (78)	*458*
Please Come Home For Christmas—Charles Brown (61)	*20*
Driftin' Blues—Bobby Bland (68)	6.9
Please Come Home For Christmas—Charles Brown (60)	*6.3*
Dan BROWN ▶ 4784 (6)	**417**
Are We Ourselves?—Fixx (84)	811
Secret Separation—Fixx (86)	629
How Much Is Enough—Fixx (91)	414
Driven Out—Fixx (89)	236
Sunshine In The Shade—Fixx (84)	96
No One Has To Cry—Fixx (91)	20
Danny Joe BROWN ▶ 6926 (1)	**128**
Flirtin' With Disaster—Molly Hatchet (79)	383
David BROWN ▶ 10412 (1)	**8.7**
Let It Shine—Santana (76)	17
Deanna BROWN [Deanna Crisp Brown, Deanna Crisp Brown Thomas] ▶ 7358 (2)	**100**
Get Up Offa That Thing—James Brown (76)	279
Bodyheat (Part 1)—James Brown (77)	22
Deidra BROWN [Deidre Yvonne Jenkins] ▶ 7359 (2)	**100**
Get Up Offa That Thing—James Brown (76)	279
Bodyheat (Part 1)—James Brown (77)	22
Devora BROWN ▶ 4303 (2)	**529**
Village Of Love—Nathaniel Mayer And The Fabulous Twilights (62)	1041
Mind Over Matter (I'm Gonna Make You Mine)—Nolan Strong (62)	8.2
Douglas Fontaine BROWN [Doug Brown, Fontaine Brown] ▶ 8725 (3)	**41**
I Got What You Need—Kim Weston (67)	64
Ready To Ride—Southwind (69)	8.6
Been So Nice—Righteous Brothers (67)	0.9
Douglas L. BROWN ▶ 6110 (1)	**205**
Give Me One More Chance—Wilmer Alexander Jr. And The Dukes (68)	205
—Ed Brown see: Edward C. BLACK	
Eddie BROWN ▶ 10055 (1)	**13**
You Were Made For Me—Irene Cara (84)	27
Edwin BROWN ▶ 7632 (2)	**84**
Wind In The Willow—Jo Stafford (57)	*335*
Wind In The Willow—Ann Reynolds (57)	*0.0*
Errol BROWN [Lester Errol Brown] ▶ 439 (10)	**9343**
Brother Louie—Stories (73)	5338
You Sexy Thing—Hot Chocolate (75)	4632
Emma—Hot Chocolate (75)	2191
Every 1's A Winner—Hot Chocolate (78)	2122
You Could Have Been A Lady—April Wine (72)	695
Disco Queen—Hot Chocolate (75)	659
Don't Stop It Now—Hot Chocolate (76)	259
Going Through The Motions—Hot Chocolate (79)	112
Are You Getting Enough Happiness—Hot Chocolate (82)	84
Think About Your Children—Mary Hopkin (70)	24
Floyd BROWN [Earthquake] ▶ 4281 (1)	**534**
Ice Ice Baby—Vanilla Ice (90)	3735
—Fontaine Brown see: Douglas Fontaine BROWN	
—Frankie Brown see: Ted DAFFAN	
Gayle Candis BROWN ▶ 6178 (1)	**197**
It's Too Late, Baby Too Late—Arthur Prysock (65)	394
George BROWN [George Garoufis] ▶ 10140 (4)	**12**
Hey, Stella! (Who Zat Down Your Cellar?)—Crew-Cuts (58)	29
Italian Jingle Bells—Lou Monte (55)	8.7
Mala Femmena—Connie Francis (63)	*5.7*
When I Hold You In My Arms—Lou Monte with Hugo Winterhalter And His Orchestra (54)	0.0
—George Brown see: Billy HILL	
George M. BROWN ▶ 591 (35) HOF	**7345**
Celebration—Kool & The Gang (80)	6016
Cherish—Kool & The Gang (85)	3699
Joanna—Kool & The Gang (83)	3511
Ladies Night—Kool & The Gang (79)	3414
Too Hot—Kool & The Gang (80)	2617
Jungle Boogie—Kool & The Gang (73)	2506
Hollywood Swinging—Kool & The Gang (74)	2079
Summertime—DJ Jazzy Jeff & The Fresh Prince (91)	1783
Misled—Kool & The Gang (84)	1436
Get Down On It—Kool & The Gang (82)	1373
Fresh—Kool & The Gang (85)	1367
Victory—Kool & The Gang (86)	1269
Tonight—Kool & The Gang (84)	1136
Take My Heart (You Can Have It If You Want It)—Kool & The Gang (81)	1077
Stone Love—Kool & The Gang (87)	994
Emergency—Kool & The Gang (85)	915
Spirit Of The Boogie—Kool & The Gang (75)	825
Let's Go Dancin' (Ooh La, La, La)—Kool & The Gang (82)	654
Big Fun—Kool & The Gang (82)	532
Funky Stuff—Kool & The Gang (73)	473
Higher Plane—Kool & The Gang (74)	446
Kool And The Gang—Kool & The Gang (69)	329
Jones Vs. Jones—Kool & The Gang (81)	316
Caribbean Festival—Kool & The Gang (75)	268
Open Sesame - Part I—Kool & The Gang (76)	252
Rhyme Tyme People—Kool & The Gang (75)	182
Holiday—Kool & The Gang (87)	126
Special Way—Kool & The Gang (87)	122
Let The Music Take Your Mind—Kool & The Gang (70)	85
Love And Understanding (Come Together)—Kool & The Gang (76)	48
Funky Man—Kool & The Gang (70)	41
The Gangs Back Again—Kool & The Gang (69)	37
Steppin' Out—Kool & The Gang (82)	6.6
Who's Gonna Take The Weight (Part One)—Kool & The Gang (71)	4.1
Summer Madness—Kool & The Gang (75)	0.0
George R. BROWN ▶ 5896 (1)	**232**
If You Don't Want My Love—Jaye P. Morgan (55)	463
Greg BROWN ▶ 7591 (1)	**87**
Baby Talk—Alisha (85)	174
Harold BROWN ▶ 1236 (21)	**3621**
Spill The Wine—Eric Burdon And War (70)	*5207*
The Cisco Kid—War (73)	4378
Why Can't We Be Friends?—War (75)	3006
Low Rider—War (75)	2369
Slippin' Into Darkness—War (71)	*2076*
The World Is A Ghetto—War (72)	1817
Gypsy Man—War (73)	1659
Summer—War (76)	1559
Me And Baby Brother—War (73)	1513
All Day Music—War (71)	704
Ballero—War (74)	472
They Can't Take Away Our Music—Eric Burdon And War Featuring Sharon Scott And The Beautiful New Born Children Of Southern California (70)	418
Spill The Wine—Isley Brothers (71)	*409*
Galaxy—War (77)	325
L.A. Sunshine—War (77)	291
Low Rider (On The Boulevard)—Latin Alliance (91)	121
Lonely Feelin'—War (71)	74
You Got The Power—War (82)	35
Slipping Into Darkness—Ramsey Lewis (72)	*35*
Good, Good Feelin'—War (79)	12
Outlaw—War (82)	10
Huford Benjamin BROWN ▶ 6317 (1)	**182**
Pass The Dutchie—Musical Youth (82)	1276
James BROWN [James Joseph Brown Jr., Jim Jam, Dessie Rozier] ▶ 52 (99) HOF	**40809**
I Got You (I Feel Good)—James Brown And The Famous Flames (65)	6412
It's A Man's Man's Man's World—James Brown And The Famous Flames (66)	2793
Cold Sweat - Part 1—James Brown And The Famous Flames (67)	2719
I Got The Feelin'—James Brown And The Famous Flames (68)	2648
Mother Popcorn (You Got To Have A Mother For Me) Part 1—James Brown (69)	2396
Papa's Got A Brand New Bag Part I—James Brown And The Famous Flames (65)	*2301*
Get On The Good Foot - Part 1—James Brown (72)	1605
Say It Loud - I'm Black And I'm Proud (Part 1)—James Brown (68)	1559
Hot Pastrami—Dartells (63)	1481
Super Bad (Part 1 & Part 2)—James Brown (70)	1478
Get Up! (Before The Night Is Over)—Technotronic (90)	1473
Hot Pants Pt. 1 (She Got To Use What She Got To Get What She Wants)—James Brown (71)	1325
Licking Stick-Licking Stick (Part 1)—James Brown And The Famous Flames (68)	1305
Get Up I Feel Like Being Like A Sex Machine (Part 1)—James Brown (70)	*913*
Make It Funky (Part 1)—James Brown (71)	869
Papa's Got A Brand New Bag—Otis Redding (68)	*821*
The Payback - Part I—James Brown (74)	817
I Don't Want Nobody To Give Me Nothing (Open Up The Door, I'll Get It Myself) (Part 1)—James Brown (69)	778

James BROWN [James Joseph Brown Jr., Jim Jam, Dessie Rozier] ▶ 52 (99) HOF *Continued*	**40809**
I Can't Stand Myself (When You Touch Me)—James Brown And The Famous Flames (67)	759
Oh Baby Don't You Weep (Part 1)—James Brown And The Famous Flames (64)	714
Ain't It Funky Now (Part 1)—James Brown (69)	694
Doing It To Death—Fred Wesley & The J.B.'s (73)	658
Soul Power Pt. 1—James Brown (71)	641
My Thang—James Brown (74)	613
It's A New Day (Part 1) & (Part 2)—James Brown (70)	587
Get It Together (Part 1)—James Brown And The Famous Flames (67)	584
I'm A Greedy Man - Part 1—James Brown (71)	557
There Was A Time—James Brown And The Famous Flames (68)	*557*
Bring It Up—James Brown And The Famous Flames (67)	556
Goodbye My Love—James Brown (68)	544
Brother Rapp (Part 1) & (Part 2)—James Brown (70)	533
King Heroin—James Brown (72)	531
Get Up, Get Into It, Get Involved Pt. 1—James Brown (70)	511
World (Part 1)—James Brown (69)	498
Ain't That A Groove Part 1—James Brown And The Famous Flames (66)	496
The Popcorn—James Brown (69)	494
Money Won't Change You Part 1—James Brown And The Famous Flames (66)	493
Let A Man Come In And Do The Popcorn Part One—James Brown (69)	488
Hot Pastrami With Mashed Potatoes - Part 1—Joey Dee & The Starliters (63)	476
Papa Don't Take No Mess - Part I—James Brown (74)	475
Let Yourself Go—James Brown And The Famous Flames (67)	473
Talking Loud And Saying Nothing - Pt. I—James Brown (72)	446
Don't Be A Drop-Out—James Brown And The Famous Flames (66)	443
I Got Ants In My Pants - Part 1 And I Want To Dance—James Brown (73)	441
Lost Someone—James Brown And The Famous Flames (61)	*417*
I Got A Bag Of My Own—James Brown (72)	398
I Guess I'll Have To Cry, Cry, Cry—James Brown And The Famous Flames (68)	395
There It Is - Part 1—James Brown (72)	389
Escape-Ism (Part 1)—James Brown (71)	378
Think (About It)—Lyn Collins (72)	362
Lowdown Popcorn—James Brown (69)	360
It Takes Two—Rob Base & D.J. E-Z Rock (88)	353
Stone To The Bone - Part 1—James Brown (73)	349
Sexy, Sexy, Sexy—James Brown (73)	336
I Cried—James Brown (71)	*335*
Part Two (Let A Man Come In And Do The Popcorn)—James Brown (69)	322
What My Baby Needs Now Is A Little More Lovin'—James Brown & Lyn Collins (72)	289
Try Me—James Brown At The Organ (65)	*270*
Funky Drummer (Part 1)—James Brown (70)	266
Try Me—James Brown And The Famous Flames (58)	*258*
Gimme Some More—J.B.'s (72)	231
America Is My Home - Pt. 1—James Brown And The Famous Flames (68)	228
You Can't Play With My Yo-Yo—Yo-Yo (91)	209
Tit For Tat (Ain't No Taking Back)—James Brown (68)	189
If Somebody Told You—Anna King (63)	183
(Do The) Mashed Potatoes (Part 1)—Nat Kendrick And The Swans (60)	*170*
I Don't Mind—James Brown And The Famous Flames (61)	149
Try Me—Jimmy Hughes (64)	*134*
There Was A Time—Gene Chandler (68)	*133*
Good, Good Lovin'—Chubby Checker (61)	130
Shout And Shimmy—James Brown And The Famous Flames (62)	119
It's My Thing (You Can't Tell Me Who To Sock It To)—Marva Whitney (69)	112
Funky President (People It's Bad)—James Brown (74)	102

Hot Pants - I'm Coming, Coming, I'm Coming—Bobby Byrd (71)	97
Coldblooded—James Brown (74)	88
My Part—James Brown (71)	76
Make It Funky (Part 3)—James Brown (71)	76
Baby, You're Right—James Brown And The Famous Flames (61)	69
Reality—James Brown (75)	56
Get Up I Feel Like Being A Sex Machine—James Brown (75)	*53*
Pass The Peas—J.B.'s (72)	48
Parrty (Part 1)—Maceo And The Macks (73)	45
This Old Heart—James Brown And The Famous Flames (60)	40
Keep On Doin' What You're Doin'—Bobby Byrd (72)	39
You've Got The Power—James Brown And The Famous Flames (60)	31
I'll Go Crazy—James Brown And The Famous Flames (66)	22
There Was A Time—Dapps Featuring Alfred Ellis (68)	*20*
You've Got To Change Your Mind—Bobby Byrd & James Brown (68)	18
Me And My Baby Got A Good Thing Going—Lyn Collins (72)	17
Mashed Potatoes U.S.A.—James Brown And The Famous Flames (62)	14
Mashed Potatoes (Part 1)—Steve Alaimo (62)	*9.3*
Soul Pride (Part 1)—James Brown (69)	7.3
Lost Someone—James Brown And The Famous Flames (66)	*6.2*
Hustle!!! (Dead On It)—James Brown (75)	4.8
Please, Please, Please—James Brown And The Famous Flames (64)	4.6
Sweet Little Baby Boy—James Brown And The Famous Flames (66)	4.6
The Soul Of J. B.—James Brown And The Famous Flames (67)	3.3
I Cried—Tammy Montgomery (63)	*0.9*
New Breed (Part 1) (The Boo-Ga-Loo)—James Brown (66)	0.5
James B. BROWN [Jimmy Brown] ▶ 5590 (2)	**267**
Dusic—Brick (77)	793
Sweat (Til You Get Wet)—Brick (81)	16
—James Hooker Brown Jr. see: James HOOKER	
—James Joseph Brown Jr. see: James BROWN	
Jeffrey Aaron BROWN ▶ 8430 (1)	**51**
Tribute (Right On)—Pasadenas (89)	304
—Jimmy Brown see: James B. BROWN	
Jocelyn BROWN ▶ 9162 (1)	**30**
Somebody Else's Guy—Jocelyn Brown (84)	60
L. Russell BROWN [Lawrence Russell Brown] ▶ 160 (32)	**18548**
Knock Three Times—Dawn (70)	9840
Tie A Yellow Ribbon Round The Ole Oak Tree—Dawn Featuring Tony Orlando (73)	*8042*
Say, Has Anybody Seen My Sweet Gypsy Rose—Dawn Featuring Tony Orlando (73)	3651
Sock It To Me-Baby!—Mitch Ryder And The Detroit Wheels (67)	3156
C'mon Marianne—4 Seasons Featuring The "Sound" Of Frankie Valli (67)	*1901*
I Woke Up In Love This Morning—Partridge Family Starring Shirley Jones & Featuring David Cassidy (71)	1847
Steppin' Out (Gonna Boogie Tonight)—Tony Orlando And Dawn (74)	1391
Who's In The Strawberry Patch With Sally—Tony Orlando And Dawn (73)	839
Watch The Flowers Grow—4 Seasons Featuring The "Sound" Of Frankie Valli (67)	765
Summer Sand—Dawn (71)	744
I Play And Sing—Dawn (71)	724
We're Free—Beverly Bremers (72)	654
The Girl I'll Never Know (Angels Never Fly This Low)—Frankie Valli (69)	525
I Hear Those Church Bells Ringing—Dusk (71)	494
C'mon Marianne—Donny Osmond (76)	*435*
Am I Losing You—Partridge Family Starring Shirley Jones & Featuring David Cassidy (72)	417
Joy—Mitch Ryder (67)	378
Angel Baby—Dusk (71)	311
Nothing Succeeds Like Success—Bill Deal & The Rhondels (70)	277

Summer And Sandy—Lesley Gore (67)	257
Number Wonderful—Rock Flowers (71)	143
It Only Hurts When I Try To Smile—Dawn Featuring Tony Orlando (74)	135
Bon Bon Vie (Gimme The Good Life)—T.S. Monk (81)	113
Use It Up And Wear It Out—Pat & Mick (90)	87
Open Up Your Door—Richard and The Young Lions (66)	71
Treat Me Like A Good Piece Of Candy—Dusk (71)	65
Fancy Dancer—Frankie Valli (79)	25
She Ain't Lovin' You—Distant Cousins (66)	20
Pow Wow—Cory Daye (79)	19
Is There Anyone Home?—Jimmy Druiett (72)	5.2
Singles Game—Jay And The Techniques (68)	4.6
Should I Tie A Yellow Ribbon Round The Ole Oak Tree? The Answer—Connie Francis (73)	*0.7*
Larry BROWN [Edwin Charles] ▶ 6388 (1)	**176**
Tear Drops—Lee Andrews And The Hearts (57)	703
Lawrence BROWN ▶ 5816 (3)	**239**
One Love In My Lifetime—Diana Ross (76)	628
In And Out Of My Life—Martha Reeves & The Vandellas (72)	52
Maria (You Were The Only One)—Jimmy Ruffin (71)	14
Lawrence Anthony BROWN ▶ 9542 (1)	**22**
You Can Call Me Blue—Michael Johnson (80)	43
—Lawrence Russell Brown see: L. Russell BROWN	
Lester L. BROWN ▶ 5245 (1)	**319**
Abilene—George Hamilton IV (63)	1276
—Lester Errol Brown see: Errol BROWN	
Lew BROWN [Louis Brownstein] ▶ 2549 (11) HOF	**1392**
Together—Connie Francis (61)	2968
I Wanna Go Where You Go, Do What You Do (Then I'll Be Happy)—Eddie Fisher (55)	382
Beer Barrel Polka—Bobby Vinton (75)	329
Life Is Just A Bowl Of Cherries—Jaye P. Morgan (55)	175
That Old Feeling—Kitty Kallen (60)	67
The Birth Of The Blues—Sammy Davis Jr. (55)	*58*
Take Everything But You—Kitty Kallen (54)	23
Best Things In Life Are Free—Richard Cannon (58)	20
It All Depends On You—Jerry Lewis (57)	19
So Blue—Vibrations (60)	19
The Birth Of The Blues—Lenny Dee (55)	*0.0*
Mark Alton BROWN [Mark Brown, Brownmark] ▶ 8894 (1)	**37**
America—Prince & The Revolution (85)	220
Marshall BROWN ▶ 6602 (3)	**153**
Banjo's Back In Town—Teresa Brewer (55)	*359*
Shoot It Again—Teresa Brewer (55)	66
Banjo's Back In Town—Swing & Sway With Sammy Kaye (55)	*0.0*
Maxine M. BROWN ▶ 3187 (3)	**959**
All In My Mind—Maxine Brown (60)	*1336*
Funny—Maxine Brown (61)	1027
All In My Mind—Dakota Staton (61)	*0.0*
Michael Martin BROWN ▶ 4512 (2)	**474**
Lizzie Borden—Chad Mitchell Trio (62)	407
The John Birch Society—Chad Mitchell Trio (62)	67
—Michael D./Mike Brown see: Michael David LOOKOFSKY	
Mick BROWN ▶ 5900 (4)	**231**
In My Dreams—Party (91)	610
Alone Again—Dokken (85)	164
Burning Like A Flame—Dokken (87)	82
In My Dreams—Dokken (86)	68
Milton S. BROWN Jr. ▶ 3723 (2)	**719**
Everybody's Everything—Santana (71)	1516
Karate—Emperor's (66)	428
Milton L. BROWN ▶ 5924 (2)	**227**
Every Which Way But Loose—Eddie Rabbitt (79)	485
Hoppy, Gene And Me—Roy Rogers (74)	197
Nacio Herb BROWN ▶ 2604 (6) HOF	**1331**
Temptation—Everly Brothers (61)	*771*
Paradise—Sammy Turner (60)	466
Should I—String-A-Longs (61)	391
Temptation—Roger Williams (60)	*286*
Temptation—Boots Randolph (67)	*29*
You Were Meant For Me—Johnston Brothers (55)	13
Nancy BROWN ▶ 11580 (1)	**1.1**
Golden Gate Park—Rejoice! (68)	2.2

Nappy BROWN [Napoleon Brown, Napoleon Brown Goodson Culp] ▶ 4980 (4)	**366**
Don't Be Angry—Nappy Brown (55)	*1091*
Night Time Is The Right Time—Rufus & Carla (64)	*3.3*
Night Time Is The Right Time—Ray Charles (59)	*2.4*
Don't Be Angry—Crew-Cuts (55)	*0.0*
Norman BROWN ▶ 9875 (1)	**16**
Pitter-Patter—Four Sportsmen (61)	31
Odell BROWN ▶ 2628 (1)	**1308**
Sexual Healing—Marvin Gaye (82)	3925
Ollie BROWN ▶ 3761 (1)	**707**
Breakin'.. There's No Stoppin' Us—Ollie And Jerry (84)	1414
Oscar BROWN Jr. ▶ 2822 (4)	**1169**
The Snake—Al Wilson (68)	769
A Young Girl—Noel Harrison (65)	535
Don't Cry My Love—Impressions (68)	174
The Lone Ranger—Oscar Brown Jr. (74)	135
Paula BROWN ▶ 3394 (1)	**868**
Mad About You—Belinda Carlisle (86)	2603
Peter H. BROWN ▶ 1315 (7)	**3370**
Material Girl—Madonna (85)	3543
Dance With Me—Peter Brown Special Background Vocals: Betty Wright (78)	2150
Do Ya Wanna Get Funky With Me—Peter Brown (77)	660
You Should Do It—Peter Brown (78)	214
Stargazer—Peter Brown (79)	58
Crank It Up (Funk Town) Pt. 1—Peter Brown (79)	39
Fantasy Love Affair—Peter Brown (79)	9.5
Peter Ronald BROWN ▶ 1526 (3)	**2802**
Sunshine Of Your Love—Cream (68)	3604
White Room—Cream (68)	3165
I Feel Free—Belinda Carlisle (88)	37
Phil BROWN ▶ 9461 (1)	**23**
It's Not You, It's Not Me—KBC Band (86)	47
Piney BROWN [Columbus Perry] ▶ 11725 (1)	**0.4**
Just A Little Bit—Little Milton (69)	3.1
Ray BROWN ▶ 6439 (1)	**169**
Gravy Waltz—Steve Allen (63)	169
Reggie BROWN ▶ 10776 (1)	**5.3**
You're My Driving Wheel—Supremes (76)	21
Richard Ian BROWN ▶ 8738 (3)	**41**
I Melt With You—Modern English (90)	*107*
I Melt With You—Modern English (83)	*88*
Hands Across The Sea—Modern English (84)	8.5
—Robert Barrisford Brown see: Bobby BROWN	
Roy BROWN ▶ 3910 (2)	**660**
Rockin' At Midnight—Honeydrippers (85)	*453*
Good Rockin' Tonight—Pat Boone (59)	*208*
Ruth BROWN [Ruth Alston Weston] ▶ 10106 (1)	**13**
When I Get You Baby—Ruth Brown (57)	25
Samantha BROWN ▶ 8573 (1)	**46**
Stop—Sam Brown (89)	138
Samuel F. BROWN III ▶ 7534 (1)	**90**
One Day In Your Life—Michael Jackson (81)	181
Sheree BROWN [Shereelynn Sarah Brown] ▶ 7717 (2)	**79**
Haven't You Heard—Patrice Rushen (80)	293
Look Up—Patrice Rushen (80)	18
—Shereelynn Sarah Brown see: Sheree BROWN	
Stanley BROWN ▶ 10033 (1)	**14**
I'm Dreamin'—Christopher Williams (91)	14
Steven James BROWN ▶ 6038 (3)	**213**
Give It To Me Good—Trixter (90)	150
Surrender—Trixter (91)	104
One In A Million—Trixter (91)	84
Teddy BROWN ▶ 6364 (1)	**178**
I Need Help (I Can't Do It Alone) (Part 1)—Bobby Byrd (70)	178
Thomas Harold BROWN ▶ 10650 (2)	**6.4**
November Snow—Rejoice! (69)	5.3
Golden Gate Park—Rejoice! (68)	2.2
Timothy BROWN [Father MC] ▶ 6890 (1)	**131**
I'll Do 4 U—Father MC (91)	522
Toni BROWN ▶ 8406 (1)	**52**
Brownsville—Joy Of Cooking (71)	155
Vincent BROWN ▶ 6156 (1)	**199**
O.P.P.—Naughty By Nature (91)	1392

Wade BROWN ▶ 3495 (4)	**818**
Love Me For A Reason—Osmonds (74)	1275
That's How Love Goes—Jermaine Jackson (72)	467
We've Come Too Far To End It Now—Smokey Robinson & The Miracles (72)	421
I Can't Stand To See You Cry—Smokey Robinson & The Miracles (72)	290
Walter BROWN ▶ 11145 (1)	**3.0**
Confessin' The Blues—Dakota Staton (58)	6.0
Walter Earl BROWN ▶ 1821 (1)	**2264**
If I Can Dream—Elvis Presley (68)	2264
—Wandra Merrell Brown see: Wandra MERRELL	
Wayne BROWN ▶ 9559 (1)	**21**
Heartache—Pepsi & Shirlie (87)	64
William C. BROWN III ▶ 7086 (1)	**116**
Son Of Shaft—Bar-Kays (71)	349
William A. BROWN ▶ 8795 (2)	**39**
Didn't I—Sylvia (73)	139
Lovely Way She Loves—Moments (70)	13
Yamma BROWN [Yamma Brown Lumar] ▶ 7360 (2)	**100**
Get Up Offa That Thing—James Brown (76)	279
Bodyheat (Part 1)—James Brown (77)	22
Al BROWNE ▶ 6923 (2)	**128**
Bad Motorcycle—Storey Sisters (58)	251
Sweetest One—Crests (57)	5.0
Hayden BROWNE ▶ 7434 (1)	**96**
Get A Life—Soul II Soul (90)	192
Jackson BROWNE ▶ 361 (20) HOF	**10599**
Somebody's Baby—Jackson Browne (82)	2571
Take It Easy—Eagles (72)	1870
Doctor My Eyes—Jackson Browne (72)	1680
Running On Empty—Jackson Browne (78)	1466
Lawyers In Love—Jackson Browne (83)	1219
Boulevard—Jackson Browne (80)	1074
Here Come Those Tears Again—Jackson Browne (77)	701
That Girl Could Sing—Jackson Browne (80)	690
Tender Is The Night—Jackson Browne (83)	646
For America—Jackson Browne (86)	494
Rock Me On The Water—Jackson Browne (72)	*403*
For A Rocker—Jackson Browne (84)	268
For A Dancer—Prelude (75)	132
James Dean—Eagles (74)	125
The Pretender—Jackson Browne (77)	122
Redneck Friend—Jackson Browne (73)	121
In The Shape Of A Heart—Jackson Browne (86)	87
Rock Me On The Water—Linda Ronstadt (72)	*16*
Hold On, Hold Out—Jackson Browne (80)	13
The Load-Out—Jackson Browne (78)	0.0
Tom BROWNE ▶ 9165 (2)	**30**
Thighs High (Grip Your Hips And Move)—Tom Browne (81)	49
Funkin' For Jamaica (N.Y.)—Tom Browne (80)	35
Barney Duke BROWNER ▶ 7544 (2)	**90**
I Got To Handle It—Capitols (66)	77
Gotta Give Her Love—Volume's (64)	13
Rudolph BROWNER ▶ 6124 (1)	**202**
Jealous Kind Of Fella—Garland Green (69)	810
Larry BROWNLEE ▶ 3869 (2)	**672**
The Sly, Slick, And The Wicked—Lost Generation (70)	1128
Michael—C.O.D.'s (65)	591
—Brownmark see: Mark Alton BROWN	
Derry BROWNSON ▶ 3102 (2)	**1010**
Unbelievable—EMF (91)	4783
Lies—EMF (91)	266
—Louis Brownstein see: Lew BROWN	
Dave BRUBECK ▶ 6109 (2)	**206**
Bossa Nova U.S.A.—Dave Brubeck Quartet (63)	150
Unsquare Dance—Dave Brubeck Quartet (61)	56
Ed BRUCE [William Edwin Bruce] ▶ 4945 (3)	**376**
Mammas Don't Let Your Babies Grow Up To Be Cowboys—Waylon & Willie (78)	268
A Working Man's Prayer—Arthur Prysock (68)	203
The Man That Turned My Mama On—Tanya Tucker (74)	79
Gary BRUCE ▶ 747 (1)	**5879**
Moody River—Pat Boone (61)	5879
Jack BRUCE ▶ 1527 (3)	**2802**
Sunshine Of Your Love—Cream (68)	3604

White Room—Cream (68)	3165
I Feel Free—Belinda Carlisle (88)	37
Michael BRUCE ▶ 2096 (9)	**1885**
School's Out—Alice Cooper (72)	*2297*
Eighteen—Alice Cooper (71)	1021
No More Mr. Nice Guy—Alice Cooper (73)	839
Elected—Alice Cooper (72)	776
Be My Lover—Alice Cooper (72)	439
Billion Dollar Babies—Alice Cooper (73)	243
Under My Wheels—Alice Cooper (71)	190
School's Out—Krokus (86)	*104*
Caught In A Dream—Alice Cooper (71)	42
Patsy BRUCE ▶ 6411 (2)	**173**
Mammas Don't Let Your Babies Grow Up To Be Cowboys—Waylon & Willie (78)	268
The Man That Turned My Mama On—Tanya Tucker (74)	79
—Robert Bruce see: Robert Byron WRIGHT	
—William Edwin Bruce see: Ed BRUCE	
Bill BRUFORD ▶ 7167 (1)	**112**
And You And I (Part I)—Yes (72)	447
Christian BRUHN ▶ 7660 (2)	**82**
Marble Breaks And Iron Bends—Drafi (66)	170
Silly Milly—Blue Swede (74)	120
Albert E. BRUMLEY Sr. ▶ 7594 (2)	**87**
Turn Your Radio On—Ray Stevens (71)	85
I'll Fly Away—Lonnie Sattin & Orchestra (60)	1.6
George BRUNIES ▶ 11445 (2)	**1.6**
Make Love To Me—Johnny Thunder & Ruby Winters (67)	*13*
Make Love To Me!—Jo Stafford (54)	*0.0*
Henry BRUNIES ▶ 10788 (1)	**5.3**
Angry—Frank Pizani (57)	21
Merritt BRUNIES ▶ 10789 (1)	**5.3**
Angry—Frank Pizani (57)	21
Anthony Michael BRUNO [Tony Bruno, Tony Rey] ▶ 8502 (1)	**48**
Love Has Taken Its Toll—Saraya (89)	144
Brenda BRUNO ▶ 6004 (2)	**217**
Tell Him I'm Not Home—Chuck Jackson (63)	568
Ask Me—Maxine Brown (63)	56
—C. Bruno see: Bruno CHERUBINI	
Tony BRUNO ▶ 4072 (4)	**604**
Last Chance To Turn Around—Gene Pitney (65)	1140
Tell Him I'm Not Home—Chuck Jackson (63)	568
Ask Me—Maxine Brown (63)	56
I Can't Take It—Mary Ann Fisher (61)	14
—Tony Bruno see also: Anthony Michael BRUNO	
George BRUNS ▶ 702 (14)	**6200**
Ballad Of Davy Crockett—Bill Hayes (55)	*6567*
Ballad Of Davy Crockett—Fess Parker (55)	*2764*
Ballad Of Davy Crockett—"Tennessee" Ernie Ford (55)	*2107*
Zorro—Chordettes (58)	653
Pancho Lopez (Davy Crockett)—Lalo Guerrero (55)	*238*
Ballad Of Davy Crockett—Walter Schumann (55)	*45*
Old Betsy (Davy Crockett's Gun)—Voices Of Walter Schumann (55)	*38*
Old Betsy (Davy Crockett's Rifle)—Fess Parker & Buddy Ebsen (55)	*38*
Duvid Crockett (The Ballad Of Davy Crockett)—Mickey Katz And His Orchestra (55)	36
Johnny Tremain—Billy Vaughn and His Orchestra (57)	6.0
Old Betsy (Davy Crockett's Gun)—Sons Of The Pioneers (55)	*0.0*
The Ballad Of Davy Crockett—Rusty Draper (55)	*0.0*
The Ballad Of Davy Crockett—Steve Allen (55)	*0.0*
Old Betsy—Burl Ives (55)	*0.0*
Gerald BRUNSKILL ▶ 9993 (1)	**14**
Victory Line—Limited Warranty (86)	71
Frank BRUNSON ▶ 4643 (1)	**446**
I Likes To Do It—People's Choice (71)	446
Dave BRYAN ▶ 7664 (1)	**82**
Only Lonely—Bon Jovi (85)	164
—Dougie Bryan see: Radcliffe BRYAN	
Radcliffe BRYAN [Dougie Bryan] ▶ 8893 (1)	**37**
Running Back—Eddie Money (80)	37
Thomas BRYAN ▶ 9578 (1)	**21**
Shirley—John Fred and the Playboys (59)	42

Boudleaux BRYANT ▶ 47 (52) HOF	**41708**
All I Have To Do Is Dream—Everly Brothers (58)	*8593*
Bye Bye Love—Everly Brothers (57)	*7746*
Wake Up Little Susie—Everly Brothers (57)	*6983*
Bird Dog—Everly Brothers (58)	6981
Problems—Everly Brothers (58)	3453
Mexico—Bob Moore And His Orch. (61)	2888
Let's Think About Living—Bob Luman (60)	2859
Love Hurts—Nazareth (75)	*2521*
Devoted To You—Everly Brothers (58)	*1872*
All I Have To Do Is Dream—Richard Chamberlain (63)	*1309*
Take A Message To Mary—Everly Brothers (59)	1270
Poor Jenny—Everly Brothers (59)	784
Like Strangers—Everly Brothers (60)	769
Have A Good Time—Sue Thompson (62)	761
All I Have To Do Is Dream— Bobbie Gentry & Glen Campbell (70)	*694*
Hawk-Eye—Frankie Laine (55)	*482*
Wake Up Little Susie—Simon and Garfunkel (82)	*477*
My Last Date (With You)—Skeeter Davis (60)	*381*
Devoted To You—Carly Simon and James Taylor (78)	*345*
Blue Boy—Jim Reeves (58)	298
Raining In My Heart—Leo Sayer (78)	*267*
My Last Date (With You)—Joni James (60)	*266*
Love Of My Life—Everly Brothers (58)	258
All I Have To Do Is Dream— Andy Gibb And Victoria Principal (81)	*206*
(All I Have To Do Is) Dream— Nitty Gritty Dirt Band (75)	*161*
Come Live With Me—Ray Charles (73)	*156*
Willie Can—Sue Thompson (63)	147
Teen Ex—Browns Featuring Jim Edward Brown (60)	126
Bye Bye Love—Webb Pierce (57)	*109*
Wake Up Little Suzie— Jive Bunny And The Mastermixers (89)	*80*
Always It's You—Everly Brothers (60)	78
I've Been Thinking—Four Lads (55)	*63*
Come Live With Me—Roy Clark (73)	*48*
Auf Wiedersehen Marlene—Bob Moore (62)	33
The Richest Man (In The World)—Eddy Arnold (55)	25
Raining In My Heart— Buddy Holly / The Crickets (59)	*13*
Brand New Heartache—Everly Brothers (60)	9.6
She Wears My Ring—Solomon King (68)	7.8
Love Hurts—Jim Capaldi (75)	*6.4*
Fall Away—Eddie Albert (65)	6.0
Bye Bye Love—Will Jordan (59)	*5.6*
My Hero (That's What You Are)—Sue Thompson (62)	4.9
Margo (The Ninth Of May)— Browns Featuring Jim Edward Brown (60)	4.7
All I Have To Do Is Dream—Everly Brothers (61)	*2.8*
Tina—Easy Riders (57)	2.4
Sweet Sugar Lips—Kalin Twins (59)	1.5
Bye Bye Love—T. Tommy (57)	*0.0*
Bye, Bye, Love—Chuck Miller (57)	*0.0*
Hawk-Eye—Chuck Miller (55)	*0.0*
Hawk-Eye—Bobby Lord (55)	*0.0*
I've Been Thinkin'—Rusty Draper (55)	*0.0*
I've Been Thinking—Eddy Arnold (55)	*0.0*
David Paul BRYANT ▶ 2841 (3)	**1161**
Don't You Want Me—Jody Watley (87)	2205
The Love In Your Eyes—Eddie Money (89)	753
Back On Holiday—Robbie Nevil (88)	525
Donald BRYANT ▶ 4177 (2)	**573**
I Can't Stand The Rain—Eruption (78)	*930*
I Can't Stand The Rain—Ann Peebles (73)	*789*
Felice BRYANT [Matilda Genevieve Scaduto] ▶ 282 (29) HOF	**12424**
Bye Bye Love—Everly Brothers (57)	*7746*
Wake Up Little Susie—Everly Brothers (57)	*6983*
Problems—Everly Brothers (58)	3453
Take A Message To Mary—Everly Brothers (59)	1270
Poor Jenny—Everly Brothers (59)	784
Have A Good Time—Sue Thompson (62)	761
I'm Not Afraid—Ricky Nelson (60)	582
Wake Up Little Susie—Simon and Garfunkel (82)	*477*
We Could—Al Martino (64)	429
Raining In My Heart—Leo Sayer (78)	*267*
Love Of My Life—Everly Brothers (58)	258
Come Live With Me—Ray Charles (73)	*156*
Willie Can—Sue Thompson (63)	147
Teen Ex—Browns Featuring Jim Edward Brown (60)	126
Bye Bye Love—Webb Pierce (57)	*109*
Wake Up Little Suzie— Jive Bunny And The Mastermixers (89)	*80*
Always It's You—Everly Brothers (60)	78
Come Live With Me—Roy Clark (73)	*48*
Auf Wiedersehen Marlene—Bob Moore (62)	33
Raining In My Heart— Buddy Holly / The Crickets (59)	*13*
Brand New Heartache—Everly Brothers (60)	9.6
She Wears My Ring—Solomon King (68)	7.8
Fall Away—Eddie Albert (65)	6.0
Bye Bye Love—Will Jordan (59)	*5.6*
My Hero (That's What You Are)—Sue Thompson (62)	4.9
Tina—Easy Riders (57)	2.4
Sweet Sugar Lips—Kalin Twins (59)	1.5
Bye Bye Love—T. Tommy (57)	*0.0*
Bye, Bye, Love—Chuck Miller (57)	*0.0*
Marty BRYANT [Lamar C. Bryant] ▶ 7880 (1)	**71**
You're A Big Girl Now—Stylistics (71)	142
Ray BRYANT ▶ 4977 (2)	**366**
Madison Time Part One—Ray Bryant Combo (60)	681
Little Susie—Ray Bryant Trio (60)	26
William BRYANT ▶ 5700 (1)	**253**
What Is Love?—Howard Jones (84)	506
Tracey BRYN [Tracey Bryn Belland, Tracey Bryn Kennedy] ▶ 8959 (1)	**35**
Monsters And Angels—Voice Of The Beehive (91)	106
Peabo BRYSON [Robert L. Bryson] ▶ 4662 (5)	**444**
Let The Feeling Flow—Peabo Bryson (81)	334
Reaching For The Sky—Peabo Bryson (78)	58
I'm So Into You—Peabo Bryson (78)	30
Slow Dancin'—Peabo Bryson (84)	21
Feel The Fire—Peabo Bryson (78)	1.2
Wally BRYSON ▶ 10051 (1)	**13**
Don't Want To Say Goodbye—Raspberries (72)	27
Mark BRZEZICKI ▶ 5169 (3)	**332**
In A Big Country—Big Country (83)	1155
Fields Of Fire—Big Country (84)	159
Wonderland—Big Country (84)	12
Chico BUARQUE DE HOLLANDA [Chico Buarque, Francisco Buarque de Hollanda] ▶ 4306 (1)	**527**
A Banda (Ah Bahn-da)— Herb Alpert & The Tijuana Brass (67)	527
Alan BUBIS ▶ 11032 (1)	**3.7**
Pipe Dreams—Jimmy Beck & His Orchestra (59)	7.4
Harriet BUBIS ▶ 11033 (1)	**3.7**
Pipe Dreams—Jimmy Beck & His Orchestra (59)	7.4
Bill BUCHANAN ▶ 2300 (7)	**1634**
The Flying Saucer (Pts. 1 & 2)— Buchanan And Goodman (56)	1700
Please Don't Ask About Barbara—Bobby Vee (62)	971
Flying Saucer The Second— Buchanan And Goodman (57)	410
Santa And The Satellite— Buchanan And Goodman (57)	116
Buchanan And Goodman On Trial— Buchanan And Goodman (56)	55
The Creature (From A Science Fiction Movie)— Buchanan & Ancell (57)	15
Cry On My Shoulder—Johnny Crawford (63)	0.4
Peter BUCHANAN ▶ 10305 (1)	**10**
Have A Drink On Me—Buddy Thomas (61)	51
—Martyn Jeryl Buchwald see: Marty BALIN	
Peter BUCK ▶ 2217 (10)	**1729**
Losing My Religion—R.E.M. (91)	2447
Stand—R.E.M. (89)	1642
Shiny Happy People—R.E.M. (91)	1294
The One I Love—R.E.M. (87)	1261
It's The End Of The World As We Know It (And I Feel Fine)—R.E.M. (88)	87
So. Central Rain (I'm Sorry)—R.E.M. (84)	50
Pop Song 89—R.E.M. (89)	43
Radio Song—R.E.M. (91)	42
Radio Free Europe—R.E.M. (83)	34
Fall On Me—R.E.M. (86)	16
Robert BUCK ▶ 9493 (1)	**23**
What's The Matter Here?—10,000 Maniacs (88)	45
—Bonnie Buckingham see: Bonnie GUITAR	
Jan BUCKINGHAM [Jan Bidewell] ▶ 3907 (4)	**661**
Modern Day Delilah—Van Stephenson (84)	823
Nice Girls—Melissa Manchester (83)	399
What The Big Girls Do—Van Stephenson (84)	297
Til You And Your Lover Are Lovers Again— Engelbert Humperdinck (83)	35
Lindsey BUCKINGHAM ▶ 548 (7)	**7848**
Trouble—Lindsey Buckingham (81)	2002
Big Love—Fleetwood Mac (87)	1784
Tusk—Fleetwood Mac (79)	1782
Go Your Own Way—Fleetwood Mac (77)	1577
Go Insane—Lindsey Buckingham (84)	671
Holiday Road—Lindsey Buckingham (83)	28
Family Man—Fleetwood Mac (88)	10
Steve BUCKINGHAM ▶ 5893 (2)	**232**
Nice Girls—Melissa Manchester (83)	399
What The Big Girls Do—Van Stephenson (84)	297
Mickey BUCKINS ▶ 2518 (5)	**1421**
Double Lovin'—Osmonds (71)	1333
Tell Me A Lie—Sami Jo (74)	844
The Feeling Is Right—Clarence Carter (69)	449
Victim Of A Foolish Heart—Bettye Swann (72)	210
Take It Off Him And Put It On Me— Clarence Carter (70)	15
—Nigel Buckle see: Nigel TWIST	
Jerry BUCKNER ▶ 3209 (2)	**951**
Pac-Man Fever—Buckner & Garcia (81)	1886
Merry Christmas In The NFL— Willis "The Guard" and Vigorish (80)	16
Paul BUFF ▶ 8909 (1)	**36**
Queen Of My Heart—René And Ray (62)	109
Wade BUFF ▶ 1687 (9)	**2485**
It's Almost Tomorrow—Dream Weavers (55)	*2855*
It's Almost Tomorrow—Jo Stafford (55)	*1089*
It's Almost Tomorrow—Snooky Lanson (55)	*494*
It's Almost Tomorrow— David Carroll And His Orchestra (55)	*371*
It's Almost Tomorrow—Jimmy Velvet (65)	*117*
Into The Night—Dream Weavers (56)	43
You're Mine—Dream Weavers (56)	0.3
It's Almost Tomorrow— Lawrence Welk & His Champagne Music (55)	*0.0*
It's Almost Tomorrow— Ray Anthony & His Orchestra with Don Durant (56)	*0.0*
Jimmy BUFFETT ▶ 1108 (10)	**4000**
Margaritaville—Jimmy Buffett (77)	2085
Come Monday—Jimmy Buffett (74)	685
Fins—Jimmy Buffett (79)	528
Cheeseburger In Paradise—Jimmy Buffett (78)	516
Changes In Latitudes, Changes In Attitudes— Jimmy Buffett (77)	333
Volcano—Jimmy Buffett (79)	155
Livingston Saturday Night—Jimmy Buffett (78)	135
Survive—Jimmy Buffett (80)	56
Manana—Jimmy Buffett (78)	33
A Pirate Looks At Forty—Jimmy Buffett (75)	1.9
Gregory BUFFORD ▶ 10159 (1)	**12**
Bounce, Rock, Skate, Roll (Part 1)— Vaughan Mason And Crew (80)	35
Dominic BUGATTI [Dominique Bugatti, Dominic Roy King] ▶ 1047 (11)	**4211**
Every Woman In The World—Air Supply (80)	3052
Heaven On The 7th Floor—Paul Nicholas (77)	*2721*
Modern Girl—Sheena Easton (81)	1013
When He Shines—Sheena Easton (82)	601
Back On My Feet Again—Babys (80)	576
Married Men—Bette Midler (79)	261
Every Home Should Have One—Patti Austin (83)	*166*
Every Home Should Have One—Patti Austin (81)	*133*
On The Strip—Paul Nicholas (78)	69
Heaven On The Seventh Floor—Mighty Pope (77)	*15*
Mystery Girl—Dukes (82)	6.7
Buddy BUIE [Perry Carlton Buie] ▶ 311 (37)	**11701**
Spooky—Classics IV (67)	*5516*
Stormy—Classics IV Featuring Dennis Yost (68)	*4909*
Traces—Classics IV Featuring Dennis Yost (69)	*4007*
So In To You—Atlanta Rhythm Section (77)	2327
Imaginary Lover—Atlanta Rhythm Section (78)	1818
I Take It Back—Sandy Posey (67)	1475
Everyday With You Girl— Classics IV Featuring Dennis Yost (69)	1298
I'm Not Gonna Let It Bother Me Tonight— Atlanta Rhythm Section (78)	932
Spooky—Atlanta Rhythm Section (79)	*887*

Buddy BUIE [Perry Carlton Buie] ▶ 311 (37)	
Continued	**11701**
Do It Or Die—Atlanta Rhythm Section (79)	861
Most Of All—B.J. Thomas (70)	718
Mighty Clouds Of Joy—B.J. Thomas (71)	675
Alien—Atlanta Rhythm Section (81)	566
What Am I Crying For?— Dennis Yost And The Classics IV (72)	559
Midnight—Dennis Yost And The Classics IV (69)	481
Stormy—Santana (78)	*450*
Mind Bender—Stillwater (77)	386
Change Of Heart— Dennis Yost And The Classics IV (69)	360
Doraville—Atlanta Rhythm Section (74)	329
The Funniest Thing— Dennis Yost And The Classics IV (70)	282
Georgia Pines—Candymen (67)	277
Traces—Lettermen (69)	*238*
Where Did All The Good Times Go— Dennis Yost And The Classics IV (70)	190
Neon Nites—Atlanta Rhythm Section (77)	181
Soul Train—Classics IV (68)	176
Champagne Jam—Atlanta Rhythm Section (78)	171
Dog Days—Atlanta Rhythm Section (77)	109
Georgia Rhythm—Atlanta Rhythm Section (77)	94
Angel (What In The World's Come Over Us)— Atlanta Rhythm Section (75)	66
Something I'll Remember—Sandy Posey (68)	57
Jukin—Atlanta Rhythm Section (76)	56
Free Spirit—Atlanta Rhythm Section (76)	53
Rosanna—Dennis Yost And The Classics IV (73)	30
I Ain't Much—Atlanta Rhythm Section (80)	29
Party Girl—Tommy Roe (64)	26
Deep In The Night—Candymen (68)	26
Back Up Against The Wall— Atlanta Rhythm Section (79)	18
Cecelia BULLARD ▶ 9120 (1)	**31**
He's My Girl—David Hallyday (87)	92
Kim BULLARD ▶ 9121 (1)	**31**
He's My Girl—David Hallyday (87)	92
Cindy BULLENS ▶ 5104 (4)	**342**
Survivor—Cindy Bullens (79)	195
Hollywood Hot—Eleventh Hour (75)	136
Street Talk (Var. III)— B. C. G. (B.C. Generation) (76)	78
Trust Me—Cindy Bullens (79)	40
James BULLINGTON ▶ 6842 (1)	**133**
Love Bug Crawl— Jimmy Edwards (57)	266
—Anna Mae Bullock see: Tina TURNER	
Vernon BULLOCK ▶ 2135 (4)	**1829**
What Does It Take (To Win Your Love)— Jr. Walker & The All Stars (69)	3648
If I Could Build My Whole World Around You— Marvin Gaye & Tammi Terrell (67)	1524
Yesterday's Dreams—Four Tops (68)	417
You And I, Pt. 1—Living Proof (78)	2.5
—Farrokh Bulsara see: Freddie MERCURY	
Pat BUNCH ▶ 6837 (1)	**134**
I'll Still Be Loving You—Restless Heart (87)	536
Sekou BUNCH ▶ 10128 (1)	**12**
Thighs High (Grip Your Hips And Move)— Tom Browne (81)	49
John BUNDRICK ▶ 5761 (2)	**244**
Stone Cold Sober—Crawler (77)	205
Wonderful—Blackwell (69)	78
Allen BUNN [Alden Bunn] ▶ 7543 (2)	**90**
Darling It's Wonderful—Lovers (57)	*79*
Darling It's Wonderful—Dale & Grace (64)	*11*
Dewey BUNNELL [Lee Martin Bunnell] ▶ 316 (7)	**11535**
A Horse With No Name—America (72)	*7299*
Tin Man—America (74)	2212
Ventura Highway—America (72)	1749
The Border—America (83)	458
Amber Cascades—America (76)	31
A Horse With No Name—Stars On 45 (81)	*12*
All Around—America (80)	4.7
—Lee Martin Bunnell see: Dewey BUNNELL	
—Bunny D. see: Elana CAGER	
—Ian Buonconsiglio see: Ian LLOYD	

David BUPP ▶ 11245 (1)	**2.6**
I Could Be So Happy—Magnificent Men (67)	5.2
—Charles Burbank see: Charles IBGUI	
Gary BURBANK [Billy Purser] ▶ 9074 (1)	**32**
Who Shot J.R.?— Gary Burbank with Band McNally (80)	95
Doc BURCH ▶ 7220 (2)	**109**
Catch A Little Moonbeam—Rinky Dinks (59)	*109*
Catch A Little Moonbeam—Doc Burch (59)	*0.0*
Don BURCH ▶ 1849 (3)	**2201**
You Cheated—Shields (58)	*1737*
You Cheated—Slades (58)	*464*
You Cheated—Del Vikings (58)	*0.0*
Fred BURCH ▶ 1070 (9)	**4119**
Tragedy—Thomas Wayne with The DeLons (59)	*2908*
P.T. 109—Jimmy Dean (62)	2113
Tragedy—Fleetwoods (61)	*1366*
Dream On Little Dreamer—Perry Como (65)	787
Tragedy—Brian Hyland (68)	*561*
Big Big World—Johnny Burnette (61)	460
He Made A Woman Out Of Me—Bobbie Gentry (70)	156
Eternally—Thomas Wayne with The DeLons (59)	30
Strange—Patsy Cline (62)	10
John BURCH [John Alexander Burchell] ▶ 10935 (1)	**4.2**
In The Meantime— Georgie Fame And The Blue Flames (65)	4.2
—John Alexander Burchell see: John BURCH	
—Jon Mark/Michael Burchell see: Jon MARK	
Charles BURCHILL ▶ 2010 (4)	**2004**
Alive And Kicking—Simple Minds (85)	3897
Sanctify Yourself—Simple Minds (86)	1088
All The Things She Said—Simple Minds (86)	507
See The Lights—Simple Minds (91)	346
Ian BURDEN ▶ 6366 (2)	**178**
Mirror Man—Human League (83)	491
Love Action (I Believe In Love)—Human League (82)	29
Eric BURDON ▶ 1935 (10)	**2084**
San Franciscan Nights— Eric Burdon And The Animals (67)	1697
Sky Pilot (Part One)— Eric Burdon & The Animals (68)	1609
When I Was Young—Eric Burdon & The Animals (67)	1085
Monterey—Eric Burdon & The Animals (67)	1017
I'm Crying—Animals (64)	920
Inside-Looking Out—Animals (66)	468
The Night—Animals (83)	309
White Houses—Eric Burdon and The Animals (68)	277
Anything—Eric Burdon & The Animals (68)	187
Soledad—Eric Burdon & Jimmy Witherspoon (71)	17
Tony BURELLO ▶ 7923 (1)	**69**
Why (Are There Things We Can't Explain)— Jane Morgan (54)	139
Douglas BURFORD ▶ 10786 (1)	**5.3**
My Faith, My Hope, My Love—Don Cornell (57)	11
Dave BURGESS ▶ 1577 (10)	**2678**
I'm Available—Margie Rayburn (57)	1267
Everlovin'—Rick Nelson (61)	1067
Too Much Tequila—Champs (60)	700
Chariot Rock—Champs (58)	167
Son-In-Law—Blossoms (61)	75
Silly Boy (She Doesn't Love You)—Lettermen (62)	56
Shy Away—Jerry Fuller (61)	36
Caramba—Champs (59)	3.7
Midnighter—Champs (58)	2.5
Limbo Dance—Champs (62)	1.8
Leroy BURGESS [Leroy O'Niel Jackson Jr.] ▶ 11354 (1)	**2.1**
You And I—Black Ivory (72)	4.3
Lord BURGESS [Irving Louis Burgie, Irving Burgie, Lord Burgie] ▶ 1834 (6) HOF	**2236**
Jamaica Farewell—Harry Belafonte (56)	1550
El Matador—Kingston Trio (60)	484
Island In The Sun—Harry Belafonte (57)	418
Cocoanut Woman—Harry Belafonte (57)	328
Don't Ever Love Me—Harry Belafonte (57)	65
Round The Bay Of Mexico—Harry Belafonte (59)	39
Richard BURGESS ▶ 9981 (1)	**14**
I've Been Lovin' You— Easy Street (76)	57

Tim BURGESS ▶ 10625 (1)	**6.7**
The Only One I Know—Charlatans UK (90)	33
—Yvonne Ann Burgess see: Jackie TRENT	
—Irving Burgie see: Lord BURGESS	
—Lord Burgie see: Lord BURGESS	
Bernadine BURKE ▶ 11323 (1)	**2.2**
The Electronic Magnetism (That's Heavy, Baby)— Solomon Burke (71)	6.7
Bobby BURKE ▶ 5349 (1)	**302**
Daddy's Little Girl—Al Martino (67)	603
Clarence BURKE Jr. ▶ 5947 (6)	**224**
All Night Thing—Invisible Man's Band (80)	278
Danger! She's A Stranger—Five Stairsteps (67)	157
Something's Missing—Five Stairsteps & Cubie (67)	101
Ain't Gonna Rest (Till I Get You)— Five Stairsteps (67)	51
From Us To You—Stairsteps (76)	6.5
Because I Love You—Five Stairsteps (70)	0.0
Clarence BURKE Sr. ▶ 4222 (5)	**556**
World Of Fantasy—Five Stairsteps (66)	565
Come Back—Five Stairsteps (66)	257
You Waited Too Long—Five Stairsteps (66)	138
Something's Missing—Five Stairsteps & Cubie (67)	101
Ain't Gonna Rest (Till I Get You)—Five Stairsteps (67)	51
—Clem Burke see: Clement A. BOZEWSKI	
Delores BURKE ▶ 5254 (2)	**317**
Got To Get You Off My Mind—Solomon Burke (65)	944
Keep Looking—Solomon Burke (66)	8.5
—J. Francis Burke see: Joseph Francis BURKE	
Joe BURKE ▶ 2238 (9) HOF	**1713**
For You—Rick Nelson (63)	2166
Tip-Toe Thru' The Tulips With Me—Tiny Tim (68)	858
Carolina Moon—Connie Francis (58)	*201*
Oh How I Miss You Tonight—Jeanne Black (60)	104
Yearning (Just For You)—Georgie Shaw (54)	45
Carolina Moon—Melody Makers (57)	*38*
On Treasure Island—Gale Storm (57)	21
(All That I'm Asking Is) Sympathy— Johnny Maddox (58)	18
It Looks Like Rain In Cherry Blossom Lane— Debbie Reynolds (60)	9.9
Joe (2) BURKE ▶ 10651 (1)	**6.4**
Love Is—Maxine Starr (62)	13
—John Francis Burke see: Johnny BURKE	
Johnny BURKE [John Francis Burke, K. C. Rogan] ▶ 1246 (13) HOF	**3601**
Misty—Johnny Mathis (59)	*1736*
Misty—Ray Stevens (75)	*1222*
Misty—Lloyd Price (63)	*848*
Swinging On A Star—Big Dee Irwin (63)	789
Pennies From Heaven—Skyliners (60)	786
You'll Always Be My Lifetime Sweetheart— Perry Como (55)	634
What's New— Linda Ronstadt & The Nelson Riddle Orchestra (83)	425
It Could Happen To You—Dinah Washington (60)	358
Misty—Vibrations (65)	*153*
Imagination—Quotations (62)	96
From The First Hello To The Last Goodbye— Jane Morgan and The 450 Collegians (57)	65
Misty—Sarah Vaughan (59)	*22*
He Cha Cha'd In—Kay Starr (58)	3.8
Joseph Francis BURKE [J. Francis Burke, Sonny Burke, Peter Fadden] ▶ 3483 (3)	**822**
They Were Doin' The Mambo— Vaughn Monroe with Orchestra (54)	1433
I Love To Dance With You—Patti Page (55)	211
Midnight Sun—Five Whispers (62)	1.2
Kenneth BURKE ▶ 11092 (1)	**3.3**
From Us To You—Stairsteps (76)	6.5
—K.S.H.S. Burke see: Selassie BURKE	
Mark BURKE ▶ 11187 (1)	**2.8**
Keep Looking—Solomon Burke (66)	8.5
Melanie BURKE ▶ 11324 (1)	**2.2**
The Electronic Magnetism (That's Heavy, Baby)— Solomon Burke (71)	6.7
Mike BURKE ▶ 5652 (1)	**260**
Suspicions—Sidekicks (66)	519
Reggie BURKE ▶ 4382 (2)	**508**
Serpentine Fire—Earth, Wind & Fire (77)	1513
(Let's Go) All The Way—Whispers (78)	24

Selassie BURKE [K.S.H.S. Burke] ▶ 7549 (1)	**89**
I Have A Dream–Donny Osmond (75)	179
Solomon BURKE [James Solomon McDonald] ▶ 2694 (11)	**1269**
Got To Get You Off My Mind–Solomon Burke (65)	944
Tonight's The Night–Solomon Burke (65)	854
Everybody Needs Somebody To Love–Wilson Pickett (67)	*511*
The Price–Solomon Burke (64)	312
Everybody Needs Somebody To Love–Solomon Burke (64)	*302*
Down In The Valley–Solomon Burke (62)	*194*
Down In The Alley–Ronnie Hawkins (70)	*110*
Love's Street And Fool's Road–Solomon Burke (72)	77
Someone Is Watching–Solomon Burke (65)	29
Keep Looking–Solomon Burke (66)	8.5
You And Your Baby Blues–Solomon Burke (75)	2.6
Solomon BURKE Jr. ▶ 6189 (3)	**196**
The Price–Solomon Burke (64)	312
I Have A Dream–Donny Osmond (75)	179
The Electronic Magnetism (That's Heavy, Baby)–Solomon Burke (71)	6.7
–Sonny Burke see: Joseph Francis BURKE	
Stanley BURKE ▶ 9232 (1)	**28**
Body Talk–Deele (84)	140
Paul BURKHARD ▶ 11598 (1)	**1.0**
Oh Mein Papa–Dick Lee (61)	3.1
Jacqueline BURKS ▶ 10563 (1)	**7.2**
Nothing Will Ever Change–Joni James (58)	14
Sascha BURLAND [Granville A. Burland] ▶ 869 (4)	**5110**
No Matter What Shape (Your Stomach's In)–T-Bones (65)	3789
Uh! Oh! (Part 2)–Nutty Squirrels (59)	*2146*
Sippin' 'N Chippin'–T-Bones (66)	212
Uh! Oh! [Part 1]–Nutty Squirrels (59)	*74*
Larry BURNETT ▶ 4562 (1)	**465**
Cinderella–Firefall (77)	465
Billy BURNETTE [Dorsey William Burnette] ▶ 8209 (1)	**58**
Don't Say No–Billy Burnette (80)	58
Billy Joe BURNETTE ▶ 6455 (2)	**167**
Teddy Bear–Red Sovine (76)	478
Teddy Bear's Last Ride–Diana Williams (76)	94
Dorsey BURNETTE ▶ 976 (10)	**4599**
It's Late–Ricky Nelson (59)	2201
Waitin' In School–Ricky Nelson (57)	965
Believe What You Say–Ricky Nelson (58)	953
(There Was A) Tall Oak Tree–Dorsey Burnette (60)	868
Hey Little One–Dorsey Burnette (60)	*456*
Hey Little One–Glen Campbell (68)	*335*
Gypsy Woman–Rick Nelson (63)	123
Here Comes That Feelin'–Brenda Lee (62)	106
Green Grass Of Texas–Texans (61)	70
Hey Little One–J. Frank Wilson And The Cavaliers (64)	*51*
–Dorsey William Burnette see: Billy BURNETTE	
Ernie BURNETTE ▶ 4494 (4)	**478**
My Melancholy Baby–Tommy Edwards (59)	*830*
My Melancholy Baby–Crazy Otto (55)	*160*
My Melancholy Baby–Marcels (62)	*123*
My Melancholy Baby–Willie Gibson & The Boys (55)	*0.0*
Johnny BURNETTE ▶ 1814 (4)	**2275**
Just A Little Too Much–Ricky Nelson (59)	1281
Waitin' In School–Ricky Nelson (57)	965
Believe What You Say–Ricky Nelson (58)	953
Green Grass Of Texas–Texans (61)	70
–Jonathan Burnette see: Rocky BURNETTE	
O'Bryan BURNETTE ▶ 7527 (1)	**91**
The Gigolo–O'Bryan (82)	182
Rocky BURNETTE [Jonathan Burnette] ▶ 2917 (1)	**1119**
Tired Of Toein' The Line–Rocky Burnette (80)	2237
Charles BURNS ▶ 9765 (1)	**17**
Painted Moon–Silencers (87)	34
Dick BURNS [Richard "Dick" Warren Burns] ▶ 10279 (1)	**11**
The Dartell Stomp–Mustangs (64)	11
–Dick Burns see: Richard BURNS	
Juana BURNS [Juana Burns-Sperling] ▶ 5521 (3)	**275**

Supersonic–J.J. Fad (88)	542
Way Out–J.J. Fad (88)	132
Is It Love–J.J. Fad (88)	69
Kenneth BURNS [Jethro] ▶ 11149 (2)	**3.0**
He'll Have To Go–Homer & Jethro (60)	*9.0*
Ground Hog–Browns Featuring Jim Edward Brown (61)	2.3
Kevin BURNS ▶ 11357 (1)	**2.1**
We Should Be Sleeping–Eddie Money (87)	8.4
Martin BURNS ▶ 11329 (1)	**2.2**
Johnny Casanova–Jaye P. Morgan (56)	6.7
Marvin Louis BURNS [Lil' Louis] ▶ 6670 (1)	**145**
French Kiss–Lil Louis (89)	145
–Morry Burns see: Moon MULLICAN	
Pete BURNS ▶ 4557 (5)	**465**
You Spin Me Round (Like A Record)–Dead Or Alive (85)	1071
Brand New Lover–Dead Or Alive (86)	1017
Come Home With Me Baby–Dead Or Alive (89)	117
Lover Come Back To Me–Dead Or Alive (85)	84
Something In My House–Dead Or Alive (87)	38
Richard BURNS [Richard Brian Burns, Dick Burns] ▶ 4939 (2)	**378**
Powder Blue Mercedes Queen–Raiders (72)	389
Good Times, Rock & Roll–Flash Cadillac & The Continental Kids (75)	248
–Richard "Dick" Warren Burns see: Dick BURNS	
–Richard Brian Burns see: Richard BURNS	
Rusty BURNS ▶ 8131 (2)	**60**
Nicole–Point Blank (81)	357
Let Me Stay With You Tonight–Point Blank (81)	5.7
–Juana Burns-Sperling see: Juana BURNS	
Gary BURR ▶ 1791 (1)	**2319**
Love's Been A Little Bit Hard On Me–Juice Newton (82)	2319
–Kirk Burrell see: Stanley BURRELL	
Louis BURRELL ▶ 5442 (1)	**288**
2 Legit 2 Quit–M.C. Hammer (91)	1441
Raymond BURRELL ▶ 6381 (2)	**177**
Gone, Gone, Gone–Bad Company (79)	159
Honey Child–Bad Company (76)	69
Stanley BURRELL [Kirk Burrell, M.C. Hammer, Hammer] ▶ 1305 (7)	**3396**
Have You Seen Her–M.C. Hammer (90)	*2337*
Pray–M.C. Hammer (90)	2147
U Can't Touch This–M.C. Hammer (90)	1930
2 Legit 2 Quit–M.C. Hammer (91)	1441
Addams Groove–M.C. Hammer (91)	996
Here Comes The Hammer–M.C. Hammer (90)	279
Love Me Just For Me–Special Generation (90)	6.8
Eddie BURRIS ▶ 6453 (1)	**167**
Okie From Muskogee–Merle Haggard (69)	334
Jim BURRIS ▶ 7638 (1)	**83**
Ballin' The Jack–Georgia Gibbs (55)	167
–Earl Solomon Burroughs see: Jack HAMMER	
James BURSTON ▶ 9873 (1)	**16**
One Eye Open–Maskman & The Agents (69)	31
Grace E. BURT ▶ 11789 (1)	**0.0**
Come Home–Eileen Barton (56)	0.0
Earl BURTNETT ▶ 3843 (1)	**680**
Sleep–Little Willie John (60)	1361
Glen BURTNICK [Glenn Burtnick] ▶ 5018 (4)	**358**
Love At First Sight–Styx (91)	751
Follow You–Glen Burtnick (87)	121
Love Is The Ritual–Styx (90)	56
Perfect World–Alias (91)	39
China BURTON ▶ 6793 (1)	**136**
Jesse–Julian Lennon (85)	136
Dorian BURTON [George Burton] ▶ 1543 (9)	**2765**
A Tear Fell–Teresa Brewer (56)	*2559*
You Don't Know What You've Got (Until You Lose It)–Ral Donner (61)	2270
A Tear Fell–Ray Charles (64)	*328*
Still–Fontane Sisters (56)	*204*
I Can't Love You Enough–LaVern Baker (56)	202
Hey, Little Girl–Foster Sylvers (73)	*24*
Still–LaVern Baker (56)	*12*
Two Innocent Hearts–Ginny Gibson (56)	11
A Tear Fell–Ivory Joe Hunter (56)	*0.0*
–George Burton see: Dorian BURTON	

Lori BURTON ▶ 3812 (4)	**691**
Baby Let's Wait–Royal Guardsmen (68)	700
I Ain't Gonna Eat Out My Heart Anymore–Young Rascals (65)	*306*
Ain't Gonna Eat Out My Heart Anymore–Angel (78)	*244*
All Or Nothing–Patti LaBelle And The Blue Belles (65)	133
Michael BURTON ▶ 1882 (2)	**2165**
Pillow Talk–Sylvia (73)	4260
Didn't I–Sylvia (73)	139
Nat BURTON [Nat Schwartz] ▶ 9883 (2)	**16**
The White Cliffs Of Dover–Righteous Brothers (66)	19
Our Waltz–Sarah Vaughan (60)	12
Ray BURTON [Raymond Doughty] ▶ 1359 (2)	**3269**
I Am Woman–Helen Reddy (72)	6487
Club Michelle–Eddie Money (84)	101
Ben BURTT ▶ 7840 (1)	**73**
Ewok Celebration–Meco (83)	218
–Raybon Owen Busby see: Buzz RABIN	
Fini BUSCH [Josefine Huber-Busch] ▶ 3245 (3)	**930**
Sailor (Your Home Is The Sea)–Lolita (60)	2661
Cowboy Jimmy Joe (Die Sterne Der Prarie)–Lolita (61)	66
(A Ship Will Come) Ein Schiff Wird Kommen–Lale Anderson (61)	*19*
–Lou Busch see: Louis F. BUSH	
Bob BUSH ▶ 9406 (1)	**24**
Broken Vow–Chordettes (60)	24
Eddie BUSH ▶ 8239 (1)	**57**
What's He Doing In My World–Eddy Arnold (65)	172
John BUSH ▶ 4893 (2)	**387**
What I Am–Edie Brickell & The New Bohemians (88)	1562
Circle–Edie Brickell & The New Bohemians (89)	371
Kate BUSH ▶ 3911 (2)	**660**
Running Up That Hill–Kate Bush (85)	645
The Man With The Child In His Eyes–Kate Bush (79)	15
Louis F. BUSH [Louis Ferdinand Busch, Lou Busch, Joe "Fingers" Carr] ▶ 1384 (4)	**3211**
Hello Mudduh, Hello Fadduh! (A Letter From Camp)–Allan Sherman (63)	*5106*
Ivory Rag (In der Alten Hafenbar)–Johnny Maddox And The Rhythmasters (55)	*1115*
Hello Mudduh, Hello Fadduh! (A Letter From Camp) (New 1964 Version)–Allan Sherman (64)	*202*
Ivory Rag (In der Alten Hafenbar)–Crazy Otto (55)	*0.0*
Joseph BUSHKIN ▶ 9428 (2)	**24**
Something Wonderful Happens In Summer–Frank Sinatra (57)	46
Oh! Look At Me Now–Modernaires (57)	1.9
Ron BUSHY ▶ 7716 (3)	**79**
Soul Experience–Iron Butterfly (69)	180
Easy Rider (Let The Wind Pay The Way)–Iron Butterfly (70)	125
In The Time Of Our Lives–Iron Butterfly (69)	5.5
Paul BUSKIRK ▶ 7519 (1)	**91**
Night Life–Rusty Draper (63)	273
Henry BUSSE ▶ 9863 (1)	**16**
Hot Lips–Grady Martin And The Slew Foot Five (55)	48
Jon BUTCHER ▶ 11089 (1)	**3.3**
Sounds Of Your Voice–Jon Butcher (85)	6.6
Anthony Earl BUTLER ▶ 5170 (3)	**332**
In A Big Country–Big Country (83)	1155
Fields Of Fire–Big Country (84)	159
Wonderland–Big Country (84)	12
Artie BUTLER ▶ 7622 (3)	**85**
Past, Present And Future–Shangri-Las (66)	169
Amanda–Dionne Warwicke (71)	45
I'm Never Gonna Say Goodbye–Billy Preston (82)	11
Billy BUTLER ▶ 2321 (7)	**1593**
Honky Tonk (Pts. 1 & 2)–Bill Doggett (56)	*5649*
Honky Tonk - Part 1–James Brown Soul Train (72)	*437*
Honky Tonk (Part 2)–Bill Doggett (61)	*113*
Honky Tonk '65–Lonnie Mack (65)	*77*
(Let's Do) The Hully Gully Twist–Bill Doggett (60)	41
Hold It–Bill Doggett (58)	7.2
Honky Tonk (pt. 2)–Rusty Bryant & The Carolyn Club Band (56)	*0.0*
–Billy Butler see: William Earl BUTLER	

Chris BUTLER ▶ 7396 (1)	**99**
I Know What Boys Like—Waitresses (82)	99
Daws BUTLER ▶ 11789 (1)	**0.0**
Point Of Order—Stan Freberg & Daws Butler (54)	0.0
Durron BUTLER ▶ 9147 (1)	**30**
Ooops Up—Snap! (90)	273
Floyd BUTLER ▶ 5634 (1)	**262**
Check It Out—Tavares (73)	524
—Geezer Butler see: Terry BUTLER	
Harry BUTLER [William Henry Butler] ▶ 6297 (1)	**184**
Sun Arise—Rolf Harris (63)	369
Jerry BUTLER ▶ 470 (32)	**8855**
He Don't Love You (Like I Love You)—Tony Orlando & Dawn (75)	*4607*
He Will Break Your Heart—Jerry Butler (60)	*3246*
Only The Strong Survive—Jerry Butler (69)	3213
Never Give You Up—Jerry Butler (68)	1243
I've Been Loving You Too Long (To Stop Now)—Otis Redding (65)	*1217*
Hey, Western Union Man—Jerry Butler (68)	1108
For Your Precious Love—Jerry Butler & The Impressions (58)	*1045*
A Brand New Me—Dusty Springfield (69)	*1011*
What's The Use Of Breaking Up—Jerry Butler (69)	960
Moody Woman—Jerry Butler (69)	921
Find Another Girl—Jerry Butler (61)	912
For Your Precious Love—Oscar Toney, Jr. (67)	*778*
For Your Precious Love—Garnet Mimms & The Enchanters (63)	*662*
I Stand Accused—Isaac Hayes (70)	*574*
Are You Happy—Jerry Butler (68)	543
I'm A Telling You—Jerry Butler (61)	496
For Your Precious Love—Jackie Wilson And Count Basie (68)	*411*
Don't Let Love Hang You Up—Jerry Butler (69)	360
Lost—Jerry Butler (67)	297
I Could Write A Book—Jerry Butler (70)	294
I Stand Accused—Jerry Butler (64)	*292*
I Wanna Do It To You—Jerry Butler (77)	203
Brand New Me—Aretha Franklin (71)	*115*
I've Been Loving You Too Long—Ike & Tina Turner (69)	*87*
He Don't Love You—Jim Croce (76)	*76*
Your Precious Love—Linda Jones (72)	*74*
A Brand New Me—Jerry Butler (69)	*12*
You—Aretha Franklin (76)	7.1
He Will Break Your Heart—Righteous Brothers (66)	*4.8*
Been A Long Time—Betty Everett (69)	4.3
Special Memory—Jerry Butler (70)	4.2
For Your Precious Love—Jerry Butler (66)	*1.4*
Jonathan BUTLER ▶ 5593 (1)	**267**
Lies—Jonathan Butler (87)	534
Larry Lee BUTLER ▶ 1645 (2)	**2553**
(Hey Won't You Play) Another Somebody Done Somebody Wrong Song—B.J. Thomas (75)	4865
Lullaby Of Love—Poppies (66)	241
Martin BUTLER ▶ 8468 (1)	**49**
Fly Little White Dove Fly—Bells (70)	98
Richard BUTLER ▶ 4694 (4)	**437**
Heartbreak Beat—Psychedelic Furs (87)	523
Love My Way—Psychedelic Furs (83)	375
Pretty In Pink—Psychedelic Furs (86)	330
The Ghost In You—Psychedelic Furs (84)	228
Terry BUTLER [Terence Michael Butler, Geezer Butler, Terence Butler] ▶ 7273 (2)	**106**
Paranoid—Black Sabbath (70)	212
Iron Man—Black Sabbath (72)	211
Tim BUTLER ▶ 4695 (4)	**437**
Heartbreak Beat—Psychedelic Furs (87)	523
Love My Way—Psychedelic Furs (83)	375
Pretty In Pink—Psychedelic Furs (86)	330
The Ghost In You—Psychedelic Furs (84)	228
William Earl BUTLER [William E.M. Butler, Billy Butler] ▶ 2323 (9)	**1591**
The Matador—Major Lance (64)	771
I Stand Accused—Isaac Hayes (70)	*574*
Bless Our Love—Gene Chandler (64)	*492*
God Bless Our Love—Ballads (68)	*313*
I Stand Accused—Jerry Butler (64)	*292*
Just As Long As You Need Me, Part I—Independents (72)	74
Let Her Love Me—Otis Leavill (65)	59
How Did We Lose It Baby—Jerry Butler (71)	24
Special Memory—Jerry Butler (70)	4.2
William Eugene BUTLER ▶ 11147 (1)	**3.0**
Night Pulse—Double Image (83)	9.0
—William E.M. Butler see: William Earl BUTLER	
—William Henry Butler see: Harry BUTLER	
Billy BUTTIER ▶ 1156 (1)	**3841**
Tighten Up—Archie Bell & The Drells (68)	7682
Glen BUXTON ▶ 3457 (4)	**840**
School's Out—Alice Cooper (72)	*2297*
Eighteen—Alice Cooper (71)	1021
Elected—Alice Cooper (72)	776
School's Out—Krokus (86)	*104*
Ray BUZZEO ▶ 11238 (1)	**2.6**
Birds Of All Nations—George McCannon III (70)	2.6
—Joy Byers see: Joy Byers JOHNSTON	
Sheri BYERS ▶ 3509 (1)	**808**
Girls Nite Out—Tyler Collins (90)	1615
Max BYGRAVES [Walter William Bygraves, Roy Erwin, Roy Irwin] ▶ 2714 (4)	**1249**
You Need Hands—Eydie Gorme (58)	*1067*
Gotta Have Rain—Eydie Gorme (58)	*182*
Gotta Have Rain—Max Bygraves (58)	*0.0*
You Need Hands—Max Bygraves (58)	*0.0*
—Walter William Bygraves see: Max BYGRAVES	
Hal BYNUM ▶ 3010 (1)	**1069**
Lucille—Kenny Rogers (77)	2138
Mark BYNUM ▶ 8415 (5)	**51**
Move Your Boogie Body—Bar-Kays (79)	270
Today Is The Day—Bar-Kays (80)	150
Freakshow On The Dance Floor—Bar-Kays (84)	79
Hit And Run—Bar-Kays (81)	23
Boogie Body Land—Bar-Kays (81)	23
Bobby BYRD ▶ 2076 (13)	**1909**
Get Up! (Before The Night Is Over)—Technotronic (90)	1473
Licking Stick-Licking Stick (Part 1)—James Brown And The Famous Flames (68)	1305
Get Up I Feel Like Being Like A Sex Machine (Part 1)—James Brown (70)	*913*
Get Up, Get Into It, Get Involved Pt. 1—James Brown (70)	511
Talking Loud And Saying Nothing - Pt. I—James Brown (72)	446
Lost Someone—James Brown And The Famous Flames (61)	*417*
I Cried—James Brown (71)	*335*
Baby Baby Baby—Anna King-Bobby Byrd (64)	273
Get Up I Feel Like Being A Sex Machine—James Brown (75)	*53*
Keep On Doin' What You're Doin'—Bobby Byrd (72)	39
You've Got To Change Your Mind—Bobby Byrd & James Brown (68)	18
Lost Someone—James Brown And The Famous Flames (66)	*6.2*
I Cried—Tammy Montgomery (63)	*0.9*
Byron BYRD ▶ 9137 (1)	**30**
Wanna Make Love (Come Flic My Bic)—Sun (76)	30
Donald BYRD [Donaldson Toussaint L'Ouverture Byrd] ▶ 3962 (2)	**639**
Happy Music—Blackbyrds (76)	580
Do It, Fluid—Blackbyrds (74)	59
Ethel BYRD ▶ 11773 (1)	**0.1**
So Strange—Jesters (57)	0.3
—Robert James Byrd see: Bobby DAY	
David BYRNE ▶ 3825 (7)	**688**
Burning Down The House—Talking Heads (83)	1439
Wild Wild Life—Talking Heads (86)	742
And She Was—Talking Heads (85)	350
This Must Be The Place (Naïve Melody)—Talking Heads (83)	156
Once In A Lifetime—Talking Heads (86)	39
Life During Wartime (This Ain't No Party.. This Ain't No Disco.. This Ain't No Foolin' Around)—Talking Heads (79)	25
Psycho Killer—Talking Heads (78)	8.0
John BYRNE ▶ 4292 (1)	**530**
Psychotic Reaction—Count Five (66)	2651
Pete BYRNE ▶ 2756 (3)	**1217**
Promises, Promises—Naked Eyes (83)	1540
When The Lights Go Out—Naked Eyes (83)	509
(What) In The Name Of Love—Naked Eyes (84)	385
Robert BYRNE ▶ 6268 (3)	**187**
Get It Up—Ronnie Milsap (79)	310
That Didn't Hurt Too Bad—Dr. Hook (81)	59
Baby Fat—Robert Byrne (79)	5.8
Simon BYRNE ▶ 10451 (1)	**8.3**
Heart And Soul—Monkees (87)	17
Michael BYRNES ▶ 8678 (1)	**43**
Can't Stop Loving You—Last Word (67)	86
Larry BYROM ▶ 4821 (3)	**405**
Hey Lawdy Mama—Steppenwolf (70)	613
Who Needs Ya—Steppenwolf (70)	365
America/Standing—Five Stairsteps (70)	93
Monty BYROM ▶ 4781 (3)	**417**
I Wanna Go Back—Eddie Money (86)	*1073*
I Wanna Go Back—Billy Satellite (84)	*89*
Satisfy Me—Billy Satellite (84)	89
Al BYRON ▶ 696 (3)	**6251**
Roses Are Red (My Love)—Bobby Vinton (62)	10687
Happy Go Lucky Me—Paul Evans (60)	1584
Long As The Rose Is Red—Florraine Darlin (62)	231
—David Byron see: David John BYRON	
David John BYRON [David Byron, David Garrick] ▶ 10508 (1)	**7.8**
Sweet Lorraine—Uriah Heep (73)	23
David Leigh BYRON ▶ 2706 (1)	**1261**
Shadows Of The Night—Pat Benatar (82)	1261

C

—Toni C. see: Toni COLANDREO	
Louis CABAZA ▶ 11365 (1)	**2.1**
From The Very Start—Children (71)	4.1
Albert CABRERA ▶ 5207 (3)	**327**
Show Me—Cover Girls (87)	459
Promise Me—Cover Girls (88)	433
Inside Outside—Cover Girls (88)	204
John CACAVAS ▶ 5863 (1)	**235**
Gallant Men—Senator Everett McKinley Dirksen (66)	471
Oscar CADENA ▶ 11385 (1)	**1.9**
Sugah Wooga—Three Playmates (58)	3.9
Frank CADY ▶ 10531 (1)	**7.5**
Red Grapes—Sammy Davis Jr. (54)	15
Irving CAESAR ▶ 4381 (4) HOF	**509**
Just A Gigolo—David Lee Roth (85)	461
Swanee—Jaye P. Morgan (55)	305
I Want To Be Happy Cha Cha—Tommy Dorsey Orchestra starring Warren Covington (58)	*153*
Tea For Two—Nino Tempo & April Stevens (64)	*99*
Sid CAESAR ▶ 11249 (1)	**2.6**
Tower Trot (And Then You Do That Step)—Dick Jacobs And His Chorus And Orchestra (57)	23
John CAFFERTY ▶ 1074 (9)	**4105**
On The Dark Side—John Cafferty And The Beaver Brown Band (84)	*1418*
Tough All Over—John Cafferty And The Beaver Brown Band (85)	718
C-I-T-Y—John Cafferty And The Beaver Brown Band (85)	688
Tender Years—John Cafferty And The Beaver Brown Band (84)	*532*
Small Town Girl—John Cafferty And The Beaver Brown Band (85)	206
Voice Of America's Sons—John Cafferty And The Beaver Brown Band (86)	195
On The Dark Side—Eddie And The Cruisers (83)	*183*
Pride & Passion—John Cafferty and the Beaver Brown Band (89)	108
Tender Years—John Cafferty And The Beaver Brown Band (84)	*57*
Charlotte CAFFEY ▶ 643 (7)	**6771**
We Got The Beat—Go-Go's (82)	4904
Vacation—Go-Go's (82)	2046
Head Over Heels—Go-Go's (84)	1413
Turn To You—Go-Go's (84)	530
Get Up And Go—Go-Go's (82)	260
Lay Down Your Arms—Graces (89)	161
I Feel The Magic—Belinda Carlisle (86)	60

Catherine CAFRA [Catherine Williamson] ► 6601 (2)	**153**
Skinny Minnie—Bill Haley And His Comets (58)	608
Whoa Mabel—Bill Haley And His Comets (58)	2.7
Earl CAGE ► 7447 (4)	**95**
Mini-Skirt Minnie—Wilson Pickett (69)	364
I'm A Fool For You—James Carr (67)	10
Scratch My Back (And Mumble In My Ear)—Clarence Carter (71)	6.3
One Wonderful Love—Ray Smith (60)	1.2
Elana CAGER [Bunny D.] ► 8566 (1)	**46**
Cars With The Boom—L'Trimm (88)	232
Joseph CAGLE [Joey Allen, Joseph Alan Cagle] ► 2468 (8)	**1454**
Heaven—Warrant (89)	3557
I Saw Red—Warrant (90)	1193
Cherry Pie—Warrant (90)	992
Sometimes She Cries—Warrant (89)	824
Down Boys—Warrant (89)	567
Uncle Tom's Cabin—Warrant (91)	71
Blind Faith—Warrant (91)	40
Big Talk—Warrant (89)	23
Sammy CAHN [Samuel Cohen] ► 273 (80) HOF	**12633**
Teach Me Tonight—DeCastro Sisters (54)	*3787*
Love And Marriage—Frank Sinatra (55)	*3059*
Hey Jealous Lover—Frank Sinatra (56)	2954
All The Way—Frank Sinatra (57)	*2520*
I'll Never Stop Loving You—Doris Day (55)	*1346*
High Hopes—Frank Sinatra "and a bunch of kids" (59)	944
(Love Is) The Tender Trap—Frank Sinatra (55)	*901*
Teach Me Tonight—George Maharis (62)	*774*
Same Old Saturday Night—Frank Sinatra (55)	754
It's A Woman's World—Four Aces (54)	*680*
Day By Day—Four Freshmen (55)	668
Somebody Up There Likes Me—Perry Como (56)	630
Pocketful Of Miracles—Frank Sinatra (61)	587
I Still Get Jealous—Louis Armstrong And The All-Stars (64)	*531*
Time After Time—Chris Montez (66)	*519*
The Second Time Around—Frank Sinatra (61)	491
Forever Darling—Ames Brothers (56)	*459*
Love And Marriage—Dinah Shore (55)	*386*
Bei Mir Bist Du Schon—Louis Prima And Keely Smith (59)	365
The Boys' Night Out—Patti Page (62)	326
Wake Me When It's Over—Andy Williams (60)	278
Written On The Wind—Four Aces (56)	261
If You Can Dream—Four Aces (56)	*256*
I Still Get Jealous—Joni James (59)	*247*
Where Love Has Gone—Jack Jones (64)	235
Time After Time—Frankie Ford (60)	*220*
Gal With The Yaller Shoes—Four Aces (56)	209
The Things We Did Last Summer—Shelley Fabares (62)	206
Call Me Irresponsible—Frank Sinatra (63)	*187*
Best Of Everything—Johnny Mathis (59)	186
Teach Me Tonight Cha Cha—DeCastro Sisters (58)	*179*
If It's The Last Thing I Do—Thelma Houston (77)	173
The Song From "Kings Go Forth" (Monique)—Frank Sinatra (58)	170
Let Me Try Again (Laisse Moi Le Temps)—Frank Sinatra (73)	148
Crazy Love—Frank Sinatra (57)	145
I Should Care—Gloria Lynne (64)	124
I'll Walk Alone—Johnny Nash (57)	105
Long Hot Summer—Jimmie Rodgers (58)	102
How Are Ya' Fixed For Love—Frank Sinatra and Keely Smith (58)	99
Call Me Irresponsible—Jack Jones (63)	*90*
So Long My Love—Frank Sinatra (57)	75
Teach Me Tonight—Al Jarreau (82)	*60*
It's Magic—Teddy Randazzo (58)	*51*
Only Trust Your Heart—Dick Roman (57)	*48*
Only Trust Your Heart—Joni James (57)	*48*
Anyone Can Fall In Love—Doris Day (54)	42
Serenade—Slim Whitman (56)	*32*
It's Magic—Platters (62)	*21*
Come Blow Your Horn—Frank Sinatra (63)	21
It's Better In The Dark—Tony Martin (56)	21

The Same Old Song And Dance—Frank Sinatra (58)	18
Be My Love—Joni James (60)	*17*
Look To Your Heart—Georgie Shaw (55)	8.7
To Love And Be Loved—Jane Morgan (58)	*7.2*
Sold To The Man With The Broken Heart—Tony Bennett with Percy Faith (57)	6.8
Dormi Dormi Dormi—Eydie Gorme (58)	6.7
Oh My Maria—Eddie Fisher (56)	6.6
Teach Me Tonight—Big Three: Sarah Vaughan/Joe Williams/Count Basie (60)	*1.5*
The Last Dance—McGuire Sisters (60)	0.8
Who Are They To Say—DeCastro Sisters (58)	0.7
To Love And Be Loved—Frank Sinatra (59)	*0.4*
Serenade—Ray Heindorf & His Orchestra with The Mellomen (56)	*0.0*
Teach Me Tonight—Modernaires Featuring Paula Kelly & George Auld (54)	*0.0*
I'll Never Stop Loving You—Les Baxter & His Orchestra (55)	*0.0*
I'll Never Stop Loving You—David Whitfield with The Roland Shaw Orchestra (55)	*0.0*
Teach Me Tonight—Jo Stafford (54)	*0.0*
Teach Me Tonight—Janet Brace (54)	*0.0*
Love And Marriage—Helen Grayco (55)	*0.0*
Be My Love—Joanie Sommers (60)	*0.0*
Forever, Darling—Desi Arnaz & His Orchestra (56)	*0.0*
If You Can Dream—Lena Horne (56)	*0.0*
Woman's World—Ray Anthony & His Orchestra (54)	*0.0*
(Love Is) The Tender Trap—Ella Fitzgerald (55)	*0.0*
Only Trust Your Heart—Dean Martin (57)	*0.0*
Only Trust Your Heart—Bob Winn (57)	*0.0*
Pete Kelly's Blues—June Christy (55)	*0.0*
Pete Kelly's Blues—Ella Fitzgerald (55)	*0.0*
Serenade—Dick Lee (56)	*0.0*
Three Coins In The Fountain—Four Aces (54)	*0.0*
Three Coins In The Fountain—Frank Sinatra (54)	*0.0*
Jonathan CAIN [John L. Friga] ► 293 (30)	**12200**
Open Arms—Journey (82)	4821
Who's Crying Now—Journey (81)	3618
Separate Ways (Worlds Apart)—Journey (83)	1982
Price Of Love—Bad English (89)	1890
Don't Stop Believin'—Journey (81)	1658
This Could Be The Night—Loverboy (86)	1219
Faithfully—Journey (83)	1200
I'll Be Alright Without You—Journey (86)	1156
Be Good To Yourself—Journey (86)	1150
Only The Young—Journey (85)	927
Girl Can't Help It—Journey (86)	779
Still They Ride—Journey (82)	754
Possession—Bad English (90)	749
Suzanne—Journey (86)	673
After The Fall—Journey (83)	628
Send Her My Love—Journey (83)	590
Straight To Your Heart—Bad English (91)	390
Holdin' On—Tané Cain (82)	376
Turn And Walk Away—Babys (80)	372
Til It's Time To Say Goodbye—Jonathan Cain (76)	319
Forget Me Not—Bad English (89)	310
Why Can't This Night Go On Forever—Journey (87)	171
Heaven Is A 4 Letter Word—Bad English (90)	169
Mega Force—707 (82)	139
Midnight Rendezvous—Babys (80)	68
Wait On Love—Michael Bolton (88)	58
Working Class Man—Jimmy Barnes (86)	53
Sing—Mickey Thomas (89)	37
Allies—Heart (83)	18
Too Much Ain't Enough Love—Jimmy Barnes (88)	5.6
Marie CAIN ► 6190 (1)	**196**
Give Me A Reason To Be Gone—Maureen McGovern (74)	196
Giorgio CALABRESE ► 5745 (5)	**246**
Softly, As I Leave You—Frank Sinatra (64)	*675*
Softly As I Leave You—Matt Monro (62)	*25*
Our Concerto—Steve Lawrence (62)	*25*
Our Concerto—Umberto Bindi (60)	*13*
Our Concerto (Il Nostro Concerto)—Al Martino (60)	*0.0*
Bob CALAME ► 8879 (1)	**37**
Wun'erful, Wun'erful! (Sides Uh-One & Uh-Two)—Stan Freberg (57)	298
—Gilberto Miguel Calderón see: Joe CUBA	
Juan Carlos CALDERÓN ► 1843 (2)	**2208**
Eres Tu (Touch The Wind)—Mocedades (73)	1772
Route 101—Herb Alpert (82)	437

Mark CALDERON ► 1749 (3)	**2368**
All 4 Love—Color Me Badd (91)	5388
I Wanna Sex You Up—Color Me Badd (91)	4560
I Adore Mi Amor—Color Me Badd (91)	4094
Bobby CALDWELL ► 1351 (9)	**3284**
The Next Time I Fall—Peter Cetera (86)	3246
What Kind Of Man Would I Be?—Chicago (89)	1631
What You Won't Do For Love—Bobby Caldwell (78)	1402
Heart Of Mine—Boz Scaggs (88)	429
Coming Down From Love—Bobby Caldwell (80)	139
All Of My Love—Bobby Caldwell (82)	98
Don't Fight The Hands (That Need You)—Hamilton, Joe Frank & Dennison (76)	53
Janet—Commodores (85)	16
Niagara Falls—Chicago (87)	8.9
Gayle CALDWELL ► 4138 (1)	**583**
Cycles—Frank Sinatra (68)	583
Gloria CALDWELL ► 3655 (3)	**747**
Don't Let Me Be Misunderstood—Santa Esmeralda Starring Larry Gomez (77)	*1226*
Don't Let Me Be Misunderstood—Animals (65)	*1016*
Don't Let Me Be Misunderstood—Nina Simone (65)	*0.0*
Nicholas CALDWELL ► 4503 (1)	**475**
Lady—Whispers (80)	475
Ronnie CALDWELL ► 5551 (2)	**272**
Soul Finger—Bar-Kays (67)	1546
Give Everybody Some—Bar-Kays (67)	97
Toy CALDWELL ► 2359 (5)	**1564**
Heard It In A Love Song—Marshall Tucker Band (77)	1453
Can't You See—Marshall Tucker Band (77)	*72*
This Ol' Cowboy—Marshall Tucker Band (75)	20
It Takes Time—Marshall Tucker Band (80)	17
Can't You See—Waylon Jennings (76)	*1.4*
J.J. CALE [John W. Cale, John Weldon Cale] ► 1493 (8)	**2914**
After Midnight—Eric Clapton (70)	*1251*
Crazy Mama—J.J. Cale (72)	778
After Midnight—J.J. Cale (72)	*392*
Lies—J.J. Cale (72)	280
The Sensitive Kind—Santana (81)	171
After Midnight—Maggie Bell (74)	*38*
Hey Baby—J.J. Cale (76)	4.9
Cocaine—Eric Clapton And His Band (80)	0.0
—John W. Cale see: J.J. CALE	
Charlie CALELLO ► 4484 (3)	**482**
New Mexican Rose—4 Seasons (63)	480
(You're Gonna) Hurt Yourself—Frankie Valli (66)	431
Across The Street—Lenny O'Henry (64)	79
—Charles Calhoun see: Jesse STONE	
Kevin CALHOUN [Kevin Calhoun Hazlett] ► 8967 (1)	**35**
When The Radio Is On—Paul Shaffer (89)	70
Ray CALHOUN ► 5895 (1)	**232**
Outstanding—Gap Band (83)	232
Richard CALHOUN ► 6258 (1)	**188**
Stay—Rufus/Chaka Khan (78)	376
Roy CALHOUN [Royalston Calhoun] ► 6389 (1)	**176**
Tear Drops—Lee Andrews And The Hearts (57)	703
William CALHOUN ► 5370 (1)	**299**
Cult Of Personality—Living Colour (89)	1195
Randy CALIFORNIA [Randy Craig Wolfe] ► 3124 (2)	**997**
I Got A Line On You—Spirit (69)	821
1984—Spirit (70)	175
Bob CALILLI ► 2290 (3)	**1645**
Walk Away Renee—Left Banke (66)	*3456*
Walk Away Renee—Four Tops (68)	*1445*
Walk Away Renee—Southside Johnny & The Jukes (86)	*32*
Ugo CALISE ► 7246 (2)	**108**
I Only Know I Love You—Four Aces (56)	*324*
I Only Know I Love You—Johnny Desmond (56)	*0.0*
Ruth CALKINS ► 10640 (1)	**6.5**
I'll Release You—Joann Bon And The Coquettes (67)	*33*
Alex CALL ► 1019 (3)	**4360**
867-5309/Jenny—Tommy Tutone (82)	3051
Perfect World—Huey Lewis and the News (88)	2263
Little Too Late—Pat Benatar (83)	571
Allen CALLAIS [Allen Collay] ► 9837 (1)	**16**
Last Chance—Collay And The Satellites (60)	16

Peter CALLANDER [Peter Robin Callander, Robin Conrad] ▶ 309 (13)	**11725**
Daddy Don't You Walk So Fast—Wayne Newton (72)	5656
Billy, Don't Be A Hero—Bo Donaldson And The Heywoods (74)	*4779*
The Night Chicago Died—Paper Lace (74)	4648
Hitchin' A Ride—Vanity Fare (70)	3768
The Ballad Of Bonnie And Clyde—Georgie Fame (68)	3288
Even The Bad Times Are Good—Tremeloes (67)	509
Suddenly You Love Me—Tremeloes (68)	490
The Black-Eyed Boys—Paper Lace (74)	343
Give Me Time (L'Amore Se Ne Va)—Dusty Springfield (67)	185
Billy--Don't Be A Hero—Paper Lace (74)	*63*
She's My Girl—Bobby Shafto (64)	22
To Make A Big Man Cry—Roy Head (66)	4.2
Who Needs It—Gene Pitney (64)	2.7
John CALLARD ▶ 9046 (1)	**32**
Caterpillar Crawl—Strangers (59)	130
Bobby CALLENDER ▶ 9252 (1)	**28**
Little Star—Bobby Callender (63)	83
George CALLENDER ▶ 2091 (3)	**1888**
Primrose Lane—Jerry Wallace with The Jewels (59)	*3631*
Life's A Holiday—Jerry Wallace (61)	130
Primrose Lane—O.C. Smith (70)	*81*
Terry CALLIER ▶ 4942 (2)	**377**
The Love We Had (Stays On My Mind)—Dells (71)	681
It's All Up To You—Dells (72)	72
Paul CALLIRIS [Thanos Kalliris] ▶ 9958 (1)	**15**
Holding My Heart—Bang (2) (90)	44
—Jo Callis see: John William CALLIS	
John William CALLIS [Jo Callis] ▶ 1169 (5)	**3806**
Don't You Want Me—Human League (82)	7286
(Keep Feeling) Fascination—Human League (83)	1946
Mirror Man—Human League (83)	491
Heart Like A Wheel—Human League (90)	398
The Lebanon—Human League (84)	82
Reggie CALLOWAY ▶ 950 (11)	**4697**
I Wanna Be Rich—Calloway (90)	3279
Casanova—Levert (87)	1899
Jump Start—Natalie Cole (87)	995
Operator—Midnight Star (84)	854
Love Overboard—Gladys Knight And The Pips (87)	739
Wet My Whistle—Midnight Star (83)	274
Freak-A-Zoid—Midnight Star (83)	253
Meeting In The Ladies Room—Klymaxx (85)	193
All The Way—Calloway (90)	152
Joy—Teddy Pendergrass (88)	62
Headlines—Midnight Star (86)	59
Vincent CALLOWAY ▶ 2150 (10)	**1813**
I Wanna Be Rich—Calloway (90)	3279
Jump Start—Natalie Cole (87)	995
Operator—Midnight Star (84)	854
Freak-A-Zoid—Midnight Star (83)	253
Meeting In The Ladies Room—Klymaxx (85)	193
All The Way—Calloway (90)	152
Joy—Teddy Pendergrass (88)	62
Scientific Love—Midnight Star (85)	60
Headlines—Midnight Star (86)	59
No Parking (On The Dance Floor)—Midnight Star (84)	46
Tom CALTON ▶ 9784 (1)	**17**
Half Moon Silver—Hotel (80)	51
Albert CALVERT ▶ 7579 (1)	**88**
My Son, My Son—Vera Lynn (54)	263
Jim CALVERT ▶ 6029 (2)	**214**
Do Something To Me—Tommy James And The Shondells (68)	*639*
Do Something To Me—? And The Mysterians (67)	*3.4*
Billie Rae CALVIN ▶ 10022 (1)	**14**
A Dream's A Dream—Soul II Soul (90)	42
Johnnie CAMACHO ▶ 9924 (1)	**15**
Bongo Guitar (Oye Negra)—Ralph Marterie & His Orchestra (54)	30
Michael CAMACHO ▶ 10762 (1)	**5.5**
Stay True—Sly Fox (86)	5.5
Salvador CAMARATA ▶ 10965 (1)	**4.0**
Goodbye To Toyland—Vonnair Sisters (62)	12
Jimmie CAMERON ▶ 7110 (2)	**115**
It's Only Love—Simply Red (89)	222
Bullish—Herb Alpert/Tijuana Brass (84)	9.1
John CAMERON ▶ 5166 (2)	**332**
1900 Yesterday—Liz Damon's Orient Express (70)	655
Different Strokes—Syl Johnson (67)	8.5
Vella CAMERON ▶ 7189 (1)	**111**
It's Only Love—Simply Red (89)	222
Tony CAMILLO ▶ 1770 (2)	**2345**
Dynomite - Part I—Tony Camillo's Bazuka (75)	1673
I Feel A Song (In My Heart)—Gladys Knight & The Pips (75)	1343
—E. Camino see: Isabel HANSEN	
Mat CAMISON ▶ 7545 (1)	**90**
Pepper Box—Peppers (74)	179
David CAMON ▶ 7589 (2)	**87**
Cry To Me—Loleatta Holloway (75)	101
Somebody's Gotta Win, Somebody's Gotta Lose—Controllers (77)	37
Hamilton CAMP ▶ 6685 (1)	**144**
Here's To You—Hamilton Camp (68)	144
—Barbara Campbell see: Sam COOKE	
—Bonnie Maureen Campbell see: Bonnie OWENS	
Buster CAMPBELL [Prince Buster, Cecil Eustace Bustamente Campbell] ▶ 5550 (1)	**272**
Ten Commandments—Prince Buster (67)	272
—Cecil Eustace Bustamente Campbell see: Buster CAMPBELL	
George CAMPBELL ▶ 2544 (4)	**1398**
Four Walls—Jim Reeves (57)	*1889*
Four Walls—Jim Lowe (57)	*881*
Four Walls—Kay Starr (62)	*26*
Four Walls—Dorothy Collins (57)	*0.0*
Glen CAMPBELL ▶ 10889 (1)	**4.6**
Little Lonely—Chad Allen (61)	9.2
—James Milton Campbell Jr. see: Milton CAMPBELL	
Jeff CAMPBELL ▶ 11129 (1)	**3.1**
Roxanne, Roxanne—UTFO (85)	28
Jimmy CAMPBELL ▶ 4000 (4)	**625**
Try A Little Tenderness—Otis Redding (66)	*946*
Try A Little Tenderness—Three Dog Night (69)	*803*
Try A Little Tenderness—Commitments (91)	*127*
Try A Little Tenderness—Aretha Franklin (62)	*0.4*
Junior CAMPBELL [William Campbell] ▶ 2494 (2)	**1437**
Reflections Of My Life—Marmalade (70)	2469
Rainbow—Marmalade (70)	405
—Linda Marie Campbell see: Linda WOMACK	
Lucie CAMPBELL ▶ 10168 (1)	**12**
He'll Understand (And Say "Well Done")—Pat Boone (57)	12
Luther CAMPBELL [Luke Skyywalker] ▶ 5378 (3)	**298**
Me So Horny—2 Live Crew (89)	729
Banned In The U.S.A.—Luke Featuring 2 Live Crew (90)	588
Pop That Coochie—2 Live Crew (91)	137
Mike CAMPBELL ▶ 952 (10)	**4688**
Stop Draggin' My Heart Around—Stevie Nicks (with Tom Petty And The Heartbreakers) (81)	3309
The Boys Of Summer—Don Henley (84)	2124
Refugee—Tom Petty And The Heartbreakers (80)	1188
You Got Lucky—Tom Petty and The Heartbreakers (82)	1111
The Heart Of The Matter—Don Henley (90)	820
Runnin' Down A Dream—Tom Petty (89)	589
Jammin' Me—Tom Petty and The Heartbreakers (87)	534
Here Comes My Girl—Tom Petty And The Heartbreakers (80)	131
Ways To Be Wicked—Lone Justice (85)	115
A Woman In Love (It's Not Me)—Tom Petty and the Heartbreakers (81)	104
Milton CAMPBELL [Little Milton, James Milton Campbell Jr.] ▶ 6686 (2)	**144**
That's What Love Will Make You Do—Little Milton (72)	141
Friend Of Mine—Little Milton (76)	9.5
Orville B. CAMPBELL ▶ 8660 (3)	**43**
The Golden Rule—'Cile Turner (59)	*123*
Teenage Queen—Johnny Dee with the Bluenotes (57)	5.1
The Golden Rule—Don Rondo (59)	*0.0*
Sterling CAMPBELL ▶ 9010 (1)	**33**
Violence Of Summer (Love's Taking Over)—Duran Duran (90)	165
Tevin CAMPBELL ▶ 3966 (1)	**636**
Tell Me What You Want Me To Do—Tevin Campbell (91)	1907
—William Campbell see: Junior CAMPBELL	
Colin CAMPSIE ▶ 4691 (2)	**438**
Another Lover—Giant Steps (88)	1147
Into You—Giant Steps (89)	166
Al CANDELARIA ▶ 6216 (1)	**192**
Honest I Do—Innocents (60)	577
Mary CANDY ▶ 3633 (1)	**756**
The Men In My Little Girl's Life—Mike Douglas (65)	2269
—Candyman see: John B. SHAFFER III	
Armand CANFORA ▶ 7174 (2)	**112**
Time, Time—Ed Ames (67)	216
Free Again—Barbra Streisand (66)	119
Brian CANHAM ▶ 6233 (1)	**191**
Living In A Dream—Pseudo Echo (87)	191
Coz CANLER ▶ 3240 (3)	**933**
Talking In Your Sleep—Romantics (83)	3966
One In A Million—Romantics (84)	404
Test Of Time—Romantics (85)	115
Warren CANN ▶ 8841 (1)	**38**
Reap The Wild Wind—Ultravox (83)	152
Richie CANNATA ▶ 9369 (1)	**25**
Remo's Theme (What If)—Tommy Shaw (85)	50
Tom CANNING ▶ 7196 (1)	**111**
Breakin' Away—Al Jarreau (81)	332
Ace CANNON ▶ 2059 (1)	**1940**
Tuff—Ace Cannon (61)	1940
Freddy CANNON [Frederick Picariello] ▶ 3088 (2)	**1015**
Tallahassee Lassie—Freddy Cannon (59)	2864
Patty Baby—Freddy Cannon (63)	242
Gus CANNON ▶ 2181 (3)	**1778**
Walk Right In—Rooftop Singers (62)	*6902*
Walk Right In—Dr. Hook (77)	*188*
Walk Right In—Moments (1) (63)	*23*
Hughie CANNON ▶ 933 (11)	**4756**
Frankie And Johnny—Sam Cooke (63)	*1389*
Won't You Come Home Bill Bailey—Bobby Darin (60)	*1030*
Frankie And Johnny—Elvis Presley (66)	*908*
Frankie And Johnny—Brook Benton (61)	*809*
Frankie's Man Johnny—Johnny Cash (59)	*364*
The New "Frankie And Johnnie" Song—Greenwood County Singers (64)	*115*
Bill Bailey, Won't You Please Come Home—Ella Fitzgerald (63)	*79*
Won'cha Come Home, Bill Bailey—Della Reese (61)	*53*
Bill Bailey Won't You Please Come Home—Brenda Lee (59)	*46*
Frankie And Johnny—Sylvia Robbins (60)	*23*
Bill Bailey, Won't You Please Come Home—Maria Marshall (56)	*17*
Michael CANOSA ▶ 4527 (2)	**470**
I Was Such A Fool (To Fall In Love With You)—Connie Francis (62)	*833*
I Was Such A Fool (To Fall In Love With You)—Flamingos (60)	*107*
Larry CANSLER ▶ 1915 (2)	**2115**
Wildfire—Michael Murphey (75)	4221
School Teacher—Kenny Rogers And The First Edition (72)	7.9
Giuseppe CANTARELLI ▶ 3204 (2)	**955**
I Still Believe—Brenda K. Starr (88)	1275
Another Night—Aretha Franklin (86)	634
Don CANTON ▶ 6452 (2)	**167**
Over The Weekend—Playboys (58)	302
Five Hundred Guys—Frank Sinatra (56)	133
William E. CANTRELL ▶ 10928 (1)	**4.3**
I'm Serious—Hilltoppers (57)	8.6
Anna CANTÙ [Mamared] ▶ 11136 (1)	**3.1**
Can't Hold Back (Your Loving)—Kano (81)	12
Jim CAPALDI ▶ 2419 (9)	**1502**
One And Only Man—Steve Winwood (90)	737
That's Love—Jim Capaldi (83)	554
It's All Right—Jim Capaldi (74)	244
Hearts On Fire—Steve Winwood (89)	205

Jim CAPALDI ▶ 2419 (9) *Continued*	**1502**
Empty Pages—Traffic (70)	166
Paper Sun—Traffic Featuring Stevie Winwood (67)	108
Living On The Edge—Jim Capaldi (83)	103
Some Come Running—Jim Capaldi (88)	19
Eve—Jim Capaldi (72)	13
Frank CAPANO ▶ 5311 (3)	**308**
You Wanted Someone To Play With (I Wanted Someone To Love)—Frankie Laine (67)	459
Tears—Bobby Vinton (66)	*382*
Tears (For Souvenirs)—Ken Dodd (66)	*5.7*
Jerry CAPEHART ▶ 609 (11)	**7073**
Turn Around, Look At Me—Vogues (68)	*3450*
Summertime Blues—Blue Cheer (68)	*2126*
Summertime Blues—Eddie Cochran (58)	*1493*
Summertime Blues—Who (70)	*976*
Dutchman's Gold—Walter Brennan With Billy Vaughn And His Orchestra (60)	578
C'mon Everybody—Eddie Cochran (58)	*493*
Turn Around, Look At Me—Glen Campbell (61)	*447*
C'mon Everybody—Jive Bunny And The Mastermixers (89)	*80*
Turn Around, Look At Me—Lettermen (62)	*9.9*
Summertime Blues—Jive Bunny & The Mastermixers (90)	*6.7*
Teenage Heaven—Eddie Cochran (59)	0.8
John CAPEK ▶ 2221 (2)	**1728**
Rhythm Of My Heart—Rod Stewart (91)	3022
Pieces Of Ice—Diana Ross (83)	434
Bobby CAPERS ▶ 11073 (1)	**3.4**
El Pussy Cat—Mongo Santamaria (65)	3.4
Cathi CAPIOLA ▶ 9800 (1)	**17**
Shiver And Shake—Silencers (80)	34
Arnold CAPITANELLI ▶ 4751 (2)	**423**
Move In A Little Closer, Baby—Mama Cass (69)	302
I Can't Live A Dream—Osmonds (76)	272
Leonard L. CAPIZZI ▶ 968 (3)	**4623**
Monster Mash—Bobby (Boris) Pickett And The Crypt-Kickers (62)	*7305*
Monster Mash—Bobby (Boris) Pickett And The Crypt-Kickers (73)	*1895*
Monster Mash—Bobby (Boris) Pickett And The Crypt-Kickers (70)	*47*
Gilbert CAPLE ▶ 3175 (2)	**971**
Last Night—Mar-Keys (61)	4476
Good Time Charlie—Bobby Bland (66)	227
Paul CAPLIN ▶ 10024 (1)	**14**
Shiny Shiny—Haysi Fantayzee (83)	42
—Aldo Caponi see: Don BACKY	
—Aldo Caporuscio see: Aldo NOVA	
Edilio CAPOTOSTI ▶ 11338 (1)	**2.2**
She Will Survive (Poland)—Bobby Vinton (82)	6.5
John CAPPELLO ▶ 9665 (1)	**19**
Ballad Of A Girl And Boy—Graduates (59)	77
Al CAPPS ▶ 1065 (2)	**4153**
Half-Breed—Cher (73)	6135
She's Just My Style—Gary Lewis And The Playboys (65)	4343
Remo CAPRA ▶ 6163 (1)	**198**
The Prophecy Of Daniel And John The Divine (Six-Six-Six)—Cowsills (69)	198
Irene CARA [Irene Cara Escalera] ▶ 984 (6)	**4547**
Flashdance...What A Feeling—Irene Cara (83)	9574
Breakdance—Irene Cara (84)	1574
Why Me?—Irene Cara (83)	1151
Anyone Can See—Irene Cara (81)	542
The Dream (Hold On To Your Dream)—Irene Cara (83)	489
You Were Made For Me—Irene Cara (84)	27
Michael CARABELLO ▶ 5810 (1)	**240**
No One To Depend On—Santana (72)	719
—Caravelli see: Claude VASORI	
Guy CARAWAN ▶ 11607 (1)	**1.0**
We Shall Overcome—Joan Baez (63)	5.0
Joey CARBONE ▶ 6185 (1)	**196**
Love You Like I Never Loved Before—John O'Banion (81)	588
Martin CARBOO ▶ 8096 (1)	**62**
Got To Get—Leila K with Rob 'N' Raz (90)	248
—Anthony E. Cardenas see: Tony MONTANA	

George CARDINI ▶ 9589 (1)	**21**
From The Bottom Of My Heart (Dammi, Dammi, Dammi)—Dean Martin (62)	41
Jack CARDWELL ▶ 5201 (1)	**328**
Jesus Is A Soul Man—Lawrence Reynolds (69)	656
Ralph CARE ▶ 8441 (2)	**50**
Goodbye Charlie—Patti Page (59)	83
I Envy—Nat "King" Cole (54)	27
Bill CAREY ▶ 11269 (1)	**2.5**
Nuevo Laredo—Les Paul and Mary Ford (56)	10
Bob CAREY ▶ 1713 (4)	**2448**
Banana Boat Song—Tarriers (56)	*4406*
Banana Boat Song—Fontane Sisters (56)	*1239*
Banana Boat Song—Steve Lawrence (56)	*939*
Banana Boat Song—Sarah Vaughan (56)	*758*
Jake CAREY ▶ 9035 (1)	**33**
Mio Amore—Flamingos (60)	196
Mariah CAREY ▶ 288 (6)	**12371**
Love Takes Time—Mariah Carey (90)	4682
Emotions—Mariah Carey (91)	4618
Vision Of Love—Mariah Carey (90)	4507
Someday—Mariah Carey (91)	4433
Can't Let Go—Mariah Carey (91)	4348
I Don't Wanna Cry—Mariah Carey (91)	3692
Tony CAREY ▶ 2406 (5)	**1516**
A Fine Fine Day—Tony Carey (84)	688
The First Day Of Summer—Tony Carey (84)	402
Why Me?—Planet P (83)	225
West Coast Summer Nights—Tony Carey (83)	147
I Won't Be Home Tonight—Tony Carey (83)	54
Zeke CAREY ▶ 8887 (2)	**37**
Mio Amore—Flamingos (60)	196
The Boogaloo Party—Flamingos (66)	13
Frank CARI [Frank Cariola] ▶ 7961 (2)	**67**
High On A Hill—Scott English (64)	90
One Heart—George Hamilton IV (58)	44
Pier Quinto CARIAGGI ▶ 10856 (1)	**4.9**
Dear Gesu Bambino—Christian Morandi (61)	9.7
Jon CARIN ▶ 8184 (2)	**59**
Learning To Fly—Pink Floyd (87)	86
State Of The Nation—Industry (83)	76
—Frank Cariola see: Frank CARI	
Billy CARL ▶ 6378 (3)	**177**
Goody Goody Gumdrops—1910 Fruitgum Co. (68)	638
(We'll Meet In The) "Yellow Forest"—Jay & The Americans (67)	32
Diane—Golden Gate (70)	4.4
Max CARL [Max C. Gronenthal] ▶ 3436 (5)	**849**
Second Chance—Thirty Eight Special (89)	1786
The Sound Of Your Voice—.38 Special (91)	423
Comin' Down Tonight—38 Special (89)	167
Rock & Roll Strategy—Thirty Eight Special (88)	163
Somewhere, Somebody—Aaron Neville (91)	73
Frankie CARLE ▶ 8951 (2)	**35**
Sunrise Serenade—Willie Mitchell (62)	33
Oh! What It Seemed To Be—Castells (62)	7.9
Bob CARLETON ▶ 9029 (1)	**33**
Ja-Da—Johnny And The Hurricanes (61)	33
Jeff CARLISI ▶ 1983 (10)	**2035**
Second Chance—Thirty Eight Special (89)	1786
Caught Up In You—38 Special (82)	1470
Like No Other Night—38 Special (86)	857
If I'd Been The One—38 Special (83)	839
Hold On Loosely—.38 Special (81)	550
The Sound Of Your Voice—.38 Special (91)	423
You Keep Runnin' Away—38 Special (82)	410
Somebody Like You—38 Special (86)	322
Fantasy Girl—.38 Special (81)	232
Comin' Down Tonight—38 Special (89)	167
Sam CARLISI ▶ 11791 (1)	**0.0**
Love I You—Gaylords (54)	0.0
Crystal CARLISLE ▶ 9393 (1)	**25**
This Time Make It Funky—Tracie Spencer (91)	123
Randall CARLISLE ▶ 6962 (1)	**125**
Please, Mr. President—Paula Webb (75)	125
—Tyran Carlo see: Billy DAVIS	
Harry CARLSON ▶ 9363 (1)	**25**
When You Took Your Love (From Me)—Jimmy Dorsey Orchestra (58)	76
—Lisa Keith Carlson see: Lisa KEITH	

John CARLTON ▶ 9192 (1)	**29**
Amerikan Music—Steve Alaimo (72)	58
Russ CARLYLE [Phillip Gantose] ▶ 6876 (4)	**131**
Stashu Pandowski (She's Not Very Much Good For Pretty)—Russ Carlyle And The Coachmen (57)	*193*
Stashu Pandowski (She's Not Very Much Good For Pretty)—Julius La Rosa (57)	*69*
Stashu Pandowski (She's Not Very Much Good For Pretty)—Toppers (57)	*0.0*
Stashu Pandowski (She's Not Very Much Good For Pretty)—Ray Henry & His Orchestra (57)	*0.0*
Brian CARMAN ▶ 1250 (1)	**3580**
Pipeline—Chantay's (63)	3580
Denny CARMASSI ▶ 8554 (1)	**46**
How Can I Refuse—Heart (83)	279
Eric CARMEN ▶ 130 (22)	**20589**
All By Myself—Eric Carmen (75)	5141
That's Rock 'N' Roll—Shaun Cassidy (77)	3524
Go All The Way—Raspberries (72)	3209
Make Me Lose Control—Eric Carmen (88)	2490
Almost Paradise...Love Theme From FOOTLOOSE—Mike Reno And Ann Wilson (84)	1939
I Wanna Be With You—Raspberries (72)	1793
Hey Deanie—Shaun Cassidy (77)	1486
Never Gonna Fall In Love Again—Eric Carmen (76)	1451
Let's Pretend—Raspberries (73)	1313
Change Of Heart—Eric Carmen (78)	983
She Did It—Eric Carmen (77)	834
Overnight Sensation (Hit Record)—Raspberries (74)	659
Sunrise—Eric Carmen (76)	490
I Wanna Hear It From Your Lips—Eric Carmen (85)	384
Tonight—Raspberries (73)	365
It Hurts Too Much—Eric Carmen (80)	64
She Did It—Michael Damian (81)	42
I'm Through With Love—Eric Carmen (85)	37
I'm A Rocker—Raspberries (73)	27
I Need You—Euclid Beach Band (79)	27
Don't Want To Say Goodbye—Raspberries (72)	27
Boats Against The Current—Eric Carmen (77)	20
—Delyle Gregory Carmichael see: C. Delyle GREGORY	
—Greg Carmichael see: C. Delyle GREGORY	
Hoagy CARMICHAEL ▶ 695 (23) HOF	**6260**
Georgia On My Mind—Ray Charles (60)	*4142*
Star Dust—Billy Ward And His Dominoes (57)	*1814*
Heart And Soul—Cleftones (61)	*1608*
Lazy River—Bobby Darin (61)	*1246*
Ole Buttermilk Sky—Bill Black's Combo (61)	701
Up A Lazy River—Si Zentner And His Orchestra (61)	*547*
Heart And Soul—Jan & Dean (61)	*515*
Stardust—Nino Tempo & April Stevens (64)	*465*
Georgia On My Mind—Michael Bolton (90)	*390*
Star Dust Mambo—Richard Maltby And His Orchestra (54)	*148*
Georgia On My Mind—Righteous Brothers (66)	*112*
Heart And Soul—Johnny Maddox (56)	*111*
Verse Of Stardust—Eddie Dexter and His Band (55)	*90*
Lazy River—Roberta Sherwood (56)	*46*
Georgia On My Mind—Willie Nelson (78)	*41*
Georgia On My Mind—Wes Montgomery (68)	*38*
Stardust—Frank Sinatra (62)	*34*
Star Dust—Connee Boswell (56)	*32*
Stardust—Nat "King" Cole (57)	*31*
Star Dust—Jaye P. Morgan And The Morgan Brothers (58)	*8.5*
Star Dust—Philip Green And His Orchestra (55)	*6.8*
Heart And Soul—Tom & Dan (56)	*0.0*
Lazy River—Cathy Ryan (56)	*0.0*
James CARMICHAEL [James Anthony Carmichael, Charlemagne] ▶ 6966 (1)	**125**
Glasshouse—Temptations (75)	499
Ralph CARMICHAEL ▶ 6558 (1)	**157**
We Love You, Call Collect—Art Linkletter (69)	314
Kim CARNES ▶ 1042 (15)	**4228**
Don't Fall In Love With A Dreamer—Kenny Rogers with Kim Carnes (80)	3393
Crazy In The Night (Barking At Airplanes)—Kim Carnes (85)	760
Draw Of The Cards—Kim Carnes (81)	564
Voyeur—Kim Carnes (82)	516
Does It Make You Remember—Kim Carnes (82)	507

Kim CARNES ▶ 1042 (15) *Continued*	**4228**
You're A Part Of Me—Gene Cotton With Kim Carnes (78)	*470*
Make No Mistake, He's Mine—Barbra Streisand (Duet With Kim Carnes) (84)	300
You Make My Heart Beat Faster (And That's All That Matters)—Kim Carnes (84)	172
It Hurts So Bad—Kim Carnes (79)	169
Invitation To Dance—Kim Carnes (85)	122
Mistaken Identity—Kim Carnes (81)	121
Abadabadango—Kim Carnes (85)	82
Divided Hearts—Kim Carnes (86)	70
You're A Part Of Me—Susan Jacks (75)	*22*
You Turned My World Around—Frank Sinatra (74)	14
John CARNEY ▶ 8921 (1)	**36**
Hands Across America—Voices Of America (86)	108
Richard CARNEY ▶ 10042 (1)	**14**
Faraway Star—Chordettes (61)	27
—Russell Caron see: Greg SCELSA	
Mercury CARONIA ▶ 8858 (1)	**38**
State Of The Nation—Industry (83)	76
Joe CARONNA ▶ 10365 (1)	**9.4**
Alimony—Frankie Ford (59)	28
Renato CAROSONE ▶ 4619 (3)	**449**
Torero—Renato Carosone (58)	*899*
Torero—Julius La Rosa (58)	*0.0*
Torero—Andrews Sisters (58)	*0.0*
Dave CARPENDER ▶ 11166 (1)	**2.9**
Every Love Song—Greg Kihn Band (82)	15
Charles CARPENTER ▶ 3159 (1)	**978**
You Can Depend On Me—Brenda Lee (61)	2935
—Clarence E. Carpenter see: Pete CARPENTER	
Marion CARPENTER ▶ 11625 (1)	**0.9**
Won't You Come On Back—Fats Domino (62)	2.8
Pete CARPENTER [Clarence E. Carpenter] ▶ 2926 (3)	**1114**
The Rockford Files—Mike Post (75)	1507
Theme From Magnum P.I.—Mike Post (82)	718
Theme From "Baa Baa Black Sheep"—Mike Post (77)	3.3
Richard CARPENTER ▶ 606 (9)	**7128**
Top Of The World—Carpenters (73)	*5097*
Yesterday Once More—Carpenters (73)	*4231*
Only Yesterday—Carpenters (75)	2333
Goodbye To Love—Carpenters (72)	1867
I Need To Be In Love—Carpenters (76)	634
Those Good Old Dreams—Carpenters (81)	93
Yesterday Once More—Spinners (81)	*84*
Top Of The World—Lynn Anderson (73)	*74*
Merry Christmas Darling—Carpenters (70)	56
Robert CARPENTER ▶ 5629 (2)	**263**
Make A Little Magic—Dirt Band (80)	684
Fire In The Sky—Dirt Band (81)	69
Brad CARR ▶ 9130 (1)	**31**
Run To Paradise—Choirboys (89)	61
Jerry CARR ▶ 5388 (2)	**296**
Rosie Lee—Mello-Tones (57)	*296*
Rosie Lee—Tunedrops (57)	*0.0*
—Joe "Fingers" Carr see: Louis F. BUSH	
Leon CARR ▶ 590 (24)	**7369**
Hey There Lonely Girl—Eddie Holman (69)	*5248*
Hotel Happiness—Brook Benton (62)	2976
Gina—Johnny Mathis (62)	2333
Clinging Vine—Bobby Vinton (64)	1138
Most People Get Married—Patti Page (62)	683
Hey There Lonely Boy—Ruby And The Romantics (63)	*635*
Hey There Lonely Girl—Robert John (80)	*523*
Another Cup Of Coffee—Brook Benton (64)	317
Our Everlasting Love—Ruby And The Romantics (64)	270
She Lets Her Hair Down (Early In The Morning)—Tokens (69)	*259*
My Shy Violet—Mills Brothers (68)	207
The Young New Mexican Puppeteer—Tom Jones (72)	177
You Don't Need Me For Anything Anymore—Brenda Lee (69)	117
My Baby's Got Such Lovin' Ways—McGuire Sisters (56)	66
Big Name Button—Royal Teens (58)	53
Two Thousand Two Hundred Twenty Three Miles—Patti Page (60)	45
She Lets Her Hair Down (Early In The Morning)—Gene Pitney (69)	*36*
I'd Do It All Again—Vikki Carr (72)	12
High On The Hill Of Hope—Patti Page (63)	9.9
Boy On Page Thirty Five—Cathy Carr (56)	6.1
Raisin' Sugar Cane—Untouchables (61)	4.3
Julie Knows—Randy Sparks (64)	0.5
She Lets Her Hair Down (Early In The Morning)—Don Young (69)	0.0
Hula Hoop—Steve Allen (58)	*0.0*
Michael CARR [Maurice Alfred Cohen] ▶ 6244 (5)	**190**
The Bandit—Johnston Brothers (54)	*349*
Dreamer—Four Aces (56)	135
The Bandit—Tex Ritter (54)	*10*
Oh! My Love (Keep Your Dreams Just For Me)—June Valli (55)	6.5
The Bandit—Frank Weir & His Orchestra (54)	*0.0*
Phyllis CARR ▶ 5954 (1)	**223**
Down The Aisle Of Love—Quin-Tones (58)	670
Robert CARR ▶ 6482 (5)	**165**
We Belong Together—Robert & Johnny (58)	*339*
We Belong Together—Jimmy Velvet (63)	*151*
I Believe In You—Robert & Johnny (58)	4.3
We Belong Together—Robert & Johnny (61)	*0.0*
We Belong Together—Belmonts (61)	*0.0*
William CARR ▶ 10933 (1)	**4.3**
I'm Gonna Make You Mine—Shadows Of Knight (66)	13
Paul CARRACK ▶ 926 (6)	**4774**
How Long—Ace (75)	*3890*
I Live By The Groove—Paul Carrack (89)	542
I Need You—Paul Carrack (82)	476
One Good Reason—Paul Carrack (88)	465
How Long—Rod Stewart (82)	*203*
Rock & Roll Runaway—Ace (75)	77
Keith CARRADINE ▶ 2457 (1)	**1467**
I'm Easy—Keith Carradine (76)	1467
Bobbie CARROL ▶ 9450 (2)	**23**
Teen Age Doll—Tommy Sands (58)	17
Talk Of The School—Sonny James (59)	12
Bert CARROLL [Bert Klamkin] ▶ 2711 (2)	**1257**
Wear My Ring Around Your Neck—Elvis Presley (58)	3714
Jimmy Love—Cathy Carroll (61)	38
—Candy Carroll see: Carolyn FRANKLIN	
David CARROLL [Nook Schrier, Ralph Sterling] ▶ 4479 (2)	**485**
Mostly Martha—Crew-Cuts (55)	544
Shish Kebab—Ralph Marterie And His Orchestra (57)	427
Earl CARROLL ▶ 6994 (1)	**123**
Ain't That Just Like Me—Searchers (64)	246
Eddie CARROLL ▶ 6091 (1)	**206**
How Is Julie?—Lettermen (62)	413
Greg CARROLL ▶ 2744 (6)	**1227**
Just One Look—Doris Troy (63)	*1890*
Just One Look—Linda Ronstadt (79)	*260*
Just One Look—Hollies (67)	*251*
Just One Look—Hollies (64)	*38*
Just One Look—Anne Murray (74)	*13*
What'cha Gonna Do About It—Doris Troy (63)	0.5
Harry CARROLL ▶ 11584 (1) HOF	**1.1**
I'm Always Chasing Rainbows—Joe Pica (58)	3.3
Jonathan CARROLL ▶ 4274 (1)	**538**
Get Closer—Linda Ronstadt (82)	538
—Ron Carroll see: Ron VOLZ	
—Roy Carroll see: Milt GABLER	
Willis CARROLL ▶ 4134 (4)	**584**
Seven Days—Crew-Cuts (56)	*658*
Seven Days—Dorothy Collins (56)	*367*
Seven Days—Clyde McPhatter (56)	*142*
Seven Days—Snooky Lanson (56)	*0.0*
David CARRON ▶ 5301 (1)	**310**
Clones (We're All)—Alice Cooper (80)	310
Jenny Lou CARSON [Virginia Lucille Overstake] ▶ 1460 (10)	**2986**
Let Me Go Lover—Joan Weber (54)	*5883*
Let Me Go Lover—Teresa Brewer with The Lancers (54)	*1376*
Jealous Heart—Connie Francis (65)	*615*
Jealous Heart—Tab Hunter (58)	*408*
Let Me Go Lover—Patti Page (54)	*216*
Period—Four Knights (54)	84
Jealous Heart—Fontane Sisters (58)	*11*
Jealous Heart—Les Paul and Mary Ford (58)	*0.0*
Let Me Go, Lover!—Sunny Gale (54)	*0.0*
Let Me Go, Lover!—Peggy Lee (55)	*0.0*
—Milton Carson see: Harold FIELDS	
—Milton Carson see: Howard Ellington Riddiford BARNES	
—Milton Carson see: Joseph RONCORONI	
—Wayne Carson see: Wayne Carson THOMPSON	
Victor CARSTARPHEN ▶ 2945 (7)	**1106**
Wake Up Everybody (Part 1)—Harold Melvin And The Blue Notes (75)	1592
Bad Luck (Part 1)—Harold Melvin And The Blue Notes (75)	*1407*
Where Are All My Friends—Harold Melvin And The Blue Notes (74)	117
Bad Luck—Ritchie Family (76)	*92*
Tell The World How I Feel About 'Cha Baby—Harold Melvin And The Blue Notes (76)	66
Let's Groove—Archie Bell & The Drells (76)	38
Bad Luck—Atlanta Disco Band (76)	*14*
Hans CARSTE [Hans Haring] ▶ 2641 (3)	**1300**
Those Lazy-Hazy-Crazy Days Of Summer—Nat King Cole (63)	2528
In The Alps (In Der Schweiz)—Lawrence Welk And His Champagne Music And The McGuire Sisters (56)	63
Continental Melody—Billy Vaughn And His Orchestra (62)	4.1
Nico CARSTENS ▶ 7050 (5)	**119**
Sadie's Shawl—Bob Sharples And His Music (56)	*293*
Kwela Kwela—Bill Hayes (55)	34
Zambezi—Lou Busch and His Orchestra (55)	26
Sadie's Shawl—Richard Hayman And Jan August (56)	*0.0*
Sadie's Shawl—Philip Green & His Gob Music (56)	*0.0*
Anita CARTER ▶ 11151 (1)	**3.0**
Rosanna's Going Wild—Johnny Cash (68)	9.0
—Barry Eugene Carter see: Barry WHITE	
Benny CARTER ▶ 8583 (2)	**46**
The Basie Twist—Count Basie and His Orchestra (61)	33
Once Upon A Time—Dean Martin (58)	25
Blanche CARTER ▶ 1310 (2)	**3382**
Devil Or Angel—Bobby Vee (60)	*3382*
Devil Or Angel—Hollywood Flames (60)	*0.0*
—Bo Carter see: Armetia CHATMAN	
—Bobby Carter see: Bobby COTTER	
Bruce CARTER ▶ 11214 (1)	**2.7**
Let's Dance (Make Your Body Move)—West Street Mob (81)	30
Buster CARTER ▶ 9419 (1)	**24**
Roll In My Sweet Baby's Arms—Hank Wilson (73)	72
Calvin CARTER ▶ 1271 (13)	**3484**
He Don't Love You (Like I Love You)—Tony Orlando & Dawn (75)	*4607*
He Will Break Your Heart—Jerry Butler (60)	*3246*
You're Looking Good—Dee Clark (60)	540
Goodnight, Sweetheart, Goodnight—McGuire Sisters (54)	*514*
Your Friends—Dee Clark (61)	511
Walk On With The Duke—Duke Of Earl (62)	86
He Don't Love You—Jim Croce (76)	*76*
The Sun Is Shining—Jimmy Reed (57)	45
Everyone's Laughing—Spaniels (57)	23
Don't Walk Away From Me—Dee Clark (61)	17
He Will Break Your Heart—Righteous Brothers (66)	*4.8*
A Lonely Soldier—Jerry Butler (60)	0.7
Goodnight, Sweetheart, Goodnight—Sunny Gale (54)	*0.0*
Carlene CARTER ▶ 5827 (1)	**238**
One Step Closer—Doobie Brothers (80)	715
Charles CARTER ▶ 10276 (1)	**11**
Snap Shot—Slave (81)	53
Chip CARTER [Fernando Alan Carter] ▶ 11614 (1)	**1.0**
Love Me Just For Me—Special Generation (90)	6.8
Clarence CARTER ▶ 2035 (10)	**1979**
Too Weak To Fight—Clarence Carter (68)	2074
Tell Mama—Etta James (67)	902
Snatching It Back—Clarence Carter (69)	884
I Can't Leave Your Love Alone—Clarence Carter (70)	597
Doin' Our Thing—Clarence Carter (69)	434
I'd Rather Be An Old Man's Sweetheart (Than A Young Man's Fool)—Candi Staton (69)	422
Sweet Feeling—Candi Staton (70)	373

Clarence CARTER ▶ 2035 (10) *Continued*	**1979**
Looking For A Fox—Clarence Carter (68)	137
Funky Fever—Clarence Carter (68)	20
Thread The Needle—Clarence Carter (67)	1.4
Colin CARTER ▶ 5057 (1)	**353**
Small Beginnings—Flash (72)	706
Darryl CARTER ▶ 4187 (5)	**569**
Woman's Gotta Have It—(The Preacher) Bobby Womack (72)	468
No Sad Songs—Joe Simon (67)	338
Back For A Taste Of Your Love—Syl Johnson (73)	70
More Than I Can Stand—Bobby Womack (70)	56
How I Miss You Baby—Bobby Womack (69)	47
Deborah CARTER [Deborah Carter Hall] ▶ 4131 (1)	**584**
Give It Up—KC (83)	1169
Don CARTER ▶ 4510 (2)	**474**
Tell Me Why—Belmonts (61)	941
(How Can I Write On Paper) What I Feel In My Heart—Jim Reeves (61)	14
Earl CARTER ▶ 10254 (1)	**11**
I've Got Love For My Baby—Young Hearts (68)	43
Edward CARTER ▶ 8550 (1)	**46**
Romeo—Mr. Big (77)	93
—Fernando Alan Carter see: Chip CARTER	
Fred CARTER ▶ 7937 (2)	**69**
It Just Happened That Way—Dean Martin (66)	57
A Million Teardrops—Conway Twitty (61)	11
Helen CARTER ▶ 7925 (2)	**69**
What Am I Supposed To Do—Ann-Margret (62)	66
Rosanna's Going Wild—Johnny Cash (68)	9.0
—Jake Carter see: Joe CARTER	
James CARTER ▶ 9444 (1)	**23**
Latin Active—A Lighter Shade Of Brown (91)	164
Jerry CARTER ▶ 5569 (1)	**270**
Take A Look Around—Smith (70)	540
Joe CARTER [Jake Carter] ▶ 6581 (1)	**154**
Keep It Comin'—Keith Sweat (91)	925
John CARTER [John Nicholas Shakespeare] ▶ 493 (16)	**8492**
Little Bit O' Soul—Music Explosion (67)	*6710*
Can't You Hear My Heartbeat—Herman's Hermits (65)	5330
Beach Baby—First Class (74)	2201
Is It True—Brenda Lee (64)	1118
Sunday For Tea—Peter And Gordon (67)	525
Sleepy Joe—Herman's Hermits (68)	276
Tossing & Turning—Ivy League (65)	220
My World Fell Down—Sagittarius (67)	154
Cowboy Convention—Ohio Express (69)	144
Peek-A-Boo—New Vaudeville Band (67)	86
Sunshine Girl—Herman's Hermits (68)	80
Dreams Are Ten A Penny—First Class (74)	69
Knock Knock Who's There—Mary Hopkin (72)	57
Little Bit O' Soul—Bullet (72)	*50*
Funny How Love Can Be—First Class (75)	37
Let's Go To San Francisco—Stars On 45 (81)	12
John S. CARTER ▶ 945 (5)	**4711**
Incense And Peppermints—Strawberry Alarm Clock (67)	7462
Don't Call Us, We'll Call You—Sugarloaf/Jerry Corbetta (74)	1633
Take The L.—Motels (82)	228
That Acapulco Gold—Rainy Daze (67)	169
Sea Shell—Strawberry Alarm Clock (68)	5.2
June CARTER [June Carter Cash] ▶ 3092 (3)	**1012**
Ring Of Fire—Johnny Cash (63)	1576
The Matador—Johnny Cash (63)	443
Rosanna's Going Wild—Johnny Cash (68)	9.0
Lonnie CARTER ▶ 11451 (1)	**1.6**
Little Turtle Dove—Otis Williams And His Charms (61)	4.9
Ralph CARTER ▶ 7547 (2)	**89**
Shakin'—Eddie Money (82)	192
Club Michelle—Eddie Money (84)	101
Robert Ashley CARTER ▶ 5905 (1)	**231**
Mama Used To Say—Junior (82)	461
Robert William CARTER ▶ 8699 (1)	**42**
I Just Can't Control Myself—Nature's Divine (79)	127

Roy CARTER ▶ 9810 (1)	**17**
Walking Into Sunshine—Central Line (81)	50
Simon Kenneth CARTER ▶ 9320 (1)	**26**
I Don't Know What It Is, But It Sure Is Funky—Ripple (73)	184
Valerie CARTER ▶ 4219 (1)	**557**
Cook With Honey—Judy Collins (73)	557
Walter CARTER ▶ 9321 (1)	**26**
I Don't Know What It Is, But It Sure Is Funky—Ripple (73)	184
Ric CARTEY ▶ 562 (7)	**7680**
Young Love—Tab Hunter (57)	*8452*
Young Love—Sonny James (56)	*5688*
Young Love—Donny Osmond (73)	*531*
Young Love—Crew-Cuts (56)	*343*
Young Love—Lesley Gore (66)	*334*
Young Love—Ray Stevens (76)	*13*
Young Love—Ric Cartey with The Jiva-Tones (56)	*0.0*
Clifford CASABON ▶ 9348 (1)	**26**
Little Becky's Christmas Wish—Becky Lamb (67)	51
Arturo CASADEI ▶ 7071 (2)	**118**
Sole Sole Sole—Siw Malmkvist - Umberto Marcato (64)	180
Kiss Me And Kiss Me And Kiss Me (Tre Volte Baciami)—Perry Como (59)	111
Art CASADO ▶ 10371 (1)	**9.4**
Because Of You—Kracker (72)	47
Jack CASADY ▶ 7318 (1)	**102**
Pretty As You Feel—Jefferson Airplane (71)	512
Jerry CASALE ▶ 3133 (2)	**992**
Whip It—Devo (80)	1829
Theme From Doctor Detroit—Devo (83)	155
Jorge CASAS ▶ 4148 (3)	**580**
Get On Your Feet—Gloria Estefan (89)	1093
Can't Forget You—Gloria Estefan (91)	423
Oye Mi Canto (Hear My Voice)—Gloria Estefan (90)	225
Jacques CASCALES ▶ 8019 (1)	**65**
In This Whole Wide World—Four Preps (61)	130
—Juan Ricardo Cascales see: Johnny RICHARDS	
John CASCELLA ▶ 7827 (1)	**73**
You're My Weakness—Faith Band (79)	73
Peter CASE ▶ 10808 (1)	**5.2**
A Million Miles Away—Plimsouls (83)	16
Sonny CASELLA ▶ 8339 (2)	**54**
Bump Me Baby Pt. 1—Dooley Silverspoon (75)	53
It's-A-Happening—Magic Mushrooms (66)	3.8
Al CASEY ▶ 2284 (3)	**1654**
Forty Miles Of Bad Road—Duane Eddy His "Twangy" guitar and The Rebels (59)	2380
Ramrod—Duane Eddy his "twangy" guitar and The Rebels (58)	462
Cookin'—Al Casey Combo (62)	7.2
Harry Wayne CASEY ▶ 137 (26)	**19986**
That's The Way (I Like It)—K.C. & The Sunshine Band (75)	*6457*
Please Don't Go—K.C. & The Sunshine Band (79)	6091
(Shake, Shake, Shake) Shake Your Booty—K C & The Sunshine Band (76)	4899
I'm Your Boogie Man—K C & The Sunshine Band (77)	4680
Get Down Tonight—K.C. & The Sunshine Band (75)	4656
Keep It Comin' Love—KC & The Sunshine Band (77)	4615
Rock Your Baby—George McCrae (74)	4499
Give It Up—KC (83)	1169
Dance Across The Floor—Jimmy "Bo" Horne (78)	502
Boogie Shoes—KC & The Sunshine Band (78)	501
I Like To Do It—KC & The Sunshine Band (76)	385
I Get Lifted—George McCrae (75)	352
Do You Wanna Go Party—KC & The Sunshine Band (79)	238
Wrap Your Arms Around Me—K C & The Sunshine Band (77)	210
I Can't Leave You Alone—George McCrae (74)	161
Who Do Ya Love—KC & The Sunshine Band (78)	115
Honey I—George McCrae (76)	106
That's The Way I Like It—Ritchie Family (76)	*92*
Queen Of Clubs—K.C. & The Sunshine Band (76)	87
Do You Feel All Right—KC & The Sunshine Band (78)	64
Where Is The Love—Betty Wright (75)	37
Shotgun Shuffle—Sunshine Band (75)	29

Don't Run (Come Back To Me)—KC & The Sunshine Band (Duet with Teri DeSario) (83)	28
Shake It (Like A White Girl)—Jesse Jaymes (91)	25
Look At You—George McCrae (75)	24
Let's Go Rock And Roll—K.C. & The Sunshine Band (80)	11
Kenneth CASEY ▶ 10429 (2)	**8.6**
Sweet Georgia Brown—Carroll Bros. (62)	*19*
Sweet Georgie Brown (Sweet Georgia Brown)—Mindy Carson (57)	*6.8*
Warren CASEY ▶ 2395 (2)	**1529**
Summer Nights—John Travolta, Olivia Newton-John & Cast (78)	2789
Greased Lightnin'—John Travolta (78)	268
Alvin CASH [Alvin Welch] ▶ 9212 (1)	**28**
Keep On Dancing—Alvin Cash (68)	114
Darryl CASH ▶ 9445 (1)	**23**
Latin Active—A Lighter Shade Of Brown (91)	164
Joe CASH ▶ 9481 (1)	**23**
Love And Desire (Part I)—Arpeggio (79)	69
Johnny CASH ▶ 608 (28)	**7095**
What Is Truth—Johnny Cash (70)	991
I Walk The Line—Johnny Cash and the Tennessee Two (56)	*840*
Don't Take Your Guns To Town—Johnny Cash (59)	802
Folsom Prison Blues—Johnny Cash (68)	687
Understand Your Man—Johnny Cash (64)	509
The Matador—Johnny Cash (63)	443
I Walk The Line—Jaye P. Morgan (60)	*439*
See Ruby Fall—Johnny Cash (69)	412
I'll Walk The Line—Don Costa And His Orchestra And Chorus (59)	*376*
All Over Again—Johnny Cash (58)	354
I Got Stripes—Johnny Cash (59)	321
Flesh And Blood—Johnny Cash (70)	304
Man In Black—Johnny Cash (71)	290
Get Rhythm—Johnny Cash (69)	267
What Do I Care—Johnny Cash (58)	225
All Mama's Children—Carl Perkins (56)	144
Katy Too—Johnny Cash And The Tennessee Two (59)	96
There You Go—Johnny Cash and the Tennessee Two (56)	84
Come In Stranger—Johnny Cash (58)	70
You Dreamer You—Johnny Cash (59)	54
Tennessee Flat-Top Box—Johnny Cash (61)	42
Home Of The Blues—Johnny Cash (57)	30
Five Feet High And Rising—Johnny Cash (59)	27
Straight A's In Love—Johnny Cash (60)	12
You're The Nearest Thing To Heaven—Johnny Cash And The Tennessee Two (58)	6.6
Next In Line—Johnny Cash (57)	0.9
I Walk The Line—Hoagy Carmichael (56)	*0.0*
I Walk The Line—Carole Bennett (56)	*0.0*
Jonas CASH ▶ 6104 (1)	**206**
Bigfoot—Bro Smith (76)	206
—June Carter Cash see: June CARTER	
Rosanne CASH ▶ 3669 (1)	**744**
Seven Year Ache—Rosanne Cash (81)	744
Steve CASH ▶ 1670 (4)	**2519**
Jackie Blue—Ozark Mountain Daredevils (75)	4157
If You Wanna Get To Heaven—Ozark Mountain Daredevils (74)	684
If I Only Knew—Ozark Mountain Daredevils (76)	128
Take You Tonight—Ozark Mountain Daredevils (80)	104
Terry CASHMAN [Dennis Minogue] ▶ 1978 (12)	**2039**
Sunday Will Never Be The Same—Spanky And Our Gang (67)	1623
Medicine Man (Part 1)—Buchanan Brothers (69)	1162
American City Suite—Cashman & West (72)	696
Son Of A Lovin' Man—Buchanan Brothers (69)	336
Songman—Cashman & West (72)	264
But For Love—Jerry Naylor (70)	252
Sausalito—Al Martino (69)	231
He'd Rather Have The Rain—Heaven Bound With Tony Scotti (71)	86
The King Of Rock 'N' Roll—Cashman & West (73)	31
Baby, Baby I Love You—Terry Cashman (76)	30
California On My Mind—Morning Mist (71)	26
A Song That Never Comes—Mama Cass Elliot (70)	2.1

Buzz CASON [James E. Cason, Garry Miles] ▶ 1115 (11)	**3984**
Sukiyaki—A Taste Of Honey (81)	*3090*
Everlasting Love—Carl Carlton (74)	*1789*
Everlasting Love—Robert Knight (67)	*1702*
Popsicle—Jan & Dean (66)	820
Sandy—Ronny & The Daytonas (65)	636
Don't Give It Up—Robbie Patton (81)	508
Everlasting Love— Rex Smith/Rachel Sweet (81)	*474*
Tennessee—Jan & Dean (62)	129
Danger—Vic Dana (63)	56
Blessed Are The Lonely—Robert Knight (68)	21
The Waiting Game—Brenda Lee (64)	14
Charles Richard CASON ▶ 8998 (1)	**34**
Come An' Get Yourself Some—Leon Haywood (75)	34
—James E. Cason see: Buzz CASON	
Peter CASPERSON ▶ 10547 (1)	**7.4**
Wild In The Streets—British Lions (78)	15
Francesco CASSANO [Franco Cassano] ▶ 6713 (1)	**142**
The Way It Used To Be—Engelbert Humperdinck (69)	711
Jules CASSARD ▶ 10790 (1)	**5.3**
Angry—Frank Pizani (57)	21
—Michael O. Cassavitis see: Tony ORLANDO	
Alphonsus CASSELL ▶ 5474 (1)	**282**
Hot Hot Hot (Radio Edit)— Buster Poindexter And His Banshees Of Blue (87)	282
Amerigo CASSELLA ▶ 8393 (1)	**52**
When Love Has Gone Away—Richard Cocciante (76)	208
—Eddie Cassen see: Ed KASSNER	
John CASSESE ▶ 9977 (2)	**14**
Where I Fell In Love—Capris (61)	71
Limbo—Capris (62)	0.9
Michel CASSEZ ▶ 10207 (1)	**11**
Hawaii Honeymoon—Waikikis (65)	22
Giuseppe CASSIA ▶ 4014 (2)	**622**
Chirpy Chirpy Cheep Cheep— Mac And Katie Kissoon (71)	*1221*
Chirpy Chirpy, Cheep Cheep—Lally Stott (71)	*23*
David CASSIDY ▶ 5876 (1)	**234**
Lyin' To Myself—David Cassidy (90)	467
Jim CASSIN ▶ 6531 (1)	**160**
D A R L I N'—Hilltoppers (55)	479
—Walden Robert Cassotto see: Bobby DARIN	
Amadee CASTENELL ▶ 10534 (1)	**7.5**
Action Speaks Louder Than Words— Chocolate Milk (75)	67
Emilio CASTILLO ▶ 2831 (7)	**1165**
So Very Hard To Go—Tower Of Power (73)	1182
You're Still A Young Man—Tower Of Power (72)	811
This Time It's Real—Tower Of Power (73)	177
Down To The Nightclub—Tower Of Power (72)	154
You Ought To Be Havin' Fun—Tower Of Power (76)	75
Time Will Tell—Tower Of Power (74)	63
What Is Hip?—Tower Of Power (74)	4.3
David CASTLE ▶ 7155 (2)	**113**
The Loneliest Man On The Moon—David Castle (77)	96
Ten To Eight—David Castle (77)	65
Boomer CASTLEMAN [Owens Boomer Castleman, Boomer Clarke] ▶ 3729 (3)	**718**
Judy Mae—Boomer Castleman (75)	493
Airplane Song (My Airplane)—Royal Guardsmen (67)	255
I Feel Good (I Feel Bad)— Lewis & Clarke Expedition (67)	195
Leonard CASTON ▶ 837 (13)	**5281**
Keep On Truckin' (Part 1)—Eddie Kendricks (73)	5698
Boogie Down—Eddie Kendricks (73)	4614
Nathan Jones—Supremes (71)	1414
Son Of Sagittarius—Eddie Kendricks (74)	630
I Had A Talk With My Man—Mitty Collier (64)	548
Tell Her Love Has Felt The Need— Eddie Kendricks (74)	456
Happy—Eddie Kendricks (75)	250
One Tear—Eddie Kendricks (74)	143
No Faith, No Love—Mitty Collier (65)	106
Hold On—Radiants (68)	92
Eddie's Love—Eddie Kendricks (72)	71
Wanted: Lover, No Experience Necessary— Laura Lee (67)	30

Girl You Need A Change Of Mind (Part 1)— Eddie Kendricks (73)	16
Jimmy CASTOR ▶ 2456 (6)	**1468**
Troglodyte (Cave Man)—Jimmy Castor Bunch (72)	3177
The Bertha Butt Boogie - Part I— Jimmy Castor Bunch (75)	916
Hey, Leroy, Your Mama's Callin' You— Jimmy Castor (66)	651
I Promise To Remember— Frankie Lymon and the Teenagers (56)	*231*
King Kong - Pt. 1—Jimmy Castor Bunch (75)	78
I Promise—Jimmy Castor & The Juniors (56)	*0.0*
Peppy CASTRO [Emil Theilheim] ▶ 3170 (2)	**972**
Breaking Away—Balance (81)	745
Falling In Love—Balance (81)	227
Vince CASTRO Jr. ▶ 10223 (1)	**11**
Bong Bong (I Love You Madly)—Vince Castro (58)	22
Leonello CASUCCI ▶ 5907 (1)	**231**
Just A Gigolo—David Lee Roth (85)	461
Vincent CATALANO ▶ 6645 (2)	**148**
Coney Island Baby—Excellents (62)	292
Gift Of Love—Van Dykes (1) (61)	5.8
Chet CATALLO ▶ 9332 (1)	**26**
Cafe Amore—Spyro Gyra (81)	26
Frank CATANA ▶ 10793 (1)	**5.3**
He Wore The Green Beret—Nancy Ames (66)	11
Tony CATCHPOLE ▶ 10064 (1)	**13**
Toyland—Alan Bown (68)	26
Earl CATE ▶ 4553 (2)	**466**
Union Man—Cate Brothers (76)	886
Can't Change My Heart—Cate Brothers (76)	45
Ernie CATE ▶ 4554 (2)	**466**
Union Man—Cate Brothers (76)	886
Can't Change My Heart—Cate Brothers (76)	45
Randy CATE ▶ 8107 (1)	**61**
Easy Love—Dionne Warwick (80)	184
Demetrius CATES [Demetrius Emery Cates, Demo Cates] ▶ 10130 (1)	**12**
Get Down People—Fabulous Counts (70)	37
—Demo Cates see: Demetrius CATES	
George CATES ▶ 6128 (5)	**202**
Weary Blues— McGuire Sisters And Lawrence Welk (56)	355
Carmen's Boogie—Crew-Cuts (55)	57
Stockholm—Lawrence Welk And His Orchestra (64)	29
A-One A-Two A-Cha Cha Cha— Lawrence Welk And His Orchestra and Chorus (61)	18
Where There's Life— George Cates And His Orchestra And Chorus (56)	16
William CATES ▶ 6633 (1)	**149**
Spread It On Thick—Gentrys (65)	447
Lee CATHY [Sid Faust, Cathy Lynn] ▶ 2808 (4)	**1185**
Angels Listened In—Crests (59)	1087
Just Between You And Me—Chordettes (57)	1055
Shape I'm In—Johnny Restivo (59)	223
Happiest Christmas Tree—Nat "King" Cole (59)	2.0
Victor CATLING ▶ 10718 (1)	**5.9**
Bad Little Woman—Shadows Of Knight (66)	30
Joe CATO ▶ 10329 (1)	**10**
Plain And Simple Girl—Garland Green (71)	10
Bob CATRON ▶ 6896 (1)	**130**
(Native Girl) Elephant Walk— Donald Jenkins & The Delighters (63)	260
—Nicholas Catsos see: Gary ROMERO	
Ben CAULEY ▶ 5552 (2)	**272**
Soul Finger—Bar-Kays (67)	1546
Give Everybody Some—Bar-Kays (67)	97
Davis CAUSEY ▶ 6756 (1)	**140**
That's Your Secret—Sea Level (78)	280
James CAUTY ▶ 3745 (3)	**713**
3 A.M. Eternal—KLF (91)	1338
Doctorin' The Tardis—Timelords (88)	159
What Time Is Love?—KLF (91)	73
Felix CAVALIERE ▶ 106 (24) HOF	**23374**
Groovin'—Young Rascals (67)	*9580*
People Got To Be Free—Rascals (68)	*9189*
A Beautiful Morning—Young Rascals (68)	5558
How Can I Be Sure—Young Rascals (67)	*4109*
A Girl Like You—Young Rascals (67)	2139

I've Been Lonely Too Long—Young Rascals (67)	1562
Carry Me Back—Rascals (69)	1185
See—Rascals (69)	1160
It's Wonderful—Young Rascals (67)	1044
A Ray Of Hope—Rascals (68)	981
Groovin'—Booker T. & The M.G.'s (67)	*957*
How Can I Be Sure—David Cassidy (72)	*939*
You Better Run—Young Rascals (66)	*833*
Heaven—Rascals (69)	815
Hold On—Rascals (69)	536
Only A Lonely Heart Sees—Felix Cavaliere (80)	417
Glory Glory—Rascals (70)	373
Come On Up—Young Rascals (66)	371
You Better Run—Pat Benatar (80)	*350*
On A Sunday Afternoon— A Lighter Shade Of Brown (91)	320
Love Me—Rascals (71)	50
People Gotta Be Free—5th Dimension (70)	*11*
Right On—Rascals (70)	3.7
Good To Have Love Back—Felix Cavaliere (80)	1.7
Dave CAVANAUGH ▶ 9816 (1)	**16**
Let There Be You—Five Keys (57)	33
James CAVANAUGH ▶ 5133 (6)	**336**
You're Nobody Till Somebody Loves You— Dean Martin (64)	*699*
Second Fiddle—Kay Starr (56)	353
You're Nobody Till Somebody Loves You— Wonder Who ? (66)	*21*
You're Nobody Till Somebody Loves You— Damita Jo (62)	*10*
You're Nobody 'Til Somebody Loves You— Mills Brothers (54)	*6.0*
You're Nobody 'til Somebody Loves You— Dinah Washington (62)	*6.0*
Jessie CAVANAUGH [Howard S. Richmond] ▶ 6408 (5)	**174**
Bonnie Blue Gal— Mitch Miller with His Orch. & Chorus (55)	*321*
Desafinado (Slightly Out Of Tune)—Pat Thomas (62)	*41*
Words—Pat Boone (60)	5.3
Bonnie Blue Gal— Lawrence Welk And His Champagne Music And The McGuire Sisters (55)	*0.0*
Desafinado (Slightly Out Of Tune)— Ella Fitzgerald (62)	*0.0*
Neal CAVANAUGH ▶ 7320 (1)	**102**
Yes—Merry Clayton (88)	306
Carlos CAVAZO ▶ 6984 (1)	**124**
Bang Your Head (Metal Health)—Quiet Riot (84)	495
Tony CAVAZO ▶ 6985 (1)	**124**
Bang Your Head (Metal Health)—Quiet Riot (84)	495
Claude CAVE ▶ 8764 (2)	**40**
Mandrill—Mandrill (71)	40
Hang Loose—Mandrill (73)	34
James CAWLEY ▶ 8264 (1)	**56**
Where Have You Been All My Life—Fotomaker (78)	56
Dorival CAYMMI ▶ 5534 (1)	**274**
...And Roses And Roses—Andy Williams (65)	547
Ken CEDAR ▶ 7857 (1)	**72**
Each And Every Time—Sweet Sensation (90)	144
—Christopher Cedzich see: Chris GANTRY	
Adriano CELENTANO ▶ 7861 (1)	**72**
Tar And Cement—Verdelle Smith (66)	359
Maurice CENAC ▶ 6151 (1)	**200**
Jam On It—Newcleus (84)	200
Nick CENCI ▶ 4683 (1)	**438**
Convention '72—Delegates (72)	877
—Peter A. Ceragioli Jr. see: Pete JOLLY	
Todd CERNEY ▶ 5981 (3)	**220**
I'll Still Be Loving You—Restless Heart (87)	536
Notorious—Loverboy (87)	386
If Ever A Love There Was—Four Tops (88)	17
Richie CERNIGLIA ▶ 7476 (3)	**93**
Together—Illusion (69)	240
How Does It Feel—Illusion (69)	31
Let's Make Each Other Happy—Illusion (70)	6.0
Raymond CERONI ▶ 2689 (2)	**1272**
I've Had It—Bell Notes (59)	*2423*
I've Had It—Fanny (74)	*121*
—Jean-Pierre/Jean Marc Cerrone see: Marc CERRONE	

Marc CERRONE [Max Berlin, Jean-Marc Cerrone, Jean-Pierre Cerrone] ▶ 5345 (5)	**302**
Got To Have Loving—Don Ray (78)	365
Love In 'C' Minor - Pt. 1—Cerrone (77)	*122*
Love In C Minor—Heart and Soul Orchestra (77)	*84*
Supernature—Cerrone (78)	27
Africanism—Kongas (78)	15
Otto CESANA ▶ 7190 (1)	**111**
Devotion—Janice Harper (58)	111
—Elio Cesare see: Tony RENIS	
Marcello CESARE ▶ 8850 (1)	**38**
Kiss You (When It's Dangerous)—Eight Seconds (87)	151
John CESARIO ▶ 5751 (1)	**245**
Endless Nights—Eddie Money (87)	735
Peter CETERA ▶ 134 (18)	**20413**
Hard To Say I'm Sorry—Chicago (82)	6596
If You Leave Me Now—Chicago (76)	5464
Glory Of Love (Theme From The Karate Kid Part II)—Peter Cetera (86)	4132
You're The Inspiration—Chicago (84)	3035
Baby, What A Big Surprise—Chicago (77)	2299
Feelin' Stronger Every Day—Chicago (73)	1808
One Good Woman—Peter Cetera (88)	1789
Wishing You Were Here—Chicago (74)	1416
No Tell Lover—Chicago (78)	1023
Stay The Night—Chicago (84)	981
Along Comes A Woman—Chicago (85)	906
Voices That Care—Voices That Care (91)	901
Love Me Tomorrow—Chicago (82)	788
Lowdown—Chicago (71)	603
Best Of Times—Peter Cetera (88)	199
Big Mistake—Peter Cetera (87)	144
Thunder And Lightning—Chicago (80)	142
Gone Long Gone—Chicago (79)	54
Robert CHABRIER ▶ 7626 (1)	**84**
Barking Dog—Crew-Cuts (54)	168
Les CHADWICK ▶ 3794 (1)	**696**
Don't Let The Sun Catch You Crying—Gerry And The Pacemakers (64)	2786
Robert CHAISSON ▶ 4184 (5)	**571**
Suzie Q (Part One)—Creedence Clearwater Revival (68)	*1687*
Susie Q—Dale Hawkins (57)	*544*
Do You Believe In Shame?—Duran Duran (89)	93
Susie-Q—Crew-Cuts (57)	*0.0*
Susie-Q—José Feliciano (70)	*0.0*
Charlotte CHAIT ▶ 9642 (1)	**20**
Bel Sante—Mitch Miller with His Orch. & Chorus (55)	40
Kevin CHALFANT ▶ 5282 (1)	**314**
I've Got A Lot To Learn About Love—Storm (91)	941
—Anthony George Chalk see: Tony COLTON	
Charlie CHALMERS ▶ 6803 (3)	**136**
City In The Sky—Staple Singers (74)	205
One Woman—Johnny Rivers (69)	62
You Can Lead Your Woman To The Altar—Oscar Toney, Jr. (67)	37
Steven CHAMBERLIN ▶ 2469 (8)	**1454**
Heaven—Warrant (89)	3557
I Saw Red—Warrant (90)	1193
Cherry Pie—Warrant (90)	992
Sometimes She Cries—Warrant (89)	824
Down Boys—Warrant (89)	567
Uncle Tom's Cabin—Warrant (91)	71
Blind Faith—Warrant (91)	40
Big Talk—Warrant (89)	23
Carl CHAMBERS ▶ 6855 (1)	**132**
Close Enough To Perfect—Alabama (82)	132
George CHAMBERS ▶ 11591 (2)	**1.1**
Love, Peace And Happiness—Chambers Brothers (70)	2.2
Funky—Chambers Brothers (71)	2.1
—James E. Chambers see: Jimmy CLIFF	
Jimmy CHAMBERS ▶ 2931 (2)	**1113**
I've Been Thinking About You—Londonbeat (91)	3755
A Better Love—Londonbeat (91)	873
Joe CHAMBERS ▶ 3310 (3)	**904**
Time Has Come Today—Chambers Brothers (68)	1807
Love, Peace And Happiness—Chambers Brothers (70)	2.2
Funky—Chambers Brothers (71)	2.1
Larry CHAMBERS ▶ 7900 (2)	**70**
A Man And A Half—Wilson Pickett (68)	273

I'm The Midnight Special—Clarence Carter (73)	8.8
Lester CHAMBERS ▶ 11592 (2)	**1.1**
Love, Peace And Happiness—Chambers Brothers (70)	2.2
Funky—Chambers Brothers (71)	2.1
—Rick Chambers see: Ritchie ADAMS	
Roland CHAMBERS ▶ 9712 (1)	**19**
Love In Them There Hills—Vibrations (68)	56
Willie CHAMBERS ▶ 3311 (3)	**904**
Time Has Come Today—Chambers Brothers (68)	1807
Love, Peace And Happiness—Chambers Brothers (70)	2.2
Funky—Chambers Brothers (71)	2.1
—Bettye Jean Champion see: Bettye SWANN	
Bill CHAMPLIN ▶ 1534 (9)	**2791**
After The Love Has Gone—Earth, Wind & Fire (79)	3559
Turn Your Love Around—George Benson (81)	2450
Is It You—Lee Ritenour (81)	902
Friends In Love—Dionne Warwick And Johnny Mathis (82)	322
Hold On—Sons Of Champlin (76)	273
Sara—Bill Champlin (82)	132
Tonight Tonight—Bill Champlin (81)	119
Here Is Where Your Love Belongs—Sons Of Champlin (77)	104
Hearts In Trouble—Chicago (90)	102
Barry CHANCE ▶ 6863 (1)	**132**
Fins—Jimmy Buffett (79)	528
Leon CHANCLER ▶ 2873 (2)	**1139**
Let It Whip—Dazz Band (82)	2147
Reach For It—George Duke (77)	261
Bodie CHANDLER ▶ 3113 (7)	**1004**
I Wonder What She's Doing Tonight—Barry And The Tamerlanes (63)	845
Glad She's A Woman—Bobby Goldsboro (69)	285
Down And Out In New York City—James Brown (73)	234
The Last Leaf—Cascades (63)	220
Roberta—Barry And The Tamerlanes (64)	77
Shy Girl—Cascades (63)	59
Seein' Is Believin'—Eddie Hodges (62)	2.2
Chas CHANDLER ▶ 7080 (1)	**117**
Inside-Looking Out—Animals (66)	468
David CHANDLER [Dean Rotherman] ▶ 8278 (1)	**56**
Praying To A New God—Wang Chung (89)	167
Gene CHANDLER [Eugene Dixon] ▶ 1171 (10)	**3799**
Duke Of Earl—Gene Chandler (62)	*9144*
I Fooled You This Time—Gene Chandler (66)	492
Good Guys Only Win In The Movies—Mel And Tim (70)	386
Girl Don't Care—Gene Chandler (67)	330
Simply Call It Love—Gene Chandler (70)	238
Walk On With The Duke—Duke Of Earl (62)	86
Duchess Of Earl—Pearlettes (62)	*50*
You're A Lady—Gene Chandler (71)	3.4
When You're #1—Gene Chandler (79)	1.2
Duchess Of Earl—Bobbie Smith & The Dreamgirls (62)	*0.0*
George CHANDLER ▶ 2932 (2)	**1113**
I've Been Thinking About You—Londonbeat (91)	3755
A Better Love—Londonbeat (91)	873
—June Deniece Chandler see: Deniece WILLIAMS	
Len CHANDLER ▶ 4136 (1)	**584**
Beans In My Ears—Serendipity Singers (64)	584
Herman CHANEY ▶ 9672 (1)	**19**
Charlena—Sevilles (61)	38
Roy CHANEY ▶ 4293 (1)	**530**
Psychotic Reaction—Count Five (66)	2651
Bruce CHANNEL [Bruce McMeans] ▶ 942 (5)	**4715**
Hey! Baby—Bruce Channel (62)	*8663*
Number One Man—Bruce Channel (62)	400
Hey! Baby—Jose Feliciano (69)	*381*
Hey Baby—Ringo Starr (76)	*116*
Come On Baby—Bruce Channel (62)	4.9
Marc CHANTEREAU ▶ 8337 (1)	**54**
Souvenirs—Voyage (79)	161
Jean CHAPEL [Opal Jean Amburgey] ▶ 4731 (3)	**429**
Lay Some Happiness On Me—Dean Martin (67)	317
To Get To You—Jerry Wallace (72)	242
Lonely Again—Eddy Arnold (67)	28
Harry CHAPIN ▶ 894 (10)	**4961**
Cat's In The Cradle—Harry Chapin (74)	4219

Taxi—Harry Chapin (72)	1100
WOLD—Harry Chapin (73)	683
Sequel—Harry Chapin (80)	488
I Wanna Learn A Love Song—Harry Chapin (75)	358
Sunday Morning Sunshine—Harry Chapin (72)	95
Better Place To Be (Parts 1 & 2)—Harry Chapin (76)	64
Could You Put Your Light On, Please—Harry Chapin (72)	33
Circles—New Seekers (72)	23
What Made America Famous—Harry Chapin (74)	7.3
Sandra CHAPIN ▶ 1921 (1)	**2110**
Cat's In The Cradle—Harry Chapin (74)	4219
Blondie CHAPLIN [William Terence Chaplin, Terence William Chaplin] ▶ 11478 (1)	**1.5**
See The Light—Flame (70)	6.1
Charles CHAPLIN ▶ 983 (9)	**4558**
This Is My Song—Petula Clark (67)	3690
Smile—Nat "King" Cole (54)	*828*
Smile—Timi Yuro (61)	*422*
Eternally—Sarah Vaughan (60)	*324*
Smile—Betty Everett & Jerry Butler (64)	*322*
Smile—Tony Bennett (59)	*207*
Limelight—Mr. Acker Bilk (62)	*93*
Smile—Ferrante & Teicher (62)	*75*
Smile—Sunny Gale (54)	*0.0*
Saul CHAPLIN [Saul Kaplan] ▶ 5720 (4) HOF	**251**
Bei Mir Bist Du Schon—Louis Prima And Keely Smith (59)	365
If It's The Last Thing I Do—Thelma Houston (77)	173
Berry Tree—Bill Hayes (55)	71
Anniversary Song—Mulcays (56)	7.0
—Terence William Chaplin see: Blondie CHAPLIN	
Gary CHAPMAN ▶ 5671 (1)	**257**
Finally—T.G. Sheppard (82)	257
Jean CHAPMAN ▶ 7727 (1)	**78**
That's Freedom—Tom Kimmel (87)	155
Mike CHAPMAN ▶ 168 (31)	**17628**
Kiss You All Over—Exile (78)	7882
Mickey—Toni Basil (82)	*5959*
Little Willy—Sweet (73)	3958
Love Is A Battlefield—Pat Benatar (83)	3131
Stumblin' In—Suzi Quatro And Chris Norman (79)	2721
Ballroom Blitz—Sweet (75)	2550
Better Be Good To Me—Tina Turner (84)	2151
Love Touch—Rod Stewart (86)	1772
Heart And Soul—Huey Lewis and the News (83)	1620
The Best—Tina Turner (89)	940
Living Next Door To Alice—Smokie (76)	937
Hanging On A Heart Attack—Device (86)	505
The Truth—Tami Show (91)	466
You Thrill Me—Exile (78)	360
She's In Love With You—Suzi Quatro (79)	354
Hands Tied—Scandal Featuring Patty Smyth (84)	338
Blockbuster—Sweet (73)	280
If You Can't Give Me Love—Suzi Quatro (79)	216
Ricky—"Weird Al" Yankovic (83)	*188*
Can The Can—Suzi Quatro (76)	167
Lipstick—Suzi Quatro (81)	166
Doctorin' The Tardis—Timelords (88)	159
Pleasure And Pain—Divinyls (86)	84
Who Says—Device (86)	81
I Engineer—Animotion (86)	39
Co-Co—Sweet (71)	22
How Could This Go Wrong—Exile (79)	8.0
48 Crash—Suzi Quatro (74)	7.6
If You Think You Know How To Love Me—Smokey (75)	4.8
Try It On—Exile (77)	3.4
Part Of Me That Needs You Most—Jay Black (80)	2.9
Tracy CHAPMAN ▶ 1785 (4)	**2326**
Fast Car—Tracy Chapman (88)	1797
Baby Can I Hold You—Tracy Chapman (88)	436
Talkin' Bout A Revolution—Tracy Chapman (88)	69
Crossroads—Tracy Chapman (89)	25
—Martine Chapot see: Martine CLÉMENCEAU	
Craig CHAQUICO ▶ 3355 (5)	**885**
Jane—Jefferson Starship (79)	1718
Find Your Way Back—Jefferson Starship (81)	493
Light The Sky On Fire—Jefferson Starship (78)	136
Layin' It On The Line—Jefferson Starship (84)	124
St. Charles—Jefferson Starship (76)	52

Moose CHARLAP [Morris I. Charlap] ▶ 6344 (8) **181**
English Muffins And Irish Stew—Sylvia Syms (56) 216
How Blue—Mills Brothers (54) 97
I Was Telling Her About You—Al Hibbler (56) 42
Town Crier—Al Hibbler (57) 20
(But As They Say) That's Life—Jack Pleis And His Orchestra (57) 9.6
Young Ideas—Gordon Jenkins & His Orchestra (55) 4.4
Young Ideas—Tony Martin (55) 4.4
Never Before—Connie Francis (58) 0.7
—Morris I. Charlap see: Moose CHARLAP
—Charlemagne see: Berry GORDY
—Charlemagne see: James CARMICHAEL
—Charlemagne see: Kathy WAKEFIELD
—Charlemagne see: Ronald Norman MILLER
Roger CHARLERY ▶ 5831 (1) **238**
Tenderness—General Public (84) 715
Beau CHARLES ▶ 4218 (1) **558**
Lies—Knickerbockers (65) 1117
—Bobby Charles see: Robert GUIDRY
Deena CHARLES [Dorothy Russo] ▶ 2789 (1) **1196**
If Wishes Came True—Sweet Sensation (90) 3587
Dick CHARLES [Richard Charles Krieg] ▶ 3508 (1) **808**
May You Always—McGuire Sisters (58) 1616
—Edwin Charles see: Larry BROWN
Gerard CHARLES ▶ 1649 (14) **2544**
Head To Toe—Lisa Lisa And Cult Jam (87) 4435
Lost In Emotion—Lisa Lisa And Cult Jam (87) 3486
Naughty Girls (Need Love Too)—Samantha Fox (88) 2531
All Cried Out—Lisa Lisa And Cult Jam With Full Force Featuring Paul Anthony And Bow Legged Lou (86) 1667
I Wanna Have Some Fun—Samantha Fox (88) 1135
I Wonder If I Take You Home—Lisa Lisa and Cult Jam with Full Force (85) 656
Thanks For My Child—Cheryl "Pepsii" Riley (88) 509
Little Jackie Wants To Be A Star—Lisa Lisa And Cult Jam (89) 441
Can You Feel The Beat—Lisa Lisa And Cult Jam (85) 231
Basketball—Kurtis Blow (85) 77
Someone To Love Me For Me—Lisa Lisa & Cult Jam (87) 52
Why Can't You Come Home—Ex-Girlfriend (91) 48
Roxanne, Roxanne—UTFO (85) 28
Go For Yours—Lisa Lisa & Cult Jam with Full Force (88) 22
Gordon CHARLES ▶ 4261 (4) **543**
My Little Angel—Four Lads (56) 577
Ring A Ding A Ding—Tommy Sands (57) 288
Groovy—Joe Dodo And The Groovers (58) 87
It's So Easy To Forget—Four Lads (57) 47
Jacques CHARLES ▶ 6799 (2) **136**
My Man—Peggy Lee (59) 340
My Man—Barbra Streisand (65) 204
—Leslie Charles see: Billy OCEAN
Ray CHARLES [Ray Charles Robinson] ▶ 485 (33) **8586**
What'd I Say (Part 1)—Ray Charles And His Orchestra (59) 2609
What'd I Say—Elvis Presley With The Jubilee Four And Carole Lombard Quartet (64) 878
I've Got A Woman Part 1—Jimmy McGriff (62) 782
Booty Butt—Ray Charles Orchestra (71) 746
What'd I Say (Part 1)—Bobby Darin (62) 618
What'd I Say—Jerry Lee Lewis And His Pumping Piano (61) 516
I Chose To Sing The Blues—Ray Charles & The Raeletts (66) 501
I Got A Sweetie—Jo Stafford (55) 471
This Little Girl Of Mine—Everly Brothers (58) 445
Them That Got—Ray Charles And His Orchestra (61) 371
I Got A Woman—Rick Nelson (63) 361
That's A Lie—Ray Charles (68) 326
Sweet Sixteen Bars—Earl Grant (62) 285
I Got A Woman—Freddie Scott (63) 269
Understanding—Ray Charles (68) 193
Swanee River Rock (Talkin' 'Bout That River)—Ray Charles (57) 179
Careless Love—Ray Charles (62) 154
If It Wasn't For Bad Luck—Ray Charles & Jimmy Lewis (69) 150
What'd I Say—Rare Earth (72) 109
I Can Make It Thru The Days (But Oh Those Lonely Nights)—Ray Charles (73) 59
I Gotta Woman (Part One)—Ray Charles And His Orchestra (65) 57
But On The Other Hand Baby—Ray Charles And His Orchestra (61) 41
Tell The Truth—Ray Charles (60) 37
Hallelujah I Love Him So—Peggy Lee (59) 27
Rockhouse (Part 2)—Ray Charles (58) 21
Ain't That Love—Micki Marlo (57) 11
Ain't That Love—Harry Belafonte (58) 11
The Brightest Smile In Town—Ray Charles And His Orchestra (63) 6.8
Who You Gonna' Love—Ray Charles And His Orchestra (60) 6.4
Hallelujah I Love Her So—Eddie Cochran (59) 3.6
What I Say—Etta James (64) 2.2
Leave My Man (Woman) Alone—Raeletts Featuring Vernita Moss (71) 0.8
What'd I Say—Jack Eubanks, His Orchestra and Singers (61) 0.0
—Ray (2) Charles see: Charles Raymond OFFENBERG
—R.B. Charles see: Randy BACHMAN
Sonny CHARLES [Charles Hemphill] ▶ 4697 (2) **436**
I'm Leavin'—Elvis Presley (71) 503
Put It In A Magazine—Sonny Charles (82) 370
Manny CHARLTON ▶ 10281 (1) **10**
Holiday—Nazareth (80) 63
Mark CHARRON ▶ 1810 (4) **2283**
Mama—B.J. Thomas (66) 978
Billy And Sue—B.J. Thomas And The Triumphs (66) 782
Woman Helping Man—Vogues (69) 423
Bring Back The Time—B.J. Thomas (66) 100
Bill CHASE ▶ 4648 (1) **446**
Get It On—Chase (71) 891
—Brandon Chase see: Gary ZEKLEY
Clifton CHASE [Clifton Nathaniel Chase, Jiggs Chase] ▶ 8308 (2) **55**
Apache—Sugar Hill Gang (82) 173
The Message—Grandmaster Flash & The Furious Five (82) 80
Ellison CHASE [Joseph LaPollo] ▶ 6116 (3) **204**
I'm Happy That Love Has Found You—Jimmy Hall (80) 568
Let's Rock—Ellison Chase (76) 27
Top Of The World (Make My Reservation)—Canyon (75) 3.3
—Jiggs Chase see: Clifton CHASE
Lincoln CHASE ▶ 366 (21) **10519**
The Name Game—Shirley Ellis (64) 4579
The Nitty Gritty—Shirley Ellis (63) 2204
The Clapping Song (Clap Pat Clap Slap)—Shirley Ellis (65) 1719
Jim Dandy—LaVern Baker and The Gliders (56) 1096
Jim Dandy—Black Oak Arkansas (73) 969
Such A Night—Elvis Presley With The Jordanaires (64) 957
The Nitty Gritty—Gladys Knight & The Pips (69) 893
Wonderland By Night—Anita Bryant (60) 792
Cinnamon Sinner—Tony Bennett with Percy Faith and His Orchestra (54) 595
The Clapping Song—Pia Zadora (82) 271
The Puzzle Song (A Puzzle In Song)—Shirley Ellis (65) 163
(That's) What The Nitty Gritty Is—Shirley Ellis (64) 129
That's All I Need—Dorothy Collins (55) 120
Attack Of The Name Game—Stacy Lattisaw (82) 54
Nitty Gritty—Ricardo Ray (68) 50
Jim Dandy Got Married—LaVern Baker (57) 39
Such A Night—Dinah Washington (62) 33
Bring Back My Love—June Valli (58) 18
That's All I Need—LaVern Baker & The Gliders (55) 0.0
That's All I Need—Rusty Draper (55) 0.0
That's All I Need—Jill Corey (55) 0.0
Kerry CHATER ▶ 4077 (6) **601**
I Know A Heartache When I See One—Jennifer Warnes (79) 894
I.O.U.—Lee Greenwood (83) 242
Love On A Shoestring—Captain & Tennille (80) 174
So Hard Livin' Without You—Airwaves (78) 89
(Want You) Back In My Life Again—Carpenters (81) 73
I'll Have To Go Away—Skylark (73) 29
Armetia CHATMAN [Bo Carter, Bo Chatman, Armenter Chatmon] ▶ 3800 (3) **696**
Corinna Corinna—Ray Peterson (60) 1744
Corrine Corrina—Joe Turner (56) 342
Corrine, Corrina—Swingin' Sam (56) 0.0
—Bo Chatman see: Armetia CHATMAN
—John Len Chatman see: Peter CHATMAN
Peter CHATMAN [John Len Chatman, Memphis Slim] ▶ 7610 (3) **85**
Every Day—Patti Page (55) 134
Every Day I Have The Blues—Billy Stewart (67) 122
Every Day—Count Basie And His Orchestra (55) 0.0
Brian CHATTON ▶ 5692 (1) **254**
I Wanna Be A Cowboy—Boys Don't Cry (86) 1016
Danny CHAUNCEY ▶ 4320 (4) **523**
I Wanna Go Back—Eddie Money (86) 1073
The Sound Of Your Voice—.38 Special (91) 423
I Wanna Go Back—Billy Satellite (84) 89
Satisfy Me—Billy Satellite (84) 89
Robert CHAUVIGNY ▶ 6365 (1) **178**
A Young Girl—Noel Harrison (65) 535
Ingrid CHAVEZ ▶ 1720 (2) **2434**
Justify My Love—Madonna (90) 3894
Do Anything—Natural Selection (91) 3407
Manuel CHAVEZ ▶ 9673 (1) **19**
Charlena—Sevilles (61) 38
Chubby CHECKER [Ernest Evans] ▶ 4132 (1) **584**
Hooka Tooka—Chubby Checker (63) 1168
Callie CHEEK ▶ 10523 (1) **7.6**
You Got To Keep On Bumpin'—Kay-Gees (74) 61
Michael CHEEK ▶ 10524 (1) **7.6**
You Got To Keep On Bumpin'—Kay-Gees (74) 61
Judy CHEEKS ▶ 9735 (1) **18**
Mellow Lovin'—Judy Cheeks (78) 54
—Cheese see: Hearlon MARTIN
Vincent CHEESMAN [Vincent Rodney Cheesman, Vincent Crane] ▶ 2410 (1) **1509**
Fire—Crazy World Of Arthur Brown (68) 6038
Phil CHEN ▶ 4220 (2) **557**
Passion—Rod Stewart (80) 2748
Somebody Special—Rod Stewart (81) 44
Gary CHERONE ▶ 1258 (2) **3558**
More Than Words—Extreme (91) 4589
Hole Hearted—Extreme (91) 2526
Neneh CHERRY [Neneh Mariann Cherry, Neneh Mariann Karlsson] ▶ 2666 (3) **1285**
Buffalo Stance—Neneh Cherry (89) 2690
Kisses On The Wind—Neneh Cherry (89) 1072
Heart—Neneh Cherry (89) 154
Rick CHERTOFF ▶ 2672 (6) **1281**
She Bop—Cyndi Lauper (84) 3432
Day By Day—Hooters (85) 759
Never Enough—Patty Smyth (87) 206
Johnny B—Hooters (87) 201
Satellite—Hooters (87) 169
Brother, Don't You Walk Away—Hooters (90) 17
Bixio CHERUBINI ▶ 4271 (1) **539**
Mama—Connie Francis (60) 2155
Bruno CHERUBINI [C. Bruno] ▶ 8075 (2) **63**
Roman Guitar (Chitarra Romana)—Lou Monte (57) 157
The Woodpecker Song—Bobby Rydell (63) 32
Jerry CHESNUT ▶ 4755 (3) **423**
T-R-O-U-B-L-E—Elvis Presley (75) 408
It's Four In The Morning—Faron Young (72) 11
Another Place Another Time—Jerry Lee Lewis (68) 3.2
Deborah CHESSLER ▶ 1967 (3) **2044**
It's Too Soon To Know—Pat Boone (58) 1737
It's Too Soon To Know—Etta James (61) 264
It's Too Soon To Know—Tony Bennett (55) 43
Christian CHEVALLIER ▶ 10270 (1) **11**
Your Heart Is Free Just Like The Wind—Vikki Carr (68) 21
Ray CHEW ▶ 7488 (1) **93**
Work That Body—Diana Ross (82) 278

Lloyd CHIATE ▶ 5541 (3)	**273**
Maybe I'm A Fool—Eddie Money (79)	715
Get A Move On—Eddie Money (79)	248
Magic Man—Robert Winters & Fall (81)	45
—George Forrest Chichester Jr. see: George FORREST	
Michele CHIEREGATO ▶ 7756 (1)	**76**
Boom Boom (Let's Go Back To My Room)— Paul Lekakis (87)	381
Desmond CHILD ▶ 252 (28) HOF	**13523**
Livin' On A Prayer—Bon Jovi (86)	5011
You Give Love A Bad Name—Bon Jovi (86)	4318
Bad Medicine—Bon Jovi (88)	3448
Born To Be My Baby—Bon Jovi (88)	3071
Angel—Aerosmith (88)	2836
How Can We Be Lovers—Michael Bolton (90)	2141
Just Like Jesse James—Cher (89)	2020
I Was Made For Lovin' You—Kiss (79)	1971
I Hate Myself For Loving You— Joan Jett and the Blackhearts (88)	1501
Poison—Alice Cooper (89)	1500
What It Takes—Aerosmith (90)	1375
Dude (Looks Like A Lady)—Aerosmith (87)	1227
We All Sleep Alone—Cher (88)	926
Little Liar—Joan Jett and the Blackhearts (88)	911
Save Up All Your Tears—Cher (91)	688
Does Anybody Really Fall In Love Anymore?— Kane Roberts (91)	452
Love On A Rooftop—Desmond Child (91)	440
These Times Are Hard For Lovers—John Waite (87)	274
Heaven's On Fire—KISS (84)	264
House Of Fire—Alice Cooper (90)	215
Calling It Love—Animotion (89)	215
Our Love Is Insane—Desmond Child And Rouge (79)	209
Reason To Live—KISS (87)	145
You're The Story Of My Life—Desmond Child (91)	135
Hide Your Heart—KISS (89)	110
Timeless Love—Saraya (89)	49
If You Were A Woman (And I Was A Man)— Bonnie Tyler (86)	33
Let's Put The X In Sex—KISS (89)	7.3
Jane CHILD [Jane Richman] ▶ 1238 (2)	**3621**
Don't Wanna Fall In Love—Jane Child (90)	3360
Welcome To The Real World—Jane Child (90)	262
—Laura Webb Childress see: Laura WEBB	
Toni CHILDS [Annette Bard] ▶ 8525 (1)	**47**
Don't Walk Away—Toni Childs (88)	95
Charlie CHIN ▶ 9024 (1)	**33**
Good Old Rock 'N Roll— Cat Mother And The All Night News Boys (69)	164
Nicky CHINN ▶ 237 (22)	**14391**
Kiss You All Over—Exile (78)	7882
Mickey—Toni Basil (82)	*5959*
Little Willy—Sweet (73)	3958
Stumblin' In—Suzi Quatro And Chris Norman (79)	2721
Ballroom Blitz—Sweet (75)	2550
Better Be Good To Me—Tina Turner (84)	2151
Heart And Soul—Huey Lewis and the News (83)	1620
Living Next Door To Alice—Smokie (76)	937
You Thrill Me—Exile (78)	360
She's In Love With You—Suzi Quatro (79)	354
Blockbuster—Sweet (73)	280
If You Can't Give Me Love—Suzi Quatro (79)	216
Ricky—"Weird Al" Yankovic (83)	*188*
Can The Can—Suzi Quatro (76)	167
Lipstick—Suzi Quatro (81)	166
Doctorin' The Tardis—Timelords (88)	159
Co-Co—Sweet (71)	22
How Could This Go Wrong—Exile (79)	8.0
48 Crash—Suzi Quatro (74)	7.6
If You Think You Know How To Love Me—Smokey (75)	4.8
Try It On—Exile (77)	3.4
Part Of Me That Needs You Most—Jay Black (80)	2.9
Elliot CHIPRUT ▶ 717 (2)	**6092**
Simon Says—1910 Fruitgum Co. (68)	5710
May I Take A Giant Step (Into Your Heart)— 1910 Fruitgum Co. (68)	382
Ed CHISOLM ▶ 2840 (2)	**1161**
Let The Music Play—Shannon (83)	1909
Give Me Tonight—Shannon (84)	413
Paul CHITEN ▶ 6339 (1)	**181**
Can't Wait Another Minute—Five Star (86)	362

Rose Marie CHIVETTI ▶ 7117 (1)	**115**
Betty In Bermudas—Dovells (63)	345
Babe CHIVIAN [Marvin Leonard Chivian, Babe Marvin] ▶ 8126 (2)	**61**
Down In The Valley—Solomon Burke (62)	*194*
Down In The Alley—Ronnie Hawkins (70)	*110*
—Marvin Leonard Chivian see: Babe CHIVIAN	
Tommy CHONG ▶ 1900 (8)	**2136**
Earache My Eye (Featuring Alice Bowie)— Cheech & Chong (74)	1634
Basketball Jones Featuring Tyrone Shoelaces— Cheech & Chong (73)	*1097*
Sister Mary Elephant (Shudd-Up!)— Cheech & Chong (73)	765
Does Your Mama Know About Me— Bobby Taylor & The Vancouvers (68)	703
Bloat On Featuring The Bloaters— Cheech & Chong (77)	*328*
Black Lassie (Featuring Johnny Stash)— Cheech & Chong (74)	262
Born In East L.A.—Cheech & Chong (85)	*256*
(How I Spent My Summer Vacation) Or A Day At The Beach With Pedro And Man - Part I—C heech & Chong (75)	184
Frederic CHOPIN ▶ 7206 (8)	**110**
To Love Again—Four Aces (56)	*408*
Till The End Of Time—Ray Charles Singers (64)	17
I'm Always Chasing Rainbows—Joe Pica (58)	3.3
Choppin' Cha Cha—Marty Ames (59)	2.6
To Love Again—Bob Manning (56)	*0.0*
To Love Again—Carmen Cavallaro (56)	*0.0*
To Love Again—Vic Damone (56)	*0.0*
To Love Again—Marc Fredericks (56)	*0.0*
Al CHORNEY ▶ 7504 (3)	**91**
Rebel—Carol Jarvis (57)	*269*
Snowbound For Christmas—DeCastro Sisters (55)	4.8
Rebel—Jill Whitney (57)	*0.0*
Betty CHOTAS ▶ 6433 (1)	**169**
Just A Little—Brenda Lee (60)	169
Randie CHOWNING ▶ 10221 (1)	**11**
Look Away—Ozark Mountain Daredevils (74)	11
Gene CHRISMAN ▶ 8292 (1)	**55**
Scratchy—Travis Wammack (64)	165
Dave CHRISTENSON ▶ 11047 (1)	**3.6**
One Simple Thing—Stabilizers (87)	7.2
Laurie CHRISTENSON ▶ 5573 (1)	**270**
In The Middle Of A Heartache—Wanda Jackson (61)	810
Arlester CHRISTIAN ▶ 1197 (7)	**3712**
Funky Broadway—Wilson Pickett (67)	*2155*
We Got More Soul—Dyke And The Blazers (69)	550
Let A Woman Be A Woman - Let A Man Be A Man— Dyke And The Blazers (69)	526
Funky Broadway Part 1—Dyke And The Blazers (67)	*286*
Funky Walk Part I (East)—Dyke And The Blazers (68)	153
Uhh—Dyke And The Blazers (70)	32
Runaway People—Dyke And The Blazers (70)	11
Chris CHRISTIAN [Lon Christian Smith] ▶ 5931 (4)	**226**
I Want You, I Need You—Chris Christian (81)	446
(Want You) Back In My Life Again—Carpenters (81)	73
All Things Are Possible—Dan Peek (79)	27
Still The Lovin' Is Fun—B.J. Thomas (77)	27
Ricky Lynn CHRISTIAN ▶ 1459 (1)	**2988**
I Don't Need You—Kenny Rogers (81)	2988
Roger CHRISTIAN ▶ 694 (18)	**6275**
The Little Old Lady (From Pasadena)— Jan & Dean (64)	3373
Dead Man's Curve—Jan & Dean (64)	2112
Drag City—Jan & Dean (63)	1652
Honolulu Lulu—Jan & Dean (63)	1484
Don't Worry Baby—B.J. Thomas (77)	*1157*
Shut Down—Beach Boys (63)	*1051*
Little Deuce Coupe—Beach Boys (63)	1016
Don't Worry Baby—Beach Boys (64)	*903*
Ride The Wild Surf—Jan & Dean (64)	823
Three Window Coupe—Rip Chords (64)	620
Sidewalk Surfin'—Jan & Dean (64)	605
The New Girl In School—Jan & Dean (64)	600
You Really Know How To Hurt A Guy— Jan & Dean (65)	519
Bucket "T"—Ronny & The Daytonas (64)	293

Shut Down—Beach Boys (81)	*240*
The Anaheim, Azusa & Cucamonga Sewing Circle, Book Review And Timing Association— Jan & Dean (64)	194
Don't Worry Baby—Tokens (70)	*89*
A Beginning From An End—Jan & Dean (66)	5.2
—Tim Christian see: Clemon Timothy RILEY	
Christine CHRISTIANSEN ▶ 10567 (1)	**7.2**
Get Serious—Cut 'N' Move (91)	36
Dean CHRISTIE ▶ 8610 (1)	**45**
Heart Breaker—Dean Christie (62)	45
Jeff CHRISTIE ▶ 2408 (2)	**1514**
Yellow River—Christie (70)	1491
San Bernadino—Christie (71)	23
Lou CHRISTIE [Lugee Sacco] ▶ 720 (10)	**6072**
Lightnin' Strikes—Lou Christie (65)	6323
Two Faces Have I—Lou Christie (63)	3221
The Gypsy Cried—Lou Christie (63)	1196
Rhapsody In The Rain—Lou Christie (66)	860
Outside The Gates Of Heaven—Lou Christie (66)	290
Are You Getting Any Sunshine?— Lou Christie (69)	154
Painter—Lou Christie (66)	93
Shake Hands And Walk Away Cryin'— Lou Christie (67)	5.4
Big Time—Lou Christie (66)	2.8
Glory River—Lou Christie (70)	0.0
Johnnie CHRISTO [John Christoforou] ▶ 2440 (5)	**1485**
Wild, Wild West—Escape Club (88)	4224
I'll Be There—Escape Club (91)	1572
Shake For The Sheik—Escape Club (88)	509
Call It Poison—Escape Club (91)	412
Walking Through Walls—Escape Club (89)	67
—John Christoforou see: Johnnie CHRISTO	
Don CHRISTOPHER ▶ 8695 (1)	**42**
The Ol' Race Track—Mills Brothers (68)	85
Gavin CHRISTOPHER [Gavin Christopher Wright] ▶ 2180 (2)	**1780**
Once You Get Started— Rufus Featuring Chaka Khan (75)	1467
Dance Wit Me—Rufus Featuring Chaka Khan (76)	313
Gretchen CHRISTOPHER ▶ 1443 (4)	**3029**
Come Softly To Me—Fleetwoods (59)	*8460*
Graduation's Here—Fleetwoods (59)	416
Come Softly To Me—Ronnie Height (59)	*196*
Come Softly To Me— New Seekers Featuring Marty Kristian (73)	*14*
Johnny CHRISTOPHER ▶ 1638 (7)	**2560**
Always On My Mind—Willie Nelson (82)	*2961*
Always On My Mind—Pet Shop Boys (88)	*1512*
No Love At All—B.J. Thomas (71)	1159
If You Talk In Your Sleep—Elvis Presley (74)	810
Pass The Apple Eve—B.J. Thomas (69)	50
Mama Liked The Roses—Elvis Presley (70)	44
Hey Hey Woman—Joe Jeffrey (69)	30
Harold CHRISTY ▶ 11384 (1)	**2.0**
Bring Back Those Rockabye Baby Days—Tiny Tim (68)	5.9
—Chuck D. see: Carlton RIDENHOUR	
Rick CHUDACOFF ▶ 2490 (1)	**1441**
Steal Away—Robbie Dupree (80)	2883
—Chung Dong-Hwa see: Towa TEI	
—Chunky A see: Arsenio HALL	
Eugene CHURCH ▶ 5942 (3)	**225**
Pretty Girls Everywhere— Eugene Church and The Fellows (58)	365
Miami—Eugene Church (59)	75
Good News—Eugene Church (60)	4.8
—Terry Noland Church see: Terry NOLAND	
—Cinthy Churchill see: Marilyn Weiss ALLEN	
Frank CHURCHILL ▶ 11100 (1)	**3.2**
Heigh-Ho—Fifth Estate (67)	6.4
Tony CHURCHILL ▶ 10747 (1)	**5.6**
Granddaddy (Part 1)—New Birth (75)	17
Carl CICCHETTI ▶ 1953 (1)	**2054**
Beep Beep—Playmates (58)	4109
Don CICCONE ▶ 2004 (3)	**2013**
Mr. Dieingly Sad—Critters (66)	1375
There's Got To Be A Word!—Innocence (66)	618
Georgianna—Princetons (66)	20

Madonna L. CICCONE [Madonna] ▶ 93 (19)	**25991**
Vogue—Madonna (90)	5025
Live To Tell—Madonna (86)	4537
Like A Prayer—Madonna (89)	4495
Open Your Heart—Madonna (86)	4274
Papa Don't Preach—Madonna (86)	4241
Justify My Love—Madonna (90)	3894
Who's That Girl—Madonna (87)	3738
Express Yourself—Madonna (89)	3109
True Blue—Madonna (86)	2906
Causing A Commotion—Madonna (87)	2831
Cherish—Madonna (89)	2774
La Isla Bonita—Madonna (87)	2230
Lucky Star—Madonna (84)	2133
Angel—Madonna (85)	1848
Keep It Together—Madonna (90)	1095
Sidewalk Talk—Jellybean (85)	895
Oh Father—Madonna (89)	816
Rescue Me—Madonna (91)	803
Hanky Panky—Madonna (90)	778
Angelo M. CIFELLI [Chubby Cifelli] ▶ 3316 (2)	**902**
Tell It To The Rain—4 Seasons Featuring The "Sound" Of Frankie Valli (66)	1614
Patch Of Blue—Frankie Valli & The 4 Seasons (70)	190
—Chubby Cifelli see: Angelo M. CIFELLI	
Phil CILIA ▶ 3809 (2)	**693**
Cry—Waterfront (89)	1294
Nature Of Love—Waterfront (89)	93
Eugene CINES ▶ 9426 (1)	**24**
Hello There—Gisele MacKenzie (57)	48
Joanne CIPOLLA ▶ 10035 (1)	**14**
When Things Go Wrong—Robin Lane & The Chartbusters (80)	27
—Mark Cipolla see: Mick SMILEY	
Mario CIPOLLINA ▶ 8425 (2)	**51**
Workin' For A Livin'—Huey Lewis and the News (82)	267
Don't Make Me Do It—Patrick Simmons (83)	38
Carl CISCO ▶ 8372 (2)	**53**
Hot Shot—Buena Vistas (66)	80
Here Come Da Judge—Buena Vistas (68)	52
Raoul CITA ▶ 7572 (2)	**88**
Life Is But A Dream—Earls (61)	118
My Memories Of You—Donnie And The Dreamers (61)	29
Paolo CITORELLO ▶ 3685 (1)	**734**
Lazy Mary (Luna Mezzo Mare)—Lou Monte (58)	1468
Jimmy CLANTON ▶ 999 (4)	**4486**
Just A Dream—Jimmy Clanton (58)	*3976*
Letter To An Angel—Jimmy Clanton (58)	689
Part Of Me—Jimmy Clanton (58)	331
Just A Dream—Margaret Whiting (58)	*0.0*
Donald CLAPS ▶ 1954 (1)	**2054**
Beep Beep—Playmates (58)	4109
Eric CLAPTON ▶ 618 (18) HOF	**7000**
Lay Down Sally—Eric Clapton (77)	3975
Sunshine Of Your Love—Cream (68)	3604
Layla—Derek And The Dominos (72)	*1552*
I Can't Stand It—Eric Clapton And His Band (81)	1242
Wonderful Tonight—Eric Clapton (78)	754
Forever Man—Eric Clapton (85)	573
Hello Old Friend—Eric Clapton (76)	542
Let It Rain—Eric Clapton (72)	390
Layla—Derek And The Dominos (71)	*359*
Watch Out For Lucy—Eric Clapton And His Band (79)	239
Badge—Cream (69)	230
Anyone For Tennis (The Savage Seven Theme)—Cream (68)	137
Comin' Home—Delaney & Bonnie And Friends Featuring Eric Clapton (70)	84
Bell Bottom Blues—Eric Clapton (73)	*45*
Another Ticket—Eric Clapton And His Band (81)	44
Bad Love—Eric Clapton (90)	38
Bell Bottom Blues—Derek And The Dominos (71)	*34*
Blues Power (Live)—Eric Clapton (80)	20
Sidney CLARE ▶ 6612 (3) HOF	**151**
I Wanna Go Where You Go, Do What You Do (Then I'll Be Happy)—Eddie Fisher (55)	382
Ma! (He's Making Eyes At Me)—Lena Zavaroni (74)	31
On The Good Ship Lollipop—Wonder Who ? (66)	16
Chris CLARK ▶ 10884 (1)	**4.7**
I Want To Go Back There Again—Chris Clark (67)	9.4

Claudine CLARK ▶ 1506 (1)	**2853**
Party Lights—Claudine Clark (62)	2853
Dave CLARK ▶ 230 (15)	**14742**
Bits And Pieces—Dave Clark Five (64)	4088
Glad All Over—Dave Clark Five (64)	3143
Because—Dave Clark Five (64)	3059
Catch Us If You Can—Dave Clark Five (65)	2966
Can't You See That She's Mine—Dave Clark Five (64)	2823
Any Way You Want It—Dave Clark Five (64)	1945
Try Too Hard—Dave Clark Five (66)	1282
At The Scene—Dave Clark Five (66)	1146
Come Home—Dave Clark Five (65)	1101
Everybody Knows (I Still Love You)—Dave Clark Five (64)	926
Please Tell Me Why—Dave Clark Five (66)	830
Nineteen Days—Dave Clark Five (66)	408
Satisfied With You—Dave Clark Five (66)	347
I've Got To Have A Reason—Dave Clark Five (67)	311
Red And Blue—Dave Clark Five (67)	106
Dave (2) CLARK ▶ 4112 (6)	**589**
Chains And Things—B.B. King (70)	463
Why I Sing The Blues—B.B. King (69)	319
Ghetto Woman—B.B. King (71)	216
I Got Some Help I Don't Need—B.B. King (72)	129
Poverty—Bobby Bland (66)	50
I'm Gonna Sit In Till You Give In—B.B. King (62)	0.5
Dee CLARK [Delectus Clark] ▶ 472 (6)	**8813**
Raindrops—Dee Clark (61)	6123
You Can't Sit Down—Dovells (63)	*3787*
You Can't Sit Down (Part 2)—Phil Upchurch Combo (61)	*956*
Nobody But You—Dee Clark (58)	936
Your Friends—Dee Clark (61)	511
I'm Going Back to School—Dee Clark (62)	234
Gary CLARK ▶ 3747 (1)	**712**
Mary's Prayer—Danny Wilson (87)	712
Gene CLARK [Harold Eugene Clark] ▶ 1729 (5)	**2407**
You Showed Me—Turtles (68)	3696
Eight Miles High—Byrds (66)	1385
Set You Free This Time—Byrds (66)	59
Full Circle—Byrds (73)	32
I'll Feel A Whole Lot Better—Byrds (65)	5.7
Graeme CLARK ▶ 8628 (1)	**45**
Wishing I Was Lucky—Wet Wet Wet (88)	178
Guy CLARK ▶ 8249 (1)	**57**
L.A. Freeway—Jerry Jeff Walker (73)	57
—Hal Clark see: Hal SOUTHERN	
—Harold Eugene Clark see: Gene CLARK	
Jerri CLARK ▶ 11490 (1)	**1.5**
Continuing Story Of Harper Valley P.T.A.—Dee Mullins (68)	*4.4*
—Lee Clark see: Lee GALLO	
Michael CLARK [Michael James Bruce Clark] ▶ 1362 (4)	**3264**
Slow Hand—Pointer Sisters (81)	4979
Heart Of The Night—Juice Newton (82)	780
The Woman In Me—Donna Summer (82)	667
Wild Again—Starship (88)	102
—Michael George Jackson Clark see: Mick JACKSON	
—Michael James Bruce Clark see: Michael CLARK	
Petula CLARK ▶ 2475 (2)	**1452**
You're The One—Vogues (65)	2706
Now That You've Gone—Connie Stevens (65)	298
Richard CLARK ▶ 11340 (1)	**2.1**
Every Day And Every Night—Trolls (66)	4.3
Rudy CLARK ▶ 203 (20)	**15486**
Good Lovin'—Young Rascals (66)	*6878*
Everybody Plays The Fool—Main Ingredient (72)	*4562*
Got My Mind Set On You—George Harrison (87)	3952
The Shoop Shoop Song (It's In His Kiss)—Betty Everett (64)	*2802*
Everybody Plays The Fool—Aaron Neville (91)	*1326*
If You Gotta Make A Fool Of Somebody—James Ray (61)	*1123*
The Shoop Shoop Song (It's In His Kiss)—Cher (90)	*450*
Itty Bitty Pieces—James Ray (62)	429
Beg Me—Chuck Jackson (64)	359
Do It Right—Brook Benton (64)	236

If You Gotta Make A Fool Of Somebody—Maxine Brown (65)	*227*
Shirl Girl—Wayne Newton & The Newton Brothers (63)	184
You Can't Stand Alone—Wilson Pickett (67)	183
It's In His Kiss (The Shoop Shoop Song)—Kate Taylor (77)	*142*
Seven Lonely Nights—Four Tops (75)	54
Good Lovin'—Olympics (65)	*51*
Put On Your Shoes And Walk—Clarence Carter (73)	45
Good Lovin'—Grateful Dead (78)	*19*
What Can A Man Do—Ben E. King (64)	18
Do The Monkey—King Curtis (63)	4.4
Steve CLARK ▶ 1590 (12)	**2655**
Pour Some Sugar On Me—Def Leppard (88)	3871
Love Bites—Def Leppard (88)	3277
Armageddon It—Def Leppard (88)	2857
Photograph—Def Leppard (83)	1231
Hysteria—Def Leppard (88)	1083
Rocket—Def Leppard (89)	1017
Rock Of Ages—Def Leppard (83)	1009
Animal—Def Leppard (87)	796
Foolin'—Def Leppard (83)	557
Bringin' On The Heartbreak—Def Leppard (84)	157
Women—Def Leppard (87)	26
Rock Brigade—Def Leppard (80)	9.8
Tena CLARK ▶ 7385 (2)	**99**
Congratulations—Vesta (89)	214
Reservations For Two—Dionne Warwick (87)	83
—Alan Clarke see: Allan CLARKE	
Allan CLARKE [Harold Allan Clarke, Alan Clarke] ▶ 853 (18)	**5206**
Long Cool Woman (In A Black Dress)—Hollies (72)	5749
On A Carousel—Hollies (67)	*2080*
Carrie-Anne—Hollies (67)	2018
Stop Stop Stop—Hollies (66)	2003
Pay You Back With Interest—Hollies (67)	*585*
Jennifer Eccles—Hollies (68)	555
Tell Me To My Face—Keith (67)	500
Dear Eloise—Hollies (67)	416
(I Will Be Your) Shadow In The Street—Allan Clarke (78)	391
King Midas In Reverse—Hollies (67)	292
On A Carousel—Glass Moon (82)	*180*
Have You Ever Loved Somebody—Searchers (66)	165
Slipstream—Allan Clarke (80)	68
Pay You Back With Interest—Gary O' (81)	*45*
Another Night—Hollies (75)	*28*
The Day That Curly Billy Shot Down Crazy Sam McGee—Hollies (73)	9.6
Another Night—Wilson Brothers (79)	*3.9*
Do The Best You Can—Hollies (68)	3.5
Anthony Ralph CLARKE ▶ 9167 (1)	**30**
Our Song—Jack Jones (67)	59
—Boomer Clarke see: Boomer CASTLEMAN	
Grant CLARKE ▶ 4135 (4)	**584**
Ragtime Cowboy Joe—David Seville And The Chipmunks (59)	852
Second Hand Rose—Barbra Streisand (65)	580
Am I Blue—Cher (73)	*17*
Am I Blue—Ray Charles (61)	*2.8*
—Harold Allan Clarke see: Allan CLARKE	
Herb CLARKE ▶ 5926 (1)	**227**
Tic Tender Love And Care—Jimmie Rodgers (60)	681
Hugh CLARKE ▶ 1650 (14)	**2544**
Head To Toe—Lisa Lisa And Cult Jam (87)	4435
Lost In Emotion—Lisa Lisa And Cult Jam (87)	3486
Naughty Girls (Need Love Too)—Samantha Fox (88)	2531
All Cried Out—Lisa Lisa And Cult Jam With Full Force Featuring Paul Anthony And Bow Legged Lou (86)	1667
I Wanna Have Some Fun—Samantha Fox (88)	1135
I Wonder If I Take You Home—Lisa Lisa and Cult Jam with Full Force (85)	656
Thanks For My Child—Cheryl "Pepsii" Riley (88)	509
Little Jackie Wants To Be A Star—Lisa Lisa And Cult Jam (89)	441
Can You Feel The Beat—Lisa Lisa And Cult Jam (85)	231
Basketball—Kurtis Blow (85)	77
Someone To Love Me For Me—Lisa Lisa & Cult Jam (87)	52
Why Can't You Come Home—Ex-Girlfriend (91)	48

Hugh CLARKE ▶ 1650 (14) *Continued*	**2544**
Roxanne, Roxanne—UTFO (85)	28
Go For Yours—Lisa Lisa & Cult Jam with Full Force (88)	22
Jeremiah CLARKE ▶ 6872 (1)	**131**
Trumpet Voluntary—Royal Philharmonic Orchestra (81)	131
Peter CLARKE ▶ 6007 (2)	**217**
Kiss Them For Me—Siouxsie And The Banshees (91)	481
Peek-A-Boo—Siouxsie & The Banshees (88)	289
Stanley CLARKE ▶ 10634 (1)	**6.6**
I'm For Real—Howard Hewett (86)	13
Tony CLARKE [Ralph Thomas Williams] ▶ 2777 (4)	**1200**
Pushover—Etta James (63)	949
The Entertainer—Tony Clarke (65)	659
Two Sides (To Every Story)—Etta James (63)	108
(The Story Of) Woman, Love And A Man (Part 1)—Tony Clarke (64)	35
Vince CLARKE [Vincent John Martin] ▶ 2766 (6)	**1210**
Chains Of Love—Erasure (88)	1086
A Little Respect—Erasure (88)	957
Only You—Yaz (83)	127
Situation—Yazoo (82)	67
Chorus—Erasure (91)	53
Stop!—Erasure (89)	2.3
Willie CLARKE ▶ 1046 (18)	**4218**
I Wanna Sex You Up—Color Me Badd (91)	4560
Clean Up Woman—Betty Wright (71)	3048
Rockin' Chair—Gwen McCrae (75)	1685
Knockin' Boots—Candyman (90)	1245
Nobody But You Babe—Clarence Reid (69)	692
Baby Sitter—Betty Wright (72)	470
Girls Can't Do What The Guys Do—Betty Wright (68)	428
Secretary—Betty Wright (74)	230
It's Hard To Stop (Doing Something When It's Good To You)—Betty Wright (73)	116
Queen Of Clubs—K.C. & The Sunshine Band (76)	87
Let Me Be Your Lovemaker—Betty Wright (73)	85
If You Love Me Like You Say You Love Me—Betty Wright (72)	41
Where Is The Love—Betty Wright (75)	37
I Love The Way You Love—Betty Wright (71)	33
Tonight Is The Night Pt. 2—Betty Wright (78)	18
The Boogaloo Party—Flamingos (66)	13
Oola La—Betty Wright (75)	8.1
You Got Your Thing On A String—J.P. Robinson (69)	3.1
—Alison Clarkson see: Betty BOO	
Tony CLARKSON ▶ 11514 (1)	**1.4**
King Croesus—World Of Oz (68)	5.5
Richard CLASKY ▶ 2673 (1)	**1281**
Image Of A Girl—Safaris With The Phantom's Band (60)	2563
Quinton CLAUNCH ▶ 6252 (4)	**189**
A Man Needs A Woman—James Carr (67)	363
I'm A Fool For You—James Carr (67)	10
I'm Serious—Hilltoppers (57)	8.6
Love Attack—James Carr (66)	2.4
Adam CLAYTON ▶ 1100 (14)	**4015**
With Or Without You—U2 (87)	4346
I Still Haven't Found What I'm Looking For—U2 (87)	3862
Desire—U2 (88)	2667
Mysterious Ways—U2 (91)	2021
Angel Of Harlem—U2 (88)	876
Where The Streets Have No Name—U2 (87)	*803*
Pride (In The Name Of Love)—U2 (84)	535
In God's Country—U2 (87)	300
New Year's Day—U2 (83)	295
When Love Comes To Town—U2 With B. B. King (89)	105
The Fly—U2 (91)	78
All I Want Is You—U2 (89)	76
I Will Follow—U2 (84)	57
Where The Streets Have No Name—Pet Shop Boys (91)	*37*
Harold CLAYTON ▶ 1939 (1)	**2083**
Take Your Time (Do It Right) (Part 1)—S.O.S. Band (80)	4167
Justin CLAYTON ▶ 4348 (1)	**515**
Valotte—Julian Lennon (84)	1544
Paul CLAYTON [Paul Clayton Worthington] ▶ 4233 (3)	**552**
Gotta Travel On—Billy Grammer (58)	*3674*
Gotta Travel On—Timi Yuro (63)	*190*
Gotta Travel On—Harry Belafonte (59)	*0.0*
—Stanley Clayton see: Bob THIELE	
David CLAYTON-THOMAS [David Henry Thomsett] ▶ 581 (6)	**7486**
Spinning Wheel—Blood, Sweat & Tears (69)	*5800*
All Or Nothing—Milli Vanilli (89)	1700
Lucretia Mac Evil—Blood, Sweat & Tears (70)	875
Go Down Gamblin'—Blood, Sweat & Tears (71)	582
Lisa, Listen To Me—Blood, Sweat & Tears (71)	117
Spinning Wheel Pt. 1—James Brown (71)	*37*
Martine CLÉMENCEAU [Martine Chapot, Clémentine] ▶ 3312 (1)	**904**
Solitaire—Laura Branigan (83)	1808
Jack H. CLEMENT ▶ 1381 (14)	**3216**
Guess Things Happen That Way—Johnny Cash And The Tennessee Two (58)	*1143*
Ballad Of A Teenage Queen—Johnny Cash and the Tennessee Two (58)	891
Miller's Cave—Bobby Bare (64)	485
The One On The Right Is On The Left—Johnny Cash (66)	302
It's Just About Time—Johnny Cash And The Tennessee Two (58)	118
Harper Valley P.T.A. (Later That Same Day)—Ben Colder (68)	*111*
Everybody Loves A Nut—Johnny Cash (66)	109
Katy Too—Johnny Cash And The Tennessee Two (59)	96
Big Brother—Dickey Lee (64)	30
California Girl (And The Tennessee Square)—Tompall & The Glaser Brothers (69)	25
Down The Street To 301—Johnny Cash (60)	18
How Blue Can You Get—B.B. King (64)	13
I Know One—Jim Reeves (60)	13
Guess Things Happen That Way—June Valli (61)	*4.7*
—Clémentine see: Martine CLÉMENCEAU	
Adrian CLEMENTS ▶ 8294 (1)	**55**
The Lonely One—Special Delivery Featuring Terry Huff (76)	110
Zeke CLEMENTS ▶ 7813 (1)	**74**
Send Me Some Money—Les Paul and Mary Ford (56)	74
Alistair CLEMINSON ▶ 10282 (1)	**10**
Holiday—Nazareth (80)	63
David CLEMINSON ▶ 11738 (1)	**0.3**
Come On Down (From The Top Of That Hill)—Jackie deShannon (67)	0.9
Clem CLEMPSON [David Clempson] ▶ 7411 (1)	**97**
Hot 'N' Nasty—Humble Pie (72)	389
—David Clempson see: Clem CLEMPSON	
James CLENCH ▶ 11464 (1)	**1.6**
Down The Road—B.T.O. (78)	6.3
N.J. CLESI [Nick Jeannine Clesi] ▶ 3386 (1)	**872**
I'm Sorry I Made You Cry—Connie Francis (58)	872
Al CLEVELAND ▶ 675 (13)	**6424**
What's Going On—Marvin Gaye (71)	*5213*
I Second That Emotion—Smokey Robinson & The Miracles (67)	4546
Baby, Baby Don't Cry—Smokey Robinson & The Miracles (69)	2458
What's Going On—Cyndi Lauper (87)	*885*
Special Occasion—Smokey Robinson & The Miracles (68)	729
Yester Love—Smokey Robinson & The Miracles (68)	664
Doggone Right—Smokey Robinson & The Miracles (69)	615
Point It Out—Smokey Robinson & The Miracles (69)	525
Here I Go Again—Smokey Robinson & The Miracles (69)	281
Malinda—Bobby Taylor & The Vancouvers (68)	254
Wholy Holy—Aretha Franklin (72)	151
Yesterday's Hero—Gene Pitney (64)	66
What's Going On—Quincy Jones (71)	*4.6*
Mike CLEVELAND ▶ 9887 (1)	**15**
Last Night A D.J. Saved My Life—Indeep (83)	15
James CLIBURN ▶ 5570 (1)	**270**
Take A Look Around—Smith (70)	540
Jimmy CLIFF [James E. Chambers] ▶ 2437 (6)	**1487**
Wonderful World, Beautiful People—Jimmy Cliff (69)	1091
Let Your Yeah Be Yeah—Brownsville Station (73)	266
Sitting In Limbo—Don Brown (78)	115
You Can Get It If You Really Want—Desmond Dekker (70)	28
Many Rivers To Cross—Nilsson (74)	26
Come Into My Life—Jimmy Cliff (70)	18
Buzz CLIFFORD [Reese Francis Clifford] ▶ 4163 (1)	**577**
Echo Park—Keith Barbour (69)	577
Gordon CLIFFORD ▶ 5620 (2)	**264**
Paradise—Sammy Turner (60)	466
I Surrender, Dear—Aretha Franklin (62)	62
—Reese Francis Clifford see: Buzz CLIFFORD	
Dennis CLIFTON ▶ 7278 (1)	**106**
Baby I Want You—Funky Communication Committee (79)	211
Paul CLIFTON ▶ 8867 (1)	**37**
Miami—Eugene Church (59)	75
Simon CLIMIE ▶ 1025 (5)	**4313**
I Knew You Were Waiting (For Me)—Aretha Franklin & George Michael (87)	3691
My Heart Can't Tell You No—Rod Stewart (88)	2425
Invincible—Pat Benatar (85)	1289
Room To Move—Animotion (89)	1179
Love Changes (Everything)—Climie Fisher (88)	651
Peggy CLINGER ▶ 5503 (1)	**277**
Rock Me Baby—David Cassidy (72)	555
Donna Lynn CLINTON ▶ 11561 (1)	**1.2**
Agony of DeFeet—Parliament (81)	3.6
George CLINTON ▶ 1364 (24)	**3258**
Tear The Roof Off The Sucker (Give Up The Funk)—Parliament (76)	*1416*
(I Wanna) Testify—Parliaments (67)	*1404*
The Humpty Dance—Digital Underground (90)	1362
One Nation Under A Groove - Part I—Funkadelic (78)	1189
Flash Light—Parliament (78)	1115
We Want The Funk—Gerardo (91)	*667*
Testify (I Wonna)—Johnnie Taylor (69)	*569*
Mama Said Knock You Out—LL Cool J (91)	473
Me Myself And I—De La Soul (89)	353
Kiss You Back—Digital Underground (91)	322
All Your Goodies Are Gone (The Loser's Seat)—Parliaments (67)	221
(Not Just) Knee Deep - Part 1—Funkadelic (79)	182
I'll Bet You—Funkadelic (69)	116
Can You Get To That—Funkadelic (71)	115
Bootzilla—Bootsy's Rubber Band (78)	87
I Wanna Know If It's Good To You?—Funkadelic (70)	65
Aqua Boogie (A Psychoalphadiscobetabioaquadoloop)—Parliament (78)	62
Up For The Down Stroke—Parliament (74)	57
You And Your Folks, Me And My Folks—Funkadelic (71)	34
Chocolate City—Parliament (75)	16
Disco To Go—Brides Of Funkenstein (78)	15
Do That Stuff—Parliament (76)	7.1
Better By The Pound—Funkadelic (75)	1.5
Theme From The Black Hole—Parliament (80)	1.0
George S. CLINTON ▶ 3900 (2)	**663**
Life And Breath—Climax Featuring Sonny Geraci (72)	604
If You Only Believe (Jesus For Tonite)—Michel Polnareff (76)	175
Larry CLINTON ▶ 4522 (2)	**471**
Calypso Melody—David Rose And His Orchestra (57)	*471*
Calypso Melody—Danny Welton (57)	*0.0*
Robert CLIVILLÉS ▶ 522 (10)	**8107**
Emotions—Mariah Carey (91)	4618
Gonna Make You Sweat—C & C Music Factory (Featuring Freedom Williams) (90)	4586
Here We Go—C & C Music Factory (Featuring Freedom Williams And Zelma Davis) (91)	3090
Things That Make You Go Hmmmm—C & C Music Factory (Featuring Freedom Williams) (91)	2086
Could This Be Love—Seduction (90)	1133
You're My One And Only (True Love)—Seduction (89)	682
Let The Beat Hit 'Em—Lisa Lisa & Cult Jam (91)	262
Just A Touch Of Love—C & C Music Factory (91)	229

Robert CLIVILLÉS ▶ 522 (10) ***Continued***	**8107**
Breakdown—Seduction (90)	46
Love Me Forever Or Love Me Not—Trilogy (91)	33
John C. CLORE ▶ 9079 (1)	**32**
I Need Love—Third Booth (68)	32
—Christopher Cloud see: Tommy BOYCE	
David CLOWNEY [Dave "Baby" Cortez] ▶ 1345 (12)	**3300**
Happy Organ—Dave "Baby" Cortez (59)	5914
Rinky Dink—Baby Cortez (62)	1807
Whistling Organ—Dave "Baby" Cortez (59)	293
Happy Weekend—Dave "Baby" Cortez (62)	189
Count Down—Dave "Baby" Cortez (66)	122
Organ Shout—Dave "Baby" Cortez (63)	93
Cat Nip—Dave "Baby" Cortez (60)	89
Hot Cakes! 1st Serving—Dave "Baby" Cortez (63)	7.0
Fiesta—Dave "Baby" Cortez (62)	3.5
Hurricane—Dave "Baby" Cortez (60)	3.0
Piano Shuffle—Dave "Baby" Cortez (59)	0.8
So Strange—Jesters (57)	0.3
Julia CLOWNEY ▶ 8544 (1)	**47**
Organ Shout—Dave "Baby" Cortez (63)	93
Jeremy CLYDE ▶ 6180 (3)	**197**
What Do You Want With Me—Chad & Jeremy (65)	355
You Are She—Chad & Jeremy (66)	38
Should I—Chad & Jeremy (65)	0.5
Theophilus COAKLEY ▶ 5793 (2)	**241**
Do What You Wanna Do—T-Connection (77)	216
At Midnight—T-Connection (79)	51
Nonne COAN ▶ 9615 (1)	**20**
Boom-A-Dip-Dip—Stan Robinson (59)	61
Carroll COATES ▶ 8125 (5)	**61**
Soft Sands—Chordettes (57)	*122*
Soft Sands—Dorothy Collins (57)	*0.0*
Soft Sands—Rover Boys (57)	*0.0*
Soft Sands—Ray Ellis & His Orchestra (57)	*0.0*
Soft Sands—Voices Of Walter Schumann (57)	*0.0*
Eric COATES ▶ 9694 (1)	**19**
Sleepy Lagoon—Platters (60)	38
Maurice COATES ▶ 4236 (2)	**551**
Dry Your Eyes—Brenda & The Tabulations (67)	1093
Just Once In A Lifetime— Brenda & The Tabulations (67)	12
Dennis COATS ▶ 10487 (1)	**7.9**
(I've Been Lookin' For) A New Way To Say I Love You— Driver (77)	24
Kurt COBAIN ▶ 3801 (1)	**695**
Smells Like Teen Spirit—Nirvana (91)	2086
Ed COBB ▶ 656 (9)	**6677**
Tainted Love—Soft Cell (82)	2403
Dirty Water—Standells (66)	*2146*
Every Little Bit Hurts—Brenda Holloway (64)	1041
Sometimes Good Guys Don't Wear White— Standells (66)	356
Dirty Water—Inmates (79)	*291*
Why Pick On Me—Standells (66)	278
Brontosaurus Stomp—Piltdown Men (60)	109
I'll Always Love You—Brenda Holloway (64)	106
Piltdown Rides Again—Piltdown Men (60)	2.5
George L. COBB ▶ 4466 (4)	**487**
Alabama Jubilee—Ferko String Band (55)	*975*
Alabama Jubilee— Cliff Steward & The San Francisco Boys (55)	*0.0*
Alabama Jubilee—Art Mooney & His Orchestra (55)	*0.0*
Alabama Jubilee—David Carroll & His Orchestra (55)	*0.0*
James E. COBB ▶ 7134 (1)	**114**
Searching For A Thrill—Starbuck (78)	229
—James B. Cobb Jr. see: J.R. COBB	
Joe COBB ▶ 2796 (8)	**1191**
Right On The Tip Of My Tongue— Brenda & The Tabulations (71)	1092
So Much Love—Faith, Hope & Charity (70)	552
Triangle Of Love (Hey Diddle Diddle)— Presidents (71)	293
And My Heart Sang (Tra La La)— Brenda & The Tabulations (70)	229
Heavy Love—David Ruffin (76)	155
A Part Of You—Brenda & The Tabulations (71)	32
The Language Of Love—Intrigues (71)	21
Baby Don't Take Your Love— Faith, Hope & Charity (70)	10

Johnny COBB ▶ 5845 (2)	**237**
Straight From The Heart—Allman Brothers Band (81)	368
Angeline—Allman Brothers Band (80)	161
Joyce COBB ▶ 7415 (1)	**97**
Dig The Gold—Joyce Cobb (79)	194
J.R. COBB [James B. Cobb Jr.] ▶ 463 (23)	**9013**
Spooky—Classics IV (67)	*5516*
Stormy—Classics IV Featuring Dennis Yost (68)	*4909*
Traces—Classics IV Featuring Dennis Yost (69)	*4007*
I Take It Back—Sandy Posey (67)	1475
Everyday With You Girl— Classics IV Featuring Dennis Yost (69)	1298
Spooky—Atlanta Rhythm Section (79)	*887*
Do It Or Die—Atlanta Rhythm Section (79)	861
Most Of All—B.J. Thomas (70)	718
What Am I Crying For?— Dennis Yost And The Classics IV (72)	559
Midnight—Dennis Yost And The Classics IV (69)	481
Stormy—Santana (78)	*450*
Be Young, Be Foolish, Be Happy—Tams (68)	375
Change Of Heart—Dennis Yost And The Classics IV (69)	360
The Funniest Thing— Dennis Yost And The Classics IV (70)	282
Traces—Lettermen (69)	*238*
Where Did All The Good Times Go— Dennis Yost And The Classics IV (70)	190
Soul Train—Classics IV (68)	176
Champagne Jam—Atlanta Rhythm Section (78)	171
Georgia Rhythm—Atlanta Rhythm Section (77)	94
Something I'll Remember—Sandy Posey (68)	57
Rosanna—Dennis Yost And The Classics IV (73)	30
I Ain't Much—Atlanta Rhythm Section (80)	29
Back Up Against The Wall— Atlanta Rhythm Section (79)	18
Margaret COBB ▶ 943 (5)	**4715**
Hey! Baby—Bruce Channel (62)	*8663*
Number One Man—Bruce Channel (62)	400
Hey! Baby—Jose Feliciano (69)	*381*
Hey Baby—Ringo Starr (76)	*116*
Come On Baby—Bruce Channel (62)	4.9
Rick COBB ▶ 7008 (1)	**122**
D.O.A.—Bloodrock (70)	733
Cy COBEN [Seymour Coben] ▶ 3957 (8)	**642**
My Treasure—Hilltoppers (55)	*288*
Lonely Little Robin— Browns Featuring Jim Edward Brown (60)	179
That Greasy Kid Stuff—Janie Grant (62)	144
I Saw Esau—Ames Brothers (56)	125
Boppin' In A Sack—Lane Brothers (58)	61
Souvenirs—Barbara Evans (59)	12
Old Piano Roll Blues— Johnny Maddox And The Rhythmasters (55)	7.5
My Treasure—Connie Francis (55)	*0.0*
—Seymour Coben see: Cy COBEN	
Robert W. COBERT ▶ 2058 (1)	**1940**
Quentin's Theme— Charles Randolph Grean Sounde (69)	1940
Ray COBURN [Raymond Alfred Cockburn] ▶ 4480 (1)	**484**
Feel It Again—Honeymoon Suite (86)	484
Richard COBURN [Reginald DeLong] ▶ 3814 (4)	**691**
Whispering—Nino Tempo & April Stevens (63)	*1526*
Whispering— Dr. Buzzard's Original "Savannah" Band (76)	*448*
Whispering—Paul Whiteman & The New Ambassador Hotel Orchestra (54)	*98*
Whispering—Bachelors (63)	*0.0*
Shelly COBURN ▶ 3641 (2)	**753**
Remember Me—Rita Pavone (64)	753
Only A Fool Breaks His Own Heart— Arthur Prysock (65)	0.5
Riccardo COCCIANTE ▶ 8394 (1)	**52**
When Love Has Gone Away—Richard Cocciante (76)	208
Bob COCHRAN ▶ 7462 (2)	**94**
Somethin' Else—Eddie Cochran (59)	188
Three Steps To Heaven—Eddie Cochran (60)	0.8
Charles E. COCHRAN ▶ 6241 (1)	**190**
Spanish Eddie—Laura Branigan (85)	381
Charles Lincoln COCHRAN ▶ 7814 (1)	**74**
Years From Now—Dr. Hook (80)	148

Dorcas COCHRAN ▶ 4471 (9)	**486**
Mostly Martha—Crew-Cuts (55)	544
Summer Dreams—McGuire Sisters (59)	230
Such A Day—Rita Raines (56)	*133*
Such A Day—Vera Lynn (56)	*55*
In The Beginning—Frankie Laine (54)	30
Again—Lettermen (62)	26
Suddenly—Jo Stafford (54)	22
Under The Bridges Of Paris—Dean Martin (55)	18
Here—Tony Martin (54)	0.0
Eddie COCHRAN ▶ 1629 (8)	**2588**
Summertime Blues—Blue Cheer (68)	*2126*
Summertime Blues—Eddie Cochran (58)	*1493*
Summertime Blues—Who (70)	*976*
C'mon Everybody—Eddie Cochran (58)	*493*
C'mon Everybody— Jive Bunny And The Mastermixers (89)	*80*
Summertime Blues— Jive Bunny & The Mastermixers (90)	*6.7*
Teenage Heaven—Eddie Cochran (59)	0.8
Three Steps To Heaven—Eddie Cochran (60)	0.8
—Garland Petty Cochran see: Hank COCHRAN	
Hank COCHRAN [Garland Petty Cochran] ▶ 264 (16)	**12906**
A Little Bitty Tear—Burl Ives (61)	*2827*
Make The World Go Away—Eddy Arnold (65)	*2430*
I Fall To Pieces—Patsy Cline (61)	2018
Funny Way Of Laughin'—Burl Ives (62)	1763
She's Got You—Patsy Cline (62)	1674
Make The World Go Away—Timi Yuro (63)	*943*
I Want To Go With You—Eddy Arnold (66)	680
Go On Home—Patti Page (61)	603
Don't Touch Me—Bettye Swann (69)	*561*
Make The World Go Away— Donny And Marie Osmond (75)	*227*
Don't Touch Me—Jeannie Seely (66)	*84*
A Little Bitty Tear—Wanda Jackson (62)	*63*
You're Stronger Than Me—Patsy Cline (62)	37
Tears Broke Out On Me—Eddy Arnold (62)	14
The Same Old Hurt—Burl Ives (63)	8.6
Make The World Go Away—Ray Price (63)	*0.4*
Steve COCHRAN ▶ 5316 (1)	**307**
Heartache Away—Don Johnson (86)	307
Todd COCHRAN [Todd Thomas Cochran, Bayété] ▶ 10942 (1)	**4.2**
My Pearl—Automatic Man (76)	17
Wayne COCHRAN ▶ 519 (3)	**8216**
Last Kiss—J. Frank Wilson And The Cavaliers (64)	*7406*
Last Kiss—Wednesday (73)	*699*
Last Kiss—J. Frank Wilson And The Cavaliers (73)	*110*
David COCHRANE ▶ 8368 (1)	**53**
Why You Wanna Try Me—Commodores (82)	106
Don COCHRANE ▶ 6949 (1)	**126**
I Love Onions—Susan Christie (66)	252
Tom COCHRANE ▶ 6209 (2)	**193**
White Hot—Red Rider (80)	163
Young Thing, Wild Dreams (Rock Me)—Red Rider (84)	112
Bruce COCKBURN ▶ 3382 (2)	**873**
Wondering Where The Lions Are— Bruce Cockburn (80)	810
If I Had A Rocket Launcher—Bruce Cockburn (85)	63
—Raymond Alfred Cockburn see: Ray COBURN	
Joe COCKER [John R. Cocker] ▶ 3621 (4)	**764**
High Time We Went—Joe Cocker (71)	871
Woman To Woman— Joe Cocker And The Chris Stainton Band (72)	346
Pardon Me Sir—Joe Cocker (73)	308
Black-Eyed Blues—Joe Cocker (71)	1.5
—John R. Cocker see: Joe COCKER	
Bud COCKRELL ▶ 6682 (1)	**145**
A Place In The Sun—Pablo Cruise (77)	289
Phil CODY ▶ 592 (8)	**7344**
Laughter In The Rain—Neil Sedaka (74)	5057
Bad Blood—Neil Sedaka (75)	4731
Doing It All For My Baby—Huey Lewis and the News (87)	1308
Should've Never Let You Go— Neil Sedaka & Dara Sedaka (80)	1041
Solitaire—Carpenters (75)	812
Love In The Shadows—Neil Sedaka (76)	796
The Immigrant—Neil Sedaka (75)	559
Steppin' Out—Neil Sedaka (76)	384

David Allan COE ▶ 5237 (1)	**320**
Would You Lay With Me (In A Field Of Stone)—Tanya Tucker (74)	320
Steve COE ▶ 6936 (1)	**127**
Shattered Glass—Laura Branigan (87)	255
Thomas J. COE [Thomas Coe, Tommy Jarrett, Coe Porter] ▶ 2640 (4)	**1300**
How The Time Flies—Jerry Wallace (58)	1203
Think His Name—Johnny Rivers (71)	181
Life's A Holiday—Jerry Wallace (61)	130
Mister Livingston—Larry Verne (60)	111
Brice COEFIELD ▶ 6952 (2)	**126**
Puddin N' Tain (Ask Me Again I'll Tell You The Same)—Alley Cats (63)	343
This Is The Nite—Valiants (57)	45
Dennis COFFEY ▶ 951 (5)	**4692**
Scorpio—Dennis Coffey And The Detroit Guitar Band (71)	3507
Taurus—Dennis Coffey And The Detroit Guitar Band (72)	1064
Ride, Sally, Ride—Dennis Coffey (72)	117
Our Faded Love—Royaltones (64)	7.7
Getting It On—Dennis Coffey (72)	0.0
Terry COFFEY ▶ 8871 (1)	**37**
Show Me—Howard Hewett (90)	112
Nelson COGANE ▶ 11410 (1)	**1.8**
Is There Somebody Else—Dream Weavers (56)	5.5
Danny COGGINS ▶ 6062 (1)	**210**
Pucker Up Buttercup—Jr. Walker & The All Stars (67)	629
Wayne COGSWELL ▶ 4931 (3)	**379**
Night Theme—Mark II (60)	338
Teensville—Chet Atkins (60)	186
The Slop—Chet Atkins (61)	24
—Alice Cohen see: Alice DeSOTO	
—Daniel Cohen see: Casey KELLY	
David COHEN ▶ 5729 (2)	**250**
Mongoose—Elephant's Memory (70)	737
Skyscraper Commando—Elephant's Memory (71)	13
—David Alexander Cohen see: David COURTNEY	
Eddie COHEN [Eddie Stuart] ▶ 9361 (2)	**25**
His Name Was Dean—Nathan Russell (56)	*51*
His Name Was Dean—Jimmy Wakely (56)	*0.0*
—Edwin Greines Cohen see: Edwin GREINES	
—Elizabeth Cohen see: Betty COMDEN	
Fred COHEN ▶ 5735 (1)	**249**
Woman Is A Man's Best Friend—Teddy And The Twilights (62)	249
—Jacob Cohen see: Rodney DANGERFIELD	
—Jean Cohen see: Bernard KESSLAIR	
Jeffrey E. COHEN ▶ 1741 (7)	**2385**
Freeway Of Love—Aretha Franklin (85)	2925
You're A Friend Of Mine—Clarence Clemons (85)	936
Jimmy Lee—Aretha Franklin (86)	439
Put Your Mouth On Me—Eddie Murphy (89)	425
Jody—Jermaine Stewart (86)	290
Baby Come To Me—Regina Belle (89)	187
Attack Of The Name Game—Stacy Lattisaw (82)	54
Jerry Allen COHEN ▶ 4509 (1)	**474**
Ain't No Stoppin' Us Now—McFadden & Whitehead (79)	1423
—Kalman Cohen see: Kal MANN	
—Leah Cohen see: Leah KUNKEL	
Leonard COHEN ▶ 5826 (2) HOF	**239**
Suzanne—Noel Harrison (67)	232
So Long, Marianne—Brian Hyland (71)	6.3
Lisa COHEN [Lisa Catherine Cohen, Tammy Hutson] ▶ 6987 (1)	**124**
Ooh La La—David Hallyday (91)	248
—Maurice Alfred Cohen see: Michael CARR	
Murray COHEN [L. White] ▶ 6626 (2)	**150**
How Can I Forget—Jimmy Holiday (63)	*389*
How Can I Forget—Ben E. King (63)	*60*
—Samuel Cohen see: Sammy CAHN	
—Stuart David Cohen see: David BLUE	
—Chester Cohn see: Chester CONN	
James M. COHN [Jim "Chopper" Cohn] ▶ 11596 (1)	**1.0**
Boy Toy—Tia (87)	3.1

Marc COHN ▶ 2259 (3)	**1686**
Walking In Memphis—Marc Cohn (91)	1284
Silver Thunderbird—Marc Cohn (91)	233
True Companion—Marc Cohn (91)	169
Cirino COLACRAI ▶ 2363 (8)	**1557**
Runaround—Fleetwoods (60)	*875*
Runaround—Three Chuckles (54)	*599*
It's Just A House Without You—Brook Benton (61)	174
Hurtin' Inside—Brook Benton (59)	33
Nothin' Shakin—Eddie Fontaine (58)	27
Foolishly—Three Chuckles (55)	*24*
Runaround—Karen Chandler (54)	*0.0*
Foolishly—Buddy Cole with The Wood Sisters (55)	*0.0*
—Antoinette Colandreo see: Toni COLANDREO	
Toni COLANDREO [Toni C., Antoinette Colandreo] ▶ 1906 (4)	**2126**
The Power—Snap! (90)	2984
Love Will Save The Day—Whitney Houston (88)	1077
Say It, Say It—E.G. Daily (86)	120
The Real Thing—Jellybean (87)	29
Domenico COLAROSSI ▶ 6943 (1)	**127**
All—James Darren (67)	507
Calvin COLBERT ▶ 7586 (1)	**87**
Alvin Stone (The Birth & Death Of A Gangster)—Fantastic Four (75)	175
John COLBERT ▶ 5518 (1)	**275**
Hearsay—Soul Children (72)	550
Elmer COLBY ▶ 10532 (1)	**7.5**
Take Everything But You—Kitty Kallen (54)	23
Robert COLBY ▶ 8626 (3)	**45**
Free Again—Barbra Streisand (66)	119
Passport To The Future—Jean Jacques Perrey (70)	20
Jilted—Teresa Brewer (54)	0.0
Nat "King" COLE [Nathaniel Adams Coles] ▶ 4521 (4)	**472**
With You On My Mind—Nat "King" Cole (57)	800
Madrid—Nat "King" Cole (59)	198
Straighten Up And Fly Right—DeJohn Sisters (58)	52
Whatcha' Gonna Do—Nat King Cole (60)	6.6
David COLE ▶ 603 (11)	**7203**
Emotions—Mariah Carey (91)	4618
Two To Make It Right—Seduction (89)	3363
We Can't Go Wrong—Cover Girls (89)	1676
Because Of You—Cover Girls (87)	694
You're My One And Only (True Love)—Seduction (89)	682
My Heart Skips A Beat—Cover Girls (89)	400
Let The Beat Hit 'Em—Lisa Lisa & Cult Jam (91)	262
All That Glitters Isn't Gold—Cover Girls (90)	242
I'm Never Gonna Give You Up—Brat Pack (90)	81
Breakdown—Seduction (90)	46
Love Me Forever Or Love Me Not—Trilogy (91)	33
Gardner COLE ▶ 1262 (9)	**3543**
Open Your Heart—Madonna (86)	4274
Everything—Jody Watley (89)	1977
Another Lover—Giant Steps (88)	1147
Strange But True—Times Two (88)	711
Most Of All—Jody Watley (88)	213
Into You—Giant Steps (89)	166
Inside A Dream—Jane Wiedlin (88)	148
How Can I Forget You—Elisa Fiorillo (88)	143
Live It Up—Gardner Cole (88)	25
Johnny COLE ▶ 10399 (1)	**8.9**
Look At Me—Dobie Gray (63)	8.9
Jude COLE ▶ 2147 (3)	**1819**
Baby, It's Tonight—Jude Cole (90)	1136
Time For Letting Go—Jude Cole (90)	492
House Full Of Reasons—Jude Cole (90)	190
—Larry Cole see: Larry STEINBACHEK	
Natalie COLE ▶ 5715 (2)	**251**
Sophisticated Lady (She's A Different Lady)—Natalie Cole (76)	730
Annie Mae—Natalie Cole (78)	7.8
Ralph COLE ▶ 7262 (1)	**107**
Take It Slow (Out In The Country)—Lighthouse (71)	320
Tony COLE [Branko Bernard Miller] ▶ 9403 (2)	**24**
Beg, Steal Or Borrow—New Seekers (72)	45
Suite: Man And Woman—Tony Cole (72)	9.3
Bud COLEMAN [Ervan Coleman] ▶ 4594 (1)	**458**
Tijuana Taxi—Herb Alpert & The Tijuana Brass (65)	458

Cy COLEMAN [Seymour Kaufman] ▶ 2387 (12) HOF	**1537**
Witchcraft—Frank Sinatra (57)	1455
Firefly—Tony Bennett (58)	1081
I'm Gonna Laugh You Right Out Of My Life—Nat "King" Cole (55)	211
Autumn Waltz—Tony Bennett with Percy Faith and His Orchestra and Chorus (56)	142
If My Friends Could See Me Now—Linda Clifford (78)	72
Real Live Girl—Steve Alaimo (65)	47
Pass Me By—Peggy Lee (65)	*29*
Where Am I Going?—Barbra Streisand (66)	12
Hey, Look Me Over—Pete King Chorale and Orchestra (61)	11
I Love My Wife—Frank Sinatra (77)	7.0
My How The Time Goes By—Patti Page (57)	5.7
Pass Me By—Mike Douglas (65)	*0.0*
David E. COLEMAN ▶ 6035 (4)	**214**
Paper Valentine—Mills Brothers (55)	*117*
The Boston Fancy—Gisele MacKenzie (55)	*97*
The Boston Fancy—Marian Caruso (55)	*0.0*
Paper Valentine—Crackerjacks (55)	*0.0*
Duke COLEMAN [Morris Lee Coleman] ▶ 8040 (1)	**64**
Southern Country Boy—Carter Brothers (65)	64
—Ervan Coleman see: Bud COLEMAN	
Jim COLEMAN ▶ 10330 (1)	**10**
Hello Fool—Ralph Emery (61)	20
Larry COLEMAN ▶ 2454 (13)	**1469**
Just As Much As Ever—Bobby Vinton (67)	*966*
Just As Much As Ever—Bob Beckham (59)	*956*
Voices—Fontane Sisters (56)	290
Good And Lonesome—Kay Starr (55)	273
Rockin' The Cha Cha—Alan Dale (55)	221
That's Ok With Me—Susan Hunter (55)	53
One Suit—"Tennessee" Ernie Ford (57)	41
I Like Them All—Dean Martin (55)	14
Wait For Tomorrow—Jill Corey (56)	12
Hummin' And Waltzin'—Les Paul and Mary Ford (57)	7.6
Hep Dee Hootie (Cutie Wootie)—Tommy Sands (57)	4.7
Big Guitar—David Hill (58)	*0.0*
Hook—Rita Robbins (54)	0.0
Lisa COLEMAN ▶ 5340 (3)	**303**
Mountains—Prince And The Revolution (86)	567
Waterfall—Wendy & Lisa (87)	232
America—Prince & The Revolution (85)	220
Lonnie COLEMAN ▶ 6118 (1)	**203**
Boom Boom Boomerang—DeCastro Sisters (55)	203
Martin COLEMAN ▶ 7433 (4)	**96**
If This Is Love (I'd Rather Be Lonely)—Precisions (67)	215
Together We Can Make Such Sweet Music—Spinners (73)	45
Greetings (This Is Uncle Sam)—Valadiers (61)	*9.2*
Greetings (This Is Uncle Sam)—Monitors (66)	*5.8*
—Morris Lee Coleman see: Duke COLEMAN	
Ron COLEMAN ▶ 2918 (1)	**1119**
Tired Of Toein' The Line—Rocky Burnette (80)	2237
—Thelma Louise Coleman see: Thelma GORDY	
Tony COLEMAN ▶ 5127 (1)	**337**
One Hundred Ways—Quincy Jones (81)	1012
Walter COLEMAN ▶ 6346 (1)	**181**
Baby Oh Baby—Shells (60)	542
—Nathaniel Adams Coles see: Nat "King" COLE	
Doris COLEY ▶ 6831 (1)	**134**
I Met Him On A Sunday (Ronde-Ronde)—Shirelles (58)	537
John Ford COLEY [John Edward Colley] ▶ 3627 (2)	**761**
Gone Too Far—England Dan & John Ford Coley (77)	712
What Can I Do With This Broken Heart—England Dan & John Ford Coley (79)	147
Michael COLICCHIO ▶ 11360 (1)	**2.1**
The Story Of Our Love—Johnny Mathis (59)	4.2
Sidney COLIN [Marvin Scott] ▶ 10177 (4)	**12**
Friends And Neighbors—Sammy Kaye & "Swing And Sway" Orchestra (54)	*8.7*
Friends And Neighbors—Plunkett Family (54)	*8.7*
Friends And Neighbors—Billy Cotton & Band (54)	*8.7*
Friends And Neighbors—Tommy Prisco (54)	*8.7*

Johnny COLLA ▶ 1216 (5)	**3665**
The Power Of Love—Huey Lewis and the News (85)	4627
The Heart Of Rock & Roll—Huey Lewis and the News (84)	2167
If This Is It—Huey Lewis and the News (84)	1977
Workin' For A Livin'—Huey Lewis and the News (82)	267
Don't Make Me Do It—Patrick Simmons (83)	38
—Allen Collay see: Allen CALLAIS	
Phil COLLEN ▶ 1887 (7)	**2155**
Pour Some Sugar On Me—Def Leppard (88)	3871
Love Bites—Def Leppard (88)	3277
Armageddon It—Def Leppard (88)	2857
Hysteria—Def Leppard (88)	1083
Rocket—Def Leppard (89)	1017
Animal—Def Leppard (87)	796
Women—Def Leppard (87)	26
David COLLETT ▶ 5304 (3)	**310**
Summer Set—Monty Kelly & His Orchestra (60)	*619*
Summer Set—Mr. Acker Bilk (60)	*0.0*
Summer Set—Ronnie Chamberlain (60)	*0.0*
—John Edward Colley see: John Ford COLEY	
Keith COLLEY ▶ 3300 (7)	**908**
Shame, Shame—Magic Lanterns (68)	996
Playgirl—Thee Prophets (69)	426
One Track Mind—Knickerbockers (66)	330
Enamorado—Keith Colley (63)	232
Groovy Summertime—Love Generation (67)	163
Father Sebastian—Ramblers (2) (64)	47
High On Love—Knickerbockers (66)	14
Linda Jo COLLEY ▶ 3740 (4)	**714**
Shame, Shame—Magic Lanterns (68)	996
Playgirl—Thee Prophets (69)	426
One Track Mind—Knickerbockers (66)	330
High On Love—Knickerbockers (66)	14
William COLLIER ▶ 10456 (1)	**8.2**
Here's A Heart—Diplomats (64)	25
Barry COLLINGS ▶ 9505 (1)	**22**
Friends—Feather (70)	112
Aaron COLLINS ▶ 1768 (6)	**2348**
Eddie My Love—Fontane Sisters with Billy Vaughn's Orchestra (56)	*1670*
Foot Stomping - Part 1—Flares (61)	1126
Eddie My Love—Chordettes (56)	*1068*
Eddie My Love—Teen Queens (56)	*856*
So All Alone—Teen Queens (56)	72
Rock And Roll Heaven—Flares (62)	1.4
Albert COLLINS ▶ 3834 (5)	**687**
Lucille—Little Richard (57)	*684*
Lucille—Everly Brothers (60)	*596*
Slippin' And Slidin' (Peepin' And Hidin')—Little Richard (56)	*180*
Slipin' And Slidin'—Sing Along With Jim And Monica (64)	*4.1*
Slippin' & Slidin'—Willie Mitchell (67)	*3.3*
Allen COLLINS ▶ 2379 (5)	**1544**
Free Bird—Will To Power (88)	*1705*
Free Bird—Lynyrd Skynyrd (74)	*716*
Free Bird (Live)—Lynyrd Skynyrd (76)	*482*
Don't Misunderstand Me—Rossington Collins Band (80)	231
Double Trouble—Lynyrd Skynyrd (76)	31
Ansel COLLINS ▶ 5181 (1)	**329**
Double Barrel—Dave And Ansil Collins (71)	987
—Bootsy Collins see: William Earl COLLINS	
Chuck COLLINS ▶ 11792 (1)	**0.0**
Judy—Prodigals (58)	0.0
Everett COLLINS ▶ 10307 (1)	**10**
You Are My Everything—Surface (89)	41
Gail COLLINS [Gail Collins Pappalardi] ▶ 9834 (1)	**16**
For Yasgur's Farm—Mountain (70)	97
—Gloria Lavern Collins see: Lyn COLLINS	
Judy COLLINS ▶ 7438 (1)	**96**
Open The Door (Song For Judith)—Judy Collins (71)	96
Larry COLLINS ▶ 1453 (3)	**3005**
Delta Dawn—Helen Reddy (73)	*5954*
Delta Dawn—Tanya Tucker (72)	*41*
You're Good For Me—Lou Rawls (68)	15
Leonard COLLINS ▶ 8151 (1)	**60**
Back Beat No. 1—Rondels (61)	240

Lyn COLLINS [Gloria Lavern Collins, Juliet Gray] ▶ 7349 (2)	**101**
What My Baby Needs Now Is A Little More Lovin'—James Brown & Lyn Collins (72)	289
Me And My Baby Got A Good Thing Going—Lyn Collins (72)	17
Mark COLLINS ▶ 10626 (1)	**6.7**
The Only One I Know—Charlatans UK (90)	33
Paul COLLINS ▶ 7652 (1)	**83**
Get A Move On—Eddie Money (79)	248
Phil COLLINS ▶ 42 (34) HOF	**44814**
Against All Odds (Take A Look At Me Now)—Phil Collins (84)	6268
Another Day In Paradise—Phil Collins (89)	5942
Easy Lover—Philip Bailey (84)	4579
One More Night—Phil Collins (85)	4350
Sussudio—Phil Collins (85)	3919
Two Hearts—Phil Collins (88)	3857
Invisible Touch—Genesis (86)	3735
In Too Deep—Genesis (87)	2454
Something Happened On The Way To Heaven—Phil Collins (90)	2309
Do You Remember?—Phil Collins (90)	2287
Tonight, Tonight, Tonight—Genesis (87)	2246
I Wish It Would Rain Down—Phil Collins (90)	2212
Throwing It All Away—Genesis (86)	2205
Land Of Confusion—Genesis (86)	2182
Don't Lose My Number—Phil Collins (85)	2148
No Son Of Mine—Genesis (91)	1981
That's All—Genesis (83)	1827
Take Me Home—Phil Collins (86)	1663
Misunderstanding—Genesis (80)	1405
In The Air Tonight—Phil Collins (81)	867
Hang In Long Enough—Phil Collins (90)	819
I Missed Again—Phil Collins (81)	812
Follow You Follow Me—Genesis (78)	761
No Reply At All—Genesis (81)	731
Paperlate—Genesis (82)	533
Abacab—Genesis (81)	451
I Don't Care Anymore—Phil Collins (83)	331
Taking It All Too Hard—Genesis (84)	331
Man On The Corner—Genesis (82)	327
Illegal Alien—Genesis (84)	277
Turn It On Again—Genesis (80)	248
Mama—Genesis (83)	137
Who Said I Would—Phil Collins (91)	100
I Cannot Believe It's True—Phil Collins (83)	54
Rodger COLLINS [Hajji Rajah Kasim Sabre] ▶ 2828 (2)	**1168**
She's Lookin' Good—Wilson Pickett (68)	*1018*
She's Looking Good—Rodger Collins (67)	*150*
Susan COLLINS ▶ 3423 (1)	**854**
Sweet Life—Paul Davis (78)	1708
Terry COLLINS ▶ 10783 (1)	**5.3**
This Is What You Mean To Me—Engelbert Humperdinck (75)	11
Tommy COLLINS [Leonhard Raymond Sipes] ▶ 6343 (1)	**181**
Carolyn—Merle Haggard And The Strangers (71)	181
William Earl COLLINS [Bootsy Collins, William Collins] ▶ 2462 (11)	**1462**
Tear The Roof Off The Sucker (Give Up The Funk)—Parliament (76)	*1416*
The Humpty Dance—Digital Underground (90)	1362
Flash Light—Parliament (78)	1115
We Want The Funk—Gerardo (91)	*667*
Mama Said Knock You Out—LL Cool J (91)	473
Bootzilla—Bootsy's Rubber Band (78)	87
Aqua Boogie (A Psychoalphadiscobetabioaquadoloop)—Parliament (78)	62
Up For The Down Stroke—Parliament (74)	57
Chocolate City—Parliament (75)	16
Disco To Go—Brides Of Funkenstein (78)	15
Theme From The Black Hole—Parliament (80)	1.0
Dom COLLURA ▶ 8559 (1)	**46**
Echo—Emotions (1) (62)	278
Michele COLLYER ▶ 5752 (1)	**245**
Endless Nights—Eddie Money (87)	735
Ornella Ferrari COLOMBI [Biri] ▶ 6809 (3)	**135**
Without You—Eddie Fisher (56)	*406*

Without You—Johnny Desmond (56)	*0.0*
Without You—Alan Dean (56)	*0.0*
Carlos COLON ▶ 9698 (1)	**19**
Within My Heart—Voyce (91)	75
Johnny COLONNA ▶ 11645 (1)	**0.9**
I Told The Stars—Lettermen (62)	1.7
Jessi COLTER [Mirriam Eddy, Mirriam Johnson] ▶ 1468 (3)	**2956**
I'm Not Lisa—Jessi Colter (75)	2753
You Ain't Never Been Loved (Like I'm Gonna Love You)—Jessi Colter (75)	145
What's Happened To Blue Eyes—Jessi Colter (75)	58
Tony COLTON [Anthony George Chalk] ▶ 6412 (3)	**173**
I'm No Angel—Gregg Allman Band (87)	200
Big Time Operator—Keith Hampshire (73)	145
Warmin' Up The Band—Don Everly (74)	6.6
Chi COLTRANE ▶ 2624 (2)	**1312**
Thunder And Lightning—Chi Coltrane (72)	1307
Go Like Elijah—Chi Coltrane (73)	5.3
Anthony COLUMBO Jr. ▶ 8046 (1)	**64**
Zip Zip—Diamonds (57)	255
Louis COLUMBO ▶ 8047 (1)	**64**
Zip Zip—Diamonds (57)	255
Russ COLUMBO [Ruggiero Eugenio di Rodolpho Colombo] ▶ 5194 (1)	**329**
Prisoner Of Love—James Brown And The Famous Flames (63)	986
Doug COLVIN ▶ 8875 (2)	**37**
Rockaway Beach—Ramones (77)	96
Sheena Is A Punk Rocker—Ramones (77)	53
Thomas COMAN [Thomas F. Coman III, Tom Donahue] ▶ 2324 (3)	**1590**
C'mon And Swim—Bobby Freeman (64)	2736
Midnight Stroll—Revels (59)	418
S-W-I-M—Bobby Freeman (64)	164
Jeffrey COMANOR ▶ 2814 (2)	**1178**
We'll Never Have To Say Goodbye Again—England Dan & John Ford Coley (78)	*1174*
Never Have To Say Goodbye Again—Deardorff & Joseph (77)	*3.9*
Betty COMDEN [Elizabeth Cohen] ▶ 5430 (11) HOF	**290**
Just In Time—Tony Bennett with Percy Faith and His Orchestra (56)	*374*
Dance Only With Me—Perry Como (58)	150
Now!—Lena Horne (63)	110
The Party's Over—Doris Day (56)	*92*
Just In Time—Dean Martin (60)	*71*
Make Someone Happy—Perry Como (60)	57
Bells Are Ringing—Jo Stafford (56)	*8.2*
Bells Are Ringing—Jeri Southern (56)	*8.2*
Just In Time—Jeri Southern (56)	*0.0*
The Party's Over—Carmen McRae (57)	*0.0*
The Party's Over—Lurlean Hunter (57)	*0.0*
Terry COMER ▶ 9660 (1)	**19**
Rock & Roll Runaway—Ace (75)	77
Carl CONASTER ▶ 6089 (1)	**207**
Reveille Rock—Johnny And The Hurricanes (59)	828
—Perry Cone see: Jack PERRICONE	
Richard CONGDON ▶ 4016 (2)	**622**
Where Are You Now?—Jimmy Harnen w/Synch (89)	*1182*
Where Are You Now?—Synch (86)	*62*
Arthur CONLEY ▶ 1636 (5)	**2563**
Sweet Soul Music—Arthur Conley (67)	*5467*
Funky Street—Arthur Conley (68)	1322
Aunt Dora's Love Soul Shack—Arthur Conley (68)	65
Whole Lotta Woman—Arthur Conley (67)	61
Sweet Soul Music—Magnificent Men (67)	*7.6*
Dave CONLEY ▶ 5441 (3)	**288**
Happy—Surface (87)	678
Don't Take It Personal—Jermaine Jackson (89)	156
You Are My Everything—Surface (89)	41
Larry CONLEY ▶ 7409 (3)	**97**
Free—Tommy Leonetti (56)	*144*
A Cottage For Sale—Little Willie John (60)	51
Free—Lancers (56)	*0.0*
Chuck CONLON ▶ 7558 (1)	**89**
The Little Black Egg—Nightcrawlers (66)	89

Chester CONN [Chester Cohn] ▶ 3152 (5)	**982**
Night Lights—Nat "King" Cole (56)	1019
Forgive My Heart—Nat "King" Cole (55)	892
That's You—Nat King Cole (60)	60
Why Should I Cry Over You—Frank Sinatra (55)	14
Make Her Mine—Nat "King" Cole (54)	0.0
Andy CONNELL [Andrew John Connell, Bootsy] ▶ 3547 (3)	**789**
Breakout—Swing Out Sister (87)	1952
Twilight World—Swing Out Sister (87)	393
Waiting Game—Swing Out Sister (89)	15
Jane CONNELL [Jane Sperry Bennett] ▶ 7432 (1)	**96**
Joey Baby—Anita And Th' So-And-So's (62)	192
Melissa CONNELL ▶ 5818 (1)	**239**
I've Never Been In Love—Suzi Quatro (79)	239
Al CONNELLY ▶ 3909 (2)	**661**
Someday—Glass Tiger (86)	1758
I Will Be There—Glass Tiger (87)	374
Reg CONNELLY ▶ 4001 (4)	**625**
Try A Little Tenderness—Otis Redding (66)	*946*
Try A Little Tenderness—Three Dog Night (69)	*803*
Try A Little Tenderness—Commitments (91)	*127*
Try A Little Tenderness—Aretha Franklin (62)	*0.4*
Brian CONNOLLY ▶ 3054 (4)	**1033**
Fox On The Run—Sweet (75)	2954
Action—Sweet (76)	1094
California Nights—Sweet (78)	63
Funk It Up (David's Song)—Sweet (77)	20
Pat CONNOLLY ▶ 2017 (7)	**2000**
Wipe Out—Surfaris (63)	*4648*
Wipe Out—Surfaris (66)	*1843*
Wipeout—Fat Boys (87)	*961*
Point Panic—Surfaris (63)	378
Surfer Joe—Surfaris (63)	236
Wipe Out—Jive Bunny & The Mastermixers (90)	*6.7*
Wipe Out—Surfaris (70)	*4.6*
Tommie CONNOR ▶ 4403 (5)	**505**
Red River Rose—Ames Brothers (58)	793
Lili Marlene—Al Martino (68)	140
Heart Without A Sweetheart—Gale Storm (56)	63
I Saw Mommy Kissing Santa Claus—Jimmy Boyd (54)	25
I Saw Mommy Do The Mambo (With You Know Who)—Jimmy Boyd (54)	15
Carol CONNORS [Annette Kleinbard] ▶ 821 (7)	**5354**
Hey Little Cobra—Rip Chords (63)	4281
Gonna Fly Now (Theme From "Rocky")—Bill Conti (77)	*4145*
With You I'm Born Again—Billy Preston & Syreeta (79)	3182
Gonna Fly Now (Theme From "Rocky")—Maynard Ferguson (77)	*595*
You Take My Heart Away—James Darren (77)	98
Rocky II Disco—Maynard Ferguson (79)	22
Theme From Rocky (Gonna Fly Now)—Rhythm Heritage (77)	*7.6*
Marshall CONNORS ▶ 1898 (1)	**2140**
Hey Little Cobra—Rip Chords (63)	4281
Con CONRAD [Conrad K. Dober] ▶ 6706 (3) HOF	**143**
Margie—Fats Domino (59)	364
Ma! (He's Making Eyes At Me)—Lena Zavaroni (74)	31
You've Got To See Mamma Every Night (Or You Can't See Mamma At All)—Peggy Lee (56)	12
Jack CONRAD ▶ 1742 (7)	**2380**
Every Time I Think Of You—Babys (78)	1477
Isn't It Time—Babys (77)	1422
The Family Of Man—Three Dog Night (72)	1414
How Much Love—Vixen (90)	308
If Looks Could Kill—Heart (86)	176
So High (Rock Me Baby And Roll Me Away)—Dave Mason (77)	52
Just For The Moment—Ray Kennedy (80)	15
—Robin Conrad see: Peter CALLANDER	
Michael CONROY ▶ 8739 (3)	**41**
I Melt With You—Modern English (90)	*107*
I Melt With You—Modern English (83)	*88*
Hands Across The Sea—Modern English (84)	8.5
—Dale Frances Consalvi see: Dale BOZZIO	

Jean Louis CONSTANTIN ▶ 11007 (1)	**3.9**
I Look At You—Lassies (56)	12
—Bob Conte see: Bob GAUDIO	
Henri CONTET ▶ 10677 (1)	**6.1**
We All Need Love—Percy Faith And His Orchestra and Chorus (56)	18
Bill CONTI ▶ 1195 (9)	**3714**
Gonna Fly Now (Theme From "Rocky")—Bill Conti (77)	*4145*
For Your Eyes Only—Sheena Easton (81)	3674
Gonna Fly Now (Theme From "Rocky")—Maynard Ferguson (77)	*595*
Theme From Dynasty—Bill Conti (82)	205
The Moment Of Truth—Survivor (84)	138
You Take My Heart Away—James Darren (77)	98
Rocky II Disco—Maynard Ferguson (79)	22
Theme From Rocky (Gonna Fly Now)—Rhythm Heritage (77)	*7.6*
Theme From "Rocky" (Gonna Fly Now)—Current (77)	*3.4*
Corrado CONTI ▶ 5315 (2)	**307**
To The Door Of The Sun (Alle Porte Del Sole)—Al Martino (74)	825
The Way It Used To Be—Engelbert Humperdinck (69)	711
Connie CONWAY [Connie Crunk] ▶ 9261 (2)	**28**
Why—Gary Lee (59)	50
A Teenager Feels It Too—Denny Reed (60)	5.0
Jim CONWAY ▶ 5037 (1)	**356**
Tomboy—Perry Como (59)	711
Neal CONWAY ▶ 4710 (1)	**433**
Gypsy Woman (She's Homeless)—Crystal Waters (91)	867
Norma CONWAY [Norma Crunk] ▶ 9262 (2)	**28**
Why—Gary Lee (59)	50
A Teenager Feels It Too—Denny Reed (60)	5.0
—Russ Conway see: Trevor STANFORD	
Talmadge CONWAY ▶ 6458 (2)	**167**
He's A Friend—Eddie Kendricks (76)	362
Ten Percent—Double Exposure (76)	92
Tommy CONWELL ▶ 9312 (1)	**27**
I'm Not Your Man—Tommy Conwell And The Young Rumblers (88)	80
Cheryl COOK ▶ 8463 (2)	**50**
Apache—Sugar Hill Gang (82)	*173*
8th Wonder—Sugarhill Gang (81)	30
—Dale Cook see: Sam COOKE	
—David Albert Cook see: David ESSEX	
Don COOK ▶ 11319 (1)	**2.3**
Somebody's Gonna Love You—Lee Greenwood (83)	4.5
—Grace Cook see: Eddie HAZEL	
Ira COOK ▶ 11690 (1)	**0.7**
Sunday Barbecue—Tennessee Ernie Ford (58)	1.4
Jeffrey COOK ▶ 6286 (1)	**186**
Must Be Love—James Gang (74)	371
Joe COOK ▶ 3272 (3)	**917**
Peanuts—Little Joe And The Thrillers (57)	*676*
Peanuts—Rick And The Keens (61)	*208*
Peanuts—Four Seasons (64)	*33*
Norman COOK [Quentin Leo Cook, Norman Quentin Cook, Fatboy Slim] ▶ 8932 (1)	**36**
Won't Talk About It—Beats International (90)	72
—Quentin Leo Cook see: Norman COOK	
Roger COOK ▶ 405 (24) HOF	**9744**
Long Cool Woman (In A Black Dress)—Hollies (72)	5749
You've Got Your Troubles—Fortunes (65)	2028
Green Grass—Gary Lewis And The Playboys (66)	1953
I'd Like To Teach The World To Sing (In Perfect Harmony)—New Seekers (71)	*1791*
Doctor's Orders—Carol Douglas (74)	1742
Here Comes That Rainy Day Feeling Again—Fortunes (71)	1705
My Baby Loves Lovin'—White Plains (70)	1636
I'd Like To Teach The World To Sing (In Perfect Harmony)—Hillside Singers (71)	*1474*
I Believe In You—Don Williams (80)	1147
Talking In Your Sleep—Crystal Gayle (78)	1069
I Was Kaiser Bill's Batman—Whistling Jack Smith (67)	1009
The Way It Used To Be—Engelbert Humperdinck (69)	711
Softly Whispering I Love You—English Congregation (72)	708

7-6-5-4-3-2-1 (Blow Your Whistle)—Gary Toms Empire (75)	546
Goin' Down (On The Road To L.A.)—Terry Black And Laurel Ward (72)	216
Years From Now—Dr. Hook (80)	148
Lovin' You Baby—White Plains (70)	121
Melting Pot—Blue Mink Featuring Madeleine Bell (70)	110
One More Chance—Ocean (72)	85
Freedom Comes, Freedom Goes—Fortunes (71)	82
What's Your Name, What's Your Number—Andrea True Connection (78)	63
This Golden Ring—Fortunes (66)	59
Good Morning Freedom—Daybreak (70)	52
We Got A Dream—Ocean (71)	44
—Samuel Cook see: Sam COOKE	
William S. COOK ▶ 1245 (8)	**3609**
You Can Have Her—Roy Hamilton (61)	*1762*
I'll Come Running Back To You—Sam Cooke (57)	732
You Can Have Her—Sam Neely (74)	*607*
Forgive This Fool—Roy Hamilton (55)	299
You Can Have Her—Righteous Brothers (65)	*115*
You Can Have Him—Dionne Warwick (65)	*74*
No Substitute For Love—Roy Hamilton (61)	12
You Can Have Him—Timi Yuro (65)	*7.6*
—Charles Cooke see: Sam COOKE	
Fabian COOKE ▶ 5014 (3)	**359**
Rico Suave—Gerardo (91)	1126
We Want The Funk—Gerardo (91)	*667*
When The Lights Go Out—Gerardo (91)	1.5
James COOKE ▶ 7853 (1)	**72**
Buzzy Brown—Tim Davis (72)	72
—Linda Cooke see: Linda WOMACK	
Sam COOKE [Barbara Campbell, Dale Cook, Samuel Cook, Charles Cooke] ▶ 25 (70) HOF	**52616**
You Send Me—Sam Cooke (57)	*6908*
Chain Gang—Sam Cooke (60)	*6849*
Sweet Soul Music—Arthur Conley (67)	*5467*
Wonderful World—Herman's Hermits (65)	*3144*
Twistin' The Night Away—Sam Cooke (62)	*2859*
Only Sixteen—Dr. Hook (76)	*2695*
Shake—Sam Cooke (65)	*2453*
Wonderful World—Sam Cooke (60)	*1801*
Another Saturday Night—Sam Cooke (63)	*1758*
Cupid—Spinners (80)	*1698*
Another Saturday Night—Cat Stevens (74)	*1628*
Cupid—Sam Cooke (61)	*1567*
Having A Party—Sam Cooke (62)	*1471*
Good News—Sam Cooke (64)	1442
Bring It On Home To Me—Eddie Floyd (68)	*1280*
Nothing Can Change This Love—Sam Cooke (62)	1270
Good Times—Sam Cooke (64)	1253
Bring It On Home To Me—Sam Cooke (62)	*1214*
(What A) Wonderful World—Art Garfunkel With James Taylor & Paul Simon (78)	*839*
Everybody Likes To Cha Cha Cha—Sam Cooke (59)	816
Cupid—Johnny Nash (69)	*801*
Love You Most Of All—Sam Cooke (58)	717
Cousin Of Mine—Sam Cooke (64)	715
Cupid—Tony Orlando & Dawn (76)	*689*
Only Sixteen—Sam Cooke (59)	*606*
When A Boy Falls In Love—Mel Carter (63)	*605*
Sugar Dumpling—Sam Cooke (65)	560
Sad Mood—Sam Cooke (60)	536
You Send Me—Teresa Brewer (57)	*505*
It's Got The Whole World Shakin'—Sam Cooke (65)	473
Bring It On Home To Me—Animals (65)	*470*
Nobody Loves Me Like You—Flamingos (60)	468
A Change Is Gonna Come—Sam Cooke (65)	*424*
I'll Bring It Home To You—Carla Thomas (62)	412
Win Your Love For Me—Sam Cooke (58)	380
Feel It—Sam Cooke (61)	*367*
Soothe Me—Sims Twins (61)	*365*
Shake—Otis Redding (67)	*331*
Twisting The Night Away—Rod Stewart (73)	*320*
Soothe Me—Sam & Dave (67)	*309*
Meet Me At The Twistin' Place—Johnnie Morisette (62)	212
Somebody Have Mercy—Sam Cooke (62)	187
Baby, Baby, Baby—Sam Cooke (63)	180
When A Boy Falls In Love—Sam Cooke (65)	*174*
You Send Me—Ponderosa Twins + One (71)	*168*

Sam COOKE [Barbara Campbell, Dale Cook, Samuel Cook, Charles Cooke] ▶ 25 (70) HOF *Continued*	**52616**
You Were Made For Me–Luther Ingram (72)	*163*
That's Where It's At–Sam Cooke (64)	137
You Send Me–Aretha Franklin (68)	*126*
Chain Gang–Jackie Wilson And Count Basie (68)	*123*
Cupid–Johnny Rivers (65)	*115*
Having a Party–Luther Vandross (82)	96
You Were Made For Me–Sam Cooke (58)	*90*
Chain Gang–Jim Croce (76)	*76*
Twistin' The Night Away–Rod Stewart (87)	*74*
Shake–British Walkers (67)	*35*
Having A Party–Ovations (73)	*34*
Soothe Me–Ovations (73)	*34*
Wonderful World–Ovations (73)	*34*
You Send Me–Manhattans (85)	*22*
(What A) Wonderful World–Johnny Nash (76)	*17*
Laughin And Clownin–Ray Charles (70)	12
A Change Is Gonna Come–5th Dimension (70)	*11*
Bring It On Home–Lou Rawls (70)	*9.8*
Sweet Soul Music–Magnificent Men (67)	*7.6*
Feel It–Sam Cooke (66)	*5.2*
It's All Right–Sam Cooke (61)	3.6
No One (Can Ever Take Your Place)–Sam Cooke (60)	2.4
Baby, We've Got Love–Johnnie Taylor (63)	1.4
With You–Sam Cooke (60)	1.0
You Send Me–Plas Johnson & His Orchestra (57)	*0.0*
–Whey Cooler see: Vincent COREA	
Eddie COOLEY ▶ 1221 (11)	**3651**
Fever–Peggy Lee (58)	*2762*
Fever–McCoys (65)	*2289*
Fever–Little Willie John (56)	*793*
Priscilla–Eddie Cooley And The Dimples (56)	*670*
Fever–Rita Coolidge (73)	*72*
Fever–Earl Grant (57)	*38*
Fever–Pete Bennett & The Embers (61)	*7.2*
Fever–Ray Peterson (57)	*0.0*
Fever–Little Willie John (58)	*0.0*
Priscilla–Julius La Rosa (56)	*0.0*
Priscilla–Les Brown & His Band Of Renown (56)	*0.0*
Priscilla COOLIDGE [Priscilla Jones, Priscilla Seibert] ▶ 8886 (2)	**37**
My Crew–Rita Coolidge (73)	72
I Need You–Maurice White (86)	2.4
Alice COOPER [Vincent Damon Furnier] ▶ 766 (18)	**5723**
School's Out–Alice Cooper (72)	*2297*
I Never Cry–Alice Cooper (76)	1991
You And Me–Alice Cooper (77)	1909
Only Women–Alice Cooper (75)	*1899*
Poison–Alice Cooper (89)	1500
How You Gonna See Me Now–Alice Cooper (78)	1236
Eighteen–Alice Cooper (71)	1021
No More Mr. Nice Guy–Alice Cooper (73)	839
Elected–Alice Cooper (72)	776
Teenage Lament '74–Alice Cooper (73)	465
Welcome To My Nightmare–Alice Cooper (75)	301
Down To The Line–Bachman-Turner Overdrive (75)	290
Billion Dollar Babies–Alice Cooper (73)	243
Department Of Youth–Alice Cooper (75)	121
Only Women Bleed–Favorite Angel (90)	*108*
School's Out–Krokus (86)	*104*
Hey Stoopid–Alice Cooper (91)	48
Only My Heart Talkin'–Alice Cooper (90)	30
Bernadette COOPER ▶ 8414 (1)	**51**
The Men All Pause–Klymaxx (86)	103
Colin COOPER ▶ 4637 (2)	**446**
Couldn't Get It Right–Climax Blues Band (77)	2219
Makin' Love–Climax Blues Band (78)	10
Dick COOPER [Willie A. Cooper] ▶ 7988 (1)	**66**
Nobody–Three Dog Night (68)	132
Gary Lee COOPER ▶ 2151 (1)	**1813**
Let's Go All The Way–Sly Fox (85)	1813
Joey COOPER ▶ 4066 (3)	**606**
I'm A Fool–Dino, Desi & Billy (65)	1193
Who Do You Think You Are–Shindogs (66)	19
If You Think I Don't Need You–Elvis Presley (64)	1.1
Kathy COOPER ▶ 9484 (1)	**23**
It's Time To Say Goodbye–Third Rail (68)	46
Les COOPER ▶ 2479 (2)	**1451**
Wiggle Wobble–Les Cooper And The Soulrockers (62)	1446
Deserie–Charts (57)	10
–Mark Cooper see: Milton GRANT	
Martin H. COOPER ▶ 3963 (1)	**637**
If You Leave–Orchestral Manoeuvres In The Dark (86)	1910
Marty COOPER ▶ 1941 (10)	**2079**
Peanut Butter–Marathons (61)	1099
Hey Harmonica Man–Stevie Wonder (64)	555
Run, Run, Look And See–Brian Hyland (66)	537
The Lonely Surfer–Jack Nitzsche (63)	487
You Can't Be A Beacon (If Your Light Don't Shine)–Donna Fargo (74)	385
I Love You Lady Dawn–Bells (71)	332
(I'm A) Yoyo Man–Rick Cunha (74)	289
A Stranger In Your Town–Shacklefords (63)	157
The Biplane, Ever More–Irish Rovers (68)	62
Mama Was A Cotton Picker–Jimmie Rodgers (64)	13
Michael V. COOPER ▶ 2474 (5)	**1453**
Ffun–Con Funk Shun (77)	819
Too Tight–Con Funk Shun (80)	413
Shake And Dance With Me–Con Funk Shun (78)	180
Chase Me–Con Funk Shun (79)	74
Got To Be Enough–Con Funk Shun (80)	9.0
Paula COOPER ▶ 11739 (1)	**0.3**
Come On Down (From The Top Of That Hill)–Jackie deShannon (67)	0.9
Richard COOPER ▶ 4631 (2)	**448**
The Dream Never Dies–Cooper Brothers (78)	363
I'll Know Her When I See Her–Cooper Brothers Band (79)	85
Sandy COOPER ▶ 6535 (1)	**159**
In The Bush–Musique (78)	318
Ted COOPER ▶ 8171 (1)	**60**
Ronnie, Call Me When You Get A Chance–Shelley Fabares (63)	119
Willie COOPER ▶ 9471 (1)	**23**
This Thing Called Love–Webs (67)	46
–Willie A. Cooper see: Dick COOPER	
J. Fred COOTS ▶ 1198 (7) HOF	**3712**
Love Letters In The Sand–Pat Boone (57)	9892
I Still Get A Thrill (Thinking Of You)–Joni James (59)	384
Santa Claus Is Coming To Town–4 Seasons (62)	*369*
Santa Claus Is Comin' To Town–Jackson 5 (70)	*36*
For All We Know–Dinah Washington (62)	34
Santa Claus Is Comin' To Town–Bing Crosby and the Andrews Sisters (54)	*3.2*
Santa Claus Is Comin' To Town–Fred Waring presents The Teen Trio (54)	*3.2*
Cowboy COPAS [Lloyd Copas] ▶ 3878 (4)	**669**
Alabam–Cowboy Copas (60)	*323*
Alabam–Pat Boone (60)	*321*
Signed, Sealed, And Delivered–James Brown And The Famous Flames (63)	*46*
Signed, Sealed And Delivered–Rusty Draper (61)	*5.4*
Julian COPE ▶ 8569 (1)	**46**
World Shut Your Mouth–Julian Cope (87)	46
LaForrest COPE ▶ 1480 (1)	**2931**
You Give Good Love–Whitney Houston (85)	2931
Allan COPELAND ▶ 9972 (3)	**14**
Darling! Darling! Darling!–Jo Stafford (55)	25
Make Love To Me–Johnny Thunder & Ruby Winters (67)	*13*
Make Love To Me!–Jo Stafford (54)	*0.0*
Greg COPELAND ▶ 5964 (1)	**222**
Buy For Me The Rain–Nitty Gritty Dirt Band (67)	443
–Allan Copelon see: Allan SHERMAN	
Bruno COQUATRIX ▶ 4504 (3)	**475**
Count Every Star–Donnie And The Dreamers (61)	*400*
Count Every Star–Linda Scott (62)	*391*
Count Every Star–Rivieras (1) (58)	*160*
Peter COR [Peter Jan Cor Belenky] ▶ 3590 (1)	**775**
Getaway–Earth, Wind & Fire (76)	1550
Gary CORBETT ▶ 3410 (1)	**858**
She Bop–Cyndi Lauper (84)	3432
Jerry CORBETTA ▶ 1858 (5)	**2194**
Green-Eyed Lady–Sugarloaf (70)	3826
Don't Call Us, We'll Call You–Sugarloaf/Jerry Corbetta (74)	1633
You're Looking Like Love To Me–Peabo Bryson/Roberta Flack (83)	224
Mother Nature's Wine–Sugarloaf (71)	22
Stars In My Eyes–Sugarloaf/Jerry Corbetta (75)	20
Gene CORBIN ▶ 10053 (1)	**13**
If I Had A Reason–Bubble Puppy (69)	27
Jack CORBITT ▶ 10019 (1)	**14**
Don't Make The Good Girls Go Bad–Della Humphrey (68)	28
Jerry CORBITT ▶ 4542 (1)	**468**
Grizzly Bear–Youngbloods (66)	468
Mike CORBY [Corby Michael John Siddons] ▶ 10890 (1)	**4.6**
If You've Got The Time–Babys (77)	18
Tom CORCORAN ▶ 6864 (1)	**132**
Fins–Jimmy Buffett (79)	528
Ritchie CORDELL [Richard Joel Rosenblatt] ▶ 177 (25)	**17103**
Mony Mony–Tommy James And The Shondells (68)	*4671*
I Think We're Alone Now–Tommy James And The Shondells (67)	*4661*
I Think We're Alone Now–Tiffany (87)	*4060*
Mony Mony "Live"–Billy Idol (87)	*3728*
Indian Giver–1910 Fruitgum Co. (69)	3435
Gimme Gimme Good Lovin'–Crazy Elephant (69)	2168
Mirage–Tommy James And The Shondells (67)	1826
Gettin' Together–Tommy James And The Shondells (67)	1135
She–Tommy James And The Shondells (69)	869
It's Only Love–Tommy James And The Shondells (66)	725
I Like The Way–Tommy James And The Shondells (67)	664
The Train–1910 Fruitgum Co. (69)	436
Out Of The Blue–Tommy James And The Shondells (67)	415
Get Out Now–Tommy James And The Shondells (68)	403
Somebody Cares–Tommy James And The Shondells (68)	397
I Think We're Alone Now–Rubinoos (77)	*327*
Church Street Soul Revival–Tommy James (70)	311
Sparkle And Shine–Clique (70)	71
When We Get Married–1910 Fruitgum Co. (69)	56
We Gotta Go Home–Music Explosion (67)	41
There's A Better Day Comin'–Crazy Elephant (69)	25
Mony Mony–Billy Idol (81)	*23*
Go Away–1910 Fruitgum Co. (70)	8.1
S.O.S. (Heart In Distress)–Christine Cooper (66)	3.4
Mony Mony–Tight Fit (81)	*0.9*
Anthony CORDER ▶ 10839 (1)	**5.0**
Walkin' Shoes–Tora Tora (89)	20
Louie CORDERO ▶ 4839 (2)	**401**
Sittin' In The Lap Of Luxury–Louie Louie (90)	734
I Wanna Get Back With You–Louie Louie (90)	136
Miguel CORDERO ▶ 9699 (1)	**19**
Within My Heart–Voyce (91)	75
Attrell CORDES [Prince Be] ▶ 2158 (1)	**1809**
Set Adrift On Memory Bliss–PM Dawn (91)	3619
Ken CORDRAY ▶ 8743 (1)	**41**
Francene–ZZ Top (72)	122
Vincent COREA [Whey Cooler] ▶ 2887 (2)	**1130**
Catch Me (I'm Falling)–Pretty Poison (87)	1846
Nightime–Pretty Poison (88)	414
John COREY [John Coury] ▶ 3774 (2)	**703**
The Last Worthless Evening–Don Henley (89)	774
You Could Take My Heart Away–Silver Condor (81)	445
–Sam Corgliano see: Ricky LAYNE	
–Corina see: Corina AYALA	
Al CORLEY ▶ 10091 (1)	**13**
Square Rooms–Al Corley (85)	39
Bob CORLEY ▶ 11423 (1)	**1.7**
Number One Street (Sides 1 & 2)–Bob Corley (55)	1.7
Ray CORMIER ▶ 11793 (1)	**0.0**
Hit And Run Affair–Perry Como (54)	0.0
Carter CORNELIUS ▶ 5585 (1)	**268**
I'm Never Gonna Be Alone Anymore–Cornelius Brothers & Sister Rose (72)	536

Don CORNELIUS ▶ 6877 (2)	**131**
The Gigolo—O'Bryan (82)	182
Soul Train "75"—Soul Train Gang (75)	81
Eddie CORNELIUS ▶ 312 (6)	**11613**
Too Late To Turn Back Now—Cornelius Brothers & Sister Rose (72)	5642
Treat Her Like A Lady—Cornelius Brothers & Sister Rose (71)	4707
Don't Ever Be Lonely (A Poor Little Fool Like Me)—Cornelius Brothers & Sister Rose (72)	912
I'm Never Gonna Be Alone Anymore—Cornelius Brothers & Sister Rose (72)	536
Let Me Down Easy—Cornelius Brothers & Sister Rose (73)	60
I Just Can't Stop Loving You—Cornelius Brothers & Sister Rose (73)	23
—Harry Cornelius see: Harold FIELDS	
Dennis CORRELL ▶ 8470 (1)	**49**
Gas Lamps And Clay—Blues Image (70)	98
Vince CORSO ▶ 5524 (3)	**274**
Ties That Bind—Brook Benton (60)	492
Silent Lips—Georgia Gibbs (57)	53
Separate Ways—Sarah Vaughan (59)	3.0
Jack CORTES ▶ 10460 (1)	**8.2**
The Mess Around—Bobby Freeman (61)	8.2
—Dave "Baby" Cortez see: David CLOWNEY	
George CORY ▶ 3563 (1)	**785**
(I Left My Heart) In San Francisco—Tony Bennett (62)	1570
Bill COSBY ▶ 3368 (6)	**878**
Little Ole Man (Uptight - Everything's Alright)—Bill Cosby (67)	*2587*
Yes, Yes, Yes—Bill Cosby (76)	290
Hooray For The Salvation Army Band—Bill Cosby (67)	*171*
Fat Albert (Hey, Hey, Hey)—Fat Albert Orchestra and Chorus (68)	32
Funky North Philly—Bill Cosby (68)	32
Hikky Burr - Part One—Bill Cosby With The Bunions Bradford Band (69)	12
Henry COSBY ▶ 241 (28) HOF	**14235**
Fingertips - Pt 2—Little Stevie Wonder (63)	*8343*
The Tears Of A Clown—Smokey Robinson & The Miracles (70)	*7441*
I Was Made To Love Her—Stevie Wonder (67)	*5544*
Uptight (Everything's Alright)—Stevie Wonder (65)	*4256*
My Cherie Amour—Stevie Wonder (69)	*3557*
Little Ole Man (Uptight - Everything's Alright)—Bill Cosby (67)	*2587*
Shoo-Be-Doo-Be-Doo-Da-Day—Stevie Wonder (68)	1997
I'm Livin' In Shame—Diana Ross And The Supremes (69)	1652
I'm Wondering—Stevie Wonder (67)	1268
Nothing's Too Good For My Baby—Stevie Wonder (66)	775
Never Had A Dream Come True—Stevie Wonder (70)	728
No Matter What Sign You Are—Diana Ross And The Supremes (69)	554
Workout Stevie, Workout—Little Stevie Wonder (63)	457
Do The Boomerang—Jr. Walker & The All Stars (65)	379
With A Child's Heart—Michael Jackson (73)	*371*
Up Tight—Ramsey Lewis (66)	*275*
Home Cookin—Jr. Walker & The All Stars (69)	223
I Was Made To Love Her—King Curtis & The Kingpins (67)	*88*
Uptight—Shalamar (77)	*80*
Uptight (Everything's Alright)—Nancy Wilson (66)	*28*
I Was Made To Love Her—Stars On 45 (82)	*27*
My Cherie Amour—Stars On 45 (82)	*27*
Uptight Everything's All Right—Stars On 45 (82)	*27*
Fingertips—Stars On 45 (82)	*27*
Tears Of A Clown—Stars On 45 (81)	*12*
My Cherie Amour—Soul Train Gang (77)	*8.1*
With A Child's Heart—Stevie Wonder (66)	*4.4*
Uptight (Everything's Alright)—Jazz Crusaders (66)	*2.8*
Patricia COSBY ▶ 10054 (1)	**13**
Tell Me That I'm Wrong—Blood, Sweat & Tears (74)	13
Lance COSGROVE ▶ 7712 (1)	**79**
Everything You Do (You're Sexing Me)—Fiona (Duet With Kip Winger) (89)	238
Sam COSLOW ▶ 1450 (9) HOF	**3012**
Everybody Loves Somebody—Dean Martin (64)	8239
Blue Mirage (Don't Go)—Les Baxter & His Orchestra (55)	*239*
Mr. Paganini (You'll Have To Swing It)—Ella Fitzgerald (61)	119
Tomorrow Night—Damita Jo (65)	27
Sing You Sinners—Tony Bennett with Percy Faith and His Orchestra (56)	22
One Kiss Away From Heaven (Malatia)—Tony Bennett with Percy Faith (57)	4.4
True Blue Lou—Tony Bennett (63)	1.3
Blue Mirage (Don't Go)—Percy Faith & His Orchestra (55)	*0.0*
Blue Mirage—Frank Chacksfield & His Orchestra (55)	*0.0*
Wilma COSMÉ [Sa-Fire] ▶ 4543 (1)	**468**
Thinking Of You—Sa-Fire (89)	1403
Fran COSMO [Francis Cosmo Migliaccio] ▶ 8189 (1)	**59**
So You Ran—Orion The Hunter (84)	118
—Domenick Costa see: Don COSTA	
Don COSTA [Domenick Costa] ▶ 1087 (2)	**4058**
Because They're Young—Duane Eddy And The Rebels (60)	3920
I Can't Believe I'm Losing You—Frank Sinatra (68)	277
Alec R. COSTANDINOS [Alexandre Kouyoumdjian] ▶ 3882 (3)	**669**
Thank God It's Friday—Love And Kisses (78)	566
Love In 'C' Minor - Pt. 1—Cerrone (77)	*122*
Love In C Minor—Heart and Soul Orchestra (77)	*84*
Elvis COSTELLO [Declan Patrick Aloysius MacManus] ▶ 2380 (7) HOF	**1544**
Veronica—Elvis Costello (89)	736
My Brave Face—Paul McCartney (89)	522
Everyday I Write The Book—Elvis Costello And The Attractions (83)	470
The Only Flame In Town—Elvis Costello & The Atractions (84)	204
Girls Talk—Dave Edmunds (79)	147
Watching The Detectives—Elvis Costello (78)	94
Alison—Elvis Costello (78)	0.0
Darren COSTIN ▶ 4961 (2)	**371**
Dance Hall Days—Wang Chung (84)	1096
Don't Be My Enemy—Wang Chung (84)	17
—Suzanne Coston see: Suzanne DePASSE	
John COTE ▶ 9558 (1)	**21**
Monster—Fred Schneider (91)	43
Elizabeth COTTEN ▶ 2903 (6)	**1125**
Freight Train—Rusty Draper (57)	*936*
Freight Train—Chas. McDevitt Skiffle Group (57)	*186*
Freight Train—Duane Eddy (70)	*2.6*
Freight Train—Liz Winters with Bob Cort & His Skiffle Group (57)	*0.0*
Freight Train—Steve Karmen (57)	*0.0*
Freight Train—Margie Rayburn (57)	*0.0*
Michael COTTEN ▶ 8493 (2)	**48**
Don't Want To Wait Anymore—Tubes (81)	377
Piece By Piece—Tubes (85)	10
Bobby COTTER [Bobby Carter, Robert L. Cotter] ▶ 10041 (1)	**14**
Saturday—Norma Jean Wright (78)	41
—Robert L. Cotter see: Bobby COTTER	
Gene COTTON ▶ 4268 (4)	**539**
Like A Sunday In Salem (The Amos & Andy Song)—Gene Cotton (78)	384
Sunshine Roses—Gene Cotton (74)	105
If I Could Get You (Into My Life)—Gene Cotton (82)	44
Bein' Here With You Tonight—Gene Cotton & American Ace (81)	5.3
Hal COTTON ▶ 8350 (3)	**54**
You Can't Be True Dear—Mary Kaye Trio (59)	*189*
You Can't Be True, Dear—Patti Page (65)	*25*
You Can't Be True Dear—Steve Lawrence & Eydie Gorme (59)	*0.0*
Paul COTTON ▶ 2420 (5)	**1501**
Heart Of The Night—Poco (79)	918
Under The Gun—Poco (80)	329
Indian Summer—Poco (77)	194
Midnight Rain—Poco (80)	31
Days Gone By—Poco (84)	30
Orville COUCH ▶ 5918 (2)	**228**
First Quarrel—Paul & Paula (63)	680
I Feel A Sin Coming On—Solomon Burke (66)	3.4
Chris COUCHOIS ▶ 10645 (1)	**6.5**
Walkin' The Fence—Couchois (79)	26
Mike COUCHOIS ▶ 10646 (1)	**6.5**
Walkin' The Fence—Couchois (79)	26
Pat COUCHOIS ▶ 10647 (1)	**6.5**
Walkin' The Fence—Couchois (79)	26
Jean COULON ▶ 10912 (1)	**4.4**
Under The Bridges Of Paris—Dean Martin (55)	18
Clarence COULTER ▶ 8026 (1)	**64**
Somebody's Gettin' It—Johnnie Taylor (76)	193
Phil COULTER ▶ 1567 (7)	**2700**
Saturday Night—Bay City Rollers (75)	4835
My Boy—Elvis Presley (75)	*838*
My Boy—Richard Harris (71)	*497*
Hi Hi Hazel—Gary And The Hornets (66)	16
Julie Ann—Ginger (76)	11
Congratulations—Cliff Richard (68)	3.7
Forever And Ever—Slik (76)	1.2
Fred COUPLAND ▶ 11794 (1)	**0.0**
Oh Yeah—Tommy Danton & The Echoes (57)	0.0
—Pierre Cour see: Pierre LeMAIRE	
Alexander COURAGE ▶ 11208 (1)	**2.8**
Theme Of Star Trek II (Main Title)—Soundtrack (82)	5.5
—C.C. Courtney see: Charles Cane COURTNEY	
Charles Cane COURTNEY [C.C. Courtney] ▶ 3195 (1)	**956**
(If You Let Me Make Love To You Then) Why Can't I Touch You?—Ronnie Dyson (70)	1912
David COURTNEY [David Alexander Cohen] ▶ 1499 (5)	**2897**
The Show Must Go On—Three Dog Night (74)	3484
Long Tall Glasses (I Can Dance)—Leo Sayer (75)	2026
Giving It All Away—Roger Daltrey (73)	175
Shooting Star—Dollar (79)	54
One Man Band—Leo Sayer (75)	1.8
Lou COURTNEY [Louis Russell Pegues] ▶ 2563 (7)	**1377**
Do The Freddie—Freddie And The Dreamers (65)	1014
Ain't It The Truth—Mary Wells (64)	486
Up And Down—McCoys (66)	342
Skate Now—Lou Courtney (67)	219
Do The Thing—Lou Courtney (67)	101
Find My Way Back Home—Nashville Teens (65)	2.4
Hey Joyce—Lou Courtney (68)	2.4
—John Preston Courville see: Johnny PRESTON	
Gary Lee COURY ▶ 10337 (1)	**9.9**
The Star Wars Stars—Force (77)	20
—John Coury see: John COREY	
Richard COUSINS ▶ 6489 (1)	**164**
Smoking Gun—Robert Cray Band (87)	491
William COUTURIE ▶ 6169 (1)	**198**
19—Paul Hardcastle (85)	792
Don COVAY [Donald James Randolph] ▶ 213 (34)	**15259**
Pony Time—Chubby Checker (61)	*8332*
Chain Of Fools—Aretha Franklin (67)	*5735*
See Saw—Aretha Franklin (68)	*1603*
Lights Out—Peter Wolf (84)	1089
Letter Full Of Tears—Gladys Knight & The Pips (61)	1047
Mercy, Mercy—Don Covay & The Goodtimers (64)	*855*
Tonight's The Night—Solomon Burke (65)	854
The Continental Walk—Hank Ballard And The Midnighters (61)	*672*
Seesaw—Don Covay & The Goodtimers (65)	*509*
I Was Checkin' Out She Was Checkin' In—Don Covay (73)	489
You're Good For Me—Solomon Burke (63)	383
Shoes—Brook Benton With The Dixie Flyers (70)	285
Pony Time—Don Covay and The Goodtimers (61)	*281*
You Threw A Lucky Punch—Gene Chandler (62)	*280*
She Said Yes—Wilson Pickett (70)	169
You Can Run (But You Can't Hide)—Jerry Butler (62)	129
Mercy, Mercy, Mercy—Phoebe Snow (81)	*121*
The Continental Walk—Rollers (61)	*81*
Gilee—Sonny Spencer (59)	64
Hey Lover—Debbie Dovale (63)	61
Crossfire Time—Dee Clark (63)	54
Chain Of Fools—Little Caesar (90)	*52*
(Boo Hoo) I'm Gonna Cry—Lloyd Price (61)	51
It's Better To Have (And Don't Need)—Don Covay (74)	48

Don COVAY [Donald James Randolph] ▶ 213 (34) *Continued*	**15259**
Demonstration—Otis Redding (70)	32
I Don't Know What You've Got But It's Got Me - Part 1—Little Richard (65)	29
Soul Meeting—Soul Clan (68)	15
Elizabeth—Dave Ford And The Hollywood Flames (62)	14
Long Tall Shorty—Tommy Tucker (64)	12
I Just Go For You—Jimmy Jones (60)	8.7
I'm Hanging Up My Heart For You—Solomon Burke (62)	8.1
Take This Hurt Off Me—Don Covay (64)	3.9
Your Memory—Five Satins (60)	3.0
Chain Of Fools (Part 1)—Jimmy Smith (68)	*0.9*
David COVERDALE ▶ 966 (10)	**4632**
Here I Go Again—Whitesnake (87)	4367
Is This Love—Whitesnake (87)	3575
The Deeper The Love—Whitesnake (90)	517
Fool For Your Loving—Whitesnake (89)	*489*
Give Me All Your Love—Whitesnake (88)	254
Fool For Your Loving—Whitesnake (80)	*207*
Still Of The Night—Whitesnake (87)	46
Might Just Take Your Life—Deep Purple (74)	27
Now You're Gone—Whitesnake (90)	24
You Can't Do It Right (With The One You Love)—Deep Purple (74)	4.3
—Julian Covey see: Philamore LINCOLN	
Joey COVINGTON [Joey Edward Michno] ▶ 4100 (2)	**593**
With Your Love—Jefferson Starship (76)	1472
Pretty As You Feel—Jefferson Airplane (71)	512
Marie COWAN ▶ 8316 (3)	**54**
Waltzing Matilda—Jimmie Rodgers (60)	*163*
Waltzing Matilda—David Carroll And His Orchestra (59)	*0.0*
Waltzing Matilda—Merrill Staton Choir (60)	*0.0*
Michael COWAN ▶ 10396 (1)	**8.9**
The Float—Hank Ballard And The Midnighters (61)	8.9
Johnny COWELL ▶ 1287 (6)	**3451**
Our Winter Love—Bill Pursell (63)	*2027*
Walk Hand In Hand—Tony Martin (56)	*1116*
Walk Hand In Hand—Andy Williams (56)	*233*
Our Winter Love—Lettermen (67)	*48*
Walk Hand In Hand—Denny Vaughn (56)	*47*
(These Are) The Young Years—Floyd Cramer (63)	3.2
Bill COWSILL ▶ 4815 (2)	**407**
We Can Fly—Cowsills (68)	950
In Need Of A Friend—Cowsills (68)	340
Bob COWSILL ▶ 4816 (2)	**407**
We Can Fly—Cowsills (68)	950
In Need Of A Friend—Cowsills (68)	340
Herbert COX ▶ 4922 (5)	**380**
Let's Turkey Trot—Little Eva (63)	947
Little Girl Of Mine—Cleftones (56)	*372*
Can't We Be Sweethearts—Cleftones (56)	59
Little Girl Of Mine—Diamonds (56)	*0.0*
Trudy—Cleftones (58)	0.0
Jimmie COX ▶ 3545 (2)	**791**
Nobody Wants You When You're Down And Out—Bobby Womack (73)	*787*
Nobody Knows You When You're Down And Out—Nina Simone (60)	*4.1*
Peter COX ▶ 2950 (5)	**1104**
King Of Wishful Thinking—Go West (90)	1534
We Close Our Eyes—Go West (85)	471
Don't Look Down - The Sequel—Go West (87)	354
Call Me—Go West (85)	289
Eye To Eye—Go West (85)	71
Roy COX ▶ 3928 (2)	**653**
Hot Smoke & Sasafrass—Bubble Puppy (69)	1280
If I Had A Reason—Bubble Puppy (69)	27
Tim COX ▶ 10849 (1)	**4.9**
Jack The Lad—3 Man Island (88)	15
Graham COXON ▶ 9675 (1)	**19**
There's No Other Way—Blur (91)	77
Steve COY ▶ 4558 (5)	**465**
You Spin Me Round (Like A Record)—Dead Or Alive (85)	1071
Brand New Lover—Dead Or Alive (86)	1017
Come Home With Me Baby—Dead Or Alive (89)	117
Lover Come Back To Me—Dead Or Alive (85)	84
Something In My House—Dead Or Alive (87)	38
—Isaac Cozerbreit see: Charles WILLIAMS	
—Vincent Eugene Craddock see: Gene VINCENT	
—Arthur S. Crafa see: Art CRAFER	
Art CRAFER [Arthur S. Crafa] ▶ 2269 (6)	**1670**
No Arms Can Ever Hold You (Like These Arms Of Mine)—Georgie Shaw (55)	*1126*
No Other Arms—Pat Boone (55)	*1053*
No Arms Can Ever Hold You—Bachelors (64)	*791*
No Arms Can Ever Hold You (Like These Arms Of Mine)—Gaylords (55)	*187*
No Arms Can Ever Hold You—Bobby Vinton (70)	*184*
No Arms Can Ever Hold You—Jimmy Young with Bob Sharples & His Music (55)	*0.0*
Morty CRAFT ▶ 2510 (7)	**1429**
Church Bells May Ring—Diamonds (56)	*981*
Alone (Why Must I Be Alone)—Shepherd Sisters (57)	*891*
Alone—4 Seasons (64)	*610*
Hide 'Nor Hair—Ray Charles And His Orchestra (62)	578
Tell Her For Me—Adam Wade (59)	302
Church Bells May Ring—Willows (56)	*210*
Alone (Why Must I Be Alone)—Brother Sisters (57)	*0.0*
Selma CRAFT ▶ 3317 (4)	**902**
Alone (Why Must I Be Alone)—Shepherd Sisters (57)	*891*
Alone—4 Seasons (64)	*610*
Tell Her For Me—Adam Wade (59)	302
Alone (Why Must I Be Alone)—Brother Sisters (57)	*0.0*
Harry CRAFTON ▶ 8421 (2)	**51**
Rock The Joint—Bill Haley With Haley's Comets (55)	*146*
Rock The Joint—Bill Haley & His Comets (57)	*6.6*
Charlie CRAIG ▶ 7721 (1)	**79**
Get That Gasoline Blues—NRBQ (74)	158
—Denise Ora Craig see: Denise LaSALLE	
Francis CRAIG ▶ 2175 (4)	**1788**
Near You—Roger Williams (58)	*1787*
Beg Your Pardon—Billy Vaughn And His Orchestra (60)	1.5
Near You—Cliffie Stone & His Orchestra (58)	*0.0*
Near You—Mulcays (58)	*0.0*
Gregory CRAIG ▶ 5970 (1)	**221**
The Word Is Out—Jermaine Stewart (85)	442
—Jimmy Craig see: Milton KELLEM	
Marvin CRAIG ▶ 9016 (1)	**33**
Fantastic Voyage—Lakeside (80)	296
Michael CRAIG ▶ 780 (10)	**5663**
Karma Chameleon—Culture Club (83)	5903
Do You Really Want To Hurt Me—Culture Club (82)	5783
Time (Clock Of The Heart)—Culture Club (83)	4056
Miss Me Blind—Culture Club (84)	2167
I'll Tumble 4 Ya—Culture Club (83)	1624
Church Of The Poison Mind—Culture Club (83)	1501
Move Away—Culture Club (86)	1007
It's A Miracle—Culture Club (84)	965
The War Song—Culture Club (84)	766
Mistake No. 3—Culture Club (84)	455
Roger CRAIG ▶ 9619 (2)	**20**
Stacy—Fortune (85)	34
You Are My Love—Liverpool Express (76)	6.4
—Edyth Craighead see: Brian HOLLAND	
—Edyth Craighead see: Eddie HOLLAND	
—Edyth Craighead see: Lamont DOZIER	
Billy CRAIN ▶ 5460 (1)	**284**
Call It Love—Poco (89)	851
Tom CRAIN ▶ 3292 (4)	**909**
The Devil Went Down To Georgia—Charlie Daniels Band (79)	*3303*
In America—Charlie Daniels Band (80)	1335
The Legend Of Wooley Swamp—Charlie Daniels Band (80)	633
The Devil Came Up To Michigan—K.M.C. Kru (91)	*243*
Floyd CRAMER ▶ 272 (10)	**12678**
Last Date—Floyd Cramer (60)	*7744*
On The Rebound—Floyd Cramer (61)	3421
Fancy Pants—Al (He's The King) Hirt Trumpet with Chorus and Orchestra (65)	478
Last Date—Lawrence Welk And His Orchestra (60)	*411*
My Last Date (With You)—Skeeter Davis (60)	*381*
My Last Date (With You)—Joni James (60)	*266*
Your Last Goodbye—Floyd Cramer (61)	245
Hot Pepper—Floyd Cramer (62)	98
Hang On—Floyd Cramer (61)	59
Flip Flop And Bop—Floyd Cramer (58)	6.5
Bill CRANDALL [Buddy Randell] ▶ 2704 (4)	**1262**
Short Shorts—Royal Teens (58)	*2815*
Lies—Knickerbockers (65)	1117
Short Shorts—Four Winds (58)	*0.0*
Short Shorts—Tiny Bradshaw & His Orchestra (58)	*0.0*
Cy CRANE [Steve Donroy, Seymour Gottlieb] ▶ 1949 (6)	**2065**
It's My Party—Lesley Gore (63)	*7824*
I'm Just A Dancing Partner—Platters (56)	118
It's My Party—Dave Stewart With Barbara Gaskin (81)	*64*
I Hear Those Bells—Dinah Washington (55)	55
What Does It Matter—Platters (59)	20
Sometimes I Wish I Were A Boy—Lesley Gore (64)	19
Jimmie CRANE [Loreto Domenico Fraieli] ▶ 401 (23)	**9860**
I Need You Now—Eddie Fisher (54)	*6888*
If I Give My Heart To You—Doris Day (54)	*4238*
Hurt—Timi Yuro (61)	*3272*
If I Give My Heart To You—Denise Lor (54)	*1609*
Every Day Of My Life—Bobby Vinton (72)	*1257*
If I Give My Heart To You—Dinah Shore (54)	*1206*
If I Give My Heart To You—Kitty Kallen (59)	*711*
I Can't Get You Out Of My Heart—Al Martino (59)	*609*
Hurt—Elvis Presley (76)	*517*
Ev'ry Day Of My Life—McGuire Sisters (56)	*516*
My Believing Heart—Joni James (55)	411
If I Give My Heart To You—Connee Boswell (54)	*402*
Come Back—Jimmy Clanton (60)	264
I Can't Say Goodbye—Fireflies Featuring Ritchie Adams (59)	245
Hurt—Little Anthony And The Imperials (66)	*222*
Hurt—Roy Hamilton (54)	*63*
Hurt—Manhattans (75)	*58*
I Need You Now—Ronnie Dove (69)	*21*
So Close To My Heart—Kathy Linden (59)	18
I Can't Get You Out Of My Heart—Al Martino (64)	*1.5*
I Need You Now—100 Strings And Joni (60)	*1.1*
I Can't Get You Out Of My Heart—Bob Carroll (59)	*0.0*
Ev'ry Day Of My Life—Vera Lynn (56)	*0.0*
Lor CRANE ▶ 1672 (5)	**2515**
Don't Just Stand There—Patty Duke (65)	2466
White On White—Danny Williams (64)	1727
Say Something Funny—Patty Duke (65)	659
Funny Little Butterflies—Patty Duke (65)	183
A Little Toy Balloon—Danny Williams (64)	56
Mitch CRANE ▶ 5853 (1)	**237**
More Than Just The Two Of Us—Sneaker (81)	473
Philip M. CRANE ▶ 8382 (1)	**52**
Little Sandy Sleighfoot—Jimmy Dean with Ray Ellis and his Orchestra (57)	105
—Vincent Crane see: Vincent CHEESMAN	
Dennis CRASWELL ▶ 3090 (1)	**1013**
Liar, Liar—Castaways (65)	2025
—Rogers Lee Craton see: Lee ROGERS	
—Cliff Crawford see: Cliff CROFFORD	
Dave CRAWFORD ▶ 1613 (9)	**2623**
Precious, Precious—Jackie Moore (70)	1320
Young Hearts Run Free—Candi Staton (76)	1234
I Like To Live The Love—B.B. King (73)	824
Call My Name, I'll Be There—Wilson Pickett (71)	440
Philadelphia—B.B. King (74)	92
Mighty High—Mighty Clouds Of Joy (76)	82
Sometimes It's Got To Rain—Jackie Moore With The Dixie Flyers (71)	37
Who Are You—B.B. King (74)	21
Victim—Candi Staton (78)	14
Helen CRAWFORD ▶ 10865 (1)	**4.8**
So Blue—Vibrations (60)	19
James CRAWFORD ▶ 4826 (3)	**404**
Iko Iko—Belle Stars (89)	*940*
Iko Iko—Dixie Cups (65)	*854*
Iko Iko—Dr. John (72)	*226*
John CRAWFORD ▶ 2785 (4)	**1198**
No More Words—Berlin (84)	847
The Metro—Berlin (83)	265
Sex (I'm A...)—Berlin (83)	166
Now It's My Turn—Berlin (84)	31
Kerry CRAWFORD ▶ 6333 (1)	**182**
Take Off—Bob & Doug McKenzie (82)	908

Robert CRAY ▶ 6490 (1)	**164**
Smoking Gun—Robert Cray Band (87)	491

Henry CREAMER ▶ 1998 (2)	**2015**
Way Down Yonder In New Orleans—Freddie Cannon (59)	4029
After You've Gone—Frankie Avalon (62)	0.5

Luigi CREATORE [Fred Lawrence, Jack Limber, Mark Markwell, Victor Paul] ▶ 387 (52)	**10182**
The Lion Sleeps Tonight—Tokens (61)	*9030*
Can't Help Falling In Love—Elvis Presley With The Jordanaires (61)	*5450*
The Lion Sleeps Tonight—Robert John (71)	*5059*
Secretly—Jimmie Rodgers (58)	*4105*
Bimbombey—Jimmie Rodgers (58)	1823
Are You Really Mine—Jimmie Rodgers (58)	1540
A Walkin' Miracle—Essex Featuring Anita Humes (63)	1442
Oh Oh I'm Falling In Love Again—Jimmie Rodgers (58)	1234
Let's Put It All Together—Stylistics (74)	*1045*
Hello Heartache, Goodbye Love—Little Peggy March (63)	666
I'm Never Gonna Tell—Jimmie Rodgers (59)	568
Heavy Fallin' Out—Stylistics (74)	552
Can't Help Falling In Love—Corey Hart (86)	*544*
I Wish I Were A Princess—Little Peggy March (63)	501
Wild In The Country—Elvis Presley With The Jordanaires (61)	471
Snoopy's Christmas—Royal Guardsmen (67)	431
And Now—Della Reese (60)	398
Make Me A Miracle—Jimmie Rodgers (58)	387
Can't Help Falling In Love—Al Martino (70)	*308*
Because You're Young—Jimmie Rodgers (59)	293
B'wa Nina (Pretty Girl)—Tokens (62)	269
The Impossible Happened—Little Peggy March (63)	258
Experience Unnecessary—Sarah Vaughan (55)	252
Secretly—Lettermen (65)	*243*
I'll Take You Home—Corsairs Featuring Jay "Bird" Uzzell (62)	240
Can't Give You Anything (But My Love)—Stylistics (75)	227
Pupalina—Gaylords (54)	*213*
Star On A TV Show—Stylistics (75)	165
Everyday—Della Reese (60)	139
Thank You Baby—Stylistics (75)	111
The Wizard—Jimmie Rodgers (58)	110
You Understand Me—Sam Cooke (60)	*99*
It Happened Again—Sarah Vaughan (56)	94
Funky Weekend—Stylistics (75)	61
You Are Beautiful—Stylistics (76)	58
A Far Far Better Thing—Della Reese (61)	53
Can't Help Falling In Love—Andy Williams (70)	*26*
The Crazy Otto Rag—Hugo & Luigi (55)	*24*
Bad Girl—Valerie Carr (58)	15
Love Is The Answer—Van Mc Coy & The Soul City Symphony (74)	13
Let's Put It All Together—Band Of Gold (84)	*12*
Dance Mr. Snowman Dance—Crew-Cuts (54)	6.0
Lulu Had A Baby—Chico Holiday (59)	3.7
Big Boat—Tokens (62)	1.8
Can't Help Falling In Love With You—Jimmy Castor (80)	*1.8*
You Understand Me—Jimmie Rodgers (58)	*1.6*
Pupalina (My Little Doll)—Guy Lombardo & His Royal Canadians (54)	*0.0*
Can't Help Falling In Love—Four Esquires (61)	*0.0*
Can't Help Falling In Love—Keely Smith (61)	*0.0*
The Crazy Otto Rag—Happy Hoagy Carmichael (55)	*0.0*
The Crazy Otto Rag—Crazy Otto (55)	*0.0*
Pupalina (My Little Doll)—Jimmy Durante (54)	*0.0*

Linda CREED [Linda Epstein] ▶ 223 (25) HOF	**15053**
You Make Me Feel Brand New—Stylistics Featurng Airrion Love & Russell Thompkins, Jr. (74)	*5023*
The Rubberband Man—Spinners (76)	4975
Greatest Love Of All—Whitney Houston (86)	*4409*
Betcha By Golly, Wow—Stylistics Featurng Airrion Love & Russell Thompkins, Jr. (72)	*3608*
You Are Everything—Stylistics (71)	2438
Break Up To Make Up—Stylistics (73)	*1985*
I'm Stone In Love With You—Stylistics (72)	1537
Rockin' Roll Baby—Stylistics (73)	1272
People Make The World Go Round—Stylistics (72)	969
I'm Coming Home—Spinners (74)	*864*
Stop, Look, Listen (To Your Heart)—Stylistics (71)	803
One Man Band (Plays All Alone)—Ronnie Dyson (73)	768
The Greatest Love Of All—George Benson (77)	*660*
Ghetto Child—Spinners (73)	517
Hold Me—Teddy Pendergrass (84)	457
Living A Little, Laughing A Little—Spinners (75)	291
Life Is A Song Worth Singing—Johnny Mathis (73)	226
I'm Coming Home—Johnny Mathis (73)	*198*
Help Me Find A Way (To Say I Love You)—Little Anthony And The Imperials (70)	106
Quick, Fast, In A Hurry—New York City (74)	75
Break Up To Make Up—Cynthia (91)	*49*
I Wanna Be A Free Girl—Dusty Springfield (70)	38
1,000 Laughs—Eloise Laws (78)	13
Betcha By Golly Wow—Band Of Gold (84)	*12*
You Make Me Feel Brand New—Band Of Gold (84)	*12*

Jim CREGAN ▶ 2418 (5)	**1502**
Passion—Rod Stewart (80)	2748
Crazy About Her—Rod Stewart (89)	1149
Forever Young—Rod Stewart (88)	1122
Tonight I'm Yours (Don't Hurt Me)—Rod Stewart (82)	845
Somebody Special—Rod Stewart (81)	44

—Hugh Anthony Cregg see: Huey LEWIS

Lol CRÈME ▶ 3383 (3)	**873**
Neanderthal Man—Hotlegs (70)	948
Cry—Godley & Creme (85)	899
Rubber Bullets—10 C. C. (73)	322

Walt CREMONINI [Valter Cremonini, Walter Cremonini] ▶ 11675 (1)	**0.7**
Keep Warm—Jinny (91)	2.2

Marshall CRENSHAW ▶ 4323 (3)	**521**
Someday, Someway—Marshall Crenshaw (82)	*425*
Someday, Someway—Robert Gordon (81)	*57*
Favorite Waste Of Time—Bette Midler (83)	40

Jim CRETECOS ▶ 1855 (2)	**2195**
Doesn't Somebody Want To Be Wanted—Partridge Family Starring Shirley Jones & Featuring David Cassidy (71)	4568
Lay A Little Lovin' On Me—Robin McNamara (70)	2016

Michael CRETU ▶ 4170 (1)	**574**
Sadeness Part 1—Enigma (91)	1723

Bob CREWE [Robert Stanley Crewe Jr.] ▶ 40 (86) HOF	**45527**
Big Girls Don't Cry—4 Seasons (62)	*10012*
Walk Like A Man—4 Seasons (63)	*8138*
Rag Doll—4 Seasons Featuring The "Sound" Of Frankie Valli (64)	7976
Can't Take My Eyes Off You—Frankie Valli (67)	*7410*
Let's Hang On!—4 Seasons Featuring The "Sound" Of Frankie Valli (65)	*6625*
My Eyes Adored You—Frankie Valli (74)	5362
Lady Marmalade—Labelle (75)	*5277*
Silhouettes—Rays (57)	*4941*
Silhouettes—Herman's Hermits (65)	*3289*
Sock It To Me-Baby!—Mitch Ryder And The Detroit Wheels (67)	3156
Tallahassee Lassie—Freddy Cannon (59)	2864
Navy Blue—Diane Renay (64)	2732
Ronnie—4 Seasons Featuring The "Sound" Of Frankie Valli (64)	2454
Swearin' To God—Frankie Valli (75)	2151
Silence Is Golden—Tremeloes (67)	2043
Save It For Me—4 Seasons Featuring The "Sound" Of Frankie Valli (64)	*1587*
Get Dancin'—Disco Tex & The Sex-O-Lettes Featuring Sir Monti Rock III (74)	1522
Bye, Bye, Baby (Baby, Goodbye)—4 Seasons Featuring The "Sound" Of Frankie Valli (65)	1453
La Dee Dah—Billy & Lillie (57)	1426
Can't Take My Eyes Off You—Lettermen (67)	*1323*
The Sun Ain't Gonna Shine (Anymore)—Walker Bros. (66)	*1271*
Lucky Ladybug—Billy & Lillie (58)	900
To Give (The Reason I Live)—Frankie Valli (67)	836
I Make A Fool Of Myself—Frankie Valli (67)	799
I Wanna Dance Wit' Choo (Doo Dat Dance)—Disco Tex & The Sex-O-Lettes Featuring Sir Monti Rock III (75)	676
The Proud One—Osmonds (75)	*633*
Jump Over—Freddy Cannon (60)	624
Girl Come Running—4 Seasons Featuring The "Sound" Of Frankie Valli (65)	604
Buzz Buzz A-Diddle-It—Freddy Cannon (61)	526
New Mexican Rose—4 Seasons (63)	480
More Than The Eye Can See—Al Martino (67)	434
(You're Gonna) Hurt Yourself—Frankie Valli (66)	431
Magic Moon (Clair De Lune)—Rays (61)	*413*
Let's Hang On—Barry Manilow (82)	*370*
Pony Express—Danny & The Juniors (61)	344
Dusty—Rag Dolls (65)	323
Okefenokee—Freddy Cannon (59)	301
Walk Like A Man—Mary Jane Girls (86)	*290*
Summer And Sandy—Lesley Gore (67)	257
Can't Take My Eyes Off You—Nancy Wilson (69)	*255*
You're Looking Like Love To Me—Peabo Bryson/Roberta Flack (83)	224
Soon (I'll Be Home Again)—4 Seasons Featuring Frankie Valli (63)	214
The Proud One—Frankie Valli (66)	*211*
Toy Soldier—4 Seasons Featuring The "Sound" Of Frankie Valli (65)	204
The Sun Ain't Gonna Shine Anymore—Nielsen/Pearson (81)	*168*
Knock! Knock! (Who's There?)—Orlons (64)	160
Bells, Bells, Bells (The Bell Song)—Billy & Lillie (59)	155
Humdinger—Freddy Cannon (60)	153
Happy Shades Of Blue—Freddie Cannon (60)	150
Eternity—Vikki Carr (69)	139
Hollywood Hot—Eleventh Hour (75)	136
Silhouettes—Diamonds (57)	*130*
Little Boy (In Grown Up Clothes)—4 Seasons (65)	113
Teen Queen Of The Week—Freddy Cannon (62)	112
Lady Marmalade—Ritchie Family (76)	*92*
Twistin' All Night Long.—Danny & The Juniors With Guest Artist Freddy Cannon (62)	86
Urge—Freddy Cannon (60)	82
Across The Street—Lenny O'Henry (64)	79
Street Talk (Var. III)—B. C. G. (B.C. Generation) (76)	78
Whatever You Want—Jerry Butler (63)	65
Don't Mention My Name—Shepherd Sisters (63)	58
That's The Only Way—4 Seasons (63)	51
Silhouettes—Steve Gibson & the Red Caps (57)	*47*
I Can't Take My Eyes Off You—Pet Shop Boys (91)	*37*
Happiness—Billy & Lillie (58)	32
Jam Band—Disco Tex & The Sex-O-Lettes (75)	26
Fancy Dancer—Frankie Valli (79)	25
Daddy Cool—Rays (57)	*21*
Daddy Cool—Diamonds (57)	*21*
Society Girl—Rag Dolls (64)	20
She Ain't Lovin' You—Distant Cousins (66)	20
(Kwa-Na-Va-Ka) Cuernavaca Choo Choo—Freddy Cannon (60)	14
Hickory—Frankie Valli And The 4 Seasons (74)	12
Birds Of Britain—Bob Crewe Generation (67)	12
You're Ready Now—Frankie Valli (66)	8.3
The Sun Ain't Gonna Shine Anymore—Fuzzy Bunnies (68)	*6.0*
Watch Out, Sally!—Diane Renay (64)	4.9
I'm Comin' Home—Sammy Davis Jr. (57)	4.7
Walk Like A Man—Gidea Park (81)	*3.7*
Let's Hang On—Gidea Park (81)	*3.7*
Big Girls Don't Cry—Gidea Park (81)	*3.7*
Elevator Operator—Rays (58)	3.1
Mediterranean Moon—Rays (60)	3.0
So Good—Eleventh Hour (74)	3.0
My Time For Cryin'—Maxine Brown (62)	1.4
Takin' All I Can Get—Mitch Ryder And The Detroit Wheels (66)	0.5

Ian Stevenson CRICHTON ▶ 6396 (2)	**175**
On The Loose—Saga (82)	675
Wind Him Up—Saga (83)	200

Jim CRICHTON ▶ 6287 (3)	**185**
On The Loose—Saga (82)	675
Wind Him Up—Saga (83)	200
The Flyer—Saga (83)	21

Arthur CRIER ▶ 3930 (3)	**652**
Nag—Halos (61)	610
Well-A, Well-A—Shirley & Lee (61)	39
Remember—Velours (58)	8.7

Keith CRIER ▶ 4904 (2)	**385**
Disco Nights (Rock-Freak)—G.Q. (79)	1528
Standing Ovation—GQ (80)	11

Mick CRIPPS ▶ 7209 (1)	**110**
The Ballad Of Jayne—L.A. Guns (90)	549

—Peter George Criscoula see: Peter CRISS

Anthony CRISS ► 6157 (1)	**199**
O.P.P.—Naughty By Nature (91)	1392
Peter CRISS [Peter George Criscoula] ► 4532 (2)	**470**
Beth—Kiss (76)	1404
Don't You Let Me Down—Peter Criss (78)	3.0
Joe CRISTOFANILLI ► 10837 (1)	**5.0**
Wanted Man—Ratt (84)	15
Steven CRISTOL ► 5490 (1)	**279**
Tomorrow Doesn't Matter Tonight—Starship (86)	558
—Yodar Critch see: Gary ZEKLEY	
Ingrid CROCE ► 11435 (1)	**1.7**
Age (Where I Started Again)—Horatio (69)	3.4
Jim CROCE ► 179 (11) HOF	**16968**
Bad, Bad Leroy Brown—Jim Croce (73)	*5404*
Time In A Bottle—Jim Croce (73)	4906
You Don't Mess Around With Jim—Jim Croce (72)	2204
I'll Have To Say I Love You In A Song—Jim Croce (74)	1744
Operator (That's Not The Way It Feels)—Jim Croce (72)	1176
Workin' At The Car Wash Blues—Jim Croce (74)	614
One Less Set Of Footsteps—Jim Croce (73)	567
It Doesn't Have To Be That Way—Jim Croce (73)	233
Lover's Cross—Melanie (74)	102
Bad, Bad Leroy Brown—Frank Sinatra (74)	*18*
Age (Where I Started Again)—Horatio (69)	3.4
—George Crockett see: G.L. CROCKETT	
G.L. CROCKETT [George Crockett] ► 7216 (1)	**110**
It's A Man Down There—G.L. Crockett (65)	219
—Howard Crockett see: Howard HAUSEY	
Cliff CROFFORD [Cliff Crawford, Clifton Thomas Crofford] ► 1594 (4)	**2652**
Old Rivers—Walter Brennan (62)	2230
Chip Chip—Gene McDaniels (62)	1262
The Puzzle—Gene McDaniels (63)	0.5
Houdini—Walter Brennan (62)	0.4
—Darrell G. Crofts see: Dash CROFTS	
Dash CROFTS [Darrell G. Crofts] ► 885 (9)	**5029**
Get Closer—Seals & Crofts (Featuring Carolyn Willis) (76)	2732
Diamond Girl—Seals & Crofts (73)	2135
Summer Breeze—Seals & Crofts (72)	*2085*
Hummingbird—Seals & Crofts (73)	1121
We May Never Pass This Way (Again)—Seals & Crofts (73)	919
I'll Play For You—Seals & Crofts (75)	885
Summer Breeze (Part 1)—Isley Brothers (74)	*173*
If You See My Love—Lenny Welch (64)	6.1
Castles In The Sand—Seals & Crofts (75)	1.8
Lenny CROHET ► 9022 (1)	**33**
Love Is Funny That Way—Jackie Wilson (71)	99
Bill CROMPTON ► 8500 (3)	**48**
House Of Bamboo—Earl Grant (60)	*80*
House Of Bamboo—Andy Williams (58)	*10*
Why—Beatles With Tony Sheridan (64)	6.1
Chad CROMWELL ► 10161 (1)	**12**
Make It Mean Something—Rob Jungklas (87)	35
Kevin CRONIN ► 186 (14)	**16611**
Keep On Loving You—REO Speedwagon (80)	5762
Can't Fight This Feeling—REO Speedwagon (85)	4755
Keep The Fire Burnin'—REO Speedwagon (82)	1759
In My Dreams—REO Speedwagon (87)	1030
Here With Me—REO Speedwagon (88)	776
That Ain't Love—REO Speedwagon (87)	658
Don't Let Him Go—REO Speedwagon (81)	590
Sweet Time—REO Speedwagon (82)	551
I Do' Wanna Know—REO Speedwagon (84)	531
Live Every Moment—REO Speedwagon (85)	400
Roll With The Changes—REO Speedwagon (78)	288
Time For Me To Fly—REO Speedwagon (78)	*170*
Time For Me To Fly—REO Speedwagon (80)	*125*
Love Is A Rock—REO Speedwagon (90)	117
Max CROOK ► 776 (6)	**5682**
Runaway—Del Shannon (61)	*10390*
Runaway—Charlie Kulis (75)	*327*
Runaway—Bonnie Raitt (77)	*294*
Runaway—Lawrence Welk And His Orchestra (62)	*146*
Runaway—Dawn Featuring Tony Orlando (72)	*124*
Runaway—Luis Cardenas (86)	*83*

David CROOKS [Dave Barker] ► 5182 (1)	**329**
Double Barrel—Dave And Ansil Collins (71)	987
Steve CROPPER ► 189 (55) HOF	**16377**
(Sittin' On) The Dock Of The Bay—Otis Redding (68)	*7420*
Knock On Wood—Amii Stewart (79)	*4967*
Green Onions—Booker T. & The M.G.'s (62)	*4924*
634-5789 (Soulsville, U.S.A)—Wilson Pickett (66)	2078
Time Is Tight—Booker T. & The M.G.'s (69)	2035
See Saw—Aretha Franklin (68)	*1603*
Soul-Limbo—Booker T. & The M.G.'s (68)	1495
Knock On Wood—Eddie Floyd (66)	*1439*
(Sittin' On) The Dock Of The Bay—Michael Bolton (88)	*1137*
In The Midnight Hour—Wilson Pickett (65)	*1036*
In The Midnight Hour—Cross Country (73)	*725*
The Happy Song (Dum-Dum)—Otis Redding (68)	722
Hip Hug-Her—Booker T. & The M.G.'s (67)	719
Hole In The Wall—Packers (65)	689
Fa-Fa-Fa-Fa-Fa (Sad Song)—Otis Redding (66)	553
Seesaw—Don Covay & The Goodtimers (65)	*509*
Can Your Monkey Do The Dog—Rufus Thomas (64)	480
You Don't Know What You Mean To Me—Sam & Dave (68)	453
On The Dock Of The Bay—Dells (69)	*452*
Knock On Wood—Otis & Carla (67)	*443*
In The Midnight Hour—Mirettes (68)	*421*
Mr. Pitiful—Otis Redding (65)	416
Ninety-Nine And A Half (Won't Do)—Wilson Pickett (66)	412
I've Got No Time To Lose—Carla Thomas (64)	384
Melting Pot—Booker T. & The M.G.'s (71)	365
Mini-Skirt Minnie—Wilson Pickett (69)	364
Don't Fight It—Wilson Pickett (65)	293
Candy—Astors (65)	239
Move 'Em Out—Delaney & Bonnie (72)	221
(Sittin' On) The Dock Of The Bay—Reddings (82)	*200*
Raise Your Hand—Eddie Floyd (67)	168
Just One More Day—Otis Redding (65)	138
A Woman's Love—Carla Thomas (64)	125
I've Got To Have Your Love—Eddie Floyd (69)	120
My Sweet Potato—Booker T. & The M.G.'s (66)	119
(Sittin' On) The Dock Of The Bay—Sergio Mendes & Brasil '66 (69)	*101*
(Sittin' On) The Dock Of The Bay—Sammy Hagar (79)	*92*
Jellybread—Booker T. & The MGs (62)	74
Slim Jenkin's Place—Booker T. & The M.G.'s (67)	64
Chinese Checkers—Booker T. & The MG's (63)	63
(Sittin' On) The Dock Of The Bay—King Curtis & The Kingpins (68)	*45*
Knucklehead—Bar-Kays (67)	34
In The Midnight Hour—Wanted (67)	*25*
Green Onions—Dick Hyman (69)	*23*
On A Saturday Night—Eddie Floyd (67)	14
Somebody Stole My Dog—Rufus Thomas (64)	14
The Hunter—Ike & Tina Turner (69)	12
In The Midnight Hour—Samantha Sang (79)	*7.5*
Soul Dressing—Booker T. & The MG's (64)	4.4
What A Fool I've Been—Carla Thomas (63)	4.0
Mo-Onions—Booker T. & The MG's (64)	3.7
Pop-Eye Stroll—Mar-Keys (62)	3.1
Puff Of Smoke—Roy Head (71)	2.1
Love Is A Doggone Good Thing—Eddie Floyd (67)	1.9
It's All Over—Wilson Pickett (65)	1.4
Bing CROSBY ► 8025 (1)	**64**
Where The Blue Of The Night—Tommy Mara (58)	193
Bob CROSBY ► 11178 (1)	**2.9**
Big Noise From Winnetka—Spaghetti Head (75)	11
David CROSBY ► 3607 (5) HOF	**769**
Eight Miles High—Byrds (66)	1385
Carry Me—David Crosby / Graham Nash (75)	199
Lady Friend—Byrds (67)	83
Music Is Love—David Crosby (71)	43
Out Of The Darkness—David Crosby / Graham Nash (76)	34
Jimmy CROSBY ► 10390 (1)	**9.0**
Kool's Back Again—Kool & The Gang (70)	18
Robbin CROSBY ► 4342 (4)	**516**
Round And Round—Ratt (84)	1127
Lay It Down—Ratt (85)	345
Dance—Ratt (87)	196
Wanted Man—Ratt (84)	15
—Ronald Clyde Crosby see: Jerry Jeff WALKER	

Billy CROSS ► 5568 (1)	**271**
Take Me Back—Bonnie Tyler (83)	271
Chris CROSS [Christopher Thomas Allen] ► 8842 (1)	**38**
Reap The Wild Wind—Ultravox (83)	152
Christopher CROSS [Christopher Charles Geppert] ► 175 (10)	**17283**
Arthur's Theme (Best That You Can Do)—Christopher Cross (81)	6911
Ride Like The Wind—Christopher Cross (80)	5337
Sailing—Christopher Cross (80)	4811
Think Of Laura—Christopher Cross (83)	1607
All Right—Christopher Cross (83)	1504
Never Be The Same—Christopher Cross (80)	1279
Say You'll Be Mine—Christopher Cross (81)	592
No Time For Talk—Christopher Cross (83)	358
Charm The Snake—Christopher Cross (85)	92
A Chance For Heaven—Christopher Cross (84)	64
Douglass CROSS ► 3564 (1)	**785**
(I Left My Heart) In San Francisco—Tony Bennett (62)	1570
Reuben CROSS ► 3305 (1)	**906**
Shame—Evelyn "Champagne" King (78)	1812
Tim CROSS ► 5529 (1)	**274**
Family Man—Daryl Hall & John Oates (83)	1641
Paul CROSTA ► 6732 (1)	**142**
Always—Firefall (83)	283
Juan CROUCIER ► 7537 (2)	**90**
Lay It Down—Ratt (85)	345
You're In Love—Ratt (85)	7.9
Bob CROWDER ► 11594 (1)	**1.0**
Stormy Monday—Latimore (73)	3.1
Rodney CROWELL ► 716 (3)	**6093**
Shame On The Moon—Bob Seger & The Silver Bullet Band (82)	4148
An American Dream—Dirt Band (79)	1475
Ashes By Now—Rodney Crowell (80)	470
J.C. CROWLEY [John Charles Crowley II] ► 1218 (3)	**3663**
Baby Come Back—Player (77)	6598
I Want You, I Need You—Chris Christian (81)	446
Prisoner Of Your Love—Player (78)	430
Arthur CRUDUP ► 3682 (2)	**736**
My Baby Left Me—Elvis Presley (56)	736
That's All Right—Steve Walsh (80)	0.2
Tyrone CRUM ► 11655 (1)	**0.8**
Riding High—Faze-O (78)	4.8
—Christopher Crummy see: Chris CURTIS	
Kirk CRUMPLER ► 7954 (1)	**67**
Girlfriend—Bobby Brown (86)	202
—Connie Crunk see: Connie CONWAY	
—Norma Crunk see: Norma CONWAY	
Bettye CRUTCHER [Bettye Jean Crutcher Barnes, Bettye Jean Crutcher] ► 2130 (13)	**1837**
Who's Making Love—Johnnie Taylor (68)	*3954*
From His Woman To You—Barbara Mason (74)	446
I Like What You're Doing (To Me)—Carla Thomas (69)	399
I Could Never Be President—Johnnie Taylor (69)	345
Who's Making Love—Blues Brothers (80)	*342*
Who's Making Love—Young-Holt Unlimited (69)	*241*
Move 'Em Out—Delaney & Bonnie (72)	221
Stop Doggin' Me—Johnnie Taylor (72)	85
My Main Man—Staple Singers (74)	74
Slum Baby—Booker T. & The M.G.'s (69)	74
Pin The Tail On The Donkey—Newcomers (71)	70
Sugar Bee—Mitch Ryder (69)	30
Somebody's Sleeping In My Bed—Johnnie Taylor (67)	9.8
Jan CRUTCHFIELD ► 4590 (4)	**460**
Dream On Little Dreamer—Perry Como (65)	787
Archie's Melody—By-Liners (62)	90
I'm Living In Two Worlds—Bonnie Guitar (66)	19
In The Room—Pat Boone (63)	2.7
Jerry CRUTCHFIELD ► 5279 (2)	**314**
My Whole World Is Falling Down—Brenda Lee (63)	623
Kid Stuff—Barbara Fairchild (73)	4.7
Michael CRUZ ► 7166 (1)	**112**
The Right Combination—Seiko & Donnie Wahlberg (90)	224
Gene CRYSLER [James Eugene Fitzwater Jr.] ► 8780 (1)	**39**
Mr. Walker, It's All Over—Billie Jo Spears (69)	39

Billy CRYSTAL ▶ 7019 (1)	**121**
You Look Marvelous—Billy Crystal (85)	242
Bob CRYSTAL ▶ 10118 (1)	**12**
Present For Bob—DeJohn Sisters (55)	37
Joe CSIDA ▶ 10584 (1)	**7.1**
1492—Betty Johnson (57)	21
Joe CUBA [Gilberto Miguel Calderón] ▶ 6242 (2)	**190**
Bang! Bang!—Joe Cuba Sextet (66)	373
El Pito (I'll Never Go Back To Georgia)—Joe Cuba Sextet (66)	8.1
Warren CUCCURULLO ▶ 4965 (4)	**370**
Destination Unknown—Missing Persons (82)	419
Words—Missing Persons (82)	351
Violence Of Summer (Love's Taking Over)—Duran Duran (90)	165
Give—Missing Persons (84)	85
John CUFFLEY ▶ 4638 (2)	**446**
Couldn't Get It Right—Climax Blues Band (77)	2219
Makin' Love—Climax Blues Band (78)	10
Don CUGINI ▶ 10795 (2)	**5.3**
Let Me Sleep Alone—Cugini (79)	15
School's Back—Philadelphia (77)	0.9
Fabrice CUITAD [David Fairstein] ▶ 4171 (1)	**574**
Sadeness Part 1—Enigma (91)	1723
Derrick CULLER ▶ 8091 (2)	**62**
Don't Take It Personal—Jermaine Jackson (89)	156
You Are My Everything—Surface (89)	41
Samuel Orvitt CULLEY ▶ 10457 (1)	**8.2**
Here's A Heart—Diplomats (64)	25
—Napoleon Brown Goodson Culp see: Nappy BROWN	
Sander CULT ▶ 10514 (2)	**7.7**
Love Songs Are Back Again—Band Of Gold (84)	*12*
Love Songs Are Back Again—Band Of Gold (84)	*12*
Bruce CULVER ▶ 6194 (1)	**195**
Desire Me—Sam Cooke (57)	195
—Barbara Lynn Cumby see: Barbara LYNN	
Burton CUMMINGS ▶ 197 (25)	**15913**
American Woman—Guess Who (70)	7040
These Eyes—Guess Who (69)	*3940*
No Time—Guess Who (69)	3320
Stand Tall—Burton Cummings (76)	2133
Laughing—Guess Who (69)	2066
Share The Land—Guess Who (70)	1836
Clap For The Wolfman—Guess Who (74)	1703
Rain Dance—Guess Who (71)	1323
These Eyes—Jr. Walker & The All Stars (69)	*1159*
Star Baby—Guess Who (74)	851
Albert Flasher—Guess Who (71)	850
Dancin' Fool—Guess Who (74)	608
Hang On To Your Life—Guess Who (71)	496
Heartbroken Bopper—Guess Who (72)	448
Sour Suite—Guess Who (71)	417
You Saved My Soul—Burton Cummings (81)	414
Follow Your Daughter Home—Guess Who (73)	172
Guns, Guns, Guns—Guess Who (72)	142
Break It To Them Gently—Burton Cummings (78)	63
I'm Scared—Burton Cummings (77)	58
Runnin' Back To Saskatoon—Guess Who (72)	45
Broken—Guess Who (71)	42
Glamour Boy—Guess Who (73)	33
My Own Way To Rock—Burton Cummings (77)	26
Seems Like I Can't Live With You, But I Can't Live Without You—Guess Who (75)	9.9
John CUMMINGS [John William Cummings, Johnny Ramone] ▶ 8876 (2)	**37**
Rockaway Beach—Ramones (77)	96
Sheena Is A Punk Rocker—Ramones (77)	53
Stephen CUMMINGS ▶ 7350 (1)	**100**
Who Listens To The Radio—Sports (79)	201
Rick CUNHA ▶ 4919 (2)	**382**
(I'm A) Yoyo Man—Rick Cunha (74)	289
When The Feeling Comes Around—Jennifer Warnes (80)	237
Gino CUNICO ▶ 3551 (1)	**787**
When I Wanted You—Barry Manilow (79)	787
B.B. CUNNINGHAM ▶ 4375 (2)	**509**
Let It Out (Let It All Hang Out)—Hombres (67)	2036

It's A Gas—Hombres (68)	1.4
Carl CUNNINGHAM ▶ 5553 (2)	**272**
Soul Finger—Bar-Kays (67)	1546
Give Everybody Some—Bar-Kays (67)	97
James CUNNINGHAM ▶ 4958 (3)	**373**
Jo Ann—Playmates (58)	*746*
Jo-Ann—Lancers (58)	*0.0*
Jo Ann—Twin-Tones (58)	*0.0*
John CUNNINGHAM ▶ 4959 (3)	**373**
Jo Ann—Playmates (58)	*746*
Jo-Ann—Lancers (58)	*0.0*
Jo Ann—Twin-Tones (58)	*0.0*
John Collins CUNNINGHAM ▶ 9099 (1)	**31**
Norma Jean Wants To Be A Movie Star—Sundown Company (76)	31
Ronnie CUNNINGHAM ▶ 9903 (1)	**15**
Wake Up—Law (75)	15
Tommy CUNNINGHAM ▶ 8629 (1)	**45**
Wishing I Was Lucky—Wet Wet Wet (88)	178
Woody CUNNINGHAM ▶ 10715 (1)	**5.9**
Get Tough—Kleeer (81)	12
Bill CUOMO ▶ 3212 (2)	**949**
Oh Sherrie—Steve Perry (84)	3231
Draw Of The Cards—Kim Carnes (81)	564
Sal CUOMO ▶ 10154 (1)	**12**
Liar—Regents (61)	12
Charles H. CUPPETT [Charles Harold] ▶ 10948 (1)	**4.2**
Nightfall—Al Hibbler (56)	13
Mike CURB ▶ 3359 (5)	**882**
Blue's Theme—Arrows Featuring Davie Allen (67)	981
Burning Bridges—Mike Curb Congregation (70)	738
Butterfly—Danyel Gérard (72)	103
Devil's Angels—Davie Allen And The Arrows (67)	1.9
Theme From The Wild Angels—Davie Allan And The Arrows (66)	1.4
Alberto CURCI ▶ 982 (2)	**4567**
Lonely Boy—Paul Anka (59)	*9133*
Lonely Boy—Donny Osmond (72)	*0.0*
Freddy CURCI ▶ 2626 (1)	**1309**
More Than Words Can Say—Alias (90)	2619
Paul CURCIO ▶ 7668 (1)	**82**
Dance With Me—Mojo Men (65)	164
Nick CURINGA ▶ 3085 (2)	**1019**
Those Oldies But Goodies (Remind Me Of You)—Little Caesar And The Romans (61)	*2037*
Those Oldies But Goodies (Remind Me Of You)—Nino and the Ebb Tides (61)	*0.0*
Cy CURNIN ▶ 2716 (10)	**1247**
One Thing Leads To Another—Fixx (83)	2676
Saved By Zero—Fixx (83)	900
Are We Ourselves?—Fixx (84)	811
Secret Separation—Fixx (86)	629
The Sign Of Fire—Fixx (83)	523
How Much Is Enough—Fixx (91)	414
Driven Out—Fixx (89)	236
Sunshine In The Shade—Fixx (84)	96
Stand Or Fall—Fixx (82)	67
No One Has To Cry—Fixx (91)	20
Alannah CURRIE ▶ 1187 (11)	**3747**
Hold Me Now—Thompson Twins (84)	3557
Lay Your Hands On Me—Thompson Twins (85)	1742
King For A Day—Thompson Twins (86)	1479
Doctor! Doctor!—Thompson Twins (84)	1247
Lies—Thompson Twins (83)	612
Sugar Daddy—Thompson Twins (89)	527
Get That Love—Thompson Twins (87)	480
You Take Me Up—Thompson Twins (84)	304
Love On Your Side—Thompson Twins (83)	286
Nothing In Common—Thompson Twins (86)	272
The Gap—Thompson Twins (84)	95
Billy CURRIE ▶ 8843 (1)	**38**
Reap The Wild Wind—Ultravox (83)	152
Jimmy CURRIE ▶ 2067 (2)	**1932**
I'll Never Fall In Love Again—Tom Jones (69)	*3450*
I'll Never Fall In Love Again—Tom Jones (67)	*413*
Justin CURRIE ▶ 6788 (1)	**137**
Kiss This Thing Goodbye—Del Amitri (90)	410
Ted CURRIER ▶ 9526 (1)	**22**
Forever Yours—Tony Terry (88)	44

Thomas CURRY ▶ 5930 (1)	**226**
Try The Impossible—Lee Andrews And The Hearts (58)	453
Tim CURRY ▶ 9498 (1)	**23**
I Do The Rock—Tim Curry (79)	45
Andrew CURTIS ▶ 11706 (1)	**0.6**
Birdman Part One (Title No. 1 Again)—Rare Bird (73)	2.8
—Antonio De Curtis see: TOTÒ	
Barry CURTIS [Curt Bartholomew] ▶ 11131 (1)	**3.1**
Don't Say No—Kingsmen (67)	6.1
Bill CURTIS ▶ 9391 (3)	**25**
I Like Girls—Fatback Band (78)	17
Backstrokin'—Fatback (80)	10
Gotta Get My Hands On Some (Money)—Fatback (80)	6.0
Cal CURTIS ▶ 4095 (1)	**595**
Second Chance—Thirty Eight Special (89)	1786
Chris CURTIS [Christopher Crummy] ▶ 9033 (1)	**33**
He's Got No Love—Searchers (65)	65
Eddie CURTIS [Memphis Eddie Curtis, Memphis Curtis] ▶ 973 (13)	**4606**
The Joker—Steve Miller Band (73)	5290
Song Of The Dreamer—Eddie Fisher (55)	*1286*
You're Gonna Miss Me—Connie Francis (59)	631
Wild Cherry—Don Cherry (56)	475
Lovey Dovey—Buddy Knox (60)	*340*
Lovey Dovey—Otis & Carla (68)	*242*
Lovey Dovey—Clyde McPhatter (59)	*214*
Lovey Dovey—Bunny Sigler (67)	*51*
Rumble Boogie—Don Cherry (56)	16
Hard Head—Louis Jordan (63)	12
Song Of The Dreamer—Bunny Paul (55)	*0.0*
Song Of The Dreamer—Johnnie Ray (55)	*0.0*
Song Of The Dreamer—Billy Brooks (55)	*0.0*
King CURTIS [Curtis Ousley] ▶ 1515 (6)	**2818**
Soul Serenade—Willie Mitchell (68)	*1399*
Soul Twist—King Curtis And The Noble Knights (62)	1269
Memphis Soul Stew—King Curtis (67)	536
Beach Party—King Curtis And The Noble Knights (62)	267
Jealous Love—Wilson Pickett (68)	266
Soul Serenade—King Curtis (64)	*183*
Loyal CURTIS ▶ 10772 (1)	**5.4**
Drifting And Dreaming—Teddy Tyle, His Saxophone and His Orch. (58)	16
Mann CURTIS [Emanuel Kurtz, Manny Kurtz] ▶ 1417 (17)	**3131**
Let It Be Me—Betty Everett & Jerry Butler (64)	*2995*
Let It Be Me—Everly Brothers (60)	*2197*
Play Me Hearts And Flowers (I Wanna Cry)—Johnny Desmond (55)	*1143*
Fooled—Perry Como (55)	819
Let It Be Me—Willie Nelson (82)	*368*
This Little Girl's Gone Rockin'—Ruth Brown (58)	285
Let It Be Me—Glen Campbell And Bobbie Gentry (69)	*224*
Christmas Auld Lang Syne—Bobby Darin (60)	186
(I Don't Care) Only Love Me—Steve Lawrence (59)	*96*
Let It Be Me—Jill Corey (57)	*87*
In The Alps (In Der Schweiz)—Lawrence Welk And His Champagne Music And The McGuire Sisters (56)	63
A Fool Of Fools—Tony Bennett (68)	11
I'm Gonna Live Till I Die—Frank Sinatra and Ray Anthony and his Orchestra (55)	10
Let It Be Me—Sweet Inspirations (67)	*6.2*
Crying Roses—Kitty Kallen (57)	5.6
Play Me Hearts And Flowers (I Wanna Cry)—Dick Jacobs & His Orchestra (55)	*0.0*
(I Don't Care) Only Love Me—Kay Starr (59)	*0.0*
—Memphis Curtis see: Eddie CURTIS	
Michael CURTIS ▶ 5096 (1)	**343**
Southern Cross—Crosby, Stills & Nash (82)	1029
Richard CURTIS ▶ 5097 (1)	**343**
Southern Cross—Crosby, Stills & Nash (82)	1029
Sonny CURTIS ▶ 425 (13)	**9485**
More Than I Can Say—Leo Sayer (80)	*5089*
Walk Right Back—Everly Brothers (61)	*2037*
I Fought The Law—Bobby Fuller Four (66)	*1813*
A Fool Never Learns—Andy Williams (63)	1401
Where Will The Words Come From—Gary Lewis And The Playboys (66)	862
The Straight Life—Bobby Goldsboro (68)	764

Sonny CURTIS ▶ 425 (13) *Continued*	**9485**
I Fought The Law—Sam Neely (75)	*288*
Hung Up In Your Eyes—Brian Hyland (67)	191
More Than I Can Say—Bobby Vee (61)	*183*
Holiday For Clowns—Brian Hyland (67)	25
Walk Right Back—Anne Murray (78)	*4.4*
I Fought The Law—Paul Stefen and the Royal Lancers (62)	*1.3*
Cross My Heart—Bobby Vee (65)	0.9
Jimmy CURTISS [Jim Stuberge, Jimmy Stulberger] ▶ 5072 (1)	**349**
Child Of Clay—Jimmie Rodgers (67)	698
Stephen CUSACK ▶ 11001 (2)	**3.9**
Maybe This Day—Kissing The Pink (83)	20
Certain Things Are Likely—K.T.P./Kissing The Pink (87)	4.3
Vince CUSANO [Vincent John Cusano, Vinnie Vincent] ▶ 5586 (2)	**268**
Tears—John Waite (84)	416
Lick It Up—KISS (83)	120
Larry CUSIMANO ▶ 8560 (1)	**46**
Echo—Emotions (1) (62)	278
Paschal CUSIMANO ▶ 9439 (2)	**23**
Bicycle Morning—Billy Sans (74)	16
Solo—Billy Sans (71)	16
—Cutfather see: Mich HANSEN	
Scott CUTLER ▶ 3264 (5)	**921**
Piano In The Dark—Brenda Russell (88)	1550
How Much Is Enough—Fixx (91)	414
Forgive Me For Dreaming—Elisa Fiorillo (88)	311
I've Been Waiting For You—Guys Next Door (90)	277
No One Has To Cry—Fixx (91)	20
Sid CUTNER ▶ 8552 (1)	**46**
Mink Schmink—Eartha Kitt (54)	93
—Regina Marie Cuttita see: Regina RICHARDS	
—Claudio Cuza see: Eduardo DAVIDSON	
Johnny CYMBAL [John Hendry Blair, Derek] ▶ 1383 (6)	**3213**
Cinnamon—Derek (68)	2256
Mr. Bass Man—Johnny Cymbal (63)	1214
Mary In The Morning—Al Martino (67)	657
Rock Me Baby—David Cassidy (72)	555
Back Door Man—Derek (69)	286
Teenage Heaven—Johnny Cymbal (63)	243
André CYMONE [André Cymone Anderson, Andre Simon Anderson] ▶ 834 (8)	**5288**
Looking For A New Love—Jody Watley (87)	4041
Real Love—Jody Watley (89)	3609
Friends—Jody Watley (89)	1337
Some Kind Of Lover—Jody Watley (88)	1295
Room At The Top—Adam Ant (90)	808
I Want You—Jody Watley (91)	205
Still A Thrill—Jody Watley (87)	148
Precious Love—Jody Watley (90)	70

D

Michael D'ABO ▶ 1059 (3)	**4167**
Build Me Up Buttercup—Foundations (68)	7390
Handbags And Gladrags—Rod Stewart (72)	*393*
Handbags And Gladrags—Chase (71)	*79*
Ernest DABON ▶ 10535 (1)	**7.5**
Action Speaks Louder Than Words—Chocolate Milk (75)	67
Robert DABON ▶ 10536 (1)	**7.5**
Action Speaks Louder Than Words—Chocolate Milk (75)	67
—Desmond Dacres see: Desmond DEKKER	
Donnie DACUS [James O. Dacus] ▶ 8015 (2)	**65**
Must Have Been Crazy—Chicago (79)	44
Turn Back The Pages—Stephen Stills (75)	43
—James O. Dacus see: Donnie DACUS	
—Daddy G see: Gene BARGE	
Robert DADE [Bob Astor, Robert Ernest Dade] ▶ 6507 (1)	**161**
Here Comes The Judge—Pigmeat Markham (68)	646
Ted DAFFAN [Frankie Brown, Theron Eugene Daffan] ▶ 1206 (9)	**3689**
I'm A Fool To Care—Les Paul and Mary Ford (54)	*1621*
I'm A Fool To Care—Joe Barry (61)	*1130*
Born To Lose—Ray Charles (62)	490
No Letter Today—Les Paul and Mary Ford (55)	240
Worried Mind—Ray Anthony (62)	232
I'm A Fool To Care—Ray Charles (65)	*71*
I'm A Fool To Care—Oscar Black (61)	*12*
Rockin', Rollin' Ocean—Hank Snow (60)	11
I've Got Five Dollars And It's Saturday Night—George & Gene; George Jones & Gene Pitney (65)	3.7
—Theda Daffan see: Theda ROUSH	
—Theron Eugene Daffan see: Ted DAFFAN	
Pierre-Alain DAHAN [Peter Arpadys] ▶ 6692 (2)	**143**
Pepper Box—Peppers (74)	179
Souvenirs—Voyage (79)	161
Steve DAHL ▶ 8651 (1)	**44**
Do You Think I'm Disco?—Steve Dahl And Teenage Radiation (79)	*131*
Patti DAHLSTROM ▶ 5435 (2)	**290**
Emotion—Helen Reddy (75)	579
He Did Me Wrong, But He Did It Right—Patti Dahlstrom (74)	0.3
Ray DAHROUGE ▶ 5397 (4)	**295**
Never Gonna Let Him Know—Debbie Taylor (69)	191
Never Get Enough Of Your Love—L.T.D. (78)	134
Gotta Find A Way—Moments (73)	113
You're My One Weakness Girl—Street People (76)	9.5
Harry DAILEY ▶ 8409 (1)	**52**
Volcano—Jimmy Buffett (79)	155
E.G. DAILY [Elizabeth Ann Guttman] ▶ 8763 (1)	**40**
Say It, Say It—E.G. Daily (86)	120
—Sharon Lee Dain see: Jackie DeSHANNON	
—Marquis Dair see: Marcus DARE	
John DAJANI ▶ 8511 (1)	**48**
Pop Goes The Weasel—3rd Bass (91)	333
Sally Jo DAKOTA [Soleil Dakota] ▶ 3967 (1)	**636**
Tell Me What You Want Me To Do—Tevin Campbell (91)	1907
—Soleil Dakota see: Sally Jo DAKOTA	
—Chip Dale see: Dino TOME	
—Chip Dale see: John WOLOSCHUK	
Dick DALE [Richard Anthony Monsour] ▶ 5871 (1)	**234**
Let's Go Trippin'—Dick Dale And The Del-Tones (61)	234
Jim DALE [James Smith] ▶ 1293 (1)	**3441**
Georgy Girl—Seekers (66)	*6883*
Angelo D'ALEO ▶ 7353 (1)	**100**
Diddle-Dee-Dum (What Happens When Your Love Has Gone)—Belmonts (62)	201
Dan DALEY ▶ 4060 (1)	**608**
Still In Saigon—Charlie Daniels Band (82)	608
Bobby DALL [Robert Harry Kuykendall] ▶ 1176 (10)	**3772**
Every Rose Has Its Thorn—Poison (88)	4813
Unskinny Bop—Poison (90)	2869
Something To Believe In—Poison (90)	2063
Nothin' But A Good Time—Poison (88)	1314
Talk Dirty To Me—Poison (87)	1055
I Won't Forget You—Poison (87)	1051
Fallen Angel—Poison (88)	903
Life Goes On—Poison (91)	401
Ride The Wind—Poison (91)	377
I Want Action—Poison (87)	240
Dick DALLAS [Richard Carroll Lamb] ▶ 7990 (1)	**66**
I Wish I Knew (How It Would Feel To Be Free)—Solomon Burke (68)	132
Sarah DALLIN ▶ 3514 (8)	**803**
I Heard A Rumour—Bananarama (87)	2288
Cruel Summer—Bananarama (84)	1392
I Can't Help It—Bananarama (87)	331
Love In The First Degree—Bananarama (88)	262
The Wild Life—Bananarama (84)	104
More Than Physical—Bananarama (86)	74
Love, Truth And Honesty—Bananarama (88)	64
Robert DeNiro's Waiting—Bananarama (84)	4.7
Miki DALLON [Michael Trevor Tinsley] ▶ 11197 (1)	**2.8**
Take A Heart—Don Fardon (68)	2.8
Bill DALTON ▶ 3760 (4)	**707**
Short Shorts—Royal Teens (58)	*2815*
Harvey's Got A Girlfriend—Royal Teens (58)	14
Short Shorts—Four Winds (58)	*0.0*
Short Shorts—Tiny Bradshaw & His Orchestra (58)	*0.0*
Jack DALTON ▶ 9093 (1)	**31**
Love Heals—Colours (68)	63
Roger DALTON ▶ 3531 (1)	**797**
Baby Don't Forget My Number—Milli Vanilli (89)	3187
Pete DAMATO ▶ 3772 (1)	**703**
Just Ask Your Heart—Frankie Avalon (59)	2110
Stan DAMERELL ▶ 9309 (3)	**27**
If—Timi Yuro (64)	*42*
If—Paragons (61)	*33*
If—Roy Hamilton (61)	*5.2*
Michael DAMIAN [Michael Damian Weir] ▶ 2994 (3)	**1074**
Was It Nothing At All—Michael Damian (89)	743
Cover Of Love—Michael Damian (89)	482
What A Price To Pay—Michael Damian (91)	210
Salvatore D'AMICO ▶ 10730 (2)	**5.7**
Why Why Why—Steve Lawrence (60)	10
Hello Enemy—Johnny Tillotson (66)	1.4
—Ciro Dammicco see: ZACAR	
—Russ Damon see: Les LEDO	
Jodi D'AMOUR ▶ 5424 (1)	**291**
No Chemise Please—Gerry Granahan (58)	872
Wally DAMRICK ▶ 5432 (1)	**290**
Old Fashioned Boy (You're The One)—Stallion (77)	290
Bill DANA [José Jimenez, William Szathmary] ▶ 4574 (1)	**463**
The Astronaut (Parts 1 & 2)—Jose Jimenez (61)	926
Vic DANA [Samuel Mendola] ▶ 10962 (1)	**4.1**
Billy, I've Got To Go To Town—Geraldine Stevens (69)	*8.1*
Walter DANA [Wladyslaw Danilowski, Danilov] ▶ 6323 (1)	**182**
Who Stole The Keeshka?—Matys Bros. (63)	364
Jimmy D'ANDA ▶ 9769 (1)	**17**
Smooth Up—Bulletboys (89)	68
—Jim Dandy see: James MANGRUM	
—Bob Dane see: Hugo PERETTI	
—Damian Dane see: Bruce BROADUS	
Rich DANGEL ▶ 5004 (3)	**360**
Tall Cool One—Wailers (59)	*532*
Tall Cool One—Wailers (64)	*507*
Mau-Mau—Wailers (59)	40
Rodney DANGERFIELD [Jacob Cohen] ▶ 9629 (1)	**20**
Rappin' Rodney—Rodney Dangerfield (83)	140
Eliot DANIEL ▶ 1614 (3)	**2623**
Lavender Blue—Sammy Turner (59)	3681
Disco Lucy (I Love Lucy Theme)—Wilton Place Street Band (77)	735
Ricky—"Weird Al" Yankovic (83)	*188*
Marcus DANIEL ▶ 2776 (5)	**1201**
Slip Away—Clarence Carter (68)	2304
Tell Mama—Etta James (67)	902
Sweet Feeling—Candi Staton (70)	373
Looking For A Fox—Clarence Carter (68)	137
Funky Fever—Clarence Carter (68)	20
Bobby DANIELS ▶ 8753 (1)	**40**
Super Bowl Shuffle—Chicago Bears Shufflin' Crew (86)	161
Charles N. DANIELS [Charles Neil Davis, Jules Lemare, Neil Moret] ▶ 5060 (5) HOF	**352**
Moonlight And Roses (Bring Mem'ries Of You)—Three Suns (54)	*522*
Moonlight And Roses (Bring Mem'ries Of You)—Vic Dana (65)	*340*
Sweet And Lovely—April Stevens & Nino Tempo (62)	49
You Tell Me Your Dream (I'll Tell You Mine)—Archie Bleyer (56)	*49*
You Tell Me Your Dream—Jerry Murad's Harmonicats (56)	*0.0*
Charlie DANIELS ▶ 1240 (11)	**3615**
The Devil Went Down To Georgia—Charlie Daniels Band (79)	*3303*
Uneasy Rider—Charlie Daniels (73)	1575
In America—Charlie Daniels Band (80)	1335

Charlie DANIELS ▶ 1240 (11) *Continued*	**3615**
The Legend Of Wooley Swamp—Charlie Daniels Band (80)	633
The South's Gonna Do It—Charlie Daniels Band (75)	604
It Hurts Me—Elvis Presley With The Jordanaires (64)	437
Long Haired Country Boy—Charlie Daniels Band (75)	263
The Devil Came Up To Michigan—K.M.C. Kru (91)	*243*
Birmingham Blues—Charlie Daniels Band (75)	19
Texas—Charlie Daniels Band (76)	17
Heaven Can Be Anywhere (Twin Pines Theme)—Charlie Daniels Band (77)	9.9
Danny DANIELS ▶ 11014 (1)	**3.8**
I'm Bewildered—DeCastro Sisters (55)	7.7
Don DANIELS ▶ 6964 (2)	**125**
Let's Be Young Tonight—Jermaine Jackson (76)	184
Down To Love Town—Originals (76)	99
Dorothy DANIELS ▶ 2995 (3)	**1074**
My Heart Belongs To Only You—Bobby Vinton (64)	*1879*
My Heart Belongs To Only You—Jackie Wilson (61)	*265*
My Heart Belongs To Only You—Mary Swan (58)	*4.5*
Eric DANIELS ▶ 10475 (1)	**8.0**
Give Me Your Heart—Vanity Kills (91)	16
Frank DANIELS ▶ 2996 (3)	**1074**
My Heart Belongs To Only You—Bobby Vinton (64)	*1879*
My Heart Belongs To Only You—Jackie Wilson (61)	*265*
My Heart Belongs To Only You—Mary Swan (58)	*4.5*
Jack DANIELS ▶ 1512 (6)	**2836**
Turn Back The Hands Of Time—Tyrone Davis (70)	4386
I'll Be Right Here—Tyrone Davis (70)	540
(I Can Feel Those Vibrations) This Love Is Real—Jackie Wilson (70)	323
It's A Man Down There—G.L. Crockett (65)	219
One-Way Ticket—Tyrone Davis (71)	167
You Keep Me Holding On—Tyrone Davis (71)	36
Lee DANIELS ▶ 11452 (1)	**1.6**
Dansero—Joni James (58)	4.9
Nelson DANIELS ▶ 11775 (1)	**0.1**
Bad, Bold And Beautiful Girl—Persuaders (73)	0.4
Ted DANIELS ▶ 10218 (1)	**11**
The Pain Gets A Little Deeper—Darrow Fletcher (66)	22
—Danilov see: Walter DANA	
—Wladyslaw Danilowski see: Walter DANA	
Rick DANKO ▶ 7851 (1)	**72**
Life Is A Carnival—Band (71)	216
Johnny DANKWORTH ▶ 10417 (1)	**8.7**
Experiments With Mice—Johnny Dankworth (56)	26
Bill DANOFF ▶ 409 (7)	**9700**
Afternoon Delight—Starland Vocal Band (76)	7037
Take Me Home, Country Roads—John Denver (71)	6363
Friends With You—John Denver (71)	636
Please, Daddy—John Denver (73)	163
Baby, You Look Good To Me Tonight—John Denver (76)	88
Hail! Hail! Rock And Roll!—Starland Vocal Band (77)	49
California Day—Starland Vocal Band (76)	29
—Mary Catherine Danoff see: Taffy DANOFF	
Sid DANOFF ▶ 6051 (4)	**211**
Dance Everyone Dance—Betty Madigan (58)	*619*
Mashuga—Louis Prima & Keely Smith (60)	15
Dance, Everyone, Dance—Les Baxter & His Orchestra (58)	*0.0*
Dance, Everyone, Dance—Hi-Liters (58)	*0.0*
Taffy DANOFF [Mary Catherine Danoff, Mary Catherine Nivert, Taffy Nivert] ▶ 1632 (5)	**2579**
Take Me Home, Country Roads—John Denver (71)	6363
Friends With You—John Denver (71)	636
Please, Daddy—John Denver (73)	163
Loving You With My Eyes—Starland Vocal Band (80)	67
Hail! Hail! Rock And Roll!—Starland Vocal Band (77)	49
Charles "Bud" DANT ▶ 10395 (2)	**8.9**
Yes Siree!!—Earl Grant (63)	21
Licorice Stick—Pete Fountain (64)	5.7
—David Dante see: David HESS	
Ron DANTE [Carmine Granito] ▶ 7619 (3)	**85**
(He's) Raining In My Sunshine—Jay & The Americans (66)	145
Midnight Show—Bobby Vinton (75)	*22*
Midnight Show—Ron Dante (75)	*3.3*

Charles DANVERS [Charles Sananes] ▶ 2192 (9)	**1758**
Til—Angels (61)	*1330*
Till—Vogues (68)	*931*
Till—Roger Williams (57)	*656*
Till—Tom Jones (71)	*445*
Till—Percy Faith And His Orchestra and Chorus (57)	*151*
Till—Tokens (68)	*1.8*
Till—Dinah Shore (57)	*0.0*
Till—Leo Diamond His Harmonica & Orch (57)	*0.0*
Till—Kay Armen (57)	*0.0*
Evelyn DANZIG [Evelyn Levine] ▶ 3384 (4)	**872**
Scarlet Ribbons (For Her Hair)—Browns (59)	*1712*
The Funky Gibbon—Goodies (75)	40
I Miss The Boy—Betty Madigan (56)	6.2
Scarlet Ribbons (For Her Hair)—Enoch Light & The Light Brigade (59)	*0.0*
Ken DARBY [Vera Matson] ▶ 924 (12)	**4781**
Love Me Tender—Elvis Presley (56)	*8241*
This Friendly World—Fabian (59)	1169
Love Me Tender—Richard Chamberlain (62)	*673*
The Bus Stop Song (A Paper Of Pins)—Four Lads (56)	*665*
Love Me Tender—Percy Sledge (67)	*405*
Poor Boy—Elvis Presley (56)	183
Love Me Tender—Henri René (56)	*108*
The Song From Desiree (We Meet Again)—Johnny Desmond (54)	*91*
The Song From Desiree (We Meet Again)—Bing Crosby And Alfred Newman (54)	*0.0*
The Song From Desiree (We Meet Again)—Jane Froman (54)	*0.0*
The Bus Stop Song (A Paper Of Pins)—Burl Ives (56)	*0.0*
The River Of No Return—Marilyn Monroe (54)	0.0
Terence Trent D'ARBY [Sananda Maitreya] ▶ 921 (5)	**4798**
Wishing Well—Terence Trent D'Arby (88)	3992
Sign Your Name—Terence Trent D'Arby (88)	2244
Dance Little Sister (Part One)—Terence Trent D'Arby (88)	428
If You Let Me Stay—Terence Trent D'Arby (87)	103
To Know Someone Deeply Is To Know Someone Softly—Terence Trent D'Arby (90)	27
Richard DARBYSHIRE ▶ 9432 (2)	**24**
Realistic—Shirley Lewis (89)	27
So The Story Goes—Living In A Box (87)	20
Marcus DARE [Marquis Dair, Marquis X. Hair] ▶ 4630 (2)	**448**
Dead Giveaway—Shalamar (83)	1143
Slow Love—Doc Box & B. Fresh (90)	200
Fred DARIAN ▶ 2251 (6)	**1704**
Mr Custer—Larry Verne (60)	4906
Mister Livingston—Larry Verne (60)	111
Little Tin Soldier—Toy Dolls (62)	52
Johnny Willow—Fred Darian (61)	41
Roll Call Company J—Balladeers (60)	3.8
Battle Of Gettysburg—Fred Darian (61)	0.5
Bobby DARIN [Walden Robert Cassotto] ▶ 121 (31) HOF	**21376**
Dream Lover—Bobby Darin (59)	*5771*
You're The Reason I'm Living—Bobby Darin (63)	4462
Splish Splash—Bobby Darin (58)	4440
Things—Bobby Darin (62)	*2406*
18 Yellow Roses—Bobby Darin (63)	1520
I'll Be There—Gerry And The Pacemakers (64)	*977*
Multiplication—Bobby Darin (61)	784
Early In The Morning—Rinky-Dinks (Dash is important) (58)	*694*
Early In The Morning—Buddy Holly / The Crickets (58)	*570*
If A Man Answers—Bobby Darin (62)	564
Treat My Baby Good—Bobby Darin (63)	497
Wait A Minute—Coasters (61)	495
Simple Song Of Freedom—Tim Hardin (69)	*399*
Somebody To Love—Bobby Darin (60)	381
This Little Girl's Gone Rockin'—Ruth Brown (58)	285
Be Mad Little Girl—Bobby Darin (63)	259
Long Line Rider—Bobby Darin (68)	228
Come September—Billy Vaughn And His Orchestra (61)	*190*
Shirl Girl—Wayne Newton & The Newton Brothers (63)	184
Beachcomber—Bobby Darin At The Piano (60)	128

Simple Song Of Freedom—Buckwheat (72)	*85*
Jailer, Bring Me Water—Trini Lopez (64)	36
The Things In This House—Bobby Darin (64)	25
Theme From Come September—Bobby Darin & His Orchestra (61)	*23*
I'll Be There—Bobby Darin (60)	*16*
Dream Lover—Paris Sisters (64)	*15*
Things—Anne Murray (76)	*11*
Do The Monkey—King Curtis (63)	4.4
Dealer In Dreams—Bobby Darin (58)	2.4
Look For My True Love—Bobby Darin (61)	0.5
Theme From "Come September"—Dick Jacobs And His Orchestra (61)	*0.0*
Joseph DARION ▶ 4055 (3)	**611**
The Impossible Dream (The Quest)—Jack Jones (66)	*685*
The Impossible Dream—Hesitations (68)	*449*
There Should Be Rules (Protecting Fools Who Fall In Love)—Betty Madigan (55)	132
Denver DARLING ▶ 9546 (1)	**22**
Choo Choo Ch'Boogie—Bill Haley And His Comets (56)	65
Erik DARLING ▶ 989 (9)	**4532**
Walk Right In—Rooftop Singers (62)	*6902*
Banana Boat Song—Tarriers (56)	*4406*
Banana Boat Song—Fontane Sisters (56)	*1239*
Banana Boat Song—Steve Lawrence (56)	*939*
Tom Cat—Rooftop Singers (63)	829
Banana Boat Song—Sarah Vaughan (56)	*758*
Mama Don't Allow—Rooftop Singers (63)	296
Walk Right In—Dr. Hook (77)	*188*
Walk Right In—Moments (1) (63)	*23*
August DARNELL [Thomas August Darnell Browder, Kid Creole] ▶ 5456 (3)	**284**
Cherchez La Femme/Se Si Bon—Dr. Buzzard's Original "Savannah" Band (76)	448
There But For The Grace Of God Go I—Machine (79)	86
I'll Play The Fool—Dr. Buzzard's Original "Savannah" Band (76)	35
Rick DARNELL ▶ 3829 (1)	**687**
The Thrill Is Gone—B.B. King (69)	1375
Shelby DARNELL [Bob Miller] ▶ 8791 (3)	**39**
There's A Star Spangled Banner Waving #2 (The Ballad Of Francis Powers)—Red River Dave (60)	*117*
There's A Star Spangled Banner Waving Somewhere—Tommy Dee (60)	*0.0*
There's A Star Spangled Banner Waving Somewhere—Betty Johnson (60)	*0.0*
Chris DARWAY [Chet Bolins] ▶ 10864 (1)	**4.8**
Little Girl—Critters (67)	4.8
Chuck DARWIN ▶ 9581 (1)	**21**
The Answer To A Maiden's Prayer—June Valli (59)	42
Ted DARYLL [Theodore Meister] ▶ 1664 (9)	**2528**
She Cried—Jay & The Americans (62)	*3516*
Country Girl - City Man—Billy Vera & Judy Clay (68)	351
Tommy—Reparata And The Delrons (65)	251
She Cried—Lettermen (70)	*222*
Good Times—Jerry Butler (65)	210
He Cried—Shangri-Las (66)	*202*
The Magic Touch—Bobby Fuller Four (66)	22
Who Are You—Stacey Cane (65)	18
The Shadow Of Your Love—Five Stairsteps & Cubie (68)	16
Julian DASH ▶ 10109 (1)	**13**
Tuxedo Junction—Frankie Avalon (60)	51
Richard DASHUT ▶ 10836 (1)	**5.0**
Family Man—Fleetwood Mac (88)	10
Clark DATCHLER ▶ 1203 (2)	**3700**
Shattered Dreams—Johnny Hates Jazz (88)	3210
I Don't Want To Be A Hero—Johnny Hates Jazz (88)	490
Doc DAUGHERTY [Ralph Edward Daugherty] ▶ 7082 (4)	**117**
I'm Confessin' (That I Love You)—Frank Ifield (63)	*333*
I'm Confessin' (That I Love You)—Terri Dean (59)	*10*
I'm Confessin' (That I Love You)—Nino Tempo & April Stevens (64)	*6.7*
I'm Confessin' That I Love You—Barbara Lantz (59)	*0.0*
Pat DAUGHERTY ▶ 11553 (1)	**1.2**
Strong Enough To Be Gentle—Black Oak Arkansas (76)	8.4
—Ralph Edward Daugherty see: Doc DAUGHERTY	

Dean DAUGHTRY ► 2220 (4)	**1729**
So In To You—Atlanta Rhythm Section (77)	2327
Imaginary Lover—Atlanta Rhythm Section (78)	1818
I'm Not Gonna Let It Bother Me Tonight—Atlanta Rhythm Section (78)	932
Dog Days—Atlanta Rhythm Section (77)	109
Sherwood Mackay DAVASHE ► 7377 (2)	**99**
Lovely Lies—Manhattan Brothers And Miriam Makeba (56)	*199*
Lovely Lies—Nick Noble (56)	*0.0*
—John Davenport see: Otis BLACKWELL	
N'Dea DAVENPORT ► 9458 (1)	**23**
Never Stop—Brand New Heavies (91)	93
—Vincent Paul Davey see: Vince ELY	
Beau DAVID ► 8866 (1)	**37**
She—Southcote (74)	37
Bobby DAVID ► 5605 (2)	**266**
Devil In The Bottle—T.G. Sheppard (75)	153
I'm Not Gonna Cry Anymore—Nancy Brooks (79)	113
—F. R. David see: Robert FITOUSSI	
Hal DAVID ► 17 (131) HOF	**64969**
Raindrops Keep Fallin' On My Head—B.J. Thomas (69)	10203
This Guy's In Love With You—Herb Alpert (68)	*9073*
(They Long To Be) Close To You—Carpenters (70)	*7620*
One Less Bell To Answer—5th Dimension (70)	7509
My Heart Is An Open Book—Carl Dobkins, Jr. (59)	5285
What's New Pussycat?—Tom Jones (65)	4965
Blue On Blue—Bobby Vinton (63)	4326
Only Love Can Break A Heart—Gene Pitney (62)	*3874*
Wishin' And Hopin'—Dusty Springfield (64)	3504
I Say A Little Prayer—Dionne Warwick (67)	*3302*
The Look Of Love—Sergio Mendes & Brasil '66 (68)	*3151*
Walk On By—Dionne Warwick (64)	*2790*
To All The Girls I've Loved Before—Julio Iglesias & Willie Nelson (84)	2750
What The World Needs Now Is Love—Jackie deShannon (65)	*2689*
Broken Hearted Melody—Sarah Vaughan (59)	2677
(The Man Who Shot) Liberty Valance—Gene Pitney (62)	2442
I'll Never Fall In Love Again—Dionne Warwick (69)	*2372*
Anyone Who Had A Heart—Dionne Warwick (63)	2092
This Girl's In Love With You—Dionne Warwick (69)	*2079*
Message To Michael—Dionne Warwick (66)	2078
Always Something There To Remind Me—Naked Eyes (83)	*1983*
Johnny Get Angry—Joanie Sommers (62)	1932
Do You Know The Way To San José—Dionne Warwick (68)	1893
Alfie—Dionne Warwick (67)	*1730*
Wives And Lovers—Jack Jones (63)	1677
I Say A Little Prayer—Aretha Franklin (68)	*1449*
Sea Of Heartbreak—Don Gibson (61)	*1296*
It Was Almost Like A Song—Ronnie Milsap (77)	1242
Don't Make Me Over—Dionne Warwick (62)	*1150*
Promises, Promises—Dionne Warwick (68)	1078
Twenty Four Hours From Tulsa—Gene Pitney (63)	977
You'll Never Get To Heaven (If You Break My Heart)—Stylistics (73)	*836*
What The World Needs Now Is Love—Tom Clay (71)	*836*
Don't Make Me Over—Sybil (89)	*835*
Magic Moments—Perry Como (57)	834
I Just Don't Know What To Do With Myself—Dionne Warwick (66)	*827*
Everybody's Out Of Town—B.J. Thomas (70)	796
Reach Out For Me—Dionne Warwick (64)	*794*
Always Something There To Remind Me—R.B. Greaves (70)	*784*
Make It Easy On Yourself—Walker Bros. (65)	*781*
True Love Never Runs Smooth—Gene Pitney (63)	775
The Look Of Love—Dusty Springfield (67)	*749*
Make It Easy On Yourself—Jerry Butler (62)	*738*
Who Is Gonna Love Me?—Dionne Warwick (68)	727
Story Of My Life—Marty Robbins (57)	692
Are You There (With Another Girl)—Dionne Warwick (65)	683
Trains And Boats And Planes—Dionne Warwick (66)	*662*
You'll Never Get To Heaven (If You Break My Heart)—Dionne Warwick (64)	*651*
Living Together, Growing Together—5th Dimension (73)	623
Make It Easy On Yourself—Dionne Warwick (70)	*617*
Outside My Window—Fleetwoods (60)	556
Alfie—Cher (66)	*533*
I'm A Better Man—Engelbert Humperdinck (69)	523
Windows Of The World—Dionne Warwick (67)	510
Let Me Go To Him—Dionne Warwick (70)	506
The Green Grass Starts To Grow—Dionne Warwick (70)	502
Paper Mache—Dionne Warwick (70)	479
The April Fools—Dionne Warwick (69)	474
Be True To Yourself—Bobby Vee (63)	466
The Love Of A Boy—Timi Yuro (62)	465
My Little Red Book—Love (66)	458
Odds And Ends—Dionne Warwick (69)	427
Heavenly Lover—Teresa Brewer (59)	425
I Wake Up Crying—Chuck Jackson (61)	415
Blue Guitar—Richard Chamberlain (63)	413
Another Night—Dionne Warwick (66)	396
(New In) The Ways Of Love—Tommy Edwards (59)	391
Walk On By—Isaac Hayes (69)	*367*
To Wait For Love—Herb Alpert (68)	365
(There's) Always Something There To Remind Me—Lou Johnson (64)	*363*
Trains And Boats And Planes—Billy J. Kramer & The Dakotas (65)	*357*
(There's) Always Something There To Remind Me—Sandie Shaw (64)	*337*
With Open Arms—Jane Morgan (59)	319
I Just Don't Know What To Do With Myself—Gary Puckett (70)	*315*
A House Is Not A Home—Dionne Warwick (64)	*286*
The First Night Of The Full Moon—Jack Jones (64)	*266*
A House Is Not A Home—Brook Benton (64)	*260*
Reach Out For Me—Lou Johnson (63)	*247*
You'll Answer To Me—Patti Page (61)	226
Long Ago Tomorrow—B.J. Thomas (71)	224
Here I Am—Dionne Warwick (65)	188
Lost Horizon—Shawn Phillips (73)	159
A Lifetime Of Loneliness—Jackie De Shannon (65)	158
Who Gets The Guy—Dionne Warwick (71)	147
(There's) Always Something There To Remind Me—Dionne Warwick (68)	*141*
Looking With My Eyes—Dionne Warwick (65)	139
(They Long To Be) Close To You—Jerry Butler Featuring Brenda Lee Eager (72)	*133*
Promise Her Anything—Tom Jones (66)	131
Don't Make Me Over—Jennifer Warnes (79)	*131*
The Charanga—Merv Griffin (61)	125
Let Me Be Lonely—Dionne Warwick (68)	112
Me Japanese Boy I Love You—Bobby Goldsboro (64)	104
Walk On By—Sybil (90)	*95*
Don't Make Me Over—Brenda & The Tabulations (70)	*95*
The Look Of Love—Isaac Hayes (71)	*94*
99 Miles From L.A.—Albert Hammond (75)	77
Send A Little Love My Way—Anne Murray (73)	67
My Baby's Got Such Lovin' Ways—McGuire Sisters (56)	66
A Whistling Tune—Elvis Presley with the Jordanaires (62)	62
Home Is Where The Heart Is—Elvis Presley with the Jordanaires (62)	62
The Breaking Point—Chuck Jackson (61)	46
I Say A Little Prayer—Glen Campbell (71)	*38*
This Empty Place—Dionne Warwick (63)	38
Come And Get Me—Jackie deShannon (66)	34
Close To You—B.T. Express (76)	*31*
The Beginning Of Loneliness—Dionne Warwick (67)	30
I Never Said I Love You—Orsa Lia (79)	26
Wendy Wendy—Four Coins (58)	26
Our Concerto—Steve Lawrence (62)	*25*
Make The Music Play—Dionne Warwick (63)	22
Saturday Sunshine—Burt Bacharach (63)	19
Many A Wonderful Moment—Rosemary Clooney (60)	17
I Just Don't Know What To Do With Myself—Tommy Hunt (62)	*13*
Our Concerto—Umberto Bindi (60)	*13*
Only Love Can Break A Heart—Margaret Whiting (67)	*13*
From Rocking Horse To Rocking Chair—Paul Anka (64)	11
Walk On By—AWB (79)	*7.4*
Boy On Page Thirty Five—Cathy Carr (56)	6.1
Alfie—Cilla Black (66)	*6.1*
When The Boys Get Together—Joanie Sommers (62)	5.7
I'll Never Fall In Love Again—Burt Bacharach (69)	*4.9*
Forgive Me (For Giving You Such A Bad Time)—Babs Tino (62)	3.5
Don't Let It Happen To Us—Shirelles (63)	3.3
Sea Of Heartbreak—Poco (82)	*3.1*
Somebody Else's Sweetheart—Wanderers (61)	1.8
It's The Love That Really Counts (In The Long Run)—Shirelles (62)	1.8
Who's Been Sleeping In My Bed?—Linda Scott (64)	1.3
Walk On By—Gloria Gaynor (75)	*1.1*
Rome Will Never Leave You—Richard Chamberlain (64)	1.0
Only Love Can Break A Heart—Bobby Vinton (77)	*0.9*
Our Concerto (Il Nostro Concerto)—Al Martino (60)	*0.0*
Hod DAVID [Hod David Schudson] ► 10780 (1)	**5.3**
If That's How Nature Made Him—Helen Grayco (77)	11
—Janice David see: Janice DAVIS	
Jean DAVID ► 9433 (1)	**24**
It's So Easy To Forget—Four Lads (57)	47
John DAVID [John David Williams] ► 11229 (1)	**2.7**
High School Nights—Dave Edmunds (85)	8.0
Lee DAVID ► 1658 (4)	**2537**
Tonight You Belong To Me—Patience and Prudence (56)	*3814*
Tonight You Belong To Me—Lawrence Welk And His Sparkling Strings (56)	*1097*
Tonight You Belong To Me—Karen Chandler & Jimmy Wakely (56)	*162*
Tonight You Belong To Me—Tracey Twins (56)	*0.0*
—Leizer David see: Lou STALLMAN	
Mack DAVID ► 359 (37) HOF	**10666**
Baby It's You—Smith (69)	*4062*
It Must Be Him—Vikki Carr (67)	3693
Baby It's You—Shirelles (61)	*2409*
It Only Hurts For A Little While—Ames Brothers (56)	1919
Bimbombey—Jimmie Rodgers (58)	1823
Hush, Hush, Sweet Charlotte—Patti Page (65)	1760
Young Emotions—Ricky Nelson (60)	1584
My Own True Love—Duprees (62)	*1002*
My Own True Love—Jimmy Clanton (59)	*781*
I've Been There—Tommy Edwards (59)	630
Hanging Tree—Marty Robbins (59)	599
The Lesson—Vikki Carr (67)	547
Walk On The Wild Side—Brook Benton (62)	*459*
The Blob—Five Blobs (58)	*331*
Seventy Seven Sunset Strip—Big Sound of Don Ralke (59)	*298*
Cherry Pink And Apple Blossom White—Alan Dale (55)	*226*
Singing Hills—Billy Vaughn and His Orchestra (58)	*216*
My Dream Sonata—Nat "King" Cole (56)	*201*
Heaven Was Never Like This—Eddie Fisher (54)	174
The Bird Man—Highwaymen (62)	144
I Don't Care If The Sun Don't Shine—Elvis Presley (56)	129
Gloria's Theme—Adam Wade (60)	123
The Wizard—Jimmie Rodgers (58)	110
Butterfly—Danyel Gérard (72)	103
She'll Be There—Vikki Carr (68)	37
Candy Cha Cha—Jan August-Richard Hayman (58)	32
Home From The Hill—Kingston Trio (60)	31
Theme From Taras Bulba (The Wishing Star)—Jerry Butler (62)	*16*
31 Flavors—Shirelles (63)	15
It's A Mad, Mad, Mad, Mad World—Shirelles (63)	6.3
Verboten! (Forbidden)—Paul Anka (58)	6.1
The Singing Hills—Don Cogan & LeRoy Holmes & His Orchestra (58)	*0.0*
My Own True Love (Tara's Theme)—Johnny Desmond (54)	*0.0*
Theme From Taras Bulba (The Wishing Star)—Maxine Starr (62)	*0.0*
My Own True Love—Four Coachmen (59)	*0.0*
Seventy Seven Sunset Strip—Frank Ortega Trio (59)	*0.0*
The Blob—Zanies (58)	*0.0*
Russ DAVID ► 10501 (1)	**7.8**
Where There's Life—George Cates And His Orchestra And Chorus (56)	16
—Scott David see: Jerry SAMUELS	

Sunny DAVID [James Faye Hall] ▶ 5450 (2)	**287**
Love Love Love—Clovers (56)	*546*
Love Love Love—Diamonds (56)	*315*
—David J. see: David HASKINS	
Aqil DAVIDSON ▶ 7783 (1)	**75**
I Wanna Get With U—Guy (90)	300
Bill DAVIDSON [William Frederick Davidson, Billy Day] ▶ 7700 (1)	**80**
Where Are You Going To My Love—Brotherhood Of Man (70)	319
Dean DAVIDSON ▶ 11673 (1)	**0.7**
Long Way To Love—Britny Fox (88)	0.7
Eduardo DAVIDSON [Claudio Cuza] ▶ 9939 (2)	**15**
La Pachanga—Audrey Arno And The Hazy Osterwald Sextet (61)	*29*
La Pachanga—Hugo & Luigi with their Children's Cho. (61)	*0.0*
Lenny DAVIDSON ▶ 1555 (5)	**2727**
Catch Us If You Can—Dave Clark Five (65)	2966
At The Scene—Dave Clark Five (66)	1146
Everybody Knows (I Still Love You)—Dave Clark Five (64)	926
I've Got To Have A Reason—Dave Clark Five (67)	311
Red And Blue—Dave Clark Five (67)	106
—David Z. see: David RIVKIN	
Bob DAVIE [Hutch Davie, Robert Bunyan Davie II] ▶ 808 (10)	**5479**
Green Door—Jim Lowe (56)	*9717*
Starlight, Starbright—Linda Scott (61)	384
By You By You By You—Jim Lowe (57)	197
It's All Because—Linda Scott (61)	181
I Feel The Beat—Jim Lowe (56)	148
Hoopa Hoola—Betty Johnson (58)	75
Rock And Roll Rhapsody—Four Aces (58)	56
Birds Of Britain—Bob Crewe Generation (67)	12
Green Door—Jerms (69)	*4.7*
Just Love Me—Jaye P. Morgan (56)	1.3
—Hutch Davie see: Bob DAVIE	
Alun DAVIES ▶ 10296 (1)	**10**
Bad Brakes—Cat Stevens (79)	21
Iva DAVIES [Ivor Arthur Davies] ▶ 2719 (6)	**1245**
Electric Blue—Icehouse (88)	1520
Crazy—Icehouse (87)	976
No Promises—Icehouse (86)	90
We Can Get Together—Icehouse (81)	82
My Obsession—Icehouse (88)	35
Touch The Fire—Icehouse (89)	15
—Ivor Arthur Davies see: Iva DAVIES	
Lew DAVIES ▶ 9255 (3)	**28**
(The Song Of) Daniel Boone (The Daddy Of Them All)—Loren Becker With Enoch Light Orch. & Chorus (55)	*55*
Daniel Boone (The Daddy Of Them All)—Ken Carson (55)	*0.0*
Daniel Boone (The Daddy Of Them All)—Dick Lee (55)	*0.0*
—Michael Philip Leslie Davies see: Mike DAVIES	
Mike DAVIES [Michael Philip Leslie Davies, Mike Leslie] ▶ 7701 (1)	**80**
Where Are You Going To My Love—Brotherhood Of Man (70)	319
Ray DAVIES ▶ 110 (29) HOF	**22760**
You Really Got Me—Kinks (64)	*2854*
Tired Of Waiting For You—Kinks (65)	2723
All Day And All Of The Night—Kinks (64)	2429
Dandy—Herman's Hermits (66)	2256
Lola—Kinks (70)	*2128*
A Well Respected Man—Kinks (65)	1793
Come Dancing—Kinks (83)	1678
Sunny Afternoon—Kinks (66)	1417
Push It—Salt-N-Pepa (87)	1049
Set Me Free—Kinks (65)	695
Apeman—Kinks (71)	457
Who'll Be The Next In Line—Kinks (65)	438
Don't Forget To Dance—Kinks (83)	421
A Rock 'N' Roll Fantasy—Kinks (78)	407
Till The End Of The Day—Kinks (66)	391
You Really Got Me—Van Halen (78)	*352*
(Wish I Could Fly Like) Superman—Kinks (79)	332
Dedicated Follower Of Fashion—Kinks (66)	321
Do It Again—Kinks (84)	293
Victoria—Kinks (70)	245

Sleepwalker—Kinks (77)	144
Mr. Pleasant—Kinks (67)	131
Deadend Street—Kinks (66)	127
Stop Your Sobbing—Pretenders (80)	103
Lola (Live Version)—Kinks (80)	*56*
Better Things—Kinks (81)	27
Destroyer—Kinks (81)	11
Juke Box Music—Kinks (77)	6.8
You Really Got Me—Tight Fit (81)	*0.9*
Rick DAVIES ▶ 750 (11)	**5849**
The Logical Song—Supertramp (79)	*2915*
It's Raining Again—Supertramp (82)	1898
Take The Long Way Home—Supertramp (79)	1451
Give A Little Bit—Supertramp (77)	1217
Goodbye Stranger—Supertramp (79)	1209
Dreamer—Supertramp (80)	1034
My Kind Of Lady—Supertramp (83)	550
Cannonball—Supertramp (85)	460
Bloody Well Right—Supertramp (75)	348
Breakfast In America—Supertramp (80)	120
The Topical Song—Barron Knights (79)	*55*
Benny DAVIS ▶ 647 (20) HOF	**6743**
Don't Break The Heart That Loves You—Connie Francis (62)	6052
There Goes My Heart—Joni James (58)	*1463*
Follow The Boys—Connie Francis (63)	1325
Baby Face—Wing And A Prayer Fife And Drum Corps. (75)	*1324*
With These Hands—Tom Jones (65)	669
I Still Get A Thrill (Thinking Of You)—Joni James (59)	384
There Goes My Heart—Four Aces (55)	*379*
Baby Face—Bobby Darin (62)	*375*
Margie—Fats Domino (59)	364
Whose Heart Are You Breaking Tonight—Connie Francis (65)	358
Baby's First Christmas—Connie Francis (61)	257
Carolina Moon—Connie Francis (58)	*201*
Baby Face—Little Richard (58)	*195*
Oh How I Miss You Tonight—Jeanne Black (60)	104
Are You Sorry—Joni James (59)	78
Yearning (Just For You)—Georgie Shaw (54)	45
Carolina Moon—Melody Makers (57)	*38*
(All That I'm Asking Is) Sympathy—Johnny Maddox (58)	18
The Biggest Sin Of All—Connie Francis (62)	9.5
Baby Face—Bobby Vee (61)	*2.0*
Bernice DAVIS ▶ 4244 (7)	**547**
Long Lonely Nights—Bobby Vinton (65)	*1021*
Long Lonely Nights—Clyde McPhatter (57)	*517*
Long Lonely Nights—Lee Andrews And The Hearts (57)	*429*
Long Lonely Nights—Dells (70)	*187*
Long Lonely Nights—4 Seasons (64)	*34*
Long, Lonely Nights—Kings (2) (57)	*0.0*
Long Lonely Nights—Kitty Kallen (57)	*0.0*
—Bill Davis see: William DOUCHETTE	
Billy DAVIS [Tyran Carlo, Roquel Davis] ▶ 604 (40)	**7202**
Lonely Teardrops—Jackie Wilson (58)	*3299*
You Got What It Takes—Marv Johnson (59)	*2631*
You Got What It Takes—Dave Clark Five (67)	*1890*
I'd Like To Teach The World To Sing (In Perfect Harmony)—New Seekers (71)	*1791*
I'd Like To Teach The World To Sing (In Perfect Harmony)—Hillside Singers (71)	*1474*
That's Why (I Love You So)—Jackie Wilson (59)	1212
We're Gonna Make It—Little Milton (65)	983
All I Could Do Was Cry—Etta James (60)	*949*
Pushover—Etta James (63)	949
I'll Be Satisfied—Jackie Wilson (59)	851
I Had A Talk With My Man—Mitty Collier (64)	548
To Be Loved—Jackie Wilson (58)	522
Recovery—Fontella Bass (65)	492
Reet Petite (The Finest Girl You Ever Want To Meet)—Jackie Wilson (57)	457
Who's Cheating Who?—Little Milton (65)	442
Lonely Teardrops—Brian Hyland (71)	*402*
Country Sunshine—Dottie West (73)	379
See Saw—Moonglows (56)	*357*
Slip-In Mules (No High Heel Sneakers)—Sugar Pie Desanto (64)	*277*
Too Pooped To Pop Casey—Chuck Berry (60)	231
Two Sides (To Every Story)—Etta James (63)	108

No Faith, No Love—Mitty Collier (65)	106
I Surrender—Fontella Bass (66)	97
Seven Day Fool—Etta James (61)	92
Pay Back—Etta James (63)	89
Jerk And Twine—Jackie Ross (65)	81
Lonely Teardrops—Narvel Felts (76)	*77*
See Saw—Don Cornell (56)	*56*
Because I Love You—Billy Stewart (66)	53
I've Got The Skill—Jackie Ross (64)	48
You'll Miss Me (When I'm Gone)—Fontella Bass & Bobby McClure (65)	42
Jim Dandy Got Married—LaVern Baker (57)	39
Your People—Little Milton (65)	25
We Have Love—Jackie Wilson (58)	23
We Got The Winning Hand—Little Milton (66)	20
All I Could Do Was Cry—Joe Tex (60)	*14*
In The Basement - Part 1—Etta James & Sugar Pie Desanto (66)	7.2
The (Bossa Nova) Bird—Dells (62)	5.3
Peak Of Love—Bobby McClure (66)	3.8
Safe And Sound—Fontella Bass (66)	0.5
—Brenda Holloway Davis see: Brenda HOLLOWAY	
Carl DAVIS ▶ 2162 (19)	**1806**
Love Makes A Woman—Barbara Acklin (68)	1694
The Matador—Major Lance (64)	771
Two Little Kids—Peaches & Herb (67)	574
Dear Lover—Mary Wells (66)	453
The Coldest Days Of My Life (Part 1)—Chi-Lites (72)	391
From The Teacher To The Preacher—Gene Chandler And Barbara Acklin (68)	379
Just Ain't No Love—Barbara Acklin (68)	305
I Love You—Otis Leavill (69)	154
I Still Love You—Jackie Wilson (69)	79
Love Song—Artistics (67)	65
I Don't Want To Lose You—Jackie Wilson (67)	60
Wrapped Up In Your Warm And Tender Love—Tyrone Davis (73)	45
Time Stopped—Marvin Smith (66)	33
All The Waiting Is Not In Vain—Tyrone Davis (69)	29
Funky Chicken—Willie Henderson And The Soul Explosions (70)	23
(I'm Just A) Fool For You—Gene Chandler (66)	13
Straight Ahead—Young-Holt Unlimited (69)	12
Helpless—Jackie Wilson (69)	8.7
There Goes The Lover—Gene Chandler (67)	7.7
Carol DAVIS ▶ 6159 (1)	**199**
Say It Again—Jermaine Stewart (88)	397
—Charles Neil Davis see: Charles N. DANIELS	
Chip DAVIS [Louis F. Davis] ▶ 1367 (4)	**3253**
Convoy—C.W. McCall (75)	5960
Wolf Creek Pass—C.W. McCall (75)	215
Old Home Filler-Up An' Keep On-A-Truckin' Cafe—C.W. McCall (74)	198
There Won't Be No Country Music (There Won't Be No Rock 'N' Roll)—C.W. McCall (76)	133
Clifton DAVIS ▶ 390 (5)	**10150**
Never Can Say Goodbye—Jackson 5 (71)	*6524*
Never Can Say Goodbye—Gloria Gaynor (74)	*1693*
Lookin' Through The Windows—Jackson 5 (72)	1025
Never Can Say Goodbye—Isaac Hayes (71)	*700*
Never Can Say Goodbye—Communards (88)	*208*
Clive DAVIS ▶ 1500 (1)	**2889**
All Out Of Love—Air Supply (80)	5778
—Denise L. Davis see: Rainy DAVIS	
Don DAVIS ▶ 587 (23)	**7400**
Disco Lady—Johnnie Taylor (76)	5946
Who's Making Love—Johnnie Taylor (68)	*3954*
I Believe In You (You Believe In Me)—Johnnie Taylor (73)	2291
Take Care Of Your Homework—Johnnie Taylor (69)	958
Jody's Got Your Girl And Gone—Johnnie Taylor (71)	731
Love Bones—Johnnie Taylor (69)	494
Condition Red—Goodees (68)	482
Toast To The Fool—Dramatics (72)	402
We're Getting Careless With Our Love—Johnnie Taylor (74)	382
I'll Love You Forever—Holidays (66)	352
Who's Making Love—Blues Brothers (80)	*342*
Baby Please Come Back Home—J.J. Barnes (67)	321
Who's Making Love—Young-Holt Unlimited (69)	*241*
Somebody's Gettin' It—Johnnie Taylor (76)	193

Don DAVIS ▶ 587 (23) *Continued*	**7400**
Pick Up The Pieces—Carla Thomas (67)	176
My Pretending Days Are Over—Dells (73)	161
Love Is Better In The A.M. (Part 1)— Johnnie Taylor (77)	96
Shake It Well—Dramatics (77)	90
I've Been Born Again—Johnnie Taylor (74)	86
Stop Doggin' Me—Johnnie Taylor (72)	85
I Have Learned To Do Without You— Mavis Staples (70)	41
I'm Satisfied— San Remo Golden Strings (65)	38
Ocean Of Thoughts And Dreams—Dramatics (78)	7.3
Ed DAVIS ▶ 11314 (1)	**2.3**
Mr. Pride—Chuck (2) Jackson (61)	4.6
Eugene DAVIS ▶ 7491 (2)	**92**
Talking About My Baby—Gloria Walker (68)	255
Please Don't Desert Me Baby— Gloria Walker & The Chevelles (69)	7.5
George DAVIS ▶ 2001 (2)	**2014**
Boy From New York City—Manhattan Transfer (81)	*2222*
The Boy From New York City—Ad Libs (65)	*1806*
George Richard DAVIS Jr. ▶ 1144 (4)	**3880**
Tell It Like It Is—Aaron Neville (66)	*6327*
Tell It Like It Is—Heart (80)	*1344*
Tell It Like It Is—Andy Williams (76)	*63*
She Took You For A Ride—Aaron Neville (67)	25
Hal DAVIS ▶ 1037 (5)	**4252**
I'll Be There—Jackson 5 (70)	9838
Dancing Machine—Jackson 5 (74)	4702
Get It Together—Jackson 5 (73)	729
Castles In The Sand—Little Stevie Wonder (64)	304
Can I—Eddie Kendricks (71)	6.3
Herman R. DAVIS ▶ 3278 (2)	**914**
Groovy Situation—Gene Chandler (70)	1714
I Need Your Loving—Human League (86)	343
James Edward DAVIS ▶ 11183 (1)	**2.8**
We Both Deserve Each Other's Love—L.T.D. (78)	5.7
James O. DAVIS ▶ 7435 (1)	**96**
Kick The Wall—Jimmy Davis & Junction (87)	96
Janice DAVIS [Janice David] ▶ 8000 (1)	**66**
Mr. Penguin - Pt. 1—Lunar Funk (72)	197
Jay DAVIS ▶ 3891 (2)	**666**
Baby Jane—Rod Stewart (83)	1035
What Am I Gonna Do (I'm So In Love With You)— Rod Stewart (83)	446
Jean H. DAVIS ▶ 8174 (1)	**60**
I'm Falling In Love With You— Little Anthony And The Imperials (74)	60
—Jeffery Davis see: Joseph HOOVEN	
Jesse Edwin DAVIS III ▶ 6910 (1)	**129**
Farther On Down The Road—Joe Simon (70)	259
Jimmie H. DAVIS ▶ 6575 (2)	**154**
Worried Mind—Ray Anthony (62)	232
There's A New Moon Over My Shoulder— Bonnie Guitar (57)	116
Jo DAVIS ▶ 6435 (2)	**169**
Bobby—Neil Scott (61)	324
I Can't Do It By Myself—Anita Bryant (61)	14
Joel DAVIS ▶ 9590 (1)	**21**
Joy—Teddy Pendergrass (88)	62
John E. DAVIS ▶ 9868 (2)	**16**
Ain't That Enough For You— John Davis And The Monster Orchestra (78)	9.4
I Just Can't Say Goodbye—Philly Devotions (75)	6.4
—Jonathan Davis see: Kamaal FAREED	
Joseph M. DAVIS ▶ 7369 (1)	**100**
I Learned A Lesson I'll Never Forget—Joe Pica (55)	100
Karl DAVIS ▶ 6282 (2)	**186**
I'm Here To Get My Baby Out Of Jail— Everly Brothers (62)	128
Kentucky—Bob Moore and His Orch. (63)	122
Katherine DAVIS ▶ 3775 (10)	**703**
The Little Drummer Boy—Harry Simeone Chorale (58)	*770*
The Little Drummer Boy—Harry Simeone Chorale (59)	*542*
The Little Drummer Boy—Harry Simeone Chorale (62)	*347*
The Little Drummer Boy—Harry Simeone Chorale (60)	*220*
The Little Drummer Boy—Harry Simeone Chorale (61)	*133*
The Little Drummer Boy—Johnny Cash (59)	*69*
Little Drummer Boy—Lou Rawls (67)	*14*

The Little Drummer Boy—Moonlion (75)	*7.4*
The Little Drummer Boy—Jack Halloran Singers (62)	*2.2*
The Little Drummer Boy—Harry Simeone Chorale (63)	*2.2*
Ken DAVIS ▶ 6658 (1)	**146**
Ain't Gonna Tell Anybody— Jimmy Gilmer and The Fireballs (64)	293
Kim DAVIS ▶ 8132 (2)	**60**
Nicole—Point Blank (81)	357
Let Me Stay With You Tonight—Point Blank (81)	5.7
Larry DAVIS [Lawrence Davis, Larry Julian, Lorin Julian] ▶ 8567 (1)	**46**
Cars With The Boom—L'Trimm (88)	232
—Lawrence Davis see: Larry DAVIS	
Lou DAVIS ▶ 9864 (1)	**16**
Hot Lips—Grady Martin And The Slew Foot Five (55)	48
—Louis F. Davis see: Chip DAVIS	
Mac DAVIS [Morris Davis, Scott Davis] ▶ 87 (29) HOF	**26634**
Baby Don't Get Hooked On Me— Mac Davis (72)	5547
In The Ghetto—Elvis Presley (69)	*5247*
Don't Cry Daddy—Elvis Presley (69)	3047
Something's Burning— Kenny Rogers And The First Edition (70)	2846
Watching Scotty Grow—Bobby Goldsboro (70)	1958
Stop And Smell The Roses—Mac Davis (74)	1785
One Hell Of A Woman—Mac Davis (74)	1579
I Believe In Music—Gallery (72)	*1440*
Clean Up Your Own Back Yard—Elvis Presley (69)	713
In The Ghetto—Candi Staton (72)	*603*
Memories—Elvis Presley (69)	*601*
It's Hard To Be Humble—Mac Davis (80)	598
Daddy's Little Man—O.C. Smith (69)	570
Everybody Loves A Love Song—Mac Davis (72)	388
Friend, Lover, Woman, Wife—O.C. Smith (69)	372
Everything A Man Could Ever Need— Glen Campbell (70)	358
Whoever Finds This, I Love You—Mac Davis (70)	274
Texas In My Rear View Mirror—Mac Davis (80)	241
Memories—Lettermen (69)	*238*
Burnin' Thing—Mac Davis (75)	201
A Little Less Conversation— Elvis Presley With The Jordanaires (68)	197
Dream Me Home—Mac Davis (73)	143
Problem Child—Mark Lindsay (70)	105
Your Side Of The Bed—Mac Davis (73)	59
Good Time Girl—Nancy Sinatra (68)	56
You're Good For Me—Lou Rawls (68)	15
I Believe In Music—Marian Love (71)	*10*
Beginning To Feel The Pain—Mac Davis (71)	5.0
God Knows I Love You—Nancy Sinatra (69)	4.6
Mark DAVIS ▶ 10673 (1)	**6.2**
Disco Rufus—Stargard (78)	12
Martha DAVIS ▶ 872 (8)	**5088**
Only The Lonely—Motels (82)	2241
Suddenly Last Summer—Motels (83)	1697
Shame—Motels (85)	605
Remember The Nights—Motels (83)	499
Take The L.—Motels (82)	228
Forever Mine—Motels (82)	167
Shock—Motels (85)	36
Don't Tell Me The Time—Martha Davis (87)	35
—Mavis Vegas Davis see: Michele ALLER	
Maxwell DAVIS ▶ 2735 (7)	**1233**
Eddie My Love— Fontane Sisters with Billy Vaughn's Orchestra (56)	*1670*
Eddie My Love—Chordettes (56)	*1068*
Eddie My Love—Teen Queens (56)	*856*
So All Alone—Teen Queens (56)	72
The Girl In My Dreams—Cliques (56)	*39*
Girl In My Dreams—Capris (61)	*4.0*
The Girl In My Dreams—Four Lovers (56)	*0.0*
Melvin DAVIS ▶ 7135 (1)	**114**
I Don't Wanna Lose You—Johnnie Taylor (71)	114
Michael DAVIS ▶ 8913 (1)	**36**
Kick Out The Jams—MC5 (69)	181
—Morris Davis see: Mac DAVIS	
Mose DAVIS ▶ 10131 (1)	**12**
Get Down People—Fabulous Counts (70)	37
Paul DAVIS ▶ 362 (15)	**10591**
I Go Crazy—Paul Davis (77)	3006

'65 Love Affair—Paul Davis (82)	2028
Sweet Life—Paul Davis (78)	1708
Cool Night—Paul Davis (81)	1310
Ride 'Em Cowboy—Paul Davis (74)	1056
Do Right—Paul Davis (80)	880
I Just Wanna Keep It Together—Paul Davis (70)	432
Superstar—Paul Davis (76)	410
Bop—Dan Seals (86)	408
Thinking Of You—Paul Davis (76)	188
Boogie Woogie Man—Paul Davis (72)	155
Keep Our Love Alive—Paul Davis (75)	39
Cry Just A Little—Paul Davis (80)	21
All The Way—Brick (80)	6.1
Do It With Feeling—Michael Zager's Moon Band Featuring Peabo Bryson (76)	5.8
Pepper DAVIS [David Asner] ▶ 8537 (1)	**47**
Baby I Do Love You—Galens (63)	141
Rainy DAVIS [Denise L. Davis, Denise Kessler] ▶ 11703 (1)	**0.6**
Spring Love—Cover Girls (87)	1.1
Richard DAVIS ▶ 5833 (2)	**238**
Church Bells May Ring—Diamonds (56)	*981*
Church Bells May Ring—Willows (56)	*210*
—Rick Davis see: Erik BRANN	
Rob DAVIS ▶ 10012 (1)	**14**
What's She Got—Liquid Gold (83)	28
—Robert Michael Davis see: Bob MONROE	
Ronald DAVIS ▶ 11522 (1)	**1.4**
Gino Is A Coward—Gino Washington (64)	1.4
—Roquel Davis see: Billy DAVIS	
—Scott Davis see: Mac DAVIS	
Sheila DAVIS ▶ 4498 (1)	**477**
Who Will Answer?—Ed Ames (67)	954
—Sheriff Tex Davis see: William DOUCHETTE	
Sherman DAVIS ▶ 11215 (1)	**2.7**
Let's Dance (Make Your Body Move)— West Street Mob (81)	30
Skeeter DAVIS [Mary Frances Penick] ▶ 6014 (2)	**216**
My Last Date (With You)—Skeeter Davis (60)	*381*
My Last Date (With You)—Joni James (60)	*266*
Spencer DAVIS ▶ 2790 (5)	**1194**
Gimme Some Lovin'—Spencer Davis Group (66)	*2448*
Gimme Some Lovin'—Blues Brothers (80)	*890*
Gimme Some Lovin' Part One—Traffic, Etc. (71)	*217*
Gimme Some Lovin'—Kongas (78)	*15*
Time Seller—Spencer Davis Group (67)	10
Stephen Allen DAVIS ▶ 2088 (3)	**1891**
Take Time To Know Her—Percy Sledge (68)	1850
Don't Girls Get Lonely—Glenn Shorrock (83)	76
Let Me Love You Goodbye—Bobby Vinton (81)	5.0
Warren DAVIS ▶ 3527 (3)	**797**
Book Of Love—Monotones (58)	*2045*
Book Of Love—Raindrops (64)	*259*
Book of Love—Nino & the Ebb Tides (61)	*88*
William DAVIS ▶ 9002 (2)	**33**
Gee—Pixies Three (64)	*90*
Gee—Jan & Dean (60)	*44*
Yvette DAVIS ▶ 8557 (1)	**46**
How Could I Let You Get Away—Spinners (72)	46
—Christopher John Davison see: Chris DE BURGH	
Daniele DAVOLI ▶ 3065 (4)	**1027**
Everybody Everybody—Black Box (90)	1472
Strike It Up—Black Box (91)	1185
I Don't Know Anybody Else—Black Box (90)	395
Gonna Catch You—Lonnie Gordon (91)	30
Charles DAWES ▶ 672 (3)	**6446**
It's All In The Game—Tommy Edwards (58)	*10634*
It's All In The Game—Four Tops (70)	*1294*
It's All In The Game—Cliff Richard (63)	*964*
—Billy Dawn see: Billy Dawn SMITH	
John C. DAWSON ▶ 11730 (1)	**0.4**
Louisiana Lady— New Riders Of The Purple Sage (71)	0.4
Arlan DAY [Alan Green] ▶ 7425 (1)	**97**
I Surrender—Arlan Day (81)	97
—Bernard Colin Day see: Bob ALLISON	
—Billy Day see: Bill DAVIDSON	
Bing DAY ▶ 11662 (1)	**0.8**
Mama's Place—Bing Day (59)	2.3

Bobby DAY [Robert James Byrd] ▶ 329 (12)	**11153**
Over And Over—Dave Clark Five (65)	*5663*
Little Bitty Pretty One—Jackson 5 (72)	*1791*
Little Bitty Pretty One—Thurston Harris (57)	*1745*
Buzz Buzz Buzz—Hollywood Flames (57)	*936*
Little Bitty Pretty One—Clyde McPhatter (62)	*583*
Little Bitty Pretty One—Frankie Lymon (60)	*420*
Over And Over—Bobby Day (58)	*263*
Little Bitty Pretty One—Bobby Day And The Satellites (57)	*172*
Gotta New Girl—Bobby Day (59)	44
Over And Over—Thurston Harris (58)	*2.9*
That's All I Want—Bobby Day (59)	1.1
Buzz Buzz Buzz—Rusty Draper (57)	*0.0*
Joey DAY [Joseph DiFrancesco] ▶ 4428 (3)	**495**
Beg, Borrow And Steal—Ohio Express (67)	957
Girl (You Captivate Me)—? & The Mysterians (67)	29
Just Another Face—Blades Of Grass (67)	4.8
Jon DAY [Jonathan Charles Baker, John Baker] ▶ 10627 (1)	**6.7**
The Only One I Know—Charlatans UK (90)	33
Michael DAY ▶ 5175 (1)	**331**
Try Again—Champaign (83)	992
Morris DAY ▶ 2740 (5)	**1230**
Jerk-Out—Time (90)	1425
Jungle Love—Time (84)	911
Fishnet—Morris Day (88)	464
The Bird—Time (85)	441
The Oak Tree—Morris Day (85)	195
Robert DAY ▶ 4284 (3)	**533**
You'll Always Be My Lifetime Sweetheart—Perry Como (55)	634
Give Us This Day—Joni James (56)	*431*
Give Us This Day—Dream Weavers (56)	*0.0*
Valerie DAY ▶ 4046 (2)	**614**
Point Of No Return—Nu Shooz (86)	764
Should I Say Yes?—Nu Shooz (88)	463
Daddio DAYLIE [Daddy-O Daylie, Holmes Daylie] ▶ 9264 (1)	**28**
Do Anything You Wanna (Part 1)—Harold Betters (64)	110
John DEACON ▶ 238 (8) HOF	**14380**
Another One Bites The Dust—Queen (80)	11623
Ice Ice Baby—Vanilla Ice (90)	3735
You're My Best Friend—Queen (76)	1464
Under Pressure—Queen & David Bowie (81)	689
Need Your Loving Tonight—Queen (80)	268
I Want It All—Queen (89)	251
One Vision—Queen (85)	249
I Want To Break Free—Queen (84)	229
—Robert Allen Deal see: Mick MARS	
Bill DEAN ▶ 10770 (1)	**5.4**
A Letter To Dad—Every Father's Teenage Son (67)	11
David DEAN ▶ 11795 (1)	**0.0**
The Freeze—Fention & The Castle Rockers (58)	0.0
Debbie DEAN [Reba Jeanette Smith, Penny Smith] ▶ 5999 (1)	**218**
I Can't Dance To That Music You're Playin'—Martha Reeves & The Vandellas (68)	435
Eddie DEAN [Edgar Dean Glosup] ▶ 3357 (2)	**883**
One Has My Name (The Other Has My Heart)—Barry Young (65)	1343
I Dreamed Of A Hill-Billy Heaven—Tex Ritter (61)	870
James Anthony DEAN ▶ 923 (11)	**4786**
You Don't Have To Be A Star (To Be In My Show)—Marilyn McCoo & Billy Davis Jr. (76)	5716
What Becomes Of The Brokenhearted—Jimmy Ruffin (66)	2895
I've Passed This Way Before—Jimmy Ruffin (66)	1244
Everything Is Good About You—Lettermen (71)	165
My Pretending Days Are Over—Dells (73)	161
I'll Say Forever My Love—Jimmy Ruffin (68)	136
It's So Hard Being A Loser—Contours (67)	136
I've Been Born Again—Johnnie Taylor (74)	86
I Hope We Get To Love In Time—Marilyn McCoo & Billy Davis Jr. (76)	81
That's The Sound That Lonely Makes—Tavares (74)	79
I Am The Man For You Baby—Edwin Starr (68)	13
Jimmy DEAN ▶ 284 (7)	**12415**
Big Bad John—Jimmy Dean (61)	*10897*
Dear Ivan—Jimmy Dean (62)	685
Little Black Book—Jimmy Dean (62)	620
I.O.U.—Jimmy Dean (76)	234
Gonna Raise A Rukus Tonight—Jimmy Dean (62)	86
The First Thing Ev'ry Morning (And The Last Thing Ev'ry Night)—Jimmy Dean (65)	19
Big Bruce—Steve Greenberg (69)	*3.1*
Lorene DEAN ▶ 4634 (1)	**448**
One Has My Name (The Other Has My Heart)—Barry Young (65)	1343
Mary DEAN [Mary Dean Lauria] ▶ 1418 (2)	**3128**
Half-Breed—Cher (73)	6135
Own The Night—Chaka Khan (85)	181
Paul DEAN ▶ 1689 (12)	**2483**
This Could Be The Night—Loverboy (86)	1219
Heaven In Your Eyes—Loverboy (86)	1186
Hot Girls In Love—Loverboy (83)	1158
Working For The Weekend—Loverboy (81)	740
When It's Over—Loverboy (82)	624
Turn Me Loose—Loverboy (81)	624
Queen Of The Broken Hearts—Loverboy (83)	453
Notorious—Loverboy (87)	386
The Kid Is Hot Tonite—Loverboy (81)	138
Lead A Double Life—Loverboy (86)	114
Jump—Loverboy (82)	67
Too Hot—Loverboy (89)	53
—Ritchie Dean see: Warren SCHATZ	
Eddie V. DEANE ▶ 1793 (9)	**2312**
The Men In My Little Girl's Life—Mike Douglas (65)	2269
Rock A Billy—Guy Mitchell (57)	1415
Small Sad Sam—Phil McLean (61)	902
Hootenanny—Glencoves (63)	488
Princess—Frank Gari (61)	302
Nee Nee Na Na Na Na Nu Nu—Dicky Doo And The Don'ts (58)	135
A Little Dog Cried—Jimmie Rodgers (61)	118
Third Finger - Left Hand—Eileen Rodgers (57)	8.2
I Like Girls—Johnny Restivo (59)	6.5
Arthur Joseph DeANGELIS ▶ 11023 (1)	**3.8**
Africa—Thundermug (72)	7.5
Joe DeANGELIS ▶ 5211 (2)	**326**
Don't Say Goodnight And Mean Goodbye—Shirelles (63)	637
A Cross Stands Alone—Jimmy Witter (61)	15
Peter DeANGELIS ▶ 458 (28)	**9118**
Why—Frankie Avalon (59)	*7611*
Painted, Tainted Rose—Al Martino (63)	1454
Dede Dinah—Frankie Avalon (57)	1252
I'll Wait For You—Frankie Avalon (58)	1197
With All My Heart—Jodie Sands (57)	*1183*
Why—Donny Osmond (72)	*1103*
Living A Lie—Al Martino (63)	963
Where Are You—Frankie Avalon (60)	784
You Are Mine—Frankie Avalon (62)	616
Always Together—Al Martino (64)	533
You Excite Me—Frankie Avalon (58)	296
Perfect Love—Frankie Avalon (60)	244
I Love My Girl—Hilltoppers (57)	*217*
What Happens Now—Mona Carol (56)	202
I Love My Girl—Cozy Morley (57)	*185*
Just Yesterday—Al Martino (66)	179
The Puppet Song—Frankie Avalon (60)	167
You, No One But You—Frankie Laine (67)	151
Swingin' On A Rainbow—Frankie Avalon (59)	84
My Cherie—Al Martino (65)	76
I'll Be There—Eddie Holman (70)	58
Will I Always Be Your Sweetheart—Mona Carol (56)	*41*
With All My Heart—Judy Scott (57)	*23*
Calypso Parakeet—Patty Brandon (57)	12
I'm Happy—Four Dates (58)	4.9
With All My Heart—Al Martino (65)	*2.8*
With All My Heart—Buddy Greco (57)	*0.0*
Will I Always Be Your Sweetheart—Kitty Kallen (56)	*0.0*
T. DeANGELO ▶ 11639 (1)	**0.9**
This Is My Country, Thank You Canada—Shelley Looney (80)	1.8
Tom DeANGELO ▶ 7971 (2)	**67**
Wait A Minute—Tim Tam And The Turn-Ons (66)	82
Little Becky's Christmas Wish—Becky Lamb (67)	51
—Elisa Dease see: Elisa FIORILLO	
Billy DEATON ▶ 10211 (3)	**11**
Louisiana Man—Bobbie Gentry (68)	*14*
Louisiana Man—Pozo Seco Singers (67)	*4.9*
Louisiana Man—Rusty & Doug (61)	*3.3*
Bobby DeBARGE ▶ 4002 (4)	**625**
There'll Never Be—Switch (78)	444
Best Beat In Town—Switch (79)	115
I Call Your Name—Switch (79)	102
Love Over And Over Again—Switch (80)	32
Bunny DeBARGE [Etterlene DeBarge, Etterlene Jordan, Etterlene Knight] ▶ 3580 (3)	**778**
Time Will Reveal—DeBarge (83)	1067
I Like It—DeBarge (83)	684
Love Over And Over Again—Switch (80)	32
Chico DeBARGE ▶ 6634 (1)	**149**
You Wear It Well—El DeBarge with DeBarge (85)	298
El DeBARGE ▶ 1584 (6)	**2669**
All This Love—DeBarge (83)	1372
Time Will Reveal—DeBarge (83)	1067
I Like It—DeBarge (83)	684
The Secret Garden (Sweet Seduction Suite)—Quincy Jones featuring Al B. Sure!, James Ingram, El DeBarge & Barry White (90)	416
You Wear It Well—El DeBarge with DeBarge (85)	298
Love Me In A Special Way—DeBarge (84)	282
—Etterlene DeBarge see: Bunny DeBARGE	
Randy DeBARGE ▶ 5922 (1)	**228**
I Like It—DeBarge (83)	684
Alice DeBUHR ▶ 6182 (1)	**196**
Charity Ball—Fanny (71)	589
Chris DE BURGH [Christopher John Davison, Chris DeBurgh] ▶ 1036 (4)	**4254**
The Lady In Red—Chris DeBurgh (87)	3227
Don't Pay The Ferryman—Chris DeBurgh (83)	544
High On Emotion—Chris DeBurgh (84)	403
Ship To Shore—Chris DeBurgh (83)	80
—Chris DeBurgh see: Chris DE BURGH	
Claude DEBUSSY ▶ 5436 (5)	**290**
Magic Moon (Clair De Lune)—Rays (61)	*413*
Moonlight Love—Perry Como (56)	337
My Claire De Lune—Steve Lawrence (61)	*68*
Moonlight Love (Clair De Lune)—Roger Williams (57)	*34*
My Clair De Lune—George Feyer (61)	*0.0*
Gary DeCARLO [Garrett Scott] ▶ 1733 (3)	**2403**
Na Na Hey Hey Kiss Him Goodbye—Steam (69)	*5814*
Kiss Him Goodbye—Nylons (87)	*977*
I've Gotta Make You Love Me—Steam (70)	418
Nick DeCARO ▶ 6165 (1)	**198**
Louie, Louie—Sandpipers (66)	*595*
Tom DeCILLIS ▶ 8060 (2)	**63**
Baby Toys—Toys (66)	86
I Was Born A Loser—Bobby Lee (66)	20
Carol DECKER ▶ 2748 (2)	**1223**
Heart And Soul—T'Pau (87)	2422
Only A Heartbeat—T'Pau (91)	24
Jeanine DECKERS [Jeanne-Paule Marie Deckers, Singing Nun, Soeur Sourire] ▶ 406 (2)	**9739**
Dominique—Singing Nun (63)	9721
Tous Les Chemins (All The Roads)—Singing Nun (Soeur Sourire) (64)	18
Mark DECLOEDT ▶ 3103 (2)	**1010**
Unbelievable—EMF (91)	4783
Lies—EMF (91)	266
—Daisy Dee see: Desiree ROLLOCKS	
Graham DEE ▶ 8498 (1)	**48**
The Loneliest Man On The Moon—David Castle (77)	96
—Jackie Dee see: Jackie DeSHANNON	
—Jean Dee see: Yvonne DEVANEY	
Joey DEE [Joseph DiNicola] ▶ 939 (5)	**4727**
Peppermint Twist - Part 1—Joey Dee & The Starliters (61)	9044
Hey, Let's Twist—Joey Dee & The Starliters (62)	528
Everytime (I Think About You) (Part 1)—Joey Dee & The Starliters (62)	51
Roly Poly—Joey Dee & The Starliters (62)	40
Baby, You're Driving Me Crazy—Joey Dee (63)	9.0
Johnnie DEE [John Richard DeGiuli] ▶ 10778 (1)	**5.3**
Love Changes Everything—Honeymoon Suite (88)	16
—Johnny Dee see: John D. LOUDERMILK	
—Kool Moe Dee see: Mohandas DeWESE	

Lenny DEE [Leonard George DeStoppelaire] ► 3381 (4)	**873**
Plantation Boogie—Lenny Dee (55)	*873*
Plantation Boogie— Georgie Auld & His Rockin' Rhythm (55)	*0.0*
Plantation Boogie— Buddy Cole with The Wood Sisters (55)	*0.0*
Plantation Boogie—Shay Torrent (55)	*0.0*
—Papa Dee see: Dan WAHLGREN	
—Prince Markie Dee see: Mark Anthony MORALES	
Sylvia DEE [Josephine Moore Proffitt] ► 907 (12)	**4872**
The End Of The World—Skeeter Davis (63)	6448
Too Young—Donny Osmond (72)	1365
House With Love In It—Four Lads (56)	738
Please Don't Talk To The Lifeguard—Diane Ray (63)	464
Moon Light Swim—Tony Perkins (57)	*335*
Moonlight Swim—Nick Noble (57)	*285*
Somebody Nobody Wants—Dion (61)	59
If Anyone Finds This I Love You—Kay Starr (55)	27
Robot Man—Jamie Horton (60)	15
I Miss The Boy—Betty Madigan (56)	6.2
Wait For Me—Rita Pavone (64)	1.8
Moonlight Swim—Joel Grey (57)	*0.0*
Tommy DEE [Tommy Donaldson] ► 2774 (2)	**1203**
Three Stars—Tommy Dee (59)	*1202*
Three Stars—Ruby Wright (59)	*0.8*
—Johnny Deerfield see: Ron HARGRAVE	
Bruce DEES ► 8279 (1)	**56**
Got To Give In To Love—Bonnie Boyer (79)	222
Lillian DEES ► 11182 (1)	**2.8**
A Woman's Way—Rozetta Johnson (70)	2.8
Rick DEES [Rigdon Osmond Dees III] ► 632 (2)	**6833**
Disco Duck (Part I)— Rick Dees And His Cast Of Idiots (76)	6774
Eat My Shorts—Rick Dees (84)	118
Sam DEES ► 2177 (6)	**1785**
One In A Million You—Larry Graham (80)	1378
Love All The Hurt Away—Aretha Franklin (81)	299
Save The Overtime (For Me)— Gladys Knight & The Pips (83)	179
Cry To Me—Loleatta Holloway (75)	101
Where Did We Go Wrong—L.T.D. (80)	37
Send For Me—Atlantic Starr (81)	6.9
William DEES ► 531 (11)	**8041**
Oh, Pretty Woman— Roy Orbison And The Candy Men (64)	*8819*
It's Over—Roy Orbison (64)	2050
(Oh) Pretty Woman—Van Halen (82)	*1208*
Ride Away—Roy Orbison (65)	995
Goodnight—Roy Orbison (65)	873
Breakin' Up Is Breakin' My Heart—Roy Orbison (66)	686
Twinkle Toes—Roy Orbison (66)	450
Crawling Back—Roy Orbison (65)	429
(Say) You're My Girl—Roy Orbison (65)	335
Communication Breakdown—Roy Orbison (66)	230
Walk On—Roy Orbison (68)	7.9
John DeFARIA ► 4986 (1)	**364**
Get On Your Feet—Gloria Estefan (89)	1093
—Michaele DeFerraro see: Michele MICHAELE	
—James DeFore see: Jimmy Dee FORE	
Chris DeGARMO ► 2586 (2)	**1347**
Silent Lucidity—Queensryche (91)	1326
Another Rainy Night (Without You)—Queensryche (91)	61
—John Richard DeGiuli see: Johnnie DEE	
Donald DeGRATE [DeVante Swing] ► 5650 (1)	**260**
Forever My Lady—Jodeci (91)	519
Willy DEHMEL ► 6813 (2)	**135**
Baciare Baciare (Kissing Kissing)— Dorothy Collins (59)	*405*
Baciare Baciare (Kissing Kissing)—Ilse Werner (59)	*0.0*
Richard DEHR ► 598 (15)	**7262**
Memories Are Made Of This—Dean Martin (55)	*8655*
Greenfields—Brothers Four (60)	*6907*
Marianne—Terry Gilkyson And The Easy Riders (57)	*3770*
Marianne—Hilltoppers (57)	*2812*
Love Is A Golden Ring— Frankie Laine with The Easy Riders (57)	891
Memories Are Made Of This—Gale Storm (55)	*785*

Memories Are Made Of This—Drifters (66)	*271*
Memories Are Made Of This—Mindy Carson (55)	*217*
Marianne—Lane Brothers (57)	*71*
Marianne—Burl Ives (57)	*45*
Green Fields—Vogues (69)	*25*
Memories Are Made Of This—Roger Williams (59)	*14*
Greenfields—Julius La Rosa (60)	*0.0*
Mary Ann—Talbot Brothers (57)	*0.0*
Mary Ann—Edmundo Ros & His Orchestra (57)	*0.0*
Luchi DeJESUS ► 3464 (2)	**835**
A Rockin' Good Way (To Mess Around And Fall In Love)—Dinah Washington & Brook Benton (60)	2398
I Want You Forever—Brook Benton (59)	106
Dux DeJOHN [Mary Ann Barcaro, Mary Ann DiGiovanni] ► 3933 (3)	**652**
No More—DeJohn Sisters (54)	*1444*
No More—McGuire Sisters (54)	*474*
Present For Bob—DeJohn Sisters (55)	37
Julie DeJOHN [Julie DiGiovanni] ► 3934 (3)	**652**
No More—DeJohn Sisters (54)	*1444*
No More—McGuire Sisters (54)	*474*
Present For Bob—DeJohn Sisters (55)	37
Leo DeJOHN [Leo DiGiovanni] ► 3961 (3)	**639**
No More—DeJohn Sisters (54)	*1444*
No More—McGuire Sisters (54)	*474*
No More—Guy Lombardo & His Royal Canadians (54)	*0.0*
Desmond DEKKER [Desmond Dacres] ► 3233 (1)	**937**
Israelites—Desmond Dekker & The Aces (69)	1874
Mike DEKLE ► 10961 (1)	**4.1**
Scarlet Fever—Kenny Rogers (83)	4.1
Jimmy DeKNIGHT [James E. Myers] ► 1013 (4)	**4382**
(We're Gonna) Rock Around The Clock— Bill Haley And His Comets (55)	*8240*
(We're Gonna) Rock Around The Clock— Bill Haley And His Comets (74)	*381*
Rock Around The Clock— Jive Bunny And The Mastermixers (89)	*80*
(We're Gonna) Rock Around The Clock— Bill Haley and His Comets (54)	*64*
René DeKNIGHT ► 8032 (1)	**64**
The Declaration—5th Dimension (70)	192
Manuel De La CALVA ► 10981 (1)	**4.0**
He Gives Me Love (La La La)—Lesley Gore (68)	12
Vince De La CRUZ ► 4863 (1)	**397**
Do You Want Crying—Katrina And The Waves (85)	397
Michael DELAHUNTY ► 2113 (4)	**1861**
Hands To Heaven—Breathe (88)	3472
How Can I Fall?—Breathe (88)	2861
Don't Tell Me Lies—Breathe (89)	1080
All This I Should Have Known—Breathe (89)	30
Leonard DELANEY ► 10015 (1)	**14**
Bustin' Surfboards—Tornadoes (62)	56
Prentice DeLANEY [Sean Delaney, Prentice John Delaney Jr.] ► 5974 (3)	**220**
Rocket Ride—Kiss (78)	389
Sing It, Shout It—Starz (77)	148
(She's Just A) Fallen Angel—Starz (76)	6.5
—Sean Delaney see: Prentice DeLANEY	
Edgar DeLANGE ► 11202 (1) HOF	**2.8**
I'll Be Worthy Of You—Cab Calloway (56)	5.6
Pierre DELANOË [Pierre Leroyer] ► 1276 (15)	**3474**
Let It Be Me—Betty Everett & Jerry Butler (64)	*2995*
Let It Be Me—Everly Brothers (60)	*2197*
The Day The Rains Came—Jane Morgan (58)	*1490*
What Now My Love—Sonny & Cher (66)	*986*
What Now My Love— Herb Alpert & The Tijuana Brass (66)	*706*
The Day The Rains Came— Raymond Lefevre and His Orchestra (58)	*623*
What Now My Love—Mitch Ryder (67)	*593*
Let It Be Me—Willie Nelson (82)	*368*
Let It Be Me—Glen Campbell And Bobbie Gentry (69)	*224*
Down By The Riverside— Les Compagnons De La Chanson (60)	*175*
Let It Be Me—Jill Corey (57)	*87*
If Only I Could Live My Life Again— Jane Morgan (59)	15
Let It Be Me—Sweet Inspirations (67)	*6.2*

What Now My Love—"Groove" Holmes (66)	*5.1*
Down By The Riverside (Qu'l Fait Bon Vivre)— Les Barclay (60)	*0.0*
Fito De La PARRA ► 8220 (1)	**58**
Time Was—Canned Heat (69)	290
—Maria Joaquia de la Portilla Torres see: Maria GREVER	
—Hollis Rudolph DeLaughter see: Red LANE	
Eddie DEL BARRIO ► 5643 (2)	**261**
Fantasy—Earth, Wind & Fire (78)	662
Star—Earth, Wind & Fire (79)	121
Andres DEL CASTILLO ► 8851 (1)	**38**
Kiss You (When It's Dangerous)—Eight Seconds (87)	151
Robert DEL DIN ► 10045 (1)	**14**
Never—Earls (63)	41
Rafael DE LEON [Roaring Lion] ► 2598 (6)	**1340**
Marianne—Terry Gilkyson And The Easy Riders (57)	*3770*
Marianne—Hilltoppers (57)	*2812*
Marianne—Lane Brothers (57)	*71*
Marianne—Burl Ives (57)	*45*
Mary Ann—Talbot Brothers (57)	*0.0*
Mary Ann—Edmundo Ros & His Orchestra (57)	*0.0*
James DeLESTON ► 6869 (1)	**132**
Do I Like It—Nat "King" Cole (58)	263
Felipe DELGADO ► 3417 (1)	**856**
Finally—Ce Ce Peniston (91)	2569
Jack DELGADO ► 11563 (1)	**1.2**
Place In The Sun—Johnny Nash (60)	4.8
—Jean Ann Del Grosso see: Laurie ALLEN	
Herbert DELL ► 11015 (1)	**3.8**
I'm Bewildered—DeCastro Sisters (55)	7.7
Alton DELMORE ► 7022 (2)	**121**
Blues (Stay Away From Me)—Ace Cannon (62)	*465*
Blues Stay Away From Me— Billy Vaughn And His Orchestra (59)	*19*
Lionel DELMORE ► 5559 (1)	**271**
Swingin'—John Anderson (83)	543
Rabon DELMORE ► 7023 (2)	**121**
Blues (Stay Away From Me)—Ace Cannon (62)	*465*
Blues Stay Away From Me— Billy Vaughn And His Orchestra (59)	*19*
—Reginald DeLong see: Richard COBURN	
Gaye DELORME ► 4254 (1)	**545**
Earache My Eye (Featuring Alice Bowie)— Cheech & Chong (74)	1634
Al DeLORY ► 2264 (5)	**1678**
Mr Custer—Larry Verne (60)	4906
Mister Livingston—Larry Verne (60)	111
Johnny Willow—Fred Darian (61)	41
Roll Call Company J—Balladeers (60)	3.8
Battle Of Gettysburg—Fred Darian (61)	0.5
Waldo DE LOS RIOS [Osvaldo Nicolas Ferraro Gutierrez] ► 4701 (1)	**435**
A Song Of Joy (Himno A La Alegria)— Miguel Rios (70)	1305
Brad DELP ► 5941 (2)	**225**
Can'tcha Say (You Believe In Me)—Boston (87)	270
Still In Love—Boston (87)	270
Paul DELPH ► 10115 (1)	**13**
Don't Want No-Body—J.D. Drews (80)	25
Michele DEL PRETE ► 7794 (2)	**75**
Tar And Cement—Verdelle Smith (66)	359
Nessuno Mi Puo' Giudcare—Gene Pitney (66)	13
—Carlos Del Rosario see: Yutaka YOKOKURA	
Dave DeLUCA ► 6417 (1)	**173**
Blame It On Love— Smokey Robinson & Barbara Mitchell (83)	345
Thomas DeLUCA ► 10010 (1)	**14**
Satisfied Man—Molly Hatchet (84)	28
Ann DeLUGG ► 10845 (1)	**5.0**
The Big Beat— Dick Jacobs And His Chorus And Orchestra (57)	9.9
Milton DeLUGG ► 4848 (7)	**399**
A Poor Man's Roses (Or A Rich Man's Gold)— Patti Page (57)	*516*
Sailor Boys Have Talk To Me In English— Rosemary Clooney (55)	*243*
Bongola—Preston Epps (60)	14
The Big Beat— Dick Jacobs And His Chorus And Orchestra (57)	9.9

Milton DeLUGG ▶ 4848 (7) *Continued*	**399**
Sailor Boys Have Talk To Me In English—5 DeMarco Sisters (55)	*0.0*
Sailor Boys Have Talk To Me In English—Helen O'Connell (55)	*0.0*
A Poor Man's Roses (Or A Rich Man's Gold)—Patsy Cline (57)	*0.0*
Steve DeMARCHI ▶ 2627 (1)	**1309**
More Than Words Can Say—Alias (90)	2619
C. DeMARINIS ▶ 8685 (3)	**43**
Pupalina—Gaylords (54)	*213*
Pupalina (My Little Doll)—Guy Lombardo & His Royal Canadians (54)	*0.0*
Pupalina (My Little Doll)—Jimmy Durante (54)	*0.0*
Bill DeMARTINES ▶ 6047 (1)	**212**
One More Night—Streek (81)	212
Warren DeMARTINI ▶ 4241 (4)	**548**
Round And Round—Ratt (84)	1127
Lay It Down—Ratt (85)	345
Dance—Ratt (87)	196
Way Cool Jr.—Ratt (88)	109
—Paul DeMaya see: Paul GIACALONE	
Shena DeMELL ▶ 8104 (6)	**62**
I Surrender—Fontella Bass (66)	97
Mountain Of Love—Billy Stewart (65)	24
We Got The Winning Hand—Little Milton (66)	20
Do I Make Myself Clear—Etta James & Sugar Pie Desanto (65)	7.2
I Can't Help It—Moments (71)	6.5
Believe In Me Baby - Part 1—Jesse James (67)	4.3
—Eddy Quintela de Mendonça see: Eddy QUINTELA	
Vincent DeMEO ▶ 8953 (1)	**35**
Stoned Cowboy—Fantasy (70)	141
Christos DEMETRIOU ▶ 6099 (2)	**206**
Step On—Happy Mondays (91)	*231*
He's Gonna Step On You Again—John Kongos (71)	*181*
Claude DeMETRIUS [Claude Demetrius] ▶ 605 (8)	**7172**
Hard Headed Woman—Elvis Presley (58)	3490
Mean Woman Blues—Roy Orbison (63)	2805
I Was The One—Elvis Presley (56)	930
Ain't That Just Like A Woman—Fats Domino (61)	670
Take Me Back Baby—Guy Mitchell (57)	277
Strictly Sentimental—June Valli (57)	27
You Were Born To Be Loved—Billy Bland (60)	4.4
Santa Bring My Baby Back To Me—Elvis Presley (57)	2.1
Tony DeMEUR [Ronnie Golden] ▶ 10345 (1)	**9.7**
Mirror Star—Fabulous Poodles (79)	19
Patrick De MEYER ▶ 9742 (1)	**18**
Crazy—Daisy Dee (91)	90
Rod DEMICK ▶ 10719 (1)	**5.9**
Bad Little Woman—Shadows Of Knight (66)	30
Otto DEMMLAR ▶ 11712 (1)	**0.5**
Sie Liebt Dich (She Loves You)—Die Beatles (64)	*1.9*
—Willy de Moor see: Bill ADOR	
Vinicius De MORAES ▶ 3350 (1)	**885**
The Girl From Ipanema—Getz/Gilberto (64)	2656
Greg DEMPSEY ▶ 5239 (3)	**320**
I Could Be So Good To You—Don And The Goodtimes (67)	218
Boogie Bands And One Night Stands—Kathy Dalton (74)	201
Roll Away The Stone—Leon Russell (70)	20
James DEMPSEY ▶ 6972 (2)	**124**
Ace In The Hole—Somethin' Smith & The Redheads (55)	*202*
Ace In The Hole—Roberta Sherwood with The Singing Waiters (60)	*47*
Terry DEMPSEY ▶ 9956 (1)	**15**
Daydreamer—C.C. & Company (76)	15
Ian DENCH ▶ 3104 (2)	**1010**
Unbelievable—EMF (91)	4783
Lies—EMF (91)	266
—Marcias DeNegri see: Kenny GEORGE	
Johanna DENEROFF ▶ 10710 (1)	**5.9**
Love On The Phone—Suzanne Fellini (80)	24
John DeNICOLA ▶ 1611 (2)	**2625**
(I've Had) The Time Of My Life—Bill Medley And Jennifer Warnes (87)	3918

Hungry Eyes—Eric Carmen (87)	2638
Homer DENISON ▶ 7897 (1)	**70**
Tell Her You Love Her—Frank Sinatra (57)	211
Paul DENMAN ▶ 6359 (1)	**179**
Paradise—Sade (88)	717
Michael DENNE ▶ 5393 (5)	**296**
Oh Honey—Delegation (79)	419
You To Me Are Everything—Real Thing (76)	*132*
I Can't Ask For Anymore Than You—Cliff Richard (76)	22
You To Me Are Everything—Broadway (76)	*15*
You To Me Are Everything (Part 1)—Revelation (76)	*1.7*
Cathy DENNIS ▶ 1695 (5)	**2479**
Touch Me (All Night Long)—Cathy Dennis (91)	2867
Too Many Walls—Cathy Dennis (91)	1507
Just Another Dream—Cathy Dennis (90)	1350
That's The Way Of The World—D Mob With Cathy Dennis (90)	184
Everybody Move—Cathy Dennis (91)	7.4
Quitman DENNIS ▶ 10767 (1)	**5.5**
A Broken Man—Malibu's (69)	16
Willie DENNIS ▶ 7334 (1)	**101**
Mind Playing Tricks On Me—Geto Boys (91)	405
Joy DENNY [Denise Eisenberg, Denise Rich] ▶ 7500 (1)	**92**
Frankie—Sister Sledge (85)	92
Philip DENNYS ▶ 6474 (1)	**165**
Dance With The Devil—Cozy Powell (74)	330
Samuel DENOFF ▶ 10491 (1)	**7.9**
Fat Albert (Hey, Hey, Hey)—Fat Albert Orchestra and Chorus (68)	32
René DENONCIN ▶ 7057 (2)	**119**
Valley Valparaiso—Percy Faith And His Orchestra and Chorus (56)	349
Kiss And Run—Peggy King (56)	6.8
David DeNOON ▶ 7959 (1)	**67**
My Daddy Is President—Little Jo Ann (62)	134
Diane DeNOTA ▶ 2405 (2)	**1517**
Just Ask Your Heart—Frankie Avalon (59)	2110
Don't Throw Away All Those Teardrops—Frankie Avalon (60)	813
John DENSMORE ▶ 516 (17)	**8288**
Light My Fire—Doors (67)	*8461*
Hello, I Love You—Doors (68)	6496
Touch Me—Doors (68)	5980
Light My Fire—Jose Feliciano (68)	*4958*
Love Her Madly—Doors (71)	1978
People Are Strange—Doors (67)	1529
Riders On The Storm—Doors (71)	1436
Love Me Two Times—Doors (67)	731
The Unknown Soldier—Doors (68)	682
Wishful Sinful—Doors (69)	464
L.A. Woman—Billy Idol (90)	208
Light My Fire—Amii Stewart (79)	*51*
The Mosquito—Doors (72)	50
Roadhouse Blues—Doors (70)	38
Light My Fire—Rhetta Hughes (69)	*33*
Light My Fire—Doors (68)	*32*
Love Street—Doors (68)	9.0
Lee DENSON ▶ 9473 (1)	**23**
The Pied Piper—Billy Williams (57)	23
Willie DENSON ▶ 1747 (4)	**2372**
Mama Said—Shirelles (61)	2972
Backstage—Gene Pitney (66)	697
A Tear—Gene McDaniels (61)	650
Stop The Music—Shirelles (62)	425
Jimmy DENTON ▶ 4418 (1)	**499**
Black Slacks—Joe Bennett And The Sparkletones (57)	998
John DENVER [Henry John Deutschendorf Jr.] ▶ 66 (29) HOF	**32965**
Leaving On A Jet Plane—Peter, Paul & Mary (69)	*7725*
Take Me Home, Country Roads—John Denver (71)	6363
I'm Sorry—John Denver (75)	5600
Annie's Song—John Denver (74)	4963
Sunshine On My Shoulders—John Denver (74)	4334
Rocky Mountain High—John Denver (72)	2566
Back Home Again—John Denver (74)	2148
Fly Away—John Denver (75)	1734
Sweet Surrender—John Denver (74)	998
My Sweet Lady—Cliff DeYoung (73)	*929*
Looking For Space—John Denver (76)	593

Shanghai Breezes—John Denver (82)	585
I'd Rather Be A Cowboy—John Denver (73)	521
How Can I Leave You Again—John Denver (77)	349
Calypso—John Denver (75)	346
My Sweet Lady—John Denver (77)	*316*
Like A Sad Song—John Denver (76)	277
Follow Me—Mary Travers (71)	260
Autograph—John Denver (80)	146
It Makes Me Giggle—John Denver (76)	140
Farewell Andromeda (Welcome To My Morning)—John Denver (73)	127
It Amazes Me—John Denver (78)	105
I Want To Live—John Denver (78)	84
Perhaps Love—Placido Domingo And John Denver (82)	70
Goodbye Again—John Denver (72)	46
Seasons Of The Heart—John Denver (82)	31
Love Again—John Denver (84)	19
Dancing With The Mountains—John Denver (80)	3.0
Leaving On A Jet Plane—Gloria Loring (69)	*2.2*
Edward Harry DEO ▶ 11393 (1)	**1.9**
Peep Peep Pop Pop—Dearly Beloveds (66)	5.7
Eumir DEODATO ▶ 2795 (7)	**1193**
Celebration—Kool & The Gang (80)	6016
Get Down On It—Kool & The Gang (82)	1373
Take My Heart (You Can Have It If You Want It)—Kool & The Gang (81)	1077
Let's Go Dancin' (Ooh La, La, La)—Kool & The Gang (82)	654
Big Fun—Kool & The Gang (82)	532
Jones Vs. Jones—Kool & The Gang (81)	316
Steppin' Out—Kool & The Gang (82)	6.6
Suzanne DePASSE [Suzanne Coston] ▶ 4007 (1)	**624**
Here Comes The Judge—Shorty Long (68)	1872
Gene DePAUL ▶ 1630 (20) HOF	**2583**
Teach Me Tonight—DeCastro Sisters (54)	*3787*
Teach Me Tonight—George Maharis (62)	*774*
Teach Me Tonight Cha Cha—DeCastro Sisters (58)	*179*
Namely You—Don Cherry (56)	*126*
Lonesome Polecat—McGuire Sisters (54)	*84*
Love In A Home—Doris Day (56)	*72*
Teach Me Tonight—Al Jarreau (82)	*60*
Please Mr Brown—Sarah Vaughan (57)	59
You Can't Run Away From It—Four Aces (56)	24
Teach Me Tonight—Big Three: Sarah Vaughan/Joe Williams/Count Basie (60)	*1.5*
Who Are They To Say—DeCastro Sisters (58)	0.7
Teach Me Tonight—Modernaires Featuring Paula Kelly & George Auld (54)	*0.0*
Lonesome Polecat—Jack Pleis and His Orchestra and Chorus (54)	*0.0*
Lonesome Polecat—Freddy Martin & His Orchestra (54)	*0.0*
Teach Me Tonight—Jo Stafford (54)	*0.0*
Teach Me Tonight—Janet Brace (54)	*0.0*
Namely You—Julius La Rosa (56)	*0.0*
Namely You—Carmen McRae (56)	*0.0*
Love In A Home—Bing Crosby (56)	*0.0*
Love In A Home—Crew-Cuts (56)	*0.0*
Lynsey DePAUL [Lynsey Mockon Rubin] ▶ 9716 (1)	**18**
Dancin' (On A Saturday Night)—Flash Cadillac & The Continental Kids (74)	37
Paula DePORES [Triune] ▶ 11086 (1)	**3.3**
Mojo Workout (Dance)—Larry Bright (60)	13
Francis Jean DEPRUCK ▶ 8157 (1)	**60**
Ca Plane Pour Moi—Plastic Bertrand (78)	179
—Thomas DeQuincey see: Jo BOGAERT	
—Derek see: Johnny CYMBAL	
Larry DERMER ▶ 3306 (3)	**906**
Bad Boy—Miami Sound Machine (86)	1668
Falling In Love (Uh-Oh)—Miami Sound Machine (86)	691
Betcha Say That—Gloria Estefan and Miami Sound Machine (87)	358
Robert DERMINER [Rob Tyner] ▶ 8914 (1)	**36**
Kick Out The Jams—MC5 (69)	181
Frank DeROSA ▶ 5948 (5)	**224**
Big Guitar—Owen Bradley Quintet (58)	*448*
Big Guitar—Sam (The Man) Taylor & His Orch. (58)	*0.0*
Big Guitar—Frank DeRosa & His D Men (58)	*0.0*
Big Guitar—Irving Ashby (58)	*0.0*
Big Guitar—David Hill (58)	*0.0*

Peter DeROSE ▶ 906 (9) HOF	**4890**
Deep Purple—Nino Tempo & April Stevens (63)	*7500*
Deep Purple—Donny And Marie Osmond (75)	*1422*
Deep Purple—Billy Ward And His Dominoes (57)	*528*
Have You Ever Been Lonely—Jerry Cooper & The Johnny Guarnieri Quintet (55)	*192*
Have You Ever Been Lonely (Have You Ever Been Blue)—Caravelles (64)	*72*
Have You Ever Been Lonely (Have You Ever Been Blue)—Teresa Brewer (60)	*44*
Nightfall—Al Hibbler (56)	13
Have You Ever Been Lonely (Have You Ever Been Blue)—Karen Chandler (55)	*12*
Have You Ever Been Lonely (Have You Ever Been Blue)—Jaye P. Morgan (55)	*0.0*
Michael DEROSIER ▶ 4712 (2)	**433**
Barracuda—Heart (77)	1624
Little Queen—Heart (77)	164
Earl DeROUEN ▶ 11732 (1)	**0.4**
Little Ghetto Boy—Donny Hathaway (72)	0.8
Candy DeROUGE [Wolfgang Detmann] ▶ 5788 (3)	**241**
Power Of Love—Laura Branigan (87)	*653*
The Power Of Love—Jennifer Rush (86)	*248*
The Power Of Love (You Are My Lady)—Air Supply (85)	*65*
Rachel De ROUGEMONT ▶ 8568 (1)	**46**
Cars With The Boom—L'Trimm (88)	232
Carl D'ERRICO ▶ 4030 (2)	**620**
It's My Life—Animals (65)	1231
I'm Gonna Make You Mine—Shadows Of Knight (66)	13
Rick DERRINGER [Rick Dean Zehringer, Richard Zehringer, Rick Zehringer] ▶ 2773 (5)	**1203**
Rock And Roll, Hoochie Koo—Rick Derringer (74)	831
Don't Worry Mother, Your Son's Heart Is Pure—McCoys (66)	227
Teenage Love Affair—Rick Derringer (74)	131
Let Me In—Derringer (76)	10
Don't Ever Say Goodbye—Rick Derringer (80)	8.9
—Vassilis Dertilis see: Billy ADAMS	
Michael Des BARRES ▶ 2729 (2)	**1237**
Obsession—Animotion (85)	2123
I Do What I Do—John Taylor (86)	527
Jeff DES ENFANTS ▶ 9236 (1)	**28**
Sailing Ships—Mesa (77)	140
Russ DeSALVO ▶ 2275 (2)	**1663**
If Wishes Came True—Sweet Sensation (90)	3587
Thinking Of You—Sa-Fire (89)	1403
Sugar Pie DeSANTO [Umpeylia Marema Balinton, Peylia Parham] ▶ 7957 (6)	**67**
I Surrender—Fontella Bass (66)	97
I Want To Know—Sugar Pie DeSanto (60)	48
Mountain Of Love—Billy Stewart (65)	24
Do I Make Myself Clear—Etta James & Sugar Pie Desanto (65)	7.2
Believe In Me Baby - Part 1—Jesse James (67)	4.3
Peak Of Love—Bobby McClure (66)	3.8
John DESAUTELS ▶ 5446 (3)	**288**
Love Theme From "Eyes Of Laura Mars" (Prisoner)—Barbra Streisand (78)	*513*
Prisoner (Captured By Your Eyes)—L.A. Jets (76)	*45*
Dancin' Thru The Night—L.A. Jets (76)	8.5
—Kenrick Des-Etages see: Lee VANDERBILT	
Jackie DeSHANNON [Sharon Lee Dain, Jackie Dee, Sharon Lee Myers] ▶ 325 (21) HOF	**11325**
Bette Davis Eyes—Kim Carnes (81)	8923
Dum Dum—Brenda Lee (61)	4104
Put A Little Love In Your Heart—Jackie DeShannon (69)	*3577*
Put A Little Love In Your Heart—Annie Lennox & Al Green (88)	*1389*
Heart In Hand—Brenda Lee (62)	1107
Come And Stay With Me—Marianne Faithfull (65)	614
(He's) The Great Imposter—Fleetwoods (61)	555
Love Will Find A Way—Jackie De Shannon (69)	529
When You Walk In The Room—Searchers (64)	*481*
Alone With You—Brenda Lee (64)	419
So Deep—Brenda Lee (62)	233
Brighton Hill—Jackie Deshannon (70)	207
Bad Water—Raeletts (71)	202
Tears From An Angel—Troy Shondell (61)	128
Don't Let The Flame Burn Out—Jackie Deshannon (77)	117
Vanilla Olay—Jackie Deshannon (72)	71
He's So Heavenly—Brenda Lee (63)	60
Breakaway—Tracey Ullman (84)	56
When You Walk In The Room—Jackie deShannon (64)	*47*
When You Walk In The Room—Paul Carrack (88)	*23*
When You Walk In The Room—Tight Fit (81)	*0.9*
Antoniette DESIMONE ▶ 11339 (1)	**2.2**
She Will Survive (Poland)—Bobby Vinton (82)	6.5
—Giovanni Alfredo De Simone see: Johnny DESMOND	
Johnny DESMOND [Giovanni Alfredo De Simone] ▶ 11796 (1)	**0.0**
Theme From "The Proud Ones"—Johnny Desmond (56)	*0.0*
Paul DESMOND [Paul Emil Breitenfield] ▶ 3162 (1)	**977**
Take Five—Dave Brubeck Quartet (61)	977
Alice DeSOTO [Alice Cohen] ▶ 9196 (1)	**29**
Look My Way—Vels (85)	87
Maximiano De SOUSA ▶ 6992 (3)	**123**
Madeira—Mitch Miller And His Orchestra (56)	*123*
Madeira—Ray Anthony (56)	*0.0*
Madeira—LeRoy Holmes & His Orchestra (56)	*0.0*
Barry DESPENZA ▶ 2117 (2)	**1850**
Can I Change My Mind—Tyrone Davis (68)	3123
Is It Something You've Got—Tyrone Davis (69)	577
Regis Gabriel DESPLANQUES ▶ 4719 (3)	**432**
Padre—Toni Arden (58)	*1727*
Padre—Valerie Carr (58)	*0.0*
Padre—Sarah Vaughan (58)	*0.0*
Norman DESROSIERS ▶ 7989 (1)	**66**
Try (Try To Fall In Love)—Cooker (74)	66
—Yves Dessca see: Yves-Jacques LAVOT	
—Leonard George DeStoppelaire see: Lenny DEE	
Jimmy DESTRI ▶ 7380 (1)	**99**
Atomic—Blondie (80)	298
Buddy DeSYLVA [George Gard DeSylva] ▶ 3022 (9) HOF	**1061**
Together—Connie Francis (61)	2968
Alabamy Bound—Les Paul and Mary Ford (55)	*84*
The Birth Of The Blues—Sammy Davis Jr. (55)	*58*
Best Things In Life Are Free—Richard Cannon (58)	20
It All Depends On You—Jerry Lewis (57)	19
So Blue—Vibrations (60)	19
If You Knew Susie—Johnston Brothers (55)	13
Alabamy Bound—Mulcays (55)	*0.0*
The Birth Of The Blues—Lenny Dee (55)	*0.0*
—George Gard DeSylva see: Buddy DeSYLVA	
—Wolfgang Detmann see: Candy DeROUGE	
—Marcella Detroit see: Marcy LEVY	
Helen DEUTSCH ▶ 6238 (2)	**191**
Take My Love—Eddie Fisher (55)	205
Hi-Lili, Hi-Lo—Richard Chamberlain (63)	*176*
—Henry John Deutschendorf Jr. see: John DENVER	
Drafi DEUTSCHER ▶ 8683 (1)	**43**
Marble Breaks And Iron Bends—Drafi (66)	170
Ian DEVANEY ▶ 2153 (4)	**1811**
All Around The World—Lisa Stansfield (90)	3201
You Can't Deny It—Lisa Stansfield (90)	830
Change—Lisa Stansfield (91)	756
This Is The Right Time—Lisa Stansfield (90)	646
Yvonne DEVANEY [Jean Dee, Yvonne McGowan] ▶ 4467 (2)	**487**
A Million And One—Dean Martin (66)	*369*
A Million And One—Vic Dana (66)	*118*
William DeVAUGHN ▶ 1233 (1)	**3624**
Be Thankful For What You Got—William Devaughn (74)	3624
Phil DeVAULT ▶ 7787 (1)	**75**
This Is Ponderous—2NU (90)	300
—Antonio DeVerdis-Mazzone see: Tony GREEN	
C.C. DeVILLE [Bruce Anthony Johannesson] ▶ 1177 (10)	**3772**
Every Rose Has Its Thorn—Poison (88)	4813
Unskinny Bop—Poison (90)	2869
Something To Believe In—Poison (90)	2063
Nothin' But A Good Time—Poison (88)	1314
Talk Dirty To Me—Poison (87)	1055
I Won't Forget You—Poison (87)	1051
Fallen Angel—Poison (88)	903
Life Goes On—Poison (91)	401
Ride The Wind—Poison (91)	377
I Want Action—Poison (87)	240
Willy DeVILLE [William Paul Borsey Jr.] ▶ 5857 (2)	**236**
I Must Be Dreaming—Giuffria (86)	220
Each Word's A Beat Of My Heart—Mink DeVille (84)	16
Antonio De VITA ▶ 5883 (2)	**233**
Softly, As I Leave You—Frank Sinatra (64)	*675*
Softly As I Leave You—Matt Monro (62)	*25*
Hank DeVITO ▶ 800 (1)	**5541**
Queen Of Hearts—Juice Newton (81)	5541
Ronnie DeVOE ▶ 3693 (1)	**733**
Do Me!—Bell Biv DeVoe (90)	2931
Frank DeVOL ▶ 1260 (7)	**3548**
The Happening—Supremes (67)	*6167*
Hush, Hush, Sweet Charlotte—Patti Page (65)	1760
Theme From My Three Sons—Lawrence Welk And His Orchestra (61)	*640*
The Happening—Herb Alpert & The Tijuana Brass (67)	*438*
The Blues From Kiss Me Deadly (I'd Rather Have The Blues)—Nat "King" Cole (55)	48
Lover Come Back—Doris Day (62)	1.3
(Theme From) My Three Sons—Bob Moore and His Orch. (61)	*0.0*
Barry De VORZON ▶ 424 (19)	**9514**
Theme From S.W.A.T.—Rhythm Heritage (75)	4799
Nadia's Theme (The Young And The Restless)—Barry De Vorzon and Perry Botkin, Jr. (76)	2470
Dreamin'—Johnny Burnette (60)	*2376*
I Wonder What She's Doing Tonight—Barry And The Tamerlanes (63)	845
Treasure Of Your Love—Eileen Rodgers (58)	598
Hey Little One—Dorsey Burnette (60)	*456*
Just Married—Marty Robbins (58)	416
How Is Julie?—Lettermen (62)	413
Hey Little One—Glen Campbell (68)	*335*
Down And Out In New York City—James Brown (73)	234
I Will Love You—Richard Chamberlain (63)	234
Dreamin'—John Schneider (82)	*169*
Roberta—Barry And The Tamerlanes (64)	77
Shy Girl—Cascades (63)	59
Hey Little One—J. Frank Wilson And The Cavaliers (64)	*51*
Bless The Beasts And Children—Carpenters (71)	*39*
Bless The Beasts And Children—Barry De Vorzon & Perry Botkin, Jr. (77)	*20*
Girls—Johnny Burnette (61)	18
The Brightest Smile In Town—Ray Charles And His Orchestra (63)	6.8
John DeVRIES ▶ 9429 (2)	**24**
Something Wonderful Happens In Summer—Frank Sinatra (57)	46
Oh! Look At Me Now—Modernaires (57)	1.9
Anton DE WAAL [George Charles Gunn] ▶ 9545 (2)	**22**
Kwela Kwela—Bill Hayes (55)	34
Zambezi—Lou Busch and His Orchestra (55)	26
Robert DEWALD ▶ 9313 (1)	**27**
I'm Not Your Man—Tommy Conwell And The Young Rumblers (88)	80
—Autry DeWalt see: Jr. WALKER	
—Allison Dewar see: Scott TURNER	
James DEWAR ▶ 9276 (1)	**27**
Caledonia—Robin Trower (76)	55
—Sidney DeWayne see: Sid JOHNSON	
—Daddy Dewdrop see: Dick MONDA	
Mohandas DeWESE [Kool Moe Dee] ▶ 6573 (2)	**154**
Wild, Wild West—Kool Moe Dee (88)	142
Go See The Doctor—Kool Moe Dee (87)	13
Nicholas DEWEY ▶ 3001 (1)	**1073**
Runaway—Jefferson Starship (78)	1073
Ray DEWEY ▶ 10198 (1)	**11**
Magic Man—Robert Winters & Fall (81)	45
Lewis DeWITT ▶ 1809 (1)	**2283**
Flowers On The Wall—Statler Brothers (65)	2283
Frank De WULF ▶ 8993 (1)	**34**
Crash (Have Some Fun)—TKA (90)	68

Al DEXTER [Clarence Albert Poindexter] ▶ 7025 (2)	**121**
Too Late To Worry - Too Blue To Cry—Glen Campbell (62)	*109*
Too Late To Worry, Too Blue To Cry—Ronnie Milsap (75)	*12*
Fred DEXTER ▶ 9556 (2)	**21**
Drive In Show—Eddie Cochran (57)	17
Paper Roses—Lola Dee (55)	13
John DEXTER ▶ 4698 (2)	**436**
Heaven In Your Eyes—Loverboy (86)	1186
We Can Last Forever—Chicago (89)	279
Richard DEY ▶ 3390 (1)	**870**
Just Like Me—Paul Revere And The Raiders Featuring Mark Lindsay (65)	1739
Dennis DeYOUNG ▶ 90 (21)	**26261**
Babe—Styx (79)	6765
Mr. Roboto—Styx (83)	4156
The Best Of Times—Styx (81)	3282
Lady—Styx (74)	2262
Come Sail Away—Styx (77)	2096
Show Me The Way—Styx (90)	1997
Don't Let It End—Styx (83)	1707
Desert Moon—Dennis DeYoung (84)	1375
Why Me—Styx (79)	807
Love At First Sight—Styx (91)	751
Lorelei—Styx (76)	614
Music Time—Styx (84)	308
Mademoiselle—Styx (76)	304
Call Me—Dennis DeYoung (86)	243
High Time—Styx (83)	197
Nothing Ever Goes As Planned—Styx (81)	166
Borrowed Time—Styx (80)	120
Best Thing—Styx (72)	57
Don't Wait For Heroes—Dennis DeYoung (84)	49
You Need Love—Styx (75)	28
This Is The Time—Dennis DeYoung (86)	26
Guy D'HARDELOT [Helen Guy, Helen Rhodes] ▶ 9586 (1)	**21**
One Love, One Heart—Four Coins (59)	62
David DIAMOND ▶ 5525 (2)	**274**
Switchin' To Glide—Kings (80)	548
This Beat Goes On—Kings (80)	0.0
David Samuel DIAMOND ▶ 8289 (1)	**55**
Sex (I'm A...)—Berlin (83)	166
Gregg DIAMOND ▶ 913 (3)	**4840**
More, More, More (Pt. 1)—Andrea True Connection (76)	4619
N.Y., You Got Me Dancing—Andrea True Connection (77)	193
Party Line—Andrea True Connection (76)	27
James DIAMOND ▶ 9767 (1)	**17**
Little Suzi—Tesla (87)	34
—Janey Diamond see: Jayney KLIMEK	
Joel DIAMOND ▶ 8933 (2)	**36**
Like A Sunday Morning—Lana Cantrell (75)	69
Calico—Tommy James (73)	4.3
Keith DIAMOND [Keith Vincent Constantine Alexander] ▶ 829 (8)	**5327**
Caribbean Queen (No More Love On The Run)—Billy Ocean (84)	4341
Loverboy—Billy Ocean (84)	2995
Suddenly—Billy Ocean (85)	2464
Object Of My Desire—Starpoint (85)	913
Mystery Lady—Billy Ocean (85)	617
He'll Never Love You (Like I Do)—Freddie Jackson (85)	531
Restless—Starpoint (86)	288
When Love Cries—Donna Summer (91)	32
Lee DIAMOND ▶ 1145 (4)	**3880**
Tell It Like It Is—Aaron Neville (66)	*6327*
Tell It Like It Is—Heart (80)	*1344*
Tell It Like It Is—Andy Williams (76)	*63*
She Took You For A Ride—Aaron Neville (67)	25
Martin DIAMOND ▶ 8748 (1)	**40**
Fool Of The Year—Georgia Gibbs (56)	81
Max DIAMOND [Al Perton] ▶ 4658 (1)	**444**
My Boomerang Won't Come Back—Charlie Drake (61)	888
Mike DIAMOND ▶ 7456 (2)	**95**
Hey Ladies—Beastie Boys (89)	302
Brass Monkey—Beastie Boys (87)	278
Neil DIAMOND ▶ 6 (68) HOF	**86693**
I'm A Believer—Monkees (66)	*13324*

You Don't Bring Me Flowers—Barbra & Neil (78)	6538
A Little Bit Me, A Little Bit You—Monkees (67)	6085
Cracklin' Rosie—Neil Diamond (70)	*5687*
Song Sung Blue—Neil Diamond (72)	5232
Love On The Rocks—Neil Diamond (80)	4576
Sweet Caroline (Good Times Never Seemed So Good)—Neil Diamond (69)	*4390*
Holly Holy—Neil Diamond (69)	*3606*
Red Red Wine—UB40 (88)	*3303*
I Am...I Said—Neil Diamond (71)	2794
Longfellow Serenade—Neil Diamond (74)	2467
Cherry, Cherry—Neil Diamond (66)	*2434*
Heartlight—Neil Diamond (82)	2132
Girl, You'll Be A Woman Soon—Neil Diamond (67)	1964
Hello Again—Neil Diamond (81)	1704
Thank The Lord For The Night Time—Neil Diamond (67)	1615
America—Neil Diamond (81)	1556
Desiree—Neil Diamond (77)	1485
September Morn'—Neil Diamond (79)	1451
Brother Love's Travelling Salvation Show—Neil Diamond (69)	1305
Yesterday's Songs—Neil Diamond (81)	1289
Play Me—Neil Diamond (72)	1261
Stones—Neil Diamond (72)	1248
Kentucky Woman—Neil Diamond (67)	*1124*
Walk On Water—Neil Diamond (72)	1119
Solitary Man—Neil Diamond (70)	*1076*
If You Know What I Mean—Neil Diamond (76)	1025
I Got The Feelin' (Oh No No)—Neil Diamond (66)	955
Shilo—Neil Diamond (70)	947
Sunday And Me—Jay & The Americans (65)	942
Forever In Blue Jeans—Neil Diamond (79)	920
You Got To Me—Neil Diamond (67)	867
Kentucky Woman—Deep Purple (68)	*648*
"Cherry Cherry" From Hot August Night—Neil Diamond (73)	*632*
And The Grass Won't Pay No Mind—Mark Lindsay (70)	626
Be—Neil Diamond (73)	605
Soolaimon (African Trilogy II)—Neil Diamond (70)	602
Do It—Neil Diamond (70)	593
If I Never Knew Your Name—Vic Dana (70)	584
Red Red Wine—UB40 (84)	*552*
I'm Alive—Neil Diamond (83)	490
On The Way To The Sky—Neil Diamond (82)	460
Solitary Man—Neil Diamond (66)	*433*
Sweet Caroline (Good Times Never Seemed So Good)—Bobby Womack & Peace (72)	*430*
Be Mine Tonight—Neil Diamond (82)	418
Sunflower—Glen Campbell (77)	418
My Babe—Ronnie Dove (67)	385
I'm A Believer—Neil Diamond (71)	*352*
Brooklyn Roads—Neil Diamond (68)	349
Ten Lonely Guys—Pat Boone (62)	*317*
Sunday Sun—Neil Diamond (68)	294
I've Been This Way Before—Neil Diamond (75)	281
Two-Bit Manchild—Neil Diamond (68)	276
Headed For The Future—Neil Diamond (86)	262
Red Red Wine—Neil Diamond (68)	*221*
Skybird—Neil Diamond (74)	212
Don't Think...Feel—Neil Diamond (76)	191
Say Maybe—Neil Diamond (79)	151
Front Page Story—Neil Diamond (83)	147
Done Too Soon—Neil Diamond (71)	137
Holly Holy—Jr. Walker & The All Stars (70)	*114*
Turn Around—Neil Diamond (84)	110
The Long Way Home—Neil Diamond (73)	98
Ten Lonely Guys—Ten Broken Hearts (62)	*81*
Red Red Wine—Vic Dana (70)	*69*
Cracklin' Rosie—Stars On 45 (81)	*12*
Solitary Man—T.G. Sheppard (76)	*5.7*
Crunchy Granola Suite—Neil Diamond (72)	0.0
Oramay DIAMOND ▶ 5567 (5)	**271**
The Wall—Patti Page (57)	*244*
She's Got Everything—Essex Featuring Anita Humes (63)	219
Next Stop Paradise—Teddy Randazzo (57)	163
The Wall—Eileen Rodgers (57)	*77*
The Wall—Brook Benton (57)	*0.0*
Steve DIAMOND ▶ 5178 (1)	**329**
I've Got A Rock N' Roll Heart—Eric Clapton (83)	988
Inez DIAZ ▶ 4902 (1)	**385**

Temptation—Corina (91)	1924
Manu DIBANGO [Emmanuel N'Djoke Dibango, Odilien Dibango] ▶ 3098 (2)	**1010**
Soul Makossa—Manu Dibango (73)	*625*
Soul Makossa—Afrique (73)	*386*
Peter DIBBENS ▶ 8937 (2)	**36**
Shady Lady—Shepstone & Dibbens (73)	53
Please Tell Him That I Said Hello—Debbie Campbell (75)	19
Eduardo DI CAPUA ▶ 1119 (4)	**3955**
It's Now Or Never—Elvis Presley With The Jordanaires (60)	*10781*
It's Now Or Never—John Schneider (81)	*781*
Ma Ma Ma Marie—Gaylords (58)	*240*
Oh Marie—Village Stompers (64)	*41*
—Bruno Ravel DiCecco see: Bruno RAVEL	
Pat DICESARE ▶ 11299 (1)	**2.4**
I'm Spinning—Kripp Johnson (57)	4.7
Richard V. DI CICCO [Richie Rome] ▶ 3583 (3)	**777**
Bobby Sox To Stockings—Frankie Avalon (59)	2192
The Best Disco In Town—Ritchie Family (76)	*92*
The Best Disco In Town—Ritchie Family (76)	*92*
Derek DICK ▶ 9795 (1)	**17**
Kayleigh—Marillion (85)	84
George DICK ▶ 10133 (1)	**12**
She's Fly—Tony Terry (87)	49
—Paul Revere Dick see: Paul REVERE	
—Dicken see: Jeffrey Robert PAIN	
—B.B. Dickerson see: Morris DICKERSON	
Clyde DICKERSON ▶ 10704 (1)	**6.0**
Jupiter-C—Pat and the Satellites (59)	18
Dez DICKERSON [Desmond D'Andrea Dickerson] ▶ 9813 (1)	**17**
Cool (Part 1)—Time (82)	33
Dub DICKERSON ▶ 3097 (2)	**1010**
Stood Up—Ricky Nelson (57)	1972
Dear Love—Sonny James (57)	24
Morris DICKERSON [Morris Dewayne Dickerson, B.B. Dickerson] ▶ 1242 (18)	**3614**
Spill The Wine—Eric Burdon And War (70)	*5207*
The Cisco Kid—War (73)	4378
Why Can't We Be Friends?—War (75)	3006
Low Rider—War (75)	2369
Slippin' Into Darkness—War (71)	*2076*
The World Is A Ghetto—War (72)	1817
Gypsy Man—War (73)	1659
Summer—War (76)	1559
Me And Baby Brother—War (73)	1513
All Day Music—War (71)	704
Ballero—War (74)	472
They Can't Take Away Our Music—Eric Burdon And War Featuring Sharon Scott And The Beautiful New Born Children Of Southern California (70)	418
Spill The Wine—Isley Brothers (71)	*409*
Galaxy—War (77)	325
L.A. Sunshine—War (77)	291
Low Rider (On The Boulevard)—Latin Alliance (91)	121
Lonely Feelin'—War (71)	74
Slipping Into Darkness—Ramsey Lewis (72)	*35*
Robert DICKERSON ▶ 7997 (1)	**66**
Contact—Edwin Starr (79)	198
Hal DICKINSON ▶ 9788 (1)	**17**
Don't Let The Kiddy Geddin—Kitty Kallen (54)	51
Vince DICOLA ▶ 3706 (3)	**727**
Far From Over—Frank Stallone (83)	1363
Heart's On Fire—John Cafferty (86)	99
Darlin'—Frank Stallone (84)	38
—Bo Diddley see: Elias McDANIEL	
Howard DIETZ ▶ 10684 (1) HOF	**6.1**
Magic Moment—Nat King Cole (61)	12
Jack DIÉVAL ▶ 3051 (2)	**1034**
The Way Of Love—Cher (72)	*2031*
The Way Of Love—Kathy Kirby (65)	*38*
Chris DIFFORD ▶ 3029 (4)	**1054**
Hourglass—Squeeze (87)	936
One Good Reason—Paul Carrack (88)	465
853-5937—Squeeze (87)	431
Tempted—Squeeze (81)	277
—Joseph DiFrancesco see: Joey DAY	

Paul DIFRANCO ▶ 3478 (1)	**825**
Life Is A Rock (But The Radio Rolled Me)—Reunion (74)	1650
John DIGAUDIO ▶ 9946 (1)	**15**
Don't Run My Life—Spys (82)	73
James Leon DIGGS ▶ 6220 (1)	**192**
Temptation 'Bout To Get Me—Knight Bros. (65)	192
—Julie DiGiovanni see: Julie DeJOHN	
—Leo DiGiovanni see: Leo DeJOHN	
—Mary Ann DiGiovanni see: Dux DeJOHN	
Joel DIGREGORIO ▶ 3293 (4)	**909**
The Devil Went Down To Georgia—Charlie Daniels Band (79)	*3303*
In America—Charlie Daniels Band (80)	1335
The Legend Of Wooley Swamp—Charlie Daniels Band (80)	633
The Devil Came Up To Michigan—K.M.C. Kru (91)	*243*
Matt DIKE ▶ 1853 (10)	**2197**
Wild Thing—Tone Loc (88)	2613
Funky Cold Medina—Tone Loc (89)	2425
Bust A Move—Young M.C. (89)	1887
Principal's Office—Young M.C. (89)	445
Hey Ladies—Beastie Boys (89)	302
I Come Off—Young M.C. (90)	147
Summer Vacation—Party (90)	*113*
Pick Up The Pace 1990—Young M.C. (90)	32
Shake It (Like A White Girl)—Jesse Jaymes (91)	25
Summer Vacation—Party (91)	*20*
Eldo DI LAZZARO ▶ 8076 (2)	**63**
Roman Guitar (Chitarra Romana)—Lou Monte (57)	157
The Woodpecker Song—Bobby Rydell (63)	32
Amber DILENA ▶ 8962 (1)	**35**
Ready Or Not—Helen Reddy (78)	70
Danny DILL [Horace Eldred Dill] ▶ 2757 (7)	**1217**
Detroit City—Bobby Bare (63)	*1484*
Detroit City—Tom Jones (67)	*748*
So Wrong—Patsy Cline (62)	182
Partners—Jim Reeves (59)	29
Detroit City—Solomon Burke (67)	*17*
Detroit City No. 2—Ben Colder (63)	*4.9*
Detroit City—Dean Martin (70)	*1.3*
—Horace Eldred Dill see: Danny DILL	
Moses DILLARD ▶ 9885 (1)	**16**
We Fell In Love While Dancing—Bill Brandon (78)	31
Clifton DILLON ▶ 8303 (1)	**55**
Housecall—Shabba Ranks (91)	329
John DILLON ▶ 4943 (2)	**377**
If You Wanna Get To Heaven—Ozark Mountain Daredevils (74)	684
Take You Tonight—Ozark Mountain Daredevils (80)	104
Will DILLON ▶ 10574 (1)	**7.1**
I Want A Girl—Bruce Hayes with Mary Mayo (60)	*14*
Sam DIMAGGIO ▶ 10504 (1)	**7.8**
Solo—Billy Sans (71)	16
Danny DIMINNO ▶ 1465 (8)	**2964**
Return To Me—Dean Martin (58)	5132
I Can't Get You Out Of My Heart—Al Martino (59)	*609*
A Voice In The Choir—Al Martino (67)	109
From The Bottom Of My Heart (Dammi, Dammi, Dammi)—Dean Martin (62)	41
Dearest (Cara)—Al Martino (60)	35
Ole Mummer's Strut—Nu Tornados (59)	13
I Can't Get You Out Of My Heart—Al Martino (64)	*1.5*
I Can't Get You Out Of My Heart—Bob Carroll (59)	*0.0*
Frank DIMINO ▶ 9290 (2)	**27**
That Magic Touch—Angel (77)	78
Flying With Broken Wings (Without You)—Angel (78)	3.6
Vince DIMIRCO ▶ 3302 (1)	**908**
Up The Ladder To The Roof—Supremes (70)	1815
Dion DIMUCCI ▶ 345 (11)	**10859**
Runaround Sue—Dion (61)	*10242*
Lovers Who Wander—Dion (62)	2550
Donna The Prima Donna—Dion (Di Muci) (63)	2208
Little Diane—Dion (62)	1399
Love Came To Me—Dion (62)	1229
Runaround Sue—Leif Garrett (77)	*949*
Sandy—Dion (63)	851
(I Was) Born To Cry—Dion (62)	384
Your Own Back Yard—Dion (70)	94
Runaround Sue—Four Preps (62)	*24*
Runaround Sue—Jive Bunny & The Mastermixers (90)	*6.7*
Mario DINAPOLI ▶ 9053 (1)	**32**
She's Got To Be A Saint—Ray Price (73)	65
—Joseph DiNicola see: Joey DEE	
Pat DINIZIO ▶ 4614 (3)	**451**
A Girl Like You—Smithereens (89)	422
Blues Before And After—Smithereens (90)	20
Only A Memory—Smithereens (88)	8.0
—Ella Lucille Dinning see: Lou DINNING	
—Eugenia Joy Dinning see: Jean DINNING	
Jean DINNING [Eugenia Joy Dinning, Jean Surrey] ▶ 1230 (3)	**3630**
Teen Angel—Mark Dinning (59)	*6926*
A Star Is Born (A Love Has Died)—Mark Dinning (60)	247
Teen Angel—Wednesday (74)	*88*
Lou DINNING [Ella Lucille Dinning, Ella Robertson] ▶ 4534 (2)	**469**
Not One Minute More—Della Reese (59)	1216
Step By Step, Little By Little—Anita Bryant (62)	63
Paul DINO ▶ 5028 (1)	**357**
Ginnie Bell—Paul Dino (61)	357
Ralph DINO [Ralph Palladino] ▶ 3918 (1)	**657**
Do What You Do—Jermaine Jackson (84)	1314
Anthony D'IORIO ▶ 10748 (1)	**5.6**
Questions—Bang (72)	17
Alfred DIPAOLA ▶ 4011 (1)	**623**
Lonely Teenager—Dion (60)	1868
Vincenzo DI PAOLA ▶ 5100 (4)	**343**
Come Prima—Tony Dallara (58)	*636*
Come Prima—Polly Bergen (58)	*524*
Come Prima—Luciano Tajoli (58)	*0.0*
Come Prima—Domenico Modugno (58)	*0.0*
Bob DIPIERO ▶ 9456 (1)	**23**
American Made—Oak Ridge Boys (83)	47
—Ruggiero Eugenio di Rodolpho Colombo see: Russ COLUMBO	
Mack DISCANT ▶ 3716 (8)	**721**
Theme From "A Summer Place"—Lettermen (65)	*1085*
Theme from A Summer Place—Dick Roman (62)	*274*
Bel Sante—Mitch Miller with His Orch. & Chorus (55)	40
Your Kisses Kill Me—Eydie Gorme (57)	31
Johnny Casanova—Jaye P. Morgan (56)	6.7
Theme From "A Summer Place"—Lolita (61)	*5.4*
Leave It To Love—Sarah Vaughan (57)	3.2
Livin' Dangerously—McGuire Sisters (60)	1.5
Enrique Santos DISCEPOLO ▶ 9918 (1)	**15**
Uno—Tony Martin (54)	45
Alan DISCHEL ▶ 9794 (2)	**17**
Girl (You Captivate Me)—? & The Mysterians (67)	29
Just Another Face—Blades Of Grass (67)	4.8
Kevin DISIMONE ▶ 10124 (1)	**12**
Take Away—Big Ric (83)	37
Nicholas DISTEFANO ▶ 8679 (1)	**43**
Shelter Me—Joe Cocker (86)	43
Sacha DISTEL ▶ 4680 (2)	**439**
The Good Life—Tony Bennett (63)	*875*
The Good Life—Kathy Keegan (63)	*2.3*
Andrew DITARANTO ▶ 10796 (2)	**5.3**
Let Me Sleep Alone—Cugini (79)	15
School's Back—Philadelphia (77)	0.9
Martin DITCHAM ▶ 3207 (1)	**952**
The Sweetest Taboo—Sade (85)	1904
Larry DI TOMASO ▶ 3919 (1)	**657**
Do What You Do—Jermaine Jackson (84)	1314
Joe DIXIE [Hans Drechsler] ▶ 10350 (5)	**9.7**
The Phonograph Song—Guy Lombardo And His Royal Canadians (56)	*19*
The Phonograph Song (Our Melody)—Billy May & His Orchestra (56)	*19*
The Phonograph Song (Our Melody)—Art Mooney & His Orchestra (56)	*0.0*
The Phonograph Song (Our Melody)—Lou Stein (56)	*0.0*
Whistlin' Willie (Our Melody)—Chordettes (56)	*0.0*
Chris DIXON ▶ 9283 (1)	**27**
Want You For My Girlfriend—4 By Four (87)	54
David George DIXON ▶ 4379 (1)	**509**
I Dig Rock And Roll Music—Peter, Paul & Mary (67)	1527
David Lincoln DIXON ▶ 5944 (1)	**225**
Tell Me Something—Indecent Obsession (90)	449
—Eugene Dixon see: Gene CHANDLER	
Jack DIXON ▶ 9568 (2)	**21**
That's Why I Cry—Buddy Knox (58)	11
Teasable, Pleasable You—Buddy Knox (59)	10
Jerry DIXON ▶ 2470 (8)	**1454**
Heaven—Warrant (89)	3557
I Saw Red—Warrant (90)	1193
Cherry Pie—Warrant (90)	992
Sometimes She Cries—Warrant (89)	824
Down Boys—Warrant (89)	567
Uncle Tom's Cabin—Warrant (91)	71
Blind Faith—Warrant (91)	40
Big Talk—Warrant (89)	23
Julius DIXON [Julius E. Dixson Sr.] ▶ 1300 (11)	**3407**
Lollipop—Chordettes (58)	*3626*
Dim, Dim The Lights (I Want Some Atmosphere)—Bill Haley And His Comets (54)	*1605*
Clouds—Spacemen (59)	603
Lollipop—Ronald And Ruby (58)	*224*
It Hurts To Be In Love—Annie Laurie (57)	47
Teenage Meeting (Gonna Rock It Up Right)—Don Cornell (56)	*24*
Reason—5 Chanels (58)	21
Love's Burning Fire—Beverly Ann Gibson (59)	19
Love's A Hurting Game—Ivory Joe Hunter (57)	12
Teenage Meeting (Gonna Rock It Up Right)—Dave Appell & His Applejacks (56)	*0.0*
Dim, Dim The Lights (I Want Some Atmosphere)—Four Tophatters (54)	*0.0*
Luther DIXON [Barney Williams] ▶ 124 (45)	**21199**
Soldier Boy—Shirelles (62)	8622
A Hundred Pounds Of Clay—Gene McDaniels (61)	7256
Sixteen Candles—Crests (58)	*5437*
Baby It's You—Smith (69)	*4062*
Mama Said—Shirelles (61)	2972
Baby It's You—Shirelles (61)	*2409*
Why Baby Why—Pat Boone (57)	2033
Love Land—Charles Wright And The Watts 103rd Street Rhythm Band (70)	1504
Soul Serenade—Willie Mitchell (68)	*1399*
Just Born (To Be Your Baby)—Perry Como (57)	1363
With This Ring—Platters (67)	1217
Irresistible You—Bobby Darin (61)	*1175*
I Love You 1000 Times—Platters (66)	858
Tonight's The Night—Shirelles (60)	*817*
A Tear—Gene McDaniels (61)	650
Welcome Home Baby—Shirelles (62)	648
I Don't Want To Cry—Chuck Jackson (61)	*610*
Angel Smile—Nat "King" Cole (57)	553
Human—Tommy Hunt (61)	463
Big Boss Man—Elvis Presley (67)	*425*
I Don't Wanna Cry—Ronnie Dyson (70)	*414*
Funk Factory—Wilson Pickett (72)	305
Beach Party—King Curtis And The Noble Knights (62)	267
Don't Believe Him, Donna—Lenny Miles (60)	263
Bahama Mama—Four Aces (57)	248
(It Never Happens) In Real Life—Chuck Jackson (61)	209
So Close—Brook Benton (59)	192
Soul Serenade—King Curtis (64)	*183*
Thank You Baby—Shirelles (64)	118
Irresistable You—Bobby Peterson (60)	*112*
Tonight's The Night—Chiffons (60)	*68*
I Don't Want To Cry—Ruby Winters (69)	*57*
Too Experienced—Eddie Lovette (69)	57
Little Gypsy—Ames Brothers (58)	56
Big Boss Man—Jimmy Reed (61)	*39*
Boys—Beatles (65)	37
The Jazz In You—Gloria Lynne (61)	26
Eternally—Chantels (63)	22
Soul Hootenanny Pt. 1—Gene Chandler (64)	*17*
In Between Tears—Lenny Miles (61)	13
Never Let Me Go—Lloyd Price And His Orchestra (60)	12
Midnight—Hugo Winterhalter's Orch. & Chorus (58)	12
Lovin' Up A Storm—Jerry Lee Lewis (59)	12
Somebody New—Chuck Jackson (64)	6.7
16 Candles—Fred Parris & The Five Satins (82)	*4.8*
Mort DIXON ▶ 4917 (3) HOF	**382**
I'll Take Care Of Your Cares—Frankie Laine (67)	560
River Stay 'Way From My Door—Frank Sinatra (60)	201
Bye Bye Blackbird—Art Mooney And His Orchestra (59)	3.9

Reather DIXON ▶ 4354 (2)	**514**
Mr Lee—Bobbettes (57)	*2273*
I Shot Mr Lee—Bobbettes (60)	*297*
Willie DIXON ▶ 760 (15) HOF	**5764**
Seventh Son—Johnny Rivers (65)	2423
Little Red Rooster—Sam Cooke (63)	1404
For My Baby—Brook Benton (61)	549
Wang Dang Doodle—Ko Ko Taylor (66)	*463*
I Just Want To Make Love To You—Foghat (77)	*412*
N-E-R-V-O-U-S!—Ian Whitcomb (65)	304
You Can't Judge A Book By The Cover— Bo Diddley (62)	282
Wang Dang Doodle—Pointer Sisters (73)	*177*
Doncha' Think It's Time—Elvis Presley (58)	159
It Do Me So Good—Ann-Margret (61)	103
I'm Your Hoochie Cooche Man—Dion Di Muci (64)	*71*
Spoonful—Etta & Harvey (60)	40
I Just Want To Make Love To You—Foghat (72)	*36*
I'm Your Hoochie Cooche Man (Part 1)— Jimmy Smith (66)	*15*
My Babe—Roy Head And The Traits (66)	0.9
Wylie DIXON ▶ 8927 (1)	**36**
You Just Can't Win (By Making The Same Mistake)— Gene & Jerry (70)	108
—DJ Eddie F see: Edward FERRELL	
—D J Pogo see: Simone Antoinette JOHNSON	
—D J Quik see: David Marvin BLAKE	
—DJ Shodal see: Towa TEI	
—Burton D'Lugoff see: Burt LONG	
Gene DOBBINS ▶ 8166 (1)	**60**
Easy As Pie—Billy "Crash" Craddock (75)	179
Georgia DOBBINS ▶ 1190 (5)	**3729**
Mashed Potato Time—Dee Dee Sharp (62)	8768
Please Mr. Postman—Marvelettes (61)	*7831*
Please Mr. Postman—Carpenters (74)	*4500*
Please Mr. Postman—Gentle Persuasion (83)	*45*
Please Mr. Postman—Beatles (64)	*6.4*
Shelley DOBBINS ▶ 5098 (1)	**343**
Non Dimenticar (Don't Forget)—Nat "King" Cole (58)	1029
—Conrad K. Dober see: Con CONRAD	
Carl DOBKINS Jr ▶ 7466 (1)	**94**
If You Don't Want My Lovin'— Carl Dobkins, Jr. (59)	94
Bill DOBSLAW ▶ 8923 (1)	**36**
Little Donna—Rivieras (2) (64)	36
Bonnie DOBSON ▶ 6548 (1)	**158**
Morning Dew—Lulu (68)	316
Bonnie DODD ▶ 4229 (1)	**554**
Be Careful Of Stones That You Throw—Dion (63)	554
Dorothy DODD ▶ 6603 (1)	**153**
Granada—Frank Sinatra (61)	305
—Ivan Wesley Dodd see: Jimmie DODD	
Jimmie DODD [Ivan Wesley Dodd] ▶ 4602 (1)	**453**
Lonely Guitar—Annette (59)	453
Bryan DODDS ▶ 9017 (1)	**33**
Fantastic Voyage—Lakeside (80)	296
Malcolm DODDS [Sibelius Williams] ▶ 3526 (2)	**798**
Two Tickets To Paradise—Brook Benton (63)	686
Hit Record—Brook Benton (62)	455
Steve DODGE ▶ 6423 (1)	**172**
Come On, React!—Fireballs (68)	172
Larry DODSON ▶ 6885 (9)	**131**
Shake Your Rump To The Funk—Bar-Kays (76)	593
Move Your Boogie Body—Bar-Kays (79)	270
Today Is The Day—Bar-Kays (80)	150
Freakshow On The Dance Floor—Bar-Kays (84)	79
Too Hot To Stop—Bar-Kays (77)	36
Hit And Run—Bar-Kays (81)	23
Boogie Body Land—Bar-Kays (81)	23
Let's Have Some Fun—Bar-Kays (78)	8.9
Shine—Bar-Kays (79)	7.7
Rich DODSON ▶ 1769 (2)	**2345**
Sweet City Woman—Stampeders (71)	2061
Devil You—Stampeders (71)	285
Venus DODSON ▶ 10869 (1)	**4.7**
Girls (Part I)—Moments And Whatnauts (75)	24
Franz DOELLE ▶ 1783 (5)	**2329**
When The White Lilacs Bloom Again— Helmut Zacharias And His Magic Violins (56)	*1098*
When The White Lilacs Bloom Again— Billy Vaughn and His Orchestra (56)	*605*
When The White Lilacs Bloom Again— Florian Zabach (56)	*295*
When The White Lilacs Bloom Again— Lawrence Welk And His Sparkling Strings (56)	*195*
When The White Lilacs Bloom Again— LeRoy Holmes And His Orchestra (56)	*137*
Craig DOERGE ▶ 3778 (3)	**702**
Cried Like A Baby—Bobby Sherman (71)	1369
Out Of The Darkness— David Crosby / Graham Nash (76)	34
Hold On, Hold Out—Jackson Browne (80)	13
Bill DOGGETT ▶ 2319 (7)	**1598**
Honky Tonk (Pts. 1 & 2)—Bill Doggett (56)	*5649*
Honky Tonk - Part 1—James Brown Soul Train (72)	*437*
Honky Tonk (Part 2)—Bill Doggett (61)	*113*
Honky Tonk '65—Lonnie Mack (65)	*77*
(Let's Do) The Hully Gully Twist—Bill Doggett (60)	41
Never Trust A Woman—B.B. King (64)	17
Honky Tonk (pt. 2)— Rusty Bryant & The Carolyn Club Band (56)	*0.0*
Ray DOGGETT ▶ 8016 (1)	**65**
That Crazy Feeling—Kenneth Rogers (58)	65
Ned DOHENY ▶ 6768 (2)	**139**
What Cha' Gonna Do For Me—Chaka Khan (81)	255
Get It Up—Ben E. King and AWB (77)	11
Dennis DOHERTY ▶ 2526 (2)	**1415**
I Saw Her Again—Mamas & The Papas (66)	2615
For The Love Of Ivy—Mamas & The Papas (68)	214
Don DOKKEN ▶ 5901 (4)	**231**
In My Dreams—Party (91)	610
Alone Again—Dokken (85)	164
Burning Like A Flame—Dokken (87)	82
In My Dreams—Dokken (86)	68
John DOLAN ▶ 5029 (2)	**357**
God, Country And My Baby—Johnny Burnette (61)	*714*
God Country And My Baby—Chico Holiday (61)	*0.0*
Thomas DOLBY [Thomas Morgan Robertson] ▶ 1960 (3)	**2050**
She Blinded Me With Science—Thomas Dolby (83)	3507
Hyperactive—Thomas Dolby (84)	172
Europa And The Pirate Twins—Thomas Dolby (83)	125
Joe DOLCE ▶ 4537 (1)	**469**
Shaddap You Face—Joe Dolce (81)	469
Micky DOLENZ ▶ 7138 (2)	**114**
Don't Do It—Micky Dolenz (67)	114
Mommy And Daddy—Monkees (69)	0.0
Morris DOLLISON [Maurice Dollison, Cash McCall] ▶ 4275 (4)	**537**
Jealous Kind Of Fella—Garland Green (69)	810
Let Me Back In—Tyrone Davis (70)	318
When You Wake Up—Cash McCall (66)	26
I'm Satisfied—Otis Clay (66)	3.0
Norman DOLPH ▶ 3425 (2)	**853**
Life Is A Rock (But The Radio Rolled Me)— Reunion (74)	1650
Don't Stop Trying—Rodway (82)	56
John Grayton DOLPHIN [John Gray] ▶ 4202 (5)	**564**
Buzz Buzz Buzz—Hollywood Flames (57)	*936*
Jivin' Around—Al Casey Combo (62)	125
All Night Long—Sandy Nelson (62)	27
Jivin' Around (Pt. 2)—Ernie Freeman Combo (56)	13
Buzz Buzz Buzz—Rusty Draper (57)	*0.0*
Sam DOMINGO ▶ 9531 (1)	**22**
Baby Baby—Eighth Wonder (89)	44
Alberto DOMINGUEZ ▶ 2539 (1)	**1405**
Perfidia—Ventures (60)	1405
Fats DOMINO [Antoine Dominique Domino Jr.] ▶ 92 (71) HOF	**26166**
Ain't That A Shame—Pat Boone (55)	*6966*
I Hear You Knocking—Gale Storm (55)	*5135*
I'm In Love Again—Fats Domino (56)	*3481*
I Hear You Knocking—Dave Edmunds (70)	*3442*
I'm Walkin'—Fats Domino (57)	*2846*
Whole Lotta Loving—Fats Domino (58)	2302
Blue Monday—Fats Domino (56)	2195
Walking To New Orleans—Fats Domino (60)	2113
I Want To Walk You Home—Fats Domino (59)	2017
Be My Guest—Fats Domino (59)	1844
My Girl Josephine—Fats Domino (60)	*1293*
Three Nights A Week—Fats Domino (60)	1103
Let The Four Winds Blow—Fats Domino (61)	*1081*
I'm Ready—Fats Domino (59)	1028
Valley Of Tears—Fats Domino (57)	1025
I'm Walkin'—Ricky Nelson (57)	*939*
Bo Weevil—Teresa Brewer (56)	*908*
I'm Gonna Be A Wheel Some Day—Fats Domino (59)	900
Don't Come Knockin'—Fats Domino (60)	760
Ain't That A Shame!— 4 Seasons Featuring Frankie Valli (63)	*760*
It Keeps Rainin'—Fats Domino (61)	735
What A Price—Fats Domino (61)	733
My Girl Josephine—Jerry Jaye (67)	*721*
Ain't It A Shame—Fats Domino (55)	*665*
Country Boy—Fats Domino (60)	600
Shu Rah—Fats Domino (61)	516
It's You I Love—Fats Domino (57)	423
Ain't That A Shame—Cheap Trick (79)	*411*
Wait And See—Fats Domino (57)	406
Natural Born Lover—Fats Domino (60)	381
I'm In Love Again—Fontane Sisters (56)	*355*
Telling Lies—Fats Domino (59)	339
When I See You—Fats Domino (57)	328
I've Been Around—Fats Domino (59)	303
I Want You To Know—Fats Domino (57)	295
Let The Four Winds Blow—Roy Brown (57)	*280*
Fell In Love On Monday—Fats Domino (61)	275
Tell Me That You Love Me—Fats Domino (60)	274
Big Beat—Fats Domino (57)	269
So Long—Fats Domino (56)	245
Bo Weevil—Fats Domino (56)	*220*
There Goes (My Heart Again)—Fats Domino (63)	215
Please Don't Leave Me—Fontane Sisters (56)	213
My Real Name—Fats Domino (62)	203
I'm In Love Again—Rick Nelson (63)	*189*
Poor Me—Fats Domino (55)	*184*
Yes My Darling—Fats Domino (58)	141
Honey Chile—Fats Domino (56)	105
Before I Grow Too Old—Fats Domino (60)	92
Little Mary—Fats Domino (58)	72
No, No—Fats Domino (58)	60
I Still Love You—Fats Domino (57)	57
Nothing New (Same Old Thing)—Fats Domino (62)	52
Lazy Lady—Fats Domino (64)	32
I Hear You Knocking—Fats Domino (61)	*29*
Rockin' Bicycle—Fats Domino (61)	22
The Rooster Song—Fats Domino (57)	19
Don't You Know I Love You—Fats Domino (58)	18
Don't Blame It On Me—Fats Domino (56)	10
Ida Jane—Fats Domino (62)	8.4
I Just Cry—Fats Domino (61)	7.0
Young School Girl—Fats Domino (58)	3.3
Won't You Come On Back—Fats Domino (62)	2.8
Heartbreak Hill—Fats Domino (64)	1.9
Dance With Mr. Domino—Fats Domino (62)	1.3
If You Need Me—Fats Domino (60)	1.1
I Hear You Knocking—Smiley Lewis (55)	*0.0*
Ain't That A Shame—Ronnie Gaylord (55)	*0.0*
Bo Weevil—Bonnie Lou (56)	*0.0*
I'm Walkin'—Larry Storch (57)	*0.0*
Poor Me—Bill Carey (55)	*0.0*
—Kevin Michael Dompe see: Kevin HASKINS	
Luigi DONADIO ▶ 10902 (1)	**4.5**
Senza Mamma (With No One)—Connie Francis (60)	8.9
Pino DONAGGIO ▶ 2111 (3)	**1862**
You Don't Have To Say You Love Me— Dusty Springfield (66)	*4119*
You Don't Have To Say You Love Me— Elvis Presley (70)	*1432*
You Don't Have To Say You Love Me— Four Sonics (68)	*36*
—Tom Donahue see: Thomas COMAN	
—David R. Donaldson Jr. see: Dee ROBB	
Lou DONALDSON ▶ 10103 (1)	**13**
Alligator Bogaloo—Lou Donaldson (67)	13
—Tommy Donaldson see: Tommy DEE	
Walter DONALDSON ▶ 1736 (18) HOF	**2402**
Love Me Or Leave Me—Sammy Davis Jr. (55)	*1367*
My Mammy—Happenings (67)	1237
My Blue Heaven—Fats Domino (56)	*919*
Makin' Whoopee—Ray Charles (64)	469

Walter DONALDSON ► 1736 (18) HOF *Cont'd*	**2402**
Yes Sir That's My Baby—Ricky Nelson (60)	*465*
Little White Lies—Betty Johnson (57)	*176*
My Blue Heaven—Duane Eddy (61)	*155*
Yes Sir That's My Baby—Four Aces (57)	*20*
Yes Sir, That's My Baby— Julius Wechter & The Baja Marimba Band (68)	*15*
My Buddy—Eddie Harris (61)	12
My Blue Heaven—Bobby Day (60)	*10*
My Blue Heaven—String-A-Longs (62)	*5.8*
Yes Sir That's My Baby— Ralph Marterie And His Orchestra (56)	*5.7*
Carolina In The Morning—Mitch Miller & his "Sing Along With Mitch" Chorus (59)	3.9
Little White Lies—Kenjolairs (63)	*0.8*
Love Me Or Leave Me— Lawrence Welk & His Champagne Music (55)	*0.0*
Love Me Or Leave Me—Billy Eckstine (55)	*0.0*
Love Me Or Leave Me—Lena Horne (55)	*0.0*
Alfredo Do NASCIMENTO ► 5455 (6)	**285**
The Bandit—Johnston Brothers (54)	*349*
The Bandit (O' Cangaciero)— Eddie Barclay and His Orch. (55)	*155*
The Bandit—Percy Faith & His Orchestra (54)	*10*
The Bandit—Tex Ritter (54)	*10*
The Bandit—Frank Weir & His Orchestra (54)	*0.0*
The Bandit—Ronald Chesney (54)	*0.0*
Bonita DONATO [Bonita Ann Andre] ► 9335 (1)	**26**
Oowee, Oowee—Perry Como (65)	104
Mona DONATO [Ramona Marie Witry] ► 9336 (1)	**26**
Oowee, Oowee—Perry Como (65)	104
—Anthony James Donegan see: Lonnie DONEGAN	
Lonnie DONEGAN [Anthony James Donegan] ► 2055 (3)	**1942**
I'll Never Fall In Love Again—Tom Jones (69)	*3450*
I'll Never Fall In Love Again—Tom Jones (67)	*413*
Have A Drink On Me—Buddy Thomas (61)	51
Joe DONG ► 2976 (2)	**1088**
Loop De Loop—Johnny Thunder (62)	*2175*
Loop De Loop—Soul Sisters (64)	*1.4*
Carlo DONIDA [Carlo Donida Labati] ► 1706 (9)	**2455**
Al Di La'—Emilio Pericoli (62)	*2344*
I (Who Have Nothing)—Tom Jones (70)	*1304*
I (Who Have Nothing)—Ben E. King (63)	*810*
Help Yourself—Tom Jones (68)	710
I (Who Have Nothing)—Terry Knight And The Pack (66)	*588*
Al-Di-La—Ray Charles Singers (64)	*518*
I (Who Have Nothing)—Sylvester (79)	*146*
Al Di La—Connie Francis (62)	*77*
I Who Have Nothing—Liquid Smoke (70)	*71*
James DONNA ► 3091 (1)	**1013**
Liar, Liar—Castaways (65)	2025
Dorothy DONNELLY ► 7424 (3)	**97**
Drink, Drink, Drink—Mario Lanza (54)	154
Serenade—Mario Lanza (56)	*39*
Silver Moon—Bing Crosby (55)	*0.0*
—Philip Donnely see: Robbie BLUNT	
—Raymond Donnez see: Don RAY	
—Steve Donroy see: Cy CRANE	
—Steve Donroy see: Herb WEINER	
—Dicky Doo see: Gerry GRANAHAN	
Charlie DORE ► 1553 (2)	**2728**
Strut—Sheena Easton (84)	2303
Pilot Of The Airwaves—Charlie Dore (80)	1577
Steve DORFF ► 2306 (8) HOF	**1624**
I Just Fall In Love Again—Anne Murray (79)	1411
Through The Years—Kenny Rogers (81)	1241
Fire In The Morning—Melissa Manchester (80)	515
Every Which Way But Loose—Eddie Rabbitt (79)	485
Let Me Love You Once—Greg Lake (81)	377
Hoppy, Gene And Me—Roy Rogers (74)	197
Easy Love—Dionne Warwick (80)	184
Pirate—Cher (77)	4.4
Françoise DORIN ► 11284 (1)	**2.4**
Venice Blue (Que C'Est Triste Venise)— Bobby Darin (65)	7.3
Jim DORIS ► 2660 (2)	**1289**
Oh Me Oh My (I'm A Fool For You Baby)—Lulu (69)	*1163*
Oh Me Oh My (I'm A Fool For You Baby)— Aretha Franklin (72)	*126*
Harold DORMAN ► 1249 (4)	**3582**
Mountain Of Love—Johnny Rivers (64)	*2068*
Mountain Of Love—Harold Dorman (60)	*1210*
Mountain Of Love—Ronnie Dove (68)	*288*
Mississippi Cotton Picking Delta Town— Charley Pride (74)	31
Lee DORMAN ► 7754 (2)	**76**
Soul Experience—Iron Butterfly (69)	180
Easy Rider (Let The Wind Pay The Way)— Iron Butterfly (70)	125
Jane DORNACKER ► 8256 (1)	**57**
Don't Touch Me There—Tubes (76)	113
Ivan DOROSCHUK ► 792 (4)	**5598**
The Safety Dance—Men Without Hats (83)	4696
Pop Goes The World—Men Without Hats (87)	860
I Like—Men Without Hats (83)	33
Moonbeam—Men Without Hats (88)	9.8
Bob DOROUGH ► 5960 (1)	**223**
Comin' Home Baby—Mel Torme (62)	446
Ray DORSET ► 925 (1)	**4780**
In The Summertime—Mungo Jerry (70)	4780
Glenn DORSEY ► 4842 (1)	**400**
Sugar Pie Guy Pt. 1—Joneses (74)	400
Lee DORSEY ► 4286 (1)	**532**
Ya Ya—Lee Dorsey (61)	2127
Thomas A. DORSEY ► 4764 (6)	**421**
(There'll Be) Peace In The Valley (For Me)— Elvis Presley (57)	*395*
(There'll Be) Peace In The Valley (For Me)— Pat Boone (57)	*12*
(There'll Be) Peace In The Valley (For Me)— Red Foley (56)	*6.9*
Standing Here Wondering Which Way To Go— Marion Williams (71)	3.3
(There'll Be) Peace In The Valley (For Me)— Elvis Presley (57)	*2.1*
Take My Hand, Precious Lord—Elvis Presley (57)	2.1
Thomas L. DORSEY ► 5118 (1)	**340**
Love Machine—O'Kaysions (68)	340
Fanny DOSHER ► 10253 (1)	**11**
With All My Love—Five Keys (58)	11
Jerry DOUCETTE ► 6565 (3)	**156**
Mama Let Him Play—Doucette (78)	150
Nobody—Doucette (79)	11
All I Wanna Do—Doucette (78)	2.3
William DOUCHETTE [Sheriff Tex Davis, Bill Davis] ► 2571 (4)	**1366**
Be Bop A Lula— Gene Vincent and His Blue Caps (56)	*2525*
Race With The Devil— Gene Vincent and His Blue Caps (56)	116
Boom-A-Dip-Dip—Stan Robinson (59)	61
Be Bop A-Lula—Everly Brothers (60)	*50*
Chuck DOUGHERTY ► 5865 (1)	**235**
Transistor Sister—Freddy Cannon (61)	471
Dan DOUGHERTY ► 6028 (1)	**214**
Glad Rag Doll—Crazy Otto (55)	428
Neal DOUGHTY ► 3331 (2)	**896**
One Lonely Night—REO Speedwagon (85)	732
Variety Tonight—REO Speedwagon (87)	165
—Raymond Doughty see: Ray BURTON	
Bert DOUGLAS ► 10872 (1)	**4.7**
When Your Old Wedding Ring Was New— Bruce Hayes with Mary Mayo (60)	14
Carl DOUGLAS ► 778 (2)	**5678**
Kung Fu Fighting—Carl Douglas (74)	5556
Dance The Kung Fu—Carl Douglas (75)	246
Chip DOUGLAS [Douglas Farthing Hatlelid] ► 10127 (1)	**12**
It's About Time—Dillards (71)	12
—George Douglas see: Bob THIELE	
Glenn DOUGLAS [Douglas Glenn Tubb] ► 10324 (1)	**10**
Home Of The Blues—Johnny Cash (57)	30
Jack DOUGLAS ► 9942 (1)	**15**
Kings And Queens—Aerosmith (78)	73
Jan DOUGLAS ► 7450 (1)	**95**
Make Me Forget—Bobby Rydell (64)	285
Keith DOUGLAS ► 10840 (1)	**5.0**
Walkin' Shoes—Tora Tora (89)	20
Lew DOUGLAS [Allen Webster] ► 3889 (8)	**667**
Have You Heard—Duprees Featuring Joey Vann (63)	1071
Why Don't You Believe Me— Duprees Featuring Joey Vann (63)	*583*
Pretend—Carl Mann (59)	*253*
When You Took Your Love (From Me)— Jimmy Dorsey Orchestra (58)	76
Clay Idol—Betty Johnson (56)	41
Pa Pa Pa—Joni James (54)	23
Why Don't You Believe Me—Vic Damone (65)	*12*
Pretend—Tab Smith, His Fabulous Alto and His Band (57)	*5.2*
Marc DOUGLAS ► 10093 (1)	**13**
Got A New Love—Good Question (88)	39
Robert DOUGLAS ► 7881 (1)	**71**
You're A Big Girl Now—Stylistics (71)	142
Sean DOUGLAS ► 10094 (1)	**13**
Got A New Love—Good Question (88)	39
Greg DOUGLASS ► 4605 (2)	**452**
Jungle Love—Steve Miller Band (77)	837
Love Never Fails—Greg Kihn Band (83)	168
Jimmy DOUGLASS ► 10277 (1)	**11**
Snap Shot—Slave (81)	53
Danny DOUMA ► 7357 (1)	**100**
A Little Love—Juice Newton (84)	301
Amadeu Do VALE ► 1621 (4)	**2602**
Lisbon Antigua— Nelson Riddle And His Orchestra (55)	*7507*
Lisbon Antigua (In Old Lisbon)— Mitch Miller & His Orchestra (56)	*298*
Lisbon Antigua— Lawrence Welk & His Champagne Music (56)	*0.0*
Lisbon Antigua (In Old Lisbon)—Alan Dale (55)	*0.0*
Maurice DOWDELL ► 11615 (1)	**1.0**
Love Me Just For Me—Special Generation (90)	6.8
Brent DOWE ► 7290 (1)	**105**
Rivers Of Babylon—Boney M (78)	419
—Horace Kirby Dowell see: Saxie DOWELL	
Saxie DOWELL [Horace Kirby Dowell] ► 3804 (4)	**695**
Playmates— Fontane Sisters with Billy Vaughn's Orchestra (55)	*393*
Three Little Fishes— Mitch Ryder And The Detroit Wheels (67)	*300*
Three Little Fishes—Buzz Clifford (61)	*1.6*
Playmates—Hack Swain (55)	*0.0*
Joe DOWEN ► 11455 (1)	**1.6**
Something In You—Manitoba (70)	1.6
Taime DOWNE [Gustav Molvik] ► 5360 (1)	**300**
House Of Pain—Faster Pussycat (90)	600
Geoffrey DOWNES ► 1535 (6)	**2789**
Heat Of The Moment—Asia (82)	2585
Don't Cry—Asia (83)	1413
Only Time Will Tell—Asia (82)	916
Go—Asia (85)	345
Video Killed The Radio Star—Buggles (79)	312
The Hunter—GTR (86)	55
Julia DOWNES ► 6447 (1)	**168**
Machinery—Sheena Easton (82)	168
Brian DOWNEY ► 9477 (1)	**23**
Cowboy Song—Thin Lizzy (76)	46
Al DOWNING ► 8090 (2)	**62**
I'll Be Holding On—Al Downing (75)	123
Heartbreak Hill—Fats Domino (64)	1.9
Kenneth DOWNING ► 9080 (2)	**32**
You've Got Another Thing Comin'—Judas Priest (82)	89
Living After Midnight—Judas Priest (80)	5.6
Rich DOWNING ► 8728 (1)	**41**
Mighty High—Mighty Clouds Of Joy (76)	82
Bobby DOYLE ► 3832 (2)	**687**
String Along—Rick Nelson (63)	*985*
String Along—Fabian (60)	*389*
—Richard Doyle see: Shamus M'COOL	
Gene DOZIER [Ugene Lloyd Dozier, Billy Jackson] ► 10657 (3)	**6.3**
International Playboy—Wilson Pickett (73)	10
Memory Lane—Minnie Riperton (79)	3.4
Hunk Of Funk— Gene Dozier And The Brotherhood (67)	2.9

Lamont DOZIER [Edyth Craighead, Edith Wayne] ▶ 15 (151) HOF	**67349**
Where Did Our Love Go—Supremes (64)	*9056*
I Can't Help Myself—Four Tops (65)	*8859*
Come See About Me—Supremes (64)	*8772*
Baby Love—Supremes (64)	8476
Stop! In The Name Of Love—Supremes (65)	*7776*
You Can't Hurry Love—Supremes (66)	*7615*
I Hear A Symphony—Supremes (65)	6983
Reach Out I'll Be There—Four Tops (66)	*6413*
You Keep Me Hangin' On—Supremes (66)	*6251*
The Happening—Supremes (67)	*6167*
Band Of Gold—Freda Payne (70)	6004
Love Is Here And Now You're Gone—Supremes (67)	5783
1-2-3—Len Barry (65)	*5700*
Reflections—Diana Ross And The Supremes (67)	5395
Back In My Arms Again—Supremes (65)	*4991*
Roll With It—Steve Winwood (88)	4539
Heat Wave—Martha & The Vandellas (63)	*4013*
Two Hearts—Phil Collins (88)	3857
You Keep Me Hangin' On—Kim Wilde (87)	*3516*
Baby I Need Your Lovin'—Johnny Rivers (67)	*3362*
My World Is Empty Without You—Supremes (66)	*3008*
It's The Same Old Song—Four Tops (65)	*2864*
Standing In The Shadows Of Love—Four Tops (66)	2566
Bernadette—Four Tops (67)	2554
Jimmy Mack—Martha & The Vandellas (67)	*2552*
How Sweet It Is To Be Loved By You—Marvin Gaye (64)	*2463*
Give Me Just A Little More Time—Chairmen Of The Board (70)	2390
How Sweet It Is (To Be Loved By You)—James Taylor (75)	*2292*
You Keep Me Hangin' On—Vanilla Fudge (68)	*2110*
Nowhere To Run—Martha & The Vandellas (65)	1982
Mickey's Monkey—Miracles (63)	1976
Heaven Must Have Sent You—Bonnie Pointer (79)	*1857*
You Can't Hurry Love—Phil Collins (82)	*1813*
Love Is Like An Itching In My Heart—Supremes (66)	1721
I'm Ready For Love—Martha & The Vandellas (66)	1702
Quicksand—Martha & The Vandellas (63)	1686
In And Out Of Love—Diana Ross And The Supremes (67)	1650
Baby I Need Your Loving—Four Tops (64)	*1637*
Take Me In Your Arms (Rock Me)—Doobie Brothers (75)	*1636*
Nothing But Heartaches—Supremes (65)	1633
Can I Get A Witness—Marvin Gaye (63)	*1429*
You're A Wonderful One—Marvin Gaye (64)	1385
7-Rooms Of Gloom—Four Tops (67)	1376
This Old Heart Of Mine (Is Weak For You)—Isley Brothers (66)	*1339*
Heat Wave—Linda Ronstadt (75)	*1210*
Forever Came Today—Diana Ross And The Supremes (68)	*1145*
Westbound #9—Flaming Ember (70)	1141
This Old Heart Of Mine—Rod Stewart (with Ronald Isley) (90)	*1125*
Something About You—Four Tops (65)	*1109*
Come And Get These Memories—Martha & The Vandellas (63)	1109
How Sweet It Is (To Be Loved By You)—Jr. Walker & The All Stars (66)	*1081*
Shake Me, Wake Me (When It's Over)—Four Tops (66)	1067
Mind, Body And Soul—Flaming Ember (69)	1044
(I'm A) Road Runner—Jr. Walker & The All Stars (66)	1035
Deeper And Deeper—Freda Payne (70)	1024
Where Did Our Love Go—Donnie Elbert (71)	*1001*
When The Lovelight Starts Shining Through His Eyes—Supremes (63)	958
(Come 'round Here) I'm The One You Need—Miracles (66)	943
You Keep Running Away—Four Tops (67)	912
The Day I Found Myself—Honey Cone (72)	906
I Can't Help Myself (Sugar Pie, Honey Bunch)—Donnie Elbert (72)	*858*
You Lost The Sweetest Boy—Mary Wells (63)	855
Come See About Me—Jr. Walker & The All Stars (67)	*794*
Baby Don't You Do It—Marvin Gaye (64)	*737*
Don't Do It—Band (72)	*698*
The Other Side—Aerosmith (90)	642
Reach Out I'll Be There—Diana Ross (71)	*619*
Invisible—Alison Moyet (85)	595
(You've Got Me) Dangling On A String—Chairmen Of The Board (70)	*558*
Strange I Know—Marvelettes (62)	557
I Gotta Dance To Keep From Crying—Miracles (63)	546
Stop In The Name Of Love—Hollies (83)	*525*
Can I Get A Witness—Lee Michaels (71)	*522*
Anything Is Possible—Debbie Gibson (90)	515
Your Unchanging Love—Marvin Gaye (67)	484
Everything's Tuesday—Chairmen Of The Board (70)	479
You Brought The Joy—Freda Payne (71)	474
Cherish What Is Dear To You (While It's Near To You)—Freda Payne (71)	473
Chairman Of The Board—Chairmen Of The Board (71)	458
Take Me In Your Arms (Rock Me A Little While)—Kim Weston (65)	*440*
Locking Up My Heart—Marvelettes (63)	428
Live Wire—Martha & The Vandellas (64)	418
I Can't Help Myself (Sugar Pie, Honey Bunch)—Bonnie Pointer (79)	*407*
It's The Same Old Song—KC & The Sunshine Band (78)	*395*
Little Darling (I Need You)—Doobie Brothers (77)	*392*
I'm In A Different World—Four Tops (68)	381
Little Darling, I Need You—Marvin Gaye (66)	*372*
In My Lonely Room—Martha & The Vandellas (64)	348
Heaven Must Have Sent You—Elgins (66)	*326*
Helpless—Kim Weston (66)	316
Why Can't We Be Lovers—Holland-Dozier (72)	313
Without The One You Love (Life's Not Worth While)—Four Tops (64)	306
Forever Came Today—Jackson 5 (75)	*305*
Crumbs Off The Table—Glass House (69)	279
Don't Leave Me Starvin' For Your Love (Part 1)—Holland-Dozier (73)	273
I Guess I'll Always Love You—Isley Brothers (66)	243
Baby, I Need Your Loving—O.C. Smith (70)	*239*
Where Did Our Love Go—J. Geils Band (76)	*205*
Darling Baby—Elgins (66)	*197*
Something About You—Le Blanc & Carr (77)	*183*
While You're Out Looking For Sugar?—Honey Cone (69)	183
Shades Of Green—Flaming Ember (70)	173
You Keep Me Hangin' On—Vanilla Fudge (67)	*165*
Just Ain't Enough Love—Eddie Holland (64)	160
Love (Makes Me Do Foolish Things)—Martha & The Vandellas (65)	154
Girls It Ain't Easy—Honey Cone (69)	149
Candy To Me—Eddie Holland (64)	141
Baby, I Need Your Lovin'—Eric Carmen (79)	*135*
You Keep Me Hanging On—Wilson Pickett (69)	*133*
One, Two, Three—Ramsey Lewis (67)	*131*
I Just Can't Walk Away—Four Tops (83)	124
If You Can Beat Me Rockin' (You Can Have My Chair)—Laura Lee (72)	122
Reach Out, I'll Be There—Gloria Gaynor (75)	*119*
Jimmy Mack—Sheena Easton (86)	*115*
Leaving Here—Eddie Holland (64)	114
This Old Heart Of Mine (Is Weak For You)—Tammi Terrell (69)	*96*
Forever—Marvelettes (63)	93
Reach Out, I'll Be There—Ritchie Family (76)	*92*
Come See About Me—Nella Dodds (64)	*92*
I Can't Help Myself (Sugar Pie, Honey Bunch)—Shalamar (77)	*80*
It's The Same Old Song—Shalamar (77)	*80*
Stop! In the Name of Love—Shalamar (77)	*80*
Reach Out—Merrilee Rush (68)	*70*
Stop! In The Name Of Love—Margie Joseph (71)	*64*
The Road We Didn't Take—Freda Payne (72)	58
I'll Turn To Stone—Four Tops (67)	58
This Old Heart Of Mine—Rod Stewart (76)	*53*
Let Me Start Tonite—Lamont Dozier (75)	48
My World Is Empty Without You—Jose Feliciano (69)	*46*
Back In My Arms Again—Genya Ravan (78)	*41*
Put Yourself In My Place—Elgins (66)	33
Take Me With You—Honey Cone (70)	28
Run, Run, Run—Supremes (64)	24
Reach Out I'll Be There—Stars On 45 (81)	*12*
Stop In The Name Of Love—Stars On 45 (81)	*12*
Without You—Peabo Bryson (88)	10
I Think You Need Love—Dionne Warwicke (73)	10
If It's Good To You (It's Good For You)—Flaming Ember (71)	9.0
You've Got Me Dangling On A String—Donny Osmond (77)	*8.4*
I Can't Help Myself—Magnificent Men (67)	*7.6*
Too Many Cooks (Spoil The Soup)—100 Proof Aged In Soul (69)	3.9
Stealing Moments From Another Woman's Life—Glass House (70)	3.7
Darling Baby—Jackie Moore (72)	*3.5*
Try My Love On For Size—Chairmen Of The Board (71)	3.4
Hear The Words, Feel The Feeling—Margie Joseph (76)	2.6
Function At The Junction—Shorty Long (66)	1.9
Take Me In Your Arms (Rock Me A Little While)—Isley Brothers (68)	*1.8*
Stop The World And Let Me Off—Flaming Ember (71)	1.2
You Keep Me Hangin' On—Jackie DeShannon (70)	*1.0*
Reach Out I'll Be There—New Seekers (74)	*0.7*
Tie A String Around Your Finger—Marvelettes (63)	0.5
Reggie DOZIER ▶ 7831 (1)	**73**
Midnight Flower—Four Tops (74)	146
Tim DOZIER ▶ 7878 (1)	**71**
Slide—Slave (77)	640
—Ugene Lloyd Dozier see: Gene DOZIER	
Willis DRAFFEN ▶ 7000 (1)	**123**
That's Not How It Goes—Bloodstone (74)	123
Charlie DRAKE ▶ 4659 (1)	**444**
My Boomerang Won't Come Back—Charlie Drake (61)	888
Ervin DRAKE ▶ 2407 (14) HOF	**1516**
I Believe—Bachelors (64)	*702*
Good Morning Heartache—Diana Ross (73)	680
It Was A Very Good Year—Frank Sinatra (65)	*634*
Al-Di-La—Ray Charles Singers (64)	*518*
Old Oaken Bucket—Tommy Sands (60)	173
Al Di La—Connie Francis (62)	*77*
Sympathetic Eyes—Ames Brothers (55)	76
My Home Town—Steve Lawrence (63)	42
I Ain't Gonna Lead This Life No More—Dean Martin (59)	17
The Father Of Girls—Perry Como (68)	8.1
I Believe—Roy Hamilton (55)	*5.6*
I Believe—Elvis Presley (57)	*2.1*
It Was A Very Good Year—Della Reese (66)	*1.4*
My Friend—Eddie Fisher (54)	0.0
Guy DRAKE ▶ 5232 (1)	**322**
Welfare Cadilac—Guy Drake (70)	322
Jimmy DRAKE [Nervous Norvus] ▶ 2733 (3)	**1235**
Transfusion—Nervous Norvus (56)	*985*
Ape Call—Nervous Norvus (56)	250
Transfusion—Four Jokers (56)	*0.0*
Milton DRAKE ▶ 6691 (5)	**144**
Bless Your Heart—Fontane Sisters with Billy Vaughn's Orchestra (54)	*282*
Mairzy Doats—Innocence (67)	*119*
Town Crier—Al Hibbler (57)	20
Mairzy Doats—Dodie Stevens (59)	*1.2*
Bless Your Heart—Bob Dini (54)	*0.0*
—Tom Drake see: Steven YATES	
Guy DRAPER ▶ 2466 (3)	**1457**
Court Of Love—Unifics (68)	846
The Beginning Of My End—Unifics (68)	567
It's A Groovy World!—Unifics (69)	44
Robert DRAPER ▶ 5407 (1)	**293**
Wiggle Wiggle—Accents (58)	293
Terry DRAPER ▶ 5058 (2)	**352**
Calling Occupants Of Interplanetary Craft—Carpenters (77)	*660*
Calling Occupants—Klaatu (77)	*45*
Richard DRAPKIN ▶ 9510 (1)	**22**
Together We Can Make Such Sweet Music—Spinners (73)	45
Clarence DRAYTON [Clarence R. Drayton, Clay Drayton] ▶ 10332 (1)	**9.9**
Love Is All You Need—High Inergy (78)	9.9
Sandra DRAYTON ▶ 5663 (1)	**258**
A Letter To Myself—Chi-Lites (73)	516
Victor DRAYTON ▶ 4846 (4)	**399**
Don't Let The Green Grass Fool You—Wilson Pickett (71)	1388
I'm Gonna Love You—Intrigues (69)	115

Victor DRAYTON ▶ 4846 (4) *Continued*	**399**
One For The Money (Part 1)—Whispers (76)	40
Just A Little Bit More—Intrigues (70)	14
—Dr. Dre see: Andre Romell YOUNG	
—L. A. Dre see: Andre BOLTON	
Jean-Paul DREAU [Jean-Paul Benchetrit] ▶ 5447 (1)	**287**
Nobody Wins—Elton John (81)	575
—Hans Drechsler see: Joe DIXIE	
Al DREDICK ▶ 6945 (2)	**126**
Nee Nee Na Na Na Na Nu Nu— Dicky Doo And The Don'ts (58)	135
A Little Dog Cried—Jimmie Rodgers (61)	118
Chris DREJA ▶ 5260 (1)	**317**
Over Under Sideways Down—Yardbirds (66)	1583
Charlie DREW ▶ 7048 (1)	**119**
The Biggest Parakeets In Town—Jud Strunk (75)	239
Dennis DREW ▶ 6554 (1)	**157**
Trouble Me—10,000 Maniacs (89)	315
Corinne DREWERY ▶ 3548 (3)	**789**
Breakout—Swing Out Sister (87)	1952
Twilight World—Swing Out Sister (87)	393
Waiting Game—Swing Out Sister (89)	15
Dave DREYER ▶ 5915 (5) HOF	**229**
The Wall—Patti Page (57)	*244*
Me And My Shadow— Frank Sinatra And Sammy Davis Jr. (62)	203
Next Stop Paradise—Teddy Randazzo (57)	163
The Wall—Eileen Rodgers (57)	*77*
The Wall—Brook Benton (57)	*0.0*
—Dr. Freeze see: Elliot STRAITE	
Jimmy DRIFTWOOD [James Corbitt Morris] ▶ 550 (10)	**7815**
Battle Of New Orleans—Johnny Horton (59)	*13064*
Battle Of Kookamonga—Homer & Jethro (59)	1052
Tennessee Stud—Eddy Arnold (59)	510
Sal's Got A Sugar Lip—Johnny Horton (59)	166
Battle Of New Orleans—Nitty Gritty Dirt Band (74)	*51*
Four Little Girls In Boston—Jimmie Rodgers (60)	41
Battle Of New Orleans—Vaughn Monroe with Norman Layden, His Orchestra and Chorus (59)	*15*
Battle Of New Orleans—Harpers Bizarre (68)	*5.3*
Battle Of New Orleans—Bert Sommer (70)	*5.3*
Sittin' By Sittin' Bull—Eddy Arnold (59)	0.8
Carl DRIGGS ▶ 3440 (2)	**848**
Get Off—Foxy (78)	1677
Because Of You—Kracker (72)	47
Riccardo DRIGO ▶ 7281 (1)	**105**
Hearts—Jackie Wilson (62)	211
Jean-Luc DRION ▶ 7142 (1)	**113**
Don Quichotte—Magazine 60 (86)	227
—Dr. John see: Mac REBENNACK	
—Marilyn Marie Droman see: Marilyn MARTIN	
James DROWN ▶ 9899 (1)	**15**
I'm Gonna Make You Love Me—Blend (78)	15
—Dr. Robert see: Bruce Robert HOWARD	
Richard DRUMMIE ▶ 2951 (5)	**1104**
King Of Wishful Thinking—Go West (90)	1534
We Close Our Eyes—Go West (85)	471
Don't Look Down - The Sequel—Go West (87)	354
Call Me—Go West (85)	289
Eye To Eye—Go West (85)	71
Burleigh DRUMMOND ▶ 10002 (1)	**14**
Nice, Nice, Very Nice—Ambrosia (75)	71
Michael DRUMMOND ▶ 7964 (1)	**67**
Misfit—Curiosity Killed The Cat (87)	336
William Ernest DRUMMOND ▶ 3746 (3)	**713**
3 A.M. Eternal—KLF (91)	1338
Doctorin' The Tardis—Timelords (88)	159
What Time Is Love?—KLF (91)	73
Roy DRUSKY ▶ 4582 (4)	**462**
Anymore—Teresa Brewer (60)	1292
Alone With You—Faron Young (58)	55
Before This Day Ends—Eddy Arnold (60)	*38*
Before This Day Ends— George Hamilton IV (60)	*0.0*
John DUARTE ▶ 5500 (3)	**278**
Radio Romance—Tiffany (89)	275
Feelings Of Forever—Tiffany (88)	203
Can I Call You My Girl—PC Quest (91)	155

Peter Anthony DUARTE ▶ 10525 (1)	**7.6**
You Got To Keep On Bumpin'—Kay-Gees (74)	61
John Joseph DUBAS ▶ 4340 (1)	**516**
She's The One—Chartbusters (64)	516
—Joe Dube see: Jeffrey Warren GROB	
Matt DUBEY [Matthew D. Dubinsky] ▶ 4392 (6)	**506**
Mutual Admiration Society—Teresa Brewer (56)	*723*
Mutual Admiration Society— Eddy Arnold And Jaye P. Morgan (56)	*279*
This Much I Know—Tony Martin (56)	5.8
If'N—Richard Hayes (57)	*1.8*
If'N—Jeannie Carson (57)	*1.8*
If'N—Jaye P. Morgan and Eddy Arnold (57)	*1.8*
Al DUBIN ▶ 1172 (8) HOF	**3799**
For You—Rick Nelson (63)	2166
I Only Have Eyes For You—Flamingos (59)	*1735*
I Only Have Eyes For You—Art Garfunkel (75)	*1357*
September In The Rain—Dinah Washington (61)	1242
Tip-Toe Thru' The Tulips With Me—Tiny Tim (68)	858
I Only Have Eyes For You—Lettermen (66)	*122*
I Only Have Eyes For You—Jerry Butler (72)	*113*
I Only Have Eyes For You—Cliff Richard (64)	*5.3*
Steven DUBIN ▶ 4519 (3)	**472**
The Love In Your Eyes—Eddie Money (89)	753
Back On Holiday—Robbie Nevil (88)	525
For Your Mind—Robbie Nevil (91)	93
—Matthew D. Dubinsky see: Matt DUBEY	
—Damita Jo DuBlanc see: Damita Jo GIBSON	
Steve DUBOFF ▶ 691 (7)	**6307**
The Rain, The Park & Other Things—Cowsills (67)	7643
The Pied Piper—Crispian St. Peters (66)	*4251*
We Can Fly—Cowsills (68)	950
Pied Piper—Changin' Times (65)	*131*
Did You Ever—Hullaballoos (65)	68
Does She Do It Like She Dances— Addrisi Brothers (77)	44
Another Page—Connie Francis (67)	2.3
Pye DUBOIS [Paul Phillip Woods] ▶ 7072 (2)	**118**
Tom Sawyer—Rush (81)	329
Go For Soda—Kim Mitchell (85)	71
Tim DuBOIS ▶ 3754 (2)	**710**
Love In The First Degree—Alabama (81)	1156
She Got The Goldmine (I Got The Shaft)— Jerry Reed (82)	132
Kevin DUBROW ▶ 6986 (1)	**124**
Bang Your Head (Metal Health)—Quiet Riot (84)	495
Willie Lee DUCKWORTH ▶ 7445 (1)	**95**
Sound-Off—Titus Turner (61)	191
Pierre DUDAN ▶ 8798 (2)	**39**
Softly, Softly—Jaye P. Morgan (55)	*117*
Softly, Softly— Guy Lombardo & His Royal Canadians (55)	*0.0*
Lyn DUDDY ▶ 1251 (3)	**3573**
Johnny Angel—Shelley Fabares (62)	7079
Let It Ring—Doris Day (55)	63
Keep Your Cotton Pickin' Paddies Offa My Heart— Teresa Brewer (56)	6.7
Anne DUDLEY ▶ 3323 (2)	**899**
Too Many Walls—Cathy Dennis (91)	1507
Paranoimia—Art Of Noise with Max Headroom (86)	437
Theodore DUDLEY ▶ 8800 (1)	**39**
Cutie Pie—One Way (82)	273
Billy DUFFY ▶ 6376 (2)	**177**
Fire Woman—Cult (89)	345
Edie (Ciao Baby)—Cult (89)	9.4
Chris DUFFY ▶ 3810 (2)	**693**
Cry—Waterfront (89)	1294
Nature Of Love—Waterfront (89)	93
Steve DUFFY ▶ 6729 (2)	**142**
He Thinks I Still Care—Connie Francis (62)	*284*
She Thinks I Still Care—Elvis Presley (76)	*0.0*
Louis DUHIG ▶ 5476 (1)	**281**
Doll House—Donnie Brooks (60)	563
—Eric Duhn see: Fred OLDÖRP	
Martin DUISER ▶ 4398 (7)	**506**
Stars On 45—Stars On 45 (81)	*442*
Stars On 45—Stars On 45 (81)	*442*
Rock And Roll Star—Champagne (77)	60
Stars On 45—Stars On 45 (82)	*27*

Stars on 45—Stars On 45 (81)	*16*
Stars On 45—Stars On 45 (81)	*12*
Stars On 45—Stars On 45 (81)	*12*
—Billy Duke see: William TESONE	
George DUKE ▶ 2595 (6)	**1342**
Sweet Baby—Stanley Clarke/George Duke (81)	909
Reach For It—George Duke (77)	261
Shine On—George Duke (82)	260
Amnesia—Shalamar (84)	152
Next Love—Deniece Williams (84)	42
Dukey Stick (Pt. 2)—George Duke (78)	11
Mike DUKE ▶ 2663 (3)	**1286**
Doing It All For My Baby— Huey Lewis and the News (87)	1308
Street Corner Serenade—Wet Willie (77)	731
Hope You Love Me Like You Say You Do— Huey Lewis and the News (82)	389
—Robert Duke see: Joe MEEK	
Vernon DUKE [Vladimir Dukelsky] ▶ 4976 (4) HOF	**367**
April In Paris—Count Basie And His Orchestra (56)	*360*
Taking A Chance On Love—Ahmad Jamal Trio (58)	5.2
April In Paris—Modernaires (56)	*2.8*
April In Paris— Count Basie Big Band with Ella Fitzgerald (56)	*0.0*
—Vladimir Dukelsky see: Vernon DUKE	
Kevin DUKES ▶ 8986 (1)	**34**
Hearts In Trouble—Chicago (90)	102
—William Dumaresq see: Max FRITH	
Daphne DUMAS ▶ 5095 (3)	**343**
Westbound #9—Flaming Ember (70)	1141
Everything's Tuesday—Chairmen Of The Board (70)	479
The Road We Didn't Take—Freda Payne (72)	58
Dennis DUNAWAY ▶ 3314 (5)	**903**
School's Out—Alice Cooper (72)	*2297*
Eighteen—Alice Cooper (71)	1021
Elected—Alice Cooper (72)	776
Under My Wheels—Alice Cooper (71)	190
School's Out—Krokus (86)	*104*
—Lowell Fillmore Dunbar see: Sly DUNBAR	
—Reggie Dunbar see: Murry WILSON	
—Richard Dunbar see: Richard KNIGHT	
Ronald DUNBAR ▶ 539 (27)	**7939**
Band Of Gold—Freda Payne (70)	6004
Patches—Clarence Carter (70)	5109
Give Me Just A Little More Time— Chairmen Of The Board (70)	2390
She's Not Just Another Woman—8th Day (71)	2012
Pay To The Piper—Chairmen Of The Board (70)	1695
Westbound #9—Flaming Ember (70)	1141
Mind, Body And Soul—Flaming Ember (69)	1044
Deeper And Deeper—Freda Payne (70)	1024
The Day I Found Myself—Honey Cone (72)	906
I'm Not My Brother's Keeper—Flaming Ember (70)	894
You've Got To Crawl (Before You Walk)—8th Day (71)	724
(You've Got Me) Dangling On A String— Chairmen Of The Board (70)	*558*
Everything's Tuesday—Chairmen Of The Board (70)	479
Crumbs Off The Table—Glass House (69)	279
While You're Out Looking For Sugar?—Honey Cone (69)	183
Shades Of Green—Flaming Ember (70)	173
Girls It Ain't Easy—Honey Cone (69)	149
If You Can Beat Me Rockin' (You Can Have My Chair)—Laura Lee (72)	122
I Can't Be You (You Can't Be Me)—Glass House (70)	60
Take Me With You—Honey Cone (70)	28
90 Day Freeze (On Her Love)— 100 Proof Aged In Soul (71)	21
Greetings (This Is Uncle Sam)—Valadiers (61)	*9.2*
You've Got Me Dangling On A String—Donny Osmond (77)	*8.4*
Greetings (This Is Uncle Sam)—Monitors (66)	*5.8*
Too Many Cooks (Spoil The Soup)— 100 Proof Aged In Soul (69)	3.9
Agony of DeFeet—Parliament (81)	3.6
Stop The World And Let Me Off—Flaming Ember (71)	1.2
Sly DUNBAR [Lowell Fillmore Dunbar] ▶ 7903 (2)	**70**
Housecall—Shabba Ranks (91)	329
Pull Up To The Bumper—Grace Jones (81)	62
Darryl DUNCAN ▶ 4717 (1)	**432**
Let Go—Sharon Bryant (89)	432

Jimmy DUNCAN ▶ 788 (8)	**5622**
My Special Angel—Bobby Helms (57)	*2619*
My Special Angel—Vogues (68)	*2083*
String Along—Rick Nelson (63)	*985*
String Along—Fabian (60)	*389*
Everybody Knows—Steve Lawrence (64)	236
I See You—Cathy And Joe (64)	76
Fool And The Angel—Bobby Helms (58)	40
My Special Angel—Sonny Land Trio (57)	*0.0*
Johnny DUNCAN [John Richard Duncan] ▶ 9474 (1)	**23**
I'd Rather Love You—Charley Pride (71)	23
Lanny DUNCAN ▶ 4429 (1)	**495**
Let's Go (pony)—Routers (62)	990
Malcolm DUNCAN ▶ 2779 (3)	**1199**
Pick Up The Pieces—AWB (74)	5059
Cut The Cake—AWB (75)	1651
School Boy Crush—AWB (75)	485
Robert DUNCAN ▶ 4430 (1)	**495**
Let's Go (pony)—Routers (62)	990
Rosetta DUNCAN ▶ 9478 (1)	**23**
Rememb'ring—Peter Lind Hayes & Mary Healy (55)	46
Vivian DUNCAN ▶ 9479 (1)	**23**
Rememb'ring—Peter Lind Hayes & Mary Healy (55)	46
Wayne DUNCAN ▶ 2589 (2)	**1346**
Wasted Days And Wasted Nights—Freddy Fender (75)	*2670*
Wasted Days And Wasted Nights—Freddy Fender (60)	*21*
Willie Joe DUNCAN ▶ 9862 (1)	**16**
Twitchy—Rene Hall's Orchestra Featuring Willie Joe (58)	16
David DUNDAS ▶ 3670 (1)	**744**
Jeans On—David Dundas (76)	1487
By DUNHAM ▶ 7417 (3)	**97**
Anyway The Wind Blows—Doris Day (60)	113
Au Revoir—Teresa Brewer (54)	100
It's A Cotton Candy World—Jerry Wallace (64)	52
George DUNING ▶ 652 (8)	**6704**
Theme From "Picnic" (Medley)—Morris Stoloff Conducting The Columbia Pictures Orchestra (56)	*4036*
Theme From "Picnic"—George Cates & His Orchestra (56)	*1975*
Picnic—McGuire Sisters (56)	*1270*
Toys In The Attic—Joe Sherman, His Orchestra And Chorus (63)	*50*
Theme From Picnic—Ralph Marterie And His Orchestra (56)	*34*
Toys In The Attic—Jack Jones (63)	*20*
Toys In The Attic—Dennis Regor (63)	*0.0*
Picnic—Buddy Bregman & His Orchestra (56)	*0.0*
Louis DUNLAP ▶ 3160 (1)	**978**
You Can Depend On Me—Brenda Lee (61)	2935
Melvin DUNLAP ▶ 5120 (2)	**339**
Do Your Thing—Watts 103rd Street Rhythm Band (69)	1496
Till You Get Enough—Watts 103rd Street Rhythm Band (69)	200
Artie DUNN ▶ 2246 (3)	**1708**
Twilight Time—Platters (58)	*6653*
Twilight Time—Dick Contino (56)	*149*
Twilight Time—Andy Williams (62)	*28*
—Chris Dunn see: Chris WATERS	
Don DUNN [Donald Lewis Dunn] ▶ 9242 (2)	**28**
Hitchcock Railway—Jose Feliciano (68)	48
Alright In The City—Dunn & McCashen (70)	8.2
Donald "Duck" DUNN [Donald V. Dunn] ▶ 2707 (7)	**1259**
Time Is Tight—Booker T. & The M.G.'s (69)	2035
Soul-Limbo—Booker T. & The M.G.'s (68)	1495
Hip Hug-Her—Booker T. & The M.G.'s (67)	719
Melting Pot—Booker T. & The M.G.'s (71)	365
Boot-Leg—Booker T. & The MG's (65)	349
Slim Jenkin's Place—Booker T. & The M.G.'s (67)	64
The Hunter—Ike & Tina Turner (69)	12
—Donald Lewis Dunn see: Don DUNN	
—Donald V. Dunn see: Donald "Duck" DUNN	
—Larry Dunn see: Lorenzo DUNN	
Lorenzo DUNN [Larry Dunn] ▶ 2198 (3) HOF	**1751**
Shining Star—Earth, Wind & Fire (75)	4991
Let Me Talk—Earth, Wind & Fire (80)	319
And Love Goes On—Earth, Wind & Fire (81)	174
Harry DUPREE ▶ 11797 (1)	**0.0**
Lisbon Antigua (In Old Lisbon)—Alan Dale (55)	*0.0*
Jack DUPREE [Champion Jack Dupree, William Thomas Dupree] ▶ 11026 (1)	**3.7**
Walking The Blues—Jack DuPree and Mr. Bear (55)	7.5
Robbie DUPREE [Robert H. Dupuis] ▶ 2491 (1)	**1441**
Steal Away—Robbie Dupree (80)	2883
—William Thomas Dupree see: Jack DUPREE	
Luis DUPREY ▶ 4903 (1)	**385**
Temptation—Corina (91)	1924
—Robert H. Dupuis see: Robbie DUPREE	
Paul DURAND ▶ 10678 (1)	**6.1**
We All Need Love—Percy Faith And His Orchestra and Chorus (56)	18
Robert DURAND ▶ 2653 (2)	**1292**
Just A Little—Beau Brummels (65)	2227
Don't Talk To Strangers—Beau Brummels (65)	357
Darrol DURANT ▶ 7339 (1)	**101**
B.B.D. (I Thought It Was Me)?—Bell Biv DeVoe (90)	504
Thomas DURDEN ▶ 1336 (4)	**3322**
Heartbreak Hotel—Elvis Presley (56)	*9660*
Heartbreak Hotel—Frijid Pink (70)	*236*
Heartbreak Hotel—Roger Miller (66)	*53*
Heartbreak Hotel—Stan Freberg (56)	*17*
Eddie DURHAM ▶ 1380 (3)	**3222**
Topsy II—Cozy Cole (58)	6164
Topsy I—Cozy Cole (58)	205
I Don't Want To Set The World On Fire—Somethin' Smith & The Redheads (58)	149
Norman DURHAM ▶ 10716 (1)	**5.9**
Get Tough—Kleeer (81)	12
John DURRILL ▶ 726 (7)	**6022**
Dark Lady—Cher (74)	4004
Western Union—Five Americans (67)	2583
I See The Light—Five Americans (65)	795
Sound Of Love—Five Americans (67)	657
I Saw A Man And He Danced With His Wife—Cher (74)	434
Zip Code—Five Americans (67)	404
Evol-Not Love—Five Americans (66)	315
Michael DURSO ▶ 5123 (4)	**339**
Petticoats Of Portugal—Dick Jacobs And His Chorus And Orchestra (56)	*982*
Petticoats Of Portugal—Billy Vaughn and His Orchestra (56)	*34*
Petticoats Of Portugal—Caesar Giovannini & Sextette (56)	*0.0*
Petticoats Of Portugal—Florian Zabach (56)	*0.0*
William Arthur DURST ▶ 11024 (1)	**3.8**
Africa—Thundermug (72)	7.5
Bev DUSHAM ▶ 5080 (1)	**346**
City Of Angels—Highlights (56)	692
Anton DVORAK ▶ 6219 (2)	**192**
The Mocking Bird—Four Lads (58)	*370*
The Mocking Bird—Four Lads (56)	*15*
—Reginald Kenneth Dwight see: Elton JOHN	
Des DYER ▶ 1773 (3)	**2340**
Sky High—Jigsaw (75)	3070
Who Do You Think You Are—Bo Donaldson And The Heywoods (74)	1150
Love Fire—Jigsaw (76)	462
Bob DYLAN ▶ 31 (55) HOF	**50201**
Mr. Tambourine Man—Byrds (65)	6122
Like A Rolling Stone—Bob Dylan (65)	*5241*
Blowin' In The Wind—Peter, Paul & Mary (63)	*4579*
Rainy Day Women #12 & 35—Bob Dylan (66)	4251
Mighty Quinn (Quinn The Eskimo)—Manfred Mann (68)	2902
Lay Lady Lay—Bob Dylan (69)	*2350*
It Ain't Me Babe—Turtles (65)	*2181*
Blowin' In The Wind—Stevie Wonder (66)	*1913*
Positively 4th Street—Bob Dylan (65)	1832
All I Really Want To Do—Cher (65)	*1745*
Don't Think Twice—Wonder Who ? (65)	*1628*
Knockin' On Heaven's Door—Bob Dylan (73)	1579
Don't Think Twice, It's All Right—Peter, Paul & Mary (63)	*1302*
Forever Young—Rod Stewart (88)	1122
If Not For You—Olivia Newton-John (71)	1107
All Along The Watchtower—Jimi Hendrix Experience (68)	944
She Belongs To Me—Rick Nelson And The Stone Canyon Band (69)	865
All I Really Want To Do—Byrds (65)	*807*
I Want You—Bob Dylan (66)	740
My Back Pages—Byrds (67)	618
Wigwam—Bob Dylan (70)	556
George Jackson—Bob Dylan (71)	551
Watching The River Flow—Bob Dylan (71)	536
Jammin' Me—Tom Petty and The Heartbreakers (87)	534
Just Like A Woman—Bob Dylan (66)	*509*
Hurricane (Part I)—Bob Dylan (75)	484
Handle With Care—Traveling Wilburys (88)	448
Gotta Serve Somebody—Bob Dylan (79)	445
Subterranean Homesick Blues—Bob Dylan (65)	438
On A Night Like This—Bob Dylan (74)	368
Too Much Of Nothing—Peter, Paul & Mary (67)	357
It Ain't Me, Babe—Johnny Cash (64)	*326*
Tangled Up In Blue—Bob Dylan (75)	319
Tonight I'll Be Staying Here With You—Bob Dylan (69)	283
Mozambique—Bob Dylan (76)	256
Can You Please Crawl Out Your Window?—Bob Dylan (66)	245
You Angel You—Manfred Mann's Earth Band (79)	199
Sweetheart Like You—Bob Dylan (83)	187
Most Likely You Go Your Way (And I'll Go Mine)—Bob Dylan / The Band (74)	177
Lay Lady Lay—Isley Brothers (71)	*173*
End Of The Line—Traveling Wilburys (89)	166
I Shall Be Released—Box Tops (69)	156
Love Minus Zero - No Limit—Turley Richards (70)	144
I Threw It All Away—Bob Dylan (69)	135
You Ain't Going Nowhere—Byrds (68)	108
Love Is Just A Four-Letter Word—Joan Baez (69)	93
Lay Lady Lay—Ferrante & Teicher (70)	*60*
When The Ship Comes In—Peter, Paul & Mary (65)	49
Leopard-Skin Pill-Box Hat—Bob Dylan (67)	48
Like A Rolling Stone—Phil Flowers & The Flower Shop (69)	*27*
One Too Many Mornings—Beau Brummels (66)	21
Something There Is About You—Bob Dylan (74)	16
Just Like A Woman—Manfred Mann (66)	*7.6*
Mr. Jones—Grass Roots (65)	7.4
If You Gotta Go, Go Now—Manfred Mann (65)	0.5
James DYRENFORTH ▶ 10120 (1)	**12**
Garden In The Rain—Vic Dana (64)	25

E

Don EARL ▶ 3137 (3)	**990**
I'm Available—Margie Rayburn (57)	1267
Teddy Bear Song—Barbara Fairchild (73)	708
Kid Stuff—Barbara Fairchild (73)	4.7
Raymond EARL ▶ 5227 (2)	**323**
I Got My Mind Made Up (You Can Get It Girl)—Instant Funk (79)	815
Let Me Party With You (Part 1) (Party, Party, Party)—Bunny Sigler (78)	204
Stacy EARL ▶ 5982 (1)	**219**
Love Me All Up—Stacy Earl (91)	658
James EARLEY ▶ 5159 (3)	**332**
2 Legit 2 Quit—M.C. Hammer (91)	1441
Go For It (Heart And Fire)—Joey B. Ellis & Tynetta Hare (90)	111
Turn It Up—Oaktown's 3.5.7 (91)	49
—Earthquake see: Floyd BROWN	
Dennis EAST [Dennis Thomas Oosthuis] ▶ 7176 (1)	**112**
Empty Beach—Tricia Leigh Fisher (90)	112
Nathan EAST ▶ 2372 (2)	**1554**
Easy Lover—Philip Bailey (84)	4579
Reservations For Two—Dionne Warwick (87)	83
—Linda Louise Eastman see: Linda McCARTNEY	
Richard EASTMAN ▶ 5363 (1)	**300**
Dominoes—Robbie Nevil (87)	899
Barry EASTMOND ▶ 917 (9)	**4815**
There'll Be Sad Songs (To Make You Cry)—Billy Ocean (86)	4280
When The Going Gets Tough, The Tough Get Going—Billy Ocean (85)	3161
Love Zone—Billy Ocean (86)	1312

Barry EASTMOND ► 917 (9) ***Continued***	**4815**
You Are My Lady—Freddie Jackson (85)	1184
Love Is Forever—Billy Ocean (86)	997
The Colour Of Love—Billy Ocean (88)	815
He'll Never Love You (Like I Do)— Freddie Jackson (85)	531
Nice 'N' Slow—Freddie Jackson (88)	207
Have You Ever Loved Somebody— Freddie Jackson (87)	143
Lynn EASTON ► 1952 (4)	**2056**
The Jolly Green Giant—Kingsmen (65)	2937
Annie Fanny—Kingsmen (65)	483
The Climb—Kingsmen (65)	299
Long Green—Fireballs (69)	295
Sheena EASTON [Sheena Shirley Orr] ► 5784 (1)	**242**
The Arms Of Orion—Prince With Sheena Easton (89)	483
Al EATON ► 7624 (1)	**84**
The Ghetto—Too Short (90)	337
Bobby EATON ► 8840 (3)	**38**
Drop By My Place—Little Carl Carlton (70)	140
You Made A Believer (Out Of Me)—Ruby Andrews (69)	22
Hey Boy Take A Chance On Love—Ruby Andrews (67)	8.4
Jimmy EATON ► 6797 (6)	**136**
Dance By The Light Of The Moon—Olympics (60)	*428*
Flamenco Love— Don Costa His Orchestra And Chorus (56)	*146*
Dance With A Dolly (With A Hole In Her Stocking)— Damita Jo (61)	*65*
Flamenco Love—Tony Martin (56)	*0.0*
Flamenco Love—Al Caiola and his Magic Guitar (56)	*0.0*
Flamenco Love—Richard Hayman (56)	*0.0*
Steve EATON ► 4073 (2)	**604**
All You Get From Love Is A Love Song— Carpenters (77)	320
Rag Doll—Sammy Johns (75)	284
—Tim Eaton see: Buster (2) BROWN	
William EATON ► 6860 (2)	**132**
I'm The One—Roberta Flack (82)	388
Be Mine (Tonight)—Grover Washington, Jr. (82)	8.6
Hubert EAVES III ► 5806 (3)	**240**
She Won't Talk To Me—Luther Vandross (89)	438
Something's On Your Mind—D Train (84)	37
You're The One For Me—"D" Train (82)	5.8
Fred EBB ► 1579 (21) HOF	**2675**
My Coloring Book—Kitty Kallen (62)	*1467*
My Coloring Book—Sandy Stewart (62)	*1420*
Little Blue Man—Betty Johnson (58)	791
Theme From New York, New York— Frank Sinatra (80)	577
Kiss Me Another—Georgia Gibbs (56)	566
Good And Lonesome—Kay Starr (55)	273
Close The Door—Jim Lowe (55)	235
Rockin' The Cha Cha—Alan Dale (55)	221
Summer Sweetheart—Ames Brothers (56)	60
That's Ok With Me—Susan Hunter (55)	53
In The Arms Of My Love—Joe Valino (57)	27
I Like Them All—Dean Martin (55)	14
Wait For Tomorrow—Jill Corey (56)	12
I'll Wait—Betty Johnson (56)	7.7
Dream World—Four Coins (58)	6.8
That Do Make It Nice—Eddy Arnold (55)	6.5
Sugar Corsage—Bonnie Scott (57)	*2.4*
Sugar Corsage—Chuck Reed (57)	*2.4*
My Coloring Book—Barbra Streisand (62)	*0.0*
My Coloring Book—George Chakiris (62)	*0.0*
Hook—Rita Robbins (54)	0.0
—Ebb Tide see: Ted HARRIS	
Gerhard EBELER ► 8351 (3)	**54**
You Can't Be True Dear—Mary Kaye Trio (59)	*189*
You Can't Be True, Dear—Patti Page (65)	*25*
You Can't Be True Dear— Steve Lawrence & Eydie Gorme (59)	*0.0*
—Margaret Louis Ebey see: Margie SINGLETON	
—Dolores Eble see: Dolores FULLER	
Odis ECHOLS ► 2022 (2)	**1998**
Sugartime—McGuire Sisters (57)	*3995*
Sugartime—Charlie Phillips (57)	*0.0*
Michael ECKART ► 8272 (1)	**56**
I Love The Bass—Bardeux (89)	168
—William Clarence Eckstein see: Billy ECKSTINE	
Billy ECKSTINE [William Clarence Eckstein, William Eckstein] ► 10844 (3)	**5.0**
Jelly, Jelly, Jelly—Bobby Bland (62)	4.9
Stormy Monday—Latimore (73)	3.1
I Want To Talk About You—Ray Charles (67)	1.5
John EDDIE ► 5710 (1)	**252**
Jungle Boy—John Eddie (86)	252
Duane EDDY ► 687 (21)	**6336**
Forty Miles Of Bad Road—Duane Eddy His "Twangy" guitar and The Rebels (59)	2380
Rebel 'rouser—Duane Eddy (58)	2375
(Dance With The) Guitar Man— Duane Eddy And The Rebelettes (62)	2041
Cannonball—Duane Eddy His "Twangy" guitar and The Rebels (58)	1147
Lonely One—Duane Eddy His "Twangy" guitar and The Rebels (59)	881
Boss Guitar—Duane Eddy And The Rebelettes (63)	722
Yep—Duane Eddy His "Twangy" guitar and The Rebels (59)	522
Some Kind A Earthquake—Duane Eddy His "Twangy" guitar and The Rebels (59)	513
Shazam—Duane Eddy His "Twangy" Guitar And The Rebels (60)	362
Kommotion—Duane Eddy (60)	345
First Love First Tears—Duane Eddy His "Twangy" guitar and The Rebels (59)	256
Quiet Three—Duane Eddy His "Twangy" guitar and The Rebels (59)	255
Ring Of Fire—Duane Eddy (61)	197
Your Baby's Gone Surfin'—Duane Eddy (63)	161
Lonely Boy, Lonely Guitar—Duane Eddy (63)	134
Drivin' Home—Duane Eddy And The Rebels (61)	92
Moovin' N' Groovin'—Duane Eddy (58)	31
The Son Of Rebel Rouser—Duane Eddy (63)	20
The Battle—Duane Eddy and The Rebels (62)	13
The Avenger—Duane Eddy And The Rebels (61)	3.8
Stretchin' Out—Duane Eddy and The Rebelettes (62)	0.4
George EDDY [George Paxton] ► 3577 (4)	**779**
The Writing On The Wall—Adam Wade (61)	2168
Let True Love Begin—Nat King Cole (61)	104
Mr. Happiness—Johnny Maestro With The Coeds (61)	61
Flying Blue Angels— George, Johnny And The Pilots (62)	3.6
—Hal Eddy see: Harry EDELSTEIN	
—Mirriam Eddy see: Jessi COLTER	
Randy EDELMAN ► 1924 (3)	**2102**
Weekend In New England—Barry Manilow (76)	2022
Everybody Wants To Find A Bluebird— Randy Edelman (75)	55
Can't It All Be Love—Randy Edelman (77)	25
Harry EDELSTEIN [Hal Eddy] ► 7448 (2)	**95**
Our Love Affair—Tommy Charles (56)	187
After School—Tommy Charles (56)	4.0
Ron EDGAR ► 11619 (1)	**1.0**
Just About The Same—Association (70)	4.8
Floyd EDGE ► 4991 (1)	**363**
Dance To The Bop— Gene Vincent and His Blue Caps (57)	363
Tracy EDMOND ► 9141 (1)	**30**
The Devil Came Up To Michigan—K.M.C. Kru (91)	*243*
Kenneth EDMONDS [Kenneth Brian Edmonds, Babyface] ► 139 (34) HOF	**19947**
I'm Your Baby Tonight—Whitney Houston (90)	3804
On Our Own—Bobby Brown (89)	3434
Every Little Step—Bobby Brown (89)	2865
The Lover In Me—Sheena Easton (88)	2763
Giving You The Benefit—Pebbles (90)	2301
Ready Or Not—After 7 (90)	2131
Roni—Bobby Brown (88)	1988
Girlfriend—Pebbles (88)	1891
The Way You Love Me—Karyn White (88)	1851
Can't Stop—After 7 (90)	1836
Secret Rendezvous—Karyn White (89)	1717
Rock Steady—Whispers (87)	1571
Whip Appeal—Babyface (90)	1497
Rock Wit'cha—Bobby Brown (89)	1460
Don't Be Cruel—Bobby Brown (88)	1445
Two Occasions—Deele (88)	1277
Superwoman—Karyn White (89)	1259
It's No Crime—Babyface (89)	1221
My, My, My—Johnny Gill (90)	1143
Miracle—Whitney Houston (91)	1127
Tender Lover—Babyface (89)	988
Dial My Heart—Boys (88)	927
Love Makes Things Happen—Pebbles (90)	846
I'd Still Say Yes—Klymaxx (87)	841
Heat Of The Moment—After 7 (90)	*780*
My Kinda Girl—Babyface (90)	508
Fairweather Friend—Johnny Gill (90)	468
Knocked Out—Paula Abdul (88)	378
Exclusivity—Damian Dame (91)	180
Nothin (that compares 2 U)—Jacksons (89)	78
Heat Of The Moment—After 7 (89)	*76*
Backyard—Pebbles (91)	59
Right Down To It—Damian Dame (91)	17
Word To The Badd!!—Jermaine Jackson (91)	11
Carl EDMONDSON ► 5911 (1)	**230**
Hey-Da-Da-Dow—Dolphins (64)	230
Robert EDMONDSON ► 9096 (1)	**31**
Easy Rider (Let The Wind Pay The Way)— Iron Butterfly (70)	125
Travis EDMONSON ► 6550 (1)	**158**
Cloudy Summer Afternoon (Raindrops)— Barry McGuire (66)	158
—Dennis Edmonton see: Mars BONFIRE	
Jerry EDMONTON [Gerald McCrohan] ► 2763 (5)	**1213**
Monster—Steppenwolf (69)	707
Hey Lawdy Mama—Steppenwolf (70)	613
Straight Shootin' Woman—Steppenwolf (74)	589
For Ladies Only—Steppenwolf (71)	190
America/Standing—Five Stairsteps (70)	93
Dave EDMUNDS ► 11230 (1)	**2.7**
High School Nights—Dave Edmunds (85)	8.0
Bernard EDWARDS ► 143 (20) HOF	**19807**
Le Freak—Chic (78)	11074
Upside Down—Diana Ross (80)	8140
Good Times—Chic (79)	6108
We Are Family—Sister Sledge (79)	4694
Dance, Dance, Dance (Yowsah, Yowsah, Yowsah)— Chic (77)	2478
I'm Coming Out—Diana Ross (80)	2369
I Want Your Love—Chic (79)	2083
He's The Greatest Dancer—Sister Sledge (79)	1848
Rapper's Delight—Sugarhill Gang (79)	551
Backfired—Debbie Harry (81)	351
Everybody Dance—Chic (78)	267
Rebels Are We—Chic (80)	112
Got To Love Somebody—Sister Sledge (80)	93
My Forbidden Lover—Chic (79)	91
Why—Carly Simon (82)	86
Soup For One—Chic (82)	43
Saturday—Norma Jean Wright (78)	41
Real People—Chic (80)	16
The Jam Was Moving—Debbie Harry (81)	11
Chip Off The Old Block—Chic (80)	0.0
Bobby EDWARDS [Robert E. Moncrief] ► 3938 (4)	**650**
You're The Reason—Bobby Edwards (61)	*2462*
You're The Reason—Joe South (61)	*136*
You're The Reason—Hank Locklin (61)	*0.0*
You're The Reason—Gerry And The Pacemakers (65)	*0.0*
Clara EDWARDS ► 4139 (2)	**582**
With The Wind And The Rain In Your Hair— Pat Boone (59)	1142
By The Bend Of The River— Joe Leahy & His Orchestra (57)	11
Daphna EDWARDS ► 10116 (1)	**13**
Don't Want No-Body—J.D. Drews (80)	25
Darrell EDWARDS ► 7901 (4)	**70**
Tender Years—George Jones (61)	*53*
Who Shot Sam—George Jones (59)	20
Tender Years—Brook Benton (63)	*11*
Why Baby Why—Red Sovine & Webb Pierce (57)	0.0
Doug EDWARDS ► 2724 (2)	**1240**
Wildflower—Skylark (73)	*2222*
Wildflower—New Birth (74)	*257*
Earl EDWARDS ► 1430 (4)	**3074**
Duke Of Earl—Gene Chandler (62)	*9144*
Walk On With The Duke—Duke Of Earl (62)	86
Duchess Of Earl—Pearlettes (62)	*50*
Duchess Of Earl—Bobbie Smith & The Dreamgirls (62)	*0.0*

Fred EDWARDS ▶ 3294 (4)	**909**
The Devil Went Down To Georgia—Charlie Daniels Band (79)	*3303*
In America—Charlie Daniels Band (80)	1335
The Legend Of Wooley Swamp—Charlie Daniels Band (80)	633
The Devil Came Up To Michigan—K.M.C. Kru (91)	*243*
Gus EDWARDS [Gus Simon] ▶ 6154 (1) HOF	**199**
By The Light Of The Silvery Moon—Jimmy Bowen With The Rhythm Orchids (58)	398
J. Vincent EDWARDS ▶ 1575 (2)	**2684**
Right Back Where We Started From—Maxine Nightingale (76)	*5350*
Right Back Where We Started From—Sinitta (89)	*18*
Jackie EDWARDS ▶ 4406 (2)	**503**
Somebody Help Me—Spencer Davis Group (67)	415
Keep On Running—Spencer Davis Group (66)	88
James EDWARDS ▶ 2292 (2)	**1642**
Sh-Boom—Crew-Cuts (54)	*7040*
Sh-Boom—Chords (54)	*1169*
Joan EDWARDS ▶ 8995 (2)	**34**
Let It Ring—Doris Day (55)	63
Keep Your Cotton Pickin' Paddies Offa My Heart—Teresa Brewer (56)	6.7
Jonathan EDWARDS ▶ 1086 (3)	**4069**
Sunshine—Jonathan Edwards (71)	4034
Train Of Glory—Jonathan Edwards (72)	24
Everybody Knows Her—Jonathan Edwards (72)	11
Kenny EDWARDS ▶ 7217 (2)	**110**
Baby Don't Go—Karla Bonoff (80)	128
The Long Way Around—Linda Ronstadt (71)	45
Lockie EDWARDS ▶ 3917 (8)	**657**
Model Girl—Johnny Maestro The Voice Of The Crests (61)	600
That's When I Cried—Jimmy Jones (60)	340
Ten Lonely Guys—Pat Boone (62)	*317*
Leave Me Alone—Baby Washington (63)	233
Mr. Wishing Well—Nat King Cole (63)	110
Ten Lonely Guys—Ten Broken Hearts (62)	*81*
Insult To Injury—Timi Yuro (63)	24
Getting Ready For The Heartbreak—Chuck Jackson (62)	18
Michael EDWARDS ▶ 4023 (3)	**621**
Once In Awhile—Chimes (60)	*1239*
Once In A While—Modernaires (57)	*1.9*
Once In A While—Clyde Stacy (58)	*0.4*
Michael James EDWARDS ▶ 836 (2)	**5282**
Right Here, Right Now—Jesus Jones (91)	3607
Real, Real, Real—Jesus Jones (91)	1675
—Patricia Louise Edwards see: Patti LaBELLE	
R. Alan EDWARDS ▶ 8444 (1)	**50**
Fantastically Foolish—Tommy Sands (57)	50
Ray EDWARDS ▶ 2607 (3)	**1328**
Get A Job—Silhouettes (58)	*5224*
Get A Job—Nino & the Ebb Tides (61)	*88*
Get A Job—Mills Brothers (58)	*0.0*
Sherman EDWARDS ▶ 431 (21)	**9438**
See You In September—Happenings (66)	*5461*
Broken Hearted Melody—Sarah Vaughan (59)	2677
Dungaree Doll—Eddie Fisher (55)	2143
Johnny Get Angry—Joanie Sommers (62)	1932
Wonderful Wonderful—Johnny Mathis (57)	*1803*
Wonderful! Wonderful!—Tymes (63)	*1667*
See You In September—Tempos (59)	*829*
Flaming Star—Elvis Presley With The Jordanaires (61)	770
Outside My Window—Fleetwoods (60)	556
Rock Right—Georgia Gibbs (56)	355
You'll Answer To Me—Patti Page (61)	226
I Am—Tony Bennett with Ray Ellis and His Orchestra (57)	190
Biology—Danny Valentino (60)	*106*
A Whistling Tune—Elvis Presley with the Jordanaires (62)	62
Home Is Where The Heart Is—Elvis Presley with the Jordanaires (62)	62
Day I Died, The—Playmates (58)	13
When The Boys Get Together—Joanie Sommers (62)	5.7
Don't Let It Happen To Us—Shirelles (63)	3.3
Crossroads Of Love—Tempos Featuring Mike Lazo (59)	1.2
Wonderful! Wonderful!—Jan Peerce with Joe Reisman & His Orchestra (57)	*0.0*
Biology—Sue Raney (60)	*0.0*
Tom EDWARDS ▶ 9381 (2)	**25**
What Is A Teenage Girl?—Tom Edwards (57)	48
What Is A Teenage Boy?—Tom Edwards (57)	1.6
Tommy EDWARDS ▶ 6046 (2)	**212**
Honestly And Truly—Tommy Edwards (59)	202
I Looked At Heaven—Tommy Edwards (59)	10
Webley EDWARDS [John Kalapana] ▶ 7992 (2)	**66**
Pearly Shells (Popo O Ewa)—Burl Ives (64)	*198*
Pearly Shells—Arthur Lyman (64)	*0.0*
—Nicholas Eede see: Nick VAN EEDE	
Joe EGAN ▶ 1723 (3)	**2420**
Stuck In The Middle With You—Stealers Wheel (73)	2928
Star—Stealers Wheel (73)	726
Everyone's Agreed That Everything Will Turn Out Fine—Stealers Wheel (73)	459
Walter EGAN ▶ 1344 (6)	**3302**
Magnet And Steel—Walter Egan (78)	1873
Hot Summer Nights—Night (79)	*852*
Fool Moon Fire—Walter Egan (83)	347
Hot Summer Nights—Walter Egan (78)	*155*
Only The Lucky—Walter Egan (77)	71
Unloved—Walter Egan (79)	3.8
Jaap EGGERMONT ▶ 4501 (6)	**476**
Stars On 45—Stars On 45 (81)	*442*
Stars On 45—Stars On 45 (81)	*442*
Stars On 45—Stars On 45 (82)	*27*
Stars on 45—Stars On 45 (81)	*16*
Stars On 45—Stars On 45 (81)	*12*
Stars On 45—Stars On 45 (81)	*12*
Arthur EGNOIAN [Art Laboe] ▶ 1409 (7)	**3147**
Teen Beat—Sandy Nelson (59)	*3896*
Bongo Rock—Preston Epps (59)	*1240*
Teen Beat '65—Sandy Nelson (64)	*535*
Bongo Rock—Incredible Bongo Band (73)	*310*
Bongo Bongo Bongo—Preston Epps (60)	200
Corrido Rock (Pt. 1)—"Handsome" Jim Balcom (58)	*113*
Corrido Rock—Jimmy Church's Magicians (58)	*0.0*
—Norma Deloris Egstrom see: Peggy LEE	
Phil EHART ▶ 4568 (2)	**465**
Point Of Know Return—Kansas (77)	905
Play The Game Tonight—Kansas (82)	814
M. Dan EHMIG ▶ 11705 (1)	**0.6**
Hungry—Lita Ford (90)	1.1
Larry EHRLICH ▶ 4234 (3)	**552**
Gotta Travel On—Billy Grammer (58)	*3674*
Gotta Travel On—Timi Yuro (63)	*190*
Gotta Travel On—Harry Belafonte (59)	*0.0*
Max EHRMANN ▶ 3718 (1)	**721**
Desiderata—Les Crane (71)	1441
Rohusuke EI [Rokusuke EI, Takeo EI] ▶ 1079 (1)	**4086**
Sukiyaki—Kyu Sakamoto (63)	*8172*
—Takeo EI see: Rohusuke EI	
—Robert Charles Elchom see: Bobby ICON	
Shirley EIKHARD ▶ 2165 (1)	**1803**
Something To Talk About—Bonnie Raitt (91)	1803
Dave EILAND ▶ 8244 (1)	**57**
I Need Your Loving—Human League (86)	343
—Eva Eln see: E. Eln LOGGINS	
Herb EISEMAN ▶ 8736 (3)	**41**
Trouble With Harry—Alfi & Harry (56)	*105*
Trouble With Harry—Les Baxter, His Chorus and Orchestra (56)	*17*
The Trouble With Harry—Jack Pleis and His Orchestra and Chorus (56)	*0.0*
—Stanley Harvey Eisen see: Paul STANLEY	
—Denise Eisenberg see: Joy DENNY	
—Stephen Geoffrey Eisenberg see: Geoffrey STEVENS	
—Sylvia Eisenberg see: Sil SEDORES	
—Lawrence Eisler see: Eddie LAWRENCE	
David Glen EISLEY ▶ 4205 (2)	**563**
Call To The Heart—Giuffria (84)	942
Lonely In Love—Giuffria (85)	185
—Renrut Eki see: Ike TURNER	
Kurtis EL KHALEEL [Kurtis Mantronik] ▶ 9894 (1)	**15**
Got To Have Your Love—Mantronix (featuring Wondress) (90)	46
Leila EL KHALIFI [Leila K] ▶ 8097 (1)	**62**
Got To Get—Leila K with Rob 'N' Raz (90)	248
Donnie ELBERT ▶ 4051 (4)	**612**
Open The Door To Your Heart—Darrell Banks (66)	936
Sweet Baby—Donnie Elbert (72)	74
What Can I Do—Donnie Elbert (57)	51
Can't Get Over Losing You—Donnie Elbert (70)	18
Harry ELDRIDGE ▶ 11062 (1)	**3.5**
High Tide Boogie—Richard Maltby And His Orchestra (55)	6.9
—Eddison Electrik see: Eddison SAINSBURY	
Dino ELEFANTE ▶ 7389 (2)	**99**
Fight Fire With Fire—Kansas (83)	110
Right Away—Kansas (82)	88
John ELEFANTE ▶ 7390 (2)	**99**
Fight Fire With Fire—Kansas (83)	110
Right Away—Kansas (82)	88
Danny ELFMAN ▶ 4896 (2)	**387**
Weird Science—Oingo Boingo (85)	310
Just Another Day—Oingo Boingo (85)	77
Edward ELGAR ▶ 5404 (1)	**293**
The Graduation Song...Pomp And Circumstance—Adrian Kimberly (61)	293
—Bob Elgin see: Stanley KAHAN	
Bobby ELI [Eli Tatarsky] ▶ 1060 (10)	**4160**
Love Won't Let Me Wait—Major Harris (75)	3713
Sideshow—Blue Magic (74)	*2571*
Just Don't Want To Be Lonely—Main Ingredient (74)	*2140*
Three Ring Circus—Blue Magic (74)	407
Just Don't Want To Be Lonely—Ronnie Dyson (73)	*210*
Mr. Magic Man—Wilson Pickett (73)	29
Sideshow—Band Of Gold (84)	*12*
This Is What You Mean To Me—Engelbert Humperdinck (75)	11
Laid Back Love—Major Harris (76)	9.1
Happy Man (Part 1)—Impact (76)	3.4
Gwynn ELIAS ▶ 7352 (2)	**100**
Love Me As I Love You—George Maharis (62)	272
And The Heavens Cried—Ronnie Savoy (60)	19
Jonathan ELIAS ▶ 6386 (1)	**176**
I Do What I Do—John Taylor (86)	527
Michael ELIAS ▶ 5374 (2)	**298**
I Cried—Patti Page (54)	*582*
I Cried—Joe Damiano (59)	*14*
T.S. ELIOT ▶ 5802 (2)	**240**
Memory—Barry Manilow (82)	*493*
Memory - The Theme From Andrew Lloyd Webber's Musical "Cats"—Barbra Streisand (82)	*228*
Edward ELISCU ▶ 8270 (5) HOF	**56**
Without A Song—Roy Hamilton (55)	*145*
Without A Song (Part 1)—James Cleveland and the Cleveland Singers (66)	*18*
More Than You Know—Platters (62)	3.2
Great Day—Sarah Vaughan (61)	1.9
Without A Song—Kay Starr (55)	*0.0*
—Tracey Elizondo see: Tracey AMOS	
Edward ELLEN ▶ 8503 (1)	**48**
Bring Back Your Heart—Del Vikings (61)	96
Collin ELLINGSON ▶ 9754 (1)	**17**
Divided Hearts—Kim Carnes (86)	70
Dave ELLINGSON ▶ 1754 (8)	**2367**
Don't Fall In Love With A Dreamer—Kenny Rogers with Kim Carnes (80)	3393
Draw Of The Cards—Kim Carnes (81)	564
Voyeur—Kim Carnes (82)	516
Does It Make You Remember—Kim Carnes (82)	507
You Make My Heart Beat Faster (And That's All That Matters)—Kim Carnes (84)	172
Invitation To Dance—Kim Carnes (85)	122
Abadabadango—Kim Carnes (85)	82
You Turned My World Around—Frank Sinatra (74)	14
Duke ELLINGTON ▶ 4196 (10) HOF	**566**
Mood Indigo—Norman Petty Trio (54)	*481*
Caravan—Santo & Johnny (60)	*396*
Don't Get Around Much Anymore—Belmonts (61)	*211*
Don't Get Around Much Anymore—Tab Hunter (57)	*101*

Duke ELLINGTON ▶ 4196 (10) HOF *Continued* 566
Caravan (pt. 1)—Cozy Cole (58) *82*
Don't Get Around Much Anymore—Jo Stafford (55) *13*
Mood Indigo Mambo—Perez Prado & Orchestra (55) *5.9*
Black And Tan Fantasy—
David Rose And His Orchestra (62) 3.5
Caravan (Part 2)—Cozy Cole (58) *1.4*
Mood Indigo—Modernaires & George Auld (54) *0.0*

Bill ELLIOT ▶ 8102 (1) 62
Costafine Town—Splinter (74) 123

Brian ELLIOT ▶ 1911 (1) 2121
Papa Don't Preach—Madonna (86) 4241

Don ELLIOT ▶ 2937 (2) 1110
Uh! Oh! (Part 2)—Nutty Squirrels (59) *2146*
Uh! Oh! [Part 1]—Nutty Squirrels (59) *74*

David Leland ELLIOTT ▶ 2946 (1) 1105
Here And Now—Luther Vandross (89) 2210

—Jack Elliott see: Irwin Elliott ZUCKER

Joe ELLIOTT ▶ 1591 (12) 2655
Pour Some Sugar On Me—Def Leppard (88) 3871
Love Bites—Def Leppard (88) 3277
Armageddon It—Def Leppard (88) 2857
Photograph—Def Leppard (83) 1231
Hysteria—Def Leppard (88) 1083
Rocket—Def Leppard (89) 1017
Rock Of Ages—Def Leppard (83) 1009
Animal—Def Leppard (87) 796
Foolin'—Def Leppard (83) 557
Bringin' On The Heartbreak—Def Leppard (84) 157
Women—Def Leppard (87) 26
Rock Brigade—Def Leppard (80) 9.8

John M. ELLIOTT ▶ 4214 (3) 561
Ivory Rag (In der Alten Hafenbar)—
Johnny Maddox And The Rhythmasters (55) *1115*
Sam's Song—Dean Martin And Sammy Davis Jr. (62) 8.0
Ivory Rag (In der Alten Hafenbar)—Crazy Otto (55) *0.0*

—Max Elliott see: Maxi PRIEST

Ron ELLIOTT ▶ 1400 (4) 3172
Just A Little—Beau Brummels (65) 2227
Laugh, Laugh—Beau Brummels (64) 1366
You Tell Me Why—Beau Brummels (65) 514
Don't Talk To Strangers—Beau Brummels (65) 357

Alfred James ELLIS ▶ 1056 (7) 4174
Cold Sweat - Part 1—
James Brown And The Famous Flames (67) 2719
Mother Popcorn (You Got To Have A Mother For Me)
Part 1—James Brown (69) 2396
Say It Loud - I'm Black And I'm Proud (Part 1)—
James Brown (68) 1559
Licking Stick-Licking Stick (Part 1)—
James Brown And The Famous Flames (68) 1305
Get It Together (Part 1)—
James Brown And The Famous Flames (67) 584
Moon Walk Part I—Joe Simon (69) 409
Soul Pride (Part 1)—James Brown (69) 7.3

Barbara ELLIS ▶ 1444 (4) 3029
Come Softly To Me—Fleetwoods (59) *8460*
Graduation's Here—Fleetwoods (59) 416
Come Softly To Me—Ronnie Height (59) *196*
Come Softly To Me—
New Seekers Featuring Marty Kristian (73) *14*

Darryl ELLIS ▶ 10285 (1) 10
In The Mood—Tyrone Davis (79) 31

—Emmitt Ellis Jr. see: Bobby RUSH

Joey B. ELLIS [Joseph Ellis, MC Breeze] ▶ 9250 (1) 28
Go For It (Heart And Fire)—
Joey B. Ellis & Tynetta Hare (90) 111

Jonah ELLIS ▶ 3970 (2) 634
Don't Stop The Music—Yarbrough & Peoples (81) 954
Don't Waste Your Time—Yarbrough & Peoples (84) 316

Ray ELLIS ▶ 10620 (1) 6.7
Very Much In Love—Johnny Mathis (59) 13

Shirley ELLIS [Shirley Elliston, Shirley Marie O'Garra] ▶ 1654 (3) 2540
The Name Game—Shirley Ellis (64) 4579
Soul Time—Shirley Ellis (67) 237
Attack Of The Name Game—Stacy Lattisaw (82) 54

Ted ELLIS [Ted Ellis Botkin] ▶ 2684 (2) 1272
Dreamin'—Johnny Burnette (60) *2376*
Dreamin'—John Schneider (82) *169*

Terry Lynn ELLIS ▶ 3870 (2) 671
Hold On—En Vogue (90) 3351
Lies—En Vogue (90) 676

William Cosby ELLIS ▶ 5762 (1) 244
Don't Treat Me Bad—Firehouse (91) 976

James R. ELLISON ▶ 7120 (2) 115
What Can I Do For You?—Labelle (75) 223
Feels Like Another One—Patti LaBelle (91) 13

John ELLISON ▶ 1673 (3) 2514
Some Kind Of Wonderful—Grand Funk (74) *2487*
Some Kind Of Wonderful—Soul Brothers Six (67) *15*
(She's) Some Kind Of Wonderful—
Fantastic Johnny C (68) *13*

Lorraine ELLISON [Marybelle Luraine Ellison] ▶ 6495 (3) 163
I Dig You Baby—Jerry Butler (67) *266*
Stay Together Young Lovers—
Brenda & The Tabulations (67) 118
I Dig You Baby—Lorraine Ellison (66) *46*

—Marybelle Luraine Ellison see: Lorraine ELLISON

Ronald ELLISON ▶ 9284 (1) 27
Jerk And Twine—Jackie Ross (65) 81

—Shirley Elliston see: Shirley ELLIS

Rolf ELLMER ▶ 9044 (1) 32
This Beat Is Hot—B.G. Prince Of Rap (91) 65

Kenn ELLNER ▶ 4294 (1) 530
Psychotic Reaction—Count Five (66) 2651

Bob ELLSWORTH ▶ 7204 (3) 110
Somebody Else Is Taking My Place—Al Martino (65) *249*
Somebody Else Is Taking My Place—Joni James (61) *66*
Somebody Else Is Taking My Place—
Jaye P. Morgan (59) *15*

Ziggy ELMAN [Harry Finkelman] ▶ 9748 (2) 18
And The Angels Sing—Three Chuckles (56) *23*
And The Angels Sing—Johnny Nash (59) *12*

—Elmo see: Garry BONNER

Lawrence ELOW ▶ 11798 (1) 0.0
Not As A Stranger—McGuire Sisters (54) 0.0

—El Sati see: Stijn LAUWERS

Harry ELSTON ▶ 2184 (1) 1769
Grazing In The Grass—Friends Of Distinction (69) *3539*

Billy ELWORTHY ▶ 2987 (3) 1082
Sweetheart—Franke & The Knockouts (81) 1388
Without You (Not Another Lonely Night)—
Franke & the Knockouts (82) 684
You're My Girl—Franke and the Knockouts (81) 478

Vince ELY [Vincent Paul Davey] ▶ 6635 (2) 149
Love My Way—Psychedelic Furs (83) 375
Pretty In Pink—Psychedelic Furs (86) 330

Billy EMERSON ▶ 5275 (3) 314
Red Hot—Sam The Sham And The Pharaohs (66) *152*
Red Hot—Robert Gordon With Link Wray (77) *111*
It Do Me So Good—Ann-Margret (61) 103

Keith EMERSON ▶ 7921 (2) 70
Touch And Go—Emerson, Lake & Powell (86) 116
Stone Of Years—Emerson, Lake & Palmer (71) 23

Lee EMERSON [Emerson Lee Bellamy] ▶ 7890 (3) 71
(Doin' The) Lovers Leap—Webb Pierce (60) 55
Love My Lady—Bobby Helms (58) 19
No Signs Of Loneliness Here—Marty Robbins (63) 6.4

Leroy EMMANUEL [Leroy Mannuel] ▶ 9525 (2) 22
Get Down People—Fabulous Counts (70) 37
Why Not Start All Over Again—Counts (72) 9.8

Les EMMERSON ▶ 660 (9) 6616
Signs—Five Man Electrical Band (71) 3062
Signs—Tesla (90) 1489
Absolutely Right—Five Man Electrical Band (71) 752
Control Of Me—Les Emmerson (72) 456
Werewolf—Five Man Electrical Band (74) 308
I'm A Stranger Here—Five Man Electrical Band (73) 210
Money Back Guarantee—
Five Man Electrical Band (72) 168
Moonshine (Friend Of Mine)—John Kay (73) 92
Julianna—Five Man Electrical Band (72) 81

Daniel Decatur EMMETT ▶ 3753 (3) HOF 710
Theme From Dixie—Duane Eddy (61) *419*
Dixie—Mickey Newbury (71) *222*
Dixie—Elvis Presley (72) *69*

Rik EMMETT ▶ 3228 (6) 940
Hold On—Triumph (79) 538
Somebody's Out There—Triumph (86) 502
Magic Power—Triumph (81) 298
Lay It On The Line—Triumph (79) 122
I Can Survive—Triumph (80) 28
Follow Your Heart—Triumph (85) 10

Bobby EMMONS ▶ 4099 (2) 594
Luckenbach, Texas (Back To The Basics Of Love)—
Waylon Jennings (77) 818
Help Me Make It (To My Rockin' Chair)—
B.J. Thomas (75) 185

Melvin ENDSLEY ▶ 214 (7) 15197
Singing The Blues—Guy Mitchell (56) *11013*
I Like Your Kind Of Love—Andy Williams (57) *1619*
Knee Deep In The Blues—Guy Mitchell (57) 962
Love Me To Pieces—Jill Corey (57) 893
Singing The Blues—Marty Robbins (56) *702*
Why I'm Walkin'—Stonewall Jackson (60) 14
I Like Your Kind Of Love—Melvin Endsley (57) *0.0*

Bill ENGELHART ▶ 7983 (1) 66
I Love An Angel—Little Bill & The Bluenotes (59) 66

Hans ENGELMANN ▶ 350 (7) 10780
Melody Of Love—Billy Vaughn and His Orchestra (54) *7273*
Melody Of Love—
David Carroll And His Orchestra (54) *2366*
Melody Of Love—Four Aces (54) *2262*
Melody Of Love—Leo Diamond (55) *10*
Melody Of Love—
Sammy Kaye & His "Swing & Sway" Orchestra (55) *0.0*
Melody Of Love—Frank Sinatra & Ray Anthony (55) *0.0*
Melody Of Love—Tony Martin & Dinah Shore (55) *0.0*

Paul ENGEMANN ▶ 9749 (1) 18
Reach Out—Giorgio Moroder (84) 53

—England Dan see: Dan SEALS

Jackie ENGLISH ▶ 11163 (1) 2.9
Once A Night—Jackie English (80) 5.9

Scott ENGLISH ▶ 707 (12) 6156
Bend Me, Shape Me—American Breed (67) *6075*
Mandy—Barry Manilow (74) *4532*
Help Me Girl—Eric Burdon And The Animals (66) *651*
Help Me Girl—Outsiders (66) *588*
I Am What I Am—Lois Fletcher (74) 263
Now I Know—Jack Jones (67) 181
Brandy—Scott English (72) *48*
(In The) Cold Light Of Day—Gene Pitney (66) 28
Help Yourself (To All Of My Lovin')—
James & Bobby Purify (68) 28
Bend Me, Shape Me—Storm (71) *13*
When Love Slips Away—Dee Dee Warwick (67) 4.8
Bend Me, Shape Me—Tight Fit (81) *0.9*

William ENGVICK ▶ 4093 (5) 596
I'll Remember Today—Patti Page (57) 847
Bonnie Blue Gal—
Mitch Miller with His Orch. & Chorus (55) *321*
All I Need Is You—Les Paul and Mary Ford (59) 19
Kiss And Run—Peggy King (56) 6.8
Bonnie Blue Gal—Lawrence Welk And His
Champagne Music And The McGuire Sisters (55) *0.0*

Bill ENIS ▶ 4119 (2) 587
Shame On Me—Bobby Bare (62) *1068*
Shame On Me—Chuck Jackson (67) *106*

Sue ENNIS ▶ 3140 (6) 989
Straight On—Heart (78) 1064
Even It Up—Heart (80) 530
Dog & Butterfly—Heart (79) 515
This Man Is Mine—Heart (82) 497
The Best Man In The World—Ann Wilson (86) 298
How Can I Refuse—Heart (83) 279

Brian ENO ▶ 10505 (1) 7.8
Once In A Lifetime—Talking Heads (86) 39

Duke ENSTON ▶ 5696 (3) 254
D A R L I N'—Hilltoppers (55) 479
Bless Your Heart—
Fontane Sisters with Billy Vaughn's Orchestra (54) *282*
Bless Your Heart—Bob Dini (54) *0.0*

Warren ENTNER ▶ 7073 (1) 118
Come On And Say It—Grass Roots (70) 353

John ENTWHISTLE ▶ 8555 (1) 46
Postcard—Who (74) 46

ENYA [Eithne Ni Bhraonain, Enya Patricia O'Brennan] ▶ 5185 (1)	**329**
Orinoco Flow—Enya (89)	658
Fangette ENZEL ▶ 7034 (1)	**120**
It's An Uphill Climb To The Bottom—Walter Jackson (66)	120
Nathaniel EPPS ▶ 8178 (1)	**59**
Rubber Biscuit—Blues Brothers (79)	297
Preston EPPS ▶ 3589 (2)	**775**
Bongo Rock—Preston Epps (59)	*1240*
Bongo Rock—Incredible Bongo Band (73)	*310*
—Linda Epstein see: Linda CREED	
Michael EQUINE ▶ 9025 (1)	**33**
Good Old Rock 'N Roll—Cat Mother And The All Night News Boys (69)	164
Richard ERBE ▶ 8065 (1)	**63**
Deep Enough For Me—Ocean (71)	126
—Hermann Erbel see: Herman RAREBELL	
Tom ERDELYI [Tomas Erdélyi, Tommy Ramone] ▶ 8877 (2)	**37**
Rockaway Beach—Ramones (77)	96
Sheena Is A Punk Rocker—Ramones (77)	53
Ernie ERDMAN ▶ 10269 (3)	**11**
Toot, Toot, Tootsie—Johnston Brothers (55)	13
Nobody's Sweetheart—Jerry Cooper with The Johnny Guarnieri Swingtet (55)	*13*
Nobody's Sweetheart—Johnnie Ray (55)	*13*
—Edward Marshall Erenberg see: Celia MARSHALL	
—Eric B. see: Eric BARRIER	
Elliot ERICKSON ▶ 2435 (2)	**1490**
Do Anything—Natural Selection (91)	3407
Hearts Don't Think (They Feel)—Natural Selection (91)	708
Jack ERICKSON ▶ 7183 (1)	**111**
May I Never Love Again—Tony Bennett with Percy Faith and His Orchestra (55)	222
—Roger Kynard Erickson see: Roky ERICKSON	
Roky ERICKSON [Roger Kynard Erickson] ▶ 4888 (1)	**387**
You're Gonna Miss Me—Thirteenth Floor Elevators (66)	387
—Holly Erlanger see: Holly KNIGHT	
Bill ERMAN ▶ 8714 (1)	**41**
Son-In-Law—Louise Brown (61)	41
Robert ERNLUND ▶ 10893 (1)	**4.5**
Rev It Up—Newcity Rockers (87)	14
Greg ERRICO ▶ 8584 (1)	**46**
BLT—Lee Oskar (76)	91
—Janet Ann Errico see: Jan ASHTON	
—John Errington see: John MILES	
—King Errison see: Errison JOHNSON	
Ahmet ERTEGUN [A. Nugetre, Nuggy] ▶ 848 (10)	**5213**
The Joker—Steve Miller Band (73)	5290
Don't Play That Song—Aretha Franklin With The Dixie Flyers (70)	*1651*
Don't Play That Song (You Lied)—Ben E. King (62)	*1588*
Somebody Touched Me—Buddy Knox with The Rhythm Orchids (58)	853
Chains Of Love—Pat Boone (56)	*798*
Lovey Dovey—Buddy Knox (60)	*340*
Chains Of Love—Bobby Bland (69)	*310*
Lovey Dovey—Otis & Carla (68)	*242*
Lovey Dovey—Clyde McPhatter (59)	*214*
Lovey Dovey—Bunny Sigler (67)	*51*
Jacqueline ERTEL [Jacqueline Everly] ▶ 6141 (1)	**200**
Bowling Green—Everly Brothers (67)	400
Bobby ERVIN ▶ 6539 (2)	**159**
I Need Love—LL Cool J (87)	765
I'm Bad—LL Cool J (87)	18
Dee ERVIN [DeFosco T. Ervin Jr., Big Dee Irwin] ▶ 4938 (8)	**378**
Seems Like I Gotta Do Wrong—Whispers (70)	340
Been So Long—Pastels (58)	226
Sweet Young Thing Like You—Ray Charles (68)	161
I Can Make It Thru The Days (But Oh Those Lonely Nights)—Ray Charles (73)	59

I Got To Tell Somebody—Betty Everett (70)	33
I'm Down To My Last Heartbreak—Wilson Pickett (63)	8.2
Willie Pass The Water—Ripple (74)	7.5
Your Love Is So Doggone Good—Whispers (71)	6.8
—DeFosco T. Ervin Jr. see: Dee ERVIN	
—Roy Erwin see: Max BYGRAVES	
—Irene Cara Escalera see: Irene CARA	
Homer ESCAMILLA ▶ 3993 (4)	**629**
Are You Satisfied—Rusty Draper (55)	*1239*
Are You Satisfied—Toni Arden (55)	*14*
Are You Satisfied—Sheb Wooley (55)	*4.8*
Are You Satisfied?—Jimmy Wakely with Gloria Wood (55)	*0.0*
Jesus ESCAMILLA [Jesse Gonzales] ▶ 6361 (2)	**179**
Happy Jose (Ching-Ching)—Jack Ross (61)	*358*
Happy Jose (Ching-Ching)—Dave Appell and his Orchestra (62)	*0.0*
Coke ESCOVEDO ▶ 5811 (1)	**240**
No One To Depend On—Santana (72)	719
—Sheila Escovedo see: SHEILA E.	
Grady ESKED ▶ 10389 (1)	**9.1**
Nobody (Tellin' Me 'Bout My Baby)—Charles Wright And The Watts 103d Street Rhythm Band (71)	18
Ralph ESKRIDGE ▶ 4434 (1)	**495**
Love Jones—Brighter Side Of Darkness (72)	*1485*
Dino ESPOSITO ▶ 1078 (6)	**4091**
I Like It—Dino (89)	1942
Romeo—Dino (90)	1433
Sunshine—Dino (89)	641
24/7—Dino (89)	336
Summergirls—Dino (88)	301
Never 2 Much Of U—Dino (89)	154
Joe ESPOSITO ▶ 1869 (6)	**2184**
Bad Girls—Donna Summer (79)	7825
Music, Harmony And Rhythm—Brooklyn Dreams (78)	156
Sad Eyes—Brooklyn Dreams (77)	114
Heart's On Fire—John Cafferty (86)	99
Can't Let Go—Stephen Stills Featuring Michael Finnigan (84)	88
Make It Last—Brooklyn Dreams (79)	70
Michael ESPOSITO ▶ 3449 (1)	**844**
(We Ain't Got) Nothin' Yet—Blues Magoos (66)	3377
Robert ESPOSITO ▶ 4400 (1)	**505**
Roses Are Red My Love—"You Know Who" Group! (64)	505
Kim ESPY ▶ 10265 (1)	**11**
Natural Love—Petula Clark (82)	43
—Esquerita see: Eskew REEDER	
Jose Augusto ESQUIBEL [Zecca Esquibel] ▶ 6086 (1)	**207**
Just So Lonely—Get Wet (81)	207
David ESSEX [David Albert Cook] ▶ 614 (3)	**7048**
Rock On—David Essex (73)	*3737*
Rock On—Michael Damian (89)	*3134*
Lamplight—David Essex (74)	177
Bernard ESTARDY [Subway] ▶ 11582 (1)	**1.1**
Chinese Kung Fu—Banzaii (75)	1.1
Emilio ESTEFAN ▶ 2271 (2)	**1669**
Coming Out Of The Dark—Gloria Estefan (91)	3801
Live For Loving You—Gloria Estefan (91)	1207
Gloria ESTEFAN [Gloria Fajardo] ▶ 180 (12)	**16927**
Anything For You—Gloria Estefan and Miami Sound Machine (88)	3939
Don't Wanna Lose You—Gloria Estefan (89)	3881
Coming Out Of The Dark—Gloria Estefan (91)	3801
1-2-3—Gloria Estefan and Miami Sound Machine (88)	2190
Rhythm Is Gonna Get You—Gloria Estefan and Miami Sound Machine (87)	1833
Words Get In The Way—Miami Sound Machine (86)	1788
Here We Are—Gloria Estefan (89)	1533
Can't Stay Away From You—Gloria Estefan and Miami Sound Machine (87)	1471
Live For Loving You—Gloria Estefan (91)	1207
Cuts Both Ways—Gloria Estefan (90)	341
Oye Mi Canto (Hear My Voice)—Gloria Estefan (90)	225
Seal Our Fate—Gloria Estefan (91)	219
Deon ESTUS ▶ 3260 (1)	**923**
Heaven Help Me—Deon Estus (89)	1845

Bob ESTY ▶ 2069 (4)	**1926**
Fight—Barbra Streisand (79)	1784
Take Me Home—Cher (79)	1769
Wasn't It Good—Cher (79)	162
Hell On Wheels—Cher (79)	137
Melissa ETHERIDGE ▶ 9988 (2)	**14**
Similar Features—Melissa Etheridge (89)	10
No Souvenirs—Melissa Etheridge (89)	4.2
Terry ETLINGER ▶ 7680 (1)	**81**
Sleepin'—Diana Ross (74)	162
Barry ETRIS ▶ 4089 (1)	**597**
Reuben James—Kenny Rogers And The First Edition (69)	1195
—Steve Ett see: Steve ETTINGER	
—James Etta see: Etta JAMES	
Steve ETTINGER [Steve Ett] ▶ 4900 (2)	**385**
I Need Love—LL Cool J (87)	765
I'm That Type Of Guy—LL Cool J (89)	696
Darrell EUBANKS [Darrell Banks] ▶ 4539 (1)	**468**
Open The Door To Your Heart—Darrell Banks (66)	936
Jerry EUBANKS ▶ 8973 (1)	**35**
Dream Lover—Marshall Tucker Band (78)	70
Bill EUCKER ▶ 6840 (1)	**134**
Pink Dominos—Crescents (63)	134
George EUGENE ▶ 10761 (1)	**5.5**
Presidential Press Conference—Sickniks (61)	22
Jane EUGENE ▶ 7463 (1)	**94**
Hangin' On A String (Contemplating)—Loose Ends (85)	282
—Bill Eustrom see: Bill NORVAS	
EVANS ▶ 11005 (1)	**3.9**
Come On Over—Strollers (61)	7.8
Chris EVANS [Trevor Beacham, Christopher Robin Evans] ▶ 11515 (1)	**1.4**
King Croesus—World Of Oz (68)	5.5
Craig EVANS ▶ 10204 (1)	**11**
I Found You—Frankie Laine (68)	11
Dale EVANS [Frances Octavia Smith] ▶ 1528 (3)	**2800**
The Bible Tells Me So—Don Cornell (55)	*2057*
The Bible Tells Me So—Nick Noble (55)	*743*
The Bible Tells Me So—Ralph Young (55)	*0.0*
Dave EVANS ▶ 1101 (14)	**4015**
With Or Without You—U2 (87)	4346
I Still Haven't Found What I'm Looking For—U2 (87)	3862
Desire—U2 (88)	2667
Mysterious Ways—U2 (91)	2021
Angel Of Harlem—U2 (88)	876
Where The Streets Have No Name—U2 (87)	*803*
Pride (In The Name Of Love)—U2 (84)	535
In God's Country—U2 (87)	300
New Year's Day—U2 (83)	295
When Love Comes To Town—U2 With B. B. King (89)	105
The Fly—U2 (91)	78
All I Want Is You—U2 (89)	76
I Will Follow—U2 (84)	57
Where The Streets Have No Name—Pet Shop Boys (91)	*37*
Don EVANS ▶ 7309 (1)	**103**
The Night—Animals (83)	309
Eddie EVANS ▶ 7555 (1)	**89**
The Fife Piper—Dynatones (66)	266
—Ernest Evans see: Chubby CHECKER	
—Glenda Joyce Evans see: Glenda HUDSON	
Gordon EVANS ▶ 11239 (1)	**2.6**
Walkin' Proud—Pete Klint Quintet (67)	5.3
H. EVANS ▶ 10351 (3)	**9.7**
The Phonograph Song—Guy Lombardo And His Royal Canadians (56)	*19*
The Phonograph Song (Our Melody)—Billy May & His Orchestra (56)	*19*
The Phonograph Song (Our Melody)—Art Mooney & His Orchestra (56)	*0.0*
Harry EVANS ▶ 11079 (1)	**3.3**
I Only Want You—Passions (60)	3.3
Jack EVANS ▶ 11735 (1)	**0.4**
Billy Boy's Tune—Three Graces (59)	0.8
Jean EVANS [Jean Evens] ▶ 8785 (1)	**39**
Welcome Home—Sammy Kaye & His Orchestra (61)	117

Joe EVANS ▶ 11355 (1)	**2.1**
Baby I Need You—Manhattans (66)	4.2
—Judy Evans see: Marilyn HOOVEN	
—Louis Evans see: Redd EVANS	
Mitchel EVANS ▶ 3395 (1)	**868**
Mad About You—Belinda Carlisle (86)	2603
Paul EVANS [Paul Rapport] ▶ 428 (14)	**9450**
Roses Are Red (My Love)—Bobby Vinton (62)	10687
When—Kalin Twins (58)	3515
Happy Go Lucky Me—Paul Evans (60)	1584
The Next Step Is Love—Elvis Presley (70)	632
Johnny Will—Pat Boone (61)	608
I Gotta Know—Elvis Presley With The Jordanaires (60)	607
Worried Guy—Johnny Tillotson (64)	523
Long As The Rose Is Red—Florraine Darlin (62)	231
Our World—Johnny Tillotson (65)	227
Summer Souvenirs—Karl Hammel, Jr. (61)	221
I Could Conquer The World—Shevelles (64)	28
I Think About You All The Time—Paul Evans (58)	26
Blue River—Elvis Presley (66)	5.3
Hushabye Little Guitar—Paul Evans (60)	4.5
Ray EVANS ▶ 279 (38) HOF	**12501**
Tammy—Debbie Reynolds (57)	*9194*
Whatever Will Be, Will Be (Que Sera, Sera)—Doris Day (56)	*6972*
Dear Heart—Andy Williams (64)	*1324*
To Each His Own—Platters (60)	*1235*
Dear Heart—Jack Jones (64)	*1154*
Mona Lisa—Carl Mann (59)	*948*
Bonanza—Al Caiola And His Orchestra (61)	*895*
Tammy—Ames Brothers (57)	*793*
Mona Lisa—Conway Twitty (59)	*581*
Que Sera, Sera (Whatever Will Be, Will Be)—High Keys (63)	*355*
Wish Me A Rainbow—Gunter Kallmann Chorus (66)	327
All The Time—Johnny Mathis (58)	327
Angel—Johnny Tillotson (65)	308
Que Sera, Sera (Whatever Will Be, Will Be)—Mary Hopkin (70)	*259*
In The Arms Of Love—Andy Williams (66)	249
Dear Heart—Henry Mancini's Orchestra And Chorus (64)	*243*
Theme From "Harlow" (Lonely Girl)—Bobby Vinton (65)	198
To Each His Own—Frankie Laine (68)	*170*
Almost In Your Arms—Johnny Nash (58)	153
Let Me Be Loved—Mantovani And His Orchestra (57)	*109*
To Each His Own—Tymes (64)	*100*
Another Time, Another Place—Patti Page (58)	82
You're So Right For Me—Tony Bennett with Ralph Sharon and his Orch. (58)	70
Silver Bells—Bing Crosby and Carol Richards (54)	*39*
Love Song From "Houseboat" (Almost In Your Arms)—Sam Cooke (58)	*36*
Never Let Me Go—Nat "King" Cole (56)	20
Silver Bells—Bing Crosby and Carol Richards (57)	*14*
Golden Earrings—Five Satins (61)	3.2
Bonanza!—Johnny Cash (62)	*3.2*
Buttons And Bows—Don Robertson (61)	0.5
Tammy—Richard Hayman, His Orchestra And Chorus (57)	*0.0*
Main Title/Tammy—Joseph Gershenson & The Universal-International Orchestra (57)	*0.0*
Whatever Will Be Will Be (Que Será Será)—Eddy Howard (56)	*0.0*
Love Song From "Houseboat" (Almost In Your Arms)—Don Costa & His Orchestra (58)	*0.0*
Love Song From "Houseboat" (Almost In Your Arms)—Les Baxter & His Orchestra (58)	*0.0*
Tammy—Pat Kirby (57)	*0.0*
Tammy—Bill Snyder & His Orchestra (57)	*0.0*
Let Me Be Loved—Eydie Gorme (57)	*0.0*
Raymond Augustus EVANS ▶ 6862 (1)	**132**
Opportunity—Jewels (64)	264
Redd EVANS [Louis Evans] ▶ 938 (7)	**4729**
There! I've Said It Again—Bobby Vinton (63)	*8758*
Don't Go To Strangers—Etta Jones (60)	*486*
There I've Said It Again—Sam Cooke (59)	*149*
Don't Go To Strangers—Vaughn Monroe with Orchestra And Chorus (56)	*107*
Not One Goodbye—Jaye P. Morgan (55)	93
Take Me Back Again—Tony Bennett (54)	92
Don't Go To Strangers—Andy Williams (60)	*0.0*
Richard L. EVANS ▶ 6432 (1)	**169**
Burning Spear—Soulful Strings (68)	169
Rick EVANS ▶ 455 (3)	**9175**
In The Year 2525 (Exordium & Terminus)—Zager & Evans (69)	9107
Mr. Turnkey—Zager & Evans (69)	68
Listen To The People—Zager & Evans (69)	0.4
Rod EVANS ▶ 11097 (2)	**3.2**
Emmaretta—Deep Purple (69)	8.7
The Bird Has Flown—Deep Purple (69)	0.9
Tolchard EVANS ▶ 7801 (4)	**74**
If—Al Hirt (69)	*48*
If—Timi Yuro (64)	*42*
If—Paragons (61)	*33*
If—Roy Hamilton (61)	*5.2*
Tom EVANS ▶ 1049 (4)	**4208**
Without You—Nilsson (71)	*7670*
Maybe Tomorrow—Iveys (69)	316
Hold On—Badfinger (81)	108
Without You—Heart (78)	*6.6*
Alicia EVELYN ▶ 2358 (6)	**1564**
Pepper Hot Baby—Jaye P. Morgan (55)	*829*
Six Nights A Week—Crests (59)	688
I Get The Sweetest Feeling—Jackie Wilson (68)	535
Pepper Hot Baby—Gisele MacKenzie (55)	*92*
Flower Of Love—Crests (59)	63
Pepper-Hot Baby—Bonnie Davis (55)	*0.0*
—Jean Evens see: Jean EVANS	
—Bill Everette see: Bill JUSTIS	
Dick EVERITT ▶ 7646 (2)	**83**
The World Through A Tear—Neil Sedaka (65)	165
The Answer To My Prayer—Neil Sedaka (66)	84
Don EVERLY ▶ 298 (10)	**12123**
Cathy's Clown—Everly Brothers (60)	9441
('til) I Kissed You—Everly Brothers (59)	4212
So Sad (To Watch Good Love Go Bad)—Everly Brothers (60)	2692
Gone, Gone, Gone—Everly Brothers (64)	522
It's All Over—Casinos (67)	149
Should We Tell Him—Everly Brothers (58)	71
Since You Broke My Heart—Everly Brothers (60)	21
Oh What A Feeling—Everly Brothers (59)	16
Nancy's Minuet—Everly Brothers (63)	14
Maybe Tomorrow—Everly Brothers (57)	5.0
—Jacqueline Everly see: Jacqueline ERTEL	
Phil EVERLY ▶ 296 (8)	**12171**
Cathy's Clown—Everly Brothers (60)	9441
When Will I Be Loved—Linda Ronstadt (75)	*3982*
When Will I Be Loved—Everly Brothers (60)	*1552*
(Girls, Girls, Girls) Made To Love—Eddie Hodges (62)	1175
Gone, Gone, Gone—Everly Brothers (64)	522
Gee But It's Lonely—Pat Boone (58)	442
Should We Tell Him—Everly Brothers (58)	71
Maybe Tomorrow—Everly Brothers (57)	5.0
Jörg EVERS ▶ 8236 (2)	**57**
Boogie Woogie Dancin' Shoes—Claudja Barry (79)	216
Dancin' Fever—Claudja Barry (78)	43
Sabu EVERTEZ ▶ 11417 (1)	**1.8**
Oh Me—Fields-Madera Orchestra (59)	5.4
Larry EVOY ▶ 862 (3)	**5159**
Last Song—Edward Bear (72)	4333
Close Your Eyes—Edward Bear (73)	700
You, Me And Mexico—Edward Bear (70)	125
Mamie EWALD ▶ 5026 (2)	**357**
Revenge—Brook Benton (61)	1071
Panic—Otis Williams And His Charms (61)	0.9
David Franklin EWER [Dave Ewer, Dave Kaffinetti] ▶ 10292 (2)	**10**
Sympathy—Rare Bird (70)	39
Birdman Part One (Title No. 1 Again)—Rare Bird (73)	2.8
Willie EWING ▶ 4330 (1)	**518**
I Love You—Volume's (62)	1037
Tom EYEN ▶ 5505 (1)	**277**
And I Am Telling You I'm Not Going—Jennifer Holliday (82)	554
Tony EYERS ▶ 3715 (2)	**723**
I'm On Fire—5000 Volts (75)	*675*
I'm On Fire—Jim Gilstrap (75)	*48*
Norman EZELL ▶ 2328 (5)	**1585**
Western Union—Five Americans (67)	2583
I See The Light—Five Americans (65)	795
Sound Of Love—Five Americans (67)	657
Zip Code—Five Americans (67)	404
Evol-Not Love—Five Americans (66)	315
Bob EZRIN ▶ 2585 (10)	**1347**
Beth—Kiss (76)	1404
Detroit Rock City—Kiss (76)	870
Shout It Out Loud—Kiss (76)	*563*
Wait For You—Bonham (89)	221
Under My Wheels—Alice Cooper (71)	190
A World Without Heroes—KISS (81)	167
Department Of Youth—Alice Cooper (75)	121
Shout It Out Loud (Live)—Kiss (77)	*104*
Learning To Fly—Pink Floyd (87)	86
Flaming Youth—Kiss (76)	41

F

Bill FABER ▶ 6011 (1)	**216**
You Were Only Fooling (While I Was Falling In Love)—Vic Damone (65)	649
—Bent Fabric see: Bent FABRICIUS-BJERRE	
Bent FABRICIUS-BJERRE [Frank Bjorn, Bent Fabric] ▶ 1437 (5)	**3042**
Alley Cat—Bent Fabric And His Piano (62)	*2839*
Chicken Feed—Bent Fabric And His Piano (62)	356
The Alley Cat Song—David Thorne (62)	*38*
The Happy Puppy—Bent Fabric (63)	7.7
The Alley Cat Song—Peggy Lee (63)	*4.1*
—Peter Fadden see: Joseph Francis BURKE	
Richard FAGAN ▶ 8238 (1)	**57**
The Good Lord Loves You—Neil Diamond (80)	57
Donald FAGEN ▶ 538 (21)	**7977**
Rikki Don't Lose That Number—Steely Dan (74)	2950
Do It Again—Steely Dan (72)	*2218*
Reeling In The Years—Steely Dan (73)	2111
Hey Nineteen—Steely Dan (80)	1601
Peg—Steely Dan (77)	1459
Deacon Blues—Steely Dan (78)	825
I.G.Y. (What A Beautiful World)—Donald Fagen (82)	732
Josie—Steely Dan (78)	619
FM (No Static At All)—Steely Dan (78)	561
Time Out Of Mind—Steely Dan (81)	531
Black Friday—Steely Dan (75)	400
Show Biz Kids—Steely Dan (73)	342
My Old School—Steely Dan (73)	211
Pretzel Logic—Steely Dan (74)	153
New Frontier—Donald Fagen (83)	118
The Fez—Steely Dan (76)	109
Don't Let Me In—Sneaker (82)	80
Century's End—Donald Fagen (88)	50
Do It Again—Club House (83)	*40*
Kid Charlemagne—Steely Dan (76)	16
Bad Sneakers—Steely Dan (75)	13
—Don Edward Fagenson see: Don WAS	
Siobhan FAHEY [Siobhan Stewart] ▶ 3540 (7)	**793**
I Heard A Rumour—Bananarama (87)	2288
Cruel Summer—Bananarama (84)	1392
I Can't Help It—Bananarama (87)	331
Love In The First Degree—Bananarama (88)	262
The Wild Life—Bananarama (84)	104
More Than Physical—Bananarama (86)	74
Robert DeNiro's Waiting—Bananarama (84)	4.7
Jörn FAHRENKROG-PETERSEN ▶ 1958 (1)	**2050**
99 Luftballons—Nena (83)	4100
Vernon FAILS ▶ 7255 (1)	**107**
Talk To Me—Anita Baker (90)	321
Sammy FAIN [Samuel E. Feinberg] ▶ 423 (37) HOF	**9523**
Love Is A Many Splendored Thing—Four Aces (55)	*8585*
April Love—Pat Boone (57)	5035
A Certain Smile—Johnny Mathis (58)	*1228*
I'll Remember Tonight—Pat Boone (58)	749
Secret Love—Freddy Fender (75)	*697*
Secret Love—Billy Stewart (66)	*556*
Love Is A Many-Splendored Thing—Don Cornell (55)	*365*

Sammy FAIN [Samuel E. Feinberg] ▶ 423 (37) HOF *Continued*	**9523**
I'll Be Seeing You—Frank Sinatra (61)	*332*
A Very Precious Love—Ames Brothers (58)	*280*
I'll Be Seeing You—Tommy Sands (59)	*273*
A Little Love Can Go A Long Long Way—Dream Weavers Featuring Wade Buff (56)	*184*
I'll Be Seeing You—Four Freshmen & Stan Kenton & Orchestra (54)	*98*
If You Wanna See Mamie Tonight—Ames Brothers (56)	97
Kiss Me And Kill Me With Love—Mills Brothers (55)	*89*
Love Is A Many-Splendored Thing—David Rose and His Orchestra (55)	*72*
That Old Feeling—Kitty Kallen (60)	67
I'll Be Seeing You—Poni-Tails (59)	*49*
Dear Hearts And Gentle People—Springfields (62)	48
Love Is A Many Splendored Thing—Woody Herman and His Orchestra (55)	*42*
I'll Be Seeing You—Five Satins (60)	*24*
Love Is A Many-Splendored Thing—Four Preps (62)	*24*
Secret Love—Jimmy Ricks (59)	*19*
Are You Havin' Any Fun—Crew-Cuts (55)	12
Love Is A Many Splendored Thing—Don, Dick N' Jimmy (55)	*2.3*
Secret Love—Richard "Groove" Holmes (66)	*1.4*
Kiss Me And Kill Me With Love—McGuire Sisters (55)	*0.0*
A Little Love Can Go A Long, Long Way—Johnny Desmond (56)	*0.0*
Wedding Bells (Are Breaking Up That Old Gang Of Mine)—Four Aces (54)	0.0
Secret Love—Doris Day (54)	*0.0*
A Certain Smile—Sunny Gale (58)	*0.0*
A Certain Smile—Milton Sparks (58)	*0.0*
A Certain Smile—Jerry Fuller (58)	*0.0*
A Certain Smile—Andy Russell (58)	*0.0*
A Very Precious Love—Doris Day (58)	*0.0*
A Very Precious Love—Bonnie Guitar (58)	*0.0*
A Very Precious Love—Johnston Brothers (58)	*0.0*
A Very Precious Love—Jack Jones (58)	0.0
Bruce FAIRBAIRN ▶ 4154 (1)	**579**
Hot Girls In Love—Loverboy (83)	1158
Dede FAIRBANKS [Dede Blythe] ▶ 11164 (1)	**2.9**
Heartbreak Harry—Alis Leslie (57)	5.9
Herman FAIRBANKS [Sy Franklin] ▶ 7607 (3)	**86**
I'm Sincere—Alan Dale (55)	*257*
I'm Sincere—Joe Barrett (55)	*0.0*
I'm Sincere—Shannon Sisters (55)	*0.0*
—Phyllis Fairbanks see: Phyllis LANDSBERG	
Fred FAIRBRASS ▶ 2642 (1)	**1299**
I'm Too Sexy—Right Said Fred (91)	3898
Richard FAIRBRASS ▶ 2643 (1)	**1299**
I'm Too Sexy—Right Said Fred (91)	3898
Werly FAIRBURN ▶ 9311 (1)	**27**
I Guess I'm Crazy—Jim Reeves (64)	27
Coventry FAIRCHILD [Lorraine Ximenes] ▶ 7613 (1)	**85**
Stop! Get A Ticket—Clefs Of Lavender Hill (66)	171
Travis FAIRCHILD [Joseph Ximenes] ▶ 7614 (1)	**85**
Stop! Get A Ticket—Clefs Of Lavender Hill (66)	171
Reuben FAIRFAX ▶ 9303 (1)	**27**
Belle—Al Green (77)	80
Jim FAIRS ▶ 4813 (4)	**408**
It Could Be We're In Love—Cryan Shames (67)	276
I Wanna Meet You—Cryan' Shames (66)	237
Greenburg, Glickstein, Charles, David Smith & Jones—Cryan' Shames (68)	65
Mr. Unreliable—Cryan' Shames (67)	0.5
—David Fairstein see: Fabrice CUITAD	
Brian FAIRWEATHER ▶ 5085 (5)	**345**
Invisible Hands—Kim Carnes (83)	454
You Make My Heart Beat Faster (And That's All That Matters)—Kim Carnes (84)	172
Invitation To Dance—Kim Carnes (85)	122
Dancing In Heaven (Orbital Be-Bop)—Q-Feel (89)	48
I Pretend—Kim Carnes (84)	41
Andy FAIRWEATHER-LOW ▶ 9151 (1)	**30**
Spider Jiving—Andy Fairweather Low (75)	30
Percy FAITH ▶ 3982 (4)	**631**
Theme For Young Lovers—Percy Faith And His Orchestra (60)	424
My Heart Cries For You—Ray Charles (64)	*368*
My Heart Cries For You—Ray Stevens (59)	*40*
My Heart Cries For You—Connie Francis (67)	*3.3*
Russell FAITH ▶ 1756 (10)	**2367**
Bobby Sox To Stockings—Frankie Avalon (59)	2192
Togetherness—Frankie Avalon (60)	981
Somewhere In Your Heart—Frank Sinatra (64)	643
Blood Is Thicker Than Water—William Devaughn (74)	294
Just Yesterday—Al Martino (66)	179
Who Else But You—Frankie Avalon (61)	95
Don't Tell Me Not To Love You—Joni James (56)	*58*
King Of Love—Fabian (60)	19
Always Keep Me In Your Heart—Four Aces (69)	3.0
Don't Tell Me Not To Love You—June Valli (56)	*0.0*
—Gloria Fajardo see: Gloria ESTEFAN	
Ron FAJERSTEIN ▶ 9103 (1)	**31**
New Thing—Enuff Z'Nuff (89)	93
John FALBO ▶ 4041 (1)	**614**
Love Came To Me—Dion (62)	1229
Peter FALCIGLIA ▶ 7355 (1)	**100**
I Need Some One—Belmonts (61)	201
FALCO [Johann Holzel] ▶ 1631 (4)	**2580**
Rock Me Amadeus—Falco (86)	4222
Der Kommissar—After The Fire (83)	*2710*
Vienna Calling—Falco (86)	751
Der Kommissar (The Commissioner)—Falco (83)	*38*
Billy FALCON [William Falcone] ▶ 3988 (2)	**629**
Power Windows—Billy Falcon (91)	521
Sometimes (It's A Bitch)—Stevie Nicks (91)	217
—William Falcone see: Billy FALCON	
—Eric Falconer see: Eric FAULKNER	
Phillipa FALLON ▶ 10453 (1)	**8.3**
Soon I'll Wed My Love—John Gary (64)	17
—Jake Falsworth see: Jake HOOKER	
Harold FALTERMEYER ▶ 454 (8)	**9193**
Hot Stuff—Donna Summer (79)	8596
Shakedown—Bob Seger (87)	4602
The Heat Is On—Glenn Frey (84)	3215
Axel F—Harold Faltermeyer (85)	2849
Cold Love—Donna Summer (80)	353
Walk Away—Donna Summer (80)	352
Bit By Bit—Stephanie Mills (85)	62
Square Rooms—Al Corley (85)	39
Rodolfo FALVO ▶ 11799 (1)	**0.0**
When I Hold You In My Arms—Lou Monte with Hugo Winterhalter And His Orchestra (54)	0.0
Georgie FAME [Clive Powell] ▶ 5603 (1)	**266**
Get Away—Georgie Fame & The Blue Flames (66)	266
Vince FAMILIO ▶ 7344 (1)	**101**
Princess—Frank Gari (61)	302
Wayne FAMOUS [Wayne McNatt] ▶ 9188 (1)	**29**
What She Does To Me (The Diana Song)—Producers (81)	117
Charles FANA ▶ 6591 (3)	**154**
Your Wild Heart—Joy Layne (57)	*308*
Your Wild Heart—Karen Chandler (57)	*0.0*
Your Wild Heart—Poni Tails (57)	*0.0*
—Giuseppe Fanciulli see: Giuseppe FUCILLI	
John FANNON ▶ 4524 (2)	**471**
Don't Ever Wanna Lose Ya—New England (79)	366
Hello, Hello, Hello—New England (79)	105
Tony FANUCCHI ▶ 10483 (1)	**8.0**
Information—Eric Martin (85)	32
Silvio FARACI ▶ 4012 (1)	**623**
Lonely Teenager—Dion (60)	1868
Jimmy FARAGHER ▶ 7179 (1)	**111**
Stay The Night—Faragher Brothers (79)	223
Tommy FARAGHER ▶ 3063 (4)	**1028**
With Every Beat Of My Heart—Taylor Dayne (89)	2568
Stay The Night—Faragher Brothers (79)	223
Under The Influence—Vanity (86)	101
Undeniable—Ms. Adventures (90)	81
Andrea FARBER ▶ 8070 (1)	**63**
Games—Phoebe Snow (81)	126
Kamaal FAREED [Jonathan Davis] ▶ 4404 (1)	**504**
Groove Is In The Heart—Deee-Lite (90)	2521
Donna FARGO [Yvonne Silver, Yvonne Vaughn] ▶ 769 (7)	**5716**
Funny Face—Donna Fargo (72)	2735
The Happiest Girl In The Whole U.S.A.—Donna Fargo (72)	2118
Superman—Donna Fargo (73)	523
Little Girl Gone—Donna Fargo (73)	227
You Were Always There—Donna Fargo (73)	99
U.S. Of A.—Donna Fargo (74)	12
It Do Feel Good—Donna Fargo (75)	2.2
Frank FARIAN [Franz Reuther] ▶ 1707 (7)	**2455**
Girl I'm Gonna Miss You—Milli Vanilli (89)	3277
Baby Don't Forget My Number—Milli Vanilli (89)	3187
All Or Nothing—Milli Vanilli (89)	1700
Rivers Of Babylon—Boney M (78)	419
Daddy Cool—Boney M (76)	60
Oh My Lord—Boney M (78)	9.7
Ma Baker—Boney M (77)	3.4
Ann FARINA ▶ 1530 (7)	**2800**
Sleep Walk—Santo & Johnny (59)	*6980*
Tear Drop—Santo & Johnny (59)	945
Twistin' Bells—Santo & Johnny (60)	*237*
Love Lost—Santo & Johnny (60)	105
Hop Scotch—Santo & Johnny (61)	92
Sleepwalk—Larry Carlton (82)	*82*
Bullseye—Santo & Johnny (60)	18
Johnny FARINA ▶ 1531 (7)	**2800**
Sleep Walk—Santo & Johnny (59)	*6980*
Tear Drop—Santo & Johnny (59)	945
Twistin' Bells—Santo & Johnny (60)	*237*
Love Lost—Santo & Johnny (60)	105
Hop Scotch—Santo & Johnny (61)	92
Sleepwalk—Larry Carlton (82)	*82*
Bullseye—Santo & Johnny (60)	18
Mimi FARINA [Margarita Mimi Baez] ▶ 5846 (1)	**237**
In The Quiet Morning (For Janis Joplin)—Joan Baez (72)	237
Peggy FARINA [Peggy Santiglia] ▶ 3799 (2)	**696**
Beggin'—4 Seasons Featuring The "Sound" Of Frankie Valli (67)	1234
Wow Wow Wee (He's The Boy For Me)—Angels (64)	394
Richard FARINA ▶ 11171 (1)	**2.9**
Hard Lovin' Loser—Judy Collins (67)	2.9
Sandy FARINA ▶ 6561 (1)	**157**
Kiss Me In The Rain—Barbra Streisand (80)	314
Santo FARINA ▶ 1532 (7)	**2800**
Sleep Walk—Santo & Johnny (59)	*6980*
Tear Drop—Santo & Johnny (59)	945
Twistin' Bells—Santo & Johnny (60)	*237*
Love Lost—Santo & Johnny (60)	105
Hop Scotch—Santo & Johnny (61)	92
Sleepwalk—Larry Carlton (82)	*82*
Bullseye—Santo & Johnny (60)	18
Eleanor FARJEON ▶ 3125 (1)	**996**
Morning Has Broken—Cat Stevens (72)	1992
Edward J. FARLEY ▶ 10420 (1)	**8.6**
Music Goes 'Round And Around—Joe Pica (54)	26
—Melville Farley see: Gordon REES	
David Anthony FARMER ▶ 11414 (1)	**1.8**
You And Me—Liner (79)	5.4
Steve FARMER ▶ 3981 (2)	**632**
Journey To The Center Of The Mind—Amboy Dukes (68)	1261
You Talk Sunshine, I Breathe Fire—Amboy Dukes (68)	3.7
Thomas Laurence FARMER ▶ 11415 (1)	**1.8**
You And Me—Liner (79)	5.4
Peter FARNAN ▶ 10982 (1)	**4.0**
Talk About It—Boom Crash Opera (91)	20
Mark FARNER ▶ 629 (12)	**6891**
Bad Time—Grand Funk (75)	2544
Shinin' On—Grand Funk (74)	947
Walk Like A Man—Grand Funk (73)	906
Closer To Home—Grand Funk Railroad (70)	847
Rock 'N Roll Soul—Grand Funk Railroad (72)	782
Footstompin' Music—Grand Funk Railroad (71)	645
Time Machine—Grand Funk Railroad (69)	454
Mean Mistreater—Grand Funk Railroad (70)	392
Heartbreaker—Grand Funk Railroad (70)	127
Upsetter—Grand Funk Railroad (72)	111
Sally—Grand Funk Railroad (76)	58
Mr. Limousine Driver—Grand Funk Railroad (69)	3.9
John FARNHAM ▶ 9106 (1)	**31**
Playing To Win—LRB (85)	217

Nancy FARNSWORTH ▶ 5063 (1)	**351**
Here Come Those Tears Again—Jackson Browne (77)	701
Lynne FARR ▶ 6900 (2)	**130**
Seems Like I Gotta Do Wrong—Whispers (70)	340
I Got To Tell Somebody—Betty Everett (70)	33
—Michael George Farr see: Mike LEANDER	
Jimmy FARRAR ▶ 11006 (1)	**3.9**
The Rambler—Molly Hatchet (81)	7.8
John FARRAR ▶ 69 (13)	**30604**
You're The One That I Want— John Travolta And Olivia Newton-John (78)	6783
Magic—Olivia Newton-John (80)	6599
Have You Never Been Mellow— Olivia Newton-John (75)	4952
A Little More Love—Olivia Newton-John (78)	3997
Hopelessly Devoted To You—Olivia Newton-John (78)	3835
Make A Move On Me—Olivia Newton-John (82)	2305
Suddenly—Olivia Newton-John & Cliff Richard (80)	1080
Something Better To Do—Olivia Newton-John (75)	1004
Sam—Olivia Newton-John (77)	638
Don't Stop Believin'—Olivia Newton-John (76)	486
Tied Up—Olivia Newton-John (83)	344
Landslide—Olivia Newton-John (82)	221
Totally Hot—Olivia Newton-John (79)	109
Joseph T. FARRELL ▶ 5038 (1)	**356**
Tomboy—Perry Como (59)	711
Wes FARRELL [Wesley Donald Fogel] ▶ 256 (27)	**13420**
Hang On Sloopy—McCoys (65)	*6827*
Doesn't Somebody Want To Be Wanted—Partridge Family Starring Shirley Jones & Featuring David Cassidy (71)	4568
Come A Little Bit Closer—Jay & The Americans (64)	4277
Come On Down To My Boat—Every Mothers' Son (67)	3309
I'll Meet You Halfway—Partridge Family Starring Shirley Jones & Featuring David Cassidy (71)	2417
Let's Lock The Door (And Throw Away The Key)— Jay & The Americans (64)	1513
Hang On Sloopy—Ramsey Lewis Trio (65)	*1400*
Could It Be Forever—David Cassidy (72)	870
I'll Make All Your Dreams Come True— Ronnie Dove (65)	859
Happy Summer Days—Ronnie Dove (66)	651
My Girl Sloopy—Vibrations (64)	*637*
Goodbye Baby (Baby Goodbye)—Solomon Burke (64)	588
Look What You've Done—Pozo-Seco Singers (66)	512
(My Girl) Sloopy— Little Caesar And The Consuls (65)	*340*
Ten Lonely Guys—Pat Boone (62)	*317*
Hello Pretty Girl—Ronnie Dove (65)	302
Think Of The Good Times—Jay & The Americans (65)	280
Why Can't You Bring Me Home— Jay & The Americans (66)	253
Everybody Do The Sloopy—Johnny Thunder (65)	163
Hang On Sloopy—Rick Derringer (75)	*96*
Ten Lonely Guys—Ten Broken Hearts (62)	*81*
Hang On Sloopy—Lettermen (70)	*42*
Friend And A Lover—Partridge Family Starring Shirley Jones & Featuring David Cassidy (73)	40
Boys—Beatles (65)	37
Run, Run, Run—Ronny Douglas (61)	31
No One Knows—Every Mother's Son (68)	12
I Can't Stop—Osmond Brothers (71)	2.1
Osvaldo FARRES ▶ 4840 (1)	**401**
Come Closer To Me (Acercate Mas)— Nat "King" Cole (58)	801
Clive FARRINGTON ▶ 4450 (2)	**492**
The Promise—When In Rome (88)	1410
Heaven Knows—When In Rome (89)	65
Bob FARRIS ▶ 9138 (1)	**30**
Boppin' In A Sack—Lane Brothers (58)	61
Andy FARRISS ▶ 521 (15)	**8139**
Need You Tonight—INXS (87)	4241
Devil Inside—INXS (88)	2910
What You Need—INXS (86)	2667
New Sensation—INXS (88)	2229
Never Tear Us Apart—INXS (88)	1469
Suicide Blonde—INXS (90)	1317
The One Thing—INXS (83)	545
Bitter Tears—INXS (91)	337
Listen Like Thieves—INXS (86)	251
Original Sin—INXS (84)	162
This Time—INXS (85)	62

I Send A Message—INXS (84)	50
Don't Change—INXS (83)	23
Shining Star—INXS (91)	20
Kiss The Dirt (Falling Down The Mountain)—INXS (86)	11
Jon FARRISS ▶ 3603 (2)	**772**
Disappear—INXS (90)	1536
Don't Change—INXS (83)	23
Tim FARRISS ▶ 11018 (1)	**3.8**
Don't Change—INXS (83)	23
Cee FARROW [Christian F. Kruzinski] ▶ 9846 (1)	**16**
Should I Love You—Cee Farrow (83)	32
—Jesse Oris Farrow see: Chet POWERS	
Larry FARROW ▶ 8280 (1)	**56**
If It Don't Fit, Don't Force It— Kellee Patterson (77)	111
Mikki FARROW ▶ 7455 (2)	**95**
Let's Make A Promise—Peaches & Herb (68)	188
Catfish—Four Tops (76)	96
Tony FASCE ▶ 8534 (1)	**47**
Your Own Back Yard—Dion (70)	94
Jack FASCINATO ▶ 10903 (2)	**4.5**
Fifty Fathoms—Jack Fascinato (56)	5.5
I Love To Sing—Jack Fascinato (56)	5.2
Barry FASMAN ▶ 11185 (1)	**2.8**
No Return—Megan McDonough (73)	5.7
Fred FASSERT ▶ 677 (3)	**6403**
Barbara Ann—Beach Boys (65)	*4402*
Barbara-Ann—Regents (61)	*1760*
Barbara Ann—Beach Boys (81)	*240*
Edries FATAAR ▶ 11479 (1)	**1.5**
See The Light—Flame (70)	6.1
Rikki FATAAR ▶ 11480 (1)	**1.5**
See The Light—Flame (70)	6.1
Steve FATAAR ▶ 11481 (1)	**1.5**
See The Light—Flame (70)	6.1
—Fatboy Slim see: Norman COOK	
—Father MC see: Timothy BROWN	
Eric FAULKNER [Eric Falconer] ▶ 3213 (1)	**948**
Money Honey—Bay City Rollers (76)	1897
—Sid Faust see: Lee CATHY	
Jackie FAUTHEREE ▶ 2572 (2)	**1366**
Cradle Of Love—Johnny Preston (60)	*2731*
Cradle Of Love—Ronnie & Robyn (66)	*0.5*
Joe FAVALE ▶ 8561 (1)	**46**
Echo—Emotions (1) (62)	278
Larry FAWCETT ▶ 11108 (1)	**3.2**
I Lied To My Heart—Enchanters (1) (61)	3.2
Mondo FAX ▶ 8187 (1)	**59**
Eat My Shorts—Rick Dees (84)	118
Eric FEARMAN ▶ 7141 (1)	**113**
Joystick—Dazz Band (84)	227
Alan FEARN ▶ 7885 (1)	**71**
All I Need Is You—Blue Train (91)	284
Carl FEASTER ▶ 2293 (2)	**1642**
Sh-Boom—Crew-Cuts (54)	*7040*
Sh-Boom—Chords (54)	*1169*
Claude FEASTER ▶ 2294 (2)	**1642**
Sh-Boom—Crew-Cuts (54)	*7040*
Sh-Boom—Chords (54)	*1169*
Tom FEHER ▶ 11439 (2)	**1.7**
Desiree'—Left Banke (67)	2.4
Ivy, Ivy—Left Banke (67)	1.0
Michael FEIN ▶ 7111 (1)	**115**
The Fonz Song—Heyettes (76)	115
—Samuel E. Feinberg see: Sammy FAIN	
—Bernard Feinstein see: Buddy FEYNE	
Buzz FEITEN [Howard R. Feiten] ▶ 3762 (1)	**706**
Who'll Be The Fool Tonight—Larsen-Feiten Band (80)	706
—Howard R. Feiten see: Buzz FEITEN	
Dino FEKARIS ▶ 261 (18)	**13041**
Reunited—Peaches & Herb (79)	*7690*
I Will Survive—Gloria Gaynor (78)	*7179*
Shake Your Groove Thing—Peaches & Herb (78)	2986
Makin' It—David Naughton (79)	2897
I Just Want To Celebrate—Rare Earth (71)	2092
Hey Big Brother—Rare Earth (71)	928
I Pledge My Love—Peaches & Herb (80)	870
I Will Survive—Sa-Fire (89)	*247*

We've Got Love—Peaches & Herb (79)	221
Let Me Know (I Have A Right)—Gloria Gaynor (79)	220
You Gotta Have Love In Your Heart— Supremes & Four Tops (71)	210
A Little Lovin' (Keeps The Doctor Away)—Raes (78)	209
That Once In A Lifetime—Demis Roussos (78)	173
She Don't Let Nobody (But Me)—Curtis Mayfield (81)	75
Mother Nature—Temptations (72)	38
Roller-Skatin' Mate (Part 1)—Peaches & Herb (79)	32
Reunited—Band Of Gold (84)	*12*
Anybody Wanna Party?—Gloria Gaynor (79)	4.6
—Marc Feld see: Marc BOLAN	
Allan FELDER ▶ 2333 (18)	**1582**
Armed And Extremely Dangerous—First Choice (73)	913
Don't Take Your Love—Manhattans (74)	457
Smarty Pants—First Choice (73)	456
Hold Back The Night—Trammps (76)	*426*
He's A Friend—Eddie Kendricks (76)	362
Doctor Love—First Choice (77)	236
Stop To Start—Blue Magic (74)	197
Walk Right Up To The Sun—Delfonics (71)	182
Good Things Don't Last Forever— Ecstasy, Passion & Pain (74)	130
The Player - Part 1—First Choice (74)	121
Let Me Make Love To You—O'Jays (75)	101
Ten Percent—Double Exposure (76)	92
Hold Back The Night— Graham Parker And The Rumour (77)	*83*
Dreamin'—Loleatta Holloway (77)	46
A Mother For My Children—Whispers (74)	16
Newsy Neighbors—First Choice (74)	11
We're On The Right Track— South Shore Commission (76)	7.7
Touch And Go— Ecstasy, Passion & Pain Featuring Barbara Roy (76)	1.4
Don FELDER ▶ 1955 (2)	**2054**
Hotel California—Eagles (77)	4658
Heavy Metal (Takin' A Ride)—Don Felder (81)	501
—Jerome Solon Felder see: Doc POMUS	
Wilton FELDER ▶ 7346 (2)	**101**
Way Back Home—Jr. Walker & The All Stars (71)	*144*
Way Back Home—Jazz Crusaders (70)	*53*
Bob FELDMAN ▶ 1033 (25)	**4262**
My Boyfriend's Back—Angels (63)	*8148*
I Want Candy—Strangeloves (65)	*1629*
Night Time—Strangeloves (66)	764
Cara-Lin—Strangeloves (65)	565
Wow Wow Wee (He's The Boy For Me)—Angels (64)	394
Ten Lonely Guys—Pat Boone (62)	*317*
Let's Stomp—Bobby Comstock (63)	288
(You Make Me Feel) So Good—McCoys (66)	259
Giving Up On Love—Jerry Butler (64)	257
Patty Baby—Freddy Cannon (63)	242
I Want Candy—Bow Wow Wow (82)	*177*
Bubble Gum Music—Rock And Roll Dubble Bubble Trading Card Co. Of Philadelphia-19141 (69)	144
What's Gonna Happen When Summer's Done— Freddy Cannon (62)	143
What Time Is It?—Jive Five (62)	103
Ten Lonely Guys—Ten Broken Hearts (62)	*81*
Out In The Sun (Hey-O)—Beach Nuts (65)	63
Sorrow—David Bowie (73)	53
Let's Put The Fun Back In Rock N Roll— Freddy Cannon & The Belmonts (81)	47
Money Music—Boys In The Band (70)	25
Thank You And Goodnight—Angels (63)	21
A Letter From Betty—Bobby Vee (63)	11
I'm On Fire—Jerry Lee Lewis (64)	2.7
I'm Tossin' And Turnin' Again—Bobby Lewis (62)	1.3
Your Boyfriend's Back— Bobby Comstock & The Counts (63)	*0.4*
Broadway—Freddy Cannon (62)	0.4
Jack FELDMAN ▶ 3398 (3)	**867**
Copacabana (At The Copa)—Barry Manilow (78)	1800
I Made It Through The Rain—Barry Manilow (80)	1325
Hey Mambo—Barry Manilow with Kid Creole And The Coconuts (88)	6.2
—Jeff Feldman see: Jeff MANN	
Nick FELDMAN ▶ 1405 (8)	**3154**
Everybody Have Fun Tonight—Wang Chung (86)	4287
Let's Go—Wang Chung (87)	1295
Dance Hall Days—Wang Chung (84)	1096

Nick FELDMAN ▶ 1405 (8) ***Continued***	**3154**
To Live And Die In L.A.—Wang Chung (85)	566
Hypnotize Me—Wang Chung (87)	403
Don't Let Go—Wang Chung (84)	335
Praying To A New God—Wang Chung (89)	167
Don't Be My Enemy—Wang Chung (84)	17
Richard FELDMAN ▶ 2896 (5)	**1127**
Promises—Eric Clapton And His Band (78)	1467
I Need You—Pointer Sisters (83)	372
A Little Love—Juice Newton (84)	301
One Lover At A Time—Atlantic Starr (87)	210
Somebody Like You—Robbie Nevil (89)	194
Steve FELDMAN ▶ 4851 (2)	**398**
Mercy—Ohio Express (69)	675
Sweeter Than Sugar—Ohio Express (69)	121
J. Nicolas FELGEN [Camillo Jean Nicolas Felgen, Jean Nicolas] ▶ 11713 (1)	**0.5**
Sie Liebt Dich (She Loves You)—Die Beatles (64)	*1.9*
Hilda FELICIANO ▶ 8192 (1)	**59**
Rain—Jose Feliciano (69)	118
Jose FELICIANO ▶ 6514 (4)	**161**
Rain—Jose Feliciano (69)	118
Destiny—Jose Feliciano (70)	87
Feliz Navidad—Jose Feliciano (70)	12
Chico And The Man (Main Theme)— José Feliciano (75)	3.2
Rose FELICIO ▶ 11175 (1)	**2.9**
The Rockin' Lady (From New Orleans)— Penny Candy (59)	5.7
John FELKER ▶ 7127 (1)	**115**
Memory Lane—Hippies (Formerly The Tams) (63)	229
Terry FELL ▶ 1926 (5)	**2098**
You're The Reason—Bobby Edwards (61)	*2462*
Sandy—Larry Hall (59)	1449
You're The Reason—Joe South (61)	*136*
You're The Reason—Hank Locklin (61)	*0.0*
You're The Reason—Gerry And The Pacemakers (65)	*0.0*
Dick FELLER ▶ 3813 (4)	**691**
Some Days Are Diamonds (Some Days Are Stones)— John Denver (81)	428
Lord, Mr. Ford—Jerry Reed (73)	228
Makin' The Best Of A Bad Situation— Dick Feller (74)	33
Biff The Friendly Purple Bear—Dick Feller (73)	3.0
Sherm FELLER ▶ 4469 (2)	**486**
Summertime Summertime—Jamies (58)	*580*
Summertime, Summertime—Jamies (62)	*393*
Suzanne FELLINI ▶ 10711 (1)	**5.9**
Love On The Phone—Suzanne Fellini (80)	24
Simon FELLOWES ▶ 9299 (1)	**27**
American Dream—Simon F. (87)	27
Steve FELLOWS ▶ 7569 (1)	**88**
You're Amazing—Robert Palmer (90)	439
Kurt FELTZ [Jonny Bartels] ▶ 6758 (3)	**140**
This Must Be Wrong (Oho-Aha)— Caterina Valente (55)	190
Stroll Me—Kay Starr (58)	184
La Pachanga— Audrey Arno And The Hazy Osterwald Sextet (61)	*29*
Andrew FENADY ▶ 11292 (1)	**2.4**
The Rebel - Johnny Yuma—Johnny Cash (61)	4.8
Don FENCETON ▶ 5601 (1)	**266**
I Am Love—Jackson 5 (75)	1065
Freddy FENDER [Baldemar Huerta] ▶ 2590 (2)	**1346**
Wasted Days And Wasted Nights—Freddy Fender (75)	*2670*
Wasted Days And Wasted Nights—Freddy Fender (60)	*21*
—Fenderella see: Joyce IRBY	
Richard FENN ▶ 5530 (1)	**274**
Family Man—Daryl Hall & John Oates (83)	1641
Anthony FENNELL ▶ 11501 (1)	**1.4**
Name And Number—Big Noise (89)	4.2
Michael FENNELLY ▶ 3183 (2)	**962**
Go Back—Crabby Appleton (70)	961
Just About The Same—Association (70)	4.8
David FENTON ▶ 3879 (1)	**669**
Turning Japanese—Vapors (80)	669
—Jack Fenton see: Jay FISHMAN	
John FENTON ▶ 11123 (1)	**3.1**
Ce Soir—Golden Earring (75)	9.4

Raymond FENWICK ▶ 5688 (1)	**254**
Touch Me—Fancy (74)	509
Francesco FEOLA ▶ 11769 (1)	**0.1**
Tic-A-Tee, Tik-A-Tay—Dean Martin (62)	0.4
Shiller Shaun FEQUIERE [Kangol Kid] ▶ 6429 (2)	**170**
Right Next To Me—Whistle (89)	167
Roxanne, Roxanne—UTFO (85)	28
—Frank Carlton Serafino Feranna see: Nikki SIXX	
Allyn FERGUSON ▶ 8062 (2)	**63**
Theme from Charlie's Angels— Henry Mancini And His Orchestra (77)	118
I'll Search My Heart—Johnny Mathis (63)	13
Bob FERGUSON ▶ 2473 (3)	**1453**
Wings Of A Dove—Ferlin Husky (60)	*1427*
The Carroll County Accident—Porter Wagoner (69)	26
Wings Of A Dove—Paul Clayton (60)	*0.0*
Dave FERGUSON ▶ 9322 (1)	**26**
I Don't Know What It Is, But It Sure Is Funky— Ripple (73)	184
Jay FERGUSON ▶ 1483 (6)	**2928**
Thunder Island—Jay Ferguson (77)	1909
Run Run Run—Jo Jo Gunne (72)	663
Shakedown Cruise—Jay Ferguson (79)	640
Mr. Skin—Spirit (73)	40
Animal Zoo—Spirit (70)	5.9
Mechanical World—Spirit (68)	4.1
Lloyd FERGUSON ▶ 6318 (1)	**182**
Pass The Dutchie—Musical Youth (82)	1276
—Maria Elena Fernadez-Vidal see: Maria VIDAL	
José FERNANDEZ DIAZ ▶ 5021 (1)	**358**
Guantanamera— Sandpipers (66)	2149
Iris FERNANDO [Iris Ann Folwell] ▶ 9560 (1)	**21**
Heartache—Pepsi & Shirlie (87)	64
Tambi FERNANDO [Jascha Tambimuttu] ▶ 9561 (1)	**21**
Heartache—Pepsi & Shirlie (87)	64
Arthur FERRANTE ▶ 10564 (1)	**7.2**
Dream Concerto—Ferrante & Teicher (59)	22
Frank FERRARA ▶ 10749 (1)	**5.6**
Questions—Bang (72)	17
Louis FERRARI [Jose Gomera] ▶ 7092 (1)	**116**
Valley Valparaiso— Percy Faith And His Orchestra and Chorus (56)	349
Richard FERRARIS ▶ 6126 (1)	**202**
Let's Love—Johnny Mathis (58)	405
—Osvaldo Nicolas Ferraro Gutierrez see: Waldo DE LOS RIOS	
Cliff FERRÉ ▶ 6521 (4)	**160**
The Money Tree—Margaret Whiting (56)	*233*
The Money Tree—Patience and Prudence (56)	*88*
The Money Tree—Frankie Lester (56)	*0.0*
The Money Tree—Annisteen Allen (56)	*0.0*
Edward FERRELL [Eddie Ferrell, DJ Eddie F] ▶ 7299 (1)	**104**
Missunderstanding—Al B. Sure! (90)	313
Stephen FERRERA ▶ 11532 (1)	**1.3**
Solitude Standing—Suzanne Vega (87)	6.4
—Roger Garfield Ferrier see: Roger HART	
Giovanni FERRIO ▶ 8325 (5)	**54**
Little Serenade—Teddy Randazzo (58)	*203*
Little Serenade—Ames Brothers (58)	*9.8*
Little Serenade (Piccolissima Serenata)— Eddie Calvert (58)	*0.0*
Little Serenade—Ted Heath & His Music (58)	*0.0*
Little Serenade—Johnston Brothers (58)	*0.0*
Steve FERRONE ▶ 7684 (1)	**81**
School Boy Crush—AWB (75)	485
Bryan FERRY ▶ 3032 (4)	**1053**
Love Is The Drug—Roxy Music (75)	789
Kiss And Tell—Bryan Ferry (88)	370
Dance Away—Roxy Music (79)	275
Over You—Roxy Music (80)	27
Buddy FEYNE [Bernard Feinstein] ▶ 10110 (1)	**13**
Tuxedo Junction—Frankie Avalon (60)	51
—Addy Fieger see: Addy BARON	

Doug FIEGER ▶ 692 (4)	**6277**
My Sharona—Knack (79)	9055
Good Girls Don't—Knack (79)	1458
Baby Talks Dirty—Knack (80)	422
Can't Put A Price On Love—Knack (80)	160
Eugene FIELD ▶ 8218 (3)	**58**
Winkin', Blinkin' And Nod—Simon Sisters (64)	*60*
Wynken, Blynken And Nod—Doobie Brothers (81)	*51*
Little Boy Blue— Billy Vaughn and His Orchestra (56)	7.6
Robert FIELD ▶ 8564 (1)	**46**
Powerful Stuff—Fabulous Thunderbirds (88)	139
Richard "Dimples" FIELDS ▶ 5580 (2)	**269**
If It Ain't One Thing...It's Another— Richard "Dimples" Fields (82)	331
All Of Me For All Of You—9.9 (85)	311
Albert FIELDS ▶ 9686 (2)	**19**
Summer Vacation—Party (90)	*113*
Summer Vacation—Party (91)	*20*
Alvin FIELDS ▶ 5129 (2)	**336**
Let's All Chant—Michael Zager Band (78)	662
Am I Losing You—Manhattans (78)	15
Dorothy FIELDS ▶ 2260 (10) HOF	**1686**
The Way You Look Tonight—Lettermen (61)	1962
Don't Blame Me—Everly Brothers (61)	702
I'm In The Mood For Love—Chimes (61)	*532*
If My Friends Could See Me Now—Linda Clifford (78)	72
I'm In The Mood For Love—Fats Domino (57)	*68*
I Can't Give You Anything But Love— Johnston Brothers (55)	*13*
Where Am I Going?—Barbra Streisand (66)	12
Fine Romance— Sammy Davis Jr. And Carmen McRae (55)	7.8
On The Sunny Side Of The Street—Modernaires (57)	1.9
I'm In The Mood For Love— Spike Jones & City Slickers (54)	*0.0*
Harold FIELDS [Milton Carson, Harold Cornelius, Harry Cornelius, Harold C. Fields, David Greer, John Jerome, Sam Lorraine] ▶ 2345 (9)	**1572**
A Blossom Fell—Nat "King" Cole (55)	*4027*
Sadie's Shawl—Bob Sharples And His Music (56)	*293*
Chincherinchee—Perry Como (56)	282
Why Not Now—Matt Monro (61)	115
A Blossom Fell—Dickie Valentine (55)	*0.0*
A Blossom Fell—Vic Barrett (55)	*0.0*
Sadie's Shawl—Richard Hayman And Jan August (56)	*0.0*
Sadie's Shawl—Philip Green & His Gob Music (56)	*0.0*
Someone Else's Roses—Doris Day (54)	0.0
Irving FIELDS ▶ 3984 (3)	**630**
Chantez-Chantez (Shan-tay, "Sing")— Dinah Shore (57)	654
Teasin'—Quaker City Boys (58)	529
Sugar Candy—Georgia Gibbs (57)	77
Lou FIELDS ▶ 7408 (1)	**98**
Peace Of Mind—Teresa Brewer (60)	98
Martin FIERRO ▶ 11543 (1)	**1.3**
It Didn't Even Bring Me Down— Sir Douglas Quintet (69)	3.8
Anton FIG ▶ 5261 (2)	**316**
New Romance (It's A Mystery)—Spider (80)	418
Calling It Love—Animotion (89)	215
Ray FIGLAR ▶ 7556 (1)	**89**
The Fife Piper—Dynatones (66)	266
Larry FIGUEIREDO ▶ 10046 (1)	**14**
Never—Earls (63)	41
Romuald FIGUIER [Romuald] ▶ 9169 (1)	**30**
Let Me Try Again (Laisse Moi Le Temps)— Frank Sinatra (73)	148
Jack FINA ▶ 4322 (2)	**522**
Bumble Boogie—B. Bumble & The Stingers (61)	*975*
Bumble Boogie—Ralph Marterie & His Orchestra (54)	*69*
Rick FINCH ▶ 149 (24)	**19388**
That's The Way (I Like It)— K.C. & The Sunshine Band (75)	*6457*
Please Don't Go—K.C. & The Sunshine Band (79)	6091
(Shake, Shake, Shake) Shake Your Booty— K C & The Sunshine Band (76)	4899
I'm Your Boogie Man—K C & The Sunshine Band (77)	4680
Get Down Tonight—K.C. & The Sunshine Band (75)	4656
Keep It Comin' Love—KC & The Sunshine Band (77)	4615

Rick FINCH ▶ 149 (24) *Continued*	**19388**
Rock Your Baby—George McCrae (74)	4499
Dance Across The Floor—Jimmy "Bo" Horne (78)	502
Boogie Shoes—KC & The Sunshine Band (78)	501
I Like To Do It—KC & The Sunshine Band (76)	385
I Get Lifted—George McCrae (75)	352
Do You Wanna Go Party— KC & The Sunshine Band (79)	238
Wrap Your Arms Around Me— K C & The Sunshine Band (77)	210
I Can't Leave You Alone—George McCrae (74)	161
Who Do Ya Love—KC & The Sunshine Band (78)	115
Honey I—George McCrae (76)	106
That's The Way I Like It—Ritchie Family (76)	*92*
Queen Of Clubs—K.C. & The Sunshine Band (76)	87
Do You Feel All Right—KC & The Sunshine Band (78)	64
Where Is The Love—Betty Wright (75)	37
Shotgun Shuffle—Sunshine Band (75)	29
Shake It (Like A White Girl)—Jesse Jaymes (91)	25
Look At You—George McCrae (75)	24
Let's Go Rock And Roll— K.C. & The Sunshine Band (80)	11
Ben FINDON ▶ 4949 (2)	**376**
Love Really Hurts Without You—Billy Ocean (76)	709
Light Up The World With Sunshine— Hamilton, Joe Frank & Dennison (76)	42
Jack Wolf FINE ▶ 7608 (3)	**86**
I'm Sincere—Alan Dale (55)	*257*
I'm Sincere—Joe Barrett (55)	*0.0*
I'm Sincere—Shannon Sisters (55)	*0.0*
Sylvia FINE ▶ 1943 (11)	**2074**
Themes From The Man With The Golden Arm— Richard Maltby And His Orchestra (56)	*1358*
Main Title And Molly O From The Man With The Golden Arm—Dick Jacobs And His Chorus And Orchestra (56)	*962*
Main Title From The Man With The Golden Arm— Elmer Bernstein And Orchestra (56)	*817*
Themes From The Man With The Golden Arm— Billy May And His Orchestra (56)	*547*
Delilah Jones—McGuire Sisters (56)	*191*
Main Title Golden Arm— Les Elgart and His Orchestra (56)	*187*
The Five Pennies—Dodie Stevens (59)	22
Main Title From "The Man With The Golden Arm"— Buddy Morrow And His Orchestra (56)	*18*
Ciu Ciu Bella—Danny Kaye (56)	13
Molly-O—Ralph Young (56)	*0.0*
Delilah Jones—Danny Kaye (56)	*0.0*
Michael FINESILVER ▶ 2411 (1)	**1509**
Fire—Crazy World Of Arthur Brown (68)	6038
Bob FINIZ [Robert J. Finizio] ▶ 7703 (3)	**80**
When You're Gone— Brenda & The Tabulations (67)	198
Walk On With The Duke—Duke Of Earl (62)	86
Just Once In A Lifetime— Brenda & The Tabulations (67)	12
—Robert J. Finizio see: Bob FINIZ	
—Catherine L. Fink see: Kay THOMPSON	
—Janis Eddy Fink see: Janis IAN	
Matt FINK ▶ 8895 (1)	**37**
America—Prince & The Revolution (85)	220
—Harry Finkelman see: Ziggy ELMAN	
John FINLEY ▶ 3172 (2)	**971**
Let Me Serenade You—Three Dog Night (73)	952
Circus—Mike Quatro Jam Band (72)	58
Neil FINN ▶ 912 (6)	**4844**
Don't Dream It's Over—Crowded House (87)	3350
Something So Strong—Crowded House (87)	1595
I Got You—Split Enz (80)	278
Better Be Home Soon—Crowded House (88)	256
World Where You Live—Crowded House (87)	120
Fall At Your Feet—Crowded House (91)	43
Tim FINN ▶ 9521 (1)	**22**
Six Months In A Leaky Boat—Split Enz (82)	22
—Larry Finnegan see: John L. FINNERAN	
John L. FINNERAN [Larry Finnegan, John Lawrence Finneran] ▶ 3482 (3)	**822**
Dear One—Larry Finnegan (62)	1573
Johnny Loves Me—Florraine Darlin (64)	26
The Other Ringo—Larry Finnegan (64)	11
Vincent FINNERAN ▶ 3556 (1)	**786**
Dear One—Larry Finnegan (62)	1573
David FINNERTY ▶ 3983 (3)	**630**
Let's Live Together—Road Apples (75)	*550*
Let's Live Together—Cazz (78)	*40*
For Love—Pousette-Dart Band (79)	40
Lance FINNEY [Lance Finnie] ▶ 3619 (2)	**764**
You're So Fine—Falcons (59)	*1478*
You're So Fine—Bunny Sigler (67)	*51*
Bob FINNICUM ▶ 7707 (1)	**79**
(The Bees Are For The Birds) The Birds Are For The Bees—Newbeats (65)	238
—Lance Finnie see: Lance FINNEY	
Elisa FIORILLO [Elisa Dease] ▶ 6577 (1)	**154**
On The Way Up—Elisa Fiorillo (90)	617
Vince FIORINO ▶ 11800 (1)	**0.0**
Skinnie Minnie (Fish Tail)—Teresa Brewer (54)	0.0
Ted FIORITO ▶ 11049 (1) HOF	**3.6**
Charley My Boy— Somethin' Smith & The Redheads (55)	7.1
André FISCHER ▶ 6034 (1)	**214**
Hollywood—Rufus Featuring Chaka Khan (77)	427
Carl T. FISCHER [Terry Harmon] ▶ 7564 (2)	**88**
We'll Be Together Again—Rosemary Clooney (54)	*171*
We'll Be Together Again— Ray Charles And Betty Carter (62)	*5.5*
Helen Ann FISCHER ▶ 11241 (1)	**2.6**
The Man On Page 602—Zoot Fenster (75)	7.9
Lisa FISCHER ▶ 4673 (2)	**442**
How Can I Ease The Pain—Lisa Fischer (91)	802
Save Me—Lisa Fischer (91)	82
George FISCHOFF ▶ 1762 (5)	**2360**
98.6—Keith (66)	2675
Lazy Day—Spanky And Our Gang (67)	1247
Ain't Gonna Lie—Keith (66)	601
Georgia Porcupine—George Fischoff (74)	80
Run To My Lovin' Arms—Lenny Welch (65)	38
Richard FISHBAUGH ▶ 6066 (1)	**210**
A Little Rain Must Fall—Epic Splendor (67)	210
Bruce FISHER ▶ 699 (4)	**6239**
Will It Go Round In Circles—Billy Preston (73)	5175
Nothing From Nothing—Billy Preston (74)	5114
You Are So Beautiful—Joe Cocker (75)	*2189*
You Are So Beautiful—Billy Preston (74)	*0.0*
Carl FISHER [Carlton James Fisher, Del Sharh] ▶ 8263 (4)	**57**
Ain't Nothin' But A House Party—Show Stoppers (68)	*46*
Mr. Magic Man—Wilson Pickett (73)	29
(Ain't Nothin' But A) House Party— J. Geils Band (76)	*21*
Storm Warning—Volcanos (65)	8.8
Dan FISHER ▶ 5928 (1)	**227**
Good Morning Heartache—Diana Ross (73)	680
Dave FISHER ▶ 8488 (1)	**48**
I'm On My Way—Highwaymen (62)	97
Doris FISHER ▶ 3171 (4)	**972**
You Always Hurt The One You Love— Clarence Henry (61)	*1553*
You Always Hurt The One You Love— Fontane Sisters (56)	*292*
You Always Hurt The One You Love— Somethin' Smith & The Redheads (57)	*96*
Into Each Life Some Rain Must Fall—Crazy Otto (56)	2.0
Floyd FISHER ▶ 9569 (1)	**21**
Summertime, Summertime—Nocera (87)	42
Fred FISHER [Albert von Breitenbach] ▶ 3388 (8) HOF	**870**
Peg O' My Heart— Seymour & His Heartbeat Trumpet (58)	*243*
Chicago—Frank Sinatra (57)	*242*
Peg O' My Heart— Robert Maxwell, His Harp And Orchestra (64)	*227*
That's When Your Heartaches Begin— Elvis Presley (57)	144
Happy Days And Lonely Nights— Fontane Sisters with Billy Vaughn's Orchestra (54)	*119*
Happy Days And Lonely Nights—Connie Francis (58)	*60*
I Found A Million Dollar Baby In A Five And Ten Cent Store—Mills Brothers (58)	39
Chicago—Grady Martin & The Slew Foot Five (57)	*0.0*
—Gail Fisher see: Gail LEVY	
Margie FISHER ▶ 8828 (1)	**38**
Op—Honeycones (58)	38
Mark FISHER ▶ 8751 (3)	**40**
Oh How I Miss You Tonight—Jeanne Black (60)	104
When You're Smiling—Bobby Freeman (59)	*12*
Everywhere You Go—Quaker City Boys (59)	5.2
Marvin FISHER ▶ 4830 (3)	**404**
Nothing Ever Changes My Love For You— Nat "King" Cole (56)	353
When Rock And Roll Come To Trinidad— Nat "King" Cole (57)	260
Open Up The Doghouse (Two Cats Are Comin' In)— Dean Martin And Nat "King" Cole (54)	195
Matthew FISHER ▶ 2760 (6)	**1216**
A Whiter Shade Of Pale—Procol Harum (67)	*3537*
A Whiter Shade Of Pale—R.B. Greaves (70)	*62*
A Whiter Shade Of Pale—Hesitations (68)	*29*
A Whiter Shade Of Pale—Procol Harum (72)	*14*
Whiter Shade Of Pale— Hagar, Schon, Aaronson, Shrieve (84)	*5.6*
A Whiter Shade Of Pale—Shorty Long (69)	*0.4*
—Patty Fisher see: Ruth FREED	
Rob FISHER ▶ 1564 (7)	**2710**
Cry For Help—Rick Astley (91)	1691
Promises, Promises—Naked Eyes (83)	1540
Room To Move—Animotion (89)	1179
Love Changes (Everything)—Climie Fisher (88)	651
When The Lights Go Out—Naked Eyes (83)	509
(What) In The Name Of Love—Naked Eyes (84)	385
Move Right Out—Rick Astley (91)	74
Roger FISHER ▶ 3950 (4)	**644**
Barracuda—Heart (77)	1624
Crazy On You—Heart (76)	*521*
Little Queen—Heart (77)	164
Crazy On You—Heart (77)	*110*
Shelley FISHER ▶ 9152 (1)	**30**
Dis-Gorilla (Part 1)— Rick Dees And His Cast Of Idiots (77)	91
Jack FISHMAN [Georges Sigara] ▶ 2775 (3)	**1203**
Why Don't They Understand— George Hamilton IV (57)	*1673*
Help Yourself—Tom Jones (68)	710
Why Don't They Understand—Bobby Vinton (70)	*23*
Jay FISHMAN [Jack Fenton] ▶ 4247 (2)	**546**
When Liking Turns To Loving—Ronnie Dove (66)	1089
Today Has Been Cancelled—Billy Meshel (69)	3.9
Paul FISHMAN ▶ 3336 (2)	**894**
The Politics Of Dancing—Re-Flex (83)	852
Hurt—Re-Flex (84)	42
John FITCH ▶ 2514 (3)	**1427**
Shame—Evelyn "Champagne" King (78)	1812
I Don't Know If It's Right— Evelyn "Champagne" King (78)	1020
Music Box—Evelyn "Champagne" King (79)	33
Robert FITOUSSI [F. R. David] ▶ 8147 (1)	**60**
Words—F.R. David (83)	180
Alan FITZGERALD ▶ 3141 (2)	**987**
Sentimental Street—Night Ranger (85)	1309
When You Close Your Eyes—Night Ranger (84)	998
Ella FITZGERALD ▶ 9535 (1)	**22**
Party Blues—Count Basie Small Band with Ella Fitzgerald and Joe Williams (57)	66
Tyrone FITZGERALD ▶ 3468 (1)	**833**
Funky Nassau - Part 1—Beginning Of The End (71)	1665
Dale FITZSIMMONS ▶ 8602 (1)	**45**
Teen Age Goodnight—Chordettes (56)	90
—James Eugene Fitzwater Jr. see: Gene CRYSLER	
Charles FIZER ▶ 6348 (1)	**180**
The Bounce—Olympics (63)	540
Torstein FLAKNE ▶ 7257 (1)	**107**
Love Cries—Stage Dolls (89)	214
Fiona FLANAGAN ▶ 7713 (1)	**79**
Everything You Do (You're Sexing Me)— Fiona (Duet With Kip Winger) (89)	238
Barry FLAST ▶ 9634 (1)	**20**
Rumor At The Honky Tonk—Spellbound (78)	20
Lester FLATT ▶ 9420 (1)	**24**
Roll In My Sweet Baby's Arms—Hank Wilson (73)	72
—Louisa Flavell see: Maewa KAIHAN	

Bobby FLAX ▶ 3858 (5)	**674**
White Lies, Blue Eyes—Bullet (71)	899
Do You Know What Time It Is?—P-Nut Gallery (71)	259
Bed And Board—Barbara Mason (72)	135
Willpower Weak, Temptation Strong—Bullet (72)	53
Another Love—Ian Lloyd & Stories (74)	2.0
—Flea see: Michael BALZARY	
Neville FLEESON ▶ 4505 (3)	**475**
(I'll Be With You In) Apple Blossom Time—Tab Hunter (59)	*730*
I'll Be With You In Apple Blossom Time—Wayne Newton (65)	*207*
(I'll Be With You) In Apple Blossom Time—Four Aces (54)	*13*
Robert FLEISCHMAN ▶ 7228 (2)	**109**
Wheel In The Sky—Journey (78)	293
Anytime—Journey (78)	54
Daniel FLEISHOUR [Daniel Dale Fleishour, Danny Flower] ▶ 6164 (2)	**198**
Play The Game Tonight—Kansas (82)	814
I Can't Stop This Feelin'—Pure Prairie League (80)	71
George FLEMING ▶ 6472 (1)	**165**
Freedom Overspill—Steve Winwood (86)	661
Kye FLEMING [Rhonda Kye Fleming, Rhonda Fleming Gill] ▶ 2115 (7)	**1858**
Nobody—Sylvia (2) (82)	1577
Smoky Mountain Rain—Ronnie Milsap (80)	1012
I Wouldn't Have Missed It For The World—Ronnie Milsap (81)	887
Years—Wayne Newton (80)	408
Got To Give In To Love—Bonnie Boyer (79)	222
Fooled By A Feeling—Barbara Mandrell (79)	14
I Was Country When Country Wasn't Cool—Barbara Mandrell (81)	3.9
—Rhonda Kye Fleming see: Kye FLEMING	
Tyrone FLEMING ▶ 5177 (2)	**330**
I Wanna Be Your Girl—Icy Blu (91)	316
Pump It (Nice An' Hard)—Icy Blu (91)	29
William FLEMISTER ▶ 8001 (1)	**66**
Mr. Penguin - Pt. 1—Lunar Funk (72)	197
Wade FLEMONS ▶ 2941 (5)	**1109**
Stay In My Corner—Dells (68)	1713
Use Your Head—Mary Wells (65)	422
Here I Stand—Rip Chords (63)	*293*
Here I Stand—Wade Flemons and the Newcomers (58)	*80*
Love Is Life—Earth, Wind & Fire (71)	72
Floyd FLESHMAN ▶ 10938 (1)	**4.2**
I Can't Get Over You—Dramatics (77)	13
Darrow FLETCHER ▶ 10219 (1)	**11**
The Pain Gets A Little Deeper—Darrow Fletcher (66)	22
Donald FLETCHER ▶ 2239 (2)	**1713**
Dancing Machine—Jackson 5 (74)	4702
Get It Together—Jackson 5 (73)	729
Edward FLETCHER ▶ 9620 (1)	**20**
The Message—Grandmaster Flash & The Furious Five (82)	80
Guy FLETCHER ▶ 4805 (6)	**410**
Fallen Angel—Frankie Valli (76)	302
I Can't Tell The Bottom From The Top—Hollies (70)	134
Dedication—Bay City Rollers (77)	129
Save Me—Merrilee Rush (77)	*125*
Don't Turn The Light Out—Cliff Richard (77)	76
Save Me—Donna McDaniel (77)	*53*
Robert FLETCHER ▶ 6632 (2)	**149**
Don't Fence Me In—Tommy Edwards (60)	*292*
Don't Fence Me In—George Maharis (63)	*6.3*
Doug FLETT ▶ 4806 (6)	**410**
Fallen Angel—Frankie Valli (76)	302
I Can't Tell The Bottom From The Top—Hollies (70)	134
Dedication—Bay City Rollers (77)	129
Save Me—Merrilee Rush (77)	*125*
Don't Turn The Light Out—Cliff Richard (77)	76
Save Me—Donna McDaniel (77)	*53*
Bob FLICK ▶ 8007 (1)	**66**
Frogg—Brothers Four (61)	328
Emil FLINDT ▶ 9929 (2)	**15**
The Waltz You Saved For Me—Ferlin Husky (61)	*28*
The Waltz You Saved For Me—Billy Vaughn and His Orchestra (55)	*11*

Shelby FLINT ▶ 3373 (3)	**877**
Angel On My Shoulder—Shelby Flint (60)	*760*
I Will Love You—Richard Chamberlain (63)	234
Angel On My Shoulder—Jerry Wallace (61)	*0.0*
B.F. FLIP [Bernie Friedman] ▶ 11042 (1)	**3.6**
Impossible—Gloria Lynne (61)	7.2
Johnny FLIPPIN ▶ 10832 (1)	**5.0**
Backstrokin'—Fatback (80)	10
Dick FLOOD ▶ 5414 (2)	**292**
The Shag (Is Totally Cool)—Billy Graves (59)	400
Gee—George Hamilton IV (59)	92
Mike FLOREALE [Michael Nuttall] ▶ 4451 (2)	**492**
The Promise—When In Rome (88)	1410
Heaven Knows—When In Rome (89)	65
—Gerald Florio see: Gerard FLORIO	
Gerard FLORIO [Gerald Florio, Danny Jordan] ▶ 5141 (3)	**335**
Jennifer Tomkins—Street People (2) (69)	899
Give Up Your Guns—Buoys (71)	67
Thank You Girl—Street People (70)	4.2
—Danny Flower see: Daniel FLEISHOUR	
Danny FLOWERS ▶ 4224 (2)	**556**
Tulsa Time—Eric Clapton And His Band (80)	*553*
Tulsa Time—Don Williams (78)	*3.1*
Herbie FLOWERS ▶ 6816 (1)	**135**
Our World—Blue Mink (70)	270
Richard FLOWERS ▶ 7870 (1)	**71**
Keep On Keeping On—N.F. Porter (71)	71
Derek FLOYD ▶ 7940 (1)	**68**
Reaching For The World—Harold Melvin And The Blue Notes (77)	68
Eddie FLOYD ▶ 771 (22)	**5709**
Knock On Wood—Amii Stewart (79)	*4967*
634-5789 (Soulsville, U.S.A)—Wilson Pickett (66)	2078
Knock On Wood—Eddie Floyd (66)	*1439*
The Breakdown (Part 1)—Rufus Thomas (71)	588
You Don't Know What You Mean To Me—Sam & Dave (68)	453
Knock On Wood—Otis & Carla (67)	*443*
I've Never Found A Girl (To Love Me Like You Do)—Eddie Floyd (68)	*437*
California Girl—Eddie Floyd (70)	426
Ninety-Nine And A Half (Won't Do)—Wilson Pickett (66)	412
Raise Your Hand—Eddie Floyd (67)	168
I've Got To Have Your Love—Eddie Floyd (69)	120
I Love You More Than Words Can Say—Otis Redding (67)	113
I'll Always Have Faith In You—Carla Thomas (67)	103
Don't Tell Your Mama (Where You've Been)—Eddie Floyd (69)	69
I've Never Found A Man (To Love Me Like You Do)—Esther Phillips (72)	*37*
Why Is The Wine Sweeter (On The Other Side)—Eddie Floyd (69)	30
Someone Is Watching—Solomon Burke (65)	29
Stop! Look What You're Doing—Carla Thomas (65)	27
On A Saturday Night—Eddie Floyd (67)	14
Never Get Enough Of Your Love—Oscar Toney, Jr. (68)	9.6
Love Is A Doggone Good Thing—Eddie Floyd (67)	1.9
Don't Rock The Boat—Eddie Floyd (67)	1.5
King FLOYD ▶ 820 (4)	**5354**
Groove Me—King Floyd (70)	*3856*
Baby Let Me Kiss You—King Floyd (71)	858
Woman Don't Go Astray—King Floyd (72)	551
Groove Me—Fern Kinney (79)	*88*
Stafford FLOYD ▶ 10777 (1)	**5.3**
You're My Driving Wheel—Supremes (76)	21
Jochem FLUITSMA ▶ 8835 (1)	**38**
Female Intuition—Mai Tai (86)	76
—Edward Flurl see: Eddie RAMBEAU	
Jimmy FLYNN ▶ 10231 (1)	**11**
Georgia Rose—Tony Bennett (66)	33
—Wesley Donald Fogel see: Wes FARRELL	
Dan FOGELBERG ▶ 206 (14)	**15422**
Longer—Dan Fogelberg (79)	4740
Leader Of The Band—Dan Fogelberg (81)	1800
Same Old Lang Syne—Dan Fogelberg (80)	1688
Hard To Say—Dan Fogelberg (81)	1608
The Language Of Love—Dan Fogelberg (84)	1015
Run For The Roses—Dan Fogelberg (82)	821

Missing You—Dan Fogelberg (82)	804
Heart Hotels—Dan Fogelberg (80)	695
The Power Of Gold—Dan Fogelberg / Tim Weisberg (78)	690
Part Of The Plan—Dan Fogelberg (74)	603
Make Love Stay—Dan Fogelberg (83)	582
Believe In Me—Dan Fogelberg (84)	272
She Don't Look Back—Dan Fogelberg (87)	62
Love Gone By—Dan Fogelberg (77)	44
John FOGERTY ▶ 36 (30) HOF	**47537**
Proud Mary—Creedence Clearwater Revival (69)	*5879*
Green River—Creedence Clearwater Revival (69)	5510
Lookin' Out My Back Door—Creedence Clearwater Revival (70)	5032
Bad Moon Rising—Creedence Clearwater Revival (69)	5009
Up Around The Bend—Creedence Clearwater Revival (70)	3742
Travelin' Band—Creedence Clearwater Revival (70)	2955
Have You Ever Seen The Rain—Creedence Clearwater Revival (71)	2885
Proud Mary—Ike & Tina Turner (71)	*2683*
Fortunate Son—Creedence Clearwater Revival (69)	2586
Sweet Hitch-Hiker—Creedence Clearwater Revival (71)	2286
Down On The Corner—Creedence Clearwater Revival (69)	2232
Who'll Stop The Rain—Creedence Clearwater Revival (70)	1390
The Old Man Down The Road—John Fogerty (84)	1278
Rockin' All Over The World—John Fogerty (75)	675
Someday Never Comes—Creedence Clearwater Revival (72)	631
Rock And Roll Girls—John Fogerty (85)	608
Proud Mary—Solomon Burke (69)	*406*
Commotion—Creedence Clearwater Revival (69)	386
Centerfield—John Fogerty (85)	356
Lodi—Al Wilson (69)	*250*
Run Through The Jungle—Creedence Clearwater Revival (70)	170
Long As I Can See The Light—Creedence Clearwater Revival (70)	161
Lodi—Creedence Clearwater Revival (69)	*128*
Almost Saturday Night—Dave Edmunds (81)	*103*
Proud Mary—Checkmates, Ltd. Featuring Sonny Charles (69)	*93*
Almost Saturday Night—John Fogerty (75)	*63*
Eye Of The Zombie—John Fogerty (86)	22
You Got The Magic—John Fogerty (76)	13
You Don't Owe Me—Blue Ridge Rangers (73)	2.9
Hey Tonight—Creedence Clearwater Revival (71)	0.0
Tom FOGERTY ▶ 9658 (2)	**19**
Joyful Resurrection—Tom Fogerty (73)	13
Goodbye Media Man (Part 1)—Tom Fogerty (71)	6.2
Dick FOLEY ▶ 8008 (1)	**66**
Frogg—Brothers Four (61)	328
Ellen FOLEY ▶ 11265 (1)	**2.5**
Keep It Confidential—Nona Hendryx (83)	7.6
—Fern Foley see: Bobby AUSTIN	
Red FOLEY [Clyde Julian Foley] ▶ 6505 (2)	**161**
Old Shep—Ralph DeMarco (59)	*144*
Old Shep—Elvis Presley (56)	*18*
Zac FOLEY ▶ 3105 (2)	**1010**
Unbelievable—EMF (91)	4783
Lies—EMF (91)	266
—Iris Ann Folwell see: Iris FERNANDO	
Boris FOMIN ▶ 1050 (1)	**4207**
Those Were The Days—Mary Hopkin (68)	8414
Michael FONFARA ▶ 6804 (1)	**136**
Apricot Brandy—Rhinoceros (69)	272
Eddie FONTAINE [Edward Henry Reardon] ▶ 10619 (1)	**6.7**
Nothin' Shakin—Eddie Fontaine (58)	27
John FOOTMAN ▶ 4708 (4)	**434**
It Must Be Love—Alton McClain & Destiny (79)	469
Look What You've Done To My Heart—Marilyn McCoo & Billy Davis Jr. (77)	199
Star Love—Cheryl Lynn (79)	181
99 1/2—Carol Lynn Townes (84)	85
Steve FORBERT ▶ 2312 (2)	**1610**
Romeo's Tune—Steve Forbert (79)	1573
Say Goodbye To Little Jo—Steve Forbert (80)	38
—Alan Bernard Forbes see: Eugene REYNOLDS	

Alexandra FORBES ▶ 2334 (1)	**1582**
Don't Rush Me—Taylor Dayne (88)	3164
—Brute Force see: Stephen FRIEDLAND	
—Aleck Ford see: Sonny Boy WILLIAMSON II	
Dave FORD ▶ 11040 (1)	**3.6**
Elizabeth—Dave Ford And The Hollywood Flames (62)	14
—Dean Ford see: Thomas McALEESE	
—Dee Dee Ford see: Wrecia HOLLOWAY	
Dwayne FORD ▶ 9438 (1)	**24**
Sherry—Keane Brothers (76)	24
Frankie FORD [Frank V. Guzzo] ▶ 10366 (1)	**9.4**
Alimony—Frankie Ford (59)	28
Jim FORD ▶ 3057 (4)	**1032**
Niki Hoeky—P.J. Proby (67)	781
Harry Hippie—Bobby Womack & Peace (72)	731
Harlan County—Jim Ford (69)	31
Up The Creek (Without A Paddle)—Temptations (76)	27
Lita FORD ▶ 3405 (3)	**863**
Close My Eyes Forever—Lita Ford (89)	1377
Shot Of Poison—Lita Ford (91)	520
Hungry—Lita Ford (90)	1.1
Mary FORD [Iris Colleen Summers] ▶ 7865 (1)	**71**
Song In Blue—Les Paul and Mary Ford (55)	214
—Naomi Ford see: Lee HAZLEWOOD	
Penny FORD ▶ 9148 (1)	**30**
Ooops Up—Snap! (90)	273
Perry FORD [Bryan Pugh] ▶ 7825 (1)	**73**
Tossing & Turning—Ivy League (65)	220
Robert Arthur FORD Jr. ▶ 8581 (3)	**46**
Rappin' Rodney—Rodney Dangerfield (83)	140
The Breaks (Part 1)—Kurtis Blow (80)	94
Basketball—Kurtis Blow (85)	77
Ronald FORD ▶ 9371 (1)	**25**
Hey Ladies—Beastie Boys (89)	302
Vincent FORD ▶ 7402 (1)	**98**
Roots, Rock, Reggae—Bob Marley & The Wailers (76)	98
Jimmy Dee FORE [James DeFore] ▶ 7752 (1)	**76**
Henrietta—Jimmy Dee And The Offbeats (58)	153
Mel FOREE ▶ 5721 (2)	**251**
No One Will Ever Know—Jimmie Rodgers (62)	490
Heartbreak Avenue—Don Gibson (59)	6.0
Christopher FOREMAN ▶ 5331 (1)	**303**
Our House—Madness (83)	2122
—James Foreman see: James MTUME	
Earl FOREST ▶ 6841 (2)	**134**
Morning After—Mar-Keys (61)	241
Next Time You See Me—Little Junior Parker (57)	26
Georgio FORLI ▶ 8072 (2)	**63**
Lazy Gondolier—Mantovani And His Orchestra (55)	*188*
Lazy Gondolier—Lawrence Welk & His Champagne Music (55)	*0.0*
Doug FORMAN ▶ 8232 (1)	**58**
It's A Night For Beautiful Girls—Fools (80)	115
—Gene Forrest see: Forrest WILSON	
George FORREST [George Forrest Chichester Jr.] ▶ 6849 (2)	**133**
Baubles Bangles And Beads—Kirby Stone Four (58)	*398*
Baubles Bangles And Beads—Jonah Jones Quartet (58)	*0.0*
Jimmy FORREST ▶ 3093 (6)	**1012**
Night Train—James Brown And The Famous Flames (62)	*656*
Night Train—Viscounts (60)	*221*
All Nite Long—Billy Vaughn And His Orchestra (59)	*91*
Night Train—Richard Hayman And His Orchestra (61)	*35*
Night Train—Ernie Englund (55)	*4.1*
Night Train Mambo—Jimmy Forrest (55)	*4.1*
—Steven William Forrest see: Steve BRONSKI	
William FORREST ▶ 11731 (1)	**0.4**
There Goes My Love—Fantastics (59)	0.4
Keith FORSEY ▶ 265 (12)	**12791**
Flashdance...What A Feeling—Irene Cara (83)	9574
Hot Stuff—Donna Summer (79)	8596
Shakedown—Bob Seger (87)	4602
Don't You (Forget About Me)—Simple Minds (85)	4351
The Heat Is On—Glenn Frey (84)	3215
Why Me?—Irene Cara (83)	1151
Beat's So Lonely—Charlie Sexton (85)	860

Never Ending Story—Limahl (85)	839
Cold Love—Donna Summer (80)	353
Boogie Woogie Dancin' Shoes—Claudja Barry (79)	216
Lady, Lady, Lady—Joe "Bean" Esposito (83)	31
Thief Of Hearts—Melissa Manchester (84)	24
Bob FORSHEE ▶ 5659 (1)	**258**
Would It Make Any Difference To You—Etta James (62)	258
—B.Y. Forster see: George David WEISS	
John FORTE ▶ 9532 (1)	**22**
Baby Baby—Eighth Wonder (89)	44
Michael FORTE ▶ 4687 (1)	**438**
Dreamin'—Vanessa Williams (89)	1314
Jeff FORTGANG ▶ 2377 (2)	**1545**
Some Guys Have All The Luck—Rod Stewart (84)	*1026*
Some Guys Have All The Luck—Persuaders (73)	*519*
Chet FORTUNE ▶ 8668 (1)	**43**
Remote Control—Reddings (80)	130
Jack FOSHEE ▶ 6843 (1)	**133**
Love Bug Crawl—Jimmy Edwards (57)	266
Ivano FOSSATI ▶ 9464 (1)	**23**
Jesahel—English Congregation (72)	70
Steve FOSSEN ▶ 9269 (1)	**27**
Little Queen—Heart (77)	164
Billy FOSTER ▶ 6002 (2)	**217**
I'd Rather Go Blind—Sydney Youngblood (90)	265
Talking About My Baby—Gloria Walker (68)	255
B.J. Cook FOSTER ▶ 5825 (1)	**239**
Let Me Go, Love—Nicolette Larson (79)	477
Bruce FOSTER ▶ 7332 (1)	**101**
Platinum Heroes—Bruce Foster (77)	101
David FOSTER ▶ 148 (43) HOF	**19473**
Hard To Say I'm Sorry—Chicago (82)	6596
St. Elmo's Fire (Man In Motion)—John Parr (85)	4824
Glory Of Love (Theme From The Karate Kid Part II)—Peter Cetera (86)	4132
After The Love Has Gone—Earth, Wind & Fire (79)	3559
You're The Inspiration—Chicago (84)	3035
Will You Still Love Me?—Chicago (86)	2842
Got To Be Real—Cheryl Lynn (78)	1732
She's A Beauty—Tubes (83)	1661
Who's Holding Donna Now—DeBarge (85)	1361
Look What You've Done To Me—Boz Scaggs (80)	1316
Heart To Heart—Kenny Loggins (82)	1312
Breakdown Dead Ahead—Boz Scaggs (80)	1220
Stay The Night—Chicago (84)	981
Love Theme From St. Elmo's Fire—David Foster (85)	968
Jojo—Boz Scaggs (80)	902
Voices That Care—Voices That Care (91)	901
What About Me?—Kenny Rogers (84)	866
Love Me Tomorrow—Chicago (82)	788
Mornin'—Jarreau (83)	668
I'll Do 4 U—Father MC (91)	522
Forever—Kenny Loggins (85)	516
I'm Alive—Neil Diamond (83)	490
Hold Me 'til The Morning Comes—Paul Anka (83)	477
Don't Want To Wait Anymore—Tubes (81)	377
Too Young—Jack Wagner (85)	340
I Am Love—Jennifer Holliday (83)	334
Friends In Love—Dionne Warwick And Johnny Mathis (82)	322
You—Earth, Wind & Fire (80)	320
Through The Fire—Chaka Khan (85)	257
The Secret Of My Success—Night Ranger (87)	179
And Love Goes On—Earth, Wind & Fire (81)	174
In The Stone—Earth, Wind & Fire (79)	161
Fly Away—Peter Allen (81)	*131*
Tonight Tonight—Bill Champlin (81)	119
Lonely Won't Leave Me Alone—Glenn Medeiros (87)	84
After All—Al Jarreau (84)	83
Lady Of My Heart—Jack Wagner (85)	77
The Best Of Me—David Foster And Olivia Newton-John (86)	69
Winter Games—David Foster (88)	42
You're The Only Love—Paul Hyde And The Payolas (85)	21
Fly Away—Stevie Woods (82)	*19*
Now And Forever (You And Me)—Anne Murray (86)	17
I'll Be There—Kenny Loggins (85)	9.0
Denzil FOSTER ▶ 3426 (4)	**853**
Hold On—En Vogue (90)	3351

Lies—En Vogue (90)	676
Why You Treat Me So Bad—Club Nouveau (87)	381
Little Walter—Tony! Toni! Toné! (88)	272
Desmond FOSTER ▶ 9090 (1)	**31**
I Can't Face The Fact—Gina Go-Go (89)	94
Fred FOSTER ▶ 1386 (3)	**3209**
Me And Bobby McGee—Janis Joplin (71)	*5615*
Me And Bobby McGee—Jerry Lee Lewis (71)	*402*
The Shag (Is Totally Cool)—Billy Graves (59)	400
Gina FOSTER ▶ 9722 (1)	**18**
Love Is A House—Force M.D.'s (87)	55
Ian FOSTER ▶ 6522 (1)	**160**
Let Me Be The One—Five Star (86)	160
Jerry FOSTER ▶ 6330 (1)	**182**
When You Say Love—Sonny & Cher (72)	545
Michael FOSTER ▶ 5763 (1)	**244**
Don't Treat Me Bad—Firehouse (91)	976
Norman FOSTER ▶ 5209 (1)	**327**
Zorro—Chordettes (58)	653
Preston FOSTER ▶ 4797 (1)	**412**
Got My Mojo Working (Part 1)—Jimmy Smith (66)	412
Stephen FOSTER ▶ 6115 (5) HOF	**205**
Swanee River Rock (Talkin' 'Bout That River)—Ray Charles (57)	*179*
Oh! Susanna—Don Charles presents the Singing Dogs, directed by Carl Weisman (55)	95
Swanee River—Ace Cannon (63)	21
Swanee River Rock—Plas Johnson & His Orchestra (57)	*0.0*
Swanee River Rock—Sanford Clark (57)	*0.0*
—Lawrence Constantine Fotinakis see: Larry FOTINE	
Larry FOTINE [Lawrence Constantine Fotinakis] ▶ 6009 (2)	**217**
You Were Only Fooling (While I Was Falling In Love)—Vic Damone (65)	649
Blue Guitar—Larry Lawrence (59)	0.9
Pete FOUNTAIN [Pierre Dewey LaFontaine Jr.] ▶ 11398 (1)	**1.9**
Licorice Stick—Pete Fountain (64)	5.7
Cheyenne FOWLER ▶ 10408 (1)	**8.8**
I've Got The Next Dance—Deniece Williams (79)	26
George FOWLER ▶ 11585 (1)	**1.1**
I've Got A Notion—Marv Johnson (61)	3.2
Gregory Keith FOWLER ▶ 4285 (4)	**532**
World Of Fantasy—Five Stairsteps (66)	565
Come Back—Five Stairsteps (66)	257
Danger! She's A Stranger—Five Stairsteps (67)	157
You Waited Too Long—Five Stairsteps (66)	138
—Kim Fowler see: Kim WILDE	
T.J. FOWLER ▶ 4544 (2)	**468**
Crossfire—Johnny And The Hurricanes (59)	816
Rocking Goose—Johnny And The Hurricanes (60)	239
Wally FOWLER ▶ 7036 (1)	**120**
That's How Much I Love You—Pat Boone (58)	361
Gloria FOWLES [Gloria Gaynor] ▶ 11011 (1)	**3.9**
You Can't Go Halfway—Johnny Nash (74)	15
Kim FOWLEY ▶ 4147 (6)	**581**
Nut Rocker—B. Bumble & The Stingers (62)	*861*
Down To The Line—Bachman-Turner Overdrive (75)	290
The Happy Girls—Helen Reddy (77)	113
Nutrocker—Emerson, Lake & Palmer (72)	*94*
All The Kids On The Street—Hollywood Stars (77)	5.5
Nut Rocker—Jack B. Nimble & Quicks (62)	*0.0*
John FOWLKES ▶ 9194 (1)	**29**
You'd Better Believe It—Manhattans (73)	58
Billy FOX ▶ 4550 (1)	**466**
One Man Band—Three Dog Night (70)	1398
Charles FOX ▶ 505 (11) HOF	**8368**
Killing Me Softly With His Song—Roberta Flack (73)	*7658*
I Got A Name—Jim Croce (73)	2549
Happy Days—Pratt & McClain (76)	2197
Ready To Take A Chance Again—Barry Manilow (78)	1827
Different Worlds—Maureen McGovern (79)	886
Making Our Dreams Come True—Cyndi Grecco (76)	709
My Fair Share—Seals & Crofts (77)	600
Eternity—Vikki Carr (69)	139
Killing Me Softly—Al B. Sure! (88)	*86*
Seasons—Charles Fox (80)	57
Deeply—Anson Williams (77)	30

Glory M. FOX ▶ 10047 (1)	**14**
Clay Idol—Betty Johnson (56)	41
Jim FOX ▶ 7061 (1)	**118**
Funk #49—James Gang (70)	355
Paul FOX ▶ 5314 (2)	**308**
Talk To Me—Chico DeBarge (86)	908
Janet—Commodores (85)	16
Robin FOX [Robin Barnett] ▶ 7223 (1)	**109**
Dream Lover—Rebel Pebbles (91)	328
Douglas FOXWORTHY ▶ 7593 (1)	**87**
Love On A Shoestring—Captain & Tennille (80)	174
Charlie FOXX ▶ 1200 (8)	**3705**
Mockingbird—Carly Simon & James Taylor (74)	*3070*
Mockingbird—Inez Foxx (63)	*2534*
She's A Heartbreaker—Gene Pitney (68)	1367
Hurt By Love—Inez Foxx (64)	312
(1-2-3-4-5-6-7) Count The Days—Inez & Charlie Foxx (67)	151
Mockingbird—Aretha Franklin (67)	*20*
He's The One You Love—Inez Foxx (63)	3.6
Hi Diddle Diddle—Inez Foxx (63)	1.4
Inez FOXX ▶ 1304 (6)	**3399**
Mockingbird—Carly Simon & James Taylor (74)	*3070*
Mockingbird—Inez Foxx (63)	*2534*
I Love You 1000 Times—Platters (66)	858
Hurt By Love—Inez Foxx (64)	312
Mockingbird—Aretha Franklin (67)	*20*
He's The One You Love—Inez Foxx (63)	3.6
Chris FRADKIN ▶ 10809 (1)	**5.2**
A Million Miles Away—Plimsouls (83)	16
George FRAGOS ▶ 11568 (1)	**1.2**
I Hear A Rhapsody—Knightsbridge Strings (60)	3.5
—Loreto Domenico Fraieli see: Jimmie CRANE	
Peter FRAMPTON ▶ 323 (8)	**11384**
I'm In You—Peter Frampton (77)	3918
Show Me The Way—Peter Frampton (75)	2813
Baby, I Love Your Way—Will To Power (88)	*1705*
Baby, I Love Your Way—Peter Frampton (76)	*1353*
Do You Feel Like We Do—Peter Frampton (76)	1212
I Can't Stand It No More—Peter Frampton (79)	917
Tried To Love—Peter Frampton (77)	273
Lying—Peter Frampton (86)	101
—Joe Francavilla see: Joe VILLA	
Paula FRANCES [Paula Ianello] ▶ 6272 (1)	**187**
My True Carrie, Love—Nat King Cole (64)	374
Connie FRANCIS [Concetta Rosa Maria Franconero] ▶ 3658 (3)	**747**
Vacation—Connie Francis (62)	1465
Plenty Good Lovin'—Connie Francis (59)	254
Senza Mamma (With No One)—Connie Francis (60)	8.9
Lipson FRANCIS ▶ 9811 (1)	**17**
Walking Into Sunshine—Central Line (81)	50
Patrick FRANCIS ▶ 10841 (1)	**5.0**
Walkin' Shoes—Tora Tora (89)	20
Claude FRANÇOIS ▶ 3612 (5)	**768**
My Boy—Elvis Presley (75)	*838*
My Way—Frank Sinatra (69)	*701*
My Way—Elvis Presley (77)	*551*
My Boy—Richard Harris (71)	*497*
My Way—Brook Benton (70)	*250*
—Concetta Rosa Maria Franconero see: Connie FRANCIS	
Chuck FRANCOUR ▶ 10372 (1)	**9.4**
Because Of You—Kracker (72)	47
Simon FRANGLEN ▶ 6764 (1)	**139**
Temple Of Love—Harriet (91)	278
David FRANK ▶ 2971 (4)	**1089**
Don't Disturb This Groove—System (87)	1797
You Are In My System—System (83)	*182*
This Is My Night—Chaka Khan (85)	157
You Are In My System—Robert Palmer (83)	*42*
Doug FRANK ▶ 8515 (1)	**47**
After You—Dionne Warwick (80)	95
Paul FRANK ▶ 10706 (1)	**6.0**
Free—Fresh Start (74)	18
—Rachel Frank see: Beverly ROSS	
Rick FRANK ▶ 5730 (2)	**250**
Mongoose—Elephant's Memory (70)	737
Skyscraper Commando—Elephant's Memory (71)	13

Sid FRANK ▶ 3343 (2)	**890**
Please Mr Sun—Tommy Edwards (59)	*1404*
Please Mr. Sun—Vogues (66)	*376*
Aretha FRANKLIN [Aretha White] ▶ 326 (12)	**11269**
(Sweet Sweet Baby) Since You've Been Gone—Aretha Franklin (68)	*3603*
Day Dreaming—Aretha Franklin (72)	2595
Think—Aretha Franklin (68)	2204
Rock Steady—Aretha Franklin (71)	1878
Who's Zoomin' Who—Aretha Franklin (85)	1671
Call Me—Aretha Franklin (70)	1509
All The King's Horses—Aretha Franklin (72)	731
Spirit In The Dark—Aretha Franklin With The Dixie Flyers (70)	680
Master Of Eyes (The Deepness Of Your Eyes)—Aretha Franklin (73)	542
Mr. D.J. (5 For The D.J.)—Aretha Franklin (75)	141
Since You've Been Gone—Ramsey Lewis (68)	*7.3*
You And Me—Aretha Franklin (70)	0.0
Carolyn FRANKLIN [Candy Carroll] ▶ 2743 (3)	**1228**
Angel—Aretha Franklin (73)	1150
Ain't No Way—Aretha Franklin (68)	520
Without Love—Aretha Franklin (74)	268
Dave FRANKLIN ▶ 4449 (3)	**493**
When My Dreamboat Comes Home—Fats Domino (56)	*937*
The Voice In My Heart—Eydie Gorme (58)	24
When My Dream Boat Comes Home—Grady Martin & His Slew Foot Five (56)	*0.0*
Michelle FRANKLIN ▶ 8974 (1)	**35**
Is It Love—J.J. Fad (88)	69
—Sy Franklin see: Herman FAIRBANKS	
Michael FRANKS ▶ 5758 (1)	**245**
Popsicle Toes—Michael Franks (76)	245
Tillman FRANKS ▶ 1883 (4)	**2163**
Sink The Bismarck—Johnny Horton (60)	3896
The Comancheros—Claude King (61)	210
When It's Springtime In Alaska (It's Forty Below)—Johnny Horton (59)	6.6
Honky-Tonk Man—Johnny Horton (62)	4.4
Chris FRANTZ ▶ 3826 (7)	**688**
Burning Down The House—Talking Heads (83)	1439
Wild Wild Life—Talking Heads (86)	742
And She Was—Talking Heads (85)	350
This Must Be The Place (Naïve Melody)—Talking Heads (83)	156
Once In A Lifetime—Talking Heads (86)	39
Life During Wartime (This Ain't No Party.. This Aint No Disco.. This Ain't No Foolin' Around)—Talking Heads (79)	25
Psycho Killer—Talking Heads (78)	8.0
Christopher FRANTZ ▶ 6853 (1)	**132**
Genius Of Love—Tom Tom Club (82)	529
Heinrich FRANTZEN ▶ 6664 (2)	**146**
Don't Cry My Love (The Faithful Hussar)—Vera Lynn (57)	*196*
Faithful Hussar—Ted Heath (56)	*80*
Jeffrey FRANZEL ▶ 2335 (1)	**1582**
Don't Rush Me—Taylor Dayne (88)	3164
Pat FRANZESE ▶ 5574 (1)	**270**
In The Middle Of A Heartache—Wanda Jackson (61)	810
Andy FRASER ▶ 1097 (8)	**4025**
All Right Now—Free (70)	*4192*
Every Kinda People—Robert Palmer (78)	1228
Fire And Water—Wilson Pickett (71)	960
Stealer—Free (70)	359
All Right Now—Rod Stewart (84)	*89*
All Right Now—Pepsi & Shirlie (88)	*85*
Biscuit's In The House—Biscuit (90)	34
All Right Now—Lea Roberts (75)	*18*
Ian FRASER ▶ 11636 (1)	**0.9**
There's No Such Thing As Love—Anthony Newley (63)	1.8
Dale FRASHUER ▶ 1734 (3)	**2403**
Na Na Hey Hey Kiss Him Goodbye—Steam (69)	*5814*
Kiss Him Goodbye—Nylons (87)	*977*
I've Gotta Make You Love Me—Steam (70)	418
Russ FRATTO ▶ 2721 (5)	**1244**
Maybellene—Chuck Berry (55)	*2343*
Maybelline—Johnny Rivers (64)	*1388*
Maybellene—Johnny Long & His Orchestra (55)	*0.0*

Maybellene—Jim Lowe (55)	*0.0*
Maybellene—Ralph Marterie & His Orchestra (55)	*0.0*
Al FRAZIER ▶ 2892 (4)	**1129**
Bird Is The Word—Trashmen (63)	*1861*
Papa Oom Mow Mow—Trashmen (63)	*1861*
Papa-Oom-Mow-Mow—Rivingtons (62)	*480*
The Bird's The Word—Rivingtons (63)	*315*
Billy FRAZIER ▶ 7782 (1)	**75**
Where Is The Party—Helena Ferguson (67)	75
Dallas FRAZIER ▶ 187 (17)	**16421**
Alley Oop—Hollywood Argyles [Gary Paxton] (60)	*6926*
Elvira—Oak Ridge Boys (81)	*4183*
Alley Oop—Danté And The Evergreens (60)	*1398*
Mohair Sam—Charlie Rich (65)	1150
Johnny One Time—Brenda Lee (69)	736
The Son Of Hickory Holler's Tramp—O.C. Smith (68)	711
There Goes My Everything—Engelbert Humperdinck (67)	*658*
There Goes My Everything—Elvis Presley (70)	*390*
Where Did They Go, Lord—Elvis Presley (71)	360
Alley Oop—Four Preps (61)	*130*
I Can't Believe That You've Stopped Loving Me—Charley Pride (70)	95
There Goes My Everything—Jack Greene (67)	*89*
Elvira—Dallas Frazier (66)	*73*
Alley Oop—Dyna-Sores (60)	*71*
All I Have To Offer You (Is Me)—Charley Pride (69)	41
(I'm So) Afraid Of Losing You Again—Charley Pride (69)	40
What's Your Mama's Name—Tanya Tucker (73)	14
Robert FRAZIER ▶ 6492 (1)	**163**
Play The Game Tonight—Kansas (82)	814
Stan FREBERG ▶ 5213 (5)	**325**
Banana Boat (Day-O)—Stan Freberg (57)	*352*
Wun'erful, Wun'erful! (Sides Uh-One & Uh-Two)—Stan Freberg (57)	298
Green ChriTma—Stan Freberg (58)	110
The Old Payola Roll Blues (Like the Beginning)—Stan Freberg Featuring Jesse White (60)	0.8
Point Of Order—Stan Freberg & Daws Butler (54)	0.0
Joey FRECHETTE ▶ 6678 (1)	**145**
Clap Your Hands—Beau-Marks (60)	578
John FRED [John Fred Gourrier] ▶ 1031 (3)	**4283**
Judy In Disguise (With Glasses)—John Fred & His Playboy Band (67)	8168
Hey Hey Bunny—John Fred & His Playboy Band (68)	355
Shirley—John Fred and the Playboys (59)	42
Mike FREDA ▶ 6171 (1)	**198**
Here Come The Judge—Magistrates (68)	396
Patrick FREDERICK ▶ 7616 (1)	**85**
Lovin' The Night Away—Dillman Band (81)	170
—Henry St. Claire Fredericks see: Taj MAHAL	
—Dennis Hardy Frederiksen see: Fergie FREDERIKSEN	
Fergie FREDERIKSEN [Dennis Hardy Frederiksen] ▶ 9859 (1)	**16**
Carrie's Gone—Le Roux (83)	48
—Ronald L. Fredianelli see: Ronnie GAYLORD	
Nan FREDRICS ▶ 5838 (1)	**238**
On An Evening In Roma—Dean Martin (59)	715
—Free see: Eric SMITH	
Alan FREED [Albert James Freed] ▶ 847 (16)	**5219**
Sincerely—McGuire Sisters (54)	*6576*
Maybellene—Chuck Berry (55)	*2343*
Maybelline—Johnny Rivers (64)	*1388*
Most Of All—Don Cornell (55)	*1147*
Sincerely—4 Seasons (64)	*115*
Sincerely—Paul Anka (69)	*86*
Teenage Meeting (Gonna Rock It Up Right)—Don Cornell (56)	*24*
Sincerely—Tokens (61)	*11*
Most Of All—Fontane Sisters with Billy Vaughn's Orchestra (55)	*0.0*
Teenage Meeting (Gonna Rock It Up Right)—Dave Appell & His Applejacks (56)	*0.0*
Sincerely—Moonglows (55)	*0.0*
Maybellene—Johnny Long & His Orchestra (55)	*0.0*
Maybellene—Jim Lowe (55)	*0.0*
Maybellene—Ralph Marterie & His Orchestra (55)	*0.0*
Most Of All—Moonglows (55)	*0.0*
Nadine—Dells (70)	0.0

Arthur FREED [Arthur Grossman] ▶ 4876 (2) HOF	**392**
Temptation—Everly Brothers (61)	*771*
You Were Meant For Me—Johnston Brothers (55)	13
Ralph FREED ▶ 5683 (5)	**256**
I Never Felt More Like Falling In Love—Tony Bennett with Ray Ellis and His Orchestra (57)	304
Adios Amigo—Jim Reeves (62)	105
You Were Made For Love—Dean Martin (59)	89
Things They Don't Teach You In School—Connie Freed (58)	20
My Last Night In Rome—Eddie Dano (56)	*3.2*
Ruth FREED [Patty Fisher] ▶ 6976 (2)	**124**
Tunnel Of Love—Doris Day (58)	245
Make A Circle—Kay Starr (63)	3.2
—David Freedman see: Dave MANN	
Max C. FREEDMAN [Ray Freeman] ▶ 1014 (4)	**4382**
(We're Gonna) Rock Around The Clock—Bill Haley And His Comets (55)	*8240*
(We're Gonna) Rock Around The Clock—Bill Haley And His Comets (74)	*381*
Rock Around The Clock—Jive Bunny And The Mastermixers (89)	*80*
(We're Gonna) Rock Around The Clock—Bill Haley and His Comets (54)	*64*
Roy FREELAND [Roy Freirich] ▶ 2559 (7)	**1385**
This Night Won't Last Forever—Michael Johnson (79)	*1098*
Another Night—Aretha Franklin (86)	634
Black Cars—Gino Vannelli (85)	400
Wild Horses—Gino Vannelli (87)	292
Brooklyn Girls—Robbie Dupree (81)	159
This Night Won't Last Forever—Bill LaBounty (78)	*134*
She Loves My Car—Ronnie Milsap (84)	52
Allan FREEMAN ▶ 11233 (1)	**2.6**
Astral Man—Nektar (75)	11
Bobby FREEMAN ▶ 666 (8)	**6505**
Do You Want To Dance—Bobby Freeman (58)	*2560*
Do You Want To Dance?—Bette Midler (72)	*1467*
Do You Wanna Dance?—Beach Boys (65)	*1224*
Betty Lou Got A New Pair Of Shoes—Bobby Freeman (58)	495
Do You Want To Dance—Del Shannon (64)	*333*
Do You Wanna Dance—Mamas & The Papas (68)	*286*
Need Your Love—Bobby Freeman (58)	118
Do You Wanna Dance—Ramones (78)	*23*
Bud FREEMAN ▶ 9584 (2)	**21**
Moonlight Mountain—Faron Young (61)	36
Moonlight Mountain—Faron Young (57)	5.7
David FREEMAN ▶ 10688 (1)	**6.1**
No More "I Love You's"—Lover Speaks (86)	12
Don FREEMAN ▶ 5111 (3)	**341**
Don't You Get So Mad—Jeffrey Osborne (83)	600
Rainbow's End—Sergio Mendes (83)	227
Discipline Of Love (Why Did You Do It)—Robert Palmer (85)	54
Ernie FREEMAN [Mike Akapoff] ▶ 3660 (5)	**746**
Percolator (Twist)—Billy Joe & The Checkmates (62)	*1188*
Jivin' Around—Al Casey Combo (62)	125
Beautiful Obsession—Sir Chauncey And His Exciting Strings (60)	68
Percolator—Hot Butter (73)	*29*
Jivin' Around (Pt. 2)—Ernie Freeman Combo (56)	13
Frederick FREEMAN ▶ 11050 (1)	**3.6**
Too Hot To Stop—Bar-Kays (77)	36
Isabelle FREEMAN ▶ 10374 (1)	**9.3**
Children's Christmas Song—Supremes (65)	9.3
John FREEMAN ▶ 3569 (2)	**784**
Just Don't Want To Be Lonely—Main Ingredient (74)	*2140*
Just Don't Want To Be Lonely—Ronnie Dyson (73)	*210*
Kenneth FREEMAN ▶ 11764 (1)	**0.2**
Run And Hide—Uniques (66)	0.5
Ned FREEMAN ▶ 10859 (1)	**4.9**
I Know What God Is—Perry Como (60)	15
—Ray Freeman see: Max C. FREEDMAN	
Roy FREEMAN ▶ 6568 (2)	**155**
Sit With The Guru—Strawberry Alarm Clock (68)	242
Barefoot In Baltimore—Strawberry Alarm Clock (68)	224
Stu FREEMAN ▶ 11540 (1)	**1.3**
It's-A-Happening—Magic Mushrooms (66)	3.8

Ticker FREEMAN ▶ 7950 (1)	**68**
You'll Always Be The One I Love—Dean Martin (64)	136
Paul FREES [Solomon Hersh Frees] ▶ 9625 (1)	**20**
I'm Drowning My Sorrows—Teresa Brewer (57)	40
—Solomon Hersh Frees see: Paul FREES	
Ace FREHLEY [Paul Daniel Frehley] ▶ 6113 (2)	**205**
Rocket Ride—Kiss (78)	389
Flaming Youth—Kiss (76)	41
David FREIBERG ▶ 4728 (1)	**429**
Jane—Jefferson Starship (79)	1718
—Guy Freidline see: Guy MAGENTA	
—Roy Freirich see: Roy FREELAND	
Don FRENCH ▶ 9390 (2)	**25**
A Child Of God (It's Hard To Believe)—Millie Jackson (71)	37
Little Blonde Girl—Don French (59)	6.1
Michael FRENCHIK ▶ 2870 (1)	**1139**
Dancing On The Ceiling—Lionel Richie (86)	3417
Matt FRENETTE ▶ 5647 (2)	**260**
Working For The Weekend—Loverboy (81)	740
Jump—Loverboy (82)	67
Chris FRETWELL ▶ 9441 (1)	**23**
This Love—Bad Company (86)	47
James FREUD [Colin McGlinchy] ▶ 4603 (1)	**453**
Out Of Mind Out Of Sight—Models (86)	453
Alan FREW ▶ 2255 (5)	**1700**
Don't Forget Me (When I'm Gone)—Glass Tiger (86)	2668
Someday—Glass Tiger (86)	1758
I'm Still Searching—Glass Tiger (88)	408
I Will Be There—Glass Tiger (87)	374
My Song—Glass Tiger (88)	41
Allen FREY ▶ 10741 (1)	**5.6**
I Wash My Hands Of The Whole Damn Deal (Part 1)—New Birth (74)	11
Glenn FREY ▶ 161 (23) HOF	**18538**
One Of These Nights—Eagles (75)	5146
Hotel California—Eagles (77)	4658
Heartache Tonight—Eagles (79)	4547
Best Of My Love—Eagles (74)	4142
New Kid In Town—Eagles (76)	4051
Lyin' Eyes—Eagles (75)	3949
You Belong To The City—Glenn Frey (85)	3346
Take It To The Limit—Eagles (75)	3081
The Long Run—Eagles (79)	2002
I Can't Tell You Why—Eagles (80)	1924
Take It Easy—Eagles (72)	1870
The One You Love—Glenn Frey (82)	1201
Smuggler's Blues—Glenn Frey (85)	1119
Life In The Fast Lane—Eagles (77)	1068
True Love—Glenn Frey (88)	970
Sexy Girl—Glenn Frey (84)	756
I Found Somebody—Glenn Frey (82)	570
All Those Lies—Glenn Frey (82)	403
Tequila Sunrise—Eagles (73)	344
Part Of Me, Part Of You—Glenn Frey (91)	267
The Allnighter—Glenn Frey (84)	171
James Dean—Eagles (74)	125
Livin' Right—Glenn Frey (89)	11
Sylvia FRICKER [Sylvia Tyson] ▶ 684 (2)	**6359**
You Were On My Mind—We Five (65)	*6094*
You Were On My Mind—Crispian St. Peters (67)	*265*
Freddy FRIDAY [Murray Sporn] ▶ 2651 (3)	**1294**
Java—Al (He's The King) Hirt Trumpet With Chorus And Orchestra (64)	*4600*
Java—Floyd Cramer (62)	*570*
Java Jones—Donna Lynn (64)	*5.7*
Langdon FRIDIE ▶ 4297 (1)	**530**
Troglodyte (Cave Man)—Jimmy Castor Bunch (72)	3177
Dennis FRIDKIN ▶ 9893 (1)	**15**
Apple Cider—Five By Five (69)	15
Gerald FRIED ▶ 7692 (1)	**80**
Theme From Roots—Quincy Jones (77)	80
Hugo FRIEDHOFER ▶ 3668 (1)	**744**
Love Theme From One Eyed Jacks—Ferrante & Teicher (61)	744
Stephen FRIEDLAND [Brute Force] ▶ 5164 (1)	**332**
Nobody Knows What's Goin' On (In My Mind But Me)—Chiffons (65)	332

Alan FRIEDMAN ▶ 8004 (1)	**66**
Let The Beat Hit 'Em—Lisa Lisa & Cult Jam (91)	262
Amy FRIEDMAN ▶ 10775 (1)	**5.4**
Then Came You—T.P.E. (91)	5.4
—Bernie Friedman see: B.F. FLIP	
Charles FRIEDMAN ▶ 6255 (1)	**189**
Kiss Me Another—Georgia Gibbs (56)	566
Dean FRIEDMAN ▶ 2922 (1)	**1116**
Ariel—Dean Friedman (77)	1116
Gary FRIEDMAN ▶ 4153 (3)	**579**
Light Sings—5th Dimension (71)	645
This World—Staple Singers (72)	*509*
This World—Sweet Inspirations (70)	*3.4*
Jud FRIEDMAN ▶ 2082 (1)	**1901**
I Don't Have The Heart—James Ingram (90)	3801
Leo FRIEDMAN ▶ 8331 (2)	**54**
Let Me Call You Sweetheart—Timi Yuro (62)	*94*
Let Me Call You Sweetheart—Bruce Hayes with Mary Mayo (60)	*14*
Rob FRIEDMAN ▶ 3602 (1)	**772**
Don't Shed A Tear—Paul Carrack (87)	1544
Ruthann FRIEDMAN ▶ 456 (2)	**9149**
Windy—Association (67)	*8778*
Windy—Wes Montgomery (67)	*371*
Cliff FRIEND ▶ 2565 (12)	**1375**
When My Dreamboat Comes Home—Fats Domino (56)	*937*
June Night—Jimmy Dorsey Orchestra and Chorus (57)	581
I Wanna Go Where You Go, Do What You Do (Then I'll Be Happy)—Eddie Fisher (55)	382
Lovesick Blues—Frank Ifield (62)	*358*
Time Waits For No One—Hilltoppers (54)	253
Trade Winds—Billy Vaughn And His Orchestra (59)	203
Lovesick Blues—Sonny James (57)	*85*
Lovesick Blues—Floyd Cramer (62)	*47*
Time—Teresa Brewer (54)	28
Don't Sweetheart Me—Bobby Dee & Rhodie-Summers (57)	5.8
When My Dream Boat Comes Home—Grady Martin & His Slew Foot Five (56)	*0.0*
Lovesick Blues—Sonny Knight (57)	*0.0*
Bill FRIES [C.W. McCall] ▶ 1368 (4)	**3253**
Convoy—C.W. McCall (75)	5960
Wolf Creek Pass—C.W. McCall (75)	215
Old Home Filler-Up An' Keep On-A-Truckin' Cafe—C.W. McCall (74)	198
There Won't Be No Country Music (There Won't Be No Rock 'N' Roll)—C.W. McCall (76)	133
Tim FRIESE-GREENE ▶ 5300 (2)	**310**
It's My Life—Talk Talk (84)	595
Life's What You Make It—Talk Talk (86)	25
—John L. Friga see: Jonathan CAIN	
Derek FRIGO ▶ 10368 (1)	**9.4**
Mother's Eyes—Enuff Z'Nuff (91)	19
Rudolf FRIML ▶ 7277 (3) HOF	**106**
Indian Love Call—Ray Stevens (75)	*140*
Indian Love Call—Ernie Freeman (58)	*59*
Some Day—Frankie Laine (54)	0.0
Robert FRIPP ▶ 10971 (1)	**4.0**
In The Court Of The Crimson King—King Crimson (70)	20
Al FRISCH ▶ 1794 (16)	**2308**
Two Different Worlds—Don Rondo (56)	*1457*
Winner Take All—Platters (56)	*635*
All Over The World—Nat King Cole (63)	603
Flowers Mean Forgiveness—Frank Sinatra (56)	582
My Love Song To You—Bob Manning (54)	464
Two Different Worlds—Roger Williams And Jane Morgan (56)	*427*
Two Different Worlds—Lenny Welch (65)	*403*
Sweet Brown Eyed Baby—Ames Brothers (55)	153
If I'm Elected—Eddie Fisher (56)	54
Two Different Worlds—Dick Haymes (56)	*11*
Language Of Love—Cindy And Lindy (57)	6.4
Monte Carlo Melody—Werner Müller And His Orchestra (56)	5.5
He Cha Cha'd In—Kay Starr (58)	3.8
Two Different Worlds—Dick Kallman (56)	*0.0*
Winner Take All—Sunny Gale (56)	*0.0*
Gingerbread—Gingersnaps (58)	0.0
Max FRITH [William Dumaresq] ▶ 11724 (1)	**0.4**
I Know A Man—Rolf Harris (63)	0.9

Donnie FRITTS ▶ 4587 (4)	**461**
Choo Choo Train—Box Tops (68)	854
You're All Around Me—Percy Sledge (68)	58
Breakfast In Bed—Dusty Springfield (69)	9.1
Ooh Ooh Ooh—Sam & Dave (69)	1.4
Lefty FRIZZELL [William Orville Frizzell] ▶ 7751 (1)	**76**
Mom And Dad's Waltz—Patti Page (61)	76
Steven FROMHOLZ ▶ 10950 (1)	**4.2**
I'd Have To Be Crazy—Willie Nelson (76)	4.2
Scott FRONSOE ▶ 10466 (1)	**8.1**
Love Is For The Best In Us—James Walsh Gypsy Band (79)	8.1
Dominic FRONTIERE ▶ 1933 (3)	**2089**
Hang 'Em High—Booker T. & The MG's (68)	*1959*
Hang 'Em High—Hugo Montenegro, His Orchestra And Chorus (68)	*115*
Felicidad—Sally Field (67)	28
Francesco FRONTINI ▶ 9088 (1)	**32**
The Little Musicians—Hugo Winterhalter's Orchestra And Chorus (56)	32
Mitchell FROOM ▶ 3462 (3)	**837**
Something So Strong—Crowded House (87)	1595
Club Michelle—Eddie Money (84)	101
Right The First Time—Gamma (82)	43
Craig FROST ▶ 7902 (1)	**70**
Take Me—Grand Funk Railroad (76)	141
—Eunice Frost see: Eunice LEVY	
Frances FROST [Frances Claire Frost, Frances Swan] ▶ 3581 (2)	**777**
What About Me—Moving Pictures (82)	*1247*
What About Me—Moving Pictures (89)	*308*
Frank FROST ▶ 11119 (1)	**3.1**
My Back Scratcher—Frank Frost (66)	6.3
Garry FROST ▶ 3579 (3)	**778**
What About Me—Moving Pictures (82)	*1247*
What About Me—Moving Pictures (89)	*308*
That's When I Think Of You—1927 (89)	0.4
Richard FROST [Rich Martin] ▶ 8824 (1)	**38**
She's Got Love—Thomas & Richard Frost (69)	77
Thomas FROST [Tom Martin] ▶ 8825 (1)	**38**
She's Got Love—Thomas & Richard Frost (69)	77
Ed FRUGÉ ▶ 9012 (1)	**33**
Heart's On Fire—John Cafferty (86)	99
John FRUSCIANTE ▶ 10603 (1)	**6.9**
Give It Away—Red Hot Chili Peppers (91)	28
Martin FRY ▶ 1588 (7)	**2661**
The Look Of Love - Part One—ABC (82)	1769
When Smokey Sings—ABC (87)	1756
Be Near Me—ABC (85)	1562
Poison Arrow—ABC (83)	732
(How To Be A) Millionaire—ABC (86)	711
Vanity Kills—ABC (86)	36
That Was Then But This Is Now—ABC (84)	12
Mike FRYE ▶ 5531 (1)	**274**
Family Man—Daryl Hall & John Oates (83)	1641
Terry FRYER ▶ 7321 (1)	**102**
Yes—Merry Clayton (88)	306
Magnus FRYKBERG ▶ 7129 (1)	**115**
My Body Says Yes—Titiyo Featuring Papa D (91)	229
Giuseppe FUCILLI [Giuseppe Fanciulli] ▶ 3688 (3)	**733**
Guaglione—Perez Prado And His Orchestra (58)	*703*
Guaglione—Mitchell Ayers and his Orchestra and Chorus (56)	*15*
Guaglione (Little Boy)—Ralph Marterie And His Orchestra (56)	*15*
Michel FUGAIN ▶ 7237 (1)	**108**
If I Only Had Time—Nick Decaro (68)	108
Billy FULGRUM ▶ 11691 (1)	**0.7**
It's Been A Long Long Time—Elgins (67)	4.3
Craig FULLER ▶ 4005 (2)	**624**
Amie—Pure Prairie League (75)	615
Let Me Down Easy—American Flyer (76)	19
—Darrell Fuller see: Dolores FULLER	
Dolores FULLER [Dolores Eble, Darrell Fuller] ▶ 3014 (5)	**1068**
Do The Clam—Elvis Presley With The Jordanaires, Jubilee Four & Carole Lombard Trio (65)	929

Rock-A-Hula Baby ("Twist" Special)—Elvis Presley With The Jordanaires (61)	854
I'll Touch A Star—Terry Stafford (64)	745
Spinout—Elvis Presley With The Jordanaires (66)	614
I Got Lucky—Elvis Presley with the Jordanaires (62)	62
Jerry FULLER ▶ 57 (18)	**36872**
Travelin' Man—Ricky Nelson (61)	8567
Young Girl—Union Gap Featuring Gary Puckett (68)	7523
Lady Willpower—Gary Puckett And The Union Gap (68)	5918
Show And Tell—Al Wilson (73)	5374
Over You—Gary Puckett And The Union Gap (68)	2707
Young World—Rick Nelson (62)	2396
It's Up To You—Rick Nelson (62)	1944
A Wonder Like You—Rick Nelson (61)	1482
If I Were You—Lulu (81)	*337*
Touch And Go—Al Wilson (74)	322
Please Don't Fight It—Dino, Desi & Billy (65)	226
Congratulations—Rick Nelson (64)	133
Son-In-Law—Blossoms (61)	75
If I Were You—Toby Beau (80)	*39*
For Your Sweet Love—Cascades (63)	27
Betty My Angel—Jerry Fuller (59)	17
Guilty Of Loving You—Jerry Fuller (61)	11
Me And You—O.C. Smith (69)	9.1
Jim FULLER ▶ 2018 (7)	**2000**
Wipe Out—Surfaris (63)	*4648*
Wipe Out—Surfaris (66)	*1843*
Wipeout—Fat Boys (87)	*961*
Point Panic—Surfaris (63)	378
Surfer Joe—Surfaris (63)	236
Wipe Out—Jive Bunny & The Mastermixers (90)	*6.7*
Wipe Out—Surfaris (70)	*4.6*
Leroy FULLYLOVE ▶ 2807 (2)	**1185**
Bumble Bee—Searchers (65)	*834*
Bumble Bee—LaVern Baker (60)	*351*
Orena D. FULMER [Orena D. Fullmer, Triune] ▶ 11087 (1)	**3.3**
Mojo Workout (Dance)—Larry Bright (60)	13
Lowell FULSOM [Lowell Fulson] ▶ 3955 (3)	**642**
Tramp—Otis & Carla (67)	*913*
Tramp—Lowell Fulsom (67)	*364*
Blue Shadows—B.B. King (65)	3.2
Don FULTON ▶ 11375 (2)	**2.1**
Straight Flush—Frantics (59)	9.1
Fog Cutter—Frantics (59)	3.1
Jack FULTON ▶ 1006 (6)	**4416**
Ivory Tower—Cathy Carr (56)	*4201*
Ivory Tower—Gale Storm (56)	*2381*
Ivory Tower—Otis Williams And His Charms (56)	*2092*
Times Two I Love You—Three Chuckles (55)	119
Peace—McGuire Sisters (59)	39
Wanted—Perry Como (54)	0.0
Kathryn FULTON ▶ 1073 (1)	**4110**
Fool #1—Brenda Lee (61)	4110
Paul FULTON ▶ 8179 (1)	**59**
Rubber Biscuit—Blues Brothers (79)	297
Johnny FUNCHES ▶ 3324 (1)	**899**
Oh, What A Night—Dells (69)	1798
Tommy FUNDERBURK ▶ 4264 (1)	**540**
It's Not Enough—Starship (89)	1080
Buddy FUNK ▶ 5468 (1)	**283**
Hey Little Girl—Techniques (57)	283
—Stanard Funsten see: Stan RIDGWAY	
—Gwen Fuqua see: Gwen GORDY	
Harvey FUQUA [Harry Pratt] ▶ 351 (27)	**10777**
Someday We'll Be Together—Diana Ross And The Supremes (69)	7492
Sincerely—McGuire Sisters (54)	*6576*
What Does It Take (To Win Your Love)—Jr. Walker & The All Stars (69)	3648
Twenty-Five Miles—Edwin Starr (69)	*2304*
My Whole World Ended (The Moment You Left Me)—David Ruffin (69)	1875
If I Could Build My Whole World Around You—Marvin Gaye & Tammi Terrell (67)	1524
Most Of All—Don Cornell (55)	*1147*
K-Jee—Nite-Liters (71)	726
If I Can't Have You—Etta & Harvey (60)	659
Pucker Up Buttercup—Jr. Walker & The All Stars (67)	629

That's What Girls Are Made For—Spinners (61)	598
Afro-Strut—Nite-Liters (72)	372
See Saw—Moonglows (56)	*357*
Cleo's Mood—Jr. Walker & The All Stars (66)	215
Sincerely—4 Seasons (64)	*115*
Sincerely—Paul Anka (69)	*86*
I Can't Believe You Love Me—Tammi Terrell (66)	70
See Saw—Don Cornell (56)	*56*
Come On And See Me—Tammi Terrell (66)	32
These Things Will Keep Me Loving You—Velvelettes (66)	17
Sincerely—Tokens (61)	*11*
Love (I'm So Glad) I Found You—Spinners (61)	4.6
It's Been A Long Long Time—Elgins (67)	4.3
Twenty-Five Miles—Mongo Santamaria (69)	*0.9*
Most Of All—Fontane Sisters with Billy Vaughn's Orchestra (55)	*0.0*
Sincerely—Moonglows (55)	*0.0*
Most Of All—Moonglows (55)	*0.0*
Richie FURAY ▶ 3637 (3)	**755**
Fallin' In Love—Souther, Hillman, Furay Band (74)	515
C'mon—Poco (71)	210
Just For Me And You—Poco (71)	30
Douglas FURBER ▶ 9808 (3)	**17**
Bells Of St Mary's—Terry & The Mellos featuring Terry Corin (60)	*33*
The Bells Of St. Mary's—Lynn Taylor & The Peachettes (60)	*0.0*
The Bells Of St. Mary's—Baysiders (60)	*0.0*
—Vincent Damon Furnier see: Alice COOPER	
Magne FURUHOLMEN ▶ 2375 (2)	**1551**
Take On Me—A-Ha (85)	4264
Cry Wolf—A-Ha (87)	259
Bobby FUSCO ▶ 9961 (1)	**14**
Feelin' That Glow—Roberta Flack (75)	72

G

Mark GABLE ▶ 9131 (1)	**31**
Run To Paradise—Choirboys (89)	61
Milt GABLER [Jimmy Brewster, Roy Carroll, Roy Ilene] ▶ 1076 (21)	**4098**
If I Give My Heart To You—Doris Day (54)	*4238*
If I Give My Heart To You—Denise Lor (54)	*1609*
Danke Schoen—Wayne Newton & The Newton Brothers (63)	1445
If I Give My Heart To You—Dinah Shore (54)	*1206*
Go On With The Wedding—Patti Page (55)	*976*
If I Give My Heart To You—Kitty Kallen (59)	*711*
Skinny Minnie—Bill Haley And His Comets (58)	608
If I Give My Heart To You—Connee Boswell (54)	*402*
Now And Forever—Bert Kaempfert And His Orchestra (61)	331
Wiederseh'n—Al Martino (66)	295
Go On With The Wedding—Kitty Kallen & Georgie Shaw (55)	*288*
I Want You All To Myself (Just You)—Kitty Kallen (54)	218
Choo Choo Ch'Boogie—Bill Haley And His Comets (56)	65
L-O-V-E—Nat King Cole (64)	29
Sweet Maria—Billy Vaughn Singers (67)	18
Someone—Billy Vaughn And His Orchestra (62)	14
Where Can You Be—Don Cherry (54)	*11*
Whoa Mabel—Bill Haley And His Comets (58)	2.7
Stay Here With Me (Resta Cu 'Mme)—Domenico Modugno (58)	1.6
Go On With The Wedding—Modernaires (56)	*0.0*
Where Can You Be—Jerry Martin (54)	*0.0*
Charles Hutchison GABRIEL ▶ 8719 (1)	**41**
Brighten The Corner Where You Are—Browns Featuring Jim Edward Brown (60)	82
Gilbert GABRIEL ▶ 2908 (2)	**1123**
Life In A Northern Town—Dream Academy (85)	1832
The Love Parade—Dream Academy (86)	413
Pascal GABRIEL ▶ 11211 (1)	**2.7**
Theme From S-Express—S-Express (88)	14
Peter GABRIEL ▶ 525 (10)	**8098**
Sledgehammer—Peter Gabriel (86)	4081
Big Time—Peter Gabriel (86)	1747
Shock The Monkey—Peter Gabriel (82)	735
In Your Eyes—Peter Gabriel (86)	*589*

Peter GABRIEL ▶ 525 (10) *Continued*	**8098**
In Your Eyes—Peter Gabriel (89)	*425*
Pop Goes The Weasel—3rd Bass (91)	333
Games Without Frontiers—Peter Gabriel (80)	269
Don't Give Up—Peter Gabriel/Kate Bush (87)	103
Solsbury Hill—Peter Gabriel (77)	*84*
Solsbury Hill—Peter Gabriel (83)	*18*
—Paul Francis Gadd see: Gary GLITTER	
Steve GADD ▶ 7161 (1)	**112**
Stuff Like That—Quincy Jones (78)	787
Jacob GADE ▶ 7510 (1)	**91**
Jalousie—Caterina Valente (55)	183
James GADSON ▶ 5121 (2)	**339**
Do Your Thing—Watts 103rd Street Rhythm Band (69)	1496
Till You Get Enough—Watts 103rd Street Rhythm Band (69)	200
Rich GAEL ▶ 8066 (1)	**63**
Deep Enough For Me—Ocean (71)	126
Peter GAGE ▶ 9727 (1)	**18**
She's Lost You—Zephyrs (65)	18
Ed GAGLIARDI ▶ 9947 (1)	**15**
Don't Run My Life—Spys (82)	73
—Guy Mitchell Gaglio see: Guy MARSHALL	
André GAGNON ▶ 11122 (1)	**3.1**
Wow—Andre Gagnon (76)	3.1
—LaDonna Adrian Gaines see: Donna SUMMER	
Rose Mary GAINES ▶ 7306 (1)	**104**
Lonely Soldier—Mike Williams (66)	207
Steve GAINES ▶ 9126 (1)	**31**
You Got That Right—Lynyrd Skynyrd (78)	61
Serge GAINSBOURG [Lucien Ginsburg] ▶ 6224 (2)	**192**
Je T'Aime...Moi Non Plus—Jane Birkin & Serge Gainsbourg (69)	*191*
Soul Je T'Aime—Sylvia & Ralfi Pagan (73)	*1.3*
Bruce GAITSCH ▶ 1948 (4)	**2068**
La Isla Bonita—Madonna (87)	2230
Don't Mean Nothing—Richard Marx (87)	2111
Boys Night Out—Timothy B. Schmit (87)	539
Nothin' To Hide—Poco (89)	179
—Gordon Galbraith see: Jean SAWYER	
Rob GALBRAITH ▶ 7647 (2)	**83**
Got To Give In To Love—Bonnie Boyer (79)	222
Damn It All—Gene Cotton (75)	28
Harold GALBREATH ▶ 9681 (1)	**19**
Young Dove's Calling—Couplings (58)	38
Michele GALDIERI ▶ 5084 (2)	**345**
Non Dimenticar (Don't Forget)—Nat "King" Cole (58)	1029
Traveling Down A Lonely Road—Teddi King (56)	6.4
Joe GALDO ▶ 3307 (3)	**906**
Bad Boy—Miami Sound Machine (86)	1668
Falling In Love (Uh-Oh)—Miami Sound Machine (86)	691
Betcha Say That—Gloria Estefan and Miami Sound Machine (87)	358
Phil GALDSTON ▶ 4992 (3)	**362**
It's Not Over ('til It's Over)—Starship (87)	1049
Fools Like Me—Lorenzo Lamas (84)	23
Reason To Try—Eric Carmen (88)	9.7
Eric GALE ▶ 7162 (1)	**112**
Stuff Like That—Quincy Jones (78)	787
Jack GALE ▶ 6485 (3)	**164**
Teenage Heaven—Johnny Cymbal (63)	243
Elephant Walk—Kings (2) (58)	*43*
Elephant Walk—Chords (59)	*0.0*
Trevor GALE ▶ 4706 (1)	**434**
Running Back To You—Vanessa Williams (91)	868
Willey GALE ▶ 7999 (1)	**66**
If I Possessed A Printing Press—George Hamilton IV (57)	66
Jose GALHARDO ▶ 1622 (4)	**2602**
Lisbon Antigua—Nelson Riddle And His Orchestra (55)	*7507*
Lisbon Antigua (In Old Lisbon)—Mitch Miller & His Orchestra (56)	*298*
Lisbon Antigua—Lawrence Welk & His Champagne Music (56)	*0.0*
Lisbon Antigua (In Old Lisbon)—Alan Dale (55)	*0.0*
—Gabriel Ruiz Galindo see: Gabriel RUIZ	
Robert GALL ▶ 5488 (4)	**279**
For Mama (La Mamma)—Connie Francis (65)	*438*
For Mama—Jerry Vale (65)	*400*
For Mama—Matt Monro (65)	*0.0*
For Mama (La Mamma)—Vic Damone (65)	*0.0*
Benny GALLAGHER ▶ 3611 (7)	**768**
When I'm Dead And Gone—McGuinness Flint (70)	565
Break Away—Art Garfunkel (75)	478
A Heart In New York—Art Garfunkel (81)	227
I Wanna Stay With You—Gallagher And Lyle (76)	160
Heart On My Sleeve—Gallagher and Lyle (76)	*87*
Heart On My Sleeve—Bryan Ferry (76)	*17*
Every Little Teardrop—Gallagher And Lyle (77)	2.5
Mark GALLAGHER ▶ 11203 (1)	**2.8**
Silly People—Litter (69)	11
Mick GALLAGHER ▶ 5336 (1)	**303**
Do You Feel Like We Do—Peter Frampton (76)	1212
Rosemary GALLAGHER ▶ 5950 (1)	**224**
Darling Lorraine—Knockouts (59)	448
—Grace Lane Gallico see: Grace LANE	
—Susan Marie Gallion see: Susan THOMAS	
Joey GALLO ▶ 4368 (4)	**511**
Dead Giveaway—Shalamar (83)	1143
Save The Overtime (For Me)—Gladys Knight & The Pips (83)	179
Show Me The Way—Regina Belle (87)	146
Full Of Fire—Shalamar (80)	136
Lee GALLO [Lee Clark, Lee A.C. Gallo] ▶ 9378 (1)	**25**
Fried Eggs—Intruders (59)	75
Sammy GALLOP ▶ 1149 (20)	**3864**
Wake The Town And Tell The People—Les Baxter His Chorus And Orchestra (55)	*2302*
Wake The Town And Tell The People—Mindy Carson (55)	*1076*
Night Lights—Nat "King" Cole (56)	1019
There Must Be A Way—Joni James (59)	*951*
Forgive My Heart—Nat "King" Cole (55)	892
Count Every Star—Donnie And The Dreamers (61)	*400*
Count Every Star—Linda Scott (62)	*391*
Half As Lovely (Twice As True)—Frank Sinatra (54)	234
Count Every Star—Rivieras (1) (58)	*160*
Somewhere Along The Way—Steve Lawrence (61)	*134*
That's You—Nat King Cole (60)	60
There Must Be A Way—Jimmy Roselli (67)	*52*
Boulevard Of Nightingales—Tony Martin (54)	47
Somewhere Along The Way—Roy Hamilton (59)	*8.9*
Maybe You'll Be There—Billy And The Essentials (62)	8.8
Devil's Highway—9 LaFalce Brothers (55)	7.0
What A Heavenly Night For Love—Lawrence Welk And His Champagne Music (56)	*2.1*
What A Heavenly Night For Love—Frankie Masters & His Orchestra (56)	*2.1*
What A Heavenly Night For Love—Dinah Shore (56)	*2.1*
Make Her Mine—Nat "King" Cole (54)	0.0
Tod GALLOWAY ▶ 8586 (1)	**45**
Whiffenpoof Song—Bob Crewe (59)	136
Angelo GALLUCCI ▶ 7812 (1)	**74**
Ever Since You Went Away—Les Elgart and His Orch. With Don Forbes (55)	74
Simon GALLUP [Simon Johnathan Gallup] ▶ 3818 (8)	**690**
Love Song—Cure (89)	2408
Just Like Heaven—Cure (87)	604
Why Can't I Be You?—Cure (87)	279
Fascination Street—Cure (89)	194
Lullaby—Cure (89)	170
Pictures Of You—Cure (90)	105
Hot Hot Hot!!!—Cure (88)	88
Never Enough—Cure (90)	68
Amos GALPIN ▶ 7850 (1)	**72**
Big Mistake—Peter Cetera (87)	144
Albhy GALUTEN [Alan Bruce Galuten] ▶ 2851 (3)	**1152**
What Kind Of Fool—Barbra Streisand & Barry Gibb (81)	1271
This Woman—Kenny Rogers (84)	574
Take The Short Way Home—Dionne Warwick (83)	460
Charles GAMBEL ▶ 9175 (1)	**29**
Tell Me Mamma—Christine Quaite (64)	88
John GAMBLE ▶ 8512 (1)	**48**
Pop Goes The Weasel—3rd Bass (91)	333
Kenneth GAMBLE ▶ 34 (128) HOF	**47753**
Me And Mrs. Jones—Billy Paul (72)	*6926*
I'm Gonna Make You Love Me—Diana Ross And The Supremes & The Temptations (68)	*6496*
Love Train—O'Jays (73)	5733
TSOP (The Sound Of Philadelphia)—MFSB Featuring The Three Degrees (74)	*5419*
You'll Never Find Another Love Like Mine—Lou Rawls (76)	4173
Don't Leave Me This Way—Thelma Houston (76)	*4138*
When Will I See You Again—Three Degrees (74)	4029
If You Don't Know Me By Now—Harold Melvin And The Blue Notes (72)	*3604*
Use Ta Be My Girl—O'Jays (78)	3380
If You Don't Know Me By Now—Simply Red (89)	*3293*
Cowboys To Girls—Intruders (68)	3286
Expressway To Your Heart—Soul Survivors (67)	3264
Only The Strong Survive—Jerry Butler (69)	3213
I Love Music (Part 1)—O'Jays (75)	*2798*
Enjoy Yourself—Jacksons (76)	2647
Drowning In The Sea Of Love—Joe Simon (71)	2257
The Love I Lost (Part 1)—Harold Melvin And The Blue Notes (73)	2070
Break Up To Make Up—Stylistics (73)	*1985*
For The Love Of Money—O'Jays (74)	*1864*
Power Of Love—Joe Simon (72)	*1856*
I Can't Stop Dancing—Archie Bell & The Drells (68)	1681
Put Your Hands Together—O'Jays (73)	1517
Engine Number 9—Wilson Pickett (70)	1414
Never Give You Up—Jerry Butler (68)	1243
Together—Tierra (80)	*1181*
Hey, Western Union Man—Jerry Butler (68)	1108
Now That We Found Love—Heavy D & The Boyz (91)	*1100*
"There's Gonna Be A" Showdown—Archie Bell & The Drells (68)	1090
A Brand New Me—Dusty Springfield (69)	*1011*
What's The Use Of Breaking Up—Jerry Butler (69)	960
Moody Woman—Jerry Butler (69)	921
Who Do You Love—Sapphires (64)	842
Close The Door—Teddy Pendergrass (78)	805
Livin' For The Weekend—O'Jays (76)	736
Thanks For Saving My Life—Billy Paul (74)	709
Forever Mine—O'Jays (79)	688
I'm Gonna Make You Love Me—Madeline Bell (68)	*687*
(Love Is Like A) Baseball Game—Intruders (68)	650
I'll Always Love My Mama (Part I)—Intruders (73)	618
Time To Get Down—O'Jays (73)	578
Hope That We Can Be Together Soon—Sharon Paige And Harold Melvin And The Blue Notes (75)	548
Are You Happy—Jerry Butler (68)	543
United—Peaches & Herb (68)	*534*
Explosion In Your Soul—Soul Survivors (67)	511
Give The People What They Want—O'Jays (75)	505
You Gonna Make Me Love Somebody Else—Jones Girls (79)	469
The 81—Candy And The Kisses (64)	457
I Don't Love You Anymore—Teddy Pendergrass (77)	428
I Miss You (Part I)—Harold Melvin And The Blue Notes (72)	423
Pool Of Bad Luck—Joe Simon (72)	415
Show You The Way To Go—Jacksons (77)	412
Do The Choo Choo—Archie Bell & The Drells (68)	386
Me And Mrs. Jones—Ron Banks And The Dramatics (75)	*371*
Don't Let Love Hang You Up—Jerry Butler (69)	360
992 Arguments—O'Jays (72)	356
If Only You Knew—Patti LaBelle (84)	347
Everybody Monkey—Freddy Cannon (63)	338
Now That We Found Love—Third World (78)	*333*
Girl You're Too Young—Archie Bell & The Drells (69)	332
Sexy—MFSB (75)	317
Watch Your Step—Brooks O'Dell (63)	309
Girl, Don't Let It Get You Down—O'Jays (80)	309
Lost—Jerry Butler (67)	297
I Could Write A Book—Jerry Butler (70)	294
You're The Reason Why—Ebonys (71)	293
Slow Drag—Intruders (68)	291
Deeper (In Love With You)—O'Jays (70)	279
Together—Intruders (67)	*266*
You're My Latest, My Greatest Inspiration—Teddy Pendergrass (81)	265
Don't Leave Me This Way—Communards (86)	*261*

Kenneth GAMBLE ▶ 34 (128) HOF *Cont'd*	**47753**
One Night Affair—Jerry Butler (72)	*239*
Goin' Places—Jacksons (77)	234
Message In Our Music—O'Jays (76)	231
Turn Off The Lights—Teddy Pendergrass (79)	225
Yesterday I Had The Blues— Harold Melvin And The Blue Notes (73)	224
Silly, Silly, Fool—Dusty Springfield (70)	203
Let's Make A Promise—Peaches & Herb (68)	188
See You When I Git There—Lou Rawls (77)	175
I Really Love You—Dee Dee Sharp (65)	171
When Love Is New—Arthur Prysock (76)	167
Baby I'm Lonely—Intruders (67)	143
I Wanna Know Your Name—Intruders (73)	140
Love Is The Message— MFSB Featuring The Three Degrees (74)	126
Impossible Mission (Mission Impossible)— Soul Survivors (68)	125
Satisfaction Guaranteed (Or Take Your Love Back)— Harold Melvin And The Blue Notes (74)	120
Brand New Me—Aretha Franklin (71)	*115*
One Night Affair—O'Jays (69)	*97*
Power Of Love—Martha Reeves (74)	*96*
I Love Music—Ritchie Family (76)	*92*
T.S.O.P.—Ritchie Family (76)	*92*
Darlin' Darlin' Baby (Sweet, Tender, Love)— O'Jays (76)	90
My Balloon's Going Up— Archie Bell & The Drells (69)	82
United (Part 1)—Music Makers (67)	*78*
This Is My Love Song—Intruders (70)	73
I'm Girl Scoutin'—Intruders (71)	71
Slow Motion (Part 1)—Johnny Williams (73)	70
Love Me—Bobby Hebb (66)	64
I Bet He Don't Love You (Like I Love You)— Intruders (71)	58
Groovy People—Lou Rawls (76)	57
Love In Them There Hills—Vibrations (68)	56
Let's Make A Baby—Billy Paul (76)	53
(We'll Be) United—Intruders (66)	*51*
Break Up To Make Up—Cynthia (91)	*49*
I'm Gonna Make You Love Me— Dee Dee Warwick (66)	*48*
I Just Love The Man—Jones Girls (81)	47
I Love My Baby—Archie Bell & The Drells (69)	43
For The Love Of Money—Bulletboys (89)	*39*
I Wanna Be A Free Girl— Dusty Springfield (70)	38
Am I Black Enough For You—Billy Paul (73)	29
Let Me Be Good To You—Lou Rawls (79)	28
Let's Clean Up The Ghetto— Philadelphia International All Stars (77)	27
A Love That's Real—Intruders (67)	26
Work On Me—O'Jays (77)	25
The Zip—MFSB (75)	20
The Boy With The Beatle Hair—Swans (64)	19
You're My Blessing—Lou Rawls (80)	19
Pray For Me—Intruders (71)	13
A Brand New Me—Jerry Butler (69)	*12*
Chains Of Love—Drifters (65)	12
Don't Let The Music Slip Away— Archie Bell & The Drells (69)	8.6
Looky Looky (Look At Me Girl)—O'Jays (70)	6.3
Now I'm A Woman—Nancy Wilson (71)	5.8
Been A Long Time—Betty Everett (69)	4.3
Finders Keepers, Losers Weepers— Nella Dodds (65)	3.8
Check Yourself— Italian Asphalt & Pavement Company (70)	2.6
Sing A Happy Song—O'Jays (79)	2.4
I Struck It Rich—Len Barry (66)	1.9
A World Without Music— Archie Bell & The Drells (70)	0.4
Albert GAMSE ▶ 5208 (1)	**327**
Chantez-Chantez (Shan-tay, "Sing")— Dinah Shore (57)	654
David GAMSON ▶ 2869 (4)	**1139**
Perfect Way—Scritti Politti (85)	1569
Love Of A Lifetime—Chaka Khan (86)	292
Sure Lookin'—Donny Osmond (91)	259
Boom! There She Was— Scritti Politti Featuring Roger (88)	245
—Christina Ganahl see: Ina WOLF	

Mark GANE ▶ 8329 (1)	**54**
Black Stations/White Stations—M+M (84)	108
Claude GANEM ▶ 6477 (1)	**165**
El Bimbo—Bimbo Jet (75)	165
Wiley GANN ▶ 9880 (1)	**16**
Mississippi Cotton Picking Delta Town— Charley Pride (74)	31
Kim GANNON ▶ 1012 (5)	**4386**
I Want To Be Wanted—Brenda Lee (60)	6284
Croce Di Oro (Cross Of Gold)—Patti Page (55)	*987*
Croce Di Oro (Cross Of Gold)—Joan Regan (55)	*257*
I'll Be Home For Christmas—Elvis Presley (57)	2.1
Croce Di Oro (Cross Of Gold)— Red Foley & Betty Foley (55)	*0.0*
Cecil GANT ▶ 5016 (1)	**359**
I Wonder—Brenda Lee (63)	717
Dean GANT ▶ 7437 (2)	**96**
All Night Thing—Invisible Man's Band (80)	278
Never Thought I'd Fall In Love—Spinners (82)	3.3
Don GANT ▶ 3020 (2)	**1062**
Run, Baby Run (Back Into My Arms)—Newbeats (65)	1760
Cry Softly Lonely One—Roy Orbison (67)	363
Kenneth GANT ▶ 10146 (1)	**12**
Scientific Love—Midnight Star (85)	60
—Milton Gant see: Milton SPARKS	
—Phillip Gantose see: Russ CARLYLE	
Chris GANTRY [Christopher Cedzich] ▶ 3328 (2)	**897**
Dreams Of The Everyday Housewife— Glen Campbell (68)	*563*
Dreams Of The Everyday Housewife— Wayne Newton (68)	*334*
George GARABEDIAN ▶ 11759 (1)	**0.2**
Mr. Grillon—Archibald Players (58)	0.4
Val GARAY ▶ 5669 (2)	**257**
Draw Of The Cards—Kim Carnes (81)	564
Say It Again—Santana (85)	347
Carlos GARCIA ▶ 10373 (1)	**9.4**
Because Of You—Kracker (72)	47
Enrique GARCIA ▶ 1269 (3)	**3505**
1-2-3— Gloria Estefan and Miami Sound Machine (88)	2190
Rhythm Is Gonna Get You— Gloria Estefan and Miami Sound Machine (87)	1833
Conga—Miami Sound Machine (85)	1494
Gary GARCIA ▶ 3210 (2)	**951**
Pac-Man Fever—Buckner & Garcia (81)	1886
Merry Christmas In The NFL— Willis "The Guard" and Vigorish (80)	16
Jerry GARCIA ▶ 3839 (5) HOF	**684**
Touch Of Grey—Grateful Dead (87)	1004
Truckin'—Grateful Dead (71)	237
Uncle John's Band—Grateful Dead (70)	142
Alabama Getaway—Grateful Dead (80)	99
Sugaree—Jerry Garcia (72)	4.8
Mickey GARCIA ▶ 9178 (1)	**29**
First True Love—Tiana (90)	59
Don GARDNER ▶ 4997 (2)	**361**
I Need Your Loving— Don Gardner And Dee Dee Ford (62)	1156
Don't You Worry— Don Gardner And Dee Dee Ford (62)	144
Joey GARDNER ▶ 9114 (1)	**31**
Louder Than Love—TKA (91)	92
Kossi GARDNER ▶ 8987 (1)	**34**
Dance With You—Carrie Lucas (79)	34
Ray GARDNER ▶ 10413 (1)	**8.7**
Let It Shine—Santana (76)	17
Stu GARDNER ▶ 6676 (1)	**145**
Yes, Yes, Yes—Bill Cosby (76)	290
George GARDOS ▶ 9835 (1)	**16**
For Yasgur's Farm—Mountain (70)	97
Gene GARF ▶ 10966 (1)	**4.0**
Goodbye To Toyland—Vonnair Sisters (62)	12
Gil GARFIELD ▶ 3848 (3)	**678**
Wonderful Summer—Robin Ward (63)	1300
I Want My Baby Back—Jimmy Cross (65)	56
Passion Flower—Caterina Valente (59)	2.0
Wayne GARFIELD ▶ 10974 (1)	**4.0**
When You Wake Up Tomorrow—Candi Staton (79)	16

Gene GARFIN ▶ 8718 (1)	**41**
That's Why I Love You—Andrew Gold (76)	82
Art GARFUNKEL ▶ 2524 (3)	**1417**
Scarborough Fair (/Canticle)— Simon & Garfunkel (68)	*1431*
Scarborough Fair—Sergio Mendes & Brasil '66 (68)	*1088*
Hey Schoolgirl—Tom & Jerry (57)	316
David GARIBALDI ▶ 8373 (2)	**53**
Down To The Nightclub—Tower Of Power (72)	154
What Is Hip?—Tower Of Power (74)	4.3
Pietro GARINEI ▶ 6073 (8)	**209**
Goodbye To Rome (Arrivederci Roma)— Georgia Gibbs (55)	*439*
Arrivederci Roma—Roger Williams (58)	*379*
Arrivederci Roma—Mario Lanza (58)	*11*
Arrivederci, Roma—Eddie Fisher (62)	*2.7*
Arrivederci Roma (Goodbye To Rome)— Three Suns (55)	*0.0*
Arrivederci Roma (Goodbye To Rome)— Ralph Young (55)	*0.0*
Arrivederci Roma (Goodbye To Rome)— Three Suns (58)	*0.0*
Arrivederci, Roma—Norman Luboff Choir (55)	*0.0*
Lou GARISTO ▶ 11300 (1)	**2.3**
Take Me Back—Frankie Laine (68)	2.3
Joe GARLAND ▶ 1095 (11)	**4029**
In The Mood—Ernie Fields Orch. (59)	*3341*
In The Mood—Henhouse Five Plus Too (76)	*400*
In The Mood—Bette Midler (74)	*323*
In The Mood—Crazy Otto (55)	*115*
In The Mood—Jive Bunny And The Mastermixers (89)	*80*
In The Mood—Jive Bunny And The Mastermixers (89)	*80*
In The Mood—Larry Elgart And His Manhattan Swing Orchestra (82)	*50*
Leap Frog—Chuck Alaimo Quartet (57)	39
In The Mood—Matys Brothers (56)	*32*
In The Mood—Frank Barber Orchestra (82)	*14*
In The Mood—Frank Barber Orchestra (82)	*14*
V. GARLIC ▶ 4654 (2)	**444**
The Walk—Jimmy McCracklin (58)	*868*
The Walk—Inmates (80)	*21*
Thomas GARLOCK ▶ 9442 (1)	**23**
Sooner Or Later—Johnny Mathis (63)	47
David GARNER ▶ 10333 (1)	**9.9**
Break My Heart—David Ruffin (79)	9.9
Erroll GARNER ▶ 1615 (6)	**2622**
Misty—Johnny Mathis (59)	*1736*
Misty—Ray Stevens (75)	*1222*
Misty—Lloyd Price (63)	*848*
Misty—"Groove" Holmes (66)	*631*
Misty—Vibrations (65)	*153*
Misty—Sarah Vaughan (59)	*22*
Kate GARNER ▶ 10025 (1)	**14**
Shiny Shiny—Haysi Fantayzee (83)	42
Robert GARNER ▶ 8115 (1)	**61**
Sockin' 1-2-3-4—John Roberts (67)	122
Willie GARNER ▶ 10885 (1)	**4.7**
Super Duper Love (Are You Diggin' On Me) Part 1— Sugar Billy (75)	4.7
Gale GARNETT ▶ 746 (3)	**5889**
We'll Sing In The Sunshine—Gale Garnett (64)	5337
Lovin' Place—Gale Garnett (64)	508
Down Here On The Ground—Lou Rawls (68)	87
Bryan GAROFALO ▶ 11801 (1)	**0.0**
The Load-Out—Jackson Browne (78)	0.0
—George Garoufis see: George BROWN	
Bob GARRETT ▶ 7568 (1)	**88**
If Looks Could Kill—Heart (86)	176
George GARRETT ▶ 4482 (1)	**483**
Bird Dance Beat—Trashmen (64)	483
John Virgo GARRETT III [Luca Anzilotti] ▶ 3073 (2)	**1025**
The Power—Snap! (90)	2984
Ooops Up—Snap! (90)	273
Lee GARRETT ▶ 1358 (7)	**3270**
Signed, Sealed, Delivered I'm Yours—Stevie Wonder (70)	*5081*
Let's Get Serious—Jermaine Jackson (80)	1855
It's A Shame—Spinners (70)	1453
Signed, Sealed, Delivered (I'm Yours)— Peter Frampton (77)	*1028*

Lee GARRETT ▶ 1358 (7) *Continued*	**3270**
Maybe I'm A Fool—Eddie Money (79)	715
It's A Shame (My Sister)—Monie Love (91)	420
You're My Everything—Lee Garrett (76)	135
Marilyn GARRETT ▶ 2550 (2)	**1392**
The Night Has A Thousand Eyes—Bobby Vee (62)	4114
(There'll Come A Day When) Ev'ry Little Bit Hurts—Bobby Vee (64)	63
Michael GARRETT ▶ 9888 (1)	**15**
Keep It Tight—Single Bullet Theory (83)	31
Peter GARRETT ▶ 5198 (3)	**328**
Beds Are Burning—Midnight Oil (88)	812
Blue Sky Mine—Midnight Oil (90)	369
The Dead Heart—Midnight Oil (88)	276
—Samuel Garrett see: Hank MILLS	
Siedah GARRETT ▶ 1860 (3)	**2191**
Man In The Mirror—Michael Jackson (88)	4127
The Secret Garden (Sweet Seduction Suite)—Quincy Jones featuring Al B. Sure!, James Ingram, El DeBarge & Barry White (90)	416
Tomorrow (A Better You, Better Me)—Quincy Jones featuring Tevin Campbell (90)	72
Snuff GARRETT [Thomas Leslie Garrett, Tom Leslie, Leslie Thomas, Lesslie] ▶ 1243 (8)	**3611**
She's Just My Style—Gary Lewis And The Playboys (65)	4343
Sukiyaki—A Taste Of Honey (81)	*3090*
Everybody Loves A Clown—Gary Lewis And The Playboys (65)	2836
(You Don't Have To) Paint Me A Picture—Gary Lewis And The Playboys (66)	967
Every Which Way But Loose—Eddie Rabbitt (79)	485
Hoppy, Gene And Me—Roy Rogers (74)	197
Someday (When I'm Gone From You)—Bobby Vee And The Crickets (62)	1.3
Cross My Heart—Bobby Vee (65)	0.9
—Thomas Leslie Garrett see: Snuff GARRETT	
William GARRETT ▶ 1114 (8)	**3986**
Mashed Potato Time—Dee Dee Sharp (62)	8768
Please Mr. Postman—Marvelettes (61)	*7831*
Please Mr. Postman—Carpenters (74)	*4500*
I Love You Madly—Fantastic Four (68)	320
You Gave Me Something (And Everything's Alright)—Fantastic Four (67)	312
Show Time—Detroit Emeralds (68)	57
Please Mr. Postman—Gentle Persuasion (83)	*45*
Please Mr. Postman—Beatles (64)	*6.4*
—David Garrick see: David John BYRON	
Hoyt GARRICK ▶ 6441 (1)	**168**
New Orleans Ladies—Louisiana's Le Roux (78)	337
Sid GARRIS ▶ 6534 (2)	**159**
Opus One—Mills Brothers (55)	*317*
Opus One—Modernaires (57)	*1.9*
Glen GARRISON ▶ 10977 (1)	**4.0**
Listen, They're Playing My Song—Ray Charles (68)	8.0
Freddie GARRITY ▶ 1374 (1)	**3238**
I'm Telling You Now—Freddie And The Dreamers (65)	6476
Mort GARSON ▶ 733 (21)	**5992**
Our Day Will Come—Ruby And The Romantics (63)	*6254*
Left Right Out Of Your Heart (Hi-Lee Hi-Lo Hi-Lup-Up-Up)—Patti Page (58)	*1703*
Our Day Will Come—Frankie Valli (75)	*1249*
My Summer Love—Ruby And The Romantics (63)	1134
Young Wings Can Fly (Higher Than You Know)—Ruby And The Romantics (63)	499
Delicious—Jim Backus & Friend (58)	235
Jacqueline—Bobby Helms (58)	228
The World Of Lonely People—Anita Bryant (64)	205
Baby Come Home—Ruby And The Romantics (64)	106
Starry Eyed—Gary Stites (59)	94
Dynamite—Brenda Lee (57)	90
Take A Chance—Jaye P. Morgan (57)	53
Tamiami—Bill Haley And His Comets (60)	52
Things I Didn't Say—Jordan Brothers (60)	21
Buttermilk—Joe Sherman, his Orchestra and Chorus (58)	*17*
Buttermilk—Fontane Sisters (58)	*17*
Pony Train—Titus Turner (61)	10
All In Good Time—Nelson Trio (60)	4.1
Salvation Rock—Marv Meredith And His Orchestra (60)	4.1

Blue Strings—Hugo Winterhalter and his Orchestra (59)	4.0
Left Right Out Of Your Heart (Hi-Lee Hi-Lo Hi-Lup-Up-Up)—Vaughn Monroe (58)	*0.0*
Terry GARTHWAITE ▶ 8407 (1)	**52**
Brownsville—Joy Of Cooking (71)	155
Green GARTSIDE [Paul Julian Strohmeyer, Gartside Paul Strohmeyer] ▶ 2997 (4)	**1074**
Perfect Way—Scritti Politti (85)	1569
Love Of A Lifetime—Chaka Khan (86)	292
Boom! There She Was—Scritti Politti Featuring Roger (88)	245
Wood Beez (pray like aretha franklin)—Scritti Politti (86)	21
Diran GARVARENTZ ▶ 8323 (1)	**54**
Yet...I Know (Et Pourtant)—Steve Lawrence (64)	163
Nick GARVEY ▶ 9118 (1)	**31**
Love And Loneliness—Motors (80)	61
Michael GARVIN ▶ 6454 (2)	**167**
Never Give Up On A Good Thing—George Benson (82)	233
Only One You—T.G. Sheppard (82)	100
Rex GARVIN ▶ 2005 (4)	**2011**
Over The Mountain Across The Sea—Johnnie & Joe (57)	*1144*
Over The Mountain (Across The Sea)—Bobby Vinton (63)	*858*
Over The Mountain; Across The Sea—Johnnie & Joe (60)	*8.6*
What'cha Gonna Do About It—Doris Troy (63)	0.5
Sam GARY ▶ 11012 (1)	**3.9**
You Can't Go Halfway—Johnny Nash (74)	15
—Ted Gary see: Milton KELLEM	
Walter GARY ▶ 9802 (1)	**17**
Always You—Betty Madigan (54)	*67*
Clarence GASKILL ▶ 5195 (1)	**329**
Prisoner Of Love—James Brown And The Famous Flames (63)	986
Barbara Jean GASKINS ▶ 6053 (2)	**211**
Ask Me—Ecstasy, Passion & Pain (74)	210
I Wouldn't Give You Up—Ecstasy, Passion & Pain (74)	0.7
David GASKINS ▶ 10520 (1)	**7.7**
You Are The One—TKA (89)	15
Greg GASKINS ▶ 11570 (1)	**1.2**
I Bet'cha (Couldn't Love Me)—Manhattans (66)	2.3
Tiberio GASPAR ▶ 8259 (1)	**57**
Pretty World—Sergio Mendes & Brasil '66 (69)	226
Dick GASPARRE ▶ 11569 (1)	**1.2**
I Hear A Rhapsody—Knightsbridge Strings (60)	3.5
Paul GASPER ▶ 8982 (1)	**34**
Still Waters Run Deep—Brook Benton (62)	69
—Édith Giovanna Gassion see: Edith PIAF	
Louis GASTÉ ▶ 1865 (7)	**2185**
Feelings—Morris Albert (75)	*3636*
To You My Love—Nick Noble (56)	*677*
To You My Love—Georgie Shaw (56)	*37*
Feelings—Walter Jackson (76)	*9.1*
Majorca—Monty Kelly & His Orchestra (55)	*3.7*
Majorca (Isle Of Love)—Bob Manning (55)	*3.7*
To You, My Love—Betty Madigan (56)	*0.0*
Pat GASTON ▶ 6922 (4)	**128**
Walking Along—Diamonds (58)	*783*
The Wedding—Solitaires (55)	*36*
The Wedding—Chordettes (55)	*13*
Walking Along—Solitaires (58)	*0.0*
Jimmy GATELEY ▶ 7395 (2)	**99**
The Minute You're Gone—Sonny James (63)	*97*
The Minute You're Gone—Cliff Richard (65)	*1.4*
Michael GATELY ▶ 5238 (5)	**320**
If You Don't Want My Love—Robert John (68)	553
When The Party Is Over—Robert John (70)	142
California Kid And Reemo—Lobo (71)	97
I Can't Move No Mountains—Blood, Sweat & Tears (72)	26
We Can Make The World—Gravy (71)	4.8
David GATES ▶ 59 (30)	**36656**
Make It With You—Bread (70)	*7490*
Popsicles And Icicles—Murmaids (63)	4903
Baby I'm-A Want You—Bread (71)	3877
Everything I Own—Bread (72)	2798
If—Bread (71)	*2641*

It Don't Matter To Me—Bread (70)	1695
Lost Without Your Love—Bread (76)	1681
Goodbye Girl—David Gates (77)	1624
The Guitar Man—Bread (72)	1419
Diary—Bread (72)	1323
Aubrey—Bread (73)	1274
Sweet Surrender—Bread (72)	1250
Let Your Love Go—Bread (70)	848
Part Time Love—Gladys Knight & The Pips (75)	706
Never Let Her Go—David Gates (74)	555
Took The Last Train—David Gates (78)	541
Mother Freedom—Bread (71)	516
Clouds—David Gates (73)	496
My One And Only, Jimmy Boy—Girlfriends (63)	305
Sail Around The World—David Gates (73)	286
Where Does The Lovin' Go—David Gates (80)	222
Hooked On You—Bread (77)	124
Been Too Long On The Road—Mark Lindsay (71)	106
Ain't Gonna Cry No More—Brenda Lee (66)	82
Take Me Now—David Gates (81)	72
Hold Tight—Vicki Sue Robinson (77)	50
Make It With You—Whispers (77)	*16*
If—Telly Savalas (74)	*14*
Make It With You—Ralfi Pagan (71)	*7.4*
Heartbreak Ahead—Murmaids (64)	4.9
Ira GATES ▶ 9213 (1)	**28**
Keep On Dancing—Alvin Cash (68)	114
Helen GATHERS ▶ 4355 (2)	**514**
Mr Lee—Bobbettes (57)	*2273*
I Shot Mr Lee—Bobbettes (60)	*297*
Larry GATLIN ▶ 10023 (2)	**14**
Delta Dirt—Larry Gatlin (74)	14
Help Me—Elvis Presley (74)	0.0
Sue GATLIN ▶ 3791 (1)	**697**
Two Of Hearts—Stacey Q (86)	2091
Timmy GATLING ▶ 3840 (5)	**683**
Make You Sweat—Keith Sweat (90)	1110
Talk To Myself—Christopher Williams (89)	406
Another Like My Lover—Jasmine Guy (91)	122
When Will I See You Smile Again?—Bell Biv DeVoe (91)	70
I Like—Guy (89)	56
Mary Glen GAUDET ▶ 5184 (1)	**329**
To A Soldier Boy—Tassels (59)	329
Bob GAUDIO [Bob Conte] ▶ 43 (53) HOF	**44746**
Big Girls Don't Cry—4 Seasons (62)	*10012*
Sherry—4 Seasons (62)	*9519*
Walk Like A Man—4 Seasons (63)	*8138*
Rag Doll—4 Seasons Featuring The "Sound" Of Frankie Valli (64)	7976
Can't Take My Eyes Off You—Frankie Valli (67)	*7410*
December, 1963 (Oh, What A Night)—Four Seasons (75)	5913
Dawn (Go Away)—4 Seasons Featuring The "Sound" Of Frankie Valli (64)	*5627*
Who Loves You—Four Seasons (75)	*3116*
Short Shorts—Royal Teens (58)	*2815*
Ronnie—4 Seasons Featuring The "Sound" Of Frankie Valli (64)	2454
Silence Is Golden—Tremeloes (67)	2043
Save It For Me—4 Seasons Featuring The "Sound" Of Frankie Valli (64)	*1587*
Bye, Bye, Baby (Baby, Goodbye)—4 Seasons Featuring The "Sound" Of Frankie Valli (65)	1453
Can't Take My Eyes Off You—Lettermen (67)	*1323*
The Sun Ain't Gonna Shine (Anymore)—Walker Bros. (66)	*1271*
Beggin'—4 Seasons Featuring The "Sound" Of Frankie Valli (67)	1234
Big Man In Town—4 Seasons Featuring The "Sound" Of Frankie Valli (64)	1113
Believe Me—Royal Teens (59)	925
To Give (The Reason I Live)—Frankie Valli (67)	836
I Make A Fool Of Myself—Frankie Valli (67)	799
The Proud One—Osmonds (75)	*633*
Girl Come Running—4 Seasons Featuring The "Sound" Of Frankie Valli (65)	604
Marlena—4 Seasons (63)	464
Walk Like A Man—Mary Jane Girls (86)	*290*
Can't Take My Eyes Off You—Nancy Wilson (69)	*255*
You're Looking Like Love To Me—Peabo Bryson/Roberta Flack (83)	224

Bob GAUDIO [Bob Conte] ▶ 43 (53) HOF *Cont'd*	**44746**
Soon (I'll Be Home Again)— 4 Seasons Featuring Frankie Valli (63)	214
The Proud One—Frankie Valli (66)	*211*
Toy Soldier—4 Seasons Featuring The "Sound" Of Frankie Valli (65)	204
Be My Girl—Four-Evers (64)	183
Silver Star—Four Seasons (76)	172
The Sun Ain't Gonna Shine Anymore— Nielsen/Pearson (81)	*168*
Saturday's Father—4 Seasons (68)	146
Little Boy (In Grown Up Clothes)—4 Seasons (65)	113
Down The Hall—Four Seasons (77)	102
Idaho—4 Seasons Featuring Frankie Valli (69)	80
Sherry—Robert John (80)	*77*
Whatever You Want—Jerry Butler (63)	65
Don't Mention My Name—Shepherd Sisters (63)	58
I Can't Take My Eyes Off You—Pet Shop Boys (91)	*37*
Harvey's Got A Girlfriend—Royal Teens (58)	14
I Would Be In Love (Anyway)—Frank Sinatra (70)	12
Spend The Night In Love—Four Seasons (80)	12
You're Ready Now—Frankie Valli (66)	8.3
The Sun Ain't Gonna Shine Anymore—Fuzzy Bunnies (68)	*6.0*
Sherry—Gidea Park (81)	*3.7*
Walk Like A Man—Gidea Park (81)	*3.7*
Big Girls Don't Cry—Gidea Park (81)	*3.7*
Dawn—Gidea Park (81)	*3.7*
Who Loves You—Gidea Park (81)	*3.7*
Something's On Her Mind— 4 Seasons Featuring Frankie Valli (69)	1.9
Short Shorts—Four Winds (58)	*0.0*
Short Shorts—Tiny Bradshaw & His Orchestra (58)	*0.0*
—Leonard François Joseph Guy Gauthier see: Hal WILLIS	
Paul GAUVIN ▶ 7985 (1)	**66**
Who Were You Thinkin' Of—Doolittle Band (80)	199
Kevin GAVIN ▶ 10028 (1)	**14**
We're Together—Hillside Singers (72)	55
Pete GAVIN ▶ 11523 (1)	**1.3**
Warmin' Up The Band—Don Everly (74)	6.6
Tommy GAWENDA ▶ 7391 (2)	**99**
The Truth—Tami Show (91)	466
She's Only 20—Tami Show (88)	17
Harold GAY ▶ 9970 (1)	**14**
Springfield Plane—Kenny O'Dell (68)	29
Noel GAY [Reginald Moxon Armitage, Stanley Hill] ▶ 2214 (1)	**1730**
Leaning On The Lamp Post—Herman's Hermits (66)	1730
Mac GAYDEN ▶ 1907 (6)	**2125**
Everlasting Love—Carl Carlton (74)	*1789*
Everlasting Love—Robert Knight (67)	*1702*
Don't Give It Up—Robbie Patton (81)	508
Everlasting Love—Rex Smith/Rachel Sweet (81)	*474*
Blessed Are The Lonely—Robert Knight (68)	21
She Shot A Hole In My Soul—Clifford Curry (67)	10
—Anna Gaye see: Anna GORDY	
Barbie GAYE ▶ 3030 (1)	**1054**
My Boy Lollipop—Millie Small (64)	4215
Marvin GAYE ▶ 96 (35) HOF	**25616**
Let's Get It On—Marvin Gaye (73)	7308
Dancing In The Street—Martha & The Vandellas (64)	*5484*
What's Going On—Marvin Gaye (71)	*5213*
Got To Give It Up Pt. I—Marvin Gaye (77)	4806
Sexual Healing—Marvin Gaye (82)	3925
Mercy Mercy Me (The Ecology)—Marvin Gaye (71)	*3682*
Baby, I'm For Real—Originals (69)	1958
Pride And Joy—Marvin Gaye (63)	1884
Inner City Blues (Make Me Wanna Holler)— Marvin Gaye (71)	1676
Trouble Man—Marvin Gaye (72)	1642
The Bells—Originals (70)	1418
Dancing In The Street— Mick Jagger & David Bowie (85)	*1333*
Beechwood 4-5789—Marvelettes (62)	*1082*
What's Going On—Cyndi Lauper (87)	*885*
Come Get To This—Marvin Gaye (73)	813
Pretty Little Baby—Marvin Gaye (65)	743
Stubborn Kind Of Fellow—Marvin Gaye (62)	594
Hitch Hike—Marvin Gaye (63)	562
Mercy Mercy Me (The Ecology)—Robert Palmer (91)	*499*
Distant Lover—Marvin Gaye (74)	438
Dancing In The Street—Van Halen (82)	*390*
You're The Man (Part 1)—Marvin Gaye (72)	372
You Sure Love To Ball—Marvin Gaye (74)	308
Wholy Holy—Aretha Franklin (72)	151
If This World Were Mine— Marvin Gaye & Tammi Terrell (68)	138
Dancin' In The Streets—Teri DeSario with K.C. (80)	*98*
Wherever I Lay My Hat (That's My Home)— Paul Young (83)	90
Dancing In The Street—Mamas & The Papas (66)	*77*
Beechwood 4-5789—Carpenters (82)	*52*
We Can Make It Baby—Originals (70)	40
After The Dance—Marvin Gaye (76)	36
Dancing In The Street—Ramsey Lewis (67)	*27*
What's Going On—Quincy Jones (71)	*4.6*
Dancing In The Street—Tight Fit (81)	*0.9*
Dancing In The Street—Dovells (74)	*0.3*
Ronnie GAYLORD [Ronald L. Fredianelli] ▶ 5856 (3)	**237**
I Will Never Pass This Way Again— Glen Campbell (72)	165
I'm No Gonna Say—Ronnie Gaylord (54)	72
Cuddle Me—Ronnie Gaylord (54)	0.0
—Gloria Gaynor see: Gloria FOWLES	
Paul GAYTEN ▶ 1620 (4)	**2602**
But I Do—Clarence Henry (61)	*4122*
My Dearest Darling—Etta James (60)	941
But I Do—Bobby Vinton (72)	*85*
Nervous Boogie—Paul Gayten (57)	28
Heino GAZE ▶ 523 (11)	**8106**
Calcutta—Lawrence Welk And His Orchestra (60)	*6283*
Was macht der alte Seemann— Johnny Maddox And The Rhythmasters (55)	*1115*
Ask Me—Nat "King" Cole (56)	*604*
Berlin Melody—Billy Vaughn And His Orchestra (61)	*342*
That's The Way It Goes—Eddie Fisher (57)	108
Calcutta—Four Preps (61)	*23*
Roses Of Rio—Four Aces (58)	6.6
Calcutta—Werner Muller (60)	*0.0*
Berlin Melody—Kurt Edelhagen (61)	*0.0*
Was macht der alte Seemann—Crazy Otto (55)	*0.0*
Ask Me (Deine Erste Liebe)—Alice Babs (56)	*0.0*
Greg GEDDES ▶ 8787 (1)	**39**
Future Shock—Hello People (75)	156
Bob GEDDINS ▶ 2267 (2)	**1674**
Haunted House—Gene Simmons (64)	1658
I Want To Know—Sugar Pie DeSanto (60)	48
—Michael Stanley Gee see: Michael STANLEY	
Adam GEIBEL ▶ 3844 (1)	**680**
Sleep—Little Willie John (60)	1361
Larry GELBART ▶ 11250 (1)	**2.6**
Tower Trot (And Then You Do That Step)— Dick Jacobs And His Chorus And Orchestra (57)	23
Stan GELBER ▶ 6605 (3)	**152**
Now I Know—Jack Jones (67)	181
The Ol' Race Track—Mills Brothers (68)	85
Brush A Little Sunshine—Tommy Roe (70)	64
Gary GELD ▶ 389 (19)	**10168**
Hurting Each Other—Carpenters (72)	4895
Sealed With A Kiss—Brian Hyland (62)	*4300*
Save Your Heart For Me— Gary Lewis And The Playboys (65)	4051
Sealed With A Kiss— Gary Lewis And The Playboys (68)	*1606*
Sealed With A Kiss—Bobby Vinton (72)	*1454*
Ginny Come Lately—Brian Hyland (62)	851
Let Me Belong To You—Brian Hyland (61)	766
Warmed Over Kisses (Left Over Love)— Brian Hyland (62)	608
The Tear Of The Year—Jackie Wilson (61)	410
He Says The Same Things To Me—Skeeter Davis (64)	408
I'm Afraid To Go Home—Brian Hyland (63)	295
The Way I Am—Jackie Wilson (61)	192
I May Not Live To See Tomorrow—Brian Hyland (62)	173
I Told You So—Jimmy Jones (61)	163
If Mary's There—Brian Hyland (63)	123
I Got Love—Melba Moore (70)	18
I'll Never Stop Wanting You—Brian Hyland (61)	8.8
The Night I Cried—Brian Hyland (61)	6.9
Sealed With A Kiss—Toys (68)	*6.3*
Bob GELDOF ▶ 4070 (3)	**605**
Do They Know It's Christmas?—Band Aid (84)	865
I Don't Like Mondays—Boomtown Rats (80)	102
This Is The World Calling—Bob Geldof (86)	70
—Jack Gellar see: Ronnie SCOTT	
Pat GENARO ▶ 10438 (1)	**8.5**
Here In My Heart—Al Martino (61)	25
Roger GENGER ▶ 9195 (1)	**29**
You'd Better Believe It—Manhattans (73)	58
Robert GENOVESE ▶ 5949 (5)	**224**
Big Guitar—Owen Bradley Quintet (58)	*448*
Big Guitar— Sam (The Man) Taylor And His Orchestra (58)	*0.0*
Big Guitar—Frank DeRosa & His D Men (58)	*0.0*
Big Guitar—Irving Ashby (58)	*0.0*
Big Guitar—David Hill (58)	*0.0*
Don GENSON [Mel Van] ▶ 11802 (1)	**0.0**
Hit And Run Affair—Perry Como (54)	0.0
Alfonso GENTILE ▶ 3223 (1)	**941**
There's A Moon Out Tonight—Capris (60)	2822
Mickey GENTILE ▶ 6625 (4)	**150**
Never, Never Leave Me—Mary Wells (65)	277
Stop Takin' Me For Granted—Mary Wells (64)	13
We Have Something More—Connie Francis (64)	9.2
Never Love A Robin—Bobby Vee (63)	0.9
—Art Gentry see: Argentry MITCHELL	
Bo GENTRY ▶ 743 (14)	**5898**
Mony Mony—Tommy James And The Shondells (68)	*4671*
Mony Mony "Live"—Billy Idol (87)	*3728*
Indian Giver—1910 Fruitgum Co. (69)	3435
Mirage—Tommy James And The Shondells (67)	1826
Make Believe—Wind (69)	1026
I Like The Way—Tommy James And The Shondells (67)	664
Special Delivery—1910 Fruitgum Co. (69)	640
Out Of The Blue— Tommy James And The Shondells (67)	415
Get Out Now—Tommy James And The Shondells (68)	403
Somebody Cares— Tommy James And The Shondells (68)	397
We Gotta Go Home—Music Explosion (67)	41
Mony Mony—Billy Idol (81)	*23*
Groovin' With Mr. Bloe—Cool Heat (70)	22
Mony Mony—Tight Fit (81)	*0.9*
Bobbie GENTRY [Roberta Lee Streeter] ▶ 299 (8)	**12119**
Ode To Billie Joe—Bobbie Gentry (67)	*10012*
Fancy—Bobbie Gentry (69)	951
Ode To Billie Joe—Kingpins (67)	*496*
Okolona River Bottom Band—Bobbie Gentry (67)	324
Mornin' Glory—Bobbie Gentry & Glen Campbell (68)	145
Ode To Billie Joe—Bobbie Gentry (76)	*135*
Ode To Billy Joe - Main Title—Bobbie Gentry (76)	*48*
Ode To Billy Joe—Ray Bryant (67)	*9.0*
Melvin GENTRY ▶ 3389 (4)	**870**
I Wanna Be Rich—Calloway (90)	3279
Body Talk—Deele (84)	140
Scientific Love—Midnight Star (85)	60
Headlines—Midnight Star (86)	59
—Will Gentry see: Ramsey KEARNEY	
—Jimmy Pete Georgantones see: Jimmy GEORGE	
Allen GEORGE ▶ 10616 (1)	**6.7**
Your Personal Touch— Evelyn "Champagne" King (86)	13
Barbara GEORGE [Barbara Ann Smith] ▶ 896 (3)	**4943**
I Know (You Don't Love Me No More)— Barbara George (61)	4711
You Talk About Love—Barbara George (62)	230
Send For Me (If You Need Some Lovin)— Barbara George (62)	2.2
—Boy George see: George O'DOWD	
Brian GEORGE ▶ 1651 (14)	**2544**
Head To Toe—Lisa Lisa And Cult Jam (87)	4435
Lost In Emotion—Lisa Lisa And Cult Jam (87)	3486
Naughty Girls (Need Love Too)—Samantha Fox (88)	2531
All Cried Out—Lisa Lisa And Cult Jam With Full Force Featuring Paul Anthony And Bow Legged Lou (86)	1667
I Wanna Have Some Fun—Samantha Fox (88)	1135
I Wonder If I Take You Home— Lisa Lisa and Cult Jam with Full Force (85)	656
Thanks For My Child—Cheryl "Pepsii" Riley (88)	509
Little Jackie Wants To Be A Star— Lisa Lisa And Cult Jam (89)	441

Brian GEORGE ▶ 1651 (14) ***Continued***	**2544**
Can You Feel The Beat–Lisa Lisa And Cult Jam (85)	231
Basketball–Kurtis Blow (85)	77
Someone To Love Me For Me–Lisa Lisa & Cult Jam (87)	52
Why Can't You Come Home–Ex-Girlfriend (91)	48
Roxanne, Roxanne–UTFO (85)	28
Go For Yours– Lisa Lisa & Cult Jam with Full Force (88)	22
Carol GEORGE ▶ 8722 (1)	**41**
Sinner Man–Sarah Dash (79)	82
Don GEORGE ▶ 719 (7)	**6075**
The Yellow Rose Of Texas– Mitch Miller with His Orch. & Chorus (55)	*9072*
The Yellow Rose Of Texas–Johnny Desmond (55)	*2853*
The Yellow Rose Of Texas–Stan Freberg (55)	*123*
You'll Always Be My Sweetheart–Bobby Van (58)	51
I Was Telling Her About You–Al Hibbler (56)	42
Angel Pie (Postillion)–Peggy King (56)	10
More Than Ever–Georgia Gibbs (54)	0.0
Dona Lyn GEORGE ▶ 3835 (1)	**686**
Love Song–Anne Murray (73)	1372
Gil GEORGE [Hazel Gilman George] ▶ 8859 (4)	**38**
Old Betsy (Davy Crockett's Gun)– Voices Of Walter Schumann (55)	*38*
Old Betsy (Davy Crockett's Rifle)– Fess Parker & Buddy Ebsen (55)	*38*
Old Betsy (Davy Crockett's Gun)– Sons Of The Pioneers (55)	*0.0*
Old Betsy–Burl Ives (55)	*0.0*
–Hazel Gilman George see: Gil GEORGE	
Jimmy GEORGE [Jimmy Pete Georgantones] ▶ 1234 (4)	**3622**
I'll Always Love You–Taylor Dayne (88)	2802
Just To See Her–Smokey Robinson (87)	1564
Don't Fight The Hands (That Need You)– Hamilton, Joe Frank & Dennison (76)	53
Magic Man–Robert Winters & Fall (81)	45
–Keni St. George see: Kenny GEORGE	
Kenny GEORGE [Marcias DeNegri, Keni St. George] ▶ 8963 (1)	**35**
Listen To The Buddha–Ozo (76)	35
Lucien GEORGE ▶ 1657 (13)	**2537**
Head To Toe–Lisa Lisa And Cult Jam (87)	4435
Lost In Emotion–Lisa Lisa And Cult Jam (87)	3486
Naughty Girls (Need Love Too)–Samantha Fox (88)	2531
All Cried Out–Lisa Lisa And Cult Jam With Full Force Featuring Paul Anthony And Bow Legged Lou (86)	1667
I Wanna Have Some Fun–Samantha Fox (88)	1135
I Wonder If I Take You Home– Lisa Lisa and Cult Jam with Full Force (85)	656
Thanks For My Child–Cheryl "Pepsii" Riley (88)	509
Little Jackie Wants To Be A Star– Lisa Lisa And Cult Jam (89)	441
Can You Feel The Beat–Lisa Lisa And Cult Jam (85)	231
Someone To Love Me For Me–Lisa Lisa & Cult Jam (87)	52
Why Can't You Come Home–Ex-Girlfriend (91)	48
Roxanne, Roxanne–UTFO (85)	28
Go For Yours– Lisa Lisa & Cult Jam with Full Force (88)	22
Paul GEORGE ▶ 1652 (14)	**2544**
Head To Toe–Lisa Lisa And Cult Jam (87)	4435
Lost In Emotion–Lisa Lisa And Cult Jam (87)	3486
Naughty Girls (Need Love Too)–Samantha Fox (88)	2531
All Cried Out– Lisa Lisa And Cult Jam With Full Force Featuring Paul Anthony And Bow Legged Lou (86)	1667
I Wanna Have Some Fun–Samantha Fox (88)	1135
I Wonder If I Take You Home– Lisa Lisa and Cult Jam with Full Force (85)	656
Thanks For My Child–Cheryl "Pepsii" Riley (88)	509
Little Jackie Wants To Be A Star– Lisa Lisa And Cult Jam (89)	441
Can You Feel The Beat–Lisa Lisa And Cult Jam (85)	231
Basketball–Kurtis Blow (85)	77
Someone To Love Me For Me–Lisa Lisa & Cult Jam (87)	52
Why Can't You Come Home–Ex-Girlfriend (91)	48
Roxanne, Roxanne–UTFO (85)	28
Go For Yours– Lisa Lisa & Cult Jam with Full Force (88)	22
Phil GEORGE ▶ 5151 (1)	**333**
For Tonight–Nancy Martinez (86)	667

Richard GEORGE ▶ 10480 (1)	**8.0**
How Many Others–Dick Roman (55)	24
Robin GEORGE [Robin Sidebotham] ▶ 8776 (2)	**40**
The Swalk–Notorious (90)	66
Heartline–Robin George (85)	6.8
Steve GEORGE ▶ 1212 (7)	**3672**
Broken Wings–Mr. Mister (85)	5158
Kyrie–Mr. Mister (85)	4320
Is It Love–Mr. Mister (86)	1255
Something Real (Inside Me/Inside You)– Mr. Mister (87)	420
Hunters Of The Night–Mr. Mister (84)	168
I Do Believe In You–Pages (79)	55
The Border–Mr. Mister (87)	8.7
–Steven Demetre Georgiou see: Cat STEVENS	
–Christopher Charles Geppert see: Christopher CROSS	
Tom GERACI ▶ 6087 (1)	**207**
Tom Cat–Rooftop Singers (63)	829
Raeford GERALD [Raymond Godfrey Gerald, Ray Godfrey] ▶ 1503 (11)	**2871**
Get Down, Get Down (Get On The Floor)– Joe Simon (75)	1761
Your Time To Cry–Joe Simon (70)	909
Step By Step–Joe Simon (73)	673
My Man, A Sweet Man–Millie Jackson (72)	613
Trouble In My Home–Joe Simon (72)	306
How Do You Feel The Morning After– Millie Jackson (74)	136
I Miss You Baby–Millie Jackson (72)	106
I Need You, You Need Me–Joe Simon (76)	64
Music In My Bones–Joe Simon (75)	58
Breakaway–Millie Jackson (73)	23
Friends Or Lovers–Act I (73)	0.8
Neil GERALDO ▶ 3034 (3)	**1049**
We Live For Love–Pat Benatar (80)	678
Promises In The Dark–Pat Benatar (81)	407
Ooh Ooh Song–Pat Benatar (85)	335
Danyel GÉRARD [Gérard Daniel Kherlakian] ▶ 9599 (1)	**21**
Butterfly–Danyel Gérard (72)	103
Greg GERARD [Gregory Gerard Guralski] ▶ 3185 (1)	**960**
Save Some Love–Keedy (91)	960
–Philippe Gerard see: Philippe Gerard BLOCH	
–Åke Gerhard see: Åke Gerhard LARSSON	
Horace GERLACH ▶ 5350 (1)	**302**
Daddy's Little Girl–Al Martino (67)	603
Richard GERMINARO ▶ 6143 (2)	**200**
I Love Makin' Love To You–Evie Sands (75)	367
You Can Do It–Dobie Gray (78)	234
Phil GERNHARD ▶ 1009 (4)	**4398**
Snoopy Vs. The Red Baron–Royal Guardsmen (66)	8083
The Return Of The Red Baron–Royal Guardsmen (67)	1016
Natural Love–Petula Clark (82)	43
Snoopy For President–Royal Guardsmen (68)	23
Marinus GERRITSEN ▶ 10590 (1)	**7.0**
Dong Dong Diki Di-Ki Dong–Super Cirkus (69)	14
George GERSHWIN ▶ 804 (22) HOF	**5506**
I Got Rhythm–Happenings (67)	5952
Summertime–Billy Stewart (66)	*1685*
I Loves You Porgy–Nina Simone (59)	1423
Love Walked In–Dinah Washington (60)	*884*
But Not For Me–Ketty Lester (62)	*383*
Swanee–Jaye P. Morgan (55)	305
Rhapsody In Blue–Deodato (73)	227
Our Love Is Here To Stay–Dinah Washington (61)	*179*
Love Walked In–Flamingos (59)	*152*
Rhapsody In Blue– Royal Philharmonic Orchestra (81)	131
Summertime–Marcels (61)	*107*
Summertime–Chris Columbo Quintet (63)	*84*
Someone To Watch Over Me–Frank Sinatra (54)	60
Summertime–Sam Cooke (57)	*20*
'S Wonderful– Ray Conniff & His Orchestra and Chorus (57)	18
Summertime–Rick Nelson (62)	*7.8*
Summertime (Part 2)–Sam Cooke (59)	*4.4*
But Not For Me–Johnny Nash (59)	*3.7*
Love Is Here To Stay–Chris Montez (68)	*2.7*

Summertime– Billy Hemmans & Clays Composite (70)	*2.1*
Summertime–Will Sanders (61)	*0.0*
Blah-Blah-Blah–Steve Lawrence (59)	0.0
Ira GERSHWIN ▶ 901 (18) HOF	**4910**
I Got Rhythm–Happenings (67)	5952
Summertime–Billy Stewart (66)	*1685*
I Loves You Porgy–Nina Simone (59)	1423
Love Walked In–Dinah Washington (60)	*884*
But Not For Me–Ketty Lester (62)	*383*
Our Love Is Here To Stay–Dinah Washington (61)	*179*
Love Walked In–Flamingos (59)	*152*
Summertime–Marcels (61)	*107*
Someone To Watch Over Me–Frank Sinatra (54)	60
The Gal That Got Away–Frank Sinatra (54)	*37*
Summertime–Sam Cooke (57)	*20*
Summertime–Rick Nelson (62)	*7.8*
Summertime (Part 2)–Sam Cooke (59)	*4.4*
But Not For Me–Johnny Nash (59)	*3.7*
Love Is Here To Stay–Chris Montez (68)	*2.7*
Summertime–Will Sanders (61)	*0.0*
The Man That Got Away–Jeri Southern (54)	*0.0*
Blah-Blah-Blah–Steve Lawrence (59)	0.0
Harvey GERST ▶ 6406 (1)	**174**
It Won't Be Wrong–Byrds (66)	348
–Linda Gertz see: Linda LAURIE	
Per GESSLE ▶ 126 (8)	**20767**
It Must Have Been Love–Roxette (90)	4505
The Look–Roxette (89)	3666
Listen To Your Heart–Roxette (89)	3652
Joyride–Roxette (91)	3467
Dangerous–Roxette (89)	3358
Fading Like A Flower (Every Time You Leave)– Roxette (91)	2624
Spending My Time–Roxette (91)	929
Dressed For Success–Roxette (89)	856
Ray GETZOV ▶ 3344 (2)	**890**
Please Mr Sun–Tommy Edwards (59)	*1404*
Please Mr. Sun–Vogues (66)	*376*
Stephen GEYER ▶ 1256 (2)	**3560**
The Theme From "The Greatest American Hero" (Believe It Or Not)–Joey Scarbury (81)	5521
Hot Rod Hearts–Robbie Dupree (80)	1599
George GHIZ ▶ 8707 (1)	**42**
Hunters Of The Night–Mr. Mister (84)	168
Paul GIACALONE [Paul DeMaya] ▶ 2337 (2)	**1581**
You Were Mine–Fireflies (59)	1499
I Can't Say Goodbye– Fireflies Featuring Ritchie Adams (59)	245
Angelo GIACOMAZZI ▶ 5477 (4)	**281**
The Italian Theme– Cyril Stapleton And His Orchestra (56)	*563*
The Italian Theme– Joe Reisman and His Orchestra (56)	*0.0*
The Italian Theme–Dorothy Collins (56)	*0.0*
The Italian Theme–Owen Bradley & His Quintet (56)	*0.0*
Marc GIACOMELLI ▶ 6334 (1)	**182**
Take Off–Bob & Doug McKenzie (82)	908
John GIAMETTA ▶ 10259 (1)	**11**
Finders Keepers–Salt Water Taffy (68)	22
Carl GIAMMARESE ▶ 6617 (1)	**150**
Music Everywhere–Tufano & Giammarese (73)	150
Leo GIANANGELO ▶ 7195 (1)	**111**
Sing–Tony Orlando & Dawn (77)	111
Bill GIANT [Billy Merman, Bill Zimmerman, Harvey Zimmerman] ▶ 1331 (10)	**3343**
(You're the) Devil In Disguise– Elvis Presley With The Jordanaires (63)	3964
Speedy Gonzales–Pat Boone (62)	*2754*
Ask Me–Elvis Presley With The Jordanaires (64)	1582
That's Old Fashioned (That's The Way Love Should Be)–Everly Brothers (62)	1204
Young And In Love–Chris Crosby (64)	357
A Time To Love-A Time To Cry (Petite Fleur)– Lou Johnson (65)	*356*
The Next Kiss (Is The Last Goodbye)– Conway Twitty (61)	170
It's Gotta Last Forever– Billy J. Kramer With The Dakotas (65)	109
Speedy Gonzales–David Dante (61)	*19*
Today, Tomorrow And Forever–Elvis Presley (64)	1.1

Andy GIBB ► 709 (4)	**6132**
Shadow Dancing—Andy Gibb (78)	10099
(Love Is) Thicker Than Water—Andy Gibb (77)	5791
Time Is Time—Andy Gibb (80)	991
Me (Without You)—Andy Gibb (81)	216
Barry GIBB ► 10 (79) HOF	**75961**
Shadow Dancing—Andy Gibb (78)	10099
Stayin' Alive—Bee Gees (77)	9872
Night Fever—Bee Gees (78)	9237
I Just Want To Be Your Everything—Andy Gibb (77)	8938
How Deep Is Your Love—Bee Gees (77)	7757
Woman In Love—Barbra Streisand (80)	7247
How Can You Mend A Broken Heart—Bee Gees (71)	6914
Too Much Heaven—Bee Gees (78)	6865
Grease—Frankie Valli (78)	6566
Islands In The Stream— Kenny Rogers Duet with Dolly Parton (83)	6346
Tragedy—Bee Gees (79)	6069
Jive Talkin'—Bee Gees (75)	5841
Emotion—Samantha Sang (77)	5831
(Love Is) Thicker Than Water—Andy Gibb (77)	5791
If I Can't Have You—Yvonne Elliman (78)	4924
Lonely Days—Bee Gees (70)	4559
You Should Be Dancing—Bee Gees (76)	4461
Love So Right—Bee Gees (76)	3669
Love You Inside Out—Bee Gees (79)	3185
I've Gotta Get A Message To You—Bee Gees (68)	3087
Guilty—Barbra Streisand & Barry Gibb (80)	2811
I Started A Joke—Bee Gees (68)	2767
Desire—Andy Gibb (80)	2687
Nights On Broadway—Bee Gees (75)	*2655*
(Our Love) Don't Throw It All Away—Andy Gibb (78)	2401
An Everlasting Love—Andy Gibb (78)	2236
Fanny (Be Tender With My Love)—Bee Gees (75)	*1717*
Heartbreaker—Dionne Warwick (82)	1606
Love Me—Yvonne Elliman (76)	1469
Run To Me—Bee Gees (72)	1396
What Kind Of Fool—Barbra Streisand & Barry Gibb (81)	1271
(The Lights Went Out In) Massachusetts— Bee Gees (67)	1232
One—Bee Gees (89)	1162
Words—Bee Gees (68)	1127
Holiday—Bee Gees (67)	1119
I Can't Help It—Andy Gibb & Olivia Newton-John (80)	1086
Boogie Child—Bee Gees (77)	1054
To Love Somebody—Bee Gees (67)	*1006*
My World—Bee Gees (72)	995
Time Is Time—Andy Gibb (80)	991
New York Mining Disaster 1941 Have You Seen My Wife, Mr. Jones—Bee Gees (67)	983
First Of May—Bee Gees (69)	706
Come On Over—Olivia Newton-John (76)	650
The Woman In You—Bee Gees (83)	642
Sweetheart—Engelbert Humperdinck (70)	604
This Woman—Kenny Rogers (84)	574
Alive—Bee Gees (72)	563
Edge Of The Universe—Bee Gees (77)	520
More Than A Woman—Tavares (77)	508
Tomorrow Tomorrow—Bee Gees (69)	469
Take The Short Way Home—Dionne Warwick (83)	460
Don't Wanna Live Inside Myself—Bee Gees (71)	414
Jumbo—Bee Gees (68)	397
You Stepped Into My Life—Melba Moore (78)	*350*
Shine Shine—Barry Gibb (84)	339
He's A Liar—Bee Gees (81)	336
Warm Ride—Rare Earth (78)	335
Living Eyes—Bee Gees (81)	310
Ain't Nothing Gonna Keep Me From You— Teri Desario (78)	304
Promises—Barbra Streisand (81)	276
Someone Belonging To Someone—Bee Gees (83)	242
Marley Purt Drive—Jose Feliciano (69)	193
Don't Forget To Remember—Bee Gees Featuring Barry Gibb, Maurice Gibb & Colin Peterson (69)	186
Chain Reaction—Diana Ross (86)	*114*
You Win Again—Bee Gees (87)	82
Saw A New Morning—Bee Gees (73)	82
If Only I Had My Mind On Something Else— Bee Gees (70)	81
Eaten Alive—Diana Ross (85)	76
To Love Somebody—Sweet Inspirations (68)	*56*
Eyes That See In The Dark—Kenny Rogers (84)	37
You Stepped Into My Life—Wayne Newton (79)	*32*

Only One Woman—Nigel Olsson (75)	31
Mr. Natural—Bee Gees (74)	22
When He's Gone—Bee Gees (91)	11
Fanny (Be Tender With My Love)—Gino Cunico (75)	*9.9*
Nights On Broadway—Candi Staton (77)	*8.1*
I.O.I.O.—Bee Gees (70)	5.1
Chain Reaction—Diana Ross (85)	*5.0*
Wouldn't I Be Someone—Bee Gees (73)	0.7
Maurice GIBB ► 55 (55) HOF	**37342**
Shadow Dancing—Andy Gibb (78)	10099
Stayin' Alive—Bee Gees (77)	9872
Night Fever—Bee Gees (78)	9237
How Deep Is Your Love—Bee Gees (77)	7757
Too Much Heaven—Bee Gees (78)	6865
Islands In The Stream— Kenny Rogers Duet with Dolly Parton (83)	6346
Tragedy—Bee Gees (79)	6069
Jive Talkin'—Bee Gees (75)	5841
If I Can't Have You—Yvonne Elliman (78)	4924
Lonely Days—Bee Gees (70)	4559
You Should Be Dancing—Bee Gees (76)	4461
Love So Right—Bee Gees (76)	3669
Love You Inside Out—Bee Gees (79)	3185
I've Gotta Get A Message To You—Bee Gees (68)	3087
Guilty—Barbra Streisand & Barry Gibb (80)	2811
I Started A Joke—Bee Gees (68)	2767
Desire—Andy Gibb (80)	2687
Nights On Broadway—Bee Gees (75)	*2655*
Fanny (Be Tender With My Love)—Bee Gees (75)	*1717*
Heartbreaker—Dionne Warwick (82)	1606
Run To Me—Bee Gees (72)	1396
(The Lights Went Out In) Massachusetts— Bee Gees (67)	1232
One—Bee Gees (89)	1162
Words—Bee Gees (68)	1127
Boogie Child—Bee Gees (77)	1054
First Of May—Bee Gees (69)	706
The Woman In You—Bee Gees (83)	642
Sweetheart—Engelbert Humperdinck (70)	604
Alive—Bee Gees (72)	563
More Than A Woman—Tavares (77)	508
Tomorrow Tomorrow—Bee Gees (69)	469
Boys Do Fall In Love—Robin Gibb (84)	424
Jumbo—Bee Gees (68)	397
You Stepped Into My Life—Melba Moore (78)	*350*
Shine Shine—Barry Gibb (84)	339
He's A Liar—Bee Gees (81)	336
Warm Ride—Rare Earth (78)	335
Living Eyes—Bee Gees (81)	310
Someone Belonging To Someone—Bee Gees (83)	242
Marley Purt Drive—Jose Feliciano (69)	193
Don't Forget To Remember—Bee Gees Featuring Barry Gibb, Maurice Gibb & Colin Peterson (69)	186
Chain Reaction—Diana Ross (86)	*114*
You Win Again—Bee Gees (87)	82
Saw A New Morning—Bee Gees (73)	82
If Only I Had My Mind On Something Else— Bee Gees (70)	81
Eaten Alive—Diana Ross (85)	76
Eyes That See In The Dark—Kenny Rogers (84)	37
You Stepped Into My Life—Wayne Newton (79)	*32*
Only One Woman—Nigel Olsson (75)	31
When He's Gone—Bee Gees (91)	11
Fanny (Be Tender With My Love)—Gino Cunico (75)	*9.9*
Nights On Broadway—Candi Staton (77)	*8.1*
I.O.I.O.—Bee Gees (70)	5.1
Chain Reaction—Diana Ross (85)	*5.0*
Wouldn't I Be Someone—Bee Gees (73)	0.7
Robin GIBB ► 29 (62) HOF	**50528**
Shadow Dancing—Andy Gibb (78)	10099
Stayin' Alive—Bee Gees (77)	9872
Night Fever—Bee Gees (78)	9237
How Deep Is Your Love—Bee Gees (77)	7757
Woman In Love—Barbra Streisand (80)	7247
How Can You Mend A Broken Heart—Bee Gees (71)	6914
Too Much Heaven—Bee Gees (78)	6865
Islands In The Stream— Kenny Rogers Duet with Dolly Parton (83)	6346
Tragedy—Bee Gees (79)	6069
Jive Talkin'—Bee Gees (75)	5841
Emotion—Samantha Sang (77)	5831
If I Can't Have You—Yvonne Elliman (78)	4924
Lonely Days—Bee Gees (70)	4559

You Should Be Dancing—Bee Gees (76)	4461
Love So Right—Bee Gees (76)	3669
Love You Inside Out—Bee Gees (79)	3185
I've Gotta Get A Message To You—Bee Gees (68)	3087
Guilty—Barbra Streisand & Barry Gibb (80)	2811
I Started A Joke—Bee Gees (68)	2767
Desire—Andy Gibb (80)	2687
Nights On Broadway—Bee Gees (75)	*2655*
Fanny (Be Tender With My Love)—Bee Gees (75)	*1717*
Heartbreaker—Dionne Warwick (82)	1606
Love Me—Yvonne Elliman (76)	1469
Run To Me—Bee Gees (72)	1396
Hold On To My Love—Jimmy Ruffin (80)	1303
(The Lights Went Out In) Massachusetts— Bee Gees (67)	1232
One—Bee Gees (89)	1162
Words—Bee Gees (68)	1127
Holiday—Bee Gees (67)	1119
Boogie Child—Bee Gees (77)	1054
To Love Somebody—Bee Gees (67)	*1006*
My World—Bee Gees (72)	995
New York Mining Disaster 1941 Have You Seen My Wife, Mr. Jones—Bee Gees (67)	983
First Of May—Bee Gees (69)	706
Come On Over—Olivia Newton-John (76)	650
The Woman In You—Bee Gees (83)	642
Edge Of The Universe—Bee Gees (77)	520
More Than A Woman—Tavares (77)	508
Boys Do Fall In Love—Robin Gibb (84)	424
Jumbo—Bee Gees (68)	397
You Stepped Into My Life—Melba Moore (78)	*350*
He's A Liar—Bee Gees (81)	336
Warm Ride—Rare Earth (78)	335
Living Eyes—Bee Gees (81)	310
Promises—Barbra Streisand (81)	276
Someone Belonging To Someone—Bee Gees (83)	242
Marley Purt Drive—Jose Feliciano (69)	193
Help Me!—Marcy Levy & Robin Gibb (80)	180
Chain Reaction—Diana Ross (86)	*114*
You Win Again—Bee Gees (87)	82
Saw A New Morning—Bee Gees (73)	82
To Love Somebody—Sweet Inspirations (68)	*56*
You Stepped Into My Life—Wayne Newton (79)	*32*
Only One Woman—Nigel Olsson (75)	31
Mr. Natural—Bee Gees (74)	22
When He's Gone—Bee Gees (91)	11
Saved By The Bell—Robin Gibb (69)	11
Fanny (Be Tender With My Love)—Gino Cunico (75)	*9.9*
Nights On Broadway—Candi Staton (77)	*8.1*
Chain Reaction—Diana Ross (85)	*5.0*
Wouldn't I Be Someone—Bee Gees (73)	0.7
Steve GIBB ► 1562 (1)	**2715**
She Believes In Me—Kenny Rogers (79)	2715
Billy GIBBONS ► 1582 (17)	**2672**
Legs—ZZ Top (84)	1701
Sleeping Bag—ZZ Top (85)	1591
Tush—ZZ Top (75)	835
La Grange—ZZ Top (74)	740
Stages—ZZ Top (86)	629
Rough Boy—ZZ Top (86)	621
Velcro Fly—ZZ Top (86)	451
Gimme All Your Lovin'—ZZ Top (83)	417
It's Only Love—ZZ Top (76)	308
Doubleback—ZZ Top (90)	295
Sharp Dressed Man—ZZ Top (83)	150
Francene—ZZ Top (72)	122
Leila—ZZ Top (81)	45
Arrested For Driving While Blind—ZZ Top (77)	43
Cheap Sunglasses—ZZ Top (80)	32
Give It Up—ZZ Top (91)	23
Enjoy And Get It On—ZZ Top (77)	14
Carroll GIBBONS ► 10121 (1)	**12**
Garden In The Rain—Vic Dana (64)	25
Steve GIBBONS ► 8260 (1)	**57**
Johnny Cool—Steve Gibbons Band (76)	57
A. Harrington GIBBS ► 10910 (1)	**4.4**
Runnin' Wild—Les Paul and Mary Ford (56)	13
Van GIBBS ► 11666 (1)	**0.8**
Falling In Love—Fat Boys (87)	3.9
Howard GIBELING ► 9367 (1)	**25**
Jay-Dee's Boogie Woogie— Jimmy Dorsey Orchestra and Chorus (57)	50

Kahlil GIBRAN ▶ 9758 (1)	**17**
Theme From "The Prophet" (Pleasure Is A Freedom Song/On Love)–Richard Harris (75)	17
Andy GIBSON [Albert Andrew Gibson, Albert Shubert] ▶ 2732 (7)	**1235**
The Hucklebuck–Chubby Checker (60)	*1494*
(I Do The) Shimmy Shimmy–Bobby Freeman (60)	*452*
Italian Huckle Buck–Lou Monte (54)	*227*
Shimmy Shimmy–Orlons (64)	*165*
Good, Good Lovin'–Chubby Checker (61)	130
Little Turtle Dove–Otis Williams And His Charms (61)	4.9
The Huckle-Buck (Italian Style)–Lou Monte (60)	*0.0*
Bill GIBSON ▶ 3371 (4)	**877**
Hip To Be Square–Huey Lewis and the News (86)	2226
Workin' For A Livin'–Huey Lewis and the News (82)	267
Give Me The Keys (And I'll Drive You Crazy)–Huey Lewis and the News (89)	253
Don't Make Me Do It–Patrick Simmons (83)	38
Bob GIBSON [Samuel Robert Gibson] ▶ 4934 (3)	**378**
Abilene–George Hamilton IV (63)	1276
Hear The Bells–Tokens (63)	148
The New "Frankie And Johnnie" Song–Greenwood County Singers (64)	*115*
Damita Jo GIBSON [Damita Jo DuBlanc] ▶ 7745 (1)	**77**
Little Loneliness–Kay Starr (57)	77
Debbie GIBSON ▶ 170 (10)	**17558**
Lost In Your Eyes–Debbie Gibson (89)	4151
Foolish Beat–Debbie Gibson (88)	3426
Shake Your Love–Debbie Gibson (87)	2628
Only In My Dreams–Debbie Gibson (87)	2432
Out Of The Blue–Debbie Gibson (88)	2187
Electric Youth–Debbie Gibson (89)	1095
No More Rhyme–Debbie Gibson (89)	738
Staying Together–Debbie Gibson (88)	558
Anything Is Possible–Debbie Gibson (90)	515
We Could Be Together–Debbie Gibson (89)	86
Don GIBSON ▶ 153 (24)	**19106**
I Can't Stop Loving You–Ray Charles (62)	*11133*
Oh Lonesome Me–Don Gibson (58)	*2509*
Sweet Dreams–Tommy McLain (66)	*1307*
Blue Blue Day–Don Gibson (58)	940
Just One Time–Don Gibson (60)	785
Who Cares–Don Gibson (59)	*418*
Sweet Dreams (Of You)–Patsy Cline (63)	*392*
Look Who's Blue–Don Gibson (58)	278
Too Soon To Know–Roy Orbison (66)	195
Far Far Away–Don Gibson (60)	189
Give Myself A Party–Don Gibson (58)	186
Who Cares–Fats Domino (63)	*185*
Don't Tell Me Your Troubles–Don Gibson (59)	121
Lonesome Number One–Don Gibson (61)	114
Lonesome Old House–Don Gibson (59)	114
Sweet Dreams–Don Gibson (60)	*92*
I Can't Stop Loving You–Count Basie (63)	*71*
Oh Lonesome Me–Bob Luman (60)	*32*
I Can't Stop Loving You–Don Gibson (58)	*30*
Oh Lonesome Me–Johnny Cash (60)	*14*
What About Me–Don Gibson (61)	0.5
I Can't Stop Loving You–Gene Ammons (62)	*0.0*
Oh Lonesome Me–Jackie Walker (58)	*0.0*
Oh! Lonesome Me–Swallows (58)	*0.0*
Douglas GIBSON ▶ 4298 (1)	**530**
Troglodyte (Cave Man)–Jimmy Castor Bunch (72)	3177
Glenn GIBSON ▶ 8811 (1)	**39**
Wonderful–Blackwell (69)	78
James GIBSON ▶ 9830 (1)	**16**
Standing On Guard–Falcons (66)	49
Jill GIBSON ▶ 6413 (1)	**173**
You Really Know How To Hurt A Guy–Jan & Dean (65)	519
Johnny GIBSON ▶ 9637 (1)	**20**
Midnight–Johnny Gibson (62)	80
–S. Gibson see: Mickey BAKER	
–Samuel Robert Gibson see: Bob GIBSON	
Steve GIBSON ▶ 6893 (1)	**130**
I Just Can't Say No To You–Parker McGee (77)	261
–Iris May Giebler see: Iris MAY	
Heinz GIETZ ▶ 6734 (3)	**142**
This Must Be Wrong (Oho-Aha)–Caterina Valente (55)	190
Stroll Me–Kay Starr (58)	184

Please Don't Go So Soon (Wenn Die Liebe Will)–Jo Stafford (55)	34
Peter GIFFORD ▶ 5858 (2)	**236**
Beds Are Burning–Midnight Oil (88)	812
Blue Sky Mine–Midnight Oil (90)	369
Roland GIFT ▶ 1039 (6)	**4245**
Good Thing–Fine Young Cannibals (89)	3616
She Drives Me Crazy–Fine Young Cannibals (89)	3569
Don't Look Back–Fine Young Cannibals (89)	994
I'm Not The Man I Used To Be–Fine Young Cannibals (89)	226
Johnny Come Home–Fine Young Cannibals (86)	56
I'm Not Satisfied–Fine Young Cannibals (90)	29
Sal GIGLIO Jr. [Plinky Giglio, Sal Plinky, Plinky] ▶ 9231 (1)	**28**
Love Is The Ritual–Styx (90)	56
Alessandro GILARDI ▶ 11676 (1)	**0.7**
Keep Warm–Jinny (91)	2.2
Cary GILBERT ▶ 1055 (8)	**4179**
Me And Mrs. Jones–Billy Paul (72)	*6926*
Don't Leave Me This Way–Thelma Houston (76)	*4138*
Livin' For The Weekend–O'Jays (76)	736
Me And Mrs. Jones–Ron Banks And The Dramatics (75)	*371*
Don't Leave Me This Way–Communards (86)	*261*
Nursery Rhymes (Part I)–People's Choice (76)	45
Let's Clean Up The Ghetto–Philadelphia International All Stars (77)	27
Don't Let The Music Slip Away–Archie Bell & The Drells (69)	8.6
Gillian GILBERT ▶ 6095 (3)	**206**
True Faith–New Order (87)	637
Round & Round–New Order (89)	209
Blue Monday 1988–New Order (88)	105
L. Wolfe GILBERT ▶ 4194 (5) HOF	**567**
Down Yonder–Johnny And The Hurricanes (60)	484
Ramona–Blue Diamonds (60)	*152*
My Mother's Eyes–Russ Hamilton (58)	5.5
Marta–Bachelors (67)	5.2
Ramona–Lancers (57)	*3.0*
Mary Hadler GILBERT ▶ 1563 (2)	**2711**
Shifting Whispering Sands–Billy Vaughn and His Orchestra (55)	*2970*
Shifting Whispering Sands–Rusty Draper (55)	*2452*
Ray GILBERT ▶ 1892 (7)	**2144**
Zip-A-Dee Doo-Dah–Bob B. Soxx And The Blue Jeans (62)	1913
Muskrat Ramble–McGuire Sisters (54)	*1322*
...And Roses And Roses–Andy Williams (65)	547
Muskrat Ramble–Freddy Cannon (61)	*259*
Muskrat Ramble–Matys Brothers (54)	*246*
Muskrat Ramble–Louis Armstrong & His All-Stars (54)	*0.0*
Muskrat Ramble–Rusty Draper (54)	*0.0*
Ronald GILBERT ▶ 3011 (4)	**1069**
(We Ain't Got) Nothin' Yet–Blues Magoos (66)	3377
Pipe Dream–Blues Magoos (67)	242
One By One–Blues Magoos (67)	150
There's A Chance We Can Make It–Blues Magoos (67)	57
Ronnie GILBERT ▶ 3235 (4)	**935**
Gotta Travel On–Billy Grammer (58)	*3674*
Kisses Sweeter Than Wine–Jimmie Rodgers (57)	2683
Gotta Travel On–Timi Yuro (63)	*190*
Gotta Travel On–Harry Belafonte (59)	*0.0*
Tim GILBERT ▶ 1165 (3)	**3818**
Incense And Peppermints–Strawberry Alarm Clock (67)	7462
That Acapulco Gold–Rainy Daze (67)	169
Sea Shell–Strawberry Alarm Clock (68)	5.2
V.C. GILBERT [Vivian Clark Gilbert, Jack V.C. Gilbert] ▶ 1536 (3)	**2787**
Shifting Whispering Sands–Billy Vaughn and His Orchestra (55)	*2970*
Shifting Whispering Sands–Rusty Draper (55)	*2452*
Chapel By The Sea–Billy Vaughn And His Orchestra (62)	77
Frank GILCKEN ▶ 10750 (1)	**5.6**
Questions–Bang (72)	17
Nick GILDER ▶ 889 (6)	**4984**
Hot Child In The City–Nick Gilder (78)	7241

The Warrior–Scandal Featuring Patty Smyth (84)	2200
Here Comes The Night–Nick Gilder (78)	320
Rock Me–Nick Gilder (79)	193
Roxy Roller–Sweeney Todd (76)	*13*
Roxy Roller (Bryan Adams)–Sweeney Todd (76)	*0.7*
Michael GILES ▶ 10972 (1)	**4.0**
In The Court Of The Crimson King–King Crimson (70)	20
Rick GILES ▶ 2390 (3)	**1532**
Wham Bam Shang-A-Lang–Silver (76)	1318
So Close–Daryl Hall & John Oates (90)	999
You Put The Beat In My Heart–Eddie Rabbitt (83)	29
Zane GILES ▶ 9897 (1)	**15**
Owwww!–Chunky A (89)	31
Terry GILKYSON ▶ 599 (15)	**7262**
Memories Are Made Of This–Dean Martin (55)	*8655*
Greenfields–Brothers Four (60)	*6907*
Marianne–Terry Gilkyson And The Easy Riders (57)	*3770*
Marianne–Hilltoppers (57)	*2812*
Love Is A Golden Ring–Frankie Laine with The Easy Riders (57)	891
Memories Are Made Of This–Gale Storm (55)	*785*
Memories Are Made Of This–Drifters (66)	*271*
Memories Are Made Of This–Mindy Carson (55)	*217*
Marianne–Lane Brothers (57)	*71*
Marianne–Burl Ives (57)	*45*
Green Fields–Vogues (69)	*25*
Memories Are Made Of This–Roger Williams (59)	*14*
Greenfields–Julius La Rosa (60)	*0.0*
Mary Ann–Talbot Brothers (57)	*0.0*
Mary Ann–Edmundo Ros & His Orchestra (57)	*0.0*
Geoff GILL ▶ 4199 (1)	**566**
Heartbreaker–Pat Benatar (79)	1131
Peter GILL ▶ 3985 (4)	**630**
Relax–Frankie Goes To Hollywood (84)	*658*
Relax (Mix)–Frankie Goes To Hollywood (85)	*583*
Two Tribes–Frankie Goes To Hollywood (84)	469
Welcome To The Pleasuredome (Trevor Horn Remix)–Frankie Goes To Hollywood (85)	239
–Rhonda Fleming Gill see: Kye FLEMING	
Vince GILL ▶ 4495 (1)	**477**
I'm Almost Ready–Pure Prairie League (80)	477
David GILLAM ▶ 2480 (1)	**1450**
Teenager's Romance–Ricky Nelson (57)	1450
Ian GILLAN ▶ 3596 (4)	**773**
Smoke On The Water–Deep Purple (73)	3242
Woman From Tokyo–Deep Purple (73)	226
Knocking At Your Back Door–Deep Purple (84)	150
Black Night–Deep Purple (70)	148
Dizzy GILLESPIE [John Birks Gillespie] ▶ 8781 (1)	**39**
Soul Sauce (Guacha Guaro)–Cal Tjader (65)	79
Haven GILLESPIE ▶ 3767 (8) HOF	**705**
That Lucky Old Sun–Ray Charles (63)	*950*
Santa Claus Is Coming To Town–4 Seasons (62)	*369*
Santa Claus Is Comin' To Town–Jackson 5 (70)	*36*
That Lucky Old Sun–Velvets (61)	*24*
It Takes So Long (To Say Goodbye)–Dean Martin (59)	23
Santa Claus Is Comin' To Town–Bing Crosby and the Andrews Sisters (54)	*3.2*
Santa Claus Is Comin' To Town–Fred Waring presents The Teen Trio (54)	*3.2*
That Lucky Old Sun–Floridians (61)	*2.2*
Jerry GILLESPIE ▶ 2878 (2)	**1136**
Somebody's Knockin'–Terri Gibbs (81)	1628
Heaven's Just A Sin Away–Kendalls (77)	322
–John Birks Gillespie see: Dizzy GILLESPIE	
Steve GILLETTE ▶ 4757 (1)	**422**
Back On The Street Again–Sunshine Company (67)	422
–Michelle Gilliam see: Michelle PHILLIPS	
Brad GILLIS ▶ 4411 (2)	**502**
When You Close Your Eyes–Night Ranger (84)	998
(You Can Still) Rock In America–Night Ranger (83)	339
Tim GILLIS ▶ 11626 (1)	**0.9**
Won't You Come On Back–Fats Domino (62)	2.8
Ray GILMORE ▶ 6123 (1)	**203**
The Dawn Of Correction–Spokesmen (65)	608
William GILMORE ▶ 3582 (2)	**777**
Cherry Hill Park–Billy Joe Royal (69)	1529
Party Girl–Tommy Roe (64)	26

David GILMOUR ▶ 6283 (3)	**186**
Blue Light—David Gilmour (84)	116
Run Like Hell—Pink Floyd (80)	96
Learning To Fly—Pink Floyd (87)	86
Jim GILMOUR ▶ 6397 (2)	**175**
On The Loose—Saga (82)	675
Wind Him Up—Saga (83)	200
James William GILREATH ▶ 3351 (2)	**885**
Little Band Of Gold—James Gilreath (63)	821
Why Not Tonight—Jimmy Hughes (67)	64
Dan GILROY ▶ 3356 (2)	**884**
Right On Track—Breakfast Club (87)	1369
Kiss And Tell—Breakfast Club (87)	199
Jonathan GILUTIN ▶ 5156 (1)	**333**
New Attitude—Patti LaBelle (85)	999
Norman GIMBEL ▶ 246 (27) HOF	**14020**
I Will Follow Him—Little Peggy March (63)	8660
Killing Me Softly With His Song—Roberta Flack (73)	*7658*
Canadian Sunset—Andy Williams (56)	*2711*
The Girl From Ipanema—Getz/Gilberto (64)	2656
I Got A Name—Jim Croce (73)	2549
Happy Days—Pratt & McClain (76)	2197
Ready To Take A Chance Again—Barry Manilow (78)	1827
Sway—Bobby Rydell (60)	*1551*
Different Worlds—Maureen McGovern (79)	886
Making Our Dreams Come True—Cyndi Grecco (76)	709
Land Of Dreams— Hugo Winterhalter's Orchestra And Chorus (54)	552
Good Friend—Mary MacGregor (79)	419
When We Come Of Age—Joni James (54)	291
Sway (Quien Sera)—Dean Martin (54)	*243*
Killing Me Softly—Al B. Sure! (88)	*86*
Constant Rain (Chove Chuva)— Sergio Mendes & Brasil '66 (66)	78
Canadian Sunset—Etta Jones (61)	*54*
Ain'tcha Cha Comin' Out T Tonight—Jo Stafford (55)	48
Deeply—Anson Williams (77)	30
Hocus Pocus—Patti Page (54)	23
Meditation (Meditaçao)—Pat Boone (63)	*11*
The Touch—Betty Johnson (54)	*5.6*
Meditation (Meditacao)—Claudine Longet (66)	*3.8*
Pine Top's Boogie—Jo Stafford (59)	*3.6*
For Me—Sergio Mendes & Brasil '66 (67)	2.9
Live For Life—Jack Jones (67)	1.4
Never Before—Connie Francis (58)	0.7
Thom GIMBEL ▶ 11090 (1)	**3.3**
Sounds Of Your Voice—Jon Butcher (85)	6.6
—Gino see: Harry GIOSASI	
Marilyn GINS ▶ 11076 (1)	**3.4**
Can't Get Over (The Bossa Nova)—Eydie Gorme (64)	10
Arnie GINSBURG ▶ 2738 (3)	**1231**
Jennie Lee—Jan & Arnie (58)	*2196*
Jennie Lee—Billy Ward And His Dominoes (58)	*187*
Gas Money—Jan & Arnie (58)	118
—Lucien Ginsburg see: Serge GAINSBOURG	
Robert GINYARD [Rob Base] ▶ 5355 (2)	**300**
It Takes Two—Rob Base & D.J. E-Z Rock (88)	353
Joy And Pain—Rob Base & D.J. E-Z Rock (89)	124
—Giorgio see: Giorgio ALLENTINI	
Harry GIOSASI [Aristides Michael Giosasi, Gino] ▶ 1537 (3)	**2785**
Sorry (I Ran All The Way Home)—Impalas (59)	4846
(It's Been A Long Time) Pretty Baby— Gino & Gina (58)	680
Oh What A Fool—Impalas (59)	43
Alessandro GIOVANNINI ▶ 6074 (8)	**209**
Goodbye To Rome (Arrivederci Roma)— Georgia Gibbs (55)	*439*
Arrivederci Roma—Roger Williams (58)	*379*
Arrivederci Roma—Mario Lanza (58)	*11*
Arrivederci, Roma—Eddie Fisher (62)	*2.7*
Arrivederci Roma (Goodbye To Rome)— Three Suns (55)	*0.0*
Arrivederci Roma (Goodbye To Rome)— Ralph Young (55)	*0.0*
Arrivederci Roma (Goodbye To Rome)— Three Suns (58)	*0.0*
Arrivederci, Roma—Norman Luboff Choir (55)	*0.0*
Caesar GIOVANNINI ▶ 10680 (1)	**6.1**
Brazilian Rhapsody Part 2— Caesar Giovannini & His Orchestra (57)	6.1
—Pat Giraldo see: Pat BENATAR	
Jim GIRARD ▶ 10385 (1)	**9.2**
There's No Surf In Cleveland— Euclid Beach Band (78)	18
Mike GIRARD ▶ 8233 (1)	**58**
It's A Night For Beautiful Girls—Fools (80)	115
Hubert GIRAUD [Gordon Rod Parker] ▶ 4106 (6)	**591**
Mammy Blue—Stories (73)	*460*
Mammy Blue—Pop-Tops (71)	*355*
Donde Esta Santa Claus? (Where Is Santa Claus?)— Augie Rios (58)	251
Mammy Blue—James Darren (71)	*112*
Willingly (Melodie Perdue)— Monty Kelly And His Orchestra (58)	*88*
Willingly (Melodie Per Due)—Johnny Desmond (58)	*0.0*
Carlos GIRONA ▶ 9124 (1)	**31**
Rockin' In The Jungle—Eternals (59)	61
Junior GISCOMBE [Norman Washington Giscombe] ▶ 5906 (1)	**231**
Mama Used To Say—Junior (82)	461
—Norman Washington Giscombe see: Junior GISCOMBE	
Keir GIST ▶ 6158 (1)	**199**
O.P.P.—Naughty By Nature (91)	1392
—Kenny Gist Jr. see: Kenny O'DELL	
—Morris Gittler see: Mack GORDON	
Gregg GIUFFRIA ▶ 4109 (4)	**590**
Call To The Heart—Giuffria (84)	942
Lonely In Love—Giuffria (85)	185
That Magic Touch—Angel (77)	78
Flying With Broken Wings (Without You)—Angel (78)	3.6
James R. GLASER ▶ 10092 (1)	**13**
Shoot Me (With Your Love)—Tasha Thomas (79)	13
James W. GLASER ▶ 1491 (2)	**2920**
Woman, Woman— Union Gap Featuring Gary Puckett (67)	5707
Who Were You Thinkin' Of—Doolittle Band (80)	199
Tompall GLASER ▶ 8003 (1)	**66**
Five Brothers—Marty Robbins (60)	66
David GLASPER ▶ 1737 (6)	**2391**
Hands To Heaven—Breathe (88)	3472
How Can I Fall?—Breathe (88)	2861
Don't Tell Me Lies—Breathe (89)	1080
Say A Prayer—Breathe (90)	741
Does She Love That Man?—Breathe (90)	478
All This I Should Have Known—Breathe (89)	30
Preston GLASS ▶ 1705 (8)	**2455**
We Don't Have To Take Our Clothes Off— Jermaine Stewart (86)	1796
Who's Zoomin' Who—Aretha Franklin (85)	1671
Miss You Like Crazy—Natalie Cole (89)	1581
Don't Make Me Wait For Love—Kenny G (87)	854
Jimmy Lee—Aretha Franklin (86)	439
Perfect Combination—Stacy Lattisaw & Johnny Gill (84)	86
Rock-A-Lott—Aretha Franklin (87)	42
He Wants My Body—Starpoint (87)	22
Art GLASSER ▶ 11344 (2)	**2.1**
Greetings (This Is Uncle Sam)—Valadiers (61)	*9.2*
Greetings (This Is Uncle Sam)—Monitors (66)	*5.8*
Dick GLASSER ▶ 974 (10)	**4602**
I Will—Dean Martin (65)	*1808*
Angels In The Sky—Crew-Cuts (55)	*1557*
Come Running Back—Dean Martin (66)	470
I Will—Vic Dana (62)	*465*
Angels In The Sky (54)—Tony Martin (54)	*208*
I'm In Love With You—Pat Boone (56)	94
Let's Go Steady For The Summer—Three G's (58)	34
I Got It—Gene Vincent and His Blue Caps (57)	12
Someday (When I'm Gone From You)— Bobby Vee And The Crickets (62)	1.3
Angels In The Sky—Tony Martin (56)	*0.0*
Steve GLASSMEYER ▶ 6048 (1)	**212**
Love Or Something Like It—Kenny Rogers (78)	424
Melvin GLAZER ▶ 5459 (2)	**284**
The Touchables—Dickie Goodman (61)	620
The Touchables In Brooklyn—Dickie Goodman (61)	231
Robert GLAZER ▶ 4860 (1)	**397**
Your Ma Said You Cried In Your Sleep Last Night— Kenny Dino (61)	795
Tom GLAZER ▶ 856 (18)	**5185**
More—Perry Como (56)	2307
Melody Of Love—Four Aces (54)	*2262*
Skokiaan—Four Lads (54)	*2000*
On Top Of Spaghetti—Tom Glazer And The Do-Re-Mi Children's Chorus (63)	*1194*
A Worried Man—Kingston Trio (59)	*993*
Pussy Cat—Ames Brothers (58)	956
Mama Guitar—Don Cornell (57)	*210*
Lovely Lies— Manhattan Brothers And Miriam Makeba (56)	*199*
A Worried Man—Four Preps (61)	*130*
Dynamite—Brenda Lee (57)	90
A Face In The Crowd— Art Mooney & His Orchestra (57)	*6.5*
A Face In The Crowd—Andy Griffith (57)	*6.5*
A Face In The Crowd—Don Cornell (57)	*6.5*
A Face In The Crowd—Dick Lee (57)	*6.5*
Mama Guitar—Julius La Rosa (57)	*2.2*
Melody Of Love— Tony Martin & Dinah Shore (55)	*0.0*
Mama Guitar—Andy Griffith (57)	*0.0*
Lovely Lies—Nick Noble (56)	*0.0*
Dick GLEASON ▶ 9489 (2)	**23**
Ready Willing And Able—Doris Day (54)	*49*
Ready, Willing And Able—Gary Crosby (54)	*19*
Artie GLENN ▶ 825 (4)	**5332**
Crying In The Chapel— Elvis Presley With The Jordanaires (65)	*5009*
Crying In The Chapel—Carol Fran (65)	*160*
Crying In The Chapel—Sonny Til & The Orioles (59)	*148*
Crying In The Chapel—Adam Wade (65)	*14*
Charles Andre GLENN [Afrika Islam] ▶ 9327 (1)	**26**
Colors—Ice-T (88)	53
Darrell GLENN ▶ 3821 (1)	**690**
Indescribably Blue—Elvis Presley With The Jordanaires And The Imperials Quartet (67)	690
Garry GLENN ▶ 5851 (1)	**237**
Caught Up In The Rapture—Anita Baker (86)	473
Joe GLENN ▶ 11720 (1)	**0.5**
Image - Part 1—Hank Levine And Orchestra (61)	1.4
—Elmo Glick see: Jerry LEIBER	
—Elmo Glick see: Mike STOLLER	
Peter GLINDEMAN ▶ 10488 (1)	**7.9**
(I've Been Lookin' For) A New Way To Say I Love You— Driver (77)	24
Gary GLITTER [Paul Francis Gadd] ▶ 1980 (5)	**2036**
Rock And Roll Part 2—Gary Glitter (72)	2384
Do You Wanna Touch Me (Oh Yeah)— Joan Jett & The Blackhearts (82)	693
I Didn't Know I Loved You (Till I Saw You Rock And Roll)—Gary Glitter (72)	533
I'm The Leader Of The Gang— Brownsville Station (74)	422
Doctorin' The Tardis—Timelords (88)	159
—Edgar Dean Glosup see: Eddie DEAN	
Corey GLOVER ▶ 5371 (1)	**299**
Cult Of Personality—Living Colour (89)	1195
Henry GLOVER [Henry Bernard, Henry Bernard Glover] ▶ 467 (30)	**8960**
Peppermint Twist - Part 1— Joey Dee & The Starliters (61)	9044
California Sun—Rivieras (2) (64)	*2473*
Let The Little Girl Dance—Billy Bland (60)	2182
Rock Love— Fontane Sisters with Billy Vaughn's Orchestra (55)	*985*
Hey, Let's Twist—Joey Dee & The Starliters (62)	528
I'm Waiting Just For You—Pat Boone (57)	*517*
Ram-Bunk-Shush—Ventures (61)	*507*
Blues (Stay Away From Me)—Ace Cannon (62)	*465*
24 Hours A Day (365 A Year)—Georgia Gibbs (55)	292
Ram Bunk Shush—Bill Doggett (57)	*214*
California Sun—Joe Jones (61)	*133*
Count Down—Dave "Baby" Cortez (66)	122
We Told You Not To Marry—Titus Turner (59)	108
Everytime (I Think About You) (Part 1)— Joey Dee & The Starliters (62)	51
Roly Poly—Joey Dee & The Starliters (62)	40
Soulville—Aretha Franklin (68)	*24*

Henry GLOVER [Henry Bernard, Henry Bernard Glover] ▶ 467 (30) *Cont'd*	**8960**
Blues Stay Away From Me—Billy Vaughn And His Orchestra (59)	*19*
Teardrops On Your Letter—Hank Ballard And The Midnighters (59)	10
Baby, You're Driving Me Crazy—Joey Dee (63)	9.0
Red's Dream—Louisiana Red (63)	8.1
Soulville—Dinah Washington (63)	*6.8*
I'll Sail My Ship Alone—Jerry Lee Lewis And His Pumping Piano (59)	3.2
Drown In My Own Tears—Don Shirley (62)	3.2
I Love You Yes I Do—Bull Moose Jackson (61)	1.8
I'm Waiting Just For You—Hoagy Carmichael & Cass Daley (57)	*0.0*
Rock Love—Elaine Gay (55)	*0.0*
Rock Love—Bill Farrell (55)	*0.0*
Rock Love—Eddie Fontaine (55)	*0.0*
Rock Love—Teresa Brewer (55)	*0.0*
Rock Love—Dolores Gray (55)	*0.0*
Jean GLOVER [Jean Monte Ray] ▶ 9159 (1)	**30**
People World—Jim & Jean (68)	30
John Henry GLOVER ▶ 1487 (3)	**2925**
You Don't Have To Be A Star (To Be In My Show)—Marilyn McCoo & Billy Davis Jr. (76)	5716
I Hope We Get To Love In Time—Marilyn McCoo & Billy Davis Jr. (76)	81
That's The Sound That Lonely Makes—Tavares (74)	79
Linda GLOVER ▶ 11052 (1)	**3.6**
Maria (You Were The Only One)—Jimmy Ruffin (71)	14
Melvin GLOVER ▶ 9225 (3)	**28**
The Message—Grandmaster Flash & The Furious Five (82)	80
Freedom—Grandmaster Flash And The Furious 5 (80)	21
Beat Street Breakdown Part I—Grandmaster Melle Mel & the Furious Five With Mr. Ness & Cowboy (84)	12
Nathaniel GLOVER ▶ 11308 (1)	**2.3**
Freedom—Grandmaster Flash And The Furious 5 (80)	21
Roger GLOVER ▶ 3298 (5)	**909**
Smoke On The Water—Deep Purple (73)	3242
Stone Cold—Rainbow (82)	407
Woman From Tokyo—Deep Purple (73)	226
Knocking At Your Back Door—Deep Purple (84)	150
Black Night—Deep Purple (70)	148
John GLUCK ▶ 1030 (12)	**4285**
It's My Party—Lesley Gore (63)	*7824*
Mecca—Gene Pitney (63)	1433
Blue Winter—Connie Francis (64)	1016
Lovers By Night, Strangers By Day—Fleetwoods (62)	581
Punish Her—Bobby Vee (62)	567
Trouble Is My Middle Name—Bobby Vinton (62)	546
Can't Wait For Summer—Steve Lawrence (57)	334
Let's Go Calypso—Rusty Draper (57)	81
It's My Party—Dave Stewart With Barbara Gaskin (81)	*64*
Nothin' Shakin—Eddie Fontaine (58)	27
Up Jumped A Rabbit—Frankie Lymon (59)	24
Your Name Is Beautiful—Carl Smith (58)	9.0
—John Raymond Goadsby see: Goldy McJOHN	
Graham GOBLE ▶ 270 (10)	**12698**
Reminiscing—Little River Band (78)	3392
The Night Owls—Little River Band (81)	2374
Lady—Little River Band (79)	2037
The Other Guy—Little River Band (82)	1805
Take It Easy On Me—Little River Band (81)	1513
We Two—Little River Band (83)	615
It's A Long Way There—Little River Band (76)	574
You're Driving Me Out Of My Mind—Little River Band (83)	393
Playing To Win—LRB (85)	217
It's Not A Wonder—Little River Band (80)	162
David GODDARD ▶ 4969 (2)	**368**
You—Aquatones (58)	*735*
You—Gale Storm (58)	*0.0*
—Stuart Leslie Goddard see: Adam ANT	
—Ray Godfrey see: Raeford GERALD	
Kevin GODLEY ▶ 3341 (4)	**891**
Neanderthal Man—Hotlegs (70)	948
Cry—Godley & Creme (85)	899
Rubber Bullets—10 C. C. (73)	322
I'm Mandy Fly Me—10cc (76)	55
Ann GODWIN [A.G. Hassan] ▶ 4486 (3)	**482**
No Matter What—George LaMond (90)	399
Do You Wanna Get Away—Shannon (85)	328
Yo' Little Brother—Nolan Thomas (85)	236
Mable GODWIN ▶ 4120 (3)	**587**
Ling Ting Tong—Five Keys (54)	*363*
Ling-Ting-Tong—Buddy Knox (61)	*120*
Ling, Ting, Tong—Charms (55)	*105*
George GOEHRING ▶ 1470 (11)	**2954**
Lipstick On Your Collar—Connie Francis (59)	3650
Half Heaven - Half Heartache—Gene Pitney (62)	1463
Hootenanny—Glencoves (63)	488
Please Don't Talk To The Lifeguard—Diane Ray (63)	464
One Of The Lucky Ones—Anita Bryant (60)	233
Our Corner Of The Night—Barbra Streisand (68)	82
Mystery Of You—Platters (57)	70
Somebody Nobody Wants—Dion (61)	59
Adonis—Terri Stevens (59)	*35*
Robot Man—Jamie Horton (60)	15
Adonis—Terri Dean (59)	*0.0*
Kermit GOELL ▶ 6444 (4)	**168**
Leave It To Your Heart—Ames Brothers (54)	201
This Must Be Wrong (Oho-Aha)—Caterina Valente (55)	190
America, The Beautiful—Charlie Rich (76)	18
Near You—Cliffie Stone & His Orchestra (58)	*0.0*
Marjorie GOETSCHIUS ▶ 8167 (2)	**60**
This Is My Confession—Joni James (55)	86
My Bambino—Tony Martin (54)	33
Ray GOETZ ▶ 7922 (1)	**69**
For Me And My Gal—Freddy Cannon (61)	208
Gary GOETZMAN ▶ 5168 (3)	**332**
Tell Me Tomorrow - Part 1—Smokey Robinson (82)	488
Old Fashioned Love—Smokey Robinson (82)	146
He's A Pretender—High Inergy (83)	30
Duke GOFF ▶ 11277 (1)	**2.5**
Run, Woman, Run—Tammy Wynette (70)	7.5
Gerry GOFFIN ▶ 19 (125) HOF	**63481**
Go Away Little Girl—Steve Lawrence (62)	*8171*
Take Good Care Of My Baby—Bobby Vee (61)	*7900*
The Loco-Motion—Little Eva (62)	*7718*
Go Away Little Girl—Donny Osmond (71)	*6840*
Will You Love Me Tomorrow—Shirelles (60)	*5738*
Run To Him—Bobby Vee (61)	5173
Theme From Mahogany (Do You Know Where You're Going To)—Diana Ross (75)	4699
The Loco-Motion—Grand Funk (74)	*4636*
Pleasant Valley Sunday—Monkees (67)	3972
Saving All My Love For You—Whitney Houston (85)	3224
Up On The Roof—Drifters (62)	*2924*
I've Got To Use My Imagination—Gladys Knight & The Pips (73)	2639
I Can't Stay Mad At You—Skeeter Davis (63)	2616
The Loco-Motion—Kylie Minogue (88)	*2519*
I'll Meet You Halfway—Partridge Family Starring Shirley Jones & Featuring David Cassidy (71)	2417
Who Put The Bomp (In The Bomp, Bomp, Bomp)—Barry Mann (61)	2389
One Fine Day—Chiffons (63)	*2130*
Don't Say Nothin' Bad (About My Baby)—Cookies (63)	2050
I'm Into Something Good—Herman's Hermits (64)	*1902*
Just Once In My Life—Righteous Brothers (65)	1850
Tonight, I Celebrate My Love—Peabo Bryson/Roberta Flack (83)	1798
Hey, Girl—Freddie Scott (63)	*1793*
A Natural Woman (You Make Me Feel Like)—Aretha Franklin (67)	1752
Hey Girl—Donny Osmond (71)	*1748*
Don't Bring Me Down—Animals (66)	1719
Keep Your Hands Off My Baby—Little Eva (62)	1642
Miss You Like Crazy—Natalie Cole (89)	1581
Her Royal Majesty—James Darren (62)	1551
Go Away Little Girl—Happenings (66)	*1386*
Nothing's Gonna Change My Love For You—Glenn Medeiros (87)	1315
Hi-De-Ho—Blood, Sweat & Tears (70)	1305
Some Kind Of Wonderful—Drifters (61)	1244
Chains—Cookies (62)	1234
Sharing You—Bobby Vee (62)	1134
One Fine Day—Carole King (80)	*1089*
I've Got Bonnie—Bobby Rydell (62)	1069
Will You Love Me Tomorrow—4 Seasons Featuring The "Sound" Of Frankie Valli (68)	*1009*
Oh No Not My Baby—Maxine Brown (64)	*960*
Let's Turkey Trot—Little Eva (63)	947
Halfway To Paradise—Bobby Vinton (68)	*936*
Halfway To Paradise—Tony Orlando (61)	*897*
Someone That I Used To Love—Natalie Cole (80)	768
Walking Proud—Steve Lawrence (63)	764
This Little Girl—Dion (63)	761
I Want To Stay Here—Steve And Eydie (63)	735
Take Good Care Of My Baby—Bobby Vinton (68)	*690*
When My Little Girl Is Smiling—Drifters (62)	*674*
Point Of No Return—Gene McDaniels (62)	648
It Might As Well Rain Until September—Carole King (62)	646
Every Breath I Take—Gene Pitney (61)	623
Girls Grow Up Faster Than Boys—Cookies (63)	591
I Can't Stop Talking About You—Steve And Eydie (63)	559
It Started All Over Again—Brenda Lee (62)	546
Up On The Roof—James Taylor (79)	*522*
Poor Little Rich Girl—Steve Lawrence (63)	492
What A Sweet Thing That Was—Shirelles (61)	486
Hey Girl—Bobby Vee (68)	*476*
He Knows I Love Him Too Much—Paris Sisters (62)	453
He's In Town—Tokens (64)	438
Will You Still Love Me Tomorrow—Dave Mason (78)	*431*
I'm Into Somethin' Good—Earl-Jean (64)	*425*
Old Smokey Locomotion—Little Eva (63)	*399*
How Many Tears—Bobby Vee (61)	395
Porpoise Song—Monkees (68)	391
At The Club—Drifters (65)	386
I Can't Hear You No More—Helen Reddy (76)	*382*
On This Side Of Goodbye—Righteous Brothers (66)	344
Hung On You—Righteous Brothers (65)	321
Forgive Me For Dreaming—Elisa Fiorillo (88)	311
Don't Try To Fight It, Baby—Eydie Gorme (63)	311
So Sad The Song—Gladys Knight & The Pips (76)	300
Why'd You Wanna Make Me Cry—Connie Stevens (62)	297
Don't Forget About Me—Dusty Springfield (69)	*270*
Don't Ask Me To Be Friends—Everly Brothers (62)	259
Oh! No Not My Baby—Rod Stewart (73)	*197*
Oh No, Not My Baby—Merry Clayton (72)	*194*
I Could Have Loved You So Well—Ray Peterson (61)	192
Will You Still Love Me Tomorrow—Roberta Flack (72)	*184*
Up On The Roof—Cryan' Shames (68)	*174*
Lovin' Touch—Mark Dinning (60)	170
Walkin' With My Angel—Bobby Vee (61)	166
Will Power—Cookies (63)	156
Will You Love Me Tomorrow?—Melanie (73)	*152*
It's Gonna Be Alright—Maxine Brown (65)	146
Keep Your Love Locked (Deep In Your Heart)—Paul Petersen (62)	141
Happy Times (Are Here To Stay)—Tony Orlando (61)	129
How Can I Meet Her?—Everly Brothers (62)	127
Goin' Back—Byrds (67)	125
One Fine Day—Rita Coolidge (79)	*116*
Long And Lasting Love (Once In A Lifetime)—Glenn Medeiros (88)	113
I Can't Hear You—Betty Everett (64)	*106*
Everybody Go Home—Eydie Gorme (63)	104
So Much Love—Ben E. King (66)	*102*
I Can't Make It Alone—Lou Rawls (69)	*99*
I Can't Make It Alone—Bill Medley (68)	*87*
Is This What I Get For Loving You?—Ronettes Featuring Veronica (65)	74
Sailor Boy—Chiffons (64)	72
I Need You—Chuck Jackson (65)	*72*
When My Little Girl Is Smiling—Steve Alaimo (71)	*71*
So Much Love—Steve Alaimo (66)	*67*
Where Does Love Go—Freddie Scott (64)	50
Don't Forget About Me—American Breed (67)	*48*
Wasn't Born To Follow—Byrds (69)	45
No One Can Make My Sunshine Smile—Everly Brothers (62)	44
Dreamin' About You—Annette And The Vonnair Sisters (61)	37
High Out Of Time—Carole King (76)	23
One Fine Day—Julie (76)	*19*
One More Chance—Diana Ross (81)	18
Sweet Sweetheart—Bobby Vee (70)	17
I Don't Think You Know Me—American Breed (67)	15

Gerry GOFFIN ▶ 19 (125) HOF *Continued*	**63481**
Hey Girl—Lettermen (70)	*14*
He's A Bad Boy—Carole King (63)	13
I Can't Say Goodbye—Bobby Vee (62)	10
Go Away Little Boy—Marlena Shaw (77)	*9.6*
Will You Love Me Tomorrow—Dana Valery (76)	*9.4*
Yours Until Tomorrow—Vivian Reed (68)	8.2
I Need You—Rationals (68)	*7.7*
Up On The Roof—Laura Nyro (70)	*7.4*
Don't Forget About Me—Barbara Lewis (66)	*7.0*
What I Gotta Do (To Make You Jealous)—Little Eva (63)	7.0
Down Home—Rick Nelson (63)	5.1
I Just Can't Say Goodbye—Bobby Rydell (64)	3.3
Dear Mr. D.J. Play It Again—Tina Robin (61)	2.7
Will You Love Me Tomorrow?—Linda Ronstadt (70)	*1.7*
Smackwater Jack—Carole King (71)	0.0
Jack GOGA ▶ 5796 (2)	**241**
You—Marvin Gaye (68)	545
Yesterday's Dreams—Four Tops (68)	417
Glenn GOINS ▶ 11599 (1)	**1.0**
Funk'N' Roll (Dancin' In The Funkshine)—Quazar (78)	2.1
Arnie GOLAND ▶ 5425 (1)	**291**
No Chemise Please—Gerry Granahan (58)	872
Andrew GOLD ▶ 1052 (5)	**4191**
Lonely Boy—Andrew Gold (77)	2863
Thank You For Being A Friend—Andrew Gold (78)	920
Right Between The Eyes—Wax (86)	380
Never Let Her Slip Away—Andrew Gold (78)	178
That's Why I Love You—Andrew Gold (76)	82
Bert GOLD ▶ 5881 (3)	**233**
Dogface Soldier—Russ Morgan & His Orchestra (55)	*467*
Dog Face Soldier—Joe Lipman (55)	*0.0*
Dogface Soldier—Stephen Make (55)	*0.0*
Ernest GOLD [Ernst Siegmund Goldner] ▶ 486 (9)	**8577**
Exodus—Ferrante & Teicher (60)	*6965*
Exodus—Eddie Harris (61)	*683*
Main Theme from Exodus (Ari's Theme)—Mantovani And His Orchestra (60)	*645*
The Exodus Song (This Land Is Mine)—Pat Boone (61)	*190*
On The Beach—Frank Chacksfield And His Orch. (59)	*180*
31 Flavors—Shirelles (63)	15
It's A Mad, Mad, Mad, Mad World—Shirelles (63)	6.3
Exodus—Medallion Strings (61)	*0.0*
On The Beach—Playmates (59)	*0.0*
Ernie GOLD [Ernest Goldberg] ▶ 3111 (2)	**1004**
Tell It To My Heart—Taylor Dayne (87)	1915
Made Up My Mind—Sa-Fire (91)	47
Fredda GOLD ▶ 4478 (1)	**485**
Twixt Twelve And Twenty—Pat Boone (59)	971
Jack GOLD ▶ 8022 (2)	**65**
Funny Little Butterflies—Patty Duke (65)	183
You'll Always Be The One (For Me)—Four Aces (55)	11
Jim GOLD ▶ 1082 (1)	**4081**
Nice To Be With You—Gallery (72)	4081
Joey GOLD ▶ 6614 (1)	**151**
In Paradise—Laissez Faire (91)	151
Julie GOLD ▶ 1204 (1)	**3697**
From A Distance—Bette Midler (90)	3697
Ken GOLD ▶ 5387 (6)	**296**
Oh Honey—Delegation (79)	419
You To Me Are Everything—Real Thing (76)	*132*
I Can't Ask For Anymore Than You—Cliff Richard (76)	22
You To Me Are Everything—Broadway (76)	*15*
You To Me Are Everything (Part 1)—Revelation (76)	*1.7*
Wasn't It Nice In New York City—Tommy Leonetti (73)	0.7
Marian GOLD [Hartwig Schierbaum] ▶ 6977 (3)	**124**
Forever Young—Alphaville (88)	*185*
Big In Japan—Alphaville (84)	180
Forever Young—Alphaville (85)	*7.2*
Marty GOLD ▶ 3738 (1)	**715**
Tell Me Why—Bobby Vinton (64)	1431
Wally GOLD ▶ 266 (24)	**12757**
It's Now Or Never—Elvis Presley With The Jordanaires (60)	*10781*
It's My Party—Lesley Gore (63)	*7824*
Good Luck Charm—Elvis Presley w/Jordanaires (62)	6862
Half Heaven - Half Heartache—Gene Pitney (62)	1463
Lucky Devil—Carl Dobkins, Jr. (59)	895
She Can't Find Her Keys—Paul Petersen (62)	821
It's Now Or Never—John Schneider (81)	*781*
Utopia—Frank Gari (60)	774
Fools Hall Of Fame—Pat Boone (59)	646
Look Homeward Angel—Monarchs (64)	*531*
Time And The River—Nat King Cole (60)	462
Hither And Thither And Yon—Brook Benton (60)	379
Look Homeward Angel—Johnnie Ray (57)	*316*
Sweet Bird Of Youth—Nat "King" Cole (59)	135
Look Homeward Angel—Four Esquires (56)	*103*
Yesterday's Hero—Gene Pitney (64)	66
It's My Party—Dave Stewart With Barbara Gaskin (81)	*64*
Follow Me—Four Esquires (57)	*38*
Questions And Answers—In Crowd (66)	33
Young In Years—Diamonds (59)	33
Follow Me—Billy Williams Quartet (57)	*28*
Land Of You And Me—Four Esquires (59)	22
Five Card Stud—Lorne Greene (66)	9.7
Lucy, Lucy—George Hamilton IV (58)	4.4
Barry GOLDBERG ▶ 2618 (1)	**1320**
I've Got To Use My Imagination—Gladys Knight & The Pips (73)	2639
—Eleanor Goldberg see: Nora BAYES	
—Ernest Goldberg see: Ernie GOLD	
Neil Brian GOLDBERG ▶ 5290 (4)	**312**
Do It In The Name Of Love—Candi Staton (73)	250
Got To Believe In Love—Robin McNamara (70)	126
The Girl Who Loved Me When—Glass Bottle (71)	58
We're All Goin' Home—Bobby Bloom (71)	9.2
Franne GOLDE ▶ 1462 (19)	**2982**
Nightshift—Commodores (85)	2649
Don't You Want Me—Jody Watley (87)	2205
Talk To Me—Chico DeBarge (86)	908
Gettin' Ready For Love—Diana Ross (77)	598
Looking For A Stranger—Pat Benatar (83)	353
Secret—Heart (91)	245
Be There—Pointer Sisters (87)	211
Goin' To The Bank—Commodores (86)	194
Own The Night—Chaka Khan (85)	181
Don't Look Any Further—Kane Gang (88)	*126*
Voice On The Radio—Conductor (82)	79
Me - U = Blue—Glenn Medeiros (90)	64
Bit By Bit—Stephanie Mills (85)	62
Over My Head—Toni Basil (84)	61
Don't Look Any Further—Dennis Edwards (84)	*49*
Let's Go Up—Diana Ross (83)	46
God Knows—Debby Boone (78)	44
Here I Go (Fallin' In Love Again)—Frannie Golde (79)	20
Janet—Commodores (85)	16
John L. GOLDEN ▶ 8869 (2)	**37**
Poor Butterfly—Sarah Vaughan (57)	*75*
Poor Butterfly—Hilltoppers (54)	*0.0*
Lotti GOLDEN ▶ 3262 (3)	**921**
With Every Beat Of My Heart—Taylor Dayne (89)	2568
Undeniable—Ms. Adventures (90)	81
Hard Times For Lovers—Jennifer Holliday (85)	77
—Ronnie Golden see: Tony DeMEUR	
Mark GOLDENBERG ▶ 1725 (5)	**2416**
Automatic—Pointer Sisters (84)	2321
Along Comes A Woman—Chicago (85)	906
Soul Kiss—Olivia Newton-John (85)	695
Real Love—Cretones (80)	79
Skin Deep—Cher (88)	59
Barry GOLDER ▶ 4750 (3)	**424**
Tear Drops—Lee Andrews And The Hearts (57)	703
Try The Impossible—Lee Andrews And The Hearts (58)	453
Why Do I—Lee Andrews And The Hearts (58)	43
Ed GOLDMAN ▶ 8934 (1)	**36**
Billy You're My Friend—Gene Pitney (68)	36
Steve GOLDMAN ▶ 4483 (1)	**483**
How Many Times Can We Say Goodbye—Dionne Warwick And Luther Vandross (83)	483
Andy GOLDMARK ▶ 1146 (15)	**3879**
Love Is A Wonderful Thing—Michael Bolton (91)	2873
You Should Be Mine (The Woo Woo Song)—Jeffrey Osborne (86)	1213
Dynamite—Jermaine Jackson (84)	933
Soul Provider—Michael Bolton (89)	784
Goldmine—Pointer Sisters (86)	495
Flames Of Paradise (Duet With Elton John)—Jennifer Rush (87)	441
Oh, People—Patti LaBelle (86)	409
Goin' To The Bank—Commodores (86)	194
Moonlight On Water—Laura Branigan (90)	*166*
All I Want Is You—Carly Simon (88)	154
Moonlight On Water—Kevin Raleigh (89)	*88*
Me - U = Blue—Glenn Medeiros (90)	64
Twist My Arm—Pointer Sisters (86)	47
Only My Heart Talkin'—Alice Cooper (90)	30
Fools Like Me—Lorenzo Lamas (84)	23
—Ernst Siegmund Goldner see: Ernest GOLD	
George GOLDNER ▶ 1167 (23)	**3812**
Why Do Fools Fall In Love—Teenagers Featuring Frankie Lymon (56)	*4057*
Why Do Fools Fall In Love—Diana Ross (81)	*2314*
Why Do Fools Fall In Love—Gale Storm (56)	*2295*
Why Do Fools Fall In Love—Diamonds (56)	*1782*
I Want You To Be My Girl—Frankie Lymon and the Teenagers (56)	1339
Maybe—Three Degrees (70)	*895*
Maybe—Chantels (58)	*847*
Why Do Fools Fall In Love—Happenings (67)	*389*
Little Girl Of Mine—Cleftones (56)	*372*
On Campus—Dickie Goodman (69)	350
Every Night (I Pray)—Chantels (58)	330
ABC's Of Love—Frankie Lymon & the Teenagers (56)	186
I Love You So—Chantels (58)	113
Batman & His Grandmother—Dickie Goodman (66)	102
Why Do Fools Fall In Love—Gloria Mann (56)	*80*
Can't We Be Sweethearts—Cleftones (56)	59
He's Gone—Chantels (57)	30
I Want You To Be My Boy—Exciters (65)	20
The Plea—Jesters (58)	14
Maybe—Shangri-Las (64)	*8.7*
Why Do Fools Fall In Love—Beach Boys (64)	*5.6*
Why Do Fools Fall In Love—Summer Wine (73)	*0.4*
Little Girl Of Mine—Diamonds (56)	*0.0*
Bobby GOLDSBORO ▶ 301 (26)	**12016**
See The Funny Little Clown—Bobby Goldsboro (64)	1705
Little Things—Bobby Goldsboro (65)	1505
Autumn Of My Life—Bobby Goldsboro (68)	1303
Summer (The First Time)—Bobby Goldsboro (73)	957
Voodoo Woman—Bobby Goldsboro (65)	788
It's Too Late—Bobby Goldsboro (66)	749
With Pen In Hand—Vikki Carr (69)	*705*
Blue Autumn—Bobby Goldsboro (66)	633
Muddy Mississippi Line—Bobby Goldsboro (69)	537
With Pen In Hand—Billy Vera (68)	*518*
I'm A Drifter—Bobby Goldsboro (69)	499
Whenever He Holds You—Bobby Goldsboro (64)	*491*
If You've Got A Heart—Bobby Goldsboro (65)	367
Broomstick Cowboy—Bobby Goldsboro (65)	294
Whenever She Holds You—Patty Duke (66)	*205*
Come Back Home—Bobby Goldsboro (71)	155
I Know You Better Than That—Bobby Goldsboro (66)	143
Can You Feel It—Bobby Goldsboro (70)	117
It Hurts Me—Bobby Goldsboro (66)	108
The Cowboy And The Lady—John Denver (81)	97
Baby's Gone—Gene Thomas (63)	89
If You Wait For Love—Bobby Goldsboro (65)	42
With Pen In Hand—Bobby Goldsboro (72)	*35*
Goodbye To All You Women—Bobby Goldsboro (67)	8.9
With Pen In Hand—Dorothy Moore (78)	*7.3*
Pledge Of Love—Bobby Goldsboro (68)	1.9
James GOLDSBOROUGH ▶ 8621 (1)	**45**
Broken Promise—Four Coins (57)	90
Cliff GOLDSMITH ▶ 2343 (12)	**1575**
Western Movies—Olympics (58)	1584
Peanut Butter—Marathons (61)	1099
Patti Ann—Johnny Crawford (62)	465
Dance By The Light Of The Moon—Olympics (60)	*428*
(Baby) Hully Gully—Olympics (60)	165
Little Pedro—Olympics (61)	100
Dedicated (To The Songs I Love)—3 Friends (61)	80
Hully Gully Again—Little Caesar And The Romans (61)	58
(I Wanna) Dance With The Teacher—Olympics (58)	26
Comic Book Crazy—Little Sammy Yates (59)	6.4
Dooley—Olympics (61)	3.2
Private Eye—Olympics (59)	2.3
—Hilliard Goldsmith see: Bob HILLIARD	
Jerry GOLDSMITH ▶ 4143 (1)	**581**
Theme From Dr. Kildare (Three Stars Will Shine Tonight)—Richard Chamberlain (62)	1744

Jonathan GOLDSMITH ▶ 6335 (1)	**182**
Take Off—Bob & Doug McKenzie (82)	908
Lenny Lee GOLDSMITH ▶ 10978 (1)	**4.0**
Spend The Night In Love—Four Seasons (80)	12
Alexander GOLDSTEIN ▶ 6818 (1)	**135**
Balboa Blue—Marketts (62)	404
Bob GOLDSTEIN ▶ 1475 (1)	**2946**
Washington Square—Village Stompers (63)	5892
—David Goldstein see: Rupert HOLMES	
—Harvey Goldstein see: Harvey BROOKS	
Jerry GOLDSTEIN ▶ 584 (38)	**7423**
My Boyfriend's Back—Angels (63)	*8148*
Come On Down To My Boat—Every Mothers' Son (67)	3309
Why Can't We Be Friends?—War (75)	3006
Low Rider—War (75)	2369
I Want Candy—Strangeloves (65)	*1629*
Summer—War (76)	1559
Night Time—Strangeloves (66)	764
All Day Music—War (71)	704
Cara-Lin—Strangeloves (65)	565
It's Nice To Be With You—Monkees (68)	437
They Can't Take Away Our Music—Eric Burdon And War Featuring Sharon Scott And The Beautiful New Born Children Of Southern California (70)	418
Wow Wow Wee (He's The Boy For Me)—Angels (64)	394
Galaxy—War (77)	325
Ten Lonely Guys—Pat Boone (62)	*317*
L.A. Sunshine—War (77)	291
Let's Stomp—Bobby Comstock (63)	288
(You Make Me Feel) So Good—McCoys (66)	259
Giving Up On Love—Jerry Butler (64)	257
Patty Baby—Freddy Cannon (63)	242
I Want Candy—Bow Wow Wow (82)	*177*
Bubble Gum Music—Rock And Roll Dubble Bubble Trading Card Co. Of Philadelphia-19141 (69)	144
What's Gonna Happen When Summer's Done—Freddy Cannon (62)	143
Low Rider (On The Boulevard)—Latin Alliance (91)	121
What Time Is It?—Jive Five (62)	103
Ten Lonely Guys—Ten Broken Hearts (62)	*81*
Out In The Sun (Hey-O)—Beach Nuts (65)	63
Sorrow—David Bowie (73)	53
You Got The Power—War (82)	35
Thank You And Goodnight—Angels (63)	21
Good, Good Feelin'—War (79)	12
A Letter From Betty—Bobby Vee (63)	11
Outlaw—War (82)	10
The Flower Children—Marcia Strassman (67)	7.4
I'm On Fire—Jerry Lee Lewis (64)	2.7
I Can't Stop—Osmond Brothers (71)	2.1
I'm Tossin' And Turnin' Again—Bobby Lewis (62)	1.3
Your Boyfriend's Back—Bobby Comstock & The Counts (63)	*0.4*
Broadway—Freddy Cannon (62)	0.4
—Lesley Sue Goldstein see: Lesley GORE	
—Michael Goldstein see: Michael GORE	
Steve GOLDSTEIN ▶ 7096 (1)	**116**
Say It Again—Santana (85)	347
Eddie GOLGA ▶ 11416 (1)	**1.8**
You And Me—Liner (79)	5.4
Benny GOLSON ▶ 6120 (1)	**203**
Killer Joe—Quincy Jones (70)	203
—Jose Gomera see: Louis FERRARI	
Gina GOMEZ ▶ 9091 (1)	**31**
I Can't Face The Fact—Gina Go-Go (89)	94
Ian GOMM ▶ 2603 (2)	**1333**
Cruel To Be Kind—Nick Lowe (79)	1413
Hold On—Ian Gomm (79)	626
Larry GONSKY ▶ 11627 (1)	**0.9**
(She's Just A) Fallen Angel—Starz (76)	6.5
Dale GONYEA ▶ 5672 (1)	**257**
I Need Your Help Barry Manilow—Ray Stevens (79)	257
—Jesse Gonzales see: Jesus ESCAMILLA	
—Luciano Gonzales see: Chano POZO	
Antonio GONZALEZ ▶ 6845 (1)	**133**
La Raza—Kid Frost (90)	399
Bob GONZALEZ ▶ 3203 (1)	**955**
Little Girl—Syndicate Of Sound (66)	1909
Tony GONZALEZ ▶ 4463 (1)	**488**
Mentirosa—Mellow Man Ace (90)	977
Al GOODHART ▶ 10393 (2)	**9.0**

I Apologize—Timi Yuro (61)	18
Serenade Of The Bells—Four Coins (60)	8.9
Jay GOODIS ▶ 7459 (1)	**94**
If You Were A Rock And Roll Record—Freddy Cannon (62)	94
John GOODISON ▶ 5885 (2)	**233**
Where Are You Going To My Love—Brotherhood Of Man (70)	319
Lady (Put The Light On Me)—Brownsville Station (77)	307
Ken GOODLOE ▶ 7654 (2)	**82**
To Be Loved (Forever)—Pentagons (61)	391
I Wonder (If Your Love Will Ever Belong To Me)—Pentagons (61)	21
Ted GOODLOE ▶ 7655 (2)	**82**
To Be Loved (Forever)—Pentagons (61)	391
I Wonder (If Your Love Will Ever Belong To Me)—Pentagons (61)	21
Al GOODMAN [Willie Albert Goodman] ▶ 2602 (8)	**1333**
Special Lady—Ray, Goodman & Brown (80)	2439
Sexy Mama—Moments (74)	858
Look At Me (I'm In Love)—Moments (75)	430
Didn't I—Sylvia (73)	139
Sho Nuff Boogie (Part 1)—Sylvia & The Moments (74)	83
Inside Of You—Ray, Goodman & Brown (80)	78
Girls (Part I)—Moments And Whatnauts (75)	24
Lovely Way She Loves—Moments (70)	13
Benny GOODMAN ▶ 9804 (1)	**17**
Don't Be That Way—Larry Elgart And His Manhattan Swing Orchestra (82)	50
Bob GOODMAN ▶ 2070 (4)	**1924**
Close To Cathy—Mike Clifford (62)	1504
Hideaway—Four Esquires (58)	1087
Give Me Your Heart For Christmas—McGuire Sisters (54)	85
One Little Kiss—Playmates (61)	1.4
Dickie GOODMAN ▶ 1005 (22)	**4430**
Mr. Jaws—Dickie Goodman (75)	3166
The Flying Saucer (Pts. 1 & 2)—Buchanan And Goodman (56)	1700
The Touchables—Dickie Goodman (61)	620
Super Fly Meets Shaft—John & Ernest (73)	483
Energy Crisis '74—Dickie Goodman (74)	413
Flying Saucer The Second—Buchanan And Goodman (57)	410
On Campus—Dickie Goodman (69)	350
Kong—Dickie Goodman (77)	246
Ben Crazy—Dickie Goodman & Dr. I.M. III (62)	241
The Touchables In Brooklyn—Dickie Goodman (61)	231
Watergrate—Dickie Goodman (73)	208
Dr. Ben Basey—Mickey Shorr And The Cutups (62)	139
Santa And The Satellite—Buchanan And Goodman (57)	116
Batman & His Grandmother—Dickie Goodman (66)	102
Buchanan And Goodman On Trial—Buchanan And Goodman (56)	55
Mr. President—Dickie Goodman (74)	54
Frankenstein Of '59—Buchanan And Goodman (59)	38
Energy Crisis '79—Dickie Goodman (79)	26
Hey, E.T.—Dickie Goodman (82)	13
Luna Trip—Dickie Goodman (69)	8.2
Russian Bandstand—Spencer & Spencer (59)	5.3
Santa & The Touchables—Dickie Goodman (61)	0.9
Dorothy GOODMAN ▶ 5267 (1)	**315**
Yes Tonight Josephine—Johnnie Ray (57)	630
Eddie GOODMAN ▶ 11482 (1)	**1.5**
Straight Flush—Frantics (59)	9.1
Fred GOODMAN ▶ 8405 (2)	**52**
Didn't It Look So Easy—Stairsteps (71)	146
Fill My Soul—Pop Explosion (68)	5.8
Henrietta GOODMAN ▶ 9647 (1)	**20**
Inside Of You—Ray, Goodman & Brown (80)	78
Larry GOODMAN [LayLaw] ▶ 4097 (1)	**594**
No More Lies—Michel'le (89)	1783
Lillian GOODMAN ▶ 5588 (1)	**268**
Cherie I Love You—Pat Boone (58)	268
Nat GOODMAN ▶ 9475 (1)	**23**
Don't Say Goodbye—Diamonds (57)	69
—Richard Goodman see: Richie SUPA	
Shirley GOODMAN ▶ 3575 (4)	**780**
Let The Good Times Roll—Shirley And Lee (56)	*870*
Let The Good Times Roll—Bunny Sigler (67)	*455*

Let The Good Times Roll—Shirley & Lee (60)	*202*
Let The Good Times Roll—Roy Orbison (65)	*34*
Steve GOODMAN ▶ 2687 (1)	**1272**
The City Of New Orleans—Arlo Guthrie (72)	1272
Susan GOODMAN ▶ 8837 (3)	**38**
Frankenstein Of '59—Buchanan And Goodman (59)	38
Energy Crisis '79—Dickie Goodman (79)	26
Hey, E.T.—Dickie Goodman (82)	13
—Willie Albert Goodman see: Al GOODMAN	
Randy GOODRUM ▶ 231 (18)	**14726**
You Needed Me—Anne Murray (78)	5512
Oh Sherrie—Steve Perry (84)	3231
Bluer Than Blue—Michael Johnson (78)	1517
Who's Holding Donna Now—DeBarge (85)	1361
I'll Be Over You—Toto (86)	1351
What Are We Doin' In Love—Dottie West (81)	1178
It's Sad To Belong—England Dan & John Ford Coley (77)	1083
Broken Hearted Me—Anne Murray (79)	1068
If She Would Have Been Faithful...—Chicago (87)	958
Foolish Heart—Steve Perry (84)	*877*
Before My Heart Finds Out—Gene Cotton (78)	800
She's Mine—Steve Perry (84)	609
If I Had My Wish Tonight—David Lasley (82)	402
20/20—George Benson (84)	309
A Lesson In Leavin'—Dottie West (80)	45
Foolish Heart—Sharon Bryant (89)	*36*
Power—Kansas (87)	28
Now And Forever (You And Me)—Anne Murray (86)	17
Buzz GOODWIN ▶ 11154 (1)	**3.0**
Ready For Love—Silverado (81)	6.0
Joe GOODWIN ▶ 4173 (4)	**574**
Billy—Kathy Linden (58)	1535
Breeze (Blow My Baby Back To Me)—Al Hibbler (55)	170
When You're Smiling—Bobby Freeman (59)	*12*
Everywhere You Go—Quaker City Boys (59)	5.2
Ron GOODWIN ▶ 4972 (4)	**367**
Swinging Sweethearts—Ron Goodwin And His Orchestra (57)	*367*
Swinging Sweethearts—Richard Hayes (57)	*0.0*
Swingin' Sweethearts—David Carroll & His Orchestra (57)	*0.0*
Swingin' Sweethearts—Hugo Winterhalter And His Orchestra (57)	*0.0*
Myles GOODWYN ▶ 2423 (6)	**1499**
Just Between You And Me—April Wine (81)	928
Roller—April Wine (79)	352
Enough Is Enough—April Wine (82)	161
This Could Be The Right One—April Wine (84)	103
I Like To Rock—April Wine (80)	28
Say Hello—April Wine (80)	4.8
Ken GOORABIAN ▶ 2332 (2)	**1584**
You Don't Want Me Anymore—Steel Breeze (82)	1063
Dreamin' Is Easy—Steel Breeze (83)	521
Chestener GORDEN ▶ 11539 (1)	**1.3**
You And I, Pt. 1—Living Proof (78)	2.5
Alan GORDON [Almo] ▶ 267 (23)	**12728**
Happy Together—Turtles (67)	*9222*
She'd Rather Be With Me—Turtles (67)	4329
My Heart Belongs To Me—Barbra Streisand (77)	2278
You Know What I Mean—Turtles (67)	1570
Celebrate—Three Dog Night (70)	1496
She's My Girl—Turtles (67)	1458
The Cat In The Window (The Bird In The Sky)—Petula Clark (67)	667
Jill—Gary Lewis And The Playboys (67)	512
Girls In Love—Gary Lewis And The Playboys (67)	472
Melancholy Music Man—Righteous Brothers (67)	338
As Long As You're Here—Zalman Yanovsky (67)	137
Happy Together (A Fantasy)—Captain & Tennille (80)	*131*
Happy Together—Dawn Featuring Tony Orlando (72)	*124*
Sad Girl—Carl Graves (77)	95
Happy Together—Nylons (87)	*56*
Me About You—Lovin' Spoonful (69)	*53*
Me About You—Mojo Men (67)	*43*
Music Is My Life—Helen Reddy (76)	32
The Dance At St. Francis—Barracuda (68)	26
Me About You—Turtles (70)	*3.8*
When The Good Sun Shines—Elmo & Almo (67)	1.9
Kitty Doyle—Dino, Desi & Billy (67)	1.9
Two In The Afternoon—Dino, Desi & Billy (67)	1.4
—Brenda Gordon see: Brenda RUSSELL	

Colis GORDON ▶ 11743 (1)	**0.2**
He'll Be Back—Players (66)	0.5
Doug GORDON ▶ 7567 (1)	**88**
On The Line—Tangier (89)	88
Greg GORDON ▶ 7661 (1)	**82**
Bringing It Back—Elvis Presley (75)	82
Hal GORDON ▶ 10433 (3)	**8.5**
Joanie—Bay Bops (58)	14
Tell Me Now—McGuire Sisters (56)	5.3
Someone Else's Boy—Connie Francis (61)	4.3
Herb GORDON ▶ 9205 (1)	**29**
It's Unbelievable—Larks(1) (61)	58
Irving GORDON ▶ 595 (16)	**7324**
Unforgettable—Dinah Washington (59)	*1993*
Mama From The Train—Patti Page (56)	1377
Delaware—Perry Como (60)	1073
Be Anything (But Be Mine)—Connie Francis (64)	*820*
The Kentuckian Song—Hilltoppers (55)	*806*
Unforgettable—Natalie Cole (91)	*804*
Unbelievable—Nat "King" Cole (54)	412
What Will I Tell My Heart—Fats Domino (57)	*163*
Walls Have Ears—Patti Page (59)	149
Be Anything (But Be Mine)—Gloria Lynne (64)	*21*
Two Brothers—David Hill (59)	19
What Will I Tell My Heart—Harptones (61)	*3.7*
The Kentuckian Song—Guy Cherney (55)	*0.0*
The Kentuckian Song—Bobby Sherwood (55)	*0.0*
The Kentuckian Song— Paul Weston & His Orchestra (55)	*0.0*
The Kentuckian Song—Eddy Arnold with Hugo Winterhalter's Orch. And Chorus (55)	*0.0*
Jim GORDON ▶ 3188 (3)	**958**
Layla—Derek And The Dominos (72)	*1552*
Layla—Derek And The Dominos (71)	*359*
Rock & Roll Stew (Part 1)—Traffic (72)	5.1
Jon GORDON [Doc Box, Jon D. Gordon III] ▶ 7973 (1)	**67**
Slow Love—Doc Box & B. Fresh (90)	200
Kelly GORDON ▶ 1833 (2)	**2239**
That's Life—Frank Sinatra (66)	*4437*
That's Life—David Lee Roth (86)	*40*
Larry GORDON ▶ 11365 (2)	**2.1**
Fifty Fathoms—Jack Fascinato (56)	5.5
Breakwater—Lawrence Welk And His Orchestra (63)	0.4
Mack GORDON [Morris Gittler] ▶ 2009 (13) HOF	**2004**
The More I See You—Chris Montez (66)	1319
At Last—Etta James (61)	*639*
There Will Never Be Another You—Chris Montez (66)	527
Never In A Million Years—Linda Scott (62)	379
With My Eyes Wide Open I'm Dreaming— Patti Page (59)	*353*
Chattanooga Choo Choo—Harpers Bizarre (67)	*339*
Chattanooga Choo Choo—Tuxedo Junction (78)	*307*
Did You Ever See A Dream Walking—Fats Domino (62)	82
Some Day Soon—Eddie Fisher (57)	22
I Can't Begin To Tell You—Jane Morgan (59)	18
You'll Never Know— Shirley Bassey with the Rita Williams Singers (61)	16
All About Love—Eddie Fisher (57)	4.4
With My Eyes Wide Open I'm Dreaming— Enoch Light & The Light Brigade (59)	*2.9*
Marc GORDON ▶ 5043 (3)	**354**
Somebody (Somewhere) Needs You—Darrell Banks (66)	334
Castles In The Sand—Little Stevie Wonder (64)	304
I'm So Thankful—Ikettes (65)	222
Margaret GORDON ▶ 11748 (1)	**0.2**
Breakwater—Lawrence Welk And His Orchestra (63)	0.4
Michael GORDON ▶ 1099 (8)	**4022**
Out Of Limits—Marketts (63)	3529
Surfer's Stomp—Mar-Kets (62)	524
Apologize—Ed Ames (68)	201
Main Street—Gary Lewis And The Playboys (68)	105
Brink Of Disaster—Lesley Gore (67)	64
Love Machine—Roosters (68)	57
Vanishing Point—Marketts (64)	12
Get The Message—Brian Hyland (67)	9.7
Paul GORDON ▶ 1319 (5)	**3363**
The Next Time I Fall—Peter Cetera (86)	3246
Friends And Lovers— Gloria Loring & Carl Anderson (86)	3079

We've Saved The Best For Last—Kenny G (89)	260
Let Me In—Eddie Money (89)	142
Watching Over You—Glenn Medeiros (87)	42
Rexton GORDON [Rexton Ralston Fernando Gordon, Shabba Ranks] ▶ 8304 (1)	**55**
Housecall—Shabba Ranks (91)	329
Rosco GORDON ▶ 4308 (3)	**527**
Just A Little Bit—Roy Head (65)	*432*
Just A Little Bit—Rosco Gordon (60)	*95*
Just A Little Bit—Little Milton (69)	3.1
Sonny GORDON ▶ 5616 (1)	**264**
Hey Now—Lesley Gore (64)	264
Steven GORDON ▶ 5061 (1)	**351**
I Want You—Shana (89)	351
Anna GORDY [Anna Gaye] ▶ 2601 (2)	**1334**
Baby, I'm For Real—Originals (69)	1958
The Bells—Originals (70)	1418
Berry GORDY [Charlemagne] ▶ 64 (64) HOF	**34098**
I'll Be There—Jackson 5 (70)	9838
ABC—Jackson 5 (70)	8551
I Want You Back—Jackson 5 (69)	7904
The Love You Save—Jackson 5 (70)	6071
You've Made Me So Very Happy— Blood, Sweat & Tears (69)	*5673*
Mama's Pearl—Jackson 5 (71)	4810
Do You Love Me—Contours (62)	*4652*
Shop Around— Miracles (Featuring Bill "Smokey" Robinson) (60)	*3656*
Lonely Teardrops—Jackie Wilson (58)	*3299*
Shop Around—Captain & Tennille (76)	*3059*
You Got What It Takes—Marv Johnson (59)	*2631*
Sugar Daddy—Jackson 5 (71)	2514
You Got What It Takes—Dave Clark Five (67)	*1890*
I Love The Way You Love—Marv Johnson (60)	1848
I'm Livin' In Shame— Diana Ross And The Supremes (69)	1652
Do You Love Me—Dave Clark Five (64)	*1594*
O.P.P.—Naughty By Nature (91)	1392
That's Why (I Love You So)—Jackie Wilson (59)	1212
Money (That's what I want)—Barrett Strong (60)	*1212*
Try It Baby—Marvin Gaye (64)	1211
Money—Kingsmen (64)	*1174*
(You've Got To) Move Two Mountains— Marv Johnson (60)	1055
Maybe Tomorrow—Jackson 5 (71)	977
Do You Love Me—Contours (88)	*953*
All I Could Do Was Cry—Etta James (60)	*949*
I'll Be Satisfied—Jackie Wilson (59)	851
Come To Me—Marv Johnson (59)	*755*
Get It Together—Jackson 5 (73)	729
No Matter What Sign You Are— Diana Ross And The Supremes (69)	554
To Be Loved—Jackie Wilson (58)	522
Glasshouse—Temptations (75)	499
Shake Sherry—Contours (62)	473
Reet Petite (The Finest Girl You Ever Want To Meet)— Jackie Wilson (57)	457
Lonely Teardrops—Brian Hyland (71)	*402*
Money (That's What I Want) Part 1— Jr. Walker & The All Stars (66)	*391*
Merry-Go-Round—Marv Johnson (61)	381
You've Made Me So Very Happy— Brenda Holloway (67)	*353*
Money—Flying Lizards (79)	*317*
Happy Days—Marv Johnson (60)	301
Bless You—Martha Reeves & The Vandellas (71)	298
I Don't Want To Take A Chance—Mary Wells (61)	294
Ain't Gonna Be That Way—Marv Johnson (60)	259
Power—Temptations (80)	231
All The Love I've Got—Marv Johnson (60)	192
Don't Let Her Be Your Baby—Contours (63)	98
Seven Day Fool—Etta James (61)	92
My Daddy Knows Best—Marvelettes (63)	90
Lonely Teardrops—Narvel Felts (76)	*77*
Let Me Go The Right Way—Supremes (62)	75
Bad Girl—Miracles (59)	65
I'm Coming Home—Marv Johnson (59)	58
I Found That Girl—Jackson 5 (70)	51
Do You Love Me—Andy Fraser (84)	*41*
We Have Love—Jackie Wilson (58)	23
All I Could Do Was Cry—Joe Tex (60)	*14*
Don't Let Him Shop Around—Debbie Dean (61)	*10*

I Want To Go Back There Again—Chris Clark (67)	9.4
How Can We Tell Him—Marv Johnson (61)	5.7
You've Made Me So Very Happy—Lou Rawls (70)	*5.5*
Everyone Was There—Bob Kayli (58)	4.9
I Need A Change—Miracles (60)	2.5
Broken Hearted—Miracles (61)	1.8
Two Wrongs Don't Make A Right—Mary Wells (63)	0.4
Come To Me—Frances Burnett (59)	*0.0*
Emory GORDY ▶ 2341 (3)	**1575**
Traces—Classics IV Featuring Dennis Yost (69)	*4007*
Midnight—Dennis Yost And The Classics IV (69)	481
Traces—Lettermen (69)	*238*
George GORDY [George Weldon Gordy, Horgay Gordy] ▶ 3618 (10)	**765**
Beechwood 4-5789—Marvelettes (62)	*1082*
Stubborn Kind Of Fellow—Marvin Gaye (62)	594
I Promise To Wait My Love— Martha Reeves & The Vandellas (68)	345
The Young Folks—Diana Ross And The Supremes (69)	126
In And Out Of My Life— Martha Reeves & The Vandellas (72)	52
Beechwood 4-5789—Carpenters (82)	*52*
Taking My Love (And Leaving Me)— Martha Reeves & The Vandellas (69)	17
Maria (You Were The Only One)—Jimmy Ruffin (71)	14
I Truly, Truly Believe—Temptations (68)	3.6
Darling Dear—Smokey Robinson & The Miracles (70)	0.4
Gwen GORDY [Gwen Fuqua] ▶ 1008 (14)	**4404**
Lonely Teardrops—Jackie Wilson (58)	*3299*
You Got What It Takes—Marv Johnson (59)	*2631*
You Got What It Takes—Dave Clark Five (67)	*1890*
That's Why (I Love You So)—Jackie Wilson (59)	1212
All I Could Do Was Cry—Etta James (60)	*949*
I'll Be Satisfied—Jackie Wilson (59)	851
That's What Girls Are Made For—Spinners (61)	598
To Be Loved—Jackie Wilson (58)	522
Distant Lover—Marvin Gaye (74)	438
Lonely Teardrops—Brian Hyland (71)	*402*
Lonely Teardrops—Narvel Felts (76)	*77*
We Have Love—Jackie Wilson (58)	23
All I Could Do Was Cry—Joe Tex (60)	*14*
Love (I'm So Glad) I Found You—Spinners (61)	4.6
—Horgay Gordy see: George GORDY	
Iris GORDY [Iris Bristol] ▶ 5041 (1)	**355**
The Bells—Originals (70)	1418
Kennedy GORDY [Rockwell] ▶ 852 (2)	**5207**
Somebody's Watching Me—Rockwell (84)	4681
Obscene Phone Caller—Rockwell (84)	526
—Margaret Gordy see: Margaret JOHNSON	
—Raynoma Gordy see: Raynoma SINGLETON	
Robert GORDY [Bob Kayli] ▶ 7780 (2)	**75**
Take Some Time Out For Love—Isley Brothers (66)	146
Everyone Was There—Bob Kayli (58)	4.9
Rosemary GORDY ▶ 11772 (1)	**0.1**
Darling Dear—Smokey Robinson & The Miracles (70)	0.4
Thelma GORDY [Thelma Louise Coleman, Thelma Louise Gordy] ▶ 5984 (2)	**219**
Can You Do It—Contours (64)	*299*
Can You Do It—Grand Funk Railroad (76)	*139*
Charlie GORE ▶ 3997 (2)	**628**
Daddy-O— Fontane Sisters with Billy Vaughn's Orchestra (55)	*1345*
Daddy-O—Bonnie Lou (55)	*539*
Lesley GORE [Lesley Sue Goldstein] ▶ 3634 (4)	**756**
Out Here On My Own—Irene Cara (80)	807
My Town, My Guy And Me—Lesley Gore (65)	538
We Know We're In Love—Lesley Gore (66)	179
I Won't Love You Anymore (Sorry)—Lesley Gore (65)	166
Martin L. GORE ▶ 843 (11)	**5240**
Enjoy The Silence—Depeche Mode (90)	1938
People Are People—Depeche Mode (85)	1005
Policy Of Truth—Depeche Mode (90)	869
Personal Jesus—Depeche Mode (89)	646
Strangelove—Depeche Mode (88)	*263*
World In My Eyes—Depeche Mode (90)	244
Never Let Me Down Again—Depeche Mode (87)	111
Behind The Wheel—Depeche Mode (88)	68
Everything Counts—Depeche Mode (89)	41
Strangelove—Depeche Mode (87)	*41*
Master And Servant—Depeche Mode (85)	15

Michael GORE [Michael Goldstein] ▶ 990 (7)	**4531**
All The Man That I Need—Whitney Houston (90)	4418
Fame—Irene Cara (80)	3098
Out Here On My Own—Irene Cara (80)	807
Red Light—Linda Clifford (80)	288
We Know We're In Love—Lesley Gore (66)	179
I Won't Love You Anymore (Sorry)—Lesley Gore (65)	166
Theme From "Terms Of Endearment"—Michael Gore (84)	52
—Kenneth Bruce Gorelick see: KENNY G	
Al GORGONI ▶ 2961 (7)	**1097**
Step Out Of Your Mind—American Breed (67)	756
I Can't Let Go—Linda Ronstadt (80)	*535*
I'll Hold Out My Hand—Clique (69)	*459*
I Can't Let Go—Hollies (66)	*384*
The Yellow Bandana—Faron Young (63)	72
I'll Hold Out My Hand—Wind (69)	*5.8*
Crazy Annie—Evie Sands (70)	5.3
Chuck GORMAN ▶ 1452 (5)	**3006**
Seventeen—Boyd Bennett And His Rockets (55)	*4540*
Seventeen—Fontane Sisters with Billy Vaughn's Orchestra (55)	*3907*
Seventeen—Rusty Draper (55)	*534*
Seventeen—Frankie Ford (61)	*37*
Seventeen—Ella Mae Morse (55)	*0.0*
Freddie GORMAN ▶ 845 (10)	**5221**
Mashed Potato Time—Dee Dee Sharp (62)	8768
Please Mr. Postman—Marvelettes (61)	*7831*
Please Mr. Postman—Carpenters (74)	*4500*
(Just Like) Romeo & Juliet—Reflections (64)	*2234*
Strange I Know—Marvelettes (62)	557
(Just Like) Romeo And Juliet—Sha Na Na (75)	*301*
Forever—Marvelettes (63)	93
Please Mr. Postman—Gentle Persuasion (83)	*45*
Like Columbus Did—Reflections (64)	30
Please Mr. Postman—Beatles (64)	*6.4*
Leigh GORMAN ▶ 9840 (1)	**16**
Do You Wanna Hold Me?—Bow Wow Wow (83)	81
Vinny GORMANN ▶ 4954 (2)	**374**
Happy—Sunshine Company (67)	*557*
Happy—Blades Of Grass (67)	*191*
Eydie GORME [Eydie Gormé, Edith Gormezano] ▶ 11077 (1)	**3.4**
Can't Get Over (The Bossa Nova)—Eydie Gorme (64)	10
—Edith Gormezano see: Eydie GORME	
Stuart GORRELL ▶ 1771 (4)	**2343**
Georgia On My Mind—Ray Charles (60)	*4142*
Georgia On My Mind—Michael Bolton (90)	*390*
Georgia On My Mind—Righteous Brothers (66)	*112*
Georgia On My Mind—Willie Nelson (78)	*41*
Alan GORRIE ▶ 2521 (4)	**1421**
Pick Up The Pieces—AWB (74)	5059
Cut The Cake—AWB (75)	1651
School Boy Crush—AWB (75)	485
Let's Go 'Round Again—Average White Band (80)	222
Bobby GOSH ▶ 1982 (1)	**2035**
A Little Bit More—Dr. Hook (76)	2035
Larry GOSHORN ▶ 9644 (1)	**20**
Two Lane Highway—Pure Prairie League (75)	20
—Bernhard Gössling see: Bernhard LLOYD	
Dick GOSTING [Richard St. John Gosting, Dick St. John] ▶ 740 (7)	**5931**
The Mountain's High—Dick And Deedee (61)	*3809*
Tell Me—Dick And Deedee (62)	967
Young And In Love—Dick And Deedee (63)	882
Yellow Balloon—Yellow Balloon (67)	647
Be My Baby—Dick And Deedee (65)	32
The Mountain's High—Four Preps (62)	*24*
Where Did The Good Times Go—Dick And Deedee (63)	3.6
Richard GOTTEHRER ▶ 1041 (24)	**4231**
My Boyfriend's Back—Angels (63)	*8148*
I Want Candy—Strangeloves (65)	*1629*
Night Time—Strangeloves (66)	764
Cara-Lin—Strangeloves (65)	565
Wow Wow Wee (He's The Boy For Me)—Angels (64)	394
Ten Lonely Guys—Pat Boone (62)	*317*
Let's Stomp—Bobby Comstock (63)	288
(You Make Me Feel) So Good—McCoys (66)	259
Giving Up On Love—Jerry Butler (64)	257
Patty Baby—Freddy Cannon (63)	242
I Want Candy—Bow Wow Wow (82)	*177*

What's Gonna Happen When Summer's Done—Freddy Cannon (62)	143
Beat The Clock—McCoys (67)	128
What Time Is It?—Jive Five (62)	103
Ten Lonely Guys—Ten Broken Hearts (62)	*81*
Out In The Sun (Hey-O)—Beach Nuts (65)	63
Sorrow—David Bowie (73)	53
Money Music—Boys In The Band (70)	25
Thank You And Goodnight—Angels (63)	21
A Letter From Betty—Bobby Vee (63)	11
I'm On Fire—Jerry Lee Lewis (64)	2.7
I'm Tossin' And Turnin' Again—Bobby Lewis (62)	1.3
Your Boyfriend's Back—Bobby Comstock & The Counts (63)	*0.4*
Broadway—Freddy Cannon (62)	0.4
Larry GOTTLIEB ▶ 3409 (4)	**859**
When She Was My Girl—Four Tops (81)	1578
Hands Across America—Voices Of America (86)	108
Voo Doo—Rachel Sweet (83)	43
Sad Hearts—Four Tops (82)	38
—Seymour Gottlieb see: Cy CRANE	
Stephan GOTTWALD ▶ 6824 (2)	**134**
Holiday—Other Ones (87)	545
We Are What We Are—Other Ones (87)	261
Barry GOUDREAU ▶ 6195 (2)	**195**
Face The Music—RTZ (91)	271
So You Ran—Orion The Hunter (84)	118
Billy GOULD ▶ 5308 (2)	**309**
Epic—Faith No More (90)	1519
Falling To Pieces—Faith No More (90)	27
Boon GOULD [Rowland Charles Gould] ▶ 3739 (2)	**715**
Something About You—Level 42 (86)	1857
Lessons In Love—Level 42 (87)	1029
Phil GOULD ▶ 4859 (3)	**397**
Something About You—Level 42 (86)	1857
Hot Water—Level 42 (86)	48
Running In The Family—Level 42 (87)	42
—Ronald Gould see: Ronald Norman MILLER	
—Rowland Charles Gould see: Boon GOULD	
Roy GOULD ▶ 7764 (2)	**76**
I'd Never Forgive Myself—Kitty Kallen (55)	*228*
I'd Never Forgive Myself—Jerry Martin (54)	*0.0*
Steve GOULD ▶ 10083 (3)	**13**
Sympathy—Rare Bird (70)	39
High School Nights—Dave Edmunds (85)	8.0
Birdman Part One (Title No. 1 Again)—Rare Bird (73)	2.8
Graham GOULDMAN ▶ 162 (21) HOF	**18502**
I'm Not In Love—10cc (75)	*4276*
Bus Stop—Hollies (66)	3402
Listen People—Herman's Hermits (66)	3334
The Things We Do For Love—10CC (77)	3173
For Your Love—Yardbirds (65)	2568
Heart Full Of Soul—Yardbirds (65)	1853
I'm Not In Love—Will To Power (90)	*1398*
East West—Herman's Hermits (66)	1015
No Milk Today—Herman's Hermits (67)	709
Look Through Any Window—Hollies (65)	672
Right Between The Eyes—Wax (86)	380
Dreadlock Holiday—10 CC (78)	364
Rubber Bullets—10 C. C. (73)	322
People In Love—10cc (77)	124
Sausalito (Is The Place to Go)—Ohio Express (69)	122
Good Morning Judge—10CC (77)	119
Art For Art's Sake—10CC (75)	88
For You And I—10cc (79)	60
I'm Mandy Fly Me—10cc (76)	55
Behind The Door—Cher (66)	41
The Wall Street Shuffle—10 C. C. (74)	11
Dale GOULETT ▶ 9994 (1)	**14**
Victory Line—Limited Warranty (86)	71
Charles GOUNOD ▶ 11282 (1)	**2.5**
Dawning—Winifred Atwell (58)	2.5
August GOUPIL ▶ 7805 (1)	**74**
My Tani—Brothers Four (60)	223
—John Fred Gourrier see: John FRED	
—Jerry Grace see: Jerry GRAZIANO	
Rocke GRACE ▶ 5368 (1)	**299**
Rocky Mountain Way—Joe Walsh (73)	1195
Don GRADY [Don Louis Agrati] ▶ 9908 (1)	**15**
Good Feelin' Time—Yellow Balloon (67)	30

Dora GRAF ▶ 6727 (1)	**142**
Blue Water Line—Brothers Four (62)	284
Thomas GRAF ▶ 7322 (1)	**102**
Yes—Merry Clayton (88)	306
George GRAFF Jr. ▶ 10873 (1)	**4.7**
When Irish Eyes Are Smiling—Bruce Hayes with Mary Mayo (60)	14
Jonny GRAFF ▶ 10866 (1)	**4.8**
Song Of The Barefoot Mailman—Billy Leach (57)	9.5
Jake GRAFFAGNINO ▶ 3459 (1)	**838**
Stop And Think It Over—Dale & Grace (64)	1676
Ray GRAFFIA ▶ 5066 (5)	**350**
Love You So Much—New Colony Six (67)	340
Can't You See Me Cry—New Colony Six (68)	322
I Confess—New Colony Six (66)	148
I Lie Awake—New Colony Six (66)	2.9
You're Gonna Be Mine—New Colony Six (67)	2.8
Alan Nicholas GRAHAM ▶ 1988 (2)	**2030**
The Flame—Cheap Trick (88)	3887
Remember My Name—House Of Lords (90)	174
Charles GRAHAM [Charles Graham Peate] ▶ 8211 (1)	**58**
Brand New Love Affair—Jigsaw (76)	117
Irvin GRAHAM ▶ 6373 (3)	**177**
I Believe—Bachelors (64)	*702*
I Believe—Roy Hamilton (55)	*5.6*
I Believe—Elvis Presley (57)	*2.1*
Larry GRAHAM ▶ 3161 (5)	**978**
Your Love—Graham Central Station (75)	483
Can You Handle It?—Graham Central Station (74)	278
The Jam—Graham Central Station (76)	114
Just Be My Lady—Larry Graham (81)	94
It's Alright—Graham Central Station (75)	9.4
Leo GRAHAM ▶ 1481 (11)	**2929**
Shining Star—Manhattans (80)	3368
Give It Up (Turn It Loose)—Tyrone Davis (76)	560
There It Is—Tyrone Davis (73)	416
Could I Forget You—Tyrone Davis (71)	305
Without You In My Life—Tyrone Davis (73)	300
I Wish It Was Me—Tyrone Davis (74)	165
Turning Point—Tyrone Davis (75)	98
This I Swear—Tyrone Davis (77)	24
Get On Up—Tyrone Davis (78)	13
What Goes Up (Must Come Down)—Tyrone Davis (74)	7.9
I'll Never Find Another (Find Another Like You)—Manhattans (80)	7.4
Nicky GRAHAM ▶ 10322 (1)	**10**
When Will I Be Famous—Bros (88)	20
Roger GRAHAM ▶ 5908 (1)	**231**
I Ain't Got Nobody—David Lee Roth (85)	461
Willis S. GRAHAM ▶ 4850 (1)	**399**
Morning—Jim Ed Brown (70)	399
David GRAHAME ▶ 1604 (1)	**2639**
To Be With You—Mr. Big (91)	5278
Gary GRAINGER ▶ 2695 (4)	**1267**
Passion—Rod Stewart (80)	2748
Ain't Love A Bitch—Rod Stewart (79)	745
I Was Only Joking—Rod Stewart (78)	675
Somebody Special—Rod Stewart (81)	44
Leonard GRAINGER ▶ 8538 (1)	**47**
Baby I Do Love You—Galens (63)	141
Michelle GRAINGER ▶ 2843 (3)	**1156**
Black Is Black—Los Bravos (66)	*3466*
Clock—Eddie Rambeau (66)	2.8
Black Is Black—Tight Fit (81)	*0.9*
Lou GRAMM [Louis A. Grammatico] ▶ 242 (19) HOF	**14198**
Waiting For A Girl Like You—Foreigner (81)	8009
Hot Blooded—Foreigner (78)	3751
Double Vision—Foreigner (78)	2677
Cold As Ice—Foreigner (77)	2348
Just Between You And Me—Lou Gramm (89)	2059
Say You Will—Foreigner (87)	1610
Midnight Blue—Lou Gramm (87)	1532
That Was Yesterday—Foreigner (85)	1231
Head Games—Foreigner (79)	1218
Dirty White Boy—Foreigner (79)	979
Blue Morning, Blue Day—Foreigner (78)	838

Lou GRAMM [Louis A. Grammatico] ▶ 242 (19) HOF *Continued*	**14198**
Long, Long Way From Home—Foreigner (77)	679
Juke Box Hero—Foreigner (82)	447
True Blue Love—Lou Gramm (90)	351
Ready Or Not—Lou Gramm (87)	229
Reaction To Action—Foreigner (85)	214
Heart Turns To Stone—Foreigner (88)	209
Down On Love—Foreigner (85)	198
Luanne—Foreigner (82)	44
Gerry GRANAHAN [Dicky Doo, Jerry Grant, Gary Williams] ▶ 4006 (7)	**624**
No Chemise Please—Gerry Granahan (58)	872
Click Clack—Dicky Doo And The Don'ts (58)	*536*
Leave Me Alone (Let Me Cry)—Dicky Doo And The Don'ts (58)	257
Tell Me Mamma—Christine Quaite (64)	88
Teardrops Will Fall—Dicky Doo And The Don'ts (59)	66
I Can't Take It—Mary Ann Fisher (61)	14
Click Clack—Boyd Bennett & His Rockets (58)	*0.0*
Rocco GRANATA ▶ 2045 (5)	**1954**
Marina—Rocco Granata and the International Quintet (59)	*1249*
Marina—Willy Alberti (59)	*673*
Marina—Jacky Noguez and His Orchestra (59)	*32*
Marina—Joe Vina (59)	*0.0*
Marina—Tony Martin (59)	*0.0*
Johnny GRANDE ▶ 6547 (2)	**158**
Birth Of The Boogie—Bill Haley And His Comets (55)	432
Lean Jean—Bill Haley And His Comets (58)	58
Ron GRANIER ▶ 9635 (1)	**20**
Doctorin' The Tardis—Timelords (88)	159
—Carmine Granito see: Ron DANTE	
Amy GRANT ▶ 827 (6)	**5330**
Baby Baby—Amy Grant (91)	4588
Every Heartbeat—Amy Grant (91)	3631
That's What Love Is For—Amy Grant (91)	2600
Place In This World—Michael W. Smith (91)	2042
Find A Way—Amy Grant (85)	555
Lead Me On—Amy Grant (88)	2.7
Bill GRANT ▶ 10591 (1)	**7.0**
Yes Siree!!—Earl Grant (63)	21
Cornelius GRANT ▶ 1574 (7)	**2686**
You're My Everything—Temptations (67)	2625
(I Know) I'm Losing You—Rare Earth (70)	*2495*
(I Know) I'm Losing You—Temptations (66)	*1880*
(I Know) I'm Losing You—Rod Stewart With Faces (71)	*942*
(I Know) I'm Losing You—Uptown (86)	*55*
You've Got To Earn It—Staple Singers (71)	39
Take Me In Your Arms And Love Me—Gladys Knight & The Pips (67)	2.9
David GRANT ▶ 6440 (1)	**169**
One Step Closer To You—Gavin Christopher (86)	674
Earl GRANT ▶ 4481 (2)	**484**
Swingin' Gently—Earl Grant (62)	477
Yes Siree!!—Earl Grant (63)	21
Eddy GRANT ▶ 549 (5)	**7826**
Electric Avenue—Eddy Grant (83)	6142
Baby, Come Back—Equals (68)	771
Romancing The Stone—Eddy Grant (84)	702
I Don't Wanna Dance—Eddy Grant (83)	206
Softly Softly—Equals (68)	6.8
Fred GRANT ▶ 10114 (1)	**13**
Golly—Four Lads (57)	50
Gerald Frederick GRANT ▶ 6155 (2)	**199**
Ring A Ling A Lario—Jimmie Rodgers (59)	492
Mystery Of You—Platters (57)	70
Harold GRANT [Harold Kirchstein] ▶ 11803 (1)	**0.0**
Here—Tony Martin (54)	0.0
James GRANT ▶ 7394 (1)	**99**
Stop To Start—Blue Magic (74)	197
James (2) GRANT ▶ 7601 (1)	**86**
Halleluiah Man—Love and Money (89)	86
Janie GRANT ▶ 3222 (2)	**942**
Triangle—Janie Grant (61)	916
Romeo—Janie Grant (61)	26
—Jerry Grant see: Gerry GRANAHAN	
—Mark Grant see: Milton GRANT	

Mickie GRANT ▶ 767 (1)	**5720**
Pink Shoe Laces—Dodie Stevens (59)	5720
Milton GRANT [Mark Cooper, Mark Grant] ▶ 3242 (4)	**931**
Rumble—Link Wray & His Ray Men (58)	*1033*
Raw Hide—Link Wray & His Ray Men (59)	629
Jack The Ripper—Link Wray & His Ray Men (63)	191
Rumble—Jack Nitzsche (63)	*9.0*
—Neil Grant see: Iain MacFADYEN	
Patrick GRANT ▶ 3129 (3)	**994**
Supernatural Thing - Part I—Ben E. King (75)	1882
Do It In The Name Of Love—Ben E. King (75)	96
Love Don't You Go Through No Changes On Me—Sister Sledge (75)	10
Rodgers GRANT ▶ 5291 (2)	**312**
Yeh, Yeh—Georgie Fame And The Blue Flames (65)	*931*
Yeh-Yeh!—Mongo Santamaria Orch. (63)	*3.9*
Guenter GRASMUCK ▶ 7239 (1)	**108**
Live Is Life—Opus (86)	541
—Sandy Grassi see: Sandy PALMER	
Richie GRASSO ▶ 2708 (5)	**1259**
Sweet Cherry Wine—Tommy James And The Shondells (69)	2151
I Can Remember—James & Bobby Purify (68)	*283*
Do Unto Me—James & Bobby Purify (68)	251
I Can Remember—Oliver (70)	*7.7*
Fill My Soul—Pop Explosion (68)	5.8
Keith GRAVENHORST ▶ 10868 (1)	**4.8**
Don't You Know—Keith Everett (66)	4.8
James GRAVES ▶ 6812 (1)	**135**
Shoot Your Shot—Jr. Walker & The All Stars (67)	405
Bruce GRAY ▶ 7032 (1)	**121**
He's A Friend—Eddie Kendricks (76)	362
Charles GRAY ▶ 8378 (1)	**52**
Mexican Radio—Wall Of Voodoo (83)	209
Chauncey GRAY ▶ 7043 (1)	**120**
Bye Bye Blues—Bert Kaempfert And His Orchestra (66)	479
Ed GRAY [Eddie Gray, Edward James Zgorecki] ▶ 1807 (2)	**2285**
Crystal Blue Persuasion—Tommy James And The Shondells (69)	6717
On A Sunday Afternoon—A Lighter Shade Of Brown (91)	320
Jerry GRAY [Generoso Graziano] ▶ 8250 (2)	**57**
String of Pearls—Larry Elgart And His Manhattan Swing Orchestra (82)	50
Pennsylvania 6-5000—Frank Barber Orchestra (82)	14
—John Gray see: John Grayton DOLPHIN	
Jonathan GRAY ▶ 8398 (1)	**52**
I Don't Love You Anymore—London Quireboys (90)	104
—Juliet Gray see: Lyn COLLINS	
Mark Eugene GRAY ▶ 3534 (4)	**796**
Take Me Down—Alabama (82)	910
Nice Girls—Melissa Manchester (83)	399
The Closer You Get—Alabama (83)	381
Til You And Your Lover Are Lovers Again—Engelbert Humperdinck (83)	35
Paul GRAY ▶ 4640 (2)	**446**
Sugar Free—Wa Wa Nee (87)	438
Stimulation—Wa Wa Nee (88)	7.9
Thomas GRAY ▶ 4423 (1)	**497**
Money Changes Everything—Cyndi Lauper (84)	497
Tony GRAY ▶ 7078 (1)	**117**
I'll Love You Forever—Holidays (66)	352
Von GRAY [Yvonne Gray] ▶ 4721 (1)	**431**
Lady Love—Lou Rawls (77)	863
Wayne GRAY ▶ 2573 (2)	**1366**
Cradle Of Love—Johnny Preston (60)	*2731*
Cradle Of Love—Ronnie & Robyn (66)	*0.5*
—Yvonne Gray see: Von GRAY	
Jay GRAYDON ▶ 1382 (12)	**3214**
After The Love Has Gone—Earth, Wind & Fire (79)	3559
Turn Your Love Around—George Benson (81)	2450
Who's Holding Donna Now—DeBarge (85)	1361
Mornin'—Jarreau (83)	668
Too Young—Jack Wagner (85)	340
Breakin' Away—Al Jarreau (81)	332
Friends In Love—Dionne Warwick And Johnny Mathis (82)	322
Twilight Zone—Manhattan Transfer (80)	258

Trouble In Paradise—Al Jarreau (83)	87
After All—Al Jarreau (84)	83
Lady Of My Heart—Jack Wagner (85)	77
Someone—El DeBarge (86)	63
Miles GRAYSON ▶ 5718 (2)	**251**
Everybody Knows About My Good Thing (Pt. 1)—Little Johnny Taylor (71)	350
Don't Make Me Pay For His Mistakes—Z.Z. Hill (71)	152
—Generoso Graziano see: Jerry GRAY	
Jerry GRAZIANO [Jerry Grace] ▶ 10886 (1)	**4.7**
No Rock 'N Roll Tonight—Dorothy Collins (56)	4.7
Charles GREAN ▶ 2137 (7)	**1828**
He'll Have To Stay—Jeanne Black (60)	*3119*
I Dreamed—Betty Johnson (56)	1476
Hoopa Hoola—Betty Johnson (58)	75
1492—Betty Johnson (57)	21
Hootenanny Granny—Jim Lowe (63)	8.7
You Can't Get To Heaven On Roller Skates—Betty Johnson (59)	*5.0*
He'll Have To Stay—Corina Minette (60)	*0.0*
Dennis GREAVES ▶ 7471 (1)	**93**
Weapons Of Love—Truth (87)	187
R.B. GREAVES ▶ 970 (1)	**4621**
Take A Letter Maria—R.B. Greaves (69)	4621
Martin GREBB ▶ 5079 (2)	**347**
Back In Love Again—Buckinghams (68)	286
What A Wonderful Thing We Have—Fabulous Rhinestones (72)	122
Rick GRECH ▶ 11271 (1)	**2.5**
Rock & Roll Stew (Part 1)—Traffic (72)	5.1
Buddy GRECO ▶ 9296 (1)	**27**
Sempre Amore—Don Cornell (59)	27
Joey GRECO ▶ 8193 (1)	**59**
You're So Easy To Love—Tommy James (81)	118
Peter GRECO ▶ 10744 (1)	**5.6**
Tiger In The Tank—Chariots (65)	17
—Robert Greco see: Bobby GREGG	
Paul GREEDUS ▶ 7084 (2)	**117**
I Eat Cannibals—Total Coelo (83)	141
My Love Is Music—Space (79)	139
John GREEK ▶ 5005 (3)	**360**
Tall Cool One—Wailers (59)	*532*
Tall Cool One—Wailers (64)	*507*
Mau-Mau—Wailers (59)	40
Adolph GREEN ▶ 5431 (11) HOF	**290**
Just In Time—Tony Bennett with Percy Faith and His Orchestra (56)	*374*
Dance Only With Me—Perry Como (58)	150
Now!—Lena Horne (63)	110
The Party's Over—Doris Day (56)	*92*
Just In Time—Dean Martin (60)	*71*
Make Someone Happy—Perry Como (60)	57
Bells Are Ringing—Jo Stafford (56)	*8.2*
Bells Are Ringing—Jeri Southern (56)	*8.2*
Just In Time—Jeri Southern (56)	*0.0*
The Party's Over—Carmen McRae (57)	*0.0*
The Party's Over—Lurlean Hunter (57)	*0.0*
Al GREEN [Albert L. Greene] ▶ 178 (22) HOF	**17102**
Let's Stay Together—Al Green (71)	*7842*
I'm Still In Love With You—Al Green (72)	5102
You Ought To Be With Me—Al Green (72)	4701
Look What You Done For Me—Al Green (72)	3798
Tired Of Being Alone—Al Green (71)	2646
Sha-La-La (Make Me Happy)—Al Green (74)	2141
Here I Am (Come And Take Me)—Al Green (73)	*1801*
Here I Am (Come And Take Me)—UB40 (91)	*1696*
Call Me (Come Back Home)—Al Green (73)	1660
L-O-V-E (Love)—Al Green (75)	1223
Livin' For You—Al Green (73)	1004
Let's Stay Together—Tina Turner (84)	*755*
Take Me To The River—Talking Heads (78)	*717*
Let's Get Married—Al Green (74)	597
Full Of Fire—Al Green (75)	526
Keep Me Cryin'—Al Green (76)	395
Let's Stay Together—Isaac Hayes (72)	*340*
Oh Me, Oh My (Dreams In My Arms)—Al Green (75)	208
Take Me To The River—Syl Johnson (75)	*193*
Love And Happiness—Earnest Jackson (73)	125
Belle—Al Green (77)	80
God Bless Our Love—Charles Brimmer (75)	19
—Alan Green see: Arian DAY	

Albert GREEN ► 10058 (2)	**13**
Jim Dandy Got Married—LaVern Baker (57)	39
You Tickle Me Baby—Royal Jokers (55)	7.0
—Barry Ian Green see: Barry BLUE	
Bernard GREEN ► 11251 (1)	**2.6**
Tower Trot (And Then You Do That Step)— Dick Jacobs And His Chorus And Orchestra (57)	23
Bud GREEN ► 3031 (11) HOF	**1054**
Once In Awhile—Chimes (60)	*1239*
I Love My Baby (My Baby Loves Me)—Jill Corey (56)	*752*
Alabamy Bound—Les Paul and Mary Ford (55)	*84*
I'll Always Be In Love With You— Jack Pleis and His Orchestra and Chorus (56)	*79*
Day After Day—Bill Cecere (58)	5.2
Once In A While—Modernaires (57)	*1.9*
Once In A While—Clyde Stacy (58)	*0.4*
Alabamy Bound—Mulcays (55)	*0.0*
I'll Always Be In Love With You—Stroll Kings (58)	*0.0*
I'll Always Be In Love With You—Rosemary June (58)	*0.0*
I Love My Baby (My Baby Loves Me)— Benny Strong & His Orchestra (57)	*0.0*
—Earl Green see: Earl GREENE	
Edward GREEN ► 7689 (1)	**80**
Good Man Is Hard To Find—Teresa Brewer (55)	80
Edward Prince GREEN ► 10843 (1)	**5.0**
Kufanya Mapenzi (Making Love)—Ramsey Lewis (73)	5.0
Florence GREEN [Florence Greenberg] ► 1027 (1)	**4311**
Soldier Boy—Shirelles (62)	8622
Garland GREEN ► 6125 (1)	**202**
Jealous Kind Of Fella—Garland Green (69)	810
George GREEN ► 957 (4)	**4668**
Hurts So Good—John Cougar (82)	6837
Crumblin' Down—John Cougar Mellencamp (83)	1614
So Close—Daryl Hall & John Oates (90)	999
Rain On The Scarecrow— John Cougar Mellencamp (86)	486
George Henry GREEN ► 9265 (1)	**28**
Do Anything You Wanna (Part 1)—Harold Betters (64)	110
Gerald GREEN ► 7539 (1)	**90**
Can'tcha Say (You Believe In Me)—Boston (87)	270
Greg GREEN ► 8801 (1)	**39**
Cutie Pie—One Way (82)	273
Ian Edward GREEN ► 6403 (1)	**175**
A Better Love—Londonbeat (91)	873
Jack GREEN ► 7846 (1)	**72**
Walking In My Sleep—Roger Daltrey (84)	145
Jimmie GREEN ► 7933 (1)	**69**
Hey Shirley (This Is Squirrely)—Shirley & Squirrely (76)	138
Johnny GREEN ► 6921 (4) HOF	**128**
(The Song Of) Raintree County—Nat "King" Cole (57)	154
Coquette—Fats Domino (58)	94
I Want To Be Loved—Dinah Washington (62)	*32*
I Wanna Be Loved—Dean And Jean (64)	*28*
Kathe GREEN ► 6088 (1)	**207**
Love's Got A Line On You—Scandal (83)	414
Leroy GREEN ► 3473 (1)	**827**
Disco Inferno—Trammps (77)	1653
Lillian GREEN ► 10956 (1)	**4.1**
Romance In The Dark—Dinah Washington (63)	4.1
—Mel Green see: Allan ROBERTS	
Perry GREEN ► 11424 (1)	**1.7**
Lollipop (I Like You)—Intruders (69)	6.9
Peter GREEN [Peter Alan Greenbaum] ► 883 (4)	**5037**
Black Magic Woman—Santana (70)	4259
Oh Well—Rockets (79)	*461*
Oh Well - Part I—Fleetwood Mac (70)	*314*
Albatross—Fleetwood Mac (69)	3.3
—Peter Charles Green see: Daniel BOONE	
Phil GREEN ► 7485 (2)	**93**
Say Wonderful Things—Patti Page (63)	*131*
Say Wonderful Things—Ronnie Carroll (63)	*55*
Ronnie GREEN ► 8796 (1)	**39**
It Might Have Been—Joe London (59)	78
Sanford GREEN ► 4182 (2)	**571**
Play Me Hearts And Flowers (I Wanna Cry)— Johnny Desmond (55)	*1143*
Play Me Hearts And Flowers (I Wanna Cry)— Dick Jacobs & His Orchestra (55)	*0.0*
Thomas GREEN ► 8702 (1)	**42**
Girl I Need You—Artistics (67)	127
Tony GREEN [Antonio DeVerdis-Mazzone] ► 3430 (2)	**851**
Come To Me—France Joli (79)	817
Why Leave Us Alone—Five Special (79)	101
Peter John GREENALL [Rupert Greenall] ► 2874 (8)	**1137**
One Thing Leads To Another—Fixx (83)	2676
Saved By Zero—Fixx (83)	900
Are We Ourselves?—Fixx (84)	811
Secret Separation—Fixx (86)	629
The Sign Of Fire—Fixx (83)	523
Driven Out—Fixx (89)	236
Sunshine In The Shade—Fixx (84)	96
Stand Or Fall—Fixx (82)	67
—Rupert Greenall see: Peter John GREENALL	
John GREENAN ► 10293 (1)	**10**
Real Wild Child—Ivan (58)	31
Roger GREENAWAY ► 433 (23) HOF	**9423**
Long Cool Woman (In A Black Dress)—Hollies (72)	5749
You've Got Your Troubles—Fortunes (65)	2028
Green Grass—Gary Lewis And The Playboys (66)	1953
I'd Like To Teach The World To Sing (In Perfect Harmony)—New Seekers (71)	*1791*
Doctor's Orders—Carol Douglas (74)	1742
Here Comes That Rainy Day Feeling Again— Fortunes (71)	1705
My Baby Loves Lovin'—White Plains (70)	1636
Jeans On—David Dundas (76)	1487
I'd Like To Teach The World To Sing (In Perfect Harmony)—Hillside Singers (71)	*1474*
Say You'll Stay Until Tomorrow—Tom Jones (76)	1231
I Was Kaiser Bill's Batman— Whistling Jack Smith (67)	1009
The Way It Used To Be— Engelbert Humperdinck (69)	711
Softly Whispering I Love You— English Congregation (72)	708
Goin' Down (On The Road To L.A.)— Terry Black And Laurel Ward (72)	216
Lovin' You Baby—White Plains (70)	121
It's Like We Never Said Goodbye—Crystal Gayle (80)	118
Melting Pot— Blue Mink Featuring Madeleine Bell (70)	110
One More Chance—Ocean (72)	85
Freedom Comes, Freedom Goes—Fortunes (71)	82
This Golden Ring—Fortunes (66)	59
Good Morning Freedom—Daybreak (70)	52
We Got A Dream—Ocean (71)	44
(Love Me) Love The Life I Lead—Fantastics (72)	40
John GREENBACH ► 9902 (1)	**15**
Sad Tomorrows—Trini Lopez (65)	30
Norman GREENBAUM ► 504 (6)	**8379**
Spirit In The Sky—Norman Greenbaum (70)	*7449*
Canned Ham—Norman Greenbaum (70)	432
The Eggplant That Ate Chicago— Dr. West's Medicine Show And Junk Band (66)	260
Spirit In The Sky—Doctor And The Medics (86)	*221*
California Earthquake—Norman Greenbaum (71)	14
Spirit In The Sky—Dorothy Morrison (70)	*2.9*
—Peter Alan Greenbaum see: Peter GREEN	
Eliot GREENBERG ► 4439 (4)	**494**
Sweet Talkin' Guy—Chiffons (66)	1814
Out Of This World—Chiffons (66)	110
Moulty—Barbarians (66)	41
Stop, Look And Listen—Chiffons (66)	9.3
—Florence Greenberg see: Florence GREEN	
Steve GREENBERG ► 437 (3)	**9395**
Funkytown—Lipps, Inc. (80)	*8061*
Funky Town—Pseudo Echo (87)	*1216*
Rock It—Lipps, Inc. (80)	119
Alan GREENE ► 5843 (1)	**238**
Turn Around—Dick And Deedee (63)	714
—Albert L. Greene see: Al GREEN	
Bernard GREENE ► 9045 (1)	**32**
This Beat Is Hot—B.G. Prince Of Rap (91)	65
Carl GREENE ► 9233 (1)	**28**
Body Talk—Deele (84)	140
Earl GREENE [Earl Green] ► 4915 (1)	**383**
Six Days On The Road—Dave Dudley (63)	765
Hal GREENE ► 7198 (1)	**110**
True True Happiness—Johnny Tillotson (59)	221
Jeanie GREENE [Mary Elizabeth Johnson Lee] ► 11729 (1)	**0.4**
Faithful And True—Z.Z. Hill (71)	1.3
Joe GREENE ► 1633 (3)	**2574**
Outa-Space—Billy Preston (72)	4684
You're So Unique—Billy Preston (73)	405
I Wrote A Simple Song—Billy Preston (72)	59
Joseph Perkins GREENE ► 11080 (1)	**3.3**
Don't Let The Sun Catch You Cryin'— Ray Charles (60)	3.3
Larry GREENE ► 11721 (1)	**0.5**
Image - Part 1—Hank Levine And Orchestra (61)	1.4
Larry Alan GREENE ► 9785 (1)	**17**
Stacy—Fortune (85)	34
Marlin GREENE ► 6690 (2)	**144**
Cover Me—Percy Sledge (67)	287
Faithful And True—Z.Z. Hill (71)	1.3
Mort GREENE ► 7054 (2)	**119**
Weary Blues— McGuire Sisters And Lawrence Welk (56)	355
Sunday Barbecue—Tennessee Ernie Ford (58)	1.4
Sandra GREENE ► 6660 (1)	**146**
Distant Lover—Marvin Gaye (74)	438
Susaye GREENE ► 5596 (1)	**267**
Free—Deniece Williams (76)	1067
Tim GREENE ► 3792 (1)	**697**
Two Of Hearts—Stacey Q (86)	2091
Howard GREENFIELD ► 41 (74) HOF	**45400**
My Heart Has A Mind Of Its Own—Connie Francis (60)	8856
Everybody's Somebody's Fool—Connie Francis (60)	8043
Breaking Up Is Hard To Do—Neil Sedaka (62)	*7494*
Love Will Keep Us Together—Captain & Tennille (75)	*6699*
Where The Boys Are—Connie Francis (61)	4771
Breakin' In A Brand New Broken Heart— Connie Francis (61)	3470
Oh Carol—Neil Sedaka (59)	2955
Foolish Little Girl—Shirelles (63)	2718
Happy Birthday, Sweet Sixteen—Neil Sedaka (61)	2559
Frankie—Connie Francis (59)	2530
It Hurts To Be In Love—Gene Pitney (64)	*2451*
Calendar Girl—Neil Sedaka (60)	2428
Crying In The Rain—Everly Brothers (62)	2402
Next Door To An Angel—Neil Sedaka (62)	2255
Stairway To Heaven—Neil Sedaka (60)	2055
Venus In Blue Jeans—Jimmy Clanton (62)	2008
Breaking Up Is Hard To Do—Neil Sedaka (75)	*1889*
You Never Done It Like That— Captain & Tennille (78)	1801
Little Devil—Neil Sedaka (61)	1797
You Mean Everything To Me—Neil Sedaka (60)	1561
Diary—Neil Sedaka (58)	1436
Stupid Cupid—Connie Francis (58)	1181
Charms—Bobby Vee (63)	1117
Another Sleepless Night—Jimmy Clanton (60)	1057
Puppet Man—Tom Jones (71)	*993*
Alice In Wonderland—Neil Sedaka (63)	979
Rumors—Johnny Crawford (62)	912
Breaking Up Is Hard To Do—Partridge Family Starring Shirley Jones & Featuring David Cassidy (72)	*734*
Puppet Man—5th Dimension (70)	*721*
Breaking Up Is Hard To Do—Lenny Welch (70)	*683*
Your Used To Be—Brenda Lee (63)	676
Run Samson Run—Neil Sedaka (60)	648
Let's Go Steady Again—Neil Sedaka (63)	640
Way Of A Clown—Teddy Randazzo (60)	617
Two Less Lonely People In The World— Air Supply (82)	593
Since You've Been Gone—Clyde McPhatter (59)	582
Bad Girl—Neil Sedaka (63)	575
Rainy Jane—Davy Jones (71)	562
I Waited Too Long—LaVern Baker (59)	546
Fallin'—Connie Francis (58)	525
I Go Ape—Neil Sedaka (59)	439
King Of Clowns—Neil Sedaka (62)	422
Time Waits For No One—Friends Of Distinction (70)	407
Don't Hide Your Love—Cher (72)	370
Breaking Up Is Hard To Do—Happenings (68)	*309*
I Wish I'd Never Been Born—Patti Page (60)	257
What Am I Gonna Do—Jimmy Clanton (61)	251
Amarillo—Neil Sedaka (77)	230

Howard GREENFIELD ▶ 41 (74) HOF *Continued*	**45400**
You Gotta Make Your Own Sunshine—Neil Sedaka (76)	220
Por Amor Viviremos—Captain & Tennille (75)	*204*
Time Marches On—Roy Hamilton (59)	164
We Had A Good Thing Goin'—Cyrkle (67)	162
Don't Read The Letter—Patti Page (60)	123
Sunny—Neil Sedaka (64)	96
I'll Make Him Love Me—Barbara Lewis (67)	89
Breaking Up Is Hard On You (a/k/a Don't Take Ma Bell Away From Me)—American Comedy Network (84)	*82*
One Day Of Your Life—Andy Williams (70)	80
Time Machine—Danté And The Evergreens (60)	65
It Hurts To Be In Love—Dan Hartman (81)	*64*
Darkest Street In Town—Jimmy Clanton (62)	55
Back To School Again—Four Tops (82)	54
Kissin' And Twistin'—Fabian (60)	40
Did You Have A Happy Birthday?—Paul Anka (63)	39
The Hungry Years—Wayne Newton (76)	35
I Was Looking For Someone To Love—Leif Garrett (80)	22
Poor Little Puppet—Cathy Carroll (62)	21
Girls, Girls, Girls—Steve Lawrence (60)	14
Hail To The Conquering Hero—James Darren (62)	14
Breaking Up Is Hard To Do—Heaven Bound with Tony Scotti (72)	*7.9*
Our Last Song Together—Bo Donaldson And The Heywoods (75)	6.4
Crying My Heart Out For You—Neil Sedaka (59)	5.2
Dear Mr. D.J. Play It Again—Tina Robin (61)	2.7
When Somebody Loves You—Frank Sinatra (65)	2.3
What's Come Over This World?—Billy Carr (65)	0.5
Lee GREENLEE ▶ 10853 (2)	**4.9**
Lullabye—Chevrons (60)	8.9
Starlight—Lee Greenlee (59)	3.9
Ellie GREENWICH ▶ 81 (59) HOF	**27087**
Chapel Of Love—Dixie Cups (64)	*8316*
Do Wah Diddy Diddy—Manfred Mann (64)	*8308*
Hanky Panky—Tommy James And The Shondells (66)	6771
Leader Of The Pack—Shangri-Las (64)	*6265*
Be My Baby—Ronettes (63)	*6059*
Da Doo Ron Ron—Shaun Cassidy (77)	*4512*
Da Doo Ron Ron (When He Walked Me Home)—Crystals (63)	*3838*
Baby, I Love You—Andy Kim (69)	*2808*
Then He Kissed Me—Crystals (63)	2734
Take Me Home Tonight—Eddie Money (86)	2098
I Wanna Love Him So Bad—Jelly Beans (64)	1628
People Say—Dixie Cups (64)	1548
Maybe I Know—Lesley Gore (64)	1454
River Deep-Mountain High—Supremes & Four Tops (70)	*1281*
Be My Baby—Andy Kim (70)	*1212*
The Kind Of Boy You Can't Forget—Raindrops (63)	1132
I Can Hear Music—Beach Boys (69)	*916*
Look Of Love—Lesley Gore (64)	848
Baby, I Love You—Ronettes (63)	*719*
Wait 'til My Bobby Gets Home—Darlene Love (63)	657
I Have A Boyfriend—Chiffons (63)	647
Why Do Lovers Break Each Other's Heart?—Bob B. Soxx And The Blue Jeans (63)	584
Give Us Your Blessings—Shangri-Las (65)	*554*
What A Guy—Raindrops (63)	549
Don't Ever Leave Me—Connie Francis (64)	442
(Today I Met) The Boy I'm Gonna Marry—Darlene Love (63)	432
River Deep-Mountain High—Deep Purple (69)	*351*
Good Night Baby—Butterflys (64)	321
Baby Be Mine—Jelly Beans (64)	308
Leader Of The Pack—Twisted Sister (85)	*289*
Little Bell—Dixie Cups (64)	276
You Should Have Seen The Way He Looked At Me—Dixie Cups (64)	270
He's Got The Power—Exciters (63)	261
That Boy John—Raindrops (63)	228
A Fine Fine Boy—Darlene Love (63)	184
Out In The Streets—Shangri-Las (65)	175
Not Too Young To Get Married—Bob B. Soxx And The Blue Jeans (63)	171
Give Us Your Blessing—Ray Peterson (63)	*149*
I'll Take You Where The Music's Playing—Drifters (65)	146
Do-Wah-Diddy—Exciters (64)	*55*

This Is It—Jay & The Americans (62)	29
Be My Baby—Cissy Houston (71)	*24*
River Deep-Mountain High—Ike & Tina Turner (66)	*23*
Little Boy—Crystals (64)	22
All Grown Up—Crystals (64)	14
Do Wah Diddy Diddy—Stars On 45 (81)	*12*
Da Doo Ron Ron (When He Walked Me Home)—Ian Matthews (72)	*7.8*
Keep It Confidential—Nona Hendryx (83)	7.6
I Wonder—Butterflys (65)	7.3
I Don't Wanna Be Left Outside—Ellie Greenwich (70)	7.2
I Can Hear Music—Ronettes Featuring Veronica (66)	*5.6*
One Boy Too Late—Mike Clifford (63)	5.2
Hickory Dickery Dock—Baby Jane And The Rock-A-Byes (63)	3.2
River Deep-Mountain High—Ike & Tina Turner (69)	*3.1*
When The Boy's Happy (The Girl's Happy Too)—Four Pennies (63)	2.7
One More Tear—Raindrops (64)	1.9
Doo Wah Diddy Diddy—Tight Fit (81)	*0.9*
He Ain't No Angel—Ad Libs (65)	0.5
Chapel Of Love—Bette Midler (73)	*0.0*
Al GREENWOOD ▶ 9948 (1)	**15**
Don't Run My Life—Spys (82)	73
Lee GREENWOOD ▶ 5126 (1)	**338**
A Love Song—Kenny Rogers (82)	338
Dan GREER ▶ 11373 (1)	**2.0**
I'm A Fool For You—James Carr (67)	10
—David Greer see: Harold FIELDS	
—David Greer see: Joseph RONCORONI	
George Daniel GREER ▶ 3567 (2)	**784**
Let Me Love You Tonight—Pure Prairie League (80)	1568
Still Right Here In My Heart—Pure Prairie League (81)	523
Ken GREER ▶ 7677 (1)	**81**
White Hot—Red Rider (80)	163
Bobby GREGG [Robert Greco] ▶ 4071 (2)	**605**
The Jam Part 1—Bobby Gregg And His Friends (62)	592
Potato Peeler—Bobby Gregg And His Friends (62)	12
—Gregorian see: Frank PETERSON	
C. Delyle GREGORY [Delyle Gregory Carmichael, Greg Carmichael] ▶ 3197 (1)	**956**
Touch Me (All Night Long)—Cathy Dennis (91)	2867
Glenn GREGORY ▶ 10038 (1)	**14**
Let Me Go—Heaven 17 (83)	41
Mickey GREGORY ▶ 8452 (1)	**50**
School Of Life—Tommy Tate (72)	100
Miles GREGORY ▶ 3696 (2)	**732**
Love Don't Live Here Anymore—Rose Royce (78)	729
Theme From S-Express—S-Express (88)	14
Dermot GREHAN ▶ 4351 (3)	**515**
What Does It Take—Honeymoon Suite (86)	387
New Girl Now—Honeymoon Suite (84)	122
Love Changes Everything—Honeymoon Suite (88)	16
Alvin GREINER ▶ 7634 (1)	**84**
Donde Esta Santa Claus? (Where Is Santa Claus?)—Augie Rios (58)	251
Edwin GREINES [Edwin Greines Cohen] ▶ 5280 (3)	**314**
Mr Success—Frank Sinatra (58)	704
Someone, Someone—Brian Poole & The Tremeloes (64)	153
Compromise—McGuire Sisters (59)	4.8
Maria GREVER [Maria Joaquia de la Portilla Torres] ▶ 1601 (4)	**2643**
What A Diff'rence A Day Makes—Dinah Washington (59)	*4151*
What A Diff'rence A Day Makes—Esther Phillips (75)	*1007*
What A Diff'rence A Day Made—Jerry Martin (55)	*128*
What A Diff'rence A Day Made—Vaughn Monroe & His Orchestra (55)	*0.0*
Clifford GREY ▶ 10184 (1)	**11**
Got A Date With An Angel—Billy Williams (57)	46
Joe GREY ▶ 10911 (1)	**4.4**
Runnin' Wild—Les Paul and Mary Ford (56)	13
Paris GREY [Shanna V. Jackson] ▶ 8686 (1)	**43**
Good Life—Inner City (89)	128
Robbie GREY ▶ 8740 (3)	**41**
I Melt With You—Modern English (90)	*107*
I Melt With You—Modern English (83)	*88*

Hands Across The Sea—Modern English (84)	8.5
Zane GREY ▶ 2615 (3)	**1323**
(Every Time I Turn Around) Back In Love Again—L.T.D. (77)	2620
Dancin'—Grey and Hanks (79)	16
Never Had A Love Like This Before—Tavares (79)	15
Pat GRIBBEN ▶ 9976 (1)	**14**
Broken Land—Adventures (88)	14
Merrill GRIDLEY ▶ 10297 (3)	**10**
Red Head—Cloverleafs (55)	*7.9*
Red Head—Cliff Steward And His Boro Lounge Boys (55)	*7.9*
Red Head—Somethin' Smith & The Redheads (56)	*4.9*
Edvard GRIEG ▶ 2935 (2)	**1112**
Asia Minor—Kokomo (61)	1962
Piano Concerto In A Minor—Royal Philharmonic Orchestra (81)	131
Robert GRIENER ▶ 10609 (1)	**6.8**
I'll Be Good—Joe Valino (57)	21
Jimmie GRIER ▶ 6479 (3)	**165**
What's The Reason I'm Not Pleasing You—Fats Domino (56)	*415*
What's The Reason—Bobby Edwards (62)	*225*
The Object Of My Affection—Pee Wee Hunt & His Orchestra (56)	15
Ronald GRIER ▶ 9833 (1)	**16**
Aunt Dora's Love Soul Shack—Arthur Conley (68)	65
Dick GRIFFEY ▶ 8749 (1)	**40**
Soul Train "75"—Soul Train Gang (75)	81
Barbara GRIFFIN ▶ 8703 (1)	**42**
Girl I Need You—Artistics (67)	127
Billy GRIFFIN ▶ 1605 (1)	**2637**
Love Machine (Part 1)—Miracles (75)	5274
Curly GRIFFIN [Curley Griffin, Howard Griffin] ▶ 6999 (1)	**123**
Boppin' The Blues—Carl Perkins (56)	246
Gene GRIFFIN ▶ 1551 (6)	**2736**
My Prerogative—Bobby Brown (88)	4142
Just Got Paid—Johnny Kemp (88)	1198
My Fantasy—Teddy Riley featuring Guy (89)	71
I Like—Guy (89)	56
Right And Hype—Abstrac' (89)	22
Don't Take My Mind On A Trip—Boy George (89)	17
—Howard Griffin see: Curly GRIFFIN	
James GRIFFIN [Arthur James] ▶ 2570 (6)	**1370**
For All We Know—Carpenters (71)	3454
Apologize—Ed Ames (68)	201
Main Street—Gary Lewis And The Playboys (68)	105
Brink Of Disaster—Lesley Gore (67)	64
Love Machine—Roosters (68)	57
Get The Message—Brian Hyland (67)	9.7
Jimmy GRIFFIN ▶ 9215 (1)	**28**
If I Say—Kingofthehill (91)	57
Ken GRIFFIN ▶ 8352 (3)	**54**
You Can't Be True Dear—Mary Kaye Trio (59)	*189*
You Can't Be True, Dear—Patti Page (65)	*25*
You Can't Be True Dear—Steve Lawrence & Eydie Gorme (59)	*0.0*
Leroy GRIFFIN ▶ 3122 (4)	**997**
Story Untold—Crew-Cuts (55)	*873*
A Story Untold—Emotions (63)	*124*
Story Untold—Nutmegs (55)	*0.0*
Story Untold—Four Coins (55)	*0.0*
Mel GRIFFIN ▶ 9069 (1)	**32**
Love Is Better In The A.M. (Part 1)—Johnnie Taylor (77)	96
Paul GRIFFIN ▶ 7338 (2)	**101**
You Can Run (But You Can't Hide)—Jerry Butler (62)	129
The Fez—Steely Dan (76)	109
Reggie GRIFFIN ▶ 10723 (1)	**5.9**
Beat Street Breakdown Part I—Grandmaster Melle Mel & the Furious Five With Mr. Ness & Cowboy (84)	12
Richard GRIFFIN ▶ 10238 (1)	**11**
If You Think You're Lonely Now—Bobby Womack (81)	44
Sylvia GRIFFIN ▶ 11190 (1)	**2.8**
Maybe This Day—Kissing The Pink (83)	20
Tommy GRIFFIN ▶ 6735 (1)	**142**
Blue Tomorrow—Billy Vaughn And His Orchestra (61)	283
Trevor GRIFFIN ▶ 3114 (1)	**1003**
Love Is Like Oxygen—Sweet (78)	2006

William GRIFFIN [William Michael Griffin Jr., Rakim] ▶ 5146 (1)	**334**
Friends—Jody Watley (89)	1337
Herman GRIFFITH ▶ 11117 (1)	**3.2**
Can I—Eddie Kendricks (71)	6.3
John GRIFFITH ▶ 8251 (1)	**57**
China—Red Rockers (83)	227
Andrei GRIGORIEV ▶ 10362 (1)	**9.5**
Try To Find Me—Gorky Park (90)	28
Rob GRILL ▶ 7074 (1)	**118**
Come On And Say It—Grass Roots (70)	353
Howard GRIMES ▶ 10074 (1)	**13**
30-60-90—Willie Mitchell (69)	66
Steve GRIMES ▶ 5514 (1)	**275**
Groovy Train—Farm (91)	551
John GRISBY ▶ 5224 (1)	**323**
That's The Way I Feel About Cha—(The Preacher) Bobby Womack (& Peace) (71)	969
Steve GRISHAM ▶ 7833 (1)	**73**
Keeping Our Love Alive—Henry Paul Band (81)	218
—William Edward Grishaw see: Zeb TURNER	
Jeffrey Warren GROB [Joe Dube] ▶ 6858 (4)	**132**
Cherry Baby—Starz (77)	510
Sing It, Shout It—Starz (77)	148
Hold On To The Night—Starz (78)	18
(She's Just A) Fallen Angel—Starz (76)	6.5
Larry GROCE ▶ 2791 (1)	**1193**
Junk Food Junkie—Larry Groce (76)	1193
Matt GROENING ▶ 8448 (1)	**50**
Deep, Deep Trouble—Simpsons (91)	100
Ferde GROFE ▶ 11036 (1) HOF	**3.7**
Daybreak—Al Hibbler (55)	7.4
Dave GROHL ▶ 3802 (1)	**695**
Smells Like Teen Spirit—Nirvana (91)	2086
Don GROLNICK ▶ 8359 (1)	**53**
Sneakin' Up Behind You—Brecker Brothers (75)	265
Myron GROMBACHER ▶ 4793 (2)	**413**
All Fired Up—Pat Benatar (88)	720
Shot Of Poison—Lita Ford (91)	520
—Max C. Gronenthal see: Max CARL	
Pierre GROSCOLAS ▶ 10644 (3)	**6.5**
Lady Lay—Wayne Newton (74)	13
Midnight Love Affair—Tony Orlando And Dawn (76)	*6.3*
Midnight Love Affair—Carol Douglas (76)	*3.7*
Barry GROSS ▶ 5090 (2)	**344**
Bella Linda—Grassroots (68)	894
The Morning Of Our Lives—Arkade (71)	185
Henry GROSS ▶ 1192 (6)	**3720**
Shannon—Henry Gross (76)	3215
Springtime Mama—Henry Gross (76)	425
Come On Say It—Henry Gross (74)	41
One More Tomorrow—Henry Gross (75)	17
Someday (I Didn't Want To Have To Be The One)—Henry Gross (76)	14
Simone—Henry Gross (74)	7.0
—Jerome David Gross see: Jerry GROSS	
Jerry GROSS [Jerome David Gross, Jerry Summers] ▶ 5799 (2)	**240**
Here Come The Judge—Magistrates (68)	396
The Jitterbug—Dovells (62)	85
Paul GROSS ▶ 9530 (1)	**22**
Gypsy—Abraham's Children (73)	22
Walter GROSS ▶ 4609 (1)	**451**
Tenderly—Bert Kaempfert And His Orchestra (61)	451
—Arthur Grossman see: Arthur FREED	
Carl GROSSMAN [Carl Groszman, Carl Keats] ▶ 4317 (1)	**523**
A Dose Of Rock 'N' Roll—Ringo Starr (76)	523
Edward GROSSMAN ▶ 10883 (1)	**4.7**
Never Again—Dinah Washington (58)	9.4
Ronnie GROSSMAN ▶ 3913 (3)	**660**
It Hurts To Be Sixteen—Andrea Carroll (63)	*363*
The Dreamer—Neil Sedaka (63)	297
It Hurts To Be Sixteen—Barbara Chandler (63)	*0.0*
—Wilhelm Grosz see: Hugh WILLIAMS	
—Carl Groszman see: Carl GROSSMAN	
Franz GROTHE ▶ 2923 (2)	**1115**
In der Nacht ist der Mensch nicht gern alleine—Johnny Maddox And The Rhythmasters (55)	*1115*
In der Nacht ist der Mensch nicht gern alleine—Crazy Otto (55)	*0.0*
Theodor GROUYA ▶ 3652 (2)	**748**
Flamingo—Herb Alpert & The Tijuana Brass (66)	*646*
Flamingo L'Amore—Gaylords (58)	*204*
Dick GROVE ▶ 10781 (1)	**5.3**
Little Bird—Pete Jolly Trio and Friends (63)	11
Arthur GROVER ▶ 10668 (1)	**6.2**
To Say You're Mine—DeCastro Sisters (55)	19
Steve GROVES ▶ 2929 (2)	**1114**
Toast And Marmalade For Tea—Tin Tin (71)	1043
Is That The Way—Tin Tin (71)	212
Franz GRUBER ▶ 7429 (13)	**96**
Silent Night (Christmas Hymn)—Bing Crosby (60)	*110*
Silent Night (Christmas Hymn)—Bing Crosby (57)	*78*
Silent Night—Elvis Presley (57)	*2.1*
Sleep In Heavenly Peace (Silent Night)—Barbra Streisand (66)	*1.4*
Silent Night, Holy Night—Mahalia Jackson (62)	*0.9*
Silent Night—Al Hibbler (56)	*0.0*
Silent Night—Pat Holliday (58)	*0.0*
Silent Night, Holy Night—Mulcays (54)	*0.0*
Silent Night, Holy Night—Mahalia Jackson (56)	*0.0*
Silent Night (Christmas Hymn)—Bing Crosby (54)	*0.0*
Silent Night (Christmas Hymn)—Bing Crosby (55)	*0.0*
Silent Night (Christmas Hymn)—Bing Crosby (56)	*0.0*
Silent Night (Christmas Hymn)—Bing Crosby (58)	*0.0*
Niki GRUBER ▶ 7240 (1)	**108**
Live Is Life—Opus (86)	541
Marian GRUDEFF ▶ 5869 (2)	**235**
All—James Darren (67)	507
Married Man—Richard Burton (65)	216
Peter GRUEN ▶ 8133 (2)	**60**
Nicole—Point Blank (81)	357
Let Me Stay With You Tonight—Point Blank (81)	5.7
Eddie GRUNDY ▶ 7009 (1)	**122**
D.O.A.—Bloodrock (70)	733
Dave GRUSIN ▶ 3313 (5)	**903**
It Might Be You—Stephen Bishop (83)	1012
Baretta's Theme ("Keep Your Eye On The Sparrow")—Rhythm Heritage (76)	*820*
Keep Your Eye On The Sparrow—Merry Clayton (75)	*280*
Thighs High (Grip Your Hips And Move)—Tom Browne (81)	49
The Ballad Of Waterhole #3 (Code Of The West)—Roger Miller (67)	7.9
Jay GRUSKA ▶ 2317 (3)	**1603**
Friends And Lovers—Gloria Loring & Carl Anderson (86)	3079
Tell Me I'm Not Dreaming—Robert Palmer (89)	150
What You're Missing—Chicago (83)	28
—Salvatore Antonio Guaragna see: Harry WARREN	
Vince GUARALDI ▶ 1265 (5)	**3523**
Cast Your Fate To The Wind—Sounds Orchestral (65)	*2195*
Cast Your Fate To The Wind—Vince Guaraldi Trio (62)	*1207*
Cast Your Fate To The Wind—Shelby Flint (66)	*231*
Cast Your Fate To The Wind—Steve Alaimo (65)	*12*
Cast Your Fate To The Wind—Martin Denny, and His Orchestra (62)	*0.0*
Dave GUARD ▶ 3847 (4)	**679**
A Worried Man—Kingston Trio (59)	*993*
A Worried Man—Four Preps (61)	*130*
Scotch And Soda—Kingston Trio (62)	*99*
Scotch And Soda—Kingston Trio (69)	*18*
James William GUERCIO ▶ 2705 (2)	**1261**
Susan—Buckinghams (67)	2292
Distant Shores—Chad & Jeremy (66)	497
Michael GUERRA [Bobby Mitchell] ▶ 6760 (1)	**139**
Midnight Stroll—Revels (59)	418
Lalo GUERRERO ▶ 7705 (1)	**79**
Pancho Lopez (Davy Crockett)—Lalo Guerrero (55)	*238*
Luis GUERRERO ▶ 5979 (1)	**220**
Peanuts (La Cacahuata)—Sunglows (65)	220
Christopher GUEST [Christopher Haden-Guest, Nigel Tufnel] ▶ 10164 (1)	**12**
Deteriorata—National Lampoon (72)	24
William GUEST ▶ 5243 (1)	**319**
I Don't Want To Do Wrong—Gladys Knight & The Pips (71)	1596
Danny GUGLIELMI ▶ 9508 (2)	**22**
La Shabla—Danny Roma (59)	*15*
The Shovel (La Shabla)—Gaylords (59)	*15*
Luis GUGLIELMI [Louiguy] ▶ 410 (5)	**9673**
Cherry Pink And Apple Blossom White—Perez Prado And His Orchestra (55)	*9278*
Cherry Pink And Apple Blossom White—Jerry Murad's Harmonicats (60)	*319*
Cherry Pink And Apple Blossom White—Alan Dale (55)	*226*
Cherry Pink And Apple Blossom White—Xavier Cugat & His Orchestra (55)	*0.0*
Cherry Pink (And Apple Blossom White)—Georgie Auld & His Auld-Stars (55)	*0.0*
Carmela GUIDA ▶ 1813 (1)	**2276**
If You Wanna Be Happy—Jimmy Soul (63)	6827
Frank GUIDA ▶ 353 (13)	**10755**
Quarter To Three—U.S. Bonds (61)	8470
If You Wanna Be Happy—Jimmy Soul (63)	6827
New Orleans—U.S. Bonds (60)	*2886*
Dear Lady Twist—Gary (U.S.) Bonds (61)	2461
Twist, Twist Senora—Gary (U.S.) Bonds (62)	1458
Not Me—Orlons (63)	1322
Twistin' Matilda (and the channel)—Jimmy Soul (62)	1194
High School Usa—Tommy Facenda (59)	625
New Orleans—Eddie Hodges (65)	*616*
New Orleans—Neil Diamond (68)	*383*
Treat 'Em Tough—Jimmy Soul (63)	42
Copy Cat—Gary (U.S.) Bonds (62)	9.2
New Orleans—Chartbusters (65)	*0.0*
Amos GUIDER ▶ 11651 (1)	**0.8**
Steppin' Out—Kool & The Gang (82)	6.6
Cindy GUIDRY ▶ 11064 (1)	**3.4**
Into My Love—Greg Guidry (82)	6.9
Greg GUIDRY ▶ 4121 (4)	**587**
Goin' Down—Greg Guidry (82)	936
Gotta Have More Love—Climax Blues Band (80)	311
In It For Love—England Dan & John Ford Coley (80)	23
Into My Love—Greg Guidry (82)	6.9
—Kim Anthony Guidry see: Kim SHARP	
Randy GUIDRY ▶ 7305 (1)	**104**
Gotta Have More Love—Climax Blues Band (80)	311
Robert GUIDRY [Bobby Charles, Robert Charles Guidry] ▶ 705 (9)	**6168**
But I Do—Clarence Henry (61)	*4122*
See You Later Alligator—Bill Haley And His Comets (56)	2750
Walking To New Orleans—Fats Domino (60)	2113
It Keeps Rainin'—Fats Domino (61)	735
On Bended Knees—Clarence Henry (61)	168
Groovin' (Out On Life)—Newbeats (69)	121
A Little Too Much—Clarence Henry (62)	93
Before I Grow Too Old—Fats Domino (60)	92
But I Do—Bobby Vinton (72)	*85*
—Robert Charles Guidry see: Robert GUIDRY	
Ronnie GUILBEAU ▶ 5461 (1)	**284**
Call It Love—Poco (89)	851
Isaac GUILLORY ▶ 9037 (1)	**33**
Greenburg, Glickstein, Charles, David Smith & Jones—Cryan' Shames (68)	65
King GUION ▶ 5780 (2)	**242**
Solitaire—Embers (61)	323
Golden Baton—Dick Jacobs And His Chorus And Orchestra (56)	135
Bonnie GUITAR [Bonnie Buckingham] ▶ 6917 (3)	**129**
Mister Fire Eyes—Bonnie Guitar (57)	151
Candy Apple Red—Bonnie Guitar (59)	37
If You See My Love Dancing—Bonnie Guitar (57)	16
—Guitar Slim see: Eddie JONES	
John GULDBERG ▶ 5284 (1)	**313**
White Horse—Laid Back (84)	627
Sam GULINO ▶ 3428 (1)	**852**
Baby Blue—Echoes (61)	1704
—Aaron Gumbinsky see: Harry VON TILZER	
—Albert Gumbinsky see: Albert VON TILZER	
John GUMMOE ▶ 712 (2)	**6116**
Rhythm Of The Rain—Cascades (63)	*5722*
Rhythm Of The Rain—Gary Lewis And The Playboys (69)	*394*

Dick GUMP ▶ 7806 (1)	**74**
My Tani–Brothers Four (60)	223
Bob GUNDRY ▶ 8384 (2)	**52**
What Can I Do With This Broken Heart–England Dan & John Ford Coley (79)	147
I Really Love You–Davy Jones (71)	3.3
–George Charles Gunn see: Anton DEWAAL	
Eythor GUNNARSSON ▶ 9354 (1)	**25**
Garden Party–Herb Alpert (83)	25
Tracii GUNS [Tracy Ulrich] ▶ 7210 (1)	**110**
The Ballad Of Jayne–L.A. Guns (90)	549
Shirley GUNTER ▶ 6026 (1)	**214**
Oop-Shoop–Crew-Cuts (54)	643
Gisela GÜNTHER ▶ 9467 (5)	**23**
Freddy–Annie Cordy (55)	*46*
Freddy–Connie Francis (55)	*46*
Fredy–Eartha Kitt & Perez Prado (55)	*0.0*
Freddy–Stan Kenton & His Orchestra (55)	*0.0*
Freddy–Guy Lombardo & His Royal Canadians (55)	*0.0*
–Gregory Gerard Guralski see: Greg GERARD	
Geoff GURD ▶ 9723 (1)	**18**
Love Is A House–Force M.D.'s (87)	55
Adrian GURVITZ ▶ 5719 (1)	**251**
The Love In Your Eyes–Eddie Money (89)	753
Paul GURVITZ ▶ 3443 (1)	**846**
Who Found Who–Jellybean (87)	846
Margo GURYAN ▶ 2362 (2)	**1559**
Sunday Mornin'–Oliver (69)	*821*
Sunday Mornin'–Spanky And Our Gang (68)	*738*
–Howard J. Gustafson see: Bart HOWARD	
Gérard GUSTIN ▶ 10208 (1)	**11**
Hawaii Honeymoon–Waikikis (65)	22
Arlo GUTHRIE ▶ 9710 (2)	**19**
Valley To Pray–Arlo Guthrie (70)	62
Alice's Rock & Roll Restaurant–Arlo Guthrie (69)	3.0
Beverly GUTHRIE ▶ 5112 (3)	**341**
Love Me Forever–Four Esquires (57)	*475*
Love Me Forever–Roger Williams (67)	*173*
Love Me Forever–Eydie Gorme (57)	*33*
Gwen GUTHRIE ▶ 2647 (4)	**1295**
Supernatural Thing - Part I–Ben E. King (75)	1882
Ain't Nothin' Goin' On But The Rent–Gwen Guthrie (86)	300
Do It In The Name Of Love–Ben E. King (75)	96
Love Don't You Go Through No Changes On Me–Sister Sledge (75)	10
Woody GUTHRIE ▶ 8271 (5) HOF	**56**
This Land Is Your Land–Paul Clayton (60)	*25*
Gypsy Davy–Arlo Guthrie (73)	20
Sally–Kingston Trio (59)	11
This Land Is Your Land–New Christy Minstrels (62)	*3.6*
This Land Is Your Land–Ketty Lester (62)	*1.8*
Glenn GUTIERREZ ▶ 6780 (1)	**138**
If You Leave Me Now–Jaya (89)	414
Louis GUTIERREZ ▶ 4737 (1)	**427**
Walking Down Your Street–Bangles (87)	1281
Robert GUTIERREZ ▶ 9446 (1)	**23**
Latin Active–A Lighter Shade Of Brown (91)	164
–Elizabeth Ann Guttman see: E.G. DAILY	
Billy GUY [Frank Phillips] ▶ 4321 (2)	**522**
Wake Me Shake Me–Coasters (60)	399
Ain't That Just Like Me–Searchers (64)	246
–Helen Guy see: Guy D'HARDELOT	
Johnny GUY ▶ 10061 (1)	**13**
Dolly–Craig Brown (58)	13
Ronnie GUY [Ronald Guy Hruska] ▶ 10630 (1)	**6.6**
Melody–David Johansen (79)	13
Sherman GUY ▶ 8696 (4)	**42**
Move Your Boogie Body–Bar-Kays (79)	270
Today Is The Day–Bar-Kays (80)	150
Hit And Run–Bar-Kays (81)	23
Boogie Body Land–Bar-Kays (81)	23
Troy GUY ▶ 8182 (1)	**59**
Forever Amo'r–D'Zyre (91)	59
Connie GUZMAN ▶ 8856 (1)	**38**
Hold Me–Sheila E. (87)	113
Ed GUZMAN ▶ 11684 (1)	**0.7**
We're Gonna Have A Good Time–Rare Earth (73)	4.3
–Frank V. Guzzo see: Frankie FORD	
Janis Lee GWIN ▶ 2697 (1)	**1266**
Chick-A-Boom (Don't Ya Jes' Love It)–Daddy Dewdrop (71)	2531
–Gary G-Wiz see: Gary RINALDO	

H

–Elizabeth Jane Haaby see: Liz ANDERSON	
Fred HABER ▶ 10203 (1)	**11**
Tommy Jones–Johnny Tillotson (67)	11
Susan HABER ▶ 5544 (1)	**272**
Please Don't Ever Leave Me–Cyrkle (66)	272
William HABERMAN ▶ 6237 (2)	**191**
I'm Happy That Love Has Found You–Jimmy Hall (80)	568
Top Of The World (Make My Reservation)–Canyon (75)	3.3
Hal HACKADY ▶ 4882 (6)	**389**
Shake Me I Rattle (Squeeze Me I Cry)–Marion Worth (62)	*486*
Without You–Eddie Fisher (56)	*406*
Shake Me I Rattle (Squeeze Me I Cry)–Lennon Sisters (57)	*14*
Wild Rosie–Four Tophatters (55)	6.6
Without You–Alan Dean (56)	*0.0*
Without You–Johnny Desmond (56)	*0.0*
–Leonard Hacker see: Buddy HACKETT	
Buddy HACKETT [Leonard Hacker] ▶ 8671 (1)	**43**
Chinese Rock And Egg Roll–Buddy Hackett (56)	43
J.J. HACKETT ▶ 8454 (1)	**50**
Primitive Love Rites–Mondo Rock (87)	100
Naimy HACKETT ▶ 4054 (2)	**611**
Tarzan Boy–Baltimora (85)	1208
Living In The Background–Baltimora (86)	15
Steve HACKETT ▶ 4670 (1)	**442**
When The Heart Rules The Mind–GTR (86)	884
–George Hackney see: Anthony NEWLEY	
Durwood HADDOCK ▶ 6060 (1)	**210**
There She Goes–Jerry Wallace (60)	631
–Christopher Haden-Guest see: Christopher GUEST	
Manos HADJIDAKIS ▶ 745 (10)	**5895**
All Alone Am I–Brenda Lee (62)	5503
Never On Sunday–Don Costa And His Orchestra And Chorus (60)	*2048*
Never On Sunday–Chordettes (61)	*1539*
The White Rose Of Athens–David Carroll And His Orchestra (62)	*316*
(A Ship Will Come) Ein Schiff Wird Kommen–Lale Anderson (61)	*19*
Never On Sunday–Raymond Lefevre (60)	*0.0*
The White Rose Of Athens–Chordettes (62)	*0.0*
The White Rose Of Athens–Nana Mouskouri (62)	*0.0*
Never On Sunday–Marty Gold & His Orchestra (60)	*0.0*
Never On Sunday–Ray Martin & His Orchestra (60)	*0.0*
Ron HAFFKINE ▶ 6227 (1)	**191**
Baby Makes Her Blue Jeans Talk–Dr. Hook (82)	574
Sammy HAGAR ▶ 580 (18)	**7495**
Why Can't This Be Love–Van Halen (86)	3498
I've Done Everything For You–Rick Springfield (81)	2093
When It's Love–Van Halen (88)	1533
Finish What Ya Started–Van Halen (88)	1115
Your Love Is Driving Me Crazy–Sammy Hagar (82)	1037
Top Of The World–Van Halen (91)	819
Love Walks In–Van Halen (86)	778
Give To Live–Sammy Hagar (87)	664
Dreams–Van Halen (86)	588
I Can't Drive 55–Sammy Hagar (84)	510
Feels So Good–Van Halen (89)	435
Two Sides Of Love–Sammy Hagar (84)	407
Black And Blue–Van Halen (88)	288
I'll Fall In Love Again–Sammy Hagar (82)	265
You Make Me Crazy–Sammy Hagar (77)	121
Eagles Fly–Sammy Hagar (87)	76
Plain Jane–Sammy Hagar (79)	50
Best Of Both Worlds–Van Halen (86)	29
Earle HAGEN ▶ 2498 (2)	**1436**
Harlem Nocturne–Viscounts (59)	*796*
Harlem Nocturne–Viscounts (65)	*640*
Merle HAGGARD ▶ 2506 (9) HOF	**1431**
If We Make It Through December–Merle Haggard (73)	544
Today I Started Loving You Again–Bettye Swann (73)	*354*
Okie From Muskogee–Merle Haggard (69)	334
From Graceland To The Promised Land–Merle Haggard (77)	212
I Started Loving You Again–Al Martino (69)	*151*
I Take A Lot Of Pride In What I Am–Dean Martin (69)	146
Everybody's Had The Blues–Merle Haggard And The Strangers (73)	103
The Fightin' Side Of Me–Merle Haggard And The Strangers (70)	6.5
Today I Started Loving You Again–Bobby Bland (76)	*1.3*
Bob HAGGART ▶ 6021 (2)	**215**
What's New–Linda Ronstadt & The Nelson Riddle Orchestra (83)	425
Big Noise From Winnetka–Spaghetti Head (75)	11
Warren HAGOOD ▶ 9357 (1)	**25**
Cross My Heart–Billy Stewart (67)	76
Albert HAGUE ▶ 8896 (2)	**37**
Young And Foolish–Jo Stafford (55)	*46*
Young And Foolish–Dean Martin (55)	*27*
Stephen HAGUE ▶ 4823 (3)	**405**
So In Love–Orchestral Manoeuvres In The Dark (85)	644
True Faith–New Order (87)	637
Love Comes Quickly–Pet Shop Boys (86)	188
–Gary Loren Hahn see: Skip HAHN	
Skip HAHN [Gary Loren Hahn] ▶ 8342 (2)	**54**
Don't Make A Fool Of Yourself–Stacey Q (88)	125
Shy Girl–Stacey Q (87)	36
Shelley HAIMS [Shelley G. Haims, Randy L. Scott] ▶ 6623 (1)	**150**
We Go Together–Jan & Dean (60)	300
Kit HAIN ▶ 6399 (1)	**175**
Dancing In The City–Marshall Hain (78)	350
–Marquis X. Hair see: Marcus DARE	
Jester HAIRSTON ▶ 5398 (4)	**295**
Mary's Boy Child–Harry Belafonte (56)	*285*
Mary's Boy Child–Boney M (78)	*9.7*
Mary's Little Boy Chile–Four Lads (56)	*0.0*
Mary's Little Boy Chile–Mahalia Jackson (56)	*0.0*
Kenni HAIRSTON ▶ 4707 (1)	**434**
Running Back To You–Vanessa Williams (91)	868
Oakley HALDEMAN ▶ 11589 (1)	**1.1**
Here Comes Santa Claus (Right Down Santa Claus Lane)–Elvis Presley (57)	2.1
Andrew HALE ▶ 6360 (1)	**179**
Paradise–Sade (88)	717
William HALE ▶ 9812 (1)	**17**
I Love The Way You Love–Betty Wright (71)	33
Léon HALÉVY ▶ 8771 (1)	**40**
Madrid–Nat "King" Cole (59)	198
Bill HALEY ▶ 2227 (12)	**1720**
R O C K–Bill Haley And His Comets (56)	737
Skinny Minnie–Bill Haley And His Comets (58)	608
Rock A Beatin' Boogie–Bill Haley And His Comets (55)	*483*
Birth Of The Boogie–Bill Haley And His Comets (55)	432
Rudy's Rock–Bill Haley And His Comets (56)	314
Hot Dog Buddy Buddy–Bill Haley And His Comets (56)	286
Two Hound Dogs–Bill Haley And His Comets (55)	175
Rockin' Through The Rye–Bill Haley And His Comets (56)	133
Rock A Beatin' Boogie–Jive Bunny And The Mastermixers (89)	*80*
Rock-A-Beatin' Boogie–Esquire Boys (54)	*15*
Up The Creek (Without A Paddle)–Matys Brothers (56)	7.2
Whoa Mabel–Bill Haley And His Comets (58)	2.7
Raymond HALEY ▶ 4249 (5)	**546**
There It Is–Tyrone Davis (73)	416
Could I Forget You–Tyrone Davis (71)	305
Without You In My Life–Tyrone Davis (73)	300
I Wish It Was Me–Tyrone Davis (74)	165
Straight Ahead–Young-Holt Unlimited (69)	12
Rob HALFORD ▶ 9081 (2)	**32**
You've Got Another Thing Comin'–Judas Priest (82)	89
Living After Midnight–Judas Priest (80)	5.6

Aaron HALL ▶ 7551 (2)	**89**
I Wanna Get With U–Guy (90)	300
I Like–Guy (89)	56
Arsenio HALL [Chunky A] ▶ 9898 (1)	**15**
Owwww!–Chunky A (89)	31
Ashley HALL ▶ 6040 (2)	**213**
How Much Is Enough–Fixx (91)	414
Dream Lover–Rebel Pebbles (91)	328
Benny HALL Jr. ▶ 11570 (1)	**1.2**
We Can't Believe You're Gone–Bobby Harris (65)	2.3
Damion HALL ▶ 7784 (1)	**75**
I Wanna Get With U–Guy (90)	300
Daryl HALL ▶ 48 (37) HOF	**41531**
Maneater–Daryl Hall & John Oates (82)	7727
I Can't Go For That (No Can Do)– Daryl Hall & John Oates (81)	7283
Private Eyes–Daryl Hall & John Oates (81)	6308
Rich Girl–Daryl Hall & John Oates (77)	5287
Kiss On My List–Daryl Hall & John Oates (81)	4868
Say It Isn't So–Daryl Hall & John Oates (83)	4686
Out Of Touch–Daryl Hall & John Oates (84)	4068
Everytime You Go Away–Paul Young (85)	4062
Sara Smile–Daryl Hall & John Oates (76)	3191
One On One–Daryl Hall & John Oates (83)	2684
She's Gone–Daryl Hall & John Oates (76)	*2526*
You Make My Dreams–Daryl Hall & John Oates (81)	2226
Everything Your Heart Desires– Daryl Hall & John Oates (88)	1949
Dreamtime–Daryl Hall (86)	1928
Method Of Modern Love– Daryl Hall & John Oates (84)	1622
Adult Education–Daryl Hall & John Oates (84)	1464
Did It In A Minute–Daryl Hall & John Oates (82)	1415
So Close–Daryl Hall & John Oates (90)	999
Wait For Me–Daryl Hall & John Oates (79)	893
Some Things Are Better Left Unsaid– Daryl Hall & John Oates (85)	835
It's A Laugh–Daryl Hall & John Oates (78)	762
Swept Away–Diana Ross (84)	735
Your Imagination–Daryl Hall & John Oates (82)	527
Do What You Want, Be What You Are– Daryl Hall & John Oates (76)	504
Foolish Pride–Daryl Hall (86)	485
Possession Obsession–Daryl Hall & John Oates (85)	431
Missed Opportunity–Daryl Hall & John Oates (88)	421
I Don't Wanna Lose You– Daryl Hall & John Oates (78)	356
Downtown Life–Daryl Hall & John Oates (88)	326
She's Gone–Daryl Hall & John Oates (74)	*306*
She's Gone–Tavares (74)	*299*
Ruthless People–Mick Jagger (86)	219
Someone Like You–Daryl Hall (87)	161
Why Do Lovers (Break Each Other's Heart?)– Daryl Hall & John Oates (77)	74
It's Uncanny–Daryl Hall & John Oates (77)	28
Good Night & Good Morning–Jim Capaldi (76)	*22*
Goodnight And Goodmorning–Cecilio & Kapono (76)	*4.8*
–Deborah Carter Hall see: Deborah CARTER	
Edward HALL ▶ 8508 (2)	**48**
Loco Motion–Irving Ashby (57)	*48*
Loco-Motion–Joe "Fingers" Carr (57)	*48*
Graeme HALL [Graeme Anthony Hall] ▶ 9913 (1)	**15**
Beg, Steal Or Borrow–New Seekers (72)	45
Horace HALL ▶ 9975 (1)	**14**
I Don't Know What You've Got But It's Got Me - Part 1–Little Richard (65)	29
J. Graydon HALL ▶ 7037 (1)	**120**
That's How Much I Love You–Pat Boone (58)	361
Jack HALL ▶ 4995 (3)	**362**
Keep On Smilin'–Wet Willie (74)	1449
Leona–Wet Willie (75)	141
Dixie Rock–Wet Willie (75)	2.9
–James Faye Hall see: Sunny DAVID	
Jimmy HALL ▶ 4068 (4)	**605**
Keep On Smilin'–Wet Willie (74)	1449
Street Corner Serenade–Wet Willie (77)	731
Leona–Wet Willie (75)	141
Dixie Rock–Wet Willie (75)	2.9
Joe HALL ▶ 11518 (1)	**1.4**
Rock Creek Park–Blackbyrds (76)	6.8

Johanna HALL ▶ 1461 (8)	**2985**
Dance With Me–Orleans (75)	2736
Still The One–Orleans (76)	2374
Let There Be Music–Orleans (75)	299
Reach–Orleans (77)	298
Crazy (Keep On Falling)–John Hall Band (81)	294
What You Do To Me–Carl Wilson (83)	92
You Sure Fooled Me–John Hall Band (82)	21
Ms. Grace–Tymes (74)	8.6
John HALL ▶ 1451 (8)	**3007**
Dance With Me–Orleans (75)	2736
Still The One–Orleans (76)	2374
Reach–Orleans (77)	298
Crazy (Keep On Falling)–John Hall Band (81)	294
Love Me Again–John Hall Band (83)	171
What You Do To Me–Carl Wilson (83)	92
You Sure Fooled Me–John Hall Band (82)	21
Ms. Grace–Tymes (74)	8.6
John (2) HALL ▶ 9064 (1)	**32**
Flyin'–Prism (78)	159
Jon Kingsley HALL [John Kingsley Hall] ▶ 11002 (2)	**3.9**
Maybe This Day–Kissing The Pink (83)	20
Certain Things Are Likely– K.T.P./Kissing The Pink (87)	4.3
–Marcel Theo Hall see: Biz MARKIE	
Nathaniel HALL ▶ 7160 (1)	**113**
Livin' In The Light–Caron Wheeler (90)	225
Oliver HALL ▶ 5031 (1)	**357**
Revenge–Brook Benton (61)	1071
Reginald HALL ▶ 2037 (3)	**1973**
You Talk Too Much–Joe Jones & His Orchestra (60)	*3885*
Lazy Lady–Fats Domino (64)	32
You Talk Too Much–Frankie Ford (60)	*29*
Rick HALL [Roe E. Hall] ▶ 1559 (8)	**2722**
Sweet And Innocent–Donny Osmond (71)	2840
Too Weak To Fight–Clarence Carter (68)	2074
Come On–Tommy Roe (64)	546
She'll Never Know–Brenda Lee (63)	376
Sweet Feeling–Candi Staton (70)	373
Looking For A Fox–Clarence Carter (68)	137
Funky Fever–Clarence Carter (68)	20
Find 'Em, Fool 'Em & Forget 'Em–Dobie Gray (76)	4.6
–Roe E. Hall see: Rick HALL	
Shirley HALL ▶ 5935 (3)	**225**
The Watusi–Vibrations (61)	657
Hot Cakes! 1st Serving–Dave "Baby" Cortez (63)	7.0
The (Bossa Nova) Bird–Dells (62)	5.3
Terry HALL ▶ 3726 (1)	**719**
Our Lips Are Sealed–Go-Go's (81)	1438
Tom T. HALL ▶ 382 (11)	**10286**
Harper Valley P.T.A.–Jeannie C. Riley (68)	*8451*
I Love–Tom T. Hall (73)	1172
The Year That Clayton Delaney Died–Tom T. Hall (71)	367
That Song Is Driving Me Crazy–Tom T. Hall (74)	154
Harper Valley P.T.A. (Later That Same Day)– Ben Colder (68)	*111*
Sneaky Snake–Tom T. Hall (75)	81
You Always Come Back (To Hurting Me)– Johnny Rodriguez (73)	11
Harper Valley P.T.A.– King Curtis & The Kingpins (68)	*9.6*
Harper Valley P.T.A.–Bobbi Martin (68)	*5.2*
Continuing Story Of Harper Valley P.T.A.– Dee Mullins (68)	*4.4*
Me And Jesus–Tom T. Hall (72)	1.9
Waldense HALL ▶ 6431 (2)	**170**
That's When I Cried–Jimmy Jones (60)	340
Ev'rybody's Cryin'–Jimmie Beaumont (61)	0.4
Willie HALL ▶ 9153 (1)	**30**
Dis-Gorilla (Part 1)– Rick Dees And His Cast Of Idiots (77)	91
Nick HALLAM ▶ 7295 (1)	**105**
Elevate My Mind–Stereo MC's (91)	209
Erwin HALLETZ ▶ 9008 (1)	**33**
Lovely Ladies Of Milano– Dick Jacobs And His Chorus And Orchestra (57)	100
Bob HALLEY ▶ 3028 (4)	**1055**
Dear Lonely Hearts–Nat King Cole (62)	1571
That's How Heartaches Are Made– Baby Washington (63)	*384*

Tell Me Baby–Garnet Mimms (64)	139
That's How Heartaches Are Made–Marvelettes (69)	*16*
Hugh HALLIDAY ▶ 7898 (1)	**70**
Tell Her You Love Her–Frank Sinatra (57)	211
Bob HALLIGAN ▶ 4337 (2)	**517**
Don't Close Your Eyes–Kix (89)	1479
Rise To It–Kiss (90)	48
Dick HALLIGAN ▶ 8208 (1)	**58**
Lisa, Listen To Me–Blood, Sweat & Tears (71)	117
David HALLYDAY [David Michael Smet] ▶ 6988 (1)	**124**
Ooh La La–David Hallyday (91)	248
–Bobby Godfrey Mitchell Halstead see: Bobby MITCHELL	
Al HAM ▶ 9937 (2)	**15**
We're Together–Hillside Singers (72)	55
I Believed It All–Pozo Seco Singers (67)	2.4
Pete HAM ▶ 319 (6)	**11477**
Without You–Nilsson (71)	*7670*
Day After Day–Badfinger (71)	4078
No Matter What–Badfinger (70)	2280
Baby Blue–Badfinger (72)	1271
Apple Of My Eye–Badfinger (74)	11
Without You–Heart (78)	*6.6*
Stuart HAMBLEN ▶ 541 (16)	**7911**
This Ole House–Rosemary Clooney (54)	*5384*
Open Up Your Heart (And Let The Sunshine In)– Cowboy Church Sunday School (54)	*1657*
(Remember Me) I'm The One Who Loves You– Dean Martin (65)	*472*
His Hands– "Tennessee" Ernie Ford (55)	*154*
Ole Pappy Time–June Valli (54)	*65*
Ole Pappy Time–Stuart Hamblen (54)	*65*
I've Got So Many Million Years (That I Can't Count Them)–Johnnie Ray (55)	46
This Ole House–Stuart Hamblen (54)	*42*
Just A Man–Tony Martin (55)	12
Go On By–Cowboy Church Sunday School (55)	6.9
(Remember Me) I'm The One Who Loves You– Fontane Sisters (57)	*5.7*
It's No Secret What God Can Do–Elvis Presley (57)	2.1
His Hands–Mahalia Jackson (55)	*0.0*
Open Up Your Heart (And Let The Sunshine In)– Lancers (55)	*0.0*
Open Up Your Heart (And Let The Sunshine In)– McGuire Sisters (55)	*0.0*
Open Up Your Heart (And Let The Sunshine In)–Little Sister Gale & Big Sister Rosemary Clooney (55)	*0.0*
Christopher HAMILL [Limahl] ▶ 3874 (3)	**671**
Too Shy–Kajagoogoo (83)	2226
Only For Love–Limahl (85)	220
Hang On Now–Kajagoogoo (83)	28
Al HAMILTON [Albert Prentis Hamilton, Al Kent] ▶ 2444 (11)	**1484**
Knockin' Boots–Candyman (90)	1245
Hungry For Love–San Remo Golden Strings (65)	680
You've Got To Pay The Price–Al Kent (67)	*605*
You Got To Pay The Price–Gloria Taylor (69)	*591*
Stop Her On Sight (S.O.S.)–Edwin Starr (66)	495
The Whole World Is A Stage–Fantastic Four (67)	345
You Gave Me Something (And Everything's Alright)– Fantastic Four (67)	312
Alvin Stone (The Birth & Death Of A Gangster)– Fantastic Four (75)	175
Real Humdinger–J.J. Barnes (66)	93
Show Time–Detroit Emeralds (68)	57
Headline News–Edwin Starr (66)	41
Ann Marie HAMILTON ▶ 1519 (2)	**2811**
Fallin' In Love–Hamilton, Joe Frank & Reynolds (75)	4594
Winners And Losers– Hamilton, Joe Frank And Reynolds (75)	1028
Arthur HAMILTON ▶ 1337 (9)	**3321**
Cry Me A River–Joe Cocker (70)	*1327*
Cry Me A River–Julie London (55)	*1315*
I Can Sing A Rainbow–Dells (69)	524
He Needs Me–Gloria Lynne (61)	116
Cry Me A River–Janice Harper (60)	*39*
Cry Me A River–Jill Corey (55)	*0.0*
Cry Me A River–Kitty White (55)	*0.0*
Cry Me A River–Julie London (60)	*0.0*
Cry Me A River–Eileen Barton (55)	*0.0*

Bob HAMILTON [Robert Harston Hamilton Jr., Rob Reeco] ▶ 2089 (7) **1891**
(Just Like) Romeo & Juliet–Reflections (64) *2234*
Am I The Man–Jackie Wilson (60) 702
Hungry For Love–San Remo Golden Strings (65) 680
(Just Like) Romeo And Juliet–Sha Na Na (75) *301*
Poor Man's Son–Reflections (65) 257
Real Humdinger–J.J. Barnes (66) 93
Like Columbus Did–Reflections (64) 30

Bobby HAMILTON ▶ 9366 (1) **25**
Crazy Eyes For You–Bobby Hamilton (58) 50

–Clyde Hamilton see: Cyril STAPLETON

Danny HAMILTON ▶ 1476 (4) **2946**
Fallin' In Love–Hamilton, Joe Frank & Reynolds (75) 4594
Winners And Losers–Hamilton, Joe Frank And Reynolds (75) 1028
Everyday Without You–Hamilton, Joe Frank & Reynolds (76) 81
Diamond Head–Ventures (65) 53

Dave HAMILTON ▶ 4636 (2) **447**
Once Upon A Time–Marvin Gaye & Mary Wells (64) 797
Pretty Little Baby–Marvin Gaye (65) 743

Eugene HAMILTON [Ronnie Savoy] ▶ 3968 (5) **635**
Knockin' Boots–Candyman (90) 1245
Hungry For Love–San Remo Golden Strings (65) 680
The Whole World Is A Stage–Fantastic Four (67) 345
You Gave Me Something (And Everything's Alright)–Fantastic Four (67) 312
Poor Man's Son–Reflections (65) 257

Frank HAMILTON ▶ 11608 (1) **1.0**
We Shall Overcome–Joan Baez (63) 5.0

Frank S. HAMILTON ▶ 7809 (2) **74**
Baby What I Mean–Drifters (66) *136*
Baby What I Mean–Spiral Starecase (68) *12*

George HAMILTON IV ▶ 8930 (1) **36**
High School Romance–George Hamilton IV (57) 36

Jimmy HAMILTON ▶ 10560 (1) **7.2**
I Wouldn't Lie–Yarbrough & Peoples (86) 29

Mike HAMILTON ▶ 8134 (2) **60**
Nicole–Point Blank (81) 357
Let Me Stay With You Tonight–Point Blank (81) 5.7

Nancy HAMILTON ▶ 8767 (2) **40**
How High The Moon–Gloria Gaynor (75) *54*
How High The Moon Part One–Ella Fitzgerald (60) *26*

Patti HAMILTON ▶ 7468 (1) **94**
How Can I Tell My Mom And Dad–Lovelites (70) 188

Ronald HAMILTON ▶ 6083 (1) **208**
In A Moment–Intrigues (69) 832

Roy HAMILTON ▶ 11346 (1) **2.1**
Come Back My Love–Jerry Butler (58) 4.3

Russ HAMILTON [Ronald Hulme] ▶ 1433 (4) **3059**
Rainbow–Russ Hamilton (57) *3053*
Wedding Ring–Russ Hamilton (57) 5.7
Rainbow–Bill Darnel (57) *0.0*
Rainbow–Bobby Breen (57) *0.0*

Tom HAMILTON ▶ 2745 (3) **1224**
Janie's Got A Gun–Aerosmith (89) 1956
Sweet Emotion–Aerosmith (75) 464
Kings And Queens–Aerosmith (78) 73

Rosie HAMLIN ▶ 1416 (3) **3135**
Angel Baby–Rosie And The Originals (60) *2325*
Angel Baby–Angelica (91) *561*
Lonely Blue Nights–Rosie Formerly With The Originals (61) 249

Marvin HAMLISCH ▶ 588 (10) HOF **7397**
The Way We Were–Barbra Streisand (73) *6902*
Nobody Does It Better–Carly Simon (77) 5897
California Nights–Lesley Gore (67) 1534
Sunshine, Lollipops And Rainbows–Lesley Gore (65) 1112
If You Remember Me–Chris Thompson & Night (79) 961
The Way We Were–Gladys Knight & The Pips (75) *957*
Theme From Ice Castles (Through The Eyes Of Love)–Melissa Manchester (79) 30
Break It To Me Gently–Aretha Franklin (77) 9.1
Wake Up–Chambers Brothers (69) 8.1
Too Little Time–Brenda Lee (66) 5.1

Fred HAMM ▶ 7044 (1) **120**
Bye Bye Blues–Bert Kaempfert And His Orchestra (66) 479

–Hammer see: Stanley BURRELL

Jack HAMMER [Earl Solomon Burroughs] ▶ 1471 (8) **2954**
Great Balls Of Fire–Jerry Lee Lewis (57) *4298*
Peek A Boo–Cadillacs (58) 590
Do I Like It–Nat "King" Cole (58) 263
Great Balls Of Fire–Tiny Tim (69) *83*
Furry Murray–Tradewinds (59) 76
Great Balls Of Fire–Jive Bunny & The Mastermixers (90) *6.7*
Great Balls Of Fire–Georgia Gibbs (57) *0.0*
Yakkity Yak–Markeys Featuring Georgie Morton (58) 0.0

Jan HAMMER ▶ 1090 (1) **4048**
Miami Vice Theme–Jan Hammer (85) 4048

Arthur HAMMERSTEIN ▶ 5666 (3) **257**
Because Of You–Sammy Davis Jr. (54) *241*
Because Of You–Chris Montez (67) *218*
Because Of You–Rome & Paris (66) *55*

Oscar HAMMERSTEIN ▶ 751 (41) HOF **5847**
I've Told Every Little Star–Linda Scott (61) 3657
Some Enchanted Evening–Jay & The Americans (65) *1354*
All At Once You Love Her–Perry Como (55) 1162
Hello Young Lovers–Paul Anka (60) 973
If I Loved You–Chad & Jeremy (65) 969
Everybody's Got A Home But Me–Eddie Fisher (55) *530*
You'll Never Walk Alone–Patti Labelle & The Blue Belles (64) *449*
You'll Never Walk Alone–Brooklyn Bridge (69) *399*
Ol' Man River–Bing Crosby And The Buddy Cole Trio (56) *345*
Everybody's Got A Home But Me–Roy Hamilton (55) *312*
When I Grow Too Old To Dream–Ed Townsend (58) *219*
Do Re Mi–Mitch Miller & his Sing Along Chorus (59) *211*
You Are Beautiful–Johnny Mathis (58) 184
You'll Never Walk Alone–Gerry And The Pacemakers (65) *184*
Indian Love Call–Ray Stevens (75) *140*
I'll Take Romance–Eydie Gorme (57) 109
Do I Love You (Because You're Beautiful)–Vic Damone (57) *106*
Ol' Man River–Earl Grant (58) *94*
Sound Of Music–Patti Page (59) *65*
Climb Ev'ry Mountain–Tony Bennett (59) *64*
Climb Every Mountain–Hesitations (68) *40*
Do I Love You (Because You're Beautiful)–Tony Martin (57) *34*
You'll Never Walk Alone–Elvis Presley With The Jordanaires (68) *25*
Do Re Mi–Anita Bryant (59) *20*
Some Enchanted Evening–Jane Olivor (77) *18*
Lover Come Back To Me–Cleftones (62) 17
Love Look Away–Tony Bennett (58) 11
The Next Time It Happens–Carmen McRae (56) 9.8
Stout-Hearted Men–Barbra Streisand (67) 8.8
Getting To Know You–Sajid Khan (68) 8.6
I Have Dreamed–Chad & Jeremy (65) 7.1
You'll Never Walk Alone–Blue Haze (73) *7.0*
You'll Never Walk Alone–Judy Garland (54) *5.4*
I Enjoy Being A Girl–Pat Suzuki (59) *3.0*
Can't Help Lovin' That Girl Of Mine–Excels (61) 0.5
Sound Of Music–Doris Day (59) *0.0*
Ol' Man River–Johnny Nash (62) *0.0*
I Enjoy Being A Girl–Doris Day (59) *0.0*
Sound Of Music–David Whitfield (60) *0.0*
When I Grow Too Old To Dream–Duke Mitchell (58) *0.0*
Do I Love You (Because You're Beautiful)–Bob Eberly with Paul Whiteman & His Orchestra (57) *0.0*

Kirk HAMMETT ▶ 4738 (2) **427**
Enter Sandman–Metallica (91) 947
The Unforgiven–Metallica (91) 334

Ronnie HAMMON ▶ 11542 (1) **1.3**
Outlaw–War (82) 10

Albert HAMMOND [Hammond Hazlewood] ▶ 210 (31) HOF **15362**
When I Need You–Leo Sayer (77) 5176
Nothing's Gonna Stop Us Now–Starship (87) 4678
It Never Rains In Southern California–Albert Hammond (72) 3547
To All The Girls I've Loved Before–Julio Iglesias & Willie Nelson (84) 2750
The Air That I Breathe–Hollies (74) 2405
I Don't Wanna Live Without Your Love–Chicago (88) 2262
Gimme Dat Ding–Pipkins (70) 2051
One Moment In Time–Whitney Houston (88) 1663
Little Arrows–Leapy Lee (68) 1529
Through The Storm–Aretha Franklin And Elton John (89) 756
I Need To Be In Love–Carpenters (76) 634
I'm A Train–Albert Hammond (74) 607
My Heart Is Failing Me–Riff (91) 501
The Free Electric Band–Albert Hammond (73) 474
Easy To Love–Leo Sayer (77) 427
It Isn't, It Wasn't, It Ain't Never Gonna Be–Aretha Franklin (89) 303
If You Gotta Break Another Heart–Albert Hammond (73) 218
One Night Stand–Magic Lanterns (70) 165
Down By The River–Albert Hammond (72) 164
Lonely Is The Night–Air Supply (86) 129
One More Chance–Ocean (72) 85
Freedom Comes, Freedom Goes–Fortunes (71) 82
99 Miles From L.A.–Albert Hammond (75) 77
The Peacemaker–Albert Hammond (73) 70
Air Disaster–Albert Hammond (74) 69
Names, Tags, Numbers & Labels–Association (73) 56
Half A Million Miles From Home–Albert Hammond (73) 54
Good Morning Freedom–Daybreak (70) 52
Love Thing–Tina Turner (91) 35
Here I Go (Fallin' In Love Again)–Frannie Golde (79) 20
Oklahoma Sunday Morning–Glen Campbell (72) 6.0

Bruce HAMMOND ▶ 9666 (1) **19**
Ballad Of A Girl And Boy–Graduates (59) 77

Clay HAMMOND ▶ 2195 (3) **1754**
Part Time Love–Little Johnny Taylor (63) *1152*
Part Time Love–Ann Peebles (70) *600*
I'm Your Part Time Love–Mitty Collier (63) *3.2*

Ronnie W. HAMMOND ▶ 5327 (2) **304**
Do It Or Die–Atlanta Rhythm Section (79) 861
Free Spirit–Atlanta Rhythm Section (76) 53

Roy C. HAMMOND ▶ 10607 (1) **6.9**
Honey I Still Love You–Mark IV (72) 6.9

Will HAMMOND Jr. ▶ 3079 (1) **1024**
Hold You Tight–Tara Kemp (91) 3071

Willie HAMMOND ▶ 11653 (1) **0.8**
Turn Loose Of My Leg–Jim Stafford (77) 1.6

Jake HAMMONDS ▶ 5744 (2) **246**
Gonna Send You Back To Georgia (A City Slick)–Timmy Shaw (64) *423*
Gonna Send You Back To Walker–Animals (64) *70*

Carl HAMPTON ▶ 1228 (10) **3631**
(If Loving You Is Wrong) I Don't Want To Be Right–Luther Ingram (72) *5399*
If You're Ready (Come Go With Me)–Staple Singers (73) 1796
(If Loving You Is Wrong) I Don't Want To Be Right–Barbara Mandrell (79) *775*
Touch A Hand, Make A Friend–Staple Singers (74) 770
I'll Be Your Shelter (In Time Of Storm)–Luther Ingram (72) 584
I've Got A Feeling (We'll Be Seeing Each Other Again)–Al Wilson (76) 445
I'll Be The Other Woman–Soul Children (74) 371
If Loving You Is Wrong I Don't Want To Be Right–Millie Jackson (75) *204*
Be What You Are–Staple Singers (73) 122
I Could Never Be Happy–Emotions (72) 21

Chasen Cord HAMPTON ▶ 9687 (2) **19**
Summer Vacation–Party (90) *113*
Summer Vacation–Party (91) *20*

Gladys HAMPTON [Gladys Riddle] ▶ 10695 (1) **6.0**
Everybody's Somebody's Fool–Heartbeats (57) 18

Lionel HAMPTON ▶ 11156 (2) **3.0**
Red Top–Teen Queens (56) 4.8
Midnight Sun–Five Whispers (62) 1.2

Paul HAMPTON [Paul Schwartz] ▶ 1801 (8)	**2292**
You Don't Know What You've Got (Until You Lose It)–Ral Donner (61)	2270
Sea Of Heartbreak–Don Gibson (61)	*1296*
I Rise, I Fall–Johnny Tillotson (64)	482
You Can't Lie To a Liar–Ketty Lester (62)	*38*
Love Me, So I'll Know–Bob Denton (57)	*3.2*
Love Me So I'll Know–Jimmy Dean with Ray Ellis and his Orchestra (57)	*3.2*
Sea Of Heartbreak–Poco (82)	*3.1*
You Can't Lie To A Liar–Barry Gordon (62)	*0.0*
Herbie HANCOCK ▶ 1823 (7)	**2260**
Groove Is In The Heart–Deee-Lite (90)	2521
Watermelon Man–Mongo Santamaria Band (63)	*1490*
Chameleon–Herbie Hancock (74)	472
Watermelon Man–Gloria Lynne (65)	*185*
Rockit–Herbie Hancock (83)	165
Watermelon Man–Xavier Cugat (63)	*0.0*
Watermelon Man–Herbie Hancock (63)	*0.0*
James S. HANCOCK [Jimmy Harper] ▶ 8520 (1)	**47**
When You Lose The One You Love–David Whitfield with Mantovani And His Orchestra (56)	142
–Osman Handani see: Otha NASH	
Georg Friederic HANDEL ▶ 6873 (1)	**131**
Hallelujah Chorus–Royal Philharmonic Orchestra (81)	131
Lou HANDMAN ▶ 753 (5) HOF	**5826**
Are You Lonesome To Night–Elvis Presley With The Jordanaires (60)	*10024*
Are You Lonesome Tonight–Donny Osmond (73)	*1054*
Are You Lonesome Tonight–Jaye P. Morgan (59)	*310*
Yes I'm Lonesome Tonight–Thelma Carpenter (60)	*149*
Yes I'm Lonesome Tonight–Dodie Stevens (60)	*116*
John HANDY ▶ 4765 (1)	**421**
Hard Work–John Handy (76)	421
Wayne HANDY ▶ 7695 (4)	**80**
Say Yeah–Wayne Handy (57)	*80*
Say Yeah–Southemers (57)	*0.0*
Say Yeah–Sammy Salvo (57)	*0.0*
Say Yeah–Ollie Shepard (57)	*0.0*
W.C. HANDY [William Christopher Handy] ▶ 3380 (10) HOF	**873**
Yellow Dog Blues–Joe Darensbourg And His Dixie Flyers (57)	*408*
St. Louis Blues Mambo–Richard Maltby And Orchestra (54)	*383*
Yellow Dog Blues–Johnny Maddox (57)	*49*
St. Louis Blues–LaVern Baker (57)	*30*
St. Louis Blues–Cousins (61)	*4.5*
Yellow Dog Blues–Pete Fountain (57)	*0.0*
Yellow Dog Blues–Bob Crosby & His Orchestra (57)	*0.0*
St. Louis Blues Mambo–Perez Prado & His Orchestra (54)	*0.0*
St. Louis Blues Mambo–Alberto Iznaga & His Orchestra (54)	*0.0*
St. Louis Blues Mambo–Les Brown & His Band Of Renown (54)	*0.0*
–William Christopher Handy see: W.C. HANDY	
Bernie HANIGHEN ▶ 5767 (3)	**244**
Baby Doll–Andy Williams (56)	*488*
Baby Doll–Ralph Young (56)	*0.0*
Baby Doll–Chuck Miller (56)	*0.0*
Len HANKS ▶ 2616 (3)	**1323**
(Every Time I Turn Around) Back In Love Again–L.T.D. (77)	2620
Dancin'–Grey and Hanks (79)	16
Never Had A Love Like This Before–Tavares (79)	15
Mike HANKS ▶ 6384 (4)	**176**
I Love You Madly–Fantastic Four (68)	320
I Want You To Have Everything–Lee Rogers (64)	27
I'm A Practical Guy–Lee Rogers (66)	9.1
Boss Love–Lee Rogers (65)	4.2
James HANLEY ▶ 3605 (7) HOF	**770**
Second Hand Rose–Barbra Streisand (65)	580
Zing Went The Strings Of My Heart–Trammps (72)	*326*
Breeze (Blow My Baby Back To Me)–Al Hibbler (55)	170
Zing Went The Strings Of My Heart–Larry Elgart And His Manhattan Swing Orchestra (82)	*50*
Zing Went The Strings Of My Heart–Kalin Twins (60)	*42*
Zing! Went The Strings Of My Heart–Furys (63)	*4.5*

Zing Went The Strings Of My Heart–Dimensions (60)	*0.0*
Gordon HANN ▶ 9119 (1)	**31**
Love And Loneliness–Motors (80)	61
Jeff HANNA ▶ 5630 (2)	**263**
Make A Little Magic–Dirt Band (80)	684
Fire In The Sky–Dirt Band (81)	69
Frank HANNON ▶ 3287 (2)	**911**
Love Song–Tesla (89)	1711
The Way It Is–Tesla (90)	222
Isabel HANSEN [E. Camino] ▶ 11463 (2)	**1.6**
Spanish Marching Song–Joe Reisman and His Orchestra (59)	*4.7*
The Spanish Marching Song–Ethel Smith (59)	*0.0*
Mich HANSEN [Mich Hedin Hansen, Cutfather] ▶ 11112 (1)	**3.2**
Wanna Dance–Yasmin (91)	16
–Mich Hedin Hansen see: Mich HANSEN	
Randy HANSEN ▶ 2421 (1)	**1500**
State Of Shock–Jacksons (84)	3000
Charles HANSON ▶ 9197 (1)	**29**
Look My Way–Vels (85)	87
Michael HANSON ▶ 6054 (2)	**211**
I'm Still Searching–Glass Tiger (88)	408
I Will Be There–Glass Tiger (87)	374
Otto HARBACH [Otto Abels Hauerbach] ▶ 734 (5) HOF	**5978**
Smoke Gets In Your Eyes–Platters (58)	*10667*
Smoke Gets In Your Eyes–Blue Haze (72)	*1048*
Indian Love Call–Ray Stevens (75)	*140*
Smoke Gets In Your Eyes–Four Preps (61)	*130*
(When Your Heart's On Fire) Smoke Gets In Your Eyes–Richard Barrett (58)	*18*
–Edgar Yipsel Harburg see: E.Y. HARBURG	
E.Y. HARBURG [Edgar Yipsel Harburg, Isadore Hochberg] ▶ 2193 (7) HOF	**1757**
Ding Dong! The Witch Is Dead–Fifth Estate (67)	1521
Over The Rainbow–Demensions (60)	*1404*
Themes From The Wizard Of Oz–Meco (78)	477
Over The Rainbow–Gary Tanner (78)	*109*
April In Paris–Modernaires (56)	*2.8*
Over The Rainbow–Baysiders (60)	*0.0*
April In Paris–Count Basie Big Band with Ella Fitzgerald (56)	*0.0*
Lula Mae HARDAWAY ▶ 1338 (8)	**3317**
I Was Made To Love Her–Stevie Wonder (67)	*5544*
Signed, Sealed, Delivered I'm Yours–Stevie Wonder (70)	*5081*
Signed, Sealed, Delivered (I'm Yours)–Peter Frampton (77)	*1028*
You Met Your Match–Stevie Wonder (68)	659
I Don't Know Why–Stevie Wonder (69)	*386*
I Don't Know Why–Rolling Stones (75)	*236*
I Was Made To Love Her–King Curtis & The Kingpins (67)	*88*
I Was Made To Love Her–Stars On 45 (82)	*27*
Paul HARDCASTLE ▶ 4251 (2)	**545**
19–Paul Hardcastle (85)	792
Rain Forest–Paul Hardcastle (85)	347
Bobby HARDEN ▶ 4795 (1)	**412**
Tippy Toeing–Harden Trio (66)	412
Mel HARDEN ▶ 3192 (1)	**957**
Backfield In Motion–Mel And Tim (69)	1914
–Charles Hardin see: Buddy HOLLY	
Ed HARDIN ▶ 11057 (1)	**3.5**
Time Seller–Spencer Davis Group (67)	10
Glen HARDIN ▶ 708 (6)	**6155**
Count Me In–Gary Lewis And The Playboys (65)	4380
My Heart's Symphony–Gary Lewis And The Playboys (66)	1158
Where Will The Words Come From–Gary Lewis And The Playboys (66)	862
Hung Up In Your Eyes–Brian Hyland (67)	191
April Again–Dean Martin (68)	78
Holiday For Clowns–Brian Hyland (67)	25
–Lillian Hardin see: Lillian Hardin ARMSTRONG	
Tim HARDIN ▶ 508 (7)	**8333**
Reason To Believe–Rod Stewart (71)	4300
If I Were A Carpenter–Bobby Darin (66)	*2328*
If I Were A Carpenter–Four Tops (68)	*924*

If I Were A Carpenter–Johnny Cash & June Carter (70)	*514*
The Lady Came From Baltimore–Bobby Darin (67)	152
If I Were A Carpenter–Bob Seger (72)	*77*
If I Were A Carpenter–Leon Russell (74)	*38*
Chuck HARDING ▶ 8862 (1)	**38**
Honky Tonk Girl–Johnny Cash (60)	75
Hagood HARDY ▶ 4240 (1)	**548**
The Homecoming–Hagood Hardy (75)	548
Tynetta HARE ▶ 9251 (1)	**28**
Go For It (Heart And Fire)–Joey B. Ellis & Tynetta Hare (90)	111
Regi HARGIS [Reginald J. Hargis, Regi Hargis Hickman] ▶ 2365 (5)	**1557**
Dazz–Brick (76)	3530
Dusic–Brick (77)	793
Ain't Gonna Hurt Nobody–Kid 'N Play (91)	*223*
Ain't Gonna' Hurt Nobody–Brick (77)	*39*
Sweat (Til You Get Wet)–Brick (81)	16
–Reginald J. Hargis see: Regi HARGIS	
Ron HARGRAVE [Johnny Deerfield] ▶ 5297 (1)	**310**
High School Confidential–Jerry Lee Lewis And His Pumping Piano (58)	621
Robert HARGREAVES ▶ 9310 (3)	**27**
If–Timi Yuro (64)	*42*
If–Paragons (61)	*33*
If–Roy Hamilton (61)	*5.2*
Linda Ann HARGROVE ▶ 5501 (1)	**277**
Let It Shine–Olivia Newton-John (75)	277
–Hans Haring see: Hans CARSTE	
Gary HARJU ▶ 6414 (2)	**173**
Fire In The Morning–Melissa Manchester (80)	515
Pirate–Cher (77)	4.4
Morten HARKET ▶ 2519 (1)	**1421**
Take On Me–A-Ha (85)	4264
Brendan HARKIN ▶ 6794 (4)	**136**
Cherry Baby–Starz (77)	510
Sing It, Shout It–Starz (77)	148
(Any Way That You Want It) I'll Be There–Starz (78)	26
(She's Just A) Fallen Angel–Starz (76)	6.5
–Kurt Harland see: Kurt VALAQUEN	
–Jack Harlen see: Britt SIMONSON	
Steve HARLEY [Stephen Nice] ▶ 10241 (2)	**11**
Somebody Special–Rod Stewart (81)	44
Make Me Smile (Come Up And See Me)–Steve Harley And Cockney Rebel (76)	3.5
Leigh HARLINE ▶ 5235 (5)	**321**
When You Wish Upon A Star–Dion And The Belmonts (60)	*609*
When You Wish Upon A Star–Joni James (55)	*33*
When You Wish Upon A Star–Cliff Edwards (55)	*0.0*
When You Wish Upon A Star–Rosemary Clooney & Harry James (55)	*0.0*
When You Wish Upon A Star–Jack Pleis and His Orchestra and Chorus (55)	*0.0*
W. Franke HARLING [William Franke Harling] ▶ 8589 (2)	**45**
Beyond The Blue Horizon–Lou Christie (74)	103
Sing You Sinners–Tony Bennett with Percy Faith and His Orchestra (56)	22
–Allen Harlow see: Allen HAWIRKO	
Charmaine HARMA ▶ 7839 (1)	**73**
Dancin' Out Of My Heart–Ronnie Dove (67)	145
–Buddy Harman see: Murrey HARMAN	
Murrey HARMAN [Buddy Harman, Murrey Mizell Harman Jr.] ▶ 6240 (1)	**190**
Boo Boo Stick Beat–Chet Atkins (59)	381
–Terry Harmon see: Carl T. FISCHER	
William HARMON ▶ 4545 (1)	**467**
The Way I Feel About You–Karyn White (91)	1868
Jesse HARMS ▶ 2226 (1)	**1722**
Walk On Water–Eddie Money (88)	1722
Jimmy HARNEN ▶ 4017 (2)	**622**
Where Are You Now?–Jimmy Harnen w/Synch (89)	*1182*
Where Are You Now?–Synch (86)	*62*
Bud HARNER ▶ 10125 (1)	**12**
Take Away–Big Ric (83)	37

Sheldon HARNICK ▶ 3728 (12) HOF	**718**
Artificial Flowers—Bobby Darin (60)	*1153*
Sunrise, Sunset—Roger Williams (67)	144
Uh-Uh Oh Yeah—Steve Lawrence (58)	*75*
Freddy—Annie Cordy (55)	*46*
Freddy—Connie Francis (55)	*46*
Til Tomorrow—Janice Harper (60)	18
Uh Yuh Oh Yeah—Bill Hayes (58)	*0.0*
Uh-Huh, Oh Yeah—Jill Corey (58)	*0.0*
Fredy—Eartha Kitt & Perez Prado (55)	*0.0*
Artificial Flowers—Phil Napoleon (60)	*0.0*
Freddy—Stan Kenton & His Orchestra (55)	*0.0*
Freddy—Guy Lombardo & His Royal Canadians (55)	*0.0*
—Charles Harold see: Charles H. CUPPETT	
William HAROLD ▶ 9548 (1)	**22**
Goofus—Carpenters (76)	65
Charles HARPER ▶ 10799 (1)	**5.3**
Give My Love A Try—Linda Jones (67)	21
—Jimmy Harper see: James S. HANCOCK	
John HARPER ▶ 4880 (5)	**391**
Learning To Love—Peggy King (55)	*391*
Learning To Love—Jean Dinning (55)	*0.0*
Learning To Love—Dori Anne Gray (55)	*0.0*
Learning To Love—Billy Williams Quartet (55)	*0.0*
Learning To Love—LaFawn Paul with The Whipporwills (55)	*0.0*
Marjorie HARPER ▶ 5281 (2)	**314**
Jealous Of You (Tango Della Gelosia)—Connie Francis (60)	784
Roman Guitar (Chitarra Romana)—Lou Monte (57)	157
Ricci HARPER ▶ 6285 (1)	**186**
Them That Got—Ray Charles And His Orchestra (61)	371
Slim HARPO [James H. Moore, James Isaac Moore] ▶ 2106 (5)	**1868**
Baby Scratch My Back—Slim Harpo (66)	1524
Rainin' In My Heart—Slim Harpo (61)	634
Shake Your Hips—Slim Harpo (66)	24
Tip On In (Part 1)—Slim Harpo (67)	4.1
I'm Your Bread Maker, Baby—Slim Harpo (66)	0.5
Vernon HARRELL ▶ 7702 (1)	**80**
Sweet, Sweet Lovin'—Platters (67)	159
Bill HARRINGTON ▶ 10763 (1)	**5.5**
My Girl—Frankie Lymon (57)	11
Jeff HARRINGTON ▶ 3463 (5)	**835**
Stranded—Heart (90)	1124
Killin' Time—Fred Knoblock & Susan Anton (80)	467
Natural Love—Petula Clark (82)	43
In The Drivers Seat—John Schneider (82)	40
Runaway Rita—Leif Garrett (81)	26
Addie HARRIS ▶ 6832 (1)	**134**
I Met Him On A Sunday (Ronde-Ronde)—Shirelles (58)	537
Art HARRIS ▶ 3164 (4)	**975**
What Am I Living For—Conway Twitty (60)	*839*
What Am I Living For—Chuck Willis (58)	*788*
What Am I Living For—Ray Charles (71)	*315*
What Am I Living For—Percy Sledge (67)	*8.1*
Barry HARRIS ▶ 4661 (2)	**444**
I Beg Your Pardon—Kon Kan (88)	849
Puss N Boots—Kon Kan (89)	78
Bob HARRIS ▶ 8399 (2)	**52**
Lolita Ya-Ya—Ventures (62)	88
Theme From "Lolita"—Orchestra Del Oro (62)	7.9
Cal HARRIS ▶ 6215 (1)	**193**
Just Want To Hold You—Jasmine Guy (91)	578
Cecil HARRIS ▶ 11527 (1)	**1.3**
Butternut—Jimmy Heap (56)	2.6
Christopher C. HARRIS Jr. ▶ 8814 (1)	**39**
Hold Back The Tears—Delacardos (61)	39
David HARRIS ▶ 7867 (1)	**71**
Gonna Make It—Sa-Fire (89)	71
Don HARRIS [Don Francis Bowman Harris, Don "Sugarcane" Harris] ▶ 635 (9)	**6818**
I'm Leaving It Up To You—Dale & Grace (63)	*7593*
The Jolly Green Giant—Kingsmen (65)	2937
I'm Leaving It (All) Up To You—Donny And Marie Osmond (74)	*2345*
Farmer John—Premiers (64)	*827*
Big Boy Pete—Olympics (60)	760
Farmer John—Tidal Waves (66)	*70*

The Letter—Sonny & Cher (65)	43
Justine—Righteous Brothers (65)	34
Surfer Street—Allisons (63)	3.7
Eddie HARRIS ▶ 5391 (3)	**296**
Listen Here—Eddie Harris (68)	*280*
It's Crazy—Eddie Harris (68)	15
Listen Here—Brian Auger & The Trinity (70)	*0.8*
Edward HARRIS Jr. ▶ 7178 (1)	**111**
I'm Just A Prisoner (Of Your Good Lovin')—Candi Staton (70)	223
Ernie HARRIS ▶ 8234 (1)	**58**
Can You Get To That—Funkadelic (71)	115
Gerald HARRIS ▶ 8625 (2)	**45**
Love Explosion—Troy Keyes (68)	87
Last Minute Miracle—Shirelles (67)	1.9
James HARRIS ▶ 6084 (1)	**208**
In A Moment—Intrigues (69)	832
James Samuel HARRIS [Jimmy Jam Harris, Jimmy Jam] ▶ 79 (41) HOF	**27420**
Escapade—Janet Jackson (90)	4680
Miss You Much—Janet Jackson (89)	4522
Human—Human League (86)	4223
Romantic—Karyn White (91)	4086
When I Think Of You—Janet Jackson (86)	3710
Love Will Never Do (Without You)—Janet Jackson (90)	3500
Rhythm Nation—Janet Jackson (89)	3288
Sensitivity—Ralph Tresvant (90)	2969
Come Back To Me—Janet Jackson (90)	2853
Let's Wait Awhile—Janet Jackson (87)	2779
Rub You The Right Way—Johnny Gill (90)	2737
I Didn't Mean To Turn You On—Robert Palmer (86)	*2661*
Control—Janet Jackson (86)	2464
Nasty—Janet Jackson (86)	2409
Alright—Janet Jackson (90)	2323
What Have You Done For Me Lately—Janet Jackson (86)	2231
If It Isn't Love—New Edition (88)	1864
Diamonds—Herb Alpert (87)	1768
Jerk-Out—Time (90)	1425
Tender Love—Force M.D.'s (86)	1303
Saturday Love—Cherrelle (86)	565
Fake—Alexander O'Neal (87)	534
Never Knew Love Like This—Alexander O'Neal (88)	468
Fishnet—Morris Day (88)	464
Making Love In The Rain—Herb Alpert (87)	379
Just Be Good To Me—S.O.S. Band (83)	*354*
I Need Your Loving—Human League (86)	343
The Finest—S.O.S. Band (86)	326
All True Man—Alexander O'Neal (91)	291
State Of The World—Janet Jackson (91)	290
Keep Your Eye On Me—Herb Alpert (87)	239
Can You Stand The Rain—New Edition (89)	227
The Heat Of Heat—Patti Austin (86)	211
Tell Me If You Still Care—S.O.S. Band (83)	173
Just The Way You Like It—S.O.S. Band (84)	155
Encore—Cheryl Lynn (84)	117
I Didn't Mean To Turn You On—Cherrelle (84)	*91*
Dub Be Good To Me—Beats International (90)	*72*
Borrowed Love—Bingoboys (91)	35
Wrap My Body Tight—Johnny Gill (91)	30
You're Not My Kind Of Girl—New Edition (88)	5.3
Jerome HARRIS ▶ 6750 (1)	**140**
There's No Living Without Your Loving—Peter And Gordon (66)	281
—Jimmy Jam Harris see: James Samuel HARRIS	
—John Harris see: Hal SHAPER	
John Earl (Sonny) HARRIS ▶ 2893 (4)	**1129**
Papa Oom Mow Mow—Trashmen (63)	*1861*
Bird Is The Word—Trashmen (63)	*1861*
Papa-Oom-Mow-Mow—Rivingtons (62)	*480*
The Bird's The Word—Rivingtons (63)	*315*
Johnny HARRIS ▶ 6747 (2)	**141**
Jubilation—Paul Anka (72)	247
Don't Leave Me In The Morning—Odia Coates (75)	35
Kenny HARRIS ▶ 10060 (1)	**13**
Darlin' I—Vanessa Williams (89)	27
Kent HARRIS ▶ 7696 (2)	**80**
Shoppin' For Clothes—Coasters (60)	116
So Far Away—Hank Jacobs (64)	82
Lew HARRIS ▶ 9451 (1)	**23**

Things I Love—Fidelity's (58)	47
Lloyd HARRIS ▶ 10537 (1)	**7.5**
Action Speaks Louder Than Words—Chocolate Milk (75)	67
—Marcene Harris see: Dimple M. JACKSON	
Mark HARRIS ▶ 9627 (1)	**20**
Joanie—Frankie Calen (61)	40
Mark L. HARRIS ▶ 9462 (1)	**23**
Don't Take The Stars—Mystics (59)	46
Norman HARRIS ▶ 2927 (13)	**1114**
Armed And Extremely Dangerous—First Choice (73)	913
Smarty Pants—First Choice (73)	456
Hold Back The Night—Trammps (76)	*426*
Doctor Love—First Choice (77)	236
Walk Right Up To The Sun—Delfonics (71)	182
Good Things Don't Last Forever—Ecstasy, Passion & Pain (74)	130
The Player - Part 1—First Choice (74)	121
Hold Back The Night—Graham Parker And The Rumour (77)	*83*
Dreamin'—Loleatta Holloway (77)	46
A Mother For My Children—Whispers (74)	16
Newsy Neighbors—First Choice (74)	11
We're On The Right Track—South Shore Commission (76)	7.7
Touch And Go—Ecstasy, Passion & Pain Featuring Barbara Roy (76)	1.4
Oscar HARRIS ▶ 10495 (1)	**7.9**
Chicken, Baby, Chicken—Tony Harris (57)	7.9
Pete HARRIS ▶ 11053 (1)	**3.5**
You'll Find Out—Jeanne Black (60)	3.5
Peter Brian HARRIS ▶ 2584 (4)	**1347**
Touch Me (I Want Your Body)—Samantha Fox (86)	2117
Parents Just Don't Understand—D.J. Jazzy Jeff & The Fresh Prince (88)	1067
A Nightmare On My Street—D.J. Jazzy Jeff & The Fresh Prince (88)	778
I Think I Can Beat Mike Tyson—D.J. Jazzy Jeff & The Fresh Prince (89)	79
Phil HARRIS ▶ 9661 (1)	**19**
Rock & Roll Runaway—Ace (75)	77
Remus HARRIS ▶ 5149 (1)	**334**
St Therese Of The Roses—Billy Ward And His Dominoes (56)	668
—Robert Harris see: Robert Patrick WESTON	
Robert Lamont HARRIS ▶ 6937 (2)	**127**
Joystick—Dazz Band (84)	227
Let It All Blow—Dazz Band (84)	27
Roberta HARRIS ▶ 6785 (1)	**137**
Lazy Elsie Molly—Chubby Checker (64)	411
Rolf HARRIS ▶ 1375 (3)	**3238**
Tie Me Kangaroo Down, Sport—Rolf Harris (63)	3050
Sun Arise—Rolf Harris (63)	369
Nick Teen And Al K. Hall—Rolf Harris (63)	2.7
Ruth HARRIS ▶ 9463 (1)	**23**
Don't Take The Stars—Mystics (59)	46
Sam HARRIS ▶ 7648 (1)	**83**
I'd Do It All Again—Sam Harris (86)	166
Schzelle HARRIS ▶ 8145 (1)	**60**
Ain't No Future In Yo' Frontin'—M.C. Breed (91)	180
Sean HARRIS ▶ 9028 (1)	**33**
The Swalk—Notorious (90)	66
Ted HARRIS [Ebb Tide] ▶ 7149 (1)	**113**
Cryin' In The Streets (Part I)—George Perkins & The Silver Stars (70)	340
Theodore C. HARRIS ▶ 4819 (1)	**406**
Crystal Chandelier—Vic Dana (65)	406
Thurston HARRIS ▶ 8186 (1)	**59**
Do What You Did—Thurston Harris (58)	59
Valmond HARRIS ▶ 9316 (1)	**26**
Across The Street—Lenny O'Henry (64)	79
Victor HARRIS ▶ 5943 (2)	**225**
Sax Fifth Avenue—Johnny Beecher And His Buckingham Road Quintet (63)	*225*
Sax Fifth Avenue—Jack Cole Quintet (63)	*0.0*
Woody HARRIS ▶ 1296 (4)	**3426**
Queen Of The Hop—Bobby Darin (58)	2086
Rock A Billy—Guy Mitchell (57)	1415
Early In The Morning—Rinky-Dinks (58)	*694*
Early In The Morning—Buddy Holly / The Crickets (58)	*570*

Benny HARRISON ▶ 6533 (1)	**159**
You're My Girl—Franke and the Knockouts (81)	478
Danny HARRISON ▶ 11045 (1)	**3.6**
(How Can I Write On Paper) What I Feel In My Heart—Jim Reeves (61)	14
George HARRISON [Nelson Wilbury] ▶ 62 (36)	**34690**
My Sweet Lord—George Harrison (70)	*9566*
Photograph—Ringo Starr (73)	5208
Something—Beatles (69)	*5157*
Give Me Love (Give Me Peace On Earth)—George Harrison (73)	4377
All Those Years Ago—George Harrison (81)	3249
What Is Life—George Harrison (71)	1765
Here Comes The Sun—Richie Havens (71)	*1210*
Blow Away—George Harrison (79)	1035
Bangla-Desh—George Harrison (71)	829
Dark Horse—George Harrison (74)	726
Crackerbox Palace—George Harrison (77)	720
You—George Harrison (75)	695
This Song—George Harrison (76)	617
Handle With Care—Traveling Wilburys (88)	448
When We Was Fab—George Harrison (88)	422
Wrack My Brain—Ringo Starr (81)	380
Ding Dong; Ding Dong—George Harrison (75)	283
Something—Shirley Bassey (70)	*247*
Badge—Cream (69)	230
Isn't It A Pity—George Harrison (70)	222
Try Some, Buy Some—Ronnie Spector (71)	173
End Of The Line—Traveling Wilburys (89)	166
Wake Up My Love—George Harrison (82)	138
For You Blue—Beatles (70)	92
Something—Booker T. & The M.G.'s (70)	*66*
My Sweet Lord—Billy Preston (71)	*28*
Something—Johnny Rodriguez (74)	*14*
Teardrops—George Harrison (81)	9.0
Taxman—Stars On 45 (81)	8.0
My Sweet Lord—Stars On 45 (81)	*8.0*
Here Comes The Sun—Stars On 45 (81)	*8.0*
While My Guitar Gently Weeps—Stars On 45 (81)	8.0
Awaiting On You All—Silver Hawk (71)	3.4
The Inner Light—Beatles (68)	2.3
Deep Blue—George Harrison (71)	0.0
Apple Scruffs—George Harrison (71)	0.0
George (2) HARRISON ▶ 11528 (1)	**1.3**
Butternut—Jimmy Heap (56)	2.6
Jerry HARRISON ▶ 3837 (6)	**686**
Burning Down The House—Talking Heads (83)	1439
Wild Wild Life—Talking Heads (86)	742
And She Was—Talking Heads (85)	350
This Must Be The Place (Naïve Melody)—Talking Heads (83)	156
Once In A Lifetime—Talking Heads (86)	39
Life During Wartime (This Ain't No Party.. This Aint No Disco.. This Ain't No Foolin' Around)—Talking Heads (79)	25
—Katherine Harrison see: Claude BAUM	
Keith HARRISON ▶ 9965 (2)	**14**
Let It All Blow—Dazz Band (84)	27
Riding High—Faze-O (78)	4.8
Larry HARRISON ▶ 2172 (5)	**1792**
Why Baby Why—Pat Boone (57)	2033
(You Don't Know) How Glad I Am—Nancy Wilson (64)	*1420*
Only Love (Can Save Me Now)—Solomon Burke (65)	58
How Glad I Am—Kiki Dee Band (75)	*55*
Nothing Goes Up (Without Coming Down)—Nat King Cole (63)	26
Neil HARRISON ▶ 3013 (1)	**1068**
I Could Never Miss You (More Than I Do)—Lulu (81)	1068
Nigel HARRISON ▶ 5617 (1)	**264**
One Way Or Another—Blondie (79)	792
Wilbert HARRISON ▶ 2242 (3)	**1709**
Let's Work Together—Canned Heat (70)	*936*
Let's Work Together (Part 1)—Wilbert Harrison (69)	*771*
My Heart Is Yours—Wilbert Harrison (71)	2.6
Deborah HARRY [Angela Tremble] ▶ 554 (9)	**7779**
Call Me—Blondie (80)	10151
Heart Of Glass—Blondie (79)	5717
Rapture—Blondie (81)	5100
One Way Or Another—Blondie (79)	792
Dreaming—Blondie (79)	716
Island Of Lost Souls—Blondie (82)	344

Atomic—Blondie (80)	298
In Love With Love—Debbie Harry (87)	99
The Hardest Part—Blondie (80)	69
—Robert L. Harshman see: Bobby HART	
Bernice HART ▶ 5566 (1)	**271**
Master Of Eyes (The Deepness Of Your Eyes)—Aretha Franklin (73)	542
Bobby HART [Robert L. Harshman] ▶ 202 (25)	**15614**
Last Train To Clarksville—Monkees (66)	8046
Valleri—Monkees (68)	5053
Come A Little Bit Closer—Jay & The Americans (64)	4277
I Wonder What She's Doing Tonite—Tommy Boyce & Bobby Hart (67)	2377
Hurt So Bad—Lettermen (69)	*2180*
Something's Wrong With Me—Austin Roberts (72)	1783
Hurt So Bad—Linda Ronstadt (80)	*1686*
Words—Monkees (67)	1659
Hurt So Bad—Little Anthony And The Imperials (65)	*1409*
Keep On Singing—Helen Reddy (74)	*1390*
Alice Long (You're Still My Favorite Girlfriend)—Tommy Boyce & Bobby Hart (68)	1025
Dominoes—Robbie Nevil (87)	899
(I'm Not Your) Steppin' Stone—Monkees (66)	668
Out And About—Tommy Boyce & Bobby Hart (67)	489
Tear Drop City—Monkees (69)	461
Lazy Elsie Molly—Chubby Checker (64)	411
Keep On Singing—Austin Roberts (73)	*409*
Goodbye Baby (I Don't Want To See You Cry)—Tommy Boyce & Bobby Hart (68)	373
Sinner Man—Trini Lopez (65)	335
Around The Corner—Duprees (65)	56
Sometimes She's A Little Girl—Tommy Boyce & Bobby Hart (67)	44
Friend And A Lover—Partridge Family Starring Shirley Jones & Featuring David Cassidy (73)	40
Words (Are Impossible)—Donny Gerrard (76)	*29*
Words (Are Impossible)—Margie Joseph (74)	*9.9*
Hurt So Bad—Jackie DeShannon (70)	*1.0*
Bruce HART ▶ 2835 (1)	**1163**
You Take My Breath Away—Rex Smith (79)	2326
Corey HART ▶ 533 (9)	**8035**
Never Surrender—Corey Hart (85)	2697
Sunglasses At Night—Corey Hart (84)	2060
It Ain't Enough—Corey Hart (84)	893
I Am By Your Side—Corey Hart (86)	681
Everything In My Heart—Corey Hart (85)	577
Boy In The Box—Corey Hart (85)	538
In Your Soul—Corey Hart (88)	292
A Little Love—Corey Hart (90)	286
Dancin' With My Mirror—Corey Hart (87)	9.6
Dick HART ▶ 9307 (1)	**27**
Six Pack To Go—Hank Thompson (60)	80
Freddie HART [Frederick Segrest] ▶ 2257 (1)	**1696**
Easy Loving—Freddie Hart (71)	1696
—Gladys Hart see: Gladys REINHARDT	
Jimmy HART ▶ 5296 (1)	**312**
Why Should I Cry—Gentrys (70)	312
Ken HART ▶ 5882 (3)	**233**
Dogface Soldier—Russ Morgan And His Orchestra (55)	*467*
Dog Face Soldier—Joe Lipman (55)	*0.0*
Dogface Soldier—Stephen Make (55)	*0.0*
Lorenz HART ▶ 653 (9) HOF	**6701**
Blue Moon—Marcels (61)	*9049*
Where Or When—Dion And The Belmonts (59)	*3185*
Glad To Be Unhappy—Mamas & The Papas (67)	649
Blue Moon—Elvis Presley (56)	*266*
Blue Moon—Herb Lance & The Classics (61)	*121*
I Didn't Know What Time It Was—Ray Charles (69)	*75*
I Didn't Know What Time It Was—Crampton Sisters (64)	*44*
Blue Moon—Jimmy Bowen With The Rhythm Orchids (58)	*12*
Where Or When—Lettermen (63)	*1.8*
Rod HART ▶ 6274 (1)	**187**
C.B. Savage—Rod Hart (76)	187
Roger HART [Roger Garfield Ferrier] ▶ 3391 (1)	**870**
Just Like Me—Paul Revere And The Raiders Featuring Mark Lindsay (65)	1739

Wilbert HART ▶ 11804 (1)	**0.0**
Hey! Love—Delfonics (71)	0.0
William HART ▶ 877 (16)	**5065**
La - La - Means I Love You—Delfonics (68)	*3448*
Didn't I (Blow Your Mind This Time)—Delfonics (70)	*1925*
Didn't I (Blow Your Mind)—New Kids On The Block (89)	*1171*
Ready Or Not Here I Come (Can't Hide From Love)—Delfonics (68)	642
You Got Yours And I'll Get Mine—Delfonics (69)	584
Break Your Promise—Delfonics (68)	575
Trying To Make A Fool Of Me—Delfonics (70)	497
I'm Sorry—Delfonics (68)	413
Over And Over—Delfonics (71)	325
La La Means I Love You—Tierra (81)	*142*
Tell Me This Is A Dream—Delfonics (72)	92
Somebody Loves You—Delfonics (69)	83
He Don't Really Love You—Delfonics (68)	30
Think It Over—Delfonics (73)	27
Funny Feeling—Delfonics (69)	24
I Don't Want To Make You Wait—Delfonics (73)	22
John HARTFORD ▶ 3929 (6)	**653**
Gentle On My Mind—Glen Campbell (68)	*182*
Gentle On My Mind—Glen Campbell (67)	*159*
California Earthquake—Mama Cass (68)	136
Gentle On My Mind—Patti Page (68)	*115*
Gentle On My Mind—Aretha Franklin (69)	*50*
Gentle On My Mind—Dean Martin (69)	*12*
Dan HARTMAN ▶ 569 (15)	**7610**
Good Vibrations—Marky Mark & The Funky Bunch (91)	3166
I Can Dream About You—Dan Hartman (84)	2178
Living In America—James Brown (85)	1992
Free Ride—Edgar Winter Group (73)	*1640*
Instant Replay—Dan Hartman (78)	827
We Are The Young—Dan Hartman (84)	641
Second Nature—Dan Hartman (85)	384
River's Risin'—Edgar Winter (74)	302
Hangin' Around—Edgar Winter Group (73)	214
Free Ride—Tavares (75)	*142*
The Love You Take—Dan Hartman And Denise Lopez (88)	49
Easy Street—Edgar Winter Group (74)	37
Heaven In Your Arms—Dan Hartman (81)	14
This Is It—Dan Hartman (79)	11
Gravity—James Brown (86)	4.8
John HARTMAN ▶ 11257 (1)	**2.6**
Wheels Of Fortune—Doobie Brothers (76)	7.7
Paul HARTWIG ▶ 9995 (1)	**14**
Victory Line—Limited Warranty (86)	71
Alex HARVEY ▶ 728 (10)	**6014**
Delta Dawn—Helen Reddy (73)	*5954*
Tell It All Brother—Kenny Rogers And The First Edition (70)	1259
Reuben James—Kenny Rogers And The First Edition (69)	1195
Rings—Cymarron (71)	*1055*
Someone Who Cares—Kenny Rogers And The First Edition (71)	389
Rings—Lobo (74)	*367*
Delta Dawn—Tanya Tucker (72)	*41*
Married To A Memory—Judy Lynn (71)	*35*
Rings—Reuben Howell (74)	*20*
Married To A Memory—Arlene Harden (71)	*16*
Bill HARVEY ▶ 10090 (1)	**13**
Next Time You See Me—Little Junior Parker (57)	26
Doni HARVEY ▶ 10943 (1)	**4.2**
My Pearl—Automatic Man (76)	17
—Jane Harvey see: Phyllis TAFF	
Sarah HARVEY ▶ 6508 (1)	**161**
Here Comes The Judge—Pigmeat Markham (68)	646
Stephen Laurence HARVEY ▶ 4772 (1)	**419**
Trouble—Nia Peeples (88)	419
Steven HARVEY ▶ 8282 (1)	**56**
Deep Blue Sea—Jimmy Dean with Ray Ellis and his Orchestra (57)	111
Iain HARVIE ▶ 6789 (1)	**137**
Kiss This Thing Goodbye—Del Amitri (90)	410
Barry HARWOOD ▶ 7735 (1)	**77**
Don't Misunderstand Me—Rossington Collins Band (80)	231

Tony HASELDEN ▶ 3935 (1)	**651**
Nobody Said It Was Easy (Lookin' For The Lights)—Le Roux (82)	651
Max HASKETT ▶ 4410 (1)	**502**
I'm Gonna Take Care Of Everything—Rubicon (78)	502
Clarence HASKINS ▶ 6564 (5)	**156**
All Your Goodies Are Gone (The Loser's Seat)—Parliaments (67)	221
I Wanna Know If It's Good To You?—Funkadelic (70)	65
Up For The Down Stroke—Parliament (74)	57
I Got A Thing, You Got A Thing, Everybody's Got A Thing—Funkadelic (70)	44
You And Your Folks, Me And My Folks—Funkadelic (71)	34
David HASKINS [David John Haskins, David J.] ▶ 3616 (2)	**765**
So Alive—Love and Rockets (89)	2251
No Big Deal—Love and Rockets (89)	44
Kevin HASKINS [Kevin Michael Dompe] ▶ 3617 (2)	**765**
So Alive—Love and Rockets (89)	2251
No Big Deal—Love and Rockets (89)	44
—A.G. Hassan see: Ann GODWIN	
—Shadee Hassan see: Allen STORY	
Earl HATCH ▶ 6523 (2)	**160**
What's The Reason I'm Not Pleasing You—Fats Domino (56)	*415*
What's The Reason—Bobby Edwards (62)	*225*
Tony HATCH [Mark Anthony, Fred Nightingale] ▶ 58 (33) HOF	**36867**
Downtown—Petula Clark (64)	*8873*
My Love—Petula Clark (65)	5229
I Know A Place—Petula Clark (65)	4624
Forget Him—Bobby Rydell (63)	3638
You're The One—Vogues (65)	2706
Don't Sleep In The Subway—Petula Clark (67)	2193
I Couldn't Live Without Your Love—Petula Clark (66)	1795
Look For A Star—Garry Miles (60)	*1432*
A Sign Of The Times—Petula Clark (66)	1306
Color My World—Petula Clark (66)	1085
Look For A Star—Billy Vaughn And His Orchestra (60)	*1083*
Call Me—Chris Montez (66)	891
Who Am I—Petula Clark (66)	811
Round Every Corner—Petula Clark (65)	798
Look For A Star—Deane Hawley (60)	*777*
You'd Better Come Home—Petula Clark (65)	758
Look For A Star Part One—Garry Mills (60)	*739*
Don't Give Up—Petula Clark (68)	589
The Other Man's Grass Is Always Greener—Petula Clark (67)	564
Crazy Downtown—Allan Sherman (65)	*524*
Sugar And Spice—Cryan' Shames (66)	*491*
You've Got To Be Loved—Montanas (68)	408
American Boys—Petula Clark (68)	362
Sugar And Spice—Searchers (64)	*320*
Love Is Me, Love Is You—Connie Francis (66)	176
Look At Mine—Petula Clark (69)	144
Roundabout—Connie Francis (65)	73
Downtown—Mrs. Miller (66)	*27*
Downtown—Dolly Parton (84)	*25*
To Show I Love You—Peter And Gordon (66)	11
If You Ever Leave Me—Jack Jones (68)	8.2
Run To Me—Montanas (68)	3.2
Look For A Star—Nicky Como (60)	*0.0*
—Charles Edwin Hatcher see: Edwin STARR	
Bobby HATFIELD ▶ 7333 (2)	**101**
My Babe—Righteous Brothers (63)	181
Bring Your Love To Me—Righteous Brothers (65)	21
Chuck HATFIELD ▶ 7477 (1)	**93**
Wizard Of Love—Ly-Dells (61)	279
Donny HATHAWAY [Donny Pitts] ▶ 7250 (3)	**108**
The Ghetto—Too Short (90)	337
The Ghetto - Part 1—Donny Hathaway (70)	38
I Thank You—Donny Hathaway And June Conquest (72)	8.8
Richard HATHAWAY ▶ 5923 (1)	**228**
Make A Little Magic—Dirt Band (80)	684
Johnny HATHCOCK ▶ 11463 (1)	**1.6**
Welcome To My World—Jim Reeves (64)	3.2

Rob HATHCOCK ▶ 10737 (1)	**5.6**
Biscuit's In The House—Biscuit (90)	34
—Douglas Farthing Hatlelid see: Chip DOUGLAS	
Ian HATTON ▶ 8636 (1)	**44**
Wait For You—Bonham (89)	221
—Otto Abels Hauerbach see: Otto HARBACH	
Felix HAUG ▶ 4615 (1)	**450**
The Captain Of Her Heart—Double (86)	901
Tim HAUSER ▶ 11610 (1)	**1.0**
Clap Your Hands—Manhattan Transfer (75)	4.0
Howard HAUSEY [Howard Crockett, Howard Elton Hausey] ▶ 10326 (2)	**10**
Old Slew Foot—Johnny Horton (61)	26
Honky-Tonk Man—Johnny Horton (62)	4.4
Carl HAUSMAN ▶ 6980 (1)	**124**
Won't Find Better (Than Me)—New Hope (70)	248
Michael HAUSMAN ▶ 4583 (3)	**462**
Voices Carry—'til tuesday (85)	1719
Looking Over My Shoulder—til tuesday (85)	115
Love In A Vacuum—'til tuesday (85)	12
Carl HAVERLIN ▶ 11577 (1)	**1.2**
Jine The Cavalry—Mitch Miller and The Gang (59)	2.3
Bess HAWES ▶ 4262 (2)	**541**
M. T. A.—Kingston Trio (59)	*1082*
The M.T.A.—Gateway Singers (59)	*0.0*
Bruce HAWES ▶ 2027 (4)	**1993**
They Just Can't Stop It the (Games People Play)—Spinners (75)	4227
Mighty Love - Pt. I—Spinners (74)	1001
Love Or Leave—Spinners (75)	438
Sadie—Spinners (75)	314
Jeanette HAWES ▶ 6269 (2)	**187**
I Don't Wanna Lose Your Love—Emotions (76)	*279*
I Don't Want To Lose Your Love—B Angie B (91)	*96*
Allen HAWIRKO [Allen Harlow] ▶ 9065 (1)	**32**
Flyin'—Prism (78)	159
Ken HAWKER [Kenneth Alan James Hawker, Ken Lewis] ▶ 622 (8)	**6958**
Little Bit O' Soul—Music Explosion (67)	*6710*
Can't You Hear My Heartbeat—Herman's Hermits (65)	5330
Is It True—Brenda Lee (64)	1118
Sunday For Tea—Peter And Gordon (67)	525
Tossing & Turning—Ivy League (65)	220
Little Bit O' Soul—Bullet (72)	*50*
Funny How Love Can Be—First Class (75)	37
Let's Go To San Francisco—Stars On 45 (81)	12
Mike HAWKER ▶ 1956 (9)	**2052**
I Only Want To Be With You—Bay City Rollers (76)	*1517*
I Only Want To Be With You—Dusty Springfield (64)	*1347*
Stay Awhile—Dusty Springfield (64)	*460*
I Only Wanna Be With You—Samantha Fox (89)	*438*
I Only Want To Be With You—Nicolette Larson (82)	*267*
Stay Awhile—Continental Miniatures (78)	*42*
I Only Want To Be With You—Tourists (80)	*20*
You Don't Know—Helen Shapiro (61)	12
Walkin' Back To Happiness—Helen Shapiro (61)	0.5
Barbara Anne HAWKINS ▶ 4827 (3)	**404**
Iko Iko—Belle Stars (89)	*940*
Iko Iko—Dixie Cups (65)	*854*
Iko Iko—Dr. John (72)	*226*
Charlotte HAWKINS ▶ 4845 (1)	**400**
With You On My Mind—Nat "King" Cole (57)	800
Dale HAWKINS ▶ 3503 (6)	**813**
Suzie Q (Part One)—Creedence Clearwater Revival (68)	*1687*
Susie Q—Dale Hawkins (57)	*544*
La Do Dada—Dale Hawkins (58)	484
Do You Believe In Shame?—Duran Duran (89)	93
Susie-Q—Crew-Cuts (57)	*0.0*
Susie-Q—José Feliciano (70)	*0.0*
Edwin HAWKINS ▶ 1083 (3)	**4078**
Oh Happy Day—Edwin Hawkins Singers Featuring: Dorothy Combs Morrison (69)	*3570*
Oh Happy Day—Glen Campbell (70)	*496*
Ain't It Like Him—Edwin Hawkins Singers (69)	12
Erskine HAWKINS ▶ 10111 (1)	**13**
Tuxedo Junction—Frankie Avalon (60)	51
—Jamesetta Hawkins see: Etta JAMES	

Kenny HAWKINS ▶ 6737 (1)	**141**
Wild And Crazy Love—Mary Jane Girls (85)	283
Michael J. HAWKINS ▶ 5841 (2)	**238**
Can This Be Real—Natural Four (73)	637
Love That Really Counts—Natural Four (74)	103
Ronnie HAWKINS ▶ 4773 (2)	**418**
Mary Lou—Ronnie Hawkins and The Hawks (59)	832
Southern Love—Ronnie Hawkins and The Hawks (59)	7.2
Rosa Lee HAWKINS ▶ 4828 (3)	**404**
Iko Iko—Belle Stars (89)	*940*
Iko Iko—Dixie Cups (65)	*854*
Iko Iko—Dr. John (72)	*226*
Roy HAWKINS ▶ 3830 (1)	**687**
The Thrill Is Gone—B.B. King (69)	1375
Screamin' Jay HAWKINS ▶ 5277 (3)	**314**
I Put A Spell On You—Creedence Clearwater Revival (68)	*292*
I Put A Spell On You—Alan Price Set (66)	*20*
I Put A Spell On You—Crazy World Of Arthur Brown (68)	*0.9*
Barry HAY ▶ 3337 (6)	**894**
Radar Love—Golden Earring (74)	*1460*
Radar Love—White Lion (89)	*180*
Candy's Going Bad—Golden Earring (74)	60
The Devil Made Me Do It—Golden Earring (83)	53
When The Lady Smiles—Golden Earring (84)	29
Ce Soir—Golden Earring (75)	9.4
Colin James HAY ▶ 228 (7)	**14865**
Down Under—Men At Work (82)	7714
Who Can It Be Now?—Men At Work (82)	5622
Overkill—Men At Work (83)	2991
It's A Mistake—Men At Work (83)	1633
Dr. Heckyll & Mr. Jive—Men At Work (83)	468
Everything I Need—Men At Work (85)	293
Hold Me—Colin James Hay (87)	0.8
Roy HAY ▶ 781 (10)	**5663**
Karma Chameleon—Culture Club (83)	5903
Do You Really Want To Hurt Me—Culture Club (82)	5783
Time (Clock Of The Heart)—Culture Club (83)	4056
Miss Me Blind—Culture Club (84)	2167
I'll Tumble 4 Ya—Culture Club (83)	1624
Church Of The Poison Mind—Culture Club (83)	1501
Move Away—Culture Club (86)	1007
It's A Miracle—Culture Club (84)	965
The War Song—Culture Club (84)	766
Mistake No. 3—Culture Club (84)	455
Tetsuji HAYASHI ▶ 10497 (1)	**7.8**
If I Have To Go Away—Jigsaw (77)	16
Peter HAYCOCK ▶ 4639 (2)	**446**
Couldn't Get It Right—Climax Blues Band (77)	2219
Makin' Love—Climax Blues Band (78)	10
Edward HAYCRAFT ▶ 7443 (1)	**95**
A Lonely Man—Chi-Lites (72)	191
—Judy Hayden see: Tex ANN	
Billy HAYES ▶ 11386 (2)	**1.9**
Blue Christmas—Elvis Presley (57)	*2.1*
Blue Christmas—Browns Featuring Jim Edward Brown (60)	*1.7*
Bonnie HAYES ▶ 5850 (1)	**237**
Have A Heart—Bonnie Raitt (90)	237
Chris HAYES ▶ 682 (8)	**6362**
Stuck With You—Huey Lewis and the News (86)	4661
The Power Of Love—Huey Lewis and the News (85)	4627
I Want A New Drug—Huey Lewis and the News (84)	2380
Couple Days Off—Huey Lewis & The News (91)	1191
I Know What I Like—Huey Lewis and the News (87)	1139
Small World—Huey Lewis and the News (88)	563
Workin' For A Livin'—Huey Lewis and the News (82)	267
Don't Make Me Do It—Patrick Simmons (83)	38
Isaac HAYES [Ed Lee] ▶ 129 (47) HOF	**20695**
Theme From Shaft—Isaac Hayes (71)	7329
Soul Man—Sam & Dave (67)	*6911*
All 4 Love—Color Me Badd (91)	5388
I Thank You—Sam & Dave (68)	*1993*
B-A-B-Y—Carla Thomas (66)	1648
Deja Vu—Dionne Warwick (79)	1382
Soul Man—Blues Brothers (78)	*1370*
Hold On! I'm A Comin'—Sam & Dave (66)	*1302*
Your Good Thing (Is About To End)—Lou Rawls (69)	*1274*
Do Your Thing—Isaac Hayes (72)	*784*
Theme From The Men—Isaac Hayes (72)	577

Isaac HAYES [Ed Lee] ▶ 129 (47) HOF *Cont'd*	**20695**
When Something Is Wrong With My Baby—Sam & Dave (67)	*545*
Show Me How—Emotions (71)	508
Soul Sister, Brown Sugar—Sam & Dave (68)	501
Joy Pt. I—Isaac Hayes (73)	499
I Thank You—ZZ Top (80)	*446*
Mind Playing Tricks On Me—Geto Boys (91)	405
Boot-Leg—Booker T. & The MG's (65)	349
Wrap It Up—Fabulous Thunderbirds (86)	*313*
You Got Me Hummin—Cold Blood (70)	*299*
I Take What I Want—James & Bobby Purify (67)	279
Candy—Astors (65)	239
You Got Me Hummin'—Sam & Dave (66)	*235*
The Sweeter He Is Part I—Soul Children (69)	232
Soul Man—Ramsey Lewis (67)	*207*
Something Good (Is Going To Happen To You)—Carla Thomas (67)	156
Let Me Be Good To You—Carla Thomas (66)	119
Said I Wasn't Gonna Tell Nobody—Sam & Dave (66)	118
Hold On I'm Coming—Chuck Jackson & Maxine Brown (67)	*90*
Chocolate Chip—Isaac Hayes (75)	83
Born Again—Sam & Dave (69)	70
You've Got Me Hummin'—Hassles (67)	*64*
Everybody Got To Believe In Somebody—Sam & Dave (68)	60
When Something Is Wrong With My Baby—Linda Ronstadt (featuring Aaron Neville) (90)	*57*
Your Good Thing (Is About To End)—Mable John (66)	*57*
Do Your Thing—James & Bobby Purify (74)	*51*
Wonderful—Isaac Hayes (74)	49
You Don't Know Like I Know—Sam & Dave (66)	44
When Something Is Wrong With My Baby—Otis & Carla (69)	*26*
Wrap It Up—Archie Bell & The Drells (70)	*25*
Baby-Baby Don't Stop Now—Sam & Dave (70)	14
How Do You Quit (Someone You Love)—Carla Thomas (65)	13
Soulsville—Isaac Hayes (72)	3.9
How Can You Mistreat The One You Love—Jean & The Darlings (67)	2.4
When Tomorrow Comes—Carla Thomas (67)	1.0
A Dime A Dozen—Carla Thomas (68)	0.9
Stealing Love—Emotions (70)	0.4
Jerry HAYES ▶ 11004 (1)	**3.9**
Rollin' With The Flow—Charlie Rich (77)	3.9
Joe HAYES ▶ 4974 (6)	**367**
A Satisfied Mind—Bobby Hebb (66)	*440*
Satisfied Mind—Ella Fitzgerald (55)	*294*
Satisfied Mind—Jack And Betty (55)	*0.0*
A Satisfied Mind—Jeffrey Clay (55)	*0.0*
Satisfied Mind—Mahalia Jackson (55)	*0.0*
A Satisfied Mind—Porter Wagoner (55)	*0.0*
Kendall L. HAYES ▶ 790 (1)	**5609**
Walk On By—Leroy Van Dyke (61)	5609
Lee HAYES ▶ 10953 (1)	**4.1**
Blue Jeans—Chocolate Milk (81)	8.2
Maurice HAYES ▶ 10561 (1)	**7.2**
I Wouldn't Lie—Yarbrough & Peoples (86)	29
Michael Peter HAYES [Mickie Most] ▶ 6475 (1)	**165**
Dance With The Devil—Cozy Powell (74)	330
Otha HAYES ▶ 3845 (3)	**679**
Shake A Tail Feather—James & Bobby Purify (67)	*829*
The Philly Freeze—Alvin Cash & The Registers (66)	531
Shake A Tail Feather—Five Du-Tones (63)	*412*
Peter Lind HAYES [Joseph Conrad Lind] ▶ 5606 (2)	**266**
Come To Me—Johnny Mathis (58)	*531*
Come To Me—Julie Wilson (58)	*0.0*
Roy HAYES ▶ 5359 (1)	**300**
I'm Gonna Be A Wheel Some Day—Fats Domino (59)	900
Thamon HAYES ▶ 11027 (1)	**3.7**
South—Johnny Maddox And The Rhythmasters (55)	7.5
Tony HAYES ▶ 2844 (3)	**1156**
Black Is Black—Los Bravos (66)	*3466*
Clock—Eddie Rambeau (66)	2.8
Black Is Black—Tight Fit (81)	*0.9*
Richard HAYMAN ▶ 11453 (1)	**1.6**
Dansero—Joni James (58)	4.9

Bob HAYMES ▶ 4305 (4)	**528**
Lipstick And Candy And Rubbersole Shoes—Julius La Rosa (56)	428
That's All—Rick Nelson (63)	193
I've Got Love—Julius La Rosa (56)	2.7
I'll Teach You How To Cry—Kitty Kallen (63)	1.4
Chapel HAYNES ▶ 7066 (1)	**118**
Rockin' Red Wing—Sammy Masters (60)	118
Eddie HAYNES ▶ 8230 (1)	**58**
Dancing To Your Music—Archie Bell & The Drells (73)	116
Henry HAYNES [Homer] ▶ 11150 (2)	**3.0**
He'll Have To Go—Homer & Jethro (60)	*9.0*
Ground Hog—Browns Featuring Jim Edward Brown (61)	2.3
Tony HAYNES ▶ 5684 (3)	**255**
Hyperactive—Robert Palmer (86)	451
She's On The Left—Jeffrey Osborne (88)	284
Under The Influence—Vanity (86)	101
Walter HAYNES ▶ 6933 (2)	**127**
8 x 10—Bill Anderson (63)	245
Girl On The Billboard—Del Reeves (65)	10
Lee HAYS ▶ 1117 (7)	**3961**
If I Had A Hammer—Trini Lopez (63)	*4407*
Gotta Travel On—Billy Grammer (58)	*3674*
Kisses Sweeter Than Wine—Jimmie Rodgers (57)	2683
If I Had A Hammer (The Hammer Song)—Peter, Paul & Mary (62)	*1319*
Bad Man Blunder—Kingston Trio (60)	326
Gotta Travel On—Timi Yuro (63)	*190*
Gotta Travel On—Harry Belafonte (59)	*0.0*
Charles HAYWARD ▶ 3295 (4)	**909**
The Devil Went Down To Georgia—Charlie Daniels Band (79)	*3303*
In America—Charlie Daniels Band (80)	1335
The Legend Of Wooley Swamp—Charlie Daniels Band (80)	633
The Devil Came Up To Michigan—K.M.C. Kru (91)	*243*
Justin HAYWARD ▶ 294 (15)	**12185**
Nights In White Satin—Moody Blues (72)	*5122*
Your Wildest Dreams—Moody Blues (86)	1305
The Story In Your Eyes—Moody Blues (71)	1159
Question—Moody Blues (70)	1138
Gemini Dream—Moody Blues (81)	1015
The Voice—Moody Blues (81)	1006
Tuesday Afternoon (Forever Afternoon)—Moody Blues (68)	840
I Know You're Out There Somewhere—Moody Blues (88)	422
I Dreamed Last Night—Justin Hayward And John Lodge (75)	229
The Other Side Of Life—Moody Blues (86)	146
Driftwood—Moody Blues (78)	118
Blue World—Moody Blues (83)	109
Never Comes The Day—Moody Blues (69)	39
Blue Guitar—Justin Hayward And John Lodge (75)	35
Nights In White Satin—Moody Blues (68)	*6.9*
Leon HAYWOOD ▶ 1474 (9)	**2949**
I Want'a Do Something Freaky To You—Leon Haywood (75)	1057
She's A Bad Mama Jama (She's Built, She's Stacked)—Carl Carlton (81)	982
Keep It In The Family—Leon Haywood (74)	352
Don't Push It Don't Force It—Leon Haywood (80)	282
It's Got To Be Mellow—Leon Haywood (67)	252
She's With Her Other Love—Leon Hayward (65)	14
Mellow Moonlight—Leon Haywood (67)	12
Believe Half Of What You See (And None Of What You Hear)—Leon Haywood (75)	2.9
Strokin'—Leon Haywood (76)	1.3
Don HAYWOODE ▶ 10687 (1)	**6.1**
Can I Come Over Tonight—Velours (57)	12
Al HAZAN ▶ 8487 (1)	**48**
Daydreams—Johnny Crawford (61)	48
Robert HAZARD [Robert Rimato] ▶ 857 (2)	**5184**
Girls Just Want To Have Fun—Cyndi Lauper (83)	4949
Escalator Of Life—Robert Hazard (83)	235
Leonard HAZE ▶ 8202 (1)	**58**
Summertime Girls—Y&T (85)	234
Eddie HAZEL [Grace Cook] ▶ 5405 (4)	**293**
Shakey Ground—Temptations (75)	*796*

I Wanna Know If It's Good To You?—Funkadelic (70)	65
Shakey Ground—Phoebe Snow (77)	*32*
Better By The Pound—Funkadelic (75)	1.5
—Kevin Calhoun Hazlett see: Kevin CALHOUN	
—Hammond Hazlewood see: Albert HAMMOND	
—Hammond Hazlewood see: Mike HAZLEWOOD	
Lee HAZLEWOOD [Naomi Ford, Naomi Shackleford] ▶ 88 (43)	**26589**
These Boots Are Made For Walkin'—Nancy Sinatra (66)	*6840*
Sugar Town—Nancy Sinatra (66)	4036
Rebel 'rouser—Duane Eddy (58)	2375
Fool—Sanford Clark (56)	*2237*
(Dance With The) Guitar Man—Duane Eddy And The Rebelettes (62)	2041
How Does That Grab You, Darlin'?—Nancy Sinatra (66)	1710
Cannonball—Duane Eddy His "Twangy" guitar and The Rebels (58)	1147
Houston—Dean Martin (65)	935
Love Eyes—Nancy Sinatra (67)	912
Lonely One—Duane Eddy His "Twangy" guitar and The Rebels (59)	881
Lightning's Girl—Nancy Sinatra (67)	749
Boss Guitar—Duane Eddy And The Rebelettes (63)	722
Not The Lovin' Kind—Dino, Desi & Billy (65)	671
Some Velvet Morning—Nancy Sinatra & Lee Hazlewood (68)	*621*
Yep—Duane Eddy His "Twangy" guitar and The Rebels (59)	522
Some Kind A Earthquake—Duane Eddy His "Twangy" guitar and The Rebels (59)	513
Lady Bird—Nancy Sinatra & Lee Hazlewood (67)	492
Surfin' Hootenanny—Al Casey with The K-C-Ettes (63)	402
Friday's Child—Nancy Sinatra (66)	363
Shazam—Duane Eddy His "Twangy" Guitar And The Rebels (60)	362
Kommotion—Duane Eddy (60)	345
This Town—Frank Sinatra (67)	336
First Love First Tears—Duane Eddy His "Twangy" guitar and The Rebels (59)	256
Quiet Three—Duane Eddy His "Twangy" guitar and The Rebels (59)	255
In Our Time—Nancy Sinatra (66)	254
Happy—Nancy Sinatra (68)	238
100 Years—Nancy Sinatra (68)	210
Fool—Gallahads (56)	*209*
Summer Wine—Nancy Sinatra With Lee Hazlewood (67)	193
Your Baby's Gone Surfin'—Duane Eddy (63)	161
A Stranger In Your Town—Shacklefords (63)	157
Lonely Boy, Lonely Guitar—Duane Eddy (63)	134
These Boots (Are Made For Walkin')—Kon Kan (89)	*78*
So Long Babe—Nancy Sinatra (65)	49
Moovin' N' Groovin'—Duane Eddy (58)	31
Tony Rome—Nancy Sinatra (67)	30
A Cheat—Sanford Clark (56)	17
Some Velvet Morning—Vanilla Fudge (69)	*16*
Baja—Astronauts (63)	15
The Battle—Duane Eddy and The Rebels (62)	13
In Some Time—Ronnie Dove (68)	12
Still As The Night—Sanford Clark (58)	7.3
Stretchin' Out—Duane Eddy and The Rebelettes (62)	0.4
Mike HAZLEWOOD [Hammond Hazlewood] ▶ 761 (17)	**5762**
It Never Rains In Southern California—Albert Hammond (72)	3547
The Air That I Breathe—Hollies (74)	2405
Gimme Dat Ding—Pipkins (70)	2051
Little Arrows—Leapy Lee (68)	1529
I'm A Train—Albert Hammond (74)	607
The Free Electric Band—Albert Hammond (73)	474
If You Gotta Break Another Heart—Albert Hammond (73)	218
One Night Stand—Magic Lanterns (70)	165
Down By The River—Albert Hammond (72)	164
One More Chance—Ocean (72)	85
Freedom Comes, Freedom Goes—Fortunes (71)	82
The Peacemaker—Albert Hammond (73)	70
Air Disaster—Albert Hammond (74)	69
Names, Tags, Numbers & Labels—Association (73)	56

Mike HAZLEWOOD [Hammond Hazlewood] ▶ 761 (17) *Continued*	**5762**
Half A Million Miles From Home–Albert Hammond (73)	54
Good Morning Freedom–Daybreak (70)	52
Oklahoma Sunday Morning–Glen Campbell (72)	6.0
Tony HAZZARD ▶ 3743 (3)	**713**
Me, The Peaceful Heart–Lulu (68)	376
Ha Ha Said The Clown–Yardbirds (67)	329
Fox On The Run–Manfred Mann (69)	8.5
–Yusuf Hazziez see: Joe TEX	
Robert HEAD ▶ 11315 (1)	**2.3**
Mr. Pride–Chuck (2) Jackson (61)	4.6
Roy HEAD ▶ 1496 (2)	**2906**
Treat Her Right–Roy Head And The Traits (65)	4680
Apple Of My Eye–Roy Head And The Traits (65)	565
–Wayne Carson Head see: Wayne Carson THOMPSON	
Nicky HEADON [Nicholas Bowen Headon, Topper Headon] ▶ 3557 (4)	**786**
Rock The Casbah–Clash (82)	1940
Train In Vain (Stand By Me)–Clash (80)	752
Should I Stay Or Should I Go?–Clash (82)	*243*
Should I Stay Or Should I Go?–Clash (83)	*210*
–Topper Headon see: Nicky HEADON	
Jeremy HEALY ▶ 10026 (1)	**14**
Shiny Shiny–Haysi Fantayzee (83)	42
Dick HEARD ▶ 2338 (3)	**1579**
Kentucky Rain–Elvis Presley (70)	1185
Tears And Roses–Al Martino (64)	1125
Abigail Beecher–Freddy Cannon (64)	849
Charles HEARNDON ▶ 4239 (2)	**549**
K-Jee–Nite-Liters (71)	726
Afro-Strut–Nite-Liters (72)	372
Johnny HEARTSMAN ▶ 10596 (2)	**7.0**
Johnny's House Party–Jimmy Beasley and The Rockers (57)	*3.5*
Johnny's House Party (pt. 1)–John Heartsman & The Gaylarks (57)	*3.5*
–Frederick Heath see: Johnny KIDD	
Hy HEATH ▶ 3227 (3)	**940**
Take These Chains From My Heart–Ray Charles With The Jack Halloran Singers And The Ray Charles Orchestra (63)	1861
I'll Never Stand In Your Way–Four Tophatters (56)	*11*
I'll Never Stand In Your Way–Jimmie Rodgers (63)	*7.3*
Joyce HEATH ▶ 11283 (1)	**2.5**
Rock And Cry–Clyde McPhatter (57)	2.5
Ted HEATH [Louis Rico] ▶ 11325 (1)	**2.2**
Cha Cha Baby–Ted Heath and His Orchestra (58)	6.7
Tommy HEATH ▶ 6830 (1)	**134**
Angel Say No–Tommy Tutone (80)	269
Bob HEATLIE ▶ 7112 (1)	**115**
Cry Just A Little Bit–Shakin' Stevens (84)	115
HEAVY D [Dwight Meyers] ▶ 6130 (1)	**202**
Is It Good To You–Heavy D & The Boyz (91)	404
Bobby HEBB ▶ 724 (3)	**6062**
Sunny–Bobby Hebb (66)	5422
A Natural Man–Lou Rawls (71)	1273
His Song Shall Be Sung–Lou Rawls (72)	5.3
Don HECHT ▶ 3927 (2)	**654**
Walkin' After Midnight–Patsy Cline (57)	*1307*
Walkin' After Midnight–Otis Williams & His Charms (57)	*0.0*
Ken HECHT ▶ 4394 (1)	**506**
No One Knows–Dion and The Belmonts (58)	1013
Neal HEFTI ▶ 1966 (5)	**2045**
Batman Theme–Marketts (66)	*1175*
Batman Theme–Neal Hefti (66)	*560*
I Knew Jesus (Before He Was A Star)–Glen Campbell (73)	486
Theme From "Harlow" (Lonely Girl)–Bobby Vinton (65)	198
The Drinking Man's Diet–Allan Sherman (65)	1.4
Rob HEGEL ▶ 4727 (2)	**430**
Just As I Am–Air Supply (85)	777
Sinner Man–Sarah Dash (79)	82
Ray HEINDORF ▶ 7347 (6)	**101**
Pete Kelly's Blues–Ray Anthony (55)	*93*
Hold Me In Your Arms–Doris Day (54)	16

Some Sunday Morning–Wayne Newton (65)	6.6
Pete Kelly's Blues–June Christy (55)	*0.0*
Pete Kelly's Blues–Ella Fitzgerald (55)	*0.0*
Pete Kelly's Blues–Ray Heindorf & The Warner Bros. Orchestra (55)	*0.0*
Marshall HELFAND ▶ 4525 (1)	**471**
Tell Me Why–Belmonts (61)	941
André HELLER ▶ 10949 (1)	**4.2**
Christmas Dream–Perry Como (74)	13
Roberta HELLER ▶ 10658 (1)	**6.3**
Speak, My Love–Vic Damone (56)	19
Fred HELLERMAN [Fred Brooks, Bob Hill] ▶ 3069 (6)	**1026**
Gotta Travel On–Billy Grammer (58)	*3674*
Kisses Sweeter Than Wine–Jimmie Rodgers (57)	2683
Gotta Travel On–Timi Yuro (63)	*190*
I'm Just A Country Boy–George McCurn (63)	*177*
I'm Just A Country Boy–Harry Belafonte (57)	*5.3*
Gotta Travel On–Harry Belafonte (59)	*0.0*
Levon HELM [Mark Lavon Helm] ▶ 7800 (2)	**75**
Life Is A Carnival–Band (71)	216
Southern Love–Ronnie Hawkins and The Hawks (59)	7.2
–Mark Lavon Helm see: Levon HELM	
Birgit HELMER ▶ 10174 (1)	**12**
Tamouré–Bill Justis (63)	46
Bobby HELMS ▶ 10354 (1)	**9.6**
Love My Lady–Bobby Helms (58)	19
Jimmy HELMS ▶ 2933 (2)	**1113**
I've Been Thinking About You–Londonbeat (91)	3755
A Better Love–Londonbeat (91)	873
Norma HELMS ▶ 5875 (1)	**234**
Saturday Night, Sunday Morning–Thelma Houston (79)	468
–Reginald Van Helsing see: Gene SIMMONS	
Thomas HEMPEL ▶ 10515 (2)	**7.7**
Love Songs Are Back Again–Band Of Gold (84)	*12*
Love Songs Are Back Again–Band Of Gold (84)	*12*
–Charles Hemphill see: Sonny CHARLES	
Robert HEMRIC ▶ 11082 (1)	**3.3**
Frustration–Zanies (62)	6.6
Alphonso HENDERSON ▶ 8941 (1)	**36**
New Jack Hustler (Nino's Theme)–Ice-T (91)	71
Brian HENDERSON ▶ 5471 (1)	**282**
Summer Nights–Marianne Faithfull (65)	565
Charles E. HENDERSON ▶ 10804 (1)	**5.2**
Hold Me In Your Arms–Doris Day (54)	16
Dave HENDERSON ▶ 9358 (1)	**25**
Cross My Heart–Billy Stewart (67)	76
Douglas HENDERSON ▶ 4245 (7)	**547**
Long Lonely Nights–Bobby Vinton (65)	*1021*
Long Lonely Nights–Clyde McPhatter (57)	*517*
Long Lonely Nights–Lee Andrews And The Hearts (57)	*429*
Long Lonely Nights–Dells (70)	*187*
Long Lonely Nights–4 Seasons (64)	*34*
Long, Lonely Nights–Kings (2) (57)	*0.0*
Long Lonely Nights–Kitty Kallen (57)	*0.0*
–Gayla Henderson see: Jamie HORTON	
Harvey HENDERSON ▶ 6886 (9)	**131**
Shake Your Rump To The Funk–Bar-Kays (76)	593
Move Your Boogie Body–Bar-Kays (79)	270
Today Is The Day–Bar-Kays (80)	150
Freakshow On The Dance Floor–Bar-Kays (84)	79
Too Hot To Stop–Bar-Kays (77)	36
Hit And Run–Bar-Kays (81)	23
Boogie Body Land–Bar-Kays (81)	23
Let's Have Some Fun–Bar-Kays (78)	8.9
Shine–Bar-Kays (79)	7.7
James David HENDERSON ▶ 11554 (1)	**1.2**
Strong Enough To Be Gentle–Black Oak Arkansas (76)	8.4
Jimmy HENDERSON ▶ 4327 (3)	**519**
I Miss You So–Paul Anka (59)	*593*
I Miss You So–Chris Connor (56)	*513*
I Miss You So–Little Anthony & The Imperials With The 101 Strings (65)	*453*
Joe Lee HENDERSON ▶ 11467 (1)	**1.6**
The Searching Is Over–Joe Henderson (62)	3.1
Johnny HENDERSON ▶ 11434 (1)	**1.7**
The Only Way Is Up–Yazz And The Plastic Population (88)	3.4
Joseph Turner HENDERSON ▶ 3400 (8)	**866**
Why Don't They Understand–George Hamilton IV (57)	*1673*

Why Don't They Understand–Bobby Vinton (70)	*23*
Trudie–Joe Henderson (58)	*17*
Janie Is Her Name–Roger Williams (63)	1.4
Trudy–Joe Bushkin (58)	*0.0*
Trudie–Eric Rogers & His Music (58)	*0.0*
Trudie–Owen Bradley And His Orchestra (58)	*0.0*
Trudie–Jorgen Ingmann with Camarata & His Orchestra (58)	*0.0*
Knox HENDERSON ▶ 5165 (1)	**332**
Shame, Shame–Magic Lanterns (68)	996
Kyle HENDERSON ▶ 9189 (1)	**29**
What She Does To Me (The Diana Song)–Producers (81)	117
Mario HENDERSON ▶ 7529 (1)	**91**
Could I Be Dreaming–Pointer Sisters (80)	272
Michael E. HENDERSON ▶ 2702 (6)	**1263**
You Are My Starship–Norman Connors (Featuring Michael Henderson And Jean Cain) (76)	693
Be My Girl–Dramatics (76)	432
Take Me I'm Yours–Michael Henderson (78)	99
Valentine Love–Norman Connors (Featuring Michael Henderson And Jean Cain) (75)	26
Wide Receiver (Part I)–Michael Henderson (80)	22
We Both Need Each Other–Norman Connors (76)	1.2
Michael James HENDERSON ▶ 8565 (1)	**46**
Powerful Stuff–Fabulous Thunderbirds (88)	139
Patrick HENDERSON ▶ 3265 (1)	**920**
Real Love–Doobie Brothers (80)	1841
Ray HENDERSON [Raymond Brost] ▶ 2764 (12) HOF	**1211**
Together–Connie Francis (61)	2968
Five Foot Two–Don Johnson (60)	194
Life Is Just A Bowl Of Cherries–Jaye P. Morgan (55)	175
Alabamy Bound–Les Paul and Mary Ford (55)	*84*
The Birth Of The Blues–Sammy Davis Jr. (55)	*58*
Best Things In Life Are Free–Richard Cannon (58)	20
It All Depends On You–Jerry Lewis (57)	19
So Blue–Vibrations (60)	19
Sittin' On Top Of The World–Jerry Mar (57)	6.0
Bye Bye Blackbird–Art Mooney And His Orchestra (59)	3.9
Alabamy Bound–Mulcays (55)	*0.0*
The Birth Of The Blues–Lenny Dee (55)	*0.0*
Rochell HENDERSON ▶ 4645 (1)	**446**
Once Upon A Time–Rochell And The Candles With Johnny Wyatt (61)	892
Wayne HENDERSON ▶ 7936 (3)	**69**
Scratch–Crusaders (74)	65
Let's Dance (Make Your Body Move)–West Street Mob (81)	30
Keep That Same Old Feeling–Side Effect (77)	1.1
William A. HENDERSON ▶ 2568 (7)	**1371**
My Girl (Gone, Gone, Gone)–Chilliwack (81)	1067
Whatcha Gonna Do–Chilliwack (82)	542
I Believe–Chilliwack (82)	381
Fly At Night–Chilliwack (77)	185
Lonesome Mary–Chilliwack (72)	79
Crazy Talk–Chilliwack (74)	11
Something Better–Chilliwack (77)	7.3
Willie HENDERSON ▶ 5747 (4)	**246**
I Had It All The Time–Tyrone Davis (72)	315
Dance Master Pt. 1–Willie Henderson (74)	153
Funky Chicken–Willie Henderson And The Soul Explosions (70)	23
Straight Ahead–Young-Holt Unlimited (69)	12
Tony HENDRA ▶ 10165 (1)	**12**
Deteriorata–National Lampoon (72)	24
Belford HENDRICKS ▶ 1281 (10)	**3465**
It's Just A Matter Of Time–Brook Benton (59)	*5155*
Looking Back–Nat "King" Cole (58)	*2318*
Call Me–Johnny Mathis (58)	1333
I'm Too Far Gone (To Turn Around)–Bobby Bland (66)	362
Early Every Morning (Early Every Evening Too)–Dinah Washington (61)	153
Looking Back–Joe Simon (68)	*62*
Nothing In The World–Nat "King" Cole (58)	31
It's Just A Matter Of Time–Sonny James, The Southern Gentleman (70)	*31*
Can't You Just See Me–Aretha Franklin (65)	14
Looking Back–Dinah Washington (60)	*5.1*

James Richard HENDRICKS ▶ 1044 (4)	**4221**
Summer Rain—Johnny Rivers (67)	1843
Long Lonesome Highway—Michael Parks (70)	1146
Look To Your Soul—Johnny Rivers (68)	669
Muddy River—Johnny Rivers (69)	562
Jon HENDRICKS ▶ 1647 (7)	**2548**
I Want You To Be My Baby—Georgia Gibbs (55)	*1122*
I Want You To Be My Baby—Lillian Briggs (55)	*999*
Yeh, Yeh—Georgie Fame And The Blue Flames (65)	*931*
I Want You To Be My Baby—Ellie Greenwich (67)	*105*
Desafinado (Slightly Out Of Tune)—Pat Thomas (62)	*41*
Sermonette—Della Reese (59)	0.8
Desafinado (Slightly Out Of Tune)—Ella Fitzgerald (62)	*0.0*
—James Marshall Hendrix see: Jimi HENDRIX	
Jimi HENDRIX [Johnny Allen Hendrix, James Marshall Hendrix] ▶ 1840 (10)	**2211**
Fire—Five By Five (68)	542
Crosstown Traffic—Jimi Hendrix Experience (68)	437
Angel—Rod Stewart (72)	362
Purple Haze—Jimi Hendrix Experience (67)	*317*
Freedom—Jimi Hendrix (71)	210
Hooray For The Salvation Army Band—Bill Cosby (67)	*171*
Foxey Lady—Jimi Hendrix (67)	95
Purple Haze—Dion (69)	*94*
Dolly Dagger—Jimi Hendrix (71)	65
Up From The Skies—Jimi Hendrix Experience (68)	31
—Johnny Allen Hendrix see: Jimi HENDRIX	
Nona HENDRYX ▶ 8120 (1)	**61**
Why Should I Cry?—Nona Hendryx (87)	183
David William HENEKER ▶ 11634 (1)	**0.9**
Irma La Douce—Karen Chandler (60)	*4.6*
Caperton HENLEY ▶ 8089 (1)	**62**
Delia Gone—Pat Boone (60)	62
Don HENLEY ▶ 147 (24) HOF	**19495**
One Of These Nights—Eagles (75)	5146
Hotel California—Eagles (77)	4658
Heartache Tonight—Eagles (79)	4547
Best Of My Love—Eagles (74)	4142
New Kid In Town—Eagles (76)	4051
Dirty Laundry—Don Henley (82)	4004
Lyin' Eyes—Eagles (75)	3949
Take It To The Limit—Eagles (75)	3081
The Boys Of Summer—Don Henley (84)	2124
The Long Run—Eagles (79)	2002
I Can't Tell You Why—Eagles (80)	1924
Witchy Woman—Eagles (72)	1716
The End Of The Innocence—Don Henley (89)	1707
Life In The Fast Lane—Eagles (77)	1068
The Heart Of The Matter—Don Henley (90)	820
The Last Worthless Evening—Don Henley (89)	774
Sunset Grill—Don Henley (85)	675
Not Enough Love In The World—Don Henley (85)	525
Johnny Can't Read—Don Henley (82)	392
New York Minute—Don Henley (90)	351
Tequila Sunrise—Eagles (73)	344
I Can't Stand Still—Don Henley (83)	339
How Bad Do You Want It?—Don Henley (90)	330
James Dean—Eagles (74)	125
Fred HENLEY [Freddie Vel] ▶ 3939 (4)	**650**
You're The Reason—Bobby Edwards (61)	*2462*
You're The Reason—Joe South (61)	*136*
You're The Reason—Hank Locklin (61)	*0.0*
You're The Reason—Gerry And The Pacemakers (65)	*0.0*
Larry HENLEY ▶ 1934 (9)	**2086**
Wind Beneath My Wings—Bette Midler (89)	*3406*
Lizzie And The Rainman—Tanya Tucker (75)	452
Wind Beneath My Wings—Lou Rawls (83)	*159*
Holdin' On For Dear Love—Lobo (79)	74
Shotgun Rider—Delbert McClinton (81)	*45*
Shotgun Rider—Joe Sun (80)	*40*
When Love Cries—Donna Summer (91)	32
If It's Alright With You—Rose Colored Glass (71)	*22*
If It's All Right With You—Dottie West (73)	*16*
Patricia HENLEY [Patricia Henley Talbert] ▶ 7951 (1)	**68**
I Wanna Do It To You—Jerry Butler (77)	203
David HENMAN ▶ 9341 (1)	**26**
This Could Be The Right One—April Wine (84)	103
Jim HENMAN ▶ 9342 (1)	**26**
This Could Be The Right One—April Wine (84)	103

Richie HENMAN ▶ 9343 (1)	**26**
This Could Be The Right One—April Wine (84)	103
Rick HENN ▶ 2823 (3)	**1169**
I Live For The Sun—Sunrays (65)	632
Andrea—Sunrays (66)	509
The Happy Girls—Helen Reddy (77)	113
Horst Heinz HENNING ▶ 10987 (2)	**4.0**
One More Time—Dean Martin (54)	*7.9*
One More Time—Ames Brothers (54)	*7.9*
John HENNING ▶ 6422 (1)	**172**
Hot Love, Cold World—Bob Welch (78)	344
Paul HENNING ▶ 4384 (1)	**508**
The Ballad Of Jed Clampett—Lester Flatt, Earl Scruggs & The Foggy Mountain Boys (62)	508
Don HENNY ▶ 6919 (1)	**128**
A Question Of Temperature—Balloon Farm (68)	385
Clarence "Frogman" HENRY ▶ 3424 (3)	**853**
Ain't Got No Home—Clarence Henry "Frog Man" (56)	*608*
Ain't Got No Home—Band (73)	*199*
A Little Too Much—Clarence Henry (62)	93
Clarence "Sonny" HENRY ▶ 1910 (2)	**2121**
Evil Ways—Santana (70)	*2005*
Evil Ways—Carlos Santana & Buddy Miles (72)	*116*
Francis HENRY ▶ 10518 (1)	**7.7**
Little Girl—Frankie Lymon (57)	15
Gary HENRY ▶ 8826 (3)	**38**
She's Fly—Tony Terry (87)	49
Forever Yours—Tony Terry (88)	44
No Frills Love—Jennifer Holliday (86)	12
Joe HENRY ▶ 9207 (1)	**29**
Brown Arms In Houston—Orpheus (69)	57
Kent HENRY [Henry Pilschke] ▶ 8517 (1)	**47**
For Ladies Only—Steppenwolf (71)	190
Norm HENRY ▶ 5756 (1)	**245**
You Better Know It—Jackie Wilson (59)	489
Pauline HENRY ▶ 10086 (1)	**13**
1-2-3—Chimes (2) (90)	39
Scott HENRY ▶ 9630 (1)	**20**
Rappin' Rodney—Rodney Dangerfield (83)	140
William HENSHALL ▶ 2934 (2)	**1113**
I've Been Thinking About You—Londonbeat (91)	3755
A Better Love—Londonbeat (91)	873
Judy HENSKE ▶ 4133 (1)	**584**
Hooka Tooka—Chubby Checker (63)	1168
Harold G. HENSLEY ▶ 9401 (1)	**24**
Muskrat—Everly Brothers (61)	98
Ken HENSLEY ▶ 3757 (3)	**709**
Easy Livin'—Uriah Heep (72)	607
Stealin'—Uriah Heep (73)	102
Blind Eye—Uriah Heep (73)	0.0
Roy HENSLEY ▶ 7314 (1)	**103**
Goodbye Babe—Castaways (65)	103
Tom HENSLEY ▶ 7583 (1)	**87**
Headed For The Future—Neil Diamond (86)	262
Denny HENSON ▶ 7026 (2)	**121**
Rain, Oh Rain—Fools Gold (76)	109
In It For Love—England Dan & John Ford Coley (80)	23
—Robert Raymond Henson see: Bob RAY	
Donald HEPBURN ▶ 11216 (1)	**2.7**
Let's Dance (Make Your Body Move)—West Street Mob (81)	30
—Dorothy Jean Heppel see: Ginger WILLIS	
John HERALD ▶ 11286 (1)	**2.4**
Up To My Neck In High Muddy Water—Linda Ronstadt And The Stone Poneys (68)	7.2
—Piet Herbert see: Marcus MEYN	
Twyla HERBERT ▶ 721 (10)	**6072**
Lightnin' Strikes—Lou Christie (65)	6323
Two Faces Have I—Lou Christie (63)	3221
The Gypsy Cried—Lou Christie (63)	1196
Rhapsody In The Rain—Lou Christie (66)	860
Outside The Gates Of Heaven—Lou Christie (66)	290
Are You Getting Any Sunshine?—Lou Christie (69)	154
Painter—Lou Christie (66)	93
Shake Hands And Walk Away Cryin'—Lou Christie (67)	5.4
Big Time—Lou Christie (66)	2.8
Glory River—Lou Christie (70)	0.0

Victor HERBERT ▶ 10967 (1) HOF	**4.0**
Goodbye To Toyland—Vonnair Sisters (62)	12
Larry HERBSTRITT ▶ 4078 (5)	**600**
I Just Fall In Love Again—Anne Murray (79)	1411
Fire In The Morning—Melissa Manchester (80)	515
Easy Love—Dionne Warwick (80)	184
Dancin' Like Lovers—Mary MacGregor (80)	26
Pirate—Cher (77)	4.4
Billy HERMAN ▶ 6707 (2)	**142**
Roll On—New Colony Six (71)	229
Barbara, I Love You—New Colony Six (69)	83
Cleve HERMAN ▶ 11529 (1)	**1.3**
A Beginning From An End—Jan & Dean (66)	5.2
Jerry HERMAN ▶ 258 (11) HOF	**13299**
Hello, Dolly!—Louis Armstrong And The All-Stars (64)	*11318*
Mame—Herb Alpert & The Tijuana Brass (66)	*999*
So Long Dearie—Louis Armstrong (64)	407
Mame—Bobby Darin (66)	*287*
Mame—Louis Armstrong (66)	*125*
Kiss Her Now—Ed Ames (68)	66
Hello, Dolly!—Bobby Darin (65)	*40*
When Mabel Comes In The Room—Michael Allen (74)	38
Milk And Honey—Limeliters (61)	15
Shalom—Eddie Fisher (61)	4.7
Hello, Dolly!—Pete King Chorale and Orchestra (64)	*0.0*
Keith HERMAN [Keith Chagall Adelsohn, Keith Herman Adelsohn] ▶ 10049 (1)	**13**
She's Got A Whole Number—Keith Herman (79)	27
Pinky HERMAN ▶ 11056 (2)	**3.5**
Where Can You Be—Don Cherry (54)	*11*
Where Can You Be—Jerry Martin (54)	*0.0*
Woody HERMAN ▶ 6757 (2)	**140**
Woodchopper's Ball—Hutch Davie And His Honky Tonkers (58)	*280*
Woodchopper's Ball—Winifred Atwell (58)	*0.0*
Patrick HERNANDEZ ▶ 2680 (1)	**1277**
Born To Be Alive—Patrick Hernandez (79)	1277
Richie HERNANDEZ [Richie Lecea] ▶ 10957 (1)	**4.1**
Some Things A Man's Gotta Do—Shango (70)	8.2
Henri HERPIN ▶ 2833 (2)	**1165**
(All Of A Sudden) My Heart Sings—Paul Anka (58)	*1888*
(All Of A Sudden) My Heart Sings—Mel Carter (65)	*442*
René HERRERA ▶ 3524 (2)	**800**
Lo Mucho Que Te Quiero (The More I Love You)—René & René (68)	1458
Angelito—René & René (64)	628
John HERRING ▶ 5607 (1)	**266**
What Have I Got Of My Own—Trini Lopez (64)	531
Bernard HERRMANN [Bernard Hermann] ▶ 5658 (2)	**259**
Twilight Zone (Theme)—Manhattan Transfer (80)	258
Mamie—Nat King Cole (64)	2.2
—Josephine Herrmann see: Joan WHITE	
Erma HERROLD ▶ 3146 (1)	**986**
Stood Up—Ricky Nelson (57)	1972
Cindy HERRON ▶ 3871 (2)	**671**
Hold On—En Vogue (90)	3351
Lies—En Vogue (90)	676
Jerry HERST ▶ 1354 (3)	**3276**
So Rare—Jimmy Dorsey with Orchestra and Chorus (57)	*6543*
So Rare—Andy Williams (62)	*5.0*
So Rare—Mavis Rivers (60)	*3.7*
Kurt HERTHA ▶ 11680 (1)	**0.7**
Come Into My Life—Al Martino (71)	2.9
Fred HERTZ ▶ 10923 (1)	**4.3**
Hootenanny Granny—Jim Lowe (63)	8.7
Peter HERZ ▶ 11334 (1)	**2.2**
Oh My Maria—Eddie Fisher (56)	6.6
Ludwig HERZER ▶ 10930 (1)	**4.3**
Yours Is My Heart Alone—Enzo Stuarti (56)	17
David HESS [David Dante, David Hill] ▶ 1294 (9)	**3441**
Speedy Gonzales—Pat Boone (62)	*2754*
I Got Stung—Elvis Presley (58)	2661
Start Movin' (In My Direction)—Sal Mineo (57)	1620
Dumb Head—Ginny Arnell (63)	383

David HESS [David Dante, David Hill] ▶ 1294 (9) *Continued*	**3441**
Rockin' Shoes—Ames Brothers (57)	227
The Next Kiss (Is The Last Goodbye)—Conway Twitty (61)	170
Speedy Gonzales—David Dante (61)	*19*
You're Singing Our Love Song To Somebody Else—Jerry Wallace (60)	18
Five Card Stud—Lorne Greene (66)	9.7
Hal HESTER ▶ 4137 (2)	**583**
The Sand And The Sea—Nat "King" Cole (55)	*1167*
The Sand And The Sea—Bob Santa Maria (55)	*0.0*
Tony HESTER ▶ 610 (15)	**7068**
In The Rain—Dramatics (72)	*3230*
Whatcha See Is Whatcha Get—Dramatics (71)	1745
With This Ring—Platters (67)	1217
Hey You! Get Off My Mountain—Dramatics (73)	438
Fell For You—Dramatics (73)	352
Washed Ashore (On A Lonely Island In The Sea)—Platters (67)	333
Door To Your Heart—Dramatics (74)	270
I Miss You—Dells (73)	220
Hijackin' Love—Johnnie Taylor (71)	191
Get Up And Get Down—Dramatics (71)	82
I'm Satisfied—San Remo Golden Strings (65)	38
(I'm Going By) The Stars In Your Eyes—Ron Banks And The Dramatics (75)	22
You're Fooling You—Dramatics (76)	17
Don't Sign The Paper Baby (I Want You Back)—Jimmy Delphs (68)	14
In The Rain—Arthur Prysock (73)	*7.2*
James HETFIELD ▶ 4110 (3)	**590**
Enter Sandman—Metallica (91)	947
The Unforgiven—Metallica (91)	334
One—Metallica (89)	326
Richard HEUBERGER ▶ 10230 (1)	**11**
Suddenly—Jo Stafford (54)	22
Howard HEWETT ▶ 7041 (3)	**120**
Amnesia—Shalamar (84)	152
Show Me—Howard Hewett (90)	112
I'm For Real—Howard Hewett (86)	13
Lonnie HEWITT ▶ 9337 (1)	**26**
Send My Baby Back—Freddie Hughes (68)	52
John HEWLETT ▶ 11500 (1)	**1.4**
Smashed! Blocked!—John's Children (67)	2.8
Paul HEWSON [Paul David Hewson, Bono] ▶ 1102 (14)	**4015**
With Or Without You—U2 (87)	4346
I Still Haven't Found What I'm Looking For—U2 (87)	3862
Desire—U2 (88)	2667
Mysterious Ways—U2 (91)	2021
Angel Of Harlem—U2 (88)	876
Where The Streets Have No Name—U2 (87)	*803*
Pride (In The Name Of Love)—U2 (84)	535
In God's Country—U2 (87)	300
New Year's Day—U2 (83)	295
When Love Comes To Town—U2 With B. B. King (89)	105
The Fly—U2 (91)	78
All I Want Is You—U2 (89)	76
I Will Follow—U2 (84)	57
Where The Streets Have No Name—Pet Shop Boys (91)	*37*
Richard HEWSON ▶ 6080 (1)	**208**
Beyond—Herb Alpert (80)	208
Edward HEYMAN ▶ 1366 (11)	**3254**
Love Letters—Ketty Lester (62)	*2808*
When I Fall In Love—Lettermen (61)	*2046*
Love Letters—Elvis Presley (66)	*886*
Blue Star (The "Medic" Theme)—Felicia Sanders (55)	*541*
When I Fall In Love—Etta Jones (61)	*98*
When I Fall In Love—Donny Osmond (73)	*77*
I Want To Be Loved—Dinah Washington (62)	*32*
I Wanna Be Loved—Dean And Jean (64)	*28*
Love Letters—Joni James (56)	*10*
When I Fall In Love—Natalie Cole (88)	*2.4*
Blue Star (The "Medic" Theme)—Charlie Applewhite with Victor Young & His Orchestra (55)	*0.0*
DuBose HEYWARD ▶ 2984 (7)	**1082**
Summertime—Billy Stewart (66)	*1685*
I Loves You Porgy—Nina Simone (59)	1423
Summertime—Marcels (61)	*107*
Summertime—Sam Cooke (57)	*20*
Summertime—Rick Nelson (62)	*7.8*
Summertime (Part 2)—Sam Cooke (59)	*4.4*
Summertime—Will Sanders (61)	*0.0*
Nicholas HEYWARD ▶ 4569 (1)	**464**
Love Plus One—Haircut One Hundred (82)	464
Eddie HEYWOOD ▶ 337 (9)	**11000**
Canadian Sunset—Hugo Winterhalter And His Orchestra (56)	*6824*
Canadian Sunset—Andy Williams (56)	*2711*
Soft Summer Breeze—Eddie Heywood (56)	*2341*
Land Of Dreams—Hugo Winterhalter's Orchestra And Chorus (54)	552
Soft Summer Breeze—Diamonds (56)	*140*
Canadian Sunset—Sounds Orchestral (65)	*106*
Canadian Sunset—Etta Jones (61)	*54*
Soft Summer Breeze—Eddie Heywood (59)	*0.4*
Soft Summer Breeze—Romaine Brown & His Romaines (56)	*0.0*
John HIATT ▶ 2313 (2)	**1608**
Angel Eyes—Jeff Healey Band (89)	1690
Sure As I'm Sittin' Here—Three Dog Night (74)	764
—Hi-C see: Crawford WILKERSON	
Ersel HICKEY [Ersel O'Hickey] ▶ 2230 (7)	**1720**
Don't Let The Rain Come Down (Crooked Little Man)—Serendipity Singers (64)	3454
Bluebirds Over The Mountain—Beach Boys (68)	*362*
Bluebirds Over The Mountain—Ersel Hickey (58)	*194*
Bluebirds Over The Mountain—Echoes (62)	*11*
Can She Give You Fever—Ernie Tucker (60)	*1.5*
Can She Give You Fever—Stan Robinson (60)	*1.5*
Can She Give Me Fever—Little Junior Lewis (60)	*0.0*
Leo HICKMAN ▶ 10545 (1)	**7.5**
Early In The Mornin'—Ray Charles (61)	22
—Regi Hargis Hickman see: Regi HARGIS	
Joe HICKS ▶ 5225 (1)	**323**
That's The Way I Feel About Cha—(The Preacher) Bobby Womack (& Peace) (71)	969
Johnnie B. HICKS ▶ 4020 (1)	**622**
Say You—Ronnie Dove (64)	622
Johnny HICKS ▶ 11270 (1)	**2.5**
Nuevo Laredo—Les Paul and Mary Ford (56)	10
Mark HICKS ▶ 7837 (2)	**73**
Slide—Slave (77)	640
Just A Touch Of Love—Slave (80)	10
Tony HICKS ▶ 1419 (14)	**3113**
On A Carousel—Hollies (67)	*2080*
Carrie-Anne—Hollies (67)	2018
Stop Stop Stop—Hollies (66)	2003
Long Dark Road—Hollies (72)	680
Pay You Back With Interest—Hollies (67)	*585*
Tell Me To My Face—Keith (67)	500
Dear Eloise—Hollies (67)	416
King Midas In Reverse—Hollies (67)	292
On A Carousel—Glass Moon (82)	*180*
Have You Ever Loved Somebody—Searchers (66)	165
Pay You Back With Interest—Gary O' (81)	*45*
Another Night—Hollies (75)	*28*
Another Night—Wilson Brothers (79)	*3.9*
Do The Best You Can—Hollies (68)	3.5
David HIDALGO ▶ 9112 (1)	**31**
Will The Wolf Survive?—Los Lobos (85)	62
Alphonso HIGDON ▶ 7671 (1)	**82**
What Good Am I Without You—Marvin Gaye & Kim Weston (64)	163
Irene HIGGINBOTHAM ▶ 5929 (1)	**227**
Good Morning Heartache—Diana Ross (73)	680
Robert HIGGINBOTHAM [Tommy Tucker] ▶ 1274 (7)	**3477**
Hi-Heel Sneakers—Tommy Tucker (64)	*1552*
Hi-Heel Sneakers—Jose Feliciano (68)	*1222*
Slip-In Mules (No High Heel Sneakers)—Sugar Pie Desanto (64)	*277*
High Heel Sneakers—Stevie Wonder (65)	*273*
Hi Heel Sneakers - Pt. 1—Ramsey Lewis Trio (66)	*233*
High Heel Sneakers—Elvis Presley (68)	*53*
High Heel Sneakers—Jerry Lee Lewis (64)	*4.7*
Alfonso HIGGINS ▶ 7762 (1)	**76**
We Have Love—Dinah Washington (60)	152
Bertie HIGGINS [Elbert Joseph Higgins] ▶ 2511 (2)	**1429**
Key Largo—Bertie Higgins (81)	2665
Just Another Day In Paradise—Bertie Higgins (82)	289
Charles HIGGINS ▶ 10991 (1)	**3.9**
Sweet Summer Music—Attitudes (76)	12
Grant HIGGINS ▶ 7259 (1)	**107**
Baby What Do You Want Me To Do—Barbara Lewis (66)	107
Monk HIGGINS [Milton Bland] ▶ 4506 (4)	**474**
Black Fox—Freddy Robinson (70)	392
Who-Dun-It?—Monk Higgins (66)	60
When You Wake Up—Cash McCall (66)	26
Gotta Be Funky—Monk Higgins & The Specialties (72)	20
—Doris Elaine Higginson see: Doris PAYNE	
—Rodney Higgs see: Jim VALLANCE	
Robin HILD ▶ 3784 (1)	**700**
You Don't Know—Scarlett & Black (88)	700
Ray HILDEBRAND ▶ 391 (3)	**10128**
Hey Paula—Paul & Paula (62)	9041
Young Lovers—Paul & Paula (63)	2050
First Day Back At School—Paul & Paula (63)	125
Herbert HILDEBRAND-WINHAUER ▶ 7235 (1)	**108**
The Witch—Rattles (70)	108
Diane HILDERBRAND [Diane Hildebrand] ▶ 2597 (3)	**1340**
Easy Come, Easy Go—Bobby Sherman (70)	2475
He Walks Like A Man—Jody Miller (64)	89
Felicidad—Sally Field (67)	28
Russell HILDRETH ▶ 1667 (1)	**2521**
One More Try—Timmy T (90)	5043
—Al Hill see: Ben WEISMAN	
—Al Hill see: Fred WISE	
—Al Hill see: Kay TWOMEY	
Alex HILL ▶ 4256 (1)	**544**
Rumors—Timex Social Club (86)	1633
Andy HILL ▶ 2426 (4)	**1498**
I'll Get By—Eddie Money (91)	1367
Peace In Our Time—Eddie Money (89)	1122
Heart Of Stone—Cher (90)	618
Give A Little Bit More—Cliff Richard (81)	345
—Arzell Hill see: Z.Z. HILL	
Beau HILL ▶ 4807 (5)	**410**
Seventeen—Winger (89)	595
Everything You Do (You're Sexing Me)—Fiona (Duet With Kip Winger) (89)	238
Dance—Ratt (87)	196
Way Cool Jr.—Ratt (88)	109
Talk To Me—Fiona (85)	93
Beverly HILL ▶ 3251 (1)	**928**
Can't We Try—Dan Hill (87)	1855
Billy HILL [George Brown, William Joseph Hill] ▶ 905 (15) HOF	**4904**
In The Chapel In The Moonlight—Kitty Kallen (54)	*2671*
In The Chapel In The Moonlight—Dean Martin (67)	*617*
Chapel In The Moonlight—Bachelors (65)	*505*
Glory Of Love—Roommates (61)	*490*
Glory Of Love—Otis Redding (67)	*322*
Have You Ever Been Lonely—Jerry Cooper & The Johnny Guarnieri Quintet (55)	*192*
That's When Your Heartaches Begin—Elvis Presley (57)	144
Have You Ever Been Lonely (Have You Ever Been Blue)—Caravelles (64)	*72*
Glory Of Love—Don Gardner And Dee Dee Ford (62)	*59*
Have You Ever Been Lonely (Have You Ever Been Blue)—Teresa Brewer (60)	*44*
The Glory Of Love—Dells (71)	*32*
Have You Ever Been Lonely (Have You Ever Been Blue)—Karen Chandler (55)	*12*
Lights Out—Billy Vaughn And His Orchestra (59)	0.4
In The Chapel In The Moonlight—Orioles (54)	*0.0*
Have You Ever Been Lonely (Have You Ever Been Blue)—Jaye P. Morgan (55)	*0.0*
—Bob Hill see: Fred HELLERMAN	
Bunker HILL [David Walker] ▶ 3191 (2)	**957**
Hide & Go Seek, Part 1—Bunker Hill (62)	*655*
Hide & Seek—Sheep (66)	*302*

Dan HILL ▶ 1130 (6)	**3928**
Sometimes When We Touch–Dan Hill (77)	4251
Can't We Try–Dan Hill (87)	1855
Never Thought (That I Could Love)–Dan Hill (87)	425
All I See Is Your Face–Dan Hill (78)	404
Growin' Up–Dan Hill (76)	42
Let The Song Last Forever–Dan Hill (78)	7.4
Darren HILL ▶ 8252 (1)	**57**
China–Red Rockers (83)	227
–David Hill see: David HESS	
Don HILL ▶ 6197 (2)	**194**
He Made A Woman Out Of Me–Bobbie Gentry (70)	156
I Want To Love You Baby– Peggy Scott & Jo Jo Benson (69)	116
Dusty HILL [Joe Michael Hill] ▶ 1609 (16)	**2631**
Legs–ZZ Top (84)	1701
Sleeping Bag–ZZ Top (85)	1591
Tush–ZZ Top (75)	835
La Grange–ZZ Top (74)	740
Stages–ZZ Top (86)	629
Rough Boy–ZZ Top (86)	621
Velcro Fly–ZZ Top (86)	451
Gimme All Your Lovin'–ZZ Top (83)	417
It's Only Love–ZZ Top (76)	308
Doubleback–ZZ Top (90)	295
Sharp Dressed Man–ZZ Top (83)	150
Leila–ZZ Top (81)	45
Arrested For Driving While Blind–ZZ Top (77)	43
Cheap Sunglasses–ZZ Top (80)	32
Give It Up–ZZ Top (91)	23
Enjoy And Get It On–ZZ Top (77)	14
Jack HILL ▶ 10649 (1)	**6.4**
That's The Way I Want Our Love–Joe Simon (70)	13
Jessie HILL ▶ 2882 (3)	**1133**
Ooh Poo Pah Doo Part Two–Jessie Hill (60)	*751*
Ooh Poo Pah Doo–Ike & Tina Turner (71)	*377*
Whip It On Me–Jessie Hill (60)	4.5
Joel Scott HILL ▶ 9047 (1)	**32**
Caterpillar Crawl–Strangers (59)	130
–Joe Michael Hill see: Dusty HILL	
John Michael HILL ▶ 3349 (3)	**886**
Are You Ready?– Pacific Gas & Electric With The Blackberries (70)	1471
I Love Onions–Susan Christie (66)	252
Thank God For You Baby–PG&E (72)	50
Lindell HILL ▶ 7515 (1)	**91**
Mini-Skirt Minnie–Wilson Pickett (69)	364
–Stanley Hill see: Noel GAY	
–Steven Bernard Hill see: STEVIE B	
Stevie HILL ▶ 7010 (1)	**122**
D.O.A.–Bloodrock (70)	733
Tommy HILL ▶ 6857 (2)	**132**
Teddy Bear–Red Sovine (76)	478
Giddyup Go–Red Sovine (66)	25
Z.Z. HILL [Arzell Hill] ▶ 8936 (2)	**36**
I Need Someone (To Love Me)–Z.Z. Hill (71)	30
You Were Wrong–Z.Z. Hill (64)	5.6
Tony HILLER [Anthony Toby Hiller] ▶ 2953 (5)	**1102**
United We Stand–Brotherhood Of Man (70)	1614
Save Your Kisses For Me–Brotherhood Of Man (76)	*391*
Where Are You Going To My Love– Brotherhood Of Man (70)	319
Reach Out Your Hand–Brotherhood Of Man (71)	78
Save Your Kisses For Me–Bobby Vinton (76)	*22*
Bob HILLIARD [Hilliard Goldsmith] ▶ 229 (48) HOF	**14779**
Our Day Will Come–Ruby And The Romantics (63)	*6254*
Moonlight Gambler–Frankie Laine (56)	*3465*
Tower Of Strength–Gene McDaniels (61)	2388
(Seven Little Girls) Sitting In The Back Seat– Paul Evans and The Curls (59)	2385
In My Little Corner Of The World–Anita Bryant (60)	1752
Any Day Now (My Wild Beautiful Bird)– Chuck Jackson (62)	*1371*
Please Stay–Drifters (61)	*1293*
Our Day Will Come–Frankie Valli (75)	*1249*
My Summer Love–Ruby And The Romantics (63)	1134
Any Day Now–Ronnie Milsap (82)	*1068*
That's What I Like–Don, Dick N' Jimmy (54)	*648*
In The Middle Of The House–Rusty Draper (56)	*584*
In The Middle Of The House– Vaughn Monroe with Joe Reisman's Orchestra (56)	*541*
A Poor Man's Roses (Or A Rich Man's Gold)– Patti Page (57)	*516*
Young Wings Can Fly (Higher Than You Know)– Ruby And The Romantics (63)	499
Don't You Believe It–Andy Williams (62)	496
Kookie Little Paradise–Jo Ann Campbell (60)	*323*
Sailor Boys Have Talk To Me In English– Rosemary Clooney (55)	*243*
From The Candy Store On The Corner To The Chapel On The Hill–Tony Bennett with Percy Faith and His Orchestra (56)	235
Jacqueline–Bobby Helms (58)	228
English Muffins And Irish Stew–Sylvia Syms (56)	216
Kookie Little Paradise–Tree Swingers (60)	*157*
Autumn Waltz–Tony Bennett with Percy Faith and His Orchestra and Chorus (56)	142
The Waiting Game–Harry Belafonte (58)	124
Love Me In The Daytime–Doris Day (59)	115
Baby Come Home–Ruby And The Romantics (64)	106
Any Day Now–Percy Sledge (69)	*91*
Being True To One Another–Tony Bennett (59)	89
You're Following Me–Perry Como (61)	83
Dancing Chandelier–Sylvia Syms (56)	63
Take A Chance–Jaye P. Morgan (57)	53
That's What I Like–Dean Martin (54)	*50*
Dear Hearts And Gentle People–Springfields (62)	48
You Don't Have To Be A Tower Of Strength– Gloria Lynne (61)	44
I've Changed My Mind A Thousand Times– Kay Starr (56)	*30*
Show Folk–Paul Evans (61)	26
Please Stay–Dave Clark Five (68)	*19*
Southern Cross–Ames Brothers (55)	17
Waiting For Charlie–Etta James (62)	*10*
The President On The Dollar– Mitch Miller & His Orchestra (56)	7.7
Waiting For Charlie To Come Home– Marlena Shaw (67)	*3.3*
Mexican Divorce–Drifters (62)	0.5
In The Middle Of The House–Milton Berle (56)	*0.0*
Money Burns A Hole In My Pocket–Dean Martin (54)	0.0
I've Changed My Mind A Thousand Times– Mills Brothers (56)	*0.0*
A Poor Man's Roses (Or A Rich Man's Gold)– Patsy Cline (57)	*0.0*
Sailor Boys Have Talk To Me In English– Helen O'Connell (55)	*0.0*
Sailor Boys Have Talk To Me In English– 5 DeMarco Sisters (55)	*0.0*
Jacqueline HILLIARD ▶ 9595 (1)	**21**
Rolling Down A Mountainside–Main Ingredient (75)	41
Chris HILLMAN ▶ 4090 (4)	**597**
So You Want To Be A Rock 'N' Roll Star–Byrds (67)	550
It Doesn't Matter–Stephen Stills (72)	312
Have You Seen Her Face–Byrds (67)	135
Safe At Home–Souther, Hillman, Furay Band (74)	31
Julie HILTON ▶ 9368 (1)	**25**
Jay-Dee's Boogie Woogie– Jimmy Dorsey Orchestra and Chorus (57)	50
Richard HIMBER ▶ 11244 (1)	**2.6**
Day After Day–Bill Cecere (58)	5.2
Rupert HINE ▶ 8964 (1)	**35**
Break Every Rule–Tina Turner (87)	70
–Brian Frederick Hines see: Denny LAINE	
Earl HINES [Earl Kenneth Hines, Fatha Hines] ▶ 3153 (3)	**982**
You Can Depend On Me–Brenda Lee (61)	2935
Jelly, Jelly, Jelly–Bobby Bland (62)	4.9
Stormy Monday–Latimore (73)	3.1
–Fatha Hines see: Earl HINES	
Henry R. HINES ▶ 10215 (1)	**11**
Gypsy Woman Told Me–Eddie Powers (64)	33
Don HINKLEY ▶ 4575 (1)	**463**
The Astronaut (Parts 1 & 2)–Jose Jimenez (61)	926
Billy HINSCHE ▶ 8884 (1)	**37**
Tell Someone You Love Them–Dino, Desi & Billy (68)	74
Jimbeau HINSON ▶ 11392 (1)	**1.9**
Fancy Free–Oak Ridge Boys (81)	3.8
Andrew HINTON ▶ 11677 (1)	**0.7**
Keep Warm–Jinny (91)	2.2
Eddie HINTON ▶ 4052 (5)	**612**
Choo Choo Train–Box Tops (68)	854
Cover Me–Percy Sledge (67)	287
You're All Around Me–Percy Sledge (68)	58
Always David–Ruby Winters (69)	24
Breakfast In Bed–Dusty Springfield (69)	9.1
Joe HINTON ▶ 4890 (1)	**387**
Gotta Hold On To This Feeling– Jr. Walker & The All Stars (70)	1160
Robert HIPPARD ▶ 5797 (1)	**240**
Don't You Write Her Off– McGuinn, Clark & Hillman (79)	481
Louise HIRAM ▶ 6275 (1)	**187**
Competition Ain't Nothin'–Little Carl Carlton (68)	374
Henry HIRSCH ▶ 9227 (1)	**28**
Stand By My Woman–Lenny Kravitz (91)	113
Ken HIRSCH ▶ 1709 (9)	**2453**
I've Never Been To Me–Charlene (82)	*3262*
Two Less Lonely People In The World–Air Supply (82)	593
Used To Be–Charlene & Stevie Wonder (82)	379
Can't We Try–Teddy Pendergrass (80)	333
No One In The World–Anita Baker (87)	326
It Ain't Easy Comin' Down–Charlene (77)	4.6
I've Never Been To Me–Charlene (77)	*3.0*
Where Have They Gone– Jimmie Beaumont And The Skyliners (75)	2.5
Freddie–Charlene (77)	2.4
Rick HIRSCH ▶ 4596 (4)	**457**
Keep On Smilin'–Wet Willie (74)	1449
Country Side Of Life–Wet Willie (74)	128
Everything That 'Cha Do (Will Come Back To You)– Wet Willie (76)	38
Dixie Rock–Wet Willie (75)	2.9
David HIRSCHFELDER ▶ 9107 (1)	**31**
Playing To Win–LRB (85)	217
Joel HIRSCHHORN ▶ 1308 (10)	**3387**
The Morning After–Maureen McGovern (73)	3712
Will You Be Staying After Sunday– Peppermint Rainbow (68)	1080
Let's Start All Over Again–Ronnie Dove (66)	941
One More Mountain To Climb–Ronnie Dove (67)	408
Why Can't You Bring Me Home– Jay & The Americans (66)	253
Your Time Hasn't Come Yet, Baby– Elvis Presley With The Jordanaires (68)	203
Stay And Love Me All Summer–Brian Hyland (69)	147
For A Friend–Bugaloos (70)	54
We May Never Love Like This Again– Maureen McGovern (75)	54
Wake Up–Chambers Brothers (69)	8.1
Clare HIRST ▶ 10578 (1)	**7.1**
Sign Of The Times–Belle Stars (83)	49
Rob HIRST ▶ 5199 (3)	**328**
Beds Are Burning–Midnight Oil (88)	812
Blue Sky Mine–Midnight Oil (90)	369
The Dead Heart–Midnight Oil (88)	276
Duane HITCHINGS ▶ 879 (9)	**5053**
Da Ya Think I'm Sexy?–Rod Stewart (78)	*8390*
Young Turks–Rod Stewart (81)	3203
Infatuation–Rod Stewart (84)	2065
Crazy About Her–Rod Stewart (89)	1149
Voyeur–Kim Carnes (82)	516
The Big Crash–Eddie Money (83)	253
Don't Look Any Further–Kane Gang (88)	*126*
Abadabadango–Kim Carnes (85)	82
Don't Look Any Further–Dennis Edwards (84)	*49*
Bob HITE ▶ 8221 (1)	**58**
Time Was–Canned Heat (69)	290
Larry HITZFELD ▶ 7753 (1)	**76**
Henrietta–Jimmy Dee And The Offbeats (58)	153
Carl HJELM ▶ 11043 (1)	**3.6**
Lapland–Baltimore And Ohio Marching Band (67)	7.2
Dave HLUBEK ▶ 6867 (2)	**132**
Flirtin' With Disaster–Molly Hatchet (79)	383
The Rambler–Molly Hatchet (81)	7.8
Cliff HOAD ▶ 11572 (1)	**1.2**
Black Leather–Kings Of The Sun (88)	2.3
Jeff HOAD ▶ 11573 (1)	**1.2**
Black Leather–Kings Of The Sun (88)	2.3
Becky HOBBS ▶ 10147 (1)	**12**
I Can't Say Goodbye To You–Helen Reddy (81)	12

David HOBBS ▶ 5379 (3)	**298**
Me So Horny—2 Live Crew (89)	729
Banned In The U.S.A.—Luke Featuring 2 Live Crew (90)	588
Pop That Coochie—2 Live Crew (91)	137
John HOBBS ▶ 6263 (2)	**188**
If I Were You—Lulu (81)	*337*
If I Were You—Toby Beau (80)	*39*
—Thomas Eugene Hobbs II see: Tom KIMMEL	
Bud HOBGOOD ▶ 3550 (6)	**788**
Get It Together (Part 1)—James Brown And The Famous Flames (67)	584
There Was A Time—James Brown And The Famous Flames (68)	*557*
Let Yourself Go—James Brown And The Famous Flames (67)	473
There Was A Time—Gene Chandler (68)	*133*
There Was A Time—Dapps Featuring Alfred Ellis (68)	*20*
The Soul Of J. B.—James Brown And The Famous Flames (67)	3.3
Curtis HOBSON ▶ 10995 (1)	**3.9**
Long Stroke—ADC Band (78)	24
—Isadore Hochberg see: E.Y. HARBURG	
Billy HOCHER ▶ 5564 (1)	**271**
No—Bulldog (72)	542
Vera HODES ▶ 7028 (1)	**121**
Ben Crazy—Dickie Goodman & Dr. I.M. III (62)	241
—Gary Hodgden see: Gary WEST	
Chris HODGE ▶ 4666 (1)	**443**
We're On Our Way—Chris Hodge (72)	443
Gary HODGE ▶ 10817 (1)	**5.1**
Werewolf—Frantics (60)	10
Gaynel HODGE ▶ 2166 (9)	**1801**
Earth Angel (Will You Be Mine)—Penguins (54)	*2284*
Earth Angel (Will You Be Mine)—Crew-Cuts (55)	*1777*
Earth Angel—New Edition (86)	*545*
Earth Angel (Will You Be Mine)—Vogues (69)	*486*
Earth Angel—Johnny Tillotson (60)	*230*
Earth Angel (Will You Be Mine)—Gloria Mann (55)	*74*
Earth Angel—Fred Parris & The Five Satins (82)	*4.8*
Earth Angel—Cleftones (61)	*2.3*
Earth Angel—Les Baxter & The Bombers (54)	*0.0*
John Philip HODGE ▶ 6419 (1)	**172**
Give A Little Bit More—Cliff Richard (81)	345
—Maurice Hodge see: Nevelle HODGE	
Nevelle HODGE [Maurice Hodge, Nevelle] ▶ 7300 (1)	**104**
Missunderstanding—Al B. Sure! (90)	313
Charles Nicholas HODGES ▶ 11522 (1)	**1.3**
Warmin' Up The Band—Don Everly (74)	6.6
Jesse D. HODGES ▶ 2587 (2)	**1347**
Mission Bell—Donnie Brooks (60)	2611
Memphis—Donnie Brooks (61)	41
Jimmie HODGES ▶ 4496 (3)	**477**
Someday (You'll Want Me To Want You)—Della Reese (60)	*402*
Someday (You'll Want Me To Want You)—Jodie Sands (58)	*72*
Someday You'll Want Me To Want You—Brook Benton (60)	*3.5*
Kenny HODGES ▶ 11321 (1)	**2.2**
And She's Mine—Spanky And Our Gang (69)	2.2
Leroy HODGES ▶ 10075 (1)	**13**
30-60-90—Willie Mitchell (69)	66
Mabon HODGES ▶ 1447 (10)	**3025**
Here I Am (Come And Take Me)—Al Green (73)	*1801*
Here I Am (Come And Take Me)—UB40 (91)	*1696*
L-O-V-E (Love)—Al Green (75)	1223
Take Me To The River—Talking Heads (78)	*717*
Full Of Fire—Al Green (75)	526
I Take What I Want—James & Bobby Purify (67)	279
Oh Me, Oh My (Dreams In My Arms)—Al Green (75)	208
Take Me To The River—Syl Johnson (75)	*193*
Love And Happiness—Earnest Jackson (73)	125
30-60-90—Willie Mitchell (69)	66
David HODGKINS ▶ 3012 (2)	**1068**
Games—Redeye (70)	964
Red Eye Blues—Redeye (71)	104
—Michael Hodgkinson see: Johnny AVERAGE	

Christine HODGSON [Christine Authors, Christine Holmes] ▶ 2425 (1)	**1498**
Devil Woman—Cliff Richard (76)	2996
Roger HODGSON ▶ 758 (11)	**5782**
The Logical Song—Supertramp (79)	*2915*
It's Raining Again—Supertramp (82)	1898
Take The Long Way Home—Supertramp (79)	1451
Give A Little Bit—Supertramp (77)	1217
Goodbye Stranger—Supertramp (79)	1209
Dreamer—Supertramp (80)	1034
My Kind Of Lady—Supertramp (83)	550
Had A Dream (Sleeping With The Enemy)—Roger Hodgson (84)	392
Bloody Well Right—Supertramp (75)	348
Breakfast In America—Supertramp (80)	120
The Topical Song—Barron Knights (79)	*55*
William HODGSON ▶ 10421 (1)	**8.6**
Music Goes 'Round And Around—Joe Pica (54)	26
Greg HOELTZEL ▶ 8873 (1)	**37**
The Teaser—Bob Kuban And The In-Men (66)	75
Martin Lee HOENES [Marty Lee Hoenes, Marty Lee] ▶ 6787 (2)	**137**
Love Is Like A Rock—Donnie Iris (81)	454
Tough World—Donnie Iris (82)	138
—Marty Lee Hoenes see: Martin Lee HOENES	
Edward R. HOERNER ▶ 11740 (1)	**0.3**
Shake A Leg—Sea Level (77)	0.3
Al HOFFMAN ▶ 239 (58) HOF	**14339**
Hot Diggity (Dog Ziggity Boom)—Perry Como (56)	5854
Allegheny Moon—Patti Page (56)	*5270*
Papa Loves Mambo—Perry Como (54)	4276
Secretly—Jimmie Rodgers (58)	*4105*
Hawaiian Wedding Song—Andy Williams (58)	3451
Are You Really Mine—Jimmie Rodgers (58)	1540
Heartaches—Marcels (61)	*1413*
O Dio Mio—Annette (60)	1390
Oh Oh I'm Falling In Love Again—Jimmie Rodgers (58)	1234
Moon Talk—Perry Como (58)	697
Mama Teach Me To Dance—Eydie Gorme (56)	*687*
I'm Never Gonna Tell—Jimmie Rodgers (59)	568
Ivy Rose—Perry Como (57)	559
Teasin'—Quaker City Boys (58)	529
Don't Stay Away Too Long—Eddie Fisher (55)	490
Belonging To Someone—Patti Page (58)	482
La Plume De Ma Tante—Hugo & Luigi (59)	398
Make Me A Miracle—Jimmie Rodgers (58)	387
Heartaches—Patsy Cline (62)	*275*
Where Will The Dimple Be—Rosemary Clooney (55)	263
Secretly—Lettermen (65)	*243*
You're Cheatin' Yourself (If You're Cheatin' On Me)—Frank Sinatra (57)	135
Santo Natale (Merry Christmas)—David Whitfield with Stanley Black And His Orchestra (54)	*129*
Mairzy Doats—Innocence (67)	*119*
Mi Casa, Su Casa (My House Is Your House)—Perry Como (57)	115
I Was Hoping You'd Ask Me—Janice Harper (58)	111
Kiss Me And Kiss Me And Kiss Me (Tre Volte Baciami)—Perry Como (59)	111
You Understand Me—Sam Cooke (60)	*99*
Heartaches—Somethin' Smith & The Redheads (56)	*75*
Ha! Ha! Ha! (Chella Lla)—Kay Armen (57)	*72*
Daydreams—Art Mooney And His Orchestra (56)	68
Gotta Lotta Love—Steve Alaimo (63)	57
I Can't Tell A Waltz From A Tango—Patti Page (54)	57
Golly—Four Lads (57)	50
Boulevard Of Nightingales—Tony Martin (54)	47
My Bambino—Tony Martin (54)	33
Heartaches—Four Preps (62)	*24*
Thirteen Going On Fourteen—Crew-Cuts (56)	23
I Apologize—Timi Yuro (61)	18
S'-All Right? S'-All Right!—Senor Wences (59)	16
Addio—Ames Brothers (54)	15
Ev'ry Night At Nine O'Clock—Somethin' Smith & The Redheads (57)	14
Do You Love Me Like You Kiss Me (Scapricciatiello)—McGuire Sisters (58)	12
I'm Gonna Live Till I Die—Frank Sinatra and Ray Anthony and his Orchestra (55)	10

Forget Her—Tony Bennett with Percy Faith and His Orchestra (56)	5.5
Lulu Had A Baby—Chico Holiday (59)	3.7
You Understand Me—Jimmie Rodgers (58)	*1.6*
Mairzy Doats—Dodie Stevens (59)	*1.2*
Heartaches—Sam Sideburn (58)	*0.8*
Torero—Julius La Rosa (58)	*0.0*
Torero—Andrews Sisters (58)	*0.0*
Santo Natale—Ronnie Gaylord (54)	*0.0*
Ha! Ha! Ha! ("Che Lla La!")—Lou Monte (57)	*0.0*
Heartaches—Ted Weems And His Orchestra (56)	*0.0*
Allegheny Moon—Grady Martin & His Slew Foot Five (56)	*0.0*
Mama, Teach Me To Dance—Bobby Madera & His Orchestra (56)	*0.0*
Gilly Gilly Ossenfeffer Katzenellen Bogen By The Sea—Four Lads (54)	0.0
HA HA HA (Chella Lla)—Sammy Kaye & His "Swing And Sway" Orchestra (57)	*0.0*
Dan HOFFMAN ▶ 11278 (1)	**2.5**
Run, Woman, Run—Tammy Wynette (70)	7.5
Henry HOFFMAN ▶ 1219 (2)	**3660**
Bobby's Girl—Marcie Blane (62)	7201
What Does A Girl Do?—Marcie Blane (63)	120
Jack HOFFMAN ▶ 8088 (5)	**62**
Dreamy Eyes—Four Preps (56)	61
Tres Chic—Geoff Gilmore & The Sheiks (59)	34
Dream Boat—Paulette Sisters (55)	*10*
Dreamboat—5 DeMarco Sisters (55)	*10*
Dreamboat—Lou Monte (55)	*0.0*
Uwe HOFFMANN ▶ 6825 (2)	**134**
Holiday—Other Ones (87)	545
We Are What We Are—Other Ones (87)	261
Susanna HOFFS ▶ 1766 (4)	**2350**
Eternal Flame—Bangles (89)	3515
In Your Room—Bangles (88)	1791
Walking Down Your Street—Bangles (87)	1281
My Side Of The Bed—Susanna Hoffs (91)	464
Donald HOGAN ▶ 2497 (5)	**1436**
When We Get Married—Dreamlovers (61)	*978*
When We Get Married—Intruders (70)	*340*
If I Should Lose You—Dreamlovers (62)	209
When We Get Married—Larry Graham (80)	*39*
Let Them Love (And Be Loved)—Dreamlovers (61)	8.6
Sam HOGIN ▶ 4174 (1)	**574**
I Believe In You—Don Williams (80)	1147
John HOIER ▶ 6497 (1)	**163**
That's The Way A Woman Is—Messengers (71)	325
John HOKE ▶ 10462 (1)	**8.1**
When You Feel Love—Bob McGilpin (78)	16
Eddie HOKENSON ▶ 2026 (2)	**1994**
Bad Girls—Donna Summer (79)	7825
Sad Eyes—Brooklyn Dreams (77)	114
Mark HOLDEN ▶ 5794 (1)	**241**
Lady Soul—Temptations (86)	241
Ron HOLDEN ▶ 1710 (1)	**2451**
Love You So—Ron Holden With The Thunderbirds (60)	2451
Jack HOLDER ▶ 10162 (1)	**12**
Make It Mean Something—Rob Jungklas (87)	35
Milton HOLDER ▶ 10169 (1)	**12**
Bermuda Shorts—Delroys (57)	35
—Neville Holder see: Noddy HOLDER	
Noddy HOLDER [Neville Holder] ▶ 1731 (9)	**2406**
Cum On Feel The Noize—Quiet Riot (83)	*2756*
Run Runaway—Slade (84)	816
My Oh My—Slade (84)	396
Mama Weer All Crazee Now—Quiet Riot (84)	*324*
Mama Weer All Crazee Now—Slade (72)	*194*
Gudbuy T' Jane—Slade (73)	186
Cum On Feel The Noize—Slade (73)	*87*
Take Me Bak 'Ome—Slade (72)	40
Little Sheila—Slade (85)	15
Mark HOLDING ▶ 2798 (1)	**1190**
C'est La Vie—Robbie Nevil (86)	3569
Lee HOLDRIDGE ▶ 5622 (2)	**264**
Moonlighting (Theme)—Al Jarreau (87)	480
Moment By Moment—Yvonne Elliman (78)	48
Chico HOLIDAY ▶ 5030 (2)	**357**
God, Country And My Baby—Johnny Burnette (61)	*714*
God Country And My Baby—Chico Holiday (61)	*0.0*

Jimmy HOLIDAY ► 1053 (14)	**4190**
Put A Little Love In Your Heart—Jackie DeShannon (69)	*3577*
All I Ever Need Is You—Sonny & Cher (71)	2452
Put A Little Love In Your Heart—Annie Lennox & Al Green (88)	*1389*
Don't Change On Me—Ray Charles (71)	751
Love Will Find A Way—Jackie De Shannon (69)	529
I Chose To Sing The Blues—Ray Charles & The Raeletts (66)	501
That's A Lie—Ray Charles (68)	326
Brighton Hill—Jackie Deshannon (70)	207
Bad Water—Raeletts (71)	202
Understanding—Ray Charles (68)	193
Baby I Love You—Little Milton (70)	*59*
Let Me Love You—Ray Charles (69)	47
Make A Little Love—Lowell Fulsom (67)	3.8
Baby I Love You—Jimmy Holiday (66)	*1.4*

Danny HOLIEN ► 6705 (1)	**143**
Colorado—Danny Holien (72)	143

Rodney HOLLAMAN ► 3664 (1)	**744**
Girl You Know It's True—Milli Vanilli (88)	3721

Brian HOLLAND [Edyth Craighead, Edith Wayne, Brianbert] ► 14 (164) HOF	**70184**
Where Did Our Love Go—Supremes (64)	*9056*
I Can't Help Myself—Four Tops (65)	*8859*
Come See About Me—Supremes (64)	*8772*
Mashed Potato Time—Dee Dee Sharp (62)	8768
Baby Love—Supremes (64)	8476
Please Mr. Postman—Marvelettes (61)	*7831*
Stop! In The Name Of Love—Supremes (65)	*7776*
You Can't Hurry Love—Supremes (66)	*7615*
I Hear A Symphony—Supremes (65)	6983
Reach Out I'll Be There—Four Tops (66)	*6413*
You Keep Me Hangin' On—Supremes (66)	*6251*
The Happening—Supremes (67)	*6167*
Band Of Gold—Freda Payne (70)	6004
Love Is Here And Now You're Gone—Supremes (67)	5783
1-2-3—Len Barry (65)	*5700*
Reflections—Diana Ross And The Supremes (67)	5395
Back In My Arms Again—Supremes (65)	*4991*
Roll With It—Steve Winwood (88)	4539
Please Mr. Postman—Carpenters (74)	*4500*
Heat Wave—Martha & The Vandellas (63)	*4013*
You Keep Me Hangin' On—Kim Wilde (87)	*3516*
Baby I Need Your Lovin'—Johnny Rivers (67)	*3362*
My World Is Empty Without You—Supremes (66)	*3008*
It's The Same Old Song—Four Tops (65)	*2864*
Standing In The Shadows Of Love—Four Tops (66)	2566
Bernadette—Four Tops (67)	2554
Jimmy Mack—Martha & The Vandellas (67)	*2552*
How Sweet It Is To Be Loved By You—Marvin Gaye (64)	*2463*
Give Me Just A Little More Time—Chairmen Of The Board (70)	2390
Playboy—Marvelettes (62)	2321
How Sweet It Is (To Be Loved By You)—James Taylor (75)	*2292*
You Keep Me Hangin' On—Vanilla Fudge (68)	*2110*
Nowhere To Run—Martha & The Vandellas (65)	1982
Mickey's Monkey—Miracles (63)	1976
Heaven Must Have Sent You—Bonnie Pointer (79)	*1857*
You Can't Hurry Love—Phil Collins (82)	*1813*
Love Is Like An Itching In My Heart—Supremes (66)	1721
I'm Ready For Love—Martha & The Vandellas (66)	1702
Quicksand—Martha & The Vandellas (63)	1686
In And Out Of Love—Diana Ross And The Supremes (67)	1650
Baby I Need Your Loving—Four Tops (64)	*1637*
Take Me In Your Arms (Rock Me)—Doobie Brothers (75)	*1636*
Nothing But Heartaches—Supremes (65)	1633
Can I Get A Witness—Marvin Gaye (63)	*1429*
You're A Wonderful One—Marvin Gaye (64)	1385
7-Rooms Of Gloom—Four Tops (67)	1376
This Old Heart Of Mine (Is Weak For You)—Isley Brothers (66)	*1339*
Heat Wave—Linda Ronstadt (75)	*1210*
Forever Came Today—Diana Ross And The Supremes (68)	*1145*
Westbound #9—Flaming Ember (70)	1141
This Old Heart Of Mine—Rod Stewart (with Ronald Isley) (90)	*1125*
Something About You—Four Tops (65)	*1109*
Come And Get These Memories—Martha & The Vandellas (63)	1109
How Sweet It Is (To Be Loved By You)—Jr. Walker & The All Stars (66)	*1081*
Shake Me, Wake Me (When It's Over)—Four Tops (66)	1067
Mind, Body And Soul—Flaming Ember (69)	1044
(I'm A) Road Runner—Jr. Walker & The All Stars (66)	1035
Deeper And Deeper—Freda Payne (70)	1024
Where Did Our Love Go—Donnie Elbert (71)	*1001*
When The Lovelight Starts Shining Through His Eyes—Supremes (63)	958
(Come 'Round Here) I'm The One You Need—Miracles (66)	943
You Keep Running Away—Four Tops (67)	912
The Day I Found Myself—Honey Cone (72)	906
I Can't Help Myself (Sugar Pie, Honey Bunch)—Donnie Elbert (72)	*858*
You Lost The Sweetest Boy—Mary Wells (63)	855
Come See About Me—Jr. Walker & The All Stars (67)	*794*
Baby Don't You Do It—Marvin Gaye (64)	*737*
Don't Do It—Band (72)	*698*
Just A Little Bit Of You—Michael Jackson (75)	683
The Other Side—Aerosmith (90)	642
Reach Out I'll Be There—Diana Ross (71)	*619*
(You've Got Me) Dangling On A String—Chairmen Of The Board (70)	*558*
Strange I Know—Marvelettes (62)	557
I Gotta Dance To Keep From Crying—Miracles (63)	546
Twistin' Postman—Marvelettes (62)	539
Stop In The Name Of Love—Hollies (83)	*525*
Can I Get A Witness—Lee Michaels (71)	*522*
Your Unchanging Love—Marvin Gaye (67)	484
Everything's Tuesday—Chairmen Of The Board (70)	479
You Brought The Joy—Freda Payne (71)	474
Cherish What Is Dear To You (While It's Near To You)—Freda Payne (71)	473
Chairman Of The Board—Chairmen Of The Board (71)	458
Take Me In Your Arms (Rock Me A Little While)—Kim Weston (65)	*440*
Locking Up My Heart—Marvelettes (63)	428
Live Wire—Martha & The Vandellas (64)	418
I Can't Help Myself (Sugar Pie, Honey Bunch)—Bonnie Pointer (79)	*407*
It's The Same Old Song—KC & The Sunshine Band (78)	*395*
Little Darling (I Need You)—Doobie Brothers (77)	*392*
I'm Gonna Let My Heart Do The Walking—Supremes (76)	385
I'm In A Different World—Four Tops (68)	381
Little Darling, I Need You—Marvin Gaye (66)	*372*
In My Lonely Room—Martha & The Vandellas (64)	348
Heaven Must Have Sent You—Elgins (66)	*326*
Helpless—Kim Weston (66)	316
Why Can't We Be Lovers—Holland-Dozier (72)	313
Without The One You Love (Life's Not Worth While)—Four Tops (64)	306
Forever Came Today—Jackson 5 (75)	*305*
We're Almost There—Michael Jackson (75)	293
Crumbs Off The Table—Glass House (69)	279
Don't Leave Me Starvin' For Your Love (Part 1)—Holland-Dozier (73)	273
Get The Cream Off The Top—Eddie Kendricks (75)	252
I Guess I'll Always Love You—Isley Brothers (66)	243
Baby, I Need Your Loving—O.C. Smith (70)	*239*
Where Did Our Love Go—J. Geils Band (76)	*205*
All I Do Is Think Of You—Troop (90)	198
Darling Baby—Elgins (66)	*197*
All The Love I've Got—Marv Johnson (60)	192
Something About You—Le Blanc & Carr (77)	*183*
While You're Out Looking For Sugar?—Honey Cone (69)	183
Shades Of Green—Flaming Ember (70)	173
You Keep Me Hangin' On—Vanilla Fudge (67)	*165*
Just Ain't Enough Love—Eddie Holland (64)	160
Love (Makes Me Do Foolish Things)—Martha & The Vandellas (65)	154
Keep Holding On—Temptations (76)	149
Girls It Ain't Easy—Honey Cone (69)	149
Candy To Me—Eddie Holland (64)	141
Baby, I Need Your Lovin'—Eric Carmen (79)	*135*
You Keep Me Hanging On—Wilson Pickett (69)	*133*
One, Two, Three—Ramsey Lewis (67)	*131*
I Just Can't Walk Away—Four Tops (83)	124
If You Can Beat Me Rockin' (You Can Have My Chair)—Laura Lee (72)	122
Reach Out, I'll Be There—Gloria Gaynor (75)	*119*
Jimmy Mack—Sheena Easton (86)	*115*
Leaving Here—Eddie Holland (64)	114
This Old Heart Of Mine (Is Weak For You)—Tammi Terrell (69)	*96*
Forever—Marvelettes (63)	93
Reach Out, I'll Be There—Ritchie Family (76)	*92*
Come See About Me—Nella Dodds (64)	*92*
It's The Same Old Song—Shalamar (77)	*80*
Stop! In the Name of Love—Shalamar (77)	*80*
I Can't Help Myself (Sugar Pie, Honey Bunch)—Shalamar (77)	*80*
Reach Out—Merrilee Rush (68)	*70*
Stop! In The Name Of Love—Margie Joseph (71)	*64*
The Road We Didn't Take—Freda Payne (72)	58
I'll Turn To Stone—Four Tops (67)	58
This Old Heart Of Mine—Rod Stewart (76)	*53*
My World Is Empty Without You—Jose Feliciano (69)	*46*
Please Mr. Postman—Gentle Persuasion (83)	*45*
Back In My Arms Again—Genya Ravan (78)	*41*
Put Yourself In My Place—Elgins (66)	33
Take Me With You—Honey Cone (70)	28
(Let's Go) All The Way—Whispers (78)	24
Run, Run, Run—Supremes (64)	24
You're My Driving Wheel—Supremes (76)	21
Reach Out I'll Be There—Stars On 45 (81)	*12*
Stop In The Name Of Love—Stars On 45 (81)	*12*
I Think You Need Love—Dionne Warwicke (73)	10
Greetings (This Is Uncle Sam)—Valadiers (61)	*9.2*
If It's Good To You (It's Good For You)—Flaming Ember (71)	9.0
You've Got Me Dangling On A String—Donny Osmond (77)	*8.4*
I Can't Help Myself—Magnificent Men (67)	*7.6*
Please Mr. Postman—Beatles (64)	*6.4*
Greetings (This Is Uncle Sam)—Monitors (66)	*5.8*
Too Many Cooks (Spoil The Soup)—100 Proof Aged In Soul (69)	3.9
Stealing Moments From Another Woman's Life—Glass House (70)	3.7
Darling Baby—Jackie Moore (72)	*3.5*
Try My Love On For Size—Chairmen Of The Board (71)	3.4
I've Got A Notion—Marv Johnson (61)	3.2
Function At The Junction—Shorty Long (66)	1.9
Take Me In Your Arms (Rock Me A Little While)—Isley Brothers (68)	*1.8*
Stop The World And Let Me Off—Flaming Ember (71)	1.2
You Keep Me Hangin' On—Jackie DeShannon (70)	*1.0*
Reach Out I'll Be There—New Seekers (74)	*0.7*
Tie A String Around Your Finger—Marvelettes (63)	0.5

Eddie HOLLAND [Edyth Craighead, Edith Wayne] ► 12 (163) HOF	**72158**
Where Did Our Love Go—Supremes (64)	*9056*
I Can't Help Myself—Four Tops (65)	*8859*
Come See About Me—Supremes (64)	*8772*
Baby Love—Supremes (64)	8476
Stop! In The Name Of Love—Supremes (65)	*7776*
You Can't Hurry Love—Supremes (66)	*7615*
I Hear A Symphony—Supremes (65)	6983
Reach Out I'll Be There—Four Tops (66)	*6413*
You Keep Me Hangin' On—Supremes (66)	*6251*
The Happening—Supremes (67)	*6167*
Band Of Gold—Freda Payne (70)	6004
Love Is Here And Now You're Gone—Supremes (67)	5783
1-2-3—Len Barry (65)	*5700*
Reflections—Diana Ross And The Supremes (67)	5395
Back In My Arms Again—Supremes (65)	*4991*
Roll With It—Steve Winwood (88)	4539
Heat Wave—Martha & The Vandellas (63)	*4013*
You Keep Me Hangin' On—Kim Wilde (87)	*3516*
Baby I Need Your Lovin'—Johnny Rivers (67)	*3362*
My World Is Empty Without You—Supremes (66)	*3008*
Beauty Is Only Skin Deep—Temptations (66)	2987
It's The Same Old Song—Four Tops (65)	*2864*
Standing In The Shadows Of Love—Four Tops (66)	2566
Bernadette—Four Tops (67)	2554
Jimmy Mack—Martha & The Vandellas (67)	*2552*
(I Know) I'm Losing You—Rare Earth (70)	*2495*
How Sweet It Is To Be Loved By You—Marvin Gaye (64)	*2463*

Eddie HOLLAND [Edyth Craighead, Edith Wayne] ▶ 12 (163) HOF *Continued*	**72158**
Give Me Just A Little More Time—Chairmen Of The Board (70)	2390
How Sweet It Is (To Be Loved By You)—James Taylor (75)	*2292*
Ain't Too Proud To Beg—Temptations (66)	*2123*
You Keep Me Hangin' On—Vanilla Fudge (68)	*2110*
Nowhere To Run—Martha & The Vandellas (65)	1982
Mickey's Monkey—Miracles (63)	1976
All I Need—Temptations (67)	1916
(I Know) I'm Losing You—Temptations (66)	*1880*
Heaven Must Have Sent You—Bonnie Pointer (79)	*1857*
You Can't Hurry Love—Phil Collins (82)	*1813*
Love Is Like An Itching In My Heart—Supremes (66)	1721
I'm Ready For Love—Martha & The Vandellas (66)	1702
Quicksand—Martha & The Vandellas (63)	1686
In And Out Of Love—Diana Ross And The Supremes (67)	1650
Baby I Need Your Loving—Four Tops (64)	*1637*
Take Me In Your Arms (Rock Me)—Doobie Brothers (75)	*1636*
Nothing But Heartaches—Supremes (65)	1633
(Loneliness Made Me Realize) It's You That I Need—Temptations (67)	1525
Can I Get A Witness—Marvin Gaye (63)	*1429*
You're A Wonderful One—Marvin Gaye (64)	1385
7-Rooms Of Gloom—Four Tops (67)	1376
This Old Heart Of Mine (Is Weak For You)—Isley Brothers (66)	*1339*
Heat Wave—Linda Ronstadt (75)	*1210*
Forever Came Today—Diana Ross And The Supremes (68)	*1145*
Westbound #9—Flaming Ember (70)	1141
This Old Heart Of Mine—Rod Stewart (with Ronald Isley) (90)	*1125*
Something About You—Four Tops (65)	*1109*
Come And Get These Memories—Martha & The Vandellas (63)	1109
How Sweet It Is (To Be Loved By You)—Jr. Walker & The All Stars (66)	*1081*
Shake Me, Wake Me (When It's Over)—Four Tops (66)	1067
Mind, Body And Soul—Flaming Ember (69)	1044
Too Many Fish In The Sea—Marvelettes (64)	*1040*
(I'm A) Road Runner—Jr. Walker & The All Stars (66)	1035
Deeper And Deeper—Freda Payne (70)	1024
Where Did Our Love Go—Donnie Elbert (71)	*1001*
When The Lovelight Starts Shining Through His Eyes—Supremes (63)	958
(Come 'Round Here) I'm The One You Need—Miracles (66)	943
(I Know) I'm Losing You—Rod Stewart With Faces (71)	*942*
You Keep Running Away—Four Tops (67)	912
The Day I Found Myself—Honey Cone (72)	906
I Can't Help Myself (Sugar Pie, Honey Bunch)—Donnie Elbert (72)	*858*
You Lost The Sweetest Boy—Mary Wells (63)	855
Ain't Too Proud To Beg—Rolling Stones (74)	*829*
Come See About Me—Jr. Walker & The All Stars (67)	*794*
Baby Don't You Do It—Marvin Gaye (64)	*737*
Don't Do It—Band (72)	*698*
Just A Little Bit Of You—Michael Jackson (75)	683
Girl (Why You Wanna Make Me Blue)—Temptations (64)	667
The Other Side—Aerosmith (90)	642
Reach Out I'll Be There—Diana Ross (71)	*619*
(You've Got Me) Dangling On A String—Chairmen Of The Board (70)	*558*
I Gotta Dance To Keep From Crying—Miracles (63)	546
You—Marvin Gaye (68)	545
Stop In The Name Of Love—Hollies (83)	*525*
Can I Get A Witness—Lee Michaels (71)	*522*
Your Unchanging Love—Marvin Gaye (67)	484
Everything's Tuesday—Chairmen Of The Board (70)	479
Take Me In Your Arms (Rock Me A Little While)—Kim Weston (65)	*440*
Locking Up My Heart—Marvelettes (63)	428
Live Wire—Martha & The Vandellas (64)	418
I Can't Help Myself (Sugar Pie, Honey Bunch)—Bonnie Pointer (79)	*407*
It's The Same Old Song—KC & The Sunshine Band (78)	*395*
Little Darling (I Need You)—Doobie Brothers (77)	*392*
I'm Gonna Let My Heart Do The Walking—Supremes (76)	385
Everybody Needs Love—Gladys Knight & The Pips (67)	383
I'm In A Different World—Four Tops (68)	381
Little Darling, I Need You—Marvin Gaye (66)	*372*
In My Lonely Room—Martha & The Vandellas (64)	348
Heaven Must Have Sent You—Elgins (66)	*326*
Helpless—Kim Weston (66)	316
Why Can't We Be Lovers—Holland-Dozier (72)	313
Without The One You Love (Life's Not Worth While)—Four Tops (64)	306
Forever Came Today—Jackson 5 (75)	*305*
Too Many Fish In The Sea—Mitch Ryder And The Detroit Wheels (67)	*300*
We're Almost There—Michael Jackson (75)	293
Crumbs Off The Table—Glass House (69)	279
Don't Leave Me Starvin' For Your Love (Part 1)—Holland-Dozier (73)	273
Get The Cream Off The Top—Eddie Kendricks (75)	252
I Guess I'll Always Love You—Isley Brothers (66)	243
Baby, I Need Your Loving—O.C. Smith (70)	*239*
Gotta See Jane—R. Dean Taylor (71)	236
Where Did Our Love Go—J. Geils Band (76)	*205*
Darling Baby—Elgins (66)	*197*
Something About You—Le Blanc & Carr (77)	*183*
While You're Out Looking For Sugar?—Honey Cone (69)	183
Shades Of Green—Flaming Ember (70)	173
He Was Really Sayin' Somethin'—Velvelettes (65)	172
You Keep Me Hangin' On—Vanilla Fudge (67)	*165*
Everything Is Good About You—Lettermen (71)	165
Just Ain't Enough Love—Eddie Holland (64)	160
Love (Makes Me Do Foolish Things)—Martha & The Vandellas (65)	154
Keep Holding On—Temptations (76)	149
Girls It Ain't Easy—Honey Cone (69)	149
Candy To Me—Eddie Holland (64)	141
Baby, I Need Your Lovin'—Eric Carmen (79)	*135*
You Keep Me Hanging On—Wilson Pickett (69)	*133*
One, Two, Three—Ramsey Lewis (67)	*131*
I Just Can't Walk Away—Four Tops (83)	124
Reach Out, I'll Be There—Gloria Gaynor (75)	*119*
Jimmy Mack—Sheena Easton (86)	*115*
Leaving Here—Eddie Holland (64)	114
This Old Heart Of Mine (Is Weak For You)—Tammi Terrell (69)	*96*
Reach Out, I'll Be There—Ritchie Family (76)	*92*
Come See About Me—Nella Dodds (64)	*92*
It's The Same Old Song—Shalamar (77)	*80*
Stop! In the Name of Love—Shalamar (77)	*80*
I Can't Help Myself (Sugar Pie, Honey Bunch)—Shalamar (77)	*80*
Reach Out—Merrilee Rush (68)	*70*
Stop! In The Name Of Love—Margie Joseph (71)	*64*
I'll Turn To Stone—Four Tops (67)	58
(I Know) I'm Losing You—Uptown (86)	*55*
This Old Heart Of Mine—Rod Stewart (76)	*53*
My World Is Empty Without You—Jose Feliciano (69)	*46*
Back In My Arms Again—Genya Ravan (78)	*41*
Put Yourself In My Place—Elgins (66)	33
Take Me With You—Honey Cone (70)	28
(Let's Go) All The Way—Whispers (78)	24
Run, Run, Run—Supremes (64)	24
The Girl's Alright With Me—Temptations (64)	23
Reach Out I'll Be There—Stars On 45 (81)	*12*
Stop In The Name Of Love—Stars On 45 (81)	*12*
I Think You Need Love—Dionne Warwicke (73)	10
If It's Good To You (It's Good For You)—Flaming Ember (71)	9.0
Ain't Too Proud To Beg—Rick Astley (89)	*8.7*
You've Got Me Dangling On A String—Donny Osmond (77)	*8.4*
I Can't Help Myself—Magnificent Men (67)	*7.6*
Ain't Too Proud To Beg—Magnificent Men (67)	*7.6*
Too Many Cooks (Spoil The Soup)—100 Proof Aged In Soul (69)	3.9
Darling Baby—Jackie Moore (72)	*3.5*
Lonely Lonely Girl Am I—Velvelettes (65)	2.8
Function At The Junction—Shorty Long (66)	1.9
Take Me In Your Arms (Rock Me A Little While)—Isley Brothers (68)	*1.8*
Stop The World And Let Me Off—Flaming Ember (71)	1.2
You Keep Me Hangin' On—Jackie DeShannon (70)	*1.0*
Reach Out I'll Be There—New Seekers (74)	*0.7*
Tie A String Around Your Finger—Marvelettes (63)	0.5
Nicky HOLLAND ▶ 8762 (1)	**40**
Advice For The Young At Heart—Tears For Fears (90)	80
Randy HOLLAND ▶ 2938 (1)	**1109**
Giving You The Best That I Got—Anita Baker (88)	3327
Steve HOLLAND ▶ 10224 (1)	**11**
Power Play—Molly Hatchet (82)	11
Fred HOLLANDER ▶ 8880 (1)	**37**
Wun'erful, Wun'erful! (Sides Uh-One & Uh-Two)—Stan Freberg (57)	298
Dick HOLLER ▶ 327 (7)	**11168**
Snoopy Vs. The Red Baron—Royal Guardsmen (66)	8083
Abraham, Martin And John—Dion (68)	*5358*
Abraham, Martin And John—Tom Clay (71)	*836*
Abraham, Martin And John—Moms Mabley (69)	*405*
Abraham, Martin And John—Smokey Robinson & The Miracles (69)	*379*
Cole, Cooke And Redding—Wilson Pickett (70)	*142*
Snoopy For President—Royal Guardsmen (68)	23
—Charles Hardin Holley see: Buddy HOLLY	
John HOLLIDAY ▶ 2441 (5)	**1485**
Wild, Wild West—Escape Club (88)	4224
I'll Be There—Escape Club (91)	1572
Shake For The Sheik—Escape Club (88)	509
Call It Poison—Escape Club (91)	412
Walking Through Walls—Escape Club (89)	67
Richard HOLLINGSWORTH ▶ 11375 (1)	**2.0**
You Got That Touch—Sonny James (58)	4.0
Laura HOLLINS ▶ 6121 (3)	**203**
Why Don't You Write Me—Jacks (55)	*203*
Why Don't You Write Me?—Buddy Greco (55)	*0.0*
Why Don't You Write Me—Snooky Lanson (55)	*0.0*
Ed HOLLIS ▶ 9472 (1)	**23**
Talk Talk—Talk Talk (82)	46
—Jesse Hollis see: Brook BENTON	
Mark HOLLIS ▶ 5094 (4)	**343**
It's My Life—Talk Talk (84)	595
Talk Talk—Talk Talk (82)	46
Life's What You Make It—Talk Talk (86)	25
Such A Shame—Talk Talk (84)	10
Robert HOLLOMAN ▶ 11776 (1)	**0.1**
Bad, Bold And Beautiful Girl—Persuaders (73)	0.4
Ken HOLLON ▶ 7905 (2)	**70**
What've I Done (To Make You Mad)—Linda Jones (67)	139
Right Now And Not Later—Shangri-Las (65)	1.9
Brenda HOLLOWAY [Brenda Holloway Davis] ▶ 2413 (3)	**1508**
You've Made Me So Very Happy—Blood, Sweat & Tears (69)	*5673*
You've Made Me So Very Happy—Brenda Holloway (67)	*353*
You've Made Me So Very Happy—Lou Rawls (70)	*5.5*
Patrice HOLLOWAY ▶ 2414 (3)	**1508**
You've Made Me So Very Happy—Blood, Sweat & Tears (69)	*5673*
You've Made Me So Very Happy—Brenda Holloway (67)	*353*
You've Made Me So Very Happy—Lou Rawls (70)	*5.5*
Wrecia HOLLOWAY [Dee Dee Ford] ▶ 10287 (1)	**10**
Let Me Down Easy—Betty LaVette (65)	21
Alton HOLLOWELL ▶ 11259 (1)	**2.5**
True Love Gone (Come On Home)—Betty Madigan (57)	13
Gerald HOLLOWELL ▶ 11260 (1)	**2.5**
True Love Gone (Come On Home)—Betty Madigan (57)	13
Ulysses HOLLOWELL ▶ 11261 (1)	**2.5**
True Love Gone (Come On Home)—Betty Madigan (57)	13

Buddy HOLLY [Charles Hardin, Charles Hardin Holley] ▶ 655 (25) HOF	**6699**
Peggy Sue—Buddy Holly / The Crickets (57)	*4478*
That'll Be The Day—Buddy Holly / The Crickets (57)	*4320*
It's So Easy—Linda Ronstadt (77)	1953
That'll Be The Day—Linda Ronstadt (76)	*1413*
True Love Ways—Peter And Gordon (65)	*1390*
Maybe Baby—Buddy Holly / The Crickets (58)	997
Love's Made A Fool Of You—Bobby Fuller Four (66)	*503*
Not Fade Away—Rolling Stones (64)	*417*
Think It Over—Buddy Holly / The Crickets (58)	325
Everyday—James Taylor (85)	*250*
Words Of Love—Diamonds (57)	194
Peggy Sue—Beach Boys (78)	*133*
True Love Ways—Mickey Gilley (80)	*74*
Well All Right—Santana (78)	67
Everyday—John Denver (72)	*64*
Not Fade Away—Tanya Tucker (78)	*54*
Everyday—Buddy Holly / The Crickets (57)	*53*
Not Fade Away—Eric Hine (81)	*40*
Love's Made A Fool Of You—Cochise (71)	*35*
Listen To Me—Buddy Holly / The Crickets (58)	23
Love Me—Buddy Holly / The Crickets (58)	6.2
That'll Be The Day—Everly Brothers (65)	*5.0*
Peggy Sue—Jackie Walker (57)	*0.0*
That'll Be The Day—Jeff Allen (57)	*0.0*
That'll Be The Day—Buddy Holly & The Three Tunes (57)	*0.0*
—Per Holm see: Per HOLM-PETERSEN	
Eddie HOLMAN ▶ 5064 (3)	**351**
This Can't Be True—Eddie Holman (66)	437
Don't Stop Now—Eddie Holman (70)	260
Am I A Loser—Eddie Holman (66)	4.3
Roy HOLMAN ▶ 8687 (1)	**43**
Good Life—Inner City (89)	128
Bob HOLMES ▶ 10020 (1)	**14**
Anywhere With You—Rubber Rodeo (84)	28
Bryan HOLMES ▶ 9190 (1)	**29**
What She Does To Me (The Diana Song)—Producers (81)	117
Carolyn HOLMES [Carol E. Holmes] ▶ 5955 (1)	**223**
Down The Aisle Of Love—Quin-Tones (58)	670
—Christine Holmes see: Christine HODGSON	
Gary HOLMES ▶ 9889 (1)	**15**
Keep It Tight—Single Bullet Theory (83)	31
Jake HOLMES ▶ 3199 (6)	**955**
So Close—Jake Holmes (70)	644
Strangers In A Strange World—Jenny Burton & Patrick Jude (84)	191
Saturday's Father—4 Seasons (68)	146
Idaho—4 Seasons Featuring Frankie Valli (69)	80
I Would Be In Love (Anyway)—Frank Sinatra (70)	12
Something's On Her Mind—4 Seasons Featuring Frankie Valli (69)	1.9
Jerry HOLMES ▶ 7444 (1)	**95**
What A Fool Was I—Georgie Shaw (56)	95
Mark HOLMES ▶ 9183 (1)	**29**
Somebody Somewhere—Platinum Blonde (86)	29
Robert HOLMES ▶ 4584 (3)	**462**
Voices Carry—'til tuesday (85)	1719
Looking Over My Shoulder—til tuesday (85)	115
Love In A Vacuum—'til tuesday (85)	12
Robert Lee HOLMES ▶ 11366 (1)	**2.1**
Tip On In (Part 1)—Slim Harpo (67)	4.1
—Robert Howard Holmes see: Bob HUDSON	
Rupert HOLMES [David Goldstein] ▶ 250 (12)	**13629**
Escape (The Pina Colada Song)—Rupert Holmes (79)	6740
You Got It All—Jets (86)	2436
Him—Rupert Holmes (80)	2192
Timothy—Buoys (70)	1236
Jennifer Tomkins—Street People (2) (69)	899
Answering Machine—Rupert Holmes (80)	363
I Don't Need You—Rupert Holmes (81)	156
Let's Get Crazy Tonight—Rupert Holmes (78)	98
Give Up Your Guns—Buoys (71)	67
Morning Man—Rupert Holmes (80)	67
Blackjack—Rupert Holmes (81)	5.5
Thank You Girl—Street People (70)	4.2
—Waldo T. Holmes see: Wally HOLMES	

Wally HOLMES [Waldo T. Holmes] ▶ 816 (4)	**5393**
Rock The Boat—Hues Corporation (74)	4482
Rockin' Soul—Hues Corporation (74)	676
Love Corporation—Hues Corporation (75)	232
I Caught Your Act—Hues Corporation (77)	4.3
Per HOLM-PETERSEN [Per Holm] ▶ 10568 (1)	**7.2**
Get Serious—Cut 'N' Move (91)	36
Lawrence HOLOFCENER ▶ 3450 (11)	**844**
Mr. Wonderful—Peggy Lee (56)	*899*
Mr. Wonderful—Sarah Vaughan (56)	*674*
Mr. Wonderful—Teddi King (56)	*459*
Too Close For Comfort—Eydie Gorme (56)	*381*
Jacques D'Iraque—Sammy Davis Jr. (56)	80
Funny—Jesse Belvin (58)	*15*
Funny—Gene McDaniels (62)	*10*
Mr. Wonderful—Mello-Larks (56)	*0.0*
Mr. Wonderful—Bette Anne Steele (56)	*0.0*
Too Close For Comfort—Lillian Briggs (56)	*0.0*
Too Close For Comfort—Sammy Davis Jr. (56)	*0.0*
David HOLT ▶ 5445 (3)	**288**
Mobile—Julius La Rosa (54)	534
Anyone Can Fall In Love—Doris Day (54)	42
Lollipop—Vince Edwards (58)	0.0
Derek HOLT ▶ 1745 (3)	**2376**
Couldn't Get It Right—Climax Blues Band (77)	2219
I Love You—Climax Blues Band (81)	1929
Makin' Love—Climax Blues Band (78)	10
Isaac HOLT [Redd Holt] ▶ 7075 (1)	**117**
Wack Wack—Young Holt Trio (66)	470
John HOLT ▶ 1545 (1)	**2753**
The Tide Is High—Blondie (80)	5506
—Patricia Louise Holt see: Patti LaBELLE	
—Redd Holt see: Isaac HOLT	
Will HOLT ▶ 2830 (5)	**1166**
Lemon Tree—Trini Lopez (65)	*795*
Light Sings—5th Dimension (71)	645
Lemon Tree—Peter, Paul & Mary (62)	*437*
Raspberries Strawberries—Kingston Trio (59)	218
Sinner Man—Les Baxter, His Chorus and Orchestra (56)	19
Scott HOLTZMAN ▶ 8388 (1)	**52**
San Francisco Girls (Return Of The Native)—Fever Tree (68)	156
Vivian HOLTZMAN ▶ 8389 (1)	**52**
San Francisco Girls (Return Of The Native)—Fever Tree (68)	156
James HOLVAY ▶ 441 (6)	**9298**
Kind Of A Drag—Buckinghams (66)	6157
Don't You Care—Buckinghams (67)	2879
Susan—Buckinghams (67)	2292
Hey Baby (They're Playing Our Song)—Buckinghams (67)	1754
Give It To Me—Mob (71)	71
I Dig Everything About You—Mob (70)	50
Wayland HOLYFIELD ▶ 5972 (2)	**221**
Could I Have This Dance—Anne Murray (80)	439
Some Broken Hearts Never Mend—Don Williams (77)	0.9
—Johann Holzel see: FALCO	
—Homer see: Henry HAYNES	
James HONEYMAN-SCOTT ▶ 3488 (1)	**820**
Brass In Pocket (I'm Special)—Pretenders (80)	1641
Alan HOOD ▶ 10415 (1)	**8.7**
Summertime Lies—Four Preps (58)	17
Oliver HOOD ▶ 1701 (8)	**2462**
You Are My Sunshine—Ray Charles With The Raeletts (62)	*2038*
You Are My Sunshine—Ferko String Band (55)	*250*
You Are My Sunshine—Mitch Ryder (67)	*123*
You Are My Sunshine—Johnny And The Hurricanes (60)	*45*
You Are My Sunshine—Dyke And The Blazers (70)	*6.2*
You Are My Sunshine—Joe Pica (55)	*0.0*
You Are My Sunshine—Bing Crosby (55)	*0.0*
You Are My Sunshine—Ames Brothers (55)	*0.0*
Jonathan HOOK ▶ 8402 (1)	**52**
Guaranteed For Life—Millions Like Us (87)	103
Peter HOOK ▶ 6096 (3)	**206**
True Faith—New Order (87)	637

Round & Round—New Order (89)	209
Blue Monday 1988—New Order (88)	105
Brian HOOKER ▶ 11805 (1)	**0.0**
Some Day—Frankie Laine (54)	0.0
Jake HOOKER [Jake Falsworth, Jerry Mamberg, Jake Hooker Richards] ▶ 1125 (2)	**3943**
I Love Rock 'N Roll—Joan Jett & The Blackhearts (82)	*7869*
I Love Rocky Road—"Weird Al" Yankovic (83)	*26*
James HOOKER [James Hooker Brown Jr.] ▶ 6473 (1)	**165**
Freedom Overspill—Steve Winwood (86)	661
John Lee HOOKER ▶ 4009 (2)	**623**
Boom Boom—Animals (64)	*433*
Boom Boom—John Lee Hooker (62)	*190*
Thomas HOOKER ▶ 7757 (1)	**76**
Boom Boom (Let's Go Back To My Room)—Paul Lekakis (87)	381
Roney HOOKS ▶ 7340 (1)	**101**
B.B.D. (I Thought It Was Me)?—Bell Biv DeVoe (90)	504
Daryl HOOPER ▶ 8661 (1)	**43**
A Thousand Shadows—Seeds (67)	130
Nellee HOOPER [Paul Andrew Hooper] ▶ 3714 (2)	**723**
Back To Life—Soul II Soul (89)	2835
A Dream's A Dream—Soul II Soul (90)	42
—Peter Hoorelbeke see: Pete RIVERA	
Peter HOOTON ▶ 5515 (1)	**275**
Groovy Train—Farm (91)	551
Jeff HOOVEN ▶ 3006 (2)	**1071**
Cindy's Birthday—Johnny Crawford (62)	1448
Your Nose Is Gonna Grow—Johnny Crawford (62)	695
Joseph HOOVEN [Jeffery Davis] ▶ 2959 (5)	**1097**
Gimme Little Sign—Brenton Wood (67)	2590
Baby You Got It—Brenton Wood (67)	486
Anyway The Wind Blows—Doris Day (60)	113
Au Revoir—Teresa Brewer (54)	100
Lovey Dovey Kinda Lovin'—Brenton Wood (68)	1.4
Marilyn HOOVEN [Judy Evans] ▶ 7883 (2)	**71**
Anyway The Wind Blows—Doris Day (60)	113
Au Revoir—Teresa Brewer (54)	100
Barry Kenneth HOPKINS ▶ 6586 (1)	**154**
Mistrusted Love—Mistress (79)	154
Kenyon HOPKINS ▶ 5766 (4)	**244**
Baby Doll—Andy Williams (56)	*488*
Baby Doll—Ralph Young (56)	*0.0*
Baby Doll—Chuck Miller (56)	*0.0*
Baby Doll—Percy Faith & His Orchestra (56)	*0.0*
Lightning HOPKINS ▶ 10189 (1)	**11**
Feel So Bad—Little Milton (67)	11
Sylvester HOPKINS ▶ 6438 (2)	**169**
Cry Baby—Bonnie Sisters (56)	*338*
Cry Baby—Billy Williams Quartet (56)	*0.0*
James HOPKINS-HARRISON ▶ 8505 (1)	**48**
Time Bomb—Lake (77)	95
Larry HOPPEN ▶ 3683 (3)	**734**
Love Takes Time—Orleans (79)	1165
Let There Be Music—Orleans (75)	299
Don't Throw Our Love Away—Orleans (79)	6.7
Sean HOPPER ▶ 3538 (3)	**793**
Hip To Be Square—Huey Lewis and the News (86)	2226
Workin' For A Livin'—Huey Lewis and the News (82)	267
Don't Make Me Do It—Patrick Simmons (83)	38
—Wesaline Hopson see: Wesaline Hopson KERR	
Bob HORN ▶ 7244 (1)	**108**
Take Me Back To Toyland—Nat "King" Cole (55)	324
Lawrence HORN ▶ 5007 (2)	**360**
Shake And Fingerpop—Jr. Walker & The All Stars (65)	674
Shoot Your Shot—Jr. Walker & The All Stars (67)	405
Trevor HORN ▶ 2075 (3)	**1911**
Owner Of A Lonely Heart—Yes (83)	6336
Leave It—Yes (84)	669
Video Killed The Radio Star—Buggles (79)	312
James HORNER ▶ 3401 (2)	**866**
Somewhere Out There—Linda Ronstadt And James Ingram (86)	2590
Theme Of Star Trek II (Main Title)—Soundtrack (82)	5.5

Bruce HORNSBY ▶ 356 (10)	**10686**
The Way It Is—Bruce Hornsby And The Range (86)	4406
Jacob's Ladder—Huey Lewis and the News (87)	3640
Mandolin Rain—Bruce Hornsby And The Range (87)	2210
The Valley Road—Bruce Hornsby & The Range (88)	1734
The End Of The Innocence—Don Henley (89)	1707
Every Little Kiss—Bruce Hornsby And The Range (87)	*895*
Across The River—Bruce Hornsby & The Range (90)	765
Look Out Any Window—Bruce Hornsby & The Range (88)	387
Every Little Kiss—Bruce Hornsby And The Range (86)	*152*
Lost Soul—Bruce Hornsby & The Range (90)	12
John HORNSBY ▶ 1017 (5)	**4368**
Jacob's Ladder—Huey Lewis and the News (87)	3640
Mandolin Rain—Bruce Hornsby And The Range (87)	2210
The Valley Road—Bruce Hornsby & The Range (88)	1734
Across The River—Bruce Hornsby & The Range (90)	765
Look Out Any Window—Bruce Hornsby & The Range (88)	387
Adam HOROVITZ ▶ 3853 (3)	**676**
(You Gotta) Fight For Your Right (To Party!)—Beastie Boys (86)	1744
Hey Ladies—Beastie Boys (89)	302
Brass Monkey—Beastie Boys (87)	278
—Paul Horowitz see: Paul TAYLOR	
Peg HORTHER ▶ 6500 (1)	**163**
Hootenanny—Glencoves (63)	488
—George Vaughn Horton see: Vaughn HORTON	
—James McKinley Horton see: McKinley HORTON	
Jamie HORTON [Gayla Henderson, Gayla Peevey] ▶ 8369 (1)	**53**
My Little Marine—Jamie Horton (60)	106
Johnny HORTON ▶ 2046 (3)	**1953**
Sink The Bismarck—Johnny Horton (60)	3896
When It's Springtime In Alaska (It's Forty Below)—Johnny Horton (59)	6.6
Honky-Tonk Man—Johnny Horton (62)	4.4
Lemon HORTON ▶ 6400 (1)	**175**
Everybody Knows About My Good Thing (Pt. 1)—Little Johnny Taylor (71)	350
—Lisa Horton see: Lisa MONTGOMERY	
McKinley HORTON [James McKinley Horton, James Horton McKinley] ▶ 8138 (2)	**60**
Don't Say No Tonight—Eugene Wilde (85)	84
Gotta Get You Home Tonight—Eugene Wilde (85)	37
Sampson HORTON ▶ 3609 (2)	**768**
Wishing For Your Love—Voxpoppers (58)	*768*
Wishing For Your Love—Clovers (58)	*0.0*
Vaughn HORTON [George Vaughn Horton, George Vaughn] ▶ 1957 (6)	**2051**
Mule Skinner Blues—Fendermen (60)	*3277*
Teardrops In My Heart—Joe Barry (61)	*209*
Teardrops In My Heart—Teresa Brewer (57)	*181*
Choo Choo Ch'Boogie—Bill Haley And His Comets (56)	65
Mule Skinner Blues—Rusty Draper (60)	*0.0*
Teardrops In My Heart—Tommy Prisco (57)	*0.0*
William HORTON ▶ 2608 (3)	**1328**
Get A Job—Silhouettes (58)	*5224*
Get A Job—Nino & the Ebb Tides (61)	*88*
Get A Job—Mills Brothers (58)	*0.0*
Zilphia HORTON ▶ 11609 (1)	**1.0**
We Shall Overcome—Joan Baez (63)	5.0
Colin HORTON-JENNINGS ▶ 6715 (1)	**142**
Magic Woman Touch—Hollies (73)	284
Arnold B. HORWITT ▶ 8897 (2)	**37**
Young And Foolish—Jo Stafford (55)	*46*
Young And Foolish—Dean Martin (55)	*27*
Athena HOSEY ▶ 11352 (1)	**2.1**
Someone Else's Boy—Connie Francis (61)	4.3
Dorothy HOSKINS ▶ 11674 (1)	**0.7**
What It Takes To Get A Good Woman (That's What It's Gonna Take To Keep Her)—Denise LaSalle (73)	2.2
Ollie HOSKINS [Ollie Nightingale] ▶ 8898 (1)	**37**
I Got A Sure Thing—Ollie & The Nightingales (68)	110
Bob HOSKO ▶ 11348 (2)	**2.1**
Straight Flush—Frantics (59)	9.1
Fog Cutter—Frantics (59)	3.1

Haruomi HOSONO ▶ 8576 (1)	**46**
Computer Game ("Theme From The Circus")—Yellow Magic Orchestra (80)	138
—A. Hott see: Joseph Louis STONE	
—A. Hott see: Paul (2) KLEIN	
—Philemon Hou see: Hugh MASEKELA	
Doris HOUCK ▶ 10642 (1)	**6.5**
Someone On Your Mind—Champ Butler (55)	13
Will HOUGH ▶ 9157 (1)	**30**
I Wonder Who's Kissing Her Now—Bobby Darin (64)	90
Stephen HOUSDEN ▶ 9108 (1)	**31**
Playing To Win—LRB (85)	217
Bob HOUSE ▶ 5980 (1)	**220**
Could I Have This Dance—Anne Murray (80)	439
Robbie HOUSE ▶ 11105 (1)	**3.2**
Bad, Bad Billy—Snuff (83)	9.5
John HOUSER ▶ 4894 (2)	**387**
What I Am—Edie Brickell & The New Bohemians (88)	1562
Circle—Edie Brickell & The New Bohemians (89)	371
Cisco HOUSTON ▶ 4869 (2)	**396**
Bad Man Blunder—Kingston Trio (60)	326
A Dollar Down—Limeliters (61)	232
George HOVEN ▶ 7153 (2)	**113**
(It's No) Sin—Duprees Featuring Joey Vann (64)	*202*
(It's No) Sin—Billy Vaughn And His Orchestra (59)	*12*
Bart HOWARD [Howard J. Gustafson] ▶ 2068 (6)	**1931**
Fly Me To The Moon - Bossa Nova—Joe Harnell And His Orchestra (62)	*1270*
Fly Me To The Moon—Bobby Womack (68)	*383*
Fly Me To The Moon (In Other Words)—Tony Bennett (65)	*137*
You Are In Love—Perry Como (59)	122
Fly Me To The Moon—LaVern Baker (65)	*16*
Fly Me To The Moon—Sam & Bill (66)	*2.8*
Bruce Robert HOWARD [Robert Bruce Howard, Dr. Robert] ▶ 3248 (1)	**929**
Digging Your Scene—Blow Monkeys (86)	929
Chesley HOWARD [Alan Kallman] ▶ 3678 (3)	**739**
She's Everything (I Wanted You To Be)—Ral Donner (61)	969
Please Don't Go—Ral Donner (61)	507
I Didn't Figure On Him (To Come Back)—Ral Donner (61)	2.8
Doug HOWARD ▶ 10275 (1)	**11**
Feet Don't Fail Me Now—Utopia (83)	42
Eddy HOWARD ▶ 10447 (1)	**8.4**
Careless—Bobby Vinton (65)	25
Edward HOWARD ▶ 11733 (1)	**0.4**
Little Ghetto Boy—Donny Hathaway (72)	0.8
Harlan HOWARD ▶ 127 (31) HOF	**20766**
Heartaches By The Number—Guy Mitchell (59)	*7361*
Busted—Ray Charles And His Orchestra (63)	4303
I Fall To Pieces—Patsy Cline (61)	2018
The Chokin' Kind—Joe Simon (69)	*1535*
Too Many Rivers—Brenda Lee (65)	1517
Call Me Mr. In-Between—Burl Ives (62)	974
I've Got A Tiger By The Tail—Buck Owens (65)	614
Heartaches By The Number—Johnny Tillotson (65)	*537*
Mary Ann Regrets—Burl Ives (62)	533
Foolin' Around—Kay Starr (61)	*492*
He Called Me Baby—Candi Staton (70)	*469*
When I Get Thru With You (You'll Love Me Too)—Patsy Cline (62)	383
No Charge—Melba Montgomery (74)	*284*
The Blizzard—Jim Reeves (61)	227
If I Cried Every Time You Hurt Me—Wanda Jackson (62)	220
Baby, Don't Be Looking In My Mind—Joe Simon (69)	214
Everglades—Kingston Trio (60)	190
Yours Love—Joe Simon (70)	168
She Called Me Baby—Charlie Rich (74)	*104*
Baby Come Home To Me—Burl Ives (63)	34
He Called Me Baby—Ella Washington (69)	*34*
I'm The Boss—Burl Ives (63)	31
Pick Me Up On Your Way Down—Pat Zill (61)	26
I Don't Believe I'll Fall In Love Today—Bobby Bare (62)	18
Chokin' Kind—Z.Z. Hill (71)	*18*
No Charge—Shirley Caesar (75)	*13*
I Won't Forget You—Jim Reeves (64)	8.1

Sally Was A Good Old Girl—Fats Domino (64)	*1.9*
Sally Was A Good Old Girl—Trini Lopez (68)	*1.8*
Foolin' Around—Buck Owens (61)	*0.0*
Heartaches By The Number—Pat Zill (65)	*0.0*
James Newton HOWARD ▶ 2712 (3)	**1251**
Everything—Jody Watley (89)	1977
Lady Love Me (One More Time)—George Benson (83)	520
Prove Me Wrong—David Pack (86)	5.6
Jerome HOWARD ▶ 7313 (4)	**103**
Midnight Lace—Ray Ellis And His Orchestra (60)	*138*
Midnight Lace Part One—Ray Conniff & His Orch. & Chorus (60)	*60*
Midnight Lace—David Carroll And His Orchestra (60)	*7.8*
Midnight Lace—Sid Feller & His Orchestra (60)	*0.0*
Joe HOWARD ▶ 9158 (1) HOF	**30**
I Wonder Who's Kissing Her Now—Bobby Darin (64)	90
John HOWARD ▶ 7533 (2)	**90**
Tears And Laughter—Dinah Washington (62)	241
Carefree Wanderer—Bill Parsons with The All-American Boy's (59)	30
Ken HOWARD [Howard Blaikley] ▶ 1981 (4)	**2035**
Have I The Right?—Honeycombs (64)	3306
I've Lost You—Elvis Presley (70)	400
I Can't Stop—Honeycombs (64)	362
Boy—Lulu (68)	3.3
—Mark Howard see: Joseph SHAPIRO	
Richard HOWARD ▶ 7205 (3)	**110**
Somebody Else Is Taking My Place—Al Martino (65)	*249*
Somebody Else Is Taking My Place—Joni James (61)	*66*
Somebody Else Is Taking My Place—Jaye P. Morgan (59)	*15*
Robert HOWARD ▶ 7580 (1)	**88**
My Son, My Son—Vera Lynn (54)	263
—Robert Bruce Howard see: Bruce Robert HOWARD	
Shane HOWARD ▶ 8059 (1)	**63**
Solid Rock—Goanna (83)	63
—Steven Howard see: Herbert NEWMAN	
Tash HOWARD [Howard Tashman] ▶ 6771 (1)	**138**
Juanita Banana—Peels (66)	277
Tod HOWARTH ▶ 8971 (1)	**35**
Mega Force—707 (82)	139
Ron HOWDEN ▶ 11234 (1)	**2.6**
Astral Man—Nektar (75)	11
—Bones Howe see: Dayton HOWE	
Brian HOWE ▶ 3281 (5)	**913**
If You Needed Somebody—Bad Company (90)	1041
Walk Through Fire—Bad Company (91)	687
This Love—Bad Company (86)	47
Shake It Up—Bad Company (89)	30
Holy Water—Bad Company (90)	20
Dayton HOWE [Bones Howe] ▶ 5839 (1)	**238**
Sting Ray—Routers (63)	476
Julia Ward HOWE ▶ 2685 (4) HOF	**1272**
Battle Hymn Of The Republic—Mormon Tabernacle Choir (59)	*1595*
Battle Hymn Of The Republic—Andy Williams With The St. Charles Borromeo Choir (68)	*658*
Battle Hymn Of The Republic—Mickey Newbury (71)	*222*
Battle Hymn Of The Republic—Elvis Presley (72)	*69*
Leslie HOWE ▶ 9549 (1)	**22**
Angel In My Pocket—One To One (86)	43
Steve HOWE ▶ 2645 (3)	**1298**
Roundabout—Yes (72)	1487
When The Heart Rules The Mind—GTR (86)	884
And You And I (Part I)—Yes (72)	447
Alphonso HOWELL ▶ 2486 (1)	**1445**
Let Me In—Sensations (62)	4334
Andy HOWELL ▶ 10452 (1)	**8.3**
Heart And Soul—Monkees (87)	17
Brad HOWELL [Brad Nail] ▶ 2752 (2)	**1222**
Baby Don't Forget My Number—Milli Vanilli (89)	3187
All Or Nothing—Milli Vanilli (89)	1700
Noah HOWELL ▶ 11059 (1)	**3.5**
You Tickle Me Baby—Royal Jokers (55)	7.0
Carlee HOYLES ▶ 4456 (2)	**491**
Heartbreak (It's Hurtin' Me)—Little Willie John (60)	*569*
Heartbreak (It's Hurtin' Me)—Jon Thomas And Orchestra (60)	*414*

Doug HOYT ► 9631 (1)	**20**
Rappin' Rodney—Rodney Dangerfield (83)	140
Dan HRDLICKA ► 7691 (1)	**80**
Stop, Wait And Listen—Circus (73)	80
—Ronald Guy Hruska see: Ronnie GUY	
Nancy HUANG ► 10108 (1)	**13**
Coming To America (Part One)—System (88)	25
—Jerry Reed Hubbard see: Jerry REED	
Raymond HUBBELL ► 8870 (2)	**37**
Poor Butterfly—Sarah Vaughan (57)	*75*
Poor Butterfly—Hilltoppers (54)	*0.0*
—Josefine Huber-Busch see: Fini BUSCH	
Mick HUCKNALL ► 1627 (4)	**2593**
Holding Back The Years—Simply Red (86)	2985
Something Got Me Started—Simply Red (91)	591
The Right Thing—Simply Red (87)	545
Stars—Simply Red (91)	260
Lorence HUD ► 6374 (1)	**177**
Sign Of The Gypsy Queen—April Wine (81)	177
Floyd HUDDLESTON ► 7722 (9)	**79**
Trouble With Harry—Alfi & Harry (56)	*105*
Ready Willing And Able—Doris Day (54)	*49*
Ready, Willing And Able—Gary Crosby (54)	*19*
Trouble With Harry— Les Baxter, His Chorus and Orchestra (56)	*17*
I'm Leavin' You—Engelbert Humperdinck (73)	11
Now Is The Time—Eileen Rodgers (55)	*4.4*
Now Is The Time—Paulette Sisters (55)	*4.4*
Swanee River Rock—Sanford Clark (57)	*0.0*
The Trouble With Harry— Jack Pleis and His Orchestra and Chorus (56)	*0.0*
Helene HUDGINS ► 5773 (1)	**243**
Mama Don't Cry At My Wedding—Joni James (54)	243
Smead HUDMAN ► 11225 (1)	**2.7**
Playing Your Game, Baby—Barry White (78)	5.3
Al HUDSON ► 8802 (1)	**39**
Cutie Pie—One Way (82)	273
Bill HUDSON ► 4515 (4)	**473**
So You Are A Star—Hudson Brothers (74)	879
Rendezvous—Hudson Brothers (75)	557
Lonely School Year—Hudson Brothers (75)	189
Coochie Coochie Coo—Hudson Brothers (75)	8.9
Bob HUDSON [Robert Howard Holmes] ► 5624 (2)	**263**
Ajax Liquor Store—Hudson and Landry (71)	435
Ajax Airlines—Hudson And Landry (71)	90
Brett HUDSON ► 4516 (4)	**473**
So You Are A Star—Hudson Brothers (74)	879
Rendezvous—Hudson Brothers (75)	557
Lonely School Year—Hudson Brothers (75)	189
Coochie Coochie Coo—Hudson Brothers (75)	8.9
—Bryan Loren Hudson see: Bryan LOREN	
Curtis HUDSON ► 3978 (1)	**632**
Holiday—Madonna (83)	1264
Glenda HUDSON [Glenda Joyce Evans] ► 8803 (1)	**39**
Cutie Pie—One Way (82)	273
Harold HUDSON ► 3595 (2)	**773**
Lady (You Bring Me Up)—Commodores (81)	2150
Painted Picture—Commodores (82)	113
James HUDSON ► 5670 (2)	**257**
Goodnight, Sweetheart, Goodnight— McGuire Sisters (54)	*514*
Goodnight, Sweetheart, Goodnight—Sunny Gale (54)	*0.0*
Jerry HUDSON ► 9998 (1)	**14**
Gillian Frank—Jerry Hudson (73)	14
Lord Tim HUDSON ► 11281 (1)	**2.5**
The Flower Children—Marcia Strassman (67)	7.4
Mark HUDSON ► 4472 (5)	**486**
So You Are A Star—Hudson Brothers (74)	879
Rendezvous—Hudson Brothers (75)	557
Lonely School Year—Hudson Brothers (75)	189
Darlin'—Frank Stallone (84)	38
Coochie Coochie Coo—Hudson Brothers (75)	8.9
Saul HUDSON [Slash] ► 1639 (7)	**2558**
Sweet Child O' Mine—Guns N' Roses (88)	4596
Patience—Guns N' Roses (89)	2050
Paradise City—Guns N' Roses (89)	1901
Don't Cry—Guns N' Roses (91)	1769
Welcome To The Jungle—Guns N' Roses (88)	1661
You Could Be Mine—Guns N' Roses (91)	289
Nightrain—Guns N' Roses (89)	9.3
Vick HUDSON ► 6650 (1)	**148**
It's The Real Thing - Pt I—Electric Express (71)	148
Will HUDSON ► 1438 (4)	**3040**
Moonglow—Morris Stoloff Conducting The Columbia Pictures Orchestra (56)	*4036*
Moonglow—George Cates & His Orchestra (56)	*1975*
The Organ Grinder's Swing—Jimmy Smith With Kenny Burrell And Grady Tate (65)	*30*
Organ Grinder's Swing— Sam (The Man) Taylor And His Orchestra (58)	*4.0*
William HUDSPETH ► 1781 (1)	**2331**
Heartbeat - It's A Lovebeat— Defranco Family Featuring Tony Defranco (73)	4662
—Baldemar Huerta see: Freddy FENDER	
Jack HUES [Jeremy Allan Ryder] ► 1406 (8)	**3154**
Everybody Have Fun Tonight—Wang Chung (86)	4287
Let's Go—Wang Chung (87)	1295
Dance Hall Days—Wang Chung (84)	1096
To Live And Die In L.A.—Wang Chung (85)	566
Hypnotize Me—Wang Chung (87)	403
Don't Let Go—Wang Chung (84)	335
Praying To A New God—Wang Chung (89)	167
Don't Be My Enemy—Wang Chung (84)	17
Dann HUFF ► 8906 (1)	**36**
I'm A Believer—Giant (89)	182
David Lyndon HUFF ► 8907 (1)	**36**
I'm A Believer—Giant (89)	182
David William HUFF ► 11630 (1)	**0.9**
Born To Get Down (Born To Get Around)— Muscle Shoals Horns (76)	1.9
Larry HUFF ► 1312 (1)	**3379**
Easier Said Than Done—Essex (63)	6758
Leon HUFF [Jerry Anthony Williams, Theresa Bell] ► 32 (127) HOF	**49276**
Me And Mrs. Jones—Billy Paul (72)	*6926*
I'm Gonna Make You Love Me—Diana Ross And The Supremes & The Temptations (68)	*6496*
Love Train—O'Jays (73)	5733
TSOP (The Sound Of Philadelphia)— MFSB Featuring The Three Degrees (74)	*5419*
Back Stabbers—O'Jays (72)	4999
You'll Never Find Another Love Like Mine— Lou Rawls (76)	4173
Don't Leave Me This Way—Thelma Houston (76)	*4138*
When Will I See You Again—Three Degrees (74)	4029
If You Don't Know Me By Now— Harold Melvin And The Blue Notes (72)	*3604*
Use Ta Be My Girl—O'Jays (78)	3380
If You Don't Know Me By Now—Simply Red (89)	*3293*
Cowboys To Girls—Intruders (68)	3286
Expressway To Your Heart—Soul Survivors (67)	3264
Only The Strong Survive—Jerry Butler (69)	3213
I Love Music (Part 1)—O'Jays (75)	*2798*
Enjoy Yourself—Jacksons (76)	2647
Drowning In The Sea Of Love—Joe Simon (71)	2257
The Love I Lost (Part 1)— Harold Melvin And The Blue Notes (73)	2070
For The Love Of Money—O'Jays (74)	*1864*
Power Of Love—Joe Simon (72)	*1856*
I Can't Stop Dancing—Archie Bell & The Drells (68)	1681
Put Your Hands Together—O'Jays (73)	1517
Do It Any Way You Wanna—People's Choice (75)	1448
Engine Number 9—Wilson Pickett (70)	1414
Never Give You Up—Jerry Butler (68)	1243
Together—Tierra (80)	*1181*
Hey, Western Union Man—Jerry Butler (68)	1108
Now That We Found Love—Heavy D & The Boyz (91)	*1100*
"There's Gonna Be A" Showdown— Archie Bell & The Drells (68)	1090
A Brand New Me—Dusty Springfield (69)	*1011*
What's The Use Of Breaking Up—Jerry Butler (69)	960
Moody Woman—Jerry Butler (69)	921
Close The Door—Teddy Pendergrass (78)	805
Livin' For The Weekend—O'Jays (76)	736
Thanks For Saving My Life—Billy Paul (74)	709
Forever Mine—O'Jays (79)	688
I'm Gonna Make You Love Me—Madeline Bell (68)	*687*
(Love Is Like A) Baseball Game—Intruders (68)	650
I'll Always Love My Mama (Part I)—Intruders (73)	618
Mixed-Up, Shook-Up, Girl—Patty & The Emblems (64)	605
Time To Get Down—O'Jays (73)	578
Hope That We Can Be Together Soon—Sharon Paige And Harold Melvin And The Blue Notes (75)	548
Are You Happy—Jerry Butler (68)	543
United—Peaches & Herb (68)	*534*
Explosion In Your Soul—Soul Survivors (67)	511
Give The People What They Want—O'Jays (75)	505
You Gonna Make Me Love Somebody Else— Jones Girls (79)	469
I Don't Love You Anymore—Teddy Pendergrass (77)	428
I Miss You (Part I)— Harold Melvin And The Blue Notes (72)	423
Pool Of Bad Luck—Joe Simon (72)	415
Show You The Way To Go—Jacksons (77)	412
Do The Choo Choo—Archie Bell & The Drells (68)	386
Me And Mrs. Jones— Ron Banks And The Dramatics (75)	*371*
Don't Let Love Hang You Up—Jerry Butler (69)	360
992 Arguments—O'Jays (72)	356
Now That We Found Love—Third World (78)	*333*
Sexy—MFSB (75)	317
Girl, Don't Let It Get You Down—O'Jays (80)	309
Lost—Jerry Butler (67)	297
I Could Write A Book—Jerry Butler (70)	294
You're The Reason Why—Ebonys (71)	293
Slow Drag—Intruders (68)	291
Deeper (In Love With You)—O'Jays (70)	279
Together—Intruders (67)	*266*
You're My Latest, My Greatest Inspiration— Teddy Pendergrass (81)	265
Don't Leave Me This Way—Communards (86)	*261*
One Night Affair—Jerry Butler (72)	*239*
Goin' Places—Jacksons (77)	234
Message In Our Music—O'Jays (76)	231
Turn Off The Lights—Teddy Pendergrass (79)	225
Yesterday I Had The Blues— Harold Melvin And The Blue Notes (73)	224
Silly, Silly, Fool—Dusty Springfield (70)	203
Hey You! Little Boo-Ga-Loo—Chubby Checker (66)	187
See You When I Git There—Lou Rawls (77)	175
When Love Is New—Arthur Prysock (76)	167
Baby I'm Lonely—Intruders (67)	143
I Wanna Know Your Name—Intruders (73)	140
At The Top Of The Stairs—Formations (68)	132
Love Is The Message— MFSB Featuring The Three Degrees (74)	126
Impossible Mission (Mission Impossible)— Soul Survivors (68)	125
Satisfaction Guaranteed (Or Take Your Love Back)— Harold Melvin And The Blue Notes (74)	120
It's Forever—Ebonys (73)	119
Brand New Me—Aretha Franklin (71)	*115*
One Night Affair—O'Jays (69)	*97*
Power Of Love—Martha Reeves (74)	*96*
T.S.O.P.—Ritchie Family (76)	*92*
I Love Music—Ritchie Family (76)	*92*
Darlin' Darlin' Baby (Sweet, Tender, Love)— O'Jays (76)	90
My Balloon's Going Up— Archie Bell & The Drells (69)	82
United (Part 1)—Music Makers (67)	*78*
This Is My Love Song—Intruders (70)	73
I'm Girl Scoutin'—Intruders (71)	71
Slow Motion (Part 1)—Johnny Williams (73)	70
It's That Time Of The Year—Len Barry (66)	64
Love Me—Bobby Hebb (66)	64
I Bet He Don't Love You (Like I Love You)— Intruders (71)	58
Groovy People—Lou Rawls (76)	57
Love In Them There Hills—Vibrations (68)	56
Let's Make A Baby—Billy Paul (76)	53
(We'll Be) United—Intruders (66)	*51*
I'm Gonna Make You Love Me—Dee Dee Warwick (66)	*48*
I Just Love The Man—Jones Girls (81)	47
Nursery Rhymes (Part I)—People's Choice (76)	45
I Love My Baby—Archie Bell & The Drells (69)	43
For The Love Of Money—Bulletboys (89)	*39*
Let's Groove—Archie Bell & The Drells (76)	38
I Wanna Be A Free Girl—Dusty Springfield (70)	38
Am I Black Enough For You—Billy Paul (73)	29
Let Me Be Good To You—Lou Rawls (79)	28
Let's Clean Up The Ghetto— Philadelphia International All Stars (77)	27

Leon HUFF [Jerry Anthony Williams, Theresa Bell] ▶ 32 (127) HOF *Continued*	**49276**
A Love That's Real—Intruders (67)	26
Work On Me—O'Jays (77)	25
The Zip—MFSB (75)	20
You're My Blessing—Lou Rawls (80)	19
Pray For Me—Intruders (71)	13
A Brand New Me—Jerry Butler (69)	*12*
Live It Up—Dusty Springfield (64)	11
Don't Let The Music Slip Away— Archie Bell & The Drells (69)	8.6
Looky Looky (Look At Me Girl)—O'Jays (70)	6.3
I Can't Live Without Your Love— Teddy Pendergrass (81)	6.2
I Wanna Be Your Baby—Three Degrees (72)	5.9
Now I'm A Woman—Nancy Wilson (71)	5.8
Been A Long Time—Betty Everett (69)	4.3
Check Yourself— Italian Asphalt & Pavement Company (70)	2.6
Sing A Happy Song—O'Jays (79)	2.4
I Struck It Rich—Len Barry (66)	1.9
A World Without Music— Archie Bell & The Drells (70)	0.4
Terry HUFF ▶ 8295 (1)	**55**
The Lonely One— Special Delivery Featuring Terry Huff (76)	110
—Brian John Hug see: Brian HUGG	
—Michael John Hug see: Mike HUGG	
Brian HUGG [Brian John Hug] ▶ 11433 (1)	**1.7**
Better Man Than I—Terry Knight And The Pack (66)	3.4
Mike HUGG [Michael John Hug] ▶ 4716 (2)	**432**
Daytime Night-Time—Keith Hampshire (72)	431
Better Man Than I—Terry Knight And The Pack (66)	3.4
Grayson HUGH ▶ 10031 (1)	**14**
Bring It All Back—Grayson Hugh (89)	14
Bill HUGHES [Bill Keith Hughes, Billie Hughes] ▶ 6264 (2)	**188**
Walking On The Chinese Wall— Philip Bailey (85)	270
Night And Day—Bette Midler (91)	195
—Billie Hughes see: Bill HUGHES	
Chris HUGHES ▶ 2283 (1)	**1657**
Everybody Wants To Rule The World— Tears For Fears (85)	4971
Fred HUGHES ▶ 8940 (1)	**36**
I Understand—Fred Hughes (70)	36
Glenn HUGHES ▶ 9572 (2)	**21**
Beg, Borrow Or Steal—Hughes/Thrall (82)	40
You Can't Do It Right (With The One You Love)— Deep Purple (74)	4.3
Glyn HUGHES ▶ 6001 (1)	**217**
(The Puppet Song) Whiskey On A Sunday— Irish Rovers (68)	217
Jimmy HUGHES ▶ 1851 (2)	**2199**
Steal Away—Jimmy Hughes (64)	*1496*
Steal Away—Johnnie Taylor (70)	*703*
John HUGHES ▶ 11083 (1)	**3.3**
Canvas Of Life—Minor Detail (83)	6.6
Joseph HUGHES ▶ 10689 (1)	**6.1**
No More "I Love You's"— Lover Speaks (86)	12
L. HUGHES ▶ 10352 (3)	**9.7**
The Phonograph Song— Guy Lombardo And His Royal Canadians (56)	*19*
The Phonograph Song (Our Melody)— Billy May & His Orchestra (56)	*19*
The Phonograph Song (Our Melody)— Art Mooney & His Orchestra (56)	*0.0*
Willie HUGHES ▶ 11084 (1)	**3.3**
Canvas Of Life—Minor Detail (83)	6.6
Jay HUGUELY ▶ 3086 (2)	**1018**
The White Knight— Cledus Maggard and The Citizen's Band (75)	1010
Kentucky Moonrunner— Cledus Maggard And The Citizen's Band (76)	16
Alan HULL ▶ 4047 (2)	**613**
Run For Home—Lindisfane (78)	525
Lady Eleanor—Lindisfarne (72)	88
Bill HULL ▶ 9323 (1)	**26**
I Don't Know What It Is, But It Sure Is Funky— Ripple (73)	184

Bunny HULL [Jeri K. Hull] ▶ 2542 (5)	**1401**
Breakdance—Irene Cara (84)	1574
Let Me Be Your Angel—Stacy Lattisaw (80)	1019
New Attitude—Patti LaBelle (85)	999
Proud—Joe Chemay Band (81)	63
Dynamite!—Stacy Lattisaw (80)	3.8
Jeff HULL ▶ 4339 (1)	**517**
Piano In The Dark—Brenda Russell (88)	1550
—Jeri K. Hull see: Bunny HULL	
—Ronald Hulme see: Russ HAMILTON	
—Eddie Humphrey see: Gregory JACOBS	
Paul HUMPHREYS ▶ 2206 (5)	**1742**
If You Leave— Orchestral Manoeuvres In The Dark (86)	1910
Dreaming—Orchestral Manoeuvres In The Dark (88)	867
(Forever) Live And Die— Orchestral Manoeuvres In The Dark (86)	740
So In Love—Orchestral Manoeuvres In The Dark (85)	644
Secret—Orchestral Manoeuvres In The Dark (85)	210
—Humpty Hump see: Gregory JACOBS	
—Ralph Uriah Hunsecker see: Ralph BLANE	
—Charles James Hunt see: Tommy HUNT	
Floyd HUNT ▶ 5210 (1)	**326**
Fool That I Am—Etta James (61)	326
Geraldine HUNT [Geraldine Milligan] ▶ 6192 (1)	**195**
Murphy's Law—Cheri (82)	390
Irvin HUNT ▶ 9128 (1)	**31**
It's So Nice—Jackie Deshannon (70)	61
Tommy HUNT [Charles James Hunt] ▶ 9036 (1)	**33**
Mio Amore—Flamingos (60)	196
—Billy Joe Hunter see: Lou BIDEU	
Don HUNTER ▶ 4951 (3)	**375**
You Met Your Match—Stevie Wonder (68)	659
I Don't Know Why—Stevie Wonder (69)	*386*
I Don't Know Why—Rolling Stones (75)	*236*
Hank HUNTER ▶ 714 (13)	**6112**
Second Hand Love—Connie Francis (62)	2008
Footsteps—Steve Lawrence (60)	1685
Just For Old Time's Sake—McGuire Sisters (61)	1660
Ginger Bread—Frankie Avalon (58)	1599
Vacation—Connie Francis (62)	1465
Tears And Roses—Al Martino (64)	1125
My Empty Arms—Jackie Wilson (61)	1110
I'm Gonna' Be Warm This Winter— Connie Francis (62)	987
Drownin' My Sorrows—Connie Francis (63)	549
Looking For Love—Connie Francis (64)	360
Jumpin' Jack—Kalin Twins (58)	105
Stranger In Your Arms—Bobby Vee (64)	31
Forever And A Day—Jackie Wilson (62)	30
Ian HUNTER [Ian Hunter Patterson] ▶ 1191 (5)	**3723**
Once Bitten Twice Shy—Great White (89)	2117
Ships—Barry Manilow (79)	1503
Just Another Night—Ian Hunter (79)	92
The Golden Age Of Rock 'N' Roll— Mott The Hoople (74)	56
One Of The Boys—Mott The Hoople (73)	1.8
Ivory Joe HUNTER ▶ 240 (26)	**14281**
I Almost Lost My Mind—Pat Boone (56)	6595
Since I Met You Baby—Ivory Joe Hunter (56)	*1846*
Ain't That Loving You Baby— Elvis Presley With The Jordanaires (64)	1406
My Wish Came True—Elvis Presley (59)	1064
Empty Arms—Teresa Brewer (57)	*992*
It May Sound Silly—McGuire Sisters (55)	*923*
Out Of Sight Out Of Mind—Five Keys (56)	*860*
Empty Arms—Ivory Joe Hunter (57)	*540*
Out Of Sight, Out Of Mind— Little Anthony And The Imperials (69)	*410*
Since I Met You Baby—Mindy Carson (56)	*318*
No Other One—Eddie Fisher (56)	315
Since I Met You Baby—Freddy Fender (75)	*270*
Since I Met You, Baby— Sonny James, The Southern Gentleman (69)	*136*
Out Of Sight - Out Of Mind— Sunny & The Sunliners (64)	*54*
I Need You So—Ted Taylor (60)	*50*
Love's A Hurting Game—Ivory Joe Hunter (57)	12

Empty Arms—Sonny James (71)	*8.7*
Since I Met You Baby—Bobby Vee (60)	*8.2*
Yes, I Want You—Ivory Joe Hunter (58)	2.6
Out Of Sight, Out Of Mind—Essex (63)	*1.7*
I Need You So—Chuck Jackson & Maxine Brown (65)	*1.4*
It May Sound Silly—Joan Weber (55)	*0.0*
Since I Met You Baby—Molly Bee (56)	*0.0*
It May Sound Silly—Dolores Gray (55)	*0.0*
It May Sound Silly—Bill Farrell (55)	*0.0*
It May Sound Silly— Ivory Joe Hunter and his Ivorytones (55)	*0.0*
Ivy Jo HUNTER [Ivy George Hunter, George Ivy Hunter] ▶ 895 (24)	**4951**
Dancing In The Street—Martha & The Vandellas (64)	*5484*
Dancing In The Street— Mick Jagger & David Bowie (85)	*1333*
My Baby Loves Me—Martha & The Vandellas (66)	*999*
Ask The Lonely—Four Tops (65)	738
You—Marvin Gaye (68)	545
Sweet Understanding Love—Four Tops (73)	476
I'll Always Love You—Spinners (65)	466
Loving You Is Sweeter Than Ever—Four Tops (66)	435
Yesterday's Dreams—Four Tops (68)	417
I'll Keep Holding On—Marvelettes (65)	405
Dancing In The Street—Van Halen (82)	*390*
Wild One—Martha & The Vandellas (64)	377
You've Been In Love Too Long— Martha & The Vandellas (65)	348
Without Love—Aretha Franklin (74)	268
Danger Heartbreak Dead Ahead—Marvelettes (65)	246
Can You Jerk Like Me—Contours (64)	228
My Baby Loves Me—David T. Walker (69)	*174*
Dancin' In The Streets—Teri DeSario with K.C. (80)	*98*
Dancing In The Street—Mamas & The Papas (66)	*77*
Truly Yours—Spinners (66)	63
Dancing In The Street—Ramsey Lewis (67)	*27*
Got To Have You Back—Isley Brothers (67)	11
Dancing In The Street—Tight Fit (81)	*0.9*
Dancing In The Street—Dovells (74)	*0.3*
—Ivy George Hunter see: Ivy Jo HUNTER	
John Martin HUNTER Jr. ▶ 4359 (1)	**513**
Tragedy—John Hunter (84)	513
John W. HUNTER ▶ 4376 (2)	**509**
Let It Out (Let It All Hang Out)—Hombres (67)	2036
It's A Gas—Hombres (68)	1.4
Kevin HUNTER ▶ 10410 (1)	**8.8**
For A While—Mary MacGregor (77)	18
Marc HUNTER ▶ 10756 (1)	**5.5**
Rain—Dragon (84)	17
Robert HUNTER ▶ 3831 (6) HOF	**687**
Touch Of Grey—Grateful Dead (87)	1004
Truckin'—Grateful Dead (71)	237
Uncle John's Band—Grateful Dead (70)	142
Alabama Getaway—Grateful Dead (80)	99
Sugar Magnolia—Grateful Dead (73)	6.1
Sugaree—Jerry Garcia (72)	4.8
Todd HUNTER ▶ 10756 (1)	**5.5**
Rain—Dragon (84)	17
Herman HUPFELD ▶ 3768 (5)	**704**
As Time Goes By—Johnny Nash (59)	*551*
As Time Goes By—Nilsson (73)	*98*
As Time Goes By—Johnnie Ray (55)	*31*
As Time Goes By—Fats Domino (57)	*19*
As Time Goes By—Bill Snyder (56)	*5.6*
Debbie HUPP ▶ 2824 (1)	**1169**
You Decorated My Life—Kenny Rogers (79)	2338
Basil HURDON ▶ 5681 (2)	**256**
Fortuneteller—Bobby Curtola (62)	498
Aladdin—Bobby Curtola (62)	13
Dyer HURDON ▶ 5682 (2)	**256**
Fortuneteller—Bobby Curtola (62)	498
Aladdin—Bobby Curtola (62)	13
John HURLEY ▶ 2071 (7)	**1924**
Son-Of-A Preacher Man— Dusty Springfield (68)	*2224*
The Land Of Milk And Honey—Vogues (66)	626
Spread It On Thick—Gentrys (65)	447
Love Of The Common People—Winstons (69)	*407*
Love Of The Common People—Paul Young (84)	*288*
A Woman Of The World—Gentrys (66)	5.6
Son Of A Preacher Man—Aretha Franklin (70)	*0.0*

Steve HURLEY ▶ 4838 (1)	**401**
Too Blind To See It—Kym Sims (91)	401
Mike HURST [Michael John Hurst Pickworth, Mike Pickworth] ▶ 5689 (1)	**254**
Touch Me—Fancy (74)	509
Jim HURT ▶ 4064 (3)	**607**
Love In The First Degree—Alabama (81)	1156
Shotgun Rider—Delbert McClinton (81)	*45*
Shotgun Rider—Joe Sun (80)	*40*
Phil HURTT ▶ 1610 (10)	**2626**
I'll Be Around—Spinners (72)	*4157*
Sweet Charlie Babe—Jackie Moore (73)	625
Ready For The '80s—Village People (79)	147
I'll Be Around—What Is This (85)	*124*
I Found My Dad—Joe Simon (72)	95
The Best Disco In Town—Ritchie Family (76)	*92*
The Best Disco In Town—Ritchie Family (76)	*92*
Sunshine (Part 2)—O'Jays (74)	81
You Call Me Back—Clyde Brown (74)	3.2
Discomania—Lovers (77)	0.6
—Sandra Elayne Hurvitz see: Essra MOHAWK	
Sadie HURWITZ ▶ 10195 (1)	**11**
I Was Meant For You (The Wah-Wah Song)—Four Knights (54)	23
Simon HUSBANDS ▶ 7886 (1)	**71**
All I Need Is You—Blue Train (91)	284
Simon HUSSEY ▶ 6696 (1)	**143**
Higher Than Hope—Daryl Braithwaite (91)	286
Wayne HUSSEY ▶ 4559 (5)	**465**
You Spin Me Round (Like A Record)—Dead Or Alive (85)	1071
Brand New Lover—Dead Or Alive (86)	1017
Come Home With Me Baby—Dead Or Alive (89)	117
Lover Come Back To Me—Dead Or Alive (85)	84
Something In My House—Dead Or Alive (87)	38
Paul HUSTON ▶ 8641 (1)	**44**
Me Myself And I—De La Soul (89)	353
—Frank Hutch/F. Hutch see: Frankie L. HUTCHISON	
Willie HUTCH [William McKinley Hutchinson, Willie M. Hutchison] ▶ 1318 (7)	**3366**
I'll Be There—Jackson 5 (70)	9838
Together Let's Find Love—5th Dimension (71)	691
Brother's Gonna Work It Out—Willie Hutch (73)	229
Let Yourself Go—Friends Of Distinction (69)	212
Slick—Willie Hutch (73)	85
California My Way—Main Ingredient (74)	24
Who Could Be Lovin' You—Al Wilson (67)	11
Michael HUTCHENCE ▶ 471 (14)	**8825**
Need You Tonight—INXS (87)	4241
Devil Inside—INXS (88)	2910
What You Need—INXS (86)	2667
New Sensation—INXS (88)	2229
Disappear—INXS (90)	1536
Never Tear Us Apart—INXS (88)	1469
Suicide Blonde—INXS (90)	1317
The One Thing—INXS (83)	545
Bitter Tears—INXS (91)	337
Listen Like Thieves—INXS (86)	251
Original Sin—INXS (84)	162
I Send A Message—INXS (84)	50
Don't Change—INXS (83)	23
Kiss The Dirt (Falling Down The Mountain)—INXS (86)	11
Susan HUTCHESON ▶ 2237 (2)	**1713**
I Love The Nightlife (Disco 'round)—Alicia Bridges (78)	3417
Body Heat—Alicia Bridges (79)	9.2
Jalil HUTCHINS ▶ 10735 (1)	**5.6**
Friends—Whodini (85)	11
Sammie HUTCHINS ▶ 10897 (1)	**4.5**
(Call Me) The Traveling Man—Masqueraders (76)	23
Ray HUTCHINSON ▶ 6679 (1)	**145**
Clap Your Hands—Beau-Marks (60)	578
Sheila HUTCHINSON ▶ 4195 (1)	**567**
So I Can Love You—Emotions (69)	567
Wanda HUTCHINSON [Wanda Vaughn] ▶ 4280 (5)	**534**
Fall In Love With Me—Earth, Wind & Fire (83)	838
I Don't Wanna Lose Your Love—Emotions (76)	*279*
Thinking Of You—Earth, Wind & Fire (88)	137
I Don't Want To Lose Your Love—B Angie B (91)	*96*
Side By Side—Earth, Wind & Fire (83)	65
Frankie L. HUTCHISON [F. Hutch, Frank Hutch] ▶ 5808 (1)	**240**
Love Power—Willie Hutch (75)	240
—Willie M. Hutchison see: Willie HUTCH	
Phil HUTH ▶ 9052 (1)	**32**
Life's Too Short—Lafayettes (62)	65
Janice HUTSON ▶ 5842 (2)	**238**
Can This Be Real—Natural Four (73)	637
Love That Really Counts—Natural Four (74)	103
Leroy HUTSON ▶ 5106 (4)	**341**
Can This Be Real—Natural Four (73)	637
The Ghetto—Too Short (90)	337
Love That Really Counts—Natural Four (74)	103
The Ghetto - Part 1—Donny Hathaway (70)	38
—Tammy Hutson see: Lisa COHEN	
Ralf HUTTER ▶ 4620 (2)	**449**
Autobahn—Kraftwerk (75)	701
Trans-Europe Express—Kraftwerk (78)	99
Danny HUTTON ▶ 5480 (1)	**280**
Roses And Rainbows—Danny Hutton (65)	280
Leo HUTTON ▶ 6291 (1)	**185**
The Funky Judge—Bull & The Matadors (68)	370
—Harry Hyams see: Gary BENSON	
Karl HYDE ▶ 7943 (2)	**68**
Stand Up—Underworld (89)	119
Underneath The Radar—Underworld (88)	85
Madeline HYDE ▶ 10519 (1)	**7.7**
Little Girl—Frankie Lymon (57)	15
Paul HYDE [Paul Reginald Nelson] ▶ 7406 (2)	**98**
Dirty Water—Rock And Hyde (87)	185
You're The Only Love—Paul Hyde And The Payolas (85)	21
Dick HYMAN ▶ 2852 (2)	**1152**
The Minotaur—Dick Hyman & His Electric Eclectics (69)	629
Turvy II—Cozy Cole (58)	523
Jeff HYMAN [Joey Ramone] ▶ 8878 (2)	**37**
Rockaway Beach—Ramones (77)	96
Sheena Is A Punk Rocker—Ramones (77)	53
Rob HYMAN ▶ 1261 (9)	**3545**
Time After Time—Cyndi Lauper (84)	4828
And We Danced—Hooters (85)	804
Day By Day—Hooters (85)	759
Where Do The Children Go—Hooters (86)	387
All You Zombies—Hooters (85)	225
Never Enough—Patty Smyth (87)	206
Johnny B—Hooters (87)	201
Satellite—Hooters (87)	169
Brother, Don't You Walk Away—Hooters (90)	17
Tony HYMAS ▶ 9768 (1)	**17**
Little Suzi—Tesla (87)	34
Chrissie HYNDE ▶ 639 (6)	**6808**
Back On The Chain Gang—Pretenders (82)	2853
Brass In Pocket (I'm Special)—Pretenders (80)	1641
Don't Get Me Wrong—Pretenders (86)	1466
Middle Of The Road—Pretenders (83)	1042
Show Me—Pretenders (84)	506
My Baby—Pretenders (87)	121

I

Janis IAN [Janis Eddy Fink] ▶ 683 (6)	**6361**
At Seventeen—Janis Ian (75)	3880
Society's Child (Baby I've Been Thinking)—Janis Ian (67)	1654
Jesse—Roberta Flack (73)	742
Under The Covers—Janis Ian (81)	51
Insanity Comes Quietly To The Structured Mind—Janis Ian (67)	32
In The Winter—Janis Ian (75)	2.7
—Paula Ianello see: Paula FRANCES	
Rick IANTOSCA ▶ 7675 (1)	**81**
Downtown Life—Daryl Hall & John Oates (88)	326
Samuel IBARRA ▶ 4473 (1)	**486**
Lo Mucho Que Te Quiero (The More I Love You)—René & René (68)	1458
Charles IBGUI [Charles Burbank] ▶ 11597 (1)	**1.0**
Boy Toy—Tia (87)	3.1
—Ice-T see: Tracy MARROW	
Bobby ICON [Robert Charles Eichorn] ▶ 7258 (1)	**107**
Love Cries—Stage Dolls (89)	214
Abraham Zevi IDELSOHN ▶ 6093 (3)	**206**
Dance Everyone Dance—Betty Madigan (58)	*619*
Dance, Everyone, Dance—Hi-Liters (58)	*0.0*
Dance, Everyone, Dance—Les Baxter & His Orchestra (58)	*0.0*
Billy IDOL [William M. A. Broad] ▶ 670 (10)	**6462**
Cradle Of Love—Billy Idol (90)	3538
Eyes Without A Face—Billy Idol (84)	3144
Hot In The City—Billy Idol (82)	*710*
Sweet Sixteen—Billy Idol (87)	569
White Wedding—Billy Idol (83)	494
Flesh For Fantasy—Billy Idol (84)	488
Rebel Yell—Billy Idol (84)	476
Don't Need A Gun—Billy Idol (87)	357
Catch My Fall—Billy Idol (84)	270
Hot In The City—Billy Idol (87)	*239*
—Dominic Ierace see: Donnie IRIS	
Walker IGLEHEART ▶ 5356 (1)	**300**
Be With You—Bangles (89)	600
Julio IGLESIAS ▶ 5319 (1)	**306**
All Of You—Julio Iglesias & Diana Ross (84)	919
Pepe IGLESIAS ▶ 11128 (1)	**3.1**
Eso Es El Amor (This Is Love)—Morty Palitz & Orchestra with the Americanos (59)	6.2
—Roy Ilene see: Milt GABLER	
Gary ILLINGWORTH ▶ 6281 (4)	**186**
I Can Remember—James & Bobby Purify (68)	*283*
Do Unto Me—James & Bobby Purify (68)	251
There's So Much Love All Around Me—Three Degrees (71)	11
I Can Remember—Oliver (70)	*7.7*
—Barry Imberman see: Barry MANN	
—John V. Imbragulio see: John VINCENT	
Mildred IMES ▶ 3940 (4)	**650**
You're The Reason—Bobby Edwards (61)	*2462*
You're The Reason—Joe South (61)	*136*
You're The Reason—Hank Locklin (61)	*0.0*
You're The Reason—Gerry And The Pacemakers (65)	*0.0*
Charles INGERSOLL ▶ 10255 (1)	**11**
I've Got Love For My Baby—Young Hearts (68)	43
Doug INGLE ▶ 3635 (5)	**756**
In-A-Gadda-Da-Vida—Iron Butterfly (68)	*606*
Soul Experience—Iron Butterfly (69)	180
Easy Rider (Let The Wind Pay The Way)—Iron Butterfly (70)	125
In-A-Gadda-Da-Vida—Iron Butterfly (69)	*70*
In The Time Of Our Lives—Iron Butterfly (69)	5.5
Jorgen INGMANN [Jorgen Ingmann Pedersen] ▶ 6370 (1)	**178**
Chicken Feed—Bent Fabric And His Piano (62)	356
Arnold INGRAM ▶ 2985 (2)	**1082**
Float On—Floaters (77)	*3048*
Bloat On Featuring The Bloaters—Cheech & Chong (77)	*328*
Butch INGRAM ▶ 9759 (1)	**17**
Motown Review—Philly Cream (79)	35
James INGRAM ▶ 3277 (3)	**915**
P.Y.T. (Pretty Young Thing)—Michael Jackson (83)	1161
Yah Mo B There—James Ingram (83)	906
Baby Come And Get It—Pointer Sisters (85)	323
John INGRAM ▶ 7279 (1)	**106**
Baby I Want You—Funky Communication Committee (79)	211
Luther INGRAM ▶ 2105 (7)	**1872**
Respect Yourself—Staple Singers (71)	*1800*
Respect Yourself—Bruce Willis (87)	*1395*
My Honey And Me—Luther Ingram (70)	*339*
Always—Luther Ingram (73)	120
Missing You—Luther Ingram (72)	69
My Honey And Me—Emotions (72)	*22*
To The Other Man—Luther Ingram (70)	1.7
Tommy INGRAM ▶ 11552 (1)	**1.2**
I Think Somebody Loves Me—Noble Downs (72)	1.2

Autry INMAN ▶ 9407 (1)	**24**
Second Honeymoon–Johnny Cash (60)	24
David INNIS ▶ 4061 (1)	**608**
Dare Me–Pointer Sisters (85)	1216
Louis INNIS ▶ 3501 (5)	**814**
Daddy-O– Fontane Sisters with Billy Vaughn's Orchestra (55)	*1345*
Daddy-O–Bonnie Lou (55)	*539*
Big Love–Joe Henderson (62)	127
I'm Learning About Love–Brenda Lee (61)	110
Portrait Of A Fool–Conway Twitty (62)	10
Paul INSETTA ▶ 6739 (2)	**141**
I Woke Up Crying–Joni James (56)	129
When I Let You Go–Jerry Vale (55)	13
—Susan Bridget Inskip see: Florrie PALMER	
—Anthony Gordon Instone see: Tony MACAULAY	
Tony IOMMI ▶ 7274 (2)	**106**
Paranoid–Black Sabbath (70)	212
Iron Man–Black Sabbath (72)	211
—Rocco Giuseppe Iosco see: Bob YOSCO	
Joyce IRBY [Fenderella] ▶ 4984 (3)	**365**
I'd Still Say Yes–Klymaxx (87)	841
The Men All Pause–Klymaxx (86)	103
I'll Be There–Joyce "Fenderella" Irby (90)	99
Maurice IRBY ▶ 964 (2)	**4654**
Apples, Peaches, Pumpkin Pie– Jay And The Techniques (67)	4150
Strawberry Shortcake–Jay And The Techniques (68)	504
Donnie IRIS [Dominic Ierace] ▶ 765 (10)	**5725**
The Rapper–Jaggerz (70)	4659
Ah! Leah!–Donnie Iris (80)	767
My Girl–Donnie Iris (82)	523
Love Is Like A Rock–Donnie Iris (81)	454
I Call My Baby Candy–Jaggerz (70)	181
Tough World–Donnie Iris (82)	138
Do You Compute?–Donnie Iris (83)	99
Sweet Merilee–Donnie Iris (81)	79
What A Bummer–Jaggerz (70)	11
Injured In The Game Of Love–Donnie Iris (85)	7.2
Eddie IRONS ▶ 2811 (2)	**1180**
Dazz–Brick (76)	3530
Sweat (Til You Get Wet)–Brick (81)	16
Weldon IRVINE ▶ 8815 (1)	**39**
To Be Young, Gifted And Black–Nina Simone (69)	77
—Big Dee Irwin see: Dee ERVIN	
—Roy Irwin see: Max BYGRAVES	
Russ IRWIN ▶ 4641 (1)	**446**
My Heart Belongs To You–Russ Irwin (91)	446
Chris ISAAK ▶ 2496 (2)	**1436**
Wicked Game–Chris Isaak (90)	1406
Don't Make Me Dream About You–Chris Isaak (91)	30
Alvertis ISBELL ▶ 630 (13)	**6854**
I'll Take You There–Staple Singers (72)	5980
Hard To Handle–Black Crowes (91)	*595*
Love Bones–Johnnie Taylor (69)	494
I've Never Found A Girl (To Love Me Like You Do)– Eddie Floyd (68)	*437*
Hard To Handle–Black Crowes (90)	*279*
Raise Your Hand–Eddie Floyd (67)	168
Hard To Handle–Otis Redding (68)	*114*
I'll Always Have Faith In You–Carla Thomas (67)	103
I've Never Found A Man (To Love Me Like You Do)– Esther Phillips (72)	*37*
Someone Is Watching–Solomon Burke (65)	29
Stop! Look What You're Doing–Carla Thomas (65)	27
Every Man Oughta Have A Woman–William Bell (68)	20
Hard To Handle–Patti Drew (68)	*7.7*
—Jeffrey Dean Isbell see: Izzy STRADLIN	
Steve ISHAM ▶ 6880 (1)	**131**
Turn Up The Radio–Autograph (84)	654
—Afrika Islam see: Charles Andre GLENN	
—Yusuf Islam see: Cat STEVENS	
Jimmy ISLE ▶ 10076 (2)	**13**
Diamond Ring–Jerry Wallace (58)	25
Little Miss Blue–Dion (60)	2.1
Ronnie ISLE ▶ 10077 (2)	**13**
Diamond Ring–Jerry Wallace (58)	25
Little Miss Blue–Dion (60)	2.1
Ernie ISLEY ▶ 2897 (20)	**1127**
Fight The Power Part 1–Isley Brothers (75)	2590
For The Love Of You (Part 1 & 2)– Isley Brothers (75)	*696*
Don't Say Goodnight (It's Time For Love) (Parts 1 & 2)–Isley Brothers (80)	378
What It Comes Down To–Isley Brothers (73)	311
Caravan Of Love–Isley Jasper Isley (85)	310
Live It Up Part 1–Isley Brothers (74)	287
Livin' In The Life–Isley Brothers (77)	278
Need A Little Taste Of Love–Doobie Brothers (89)	273
Harvest For The World–Isley Brothers (76)	239
Who Loves You Better - Part 1–Isley Brothers (76)	186
Hurry Up And Wait–Isley Brothers (81)	171
Kiss And Tell–Isley, Jasper, Isley (85)	162
The Pride (Part 1)–Isley Brothers (77)	104
Take Me To The Next Phase–Isley Brothers (78)	92
Midnight Sky (Part 1)–Isley Brothers (75)	81
Warpath–Isley Brothers (71)	53
I Wanna Be With You (Part I)–Isley Brothers (79)	40
Inside You (Part 1)–Isley Brothers (81)	14
For The Love Of You–Houston Person (76)	*6.4*
It's A Disco Night (Rock Don't Stop)– Isley Brothers (79)	5.8
Marvin ISLEY ▶ 2920 (19)	**1116**
Fight The Power Part 1–Isley Brothers (75)	2590
For The Love Of You (Part 1 & 2)– Isley Brothers (75)	*696*
Don't Say Goodnight (It's Time For Love) (Parts 1 & 2)–Isley Brothers (80)	378
What It Comes Down To–Isley Brothers (73)	311
Caravan Of Love–Isley Jasper Isley (85)	310
Live It Up Part 1–Isley Brothers (74)	287
Livin' In The Life–Isley Brothers (77)	278
Need A Little Taste Of Love–Doobie Brothers (89)	273
Harvest For The World–Isley Brothers (76)	239
Who Loves You Better - Part 1–Isley Brothers (76)	186
Hurry Up And Wait–Isley Brothers (81)	171
Kiss And Tell–Isley, Jasper, Isley (85)	162
The Pride (Part 1)–Isley Brothers (77)	104
Take Me To The Next Phase–Isley Brothers (78)	92
Midnight Sky (Part 1)–Isley Brothers (75)	81
I Wanna Be With You (Part I)–Isley Brothers (79)	40
Inside You (Part 1)–Isley Brothers (81)	14
For The Love Of You–Houston Person (76)	*6.4*
It's A Disco Night (Rock Don't Stop)– Isley Brothers (79)	5.8
O'Kelly ISLEY ▶ 561 (41)	**7707**
It's Your Thing–Isley Brothers (69)	6205
That Lady (Part 1)–Isley Brothers (73)	3068
Nobody But Me–Human Beinz (67)	3029
Fight The Power Part 1–Isley Brothers (75)	2590
Shout - Part 1–Joey Dee & The Starliters (62)	*2111*
Respectable–Outsiders (66)	*1172*
I Turned You On–Isley Brothers (69)	1108
Pop That Thang–Isley Brothers (72)	972
For The Love Of You (Part 1 & 2)– Isley Brothers (75)	*696*
Shout Part One–Isley Brothers (59)	*544*
Lay-Away–Isley Brothers (72)	409
Don't Say Goodnight (It's Time For Love) (Parts 1 & 2)–Isley Brothers (80)	378
Work To Do–Isley Brothers (72)	364
Twistin' With Linda–Isley Brothers (62)	320
What It Comes Down To–Isley Brothers (73)	311
Live It Up Part 1–Isley Brothers (74)	287
Livin' In The Life–Isley Brothers (77)	278
Need A Little Taste Of Love–Doobie Brothers (89)	273
Harvest For The World–Isley Brothers (76)	239
Keep On Doin'–Isley Brothers (70)	232
Freedom–Isley Brothers (71)	215
Who Loves You Better - Part 1–Isley Brothers (76)	186
Hurry Up And Wait–Isley Brothers (81)	171
Was It Good To You–Isley Brothers (69)	169
Black Berries - Pt. 1–Isley Brothers (69)	145
Girls Will Be Girls, Boys Will Be Boys– Isley Brothers (70)	116
The Pride (Part 1)–Isley Brothers (77)	104
Take Me To The Next Phase–Isley Brothers (78)	92
Midnight Sky (Part 1)–Isley Brothers (75)	81
Warpath–Isley Brothers (71)	53
Shout–Lulu And The Luvers (64)	*42*
I Wanna Be With You (Part I)–Isley Brothers (79)	40
Respectable–Chants (61)	*24*
Shout! - Part 1–Chambers Brothers (68)	*21*
Get Into Something–Isley Brothers (70)	18
Inside You (Part 1)–Isley Brothers (81)	14
Respectable–Isley Brothers (60)	*14*
Shout - Part 1–Isley Brothers (62)	*8.8*
For The Love Of You–Houston Person (76)	*6.4*
Shout–Lulu (67)	*6.1*
It's A Disco Night (Rock Don't Stop)– Isley Brothers (79)	5.8
Ronald ISLEY ▶ 573 (40)	**7562**
It's Your Thing–Isley Brothers (69)	6205
That Lady (Part 1)–Isley Brothers (73)	3068
Nobody But Me–Human Beinz (67)	3029
Fight The Power Part 1–Isley Brothers (75)	2590
Shout - Part 1–Joey Dee & The Starliters (62)	*2111*
Respectable–Outsiders (66)	*1172*
I Turned You On–Isley Brothers (69)	1108
Pop That Thang–Isley Brothers (72)	972
For The Love Of You (Part 1 & 2)– Isley Brothers (75)	*696*
Shout Part One–Isley Brothers (59)	*544*
Lay-Away–Isley Brothers (72)	409
Don't Say Goodnight (It's Time For Love) (Parts 1 & 2)–Isley Brothers (80)	378
Work To Do–Isley Brothers (72)	364
Twistin' With Linda–Isley Brothers (62)	320
What It Comes Down To–Isley Brothers (73)	311
Live It Up Part 1–Isley Brothers (74)	287
Livin' In The Life–Isley Brothers (77)	278
Need A Little Taste Of Love–Doobie Brothers (89)	273
Harvest For The World–Isley Brothers (76)	239
Keep On Doin'–Isley Brothers (70)	232
Freedom–Isley Brothers (71)	215
Who Loves You Better - Part 1–Isley Brothers (76)	186
Hurry Up And Wait–Isley Brothers (81)	171
Was It Good To You–Isley Brothers (69)	169
Girls Will Be Girls, Boys Will Be Boys– Isley Brothers (70)	116
The Pride (Part 1)–Isley Brothers (77)	104
Take Me To The Next Phase–Isley Brothers (78)	92
Midnight Sky (Part 1)–Isley Brothers (75)	81
Warpath–Isley Brothers (71)	53
Shout–Lulu And The Luvers (64)	*42*
I Wanna Be With You (Part I)–Isley Brothers (79)	40
Respectable–Chants (61)	*24*
Shout! - Part 1–Chambers Brothers (68)	*21*
Get Into Something–Isley Brothers (70)	18
Inside You (Part 1)–Isley Brothers (81)	14
Respectable–Isley Brothers (60)	*14*
Shout - Part 1–Isley Brothers (62)	*8.8*
For The Love Of You–Houston Person (76)	*6.4*
Shout–Lulu (67)	*6.1*
It's A Disco Night (Rock Don't Stop)– Isley Brothers (79)	5.8
Rudolph ISLEY ▶ 574 (40)	**7562**
It's Your Thing–Isley Brothers (69)	6205
That Lady (Part 1)–Isley Brothers (73)	3068
Nobody But Me–Human Beinz (67)	3029
Fight The Power Part 1–Isley Brothers (75)	2590
Shout - Part 1–Joey Dee & The Starliters (62)	*2111*
Respectable–Outsiders (66)	*1172*
I Turned You On–Isley Brothers (69)	1108
Pop That Thang–Isley Brothers (72)	972
For The Love Of You (Part 1 & 2)– Isley Brothers (75)	*696*
Shout Part One–Isley Brothers (59)	*544*
Lay-Away–Isley Brothers (72)	409
Don't Say Goodnight (It's Time For Love) (Parts 1 & 2)–Isley Brothers (80)	378
Work To Do–Isley Brothers (72)	364
Twistin' With Linda–Isley Brothers (62)	320
What It Comes Down To–Isley Brothers (73)	311
Live It Up Part 1–Isley Brothers (74)	287
Livin' In The Life–Isley Brothers (77)	278
Need A Little Taste Of Love–Doobie Brothers (89)	273
Harvest For The World–Isley Brothers (76)	239
Keep On Doin'–Isley Brothers (70)	232
Freedom–Isley Brothers (71)	215
Who Loves You Better - Part 1–Isley Brothers (76)	186
Hurry Up And Wait–Isley Brothers (81)	171
Was It Good To You–Isley Brothers (69)	169
Girls Will Be Girls, Boys Will Be Boys– Isley Brothers (70)	116
The Pride (Part 1)–Isley Brothers (77)	104

Rudolph ISLEY ► 574 (40) *Continued*	**7562**
Take Me To The Next Phase—Isley Brothers (78)	92
Midnight Sky (Part 1)—Isley Brothers (75)	81
Warpath—Isley Brothers (71)	53
Shout—Lulu And The Luvers (64)	*42*
I Wanna Be With You (Part I)—Isley Brothers (79)	40
Respectable—Chants (61)	*24*
Shout! - Part 1—Chambers Brothers (68)	*21*
Get Into Something—Isley Brothers (70)	18
Inside You (Part 1)—Isley Brothers (81)	14
Respectable—Isley Brothers (60)	*14*
Shout - Part 1—Isley Brothers (62)	*8.8*
For The Love Of You—Houston Person (76)	*6.4*
Shout—Lulu (67)	*6.1*
It's A Disco Night (Rock Don't Stop)— Isley Brothers (79)	5.8
Jesse Eric ITZLER [Jesse Jaymes] ► 10671 (1)	**6.2**
Shake It (Like A White Girl)—Jesse Jaymes (91)	25
Iosef IVANOVICI ► 11302 (1)	**2.3**
Anniversary Song—Mulcays (56)	7.0
Peter IVERS ► 9485 (1)	**23**
Let's Go Up—Diana Ross (83)	46
Burl IVES ► 10449 (1)	**8.3**
Curry Road—Burl Ives (63)	17
Chet IVEY ► 11716 (1)	**0.5**
Shake A Poo Poo— Chet "Poison" Ivey And His Fabulous Avengers (69)	0.5
Clayton IVEY ► 3321 (1)	**900**
Angel In Your Arms—Hot (77)	2701
Geoff IWAMOTO ► 8427 (1)	**51**
Your Daddy Don't Know—Toronto (82)	101
Debora IYALL ► 7088 (1)	**116**
A Girl In Trouble (Is A Temporary Thing)— Romeo Void (84)	466
Sal IZZO ► 8085 (2)	**62**
Kid Stuff—McGuire Sisters (57)	*125*
Kid Stuff—Bernadine Read (57)	*0.0*

J

Paul JABARA ► 514 (6)	**8296**
No More Tears (Enough Is Enough)— Barbra Streisand/Donna Summer (79)	5346
Last Dance—Donna Summer (78)	3589
Fight—Barbra Streisand (79)	1784
Main Event—Barbra Streisand (79)	1784
It's Raining Men—Weather Girls (83)	316
Work That Body—Diana Ross (82)	278
Steve JABLECKI ► 1940 (2)	**2082**
Sweet Mary—Wadsworth Mansion (70)	2080
Michigan Harry Slaughter—Wadsworth Mansion (71)	1.7
Terry JACKS ► 690 (7)	**6312**
Which Way You Goin' Billy?— Poppy Family (Featuring Susan Jacks) (70)	4709
That's Where I Went Wrong— Poppy Family (Featuring Susan Jacks) (70)	1015
Where Evil Grows— Poppy Family Vocal: Susan And Terry Jacks (71)	504
You Don't Know What Love Is— Susan Jacks And The Poppy Family (73)	37
Good Friends?— Poppy Family Vocal: Susan Jacks (72)	30
I Was Wondering— Poppy Family Vocal: Susan Jacks (71)	18
Christina—Terry Jacks (75)	18
Adam JACKSON ► 11774 (1)	**0.1**
So Strange—Jesters (57)	0.3
Al JACKSON ► 348 (24)	**10822**
Let's Stay Together—Al Green (71)	*7842*
I'm Still In Love With You—Al Green (72)	5102
Green Onions—Booker T. & The M.G.'s (62)	*4924*
You Ought To Be With Me—Al Green (72)	4701
Look What You Done For Me—Al Green (72)	3798
Time Is Tight—Booker T. & The M.G.'s (69)	2035
Call Me (Come Back Home)—Al Green (73)	1660
Soul-Limbo—Booker T. & The M.G.'s (68)	1495
Let's Stay Together—Tina Turner (84)	*755*
Hip Hug-Her—Booker T. & The M.G.'s (67)	719
Hole In The Wall—Packers (65)	689
Melting Pot—Booker T. & The M.G.'s (71)	365
Let's Stay Together—Isaac Hayes (72)	*340*
Cold Feet—Albert King (68)	159
My Sweet Potato—Booker T. & The M.G.'s (66)	119
Jellybread—Booker T. & The MGs (62)	74
Slim Jenkin's Place—Booker T. & The M.G.'s (67)	64
Chinese Checkers—Booker T. & The MG's (63)	63
Breaking Up Somebody's Home— Ann Peebles (72)	*29*
Green Onions—Dick Hyman (69)	*23*
The Hunter—Ike & Tina Turner (69)	12
Breaking Up Somebody's Home—Albert King (73)	*12*
Soul Dressing—Booker T. & The MG's (64)	4.4
Mo-Onions—Booker T. & The MG's (64)	3.7
Anthony JACKSON ► 3969 (2)	**634**
For The Love Of Money—O'Jays (74)	*1864*
For The Love Of Money—Bulletboys (89)	*39*
Bernard Leon JACKSON ► 916 (5)	**4826**
The First Time—Surface (90)	4220
Shower Me With Your Love—Surface (89)	1746
Happy—Surface (87)	678
Never Gonna Let You Down—Surface (91)	640
Closer Than Friends—Surface (89)	207
Betty JACKSON ► 11746 (1)	**0.2**
Hey Lonely One—Baby Washington (63)	0.4
—Billy Jackson see: Gene DOZIER	
Charles Henry JACKSON Jr. [Chuck Jackson] ► 646 (20)	**6763**
Where Do Broken Hearts Go—Whitney Houston (88)	3452
I've Got Love On My Mind—Natalie Cole (77)	3003
This Will Be—Natalie Cole (75)	2336
Our Love—Natalie Cole (77)	1689
Inseparable—Natalie Cole (75)	745
Sophisticated Lady (She's A Different Lady)— Natalie Cole (76)	730
Baby I've Been Missing You—Independents (73)	372
Mr. Melody—Natalie Cole (76)	277
The More You Do It (The More I Like It Done To Me)— Ronnie Dyson (76)	243
United Together—Aretha Franklin (80)	205
If It's Real What I Feel— Jerry Butler Featuring Brenda Lee [Eager] (71)	128
Same Thing It Took—Impressions (75)	115
Let This Be A Lesson To You—Independents (74)	97
It's All Over—Independents (73)	79
Just As Long As You Need Me, Part I— Independents (72)	74
It's Cool—Tymes (76)	55
Want You For My Girlfriend—4 By Four (87)	54
Loving Power—Impressions (76)	31
Walk Easy My Son—Jerry Butler (71)	15
You—Aretha Franklin (76)	7.1
Christopher JACKSON ► 3037 (1)	**1049**
You Little Trustmaker—Tymes (74)	1049
Chuck JACKSON ► 4259 (4)	**544**
I Don't Want To Cry—Chuck Jackson (61)	*610*
I Don't Wanna Cry—Ronnie Dyson (70)	*414*
I Don't Want To Cry—Ruby Winters (69)	*57*
Tears Of Joy—Chuck Jackson (63)	7.5
—Chuck Jackson see: Charles Henry JACKSON Jr.	
Dave JACKSON [David-John Jackson-Rich] ► 7325 (2)	**102**
Blame It On The Boogie—Jacksons (78)	*217*
Blame It On The Boogie—Mick Jackson (78)	*89*
David P. JACKSON ► 2253 (1)	**1703**
No No Song—Ringo Starr (75)	3406
—David Ian Jackson see: Joe JACKSON	
—David Waymond Jackson see: Stonewall JACKSON	
Deon JACKSON ► 2103 (3)	**1880**
Love Makes The World Go Round—Deon Jackson (66)	*1783*
Love Makes The World Go Round—Odds & Ends (71)	*77*
Love Makes The World Go Round—Kiki Dee (71)	*21*
Dimple M. JACKSON [Marcene Harris] ► 8261 (1)	**57**
Tell Me The Truth—Nancy Wilson (63)	113
Eddie JACKSON ► 9606 (1)	**20**
Another Rainy Night (Without You)— Queensryche (91)	61
Eddie L. JACKSON ► 6468 (1)	**166**
The Touch Of You—Brenda & The Tabulations (70)	331
Fred JACKSON [Thomas Marlowe] ► 8011 (1)	**65**
Don't Cry My Love (The Faithful Hussar)— Vera Lynn (57)	*196*
Freddie JACKSON ► 4968 (2)	**368**
Jam Tonight—Freddie Jackson (87)	446
Tasty Love—Freddie Jackson (86)	290
Gary JACKSON ► 1566 (5)	**2701**
(Your Love Has Lifted Me) Higher And Higher— Rita Coolidge (77)	*5006*
(Your Love Keeps Lifting Me) Higher And Higher— Jackie Wilson (67)	*2626*
Since You Showed Me How To Be Happy— Jackie Wilson (67)	461
Higher And Higher—Canada Goose (70)	*9.9*
You Brought About A Change In Me— Jackie Wilson (68)	0.0
George Harold JACKSON [Harold Jackson] ► 8262 (1)	**57**
Tell Me The Truth—Nancy Wilson (63)	113
George Henry JACKSON ► 297 (24)	**12143**
One Bad Apple—Osmonds (70)	8155
Too Weak To Fight—Clarence Carter (68)	2074
Double Lovin'—Osmonds (71)	1333
Snatching It Back—Clarence Carter (69)	884
I Can't Leave Your Love Alone—Clarence Carter (70)	597
Old Time Rock & Roll— Bob Seger & The Silver Bullet Band (79)	*498*
It's All In Your Mind—Clarence Carter (70)	460
The Feeling Is Right—Clarence Carter (69)	449
I'd Rather Be An Old Man's Sweetheart (Than A Young Man's Fool)—Candi Staton (69)	422
Mini-Skirt Minnie—Wilson Pickett (69)	364
Old Time Rock & Roll— Bob Seger & The Silver Bullet Band (83)	*336*
Make You Feel Love Again—Wet Willie (78)	314
A Man And A Half—Wilson Pickett (68)	273
This Is The Way That I Feel—Marie Osmond (77)	265
I'm Just A Prisoner (Of Your Good Lovin')— Candi Staton (70)	223
Victim Of A Foolish Heart—Bettye Swann (72)	210
Slipped, Tripped And Fell In Love— Clarence Carter (71)	174
Whatever Turns You On—Travis Wammack (72)	131
Take It Off Him And Put It On Me— Clarence Carter (70)	15
I'm A Fool For You—James Carr (67)	10
I'm The Midnight Special—Clarence Carter (73)	8.8
Find 'Em, Fool 'Em & Forget 'Em—Dobie Gray (76)	4.6
The Only Way Is Up— Yazz And The Plastic Population (88)	3.4
Love Attack—James Carr (66)	2.4
Gerald JACKSON ► 3498 (1)	**816**
Turn The Beat Around—Vicki Sue Robinson (76)	1632
—Harold Jackson see: George Harold JACKSON	
Herb JACKSON ► 10416 (1)	**8.7**
There Stands The Door—We Five (66)	8.7
Jackie JACKSON [Sigmund Esco Jackson] ► 4597 (3)	**456**
Torture—Jacksons (84)	784
Can You Feel It—Jacksons (81)	80
Walk Right Now—Jacksons (81)	71
Janet JACKSON ► 524 (7)	**8100**
Escapade—Janet Jackson (90)	4680
Rhythm Nation—Janet Jackson (89)	3288
Black Cat—Janet Jackson (90)	2927
Come Back To Me—Janet Jackson (90)	2853
Let's Wait Awhile—Janet Jackson (87)	2779
Alright—Janet Jackson (90)	2323
State Of The World—Janet Jackson (91)	290
Jermaine JACKSON [Muhammad Abdul Aziz] ► 3360 (8)	**882**
I Think It's Love—Jermaine Jackson (86)	892
Let Me Tickle Your Fancy—Jermaine Jackson (82)	820
You Like Me Don't You—Jermaine Jackson (81)	195
I'm Just Too Shy—Jermaine Jackson (81)	176
(Closest Thing To) Perfect—Jermaine Jackson (85)	139
Lonely Won't Leave Me Alone—Glenn Medeiros (87)	84
Do You Remember Me?—Jermaine Jackson (86)	81
Word To The Badd!!—Jermaine Jackson (91)	11
Jerry JACKSON ► 10889 (1)	**4.6**
Little Lonely—Chad Allen (61)	9.2

Jill JACKSON ▶ 2977 (2)	**1087**
Young Lovers—Paul & Paula (63)	2050
First Day Back At School—Paul & Paula (63)	125
J.J. JACKSON [J. L. Jackson, Jerome Louis Jackson] ▶ 3230 (5)	**939**
But It's Alright—J.J. Jackson (66)	*1049*
Long Live Our Love—Shangri-Las (66)	433
But It's Alright—J.J. Jackson (69)	*334*
Four Walls (Three Windows And Two Doors)— J.J. Jackson (67)	48
Me Without You—Mary Wells (65)	16
—J. L. Jackson see: J.J. JACKSON	
—Joanne Jackson see: Joanne BRATTON	
Joe JACKSON [David Ian Jackson] ▶ 706 (6)	**6167**
Steppin' Out—Joe Jackson (82)	2983
Is She Really Going Out With Him?—Joe Jackson (79)	1076
Breaking Us In Two—Joe Jackson (83)	1020
You Can't Get What You Want (Till You Know What You Want)—Joe Jackson (84)	909
Happy Ending—Joe Jackson (84)	162
Memphis—Joe Jackson (83)	17
June JACKSON ▶ 4159 (2)	**577**
Show Business—Lou Rawls (67)	384
Oh My Angel—Bertha Tillman (62)	194
LaToya JACKSON ▶ 7795 (1)	**75**
Heart Don't Lie—La Toya Jackson (84)	224
Lee JACKSON ▶ 11747 (1)	**0.2**
Father Knows Best—Radiants (62)	0.4
—Leroy O'Niel Jackson Jr. see: Leroy BURGESS	
Mark JACKSON ▶ 9562 (1)	**21**
It Don't Hurt No More—Nappy Brown (58)	43
Marlon JACKSON ▶ 6019 (1)	**215**
Body—Jacksons (84)	215
Martin JACKSON ▶ 3572 (2)	**781**
Breakout—Swing Out Sister (87)	1952
Twilight World—Swing Out Sister (87)	393
Maybelle JACKSON ▶ 10378 (1)	**9.2**
Heeby Jeebies—Little Richard (56)	18
McKinley JACKSON ▶ 3236 (5)	**935**
Trying To Hold On To My Woman—Lamont Dozier (73)	1176
Fish Ain't Bitin'—Lamont Dozier (74)	544
Midnight Flower—Four Tops (74)	146
Treat 'Em Right—Chubb Rock (91)	4.7
Hear The Words, Feel The Feeling— Margie Joseph (76)	2.6
Michael JACKSON [Michael Joe Jackson] ▶ 18 (27) HOF	**63846**
Say Say Say— Paul McCartney and Michael Jackson (83)	8900
Billie Jean—Michael Jackson (83)	*8153*
Beat It—Michael Jackson (83)	*6897*
We Are The World—USA for Africa (85)	6108
Black Or White—Michael Jackson (91)	5300
The Girl Is Mine— Michael Jackson/Paul McCartney (82)	5033
Don't Stop 'til You Get Enough— Michael Jackson (79)	4819
I Just Can't Stop Loving You—Michael Jackson (87)	3560
Shake Your Body (Down To The Ground)—Jacksons (79)	3398
The Way You Make Me Feel—Michael Jackson (87)	3330
Bad—Michael Jackson (87)	*3156*
Dirty Diana—Michael Jackson (88)	3087
State Of Shock—Jacksons (84)	3000
Wanna Be Startin' Somethin'—Michael Jackson (83)	2168
Muscles—Diana Ross (82)	1868
Smooth Criminal—Michael Jackson (88)	1503
Eat It—"Weird Al" Yankovic (84)	*1414*
Lovely One—Jacksons (80)	1367
Centipede—Rebbie Jackson (84)	937
Another Part Of Me—Michael Jackson (88)	934
Heartbreak Hotel—Jacksons (80)	803
Do The Bartman—Simpsons (90)	139
Can You Feel It—Jacksons (81)	80
Eaten Alive—Diana Ross (85)	76
Walk Right Now—Jacksons (81)	71
Billie Jean—Club House (83)	*40*
Fat—"Weird Al" Yankovic (88)	*12*
—Michael Joe Jackson see: Michael JACKSON	
Mick JACKSON [Michael George Jackson Clark] ▶ 4950 (3)	**375**
Weekend—Wet Willie (79)	546

Blame It On The Boogie—Jacksons (78)	*217*
Blame It On The Boogie—Mick Jackson (78)	*89*
Millie JACKSON ▶ 4242 (3)	**547**
Ask Me What You Want—Millie Jackson (72)	1028
A Child Of God (It's Hard To Believe)— Millie Jackson (71)	37
I Got To Try It One Time—Millie Jackson (74)	30
Paul M. JACKSON Jr. ▶ 5403 (2)	**293**
Let Me Tickle Your Fancy—Jermaine Jackson (82)	820
I'm Just Too Shy—Jermaine Jackson (81)	176
Paul J. JACKSON ▶ 7068 (1)	**118**
Chameleon—Herbie Hancock (74)	472
Pete JACKSON ▶ 3499 (1)	**816**
Turn The Beat Around—Vicki Sue Robinson (76)	1632
Randall Darnell JACKSON ▶ 10388 (2)	**9.1**
Information—Eric Martin (85)	32
Too Much Ain't Enough Love—Jimmy Barnes (88)	5.6
Randolph Lynch JACKSON ▶ 6819 (1)	**135**
Who's Behind The Door?—Zebra (83)	135
Ray JACKSON ▶ 10618 (1)	**6.7**
Who Shot Sam—George Jones (59)	20
Raymond Earl JACKSON ▶ 880 (18)	**5049**
(If Loving You Is Wrong) I Don't Want To Be Right— Luther Ingram (72)	*5399*
Who's Making Love—Johnnie Taylor (68)	*3954*
If You're Ready (Come Go With Me)—Staple Singers (73)	1796
Take Care Of Your Homework—Johnnie Taylor (69)	958
(If Loving You Is Wrong) I Don't Want To Be Right— Barbara Mandrell (79)	*775*
Touch A Hand, Make A Friend—Staple Singers (74)	770
I'll Be Your Shelter (In Time Of Storm)— Luther Ingram (72)	584
I Like What You're Doing (To Me)—Carla Thomas (69)	399
I Could Never Be President—Johnnie Taylor (69)	345
Who's Making Love—Blues Brothers (80)	*342*
Can't You Find Another Way (Of Doing It)— Sam & Dave (68)	318
Who's Making Love—Young-Holt Unlimited (69)	*241*
If Loving You Is Wrong I Don't Want To Be Right— Millie Jackson (75)	*204*
Be What You Are—Staple Singers (73)	122
Slum Baby—Booker T. & The M.G.'s (69)	74
Sugar Bee—Mitch Ryder (69)	30
I Could Never Be Happy—Emotions (72)	21
Too Many Lovers—Shack (71)	20
Rudy JACKSON ▶ 1127 (5)	**3938**
Hearts Of Stone— Fontane Sisters with Billy Vaughn's Orchestra (54)	*5978*
Hearts Of Stone—Charms (54)	*1329*
Hearts Of Stone—Blue Ridge Rangers (73)	*570*
Hearts Of Stone—Vicki Young (54)	*0.0*
Hearts Of Stone—McGuire Sisters (55)	*0.0*
—Shanna V. Jackson see: Paris GREY	
—Sigmund Esco Jackson see: Jackie JACKSON	
Steven Randall JACKSON ▶ 1730 (3)	**2406**
Shake Your Body (Down To The Ground)—Jacksons (79)	3398
Lovely One—Jacksons (80)	1367
Walk Right Now—Jacksons (81)	71
Stonewall JACKSON [David Waymond Jackson] ▶ 10576 (1)	**7.1**
Why I'm Walkin'—Stonewall Jackson (60)	14
Sylvester JACKSON ▶ 3082 (1)	**1022**
I Love Your Smile—Shanice (91)	4090
—Thomas Gregory Jackson see: Tommy JAMES	
Wanda JACKSON ▶ 1896 (5)	**2141**
Right Or Wrong—Ronnie Dove (64)	*1192*
In The Middle Of A Heartache—Wanda Jackson (61)	810
Right Or Wrong—Wanda Jackson (61)	*673*
Mean Mean Man—Wanda Jackson (60)	7.2
Right Or Wrong—Debbie Reynolds (61)	*0.0*
Wayne JACKSON ▶ 7449 (2)	**95**
Boot-Leg—Booker T. & The MG's (65)	349
Always David—Ruby Winters (69)	24
William JACKSON ▶ 11041 (1)	**3.6**
Don't Be Afraid (Do As I Say)— Frankie Karl & The Dreams (68)	3.6
William E. JACKSON III ▶ 1408 (12)	**3151**
So Much In Love—Tymes (63)	*6568*
Don't Throw Your Love Away—Searchers (64)	1264
Midnight Stroll—Revels (59)	418
So Much In Love—Timothy B. Schmit (82)	*197*

Groovy Baby—Billy Abbott And The Jewels (63)	188
Here She Comes—Tymes (64)	39
The Boy With The Beatle Hair—Swans (64)	19
Let's Make Love Tonight—Bobby Rydell (63)	12
Rosie—Chubby Checker (64)	9.6
Leroy—Norma Tracey And The Cinderella Kids (65)	4.6
Willyam, Willyam—Dee Dee Sharp (64)	1.8
The Magic Of Our Summer Love—Tymes (64)	0.9
Wyn JACKSON [Yonah] ▶ 11258 (1)	**2.6**
After The First One—Yonah (79)	2.6
Wynn JACKSON ▶ 10338 (1)	**9.9**
The Star Wars Stars—Force (77)	20
—David-John Jackson-Rich see: Dave JACKSON	
Al JACOBS ▶ 419 (20)	**9576**
I Need You Now—Eddie Fisher (54)	*6888*
If I Give My Heart To You—Doris Day (54)	*4238*
Hurt—Timi Yuro (61)	*3272*
If I Give My Heart To You—Denise Lor (54)	*1609*
Every Day Of My Life—Bobby Vinton (72)	*1257*
If I Give My Heart To You—Dinah Shore (54)	*1206*
If I Give My Heart To You—Kitty Kallen (59)	*711*
Hurt—Elvis Presley (76)	*517*
Ev'ry Day Of My Life—McGuire Sisters (56)	*516*
My Believing Heart—Joni James (55)	411
If I Give My Heart To You—Connee Boswell (54)	*402*
Hurt—Little Anthony And The Imperials (66)	*222*
Just One More Time—Eddie Fisher (55)	208
Hurt—Roy Hamilton (54)	*63*
Hurt—Manhattans (75)	*58*
It All Started With Your Kiss—Micki Marlo (57)	54
I Need You Now—Ronnie Dove (69)	*21*
So Close To My Heart—Kathy Linden (59)	18
I Need You Now—100 Strings And Joni (60)	*1.1*
Ev'ry Day Of My Life—Vera Lynn (56)	*0.0*
Dick JACOBS ▶ 10316 (1)	**10**
Just Because—McGuire Sisters (61)	30
Gregory JACOBS [MC Blowfish, Eddie Humphrey, Gregory Edward Jacobs, Humpty Hump, Shock G] ▶ 4514 (3)	**474**
The Humpty Dance—Digital Underground (90)	1362
Mama Said Knock You Out—LL Cool J (91)	473
Kiss You Back—Digital Underground (91)	322
Henry JACOBS ▶ 8724 (1)	**41**
So Far Away—Hank Jacobs (64)	82
Jack JACOBS ▶ 10612 (1)	**6.8**
Take Me Home—Balcones Fault (77)	6.8
Jacob JACOBS [Yakov Yakubovitsh] ▶ 7512 (1)	**91**
Bei Mir Bist Du Schon— Louis Prima And Keely Smith (59)	365
Jim JACOBS ▶ 2396 (2)	**1529**
Summer Nights— John Travolta, Olivia Newton-John & Cast (78)	2789
Greased Lightnin'—John Travolta (78)	268
Randy JACOBS ▶ 4518 (2)	**473**
Walk The Dinosaur—Was (Not Was) (89)	1386
Wide Receiver (Part I)—Michael Henderson (80)	22
Roy JACOBS ▶ 8214 (1)	**58**
I'm Gonna Move To The Outskirts Of Town— Ray Charles (61)	116
Ted JACOBS ▶ 10303 (1)	**10**
Don't You Wanna Be Mine—Denise Lopez (90)	21
Willie JACOBS ▶ 11718 (1)	**0.5**
If You Can't Rock Me—Ricky Nelson (63)	0.5
—Fred Jacobsen see: Fred JAY	
—Yasmin Jacobsen see: Yasmin Elvira STEENHOLDT	
Arthur JACOBSON ▶ 6249 (1)	**189**
I'm Happy That Love Has Found You—Jimmy Hall (80)	568
—Friedrich Alex Jacobson see: Fred JAY	
Kenny JACOBSON ▶ 4075 (7)	**603**
Put A Light In The Window—Four Lads (57)	768
Ding Dong—McGuire Sisters (58)	351
Don't Tell Me Your Troubles— Jimmy Bowen With The Rhythm Orchids (57)	31
Every Day—Joni James (54)	26
Born To Love—Teresa Brewer (57)	14
Easy Does It—Jaye P. Morgan (58)	1.2
The Swingin' Shepherd Blues— Ella Fitzgerald & Her Shepherds (58)	*0.0*

Sid JACOBSON ► 1284 (10)	**3456**
(At) The End (Of A Rainbow)—Earl Grant (58)	2879
Yogi—Ivy Three (60)	1816
Boy Without A Girl—Frankie Avalon (59)	1218
I've Come Of Age—Billy Storm (59)	776
Don't Pity Me—Dion and The Belmonts (58)	662
Wonderful You—Jimmie Rodgers (59)	120
Presidential Press Conference—Sickniks (61)	22
Anniversary Of Love—Caslons (61)	21
Yen Yet Song—Gary Cane And His Friends (60)	8.2
You Don't Know Girls—Kathy Linden (59)	7.0
Tony JAFFE ► 11546 (1)	**1.2**
They Don't Make 'Em Like That Any More—Reunion (75)	3.7
Mick JAGGER ► 22 (71) HOF	**58528**
Honky Tonk Women—Rolling Stones (69)	10430
(I Can't Get No) Satisfaction—Rolling Stones (65)	*10038*
Paint It, Black—Rolling Stones (66)	7253
Ruby Tuesday—Rolling Stones (67)	*7240*
Get Off Of My Cloud—Rolling Stones (65)	6209
Brown Sugar—Rolling Stones (71)	6055
19th Nervous Breakdown—Rolling Stones (66)	5987
Jumpin' Jack Flash—Rolling Stones (68)	*5867*
Miss You—Rolling Stones (78)	5848
Angie—Rolling Stones (73)	5117
Start Me Up—Rolling Stones (81)	4381
Emotional Rescue—Rolling Stones (80)	3524
Mother's Little Helper—Rolling Stones (66)	3076
As Tears Go By—Rolling Stones (65)	*2591*
Have You Seen Your Mother, Baby, Standing In The Shadow?—Rolling Stones (66)	2548
Tumbling Dice—Rolling Stones (72)	*2232*
Mixed Emotions—Rolling Stones (89)	1864
The Last Time—Rolling Stones (65)	*1655*
Dandelion—Rolling Stones (67)	1620
Beast Of Burden—Rolling Stones (78)	*1440*
Undercover Of The Night—Rolling Stones (83)	1367
Just Another Night—Mick Jagger (85)	1161
She's A Rainbow—Rolling Stones (67)	1131
Heart Of Stone—Rolling Stones (65)	1125
Waiting On A Friend—Rolling Stones (81)	1065
Doo Doo Doo Doo Doo (Heartbreaker)—Rolling Stones (74)	973
It's Only Rock 'N Roll (But I Like It)—Rolling Stones (74)	936
As Tears Go By—Marianne Faithfull (64)	*926*
Happy—Rolling Stones (72)	891
Tell Me (You're Coming Back)—Rolling Stones (64)	793
Fool To Cry—Rolling Stones (76)	750
Rock And A Hard Place—Rolling Stones (89)	727
Wild Horses—Rolling Stones (71)	724
Satisfaction—Otis Redding (66)	*624*
She's So Cold—Rolling Stones (80)	599
Hot Stuff—Rolling Stones (76)	567
Let's Spend The Night Together—Rolling Stones (67)	*544*
Jumpin' Jack Flash—Aretha Franklin (86)	*527*
Hang Fire—Rolling Stones (82)	495
Shattered—Rolling Stones (78)	473
Street Fighting Man—Rolling Stones (68)	467
You Can't Always Get What You Want—Rolling Stones (73)	*462*
One Hit (To The Body)—Rolling Stones (86)	449
Lady Jane—Rolling Stones (66)	445
Ruby Tuesday—Melanie (70)	*414*
Lucky In Love—Mick Jagger (85)	377
We Love You—Rolling Stones (67)	336
That Girl Belongs To Yesterday—Gene Pitney (64)	317
Tumbling Dice—Linda Ronstadt (78)	*309*
Let's Work—Mick Jagger (87)	291
Waiting For That Day—George Michael (91)	248
You Can't Always Get What You Want—George Michael (91)	*248*
She Was Hot—Rolling Stones (84)	242
Ruthless People—Mick Jagger (86)	219
Almost Hear You Sigh—Rolling Stones (90)	209
Gimme Shelter—Grand Funk Railroad (71)	*207*
Highwire—Rolling Stones (91)	174
Throwaway—Mick Jagger (87)	113
Gimme Shelter—Merry Clayton (70)	*105*
Out Of Time—Rolling Stones (75)	74
Beast Of Burden—Bette Midler (84)	*71*
I'm Free—Soup Dragons (90)	48

All Down The Line—Rolling Stones (72)	43
The Last Time—Buchanan Brothers (69)	*38*
Sittin' On A Fence—Twice As Much (66)	19
Jumpin' Jack Flash—Johnny Winter (71)	*15*
Let's Spend The Night Together—David Bowie (73)	*7.4*
Play With Fire—Rolling Stones (65)	2.3
Under My Thumb—Del Shannon (66)	*1.4*
Under My Thumb—Hounds (80)	*1.0*
(I Can't Get No) Satisfaction—Tight Fit (81)	*0.9*
—Jim Jam see: James BROWN	
—Jimmy Jam see: James Samuel HARRIS	
James JAMERSON Jr. ► 4671 (1)	**442**
Don't Hold Back—Chanson (78)	884
Alex JAMES ► 9676 (1)	**19**
There's No Other Way—Blur (91)	77
—Arthur James see: James GRIFFIN	
Bob JAMES ► 8029 (3)	**64**
Celebrate Me Home—Kenny Loggins (78)	77
Theme From "Taxi" (Angela)—Bob James (79)	23
The Chicago Theme (Love Loop)—Hubert Laws (75)	3.2
Casey JAMES ► 2229 (6)	**1720**
Mama Can't Buy You Love—Elton John (79)	2115
Livin' It Up (Friday Night)—Bell & James (79)	1206
If You Wanna Do A Dance—Spinners (78)	168
Heaven On Earth (So Fine)—Spinners (77)	12
Easy Come, Easy Go—Spinners (78)	8.8
This Time Baby—Jackie Moore (79)	6.1
Cheryl JAMES [Salt] ► 3856 (2)	**674**
Expression—Salt-N-Pepa (90)	655
Backyard—Pebbles (91)	59
—Chris D. James see: Chris BOSTOCK	
Doug JAMES [Douglas Thomas James] ► 1547 (3)	**2751**
How Am I Supposed To Live Without You—Michael Bolton (89)	*4042*
How Am I Supposed To Live Without You—Laura Branigan (83)	*1366*
After You—Dionne Warwick (80)	95
—Douglas Thomas James see: Doug JAMES	
Elmore JAMES [Elmore Brooks] ► 10459 (2)	**8.2**
One Way Out—Allman Brothers Band (72)	18
It Hurts Me Too—Elmore James (65)	4.6
Etta JAMES [James Etta, Jamesetta Hawkins] ► 1787 (8)	**2326**
Dance With Me Henry (Wallflower)—Georgia Gibbs (55)	*5087*
Something's Got A Hold On Me—Etta James (62)	899
If I Can't Have You—Etta & Harvey (60)	659
Dance With Me Georgie—Bobbettes (60)	*2.5*
The Wallflower—Three Rays (55)	*0.0*
The Wallflower—Etta James & The Peaches (55)	*0.0*
The Wallflower (Dance With Me Henry)—Lee Winters (55)	*0.0*
The Italian Wallflower (I'll Dance With Her Henry)—Lou Monte (55)	*0.0*
—Freddy James see: Teddy POWELL	
Inez JAMES ► 6245 (3)	**190**
Vaya Con Dios—Drifters (64)	*412*
Vaya Con Dios—Dawn Featuring Tony Orlando (72)	*82*
Vaya Con Dios—Freddy Fender (76)	*75*
Jamie JAMES ► 7188 (1)	**111**
My Mistake—Kingbees (80)	111
Jesse JAMES ► 480 (9)	**8687**
The Horse—Cliff Nobles & Co. (68)	4506
Boogaloo Down Broadway—Fantastic Johnny C (67)	2711
Hitch It To The Horse—Fantastic Johnny C (68)	548
I Know I'm In Love—Chee-Chee And Peppy (71)	544
Got What You Need—Fantastic Johnny C (68)	256
Horse Fever—Cliff Nobles & Co. (68)	53
The Mule—James Boys (68)	50
Switch It On—Cliff Nobles & Co. (69)	18
Feel Good—Ike & Tina Turner (72)	4.4
Jimmy JAMES [Michael Francis James] ► 8478 (1)	**49**
Come To Me Softly—Jimmy James & The Vagabonds (68)	49
—Marguerite James see: Teddy POWELL	
Mark JAMES [Francis Zambon] ► 136 (19) HOF	**20012**
Suspicious Minds—Elvis Presley (69)	*6269*

Hooked On A Feeling—Blue Swede (74)	*5017*
Hooked On A Feeling—B.J. Thomas (68)	*3334*
Always On My Mind—Willie Nelson (82)	*2961*
One Hell Of A Woman—Mac Davis (74)	1579
Always On My Mind—Pet Shop Boys (88)	*1512*
The Eyes Of A New York Woman—B.J. Thomas (68)	893
It's Only Love—B.J. Thomas (69)	*616*
Moody Blue—Elvis Presley (76)	534
Raised On Rock—Elvis Presley (73)	463
Turn On A Dream—Box Tops (69)	449
Everybody Loves A Rain Song—B.J. Thomas (78)	280
It's Only Love—Elvis Presley (71)	*276*
Suspicious Minds—Dee Dee Warwick (71)	*123*
Pass The Apple Eve—B.J. Thomas (69)	50
Suspicious Minds—Elvis Presley (82)	*23*
Loving You Is A Natural Thing—Ronnie Milsap (70)	8.4
Sunday Sunrise—Anne Murray (75)	8.0
Roller Coaster—Blood, Sweat & Tears (73)	5.7
—Michael Francis James see: Jimmy JAMES	
Palmer JAMES ► 4629 (2)	**448**
Back Up Train—Al Greene & The Soul Mate's (67)	806
Hot Wire—Al Green (73)	45
Rick JAMES [James A. Johnson] ► 291 (18)	**12252**
Party All The Time—Eddie Murphy (85)	4492
In My House—Mary Jane Girls (85)	2199
U Can't Touch This—M.C. Hammer (90)	1930
Super Freak (Part I)—Rick James (81)	1318
You And I—Rick James (78)	1255
Give It To Me Baby—Rick James (81)	501
17—Rick James (84)	471
Cold Blooded—Rick James (83)	460
Ebony Eyes—Rick James feat. Smokey Robinson (83)	384
Mary Jane—Rick James (78)	364
Wild And Crazy Love—Mary Jane Girls (85)	283
Can't Stop—Rick James (85)	219
Dance Wit' Me - Part 1—Rick James (82)	191
Standing On The Top Part 1—Temptations Featuring Rick James (82)	125
Bustin' Out—Rick James (79)	82
High On Your Love Suite—Rick James (79)	39
Love Gun—Rick James (79)	18
I'm A Sucker For Your Love—Teena Marie (79)	8.7
Sonny JAMES [James Hugh Loden] ► 3505 (5)	**811**
Satin Pillows—Bobby Vinton (65)	985
Young Ideas—Chico Holiday (59)	294
You're The Only World I Know—Sonny James "The Southern Gentleman" (64)	33
Talk Of The School—Sonny James (59)	12
You Got That Touch—Sonny James (58)	4.0
Sylvester JAMES [Sylvester] ► 6445 (2)	**168**
You Make Me Feel (Mighty Real)—Sylvester (78)	*305*
You Make Me Feel (Mighty Real)—Jimmy Somerville (90)	*32*
Tim JAMES [Timothy James Auringer] ► 3095 (3)	**1012**
All This Time—Tiffany (88)	1620
After The Summer's Gone—PC Quest (91)	326
Can I Call You My Girl—PC Quest (91)	155
Tommy JAMES [Thomas Gregory Jackson] ► 156 (31)	**18872**
Crimson And Clover—Tommy James And The Shondells (68)	*9176*
Crystal Blue Persuasion—Tommy James And The Shondells (69)	6717
Draggin' The Line—Tommy James (71)	5158
Mony Mony—Tommy James And The Shondells (68)	*4671*
Mony Mony "Live"—Billy Idol (87)	*3728*
Tighter, Tighter—Alive And Kicking (70)	3353
Sweet Cherry Wine—Tommy James And The Shondells (69)	2151
Crimson And Clover—Joan Jett & The Blackhearts (82)	*1672*
Ball Of Fire—Tommy James And The Shondells (69)	1168
Sugar On Sunday—Clique (69)	1154
Three Times In Love—Tommy James (80)	1053
She—Tommy James And The Shondells (69)	869
Nothing To Hide—Tommy James (71)	663
Gotta Get Back To You—Tommy James And The Shondells (70)	636
I'm Comin' Home—Tommy James (71)	603
Come To Me—Tommy James And The Shondells (70)	437

Tommy JAMES [Thomas Gregory Jackson] ▶ 156 (31) *Continued*	**18872**
Love Song—Tommy James (72)	331
Ball And Chain—Tommy James (70)	327
Cat's Eye In The Window—Tommy James (72)	327
On A Sunday Afternoon— A Lighter Shade Of Brown (91)	320
Church Street Soul Revival—Tommy James (70)	311
Boo, Boo, Don't 'Cha Be Blue—Tommy James (73)	288
Tell 'Em Willie Boy 's A'Comin'—Tommy James (72)	159
You're So Easy To Love—Tommy James (81)	118
I'm Alive—Blue Swede (75)	92
Sparkle And Shine—Clique (70)	71
Celebration—Tommy James (72)	68
Mony Mony—Billy Idol (81)	*23*
Adrienne—Tommy James (71)	21
Calico—Tommy James (73)	4.3
Mony Mony—Tight Fit (81)	*0.9*
—Walter James see: Jim WALTERS	
Nick JAMESON ▶ 7749 (2)	**76**
Weatherman Says—Jack Wagner (87)	*120*
Weatherman—Nick Jameson (86)	*33*
Tom JAMESON ▶ 4470 (2)	**486**
Summertime Summertime—Jamies (58)	*580*
Summertime, Summertime—Jamies (62)	*393*
Henry JAMIPH ▶ 7238 (1)	**108**
Swing—Tokens (64)	108
Jimi JAMISON ▶ 9950 (1)	**15**
Man Against The World—Survivor (87)	44
Roosevelt JAMISON ▶ 8140 (1)	**60**
That's How Strong My Love Is—Otis Redding (65)	60
—Jam Master Jay see: Jason MIZELL	
—Lu Janis see: Dick MONDA	
Chaz JANKEL ▶ 5755 (1)	**245**
Ai No Corrida (I-No-Ko-ree-da)—Quincy Jones (81)	489
Horst JANKOWSKI ▶ 2062 (2)	**1939**
A Walk In The Black Forest—Horst Jankowski (65)	1860
Simpel Gimpel—Horst Jankowski (65)	158
Tom JANS ▶ 3269 (4)	**919**
My Mother's Eyes—Bette Midler (80)	451
Loving Arms—Doble Gray (73)	*435*
Satisfied Man—Molly Hatchet (84)	28
Loving Arms— Kris Kristofferson & Rita Coolidge (74)	*20*
Hans JANSEN ▶ 11376 (1)	**2.0**
Grasshopper—Spin (76)	4.0
Danny JANSSEN ▶ 363 (11)	**10583**
Little Woman—Bobby Sherman (69)	5391
La La La (If I Had You)—Bobby Sherman (69)	1986
Something's Wrong With Me—Austin Roberts (72)	1783
Keep On Singing—Helen Reddy (74)	*1390*
Could It Be Forever—David Cassidy (72)	870
Hey, Mister Sun—Bobby Sherman (70)	795
Sherry Don't Go—Lettermen (68)	477
Keep On Singing—Austin Roberts (73)	*409*
Friend And A Lover—Partridge Family Starring Shirley Jones & Featuring David Cassidy (73)	40
Words (Are Impossible)—Donny Gerrard (76)	*29*
Words (Are Impossible)—Margie Joseph (74)	*9.9*
—Hubert Janssen see: Jean SENN	
Myrna JANSSEN ▶ 6537 (1)	**159**
Sherry Don't Go—Lettermen (68)	477
Karin JANSSON ▶ 5644 (1)	**261**
Under The Milky Way—Church (88)	522
Ken JANZ ▶ 8979 (1)	**34**
Leaving L.A.—Deliverance (80)	69
Paul JANZ ▶ 8980 (1)	**34**
Leaving L.A.—Deliverance (80)	69
Herbert JARCZYK [Joe Jenkins] ▶ 6597 (3)	**153**
(I'm Always Hearing) Wedding Bells— Eddie Fisher (55)	*459*
(I'm Always Hearing) Wedding Bells— Frankie Lester (55)	*0.0*
(I'm Always Hearing) Wedding Bells— Guy Lombardo & His Royal Canadians (55)	*0.0*
—Max Jarczyk see: Michael JARY	
Alan JARDINE ▶ 5415 (3)	**292**
Almost Summer— Celebration Featuring Mike Love (78)	501
Friends—Beach Boys (68)	422

California Saga (On My Way To Sunny Californ-I-A)— Beach Boys (73)	19
Maurice JARRE ▶ 2829 (6)	**1168**
Somewhere, My Love— Ray Conniff And The Singers (66)	*1994*
Lara's Theme from "Dr. Zhivago"— Roger Williams (66)	*75*
Theme From Lawrence Of Arabia— Ferrante & Teicher (63)	*70*
Love Theme From Shogun (Mariko's Theme)— Meco (80)	25
Theme From Lawrence Of Arabia— Bernie Leighton (63)	*0.0*
Theme From Lawrence Of Arabia— Percy Faith and his Orchestra (63)	*0.0*
Al JARREAU ▶ 3943 (5)	**648**
Mornin'—Jarreau (83)	668
Moonlighting (Theme)—Al Jarreau (87)	480
Breakin' Away—Al Jarreau (81)	332
Boogie Down—Al Jarreau (83)	94
After All—Al Jarreau (84)	83
Phil JARRELL ▶ 1321 (1)	**3359**
Torn Between Two Lovers—Mary MacGregor (76)	6718
Earl JARRETT ▶ 7958 (1)	**67**
Another Puff—Jerry Reed (72)	134
Michael JARRETT ▶ 5712 (1)	**251**
I'm Leavin'—Elvis Presley (71)	503
Ted JARRETT ▶ 6347 (1)	**180**
You Can Make It If You Try—Gene Allison (57)	180
—Tommy Jarrett see: Thomas J. COE	
Felton JARVIS ▶ 10375 (1)	**9.3**
Piddle De Pat—Tommy Roe (62)	19
John JARVIS ▶ 9077 (1)	**32**
The Greatest Gift Of All— Kenny Rogers & Dolly Parton (84)	32
Michael JARY [Max Jarczyk, Maximilian Jarczyk] ▶ 2924 (2)	**1115**
Das Machen Nur Die Beine Von Dolores— Johnny Maddox And The Rhythmasters (55)	*1115*
Das Machen Nur Die Beine Von Dolores— Crazy Otto (55)	*0.0*
Peter JASON ▶ 11672 (1)	**0.7**
Marnie—Nat King Cole (64)	2.2
Chris JASPER ▶ 2921 (19)	**1116**
Fight The Power Part 1—Isley Brothers (75)	2590
For The Love Of You (Part 1 & 2)— Isley Brothers (75)	*696*
Don't Say Goodnight (It's Time For Love) (Parts 1 & 2)—Isley Brothers (80)	378
What It Comes Down To—Isley Brothers (73)	311
Caravan Of Love—Isley Jasper Isley (85)	310
Live It Up Part 1—Isley Brothers (74)	287
Livin' In The Life—Isley Brothers (77)	278
Need A Little Taste Of Love—Doobie Brothers (89)	273
Harvest For The World—Isley Brothers (76)	239
Who Loves You Better - Part 1—Isley Brothers (76)	186
Hurry Up And Wait—Isley Brothers (81)	171
Kiss And Tell—Isley, Jasper, Isley (85)	162
The Pride (Part 1)—Isley Brothers (77)	104
Take Me To The Next Phase—Isley Brothers (78)	92
Midnight Sky (Part 1)—Isley Brothers (75)	81
I Wanna Be With You (Part I)—Isley Brothers (79)	40
Inside You (Part 1)—Isley Brothers (81)	14
For The Love Of You—Houston Person (76)	*6.4*
It's A Disco Night (Rock Don't Stop)— Isley Brothers (79)	5.8
Joan JAVITS ▶ 7180 (5)	**111**
I Want Eddie Fisher For Christmas— Betty Johnson (54)	*176*
This Year's Santa Baby—Eartha Kitt (54)	51
My Bewildered Heart—Jaye P. Morgan (56)	11
Kitty Who—Kitty Kallen (55)	5.3
I Want Eddie Fisher For Christmas— Spike Jones with Linda Strangis (54)	*0.0*
—Sid Jaxon see: Sid WYCHE	
Eve JAY [Eve Jay Zeserson] ▶ 8783 (1)	**39**
You Forgot All The Words—Frank Sinatra (56)	79
Fred JAY [Fred Jacobsen, Friedrich Alex Jacobson] ▶ 1264 (12)	**3538**
I Cried A Tear—LaVern Baker (58)	2588
The Wedding—Julie Rogers (64)	1833

What Am I Living For—Conway Twitty (60)	*839*
What Am I Living For—Chuck Willis (58)	*788*
When A Child Is Born—Michael Holm (74)	369
Things I Didn't Do—Perry Como (54)	320
What Am I Living For—Ray Charles (71)	*315*
Give Me Your Love—Don Cornell (55)	148
Johnny Be Smart—Sarah Vaughan (55)	19
Oh My Lord—Boney M (78)	9.7
What Am I Living For—Percy Sledge (67)	*8.1*
Ma Baker—Boney M (77)	3.4
Michael JAY [Michael Jay Margules] ▶ 1820 (8)	**2268**
Toy Soldiers—Martika (89)	2662
More Than You Know—Martika (88)	867
Cross My Heart—Eighth Wonder (88)	325
The Right Combination— Seiko & Donnie Wahlberg (90)	224
Bounce Back—Alisha (90)	172
Dancing Under A Latin Moon—Candi (88)	163
If I Say Yes—Five Star (86)	120
Don't You Wanna Be Mine—Denise Lopez (90)	21
Penny JAY ▶ 9655 (1)	**19**
Don't Let Me Cross Over—Carl Butler (63)	19
—Jesse Jaymes see: Jesse Eric ITZLER	
—Jazzy Jeff see: Jeff TOWNES	
Jonathan JECZALIK ▶ 6665 (1)	**146**
Paranoimia— Art Of Noise with Max Headroom (86)	437
Dorothy JEFFERS ▶ 11180 (1)	**2.8**
Forty Two—Rusty Draper (56)	5.7
Joseph JEFFERSON ▶ 1023 (11)	**4317**
They Just Can't Stop It the (Games People Play)— Spinners (75)	4227
One Of A Kind (Love Affair)—Spinners (73)	1793
Mighty Love - Pt. I—Spinners (74)	1001
Love Don't Love Nobody - Pt. I—Spinners (74)	724
Love Or Leave—Spinners (75)	438
Sadie—Spinners (75)	314
Jealousy—Major Harris (76)	97
Aiming At Your Heart—Temptations (81)	85
Brandy—O'Jays (78)	85
Once You Hit The Road—Dionne Warwick (75)	84
I Got Over Love—Major Harris (76)	15
Lawrence JEFFERSON ▶ 9582 (1)	**21**
The Answer To A Maiden's Prayer—June Valli (59)	42
Thomas JEFFERSON ▶ 8033 (1)	**64**
The Declaration—5th Dimension (70)	192
William JEFFERY [William Jeffrey] ▶ 9608 (1)	**20**
Very Special—Debra Laws (81)	41
Frances JEFFORDS [Frances Adair] ▶ 9278 (2)	**27**
How Will I Know My Love—Annette (58)	*82*
How Will I Know My Love?—Lennon Sisters (58)	*0.0*
—Allan Jeffrey see: Irwin PINCUS	
—Joe Jeffrey see: Joe STAFFORD Jr.	
Nat JEFFREY ▶ 8216 (1)	**58**
Elena—Marc Tanner Band (79)	174
—William Jeffrey see: William JEFFERY	
Alan JEFFREYS ▶ 3817 (3)	**690**
Hopeless—Andy Williams (63)	1311
Sooner Or Later—Johnny Mathis (63)	47
I Feel That I've Known You Forever— Elvis Presley With The Jordanaires (65)	23
Garland JEFFREYS ▶ 10548 (1)	**7.4**
Wild In The Streets—British Lions (78)	15
—Jacek Jelen' see: Jack YELLEN	
Gerald JEMMOTT ▶ 6856 (1)	**132**
So Excited—B.B. King (70)	265
Barry JENKINS ▶ 2914 (5)	**1119**
San Franciscan Nights— Eric Burdon And The Animals (67)	1697
Sky Pilot (Part One)— Eric Burdon & The Animals (68)	1609
When I Was Young— Eric Burdon & The Animals (67)	1085
Monterey—Eric Burdon & The Animals (67)	1017
Anything—Eric Burdon & The Animals (68)	187
Craig JENKINS ▶ 11403 (1)	**1.9**
Trade Winds, Trade Winds—Aki Aleong (61)	5.6

David JENKINS ▶ 1180 (7)	**3761**
Whatcha Gonna Do?—Pablo Cruise (77)	2803
Love Will Find A Way—Pablo Cruise (78)	2597
Cool Love—Pablo Cruise (81)	1056
I Want You Tonight—Pablo Cruise (79)	841
Don't Want To Live Without It—Pablo Cruise (78)	793
Never Had A Love—Pablo Cruise (78)	42
Slip Away—Pablo Cruise (81)	35
—Deidre Yvonne Jenkins see: Deidra BROWN	
Derek JENKINS ▶ 8362 (1)	**53**
Got A Love For You—Jomanda (91)	318
Donald JENKINS ▶ 6897 (1)	**130**
(Native Girl) Elephant Walk—Donald Jenkins & The Delighters (63)	260
—Frances Ralston Jenkins see: Mike TERRY	
Gordon JENKINS ▶ 3100 (13) HOF	**1010**
This Is All I Ask—Tony Bennett (63)	*298*
This Is All I Ask—Burl Ives (63)	*221*
Repeat After Me—Patti Page (56)	*160*
Never Leave Me—Dick Roman (56)	*99*
Never Leave Me—Dick Haymes (56)	*99*
New York's My Home—Sammy Davis Jr. (56)	86
Married I Can Always Get—Teddi King (56)	*35*
Good-Bye—Bob Manning (55)	11
P. S. I Love You—Classics (2) (63)	2.7
Never Leave Me—Lancers (56)	*0.0*
Married I Can Always Get—Jeri Southern (56)	*0.0*
Repeat After Me—Gordon Jenkins & His Orchestra (56)	*0.0*
Married I Can Always Get—Gordon Jenkins & His Orchestra (56)	*0.0*
Gus JENKINS ▶ 5657 (4)	**259**
Tricky—Ralph Marterie And His Orchestra (57)	*228*
Chittlins—Gus Jenkins (64)	23
Tricky—Gus Jenkins (56)	*7.0*
Tricky—Rhythm Rockers Featuring Chet Atkins (57)	*0.0*
—Harold L. Jenkins see: Conway TWITTY	
—Joe Jenkins see: Herbert JARCZYK	
Marsha JENKINS ▶ 7200 (1)	**110**
Kissing You—Keith Washington (91)	331
Steve JENKINS ▶ 7688 (1)	**80**
Brown Paper Bag—Syndicate Of Sound (70)	80
Tomi JENKINS ▶ 2482 (6)	**1447**
Word Up—Cameo (86)	1982
Candy—Cameo (86)	604
She's Strange—Cameo (84)	325
Back And Forth—Cameo (87)	195
Freaky Dancin'—Cameo (81)	40
We're Goin' Out Tonight—Cameo (80)	13
Bob JENNINGS ▶ 6540 (1)	**159**
Lay Some Happiness On Me—Dean Martin (67)	317
Dick JENNINGS ▶ 6293 (2)	**185**
Little Ole Wine Drinker, Me—Dean Martin (67)	*365*
Little Old Wine Drinker Me—Robert Mitchum (67)	*3.9*
Waylon JENNINGS ▶ 2007 (4)	**2007**
Theme From The Dukes Of Hazzard (Good Ol' Boys)—Waylon (80)	1454
Good Hearted Woman—Waylon & Willie (76)	653
Are You Sure Hank Done It This Way—Waylon Jennings (75)	156
Just To Satisfy You—Waylon & Willie (82)	141
Will JENNINGS ▶ 183 (23) HOF	**16704**
Up Where We Belong—Joe Cocker and Jennifer Warnes (82)	5012
Higher Love—Steve Winwood (86)	4547
Roll With It—Steve Winwood (88)	4539
Didn't We Almost Have It All—Whitney Houston (87)	3593
I'll Never Love This Way Again—Dionne Warwick (79)	3458
Looks Like We Made It—Barry Manilow (77)	3436
The Finer Things—Steve Winwood (87)	1736
Don't You Know What The Night Can Do?—Steve Winwood (88)	1713
While You See A Chance—Steve Winwood (81)	1658
Valerie—Steve Winwood (87)	1522
Somewhere In The Night—Barry Manilow (78)	*1230*
Holding On—Steve Winwood (88)	1174
Back In The High Life Again—Steve Winwood (87)	1076
Somewhere In The Night—Helen Reddy (75)	*918*
No Night So Long—Dionne Warwick (80)	723
Freedom Overspill—Steve Winwood (86)	661
Boys Night Out—Timothy B. Schmit (87)	539

Still In The Game—Steve Winwood (82)	300
Talking Back To The Night—Steve Winwood (88)	228
Somewhere In The Night—Batdorf & Rodney (75)	*94*
Valerie—Steve Winwood (82)	86
If Love Must Go—Dobie Gray (76)	34
I'm So Glad I'm Standing Here Today—Crusaders (81)	3.1
Harry JENSEN ▶ 4299 (1)	**530**
Troglodyte (Cave Man)—Jimmy Castor Bunch (72)	3177
Henry JEROME [Al Mortimer] ▶ 2713 (3)	**1251**
For The Love Of Him—Bobbi Martin (70)	2119
Give A Woman Love—Bobbi Martin (70)	128
I Love You So—Bobbi Martin (65)	127
—John Jerome see: Harold FIELDS	
—John Jerome see: Howard Ellington Riddiford BARNES	
M.K. JEROME ▶ 11331 (1)	**2.2**
Some Sunday Morning—Wayne Newton (65)	6.6
Patti JEROME ▶ 7907 (1)	**70**
What You See Is What You Get—Stoney And Meatloaf (71)	140
Ray JESSEL ▶ 5870 (2)	**235**
All—James Darren (67)	507
Married Man—Richard Burton (65)	216
—Nick Jesson see: Nick LOCKWOOD	
Philip JESSON ▶ 8733 (1)	**41**
Burning Flame—Vitamin Z (85)	122
Jack JESSUP ▶ 5609 (3)	**265**
What A Price—Fats Domino (61)	733
Nothing New (Same Old Thing)—Fats Domino (62)	52
Rockin' Bicycle—Fats Domino (61)	22
—Jethro see: Kenneth BURNS	
Joan JETT [Joan Marie Larkin] ▶ 2366 (5)	**1557**
I Hate Myself For Loving You—Joan Jett and the Blackhearts (88)	1501
Little Liar—Joan Jett and the Blackhearts (88)	911
Fake Friends—Joan Jett & The Blackhearts (83)	407
House Of Fire—Alice Cooper (90)	215
Good Music—Joan Jett And The Blackhearts (86)	80
Mark JIARAS ▶ 7480 (1)	**93**
The Truth—Tami Show (91)	466
Jimmie JILES ▶ 4448 (1)	**493**
Leaving Me—Independents (73)	986
Charlie JIMENEZ ▶ 6450 (1)	**168**
Dream Boy-Dream Girl—Cynthia & Johnny O. (90)	168
—José Jimenez see: Bill DANA	
Virginia JIRIK ▶ 11063 (1)	**3.5**
High Tide Boogie—Richard Maltby And His Orchestra (55)	6.9
—Jivin' Gene see: Gene BOURGEOIS	
Lionel JOB ▶ 6582 (1)	**154**
Keep It Comin'—Keith Sweat (91)	925
Steve JOBE ▶ 5467 (1)	**283**
Where Were You When I Was Falling In Love—Lobo (79)	848
Chuck JOBES ▶ 9248 (1)	**28**
Barbara, I Love You—New Colony Six (69)	83
Antonio Carlos JOBIM ▶ 1440 (10) HOF	**3034**
The Girl From Ipanema—Getz/Gilberto (64)	2656
Desafinado—Stan Getz/Charlie Byrd (62)	*1912*
Meditation (Meditaçao)—Charlie Byrd (63)	*207*
Desafinado (Slightly Out Of Tune)—Pat Thomas (62)	*41*
Quiet Nights Of Quiet Stars—Andy Williams (65)	23
Meditation (Meditaçao)—Pat Boone (63)	*11*
Meditation (Meditacao)—Claudine Longet (66)	*3.8*
Desafinado—Si Zentner And His Orchestra (62)	*0.0*
Desafinado (Slightly Out Of Tune)—Ella Fitzgerald (62)	*0.0*
Meditation (Meditaçao)—Billy Vaughn And His Orchestra (63)	*0.0*
Billy JOEL ▶ 27 (37) HOF	**52367**
It's Still Rock And Roll To Me—Billy Joel (80)	7270
My Life—Billy Joel (78)	4667
Uptown Girl—Billy Joel (83)	4498
Just The Way You Are—Billy Joel (77)	4420
We Didn't Start The Fire—Billy Joel (89)	4142
Tell Her About It—Billy Joel (83)	3772
You May Be Right—Billy Joel (80)	1981
I Go To Extremes—Billy Joel (90)	1511
Allentown—Billy Joel (82)	1460

The Longest Time—Billy Joel (84)	1317
An Innocent Man—Billy Joel (83)	1301
You're Only Human (Second Wind)—Billy Joel (85)	1244
Modern Woman—Billy Joel (86)	1098
A Matter Of Trust—Billy Joel (86)	1071
Movin' Out (Anthony's Song)—Billy Joel (78)	980
She's Always A Woman—Billy Joel (78)	976
Don't Ask Me Why—Billy Joel (80)	916
Piano Man—Billy Joel (74)	912
Big Shot—Billy Joel (79)	911
This Is The Time—Billy Joel (86)	868
Say Goodbye To Hollywood—Billy Joel (81)	803
Keeping The Faith—Billy Joel (85)	743
Pressure—Billy Joel (82)	742
Honesty—Billy Joel (79)	695
Only The Good Die Young—Billy Joel (78)	644
She's Got A Way—Billy Joel (81)	621
Leave A Tender Moment Alone—Billy Joel (84)	590
The Entertainer—Billy Joel (74)	528
The Night Is Still Young—Billy Joel (85)	373
Sometimes A Fantasy—Billy Joel (80)	351
And So It Goes—Billy Joel (90)	300
The Downeaster "Alexa"—Billy Joel (90)	165
Goodnight Saigon—Billy Joel (83)	130
That's Not Her Style—Billy Joel (90)	129
Travelin' Prayer—Billy Joel (74)	117
Baby Grand—Billy Joel (87)	60
Worse Comes To Worst—Billy Joel (74)	59
—Bruce Anthony Johannesson see: C.C. DeVILLE	
David JOHANSEN ▶ 10631 (1)	**6.6**
Melody—David Johansen (79)	13
Darlynn JOHN ▶ 6704 (1)	**143**
Walk Slow—Little Willie John (60)	285
—Dominic John see: Joseph RONCORONI	
Elton JOHN [Reginald Kenneth Dwight, Ann Orson] ▶ 37 (51) HOF	**46707**
Crocodile Rock—Elton John (72)	6901
Philadelphia Freedom—Elton John Band (75)	6474
Don't Go Breaking My Heart—Elton John And Kiki Dee (76)	6364
Island Girl—Elton John (75)	5893
Bennie And The Jets—Elton John (74)	5459
Little Jeannie—Elton John (80)	4655
Goodbye Yellow Brick Road—Elton John (73)	4555
Daniel—Elton John (73)	4279
Don't Let The Sun Go Down On Me—Elton John (74)	*4278*
Someone Saved My Life Tonight—Elton John (75)	3538
Don't Let The Sun Go Down On Me—George Michael (91)	*3346*
I Don't Wanna Go On With You Like That—Elton John (88)	2894
I Guess That's Why They Call It The Blues—Elton John (83)	2690
Your Song—Elton John (70)	2412
The Bitch Is Back—Elton John (74)	2289
Sorry Seems To Be The Hardest Word—Elton John (76)	2125
Rocket Man—Elton John (72)	2111
Sad Songs (Say So Much)—Elton John (84)	1892
Candle In The Wind—Elton John (87)	1744
Saturday Night's Alright For Fighting—Elton John (73)	1637
Nikita—Elton John (86)	1603
Blue Eyes—Elton John (82)	1448
I'm Still Standing—Elton John (83)	1238
Honky Cat—Elton John (72)	1232
Empty Garden (Hey Hey Johnny)—Elton John (82)	1190
Healing Hands—Elton John (89)	1070
Levon—Elton John (71)	875
Sacrifice—Elton John (90)	860
Wrap Her Up—Elton John (85)	852
Part-Time Love—Elton John (78)	822
Grow Some Funk Of Your Own—Elton John (76)	803
Friends—Elton John (71)	742
Who Wears These Shoes?—Elton John (84)	739
A Word In Spanish—Elton John (88)	673
Border Song (Holy Moses)—Aretha Franklin (70)	*643*
Kiss The Bride—Elton John (83)	583
Club At The End Of The Street—Elton John (90)	549
Tiny Dancer—Elton John (72)	461
In Neon—Elton John (84)	451
Chloe—Elton John (81)	446
Ego—Elton John (78)	432

Elton JOHN [Reginald Kenneth Dwight, Ann Orson] ▶ 37 (51) HOF *Continued*	**46707**
I Feel Like A Bullet (In The Gun Of Robert Ford)—Elton John (76)	423
You Gotta Love Someone—Elton John (90)	372
Bite Your Lip (Get Up And Dance!)—Elton John (77)	320
(Sartorial Eloquence) Don't Ya Wanna Play This Game No More?—Elton John (80)	310
Heartache All Over The World—Elton John (86)	221
Border Song—Elton John (70)	*98*
The Rumour—Olivia Newton-John (88)	97
Step Into Christmas—Elton John (73)	40
Bad Side Of The Moon—April Wine (72)	19
Snookeroo—Ringo Starr (75)	0.0
Little Willie JOHN ▶ 5638 (4)	**262**
Walk Slow—Little Willie John (60)	285
Leave My Kitten Alone—Little Willie John (61)	*154*
Leave My Kitten Alone—Johnny Preston (61)	*113*
Leave My Kitten Alone—Little Willie John (59)	*91*
Mertis JOHN ▶ 10666 (1)	**6.3**
Take My Love (I Want To Give It All To You)—Little Willie John (61)	6.3
Robert JOHN [Robert John Pedrick] ▶ 631 (7)	**6852**
Sad Eyes—Robert John (79)	6529
If You Don't Want My Love—Robert John (68)	553
When The Party Is Over—Robert John (70)	142
California Kid And Reemo—Lobo (71)	97
I Can't Move No Mountains—Blood, Sweat & Tears (72)	26
Give A Little—Robert John (78)	8.6
We Can Make The World—Gravy (71)	4.8
Djuana JOHNICAN [Suhayla Sabir, Sweet L.D.] ▶ 9824 (1)	**16**
Turn It Up—Oaktown's 3.5.7 (91)	49
Carolyn JOHNS ▶ 8281 (1)	**56**
If It Don't Fit, Don't Force It—Kellee Patterson (77)	111
Sammy JOHNS ▶ 1501 (2)	**2877**
Chevy Van—Sammy Johns (75)	2456
Early Morning Love—Sammy Johns (74)	421
Julius JOHNSEN ▶ 8034 (1)	**64**
The Declaration—5th Dimension (70)	192
Alvin JOHNSON ▶ 8109 (1)	**61**
Castin' My Spell—Johnny Otis Show (59)	123
—Anne Spear Johnson see: Anne SPEAR	
Arnold JOHNSON ▶ 11301 (1)	**2.3**
Does Your Heart Beat For Me—Betty Johnson (59)	7.0
Augie JOHNSON ▶ 11217 (1)	**2.7**
Let's Dance (Make Your Body Move)—West Street Mob (81)	30
Austin JOHNSON ▶ 11224 (1)	**2.7**
Playing Your Game, Baby—Barry White (78)	5.3
Bill JOHNSON ▶ 11013 (1)	**3.9**
You Can't Go Halfway—Johnny Nash (74)	15
—Bob Johnson see: Robert White JOHNSON	
Brenda JOHNSON [Brenda L. Thompson] ▶ 9452 (1)	**23**
Back For A Taste Of Your Love—Syl Johnson (73)	70
Brian JOHNSON ▶ 4831 (4)	**403**
You Shook Me All Night Long—AC/DC (80)	530
Back In Black—AC/DC (80)	471
Let's Get It Up—AC/DC (82)	184
Guns For Hire—AC/DC (83)	25
—Brooks O'Dell Johnson see: Brooks O'DELL	
—Bubber Johnson see: Robert Bubber JOHNSON	
Bud JOHNSON Jr. ▶ 5925 (1)	**227**
No, No, No—Chanters (61)	227
Candy JOHNSON ▶ 10081 (1)	**13**
Blip Blop—Bill Doggett (58)	13
Charles Icarus JOHNSON [Charles Foster Johnson] ▶ 8013 (1)	**65**
Reach For It—George Duke (77)	261
—Charles Foster Johnson see: Charles Icarus JOHNSON	
Clarence JOHNSON ▶ 8499 (2)	**48**
In My Heart—Timetones (61)	86
Deserie—Charts (57)	10
Clarence JOHNSON Jr. ▶ 4113 (2)	**589**
Love Jones—Brighter Side Of Darkness (72)	*1485*
How Can I Tell My Mom And Dad—Lovelites (70)	188

Claude JOHNSON ▶ 1688 (4)	**2484**
What's Your Name—Don & Juan (62)	*2292*
Who's That Knocking—Genies (59)	272
What's Your Name—Andy & David Williams (74)	*44*
Magic Wand—Don & Juan (62)	12
Cliff JOHNSON ▶ 5849 (1)	**237**
Stay In Time—Off Broadway USA (80)	237
Donna JOHNSON ▶ 7796 (1)	**75**
Heart Don't Lie—La Toya Jackson (84)	224
Doug JOHNSON ▶ 9683 (1)	**19**
Lead A Double Life—Loverboy (86)	114
—Dr. Marguerite Ann Johnson see: Maya ANGELOU	
Earl King JOHNSON [Earl Silas Johnson IV, Earl King, Pearl King] ▶ 793 (10)	**5598**
I Hear You Knocking—Gale Storm (55)	*5135*
One Night—Elvis Presley (58)	4905
I Hear You Knocking—Dave Edmunds (70)	*3442*
What A Party—Fats Domino (61)	553
Do-Re-Mi—Lee Dorsey (61)	553
Witchcraft—Elvis Presley With The Jordanaires (63)	500
I Hear You Knocking—Fats Domino (61)	*29*
Teasin' You—Willie Tee (65)	14
My Heart Is Bleeding—Fats Domino (62)	1.6
I Hear You Knocking—Smiley Lewis (55)	*0.0*
Edwin JOHNSON ▶ 8110 (1)	**61**
Castin' My Spell—Johnny Otis Show (59)	123
Emanuel JOHNSON ▶ 5174 (2)	**331**
Gloria—Enchantment (77)	511
Sunshine—Enchantment (77)	151
Enotris JOHNSON ▶ 2014 (6)	**2001**
Long Tall Sally—Little Richard (56)	*1982*
Long Tall Sally—Pat Boone (56)	*1222*
Jenny Jenny—Little Richard (57)	*932*
Jenny, Jenny—Mitch Ryder And The Detroit Wheels (65)	*728*
Long Tall Sally—Cat Mother And The All Night News Boys (69)	*164*
Miss Ann—Little Richard (57)	97
Eric JOHNSON ▶ 7577 (2)	**88**
Ain't Gonna Hurt Nobody—Kid 'N Play (91)	*223*
All Through The Night—Tone Loc (91)	39
Errison JOHNSON [King Errison, Errison Pallman Johnson] ▶ 9611 (1)	**20**
Darling Come Back Home—Eddie Kendricks (73)	61
—Errison Pallman Johnson see: Errison JOHNSON	
Frank L. JOHNSON ▶ 6236 (1)	**191**
We're Getting Careless With Our Love—Johnnie Taylor (74)	382
Fred JOHNSON ▶ 3587 (5)	**775**
All In My Mind—Maxine Brown (60)	*1336*
Stop The Wedding—Etta James (62)	706
Old Spanish Town—Bell Notes (59)	183
Don't Stop The Wedding—Ann Cole (62)	10
All In My Mind—Dakota Staton (61)	*0.0*
—Frederic Homer Johnson Jr. see: Keg JOHNSON	
Garry JOHNSON [Jellybean Johnson] ▶ 7007 (2)	**122**
Why Should I Cry?—Nona Hendryx (87)	183
Criticize—Alexander O'Neal (87)	122
General JOHNSON [Norman Earl Johnson] ▶ 443 (21)	**9287**
Want Ads—Honey Cone (71)	6401
Patches—Clarence Carter (70)	5109
Somebody's Been Sleeping—100 Proof Aged In Soul (70)	2587
Bring The Boys Home—Freda Payne (71)	2168
Stick-Up—Honey Cone (71)	2010
Pay To The Piper—Chairmen Of The Board (70)	1695
One Monkey Don't Stop No Show Part 1—Honey Cone (71)	1447
The Day I Found Myself—Honey Cone (72)	906
You've Got To Crawl (Before You Walk)—8th Day (71)	724
It Will Stand—Showmen (61)	*391*
Everything Good Is Bad—100 Proof Aged In Soul (72)	364
Finder's Keepers—Chairmen Of The Board (73)	201
If I Could See The Light—8th Day (71)	97
Men Are Getting Scarce—Chairmen Of The Board (71)	66
I Can't Be You (You Can't Be Me)—Glass House (70)	60
One Man's Leftovers (Is Another Man's Feast)—100 Proof Aged In Soul (71)	54

Let's Fool Around—General Johnson (77)	45
It Will Stand—Showmen (64)	*30*
Sittin' On A Time Bomb (Waitin' For The Hurt To Come)—Honey Cone (72)	23
39-21-46—Showmen (67)	12
Crying Like A Baby—Jive Five (67)	3.3
George JOHNSON ▶ 1972 (8)	**2043**
I'll Be Good To You—Brothers Johnson (76)	*2385*
Stomp!—Brothers Johnson (80)	1785
I'll Be Good To You—Quincy Jones (89)	*782*
Get The Funk Out Ma Face—Brothers Johnson (76)	586
Struttin'—Billy Preston (74)	553
Is It Love That We're Missin'—Quincy Jones (75)	141
The Real Thing—Brothers Johnson (81)	133
Tomorrow (A Better You, Better Me)—Quincy Jones featuring Tevin Campbell (90)	72
—Grace Johnson see: Grace SLICK	
Gregory JOHNSON ▶ 9826 (2)	**16**
I Just Want To Be—Cameo (79)	31
It's Serious—Cameo (78)	1.8
Harold JOHNSON ▶ 4927 (1)	**379**
You're A Special Part Of Me—Diana Ross & Marvin Gaye (73)	1138
Hazel JOHNSON ▶ 6179 (1)	**197**
It's Too Late, Baby Too Late—Arthur Prysock (65)	394
Hiram JOHNSON ▶ 4520 (3)	**472**
Could This Be Magic—Dubs (57)	551
Baby Oh Baby—Shells (60)	542
Don't Ask Me (To Be Lonely)—Dubs (57)	32
Holly JOHNSON ▶ 3672 (5)	**741**
Relax—Frankie Goes To Hollywood (84)	*658*
Relax (Mix)—Frankie Goes To Hollywood (85)	*583*
Two Tribes—Frankie Goes To Hollywood (84)	469
Welcome To The Pleasuredome (Trevor Horn Remix)—Frankie Goes To Hollywood (85)	239
Love Train—Holly Johnson (89)	111
Horace JOHNSON ▶ 10299 (1)	**10**
Who Are You—B.B. King (74)	21
Howard JOHNSON ▶ 9594 (3) HOF	**21**
What Do You Want To Make Those Eyes At Me For—Ray Peterson (60)	*62*
What Do You Want To Make Those Eyes At Me For?—Sunny Gale (60)	*0.0*
What Do You Want To Make Those Eyes At Me For—Kenny Rankin (60)	*0.0*
Howard Williams JOHNSON ▶ 6762 (1)	**139**
If You Want It—Niteflyte (79)	278
Hoyt JOHNSON ▶ 11337 (1)	**2.2**
You're The Nearest Thing To Heaven—Johnny Cash And The Tennessee Two (58)	6.6
J. George JOHNSON ▶ 10260 (1)	**11**
Only The Broken Hearted—Bob Beckham (60)	21
James E. JOHNSON ▶ 2982 (5)	**1084**
Stranded In The Jungle—Cadets (56)	*810*
The Watusi—Vibrations (61)	657
Stranded In The Jungle—Jayhawks (56)	*531*
Stranded In The Jungle—Gadabouts (56)	*198*
Feel So Bad—Ray Charles (71)	190
James P. JOHNSON ▶ 5270 (4) HOF	**315**
The Charleston—Ernie Fields Orch. (61)	*411*
Don't Cry, Baby—Etta James (61)	*323*
Don't Cry, Baby—Aretha Franklin (62)	*4.0*
Charleston—Cozy Cole (61)	*0.0*
—James A. Johnson see: Rick JAMES	
Janice JOHNSON ▶ 1147 (2)	**3876**
Boogie Oogie Oogie—A Taste Of Honey (78)	7729
Do It Good—Taste Of Honey (79)	23
Jay JOHNSON ▶ 11387 (2)	**1.9**
Blue Christmas—Elvis Presley (57)	*2.1*
Blue Christmas—Browns Featuring Jim Edward Brown (60)	*1.7*
—Jellybean Johnson see: Garry JOHNSON	
Jesse Woods JOHNSON ▶ 1994 (7)	**2022**
Jungle Love—Time (84)	911
Everybody Dance—Ta Mara & The Seen (85)	794
Nights Like This—After 7 (91)	402
Crazay—Jesse Johnson (86)	330
Be Your Man—Jesse Johnson's Revue (85)	248
Love Struck—Jesse Johnson (88)	75
I Want My Girl—Jesse Johnson's Revue (85)	72

Jimmy JOHNSON [James Earl Thompson] ▶ 6266 (1)	**188**
Don't Answer The Door Part 1—B.B. King (66)	375
—Jimmy Johnson see: Jimmy Ray JOHNSON	
Jimmy Ray JOHNSON [Jimmy Johnson] ▶ 10153 (1)	**12**
Up Tight, Good Man—Laura Lee (67)	36
J.J. JOHNSON ▶ 7016 (1)	**121**
Across 110th Street— (Performed By Bobby Womack & Peace) (73)	243
Joan Marie JOHNSON ▶ 4829 (3)	**404**
Iko Iko—Belle Stars (89)	*940*
Iko Iko—Dixie Cups (65)	*854*
Iko Iko—Dr. John (72)	*226*
Joe JOHNSON ▶ 10030 (1)	**14**
Rock-A-Lott—Aretha Franklin (87)	42
Keg JOHNSON [Frederic Homer Johnson Jr.] ▶ 10409 (1)	**8.8**
I've Got The Next Dance—Deniece Williams (79)	26
Kevin JOHNSON ▶ 2964 (3)	**1094**
Rock N' Roll (I Gave You The Best Years Of My Life)— Mac Davis (74)	*949*
Rock 'N Roll (I Gave You The Best Years Of My Life)— Kevin Johnson (73)	*135*
Rock 'N Roll (I Gave You The Best Years Of My Life)— Terry Jacks (74)	*9.0*
Kinrod Charles JOHNSON ▶ 8180 (1)	**59**
Rubber Biscuit—Blues Brothers (79)	297
Larry JOHNSON ▶ 6221 (2)	**192**
I'm Gonna Miss You—Artistics (66)	479
Love Song—Artistics (67)	65
—Larry Curtis Johnson see: Maurice STARR	
Leonerist JOHNSON ▶ 6946 (1)	**126**
"B" Girls—Young & Restless (90)	253
Louis A. JOHNSON ▶ 4652 (1)	**445**
Sweet Love—Anita Baker (86)	1336
Louis E. JOHNSON ▶ 2038 (7)	**1972**
I'll Be Good To You—Brothers Johnson (76)	*2385*
Stomp!—Brothers Johnson (80)	1785
I'll Be Good To You—Quincy Jones (89)	*782*
Get The Funk Out Ma Face—Brothers Johnson (76)	586
Struttin'—Billy Preston (74)	553
The Real Thing—Brothers Johnson (81)	133
Tomorrow (A Better You, Better Me)— Quincy Jones featuring Tevin Campbell (90)	72
L.V. JOHNSON ▶ 8902 (1)	**36**
Are You Serious—Tyrone Davis (82)	73
Margaret JOHNSON [Margaret Gordy] ▶ 7584 (2)	**87**
I Promise To Wait My Love— Martha Reeves & The Vandellas (68)	345
I Truly, Truly Believe—Temptations (68)	3.6
Martha JOHNSON ▶ 8330 (1)	**54**
Black Stations/White Stations—M+M (84)	108
Marv JOHNSON ▶ 3289 (4)	**911**
Give Your Baby A Standing Ovation—Dells (73)	807
Come To Me—Marv Johnson (59)	*755*
Ain't Gonna Be That Way—Marv Johnson (60)	259
Come To Me—Frances Burnett (59)	*0.0*
—Michael Edwin Johnson see: Michael JONZUN	
—Mirriam Johnson see: Jessi COLTER	
—Norman Earl Johnson see: General JOHNSON	
Paul Morais JOHNSON ▶ 11502 (1)	**1.4**
Name And Number—Big Noise (89)	4.2
Ralph JOHNSON ▶ 8356 (1)	**53**
Let Me Talk—Earth, Wind & Fire (80)	319
Raymond JOHNSON ▶ 9000 (1)	**34**
Why Leave Us Alone—Five Special (79)	101
—Rick Johnson see: Gordon RITTER	
Robert JOHNSON ▶ 3256 (1)	**924**
Crossroads—Cream (69)	924
—Robert Johnson see: Robert Bubber JOHNSON	
Robert Bubber JOHNSON [Bubber Johnson, Robert Johnson] ▶ 9990 (3)	**14**
Come Home—Bubber Johnson (55)	*14*
Come Home—Eydie Gorme (56)	*0.0*
Come Home—Arthur Prysock (56)	*0.0*
Robert Earl JOHNSON ▶ 7079 (1)	**117**
I'll Love You Forever—Holidays (66)	352

Robert White JOHNSON [, Bob Johnson, Robert Albin Johnson] ▶ 2566 (4)	**1375**
Where Does My Heart Beat Now—Celine Dion (90)	2564
Comin' Down Tonight—38 Special (89)	167
99 Worlds—Peter Wolf (90)	104
It's Gettin' Late—Beach Boys (85)	48
—Robert Albin Johnson see: Robert White JOHNSON	
Roy Lee JOHNSON ▶ 8868 (1)	**37**
Mr. Moonlight—Beatles (65)	37
Sid JOHNSON [Sidney DeWayne, Sidney DeWayne Johnson] ▶ 4743 (1)	**426**
Two Occasions—Deele (88)	1277
Simone Antoinette JOHNSON [Monie Love, Simone Wilson, D J Pogo] ▶ 7627 (1)	**84**
It's A Shame (My Sister)—Monie Love (91)	420
Steve JOHNSON ▶ 11519 (1)	**1.4**
Rock Creek Park—Blackbyrds (76)	6.8
Syl JOHNSON [Sylvester Johnson, Sylvester Thompson] ▶ 8170 (3)	**60**
Is It Because I'm Black—Syl Johnson (69)	95
Back For A Taste Of Your Love—Syl Johnson (73)	70
Come On Sock It To Me—Syl Johnson (67)	14
Ted JOHNSON ▶ 9684 (1)	**19**
Lead A Double Life—Loverboy (86)	114
Terry JOHNSON ▶ 2911 (5)	**1121**
Baby, Baby Don't Cry— Smokey Robinson & The Miracles (69)	2458
Here I Go Again— Smokey Robinson & The Miracles (69)	281
Malinda—Bobby Taylor & The Vancouvers (68)	254
Lovers Never Say Goodbye—Flamingos (58)	228
Mio Amore—Flamingos (60)	196
Thurlene JOHNSON ▶ 10427 (1)	**8.6**
Honey I'm Rich—Raydio (78)	17
Tommy JOHNSON ▶ 4416 (1)	**500**
On The Road Again—Canned Heat (68)	1500
Troy JOHNSON ▶ 7030 (1)	**121**
Cover Of Love—Michael Damian (89)	482
Valerie JOHNSON ▶ 4642 (1)	**446**
Stomp!—Brothers Johnson (80)	1785
Virgil JOHNSON ▶ 3285 (1)	**912**
Tonight (Could Be The Night)—Velvets (61)	912
Walter JOHNSON ▶ 4677 (1)	**440**
Your Love—Marilyn McCoo And Billy Davis Jr. (77)	879
William Luther JOHNSON ▶ 10112 (1)	**13**
Tuxedo Junction—Frankie Avalon (60)	51
Woodrow Buddy JOHNSON ▶ 898 (8)	**4934**
Since I Fell For You—Lenny Welch (63)	*4149*
Baby, Don't You Cry (The New Swingova Rhythm)— Ray Charles And His Orchestra (64)	390
Since I Fell For You—Laura Lee (72)	*258*
Since I Fell For You—Charlie Rich (76)	*83*
I Don't Want Nobody (To Have My Love But You)— Woody Herman and His Orchestra (56)	*28*
I Don't Want Nobody (To Have My Love But You)—Ella Johnson With Buddy Johnson And His Orchestra (60)	*20*
Since I Fell For You—Hodges, James & Smith (77)	*3.9*
It's Ordacious— Buddy Johnson and His Orchestra (55)	2.0
Steve JOHNSTAD ▶ 7790 (1)	**75**
I Wanna Be Loved—House Of Lords (88)	150
Arthur JOHNSTON ▶ 4874 (1) HOF	**393**
Pennies From Heaven—Skyliners (60)	786
Bob JOHNSTON ▶ 5664 (2)	**257**
Look What You've Done—Pozo-Seco Singers (66)	512
Pretty Little Pearly—Click-Clacks (58)	2.5
Bruce JOHNSTON ▶ 577 (5)	**7508**
I Write The Songs—Barry Manilow (75)	7247
Rendezvous—Hudson Brothers (75)	557
Beach Girl—Pat Boone (64)	119
Gee, But I'm Lonesome—Ron Holden (60)	43
Gone—Rip Chords (63)	38
Diane JOHNSTON ▶ 11548 (1)	**1.2**
Pretty Little Pearly—Click-Clacks (58)	2.5
—John Harold Johnston see: Johnny REINE	
Joy Byers JOHNSTON [Joy Byers] ▶ 1903 (11)	**2132**
What's A Matter Baby (Is It Hurting You)—Timi Yuro (62)	*1256*
Ring Dang Doo— Sam The Sham And The Pharaohs (65)	725

It Hurts Me— Elvis Presley With The Jordanaires (64)	437
When You Loved Me—Brenda Lee (64)	397
Wishing It Was You—Connie Francis (65)	313
Let Yourself Go— Elvis Presley With The Jordanaires (68)	263
Please Don't Stop Loving Me—Elvis Presley (66)	237
Here Comes Heaven—Eddy Arnold (67)	104
What's A Matter Baby—Ellen Foley (79)	*31*
C'mon Everybody—Elvis Presley (64)	1.1
(No, No) I'm Losing You—Aretha Franklin (65)	0.5
—Karen Michelle Johnston see: Michelle SHOCKED	
Robert L. JOHNSTON ▶ 10632 (1)	**6.6**
Carrie's Gone—J.C. Stone (74)	6.6
Tom JOHNSTON ▶ 624 (9)	**6925**
Long Train Runnin'—Doobie Brothers (73)	1978
China Grove—Doobie Brothers (73)	1533
Listen To The Music—Doobie Brothers (72)	1453
The Doctor—Doobie Brothers (89)	977
Another Park, Another Sunday—Doobie Brothers (74)	568
Savannah Nights—Tom Johnston (79)	473
Eyes Of Silver—Doobie Brothers (74)	304
Sweet Maxine—Doobie Brothers (75)	259
Nobody—Doobie Brothers (74)	161
Davey JOHNSTONE ▶ 2631 (3)	**1306**
I Guess That's Why They Call It The Blues— Elton John (83)	2690
Wrap Her Up—Elton John (85)	852
Grow Some Funk Of Your Own—Elton John (76)	803
Phil JOHNSTONE ▶ 5053 (3)	**353**
Tall Cool One—Robert Plant (88)	586
Hurting Kind (I've Got My Eyes On You)— Robert Plant (90)	248
Ship Of Fools—Robert Plant (88)	22
Craig JOINER ▶ 6631 (3)	**149**
Heaven In The Back Seat—Eddie Money (91)	176
Don't Break My Heart—Romeo's Daughter (88)	105
I Cry Myself To Sleep At Night— Romeo's Daughter (89)	26
James JOINER ▶ 2446 (4)	**1483**
Fallen Star—Jimmy Newman (57)	*636*
Fallen Star—Ferlin Husky (57)	*536*
Fallen Star—Hilltoppers (57)	*311*
Fallen Star—Nick Noble (57)	*0.0*
—Jokern see: Nils PERNE	
David JOLICOEUR ▶ 8642 (1)	**44**
Me Myself And I—De La Soul (89)	353
Bernard JOLIVETTE ▶ 3766 (1)	**706**
This Should Go On Forever—Rod Bernard (59)	1411
Steve JOLLEY ▶ 4808 (6)	**409**
Cruel Summer—Bananarama (84)	1392
A Trick Of The Night—Bananarama (86)	115
The Wild Life—Bananarama (84)	104
Shy Boy (Don't It Make You Feel Good)— Bananarama (83)	74
Love Resurrection—Alison Moyet (85)	44
Robert DeNiro's Waiting—Bananarama (84)	4.7
Keith JOLLIMORE ▶ 7263 (1)	**107**
Take It Slow (Out In The Country)—Lighthouse (71)	320
Pete JOLLY [Peter A. Ceragioli Jr.] ▶ 10782 (1)	**5.3**
Little Bird—Pete Jolly Trio and Friends (63)	11
Al JOLSON ▶ 7904 (2)	**70**
Me And My Shadow— Frank Sinatra And Sammy Davis Jr. (62)	203
Anniversary Song—Mulcays (56)	7.0
Addie Williams JONES ▶ 9750 (1)	**18**
Hey America— James Brown And The Famous Flames (70)	35
—Agnes Jones see: Bobby SHARP	
Al JONES ▶ 10585 (1)	**7.1**
Old Enough To Love—Rick Nelson (63)	21
Allen Alvoid JONES Jr. ▶ 2215 (18)	**1730**
Keep On Dancing—Gentrys (65)	3698
Hard To Handle—Black Crowes (91)	*595*
Ain't That Loving You (For More Reasons Than One)— Luther Ingram (70)	*442*
Son Of Shaft—Bar-Kays (71)	349
Hard To Handle—Black Crowes (90)	*279*
Move Your Boogie Body—Bar-Kays (79)	270

Allen Alvoid JONES Jr. ▶ 2215 (18) *Cont'd*	**1730**
Today Is The Day—Bar-Kays (80)	150
Hard To Handle—Otis Redding (68)	*114*
Ain't That Loving You (For More Reasons Than One)—Isaac Hayes & David Porter (72)	*110*
Freakshow On The Dance Floor—Bar-Kays (84)	79
Don't Have To Shop Around—Mad Lads (65)	78
Hit And Run—Bar-Kays (81)	23
Boogie Body Land—Bar-Kays (81)	23
Somebody's Sleeping In My Bed—Johnnie Taylor (67)	9.8
Let's Have Some Fun—Bar-Kays (78)	8.9
Hard To Handle—Patti Drew (68)	*7.7*
Shine—Bar-Kays (79)	7.7
Memphis At Sunrise—Bar-Kays (72)	7.6
Andrew JONES ▶ 3174 (3)	**971**
When You Dance—Turbans (55)	*672*
When You Dance—Jay & The Americans (69)	*299*
When You Dance—Laurie Sisters (55)	*0.0*
Biff JONES ▶ 2145 (5)	**1819**
Suddenly There's A Valley—Gogi Grant (55)	*1757*
Suddenly There's A Valley—Jo Stafford (55)	*1118*
Suddenly There's A Valley—Julius La Rosa (55)	*522*
Suddenly There's A Valley—Mills Brothers (55)	*194*
Suddenly There's A Valley—Patty Andrews (55)	*47*
Bill JONES ▶ 10586 (1)	**7.1**
Old Enough To Love—Rick Nelson (63)	21
—Billy Jones see: Billy STORM	
Bob JONES ▶ 10467 (1)	**8.1**
Boss—Rumblers (63)	48
Booker T. JONES Jr. ▶ 1004 (33)	**4437**
Green Onions—Booker T. & The M.G.'s (62)	*4924*
Time Is Tight—Booker T. & The M.G.'s (69)	2035
To Be A Lover—Billy Idol (86)	1625
Soul-Limbo—Booker T. & The M.G.'s (68)	1495
Hip Hug-Her—Booker T. & The M.G.'s (67)	719
Hole In The Wall—Packers (65)	689
I Forgot To Be Your Lover—William Bell (69)	558
I've Never Found A Girl (To Love Me Like You Do)—Eddie Floyd (68)	*437*
California Girl—Eddie Floyd (70)	426
Melting Pot—Booker T. & The M.G.'s (71)	365
My Sweet Potato—Booker T. & The M.G.'s (66)	119
I Love You More Than Words Can Say—Otis Redding (67)	113
I Got A Sure Thing—Ollie & The Nightingales (68)	110
Private Number—Judy Clay & William Bell (68)	99
Jellybread—Booker T. & The MGs (62)	74
My Crew—Rita Coolidge (73)	72
Don't Tell Your Mama (Where You've Been)—Eddie Floyd (69)	69
A Tribute To A King—William Bell (68)	66
Slim Jenkin's Place—Booker T. & The M.G.'s (67)	64
Chinese Checkers—Booker T. & The MG's (63)	63
Everybody Loves A Winner—William Bell (67)	39
I've Never Found A Man (To Love Me Like You Do)—Esther Phillips (72)	*37*
Knucklehead—Bar-Kays (67)	34
Why Is The Wine Sweeter (On The Other Side)—Eddie Floyd (69)	30
Green Onions—Dick Hyman (69)	*23*
Every Man Oughta Have A Woman—William Bell (68)	20
The Hunter—Ike & Tina Turner (69)	12
All God's Children Got Soul—Dorothy Morrison (69)	8.0
Evergreen—Booker T. (74)	7.6
Soul Dressing—Booker T. & The MG's (64)	4.4
Mo-Onions—Booker T. & The MG's (64)	3.7
Pop-Eye Stroll—Mar-Keys (62)	3.1
Born Under A Bad Sign—William Bell (69)	0.5
Brenda Lee JONES ▶ 4104 (2)	**591**
Tra La La La Suzy—Dean And Jean (63)	718
The Majestic—Dion (61)	465
Brian JONES ▶ 11714 (1)	**0.5**
Play With Fire—Rolling Stones (65)	2.3
—Brian Keith Jones see: Hakim Rashad MUHAMMAD	
Bucky JONES ▶ 8446 (1)	**50**
Only One You—T.G. Sheppard (82)	100
Charles JONES ▶ 10166 (1)	**12**
How Did We Lose It Baby—Jerry Butler (71)	24
Charles R. JONES ▶ 5874 (1)	**234**
I Love You Madly—Four Coins (54)	234

—Charlie Jones see: Stephen Charles JONES	
Chico JONES ▶ 8027 (1)	**64**
Somebody's Gettin' It—Johnnie Taylor (76)	193
Clarence JONES ▶ 11631 (1)	**0.9**
Born To Get Down (Born To Get Around)—Muscle Shoals Horns (76)	1.9
Columbia JONES ▶ 7428 (1)	**96**
Just Another Day In Paradise—Bertie Higgins (82)	289
—Curt Jones see: George Curtis JONES	
Darrell JONES ▶ 7287 (1)	**105**
Heroes—Commodores (80)	211
David H. JONES ▶ 3496 (4)	**818**
Love Me For A Reason—Osmonds (74)	1275
That's How Love Goes—Jermaine Jackson (72)	467
We've Come Too Far To End It Now—Smokey Robinson & The Miracles (72)	421
I Can't Stand To See You Cry—Smokey Robinson & The Miracles (72)	290
David P. JONES ▶ 6552 (5)	**157**
Soldier Boy—Ella Fitzgerald (55)	*315*
Soldier Boy—Pat O'Day (55)	*0.0*
Soldier Boy—Sunny Gale (55)	*0.0*
Soldier Boy—Eydie Gorme (55)	*0.0*
Soldier Boy—Four Fellows (55)	*0.0*
—David Robert Jones see: David BOWIE	
Don JONES ▶ 10263 (1)	**11**
Happy Feet Time—Monclairs (65)	11
Dory JONES ▶ 8900 (1)	**36**
Rubberneckin'—Elvis Presley (69)	73
Eddie JONES [Guitar Slim] ▶ 10431 (2)	**8.6**
The Things That I Used To Do—James Brown (64)	5.8
If My Heart Could Speak—Manhattans (70)	5.6
Elvin JONES ▶ 7893 (1)	**71**
It's Wonderful To Be In Love—Ovations (Featuring Louis Wiliams) (65)	212
Emridge JONES [Blitz] ▶ 6722 (1)	**142**
Serious—Donna Allen (87)	852
Evan JONES ▶ 5408 (1)	**293**
Pushbike Song—Mixtures (71)	585
Floyd JONES ▶ 4407 (2)	**503**
On The Road Again—Canned Heat (68)	1500
Help For My Waiting—Dorians (71)	9.0
Fred O. JONES ▶ 6796 (1)	**136**
Who's That Knocking—Genies (59)	272
—Frederick Joseph Jones see: Rick JONES	
—Gale Jones see: Ramona REDD	
George JONES [George Glenn Jones] ▶ 10288 (3)	**10**
Who Shot Sam—George Jones (59)	20
Take Me—Brenda Lee (67)	7.4
Why Baby Why—Red Sovine & Webb Pierce (57)	0.0
George Wydell JONES Jr. [George Jones Jr.] ▶ 3369 (1)	**877**
Rama Lama Ding Dong—Edsels (61)	877
George Curtis JONES [Curt Jones] ▶ 9333 (1)	**26**
Make Up Your Mind—Aurra (82)	78
—George Jones Jr. see: George Wydell JONES Jr.	
Glenn JONES ▶ 7873 (1)	**71**
We've Only Just Begun (The Romance Is Not Over)—Glenn Jones (87)	143
Gloria JONES [LaVerne Ware] ▶ 1835 (5)	**2230**
If I Were Your Woman—Gladys Knight & The Pips (70)	2652
My Mistake (Was To Love You)—Diana Ross & Marvin Gaye (74)	961
Just Seven Numbers (Can Straighten Out My Life)—Four Tops (71)	547
Haven't Stopped Dancing Yet—Gonzalez (79)	457
Take Me Girl, I'm Ready—Jr. Walker & The All Stars (71)	403
Gordon JONES ▶ 7818 (1)	**74**
Innocent—Whispers (90)	221
Grace JONES ▶ 7087 (4)	**116**
I'm Not Perfect (But I'm Perfect For You)—Grace Jones (86)	168
Pull Up To The Bumper—Grace Jones (81)	62
Sorry—Grace Jones (77)	17
That's The Trouble—Grace Jones (77)	17
Harold JONES ▶ 5628 (1)	**263**
Special Someone—Heywoods (72)	263

Herman JONES ▶ 11125 (1)	**3.1**
Take It Off Him And Put It On Me—Clarence Carter (70)	15
Hilliard JONES ▶ 5329 (1)	**304**
Daughter—Blenders (63)	304
Howard JONES ▶ 436 (10)	**9405**
No One Is To Blame—Howard Jones (86)	2569
Things Can Only Get Better—Howard Jones (85)	2132
You Know I Love You...Don't You?—Howard Jones (86)	1128
Everlasting Love—Howard Jones (89)	1092
Life In One Day—Howard Jones (85)	695
New Song—Howard Jones (84)	629
The Prisoner—Howard Jones (89)	557
What Is Love?—Howard Jones (84)	506
Like To Get To Know You Well—Howard Jones (85)	267
All I Want—Howard Jones (87)	84
Idris JONES ▶ 5409 (1)	**293**
Pushbike Song—Mixtures (71)	585
Isham JONES ▶ 4770 (5) HOF	**419**
I'll See You In My Dreams—Pat Boone (62)	*540*
There Is No Greater Love—Wanderers (62)	133
On The Alamo—Norman Petty Trio (54)	77
Swingin' Down The Lane—Jerry Wallace (60)	44
I'll See You In My Dreams—Seymour & His Heartbeat Trumpet (58)	*44*
James Leonard JONES ▶ 4511 (4)	**474**
The Philly Freeze—Alvin Cash & The Registers (66)	531
Alvin's Boo-Ga-Loo—Alvin Cash & The Registers (66)	155
Is It Because I'm Black—Syl Johnson (69)	95
Tired Of Being Lonely—Sharpees (66)	44
Jerry JONES ▶ 6469 (1)	**166**
The Touch Of You—Brenda & The Tabulations (70)	331
Jill JONES ▶ 5572 (1)	**270**
Get Me To The World On Time—Electric Prunes (67)	540
Jimmy JONES ▶ 1715 (3)	**2447**
Handy Man—Jimmy Jones (59)	*5670*
Handy Man—James Taylor (77)	*3089*
Handy Man—Del Shannon (64)	*1029*
Joe JONES ▶ 2044 (2)	**1957**
You Talk Too Much—Joe Jones & His Orchestra (60)	*3885*
You Talk Too Much—Frankie Ford (60)	*29*
Joe C. JONES ▶ 7656 (2)	**82**
To Be Loved (Forever)—Pentagons (61)	391
I Wonder (If Your Love Will Ever Belong To Me)—Pentagons (61)	21
John Paul JONES [John Paul Baldwin, John Baldwin] ▶ 1602 (11)	**2640**
Whole Lotta Love—Led Zeppelin (69)	*4704*
Black Dog—Led Zeppelin (71)	*1455*
D'yer Mak'er—Led Zeppelin (73)	1260
Fool In The Rain—Led Zeppelin (79)	673
Trampled Under Foot—Led Zeppelin (75)	436
Rock And Roll—Led Zeppelin (72)	411
Whole Lotta Love—C.C.S. (71)	*247*
Whole Lotta Love—King Curtis & The Kingpins (71)	*230*
Good Times Bad Times—Led Zeppelin (69)	160
Black Dog—Newcity Rockers (87)	*89*
Whole Lotta Love—Wonder Band (79)	*8.7*
—Juggy Jones see: Henry MURRAY	
Kevin JONES [Kevin T. Jones, Kipper Jones] ▶ 6462 (2)	**166**
The Right Stuff—Vanessa Williams (88)	233
The Comfort Zone—Vanessa Williams (91)	99
—Kipper Jones see: Kevin JONES	
Lee JONES ▶ 8068 (2)	**63**
I Ain't Got To Love Nobody Else—Masqueraders (68)	175
(Call Me) The Traveling Man—Masqueraders (76)	23
Marshall JONES ▶ 1873 (15)	**2174**
Love Rollercoaster—Ohio Players (75)	5251
Fire—Ohio Players (74)	4114
Funky Worm—Ohio Players (73)	1438
Skin Tight—Ohio Players (74)	1151
Who'd She Coo?—Ohio Players (76)	885
Ecstasy—Ohio Players (73)	621
Sweet Sticky Thing—Ohio Players (75)	411
Fopp—Ohio Players (76)	398
I Want To Be Free—Ohio Players (75)	335
Jive Turkey (Part 1)—Ohio Players (74)	245
Pain (Part 1)—Ohio Players (71)	208
O-H-I-O—Ohio Players (77)	144

Marshall JONES ▶ 1873 (15) *Continued*	**2174**
Feel The Beat (Everybody Disco)—Ohio Players (77)	42
Got Pleasure—Ohio Players (72)	14
Rattlesnake—Ohio Players (76)	12
Maxine JONES ▶ 3872 (2)	**671**
Hold On—En Vogue (90)	3351
Lies—En Vogue (90)	676
Michael JONES [Kashif Saleem, Kashif] ▶ 2144 (4)	**1821**
Love Come Down—Evelyn King (82)	732
I'm In Love—Evelyn King (81)	420
Inside Love (So Personal)—George Benson (83)	350
Betcha She Don't Love You—Evelyn King (83)	319
Michael Geoffrey JONES ▶ 3558 (4)	**786**
Rock The Casbah—Clash (82)	1940
Train In Vain (Stand By Me)—Clash (80)	752
Should I Stay Or Should I Go?—Clash (82)	*243*
Should I Stay Or Should I Go?—Clash (83)	*210*
Michael Leslie JONES ▶ 97 (23) HOF	**25188**
Waiting For A Girl Like You—Foreigner (81)	8009
I Want To Know What Love Is—Foreigner (84)	4867
Hot Blooded—Foreigner (78)	3751
Urgent—Foreigner (81)	3141
Double Vision—Foreigner (78)	2677
Feels Like The First Time—Foreigner (77)	2362
Cold As Ice—Foreigner (77)	2348
Say You Will—Foreigner (87)	1610
I Don't Want To Live Without You—Foreigner (88)	1495
That Was Yesterday—Foreigner (85)	1231
Head Games—Foreigner (79)	1218
Dirty White Boy—Foreigner (79)	979
Blue Morning, Blue Day—Foreigner (78)	838
Long, Long Way From Home—Foreigner (77)	679
Rush—Big Audio Dynamite II (91)	464
Break It Up—Foreigner (82)	452
Juke Box Hero—Foreigner (82)	447
Women—Foreigner (80)	275
Reaction To Action—Foreigner (85)	214
Heart Turns To Stone—Foreigner (88)	209
Down On Love—Foreigner (85)	198
Luanne—Foreigner (82)	44
Bad Love—Eric Clapton (90)	38
Mike JONES ▶ 8960 (1)	**35**
Monsters And Angels—Voice Of The Beehive (91)	106
Monroe JONES ▶ 5635 (1)	**262**
Yeah, Yeah, Yeah—Judson Spence (88)	524
Nat JONES ▶ 2942 (8)	**1109**
Bring It Up—James Brown And The Famous Flames (67)	556
Ain't That A Groove Part 1—James Brown And The Famous Flames (66)	496
Money Won't Change You Part 1—James Brown And The Famous Flames (66)	493
Don't Be A Drop-Out—James Brown And The Famous Flames (66)	443
Tit For Tat (Ain't No Taking Back)—James Brown (68)	189
Hey America—James Brown And The Famous Flames (70)	35
Sweet Little Baby Boy—James Brown And The Famous Flames (66)	4.6
New Breed (Part 1) (The Boo-Ga-Loo)—James Brown (66)	0.5
Ollie JONES ▶ 499 (18)	**8449**
Tiger—Fabian (59)	*2838*
Send For Me—Nat "King" Cole And The Four Knights (57)	2670
Step By Step—Crests (60)	1484
I'll Be There—Damita Jo (61)	897
Model Girl—Johnny Maestro The Voice Of The Crests (61)	600
Love Makes The World Go 'round—Perry Como (58)	570
My Love—Nat King Cole-Stan Kenton (60)	568
Build Your Love (On A Strong Foundation)—Johnnie Ray (57)	390
(It Never Happens) In Real Life—Chuck Jackson (61)	209
My Anxious Heart—Four Coins (55)	36
Teenage Meeting (Gonna Rock It Up Right)—Don Cornell (56)	*24*
Midnight—Hugo Winterhalter's Orch. & Chorus (58)	12
Love's A Hurting Game—Ivory Joe Hunter (57)	12
Impossible—Gloria Lynne (61)	7.2
Happy Pair—Ames Brothers (60)	5.0
Cross Over—Jimmy Bowen With The Rhythm Orchids (57)	4.6
Tiger—Nick Todd (59)	*0.0*
Teenage Meeting (Gonna Rock It Up Right)—Dave Appell & His Applejacks (56)	*0.0*
—Ora Denise Jones see: Denise LaSALLE	
—Paul Laurence Jones see: Paul LAURENCE	
Phalon JONES ▶ 5554 (2)	**272**
Soul Finger—Bar-Kays (67)	1546
Give Everybody Some—Bar-Kays (67)	97
—Priscilla Jones see: Priscilla COOLIDGE	
Quincy JONES ▶ 1850 (12)	**2200**
Love Is In Control (Finger On The Trigger)—Donna Summer (82)	1455
P.Y.T. (Pretty Young Thing)—Michael Jackson (83)	1161
Yah Mo B There—James Ingram (83)	906
Stuff Like That—Quincy Jones (78)	787
Get The Funk Out Ma Face—Brothers Johnson (76)	586
In The Heat Of The Night—Ray Charles (67)	495
The Secret Garden (Sweet Seduction Suite)—Quincy Jones featuring Al B. Sure!, James Ingram, El DeBarge & Barry White (90)	416
You Put It On Me—B.B. King (68)	159
Money Runner—Quincy Jones (72)	152
Motherland—Quincy Jones (77)	80
The B.B. Jones—B.B. King (68)	26
Hikky Burr - Part One—Bill Cosby With The Bunions Bradford Band (69)	12
Ralph JONES ▶ 9971 (1)	**14**
Lean Jean—Bill Haley And His Comets (58)	58
Ray JONES ▶ 9649 (1)	**20**
Operator—Gladys Knight & The Pips (62)	59
Raymond C. JONES ▶ 2781 (2)	**1199**
Stay With Me Tonight—Jeffrey Osborne (83)	831
The Borderlines—Jeffrey Osborne (85)	368
Reginald JONES ▶ 9013 (1)	**33**
I'll Be There—Joyce "Fenderella" Irby (90)	99
Richard M. JONES ▶ 8892 (2)	**37**
Trouble In Mind—Aretha Franklin (62)	*24*
Trouble In Mind—Nina Simone (61)	*12*
Rick JONES [Frederick Joseph Jones] ▶ 2538 (2)	**1406**
Couldn't Get It Right—Climax Blues Band (77)	2219
I Can Take Or Leave Your Loving—Herman's Hermits (68)	962
Rickie Lee JONES ▶ 1341 (5)	**3305**
Chuck E.'s In Love—Rickie Lee Jones (79)	2790
Young Blood—Rickie Lee Jones (79)	326
A Lucky Guy—Rickie Lee Jones (81)	158
The Real End—Rickie Lee Jones (84)	21
Danny's All-Star Joint—Rickie Lee Jones (79)	9.6
Rose Ella JONES ▶ 6052 (3)	**211**
Virgin Man—Smokey Robinson (74)	213
Quiet Storm—Smokey Robinson (76)	112
Daylight And Darkness—Smokey Robinson (78)	97
—Ruth Lee Jones see: Dinah WASHINGTON	
Shanti JONES ▶ 5036 (1)	**356**
Strange But True—Times Two (88)	711
Stan JONES ▶ 1350 (9)	**3284**
Wringle Wrangle—Fess Parker (57)	*823*
(Ghost) Riders In The Sky—Ramrods (60)	*803*
Wringle Wrangle—Bill Hayes (57)	*750*
(Ghost) Riders In The Sky—Outlaws (80)	*437*
Ghost Riders In The Sky—Baja Marimba Band (66)	*294*
Riders In The Sky—Lawrence Welk And His Orchestra and Chorus (61)	*177*
Wringle Wrangle—Rex Allen (57)	*0.0*
Wringle Wrangle—Merv Griffin (57)	*0.0*
Wringle Wrangle—Vaughn Monroe (57)	*0.0*
Stephen JONES ▶ 4820 (2)	**405**
Take It Easy—Andy Taylor (86)	695
When The Rain Comes Down—Andy Taylor (86)	116
Stephen Charles JONES [Charlie Jones] ▶ 8462 (1)	**50**
Hurting Kind (I've Got My Eyes On You)—Robert Plant (90)	248
Steven Leslie JONES ▶ 6410 (1)	**173**
Days Like These—Asia (90)	173
Thomas Earl JONES III ▶ 4175 (3)	**574**
Old Time Rock & Roll—Bob Seger & The Silver Bullet Band (79)	*498*
Old Time Rock & Roll—Bob Seger & The Silver Bullet Band (83)	*336*
Make You Feel Love Again—Wet Willie (78)	314
Tom JONES ▶ 2209 (5) HOF	**1738**
My Cup Runneth Over—Ed Ames (67)	2403
Try To Remember—Gladys Knight & The Pips (75)	*957*
Try To Remember—Ed Ames (65)	*101*
Try To Remember—Brothers Four (65)	*8.3*
Try To Remember—Roger Williams (65)	*6.9*
William Harlin JONES ▶ 11268 (1)	**2.5**
Take It Any Way You Want It—Outlaws (78)	5.1
—William Hamlin Jones see: Billy STORM	
Michael JONZUN [Michael Edwin Johnson] ▶ 4818 (4)	**406**
Candy Girl—New Edition (83)	387
You Better Dance—Jets (89)	167
Oo-Ee-Diddley-Bop!—Peter Wolf (85)	107
Is This The End—New Edition (83)	20
Janis JOPLIN ▶ 4458 (4)	**491**
Kozmic Blues—Janis Joplin (69)	435
Down On Me—Big Brother And The Holding Company (68)	*395*
(Oh Lord Won't You Buy Me A) Mercedes Benz—Goose Creek Symphony (72)	152
Down On Me—Janis Joplin (72)	*51*
Scott JOPLIN ▶ 1107 (1) HOF	**4001**
The Entertainer—Marvin Hamlisch (74)	4001
Archie JORDAN ▶ 3676 (4)	**740**
It Was Almost Like A Song—Ronnie Milsap (77)	1242
It's All I Can Do—Anne Murray (81)	158
What A Difference You've Made In My Life—Ronnie Milsap (77)	27
I Never Said I Love You—Orsa Lia (79)	26
Brad JORDAN ▶ 7335 (1)	**101**
Mind Playing Tricks On Me—Geto Boys (91)	405
Danny JORDAN ▶ 9486 (1)	**23**
Ann-Marie—Belmonts (63)	46
—Danny Jordan see: Gerard FLORIO	
Dave JORDAN ▶ 7528 (1)	**91**
One More Minute—Saint Tropez (79)	182
David JORDAN ▶ 10032 (2)	**14**
I Have Learned To Do Without You—Mavis Staples (70)	41
I Don't Wanna Leave You—Debbie Taylor (76)	0.4
Dazz JORDAN [John Bernard Toorish] ▶ 4489 (3)	**481**
My Little Angel—Four Lads (56)	577
The Mocking Bird—Four Lads (58)	*370*
The Mocking Bird—Four Lads (56)	*15*
Ellington JORDAN ▶ 6003 (2)	**217**
I'd Rather Go Blind—Sydney Youngblood (90)	265
Talking About My Baby—Gloria Walker (68)	255
—Etterlene Jordan see: Bunny DeBARGE	
Fred JORDAN ▶ 9304 (1)	**27**
Belle—Al Green (77)	80
Joe JORDAN [Robert Joseph Jordan, Ronnie Jordan] ▶ 3755 (3)	**709**
Ka Ding Dong—Hilltoppers (56)	*506*
Ka Ding Dong—G-Clefs (56)	*467*
Ka Ding Dong—Diamonds (56)	*445*
Juanita JORDAN ▶ 4161 (2)	**577**
Daisy Petal Pickin'—Jimmy Gilmer And The Fireballs (63)	1293
Ain't Gonna Tell Anybody—Jimmy Gilmer and The Fireballs (64)	293
—Leroy Jordan see: Lonnie JORDAN	
Lonnie JORDAN [Leroy Jordan] ▶ 1237 (21)	**3621**
Spill The Wine—Eric Burdon And War (70)	*5207*
The Cisco Kid—War (73)	4378
Why Can't We Be Friends?—War (75)	3006
Low Rider—War (75)	2369
Slippin' Into Darkness—War (71)	*2076*
The World Is A Ghetto—War (72)	1817
Gypsy Man—War (73)	1659
Summer—War (76)	1559
Me And Baby Brother—War (73)	1513
All Day Music—War (71)	704

Lonnie JORDAN [Leroy Jordan] ▶ 1237 (21) *Continued*	**3621**
Ballero—War (74)	472
They Can't Take Away Our Music—Eric Burdon And War Featuring Sharon Scott And The Beautiful New Born Children Of Southern California (70)	418
Spill The Wine—Isley Brothers (71)	*409*
Galaxy—War (77)	325
L.A. Sunshine—War (77)	291
Low Rider (On The Boulevard)—Latin Alliance (91)	121
Lonely Feelin'—War (71)	74
You Got The Power—War (82)	35
Slipping Into Darkness—Ramsey Lewis (72)	*35*
Good, Good Feelin'—War (79)	12
Outlaw—War (82)	10
Louis JORDAN ▶ 8984 (3)	**34**
Is You Is Or Is You Ain't My Baby—Buster Brown (60)	37
Early In The Mornin'—Ray Charles (61)	22
Never Trust A Woman—B.B. King (64)	17
Marc JORDAN ▶ 2222 (2)	**1728**
Rhythm Of My Heart—Rod Stewart (91)	3022
Pieces Of Ice—Diana Ross (83)	434
Max JORDAN ▶ 11341 (1)	**2.1**
Every Day And Every Night—Trolls (66)	4.3
Perry JORDAN ▶ 9272 (1)	**27**
Music Eyes—Heartsfield (74)	27
—Ronnie Jordan see: Joe JORDAN	
Roy JORDAN ▶ 7164 (3)	**112**
The Greatest Feeling In The World—Four Tunes (54)	184
I'll Never Know—Four Lads (56)	33
My Love's A Gentle Man—Dorothy Collins (55)	7.7
Steve JORDAN ▶ 7916 (1)	**70**
Almost Hear You Sigh—Rolling Stones (90)	209
—Terrence P. Jordan see: Terry MELCHER	
Thomas J. JORDAN ▶ 10298 (3)	**10**
Red Head—Cloverleafs (55)	*7.9*
Red Head—Cliff Steward And His Boro Lounge Boys (55)	*7.9*
Red Head—Somethin' Smith & The Redheads (56)	*4.9*
—Jörn K see: Joern Volsgaard KRISTENSEN	
Joe JOSEA [Joe Bihari] ▶ 2980 (14)	**1085**
Cherry Pie—Skip & Flip (60)	1582
Oop-Shoop—Crew-Cuts (54)	643
Rock Me Baby—B.B. King (64)	519
Sweet Sixteen—B.B. King (72)	98
The Girl In My Dreams—Cliques (56)	*39*
The Woman I Love—B.B. King (68)	19
The Jungle—B.B. King (67)	11
Truly—Dinning Sisters Featuring Jean Dinning (55)	9.6
Partin' Time—B.B. King (60)	5.1
Girl In My Dreams—Capris (61)	*4.0*
That Evil Child—B.B. King (71)	3.0
Be Careful With A Fool—B.B. "Blues Boy" King and His Orchestra (57)	1.8
Got A Right To Love My Baby—B.B. King (60)	0.4
The Girl In My Dreams—Four Lovers (56)	*0.0*
Daniel JOSEPH ▶ 6193 (1)	**195**
Murphy's Law—Cheri (82)	390
Joe JOSEPH ▶ 9331 (2)	**26**
Baby You're So Fine—Mickey And Sylvia (61)	*100*
Gee Baby—Joe & Ann (60)	*2.4*
Quinton JOSEPH ▶ 5912 (3)	**230**
We Need Order—Chi-Lites (72)	206
Dance Master Pt. 1—Willie Henderson (74)	153
We Are Neighbors—Chi-Lites (71)	100
—Ray Joseph see: Larry SHAYNE	
Tony JOSEPH ▶ 10068 (1)	**13**
All Through The Night—Tone Loc (91)	39
Curtis JOSEPHS ▶ 7067 (1)	**118**
Yo' Little Brother—Nolan Thomas (85)	236
Lou JOSIE ▶ 953 (4)	**4681**
Midnight Confessions—Grass Roots (68)	3992
Hey Harmonica Man—Stevie Wonder (64)	555
We Can Make Music—Tommy Roe (70)	397
What Makes Little Girls Cry—Victorians (63)	14
Marty JOURARD ▶ 7768 (1)	**76**
Take The L.—Motels (82)	228
Michel JOURDAN ▶ 8922 (4)	**36**
Let Me Try Again (Laisse Moi Le Temps)—Frank Sinatra (73)	148
Lady Lay—Wayne Newton (74)	13
Midnight Love Affair—Tony Orlando And Dawn (76)	*6.3*
Midnight Love Affair—Carol Douglas (76)	*3.7*
Nick JOVAN ▶ 4653 (2)	**445**
City Of Angels—Highlights (56)	692
Class Cutter (Yeah Yeah)—Dale Hawkins (59)	297
Jeannie JOY [Jean A. Koons] ▶ 10686 (1)	**6.1**
Pickle Up A Doodle—Teresa Brewer (58)	6.1
Leonard JOY ▶ 6466 (4)	**166**
Foolishly Yours—Doris Day (55)	*166*
Foolishly Yours—Kay Starr (55)	*166*
Foolishly Yours—Four Knights (55)	*0.0*
Foolishly Yours—Lee Raymond with The Costello Sisters (55)	*0.0*
—Barbara Joyce see: Barbara LOMAS	
Dorothea JOYCE ▶ 2622 (1)	**1315**
Love's Lines, Angles And Rhymes—5th Dimension (71)	1315
Jerry JOYCE ▶ 6991 (5)	**124**
The Lord Is A Busy Man—Merry Macs (55)	*247*
The Lord Is A Busy Man—Nan Wynn (55)	*0.0*
The Lord Is A Busy Man—Ralph Young (55)	*0.0*
The Lord Is A Busy Man—Steve Lawrence (55)	*0.0*
The Lord Is A Busy Man—Mahalia Jackson (55)	*0.0*
Miranda JOYCE ▶ 10579 (1)	**7.1**
Sign Of The Times—Belle Stars (83)	49
Roger JOYCE ▶ 8268 (1)	**56**
It Feels So Good To Be Loved So Bad—Manhattans (77)	169
Carole JOYNER ▶ 563 (7)	**7680**
Young Love—Tab Hunter (57)	*8452*
Young Love—Sonny James (56)	*5688*
Young Love—Donny Osmond (73)	*531*
Young Love—Crew-Cuts (56)	*343*
Young Love—Lesley Gore (66)	*334*
Young Love—Ray Stevens (76)	*13*
Young Love—Ric Cartey with The Jiva-Tones (56)	*0.0*
Michael JUDKINS ▶ 10996 (1)	**3.9**
Long Stroke—ADC Band (78)	24
—Steven Judkins see: Stevie WONDER	
Al JULIA ▶ 2649 (1)	**1294**
I Cried A Tear—LaVern Baker (58)	2588
Don JULIAN ▶ 1511 (1)	**2839**
The Jerk—Larks (2) (64)	2839
—Lorin/Larry Julian see: Larry DAVIS	
Michael JULIEN ▶ 3397 (3)	**867**
Let's Live For Today—Grass Roots (67)	2587
He Gives Me Love (La La La)—Lesley Gore (68)	12
(Kiss Me) Honey, Honey (Kiss Me)—Gogi Grant (59)	1.3
Rob JUNGKLAS ▶ 10163 (1)	**12**
Make It Mean Something—Rob Jungklas (87)	35
Marvin JUNIOR ▶ 3325 (1)	**899**
Oh, What A Night—Dells (69)	1798
Dick JURGENS ▶ 10448 (1)	**8.4**
Careless—Bobby Vinton (65)	25
Udo JÜRGENS [Udo Jürgen Bockelman] ▶ 4861 (1)	**397**
Walk Away—Matt Monro (64)	794
Gerhard JUSSENHOVEN ▶ 10823 (1)	**5.1**
Angel Pie (Postillion)—Peggy King (56)	10
Bill JUSTIS [Bill Everette, William Everett Justis] ▶ 718 (10)	**6083**
Raunchy—Bill Justis (57)	*5369*
Raunchy—Ernie Freeman (57)	*2380*
Gitarzan—Ray Stevens (69)	2376
Raunchy—Billy Vaughn and His Orchestra (57)	*999*
Ways Of A Woman In Love—Johnny Cash And The Tennessee Two (58)	454
College Man—Bill Justis (58)	*282*
Tamouré—Bill Justis (63)	46
One Wonderful Love—Ray Smith (60)	1.2
Raunchy—Muvva "Guitar" Hubbard (57)	*0.0*
College Man—Ralph Marterie & His Orchestra (58)	*0.0*
—William Everett Justis see: Bill JUSTIS	
Paul JUSTMAN ▶ 7977 (1)	**67**
Concealed Weapons—J. Geils Band (84)	133
Seth JUSTMAN ▶ 287 (16)	**12389**
Centerfold—J. Geils Band (81)	8445
Freeze-Frame—J. Geils Band (82)	3225
Must Of Got Lost—J. Geils Band (74)	1063
Give It To Me—J. Geils Band (73)	1008
Come Back—J. Geils Band (80)	540
One Last Kiss—J. Geils Band (78)	468
Love Stinks—J. Geils Band (80)	428
Angel In Blue—J. Geils Band (82)	408
Concealed Weapons—J. Geils Band (84)	133
Take It Back—J. Geils Band (79)	82
Just Can't Wait—J. Geils Band (80)	52
Make Up Your Mind—J. Geils Band (73)	39
You're The Only One—Geils (77)	15
Givin' It All Up—J. Geils Band (75)	11
Nightgown—Candyman (91)	10
Flamethrower—J. Geils Band (82)	0.0

K

—Norman Kaaihue see: Norman KAYE	
—Ernest Kador see: Ernie K-DOE	
Fudgie KAE [Fudgie Kae Solomon] ▶ 10732 (1)	**5.7**
Mandrill—Mandrill (71)	40
Bert KAEMPFERT [Bernd Bertie, Mark Bones, Berthold Kaempfert] ▶ 518 (20) HOF	**8228**
Strangers In The Night—Frank Sinatra (66)	6342
Wooden Heart—Joe Dowell (61)	*6334*
Spanish Eyes—Al Martino (65)	*1721*
A Swingin' Safari—Billy Vaughn And His Orchestra (62)	1453
Danke Schoen—Wayne Newton & The Newton Brothers (63)	1445
Lady—Jack Jones (67)	730
The World We Knew (Over And Over)—Frank Sinatra (67)	690
Afrikaan Beat—Bert Kaempfert And His Orchestra (62)	650
Only Those In Love—Baby Washington (65)	402
Moon Over Naples—Bert Kaempfert And His Orchestra (65)	*344*
Now And Forever—Bert Kaempfert And His Orchestra (61)	331
Wiederseh'n—Al Martino (66)	295
My Way Of Life—Frank Sinatra (68)	214
Wooden Heart—Bobby Vinton (75)	*108*
Remember When—Wayne Newton (65)	80
L-O-V-E—Nat King Cole (64)	29
Sweet Maria—Billy Vaughn Singers (67)	18
You Turned My World Around—Frank Sinatra (74)	14
Someone—Billy Vaughn And His Orchestra (62)	14
Lonely Is The Name—Sammy Davis Jr. (68)	7.6
—Dave Kaffinetti see: David Franklin EWER	
David KAGAN ▶ 8716 (1)	**41**
Never Enough—Patty Smyth (87)	206
Eric KAGNA ▶ 3952 (2)	**643**
Straight From The Heart—Bryan Adams (83)	1225
Can't Wait All Night—Juice Newton (84)	92
Irving KAHAL ▶ 4886 (6) HOF	**388**
I'll Be Seeing You—Frank Sinatra (61)	*332*
I'll Be Seeing You—Tommy Sands (59)	*273*
I'll Be Seeing You—Four Freshmen & Stan Kenton & Orchestra (54)	*98*
I'll Be Seeing You—Poni-Tails (59)	*49*
I'll Be Seeing You—Five Satins (60)	*24*
Wedding Bells (Are Breaking Up That Old Gang Of Mine)—Four Aces (54)	0.0
Stanley KAHAN [Bob Elgin, Stanley J. Kahan] ▶ 944 (16)	**4713**
A Hundred Pounds Of Clay—Gene McDaniels (61)	7256
Killer Joe—Rocky Fellers (63)	*1215*
Last Chance To Turn Around—Gene Pitney (65)	1140
Girl With The Golden Braids—Perry Como (57)	770
Big Cold Wind—Pat Boone (61)	765
Talk To Me—Frank Sinatra (59)	656
My Town, My Guy And Me—Lesley Gore (65)	538
Come Tomorrow—Manfred Mann (65)	340
Ten Lonely Guys—Pat Boone (62)	*317*
Like The Big Guys Do—Rocky Fellers (63)	199
Killer Joe—Kingsmen (66)	*94*
Ten Lonely Guys—Ten Broken Hearts (62)	*81*
Bitter With The Sweet—Billy Eckstine (56)	69
Operator—Gladys Knight & The Pips (62)	59
In Between Tears—Lenny Miles (61)	13
Ancient History—Les Brown and His Band of Renown (56)	4.6

Elroy KAHANEK ▶ 11168 (1)	**2.9**
Tryin' To Beat The Morning Home—T.G. Sheppard (75)	8.7
Andy KAHN ▶ 7388 (1)	**99**
Hot Shot—Karen Young (78)	198
Bernard KAHN ▶ 10821 (1)	**5.1**
Because Of My Pride—Fireflies (60)	15
Donald KAHN ▶ 9733 (1)	**18**
Beautiful Friendship—Ella Fitzgerald (56)	36
Gus KAHN ▶ 1735 (23)	**2402**
Dream A Little Dream Of Me—Mama Cass With The Mamas & The Papas (68)	1936
Love Me Or Leave Me—Sammy Davis Jr. (55)	*1367*
I'll See You In My Dreams—Pat Boone (62)	*540*
Makin' Whoopee—Ray Charles (64)	469
Yes Sir That's My Baby—Ricky Nelson (60)	*465*
To A Sleeping Beauty—Jimmy Dean (62)	445
Coquette—Fats Domino (58)	94
On The Alamo—Norman Petty Trio (54)	77
Goofus—Carpenters (76)	65
Swingin' Down The Lane—Jerry Wallace (60)	44
I'll See You In My Dreams—Seymour & His Heartbeat Trumpet (58)	*44*
The Waltz You Saved For Me—Ferlin Husky (61)	*28*
Yes Sir That's My Baby—Four Aces (57)	*20*
Yes Sir, That's My Baby—Julius Wechter & The Baja Marimba Band (68)	*15*
When You Come To The End Of The Day—Red Foley (55)	13
Toot, Toot, Tootsie—Johnston Brothers (55)	13
Nobody's Sweetheart—Johnnie Ray (55)	*13*
Nobody's Sweetheart—Jerry Cooper with The Johnny Guarnieri Swingtet (55)	*13*
Guilty—Crests (62)	9.8
Charley My Boy—Somethin' Smith & The Redheads (55)	7.1
Carolina In The Morning—Mitch Miller & his "Sing Along With Mitch" Chorus (59)	3.9
Love Me Or Leave Me—Lena Horne (55)	*0.0*
Love Me Or Leave Me—Billy Eckstine (55)	*0.0*
Marvin KAHN [Muri Kahn] ▶ 4956 (6)	**373**
Petticoats Of Portugal—Dick Jacobs And His Chorus And Orchestra (56)	*982*
Take Me Back Again—Tony Bennett (54)	92
Petticoats Of Portugal—Billy Vaughn and His Orchestra (56)	*34*
You'll Always Be The One (For Me)—Four Aces (55)	11
Petticoats Of Portugal—Florian Zabach (56)	*0.0*
Petticoats Of Portugal—Caesar Giovannini & Sextette (56)	*0.0*
—Muri Kahn see: Marvin KAHN	
David KAHNE ▶ 4079 (3)	**600**
Walking Down Your Street—Bangles (87)	1281
A Girl In Trouble (Is A Temporary Thing)—Romeo Void (84)	466
China—Red Rockers (83)	227
Maewa KAIHAN [Louisa Flavell] ▶ 9387 (1)	**25**
Now Is The Hour—Gale Storm (56)	74
—Mauricio Alberto Kaiserman see: Morris ALBERT	
Bob KALAMASZ ▶ 10699 (1)	**6.0**
Back To The River—Damnation Of Adam Blessing (70)	30
—John Kalapana see: Webley EDWARDS	
Jim KALE ▶ 2190 (1)	**1760**
American Woman—Guess Who (70)	7040
Marvin KALFIN ▶ 4723 (1)	**431**
Just To Be With You—Passions (59)	431
Harold KALIN ▶ 8314 (2)	**54**
Walkin' To School—Kalin Twins (58)	83
Oh My Goodness—Kalin Twins (59)	26
Herbie KALIN ▶ 8315 (2)	**54**
Walkin' To School—Kalin Twins (58)	83
Oh My Goodness—Kalin Twins (59)	26
—Thanos Kalliris see: Paul CALLIRIS	
—Alan Kallman see: Chesley HOWARD	
Martin KALMANOFF ▶ 3255 (4)	**924**
First Name Initial—Annette With The Afterbeats (59)	1207
Utopia—Frank Gari (60)	774
Pictures In The Fire—Pat Boone (62)	102
Young Dreams—Elvis Presley with the Jordanaires (58)	24

Bert KALMAR ▶ 2356 (2) HOF	**1566**
Who's Sorry Now—Connie Francis (58)	*4383*
Who's Sorry Now—Marie Osmond (75)	*314*
Patrick KALOUSTIAN ▶ 11498 (1)	**1.4**
Nite Rock (Lonely Train)—Nite Rockers (58)	4.3
Wayne KAMBES [Wayne Kramer] ▶ 8915 (1)	**36**
Kick Out The Jams—MC5 (69)	181
Michael KAMEN ▶ 1861 (2)	**2191**
(Everything I Do) I Do It For You—Bryan Adams (91)	6505
I Do The Rock—Tim Curry (79)	45
—Melvin Kaminsky see: Mel BROOKS	
Peter KAMINSKY ▶ 6329 (1)	**182**
First Time Love—Livingston Taylor (80)	364
Manuela KAMOSI [Manuela Barbra Monasco Kamosi, Ya Kid K] ▶ 1847 (4)	**2203**
Pump Up The Jam—Technotronic (89)	3746
Get Up! (Before The Night Is Over)—Technotronic (90)	1473
Spin That Wheel—Hi Tek 3 featuring Ya Kid K (90)	98
Rockin' Over The Beat—Technotronic (90)	5.2
John KANDER ▶ 2114 (7) HOF	**1859**
My Coloring Book—Kitty Kallen (62)	*1467*
My Coloring Book—Sandy Stewart (62)	*1420*
Theme From New York, New York—Frank Sinatra (80)	577
Cabaret—Herb Alpert & The Tijuana Brass (68)	*124*
Cabaret—King Richard's Fluegel Knights (67)	*2.8*
My Coloring Book—George Chakiris (62)	*0.0*
My Coloring Book—Barbra Streisand (62)	*0.0*
Harriet KANE ▶ 8797 (1)	**39**
It Might Have Been—Joe London (59)	78
Jim KANE ▶ 11204 (1)	**2.8**
Silly People—Litter (69)	11
Murray KANE [Moses Simon Kaplan] ▶ 10119 (2)	**12**
Just Because—McGuire Sisters (61)	30
Compromise—McGuire Sisters (59)	4.8
—Peter T. Kane see: King PALMER	
—Peter T. Kane see: Richard MULLAN	
—Sandra Kane see: Jeff KATZ	
—Sandra Kane see: Jerry KASENETZ	
Terrence KANE ▶ 11456 (1)	**1.6**
Take Your Love (And Shove It)—Kane's Cousins (69)	3.2
—Kangol Kid see: Shiller Shaun FEQUIERE	
Paul KANTNER ▶ 2303 (8)	**1633**
Jane—Jefferson Starship (79)	1718
Ballad Of You & Me & Pooneil—Jefferson Airplane (67)	492
Volunteers—Jefferson Airplane (69)	345
Watch Her Ride—Jefferson Airplane (67)	310
Girl With The Hungry Eyes—Jefferson Starship (80)	124
Crown Of Creation—Jefferson Airplane (68)	89
St. Charles—Jefferson Starship (76)	52
Ride The Tiger—Jefferson Starship (74)	17
Bronislaw KAPER ▶ 3239 (9)	**934**
Somebody Up There Likes Me—Perry Como (56)	630
Forever Darling—Ames Brothers (56)	*459*
Take My Love—Eddie Fisher (55)	205
Hi-Lili, Hi-Lo—Richard Chamberlain (63)	*176*
Gloria's Theme—Adam Wade (60)	123
Hi Lili Hi Lo—Dick Hyman Trio (56)	*83*
Hi Lili Hi Lo—Roger Williams (56)	*39*
Home From The Hill—Kingston Trio (60)	31
Forever, Darling—Desi Arnaz & His Orchestra (56)	*0.0*
Art KAPLAN ▶ 8989 (1)	**34**
That's How Much—Brian Hyland (60)	102
Gabe KAPLAN ▶ 10069 (1)	**13**
Up Your Nose—Gabriel Kaplan (77)	39
—Gilbert Edward Kaplan see: Gilbert E. KENNINGTON	
—Moses Simon Kaplan see: Murray KANE	
Sammy KAPLAN ▶ 4725 (2)	**430**
Karate-Boo-Ga-Loo—Jerryo (67)	432
Boo-Ga-Loo—Tom & Jerrio (65)	427
—Saul Kaplan see: Saul CHAPLIN	
Sy KAPLAN ▶ 6174 (1)	**197**
Bongo Stomp—Little Joey And The Flips (62)	592
—David Kapp see: Mickey LEADER	
George KARAK [George Nick Karakoglou] ▶ 5927 (1)	**227**
Runaway—Bon Jovi (84)	454

Anton KARAS ▶ 5132 (2)	**336**
3rd Man Theme—Herb Alpert & The Tijuana Brass (65)	*287*
Harry Lime Theme—Crazy Otto (55)	*49*
Paul KARAS ▶ 11707 (1)	**0.6**
Birdman Part One (Title No. 1 Again)—Rare Bird (73)	2.8
Ruth KARDON ▶ 11420 (1)	**1.8**
Tell Me Now—McGuire Sisters (56)	5.3
Kenny KAREN [Chaim Hillel Teicher] ▶ 9270 (1)	**27**
Darkest Street In Town—Jimmy Clanton (62)	55
Tommy KAREN ▶ 10266 (1)	**11**
More And More—Andy Williams (67)	32
Fred KARGER ▶ 5233 (3)	**321**
Gidget—James Darren (59)	*542*
Don't Knock The Rock—Bill Haley And His Comets (56)	85
Gidget—Four Preps (58)	*15*
Carlo KARGES ▶ 1959 (1)	**2050**
99 Luftballons—Nena (83)	4100
—Raymond Karl see: Irving TAYLOR	
—Florence Karlen see: Florence KAYE	
Fred KARLIN ▶ 2133 (2)	**1834**
For All We Know—Carpenters (71)	3454
Come Saturday Morning—Sandpipers (69)	1366
Steve KARLISKI ▶ 5769 (2)	**244**
Molly—Bobby Goldsboro (62)	220
The Yellow Bandana—Faron Young (63)	72
—Neneh Mariann Karlsson see: Neneh CHERRY	
Steve KARMEN ▶ 6331 (1)	**182**
When You Say Love—Sonny & Cher (72)	545
Harold KARR ▶ 4393 (6)	**506**
Mutual Admiration Society—Teresa Brewer (56)	*723*
Mutual Admiration Society—Eddy Arnold And Jaye P. Morgan (56)	*279*
This Much I Know—Tony Martin (56)	5.8
If'N—Richard Hayes (57)	*1.8*
If'N—Jeannie Carson (57)	*1.8*
If'N—Jaye P. Morgan and Eddy Arnold (57)	*1.8*
Gilbert KARSON ▶ 9185 (1)	**29**
Le Spank—Le Pamplemousse (77)	117
—John Kasandra see: John W. ANDERSON	
Jerry KASENETZ [Sandra Kane] ▶ 4124 (9)	**585**
She—Tommy James And The Shondells (69)	869
Goody Goody Gumdrops—1910 Fruitgum Co. (68)	638
The Train—1910 Fruitgum Co. (69)	436
Pinch Me (Baby, Convince Me)—Ohio Express (69)	144
Free As The Wind—Brooklyn Bridge (70)	72
Sunshine, Red Wine—Crazy Elephant (69)	64
Gimme Some More—Crazy Elephant (69)	42
There's A Better Day Comin'—Crazy Elephant (69)	25
Go Away—1910 Fruitgum Co. (70)	8.1
Al KASHA ▶ 812 (17)	**5426**
The Morning After—Maureen McGovern (73)	3712
Irresistible You—Bobby Darin (61)	*1175*
My Empty Arms—Jackie Wilson (61)	1110
Will You Be Staying After Sunday—Peppermint Rainbow (68)	1080
Let's Start All Over Again—Ronnie Dove (66)	941
I'm Comin' On Back To You—Jackie Wilson (61)	687
Don't Wake Me Up In The Morning, Michael—Peppermint Rainbow (69)	475
One More Mountain To Climb—Ronnie Dove (67)	408
Why Can't You Bring Me Home—Jay & The Americans (66)	253
Your Time Hasn't Come Yet, Baby—Elvis Presley With The Jordanaires (68)	203
Stay And Love Me All Summer—Brian Hyland (69)	147
Irresistable You—Bobby Peterson (60)	*112*
For A Friend—Bugaloos (70)	54
We May Never Love Like This Again—Maureen McGovern (75)	54
Forever And A Day—Jackie Wilson (62)	30
Lonely Life—Jackie Wilson (61)	13
Wake Up—Chambers Brothers (69)	8.1
Phyllis KASHA ▶ 11536 (1)	**1.3**
Sweet September—Lettermen (65)	3.8
—Kashif see: Michael JONES	
Tommy KASPAR ▶ 10321 (1)	**10**
You Mean Everything To Me—Fleetwoods (59)	10
—Klaus Karl Kassbaum see: Nick ST. NICHOLAS	

Art KASSEL ▶ 6181 (4)	**196**
The Ship That Never Sailed—David Carroll And His Orchestra (57)	*177*
The Ship That Never Sailed—Billy Vaughn and His Orchestra (57)	*19*
The Ship That Never Sailed—Johnny Ridge (57)	*0.0*
The Ship That Never Sailed—Sammy Kaye & His "Swing And Sway" Orchestra (57)	*0.0*
Ed KASSNER [Eddie Cassen, Edward Kassner] ▶ 9857 (1)	**16**
How Lucky You Are—Joni James (56)	32
Andrew KASTNER ▶ 9399 (1)	**24**
Somewhere, Somebody—Aaron Neville (91)	73
Tolga KATAS ▶ 2793 (2)	**1193**
Sending All My Love—Linear (90)	2325
Don't You Come Cryin'—Linear (90)	91
Gabriel KATONA ▶ 11148 (1)	**3.0**
Night Pulse—Double Image (83)	9.0
George KATSAKIS ▶ 7685 (2)	**81**
Flamingo Express—Royaltones (60)	231
Our Faded Love—Royaltones (64)	7.7
Bill KATZ ▶ 6277 (6)	**187**
Endless—McGuire Sisters (56)	*244*
What Is A Wife—Steve Allen (55)	161
I Love Mickey—Mickey Mantle And Teresa Brewer (56)	24
Rock Bottom—McGuire Sisters (57)	5.5
Endless—Honey Bees (56)	*0.0*
What Is A Husband?—Jane Meadows (56)	0.0
Jeff KATZ [Sandra Kane] ▶ 4125 (9)	**585**
She—Tommy James And The Shondells (69)	869
Goody Goody Gumdrops—1910 Fruitgum Co. (68)	638
The Train—1910 Fruitgum Co. (69)	436
Pinch Me (Baby, Convince Me)—Ohio Express (69)	144
Free As The Wind—Brooklyn Bridge (70)	72
Sunshine, Red Wine—Crazy Elephant (69)	64
Gimme Some More—Crazy Elephant (69)	42
There's A Better Day Comin'—Crazy Elephant (69)	25
Go Away—1910 Fruitgum Co. (70)	8.1
Mickey KATZ ▶ 10145 (1)	**12**
Duvid Crockett (The Ballad Of Davy Crockett)—Mickey Katz And His Orchestra (55)	36
Charles E. KAUFMAN [Charlie Kaufman, Charlie Midnight] ▶ 2131 (5)	**1837**
Living In America—James Brown (85)	1992
The Doctor—Doobie Brothers (89)	977
We Are The Young—Dan Hartman (84)	641
Second Nature—Dan Hartman (85)	384
Gravity—James Brown (86)	4.8
Murray KAUFMAN [Murray the K] ▶ 2447 (1)	**1480**
Splish Splash—Bobby Darin (58)	4440
Paul KAUFMAN ▶ 1436 (3)	**3044**
Poetry In Motion—Johnny Tillotson (60)	5448
My Town, My Guy And Me—Lesley Gore (65)	538
There's No Living Without Your Loving—Peter And Gordon (66)	281
—Sam Kaufman see: C.B. SAMUEL	
—Seymour Kaufman see: Cy COLEMAN	
—Walter Maurice Kaufman see: Walter KENT	
Jorma KAUKONEN ▶ 7319 (1)	**102**
Pretty As You Feel—Jefferson Airplane (71)	512
Dietmar KAWOHL ▶ 2967 (1)	**1092**
Girl I'm Gonna Miss You—Milli Vanilli (89)	3277
Dean KAY [Dean Thompson, Dean Kermit Thompson] ▶ 1826 (3)	**2248**
That's Life—Frank Sinatra (66)	*4437*
That's Life—David Lee Roth (86)	*40*
The Ballad Of Evel Knievel—John Culliton Mahoney (74)	18
John KAY [Joachim Fritz Krauledat] ▶ 693 (10)	**6275**
Magic Carpet Ride—Steppenwolf (68)	4838
Rock Me—Steppenwolf (69)	2080
Move Over—Steppenwolf (69)	918
Monster—Steppenwolf (69)	707
Hey Lawdy Mama—Steppenwolf (70)	613
Who Needs Ya—Steppenwolf (70)	365
It's Never Too Late—Steppenwolf (69)	342
Screaming Night Hog—Steppenwolf (70)	340
For Ladies Only—Steppenwolf (71)	190

America/Standing—Five Stairsteps (70)	93
Barry KAYE ▶ 8048 (1)	**64**
Zip Zip—Diamonds (57)	255
Buddy KAYE [Jules Leonard Kaye] ▶ 1327 (37)	**3350**
Speedy Gonzales—Pat Boone (62)	*2754*
The Old Songs—Barry Manilow (81)	1046
All Cried Out—Dusty Springfield (64)	540
Rhythm 'N' Blues (Mama's Got The Rhythm—Papa's Got The Blues)—McGuire Sisters (55)	437
Sweet William—Millie Small (64)	432
Give Us This Day—Joni James (56)	*431*
Not As A Stranger—Frank Sinatra (55)	*311*
The Star You Wished Upon Last Night—Gisele MacKenzie (56)	*298*
Girls Ain't Nothing But Trouble—D.J. Jazzy Jeff & The Fresh Prince (88)	241
Delicious—Jim Backus & Friend (58)	235
The World Of Lonely People—Anita Bryant (64)	205
Sweet Song Of India—McGuire Sisters (55)	182
The Next Kiss (Is The Last Goodbye)—Conway Twitty (61)	170
This Is My Prayer—Ray Charles Singers (65)	124
Banjo Boy—Dorothy Collins (60)	*92*
(Baby, Baby) Be Good To Me—McGuire Sisters (56)	85
Christmas Alphabet—McGuire Sisters (54)	62
Big Name Button—Royal Teens (58)	53
What Is A Teenage Girl?—Tom Edwards (57)	48
Hello There—Gisele MacKenzie (57)	48
June July And August—Rusty Draper (58)	45
Move Me, O Wondrous Music—Ray Charles Singers (70)	22
Mambo In The Moonlight—Gary Crosby And The Cheer Leaders (54)	21
Speedy Gonzales—David Dante (61)	*19*
Till The End Of Time—Ray Charles Singers (64)	17
Till The End Of Time—Nobles (58)	9.2
Banjo Boy—Art Mooney And His Orchestra (60)	*3.6*
What Is A Teenage Boy?—Tom Edwards (57)	1.6
Welcome Home—Shelley Fabares (63)	0.4
Hula Hoop—Steve Allen (58)	0.0
Give Us This Day—Dream Weavers (56)	*0.0*
The Italian Theme—Dorothy Collins (56)	*0.0*
A Carnival In Venice—Mills Brothers (54)	0.0
Not As A Stranger—Henri René & His Orchestra (55)	*0.0*
The Italian Theme—Owen Bradley & His Quintet (56)	*0.0*
The Star You Wished Upon Last Night—Nick Noble (56)	*0.0*
The Star You Wished Upon Last Night—Jeannie Carson (56)	*0.0*
Florence KAYE [Florence Karlen] ▶ 1711 (7)	**2448**
(You're the) Devil In Disguise—Elvis Presley With The Jordanaires (63)	3964
Ask Me—Elvis Presley With The Jordanaires (64)	1582
That's Old Fashioned (That's The Way Love Should Be)—Everly Brothers (62)	1204
Young And In Love—Chris Crosby (64)	357
A Time To Love-A Time To Cry (Petite Fleur)—Lou Johnson (65)	*356*
Held For Questioning—Rusty Draper (56)	244
Today, Tomorrow And Forever—Elvis Presley (64)	1.1
—Jules Leonard Kaye see: Buddy KAYE	
Norman KAYE [Norman Kaaihue] ▶ 5001 (3)	**360**
Let's Love—Johnny Mathis (58)	405
I Keep Crying—Hurricanes (54)	147
Somebody Else's Love Song—Georgie Shaw (54)	21
Tommy KAYE ▶ 4551 (1)	**466**
One Man Band—Three Dog Night (70)	1398
Tony KAYE [Anthony John Selvidge] ▶ 8093 (1)	**62**
Rhythm Of Love—Yes (87)	310
—Kayel see: Louis SHARPE	
Howard KAYLAN ▶ 3731 (4)	**717**
Elenore—Turtles (68)	2721
Sound Asleep—Turtles (68)	382
You Don't Have To Walk In The Rain—Turtles (69)	301
Love In The City—Turtles (69)	183
—Bob Kayli see: Robert GORDY	
—Kayo see: Kevin ROBERSON	
Eric KAZ ▶ 1668 (7)	**2520**
Heartbeat—Don Johnson (86)	2057

That's What Love Is All About—Michael Bolton (87)	1008
Hearts On Fire—Randy Meisner (81)	862
Deep Inside My Heart—Randy Meisner (80)	694
Love Has No Pride—Linda Ronstadt (73)	392
Let Me Down Easy—American Flyer (76)	19
Gotta Get Away—Randy Meisner (81)	12
Ernie K-DOE [Ernest Kador] ▶ 5668 (2)	**257**
Te-Ta-Te-Ta-Ta—Ernie K-Doe (61)	256
Popeye Joe—Ernie K-Doe (62)	0.9
Kelly KEAGY ▶ 1763 (2)	**2360**
Sister Christian—Night Ranger (84)	2250
Sing Me Away—Night Ranger (83)	221
Tom KEANE ▶ 2955 (4)	**1099**
Will You Still Love Me?—Chicago (86)	2842
Through The Fire—Chaka Khan (85)	257
The Secret Of My Success—Night Ranger (87)	179
Lonely Won't Leave Me Alone—Glenn Medeiros (87)	84
Ramsey KEARNEY [Will Gentry] ▶ 2427 (1)	**1497**
Emotions—Brenda Lee (60)	2994
—Carl Keats see: Carl GROSSMAN	
Ruth KEDDINGTON ▶ 11806 (1)	**0.0**
Theme From "The Proud Ones"—Johnny Desmond (56)	*0.0*
Arrett KEEFER [Rusty Keefer] ▶ 4564 (4)	**465**
R O C K—Bill Haley And His Comets (56)	737
Skinny Minnie—Bill Haley And His Comets (58)	608
Rockin' Through The Rye—Bill Haley And His Comets (56)	133
Whoa Mabel—Bill Haley And His Comets (58)	2.7
—Rusty Keefer see: Arrett KEEFER	
Ruth KEEFER ▶ 5748 (1)	**246**
R O C K—Bill Haley And His Comets (56)	737
—Dorothy Jacqueline Keely see: Keely SMITH	
—John David Keen see: Speedy KEEN	
Speedy KEEN [John David Keen] ▶ 4248 (1)	**546**
Something In The Air—Thunderclap Newman (69)	546
Don KEENE ▶ 8422 (2)	**51**
Rock The Joint—Bill Haley With Haley's Comets (55)	*146*
Rock The Joint—Bill Haley & His Comets (57)	*6.6*
Clarence KEHNER ▶ 2890 (6)	**1130**
Bobby Sox To Stockings—Frankie Avalon (59)	2192
Somewhere In Your Heart—Frank Sinatra (64)	643
Who Else But You—Frankie Avalon (61)	95
Don't Tell Me Not To Love You—Joni James (56)	*58*
Always Keep Me In Your Heart—Four Aces (69)	3.0
Don't Tell Me Not To Love You—June Valli (56)	*0.0*
Don KEHR ▶ 9762 (1)	**17**
Running Back—Urgent (85)	52
Michael KEHR ▶ 9763 (1)	**17**
Running Back—Urgent (85)	52
Steve KEHR ▶ 9764 (1)	**17**
Running Back—Urgent (85)	52
Tom KEIFER ▶ 1075 (8)	**4103**
Don't Know What You Got (Till It's Gone)—Cinderella (88)	1150
Nobody's Fool—Cinderella (86)	1011
Coming Home—Cinderella (89)	744
Shelter Me—Cinderella (90)	427
The Last Mile—Cinderella (89)	338
Heartbreak Station—Cinderella (91)	238
Somebody Save Me—Cinderella (87)	109
Gypsy Road—Cinderella (89)	85
—Neville Keighley see: Belouis SOME	
Barbara KEITH ▶ 8269 (1)	**56**
Free The People—Delaney & Bonnie & Friends (70)	56
Brian KEITH [Brian O'Shea] ▶ 9465 (1)	**23**
Jesahel—English Congregation (72)	70
Bubba KEITH ▶ 8135 (2)	**60**
Nicole—Point Blank (81)	357
Let Me Stay With You Tonight—Point Blank (81)	5.7
Jeff KEITH ▶ 3288 (2)	**911**
Love Song—Tesla (89)	1711
The Way It Is—Tesla (90)	222
Larry KEITH ▶ 2910 (5)	**1121**
Better Love Next Time—Dr. Hook (79)	1340
This Time I'm In It For Love—Player (78)	1215
Don't Stop Me Baby (I'm On Fire)—Boys Band (82)	122
Blaze Of Glory—Kenny Rogers (81)	97
Mary Anne—Fallenrock (75)	8.4

Lisa KEITH [Lisa Bernard, Lisa Keith Carlson] ▶ 8121 (1) **61**
Why Should I Cry?—Nona Hendryx (87) 183
—Marilyn Keith see: Marilyn BERGMAN
Randall KEITH ▶ 9259 (1) **28**
Voodoo Woman—Simon Stokes & The Nighthawks (69) 55
Vivian KEITH ▶ 1680 (1) **2505**
Before The Next Teardrop Falls—Freddy Fender (75) 5010
Michael KELISHES ▶ 10468 (1) **8.1**
Boss—Rumblers (63) 48
Milton KELLEM [Jimmy Craig, Ted Gary] ▶ 1808 (5) **2284**
Gonna Get Along Without Ya Now—Patience and Prudence (56) *1384*
Gonna Get Along Without You Now—Skeeter Davis (64) *435*
Gonna' Get Along Without You Now—Tracey Dey (64) *414*
House Of Love—Scott Garrett (59) 31
Gonna Get Along Without Ya' Now—Trini Lopez (67) *20*
Ted KELLEM [Victor Aronson] ▶ 6112 (1) **205**
From A School Ring To A Wedding Ring—Rover Boys (56) 205
Jack KELLER ▶ 152 (35) **19153**
My Heart Has A Mind Of Its Own—Connie Francis (60) 8856
Everybody's Somebody's Fool—Connie Francis (60) 8043
Run To Him—Bobby Vee (61) 5173
Breakin' In A Brand New Broken Heart—Connie Francis (61) 3470
Easy Come, Easy Go—Bobby Sherman (70) 2475
Venus In Blue Jeans—Jimmy Clanton (62) 2008
Just For Old Time's Sake—McGuire Sisters (61) 1660
Just Between You And Me—Chordettes (57) 1055
Please Don't Ask About Barbara—Bobby Vee (62) 971
Let's Turkey Trot—Little Eva (63) 947
Your Used To Be—Brenda Lee (63) 676
Girls Grow Up Faster Than Boys—Cookies (63) 591
Seattle—Perry Como (69) 550
It Started All Over Again—Brenda Lee (62) 546
Don't Try To Fight It, Baby—Eydie Gorme (63) 311
Beats There A Heart So True—Perry Como (58) 268
Don't Ask Me To Be Friends—Everly Brothers (62) 259
I Wish I'd Never Been Born—Patti Page (60) 257
Lovin' Touch—Mark Dinning (60) 170
How Can I Meet Her?—Everly Brothers (62) 127
Don't Read The Letter—Patti Page (60) 123
That's How Much—Brian Hyland (60) 102
It's So Easy To Say—Johnny Nash (58) 88
Ready Or Not—Helen Reddy (78) 70
Gotta Have Your Love—Sapphires (65) 45
No One Can Make My Sunshine Smile—Everly Brothers (62) 44
Seven Minutes In Heaven—Poni-Tails (58) 35
I Can't Sit Down—Marie & Rex (59) 34
Poor Little Puppet—Cathy Carroll (62) 21
All The Grey Haired Men—Lettermen (68) 7.3
Your Second Choice—Clyde McPhatter (61) 6.1
(One Of These Days) Sunday's Gonna' Come On Tuesday—New Establishment (69) 6.0
When Somebody Loves You—Frank Sinatra (65) 2.3
What's Come Over This World?—Billy Carr (65) 0.5
Cry On My Shoulder—Johnny Crawford (63) 0.4
Jerry KELLER ▶ 2171 (5) **1792**
Turn-Down Day—Cyrkle (66) 1047
Here Comes Summer—Jerry Keller (59) *973*
Here Comes Summer—Wildfire (77) *226*
Almost There—Andy Williams (64) 131
A Man And A Woman—Tamiko Jones With Herbie Mann (66) 12
Jim KELLER ▶ 2279 (2) **1660**
867-5309/Jenny—Tommy Tutone (82) 3051
Angel Say No—Tommy Tutone (80) 269
Sheldon KELLER ▶ 11252 (1) **2.6**
Tower Trot (And Then You Do That Step)—Dick Jacobs And His Chorus And Orchestra (57) 23
Chet KELLEY ▶ 2156 (2) **1810**
Time Won't Let Me—Outsiders (66) 2793
Girl In Love—Outsiders (66) 826
Ernest KELLEY ▶ 7732 (3) **77**
Satisfied (Part 2)—Cashmeres (60) *120*
Bermuda Shorts—Delroys (57) 35
Satisfied (Part 2)—Debbie Reynolds (60) *10*
Herman Wesley KELLEY ▶ 6117 (3) **204**
Pop That Thang—Isley Brothers (72) 972
Get Serious—Cut 'N' Move (91) 36
I Spy (For The FBI)—Jamo Thomas & His Party Brothers Orchestra (66) 5.2
Kenneth KELLEY ▶ 11201 (1) **2.8**
If My Heart Could Speak—Manhattans (70) 5.6
Richard KELLIS ▶ 4088 (1) **597**
That's Life (That's Tough)—Gabriel And The Angels (62) 597
Casey KELLY [Daniel Cohen] ▶ 5861 (1) **236**
Poor Boy—Casey Kelly (72) 236
Charles KELLY ▶ 11440 (1) **1.7**
Happy Man (Part 1)—Impact (76) 3.4
Eban KELLY ▶ 6929 (1) **128**
You And Me Tonight—Deja (87) 255
Fred KELLY ▶ 11708 (1) **0.6**
Birdman Part One (Title No. 1 Again)—Rare Bird (73) 2.8
George KELLY ▶ 10964 (1) **4.1**
So Will I—Ames Brothers (55) 8.1
James KELLY ▶ 4825 (1) **404**
Miss America—Mark Lindsay (70) 404
Mark KELLY ▶ 9796 (1) **17**
Kayleigh—Marillion (85) 84
Michael KELLY ▶ 5160 (3) **332**
2 Legit 2 Quit—M.C. Hammer (91) 1441
Go For It (Heart And Fire)—Joey B. Ellis & Tynetta Hare (90) 111
Turn It Up—Oaktown's 3.5.7 (91) 49
Paul KELLY ▶ 2265 (4) **1676**
Personally—Karla Bonoff (82) 1267
Stealing In The Name Of The Lord—Paul Kelly (70) 373
Don't Burn Me—Paul Kelly (73) 24
Love Me Now—Ruby Winters (74) 12
Rick KELLY ▶ 2862 (2) **1147**
Make It Real—Jets (88) 2361
I Do You—Jets (87) 720
Robert KELLY ▶ 9790 (1) **17**
It Won't Be This Way (Always)—King Pins (63) 34
Sherman KELLY ▶ 2081 (2) **1901**
Dancing In The Moonlight—King Harvest (72) 1878
A Little Bit Like Magic—King Harvest (73) 67
Thomas KELLY ▶ 5812 (1) **240**
Take Care Of Your Homework—Johnnie Taylor (69) 958
Thomas F. KELLY ▶ 257 (16) HOF **13380**
Like A Virgin—Madonna (84) *6377*
Alone—Heart (87) 4753
So Emotional—Whitney Houston (87) 3671
True Colors—Cyndi Lauper (86) 3546
Eternal Flame—Bangles (89) 3515
In Your Room—Bangles (88) 1791
I Drove All Night—Cyndi Lauper (89) 1573
In My Dreams—REO Speedwagon (87) 1030
Fire And Ice—Pat Benatar (81) 1023
Sex As A Weapon—Pat Benatar (85) 583
My Side Of The Bed—Susanna Hoffs (91) 464
Like A Surgeon—"Weird Al" Yankovic (85) *257*
I Want You So Bad—Heart (88) 224
Jackie—Blue Zone U.K. (88) 200
My First Night Without You—Cyndi Lauper (89) 149
Hey Mambo—Barry Manilow with Kid Creole And The Coconuts (88) 6.2
Tom KELLY ▶ 4369 (1) **510**
I Touch Myself—Divinyls (91) 2042
Hubert KEMMLER ▶ 7810 (1) **74**
The Different Story (World Of Lust And Crime)—Peter Schilling (89) 222
Gary KEMP ▶ 697 (5) **6249**
Set Adrift On Memory Bliss—PM Dawn (91) 3619
True—Spandau Ballet (83) 3310
Gold—Spandau Ballet (83) 572
Only When You Leave—Spandau Ballet (84) 459
Communication—Spandau Ballet (84) 100
Johnny KEMP ▶ 4081 (1) **599**
Just Got Paid—Johnny Kemp (88) 1198
Tara KEMP ▶ 4586 (2) **461**
Piece Of My Heart—Tara Kemp (91) 1377
Too Much—Tara Kemp (91) 4.1
Thomas KEMP ▶ 6200 (2) **194**
I've Lost Everything I've Ever Loved—David Ruffin (69) 242
Take Some Time Out For Love—Isley Brothers (66) 146
Wayne KEMP ▶ 4272 (2) **539**
One Piece At A Time—Johnny Cash And The Tennessee Three (76) 398
Love Bug—Jack Jones (65) 281
Rolf KEMPF ▶ 4074 (1) **604**
Hello Hurray—Alice Cooper (73) 604
—Jaan Kenbrovin see: James KENDIS
Mark KENDALL ▶ 4855 (3) **398**
The Angel Song—Great White (89) 604
Rock Me—Great White (87) 217
Call It Rock 'N Roll—Great White (91) 208
Robert KENDALL ▶ 9386 (1) **25**
Walking On Back—Edward Bear (73) 25
James KENDIS [James Brockman, Jaan Kenbrovin, Nat Vincent] ▶ 4365 (1) **512**
Billy—Kathy Linden (58) 1535
—Edward James Kendrick see: Eddie KENDRICKS
Kevin KENDRICK ▶ 8477 (1) **49**
Back And Forth—Cameo (87) 195
Eddie KENDRICKS [Edward James Kendrick] ▶ 11624 (1) **0.9**
Lonely Lonely Girl Am I—Velvelettes (65) 2.8
—John Henry Kendricks see: Hank BALLARD
Billy KENNEDY ▶ 9555 (1) **21**
I Need You, You Need Me—Joe Simon (76) 64
Jerry KENNEDY ▶ 9040 (3) **33**
Everybody's Twisting Down In Mexico—Billy Vaughn And His Orchestra (61) 43
Kentucky Moonrunner—Cledus Maggard And The Citizen's Band (76) 16
Golden Wildwood Flower—Tom & Jerry (61) 10
Jimmy KENNEDY ▶ 671 (18) HOF **6450**
My Prayer—Platters (56) *8202*
Harbor Lights—Platters (60) *2551*
Red Sails In The Sunset—Platters Featuring Tony Williams (60) *574*
Red Sails In The Sunset—Fats Domino (63) *526*
Sweet Heartaches—Eddie Fisher (56) 341
My Prayer—Ray, Goodman & Brown (80) *266*
The Magic Tango—Hugo Winterhalter & Orchestra (54) 210
Red Sails In The Sunset—Tab Hunter (57) *70*
Under The Sun Valley Moon—Patti Page (59) 69
My Prayer—Johnny Thunder (66) *34*
Oh Pain! Oh Agony! (Know What I Mean Jelly Bean)—Gisele MacKenzie (57) 17
Harbor Lights—Mulcays (55) *13*
My Arms Are A House—Hank Snow (57) 11
Write To Me From Naples—Dean Martin (57) 10
Did You Ever Get The Roses—Ames Brothers (57) 5.3
Harbor Lights—Seymour & His Heartbeat Trumpet (59) *1.6*
My Prayer—Ink Spots (56) *0.0*
Isle Of Capri—Gaylords (54) *0.0*
Joy KENNEDY ▶ 10861 (1) **4.8**
I'll Love You Till The Cows Come Home—Clyde McPhatter (61) 4.8
Joyce KENNEDY [Joyce Washington] ▶ 11436 (1) **1.7**
Fire—Mother's Finest (76) 5.1
Mary Ann KENNEDY ▶ 6838 (1) **134**
I'll Still Be Loving You—Restless Heart (87) 536
Michael KENNEDY ▶ 1782 (1) **2331**
Heartbeat - It's A Lovebeat—Defranco Family Featuring Tony Defranco (73) 4662
Ray KENNEDY ▶ 2361 (6) **1560**
Every Time I Think Of You—Babys (78) 1477
Isn't It Time—Babys (77) 1422
Sail On Sailor—Beach Boys (75) *268*
Tonight Tonight—Bill Champlin (81) 119
Sail On Sailor—Beach Boys (73) *49*
Just For The Moment—Ray Kennedy (80) 15
Sam KENNEDY ▶ 4913 (1) **383**
Kisses Sweeter Than Wine—Jimmie Rodgers (57) 2683
Steve KENNEDY ▶ 3656 (1) **747**
When I Die—Motherlode (69) 1495
—Tracey Bryn Kennedy see: Tracey BRYN

Philip KENNEMORE ▶ 8203 (1)	**58**
Summertime Girls—Y&T (85)	234
Chris KENNER ▶ 334 (16)	**11052**
I Like It Like That, Part 1—Chris Kenner (61)	*5095*
I Like It Like That—Dave Clark Five (65)	*2277*
Land Of 1000 Dances—Wilson Pickett (66)	*2102*
Land Of 1000 Dances— Cannibal And The Headhunters (65)	*1096*
Something You Got— Chuck Jackson & Maxine Brown (65)	*414*
Something You Got—Alvin Robinson (64)	*294*
Sick And Tired—Fats Domino (58)	248
Something You Got—Ramsey Lewis Trio (64)	*186*
Land Of A Thousand Dances Part I— Thee Midniters (65)	*156*
Land Of 1000 Dances—Electric Indian (69)	*146*
Land Of A Thousand Dances—J. Geils Band (83)	*136*
Land Of 1000 Dances—Chris Kenner (63)	*93*
I Don't Like It Like That—Bobbettes (61)	*53*
I Like It Like That—Loggins & Messina (75)	*19*
A Very True Story—Chris Kenner (61)	9.0
Land Of 1000 Dances—Round Robin (65)	*0.0*
—Alan Kenneth see: Alan BERNSTEIN	
Gilbert E. KENNINGTON [Gilbert Edward Kaplan] ▶ 10066 (1)	**13**
Come Share The Good Times With Me— Julie Monday (66)	26
Charles KENNY ▶ 1162 (5)	**3830**
Love Letters In The Sand—Pat Boone (57)	9892
There's A Gold Mine In The Sky—Pat Boone (57)	*1031*
Cathedal In The Pines—Pat Boone (57)	20
There's A Gold Mine In The Sky— Nat "King" Cole (57)	*15*
There's A Gold Mine In The Sky—Bing Crosby (57)	*0.0*
Gerard KENNY ▶ 5537 (2)	**273**
I Made It Through The Rain—Barry Manilow (80)	1325
Everybody But Me—G.W. Kenny (73)	8.2
James KENNY ▶ 10753 (1)	**5.5**
Gypsy Spirit—Pendulum (80)	17
Nick KENNY ▶ 1163 (5)	**3830**
Love Letters In The Sand—Pat Boone (57)	9892
There's A Gold Mine In The Sky—Pat Boone (57)	*1031*
Cathedral In The Pines—Pat Boone (57)	20
There's A Gold Mine In The Sky— Nat "King" Cole (57)	*15*
There's A Gold Mine In The Sky—Bing Crosby (57)	*0.0*
KENNY G [Kenneth Bruce Gorelick] ▶ 1173 (3)	**3785**
Songbird—Kenny G (87)	2605
Silhouette—Kenny G (88)	1085
Going Home—Kenny G (89)	189
—Al Kent see: Al HAMILTON	
Arthur KENT ▶ 893 (12)	**4970**
The End Of The World—Skeeter Davis (63)	6448
Take Good Care Of Her—Adam Wade (61)	*2184*
Ring A Ling A Lario—Jimmie Rodgers (59)	492
Don't Go To Strangers—Etta Jones (60)	*486*
Dearer Than Life—Brook Benton (63)	286
Tonight I Won't Be There—Adam Wade (61)	194
Don't Go To Strangers— Vaughn Monroe with Orchestra And Chorus (56)	*107*
Take Good Care Of Her—Mel Carter (66)	*56*
Take Good Care Of Her—Elvis Presley (74)	*41*
It's Good To Have You Back With Me— Adam Wade (62)	5.8
Wait For Me—Rita Pavone (64)	1.8
Don't Go To Strangers—Andy Williams (60)	*0.0*
George KENT ▶ 11046 (1)	**3.6**
(How Can I Write On Paper) What I Feel In My Heart— Jim Reeves (61)	14
Gerald KENT ▶ 10099 (1)	**13**
Wake Up And Be Somebody—Brainstorm (77)	13
Jeff KENT ▶ 11266 (1)	**2.5**
Keep It Confidential—Nona Hendryx (83)	7.6
Melvin KENT ▶ 10367 (1)	**9.4**
You Can Call Me Rover—Main Ingredient (73)	28
Michael KENT ▶ 7931 (1)	**69**
(I Remember) Summer Morning—Vanity Fare (70)	138
Robert E. KENT ▶ 8694 (1)	**42**
Don't Knock The Rock— Bill Haley And His Comets (56)	85

Walter KENT [Walter Maurice Kaufman] ▶ 10052 (3)	**13**
The White Cliffs Of Dover—Righteous Brothers (66)	19
I'm Gonna Live Till I Die—Frank Sinatra and Ray Anthony and his Orchestra (55)	10
I'll Be Home For Christmas—Elvis Presley (57)	2.1
—Wayne Douglas Kent see: Artie WAYNE	
Murray KENTON ▶ 6772 (1)	**138**
Juanita Banana—Peels (66)	277
Peter KER ▶ 2412 (1)	**1509**
Fire—Crazy World Of Arthur Brown (68)	6038
—June Williams Kerenhappuch see: June Watson WILLIAMS	
Lenny KERLEY ▶ 6777 (2)	**138**
It Could Be We're In Love—Cryan Shames (67)	276
Mr. Unreliable—Cryan' Shames (67)	0.5
Jerome KERN ▶ 464 (12) HOF	**8995**
Smoke Gets In Your Eyes—Platters (58)	*10667*
I've Told Every Little Star—Linda Scott (61)	3657
The Way You Look Tonight—Lettermen (61)	1962
Smoke Gets In Your Eyes—Blue Haze (72)	*1048*
Ol' Man River— Bing Crosby And The Buddy Cole Trio (56)	*345*
Smoke Gets In Your Eyes—Four Preps (61)	*130*
Ol' Man River—Earl Grant (58)	*94*
Ol' Man River—Jimmy Smith (62)	*30*
(When Your Heart's On Fire) Smoke Gets In Your Eyes—Richard Barrett (58)	*18*
Fine Romance— Sammy Davis Jr. And Carmen McRae (55)	7.8
Can't Help Lovin' That Girl Of Mine—Excels (61)	0.5
Ol' Man River—Johnny Nash (62)	*0.0*
George KERR ▶ 4523 (9)	**471**
A Love So Fine—Chiffons (63)	466
All I Have—Moments (70)	247
Look Over Your Shoulder—O'Jays (68)	159
I'll Erase Away Your Pain—Whatnauts (71)	140
What've I Done (To Make You Mad)—Linda Jones (67)	139
Love Explosion—Troy Keyes (68)	87
Lucky Me—Moments (71)	11
Last Minute Miracle—Shirelles (67)	1.9
We're Friends By Day (And Lovers By Night)— Whatnauts (71)	0.4
Jim KERR ▶ 2011 (4)	**2004**
Alive And Kicking—Simple Minds (85)	3897
Sanctify Yourself—Simple Minds (86)	1088
All The Things She Said—Simple Minds (86)	507
See The Lights—Simple Minds (91)	346
Jo KERR [Jonathan Michael Kerr] ▶ 2196 (1)	**1753**
She Blinded Me With Science—Thomas Dolby (83)	3507
—Jonathan Michael Kerr see: Jo KERR	
Richard KERR ▶ 565 (13)	**7657**
Mandy—Barry Manilow (74)	*4532*
I'll Never Love This Way Again—Dionne Warwick (79)	3458
Looks Like We Made It—Barry Manilow (77)	3436
Somewhere In The Night—Barry Manilow (78)	*1230*
Somewhere In The Night—Helen Reddy (75)	*918*
No Night So Long—Dionne Warwick (80)	723
Shine On—L.T.D. (80)	538
I Am What I Am—Lois Fletcher (74)	263
I'm Dreaming—Jennifer Warnes (77)	220
Somewhere In The Night—Batdorf & Rodney (75)	*94*
Brandy—Scott English (72)	*48*
A Little Bit Of Heaven—Natalie Cole (85)	23
Where Did We Go Wrong— Frankie Valli Introducing Chris Forde (80)	10
Wesaline Hopson KERR [Wesaline Hopson, Wesaline Kerr] ▶ 6672 (2)	**145**
Is This The Way To Treat A Girl (You Bet It Is)— Hesitations (69)	142
Instigating (Trouble Making Fool)— Whatnauts (73)	3.3
Larry KERRIN ▶ 5295 (4)	**312**
Hunch—Bobby Peterson Quintet (59)	*301*
Hunch—Paul Gayten (59)	*281*
The Big Time Spender (Part I)— Cornbread & Biscuits (60)	34
Come On Over—Strollers (61)	7.8
Ron KERSEY ▶ 6566 (2)	**156**
Don't Take Your Love—Manhattans (74)	457
Send For Me—Atlantic Starr (81)	6.9

Tyrone G. KERSEY ▶ 3474 (1)	**827**
Disco Inferno—Trammps (77)	1653
Doug KERSHAW ▶ 7218 (4)	**110**
Shake Hands (And Come Out Crying)—Newbeats (66)	98
Louisiana Man—Bobbie Gentry (68)	*14*
Louisiana Man—Pozo Seco Singers (67)	*4.9*
Louisiana Man—Rusty & Doug (61)	*3.3*
Nik KERSHAW ▶ 2304 (2)	**1632**
The One And Only—Chesney Hawkes (91)	1298
Wouldn't It Be Good—Nik Kershaw (84)	334
Walt KESKE ▶ 6538 (1)	**159**
Sherry Don't Go—Lettermen (68)	477
Stanley A. KESLER ▶ 3980 (2)	**632**
Playing For Keeps—Elvis Presley (57)	368
If I'm A Fool For Loving You—Bobby Wood (64)	265
Barney KESSEL ▶ 5250 (1)	**318**
You're My One And Only Love—Ricky Nelson (57)	636
Bernard KESSLAIR [Jean Cohen] ▶ 5258 (1)	**317**
Love In Every Room (Meme Si Tu Revenais)— Paul Mauriat And His Orchestra (68)	317
—Danny Kessler see: Marilyn SCHACK	
—Denise Kessler see: Rainy DAVIS	
Mary Alice KESSLER ▶ 5536 (1)	**274**
Do It For Love—Sheena Easton (85)	547
Mary E. KESSLER ▶ 4350 (2)	**515**
Baby Love—Regina (86)	1461
Like A Child—Noel (88)	83
—Peter Kessler see: Pete WARNER	
Albert W. KETELBEY ▶ 11098 (1)	**3.2**
In A Persian Market— LeRoy Holmes And His Orchestra (58)	3.2
Alfons KETTNER ▶ 3782 (1)	**701**
What You Won't Do For Love—Bobby Caldwell (78)	1402
Ian KEWLEY ▶ 5654 (2)	**259**
Everything Must Change—Paul Young (85)	305
Some People—Paul Young (86)	214
Francis Scott KEY ▶ 4333 (2) HOF	**518**
The Star-Spangled Banner—Jose Feliciano (68)	259
The Star Spangled Banner—Whitney Houston (91)	259
Jimmy KEY ▶ 9718 (1)	**18**
You're Stronger Than Me—Patsy Cline (62)	37
Baron KEYES ▶ 9292 (1)	**27**
Sweet Someone—Eddie And Betty (59)	54
Bert KEYES ▶ 1817 (7)	**2272**
Love On A Two-Way Street—Moments (70)	*3309*
Love On A Two Way Street—Stacy Lattisaw (81)	*768*
Angel Smile—Nat "King" Cole (57)	553
Little Gypsy—Ames Brothers (58)	56
Sunday—Moments (2) (69)	43
Isn't It Amazing— Crests Featuring Johnny Maestro (60)	12
Happy Pair—Ames Brothers (60)	5.0
James C. KEYES ▶ 2295 (2)	**1642**
Sh-Boom—Crew-Cuts (54)	*7040*
Sh-Boom—Chords (54)	*1169*
John KEYES ▶ 4329 (1)	**519**
Too Weak To Fight—Clarence Carter (68)	2074
Chaka KHAN [Carole Yvette Marie Stevens, Yvette Stevens] ▶ 1690 (3)	**2482**
Sweet Thing—Rufus Featuring Chaka Khan (75)	3041
You Got The Love—Rufus Featuring Chaka Khan (74)	1547
Stay—Rufus/Chaka Khan (78)	376
Allyson KHENT ▶ 1267 (6)	**3515**
Sixteen Candles—Crests (58)	*5437*
Trouble In Paradise—Crests (60)	1055
Year Ago Tonight—Crests (59)	493
Journey Of Love— Crests Featuring Johnny Maestro (60)	42
Lovin' Up A Storm—Jerry Lee Lewis (59)	12
16 Candles—Fred Parris & The Five Satins (82)	*4.8*
—Gérard Daniel Kherlakian see: Danyel GÉRARD	
George KHOURY ▶ 960 (5)	**4662**
Sea Of Love—Phil Phillips with The Twilights (59)	*5548*
Sea Of Love—Honeydrippers (84)	*3169*
Sea Of Love—Del Shannon (81)	*406*
Matilda Has Finally Come Back— Cookie & His Cupcakes (59)	189
Verdie Mae—Phil Phillips (59)	11
Bob KHOZOURI ▶ 7125 (1)	**115**
Show Me—Cover Girls (87)	459

Perry KIBBLE [Perry McBride] ► 1148 (2)	**3876**
Boogie Oogie Oogie—A Taste Of Honey (78)	7729
Do It Good—Taste Of Honey (79)	23
—Kid Creole see: August DARNELL	
Johnny KIDD [Frederick Albert Heath, Frederick Heath] ► 2848 (1)	**1155**
Shakin' All Over—Guess Who? (65)	1155
Wendy KIDD ► 4186 (2)	**570**
Yesterday's Gone—Chad Stuart & Jeremy Clyde (64)	*815*
Yesterday's Gone—Overlanders (64)	*325*
—Kid Frost see: Arturo MOLINA Jr.	
Anthony KIEDIS ► 10604 (1)	**6.9**
Give It Away—Red Hot Chili Peppers (91)	28
Greg KIHN ► 1693 (8)	**2479**
Jeopardy—Greg Kihn Band (83)	*3516*
The Breakup Song (They Don't Write 'Em)—Greg Kihn Band (81)	1125
Lucky—Greg Kihn (85)	449
Love Never Fails—Greg Kihn Band (83)	168
Happy Man—Greg Kihn Band (82)	135
I Lost On Jeopardy—"Weird Al" Yankovic (84)	*18*
Every Love Song—Greg Kihn Band (82)	15
Love And Rock And Roll—Greg Kihn (86)	12
Steve KILBEY ► 5645 (1)	**261**
Under The Milky Way—Church (88)	522
Duncan KILBURN ► 8296 (1)	**55**
Pretty In Pink—Psychedelic Furs (86)	330
Merle KILGORE ► 1185 (11)	**3749**
Wolverton Mountain—Claude King (62)	*3425*
Ring Of Fire—Johnny Cash (63)	1576
She Understands Me—Johnny Tillotson (64)	*808*
Dum-De-Da—Bobby Vinton (66)	*465*
(I'm The Girl From) Wolverton Mountain—Jo Ann Campbell (62)	*453*
Not Too Long Ago—Uniques Featuring Joe Stampley (65)	240
Johnny Reb—Johnny Horton (59)	123
Dianne, Dianne—Ronny & The Daytonas (66)	118
The Man—Lorne Greene (65)	49
The Folk Singer—Tommy Roe (63)	28
Old Enough To Love—Rick Nelson (63)	21
Buddy KILLEN [William D. Killen] ► 665 (13)	**6516**
Just Walking In The Rain—Johnnie Ray (56)	7908
Forever—Little Dippers (60)	*1643*
Ain't Gonna Bump No More (With No Big Fat Woman)—Joe Tex (77)	1347
Forever—Pete Drake And His Talking Steel Guitar (64)	*954*
Sugar Lips—Al (He's The King) Hirt Trumpet with Chorus and Orchestra (64)	642
Ballad Of Two Brothers—Autry Inman (68)	334
Forever—Mercy (69)	*96*
Losing Your Love—Jim Reeves (61)	60
Everybody's Twisting Down In Mexico—Billy Vaughn And His Orchestra (61)	43
I Can't Wait Any Longer—Bill Anderson (78)	16
Cry Softly—Nancy Ames (66)	16
Forever—Billy Walker (60)	*13*
Portrait Of A Fool—Conway Twitty (62)	10
—William D. Killen see: Buddy KILLEN	
—Ronald Killette see: Buck TRAIL	
Keith KILLGO ► 7776 (3)	**76**
Flying High—Blackbyrds (75)	71
Rock Creek Park—Blackbyrds (76)	6.8
Time Is Movin'—Blackbyrds (77)	3.4
Joyce KILMER ► 6995 (2)	**123**
Trees—Platters (61)	*224*
Trees—Al Hibbler (57)	*21*
Andy KIM [Andrew Youakim] ► 212 (18)	**15266**
Sugar, Sugar—Archies (69)	*12247*
Rock Me Gently—Andy Kim (74)	4233
Jingle Jangle—Archies (69)	2684
How'd We Ever Get This Way—Andy Kim (68)	1172
Sugar Sugar—Wilson Pickett (70)	*1116*
So Good Together—Andy Kim (69)	785
Shoot 'em Up, Baby—Andy Kim (68)	590
Feelin' So Good (S.k.o.o.b.y.-D.o.o.)—Archies (68)	552
Who's Your Baby?—Archies (70)	546
Fire, Baby I'm On Fire—Andy Kim (74)	487
Sugar Sugar—Stars On 45 (81)	*442*
Rainbow Ride—Andy Kim (68)	351
I Wish I Were—Andy Kim (71)	219
A Friend In The City—Andy Kim (70)	140
It's Your Life—Andy Kim (70)	116
You Got Style—Jon & Robin (68)	92
I Been Moved—Andy Kim (71)	32
Oh My My—Monkees (70)	7.4
Bobby KIMBALL ► 9127 (1)	**31**
Waiting For Your Love—Toto (83)	61
Jennifer KIMBALL ► 4019 (2)	**622**
Almost Over You—Sheena Easton (83)	835
Bop—Dan Seals (86)	408
Linda J. KIMBALL ► 7778 (1)	**75**
I've Been Waiting For You All Of My Life—Paul Anka (81)	151
Edwin KIMMEL ► 11195 (1)	**2.8**
Take A Bow—Alan Dean (56)	5.6
Tom KIMMEL [Thomas Eugene Hobbs II] ► 7728 (1)	**78**
That's Freedom—Tom Kimmel (87)	155
Greg KIMPLE ► 8954 (1)	**35**
Stoned Cowboy—Fantasy (70)	141
Jan KINCAID ► 9459 (1)	**23**
Never Stop—Brand New Heavies (91)	93
Jesse Lee KINCAID ► 4718 (1)	**432**
Baby You Come Rollin' Across My Mind—Peppermint Trolley Company (68)	432
William KINDT ► 10920 (1)	**4.4**
Wabash Cannonball—Rusty Draper (56)	4.4
Adrian KING ► 11246 (1)	**2.6**
I Could Be So Happy—Magnificent Men (67)	5.2
Alan KING ► 9662 (1)	**19**
Rock & Roll Runaway—Ace (75)	77
Albert KING [Albert Nelson] ► 7704 (1)	**79**
Cold Feet—Albert King (68)	159
Anna KING [Anna Delores Williams] ► 6791 (1)	**137**
Baby Baby Baby—Anna King-Bobby Byrd (64)	273
Anthony KING [Anthony Frederick Lilly] ► 11207 (1)	**2.8**
You Know How It Is With A Woman—Jefferson (70)	5.5
B.B. KING [Riley B. King] ► 1676 (25)	**2508**
Rock Me Baby—B.B. King (64)	519
Paying The Cost To Be The Boss—B.B. King (68)	477
Ask Me No Questions—B.B. King (71)	469
Chains And Things—B.B. King (70)	463
Don't Answer The Door Part 1—B.B. King (66)	375
Why I Sing The Blues—B.B. King (69)	319
So Excited—B.B. King (70)	265
Ghetto Woman—B.B. King (71)	216
Get Off My Back Woman—B.B. King (69)	144
I Got Some Help I Don't Need—B.B. King (72)	129
Just A Little Love—B.B. King (69)	100
Sweet Sixteen—B.B. King (72)	98
I'm Gonna Do What They Do To Me—B.B. King (68)	87
Beautician Blues—B.B. King (64)	62
I Want You So Bad—B.B. King (69)	44
Let Me Love You—B.B. King (64)	21
The Woman I Love—B.B. King (68)	19
The Jungle—B.B. King (67)	11
Partin' Time—B.B. King (60)	5.1
I Need You So Bad—B.B. "Blues Boy" King and his orchestra (57)	5.1
That Evil Child—B.B. King (71)	3.0
You're Gonna Miss Me—B.B. King (64)	2.6
Be Careful With A Fool—B.B. "Blues Boy" King and His Orchestra (57)	1.8
I'm Gonna Sit In Till You Give In—B.B. King (62)	0.5
Got A Right To Love My Baby—B.B. King (60)	0.4
Ben E. KING [Benjamin Earl Nelson] ► 918 (13)	**4812**
There Goes My Baby—Drifters (59)	*4700*
Stand By Me—Ben E. King (61)	*3409*
Stand By Me—Ben E. King (86)	*1763*
Stand By Me—Spyder Turner (66)	*1730*
Stand By Me—Mickey Gilley (80)	*1122*
I'll Be There—Damita Jo (61)	897
There Goes My Baby—Donna Summer (84)	*674*
Stand By Me—John Lennon (75)	*647*
Seven Letters—Ben E. King (64)	398
Stand By Me—Maurice White (85)	*304*
Stand By Me—David & Jimmy Ruffin (70)	*227*
Stand By Me—Earl Grant (65)	*129*
Stand By Me—Cassius Clay (64)	*14*
Carl KING ► 8056 (1)	**63**
Over And Over—Timmy -T- (91)	63
Carole KING [Carol Klein] ► 13 (127) HOF	**71479**
It's Too Late—Carole King (71)	*8487*
Go Away Little Girl—Steve Lawrence (62)	*8171*
Take Good Care Of My Baby—Bobby Vee (61)	*7900*
The Loco-Motion—Little Eva (62)	*7718*
Go Away Little Girl—Donny Osmond (71)	*6840*
You've Got A Friend—James Taylor (71)	*6010*
Will You Love Me Tomorrow—Shirelles (60)	*5738*
The Loco-Motion—Grand Funk (74)	*4636*
Jazzman—Carole King (74)	4084
Pleasant Valley Sunday—Monkees (67)	3972
Up On The Roof—Drifters (62)	*2924*
I Can't Stay Mad At You—Skeeter Davis (63)	2616
The Loco-Motion—Kylie Minogue (88)	*2519*
Crying In The Rain—Everly Brothers (62)	2402
One Fine Day—Chiffons (63)	*2130*
Don't Say Nothin' Bad (About My Baby)—Cookies (63)	2050
I'm Into Something Good—Herman's Hermits (64)	*1902*
Just Once In My Life—Righteous Brothers (65)	1850
Hey, Girl—Freddie Scott (63)	*1793*
A Natural Woman (You Make Me Feel Like)—Aretha Franklin (67)	1752
Hey Girl—Donny Osmond (71)	*1748*
Don't Bring Me Down—Animals (66)	1719
Sweet Seasons—Carole King (72)	1709
So Far Away—Carole King (71)	1658
Keep Your Hands Off My Baby—Little Eva (62)	1642
Her Royal Majesty—James Darren (62)	1551
Go Away Little Girl—Happenings (66)	*1386*
Hi-De-Ho—Blood, Sweat & Tears (70)	1305
Some Kind Of Wonderful—Drifters (61)	1244
Chains—Cookies (62)	1234
Sharing You—Bobby Vee (62)	1134
It's Going To Take Some Time—Carpenters (72)	1120
One Fine Day—Carole King (80)	*1089*
I've Got Bonnie—Bobby Rydell (62)	1069
Will You Love Me Tomorrow—4 Seasons Featuring The "Sound" Of Frankie Valli (68)	*1009*
Nightingale—Carole King (74)	978
Oh No Not My Baby—Maxine Brown (64)	*960*
Halfway To Paradise—Bobby Vinton (68)	*936*
You've Got A Friend—Roberta Flack & Donny Hathaway (71)	*909*
Halfway To Paradise—Tony Orlando (61)	*897*
Been To Canaan—Carole King (72)	887
Walking Proud—Steve Lawrence (63)	764
This Little Girl—Dion (63)	761
I Want To Stay Here—Steve And Eydie (63)	735
Take Good Care Of My Baby—Bobby Vinton (68)	*690*
When My Little Girl Is Smiling—Drifters (62)	*674*
Point Of No Return—Gene McDaniels (62)	648
It Might As Well Rain Until September—Carole King (62)	646
Every Breath I Take—Gene Pitney (61)	623
I Can't Stop Talking About You—Steve And Eydie (63)	559
Believe In Humanity—Carole King (73)	547
Only Love Is Real—Carole King (76)	541
Up On The Roof—James Taylor (79)	*522*
Corazon—Carole King (73)	515
Poor Little Rich Girl—Steve Lawrence (63)	492
What A Sweet Thing That Was—Shirelles (61)	486
Hey Girl—Bobby Vee (68)	*476*
Hard Rock Cafe—Carole King (77)	476
He Knows I Love Him Too Much—Paris Sisters (62)	453
He's In Town—Tokens (64)	438
Will You Still Love Me Tomorrow—Dave Mason (78)	*431*
I Feel The Earth Move—Martika (89)	*430*
I'm Into Somethin' Good—Earl-Jean (64)	*425*
Where You Lead—Barbra Streisand (71)	*423*
Old Smokey Locomotion—Little Eva (63)	*399*
How Many Tears—Bobby Vee (61)	395
Porpoise Song—Monkees (68)	391
At The Club—Drifters (65)	386
I Can't Hear You No More—Helen Reddy (76)	*382*

Carole KING ▶ 13 (127) HOF *Continued*	**71479**
No Sad Song—Helen Reddy (71)	356
On This Side Of Goodbye—Righteous Brothers (66)	344
Hung On You—Righteous Brothers (65)	321
One To One—Carole King (82)	319
What Am I Gonna Do—Smith (70)	307
Why'd You Wanna Make Me Cry—Connie Stevens (62)	297
Where You Lead—Barbra Streisand (72)	*280*
Don't Forget About Me—Dusty Springfield (69)	*270*
Oh! No Not My Baby—Rod Stewart (73)	*197*
Oh No, Not My Baby—Merry Clayton (72)	*194*
After All This Time—Merry Clayton (71)	188
Will You Still Love Me Tomorrow—Roberta Flack (72)	*184*
Up On The Roof—Cryan' Shames (68)	*174*
Walkin' With My Angel—Bobby Vee (61)	166
Will Power—Cookies (63)	156
Will You Love Me Tomorrow?—Melanie (73)	*152*
It's Gonna Be Alright—Maxine Brown (65)	146
Keep Your Love Locked (Deep In Your Heart)—Paul Petersen (62)	141
Happy Times (Are Here To Stay)—Tony Orlando (61)	129
Goin' Back—Byrds (67)	125
One Fine Day—Rita Coolidge (79)	*116*
I Can't Hear You—Betty Everett (64)	*106*
Everybody Go Home—Eydie Gorme (63)	104
So Much Love—Ben E. King (66)	*102*
I Can't Make It Alone—Lou Rawls (69)	*99*
I Can't Make It Alone—Bill Medley (68)	*87*
You Light Up My Life—Carole King (73)	83
Is This What I Get For Loving You?—Ronettes Featuring Veronica (65)	74
I Need You—Chuck Jackson (65)	*72*
When My Little Girl Is Smiling—Steve Alaimo (71)	*71*
So Much Love—Steve Alaimo (66)	*67*
Where Does Love Go—Freddie Scott (64)	50
Don't Forget About Me—American Breed (67)	*48*
Wasn't Born To Follow—Byrds (69)	45
Dreamin' About You—Annette And The Vonnair Sisters (61)	37
It's Too Late—Bill Deal & The Rhondels (72)	*29*
High Out Of Time—Carole King (76)	23
Help Me—Andy Williams (62)	19
One Fine Day—Julie (76)	*19*
Sweet Sweetheart—Bobby Vee (70)	17
I Don't Think You Know Me—American Breed (67)	15
Hey Girl—Lettermen (70)	*14*
He's A Bad Boy—Carole King (63)	13
I Can't Say Goodbye—Bobby Vee (62)	10
Go Away Little Boy—Marlena Shaw (77)	*9.6*
Will You Love Me Tomorrow—Dana Valery (76)	*9.4*
Yours Until Tomorrow—Vivian Reed (68)	8.2
I Need You—Rationals (68)	*7.7*
Up On The Roof—Laura Nyro (70)	*7.4*
Don't Forget About Me—Barbara Lewis (66)	*7.0*
What I Gotta Do (To Make You Jealous)—Little Eva (63)	7.0
Down Home—Rick Nelson (63)	5.1
I Just Can't Say Goodbye—Bobby Rydell (64)	3.3
Dear Mr. D.J. Play It Again—Tina Robin (61)	2.7
Will You Love Me Tomorrow?—Linda Ronstadt (70)	*1.7*
As We Go Along—Monkees (68)	0.0
Smackwater Jack—Carole King (71)	0.0
I Feel The Earth Move—Carole King (71)	*0.0*
Charles KING ▶ 2856 (1)	**1150**
Hawaiian Wedding Song—Andy Williams (58)	3451
Claude KING ▶ 2061 (2)	**1939**
Wolverton Mountain—Claude King (62)	*3425*
(I'm The Girl From) Wolverton Mountain—Jo Ann Campbell (62)	*453*
—Dominic Roy King see: Dominic BUGATTI	
Doug KING ▶ 7336 (1)	**101**
Mind Playing Tricks On Me—Geto Boys (91)	405
—Earl King see: Earl King JOHNSON	
Earl Kenneth KING Jr. ▶ 7302 (1)	**104**
Honey, Honey—David Hudson (80)	104
Ed KING ▶ 2187 (6)	**1763**
Sweet Home Alabama—Lynyrd Skynyrd (74)	2031
Tomorrow—Strawberry Alarm Clock (67)	1241
Saturday Night Special—Lynyrd Skynyrd (75)	407
Sit With The Guru—Strawberry Alarm Clock (68)	242
Barefoot In Baltimore—Strawberry Alarm Clock (68)	224
I Dig Girls—J.J. Jackson (66)	107
Erwin KING ▶ 9364 (1)	**25**
When You Took Your Love (From Me)—Jimmy Dorsey Orchestra (58)	76
Freddy KING ▶ 5623 (3)	**264**
Hide Away—Freddy King (61)	460
San-Ho-Zay—Freddy King (61)	62
You've Got To Love Her With A Feeling—Freddy King (61)	5.2
Gail "Sky" KING ▶ 9298 (1)	**27**
Cool As Ice (Everybody Get Loose)—Vanilla Ice (91)	81
Gary KING [Blitz] ▶ 6723 (1)	**142**
Serious—Donna Allen (87)	852
Gil KING ▶ 9145 (1)	**30**
In Time—Engelbert Humperdinck (72)	121
Harry Francis KING ▶ 5143 (1)	**334**
General Hospi-Tale—Afternoon Delights (81)	669
Harry J. KING [Blitz] ▶ 6724 (1)	**142**
Serious—Donna Allen (87)	852
Jay KING ▶ 6940 (1)	**127**
Why You Treat Me So Bad—Club Nouveau (87)	381
Jimmy KING ▶ 5555 (2)	**272**
Soul Finger—Bar-Kays (67)	1546
Give Everybody Some—Bar-Kays (67)	97
John KING ▶ 9372 (1)	**25**
Hey Ladies—Beastie Boys (89)	302
Jonathan KING [Kenneth George King] ▶ 1914 (4)	**2115**
Everyone's Gone To The Moon—Jonathan King (65)	1523
It's Good News Week—Hedgehoppers Anonymous (65)	482
Where The Sun Has Never Shone—Jonathan King (65)	107
Don't Push Me—Hedgehoppers Anonymous (66)	2.4
—Kenneth George King see: Jonathan KING	
Mark KING ▶ 3675 (4)	**740**
Something About You—Level 42 (86)	1857
Lessons In Love—Level 42 (87)	1029
Hot Water—Level 42 (86)	48
Running In The Family—Level 42 (87)	42
Martin Luther KING ▶ 9711 (1)	**19**
I Have A Dream—Rev. Martin Luther King (68)	19
Marva KING ▶ 7819 (1)	**74**
Innocent—Whispers (90)	221
Paul KING ▶ 6651 (1)	**147**
Love And Pride—King (85)	295
—Pearl King see: Earl King JOHNSON	
Pee Wee KING [Julius Frank Anthony Kuczynski] ▶ 2577 (8)	**1355**
You Belong To Me—Duprees (62)	*1989*
Tennessee Waltz—Sam Cooke (64)	*546*
Tennessee Waltz—Bobby Comstock & The Counts (59)	*385*
Bonaparte's Retreat—Billy Grammer (59)	342
Tennessee Waltz—Jerry Fuller (59)	*177*
You Belong To Me—100 Strings & Joni (60)	*46*
Tennessee Waltz—Don Robertson (61)	*8.4*
Tennessee Waltz—Jupiter Serenaders (59)	*0.0*
Richard KING ▶ 8287 (1)	**55**
Put This Love To The Test—Jon Astley (88)	111
—Riley B. King see: B.B. KING	
Robert L. KING ▶ 700 (15)	**6215**
Draggin' The Line—Tommy James (71)	5158
Tighter, Tighter—Alive And Kicking (70)	3353
Nothing To Hide—Tommy James (71)	663
Gotta Get Back To You—Tommy James And The Shondells (70)	636
I'm Comin' Home—Tommy James (71)	603
Come To Me—Tommy James And The Shondells (70)	437
Love Song—Tommy James (72)	331
Ball And Chain—Tommy James (70)	327
Cat's Eye In The Window—Tommy James (72)	327
Boo, Boo, Don't 'Cha Be Blue—Tommy James (73)	288
Tell 'Em Willie Boy 's A'Comin'—Tommy James (72)	159
Sparkle And Shine—Clique (70)	71
Celebration—Tommy James (72)	68
There's A Better Day Comin'—Crazy Elephant (69)	25
Adrienne—Tommy James (71)	21
Shirley KING ▶ 3734 (1)	**717**
Lady (You Bring Me Up)—Commodores (81)	2150
Thomas R. KING ▶ 2157 (2)	**1810**
Time Won't Let Me—Outsiders (66)	2793
Girl In Love—Outsiders (66)	826
Tom KING [Harry Balk] ▶ 1925 (8)	**2101**
Red River Rock—Johnny And The Hurricanes (59)	3410
Beatnik Fly—Johnny And The Hurricanes (60)	1493
Reveille Rock—Johnny And The Hurricanes (59)	828
Crossfire—Johnny And The Hurricanes (59)	816
Am I The Man—Jackie Wilson (60)	702
Rocking Goose—Johnny And The Hurricanes (60)	239
Midnight—Johnny Gibson (62)	80
Casanova Brown—Young Sisters (62)	3.6
Warren KING ▶ 9801 (1)	**17**
Shiver And Shake—Silencers (80)	34
Wayne KING ▶ 3299 (4)	**908**
Josephine—Bill Black's Combo (60)	1744
Goofus—Carpenters (76)	65
The Waltz You Saved For Me—Ferlin Husky (61)	*28*
The Waltz You Saved For Me—Billy Vaughn and His Orchestra (55)	*11*
William KING ▶ 2898 (3)	**1127**
Lady (You Bring Me Up)—Commodores (81)	2150
Brick House—Commodores (77)	1962
Too Hot Ta Trot—Commodores (77)	499
Windsor KING ▶ 6646 (5)	**148**
Satisfied (Part 2)—Cashmeres (60)	*120*
Four Walls (Three Windows And Two Doors)—J.J. Jackson (67)	48
Ask Me—Inez Foxx (64)	45
Dance, Dance, Dance—Joey Dee (63)	28
Satisfied (Part 2)—Debbie Reynolds (60)	*10*
—King Radio see: Norman SPAN	
Peter KINGSBERY ▶ 4335 (1)	**517**
When Your Heart Is Weak—Cock Robin (85)	517
Christopher KINGSLEY ▶ 4788 (1)	**416**
Long Haired Lover From Liverpool—Little Jimmy Osmond (72)	416
Gershon KINGSLEY [Götz Gustav Ksinski] ▶ 1812 (1)	**2281**
Popcorn—Hot Butter (72)	2281
Larry KINGSTON ▶ 9539 (2)	**22**
When The Ship Hit The Sand—"Little" Jimmy Dickens (66)	16
Thank God And Greyhound—Roy Clark (70)	12
Robert KINGSTON [Barry White] ▶ 7252 (1)	**107**
Mary Hartman, Mary Hartman—Deadly Nightshade (76)	107
—Philip Kinorra see: Philamore LINCOLN	
Billy KINSLEY ▶ 11099 (1)	**3.2**
You Are My Love—Liverpool Express (76)	6.4
John Leroy KINYON ▶ 10202 (1)	**11**
Stand Or Fall—Fixx (82)	67
David KINZIE [Dave York] ▶ 10348 (1)	**9.7**
Beach Party—Dave York And The Beachcombers (62)	19
Randall KIPER ▶ 3186 (1)	**960**
Tic-Tac-Toe—Kyper (90)	960
Nat KIPNER ▶ 1702 (3)	**2461**
Too Much, Too Little, Too Late—Johnny Mathis/Deniece Williams (78)	4728
Cheryl Moana Marie—John Rowles (71)	166
We're Together—Hillside Singers (72)	55
Steve KIPNER ▶ 263 (12)	**12953**
Physical—Olivia Newton-John (81)	11192
Heart Attack—Olivia Newton-John (82)	3891
Hard Habit To Break—Chicago (84)	3593
Twist Of Fate—Olivia Newton-John (83)	2773
Impulsive—Wilson Phillips (90)	2616
If She Would Have Been Faithful...—Chicago (87)	958
Too Young—Jack Wagner (85)	340
20/20—George Benson (84)	309
Is That The Way—Tin Tin (71)	212
Moonlight On Water—Laura Branigan (90)	*166*
Moonlight On Water—Kevin Raleigh (89)	*88*
Niagara Falls—Chicago (87)	8.9
Charles KIPPS ▶ 1970 (2)	**2044**
Walk Away From Love—David Ruffin (75)	2040
Just Let Me Hold You For A Night—David Ruffin (77)	3.6
Dave KIRBY ▶ 8756 (1)	**40**
Is Anybody Goin' To San Antone—Charley Pride (70)	80
Harold KIRBY ▶ 9048 (1)	**32**
Caterpillar Crawl—Strangers (59)	130

Kier KIRBY ▶ 4102 (2)	**593**
Groove Is In The Heart—Deee-Lite (90)	2521
Power Of Love—Deee-Lite (90)	266
—Harold Kirchstein see: Harold GRANT	
Curt KIRK ▶ 8078 (1)	**63**
I Wouldn't Trade You For The World—Bachelors (64)	188
Eddie KIRK ▶ 7453 (1)	**95**
Bright Lights And Blonde Haired Women—"Tennessee" Ernie Ford (56)	95
Jim KIRK [John R. Mann] ▶ 8387 (1)	**52**
Voice Of Freedom—Jim Kirk And The TM Singers (80)	52
Steve KIRK [Jaap Streefkerk] ▶ 9468 (5)	**23**
Freddy—Annie Cordy (55)	*46*
Freddy—Connie Francis (55)	*46*
Fredy—Eartha Kitt & Perez Prado (55)	*0.0*
Freddy—Stan Kenton & His Orchestra (55)	*0.0*
Freddy—Guy Lombardo & His Royal Canadians (55)	*0.0*
Simon KIRKE ▶ 9760 (1)	**17**
Honey Child—Bad Company (76)	69
Billy KIRKLAND ▶ 7236 (1)	**108**
Memorize Your Number—Leif Garrett (79)	108
John KIRKLAND ▶ 10469 (1)	**8.1**
Boss—Rumblers (63)	48
Leroy KIRKLAND ▶ 2783 (10)	**1199**
All In My Mind—Maxine Brown (60)	*1336*
Something's Got A Hold On Me—Etta James (62)	899
Stop The Wedding—Etta James (62)	706
Next Door To The Blues—Etta James (62)	219
Old Spanish Town—Bell Notes (59)	183
It's A Mean Old Man's World—Dinah Washington (62)	26
Don't Stop The Wedding—Ann Cole (62)	10
Give A Little Time—Ella Mae Morse (54)	7.1
There's Nothing Like Love—Jackie Wilson And Linda Hopkins (62)	4.3
All In My Mind—Dakota Staton (61)	*0.0*
Mike KIRKLAND ▶ 8009 (1)	**66**
Frogg—Brothers Four (61)	328
Terry KIRKMAN ▶ 260 (5)	**13075**
Cherish—Association (66)	*7384*
Cherish—David Cassidy (71)	*3572*
Everything That Touches You—Association (68)	1677
Six Man Band—Association (68)	441
Requiem For The Masses—Association (67)	1.0
Art KIRKPATRICK ▶ 11692 (1)	**0.7**
It's Been A Long Long Time—Elgins (67)	4.3
Don KIRKPATRICK ▶ 9134 (1)	**31**
Who's Afraid Of Virginia Woolf? (Part 1)—Jimmy Smith (64)	61
Wayne KIRKPATRICK ▶ 1977 (5)	**2039**
Every Heartbeat—Amy Grant (91)	3631
Place In This World—Michael W. Smith (91)	2042
For You—Michael W. Smith (91)	241
Wise Up—Amy Grant (85)	134
Lead Me On—Amy Grant (88)	2.7
Randell KIRSCH ▶ 8757 (1)	**40**
Blue Kiss—Jane Wiedlin (85)	80
Don KIRSHNER ▶ 4909 (3)	**385**
Wait A Minute—Coasters (61)	495
Warm Up To Me Baby—Jimmy Bowen With The Rhythm Orchids (57)	272
Dealer In Dreams—Bobby Darin (58)	2.4
Lonnie KIRTZ ▶ 9632 (1)	**20**
What's Too Much—Smokey Robinson (87)	80
Inez J. KITTS ▶ 11363 (1)	**2.1**
Ronnie's Rapp—Ron And The D.C. Crew (87)	8.3
—Bert Klamkin see: Bert CARROLL	
Irmgard KLARMANN ▶ 5738 (1)	**247**
Symptoms Of True Love—Tracie Spencer (88)	494
—Daniel Robert Klawon see: Denny KLAWSON	
Denny KLAWSON [Daniel Robert Klawon] ▶ 5173 (1)	**331**
It's Cold Outside—Choir (67)	331
Gary KLEBE ▶ 8177 (1)	**59**
Too Late—Shoes (79)	59
Gary KLEIN ▶ 1209 (4)	**3680**
Bobby's Girl—Marcie Blane (62)	7201
What Does A Girl Do?—Marcie Blane (63)	120
Baby You're So Right For Me—Brenda & The Tabulations (68)	33
Guess Who?—Dusty Springfield (64)	5.8
—Gene Klein see: Gene SIMMONS	
George KLEIN ▶ 11198 (1)	**2.8**
Loving You Is A Natural Thing—Ronnie Milsap (70)	8.4
Jim KLEIN ▶ 6362 (3)	**179**
Over And Over—Pajama Party (89)	171
Hide And Seek—Pajama Party (90)	119
Yo No Se—Pajama Party (89)	68
John M. KLEIN ▶ 11778 (2)	**0.0**
Break My Heart Gently—Dorothy Collins (54)	0.0
Can This Be The End Of A Dream—Dorothy Collins (54)	0.0
—Miriam Klein see: Miriam UNIMAN	
Paul KLEIN ▶ 3647 (14)	**751**
Little Blue Man—Betty Johnson (58)	791
Good And Lonesome—Kay Starr (55)	273
Close The Door—Jim Lowe (55)	235
Rockin' The Cha Cha—Alan Dale (55)	221
Summer Sweetheart—Ames Brothers (56)	60
That's Ok With Me—Susan Hunter (55)	53
In The Arms Of My Love—Joe Valino (57)	27
I Like Them All—Dean Martin (55)	14
Wait For Tomorrow—Jill Corey (56)	12
I'll Wait—Betty Johnson (56)	7.7
That Do Make It Nice—Eddy Arnold (55)	6.5
Sugar Corsage—Chuck Reed (57)	*2.4*
Sugar Corsage—Bonnie Scott (57)	*2.4*
Hook—Rita Robbins (54)	0.0
Paul (2) KLEIN [A. Hott] ▶ 8485 (2)	**48**
Cars With The Boom—L'Trimm (88)	232
Ronnie's Rapp—Ron And The D.C. Crew (87)	8.3
—Annette Kleinbard see: Carol CONNORS	
Neil KLEINHANDLER ▶ 6198 (1)	**194**
Barbara—Temptations (2) (60)	582
Richard KLENDER ▶ 6944 (1)	**126**
Dear Mr. Jesus—Powersource (87)	126
John KLENNER ▶ 3338 (5)	**894**
Heartaches—Marcels (61)	*1413*
Heartaches—Patsy Cline (62)	*275*
Heartaches—Somethin' Smith & The Redheads (56)	*75*
Heartaches—Four Preps (62)	*24*
Heartaches—Sam Sideburn (58)	*0.8*
Alf KLIMEK ▶ 6826 (2)	**134**
Holiday—Other Ones (87)	545
We Are What We Are—Other Ones (87)	261
Jayney KLIMEK [Janey Diamond] ▶ 6827 (2)	**134**
Holiday—Other Ones (87)	545
We Are What We Are—Other Ones (87)	261
Johnny KLIMEK ▶ 6828 (2)	**134**
Holiday—Other Ones (87)	545
We Are What We Are—Other Ones (87)	261
Mark KLINGMAN ▶ 6203 (1)	**194**
Friends—Bette Midler (73)	387
—Mary Klopprogge see: Mary APPLEGATE	
Othmar KLOSE ▶ 11470 (1)	**1.6**
(Hear My Song) Violetta—Ray Adams And Orchestra (62)	6.2
Jean Joseph KLUGER ▶ 9960 (2)	**15**
Cuba—Gibson Brothers (79)	22
Stories??—Chakachas (72)	7.0
Skip KNAPÉ ▶ 4441 (1)	**494**
God, Love And Rock & Roll—Teegarden & Van Winkle (70)	987
—Richard Terrance Knapp see: Terry KNIGHT	
Larry KNECHTEL ▶ 5262 (2)	**316**
Took The Last Train—David Gates (78)	541
Drivin' Home—Duane Eddy And The Rebels (61)	92
Baker KNIGHT ▶ 169 (20)	**17593**
Lonesome Town—Ricky Nelson (58)	3442
Never Be Anyone Else But You—Ricky Nelson (59)	3103
The Wonder Of You—Elvis Presley (70)	*2415*
I Got A Feeling—Ricky Nelson (58)	2224
Sweeter Than You—Ricky Nelson (59)	1336
The Wonder Of You—Ray Peterson (59)	*1077*
I Wanna Be Loved—Ricky Nelson (59)	829
Somewhere There's A Someone—Dean Martin (66)	556
You Are The One—Sugar Bears (72)	453
Not Enough Indians—Dean Martin (68)	409
You Are The Only One—Ricky Nelson (60)	406
Anytime At All—Frank Sinatra (65)	324
Mighty Good—Ricky Nelson (59)	316
Nobody's Baby Again—Dean Martin (66)	289
If You Want This Love—Sonny Knight (64)	129
Right By My Side—Ricky Nelson (60)	112
The Wonder Of You—Ray Peterson (64)	*69*
Cowboy Boots—Dave Dudley (63)	43
I Need You—Rick Nelson (62)	32
One Cup Of Happiness (And One Peace Of Mind)—Dean Martin (69)	30
—Etterlene Knight see: Bunny DeBARGE	
Frederick KNIGHT ▶ 582 (6)	**7482**
Ring My Bell—Anita Ward (79)	*6932*
Ring My Bell—DJ Jazzy Jeff & The Fresh Prince (91)	*521*
Trouble—Frederick Knight (72)	21
Don't Drop My Love—Anita Ward (79)	13
It Ain't No Fun—Shirley Brown (75)	4.0
Trying To Slip (Away)—Lloyd Price (73)	3.7
Gary KNIGHT [Gary Temkin, Harold Temkin, Gary Weston] ▶ 2393 (8)	**1530**
Vacation—Connie Francis (62)	1465
The River Is Wide—Grassroots (69)	*1304*
The River Is Wide—Forum (67)	*441*
Break Out—Mitch Ryder And The Detroit Wheels (66)	164
Too Many Rules—Connie Francis (61)	160
Music To My Heart—Obsession (70)	8.0
It's The Same Old Love—Courtship (72)	7.3
Takin' All I Can Get—Mitch Ryder And The Detroit Wheels (66)	0.5
Gladys KNIGHT ▶ 3651 (4)	**748**
I Don't Want To Do Wrong—Gladys Knight & The Pips (71)	1596
Daddy Could Swear, I Declare—Gladys Knight & The Pips (73)	1036
Save The Overtime (For Me)—Gladys Knight & The Pips (83)	179
Way Back Home—Jr. Walker & The All Stars (71)	*144*
Holly KNIGHT [Holly Erlanger] ▶ 328 (26) HOF	**11161**
Love Is A Battlefield—Pat Benatar (83)	3131
Never—Heart (85)	2388
The Warrior—Scandal Featuring Patty Smyth (84)	2200
Better Be Good To Me—Tina Turner (84)	2151
Obsession—Animotion (85)	2123
Just Between You And Me—Lou Gramm (89)	2059
Love Touch—Rod Stewart (86)	1772
Invincible—Pat Benatar (85)	1289
There's The Girl—Heart (87)	1044
The Best—Tina Turner (89)	940
One Of The Living—Tina Turner (85)	879
Rag Doll—Aerosmith (88)	789
Hanging On A Heart Attack—Device (86)	505
My Heart Is Failing Me—Riff (91)	501
New Romance (It's A Mystery)—Spider (80)	418
Hands Tied—Scandal Featuring Patty Smyth (84)	338
Change—John Waite (85)	238
It Didn't Take Long—Spider (81)	226
Little Darlin'—Sheila (81)	206
Heart Don't Fail Me Now—Holly Knight (88)	180
Hide Your Heart—KISS (89)	110
Pleasure And Pain—Divinyls (86)	84
Who Says—Device (86)	81
I Engineer—Animotion (86)	39
Love Thing—Tina Turner (91)	35
Everything Is Alright—Spider (80)	8.7
Jerry KNIGHT ▶ 2015 (4)	**2001**
Crush On You—Jets (86)	2253
Breakin'.. There's No Stoppin' Us—Ollie And Jerry (84)	1414
Private Number—Jets (86)	291
Tonight—Whispers (83)	21
Jordan KNIGHT ▶ 3107 (1)	**1006**
I'll Be Your Everything—Tommy Page (90)	3017
Merald KNIGHT ▶ 3785 (3)	**700**
I Don't Want To Do Wrong—Gladys Knight & The Pips (71)	1596
Daddy Could Swear, I Declare—Gladys Knight & The Pips (73)	1036
Save The Overtime (For Me)—Gladys Knight & The Pips (83)	179
Posie KNIGHT ▶ 4318 (1)	**523**
I've Been Lonely For So Long—Frederick Knight (72)	1046

Richard KNIGHT [Richard Dunbar] ▶ 8312 (4)	**55**
Drop By My Place—Little Carl Carlton (70)	140
We All Gotta Stick Together—Four Tops (75)	66
You Made A Believer (Out Of Me)—Ruby Andrews (69)	22
Hey Boy Take A Chance On Love—Ruby Andrews (67)	8.4
Stan KNIGHT ▶ 11555 (1)	**1.2**
Strong Enough To Be Gentle— Black Oak Arkansas (76)	8.4
Terry KNIGHT [Richard Terrance Knapp] ▶ 7975 (2)	**67**
A Change On The Way— Terry Knight And The Pack (66)	57
Love Love Love Love Love— Terry Knight And The Pack (67)	10
Dick KNISS ▶ 2488 (1)	**1445**
Sunshine On My Shoulders—John Denver (74)	4334
Fred KNOBLOCK [James Frederick Knobloch] ▶ 5248 (1)	**318**
Why Not Me—Fred Knoblock (80)	637
Gladys KNOCHELMAN ▶ 11583 (1)	**1.1**
The Soul Of J. B.— James Brown And The Famous Flames (67)	3.3
Mark KNOPFLER ▶ 427 (8)	**9463**
Money For Nothing—Dire Straits (85)	5636
Sultans Of Swing—Dire Straits (79)	2301
Walk Of Life—Dire Straits (85)	1757
Private Dancer—Tina Turner (85)	1524
So Far Away—Dire Straits (86)	783
Lady Writer—Dire Straits (79)	179
Skateaway—Dire Straits (80)	70
Industrial Disease—Dire Straits (83)	30
Joe KNOTT ▶ 7502 (1)	**91**
Add Some Music To Your Day—Beach Boys (70)	274
Buddy KNOX ▶ 1542 (15)	**2773**
Party Doll—Buddy Knox with The Rhythm Orchids (57)	*4735*
Party Doll—Steve Lawrence (57)	*1892*
Hula Love—Buddy Knox with The Rhythm Orchids (57)	1598
I'm Stickin' With You— Jimmy Bowen With The Rhythm Orchids (57)	*1396*
Rock Your Little Baby To Sleep— Buddy Knox with The Rhythm Orchids (57)	698
Swingin' Daddy— Buddy Knox with The Rhythm Orchids (58)	174
Party Doll— Cat Mother And The All Night News Boys (69)	*164*
I Think I'm Gonna Kill Myself—Buddy Knox (59)	141
Party Doll—Wingy Manone And His Orchestra (57)	*133*
I Trusted You— Jimmy Bowen With The Rhythm Orchids (57)	76
Ever Lovin' Fingers— Jimmy Bowen With The Rhythm Orchids (57)	44
I'm Stickin' With You—Fontane Sisters (57)	*36*
C'mon Baby— Buddy Knox with The Rhythm Orchids (58)	13
Party Doll—Roy Brown (57)	*7.0*
I'm Stickin' With You—Roy Brown (57)	*0.0*
Kevin KNOX ▶ 9135 (1)	**31**
Who's Afraid Of Virginia Woolf? (Part 1)— Jimmy Smith (64)	61
—Shanice Knox see: Shanice WILSON	
Keith KNUDSEN ▶ 5828 (1)	**238**
One Step Closer—Doobie Brothers (80)	715
Michael KNUST ▶ 8390 (1)	**52**
San Francisco Girls (Return Of The Native)— Fever Tree (68)	156
John James KOCH ▶ 7225 (1)	**109**
I Want You All To Myself (Just You)— Kitty Kallen (54)	218
Frank KOCIAN [Pavel] ▶ 9831 (1)	**16**
Standing On Guard—Falcons (66)	49
Cub KODA ▶ 1758 (5)	**2365**
Smokin' In The Boy's Room—Brownsville Station (73)	*3499*
Smokin' In The Boys Room—Mötley Crüe (85)	*773*
Kings Of The Party—Brownsville Station (74)	474
The Martian Boogie—Brownsville Station (77)	180
Mama Don't Allow No Parkin'— Brownsville Station (74)	50
Ted KOEHLER ▶ 4791 (7)	**413**
Let's Fall In Love—Peaches & Herb (66)	*707*
Ev'rybody's Twistin'—Frank Sinatra (62)	90

Don't Worry 'Bout Me—Vincent Edwards (62)	18
Some Sunday Morning—Wayne Newton (65)	6.6
Ev'ry Night About This Time—Diamonds (56)	5.5
Let's Fall In Love—Linda Scott (63)	*1.8*
Don't Worry About Me—Frank Sinatra (54)	0.0
Peter KOELEWIJN ▶ 8469 (1)	**49**
Black Kisses (Never Make You Blue)— Curtie And The Boombox (85)	49
Edmund KOETSCHER ▶ 3374 (2)	**876**
Liechtensteiner Polka— Will Glahe And His Orchestra And Chorus (57)	*1644*
Liechtensteiner Polka— Lawrence Welk And His Champagne Music (57)	*109*
Moe KOFFMAN ▶ 2072 (6)	**1923**
The Swingin' Shepherd Blues— Moe Koffman Quartette (58)	*892*
Swinging Shepherd Blues—Johnny Pate Quintet (58)	*654*
Swinging Shepherd Blues— David Rose And His Orchestra (58)	*376*
Swingin' Shepherd Blues Twist—Moe Koffman (62)	*1.8*
Swingin' Shepherd Blues— David Terry & His Orchestra (58)	*0.0*
The Swingin' Shepherd Blues— Ella Fitzgerald & Her Shepherds (58)	*0.0*
Géo KOGER [Georges Konyn] ▶ 11507 (1)	**1.4**
Vieni Vieni—Terri Stevens (59)	*5.6*
Alan KOHAN [Buz Kohan] ▶ 5069 (1)	**350**
One More Time—Ray Charles Singers (64)	701
—D.J. Kohler see: James TESTA	
—Donna Kohler see: James TESTA	
Churchill KOHLMAN ▶ 2047 (6)	**1951**
Cry—Ronnie Dove (66)	*1106*
Cry—Knightsbridge Strings (59)	*575*
Cry—Ray Charles (65)	*172*
Cry—Lynn Anderson (72)	*98*
Cry—Paul Anka (62)	*0.4*
Cry—Cavril Payne (65)	*0.0*
Larry KOLBER ▶ 736 (10)	**5969**
Patches—Dickey Lee (62)	4183
I Love How You Love Me—Bobby Vinton (68)	*3635*
I Love How You Love Me—Paris Sisters (61)	*2552*
Forget Me Not—Kalin Twins (58)	897
Sweet Little You—Neil Sedaka (61)	354
Someone Loves You Joe—Singing Belles (60)	168
The Yellow Bandana—Faron Young (63)	72
Let Me Be The One—Peaches & Herb (69)	*68*
Let Me Be The One—Paris Sisters (62)	*26*
Your Second Choice—Clyde McPhatter (61)	6.1
Diane KOLBY ▶ 6300 (1)	**184**
Holy Man—Diane Kolby (70)	184
Jerry KOLLENBURG [Gerald Van Kollenburg] ▶ 4535 (6)	**469**
Love You So Much—New Colony Six (67)	340
Can't You See Me Cry—New Colony Six (68)	322
Roll On—New Colony Six (71)	229
I Confess—New Colony Six (66)	148
Long Time To Be Alone—New Colony Six (71)	15
I Lie Awake—New Colony Six (66)	2.9
Fred KOLLER ▶ 3445 (1)	**845**
Angel Eyes—Jeff Healey Band (89)	1690
Otto KOLLMAN [Gerhard Altstedt, Otto Kollmann] ▶ 9496 (1)	**23**
Try Again—Dean Martin (54)	68
Dag KOLSRUD ▶ 6661 (1)	**146**
Downtown—One 2 Many (89)	438
Leslie KONG ▶ 3234 (1)	**937**
Israelites—Desmond Dekker & The Aces (69)	1874
John KONGOS ▶ 6100 (2)	**206**
Step On—Happy Mondays (91)	*231*
He's Gonna Step On You Again—John Kongos (71)	*181*
Frank KONTE ▶ 2148 (2)	**1817**
Ride Captain Ride—Blues Image (70)	3535
Gas Lamps And Clay—Blues Image (70)	98
—Georges Konyn see: Géo KOGER	
—Jean A. Koons see: Jeannie JOY	
Al KOOPER ▶ 1420 (6)	**3112**
This Diamond Ring— Gary Lewis And The Playboys (65)	7757
I Must Be Seeing Things—Gene Pitney (65)	593
I Love You More Than You'll Ever Know— Donny Hathaway (72)	211

I Can't Quit Her—Arbors (69)	85
No Time Like The Right Time—Blues Project (67)	69
Just One Minute More—Mike Finnigan (78)	13
George KOOYMANS ▶ 1625 (8)	**2599**
Twilight Zone—Golden Earring (82)	1697
Radar Love—Golden Earring (74)	*1460*
Radar Love—White Lion (89)	*180*
Candy's Going Bad—Golden Earring (74)	60
The Devil Made Me Do It—Golden Earring (83)	53
When The Lady Smiles—Golden Earring (84)	29
Dong Dong Diki Di-Ki Dong—Super Cirkus (69)	14
Ce Soir—Golden Earring (75)	9.4
Charles KOPPELMAN ▶ 4067 (1)	**605**
Yogi—Ivy Three (60)	1816
Arthur KORB ▶ 4971 (5)	**367**
Go On With The Wedding—Patti Page (55)	*976*
Go On With The Wedding— Kitty Kallen & Georgie Shaw (55)	*288*
Fool Of The Year—Georgia Gibbs (56)	81
Prince Of Players— Tommy Frederick and the Hi-Notes (58)	22
Go On With The Wedding—Modernaires (56)	*0.0*
—Nathan Korb see: Francis LEMARQUE	
Jürgen KORDULETSCH ▶ 8237 (2)	**57**
Boogie Woogie Dancin' Shoes—Claudja Barry (79)	216
Dancin' Fever—Claudja Barry (78)	43
Artie KORNFELD ▶ 593 (11)	**7337**
The Rain, The Park & Other Things— Cowsills (67)	7643
The Pied Piper—Crispian St. Peters (66)	*4251*
Dead Man's Curve—Jan & Dean (64)	2112
We Can Fly—Cowsills (68)	950
I Adore Him—Angels (63)	742
Tonight You're Gonna Fall In Love With Me— Shirelles (64)	296
Pied Piper—Changin' Times (65)	*131*
Did You Ever—Hullaballoos (65)	68
Judy Loves Me—Johnny Crawford (64)	7.8
Guess Who?—Dusty Springfield (64)	5.8
Another Page—Connie Francis (67)	2.3
Danny KORTCHMAR ▶ 688 (13)	**6334**
Dirty Laundry—Don Henley (82)	4004
Somebody's Baby—Jackson Browne (82)	2571
All She Wants To Do Is Dance—Don Henley (85)	1505
So Close—Daryl Hall & John Oates (90)	999
Sunset Grill—Don Henley (85)	675
Tender Is The Night—Jackson Browne (83)	646
Not Enough Love In The World—Don Henley (85)	525
Johnny Can't Read—Don Henley (82)	392
New York Minute—Don Henley (90)	351
I Can't Stand Still—Don Henley (83)	339
How Bad Do You Want It?—Don Henley (90)	330
If Anybody Had A Heart—John Waite (86)	98
Honey Don't Leave L.A.—James Taylor (78)	85
—Kevin Valentine Kosec see: Kevin VALENTINE	
Jonah KOSLEN ▶ 8817 (1)	**39**
Takin' It Back—Breathless (79)	39
Ira KOSLOFF ▶ 1848 (7)	**2202**
I Want You I Need You I Love You— Elvis Presley (56)	3831
Things I Didn't Do—Perry Como (54)	320
Love Me As I Love You—George Maharis (62)	272
Five Hundred Guys—Frank Sinatra (56)	133
I Spoke Too Soon—Crew-Cuts (54)	38
Bring Back My Baby To Me—Ella Mae Morse (54)	6.5
Place In The Sun—Johnny Nash (60)	4.8
Joseph KOSMA ▶ 372 (9)	**10449**
Autumn Leaves—Roger Williams (55)	*9865*
Autumn Leaves— Victor Young And His Singing Strings (55)	*192*
Autumn Leaves—Jackie Gleason (55)	*170*
Autumn Leaves—Mitch Miller & His Orchestra (55)	*162*
Autumn Leaves—Steve Allen (55)	*147*
Autumn Leaves—Ray Charles Singers (55)	*37*
Autumn Leaves - 1965—Roger Williams (65)	*8.9*
Autumn Leaves—Keely Smith (57)	*0.0*
Autumn Leaves—Bette McLaurin with Ray Ellis' Orch. And Chorus (57)	*0.0*
Ron KOSS ▶ 10692 (1)	**6.0**
Come On Down—Savage Grace (70)	6.0
Paul KOSSOFF ▶ 7040 (1)	**120**
Stealer—Free (70)	359

Nick KOUSALEOUS ▶ 4684 (1)	**438**
Convention '72—Delegates (72)	877
—Alexandre Kouyoumdjian see: Alec R. COSTANDINOS	
—Kovall see: Koenraad VAN-LISHOUT	
Paul KOY ▶ 9210 (1)	**29**
Many A Time—Steve Lawrence (58)	57
Peter KRAEMER ▶ 4872 (3)	**393**
Hello Hello—Sopwith "Camel" (66)	*746*
Postcard From Jamaica—Sopwith "Camel" (67)	36
Hello, Hello—Claudine Longet (67)	*4.7*
Ivan KRAL ▶ 6289 (1)	**185**
Every Step Of The Way—John Waite (85)	556
Alex KRAMER ▶ 3905 (9)	**662**
No Other Arms No Other Lips—Chordettes (59)	*741*
Cool Shake—Del Vikings (57)	461
Pupalina—Gaylords (54)	*213*
How Lonely Can I Get—Kitty Kallen (55)	*182*
No Other Arms No Other Lips—Four Aces (59)	*119*
Candy Cha Cha—Jan August-Richard Hayman (58)	32
How Lonely Can I Get?—Lancers (55)	*0.0*
Pupalina (My Little Doll)—Jimmy Durante (54)	*0.0*
Pupalina (My Little Doll)— Guy Lombardo & His Royal Canadians (54)	*0.0*
—Hans Herman Stein Kramer see: Mark STEIN	
Joey KRAMER ▶ 9943 (1)	**15**
Kings And Queens—Aerosmith (78)	73
Ron KRAMER ▶ 10402 (1)	**8.9**
The Ballad Of Evel Knievel— John Culliton Mahoney (74)	18
Russ KRAMER ▶ 4709 (1)	**434**
Lost In Love—New Edition (85)	434
—Wayne Kramer see: Wayne KAMBES	
Craig KRAMPF ▶ 3231 (2)	**939**
Oh Sherrie—Steve Perry (84)	3231
Strung Out—Steve Perry (84)	393
Dale KRANTZ [Dale Krantz Rossington] ▶ 7736 (1)	**77**
Don't Misunderstand Me— Rossington Collins Band (80)	231
Bob KRASNOW ▶ 8605 (1)	**45**
Report To The Nation—Winkly & Nutly (60)	45
—Joachim Fritz Krauledat see: John KAY	
Lenny KRAVITZ ▶ 1154 (4)	**3846**
Justify My Love—Madonna (90)	3894
It Ain't Over Til It's Over—Lenny Kravitz (91)	2491
Stand By My Woman—Lenny Kravitz (91)	113
Let Love Rule—Lenny Kravitz (90)	29
Mark KREIDER ▶ 5032 (1)	**357**
Such A Woman—Tycoon (79)	714
Lothar KRELL ▶ 9847 (1)	**16**
Should I Love You—Cee Farrow (83)	32
John KRENSKI ▶ 2581 (2)	**1351**
The Cheater—Bob Kuban And The In-Men (66)	1314
The Teaser—Bob Kuban And The In-Men (66)	75
Helmy KRESA ▶ 8183 (2)	**59**
That's My Desire—Yvonne Baker And The Sensations (62)	*118*
That's My Desire—Pat Boone (61)	*1.0*
Robert KRETSCHMER ▶ 4887 (3)	**388**
Crazy—Icehouse (87)	976
No Promises—Icehouse (86)	90
My Obsession—Icehouse (88)	35
Herbert KRETZMER ▶ 3597 (4)	**773**
Yesterday, When I Was Young—Roy Clark (69)	1095
In The Summer Of His Years—Connie Francis (63)	*423*
In The Summer Of His Years—Millicent Martin (63)	*22*
In The Summer Of His Years—Toni Arden (63)	*5.5*
—Peter Kreuder see: Peter PAN	
Oliver KREYSSIG ▶ 8546 (1)	**47**
The Great Commandment—Camouflage (88)	140
—Richard Charles Krieg see: Dick CHARLES	
Henry KRIEGER ▶ 5506 (1)	**277**
And I Am Telling You I'm Not Going— Jennifer Holliday (82)	554
Robby KRIEGER ▶ 453 (20)	**9220**
Light My Fire—Doors (67)	*8461*
Hello, I Love You—Doors (68)	6496
Touch Me—Doors (68)	5980
Light My Fire—Jose Feliciano (68)	*4958*
Love Her Madly—Doors (71)	1978

People Are Strange—Doors (67)	1529
Riders On The Storm—Doors (71)	1436
Love Me Two Times—Doors (67)	731
The Unknown Soldier—Doors (68)	682
Tell All The People—Doors (69)	500
Wishful Sinful—Doors (69)	464
Runnin' Blue—Doors (69)	354
L.A. Woman—Billy Idol (90)	208
Tightrope Ride—Doors (71)	155
Light My Fire—Amii Stewart (79)	*51*
The Mosquito—Doors (72)	50
Roadhouse Blues—Doors (70)	38
Light My Fire—Rhetta Hughes (69)	*33*
Light My Fire—Doors (68)	*32*
Love Street—Doors (68)	9.0
Jim KRIEGSMANN ▶ 1932 (5)	**2093**
Happy Organ—Dave "Baby" Cortez (59)	5914
Whistling Organ—Dave "Baby" Cortez (59)	293
Always You—Betty Madigan (54)	*67*
Red Roses—John Laurenz (55)	14
Joey—Betty Madigan (54)	0.0
Steve KRIKORIAN ▶ 9656 (1)	**19**
Perfect World—Alias (91)	39
Joern Volsgaard KRISTENSEN [Jörn K] ▶ 10569 (1)	**7.2**
Get Serious—Cut 'N' Move (91)	36
Kris KRISTOFFERSON ▶ 304 (21) HOF	**11912**
Me And Bobby McGee—Janis Joplin (71)	*5615*
Help Me Make It Through The Night—Sammi Smith (71)	*2203*
For The Good Times—Ray Price (70)	1883
Why Me—Kris Kristofferson (73)	1828
Loving Her Was Easier (Than Anything I'll Ever Do Again)—Kris Kristofferson (71)	829
Help Me Make It Through The Night— Gladys Knight & The Pips (72)	*483*
Sunday Morning Coming Down—Johnny Cash (70)	*405*
Me And Bobby McGee—Jerry Lee Lewis (71)	*402*
A Song I'd Like To Sing— Kris Kristofferson & Rita Coolidge (73)	339
One Day At A Time—Marilyn Sellars (74)	224
Help Me Make It Through The Night—Joe Simon (71)	*193*
I'd Rather Be Sorry—Ray Price (71)	155
Josie—Kris Kristofferson (72)	133
I've Got To Have You—Sammi Smith (72)	111
Nobody Wins—Brenda Lee (73)	62
Sunday Mornin' Comin' Down—Ray Stevens (69)	*55*
Help Me Make It Through The Night—O.C. Smith (71)	*36*
Jesus Was A Capricorn—Kris Kristofferson (72)	31
Stranger—Johnny Duncan (76)	28
The Taker—Waylon Jennings (70)	22
Please Don't Tell Me How The Story Ends— Ronnie Milsap (74)	7.6
Anthony KRIZAN ▶ 9228 (1)	**28**
Stand By My Woman—Lenny Kravitz (91)	113
Elmar KROHN ▶ 7326 (2)	**102**
Blame It On The Boogie—Jacksons (78)	*217*
Blame It On The Boogie—Mick Jackson (78)	*89*
Bobby KROLL ▶ 9440 (1)	**23**
Foolishly—Vic Damone (55)	47
Jimmy KRONDES ▶ 2376 (2)	**1550**
(At) The End (Of A Rainbow)—Earl Grant (58)	2879
Summer Souvenirs—Karl Hammel, Jr. (61)	221
Jim KRUEGER ▶ 2758 (2)	**1217**
We Just Disagree—Dave Mason (77)	1141
Save Me—Dave Mason (80)	76
Jim KRUM ▶ 10499 (1)	**7.8**
Pa Pa Pa—Joni James (54)	23
—Christian F. Kruzinski see: Cee FARROW	
—Götz Gustav Ksinski see: Gershon KINGSLEY	
David KUBINEC ▶ 11516 (1)	**1.4**
King Croesus—World Of Oz (68)	5.5
—Deborah Kucan see: Debbie WITKOWSKI	
—Julius Frank Anthony Kuczynski see: Pee Wee KING	
Jan KUEHNEMUND ▶ 7310 (1)	**103**
How Much Love—Vixen (90)	308
Robert KUHN ▶ 6630 (2)	**149**
That's My Little Suzie—Ritchie Valens (59)	291
Little Girl—Ritchie Valens (59)	7.8
F. KULAGA ▶ 11389 (1)	**1.9**
Gift Of Love—Van Dykes (1) (61)	5.8

Andrew KULBERG ▶ 5612 (1)	**265**
13 Questions—Seatrain (71)	529
Bruce KULICK ▶ 8863 (1)	**38**
Love Me Tonight—Blackjack (79)	113
Robert KULICK ▶ 8864 (1)	**38**
Love Me Tonight—Blackjack (79)	113
Les KUMMEL ▶ 2231 (4)	**1717**
Things I'd Like To Say—New Colony Six (68)	1717
I Will Always Think About You—New Colony Six (68)	1256
I Want You To Know—New Colony Six (69)	202
Barbara, I Love You—New Colony Six (69)	83
Leah KUNKEL [Leah Cohen] ▶ 7743 (1)	**77**
Straight From The Heart (Into Your Life)— Coyote Sisters (84)	153
Margot KUNKEL ▶ 9005 (1)	**33**
Loving You With My Eyes—Starland Vocal Band (80)	67
Russ KUNKEL ▶ 6022 (1)	**215**
Tender Is The Night—Jackson Browne (83)	646
—Michael Kunze see: Stephan PRAGER	
—Marty Kupersmith see: Marty SANDERS	
Steve KUPKA ▶ 2832 (7)	**1165**
So Very Hard To Go—Tower Of Power (73)	1182
You're Still A Young Man—Tower Of Power (72)	811
This Time It's Real—Tower Of Power (73)	177
Down To The Nightclub—Tower Of Power (72)	154
You Ought To Be Havin' Fun—Tower Of Power (76)	75
Time Will Tell—Tower Of Power (74)	63
What Is Hip?—Tower Of Power (74)	4.3
Marty KUPPS ▶ 4370 (1)	**510**
Two Divided By Love—Grass Roots (71)	1531
Kathy KURASCH ▶ 9755 (1)	**17**
Divided Hearts—Kim Carnes (86)	70
—January Kurta see: January TYME	
—Emanuel Kurtz see: Mann CURTIS	
Gene KURTZ ▶ 1775 (1)	**2340**
Treat Her Right—Roy Head And The Traits (65)	4680
—Manny Kurtz see: Mann CURTIS	
Larry KUSIK ▶ 2042 (18)	**1964**
As If I Didn't Know—Adam Wade (61)	958
Lady—Jack Jones (67)	730
Games That Lovers Play—Eddie Fisher (66)	*696*
Happy Summer Days—Ronnie Dove (66)	651
Love Theme From "The Godfather" (Speak Softly Love)—Andy Williams (72)	*619*
Making Memories—Frankie Laine (67)	564
People Like You—Eddie Fisher (67)	107
Games That Lovers Play—Wayne Newton (66)	*91*
Speak Softly Love—Al Martino (72)	*91*
A Happy Guy—Rick Nelson (64)	81
Fiddle Around—Jan & Dean (66)	59
When The Snow Is On The Roses—Ed Ames (67)	52
It's Not The Same— Anthony And The Imperials (66)	36
Run, Run, Run—Ronny Douglas (61)	31
Love Theme From "Romeo And Juliet" (A Time For Us)—Johnny Mathis (69)	*30*
Don't Take It Out On Me—Bobbi Martin (66)	13
No One Knows—Every Mother's Son (68)	12
More Than A Miracle—Roger Williams (67)	0.5
William S. KUTNER ▶ 11574 (1)	**1.2**
Gretchen—Diamonds (59)	2.3
Norma KUTZER ▶ 11560 (1)	**1.2**
I'm The Sky—Eddie Rambeau (66)	2.4
—June Evelyn Kuykendall see: Rickie PAGE	
—Robert Harry Kuykendall see: Bobby DALL	
Jaime KYLE ▶ 4211 (1)	**562**
Stranded—Heart (90)	1124
Dwania KYLES ▶ 9397 (1)	**24**
Special Way—Kool & The Gang (87)	122
Ben KYNARD ▶ 11291 (1)	**2.4**
Red Top—Teen Queens (56)	4.8

L

—Carlo Donida Labati see: Carlo DONIDA	
Patti LaBELLE [Patricia Louise Edwards, Patricia Louise Holt] ▶ 11095 (1)	**3.3**
Feels Like Another One—Patti LaBelle (91)	13
—Art Laboe see: Arthur EGNOIAN	

Dorothy LaBOSTRIE ▶ 3653 (5)	**748**
Tutti Frutti—Pat Boone (56)	*1434*
Tutti Frutti—Little Richard (56)	*649*
Tutti-Frutti—Jive Bunny And The Mastermixers (89)	*80*
Tutti Frutti—Jive Bunny And The Mastermixers (89)	*80*
Tutti-Frutti—Art Mooney & His Orchestra (56)	*0.0*
Bill LaBOUNTY ▶ 2403 (5)	**1521**
Hot Rod Hearts—Robbie Dupree (80)	1599
This Night Won't Last Forever—Michael Johnson (79)	*1098*
Brooklyn Girls—Robbie Dupree (81)	159
This Night Won't Last Forever—Bill LaBounty (78)	*134*
She Loves My Car—Ronnie Milsap (84)	52
Ed LaBUNSKI ▶ 7095 (1)	**116**
That's Why You Remember—Kenny Karen (73)	116
Joseph M. LaCALLE ▶ 5395 (1)	**295**
Amapola—Jacky Noguez And His Orchestra (60)	295
—Solomon Lachoff see: Sol LAKE	
Yves LACOMBLEZ [Pipou Pipokas] ▶ 8158 (1)	**60**
Ca Plane Pour Moi—Plastic Bertrand (78)	179
—Geertjan Lacunes see: Jerry RIX	
Dan LADEMACHER ▶ 6161 (1)	**199**
Saturdaynight—Herman Brood (79)	397
David LAFLAMME [Gary Posie] ▶ 9729 (1)	**18**
White Bird—David Laflamme (76)	36
Linda LAFLAMME [Linda Baker] ▶ 9730 (1)	**18**
White Bird—David Laflamme (76)	36
—Pierre Dewey LaFontaine Jr. see: Pete FOUNTAIN	
Valerien LAGUEUX ▶ 3429 (1)	**852**
Baby Blue—Echoes (61)	1704
Kenny LAGUNA ▶ 5722 (3)	**251**
Fake Friends—Joan Jett & The Blackhearts (83)	407
Good Music—Joan Jett And The Blackhearts (86)	80
Groovin' With Mr. Bloe—Cool Heat (70)	22
Francis LAI ▶ 1280 (6)	**3465**
(Where Do I Begin) Love Story—Andy Williams (71)	*2200*
(Theme From) Love Story—Henry Mancini, His Orchestra & Chorus Henry Mancini, Piano Soloist (71)	*1533*
Theme From Love Story—Francis Lai And His Orchestra (71)	*616*
I Think Of You—Perry Como (71)	422
A Man And A Woman—Tamiko Jones With Herbie Mann (66)	12
Live For Life—Jack Jones (67)	1.4
Denny LAINE [Brian Frederick Hines] ▶ 4733 (5)	**429**
Girls' School—Wings (77)	469
London Town—Wings (78)	286
From The Bottom Of My Heart (I Love You)—Moody Blues (65)	69
Stop!—Moody Blues (66)	34
Mull Of Kintyre—Wings (77)	0.0
Frankie LAINE [Francesco Paolo LoVecchio] ▶ 7565 (2)	**88**
We'll Be Together Again—Rosemary Clooney (54)	*171*
We'll Be Together Again—Ray Charles And Betty Carter (62)	*5.5*
Corky LAING [Laurence Gordon Laing] ▶ 5417 (2)	**291**
Mississippi Queen—Mountain (70)	1100
For Yasgur's Farm—Mountain (70)	97
—Laurence Gordon Laing see: Corky LAING	
Nick LAIRD-CLOWES ▶ 2909 (2)	**1123**
Life In A Northern Town—Dream Academy (85)	1832
The Love Parade—Dream Academy (86)	413
Greg LAKE ▶ 2746 (8)	**1224**
From The Beginning—Emerson, Lake & Palmer (72)	568
Lucky Man—Emerson, Lake & Palmer (71)	*341*
Lucky Man—Emerson, Lake & Palmer (72)	*227*
Touch And Go—Emerson, Lake & Powell (86)	116
Stone Of Years—Emerson, Lake & Palmer (71)	23
In The Court Of The Crimson King—King Crimson (70)	20
I Believe In Father Christmas—Greg Lake (75)	18
C'est La Vie—Greg Lake (77)	16
Sol LAKE [Solomon Lachoff] ▶ 1504 (3)	**2862**
The Lonely Bull (El Solo Torro)—Herb Alpert & The Tijuana Brass (62)	2829
The Mexican Shuffle—Herb Alpert's Tijuana Brass (64)	25
Marching Thru Madrid—Herb Alpert's Tijuana Brass (63)	8.1

Joe LALA ▶ 10914 (1)	**4.4**
Cuban Bluegrass—Stephen Stills -- Manassas (72)	8.8
Gaetano LAMA ▶ 11770 (1)	**0.1**
Tic-A-Tee, Tik-A-Tay—Dean Martin (62)	0.4
Kevin LAMB ▶ 7501 (2)	**92**
On The Wrong Track—Kevin Lamb (78)	73
Right Feeling At The Wrong Time—Hot (77)	37
—Richard Carroll Lamb see: Dick DALLAS	
Dennis LAMBERT ▶ 199 (52)	**15739**
Don't Pull Your Love—Hamilton, Joe Frank & Reynolds (71)	*4833*
We Built This City—Starship (85)	4638
Ain't No Woman (Like The One I've Got)—Four Tops (73)	3986
Nightshift—Commodores (85)	2649
It Only Takes A Minute—Tavares (75)	1975
Keeper Of The Castle—Four Tops (72)	1655
Two Divided By Love—Grass Roots (71)	1531
Country Boy (You Got Your Feet In L.A.)—Glen Campbell (75)	1187
Are You Man Enough—Four Tops (73)	1185
Do The Freddie—Freddie And The Dreamers (65)	1014
Look In My Eyes Pretty Woman—Tony Orlando And Dawn (74)	930
One Tin Soldier The Legend Of Billy Jack—Coven (71)	*917*
This Heart—Gene Redding (74)	878
One Tin Soldier—Original Caste (69)	*801*
Remember What I Told You To Forget—Tavares (75)	694
It's A Cryin' Shame—Gayle McCormick (71)	608
Daisy Mae—Hamilton, Joe Frank & Reynolds (71)	605
The Runway—Grass Roots (72)	555
Give It To The People—Righteous Brothers (74)	537
Dream On—Righteous Brothers (74)	479
One Chain Don't Make No Prison—Four Tops (74)	*371*
Up And Down—McCoys (66)	342
Ashes To Ashes—5th Dimension (73)	307
I Just Can't Get You Out Of My Mind—Four Tops (74)	288
I Dig You Baby—Jerry Butler (67)	*266*
You Brought The Woman Out Of Me—Evie Sands (75)	*254*
Don't Pull Your Love—Glen Campbell (76)	*228*
If Looks Could Kill—Player (82)	197
Goin' To The Bank—Commodores (86)	194
Too Late—Tavares (74)	193
One Tin Soldier (The Legend Of Billy Jack)—Coven (73)	*143*
The Moment Of Truth—Survivor (84)	138
Love Music—Raiders (73)	*131*
Don't Look Any Further—Kane Gang (88)	*126*
One Chain (Don't Make No Prison)—Santana (79)	*117*
One Tin Soldier The Legend Of Billy Jack—Coven (73)	*111*
Put A Little Love Away—Emotions (74)	91
Gonna Be Alright Now—Gayle McCormick (71)	65
You Brought The Woman Out Of Me—Hot (78)	*52*
Don't Look Any Further—Dennis Edwards (84)	*49*
I Dig You Baby—Lorraine Ellison (66)	*46*
Once A Fool—Kiki Dee (76)	37
To Love You—Country Store (70)	16
Love On My Mind Tonight—Temptations (83)	13
Don't Pull Your Love—Sam & Dave (71)	*11*
The House On Telegraph Hill—Bo Donaldson And The Heywoods (75)	7.0
Who Gets Your Love—Dusty Springfield (73)	6.5
Find My Way Back Home—Nashville Teens (65)	2.4
If That's The Way You Want It—Diamond Head (73)	2.2
One Good Woman—Hamilton, Joe Frank & Reynolds (72)	1.6
Love Music—Sergio Mendes & Brasil '77 (73)	*0.7*
My Ship—Tavares (75)	0.0
Jennie Lee LAMBERT ▶ 6629 (3)	**149**
Never, Never Leave Me—Mary Wells (65)	277
Stop Takin' Me For Granted—Mary Wells (64)	13
We Have Something More—Connie Francis (64)	9.2
Lanny LAMBERT ▶ 3859 (5)	**674**
White Lies, Blue Eyes—Bullet (71)	899
Do You Know What Time It Is?—P-Nut Gallery (71)	259
Bed And Board—Barbara Mason (72)	135
Willpower Weak, Temptation Strong—Bullet (72)	53
Another Love—Ian Lloyd & Stories (74)	2.0
Robert LAMBERT ▶ 6968 (1)	**125**
Stand By—Roman Holliday (83)	249

Steve LAMBERT ▶ 6969 (1)	**125**
Stand By—Roman Holliday (83)	249
Robin LAMBLE ▶ 9701 (1)	**19**
Playing With Lightning—Shot In The Dark (81)	38
—Danny Lamego see: Danny PEPPERMINT	
Robert LAMM ▶ 227 (12) HOF	**14885**
Saturday In The Park—Chicago (72)	3007
Does Anybody Really Know What Time It Is?—Chicago (70)	2918
25 Or 6 To 4—Chicago (70)	*2800*
Beginnings—Chicago (71)	1946
Questions 67 And 68—Chicago (71)	*1060*
Harry Truman—Chicago (75)	823
Free—Chicago (71)	728
Dialogue (Parts I & II)—Chicago (72)	711
Another Rainy Day In New York City—Chicago (76)	541
25 Or 6 To 4—Chicago (86)	*254*
Thunder And Lightning—Chicago (80)	142
Questions 67 And 68—Chicago (69)	*49*
Joe LAMONT ▶ 10589 (1)	**7.0**
Fright Night—J. Geils Band (85)	7.0
—Olivier René Marie Lamotte d'Incamps see: Chico De OLIVEIRA	
Diane LAMPERT ▶ 1548 (10)	**2750**
Break It To Me Gently—Brenda Lee (62)	*3448*
Break It To Me Gently—Juice Newton (82)	*1424*
Can't Wait For Summer—Steve Lawrence (57)	334
The Worryin' Kind—Tommy Sands (58)	92
Blue Ribbon Baby—Tommy Sands And The Raiders (58)	90
Let's Go Calypso—Rusty Draper (57)	81
Nothin' Shakin—Eddie Fontaine (58)	27
Touch Of Pink—Jerry Wallace (59)	*9.7*
Your Name Is Beautiful—Carl Smith (58)	9.0
A Touch Of Pink—Dick Jacobs & His Orchestra (59)	*0.0*
Bobby LANCE ▶ 3070 (1)	**1025**
The House That Jack Built—Aretha Franklin (68)	2051
Herb LANCE ▶ 10273 (4)	**11**
Mama (He Treats Your Daughter Mean)—Dinning Sisters Featuring Jean Dinning (55)	*31*
Mama (He Treats Your Daughter Mean)—Ruth Brown (62)	*0.9*
(Mama) He Treats Your Daughter Mean—Ruth Brown (55)	*0.0*
Mama (He Treats Your Daughter Mean)—Bette Anne Steele (55)	*0.0*
Major LANCE ▶ 5665 (1)	**257**
The Matador—Major Lance (64)	771
Al LANCELLOTTI ▶ 4035 (1)	**619**
Tonight—New Kids On The Block (90)	1237
—Harry Land see: Bernie LOWE	
—Leon Land see: Leon LANDGREN	
Mike LANDAU ▶ 8616 (1)	**45**
The Secret Of My Success—Night Ranger (87)	179
William LANDAU ▶ 4705 (2)	**434**
Sacred—Castells (61)	866
Make Believe Wedding—Castells (61)	1.8
Bernie LANDES ▶ 7272 (1)	**106**
Elephants Tango—Commanders With Eddie Grady (55)	106
Leon LANDGREN [Leon Land] ▶ 5135 (3)	**336**
Lay Down Your Arms—Chordettes (56)	*814*
Lay Down Your Arms—Anne Shelton (56)	*193*
Lay Down Your Arms—Russ Morgan & His Orchestra (56)	*0.0*
—Jerry Landis see: Paul SIMON	
Richard LANDIS ▶ 10327 (1)	**10**
A Man Who Sings—Richard Landis (72)	20
Ron LANDRY ▶ 5625 (2)	**263**
Ajax Liquor Store—Hudson and Landry (71)	435
Ajax Airlines—Hudson And Landry (71)	90
Phyllis LANDSBERG [Phyllis Fairbanks] ▶ 5385 (1)	**297**
The "A" Team—SSgt. Barry Sadler (66)	891
Bernie LANE [Bernard Schrieber] ▶ 5759 (1)	**245**
Shaggy Dog—Mickey Lee Lane (64)	489
Bill LANE ▶ 3546 (1)	**791**
Times Of Your Life—Paul Anka (75)	1582

Burton LANE [Burton Levy] ▶ 9509 (3) HOF	**22**
Too Late Now—DeCastro Sisters (55)	37
Everything I Have Is Yours—Dorothy Collins (59)	5.4
On A Clear Day You Can See Forever— Johnny Mathis (65)	2.4
Calvin LANE ▶ 9512 (1)	**22**
I'm Yours (Use Me Anyway You Wanna)— Ike & Tina Turner (71)	44
Grace LANE [Grace Lane Gallico] ▶ 4921 (2)	**382**
Clinging Vine—Bobby Vinton (64)	1138
Salvation Rock—Marv Meredith And His Orchestra (60)	4.1
Herb LANE ▶ 4905 (2)	**385**
Disco Nights (Rock-Freak)—G.Q. (79)	1528
Standing Ovation—GQ (80)	11
—Jani Lane see: John OSWALD	
—Jay Arthur/James A. Lane see: Jimmy ROGERS	
Ken LANE [Kermit Lane] ▶ 1549 (1)	**2746**
Everybody Loves Somebody—Dean Martin (64)	8239
—Kermit Lane see: Ken LANE	
Mickey Lee LANE [Solomon M Schreiber, Sholom Schreiber] ▶ 5390 (2)	**296**
Shaggy Dog—Mickey Lee Lane (64)	489
Where Are We Going—Bobby Bloom (70)	103
Peter LANE ▶ 11474 (1)	**1.5**
Big Boat—Peter, Paul & Mary (62)	6.2
Red LANE [Hollis Rudolph DeLaughter] ▶ 4925 (2)	**380**
The Court Room—Clarence Carter (71)	314
They Don't Make Love Like They Used To— Eddy Arnold (68)	66
Robin LANE ▶ 10036 (1)	**14**
When Things Go Wrong— Robin Lane & The Chartbusters (80)	27
Ronnie LANE ▶ 3276 (2)	**915**
Itchycoo Park—Small Faces (67)	1634
Tin Soldier—Small Faces (68)	196
Tom LANE ▶ 7119 (1)	**115**
Please Don't Sell My Daddy No More Wine— Greenwoods (66)	115
Luther King LANEY ▶ 6050 (3)	**212**
Why Don't You Believe Me— Duprees Featuring Joey Vann (63)	*583*
Clay Idol—Betty Johnson (56)	41
Why Don't You Believe Me—Vic Damone (65)	*12*
Hans LANG ▶ 11335 (1)	**2.2**
Oh My Maria—Eddie Fisher (56)	6.6
Herman LANG ▶ 8146 (1)	**60**
Ain't No Future In Yo' Frontin'—M.C. Breed (91)	180
John LANG ▶ 1213 (7)	**3672**
Broken Wings—Mr. Mister (85)	5158
Kyrie—Mr. Mister (85)	4320
Is It Love—Mr. Mister (86)	1255
Something Real (Inside Me/Inside You)— Mr. Mister (87)	420
Hunters Of The Night—Mr. Mister (84)	168
I Do Believe In You—Pages (79)	55
The Border—Mr. Mister (87)	8.7
—Dorothy Veronica Langan see: Dory PREVIN	
Gary LANGAN ▶ 6666 (1)	**146**
Paranoimia—Art Of Noise with Max Headroom (86)	437
—Dory Langdon see: Dory PREVIN	
Henry LANGE ▶ 9865 (1)	**16**
Hot Lips—Grady Martin And The Slew Foot Five (55)	48
Johnny LANGE ▶ 8772 (1)	**40**
Madrid—Nat "King" Cole (59)	198
Larry LANGE ▶ 6152 (1)	**199**
No Matter What—George LaMond (90)	399
—Lee Lange see: Bunny LEWIS	
Mutt LANGE [Robert John Lange] ▶ 164 (26)	**17872**
(Everything I Do) I Do It For You—Bryan Adams (91)	6505
Get Outta My Dreams, Get Into My Car— Billy Ocean (88)	4022
Pour Some Sugar On Me—Def Leppard (88)	3871
All I Wanna Do Is Make Love To You—Heart (90)	3718
Can't Stop This Thing We Started—Bryan Adams (91)	3455
Love Bites—Def Leppard (88)	3277
When The Going Gets Tough, The Tough Get Going— Billy Ocean (85)	3161
Loverboy—Billy Ocean (84)	2995
Armageddon It—Def Leppard (88)	2857
Do You Believe In Love— Huey Lewis and the News (82)	1493
Lovin' Every Minute Of It—Loverboy (85)	1301
Photograph—Def Leppard (83)	1231
Hysteria—Def Leppard (88)	1083
Rocket—Def Leppard (89)	1017
Rock Of Ages—Def Leppard (83)	1009
There Will Never Be Another Tonight— Bryan Adams (91)	822
Animal—Def Leppard (87)	796
It Hit Me Like A Hammer— Huey Lewis & The News (91)	695
Foolin'—Def Leppard (83)	557
Licence To Chill—Billy Ocean (89)	405
Heaven In The Back Seat—Eddie Money (91)	176
Don't Break My Heart—Romeo's Daughter (88)	105
I Didn't Mean To Stay All Night—Starship (89)	43
One Foot Back In Your Door—Roman Holliday (85)	28
Women—Def Leppard (87)	26
I Cry Myself To Sleep At Night— Romeo's Daughter (89)	26
Pascal LANGUIRAND ▶ 6377 (1)	**177**
Living On Video—Trans-X (86)	177
Allen LANIER ▶ 9163 (1)	**30**
In Thee—Blue Oyster Cult (79)	30
Donnie LANIER ▶ 1329 (15)	**3347**
Party Doll—Buddy Knox with The Rhythm Orchids (57)	*4735*
Party Doll—Steve Lawrence (57)	*1892*
Hula Love—Buddy Knox with The Rhythm Orchids (57)	1598
Here We Go Again—Ray Charles (67)	*1452*
I'm Stickin' With You— Jimmy Bowen With The Rhythm Orchids (57)	*1396*
Rock Your Little Baby To Sleep— Buddy Knox with The Rhythm Orchids (57)	698
Swingin' Daddy— Buddy Knox with The Rhythm Orchids (58)	174
Party Doll— Cat Mother And The All Night News Boys (69)	*164*
Party Doll—Wingy Manone And His Orchestra (57)	*133*
I Trusted You— Jimmy Bowen With The Rhythm Orchids (57)	76
Ever Lovin' Fingers— Jimmy Bowen With The Rhythm Orchids (57)	44
I'm Stickin' With You—Fontane Sisters (57)	*36*
Party Doll—Roy Brown (57)	*7.0*
Here We Go Again—Nancy Sinatra (69)	*2.6*
I'm Stickin' With You—Roy Brown (57)	*0.0*
Verdell LANIER ▶ 5959 (2)	**223**
It's You That I Need—Enchantment (78)	430
If You're Ready (Here It Comes)—Enchantment (78)	16
Arnold LANNI ▶ 1232 (3)	**3630**
When I'm With You—Sheriff (88)	*3279*
When I'm With You—Sheriff (83)	*188*
Should I See—Frozen Ghost (87)	164
Paul LANNOY ▶ 8994 (1)	**34**
Crash (Have Some Fun)—TKA (90)	68
John William LANTZ ▶ 9751 (1)	**18**
After Loving You—Della Reese (65)	35
Anthony La PEAU ▶ 7097 (1)	**116**
Say It Again—Santana (85)	347
Douglas LAPHAM ▶ 3679 (3)	**739**
She's Everything (I Wanted You To Be)— Ral Donner (61)	969
Please Don't Go—Ral Donner (61)	507
I Didn't Figure On Him (To Come Back)— Ral Donner (61)	2.8
Neil LAPIDUS ▶ 6199 (1)	**194**
Barbara—Temptations (2) (60)	582
—Joseph LaPollo see: Ellison CHASE	
Ronald LaPREAD ▶ 4180 (5)	**572**
Brick House—Commodores (77)	1962
Too Hot Ta Trot—Commodores (77)	499
Fancy Dancer—Commodores (76)	271
I Feel Sanctified—Commodores (74)	83
8th Wonder—Sugarhill Gang (81)	30
Agustin LARA ▶ 6604 (1)	**153**
Granada—Frank Sinatra (61)	305
Maria Teresa LARA ▶ 9139 (1)	**30**
Be Mine Tonight—Andy Williams (58)	61
Dennis LARDEN ▶ 5365 (2)	**299**
Put Your Mind At Ease—Every Mothers' Son (67)	475
Pony With The Golden Mane— Every Mothers' Son (67)	124
Lary LARDEN ▶ 5366 (2)	**299**
Put Your Mind At Ease—Every Mothers' Son (67)	475
Pony With The Golden Mane— Every Mothers' Son (67)	124
Michael LARDIE ▶ 7146 (3)	**113**
Rock Me—Great White (87)	217
Call It Rock 'N Roll—Great White (91)	208
House Of Broken Love—Great White (90)	52
Chris LARKIN ▶ 9198 (1)	**29**
Look My Way—Vels (85)	87
—Joan Marie Larkin see: Joan JETT	
Julius La ROSA ▶ 9434 (1)	**24**
Eh! Cumpari—Gaylord & Holiday (76)	71
Jens Kjaer LARSEN [M.C. Zipp] ▶ 10570 (1)	**7.2**
Get Serious—Cut 'N' Move (91)	36
Chuck LARSON ▶ 11107 (1)	**3.2**
Bad, Bad Billy—Snuff (83)	9.5
Glen LARSON ▶ 1111 (8)	**3994**
26 Miles (Santa Catalina)—Four Preps (58)	2990
Big Man—Four Preps (58)	2564
Down By The Station—Four Preps (59)	1665
Got A Girl—Four Preps (60)	514
More Money For You And Me—Four Preps (61)	130
Cinderella—Four Preps (58)	64
A Letter To The Beatles—Four Preps (64)	55
The Big Draft—Four Preps (62)	24
—Kurt Larson see: Kurt VALAQUEN	
Mel LARSON ▶ 4193 (3)	**567**
I Am Love—Jackson 5 (75)	1065
Get It Together—Jackson 5 (73)	729
Whatever You Got, I Want—Jackson 5 (74)	465
—Rolf Magnus Joakim Larson see: Joey TEMPEST	
Åke Gerhard LARSSON [Åke Gerhard] ▶ 5136 (3)	**336**
Lay Down Your Arms—Chordettes (56)	*814*
Lay Down Your Arms—Anne Shelton (56)	*193*
Lay Down Your Arms— Russ Morgan & His Orchestra (56)	*0.0*
D.C. LaRUE [David Charles L'Heureux] ▶ 11383 (1)	**2.0**
Cathedrals—D.C. LaRue (76)	4.0
—Jacques Larue see: Marcel AGERON	
Andrea LaRUSSO ▶ 3520 (1)	**801**
Dress You Up—Madonna (85)	1602
Denise LaSALLE [Denise Ora Craig, Ora Denise Jones] ▶ 1525 (6)	**2805**
Trapped By A Thing Called Love—Denise LaSalle (71)	1686
Now Run And Tell That—Denise LaSalle (72)	587
Man Sized Job—Denise LaSalle (72)	456
Love Me Right—Denise LaSalle (78)	60
Married But Not To Each Other—Denise LaSalle (76)	16
Get Your Lie Straight—Bill Coday (71)	7.1
Martin LASCELLES ▶ 9724 (1)	**18**
Love Is A House—Force M.D.'s (87)	55
David LASLEY ▶ 2051 (4)	**1949**
Lead Me On—Maxine Nightingale (79)	3179
Jojo—Boz Scaggs (80)	902
Love Me Again—Rita Coolidge (78)	73
The Blue Side—Crystal Gayle (80)	44
Albert LASRY ▶ 3154 (3)	**982**
Beyond The Sea—Bobby Darin (60)	*2565*
La Mer (Beyond The Sea)—Roger Williams (56)	*248*
La Mer—Trade Martin (59)	*5.2*
—Hans Last see: James LAST	
James LAST [Hans Last] ▶ 3372 (9)	**877**
Happy Heart—Andy Williams (69)	*836*
Games That Lovers Play—Eddie Fisher (66)	*696*
Now I Know—Jack Jones (67)	181
Happy Heart—Petula Clark (69)	*152*
Games That Lovers Play—Wayne Newton (66)	*91*
When The Snow Is On The Roses—Ed Ames (67)	52
Music From Across The Way—James Last (72)	40
Games That Lovers Play— Mantovani And His Orchestra (66)	*25*
Fool—Elvis Presley (73)	25

Werner LAST ▶ 11461 (1)	**1.6**
The Happy Cowboy—Billy Vaughn And His Orchestra (63)	3.2
Bill LASWELL ▶ 8300 (1)	**55**
Rockit—Herbie Hancock (83)	165
Marie LATIMER ▶ 5774 (1)	**243**
Age For Love—Jimmy Charles (60)	486
Benny LATIMORE ▶ 3246 (4)	**929**
Let's Straighten It Out—Latimore (74)	635
Somethin' 'Bout 'Cha—Latimore (77)	283
All The Way Lover—Millie Jackson (78)	10
Keep The Home Fire Burnin'—Latimore (75)	1.2
William LaTOUR ▶ 4973 (1)	**367**
People Are Still Having Sex—LaTour (91)	367
—Phoebe Ann Laub see: Phoebe SNOW	
Terry LAUBER ▶ 7847 (1)	**72**
Martha (Your Lovers Come And Go)—Gabriel (78)	72
Cyndi LAUPER ▶ 911 (7) HOF	**4847**
Time After Time—Cyndi Lauper (84)	4828
She Bop—Cyndi Lauper (84)	3432
Change Of Heart—Cyndi Lauper (86)	2182
The Goonies 'r' Good Enough—Cyndi Lauper (85)	1031
My First Night Without You—Cyndi Lauper (89)	149
Steady—Jules Shear (85)	142
Boy Blue—Cyndi Lauper (87)	59
Paul LAURENCE [Paul Laurence Jones] ▶ 2818 (4)	**1172**
Rock Me Tonight (For Old Times Sake)—Freddie Jackson (85)	800
Jam Tonight—Freddie Jackson (87)	446
Tasty Love—Freddie Jackson (86)	290
(You're Puttin') A Rush On Me—Stephanie Mills (87)	9.7
—Mary Dean Lauria see: Mary DEAN	
Linda LAURIE [Linda Gertz] ▶ 1028 (5)	**4307**
Leave Me Alone (Ruby Red Dress)—Helen Reddy (73)	4039
Ambrose (Part Five)—Linda Laurie (59)	337
You Got It—Diana Ross (78)	191
I'm In Love Again—Pia Zadora (82)	161
Just Keep Walkin' Ambrose—Jimmy Valentine & His Orchestra (59)	21
Stijn LAUWERS [Stijn Willem Jozef Lauwers, El Sati] ▶ 9038 (1)	**33**
Spin That Wheel—Hi Tek 3 featuring Ya Kid K (90)	98
—Jean-Pierre Lauzon see: Jean-Pierre PAQUIN	
Frank LAVERE ▶ 4758 (3)	**422**
Have You Heard—Duprees Featuring Joey Vann (63)	1071
Pretend—Carl Mann (59)	*253*
Pretend—Tab Smith His Fabulous Alto and His Band (57)	*5.2*
Clint LAVERT ▶ 4881 (2)	**390**
When A Boy Falls In Love—Mel Carter (63)	*605*
When A Boy Falls In Love—Sam Cooke (65)	*174*
Frank LAVIGNE ▶ 8852 (1)	**38**
Kiss You (When It's Dangerous)—Eight Seconds (87)	151
Kent LaVOIE [Roland Kent LaVoie, Lobo] ▶ 271 (12)	**12684**
I'd Love You To Want Me—Lobo (72)	4468
Me And You And A Dog Named Boo—Lobo (71)	2375
Don't Expect Me To Be Your Friend—Lobo (72)	2285
How Can I Tell Her—Lobo (73)	947
It Sure Took A Long, Long Time—Lobo (73)	597
Don't Tell Me Goodnight—Lobo (75)	501
She Didn't Do Magic—Lobo (71)	439
Standing At The End Of The Line—Lobo (74)	423
A Simple Man—Lobo (72)	368
There Ain't No Way—Lobo (73)	187
I'm The Only One—Lobo (71)	94
Love Me For What I Am—Lobo (73)	0.0
—Roland Kent LaVoie see: Kent LaVOIE	
Yves-Jacques LAVOT [Pierre Brancourt, Yves Dessca, Yves Lavot, Yves Lavot-Dessca, Guy Marfontaine] ▶ 5035 (4)	**357**
My Boy—Elvis Presley (75)	*838*
My Boy—Richard Harris (71)	*497*
Do I Love You—Paul Anka (71)	*446*
Do I Love You (Yes In Every Way)—Donna Fargo (78)	*2.7*
Simon LAW ▶ 3758 (1)	**709**
Back To Life—Soul II Soul (89)	2835
Mike LAWLER ▶ 8344 (1)	**54**
Angeline—Allman Brothers Band (80)	161
Lynda LAWLEY ▶ 11378 (1)	**2.0**
How Could This Go Wrong—Exile (79)	8.0
—Samuel T. Lawmaster see: Sammy MASTERS	
Eddie LAWRENCE [Lawrence Eisler] ▶ 4878 (2)	**391**
Old Philosopher—Eddie Lawrence (56)	385
New Philosopher—Eddie Lawrence (56)	6.0
—Fred Lawrence see: Luigi CREATORE	
Jack LAWRENCE [Jacob Lewis Schwartz] ▶ 667 (20) HOF	**6498**
Beyond The Sea—Bobby Darin (60)	*2565*
Hold My Hand—Don Cornell (54)	*2528*
If I Didn't Care—Connie Francis (59)	*1230*
With The Wind And The Rain In Your Hair—Pat Boone (59)	1142
Linda—Jan & Dean (63)	*866*
To You My Love—Nick Noble (56)	*677*
If I Didn't Care—Platters (61)	*495*
If I Didn't Care—Moments (70)	*391*
If I Didn't Care—Hilltoppers (54)	*255*
What Will I Tell My Heart—Fats Domino (57)	*163*
The Peddler Man (Ten I Loved)—Dean Martin (54)	123
Linda—Adam Wade (61)	*55*
Sleepy Lagoon—Platters (60)	38
To You My Love—Georgie Shaw (56)	*37*
No One But You—Charlie Applewhite (54)	22
Symphony—Sammy Turner (59)	16
Do, Do, Do (What Your Heart Says)—Tony Martin (55)	15
What Will I Tell My Heart—Harptones (61)	*3.7*
To You, My Love—Betty Madigan (56)	*0.0*
Hold My Hand—Guy Lombardo & His Royal Canadians (54)	*0.0*
—James Everett Lawrence see: Rhett LAWRENCE	
Karen LAWRENCE ▶ 5492 (2)	**279**
Love Theme From "Eyes Of Laura Mars" (Prisoner)—Barbra Streisand (78)	*513*
Prisoner (Captured By Your Eyes)—L.A. Jets (76)	*45*
Rhett LAWRENCE [James Everett Lawrence] ▶ 5754 (1)	**245**
Birthday Suit—Johnny Kemp (89)	490
—Ronald Lawrence see: Ronald ANDRE	
Stephen LAWRENCE ▶ 2836 (1)	**1163**
You Take My Breath Away—Rex Smith (79)	2326
Steve LAWRENCE [Sydney Leibowitz] ▶ 9696 (2)	**19**
Your Kisses Kill Me—Eydie Gorme (57)	31
Can't Get Over (The Bossa Nova)—Eydie Gorme (64)	10
Trevor LAWRENCE ▶ 3995 (4)	**628**
I'm So Excited '84—Pointer Sisters (84)	*1499*
I'm So Excited—Pointer Sisters (82)	*597*
Could I Be Dreaming—Pointer Sisters (80)	272
All The Way Down—Etta James (73)	40
Billy LAWRIE ▶ 7891 (1)	**71**
Is That The Way—Tin Tin (71)	212
Charlotte LAWS ▶ 9962 (1)	**14**
Feelin' That Glow—Roberta Flack (75)	72
Ronnie LAWS ▶ 5286 (3)	**313**
Stay Awake—Ronnie Laws (81)	252
Love Is Here—Ronnie Laws (78)	59
Every Generation—Ronnie Laws (80)	1.6
R.W. LAWS [Richard W. Laws] ▶ 9930 (1)	**15**
Mean Little Woman, Rosalie—Tommy Roe (72)	15
Gene LAWSON ▶ 9030 (1)	**33**
Free Me—Otis Redding (69)	131
—LayLaw see: Larry GOODMAN	
Ricky LAYNE [Sam Corgliano] ▶ 10336 (1)	**9.9**
Where Can You Go (For A Broken Heart)—George Maharis (63)	9.9
J. Turner LAYTON ▶ 1999 (2)	**2015**
Way Down Yonder In New Orleans—Freddie Cannon (59)	4029
After You've Gone—Frankie Avalon (62)	0.5
Richard LAYTON ▶ 8665 (1)	**43**
Baby Toys—Toys (66)	86
Dave LAZAR ▶ 4235 (3)	**552**
Gotta Travel On—Billy Grammer (58)	*3674*
Gotta Travel On—Timi Yuro (63)	*190*
Gotta Travel On—Harry Belafonte (59)	*0.0*
Tom LAZAROS ▶ 2838 (3)	**1162**
Big City Miss Ruth Ann—Gallery (72)	1104
City Of Windows—Stephen Monahan (67)	86
Somewhere Between Love And Tomorrow—Roy Clark (73)	31
Jim LEA ▶ 1732 (9)	**2406**
Cum On Feel The Noize—Quiet Riot (83)	*2756*
Run Runaway—Slade (84)	816
My Oh My—Slade (84)	396
Mama Weer All Crazee Now—Quiet Riot (84)	*324*
Mama Weer All Crazee Now—Slade (72)	*194*
Gudbuy T' Jane—Slade (73)	186
Cum On Feel The Noize—Slade (73)	*87*
Take Me Bak 'Ome—Slade (72)	40
Little Sheila—Slade (85)	15
Billy LEACH ▶ 10867 (1)	**4.8**
Song Of The Barefoot Mailman—Billy Leach (57)	9.5
—Leadbelly see: Huddie LEDBETTER	
Mickey LEADER [David Kapp, Alan Hold] ▶ 3165 (3)	**975**
Sailor (Your Home Is The Sea)—Lolita (60)	2661
Dance By The Light Of The Moon—Olympics (60)	*428*
Dance With A Dolly (With A Hole In Her Stocking)—Damita Jo (61)	*65*
Bernie LEADON ▶ 3411 (1)	**858**
Witchy Woman—Eagles (72)	1716
Joe LEAHY ▶ 9301 (2)	**27**
Sunshine And Rain—Teddy Bart (57)	*53*
Sunshine And Rain—Bob Whalen (57)	*0.0*
Melvin LEAKES ▶ 7941 (1)	**68**
A Man And A Half—Wilson Pickett (68)	273
Mike LEANDER [Michael George Farr] ▶ 772 (13)	**5700**
Lady Godiva—Peter And Gordon (66)	2817
Rock And Roll Part 2—Gary Glitter (72)	2384
Early In The Morning—Vanity Fare (69)	2096
Knight In Rusty Armour—Peter And Gordon (66)	1175
I Ain't Got Time Anymore—Glass Bottle Featuring Gary Criss (71)	697
Do You Wanna Touch Me (Oh Yeah)—Joan Jett & The Blackhearts (82)	693
I Didn't Know I Loved You (Till I Saw You Rock And Roll)—Gary Glitter (72)	533
Another Time, Another Place—Engelbert Humperdinck (71)	432
I'm The Leader Of The Gang—Brownsville Station (74)	422
Doctorin' The Tardis—Timelords (88)	159
It's All Over—Ben E. King (64)	100
Makes You Blind—Glitter Band (76)	16
The Jokers—Peter And Gordon (67)	2.4
Otis LEAVILL ▶ 11016 (1)	**3.8**
There Goes The Lover—Gene Chandler (67)	7.7
—Louis Leazer see: Lew POLLACK	
Lewis LEBISH ▶ 5483 (1)	**280**
Dance With Me—Drifters (59)	1398
Emanuel Rahiem LeBLANC ▶ 4906 (2)	**385**
Disco Nights (Rock-Freak)—G.Q. (79)	1528
Standing Ovation—GQ (80)	11
Lenny LeBLANC ▶ 3500 (3)	**815**
Falling—Le Blanc & Carr (77)	1481
Somebody Send My Baby Home—Lenny LeBlanc (81)	136
Midnight Light—Le Blanc & Carr (78)	13
Simon Le BON ▶ 501 (18)	**8432**
The Reflex—Duran Duran (84)	5082
Union Of The Snake—Duran Duran (83)	4545
The Wild Boys—Duran Duran (84)	4449
A View To A Kill—Duran Duran (85)	4032
Hungry Like The Wolf—Duran Duran (82)	3924
Notorious—Duran Duran (86)	3404
I Don't Want Your Love—Duran Duran (88)	2410
Is There Something I Should Know—Duran Duran (83)	2395
Election Day—Arcadia (85)	1950
New Moon On Monday—Duran Duran (84)	1339
Rio—Duran Duran (83)	946
Save A Prayer—Duran Duran (85)	773
All She Wants Is—Duran Duran (88)	486
Goodbye Is Forever—Arcadia (86)	432
Skin Trade—Duran Duran (87)	308
Violence Of Summer (Love's Taking Over)—Duran Duran (90)	165
Do You Believe In Shame?—Duran Duran (89)	93
Meet El Presidente—Duran Duran (87)	78

Stan LEBOWSKY ▶ 737 (11)	**5962**
The Wayward Wind—Gogi Grant (56)	*9460*
Tic Tender Love And Care—Jimmie Rodgers (60)	681
Don't Go Home—Playmates (58)	*635*
The Wayward Wind—Tex Ritter (56)	*406*
Every Little Thing I Do—Dion and The Belmonts (59)	373
The Most Beautiful Words—Della Reese (61)	238
The Wayward Wind—Gogi Grant (61)	*211*
You're Looking At Me—Johnny Nash (58)	127
Don't Go Home (My Little Darlin')—Shirelles (67)	*17*
Dancin' In The Streets—Ames Brothers (59)	2.6
Man That's Choice— Sam (The Man) Taylor And His Orchestra (58)	0.4
Angel LEBRON ▶ 9700 (1)	**19**
Within My Heart—Voyce (91)	75
—Richie Lecea see: Richie HERNANDEZ	
Ernesto LECUONA ▶ 2429 (9) HOF	**1493**
The Breeze And I (Andalucia)—Caterina Valente (55)	*1684*
Malaguena—Caterina Valente (55)	*434*
Malagueña—Connie Francis (60)	*281*
Always In My Heart—Los Indios Tabajaras (64)	103
Jungle Drums—Clyde Otis (61)	28
The Breeze And I—Santo & Johnny (60)	*20*
Siboney—Caterina Valente (56)	3.7
Heartless—Tommy Leonetti (55)	0.6
Malaguena—Stan Kenton & His Orchestra (55)	*0.0*
Margarita LECUONA ▶ 5549 (1)	**272**
Taboo—Arthur Lyman (59)	272
Huddie LEDBETTER [Leadbelly] ▶ 1122 (8) HOF	**3951**
Kisses Sweeter Than Wine—Jimmie Rodgers (57)	2683
Cotton Fields—Highwaymen (61)	*2196*
Black Betty—Ram Jam (77)	1183
Cottonfields—Ace Cannon (63)	*119*
Goodnight, Irene—Jerry Reed & The Hully Girlies (62)	*84*
Have A Drink On Me—Buddy Thomas (61)	51
Goodnight Irene—Billy Williams (59)	*22*
Cottonfields—Beach Boys (70)	*6.1*
Ish LEDESMA [Ish Angel, Ismael Angel Ledesma] ▶ 1522 (4)	**2805**
Get Off—Foxy (78)	1677
Fascinated—Company B (87)	694
Hot Number—Foxy (79)	652
Whirly Girl—Oxo (83)	621
—Ismael Angel Ledesma see: Ish LEDESMA	
Les LEDO [Russ Damon, Lester Lopez] ▶ 2188 (2)	**1761**
Cotton Candy—Al Hirt (64)	1570
It's Just A Little Bit Too Late— Wayne Fontana & The Mind-Benders (65)	381
Jack LEDRU ▶ 11317 (1)	**2.3**
Kiss And Run—Peggy King (56)	6.8
Albert LEE ▶ 11525 (1)	**1.3**
Warmin' Up The Band—Don Everly (74)	6.6
Allyn LEE ▶ 6674 (1)	**145**
Doin' Our Thing—Clarence Carter (69)	434
Alvin LEE ▶ 3215 (4)	**948**
I'd Love To Change The World—Ten Years After (71)	727
Baby Won't You Let Me Rock 'N Roll You— Ten Years After (72)	138
Love Like A Man—Ten Years After (70)	69
Choo Choo Mama—Ten Years After (72)	14
Arthur Taylor LEE ▶ 3941 (1)	**649**
7 And 7 Is—Love (66)	649
Beverly LEE ▶ 6208 (2)	**193**
I Met Him On A Sunday (Ronde-Ronde)— Shirelles (58)	537
Thank You Baby—Shirelles (64)	118
—Bob Lee see: Aaron SCHROEDER	
Booker LEE ▶ 11161 (1)	**3.0**
Lullabye—Chevrons (60)	8.9
Byron LEE ▶ 10314 (2)	**10**
Groovin'—UB40 (91)	12
Jamaica Ska—Ska Kings (64)	4.1
Curtis LEE ▶ 2661 (2)	**1287**
Pretty Little Angel Eyes—Curtis Lee (61)	2252
Under The Moon Of Love—Curtis Lee (61)	323
David LEE ▶ 5934 (3)	**225**
In The Summer Of His Years—Connie Francis (63)	*423*
In The Summer Of His Years—Millicent Martin (63)	*22*

In The Summer Of His Years—Toni Arden (63)	*5.5*
Dickey LEE [Dickey Lee Lipscomb] ▶ 2872 (7)	**1139**
I Saw Linda Yesterday—Dickey Lee (62)	1731
He Thinks I Still Care—Connie Francis (62)	*284*
Don't Wanna Think About Paula—Dickey Lee (63)	112
The Girl From Peyton Place—Dickey Lee (65)	79
The Dodo—Jumpin' Gene Simmons (64)	77
Big Brother—Dickey Lee (64)	30
She Thinks I Still Care—Elvis Presley (76)	*0.0*
—Ed Lee see: Isaac HAYES	
Geddy LEE [Gary Lee Weinrib] ▶ 4185 (9)	**571**
New World Man—Rush (82)	554
The Big Money—Rush (85)	372
Tom Sawyer—Rush (81)	329
The Spirit Of Radio—Rush (80)	242
Limelight—Rush (81)	159
Closer To The Heart—Rush (81)	*89*
Closer To The Heart—Rush (77)	*67*
In The Mood—Rush (77)	4.7
Fly By Night—Rush (77)	4.7
Hamza LEE ▶ 3492 (1)	**819**
I Adore Mi Amor—Color Me Badd (91)	4094
Ira LEE [Robert Sadoff] ▶ 9172 (2)	**29**
I Hear Those Bells—Dinah Washington (55)	55
The Rockin' Ghost—Archie Bleyer (56)	22
—Irma Lee see: Irma THOMAS	
Jack LEE [Lee Abbott, Jack Nathan Lee] ▶ 3699 (1)	**730**
Come Back And Stay—Paul Young (84)	730
—Jackie Lee see: Earl NELSON	
—Jack Nathan Lee see: Jack LEE	
James LEE ▶ 985 (8)	**4547**
Let's Dance—Chris Montez (62)	*3019*
Love Land—Charles Wright And The Watts 103rd Street Rhythm Band (70)	1504
In A Moment—Intrigues (69)	832
Happy Birthday Blues— Kathy Young With The Innocents (61)	682
Some Kinda Fun—Chris Montez (62)	403
Let's Dance—Ola & The Janglers (69)	*29*
Magic Is The Night— Kathy Young With The Innocents (61)	24
Let's Dance—Jive Bunny & The Mastermixers (90)	*6.7*
James (2) LEE ▶ 9133 (1)	**31**
Chip Off The Old Block—Eddy Arnold (59)	31
Jay LEE ▶ 6016 (1)	**216**
Yellow Balloon—Yellow Balloon (67)	647
Joyce LEE ▶ 3491 (1)	**819**
Please Tell Me Why—Jackie Wilson (61)	819
Juanita LEE ▶ 7230 (1)	**108**
Supersonic—J.J. Fad (88)	542
Larry Michael LEE ▶ 1767 (4)	**2349**
Jackie Blue—Ozark Mountain Daredevils (75)	4157
You Know Like I Know— Ozark Mountain Daredevils (77)	171
If I Only Knew—Ozark Mountain Daredevils (76)	128
Take You Tonight—Ozark Mountain Daredevils (80)	104
Laura LEE [Laura Lee Newton, Laura Lee Rundless] ▶ 10063 (1)	**13**
As Long As I Got You—Laura Lee (68)	26
Lawrence H. LEE Jr. ▶ 8571 (1)	**46**
Best Of Luck To You—Earl Gains (66)	46
Leonard LEE ▶ 1376 (9)	**3236**
Feel So Fine—Johnny Preston (60)	*1673*
Let The Good Times Roll—Shirley And Lee (56)	*870*
Feel So Good—Bunny Sigler (67)	*455*
Let The Good Times Roll—Bunny Sigler (67)	*455*
What Would I Do—Mickey And Sylvia (60)	336
Let The Good Times Roll—Shirley & Lee (60)	*202*
I Feel Good—Shirley & Lee (56)	170
I've Been Loved Before—Shirley & Lee (60)	46
Let The Good Times Roll—Roy Orbison (65)	*34*
Lester LEE ▶ 8745 (7)	**40**
Man From Laramie—Voices Of Walter Schumann (55)	*47*
Fire Down Below—Jeri Southern (57)	*8.4*
Fire Down Below—Roger King Mozian (57)	*8.4*
Fire Down Below— Gordon Jenkins & His Orchestra (57)	*8.4*
The Man From Laramie—Al Martino (55)	*0.0*

The Man From Laramie—Ralph Young (55)	*0.0*
The Man From Laramie— Eddy Howard & His Orchestra (55)	*0.0*
Martin LEE [Martin Barnes] ▶ 6781 (2)	**138**
Save Your Kisses For Me— Brotherhood Of Man (76)	*391*
Save Your Kisses For Me—Bobby Vinton (76)	*22*
—Marty Lee see: Martin Lee HOENES	
—Mary Elizabeth Johnson Lee see: Jeanie GREENE	
—Myron Lee see: Myron WACHENDORF	
Nancy LEE ▶ 2056 (3)	**1942**
The Stroll—Diamonds (57)	*3877*
No Wheels—Chordettes (59)	6.1
The Stroll—Lancers (57)	*0.0*
Nikki LEE [Michael Mozart] ▶ 5051 (1)	**354**
Notice Me—Nikki (90)	707
Peggy LEE [Norma Deloris Egstrom] ▶ 9100 (3) HOF	**31**
Tom Thumb's Tune—Russ Tamblyn (59)	*27*
I Don't Know Enough About You—Peggy Lee (56)	8.4
Tom Thumb's Tune—Patience & Prudence (59)	*0.0*
—Regina Marie Lee see: Regina RICHARDS	
Stella LEE ▶ 7368 (3)	**100**
Queen Of The Senior Prom—Mills Brothers (57)	*255*
Lean Jean—Bill Haley And His Comets (58)	58
Queen Of The Senior Prom—Mills Brothers (62)	*1.4*
Sydney LEE ▶ 4044 (2)	**614**
My Love, Forgive Me (Amore, Scusami)— Robert Goulet (64)	1802
Begin To Love (Cominciamo Ad Amarci)— Robert Goulet (65)	40
Tommy LEE [Thomas Lee Bass] ▶ 3578 (6)	**778**
Girls, Girls, Girls—Mötley Crüe (87)	1018
Home Sweet Home '91—Mötley Crüe (91)	*651*
Same Ol' Situation (S.O.S.)—Mötley Crüe (90)	148
Home Sweet Home—Mötley Crüe (85)	*70*
Primal Scream—Mötley Crüe (91)	60
All I Need—Mötley Crüe (87)	52
Will LEE ▶ 8360 (1)	**53**
Sneakin' Up Behind You—Brecker Brothers (75)	265
Hattie LEEPER ▶ 7307 (1)	**104**
Lonely Soldier—Mike Williams (66)	207
Gene LEES ▶ 10008 (2)	**14**
Quiet Nights Of Quiet Stars—Andy Williams (65)	23
Venice Blue (Que C'Est Triste Venise)— Bobby Darin (65)	7.3
Howard LEESE ▶ 7816 (2)	**74**
How Can I Refuse—Heart (83)	279
Little Queen—Heart (77)	164
Mike LEESON ▶ 1780 (6)	**2336**
For Your Eyes Only—Sheena Easton (81)	3674
Take Me Home Tonight—Eddie Money (86)	2098
I Wouldn't Beg For Water—Sheena Easton (82)	149
Everybody Move—Cathy Dennis (91)	7.4
My One Temptation—Mica Paris (89)	4.6
Into My Secret—Alisha (87)	1.5
Joe LEEWAY ▶ 1423 (8)	**3108**
Hold Me Now—Thompson Twins (84)	3557
Lay Your Hands On Me—Thompson Twins (85)	1742
King For A Day—Thompson Twins (86)	1479
Doctor! Doctor!—Thompson Twins (84)	1247
Lies—Thompson Twins (83)	612
You Take Me Up—Thompson Twins (84)	304
Love On Your Side—Thompson Twins (83)	286
The Gap—Thompson Twins (84)	95
Jerry LeFORS ▶ 10242 (1)	**11**
Try Again—Patsy Cline (57)	22
Nathan LEFTENANT ▶ 6833 (3)	**134**
She's Strange—Cameo (84)	325
Back And Forth—Cameo (87)	195
We're Goin' Out Tonight—Cameo (80)	13
Steve LeGASSICK ▶ 4166 (1)	**576**
One Heartbeat—Smokey Robinson (87)	1151
Sonny LeGLAIRE [Sophie LeGlaire] ▶ 10454 (1)	**8.3**
Fool's Paradise—Buddy Holly / The Crickets (58)	25
—Sophie LeGlaire see: Sonny LeGLAIRE	
Alain Le GOVIC ▶ 7540 (2)	**90**
Do I Love You—Paul Anka (71)	*446*
Do I Love You (Yes In Every Way)—Donna Fargo (78)	*2.7*

Michel LEGRAND ▶ 1825 (7) HOF	**2258**
Theme From "Summer Of '42"—Peter Nero (71)	*944*
The Windmills Of Your Mind—Dusty Springfield (69)	646
How Do You Keep The Music Playing— James Ingram And Patti Austin (83)	610
The Way He Makes Me Feel—Barbra Streisand (83)	554
Brian's Song—Michel LeGrand (72)	307
Happy—Bobby Darin (72)	282
Summer Of '42—Biddu Orchestra (75)	*263*
Franz LEHÁR ▶ 5502 (2)	**277**
Fooled—Perry Como (55)	819
Yours Is My Heart Alone—Enzo Stuarti (56)	17
Kenny LEHMAN ▶ 3476 (1)	**826**
Dance, Dance, Dance (Yowsah, Yowsah, Yowsah)— Chic (77)	2478
Johnny LEHMANN ▶ 817 (11)	**5380**
Night—Jackie Wilson (60)	4933
Alone At Last—Jackie Wilson (60)	1975
Tic Tender Love And Care—Jimmie Rodgers (60)	681
Don't Go Home—Playmates (58)	*635*
The Most Beautiful Words—Della Reese (61)	238
First Born—"Tennessee" Ernie Ford (56)	201
You're Looking At Me—Johnny Nash (58)	127
Don't Go Home (My Little Darlin')—Shirelles (67)	*17*
Majorca (Isle Of Love)—Bob Manning (55)	*3.7*
Dancin' In The Streets—Ames Brothers (59)	2.6
Man That's Choice— Sam (The Man) Taylor And His Orchestra (58)	0.4
Ted LEHRMAN ▶ 5800 (1)	**240**
No Man Is An Island—Don Cornell (54)	480
Jerry LEIBER [Elmo Glick, Jed Peters, Gaby Rodgers] ▶ 24 (122) HOF	**54926**
Jailhouse Rock—Elvis Presley (57)	*8238*
Kansas City—Wilbert Harrison (59)	*6968*
Charlie Brown—Coasters (59)	6481
Hound Dog—Elvis Presley (56)	*6329*
Ruby Baby—Dion (63)	*6167*
Love Potion Number Nine—Searchers (64)	*5796*
Yakety Yak—Coasters (58)	5603
Spanish Harlem—Aretha Franklin (71)	*4882*
There Goes My Baby—Drifters (59)	*4700*
Don't—Elvis Presley (58)	4291
Stand By Me—Ben E. King (61)	*3409*
She's Not You— Elvis Presley With The Jordanaires (62)	3394
I Keep Forgettin'—Michael McDonald (82)	*3365*
Searchin'—Coasters (57)	*3311*
Poison Ivy—Coasters (59)	2586
Drip Drop—Dion Di Muci (63)	*2250*
Reverend Mr. Black—Kingston Trio (63)	2205
Spanish Harlem—Ben E. King (60)	*2014*
Love Me—Elvis Presley (56)	*1990*
On Broadway—George Benson (78)	*1964*
Bossa Nova Baby— Elvis Presley With The Jordanaires (63)	1871
Stand By Me—Ben E. King (86)	*1763*
Along Came Jones—Coasters (59)	*1746*
Stand By Me—Spyder Turner (66)	*1730*
Black Denim Trousers And Motorcycle Boots— Cheers (55)	*1536*
Is That All There Is—Peggy Lee (69)	1534
Jackson—Nancy Sinatra & Lee Hazlewood (67)	1499
Dance With Me—Drifters (59)	1398
On Broadway—Drifters (63)	*1347*
I (Who Have Nothing)—Tom Jones (70)	*1304*
Young Blood—Coasters (57)	*1268*
D.W. Washburn—Monkees (68)	1160
Stand By Me—Mickey Gilley (80)	*1122*
Love Potion Number Nine—Clovers (59)	*1042*
Bobbie Sue—Oak Ridge Boys (82)	1000
I'll Be There—Damita Jo (61)	897
I'm A Woman—Maria Muldaur (74)	*842*
Kansas City—Trini Lopez (63)	*840*
Little Egypt (Ying-Yang)—Coasters (61)	823
I (Who Have Nothing)—Ben E. King (63)	*810*
Only In America—Jay & The Americans (63)	804
(Bazoom) I Need Your Lovin'—Cheers (54)	*802*
Young Blood—Bad Company (76)	*795*
Loving You—Elvis Presley (57)	733
There Goes My Baby—Donna Summer (84)	*674*
Along Came Jones—Ray Stevens (69)	*668*
Stand By Me—John Lennon (75)	*647*
Lucky Lips—Ruth Brown (57)	*626*
I (Who Have Nothing)—Terry Knight And The Pack (66)	*588*
(How Bout A Little Hand For) The Boys In The Band— Boys In The Band (70)	572
What About Us—Coasters (59)	504
(When She Needs Good Lovin') She Comes To Me— Chicago Loop (66)	*428*
Run Red Run—Coasters (59)	418
I'm A Woman—Peggy Lee (62)	*394*
Framed—Cheech & Chong (76)	335
Saved—LaVern Baker (61)	327
Stand By Me—Maurice White (85)	*304*
Kansas City— James Brown And The Famous Flames (67)	*301*
Ruby, Baby—Billy "Crash" Craddock (74)	*300*
Treat Me Nice—Elvis Presley (57)	295
I Keep Forgettin'—Chuck Jackson (62)	*295*
Just Tell Her Jim Said Hello— Elvis Presley With The Jordanaires (62)	251
Stand By Me—David & Jimmy Ruffin (70)	*227*
King Creole— Elvis Presley with the Jordanaires (58)	192
(You're So Square) Baby, I Don't Care— Joni Mitchell (82)	189
Lucky Lips—Cliff Richard (63)	*180*
Past, Present And Future—Shangri-Las (66)	169
What To Do With Laurie—Mike Clifford (62)	165
Searching— Jack Eubanks And The Sound Of The South (61)	*149*
I (Who Have Nothing)—Sylvester (79)	*146*
I'm A Hog For You—Coasters (59)	133
Black Denim Trousers And Motorcycle Boots— Vaughn Monroe with Chorus And Orchestra (55)	*132*
Stand By Me—Earl Grant (65)	*129*
Kansas City—Hank Ballard And The Midnighters (59)	*119*
Shoppin' For Clothes—Coasters (60)	116
Rat Race—Drifters (63)	115
Love Potion Number Nine—Coasters (71)	*97*
Hound Dog—Jive Bunny And The Mastermixers (89)	*80*
Jailhouse Rock— Jive Bunny And The Mastermixers (89)	*80*
Searchin'—Jim Croce (76)	*76*
You're The Boss—Lavern Baker & Jimmy Ricks (61)	75
Young Blood—Bruce Willis (87)	*71*
I Who Have Nothing—Liquid Smoke (70)	*71*
My Claire De Lune—Steve Lawrence (61)	*68*
Dancin'—Perry Como (57)	61
Searchin'—Ace Cannon (64)	*59*
Blues For Me—Eddie Fisher (57)	51
Lucky Lips—Gale Storm (57)	*50*
Idol With The Golden Head—Coasters (57)	45
Kansas City—Rocky Olson (59)	*40*
Love Me—5 DeMarco Sisters (54)	*39*
One Kiss Led To Another—Coasters (56)	*37*
Spanish Harlem—Santo & Johnny (62)	*30*
(When She Wants Good Lovin') My Baby Comes To Me—Coasters (57)	*29*
Fools Fall In Love—Drifters (57)	*29*
Get Him—Exciters (63)	26
Trouble—Elvis Presley with the Jordanaires (58)	24
Hound Dog—Elvis Presley (82)	*23*
Jailhouse Rock—Elvis Presley (82)	*23*
Dirty, Dirty Feeling— Elvis Presley With The Jordanaires (65)	23
Jack O' Diamonds—Ruth Brown (59)	22
Kansas City—Beatles (65)	*22*
Drip Drop—Drifters (58)	*21*
Girls Girls Girls (Part II)—Coasters (61)	21
Blueberries—Georgia Gibbs (55)	20
Spanish Harlem—King Curtis (65)	*15*
Stand By Me—Cassius Clay (64)	*14*
Searchin' (Medley)—Johnny Rivers (73)	*12*
Do Your Own Thing—Brook Benton (68)	8.6
Smokey Joe's Café—Robins (55)	6.4
Shadow Knows—Coasters (58)	4.6
Kansas City—Little Richard (59)	*3.8*
Santa Claus Is Back In Town—Elvis Presley (57)	2.1
Lovey—Clovers (60)	1.3
Drums—Kenny Chandler (61)	0.5
Fools Fall In Love—Elvis Presley (67)	*0.5*
Love Me—Georgia Gibbs (54)	*0.0*
Love Me—Connie Russell (54)	*0.0*
My Clair De Lune—George Feyer (61)	*0.0*
Love Me—Billy Williams Quartet (54)	*0.0*
One Kiss Led To Another—Sunny Gale (56)	*0.0*
Bazoom! (I Need Your Lovin')— Les Elgart & His Orchestra (54)	*0.0*
Oliver LEIBER ▶ 331 (4)	**11097**
Opposites Attract—Paula Abdul (89)	4258
Forever Your Girl—Paula Abdul (89)	3369
(It's Just) The Way That You Love Me— Paula Abdul (88)	*1918*
(It's Just) The Way That You Love Me— Paula Abdul (89)	*1553*
—Sydney Leibowitz see: Steve LAWRENCE	
—Amanda Blue Leigh see: Amanda BLUE	
Carolyn LEIGH ▶ 2129 (13) HOF	**1838**
Witchcraft—Frank Sinatra (57)	1455
Firefly—Tony Bennett (58)	1081
(How Little It Matters) How Little We Know— Frank Sinatra (56)	663
I'm Waiting Just For You—Pat Boone (57)	*517*
Real Live Girl—Steve Alaimo (65)	47
Stay With Me—Frank Sinatra (64)	39
Pass Me By—Peggy Lee (65)	*29*
Hey, Look Me Over— Pete King Chorale and Orchestra (61)	11
My How The Time Goes By—Patti Page (57)	5.7
Pass Me By—Mike Douglas (65)	*0.0*
Young At Heart—Frank Sinatra (54)	0.0
Swinging Sweethearts—Richard Hayes (57)	*0.0*
I'm Waiting Just For You— Hoagy Carmichael & Cass Daley (57)	*0.0*
Mitch LEIGH [Irwin Michnick] ▶ 2638 (4)	**1301**
The Impossible Dream (The Quest)—Jack Jones (66)	*685*
The Impossible Dream—Hesitations (68)	*449*
The Dis-Advantages Of You— Brass Ring Featuring Phil Bodner (67)	405
The Impossible Dream—Roger Williams (68)	*330*
Richard LEIGH ▶ 725 (3)	**6032**
Don't It Make My Brown Eyes Blue— Crystal Gayle (77)	5908
It's All I Can Do—Anne Murray (81)	158
I'll Get Over You—Crystal Gayle (76)	45
Elly LEIGHTON ▶ 11038 (1)	**3.7**
If Only I Could Live My Life Again— Jane Morgan (59)	15
Molly Ann LEIKIN ▶ 5997 (3)	**218**
Let Me Love You Once—Greg Lake (81)	377
Moment By Moment—Yvonne Elliman (78)	48
I'm Never Gonna Say Goodbye—Billy Preston (82)	11
—Leila K see: Leila EL KHALIFI	
Bob LEINBACH ▶ 7653 (3)	**83**
Crazy (Keep On Falling)—John Hall Band (81)	294
You Sure Fooled Me—John Hall Band (82)	21
Don't Throw Our Love Away—Orleans (79)	6.7
Hans LEIP ▶ 8541 (1)	**47**
Lili Marlene—Al Martino (68)	140
Eric LEISER ▶ 3642 (1)	**753**
Till Death Do Us Part—Bob Braun (62)	753
Jim LEISY ▶ 10904 (1)	**4.5**
Please Tell Me Why—Betty Johnson (56)	4.5
Donovan LEITCH ▶ 94 (20) HOF	**25987**
Sunshine Superman—Donovan (66)	*5806*
Mellow Yellow—Donovan (66)	*5582*
Hurdy Gurdy Man—Donovan (68)	3670
Atlantis—Donovan (69)	2086
There Is A Mountain—Donovan (67)	1569
Epistle To Dippy—Donovan (67)	1323
Jennifer Juniper—Donovan (68)	945
Catch The Wind—Donovan (65)	836
Wear Your Love Like Heaven—Donovan (67)	733
Lalena—Donovan (68)	568
Goo Goo Barabajagal (Love Is Hot)— Donovan (With The Jeff Beck Group) (69)	548
To Susan On The West Coast Waiting—Donovan (69)	538
Museum—Herman's Hermits (67)	523
Riki Tiki Tavi—Donovan (70)	444
Colours—Donovan (65)	349
I Like You—Donovan (73)	234
Season Of The Witch, Pt. 1—Vanilla Fudge (68)	133
Celia Of The Seals—Donovan (71)	100
Sunshine Superman—Willie Bobo (66)	*1.4*
Mellow Yellow—Senator Bobby & Senator McKinley (67)	*1.0*

Paul LEKA ▶ 668 (6)	**6485**
Green Tambourine—Lemon Pipers (67)	7211
Na Na Hey Hey Kiss Him Goodbye—Steam (69)	*5814*
Kiss Him Goodbye—Nylons (87)	*977*
Rice Is Nice—Lemon Pipers (68)	521
Jelly Jungle (Of Orange Marmalade)— Lemon Pipers (68)	431
I've Gotta Make You Love Me—Steam (70)	418
Prince LELEIOHOKU [William Pitt Leleiohoku II Kalaho'olewa] ▶ 7559 (1)	**88**
Hawaiian War Chant— Billy Vaughn And His Orchestra (59)	177
—William Pitt Leleiohoku II Kalaho'olewa see: Prince LELEIOHOKU	
Pierre LeMAIRE [Pierre Cour, Pierre Louis Lemaire] ▶ 5274 (4)	**314**
Love Is Blue—Dells (69)	*524*
Love Is Blue (L'Amour Est Bleu)—Al Martino (68)	*302*
Love Is Blue (L'Amour Est Bleu)— Claudine Longet (68)	*75*
Love Is Blue (L'Amour Est Bleu)— Manny Kellem, His Orchestra And Voices (68)	*2.7*
Tony LeMANS ▶ 7600 (1)	**86**
Sure Lookin'—Donny Osmond (91)	259
Edwin LEMARE ▶ 5449 (2)	**287**
Moonlight And Roses (Bring Mem'ries Of You)— Three Suns (54)	*522*
Moonlight And Roses (Bring Mem'ries Of You)— Vic Dana (65)	*340*
—Jules Lemare see: Charles N. DANIELS	
Francis LEMARQUE [Nathan Korb] ▶ 4127 (4)	**585**
Little Shoemaker—Gaylords (54)	*1620*
Little Shoemaker— Hugo Winterhalter And His Orchestra (54)	*307*
Someone To Love—Four Aces (56)	186
Marjolaina—Gogi Grant (58)	31
Harvey LEMBECK ▶ 11144 (1)	**3.0**
True, True Love—Frankie Avalon (61)	9.1
Billy LEMMONS ▶ 10794 (1)	**5.3**
Six Packs A Day—Billy Lemmons (77)	5.3
Eugene LEMON ▶ 7674 (1)	**81**
Day By Day (Every Minute Of The Hour)— Continental 4 (71)	163
Mike LENDELL [Michael Charles Rashkow] ▶ 5163 (2)	**332**
Mary In The Morning—Al Martino (67)	657
I Don't Wanna Be Left Outside—Ellie Greenwich (70)	7.2
Pearl LENDHURST ▶ 1716 (1)	**2445**
Be Bop Baby—Ricky Nelson (57)	2445
Lea LENDON ▶ 9773 (1)	**17**
The Big Time Spender (Part I)— Cornbread & Biscuits (60)	34
Barry LENG ▶ 9352 (1)	**25**
137 Disco Heaven—Amii Stewart (79)	51
Ron LENHOFF ▶ 3554 (4)	**787**
Get Up! (Before The Night Is Over)— Technotronic (90)	1473
Get Up I Feel Like Being Like A Sex Machine (Part 1)— James Brown (70)	*913*
Get Up, Get Into It, Get Involved Pt. 1—James Brown (70)	511
Get Up I Feel Like Being A Sex Machine— James Brown (75)	*53*
John LENNON ▶ 2 (163) HOF	**166587**
Hey Jude—Beatles (68)	*14634*
I Want To Hold Your Hand—Beatles (64)	*14194*
She Loves You—Beatles (64)	*10567*
Get Back—Beatles With Billy Preston (69)	*8698*
Let It Be—Beatles (70)	*8679*
We Can Work It Out—Beatles (65)	*8664*
A Hard Day's Night—Beatles (64)	*8359*
Can't Buy Me Love—Beatles (64)	8269
I Feel Fine—Beatles (64)	8162
Hello Goodbye—Beatles (67)	8134
Yesterday—Beatles (65)	*7927*
Help!—Beatles (65)	7847
(Just Like) Starting Over—John Lennon (80)	7652
Love Me Do—Beatles (64)	7070
All You Need Is Love—Beatles (67)	*6800*
Ticket To Ride—Beatles (65)	*6556*
Paperback Writer—Beatles (66)	6493
A World Without Love—Peter And Gordon (64)	*6461*
Come Together—Beatles (69)	*6145*
Eight Days A Week—Beatles (65)	6070
Fame—David Bowie (75)	5730
Instant Karma (We All Shine On)—John Ono Lennon (70)	5666
Woman—John Lennon (81)	5501
Yellow Submarine—Beatles (66)	5464
The Long And Winding Road—Beatles (70)	5434
Penny Lane—Beatles (67)	5144
Lady Madonna—Beatles (68)	*5119*
Nowhere Man—Beatles (66)	*5024*
Please Please Me—Beatles (64)	*4866*
Do You Want To Know A Secret—Beatles (64)	*4830*
Imagine—John Lennon Plastic Ono Band (71)	*4677*
Lucy In The Sky With Diamonds—Elton John (74)	4586
Whatever Gets You Thru The Night—John Lennon With The Plastic Ono Nuclear Band (74)	3620
Got To Get You Into My Life—Beatles (76)	*2422*
The Fool On The Hill— Sergio Mendes & Brasil '66 (68)	2327
She's A Woman—Beatles (64)	2317
You Won't See Me—Anne Murray (74)	1945
Day Tripper—Beatles (65)	*1881*
Revolution—Beatles (68)	1855
Nobody Told Me—John Lennon (84)	1854
The Ballad Of John And Yoko—Beatles (69)	1848
Strawberry Fields Forever—Beatles (67)	1798
Watching The Wheels—John Lennon (81)	1527
We Can Work It Out—Stevie Wonder (71)	*1496*
Bad To Me—Billy J. Kramer With The Dakotas (64)	1411
You've Got To Hide Your Love Away—Silkie (65)	*1392*
Give Peace A Chance—Plastic Ono Band (69)	*1367*
Power To The People— John Lennon Plastic Ono Band (71)	1340
P.S. I Love You—Beatles (64)	1327
Goodbye—Mary Hopkin (69)	1267
Nobody I Know—Peter And Gordon (64)	1242
Mind Games—John Lennon (73)	1241
Got To Get You Into My Life— Earth, Wind & Fire (78)	*1210*
#9 Dream—John Lennon (74)	1210
Eleanor Rigby—Beatles (66)	*1186*
I Saw Him Standing There—Tiffany (88)	*1114*
Michelle—David & Jonathan (66)	*1048*
Birthday—Underground Sunshine (69)	1006
Hey Jude—Wilson Pickett (68)	*933*
I Don't Want To See You Again— Peter And Gordon (64)	871
And I Love Her—Beatles (64)	*866*
Eleanor Rigby—Aretha Franklin (69)	*807*
Yesterday—Ray Charles (67)	*797*
Cold Turkey—Plastic Ono Band (69)	784
She Came In Through The Bathroom Window— Joe Cocker (69)	697
From A Window— Billy J. Kramer With The Dakotas (64)	*694*
Eleanor Rigby—Ray Charles (68)	*673*
Come Together—Aerosmith (78)	*659*
I Saw Her Standing There—Beatles (64)	*638*
I'll Cry Instead—Beatles (64)	638
Oh! Darling—Robin Gibb (78)	626
Mother—John Lennon/Plastic Ono Band (71)	*622*
Love—Lettermen (71)	589
A Hard Day's Night—Ramsey Lewis Trio (66)	*532*
Rain—Beatles (66)	508
All My Loving—Beatles (64)	*480*
Thank You Girl—Beatles (64)	466
No Reply—Stars On 45 (81)	442
Nowhere Man—Stars On 45 (81)	*442*
Drive My Car—Stars On 45 (81)	*442*
I'll Be Back—Stars On 45 (81)	442
We Can Work It Out—Stars On 45 (81)	*442*
I Should Have Known Better—Stars On 45 (81)	*442*
Do You Want To Know A Secret—Stars On 45 (81)	*442*
You're Going To Lose That Girl—Stars On 45 (81)	442
Let It Be—Joan Baez (71)	*435*
And I Love Him—Esther Phillips (65)	*406*
Ringo's Theme (This Boy)— George Martin And His Orch. (64)	*389*
I'll Keep You Satisfied— Billy J. Kramer With The Dakotas (64)	373
And I Love Her—George Martin And His Orch. (64)	*352*
Come Together—Ike & Tina Turner & The Ikettes (70)	*348*
From Me To You—Beatles (64)	*345*
It's All Down To Goodnight Vienna—Ringo Starr (75)	340
It's For You—Springwell (71)	*334*
I Am The Walrus—Beatles (67)	317
Ob-La-Di, Ob-La-Da—Arthur Conley (68)	*282*
If I Fell—Beatles (64)	277
With A Little Help From My Friends—Joe Cocker (68)	*272*
Magical Mystery Tour—Ambrosia (77)	*262*
Baby You're A Rich Man—Beatles (67)	258
Ob-La-Di, Ob-La-Da—Beatles (76)	*224*
I Don't Want To Spoil The Party—Beatles (65)	221
Ticket To Ride—Carpenters (70)	*196*
Don't Let Me Down—Beatles With Billy Preston (69)	194
Michelle—Billy Vaughn His Orchestra & Chorus (66)	*188*
Dear Prudence—Katfish (75)	*186*
I Want To Hold Your Hand—Boston Pops Orchestra Arthur Fiedler Conductor (64)	*184*
Day Tripper—Anne Murray (74)	*181*
Happy Xmas (War Is Over)—John & Yoko & Plastic Ono Band with Harlem Community Choir (71)	177
I Should Have Known Better—Beatles (64)	*172*
I'm Stepping Out—John Lennon (84)	146
Julia—Ramsey Lewis (69)	145
Yes It Is—Beatles (65)	137
Get Back—Beatles (82)	*134*
Ticket To Ride—Beatles (82)	*134*
A Hard Day's Night—Beatles (82)	*134*
All You Need Is Love—Beatles (82)	*134*
Magical Mystery Tour—Beatles (82)	*134*
I Should Have Known Better—Beatles (82)	*134*
You've Got To Hide Your Love Away—Beatles (82)	*134*
Mother—Barbra Streisand (71)	*130*
Got To Get You Into My Life— Blood, Sweat & Tears (75)	*128*
You Can't Do That—Beatles (64)	*126*
Michelle—Bud Shank (66)	*116*
Dear Prudence—Five Stairsteps (70)	*110*
From Me To You—Del Shannon (63)	*110*
A World Without Love—Bobby Rydell (64)	*99*
Woman Is The Nigger Of The World— John Lennon/Plastic Ono Band With Elephant's Memory And The Invisible Strings (72)	86
Jealous Guy—John Lennon (88)	76
Back In The U.S.S.R.—Chubby Checker (69)	70
Day Tripper—Ramsey Lewis (66)	*70*
I'm Happy Just To Dance With You—Anne Murray (80)	*59*
Here, There And Everywhere—Emmylou Harris (76)	*55*
Drive My Car—Gary Toms Empire (75)	*52*
Give Peace A Chance—Peace Choir (91)	*49*
From A Window—Chad & Jeremy (65)	*45*
I'm A Loser—Beatles (65)	37
Imagine—Tracie Spencer (89)	*35*
It's For You—Cilla Black (64)	*34*
With A Little Help From My Friends—Beatles (78)	*24*
Sgt. Pepper's Lonely Hearts Club Band—Beatles (78)	24
You Can't Do That—Nilsson (67)	*23*
Lady Madonna—Fats Domino (68)	*16*
What Goes On—Beatles (66)	16
There's A Place—Beatles (64)	13
Here, There And Everywhere—Fourmost (66)	*12*
I'm Happy Just To Dance With You—Beatles (64)	*12*
Step Inside Love—Cilla Black (68)	11
Drive My Car—Bob Kuban And The In-Men (66)	*11*
She's A Woman—José Feliciano (69)	9.6
Get Back—Billy Preston (78)	*9.4*
From Me To You—Stars On 45 (81)	*8.0*
Please Please Me—Stars On 45 (81)	*8.0*
Good Day Sunshine—Stars On 45 (81)	*8.0*
A Hard Day's Night—Stars On 45 (81)	*8.0*
I Want To Hold Your Hand—Stars On 45 (81)	*8.0*
This Boy—Beatles (64)	*6.4*
All My Loving—Beatles (64)	*6.4*
Rocky Raccoon—Richie Havens (69)	4.0
All My Loving—Hollyridge Strings (64)	*3.8*
Day Tripper—Vontastics (66)	*2.4*
Sie Liebt Dich (She Loves You)—Die Beatles (64)	*1.9*
Good Day Sunshine—Claudine Longet (67)	*0.9*
Julian LENNON ▶ 1289 (5)	**3449**
Too Late For Goodbyes—Julian Lennon (85)	1838
Valotte—Julian Lennon (84)	1544
Say You're Wrong—Julian Lennon (85)	614
Stick Around—Julian Lennon (86)	454
Now You're In Heaven—Julian Lennon (89)	57

Sean Ono LENNON ▶ 10139 (1)	**12**
Give Peace A Chance—Peace Choir (91)	*49*
Annie LENNOX ▶ 546 (15)	**7885**
Sweet Dreams (Are Made Of This)—Eurythmics (83)	6027
Here Comes The Rain Again—Eurythmics (84)	2759
Would I Lie To You?—Eurythmics (85)	2003
Missionary Man—Eurythmics (86)	989
Who's That Girl?—Eurythmics (84)	681
Sisters Are Doin' It For Themselves—Eurythmics And Aretha Franklin (85)	674
Love Is A Stranger—Eurythmics (83)	634
There Must Be An Angel (Playing With My Heart)—Eurythmics (85)	546
Right By Your Side—Eurythmics (84)	489
Don't Ask Me Why—Eurythmics (89)	350
I Need A Man—Eurythmics (87)	231
Thorn In My Side—Eurythmics (86)	152
You Have Placed A Chill In My Heart—Eurythmics (88)	149
It's Alright (Baby's Coming Back)—Eurythmics (86)	62
Sexcrime (Nineteen Eighty-Four)—Eurythmics (84)	23
Evelyne LENTON [Evelyne Verrecchia] ▶ 11068 (1)	**3.4**
Miss Broadway—Belle Epoque (78)	6.8
Bernard LENTZ ▶ 7446 (1)	**95**
Sound-Off—Titus Turner (61)	191
Josh LEO ▶ 9866 (1)	**16**
Baby, What About You—Crystal Gayle (83)	32
—Dave Leon see: Dave APPELL	
Anita LEONARD [Anita Leonard Nye] ▶ 10318 (4)	**10**
A Sunday Kind Of Love—Lenny Welch (72)	*26*
A Sunday Kind Of Love—Jan & Dean (62)	*7.3*
Sunday Kind Of Love—Etta James (61)	*5.7*
Sunday Kind Of Love—Fran Warren (58)	*0.8*
—Jack Leonard see: Jack LITTLE	
Mark LEONARD ▶ 2119 (1)	**1848**
Missing You—John Waite (84)	5545
Michael LEONARD ▶ 7935 (2)	**69**
Why Did I Choose You—Barbra Streisand (65)	126
I Was A Boy (When You Needed A Man)—Billy Shields (69)	11
Patrick LEONARD ▶ 7345 (1)	**101**
Princess—Frank Gari (61)	302
Patrick Raymond LEONARD ▶ 374 (10)	**10412**
Live To Tell—Madonna (86)	4537
Like A Prayer—Madonna (89)	4495
Who's That Girl—Madonna (87)	3738
Cherish—Madonna (89)	2774
La Isla Bonita—Madonna (87)	2230
One Good Woman—Peter Cetera (88)	1789
Oh Father—Madonna (89)	816
Hanky Panky—Madonna (90)	778
Most Of All—Jody Watley (88)	213
Best Of Times—Peter Cetera (88)	199
Steve LEONARD ▶ 3217 (1)	**946**
Penetration—Pyramids (64)	946
Diego Maria LEONI ▶ 9219 (1)	**28**
Don't You Love Me—49ers (90)	85
Glenn LEOPOLD ▶ 3518 (1)	**802**
Back When My Hair Was Short—Gunhill Road (73)	802
Cory LERIOS ▶ 1140 (7)	**3894**
Whatcha Gonna Do?—Pablo Cruise (77)	2803
Love Will Find A Way—Pablo Cruise (78)	2597
Cool Love—Pablo Cruise (81)	1056
I Want You Tonight—Pablo Cruise (79)	841
Don't Want To Live Without It—Pablo Cruise (78)	793
A Place In The Sun—Pablo Cruise (77)	289
Never Had A Love—Pablo Cruise (78)	42
Alan Jay LERNER ▶ 1348 (26) HOF	**3292**
On The Street Where You Live—Vic Damone (56)	*2704*
I Could Have Danced All Night—Sylvia Syms (56)	*921*
On The Street Where You Live—Andy Williams (64)	*563*
I Could Have Danced All Night—Rosemary Clooney (56)	*544*
On The Street Where You Live—Eddie Fisher (56)	*487*
Almost Like Being In Love—Michael Johnson (78)	477
I've Grown Accustomed To Your Face—Rosemary Clooney (56)	*394*
Gigi—Vic Damone (58)	*216*
How To Handle A Woman—Johnny Mathis (60)	85

I Could Have Danced All Night—Ben E. King (63)	*38*
I've Grown Accustomed To Your Face—Gordon MacRae (56)	*37*
Too Late Now—DeCastro Sisters (55)	37
I Could Have Danced All Night—Dinah Shore (56)	*36*
With A Little Bit Of Luck—Jo Stafford (56)	*28*
Get Me To The Church On Time—Julius La Rosa (56)	11
On The Street Where You Live—Lawrence Welk And His Champagne Music (56)	*3.3*
On A Clear Day You Can See Forever—Johnny Mathis (65)	2.4
Gigi—Bing Crosby (58)	*0.0*
Gigi—Tony Martin (58)	*0.0*
Gigi—Billy Eckstine (58)	*0.0*
Gigi—Strollers Featuring Artie Malvin (58)	*0.0*
I've Grown Accustomed To Her Face—Sid Feller & His Orchestra (56)	*0.0*
I Could Have Danced All Night—Lawrence Welk & His Champagne Music (56)	*0.0*
I've Grown Accustomed To Her Face—Lawrence Welk & His Champagne Music (56)	*0.0*
I've Grown Accustomed To Her Face—Sammy Kaye & His "Swing And Sway" Orchestra (56)	*0.0*
I've Grown Accustomed To Your Face—Bob Eberly with Enoch Light & His Orchestra (56)	*0.0*
James LEROY ▶ 9050 (1)	**32**
Touch Of Magic—James Leroy (73)	32
—Jean Marcel Leroy see: Jean-Jacques PERREY	
—Pierre Leroyer see: Pierre DELANOË	
Phil LESH ▶ 8185 (1)	**59**
Truckin'—Grateful Dead (71)	237
Katrina LESKANICH ▶ 5153 (1)	**333**
That's The Way—Katrina And The Waves (89)	667
Edgar LESLIE ▶ 2458 (6) HOF	**1466**
Among My Souvenirs—Connie Francis (59)	2593
For Me And My Gal—Freddy Cannon (61)	208
Last Song And Dance—Kay Starr (58)	72
The Moon Was Yellow—Frank Sinatra (62)	26
On Treasure Island—Gale Storm (57)	21
It Looks Like Rain In Cherry Blossom Lane—Debbie Reynolds (60)	9.9
—Mike Leslie see: Mike DAVIES	
—Tom Leslie see: Snuff GARRETT	
Tony LESTER ▶ 9349 (1)	**26**
One Way Love—Bandit (79)	26
Walter LESTER ▶ 3884 (9)	**667**
Since I Don't Have You—Skyliners (59)	*2364*
This I Swear—Skyliners (59)	743
Since I Don't Have You—Don McLean (81)	*545*
Since I Don't Have You—Chuck Jackson (64)	*403*
It Happened Today—Skyliners (59)	229
Since I Don't Have You—Art Garfunkel (79)	*180*
Since I Don't Have You—Eddie Holman (70)	*160*
Since I Don't Have You—Fred Parris & The Five Satins (82)	*4.8*
How Much—Skyliners (60)	1.5
—Henry Robert Merrill Levan see: Bob MERRILL	
Sylvester LEVAY [Lévay Szilveszter] ▶ 703 (11)	**6200**
Fly, Robin, Fly—Silver Convention (75)	*5615*
Get Up And Boogie (That's Right)—Silver Convention (76)	5492
Victim Of Love—Elton John (79)	357
Body Rock—Maria Vidal (84)	320
Who Do You Think You're Foolin'—Donna Summer (81)	312
Lady Bump—Penny McLean (76)	*216*
No, No, Joe—Silver Convention (76)	96
Lady Bump—Ritchie Family (76)	*92*
Fly, Robin, Fly—Ritchie Family (76)	*92*
Fools Like Me—Lorenzo Lamas (84)	23
Save Me—Silver Convention (75)	14
Raymond LEVEEN ▶ 5017 (1)	**359**
I Wonder—Brenda Lee (63)	717
Mel LEVEN ▶ 8715 (3)	**41**
Carmen's Boogie—Crew-Cuts (55)	57
How Many Others—Dick Roman (55)	24
Don't Call Me Sweetie (Cause I'm Bitter)—Eileen Rodgers (57)	9.7
Lowell LEVENGER ▶ 11454 (1)	**1.6**
Hippie From Olema—Youngbloods (70)	1.6

Neil LEVENSON ▶ 2140 (2)	**1825**
Denise—Randy And The Rainbows (63)	1818
Why Do Kids Grow Up—Randy And The Rainbows (63)	6.9
Tim LEVER ▶ 4560 (5)	**465**
You Spin Me Round (Like A Record)—Dead Or Alive (85)	1071
Brand New Lover—Dead Or Alive (86)	1017
Come Home With Me Baby—Dead Or Alive (89)	117
Lover Come Back To Me—Dead Or Alive (85)	84
Something In My House—Dead Or Alive (87)	38
Eddie LEVERT ▶ 6191 (3)	**195**
Lonely Drifter—Pieces Of Eight (67)	*357*
Lonely Drifter—O'Jays (63)	*18*
Stand In For Love—O'Jays (66)	8.1
Bill LEVERTY ▶ 2463 (3)	**1459**
Love Of A Lifetime—Firehouse (91)	2055
Don't Treat Me Bad—Firehouse (91)	976
All She Wrote—Firehouse (91)	374
Ira LEVIN ▶ 6222 (1)	**192**
He Touched Me—Barbra Streisand (65)	384
Marc LEVIN ▶ 6175 (1)	**197**
Bongo Stomp—Little Joey And The Flips (62)	592
Bob LEVINE ▶ 8983 (3)	**34**
Sunshine, Red Wine—Crazy Elephant (69)	64
Gimme Some More—Crazy Elephant (69)	42
Should Anybody Ask—Garry Bonner (74)	15
—Evelyn Levine see: Evelyn DANZIG	
Hank LEVINE ▶ 7158 (2)	**113**
(Theme From) Silver City—Ventures (61)	89
What Are We Going To Do?—David Jones (65)	71
Ian LEVINE ▶ 9966 (2)	**14**
High Energy—Evelyn Thomas (84)	20
So Many Men, So Little Time—Miquel Brown (83)	8.9
Irwin LEVINE ▶ 112 (34)	**22423**
Knock Three Times—Dawn (70)	9840
Tie A Yellow Ribbon Round The Ole Oak Tree—Dawn Featuring Tony Orlando (73)	*8042*
This Diamond Ring—Gary Lewis And The Playboys (65)	7757
Candida—Dawn (70)	4981
Say, Has Anybody Seen My Sweet Gypsy Rose—Dawn Featuring Tony Orlando (73)	3651
Black Pearl—Sonny Charles And The Checkmates, Ltd. (69)	1971
I Woke Up In Love This Morning—Partridge Family Starring Shirley Jones & Featuring David Cassidy (71)	1847
Steppin' Out (Gonna Boogie Tonight)—Tony Orlando And Dawn (74)	1391
Who's In The Strawberry Patch With Sally—Tony Orlando And Dawn (73)	839
Talk It Over—Grayson Hugh (89)	793
Summer Sand—Dawn (71)	744
I Play And Sing—Dawn (71)	724
What Are You Doing Sunday—Dawn Featuring Tony Orlando (71)	683
We're Free—Beverly Bremers (72)	654
A Thing Of The Past—Shirelles (61)	654
I Must Be Seeing Things—Gene Pitney (65)	593
I Hear Those Church Bells Ringing—Dusk (71)	494
Your Husband - My Wife—Brooklyn Bridge (69)	462
Am I Losing You—Partridge Family Starring Shirley Jones & Featuring David Cassidy (72)	417
Little Lonely One—Tom Jones (65)	381
Angel Baby—Dusk (71)	311
Let's Call It A Day Girl—Razor's Edge (66)	*270*
Mr. And Mrs. Untrue—Candi Staton (71)	150
Number Wonderful—Rock Flowers (71)	143
It Only Hurts When I Try To Smile—Dawn Featuring Tony Orlando (74)	135
You're Gonna Need Magic—Roy Hamilton (61)	131
I Can't Quit Her—Arbors (69)	85
Treat Me Like A Good Piece Of Candy—Dusk (71)	65
I Think I Love You Again—Brenda Lee (70)	40
You Came, You Saw, You Conquered!—Ronettes, featuring Veronica (69)	18
Let's Call It A Day Girl—Bobby Vee (69)	*11*
Holly Go Softly—Cornerstone (70)	7.3
Is There Anyone Home?—Jimmy Druiett (72)	5.2
Should I Tie A Yellow Ribbon Round The Ole Oak Tree? The Answer—Connie Francis (73)	*0.7*

Joey LEVINE ▶ 657 (19)	**6663**
Yummy Yummy Yummy—Ohio Express (68)	4175
Chewy Chewy—Ohio Express (68)	2224
Gimme Gimme Good Lovin'—Crazy Elephant (69)	2168
Make Believe—Wind (69)	1026
Quick Joey Small (Run Joey Run)— Kasenetz-Katz Singing Orchestral Circus (68)	1017
Down At Lulu's—Ohio Express (68)	793
Mercy—Ohio Express (69)	675
Shake—Shadows Of Knight (68)	446
Run, Run, Run—Third Rail (67)	409
You Got The Love— Professor Morrison's Lollipop (68)	178
Try It—Ohio Express (68)	125
Sweeter Than Sugar—Ohio Express (69)	121
I'm In Love With You— Kasenetz-Katz Super Cirkus (69)	46
All's Quiet On West 23rd—Julie Budd (68)	31
Bye Bye Baby—U.S. 1 (75)	17
They Don't Make 'Em Like That Any More— Reunion (75)	3.7
That's The Tune—Vogues (66)	2.9
Yes Sir—Music Explosion (68)	2.3
Down In Tennessee— Kasenetz-Katz Singing Orchestral Circus (68)	1.3
Mike LEVINE ▶ 5485 (4)	**279**
Somebody's Out There—Triumph (86)	502
Magic Power—Triumph (81)	298
I Can Survive—Triumph (80)	28
Follow Your Heart—Triumph (85)	10
—Samuel M. Levine see: Sam LEWIS	
Warren LEVINE ▶ 6998 (1)	**123**
I Stand Accused (Of Loving You)—Glories (67)	123
Blake LEVINSOHN ▶ 5921 (1)	**228**
Without You (Not Another Lonely Night)— Franke & the Knockouts (82)	684
Anthony LEVINSON ▶ 3470 (1)	**832**
Down The Aisle (Wedding Song)— Patti Labelle And The Blue Belles (63)	832
—Gerald Levinson see: Jerry LIVINGSTON	
Lou LEVINSON ▶ 10439 (1)	**8.5**
Here In My Heart—Al Martino (61)	25
Marsha LEVINSON ▶ 8968 (2)	**35**
I Found A New Love—Blue Belles (62)	45
Work Out, Part I & II—Ricky Dee & the Embers (62)	24
Richard LEVINSON ▶ 9345 (1)	**26**
Let's Do Something Cheap And Superficial— Burt Reynolds (80)	26
Carroll LEVIS ▶ 11326 (1)	**2.2**
Cha Cha Baby—Ted Heath and His Orchestra (58)	6.7
—William S. Levise Jr. see: Mitch RYDER	
Cy LEVITAN [Seymour Levittan] ▶ 11736 (1)	**0.4**
Billy Boy's Tune—Three Graces (59)	0.8
—Lee Oskar Levitin see: Lee OSKAR	
Estelle LEVITT [Estelle Loring, Ben Yardley] ▶ 2050 (10)	**1949**
Don't Say You Don't Remember— Beverly Bremers (71)	1640
This Door Swings Both Ways—Herman's Hermits (66)	1482
I Can't Grow Peaches On A Cherry Tree—Just Us (66)	611
Isn't It Lonely Together—Stark & McBrien (75)	73
Going Nowhere—Los Bravos (66)	65
Doin' The Do—Betty Boo (90)	29
Midnight Love Affair—Tony Orlando And Dawn (76)	*6.3*
All I Know Is The Way I Feel—Pointer Sisters (87)	4.3
Midnight Love Affair—Carol Douglas (76)	*3.7*
Captain Of Your Ship—Reparata And The Delrons (68)	1.9
—Seymour Levittan see: Cy LEVITAN	
Adam LEVY ▶ 4998 (1)	**361**
A Walkin' Miracle—Essex Featuring Anita Humes (63)	1442
Albert R. LEVY ▶ 8585 (1)	**46**
Are You Nervous?—Instrumentals (58)	46
Andrew LEVY ▶ 9460 (1)	**23**
Never Stop—Brand New Heavies (91)	93
—Burton Levy see: Burton LANE	
Eunice LEVY [Eunice Frost] ▶ 2350 (7)	**1569**
Ko Ko Mo (I Love You So)—Perry Como (55)	*3070*
Ko Ko Mo (I Love You So)—Crew-Cuts (55)	*1319*
Poco Loco—Gene & Eunice (59)	211
This Is My Story—Mickey And Sylvia (60)	0.4
Ko Ko Mo—Dooley Sisters (55)	*0.0*

Ko Ko Mo (I Love You So)—Hutton Sisters (55)	*0.0*
Ko Ko Mo (I Love You So)— Bill Darnel & Betty Clooney (55)	*0.0*
Gail LEVY [Gail Fisher] ▶ 3008 (3)	**1070**
Mercy, Mercy, Mercy—Buckinghams (67)	*2966*
Mercy, Mercy, Mercy—Marlena Shaw (67)	*209*
Mercy, Mercy, Mercy— Larry Williams & Johnny Watson (67)	*34*
Hal LEVY ▶ 9166 (1)	**30**
Bluejean Bop—Gene Vincent and His Blue Caps (56)	60
Jacques LEVY ▶ 4953 (3)	**374**
Hurricane (Part I)—Bob Dylan (75)	484
Mozambique—Bob Dylan (76)	256
Chestnut Mare—Byrds (70)	7.5
Marcy LEVY [Marcella Detroit, Marcella Levy] ▶ 2525 (2)	**1415**
Lay Down Sally—Eric Clapton (77)	3975
Walking On The Chinese Wall—Philip Bailey (85)	270
Morris LEVY ▶ 651 (40)	**6723**
My Boy Lollipop—Millie Small (64)	4215
Why Do Fools Fall In Love— Teenagers Featuring Frankie Lymon (56)	*4057*
California Sun—Rivieras (2) (64)	*2473*
Why Do Fools Fall In Love—Diana Ross (81)	*2314*
Why Do Fools Fall In Love—Gale Storm (56)	*2295*
Ya Ya—Lee Dorsey (61)	2127
Why Do Fools Fall In Love—Diamonds (56)	*1782*
I Want You To Be My Girl— Frankie Lymon and the Teenagers (56)	1339
Let's Turkey Trot—Little Eva (63)	947
It's Only Love—Tommy James And The Shondells (66)	725
Hey, Let's Twist—Joey Dee & The Starliters (62)	528
Why Do Fools Fall In Love—Happenings (67)	*389*
Little Girl Of Mine—Cleftones (56)	*372*
Do Unto Me—James & Bobby Purify (68)	251
ABC's Of Love— Frankie Lymon and the Teenagers (56)	186
California Sun—Joe Jones (61)	*133*
Count Down—Dave "Baby" Cortez (66)	122
I Love You So—Chantels (58)	113
Tonight My Heart Will Be Crying—Eddie Fisher (57)	*105*
Gee—Pixies Three (64)	*90*
Little Star—Bobby Callender (63)	83
Why Do Fools Fall In Love—Gloria Mann (56)	*80*
You Don't Know What It Means—Jackie Wilson (61)	71
Can't We Be Sweethearts—Cleftones (56)	59
Everytime (I Think About You) (Part 1)— Joey Dee & The Starliters (62)	51
Gee—Jan & Dean (60)	*44*
Roly Poly—Joey Dee & The Starliters (62)	40
Dance, Dance, Dance—Joey Dee (63)	28
Soulville—Aretha Franklin (68)	*24*
I Want You To Be My Boy—Exciters (65)	20
Baby, You're Driving Me Crazy—Joey Dee (63)	9.0
Red's Dream—Louisiana Red (63)	8.1
Soulville—Dinah Washington (63)	*6.8*
Why Do Fools Fall In Love—Beach Boys (64)	*5.6*
Spanish Marching Song— Joe Reisman and His Orchestra (59)	*4.7*
Why Do Fools Fall In Love—Summer Wine (73)	*0.4*
Little Girl Of Mine—Diamonds (56)	*0.0*
The Spanish Marching Song—Ethel Smith (59)	*0.0*
Tonight My Heart She Is Crying—Shirley Bassey (57)	*0.0*
Tonight My Heart She Is Crying— El Boy with The Ralph Sayho Calypso Singers (57)	*0.0*
Vincent LEVY ▶ 3009 (3)	**1070**
Mercy, Mercy, Mercy—Buckinghams (67)	*2966*
Mercy, Mercy, Mercy—Marlena Shaw (67)	*209*
Mercy, Mercy, Mercy— Larry Williams & Johnny Watson (67)	*34*
Dennis LEWIN ▶ 8912 (1)	**36**
Sweet Rachel—Beau Coup (87)	36
Richard LEWINE ▶ 10726 (1)	**5.8**
Hootenanny Saturday Night— Brothers Four (63)	12
Al LEWIS ▶ 1011 (15)	**4393**
Blueberry Hill—Fats Domino (56)	*5648*
Tears On My Pillow— Little Anthony And The Imperials (58)	*3214*
I'm Ready—Fats Domino (59)	1028
The Finger Of Suspicion— Dickie Valentine With The Stargazers (55)	*599*

Blueberry Hill—Louis Armstrong and Gordon Jenkins and His Orchestra And Chorus (56)	*265*
Wishful Thinking— Little Anthony And The Imperials (59)	138
Uh Huh Mm—Sonny James (57)	100
Walkin' Home From School— Gene Vincent and His Blue Caps (58)	73
Whispering Heart—Sherry Parsons (56)	14
Slowly But Surely— Gordon Jenkins And His Orchestra and Chorus (54)	8.9
Tears On My Pillow—Johnny Tillotson (69)	*7.6*
Tears On My Pillow— Fred Parris & The Five Satins (82)	*4.8*
The Finger Of Suspicion—Dolores Gray (55)	*0.0*
The Finger Of Suspicion Points At You— Jane Froman (55)	*0.0*
The Finger Of Suspicion— Eddy Howard & His Orchestra (55)	*0.0*
Barbara LEWIS ▶ 819 (4)	**5364**
Hello Stranger—Barbara Lewis (63)	*3938*
Hello Stranger—Yvonne Elliman (77)	*949*
Puppy Love—Barbara Lewis (64)	472
Hello Stranger—Fire And Rain (73)	*4.5*
Bobby LEWIS ▶ 4576 (2)	**462**
One Track Mind—Bobby Lewis (61)	895
Oh Baby—Cathy Carr (56)	44
Brian LEWIS ▶ 10380 (1)	**9.2**
Shape Of Things To Come—Headboys (79)	37
—Bridges George McGibbon Lewis see: Bunny LEWIS	
Bunny LEWIS [Lee Lange, Bridges George McGibbon Lewis] ▶ 1583 (3)	**2670**
Cara, Mia—Jay & The Americans (65)	*3711*
Cara Mia—David Whitfield with Mantovani And His Orchestra (54)	*1531*
Milord—Teresa Brewer (61)	*149*
Calvin LEWIS ▶ 813 (4)	**5401**
When A Man Loves A Woman—Percy Sledge (66)	*6157*
When A Man Loves A Woman—Michael Bolton (91)	*4080*
When A Man Loves A Woman—Bette Midler (80)	*398*
When A Woman Loves A Man—Esther Phillips (66)	*166*
Clarence L. LEWIS ▶ 3023 (4)	**1060**
Ya Ya—Lee Dorsey (61)	2127
I Need Your Loving— Don Gardner And Dee Dee Ford (62)	1156
Fannie Mae—Buster Brown (60)	*717*
Fannie Mae—Mighty Sam (66)	*1.9*
Curtis Reginald LEWIS ▶ 6420 (2)	**172**
Teenager's Mother (Are You Right?)— Bill Haley And His Comets (56)	264
Today I Sing The Blues— Aretha Franklin (60)	40
David E. LEWIS ▶ 1369 (7)	**3249**
Always—Atlantic Starr (87)	4301
Secret Lovers—Atlantic Starr (85)	3103
Circles—Atlantic Starr (82)	338
When Love Calls—Atlantic Starr (81)	69
Love Crazy—Atlantic Starr (91)	54
Touch A Four Leaf Clover—Atlantic Starr (83)	34
Freak-A-Ristic—Atlantic Starr (85)	16
—Debravon Lewis see: Fizzy QWICK	
Eddie LEWIS ▶ 6349 (1)	**180**
The Bounce—Olympics (63)	540
Edna LEWIS ▶ 1124 (4)	**3944**
Lipstick On Your Collar— Connie Francis (59)	3650
Judy's Turn To Cry—Lesley Gore (63)	3021
I Wish That We Were Married— Ronnie And The Hi-Lites (62)	1197
Just Because—McGuire Sisters (61)	30
Eloise LEWIS ▶ 8377 (1)	**52**
Chi Chi Merengue—Eloise Trio (60)	52
Fred LEWIS ▶ 10384 (1)	**9.2**
It's All The Way Live—Lakeside (79)	9.2
Furry LEWIS [Walter Lewis] ▶ 8408 (1)	**52**
Brownsville—Joy Of Cooking (71)	155
Gary LEWIS ▶ 1987 (2)	**2031**
She's Just My Style— Gary Lewis And The Playboys (65)	4343
Everybody Loves A Clown— Gary Lewis And The Playboys (65)	2836

Huey LEWIS [Hugh Anthony Cregg] ▶ 416 (13)	**9608**
Stuck With You—Huey Lewis and the News (86)	4661
The Power Of Love—Huey Lewis and the News (85)	4627
I Want A New Drug—Huey Lewis and the News (84)	2380
Hip To Be Square—Huey Lewis and the News (86)	2226
The Heart Of Rock & Roll— Huey Lewis and the News (84)	2167
If This Is It—Huey Lewis and the News (84)	1977
Couple Days Off—Huey Lewis & The News (91)	1191
I Know What I Like—Huey Lewis and the News (87)	1139
It Hit Me Like A Hammer—Huey Lewis & The News (91)	695
Small World—Huey Lewis and the News (88)	563
Workin' For A Livin'—Huey Lewis and the News (82)	267
Give Me The Keys (And I'll Drive You Crazy)— Huey Lewis and the News (89)	253
Don't Make Me Do It—Patrick Simmons (83)	38
Jack LEWIS ▶ 2064 (1)	**1936**
Teen Age Idol—Rick Nelson (62)	1936
James E. LEWIS ▶ 3511 (4)	**807**
If You Were Mine—Ray Charles (70)	696
If It Wasn't For Bad Luck— Ray Charles & Jimmy Lewis (69)	150
We Can Make It—Ray Charles (69)	28
Careful Man—John Edwards (74)	8.5
Jerry Lee LEWIS ▶ 5298 (1)	**310**
High School Confidential— Jerry Lee Lewis And His Pumping Piano (58)	621
Jimmy LEWIS ▶ 10107 (1)	**13**
When I Get You Baby—Ruth Brown (57)	25
Joe LEWIS ▶ 11110 (1)	**3.2**
Friend Of Mine—Little Milton (76)	9.5
Jonathan LEWIS ▶ 2502 (1)	**1434**
Always—Atlantic Starr (87)	4301
Joseph S. LEWIS ▶ 9059 (1)	**32**
Song For The Lonely—Platters (61)	64
Keith LEWIS ▶ 6138 (1)	**201**
Nights Like This—After 7 (91)	402
—Ken Lewis see: Ken HAWKER	
Kenny Lee LEWIS ▶ 6284 (2)	**186**
Cool Magic—Steve Miller Band (82)	190
Shangri-La—Steve Miller Band (84)	182
Leroy LEWIS ▶ 7265 (1)	**107**
Getting The Corners—T.S.U. Toronadoes (69)	107
Lynn LEWIS ▶ 7416 (1)	**97**
Dig The Gold—Joyce Cobb (79)	194
Margaret LEWIS ▶ 2552 (11)	**1392**
Reconsider Me—Johnny Adams (69)	*820*
Soulshake—Peggy Scott & Jo Jo Benson (69)	*539*
The Girl Most Likely—Jeannie C. Riley (68)	427
Soul Shake—Delaney & Bonnie & Friends (70)	*392*
Oh, Singer—Jeannie C. Riley (71)	236
Buffalo Soldier—Flamingos (70)	165
There Never Was A Time—Jeannie C. Riley (69)	137
Reconsider Me—Narvel Felts (75)	*53*
I Can't Be All Bad—Johnny Adams (69)	34
The Wedding Cake—Connie Francis (69)	28
I Almost Called Your Name—Margaret Whiting (67)	8.1
Mike LEWIS ▶ 5328 (2)	**304**
Ain't It True—Andy Williams (65)	519
Come Back Baby—Roddie Joy (65)	90
Miriam LEWIS ▶ 7461 (2)	**94**
Tears And Laughter—Dinah Washington (62)	241
Journey Of Love—Crests Feat. Johnny Maestro (60)	42
Morgan LEWIS ▶ 7588 (4)	**87**
How High The Moon—Gloria Gaynor (75)	*54*
How High The Moon— David Rose and His Orchestra (59)	*31*
How High The Moon Part One—Ella Fitzgerald (60)	*26*
How High The Moon—Floyd Cramer (63)	*16*
Nathaniel LEWIS ▶ 7894 (1)	**71**
It's Wonderful To Be In Love— Ovations (Featuring Louis Wiliams) (65)	212
Philip F. LEWIS ▶ 7211 (1)	**110**
The Ballad Of Jayne—L.A. Guns (90)	549
Randy LEWIS ▶ 6253 (1)	**189**
Alien—Atlanta Rhythm Section (81)	566
Ray LEWIS ▶ 7094 (2)	**116**
Love Gonna Pack Up (And Walk Out)—Persuaders (71)	443
Give My Love A Try—Linda Jones (67)	21

Richard LEWIS ▶ 2609 (3)	**1328**
Get A Job—Silhouettes (58)	*5224*
Get A Job—Nino & the Ebb Tides (61)	*88*
Get A Job—Mills Brothers (58)	*0.0*
Robert LEWIS ▶ 5264 (1)	**316**
Bristol Twistin' Annie—Dovells (62)	632
Ronnie LEWIS ▶ 5226 (1)	**323**
She Blew A Good Thing—Poets (66)	646
Russ LEWIS ▶ 3415 (1)	**857**
Groovy Situation—Gene Chandler (70)	1714
Sam LEWIS [Samuel M. Levine] ▶ 2189 (13) HOF	**1761**
Rock A Bye Your Baby With A Dixie Melody— Jerry Lewis (56)	*2560*
My Mammy—Happenings (67)	1237
Rock-A-Bye Your Baby With A Dixie Melody— Aretha Franklin (61)	*786*
In A Little Spanish Town ('twas On A Night Like This)— Bing Crosby And The Buddy Cole Trio (56)	*365*
Five Foot Two—Don Johnson (60)	194
For All We Know—Dinah Washington (62)	34
In A Little Spanish Town—Smith Brothers (54)	*30*
In A Little Spanish Town—Blue Diamonds (61)	*23*
Sam, You Made The Pants Too Long— Barbra Streisand (66)	21
Nightfall—Al Hibbler (56)	13
Sittin' On Top Of The World—Jerry Mar (57)	6.0
Rock A Bye Your Baby With A Dixie Melody— Judy Garland (61)	*0.0*
In A Little Spanish Town ('Twas On A Night Like This)— Lawrence Welk & His Sparklers (54)	*0.0*
Stanley J. LEWIS ▶ 1691 (10)	**2480**
I'll Be Home—Pat Boone (56)	*3005*
Suzie Q (Part One)— Creedence Clearwater Revival (68)	*1687*
Susie Q—Dale Hawkins (57)	*544*
La Do Dada—Dale Hawkins (58)	484
Boom Boom (Out Go The Lights)—Pat Travers (79)	159
Do You Believe In Shame?—Duran Duran (89)	93
I'll Be Home—Platters (66)	*10*
Susie-Q—Crew-Cuts (57)	*0.0*
Susie-Q—José Feliciano (70)	*0.0*
I'll Be Home—Flamingos (56)	*0.0*
Steve LEWIS ▶ 7623 (1)	**84**
Give Me The Keys (And I'll Drive You Crazy)— Huey Lewis and the News (89)	253
Steve (2) LEWIS ▶ 6820 (1)	**135**
What A Surprise— Johnny Maestro The Voice Of The Crests (61)	404
Terry LEWIS ▶ 80 (41) HOF	**27420**
Escapade—Janet Jackson (90)	4680
Miss You Much—Janet Jackson (89)	4522
Human—Human League (86)	4223
Romantic—Karyn White (91)	4086
When I Think Of You—Janet Jackson (86)	3710
Love Will Never Do (Without You)— Janet Jackson (90)	3500
Rhythm Nation—Janet Jackson (89)	3288
Sensitivity—Ralph Tresvant (90)	2969
Come Back To Me—Janet Jackson (90)	2853
Let's Wait Awhile—Janet Jackson (87)	2779
Rub You The Right Way—Johnny Gill (90)	2737
I Didn't Mean To Turn You On—Robert Palmer (86)	*2661*
Control—Janet Jackson (86)	2464
Nasty—Janet Jackson (86)	2409
Alright—Janet Jackson (90)	2323
What Have You Done For Me Lately— Janet Jackson (86)	2231
If It Isn't Love—New Edition (88)	1864
Diamonds—Herb Alpert (87)	1768
Jerk-Out—Time (90)	1425
Tender Love—Force M.D.'s (86)	1303
Saturday Love—Cherrelle (86)	565
Fake—Alexander O'Neal (87)	534
Never Knew Love Like This—Alexander O'Neal (88)	468
Fishnet—Morris Day (88)	464
Making Love In The Rain—Herb Alpert (87)	379
Just Be Good To Me—S.O.S. Band (83)	*354*
I Need Your Loving—Human League (86)	343
The Finest—S.O.S. Band (86)	326
All True Man—Alexander O'Neal (91)	291
State Of The World—Janet Jackson (91)	290

Keep Your Eye On Me—Herb Alpert (87)	239
Can You Stand The Rain—New Edition (89)	227
The Heat Of Heat—Patti Austin (86)	211
Tell Me If You Still Care—S.O.S. Band (83)	173
Just The Way You Like It—S.O.S. Band (84)	155
Encore—Cheryl Lynn (84)	117
I Didn't Mean To Turn You On—Cherrelle (84)	*91*
Dub Be Good To Me—Beats International (90)	*72*
Borrowed Love—Bingoboys (91)	35
Wrap My Body Tight—Johnny Gill (91)	30
You're Not My Kind Of Girl—New Edition (88)	5.3
—Travis Lewis see: Michael MURPHEY	
W. Michael LEWIS ▶ 7020 (3)	**121**
Cocomotion—El Coco (77)	261
Le Spank—Le Pamplemousse (77)	117
Dancing In Paradise—El Coco (78)	15
Wally LEWIS ▶ 10587 (1)	**7.1**
Kathleen—Wally Lewis (58)	14
—Walter Lewis see: Furry LEWIS	
Wayne I. LEWIS ▶ 1377 (7)	**3235**
Always—Atlantic Starr (87)	4301
Secret Lovers—Atlantic Starr (85)	3103
Circles—Atlantic Starr (82)	338
When Love Calls—Atlantic Starr (81)	69
Love Crazy—Atlantic Starr (91)	54
Touch A Four Leaf Clover—Atlantic Starr (83)	34
Stand Up—Atlantic Starr (78)	1.5
Bobby LEXING ▶ 7763 (1)	**76**
Don't Make Me Pay For His Mistakes—Z.Z. Hill (71)	152
Jan LEYERS ▶ 6326 (1)	**182**
The Way To Your Heart—Soulsister (89)	364
—Mik Lezan see: Kim NAZEL	
—David Charles L'Heureux see: D.C. LaRUE	
Eric LI ▶ 5439 (2)	**289**
Sayin' Sorry (Don't Make It Right)— Denise Lopez (88)	523
If You Feel It—Denise Lopez (88)	28
Dee LIBBEY ▶ 5206 (3)	**327**
Mangos—Rosemary Clooney (57)	*654*
Mangos—Roger King Mozian (57)	*0.0*
Mangos—Buddy Morrow & His Orchestra (57)	*0.0*
David LIBERT ▶ 10142 (1)	**12**
Randy—Happenings (68)	24
Mark LICKLEY ▶ 6306 (1)	**183**
Poison Arrow—ABC (83)	732
Charles LIDDELL ▶ 9717 (1)	**18**
Teen Prayer—Velveteens (61)	18
—Geoffrey Brillhart Lieb see: Jeff PARIS	
Howard LIEBLING ▶ 2610 (3)	**1326**
California Nights—Lesley Gore (67)	1534
Sunshine, Lollipops And Rainbows—Lesley Gore (65)	1112
Too Little Time—Brenda Lee (66)	5.1
Oscar LIESE ▶ 10167 (1)	**12**
Happy Years—Diamonds (58)	35
Ted LIFE [Theodore Life Jr.] ▶ 4324 (2)	**521**
I Don't Know If It's Right— Evelyn "Champagne" King (78)	1020
Music Box—Evelyn "Champagne" King (79)	33
Alex LIFESON [Alex Zivojinovich] ▶ 4203 (7)	**564**
New World Man—Rush (82)	554
The Big Money—Rush (85)	372
Tom Sawyer—Rush (81)	329
The Spirit Of Radio—Rush (80)	242
Limelight—Rush (81)	159
Closer To The Heart—Rush (81)	*89*
Closer To The Heart—Rush (77)	*67*
Alex LIGERTWOOD ▶ 6656 (3)	**147**
You Know That I Love You—Santana (79)	554
Searchin'—Santana (81)	19
All I Ever Wanted—Santana (80)	10
Joseph LIGGINS ▶ 7165 (2)	**112**
I've Got A Right To Cry—Eydie Gorme (56)	*56*
I've Got A Right To Cry—Bob Carroll (56)	*56*
Enoch LIGHT ▶ 9256 (3)	**28**
(The Song Of) Daniel Boone (The Daddy Of Them All)— Loren Becker With Enoch Light Orch. & Chorus (55)	*55*
Daniel Boone (The Daddy Of Them All)—Dick Lee (55)	*0.0*
Daniel Boone (The Daddy Of Them All)— Ken Carson (55)	*0.0*

Jerry LIGHT ▶ 11345 (2)	**2.1**
Greetings (This Is Uncle Sam)—Valadiers (61)	*9.2*
Greetings (This Is Uncle Sam)—Monitors (66)	*5.8*
Gordon LIGHTFOOT ▶ 209 (16) HOF	**15368**
Sundown—Gordon Lightfoot (74)	4789
The Wreck Of The Edmund Fitzgerald—Gordon Lightfoot (76)	4005
If You Could Read My Mind—Gordon Lightfoot (70)	2874
Carefree Highway—Gordon Lightfoot (74)	1133
For Lovin' Me—Peter, Paul & Mary (65)	616
Rainy Day People—Gordon Lightfoot (75)	556
The Circle Is Small (I Can See It In Your Eyes)—Gordon Lightfoot (78)	503
The Last Time I Saw Her—Glen Campbell (71)	240
Beautiful—Gordon Lightfoot (72)	230
Talking In Your Sleep—Gordon Lightfoot (71)	196
Baby Step Back—Gordon Lightfoot (82)	100
Race Among The Ruins—Gordon Lightfoot (77)	54
Cotton Jenny—Anne Murray (72)	45
Early Morning Rain—Peter, Paul & Mary (65)	16
I Can't Make It Anymore—Spyder Turner (67)	11
Summer Side Of Life—Gordon Lightfoot (71)	2.0
—Raynoma Liles see: Raynoma SINGLETON	
Marcus LILLINGTON ▶ 1738 (6)	**2391**
Hands To Heaven—Breathe (88)	3472
How Can I Fall?—Breathe (88)	2861
Don't Tell Me Lies—Breathe (89)	1080
Say A Prayer—Breathe (90)	741
Does She Love That Man?—Breathe (90)	478
All This I Should Have Known—Breathe (89)	30
—Lil' Louis see: Marvin Louis BURNS	
—Anthony Frederick Lilly see: Anthony KING	
—Limahl see: Christopher HAMILL	
—Jorge Lima Menezes see: Jorge BEN	
—Jack Limber see: Luigi CREATORE	
Sonny LIMBO ▶ 2476 (3)	**1452**
Key Largo—Bertie Higgins (81)	2665
Just Another Day In Paradise—Bertie Higgins (82)	289
What If (I Said I Love You)—Unipop (82)	70
Mirko LIMONI ▶ 3066 (4)	**1027**
Everybody Everybody—Black Box (90)	1472
Strike It Up—Black Box (91)	1185
I Don't Know Anybody Else—Black Box (90)	395
Gonna Catch You—Lonnie Gordon (91)	30
Philamore LINCOLN [Robert Anson, Julian Covey, Philip Kinorra] ▶ 4437 (1)	**494**
Temma Harbour—Mary Hopkin (70)	494
Shedrick LINCOLN ▶ 8181 (1)	**59**
Rubber Biscuit—Blues Brothers (79)	297
Bob LIND ▶ 1482 (3)	**2929**
Elusive Butterfly—Bob Lind (66)	2688
Remember The Rain—Bob Lind (66)	137
Truly Julie's Blues (I'll Be There)—Bob Lind (66)	104
Jon LIND ▶ 1159 (5)	**3833**
Crazy For You—Madonna (85)	5216
Boogie Wonderland—Earth, Wind & Fire With The Emotions (79)	2219
Sun Goddess—Ramsey Lewis And Earth, Wind & Fire (75)	162
Skin Deep—Cher (88)	59
Reason To Try—Eric Carmen (88)	9.7
—Joseph Conrad Lind see: Peter Lind HAYES	
Solomon LINDA ▶ 1516 (2)	**2818**
The Lion Sleeps Tonight—Tokens (61)	*9030*
The Lion Sleeps Tonight—Robert John (71)	*5059*
Dennis LINDE ▶ 886 (6)	**5022**
Burning Love—Elvis Presley (72)	*4697*
Mornin' Mornin'—Bobby Goldsboro (69)	188
I'm Her Fool—Billy Swan (75)	115
Down To The Station—B.W. Stevenson (77)	56
Burning Love—Elvis Presley (82)	*23*
For The Heart—Elvis Presley (76)	0.0
John LINDE ▶ 5653 (4)	**259**
What Are Boys Made Of—Percells (63)	319
Where Are We Going—Bobby Bloom (70)	103
Night Time—Pete Antell (62)	93
Yo Me Pregunto—Valrays (64)	4.5
Edith LINDEMAN ▶ 3816 (6)	**690**
I Know—Perry Como (59)	531
Little Things Mean A Lot—Joni James (59)	*461*
Kissing Tree—Billy Grammer (59)	249

Goodnight Sweet Dreams—Gordon Jenkins And His Orchestra (55)	211
Little Things Mean A Lot—John Gary (59)	*0.0*
Little Things Mean A Lot—Kitty Kallen (54)	*0.0*
Dave LINDEN ▶ 3592 (1)	**775**
Love Is A Hurtin' Thing—Lou Rawls (66)	1550
Alan LINDGREN ▶ 3229 (2)	**940**
Hello Again—Neil Diamond (81)	1704
Headed For The Future—Neil Diamond (86)	262
—Bryan Eugene Lindsay see: Gene LYND	
Mark LINDSAY ▶ 399 (17)	**9886**
Good Thing—Paul Revere And The Raiders Featuring Mark Lindsay (66)	3322
Him Or Me - What's It Gonna Be?—Paul Revere And The Raiders Featuring Mark Lindsay (67)	2110
Let Me—Paul Revere And The Raiders Featuring Mark Lindsay (69)	1361
Mr. Sun, Mr. Moon—Paul Revere And The Raiders Featuring Mark Lindsay (69)	1349
I Had A Dream—Paul Revere And The Raiders Featuring Mark Lindsay (67)	1319
Too Much Talk—Paul Revere And The Raiders Featuring Mark Lindsay (68)	1211
Ups And Downs—Paul Revere And The Raiders (67)	879
Don't Take It So Hard—Paul Revere And The Raiders Featuring Mark Lindsay (68)	876
The Great Airplane Strike—Paul Revere And The Raiders Featuring Mark Lindsay (66)	812
Steppin' Out—Paul Revere And The Raiders (65)	473
Peace Of Mind—Paul Revere And The Raiders Featuring Mark Lindsay (67)	433
Powder Blue Mercedes Queen—Raiders (72)	389
Cinderella Sunshine—Paul Revere And The Raiders Featuring Mark Lindsay (68)	268
Just Seventeen—Raiders (70)	88
Melody For An Unknown Girl—Unknowns (66)	78
Amanda—Dionne Warwicke (71)	45
Gone Movin' On—Raiders (70)	4.0
Theresa LINDSEY ▶ 8812 (1)	**39**
I'll Bet You—Funkadelic (69)	116
Rudi LINDT [Rudi Von der Dovenmuehle] ▶ 3346 (9)	**888**
Liechtensteiner Polka—Will Glahe And His Orchestra And Chorus (57)	*1644*
Liechtensteiner Polka—Lawrence Welk And His Champagne Music (57)	*109*
The Phonograph Song—Guy Lombardo And His Royal Canadians (56)	*19*
The Phonograph Song (Our Melody)—Billy May & His Orchestra (56)	*19*
Santo Domingo—Sandpipers (70)	5.5
Whistlin' Willie (Our Melody)—Chordettes (56)	*0.0*
The Phonograph Song (Our Melody)—Lou Stein (56)	*0.0*
Liechtensteiner Polka—Horst Wende & His Polka Boys (57)	*0.0*
The Phonograph Song (Our Melody)—Art Mooney & His Orchestra (56)	*0.0*
Mike LINDUP ▶ 4912 (2)	**383**
Something About You—Level 42 (86)	1857
Hot Water—Level 42 (86)	48
Rasmus LINDWALL ▶ 8098 (1)	**62**
Got To Get—Leila K with Rob 'N' Raz (90)	248
Peter G.D. LING ▶ 8832 (1)	**38**
Why Not Now—Matt Monro (61)	115
Sam LING [Saul Samuel Bihari] ▶ 2718 (9)	**1246**
Eddie My Love—Fontane Sisters with Billy Vaughn's Orchestra (56)	*1670*
Eddie My Love—Chordettes (56)	*1068*
Eddie My Love—Teen Queens (56)	*856*
So All Alone—Teen Queens (56)	72
The Girl In My Dreams—Cliques (56)	*39*
Let Me Love You—B.B. King (64)	21
I Need You So Bad—B.B. "Blues Boy" King and his orchestra (57)	5.1
Girl In My Dreams—Capris (61)	*4.0*
The Girl In My Dreams—Four Lovers (56)	*0.0*
Buzzy LINHART ▶ 6204 (1)	**194**
Friends—Bette Midler (73)	387
Harry LINK [John Henry Linkey] ▶ 8080 (1)	**62**
These Foolish Things—James Brown And The Famous Flames (63)	187

Peter LINK ▶ 3196 (1)	**956**
(If You Let Me Make Love To You Then) Why Can't I Touch You?—Ronnie Dyson (70)	1912
—John Henry Linkey see: Harry LINK	
Roger LINN ▶ 3686 (1)	**733**
Promises—Eric Clapton And His Band (78)	1467
Elbert LINNEAR ▶ 3418 (1)	**856**
Finally—Ce Ce Peniston (91)	2569
—Joseph Linquito see: Joe Lynn TURNER	
—Horace Linsky see: Horace LINSLEY	
Horace LINSLEY [Horace Linsky] ▶ 10319 (2)	**10**
Fool's Paradise—Buddy Holly / The Crickets (58)	25
Tell Me Now—McGuire Sisters (56)	5.3
William LINTON ▶ 1313 (1)	**3379**
Easier Said Than Done—Essex (63)	6758
Sandy LINZER ▶ 222 (45)	**15092**
A Lover's Concerto—Toys (65)	*6662*
Let's Hang On!—4 Seasons Featuring The "Sound" Of Frankie Valli (65)	*6625*
Dawn (Go Away)—4 Seasons Featuring The "Sound" Of Frankie Valli (64)	*5627*
Working My Way Back To You—Spinners (79)	*2453*
Keep The Ball Rolling—Jay And The Techniques (67)	*1852*
Working My Way Back To You—4 Seasons Featuring The "Sound" Of Frankie Valli (66)	*1672*
Opus 17 (Don't You Worry 'Bout Me)—4 Seasons Featuring The "Sound" Of Frankie Valli (66)	*1584*
Fresh—Kool & The Gang (85)	1367
Native New Yorker—Odyssey (77)	1155
Attack—Toys (65)	1083
Mornin' Beautiful—Tony Orlando & Dawn (75)	898
Talk It Over—Grayson Hugh (89)	793
Electric Stories—4 Seasons Featuring The "Sound" Of Frankie Valli (68)	417
Goodnight My Love—Happenings (66)	*397*
The Mouse—Soupy Sales (65)	379
Let's Hang On—Barry Manilow (82)	*370*
Can't Get Enough Of You, Baby—? And The Mysterians (67)	355
Baby Make Your Own Sweet Music—Jay And The Techniques (68)	333
Dusty—Rag Dolls (65)	323
A Lover's Concerto—Sarah Vaughan (66)	*208*
You Can Do Magic—Limmie & Family Cookin' (72)	207
You Keep Me Dancing—Samantha Sang (78)	168
Penny Arcade—Cyrkle (67)	149
Love Has Taken Its Toll—Saraya (89)	144
Weekend Lover—Odyssey (78)	124
Back To The Bullet—Saraya (89)	119
Bon Bon Vie (Gimme The Good Life)—T.S. Monk (81)	113
Use It Up And Wear It Out—Pat & Mick (90)	87
Goodnight My Love—Duprees (68)	*54*
Society Girl—Rag Dolls (64)	20
Pow Wow—Cory Daye (79)	19
May My Heart Be Cast Into Stone—Toys (66)	18
A Lover's Concerto—Stars On 45 (81)	*12*
House Of Strangers—Jim Gilstrap (75)	12
A Lover's Concerto—Mrs. Miller (66)	*9.1*
Watch Out, Sally!—Diane Renay (64)	4.9
Betrayed—4 Seasons (65)	4.6
Dawn—Gidea Park (81)	*3.7*
Opus 17—Gidea Park (81)	*3.7*
Let's Hang On—Gidea Park (81)	*3.7*
Working My Way Back To You—Gidea Park (81)	*3.7*
Hallelujah—Invitations (65)	3.7
Can I Carry Your Balloon—Swampseeds (68)	0.5
Breakin' Down The Walls Of Heartache—Bandwagon (68)	0.5
Keep The Ball Rollin'—Al Hirt (68)	*0.5*
—John Lione see: Trade MARTIN	
—Steven Barry Lipkin see: Steve BARRI	
Sid LIPPMAN ▶ 2999 (4)	**1073**
Too Young—Donny Osmond (72)	1365
House With Love In It—Four Lads (56)	738
If Anyone Finds This I Love You—Kay Starr (55)	27
Many A Wonderful Moment—Rosemary Clooney (60)	17
Belinda LIPSCOMB ▶ 3027 (4)	**1055**
I Wanna Be Rich—Calloway (90)	3279
Operator—Midnight Star (84)	854
Scientific Love—Midnight Star (85)	60
Headlines—Midnight Star (86)	59
—Dickey Lee Lipscomb see: Dickey LEE	
—Max K. Lipscomb see: Scotty McKAY	

Fred LIPSIUS ▶ 5420 (1)	**291**
Go Down Gamblin'—Blood, Sweat & Tears (71)	582
—Beverly Bremers Lipton see: Beverly BREMERS	
Leonard LIPTON ▶ 1514 (1)	**2828**
Puff (The Magic Dragon)—Peter, Paul & Mary (63)	5656
Steve LIRONI ▶ 8086 (1)	**62**
I Won't Give Up On You—TKA (90)	125
Ricky LISI ▶ 8615 (1)	**45**
Come Back Baby—Roddie Joy (65)	90
Mick LISTER ▶ 7472 (1)	**93**
Weapons Of Love—Truth (87)	187
Jack LITTLE [Jack Leonard, Little Jack Little] ▶ 5509 (4)	**276**
In A Shanty In Old Shanty Town—Somethin' Smith & The Redheads (56)	*566*
Hold Me—Baskerville Hounds (69)	*154*
Hold Me—P.J. Proby (64)	*108*
In A Shanty In Old Shanty Town—Johnny Long & His Orchestra (56)	*0.0*
—Little Steven see: Steven VAN ZANDT	
Julian LITTMAN ▶ 2853 (1)	**1151**
Strut—Sheena Easton (84)	2303
Kerry LIVGREN ▶ 680 (8)	**6371**
Dust In The Wind—Kansas (78)	2712
Carry On Wayward Son—Kansas (76)	2105
Play The Game Tonight—Kansas (82)	814
People Of The South Wind—Kansas (79)	611
Hold On—Kansas (80)	376
Reason To Be—Kansas (79)	267
Portrait (He Knew)—Kansas (78)	238
What's On My Mind—Kansas (77)	16
John LIVIGNI [John Valenti] ▶ 5699 (2)	**253**
Anything You Want—John Valenti (76)	463
Machines—John Livigni (75)	44
Jay LIVINGSTON ▶ 280 (38) HOF	**12501**
Tammy—Debbie Reynolds (57)	*9194*
Whatever Will Be, Will Be (Que Sera, Sera)—Doris Day (56)	*6972*
Dear Heart—Andy Williams (64)	*1324*
To Each His Own—Platters (60)	*1235*
Dear Heart—Jack Jones (64)	*1154*
Mona Lisa—Carl Mann (59)	*948*
Bonanza—Al Caiola And His Orchestra (61)	*895*
Tammy—Ames Brothers (57)	*793*
Mona Lisa—Conway Twitty (59)	*581*
Que Sera, Sera (Whatever Will Be, Will Be)—High Keys (63)	*355*
Wish Me A Rainbow—Gunter Kallmann Chorus (66)	327
All The Time—Johnny Mathis (58)	327
Angel—Johnny Tillotson (65)	308
Que Sera, Sera (Whatever Will Be, Will Be)—Mary Hopkin (70)	*259*
In The Arms Of Love—Andy Williams (66)	249
Dear Heart—Henry Mancini's Orchestra And Chorus (64)	*243*
Theme From "Harlow" (Lonely Girl)—Bobby Vinton (65)	198
To Each His Own—Frankie Laine (68)	*170*
Almost In Your Arms—Johnny Nash (58)	153
Let Me Be Loved—Mantovani And His Orchestra (57)	*109*
To Each His Own—Tymes (64)	*100*
Another Time, Another Place—Patti Page (58)	82
You're So Right For Me—Tony Bennett with Ralph Sharon and his Orch. (58)	70
Silver Bells—Bing Crosby and Carol Richards (54)	*39*
Love Song From "Houseboat" (Almost In Your Arms)—Sam Cooke (58)	*36*
Never Let Me Go—Nat "King" Cole (56)	20
Silver Bells—Bing Crosby and Carol Richards (57)	*14*
Golden Earrings—Five Satins (61)	3.2
Bonanza!—Johnny Cash (62)	*3.2*
Buttons And Bows—Don Robertson (61)	0.5
Tammy—Pat Kirby (57)	*0.0*
Let Me Be Loved—Eydie Gorme (57)	*0.0*
Tammy—Bill Snyder & His Orchestra (57)	*0.0*
Tammy—Richard Hayman, His Orchestra And Chorus (57)	*0.0*
Whatever Will Be Will Be (Que Será Sérá)—Eddy Howard (56)	*0.0*
Love Song From "Houseboat" (Almost In Your Arms)—Don Costa & His Orchestra (58)	*0.0*
Main Title/Tammy—Joseph Gershenson & The Universal-International Orchestra (57)	*0.0*
Love Song From "Houseboat" (Almost In Your Arms)—Les Baxter & His Orchestra (58)	*0.0*
Jerry LIVINGSTON [Gerald Levinson] ▶ 786 (32) HOF	**5629**
Wake The Town And Tell The People—Les Baxter His Chorus And Orchestra (55)	*2302*
The Twelfth Of Never—Donny Osmond (73)	*2152*
Young Emotions—Ricky Nelson (60)	1584
Wake The Town And Tell The People—Mindy Carson (55)	*1076*
Hanging Tree—Marty Robbins (59)	599
Fairy Tale—Frank Sinatra (55)	561
Amukiriki (The Lord Willing)—Les Paul and Mary Ford (55)	468
The Twelfth Of Never—Johnny Mathis (57)	*421*
Unbelievable—Nat "King" Cole (54)	412
They Say You're Laughing At Me (While I'm Crying For You)—Al Hibbler (55)	318
Seventy Seven Sunset Strip—Big Sound of Don Ralke (59)	*298*
Veni-Vidi-Vici (I Came, I Saw, I Conquered)—Gaylords (54)	256
Shenandoah Rose—Hugo & Luigi (57)	*197*
I'd Give A Million Tomorrows (For Just One Yesterday)—Billy Vaughn and His Orchestra (55)	*153*
Mairzy Doats—Innocence (67)	*119*
Adios Amigo—Jim Reeves (62)	105
Sweet Thursday—Johnny Mathis (62)	90
Who Are We—Gogi Grant (56)	64
You Too Can Be A Dreamer—Patti Page (55)	55
The Fountain Of Youth—Four Lads (59)	37
Laurie, My Love—Johnny Mathis (61)	17
Bluebell—Mitch Miller and His Orchestra and Chorus (58)	*5.9*
My Last Night In Rome—Motifs (56)	*3.2*
My Last Night In Rome—Eddie Dano (56)	*3.2*
Mairzy Doats—Dodie Stevens (59)	*1.2*
Blue Bell—Scott Engel (58)	*0.0*
Shenandoah Rose—Peter Hanley (57)	*0.0*
Shenandoah Rose—Johnny Desmond (57)	*0.0*
Shenandoah Rose—Jack Halloran Singers (57)	*0.0*
Seventy Seven Sunset Strip—Frank Ortega Trio (59)	*0.0*
I'd Give A Million Tomorrows (For Just One Yesterday)—Frank Verna (55)	*0.0*
I'd Give A Million Tomorrows (For Just One Yesterday)—Arthur Godfrey (56)	*0.0*
Neville LIVINGSTON [Bunny Livingstone, Bunny Wailer] ▶ 5513 (1)	**276**
Electric Boogie—Marcia Griffiths (89)	276
—Bunny Livingstone see: Neville LIVINGSTON	
Roberto LIVRAGHI ▶ 5697 (1)	**254**
A Man Without Love (Quando M'innamoro)—Engelbert Humperdinck (68)	1014
Billy LIVSEY ▶ 7251 (4)	**108**
She's Trouble—Musical Youth (83)	177
Take No Prisoners (In The Game Of Love)—Peabo Bryson (85)	58
No One Can Love You More Than Me—Melissa Manchester (83)	32
Button Off My Shirt—Paul Carrack (88)	6.5
—LL Cool J see: James Todd SMITH	
Bernhard LLOYD [Bernhard Gössling] ▶ 6978 (3)	**124**
Forever Young—Alphaville (88)	*185*
Big In Japan—Alphaville (84)	180
Forever Young—Alphaville (85)	*7.2*
George LLOYD ▶ 10470 (1)	**8.1**
Boss—Rumblers (63)	48
Harry LLOYD ▶ 3413 (4)	**857**
I Just Fall In Love Again—Anne Murray (79)	1411
He Did With Me—Vicki Lawrence (73)	360
It Could Have Been Me—Sami Jo (74)	344
I Believe I'm Gonna Love You—Frank Sinatra (75)	306
Ian LLOYD [Ian Buonconsiglio] ▶ 5294 (1)	**312**
I'm Coming Home—Stories (72)	624
Jack LLOYD ▶ 10102 (1)	**13**
Darling! Darling! Darling!—Jo Stafford (55)	25
Michael LLOYD ▶ 2211 (3)	**1737**
I Was Made For Dancin'—Leif Garrett (78)	1415
Kiss In The Dark—Pink Lady (79)	311
I Was Looking For Someone To Love—Leif Garrett (80)	22
Tom LLOYD ▶ 9791 (1)	**17**
I Still Want You—Del Fuegos (86)	34
—Lobo see: Kent LaVOIE	
Edu LOBO ▶ 11497 (1)	**1.4**
For Me—Sergio Mendes & Brasil '66 (67)	2.9
Albert LOCKE ▶ 9587 (1)	**21**
One Love, One Heart—Four Coins (59)	62
James LOCKE ▶ 10087 (1)	**13**
1-2-3—Chimes (2) (90)	39
Ruben LOCKE Jr. ▶ 10286 (1)	**10**
In The Mood—Tyrone Davis (79)	31
Anthony LOCKETT ▶ 10056 (2)	**13**
Sparkle—Cameo (79)	17
Keep it Hot—Cameo (81)	9.7
Tom LOCKETT ▶ 7838 (2)	**73**
Slide—Slave (77)	640
Just A Touch Of Love—Slave (80)	10
Eugene LOCKHART ▶ 7562 (1)	**88**
The World Is Waiting For The Sunrise—Don Gibson (61)	177
Hank LOCKLIN ▶ 1837 (4)	**2222**
Send Me The Pillow You Dream On—Johnny Tillotson (62)	*1043*
Send Me The Pillow You Dream On—Dean Martin (65)	*818*
Send Me The Pillow You Dream On—Browns Featuring Jim Edward Brown (60)	*345*
Send Me The Pillow You Dream On—Hank Locklin (58)	*16*
Nick LOCKWOOD [Nick Jesson] ▶ 8734 (1)	**41**
Burning Flame—Vitamin Z (85)	122
Malcolm LOCKYER ▶ 10178 (4)	**12**
Friends And Neighbors—Tommy Prisco (54)	*8.7*
Friends And Neighbors—Plunkett Family (54)	*8.7*
Friends And Neighbors—Billy Cotton & Band (54)	*8.7*
Friends And Neighbors—Sammy Kaye & "Swing And Sway" Orchestra (54)	*8.7*
Dennis LOCORRIERE ▶ 4962 (2)	**371**
Baby Makes Her Blue Jeans Talk—Dr. Hook (82)	574
If Not You—Dr. Hook (76)	179
—James Hugh Loden see: Sonny JAMES	
David LODGE ▶ 3352 (2)	**885**
Major Tom (Coming Home)—Peter Schilling (83)	1428
Savin' Myself—Eria Fachin (88)	171
John LODGE ▶ 1069 (7)	**4126**
I'm Just A Singer (In A Rock And Roll Band)—Moody Blues (73)	1595
Gemini Dream—Moody Blues (81)	1015
Isn't Life Strange—Moody Blues (72)	828
Sitting At The Wheel—Moody Blues (83)	459
Ride My See-Saw—Moody Blues (68)	324
Steppin' In A Slide Zone—Moody Blues (78)	247
Talking Out Of Turn—Moody Blues (81)	165
Fritz LOEHNER-BEDA ▶ 10931 (1)	**4.3**
Yours Is My Heart Alone—Enzo Stuarti (56)	17
Frank LOESSER ▶ 482 (27) HOF	**8678**
Standing On The Corner—Four Lads (56)	*3973*
Heart And Soul—Cleftones (61)	*1608*
A Woman In Love—Four Aces (55)	*1464*
A Woman In Love—Frankie Laine (55)	*1141*
Heart And Soul—Jan & Dean (61)	*515*
Standing On The Corner—Dean Martin (56)	*481*
I Don't Want To Walk Without You—Barry Manilow (80)	*396*
Wun'erful, Wun'erful! (Sides Uh-One & Uh-Two)—Stan Freberg (57)	298
Standing On The Corner—Mills Brothers (56)	*122*
I Don't Want To Walk Without You—Phyllis McGuire (64)	*58*
Pet Me, Pappa—Rosemary Clooney (55)	44
Faraway Boy—Della Reese (60)	22
Joey, Joey, Joey—Peggy Lee (56)	17
Baby It's Cold Outside—Ray Charles And Betty Carter (62)	16
If I Were A Bell—Big Three: Sarah Vaughan/Joe Williams/Count Basie (60)	12
Big D—Jo Stafford (56)	*10*
Big D—DeJohn Sisters (56)	*10*
I'll Know—Sammy Davis Jr. (55)	9.9
Don't Cry—Frankie Laine (56)	6.7
Somebody Somewhere—Doris Day (56)	*6.2*
Somebody Somewhere—Pat Kirby (56)	*6.2*

Frank LOESSER ▶ 482 (27) HOF *Continued*	**8678**
Somebody Somewhere—Roy Hamilton (56)	*6.2*
Have I Stayed Away Too Long—Bobby Bare (64)	3.3
Music Of Home—Bing Crosby (60)	2.4
A Woman In Love—Gordon MacRae (55)	*0.0*
Standing On The Corner—Andy Griffith (56)	*0.0*
Standing On The Corner—Neal Hefti Singers (56)	*0.0*
Frederick LOEWE ▶ 1247 (29) HOF	**3598**
On The Street Where You Live—Vic Damone (56)	*2704*
I Could Have Danced All Night—Sylvia Syms (56)	*921*
On The Street Where You Live—Andy Williams (64)	*563*
I Could Have Danced All Night— Rosemary Clooney (56)	*544*
On The Street Where You Live—Eddie Fisher (56)	*487*
Almost Like Being In Love—Michael Johnson (78)	477
I've Grown Accustomed To Your Face— Rosemary Clooney (56)	*394*
I Talk To The Trees— Edmundo Ros and His Orchestra (58)	285
Gigi—Vic Damone (58)	*216*
How To Handle A Woman—Johnny Mathis (60)	85
I Could Have Danced All Night—Ben E. King (63)	*38*
I've Grown Accustomed To Your Face— Gordon MacRae (56)	*37*
I Could Have Danced All Night—Dinah Shore (56)	*36*
With A Little Bit Of Luck—Jo Stafford (56)	*28*
With A Little Bit Of Luck— Percy Faith And His Orchestra (56)	*26*
I Could Have Danced All Night—Biddu Orchestra (76)	*15*
Get Me To The Church On Time—Julius La Rosa (56)	11
On The Street Where You Live— Lawrence Welk And His Champagne Music (56)	*3.3*
Gigi—Bing Crosby (58)	*0.0*
Gigi—Tony Martin (58)	*0.0*
Gigi—Billy Eckstine (58)	*0.0*
Gigi—Charles Margulis (58)	*0.0*
Gigi—Strollers Featuring Artie Malvin (58)	*0.0*
I've Grown Accustomed To Her Face— Sid Feller & His Orchestra (56)	*0.0*
I Could Have Danced All Night— Lawrence Welk & His Champagne Music (56)	*0.0*
I've Grown Accustomed To Her Face— Lawrence Welk & His Champagne Music (56)	*0.0*
I Could Have Danced All Night—Sammy Kaye & His "Swing And Sway" Orchestra (56)	*0.0*
I've Grown Accustomed To Her Face—Sammy Kaye & His "Swing And Sway" Orchestra (56)	*0.0*
I've Grown Accustomed To Your Face— Bob Eberly with Enoch Light & His Orchestra (56)	*0.0*
Nils LOFGREN ▶ 7234 (1)	**108**
White Lies—Grin (72)	108
Harold LOGAN ▶ 278 (19)	**12506**
Stagger Lee—Lloyd Price (58)	*7844*
Personality—Lloyd Price (59)	*7779*
I'm Gonna Get Married—Lloyd Price (59)	4720
Lady Luck—Lloyd Price And His Orchestra (60)	1501
Come Into My Heart—Lloyd Price (59)	1300
Stagger Lee—Tommy Roe (71)	*1051*
Where Were You (On Our Wedding Day)?—Lloyd Price (59)	933
Question—Lloyd Price And His Orchestra (60)	887
Stag-O-Lee—Wilson Pickett (67)	*785*
Wont'Cha Come Home—Lloyd Price (59)	615
No If's No And's— Lloyd Price And His Orchestra (60)	337
For Love—Lloyd Price And His Orchestra (60)	335
(You Better) Know What You're Doin'— Lloyd Price And His Orchestra (60)	180
Just Call Me (And I'll Understand)— Lloyd Price And His Orchestra (60)	137
(You've Got) Personality—Mitch Ryder (68)	*83*
Three Little Pigs—Lloyd Price (59)	31
Billie Baby—Lloyd Price (64)	26
Who Coulda' Told You (They Lied)— Lloyd Price (60)	6.1
Mary And Man-O— Lloyd Price And His Great Orchestra (61)	1.5
LOGANKOYA ▶ 7592 (1)	**87**
Baby Talk—Alisha (85)	174
Dan LOGGINS ▶ 9101 (1)	**31**
Vahevala (Pronounced Va-Hēē-Va-La)— Kenny Loggins With Jim Messina (72)	62
Dave LOGGINS ▶ 1040 (7)	**4245**
Please Come To Boston—Dave Loggins (74)	2238
Pieces Of April—Three Dog Night (72)	1008
Til The World Ends—Three Dog Night (75)	542
If I Had My Wish Tonight—David Lasley (82)	402
Someday—Dave Loggins (74)	144
Morning Desire—Kenny Rogers (85)	76
Jasper—Jim Stafford (76)	72
E. Ein LOGGINS [Eva Ein] ▶ 4536 (3)	**469**
Vox Humana—Kenny Loggins (85)	512
Keep The Fire—Kenny Loggins (80)	419
I'll Be There—Kenny Loggins (85)	9.0
Kenny LOGGINS ▶ 123 (28)	**21287**
Footloose—Kenny Loggins (84)	6174
What A Fool Believes—Doobie Brothers (79)	5311
Your Mama Don't Dance— Kenny Loggins With Jim Messina (72)	*3088*
Whenever I Call You "Friend"—Kenny Loggins (78)	2897
Danny's Song—Anne Murray (72)	2772
I'm Alright—Kenny Loggins (80)	2369
This Is It—Kenny Loggins (79)	2064
Love Song—Anne Murray (73)	1372
Nobody's Fool—Kenny Loggins (88)	1325
Heart To Heart—Kenny Loggins (82)	1312
Your Mama Don't Dance—Poison (89)	*1055*
My Music—Loggins & Messina (73)	1015
Don't Fight It—Kenny Loggins with Steve Perry (82)	851
I'm Free (Heaven Helps The Man)— Kenny Loggins (84)	726
Welcome To Heartlight—Kenny Loggins (83)	649
House At Pooh Corner—Nitty Gritty Dirt Band (71)	542
Forever—Kenny Loggins (85)	516
Vox Humana—Kenny Loggins (85)	512
I Gotta Try—Michael McDonald (82)	495
No Lookin' Back—Michael McDonald (85)	461
Keep The Fire—Kenny Loggins (80)	419
Growin'—Loggins & Messina (75)	341
Conviction Of The Heart—Kenny Loggins (91)	291
I Believe In Love—Kenny Loggins (77)	268
Playing With The Boys—Kenny Loggins (86)	204
Watching The River Run—Loggins & Messina (74)	164
Celebrate Me Home—Kenny Loggins (78)	77
I'll Be There—Kenny Loggins (85)	9.0
—Michael Logiudice see: Mike ANTHONY	
Manny LOIACONO ▶ 9454 (1)	**23**
What If (I Said I Love You)—Unipop (82)	70
Phyllis LOIACONO ▶ 9455 (1)	**23**
What If (I Said I Love You)—Unipop (82)	70
Jules LOMAN ▶ 5676 (3)	**256**
Rhythm 'N' Blues (Mama's Got The Rhythm— Papa's Got The Blues)—McGuire Sisters (55)	437
Christmas Alphabet—McGuire Sisters (54)	62
Mambo In The Moonlight— Gary Crosby And The Cheer Leaders (54)	21
Barbara LOMAS [Barbara Joyce] ▶ 5187 (2)	**329**
Express—B.T. Express (75)	*2209*
Express—Ritchie Family (76)	*92*
Alan LOMAX ▶ 6934 (2)	**127**
Inside-Looking Out—Animals (66)	468
Have A Drink On Me—Buddy Thomas (61)	51
John LOMAX ▶ 8058 (3)	**63**
Goodnight, Irene— Jerry Reed And The Hully Girlies (62)	*84*
Have A Drink On Me—Buddy Thomas (61)	51
Goodnight Irene—Billy Williams (59)	*22*
Carmen LOMBARDO ▶ 1617 (4)	**2619**
Return To Me—Dean Martin (58)	5132
Coquette—Fats Domino (58)	94
Sweethearts On Parade— Billy Ward & The Dominoes (55)	*22*
Sweethearts On Parade— Dick Jacobs And His Chorus And Orchestra (55)	*22*
John LOMBARDO ▶ 8447 (2)	**50**
Can't Stop Loving You—Last Word (67)	86
One Woman Band—Carol Chase (75)	7.4
Mark LONDON ▶ 797 (3)	**5566**
To Sir With Love—Lulu (67)	*10546*
Best Of Both Worlds—Lulu (67)	579
To Sir, With Love—Herbie Mann (67)	*3.8*
—Timothy London see: Tim BRINKHURST	
Burt LONG [Burton D'Lugoff] ▶ 1947 (2)	**2069**
Cindy Oh Cindy—Eddie Fisher (56)	*2225*
Cindy Oh Cindy—Vince Martin with The Tarriers (56)	*1914*
Frederick LONG [Frederick Earl Long, Shorty Long] ▶ 1908 (6)	**2122**
Devil With A Blue Dress On— Mitch Ryder And The Detroit Wheels (66)	*2815*
Here Comes The Judge—Shorty Long (68)	1872
Night Fo' Last—Shorty Long (68)	143
Devil With A Blue Dress—Pratt & McClain (76)	*34*
Function At The Junction—Shorty Long (66)	1.9
I Had A Dream—Shorty Long (69)	1.8
—Frederick Earl Long see: Frederick LONG	
Mark LONG ▶ 6649 (1)	**148**
Are You Sure—So (88)	295
Shorty LONG [Emidio Vagnoni] ▶ 9117 (1)	**31**
(I've Got) Spring Fever—Little Willie John (61)	61
—Shorty Long see: Frederick LONG	
Henry Wadsworth LONGFELLOW ▶ 9552 (1)	**21**
I Heard The Bells On Christmas Day—Bing Crosby (56)	43
Richard LONOW ▶ 5462 (1)	**284**
Call It Love—Poco (89)	851
Michael David LOOKOFSKY [Michael D. Brown, Mike Brown] ▶ 1282 (8)	**3464**
Walk Away Renee—Left Banke (66)	*3456*
Walk Away Renee—Four Tops (68)	*1445*
Pretty Ballerina—Left Banke (66)	1285
I'm Coming Home—Stories (72)	624
And Suddenly—Cherry People (68)	442
Walk Away Renee— Southside Johnny & The Jukes (86)	*32*
Desiree'—Left Banke (67)	2.4
Ivy, Ivy—Left Banke (67)	1.0
Shelley LOONEY ▶ 11640 (1)	**0.9**
This Is My Country, Thank You Canada— Shelley Looney (80)	1.8
Rudolf LOOSE ▶ 8684 (1)	**43**
Marble Breaks And Iron Bends—Drafi (66)	170
Lisa LOPES ▶ 11332 (1)	**2.2**
Word To The Badd!!—Jermaine Jackson (91)	11
Gilbert LOPEZ ▶ 3049 (4)	**1035**
Happy Happy Birthday Baby—Tune Weavers (57)	*2066*
Happy Happy Birthday—Wanda Jackson (60)	*3.5*
Happy, Happy Birthday Baby—Kay Cee Jones (57)	*0.0*
Happy, Happy Birthday Baby—Dottie Ferguson (57)	*0.0*
—Lester Lopez see: Les LEDO	
Trini LOPEZ ▶ 5470 (2)	**282**
I'm Comin' Home, Cindy—Trini Lopez (66)	431
Sinner Man—Trini Lopez (65)	335
Alan LORBER ▶ 11719 (1)	**0.5**
He's A Fool—Jackie Wilson (63)	1.4
Sam LORBER ▶ 3119 (4)	**1000**
Dare Me—Pointer Sisters (85)	1216
Where Were You When I Was Falling In Love—Lobo (79)	848
Wild Women Do—Natalie Cole (90)	292
Secrets—Mac Davis (81)	37
Jon LORD ▶ 3690 (6)	**733**
Smoke On The Water—Deep Purple (73)	3242
Woman From Tokyo—Deep Purple (73)	226
Black Night—Deep Purple (70)	148
Might Just Take Your Life—Deep Purple (74)	27
Emmaretta—Deep Purple (69)	8.7
The Bird Has Flown—Deep Purple (69)	0.9
Peter LORD [Peter Lord Moreland] ▶ 459 (4)	**9099**
Rush Rush—Paula Abdul (91)	5506
The Promise Of A New Day—Paula Abdul (91)	3398
Blowing Kisses In The Wind—Paula Abdul (91)	2686
Going Through The Motions—Aftershock (91)	172
Jerry LORDAN ▶ 914 (8)	**4829**
Apache—Jorgen Ingmann And His Guitar (61)	*4380*
A House A Car And A Wedding Ring— Dale Hawkins (58)	*189*
Apache—Sugar Hill Gang (82)	*173*
Apache '65—Arrows Featuring Davie Allan (65)	*139*
House A Car And A Wedding Ring—Mike Preston (58)	*40*
Scarlett O'Hara—Lawrence Welk And His Orchestra (63)	*30*
Apache—Sonny James (61)	*17*
Scarlet O'Hara—Bobby Gregg (63)	*0.0*
Bryan LOREN [Bryan Loren Hudson, Bryan Hudson] ▶ 4883 (2)	**388**
(Baby Tell Me) Can You Dance—Shanice Wilson (87)	319
Do The Bartman—Simpsons (90)	139
—Estelle Loring see: Estelle LEVITT	

Jet LORING ▶ 5705 (1) **252**
Lovin' Things—Grassroots (69) 504

Richard LORING ▶ 9938 (4) **15**
Summertime Lies—Four Preps (58) 17
Touch Of Pink—Jerry Wallace (59) *9.7*
Gretchen—Diamonds (59) 2.3
A Touch Of Pink—Dick Jacobs & His Orchestra (59) *0.0*

—Sam Lorraine see: Harold FIELDS

Chuck LORRE ▶ 5464 (1) **283**
French Kissin—Debbie Harry (86) 283

Debora LOSAK ▶ 7426 (1) **97**
The Loser—Skyliners (65) 193

—Antonino Lo Tempio see: Nino TEMPO

—Carol Lo Tempio see: April STEVENS

Dann LOTTERMOSER ▶ 9102 (1) **31**
Vahevala (Pronounced Va-Hēē-Va-La)—Kenny Loggins With Jim Messina (72) 62

—Charles Elzer Loudermilk see: Charlie LOUVIN

Gwen LOUDERMILK ▶ 7828 (1) **73**
Road Hog—John D. Loudermilk (62) 146

—Ira Lonnie Loudermilk see: Ira LOUVIN

John D. LOUDERMILK [Johnny Dee] ▶ 39 (47) **46403**
Indian Reservation (The Lament Of The Cherokee)—Raiders (71) *8111*
Waterloo—Stonewall Jackson (59) 4628
Norman—Sue Thompson (61) 4395
Then You Can Tell Me Goodbye—Casinos (67) *3592*
Sad Movies (Make Me Cry)—Sue Thompson (61) *3359*
A Rose And A Baby Ruth—George Hamilton IV (56) *2627*
Ebony Eyes—Everly Brothers (61) 2520
Talk Back Trembling Lips—Johnny Tillotson (63) *2470*
Tobacco Road—Nashville Teens (64) *1529*
Thou Shalt Not Steal—Dick And Deedee (64) *1357*
Torture—Kris Jensen (62) 1250
Paper Tiger—Sue Thompson (64) 1166
Everything's Alright—Newbeats (64) 1158
(He's My) Dreamboat—Connie Francis (61) 1158
(The Lament Of The Cherokee) Indian Reservation—Don Fardon (68) *1027*
James (Hold The Ladder Steady)—Sue Thompson (62) 865
Sittin' In The Balcony—Eddie Cochran (57) *856*
I Wanna Live—Glen Campbell (68) 804
Stayin' In—Bobby Vee (61) 743
Angela Jones—Johnny Ferguson (60) 718
Language Of Love—John D. Loudermilk (61) 692
Hollywood—Connie Francis (61) 569
What A Woman In Love Won't Do—Sandy Posey (67) 513
This Little Bird—Marianne Faithfull (65) 498
Sittin' In The Balcony—Johnny Dee (57) *432*
Boo Boo Stick Beat—Chet Atkins (59) 381
Sad Movies (Make Me Cry)—Lennon Sisters (61) *303*
Then You Can Tell Me Goodbye—Toby Beau (79) *257*
Then You Can Tell Me Goodbye—Glen Campbell (76) *228*
Top Forty, News, Weather And Sports—Mark Dinning (61) 160
Road Hog—John D. Loudermilk (62) 146
Then You Can Tell Me Goodbye—Eddy Arnold (68) *137*
Midnight Bus—Billy Graves (59) 78
Half-Breed—Marvin Rainwater (59) 72
Thou Shalt Not Steal—John D. Loudermilk (62) *61*
My Big Brother's Friend—Cecelia Batten (57) *53*
Callin' Doctor Casey—John D. Loudermilk (62) 25
One Thousand Concrete Blocks—Johnny Dee (57) 23
Tobacco Road—Jamul (70) *6.9*
Teenage Queen—Johnny Dee with the Bluenotes (57) 5.1
The Great Snow Man—Bob Luman (61) 4.5
Break My Mind—Bobby Wood (67) 3.3
Windy And Warm—Boots Randolph & His Combo (63) 2.2
Sittin' In The Balcony—Don Cornell (57) *0.0*
My Big Brother's Friend—Carol Hughes (57) *0.0*
A Rose And A Baby Ruth—Eddie Fontaine (56) *0.0*
Talk Back Trembling Lips—Ernest Ashworth (63) *0.0*

Bill LOUGHBOROUGH ▶ 7520 (1) **91**
Coocoo U—Kingston Trio (59) 182

Lee LOUGHNANE ▶ 2163 (2) **1805**
Call On Me—Chicago (74) 1464
No Tell Lover—Chicago (78) 1023

—Louiguy see: Luis GUGLIELMI

Guy LOUIS ▶ 2623 (2) **1315**
Don't Forget I Still Love You—Bobbi Martin (64) 1093
I Can't Stop Thinking Of You—Bobbi Martin (65) 444

Charlie LOUVIN [Charles Elzer Loudermilk] ▶ 7640 (2) **83**
If I Could Only Win Your Love—Emmylou Harris (75) 167
When I Stop Dreaming—Ray Charles & Jimmy Lewis (69) 0.0

Ira LOUVIN [Ira Lonnie Loudermilk] ▶ 7641 (2) **83**
If I Could Only Win Your Love—Emmylou Harris (75) 167
When I Stop Dreaming—Ray Charles & Jimmy Lewis (69) 0.0

Andrew LOVE ▶ 3219 (2) **944**
Keep On Dancing—Gentrys (65) 3698
Don't Have To Shop Around—Mad Lads (65) 78

Mike LOVE ▶ 82 (51) **26865**
I Get Around—Beach Boys (64) *8633*
Good Vibrations—Beach Boys (66) *8071*
Help Me, Rhonda—Beach Boys (65) *6345*
California Girls—Beach Boys (65) *3984*
Kokomo—Beach Boys (88) 3513
Fun, Fun, Fun—Beach Boys (64) *2657*
California Girls—David Lee Roth (85) *2548*
Be True To Your School—Beach Boys (63) 2214
Little Honda—Hondells (64) *2173*
Wouldn't It Be Nice—Beach Boys (66) *2149*
Do It Again—Beach Boys (68) 2041
Surfin' Safari—Beach Boys (62) *2024*
When I Grow Up (To Be A Man)—Beach Boys (64) 1865
Dance, Dance, Dance—Beach Boys (64) *1784*
Darlin'—Beach Boys (67) *1159*
Wild Honey—Beach Boys (67) 622
Help Me Rhonda—Johnny Rivers (75) *596*
Getcha Back—Beach Boys (85) 528
Almost Summer—Celebration Featuring Mike Love (78) 501
It's O.K.—Beach Boys (76) 446
Good Vibrations—Todd Rundgren (76) *391*
Wendy—Beach Boys (64) 286
Add Some Music To Your Day—Beach Boys (70) 274
I Get Around—Beach Boys (81) *240*
Fun, Fun, Fun—Beach Boys (81) *240*
Surfin' Safari—Beach Boys (81) *240*
Help Me Rhonda—Beach Boys (81) *240*
Good Vibrations—Beach Boys (81) *240*
Darlin'—Paul Davis Featuring Susan Collins (78) *215*
Here Comes The Night—Beach Boys (79) 195
Please Let Me Wonder—Beach Boys (65) 178
Rock 'N' Roll To The Rescue—Beach Boys (86) 99
Little Honda—Beach Boys (64) *90*
Darlin'—Yipes!! (80) *80*
Surfin'—Beach Boys (62) 65
Don't Back Down—Beach Boys (64) 25
Little Saint Nick—Beach Boys (63) 23
Good Vibrations—Hugo Montenegro, His Orchestra And Chorus (69) *23*
Custom Machine—Bruce And Terry (64) 14
Goin' On—Beach Boys (80) 12
409—Beach Boys (62) *11*
Still Cruisin'—Beach Boys (89) 6.4
She Knows Me Too Well—Beach Boys (64) 5.0
409—Cantina Band (81) *1.5*
I Get Around—Cantina Band (81) *1.5*
Fun, Fun, Fun—Cantina Band (81) *1.5*
Help Me Rhonda—Cantina Band (81) *1.5*
Good Vibrations—Cantina Band (81) *1.5*
California Girls—Cantina Band (81) *1.5*
Wouldn't It Be Nice—Cantina Band (81) *1.5*
Dance, Dance, Dance—Cantina Band (81) *1.5*

Milton LOVE ▶ 7169 (2) **112**
Walking Along—Diamonds (58) *783*
Walking Along—Solitaires (58) *0.0*

—Monie Love see: Simone Antoinette JOHNSON

Rudy LOVE ▶ 11070 (1) **3.4**
Your Love Is So Doggone Good—Whispers (71) 6.8

—Francesco Paolo LoVecchio see: Frankie LAINE

Carroll LOVEDAY ▶ 7582 (3) **87**
That's My Desire—Yvonne Baker And The Sensations (62) *118*
Shrine Of St. Cecilia—Faron Young (57) 56
That's My Desire—Pat Boone (61) *1.0*

Bobby LOVELACE ▶ 9360 (2) **25**
Headlines—Midnight Star (86) 59
No Parking (On The Dance Floor)—Midnight Star (84) 46

Royal LOVELL ▶ 10477 (1) **8.0**
Anchors Aweigh—Four Preps (62) 24

—Michael Lovesmith see: Michael Larry SMITH

Leroy LOVETT ▶ 4364 (3) **512**
After The Lights Go Down Low—Al Hibbler (56) *1362*
All At Once—Don Cornell (54) 114
After The Lights Go Down Low—George Maharis (62) *3.1*

Robert John LOVETT ▶ 11807 (1) **0.0**
When There's No Love Left—New Seekers featuring Eve Graham (70) 0.0

Winfred LOVETT ▶ 664 (6) **6544**
Kiss And Say Goodbye—Manhattans (76) *6161*
I Kinda Miss You—Manhattans (76) 175
I Wanna Be (Your Everything)—Manhattans (65) 115
One Life To Live—Manhattans (72) 80
Kiss And Say Goodbye—Band Of Gold (84) *12*
I Bet'cha (Couldn't Love Me)—Manhattans (66) 2.3

—Lene Lovich see: Lili PREMILOVICH

Albert LOWE ▶ 8712 (2) **41**
Greenwood Mississippi—Little Richard (70) 81
What It Takes To Get A Good Woman (That's What It's Gonna Take To Keep Her)—Denise LaSalle (73) 2.2

Bernie LOWE [Harry Land, Bernard Lowenthal, Anthony September] ▶ 151 (43) **19215**
Mashed Potato Time—Dee Dee Sharp (62) 8768
(Let Me Be Your) Teddy Bear—Elvis Presley (57) *7775*
Wild One—Bobby Rydell (60) 4945
Butterfly—Andy Williams (57) *4791*
We Got Love—Bobby Rydell (59) 3621
Swingin' School—Bobby Rydell (60) 2224
Butterfly—Charlie Gracie (57) *2197*
Good Time Baby—Bobby Rydell (61) 1828
Teen Age Prayer—Gale Storm (55) *1780*
Kissin' Time—Bobby Rydell (59) 1393
Remember You're Mine—Pat Boone (57) 1255
Ding A Ling—Bobby Rydell (60) 936
Twenty Miles—Chubby Checker (63) 929
Ninety Nine Ways—Tab Hunter (57) *920*
The Fish—Bobby Rydell (61) 799
I Wanna Thank You—Bobby Rydell (61) 781
Fabulous—Charlie Gracie (57) *709*
Teen Age Prayer—Gloria Mann (55) *625*
Back To School Again—Timmie "Oh Yeah" Rogers (57) 476
Take Me Back To Toyland—Nat "King" Cole (55) 324
Put Me In The Mood—Fontane Sisters with Billy Vaughn's Orchestra (55) 317
You're The Greatest—Billy Scott (57) *181*
A Crazy Little Palace (That's My Home)—Billy Williams Quartet (56) 172
Lose Her—Bobby Rydell (62) 140
Party Time—Sal Mineo (57) 112
Just Like In The Movies—Upbeats (58) 102
Follow Your Heart—Four Coins (57) 94
Cherié—Bobby Rydell (61) 89
The Greatest Thing—Georgia Gibbs (56) 85
Butterfly—Bob Carroll (57) *81*
Fabulous—Steve Lawrence (57) *80*
The Door To Paradise—Bobby Rydell (61) 72
Teen Age Prayer—Kitty White (55) *63*
Kissin' Time—Kiss (74) 56
Groovy Tonight—Bobby Rydell (60) 23
(Let Me Be Your) Teddy Bear—Elvis Presley (82) *23*
I'm Still A King To You—Don Cherry (56) 17
Wanderin' Eyes—Charlie Gracie (57) 5.7
Beat—Billy May And His Orchestra (56) 5.0
Gee, It's Wonderful—Bobby Rydell (62) 2.2
Butterfly—Billy Williams (57) *0.0*
Ninety-Nine Ways—Charlie Gracie (57) *0.0*
You're The Greatest—Valerie Carr (57) *0.0*

Chris LOWE ▶ 881 (10) **5040**
West End Girls—Pet Shop Boys (86) 4375
What Have I Done To Deserve This?—Pet Shop Boys And Dusty Springfield (87) 3210
It's A Sin—Pet Shop Boys (87) 1228
Opportunities (Let's Make Lots Of Money)—Pet Shop Boys (86) 1174
Domino Dancing—Pet Shop Boys (88) 721
Love Comes Quickly—Pet Shop Boys (86) 188
Suburbia—Pet Shop Boys (86) 159
So Hard—Pet Shop Boys (90) 120
Left To My Own Devices—Pet Shop Boys (89) 35
How Can You Expect To Be Taken Seriously—Pet Shop Boys (91) 4.1

Danny LOWE ▶ 7673 (1)	**82**
West Coast Woman—Painter (73)	163
Jim LOWE ▶ 6459 (2)	**166**
Talkin' To The Blues—Jim Lowe (57)	328
Nuevo Laredo—Les Paul and Mary Ford (56)	10
Johnny LOWE ▶ 9308 (1)	**27**
Six Pack To Go—Hank Thompson (60)	80
Nick LOWE ▶ 3283 (3)	**912**
Cruel To Be Kind—Nick Lowe (79)	1413
I Need You—Paul Carrack (82)	476
I Knew The Bride (When She Used To Rock 'N Roll)—Nick Lowe (85)	47
Ruth LOWE ▶ 3921 (4)	**656**
I'll Never Smile Again—Platters (61)	*630*
I'll Never Smile Again—Four Preps (62)	*24*
I'll Never Smile Again—Modernaires (57)	*1.9*
I'll Never Smile Again—Wanderers (61)	*0.0*
Sammy LOWE ▶ 9574 (1)	**21**
Hear The Bells—Tokens (63)	148
Eric LOWEN [David Eric Lowen] ▶ 2547 (2)	**1396**
We Belong—Pat Benatar (84)	2339
You Don't Have To Go Home Tonight—Triplets (91)	1130
—Bernard Lowenthal see: Bernie LOWE	
Bert LOWN ▶ 7045 (1)	**120**
Bye Bye Blues—Bert Kaempfert And His Orchestra (66)	479
Greg LOWRY ▶ 11358 (1)	**2.1**
We Should Be Sleeping—Eddie Money (87)	8.4
Keath LOWRY ▶ 10521 (1)	**7.7**
You Are The One—TKA (89)	15
Doug LUBAHN ▶ 3931 (1)	**652**
Treat Me Right—Pat Benatar (81)	1304
Al LUBAR ▶ 6541 (1)	**159**
Put Me In The Mood—Fontane Sisters with Billy Vaughn's Orchestra (55)	317
Jeremy LUBBOCK ▶ 9476 (1)	**23**
The Best Of Me—David Foster And Olivia Newton-John (86)	69
Marco LUBERTI ▶ 8395 (1)	**52**
When Love Has Gone Away—Richard Cocciante (76)	208
Joe LUBIN [Joe Lubinsky] ▶ 2079 (18)	**1901**
Tutti Frutti—Pat Boone (56)	*1434*
Secret—Gordon MacRae (58)	*824*
Cha Hua Hua—Pets (58)	*657*
Tutti Frutti—Little Richard (56)	*649*
Teacher's Pet—Doris Day (58)	241
Midnight Lace—Ray Ellis And His Orchestra (60)	*138*
Cha Hua Hua—Eddie Platt And His Orchestra (58)	*102*
Tutti-Frutti—Jive Bunny And The Mastermixers (89)	*80*
Tutti Frutti—Jive Bunny And The Mastermixers (89)	*80*
Midnight Lace Part One—Ray Conniff & His Orch. & Chorus (60)	*60*
The Careless Years—Sue Raney (57)	*12*
Out Of The Picture—Crew-Cuts (56)	12
Midnight Lace—David Carroll And His Orchestra (60)	*7.8*
Secret—Gainors (58)	*0.0*
Cha Hua Hua—Hugo & Luigi (58)	*0.0*
The Careless Years—Duke Mitchell (57)	*0.0*
Tutti-Frutti—Art Mooney & His Orchestra (56)	*0.0*
Midnight Lace—Sid Feller & His Orchestra (60)	*0.0*
—Joe Lubinsky see: Joe LUBIN	
Norman LUBOFF ▶ 1299 (3)	**3410**
Yellow Bird—Arthur Lyman Group (61)	*3220*
Yellow Bird—Lawrence Welk And His Orchestra (61)	*154*
Yellow Bird—Mills Brothers (58)	*107*
Doug LUCAS ▶ 11643 (1)	**0.9**
Tonight's The Night—S.S.O. (76)	1.8
Frank LUCAS ▶ 8443 (1)	**50**
Good Thing Man—Frank Lucas (77)	101
Huw LUCAS ▶ 11503 (1)	**1.4**
Name And Number—Big Noise (89)	4.2
—Lemeul Eugene Lucas see: Gene AUSTIN	
Reggie LUCAS ▶ 741 (9)	**5910**
The Closer I Get To You—Roberta Flack With Donny Hathaway (78)	4396
Never Knew Love Like This Before—Stephanie Mills (80)	2443
Borderline—Madonna (84)	1870
What Cha Gonna Do With My Lovin'—Stephanie Mills (79)	*611*
Two Hearts—Stephanie Mills featuring Teddy Pendergrass (81)	378
Sweet Sensation—Stephanie Mills (80)	171
Back Together Again—Roberta Flack with Donny Hathaway (80)	111
Whatcha Gonna Do With My Lovin'—Inner City (90)	*82*
You Know How To Love Me—Phyllis Hyman (79)	12
Tammy LUCAS ▶ 11379 (1)	**2.0**
All About You—Pretty In Pink (91)	4.0
Roger LUCCHESI ▶ 11808 (1)	**0.0**
The Portuguese Washerwomen (Les Lavandieres Du Portugal)—Jacqueline François with Michel Legrand & His Orchestra (56)	*0.0*
Joseph LUCCISANO ▶ 3224 (1)	**941**
There's A Moon Out Tonight—Capris (60)	2822
Troy LUCCKETTA ▶ 8285 (1)	**55**
The Way It Is—Tesla (90)	222
Peter LUCIA ▶ 809 (5)	**5473**
Crimson And Clover—Tommy James And The Shondells (68)	*9176*
Crimson And Clover—Joan Jett & The Blackhearts (82)	*1672*
I'm Alive—Blue Swede (75)	92
Calico—Tommy James (73)	4.3
Happy—Hog Heaven (71)	3.0
Frank LUGO ▶ 6309 (1)	**183**
I Need Somebody—? & The Mysterians (66)	913
Steve LUKATHER ▶ 1332 (4)	**3335**
Turn Your Love Around—George Benson (81)	2450
She's A Beauty—Tubes (83)	1661
I'll Be Over You—Toto (86)	1351
I Won't Hold You Back—Toto (83)	1289
Robin LUKE ▶ 1066 (3)	**4143**
Susie Darlin'—Robin Luke (58)	*3684*
Susie Darlin'—Tommy Roe (62)	*452*
Chicka Chicka Honey—Robin Luke with The Jolly Drifters (58)	7.8
Rudolf LUKESCH ▶ 11470 (1)	**1.6**
(Hear My Song) Violetta—Ray Adams And Orchestra (62)	6.2
—Yamma Brown Lumar see: Yamma BROWN	
Gabriel LUNA ▶ 8354 (1)	**53**
Time Was—Flamingos (61)	160
Lynn LUNDGREN ▶ 10958 (1)	**4.1**
Some Things A Man's Gotta Do—Shango (70)	8.2
Orville LUNSFORD ▶ 3155 (1)	**981**
All American Boy—Bill Parsons And His Orchestra (58)	2944
Stephen LUNT [Stephen Broughton, Steve Broughton, Stephen Broughton Lunt] ▶ 2110 (6)	**1864**
She Bop—Cyndi Lauper (84)	3432
The Goonies 'r' Good Enough—Cyndi Lauper (85)	1031
What You See Is What You Get—Brenda K. Starr (88)	570
5.7.0.5.—City Boy (78)	419
Nail It To The Wall—Stacy Lattisaw (86)	296
Boy Blue—Cyndi Lauper (87)	59
Elliot LURIE ▶ 559 (4)	**7725**
Brandy (You're A Fine Girl)—Looking Glass (72)	6917
Jimmy Loves Mary-Anne—Looking Glass (73)	*760*
Golden Rainbow—Looking Glass (72)	29
Jimmy Loves Maryann—Josie Cotton (84)	*20*
Mauro LUSINI ▶ 10205 (1)	**11**
Son Of A Travelin' Man—Ed Ames (69)	22
—Dennis/Deke Lussier see: Deke RICHARDS	
Chuck LUTZ ▶ 10173 (1)	**12**
Slip Away—Pablo Cruise (81)	35
Michael LUTZ ▶ 1759 (5)	**2365**
Smokin' In The Boy's Room—Brownsville Station (73)	*3499*
Smokin' In The Boys Room—Mötley Crüe (85)	*773*
Kings Of The Party—Brownsville Station (74)	474
The Martian Boogie—Brownsville Station (77)	180
Mama Don't Allow No Parkin'—Brownsville Station (74)	50
Annabella LWIN [Myint Myint Aye] ▶ 9841 (1)	**16**
Do You Wanna Hold Me?—Bow Wow Wow (83)	81
Billy LYALL ▶ 2515 (2)	**1425**
Magic—Pilot (75)	2804
Just A Smile—Pilot (75)	47
Graham LYLE ▶ 536 (15)	**8007**
What's Love Got To Do With It—Tina Turner (84)	6553
We Don't Need Another Hero (Thunderdome)—Tina Turner (85)	3300
Typical Male—Tina Turner (86)	3200
What You Get Is What You See—Tina Turner (87)	776
When I'm Dead And Gone—McGuinness Flint (70)	565
Two People—Tina Turner (86)	493
Break Away—Art Garfunkel (75)	478
A Heart In New York—Art Garfunkel (81)	227
I Wanna Stay With You—Gallagher And Lyle (76)	160
Soul Inspiration—Anita Baker (90)	129
Heart On My Sleeve—Gallagher and Lyle (76)	*87*
A Little Bit Of Heaven—Natalie Cole (85)	23
Heart On My Sleeve—Bryan Ferry (76)	*17*
Button Off My Shirt—Paul Carrack (88)	6.5
Every Little Teardrop—Gallagher And Lyle (77)	2.5
Kevin LYLES ▶ 3665 (1)	**744**
Girl You Know It's True—Milli Vanilli (88)	3721
Arthur LYMAN ▶ 10679 (1)	**6.1**
Honolulu Nites—Arthur Lyman Group (61)	6.1
Frankie LYMON ▶ 1866 (8)	**2184**
Why Do Fools Fall In Love—Teenagers Featuring Frankie Lymon (56)	*4057*
Why Do Fools Fall In Love—Diana Ross (81)	*2314*
Why Do Fools Fall In Love—Gale Storm (56)	*2295*
Why Do Fools Fall In Love—Diamonds (56)	*1782*
Why Do Fools Fall In Love—Happenings (67)	*389*
Why Do Fools Fall In Love—Gloria Mann (56)	*80*
Why Do Fools Fall In Love—Beach Boys (64)	*5.6*
Why Do Fools Fall In Love—Summer Wine (73)	*0.4*
Robert LYN ▶ 6319 (1)	**182**
Pass The Dutchie—Musical Youth (82)	1276
Bernie LYNCH ▶ 6437 (1)	**169**
Heaven (Must Be There)—Eurogliders (84)	169
Bruce LYNCH ▶ 8118 (1)	**61**
Was Dog A Doughnut—Cat Stevens (77)	183
George LYNCH ▶ 5902 (4)	**231**
In My Dreams—Party (91)	610
Alone Again—Dokken (85)	164
Burning Like A Flame—Dokken (87)	82
In My Dreams—Dokken (86)	68
Kenny LYNCH ▶ 4923 (3)	**380**
Long Dark Road—Hollies (72)	680
It's Gotta Last Forever—Billy J. Kramer With The Dakotas (65)	109
Follow Me—Drifters (65)	8.3
Larry LYNCH ▶ 8899 (2)	**37**
Love Never Fails—Greg Kihn Band (83)	168
Every Love Song—Greg Kihn Band (82)	15
Luther LYNCH ▶ 7948 (1)	**68**
How Do You Feel The Morning After—Millie Jackson (74)	136
Ron LYNCH ▶ 9049 (1)	**32**
Caterpillar Crawl—Strangers (59)	130
Stan LYNCH ▶ 4967 (2)	**368**
The Last Worthless Evening—Don Henley (89)	774
How Bad Do You Want It?—Don Henley (90)	330
Steve LYNCH ▶ 6881 (1)	**131**
Turn Up The Radio—Autograph (84)	654
Gene LYND [Bryan Eugene Lindsay] ▶ 11649 (1)	**0.8**
Soul Dance—Tommy Leonetti (64)	0.8
Gary LYNES ▶ 5113 (3)	**341**
Love Me Forever—Four Esquires (57)	*475*
Love Me Forever—Roger Williams (67)	*173*
Love Me Forever—Eydie Gorme (57)	*33*
Barbara LYNN [Barbara Lynn Cumby, Barbara Linda Ozen, Barbara Lynn Ozen] ▶ 2098 (8)	**1882**
You'll Lose A Good Thing—Barbara Lynn (62)	*2239*
You'll Lose A Good Thing—Freddy Fender (76)	*443*
Second Fiddle Girl—Barbara Lynn (62)	222
Oh! Baby (We Got A Good Thing Goin')—Barbara Lynn (64)	150
You're Gonna Need Me—Barbara Lynn (62)	109
This Is The Thanks I Get—Barbara Lynn (68)	38
It's Better To Have It—Barbara Lynn (65)	21
(Until Then) I'll Suffer—Barbara Lynn (71)	1.3
—Cathy Lynn see: Lee CATHY	

Cheryl LYNN [Linda Cheryl Smith] ▶ 3759 (2) **708**
Got To Be Real—Cheryl Lynn (78) 1732
I'll Do 4 U—Father MC (91) 522

Loretta LYNN ▶ 9095 (2) HOF **31**
Coal Miner's Daughter—Loretta Lynn (70) 25
I Wanna Be Free—Loretta Lynn (71) 6.0

Gloria LYNNE [Gloria Mia Wilson] ▶ 7490 (1) **93**
Watermelon Man—Gloria Lynne (65) 185

Jeff LYNNE [Otis Wilbury] ▶ 70 (39) **30101**
Don't Bring Me Down—Electric Light Orchestra (79) 3165
Telephone Line—Electric Light Orchestra (77) 2479
Evil Woman—Electric Light Orchestra (75) 2071
Xanadu—Olivia Newton-John/Electric Light Orchestra (80) 1996
Shine A Little Love—Electric Light Orchestra (79) 1849
Free Fallin'—Tom Petty (89) 1714
Hold On Tight—ELO (81) 1704
Livin' Thing—Electric Light Orchestra (76) 1658
Can't Get It Out Of My Head—Electric Light Orchestra (74) 1435
All Over The World—Electric Light Orchestra (80) 1406
Turn To Stone—Electric Light Orchestra (77) 1324
Strange Magic—Electric Light Orchestra (76) 1258
You Got It—Roy Orbison (89) 1104
I Won't Back Down—Tom Petty (89) 1038
I'm Alive—Electric Light Orchestra (80) 1029
Sweet Talkin' Woman—Electric Light Orchestra (78) 943
Rock 'N' Roll Is King—ELO (83) 790
Do Ya—Electric Light Orchestra (77) 725
Calling America—Electric Light Orchestra (86) 665
Runnin' Down A Dream—Tom Petty (89) 589
Slipping Away—Dave Edmunds (83) 521
Mr. Blue Sky—Electric Light Orchestra (78) 499
Learning To Fly—Tom Petty and the Heartbreakers (91) 469
Handle With Care—Traveling Wilburys (88) 448
When We Was Fab—George Harrison (88) 422
Last Train To London—Electric Light Orchestra (79) 419
Showdown—Electric Light Orchestra (73) 374
Twilight—ELO (81) 367
Confusion—Electric Light Orchestra (79) 313
A Face In The Crowd—Tom Petty (90) 225
End Of The Line—Traveling Wilburys (89) 166
Showdown—Odia Coates (75) 152
Daybreaker—Electric Light Orchestra (74) 104
Showdown—Electric Light Orchestra (76) 101
Into The Great Wide Open—Tom Petty and the Heartbreakers (91) 79
Do Ya—Move (72) 36
It's Over—Electric Light Orchestra (78) 29
Video—Jeff Lynne (84) 17
Four Little Diamonds—ELO (83) 12

Phil LYNOTT ▶ 2400 (3) **1523**
The Boys Are Back In Town—Thin Lizzy (76) 1492
Cowboy Song—Thin Lizzy (76) 46
Dancing In The Moonlight (It's Caught Me In Its Spotlight)—Thin Lizzy (77) 7.6

Del LYON ▶ 7361 (1) **100**
The One Rose (That's Left In My Heart)—Teresa Brewer (58) 200

Jimmy LYON ▶ 3211 (2) **949**
Baby Hold On—Eddie Money (78) 1814
Let's Be Lovers Again—Eddie Money with Valerie Carter (80) 85

George LYONS ▶ 11028 (1) **3.7**
Spaghetti Rag—Johnny Maddox And The Rhythmasters (55) 7.5

James LYONS ▶ 7247 (1) **108**
Listen Lonely Girl—Johnny Mathis (64) 323

Ruth LYONS [Ruth Evelyn Reeves] ▶ 8453 (3) **50**
Let's Light The Christmas Tree—Ruby Wright (57) 44
Wasn't The Summer Short?—Johnny Mathis (61) 5.6
Let's Light The Christmas Tree—Lennon Sisters (57) 0.0

—Lyric see: Mervin STEALS

Johnny LYTLE ▶ 6663 (1) **146**
The Loop—Johnny Lytle (66) 146

Marshall LYTLE ▶ 9638 (1) **20**
Let's All Rock Together—Jodimars (56) 40

M

Lea MAALFRID ▶ 2741 (1) **1230**
You Could Have Been With Me—Sheena Easton (81) 1230

Lemmy MABASO ▶ 5889 (1) **233**
Puffin' On Down The Track—Hugh Masekela (68) 233

Lenny MACALUSO ▶ 9305 (1) **27**
Night Dancin'—Taka Boom (79) 53

Tony MACAULAY [Anthony Gordon Instone] ▶ 138 (28) **19958**
Build Me Up Buttercup—Foundations (68) 7390
Don't Give Up On Us—David Soul (77) 4733
Love Grows (Where My Rosemary Goes)—Edison Lighthouse (70) 4513
Smile A Little Smile For Me—Flying Machine (69) 3331
(Last Night) I Didn't Get To Sleep At All—5th Dimension (72) 2475
Baby, Now That I've Found You—Foundations (67) 2250
Here Comes That Rainy Day Feeling Again—Fortunes (71) 1705
Baby Take Me In Your Arms—Jefferson (69) 1242
Alibis—Sergio Mendes (84) 727
My Marie—Engelbert Humperdinck (70) 564
In The Bad, Bad Old Days (Before You Loved Me)—Foundations (69) 510
That Same Old Feeling—Pickettywitch (70) 493
Letter To Lucille—Tom Jones (73) 372
Sorry Suzanne—Hollies (69) 353
That Same Old Feeling—Fortunes (70) 298
Silver Lady—David Soul (77) 289
Back On My Feet Again—Foundations (68) 278
Going In With My Eyes Open—David Soul (77) 266
Falling Apart At The Seams—Marmalade (76) 234
My Little Chickadee—Foundations (69) 79
It's A Better Than Good Time—Gladys Knight & The Pips (78) 49
You Won't Find Another Fool Like Me—New Seekers Featuring Lyn Paul (74) 42
(Love Me) Love The Life I Lead—Fantastics (72) 40
Melanie Makes Me Smile—Tony Burrows (70) 31
Let The Heartaches Begin—Long John Baldry (68) 28
Baby Make It Soon—Flying Machine (70) 26
Melanie Makes Me Smile—Terry Williams (72) 10
Oklahoma Sunday Morning—Glen Campbell (72) 6.0

Ewan MacCOLL [James Henry Miller] ▶ 442 (1) **9289**
The First Time Ever I Saw Your Face—Roberta Flack (72) 9289

Kirsty MacCOLL ▶ 2432 (1) **1490**
They Don't Know—Tracey Ullman (84) 1490

Galt MacDERMOT ▶ 371 (17) HOF **10457**
Hair—Cowsills (69) 8011
Aquarius—5th Dimension (69) 5902
Let The Sunshine In (The Flesh Failures)—5th Dimension (69) 5902
Easy To Be Hard—Three Dog Night (69) 5385
Good Morning Starshine—Oliver (69) 4408
African Waltz—Cannonball Adderley Orchestra (61) 383
Where Do I Go—Happenings (69) 209
Be-In (Hare Krishna)—Happenings (69) 209
Easy To Be Hard—Hair (Original Soundtrack)/Cheryl Barnes (79) 76
Where Do I Go—Carla Thomas (68) 45
Good Morning Starshine—Strawberry Alarm Clock (69) 45
I Got Life—Nina Simone (69) 6.9
Ain't Got No—Nina Simone (69) 6.9
Aquarius—Dick Hyman (69) 4.7
I Know A Man—Rolf Harris (63) 0.9
African Waltz—Ian Fraser (61) 0.0
African Waltz—Johnny Dankworth and His Orchestra (61) 0.0

Ballard MacDONALD ▶ 8112 (2) HOF **61**
Breeze (Blow My Baby Back To Me)—Al Hibbler (55) 170
Clap Hands, Here Comes Charlie—Ella Fitzgerald (61) 13

Eddie MacDONALD ▶ 6234 (4) **191**
Sold Me Down The River—Alarm (89) 218
Strength—Alarm (85) 120
Rain In The Summertime—Alarm (87) 89
Presence Of Love—Alarm (88) 59

Pat MacDONALD ▶ 3504 (1) **811**
The Future's So Bright, I Gotta Wear Shades—Timbuk 3 (86) 811

Ralph MacDONALD ▶ 1469 (7) **2955**
Just The Two Of Us—Grover Washington, Jr. (81) 3799
Where Is The Love—Roberta Flack & Donny Hathaway (72) 2619
Stuff Like That—Quincy Jones (78) 787
I'm The One—Roberta Flack (82) 388
In The Name Of Love—Ralph MacDonald (with Bill Withers) (84) 200
Mister Magic—Grover Washington, Jr. (75) 135
Be Mine (Tonight)—Grover Washington, Jr. (82) 8.6

Iain MacFADYEN [Neil Grant] ▶ 10331 (1) **9.9**
Donald Where's Your Troosers?—Andy Stewart (61) 20

Robert MacGIMSEY ▶ 3833 (1) **687**
Shadrack—Brook Benton (62) 687

Mary MacGREGOR ▶ 7663 (1) **82**
This Girl (Has Turned Into A Woman)—Mary MacGregor (77) 164

Cecil MACK [Richard Cecil McPherson] ▶ 6111 (2) **205**
The Charleston—Ernie Fields Orch. (61) 411
Charleston—Cozy Cole (61) 0.0

Geoff MACK [Albert Geoffrey McElhinney] ▶ 6753 (1) **140**
I've Been Everywhere—Hank Snow (62) 140

Ira MACK [Irving Micahnik] ▶ 2877 (5) **1136**
Red River Rock—Johnny And The Hurricanes (59) 3410
Beatnik Fly—Johnny And The Hurricanes (60) 1493
Rocking Goose—Johnny And The Hurricanes (60) 239
Midnight—Johnny Gibson (62) 80
Casanova Brown—Young Sisters (62) 3.6

Keith MACK ▶ 6971 (1) **124**
Beat Of A Heart—Scandal Featuring Patty Smyth (85) 373

Lonnie MACK [Lonnie McIntosh] ▶ 4160 (1) **577**
Wham!—Lonnie Mack (63) 577

Ronnie MACK ▶ 445 (4) **9271**
He's So Fine—Chiffons (63) 8687
He's So Fine—Jody Miller (71) 413
He's So Fine—Jane Olivor (78) 110
He's So Fine—Kristy And Jimmy McNichol (78) 62

—Warner Mack see: Warner McPHERSON

Andy MACKAY ▶ 4870 (1) **395**
Love Is The Drug—Roxy Music (75) 789

David MACKEY ▶ 9365 (1) **25**
At Midnight—T-Connection (79) 51

Bryan MacLEAN ▶ 10759 (1) **5.5**
Alone Again Or—Love (70) 5.5

Gene MacLELLAN ▶ 527 (3) **8090**
Put Your Hand In The Hand—Ocean (71) 5324
Snowbird—Anne Murray (70) 2746
The Call—Anne Murray (76) 20

Brian MacLEOD ▶ 3378 (3) **874**
My Girl (Gone, Gone, Gone)—Chilliwack (81) 1067
Whatcha Gonna Do—Chilliwack (82) 542
Just One More Time—Headpins (83) 140

John MacLEOD ▶ 1628 (8) **2589**
Baby, Now That I've Found You—Foundations (67) 2250
Baby Take Me In Your Arms—Jefferson (69) 1242
In The Bad, Bad Old Days (Before You Loved Me)—Foundations (69) 510
That Same Old Feeling—Pickettywitch (70) 493
That Same Old Feeling—Fortunes (70) 298
Back On My Feet Again—Foundations (68) 278
My Little Chickadee—Foundations (69) 79
Let The Heartaches Begin—Long John Baldry (68) 28

Murray MacLEOD ▶ 5703 (2) **253**
Sunshine Girl—Parade (67) 687
What Are We Going To Do?—David Jones (65) 71

Sean MacLEOD ▶ 9909 (1) **15**
Takin' It Easy—Seals & Crofts (78) 30

—Declan Patrick Aloysius MacManus see: Elvis COSTELLO

Dan MacMASTER ▶ 8637 (1) **44**
Wait For You—Bonham (89) 221

Kevin MacMICHAEL ▶ 8847 (1) **38**
(Between A) Rock And A Hard Place—Cutting Crew (89) 76

Michael MacNEIL ▶ 2134 (3)	**1831**
Alive And Kicking—Simple Minds (85)	3897
Sanctify Yourself—Simple Minds (86)	1088
All The Things She Said—Simple Minds (86)	507
Terry MacNEIL ▶ 4873 (3)	**393**
Hello Hello—Sopwith "Camel" (66)	*746*
Postcard From Jamaica—Sopwith "Camel" (67)	36
Hello, Hello—Claudine Longet (67)	*4.7*
—Warner MacPherson see: Warner McPHERSON	
Fred Aylor MacRAE [Johnny MacRae] ▶ 7530 (2)	**91**
Little Eeefin Annie—Joe Perkins (63)	154
You're Just About To Lose Your Clown—Ray Charles (66)	13
—Johnny MacRae see: Fred Aylor MacRAE	
Joe MACRE ▶ 10445 (2)	**8.4**
Reggae Rock 'N Roll—B. E. Taylor Group (85)	22
Karen—B. E. Taylor Group (86)	3.1
—Gonzalvo Macrillo see: Junie McCREE	
John MADARA [John L. Madora] ▶ 411 (23)	**9670**
At The Hop—Danny & The Juniors (57)	*8260*
You Don't Own Me—Lesley Gore (63)	5712
1-2-3—Len Barry (65)	*5700*
The Fly—Chubby Checker (61)	2626
Like A Baby—Len Barry (65)	1065
The Boy Next Door—Secrets (63)	798
The Dawn Of Correction—Spokesmen (65)	608
Birthday Party—Pixies Three (63)	455
Pop Pop Pop-Pie—Sherrys (62)	435
442 Glenwood Avenue—Pixies Three (64)	344
Hey You! Little Boo-Ga-Loo—Chubby Checker (66)	187
Dottie—Danny And The Juniors (58)	180
One, Two, Three—Ramsey Lewis (67)	*131*
At The Hop—Jive Bunny And The Mastermixers (89)	*80*
It's That Time Of The Year—Len Barry (66)	64
At The Hop—Nick Todd (57)	*54*
Cold Cold Winter—Pixies Three (63)	45
Lip Sync (To The Tongue Twisters)—Len Barry (65)	36
Dancin' The Strand—Maureen Gray (62)	33
Oo-La-La-Limbo—Danny & The Juniors (63)	16
Doin' The Continental Walk—Danny & The Juniors (62)	3.6
At The Shore—Johnny Caswell (63)	3.1
Slop Time—Sherrys (63)	1.8
Edward MADDEN ▶ 4201 (5) HOF	**565**
Hula Love—Buddy Knox with The Rhythm Orchids (57)	1598
By The Light Of The Silvery Moon—Jimmy Bowen With The Rhythm Orchids (58)	398
Moonlight Bay—Drifters (58)	*199*
Moonlight Bay—Joe Leahy & His Orchestra (58)	*0.0*
Moonlight Bay—Jimmie Haskell & His Orchestra (58)	*0.0*
John MADDEN ▶ 11647 (1)	**0.9**
Down Where The Winds Blow (Chilly Winds)—Serendipity Singers (64)	2.6
—Chauki Maddi see: Tito MADI	
James MADDOX ▶ 10997 (1)	**3.9**
Long Stroke—ADC Band (78)	24
Rose MADDOX ▶ 9855 (1)	**16**
I've Got Four Big Brothers (To Look After Me)—Four Lads & Cathy Johnson (55)	32
—Murphy Monroe Maddux Jr. see: Pee Wee MADDUX	
Pee Wee MADDUX [Murphy Monroe Maddux Jr.] ▶ 5610 (3)	**265**
What A Price—Fats Domino (61)	733
Nothing New (Same Old Thing)—Fats Domino (62)	52
Rockin' Bicycle—Fats Domino (61)	22
Frank MADER ▶ 9211 (1)	**29**
Many A Time—Steve Lawrence (58)	57
Bobby MADERA [Bobby Woodlen] ▶ 11418 (1)	**1.8**
Oh Me—Fields-Madera Orchestra (59)	5.4
Robert MADERIOS ▶ 11499 (1)	**1.4**
Nite Rock (Lonely Train)—Nite Rockers (58)	4.3
Tito MADI [Chauki Maddi] ▶ 6168 (3)	**198**
I Wish—Platters (58)	*322*
It's Raining Outside—Platters (58)	74
I Wish—Della Reese (58)	*0.0*
—Fred Madison see: Fred MENDELSOHN	

Lee MADISON ▶ 6774 (1)	**138**
Tears Keep On Falling—Jerry Vale (65)	138
—Madonna see: Madonna L. CICCONE	
—John L. Madora see: John MADARA	
Carl MADURI ▶ 5220 (2)	**323**
Hula Hoop Song—Georgia Gibbs (58)	*395*
Hula Hoop Song—Teresa Brewer (58)	*251*
Ron MAEL ▶ 5512 (4)	**276**
Cool Places—Sparks And Jane Wiedlin (83)	386
I Predict—Sparks (82)	106
Wonder Girl—Sparks (72)	24
Yes Or No—Go-Go's (84)	16
Russell MAEL ▶ 5711 (3)	**252**
Cool Places—Sparks And Jane Wiedlin (83)	386
I Predict—Sparks (82)	106
Yes Or No—Go-Go's (84)	16
Brian MAES ▶ 6806 (1)	**136**
Face The Music—RTZ (91)	271
—Richard Maes see: Tracy Lee ALEXANDER	
—Johnny Maestro see: John MASTRANGELO	
Rocky MAFFIT ▶ 5176 (1)	**331**
Try Again—Champaign (83)	992
Guy MAGENTA [Guy Freidline] ▶ 11295 (1)	**2.4**
Don't Tell Me Why (Pitie Senorita)—Tony Bennett with Percy Faith and His Orchestra (55)	7.1
Herb MAGIDSON ▶ 9872 (1) HOF	**16**
Gone With The Wind—Duprees Featuring Joey Vann (63)	31
Jacqueline MAGILL ▶ 4774 (2)	**418**
Mary Lou—Ronnie Hawkins and The Hawks (59)	832
Southern Love—Ronnie Hawkins and The Hawks (59)	7.2
Michel MAGNE ▶ 11328 (1)	**2.2**
Theme From Any Number Can Win—Jimmy Smith (63)	2.2
Clif MAGNESS ▶ 1743 (3)	**2378**
All I Need—Jack Wagner (84)	3171
Impulsive—Wilson Phillips (90)	2616
It's Gonna Be Special—Patti Austin (84)	25
Eaton MAGOON ▶ 8524 (1)	**47**
You Set My Heart To Music—Johnny Mathis (61)	47
Leo MAGUIRE ▶ 2709 (2)	**1258**
Don't Let The Sun Catch You Crying—Gerry And The Pacemakers (64)	2786
The Gypsy Rover—Highwaymen (61)	562
Taj MAHAL [Henry St. Claire Fredericks] ▶ 6911 (1)	**129**
Farther On Down The Road—Joe Simon (70)	259
Patsy MAHARAM ▶ 9500 (3)	**22**
"Kid" Santa Claus—Patsy (85)	*9.8*
"Kid" Santa Claus —Patsy (84)	*9.6*
"Kid" Santa Claus —Patsy (83)	*3.0*
Brent MAHER ▶ 9503 (1)	**22**
A Lesson In Leavin'—Dottie West (80)	45
—John Martin Maher see: Johnny MARR	
Lamar MAHONE ▶ 6639 (1)	**149**
Summertime—DJ Jazzy Jeff & The Fresh Prince (91)	1783
—Edward J. Mahoney see: Eddie MONEY	
Tony MAIDEN ▶ 2160 (2)	**1809**
Sweet Thing—Rufus Featuring Chaka Khan (75)	3041
At Midnight (My Love Will Lift You Up)—Rufus Featuring Chaka Khan (77)	577
Heiko MAILE ▶ 8547 (1)	**47**
The Great Commandment—Camouflage (88)	140
Richard MAINEGRA ▶ 3519 (4)	**801**
Separate Ways—Elvis Presley (72)	1102
Let's Give Adam And Eve Another Chance—Gary Puckett And The Union Gap (70)	446
Here's Some Love—Tanya Tucker (76)	30
Valerie—Cymarron (71)	13
Mike MAINIERI ▶ 2891 (2)	**1129**
Jesse—Carly Simon (80)	2247
You Know What To Do—Carly Simon (83)	25
—Sananda Maitreya see: Terence Trent D'ARBY	
Miriam MAKEBA ▶ 3465 (3)	**835**
Pata Pata—Miriam Makeba (67)	1428
Malayisha—Miriam Makeba (68)	159
The Click Song Number One—Cher (68)	41
Mauro MALAVASI ▶ 8392 (5)	**52**
Paradise—Change (81)	92
The Very Best In You—Change (82)	26

On The Beat—B. B. & Q Band (81)	12
Hold Tight—Change (81)	6.5
Searching—Change (80)	1.4
Frankie MALAVE ▶ 7401 (1)	**98**
Together Forever—Lisette Melendez (91)	295
Romany MALCO ▶ 10798 (1)	**5.3**
Skat Strut—M.C. Skat Kat And The Stray Mob (91)	16
Calum MALCOLM ▶ 10381 (1)	**9.2**
Shape Of Things To Come—Headboys (79)	37
Vlad MALECKAR ▶ 9533 (2)	**22**
Borrowed Dreams—Bobby Helms (58)	29
Yea, Yea—Kendall Sisters (58)	15
Gualtiero MALGONI ▶ 8324 (2)	**54**
That's The Way With Love—Piero Soffici (61)	*135*
That's The Way With Love—Don Costa And His Orchestra And Chorus (61)	*27*
Jody Cameron MALIS ▶ 6844 (1)	**133**
O Falling Star—Four Knights (58)	133
Norman MALKIN ▶ 3158 (9)	**979**
Hey Mr Banjo—Sunnysiders (55)	*1568*
Happy Jose (Ching-Ching)—Jack Ross (61)	*358*
Banjo Woogie—Ban-Joes (55)	*16*
Banjo Woogie—Sunnysiders (55)	*16*
Banjo Woogie—Georgie Shaw (55)	*16*
Hey, Mr. Banjo—Banjo Boys (55)	*0.0*
Hey, Mr. Banjo—Guy Lombardo & His Royal Canadians (55)	*0.0*
Hey, Mr. Banjo—Lawrence Welk & His Champagne Music (55)	*0.0*
Happy Jose (Ching-Ching)—Dave Appell and his Orchestra (62)	*0.0*
Gary MALLABER ▶ 7454 (1)	**95**
Cool Magic—Steve Miller Band (82)	190
Linda MALLAH ▶ 2620 (4)	**1317**
Make It Real—Jets (88)	2361
I Do You—Jets (87)	720
That's Why—Party (91)	288
Sendin' All My Love—Jets (88)	52
Wanda MALLETTE ▶ 3120 (1)	**999**
Lookin' For Love—Johnny Lee (80)	2996
Steven Christopher MALLON ▶ 9602 (1)	**21**
Drag My Bad Name Down—4 Of Us (90)	82
Lee MALLORY ▶ 11620 (1)	**1.0**
Just About The Same—Association (70)	4.8
David MALLOY ▶ 954 (11)	**4676**
I Love A Rainy Night—Eddie Rabbitt (80)	4947
Drivin' My Life Away—Eddie Rabbitt (80)	3070
Step By Step—Eddie Rabbitt (81)	2893
Love Will Turn You Around—Kenny Rogers (82)	1322
Suspicions—Eddie Rabbitt (79)	1079
Someone Could Lose A Heart Tonight—Eddie Rabbitt (81)	961
You Can't Run From Love—Eddie Rabbitt (83)	181
Loveline—Dr. Hook (82)	132
Gone Too Far—Eddie Rabbitt (80)	23
Love Gets Rough—Troy Newman (91)	9.4
Real Love—Dolly Parton (Duet With Kenny Rogers) (85)	6.7
Joseph E. MALLOY ▶ 2717 (6)	**1246**
Sincerely Yours—Sweet Sensation (89)	924
Hooked On You—Sweet Sensation (89)	*673*
Take It While It's Hot—Sweet Sensation (88)	265
Hooked On You—Sweet Sensation (87)	*152*
Never Let You Go—Sweet Sensation (88)	101
Biscuit's In The House—Biscuit (90)	34
Matt MALNECK ▶ 1902 (7)	**2134**
Shangri-La—Robert Maxwell, His Harp And Orchestra (64)	*1946*
Shangri La—Four Coins (57)	*1206*
Shangri-La—Vic Dana (64)	*878*
Goody Goody—Frankie Lymon (57)	*763*
Shangri-La—Lettermen (69)	*254*
Goody, Goody—Jane Grant (57)	*0.0*
Goody Goody—Ella Fitzgerald (57)	*0.0*
Dan MALONE ▶ 9986 (1)	**14**
Gimme Your Good Lovin'—Diving For Pearls (89)	29
Deadric MALONE [Don D. Robey] ▶ 358 (58)	**10672**
Share Your Love With Me—Aretha Franklin (69)	*1587*
Pledging My Love—Johnny Ace (55)	*1021*
Share Your Love With Me—Kenny Rogers (81)	*993*

Deadric MALONE [Don D. Robey] ▶ 358 (58) ***Continued***	**10672**
Ain't Nothing You Can Do—Bobby Bland (64)	914
Call On Me—Bobby Bland (63)	892
Gonzo—James Booker (60)	722
Turn On Your Love Light—Bobby Bland (61)	*708*
Ain't Doing Too Bad (Part 1)—Bobby Bland (64)	650
That's The Way Love Is—Bobby Bland (63)	640
Pledging My Love—Roy Hamilton (58)	*609*
Share Your Love With Me—Bobby Bland (64)	*534*
This Time I'm Gone For Good—Bobby Blue Bland (73)	500
Rockin' In The Same Old Boat—Bobby Bland (68)	392
Ace Of Spade—O.V. Wright (70)	379
I Pity The Fool—Bobby Bland (61)	*365*
These Hands (Small But Mighty)—Bobby Bland (65)	363
Annie Get Your Yo-Yo—Little Junior Parker (62)	356
Yield Not To Temptation—Bobby Bland (62)	283
Blind Man—Bobby Bland (64)	*282*
Don't Cry No More—Bobby Bland (61)	245
Cry Cry Cry—Bobby Bland (60)	240
Good Time Charlie—Bobby Bland (66)	227
Blind Man—Little Milton (64)	*226*
Pledging My Love—Johnny Tillotson (60)	*221*
You're Gonna Make Me Cry—O.V. Wright (65)	205
Eight Men, Four Women—O.V. Wright (67)	203
Farther Up The Road— Bobby "Blue" Bland, Bill Harvey Orchestra (57)	198
Do What You Set Out To Do—Bobby Bland (72)	189
Sometimes You Gotta Cry A Little—Bobby Bland (63)	186
Just To Hold My Hand—Clyde McPhatter (57)	170
Pledging My Love—Teresa Brewer (55)	*160*
Turn On Your Love Light—Oscar Toney, Jr. (67)	*156*
Turn On Your Love Light—Human Beinz (68)	*141*
Think—Jimmy McCracklin (65)	127
Turn On Your Love Light—Bill Black's Combo (68)	*103*
If You've Got A Heart—Bobby Bland (70)	99
To Share Your Love—Fantastic Four (67)	*63*
I Pity The Fool—Ann Peebles (71)	*53*
A Thousand Cups Of Happiness—Joe Hinton (64)	37
You Know It Ain't Right—Joe Hinton (63)	36
Gotta Get To Know You—Bobby Bland (69)	25
If Love Ruled The World—Bobby Bland (70)	24
My Answer—Jimmy McCracklin (66)	17
Ain't That Loving You—Bobby Bland (62)	13
The Feeling Is Gone—Bobby Bland (63)	11
Ain't No Telling—Bobby Bland (65)	6.9
Better To Give Than Receive—Joe Hinton (63)	5.8
Hold Me Tenderly—Bobby Bland (60)	4.9
Turn On Your Love Light—Jerry Lee Lewis (72)	*4.6*
As The Years Go Passing By—Albert King (69)	3.4
I Can't Stop Singing—Bobby Bland (64)	1.3
Dust Got In Daddy's Eyes—Bobby Bland (65)	0.9
Lead Me On—Bobby Bland (60)	0.8
Pledging My Love—Four Lads (55)	*0.0*
Pledging My Love—Tommy Mara (55)	*0.0*
Pledging My Love—Jesse Belvin (58)	*0.0*
Pledging My Love—Sanford Clark (60)	*0.0*
Pledging My Love—Ronnie Gaylord (55)	*0.0*
George MALONE ▶ 3528 (3)	**797**
Book Of Love—Monotones (58)	*2045*
Book Of Love—Raindrops (64)	*259*
Book of Love—Nino & the Ebb Tides (61)	*88*
Johnnie MALONE ▶ 1561 (3)	**2717**
Please Love Me Forever—Bobby Vinton (67)	*3277*
Please Love Me Forever— Cathy Jean And The Roommates (61)	*2128*
Please Love Me Forever—Tommy Edwards (58)	*29*
Kurt MALOO [Kurt Meier] ▶ 4616 (1)	**450**
The Captain Of Her Heart—Double (86)	901
Lynn MALSBY ▶ 1719 (1)	**2434**
I Miss You—Klymaxx (85)	2434
Tony MALTESE ▶ 8562 (1)	**46**
Echo—Emotions (1) (62)	278
—Mamared see: Anna CANTU	
—Jerry Mamberg see: Jake HOOKER	
—Steve Mancha see: Clyde WILSON	
Melissa MANCHESTER ▶ 1340 (10)	**3312**
Whenever I Call You "Friend"—Kenny Loggins (78)	2897
Midnight Blue—Melissa Manchester (75)	2399
Just Too Many People—Melissa Manchester (75)	632
Just You And I—Melissa Manchester (76)	346

Lovers After All— Melissa Manchester And Peabo Bryson (81)	149
Mathematics—Melissa Manchester (85)	70
Better Days—Melissa Manchester (76)	54
Come In From The Rain—Captain & Tennille (77)	54
Party Music—Pat Lundi (75)	30
Thief Of Hearts—Melissa Manchester (84)	24
Henry MANCINI [Enrico Nicola Mancini] ▶ 275 (45) HOF	**12605**
Moon River— Henry Mancini, His Orchestra And Chorus (61)	*3649*
Moon River—Jerry Butler (61)	*3029*
Peter Gunn—Ray Anthony (58)	*2546*
Days of Wine And Roses— Henry Mancini His Orchestra & Chorus (63)	*1363*
Dear Heart—Andy Williams (64)	*1324*
Dear Heart—Jack Jones (64)	*1154*
Mr. Lucky—Henry Mancini And His Orchestra (60)	*1007*
Days Of Wine And Roses—Andy Williams (63)	*942*
Peter Gunn—Duane Eddy His "Twangy" Guitar And The Rebels (60)	*748*
Charade— Henry Mancini And His Orchestra and Chorus (63)	*631*
Baby Elephant Walk— Lawrence Welk And His Orchestra (62)	*600*
(I Love You) Don't You Forget It—Perry Como (63)	521
The Pink Panther Theme— Henry Mancini And His Orchestra (64)	465
Charade—Sammy Kaye And His Orchestra (64)	*443*
Peter Gunn—Art Of Noise featuring Duane Eddy (86)	*267*
In The Arms Of Love—Andy Williams (66)	249
Dear Heart— Henry Mancini's Orchestra And Chorus (64)	*243*
Fallout—Henry Mancini And His Orchestra (59)	139
Sweetheart Tree—Johnny Mathis (65)	*111*
Theme From "Hatari!"— Henry Mancini And His Orchestra (62)	*85*
Send A Little Love My Way—Anne Murray (73)	67
Theme from The Great Imposter— Henry Mancini And His Orchestra (61)	*47*
Sweetheart Tree—Henry Mancini & His Orchestra (65)	*43*
Baby Elephant Walk—Miniature Men (62)	*30*
Moonlight Sonata— Henry Mancini And His Orchestra (69)	26
Peter Gunn—Deodato (76)	*20*
Banzai Pipeline— Henry Mancini And His Orchestra (63)	11
All His Children—Charley Pride/Henry Mancini (72)	9.5
Toy Tiger—Les Baxter & His Orchestra (55)	*3.8*
Toy Tiger—Johnny Long & His Orchestra (55)	*3.8*
Toy Tiger—Ralph Marterie & His Orchestra (55)	*3.8*
Toy Tiger—Victor Young And His Singing Strings (55)	*3.8*
A Shot In The Dark— Henry Mancini And His Orchestra (64)	3.8
Walkin' to Mother's— Ray Anthony and his Orchestra (59)	1.9
Charade—Andy Williams (64)	*0.5*
Charade—Adam Wade (63)	*0.0*
Charade—Four Freshmen (63)	*0.0*
Mr. Lucky—Georgie Auld (60)	*0.0*
Moon River—Jean Thomas (62)	*0.0*
Moon River—Fuller Brothers (61)	*0.0*
Great Imposter—Piltdown Men (61)	*0.0*
Baby Elephant Walk—Kai Winding (62)	*0.0*
Theme From Hatari—Roger Williams (62)	*0.0*
Days Of Wine And Roses—Pat Boone (63)	*0.0*
Peter Gunn Theme— Henry Mancini And His Orchestra (59)	*0.0*
Tony MANCUSO ▶ 9667 (1)	**19**
Ballad Of A Girl And Boy—Graduates (59)	77
Fred MANDEL ▶ 6718 (1)	**142**
Wrap Her Up—Elton John (85)	852
Johnny MANDEL ▶ 5733 (3) HOF	**249**
Song From M*A*S*H—Al DeLory (70)	224
The Shadow Of Your Smile—Boots Randolph (66)	*39*
Love Theme From "The Sandpiper" (The Shadow Of Your Smile)—Tony Bennett (65)	*10*
Julie MANDEL ▶ 7629 (1)	**84**
Back In My Arms—Nat "King" Cole (57)	168
Mel MANDEL ▶ 9968 (1)	**14**
In My Father's Footsteps—Terry Jacks (76)	29
Jerry MANFREDI ▶ 10034 (1)	**14**

I Do Believe In You—Pages (79)	55
John D. MANGIAGLI ▶ 10636 (1)	**6.6**
(You Got) The Gamma Goochee—Kingsmen (65)	6.6
Cayet MANGIARACINA ▶ 2656 (2)	**1290**
Hello Mary Lou—Ricky Nelson (61)	2471
Mary, Mary Lou—Bill Haley & His Comets (57)	55
Chuck MANGIONE ▶ 1094 (5)	**4031**
Feels So Good—Chuck Mangione (78)	2926
Give It All You Got—Chuck Mangione (80)	923
Hill Where The Lord Hides—Chuck Mangione (71)	166
Land Of Make Believe—Chuck Mangione (77)	11
Chase The Clouds Away—Chuck Mangione (75)	4.8
Mark MANGOLD ▶ 3480 (5)	**823**
I Found Someone—Cher (87)	*1409*
(Call Me) When The Spirit Moves You—Touch (80)	76
Don't You Know What Love Is—Touch (81)	53
I Found Someone—Laura Branigan (86)	*43*
Fool's Game—Michael Bolton (83)	20
—Anna Mangravito see: Anna VITO	
James MANGRUM [Jim Dandy] ▶ 11556 (1)	**1.2**
Strong Enough To Be Gentle—Black Oak Arkansas (76)	8.4
Michael MANI ▶ 10484 (1)	**8.0**
Information—Eric Martin (85)	32
Robert MANIGAULT ▶ 4300 (1)	**530**
Troglodyte (Cave Man)—Jimmy Castor Bunch (72)	3177
Alex MANIGO ▶ 5217 (1)	**324**
Lover's Island—Blue Jays (61)	647
—Pedro Manilla see: Angelo PICCIONI	
—Pedro Manilla see: MANTOVANI	
Barry MANILOW [Barry Alan Pincus] ▶ 1010 (13) HOF	**4394**
Could It Be Magic—Barry Manilow (75)	*2240*
Copacabana (At The Copa)—Barry Manilow (78)	1800
It's A Miracle—Barry Manilow (75)	1361
I Made It Through The Rain—Barry Manilow (80)	1325
Even Now—Barry Manilow (78)	813
This One's For You—Barry Manilow (76)	608
Some Kind Of Friend—Barry Manilow (83)	602
Daybreak—Barry Manilow (77)	595
Street Singin'—Lady Flash (76)	532
In The Mood—Bette Midler (74)	*323*
Could It Be Magic—Donna Summer (76)	*102*
I'm Your Man—Barry Manilow (86)	60
Hey Mambo—Barry Manilow with Kid Creole And The Coconuts (88)	6.2
Mike MANISCALCO ▶ 7535 (2)	**90**
Together—Illusion (69)	240
How Does It Feel—Illusion (69)	31
Sid MANKER ▶ 1016 (4)	**4375**
Raunchy—Bill Justis (57)	*5369*
Raunchy—Ernie Freeman (57)	*2380*
Raunchy—Billy Vaughn and His Orchestra (57)	*999*
Raunchy—Muvva "Guitar" Hubbard (57)	*0.0*
Earle MANKEY ▶ 9224 (1)	**28**
The Happy Girls—Helen Reddy (77)	113
Charles MANLEY ▶ 10436 (1)	**8.5**
(Mama Come Quick, And Bring Your) Lickin' Stick— George Torrence & The Naturals (68)	17
Aimee MANN ▶ 2782 (6)	**1199**
Voices Carry—'til tuesday (85)	1719
What About Love—'til tuesday (86)	553
Coming Up Close—'Til Tuesday (87)	181
Looking Over My Shoulder—til tuesday (85)	115
Love In A Vacuum—'til tuesday (85)	12
(Believed You Were) Lucky—'Til Tuesday (89)	5.7
Andrew MANN [Andrew Ramsbottom] ▶ 4452 (2)	**492**
The Promise—When In Rome (88)	1410
Heaven Knows—When In Rome (89)	65
Barry MANN [Barry Imberman] ▶ 30 (104) HOF	**50481**
You've Lost That Lovin' Feelin'— Righteous Brothers (64)	*9450*
(You're My) Soul And Inspiration— Righteous Brothers (66)	*7442*
Don't Know Much—Linda Ronstadt (89)	*4540*
Sometimes When We Touch—Dan Hill (77)	4251
Patches—Dickey Lee (62)	4183
Kicks—Paul Revere And The Raiders Featuring Mark Lindsay (66)	4107

Barry MANN [Barry Imberman] ► 30 (104) HOF *Continued* — **50481**

Never Gonna Let You Go—Sergio Mendes (83)	3746
I Love How You Love Me—Bobby Vinton (68)	*3635*
Blame It On The Bossa Nova—Eydie Gorme (63)	3142
Here You Come Again—Dolly Parton (77)	2755
Somewhere Out There— Linda Ronstadt And James Ingram (86)	2590
I Love How You Love Me—Paris Sisters (61)	*2552*
My Dad—Paul Petersen (62)	2461
Who Put The Bomp (In The Bomp, Bomp, Bomp)— Barry Mann (61)	2389
On Broadway—George Benson (78)	*1964*
Hungry—Paul Revere And The Raiders Featuring Mark Lindsay (66)	1931
I'm Gonna Be Strong—Gene Pitney (64)	1883
You've Lost That Lovin' Feeling— Daryl Hall & John Oates (80)	*1839*
I Just Can't Help Believing—B.J. Thomas (70)	1786
Footsteps—Steve Lawrence (60)	1685
Uptown—Crystals (62)	1673
Walkin' In The Rain—Jay And The Americans (69)	*1583*
Just Once— Quincy Jones Featuring James Ingram (81)	1525
Rock And Roll Lullaby—B.J. Thomas (72)	1491
We Gotta Get Out Of This Place—Animals (65)	1474
On Broadway—Drifters (63)	*1347*
You've Lost That Lovin' Feeling— Dionne Warwick (69)	*1346*
Bless You—Tony Orlando (61)	1332
He's Sure The Boy I Love—Crystals (62)	1298
She Say (Oom Dooby Doom)—Diamonds (59)	1292
Shape Of Things To Come— Max Frost And The Troopers (68)	1289
I'll Never Dance Again—Bobby Rydell (62)	1211
Conscience—James Darren (62)	1112
It's Getting Better—Mama Cass (69)	1101
How Much Love—Leo Sayer (77)	1081
Come Back Silly Girl—Lettermen (62)	1027
Magic Town—Vogues (66)	1013
Saturday Night At The Movies—Drifters (64)	974
The Grass Is Greener—Brenda Lee (63)	899
Walking In The Rain—Ronettes (64)	*887*
Only In America—Jay & The Americans (63)	804
I'll Take You Home—Drifters (63)	758
Make Your Own Kind Of Music— Mama Cass Elliot (69)	*735*
Don't Be Afraid, Little Darlin'— Steve Lawrence (63)	735
Brown Eyed Woman—Bill Medley (68)	662
Looking Through The Eyes Of Love—Gene Pitney (65)	*646*
Johnny Loves Me—Shelley Fabares (62)	624
Way Of A Clown—Teddy Randazzo (60)	617
Looking Through The Eyes Of Love—Partridge Family Starring Shirley Jones & Featuring David Cassidy (72)	*611*
New World Coming—Mama Cass Elliot (70)	562
Proud—Johnny Crawford (62)	547
If A Woman Answers (Hang Up The Phone)— Leroy Van Dyke (62)	496
When You Get Right Down To It—Delfonics (70)	*465*
Home Of The Brave—Jody Miller (65)	*446*
(You're My) Soul And Inspiration— Donny & Marie (77)	*407*
I Want You To Meet My Baby—Eydie Gorme (64)	389
The Last Time I Made Love— Joyce Kennedy & Jeffrey Osborne (84)	369
So Long Dixie—Blood, Sweat & Tears (72)	360
Sweet Little You—Neil Sedaka (61)	354
Heart—Kenny Chandler (63)	*340*
Mary's Little Lamb—James Darren (62)	330
We're Going All The Way—Jeffrey Osborne (84)	325
Baby Come And Get It—Pointer Sisters (85)	323
Peace Brother Peace—Bill Medley (68)	316
Don't Make My Baby Blue—Frankie Laine (63)	305
Born To Be Together— Ronettes Featuring Veronica (65)	252
You've Lost That Lovin' Feelin'— Roberta Flack & Donny Hathaway (71)	*248*
It's Gonna Be Fine—Glenn Yarbrough (65)	234
There's No Easy Way—James Ingram (84)	195
I Could Have Loved You So Well—Ray Peterson (61)	192
A Girl Has To Know—G-Clefs (62)	174
Amy—Paul Petersen (63)	164
Right Here And Now—Bill Medley (82)	158
Olympia—Sergio Mendes (84)	145
Come On Over To My Place—Drifters (65)	144
Where Have You Been (All My Life)— Arthur Alexander (62)	130
Heart! (I Hear You Beating)—Wayne Newton (63)	*116*
Mamacita—Grass Roots (75)	101
It's A Happening World—Tokens (67)	96
Cindy's Gonna Cry—Johnny Crawford (63)	77
Angelica—Oliver (70)	*76*
Let Me Be The One—Peaches & Herb (69)	*68*
Home Of The Brave—Bonnie And The Treasures (65)	*67*
Time Machine—Danté And The Evergreens (60)	65
Little Miss U.S.A.—Barry Mann (61)	61
All I Need To Know (Don't Know Much)— Bette Midler (83)	*59*
Young As We Are—Sal Mineo (59)	58
Heart To Heart—Errol Sober (79)	56
Feelings—Barry Mann (70)	53
The Princess And The Punk—Barry Mann (76)	43
Kissin' And Twistin'—Fabian (60)	40
Hold On To The Night—Hotel (79)	39
It's Not Easy—Will-O-Bees (68)	33
Don't Destroy Me—Crash Craddock (59)	31
When You Get Right Down To It—Ronnie Dyson (71)	*30*
Let Me Be The One—Paris Sisters (62)	*26*
Don't Know Much—Bill Medley (81)	*22*
You've Lost That Lovin' Feelin'— Long John Baldry & Kathi MacDonald (79)	*16*
Girls, Girls, Girls—Steve Lawrence (60)	14
When You Get Right Down To It—Barry Mann (72)	*12*
Let The Song Last Forever—Dan Hill (78)	7.4
Talk To Me Baby—Barry Mann (64)	6.2
Make Your Own Kind Of Music—Barbra Streisand (72)	*5.7*
Angelica—Barry Mann (66)	*3.4*

Charles MANN ► 4796 (1) — **412**

I Like To Live The Love—B.B. King (73)	824

Dave MANN [David Freedman, David A. Mann] ► 961 (6) — **4660**

There! I've Said It Again—Bobby Vinton (63)	*8758*
Don't Go To Strangers—Etta Jones (60)	*486*
There I've Said It Again—Sam Cooke (59)	*149*
Don't Go To Strangers— Vaughn Monroe with Orchestra And Chorus (56)	*107*
Southern Cross—Ames Brothers (55)	17
Don't Go To Strangers—Andy Williams (60)	*0.0*

—David A. Mann see: Dave MANN

Herbie MANN [Herbert Jay Solomon] ► 5939 (2) — **225**

Memphis Underground—Herbie Mann (69)	223
It's A Funky Thing-Right On (Part 1)— Herbie Mann (69)	5.2

Jeff MANN [Jeff Feldman] ► 8969 (1) — **35**

One Way Love—TKA (86)	70

Johnny MANN ► 10212 (1) — **11**

Texas Lady—Les Paul and Mary Ford (55)	22

—John R. Mann see: Jim KIRK

Kal MANN [Kalman Cohen, Cal Rotherman, Anthony September, Jon Sheldon] ► 26 (89) — **52570**

Limbo Rock—Chubby Checker (62)	*9002*
Mashed Potato Time—Dee Dee Sharp (62)	8768
(Let Me Be Your) Teddy Bear—Elvis Presley (57)	*7775*
Bristol Stomp—Dovells (61)	6389
The Wah-Watusi—Orlons (62)	5536
Wild One—Bobby Rydell (60)	4945
Butterfly—Andy Williams (57)	*4791*
Slow Twistin'—Chubby Checker (62)	4455
You Can't Sit Down—Dovells (63)	*3787*
Let's Twist Again—Chubby Checker (61)	*3771*
South Street—Orlons (63)	3753
We Got Love—Bobby Rydell (59)	3621
Don't Hang Up—Orlons (62)	3423
Swingin' School—Bobby Rydell (60)	2224
Butterfly—Charlie Gracie (57)	*2197*
Ride!—Dee Dee Sharp (62)	2161
Popeye The Hitchhiker—Chubby Checker (62)	1843
Good Time Baby—Bobby Rydell (61)	1828
Gravy (For My Mashed Potatoes)—Dee Dee Sharp (62)	1715
Loddy Lo—Chubby Checker (63)	1447
Do The Bird—Dee Dee Sharp (63)	1407
The Cha-Cha-Cha—Bobby Rydell (62)	1405
Kissin' Time—Bobby Rydell (59)	1393
Remember You're Mine—Pat Boone (57)	1255
Dancin' Party—Chubby Checker (62)	1242
Let's Limbo Some More—Chubby Checker (63)	1110
Birdland—Chubby Checker (63)	1076
Mexican Hat Rock—Applejacks (S) (58)	961
Ding A Ling—Bobby Rydell (60)	936
Twenty Miles—Chubby Checker (63)	929
Ninety Nine Ways—Tab Hunter (57)	*920*
Dance The Mess Around—Chubby Checker (61)	912
Hey, Bobba Needle—Chubby Checker (64)	888
Hully Gully Baby—Dovells (62)	838
Crossfire!—Orlons (63)	821
The Fish—Bobby Rydell (61)	799
I Wanna Thank You—Bobby Rydell (61)	781
Butterfly Baby—Bobby Rydell (63)	757
Fabulous—Charlie Gracie (57)	*709*
Dinner With Drac (Pt. 1)—John Zacherle (58)	678
Wildwood Days—Bobby Rydell (63)	674
Twist It Up—Chubby Checker (63)	596
Wild!—Dee Dee Sharp (63)	555
Twistin' USA—Danny & The Juniors (60)	*553*
Do The New Continental—Dovells (62)	542
Back To School Again— Timmie "Oh Yeah" Rogers (57)	476
Rocka Conga—Applejacks (S) (58)	423
Class—Chubby Checker (59)	387
Rock Me In The Cradle Of Love—Dee Dee Sharp (63)	350
Betty In Bermudas—Dovells (63)	345
Take Me Back To Toyland—Nat "King" Cole (55)	324
Bon-Doo-Wah—Orlons (63)	289
Surf Party—Chubby Checker (63)	241
She Wants T' Swim—Chubby Checker (64)	241
Nine More Miles (The "Faster-Faster" Song)— Georgie Young And The Rockin' Bocs (58)	235
The Popeye Waddle—Don Covay (62)	223
You're The Greatest—Billy Scott (57)	*181*
A Crazy Little Palace (That's My Home)— Billy Williams Quartet (56)	172
Lose Her—Bobby Rydell (62)	140
Party Time—Sal Mineo (57)	112
Just Like In The Movies—Upbeats (58)	102
Rules Of Love—Orlons (64)	97
Follow Your Heart—Four Coins (57)	94
Cherié—Bobby Rydell (61)	89
The Greatest Thing—Georgia Gibbs (56)	85
Teach Me To Twist— Bobby Rydell - Chubby Checker (62)	84
Butterfly—Bob Carroll (57)	*81*
Let's Twist Again— Jive Bunny And The Mastermixers (89)	*80*
Fabulous—Steve Lawrence (57)	*80*
The Door To Paradise—Bobby Rydell (61)	72
Kissin' Time—Kiss (74)	56
Twistin' U.S.A.—Chubby Checker (61)	*46*
Where Did I Go Wrong—Dee Dee Sharp (64)	39
I'll Be True—Orlons (61)	38
Groovy Tonight—Bobby Rydell (60)	23
(Let Me Be Your) Teddy Bear—Elvis Presley (82)	*23*
La Paloma Twist—Chubby Checker (62)	23
Mother, Please!—Jo Ann Campbell (63)	20
I'm Still A King To You—Don Cherry (56)	17
Lets Twist Again— Jive Bunny & The Mastermixers (90)	*6.7*
Stop Monkeyin' Aroun'—Dovells (63)	6.3
Wanderin' Eyes—Charlie Gracie (57)	5.7
Beat—Billy May And His Orchestra (56)	5.0
Jingle Bells Imitations— Bobby Rydell - Chubby Checker (61)	*3.3*
Mexican Hat Twist—Applejacks (S) (61)	2.8
Gee, It's Wonderful—Bobby Rydell (62)	2.2
Butterfly—Billy Williams (57)	*0.0*
Ninety-Nine Ways—Charlie Gracie (57)	*0.0*
You're The Greatest—Valerie Carr (57)	*0.0*

Lois MANN [Sydney Nathan] ► 9317 (3) — **26**

Signed, Sealed, And Delivered— James Brown And The Famous Flames (63)	*46*
Signed, Sealed And Delivered—Rusty Draper (61)	*5.4*
I'll Sail My Ship Alone— Jerry Lee Lewis And His Pumping Piano (59)	3.2

Lorene MANN ► 3431 (2) — **850**

Don't Go Near The Indians—Rex Allen (62)	*732*
Don't Go Near The Eskimos—Ben Colder (62)	*235*

Nick MANN ▶ 8669 (1)	**43**
Remote Control—Reddings (80)	130
Paul MANN [Paul Wechselmann] ▶ 5364 (4)	**300**
The Finger Of Suspicion—Dickie Valentine With The Stargazers (55)	*599*
The Finger Of Suspicion—Dolores Gray (55)	*0.0*
The Finger Of Suspicion Points At You—Jane Froman (55)	*0.0*
The Finger Of Suspicion—Eddy Howard & His Orchestra (55)	*0.0*
Steve MANN ▶ 8141 (1)	**60**
Anytime—McAuley Schenker Group (90)	120
Sy MANN ▶ 6063 (1)	**210**
Lullaby Of Love—Frank Gari (61)	629
—Gerry Manners see: Bill ANSON	
Dick MANNING [Samuel Medoff] ▶ 193 (53)	**16196**
Hot Diggity (Dog Ziggity Boom)—Perry Como (56)	5854
Allegheny Moon—Patti Page (56)	*5270*
Papa Loves Mambo—Perry Como (54)	4276
Secretly—Jimmie Rodgers (58)	*4105*
Hawaiian Wedding Song—Andy Williams (58)	3451
Fascination—Jane Morgan with the Troubadors (57)	*2924*
Morning Side Of The Mountain—Donny And Marie Osmond (74)	*1717*
Are You Really Mine—Jimmie Rodgers (58)	1540
O Dio Mio—Annette (60)	1390
Oh Oh I'm Falling In Love Again—Jimmie Rodgers (58)	1234
Johnny Jingo—Hayley Mills (62)	728
Moon Talk—Perry Como (58)	697
Mama Teach Me To Dance—Eydie Gorme (56)	*687*
Morning Side Of The Mountain—Tommy Edwards (59)	*606*
I'm Never Gonna Tell—Jimmie Rodgers (59)	568
Ivy Rose—Perry Como (57)	559
Don't Stay Away Too Long—Eddie Fisher (55)	490
Belonging To Someone—Patti Page (58)	482
La Plume De Ma Tante—Hugo & Luigi (59)	398
Make Me A Miracle—Jimmie Rodgers (58)	387
Fascination—Dick Jacobs And His Chorus And Orchestra (57)	*327*
Secretly—Lettermen (65)	*243*
(I Cried at) Laura's Wedding—Barbara Lynn (63)	184
You're Cheatin' Yourself (If You're Cheatin' On Me)—Frank Sinatra (57)	135
Santo Natale (Merry Christmas)—David Whitfield with Stanley Black And His Orchestra (54)	*129*
Mi Casa, Su Casa (My House Is Your House)—Perry Como (57)	115
I Was Hoping You'd Ask Me—Janice Harper (58)	111
Kiss Me And Kiss Me And Kiss Me (Tre Volte Baciami)—Perry Como (59)	111
You Understand Me—Sam Cooke (60)	*99*
Ha! Ha! Ha! (Chella Lla)—Kay Armen (57)	*72*
Daydreams—Art Mooney And His Orchestra (56)	68
Gotta Lotta Love—Steve Alaimo (63)	57
I Can't Tell A Waltz From A Tango—Patti Page (54)	57
Golly—Four Lads (57)	50
Thirteen Going On Fourteen—Crew-Cuts (56)	23
S'-All Right? S'-All Right!—Senor Wences (59)	16
Addio—Ames Brothers (54)	15
Fascination—Nat "King" Cole (57)	*15*
Do You Love Me Like You Kiss Me (Scapricciatiello)—McGuire Sisters (58)	12
Forget Her—Tony Bennett with Percy Faith and His Orchestra (56)	5.5
Lulu Had A Baby—Chico Holiday (59)	3.7
Fascination—Dinah Shore (57)	*1.9*
You Understand Me—Jimmie Rodgers (58)	*1.6*
Jilted—Teresa Brewer (54)	0.0
Torero—Julius La Rosa (58)	*0.0*
Torero—Andrews Sisters (58)	*0.0*
Santo Natale—Ronnie Gaylord (54)	*0.0*
A Carnival In Venice—Mills Brothers (54)	0.0
Ha! Ha! Ha! ("Che Lla La!")—Lou Monte (57)	*0.0*
Allegheny Moon—Grady Martin & His Slew Foot Five (56)	*0.0*
Mama, Teach Me To Dance—Bobby Madera & His Orchestra (56)	*0.0*
Gilly Gilly Ossenfeffer Katzenellen Bogen By The Sea—Four Lads (54)	0.0
HA HA HA (Chella Lla)—Sammy Kaye & His "Swing And Sway" Orchestra (57)	*0.0*
Martin MANNING ▶ 7271 (1)	**106**
Big River—Buddy Brennan Quartet (59)	106

Sam MANNING ▶ 7946 (1)	**68**
Shake Shake Sonora—Lord Flea and His Calypsonians (57)	68
Dana MANNO ▶ 9891 (1)	**15**
Pull Up To The Bumper—Grace Jones (81)	62
Lena M. MANNS ▶ 7508 (1)	**91**
I'm Gonna Hold On Long As I Can—Marvelettes (69)	183
—Lucylle Manns see: Roberta TWAIN	
—Leroy Mannuel see: Leroy EMMANUEL	
Jim MANOLIDES ▶ 11349 (2)	**2.1**
Straight Flush—Frantics (59)	9.1
Fog Cutter—Frantics (59)	3.1
Alan MANSFIELD ▶ 7570 (1)	**88**
You're Amazing—Robert Palmer (90)	439
—Frere Manston see: Marty WILDE	
MANTOVANI [Annunzio Paolo Mantovani, Paul Remy, Pedro Manilla, Tulio Trapani] ▶ 1576 (4)	**2684**
Cara, Mia—Jay & The Americans (65)	*3711*
Cara Mia—David Whitfield with Mantovani And His Orchestra (54)	*1531*
Lazy Gondolier—Mantovani And His Orchestra (55)	*188*
Lazy Gondolier—Lawrence Welk & His Champagne Music (55)	*0.0*
—Kurtis Mantronik see: Kurtis EL KHALEEL	
Nancie MANTZ ▶ 2885 (4)	**1132**
I Had Too Much To Dream (Last Night)—Electric Prunes (66)	1627
Green Light—American Breed (68)	587
Father Sebastian—Ramblers (2) (64)	47
Dr. Do-Good—Electric Prunes (67)	2.4
Bobby MANUEL ▶ 8474 (2)	**49**
Dis-Gorilla (Part 1)—Rick Dees And His Cast Of Idiots (77)	91
My Main Man—Staple Singers (74)	74
Phil MANZANERA [Philip Geoffrey Targett-Adams] ▶ 10048 (1)	**13**
Over You—Roxy Music (80)	27
Armando MANZANERO ▶ 2677 (2)	**1278**
It's Impossible—Perry Como (70)	*2155*
It's Impossible—New Birth (71)	*400*
Ray MANZAREK ▶ 506 (18)	**8366**
Light My Fire—Doors (67)	*8461*
Hello, I Love You—Doors (68)	6496
Touch Me—Doors (68)	5980
Light My Fire—Jose Feliciano (68)	*4958*
Love Her Madly—Doors (71)	1978
People Are Strange—Doors (67)	1529
Riders On The Storm—Doors (71)	1436
Love Me Two Times—Doors (67)	731
The Unknown Soldier—Doors (68)	682
Wishful Sinful—Doors (69)	464
L.A. Woman—Billy Idol (90)	208
Tightrope Ride—Doors (71)	155
Light My Fire—Amii Stewart (79)	*51*
The Mosquito—Doors (72)	50
Roadhouse Blues—Doors (70)	38
Light My Fire—Rhetta Hughes (69)	*33*
Light My Fire—Doors (68)	*32*
Love Street—Doors (68)	9.0
Rob MANZOLI ▶ 2644 (1)	**1299**
I'm Too Sexy—Right Said Fred (91)	3898
Norman MAPP ▶ 7686 (2)	**81**
Rock And Stroll Room—Mickey & Sylvia (58)	79
I Worry About You—Joe Simon (68)	1.4
Dominic MARABETI ▶ 7546 (1)	**90**
Look Into My Eyes—George LaMond (90)	179
—Dee Marak see: Paul ANKA	
John MARASCALCO ▶ 811 (25)	**5429**
Good Golly Miss Molly—Mitch Ryder And The Detroit Wheels (66)	*2815*
Be My Guest—Fats Domino (59)	1844
Send Me Some Lovin'—Sam Cooke (63)	*1153*
Rip It Up—Little Richard (56)	*1068*
Goodnight My Love—Paul Anka (68)	*813*
Good Golly Miss Molly—Little Richard (58)	*791*
Rip It Up—Bill Haley And His Comets (56)	*751*
Goodnight My Love—Fleetwoods (63)	*496*
Goodnight My Love Pleasant Dreams—McGuire Sisters (56)	*434*

Goodnight My Love (Pleasant Dreams)—Ray Peterson (59)	*311*
Good Golly Miss Molly—Swinging Blue Jeans (64)	*269*
Ready Teddy—Little Richard (56)	244
Bertha Lou—Clint Miller (57)	*138*
Send Me Some Lovin' (Peepin' and Hidin')—Little Richard (57)	*90*
Goodnight My Love—Ben E. King (66)	*81*
Heeby Jeebies—Little Richard (56)	18
Good Golly Miss Molly—Jive Bunny & The Mastermixers (90)	*6.7*
She's Got It—Little Richard (57)	5.0
Love Like A Fool—Georgettes (58)	*2.9*
Love Like A Fool—Fontane Sisters (58)	*2.9*
Bertha Lou—Johnny Faire (57)	*0.0*
Good Golly Miss Molly—Valiants (58)	*0.0*
Goodnight My Love, Pleasant Dreams—Earl Grant (56)	*0.0*
Goodnight My Love Pleasant Dreams—Jesse Belvin (56)	*0.0*
Goodnight My Love (Pleasant Dreams)—Mindy Carson (56)	*0.0*
Guido MARASCO ▶ 11152 (1)	**3.0**
Help For My Waiting—Dorians (71)	9.0
Rolf MARBOT [Friedel Albrecht Marcuse] ▶ 8656 (2)	**44**
Down By The Riverside—Les Compagnons De La Chanson (60)	*175*
Down By The Riverside (Qu'l Fait Bon Vivre)—Les Barclay (60)	*0.0*
Ernest MARBRAY ▶ 9338 (1)	**26**
Send My Baby Back—Freddie Hughes (68)	52
Gene MARCELLINO ▶ 6572 (1)	**155**
Whatever You Got, I Want—Jackson 5 (74)	465
Jerry MARCELLINO ▶ 4140 (4)	**582**
I Am Love—Jackson 5 (75)	1065
Get It Together—Jackson 5 (73)	729
Whatever You Got, I Want—Jackson 5 (74)	465
Sad Tomorrows—Trini Lopez (65)	30
Myrna MARCH ▶ 4282 (3)	**533**
I Do Take You—Three Degrees (70)	436
I Can Remember—James & Bobby Purify (68)	*283*
I Can Remember—Oliver (70)	*7.7*
Peggy MARCH [Margaret Annemarie Battavio, Little Peggy March] ▶ 7643 (1)	**83**
When The Rain Begins To Fall—Jermaine Jackson And Pia Zadora (85)	250
Donny MARCHAND ▶ 11102 (1)	**3.2**
Lady Lay—Wayne Newton (74)	13
Dante MARCHETTI ▶ 2205 (8)	**1745**
Fascination—Jane Morgan with the Troubadors (57)	*2924*
Fascination—Dick Jacobs And His Chorus And Orchestra (57)	*327*
Fascination—David Carroll Orch. And Chorus (57)	*111*
Fascination—Nat "King" Cole (57)	*15*
Fascination—Dinah Shore (57)	*1.9*
Fascination—Ethel Smith (57)	*0.0*
Fascination—Big Al Sears (57)	*0.0*
Fascination—Ray Ellis & His Gypsies (57)	*0.0*
Sano MARCO ▶ 7184 (1)	**111**
May I Never Love Again—Tony Bennett with Percy Faith and His Orchestra (55)	222
Bob MARCUCCI ▶ 570 (21)	**7572**
Why—Frankie Avalon (59)	*7611*
Dede Dinah—Frankie Avalon (57)	1252
I'll Wait For You—Frankie Avalon (58)	1197
With All My Heart—Jodie Sands (57)	*1183*
Why—Donny Osmond (72)	*1103*
Where Are You—Frankie Avalon (60)	784
You Are Mine—Frankie Avalon (62)	616
You Excite Me—Frankie Avalon (58)	296
Perfect Love—Frankie Avalon (60)	244
I Love My Girl—Hilltoppers (57)	*217*
What Happens Now—Mona Carol (56)	202
I Love My Girl—Cozy Morley (57)	*185*
The Puppet Song—Frankie Avalon (60)	167
Swingin' On A Rainbow—Frankie Avalon (59)	84
Will I Always Be Your Sweetheart—Mona Carol (56)	*41*
With All My Heart—Judy Scott (57)	*23*
Calypso Parakeet—Patty Brandon (57)	12
I'm Happy—Four Dates (58)	4.9
With All My Heart—Al Martino (65)	*2.8*
With All My Heart—Buddy Greco (57)	*0.0*
Will I Always Be Your Sweetheart—Kitty Kallen (56)	*0.0*

Bob MARCUS ▶ 11779 (2)	**0.0**
Patricia—Jerry Martin (58)	*0.0*
Patricia—Ray Peterson (58)	*0.0*
Larry MARCUS ▶ 3571 (1)	**782**
Written All Over Your Face—Rude Boys (91)	782
Sol MARCUS [Fred Stevens] ▶ 2433 (12)	**1490**
Don't Let Me Be Misunderstood— Santa Esmeralda Starring Larry Gomez (77)	*1226*
Don't Let Me Be Misunderstood—Animals (65)	*1016*
Till Then—Classics (2) (63)	909
Fabulous Character—Sarah Vaughan (56)	386
Lonely Man—Elvis Presley With The Jordanaires (61)	232
I Don't Want To Set The World On Fire— Somethin' Smith & The Redheads (58)	149
Goodbye Charlie—Patti Page (59)	83
You're All I Want For Christmas—Brook Benton (63)	41
Of This I'm Sure—Four Aces (55)	37
I Envy—Nat "King" Cole (54)	27
Thanks To The Fool—Brook Benton (62)	9.6
Don't Let Me Be Misunderstood—Nina Simone (65)	*0.0*
—Friedel Albrecht Marcuse see: Rolf MARBOT	
—Marcy Jo see: Marcy SOCKEL	
Arif MARDIN ▶ 10551 (1)	**7.3**
Tranquillo—Carly Simon (78)	22
Benny MARDONES ▶ 2866 (2)	**1146**
Into The Night—Benny Mardones (80)	*1652*
Into The Night—Benny Mardones (89)	*640*
Paul MARES ▶ 11446 (2)	**1.6**
Make Love To Me— Johnny Thunder & Ruby Winters (67)	*13*
Make Love To Me!—Jo Stafford (54)	*0.0*
Ernie MARESCA ▶ 172 (18)	**17423**
Runaround Sue—Dion (61)	*10242*
The Wanderer—Dion (61)	*5291*
Lovers Who Wander—Dion (62)	2550
Donna The Prima Donna—Dion (Di Muci) (63)	2208
Shout! Shout! (Knock Yourself Out)— Ernie Maresca (62)	1995
No One Knows—Dion and The Belmonts (58)	1013
Runaround Sue—Leif Garrett (77)	*949*
Come On Little Angel—Belmonts (62)	817
Child Of Clay—Jimmie Rodgers (67)	698
Runaround—Regents (61)	559
Whenever A Teenager Cries— Reparata And The Delrons (64)	506
Party Girl—Bernadette Carroll (64)	432
Hey Jean, Hey Dean—Dean And Jean (64)	362
Lover's Prayer—Dion and The Belmonts (59)	216
The Wanderer—Leif Garrett (78)	*182*
Runaround Sue—Four Preps (62)	*24*
Mary Jane—Ernie Maresca (62)	22
Runaround Sue—Jive Bunny & The Mastermixers (90)	*6.7*
—Guy Marfontaine see: Yves-Jacques LAVOT	
Mitch MARGO ▶ 3629 (6)	**760**
Tonight I Fell In Love—Tokens (61)	1434
I Hear Trumpets Blow—Tokens (66)	601
A Love So Fine—Chiffons (63)	466
Hear The Bells—Tokens (63)	148
When I Go To Sleep At Night—Tokens (61)	69
High On Love—Elliott Randall (77)	10
Phil MARGO ▶ 3650 (5)	**750**
Tonight I Fell In Love—Tokens (61)	1434
I Hear Trumpets Blow—Tokens (66)	601
A Love So Fine—Chiffons (63)	466
Hear The Bells—Tokens (63)	148
When I Go To Sleep At Night—Tokens (61)	69
Stuart MARGOLIN ▶ 7371 (1)	**100**
Day After Day (It's Slippin' Away)—Shango (69)	299
—Michael Jay Margules see: Michael JAY	
Ben MARGULIES ▶ 638 (3)	**6811**
Love Takes Time—Mariah Carey (90)	4682
Vision Of Love—Mariah Carey (90)	4507
Someday—Mariah Carey (91)	4433
—Norman Margulies see: Jerry RAGOVOY	
Detto MARIANO ▶ 9146 (1)	**30**
In Time—Engelbert Humperdinck (72)	121
Teena MARIE [Mary Christine Brockert] ▶ 1407 (5)	**3153**
Lovergirl—Teena Marie (84)	2474
I Need Your Lovin'—Teena Marie (80)	468
Square Biz—Teena Marie (81)	363
Ooo La La La—Teena Marie (88)	20
Jammin—Teena Marie (85)	19
Cheech MARIN ▶ 2178 (7)	**1784**
Earache My Eye (Featuring Alice Bowie)— Cheech & Chong (74)	1634
Basketball Jones Featuring Tyrone Shoelaces— Cheech & Chong (73)	*1097*
Sister Mary Elephant (Shudd-Up!)— Cheech & Chong (73)	765
Bloat On Featuring The Bloaters— Cheech & Chong (77)	*328*
Black Lassie (Featuring Johnny Stash)— Cheech & Chong (74)	262
Born In East L.A.—Cheech & Chong (85)	*256*
(How I Spent My Summer Vacation) Or A Day At The Beach With Pedro And Man - Pt I—Cheech & Chong (75)	184
—Terrence Richard Marinan see: Terry RICHARDS	
LeRoy MARINELL ▶ 5587 (1)	**268**
Werewolves Of London—Warren Zevon (78)	804
Marino MARINI ▶ 11228 (1)	**2.7**
Play Some Music For Broken Hearts—Don Cornell (58)	5.3
Frank MARINO ▶ 9708 (1)	**19**
A New Rock And Roll—Mahogany Rush (74)	19
—Rinaldo R. Marino see: Lennie MARTIN	
Jimmy MARINOS ▶ 2860 (4)	**1148**
Talking In Your Sleep—Romantics (83)	3966
What I Like About You—Michael Morales (89)	*543*
One In A Million—Romantics (84)	404
What I Like About You—Romantics (80)	*218*
Johnny MARIO ▶ 9803 (1)	**17**
Always You—Betty Madigan (54)	*67*
Eddie MARION ▶ 5561 (3)	**271**
Woman To Woman—Shirley Brown (74)	*767*
Don't Take My Kindness For Weakness— Soul Children (72)	46
Woman To Woman—Barbara Mandrell (78)	*12*
Jon MARK [Jon Mark Burchell, Jon Michael Burchell] ▶ 7469 (2)	**94**
Go Away From My World—Marianne Faithfull (65)	80
One Way Sunday—Mark-Almond (72)	13
—Spiros D. Markantonatos see: Spiro MARKS	
Larry MARKES ▶ 2692 (4)	**1269**
May You Always—McGuire Sisters (58)	1616
To A Sleeping Beauty—Jimmy Dean (62)	445
Like I Love You—Edd Byrnes And Friend (59)	392
I.O.U.—Jimmy Dean (76)	234
—Dewey Markham see: Pigmeat MARKHAM	
Pigmeat MARKHAM [Dewey Markham] ▶ 6509 (1)	**161**
Here Comes The Judge—Pigmeat Markham (68)	646
Biz MARKIE [Marcel Theo Hall] ▶ 2975 (1)	**1088**
Just A Friend—Biz Markie (90)	1088
Marty MARKIEWICZ ▶ 10358 (2)	**9.5**
Memories Of Days Gone By— Fred Parris & The Five Satins (82)	*4.8*
Memories Of Days Gone By— Fred Parris & The Five Satins (82)	*4.8*
Bob MARKLEY ▶ 6807 (1)	**135**
Smell Of Incense—Southwest F.O.B. (68)	271
Donald MARKOWITZ ▶ 2632 (1)	**1306**
(I've Had) The Time Of My Life— Bill Medley And Jennifer Warnes (87)	3918
Richard MARKOWITZ ▶ 11293 (1)	**2.4**
The Rebel - Johnny Yuma—Johnny Cash (61)	4.8
—David Marks see: Spiro MARKS	
Gerald MARKS ▶ 8600 (1)	**45**
It's A Wonderful Thing To Be Loved—Gogi Grant (57)	90
Guy MARKS [Mario Scarpa] ▶ 4792 (1)	**413**
Loving You Has Made Me Bananas—Guy Marks (68)	413
Howard MARKS ▶ 7854 (1)	**72**
Paper Love—Jack Gandy Trio (55)	72
Johnny MARKS ▶ 2517 (22) HOF	**1421**
Rockin' Around The Christmas Tree—Brenda Lee (60)	*452*
Rudolph The Red Nosed Reindeer— David Seville And The Chipmunks (60)	*215*
Free—Tommy Leonetti (56)	*144*
Anyone Can Move A Mountain—Don Anthony (70)	130
Rockin' Around The Christmas Tree—Brenda Lee (62)	*116*
Rockin' Around The Christmas Tree—Brenda Lee (61)	*108*
Rudolph The Red Nosed Reindeer—Melodeers (60)	*88*
Rudolph The Red Nosed Reindeer— David Seville And The Chipmunks (61)	*80*
I Wouldn't Know Where To Begin—Eddy Arnold (56)	59
Rudolph The Red Nosed Reindeer— David Seville And The Chipmunks (62)	*45*
I Heard The Bells On Christmas Day—Bing Crosby (56)	43
Run, Rudolph, Run—Chuck Berry (58)	30
Rudolph The Red-Nosed Reindeer—Gene Autry (57)	*19*
Free—Lancers (56)	*0.0*
Rudolph The Red Nosed Reindeer—Mulcays (54)	*0.0*
Rudolph The Red Nosed Reindeer—Mulcays (55)	*0.0*
Rudolph The Red Nosed Reindeer—Paul Anka (60)	*0.0*
Rudolph The Red Nosed Reindeer—Gene Autry (54)	*0.0*
Rudolph The Red-Nosed Reindeer— Les Paul & Mary Ford (55)	*0.0*
Rudolph The Red-Nosed Reindeer Cha Cha— Hernando Hopkins (58)	*0.0*
Rudolph, The Red-Nosed Reindeer— Gene Autry & The Pinafores (55)	*0.0*
Rudolph The Red Nosed Reindeer Cha Cha— Hugo Winterhalter and his Orchestra (58)	*0.0*
Larry MARKS ▶ 9554 (1)	**21**
L.A. Breakdown—Larry Marks (68)	21
Rose MARKS ▶ 6131 (3)	**202**
Sixty Minute Man—Clarence Carter (73)	*349*
Sixty Minute Man—Rufus Thomas (70)	*53*
Sixty Minute Man—Bill Darnel (60)	*1.6*
Spiro MARKS [Spiros D. Markantonatos, David Marks] ▶ 2386 (2)	**1538**
Master Jack—Four Jacks And A Jill (68)	1535
Mister Nico—Four Jacks And A Jill (68)	3.6
Walter MARKS ▶ 1828 (1)	**2244**
I've Gotta Be Me—Sammy Davis Jr. (68)	2244
—Mark Markwell see: Hugo PERETTI	
—Mark Markwell see: Luigi CREATORE	
—Marley Marl see: Marion WILLIAMS	
Bob MARLETTE ▶ 5283 (1)	**314**
I've Got A Lot To Learn About Love—Storm (91)	941
Bob MARLEY [Robert Nesta Marley Booker] ▶ 679 (5) HOF	**6391**
I Shot The Sheriff—Eric Clapton (74)	4537
Stir It Up—Johnny Nash (73)	1617
Is This Love—Pat Travers Band (80)	209
Guava Jelly—Capers & Carson (73)	*16*
Guava Jelly—Barbra Streisand (75)	*13*
Cedella MARLEY ▶ 10571 (1)	**7.1**
Good Time—Ziggy Marley (91)	29
—David Nesta Marley see: Ziggy MARLEY	
Sharon MARLEY ▶ 10572 (1)	**7.1**
Good Time—Ziggy Marley (91)	29
Stephen MARLEY ▶ 10573 (1)	**7.1**
Good Time—Ziggy Marley (91)	29
Ziggy MARLEY [David Nesta Marley] ▶ 4979 (2)	**366**
Tomorrow People— Ziggy Marley And The Melody Makers (88)	359
Good Time—Ziggy Marley (91)	29
Ric MARLOW [Sanford Phillip Schafler] ▶ 8219 (1)	**58**
A Taste Of Honey—Tony Bennett (64)	*116*
Kenny MARLOWE ▶ 11684 (1)	**0.7**
Little Miss Blue—Dion (60)	2.1
—Thomas Marlowe see: Fred JACKSON	
—Thomas Marlowe see: W. Albert POSER	
Jeff MARMELZAT ▶ 11579 (1)	**1.1**
All Roads (Lead Back To You)—Donny Most (76)	2.3
Didier MAROUANI ▶ 7913 (1)	**70**
My Love Is Music—Space (79)	139
Hank MARR ▶ 9204 (1)	**29**
The Greasy Spoon—Hank Marr (63)	58
Johnny MARR [John Martin Maher] ▶ 4279 (2)	**534**
Hippychick—Soho (90)	797
Getting Away With It—Electronic (90)	407
—Marta Marrero see: MARTIKA	
Steve MARRIOTT ▶ 2983 (4)	**1083**
Itchycoo Park—Small Faces (67)	1634
Hot 'N' Nasty—Humble Pie (72)	389
Tin Soldier—Small Faces (68)	196
Fool For A Pretty Face (Hurt By Love)—Humble Pie (80)	141

Tracy MARROW [Ice-T] ▶ 8095 (2)	**62**
New Jack Hustler (Nino's Theme)—Ice-T (91)	71
Colors—Ice-T (88)	53
Mick MARS [Robert Allen Deal] ▶ 1890 (6)	**2150**
Dr. Feelgood—Mötley Crüe (89)	1482
Without You—Mötley Crüe (90)	1295
Girls, Girls, Girls—Mötley Crüe (87)	1018
Don't Go Away Mad (Just Go Away)—Mötley Crüe (90)	741
Same Ol' Situation (S.O.S.)—Mötley Crüe (90)	148
Primal Scream—Mötley Crüe (91)	60
Joe MARSALA ▶ 11809 (1)	**0.0**
More Than Ever—Georgia Gibbs (54)	0.0
Bernie MARSDEN ▶ 1726 (3)	**2416**
Here I Go Again—Whitesnake (87)	4367
Fool For Your Loving—Whitesnake (89)	*489*
Fool For Your Loving—Whitesnake (80)	*207*
Fred MARSDEN ▶ 3795 (1)	**696**
Don't Let The Sun Catch You Crying—Gerry And The Pacemakers (64)	2786
Gerry MARSDEN ▶ 1029 (6)	**4297**
Don't Let The Sun Catch You Crying—Gerry And The Pacemakers (64)	2786
Ferry Cross The Mersey—Gerry And The Pacemakers (65)	2710
It's Gonna Be Alright—Gerry And The Pacemakers (65)	704
Give All Your Love To Me—Gerry And The Pacemakers (65)	143
La La La—Gerry And The Pacemakers (66)	31
I'm The One—Gerry And The Pacemakers (64)	12
Doyle MARSH ▶ 5384 (1)	**297**
The Days Of Sand And Shovels—Bobby Vinton (69)	595
Ethel MARSH ▶ 10264 (1)	**11**
Somebody Else's Love Song—Georgie Shaw (54)	21
Ian Craig MARSH ▶ 10039 (1)	**14**
Let Me Go—Heaven 17 (83)	41
Peter MARSH ▶ 9982 (1)	**14**
I've Been Lovin' You—Easy Street (76)	57
—Richard Elvern Marsh see: Sky SAXON	
Bob MARSHALL ▶ 5604 (2)	**266**
Slowdown—John Miles (77)	279
Highfly—John Miles (76)	253
Celia MARSHALL [Edward Marshall Erenberg] ▶ 3998 (3)	**626**
A Wonderful Dream—Majors (62)	878
A Little Bit Now—Dave Clark Five (67)	*209*
A Little Bit Now (A Little Bit Later)—Majors (62)	*165*
Ed MARSHALL ▶ 369 (4)	**10471**
Venus—Frankie Avalon (59)	*9989*
Venus—Frankie Avalon (76)	*473*
I'll Be Good—Joe Valino (57)	21
Venus—Johnny Mathis (68)	*2.7*
Guy MARSHALL [Guy Mitchell Gaglio] ▶ 7140 (1)	**114**
Le Bel Age (The Best Years)—Pat Benatar (86)	227
Jack MARSHALL ▶ 5251 (1)	**318**
You're My One And Only Love—Ricky Nelson (57)	636
James W. MARSHALL ▶ 3296 (4)	**909**
The Devil Went Down To Georgia—Charlie Daniels Band (79)	*3303*
In America—Charlie Daniels Band (80)	1335
The Legend Of Wooley Swamp—Charlie Daniels Band (80)	633
The Devil Came Up To Michigan—K.M.C. Kru (91)	*243*
Julian MARSHALL ▶ 4769 (3)	**419**
Nice Girls—Eye To Eye (82)	477
Dancing In The City—Marshall Hain (78)	350
Lucky—Eye To Eye (83)	11
Michael MARSHALL [Mike Meezy] ▶ 4257 (1)	**544**
Rumors—Timex Social Club (86)	1633
Ron MARSHALL ▶ 10771 (1)	**5.4**
A Letter To Dad—Every Father's Teenage Son (67)	11
Sherman MARSHALL ▶ 1201 (6)	**3702**
Then Came You—Dionne Warwicke And Spinners (74)	4589
I'm Doin' Fine Now—New York City (73)	1697
Lady Love—Lou Rawls (77)	863
You're Throwing A Good Love Away—Spinners (77)	144
Wake Up Susan—Spinners (76)	104

The Whole Town's Laughing At Me—Teddy Pendergrass (77)	7.2
Allen MARTANCIK [Allen Martin] ▶ 5216 (2)	**324**
Just Let It Come—Alive And Kicking (70)	275
Didn't It Look So Easy—Stairsteps (71)	146
Vince MARTELL [Vincent James Martemucci] ▶ 9537 (2)	**22**
Where Is My Mind—Vanilla Fudge (68)	71
Need Love—Vanilla Fudge (69)	16
—Vincent James Martemucci see: Vince MARTELL	
Jose MARTI ▶ 5022 (1)	**358**
Guantanamera—Sandpipers (66)	2149
MARTIKA [Marta Marrero] ▶ 1888 (3)	**2153**
Toy Soldiers—Martika (89)	2662
Love... Thy Will Be Done—Martika (91)	1066
More Than You Know—Martika (88)	867
—Allen Martin see: Allen MARTANCIK	
Angela MARTIN ▶ 6229 (1)	**191**
L. David Sloane—Michele Lee (68)	383
Billy MARTIN ▶ 10557 (1)	**7.2**
Five—Sammy Davis Jr. (56)	14
Bobbi MARTIN ▶ 2905 (2)	**1123**
For The Love Of Him—Bobbi Martin (70)	2119
Give A Woman Love—Bobbi Martin (70)	128
Bobby MARTIN ▶ 6687 (5)	**144**
Day By Day (Every Minute Of The Hour)—Continental 4 (71)	163
Tear After Tear—Patty LaBelle & Her Blue Belles (62)	50
I Found A New Love—Blue Belles (62)	45
Work Out, Part I & II—Ricky Dee & the Embers (62)	24
Take All Of My Life—Carrie Grant And The Grandeurs (62)	5.8
Cedric MARTIN ▶ 9973 (1)	**14**
Baby I'm Hooked—Con Funk Shun (84)	29
David MARTIN ▶ 1928 (4)	**2096**
Can't Smile Without You—Barry Manilow (78)	5240
Annabella—Hamilton, Joe Frank & Reynolds (71)	460
Can't You Hear The Song?—Wayne Newton (72)	435
It's Up To You Petula—Edison Lighthouse (71)	153
David (2) MARTIN ▶ 10043 (1)	**14**
Faraway Star—Chordettes (61)	27
David C. MARTIN ▶ 4538 (1)	**468**
Goin' Down—Greg Guidry (82)	936
David Ellis MARTIN ▶ 10104 (1)	**13**
Thinking Of You—Grandmaster Slice (91)	25
Dean MARTIN Jr. [Dino Martin] ▶ 8885 (1)	**37**
Tell Someone You Love Them—Dino, Desi & Billy (68)	74
—Dino Martin see: Dean MARTIN Jr.	
Eric MARTIN ▶ 1597 (2)	**2647**
To Be With You—Mr. Big (91)	5278
Information—Eric Martin (85)	32
Glenn MARTIN ▶ 5545 (3)	**272**
If You're Not Back In Love By Monday—Millie Jackson (77)	453
Is Anybody Goin' To San Antone—Charley Pride (70)	80
I'm Just Me—Charley Pride (71)	5.8
Grady MARTIN ▶ 2736 (4)	**1232**
Snap Your Fingers—Joe Henderson (62)	*2221*
Snap Your Fingers—Barbara Lewis (63)	*120*
I'm Learning About Love—Brenda Lee (61)	110
Let's Go—Floyd Cramer (62)	6.2
Hearlon MARTIN [Cheese] ▶ 10340 (1)	**9.8**
Keep On Doin' What You're Doin'—Bobby Byrd (72)	39
Herb MARTIN ▶ 8067 (1)	**63**
Why Did I Choose You—Barbra Streisand (65)	126
Hugh MARTIN ▶ 10181 (2) HOF	**12**
An Occasional Man—Jeri Southern (55)	*23*
An Occasional Man—Billy May & His Orchestra with Ella Mae Morse (55)	*0.0*
James "Petey" MARTIN ▶ 10825 (1)	**5.1**
Don't Forget I Love You—Butanes (61)	5.1
Jay MARTIN ▶ 9953 (1)	**15**
You Can't Get Away—Shana (90)	44
Jim MARTIN ▶ 5309 (2)	**309**
Epic—Faith No More (90)	1519
Falling To Pieces—Faith No More (90)	27
—John David Martin see: Moon MARTIN	
Joseph MARTIN ▶ 5834 (2)	**238**
Church Bells May Ring—Diamonds (56)	*981*

Church Bells May Ring—Willows (56)	*210*
Joseph C. MARTIN ▶ 8127 (2)	**61**
Down In The Valley—Solomon Burke (62)	*194*
Down In The Alley—Ronnie Hawkins (70)	*110*
Kenny MARTIN ▶ 7374 (2)	**100**
I Need Your Lovin'—Roy Hamilton (59)	*299*
I Need Your Lovin'—Clarence Paul (59)	*0.0*
Kip MARTIN ▶ 6546 (1)	**158**
Rambling—Ramblers (1) (60)	317
Larry MARTIN ▶ 4625 (1)	**449**
Forget Me Not—Kalin Twins (58)	897
Larry (2) MARTIN ▶ 10558 (1)	**7.2**
Five—Sammy Davis Jr. (56)	14
Lennie MARTIN [Rinaldo R. Marino, Lenny Martin] ▶ 3994 (7)	**629**
Since I Don't Have You—Skyliners (59)	*2364*
This I Swear—Skyliners (59)	743
Since I Don't Have You—Don McLean (81)	*545*
Since I Don't Have You—Chuck Jackson (64)	*403*
Since I Don't Have You—Art Garfunkel (79)	*180*
Since I Don't Have You—Eddie Holman (70)	*160*
Since I Don't Have You—Fred Parris & The Five Satins (82)	*4.8*
—Lenny Martin see: Lennie MARTIN	
Linda MARTIN ▶ 2698 (1)	**1266**
Chick-A-Boom (Don't Ya Jes' Love It)—Daddy Dewdrop (71)	2531
Liz MARTIN ▶ 5872 (2)	**234**
La La Peace Song—Al Wilson (74)	*389*
La La Peace Song—O.C. Smith (74)	*80*
Marilyn MARTIN [Marilyn Marie Droman] ▶ 5266 (1)	**316**
Night Moves—Marilyn Martin (86)	631
Matty MARTIN ▶ 7765 (2)	**76**
I'd Never Forgive Myself—Kitty Kallen (55)	*228*
I'd Never Forgive Myself—Jerry Martin (54)	*0.0*
Moon MARTIN [John David Martin] ▶ 1784 (4)	**2329**
Bad Case Of Loving You (Doctor, Doctor)—Robert Palmer (79)	1539
Rolene—Moon Martin (79)	512
No Chance—Moon Martin (79)	215
Dreamer—Association (81)	63
Ralph MARTIN ▶ 5835 (2)	**238**
Church Bells May Ring—Diamonds (56)	*981*
Church Bells May Ring—Willows (56)	*210*
—Raymond Stuart Martin see: Lester POWELL	
—Rich Martin see: Richard FROST	
Sam MARTIN ▶ 8779 (1)	**40**
You Call Everybody Darlin'—Mildred & Jimmie Mulcay (60)	119
Steve MARTIN ▶ 2846 (3)	**1156**
King Tut—Steve Martin And The Toot Uncommons (78)	1066
Grandmother's Song—Steve Martin (77)	68
Cruel Shoes—Steve Martin (79)	22
—T. Martin see: Martin MONTAGUE	
Timothy D. MARTIN ▶ 5154 (1)	**333**
Abra-Ca-Dabra—Defranco Family Featuring Tony Defranco (73)	666
Tom MARTIN ▶ 7788 (1)	**75**
This Is Ponderous—2NU (90)	300
—Tom Martin see: Thomas FROST	
Trade MARTIN [John Lione] ▶ 4730 (2)	**429**
Take Me For A Little While—Vanilla Fudge (68)	*395*
Take Me For A Little While—Patti LaBelle And The Blue Belles (66)	*34*
—Vincent John Martin see: Vince CLARKE	
William Rever MARTIN ▶ 9125 (1)	**31**
Rockin' In The Jungle—Eternals (59)	61
William Wylie MacPherson MARTIN ▶ 1568 (7)	**2700**
Saturday Night—Bay City Rollers (75)	4835
My Boy—Elvis Presley (75)	*838*
My Boy—Richard Harris (71)	*497*
Hi Hi Hazel—Gary And The Hornets (66)	16
Julie Ann—Ginger (76)	11
Congratulations—Cliff Richard (68)	3.7
Forever And Ever—Slik (76)	1.2

Willie MARTIN ► 6536 (2)	**159**
Call My Name, I'll Be There—Wilson Pickett (71)	440
Sometimes It's Got To Rain— Jackie Moore With The Dixie Flyers (71)	37
—Yvonne Martin see: Yvonne BAKER	
Layng MARTINE Jr. ► 1168 (7)	**3810**
Way Down—Elvis Presley (77)	1351
Should I Do It—Pointer Sisters (82)	1049
Rub It In—Billy "Crash" Craddock (74)	*962*
Rub It In—Layng Martine (71)	*360*
A Corner In The Sun—Walter Jackson (66)	99
Come On Over To My House—Layng Martine (71)	24
Everybody Needs A Rainbow—Ray Stevens (74)	15
Lewis MARTINÉE [Luiz Antonio Martinez] ► 283 (8)	**12422**
Seasons Change—Exposé (87)	3131
Come Go With Me—Exposé (87)	1928
Point Of No Return—Exposé (87)	1792
Let Me Be The One—Exposé (87)	1645
What You Don't Know—Exposé (89)	1393
Tell Me Why—Exposé (89)	1326
When I Looked At Him—Exposé (89)	1194
You Can't Get Away—Shana (90)	44
Armando MARTINEZ ► 7942 (1)	**68**
Por Amor Viviremos—Captain & Tennille (75)	*204*
Eddie MARTINEZ ► 10801 (1)	**5.2**
Kid Stuff—Lenny White (80)	21
—Luiz Antonio Martinez see: Lewis MARTINÉE	
—Mariano Martinez see: Marianito MORES	
Nigel MARTINEZ ► 9544 (1)	**22**
Night (Feel Like Getting Down)—Billy Ocean (81)	43
Paul MARTINEZ ► 6580 (1)	**154**
In The Mood—Robert Plant (83)	463
Ray MARTINEZ ► 6711 (1)	**142**
The Only Way Out—Cliff Richard (82)	142
—Robert Martinez see: Rudy MARTINEZ	
Rudy MARTINEZ [Robert Martinez] ► 543 (4)	**7895**
96 Tears—? (Question Mark) & The Mysterians (66)	*7647*
I Need Somebody—? & The Mysterians (66)	913
96 Tears—Garland Jeffreys (81)	*50*
96 Tears—Big Maybelle (67)	*15*
Carlos MARTINOLI ► 9623 (1)	**20**
Cuando Calienta El Sol (When The Sun Is Hot)—Steve Allen And His Orchestra With The Copacabana Trio (63)	*60*
David Anthony MARTINS ► 5062 (1)	**351**
Steel Men—Jimmy Dean (62)	351
—Gene Martyn see: Marcel STELLMAN	
Holt MARVELL [Albert Eric Maschwitz, Eric Maschwitz] ► 8081 (1)	**62**
These Foolish Things— James Brown And The Famous Flames (63)	187
—Babe Marvin see: Babe CHIVIAN	
Hank MARVIN [Hank Brian Marvin, Brian Robson Rankin] ► 6025 (2)	**215**
Sam—Olivia Newton-John (77)	638
Don't It Make You Feel Good—Overlanders (64)	5.0
Johnny MARVIN ► 10979 (1)	**4.0**
Goodby Little Darlin'—Johnny Cash (59)	8.0
Richard MARX ► 104 (16)	**23958**
Right Here Waiting—Richard Marx (89)	3809
Satisfied—Richard Marx (89)	3313
Hold On To The Nights—Richard Marx (88)	2976
Endless Summer Nights—Richard Marx (88)	2818
Angelia—Richard Marx (89)	2631
Should've Known Better—Richard Marx (87)	2630
Don't Mean Nothing—Richard Marx (87)	2111
Keep Coming Back—Richard Marx (91)	1893
Surrender To Me—Ann Wilson and Robin Zander (88)	1279
Children Of The Night—Richard Marx (90)	1029
Too Late To Say Goodbye—Richard Marx (90)	919
What About Me?—Kenny Rogers (84)	866
Edge Of A Broken Heart—Vixen (88)	570
Nothin' To Hide—Poco (89)	179
The Best Of Me— David Foster And Olivia Newton-John (86)	69
Crazy—Kenny Rogers (85)	41
Norman MARZANO ► 6030 (2)	**214**
Do Something To Me— Tommy James And The Shondells (68)	*639*
Do Something To Me—? And The Mysterians (67)	*3.4*

Robert MARZELL ► 11531 (1)	**1.3**
Choppin' Cha Cha—Marty Ames (59)	2.6
Carolyne MAS ► 7532 (1)	**90**
Stillsane—Carolyne Mas (79)	90
Pietro MASCAGNI ► 9697 (1)	**19**
Theme From Raging Bull (Cavalleria Rusticana)— Joel Diamond (81)	19
Eddie MASCARI ► 3441 (4)	**847**
I Got A Wife—Mark IV (59)	1423
My Wife, The Dancer—Eddie & Dutch (70)	195
(Make With) The Shake—Mark IV (58)	71
Move Over Rover—Mark IV (59)	5.1
Vittorio MASCHERONI ► 3479 (6)	**824**
Jealous Of You (Tango Della Gelosia)— Connie Francis (60)	784
My One Sin—Four Coins (57)	*690*
My One Sin—Nat "King" Cole (55)	*594*
Without You—Eddie Fisher (56)	*406*
Without You—Alan Dean (56)	*0.0*
Without You—Johnny Desmond (56)	*0.0*
—Albert Eric Maschwitz see: Holt MARVELL	
—Eric Maschwitz see: Holt MARVELL	
Hugh MASEKELA [Philemon Hou] ► 553 (4)	**7786**
Grazing In The Grass—Hugh Masekela (68)	*5702*
Grazing In The Grass—Friends Of Distinction (69)	*3539*
Riot—Hugh Masekela (69)	305
Son Of Ice Bag—Hugh Masekela (67)	9.7
—Maskman see: Harmon BETHEA	
Peter MASLEN ► 10983 (1)	**4.0**
Talk About It—Boom Crash Opera (91)	20
Barbara MASON ► 466 (8)	**8967**
Yes, I'm Ready—Teri DeSario with K.C. (79)	*4280*
Yes, I'm Ready—Barbara Mason (65)	*3873*
Sad, Sad Girl—Barbara Mason (65)	625
Oh, How It Hurts—Barbara Mason (67)	335
If You Don't (Love Me, Tell Me So)— Barbara Mason (65)	11
Is It Me?—Barbara Mason (66)	7.1
I Need Love—Barbara Mason (66)	2.9
(I Can Feel Your Love) Slipping Away— Barbara Mason (68)	1.7
Barry MASON ► 537 (17)	**8002**
Love Grows (Where My Rosemary Goes)— Edison Lighthouse (70)	4513
Love Me Tonight—Tom Jones (69)	2125
Kiss Me Goodbye—Petula Clark (68)	1753
Winter World Of Love—Engelbert Humperdinck (69)	1474
Delilah—Tom Jones (68)	1459
Say You'll Stay Until Tomorrow—Tom Jones (76)	1231
A Man Without Love (Quando M'innamoro)— Engelbert Humperdinck (68)	1014
The Last Waltz—Engelbert Humperdinck (67)	892
Les Bicyclettes De Belsize— Engelbert Humperdinck (68)	766
My Marie—Engelbert Humperdinck (70)	564
Here It Comes Again—Fortunes (65)	517
Everybody Knows—Dave Clark Five (67)	437
I'm Coming Home—Tom Jones (67)	237
I Never Said Goodbye—Engelbert Humperdinck (72)	187
Melanie Makes Me Smile—Tony Burrows (70)	*31*
Melanie Makes Me Smile—Terry Williams (72)	*10*
Love Is All—Engelbert Humperdinck (73)	9.8
Dave MASON ► 1488 (9)	**2921**
Only You Know And I Know—Delaney & Bonnie (71)	*979*
Feeling Alright—Joe Cocker (72)	*553*
Only You Know And I Know—Dave Mason (70)	*499*
Feelin' Alright—Grand Funk Railroad (71)	*334*
Let It Go, Let It Flow—Dave Mason (78)	288
Feeling Alright—Joe Cocker (69)	*153*
Paper Sun—Traffic Featuring Stevie Winwood (67)	108
Satin Red And Black Velvet Woman— Dave Mason (70)	84
Feeling Alright—Mongo Santamaria (69)	*3.9*
Harvey MASON ► 7069 (1)	**118**
Chameleon—Herbie Hancock (74)	472
James MASON ► 11370 (1)	**2.0**
Ya Mama—Wuf Ticket (83)	8.1
James Howard MASON ► 4380 (1)	**509**
I Dig Rock And Roll Music—Peter, Paul & Mary (67)	1527
Lol MASON ► 6067 (1)	**209**
5.7.0.5.—City Boy (78)	419

Marilyn MASON ► 4128 (2)	**585**
Love Takes Time—Orleans (79)	1165
Don't Throw Our Love Away—Orleans (79)	6.7
Melvin MASON ► 5820 (2)	**239**
I Do (Live Version)—J. Geils Band (82)	*637*
I Do—Marvelows (65)	*556*
—Sandy Mason see: Sandy THEORET	
Vaughan MASON ► 10160 (1)	**12**
Bounce, Rock, Skate, Roll (Part 1)— Vaughan Mason And Crew (80)	35
Vincent MASON ► 8643 (1)	**44**
Me Myself And I—De La Soul (89)	353
Wilton MASON ► 8730 (2)	**41**
The Golden Rule—'Cile Turner (59)	*123*
The Golden Rule—Don Rondo (59)	*0.0*
—B. Masona see: Charles SOUZA	
Giuseppe MASSARA ► 11220 (1)	**2.7**
Cappuccina—Nat King Cole (61)	11
Laurel MASSE ► 11611 (1)	**1.0**
Clap Your Hands—Manhattan Transfer (75)	4.0
Michael MASSER ► 201 (20) HOF	**15646**
Touch Me In The Morning—Diana Ross (73)	4788
Theme From Mahogany (Do You Know Where You're Going To)—Diana Ross (75)	4699
Greatest Love Of All—Whitney Houston (86)	*4409*
Didn't We Almost Have It All—Whitney Houston (87)	3593
Saving All My Love For You—Whitney Houston (85)	3224
Tonight, I Celebrate My Love— Peabo Bryson/Roberta Flack (83)	1798
If Ever You're In My Arms Again—Peabo Bryson (84)	1625
Miss You Like Crazy—Natalie Cole (89)	1581
It's My Turn—Diana Ross (80)	1404
Last Time I Saw Him—Diana Ross (73)	1347
Nothing's Gonna Change My Love For You— Glenn Medeiros (87)	1315
Someone That I Used To Love—Natalie Cole (80)	768
The Greatest Love Of All—George Benson (77)	*660*
Hold Me—Teddy Pendergrass (84)	457
So Sad The Song—Gladys Knight & The Pips (76)	300
I Thought It Took A Little Time (But Today I Fell In Love)—Diana Ross (76)	133
Long And Lasting Love (Once In A Lifetime)— Glenn Medeiros (88)	113
Some Changes Are For Good—Dionne Warwick (81)	107
Sorry Doesn't Always Make It Right— Diana Ross (75)	20
One More Chance—Diana Ross (81)	18
Bill MASSEY ► 5313 (2)	**308**
(I Do The) Shimmy Shimmy— Bobby Freeman (60)	*452*
Shimmy Shimmy—Orlons (64)	*165*
Cathy MASSEY ► 7392 (2)	**99**
The Truth—Tami Show (91)	466
She's Only 20—Tami Show (88)	17
Claire MASSEY ► 7393 (2)	**99**
The Truth—Tami Show (91)	466
She's Only 20—Tami Show (88)	17
Guy MASSEY ► 10635 (1)	**6.5**
Prisoner's Song—Warren Storm (58)	13
Howard MASSEY ► 8697 (1)	**42**
Red Hot—Herb Alpert (83)	42
Robert MASSEY ► 10638 (1)	**6.5**
Prisoner's Song—Warren Storm (58)	13
Pat MASTELOTTO ► 5278 (1)	**314**
Is It Love—Mr. Mister (86)	1255
Frankie MASTERS ► 11104 (3)	**3.2**
What A Heavenly Night For Love—Dinah Shore (56)	*2.1*
What A Heavenly Night For Love— Frankie Masters & His Orchestra (56)	*2.1*
What A Heavenly Night For Love— Lawrence Welk And His Champagne Music (56)	*2.1*
Jerry MASTERS ► 4377 (2)	**509**
Let It Out (Let It All Hang Out)—Hombres (67)	2036
It's A Gas—Hombres (68)	1.4
—Joe Medwick Masters see: Joe VEASEY	
Sammy MASTERS [Samuel T. Lawmaster, Johnny Todd] ► 11629 (1)	**0.9**
Who Can I Count On—Patsy Cline (61)	0.9
Carlo MASTRANGELO ► 7356 (1)	**100**
I Need Some One—Belmonts (61)	201

John MASTRANGELO [Johnny Maestro] ▶ 11279 (1)	**2.5**
Sweetest One—Crests (57)	5.0
Alex MASUCCI ▶ 7489 (1)	**93**
All Night Thing—Invisible Man's Band (80)	278
Silvano MATADIN ▶ 7523 (1)	**91**
Deeper Shade Of Soul—Urban Dance Squad (90)	545
Cosimo MATASSA ▶ 4371 (2)	**510**
Letter To An Angel—Jimmy Clanton (58)	689
Part Of Me—Jimmy Clanton (58)	331
Robert MATHER ▶ 2849 (1)	**1154**
Sexy Eyes—Dr. Hook (80)	3462
Greg MATHIESON ▶ 2126 (5)	**1843**
Heaven Knows—Donna Summer With Brooklyn Dreams (79)	3027
Telefone (Long Distance Love Affair)—Sheena Easton (83)	1957
Just Can't Win 'Em All—Stevie Woods (82)	274
Trouble In Paradise—Al Jarreau (83)	87
Devil In A Fast Car—Sheena Easton (84)	22
Louis MATHIS [Louis Al, Louis Aldine Mathis] ▶ 5241 (2)	**319**
Break Away (From That Boy)—Newbeats (65)	488
The Loneliest Night—Dale & Grace (64)	150
—Louis Aldine Mathis see: Louis MATHIS	
Marc MATHIS ▶ 5242 (2)	**319**
Break Away (From That Boy)—Newbeats (65)	488
The Loneliest Night—Dale & Grace (64)	150
—Ross G. Matico see: Bud ROSS	
Michael MATIJEVIC ▶ 3178 (2)	**966**
I'll Never Let You Go—Steelheart (91)	797
She's Gone (Lady)—Steelheart (91)	169
Dennis MATKOSKY ▶ 1229 (6)	**3631**
Maniac—Michael Sembello (83)	5111
Mirror, Mirror—Diana Ross (82)	1481
Heart Of Mine—Boz Scaggs (88)	429
We've Saved The Best For Last—Kenny G (89)	260
Let Me In—Eddie Money (89)	142
Hearts In Trouble—Chicago (90)	102
—Vera Matson see: Ken DARBY	
Sam A. MATTER ▶ 7150 (1)	**113**
Cryin' In The Streets (Part I)—George Perkins & The Silver Stars (70)	340
—Willy Mattes see: Charles WILDMAN	
Wayne MATTESON ▶ 10471 (1)	**8.1**
Boss—Rumblers (63)	48
Eric MATTHEW [Joseph William Tucci] ▶ 5778 (2)	**243**
Keep On Dancin'—Gary's Gang (79)	480
Let's Lovedance Tonight—Gary's Gang (79)	4.6
Stuart MATTHEWMAN ▶ 4058 (3)	**609**
Paradise—Sade (88)	717
Never As Good As The First Time—Sade (86)	603
Your Love Is King—Sade (85)	257
Artie MATTHEWS ▶ 7063 (1)	**118**
Weary Blues—McGuire Sisters And Lawrence Welk (56)	355
Artwell MATTHEWS ▶ 10998 (1)	**3.9**
Long Stroke—ADC Band (78)	24
—Audrey Matthews see: Kalya MATTHEWS	
Charles (Pete) MATTHEWS ▶ 5396 (1)	**295**
Michael—C.O.D.'s (65)	591
Charles Ezra MATTHEWS ▶ 5499 (1)	**278**
The Cat Walk—Village Soul Choir (70)	278
Charles G. MATTHEWS ▶ 1277 (6)	**3474**
White Silver Sands—Don Rondo (57)	*2977*
White Silver Sands—Bill Black's Combo (60)	*2957*
White Silver Sands—Dave Gardner (57)	*795*
-twistin'-White Silver Sands—Bill Black's Combo (62)	*118*
White Silver Sands—Owen Bradley Quintet (57)	*101*
White Silver Sands—Lennon Sisters (57)	*0.0*
David MATTHEWS ▶ 4747 (4)	**425**
King Heroin—James Brown (72)	531
Escape-Ism (Part 1)—James Brown (71)	378
What My Baby Needs Now Is A Little More Lovin'—James Brown & Lyn Collins (72)	289
Could Heaven Ever Be Like This (Part 1)—Idris Muhammad (77)	14

Denise MATTHEWS [Denise Katrina Smith, Vanity] ▶ 8327 (1)	**54**
Pretty Mess—Vanity (84)	108
Johnnie MATTHEWS ▶ 5737 (3)	**247**
Gonna Send You Back To Georgia (A City Slick)—Timmy Shaw (64)	*423*
Gonna Send You Back To Walker—Animals (64)	*70*
My Man--He's A Lovin' Man—Betty LaVett (63)	1.6
Kalya MATTHEWS [Audrey Matthews] ▶ 10999 (1)	**3.9**
Long Stroke—ADC Band (78)	24
Neal MATTHEWS ▶ 11810 (1)	**0.0**
Greenback Dollar—Merry Melody Singers (63)	0.0
Patricia MATTHEWS ▶ 11304 (1)	**2.3**
Copy Cat—Gary (U.S.) Bonds (62)	9.2
Sherlie Mae MATTHEWS ▶ 6145 (3)	**200**
Mine Exclusively—Olympics (66)	124
Baby, Do The Philly Dog—Olympics (66)	116
Your P-E-R-S-O-N-A-L-I-T-Y—Jackie Lee (2) (66)	113
Timothy MATTHEWS ▶ 9617 (2)	**20**
Breaking Up Somebody's Home—Ann Peebles (72)	*29*
Breaking Up Somebody's Home—Albert King (73)	*12*
—Eugenie Theresa Matthias see: Theresa MATTHIAS	
Theresa MATTHIAS [Jenny Bellestar, Eugenie Theresa Matthias, Jenny McKeown] ▶ 10580 (1)	**7.1**
Sign Of The Times—Belle Stars (83)	49
David MATTIS ▶ 7699 (1)	**80**
My Song—Aretha Franklin (68)	160
Ed MATTSON ▶ 9621 (1)	**20**
Rich Man—Terri Gibbs (81)	20
Mikhail MATUSOVSKIJ ▶ 1683 (2)	**2490**
Midnight In Moscow—Kenny Ball And His Jazzmen (62)	*4981*
Midnight In Moscow—Jan Burgens & His New Orleans Syncopators (62)	*0.0*
John MATYS ▶ 7918 (1)	**70**
Rummy Polka—Matys Bros. (59)	139
Walt MATYS ▶ 7919 (1)	**70**
Rummy Polka—Matys Bros. (59)	139
Frank MAUDSLEY ▶ 3702 (4)	**728**
I Ran (So Far Away)—A Flock Of Seagulls (82)	1474
Space Age Love Song—A Flock Of Seagulls (82)	637
Wishing (If I Had A Photograph Of You)—A Flock Of Seagulls (83)	612
The More You Live, The More You Love—A Flock Of Seagulls (84)	187
Rudi MAUGERI ▶ 11811 (1)	**0.0**
Crazy 'Bout Ya Baby—Crew-Cuts (54)	0.0
Joe MAULDIN ▶ 6654 (4)	**147**
I'm Gonna Love You Too—Hullaballoos (64)	*366*
Well All Right—Santana (78)	67
I'm Gonna Love You Too—Buddy Holly / The Crickets (58)	*13*
I'm Gonna Love You Too—Terry Jacks (73)	*11*
Bennie MAUPIN ▶ 7070 (1)	**118**
Chameleon—Herbie Hancock (74)	472
Mat MAURER ▶ 6636 (2)	**149**
Leave Me Alone—Baby Washington (63)	233
Come Dance With Me—Jay & The Americans (63)	142
Paul MAURIAT [Del Roma] ▶ 1880 (2)	**2170**
I Will Follow Him—Little Peggy March (63)	8660
Passport To The Future—Jean Jacques Perrey (70)	20
Lee MAVERS ▶ 5727 (1)	**250**
There She Goes—La's (91)	250
Christopher MAX [Christopher McDaniels] ▶ 8061 (1)	**63**
Serious Kinda Girl—Christopher Max (89)	127
Arnold MAXIN ▶ 10197 (1)	**11**
Shirley—Schoolboys (57)	23
Billy MAXTED ▶ 2090 (2)	**1890**
Manhattan Spiritual—Reg Owen And His Orchestra (58)	*1736*
Manhattan Spiritual—Mike Post (75)	*154*
Duris MAXWELL ▶ 10755 (1)	**5.5**
Nobody—Doucette (79)	11

Ray MAXWELL [René Jan van Hoogten] ▶ 10141 (2)	**12**
Step Right Up (And Say You Love Me)—Nat King Cole (62)	*36*
Step Right Up (And Say You Love Me)—Teresa Brewer (62)	*0.0*
Robert MAXWELL ▶ 936 (12)	**4743**
Ebb Tide—Righteous Brothers (65)	*2977*
Shangri-La—Robert Maxwell, His Harp And Orchestra (64)	*1946*
Shangri La—Four Coins (57)	*1206*
Shangri-La—Vic Dana (64)	*878*
Ebb Tide—Lenny Welch (64)	*842*
Little Dipper—Mickey Mozart Quintet (59)	716
Ebb Tide—Platters Featuring Tony Williams (60)	*357*
Ebb Tide—Bobby Freeman (59)	*283*
Shangri-La—Lettermen (69)	*254*
Song Of The Nairobi Trio—Fortune Tellers (61)	46
Ebb Tide—Roy Hamilton (54)	*0.0*
Ebb Tide—Roy Hamilton (59)	*0.0*
Brian MAY ▶ 2243 (9) HOF	**1708**
Ice Ice Baby—Vanilla Ice (90)	3735
Under Pressure—Queen & David Bowie (81)	689
Fat Bottomed Girls—Queen (78)	366
Flash's Theme AKA Flash—Queen (81)	290
I Want It All—Queen (89)	251
One Vision—Queen (85)	249
Tie Your Mother Down—Queen (77)	168
It's Late—Queen (78)	81
Keep Yourself Alive—Queen (75)	7.4
Ellen MAY ▶ 9176 (1)	**29**
Tell Me Mamma—Christine Quaite (64)	88
Iris MAY [Iris May Giebler] ▶ 8212 (1)	**58**
Brand New Love Affair—Jigsaw (76)	117
Johnny MAY ▶ 9497 (1)	**23**
Try Again—Dean Martin (54)	68
Simon MAY ▶ 9353 (1)	**25**
137 Disco Heaven—Amii Stewart (79)	51
John MAYALL ▶ 6350 (2)	**180**
Don't Waste My Time—John Mayall (69)	164
Room To Move—John Mayall (69)	16
—Raynoma Mayberry see: Raynoma SINGLETON	
Hans-Jörg MAYER [George Reyam] ▶ 6798 (3)	**136**
Rivers Of Babylon—Boney M (78)	419
Daddy Cool—Boney M (76)	60
Ma Baker—Boney M (77)	3.4
Henry MAYER [Heinz Meier] ▶ 2008 (6)	**2006**
My Melody Of Love—Bobby Vinton (74)	3485
Summer Wind—Frank Sinatra (66)	*685*
Summer Wind—Wayne Newton (65)	*84*
Rosemarie—Pat Boone (64)	10
Summer Wind—Roger Williams & The Harry Simeone Chorale (65)	*4.2*
Come Into My Life—Al Martino (71)	2.9
Jean MAYER ▶ 7739 (1)	**77**
Power—Temptations (80)	231
Nathaniel MAYER ▶ 4325 (1)	**521**
Village Of Love—Nathaniel Mayer And The Fabulous Twilights (62)	1041
Tim MAYER ▶ 4693 (1)	**438**
Come As You Are—Peter Wolf (87)	875
Tommy MAYER ▶ 5538 (1)	**273**
Weekend—Wet Willie (79)	546
Curtis MAYFIELD ▶ 20 (101) HOF	**62945**
He Don't Love You (Like I Love You)—Tony Orlando & Dawn (75)	*4607*
Let's Do It Again—Staple Singers (75)	4477
Gypsy Woman—Brian Hyland (70)	*4320*
It's All Right—Impressions (63)	4057
He Will Break Your Heart—Jerry Butler (60)	*3246*
Um, Um, Um, Um, Um, Um—Major Lance (63)	*3173*
Freddie's Dead (Theme From "Superfly")—Curtis Mayfield (72)	2694
Superfly—Curtis Mayfield (72)	2431
The Monkey Time—Major Lance (63)	*2079*
On And On—Gladys Knight & The Pips (74)	1927
Keep On Pushing—Impressions (64)	1886
We're A Winner—Impressions (67)	1868

Curtis MAYFIELD ▶ 20 (101) HOF *Continued*	**62945**
Mama Didn't Lie—Jan Bradley (63)	*1796*
Gypsy Woman—Impressions (61)	*1491*
You Must Believe Me—Impressions (64)	1346
Talking About My Baby—Impressions (64)	1342
I'm So Proud—Impressions (64)	*1332*
Nothing Can Stop Me—Gene Chandler (65)	1179
Hey Little Girl—Major Lance (63)	1127
Choice Of Colors—Impressions (69)	1120
Fool For You—Impressions (68)	1096
Just Be True—Gene Chandler (64)	1087
Check Out Your Mind—Impressions (70)	947
Find Another Girl—Jerry Butler (61)	912
People Get Ready—Impressions (65)	*903*
This Is My Country—Impressions (68)	827
Give Me Your Love—Barbara Mason (72)	827
Need To Belong—Jerry Butler (63)	821
Rhythm—Major Lance (64)	818
Something He Can Feel—Aretha Franklin (76)	771
(Don't Worry) If There's A Hell Below We're All Going To Go—Curtis Mayfield (70)	753
You've Been Cheatin'—Impressions (65)	676
I'm So Proud—Main Ingredient (70)	*589*
Kung Fu—Curtis Mayfield (74)	562
What Now—Gene Chandler (64)	545
Woman's Got Soul—Impressions (65)	537
I'm A Telling You—Jerry Butler (61)	496
Rainbow—Gene Chandler (63)	*424*
Curious Mind (Um, Um, Um, Um, Um, Um)—Johnny Rivers (77)	*422*
Future Shock—Curtis Mayfield (73)	408
Come See—Major Lance (65)	405
We're Rolling On (Part 1)—Impressions (68)	388
Sometimes I Wonder—Major Lance (64)	372
(Baby) Turn On To Me—Impressions (70)	348
Meeting Over Yonder—Impressions (65)	348
I Loved And I Lost—Impressions (68)	335
People Get Ready—Jeff Beck And Rod Stewart (85)	*304*
Ain't Got Time—Impressions (71)	286
Can't Satisfy—Impressions (66)	274
I Need You—Impressions (65)	272
It's All Over—Walter Jackson (64)	261
Get Down—Curtis Mayfield (71)	238
I Can't Work No Longer—Billy Butler & The Chanters (65)	236
Say You Love Me—Impressions (69)	219
Man's Temptation—Gene Chandler (63)	215
It Ain't No Use—Major Lance (64)	211
Don't Change Your Love—Five Stairsteps & Cubie (68)	197
Don't Cry My Love—Impressions (68)	174
So In Love—Curtis Mayfield (75)	167
Danger! She's A Stranger—Five Stairsteps (67)	157
Stay Away From Me (I Love You Too Much)—Major Lance (70)	134
Just One Kiss From You—Impressions (65)	133
Rainbow '65 Part I—Gene Chandler (65)	*132*
New Orleans—Staple Singers (76)	132
Girls—Major Lance (64)	110
Since I Lost The One I Love—Impressions (66)	104
I Can't Stay Away From You—Impressions (67)	87
Jump—Aretha Franklin (76)	77
He Don't Love You—Jim Croce (76)	*76*
She Don't Let Nobody (But Me)—Curtis Mayfield (81)	75
The Monkey Time—Tubes (83)	*72*
Girls Are Out To Get You—Fascinations (67)	69
I'm The One Who Loves You—Impressions (63)	69
Seven Years—Impressions (69)	55
Ain't It A Shame—Major Lance (65)	52
Look Into Your Heart—Aretha Franklin (77)	50
We Must Be In Love—Five Stairsteps & Cubie (69)	46
You Always Hurt Me—Impressions (67)	45
My Deceiving Heart—Impressions (69)	45
Can't Say Nothin'—Curtis Mayfield (73)	35
If I Were Only A Child Again—Curtis Mayfield (73)	35
Sad, Sad Girl And Boy—Impressions (63)	26
Too Slow—Impressions (66)	24
You Can't Hurt Me No More—Gene Chandler (65)	21
Good Times—Gene Chandler (65)	20
Baby Make Me Feel So Good—Five Stairsteps & Cubie (69)	19
Never Too Much Love—Bards (67)	17
I've Been Trying—Impressions (65)	17

Love Me—Impressions (71)	16
We Got To Have Peace—Curtis Mayfield (72)	13
I Thank You—Donny Hathaway And June Conquest (72)	8.8
Stay Close To Me—Five Stairsteps & Cubie (68)	7.2
Minstrel And Queen—Impressions (62)	6.1
Isle Of Sirens—Jerry Butler (62)	5.4
He Will Break Your Heart—Righteous Brothers (66)	*4.8*
Between You Baby And Me Love—Curtis Mayfield & Linda Clifford (79)	3.9
Little Young Lover—Impressions (62)	2.2
Grow Closer Together—Impressions (62)	0.9
I Just Can't Help It—Major Lance (65)	0.5
Mama Didn't Lie—Fasinations (63)	*0.0*
Hooked On Your Love—Aretha Franklin (76)	0.0
Percy MAYFIELD ▶ 489 (9)	**8542**
Hit The Road Jack—Ray Charles And His Orchestra With The Raeletts (61)	*7180*
Hide 'Nor Hair—Ray Charles And His Orchestra (62)	578
Hit The Road Jack—Stampeders (76)	*434*
At The Club—Ray Charles And His Orchestra (62)	377
My Baby Don't Dig Me—Ray Charles And His Orchestra With The Raelettes (64)	195
But On The Other Hand Baby—Ray Charles And His Orchestra (61)	41
Please Send Me Someone To Love—Moonglows (57)	39
Strange Things Happening—Little Junior Parker (64)	6.3
River's Invitation—Percy Mayfield (63)	0.9
Billy MAYHEW ▶ 1819 (4)	**2269**
It's A Sin To Tell A Lie—Somethin' Smith & The Redheads (55)	*2189*
It's A Sin To Tell A Lie—Tony Bennett (64)	*70*
It's A Sin To Tell A Lie—Dave "Baby" Cortez (59)	*11*
It's A Sin To Tell A Lie—Johnny Desmond (55)	*0.0*
Walter MAYNARD ▶ 10656 (1)	**6.3**
Late Date—Parkays (61)	6.3
Walter P. MAYNARD Jr. ▶ 11812 (1)	**0.0**
Skinny Minnie—Sprouts (58)	0.0
Lincoln MAYORGA ▶ 8284 (2)	**56**
Brontosaurus Stomp—Piltdown Men (60)	109
Piltdown Rides Again—Piltdown Men (60)	2.5
Lyle MAYS ▶ 6294 (1)	**185**
This Is Not America—David Bowie/Pat Metheny Group (85)	554
—Mark Maytorena see: Marq TORIEN	
Elaine MAZLISH ▶ 7431 (1)	**96**
Not Yet—Susan Hunter (55)	289
Emmanuele MAZZUCCHI ▶ 8149 (1)	**60**
Ma Ma Ma Marie—Gaylords (58)	*240*
—MC Hammer see: Stanley BURRELL	
Thomas McALEESE [Dean Ford] ▶ 2495 (2)	**1437**
Reflections Of My Life—Marmalade (70)	2469
Rainbow—Marmalade (70)	405
Maurice McALISTER ▶ 5866 (2)	**235**
Voice Your Choice—Radiants (64)	469
Father Knows Best—Radiants (62)	0.4
—James McAllister see: Smokey McALLISTER	
Smokey McALLISTER [James McAllister] ▶ 4655 (3)	**444**
I Can't Stand It—Soul Sisters (64)	442
Good Time Tonight—Soul Sisters (64)	1.4
Just A Moment Ago—Soul Sisters (64)	0.5
Lillie McALPIN ▶ 10325 (1)	**10**
Home Of The Blues—Johnny Cash (57)	30
Vic McALPIN ▶ 4664 (3)	**443**
Anymore—Teresa Brewer (60)	1292
Before This Day Ends—Eddy Arnold (60)	*38*
Before This Day Ends—George Hamilton IV (60)	*0.0*
Mac McANALLY ▶ 4092 (3)	**596**
Minimum Love—Mac McAnally (83)	435
It's A Crazy World—Mac McAnally (77)	248
It's My Job—Jimmy Buffett (81)	131
Robin McAULEY ▶ 8142 (1)	**60**
Anytime—McAuley Schenker Group (90)	120
Leon McAULIFFE ▶ 11118 (1)	**3.1**
Steel Guitar Rag—Dynatones (2) (59)	3.1
Bob McAVOY ▶ 7766 (2)	**76**
I'd Never Forgive Myself—Kitty Kallen (55)	*228*
I'd Never Forgive Myself—Jerry Martin (54)	*0.0*
—MC Blowfish see: Gregory JACOBS	

—MC Bones see: Walfried BÖCKER	
—MC Breed see: Eric BREED	
—MC Breeze see: Joey B. ELLIS	
Bob McBRIDE ▶ 10486 (1)	**8.0**
I Just Wanna Be Your Friend—Lighthouse (72)	16
Jimmy Ray McBRIDE ▶ 6570 (1)	**155**
Bet Your Heart On Me—Johnny Lee (81)	155
Pat McBRIDE ▶ 5107 (4)	**341**
I Could Never Lie To You—New Colony Six (69)	444
Love You So Much—New Colony Six (67)	340
Long Time To Be Alone—New Colony Six (71)	15
I Lie Awake—New Colony Six (66)	2.9
—Perry McBride see: Perry KIBBLE	
Rod McBRIEN ▶ 8519 (2)	**47**
Isn't It Lonely Together—Stark & McBrien (75)	73
Finders Keepers—Salt Water Taffy (68)	22
Amanda McBROOM ▶ 729 (1)	**6013**
The Rose—Bette Midler (80)	6013
Dan McCAFFERTY ▶ 10283 (1)	**10**
Holiday—Nazareth (80)	63
Tiemeyer McCAIN ▶ 9018 (1)	**33**
Fantastic Voyage—Lakeside (80)	296
Eric McCAINE ▶ 8168 (1)	**60**
All Nite—Entouch featuring Keith Sweat (90)	119
—Cash McCall see: Morris DOLLISON	
—C.W. McCall see: Bill FRIES	
Marti McCALL ▶ 10148 (1)	**12**
Love Light—Yutaka (81)	24
Romeo McCALL [Romeo "Breath" McCall, DeWayne Sweet] ▶ 10945 (1)	**4.2**
Flashes—Tiggi Clay (84)	13
Toussaint McCALL ▶ 4622 (3)	**449**
Nothing Takes The Place Of You—Toussaint McCall (67)	*613*
Nothing Can Take The Place Of You—Brook Benton (69)	*195*
I'll Do It For You—Toussaint McCall (67)	89
—William Aubry McCall see: W.S. STEVENSON	
David McCALLUM ▶ 11400 (1)	**1.9**
Communication—David McCallum (66)	3.8
Peter McCANN ▶ 1024 (2)	**4315**
Do You Wanna Make Love—Peter McCann (77)	2291
Right Time Of The Night—Jennifer Warnes (77)	2024
Clemmi McCANTS ▶ 6675 (1)	**145**
Doin' Our Thing—Clarence Carter (69)	434
James McCANTS ▶ 8375 (1)	**53**
Mama Said Knock You Out—LL Cool J (91)	473
Leroy McCANTS ▶ 8376 (1)	**53**
Mama Said Knock You Out—LL Cool J (91)	473
Leo McCAREY ▶ 5614 (6)	**265**
An Affair To Remember (Our Love Affair)—Vic Damone (57)	*779*
An Affair To Remember (Our Love Affair)—Nat "King" Cole (57)	*15*
An Affair To Remember—ViVienne (57)	*0.0*
An Affair To Remember—Pete King & His Orchestra (57)	*0.0*
An Affair To Remember (Our Love Affair)—Angela Drake (57)	*0.0*
An Affair To Remember (Our Love Affair)—Carmen Cavallaro (57)	*0.0*
Martin McCARRICK ▶ 7035 (1)	**120**
Kiss Them For Me—Siouxsie And The Banshees (91)	481
Charles McCARTHY ▶ 10874 (1)	**4.7**
When Your Old Wedding Ring Was New—Bruce Hayes with Mary Mayo (60)	14
Charlotte McCARTHY ▶ 3263 (1)	**921**
I Don't Want To Be Hurt Anymore—Nat King Cole (64)	921
Dennis McCARTHY ▶ 8049 (1)	**64**
My Country—Jud Strunk (74)	128
Joseph McCARTHY ▶ 5577 (5) HOF	**270**
You Made Me Love You—Nat "King" Cole (59)	496
What Do You Want To Make Those Eyes At Me For—Ray Peterson (60)	*62*
I'm Always Chasing Rainbows—Joe Pica (58)	3.3
What Do You Want To Make Those Eyes At Me For?—Sunny Gale (60)	*0.0*
What Do You Want To Make Those Eyes At Me For—Kenny Rankin (60)	*0.0*

Joseph Allen McCARTHY ► 7280 (1) — 105

I'm Gonna Laugh You Right Out Of My Life—Nat "King" Cole (55) 211

Linda McCARTNEY [Linda Louise Eastman] ► 89 (22) — 26327

Silly Love Songs—Wings (76) 7833
My Love—Paul McCartney & Wings (73) 7686
Listen To What The Man Said—Wings (75) 5030
Live And Let Die—Wings (73) 4780
Band On The Run—Paul McCartney & Wings (74) 4486
Uncle Albert/Admiral Halsey—Paul & Linda McCartney (71) 4182
Let 'Em In—Wings (76) 3857
Junior's Farm—Paul McCartney & Wings (74) 3216
Another Day—Paul McCartney (71) 2814
Jet—Paul McCartney & Wings (74) 2272
Helen Wheels—Paul McCartney & Wings (73) 2098
Hi, Hi, Hi—Wings (72) 1491
Venus And Mars Rock Show—Wings (75) 748
Give Ireland Back To The Irish—Wings (72) 518
Live And Let Die—Guns N' Roses (91) 506
Mary Had A Little Lamb—Wings (72) 378
Letting Go—Wings (75) 234
Seaside Woman—Suzy And The Red Stripes (77) 135
Sally G—Paul McCartney & Wings (74) 133
My Love—Margie Joseph (74) 114
Mine For Me—Rod Stewart (74) 6.2
Little Woman Love—Wings (72) 4.6

Paul McCARTNEY [Bernard Webb] ► 1 (192) HOF — 195949

Hey Jude—Beatles (68) 14634
I Want To Hold Your Hand—Beatles (64) 14194
She Loves You—Beatles (64) 10567
Say Say Say—Paul McCartney and Michael Jackson (83) 8900
Get Back—Beatles With Billy Preston (69) 8698
Let It Be—Beatles (70) 8679
We Can Work It Out—Beatles (65) 8664
Ebony And Ivory—Paul McCartney (82) 8546
A Hard Day's Night—Beatles (64) 8359
Can't Buy Me Love—Beatles (64) 8269
I Feel Fine—Beatles (64) 8162
Hello Goodbye—Beatles (67) 8134
Yesterday—Beatles (65) 7927
Help!—Beatles (65) 7847
Silly Love Songs—Wings (76) 7833
My Love—Paul McCartney & Wings (73) 7686
Love Me Do—Beatles (64) 7070
All You Need Is Love—Beatles (67) 6800
Ticket To Ride—Beatles (65) 6556
Paperback Writer—Beatles (66) 6493
Coming Up (Live At Glasgow)—Paul McCartney & Wings (80) 6470
A World Without Love—Peter And Gordon (64) 6461
Come Together—Beatles (69) 6145
Eight Days A Week—Beatles (65) 6070
Yellow Submarine—Beatles (66) 5464
The Long And Winding Road—Beatles (70) 5434
Penny Lane—Beatles (67) 5144
Lady Madonna—Beatles (68) 5119
Listen To What The Man Said—Wings (75) 5030
Nowhere Man—Beatles (66) 5024
With A Little Luck—Wings (78) 4974
Please Please Me—Beatles (64) 4866
Do You Want To Know A Secret—Beatles (64) 4830
Live And Let Die—Wings (73) 4780
Lucy In The Sky With Diamonds—Elton John (74) 4586
Band On The Run—Paul McCartney & Wings (74) 4486
Uncle Albert/Admiral Halsey—Paul & Linda McCartney (71) 4182
Let 'Em In—Wings (76) 3857
Junior's Farm—Paul McCartney & Wings (74) 3216
Come And Get It—Badfinger (70) 3078
Another Day—Paul McCartney (71) 2814
Goodnight Tonight—Wings (79) 2537
Got To Get You Into My Life—Beatles (76) 2422
The Fool On The Hill—Sergio Mendes & Brasil '66 (68) 2327
She's A Woman—Beatles (64) 2317
Jet—Paul McCartney & Wings (74) 2272
Helen Wheels—Paul McCartney & Wings (73) 2098
You Won't See Me—Anne Murray (74) 1945
Day Tripper—Beatles (65) 1881
Revolution—Beatles (68) 1855
The Ballad Of John And Yoko—Beatles (69) 1848
Take It Away—Paul McCartney (82) 1842
Strawberry Fields Forever—Beatles (67) 1798
No More Lonely Nights—Paul McCartney (84) 1763
We Can Work It Out—Stevie Wonder (71) 1496
Hi, Hi, Hi—Wings (72) 1491
Spies Like Us—Paul McCartney (85) 1442
Woman—Peter And Gordon (66) 1438
Bad To Me—Billy J. Kramer With The Dakotas (64) 1411
You've Got To Hide Your Love Away—Silkie (65) 1392
Give Peace A Chance—Plastic Ono Band (69) 1367
P.S. I Love You—Beatles (64) 1327
Goodbye—Mary Hopkin (69) 1267
Nobody I Know—Peter And Gordon (64) 1242
Maybe I'm Amazed—Wings (77) 1214
Got To Get You Into My Life—Earth, Wind & Fire (78) 1210
Eleanor Rigby—Beatles (66) 1186
I Saw Him Standing There—Tiffany (88) 1114
Michelle—David & Jonathan (66) 1048
Birthday—Underground Sunshine (69) 1006
Hey Jude—Wilson Pickett (68) 933
I Don't Want To See You Again—Peter And Gordon (64) 871
And I Love Her—Beatles (64) 866
Eleanor Rigby—Aretha Franklin (69) 807
Yesterday—Ray Charles (67) 797
Venus And Mars Rock Show—Wings (75) 748
Veronica—Elvis Costello (89) 736
So Bad—Paul McCartney (83) 703
She Came In Through The Bathroom Window—Joe Cocker (69) 697
From A Window—Billy J. Kramer With The Dakotas (64) 694
Eleanor Rigby—Ray Charles (68) 673
Come Together—Aerosmith (78) 659
Getting Closer—Wings (79) 640
I Saw Her Standing There—Beatles (64) 638
I'll Cry Instead—Beatles (64) 638
Oh! Darling—Robin Gibb (78) 626
Press—Paul McCartney (86) 561
A Hard Day's Night—Ramsey Lewis Trio (66) 532
My Brave Face—Paul McCartney (89) 522
Give Ireland Back To The Irish—Wings (72) 518
Rain—Beatles (66) 508
Live And Let Die—Guns N' Roses (91) 506
I've Had Enough—Wings (78) 499
All My Loving—Beatles (64) 480
Girls' School—Wings (77) 469
Thank You Girl—Beatles (64) 466
Arrow Through Me—Wings (79) 446
No Reply—Stars On 45 (81) 442
Nowhere Man—Stars On 45 (81) 442
Drive My Car—Stars On 45 (81) 442
I'll Be Back—Stars On 45 (81) 442
We Can Work It Out—Stars On 45 (81) 442
I Should Have Known Better—Stars On 45 (81) 442
Do You Want To Know A Secret—Stars On 45 (81) 442
You're Going To Lose That Girl—Stars On 45 (81) 442
Let It Be—Joan Baez (71) 435
And I Love Him—Esther Phillips (65) 406
Ringo's Theme (This Boy)—George Martin And His Orch. (64) 389
Mary Had A Little Lamb—Wings (72) 378
I'll Keep You Satisfied—Billy J. Kramer With The Dakotas (64) 373
And I Love Her—George Martin And His Orch. (64) 352
Come Together—Ike & Tina Turner & The Ikettes (70) 348
From Me To You—Beatles (64) 345
It's For You—Springwell (71) 334
I Am The Walrus—Beatles (67) 317
London Town—Wings (78) 286
Ob-La-Di, Ob-La-Da—Arthur Conley (68) 282
If I Fell—Beatles (64) 277
With A Little Help From My Friends—Joe Cocker (68) 272
On The Wings Of A Nightingale—Everly Brothers (84) 269
Magical Mystery Tour—Ambrosia (77) 262
Baby You're A Rich Man—Beatles (67) 258
Letting Go—Wings (75) 234
Ob-La-Di, Ob-La-Da—Beatles (76) 224
I Don't Want To Spoil The Party—Beatles (65) 221
Ticket To Ride—Carpenters (70) 196
Don't Let Me Down—Beatles With Billy Preston (69) 194
Michelle—Billy Vaughn His Orchestra & Chorus (66) 188
Dear Prudence—Katfish (75) 186
I Want To Hold Your Hand—Boston Pops Orchestra Arthur Fiedler Conductor (64) 184
Day Tripper—Anne Murray (74) 181
Tug Of War—Paul McCartney (82) 175
I Should Have Known Better—Beatles (64) 172
Julia—Ramsey Lewis (69) 145
Yes It Is—Beatles (65) 137
Get Back—Beatles (82) 134
Ticket To Ride—Beatles (82) 134
A Hard Day's Night—Beatles (82) 134
All You Need Is Love—Beatles (82) 134
Magical Mystery Tour—Beatles (82) 134
I Should Have Known Better—Beatles (82) 134
You've Got To Hide Your Love Away—Beatles (82) 134
Sally G—Paul McCartney & Wings (74) 133
Got To Get You Into My Life—Blood, Sweat & Tears (75) 128
You Can't Do That—Beatles (64) 126
Michelle—Bud Shank (66) 116
My Love—Margie Joseph (74) 114
Dear Prudence—Five Stairsteps (70) 110
From Me To You—Del Shannon (63) 110
A World Without Love—Bobby Rydell (64) 99
Oh Woman Oh Why—Paul McCartney (71) 78
Back In The U.S.S.R.—Chubby Checker (69) 70
Day Tripper—Ramsey Lewis (66) 70
Stranglehold—Paul McCartney (86) 60
I'm Happy Just To Dance With You—Anne Murray (80) 59
Here, There And Everywhere—Emmylou Harris (76) 55
Drive My Car—Gary Toms Empire (75) 52
Give Peace A Chance—Peace Choir (91) 49
From A Window—Chad & Jeremy (65) 45
I'm A Loser—Beatles (65) 37
It's For You—Cilla Black (64) 34
With A Little Help From My Friends—Beatles (78) 24
Sgt. Pepper's Lonely Hearts Club Band—Beatles (78) 24
You Can't Do That—Nilsson (67) 23
Wonderful Christmastime—Paul McCartney (79) 20
Lady Madonna—Fats Domino (68) 16
What Goes On—Beatles (66) 16
This One—Paul McCartney (89) 15
Waterfalls—Paul McCartney (80) 14
There's A Place—Beatles (64) 13
Here, There And Everywhere—Fourmost (66) 12
I'm Happy Just To Dance With You—Beatles (64) 12
Step Inside Love—Cilla Black (68) 11
Drive My Car—Bob Kuban And The In-Men (66) 11
Figure Of Eight—Paul McCartney (90) 11
She's A Woman—José Feliciano (69) 9.6
Get Back—Billy Preston (78) 9.4
From Me To You—Stars On 45 (81) 8.0
Please Please Me—Stars On 45 (81) 8.0
Good Day Sunshine—Stars On 45 (81) 8.0
A Hard Day's Night—Stars On 45 (81) 8.0
I Want To Hold Your Hand—Stars On 45 (81) 8.0
This Boy—Beatles (64) 6.4
All My Loving—Beatles (64) 6.4
Mine For Me—Rod Stewart (74) 6.2
Little Woman Love—Wings (72) 4.6
Rocky Raccoon—Richie Havens (69) 4.0
All My Loving—Hollyridge Strings (64) 3.8
Day Tripper—Vontastics (66) 2.4
Sie Liebt Dich (She Loves You)—Die Beatles (64) 1.9
Good Day Sunshine—Claudine Longet (67) 0.9
Mull Of Kintyre—Wings (77) 0.0

—Peter Michael McCartney see: Mike McGEAR

Chris McCARTY ► 4287 (2) — 532

Swingtown—Steve Miller Band (77) 1016
Bongo Bongo—Steve Miller Band (85) 47

Jim McCARTY ► 3002 (3) — 1072

Shapes Of Things—Yardbirds (66) 1778
Over Under Sideways Down—Yardbirds (66) 1583
Happenings Ten Years Time Ago—Yardbirds (66) 652

Tony McCASHEN ► 9243 (2) — 28

Hitchcock Railway—Jose Feliciano (68) 48
Alright In The City—Dunn & McCashen (70) 8.2

Albritton McCLAIN ► 7516 (1) — 91

Love Is Like A Rock—Donnie Iris (81) 454

Marlon McCLAIN ▶ 11218 (1)	**2.7**
Let's Dance (Make Your Body Move)—West Street Mob (81)	30
Jim McCLARTY ▶ 7330 (2)	**101**
Mega Force—707 (82)	139
I Could Be Good For You—707 (80)	133
Thomas McCLARY ▶ 3173 (5)	**971**
Brick House—Commodores (77)	1962
Slippery When Wet—Commodores (75)	793
Too Hot Ta Trot—Commodores (77)	499
Flying High—Commodores (78)	306
I Feel Sanctified—Commodores (74)	83
James McCLENDON ▶ 5968 (1)	**221**
If U Were Mine—U-Krew (90)	663
Steve McCLINTOCK ▶ 3437 (2)	**849**
All This Time—Tiffany (88)	1620
Can I Call You My Girl—PC Quest (91)	155
Delbert McCLINTON ▶ 7301 (2)	**104**
I Received A Letter—Delbert & Glen (72)	78
If You Really Want Me To, I'll Go—Ron-Dels (65)	26
O.B. McCLINTON [Osbie Burnett McClinton, Obie McClinton] ▶ 4760 (3)	**422**
A Man Needs A Woman—James Carr (67)	363
You've Got My Mind Messed Up—James Carr (66)	240
What It Takes To Get A Good Woman (That's What It's Gonna Take To Keep Her)—Denise LaSalle (73)	2.2
—Osbie Burnett McClinton see: O.B. McCLINTON	
Clarence McCLOUD ▶ 10359 (1)	**9.5**
I'm Satisfied—San Remo Golden Strings (65)	38
Doug McCLURE ▶ 10944 (1)	**4.2**
The Boogaloo Party—Flamingos (66)	13
Michael McCLURE ▶ 8434 (1)	**51**
(Oh Lord Won't You Buy Me A) Mercedes Benz—Goose Creek Symphony (72)	152
Marlon McCLURG ▶ 4682 (1)	**438**
My Bonnie Lassie—Ames Brothers (55)	1315
Andrew McCLUSKEY ▶ 2665 (3)	**1285**
If You Leave—Orchestral Manoeuvres In The Dark (86)	1910
Dreaming—Orchestral Manoeuvres In The Dark (88)	867
So In Love—Orchestral Manoeuvres In The Dark (85)	644
Deborah McCOLL ▶ 6865 (1)	**132**
Fins—Jimmy Buffett (79)	528
Jay McCONLOGUE ▶ 5556 (1)	**272**
Rain, Rain, Rain—Frankie Laine & The Four Lads with The Buddy Cole Quartet (54)	272
George McCONNELL ▶ 7122 (1)	**115**
You Wanted Someone To Play With (I Wanted Someone To Love)—Frankie Laine (67)	459
—Timothy Scott McConnell see: Tim SCOTT	
Jonas McCORD ▶ 6170 (1)	**198**
19—Paul Hardcastle (85)	792
Kevin McCORD ▶ 10220 (1)	**11**
Push—One Way (81)	11
—William Patrick McCord see: Billy VERA	
George McCORKLE ▶ 3697 (3)	**731**
Fire On The Mountain—Marshall Tucker Band (75)	387
Last Of The Singing Cowboys—Marshall Tucker Band (79)	310
Dream Lover—Marshall Tucker Band (78)	70
Keith McCORMACK ▶ 762 (2)	**5747**
Sugar Shack—Jimmy Gilmer And The Fireballs (63)	10632
Daisy Petal Pickin'—Jimmy Gilmer And The Fireballs (63)	1293
Charles E. McCORMICK ▶ 1572 (2)	**2692**
Natural High—Bloodstone (73)	2415
My Little Lady—Bloodstone (75)	277
Danny McCORMICK ▶ 10191 (1)	**11**
Pouring Water On A Drowning Man—James Carr (66)	23
Douglas McCORMICK ▶ 11221 (1)	**2.7**
Brought Up In New York (Brought Down In L.A.)—Paul Anka (78)	5.4
Randy McCORMICK ▶ 5548 (2)	**272**
Suspicions—Eddie Rabbitt (79)	1079
Real Love—Dolly Parton (Duet With Kenny Rogers) (85)	6.7
Ronel McCOWN ▶ 10533 (1)	**7.5**
What Time Of Day—Billy Thunderkloud & The Chieftones (75)	7.5

Charlie McCOY ▶ 8820 (1)	**39**
Cherry Berry Wine—Charlie McCoy (61)	116
Freddie McCOY ▶ 10419 (1)	**8.6**
Peas 'N' Rice—Freddie McCoy (67)	8.6
Jacqueline McCOY ▶ 9819 (2)	**16**
The Wedding—Solitaires (55)	*36*
The Wedding—Chordettes (55)	*13*
Rose Marie McCOY ▶ 1454 (24)	**3005**
If I May—Nat "King" Cole And The Four Knights (55)	1803
I Beg Of You—Elvis Presley (58)	1174
Don't Be Angry—Nappy Brown (55)	*1091*
My Personal Possession—Nat "King" Cole And The Four Knights (57)	*575*
Little By Little—Nappy Brown (57)	*502*
Piddily Patter Patter—Patti Page (55)	*278*
Genuine Love—Les Paul and Mary Ford (55)	271
Little By Little—Micki Marlo (57)	*228*
Got To See If I Can't Get Mommy (To Come Back Home)—Jerry Butler (70)	210
We'll Cry Together—Maxine Brown (69)	120
Mambo Baby—Ruth Brown And Her Rhythmakers with Orchestra (54)	*58*
Mambo Baby—Georgia Gibbs (54)	*15*
I'd Better Be Careful—Bob Manning (55)	14
Slam! Bam!—Crew-Cuts (55)	12
One Night Only—Otis Williams And His Charms (56)	7.2
Honey Bunch—Four Knights (55)	5.0
I Wouldn't Know (What To Do)—Dinah Washington (62)	4.9
Don't Be Angry—Crew-Cuts (55)	*0.0*
Piddily Patter—Nappy Brown (55)	*0.0*
Little By Little—Crew-Cuts (57)	*0.0*
Little By Little—Toni Arden (57)	*0.0*
My Personal Possession—Andy Bey (57)	*0.0*
Piddily Patter Patter—Helene Dixon (55)	*0.0*
Piddily Patter Patter—Burton Sisters (55)	*0.0*
Van McCOY ▶ 224 (46)	**15036**
The Hustle—Van Mc Coy & The Soul City Symphony (75)	4937
Baby, I'm Yours—Barbara Lewis (65)	*1904*
Before And After—Chad & Jeremy (65)	1114
Right On The Tip Of My Tongue—Brenda & The Tabulations (71)	1092
When You're Young And In Love—Marvelettes (67)	*757*
Let's Kiss And Make Up—Bobby Vinton (62)	647
To Each His Own—Faith, Hope & Charity (75)	578
The Sweetest Thing This Side Of Heaven—Chris Bartley (67)	577
So Much Love—Faith, Hope & Charity (70)	552
I Get The Sweetest Feeling—Jackie Wilson (68)	535
Giving Up—Gladys Knight & The Pips (64)	*499*
I Don't Wanna Lose You Baby—Chad & Jeremy (65)	444
Stop The Music—Shirelles (62)	425
Change With The Times—Van McCoy (75)	340
When You're Young And In Love—Ruby And The Romantics (64)	*326*
Triangle Of Love (Hey Diddle Diddle)—Presidents (71)	293
Baby Don't Change Your Mind—Gladys Knight & The Pips (77)	248
And My Heart Sang (Tra La La)—Brenda & The Tabulations (70)	229
Everything's Coming Up Love—David Ruffin (76)	185
He's My Guy—Irma Thomas (64)	181
Heavy Love—David Ruffin (76)	155
Getting Mighty Crowded—Betty Everett (64)	142
I've Lost You—Jackie Wilson (67)	140
Rat Race—Drifters (63)	115
Party—Van McCoy (76)	111
She's A Troublemaker—Majors (62)	89
For You—Spellbinders (65)	68
Giving Up—Donny Hathaway (72)	*66*
Shabby Little Hut—Reflections (65)	65
Baby, I'm Yours—Jody Miller (71)	*55*
Keep On Trying—Bobby Vee (65)	46
On And Off (Part 1)—Anacostia (72)	42
A Part Of You—Brenda & The Tabulations (71)	32
Lovers Always Forgive—Gladys Knight & The Pips (64)	29
Suddenly I'm All Alone—Walter Jackson (65)	24
The Language Of Love—Intrigues (71)	21
Don't Pity Me—Faith, Hope & Charity (78)	18
This Is It—Melba Moore (76)	17

Maybe Tonight—Shirelles (64)	12
Baby Don't Take Your Love—Faith, Hope & Charity (70)	10
Times Have Changed—Irma Thomas (64)	9.6
When You're Young And In Love—Choice Four (75)	*9.1*
When You're Young And In Love—Ralph Carter (75)	*6.3*
Night Walk—Van McCoy (76)	3.1
Everybody Loves A Good Time—Major Lance (65)	1.9
Baby, I'm Yours—Debby Boone (78)	*0.0*
Jimmy McCRACKLIN [James David Walker] ▶ 2613 (10)	**1324**
Tramp—Otis & Carla (67)	*913*
The Walk—Jimmy McCracklin (58)	*868*
Tramp—Lowell Fulsom (67)	*364*
Just Got To Know—Jimmy McCracklin (61)	133
Think—Jimmy McCracklin (65)	127
Every Night, Every Day—Jimmy McCracklin (65)	30
The Walk—Inmates (80)	*21*
My Answer—Jimmy McCracklin (66)	17
Get Back—Roy Head (66)	7.0
Just A Little Bit—Little Milton (69)	3.1
Alfred McCRARY ▶ 7114 (1)	**115**
You—McCrarys (78)	346
Linda McCRARY ▶ 7115 (1)	**115**
You—McCrarys (78)	346
Sam McCRARY ▶ 7116 (1)	**115**
You—McCrarys (78)	346
Junie McCREE [Gonzalvo Macrillo] ▶ 7005 (2)	**122**
Put Your Arms Around Me Honey—Fats Domino (60)	*230*
Put Your Arms Around Me Honey—Ray Smith (60)	*15*
—Dennis McCrohan see: Mars BONFIRE	
—Gerald McCrohan see: Jerry EDMONTON	
Arnold McCULLER ▶ 10846 (1)	**5.0**
Never Had A Love Like This Before—Tavares (79)	15
Danny McCULLOCH ▶ 2915 (5)	**1119**
San Franciscan Nights—Eric Burdon And The Animals (67)	1697
Sky Pilot (Part One)—Eric Burdon & The Animals (68)	1609
When I Was Young—Eric Burdon & The Animals (67)	1085
Monterey—Eric Burdon & The Animals (67)	1017
Anything—Eric Burdon & The Animals (68)	187
James McCULLOCH ▶ 1142 (5)	**3884**
Hot Child In The City—Nick Gilder (78)	7241
Here Comes The Night—Nick Gilder (78)	320
Rock Me—Nick Gilder (79)	193
Roxy Roller—Sweeney Todd (76)	*13*
Roxy Roller (Bryan Adams)—Sweeney Todd (76)	*0.7*
James McCULLOUGH ▶ 5124 (1)	**339**
The Return Of The Red Baron—Royal Guardsmen (67)	1016
John McCULLOUGH ▶ 5125 (1)	**339**
The Return Of The Red Baron—Royal Guardsmen (67)	1016
John McCURRY ▶ 4304 (2)	**528**
Poison—Alice Cooper (89)	1500
Now You're In Heaven—Julian Lennon (89)	57
Eric McCUSKER ▶ 5989 (1)	**219**
State Of The Heart—Rick Springfield (85)	656
Elias McDANIEL [Elias Otha Bates, Bo Diddley, Ethel Smith] ▶ 992 (20)	**4522**
Love Is Strange—Mickey & Sylvia (56)	*2019*
Love Is Strange—Peaches & Herb (67)	*1374*
I'm A Man—Yardbirds (65)	919
Say Man—Bo Diddley (59)	883
Road Runner—Gants (65)	*504*
Oh Yeah—Shadows Of Knight (66)	423
Bo Diddley—Bo Diddley (55)	*280*
Dearest—Mickey & Sylvia (57)	135
Crackin' Up—Bo Diddley (59)	67
Who Do You Love—Woolies (67)	*58*
Gun Slinger—Bo Diddley (60)	41
Ooh Baby—Bo Diddley (67)	39
Who Do You Love—George Thorogood And The Destroyers (79)	*34*
Road Runner—Bo Diddley (60)	*32*
Say Man Back Again—Bo Diddley (59)	26
Bo Diddley—Joe Reisman and His Orchestra And Chorus (55)	*23*

Elias McDANIEL [Elias Otha Bates, Bo Diddley, Ethel Smith] ▶ 992 (20)	**4522**
Continued	
Who Do You Love—Quicksilver Messenger Service (69)	*12*
Love Is Strange—Buddy Holly / The Crickets (69)	*11*
Love Is Strange—Everly Brothers (65)	*3.4*
Bo Diddley—Jerry Murad's Harmonicats (55)	*0.0*
—Christopher McDaniels see: Christopher MAX	
Darryl McDANIELS ▶ 8690 (1)	**42**
It's Tricky—Run-D.M.C. (87)	170
Gene McDANIELS ▶ 920 (7)	**4806**
Feel Like Makin' Love—Roberta Flack (74)	*4150*
River—Joe Simon (73)	306
Money—Gladys Knight & The Pips (75)	295
Feelin' That Glow—Roberta Flack (75)	72
Compared To What—Les McCann & Eddie Harris (70)	24
25th Of Last December—Roberta Flack (77)	8.7
Feel Like Making Love—Bob James (74)	*6.5*
Jack McDERMOTT ▶ 3756 (3)	**709**
Ka Ding Dong—Hilltoppers (56)	*506*
Ka Ding Dong—G-Clefs (56)	*467*
Ka Ding Dong—Diamonds (56)	*445*
Bob McDILL ▶ 5322 (2)	**306**
Black Sheep—Sam The Sham And The Pharaohs (67)	209
Amanda—Waylon (79)	97
Clarence McDONALD ▶ 7105 (1)	**116**
Silly—Deniece Williams (81)	347
Ian McDONALD ▶ 5910 (2)	**230**
Long, Long Way From Home—Foreigner (77)	679
In The Court Of The Crimson King—King Crimson (70)	20
—James Solomon McDonald see: Solomon BURKE	
Joe McDONALD ▶ 9583 (2)	**21**
Breakfast For Two—Country Joe McDonald (75)	15
Not So Sweet Martha Lorraine—Country Joe And The Fish (67)	5.7
Michael McDONALD ▶ 368 (19)	**10489**
What A Fool Believes—Doobie Brothers (79)	5311
I Keep Forgettin'—Michael McDonald (82)	*3365*
This Is It—Kenny Loggins (79)	2064
You Belong To Me—Carly Simon (78)	*1970*
Real Love—Doobie Brothers (80)	1841
Heart To Heart—Kenny Loggins (82)	1312
Minute By Minute—Doobie Brothers (79)	1123
Takin' It To The Streets—Doobie Brothers (76)	1049
Yah Mo B There—James Ingram (83)	906
Dependin' On You—Doobie Brothers (79)	622
I Gotta Try—Michael McDonald (82)	495
Let Me Go, Love—Nicolette Larson (79)	477
No Lookin' Back—Michael McDonald (85)	461
It Keeps You Runnin'—Doobie Brothers (76)	*406*
It Keeps You Runnin'—Carly Simon (76)	*251*
Keep This Train A-Rollin'—Doobie Brothers (81)	83
Here To Love You—Doobie Brothers (82)	70
You Belong To Me—Doobie Brothers (83)	*23*
Take It To Heart—Michael McDonald (90)	19
Megan McDONOUGH ▶ 11186 (1)	**2.8**
No Return—Megan McDonough (73)	5.7
James McDOUGAL ▶ 4146 (6)	**581**
I Need Your Loving—Don Gardner And Dee Dee Ford (62)	1156
People Sure Act Funny—Arthur Conley (68)	325
Leave My Kitten Alone—Little Willie John (61)	*154*
Leave My Kitten Alone—Johnny Preston (61)	*113*
Leave My Kitten Alone—Little Willie John (59)	*91*
Let Me Down Easy—Betty LaVette (65)	21
Don McDOUGALL ▶ 8977 (1)	**34**
Follow Your Daughter Home—Guess Who (73)	172
Rich McDOUGALL ▶ 9573 (1)	**21**
You've Got The Power—Esquires (68)	21
Gary McDOWELL ▶ 8741 (3)	**41**
I Melt With You—Modern English (90)	*107*
I Melt With You—Modern English (83)	*88*
Hands Across The Sea—Modern English (84)	8.5
Ronnie McDOWELL ▶ 4326 (2)	**520**
The King Is Gone—Ronnie McDowell (77)	1012
I Love You, I Love You, I Love You—Ronnie McDowell (78)	14
Eddie McDUFF ▶ 5919 (2)	**228**
First Quarrel—Paul & Paula (63)	680
I Feel A Sin Coming On—Solomon Burke (66)	3.4
Jack McDUFF [Brother Jack McDuff, Eugene McDuffy] ▶ 10811 (1)	**5.2**
Theme From Electric Surfboard—Brother Jack McDuff (69)	5.2
—Eugene McDuffy see: Jack McDUFF	
—Albert Geoffrey McElhinney see: Geoff MACK	
Johnny McELHONE ▶ 6303 (2)	**184**
The Honeythief—Hipsway (87)	639
I Don't Want A Lover—Texas (89)	47
Ethon McELROY ▶ 9087 (1)	**32**
Can't Help But Love You—Standells (67)	63
Thomas McELROY ▶ 3427 (4)	**853**
Hold On—En Vogue (90)	3351
Lies—En Vogue (90)	676
Why You Treat Me So Bad—Club Nouveau (87)	381
Little Walter—Tony! Toni! Toné! (88)	272
—Van McElvain see: Van McLAIN	
Dave McENERY [Red River Dave] ▶ 8792 (3)	**39**
There's A Star Spangled Banner Waving #2 (The Ballad Of Francis Powers)—Red River Dave (60)	*117*
There's A Star Spangled Banner Waving Somewhere—Tommy Dee (60)	*0.0*
There's A Star Spangled Banner Waving Somewhere—Betty Johnson (60)	*0.0*
Mark McENTEE ▶ 4345 (2)	**516**
I Touch Myself—Divinyls (91)	2042
Make Out Alright—Divinyls (91)	16
Gary McEWEN ▶ 4378 (2)	**509**
Let It Out (Let It All Hang Out)—Hombres (67)	2036
It's A Gas—Hombres (68)	1.4
Duke McFADDEN ▶ 7976 (1)	**67**
I Could Be Good For You—707 (80)	133
Gene McFADDEN ▶ 1302 (10)	**3401**
Back Stabbers—O'Jays (72)	4999
Wake Up Everybody (Part 1)—Harold Melvin And The Blue Notes (75)	1592
Ain't No Stoppin' Us Now—McFadden & Whitehead (79)	1423
Bad Luck (Part 1)—Harold Melvin And The Blue Notes (75)	*1407*
I'll Always Love My Mama (Part I)—Intruders (73)	618
Where Are All My Friends—Harold Melvin And The Blue Notes (74)	117
Bad Luck—Ritchie Family (76)	*92*
Tell The World How I Feel About 'Cha Baby—Harold Melvin And The Blue Notes (76)	66
Let's Groove—Archie Bell & The Drells (76)	38
Bad Luck—Atlanta Disco Band (76)	*14*
Theresa McFADDIN ▶ 4296 (4)	**530**
Forget Me Nots—Patrice Rushen (82)	752
One Love In My Lifetime—Diana Ross (76)	628
Look What You've Done To My Heart—Marilyn McCoo & Billy Davis Jr. (77)	199
Somebody Loves You—Whispers (73)	7.9
Gary McFARLAND ▶ 10838 (1)	**5.0**
Balanco No Samba—Stan Getz (63)	5.0
J. Leslie McFARLAND ▶ 681 (12)	**6367**
Stuck On You—Elvis Presley With The Jordanaires (60)	8364
Little Children—Billy J. Kramer With The Dakotas (64)	2943
My Honey And Me—Luther Ingram (70)	*339*
Long Legged Girl (With The Short Dress On)—Elvis Presley With The Jordanaires (67)	332
Teenager's Mother (Are You Right?)—Bill Haley And His Comets (56)	264
The Wang Dang Taffy-Apple Tango (Mambo Cha Cha Cha)—Pat Boone (59)	116
(You Hit The Wrong Note) Billy Goat—Bill Haley And His Comets (57)	109
Missing You—Luther Ingram (72)	69
Won't Be Long—Aretha Franklin (61)	27
My Honey And Me—Emotions (72)	*22*
Love Is The Only Thing—Mickey And Sylvia (61)	4.3
Rough Lover—Aretha Franklin (62)	3.1
Fred McFARLANE ▶ 10617 (1)	**6.7**
Your Personal Touch—Evelyn "Champagne" King (86)	13
George McFARLANE ▶ 4692 (2)	**438**
Another Lover—Giant Steps (88)	1147
Into You—Giant Steps (89)	166
John McFEE ▶ 5829 (1)	**238**
One Step Closer—Doobie Brothers (80)	715
Bobby McFERRIN ▶ 1333 (1)	**3324**
Don't Worry Be Happy (Edit)—Bobby McFerrin (88)	3324
Earl McFIELD ▶ 11371 (1)	**2.0**
Ya Mama—Wuf Ticket (83)	8.1
Mike McGEAR [Peter Michael McCartney] ▶ 5734 (1)	**249**
Thank U Very Much—Scaffold (68)	249
Parker McGEE ▶ 611 (5)	**7065**
I'd Really Love To See You Tonight—England Dan & John Ford Coley (76)	4120
Nights Are Forever Without You—England Dan & John Ford Coley (76)	1547
American Music—Pointer Sisters (82)	956
You've Got Me Runnin'—Gene Cotton (76)	312
I Just Can't Say No To You—Parker McGee (77)	261
Charles McGHEE ▶ 11813 (1)	**0.0**
Trudy—Cleftones (58)	0.0
Edward McGHEE ▶ 10939 (1)	**4.2**
I Can't Get Over You—Dramatics (77)	13
Granville McGHEE ▶ 5362 (1)	**300**
Drinking Wine Spo-Dee O'dee—Jerry Lee Lewis (73)	599
—Joe McGhee see: Joe SENECA	
John McGHEE ▶ 6015 (1)	**216**
Holding On (When Love Is Gone)—L.T.D. (78)	431
Michael McGILL ▶ 4288 (1)	**531**
Oh What A Day—Dells (70)	531
Bob McGILPIN ▶ 10463 (1)	**8.1**
When You Feel Love—Bob McGilpin (78)	16
Carl McGINNIS ▶ 7657 (2)	**82**
To Be Loved (Forever)—Pentagons (61)	391
I Wonder (If Your Love Will Ever Belong To Me)—Pentagons (61)	21
Don McGINNIS ▶ 9422 (2)	**24**
Cosmic Sea—Mystic Moods (73)	51
Honey Trippin'—Mystic Moods (75)	21
M. McGINNIS ▶ 11103 (1)	**3.2**
Lady Lay—Wayne Newton (74)	13
Michael McGINNIS ▶ 9645 (1)	**20**
Happiness Train—Sugar Bears (72)	20
—Andrew Esmond Sheridan McGinnity see: Tony SHERIDAN	
Bennie McGINTY ▶ 3861 (1)	**674**
Ain't Gonna Bump No More (With No Big Fat Woman)—Joe Tex (77)	1347
—Colin McGlinchy see: James FREUD	
—Yvonne McGowan see: Yvonne DEVANEY	
Paul McGRANE ▶ 8648 (1)	**44**
Juke Box Saturday Night—Nino & the Ebb Tides (61)	88
George McGRAW ▶ 3142 (1)	**987**
Woo Hoo—Rock-A-Teens (59)	987
George McGREGOR ▶ 10360 (1)	**9.5**
I'm Satisfied—San Remo Golden Strings (65)	38
Allen McGRIER ▶ 6226 (2)	**192**
Square Biz—Teena Marie (81)	363
Ooo La La La—Teena Marie (88)	20
Jimmy McGRIFF ▶ 4686 (4)	**438**
All About My Girl—Jimmy McGriff (63)	332
Kiko—Jimmy McGriff (64)	73
M.G. Blues—Jimmy McGriff (62)	27
The Last Minute Pt. I—Jimmy McGriff (63)	6.3
Ralston McGRIFF [Frank Bendinelli] ▶ 5342 (1)	**302**
Mixed-Up, Shook-Up, Girl—Patty & The Emblems (64)	605
Bill McGUFFIE ▶ 11537 (1)	**1.3**
Sweet September—Lettermen (65)	3.8
—Jim McGuinn see: Roger McGUINN	
Roger McGUINN [James Roger McGuinn, Jim McGuinn, James Joseph McGuinn III] ▶ 1105 (9)	**4009**
You Showed Me—Turtles (68)	3696
Eight Miles High—Byrds (66)	1385
So You Want To Be A Rock 'N' Roll Star—Byrds (67)	550
Mr. Spaceman—Byrds (66)	527

Roger McGUINN [James Roger McGuinn, Jim McGuinn, James Joseph McGuinn III] ▶ 1105 (9) *Continued*	**4009**
Don't You Write Her Off—McGuinn, Clark & Hillman (79)	481
5 D (Fifth Dimension)—Byrds (66)	387
It Won't Be Wrong—Byrds (66)	348
Ballad Of Easy Rider—Byrds (69)	92
Chestnut Mare—Byrds (70)	7.5
Barry McGUIRE ▶ 3877 (1)	**670**
Green, Green—New Christy Minstrels (63)	1340
Ra McGUIRE ▶ 7378 (1)	**99**
Raise A Little Hell—Trooper (78)	199
—M.C. Hammer see: Stanley BURRELL	
Don McHAN ▶ 8207 (1)	**58**
The Pill—Loretta Lynn (75)	175
David McHUGH ▶ 5904 (1)	**231**
Freedom—Pointer Sisters (85)	231
Jimmy McHUGH ▶ 2261 (19) HOF	**1685**
Where Are You—Dinah Washington (62)	*816*
Too Young To Go Steady—Nat "King" Cole (56)	*779*
Don't Blame Me—Everly Brothers (61)	702
I'm In The Mood For Love—Chimes (61)	*532*
The Star You Wished Upon Last Night—Gisele MacKenzie (56)	*298*
I'm In The Mood For Love—Fats Domino (57)	*68*
Too Young To Go Steady—Connie Stevens (60)	*53*
Too Young To Go Steady—Patti Page (56)	*41*
You're A Sweetheart—Little Willie John (58)	*24*
Louella—Pat Boone (57)	20
I Can't Give You Anything But Love—Johnston Brothers (55)	*13*
Where Are You—Duprees featuring Joey Vann (64)	*11*
I Can't Give You Anything But Love—Bert Kaempfert And His Orchestra (66)	*3.8*
You're A Sweetheart—Dinah Washington (62)	*2.7*
On The Sunny Side Of The Street—Modernaires (57)	1.9
Love Me As Though There Were No Tomorrow—Sonny Knight (65)	0.5
The Star You Wished Upon Last Night—Nick Noble (56)	*0.0*
The Star You Wished Upon Last Night—Jeannie Carson (56)	*0.0*
I'm In The Mood For Love—Spike Jones & City Slickers (54)	*0.0*
Anne McIAN [Anne Black Montgomery] ▶ 7253 (1)	**107**
Solitaire—Peter McIan (80)	214
Peter McIAN ▶ 5219 (3)	**323**
Looking For A Stranger—Pat Benatar (83)	353
Solitaire—Peter McIan (80)	214
Voice On The Radio—Conductor (82)	79
Carl McINTOSH ▶ 7464 (1)	**94**
Hangin' On A String (Contemplating)—Loose Ends (85)	282
—Lonnie McIntosh see: Lonnie MACK	
Robbie McINTOSH ▶ 2919 (2)	**1118**
Pick Up The Pieces—AWB (74)	5059
Cut The Cake—AWB (75)	1651
Fritz McINTYRE ▶ 5394 (1)	**296**
Something Got Me Started—Simply Red (91)	591
Lani McINTYRE ▶ 7362 (1)	**100**
The One Rose (That's Left In My Heart)—Teresa Brewer (58)	200
Mark McINTYRE ▶ 4517 (9)	**473**
Tucumcari—Jimmie Rodgers (59)	467
The Money Tree—Margaret Whiting (56)	*233*
Trouble With Harry—Alfi & Harry (56)	*105*
The Money Tree—Patience and Prudence (56)	*88*
Jenny Lou—Sonny James (60)	78
Trouble With Harry—Les Baxter, His Chorus and Orchestra (56)	*17*
The Money Tree—Frankie Lester (56)	*0.0*
The Money Tree—Annisteen Allen (56)	*0.0*
The Trouble With Harry—Jack Pleis and His Orchestra and Chorus (56)	*0.0*
Onnie McINTYRE ▶ 2780 (3)	**1199**
Pick Up The Pieces—AWB (74)	5059
Cut The Cake—AWB (75)	1651
School Boy Crush—AWB (75)	485

Goldy McJOHN [John Raymond Goadsby] ▶ 8518 (1)	**47**
For Ladies Only—Steppenwolf (71)	190
Duff McKAGAN ▶ 1640 (7)	**2558**
Sweet Child O' Mine—Guns N' Roses (88)	4596
Patience—Guns N' Roses (89)	2050
Paradise City—Guns N' Roses (89)	1901
Don't Cry—Guns N' Roses (91)	1769
Welcome To The Jungle—Guns N' Roses (88)	1661
You Could Be Mine—Guns N' Roses (91)	289
Nightrain—Guns N' Roses (89)	9.3
Albert Philip McKAY ▶ 662 (9) HOF	**6551**
Best Of My Love—Emotions (77)	7303
September—Earth, Wind & Fire (78)	2728
Sing A Song—Earth, Wind & Fire (75)	2498
Do Your Thing—Watts 103rd Street Rhythm Band (69)	1496
Saturday Nite—Earth, Wind & Fire (76)	856
Let Me Talk—Earth, Wind & Fire (80)	319
Till You Get Enough—Watts 103rd Street Rhythm Band (69)	200
Flowers—Emotions (76)	93
Smile—Emotions (78)	33
Scotty McKAY [Max K. Lipscomb] ▶ 6524 (1)	**160**
Summer's Comin'—Kirby St. Romain (63)	320
Jeffrey Markus McKEE ▶ 7981 (1)	**66**
Evil Boll-Weevil—Grand Canyon (74)	133
Maria McKEE ▶ 5855 (3)	**237**
Shelter—Lone Justice (87)	297
A Good Heart—Feargal Sharkey (86)	71
Sweet, Sweet Baby (I'm Falling)—Lone Justice (85)	53
Fran McKENDREE ▶ 9728 (1)	**18**
Because It's Time—McKendree Spring (71)	18
Edward McKENDRY ▶ 7186 (2)	**111**
The Last Leaf—Cascades (63)	220
Seein' Is Believin'—Eddie Hodges (62)	2.2
Danny McKENNA ▶ 3644 (1)	**752**
My Angel Baby—Toby Beau (78)	1504
Stan McKENNEY ▶ 6076 (3)	**209**
Homely Girl—Chi-Lites (74)	214
Who Is He And What Is He To You—Creative Source (74)	171
My Heart Just Keeps On Breakin'—Chi-Lites (73)	33
Maron McKENZIE ▶ 3226 (3)	**941**
Little Town Flirt—Del Shannon (62)	1561
Two Kinds Of Teardrops—Del Shannon (63)	319
Casanova Brown—Young Sisters (62)	3.6
Scott McKENZIE [Philip Wallach Blondheim] ▶ 2759 (2)	**1216**
Kokomo—Beach Boys (88)	3513
What About Me—Anne Murray (73)	338
—Jenny McKeown see: Theresa MATTHIAS	
—James Horton McKinley see: McKinley HORTON	
Maurice McKINLEY ▶ 9963 (1)	**14**
Feelin' That Glow—Roberta Flack (75)	72
Ray McKINLEY ▶ 9201 (1)	**29**
Beat Me Daddy Eight To The Bar—Commander Cody And His Lost Planet Airmen (72)	116
Wilfred McKINLEY ▶ 3416 (3)	**857**
Selfish One—Jackie Ross (64)	1658
I've Got The Skill—Jackie Ross (64)	48
(The Story Of) Woman, Love And A Man (Part 1)—Tony Clarke (64)	35
Al McKINNEY ▶ 9821 (1)	**16**
Come Go With Me—Pockets (77)	49
Sami McKINNEY ▶ 5325 (1)	**304**
Just Because—Anita Baker (89)	913
—Perri McKissack see: Perri Arlette REID	
Alma McKNIGHT ▶ 6616 (1)	**150**
Happy Days—Marv Johnson (60)	301
Billy Wade McKNIGHT ▶ 9912 (1)	**15**
Take Me To Your Heart—Monkey Meeks (73)	15
Rod McKUEN ▶ 355 (12)	**10740**
Seasons In The Sun—Terry Jacks (74)	6335
Jean—Oliver (69)	5653
I Think Of You—Perry Como (71)	422
The World I Used To Know—Jimmie Rodgers (64)	395
Mummy—Bob McFadden & Dor (59)	374
If You Go Away—Damita Jo (66)	*275*

Ally Ally Oxen Free—Kingston Trio (63)	231
If You Go Away—Terry Jacks (74)	*227*
Sing Boy Sing—Tommy Sands (58)	220
Love's Been Good To Me—Frank Sinatra (69)	209
Oliver Twist—Rod McKuen (62)	188
Two-Ten, Six-Eighteen (Doesn't Anybody Know My Name)—Jimmie Rodgers (63)	159
Van McLAIN [Van McElvain] ▶ 6759 (3)	**140**
You've Got What I Need—Shooting Star (80)	87
Hollywood—Shooting Star (82)	65
Touch Me Tonight—Shooting Star (89)	64
Malcolm McLAREN ▶ 9842 (1)	**16**
Do You Wanna Hold Me?—Bow Wow Wow (83)	81
Jerome McLAUGHLIN ▶ 11020 (1)	**3.8**
Memphis At Sunrise—Bar-Kays (72)	7.6
—Mark McLaughlin see: Marti PELLOW	
Don McLEAN ▶ 217 (10) HOF	**15165**
American Pie—Don McLean (71)	10747
Vincent—Don McLean (72)	1615
And I Love You So—Perry Como (73)	*1090*
Dreidel—Don McLean (72)	929
Castles In The Air—Don McLean (81)	*489*
If We Try—Don McLean (73)	239
And I Love You So—Bobby Goldsboro (71)	*36*
Wonderful Baby—Don McLean (75)	12
It's Just The Sun—Don McLean (81)	9.3
Castles In The Air—Don McLean (72)	*0.0*
Ali McLEOD ▶ 6526 (1)	**160**
The Honeythief—Hipsway (87)	639
Marilyn McLEOD ▶ 1123 (7)	**3948**
Love Hangover—Diana Ross (76)	*5162*
You Can't Turn Me Off (In The Middle Of Turning Me On)—High Inergy (77)	1358
Let Me Tickle Your Fancy—Jermaine Jackson (82)	820
Walk In The Night—Jr. Walker & The All Stars (72)	398
Same Ole Love (365 Days A Year)—Anita Baker (87)	363
Pops, We Love You (A Tribute To Father)—Diana Ross, Marvin Gaye, Smokey Robinson & Stevie Wonder (79)	165
Love Hangover—5th Dimension (76)	*40*
Oscar McLOLLIE ▶ 9591 (1)	**21**
Hey Girl-Hey Boy—Oscar McLollie and Jeannette Baker (58)	41
Annie McLOONE ▶ 9940 (1)	**15**
Ooo-eee—Nicolette Larson (81)	15
Sharon McMAHAN ▶ 3608 (2)	**769**
Some Day We're Gonna Love Again—Searchers (64)	461
Straighten Up Your Heart—Barbara Lewis (63)	308
Gerard McMAHON ▶ 5373 (3)	**299**
Bad Times—Tavares (80)	198
Give Me All Night—Carly Simon (87)	174
Count On Me—Gerard McMahon (83)	14
Patrick J. McMANUS ▶ 6667 (3)	**146**
Baby, Hang Up The Phone—Carl Graves (74)	244
American Made—Oak Ridge Boys (83)	47
No Love In The Room—5th Dimension (75)	0.7
—Bruce McMeans see: Bruce CHANNEL	
Edwin McMULLEN ▶ 10800 (1)	**5.2**
Frivolette—Hilltoppers (55)	16
Stan McMULLEN ▶ 8593 (1)	**45**
It's So Hard Being A Loser—Contours (67)	136
Clay McMURRAY ▶ 2108 (3)	**1865**
If I Were Your Woman—Gladys Knight & The Pips (70)	2652
Make Me The Woman That You Go Home To—Gladys Knight & The Pips (71)	785
God Bless Whoever Sent You—Originals (70)	393
Robert Ian McNABB ▶ 4790 (1)	**415**
Whisper To A Scream (Birds Fly)—Icicle Works (84)	415
Larry John McNALLY ▶ 2639 (3)	**1301**
The Motown Song—Rod Stewart (91)	1268
Somewhere, Somebody—Aaron Neville (91)	73
Just Like Paradise—Larry John McNally (81)	8.2
Robin McNAMARA ▶ 3867 (1)	**672**
Lay A Little Lovin' On Me—Robin McNamara (70)	2016
Ted McNAMARA ▶ 5044 (1)	**354**
Sooner Or Later—Grass Roots (71)	1771
—Wayne McNatt see: Wayne FAMOUS	
James McNAUGHTON ▶ 7291 (1)	**105**
Rivers Of Babylon—Boney M (78)	419

Cecil (Big Jay) McNEELY ▶ 2635 (3)	**1303**
There Is Something On Your Mind Part Two—Bobby Marchan (60)	*767*
There Is Something On Your Mind—Big Jay McNeely and Band (59)	*450*
There's Something On Your Mind—Baby Ray (66)	*86*
Doris McNEIL ▶ 5686 (2)	**255**
What Is A Man—Four Tops (69)	266
I'm Still A Struggling Man—Edwin Starr (69)	243
Landy McNEIL ▶ 5197 (2)	**328**
On The Beach (In The Summertime)—5th Dimension (70)	325
One Light Two Lights—Satisfactions (70)	3.3
Randall McNEILL ▶ 2073 (1)	**1920**
If I Could Reach You—5th Dimension (72)	1920
Robert McNELLEY ▶ 11285 (1)	**2.4**
Start It All Over—McGuffey Lane (82)	2.4
Steve McNICOL ▶ 3043 (1)	**1039**
You, I—Rugbys (69)	1039
Frank McNULTY ▶ 10404 (2)	**8.8**
To Be With You—Highlights (57)	5.3
Bye Bye Baby Goodbye—Teresa Brewer (59)	3.6
Shamus M'COOL [Richard Doyle] ▶ 9641 (1)	**20**
American Memories—Shamus M'Cool (81)	20
Prentiss McPHAIL ▶ 8293 (1)	**55**
Scratchy—Travis Wammack (64)	165
Clyde McPHATTER ▶ 3720 (9)	**720**
Ta Ta—Clyde McPhatter (60)	1080
Honey Love—Bunny Paul with The Harptones (54)	*177*
I Never Knew—Clyde McPhatter (61)	120
Psycho—Bobby Hendricks (60)	49
Honey Love—Four Lovers (56)	*5.6*
Honey Love—Narvel Felts (60)	*4.8*
Just Give Me A Ring—Clyde McPhatter (60)	2.3
Honey Love—Vicki Young (54)	*0.0*
Honey Love—Drifters Featuring Clyde McPhatter (54)	*0.0*
Donald McPHERSON ▶ 5087 (4)	**345**
Spinning Around (I Must Be Falling In Love)—Main Ingredient (71)	489
You've Been My Inspiration—Main Ingredient (70)	362
Black Seeds Keep On Growing—Main Ingredient (71)	51
I'm Better Off Without You—Main Ingredient (70)	31
—Donna McPherson see: Wyatt McPHERSON	
Graham McPHERSON ▶ 5332 (1)	**303**
Our House—Madness (83)	2122
Jim McPHERSON ▶ 4729 (1)	**429**
Jane—Jefferson Starship (79)	1718
—Richard Cecil McPherson see: Cecil MACK	
Tim McPHERSON ▶ 3193 (1)	**957**
Backfield In Motion—Mel And Tim (69)	1914
Warner McPHERSON [Warner Mack, Warner MacPherson] ▶ 5352 (4)	**301**
Roc A Chicka—Warner Mack (57)	*205*
Is It Wrong (For Loving You)—Warner Mack (57)	*65*
Is It Wrong (For Loving You)—Webb Pierce (60)	*31*
Rock-A-Chicka—Jim Lowe (57)	*0.0*
Wyatt McPHERSON [Donna McPherson] ▶ 11575 (1)	**1.2**
Here's My Confession—Wyatt (Earp) McPherson (61)	2.3
Rod McQUEEN [David William Balfe] ▶ 2336 (4)	**1581**
Beautiful Sunday—Daniel Boone (72)	1614
Did You Boogie (With Your Baby)—Flash Cadillac & The Continental Kids (76)	699
Annabelle—Daniel Boone (72)	146
Run Tell The People—Daniel Boone (75)	4.6
Tim McQUEEN ▶ 7832 (1)	**73**
Make Me Twice The Man—New York City (73)	73
Floyd F. McRAE ▶ 2296 (2)	**1642**
Sh-Boom—Crew-Cuts (54)	*7040*
Sh-Boom—Chords (54)	*1169*
Ted McRAE [Teddy Bear, Teddy McRae, Theodore McRae] ▶ 5422 (3)	**291**
Love Love Love—Clovers (56)	*546*
Love Love Love—Diamonds (56)	*315*
Walking The Blues—Jack DuPree and Mr. Bear (55)	7.5
Steve McRAY ▶ 6254 (1)	**189**
Alien—Atlanta Rhythm Section (81)	566
Bob McREE ▶ 3842 (2)	**681**
Lover's Holiday—Peggy Scott & Jo Jo Benson (68)	1147
Pickin' Wild Mountain Berries—Peggy Scott & Jo Jo Benson (68)	897
Griffith McREE ▶ 7889 (1)	**71**
Ch Ch Cherie—Johnny Average Band (81)	142
Jay McSHANN ▶ 6574 (6)	**154**
Keep Your Hands Off Of Him—Damita Jo (61)	*114*
Hands Off—Johnny Maddox Orchestra (55)	*95*
Hands Off—Jay McShann's Orchestra (55)	*95*
Confessin' The Blues—Dakota Staton (58)	6.0
Hands Off—Nan Wynn (55)	*0.0*
Hands Off—Frankie Castro (55)	*0.0*
Cameron McVEY ▶ 2667 (3)	**1285**
Buffalo Stance—Neneh Cherry (89)	2690
Kisses On The Wind—Neneh Cherry (89)	1072
Heart—Neneh Cherry (89)	154
Mark McVEY [Mark Ashton Vey] ▶ 10341 (1)	**9.8**
Sympathy—Rare Bird (70)	39
Christine McVIE [Christine Anne Perfect] ▶ 233 (13)	**14484**
Hold Me—Fleetwood Mac (82)	4430
Don't Stop—Fleetwood Mac (77)	3731
Little Lies—Fleetwood Mac (87)	1985
Say You Love Me—Fleetwood Mac (76)	1673
You Make Loving Fun—Fleetwood Mac (77)	1536
Got A Hold On Me—Christine McVie (84)	1295
Everywhere—Fleetwood Mac (87)	1062
Over My Head—Fleetwood Mac (75)	928
Think About Me—Fleetwood Mac (80)	753
Love In Store—Fleetwood Mac (82)	668
Love Will Show Us How—Christine McVie (84)	430
As Long As You Follow—Fleetwood Mac (88)	414
Save Me—Fleetwood Mac (90)	380
Carl McVOY ▶ 3920 (2)	**656**
Do It - Rat Now—Bill Black's Combo (63)	425
Monkey-Shine—Bill Black And His Combo (63)	232
Wes McWAIN ▶ 7052 (2)	**119**
Ambrose (Part Five)—Linda Laurie (59)	337
Just Keep Walkin' Ambrose—Jimmy Valentine & His Orchestra (59)	21
—M.C. Zipp see: Jens Kjaer LARSEN	
Frank W. MEACHAM ▶ 8041 (2)	**64**
American Patrol—Larry Elgart And His Manhattan Swing Orchestra (82)	*50*
American Patrol—Frank Barber Orchestra (82)	*14*
—Norman Meade see: Jerry RAGOVOY	
—Edwin Lionel Meadows see: Punky MEADOWS	
Fred MEADOWS ▶ 6012 (1)	**216**
You Were Only Fooling (While I Was Falling In Love)—Vic Damone (65)	649
Jon MEADOWS ▶ 8804 (1)	**39**
Cutie Pie—One Way (82)	273
Punky MEADOWS [Edwin Lionel Meadows] ▶ 9291 (2)	**27**
That Magic Touch—Angel (77)	78
Flying With Broken Wings (Without You)—Angel (78)	3.6
Gary MEARS ▶ 4362 (2)	**512**
So Tough—Original Casuals (58)	*457*
So Tough—Kuf-Linx (58)	*56*
—Meat Loaf see: Marvin Lee ADAY	
Huey P. MEAUX ▶ 1618 (7)	**2609**
You'll Lose A Good Thing—Barbara Lynn (62)	*2239*
The Rains Came—Sir Douglas Quintet (66)	*730*
You'll Lose A Good Thing—Freddy Fender (76)	*443*
Breaking Up Is Hard To Do—Jivin' Gene And The Jokers (59)	371
Neighbor, Neighbor—Jimmy Hughes (66)	212
The Rains Came—Big Sambo And The House Wreckers (62)	*138*
Going Out With The Tide—Jivin' Gene (60)	5.2
Dudley MECUM ▶ 10791 (1)	**5.3**
Angry—Frank Pizani (57)	21
Leon MEDICA ▶ 6442 (1)	**168**
New Orleans Ladies—Louisiana's Le Roux (78)	337
Bill MEDLEY ▶ 1718 (6)	**2438**
Little Latin Lupe Lu—Mitch Ryder And The Detroit Wheels (66)	*1093*
Go Ahead And Cry—Righteous Brothers (66)	550
Little Latin Lupe Lu—Kingsmen (64)	*362*
Little Latin Lupe Lu—Righteous Brothers (63)	*332*
My Babe—Righteous Brothers (63)	181
Bring Your Love To Me—Righteous Brothers (65)	21
Phil MEDLEY ▶ 452 (13)	**9224**
Twist And Shout—Beatles (64)	*6394*
A Million To One—Jimmy Charles And The Revellettes (60)	*3389*
Twist And Shout—Isley Brothers (62)	*2072*
Killer Joe—Rocky Fellers (63)	*1215*
Twist And Shout—Beatles (86)	*529*
A Million To One—Donny Osmond (73)	*296*
If I Didn't Have A Dime (To Play The Jukebox)—Gene Pitney (62)	279
A Million To One—Five Stairsteps & Cubie (68)	*242*
These Worldly Wonders—Patti Page (58)	152
Killer Joe—Kingsmen (66)	*94*
A Million To One—Brian Hyland (69)	*64*
Push Push—Austin Taylor (60)	9.6
Love Me My Love—Dean Martin (60)	7.7
Rick MEDLOCKE ▶ 4864 (2)	**397**
Highway Song—Blackfoot (79)	543
Fly Away—Blackfoot (81)	250
Shorty MEDLOCKE ▶ 4383 (1)	**508**
Train, Train—Blackfoot (79)	508
—Samuel Medoff see: Dick MANNING	
Hank MEDRESS ▶ 3179 (6)	**966**
Tonight I Fell In Love—Tokens (61)	1434
I Have A Boyfriend—Chiffons (63)	647
I Hear Trumpets Blow—Tokens (66)	601
A Love So Fine—Chiffons (63)	466
Hear The Bells—Tokens (63)	148
When I Go To Sleep At Night—Tokens (61)	69
—Joe Medwick see: Joe VEASEY	
Danny MEEHAN ▶ 8449 (2)	**50**
Where Are You Going—Jerry Butler (70)	56
Machines—John Livigni (75)	44
Joe MEEK [Robert Duke, Robert George Meek] ▶ 465 (3)	**8993**
Telstar—Tornadoes (62)	8395
Put A Ring On My Finger—Les Paul and Mary Ford (58)	588
Globetrottin'—Tornadoes (63)	9.8
—Robert George Meek see: Joe MEEK	
—Mike Meezy see: Michael MARSHALL	
Tim MEHER ▶ 9376 (1)	**25**
Century's End—Donald Fagen (88)	50
Rose MEHLMAN ▶ 9585 (1)	**21**
My Boyfriend Got A Beatle Haircut—Donna Lynn (64)	62
—Heinz Meier see: Henry MAYER	
—Kurt Meier see: Kurt MALOO	
Henri MEILHAC ▶ 8773 (1)	**40**
Madrid—Nat "King" Cole (59)	198
Klaus MEINE ▶ 1586 (6)	**2666**
Wind Of Change—Scorpions (91)	1981
Rock You Like A Hurricane—Scorpions (84)	725
Send Me An Angel—Scorpions (91)	610
Still Loving You—Scorpions (84)	122
No One Like You—Scorpions (82)	103
Rhythm Of Love—Scorpions (88)	51
Fred MEINKEN ▶ 7303 (2)	**104**
Wabash Blues—Viscounts (60)	*88*
Wabash Blues—Billy Vaughn and his Orchestra (59)	*16*
Randy MEISNER ▶ 2161 (4)	**1809**
Take It To The Limit—Eagles (75)	3081
Hearts On Fire—Randy Meisner (81)	862
Deep Inside My Heart—Randy Meisner (80)	694
Gotta Get Away—Randy Meisner (81)	12
—Theodore Meister see: Ted DARYLL	
Gerardo MEJIA ▶ 5015 (3)	**359**
Rico Suave—Gerardo (91)	1126
We Want The Funk—Gerardo (91)	*667*
When The Lights Go Out—Gerardo (91)	1.5
Gabriel MEKLER ▶ 2311 (5)	**1613**
Cool Aid—Paul Humphrey & His Cool Aid Chemists (71)	918
Move Over—Steppenwolf (69)	918
Kozmic Blues—Janis Joplin (69)	435
All The Way Down—Etta James (73)	40
If I Could Only Be Sure—Nolan Porter (73)	9.5
Vince MELAMED ▶ 8071 (1)	**63**
Games—Phoebe Snow (81)	126

Terry MELCHER [Terrence P. Jordan] ► 796 (13)	**5578**
Kokomo—Beach Boys (88)	3513
Good Thing—Paul Revere And The Raiders Featuring Mark Lindsay (66)	3322
Him Or Me - What's It Gonna Be?—Paul Revere And The Raiders Featuring Mark Lindsay (67)	2110
I Had A Dream—Paul Revere And The Raiders Featuring Mark Lindsay (67)	1319
Ups And Downs—Paul Revere And The Raiders (67)	879
The Great Airplane Strike—Paul Revere And The Raiders Featuring Mark Lindsay (66)	812
Getcha Back—Beach Boys (85)	528
Peace Of Mind—Paul Revere And The Raiders Featuring Mark Lindsay (67)	433
Beach Girl—Pat Boone (64)	119
Rock 'N' Roll To The Rescue—Beach Boys (86)	99
Gone—Rip Chords (63)	38
Still Cruisin'—Beach Boys (89)	6.4
Gone Movin' On—Raiders (70)	4.0
Peter MELDGAARD ► 11113 (1)	**3.2**
Wanna Dance—Yasmin (91)	16
Chris MELDON ► 9274 (1)	**27**
Rain In May—Max Werner (81)	55
Lisette MELENDEZ ► 7740 (1)	**77**
A Day In My Life (Without You)—Lisette Melendez (91)	230
Pietro MELFA ► 8100 (1)	**62**
Give Me Time (L'Amore Se Ne Va)—Dusty Springfield (67)	185
Johnny MELFI ► 10955 (1)	**4.1**
Sun, Sun, Sun (Part 1)—Ja-Kki (76)	4.1
Ray MELINA ► 11205 (1)	**2.8**
Silly People—Litter (69)	11
Arthur MELKONIAN ► 7599 (2)	**87**
Harem Dance—Armenian Jazz Sextet (57)	*173*
Harem Dance—Roger King Mozian (57)	*0.0*
John MELLENCAMP ► 74 (22) HOF	**29412**
Jack & Diane—John Cougar (82)	7228
Hurts So Good—John Cougar (82)	6837
R.O.C.K. In The U.S.A. (A Salute To 60's Rock)—John Cougar Mellencamp (86)	2666
Small Town—John Cougar Mellencamp (85)	1961
Crumblin' Down—John Cougar Mellencamp (83)	1614
Lonely Ol' Night—John Cougar Mellencamp (85)	1590
Pink Houses—John Cougar Mellencamp (83)	1265
Cherry Bomb—John Cougar Mellencamp (87)	1224
Paper In Fire—John Cougar Mellencamp (87)	1165
Ain't Even Done With The Night—John Cougar (81)	1135
Authority Song—John Cougar Mellencamp (84)	1049
Hand To Hold On To—John Cougar (82)	920
Pop Singer—John Cougar Mellencamp (89)	845
Get A Leg Up—John Mellencamp (91)	835
Check It Out—John Cougar Mellencamp (88)	788
This Time—John Cougar (80)	740
I Need A Lover—John Cougar (79)	646
Rumbleseat—John Cougar Mellencamp (86)	494
Rain On The Scarecrow—John Cougar Mellencamp (86)	486
Jackie Brown—John Cougar Mellencamp (89)	208
Rooty Toot Toot—John Cougar Mellencamp (88)	134
Small Paradise—John Cougar (80)	50
Pat MELLIN ► 10073 (1)	**13**
Lost In The Shuffle—Jaye P. Morgan (56)	26
Robert MELLIN [Israel Melnikoff] ► 1330 (20)	**3343**
Stranger On The Shore—Andy Williams (62)	*1127*
It Isn't Right—Platters (56)	986
My One Sin—Four Coins (57)	*690*
My One Sin—Nat "King" Cole (55)	*594*
No One But You (In My Heart)—Ames Brothers (58)	468
(I'm Always Hearing) Wedding Bells—Eddie Fisher (55)	*459*
Hopelessly—Ames Brothers (54)	367
You You You—Mel Carter (66)	355
Not Yet—Susan Hunter (55)	289
Missing—McGuire Sisters (56)	284
Moment I Saw You—Joni James (55)	154
You're Mine—Four Aces (57)	145
Stranger On The Shore—Drifters (62)	*88*
Cornbelt Symphony—Bing & Gary Crosby (54)	28
Lost In The Shuffle—Jaye P. Morgan (56)	26

Just Between Friends—Kitty Kallen (55)	8.1
My One And Only Love—Roy Hamilton (58)	1.1
The Man With The Banjo—Ames Brothers (54)	0.0
(I'm Always Hearing) Wedding Bells—Frankie Lester (55)	*0.0*
(I'm Always Hearing) Wedding Bells—Guy Lombardo & His Royal Canadians (55)	*0.0*
—John Graham Mellor see: Joe STRUMMER	
—Mellow Man Ace see: Sergio REYES	
—Israel Melnikoff see: Robert MELLIN	
Lord MELODY [Fitzroy Alexander] ► 2274 (4)	**1664**
Mama Look At Bubu—Harry Belafonte (57)	*1664*
Mama Looka Boo Boo—Robert Mitchum (57)	*0.0*
Mama Look A Booboo—Marty Franklin (57)	*0.0*
Mama, Looka Boo Boo (Boo Boo Man)—Calypso Carnival Featuring King Flash (57)	*0.0*
Walter MELROSE ► 11447 (2)	**1.6**
Make Love To Me—Johnny Thunder & Ruby Winters (67)	*13*
Make Love To Me!—Jo Stafford (54)	*0.0*
Irving MELSHER ► 11749 (1)	**0.2**
I May Never Pass This Way Again—Perry Como (59)	0.4
Joe MELSON ► 192 (19)	**16206**
Crying—Roy Orbison (61)	*6223*
Running Scared—Roy Orbison (61)	*6095*
Only The Lonely (Know How I Feel)—Roy Orbison (60)	*5979*
Blue Bayou—Linda Ronstadt (77)	*4470*
Crying—Don McLean (81)	*2185*
Run, Baby Run (Back Into My Arms)—Newbeats (65)	1760
Blue Angel—Roy Orbison (60)	1636
Blue Bayou—Roy Orbison (63)	*1151*
The Crowd—Roy Orbison (62)	908
Crying—Jay & The Americans (66)	*569*
I'm Hurtin'—Roy Orbison (60)	410
Cry Softly Lonely One—Roy Orbison (67)	363
Memories Of Maria—Music Of Jerry Byrd (62)	244
Running Scared—Fools (81)	*170*
Up Town—Roy Orbison (59)	161
Laugh—Velvets (61)	55
Only the Lonely—Sonny James (The Southern Gentleman) (69)	*23*
Actress—Roy Orbison (62)	9.5
Lana—Gene McCannon (63)	0.5
Joan MELTZER ► 10328 (1)	**10**
A Man Who Sings—Richard Landis (72)	20
Rich MELTZER ► 5661 (1)	**258**
Burnin' For You—Blue Öyster Cult (81)	516
Wendy MELVOIN ► 5341 (3)	**303**
Mountains—Prince And The Revolution (86)	567
Waterfall—Wendy & Lisa (87)	232
America—Prince & The Revolution (85)	220
Jackie MEMBERS ► 3624 (6)	**762**
Thin Line Between Love And Hate—Persuaders (71)	*1568*
I'll Be Sweeter Tomorrow (Than I Was Today)—O'Jays (67)	458
Love Gonna Pack Up (And Walk Out)—Persuaders (71)	443
Thin Line Between Love And Hate—Pretenders (84)	*29*
Peace In The Valley Of Love—Persuaders (72)	12
Bad, Bold And Beautiful Girl—Persuaders (73)	0.4
—Memphis Slim see: Peter CHATMAN	
Gail MENAFEE ► 11505 (1)	**1.4**
You're So Nice To Be Near—Loreleis (55)	2.8
—Murray Mencher see: Ted MURRY	
Gunther MENDE ► 5789 (3)	**241**
Power Of Love—Laura Branigan (87)	*653*
The Power Of Love—Jennifer Rush (86)	*248*
The Power Of Love (You Are My Lady)—Air Supply (85)	*65*
Fred MENDELSOHN [Fred Madison] ► 3040 (3)	**1046**
Red River Rock—Johnny And The Hurricanes (59)	3410
Don't Be Angry—Nappy Brown (55)	*1091*
Don't Be Angry—Crew-Cuts (55)	*0.0*
—Jack Mendelsohn see: Jimmy SHIRL	
Felix MENDELSSOHN ► 9944 (1)	**15**
Mendelssohn's 4th (Second Movement)—Apollo 100 (72)	15
Peppino MENDES ► 5641 (1)	**261**
Jealous Of You (Tango Della Gelosia)—Connie Francis (60)	784

Ricardo Lopez MENDEZ ► 5089 (1)	**344**
Amor—Ben E. King (61)	*1033*
—Samuel Mendola see: Vic DANA	
Newton MENDONÇA ► 10308 (2)	**10**
Desafinado (Slightly Out Of Tune)—Pat Thomas (62)	*41*
Desafinado (Slightly Out Of Tune)—Ella Fitzgerald (62)	*0.0*
Norma MENDOZA [Norma Bender] ► 3855 (2)	**676**
Somewhere—Tymes (63)	1065
Living A Lie—Al Martino (63)	963
Dave MENIKETTI ► 8204 (1)	**58**
Summertime Girls—Y&T (85)	234
Dale MENTEN ► 4402 (1)	**505**
Run, Run, Run—Gestures (64)	505
Johnny MERCER ► 167 (67) HOF	**17642**
Moon River—Henry Mancini, His Orchestra And Chorus (61)	*3649*
Moon River—Jerry Butler (61)	*3029*
Something's Gotta Give—McGuire Sisters (55)	*2681*
You Must Have Been A Beautiful Baby—Bobby Darin (61)	*2364*
I Remember You—Frank Ifield (62)	2162
Fools Rush In—Rick Nelson (63)	*1909*
I Wanna Be Around—Tony Bennett (63)	1585
That Old Black Magic—Louis Prima And Keely Smith (58)	*1560*
Days of Wine And Roses—Henry Mancini His Orchestra & Chorus (63)	*1363*
Fools Rush In (Where Angels Fear To Tread)—Brook Benton (60)	*1092*
Days Of Wine And Roses—Andy Williams (63)	*942*
The Bilbao Song—Andy Williams (61)	936
That Old Black Magic—Bobby Rydell (61)	*886*
Bernardine—Pat Boone (57)	859
Goody Goody—Frankie Lymon (57)	*763*
Summer Wind—Frank Sinatra (66)	*685*
Charade—Henry Mancini And His Orchestra and Chorus (63)	*631*
That Old Black Magic—Sammy Davis Jr. (55)	*614*
Dream—Four Aces (54)	*535*
You Must Have Been A Beautiful Baby—Dave Clark Five (67)	*455*
Love With The Proper Stranger—Jack Jones (64)	341
Dream—Etta James (61)	*263*
One For My Baby (And One More For The Road)—Tony Bennett with Ray Conniff (57)	254
Dream—Betty Johnson (58)	*235*
Autumn Leaves—Mitch Miller & His Orchestra (55)	*162*
Come Rain Or Come Shine—Ray Charles (60)	*160*
Namely You—Don Cherry (56)	*126*
Come Rain Or Come Shine—Jerry Lewis (56)	*124*
Come Rain Or Come Shine—Rosemary Clooney (56)	*124*
Sweetheart Tree—Johnny Mathis (65)	*111*
Sluefoot—Four Aces (55)	*111*
Lonesome Polecat—McGuire Sisters (54)	*84*
Summer Wind—Wayne Newton (65)	*84*
Love In A Home—Doris Day (56)	*72*
Sweetheart Tree—Henry Mancini And His Orchestra (65)	*43*
Dream—Dinah Washington (62)	*38*
Autumn Leaves—Ray Charles Singers (55)	*37*
You Can't Run Away From It—Four Aces (56)	24
And The Angels Sing—Three Chuckles (56)	*23*
Technique—Pat Boone (57)	20
Fools Rush In—Etta James (62)	*14*
And The Angels Sing—Johnny Nash (59)	*12*
Old Black Magic—Clovers (59)	*4.4*
Summer Wind—Roger Williams & The Harry Simeone Chorale (65)	*4.2*
P. S. I Love You—Classics (2) (63)	2.7
Come Rain Or Come Shine—Ray Charles (68)	*1.8*
Charade—Andy Williams (64)	*0.5*
Dream—Mulcays (54)	*0.0*
Charade—Adam Wade (63)	*0.0*
Sluefoot—Ray Anthony (55)	*0.0*
Slue Foot—Modernaires (55)	*0.0*
Charade—Four Freshmen (63)	*0.0*
Moon River—Jean Thomas (62)	*0.0*
Goody, Goody—Jane Grant (57)	*0.0*
Namely You—Carmen McRae (56)	*0.0*
Love In A Home—Crew-Cuts (56)	*0.0*

Johnny MERCER ▶ 167 (67) HOF *Continued*	**17642**
Namely You—Julius La Rosa (56)	*0.0*
Autumn Leaves—Keely Smith (57)	*0.0*
Love In A Home—Bing Crosby (56)	*0.0*
Moon River—Fuller Brothers (61)	*0.0*
Goody Goody—Ella Fitzgerald (57)	*0.0*
Days Of Wine And Roses—Pat Boone (63)	*0.0*
Something's Gotta Give—Ray Anthony (55)	*0.0*
Something's Gotta Give—Sammy Davis Jr. (55)	*0.0*
Lonesome Polecat— Freddy Martin & His Orchestra (54)	*0.0*
Lonesome Polecat— Jack Pleis and His Orchestra and Chorus (54)	*0.0*
Autumn Leaves—Bette McLaurin with Ray Ellis' Orch. And Chorus (57)	*0.0*
Kelvin MERCER ▶ 8644 (1)	**44**
Me Myself And I—De La Soul (89)	353
Jimmy MERCHANT ▶ 1867 (8)	**2184**
Why Do Fools Fall In Love— Teenagers Featuring Frankie Lymon (56)	*4057*
Why Do Fools Fall In Love—Diana Ross (81)	*2314*
Why Do Fools Fall In Love—Gale Storm (56)	*2295*
Why Do Fools Fall In Love—Diamonds (56)	*1782*
Why Do Fools Fall In Love—Happenings (67)	*389*
Why Do Fools Fall In Love—Gloria Mann (56)	*80*
Why Do Fools Fall In Love—Beach Boys (64)	*5.6*
Why Do Fools Fall In Love—Summer Wine (73)	*0.4*
Michael MERCHANT ▶ 5073 (2)	**348**
Time—Pozo-Seco Singers (66)	338
I'll Be Gone—Pozo-Seco Singers (66)	9.9
Natalie MERCHANT ▶ 5640 (3)	**261**
Trouble Me—10,000 Maniacs (89)	315
Like The Weather—10,000 Maniacs (88)	81
What's The Matter Here?—10,000 Maniacs (88)	45
Eric MERCURY ▶ 7245 (1)	**108**
You Are My Heaven— Roberta Flack With Donny Hathaway (80)	216
Freddie MERCURY [Farrokh Bulsara] ▶ 118 (16) HOF	**21680**
Crazy Little Thing Called Love—Queen (79)	7923
We Are The Champions—Queen (77)	4996
Ice Ice Baby—Vanilla Ice (90)	3735
Bohemian Rhapsody—Queen (75)	3141
Killer Queen—Queen (75)	1486
Somebody To Love—Queen (76)	1314
Body Language—Queen (82)	1067
Under Pressure—Queen & David Bowie (81)	689
Bicycle Race—Queen (78)	366
Play The Game—Queen (80)	359
I Want It All—Queen (89)	251
One Vision—Queen (85)	249
Love Kills—Freddie Mercury (84)	125
I Was Born To Love You—Freddie Mercury (85)	64
It's A Hard Life—Queen (84)	62
Don't Stop Me Now—Queen (79)	45
Charles MERENSTEIN ▶ 1704 (4)	**2458**
Handy Man—Jimmy Jones (59)	*5670*
Handy Man—James Taylor (77)	*3089*
Handy Man—Del Shannon (64)	*1029*
Bong Bong (I Love You Madly)—Vince Castro (58)	22
Dana MERINO ▶ 3923 (3)	**655**
You Need A Woman Tonight—Captain & Tennille (78)	343
Looks Like Love Again—Dann Rogers (79)	312
K.I.S.S.I.N.G.—Siedah Garrett (88)	1.5
Michael MERLO [Michel Merlo] ▶ 5323 (3)	**305**
Fibbin'—Patti Page (58)	569
My Empty Room— Little Anthony And The Imperials (60)	39
Nine O'Clock—McGuire Sisters (60)	2.5
—Michel Merlo see: Michael MERLO	
—Billy Merman see: Bill GIANT	
Ray MERRELL ▶ 7451 (1)	**95**
Make Me Forget—Bobby Rydell (64)	285
Wandra MERRELL [Wandra Merrell Brown] ▶ 2527 (10)	**1415**
Pepino The Italian Mouse—Lou Monte (62)	2271
Pepino's Friend Pasqual (The Italian Pussy-cat)— Lou Monte (63)	202
Eh Marie Eh Marie—Lou Monte (58)	80
Calypso Italiano—Lou Monte (57)	77
That's How It Goes—George Maharis (63)	48

Hey, Stella! (Who Zat Down Your Cellar?)— Crew-Cuts (58)	29
Spanish Nights And You—Connie Francis (66)	28
Dominick The Donkey— Lou Monte with Joe Reisman's Orch. & Chorus (60)	14
First Love—Playmates (59)	12
Marianna—Lou Monte (58)	5.5
—Johnny Lamont Merrett see: Little Johnny TAYLOR	
Charles D. MERRIAM ▶ 8822 (1)	**38**
Love For You—Sonoma (73)	38
Mahlon MERRICK ▶ 7159 (1)	**113**
Look Sharp—Be Sharp—Boston Pops Orchestra (54)	113
Alan MERRILL [Allan Preston Sachs] ▶ 1126 (2)	**3943**
I Love Rock 'N Roll— Joan Jett & The Blackhearts (82)	*7869*
I Love Rocky Road—"Weird Al" Yankovic (83)	*26*
Bob MERRILL [Henry Robert Merrill Levan] ▶ 117 (49) HOF	**21718**
Honeycomb—Jimmie Rodgers (57)	*5979*
You Don't Have To Be A Baby To Cry—Caravelles (63)	*3609*
People—Barbra Streisand (64)	*3349*
Tina Marie—Perry Como (55)	2680
Make Yourself Comfortable—Sarah Vaughan (54)	*2261*
Sweet Old Fashioned Girl—Teresa Brewer (56)	2000
Mambo Italiano—Rosemary Clooney (54)	1529
Miracle Of Love—Eileen Rodgers (56)	*881*
Funny Girl—Barbra Streisand (64)	448
People—Tymes (68)	*422*
When The Boys Talk About The Girls— Valerie Carr (58)	394
Above The Stars—Mr. Acker Bilk (62)	363
Where Will The Dimple Be—Rosemary Clooney (55)	263
Tell Me Tell Me—June Valli (54)	252
Madonna, Madonna—Tony Bennett with Percy Faith and His Orchestra (54)	175
How Much Is That Doggie In The Window— Baby Jane & The Rockabyes (63)	168
A Rusty Old Halo— Mahalia Jackson & The Falls-Jones Ensemble (55)	*144*
Give Me—Eileen Rodgers (56)	89
Miracle Of Love—Ginny Gibson (56)	*85*
Yes You Are—Mills Brothers (55)	84
People—Nat King Cole (64)	*76*
Bubbles—Frankie Laine (55)	*69*
Moon Is On Fire—Teresa Brewer (54)	58
Walk Along With Kings—Johnnie Ray (56)	*50*
Walk Along With Kings—Roy Hamilton (56)	*50*
Chow Mein—Gaylords (55)	47
Take Me Along—Ames Brothers (59)	*45*
Take Me Along—Lonnie Sattin (59)	*45*
Make Yourself Comfortable—Peggy King (54)	*44*
Make Yourself Comfortable—Andy Griffith (55)	*32*
You Don't Have To Be A Baby To Cry— "Tennessee" Ernie Ford (56)	*31*
Punch And Judy Love— Tony Bennett with Percy Faith and His Orchestra (55)	25
Promise Me A Rose (A Slight Detail)— Anita Bryant (59)	21
Ooh Bang Jiggilly Jang—Doris Day (55)	12
The Key To My Heart—Rosemary Clooney (56)	9.2
In The Middle Of A Dark Dark Night— Guy Mitchell (57)	8.2
I Am Woman—Barbra Streisand (64)	5.3
(Theme From "Carnival") Love Makes The World Go Round—Jane Morgan (61)	4.0
When All The Streets Are Dark— Somethin' Smith & The Redheads (55)	3.1
Sunshine Girl—Eddie Fisher (57)	2.1
Look At 'Er—Ralph Young (57)	*2.0*
Look At 'Er—Tony Martin (57)	*2.0*
Look At 'Er— Tommy Leonetti with The Ray Ellis Orchestra (57)	*2.0*
Theme From "The Wonderful World Of The Brothers Grimm"—David Rose And His Orchestra (62)	0.4
Honeycomb—Georgie Shaw (57)	*0.0*
Bubbles—Josephine Premice (55)	*0.0*
A Rusty Old Halo—Pat O'Day (55)	*0.0*
Miracle Of Love—Bonnie Lake & Her Beaus (56)	*0.0*
Make Yourself Comfortable— Eydie Gorme & Steve Lawrence (54)	*0.0*

George MERRILL ▶ 774 (5)	**5684**
I Wanna Dance With Somebody (Who Loves Me)— Whitney Houston (87)	4874
How Will I Know—Whitney Houston (85)	4102
Waiting For A Star To Fall—Boy Meets Girl (88)	3061
Oh Girl—Boy Meets Girl (85)	428
Bring Down The Moon—Boy Meets Girl (89)	270
Neal MERRITT ▶ 3403 (1)	**864**
May The Bird Of Paradise Fly Up Your Nose— "Little" Jimmy Dickens (65)	864
Oliver MERRITT ▶ 4431 (4)	**495**
Bon Voyage—Janice Harper (57)	689
That's Why I Was Born—Janice Harper (57)	*301*
That's Why I Was Born—Billy Scott (57)	*0.0*
That's Why I Was Born—Margaret Whiting (57)	*0.0*
Maceo MERRIWEATHER ▶ 10769 (1)	**5.4**
Worried Life Blues— Ray Charles And His Orchestra (60)	5.4
Norman MERSHON ▶ 5033 (1)	**357**
Such A Woman—Tycoon (79)	714
Frank MERTENS [Frank Sorgatz] ▶ 6979 (3)	**124**
Forever Young—Alphaville (88)	*185*
Big In Japan—Alphaville (84)	180
Forever Young—Alphaville (85)	*7.2*
Omar MESA ▶ 10733 (1)	**5.7**
Mandrill—Mandrill (71)	40
Gino MESCOLI ▶ 4045 (2)	**614**
My Love, Forgive Me (Amore, Scusami)— Robert Goulet (64)	1802
Begin To Love (Cominciamo Ad Amarci)— Robert Goulet (65)	40
Wilbur MESHEL [Sammy Bella, Sol H. Meshel, Billy Meshel] ▶ 5891 (6)	**233**
L. David Sloane—Michele Lee (68)	383
Around The Corner—Duprees (65)	56
Dear Mrs. Applebee—Flip Cartridge (66)	33
You're Running Out Of Kisses— Chuck Foote (61)	21
Today Has Been Cancelled—Billy Meshel (69)	3.9
Hello Enemy—Johnny Tillotson (66)	1.4
Walt MESKELL ▶ 5155 (1)	**333**
Abra-Ca-Dabra— Defranco Family Featuring Tony Defranco (73)	666
Jack MESKILL ▶ 8874 (1)	**37**
All The Way 'round The World—Mills Brothers (56)	75
—Edward Mesner see: Billy NESS	
Howard MESSER ▶ 10648 (1)	**6.5**
Walkin' The Fence—Couchois (79)	26
Jim MESSINA ▶ 1048 (8)	**4209**
Your Mama Don't Dance— Kenny Loggins With Jim Messina (72)	*3088*
Thinking Of You—Loggins & Messina (73)	1259
Your Mama Don't Dance—Poison (89)	*1055*
My Music—Loggins & Messina (73)	1015
Watching The River Run— Loggins & Messina (74)	164
Changes—Loggins & Messina (75)	115
You Better Think Twice—Poco (70)	112
Nobody But You— Kenny Loggins With Jim Messina (72)	63
Clive METCALFE ▶ 3600 (1)	**772**
A Summer Song—Chad Stuart & Jeremy Clyde (64)	2316
Pat METHENY ▶ 6295 (1)	**185**
This Is Not America— David Bowie/Pat Metheny Group (85)	554
Frank METIS ▶ 3574 (2)	**781**
Enchanted Sea—Islanders (59)	*1112*
Enchanted Sea— Exotic Sounds Of Martin Denny (59)	*450*
Gilbert METTERS ▶ 8821 (1)	**39**
Cherry Berry Wine—Charlie McCoy (61)	116
Chuck MEYER ▶ 2146 (5)	**1819**
Suddenly There's A Valley—Gogi Grant (55)	*1757*
Suddenly There's A Valley—Jo Stafford (55)	*1118*
Suddenly There's A Valley—Julius La Rosa (55)	*522*
Suddenly There's A Valley—Mills Brothers (55)	*194*
Suddenly There's A Valley—Patty Andrews (55)	*47*
George MEYER ▶ 7908 (2) HOF	**70**
For Me And My Gal—Freddy Cannon (61)	208
There Are Such Things—Modernaires (57)	1.9

Joseph MEYER ▶ 9757 (4) HOF	**17**
Clap Hands, Here Comes Charlie—Ella Fitzgerald (61)	13
If You Knew Susie—Johnston Brothers (55)	13
A Fool Of Fools—Tony Bennett (68)	11
On The Way Out—Walter Scott (58)	1.6
Michael MEYER ▶ 7791 (1)	**75**
I Wanna Be Loved—House Of Lords (88)	150
Richard E. MEYER ▶ 8754 (1)	**40**
Super Bowl Shuffle—Chicago Bears Shufflin' Crew (86)	161
Billy MEYERS ▶ 9491 (3)	**23**
Bugle Call Rag—Crazy Otto (55)	49
Nobody's Sweetheart—Johnnie Ray (55)	*13*
Nobody's Sweetheart—Jerry Cooper with The Johnny Guarnieri Swingtet (55)	*13*
Dana MEYERS ▶ 4756 (3)	**422**
It's A Love Thing—Whispers (81)	621
A Night To Remember—Shalamar (82)	260
Action—Evelyn "Champagne" King (84)	50
David Victor MEYERS ▶ 11513 (1)	**1.4**
Open Up Your Heart—Rainbow (72)	2.7
—Dwight Meyers see: HEAVY D	
Helmut MEYERS [Tim Benjamin] ▶ 9743 (1)	**18**
Crazy—Daisy Dee (91)	90
Marcus MEYN [Piet Herbert] ▶ 8548 (1)	**47**
The Great Commandment—Camouflage (88)	140
Elena MEZZETTI ▶ 7365 (3)	**100**
Stewball—Peter, Paul & Mary (63)	466
A 'Soalin'—Peter, Paul & Mary (63)	16
Big Boat—Peter, Paul & Mary (62)	6.2
—Miami Steve see: Steven VAN ZANDT	
—Irving Micahnik see: Ira MACK	
George MICHAEL [Georgios Kyriacos Panayiotou] ▶ 35 (19)	**47568**
Careless Whisper—Wham! Featuring George Michael (84)	5730
Faith—George Michael (87)	5246
Wake Me Up Before You Go-Go—Wham! (84)	5124
One More Try—George Michael (88)	4517
Everything She Wants—Wham! (85)	4018
Father Figure—George Michael (88)	4015
I Want Your Sex—George Michael (87)	3713
Monkey—George Michael (88)	3533
Praying For Time—George Michael (90)	3197
I'm Your Man—Wham! (85)	2644
Heaven Help Me—Deon Estus (89)	1845
Kissing A Fool—George Michael (88)	1710
Freedom—Wham! (85)	*1704*
A Different Corner—George Michael (86)	1473
Freedom—George Michael (90)	*1311*
The Edge Of Heaven—Wham! (86)	1111
Bad Boys—Wham! U.K. (83)	251
Waiting For That Day—George Michael (91)	248
Mother's Pride—George Michael (91)	130
John MICHAEL ▶ 5675 (1)	**256**
Angel Baby—Dean Martin (58)	513
William MICHAEL ▶ 2633 (1)	**1305**
Mission Bell—Donnie Brooks (60)	2611
Michele MICHAELE [Michaele DeFerraro, Jacqueline Misrahi] ▶ 7769 (2)	**76**
First...Be A Woman—Lenore O'Malley (80)	196
He—Today's People (73)	32
Mic MICHAELI ▶ 2726 (1)	**1239**
Carrie—Europe (87)	2479
Bret MICHAELS [Bret Michael Sychak] ▶ 1178 (10)	**3772**
Every Rose Has Its Thorn—Poison (88)	4813
Unskinny Bop—Poison (90)	2869
Something To Believe In—Poison (90)	2063
Nothin' But A Good Time—Poison (88)	1314
Talk Dirty To Me—Poison (87)	1055
I Won't Forget You—Poison (87)	1051
Fallen Angel—Poison (88)	903
Life Goes On—Poison (91)	401
Ride The Wind—Poison (91)	377
I Want Action—Poison (87)	240
Lee Eugene MICHAELS [Michael Olsen] ▶ 1347 (2)	**3295**
Do You Know What I Mean—Lee Michaels (71)	3276

Heighty Hi—Lee Michaels (69)	20
Roy MICHAELS [Shorty Miller] ▶ 9026 (1)	**33**
Good Old Rock 'N Roll—Cat Mother And The All Night News Boys (69)	164
Stephen MICHAELS [Stephen Michael] ▶ 2992 (1)	**1075**
Someone You Love—Nat "King" Cole (55)	1075
Tony MICHAELS ▶ 4955 (2)	**374**
Happy—Sunshine Company (67)	*557*
Happy—Blades Of Grass (67)	*191*
Don MICHALS ▶ 6064 (1)	**210**
Lullaby Of Love—Frank Gari (61)	629
John MICHALSKI ▶ 4295 (1)	**530**
Psychotic Reaction—Count Five (66)	2651
Paul MICHIELS ▶ 6327 (1)	**182**
The Way To Your Heart—Soulsister (89)	364
—Irwin Michnick see: Mitch LEIGH	
—Joey Edward Michno see: Joey COVINGTON	
Robert MICKENS ▶ 1857 (21)	**2194**
Celebration—Kool & The Gang (80)	6016
Jungle Boogie—Kool & The Gang (73)	2506
Hollywood Swinging—Kool & The Gang (74)	2079
Summertime—DJ Jazzy Jeff & The Fresh Prince (91)	1783
Get Down On It—Kool & The Gang (82)	1373
Emergency—Kool & The Gang (85)	915
Spirit Of The Boogie—Kool & The Gang (75)	825
Let's Go Dancin' (Ooh La, La, La)—Kool & The Gang (82)	654
Big Fun—Kool & The Gang (82)	532
Funky Stuff—Kool & The Gang (73)	473
Higher Plane—Kool & The Gang (74)	446
Kool And The Gang—Kool & The Gang (69)	329
Jones Vs. Jones—Kool & The Gang (81)	316
Caribbean Festival—Kool & The Gang (75)	268
Rhyme Tyme People—Kool & The Gang (75)	182
Let The Music Take Your Mind—Kool & The Gang (70)	85
Funky Man—Kool & The Gang (70)	41
The Gangs Back Again—Kool & The Gang (69)	37
Steppin' Out—Kool & The Gang (82)	6.6
Who's Gonna Take The Weight (Part One)—Kool & The Gang (71)	4.1
Summer Madness—Kool & The Gang (75)	0.0
Milton MIDDLEBROOK ▶ 5701 (1)	**253**
Casonova (Your Playing Days Are Over)—Ruby Andrews (67)	506
Harry MIDDLEBROOKS ▶ 2233 (4)	**1716**
Spooky—Classics IV (67)	*5516*
Spooky—Atlanta Rhythm Section (79)	*887*
Spooky—Mike Sharpe (67)	*224*
The "U-T"—Harry M. And The Marvels (61)	3.2
Ralph MIDDLEBROOKS ▶ 1874 (15)	**2174**
Love Rollercoaster—Ohio Players (75)	5251
Fire—Ohio Players (74)	4114
Funky Worm—Ohio Players (73)	1438
Skin Tight—Ohio Players (74)	1151
Who'd She Coo?—Ohio Players (76)	885
Ecstasy—Ohio Players (73)	621
Sweet Sticky Thing—Ohio Players (75)	411
Fopp—Ohio Players (76)	398
I Want To Be Free—Ohio Players (75)	335
Jive Turkey (Part 1)—Ohio Players (74)	245
Pain (Part 1)—Ohio Players (71)	208
O-H-I-O—Ohio Players (77)	144
Feel The Beat (Everybody Disco)—Ohio Players (77)	42
Got Pleasure—Ohio Players (72)	14
Rattlesnake—Ohio Players (76)	12
Anthony MIDDLETON ▶ 5836 (2)	**238**
Church Bells May Ring—Diamonds (56)	*981*
Church Bells May Ring—Willows (56)	*210*
Chuck MIDDLETON ▶ 8639 (1)	**44**
There You Go—Edwin Starr (73)	88
Bette MIDLER ▶ 5993 (4)	**219**
In The Mood—Bette Midler (74)	*323*
You're Movin' Out Today—Bette Midler (77)	*215*
You're Moving Out Today—Carole Bayer Sager (77)	*188*
I Could Have Loved You—Moments (78)	10
—Charlie Midnight see: Charles E. KAUFMAN	
—Mighty Hannibal see: James T. SHAW	
Franco MIGLIACCI ▶ 601 (9)	**7245**
Nel Blu Dipinto Di Blu (Volare)—Domenico Modugno (58)	*10773*

Volare—Bobby Rydell (60)	*3928*
Volare (Nel Blu Dipinto Di Blu)—Dean Martin (58)	*1266*
Volare—Al Martino (75)	*365*
Volare (Nel Blu Di Pinto Di Blu)—McGuire Sisters (58)	*17*
Nel Blu Dipinto Di Blu—Rosa Linda (58)	*0.0*
Volare (Nel Blu, Dipinto Di Blu)—Alan Dale (58)	*0.0*
Volare (Nel Blu Dipinto Di Blu)—Jesse Belvin (58)	*0.0*
(Nel Blu Dipinto Di Blu) Volare—Umberto Marcato (58)	*0.0*
—Francis Cosmo Migliaccio see: Fran COSMO	
—Mikaljon see: Al ABRAMS	
—Mikaljon see: John O'DEN	
—Mikaljon see: Stanley OSSMAN	
Fred MIKESELL ▶ 10349 (1)	**9.7**
Beach Party—Dave York And The Beachcombers (62)	19
Joe MIKOLAS ▶ 9154 (2)	**30**
Mexican Pearls—Billy Vaughn And His Orchestra (65)	*60*
Mexican Pearls—Don Randi (65)	*0.0*
Fred MILANO ▶ 7354 (1)	**100**
Diddle-Dee-Dum (What Happens When Your Love Has Gone)—Belmonts (62)	201
—Malvina Milder see: Malvina REYNOLDS	
Alfred Hart MILES ▶ 10478 (1)	**8.0**
Anchors Aweigh—Four Preps (62)	24
Buddy MILES ▶ 4996 (5)	**361**
Them Changes—Buddy Miles (71)	*206*
We Got To Live Together - Part I—Buddy Miles (70)	59
Rockin' And Rollin' On The Streets Of Hollywood—Buddy Miles (75)	53
Them Changes—Buddy Miles & The Freedom Express (70)	*43*
Them Changes—Carlos Santana & Buddy Miles (72)	*0.0*
Dick MILES ▶ 11460 (1)	**1.6**
Leave It To Love—Sarah Vaughan (57)	3.2
—Garry Miles see: Buzz CASON	
—Jean Miles see: Buck RAM	
John MILES [John Errington] ▶ 5454 (3)	**285**
Slowdown—John Miles (77)	279
Highfly—John Miles (76)	253
Music—John Miles (76)	19
—Junior Miles see: Edgar BRONFMAN	
—Otis Miles Jr. see: Otis Clayburne WILLIAMS	
Shiri MILETE ▶ 4999 (1)	**360**
Life—Elvis Presley (71)	360
Bubber MILEY [James Wesley Miley] ▶ 11422 (1)	**1.8**
Black And Tan Fantasy—David Rose And His Orchestra (62)	3.5
—James Wesley Miley see: Bubber MILEY	
Francis Philip MILITARY [Frank Military, Francis Philip] ▶ 7405 (2)	**98**
Christmas Auld Lang Syne—Bobby Darin (60)	186
Joanie—Bay Bops (58)	14
—Frank Military see: Francis Philip MILITARY	
Scott MILKS ▶ 8853 (1)	**38**
Kiss You (When It's Dangerous)—Eight Seconds (87)	151
Duncan MILLAR ▶ 8334 (1)	**54**
I Want To Be Your Property—Blue Mercedes (88)	108
Larry MILLAS ▶ 6745 (1)	**141**
You Wouldn't Listen—I'des Of March (66)	423
—Alex Miller see: Sonny Boy WILLIAMSON II	
Alonzo H. MILLER ▶ 2637 (2)	**1303**
U Can't Touch This—M.C. Hammer (90)	1930
Super Freak (Part I)—Rick James (81)	1318
Art MILLER ▶ 7397 (1)	**98**
Up-Hard—Willie Mitchell (68)	98
Bernard MILLER ▶ 4178 (2)	**573**
I Can't Stand The Rain—Eruption (78)	*930*
I Can't Stand The Rain—Ann Peebles (73)	*789*
—Bob Miller see: Shelby DARNELL	
—Branko Bernard Miller see: Tony COLE	
Byron Lee MILLER ▶ 8014 (1)	**65**
Reach For It—George Duke (77)	261
Charles MILLER ▶ 1241 (19)	**3615**
Spill The Wine—Eric Burdon And War (70)	*5207*
The Cisco Kid—War (73)	4378
Why Can't We Be Friends?—War (75)	3006
Low Rider—War (75)	2369

Charles MILLER ▶ 1241 (19) *Continued*	**3615**
Slippin' Into Darkness—War (71)	*2076*
The World Is A Ghetto—War (72)	1817
Gypsy Man—War (73)	1659
Summer—War (76)	1559
Me And Baby Brother—War (73)	1513
All Day Music—War (71)	704
Ballero—War (74)	472
They Can't Take Away Our Music— Eric Burdon And War Featuring Sharon Scott And The Beautiful New Born Children Of Southern California (70)	418
Spill The Wine—Isley Brothers (71)	*409*
Galaxy—War (77)	325
L.A. Sunshine—War (77)	291
Low Rider (On The Boulevard)—Latin Alliance (91)	121
Lonely Feelin'—War (71)	74
Slipping Into Darkness—Ramsey Lewis (72)	*35*
Good, Good Feelin'—War (79)	12
Denzil MILLER ▶ 10802 (1)	**5.2**
Kid Stuff—Lenny White (80)	21
Ed E. MILLER ▶ 2854 (1)	**1151**
Don't Let The Rain Come Down (Crooked Little Man)—Serendipity Singers (64)	3454
Eddie MILLER ▶ 1509 (10)	**2847**
Release Me (And Let Me Love Again)— Engelbert Humperdinck (67)	*4487*
Release Me—Esther Phillips "Little Esther" (62)	*2523*
There She Goes—Jerry Wallace (60)	631
Thanks A Lot—Brenda Lee (65)	475
Three Cigarettes In An Ashtray—Patsy Cline (57)	43
After Loving You—Della Reese (65)	35
I'll Release You—Joann Bon And The Coquettes (67)	*33*
Release Me—Johnny Adams (68)	*29*
Release Me—Jivin' Gene (60)	*13*
Release Me—Esther Phillips (67)	*7.2*
Floyd MILLER ▶ 7670 (2)	**82**
Slide—Slave (77)	640
Snap Shot—Slave (81)	53
Frances H. MILLER ▶ 10500 (1)	**7.8**
Married But Not To Each Other—Denise LaSalle (76)	16
Francis John MILLER ▶ 5914 (2)	**229**
To Dream The Dream—Frankie Miller (82)	153
The Doodle Song—Frankie Miller (77)	76
Frank MILLER ▶ 600 (15)	**7262**
Memories Are Made Of This—Dean Martin (55)	*8655*
Greenfields—Brothers Four (60)	*6907*
Marianne—Terry Gilkyson And The Easy Riders (57)	*3770*
Marianne—Hilltoppers (57)	*2812*
Love Is A Golden Ring— Frankie Laine with The Easy Riders (57)	891
Memories Are Made Of This—Gale Storm (55)	*785*
Memories Are Made Of This—Drifters (66)	*271*
Memories Are Made Of This—Mindy Carson (55)	*217*
Marianne—Lane Brothers (57)	*71*
Marianne—Burl Ives (57)	*45*
Green Fields—Vogues (69)	*25*
Memories Are Made Of This—Roger Williams (59)	*14*
Mary Ann—Talbot Brothers (57)	*0.0*
Greenfields—Julius La Rosa (60)	*0.0*
Mary Ann—Edmundo Ros & His Orchestra (57)	*0.0*
Frankie MILLER ▶ 6861 (2)	**132**
Black Land Farmer—Frankie Miller (61)	*91*
Black Land Farmer—Wink Martindale (61)	*41*
Glenn MILLER ▶ 6416 (4)	**173**
Moonlight Serenade—Rivieras (1) (59)	*316*
Moonlight Serenade—Frank Barber Orchestra (82)	*14*
Moonlight Serenade—Bobby Vinton (76)	*2.1*
Moonlight Serenade—Tommy Leonetti (59)	*0.0*
Helen MILLER ▶ 754 (16)	**5823**
Foolish Little Girl—Shirelles (63)	2718
It Hurts To Be In Love—Gene Pitney (64)	*2451*
Don't Say You Don't Remember— Beverly Bremers (71)	1640
Make Me Your Baby—Barbara Lewis (65)	1276
Charms—Bobby Vee (63)	1117
Rumors—Johnny Crawford (62)	912
Princess In Rags—Gene Pitney (65)	570
You're My Baby (And Don't You Forget It)— Vacels (65)	232
Got To See If I Can't Get Mommy (To Come Back Home)—Jerry Butler (70)	210
All Of My Life—Lesley Gore (65)	121

We'll Cry Together—Maxine Brown (69)	120
Love Takes A Long Time Growing—Deon Jackson (66)	111
I'll Make Him Love Me—Barbara Lewis (67)	89
It Hurts To Be In Love—Dan Hartman (81)	*64*
The Door Is Open—Tommy Hunt (62)	61
Can't Let You Out Of My Sight— Chuck Jackson & Maxine Brown (65)	32
Herbert L. MILLER ▶ 1607 (3)	**2633**
Night—Jackie Wilson (60)	4933
Never Turn Back—Al Hibbler (56)	292
Young Love—Rover Boys (56)	40
—James Henry Miller see: Ewan MacCOLL	
—J. D. Miller see: Jerry WEST	
Jerry MILLER ▶ 7666 (3)	**82**
Japanese Rhumba—Jayne and Audrey Meadows (55)	*79*
Hey Grandma—Moby Grape (67)	5.1
Japanese Rhumba—Twin-Tunes (55)	*0.0*
Jimmy MILLER ▶ 3329 (2)	**897**
I'm A Man—Spencer Davis Group (67)	*1717*
I'm A Man—Chicago (71)	*78*
John A. MILLER [Lost John Miller] ▶ 5091 (1)	**344**
Rainbow At Midnight—Jimmie Rodgers (62)	344
—Joseph D. Miller see: Jerry WEST	
Kim MILLER ▶ 5228 (2)	**323**
I Got My Mind Made Up (You Can Get It Girl)— Instant Funk (79)	815
Let Me Party With You (Part 1) (Party, Party, Party)— Bunny Sigler (78)	204
Lesley MILLER ▶ 9208 (1)	**29**
Brown Arms In Houston—Orpheus (69)	57
—Lonnie Vincent Miller see: Lonnie VENCENT	
—Lost John Miller see: John A. MILLER	
Marcus MILLER ▶ 1885 (9)	**2158**
Don't Want To Be A Fool—Luther Vandross (91)	1159
Power Of Love—Luther Vandross (91)	1062
Jump To It—Aretha Franklin (82)	552
Til My Baby Comes Home—Luther Vandross (85)	534
Da' Butt—E.U. (88)	387
Any Love—Luther Vandross (88)	306
Get It Right—Aretha Franklin (83)	150
Bad Boy—Luther Vandross (82)	96
The Rush—Luther Vandross (91)	71
Margaret MILLER ▶ 9575 (2)	**21**
(Theme From) Song Of The Sparrow (Instrumental)— Mitch Miller And His Orchestra (56)	36
(Theme From) Song Of The Sparrow (vocal) (Vocal)— Mitch Miller And His Orchestra (56)	6.6
Mike MILLER ▶ 9576 (2)	**21**
(Theme From) Song Of The Sparrow (Instrumental)— Mitch Miller And His Orchestra (56)	36
(Theme From) Song Of The Sparrow (vocal) (Vocal)— Mitch Miller And His Orchestra (56)	6.6
Nathan MILLER [Ned Miller] ▶ 10601 (1)	**6.9**
Why Should I Cry Over You—Frank Sinatra (55)	14
Ned MILLER ▶ 415 (8)	**9623**
Dark Moon—Gale Storm (57)	*3904*
From A Jack To A King—Ned Miller (62)	2789
Dark Moon—Bonnie Guitar (57)	*1914*
Invisible Tears—Ray Conniff Singers (64)	528
Do What You Do Do Well—Ned Miller (64)	387
Snow Flake—Jim Reeves (66)	266
Mister Fire Eyes—Bonnie Guitar (57)	151
One Among The Many—Ned Miller (63)	23
—Ned Miller see also: Nathan MILLER	
—Perry Miller see: Jesse Colin YOUNG	
Robert MILLER ▶ 5589 (1)	**267**
If Walls Could Talk—Little Milton (70)	267
Robert Eugene MILLER ▶ 1227 (10)	**3634**
Stay In My Corner—Dells (68)	1713
There Is—Dells (68)	962
Always Together—Dells (68)	562
Does Anybody Know I'm Here—Dells (68)	465
Wear It On Our Face—Dells (68)	463
Open Up My Heart—Dells (70)	361
O-O, I Love You—Dells (67)	356
Dirty Man—Laura Lee (67)	316
Hallways Of My Mind—Dells (69)	49
I Can't Do Enough—Dells (69)	9.8
Roger MILLER ▶ 157 (22)	**18712**
King Of The Road—Roger Miller (65)	*4807*

Dang Me—Roger Miller (64)	2544
Chug-A-Lug—Roger Miller (64)	2375
England Swings—Roger Miller (65)	2272
Engine Engine #9—Roger Miller (65)	1891
Queen Of The House—Jody Miller (65)	*931*
Husbands And Wives—Roger Miller (66)	*714*
Do-Wacka-Do—Roger Miller (64)	534
Walkin' In The Sunshine—Roger Miller (67)	515
Kansas City Star—Roger Miller (65)	515
One Dyin' And A Buryin'—Roger Miller (65)	459
The Last Word In Lonesome Is Me—Eddy Arnold (66)	457
You Can't Roller Skate In A Buffalo Herd— Roger Miller (66)	352
You Don't Want My Love—Andy Williams (60)	*317*
My Uncle Used To Love Me But She Died— Roger Miller (66)	278
The Swiss Maid—Del Shannon (62)	136
It Happened Just That Way—Roger Miller (65)	63
I've Been A Long Time Leavin' (But I'll Be A Long Time Gone)—Roger Miller (66)	9.6
Invitation To The Blues—Ray Price (58)	3.3
Billy Bayou—Jim Reeves (58)	2.3
Husbands And Wives—Wayne Newton (68)	*1.9*
You Don't Want My Love—Roger Miller (60)	*0.0*
Ronald Alonzo MILLER ▶ 4024 (7)	**621**
Mercy, Mercy—Don Covay & The Goodtimers (64)	*855*
Gotta See Jane—R. Dean Taylor (71)	236
Mercy, Mercy, Mercy—Phoebe Snow (81)	*121*
He's A Lover—Mary Wells (65)	104
Handful Of Memories—Baby Washington (62)	3.6
Not For All The Money In The World—Shirelles (63)	0.4
Don't Burn Down The Bridge— Gladys Knight & The Pips (75)	0.0
Ronald Dean MILLER ▶ 8417 (1)	**51**
I'll Do Anything For You—Denroy Morgan (81)	102
Ronald Norman MILLER [Charlemagne, Ronald Norman Gould] ▶ 305 (19)	**11860**
For Once In My Life—Stevie Wonder (68)	*5883*
Touch Me In The Morning—Diana Ross (73)	4788
I've Never Been To Me—Charlene (82)	*3262*
Yester-Me, Yester-You, Yesterday— Stevie Wonder (69)	*2495*
A Place In The Sun—Stevie Wonder (66)	1928
Heaven Help Us All—Stevie Wonder (70)	1758
Glasshouse—Temptations (75)	499
Travlin' Man—Stevie Wonder (67)	458
Used To Be—Charlene & Stevie Wonder (82)	379
Can't We Try—Teddy Pendergrass (80)	333
Sleepin'—Diana Ross (74)	162
For Once In My Life—Jackie Wilson (68)	*148*
For Once In My Life—Tony Bennett (67)	*50*
For Once In My Life—Stars On 45 (82)	*27*
Yester-Me, Yester-You, Yesterday—Stars On 45 (82)	*27*
It Ain't Easy Comin' Down—Charlene (77)	4.6
Take This Hurt Off Me—Don Covay (64)	3.9
I've Never Been To Me—Charlene (77)	*3.0*
Freddie—Charlene (77)	2.4
Scottie MILLER ▶ 5229 (2)	**323**
I Got My Mind Made Up (You Can Get It Girl)— Instant Funk (79)	815
Let Me Party With You (Part 1) (Party, Party, Party)— Bunny Sigler (78)	204
—Shorty Miller see: Roy MICHAELS	
Sonny MILLER ▶ 10185 (1)	**11**
Got A Date With An Angel—Billy Williams (57)	46
Steve MILLER ▶ 115 (15)	**21994**
Abracadabra—Steve Miller Band (82)	8881
The Joker—Steve Miller Band (73)	5290
Rock'n Me—Steve Miller (76)	4565
Fly Like An Eagle—Steve Miller (76)	3481
Take The Money And Run—Steve Miller (76)	1410
Swingtown—Steve Miller Band (77)	1016
Heart Like A Wheel—Steve Miller Band (81)	582
Living In The U.S.A.—Steve Miller Band (74)	*305*
Shangri-La—Steve Miller Band (84)	182
Give It Up—Steve Miller Band (82)	166
Going To The Country—Steve Miller Band (70)	110
Living In The U.S.A.—Steve Miller Band (68)	*76*
Circle Of Love—Steve Miller Band (82)	59
Bongo Bongo—Steve Miller Band (85)	47
I Want To Make The World Turn Around— Steve Miller Band (86)	28

Sue MILLER ▶ 5619 (1)	**264**
Invisible Tears—Ray Conniff Singers (64)	528
William Henry MILLER ▶ 1864 (8)	**2187**
Daddy's Home—Shep And The Limelites (61)	*4846*
Daddy's Home—Jermaine Jackson (72)	*2516*
Daddy's Home—Cliff Richard (82)	*659*
A Thousand Miles Away—Heartbeats (56)	*342*
Daddy's Home—Chuck Jackson & Maxine Brown (67)	*29*
A Thousand Miles Away— Fred Parris & The Five Satins (82)	*4.8*
A Thousand Miles Away—Heartbeats (60)	*2.1*
A Thousand Miles Away—Diamonds (56)	*0.0*
William Roderick MILLER ▶ 10150 (1)	**12**
I Feel Sanctified—Commodores (74)	83
—Geraldine Milligan see: Geraldine HUNT	
Trish MILLIKEN ▶ 10021 (1)	**14**
Anywhere With You—Rubber Rodeo (84)	28
Lucky MILLINDER [Lucius Venable Millinder] ▶ 4794 (4)	**413**
I'm Waiting Just For You—Pat Boone (57)	*517*
Ram-Bunk-Shush—Ventures (61)	*507*
Ram Bunk Shush—Bill Doggett (57)	*214*
I'm Waiting Just For You— Hoagy Carmichael & Cass Daley (57)	*0.0*
David MILLINER ▶ 8431 (1)	**51**
Tribute (Right On)—Pasadenas (89)	304
Michael MILLINER ▶ 8432 (1)	**51**
Tribute (Right On)—Pasadenas (89)	304
Jean MILLINGTON ▶ 3493 (2)	**818**
Butter Boy—Fanny (75)	622
Charity Ball—Fanny (71)	589
June MILLINGTON ▶ 6183 (1)	**196**
Charity Ball—Fanny (71)	589
Vic MILLROSE ▶ 1852 (5)	**2198**
This Girl Is A Woman Now— Gary Puckett And The Union Gap (69)	3064
Last Chance To Turn Around—Gene Pitney (65)	1140
I'll Try Anything—Dusty Springfield (67)	508
I'm Indestructible—Jack Jones (67)	61
When Love Slips Away—Dee Dee Warwick (67)	4.8
Charles MILLS ▶ 2024 (3)	**1997**
Lady Godiva—Peter And Gordon (66)	2817
Knight In Rusty Armour—Peter And Gordon (66)	1175
The Jokers—Peter And Gordon (67)	2.4
Darby MILLS ▶ 7912 (1)	**70**
Just One More Time—Headpins (83)	140
Frank MILLS ▶ 890 (3)	**4978**
Music Box Dancer—Frank Mills (79)	4307
Love Me, Love Me Love—Frank Mills (72)	428
Peter Piper—Frank Mills (79)	242
Gordon MILLS ▶ 2309 (4)	**1620**
It's Not Unusual—Tom Jones (65)	2045
A Little You—Freddie And The Dreamers (65)	421
Not Responsible—Tom Jones (66)	162
I'm The Lonely One—Cliff Richard (64)	14
Hank MILLS [Samuel Garrett] ▶ 5772 (4)	**243**
Little Ole Wine Drinker, Me—Dean Martin (67)	*365*
Kay—John Wesley Ryles I (68)	54
Girl On The Billboard—Del Reeves (65)	10
Little Old Wine Drinker Me—Robert Mitchum (67)	*3.9*
Irving MILLS ▶ 1295 (10)	**3439**
Moonglow—Morris Stoloff Conducting The Columbia Pictures Orchestra (56)	*4036*
Moonglow—George Cates & His Orchestra (56)	*1975*
Mood Indigo—Norman Petty Trio (54)	*481*
Lovesick Blues—Frank Ifield (62)	*358*
Lovesick Blues—Sonny James (57)	*85*
Straighten Up And Fly Right—DeJohn Sisters (58)	52
Lovesick Blues—Floyd Cramer (62)	*47*
Mood Indigo Mambo— Perez Prado And His Orchestra (55)	*5.9*
Lovesick Blues—Sonny Knight (57)	*0.0*
Mood Indigo—Modernaires & George Auld (54)	*0.0*
Mike MILLS ▶ 2218 (10)	**1729**
Losing My Religion—R.E.M. (91)	2447
Stand—R.E.M. (89)	1642
Shiny Happy People—R.E.M. (91)	1294
The One I Love—R.E.M. (87)	1261
It's The End Of The World As We Know It (And I Feel Fine)—R.E.M. (88)	87
So. Central Rain (I'm Sorry)—R.E.M. (84)	50

Pop Song 89—R.E.M. (89)	43
Radio Song—R.E.M. (91)	42
Radio Free Europe—R.E.M. (83)	34
Fall On Me—R.E.M. (86)	16
Stan MILLS ▶ 11538 (1)	**1.3**
Sweet September—Lettermen (65)	3.8
Ted "Wizard" MILLS ▶ 10595 (1)	**7.0**
What's Come Over Me— Margie Joseph & Blue Magic (75)	7.0
—Yvonne Mills see: Yvonne BAKER	
Billy MILNE ▶ 9949 (1)	**15**
Don't Run My Life—Spys (82)	73
—Little Milton see: Milton CAMPBELL	
Garnet MIMMS ▶ 10976 (1)	**4.0**
Anytime You Want Me—Garnet Mimms (64)	8.0
Charles MIMS ▶ 7718 (2)	**79**
Haven't You Heard—Patrice Rushen (80)	293
Look Up—Patrice Rushen (80)	18
Gerald MIMS ▶ 4739 (1)	**427**
Gentle—Dino (90)	427
Joe MIMS ▶ 4278 (1)	**535**
Get On The Good Foot - Part 1— James Brown (72)	1605
Ted MINAR ▶ 8456 (1)	**50**
Beat—Rockin' R's (59)	149
Mike MINCIELI ▶ 9978 (2)	**14**
Where I Fell In Love—Capris (61)	71
Limbo—Capris (62)	0.9
Dwain MINCY ▶ 8918 (1)	**36**
Think His Name—Johnny Rivers (71)	181
Wayne MINCY ▶ 8919 (1)	**36**
Think His Name—Johnny Rivers (71)	181
Dave MINDEL ▶ 7182 (1)	**111**
Whenever I'm Away From You—John Travolta (76)	222
Raynard MINER ▶ 731 (16)	**6009**
(Your Love Has Lifted Me) Higher And Higher— Rita Coolidge (77)	*5006*
Rescue Me—Fontella Bass (65)	*4146*
(Your Love Keeps Lifting Me) Higher And Higher— Jackie Wilson (67)	*2626*
We're Gonna Make It—Little Milton (65)	983
There Is—Dells (68)	962
I'm Not My Brother's Keeper—Flaming Ember (70)	894
Recovery—Fontella Bass (65)	492
Who's Cheating Who?—Little Milton (65)	442
Because I Love You—Billy Stewart (66)	53
Rescue Me—Cher (75)	*25*
Your People—Little Milton (65)	25
Rescue Me—Melissa Manchester (76)	*19*
Higher And Higher—Canada Goose (70)	*9.9*
In The Basement - Part 1— Etta James & Sugar Pie Desanto (66)	7.2
I'm Learnin'—Mary Wells (65)	2.3
Safe And Sound—Fontella Bass (66)	0.5
Roger MINER ▶ 8903 (1)	**36**
Are You Serious—Tyrone Davis (82)	73
Eddie MININFIELD ▶ 8857 (1)	**38**
Hold Me—Sheila E. (87)	113
Meade MINNIGERODE ▶ 8587 (1)	**45**
Whiffenpoof Song—Bob Crewe (59)	136
—Dennis Minogue see: Terry CASHMAN	
George MINOR ▶ 2487 (1)	**1445**
Let Me In—Sensations (62)	4334
Ulpio MINUCCI ▶ 4062 (4)	**607**
Domani (Tomorrow)—Julius La Rosa (55)	*1174*
I'll Never Know—Four Lads (56)	33
My Love's A Gentle Man—Dorothy Collins (55)	7.7
Domani (Tomorrow)—Tony Martin (55)	*0.0*
Ettore MIONORETTI ▶ 6708 (6)	**142**
Chee Chee-oo Chee (Sang The Little Bird)— Perry Como & Jaye P. Morgan (55)	*570*
Chee Chee-Oo Chee—Dennis Hale (55)	*0.0*
Chee Chee-Oo Chee (Sang The Little Bird)— Gaylords (55)	*0.0*
Chee Chee-Oo Chee (Sang The Little Birds)— Mariners (55)	*0.0*
Chee Chee Oo Chee (Sang The Little Bird)— Dean Martin (55)	*0.0*
Chee Chee-Oo Chee (Sang The Little Bird)— Johnston Brothers (55)	*0.0*

Ralph MIRANDA ▶ 4422 (2)	**498**
Girl On A Swing—Gerry And The Pacemakers (66)	486
Randy—Happenings (68)	24
—Robert Miskiewicz see: Robert STEELE	
—Jacqueline Misrahi see: Michele MICHAELE	
Adam MITCHELL ▶ 5611 (3)	**265**
Tears—John Waite (84)	416
Crazy Crazy Nights—KISS (87)	92
Dancin' Round And Round—Olivia Newton-John (79)	11
Alonso MITCHELL ▶ 7100 (1)	**116**
Too Pooped To Pop Casey—Chuck Berry (60)	231
Argentry MITCHELL [Art Gentry, Art Mitchell] ▶ 11333 (1)	**2.2**
I'm The Midnight Special—Clarence Carter (73)	8.8
—Art Mitchell see: Argentry MITCHELL	
Bobby MITCHELL [Bobby Godfrey Mitchell Halstead] ▶ 1886 (3)	**2158**
The Flame—Cheap Trick (88)	3887
Shattered Glass—Laura Branigan (87)	255
Remember My Name—House Of Lords (90)	174
—Bobby Mitchell see: Michael GUERRA	
George MITCHELL ▶ 6973 (2)	**124**
Ace In The Hole— Somethin' Smith & The Redheads (55)	*202*
Ace In The Hole— Roberta Sherwood with The Singing Waiters (60)	*47*
George (2) MITCHELL ▶ 9379 (1)	**25**
Fried Eggs—Intruders (59)	75
James MITCHELL ▶ 7676 (2)	**81**
Can't Nobody Love You—Solomon Burke (63)	68
30-60-90—Willie Mitchell (69)	66
—James Mitchell see: Ronny MITCHELL	
James MITCHELL Jr. ▶ 2530 (4)	**1410**
Float On—Floaters (77)	*3048*
Do Me Right—Detroit Emeralds (71)	579
Bloat On Featuring The Bloaters— Cheech & Chong (77)	*328*
Wear This Ring (With Love)—Detroit Emeralds (71)	78
John MITCHELL ▶ 3793 (1)	**697**
Two Of Hearts—Stacey Q (86)	2091
Johnny MITCHELL ▶ 6483 (5)	**165**
We Belong Together—Robert & Johnny (58)	*339*
We Belong Together—Jimmy Velvet (63)	*151*
I Believe In You—Robert & Johnny (58)	4.3
We Belong Together—Belmonts (61)	*0.0*
We Belong Together—Robert & Johnny (61)	*0.0*
Joni MITCHELL ▶ 343 (19) HOF	**10915**
Help Me—Joni Mitchell (74)	2154
Both Sides Now—Judy Collins (68)	*2125*
Woodstock—Crosby, Stills, Nash & Young (70)	*1624*
Woodstock—Matthews' Southern Comfort (71)	*1236*
You Turn Me On, I'm A Radio—Joni Mitchell (72)	1075
Free Man In Paris—Joni Mitchell (74)	755
Big Yellow Taxi—Neighborhood (70)	*669*
Big Yellow Taxi—Joni Mitchell (74)	*528*
Raised On Robbery—Joni Mitchell (73)	289
In France They Kiss On Main Street— Joni Mitchell (76)	148
Woodstock—Assembled Multitude (70)	*120*
Big Yellow Taxi—Joni Mitchell (70)	*54*
Case Of You—Frank Stallone (80)	52
Chelsea Morning—Judy Collins (69)	42
Good Friends—Joni Mitchell (85)	17
Carey—Joni Mitchell (71)	13
From Both Sides Now—Dion (69)	*8.9*
Circle Game—Buffy Sainte-Marie (70)	6.3
Both Sides Now—Johnstons (68)	*0.0*
Kim MITCHELL ▶ 8942 (1)	**36**
Go For Soda—Kim Mitchell (85)	71
Lindsay MITCHELL ▶ 9066 (1)	**32**
Flyin'—Prism (78)	159
Mel MITCHELL ▶ 4276 (8)	**536**
Petticoats Of Portugal— Dick Jacobs And His Chorus And Orchestra (56)	*982*
Passing Strangers— Sarah Vaughan & Billy Eckstine (57)	328
Lovely Ladies Of Milano— Dick Jacobs And His Chorus And Orchestra (57)	100
Petticoats Of Portugal— Billy Vaughn and His Orchestra (56)	*34*
Poor Boy—Cardigans (58)	*0.0*

Mel MITCHELL ▶ 4276 (8) *Continued*	**536**
Little Pixie—Frank D'Rone (58)	*0.0*
Petticoats Of Portugal—Florian Zabach (56)	*0.0*
Petticoats Of Portugal—Caesar Giovannini & Sextette (56)	*0.0*
Neil MITCHELL ▶ 8630 (1)	**45**
Wishing I Was Lucky—Wet Wet Wet (88)	178
Paul MITCHELL ▶ 3553 (1)	**787**
Tryin' To Love Two—William Bell (77)	1573
Phillip MITCHELL ▶ 1324 (8)	**3355**
Starting All Over Again—Mel And Tim (72)	1419
Hurts So Good—Millie Jackson (73)	886
Oh La De Da—Staple Singers (73)	458
As Long As He Takes Care Of Home—Candi Staton (74)	300
After I Cry Tonight—Lanier and Co. (82)	181
Dancing To Your Music—Archie Bell & The Drells (73)	116
Leftovers—Millie Jackson (75)	47
Carry Me—Joe Simon (74)	14
Ronny MITCHELL [James Mitchell, Ronnie Mitchell] ▶ 6878 (1)	**131**
Loving You More Every Day—Etta James (64)	131
Stephen MITCHELL ▶ 2809 (2)	**1185**
Jump (For My Love)—Pointer Sisters (84)	3301
Dangerous—Natalie Cole (85)	253
Tony MITCHELL ▶ 7482 (2)	**93**
Howzat—Sherbet (76)	149
I Have The Skill—Sherbs (81)	55
Willie MITCHELL ▶ 384 (19)	**10273**
Let's Stay Together—Al Green (71)	*7842*
I'm Still In Love With You—Al Green (72)	5102
You Ought To Be With Me—Al Green (72)	4701
Look What You Done For Me—Al Green (72)	3798
Call Me (Come Back Home)—Al Green (73)	1660
L-O-V-E (Love)—Al Green (75)	1223
Livin' For You—Al Green (73)	1004
Let's Stay Together—Tina Turner (84)	*755*
20-75—Willie Mitchell (64)	579
Full Of Fire—Al Green (75)	526
Keep Me Cryin'—Al Green (76)	395
Let's Stay Together—Isaac Hayes (72)	*340*
Oh Me, Oh My (Dreams In My Arms)—Al Green (75)	208
Comin' On—Bill Black's Combo (64)	161
Echoes Of Love—Doobie Brothers (77)	101
30-60-90—Willie Mitchell (69)	66
Bad Eye—Willie Mitchell (66)	57
God Bless Our Love—Charles Brimmer (75)	19
Buster Browne—Willie Mitchell (65)	13
Robert MITCHUM ▶ 6354 (3)	**180**
The Ballad Of Thunder Road—Robert Mitchum (62)	*250*
Ballad Of Thunder Road—Robert Mitchum (58)	*85*
Whippoorwill—Keely Smith (58)	24
Anthony MITMAN ▶ 10425 (1)	**8.6**
I Cry Myself To Sleep At Night—Romeo's Daughter (89)	26
Jackie MITTOO ▶ 6320 (1)	**182**
Pass The Dutchie—Musical Youth (82)	1276
—Autry DeWalt Mixon Jr. see: Jr. WALKER	
Buddy MIZE ▶ 4668 (1)	**443**
(You Keep Me) Hangin' On—Joe Simon (68)	885
Fonce MIZELL ▶ 535 (11)	**8025**
ABC—Jackson 5 (70)	8551
I Want You Back—Jackson 5 (69)	7904
The Love You Save—Jackson 5 (70)	6071
Mama's Pearl—Jackson 5 (71)	4810
Sugar Daddy—Jackson 5 (71)	2514
O.P.P.—Naughty By Nature (91)	1392
Maybe Tomorrow—Jackson 5 (71)	977
Bless You—Martha Reeves & The Vandellas (71)	298
You're In Good Hands—Jermaine Jackson (73)	61
I Found That Girl—Jackson 5 (70)	51
Love To The World—L.T.D. (77)	5.2
Jason MIZELL [Jam Master Jay] ▶ 5716 (2)	**251**
You Be Illin'—Run-D.M.C. (86)	626
It's Tricky—Run-D.M.C. (87)	170
Larry MIZELL ▶ 6913 (3)	**129**
Black Byrd—Donald Byrd (73)	97
You're In Good Hands—Jermaine Jackson (73)	61
Love To The World—L.T.D. (77)	5.2

Rodney MIZELL ▶ 11430 (1)	**1.7**
Love To The World—L.T.D. (77)	5.2
Vic MIZZY ▶ 5167 (1)	**332**
Addams Groove—M.C. Hammer (91)	996
John MOBLEY ▶ 9876 (1)	**16**
Pitter-Patter—Four Sportsmen (61)	31
Cyril MOCKRIDGE ▶ 5119 (2)	**340**
It's A Woman's World—Four Aces (54)	*680*
Woman's World—Ray Anthony & His Orchestra (54)	*0.0*
Joseph MODELISTE ▶ 4207 (7)	**562**
Cissy Strut—Meters (69)	731
Sophisticated Cissy—Meters (69)	475
Chicken Strut—Meters (70)	361
Look-Ka Py Py—Meters (69)	346
Ease Back—Meters (69)	213
Hand Clapping Song—Meters (70)	94
Be My Lady—Meters (77)	36
Domenico MODUGNO ▶ 473 (16)	**8812**
Nel Blu Dipinto Di Blu (Volare)—Domenico Modugno (58)	*10773*
Volare—Bobby Rydell (60)	*3928*
Ask Me—Elvis Presley With The Jordanaires (64)	1582
Volare (Nel Blu Dipinto Di Blu)—Dean Martin (58)	*1266*
Ciao Ciao Bambina—Jacky Noguez And His Orchestra (59)	*1101*
Volare—Al Martino (75)	*365*
Volare—Ace Cannon (62)	*52*
Le Petit Reveil (The Little Clock)—Domenico Modugno (58)	17
Volare (Nel Blu Di Pinto Di Blu)—McGuire Sisters (58)	*17*
Stay Here With Me (Resta Cu 'Mme)—Domenico Modugno (58)	1.6
Ciao Ciao Bambina—Domenico Modugno (59)	*1.5*
Nel Blu Dipinto Di Blu—Rosa Linda (58)	*0.0*
Volare (Nel Blu, Dipinto Di Blu)—Alan Dale (58)	*0.0*
Volare (Nel Blu Dipinto Di Blu)—Jesse Belvin (58)	*0.0*
Ciao Ciao Bambina—Jos Cleber & His Orchestra (59)	*0.0*
(Nel Blu Dipinto Di Blu) Volare—Umberto Marcato (58)	*0.0*
Tommy MOELLER ▶ 3115 (3)	**1002**
Concrete And Clay—Unit Four Plus Two (65)	*1070*
Concrete And Clay—Eddie Rambeau (65)	*928*
You've Never Been In Love Like This Before—Unit Four Plus Two (65)	5.2
John V. MOEN ▶ 10117 (1)	**12**
Once Upon A Time—Dean Martin (58)	25
Pamela MOFFETT ▶ 5579 (2)	**269**
Baby Come Close—Smokey Robinson (73)	768
Open—Smokey Robinson (76)	40
Marie S. MOFFIT ▶ 10917 (1)	**4.4**
Fee-Fi-Fo-Fum—Hungry Tiger (69)	4.4
Ken MOFFITT ▶ 2368 (4)	**1555**
Oh Julie—Crescendos (57)	*2335*
Letter From Sherry—Dale Ward (63)	749
Oh Julie—Sammy Salvo (57)	*27*
Oh Julie—Otis Williams & His Charms (58)	*0.0*
Phil MOGG ▶ 11458 (1)	**1.6**
Too Hot To Handle—UFO (77)	3.2
James MOGINIE ▶ 5200 (3)	**328**
Beds Are Burning—Midnight Oil (88)	812
Blue Sky Mine—Midnight Oil (90)	369
The Dead Heart—Midnight Oil (88)	276
—Mogol see: Giulio RAPETTI	
—Ivan Mogull see: Phil BELMONTE	
Essra MOHAWK [Sandra Elayne Hurvitz] ▶ 2968 (1)	**1091**
Change Of Heart—Cyndi Lauper (86)	2182
Josef MOHR ▶ 7430 (12)	**96**
Silent Night (Christmas Hymn)—Bing Crosby (60)	*110*
Silent Night (Christmas Hymn)—Bing Crosby (57)	*78*
Silent Night—Elvis Presley (57)	*2.1*
Sleep In Heavenly Peace (Silent Night)—Barbra Streisand (66)	*1.4*
Silent Night, Holy Night—Mahalia Jackson (62)	*0.9*
Silent Night—Al Hibbler (56)	*0.0*
Silent Night—Pat Holliday (58)	*0.0*
Silent Night, Holy Night—Mahalia Jackson (56)	*0.0*
Silent Night (Christmas Hymn)—Bing Crosby (54)	*0.0*
Silent Night (Christmas Hymn)—Bing Crosby (55)	*0.0*
Silent Night (Christmas Hymn)—Bing Crosby (56)	*0.0*

Silent Night (Christmas Hymn)—Bing Crosby (58)	*0.0*
Monte MOIR ▶ 2906 (1)	**1123**
The Pleasure Principle—Janet Jackson (87)	1123
Charles MOLE ▶ 10037 (1)	**14**
Realistic—Shirley Lewis (89)	27
Arturo MOLINA Jr. [Kid Frost] ▶ 6697 (2)	**143**
La Raza—Kid Frost (90)	399
Low Rider (On The Boulevard)—Latin Alliance (91)	121
Elvin MOLINA ▶ 9179 (1)	**29**
First True Love—Tiana (90)	59
Joey MOLLAND ▶ 8445 (1)	**50**
Love Is Gonna Come At Last—Badfinger (79)	50
Friedrich W. MÖLLER ▶ 11780 (2)	**0.0**
The Happy Wanderer—Henri René's Musette (54)	*0.0*
The Happy Wanderer—Frank Weir & His Orchestra (54)	*0.0*
Fred MOLLIN ▶ 11600 (1)	**1.0**
Santa Jaws (Part I)—Homemade Theatre (76)	3.1
Larry MOLLIN [Lawrence Molomoflavich] ▶ 11601 (1)	**1.0**
Santa Jaws (Part I)—Homemade Theatre (76)	3.1
—Lawrence Molomoflavich see: Larry MOLLIN	
—Gustav Molvik see: Taime DOWNE	
Chips MOMAN [Lincoln Wayne Moman] ▶ 575 (9)	**7558**
(Hey Won't You Play) Another Somebody Done Somebody Wrong Song—B.J. Thomas (75)	4865
Last Night—Mar-Keys (61)	4476
This Time—Troy Shondell (61)	*3567*
Luckenbach, Texas (Back To The Basics Of Love)—Waylon Jennings (77)	818
Everybody Loves A Rain Song—B.J. Thomas (78)	280
The Dark End Of The Street—James Carr (67)	96
This Time—Thomas Wayne (59)	*48*
Big Party—Barbara And The Browns (64)	14
Promises—Carla Thomas (61)	11
James V. MONACO ▶ 4216 (7) HOF	**560**
I'll Take Care Of Your Cares—Frankie Laine (67)	560
You Made Me Love You—Nat "King" Cole (59)	496
What Do You Want To Make Those Eyes At Me For—Ray Peterson (60)	*62*
I Can't Begin To Tell You—Jane Morgan (59)	18
Ev'ry Night About This Time—Diamonds (56)	5.5
What Do You Want To Make Those Eyes At Me For?—Sunny Gale (60)	*0.0*
What Do You Want To Make Those Eyes At Me For—Kenny Rankin (60)	*0.0*
Stephen MONAHAN ▶ 8673 (1)	**43**
City Of Windows—Stephen Monahan (67)	86
—Robert E. Moncrief see: Bobby EDWARDS	
Dick MONDA [Daddy Dewdrop, Lu Janis] ▶ 5709 (4)	**252**
Soul Drippin'—Mauds (68)	182
Dammit Isn't God's Last Name—Frankie Laine (69)	39
Fox Huntin' (On The Weekend)—Daddy Dewdrop (71)	20
Nanu, Nanu, (I Wanna Get Funky Wich You)—Daddy Dewdrop (79)	11
Jeff MONDAY [Jeffrey Steven Mundy] ▶ 8217 (1)	**58**
Elena—Marc Tanner Band (79)	174
Ray MONETTE ▶ 11687 (1)	**0.7**
We're Gonna Have A Good Time—Rare Earth (73)	4.3
Eddie MONEY [Edward J. Mahoney] ▶ 1363 (12)	**3261**
Baby Hold On—Eddie Money (78)	1814
I'll Get By—Eddie Money (91)	1367
Think I'm In Love—Eddie Money (82)	1049
Two Tickets To Paradise—Eddie Money (78)	817
Maybe I'm A Fool—Eddie Money (79)	715
The Big Crash—Eddie Money (83)	253
Get A Move On—Eddie Money (79)	248
Shakin'—Eddie Money (82)	192
Can't Keep A Good Man Down—Eddie Money (79)	106
Club Michelle—Eddie Money (84)	101
Let's Be Lovers Again—Eddie Money with Valerie Carter (80)	85
We Should Be Sleeping—Eddie Money (87)	8.4
Anthony MONN ▶ 9736 (1)	**18**
Mellow Lovin'—Judy Cheeks (78)	54

Marguerite MONNOT ▶ 447 (15)	**9259**
The Poor People Of Paris (La Goualante Du Pauvre Jean)—Les Baxter His Chorus And Orchestra (56)	*8007*
Milord—Bobby Darin (64)	*473*
Just Come Home—Hugo & Luigi (59)	435
The Poor People Of Paris—Russ Morgan (56)	*368*
The Poor People Of Paris—Lawrence Welk And His Champagne Music (56)	*238*
Milord—Teresa Brewer (61)	*149*
Everyday—Della Reese (60)	139
The Poor People Of Paris—Chet Atkins (56)	*72*
Milord—Edith Piaf (61)	*32*
If You Love Me—LaVern Baker (59)	*9.9*
Irma La Douce—Karen Chandler (60)	*4.6*
Irma La Douce—Mantovani And His Orchestra (60)	*4.6*
The Poor People Of Paris—Winifred Atwell (56)	*0.0*
If You Love Me (Really Love Me)—Kay Starr (54)	*0.0*
If You Love Me (Really Love Me)—Vera Lynn (54)	*0.0*
Bill MONROE ▶ 11623 (1)	**0.9**
Blue Moon Of Kentucky—Dick Haiman And the Dial Tones (61)	0.9
Bob MONROE [Robert Michael Davis] ▶ 5840 (1)	**238**
What Do All The People Know—Monroes (82)	238
—Richard Anthony Monsour see: Dick DALE	
—Magnificent Montague see: Nathaniel NATHAN	
Martin MONTAGUE [T. Martin] ▶ 6428 (1)	**171**
Precious Memories—Romeos (67)	171
—Nathaniel Montague see: Nathaniel NATHAN	
Chris MONTAN ▶ 9041 (1)	**33**
All Night With Me—Laura Branigan (82)	33
Tony MONTANA [Anthony E. Cardenas] ▶ 8709 (1)	**42**
Call It Rock 'N Roll—Great White (91)	208
Vincent MONTANA ▶ 5093 (6)	**344**
Nice 'N' Naasty—Salsoul Orchestra (76)	246
The Game Is Over (What's The Matter With You)—Brown Sugar (76)	54
Salsoul Hustle—Salsoul Orchestra (75)	43
#1 Dee Jay—Goody Goody (78)	35
You're Just The Right Size—Salsoul Orchestra (76)	16
Ritzy Mambo—Salsoul Orchestra (77)	0.6
—Ezekiel Christopher Montanez see: Chris MONTEZ	
Camille MONTE ▶ 4425 (2)	**497**
I Can't Grow Peaches On A Cherry Tree—Just Us (66)	611
Dumb Head—Ginny Arnell (63)	383
Lou MONTE [Louis Scaglione] ▶ 3588 (3)	**775**
Lazy Mary (Luna Mezzo Mare)—Lou Monte (58)	1468
Calypso Italiano—Lou Monte (57)	77
Italian Jingle Bells—Lou Monte (55)	8.7
Ralph MONTELLO ▶ 6766 (1)	**139**
Pin A Medal On Joey—James Darren (63)	277
Hugo MONTENEGRO ▶ 5771 (2)	**243**
Seattle—Perry Como (69)	550
Girls Ain't Nothing But Trouble—D.J. Jazzy Jeff & The Fresh Prince (88)	241
Chris MONTEZ [Ezekiel Christopher Montanez] ▶ 6132 (1)	**202**
Some Kinda Fun—Chris Montez (62)	403
—Anne Black Montgomery see: Anne McIAN	
Bob MONTGOMERY ▶ 802 (8)	**5521**
Misty Blue—Dorothy Moore (76)	*4394*
Two Of A Kind—Sue Thompson (62)	516
Love's Made A Fool Of You—Bobby Fuller Four (66)	*503*
Misty Blue—Eddy Arnold (67)	*448*
Misty Blue—Joe Simon (72)	*115*
Heartbeat—Buddy Holly / The Crickets (58)	69
Love's Made A Fool Of You—Cochise (71)	*35*
Back In Baby's Arms—Patsy Cline (63)	1.4
Carl MONTGOMERY ▶ 4916 (1)	**383**
Six Days On The Road—Dave Dudley (63)	765
Earl MONTGOMERY ▶ 10611 (1)	**6.8**
What's Your Mama's Name—Tanya Tucker (73)	14
Gary MONTGOMERY ▶ 9094 (1)	**31**
Love Heals—Colours (68)	63
Lisa MONTGOMERY [Lisa Horton] ▶ 4688 (1)	**438**
Dreamin'—Vanessa Williams (89)	1314
Marvin MONTGOMERY [Marvin Wetter] ▶ 6114 (4)	**205**
Number One Man—Bruce Channel (62)	400
Something Old, Something New—Paul & Paula (63)	136
Come On Baby—Bruce Channel (62)	4.9
Six Boys—J. Frank Wilson (65)	4.1
Stefano MONTIN ▶ 7758 (1)	**76**
Boom Boom (Let's Go Back To My Room)—Paul Lekakis (87)	381
Percy MONTROSE ▶ 5427 (2)	**290**
Clementine—Bobby Darin (60)	*1036*
Clementine—Jan & Dean (60)	*125*
Ronnie MONTROSE ▶ 9991 (1)	**14**
Right The First Time—Gamma (82)	43
Micky MOODY ▶ 5892 (2)	**232**
Fool For Your Loving—Whitesnake (89)	*489*
Fool For Your Loving—Whitesnake (80)	*207*
Russell MOODY ▶ 2728 (1)	**1238**
Wear My Ring Around Your Neck—Elvis Presley (58)	3714
—Walter R. Moody see: Ken WOOD	
Christopher MOON ▶ 9328 (1)	**26**
Soft And Wet—Prince (78)	53
Hal MOONEY ▶ 5690 (1)	**254**
If You Leave Me Tonight I'll Cry—Jerry Wallace (72)	508
Ralph MOONEY ▶ 5343 (4)	**302**
Crazy Arms—Bob Beckham (60)	*584*
Crazy Arms—Ray Price (56)	*10*
Crazy Arms—Andrews Sisters (56)	*10*
Crazy Arms—Karen Chandler & Jimmy Wakely (56)	*0.0*
Alan MOORE ▶ 10664 (1)	**6.3**
Lonesome Whistle Blues—Freddy King (61)	19
Anthony MOORE ▶ 9551 (1)	**22**
Learning To Fly—Pink Floyd (87)	86
Billy Joe MOORE ▶ 8240 (1)	**57**
What's He Doing In My World—Eddy Arnold (65)	172
Bob L. MOORE ▶ 7731 (1)	**77**
Little Eeefin Annie—Joe Perkins (63)	154
Bobby MOORE ▶ 3309 (2)	**905**
Searching For My Love—Bobby Moore & The Rhythm Aces (66)	893
Try My Love Again—Bobby Moore's Rhythm Aces Featuring Chico (66)	12
Charlie Lee MOORE ▶ 8210 (1)	**58**
I Ain't Got To Love Nobody Else—Masqueraders (68)	175
Daniel MOORE ▶ 698 (5)	**6245**
Shambala—Three Dog Night (73)	*4476*
My Maria—B.W. Stevenson (73)	1909
Put Out The Light—Joe Cocker (74)	371
The River Of Love—B.W. Stevenson (73)	332
Shambala—B.W. Stevenson (73)	*113*
Debra Mae MOORE [Deborah Mae Moore, Mae Moore] ▶ 5386 (1)	**297**
Heaven In Your Eyes—Loverboy (86)	1186
Derek MOORE ▶ 11235 (1)	**2.6**
Astral Man—Nektar (75)	11
Errol MOORE ▶ 9782 (1)	**17**
Electric Kingdom—Twilight 22 (83)	51
Fleecie MOORE ▶ 4964 (3)	**370**
Ain't That Just Like A Woman—Fats Domino (61)	670
Caldonia—James Brown (64)	25
Let The Good Times Roll—Ray Charles (60)	20
Gary MOORE ▶ 11031 (1)	**3.7**
Still Got The Blues—Gary Moore (91)	3.7
Gil MOORE ▶ 5486 (4)	**279**
Somebody's Out There—Triumph (86)	502
Magic Power—Triumph (81)	298
I Can Survive—Triumph (80)	28
Follow Your Heart—Triumph (85)	10
Glen MOORE ▶ 6925 (1)	**128**
You Wanted To Change Me—Roy Hamilton (55)	128
Hayward MOORE ▶ 7137 (1)	**114**
America Is My Home - Pt. 1—James Brown And The Famous Flames (68)	228
Jackie MOORE ▶ 3864 (2)	**673**
Precious, Precious—Jackie Moore (70)	1320
Sometimes It's Got To Rain—Jackie Moore With The Dixie Flyers (71)	37
James B. MOORE ▶ 8582 (3)	**46**
Rappin' Rodney—Rodney Dangerfield (83)	140
The Breaks (Part 1)—Kurtis Blow (80)	94
Basketball—Kurtis Blow (85)	77
James Leon MOORE ▶ 10256 (1)	**11**
I've Got Love For My Baby—Young Hearts (68)	43
—James H. Moore see: Slim HARPO	
—James Isaac Moore see: Slim HARPO	
Jennece MOORE ▶ 6783 (2)	**138**
How To Dance—Bingoboys (91)	554
Cool As Ice (Everybody Get Loose)—Vanilla Ice (91)	81
John C. MOORE ▶ 2505 (4)	**1432**
At My Front Door (Crazy Little Mama)—Pat Boone (55)	*1950*
At My Front Door (Crazy Little Mama)—El Dorados And Magnificents (55)	*653*
At My Front Door—Dee Clark (60)	*260*
(Crazy Little Mama Song) At My Front Door—Modernaires (55)	*0.0*
John E. MOORE ▶ 7662 (1)	**82**
We Did It—Syl Johnson (73)	82
John Edward MOORE [Johnny Moore, Bonnie Thompson] ▶ 1556 (5)	**2726**
Turn Back The Hands Of Time—Tyrone Davis (70)	4386
I'll Be Right Here—Tyrone Davis (70)	540
(I Can Feel Those Vibrations) This Love Is Real—Jackie Wilson (70)	323
One-Way Ticket—Tyrone Davis (71)	167
You Keep Me Holding On—Tyrone Davis (71)	36
Johnny MOORE ▶ 10098 (1)	**13**
Merry Christmas Baby—Chuck Berry (58)	26
—Johnny Moore see: John Edward MOORE	
Johnny Dudley MOORE ▶ 11303 (1)	**2.3**
Driftin' Blues—Bobby Bland (68)	6.9
Josephine Burke MOORE ▶ 4771 (2)	**419**
Got To Get You Off My Mind—Solomon Burke (65)	944
The Price—Solomon Burke (64)	312
—Mae Moore see: Debra Mae MOORE	
Mark MOORE ▶ 11212 (1)	**2.7**
Theme From S-Express—S-Express (88)	14
Marvin MOORE ▶ 555 (18)	**7747**
Green Door—Jim Lowe (56)	*9717*
Four Walls—Jim Reeves (57)	*1889*
I Dreamed—Betty Johnson (56)	1476
Four Walls—Jim Lowe (57)	*881*
Little Red Rented Rowboat—Joe Dowell (62)	637
Talkin' To The Blues—Jim Lowe (57)	328
By You By You By You—Jim Lowe (57)	197
I Feel The Beat—Jim Lowe (56)	148
Dum Dum Dee Dum—Johnny Cymbal (63)	100
Rock And Roll Rhapsody—Four Aces (58)	56
Four Walls—Kay Starr (62)	*26*
1492—Betty Johnson (57)	21
Where Were You When I Needed You—Jerry Vale (65)	11
Nuevo Laredo—Les Paul and Mary Ford (56)	10
You Can't Get To Heaven On Roller Skates—Betty Johnson (59)	*5.0*
Green Door—Jerms (69)	*4.7*
Just Love Me—Jaye P. Morgan (56)	1.3
Four Walls—Dorothy Collins (57)	*0.0*
Matthew MOORE ▶ 9427 (1)	**24**
Space Captain—Barbra Streisand (71)	24
Raymond MOORE ▶ 4360 (7)	**513**
It's All In Your Mind—Clarence Carter (70)	460
I'd Rather Be An Old Man's Sweetheart (Than A Young Man's Fool)—Candi Staton (69)	422
A Man And A Half—Wilson Pickett (68)	273
Whatever Turns You On—Travis Wammack (72)	131
How Do You Quit (Someone You Love)—Carla Thomas (65)	13
I'm The Midnight Special—Clarence Carter (73)	8.8
Scratch My Back (And Mumble In My Ear)—Clarence Carter (71)	6.3
René MOORE ▶ 5736 (5)	**248**
I'll Be Good—René and Angela (85)	253
Young Love—Janet Jackson (82)	110
You Don't Have To Cry—René and Angela (86)	66
Your Smile—René and Angela (86)	60
I Love You More—René & Angela (81)	6.6
Robin MOORE ▶ 922 (1)	**4789**
The Ballad Of The Green Berets—SSgt. Barry Sadler (66)	9577

Tim MOORE ▶ 2576 (7)	**1356**
Rock And Roll Love Letter—Bay City Rollers (76)	546
Second Avenue—Garfunkel (74)	*396*
Second Avenue—Tim Moore (74)	*227*
In The Middle—Tim Moore (77)	76
Charmer—Tim Moore (75)	50
Second Avenue—Tim Moore (77)	*31*
Fool Like You—Tim Moore (73)	29
Wade MOORE ▶ 7871 (1)	**71**
Ooby Dooby—Roy Orbison And Teen Kings (56)	143
Warren MOORE ▶ 418 (25)	**9592**
Love Machine (Part 1)—Miracles (75)	5274
Ain't That Peculiar—Marvin Gaye (65)	*2266*
I'll Be Doggone—Marvin Gaye (65)	2041
Ooh Baby Baby—Linda Ronstadt (78)	*1786*
Going To A Go-Go—Miracles (65)	*1646*
The Tracks Of My Tears—Johnny Rivers (67)	*1537*
The Tracks Of My Tears—Miracles (65)	*1351*
Ooo Baby Baby—Miracles (65)	*1254*
Since I Lost My Baby—Temptations (65)	1058
My Baby—Temptations (65)	1007
It's Growing—Temptations (65)	994
My Girl Has Gone—Miracles (65)	946
Tracks Of My Tears—Linda Ronstadt (75)	*724*
One More Heartache—Marvin Gaye (66)	662
Going To A Go-Go—Rolling Stones (82)	*594*
Take This Heart Of Mine—Marvin Gaye (66)	568
That's What Love Is Made Of—Miracles (64)	416
Ain't That Peculiar—Diamond Reo (74)	*361*
Here I Go Again—Smokey Robinson & The Miracles (69)	281
Come On Do The Jerk—Miracles (64)	273
Oooh, Baby Baby—Five Stairsteps (67)	*252*
Tracks Of My Tears—Aretha Franklin (69)	*81*
Going to a Go-Go—Shalamar (77)	*80*
Ain't That Peculiar—Fanny (72)	*29*
Ooh Baby Baby—Magnificent Men (67)	*7.6*
Gilbert MOORER ▶ 3375 (2)	**875**
Get On Up—Esquires (67)	1521
And Get Away—Esquires (67)	736
Ronny MOORINGS ▶ 9827 (1)	**16**
Imagination—Xymox (90)	33
Carlton MORALES ▶ 4349 (1)	**515**
Valotte—Julian Lennon (84)	1544
Mark Anthony MORALES [Prince Markie Dee] ▶ 11665 (1)	**0.8**
Falling In Love—Fat Boys (87)	3.9
Michael MORALES ▶ 2978 (3)	**1086**
Who Do You Give Your Love To?—Michael Morales (89)	984
I Don't Wanna See You—Michael Morales (91)	76
I Don't Know—Michael Morales (89)	27
Noro MORALES ▶ 9925 (1)	**15**
Bongo Guitar (Oye Negra)—Ralph Marterie & His Orchestra (54)	30
Jacques MORALI ▶ 1084 (10)	**4076**
Y.M.C.A.—Village People (78)	7239
In The Navy—Village People (79)	3766
Macho Man—Village People (78)	679
Go West—Village People (79)	259
I'm In Love Again—Pia Zadora (82)	161
Ready For The '80s—Village People (79)	147
The Best Disco In Town—Ritchie Family (76)	*92*
The Best Disco In Town—Ritchie Family (76)	*92*
I Want To Dance With You (Dance With Me)—Ritchie Family (75)	45
Discomania—Lovers (77)	0.6
Jack MORAN ▶ 9987 (1)	**14**
Gimme Your Good Lovin'—Diving For Pearls (89)	29
Jack (2) MORAN ▶ 4048 (1)	**612**
Skip A Rope—Henson Cargill (67)	1224
Tony MORAN ▶ 3144 (5)	**987**
We Can't Go Wrong—Cover Girls (89)	1676
Show Me—Cover Girls (87)	459
Promise Me—Cover Girls (88)	433
Inside Outside—Cover Girls (88)	204
Funk Boutique—Cover Girls (91)	202
Rick MORANIS ▶ 6336 (1)	**182**
Take Off—Bob & Doug McKenzie (82)	908
Julian Bensley MORE ▶ 11635 (1)	**0.9**
Irma La Douce—Karen Chandler (60)	*4.6*
Mike MORE [Michael David Munves] ▶ 7296 (1)	**104**
Everyotherday—Or-N-More (91)	209
Georges MOREAU ▶ 8759 (1)	**40**
If She Should Come To You (La Montana)—Anthony Newley (60)	*120*
George MOREL ▶ 4530 (1)	**470**
Wiggle It—2 In A Room (90)	939
Marc MORELAND ▶ 8379 (1)	**52**
Mexican Radio—Wall Of Voodoo (83)	209
—Peter Lord Moreland see: Peter LORD	
—Wenceslao Moreno see: Señor WENCES	
Marianito MORES [Mariano Martinez, Mariano Mores] ▶ 9919 (1)	**15**
Uno—Tony Martin (54)	45
—Neil Moret see: Charles N. DANIELS	
Rushton MOREVE [John Russell Morgan] ▶ 1724 (1)	**2419**
Magic Carpet Ride—Steppenwolf (68)	4838
Larry MOREY ▶ 2125 (2)	**1844**
Lavender Blue—Sammy Turner (59)	3681
Heigh-Ho—Fifth Estate (67)	6.4
Bob MORGAN ▶ 11425 (1)	**1.7**
Lollipop (I Like You)—Intruders (69)	6.9
Charlie MORGAN ▶ 6719 (1)	**142**
Wrap Her Up—Elton John (85)	852
David MORGAN ▶ 9543 (1)	**22**
You Can Call Me Blue—Michael Johnson (80)	43
Dennis W. MORGAN ▶ 801 (11)	**5526**
I Knew You Were Waiting (For Me)—Aretha Franklin & George Michael (87)	3691
My Heart Can't Tell You No—Rod Stewart (88)	2425
Nobody—Sylvia (2) (82)	1577
Room To Move—Animotion (89)	1179
Smoky Mountain Rain—Ronnie Milsap (80)	1012
I Wouldn't Have Missed It For The World—Ronnie Milsap (81)	887
Love Changes (Everything)—Climie Fisher (88)	651
Years—Wayne Newton (80)	408
Got To Give In To Love—Bonnie Boyer (79)	222
Fooled By A Feeling—Barbara Mandrell (79)	14
I Was Country When Country Wasn't Cool—Barbara Mandrell (81)	3.9
Dorinda MORGAN ▶ 3648 (5)	**750**
Confidential—Sonny Knight (56)	*750*
Confidential—Rusty Draper (56)	*0.0*
Confidential—Charles Brown (56)	*0.0*
The Man Upstairs—Kay Starr (54)	0.0
Confidential—Bubber Johnson (56)	*0.0*
Edward Lee MORGAN ▶ 9287 (1)	**27**
The Sidewinder, Part 1—Lee Morgan (64)	27
Freddy MORGAN [Hasegawa Yoshida] ▶ 3320 (11)	**901**
Hey Mr Banjo—Sunnysiders (55)	*1568*
The Japanese Farewell Song—Kay Cee Jones (55)	*101*
The Japanese Farewell Song—Kay Cee Jones (55)	*101*
Banjo Woogie—Ban-Joes (55)	*16*
Banjo Woogie—Sunnysiders (55)	*16*
Banjo Woogie—Georgie Shaw (55)	*16*
Hey, Mr. Banjo—Banjo Boys (55)	*0.0*
The Japanese Farewell Song—Lois Winters (56)	*0.0*
The Japanese Farewell Song—Lois Winters (56)	*0.0*
Hey, Mr. Banjo—Guy Lombardo & His Royal Canadians (55)	*0.0*
Hey, Mr. Banjo—Lawrence Welk & His Champagne Music (55)	*0.0*
Jamie MORGAN ▶ 3866 (1)	**672**
Buffalo Stance—Neneh Cherry (89)	2690
—John Russell Morgan see: Rushton MOREVE	
Lee MORGAN ▶ 4396 (1)	**506**
The King Is Gone—Ronnie McDowell (77)	1012
Michael MORGAN ▶ 6498 (1)	**163**
That's The Way A Woman Is—Messengers (71)	325
Ron MORGAN ▶ 6808 (1)	**135**
Smell Of Incense—Southwest F.O.B. (68)	271
Russ MORGAN ▶ 5008 (9)	**360**
You're Nobody Till Somebody Loves You—Dean Martin (64)	*699*
Somebody Else Is Taking My Place—Al Martino (65)	*249*
Somebody Else Is Taking My Place—Joni James (61)	*66*
You're Nobody Till Somebody Loves You—Wonder Who ? (66)	*21*
Somebody Else Is Taking My Place—Jaye P. Morgan (59)	*15*
You're Nobody Till Somebody Loves You—Damita Jo (62)	*10*
Does Your Heart Beat For Me—Betty Johnson (59)	7.0
You're Nobody 'Til Somebody Loves You—Mills Brothers (54)	*6.0*
You're Nobody 'til Somebody Loves You—Dinah Washington (62)	*6.0*
Terry MORGAN ▶ 8805 (1)	**39**
Cutie Pie—One Way (82)	273
John MORIER ▶ 3671 (1)	**744**
Making Every Minute Count—Spanky And Our Gang (67)	744
Frank MORIN ▶ 11544 (1)	**1.3**
It Didn't Even Bring Me Down—Sir Douglas Quintet (69)	3.8
Luke MORLEY ▶ 6057 (1)	**211**
Dirty Love—Thunder (91)	211
Giorgio MORODER ▶ 120 (35)	**21403**
Call Me—Blondie (80)	10151
Flashdance...What A Feeling—Irene Cara (83)	9574
Love To Love You Baby—Donna Summer (75)	*4573*
The Wanderer—Donna Summer (80)	4199
Take My Breath Away (Love Theme From TOP GUN)—Berlin (86)	4143
On The Radio—Donna Summer (80)	3402
Heaven Knows—Donna Summer With Brooklyn Dreams (79)	3027
I Feel Love—Donna Summer (77)	2815
Danger Zone—Kenny Loggins (86)	2682
Breakdance—Irene Cara (84)	1574
Meet Me Half Way—Kenny Loggins (87)	1448
Why Me?—Irene Cara (83)	1151
Never Ending Story—Limahl (85)	839
The Seduction (Love Theme)—James Last Band (80)	645
Chase—Giorgio Moroder (79)	511
The Dream (Hold On To Your Dream)—Irene Cara (83)	489
Son Of My Father—Giorgio (72)	*486*
I Love You—Donna Summer (77)	469
Winter Melody—Donna Summer (77)	276
Winner Takes It All—Sammy Hagar (87)	250
Cat People (Putting Out Fire)—David Bowie (82)	154
Love Kills—Freddie Mercury (84)	125
Rumour Has It—Donna Summer (78)	113
Crazy World—Big Trouble (87)	102
Love To Love You Baby—Ritchie Family (76)	*92*
Spring Affair—Donna Summer (76)	*84*
Here She Comes—Bonnie Tyler (84)	61
Reach Out—Giorgio Moroder (84)	53
You Can—Madleen Kane (81)	45
Try Me, I Know We Can Make It—Donna Summer (76)	34
Son Of My Father—Chicory (72)	*31*
Lady, Lady, Lady—Joe "Bean" Esposito (83)	31
Thief Of Hearts—Melissa Manchester (84)	24
Giving Up, Giving In—3° Degrees (79)	4.6
Spring Affair—Donna Summer (77)	*0.0*
Tom MOROLDA ▶ 7746 (1)	**77**
Ballad Of Youth—Richie Sambora (91)	153
Jerome MOROSS ▶ 9643 (1)	**20**
Stay With Me—Frank Sinatra (64)	39
Barbara MORR ▶ 10819 (1)	**5.1**
Am I Losing You—Manhattans (78)	15
Ennio MORRICONE ▶ 865 (2)	**5125**
The Good, The Bad And The Ugly—Hugo Montenegro, His Orchestra And Chorus (68)	*5078*
The Good, The Bad And The Ugly—Meco (82)	*47*
Kent MORRILL ▶ 5006 (3)	**360**
Tall Cool One—Wailers (59)	*532*
Tall Cool One—Wailers (64)	*507*
Mau-Mau—Wailers (59)	40
Andy MORRIS ▶ 2154 (4)	**1811**
All Around The World—Lisa Stansfield (90)	3201
You Can't Deny It—Lisa Stansfield (90)	830
Change—Lisa Stansfield (91)	756
This Is The Right Time—Lisa Stansfield (90)	646
Bob MORRIS ▶ 5240 (1)	**319**
Buckaroo—Buck Owens & His Buckaroos (65)	319
Del MORRIS ▶ 11442 (1)	**1.7**
Toni—Tradewinds (59)	3.3

Douglas MORRIS ▶ 4022 (5)	**621**
Sweet Talkin' Guy—Chiffons (66)	1814
Are You A Boy Or Are You A Girl—Barbarians (65)	255
Out Of This World—Chiffons (66)	110
Moulty—Barbarians (66)	41
Stop, Look And Listen—Chiffons (66)	9.3
Eddie MORRIS ▶ 11309 (1)	**2.3**
Freedom—Grandmaster Flash And The Furious 5 (80)	21
Freddie MORRIS ▶ 6736 (1)	**142**
Blue Tomorrow—Billy Vaughn And His Orchestra (61)	283
Hayward MORRIS ▶ 8411 (1)	**51**
Auctioneer (I'll Buy That Dream)— Les Paul & Mary Ford (54)	103
—James Corbitt Morris see: Jimmy DRIFTWOOD	
Joe MORRIS ▶ 4332 (4)	**518**
Shake A Hand—Jackie Wilson And Linda Hopkins (63)	*434*
Shake A Hand—Ruth Brown (62)	*38*
Shake A Hand—Mike Pedicin Quintet (58)	*36*
Shake A Hand—LaVern Baker (60)	*9.1*
Ken MORRIS ▶ 10975 (1)	**4.0**
When You Wake Up Tomorrow—Candi Staton (79)	16
Lee MORRIS [Maurice Zeserson] ▶ 941 (3)	**4719**
Blue Velvet—Bobby Vinton (63)	*8754*
I Don't Want To See Tomorrow—Nat King Cole (64)	637
Blue Velvet—Statues (60)	*46*
Margie MORRIS ▶ 7123 (1)	**115**
You Wanted Someone To Play With (I Wanted Someone To Love)—Frankie Laine (67)	459
Marlowe MORRIS ▶ 9184 (1)	**29**
Play The Thing—Marlowe Morris Quintet (62)	29
Nathan MORRIS ▶ 3353 (2)	**885**
Motownphilly—Boyz II Men (91)	2776
Uhh Ahh—Boyz II Men (91)	572
Richard MORRIS ▶ 2289 (8)	**1649**
Honey Chile—Martha Reeves & The Vandellas (67)	1767
Love Bug Leave My Heart Alone— Martha & The Vandellas (67)	707
Stop Her On Sight (S.O.S.)—Edwin Starr (66)	495
(We've Got) Honey Love— Martha Reeves & The Vandellas (69)	249
Real Humdinger—J.J. Barnes (66)	93
Sweet Darlin'—Martha Reeves & The Vandellas (68)	75
Headline News—Edwin Starr (66)	41
Forget Me Not—Martha Reeves & The Vandellas (68)	6.2
Roger MORRIS ▶ 8297 (1)	**55**
Pretty In Pink—Psychedelic Furs (86)	330
Ron MORRIS ▶ 6932 (1)	**127**
Are You A Boy Or Are You A Girl—Barbarians (65)	255
Stephen MORRIS ▶ 6097 (3)	**206**
True Faith—New Order (87)	637
Round & Round—New Order (89)	209
Blue Monday 1988—New Order (88)	105
—Steviand Hardaway Morris see: Stevie WONDER	
Tracie MORRIS ▶ 8935 (1)	**36**
Open Letter (To A Landlord)—Living Colour (89)	71
Walter Lee MORRIS [Lee Walter] ▶ 3157 (4)	**981**
Special Lady—Ray, Goodman & Brown (80)	2439
Look At Me (I'm In Love)—Moments (75)	430
Inside Of You—Ray, Goodman & Brown (80)	78
Girls (Part I)—Moments And Whatnauts (75)	24
Wanya MORRIS ▶ 6239 (1)	**191**
Uhh Ahh—Boyz II Men (91)	572
Bob MORRISON ▶ 1520 (4)	**2810**
Lookin' For Love—Johnny Lee (80)	2996
You Decorated My Life—Kenny Rogers (79)	2338
Love The World Away—Kenny Rogers (80)	1217
Make Believe It's Your First Time— Bobby Vinton (79)	68
Danny MORRISON ▶ 8860 (2)	**38**
Blaze Of Glory—Kenny Rogers (81)	97
You've Got A Good Love Coming— Van Stephenson (81)	16
Dave MORRISON ▶ 9941 (1)	**15**
Pin The Tail On The Donkey—Paul Peek (66)	29
Eddie MORRISON ▶ 5114 (1)	**340**
Madison Time Part One—Ray Bryant Combo (60)	681
Gary MORRISON ▶ 11167 (1)	**2.9**
Remember—Velours (58)	8.7
Jim MORRISON ▶ 481 (17)	**8680**
Light My Fire—Doors (67)	*8461*

Hello, I Love You—Doors (68)	6496
Touch Me—Doors (68)	5980
Light My Fire—Jose Feliciano (68)	*4958*
Love Her Madly—Doors (71)	1978
People Are Strange—Doors (67)	1529
Riders On The Storm—Doors (71)	1436
Love Me Two Times—Doors (67)	731
The Unknown Soldier—Doors (68)	682
Wishful Sinful—Doors (69)	464
You Make Me Real—Doors (70)	408
L.A. Woman—Billy Idol (90)	208
Light My Fire—Amii Stewart (79)	*51*
Roadhouse Blues—Doors (70)	38
Light My Fire—Rhetta Hughes (69)	*33*
Light My Fire—Doors (68)	*32*
Love Street—Doors (68)	9.0
Van MORRISON ▶ 303 (24) HOF	**11956**
Brown Eyed Girl—Van Morrison (67)	*2318*
Gloria—Shadows Of Knight (66)	*2124*
Domino—Van Morrison (70)	1719
Blue Money—Van Morrison (71)	1076
Wild Night—Van Morrison (71)	719
I Shall Sing—Garfunkel (73)	594
Crazy Love—Helen Reddy (71)	585
Mystic Eyes—Them (65)	580
Into The Mystic—Johnny Rivers (70)	448
Come Running—Van Morrison (70)	438
Tupelo Honey—Van Morrison (71)	400
Brown Eyed Girl—El Chicano (72)	*307*
Wavelength—Van Morrison (78)	280
Jackie Wilson Said (I'm In Heaven When You Smile)— Van Morrison (72)	130
Gloria—Doors (83)	*68*
Gloria—Them (66)	*60*
Moondance—Van Morrison (77)	31
Gloria—Them (65)	*23*
Gypsy—Van Morrison (73)	19
He Ain't Give You None—Freddie Scott (67)	15
Chick-A-Boom—Van Morrison (67)	12
Redwood Tree—Van Morrison (72)	7.1
Call Me Up In Dreamland—Van Morrison (71)	3.8
Ro Ro Rosey—Van Morrison (67)	1.9
Vernon MORRISON ▶ 6188 (1)	**196**
Rockin' In The Same Old Boat—Bobby Bland (68)	392
Voni MORRISON ▶ 5582 (1)	**269**
Act Naturally—Beatles (65)	538
Walter MORRISON [J.S. Theracon] ▶ 2991 (9)	**1077**
Funky Worm—Ohio Players (73)	1438
The Humpty Dance—Digital Underground (90)	1362
One Nation Under A Groove - Part I— Funkadelic (78)	1189
Ecstasy—Ohio Players (73)	621
Mama Said Knock You Out—LL Cool J (91)	473
Pain (Part 1)—Ohio Players (71)	208
Got Pleasure—Ohio Players (72)	14
Rattlesnake—Ohio Players (76)	12
Theme From The Black Hole—Parliament (80)	1.0
Geoff MORROW ▶ 1929 (4)	**2096**
Can't Smile Without You—Barry Manilow (78)	5240
Annabella—Hamilton, Joe Frank & Reynolds (71)	460
Can't You Hear The Song?—Wayne Newton (72)	435
It's Up To You Petula—Edison Lighthouse (71)	153
Glen MORROW ▶ 11761 (1)	**0.2**
Make My Life A Little Bit Brighter—Chester (73)	0.4
Jack MORROW ▶ 8052 (1)	**64**
You're The Reason I'm In Love—Sonny James (56)	64
Marvin MORROW ▶ 4960 (3)	**372**
More Than You Know—Martika (88)	867
If I Say Yes—Five Star (86)	120
Simple—Johnny Mathis (84)	46
Dolly MORSE ▶ 11401 (1)	**1.9**
Siboney—Caterina Valente (56)	3.7
Steve MORSE ▶ 4767 (3)	**420**
All I Wanted—Kansas (86)	801
Power—Kansas (87)	28
Take It Off The Top—Dixie Dregs (78)	9.9
—Theodora Morse see: Dorothy TERRISS	
—Al Mortimer see: Henry JEROME	
—David Mortimer see: David AUSTIN	
—George Morton see: Shadow MORTON	

Shadow MORTON [George Morton] ▶ 408 (8)	**9709**
Leader Of The Pack—Shangri-Las (64)	*6265*
Remember (Walkin' In The Sand)—Shangri-Las (64)	*3787*
I Can Never Go Home Anymore—Shangri-Las (65)	2186
Give Him A Great Big Kiss—Shangri-Las (64)	1055
Remember (Walking In The Sand)—Louise Goffin (79)	*333*
Leader Of The Pack—Twisted Sister (85)	*289*
Past, Present And Future—Shangri-Las (66)	169
Remember (Walking In The Sand)—Aerosmith (79)	*106*
Ronald MOSELEY ▶ 7767 (2)	**76**
Broken Heart—Fiestas (62)	151
Right Now And Not Later—Shangri-Las (65)	1.9
Robert MOSELY ▶ 2013 (14)	**2001**
Sha La La—Manfred Mann (64)	*1755*
If My Pillow Could Talk—Connie Francis (63)	984
Big Cold Wind—Pat Boone (61)	765
Midnight Flyer—Nat "King" Cole (59)	597
Goodbye My Lover Goodbye—Searchers (65)	344
Sha-La-La—Shirelles (64)	*143*
Give Me Your Love—Nat "King" Cole (59)	74
Hand It Over—Chuck Jackson (64)	56
Ooh What A Day—Sarah Vaughan (60)	28
Truly Love—Johnny Nash (58)	22
Point Of No Return—Adam Wade (61)	21
Somebody New—Chuck Jackson (64)	6.7
Since I Made You Cry—Rivieras (1) (60)	6.2
A City Girl Stole My Country Boy—Patti Page (61)	5.0
—Mickey Moses see: Mickey SHORR	
Ian MOSLEY ▶ 9797 (1)	**17**
Kayleigh—Marillion (85)	84
Bill MOSS ▶ 7003 (1)	**123**
Everything Is Going To Be Alright— Teegarden & Van Winkle (70)	123
Earl MOSS ▶ 10510 (1)	**7.7**
You're Gonna Make It—Festivals (70)	23
Jeffrey MOSS ▶ 2868 (1)	**1142**
Rubber Duckie—Ernie (Jim Henson) (70)	1142
Jon MOSS ▶ 782 (10)	**5663**
Karma Chameleon—Culture Club (83)	5903
Do You Really Want To Hurt Me—Culture Club (82)	5783
Time (Clock Of The Heart)—Culture Club (83)	4056
Miss Me Blind—Culture Club (84)	2167
I'll Tumble 4 Ya—Culture Club (83)	1624
Church Of The Poison Mind—Culture Club (83)	1501
Move Away—Culture Club (86)	1007
It's A Miracle—Culture Club (84)	965
The War Song—Culture Club (84)	766
Mistake No. 3—Culture Club (84)	455
Neil MOSS ▶ 2430 (1)	**1493**
Holding Back The Years—Simply Red (86)	2985
Tyrone MOSS ▶ 3724 (2)	**719**
Everybody's Everything—Santana (71)	1516
Karate—Emperor's (66)	428
Mark MOSSELEY ▶ 11364 (1)	**2.1**
Ronnie's Rapp—Ron And The D.C. Crew (87)	8.3
Peter MÖSSER ▶ 2078 (5)	**1906**
Morgen—Ivo Robic and The Song-Masters (59)	*1693*
Happy Muleteer—Ivo Robic (60)	228
Tango Of The Drums— Les Baxter His Chorus And Orchestra (56)	198
Morgen (One More Sunrise)— Leslie Uggams (59)	*1.1*
Morgen (One More Sunrise)—Rex Allen (59)	*0.0*
Ted MOSSMAN ▶ 10309 (2)	**10**
Till The End Of Time—Ray Charles Singers (64)	17
Till The End Of Time—Nobles (58)	9.2
—Mickie Most see: Michael Peter HAYES	
Bennie MOTEN ▶ 11029 (1)	**3.7**
South—Johnny Maddox And The Rhythmasters (55)	7.5
Patrick L. MOTEN ▶ 8985 (2)	**34**
Love Has Finally Come At Last— Bobby Womack and Patti LaBelle (84)	46
If You Think You're Lonely Now— Bobby Womack (81)	44
Mark MOTHERSBAUGH ▶ 3134 (2)	**992**
Whip It—Devo (80)	1829
Theme From Doctor Detroit—Devo (83)	155
Forere MOTLOHELOA ▶ 9935 (1)	**15**
The Boy In The Bubble—Paul Simon (87)	29
Buddy MOTOLA ▶ 10209 (1)	**11**
Tres Chic—Geoff Gilmore & The Sheiks (59)	34

George MOTOLA ▶ 2720 (16)	**1245**
Goodnight My Love—Paul Anka (68)	*813*
Goodnight My Love—Fleetwoods (63)	*496*
Goodnight My Love Pleasant Dreams—McGuire Sisters (56)	*434*
Goodnight My Love (Pleasant Dreams)—Ray Peterson (59)	*311*
Donnie—Bermudas (64)	282
Goodnight My Love—Ben E. King (66)	*81*
Rock And Roll Wedding—Sunny Gale (56)	*53*
Every Time I Hear Your Name—Patti Page (62)	15
Love Like A Fool—Georgettes (58)	*2.9*
Love Like A Fool—Fontane Sisters (58)	*2.9*
Jeannie, Jeannie, Jeannie—Eddie Cochran (58)	2.3
Rock And Roll Wedding—Helen Grayco (56)	*0.0*
Rock And Roll Wedding—Ella Mae Morse (56)	*0.0*
Goodnight My Love, Pleasant Dreams—Earl Grant (56)	*0.0*
Goodnight My Love Pleasant Dreams—Jesse Belvin (56)	*0.0*
Goodnight My Love (Pleasant Dreams)—Mindy Carson (56)	*0.0*
Ken MOULE [Louis Rico] ▶ 11327 (1)	**2.2**
Cha Cha Baby—Ted Heath and His Orchestra (58)	6.7
Jean-Pierre MOULIN ▶ 10598 (2)	**7.0**
Charleston Parisien—Leo Clarens & His Orchestra (56)	*3.5*
Charleston Parisien—Guy Lombardo & His Royal Canadians (56)	*3.5*
Rob MOUNSEY ▶ 6931 (1)	**128**
So Close—Diana Ross (83)	383
—Georges Moustaki see: Giuseppe MUSTACCHI	
Melvin MOY ▶ 7807 (1)	**74**
Home Cookin—Jr. Walker & The All Stars (69)	223
Sylvia MOY ▶ 421 (32) HOF	**9546**
I Was Made To Love Her—Stevie Wonder (67)	*5544*
Uptight (Everything's Alright)—Stevie Wonder (65)	*4256*
My Cherie Amour—Stevie Wonder (69)	*3557*
Little Ole Man (Uptight - Everything's Alright)—Bill Cosby (67)	*2587*
Shoo-Be-Doo-Be-Doo-Da-Day—Stevie Wonder (68)	1997
Honey Chile—Martha Reeves & The Vandellas (67)	1767
This Old Heart Of Mine (Is Weak For You)—Isley Brothers (66)	*1339*
I'm Wondering—Stevie Wonder (67)	1268
This Old Heart Of Mine—Rod Stewart (with Ronald Isley) (90)	*1125*
It Takes Two—Marvin Gaye & Kim Weston (67)	1078
My Baby Loves Me—Martha & The Vandellas (66)	*999*
Nothing's Too Good For My Baby—Stevie Wonder (66)	775
Never Had A Dream Come True—Stevie Wonder (70)	728
Love Bug Leave My Heart Alone—Martha & The Vandellas (67)	707
With A Child's Heart—Michael Jackson (73)	*371*
Up Tight—Ramsey Lewis (66)	*275*
(We've Got) Honey Love—Martha Reeves & The Vandellas (69)	249
My Baby Loves Me—David T. Walker (69)	*174*
What Am I Going To Do Without Your Love—Martha & The Vandellas (66)	135
This Old Heart Of Mine (Is Weak For You)—Tammi Terrell (69)	*96*
I Was Made To Love Her—King Curtis & The Kingpins (67)	*88*
Uptight—Shalamar (77)	*80*
This Old Heart Of Mine—Rod Stewart (76)	*53*
Uptight (Everything's Alright)—Nancy Wilson (66)	*28*
My Cherie Amour—Stars On 45 (82)	*27*
I Was Made To Love Her—Stars On 45 (82)	*27*
Uptight Everything's All Right—Stars On 45 (82)	*27*
My Cherie Amour—Soul Train Gang (77)	*8.1*
Forget Me Not—Martha Reeves & The Vandellas (68)	6.2
With A Child's Heart—Stevie Wonder (66)	*4.4*
Uptight (Everything's Alright)—Jazz Crusaders (66)	*2.8*
I Had A Dream—Shorty Long (69)	1.8
Alison MOYET ▶ 8489 (2)	**48**
Situation—Yazoo (82)	67
Love Resurrection—Alison Moyet (85)	44
—Michael Mozart see: Nikki LEE	
Wolfgang Amadeus MOZART ▶ 3366 (4)	**880**
Somewhere—Tymes (63)	1065
Mozart Symphony No. 40 In G Minor K.550, 1st Movement—Waldo De Los Rios (71)	*262*
Symphony No. 40 In G Minor—Royal Philharmonic Orchestra (81)	*131*
Aria From The Marriage Of Figaro—Royal Philharmonic Orchestra (81)	131
August MSARURGWA ▶ 749 (5)	**5863**
Skokiaan—Ralph Marterie And His Orchestra (54)	*4114*
Skokiaan—Four Lads (54)	*2000*
Skokiaan—Bulawayo Sweet Rhythms Band (54)	*663*
Skokiaan (South African Song)—Bill Haley And His Comets (60)	*87*
Skokiaan—Ray Anthony & His Orchestra (54)	*0.0*
James MTUME [James Foreman] ▶ 1001 (10)	**4480**
The Closer I Get To You—Roberta Flack With Donny Hathaway (78)	4396
Never Knew Love Like This Before—Stephanie Mills (80)	2443
What Cha Gonna Do With My Lovin'—Stephanie Mills (79)	*611*
Juicy Fruit—Mtume (83)	415
Two Hearts—Stephanie Mills featuring Teddy Pendergrass (81)	378
Sweet Sensation—Stephanie Mills (80)	171
Back Together Again—Roberta Flack with Donny Hathaway (80)	111
Whatcha Gonna Do With My Lovin'—Inner City (90)	*82*
You, Me And He—Mtume (84)	26
You Know How To Love Me—Phyllis Hyman (79)	12
Mark MUELLER ▶ 1993 (5)	**2023**
That's What Love Is For—Amy Grant (91)	2600
Nothin' At All—Heart (86)	1114
Someone—El DeBarge (86)	63
I Don't Want To Be Lonely—Dana Valery (80)	18
I Wasn't The One (Who Said Goodbye)—Agnetha Faltskog (88)	6.1
Hakim Rashad MUHAMMAD [Brian Keith Jones] ▶ 5969 (1)	**221**
If U Were Mine—U-Krew (90)	663
Meekaaeel MUHAMMED ▶ 4740 (1)	**427**
Ladies Night—Kool & The Gang (79)	3414
Lewis MUIR ▶ 5458 (1) HOF	**284**
Ragtime Cowboy Joe—David Seville And The Chipmunks (59)	852
Jimmy MULCAY ▶ 9384 (2)	**25**
Te Amo—Dick Jacobs And His Chorus And Orchestra (56)	*50*
Te Amo—Mulcays (56)	*0.0*
Mildred MULCAY ▶ 9385 (2)	**25**
Te Amo—Dick Jacobs And His Chorus And Orchestra (56)	*50*
Te Amo—Mulcays (56)	*0.0*
Cornell MULDROW ▶ 2675 (3)	**1280**
You Can't Sit Down—Dovells (63)	*3787*
You Can't Sit Down (Part 2)—Phil Upchurch Combo (61)	*956*
Love Will Make You Fail In School—Mickey And Sylvia (57)	30
Richard MULLAN [Peter T. Kane] ▶ 1132 (5)	**3923**
He—Al Hibbler (55)	*4351*
He—McGuire Sisters (55)	*1919*
He—Righteous Brothers (66)	*1116*
I'm Free—Al Hibbler (56)	218
A Dollar A Nickel And A Dime—Danny Machin (54)	22
Larry MULLEN ▶ 1103 (14)	**4015**
With Or Without You—U2 (87)	4346
I Still Haven't Found What I'm Looking For—U2 (87)	3862
Desire—U2 (88)	2667
Mysterious Ways—U2 (91)	2021
Angel Of Harlem—U2 (88)	876
Where The Streets Have No Name—U2 (87)	*803*
Pride (In The Name Of Love)—U2 (84)	535
In God's Country—U2 (87)	300
New Year's Day—U2 (83)	295
When Love Comes To Town—U2 With B. B. King (89)	105
The Fly—U2 (91)	78
All I Want Is You—U2 (89)	76
I Will Follow—U2 (84)	57
Where The Streets Have No Name—Pet Shop Boys (91)	*37*
Steve MULLEN ▶ 5753 (1)	**245**
Endless Nights—Eddie Money (87)	735
—A. Muller see: Warner WILDER	
Randy MULLER ▶ 2681 (4)	**1273**
Movin'—Brass Construction (76)	1268
Call Me—Skyy (81)	490
Ha Cha Cha (Funktion)—Brass Construction (76)	143
High—Skyy (80)	6.4
Susanne MÜLLER-PI [Susanne Sigl] ▶ 7811 (1)	**74**
The Different Story (World Of Lust And Crime)—Peter Schilling (89)	222
Moon MULLICAN [Morry Burns, Aubrey Wilson Mullican] ▶ 7375 (2)	**100**
Jole Blon—Gary U.S. Bonds (81)	99
I'll Sail My Ship Alone—Jerry Lee Lewis And His Pumping Piano (59)	3.2
Cameron L. MULLINS ▶ 5814 (1)	**239**
I Won't Mention It Again—Ray Price (71)	479
Ted MULRY ▶ 9886 (1)	**16**
Lazy Eyes—T.M.G. (79)	16
Ted MUNDA ▶ 6418 (1)	**173**
Blame It On Love—Smokey Robinson & Barbara Mitchell (83)	345
—Jeffrey Steven Mundy see: Jeff MONDAY	
Jim MUNDY ▶ 5798 (2)	**240**
Ram-Bunk-Shush—Ventures (61)	*507*
Ram Bunk Shush—Bill Doggett (57)	*214*
Nick MUNDY ▶ 3681 (3)	**736**
Talk To Me—Chico DeBarge (86)	908
What Comes Naturally—Sheena Easton (91)	804
I Can't Face The Fact—Gina Go-Go (89)	94
Gregg MUNIER ▶ 8774 (1)	**40**
Back To The Bullet—Saraya (89)	119
Mark MUNIZ [Marc Anthony, Mark Anthony, Mark Anthony Muniz, Marco Antonio Muniz] ▶ 5680 (1)	**256**
Boy, I've Been Told—Sa-Fire (88)	256
—Mark Anthony/Marco Antonio Muniz see: Mark MUNIZ	
Raphael MUNNINGS ▶ 3469 (1)	**833**
Funky Nassau - Part 1—Beginning Of The End (71)	1665
Rafael MUNOZ Sr. ▶ 10156 (1)	**12**
Tropical Merengue—Percy Faith And His Orchestra (55)	12
Bill MUNRO ▶ 11488 (1)	**1.5**
When My Baby Smiles At Me—Crazy Otto (56)	1.5
Carlis MUNRO ▶ 9832 (1)	**16**
Standing On Guard—Falcons (66)	49
Otis MUNSON ▶ 7658 (2)	**82**
To Be Loved (Forever)—Pentagons (61)	391
I Wonder (If Your Love Will Ever Belong To Me)—Pentagons (61)	21
—Michael David Munves see: Mike MORE	
—Michael Münzing see: Benito BENITES	
Orlando MURDEN ▶ 1434 (4)	**3054**
For Once In My Life—Stevie Wonder (68)	*5883*
For Once In My Life—Jackie Wilson (68)	*148*
For Once In My Life—Tony Bennett (67)	*50*
For Once In My Life—Stars On 45 (82)	*27*
Glenn MURDOCK ▶ 11437 (1)	**1.7**
Fire—Mother's Finest (76)	5.1
Billy MURE ▶ 3058 (12)	**1031**
Got A Match—Daddy-O's (58)	*379*
Gazachstahagen—Wild-Cats (59)	*235*
String Of Trumpets—Trumpeteers (59)	228
Got A Match—Frank Gallop (58)	*215*
There's Only You—Don Rondo (57)	*186*
When Will I Know—George Hamilton IV (58)	142
Trumpet Cha-Cha-Cha—Danny Davis (58)	8.6
Wild Rosie—Four Tophatters (55)	6.6
Blonde Bombshell—Don Rondo (58)	5.0
Gazachstahagen—Keymen (59)	*0.0*
Got A Match—Lou Stein (58)	*0.0*
There's Only You—Don Cornell (57)	*0.0*
Frankie MURIEL ▶ 9216 (1)	**28**
If I Say—Kingofthehill (91)	57
Randolph MURPH ▶ 4435 (1)	**495**
Love Jones—Brighter Side Of Darkness (72)	*1485*

Michael MURPHEY [Travis Lewis, Michael Martin Murphey] ▶ 1175 (8)	**3781**
Wildfire—Michael Murphey (75)	4221
Carolina In The Pines—Michael Murphey (75)	818
Geronimo's Cadillac—Michael Murphey (72)	478
Renegade—Michael Murphey (76)	344
Airplane Song (My Airplane)—Royal Guardsmen (67)	255
I Feel Good (I Feel Bad)— Lewis & Clarke Expedition (67)	195
Still Taking Chances—Michael Martin Murphey (83)	41
School Teacher— Kenny Rogers And The First Edition (72)	7.9
Audie MURPHY ▶ 4426 (1)	**497**
Shutters And Boards—Jerry Wallace (62)	993
Barry MURPHY ▶ 4966 (1)	**368**
We Can't Hide It Anymore—Larry Santos (76)	368
Brendan Philip MURPHY ▶ 9603 (1)	**21**
Drag My Bad Name Down—4 Of Us (90)	82
Declan Joseph MURPHY ▶ 9604 (1)	**21**
Drag My Bad Name Down—4 Of Us (90)	82
Eddie MURPHY ▶ 6731 (1)	**142**
Put Your Mouth On Me—Eddie Murphy (89)	425
Jean Sharp MURPHY [Jean Sharp] ▶ 4957 (2)	**373**
Sting Ray—Routers (63)	476
Balboa Blue—Marketts (62)	404
Kevin MURPHY ▶ 10423 (1)	**8.6**
Sharing The Love—Rufus With Chaka Khan (81)	8.6
Mic MURPHY ▶ 2972 (4)	**1089**
Don't Disturb This Groove—System (87)	1797
You Are In My System—System (83)	*182*
This Is My Night—Chaka Khan (85)	157
You Are In My System—Robert Palmer (83)	*42*
Paul Gerard MURPHY ▶ 9605 (1)	**21**
Drag My Bad Name Down—4 Of Us (90)	82
Peter MURPHY ▶ 7413 (1)	**97**
Cuts You Up—Peter Murphy (90)	195
Ralph MURPHY ▶ 3555 (3)	**786**
Half The Way—Crystal Gayle (79)	1014
Good Enough To Be Your Wife—Jeannie C. Riley (71)	191
He Got You—Ronnie Milsap (82)	178
Rita MURPHY ▶ 11757 (1)	**0.2**
Sweet Annie Laurie— Sammy Turner and The Twisters (59)	0.4
Walter MURPHY ▶ 1307 (2)	**3389**
A Fifth Of Beethoven— Walter Murphy & The Big Apple Band (76)	6361
Flight '76—Walter Murphy Band (76)	418
Willie MURPHY ▶ 11753 (1)	**0.2**
One Wonderful Love—Ray Smith (60)	1.2
Roger MURRAH ▶ 3977 (1)	**632**
We're In This Love Together—Al Jarreau (81)	1265
Fred MURRAY ▶ 1272 (1)	**3481**
I'm Henry VIII, I Am—Herman's Hermits (65)	6962
Henry MURRAY [Juggy Jones] ▶ 5222 (2)	**323**
She Blew A Good Thing—Poets (66)	646
Hey Lonely One—Baby Washington (63)	0.4
Jean MURRAY ▶ 2448 (1)	**1480**
Splish Splash—Bobby Darin (58)	4440
Jerry MURRAY ▶ 4726 (2)	**430**
Karate-Boo-Ga-Loo—Jerryo (67)	432
Boo-Ga-Loo—Tom & Jerrio (65)	427
Larry MURRAY ▶ 6967 (1)	**125**
Six White Horses—Tommy Cash (69)	125
Lyn MURRAY [Lionel Breeze] ▶ 6924 (1)	**128**
Dancing With My Shadow—Four Voices (58)	256
Mitch MURRAY [Lionel Michael Stitcher] ▶ 208 (12)	**15374**
I'm Telling You Now—Freddie And The Dreamers (65)	6476
Billy, Don't Be A Hero— Bo Donaldson And The Heywoods (74)	*4779*
The Night Chicago Died—Paper Lace (74)	4648
Hitchin' A Ride—Vanity Fare (70)	3768
The Ballad Of Bonnie And Clyde—Georgie Fame (68)	3288
How Do You Do It?—Gerry And The Pacemakers (64)	1557
I Like It—Gerry And The Pacemakers (64)	859
You Were Made For Me— Freddie And The Dreamers (65)	856
Even The Bad Times Are Good—Tremeloes (67)	509
The Black-Eyed Boys—Paper Lace (74)	343

I Knew It All The Time—Dave Clark Five (64)	164
Billy--Don't Be A Hero—Paper Lace (74)	*63*
Rachel MURRAY ▶ 7224 (1)	**109**
Dream Lover—Rebel Pebbles (91)	328
Russell MURRAY ▶ 6434 (2)	**169**
Mr. Songwriter—Connie Stevens (62)	335
A City Girl Stole My Country Boy—Patti Page (61)	5.0
Tom MURRAY ▶ 11206 (1)	**2.8**
Silly People—Litter (69)	11
Tom (2) MURRAY ▶ 7924 (1)	**69**
Why (Are There Things We Can't Explain)— Jane Morgan (54)	139
—Murray the K see: Murray KAUFMAN	
Norman MURRELLS ▶ 8609 (2)	**45**
House Of Bamboo—Earl Grant (60)	*80*
House Of Bamboo—Andy Williams (58)	*10*
Ted MURRY [Murray Mencher] ▶ 1109 (5)	**4000**
Don't Break The Heart That Loves You— Connie Francis (62)	6052
Follow The Boys—Connie Francis (63)	1325
Whose Heart Are You Breaking Tonight— Connie Francis (65)	358
Baby's First Christmas—Connie Francis (61)	257
The Biggest Sin Of All—Connie Francis (62)	9.5
Patrick MURTAGH ▶ 11709 (1)	**0.5**
Passion Flower—Caterina Valente (59)	2.0
Valerie MURTAGH [Valerie Avon] ▶ 9511 (1)	**22**
Desdemona—Searchers (71)	45
Bob MUSEL ▶ 1523 (8)	**2805**
Band Of Gold—Don Cherry (55)	*3488*
Band Of Gold—Kit Carson (55)	*1174*
Band Of Gold—Mel Carter (66)	*521*
Earthbound—Sammy Davis Jr. (56)	*404*
Earthbound—Mario Lanza (56)	*123*
Band Of Gold—Roommates (61)	*70*
Band Of Gold—Hi-Fi Four (55)	*4.8*
Earthbound—Roberto & His Orchestra (56)	*0.0*
Frank MUSKER ▶ 1134 (10)	**3911**
Every Woman In The World—Air Supply (80)	3052
Heaven On The 7th Floor—Paul Nicholas (77)	*2721*
Modern Girl—Sheena Easton (81)	1013
Back On My Feet Again—Babys (80)	576
Married Men—Bette Midler (79)	261
Every Home Should Have One—Patti Austin (83)	*166*
Every Home Should Have One—Patti Austin (81)	*133*
On The Strip—Paul Nicholas (78)	69
Heaven On The Seventh Floor—Mighty Pope (77)	*15*
Mystery Girl—Dukes (82)	6.7
Sy MUSKIN ▶ 6065 (1)	**210**
Lullaby Of Love—Frank Gari (61)	629
Giuseppe MUSTACCHI [Georges Moustaki] ▶ 5347 (3)	**302**
Milord—Bobby Darin (64)	*473*
Milord—Teresa Brewer (61)	*149*
Milord—Edith Piaf (61)	*32*
Elizabeth MYERS ▶ 8031 (1)	**64**
Shakin'—Eddie Money (82)	192
Frank MYERS ▶ 1862 (1)	**2189**
You And I—Eddie Rabbitt with Crystal Gayle (82)	2189
—James E. Myers see: Jimmy DeKNIGHT	
Randy MYERS ▶ 2041 (5)	**1968**
Put A Little Love In Your Heart— Jackie DeShannon (69)	*3577*
Put A Little Love In Your Heart— Annie Lennox & Al Green (88)	*1389*
Love Will Find A Way— Jackie De Shannon (69)	529
Brighton Hill—Jackie Deshannon (70)	207
Bad Water—Raeletts (71)	202
Richard MYERS ▶ 2700 (2)	**1264**
Hold My Hand—Don Cornell (54)	*2528*
Hold My Hand— Guy Lombardo & His Royal Canadians (54)	*0.0*
—Sharon Lee Myers see: Jackie DeSHANNON	
Billy MYLES [William Myles Nobles] ▶ 1068 (11)	**4129**
(You Were Made For) All My Love—Jackie Wilson (60)	1762
The Joker (That's What They Call Me)— Billy Myles (57)	*841*
Hoochi Coochi Coo— Hank Ballard And The Midnighters (60)	741

The Greatest Hurt—Jackie Wilson (62)	662
The Joker (That's What They Call Me)— Hilltoppers (57)	*630*
Your One And Only Love—Jackie Wilson (61)	350
No Love (But Your Love)—Johnny Mathis (57)	342
Let's Go Again (Where We Went Last Night)— Hank Ballard And The Midnighters (61)	315
Chapel Of Dreams—Dubs (59)	34
Tonite, Tonite—Mello-Kings (57)	*33*
Tonite, Tonite—Mello-Kings (61)	*2.7*
—David Luke Myrick see: T. Texas TYLER	
Josef MYROW ▶ 10072 (2)	**13**
Some Day Soon—Eddie Fisher (57)	22
All About Love—Eddie Fisher (57)	4.4
George MYSELS ▶ 11296 (1)	**2.4**
Father Time—Poni-Tails (59)	4.7
Maurice MYSELS ▶ 2074 (1)	**1916**
I Want You I Need You I Love You— Elvis Presley (56)	3831
Sammy MYSELS ▶ 7815 (3)	**74**
Singing Hills—Billy Vaughn and His Orchestra (58)	*216*
Is There Somebody Else—Dream Weavers (56)	5.5
The Singing Hills— Don Cogan & LeRoy Holmes & His Orchestra (58)	*0.0*
—Mystro see: Melvin STEALS	

N

Jimmie NABBIE ▶ 2212 (2)	**1736**
You Are My Love—Joni James (55)	*1736*
You Are My Love—Four Tunes (55)	*0.0*
—Vince Nacardo see: Vinny NACCARATO	
Vinny NACCARATO [Vince Nacardo] ▶ 9979 (2)	**14**
Where I Fell In Love—Capris (61)	71
Limbo—Capris (62)	0.9
Brad NACK ▶ 8961 (1)	**35**
Monsters And Angels—Voice Of The Beehive (91)	106
—Warren Nadel see: Randy STARR	
Neval NADER ▶ 2298 (7)	**1639**
Mecca—Gene Pitney (63)	1433
Lovers By Night, Strangers By Day— Fleetwoods (62)	581
Punish Her—Bobby Vee (62)	567
Trouble Is My Middle Name—Bobby Vinton (62)	546
Fly By Night—Andy Williams (61)	101
Open Up Your Door— Richard and The Young Lions (66)	71
Pretty Boy Lonely—Patti Page (63)	4.1
Ron NAGLE ▶ 8257 (1)	**57**
Don't Touch Me There—Tubes (76)	113
Irving NAHAN ▶ 4875 (4)	**393**
Dance With Me—Drifters (59)	1398
Dumplin's—Doc Bagby (57)	*116*
Dumplin's—Ernie Freeman (57)	*91*
Walk On With The Duke—Duke Of Earl (62)	86
—Brad Nall see: Brad HOWELL	
Philip NAISH ▶ 8908 (1)	**36**
I'm A Believer—Giant (89)	182
Hachidai NAKAMURA ▶ 868 (2)	**5116**
Sukiyaki—Kyu Sakamoto (63)	*8172*
Sukiyaki—A Taste Of Honey (81)	*3090*
—Dolores Nance see: Jody REYNOLDS	
Jack NANCE ▶ 839 (5)	**5258**
It's Only Make Believe—Conway Twitty (58)	*7964*
It's Only Make Believe—Glen Campbell (70)	*1910*
Story Of My Love—Conway Twitty (59)	640
She's Mine—Conway Twitty (60)	1.2
When I'm Not With You—Conway Twitty (59)	1.2
Kevin NANCE ▶ 8670 (1)	**43**
There But For The Grace Of God Go I— Machine (79)	86
Joe NANINI ▶ 8380 (1)	**52**
Mexican Radio—Wall Of Voodoo (83)	209
Bruce NAPIER ▶ 5451 (5)	**287**
Funky Worm—Ohio Players (73)	1438
Ecstasy—Ohio Players (73)	621
Pain (Part 1)—Ohio Players (71)	208
Got Pleasure—Ohio Players (72)	14
Rattlesnake—Ohio Players (76)	12

Simon NAPIER-BELL ► 2109 (4)	**1864**
You Don't Have To Say You Love Me—Dusty Springfield (66)	*4119*
You Don't Have To Say You Love Me—Elvis Presley (70)	*1432*
You Don't Have To Say You Love Me—Four Sonics (68)	*36*
Smashed! Blocked!—John's Children (67)	2.8
—Napoleon XIV see: Jerry SAMUELS	
Johnette Lin NAPOLITANO ► 3585 (2)	**777**
Joey—Concrete Blonde (90)	750
Caroline—Concrete Blonde (90)	27
Belle NARDONE ► 8677 (2)	**43**
Santo Natale (Merry Christmas)—David Whitfield with Stanley Black And His Orchestra (54)	*129*
Santo Natale—Ronnie Gaylord (54)	*0.0*
Mario NASCIMBENE ► 3303 (4)	**907**
Song Of The Barefoot Contessa—Hugo Winterhalter's Orchestra And Chorus (54)	882
Sons And Lovers—Percy Faith (60)	22
A Farewell To Arms—Gale Storm (58)	*3.1*
A Farewell To Arms—Marty Gold & His Orchestra (58)	*3.1*
Brian NASH ► 8160 (1)	**60**
Welcome To The Pleasuredome (Trevor Horn Remix)—Frankie Goes To Hollywood (85)	239
Graham NASH ► 330 (23) HOF	**11145**
On A Carousel—Hollies (67)	*2080*
Carrie-Anne—Hollies (67)	2018
Stop Stop Stop—Hollies (66)	2003
Wasted On The Way—Crosby, Stills & Nash (82)	1842
Just A Song Before I Go—Crosby, Stills & Nash (77)	1751
Teach Your Children—Crosby, Stills, Nash & Young (70)	1295
Chicago—Graham Nash (71)	826
Our House—Crosby, Stills, Nash & Young (70)	824
Marrakesh Express—Crosby, Stills & Nash (69)	815
Pay You Back With Interest—Hollies (67)	*585*
Jennifer Eccles—Hollies (68)	555
Immigration Man—Graham Nash & David Crosby (72)	539
Tell Me To My Face—Keith (67)	500
Dear Eloise—Hollies (67)	416
King Midas In Reverse—Hollies (67)	292
On A Carousel—Glass Moon (82)	*180*
Have You Ever Loved Somebody—Searchers (66)	165
Military Madness—Graham Nash (71)	147
Pay You Back With Interest—Gary O' (81)	*45*
Music Is Love—David Crosby (71)	43
Southbound Train—David Crosby & Graham Nash (72)	40
Out Of The Darkness—David Crosby / Graham Nash (76)	34
Do The Best You Can—Hollies (68)	3.5
Johnny NASH ► 381 (7)	**10298**
I Can See Clearly Now—Johnny Nash (72)	5586
Hold Me Tight—Johnny Nash (68)	3039
What Kind Of Love Is This—Joey Dee & The Starliters (62)	1073
You Got Soul—Johnny Nash (68)	257
I Lost My Baby—Joey Dee (62)	255
She Said Yes—Wilson Pickett (70)	169
My Merry-Go-Round—Johnny Nash (73)	134
Margaret NASH ► 5894 (2)	**232**
Let's Move & Groove (Together)—Johnny Nash (65)	228
You Can't Go Halfway—Johnny Nash (74)	15
Michael NASH ► 10674 (1)	**6.2**
Disco Rufus—Stargard (78)	12
Otha NASH [Osman Handani] ► 6959 (2)	**125**
Spirit Of The Boogie—Kool & The Gang (75)	825
Caribbean Festival—Kool & The Gang (75)	268
Pete NASH [Peter Nash, Prime Minister Pete Nice] ► 8513 (1)	**48**
Pop Goes The Weasel—3rd Bass (91)	333
—Peter Nash see: Pete NASH	
—N. Nathan see: Nathaniel NATHAN	
Nathaniel NATHAN [Magnificent Montague, Nathaniel Montague, N. Nathan] ► 5110 (7)	**341**
Hole In The Wall—Packers (65)	689
Spreadin' Honey—Watts 103rd Street Rhythm Band (67)	224
Keep On Dancing—Hank Ballard And The Midnighters (61)	70
Do You Know How To Twist—Hank Ballard (62)	23
She's With Her Other Love—Leon Hayward (65)	14
Up On The Mountain—Magnificents (56)	11
Grits 'N Corn Bread—Soul Runners (67)	3.3
—Sydney Nathan see: Lois MANN	
Paul NAUMANN ► 4599 (4)	**455**
Ball Of Fire—Tommy James And The Shondells (69)	1168
Do Something To Me—Tommy James And The Shondells (68)	*639*
Groovin' With Mr. Bloe—Cool Heat (70)	22
Do Something To Me—? And The Mysterians (67)	*3.4*
Dan NAVARRO ► 2465 (3)	**1458**
We Belong—Pat Benatar (84)	2339
You Don't Have To Go Home Tonight—Triplets (91)	1130
I Won't Give Up On You—TKA (90)	125
Esther NAVARRO ► 3533 (4)	**796**
Speedoo—Cadillacs (55)	*764*
Zoom—Cadillacs (56)	32
Speedo—Commodores (2) (56)	*0.0*
Speedoo—Steve Lawrence (56)	*0.0*
Charles NAYLOR ► 5725 (2)	**250**
Shake Me I Rattle (Squeeze Me I Cry)—Marion Worth (62)	*486*
Shake Me I Rattle (Squeeze Me I Cry)—Lennon Sisters (57)	*14*
Bruce NAZARIAN ► 8608 (1)	**45**
The Martian Boogie—Brownsville Station (77)	180
Kim NAZEL [Mik Lezan, Kim Renard Nazel, Arabian Prince] ► 7231 (1)	**108**
Supersonic—J.J. Fad (88)	542
Robert NEAL Jr. ► 11656 (1)	**0.8**
Riding High—Faze-O (78)	4.8
Stuart NEALE ► 4612 (2)	**451**
Too Shy—Kajagoogoo (83)	2226
Hang On Now—Kajagoogoo (83)	28
Michael NEALY ► 7789 (1)	**75**
This Is Ponderous—2NU (90)	300
Brian NEARY ► 4301 (2)	**529**
Fool In Love With You—Jim Photoglo (81)	651
We Were Meant To Be Lovers—Photoglo (80)	408
Jimmy NEBB [James H. Nebbergall] ► 2270 (6)	**1670**
No Arms Can Ever Hold You (Like These Arms Of Mine)—Georgie Shaw (55)	*1126*
No Other Arms—Pat Boone (55)	*1053*
No Arms Can Ever Hold You—Bachelors (64)	*791*
No Arms Can Ever Hold You (Like These Arms Of Mine)—Gaylords (55)	*187*
No Arms Can Ever Hold You—Bobby Vinton (70)	*184*
No Arms Can Ever Hold You—Jimmy Young with Bob Sharples & His Music (55)	*0.0*
—James H. Nebbergall see: Jimmy NEBB	
Sam NEELY ► 3074 (3)	**1025**
Loving You Just Crossed My Mind—Sam Neely (72)	702
Rosalie—Sam Neely (73)	307
Sadie Take A Lover—Sam Neely (74)	16
Chuck NEESE ► 10830 (1)	**5.0**
She Shot A Hole In My Soul—Clifford Curry (67)	10
Morty NEFF ► 11297 (1)	**2.4**
Father Time—Poni-Tails (59)	4.7
Joe NEGRO [Joe Nigro] ► 8563 (1)	**46**
Echo—Emotions (1) (62)	278
Steve NEGUS ► 6398 (2)	**175**
On The Loose—Saga (82)	675
Wind Him Up—Saga (83)	200
Harry NEHLS ► 11051 (1)	**3.6**
Too Hot To Stop—Bar-Kays (77)	36
Al NEIBURG [Allen J. Neiburg] ► 7047 (5)	**119**
I'm Confessin' (That I Love You)—Frank Ifield (63)	*333*
I'm Confessin' (That I Love You)—Terri Dean (59)	*10*
I'm Confessin' (That I Love You)—Nino Tempo & April Stevens (64)	*6.7*
Play Some Music For Broken Hearts—Don Cornell (58)	5.3
I'm Confessin' That I Love You—Barbara Lantz (59)	*0.0*
Rick NEIGHER ► 8721 (2)	**41**
I Want You—Animotion (86)	57
Got A New Love—Good Question (88)	39
Christopher NEIL ► 2825 (3)	**1169**
All I Need Is A Miracle—Mike + The Mechanics (86)	1677
Taken In—Mike + The Mechanics (86)	539
Word Of Mouth—Mike + The Mechanics (91)	122
Fred NEIL ► 1361 (4)	**3267**
Everybody's Talkin'—Nilsson (69)	*2550*
Candy Man—Roy Orbison (61)	1091
Everybody's Talkin'—Nilsson (68)	*171*
The Other Side Of This Life—Peter, Paul & Mary (66)	0.5
Vince NEIL [Vincent Neil Wharton] ► 8391 (2)	**52**
Same Ol' Situation (S.O.S.)—Mötley Crüe (90)	148
Primal Scream—Mötley Crüe (91)	60
Francine NEIMAN ► 10973 (1)	**4.0**
Music To My Heart—Obsession (70)	8.0
—Albert Nelson see: Albert KING	
—Benjamin Earl Nelson see: Ben E. KING	
Betty NELSON ► 2310 (2)	**1619**
Don't Play That Song—Aretha Franklin With The Dixie Flyers (70)	*1651*
Don't Play That Song (You Lied)—Ben E. King (62)	*1588*
Billy NELSON ► 7399 (3)	**98**
All Your Goodies Are Gone (The Loser's Seat)—Parliaments (67)	221
I Wanna Know If It's Good To You?—Funkadelic (70)	65
You And Your Folks, Me And My Folks—Funkadelic (71)	34
Dennis NELSON ► 6615 (1)	**150**
Hyperactive—Robert Palmer (86)	451
Earl NELSON [Jackie Lee] ► 1963 (8)	**2048**
Harlem Shuffle—Rolling Stones (86)	*1790*
The Duck—Jackie Lee (2) (65)	1646
Harlem Shuffle—Bob & Earl (63)	*494*
Your P-E-R-S-O-N-A-L-I-T-Y—Jackie Lee (2) (66)	113
Harlem Shuffle—Traits (66)	*32*
Funky North Philly—Bill Cosby (68)	32
Don't Ever Leave Me—Bob & Earl (62)	20
Happy Vacation—Jackie Lee (1) (59)	3.0
Ed NELSON ► 10691 (1)	**6.0**
I Apologize—Timi Yuro (61)	18
Eve NELSON ► 10653 (1)	**6.3**
When Love Cries—Donna Summer (91)	32
Gerald NELSON ► 1541 (7)	**2773**
Tragedy—Thomas Wayne with The DeLons (59)	*2908*
Tragedy—Fleetwoods (61)	*1366*
Tragedy—Brian Hyland (68)	*561*
Big Big World—Johnny Burnette (61)	460
Save All Your Lovin' For Me—Brenda Lee (62)	284
Archie's Melody—By-Liners (62)	90
Eternally—Thomas Wayne with The DeLons (59)	30
Gunnar NELSON ► 1904 (4)	**2129**
Can't Live Without Your) Love And Affection—Nelson (90)	3603
After The Rain—Nelson (90)	1789
More Than Ever—Nelson (91)	1085
Only Time Will Tell—Nelson (91)	479
Karen NELSON ► 9916 (1)	**15**
Love Me One More Time (Just For Old Times Sake)—Karen Nelson And Billy T (77)	30
Matthew NELSON ► 1905 (4)	**2129**
(Can't Live Without Your) Love And Affection—Nelson (90)	3603
After The Rain—Nelson (90)	1789
More Than Ever—Nelson (91)	1085
Only Time Will Tell—Nelson (91)	479
Miriam NELSON ► 10806 (1)	**5.2**
You're The Only Love—Paul Hyde And The Payolas (85)	21
Nate NELSON ► 8957 (2)	**35**
Mio Amore—Flamingos (60)	196
If You Try—Chantels (58)	5.1
Oliver NELSON ► 6993 (1)	**123**
Hobo Flats - Part I—Jimmy Smith (63)	123
—Paul Reginald Nelson see: Paul HYDE	
Phyllis NELSON ► 6017 (1)	**216**
I Like You—Phyllis Nelson (86)	216
—Prince Rogers Nelson see: PRINCE	
Rick NELSON ► 1253 (4)	**3564**
Garden Party—Rick Nelson & The Stone Canyon Band (72)	3139
Easy To Be Free—Rick Nelson (70)	298
Palace Guard—Rick Nelson And The Stone Canyon Band (73)	91
You Just Can't Quit—Rick Nelson (66)	36

Robert H. NELSON ▶ 9707 (1)	**19**
You Don't Know What Love Is—Susan Jacks And The Poppy Family (73)	37
Sandy NELSON ▶ 1138 (8)	**3895**
Teen Beat—Sandy Nelson (59)	*3896*
Let There Be Drums—Sandy Nelson (61)	*2590*
Teen Beat '65—Sandy Nelson (64)	*535*
Drums Are My Beat—Sandy Nelson (62)	339
...And Then There Were Drums—Sandy Nelson (62)	52
Drum Stomp—Sandy Nelson (62)	13
The Birth Of The Beat—Sandy Nelson (62)	11
Let There Be Drums—Incredible Bongo Band (73)	*4.3*
Stephen NELSON ▶ 5807 (1)	**240**
Songbird—Barbra Streisand (78)	480
Wayne NELSON ▶ 9109 (1)	**31**
Playing To Win—LRB (85)	217
Willie NELSON ▶ 394 (14) HOF	**10064**
Hello Walls—Faron Young (61)	*2385*
Funny—Joe Hinton (64)	*1910*
Crazy—Patsy Cline (61)	1794
On The Road Again—Willie Nelson (80)	1071
Pretty Paper—Roy Orbison (63)	1034
Funny How Time Slips Away—Jimmy Elledge (61)	*851*
Good Hearted Woman—Waylon & Willie (76)	653
Night Life—Rusty Draper (63)	273
Funny How Time Slips Away—Johnny Tillotson (63)	*249*
Funny How Time Slips Away—Spinners (82)	*193*
Funny How Time Slips Away—Dorothy Moore (76)	*142*
Hello Fool—Ralph Emery (61)	20
Hello Wall No. 2—Ben Colder (63)	*16*
Permanently Lonely—Timi Yuro (64)	1.8
Elmer NEMETH ▶ 5203 (1)	**328**
Cinderella—Jack Ross (62)	655
Henry NEMO ▶ 8176 (3)	**59**
Don't Take Your Love From Me—Gloria Lynne (64)	*29*
Don't Take Your Love From Me—Grady Martin And The Slew Foot Five (56)	*25*
Don't Take Your Love From Me—Joni James (56)	*5.7*
Neil NEPHEW [Neil Bernstein] ▶ 8845 (1)	**38**
Eighteen—Connie Francis (57)	76
Freida NERANGIS ▶ 4854 (3)	**398**
Dreaming A Dream—Crown Heights Affair (75)	514
Foxy Lady—Crown Heights Affair (76)	250
Every Beat Of My Heart—Crown Heights Affair (75)	32
—Nervous Norvus see: Jimmy DRAKE	
Michael NESMITH ▶ 838 (12)	**5261**
Different Drum—Stone Poneys Featuring Linda Ronstadt (67)	2273
Joanne—Michael Nesmith & The First National Band (70)	1122
Silver Moon—Michael Nesmith & The First National Band (70)	528
Tapioca Tundra—Monkees (68)	358
Listen To The Band—Monkees (69)	298
Some Of Shelly's Blues—Nitty Gritty Dirt Band (71)	*241*
The Girl I Knew Somewhere—Monkees (67)	162
Nevada Fighter—Michael Nesmith & The First National Band (71)	119
Good Clean Fun—Monkees (69)	86
Mary, Mary—Run-D.M.C. (88)	46
I've Just Begun To Care—Michael Nesmith & The First National Band (71)	24
Some Of Shelly's Blues—Nitty Gritty Dirt Band (69)	*4.1*
Billy NESS [Edward Mesner, Billy J. Ross] ▶ 9084 (1)	**32**
Chills And Fever—Ronnie Love And His Orchestra (61)	63
Larry NESTOR ▶ 9529 (1)	**22**
Tired Of Being Lonely—Sharpees (66)	44
Jon NETTLESBEY ▶ 8872 (1)	**37**
Show Me—Howard Hewett (90)	112
—Lawrence Thomas Netto see: Loz NETTO	
Loz NETTO [Lawrence Thomas Netto] ▶ 8594 (1)	**45**
Fade Away—Loz Netto (83)	45
Ernst NEUBACH ▶ 5429 (1)	**290**
In Heaven There Is No Beer—Clean Living (72)	580
Matt NEUMAN ▶ 11494 (1)	**1.5**
A European (Speaks Up For The U. S.)—Guido Sarducci (74)	2.9
Klaus-Günter NEUMANN ▶ 422 (4)	**9523**
Wonderland By Night—Bert Kaempfert And His Orchestra (60)	*7899*
Wonderland By Night—Louis Prima (60)	*1224*
Wonderland By Night—Anita Bryant (60)	*792*
The Dudelsack Song (Play To Me My Darling)—Chordettes (55)	8.4
Martin NEUMAYER ▶ 7192 (1)	**111**
How To Dance—Bingoboys (91)	554
Bob NEUWIRTH ▶ 8435 (1)	**51**
(Oh Lord Won't You Buy Me A) Mercedes Benz—Goose Creek Symphony (72)	152
—Nevelle see: Nevelle HODGE	
Rich NEVENS ▶ 11048 (1)	**3.6**
One Simple Thing—Stabilizers (87)	7.2
Robbie NEVIL ▶ 1371 (11)	**3248**
C'est La Vie—Robbie Nevil (86)	3569
It's Not Over ('til It's Over)—Starship (87)	1049
Wot's It To Ya—Robbie Nevil (87)	988
Dominoes—Robbie Nevil (87)	899
Just Like You—Robbie Nevil (91)	551
Back On Holiday—Robbie Nevil (88)	525
Somebody Like You—Robbie Nevil (89)	194
Under The Influence—Vanity (86)	101
For Your Mind—Robbie Nevil (91)	93
Mathematics—Melissa Manchester (85)	70
Someone—El DeBarge (86)	63
Art NEVILLE ▶ 4208 (7)	**562**
Cissy Strut—Meters (69)	731
Sophisticated Cissy—Meters (69)	475
Chicken Strut—Meters (70)	361
Look-Ka Py Py—Meters (69)	346
Ease Back—Meters (69)	213
Hand Clapping Song—Meters (70)	94
Be My Lady—Meters (77)	36
Christopher NEVILLE ▶ 8591 (1)	**45**
Forgive Me—Kitty Kallen (55)	91
Cyril NEVILLE ▶ 10566 (1)	**7.2**
Be My Lady—Meters (77)	36
Ivan NEVILLE ▶ 3836 (2)	**686**
Not Just Another Girl—Ivan Neville (88)	660
Falling Out Of Love—Ivan Neville (89)	26
—Naomi Neville see: Allen TOUSSAINT	
Ethelbert NEVIN ▶ 11017 (1) HOF	**3.8**
The Happy Puppy—Bent Fabric (63)	7.7
Mark NEVIN ▶ 8128 (1)	**61**
Perfect—Fairground Attraction (88)	61
Al NEVINS [Albert Tepper] ▶ 2247 (3)	**1708**
Twilight Time—Platters (58)	*6653*
Twilight Time—Dick Contino (56)	*149*
Twilight Time—Andy Williams (62)	*28*
Morty NEVINS ▶ 2241 (4)	**1709**
Twilight Time—Platters (58)	*6653*
Twilight Time—Dick Contino (56)	*149*
Twilight Time—Andy Williams (62)	*28*
These Things I Offer You (For A Lifetime)—Playmates (60)	5.7
Ira NEWBORN ▶ 11612 (1)	**1.0**
Clap Your Hands—Manhattan Transfer (75)	4.0
Mickey NEWBURY ▶ 1143 (7)	**3884**
Just Dropped In (To See What Condition My Condition Was In)—First Edition (68)	2865
Mister Can't You See—Buffy Sainte-Marie (72)	442
Funny Familiar Forgotten Feelings—Tom Jones (67)	379
Here Comes The Rain, Baby—Eddy Arnold (68)	228
Sunshine—Mickey Newbury (73)	111
Sweet Memories—Andy Williams (68)	73
Just Between Us—Bill Woody (79)	7.2
Norman NEWELL [David West] ▶ 1755 (19)	**2367**
Portrait Of My Love—Steve Lawrence (61)	*2254*
To The Door Of The Sun (Alle Porte Del Sole)—Al Martino (74)	825
More—Vic Dana (63)	*633*
Portrait Of My Love—Tokens (67)	*626*
Never, Never, Never (Grande, Grande, Grande)—Shirley Bassey (73)	433
Now That You've Gone—Connie Stevens (65)	298
Someone To Love—Four Aces (56)	186
Forget Domani—Connie Francis (65)	*140*
Say Wonderful Things—Patti Page (63)	*131*
Forget Domani—Frank Sinatra (65)	*126*
In Time—Engelbert Humperdinck (72)	121
Say Wonderful Things—Ronnie Carroll (63)	*55*
Time Alone Will Tell—Connie Francis (67)	*3.3*
Time Alone Will Tell (Non Pensare A Me)—Jerry Vale (67)	*2.8*
The White Rose Of Athens—Chordettes (62)	*0.0*
The White Rose Of Athens—Nana Mouskouri (62)	*0.0*
More (Theme From "Mondo Cane")—Della Reese (63)	*0.0*
More (From The Film "Mondo Cane")—Danny Williams (63)	*0.0*
More (Theme From The Film "Mondo Cane")—Steve Lawrence (63)	*0.0*
Anthony NEWLEY [George Hackney] ▶ 840 (17) HOF	**5258**
The Candy Man—Sammy Davis, Jr. With The Mike Curb Congregation (72)	5982
Goldfinger—Shirley Bassey (65)	*2651*
What Kind Of Fool Am I—Sammy Davis Jr. (62)	*1653*
Who Can I Turn To (When Nobody Needs Me)—Tony Bennett (64)	*814*
Who Can I Turn To—Dionne Warwick (65)	*151*
What Kind Of Fool Am I—Anthony Newley (62)	*57*
The People Tree—Sammy Davis, Jr. With The Mike Curb Congregation (72)	32
What Kind Of Fool Am I—Robert Goulet (62)	*31*
Tribute—Anthony Newley (64)	13
There's No Such Thing As Love—Anthony Newley (63)	1.8
What Kind Of Fool Am I—Cordials (62)	*0.0*
What Kind Of Fool Am I—Vic Damone (62)	*0.0*
What Kind Of Fool Am I—Burt Farber (62)	*0.0*
What Kind Of Fool Am I—Billy Daniels (62)	*0.0*
What Kind Of Fool Am I—Billy Eckstine (62)	*0.0*
What Kind Of Fool Am I—Ronnie Aldrich (62)	*0.0*
What Kind Of Fool Am I—Mantovani And His Orchestra (62)	*0.0*
Alfred NEWMAN ▶ 2747 (13)	**1224**
Anastasia—Pat Boone (56)	*671*
Airport Love Theme (Gwen And Vern)—Vincent Bell (70)	603
Best Of Everything—Johnny Mathis (59)	186
The Song From Desiree (We Meet Again)—Johnny Desmond (54)	*91*
The Song From Desiree (We Meet Again)—Paul Weston And His Orchestra (54)	*91*
20th Century Fox Trademark—Meco (82)	47
Marianna—Johnny Mathis (62)	20
Anastasia—Roger Williams (56)	*0.0*
Anastasia—LeRoy Holmes & His Orchestra (56)	*0.0*
Anastasia—Victor Young Singing Strings (56)	*0.0*
Anastasia—Guy Lombardo & His Royal Canadians (56)	*0.0*
The Song From Desiree (We Meet Again)—Jane Froman (54)	*0.0*
The Song From Desiree (We Meet Again)—Bing Crosby And Alfred Newman (54)	*0.0*
Charles NEWMAN ▶ 9547 (2)	**22**
Sweethearts On Parade—Billy Ward & The Dominoes (55)	*22*
Sweethearts On Parade—Dick Jacobs And His Chorus And Orchestra (55)	*22*
Floyd NEWMAN ▶ 3334 (1)	**895**
Last Night—Mar-Keys (61)	4476
Herbert NEWMAN [Steven Howard, Barry Stuart] ▶ 320 (10)	**11433**
The Wayward Wind—Gogi Grant (56)	*9460*
The Birds And The Bees—Jewel Akens (65)	5300
So This Is Love—Castells (62)	808
The Wayward Wind—Tex Ritter (56)	*406*
The Wayward Wind—Gogi Grant (61)	*211*
Georgie Porgie—Jewel Akens (65)	179
When The Tide Is High—Gogi Grant (56)	137
You're In Love—Gogi Grant (56)	65
Heartbreak Harry—Alis Leslie (57)	5.9
Ghost Of Billy Malloo—Dorsey Burnette (60)	3.4
Jon Erik NEWMAN ▶ 9996 (1)	**14**
Victory Line—Limited Warranty (86)	71
Lionel NEWMAN ▶ 4419 (10)	**499**
Theme From The Proud Ones—Nelson Riddle And His Orchestra (56)	*424*
Theme From Adventures In Paradise—Jerry Byrd And His Steel Guitar (60)	48

Lionel NEWMAN ▶ 4419 (10) *Continued*	**499**
Again—Lettermen (62)	26
Theme From "The Proud Ones"—Lionel Newman & His Orchesra (56)	*9.5*
Theme From The Proud Ones—LeRoy Holmes And His Orchestra (56)	*4.0*
The River Of No Return—Marilyn Monroe (54)	0.0
Theme From "The Proud Ones"—Three Suns (56)	*0.0*
(Theme From) The Proud Ones—Fred Lowery (56)	*0.0*
Theme From "The Proud Ones"—Johnny Desmond (56)	*0.0*
Theme From "The Proud Ones"—Buddy Morrow & His Orchestra (56)	*0.0*
Ralph NEWMAN ▶ 11711 (1)	**0.5**
Help Me (Get Myself Back Together Again)—Spellbinders (66)	0.9
Randy NEWMAN ▶ 274 (11) HOF	**12611**
Mama Told Me (Not To Come)—Three Dog Night (70)	*7392*
Short People—Randy Newman (77)	4354
The Blues—Randy Newman and Paul Simon (83)	258
It's Money That Matters—Randy Newman (88)	251
Anyone Who Knows What Love Is (Will Understand)—Irma Thomas (64)	231
Just One Smile—Gene Pitney (66)	146
Living Without You—Manfred Mann's Earth Band (72)	108
Mama Told Me Not To Come—Wilson Pickett (72)	*23*
I Don't Want To Hear It Anymore—Dusty Springfield (69)	*11*
I'll Be Home—Vikki Carr (71)	7.1
I Don't Want To Hear Anymore—Jerry Butler (64)	*4.2*
Troy NEWMAN ▶ 10878 (1)	**4.7**
Love Gets Rough—Troy Newman (91)	9.4
Ed NEWMARK ▶ 9209 (1)	**29**
Seasons—Charles Fox (80)	57
Betty Jean NEWSOME ▶ 2546 (1)	**1396**
It's A Man's Man's Man's World—James Brown And The Famous Flames (66)	2793
Bobby NEWSOME ▶ 8404 (1)	**52**
Standing In For Jody—Johnnie Taylor (72)	103
Ernest NEWSON ▶ 4331 (1)	**518**
I Love You—Volume's (62)	1037
John NEWTON ▶ 3565 (1)	**784**
Amazing Grace—Judy Collins (70)	*1569*
Juice NEWTON ▶ 6024 (1)	**215**
Sweet, Sweet Smile—Carpenters (78)	430
—Laura Lee Newton see: Laura LEE	
Slim NEWTON ▶ 9577 (1)	**21**
The Red Back Spider—Brownsville Station (72)	21
Wood NEWTON ▶ 6146 (1)	**200**
Bobbie Sue—Oak Ridge Boys (82)	1000
—Prime Minister Pete Nice see: Pete NASH	
—Stephen Nice see: Steve HARLEY	
Al NICHOL ▶ 3662 (5)	**745**
Elenore—Turtles (68)	2721
Sound Asleep—Turtles (68)	382
You Don't Have To Walk In The Rain—Turtles (69)	301
Love In The City—Turtles (69)	183
Grim Reaper Of Love—Turtles (66)	55
Steve NICHOL ▶ 7465 (1)	**94**
Hangin' On A String (Contemplating)—Loose Ends (85)	282
William Morris NICHOLLS ▶ 3477 (1)	**826**
Without Your Love—Roger Daltrey (80)	826
Billy NICHOLS ▶ 1188 (4)	**3739**
Do It ('til You're Satisfied)—B.T. Express (74)	3148
Ask Me What You Want—Millie Jackson (72)	1028
Can't Stop Groovin' Now, Wanna Do It Some More—B.T. Express (76)	74
Shout It Out—B.T. Express (78)	8.2
Roger NICHOLS ▶ 477 (13)	**8734**
We've Only Just Begun—Carpenters (70)	7395
Rainy Days And Mondays—Carpenters (71)	5070
Times Of Your Life—Paul Anka (75)	1582
I Won't Last A Day Without You—Carpenters (74)	*1455*
Out In The Country—Three Dog Night (70)	1391
Talk It Over In The Morning—Anne Murray (71)	172
So Many People—Chase (71)	118
I Won't Last A Day Without You—Maureen McGovern (73)	*68*
Let Me Be The One—Al Wilson (75)	65
I Won't Last A Day Without You—Al Wilson (75)	*65*

Someday Man—Monkees (69)	44
Traveling Boy—Garfunkel (74)	28
Only Me—First Edition (68)	15
Hugh NICHOLSON ▶ 9355 (1)	**25**
Capture Your Heart—Blue (77)	25
David NICHTERN ▶ 1502 (1)	**2877**
Midnight At The Oasis—Maria Muldaur (74)	2877
Kelly NICKELS [Henri Perret] ▶ 7212 (1)	**110**
The Ballad Of Jayne—L.A. Guns (90)	549
Stevie NICKS ▶ 196 (16)	**16028**
Dreams—Fleetwood Mac (77)	4725
Stand Back—Stevie Nicks (83)	2238
Leather And Lace—Stevie Nicks (with Don Henley) (81)	2103
Sara—Fleetwood Mac (79)	1897
Rhiannon (Will You Ever Win)—Fleetwood Mac (76)	1752
Gypsy—Fleetwood Mac (82)	1038
If Anyone Falls—Stevie Nicks (83)	979
Edge Of Seventeen (Just Like The White Winged Dove)—Stevie Nicks (82)	967
I Can't Wait—Stevie Nicks (86)	860
Rooms On Fire—Stevie Nicks (89)	817
Seven Wonders—Fleetwood Mac (87)	683
Nightbird—Stevie Nicks (83)	497
After The Glitter Fades—Stevie Nicks (82)	459
Has Anyone Ever Written Anything For You—Stevie Nicks (86)	135
Fireflies—Fleetwood Mac (81)	115
Sisters Of The Moon—Fleetwood Mac (80)	11
Ken NICOL ▶ 9983 (1)	**14**
I've Been Lovin' You—Easy Street (76)	57
—Jean Nicolas see: J. Nicolas FELGEN	
Joseph NICOLETTI ▶ 9437 (1)	**24**
Let's Put The Fun Back In Rock N Roll—Freddy Cannon & The Belmonts (81)	47
Roy NICOLSON ▶ 8533 (1)	**47**
I Eat Cannibals—Total Coelo (83)	141
Reed NIELSEN ▶ 6460 (1)	**166**
If You Should Sail—Nielsen/Pearson (80)	332
Rick NIELSEN ▶ 742 (11)	**5901**
I Want You To Want Me—Cheap Trick (79)	3027
Can't Stop Falling Into Love—Cheap Trick (90)	1076
Ghost Town—Cheap Trick (88)	641
Voices—Cheap Trick (79)	575
Dream Police—Cheap Trick (79)	501
Tonight It's You—Cheap Trick (85)	422
If You Want My Love—Cheap Trick (82)	336
Stop This Game—Cheap Trick (80)	334
Everything Works If You Let It—Cheap Trick (80)	311
Surrender—Cheap Trick (78)	128
She's Tight—Cheap Trick (82)	71
—Carl Niessen see: Charly NIESSEN	
Charly NIESSEN [Carl Niessen, Carl Niessen-Reisfeld] ▶ 3904 (5)	**662**
Angel Baby—Dean Martin (58)	513
Banjo Boy—Jan And Kjeld (60)	*358*
Banjo Boy—Dorothy Collins (60)	*92*
Banjo Boy—Art Mooney And His Orchestra (60)	*3.6*
Ask Me (Deine Erste Liebe)—Alice Babs (56)	*0.0*
Joe NIESSEN ▶ 6814 (2)	**135**
Baciare Baciare (Kissing Kissing)—Dorothy Collins (59)	*405*
Baciare Baciare (Kissing Kissing)—Ilse Werner (59)	*0.0*
—Fred Nightingale see: Tony HATCH	
—Ollie Nightingale see: Ollie HOSKINS	
—Joe Nigro see: Joe NEGRO	
—Laura Nigro see: Laura NYRO	
Harry NILSSON ▶ 292 (12)	**12220**
One—Three Dog Night (69)	5700
Coconut—Nilsson (72)	1661
Me And My Arrow—Nilsson (71)	1037
Spaceman—Nilsson (72)	749
Jump Into The Fire—Nilsson (72)	708
Daybreak—Nilsson (74)	539
I Guess The Lord Must Be In New York City—Nilsson (69)	447
Remember (Christmas)—Nilsson (72)	418
Without Her—Herb Alpert (69)	406
The Story Of Rock And Roll—Turtles (68)	403
Ten Little Indians—Yardbirds (67)	141
1941—Tom Northcott (68)	12

Walter NIMS ▶ 867 (1)	**5122**
Precious And Few—Climax (71)	5122
Luciano NINZATTI ▶ 11137 (1)	**3.1**
Can't Hold Back (Your Loving)—Kano (81)	12
—Nisa see: Nicola SALERNO	
Gloria NISSENSON ▶ 10833 (1)	**5.0**
One Life To Live—Wayne Massey (80)	10
Jack NITZSCHE ▶ 1391 (8)	**3192**
Up Where We Belong—Joe Cocker and Jennifer Warnes (82)	5012
Needles And Pins—Searchers (64)	*1639*
The Lonely Surfer—Jack Nitzsche (63)	487
Needles And Pins—Tom Petty and The Heartbreakers (86)	*317*
I Could Be So Good To You—Don And The Goodtimes (67)	218
Bongo Bongo Bongo—Preston Epps (60)	200
Needles And Pins—Jackie de Shannon (63)	*136*
Needles And Pins—Smokie (77)	*47*
Alan NIVEN ▶ 4789 (4)	**415**
The Angel Song—Great White (89)	604
Rock Me—Great White (87)	217
Call It Rock 'N Roll—Great White (91)	208
House Of Broken Love—Great White (90)	52
—Mary Catherine Nivert see: Taffy DANOFF	
—Taffy Nivert see: Taffy DANOFF	
Don NIX ▶ 5674 (2)	**256**
The Loser (With A Broken Heart)—Gary Lewis And The Playboys (67)	478
Olena—Don Nix (71)	18
Ed NIX ▶ 10672 (1)	**6.2**
Thank God And Greyhound—Roy Clark (70)	12
Kenton NIX ▶ 2979 (2)	**1086**
Heartbeat—Seduction (90)	*1030*
Heartbeat—Taana Gardner (81)	*55*
Larry NIX ▶ 9709 (1)	**19**
My Main Man—Staple Singers (74)	74
Robert NIX ▶ 1389 (14)	**3195**
So In To You—Atlanta Rhythm Section (77)	2327
Imaginary Lover—Atlanta Rhythm Section (78)	1818
Cherry Hill Park—Billy Joe Royal (69)	1529
I'm Not Gonna Let It Bother Me Tonight—Atlanta Rhythm Section (78)	932
Mighty Clouds Of Joy—B.J. Thomas (71)	675
Doraville—Atlanta Rhythm Section (74)	329
Neon Nites—Atlanta Rhythm Section (77)	181
Champagne Jam—Atlanta Rhythm Section (78)	171
Dog Days—Atlanta Rhythm Section (77)	109
Georgia Rhythm—Atlanta Rhythm Section (77)	94
Angel (What In The World's Come Over Us)—Atlanta Rhythm Section (75)	66
Jukin—Atlanta Rhythm Section (76)	56
Free Spirit—Atlanta Rhythm Section (76)	53
Deep In The Night—Candymen (68)	26
Sally NIX ▶ 11637 (1)	**0.9**
I Love You Yes I Do—Bull Moose Jackson (61)	1.8
Joe NIXON ▶ 11380 (1)	**2.0**
Right Or Left At Oak Street—Roy Clark (69)	4.0
Nick NIXON ▶ 5046 (1)	**354**
Teddy Bear Song—Barbara Fairchild (73)	708
Tom NIXON ▶ 8044 (1)	**64**
Do The Funky Penguin Part 1—Rufus Thomas (71)	256
Eddie NOACK ▶ 6587 (5)	**154**
These Hands—Len Dresslar (56)	*154*
These Hands—Tex Ritter (56)	*0.0*
These Hands—Jeffrey Clay (56)	*0.0*
These Hands—Johnny Oliver (56)	*0.0*
These Hands—Hank Snow The Singing Ranger And The Rainbow Ranch Boys (56)	*0.0*
Gip NOBLE ▶ 6372 (1)	**178**
Love T.K.O.—Teddy Pendergrass (80)	533
Harry NOBLE ▶ 1922 (1)	**2107**
Hold Me, Thrill Me, Kiss Me—Mel Carter (65)	2107
James NOBLE ▶ 10300 (1)	**10**
Blue Flame—Billy Vaughn And His Orchestra (62)	21
Johnny NOBLE ▶ 6496 (2)	**163**
My Tani—Brothers Four (60)	223
Hawaiian War Chant—Billy Vaughn And His Orchestra (59)	177

Keith NOBLE ► 3601 (1)	**772**
A Summer Song—Chad Stuart & Jeremy Clyde (64)	2316
Matt NOBLE ► 8861 (2)	**38**
When The Radio Is On—Paul Shaffer (89)	70
Theme From S-Express—S-Express (88)	14
Mike NOBLE ► 10135 (1)	**12**
Secrets—Mac Davis (81)	37
Ray NOBLE ► 3177 (4) HOF	**969**
The Very Thought Of You—Rick Nelson (64)	*738*
Love Is The Sweetest Thing—Saverio Saridis (62)	116
The Very Thought Of You—Little Willie John (61)	*65*
Cherokee—Larry Elgart And His Manhattan Swing Orchestra (82)	50
—William Myles Nobles see: Billy MYLES	
Leo NOCENTELLI ► 4209 (7)	**562**
Cissy Strut—Meters (69)	731
Sophisticated Cissy—Meters (69)	475
Chicken Strut—Meters (70)	361
Look-Ka Py Py—Meters (69)	346
Ease Back—Meters (69)	213
Hand Clapping Song—Meters (70)	94
Be My Lady—Meters (77)	36
Maria NOCERA ► 9570 (1)	**21**
Summertime, Summertime—Nocera (87)	42
Dale NOE ► 4424 (1)	**497**
Missing You—Ray Peterson (61)	994
Joseph NOEL ► 3460 (1)	**838**
Stop And Think It Over—Dale & Grace (64)	1676
Bob NOLAN ► 3060 (5)	**1030**
Tumbling Tumbleweeds—Billy Vaughn and His Orchestra (58)	*612*
Cool Water—Jack Scott (60)	*212*
Tumbling Tumbleweeds—Roger Williams (56)	*142*
Cool Water—Blue Belles (63)	*36*
Cool Water—Frankie Laine (55)	*27*
Bobby NOLAN ► 7373 (1)	**100**
The Crusher—Novas (65)	100
Kenny NOLAN ► 269 (16)	**12699**
My Eyes Adored You—Frankie Valli (74)	5362
Lady Marmalade—Labelle (75)	*5277*
I Like Dreamin'—Kenny Nolan (76)	3711
Get Dancin'—Disco Tex & The Sex-O-Lettes Featuring Sir Monti Rock III (74)	1522
Love's Grown Deep—Kenny Nolan (77)	893
A Penny For Your Thoughts—Tavares (82)	864
Us And Love (We Go Together)—Kenny Nolan (80)	275
Lonely Together—Barry Manilow (81)	273
Swing Your Daddy—Jim Gilstrap (75)	268
Hey There Little Firefly Part I—Firefly (75)	119
Dancin' Kid—Disco Tex & The Sex-O-Lettes Featuring Sir Monti Rock III (76)	109
Lady Marmalade—Ritchie Family (76)	*92*
Back To Dreamin' Again—Pat Shannon (70)	50
Hickory—Frankie Valli And The 4 Seasons (74)	12
My Eyes Get Blurry—Kenny Nolan (77)	3.0
So Good—Eleventh Hour (74)	3.0
Andrew NOLAND [Clarence Satchell] ► 1871 (16)	**2175**
Love Rollercoaster—Ohio Players (75)	5251
Fire—Ohio Players (74)	4114
Funky Worm—Ohio Players (73)	1438
Skin Tight—Ohio Players (74)	1151
Who'd She Coo?—Ohio Players (76)	885
Ecstasy—Ohio Players (73)	621
Sweet Sticky Thing—Ohio Players (75)	411
Fopp—Ohio Players (76)	398
I Want To Be Free—Ohio Players (75)	335
Jive Turkey (Part 1)—Ohio Players (74)	245
Pain (Part 1)—Ohio Players (71)	208
O-H-I-O—Ohio Players (77)	144
Feel The Beat (Everybody Disco)—Ohio Players (77)	42
Got Pleasure—Ohio Players (72)	14
Rattlesnake—Ohio Players (76)	12
Riding High—Faze-O (78)	4.8
Terry NOLAND [Terry Noland Church] ► 10442 (2)	**8.4**
Hypnotized—Drifters (57)	13
There Was A Fungus Among Us—Hugh Barrett and The Victors (61)	2.0
Kinder NOLEN ► 11394 (1)	**1.9**
Peep Peep Pop Pop—Dearly Beloveds (66)	5.7

Steve NOONAN ► 5965 (1)	**222**
Buy For Me The Rain—Nitty Gritty Dirt Band (67)	443
Peter NOONE ► 9955 (1)	**15**
God Knows—Debby Boone (78)	44
—Bob Norberg see: Bob NORMAN	
Carl-Henrik NORIN ► 7659 (1)	**82**
Zero-Zero—Lawrence Welk (62)	82
Bob NORMAN [Bob Norberg] ► 6622 (1)	**150**
The New Girl In School—Jan & Dean (64)	600
Chris NORMAN ► 8809 (1)	**39**
Run To Me—Savoy Brown (81)	78
Jimmy NORMAN ► 2378 (1)	**1544**
Time Is On My Side—Rolling Stones (64)	3088
Joe NORMAN ► 4978 (1)	**366**
Brenda—Cupids (63)	366
Monty NORMAN ► 5214 (3)	**324**
The James Bond Theme—Billy Strange (64)	*277*
The James Bond Theme—Meco (82)	*47*
Irma La Douce—Karen Chandler (60)	*4.6*
—Bessie Norris see: Betty WRIGHT	
Clyde NORRIS ► 6463 (1)	**166**
About This Thing Called Love—Fabian (60)	498
Joan NORRIS ► 3017 (1)	**1063**
Too Much—Elvis Presley (57)	4251
Alex NORTH [Isadore Soifer] ► 360 (17)	**10613**
Unchained Melody—Les Baxter His Chorus And Orchestra (55)	*8661*
Unchained Melody—Al Hibbler (55)	*4376*
Unchained Melody—Righteous Brothers (65)	*3432*
Unchained Melody—Roy Hamilton (55)	*2241*
Unchained Melody—Righteous Brothers (90)	*1154*
Unchained Melody (1990)—Righteous Brothers (90)	*502*
Unchained Melody—Vito & The Salutations (63)	*312*
Long Hot Summer—Jimmie Rodgers (58)	102
The Misfits—Don Costa And His Orchestra And Chorus (61)	86
Unchained Melody—Sweet Inspirations (68)	*70*
Unchained Melody—Blackwells (60)	*47*
Unchained Melody—June Valli (55)	*44*
I Belong To You—Ralph Flanagan and his Orchestra (55)	33
Antony And Cleopatra Theme—Ferrante & Teicher (63)	*29*
Unchained Melody (Live)—Heart (81)	*10*
Anthony And Cleopatra Theme—Alex North (63)	*5.9*
Unchained Melody—LeRoy Holmes & His Orchestra (55)	*0.0*
Christopher NORTH ► 10003 (1)	**14**
Nice, Nice, Very Nice—Ambrosia (75)	71
Geoffrey NORTH ► 9920 (1)	**15**
Uno—Tony Martin (54)	45
Johnny NORTHERN ► 7797 (2)	**75**
One Hurt Deserves Another—Raeletts (67)	223
To The Other Man—Luther Ingram (70)	1.7
Daniel NORTON [Sonny Norton] ► 7876 (3)	**71**
I Love You So—Chantels (58)	113
Gee—Pixies Three (64)	*90*
Gee—Jan & Dean (60)	*44*
George NORTON ► 5252 (3)	**318**
My Melancholy Baby—Tommy Edwards (59)	*830*
My Melancholy Baby—Marcels (62)	*123*
My Melancholy Baby—Willie Gibson & The Boys (55)	*0.0*
—Sonny Norton see: Daniel NORTON	
Bill NORVAS [Bill Roy Eustrom, Bill Eustrom, William H. Norvas, Roy Yustrom] ► 6457 (6)	**167**
Watermelon Song—"Tennessee" Ernie Ford (57)	80
I Pledge Allegiance To Your Heart—Ginny Gibson (57)	*28*
I Pledge Allegiance To Your Heart—Monique Cadou (57)	*28*
I Pledge Allegiance To Your Heart—Jaye P. Morgan (57)	*28*
Make Love To Me—Johnny Thunder & Ruby Winters (67)	*13*
Make Love To Me!—Jo Stafford (54)	*0.0*
Cynthia NORWOOD ► 11134 (1)	**3.1**
Down The Aisle—Ike Clanton (60)	6.1
Dennise NORWOOD ► 2401 (3)	**1523**
Garden Of Eden—Joe Valino (56)	*1523*
Garden Of Eden—Winifred Atwell (57)	*0.0*
Skinnie Minnie (Fish Tail)—Teresa Brewer (54)	0.0

Dorothy NORWOOD ► 7947 (1)	**68**
There's Got To Be Rain In Your Life (To Appreciate The Sunshine)—Dorothy Norwood (74)	68
Jack NORWORTH ► 5996 (2) HOF	**218**
Shine On Harvest Moon—Four Aces (55)	*424*
Shine On Harvest Moon—Googie René And His Band (58)	*13*
Nikolai NOSKOV ► 10363 (1)	**9.5**
Try To Find Me—Gorky Park (90)	28
Carmine NOTARO ► 9237 (1)	**28**
Sailing Ships—Mesa (77)	140
—C. Noteignis see: Charles SINGLETON	
Pat NOTO ► 5268 (3)	**315**
Sweet Kentucky Rose—Kitty Kallen (55)	*315*
Sweet Kentucky Rose—Red Foley (55)	*0.0*
Sweet Kentucky Rose—Jeffrey Clay (55)	*0.0*
Aldo NOVA [Aldo Caporuscio] ► 3654 (2)	**747**
Fantasy—Aldo Nova (82)	643
Foolin' Yourself—Aldo Nova (82)	104
Don NOVELLO [Father Guido Sarducci] ► 11495 (1)	**1.5**
A European (Speaks Up For The U. S.)—Guido Sarducci (74)	2.9
Chris NOVOSELIC ► 3803 (1)	**695**
Smells Like Teen Spirit—Nirvana (91)	2086
Rick NOWELS ► 1088 (6)	**4053**
Heaven Is A Place On Earth—Belinda Carlisle (87)	4006
Circle In The Sand—Belinda Carlisle (88)	1402
Leave A Light On—Belinda Carlisle (89)	1186
I Can't Wait—Stevie Nicks (86)	860
Rooms On Fire—Stevie Nicks (89)	817
Do You Feel Like I Feel—Belinda Carlisle (91)	124
—Rosetta Nubin see: Rosetta THARPE	
Paul NUCKLES ► 10387 (1)	**9.2**
The Scavenger—Dick Dale And The Del-Tones (63)	18
Ted NUGENT ► 1456 (11)	**2995**
High Enough—Damn Yankees (90)	3426
Journey To The Center Of The Mind—Amboy Dukes (68)	1261
Cat Scratch Fever—Ted Nugent (77)	807
Come Again—Damn Yankees (91)	327
Coming Of Age—Damn Yankees (90)	237
Yank Me, Crank Me—Ted Nugent (78)	154
Home Bound—Ted Nugent (78)	24
Dog Eat Dog—Ted Nugent (76)	22
Need You Bad—Ted Nugent (79)	14
Wango Tango—Ted Nugent (80)	12
You Talk Sunshine, I Breathe Fire—Amboy Dukes (68)	3.7
—A. Nugetre see: Ahmet ERTEGUN	
—Nuggy see: Ahmet ERTEGUN	
Cecil NULL ► 9825 (1)	**16**
I Forgot More Than You'll Ever Know—Sonny James (60)	16
Gary NUMAN [Gary Anthony James Webb] ► 1432 (2)	**3061**
Cars—Gary Numan (80)	3057
Are 'Friends' Electric?—Gary Numan & Tubeway Army (80)	4.3
Bobby NUNN ► 2176 (1)	**1786**
Rocket 2 U—Jets (88)	1786
Terri NUNN ► 8290 (1)	**55**
Sex (I'm A...)—Berlin (83)	166
Trevor NUNN ► 5803 (2)	**240**
Memory—Barry Manilow (82)	*493*
Memory - The Theme From Andrew Lloyd Webber's Musical ''Cats''—Barbra Streisand (82)	*228*
Stu NUNNERY ► 7033 (2)	**120**
Sally From Syracuse—Stu Nunnery (73)	86
Madelaine—Stu Nunnery (74)	34
—Michael Nuttall see: Mike FLOREALE	
Carl NUTTER ► 7249 (1)	**108**
Solitaire—Embers (61)	323
—Anita Leonard Nye see: Anita LEONARD	
Laura NYRO [Laura Nigro] ► 91 (13) HOF	**26210**
Wedding Bell Blues—5th Dimension (69)	*7706*
And When I Die—Blood, Sweat & Tears (69)	5381
Stoned Soul Picnic—5th Dimension (68)	4130
Eli's Coming—Three Dog Night (69)	2845
Stoney End—Barbra Streisand (70)	2206
Sweet Blindness—5th Dimension (68)	1393

Laura NYRO [Laura Nigro] ▶ 91 (13) HOF *Continued*	**26210**
Blowing Away—5th Dimension (70)	1089
Save The Country—5th Dimension (70)	*788*
Time And Love—Barbra Streisand (71)	356
Save The Country—Thelma Houston (70)	*131*
Flim Flam Man—Barbra Streisand (71)	104
Lu—Peggy Lipton (69)	76
Wedding Bell Blues—Laura Nyro (66)	*5.1*
James NYX ▶ 3412 (2)	**858**
Inner City Blues (Make Me Wanna Holler)— Marvin Gaye (71)	1676
We Can Make It Baby—Originals (70)	40

O

Philip OAKEY ▶ 1239 (5)	**3621**
Don't You Want Me—Human League (82)	7286
(Keep Feeling) Fascination—Human League (83)	1946
Mirror Man—Human League (83)	491
The Lebanon—Human League (84)	82
Love Action (I Believe In Love)—Human League (82)	29
Ben OAKLAND ▶ 8310 (1)	**55**
I'll Take Romance—Eydie Gorme (57)	109
John OATES ▶ 245 (19) HOF	**14026**
Maneater—Daryl Hall & John Oates (82)	7727
I Can't Go For That (No Can Do)— Daryl Hall & John Oates (81)	7283
Out Of Touch—Daryl Hall & John Oates (84)	4068
Sara Smile—Daryl Hall & John Oates (76)	3191
She's Gone—Daryl Hall & John Oates (76)	*2526*
You Make My Dreams—Daryl Hall & John Oates (81)	2226
Electric Blue—Icehouse (88)	1520
Adult Education—Daryl Hall & John Oates (84)	1464
Back Together Again—Daryl Hall & John Oates (77)	568
Do What You Want, Be What You Are— Daryl Hall & John Oates (76)	504
How Does It Feel To Be Back— Daryl Hall & John Oates (80)	461
Possession Obsession—Daryl Hall & John Oates (85)	431
Missed Opportunity—Daryl Hall & John Oates (88)	421
I Don't Wanna Lose You—Daryl Hall & John Oates (78)	356
Downtown Life—Daryl Hall & John Oates (88)	326
She's Gone—Daryl Hall & John Oates (74)	*306*
She's Gone—Tavares (74)	*299*
Good Night & Good Morning—Jim Capaldi (76)	*22*
Goodnight And Goodmorning—Cecilio & Kapono (76)	*4.8*
—Enya Patricia O'Brennan see: ENYA	
—Dionysius P. A. O'Brien see: Tom SPRINGFIELD	
Gerald O'BRIEN ▶ 7207 (1)	**110**
Don't Hold Back Your Love—Daryl Hall & John Oates (90)	330
Mary O'BRIEN ▶ 7761 (1)	**76**
Castles In The Sand—Little Stevie Wonder (64)	304
Timothy O'BRIEN ▶ 8320 (1)	**54**
Sally Had A Party—Flavor (68)	109
Jeannette OBSTOJ ▶ 6754 (2)	**140**
Secret Separation—Fixx (86)	629
Break Every Rule—Tina Turner (87)	70
Nan O'BYRNE ▶ 6058 (2)	**211**
I Need You—Pointer Sisters (83)	372
You Might Need Somebody—Turley Richards (80)	173
Ric OCASEK [Richard T. Otcasek] ▶ 150 (22)	**19289**
Shake It Up—Cars (81)	3778
Drive—Cars (84)	3300
You Might Think—Cars (84)	1739
Tonight She Comes—Cars (85)	1551
Let's Go—Cars (79)	1262
Magic—Cars (84)	1164
Emotion In Motion—Ric Ocasek (86)	855
Hello Again—Cars (84)	841
You Are The Girl—Cars (87)	793
Just What I Needed—Cars (78)	702
My Best Friend's Girl—Cars (78)	530
Why Can't I Have You—Cars (85)	496
I'm Not The One—Cars (86)	460
Touch And Go—Cars (80)	411
It's All I Can Do—Cars (79)	297
Since You're Gone—Cars (82)	256
Something To Grab For—Ric Ocasek (83)	242
Good Times Roll—Cars (79)	229

Slip Away—Ian Lloyd (79)	166
True To You—Ric Ocasek (86)	127
Coming Up You—Cars (88)	55
Strap Me In—Cars (87)	33
Billy OCEAN [Leslie Charles] ▶ 376 (13)	**10387**
Caribbean Queen (No More Love On The Run)— Billy Ocean (84)	4341
There'll Be Sad Songs (To Make You Cry)— Billy Ocean (86)	4280
Get Outta My Dreams, Get Into My Car— Billy Ocean (88)	4022
When The Going Gets Tough, The Tough Get Going— Billy Ocean (85)	3161
Loverboy—Billy Ocean (84)	2995
Suddenly—Billy Ocean (85)	2464
Love Zone—Billy Ocean (86)	1312
Love Is Forever—Billy Ocean (86)	997
The Colour Of Love—Billy Ocean (88)	815
Love Really Hurts Without You—Billy Ocean (76)	709
Mystery Lady—Billy Ocean (85)	617
Licence To Chill—Billy Ocean (89)	405
Night (Feel Like Getting Down)—Billy Ocean (81)	43
Phil OCHS ▶ 3888 (2)	**667**
There But For Fortune—Joan Baez (65)	500
Changes—Crispian St. Peters (66)	167
Desmond O'CONNOR ▶ 9858 (1)	**16**
How Lucky You Are—Joni James (56)	32
Gary O'CONNOR ▶ 4025 (1)	**621**
Back Where You Belong—38 Special (84)	621
Greg O'CONNOR ▶ 10984 (1)	**4.0**
Talk About It—Boom Crash Opera (91)	20
Robert O'CONNOR ▶ 6611 (1)	**151**
Move In A Little Closer, Baby—Mama Cass (69)	302
Sinead O'CONNOR ▶ 6225 (1)	**192**
The Emperor's New Clothes— Sinead O'Connor (90)	192
Randy ODA ▶ 4313 (1)	**525**
Think I'm In Love—Eddie Money (82)	1049
Alan O'DAY ▶ 244 (11)	**14111**
Undercover Angel—Alan O'Day (77)	6623
Angie Baby—Helen Reddy (74)	4137
Rock And Roll Heaven—Righteous Brothers (74)	3330
Train Of Thought—Cher (74)	751
The Drum—Bobby Sherman (71)	748
Are You Old Enough—Mark Lindsay (71)	65
Easy Evil—Travis Wammack (75)	*57*
Flashback—5th Dimension (73)	*55*
Started Out Dancing, Ended Up Making Love— Alan O'Day (77)	31
Easy Evil—John Kay (73)	*7.3*
Flashback—Paul Anka (73)	*0.3*
Bill ODDIE ▶ 10067 (1)	**13**
The Funky Gibbon—Goodies (75)	40
Brooks O'DELL [Brooks O'Dell Johnson] ▶ 8439 (1)	**50**
(1-2-3-4-5-6-7) Count The Days— Inez & Charlie Foxx (67)	151
Kenny O'DELL [Kenny Gist Jr.] ▶ 1035 (10)	**4254**
Behind Closed Doors—Charlie Rich (73)	1454
Next Plane To London—Rose Garden (67)	1270
Beautiful People—Bobby Vee And The Strangers (67)	*603*
Beautiful People—Kenny O'Dell (67)	*513*
Lizzie And The Rainman—Tanya Tucker (75)	452
Thanks For The Smiles—Charlie Ross (75)	142
Springfield Plane—Kenny O'Dell (68)	29
If It's Alright With You—Rose Colored Glass (71)	*22*
If It's All Right With You—Dottie West (73)	*16*
If My World Falls Through—Rose Garden (68)	13
James B. ODEN ▶ 7631 (3)	**84**
Goin' Down Slow—Bobby Blue Bland (74)	82
Night Time Is The Right Time—Rufus & Carla (64)	*3.3*
Night Time Is The Right Time—Ray Charles (59)	*2.4*
John O'DEN [Mikaljon] ▶ 4580 (1)	**462**
I Love The Way You Love—Marv Johnson (60)	1848
Jim ODOM ▶ 9860 (1)	**16**
Carrie's Gone—Le Roux (83)	48
Roger O'DONNELL ▶ 4492 (4)	**479**
Love Song—Cure (89)	2408
Fascination Street—Cure (89)	194
Lullaby—Cure (89)	170
Pictures Of You—Cure (90)	105

George O'DOWD [Boy George] ▶ 783 (10)	**5663**
Karma Chameleon—Culture Club (83)	5903
Do You Really Want To Hurt Me— Culture Club (82)	5783
Time (Clock Of The Heart)—Culture Club (83)	4056
Miss Me Blind—Culture Club (84)	2167
I'll Tumble 4 Ya—Culture Club (83)	1624
Church Of The Poison Mind— Culture Club (83)	1501
Move Away—Culture Club (86)	1007
It's A Miracle—Culture Club (84)	965
The War Song—Culture Club (84)	766
Mistake No. 3—Culture Club (84)	455
—Bonnie Lynn O'Farrell see: Bonnie BRAMLETT	
Charles Raymond OFFENBERG [Ray (2) Charles] ▶ 10237 (1)	**11**
Move Me, O Wondrous Music— Ray Charles Singers (70)	22
—Shirley Marie O'Garra see: Shirley ELLIS	
Ina Duley OGDON ▶ 8720 (1)	**41**
Brighten The Corner Where You Are— Browns Featuring Jim Edward Brown (60)	82
Klaus OGERMAN ▶ 4704 (2)	**435**
Your Other Love—Connie Francis (63)	744
Just Yesterday—Jack Jones (65)	126
Michael O'HARA ▶ 5326 (1)	**304**
Just Because—Anita Baker (89)	913
Patrick O'HEARN ▶ 9565 (1)	**21**
Give—Missing Persons (84)	85
—Ersel O'Hickey see: Ersel HICKEY	
John O'KANE ▶ 8403 (1)	**52**
Guaranteed For Life—Millions Like Us (87)	103
Danny O'KEEFE ▶ 2302 (1)	**1633**
Good Time Charlie's Got The Blues— Danny O'Keefe (72)	1633
John O'KEEFE ▶ 10294 (1)	**10**
Real Wild Child—Ivan (58)	31
Milton OKUN ▶ 6150 (3)	**200**
Tell It On The Mountain—Peter, Paul & Mary (64)	526
Stewball—Peter, Paul & Mary (63)	466
Big Boat—Peter, Paul & Mary (62)	6.2
Pamela Phillips OLAND ▶ 10450 (1)	**8.3**
If Ever A Love There Was—Four Tops (88)	17
Michael OLATUNJI ▶ 4908 (1)	**385**
Jingo—Santana (69)	385
—Ade Olayinka see: Melvin ANDERSON	
Chauncey OLCOTT ▶ 10875 (1) HOF	**4.7**
When Irish Eyes Are Smiling— Bruce Hayes with Mary Mayo (60)	14
Mike OLDFIELD ▶ 1669 (4)	**2520**
Tubular Bells—Mike Oldfield (74)	*2047*
Family Man—Daryl Hall & John Oates (83)	1641
19—Paul Hardcastle (85)	792
Tubular Bells—Champs' Boys Orchestra (76)	*1.4*
Andrew Loog OLDHAM ▶ 2819 (2)	**1172**
As Tears Go By—Rolling Stones (65)	*2591*
As Tears Go By—Marianne Faithfull (64)	*926*
Spooner OLDHAM [Dewey Lindon Oldham Jr.] ▶ 617 (13)	**7034**
Cry Like A Baby—Box Tops (68)	*6020*
I'm Your Puppet—James & Bobby Purify (66)	2932
It Tears Me Up—Percy Sledge (66)	1461
Sweet Inspiration—Sweet Inspirations (68)	*1368*
I Met Her In Church—Box Tops (68)	462
Wish You Didn't Have To Go— James & Bobby Purify (67)	428
Out Of Left Field—Percy Sledge (67)	342
Sweet Inspiration—Barbra Streisand (72)	*280*
Take Me (Just As I Am)—Solomon Burke (67)	265
Cry Like A Baby—Kim Carnes (80)	*249*
Are You Never Coming Home—Sandy Posey (67)	214
Up Tight, Good Man—Laura Lee (67)	36
Toys Are Made For Children—Uniques (69)	22
Fred OLDÖRP [Eric Duhn] ▶ 9905 (1)	**15**
Schweizer Kanton Polka— Will Glahe And His Orchestra (57)	30
Kim O'LEARY ▶ 7750 (2)	**76**
Weatherman Says—Jack Wagner (87)	*120*
Weatherman—Nick Jameson (86)	*33*

Lotar OLIAS ▶ 3168 (12)	**973**
Blue Mirage (Don't Go)— Guy Lombardo And His Royal Canadians (55)	*376*
You You You—Mel Carter (66)	355
Blue Mirage (Don't Go)— Les Baxter & His Orchestra (55)	*239*
Tango Of The Drums— Les Baxter His Chorus And Orchestra (56)	198
Blue Mirage (Don't Go)— Ralph Marterie And His Orchestra (55)	*137*
Such A Day—Rita Raines (56)	*133*
Such A Day—Vera Lynn (56)	*55*
The Tipsy Piano—Helmut Zacharias (59)	1.2
Blue Mirage—Frank Chacksfield & His Orchestra (55)	*0.0*
Your Heart - My Heart (Sehnsucht)— Frankie Laine (54)	0.0
Blue Mirage (Don't Go)— Percy Faith & His Orchestra (55)	*0.0*
Blue Mirage—Monty Kelly & His Orchestra with Dr. Samuel Hoffman (55)	*0.0*
Chico De OLIVEIRA [Olivier René Marie Lamotte d'Incamps] ▶ 5563 (1)	**271**
Lambada—Kaoma (90)	271
—Oliver see: Bill SWOFFORD	
Billy OLIVER ▶ 11723 (1)	**0.4**
Panic—Otis Williams And His Charms (61)	0.9
David OLIVER ▶ 10929 (1)	**4.3**
Ms.—David Oliver (78)	8.6
Jimmy OLIVER ▶ 2884 (5)	**1132**
Ta Ta—Clyde McPhatter (60)	1080
Itchy Twitchy Feeling—Bobby Hendricks (58)	*507*
I Never Knew—Clyde McPhatter (61)	120
Psycho—Bobby Hendricks (60)	49
Itchy Twitchy Feeling—Swallows (58)	*0.5*
Marion OLIVER ▶ 5571 (1)	**270**
You're Looking Good—Dee Clark (60)	540
Sean OLIVER ▶ 2025 (1)	**1996**
Wishing Well—Terence Trent D'Arby (88)	3992
Sy OLIVER ▶ 5130 (5)	**336**
Opus One—Mills Brothers (55)	*317*
Yes Indeed—Pete Fountain (62)	*125*
Opus #1—Larry Elgart And His Manhattan Swing Orchestra (82)	*50*
Opus One—Modernaires (57)	*1.9*
Yes Indeed—Modernaires (57)	*1.9*
Nino OLIVIERO ▶ 2325 (7)	**1589**
More—Kai Winding & Orchestra (63)	*2503*
More—Vic Dana (63)	*633*
All—James Darren (67)	507
More Theme From Mondo Cane—Martin Denny (63)	*0.0*
More (Theme From "Mondo Cane")— Della Reese (63)	*0.0*
More (From The Film "Mondo Cane")— Danny Williams (63)	*0.0*
More (Theme From The Film "Mondo Cane")— Steve Lawrence (63)	*0.0*
Marco OLIVO ▶ 8970 (1)	**35**
One Way Love—TKA (86)	70
Abe OLMAN ▶ 9779 (3)	**17**
Oh Johnny—Janie Grant (62)	*15*
Oh Johnny Oh—Kathy Linden (58)	*9.4*
Oh Johnny!—Sparkley Betty Barkley (58)	*9.4*
William OLOFSON ▶ 5547 (2)	**272**
Tucumcari—Jimmie Rodgers (59)	467
Jenny Lou—Sonny James (60)	78
Paul O'LONE ▶ 7478 (1)	**93**
Wizard Of Love—Ly-Dells (61)	279
Ed O'LOUGHLIN ▶ 10143 (1)	**12**
A Hurricane Is Coming Tonite—Carol Douglas (75)	24
Keith OLSEN ▶ 6211 (2)	**193**
Never Give Up—Sammy Hagar (83)	250
Has Anyone Ever Written Anything For You— Stevie Nicks (86)	135
—Michael Olsen see: Lee Eugene MICHAELS	
Arlyn Eric OLSON ▶ 11659 (1)	**0.8**
All I Wanna Do—Doucette (78)	2.3
Estella OLSON ▶ 8117 (1)	**61**
Think Of Me— Buck Owens And The Buckaroos (66)	122
Mark OLSON ▶ 11688 (1)	**0.7**
We're Gonna Have A Good Time—Rare Earth (73)	4.3
Mats OLSSON ▶ 11044 (1)	**3.6**
Lapland—Baltimore And Ohio Marching Band (67)	7.2
—Samuel Henry Olusegun Adeola see: SEAL	
Michael OMARTIAN ▶ 1021 (16)	**4331**
She Works Hard For The Money—Donna Summer (83)	4225
That's What Love Is For—Amy Grant (91)	2600
Get Used To It—Roger Voudouris (79)	971
I Think It's Love—Jermaine Jackson (86)	892
Unconditional Love—Donna Summer (83)	302
Hollywood—Boz Scaggs (78)	186
Tell Me I'm Not Dreaming—Robert Palmer (89)	150
(Closest Thing To) Perfect—Jermaine Jackson (85)	139
Boogie Down—Al Jarreau (83)	94
Charm The Snake—Christopher Cross (85)	92
Do You Remember Me?—Jermaine Jackson (86)	81
Supernatural Love—Donna Summer (84)	76
Love Has A Mind Of Its Own—Donna Summer (84)	71
Fool For Your Love—Jimmy Hall (82)	56
I Wouldn't Treat A Dog (The Way You Treated Me)— Bobby Bland (74)	39
Part Time Love—Kerry Chater (77)	22
Stormie OMARTIAN ▶ 10246 (1)	**11**
Part Time Love—Kerry Chater (77)	22
Alexander O'NEAL ▶ 8111 (1)	**61**
Criticize—Alexander O'Neal (87)	122
Brian O'NEAL ▶ 9070 (1)	**32**
Cleanin' Up The Town—Bus Boys (84)	64
Kevin O'NEAL ▶ 9071 (1)	**32**
Cleanin' Up The Town—Bus Boys (84)	64
Bobby O'NEIL ▶ 10834 (1)	**5.0**
Don't Spread It Around—Barbara Lynn (64)	10
Leo O'NEIL ▶ 10835 (1)	**5.0**
Don't Spread It Around—Barbara Lynn (64)	10
James O'NEILL ▶ 9766 (1)	**17**
Painted Moon—Silencers (87)	34
Yoko ONO ▶ 4713 (5)	**433**
Walking On Thin Ice—Yoko Ono (81)	267
Happy Xmas (War Is Over)—John & Yoko & Plastic Ono Band with Harlem Community Choir (71)	177
Woman Is The Nigger Of The World— John Lennon/Plastic Ono Band With Elephant's Memory And The Invisible Strings (72)	86
Give Peace A Chance—Peace Choir (91)	*49*
Mrs. Lennon—Yoko Ono (71)	22
Henry ONORATI ▶ 3776 (10)	**703**
The Little Drummer Boy— Harry Simeone Chorale (58)	*770*
The Little Drummer Boy—Harry Simeone Chorale (59)	*542*
The Little Drummer Boy—Harry Simeone Chorale (62)	*347*
The Little Drummer Boy—Harry Simeone Chorale (60)	*220*
The Little Drummer Boy—Harry Simeone Chorale (61)	*133*
The Little Drummer Boy—Johnny Cash (59)	*69*
Little Drummer Boy—Lou Rawls (67)	*14*
The Little Drummer Boy—Moonlion (75)	*7.4*
The Little Drummer Boy—Jack Halloran Singers (62)	*2.2*
The Little Drummer Boy— Harry Simeone Chorale (63)	*2.2*
—Dennis Thomas Oosthuis see: Dennis EAST	
David OPPENHEIM ▶ 7587 (2)	**87**
Hold Me—Baskerville Hounds (69)	*154*
Hold Me—P.J. Proby (64)	*108*
Allen ORANGE ▶ 8925 (2)	**36**
It's Hard To Get Along—Joe Simon (69)	35
Strain On My Heart—Roscoe Shelton (65)	18
Richard ORANGE ▶ 6149 (1)	**200**
Hole In My Heart (All The Way To China)— Cyndi Lauper (88)	200
Walter ORANGE ▶ 2191 (6)	**1758**
Nightshift—Commodores (85)	2649
Brick House—Commodores (77)	1962
Slippery When Wet—Commodores (75)	793
Too Hot Ta Trot—Commodores (77)	499
Painted Picture—Commodores (82)	113
I Feel Sanctified—Commodores (74)	83
Roy ORBISON ▶ 76 (40) HOF	**29154**
Oh, Pretty Woman— Roy Orbison And The Candy Men (64)	*8819*
Crying—Roy Orbison (61)	*6223*
Running Scared—Roy Orbison (61)	*6095*
Only The Lonely (Know How I Feel)—Roy Orbison (60)	*5979*
Blue Bayou—Linda Ronstadt (77)	*4470*
In Dreams—Roy Orbison (63)	2497
Crying—Don McLean (81)	*2185*
It's Over—Roy Orbison (64)	2050
Blue Angel—Roy Orbison (60)	1636
(Oh) Pretty Woman—Van Halen (82)	*1208*
Blue Bayou—Roy Orbison (63)	*1151*
You Got It—Roy Orbison (89)	1104
Ride Away—Roy Orbison (65)	995
The Crowd—Roy Orbison (62)	908
Goodnight—Roy Orbison (65)	873
Falling—Roy Orbison (63)	835
Workin' For The Man—Roy Orbison (62)	803
Leah—Roy Orbison (62)	713
Breakin' Up Is Breakin' My Heart—Roy Orbison (66)	686
Crying—Jay & The Americans (66)	*569*
Twinkle Toes—Roy Orbison (66)	450
Handle With Care—Traveling Wilburys (88)	448
Crawling Back—Roy Orbison (65)	429
See Ruby Fall—Johnny Cash (69)	412
I'm Hurtin'—Roy Orbison (60)	410
(Say) You're My Girl—Roy Orbison (65)	335
Claudette—Everly Brothers (58)	287
Memories Of Maria—Music Of Jerry Byrd (62)	244
Communication Breakdown—Roy Orbison (66)	230
That Lovin' You Feelin' Again— Roy Orbison & Emmylou Harris (80)	173
Running Scared—Fools (81)	*170*
End Of The Line—Traveling Wilburys (89)	166
Up Town—Roy Orbison (59)	161
Baby's Gone—Gene Thomas (63)	89
Laugh—Velvets (61)	55
Only the Lonely— Sonny James (The Southern Gentleman) (69)	*23*
So Long I'm Gone—Warren Smith (57)	12
Actress—Roy Orbison (62)	9.5
Walk On—Roy Orbison (68)	7.9
Lana—Gene McCannon (63)	0.5
ORFEH ▶ 7297 (1)	**104**
Everyotherday—Or-N-More (91)	209
Don ORIOLO ▶ 10078 (1)	**13**
S.T.O.P. (Stop)—Lorelei (72)	26
—Johnny Orlando see: Hugo PERETTI	
Tony ORLANDO [Michael Anthony Orlando Cassavitis] ▶ 10244 (1)	**11**
Soul Struttin'—Jamie Lyons (67)	22
—Anne Orlowski see: Gene PITNEY	
Cyril ORNADEL ▶ 2263 (3)	**1679**
Portrait Of My Love—Steve Lawrence (61)	*2254*
Portrait Of My Love—Tokens (67)	*626*
If I Ruled The World—Tony Bennett (65)	478
René ORNELAS ▶ 3525 (2)	**800**
Lo Mucho Que Te Quiero (The More I Love You)— René & René (68)	1458
Angelito—René & René (64)	628
Benjamin ORR [Benjamin Orzechowski] ▶ 4600 (1)	**454**
Stay The Night—Benjamin Orr (86)	908
—Sheena Shirley Orr see: Sheena EASTON	
Robert Ellis ORRALL ▶ 4715 (1)	**433**
I Couldn't Say No— Robert Ellis Orrall With Carlene Carter (83)	433
Victor ORSBORN ▶ 4606 (1)	**452**
Dance (Disco Heat)—Sylvester (78)	904
—Ann Orson see: Elton JOHN	
Julian ORSON ▶ 5023 (1)	**358**
Guantanamera—Sandpipers (66)	2149
Carlos ORTEGA ▶ 6166 (1)	**198**
Louie, Louie—Sandpipers (66)	*595*
Luis ORTIZ ▶ 9447 (1)	**23**
Latin Active—A Lighter Shade Of Brown (91)	164
Riz ORTOLANI ▶ 2374 (8)	**1552**
More—Kai Winding & Orchestra (63)	*2503*
More—Vic Dana (63)	*633*
Forget Domani—Connie Francis (65)	*140*
Forget Domani—Frank Sinatra (65)	*126*
More Theme From Mondo Cane—Martin Denny (63)	*0.0*
More (Theme From "Mondo Cane")—Della Reese (63)	*0.0*
More (From The Film "Mondo Cane")— Danny Williams (63)	*0.0*
More (Theme From The Film "Mondo Cane")— Steve Lawrence (63)	*0.0*

Edward ORY ▶ 3279 (5)	**914**
Muskrat Ramble—McGuire Sisters (54)	*1322*
Muskrat Ramble—Freddy Cannon (61)	*259*
Muskrat Ramble—Matys Brothers (54)	*246*
Muskrat Ramble—Rusty Draper (54)	*0.0*
Muskrat Ramble— Louis Armstrong & His All-Stars (54)	*0.0*
Roland ORZABAL [Roland Jaime Orzabal de la Quintana] ▶ 557 (8)	**7738**
Everybody Wants To Rule The World— Tears For Fears (85)	4971
Shout—Tears For Fears (85)	4675
Sowing The Seeds Of Love—Tears For Fears (89)	2998
Head Over Heels—Tears For Fears (85)	2858
Mothers Talk—Tears For Fears (86)	541
Woman In Chains—Tears For Fears (89)	410
Change—Tears For Fears (83)	95
Advice For The Young At Heart—Tears For Fears (90)	80
—Benjamin Orzechowski see: Benjamin ORR	
Joe OSBORN ▶ 7121 (2)	**115**
Gypsy Woman—Rick Nelson (63)	123
Here Comes That Feelin'—Brenda Lee (62)	106
Robert Eugene OSBORN [Bob Osburn, Robert Eugene Osborne, Bobby Van Osbourne,] ▶ 9761 (1)	**17**
Going Back To Louisiana—Bruce Channel (64)	17
Anthony C. OSBORNE ▶ 7887 (1)	**71**
All I Need Is You—Blue Train (91)	284
Billy OSBORNE ▶ 4674 (2)	**441**
Shine On—L.T.D. (80)	538
Check It Out—Tavares (73)	524
Gary OSBORNE ▶ 1018 (10)	**4365**
Little Jeannie—Elton John (80)	4655
Blue Eyes—Elton John (82)	1448
Part-Time Love—Elton John (78)	822
Nobody Wins—Elton John (81)	575
Forever Autumn—Justin Hayward (78)	531
Chloe—Elton John (81)	446
Men Of Learning—Vigrass & Osborne (72)	249
I'm Dreaming—Jennifer Warnes (77)	220
On The Other Side—Seekers (67)	52
Curly—Jimmy Clanton (69)	4.9
Jeffrey OSBORNE ▶ 2650 (9)	**1294**
On The Wings Of Love—Jeffrey Osborne (82)	873
Don't You Get So Mad—Jeffrey Osborne (83)	600
Shine On—L.T.D. (80)	538
Holding On (When Love Is Gone)—L.T.D. (78)	431
I Really Don't Need No Light—Jeffrey Osborne (82)	334
She's On The Left—Jeffrey Osborne (88)	284
Where Did We Go Wrong—L.T.D. (80)	37
Stranger—L.T.D. (79)	6.1
We Both Deserve Each Other's Love—L.T.D. (78)	5.7
Michael OSBORNE ▶ 11320 (1)	**2.2**
I Think You'll Remember Tonight—Axe (83)	4.5
Nat OSBORNE ▶ 7124 (1)	**115**
You Wanted Someone To Play With (I Wanted Someone To Love)—Frankie Laine (67)	459
—Bobby Van Osbourne see: Robert Eugene OSBORN	
—John Michael Osbourne see: Ozzy OSBOURNE	
Ozzy OSBOURNE [John Michael Osbourne] ▶ 3404 (5)	**863**
Close My Eyes Forever—Lita Ford (89)	1377
Paranoid—Black Sabbath (70)	212
Iron Man—Black Sabbath (72)	211
Shot In The Dark—Ozzy Osbourne (86)	88
No More Tears—Ozzy Osbourne (91)	74
—Bob Osburn see: Robert Eugene OSBORN	
Charles OSGOOD [Charles Osgood Wood] ▶ 5864 (1)	**235**
Gallant Men—Senator Everett McKinley Dirksen (66)	471
—Brian O'Shea see: Brian KEITH	
Shad O'SHEA ▶ 9150 (1)	**30**
Colorado Call—Shad O'Shea & The 18 Wheelers (76)	30
Lee OSKAR [Lee Oskar Levitin] ▶ 1215 (22)	**3667**
Spill The Wine—Eric Burdon And War (70)	*5207*
The Cisco Kid—War (73)	4378
Why Can't We Be Friends?—War (75)	3006
Low Rider—War (75)	2369
Slippin' Into Darkness—War (71)	*2076*
The World Is A Ghetto—War (72)	1817
Gypsy Man—War (73)	1659
Summer—War (76)	1559
Me And Baby Brother—War (73)	1513
All Day Music—War (71)	704
Ballero—War (74)	472
They Can't Take Away Our Music— Eric Burdon And War Featuring Sharon Scott And The Beautiful New Born Children Of Southern California (70)	418
Spill The Wine—Isley Brothers (71)	*409*
Galaxy—War (77)	325
L.A. Sunshine—War (77)	291
Low Rider (On The Boulevard)—Latin Alliance (91)	121
BLT—Lee Oskar (76)	91
Lonely Feelin'—War (71)	74
You Got The Power—War (82)	35
Slipping Into Darkness—Ramsey Lewis (72)	*35*
Good, Good Feelin'—War (79)	12
Outlaw—War (82)	10
Alan OSMOND ▶ 1401 (6)	**3158**
Down By The Lazy River—Osmonds (72)	4017
Hold Her Tight—Osmonds (72)	1163
Crazy Horses—Osmonds (72)	882
Let Me In—Osmonds (73)	668
Goin' Home—Osmonds (73)	522
We Can Make It Together— Steve & Eydie Featuring The Osmonds (72)	215
Donny OSMOND ▶ 6044 (4)	**213**
Too Young—Jack Wagner (85)	340
Sure Lookin'—Donny Osmond (91)	259
Hold On—Donny Osmond (89)	96
Love Will Survive—Donny Osmond (91)	27
Merrill OSMOND ▶ 1402 (6)	**3158**
Down By The Lazy River—Osmonds (72)	4017
Hold Her Tight—Osmonds (72)	1163
Crazy Horses—Osmonds (72)	882
Let Me In—Osmonds (73)	668
Goin' Home—Osmonds (73)	522
We Can Make It Together— Steve & Eydie Featuring The Osmonds (72)	215
Wayne OSMOND ▶ 2857 (5)	**1150**
Hold Her Tight—Osmonds (72)	1163
Crazy Horses—Osmonds (72)	882
Let Me In—Osmonds (73)	668
Goin' Home—Osmonds (73)	522
We Can Make It Together— Steve & Eydie Featuring The Osmonds (72)	215
—Mike Ossman see: Stanley OSSMAN	
Stanley OSSMAN [Mike Ossman, Mikaljon] ▶ 4581 (1)	**462**
I Love The Way You Love—Marv Johnson (60)	1848
—James Newell Osterberg Jr. see: Iggy POP	
Clay OSTWALD ▶ 4149 (3)	**580**
Get On Your Feet—Gloria Estefan (89)	1093
Can't Forget You—Gloria Estefan (91)	423
Oye Mi Canto (Hear My Voice)—Gloria Estefan (90)	225
Gilbert O'SULLIVAN [Raymond Edward O'Sullivan] ▶ 146 (9)	**19552**
Alone Again (Naturally)—Gilbert O'Sullivan (72)	9416
Clair—Gilbert O'Sullivan (72)	4683
Get Down—Gilbert O'Sullivan (73)	2942
Out Of The Question—Gilbert O'Sullivan (73)	1000
Ooh Baby—Gilbert O'Sullivan (73)	797
Who Was It?—Hurricane Smith (73)	368
Happiness Is Me And You—Gilbert O'Sullivan (74)	334
Christmas Song—Gilbert O'Sullivan (75)	5.9
You Are You—Gilbert O'Sullivan (75)	5.4
Jacquie O'SULLIVAN ▶ 10262 (1)	**11**
Love, Truth And Honesty—Bananarama (88)	64
—Raymond O'Sullivan see: Gilbert O'SULLIVAN	
—Osunlade see: Christian WARREN	
John OSWALD [Jani Lane, John Kennedy Oswald] ▶ 2471 (8)	**1454**
Heaven—Warrant (89)	3557
I Saw Red—Warrant (90)	1193
Cherry Pie—Warrant (90)	992
Sometimes She Cries—Warrant (89)	824
Down Boys—Warrant (89)	567
Uncle Tom's Cabin—Warrant (91)	71
Blind Faith—Warrant (91)	40
Big Talk—Warrant (89)	23
—Richard T. Otcasek see: Ric OCASEK	
—Clive Otis see: Clyde OTIS	
Clyde OTIS [Clyde Lovern Otis, Clive Otis, Cliff Owens] ▶ 111 (66)	**22458**
The Boll Weevil Song—Brook Benton (61)	7091
It's Just A Matter Of Time—Brook Benton (59)	*5155*
Kiddio—Brook Benton (60)	3969
The Stroll—Diamonds (57)	*3877*
Baby (You've Got What It Takes)— Dinah Washington & Brook Benton (60)	3840
A Rockin' Good Way (To Mess Around And Fall In Love)—Dinah Washington & Brook Benton (60)	2398
Looking Back—Nat "King" Cole (58)	*2318*
Think Twice—Brook Benton (61)	2316
That's All There Is To That— Nat "King" Cole And The Four Knights (56)	1674
Thank You Pretty Baby—Brook Benton (59)	1669
Endlessly—Brook Benton (59)	*1535*
Ain't That Loving You Baby— Elvis Presley With The Jordanaires (64)	1406
Call Me—Johnny Mathis (58)	1333
Same One—Brook Benton (60)	1295
What's A Matter Baby (Is It Hurting You)— Timi Yuro (62)	*1256*
This Bitter Earth—Dinah Washington (60)	*983*
Pop That Thang—Isley Brothers (72)	972
Out Of Sight Out Of Mind—Five Keys (56)	*860*
For My Baby—Brook Benton (61)	549
Smooth Operator—Sarah Vaughan (59)	503
Ties That Bind—Brook Benton (60)	492
Out Of Sight, Out Of Mind— Little Anthony And The Imperials (69)	*410*
Too Late To Turn Back Now—Brook Benton (64)	393
Mother Nature, Father Time—Brook Benton (65)	375
I'm Too Far Gone (To Turn Around)— Bobby Bland (66)	362
No Other One—Eddie Fisher (56)	315
Wishing It Was You—Connie Francis (65)	313
Patsy—Jack Scott (60)	287
Take A Look—Aretha Franklin (67)	284
Anyway You Want Me (That's How I Will Be)— Elvis Presley (56)	275
The Wall—Patti Page (57)	*244*
So Close—Brook Benton (59)	192
This Time Of The Year—Brook Benton (59)	*185*
It's Just A House Without You—Brook Benton (61)	174
Next Stop Paradise—Teddy Randazzo (57)	163
Doncha' Think It's Time—Elvis Presley (58)	159
Early Every Morning (Early Every Evening Too)— Dinah Washington (61)	153
You're My Baby—Sarah Vaughan (60)	112
I Want You Forever—Brook Benton (59)	106
The Wall—Eileen Rodgers (57)	*77*
Looking Back—Joe Simon (68)	*62*
Out Of Sight - Out Of Mind— Sunny & The Sunliners (64)	*54*
Silent Lips—Georgia Gibbs (57)	53
Happy Years—Diamonds (58)	35
Hurtin' Inside—Brook Benton (59)	33
Mother's Love—Diamonds (59)	33
What's A Matter Baby—Ellen Foley (79)	*31*
Nothing In The World—Nat "King" Cole (58)	31
It's Just A Matter Of Time— Sonny James, The Southern Gentleman (70)	*31*
Nothing Goes Up (Without Coming Down)— Nat King Cole (63)	26
This Bitter Earth—Satisfactions (70)	*24*
This Time Of The Year—Brook Benton (60)	*22*
Endlessly—Mavis Staples (72)	*14*
Can't You Just See Me—Aretha Franklin (65)	14
I Ain't Giving Up Nothing—Ben Hewitt (59)	13
Looking Back—Dinah Washington (60)	*5.1*
Endlessly—Sonny James (70)	*5.1*
I Just Want To Love You—Clyde McPhatter (60)	5.0
She Really Loves You—Timi Yuro (61)	5.0
Come Back My Love—Jerry Butler (58)	4.3
There You Are—Johnny Mathis (61)	3.8
Only A Girl Like You—Brook Benton (66)	3.7
Separate Ways—Sarah Vaughan (59)	3.0
Out Of Sight, Out Of Mind—Essex (63)	*1.7*
The Stroll—Lancers (57)	*0.0*
The Wall—Brook Benton (57)	*0.0*

Johnny OTIS [Phyliss Otis, Ioannis Alexandres Veliotes] ▶ 509 (19) **8330**

Dance With Me Henry (Wallflower)—Georgia Gibbs (55) *5087*
Every Beat Of My Heart—Pips (61) *2145*
So Fine—Fiestas (59) *1748*
Willie And The Hand Jive—Johnny Otis Show (58) *1711*
Willie And The Hand Jive—Eric Clapton (74) *493*
Every Beat Of My Heart—Gladys Knight & The Pips (61) *266*
Willie And The Hand Jive—George Thorogood & The Destroyers (85) *152*
So Fine—Oak Ridge Boys (82) *57*
Willie Did The Cha Cha—Johnny Otis Show (58) 18
Mumblin' Mosie—Johnny Otis Show (60) 15
So Fine (Medley)—Johnny Rivers (73) *12*
Crazy Country Hop—Johnny Otis Show (58) 12
Hand Jive—Strangeloves (66) *3.3*
Dance With Me Georgie—Bobbettes (60) *2.5*
Every Beat Of My Heart—James Brown And The Famous Flames (63) *0.9*
The Wallflower—Three Rays (55) *0.0*
The Wallflower—Etta James & The Peaches (55) *0.0*
The Wallflower (Dance With Me Henry)—Lee Winters (55) *0.0*
The Italian Wallflower (I'll Dance With Her Henry)—Lou Monte (55) *0.0*

—Johnny Otis Jr. see: Shuggie OTIS

—Phyliss Otis see: Johnny OTIS

Shuggie OTIS [Johnny Otis Jr., Johnny Alexander Veliotes Jr.] ▶ 2066 (1) **1933**

Strawberry Letter 23—Brothers Johnson (77) 1933

Mark O'TOOLE ▶ 3986 (4) **630**

Relax—Frankie Goes To Hollywood (84) *658*
Relax (Mix)—Frankie Goes To Hollywood (85) *583*
Two Tribes—Frankie Goes To Hollywood (84) 469
Welcome To The Pleasuredome (Trevor Horn Remix)—Frankie Goes To Hollywood (85) 239

Horace OTT ▶ 3348 (8) **887**

I'm Comin' On Back To You—Jackie Wilson (61) 687
You're Good For Me—Solomon Burke (63) 383
Years From Now—Jackie Wilson (61) 299
Like The Big Guys Do—Rocky Fellers (63) 199
We're Doing Fine—Dee Dee Warwick (65) 91
Three Fools—Patti Page (62) 55
Crossfire Time—Dee Clark (63) 54
Don't Walk Away From Me—Dee Clark (61) 17

Ted OTTAVIANO ▶ 9143 (2) **30**

Alice Everyday—Book Of Love (91) 18
Pretty Boys And Pretty Girls—Book Of Love (88) 12

Hans OTTEN ▶ 8353 (3) **54**

You Can't Be True Dear—Mary Kaye Trio (59) *189*
You Can't Be True, Dear—Patti Page (65) *25*
You Can't Be True Dear—Steve Lawrence & Eydie Gorme (59) *0.0*

—Curtis Ousley see: King CURTIS

Danny OVERBEA ▶ 6476 (1) **165**

Forty Cups Of Coffee—Bill Haley And His Comets (57) 165

Buzz OVERMAN ▶ 10629 (1) **6.6**

Happy And Me—Don And The Goodtimes (67) 6.6

—Virginia Lucille Overstake see: Jenny Lou CARSON

Jan OVLAND ▶ 6662 (1) **146**

Downtown—One 2 Many (89) 438

Fuzzy OWEN ▶ 5707 (2) **252**

Dear John—Pat Boone (60) 389
Same Old Me—Guy Mitchell (60) 122

Randy OWEN ▶ 3247 (2) **929**

Feels So Right—Alabama (81) 883
Lady Down On Love—Alabama (83) 46

Sarah Jane OWEN ▶ 10581 (1) **7.1**

Sign Of The Times—Belle Stars (83) 49

A.L. "Doodle" OWENS ▶ 3965 (5) **636**

Johnny One Time—Brenda Lee (69) 736
Where Did They Go, Lord—Elvis Presley (71) 360
I Can't Believe That You've Stopped Loving Me—Charley Pride (70) 95
All I Have To Offer You (Is Me)—Charley Pride (69) 41
(I'm So) Afraid Of Losing You Again—Charley Pride (69) 40

Bonnie OWENS [Bonnie Maureen Campbell] ▶ 5702 (3) **253**

Today I Started Loving You Again—Bettye Swann (73) *354*
I Started Loving You Again—Al Martino (69) *151*
Today I Started Loving You Again—Bobby Bland (76) *1.3*

Buck OWENS ▶ 1054 (13) **4182**

Crying Time—Ray Charles With The Jack Halloran Singers And The Ray Charles Orchestra With The Raelettes (65) 2462
Together Again—Ray Charles (66) 799
I've Got A Tiger By The Tail—Buck Owens (65) 614
Foolin' Around—Kay Starr (61) *492*
Under Your Spell Again—Johnny Rivers (65) 434
Waitin' In Your Welfare Line—Buck Owens (66) 224
Before You Go—Buck Owens (65) 61
I Don't Care (Just As Long As You Love Me)—Buck Owens (64) 32
Sam's Place—Buck Owens And The Buckaroos (67) 10
Santa Looked A Lot Like Daddy—Buck Owens (65) 4.7
Big In Vegas—Buck Owens And The Buckaroos (69) 4.0
My Heart Skips A Beat—Buck Owens (64) 3.8
Foolin' Around—Buck Owens (61) *0.0*

—Cliff Owens see: Clyde OTIS

David OWENS ▶ 10295 (1) **10**

Real Wild Child—Ivan (58) 31

Kelly OWENS ▶ 2174 (6) **1789**

That's All There Is To That—Nat "King" Cole And The Four Knights (56) 1674
I Beg Of You—Elvis Presley (58) 1174
Little By Little—Nappy Brown (57) *502*
Little By Little—Micki Marlo (57) *228*
Little By Little—Crew-Cuts (57) *0.0*
Little By Little—Toni Arden (57) *0.0*

Melvin OWENS ▶ 8755 (1) **40**

Super Bowl Shuffle—Chicago Bears Shufflin' Crew (86) 161

Monte OWENS ▶ 7170 (2) **112**

Walking Along—Diamonds (58) *783*
Walking Along—Solitaires (58) *0.0*

Robert OWENS ▶ 11126 (1) **3.1**

Take It Off Him And Put It On Me—Clarence Carter (70) 15

Shirley OWENS [Shirley Reeves] ▶ 4164 (3) **577**

Tonight's The Night—Shirelles (60) *817*
I Met Him On A Sunday (Ronde-Ronde)—Shirelles (58) 537
Tonight's The Night—Chiffons (60) *68*

Tex OWENS ▶ 4215 (2) **560**

The Cattle Call—Eddy Arnold with Hugo Winterhalter's Orch. And Chorus (55) *558*
The Cattle Call—Dinah Shore (57) *2.7*

William OWSLEY ▶ 7690 (1) **80**

For You—Michael W. Smith (91) 241

—Barbara Lynn Ozen see: Barbara LYNN

P

Daniele PACE ▶ 4260 (4) **544**

A Man Without Love (Quando M'innamoro)—Engelbert Humperdinck (68) 1014
To The Door Of The Sun (Alle Porte Del Sole)—Al Martino (74) 825
Suddenly You Love Me—Tremeloes (68) 490
Nessuno Mi Puo' Giudcare—Gene Pitney (66) 13

Evan PACE ▶ 9238 (1) **28**

Sailing Ships—Mesa (77) 140

Louis PACE ▶ 6725 (1) **142**

Serious—Donna Allen (87) 852

Elis PACHECO ▶ 6519 (2) **161**

Love Desire—Sandee (91) 121
There's A Party Going On—Yvonne (90) 40

Johann PACHELBEL ▶ 8523 (2) **47**

Oh Lord, Why Lord—Los Pop Tops (68) 125
Theme From Ordinary People—Marvin Hamlisch (80) 5.6

Donna PACIFICI ▶ 5152 (1) **333**

For Tonight—Nancy Martinez (86) 667

David PACK ▶ 354 (10) **10752**

Biggest Part Of Me—Ambrosia (80) 4139
How Much I Feel—Ambrosia (78) 3587
All I Need—Jack Wagner (84) 3171
You're The Only Woman (You And I)—Ambrosia (80) *1145*
Holdin' On To Yesterday—Ambrosia (75) 973
You're The Only Woman—Brat Pack (90) *293*
Nice, Nice, Very Nice—Ambrosia (75) 71
How Can You Love Me—Ambrosia (82) 21
Can't Let A Woman—Ambrosia (76) 17
Prove Me Wrong—David Pack (86) 5.6

Vance PACKARD ▶ 11564 (1) **1.2**

Place In The Sun—Johnny Nash (60) 4.8

Larry PACKER ▶ 9027 (1) **33**

Good Old Rock 'N Roll—Cat Mother And The All Night News Boys (69) 164

Frank PADEN ▶ 5821 (2) **239**

I Do (Live Version)—J. Geils Band (82) *637*
I Do—Marvelows (65) *556*

Johnny PADEN ▶ 5822 (2) **239**

I Do (Live Version)—J. Geils Band (82) *637*
I Do—Marvelows (65) *556*

Noel PAGAN ▶ 4513 (2) **474**

Silent Morning—Noel (87) 446
Like A Child—Noel (88) 83

Ricardo PAGAN ▶ 4578 (1) **462**

Sincerely Yours—Sweet Sensation (89) 924

Billy PAGE ▶ 704 (6) **6194**

The "In" Crowd—Ramsey Lewis Trio (65) *4538*
The "In" Crowd—Dobie Gray (65) *1237*
Black Lassie (Featuring Johnny Stash)—Cheech & Chong (74) 262
See You At The "Go-Go"—Dobie Gray (65) 217
Sugar Lump—Leon Haywood (74) 117
Some Beautiful—Jack Wild (70) 18

Diane PAGE ▶ 4601 (1) **454**

Stay The Night—Benjamin Orr (86) 908

Gene PAGE ▶ 8006 (1) **66**

Black Lassie (Featuring Johnny Stash)—Cheech & Chong (74) 262

Ian PAGE ▶ 6989 (1) **124**

(If You Add) All The Love In The World—Mac Davis (75) 124

Jimmy PAGE ▶ 1110 (18) **3998**

Whole Lotta Love—Led Zeppelin (69) *4704*
Immigrant Song—Led Zeppelin (70) 1706
Black Dog—Led Zeppelin (71) *1455*
D'yer Mak'er—Led Zeppelin (73) 1260
Fool In The Rain—Led Zeppelin (79) 673
Happenings Ten Years Time Ago—Yardbirds (66) 652
Over The Hills And Far Away—Led Zeppelin (73) 487
Trampled Under Foot—Led Zeppelin (75) 436
Rock And Roll—Led Zeppelin (72) 411
Whole Lotta Love—C.C.S. (71) *247*
Whole Lotta Love—King Curtis & The Kingpins (71) *230*
Good Times Bad Times—Led Zeppelin (69) 160
Black Dog—Newcity Rockers (87) *89*
Puss N Boots—Kon Kan (89) 78
Satisfaction Guaranteed—Firm (85) 62
Livin' Lovin' Maid—Led Zeppelin (70) 58
Stairway To Heaven—Far Corporation (86) 38
Whole Lotta Love—Wonder Band (79) *8.7*

—June Page see: Rickie PAGE

Martin PAGE ▶ 846 (14) **5220**

We Built This City—Starship (85) 4638
These Dreams—Heart (86) 4304
King Of Wishful Thinking—Go West (90) 1534
It's Not Enough—Starship (89) 1080
Invisible Hands—Kim Carnes (83) 454
Animal Instinct—Commodores (85) 253
You Make My Heart Beat Faster (And That's All That Matters)—Kim Carnes (84) 172
Magnetic—Earth, Wind & Fire (83) 172
Invitation To Dance—Kim Carnes (85) 122
Good Heart—Starship (91) 69
Dancing In Heaven (Orbital Be-Bop)—Q-Feel (89) 48
I Pretend—Kim Carnes (84) 41
Sing—Mickey Thomas (89) 37
Sunrise—Triplets (91) 28

Richard PAGE ▶ 1174 (8) **3782**

Broken Wings—Mr. Mister (85) 5158
Kyrie—Mr. Mister (85) 4320
Is It Love—Mr. Mister (86) 1255
Something Real (Inside Me/Inside You)—Mr. Mister (87) 420

Richard PAGE ▶ 1174 (8) *Continued*	**3782**
Don't Hold Back Your Love—Daryl Hall & John Oates (90)	330
Hunters Of The Night—Mr. Mister (84)	168
I Do Believe In You—Pages (79)	55
The Border—Mr. Mister (87)	8.7
Rickie PAGE [June Evelyn Kuykendall, June Page] ▶ 6628 (3)	**149**
Donnie—Bermudas (64)	282
Every Time I Hear Your Name—Patti Page (62)	15
Jeannie, Jeannie, Jeannie—Eddie Cochran (58)	2.3
Tommy PAGE ▶ 1951 (3)	**2062**
I'll Be Your Everything—Tommy Page (90)	3017
A Shoulder To Cry On—Tommy Page (89)	646
When I Dream Of You—Tommy Page (90)	411
Roger PAGLIA ▶ 9239 (1)	**28**
Sailing Ships—Mesa (77)	140
Ian PAICE ▶ 3700 (4)	**730**
Smoke On The Water—Deep Purple (73)	3242
Woman From Tokyo—Deep Purple (73)	226
Black Night—Deep Purple (70)	148
Might Just Take Your Life—Deep Purple (74)	27
David PAICH ▶ 141 (21)	**19931**
Rosanna—Toto (82)	5845
Lowdown—Boz Scaggs (76)	4316
Africa—Toto (82)	4097
Hold The Line—Toto (78)	2989
Got To Be Real—Cheryl Lynn (78)	1732
Lido Shuffle—Boz Scaggs (77)	1677
99—Toto (79)	1082
Miss Sun—Boz Scaggs (80)	975
Pamela—Toto (88)	655
Make Believe—Toto (82)	635
Stranger In Town—Toto (84)	580
I'll Do 4 U—Father MC (91)	522
Lady Love Me (One More Time)—George Benson (83)	520
It's Over—Boz Scaggs (76)	402
Georgy Porgy—Toto (79)	384
I'll Supply The Love—Toto (79)	361
Without Your Love—Toto (86)	357
What Can I Say—Boz Scaggs (76)	323
Houston (I'm Comin' To See You)—Glen Campbell (74)	226
Holyanna—Toto (85)	104
Waiting For Your Love—Toto (83)	61
Kevin PAIGE ▶ 2501 (2)	**1434**
Don't Shut Me Out—Kevin Paige (89)	1019
Anything I Want—Kevin Paige (90)	415
Duncan PAIN ▶ 2799 (1)	**1190**
C'est La Vie—Robbie Nevil (86)	3569
Jeffrey Robert PAIN [Dicken] ▶ 8551 (1)	**46**
Romeo—Mr. Big (77)	93
Bobby PAINE [Robert Barnard] ▶ 8224 (1)	**58**
He Could Be The One—Josie Cotton (82)	116
John PAINE ▶ 8010 (1)	**66**
Frogg—Brothers Four (61)	328
Larson PAINE [Lawrence Barnard] ▶ 8225 (1)	**58**
He Could Be The One—Josie Cotton (82)	116
Leonard PAKULA ▶ 7994 (1)	**66**
When You're Gone—Brenda & The Tabulations (67)	198
—Wally Palamarchuk see: Wally PALMAR	
Herman PALEY ▶ 4366 (1)	**512**
Billy—Kathy Linden (58)	1535
—Ralph Palladino see: Ralph DINO	
Vito PALLAVICINI ▶ 4040 (3)	**616**
My Love, Forgive Me (Amore, Scusami)—Robert Goulet (64)	1802
Begin To Love (Cominciamo Ad Amarci)—Robert Goulet (65)	40
Cappuccina—Nat King Cole (61)	11
Wally PALMAR [Wally Palamarchuk] ▶ 2804 (5)	**1187**
Talking In Your Sleep—Romantics (83)	3966
What I Like About You—Michael Morales (89)	*543*
One In A Million—Romantics (84)	404
What I Like About You—Romantics (80)	*218*
Test Of Time—Romantics (85)	115
—Cedric King Palmer see: King PALMER	
David PALMER ▶ 1558 (4)	**2725**
Jazzman—Carole King (74)	4084

Nightingale—Carole King (74)	978
Spanish Eddie—Laura Branigan (85)	381
Saved By The Grace Of Your Love—Sons Of Champlin (77)	7.6
David Gerald PALMER ▶ 4669 (1)	**442**
The Look Of Love - Part One—ABC (82)	1769
Earl PALMER ▶ 6304 (2)	**184**
Telling Lies—Fats Domino (59)	339
I Still Love You—Fats Domino (57)	57
Florrie PALMER [Susan Bridget Inskip] ▶ 727 (2)	**6022**
Morning Train (Nine To Five)—Sheena Easton (81)	5721
When He Shines—Sheena Easton (82)	601
Geoffrey PALMER ▶ 4862 (1)	**397**
Couple Days Off—Huey Lewis & The News (91)	1191
Jack PALMER ▶ 7039 (5)	**120**
Silver Dollar—Teresa Brewer (55)	*205*
Silver Dollar—Barry Darvell (62)	*24*
Everybody Loves My Baby—Dinah Washington with Eddie Chamblee & His Orch. (57)	5.9
I Found A New Baby—Bobby Darin (62)	4.9
Silver Dollar—Johnny Long (55)	*0.0*
King PALMER [Peter T. Kane, Cedric King Palmer] ▶ 3625 (4)	**761**
Eleventh Hour Melody—Al Hibbler (56)	*952*
Eleventh Hour Melody—Lou Busch and His Orchestra (56)	*548*
A Dollar A Nickel And A Dime—Danny Machin (54)	22
11th Hour Melody—Bill Snyder (56)	*0.0*
Phil PALMER ▶ 7370 (1)	**100**
I'm No Angel—Gregg Allman Band (87)	200
Robert PALMER ▶ 475 (10)	**8742**
Addicted To Love—Robert Palmer (86)	4258
Simply Irresistible—Robert Palmer (88)	3285
Some Like It Hot—Power Station (85)	1943
Hyperactive—Robert Palmer (86)	451
You're Amazing—Robert Palmer (90)	439
Communication—Power Station (85)	401
You're Gonna Get What's Coming—Bonnie Raitt (79)	118
Give Me An Inch—Ian Matthews (79)	*79*
Give Me An Inch Girl—Robert Palmer (76)	*14*
Sweet Lies—Robert Palmer (88)	4.4
—Sandra L. Palmer see: Sandy PALMER	
Sandy PALMER [Sandy Grassl, Sandra L. Palmer] ▶ 8691 (1)	**42**
The Animal Trainer And The Toad—Mountain (71)	85
John PALUMBO ▶ 4445 (1)	**493**
Don't Close Your Eyes—Kix (89)	1479
Damon Philip PAMPOLINA ▶ 9688 (2)	**19**
Summer Vacation—Party (90)	*113*
Summer Vacation—Party (91)	*20*
Peter PAN [Peter Kreuder] ▶ 9469 (5)	**23**
Freddy—Annie Cordy (55)	*46*
Freddy—Connie Francis (55)	*46*
Fredy—Eartha Kitt & Perez Prado (55)	*0.0*
Freddy—Stan Kenton & His Orchestra (55)	*0.0*
Freddy—Guy Lombardo & His Royal Canadians (55)	*0.0*
—Georgios Kyriacos Panayiotou see: George MICHAEL	
Hermisendo PANIAGUA ▶ 9926 (1)	**15**
Marimba Charleston—Marimba Chiapas (56)	15
James PANKOW ▶ 289 (9) HOF	**12336**
Just You 'N' Me—Chicago (73)	4058
(I've Been) Searchin' So Long—Chicago (74)	2030
Make Me Smile—Chicago (70)	1930
Old Days—Chicago (75)	1809
Feelin' Stronger Every Day—Chicago (73)	1808
Alive Again—Chicago (78)	1171
You Are On My Mind—Chicago (77)	182
Brand New Love Affair Part I & II—Chicago (75)	159
Colour My World—Chicago (71)	91
—George Pantazi see: Georges BOULANGER	
Marty PANZER ▶ 1997 (5)	**2017**
It's A Miracle—Barry Manilow (75)	1361
Through The Years—Kenny Rogers (81)	1241
Even Now—Barry Manilow (78)	813
This One's For You—Barry Manilow (76)	608
Where Did We Go Wrong—Frankie Valli Introducing Chris Forde (80)	10

Mario PANZERI ▶ 2320 (9)	**1595**
Love Me Tonight—Tom Jones (69)	2125
A Man Without Love (Quando M'innamoro)—Engelbert Humperdinck (68)	1014
To The Door Of The Sun (Alle Porte Del Sole)—Al Martino (74)	825
Come Prima—Tony Dallara (58)	*636*
Come Prima—Polly Bergen (58)	*524*
Suddenly You Love Me—Tremeloes (68)	490
Nessuno Mi Puo' Giudcare—Gene Pitney (66)	13
Come Prima—Luciano Tajoli (58)	*0.0*
Come Prima—Domenico Modugno (58)	*0.0*
Virgilio PANZUTI ▶ 8497 (2)	**48**
(I Don't Care) Only Love Me—Steve Lawrence (59)	*96*
(I Don't Care) Only Love Me—Kay Starr (59)	*0.0*
—Teodoro Paoletta see: Teddy POWELL	
Gino PAOLI ▶ 2767 (5)	**1209**
You're My World—Helen Reddy (77)	*1277*
You're My World—Cilla Black (64)	*591*
The Phoenix Love Theme (Senza Fine)—Brass Ring Featuring Phil Bodner (66)	557
This World We Love In (Il Cielo In Una Stanza)—Mina (61)	*29*
This World We Love In—June Valli (61)	*0.0*
Nicola PAONE ▶ 4804 (2)	**410**
Blah Blah Blah—Nicola Paone (59)	313
Mama Rosa—Julius La Rosa (55)	98
Anthony PAPA ▶ 10860 (1)	**4.8**
Let Me Sleep Alone—Cugini (79)	15
Pierre PAPADIAMANDIS ▶ 9200 (3)	**29**
I Need A Man—Grace Jones (77)	24
Sorry—Grace Jones (77)	17
That's The Trouble—Grace Jones (77)	17
—Evangelos Papathanassiou see: VANGELIS	
—Richard Papazaian see: Dick RICHARDS	
—Peter Papini see: Peter YELLOWSTONE	
Felix PAPPALARDI ▶ 5418 (2)	**291**
Mississippi Queen—Mountain (70)	1100
For Yasgur's Farm—Mountain (70)	97
—Gail Collins Pappalardi see: Gail COLLINS	
Jean-Pierre PAQUIN [Jean-Pierre Lauzon] ▶ 8947 (1)	**36**
Day And Night—Wackers (72)	107
Louis PARDINI ▶ 3393 (2)	**869**
Just To See Her—Smokey Robinson (87)	1564
We've Saved The Best For Last—Kenny G (89)	260
Charlie PARDO ▶ 10734 (1)	**5.7**
Mandrill—Mandrill (71)	40
—Zoe Parentau see: Joan WHITNEY	
Edward PARENTE ▶ 5951 (1)	**224**
Darling Lorraine—Knockouts (59)	448
Harry PARESS [Harry Perzigian] ▶ 8944 (1)	**36**
Love Is A Killer—Vixen (90)	71
—Peylia Parham see: Sugar Pie DeSANTO	
Adeneyi PARIS ▶ 5045 (1)	**354**
Sooner Or Later—Grass Roots (71)	1771
Bobby PARIS ▶ 6000 (2)	**218**
Put It In A Magazine—Sonny Charles (82)	370
Per-So-Nal-Ly—Bobby Paris (68)	33
Ekundayo PARIS ▶ 2450 (2)	**1477**
It's Ecstasy When You Lay Down Next To Me—Barry White (77)	2246
Sooner Or Later—Grass Roots (71)	1771
Jeff PARIS [Geoffrey Brillhart Lieb] ▶ 3573 (2)	**781**
Waiting For Love—Alias (91)	975
Cryin'—Vixen (89)	587
—Johnny Paris see: John POCISK	
—Noel Paris see: Noel REGNEY	
Mitchell PARISH ▶ 430 (30) HOF	**9442**
Deep Purple—Nino Tempo & April Stevens (63)	*7500*
Volare—Bobby Rydell (60)	*3928*
Star Dust—Billy Ward And His Dominoes (57)	*1814*
Corinna Corinna—Ray Peterson (60)	*1744*
Deep Purple—Donny And Marie Osmond (75)	*1422*
Volare (Nel Blu Dipinto Di Blu)—Dean Martin (58)	*1266*
Ruby—Ray Charles Orchestra & Chorus (60)	*781*
Deep Purple—Billy Ward And His Dominoes (57)	*528*
Stardust—Nino Tempo & April Stevens (64)	*465*
Ruby—Adam Wade (60)	*396*

Mitchell PARISH ▶ 430 (30) HOF *Continued*	**9442**
Volare—Al Martino (75)	*365*
Corrine Corrina—Joe Turner (56)	*342*
Moonlight Love—Perry Como (56)	337
Moonlight Serenade—Rivieras (1) (59)	*316*
Serenata—Sarah Vaughan (60)	112
You Too Can Be A Dreamer—Patti Page (55)	55
Don't Be That Way—Larry Elgart And His Manhattan Swing Orchestra (82)	50
Stardust—Frank Sinatra (62)	*34*
Star Dust—Connee Boswell (56)	*32*
Stardust—Nat "King" Cole (57)	*31*
Volare (Nel Blu Di Pinto Di Blu)— McGuire Sisters (58)	*17*
Blue Skirt Waltz— Luther Brandon And His All American Boys (59)	16
Star Dust— Jaye P. Morgan And The Morgan Brothers (58)	*8.5*
Does Your Heart Beat For Me—Betty Johnson (59)	7.0
Moonlight Serenade—Bobby Vinton (76)	*2.1*
Ruby—Bobby Milano (60)	*0.0*
Corrine, Corrina—Swingin' Sam (56)	*0.0*
Moonlight Serenade—Tommy Leonetti (59)	*0.0*
Volare (Nel Blu, Dipinto Di Blu)—Alan Dale (58)	*0.0*
Volare (Nel Blu Dipinto Di Blu)—Jesse Belvin (58)	*0.0*
Robert PARISSI ▶ 407 (7)	**9733**
Play That Funky Music—Wild Cherry (76)	*7145*
Play That Funky Music—Vanilla Ice (90)	*1923*
Baby Don't You Know—Wild Cherry (77)	288
Hold On—Wild Cherry (77)	185
Play That Funky Music—Roxanne (88)	*109*
I Love My Music—Wild Cherry (78)	79
Hot To Trot—Wild Cherry (77)	3.6
Alan PARKER ▶ 7711 (1)	**79**
Comin' Back To Me (Ooh Baby)—Smith (70)	79
Barry PARKER [Sol Parker] ▶ 2973 (8)	**1089**
The Sand And The Sea—Nat "King" Cole (55)	*1167*
Your Love For Me—Frank Sinatra (57)	406
Tell Her You Love Her—Frank Sinatra (57)	211
To Ev'ry Girl—To Ev'ry Boy (The Meaning Of Love)— Johnnie Ray (54)	44
This Love Of Mine—5 DeMarco Sisters (55)	*14*
Dansero—Joni James (58)	4.9
This Love Of Mine—Modernaires (57)	*1.9*
The Sand And The Sea—Bob Santa Maria (55)	*0.0*
Brian PARKER ▶ 3116 (3)	**1002**
Concrete And Clay—Unit Four Plus Two (65)	*1070*
Concrete And Clay—Eddie Rambeau (65)	*928*
You've Never Been In Love Like This Before— Unit Four Plus Two (65)	5.2
—Clarke Ross Parker see: Ross PARKER	
David E. PARKER ▶ 9350 (1)	**26**
Pushin' Your Luck—Sleepy King (61)	51
—Deanie Parker see: Willia Dean PARKER	
Donald PARKER ▶ 11485 (1)	**1.5**
I'm A Practical Guy—Lee Rogers (66)	9.1
Eric PARKER ▶ 7821 (1)	**74**
Crazy (Keep On Falling)—John Hall Band (81)	294
Eula PARKER ▶ 1992 (3)	**2024**
The Village Of St. Bernadette—Andy Williams (59)	*2024*
The Village Of St. Bernadette—Toni Arden (59)	*0.0*
The Village Of St. Bernadette—Rosemary June (59)	*0.0*
—Gordon Rod Parker see: Hubert GIRAUD	
Graham PARKER ▶ 4918 (2)	**382**
Wake Up (Next To You)— Graham Parker And The Shot (85)	377
Life Gets Better—Graham Parker (83)	5.3
—Herman Parker see: Junior PARKER	
John Lewis PARKER ▶ 1990 (3)	**2025**
Hard Habit To Break—Chicago (84)	3593
Staying With It—Firefall (81)	320
If You Wanna Get Back Your Lady— Pointer Sisters (83)	137
Johnny PARKER ▶ 1570 (3)	**2695**
Baby Sittin' Boogie—Buzz Clifford (61)	2355
Tra La La—Georgia Gibbs (56)	*334*
Tra La La—LaVern Baker (56)	*6.2*
Judy PARKER ▶ 963 (6)	**4657**
December, 1963 (Oh, What A Night)— Four Seasons (75)	5913
Who Loves You—Four Seasons (75)	*3116*

Silver Star—Four Seasons (76)	172
Down The Hall—Four Seasons (77)	102
Spend The Night In Love—Four Seasons (80)	12
Who Loves You—Gidea Park (81)	*3.7*
Junior PARKER [Herman Parker] ▶ 10089 (2)	**13**
Stand By Me—Little Junior Parker (60)	10
Someone Somewhere—Junior Parker (63)	2.7
Michael PARKER ▶ 8854 (1)	**38**
Lonely School Year—Hudson Brothers (75)	189
Ray PARKER Jr. ▶ 101 (18)	**24648**
Ghostbusters—Ray Parker Jr. (84)	6188
The Other Woman—Ray Parker Jr. (82)	3607
A Woman Needs Love (Just Like You Do)— Ray Parker Jr. & Raydio (81)	2942
Jack And Jill—Raydio (77)	2865
You Can't Change That—Raydio (79)	2024
You Got The Love—Rufus Featuring Chaka Khan (74)	1547
I Still Can't Get Over Loving You— Ray Parker Jr. (83)	1165
Mr. Telephone Man—New Edition (84)	1152
Jamie—Ray Parker Jr. (84)	949
Two Places At The Same Time— Ray Parker Jr. and Raydio (80)	683
That Old Song—Ray Parker Jr. And Raydio (81)	596
Bad Boy—Ray Parker Jr. (82)	563
Girls Are More Fun—Ray Parker Jr. (85)	456
All I'm Missing Is You—Glenn Medeiros (90)	439
Let Me Go—Ray Parker Jr. (82)	278
I Don't Think That Man Should Sleep Alone— Ray Parker Jr. (87)	137
(Bringing Out) The Girl In Me— Maxine Nightingale (79)	42
Honey I'm Rich—Raydio (78)	17
Richard PARKER ▶ 3045 (5)	**1038**
Oo Wee Baby, I Love You—Fred Hughes (65)	784
I Had It All The Time—Tyrone Davis (72)	315
Young Boy—Barbara Greene (68)	51
Wrapped Up In Your Warm And Tender Love— Tyrone Davis (73)	45
You Can't Take It Away—Fred Hughes (65)	23
—Richard Parker see: Richard Lee WOLD	
Robert PARKER ▶ 1950 (2)	**2063**
Barefootin'—Robert Parker (66)	2044
Tip Toe—Robert Parker (67)	20
Robert Lee PARKER ▶ 8612 (1)	**45**
Watch Your Step—Bobby Parker (61)	90
Roger PARKER ▶ 11657 (1)	**0.8**
Riding High—Faze-O (78)	4.8
Ross PARKER [Clarke Ross Parker] ▶ 4702 (1)	**435**
A Song Of Joy (Himno A La Alegria)— Miguel Rios (70)	1305
—Sol Parker see: Barry PARKER	
Wayne PARKER ▶ 7793 (1)	**75**
I Will Be There—Glass Tiger (87)	374
Willia Dean PARKER [Willia Dean Parker, Deanie Parker] ▶ 5631 (2)	**262**
I've Got No Time To Lose—Carla Thomas (64)	384
I Want Someone—Mad Lads (66)	141
C. Carson PARKS ▶ 385 (2)	**10263**
Somethin' Stupid— Nancy Sinatra & Frank Sinatra (67)	9108
Cab Driver—Mills Brothers (68)	1155
Dean PARKS ▶ 2353 (1)	**1567**
Dancing Machine—Jackson 5 (74)	4702
Larry PARKS ▶ 1396 (3)	**3184**
Bread And Butter—Newbeats (64)	*6160*
(The Bees Are For The Birds) The Birds Are For The Bees—Newbeats (65)	238
Bread And Butter—Robert John (83)	*50*
Van Dyke PARKS ▶ 2867 (4)	**1144**
Heroes And Villains—Beach Boys (67)	1373
Come To The Sunshine—Harpers Bizarre (67)	394
Sail On Sailor—Beach Boys (75)	*268*
Sail On Sailor—Beach Boys (73)	*49*
Robert PARLEE [Robere Parlez] ▶ 10676 (1)	**6.2**
Am I Forgiven—Isle Of Man (86)	12
—Robere Parlez see: Robert PARLEE	
Cliff PARMAN [Mel Stark] ▶ 6448 (5)	**168**
Pretend—Carl Mann (59)	*253*
Our Love Affair—Tommy Charles (56)	187

Pa Pa Pa—Joni James (54)	23
Pretend— Tab Smith His Fabulous Alto and His Band (57)	*5.2*
After School—Tommy Charles (56)	4.0
Paul PARNES ▶ 4663 (3)	**444**
The Next Step Is Love—Elvis Presley (70)	632
Our World—Johnny Tillotson (65)	227
I Could Conquer The World—Shevelles (64)	28
John PARR ▶ 1268 (6)	**3508**
St. Elmo's Fire (Man In Motion)—John Parr (85)	4824
Naughty Naughty—John Parr (84)	680
Night Moves—Marilyn Martin (86)	631
Magical—John Parr (85)	81
Love Grammar—John Parr (85)	34
Blame It On The Radio—John Parr (86)	25
Fred PARRIS ▶ 2596 (10)	**1341**
In The Still Of The Nite—Five Satins (56)	*623*
Cry Baby—Bonnie Sisters (56)	*338*
I'll Remember (In The Still Of The Night)— Santo & Johnny (64)	*248*
In The Still Of The Night—Paul Anka (69)	*233*
Shadows—Five Satins (59)	35
In The Still Of The Nite—Five Satins (60)	*20*
Tears, Tears, Tears—Ben E. King (67)	7.6
In The Still Of The Night— Fred Parris & The Five Satins (82)	*4.8*
In The Still Of The Nite/"I'll Remember"— Five Satins (61)	*0.9*
Cry Baby—Billy Williams Quartet (56)	*0.0*
Avery PARRISH ▶ 9670 (1)	**19**
After Hours—Lew Douglas & His Orchestra (59)	19
Sue PARRISH ▶ 11124 (1)	**3.1**
Love Me—Buddy Holly / The Crickets (58)	6.2
Charlotte PARSON ▶ 11710 (1)	**0.5**
Hello Enemy—Johnny Tillotson (66)	1.4
Alan PARSONS ▶ 855 (17)	**5197**
Eye In The Sky—Alan Parsons Project (82)	3993
Time—Alan Parsons Project (81)	1286
Games People Play—Alan Parsons Project (80)	1174
Don't Answer Me—Alan Parsons Project (84)	875
Damned If I Do—Alan Parsons Project (79)	718
I Wouldn't Want To Be Like You—Alan Parsons (77)	546
Prime Time—Alan Parsons Project (84)	415
(The System Of) Doctor Tarr And Professor Fether— Alan Parsons Project (76)	292
Let's Talk About Me—Alan Parsons Project (85)	260
Psychobabble—Alan Parsons Project (82)	257
You Don't Believe—Alan Parsons Project (83)	240
Don't Let It Show—Alan Parsons Project (77)	136
Stereotomy—Alan Parsons Project (86)	65
Days Are Numbers (The Traveller)— Alan Parsons Project (85)	63
Snake Eyes—Alan Parsons Project (81)	44
Raven—Alan Parsons (76)	22
What Goes Up—Alan Parsons Project (78)	8.2
Bill PARSONS ▶ 3156 (1)	**981**
All American Boy— Bill Parsons And His Orchestra (58)	2944
Geoffrey PARSONS ▶ 2560 (21)	**1383**
Little Shoemaker—Gaylords (54)	*1620*
Smile—Nat "King" Cole (54)	*828*
Chee Chee-oo Chee (Sang The Little Bird)— Perry Como & Jaye P. Morgan (55)	*570*
Smile—Timi Yuro (61)	*422*
Eternally—Sarah Vaughan (60)	*324*
Smile—Betty Everett & Jerry Butler (64)	*322*
Little Shoemaker— Hugo Winterhalter And His Orchestra (54)	*307*
Smile—Tony Bennett (59)	*207*
Little Serenade—Teddy Randazzo (58)	*203*
If You Love Me—LaVern Baker (59)	*9.9*
Little Serenade—Ames Brothers (58)	*9.8*
Oh Mein Papa—Dick Lee (61)	3.1
Smile—Sunny Gale (54)	*0.0*
Chee Chee-Oo Chee—Dennis Hale (55)	*0.0*
Little Serenade—Johnston Brothers (58)	*0.0*
If You Love Me (Really Love Me)—Kay Starr (54)	*0.0*
If You Love Me (Really Love Me)—Vera Lynn (54)	*0.0*
Chee Chee-Oo Chee (Sang The Little Bird)— Gaylords (55)	*0.0*
Chee Chee-Oo Chee (Sang The Little Birds)— Mariners (55)	*0.0*

Geoffrey PARSONS ▶ 2560 (21) *Continued*	**1383**
Chee Chee Oo Chee (Sang The Little Bird)—Dean Martin (55)	*0.0*
Chee Chee-Oo Chee (Sang The Little Bird)—Johnston Brothers (55)	*0.0*
John PARSONS ▶ 10346 (1)	**9.7**
Mirror Star—Fabulous Poodles (79)	19
Judy PARSONS ▶ 10581 (1)	**7.1**
Sign Of The Times—Belle Stars (83)	49
Charles PARTEE ▶ 5247 (1)	**318**
Don't Say Goodnight And Mean Goodbye—Shirelles (63)	637
Chris PARTLAND ▶ 5539 (1)	**273**
Soul City—Partland Brothers (87)	546
George PARTLAND ▶ 5540 (1)	**273**
Soul City—Partland Brothers (87)	546
David PARTON ▶ 3198 (1)	**955**
Sad Sweet Dreamer—Sweet Sensation (75)	955
Dolly PARTON ▶ 511 (7) HOF	**8312**
9 To 5—Dolly Parton (80)	6659
Two Doors Down—Dolly Parton (78)	652
Baby I'm Burnin'—Dolly Parton (78)	509
I Will Always Love You—Dolly Parton (82)	343
Jolene—Dolly Parton (73)	117
Light Of A Clear Blue Morning—Dolly Parton (77)	18
The Seeker—Dolly Parton (75)	14
Andy PARTRIDGE ▶ 7285 (1)	**105**
The Mayor Of Simpleton—XTC (89)	105
Milton PASCAL ▶ 8601 (1)	**45**
It's A Wonderful Thing To Be Loved—Gogi Grant (57)	90
Steve PASCH ▶ 9229 (1)	**28**
Stand By My Woman—Lenny Kravitz (91)	113
Geneva PASCHAL ▶ 4689 (1)	**438**
Dreamin'—Vanessa Williams (89)	1314
Jim PASH ▶ 7773 (1)	**76**
Point Panic—Surfaris (63)	378
Warren PASH ▶ 2340 (1)	**1577**
Private Eyes—Daryl Hall & John Oates (81)	6308
Alan PASQUA ▶ 3798 (5)	**696**
I'll See You In My Dreams—Giant (90)	782
You Know That I Love You—Santana (79)	554
Never Give Up—Sammy Hagar (83)	250
I'm A Believer—Giant (89)	182
Searchin'—Santana (81)	19
Joe PASQUALE ▶ 2316 (1)	**1604**
I Remember Holding You—Boys Club (88)	1604
Sal PASSANTINO ▶ 5786 (1)	**241**
Super Fly Meets Shaft—John & Ernest (73)	483
Kenny PASSARELLI ▶ 4373 (2)	**510**
Rocky Mountain Way—Joe Walsh (73)	1195
A Life Of Illusion—Joe Walsh (81)	422
Ray PASSMAN ▶ 10176 (3)	**12**
Get Him—Exciters (63)	26
Johnny Casanova—Jaye P. Morgan (56)	6.7
I'm Gonna Love You—Ames Brothers (56)	5.9
Dave PASTERNACK ▶ 6821 (1)	**135**
What A Surprise—Johnny Maestro The Voice Of The Crests (61)	404
Joe PASTERNAK ▶ 10550 (1)	**7.3**
Do, Do, Do (What Your Heart Says)—Tony Martin (55)	15
Johnny PATE ▶ 10304 (1)	**10**
Bacardi—Ralph Marterie (61)	10
Peter T. PATERNO ▶ 9689 (2)	**19**
Summer Vacation—Party (90)	*113*
Summer Vacation—Party (91)	*20*
Yolanda PATERNO ▶ 9563 (1)	**21**
It Don't Hurt No More—Nappy Brown (58)	43
Jimmy PATERSON ▶ 2202 (2)	**1748**
Come On Eileen—Dexys Midnight Runners (83)	5225
The Celtic Soul Brothers—Dexys Midnight Runners (83)	19
David PATON ▶ 2460 (3)	**1465**
Magic—Pilot (75)	2804
Just A Smile—Pilot (75)	47
January—Pilot (76)	40
Charles PATRICK ▶ 3529 (3)	**797**
Book Of Love—Monotones (58)	*2045*
Book Of Love—Raindrops (64)	*259*
Book of Love—Nino & the Ebb Tides (61)	*88*
Deeda PATRICK ▶ 8807 (2)	**39**
It Shall Come To Pass—Four Aces (54)	69
Kookie's Mad Pad—Edd Byrnes (59)	8.6
Fred PATRICK ▶ 8450 (1)	**50**
Hot Potato (Mambo)—Jayne and Audrey Meadows (55)	100
Pat PATRICK ▶ 5292 (2)	**312**
Yeh, Yeh—Georgie Fame And The Blue Flames (65)	*931*
Yeh-Yeh!—Mongo Santamaria Orch. (63)	*3.9*
A.B. PATTERSON ▶ 8317 (3)	**54**
Waltzing Matilda—Jimmie Rodgers (60)	*163*
Waltzing Matilda—Merrill Staton Choir (60)	*0.0*
Waltzing Matilda—David Carroll And His Orchestra (59)	*0.0*
Berman PATTERSON ▶ 10334 (2)	**9.9**
You Baby You—Cleftones (56)	*20*
You Baby You—Diamonds (56)	*0.0*
—Ian Hunter Patterson see: Ian HUNTER	
John PATTERSON ▶ 10842 (1)	**5.0**
Walkin' Shoes—Tora Tora (89)	20
Lover PATTERSON ▶ 2993 (2)	**1075**
There Goes My Baby—Drifters (59)	*4700*
There Goes My Baby—Donna Summer (84)	*674*
Mark PATTERSON ▶ 11000 (1)	**3.9**
Long Stroke—ADC Band (78)	24
—Pat Patterson see: Leon PAYNE	
Patrick PATTERSON ▶ 6042 (2)	**213**
The Message—Cymande (73)	420
Bra—Cymande (73)	5.5
Wiley PATTERSON ▶ 8247 (1)	**57**
That's My Heart Strings (That's My Boy)—Burl Ives (56)	114
John PATTON ▶ 3857 (2)	**674**
Where Were You (On Our Wedding Day)?—Lloyd Price (59)	933
Big John—Shirelles (61)	727
Michael PATTON ▶ 5310 (2)	**309**
Epic—Faith No More (90)	1519
Falling To Pieces—Faith No More (90)	27
Robbie PATTON ▶ 1685 (3)	**2490**
Hold Me—Fleetwood Mac (82)	4430
Don't Give It Up—Robbie Patton (81)	508
Smiling Islands—Robbie Patton (83)	295
Alan PAUL ▶ 6916 (1)	**129**
Twilight Zone—Manhattan Transfer (80)	258
Clarence PAUL [Clarence Pauling] ▶ 620 (17)	**6968**
Fingertips - Pt 2—Little Stevie Wonder (63)	*8343*
Until You Come Back To Me (That's What I'm Gonna Do)—Aretha Franklin (73)	*3181*
What's The Matter With You Baby—Marvin Gaye & Mary Wells (64)	929
Once Upon A Time—Marvin Gaye & Mary Wells (64)	797
Pretty Little Baby—Marvin Gaye (65)	743
Hitch Hike—Marvin Gaye (63)	562
Workout Stevie, Workout—Little Stevie Wonder (63)	457
You've Been In Love Too Long—Martha & The Vandellas (65)	348
I Need Your Lovin'—Roy Hamilton (59)	*299*
Danger Heartbreak Dead Ahead—Marvelettes (65)	246
La La La La La—Blendells (64)	230
Night Fo' Last—Shorty Long (68)	143
Hey Love—Stevie Wonder (67)	53
Fingertips—Stars On 45 (82)	*27*
Just A Little Misunderstanding—Contours (66)	26
Until You Come Back To Me (That's What I'm Gonna Do) (Medley)—Luther Vandross (84)	*7.6*
I Need Your Lovin'—Clarence Paul (59)	*0.0*
Henry PAUL ▶ 7834 (1)	**73**
Keeping Our Love Alive—Henry Paul Band (81)	218
Jad PAUL ▶ 9852 (3)	**16**
Banjo Woogie—Ban-Joes (55)	*16*
Banjo Woogie—Sunnysiders (55)	*16*
Banjo Woogie—Georgie Shaw (55)	*16*
Les PAUL [Lester William Polsfuss] ▶ 3953 (5)	**643**
Jura (I Swear I Love You)—Les Paul and Mary Ford (61)	277
Mandolino—Les Paul and Mary Ford (54)	218
Song In Blue—Les Paul and Mary Ford (55)	214
Magic Melody—Les Paul and Mary Ford (55)	205
All I Need Is You—Les Paul and Mary Ford (59)	19
Louis E. PAUL ▶ 6954 (1)	**126**
I Don't Believe—Guilloteens (65)	126
—Lynn Paul see: Buck RAM	
Mark PAUL [Robin Scutt] ▶ 8799 (2)	**39**
Softly, Softly—Jaye P. Morgan (55)	*117*
Softly, Softly—Guy Lombardo & His Royal Canadians (55)	*0.0*
Mark E. PAUL ▶ 5817 (2)	**239**
Radio Romance—Tiffany (89)	275
Feelings Of Forever—Tiffany (88)	203
Marshall PAUL ▶ 3318 (4)	**901**
Ten Commandments Of Love—Harvey and The Moonglows (58)	*560*
The Ten Commandments Of Love—Peaches & Herb (68)	*249*
The Ten Commandments Of Love—Little Anthony And The Imperials (69)	*65*
The Ten Commandments Of Love—James Macarthur (63)	*27*
—Victor Paul see: Luigi CREATORE	
—Clarence Pauling see: Clarence PAUL	
Lowman PAULING ▶ 807 (12)	**5491**
Dedicated To The One I Love—Mamas & The Papas (67)	*5052*
Dedicated To The One I Love—Shirelles (61)	*5044*
Think—James Brown And The Famous Flames (60)	*194*
Dedicated To The One I Love—Shirelles (59)	*96*
Dedicated To The One I Love—Bernadette Peters (81)	*90*
Dedicated To The One I Love—Temprees (72)	*59*
Dedicated To The One I Love—"5" Royales (61)	*58*
Think—5 Royales (57)	*56*
Think—James Brown (73)	*24*
Think—James Brown (73)	*14*
Think—Vicki Anderson And James Brown (67)	*1.9*
I'm With You—"5" Royales (60)	1.5
Joseph PAULINI ▶ 9054 (1)	**32**
She's Got To Be A Saint—Ray Price (73)	65
Jimmy Ray PAULMAN ▶ 10628 (1)	**6.7**
I Need Your Lovin'—Conway Twitty (57)	13
—Pavel see: Frank KOCIAN	
Peter PAVEY ▶ 11071 (1)	**3.4**
Lonely One—Kai Winding (63)	6.8
Gary S. PAXTON ▶ 2142 (4)	**1822**
It Was I—Skip & Flip (59)	1753
Quarter To Four Stomp—Stompers (62)	68
Fancy Nancy—Skip & Flip (59)	54
The Scavenger—Dick Dale And The Del-Tones (63)	18
—George Paxton see: George EDDY	
Tom PAXTON ▶ 1270 (4)	**3494**
Bottle Of Wine—Fireballs (67)	2264
Wasn't That A Party—Rovers (81)	544
The Marvelous Toy—Chad Mitchell Trio (63)	444
The Last Thing On My Mind—Neil Diamond (73)	242
Bill PAYNE ▶ 10401 (1)	**8.9**
Oh Atlanta—Little Feat (78)	8.9
Doris PAYNE [Doris Elaine Higginson, Doris Troy] ▶ 2360 (7)	**1561**
Just One Look—Doris Troy (63)	*1890*
How About That—Dee Clark (59)	668
Just One Look—Linda Ronstadt (79)	*260*
Just One Look—Hollies (67)	*251*
Just One Look—Hollies (64)	*38*
Just One Look—Anne Murray (74)	*13*
What'cha Gonna Do About It—Doris Troy (63)	0.5
Harold PAYNE ▶ 8958 (2)	**35**
Daylight—Vicki Sue Robinson (76)	*54*
Daylight—Bobby Womack (76)	*16*
Jimmy PAYNE ▶ 1505 (1)	**2853**
Woman, Woman—Union Gap Featuring Gary Puckett (67)	5707
Leon PAYNE [Pat Patterson, Leon Roger Payne] ▶ 849 (6)	**5210**
I Love You Because—Al Martino (63)	*4381*
You've Still Got A Place In My Heart—Dean Martin (68)	336
Blue Side Of Lonesome—Jim Reeves (66)	274
T'Ain't Nothin' To Me—Coasters (64)	204
I Love You Because—Johnny Cash (60)	*12*
Take Me—Brenda Lee (67)	7.4

Scherrie PAYNE ▶ 8276 (1)	**56**
Crumbs Off The Table—Glass House (69)	279
Brenda J. PAYTON ▶ 4237 (2)	**551**
Dry Your Eyes—Brenda & The Tabulations (67)	1093
Just Once In A Lifetime— Brenda & The Tabulations (67)	12
Denny PAYTON ▶ 4940 (2)	**377**
Nineteen Days—Dave Clark Five (66)	408
Satisfied With You—Dave Clark Five (66)	347
Lawrence PAYTON ▶ 8479 (2)	**49**
Catfish—Four Tops (76)	96
We All Gotta Stick Together—Four Tops (75)	66
John PEABODY ▶ 9253 (1)	**28**
Little Star—Bobby Callender (63)	83
Geoffrey PEACEY ▶ 8506 (1)	**48**
Time Bomb—Lake (77)	95
Billy PEACHES [William Peaches, Hilary Thompson] ▶ 10946 (1)	**4.2**
Flashes—Tiggi Clay (84)	13
—William Peaches see: Billy PEACHES	
Brian PEACOCK ▶ 11814 (1)	**0.0**
When There's No Love Left— New Seekers featuring Eve Graham (70)	0.0
Charlie PEACOCK [Charles William Ashworth] ▶ 2765 (1)	**1210**
Every Heartbeat—Amy Grant (91)	3631
Trevor PEACOCK ▶ 507 (1)	**8352**
Mrs. Brown You've Got A Lovely Daughter— Herman's Hermits (65)	8352
Sam PEAKE ▶ 10240 (1)	**11**
Music Box—Evelyn "Champagne" King (79)	33
Stephen PEARCY ▶ 4221 (6)	**556**
Round And Round—Ratt (84)	1127
Lay It Down—Ratt (85)	345
Dance—Ratt (87)	196
Way Cool Jr.—Ratt (88)	109
Wanted Man—Ratt (84)	15
You're In Love—Ratt (85)	7.9
Leslie PEARL ▶ 3238 (2)	**934**
If The Love Fits Wear It—Leslie Pearl (82)	709
Girls Can Get It—Dr. Hook (80)	579
Eugene PEARSON ▶ 892 (1)	**4973**
A Thousand Stars— Kathy Young With The Innocents (60)	4973
Mark PEARSON ▶ 6461 (1)	**166**
If You Should Sail—Nielsen/Pearson (80)	332
Neil PEART ▶ 4198 (8)	**566**
New World Man—Rush (82)	554
The Big Money—Rush (85)	372
Tom Sawyer—Rush (81)	329
The Spirit Of Radio—Rush (80)	242
Limelight—Rush (81)	159
Closer To The Heart—Rush (81)	*89*
Closer To The Heart—Rush (77)	*67*
Fly By Night—Rush (77)	4.7
Harry PEASE ▶ 6904 (1)	**130**
The French Song (Quand Le Soleil Dit Bonjour Aux Montagnes)—Lucille Starr (64)	389
—Charles Graham Peate see: Charles GRAHAM	
—Benjamin Franklin Peay see: Brook BENTON	
—Pebbles see: Perri Arlette REID	
—James William Pebworth see: Dub WILLIAMS	
—Herman Peckar see: Bobby RACKEP	
Robert PECKMAN ▶ 4036 (1)	**619**
Dancin' Man—Q (77)	619
A.R. PEDDY ▶ 9501 (1)	**22**
I'm Tired—Ray Peterson (61)	67
Mike PEDEN ▶ 10088 (1)	**13**
1-2-3—Chimes (2) (90)	39
Ivan PEDERSEN ▶ 8634 (1)	**44**
Love In Siberia—Laban (86)	44
—Jorgen Ingmann Pedersen see: Jorgen INGMANN	
—Robert John Pedrick see: Robert JOHN	
Tom PEDRICK ▶ 11173 (1)	**2.9**
Give A Little—Robert John (78)	8.6
Lefty PEDROSKI ▶ 6338 (3)	**181**
Baby, Hang Up The Phone—Carl Graves (74)	244
Brooklyn—Cody Jameson (77)	59

No Love In The Room—5th Dimension (75)	0.7
Ann PEEBLES ▶ 4179 (2)	**573**
I Can't Stand The Rain—Eruption (78)	*930*
I Can't Stand The Rain—Ann Peebles (73)	*789*
Catherine PEEK ▶ 3194 (1)	**956**
Lonely People—America (74)	1912
Dan PEEK ▶ 1653 (5)	**2543**
Lonely People—America (74)	1912
Today's The Day—America (76)	628
Don't Cross The River—America (73)	617
Woman Tonight—America (75)	328
All Things Are Possible—Dan Peek (79)	27
Paul PEEK ▶ 9844 (1)	**16**
Brother-In-Law (He's A Moocher)—Paul Peek (61)	16
Leon PEELS ▶ 5218 (1)	**324**
Lover's Island—Blue Jays (61)	647
—Gayla Peevey see: Jamie HORTON	
—Louis Russell Pegues see: Lou COURTNEY	
Bob PELANDER ▶ 7548 (1)	**89**
Falling In Love Again—Michael Stanley Band (81)	179
Michel PELAY ▶ 7541 (2)	**90**
Do I Love You—Paul Anka (71)	*446*
Do I Love You (Yes In Every Way)—Donna Fargo (78)	*2.7*
Cathie PELLETIER ▶ 7986 (1)	**66**
Who Were You Thinkin' Of—Doolittle Band (80)	199
Marti PELLOW [Mark McLaughlin] ▶ 8631 (1)	**45**
Wishing I Was Lucky—Wet Wet Wet (88)	178
Don PELOSI ▶ 8521 (1)	**47**
When You Lose The One You Love—David Whitfield with Mantovani And His Orchestra (56)	142
Allen PELTIER ▶ 4386 (1)	**507**
Day For Decision—Johnny Sea (66)	507
Paul PENA ▶ 1746 (1)	**2374**
Jet Airliner—Steve Miller Band (77)	2374
Leon PENDARVIS ▶ 9964 (1)	**14**
Feelin' That Glow—Roberta Flack (75)	72
Mike PENDER [Michael John Prendergast] ▶ 9034 (1)	**33**
He's Got No Love—Searchers (65)	65
Andrew PENDLEBURY ▶ 7351 (1)	**100**
Who Listens To The Radio—Sports (79)	201
Kirk PENGILLY ▶ 11019 (1)	**3.8**
Don't Change—INXS (83)	23
—Mary Frances Penick see: Skeeter DAVIS	
Ce Ce PENISTON ▶ 3419 (1)	**856**
Finally—Ce Ce Peniston (91)	2569
Dan PENN [Wallace Daniel Pennington, Daniel Pennington] ▶ 529 (20)	**8061**
Cry Like A Baby—Box Tops (68)	*6020*
I'm Your Puppet—James & Bobby Purify (66)	2932
It Tears Me Up—Percy Sledge (66)	1461
Sweet Inspiration—Sweet Inspirations (68)	*1368*
Is A Blue Bird Blue—Conway Twitty (60)	611
Come On—Tommy Roe (64)	546
I Met Her In Church—Box Tops (68)	462
Wish You Didn't Have To Go— James & Bobby Purify (67)	428
Out Of Left Field—Percy Sledge (67)	342
Sweet Inspiration—Barbra Streisand (72)	*280*
Take Me (Just As I Am)—Solomon Burke (67)	265
Cry Like A Baby—Kim Carnes (80)	*249*
Are You Never Coming Home—Sandy Posey (67)	214
Nine Pound Steel—Joe Simon (67)	115
The Dark End Of The Street—James Carr (67)	96
My Dreams—Brenda Lee (64)	59
Up Tight, Good Man—Laura Lee (67)	36
Always David—Ruby Winters (69)	24
Toys Are Made For Children—Uniques (69)	22
Faithful And True—Z.Z. Hill (71)	1.3
Michael PENN ▶ 2772 (2)	**1204**
No Myth—Michael Penn (90)	1015
This & That—Michael Penn (90)	189
Charlie PENNACHIO ▶ 2794 (2)	**1193**
Sending All My Love—Linear (90)	2325
Don't You Come Cryin'—Linear (90)	91
Dick PENNER ▶ 7872 (1)	**71**
Ooby Dooby—Roy Orbison And Teen Kings (56)	143
Ed PENNEY ▶ 3084 (4)	**1022**
Somebody's Knockin'—Terri Gibbs (81)	1628
Hopelessly—Ames Brothers (54)	367

Queen Of The Senior Prom—Mills Brothers (57)	*255*
Queen Of The Senior Prom—Mills Brothers (62)	*1.4*
Jeff PENNIG ▶ 5542 (4)	**273**
Killin' Time—Fred Knoblock & Susan Anton (80)	467
Natural Love—Petula Clark (82)	43
In The Drivers Seat—John Schneider (82)	40
Runaway Rita—Leif Garrett (81)	26
Richard PENNIMAN [Little Richard] ▶ 875 (24) HOF	**5083**
Long Tall Sally—Little Richard (56)	*1982*
Tutti Frutti—Pat Boone (56)	*1434*
Keep A Knockin'—Little Richard (57)	1277
Long Tall Sally—Pat Boone (56)	*1222*
Jenny Jenny—Little Richard (57)	*932*
Jenny, Jenny— Mitch Ryder And The Detroit Wheels (65)	*728*
Lucille—Little Richard (57)	*684*
Tutti Frutti—Little Richard (56)	*649*
Lucille—Everly Brothers (60)	*596*
Great Gosh A'mighty—Little Richard (86)	300
Ooh My Soul—Little Richard (58)	202
Slippin' And Slidin' (Peepin' And Hidin')— Little Richard (56)	*180*
Long Tall Sally— Cat Mother And The All Night News Boys (69)	*164*
Miss Ann—Little Richard (57)	97
Tutti-Frutti—Jive Bunny And The Mastermixers (89)	*80*
Tutti Frutti—Jive Bunny And The Mastermixers (89)	*80*
Rockin' With The King—Canned Heat (72)	32
True, Fine Mama—Little Richard (58)	24
Bama Lama Bama Loo—Little Richard (64)	21
He's Not Just A Soldier—Little Richard (61)	9.9
She's Got It—Little Richard (57)	5.0
Slipin' And Slidin'— Sing Along With Jim And Monica (64)	*4.1*
Slippin' & Slidin'—Willie Mitchell (67)	*3.3*
Tutti-Frutti—Art Mooney & His Orchestra (56)	*0.0*
—Daniel Pennington see: Dan PENN	
Harrison PENNINGTON ▶ 10272 (1)	**11**
Warpath—Isley Brothers (71)	53
James P. PENNINGTON ▶ 3771 (4)	**703**
Take Me Down—Alabama (82)	910
The Closer You Get—Alabama (83)	381
You And Me—Rockie Robbins (80)	56
How Could This Go Wrong—Exile (79)	8.0
Ray PENNINGTON [Ramon Daniel Pennington, Ray Starr] ▶ 5909 (4)	**230**
Three Hearts In A Tangle—Roy Drusky (61)	*284*
I'm A Ramblin' Man—Waylon Jennings (74)	66
Stay Away From My Baby—Ted Taylor (65)	18
Three Hearts In A Tangle— James Brown And The Famous Flames (62)	*8.1*
Stan PENRIDGE ▶ 4533 (2)	**470**
Beth—Kiss (76)	1404
Don't You Let Me Down—Peter Criss (78)	3.0
Rodger PENZABENE ▶ 1133 (8)	**3917**
I Wish It Would Rain—Temptations (68)	*5041*
You're My Everything—Temptations (67)	2625
I Could Never Love Another (After Loving You)— Temptations (68)	1576
The End Of Our Road—Gladys Knight & The Pips (68)	*1369*
The End Of Our Road—Marvin Gaye (70)	*504*
I Wish It Would Rain—Gladys Knight & The Pips (68)	*449*
Don't You Miss Me A Little Bit Baby— Jimmy Ruffin (67)	184
Take Me In Your Arms And Love Me— Gladys Knight & The Pips (67)	2.9
Alisa PEOPLES [Alisa Peoples Yarbrough] ▶ 5249 (1)	**318**
Don't Stop The Music—Yarbrough & Peoples (81)	954
Josephine PEOPLES ▶ 6385 (2)	**176**
Crazy With Love—Guy Mitchell (56)	*269*
Crazy With Love—Teresa Brewer (56)	*83*
Vic PEPE ▶ 10151 (1)	**12**
Hey Stoopid—Alice Cooper (91)	48
—Jacques Pépino see: James BOLDEN	
Buddy PEPPER [Jack Retherford Starkey, Jack Starkey] ▶ 6246 (3)	**190**
Vaya Con Dios—Drifters (64)	*412*
Vaya Con Dios—Dawn Featuring Tony Orlando (72)	*82*
Vaya Con Dios—Freddy Fender (76)	*75*

Harry PEPPER ▶ 11472 (1)	**1.6**
(Hear My Song) Violetta—Ray Adams And Orchestra (62)	6.2
Jim PEPPER ▶ 5633 (1)	**262**
Witchi Tai To—Everything Is Everything (69)	262
Danny PEPPERMINT [Danny Lamego] ▶ 8053 (1)	**64**
The Peppermint Twist—Danny Peppermint And The Jumping Jacks (61)	64
Bill PEPPERS ▶ 5890 (1)	**233**
I Was The One—Elvis Presley (56)	930
Frank PEPPIATT ▶ 6516 (1)	**161**
The Ballad Of Irving—Frank Gallop (66)	483
—L.R. Peques see: Mary WELLS	
—Marvin Karlton Percy see: Marvin RAINWATER	
Mike PERCY ▶ 4561 (5)	**465**
You Spin Me Round (Like A Record)—Dead Or Alive (85)	1071
Brand New Lover—Dead Or Alive (86)	1017
Come Home With Me Baby—Dead Or Alive (89)	117
Lover Come Back To Me—Dead Or Alive (85)	84
Something In My House—Dead Or Alive (87)	38
Dennis PERECA ▶ 8746 (1)	**40**
Say Hello To Ronnie—Janey Street (84)	81
Hugo PERETTI [Bob Dane, Mark Markwell, Johnny Orlando, Emil Trent] ▶ 388 (52)	**10182**
The Lion Sleeps Tonight—Tokens (61)	*9030*
Can't Help Falling In Love—Elvis Presley With The Jordanaires (61)	*5450*
The Lion Sleeps Tonight—Robert John (71)	*5059*
Secretly—Jimmie Rodgers (58)	*4105*
Bimbombey—Jimmie Rodgers (58)	1823
Are You Really Mine—Jimmie Rodgers (58)	1540
A Walkin' Miracle—Essex Featuring Anita Humes (63)	1442
Oh Oh I'm Falling In Love Again—Jimmie Rodgers (58)	1234
Let's Put It All Together—Stylistics (74)	*1045*
Hello Heartache, Goodbye Love—Little Peggy March (63)	666
I'm Never Gonna Tell—Jimmie Rodgers (59)	568
Heavy Fallin' Out—Stylistics (74)	552
Can't Help Falling In Love—Corey Hart (86)	*544*
I Wish I Were A Princess—Little Peggy March (63)	501
Wild In The Country—Elvis Presley With The Jordanaires (61)	471
Snoopy's Christmas—Royal Guardsmen (67)	431
And Now—Della Reese (60)	398
Make Me A Miracle—Jimmie Rodgers (58)	387
Can't Help Falling In Love—Al Martino (70)	*308*
Because You're Young—Jimmie Rodgers (59)	293
B'wa Nina (Pretty Girl)—Tokens (62)	269
The Impossible Happened—Little Peggy March (63)	258
Experience Unnecessary—Sarah Vaughan (55)	252
Secretly—Lettermen (65)	*243*
I'll Take You Home—Corsairs Featuring Jay "Bird" Uzzell (62)	240
Can't Give You Anything (But My Love)—Stylistics (75)	227
Pupalina—Gaylords (54)	*213*
Star On A TV Show—Stylistics (75)	165
Everyday—Della Reese (60)	139
Thank You Baby—Stylistics (75)	111
The Wizard—Jimmie Rodgers (58)	110
You Understand Me—Sam Cooke (60)	*99*
It Happened Again—Sarah Vaughan (56)	94
Funky Weekend—Stylistics (75)	61
You Are Beautiful—Stylistics (76)	58
A Far Far Better Thing—Della Reese (61)	53
Can't Help Falling In Love—Andy Williams (70)	*26*
The Crazy Otto Rag—Hugo & Luigi (55)	*24*
Bad Girl—Valerie Carr (58)	15
Love Is The Answer—Van Mc Coy & The Soul City Symphony (74)	13
Let's Put It All Together—Band Of Gold (84)	*12*
Dance Mr. Snowman Dance—Crew-Cuts (54)	6.0
Lulu Had A Baby—Chico Holiday (59)	3.7
Big Boat—Tokens (62)	1.8
Can't Help Falling In Love With You—Jimmy Castor (80)	*1.8*
You Understand Me—Jimmie Rodgers (58)	*1.6*
The Crazy Otto Rag—Crazy Otto (55)	*0.0*
Can't Help Falling In Love—Keely Smith (61)	*0.0*
Pupalina (My Little Doll)—Jimmy Durante (54)	*0.0*
Can't Help Falling In Love—Four Esquires (61)	*0.0*
The Crazy Otto Rag—Happy Hoagy Carmichael (55)	*0.0*
Pupalina (My Little Doll)—Guy Lombardo & His Royal Canadians (54)	*0.0*
—June Peretti see: June WINTERS	
Louie PEREZ ▶ 9113 (1)	**31**
Will The Wolf Survive?—Los Lobos (85)	62
—Christine Anne Perfect see: Christine McVIE	
Barney PERKINS ▶ 1901 (1)	**2134**
Want Ads—Honey Cone (71)	6401
Carl PERKINS ▶ 457 (18)	**9139**
Blue Suede Shoes—Carl Perkins (56)	*5839*
Matchbox—Beatles (64)	876
Blue Suede Shoes—Johnny Rivers (73)	*604*
Blue Suede Shoes—Elvis Presley (56)	*530*
Daddy Sang Bass—Johnny Cash (68)	446
Boppin' The Blues—Carl Perkins (56)	246
Blue Suede Shoes—Boyd Bennett And His Rockets (56)	*219*
So Wrong—Patsy Cline (62)	182
Blue Suede Shoes—Cat Mother And The All Night News Boys (69)	*164*
All Mama's Children—Carl Perkins (56)	144
Jive After Five—Carl Perkins (58)	60
Honey Don't—Beatles (65)	37
Everybody's Trying To Be My Baby—Beatles (65)	37
Your True Love—Carl Perkins (57)	36
Pink Pedal Pushers—Carl Perkins (58)	22
Pointed Toe Shoes—Carl Perkins (59)	12
Blue Suede Shoes—Jim Lowe (56)	*0.0*
Blue Suede Shoes—Bob Roubian (56)	*0.0*
Nils PERNE [Jokern] ▶ 9230 (1)	**28**
Shrine Of St. Cecilia—Faron Young (57)	56
PEROTTI ▶ 10659 (1)	**6.3**
Speak, My Love—Vic Damone (56)	19
Bob PERPER ▶ 7423 (3)	**97**
Kid Stuff—McGuire Sisters (57)	*125*
Still Waters Run Deep—Brook Benton (62)	69
Kid Stuff—Bernadine Read (57)	*0.0*
Freddie PERREN ▶ 77 (33)	**29120**
ABC—Jackson 5 (70)	8551
I Want You Back—Jackson 5 (69)	7904
Reunited—Peaches & Herb (79)	*7690*
I Will Survive—Gloria Gaynor (78)	*7179*
The Love You Save—Jackson 5 (70)	6071
Boogie Fever—Sylvers (76)	6020
It's So Hard To Say Goodbye To Yesterday—Boyz II Men (91)	4853
Mama's Pearl—Jackson 5 (71)	4810
Hot Line—Sylvers (76)	3594
Shake Your Groove Thing—Peaches & Herb (78)	2986
Makin' It—David Naughton (79)	2897
Sugar Daddy—Jackson 5 (71)	2514
Heaven Must Be Missing An Angel (Part 1)—Tavares (76)	1546
Do It Baby—Miracles (74)	1443
O.P.P.—Naughty By Nature (91)	1392
Maybe Tomorrow—Jackson 5 (71)	977
Whodunit—Tavares (77)	926
I Pledge My Love—Peaches & Herb (80)	870
Hallelujah Day—Jackson 5 (73)	582
Don't Take Away The Music—Tavares (76)	416
Bless You—Martha Reeves & The Vandellas (71)	298
I Will Survive—Sa-Fire (89)	*247*
We've Got Love—Peaches & Herb (79)	221
Let Me Know (I Have A Right)—Gloria Gaynor (79)	220
A Little Lovin' (Keeps The Doctor Away)—Raes (78)	209
That Once In A Lifetime—Demis Roussos (78)	173
Don't Cha Love It—Miracles (74)	108
Don't Let It End ('til You Let It Begin)—Miracles (73)	105
Cotton Candy—Sylvers (76)	95
I Found That Girl—Jackson 5 (70)	51
Roller-Skatin' Mate (Part 1)—Peaches & Herb (79)	32
Reunited—Band Of Gold (84)	*12*
Anybody Wanna Party?—Gloria Gaynor (79)	4.6
—Henri Perret see: Kelly NICKELS	
Jean-Jacques PERREY [Jean Marcel Leroy] ▶ 10829 (1)	**5.1**
Passport To The Future—Jean Jacques Perrey (70)	20
Jack PERRICONE [Perry Cone] ▶ 2232 (3)	**1716**
Run Joey Run—David Geddes (75)	3075
Without Your Love (Mr. Jordan)—Charlie Ross (76)	352
What I Wouldn't Do (For The Love Of You)—Angela Bofill (80)	5.7
—Christine Perrin see: Christine YARIAN	
Steve PERRON ▶ 8681 (2)	**43**
Francene—ZZ Top (72)	122
From The Very Start—Children (71)	4.1
Alfred Kealoha PERRY ▶ 7554 (1)	**89**
The First Night Of The Full Moon—Jack Jones (64)	*266*
Andy PERRY ▶ 8050 (1)	**64**
Come Out Fighting—Easterhouse (89)	64
Barney PERRY ▶ 1976 (1)	**2039**
Walking In Rhythm—Blackbyrds (75)	2039
—Columbus Perry see: Piney BROWN	
Greg PERRY ▶ 735 (13)	**5970**
Want Ads—Honey Cone (71)	6401
Somebody's Been Sleeping—100 Proof Aged In Soul (70)	2587
Bring The Boys Home—Freda Payne (71)	2168
Stick-Up—Honey Cone (71)	2010
Pay To The Piper—Chairmen Of The Board (70)	1695
One Monkey Don't Stop No Show Part 1—Honey Cone (71)	1447
You've Got To Crawl (Before You Walk)—8th Day (71)	724
Everything Good Is Bad—100 Proof Aged In Soul (72)	364
If I Could See The Light—8th Day (71)	97
Men Are Getting Scarce—Chairmen Of The Board (71)	66
I Can't Be You (You Can't Be Me)—Glass House (70)	60
One Man's Leftovers (Is Another Man's Feast)—100 Proof Aged In Soul (71)	54
Sittin' On A Time Bomb (Waitin' For The Hurt To Come)—Honey Cone (72)	23
Joe PERRY ▶ 1091 (8) HOF	**4044**
Walk This Way—Aerosmith (76)	*1949*
Love In An Elevator—Aerosmith (89)	1738
Walk This Way—Run-D.M.C. (86)	*1705*
What It Takes—Aerosmith (90)	1375
Dude (Looks Like A Lady)—Aerosmith (87)	1227
Rag Doll—Aerosmith (88)	789
Draw The Line—Aerosmith (77)	371
Back In The Saddle—Aerosmith (77)	195
Leonard O. PERRY ▶ 6059 (2)	**210**
One Love In My Lifetime—Diana Ross (76)	628
Love Don't Come No Stronger (Yours And Mine)—Jeff Perry (75)	2.3
Oscar PERRY ▶ 5726 (1)	**250**
This Time I'm Gone For Good—Bobby Blue Bland (73)	500
Phil PERRY ▶ 7311 (1)	**103**
United Together—Aretha Franklin (80)	205
Steve PERRY ▶ 253 (27)	**13491**
Open Arms—Journey (82)	4821
Who's Crying Now—Journey (81)	3618
Oh Sherrie—Steve Perry (84)	3231
Separate Ways (Worlds Apart)—Journey (83)	1982
Don't Stop Believin'—Journey (81)	1658
Lovin', Touchin', Squeezin'—Journey (79)	1571
I'll Be Alright Without You—Journey (86)	1156
Be Good To Yourself—Journey (86)	1150
Only The Young—Journey (85)	927
Foolish Heart—Steve Perry (84)	*877*
Don't Fight It—Kenny Loggins with Steve Perry (82)	851
Girl Can't Help It—Journey (86)	779
Any Way You Want It—Journey (80)	771
Still They Ride—Journey (82)	754
Suzanne—Journey (86)	673
After The Fall—Journey (83)	628
She's Mine—Steve Perry (84)	609
Send Her My Love—Journey (83)	590
Walks Like A Lady—Journey (80)	520
The Party's Over (Hopelessly In Love)—Journey (81)	425
Strung Out—Steve Perry (84)	393
Why Can't This Night Go On Forever—Journey (87)	171
Lights—Journey (78)	165
Too Late—Journey (79)	96
Stay Awhile—Journey (80)	95
Good Morning Girl—Journey (80)	95
Foolish Heart—Sharon Bryant (89)	*36*
Paul PERRYMAN ▶ 7618 (1)	**85**
Just To Hold My Hand—Clyde McPhatter (57)	170

Willie PERRYMAN [P. Red, Piano Red] ▶ 9653 (1)	**20**
Right String But The Wrong Yo-Yo—Dr. Feelgood And The Interns (62)	20
William Allan PERSKY ▶ 10492 (1)	**7.9**
Fat Albert (Hey, Hey, Hey)—Fat Albert Orchestra and Chorus (68)	32
Mats PERSSON ▶ 1802 (2)	**2291**
Listen To Your Heart—Roxette (89)	3652
Spending My Time—Roxette (91)	929
Morris PERT ▶ 5532 (1)	**274**
Family Man—Daryl Hall & John Oates (83)	1641
—Al Perton see: Max DIAMOND	
—Harry Perzigian see: Harry PARESS	
Joey PESCE ▶ 4585 (3)	**462**
Voices Carry—'til tuesday (85)	1719
Looking Over My Shoulder—til tuesday (85)	115
Love In A Vacuum—'til tuesday (85)	12
Jeff PESCETTO ▶ 5698 (3)	**253**
One Step Closer To You—Gavin Christopher (86)	674
Somebody Like You—Robbie Nevil (89)	194
I'm Gonna Miss You—Kenny Loggins (88)	60
André PESSIS ▶ 4910 (1)	**384**
Walking On A Thin Line—Huey Lewis and the News (84)	768
—Frank Peter see: Frank PETERSON	
Jim PETERIK ▶ 200 (30)	**15705**
Eye Of The Tiger—Survivor (82)	9112
Burning Heart—Survivor (85)	3695
Vehicle—Ides Of March (70)	3547
The Search Is Over—Survivor (85)	1879
Is This Love—Survivor (86)	1596
Caught Up In You—38 Special (82)	1470
I Can't Hold Back—Survivor (84)	1376
High On You—Survivor (85)	1072
American Heartbeat—Survivor (82)	655
Hold On Loosely—.38 Special (81)	550
You Wouldn't Listen—I'des Of March (66)	423
The Sound Of Your Voice—.38 Special (91)	423
Poor Man's Son—Survivor (81)	418
You Keep Runnin' Away—38 Special (82)	410
Rockin' Into The Night—38 Special (79)	347
How Much Love—Survivor (87)	239
Fantasy Girl—.38 Special (81)	232
Superman—Ides Of March (70)	223
Keeping Our Love Alive—Henry Paul Band (81)	218
First Night—Survivor (85)	210
Didn't Know It Was Love—Survivor (88)	197
L.A. Goodbye—Ides Of March (71)	130
Summer Nights—Survivor (82)	124
Ever Since The World Began—Tommy Shaw (88)	102
Across The Miles—Survivor (89)	93
Somewhere In America—Survivor (80)	82
Caught In The Game—Survivor (83)	71
The One That Really Matters—Survivor (83)	46
Man Against The World—Survivor (87)	44
Roller Coaster—Ides Of March (66)	4.3
Ben PETERS ▶ 977 (7)	**4593**
Before The Next Teardrop Falls—Freddy Fender (75)	5010
Kiss An Angel Good Mornin'—Charley Pride (71)	1193
Daytime Friends—Kenny Rogers (77)	506
Turn The World Around—Eddy Arnold (67)	267
San Francisco Is A Lonely Town—Joe Simon (69)	65
Living It Down—Freddy Fender (76)	53
All Over Me—Charlie Rich (75)	5.0
Dale PETERS ▶ 7062 (1)	**118**
Funk #49—James Gang (70)	355
—Jed Peters see: Jerry LEIBER	
—Jed Peters see: Mike STOLLER	
Jerry PETERS ▶ 1803 (6)	**2290**
Love Or Let Me Be Lonely—Friends Of Distinction (70)	*2597*
Going In Circles—Friends Of Distinction (69)	1646
Love Or Let Me Be Lonely—Paul Davis (82)	*351*
One More Time For Love—Billy Preston & Syreeta (80)	289
I Need You—Friends Of Distinction (71)	193
Let's Dance (Make Your Body Move)—West Street Mob (81)	30
Lee PETERS ▶ 7955 (1)	**67**
Girlfriend—Bobby Brown (86)	202
Lisa PETERS ▶ 9609 (1)	**20**
Very Special—Debra Laws (81)	41
Mike PETERS ▶ 6235 (4)	**191**
Sold Me Down The River—Alarm (89)	218
Strength—Alarm (85)	120
Rain In The Summertime—Alarm (87)	89
Presence Of Love—Alarm (88)	59
Wolf PETERSEN ▶ 10175 (1)	**12**
Tamouré—Bill Justis (63)	46
Betty PETERSON [Betty Blasco] ▶ 1458 (2)	**2990**
My Happiness—Connie Francis (58)	*5960*
My Happiness—Fats Domino (57)	*19*
Debbi PETERSON ▶ 5357 (1)	**300**
Be With You—Bangles (89)	600
—Dick Peterson see: Nicholas RICHARDSON	
Dickie PETERSON ▶ 7400 (1)	**98**
Just A Little Bit—Blue Cheer (68)	98
Frank PETERSON [F. Gregorian, Frank Peter, Gregorian] ▶ 4172 (1)	**574**
Sadeness Part 1—Enigma (91)	1723
Garry PETERSON ▶ 2169 (2)	**1794**
American Woman—Guess Who (70)	7040
Follow Your Daughter Home—Guess Who (73)	172
Kenneth Edward PETERSON ▶ 6914 (1)	**129**
Your Love Is So Good For Me—Diana Ross (78)	129
Paul PETERSON [St. Paul] ▶ 7723 (1)	**79**
Stranger To Love—St. Paul (90)	236
Ray PETERSON ▶ 6436 (1)	**169**
Night Theme—Mark II (60)	338
Ray A. PETERSON ▶ 10138 (1)	**12**
Sweet Little Kathy—Ray Peterson (61)	24
Ron PETERSON ▶ 11350 (2)	**2.1**
Straight Flush—Frantics (59)	9.1
Fog Cutter—Frantics (59)	3.1
Ronald Robert PETERSON ▶ 9874 (1)	**16**
Touch The Hand—Conway Twitty (75)	31
Spencer PETERSON ▶ 8726 (1)	**41**
Minnesota—Northern Light (75)	82
Thomas John PETERSON [Tom Petersson] ▶ 4783 (2)	**417**
Can't Stop Falling Into Love—Cheap Trick (90)	1076
Never Had A Lot To Lose—Cheap Trick (89)	116
—Tom Petersson see: Thomas John PETERSON	
Bernice PETKERE ▶ 3932 (2)	**652**
Close Your Eyes—Tony Bennett (55)	547
Lullaby Of The Leaves—Ventures (61)	105
—Anthony Petolino see: Don STIRLING	
Angelo PETRAGLIA ▶ 4573 (1)	**463**
10-9-8—Face To Face (84)	463
Mike PETRILLO ▶ 2936 (3)	**1110**
Tell It To The Rain—4 Seasons Featuring The "Sound" Of Frankie Valli (66)	1614
Electric Stories—4 Seasons Featuring The "Sound" Of Frankie Valli (68)	417
Patch Of Blue—Frankie Valli & The 4 Seasons (70)	190
Rick PETRONE ▶ 10827 (1)	**5.1**
Don't Let Love Pass Me By—Frankie Avalon (60)	10
Roxy PETRUCCI ▶ 8945 (1)	**36**
Love Is A Killer—Vixen (90)	71
William PETTAWAY ▶ 3666 (1)	**744**
Girl You Know It's True—Milli Vanilli (88)	3721
Shep PETTIBONE ▶ 1494 (2)	**2914**
Vogue—Madonna (90)	5025
Rescue Me—Madonna (91)	803
Jack PETTIS ▶ 9823 (1)	**16**
Bugle Call Rag—Crazy Otto (55)	49
Daryl PETTY ▶ 9922 (1)	**15**
A Million Miles From Nowhere—Brook Benton (58)	15
Norman PETTY ▶ 426 (35)	**9483**
Peggy Sue—Buddy Holly / The Crickets (57)	*4478*
That'll Be The Day—Buddy Holly / The Crickets (57)	*4320*
It's So Easy—Linda Ronstadt (77)	1953
Oh Boy—Buddy Holly / The Crickets (57)	1552
That'll Be The Day—Linda Ronstadt (76)	*1413*
True Love Ways—Peter And Gordon (65)	*1390*
Almost Paradise—Roger Williams (57)	*1031*
Maybe Baby—Buddy Holly / The Crickets (58)	997
Almost Paradise—Lou Stein (57)	*590*
Brass Buttons—String-A-Longs (61)	489
Not Fade Away—Rolling Stones (64)	*417*
I'm Gonna Love You Too—Hullaballoos (64)	*366*
Almost Paradise—Norman Petty Trio (57)	*353*
Think It Over—Buddy Holly / The Crickets (58)	325
Everyday—James Taylor (85)	*250*
Rave On—Buddy Holly / The Crickets (58)	184
Peggy Sue—Beach Boys (78)	*133*
True Love Ways—Mickey Gilley (80)	*74*
Heartbeat—Buddy Holly / The Crickets (58)	69
Well All Right—Santana (78)	67
Everyday—John Denver (72)	*64*
Not Fade Away—Tanya Tucker (78)	*54*
Everyday—Buddy Holly / The Crickets (57)	*53*
Not Fade Away—Eric Hine (81)	*40*
Fool's Paradise—Buddy Holly / The Crickets (58)	25
Vaquero (Cowboy)—Fireballs (60)	24
Listen To Me—Buddy Holly / The Crickets (58)	23
The First Kiss—Norman Petty Trio (57)	17
Hypnotized—Drifters (57)	13
I'm Gonna Love You Too—Buddy Holly / The Crickets (58)	*13*
I'm Gonna Love You Too—Terry Jacks (73)	*11*
That'll Be The Day—Everly Brothers (65)	*5.0*
Peggy Sue—Jackie Walker (57)	*0.0*
That'll Be The Day—Jeff Allen (57)	*0.0*
That'll Be The Day—Buddy Holly & The Three Tunes (57)	*0.0*
Ray PETTY ▶ 8164 (1)	**60**
Goodbye Dad—Castle Sisters (62)	119
Stella PETTY ▶ 11511 (1)	**1.4**
No Rebate On Love—Dramatics (75)	2.8
Tom PETTY ▶ 373 (25) HOF	**10424**
Stop Draggin' My Heart Around—Stevie Nicks (with Tom Petty And The Heartbreakers) (81)	3309
Don't Do Me Like That—Tom Petty And The Heartbreakers (79)	1837
Free Fallin'—Tom Petty (89)	1714
Refugee—Tom Petty And The Heartbreakers (80)	1188
You Got Lucky—Tom Petty and The Heartbreakers (82)	1111
You Got It—Roy Orbison (89)	1104
Don't Come Around Here No More—Tom Petty and The Heartbreakers (85)	1060
I Won't Back Down—Tom Petty (89)	1038
The Waiting—Tom Petty and the Heartbreakers (81)	803
Runnin' Down A Dream—Tom Petty (89)	589
Breakdown—Tom Petty And The Heartbreakers (77)	566
Jammin' Me—Tom Petty and The Heartbreakers (87)	534
Change Of Heart—Tom Petty and The Heartbreakers (83)	522
Learning To Fly—Tom Petty and the Heartbreakers (91)	469
Handle With Care—Traveling Wilburys (88)	448
I Need To Know—Tom Petty And The Heartbreakers (78)	292
A Face In The Crowd—Tom Petty (90)	225
Make It Better (Forget About Me)—Tom Petty and The Heartbreakers (85)	194
End Of The Line—Traveling Wilburys (89)	166
Here Comes My Girl—Tom Petty And The Heartbreakers (80)	131
Ways To Be Wicked—Lone Justice (85)	115
Listen To Her Heart—Tom Petty And The Heartbreakers (78)	107
A Woman In Love (It's Not Me)—Tom Petty and the Heartbreakers (81)	104
Into The Great Wide Open—Tom Petty and the Heartbreakers (91)	79
Rebels—Tom Petty and The Heartbreakers (85)	63
Violet PETTY ▶ 7747 (1)	**76**
Someone, Someone—Brian Poole & The Tremeloes (64)	153
James PETZE ▶ 8152 (1)	**60**
Back Beat No. 1—Rondels (61)	240
Leonard PETZE ▶ 8153 (1)	**60**
Back Beat No. 1—Rondels (61)	240
Dave PEVERETT ▶ 1288 (7)	**3449**
Slow Ride—Foghat (75)	1435
Third Time Lucky (First Time I Was A Fool)—Foghat (79)	1012
Drivin' Wheel—Foghat (76)	544
Stone Blue—Foghat (78)	341
Fool For The City—Foghat (76)	309
I'll Be Standing By—Foghat (77)	59
Stranger In My Home Town—Foghat (80)	51

Slim PEZIN ▶ 8338 (1)	**54**
Souvenirs—Voyage (79)	161
—Paul Pfab see: Peter PFAB	
Peter PFAB [Paul Pfab] ▶ 7193 (1)	**111**
How To Dance—Bingoboys (91)	554
Bob PFEIFER ▶ 10152 (1)	**12**
Hey Stoopid—Alice Cooper (91)	48
Michael PFEIFER ▶ 8543 (1)	**47**
Talk To Me—Fiona (85)	93
Ewald PFLEGER ▶ 7241 (1)	**108**
Live Is Life—Opus (86)	541
Don PFRIMMER ▶ 9952 (1)	**15**
You Put The Beat In My Heart—Eddie Rabbitt (83)	29
—Francis Philip see: Francis Philip MILITARY	
Gary PHILIPPET [Gary Edmund Philippet, Gary Phillips] ▶ 4799 (3)	**411**
The Breakup Song (They Don't Write 'Em)—Greg Kihn Band (81)	1125
Love Never Fails—Greg Kihn Band (83)	168
Every Love Song—Greg Kihn Band (82)	15
Terry PHILIPS [Phil Teitelbaum] ▶ 8527 (2)	**47**
Kissin' Game—Dion (61)	83
Some Of Your Lovin'—Johnny Nash (61)	12
Greg PHILLINGANES ▶ 3458 (3)	**839**
Love Will Conquer All—Lionel Richie (86)	1538
Se La—Lionel Richie (87)	642
Where's Your Angel?—Lani Hall (81)	11
Bob PHILLIPS ▶ 9910 (1)	**15**
Takin' It Easy—Seals & Crofts (78)	30
Charlie PHILLIPS ▶ 2023 (2)	**1998**
Sugartime—McGuire Sisters (57)	*3995*
Sugartime—Charlie Phillips (57)	*0.0*
Chynna PHILLIPS ▶ 1181 (4)	**3759**
Hold On—Wilson Phillips (90)	4433
Release Me—Wilson Phillips (90)	3701
You're In Love—Wilson Phillips (91)	3185
The Dream Is Still Alive—Wilson Phillips (91)	1006
Dolores PHILLIPS ▶ 7145 (1)	**113**
Come Tomorrow—Manfred Mann (65)	340
Eddie PHILLIPS ▶ 7270 (1)	**106**
Teacher Teacher—Rockpile (80)	212
Ernesto PHILLIPS ▶ 4626 (2)	**448**
Object Of My Desire—Starpoint (85)	913
Restless—Starpoint (86)	288
Ethel PHILLIPS ▶ 11181 (1)	**2.8**
Forty Two—Rusty Draper (56)	5.7
—Frank Phillips see: Billy GUY	
—Gary Phillips see: Gary PHILIPPET	
—James Phillips see: John TURNER	
—James John Turner Phillips see: John TURNER	
John PHILLIPS ▶ 84 (22)	**26672**
Monday, Monday—Mama's & The Papa's (66)	*7870*
California Dreamin'—Mama's & The Papa's (66)	*4824*
San Francisco (Be Sure To Wear Flowers In Your Hair)—Scott McKenzie (67)	*4181*
Kokomo—Beach Boys (88)	3513
Words Of Love—Mamas & The Papas (66)	3061
I Saw Her Again—Mamas & The Papas (66)	2615
Creeque Alley—Mamas & The Papas (67)	2486
Go Where You Wanna Go—5th Dimension (67)	1133
Twelve Thirty (Young Girls Are Coming To The Canyon)—Mamas & The Papas (67)	997
Look Through My Window—Mamas & The Papas (66)	842
Mississippi—John Phillips (70)	744
Like An Old Time Movie—Scott McKenzie (67)	632
California Dreamin'—Bobby Womack (68)	*442*
Safe In My Garden—Mamas & The Papas (68)	407
Dancing Bear—Mamas & The Papas (67)	381
California Dreamin'—Beach Boys (86)	249
For The Love Of Ivy—Mamas & The Papas (68)	214
California Dreamin'—America (79)	*142*
Step Out—Mamas & The Papas (72)	24
San Francisco (Wear Some Flowers In Your Hair)—Paul Mauriat and His Orchestra (68)	*17*
Monday, Monday—Stars On 45 (81)	*12*
Holy Man—Scott McKenzie (68)	7.0
John C. PHILLIPS ▶ 2668 (2)	**1283**
Green-Eyed Lady—Sugarloaf (70)	3826
Mother Nature's Wine—Sugarloaf (71)	22
Lee PHILLIPS ▶ 11256 (1)	**2.6**
International Playboy—Wilson Pickett (73)	10
Marc PHILLIPS ▶ 5967 (4)	**221**
You've Got Another Thing Coming—Hotel (79)	151
You'll Love Again—Hotel (78)	110
Half Moon Silver—Hotel (80)	51
Hold On To The Night—Hotel (79)	39
Marvin PHILLIPS ▶ 4307 (1)	**527**
Cherry Pie—Skip & Flip (60)	1582
Mel PHILLIPS ▶ 11443 (1)	**1.7**
Toni—Tradewinds (59)	3.3
Michelle PHILLIPS [Michelle Gilliam] ▶ 1085 (5)	**4072**
California Dreamin'—Mama's & The Papa's (66)	*4824*
Creeque Alley—Mamas & The Papas (67)	2486
California Dreamin'—Bobby Womack (68)	*442*
California Dreamin'—Beach Boys (86)	249
California Dreamin'—America (79)	*142*
Mike PHILLIPS ▶ 1080 (2)	**4083**
North To Alaska—Johnny Horton (60)	4054
Big River, Big Man—Claude King (61)	29
Mildred PHILLIPS ▶ 5273 (2)	**314**
Mambo Rock—Bill Haley And His Comets (55)	*943*
Mambo Rock—Mike Pedicin Quintette (55)	*0.0*
Nathaniel PHILLIPS ▶ 8122 (2)	**61**
Glide—Pleasure (79)	116
Let's Dance (Make Your Body Move)—West Street Mob (81)	30
—Phil Phillips see: Phil BAPTISTE	
Ricky PHILLIPS ▶ 5731 (1)	**250**
Possession—Bad English (90)	749
Sam PHILLIPS ▶ 10714 (1)	**5.9**
So Long I'm Gone—Warren Smith (57)	12
Shawn PHILLIPS ▶ 10397 (1)	**8.9**
We—Shawn Phillips (73)	8.9
Peter PHIPPS ▶ 10813 (1)	**5.2**
Makes You Blind—Glitter Band (76)	16
Jim PHOTOGLO [James G. Photoglo, Jim Photoglou] ▶ 4302 (2)	**529**
Fool In Love With You—Jim Photoglo (81)	651
We Were Meant To Be Lovers—Photoglo (80)	408
—Jim Photoglou see: Jim PHOTOGLO	
Edith PIAF [Édith Giovanna Gassion] ▶ 4741 (4)	**427**
I'll Remember Today—Patti Page (57)	847
If You Love Me—LaVern Baker (59)	*9.9*
If You Love Me (Really Love Me)—Kay Starr (54)	*0.0*
If You Love Me (Really Love Me)—Vera Lynn (54)	*0.0*
Anthony PIANO ▶ 11361 (1)	**2.1**
The Story Of Our Love—Johnny Mathis (59)	4.2
Michael PIANO ▶ 11408 (1)	**1.8**
Santo Domingo—Sandpipers (70)	5.5
—Piano Red see: Willie PERRYMAN	
—John Campbell Picard see: Aryan ZERO	
—Thomas R. Picardo see: Tommy WEST	
—Frederick Picariello see: Freddy CANNON	
Angelo PICCIONI [Pedro Manilla, Angelo Ferdinando Piccioni] ▶ 8073 (2)	**63**
Lazy Gondolier—Mantovani And His Orchestra (55)	*188*
Lazy Gondolier—Lawrence Welk & His Champagne Music (55)	*0.0*
Gian PICCIONI ▶ 11766 (1)	**0.2**
More Than A Miracle—Roger Williams (67)	0.5
—Albert Piccirilli see: Al REX	
Mike PICCIRILLO ▶ 3163 (6)	**976**
Tell Me Tomorrow - Part 1—Smokey Robinson (82)	488
Lonely Eyes—Robert John (79)	478
After The Summer's Gone—PC Quest (91)	326
Old Fashioned Love—Smokey Robinson (82)	146
He's A Pretender—High Inergy (83)	30
Give A Little—Robert John (78)	8.6
Steve PICCOLO ▶ 3249 (1)	**928**
Self Control—Laura Branigan (84)	2784
Lee PICKENS ▶ 7011 (1)	**122**
D.O.A.—Bloodrock (70)	733
Bobby PICKETT ▶ 969 (3)	**4623**
Monster Mash—Bobby (Boris) Pickett And The Crypt-Kickers (62)	*7305*
Monster Mash—Bobby (Boris) Pickett And The Crypt-Kickers (73)	*1895*
Monster Mash—Bobby (Boris) Pickett And The Crypt-Kickers (70)	*47*
Ken PICKETT ▶ 5792 (2)	**241**
Our World—Blue Mink (70)	270
Teacher Teacher—Rockpile (80)	212
Phil PICKETT ▶ 2342 (3)	**1575**
Karma Chameleon—Culture Club (83)	5903
Move Away—Culture Club (86)	1007
It's A Miracle—Culture Club (84)	965
Wilson PICKETT ▶ 1002 (20)	**4455**
Don't Knock My Love - Pt. I—Wilson Pickett (71)	*2128*
In The Midnight Hour—Wilson Pickett (65)	*1036*
If You Need Me—Solomon Burke (63)	*786*
In The Midnight Hour—Cross Country (73)	*725*
I'm A Midnight Mover—Wilson Pickett (68)	706
It's Too Late—Wilson Pickett (63)	544
I Found A Love - Part 1—Wilson Pickett (67)	*487*
In The Midnight Hour—Mirettes (68)	*421*
Ninety-Nine And A Half (Won't Do)—Wilson Pickett (66)	412
Don't Knock My Love—Diana Ross & Marvin Gaye (74)	*354*
Funk Factory—Wilson Pickett (72)	305
Don't Fight It—Wilson Pickett (65)	293
If You Need Me—Wilson Pickett (63)	*279*
I Found A Love—Falcons & Band (Ohio Untouchables) (62)	*276*
She Said Yes—Wilson Pickett (70)	169
Soul Dance Number Three—Wilson Pickett (67)	117
Take A Closer Look At The Woman You're With—Wilson Pickett (73)	113
In The Midnight Hour—Wanted (67)	*25*
In The Midnight Hour—Samantha Sang (79)	*7.5*
It's All Over—Wilson Pickett (65)	1.4
—Mike Pickworth see: Mike HURST	
Vito PICONE ▶ 1196 (2)	**3714**
Little Star—Elegants (58)	7398
Please Believe Me—Elegants (58)	15
Darryl PIERCE ▶ 6600 (1)	**153**
I Need Love—LL Cool J (87)	765
John PIERCE ▶ 4988 (2)	**364**
Cool Love—Pablo Cruise (81)	1056
Slip Away—Pablo Cruise (81)	35
Larry PIERCE ▶ 11127 (1)	**3.1**
Take It Off Him And Put It On Me—Clarence Carter (70)	15
Les PIERCE ▶ 4975 (1)	**367**
Sittin' In The Lap Of Luxury—Louie Louie (90)	734
Marvin PIERCE ▶ 1875 (15)	**2174**
Love Rollercoaster—Ohio Players (75)	5251
Fire—Ohio Players (74)	4114
Funky Worm—Ohio Players (73)	1438
Skin Tight—Ohio Players (74)	1151
Who'd She Coo?—Ohio Players (76)	885
Ecstasy—Ohio Players (73)	621
Sweet Sticky Thing—Ohio Players (75)	411
Fopp—Ohio Players (76)	398
I Want To Be Free—Ohio Players (75)	335
Jive Turkey (Part 1)—Ohio Players (74)	245
Pain (Part 1)—Ohio Players (71)	208
O-H-I-O—Ohio Players (77)	144
Feel The Beat (Everybody Disco)—Ohio Players (77)	42
Got Pleasure—Ohio Players (72)	14
Rattlesnake—Ohio Players (76)	12
Tim PIERCE ▶ 5990 (1)	**219**
State Of The Heart—Rick Springfield (85)	656
Tony PIERCE ▶ 3643 (1)	**752**
Cross My Broken Heart—Jets (87)	1505
Webb PIERCE ▶ 4414 (4)	**501**
I Ain't Never—Webb Pierce (59)	*807*
Leavin' On Your Mind—Patsy Cline (63)	126
Bop-A-Lena—Ronnie Self (58)	59
I Ain't Never—Four Preps (59)	*8.8*
Andrew PIERCY ▶ 3284 (2)	**912**
Der Kommissar—After The Fire (83)	*2710*
Dancing In The Shadows—After The Fire (83)	17

James Lord PIERPONT ▶ 5884 (11) HOF	**233**
Twistin' Bells—Santo & Johnny (60)	*237*
Jingle Bells—Singing Dogs (55)	*48*
Jingle Bells—Four Aces Featuring Al Alberts (55)	*27*
Jingle Bells— Bing Crosby and The Andrews Sisters (55)	*27*
Jingle Bells—Gisele MacKenzie (57)	*22*
Jingle Bells— Bing Crosby and The Andrews Sisters (57)	*22*
Jingle Bells—Perry Como (57)	*13*
Jingle Bells— Don Charles Presents The Singing Dogs Directed By Carl Weissman With Instrumental Accomp. (72)	*12*
Italian Jingle Bells—Lou Monte (55)	8.7
Jingle Bells Imitations— Bobby Rydell - Chubby Checker (61)	*3.3*
Jingle Bells—Ella Fitzgerald (60)	*1.0*
Kate PIERSON ▶ 2532 (6)	**1409**
Love Shack—B-52's (89)	2771
Roam—B-52's (89)	2734
Deadbeat Club—B-52's (90)	458
Rock Lobster—B-52's (80)	143
Private Idaho—B-52's (80)	70
Legal Tender—B-52's (83)	52
Nelson PIGFORD ▶ 2907 (1)	**1123**
It's Ecstasy When You Lay Down Next To Me— Barry White (77)	2246
Johanna PIGOTT ▶ 10758 (1)	**5.5**
Rain—Dragon (84)	17
Steve PIGOTT ▶ 5076 (1)	**347**
Living In A Box—Living In A Box (87)	694
Victoria PIKE ▶ 4944 (9)	**377**
Better Use Your Head— Little Anthony And The Imperials (66)	308
Rain In My Heart—Frank Sinatra (68)	289
It Feels So Good To Be Loved So Bad— Manhattans (77)	169
It's Not The Same—Anthony And The Imperials (66)	36
Salty Tears—Mara Lynn Brown (73)	12
Boomerang—Frankie Valli (76)	9.9
Don't Tie Me Down—Anthony & The Imperials (67)	3.3
I'm Hypnotized—Anthony And The Imperials (68)	1.4
Forget To Remember—Frank Sinatra (69)	0.0
Lorenzo PILAT ▶ 3126 (3)	**996**
Love Me Tonight—Tom Jones (69)	2125
To The Door Of The Sun (Alle Porte Del Sole)— Al Martino (74)	825
Suddenly You Love Me—Tremeloes (68)	490
Felton PILATE ▶ 3901 (5)	**663**
2 Legit 2 Quit—M.C. Hammer (91)	1441
Addams Groove—M.C. Hammer (91)	996
Chase Me—Con Funk Shun (79)	74
Got To Be Enough—Con Funk Shun (80)	9.0
Love Me Just For Me—Special Generation (90)	6.8
Chris PILGRAM ▶ 9275 (1)	**27**
Rain In May—Max Werner (81)	55
John PILLA ▶ 9881 (1)	**16**
Valley To Pray—Arlo Guthrie (70)	62
Gene PILLER ▶ 8346 (2)	**54**
What Is A Wife—Steve Allen (55)	161
What Is A Husband?—Jane Meadows (56)	0.0
Jeff PILSON ▶ 5903 (4)	**231**
In My Dreams—Party (91)	610
Alone Again—Dokken (85)	164
Burning Like A Flame—Dokken (87)	82
In My Dreams—Dokken (86)	68
Sid PINCHBACK ▶ 9359 (1)	**25**
Cross My Heart—Billy Stewart (67)	76
—Barry Alan Pincus see: Barry MANILOW	
Irwin PINCUS [Allan Jeffrey] ▶ 3451 (5)	**843**
Old Cape Cod—Patti Page (57)	2136
Stashu Pandowski (She's Not Very Much Good For Pretty)—Russ Carlyle And The Coachmen (57)	*193*
Stashu Pandowski (She's Not Very Much Good For Pretty)—Julius La Rosa (57)	*69*
Stashu Pandowski (She's Not Very Much Good For Pretty)—Toppers (57)	*0.0*
Stashu Pandowski (She's Not Very Much Good For Pretty)—Ray Henry & His Orchestra (57)	*0.0*
Lee PINCUS ▶ 10760 (1)	**5.5**
Two Innocent Hearts—Ginny Gibson (56)	11

Mike PINDER ▶ 7348 (3)	**101**
From The Bottom Of My Heart (I Love You)— Moody Blues (65)	69
A Simple Game—Four Tops (72)	49
Stop!—Moody Blues (66)	34
Mike PINERA ▶ 2087 (2)	**1892**
Ride Captain Ride—Blues Image (70)	3535
Goodnight My Love—Mike Pinera (79)	124
Lee PINES ▶ 10906 (1)	**4.4**
Man In The Phone Booth—Wanderer (57)	8.9
Rick PINETTE ▶ 4399 (2)	**505**
King Of The Hill—Rick Pinette And Oak (80)	341
This Is Love—Oak (79)	165
Frank PINGATORE ▶ 4987 (5)	**364**
Happy Baby—Bill Haley And His Comets (54)	*243*
Two Hound Dogs—Bill Haley And His Comets (55)	175
Let's All Rock Together—Jodimars (56)	40
Everybody Out'ta The Pool—Lifeguards (59)	13
Happy Baby—Les Baxter & The Bombers (54)	*0.0*
Maceo PINKARD ▶ 10430 (2) HOF	**8.6**
Sweet Georgia Brown—Carroll Bros. (62)	*19*
Sweet Georgie Brown Sweet Georgia Brown— Mindy Carson (57)	*6.8*
Sandy PINKARD ▶ 6907 (1)	**130**
Blessed Are The Believers—Anne Murray (81)	389
Kathi PINTO ▶ 6186 (1)	**196**
Love You Like I Never Loved Before— John O'Banion (81)	588
Shelley PINZ ▶ 1081 (3)	**4082**
Green Tambourine—Lemon Pipers (67)	7211
Rice Is Nice—Lemon Pipers (68)	521
Jelly Jungle (Of Orange Marmalade)— Lemon Pipers (68)	431
Maxime PIOLOT ▶ 7542 (2)	**90**
Do I Love You—Paul Anka (71)	*446*
Do I Love You (Yes In Every Way)—Donna Fargo (78)	*2.7*
Chester PIPKIN ▶ 10192 (1)	**11**
This Is The Nite—Valiants (57)	45
Gary PIPKIN ▶ 7133 (1)	**114**
Puddin N' Tain (Ask Me Again I'll Tell You The Same)—Alley Cats (63)	343
—Pipou Pipokas see: Yves LACOMBLEZ	
Salvatore PIPPA ▶ 4013 (1)	**623**
Lonely Teenager—Dion (60)	1868
Donald PIPPIN ▶ 10805 (1)	**5.2**
Hold Me In Your Arms—Doris Day (54)	16
Steve PIPPIN ▶ 2930 (5)	**1114**
Better Love Next Time—Dr. Hook (79)	1340
This Time I'm In It For Love—Player (78)	1215
Don't Stop Me Baby (I'm On Fire)—Boys Band (82)	122
Holdin' On For Dear Love—Lobo (79)	74
Mary Anne—Fallenrock (75)	8.4
Joe PIROLLO ▶ 10356 (1)	**9.6**
Walk On With The Duke—Duke Of Earl (62)	86
Armond J. PIRON ▶ 4129 (1)	**585**
Shimmy Like Kate—Olympics (60)	585
Marco PIRRONI ▶ 2593 (4)	**1345**
Goody Two Shoes—Adam Ant (82)	1666
Room At The Top—Adam Ant (90)	808
Strip—Adam Ant (84)	350
Desperate But Not Serious—Adam Ant (83)	135
Eugene PISTILLI ▶ 2451 (7)	**1474**
Sunday Will Never Be The Same— Spanky And Our Gang (67)	1623
Medicine Man (Part 1)—Buchanan Brothers (69)	1162
Son Of A Lovin' Man—Buchanan Brothers (69)	336
But For Love—Jerry Naylor (70)	252
Sausalito—Al Martino (69)	231
Richard And Me—Gene & Tommy (67)	2.8
A Song That Never Comes—Mama Cass Elliot (70)	2.1
Dean PITCHFORD ▶ 190 (17)	**16314**
Footloose—Kenny Loggins (84)	6174
Let's Hear It For The Boy—Deniece Williams (84)	5139
All The Man That I Need—Whitney Houston (90)	4418
You Should Hear How She Talks About You— Melissa Manchester (82)	3680
Fame—Irene Cara (80)	3098
Make Me Lose Control—Eric Carmen (88)	2490
Almost Paradise...Love Theme From FOOTLOOSE— Mike Reno And Ann Wilson (84)	1939

After All (Love Theme From CHANCES ARE)— Cher and Peter Cetera (89)	1696
Dancing In The Sheets—Shalamar (84)	1023
Don't Fight It—Kenny Loggins with Steve Perry (82)	851
I'm Free (Heaven Helps The Man)— Kenny Loggins (84)	726
Birthday Suit—Johnny Kemp (89)	490
Holding Out For A Hero—Bonnie Tyler (84)	489
I Wanna Hear It From Your Lips—Eric Carmen (85)	384
Red Light—Linda Clifford (80)	288
Sing—Mickey Thomas (89)	37
One Sunny Day/Dueling Bikes From Quicksilver— Ray Parker Jr. (86)	4.3
Gene PITNEY [Anne Orlowski] ▶ 417 (12)	**9599**
He's A Rebel—Crystals (62)	*6361*
Hello Mary Lou—Ricky Nelson (61)	2471
Rubber Ball—Bobby Vee (60)	2133
(I Wanna) Love My Life Away—Gene Pitney (61)	*650*
Today's Teardrops—Rick Nelson (63)	261
Bandit Of My Dreams—Eddie Hodges (62)	185
Love My Life Away—Hagers (74)	*41*
Louisiana Mama—Gene Pitney (61)	11
Harmony—Billy Bland (60)	7.2
Blue Heartaches—Tommy Edwards (60)	2.5
Across The Street (Is A Million Miles Away)— Ray Peterson (65)	1.4
He's A Rebel—Vikki Carr (62)	*0.0*
Eugene PITT ▶ 3273 (2)	**916**
My True Story—Jive Five (61)	2624
Never, Never—Jive Five (61)	83
William P. PITT ▶ 10852 (1)	**4.9**
He's Not Just A Soldier—Little Richard (61)	9.9
Wayne PITTMAN ▶ 2122 (1)	**1846**
Girl Watcher—O'Kaysions (68)	3691
Clyde PITTS ▶ 11039 (1)	**3.7**
Even The Bad Times Are Good—Jerry Wallace (64)	7.3
—Donny Pitts see: Donny HATHAWAY	
Amos PIZZEY ▶ 3446 (1)	**845**
Wild, Wild West—Escape Club (88)	4224
Ray PIZZI ▶ 8154 (1)	**60**
Back Beat No. 1—Rondels (61)	240
Mary Kay PLACE ▶ 5618 (1)	**264**
Baby Boy—Mary Kay Place as Loretta Haggers (76)	264
Robert PLAISTED ▶ 6401 (1)	**175**
Happy Reindeer—Dancer, Prancer And Nervous (59)	350
Robert PLANT ▶ 910 (24)	**4854**
Whole Lotta Love—Led Zeppelin (69)	*4704*
Immigrant Song—Led Zeppelin (70)	1706
Black Dog—Led Zeppelin (71)	*1455*
D'yer Mak'er—Led Zeppelin (73)	1260
Big Log—Robert Plant (83)	830
Fool In The Rain—Led Zeppelin (79)	673
Tall Cool One—Robert Plant (88)	586
Over The Hills And Far Away—Led Zeppelin (73)	487
In The Mood—Robert Plant (83)	463
Trampled Under Foot—Led Zeppelin (75)	436
Little By Little—Robert Plant (85)	418
Rock And Roll—Led Zeppelin (72)	411
Hurting Kind (I've Got My Eyes On You)— Robert Plant (90)	248
Whole Lotta Love—C.C.S. (71)	*247*
Whole Lotta Love— King Curtis & The Kingpins (71)	*230*
Good Times Bad Times—Led Zeppelin (69)	160
Black Dog—Newcity Rockers (87)	*89*
Burning Down One Side—Robert Plant (82)	89
Puss N Boots—Kon Kan (89)	78
Livin' Lovin' Maid—Led Zeppelin (70)	58
Pledge Pin—Robert Plant (82)	54
Stairway To Heaven—Far Corporation (86)	38
Ship Of Fools—Robert Plant (88)	22
Whole Lotta Love—Wonder Band (79)	*8.7*
Richard PLEASANCE ▶ 10985 (1)	**4.0**
Talk About It—Boom Crash Opera (91)	20
David PLEHN ▶ 7457 (1)	**95**
Easy Driver—Kenny Loggins (78)	189
Jack PLEIS ▶ 10863 (1)	**4.8**
(But As They Say) That's Life— Jack Pleis And His Orchestra (57)	9.6
—Sal Pliny see: Sal GIGLIO Jr.	
—Henry Plischke see: Kent HENRY	

Kurt PLISNIER ▶ 7242 (1)	**108**
Live Is Life—Opus (86)	541
Neely PLUMB ▶ 8156 (1)	**60**
Paco Peco—Limeliters (61)	60
Howard PLUMMER ▶ 6394 (3)	**175**
Still—Fontane Sisters (56)	*204*
I Can't Love You Enough—LaVern Baker (56)	202
Still—LaVern Baker (56)	*12*
Steve PLUNKETT ▶ 5878 (2)	**234**
Turn Up The Radio—Autograph (84)	654
How Much Love—Vixen (90)	308
William PLUNKETT ▶ 5289 (1)	**313**
Velvet Waters—Megatrons (59)	313
Leon POBER ▶ 3576 (6)	**780**
Tiny Bubbles—Don Ho And The Aliis (66)	386
Evening Rain—Earl Grant (59)	307
Pearly Shells (Popo O Ewa)—Burl Ives (64)	*198*
Moonlight Mountain—Faron Young (61)	36
Moonlight Mountain—Faron Young (57)	5.7
Pearly Shells—Arthur Lyman (64)	*0.0*
John POCISK [Johnny Paris] ▶ 2594 (6)	**1343**
Red River Rock—Johnny And The Hurricanes (59)	3410
Beatnik Fly—Johnny And The Hurricanes (60)	1493
Reveille Rock—Johnny And The Hurricanes (59)	828
Rocking Goose—Johnny And The Hurricanes (60)	239
Midnight—Johnny Gibson (62)	80
Casanova Brown—Young Sisters (62)	3.6
Lee POCKRISS ▶ 114 (39)	**22271**
Itsy Bitsy Teenie Weenie Yellow Polkadot Bikini—Brian Hyland (60)	*7476*
Johnny Angel—Shelley Fabares (62)	7079
My Heart Is An Open Book—Carl Dobkins, Jr. (59)	5285
Playground In My Mind—Clint Holmes (73)	5118
Catch A Falling Star—Perry Como (57)	3980
Tracy—Cuff Links (69)	2946
(Seven Little Girls) Sitting In The Back Seat—Paul Evans and The Curls (59)	2385
In My Little Corner Of The World—Anita Bryant (60)	1752
What Is Love—Playmates (59)	1121
Leader Of The Laundromat—Detergents (64)	1105
Jimmy's Girl—Johnny Tillotson (61)	894
When Julie Comes Around—Cuff Links (69)	724
Starbright—Johnny Mathis (60)	700
Wait For Me—Playmates (60)	690
Little Miss Stuck-Up—Playmates (61)	392
(New In) The Ways Of Love—Tommy Edwards (59)	391
Run Sally Run—Cuff Links (70)	364
Tar And Cement—Verdelle Smith (66)	359
Kookie Little Paradise—Jo Ann Campbell (60)	*323*
Hot Pants—Salvage (71)	303
In My Room (El Amor)—Verdelle Smith (66)	234
No—Dodie Stevens (60)	202
Walk Tall—2 Of Clubs (66)	193
Kookie Little Paradise—Tree Swingers (60)	*157*
Go Chase A Moonbeam—Jerry Vale (58)	109
Double-O-Seven—Detergents (65)	108
The Cheer Leader—Paul Petersen (63)	99
There Won't Be Any Snow (Christmas In The Jungle)—Derrik Roberts (65)	89
It's Only The Good Times—Tommy Edwards (59)	71
(The Clickity Clack Song) Four Little Heels—Brian Hyland (60)	62
The Prettiest Girl In School—Randy Starr (58)	37
Big Daddy—Jill Corey (58)	30
Calcutta—Four Preps (61)	*23*
The Chick—Lee And Paul (59)	13
Shake Hands With A Fool—June Valli (58)	11
Oliver Cool—Oliver Cool (60)	6.5
Dommage, Dommage (Too Bad, Too Bad)—Jerry Vale (66)	*6.1*
Dommage, Dommage (Too Bad, Too Bad)—Paul Vance (66)	*3.7*
Itsy Bitsy Teenie Weenie Yellow Polkadot Bikini—Buddy Hackett (60)	*0.0*
Art PODELL ▶ 11593 (1)	**1.1**
Miss Katy Cruel—New Christy Minstrels (64)	3.2
Richard PODOLOR ▶ 2523 (6)	**1417**
Let There Be Drums—Sandy Nelson (61)	*2590*
Drummin' Up A Storm—Sandy Nelson (62)	79
...And Then There Were Drums—Sandy Nelson (62)	52
Drum Stomp—Sandy Nelson (62)	13
Stranger From Durango—Richie Allen (60)	8.8
Let There Be Drums—Incredible Bongo Band (73)	*4.3*
Coy POE ▶ 6480 (3)	**165**
What's The Reason I'm Not Pleasing You—Fats Domino (56)	*415*
What's The Reason—Bobby Edwards (62)	*225*
The Object Of My Affection—Pee Wee Hunt & His Orchestra (56)	15
—Clarence Albert Poindexter see: Al DEXTER	
Richard POINDEXTER ▶ 2820 (7)	**1170**
Thin Line Between Love And Hate—Persuaders (71)	*1568*
Hypnotized—Linda Jones (67)	1035
Love Gonna Pack Up (And Walk Out)—Persuaders (71)	443
Thin Line Between Love And Hate—Pretenders (84)	*29*
Give My Love A Try—Linda Jones (67)	21
Peace In The Valley Of Love—Persuaders (72)	12
Bad, Bold And Beautiful Girl—Persuaders (73)	0.4
Robert POINDEXTER ▶ 3614 (7)	**767**
Thin Line Between Love And Hate—Persuaders (71)	*1568*
I'll Be Sweeter Tomorrow (Than I Was Today)—O'Jays (67)	458
Love Gonna Pack Up (And Walk Out)—Persuaders (71)	443
Thin Line Between Love And Hate—Pretenders (84)	*29*
Give My Love A Try—Linda Jones (67)	21
Peace In The Valley Of Love—Persuaders (72)	12
Bad, Bold And Beautiful Girl—Persuaders (73)	0.4
Stan POINDEXTER ▶ 7131 (1)	**114**
I'll Be Sweeter Tomorrow (Than I Was Today)—O'Jays (67)	458
Anita POINTER ▶ 2562 (6)	**1382**
I'm So Excited '84—Pointer Sisters (84)	*1499*
How Long (Betcha' Got A Chick On The Side)—Pointer Sisters (75)	1309
Fairytale—Pointer Sisters (74)	973
I'm So Excited—Pointer Sisters (82)	*597*
Could I Be Dreaming—Pointer Sisters (80)	272
Live Your Life Before You Die—Pointer Sisters (75)	57
Bonnie POINTER [Patricia Eva Pointer] ▶ 3613 (3)	**767**
How Long (Betcha' Got A Chick On The Side)—Pointer Sisters (75)	1309
Fairytale—Pointer Sisters (74)	973
Live Your Life Before You Die—Pointer Sisters (75)	57
June POINTER ▶ 3561 (3)	**786**
I'm So Excited '84—Pointer Sisters (84)	*1499*
How Long (Betcha' Got A Chick On The Side)—Pointer Sisters (75)	1309
I'm So Excited—Pointer Sisters (82)	*597*
—Patricia Eva Pointer see: Bonnie POINTER	
Ruth POINTER ▶ 3562 (3)	**786**
I'm So Excited '84—Pointer Sisters (84)	*1499*
How Long (Betcha' Got A Chick On The Side)—Pointer Sisters (75)	1309
I'm So Excited—Pointer Sisters (82)	*597*
Danny POKU ▶ 1846 (3)	**2204**
C'mon And Get My Love—D Mob Introducing Cathy Dennis (89)	1437
Just Another Dream—Cathy Dennis (90)	1350
That's The Way Of The World—D Mob With Cathy Dennis (90)	184
Edward POLA [Eddie Pola, Sidney Edward Pollacsek] ▶ 3118 (2)	**1001**
Longest Walk—Jaye P. Morgan (55)	1916
This Is My Confession—Joni James (55)	86
Paul POLITI ▶ 2754 (5)	**1217**
Those Oldies But Goodies (Remind Me Of You)—Little Caesar And The Romans (61)	*2037*
It May Be Winter Outside (But In My Heart It's Spring)—Felice Taylor (67)	*308*
Under The Influence Of Love—Love Unlimited (74)	53
It May Be Winter Outside (But In My Heart It's Spring)—Love Unlimited (73)	*36*
Those Oldies But Goodies (Remind Me Of You)—Nino and the Ebb Tides (61)	*0.0*
Herscholt POLK ▶ 4273 (1)	**538**
Ain't Understanding Mellow—Jerry Butler And Brenda Lee Eager (71)	1077
Prentice Herman POLK Jr. ▶ 8604 (1)	**45**
Dearest—Mickey & Sylvia (57)	135
Peter POLL [Friedel Berlipp] ▶ 11409 (1)	**1.8**
Santo Domingo—Sandpipers (70)	5.5
Ben POLLACK ▶ 11448 (2)	**1.6**
Make Love To Me—Johnny Thunder & Ruby Winters (67)	*13*
Make Love To Me!—Jo Stafford (54)	*0.0*
Lew POLLACK [Louis Leazer] ▶ 3109 (5) HOF	**1005**
Diane—Bachelors (64)	*1826*
Diane—Joe Harnell And His Orchestra (63)	*86*
Charmaine—Four Freshmen (55)	*55*
Charmaine—Four Preps (63)	*27*
Charmaine—Bachelors (63)	*17*
—Sidney Edward Pollacsek see: Edward POLA	
Jeff POLLARD ▶ 7785 (1)	**75**
The Last Safe Place On Earth—Le Roux (82)	75
Channing POLLOCK ▶ 6800 (2)	**136**
My Man—Peggy Lee (59)	*340*
My Man—Barbra Streisand (65)	*204*
David POLLOCK ▶ 9098 (1)	**31**
I'm New At The Game Of Romance—Jane Morgan with the Troubadors (57)	62
Jeanne POLLOCK ▶ 11815 (1)	**0.0**
La Pachanga—Hugo & Luigi with their Children's Cho. (61)	*0.0*
Michel POLNAREFF ▶ 3649 (3)	**750**
Soul Coaxing (Ame Caline)—Raymond Lefevre And His Orchestra (68)	621
If You Only Believe (Jesus For Tonite)—Michel Polnareff (76)	175
Lipstick—Michel Polnareff (76)	70
—Lester William Polsfuss see: Les PAUL	
Sue POMERANTZ ▶ 8481 (1)	**49**
Show Me The Way—Regina Belle (87)	146
David POMERANZ ▶ 1796 (3)	**2308**
Tryin' To Get The Feeling Again—Barry Manilow (76)	1698
The Old Songs—Barry Manilow (81)	1046
Storybook Children (Daybreak)—Bette Midler (78)	174
George POMEROY ▶ 8588 (1)	**45**
Whiffenpoof Song—Bob Crewe (59)	136
Rudy POMPILLI ▶ 6105 (3)	**206**
Rudy's Rock—Bill Haley And His Comets (56)	314
Week End—Kingsmen (58)	102
Lean Jean—Bill Haley And His Comets (58)	58
Doc POMUS [Jerome Solon Felder, Jerome Pomus] ▶ 63 (73) HOF	**34552**
Save The Last Dance For Me—Drifters (60)	*8918*
Surrender—Elvis Presley With The Jordanaires (61)	8380
Can't Get Used To Losing You—Andy Williams (63)	6431
Suspicion—Terry Stafford (64)	4565
This Magic Moment—Jay & The Americans (68)	*3753*
A Teenager In Love—Dion and The Belmonts (59)	*3450*
She's Not You—Elvis Presley With The Jordanaires (62)	3394
Little Sister—Elvis Presley (61)	3379
Go Jimmy Go—Jimmy Clanton (59)	2546
Turn Me Loose—Fabian (59)	2176
Hound Dog Man—Fabian (59)	1730
Marie's The Name His Latest Flame—Elvis Presley (61)	1319
Hopeless—Andy Williams (63)	1311
I'll Save The Last Dance For You—Damita Jo (60)	1268
Young Blood—Coasters (57)	*1268*
Sweets For My Sweet—Drifters (61)	*1182*
Hushabye—Mystics (59)	*1163*
This Magic Moment—Drifters (60)	*1087*
I Count The Tears—Drifters (60)	913
Save The Last Dance For Me—Defranco Family Featuring Tony Defranco (74)	*886*
Viva Las Vegas—Elvis Presley With The Jordanaires (64)	799
Young Blood—Bad Company (76)	*795*
Wrong For Each Other—Andy Williams (64)	698
No One—Ray Charles With The Raeletts (63)	*684*
(If You Cry) True Love, True Love—Drifters (59)	652
I'm A Man—Fabian (58)	597
Spanish Lace—Gene McDaniels (62)	495
Plain Jane—Bobby Darin (59)	492
Let's Do The Freddie—Chubby Checker (65)	474
Kiss Me Quick—Elvis Presley With The Jordanaires (64)	450
Angel Face—James Darren (59)	443

Doc POMUS [Jerome Solon Felder, Jerome Pomus] ▶ 63 (73) HOF *Continued*	**34552**
Seven Day Weekend—Gary (U.S.) Bonds (62)	409
No One—Connie Francis (61)	*403*
Save The Last Dance For Me—Dolly Parton (83)	*379*
Hushabye—Jay & The Americans (69)	*368*
Havin' Fun—Dion (61)	329
Mess Of Blues—Elvis Presley With The Jordanaires (60)	287
(You Make Me Feel) So Good—McCoys (66)	259
Ecstasy—Ben E. King (62)	250
Lonely Winds—Drifters (60)	241
Your Other Love—Flamingos (60)	230
I Dig Girls—Bobby Rydell (59)	218
Sweets For My Sweet—Tony Orlando (79)	*198*
A Texan And A Girl From Mexico—Anita Bryant (61)	195
First Taste Of Love—Ben E. King (60)	173
Young Boy Blues—Ben E. King (61)	160
Room Full Of Tears—Drifters (61)	152
Yum Yum—Fontane Sisters (56)	139
It's A Lonely Town (Lonely Without You)—Gene McDaniels (63)	136
A Teenager In Love—Four Preps (61)	*130*
Petticoat White (Summer Sky Blue)—Bobby Vinton (66)	114
Two Fools—Frankie Avalon (59)	99
Hushabye—Robert John (72)	*79*
Young Blood—Bruce Willis (87)	*71*
Teenage Heartache—Ray Peterson (60)	46
White Bucks And Saddle Shoes—Bobby Pedrick, Jr. (58)	40
Strollin' In The Springtime—Fabian (60)	26
Hushabye—Beach Boys (64)	*25*
Night Rider—Elvis Presley With The Jordanaires (65)	23
I Feel That I've Known You Forever—Elvis Presley With The Jordanaires (65)	23
Here Comes The Night—Ben E. King (61)	17
Carrying That Load—Ray Charles (63)	10
This Magic Moment—Richie Furay (78)	*8.2*
Wait—Jimmy Clanton (60)	7.3
Heart Of Gold—Twins (60)	6.8
No One—Brenda Lee (65)	*4.2*
Sweets For My Sweet—Central Park West (69)	*3.9*
Boogie Woogie Country Girl—Southwind (70)	3.1
Where Have They Gone—Jimmie Beaumont And The Skyliners (75)	2.5
(It's A) Long Lonely Highway—Elvis Presley (65)	2.4
Bimini Bimbo (Doin' The Limbo)—Teddy And The Twilights (62)	1.4
I Need Somebody To Lean On—Elvis Presley (64)	1.1
I Ain't Sharin' Sharon—Buddy Knox (59)	0.4
Vini PONCIA ▶ 722 (15)	**6066**
You Make Me Feel Like Dancing—Leo Sayer (76)	5541
Oh My My—Ringo Starr (74)	2014
I Was Made For Lovin' You—Kiss (79)	1971
Just Too Many People—Melissa Manchester (75)	632
New York's A Lonely Town—Trade Winds (65)	551
Do I Love You?—Ronettes (64)	*462*
(The Best Part Of) Breakin' Up—Ronettes (64)	369
Mind Excursion—Trade Winds (66)	367
Sure Know Something—Kiss (79)	365
Bad Misunderstanding—Critters (66)	321
Shandi—Kiss (80)	273
Mister Lonely—Videls (60)	152
Do I Love You?—Magic Ring (68)	*56*
Now That Summer Is Here—Videls (60)	13
Oo-Wee—Ringo Starr (75)	0.0
John PONDEL ▶ 10126 (1)	**12**
Take Away—Big Ric (83)	37
Robert PONGER ▶ 3261 (2)	**922**
Der Kommissar—After The Fire (83)	*2710*
Der Kommissar (The Commissioner)—Falco (83)	*38*
Jim PONS ▶ 3732 (4)	**717**
Elenore—Turtles (68)	2721
Sound Asleep—Turtles (68)	382
You Don't Have To Walk In The Rain—Turtles (69)	301
Love In The City—Turtles (69)	183
Jack PONTI [Giacomo Pontoriero] ▶ 7841 (2)	**72**
Follow You—Glen Burtnick (87)	121
Hey Stoopid—Alice Cooper (91)	48
Sal PONTI ▶ 7969 (1)	**67**
What Little Girl—Frankie Avalon (58)	134
—Giacomo Pontoriero see: Jack PONTI	

Frank POOLER ▶ 9246 (1)	**28**
Merry Christmas Darling—Carpenters (70)	56
Iggy POP [James Newell Osterberg Jr.] ▶ 2516 (3)	**1424**
China Girl—David Bowie (83)	1598
Candy—Iggy Pop (90)	490
Tonight—David Bowie (84)	269
Carole POPE ▶ 7842 (1)	**72**
All Touch—Rough Trade (82)	145
Greg POPOFF ▶ 7737 (1)	**77**
Flamingo Express—Royaltones (60)	231
Mike POPOFF ▶ 7738 (1)	**77**
Flamingo Express—Royaltones (60)	231
André POPP ▶ 290 (10)	**12280**
Love Is Blue (L'Amour Est Bleu)—Paul Mauriat And His Orchestra (67)	*11159*
The Portuguese Washerwomen—Joe "Fingers" Carr (56)	*791*
Love Is Blue—Dells (69)	*524*
Love Is Blue (L'Amour Est Bleu)—Al Martino (68)	*302*
Love Is Blue (L'Amour Est Bleu)—Claudine Longet (68)	*75*
Song For Anna (Chanson D'Anna)—Herb Ohta (74)	14
Love Is Blue (L'Amour Est Bleu)—Manny Kellem, His Orchestra And Voices (68)	*2.7*
The Portuguese Washerwomen—Baja Marimba Band (66)	*1.9*
Portuguese Washerwomen—Joe Sherman, his Orchestra and Chorus (56)	*0.0*
The Portuguese Washerwomen (Les Lavandieres Du Portugal)—Jacqueline François with Michel Legrand & His Orchestra (56)	*0.0*
Jeff PORCARO ▶ 1739 (3)	**2390**
Africa—Toto (82)	4097
Stranger In Town—Toto (84)	580
Holyanna—Toto (85)	104
Steve PORCARO ▶ 3623 (1)	**762**
Human Nature—Michael Jackson (83)	1523
Anita POREE ▶ 806 (8)	**5496**
Keep On Truckin' (Part 1)—Eddie Kendricks (73)	5698
Boogie Down—Eddie Kendricks (73)	4614
Love Or Let Me Be Lonely—Friends Of Distinction (70)	*2597*
Going In Circles—Friends Of Distinction (69)	1646
Son Of Sagittarius—Eddie Kendricks (74)	630
Love Or Let Me Be Lonely—Paul Davis (82)	*351*
Eddie's Love—Eddie Kendricks (72)	71
Girl You Need A Change Of Mind (Part 1)—Eddie Kendricks (73)	16
Otilio PORTAL ▶ 3862 (4)	**673**
Sweet And Gentle—Alan Dale (55)	*1346*
Sweet And Gentle—Georgia Gibbs (55)	*0.0*
Sweet And Gentle (Me Lo Dijo Adela)—Eartha Kitt & Perez Prado (55)	*0.0*
Sweet And Gentle (Me Lo Dijo Adela)—Merv Griffin & Xavier Cugat (55)	*0.0*
Raul PORTELA ▶ 1623 (4)	**2602**
Lisbon Antigua—Nelson Riddle And His Orchestra (55)	*7507*
Lisbon Antigua (In Old Lisbon)—Mitch Miller & His Orchestra (56)	*298*
Lisbon Antigua (In Old Lisbon)—Alan Dale (55)	*0.0*
Lisbon Antigua—Lawrence Welk & His Champagne Music (56)	*0.0*
Andrew PORTER ▶ 4928 (1)	**379**
You're A Special Part Of Me—Diana Ross & Marvin Gaye (73)	1138
B.L. PORTER ▶ 6259 (3)	**188**
Bobby—Neil Scott (61)	324
The Secret—Clint Ballard Jr. (61)	19
I Can't Do It By Myself—Anita Bryant (61)	14
—Coe Porter see: Thomas J. COE	
Cole PORTER ▶ 365 (29) HOF	**10538**
True Love—Bing Crosby and Grace Kelly (56)	*5139*
I've Got You Under My Skin—4 Seasons Featuring The "Sound" Of Frankie Valli (66)	*1865*
True Love—Jane Powell (56)	*939*
Love For Sale—Arthur Lyman Group (63)	477
Anything Goes—Harpers Bizarre (67)	456
In The Still Of The Night—Dion And The Belmonts (60)	425

Don't Fence Me In—Tommy Edwards (60)	*292*
You're Sensational—Frank Sinatra (56)	*239*
Silk Stockings—Perry Como (54)	*223*
All Of You—Tony Martin (55)	*202*
Ca C'est L'Amour—Tony Bennett with Neal Hefti and his Orch. (57)	*196*
I've Got You Under My Skin—Louis Prima And Keely Smith (59)	*116*
Night And Day—Sergio Mendes & Brasil '66 (67)	*46*
Now You Has Jazz—Bing Crosby and Louis Armstrong (56)	25
All Of You—Sammy Davis Jr. (55)	*23*
Don't Fence Me In—George Maharis (63)	*6.3*
Night And Day—Louis Prima And Keely Smith (59)	*5.5*
Well Did You Evah—Bing Crosby (56)	5.1
I've Got You Under My Skin—Gidea Park (81)	*3.7*
I'm In Love Again—Deb-Tones (59)	3.2
True Love—Richard Chamberlain (63)	*1.3*
All Of You—Mel Torme (55)	*0.0*
Silk Stockings—Vic Damone (54)	*0.0*
True Love—Margaret Whiting (56)	*0.0*
Ca C'est L'Amour—Tina Robin (57)	*0.0*
You're Sensational—Nick Noble (56)	*0.0*
You're Sensational—Sammy Davis Jr. (56)	*0.0*
Silk Stockings—Fred Waring's Pennsylvanians (54)	*0.0*
Ca C'est L'Amour—Freddy Martin & His Orchestra (57)	*0.0*
David PORTER ▶ 432 (35) HOF	**9436**
Soul Man—Sam & Dave (67)	*6911*
I Thank You—Sam & Dave (68)	*1993*
B-A-B-Y—Carla Thomas (66)	1648
Soul Man—Blues Brothers (78)	*1370*
Hold On! I'm A Comin'—Sam & Dave (66)	*1302*
Your Good Thing (Is About To End)—Lou Rawls (69)	*1274*
When Something Is Wrong With My Baby—Sam & Dave (67)	*545*
Show Me How—Emotions (71)	508
Soul Sister, Brown Sugar—Sam & Dave (68)	501
I Thank You—ZZ Top (80)	*446*
Wrap It Up—Fabulous Thunderbirds (86)	*313*
You Got Me Hummin—Cold Blood (70)	*299*
I Take What I Want—James & Bobby Purify (67)	279
You Got Me Hummin'—Sam & Dave (66)	*235*
The Sweeter He Is Part I—Soul Children (69)	232
Soul Man—Ramsey Lewis (67)	*207*
Something Good (Is Going To Happen To You)—Carla Thomas (67)	156
Let Me Be Good To You—Carla Thomas (66)	119
Said I Wasn't Gonna Tell Nobody—Sam & Dave (66)	118
Give Everybody Some—Bar-Kays (67)	97
Hold On I'm Coming—Chuck Jackson & Maxine Brown (67)	*90*
Born Again—Sam & Dave (69)	70
You've Got Me Hummin'—Hassles (67)	*64*
Everybody Got To Believe In Somebody—Sam & Dave (68)	60
When Something Is Wrong With My Baby—Linda Ronstadt (featuring Aaron Neville) (90)	*57*
Your Good Thing (Is About To End)—Mable John (66)	*57*
You Don't Know Like I Know—Sam & Dave (66)	44
When Something Is Wrong With My Baby—Otis & Carla (69)	*26*
Wrap It Up—Archie Bell & The Drells (70)	*25*
Baby-Baby Don't Stop Now—Sam & Dave (70)	14
How Do You Quit (Someone You Love)—Carla Thomas (65)	13
How Can You Mistreat The One You Love—Jean & The Darlings (67)	2.4
When Tomorrow Comes—Carla Thomas (67)	1.0
A Dime A Dozen—Carla Thomas (68)	0.9
Stealing Love—Emotions (70)	0.4
Garth PORTER ▶ 7483 (2)	**93**
Howzat—Sherbet (76)	149
I Have The Skill—Sherbs (81)	55
George PORTER ▶ 4210 (7)	**562**
Cissy Strut—Meters (69)	731
Sophisticated Cissy—Meters (69)	475
Chicken Strut—Meters (70)	361
Look-Ka Py Py—Meters (69)	346
Ease Back—Meters (69)	213
Hand Clapping Song—Meters (70)	94
Be My Lady—Meters (77)	36

Jake PORTER ▶ 2461 (5)	**1463**
Ko Ko Mo (I Love You So)—Perry Como (55)	*3070*
Ko Ko Mo (I Love You So)—Crew-Cuts (55)	*1319*
Ko Ko Mo—Dooley Sisters (55)	*0.0*
Ko Ko Mo (I Love You So)—Hutton Sisters (55)	*0.0*
Ko Ko Mo (I Love You So)— Bill Darnel & Betty Clooney (55)	*0.0*
Kerry PORTER ▶ 7151 (1)	**113**
Cryin' In The Streets (Part I)— George Perkins & The Silver Stars (70)	340
Lee PORTER ▶ 8326 (3)	**54**
He's A Lover—Mary Wells (65)	104
Handful Of Memories—Baby Washington (62)	3.6
Not For All The Money In The World—Shirelles (63)	0.4
Nolan PORTER ▶ 6068 (3)	**209**
I Like What You Give—Nolan (71)	201
If I Could Only Be Sure—Nolan Porter (73)	9.5
Funky L.A.— Paul Humphrey & His Cool Aid Chemists (71)	3.3
Gary PORTNOY ▶ 9652 (1)	**20**
Theme from the TV Show Cheers (Where Everybody Knows Your Name)—Gary Portnoy (83)	39
Charles PORTZ ▶ 9271 (1)	**27**
Grim Reaper Of Love—Turtles (66)	55
W. Albert POSER [Thomas Marlowe] ▶ 8012 (1)	**65**
Don't Cry My Love (The Faithful Hussar)— Vera Lynn (57)	*196*
Art POSEY ▶ 6710 (2)	**142**
I'm So Glad I Fell For You—David Ruffin (69)	277
(Let's Go) All The Way—Whispers (78)	24
—Gary Posie see: David LAFLAMME	
Bill POST ▶ 2100 (3)	**1881**
Sixteen Reasons—Connie Stevens (60)	*3679*
Sixteen Reasons—Laverne & Shirley (76)	*84*
Rawhide—Bill & Doree Post (59)	0.0
Doree POST ▶ 2101 (3)	**1881**
Sixteen Reasons—Connie Stevens (60)	*3679*
Sixteen Reasons—Laverne & Shirley (76)	*84*
Rawhide—Bill & Doree Post (59)	0.0
Jim POST ▶ 1507 (2)	**2848**
Reach Out Of The Darkness—Friend And Lover (68)	2689
If Love Is In Your Heart—Friend And Lover (68)	159
Mike POST [Michael Postil] ▶ 850 (5)	**5210**
The Theme From "The Greatest American Hero" (Believe It Or Not)—Joey Scarbury (81)	5521
The Rockford Files—Mike Post (75)	1507
The Theme From Hill Street Blues—Mike Post (81)	1335
Theme From Magnum P.I.—Mike Post (82)	718
Theme From "Baa Baa Black Sheep"— Mike Post (77)	3.3
—Michael Postil see: Mike POST	
Brian POTTER ▶ 268 (40)	**12708**
Don't Pull Your Love— Hamilton, Joe Frank & Reynolds (71)	*4833*
Ain't No Woman (Like The One I've Got)— Four Tops (73)	3986
It Only Takes A Minute—Tavares (75)	1975
Keeper Of The Castle—Four Tops (72)	1655
Two Divided By Love—Grass Roots (71)	1531
Country Boy (You Got Your Feet In L.A.)— Glen Campbell (75)	1187
Are You Man Enough—Four Tops (73)	1185
Look In My Eyes Pretty Woman— Tony Orlando And Dawn (74)	930
One Tin Soldier The Legend Of Billy Jack— Coven (71)	*917*
This Heart—Gene Redding (74)	878
One Tin Soldier—Original Caste (69)	*801*
Remember What I Told You To Forget—Tavares (75)	694
It's A Cryin' Shame—Gayle McCormick (71)	608
Daisy Mae—Hamilton, Joe Frank & Reynolds (71)	605
The Runway—Grass Roots (72)	555
Give It To The People—Righteous Brothers (74)	537
Dream On—Righteous Brothers (74)	479
One Chain Don't Make No Prison—Four Tops (74)	*371*
Ashes To Ashes—5th Dimension (73)	307
I Just Can't Get You Out Of My Mind—Four Tops (74)	288
You Brought The Woman Out Of Me—Evie Sands (75)	*254*
Don't Pull Your Love—Glen Campbell (76)	*228*
Too Late—Tavares (74)	193

One Tin Soldier (The Legend Of Billy Jack)— Coven (73)	*143*
If You Wanna Get Back Your Lady— Pointer Sisters (83)	137
Love Music—Raiders (73)	*131*
One Chain (Don't Make No Prison)—Santana (79)	*117*
One Tin Soldier The Legend Of Billy Jack— Coven (73)	*111*
Put A Little Love Away—Emotions (74)	91
Gonna Be Alright Now—Gayle McCormick (71)	65
You Brought The Woman Out Of Me—Hot (78)	*52*
Once A Fool—Kiki Dee (76)	37
To Love You—Country Store (70)	16
Don't Pull Your Love—Sam & Dave (71)	*11*
The House On Telegraph Hill— Bo Donaldson And The Heywoods (75)	7.0
Who Gets Your Love—Dusty Springfield (73)	6.5
If That's The Way You Want It—Diamond Head (73)	2.2
One Good Woman— Hamilton, Joe Frank & Reynolds (72)	1.6
Love Music—Sergio Mendes & Brasil '77 (73)	*0.7*
My Ship—Tavares (75)	0.0
Duane POTTER ▶ 11604 (1)	**1.0**
Granny's Pad—Viceroys (63)	5.1
Greg POTTS ▶ 3964 (1)	**637**
Digital Display—Ready For The World (85)	637
Wardell POTTS ▶ 6494 (3)	**163**
Second Chance—Tyler Collins (90)	213
Show Me The Way—Regina Belle (87)	146
What's It Gonna Be—Jellybean (91)	16
Bryan POTVIN ▶ 7987 (1)	**66**
She Ain't Pretty—Northern Pikes (91)	66
Emma POUGHT ▶ 4356 (2)	**514**
Mr Lee—Bobbettes (57)	*2273*
I Shot Mr Lee—Bobbettes (60)	*297*
Jannie POUGHT ▶ 4357 (2)	**514**
Mr Lee—Bobbettes (57)	*2273*
I Shot Mr Lee—Bobbettes (60)	*297*
George R. POULTON ▶ 1411 (4)	**3143**
Love Me Tender—Elvis Presley (56)	*8241*
Love Me Tender—Richard Chamberlain (62)	*673*
Love Me Tender—Percy Sledge (67)	*405*
Love Me Tender—Henri René (56)	*108*
Raymond POUNDS ▶ 8529 (1)	**47**
Eenie Meenie—Jeffrey Osborne (83)	94
Franck POURCEL [J. W. Stole] ▶ 1881 (1)	**2165**
I Will Follow Him—Little Peggy March (63)	8660
Archie POWELL ▶ 3048 (2)	**1037**
5-10-15-20 (25-30 Years Of Love)—Presidents (70)	2074
That's How Long—Chi-Lites (75)	0.0
—Clive Powell see: Georgie FAME	
Don POWELL ▶ 3552 (1)	**787**
Make It Real—Jets (88)	2361
Eddie POWELL ▶ 9739 (2)	**18**
Teacher—Falcons (60)	25
You're Mine—Falcons (59)	11
Josef POWELL ▶ 10968 (1)	**4.0**
(Let's Go) All The Way—Whispers (78)	24
Lester POWELL [Chris Armstrong, Raymond Stuart Martin, Marshall Ross] ▶ 7298 (1)	**104**
You Are My First Love—Nat "King" Cole (57)	209
Michael POWELL ▶ 7256 (1)	**107**
Talk To Me—Anita Baker (90)	321
Roger POWELL ▶ 6305 (3)	**184**
Set Me Free—Utopia (80)	641
The Very Last Time—Utopia (80)	51
Feet Don't Fail Me Now—Utopia (83)	42
Teddy POWELL [Freddy James, Marguerite James, Teodoro Paoletta] ▶ 1822 (18)	**2260**
Unchain My Heart— Ray Charles And His Orchestra (61)	*1906*
Don't Set Me Free—Ray Charles And His Orchestra With The Raelettes (63)	713
Unsuspecting Heart—Terri Stevens (54)	*610*
D A R L I N'—Hilltoppers (55)	479
Over The Weekend—Playboys (58)	302
Bewildered—Mickey & Sylvia (58)	*205*
Bewildered— James Brown And The Famous Flames (61)	*187*
Whose Heart Are You Breaking Now— Johnny Love (58)	142

Walk With Faith In Your Heart—Johnny Nash (59)	*121*
Unsuspecting Heart—Sunny Gale (54)	*120*
Unchain My Heart—Herbie Mann (68)	*73*
One Love, One Heart—Four Coins (59)	62
Lonely Lips—Chordettes (55)	58
Walk With Faith In Your Heart—Bachelors (66)	*34*
Teen Ager's Waltz— Eddy Howard And His Orchestra (55)	17
Frivolette—Hilltoppers (55)	16
Hot And Cold Running Tears—Sarah Vaughan (56)	5.6
Unsuspecting Heart—Georgie Shaw (54)	*0.0*
Chet POWERS [Jesse Oris Farrow, Chester William Powers Jr., Dino Valenti] ▶ 899 (5)	**4922**
Get Together—Youngbloods (69)	*3851*
Let's Get Together—We Five (65)	*514*
Fresh Air—Quicksilver Messenger Service (70)	320
Get Together—Youngbloods (67)	*236*
What About Me—Quicksilver Messenger Service (71)	0.8
Tom POWERS ▶ 7650 (2)	**83**
Summer Sun—Jamestown Massacre (72)	73
It Ain't Love—Tom Powers (77)	9.8
Tony POWERS [Howard Stanley Puris] ▶ 1390 (13)	**3195**
98.6—Keith (66)	2675
Lazy Day—Spanky And Our Gang (67)	1247
Remember Then—Earls (62)	822
Ain't Gonna Lie—Keith (66)	601
Why Do Lovers Break Each Other's Heart?— Bob B. Soxx And The Blue Jeans (63)	584
(Today I Met) The Boy I'm Gonna Marry— Darlene Love (63)	432
He's Got The Power—Exciters (63)	261
Come Dance With Me—Jay & The Americans (63)	142
All Of My Life—Lesley Gore (65)	121
Gotta Have Your Love—Sapphires (65)	45
Run To My Lovin' Arms—Lenny Welch (65)	38
This Is It—Jay & The Americans (62)	29
One Boy Too Late—Mike Clifford (63)	5.2
Chano POZO [Luciano Gonzales] ▶ 8782 (1)	**39**
Soul Sauce (Guacha Guaro)—Cal Tjader (65)	79
Miguel PRADO ▶ 8355 (1)	**53**
Time Was—Flamingos (61)	160
Perez PRADO ▶ 462 (10)	**9047**
Patricia—Perez Prado And His Orchestra (58)	*8711*
Seven Eleven—Gone All Stars (58)	*139*
Patricia - Twist— Perez Prado And His Orchestra (62)	*80*
Marilyn Monroe Mambo— Perez Prado And His Orchestra (54)	75
Millionaire—Perez Prado And His Orchestra (59)	39
Paris—Perez Prado And His Orchestra (58)	2.3
Patricia—Jerry Martin (58)	*0.0*
Patricia—Ray Peterson (58)	*0.0*
Patricia—Morty Craft & His Orchestra (58)	*0.0*
7-11 (Mambo #5)—Dick Jacobs & His Orchestra (58)	*0.0*
Stephan PRAGER [Michael Kunze] ▶ 755 (7)	**5809**
Fly, Robin, Fly—Silver Convention (75)	*5615*
Get Up And Boogie (That's Right)— Silver Convention (76)	5492
Lady Bump—Penny McLean (76)	*216*
No, No, Joe—Silver Convention (76)	96
Lady Bump—Ritchie Family (76)	*92*
Fly, Robin, Fly—Ritchie Family (76)	*92*
Save Me—Silver Convention (75)	14
Andy PRATT ▶ 5917 (2)	**229**
Avenging Annie—Andy Pratt (73)	*189*
Avenging Annie—Roger Daltrey (77)	*40*
Bill PRATT ▶ 10707 (1)	**6.0**
Free—Fresh Start (74)	18
Guy PRATT ▶ 7571 (1)	**88**
You're Amazing—Robert Palmer (90)	439
—Harry Pratt see: Harvey FUQUA	
Michael PRATT ▶ 7621 (1)	**85**
Suddenly—Nicky DeMatteo (60)	85
Tom PRAY ▶ 11565 (1)	**1.2**
Place In The Sun—Johnny Nash (60)	4.8
—P. Red see: Willie PERRYMAN	
Lili PREMILOVICH [Lene Lovich, Lili Marlene Premilovich] ▶ 10391 (1)	**9.0**
Supernature—Cerrone (78)	27
—John Barry Prendergast see: John BARRY	

—Michael John Prendergast see: Mike PENDER	
Elvis PRESLEY ▶ 159 (20)	**18585**
Don't Be Cruel—Elvis Presley (56)	*10167*
Heartbreak Hotel—Elvis Presley (56)	*9660*
All Shook Up—Elvis Presley (57)	*9084*
Love Me Tender—Elvis Presley (56)	*8241*
Don't Be Cruel—Bill Black's Combo (60)	*2335*
Don't Be Cruel—Cheap Trick (88)	*2074*
Love Me Tender—Richard Chamberlain (62)	*673*
Love Me Tender—Percy Sledge (67)	*405*
Heartbreak Hotel—Frijid Pink (70)	*236*
Poor Boy—Elvis Presley (56)	183
All Shook Up—Suzi Quatro (74)	*154*
Love Me Tender—Henri René (56)	*108*
All Shook Up—Jive Bunny And The Mastermixers (89)	*80*
Don't Be Cruel—Barbara Lynn (63)	*74*
Paralyzed—Elvis Presley (56)	62
Heartbreak Hotel—Roger Miller (66)	*53*
Don't Be Cruel (To A Heart That's True)—Elvis Presley (82)	*23*
Heartbreak Hotel—Stan Freberg (56)	*17*
That's Someone You Never Forget—Elvis Presley With The Jordanaires (67)	4.3
Only Believe—Elvis Presley (71)	0.0
Reg PRESLEY [Reginald Maurice Ball] ▶ 1372 (4)	**3244**
Love Is All Around—Troggs (68)	2268
With A Girl Like You—Troggs (66)	576
I Can't Control Myself—Troggs (66)	383
You Can Cry If You Want To—Troggs (68)	18
Eric PRESSLY ▶ 5452 (1)	**287**
I Can't Wait—Stevie Nicks (86)	860
Billy PRESTON ▶ 285 (13)	**12402**
Will It Go Round In Circles—Billy Preston (73)	5175
Nothing From Nothing—Billy Preston (74)	5114
Outa-Space—Billy Preston (72)	4684
Space Race—Billy Preston (73)	2646
You Are So Beautiful—Joe Cocker (75)	*2189*
Struttin'—Billy Preston (74)	553
Slaughter—Billy Preston (72)	412
You're So Unique—Billy Preston (73)	405
That's The Way God Planned It—Billy Preston (69)	*193*
That's The Way God Planned It—Billy Preston (72)	*124*
Fancy Lady—Billy Preston (75)	60
I Wrote A Simple Song—Billy Preston (72)	59
You Are So Beautiful—Billy Preston (74)	*0.0*
Johnny PRESTON [John Preston Courville] ▶ 6177 (1)	**197**
Charming Billy—Johnny Preston (60)	197
Greg PRESTOPINO ▶ 1991 (4)	**2025**
Break My Stride—Matthew Wilder (83)	3738
Wild Women Do—Natalie Cole (90)	292
What Love Is—Marty Balin (83)	90
Up Your Nose—Gabriel Kaplan (77)	39
Stephen PRESTVICH ▶ 9110 (1)	**31**
Playing To Win—LRB (85)	217
Hugh PRESTWOOD ▶ 6520 (2)	**160**
Hard Times For Lovers—Judy Collins (79)	131
The Sound Of Goodbye—Crystal Gayle (83)	30
Rob PREUSS ▶ 10779 (1)	**5.3**
Love Changes Everything—Honeymoon Suite (88)	16
Anne PREVEN ▶ 8288 (2)	**55**
I Found Love—Party (90)	47
What's It Gonna Be—Jellybean (91)	16
Jacques PREVERT ▶ 7982 (4)	**66**
Autumn Leaves—Mitch Miller & His Orchestra (55)	*162*
Autumn Leaves—Ray Charles Singers (55)	*37*
Autumn Leaves—Keely Smith (57)	*0.0*
Autumn Leaves—Bette McLaurin with Ray Ellis' Orch. And Chorus (57)	*0.0*
André PREVIN [Andreas Ludwig Priwin] ▶ 1291 (4)	**3447**
(Theme From) Valley Of The Dolls—Dionne Warwick (68)	*5758*
Like Young—Andre Previn & David Rose (59)	553
Valley Of The Dolls—King Curtis & The Kingpins (68)	*8.8*
Look Again—Roger Williams (63)	6.7

Dory PREVIN [Dorothy Veronica Langan, Dory Langdon, Dory V. Shannon Previn] ▶ 1254 (2)	**3562**
(Theme From) Valley Of The Dolls—Dionne Warwick (68)	*5758*
Come Saturday Morning—Sandpipers (69)	1366
Franke PREVITE ▶ 1199 (5)	**3707**
(I've Had) The Time Of My Life—Bill Medley And Jennifer Warnes (87)	3918
Hungry Eyes—Eric Carmen (87)	2638
Sweetheart—Franke & The Knockouts (81)	1388
Without You (Not Another Lonely Night)—Franke & the Knockouts (82)	684
You're My Girl—Franke and the Knockouts (81)	478
Ronald PREYER ▶ 10257 (1)	**11**
I've Got Love For My Baby—Young Hearts (68)	43
Alan PRICE ▶ 4589 (1)	**460**
I'm Crying—Animals (64)	920
Chilton PRICE [Chilton Searcy] ▶ 3846 (4)	**679**
You Belong To Me—Duprees (62)	*1989*
You Belong To Me—100 Strings & Joni (60)	*46*
All Night Long—Jo Stafford (56)	0.7
Please Driver (Once Around The Park Again)—Tony Bennett (54)	0.0
Chris PRICE ▶ 7595 (1)	**87**
That Lovin' You Feelin' Again—Roy Orbison & Emmylou Harris (80)	173
Dock PRICE ▶ 5339 (1)	**303**
Your Time To Cry—Joe Simon (70)	909
Harvey PRICE [Michael Price] ▶ 1442 (16)	**3030**
Temptation Eyes—Grass Roots (70)	1969
Heaven Knows—Grass Roots (69)	1417
Glory Bound—Grass Roots (72)	745
Baby Hold On—Grass Roots (70)	728
Love Is What You Make It—Grass Roots (73)	477
Love Pains—Yvonne Elliman (79)	404
Indestructible—Four Tops (88)	359
The Heartbreak Kid—Bo Donaldson And The Heywoods (74)	198
The Morning Of Our Lives—Arkade (71)	185
Save The Night For Me—Maureen Steele (85)	68
My Blue Angel—Michael Learns To Rock (91)	49
I Wouldn't Treat A Dog (The Way You Treated Me)—Bobby Bland (74)	39
Ain't No Love In The Heart Of The City—Bobby Bland (74)	35
Where There's Smoke There's Fire—Grass Roots (73)	16
Deeper And Deeper—Bo Donaldson And The Heywoods (74)	4.6
Sing Out The Love (In My Heart)—Arkade (70)	0.8
Jim PRICE ▶ 10768 (1)	**5.5**
I Can Stand A Little Rain—Joe Cocker (74)	5.5
Leo PRICE ▶ 4021 (2)	**622**
Send Me Some Lovin'—Sam Cooke (63)	*1153*
Send Me Some Lovin' (Peepin' and Hidin')—Little Richard (57)	*90*
Lloyd PRICE ▶ 247 (26)	**14016**
Stagger Lee—Lloyd Price (58)	*7844*
Personality—Lloyd Price (59)	*7779*
I'm Gonna Get Married—Lloyd Price (59)	4720
Lady Luck—Lloyd Price And His Orchestra (60)	1501
Come Into My Heart—Lloyd Price (59)	1300
Stagger Lee—Tommy Roe (71)	*1051*
Where Were You (On Our Wedding Day)?—Lloyd Price (59)	933
Just Because—Lloyd Price (57)	*889*
Question—Lloyd Price And His Orchestra (60)	887
Stag-O-Lee—Wilson Pickett (67)	*785*
Wont'Cha Come Home—Lloyd Price (59)	615
Laudy Miss Claudy—Buckinghams (67)	*435*
No If's No And's—Lloyd Price And His Orchestra (60)	337
For Love—Lloyd Price And His Orchestra (60)	335
(You Better) Know What You're Doin'—Lloyd Price And His Orchestra (60)	180
Lawdy Miss Clawdy—Gary Stites (60)	*164*
Just Call Me (And I'll Understand)—Lloyd Price And His Orchestra (60)	137
(You've Got) Personality—Mitch Ryder (68)	*83*
(Boo Hoo) I'm Gonna Cry—Lloyd Price (61)	51
Three Little Pigs—Lloyd Price (59)	31
Billie Baby—Lloyd Price (64)	26

Who Coulda' Told You (They Lied)—Lloyd Price (60)	6.1
Lonely Chair—Lloyd Price (57)	4.2
Trying To Slip (Away)—Lloyd Price (73)	3.7
Mary And Man-O—Lloyd Price And His Great Orchestra (61)	1.5
Just Because—Larry Williams (57)	*0.0*
—Michael Price see: Harvey PRICE	
Ray PRICE ▶ 9502 (1)	**22**
I'm Tired—Ray Peterson (61)	67
Roderick PRICE ▶ 5074 (3)	**348**
Drivin' Wheel—Foghat (76)	544
I'll Be Standing By—Foghat (77)	59
What A Shame—Foghat (73)	47
—Ronald K. Price see: Ronn PRICE	
Ronn PRICE [Ronald K. Price] ▶ 6786 (1)	**137**
Where Will Your Heart Take You—Buckeye (79)	137
Vaughn PRICE ▶ 10511 (1)	**7.7**
You're Gonna Make It—Festivals (70)	23
Willard PRICE ▶ 8891 (1)	**37**
Come To Me—Aretha Franklin (81)	37
Woody PRICE ▶ 10512 (1)	**7.7**
You're Gonna Make It—Festivals (70)	23
—Gertrude Pridgett see: Ma RAINEY	
Hartmut PRIESS ▶ 8766 (1)	**40**
Silly Milly—Blue Swede (74)	120
Maxi PRIEST [Max Elliott] ▶ 2800 (2)	**1188**
Close To You—Maxi Priest (90)	3399
Housecall—Shabba Ranks (91)	329
Stephen PRIEST ▶ 3055 (4)	**1033**
Fox On The Run—Sweet (75)	2954
Action—Sweet (76)	1094
California Nights—Sweet (78)	63
Funk It Up (David's Song)—Sweet (77)	20
Joaquin PRIETO ▶ 3130 (2)	**994**
The Wedding—Julie Rogers (64)	1833
In My Room (El Amor)—Verdelle Smith (66)	234
Gary PRIM ▶ 7386 (2)	**99**
Congratulations—Vesta (89)	214
Reservations For Two—Dionne Warwick (87)	83
Louis PRIMA ▶ 5830 (6)	**238**
Sing Sing Sing—Bernie Lowe Orchestra (58)	*178*
Sing, Sing, Sing—Larry Elgart And His Manhattan Swing Orchestra (82)	*50*
A Sunday Kind Of Love—Lenny Welch (72)	*26*
A Sunday Kind Of Love—Jan & Dean (62)	*7.3*
Sunday Kind Of Love—Etta James (61)	*5.7*
Sunday Kind Of Love—Fran Warren (58)	*0.8*
PRINCE [Prince Rogers Nelson] ▶ 8 (60)	**82519**
When Doves Cry—Prince (84)	7299
Let's Go Crazy—Prince and the Revolution (84)	5302
Nothing Compares 2 U—Sinead O'Connor (90)	4985
I Feel For You—Chaka Khan (84)	4722
Kiss—Prince And The Revolution (86)	*4594*
Cream—Prince (91)	4005
Purple Rain—Prince and the Revolution (84)	3842
Raspberry Beret—Prince and the Revolution (85)	3815
Batdance—Prince (89)	3386
Diamonds And Pearls—Prince (91)	3313
Manic Monday—Bangles (86)	2853
U Got The Look—Prince (87)	2827
Little Red Corvette—Prince (83)	2526
Thieves In The Temple—Prince (90)	2400
Sign O' The Times—Prince (87)	2331
Stand Back—Stevie Nicks (83)	2238
Pray—M.C. Hammer (90)	2147
The Glamorous Life—Sheila E. (84)	2003
Sugar Walls—Sheena Easton (84)	1802
Delirious—Prince (83)	1770
1999—Prince (82)	1649
I Wanna Be Your Lover—Prince (79)	1540
Round And Round—Tevin Campbell (90)	1444
Jerk-Out—Time (90)	1425
Pop Life—Prince & the Revolution (85)	1367
A Love Bizarre—Sheila E. (85)	1233
I Could Never Take The Place Of Your Man—Prince (87)	1224
Alphabet St.—Prince (88)	1202
I Would Die 4 U—Prince and the Revolution (84)	1201
Love... Thy Will Be Done—Martika (91)	1066
Jungle Love—Time (84)	911
Partyman—Prince (89)	675

PRINCE [Prince Rogers Nelson] ▶ 8 (60) *Continued*	**82519**
On The Way Up—Elisa Fiorillo (90)	617
Take Me With U—Prince and the Revolution (85)	584
Mountains—Prince And The Revolution (86)	567
The Belle Of St. Mark—Sheila E. (84)	555
The Arms Of Orion—Prince With Sheena Easton (89)	483
The Bird—Time (85)	441
Kiss—Art Of Noise featuring Tom Jones (88)	*387*
Do Me Baby—Meli'sa Morgan (86)	370
Gett Off—Prince (91)	289
Let's Pretend We're Married—Prince (83)	285
Controversy—Prince (81)	228
America—Prince & The Revolution (85)	220
Anotherloverholenyohead—Prince And The Revolution (86)	163
New Power Generation—Prince (90)	150
Hot Thing—Prince (88)	122
The Screams Of Passion—Family (85)	105
If I Was Your Girlfriend—Prince (87)	88
Soft And Wet—Prince (78)	53
Get It Up—Time (81)	49
Martika's Kitchen—Martika (91)	40
Insatiable—Prince (91)	38
Cool (Part 1)—Time (82)	33
Sex Shooter—Apollonia 6 (84)	33
Uptown—Prince (80)	29
When You Were Mine—Mitch Ryder (83)	15
777-9311—Time (82)	12
Nightgown—Candyman (91)	10
Oooh This I Need—Elisa Fiorillo (91)	9.0
—Arabian Prince see: Kim NAZEL	
Charles PRINCE ▶ 8494 (2)	**48**
Don't Want To Wait Anymore—Tubes (81)	377
Piece By Piece—Tubes (85)	10
—Fresh Prince see: Will SMITH	
Hughie PRINCE ▶ 3041 (2)	**1045**
Boogie Woogie Bugle Boy—Bette Midler (73)	2032
Beat Me Daddy Eight To The Bar—Commander Cody And His Lost Planet Airmen (72)	116
Ian PRINCE ▶ 2664 (1)	**1286**
She Ain't Worth It—Glenn Medeiros featuring Bobby Brown (90)	3857
Rod PRINCE ▶ 3960 (1)	**640**
Hot Smoke & Sasafrass—Bubble Puppy (69)	1280
—Prince Be see: Attrell CORDES	
—Prince Buster see: Buster CAMPBELL	
John PRITCHARD ▶ 4778 (1)	**418**
Can't Stop Dancin'—Captain & Tennille (77)	837
—Roger Pritchard see: Lee SHERIDEN	
Travis PRITCHETT ▶ 1974 (4)	**2042**
Tell Him No—Travis & Bob (59)	*1788*
Tell Him No—Dean & Marc (59)	*249*
Little Bitty Johnny—Travis & Bob (59)	4.3
Tell Him No—Jackson Brothers (59)	*0.0*
—Andreas Ludwig Priwin see: André PREVIN	
—P.J. Proby see: James Marcus SMITH	
—Orville Proctor see: Hank THOMPSON	
—Salek Profesorski see: Spencer PROFFER	
Spencer PROFFER [Salek Profesorski] ▶ 5465 (4)	**283**
Children Of The Sun—Billy Thorpe (79)	328
Playing To Win—LRB (85)	217
Storybook Children (Daybreak)—Bette Midler (78)	174
All Roads (Lead Back To You)—Donny Most (76)	2.3
—Josephine Moore Proffitt see: Sylvia DEE	
Sergei PROKOFIEV ▶ 4703 (3)	**435**
Russians—Sting (86)	832
I Believe In Father Christmas—Greg Lake (75)	18
Peter And The Wolf—Charles Randolph Grean Sounde (70)	13
Skip PROKOP [Ronald Harry Prokop, Ronn Prokop] ▶ 1786 (4)	**2326**
One Fine Morning—Lighthouse (71)	1259
Sunny Days—Lighthouse (72)	578
Pretty Lady—Lighthouse (73)	481
I Just Wanna Be Your Friend—Lighthouse (72)	16
Sid PROSEN ▶ 11176 (1)	**2.9**
The Rockin' Lady (From New Orleans)—Penny Candy (59)	5.7
Brian PROTHEROE ▶ 7440 (1)	**96**
Pinball—Brian Protheroe (75)	96
Aldo PROVENZANO ▶ 5318 (2)	**306**
Darling I Love You—Al Martino (59)	286
Little Girl, Little Boy—Al Martino (61)	20
Dennis PROVISOR ▶ 3342 (3)	**891**
Glory Bound—Grass Roots (72)	745
Walking Through The Country—Grass Roots (70)	587
Come On And Say It—Grass Roots (70)	353
Oscar PRUDENTE ▶ 9466 (1)	**23**
Jesahel—English Congregation (72)	70
Johnny PRUITT ▶ 3481 (3)	**823**
The Bertha Butt Boogie - Part I—Jimmy Castor Bunch (75)	916
Hey, Leroy, Your Mama's Callin' You—Jimmy Castor (66)	651
King Kong - Pt. 1—Jimmy Castor Bunch (75)	78
Red PRYSOCK ▶ 9425 (1)	**24**
Hand Clappin'—Red Prysock (55)	24
Giacomo PUCCINI ▶ 1153 (2)	**3849**
Don't You Know—Della Reese (59)	7675
Dearest (Cara)—Al Martino (60)	35
Jerry PUCKETT ▶ 11111 (1)	**3.2**
Friend Of Mine—Little Milton (76)	9.5
Tito PUENTE ▶ 2753 (1)	**1218**
Oye Como Va—Santana (71)	1218
Joe PUERTA ▶ 4367 (3)	**511**
Holdin' On To Yesterday—Ambrosia (75)	973
Nice, Nice, Very Nice—Ambrosia (75)	71
How Can You Love Me—Ambrosia (82)	21
—Bryan Pugh see: Perry FORD	
Phil PUGH ▶ 1799 (1)	**2295**
Then Came You—Dionne Warwicke And Spinners (74)	4589
—Virginia Wynette Pugh see: Tammy WYNETTE	
—Luigi Pulci see: Gino REDI	
Stefano PULGA ▶ 11138 (1)	**3.1**
Can't Hold Back (Your Loving)—Kano (81)	12
Arthur PULLAM ▶ 7998 (1)	**66**
Contact—Edwin Starr (79)	198
Leroy PULLINS ▶ 6041 (1)	**213**
I'm A Nut—Leroy Pullins (66)	213
John PURDELL ▶ 9395 (1)	**25**
No More Tears—Ozzy Osbourne (91)	74
Bernard PURDIE ▶ 9747 (1)	**18**
Funky Donkey—Pretty Purdie (67)	18
—Howard Stanley Puris see: Tony POWERS	
Donnie PURNELL ▶ 4446 (1)	**493**
Don't Close Your Eyes—Kix (89)	1479
—Billy Purser see: Gary BURBANK	
Bob PURVIS ▶ 8103 (1)	**62**
Costafine Town—Splinter (74)	123
Charlie PURVIS ▶ 5263 (3)	**316**
Go On With The Wedding—Patti Page (55)	*976*
Go On With The Wedding—Kitty Kallen & Georgie Shaw (55)	*288*
Go On With The Wedding—Modernaires (56)	*0.0*
—Claude Putman Jr. see: Curly PUTMAN	
Curly PUTMAN [Claude Putman Jr.] ▶ 1816 (7)	**2274**
Green, Green Grass Of Home—Tom Jones (66)	1685
My Elusive Dreams—Bobby Vinton (70)	*548*
Ballad Of Two Brothers—Autry Inman (68)	334
My Elusive Dreams—Charlie Rich (75)	*205*
D-I-V-O-R-C-E—Tammy Wynette (68)	81
Blood Red And Goin' Down—Tanya Tucker (73)	44
My Elusive Dreams—David Houston And Tammy Wynette (67)	*33*
Richard PUTNAM ▶ 9182 (1)	**29**
Too Good To Turn Back Now—Rick Bowles (82)	59
Joe PYATT ▶ 5421 (2)	**291**
Hunch—Bobby Peterson Quintet (59)	*301*
Hunch—Paul Gayten (59)	*281*

Q

Lew QUADLING ▶ 10123 (2)	**12**
Careless—Bobby Vinton (65)	25
Sam's Song—Dean Martin And Sammy Davis Jr. (62)	8.0
Larry QUALIANO ▶ 11074 (1)	**3.4**
Harvey's Got A Girlfriend—Royal Teens (58)	14
Diane QUANDER ▶ 5852 (1)	**237**
Caught Up In The Rapture—Anita Baker (86)	473
Charles QUARTO ▶ 5819 (1)	**239**
Geronimo's Cadillac—Michael Murphey (72)	478
Sol QUASHA ▶ 4107 (4)	**591**
Chain Gang—Bobby Scott (55)	*1174*
Chain Gang—Len Dresslar (56)	*7.2*
Chain Gang—Johnny Oliver (56)	*0.0*
Chain Gang—Lawrence Welk & His Champagne Music (56)	*0.0*
Bill QUATEMAN ▶ 8459 (1)	**50**
Only Love—Bill Quateman (73)	50
Mike QUATRO ▶ 9663 (1)	**19**
Circus—Mike Quatro Jam Band (72)	58
Suzi QUATRO [Susan Kay Quattrochio] ▶ 9664 (1)	**19**
Circus—Mike Quatro Jam Band (72)	58
—Susan Kay Quattrochio see: Suzi QUATRO	
Mac QUAYLE ▶ 9115 (1)	**31**
Louder Than Love—TKA (91)	92
Wardell QUEZERGUE ▶ 10600 (1)	**7.0**
99 + 1—J. Gardner (65)	7.0
Clarence QUICK ▶ 676 (6)	**6419**
Come Go With Me—Dell-Vikings (57)	*3709*
Whispering Bells—Dell-Vikings (57)	1742
Come Go With Me—Beach Boys (81)	*693*
Come Go With Me—Dion (63)	*244*
Come Go With Me—Del Vikings (73)	*31*
Come Go With Me—Sunny Gale (57)	*0.0*
Arline J. QUIER ▶ 11413 (1)	**1.8**
Salt Water Taffy—Morty Jay And The Surferin' Cats (63)	3.6
Charles QUILLEN ▶ 5392 (1)	**296**
I Wouldn't Have Missed It For The World—Ronnie Milsap (81)	887
Don QUINN ▶ 10736 (1)	**5.6**
Yancy Derringer—Tommy Mara (59)	11
Jim QUINN ▶ 10700 (1)	**6.0**
Back To The River—Damnation Of Adam Blessing (70)	30
Peter QUINN ▶ 3117 (1)	**1001**
The Curly Shuffle—Jump 'N the Saddle (83)	1001
Ray QUINONES ▶ 8910 (1)	**36**
Queen Of My Heart—René And Ray (62)	109
David QUINTANA ▶ 10754 (1)	**5.5**
Gypsy Spirit—Pendulum (80)	17
Eddy QUINTELA [Eddy Quintela de Mendonça, Eddy Quintela Mendonca] ▶ 2554 (3)	**1390**
Little Lies—Fleetwood Mac (87)	1985
As Long As You Follow—Fleetwood Mac (88)	414
Save Me—Fleetwood Mac (90)	380
—Eddy Quintela Mendonca see: Eddy QUINTELA	
Eddie QUINTEROS ▶ 8865 (1)	**37**
Come Dance With Me—Eddie Quinteros (60)	37
Martin QUITTENTON ▶ 1404 (2)	**3158**
Maggie May—Rod Stewart (71)	5183
You Wear It Well—Rod Stewart (72)	1133
Andy QUNTA ▶ 5105 (2)	**341**
Crazy—Icehouse (87)	976
You're The Voice—John Farnham (90)	64
Fizzy QWICK [Debravon Lewis] ▶ 10947 (1)	**4.2**
Flashes—Tiggi Clay (84)	13

R

Luther RABB ▶ 4485 (5)	**482**
Bust A Move—Young M.C. (89)	1887
You Got The Power—War (82)	35
Good, Good Feelin'—War (79)	12
Outlaw—War (82)	10
Super Highway—Ballin' Jack (71)	5.3
Eddie RABBITT ▶ 882 (12)	**5040**
I Love A Rainy Night—Eddie Rabbitt (80)	4947
Drivin' My Life Away—Eddie Rabbitt (80)	3070
Step By Step—Eddie Rabbitt (81)	2893
Kentucky Rain—Elvis Presley (70)	1185
Suspicions—Eddie Rabbitt (79)	1079

Eddie RABBITT ▶ 882 (12) *Continued*	**5040**
Someone Could Lose A Heart Tonight—Eddie Rabbitt (81)	961
You Can't Run From Love—Eddie Rabbitt (83)	181
Loveline—Dr. Hook (82)	132
Rocky Mountain Music—Eddie Rabbitt (76)	87
I Can't Help Myself—Eddie Rabbitt (77)	42
Gone Too Far—Eddie Rabbitt (80)	23
Patch It Up—Elvis Presley (70)	0.0
Bernd RABE ▶ 7719 (1)	**79**
Simpel Gimpel—Horst Jankowski (65)	158
Buzz RABIN [Raybon Owen Busby] ▶ 7576 (1)	**88**
Beaucoups Of Blues—Ringo Starr (70)	88
Trevor RABIN [Trevor Charles Rabin, Trevor Charles Rabinowitz] ▶ 1677 (6)	**2507**
Owner Of A Lonely Heart—Yes (83)	6336
Leave It—Yes (84)	669
Love Will Find A Way—Yes (87)	541
Rhythm Of Love—Yes (87)	310
It Can Happen—Yes (84)	168
Lift Me Up—Yes (91)	82
—Sydney Rabinowitz see: Sid ROBIN	
Michael RABON ▶ 2329 (5)	**1585**
Western Union—Five Americans (67)	2583
I See The Light—Five Americans (65)	795
Sound Of Love—Five Americans (67)	657
Zip Code—Five Americans (67)	404
Evol-Not Love—Five Americans (66)	315
—Andrew Racheck see: Bud REHAK	
Sergei RACHMANINOFF ▶ 1346 (2)	**3296**
All By Myself—Eric Carmen (75)	5141
Never Gonna Fall In Love Again—Eric Carmen (76)	1451
Bobby RACKEP [Herman Peckar] ▶ 9085 (1)	**32**
Chills And Fever—Ronnie Love And His Orchestra (61)	63
Jimmy RADCLIFFE ▶ 6045 (5)	**212**
She's Got Everything—Essex Featuring Anita Humes (63)	219
My Block—Four Pennies (63)	130
Deep In The Heart Of Harlem—Clyde McPhatter (64)	*112*
Pretty Boy Lonely—Patti Page (63)	4.1
Deep In The Heart Of Harlem—Walter Jackson (67)	*3.3*
Peter RADCLIFFE ▶ 2391 (1)	**1532**
You're The First, The Last, My Everything—Barry White (74)	4597
—Milan Radenkovich see: Rick RODELL	
Paul RADER ▶ 11816 (1)	**0.0**
Only Believe—Elvis Presley (71)	0.0
Mark RADICE ▶ 7284 (1)	**105**
Tonight It's You—Cheap Trick (85)	422
James RADO [James Radomski] ▶ 392 (12) HOF	**10069**
Hair—Cowsills (69)	8011
Aquarius—5th Dimension (69)	*5902*
Let The Sunshine In (The Flesh Failures)—5th Dimension (69)	5902
Easy To Be Hard—Three Dog Night (69)	*5385*
Good Morning Starshine—Oliver (69)	*4408*
Where Do I Go—Happenings (69)	*209*
Be-In (Hare Krishna)—Happenings (69)	209
Easy To Be Hard—Hair (Original Soundtrack)/Cheryl Barnes (79)	*76*
Where Do I Go—Carla Thomas (68)	*45*
Good Morning Starshine—Strawberry Alarm Clock (69)	*45*
I Got Life—Nina Simone (69)	6.9
Ain't Got No—Nina Simone (69)	6.9
—James Radomski see: James RADO	
Jackie RAE ▶ 3808 (3)	**693**
Happy Heart—Andy Williams (69)	*836*
When There's No You—Engelbert Humperdinck (71)	399
Happy Heart—Petula Clark (69)	*152*
Peter RAFELSON ▶ 1962 (2)	**2048**
Open Your Heart—Madonna (86)	4274
Rush Hour—Jane Wiedlin (88)	1247
Gerry RAFFERTY ▶ 295 (8)	**12177**
Baker Street—Gerry Rafferty (78)	6557
Stuck In The Middle With You—Stealers Wheel (73)	2928
Right Down The Line—Gerry Rafferty (78)	1565
Get It Right Next Time—Gerry Rafferty (79)	772
Days Gone Down (Still Got The Light In Your Eyes)—Gerry Rafferty (79)	714
Home And Dry—Gerry Rafferty (78)	687
Everyone's Agreed That Everything Will Turn Out Fine—Stealers Wheel (73)	459
The Royal Mile (Sweet Darlin')—Gerry Rafferty (80)	188
Melvin RAGIN ▶ 10188 (2)	**11**
(Let's Go) All The Way—Whispers (78)	24
Magic Man—Herb Alpert (81)	22
Gerome RAGNI ▶ 393 (12) HOF	**10069**
Hair—Cowsills (69)	8011
Aquarius—5th Dimension (69)	*5902*
Let The Sunshine In (The Flesh Failures)—5th Dimension (69)	5902
Easy To Be Hard—Three Dog Night (69)	*5385*
Good Morning Starshine—Oliver (69)	*4408*
Where Do I Go—Happenings (69)	*209*
Be-In (Hare Krishna)—Happenings (69)	209
Easy To Be Hard—Hair (Original Soundtrack)/Cheryl Barnes (79)	*76*
Where Do I Go—Carla Thomas (68)	*45*
Good Morning Starshine—Strawberry Alarm Clock (69)	*45*
I Got Life—Nina Simone (69)	6.9
Ain't Got No—Nina Simone (69)	6.9
Jerry RAGOVOY [Norman Margulies, Norman Meade, Jordan Ragovoy] ▶ 474 (36)	**8758**
Cry Baby—Garnet Mimms & The Enchanters (63)	*3220*
Time Is On My Side—Rolling Stones (64)	3088
Piece Of My Heart—Big Brother And The Holding Company (68)	*1544*
Pata Pata—Miriam Makeba (67)	1428
A Wonderful Dream—Majors (62)	878
Cry Baby—Janis Joplin (71)	*651*
Let's Kiss And Make Up—Bobby Vinton (62)	647
I'll Take Good Care Of You—Garnet Mimms (66)	619
Baby Don't You Weep—Garnet Mimms & The Enchanters (63)	567
About This Thing Called Love—Fabian (60)	498
Ain't Nobody Home—B.B. King (71)	*487*
What's It Gonna Be—Dusty Springfield (67)	345
Ain't Nobody Home—Howard Tate (66)	*300*
Look At Granny Run, Run—Howard Tate (66)	271
Stay With Me—Lorraine Ellison (66)	261
Piece Of My Heart—Erma Franklin (67)	*223*
A Little Bit Now—Dave Clark Five (67)	*209*
You Got It—Diana Ross (78)	191
One Way Love—Drifters (64)	169
A Quiet Place—Garnet Mimms & The Enchanters (64)	166
A Little Bit Now (A Little Bit Later)—Majors (62)	*165*
Get It While You Can—Janis Joplin (71)	159
Malayisha—Miriam Makeba (68)	159
Stop—Howard Tate (68)	155
Look Away—Garnet Mimms (64)	127
One Girl—Garnet Mimms (64)	120
She's A Troublemaker—Majors (62)	89
Try (Just A Little Bit Harder)—Janis Joplin (70)	52
Piece Of My Heart—Sammy Hagar (82)	*31*
Take It From Me—Dionne Warwicke (75)	15
Heart Be Still—Lorraine Ellison (67)	11
I Wanna Thank You—Enchanters (2) (64)	10
I Can't Wait Until I See My Baby—Justine Washington (64)	8.0
Anytime You Want Me—Garnet Mimms (64)	8.0
All I Know Is The Way I Feel—Pointer Sisters (87)	4.3
I'll Be There (To Bring You Love)—Majors (64)	3.4
—Jordan Ragovoy see: Jerry RAGOVOY	
—Harold Ray Ragsdale see: Ray STEVENS	
Derf Reklaw RAHEEM [Derf Reklaw, Fred Walker] ▶ 9870 (1)	**16**
What's The Name Of This Funk (Spider Man)—Ramsey Lewis (76)	47
Joe RAINEY ▶ 10940 (1)	**4.2**
I Love My Truck—Glen Campbell (81)	4.2
Lloyd RAINEY ▶ 11272 (1)	**2.5**
Gale Winds—Egyptian Combo (64)	5.0
Ma RAINEY [Gertrude Pridgett] ▶ 2006 (5)	**2008**
See See Rider—Eric Burdon And The Animals (66)	*1714*
C C Rider—Chuck Willis (57)	*806*
C. C. Rider—Mitch Ryder And The Detroit Wheels (65)	*728*
See See Rider—LaVern Baker (62)	*629*
C.C. Rider—Bobby Powell (65)	*408*
Ralph RAINGER [Ralph Reichenthal] ▶ 3523 (3) HOF	**800**
Blue Hawaii—Billy Vaughn And His Orchestra (58)	662
Wun'erful, Wun'erful! (Sides Uh-One & Uh-Two)—Stan Freberg (57)	298
Please—Frank Ifield (63)	200
Marvin RAINWATER [Marvin Karlton Percy] ▶ 2574 (7)	**1365**
Gonna Find Me A Bluebird—Marvin Rainwater (57)	*895*
I Gotta Go Get My Baby—Teresa Brewer (55)	308
Whole Lotta Woman—Marvin Rainwater (58)	160
Gonna Find Me A Bluebird—Eddy Arnold (57)	*83*
My Love Is Real—Marvin Rainwater (57)	47
Gonna Find Me A Bluebird—Joyce Hahn (57)	*21*
I Dig You Baby—Marivn Rainwater (58)	11
Bonnie RAITT ▶ 8658 (1)	**43**
Nick Of Time—Bonnie Raitt (90)	43
—Milton Rajonsky see: Boots BROWN	
Palmer C. RAKES ▶ 6039 (2)	**213**
Blood Is Thicker Than Water—William Devaughn (74)	294
When You're Gone—Brenda & The Tabulations (67)	198
—Rakim see: William GRIFFIN	
David RAKSIN ▶ 3951 (1)	**643**
Theme From Ben Casey—Valjean (62)	643
Ben RALEIGH ▶ 313 (31)	**11609**
She's A Fool—Lesley Gore (63)	3745
Tell Laura I Love Her—Ray Peterson (60)	*2552*
Dungaree Doll—Eddie Fisher (55)	2143
Love Is All We Need—Tommy Edwards (58)	*1872*
Midnight Mary—Joey Powers (63)	1854
Wonderful Wonderful—Johnny Mathis (57)	*1803*
Wonderful! Wonderful!—Tymes (63)	*1667*
Love Is A Hurtin' Thing—Lou Rawls (66)	1550
That's The Way Boys Are—Lesley Gore (64)	1325
Blue Winter—Connie Francis (64)	1016
Your Other Love—Connie Francis (63)	744
You Can Bring Me All Your Heartaches—Lou Rawls (66)	397
That's How Heartaches Are Made—Baby Washington (63)	*384*
Dead End Street—Lou Rawls (67)	375
Love Is All We Need—Mel Carter (66)	*369*
Rock Right—Georgia Gibbs (56)	355
I Don't Wanna Be A Loser—Lesley Gore (64)	327
Love Is All We Need—Vic Dana (64)	*201*
Bring A Little Sunshine (To My Heart)—Vic Dana (65)	185
Exclusively Yours—Carl Dobkins, Jr. (60)	121
Let's Be Lovers—Playmates (58)	103
Mary Ann Thomas—Bobby Freeman (59)	*31*
Tell Laura I Love Her—Johnny T. Angel (74)	*27*
Majesty Of Love—Marvin Rainwater and Connie Francis (57)	22
Love Is A Sacred Thing—Kitty Kallen (58)	18
That's How Heartaches Are Made—Marvelettes (69)	*16*
If That's How Nature Made Him—Helen Grayco (77)	11
Just Let Me Cry—Lesley Gore (63)	3.2
How Do You Know It's Love—Teresa Brewer (60)	2.1
Mary Ann Thomas—Buddy Heart (59)	*0.0*
Wonderful! Wonderful!—Jan Peerce with Joe Reisman & His Orchestra (57)	*0.0*
Kevin RALEIGH ▶ 3823 (3)	**689**
He Can't Love You—Michael Stanley Band (80)	615
Someone Like You—Michael Stanley Band (83)	41
When I'm Holding You Tight—Michael Stanley Band (82)	32
Don RALKE ▶ 5848 (4)	**237**
Like I Love You—Edd Byrnes And Friend (59)	392
It Shall Come To Pass—Four Aces (54)	69
Kookie's Mad Pad—Edd Byrnes (59)	8.6
Zooba!—Big Sound of Don Ralke (59)	2.3
Mick RALPHS ▶ 887 (6)	**5015**
Can't Get Enough—Bad Company (74)	3085
Feel Like Makin' Love—Bad Company (75)	1611
Movin' On—Bad Company (75)	659
Good Lovin' Gone Bad—Bad Company (75)	447
Honey Child—Bad Company (76)	69
One Of The Boys—Mott The Hoople (73)	1.8

Buck RAM [Jean Miles, Lynn Paul, Samuel Ram, Ande Rand] ▶ 72 (43)	**29842**
The Great Pretender—Platters (55)	*7497*
Twilight Time—Platters (58)	*6653*
Only You (And You Alone)—Platters (55)	*4611*
(You've Got) The Magic Touch—Platters (56)	3314
Only You—Franck Pourcel (59)	*2646*
Only You (And You Alone)—Hilltoppers (55)	*2041*
Only You—Ringo Starr (74)	*1985*
Enchanted—Platters (59)	1614
You'll Never Never Know—Platters (56)	1488
I'm Sorry—Platters (57)	1021
On My Word Of Honor—Platters (56)	795
My Dream—Platters (57)	654
He's Mine—Platters (57)	629
Remember When—Platters (59)	624
Come Prima—Polly Bergen (58)	*524*
Adorable—Fontane Sisters with Billy Vaughn's Orchestra (55)	*444*
One In A Million—Platters (56)	416
Where—Platters (59)	364
I Wish—Platters (58)	*322*
Helpless—Platters (58)	231
Heaven On Earth—Platters (56)	222
Only Because—Platters (57)	187
Twilight Time—Dick Contino (56)	*149*
I Wanna—Platters (57)	102
She Loves To Rock—Cornel Gunter and The Flairs (56)	75
It's Raining Outside—Platters (58)	74
Wish It Were Me—Platters (59)	63
Your Place In The Sun—Tony Martin (56)	61
Twilight Time—Andy Williams (62)	*28*
Sleepless Nights—Tony Williams (61)	27
Only You (And You Alone)—Mr. Acker Bilk (63)	*27*
Only You (And You Alone)—Bobby Hatfield (69)	*14*
Only You—Wayne Newton (64)	*12*
Only You—Fred Parris & The Five Satins (82)	*4.8*
I'll Be Home For Christmas—Elvis Presley (57)	2.1
Rock And Roll Heaven—Flares (62)	1.4
My Secret—Platters (59)	1.1
Adorable—Colts (55)	*0.0*
Adorable—Drifters (55)	*0.0*
I Wish—Della Reese (58)	*0.0*
The Great Pretender—Jackie Riggs (55)	*0.0*
The Great Pretender—Stan Freberg (56)	*0.0*
Only You (And You Alone)—Lola Dee (55)	*0.0*
—Samuel Ram see: Buck RAM	
Phil RAMACON [Phil Ramocon] ▶ 3721 (2)	**720**
Buffalo Stance—Neneh Cherry (89)	2690
Don't Walk Away—Toni Childs (88)	95
Serge RAMAEKERS ▶ 6619 (1)	**150**
Feel The Groove—Cartouche (91)	150
—Bellino Ramaglia see: Bill RAMAL	
Bill RAMAL [Bellino Ramaglia] ▶ 2141 (3)	**1823**
Mr. Jaws—Dickie Goodman (75)	3166
On Campus—Dickie Goodman (69)	350
Kong—Dickie Goodman (77)	246
Eddie RAMBEAU [Edward Fluri] ▶ 2477 (5)	**1451**
Navy Blue—Diane Renay (64)	2732
Kiss Me Sailor—Diane Renay (64)	606
The Push And Kick—Mark Valentino (62)	594
Here Comes The Boy—Tracey Dey (63)	47
Big-Town Boy—Shirley Matthews & The Big Town Girls (64)	32
Sid RAMIN ▶ 2116 (2)	**1854**
Music To Watch Girls By—Bob Crewe Generation (66)	*1621*
Music To Watch Girls By—Andy Williams (67)	*466*
Bobby RAMIREZ ▶ 9448 (1)	**23**
Latin Active—A Lighter Shade Of Brown (91)	164
—John Henry Ramistella see: Johnny RIVERS	
—Phil Ramocon see: Phil RAMACON	
—Joey Ramone see: Jeff HYMAN	
—Johnny Ramone see: John CUMMINGS	
—Tommy Ramone see: Tom ERDELYI	
Duran RAMOS ▶ 8005 (1)	**66**
Let The Beat Hit 'Em—Lisa Lisa & Cult Jam (91)	262
Silvano R. RAMOS ▶ 3689 (1)	**733**
El Rancho Rock—Champs (58)	733

Tito RAMOS ▶ 9745 (1)	**18**
The Meditation—TNT Band (69)	36
—Andrew Ramsbottom see: Andrew MANN	
Nico RAMSDEN ▶ 5693 (1)	**254**
I Wanna Be A Cowboy—Boys Don't Cry (86)	1016
Chuck RAMSEY ▶ 9266 (1)	**28**
Do Anything You Wanna (Part 1)—Harold Betters (64)	110
Jay RAMSEY ▶ 11817 (1)	**0.0**
We Can Make The Morning—Elvis Presley (72)	0.0
Ken RAMSEY ▶ 4390 (2)	**507**
Greenback Dollar—Kingston Trio (63)	*1014*
Greenback Dollar—Virginians (63)	*0.0*
Willis Alan RAMSEY ▶ 815 (3)	**5400**
Muskrat Love—Captain & Tennille (76)	*5059*
Muskrat Love—America (73)	*292*
Satin Sheets—Bellamy Brothers (76)	50
Rod RANCIFER ▶ 5602 (1)	**266**
I Am Love—Jackson 5 (75)	1065
—Ande Rand see: Buck RAM	
Randy RAND ▶ 6882 (1)	**131**
Turn Up The Radio—Autograph (84)	654
Robin RANDALL ▶ 5491 (1)	**279**
Tomorrow Doesn't Matter Tonight—Starship (86)	558
Teddy RANDAZZO ▶ 451 (38) HOF	**9235**
Goin' Out Of My Head—Little Anthony And The Imperials (64)	*3749*
Pretty Blue Eyes—Steve Lawrence (59)	2838
Hurt So Bad—Lettermen (69)	*2180*
Hurt So Bad—Linda Ronstadt (80)	*1686*
Hurt So Bad—Little Anthony And The Imperials (65)	*1409*
Goin' Out Of My Head—Lettermen (67)	*1323*
I'm On The Outside (Looking In)—Little Anthony And The Imperials (64)	1253
It's Gonna Take A Miracle—Deniece Williams (82)	*1178*
Take Me Back—Little Anthony And The Imperials (65)	1013
Have You Looked Into Your Heart—Jerry Vale (64)	860
It's Gonna Take A Miracle—Royalettes (65)	*576*
Big Wide World—Teddy Randazzo (63)	423
You Better Go—Derek Martin (65)	392
Sinner Man—Trini Lopez (65)	335
Better Use Your Head—Little Anthony And The Imperials (66)	308
Rain In My Heart—Frank Sinatra (68)	289
In Time—Steve Lawrence (61)	214
It's Just A House Without You—Brook Benton (61)	174
I Want To Meet Him—Royalettes (65)	172
It Feels So Good To Be Loved So Bad—Manhattans (77)	169
A Miracle—Frankie Avalon (62)	65
Still Thinking Of You—Three Chuckles (55)	63
Around The Corner—Duprees (65)	56
Goin' Out Of My Head—Frank Sinatra (69)	*36*
It's Not The Same—Anthony And The Imperials (66)	36
Hurtin' Inside—Brook Benton (59)	33
Dear Heart—Teddy Randazzo (63)	13
Salty Tears—Mara Lynn Brown (73)	12
Why Why Why—Steve Lawrence (60)	10
Boomerang—Frankie Valli (76)	9.9
Poor Boy—Royalettes (65)	7.8
Love Vibration—Joe Simon (79)	4.4
Lies—Teddy Randazzo (59)	4.2
Don't Tie Me Down—Anthony & The Imperials (67)	3.3
I'm Hypnotized—Anthony And The Imperials (68)	1.4
Hurt So Bad—Jackie DeShannon (70)	*1.0*
The Weekend—Jack Jones (66)	0.5
Forget To Remember—Frank Sinatra (69)	0.0
—Buddy Randell see: Bill CRANDALL	
Denny RANDELL ▶ 300 (35)	**12068**
A Lover's Concerto—Toys (65)	*6662*
Let's Hang On!—4 Seasons Featuring The "Sound" Of Frankie Valli (65)	*6625*
Working My Way Back To You—Spinners (79)	*2453*
Swearin' To God—Frankie Valli (75)	2151
Keep The Ball Rolling—Jay And The Techniques (67)	*1852*
Working My Way Back To You—4 Seasons Featuring The "Sound" Of Frankie Valli (66)	*1672*
Opus 17 (Don't You Worry 'Bout Me)—4 Seasons Featuring The "Sound" Of Frankie Valli (66)	*1584*
Native New Yorker—Odyssey (77)	1155
Attack—Toys (65)	1083
I Wanna Dance Wit' Choo (Doo Dat Dance)—Disco Tex & The Sex-O-Lettes Featuring Sir Monti Rock III (75)	676

Goodnight My Love—Happenings (66)	*397*
The Mouse—Soupy Sales (65)	379
Let's Hang On—Barry Manilow (82)	*370*
Can't Get Enough Of You, Baby—? And The Mysterians (67)	355
Baby Make Your Own Sweet Music—Jay And The Techniques (68)	333
Dusty—Rag Dolls (65)	323
A Lover's Concerto—Sarah Vaughan (66)	*208*
You Keep Me Dancing—Samantha Sang (78)	168
Penny Arcade—Cyrkle (67)	149
Weekend Lover—Odyssey (78)	124
Goodnight My Love—Duprees (68)	*54*
Jam Band—Disco Tex & The Sex-O-Lettes (75)	26
Society Girl—Rag Dolls (64)	20
May My Heart Be Cast Into Stone—Toys (66)	18
A Lover's Concerto—Stars On 45 (81)	*12*
A Lover's Concerto—Mrs. Miller (66)	*9.1*
Watch Out, Sally!—Diane Renay (64)	4.9
Betrayed—4 Seasons (65)	4.6
Opus 17—Gidea Park (81)	*3.7*
Let's Hang On—Gidea Park (81)	*3.7*
Working My Way Back To You—Gidea Park (81)	*3.7*
Hallelujah—Invitations (65)	3.7
Can I Carry Your Balloon—Swampseeds (68)	0.5
Breakin' Down The Walls Of Heartache—Bandwagon (68)	0.5
Keep The Ball Rollin'—Al Hirt (68)	*0.5*
Don RANDI ▶ 9155 (2)	**30**
Mexican Pearls—Billy Vaughn And His Orchestra (65)	*60*
Mexican Pearls—Don Randi (65)	*0.0*
Earl RANDLE ▶ 2904 (3)	**1124**
I'm Gonna Tear Your Playhouse Down—Paul Young (85)	1084
Echoes Of Love—Doobie Brothers (77)	101
God Bless Our Love—Charles Brimmer (75)	19
Bill RANDOLPH ▶ 8136 (2)	**60**
Nicole—Point Blank (81)	357
Let Me Stay With You Tonight—Point Blank (81)	5.7
Boots RANDOLPH ▶ 4852 (3)	**398**
Yakety Sax—Boots Randolph (63)	*699*
Hey, Mr. Sax Man—Boots Randolph (64)	118
Yakety Axe—Chet Atkins (65)	*19*
—Donald James Randolph see: Don COVAY	
Eugene RANDOLPH ▶ 2481 (4)	**1449**
A Tear Fell—Teresa Brewer (56)	*2559*
A Tear Fell—Ray Charles (64)	*328*
Hey, Little Girl—Foster Sylvers (73)	*24*
A Tear Fell—Ivory Joe Hunter (56)	*0.0*
Jimi RANDOLPH ▶ 6930 (1)	**128**
You And Me Tonight—Deja (87)	255
Richard RANDOLPH ▶ 8598 (1)	**45**
Full Of Fire—Shalamar (80)	136
Wayne RANEY ▶ 7024 (2)	**121**
Blues (Stay Away From Me)—Ace Cannon (62)	*465*
Blues Stay Away From Me—Billy Vaughn And His Orchestra (59)	*19*
Katyna RANIERI ▶ 7553 (2)	**89**
Forget Domani—Connie Francis (65)	*140*
Forget Domani—Frank Sinatra (65)	*126*
Billy RANKIN ▶ 5765 (1)	**244**
Baby Come Back—Billy Rankin (84)	244
—Brian Robson Rankin see: Hank MARVIN	
Kenny RANKIN ▶ 2352 (2)	**1568**
Peaceful—Helen Reddy (73)	1528
A Happy Guy—Rick Nelson (64)	81
—Shabba Ranks see: Rexton GORDON	
Richie RANNO ▶ 6859 (4)	**132**
Cherry Baby—Starz (77)	510
Sing It, Shout It—Starz (77)	148
Hold On To The Night—Starz (78)	18
(She's Just A) Fallen Angel—Starz (76)	6.5
Robert RANS ▶ 1342 (5)	**3303**
Material Girl—Madonna (85)	3543
Dance With Me—Peter Brown Special Background Vocals: Betty Wright (78)	2150
Do Ya Wanna Get Funky With Me—Peter Brown (77)	660
You Should Do It—Peter Brown (78)	214
Crank It Up (Funk Town) Pt. 1—Peter Brown (79)	39

Ray RANSOM ▶ 2489 (3)	**1444**
Dazz—Brick (76)	3530
Dusic—Brick (77)	793
Sweat (Til You Get Wet)—Brick (81)	16
—Renato Ranucci see: Renato RASCEL	
Emo RAPEÉ ▶ 3110 (5)	**1005**
Diane—Bachelors (64)	*1826*
Diane—Joe Harnell And His Orchestra (63)	*86*
Charmaine—Four Freshmen (55)	*55*
Charmaine—Four Preps (63)	*27*
Charmaine—Bachelors (63)	*17*
Giulio RAPETTI [Mogol] ▶ 1467 (9)	**2963**
Let's Live For Today—Grass Roots (67)	2587
Al Di La'—Emilio Pericoli (62)	*2344*
I (Who Have Nothing)—Tom Jones (70)	*1304*
I (Who Have Nothing)—Ben E. King (63)	*810*
I (Who Have Nothing)— Terry Knight And The Pack (66)	*588*
Al-Di-La—Ray Charles Singers (64)	*518*
I (Who Have Nothing)—Sylvester (79)	*146*
Al Di La—Connie Francis (62)	*77*
I Who Have Nothing—Liquid Smoke (70)	*71*
Joe RAPOSO ▶ 1309 (2)	**3384**
Sing—Carpenters (73)	*3378*
Sing A Song—Barbra Streisand (72)	*5.7*
Robert RAPPAPORT ▶ 4656 (1)	**444**
Martian Hop—Ran-Dells (63)	1332
Steve RAPPAPORT ▶ 4657 (1)	**444**
Martian Hop—Ran-Dells (63)	1332
Leon RAPPOLO ▶ 11449 (2)	**1.6**
Make Love To Me— Johnny Thunder & Ruby Winters (67)	*13*
Make Love To Me!—Jo Stafford (54)	*0.0*
—Paul Rapport see: Paul EVANS	
Herman RAREBELL [Hermann Erbel] ▶ 5783 (1)	**242**
Rock You Like A Hurricane—Scorpions (84)	725
Oscar RASBACH ▶ 6996 (2)	**123**
Trees—Platters (61)	*224*
Trees—Al Hibbler (57)	*21*
Renato RASCEL [Renato Ranucci] ▶ 6072 (9)	**209**
Goodbye To Rome (Arrivederci Roma)— Georgia Gibbs (55)	*439*
Arrivederci Roma—Roger Williams (58)	*379*
Arrivederci Roma—Mario Lanza (58)	*11*
Arrivederci, Roma—Eddie Fisher (62)	*2.7*
Arrivederci, Roma—Norman Luboff Choir (55)	*0.0*
Arrivederci Roma (Goodbye To Rome)— Three Suns (55)	*0.0*
Arrivederci Roma (Goodbye To Rome)— Three Suns (58)	*0.0*
Arrivederci Roma (Goodbye To Rome)— Ralph Young (55)	*0.0*
Arrivederci Roma— Frank Chacksfield & His Orchestra (58)	*0.0*
—Michael Charles Rashkow see: Mike LENDELL	
Gene RASKIN ▶ 1051 (1)	**4207**
Those Were The Days—Mary Hopkin (68)	8414
William RASKIN ▶ 8501 (2)	**48**
That's When Your Heartaches Begin— Elvis Presley (57)	144
Wedding Bells (Are Breaking Up That Old Gang Of Mine)—Four Aces (54)	0.0
Larry RASPBERRY ▶ 7329 (1)	**102**
Tired Of Being Blonde—Carly Simon (85)	102
Lisa RATNER [Elisa Blumberg] ▶ 6562 (1)	**157**
Kiss Me In The Rain—Barbra Streisand (80)	314
George RATZLAFF ▶ 5479 (1)	**281**
Cheer—Potliquor (72)	281
Fred RAUCH ▶ 6598 (3)	**153**
(I'm Always Hearing) Wedding Bells— Eddie Fisher (55)	*459*
(I'm Always Hearing) Wedding Bells— Frankie Lester (55)	*0.0*
(I'm Always Hearing) Wedding Bells— Guy Lombardo & His Royal Canadians (55)	*0.0*
Marci RAUER [Marcy Rauer, Marcy Debra Wagman] ▶ 9314 (1)	**27**
I'm Not Your Man— Tommy Conwell And The Young Rumblers (88)	80
—Marcy Rauer see: Marci RAUER	

—Raun see: Ron ANIELLO	
Bruno RAVEL [Bruno Ravel DiCecco] ▶ 6700 (1)	**143**
Bang Bang—Danger Danger (90)	286
Maurice RAVEL ▶ 7844 (1)	**72**
Ravel's Bolero— Henry Mancini And His Orchestra (80)	72
Eraldo RAVIOLO [Ero Valladi] ▶ 10660 (1)	**6.3**
Speak, My Love—Vic Damone (56)	19
Lou RAWLS ▶ 4952 (1)	**375**
Dead End Street Monologue—Lou Rawls (67)	375
Alan RAY ▶ 7474 (1)	**93**
You Don't Love Me Anymore—Eddie Rabbitt (78)	187
Amy RAY ▶ 7495 (1)	**92**
Closer To Fine—Indigo Girls (89)	185
Anthony RAY [Sir Mix-A-Lot] ▶ 7724 (1)	**78**
Posse' On Broadway—Sir Mix-A-Lot (88)	78
Bob RAY [Robert Raymond Henson] ▶ 5412 (1)	**292**
Right Relations—Johnny Rivers (68)	292
Brian RAY ▶ 4167 (1)	**576**
One Heartbeat—Smokey Robinson (87)	1151
Don RAY [Raymond Donnez] ▶ 6243 (2)	**190**
Got To Have Loving—Don Ray (78)	365
Africanism—Kongas (78)	15
Eddy RAY ▶ 902 (6)	**4909**
Hearts Of Stone— Fontane Sisters with Billy Vaughn's Orchestra (54)	*5978*
Hearts Of Stone—Charms (54)	*1329*
Hearts Of Stone—Bill Black's Combo (61)	*971*
Hearts Of Stone—Blue Ridge Rangers (73)	*570*
Hearts Of Stone—Vicki Young (54)	*0.0*
Hearts Of Stone—McGuire Sisters (55)	*0.0*
Harry RAY ▶ 2648 (6)	**1294**
Special Lady—Ray, Goodman & Brown (80)	2439
Sexy Mama—Moments (74)	858
Look At Me (I'm In Love)—Moments (75)	430
Sho Nuff Boogie (Part 1)—Sylvia & The Moments (74)	83
Inside Of You—Ray, Goodman & Brown (80)	78
Girls (Part I)—Moments And Whatnauts (75)	24
—Jean Monte Ray see: Jean GLOVER	
Johnnie RAY ▶ 6970 (3)	**125**
I'll Never Fall In Love Again—Johnnie Ray (59)	90
Paths Of Paradise—Johnnie Ray (55)	32
The Little White Cloud That Cried— Wayne Newton (64)	1.9
Michael RAY ▶ 5231 (4)	**322**
Tonight—Kool & The Gang (84)	1136
Emergency—Kool & The Gang (85)	915
Let's Go Dancin' (Ooh La, La, La)—Kool & The Gang (82)	654
Big Fun—Kool & The Gang (82)	532
Randy RAY ▶ 11641 (1)	**0.9**
Dance, Everybody, Dance—Dartells (63)	0.9
Don RAYE [Donald MacRae Wilhoite] ▶ 1533 (15) HOF	**2797**
Boogie Woogie Bugle Boy—Bette Midler (73)	2032
They Were Doin' The Mambo— Vaughn Monroe with Orchestra (54)	1433
The House Of Blue Lights—Chuck Miller (55)	*1312*
The Ballad Of Thunder Road—Robert Mitchum (62)	*250*
I Love To Dance With You—Patti Page (55)	211
Yet...I Know (Et Pourtant)—Steve Lawrence (64)	163
Beat Me Daddy Eight To The Bar— Commander Cody And His Lost Planet Airmen (72)	116
Ballad Of Thunder Road—Robert Mitchum (58)	*85*
Please Mr Brown—Sarah Vaughan (57)	59
Whippoorwill—Keely Smith (58)	24
I Know What God Is—Perry Como (60)	15
Struttin' With Some Barbecue— Louis Armstrong and Gary Crosby (55)	7.0
Traveling Down A Lonely Road—Teddi King (56)	6.4
This World We Love In—June Valli (61)	*0.0*
The House Of Blue Lights—Pat Morrisey (55)	*0.0*
Joe RAYE [Joseph R. Bochenek, Joseph Raye Bochenek] ▶ 6380 (1)	**177**
Heart Hideaway—Cathy Carr (56)	177
John RAYFORD ▶ 5122 (2)	**339**
Do Your Thing—Watts 103rd Street Rhythm Band (69)	1496
Till You Get Enough— Watts 103rd Street Rhythm Band (69)	200

Jeff RAYMOND ▶ 7475 (1)	**93**
You Don't Love Me Anymore—Eddie Rabbitt (78)	187
Julian RAYMOND ▶ 9690 (2)	**19**
Summer Vacation—Party (90)	*113*
Summer Vacation—Party (91)	*20*
Paul RAYMOND ▶ 9285 (1)	**27**
Tell Mama—Savoy Brown (71)	54
Ivor RAYMONDE ▶ 1965 (7)	**2046**
I Only Want To Be With You—Bay City Rollers (76)	*1517*
I Only Want To Be With You—Dusty Springfield (64)	*1347*
Stay Awhile—Dusty Springfield (64)	*460*
I Only Wanna Be With You—Samantha Fox (89)	*438*
I Only Want To Be With You—Nicolette Larson (82)	*267*
Stay Awhile—Continental Miniatures (78)	*42*
I Only Want To Be With You—Tourists (80)	*20*
Don RAYSOR ▶ 10599 (1)	**7.0**
Girl's Work Is Never Done—Chordettes (59)	14
Andy RAZAF [Adreamentania Paul Razafkeriefo] ▶ 3319 (7) HOF	**901**
Memories Of You—Four Coins (55)	*1002*
In The Mood—Henhouse Five Plus Too (76)	*400*
In The Mood—Bette Midler (74)	*323*
Memories Of You— Benny Goodman Trio with Rosemary Clooney (55)	*204*
In The Mood—Matys Brothers (56)	*32*
Ain't Misbehavin'—Johnnie Ray (56)	4.6
Memories Of You—Ink Spots (55)	*0.0*
—Adreamentania Paul Razafkeriefo see: Andy RAZAF	
Chris REA ▶ 2179 (6)	**1782**
Fool (If You Think It's Over)—Chris Rea (78)	1280
Diamonds—Chris Rea (79)	244
Working On It—Chris Rea (89)	111
Whatever Happened To Benny Santini?— Chris Rea (78)	73
Let's Dance—Chris Rea (87)	43
Loving You—Chris Rea (82)	32
Dave REA ▶ 5419 (2)	**291**
Mississippi Queen—Mountain (70)	1100
For Yasgur's Farm—Mountain (70)	97
Alice REACH ▶ 9518 (1)	**22**
Spring In Manhattan—Tony Bennett (63)	44
John Dawson READ ▶ 7064 (1)	**118**
A Friend Of Mine Is Going Blind— John Dawson Read (75)	118
—Richard Allan Ream see: Rikki ROCKETT	
—Edward Henry Reardon see: Eddie FONTAINE	
Frank REARDON ▶ 4766 (2)	**420**
Same Old Saturday Night—Frank Sinatra (55)	754
I'd Rather Be Here In Your Arms—Duprees (63)	86
Jack REARDON ▶ 1681 (6)	**2500**
When—Kalin Twins (58)	3515
The Good Life—Tony Bennett (63)	*875*
Worried Guy—Johnny Tillotson (64)	523
La Strada Del' Amore—Caterina Valente (59)	30
I Think About You All The Time—Paul Evans (58)	26
The Good Life—Kathy Keegan (63)	*2.3*
Joe REAVES ▶ 9344 (1)	**26**
Love That Really Counts—Natural Four (74)	103
David REAY ▶ 11517 (1)	**1.4**
King Croesus—World Of Oz (68)	5.5
Mac REBENNACK [Malcolm John Rebennack, Dr. John] ▶ 1686 (4)	**2486**
Right Place Wrong Time—Dr. John (73)	2006
Such A Night—Dr. John (73)	395
(Everybody Wanna Get Rich) Rite Away—Dr. John (74)	79
More And More—Carly Simon (75)	11
Jim RECOR ▶ 5147 (1)	**334**
Love In Store—Fleetwood Mac (82)	668
Eugene RECORD ▶ 165 (40)	**17833**
Oh Girl—Chi-Lites (72)	*6321*
Have You Seen Her—Chi-Lites (71)	*5172*
Soulful Strut—Young-Holt Unlimited (68)	*4727*
Have You Seen Her—M.C. Hammer (90)	*2337*
Love Makes A Woman—Barbara Acklin (68)	1694
Oh Girl—Paul Young (90)	*1496*
There'll Come A Time—Betty Everett (69)	714
(For God's Sake) Give More Power To The People— Chi-Lites (71)	678
Two Little Kids—Peaches & Herb (67)	574

Eugene RECORD ▶ 165 (40) *Continued*	**17833**
A Letter To Myself—Chi-Lites (73)	516
Stoned Out Of My Mind—Chi-Lites (73)	514
The Coldest Days Of My Life (Part 1)—Chi-Lites (72)	391
From The Teacher To The Preacher—Gene Chandler And Barbara Acklin (68)	379
Just Ain't No Love—Barbara Acklin (68)	305
Homely Girl—Chi-Lites (74)	214
We Need Order—Chi-Lites (72)	206
I Found Sunshine—Chi-Lites (73)	196
Am I The Same Girl—Barbara Acklin (69)	*192*
A Lonely Man—Chi-Lites (72)	191
I Like Your Lovin' (Do You Like Mine)—Chi-Lites (70)	185
Love Uprising—Otis Leaville (70)	159
Are You My Woman? (Tell Me So)—Chi-Lites (70)	155
I Love You—Otis Leavill (69)	154
Give It Away—Chi-Lites (69)	135
We Are Neighbors—Chi-Lites (71)	100
There Will Never Be Any Peace (Until God Is Seated At The Conference Table)—Chi-Lites (74)	94
You Got To Be The One—Chi-Lites (74)	90
There It Goes Again—Barbara And The Uniques (70)	87
I Still Love You—Jackie Wilson (69)	79
I Want To Pay You Back (For Loving Me)—Chi-Lites (71)	54
Toby—Chi-Lites (75)	48
Let This Be A Letter (To My Baby)—Jackie Wilson (70)	46
My Heart Just Keeps On Breakin'—Chi-Lites (73)	33
All The Waiting Is Not In Vain—Tyrone Davis (69)	29
You Got Me Walking—Jackie Wilson (72)	17
Have You Seen Her—Band Of Gold (84)	*12*
Helpless—Jackie Wilson (69)	8.7
Let Me Be The Man My Daddy Was—Chi-Lites (69)	7.6
It's Time For Love—Chi-Lites (75)	4.3
The Man & The Woman—Chi-Lites (72)	0.0
—Clarence Eugene Redd Jr. see: Gene REDD Sr.	
—Gail Redd see: Ramona REDD	
Gene REDD Jr. [Clarence Eugene Redd III] ▶ 9258 (5)	**28**
Let The Music Take Your Mind—Kool & The Gang (70)	85
Funky Man—Kool & The Gang (70)	41
The Gangs Back Again—Kool & The Gang (69)	37
Kool's Back Again—Kool & The Gang (70)	18
Who's Gonna Take The Weight (Part One)—Kool & The Gang (71)	4.1
Gene REDD Sr. [Clarence Eugene Redd Jr.] ▶ 4982 (7)	**365**
Please Come Home For Christmas—Eagles (78)	*458*
Broken Heart—Fiestas (62)	151
The Greasy Spoon—Hank Marr (63)	58
Shirley—Schoolboys (57)	23
Do You Know How To Twist—Hank Ballard (62)	23
Please Come Home For Christmas—Charles Brown (61)	*20*
Please Come Home For Christmas—Charles Brown (60)	*6.3*
Henry REDD ▶ 5597 (1)	**267**
Free—Deniece Williams (76)	1067
Ramona REDD [Gale Jones, Gail Redd, Gail Redd Torok] ▶ 1805 (9)	**2286**
Pledge Of Love—Ken Copeland (57)	*961*
Pledge Of Love—Mitchell Torok (57)	*556*
Pledge Of Love—Dick Contino (57)	*389*
Pink Chiffon—Mitchell Torok (60)	347
(Open Up The Door) Let The Good Times In—Dean Martin (66)	293
Pledge Of Love—Johnny Janis (57)	*52*
Face In A Crowd—Jimmie Rodgers (63)	*15*
Pledge Of Love—Penguins (57)	*0.0*
Face In A Crowd—Dean Martin (63)	*0.0*
James REDDICK ▶ 3407 (2)	**860**
Trying To Hold On To My Woman—Lamont Dozier (73)	1176
Fish Ain't Bitin'—Lamont Dozier (74)	544
—Clarence Eugene Redd III see: Gene REDD Jr.	
Otis REDDING ▶ 133 (36) HOF	**20457**
Respect—Aretha Franklin (67)	*8397*
(Sittin' On) The Dock Of The Bay—Otis Redding (68)	*7420*
Sweet Soul Music—Arthur Conley (67)	*5467*
I've Been Loving You Too Long (To Stop Now)—Otis Redding (65)	*1217*

(Sittin' On) The Dock Of The Bay—Michael Bolton (88)	*1137*
The Happy Song (Dum-Dum)—Otis Redding (68)	722
Respect—Otis Redding (65)	*680*
Hard To Handle—Black Crowes (91)	*595*
Security—Etta James (68)	*589*
Fa-Fa-Fa-Fa-Fa (Sad Song)—Otis Redding (66)	553
I Can't Turn You Loose—Chambers Brothers (68)	*526*
I've Got Dreams To Remember—Otis Redding (68)	459
On The Dock Of The Bay—Dells (69)	*452*
Mr. Pitiful—Otis Redding (65)	416
Shout Bamalama—Mickey Murray (67)	391
My Lover's Prayer—Otis Redding (66)	339
Chained And Bound—Otis Redding (64)	329
Hard To Handle—Black Crowes (90)	*279*
(Sittin' On) The Dock Of The Bay—Reddings (82)	*200*
Love Man—Otis Redding (69)	191
Wholesale Love—Buddy Miles (71)	138
Just One More Day—Otis Redding (65)	138
Free Me—Otis Redding (69)	131
Hard To Handle—Otis Redding (68)	*114*
(Sittin' On) The Dock Of The Bay—Sergio Mendes & Brasil '66 (69)	*101*
(Sittin' On) The Dock Of The Bay—Sammy Hagar (79)	*92*
Come To Me—Otis Redding (64)	89
I've Been Loving You Too Long—Ike & Tina Turner (69)	*87*
These Arms Of Mine—Otis Redding (63)	86
Respect—Rationals (66)	*74*
I Can't Turn You Loose—Edgar Winter's White Trash (72)	*46*
(Sittin' On) The Dock Of The Bay—King Curtis & The Kingpins (68)	*45*
Demonstration—Otis Redding (70)	32
Hard To Handle—Patti Drew (68)	*7.7*
Sweet Soul Music—Magnificent Men (67)	*7.6*
Security—Otis Redding (64)	*1.9*
Van Ross REDDING ▶ 9974 (1)	**14**
Baby I'm Hooked—Con Funk Shun (84)	29
Zelma REDDING ▶ 6599 (1)	**153**
I've Got Dreams To Remember—Otis Redding (68)	459
Helen REDDY [Helen Reddy Wald] ▶ 1356 (2)	**3272**
I Am Woman—Helen Reddy (72)	6487
The Happy Girls—Helen Reddy (77)	113
Margaret REDDY ▶ 11008 (1)	**3.9**
Itchin'—Jimmy Jones (60)	12
—Teddy Redell see: Teddy DeLano RIEDEL	
Gino REDI [Luigi Pulci, P. G. Redi] ▶ 5099 (1)	**343**
Non Dimenticar (Don't Forget)—Nat "King" Cole (58)	1029
—P. G. Redi see: Gino REDI	
Howard REDMON ▶ 10954 (1)	**4.1**
Blue Jeans—Chocolate Milk (81)	8.2
Gus REDMOND ▶ 4946 (1)	**376**
The Sly, Slick, And The Wicked—Lost Generation (70)	1128
John REDMOND ▶ 7560 (1)	**88**
Second Fiddle—Kay Starr (56)	353
Lewis REDNER ▶ 11590 (1)	**1.1**
Oh Little Town Of Bethlehem—Elvis Presley (57)	2.1
—Elvets Rednow see: Stevie WONDER	
—Red River Dave see: Dave McENERY	
Phil REDROW ▶ 5040 (1)	**355**
If The Love Fits Wear It—Leslie Pearl (82)	709
Michael REDWAY ▶ 6835 (1)	**134**
Good Morning—Michael Redway (73)	134
—Rob Reeco see: Bob HAMILTON	
Al REED ▶ 7254 (2)	**107**
Message From Maria—Joe Simon (68)	107
Men Of War—Rouzan Sisters (66)	0.5
Bernard REED ▶ 10959 (1)	**4.1**
Just Be Sincere—Jackie Wilson (67)	12
Dan Edward REED ▶ 5504 (1)	**277**
Ritual—Dan Reed Network (88)	277
Daniel REED ▶ 8556 (2)	**46**
Girl I Need You—Artistics (67)	127
Just Be Sincere—Jackie Wilson (67)	12
Dean REED ▶ 11390 (1)	**1.9**
Search—Dean Reed (59)	1.9

Don REED ▶ 10481 (1)	**8.0**
How Many Others—Dick Roman (55)	24
Jerry REED [Jerry Reed Hubbard, Jerry Reid Hubbard] ▶ 469 (13)	**8857**
Amos Moses—Jerry Reed (70)	2595
When You're Hot, You're Hot—Jerry Reed (71)	2062
That's All You Gotta Do—Brenda Lee (60)	1905
U.S. Male—Elvis Presley With The Jordanaires (68)	818
Guitar Man—Elvis Presley (81)	*502*
Guitar Man—Elvis Presley (68)	*386*
Ko-Ko Joe—Jerry Reed (71)	336
Alabama Wild Man—Jerry Reed (72)	145
Another Puff—Jerry Reed (72)	134
Eefananny—Ardells (63)	19
The Crude Oil Blues—Jerry Reed (74)	17
Born To Be By Your Side—Brenda Lee (67)	3.7
Hully Gully Guitar—Jerry Reed And The Hully Girlies (62)	0.9
Jimmy REED ▶ 2658 (15)	**1289**
Baby What You Want Me To Do—Jimmy Reed (60)	*382*
Shame, Shame, Shame—Jimmy Reed (63)	285
Honest I Do—Jimmy Reed (57)	207
Bright Lights Big City—Jimmy Reed (61)	*193*
Close Together—Jimmy Reed (61)	112
Hush Hush—Jimmy Reed (60)	80
Found Love—Jimmy Reed (60)	50
The Sun Is Shining—Jimmy Reed (57)	45
Baby What You Want Me To Do—Etta James (64)	*23*
Aw Shucks, Hush Your Mouth—Jimmy Reed (62)	16
Peepin' 'n Hidin'—Count Victors Featuring Danny Harrison (62)	12
Bright Lights, Big City—Sonny James (71)	*7.4*
Down In Virginia—Jimmy Reed (58)	4.6
Ain't That Loving You Baby—Betty Everett & Jerry Butler (64)	4.4
Baby, What's Wrong—Lonnie Mack (63)	3.6
Les REED ▶ 498 (17)	**8457**
There's A Kind Of Hush—Herman's Hermits (67)	*3675*
It's Not Unusual—Tom Jones (65)	2045
Kiss Me Goodbye—Petula Clark (68)	1753
Daughter Of Darkness—Tom Jones (70)	1619
Winter World Of Love—Engelbert Humperdinck (69)	1474
Delilah—Tom Jones (68)	1459
There's A Kind Of Hush (All Over The World)—Carpenters (76)	*1207*
The Last Waltz—Engelbert Humperdinck (67)	892
Les Bicyclettes De Belsize—Engelbert Humperdinck (68)	766
Here It Comes Again—Fortunes (65)	517
Everybody Knows—Dave Clark Five (67)	437
When There's No You—Engelbert Humperdinck (71)	399
I'm Coming Home—Tom Jones (67)	237
Everybody Knows—Steve Lawrence (64)	236
I Never Said Goodbye—Engelbert Humperdinck (72)	187
Love Is All—Engelbert Humperdinck (73)	9.8
To Make A Big Man Cry—Roy Head (66)	4.2
Lou REED ▶ 2168 (5)	**1796**
Wildside—Marky Mark & The Funky Bunch (91)	*1432*
Walk On The Wild Side—Lou Reed (73)	*996*
A World Without Heroes—KISS (81)	167
Rock 'N Roll—Detroit featuring Mitch Ryder (72)	22
Sweet Jane—Cowboy Junkies (89)	20
Mary Lee REED ▶ 8706 (2)	**42**
Good Lover—Jimmy Reed (62)	41
Down In Virginia—Jimmy Reed (58)	4.6
Ron REED ▶ 9075 (1)	**32**
Who Shot J.R.?—Gary Burbank with Band McNally (80)	95
—Buck Reeder see: Jan SAVAGE	
Eskew REEDER [Steven Quincy Reeder, Esquerita] ▶ 5678 (1)	**256**
Freedom Blues—Little Richard (70)	256
Raymond REEDER ▶ 3291 (1)	**909**
With You—Tony Terry (91)	909
—Steven Quincy Reeder see: Eskew REEDER	
Gordon REES [Melville Farley] ▶ 7581 (1)	**88**
My Son, My Son—Vera Lynn (54)	263
Philip REESE ▶ 9513 (1)	**22**
I'm Yours (Use Me Anyway You Wanna)—Ike & Tina Turner (71)	44

Ivan REEVE ▶ 6302 (1)	**184**
Don't Blame The Children—Sammy Davis Jr. (67)	367
C.P. REEVES ▶ 8693 (1)	**42**
Black Hands White Cotton—Caboose (70)	127
Eddie REEVES ▶ 1788 (5)	**2323**
All I Ever Need Is You—Sonny & Cher (71)	2452
Rings—Cymarron (71)	*1055*
Don't Change On Me—Ray Charles (71)	751
Rings—Lobo (74)	*367*
Rings—Reuben Howell (74)	*20*
Frederick Douglass REEVES ▶ 3722 (2)	**719**
Romeo—Dino (90)	1433
Roxanne, Roxanne—UTFO (85)	28
Jim REEVES ▶ 2183 (6)	**1771**
Am I Losing You—Jim Reeves (60)	823
I'm Gettin' Better—Jim Reeves (60)	599
What Would You Do?—Jim Reeves (61)	182
Is It Really Over?—Jim Reeves (65)	159
(How Can I Write On Paper) What I Feel In My Heart—Jim Reeves (61)	14
Need Me—Kitty Kallen (60)	4.0
—Ruth Evelyn Reeves see: Ruth LYONS	
—Shirley Reeves see: Shirley OWENS	
Russ REGAN [Harold Rustigan] ▶ 2787 (4)	**1197**
The Cinnamon Cinder (It's A Very Nice Dance)—Pastel Six (62)	850
The Dedication Song—Freddy Cannon (66)	337
The Flower Children—Marcia Strassman (67)	7.4
Junior Junior Junior—Russ Regan-Laura Lane (58)	7.4
Domenico REGIACORTE [Dominique Regia-Corte] ▶ 7143 (1)	**113**
Don Quichotte—Magazine 60 (86)	227
Noel REGNEY [Noel Paris, Léon Schlienger] ▶ 3661 (6)	**745**
Rain Rain Go Away—Bobby Vinton (62)	1134
What's The Use Of Cryin'—Eddie Fisher (58)	159
Judy—Frankie Vaughan (58)	113
Do You Hear What I Hear—Harry Simeone Chorale (62)	*38*
Cuddly Baby—Deb-Tones (58)	27
Do You Hear What I Hear?—Bing Crosby (63)	*20*
Bud REHAK [Andrew Racheck] ▶ 2478 (5)	**1451**
Navy Blue—Diane Renay (64)	2732
Kiss Me Sailor—Diane Renay (64)	606
The Push And Kick—Mark Valentino (62)	594
Here Comes The Boy—Tracey Dey (63)	47
Big-Town Boy—Shirley Matthews & The Big Town Girls (64)	32
Herbert REHBEIN ▶ 4043 (8) HOF	**614**
Lady—Jack Jones (67)	730
The World We Knew (Over And Over)—Frank Sinatra (67)	690
Wiederseh'n—Al Martino (66)	295
My Way Of Life—Frank Sinatra (68)	214
Remember When—Wayne Newton (65)	80
Sweet Maria—Billy Vaughn Singers (67)	18
You Turned My World Around—Frank Sinatra (74)	14
Lonely Is The Name—Sammy Davis Jr. (68)	7.6
Richard REICHEG ▶ 7002 (2)	**123**
Capture The Moment—Jay And The Americans (70)	340
Touch And Gone—Gary Wright (78)	19
—Ralph Reichenthal see: Ralph RAINGER	
Bickley REICHNER ▶ 995 (11)	**4503**
Papa Loves Mambo—Perry Como (54)	4276
I Need Your Love Tonight—Elvis Presley (59)	2712
Teen Age Prayer—Gale Storm (55)	*1780*
Mambo Rock—Bill Haley And His Comets (55)	*943*
Teen Age Prayer—Gloria Mann (55)	*625*
Dixie Danny—Laurie Sisters (55)	210
A Crazy Little Palace (That's My Home)—Billy Williams Quartet (56)	172
Teen Age Prayer—Kitty White (55)	*63*
The Large Large House—Mike Pedicin Quintet (56)	7.2
Up The Creek (Without A Paddle)—Matys Brothers (56)	7.2
Mambo Rock—Mike Pedicin Quintette (55)	*0.0*
Antonio REID [Antonio M. Reid, L.A. Reid] ▶ 243 (29)	**14187**
I'm Your Baby Tonight—Whitney Houston (90)	3804
On Our Own—Bobby Brown (89)	3434
Every Little Step—Bobby Brown (89)	2865
The Lover In Me—Sheena Easton (88)	2763
Giving You The Benefit—Pebbles (90)	2301
Girlfriend—Pebbles (88)	1891
The Way You Love Me—Karyn White (88)	1851
Can't Stop—After 7 (90)	1836
Secret Rendezvous—Karyn White (89)	1717
Rock Steady—Whispers (87)	1571
Don't Be Cruel—Bobby Brown (88)	1445
Superwoman—Karyn White (89)	1259
It's No Crime—Babyface (89)	1221
Miracle—Whitney Houston (91)	1127
Tender Lover—Babyface (89)	988
Dial My Heart—Boys (88)	927
Love Makes Things Happen—Pebbles (90)	846
Heat Of The Moment—After 7 (90)	*780*
My Kinda Girl—Babyface (90)	508
Fairweather Friend—Johnny Gill (90)	468
Knocked Out—Paula Abdul (88)	378
Stone Cold Gentleman—Ralph Tresvant (91)	369
Exclusivity—Damian Dame (91)	180
Body Talk—Deele (84)	140
Nothin (that compares 2 U)—Jacksons (89)	78
Heat Of The Moment—After 7 (89)	*76*
Backyard—Pebbles (91)	59
Right Down To It—Damian Dame (91)	17
Word To The Badd!!—Jermaine Jackson (91)	11
—Antonio M. Reid see: Antonio REID	
Bert REID ▶ 8418 (1)	**51**
I'll Do Anything For You—Denroy Morgan (81)	102
Billy REID ▶ 11381 (1)	**2.0**
I'm Walking Behind You—Crazy Otto (56)	2.0
Christopher REID ▶ 7802 (1)	**74**
Ain't Gonna Hurt Nobody—Kid 'N Play (91)	*223*
Clarence REID ▶ 1326 (15)	**3352**
Clean Up Woman—Betty Wright (71)	3048
Rockin' Chair—Gwen McCrae (75)	1685
Nobody But You Babe—Clarence Reid (69)	692
Baby Sitter—Betty Wright (72)	470
Girls Can't Do What The Guys Do—Betty Wright (68)	428
Secretary—Betty Wright (74)	230
It's Hard To Stop (Doing Something When It's Good To You)—Betty Wright (73)	116
Let Me Be Your Lovemaker—Betty Wright (73)	85
If You Love Me Like You Say You Love Me—Betty Wright (72)	41
Make Me Feel Like A Woman—Jackie Moore (75)	40
Don't Make The Good Girls Go Bad—Della Humphrey (68)	28
Ooola La—Betty Wright (75)	8.1
Funky Party—Clarence Reid (74)	6.5
You Got Your Thing On A String—J.P. Robinson (69)	3.1
I'm Gonna Tear You A New Heart—Clarence Reid (69)	1.8
Don REID ▶ 11818 (1)	**0.0**
The Green Years—Eddie Fisher (54)	0.0
Don S. REID ▶ 10236 (1)	**11**
I'll Go To My Grave Loving You—Statler Brothers (75)	11
Duke REID ▶ 1546 (1)	**2753**
The Tide Is High—Blondie (80)	5506
Harold REID ▶ 5205 (1)	**327**
Bed Of Rose's—Statler Brothers (71)	327
Ida REID ▶ 11407 (1)	**1.8**
You Gave Me Love—Crown Heights Affair (80)	1.8
Irving REID ▶ 5381 (8)	**298**
Things I Didn't Do—Perry Como (54)	320
Love Me As I Love You—George Maharis (62)	272
Give Me Your Love—Don Cornell (55)	148
Tonight My Heart Will Be Crying—Eddie Fisher (57)	*105*
And The Heavens Cried—Ronnie Savoy (60)	19
Johnny Be Smart—Sarah Vaughan (55)	19
Tonight My Heart She Is Crying—Shirley Bassey (57)	*0.0*
Tonight My Heart She Is Crying—El Boy with The Ralph Sayho Calypso Singers (57)	*0.0*
John REID ▶ 9494 (2)	**23**
It Hurts A Little Even Now—John Reid (75)	22
Ooh Ooh Ooh—Sam & Dave (69)	1.4
Keith REID ▶ 2034 (9)	**1980**
A Whiter Shade Of Pale—Procol Harum (67)	*3537*
Conquistador—Procol Harum (72)	1102
Homburg—Procol Harum (67)	393
You're The Voice—John Farnham (90)	64
A Whiter Shade Of Pale—R.B. Greaves (70)	*62*
A Whiter Shade Of Pale—Hesitations (68)	*29*
A Whiter Shade Of Pale—Procol Harum (72)	*14*
Whiter Shade Of Pale—Hagar, Schon, Aaronson, Shrieve (84)	*5.6*
A Whiter Shade Of Pale—Shorty Long (69)	*0.4*
—L.A. Reid see: Antonio REID	
Mike REID ▶ 2545 (2)	**1397**
I Can't Make You Love Me—Bonnie Raitt (91)	1228
Stranger In My House—Ronnie Milsap (83)	783
Perri Arlette REID [Perri McKissack, Pebbles] ▶ 1297 (3)	**3422**
Mercedes Boy—Pebbles (88)	2344
Whip Appeal—Babyface (90)	1497
Tender Lover—Babyface (89)	988
Sam REID ▶ 2928 (4)	**1114**
Don't Forget Me (When I'm Gone)—Glass Tiger (86)	2668
I'm Still Searching—Glass Tiger (88)	408
I Will Be There—Glass Tiger (87)	374
My Song—Glass Tiger (88)	41
Vernon REID ▶ 3444 (3)	**846**
Cult Of Personality—Living Colour (89)	1195
Glamour Boys—Living Colour (89)	511
Open Letter (To A Landlord)—Living Colour (89)	71
Teddy REIG ▶ 11222 (1)	**2.7**
Red's Dream—Louisiana Red (63)	8.1
Maggie REILLY ▶ 5533 (1)	**274**
Family Man—Daryl Hall & John Oates (83)	1641
Mike REILLY ▶ 9073 (1)	**32**
1927 Kansas City—Mike Reilly (71)	32
Frank REINA ▶ 9980 (2)	**14**
Where I Fell In Love—Capris (61)	71
Limbo—Capris (62)	0.9
Peggy REINAGLE ▶ 11506 (1)	**1.4**
You're So Nice To Be Near—Loreleis (55)	2.8
Johnny REINE [John Harold Johnston] ▶ 4866 (1)	**396**
Red River Rose—Ames Brothers (58)	793
Gladys REINHARDT [Gladys Hart] ▶ 1278 (6)	**3474**
White Silver Sands—Don Rondo (57)	*2977*
White Silver Sands—Bill Black's Combo (60)	*2957*
White Silver Sands—Dave Gardner (57)	*795*
-twistin'-White Silver Sands—Bill Black's Combo (62)	*118*
White Silver Sands—Owen Bradley Quintet (57)	*101*
White Silver Sands—Lennon Sisters (57)	*0.0*
Maurice J. REIS ▶ 8248 (1)	**57**
That's My Heart Strings (That's My Boy)—Burl Ives (56)	114
Bert REISFELD ▶ 978 (4)	**4588**
The Three Bells—Browns (59)	*8482*
Baciare Baciare (Kissing Kissing)—Dorothy Collins (59)	*405*
The Three Bells—Dick Flood (59)	*386*
The Three Bells—Tokens (65)	*36*
Richard REISING ▶ 10386 (1)	**9.2**
There's No Surf In Cleveland—Euclid Beach Band (78)	18
Joe REISMAN [George Armand] ▶ 3452 (3)	**842**
Joey's Song—Bill Haley And His Comets (59)	*653*
Ring A Ling A Lario—Jimmie Rodgers (59)	492
Joey's Song—Bill Black's Combo (62)	*26*
Ed REKERS ▶ 9240 (1)	**28**
Sailing Ships—Mesa (77)	140
—Derf Reklaw see: Derf Reklaw RAHEEM	
Bob RELF ▶ 2827 (4)	**1168**
Harlem Shuffle—Rolling Stones (86)	*1790*
Harlem Shuffle—Bob & Earl (63)	*494*
Harlem Shuffle—Traits (66)	*32*
Don't Ever Leave Me—Bob & Earl (62)	20
Keith RELF ▶ 3003 (3)	**1072**
Shapes Of Things—Yardbirds (66)	1778
Over Under Sideways Down—Yardbirds (66)	1583
Happenings Ten Years Time Ago—Yardbirds (66)	652
Emidio REMIGI ▶ 7006 (1)	**122**
Can I Trust You?—Bachelors (66)	366
—Paul Remy see: MANTOVANI	
Jean RENARD ▶ 2731 (1)	**1236**
Losing You—Brenda Lee (63)	2471
—Google René see: Rafael RENÉ	

Leon RENÉ [Jimmie Thomas] ▶ 302 (10)	**11967**
Rockin' Robin—Michael Jackson (72)	*5891*
Rock In Robin—Bobby Day (58)	*4824*
I Sold My Heart To The Junkman— Patti Labelle And The Blue Belles (62)	1375
Gee Whiz—Innocents (60)	*512*
When The Swallows Come Back To Capistrano— Pat Boone (57)	174
Bluebird The Buzzard And The Oriole—Bobby Day (58)	85
Hey Girl-Hey Boy— Oscar McLollie and Jeannette Baker (58)	41
Rockin' Robin—Rivieras (2) (64)	*18*
Wiggle-Tail (Pts. 1 & 2)—Googie René (58)	12
Gee Whiz—Bobby Day (with Earl Nelson) (60)	*0.0*
Malou RENÉ ▶ 663 (5)	**6547**
Tossin' And Turnin'—Bobby Lewis (61)	*12039*
One Track Mind—Bobby Lewis (61)	895
Never, Never—Jive Five (61)	83
What A Walk—Bobby Lewis (61)	73
Tossin' And Turnin'—Bunny Sigler (73)	*2.2*
Otis RENÉ ▶ 3828 (1)	**688**
I Sold My Heart To The Junkman— Patti Labelle And The Blue Belles (62)	1375
Rafael RENÉ [Rafael L. "Google" René, Rafael Leon René, Google René, Jeanne Vikki] ▶ 4759 (6)	**422**
Gee Whiz—Innocents (60)	*512*
Beautiful Weekend—Ernie Freeman (57)	*122*
Smokey Joe's La La—Googie René Combo (66)	44
Beautiful Weekend—Googie René (57)	*0.0*
Beautiful Weekend—Andy Anderson (57)	*0.0*
Gee Whiz—Bobby Day (with Earl Nelson) (60)	*0.0*
Bud RENEAU ▶ 4635 (5)	**447**
The Days Of Sand And Shovels—Bobby Vinton (69)	595
All I Need Is Time—Gladys Knight & The Pips (73)	125
Somewhere Between Love And Tomorrow— Roy Clark (73)	31
Sweet Summer Lovin'—Dolly Parton (79)	17
Big Bruce—Steve Greenberg (69)	*3.1*
—Jerry Renewych see: Bob BILYK	
Tony RENIS [Elio Cesare] ▶ 3908 (4)	**661**
All Of You—Julio Iglesias & Diana Ross (84)	919
Never, Never, Never (Grande, Grande, Grande)— Shirley Bassey (73)	433
Tonight I'll Say A Prayer—Eydie Gorme (69)	420
Quando, Quando, Quando (Tell Me When)— Pat Boone (62)	2.6
—Jerry Reno see: Gerry ROBINSON	
Mike RENO ▶ 2132 (10)	**1835**
This Could Be The Night—Loverboy (86)	1219
Heaven In Your Eyes—Loverboy (86)	1186
Working For The Weekend—Loverboy (81)	740
When It's Over—Loverboy (82)	624
Turn Me Loose—Loverboy (81)	624
Queen Of The Broken Hearts—Loverboy (83)	453
Notorious—Loverboy (87)	386
Lead A Double Life—Loverboy (86)	114
Jump—Loverboy (82)	67
Too Hot—Loverboy (89)	53
Tim RENWICK ▶ 9382 (1)	**25**
Keep On Running Away—Lazy Racer (79)	50
Louise RENY ▶ 9550 (1)	**22**
Angel In My Pocket—One To One (86)	43
Joe RENZETTI ▶ 10862 (1)	**4.8**
The Boy With The Beatle Hair—Swans (64)	19
Artie RESNICK ▶ 346 (19)	**10856**
Good Lovin'—Young Rascals (66)	*6878*
Under The Boardwalk—Drifters (64)	*4327*
Yummy Yummy Yummy—Ohio Express (68)	4175
One Kiss For Old Times' Sake—Ronnie Dove (65)	1675
A Little Bit Of Heaven—Ronnie Dove (65)	1532
Chip Chip—Gene McDaniels (62)	1262
Quick Joey Small (Run Joey Run)— Kasenetz-Katz Singing Orchestral Circus (68)	1017
I've Got Sand In My Shoes—Drifters (64)	540
Run, Run, Run—Third Rail (67)	409
I Left My Heart In The Balcony—Linda Scott (62)	134
Under The Boardwalk—Bruce Willis (87)	*110*
Under The Boardwalk—Billy Joe Royal (78)	*71*
Good Lovin'—Olympics (65)	*51*
All's Quiet On West 23rd—Julie Budd (68)	31
The Record (Baby, I Love You)—Ben E. King (65)	22
Good Lovin'—Grateful Dead (78)	*19*
I Found A Daisy In The City—Barry Darvell (65)	11
That's The Tune—Vogues (66)	2.9
Never Love A Robin—Bobby Vee (63)	0.9
Kris RESNICK ▶ 2033 (8)	**1982**
Chewy Chewy—Ohio Express (68)	2224
Down At Lulu's—Ohio Express (68)	793
Shake—Shadows Of Knight (68)	446
Run, Run, Run—Third Rail (67)	409
You Got The Love— Professor Morrison's Lollipop (68)	178
I'm In Love With You— Kasenetz-Katz Super Cirkus (69)	46
Yes Sir—Music Explosion (68)	2.3
Down In Tennessee— Kasenetz-Katz Singing Orchestral Circus (68)	1.3
Pam RESWICK ▶ 4898 (3)	**385**
I Live For Your Love—Natalie Cole (87)	1072
I'm Gonna Miss You—Kenny Loggins (88)	60
If You're Serious—Riff (91)	15
Allan REUSS ▶ 10267 (1)	**11**
More And More—Andy Williams (67)	32
—Franz Reuther see: Frank FARIAN	
—Jacques Revaud see: Jacques REVAUX	
Jacques REVAUX [Jacques Revaud] ▶ 4413 (3)	**501**
My Way—Frank Sinatra (69)	*701*
My Way—Elvis Presley (77)	*551*
My Way—Brook Benton (70)	*250*
Harry REVEL ▶ 4812 (4) HOF	**408**
Never In A Million Years—Linda Scott (62)	379
With My Eyes Wide Open I'm Dreaming— Patti Page (59)	*353*
Did You Ever See A Dream Walking—Fats Domino (62)	82
With My Eyes Wide Open I'm Dreaming— Enoch Light & The Light Brigade (59)	*2.9*
Paul REVERE [Paul Revere Dick] ▶ 3075 (4)	**1024**
The Great Airplane Strike—Paul Revere And The Raiders Featuring Mark Lindsay (66)	812
Like, Long Hair—Paul Revere And The Raiders (61)	478
Steppin' Out—Paul Revere And The Raiders (65)	473
Melody For An Unknown Girl—Unknowns (66)	78
Rudi REVIL ▶ 4420 (4)	**499**
Little Shoemaker—Gaylords (54)	*1620*
Little Shoemaker— Hugo Winterhalter And His Orchestra (54)	*307*
Marjolaina—Gogi Grant (58)	31
The Water Tumbler Tune— Henri René And His Orchestra And Chorus (55)	13
Kimberly REW ▶ 2032 (4)	**1986**
Walking On Sunshine—Katrina And The Waves (85)	1470
That's The Way—Katrina And The Waves (89)	667
Que Te Quiero—Katrina And The Waves (85)	100
Is That It?—Katrina And The Waves (86)	83
Al REX [Albert Piccirilli] ▶ 9989 (1)	**14**
Blue Comet Blues—Bill Haley And His Comets (56)	29
Stephen REXFORD ▶ 10489 (1)	**7.9**
(I've Been Lookin' For) A New Way To Say I Love You— Driver (77)	24
—Tony Rey see: Anthony Michael BRUNO	
—George Reyam see: Hans-Jörg MAYER	
Evangelina REYES ▶ 10059 (1)	**13**
Tic Toc Polly Woc— Perez Prado And His Orchestra (59)	13
Franc REYES ▶ 4217 (3)	**560**
Temptation—Corina (91)	1924
Together Forever—Lisette Melendez (91)	295
A Day In My Life (Without You)— Lisette Melendez (91)	230
Sergio REYES [Mellow Man Ace] ▶ 4421 (2)	**498**
Mentirosa—Mellow Man Ace (90)	977
Low Rider (On The Boulevard)—Latin Alliance (91)	121
Allen REYNOLDS ▶ 831 (7)	**5314**
Five O'Clock World—Vogues (65)	4152
I Saw Linda Yesterday—Dickey Lee (62)	1731
Ready For The Times To Get Better— Crystal Gayle (78)	165
Don't Wanna Think About Paula—Dickey Lee (63)	112
The Girl From Peyton Place—Dickey Lee (65)	79
The Dodo—Jumpin' Gene Simmons (64)	77
Big Brother—Dickey Lee (64)	30
Art REYNOLDS ▶ 4084 (3)	**599**
Jesus Is Just Alright—Doobie Brothers (72)	*517*
Jesus Is Just Alright—Byrds (70)	*54*
Glory, Glory—Byrds (71)	28
Chris REYNOLDS ▶ 10345 (1)	**9.7**
Russian Radio—Red Flag (89)	19
Curtis REYNOLDS ▶ 9324 (1)	**26**
I Don't Know What It Is, But It Sure Is Funky— Ripple (73)	184
Dick REYNOLDS ▶ 3790 (4)	**698**
Silver Threads And Golden Needles— Springfields (62)	*905*
Silver Threads And Golden Needles—Cowsills (69)	*233*
Silver Threads And Golden Needles—Jody Miller (65)	*200*
Silver Threads And Golden Needles— Linda Ronstadt (74)	*58*
Ellis REYNOLDS ▶ 7083 (4)	**117**
I'm Confessin' (That I Love You)—Frank Ifield (63)	*333*
I'm Confessin' (That I Love You)—Terri Dean (59)	*10*
I'm Confessin' (That I Love You)— Nino Tempo & April Stevens (64)	*6.7*
I'm Confessin' That I Love You—Barbara Lantz (59)	*0.0*
Eugene REYNOLDS [Alan Bernard Forbes] ▶ 6153 (1)	**199**
Heart Like A Wheel—Human League (90)	398
Jack REYNOLDS ▶ 10029 (1)	**14**
Time—Teresa Brewer (54)	28
J.J. REYNOLDS ▶ 4250 (2)	**545**
Battle Of Kookamonga—Homer & Jethro (59)	1052
Jimmy Love—Cathy Carroll (61)	38
Jody REYNOLDS [Dolores Nance] ▶ 1884 (4)	**2158**
Endless Sleep—Jody Reynolds (58)	*2075*
Endless Sleep—Hank Williams, Jr. (64)	*69*
Fire Of Love—Jody Reynolds (58)	30
Endless Sleep—Gene Ross (58)	*0.0*
Lawrence REYNOLDS ▶ 5202 (1)	**328**
Jesus Is A Soul Man—Lawrence Reynolds (69)	656
Malvina REYNOLDS [Malvina Milder] ▶ 2548 (6)	**1393**
Turn Around—Dick And Deedee (63)	714
What Have They Done To The Rain—Searchers (65)	570
Morningtown Ride—Seekers (67)	391
Little Boxes—Pete Seeger (64)	*168*
Little Boxes—Womenfolk (64)	*21*
Sally—Kingston Trio (59)	11
Mark REYNOLDS ▶ 10344 (1)	**9.7**
Russian Radio—Red Flag (89)	19
Paul REYNOLDS ▶ 3703 (4)	**728**
I Ran (So Far Away)—A Flock Of Seagulls (82)	1474
Space Age Love Song—A Flock Of Seagulls (82)	637
Wishing (If I Had A Photograph Of You)— A Flock Of Seagulls (83)	612
The More You Live, The More You Love— A Flock Of Seagulls (84)	187
Rickie REYNOLDS ▶ 11555 (1)	**1.2**
Strong Enough To Be Gentle— Black Oak Arkansas (76)	8.4
Thomas REYNOLDS ▶ 7372 (1)	**100**
Day After Day (It's Slippin' Away)—Shango (69)	299
Clifford RHODES ▶ 4080 (1)	**600**
Why Do I Love You So—Johnny Tillotson (60)	600
Donna RHODES ▶ 7917 (2)	**70**
City In The Sky—Staple Singers (74)	205
Scandal—RCR (80)	4.2
Doug RHODES ▶ 11621 (1)	**1.0**
Just About The Same—Association (70)	4.8
Dusty RHODES ▶ 6005 (1)	**217**
Under Your Spell Again—Johnny Rivers (65)	434
Emitt RHODES ▶ 3274 (4)	**915**
Fresh As A Daisy—Emitt Rhodes (70)	513
Live—Merry-Go-Round (67)	252
(She's A) Very Lovely Woman—Linda Ronstadt (71)	*102*
You're A Very Lovely Woman—Merry-Go-Round (67)	*50*
—Helen Rhodes see: Guy D'HARDELOT	
Jack RHODES ▶ 2879 (11)	**1134**
Silver Threads And Golden Needles— Springfields (62)	*905*
A Satisfied Mind—Bobby Hebb (66)	*440*
Satisfied Mind—Ella Fitzgerald (55)	*294*

Jack RHODES ▶ 2879 (11) *Continued*	**1134**
Silver Threads And Golden Needles—Cowsills (69)	*233*
Silver Threads And Golden Needles—Jody Miller (65)	*200*
Woman Love—Gene Vincent and His Blue Caps (56)	69
Silver Threads And Golden Needles— Linda Ronstadt (74)	*58*
Satisfied Mind—Jack And Betty (55)	*0.0*
A Satisfied Mind—Jeffrey Clay (55)	*0.0*
Satisfied Mind—Mahalia Jackson (55)	*0.0*
A Satisfied Mind—Porter Wagoner (55)	*0.0*
Nick RHODES [Nicholas James Bates] ▶ 502 (18)	**8432**
The Reflex—Duran Duran (84)	5082
Union Of The Snake—Duran Duran (83)	4545
The Wild Boys—Duran Duran (84)	4449
A View To A Kill—Duran Duran (85)	4032
Hungry Like The Wolf—Duran Duran (82)	3924
Notorious—Duran Duran (86)	3404
I Don't Want Your Love—Duran Duran (88)	2410
Is There Something I Should Know—Duran Duran (83)	2395
Election Day—Arcadia (85)	1950
New Moon On Monday—Duran Duran (84)	1339
Rio—Duran Duran (83)	946
Save A Prayer—Duran Duran (85)	773
All She Wants Is—Duran Duran (88)	486
Goodbye Is Forever—Arcadia (86)	432
Skin Trade—Duran Duran (87)	308
Violence Of Summer (Love's Taking Over)— Duran Duran (90)	165
Do You Believe In Shame?—Duran Duran (89)	93
Meet El Presidente—Duran Duran (87)	78
Perry RHODES ▶ 11504 (1)	**1.4**
Scandal—RCR (80)	4.2
Sandra RHODES ▶ 7292 (4)	**105**
City In The Sky—Staple Singers (74)	205
One Woman—Johnny Rivers (69)	62
Scandal—RCR (80)	4.2
How Much Can A Lonely Heart Stand— Skeeter Davis (64)	4.1
Stan RHODES ▶ 8423 (5)	**51**
Our Corner Of The Night—Barbra Streisand (68)	82
A Sunday Kind Of Love—Lenny Welch (72)	*26*
A Sunday Kind Of Love—Jan & Dean (62)	*7.3*
Sunday Kind Of Love—Etta James (61)	*5.7*
Sunday Kind Of Love—Fran Warren (58)	*0.8*
Taylor RHODES ▶ 2621 (2)	**1317**
Where Does My Heart Beat Now—Celine Dion (90)	2564
99 Worlds—Peter Wolf (90)	104
John RHYS ▶ 8647 (1)	**44**
Happiness—Shades Of Blue (66)	44
Roman RICARDO ▶ 9254 (1)	**28**
Like A Child—Noel (88)	83
Enrico RICCARDI ▶ 9415 (3)	**24**
Words (Are Impossible)—Donny Gerrard (76)	*29*
Vado Via—Drupi (73)	*22*
Words (Are Impossible)—Margie Joseph (74)	*9.9*
Joe RICCI ▶ 3773 (1)	**703**
Just Ask Your Heart—Frankie Avalon (59)	2110
Bill RICE ▶ 6172 (2)	**198**
When You Say Love—Sonny & Cher (72)	545
Wonder Could I Live There Anymore— Charley Pride (70)	16
Bonny RICE [Sir Mack Rice, Mack Rice] ▶ 1155 (9)	**3842**
Respect Yourself—Staple Singers (71)	*1800*
Respect Yourself—Bruce Willis (87)	*1395*
Mustang Sally—Wilson Pickett (66)	1089
Cheaper To Keep Her—Johnnie Taylor (73)	876
The Breakdown (Part 1)—Rufus Thomas (71)	588
Do The Funky Penguin Part 1—Rufus Thomas (71)	256
My Main Man—Staple Singers (74)	74
Puff Of Smoke—Roy Head (71)	2.1
Memphis Train—Buddy Miles Express (69)	0.4
—David Rice see: Josh RICE	
Eddie RICE [Stephen Rice] ▶ 10247 (1)	**11**
One In A Million—Eddie And The Tide (85)	11
Howard Lee RICE ▶ 7055 (2)	**119**
Hold Me—Menudo (85)	198
I'm Your Man—Barry Manilow (86)	60
Josh RICE [David Rice] ▶ 11541 (1)	**1.3**
It's-A-Happening—Magic Mushrooms (66)	3.8

Ronnie RICE ▶ 2235 (5)	**1715**
Things I'd Like To Say—New Colony Six (68)	1717
I Will Always Think About You—New Colony Six (68)	1256
I Could Never Lie To You—New Colony Six (69)	444
Long Time To Be Alone—New Colony Six (71)	15
You're Gonna Be Mine—New Colony Six (67)	2.8
—Sir Mack Rice see: Bonny RICE	
—Stephen Rice see: Eddie RICE	
Tim RICE ▶ 1210 (16) HOF	**3673**
One Night In Bangkok—Murray Head (85)	*2683*
Superstar— Murray Head With The Trinidad Singers (69)	*1860*
I Don't Know How To Love Him—Helen Reddy (71)	*1613*
I Don't Know How To Love Him—Yvonne Elliman (71)	*783*
Superstar - Jesus Christ Superstar— Murray Head (71)	*656*
All Time High—Rita Coolidge (83)	493
Don't Cry For Me Argentina—Festival (80)	63
One Night In Bangkok—Robey (85)	*55*
Everything's Alright—Yvonne Elliman (71)	*28*
Christmas Dream—Perry Como (74)	13
Superstar—Assembled Multitude (71)	*4.1*
The Temple—Assembled Multitude (71)	4.1
Simon Zealotes—Assembled Multitude (71)	4.1
Everything's Alright—Assembled Multitude (71)	*4.1*
Everything's Alright—Kimberlys (71)	*0.4*
I Don't Know How To Love Him—Kimberlys (71)	*0.4*
Verlie RICE ▶ 2786 (3)	**1197**
Twine Time—Alvin Cash & The Crawlers (65)	1567
Shake A Tail Feather—James & Bobby Purify (67)	*829*
Shake A Tail Feather—Five Du-Tones (63)	*412*
Allan RICH [Allan Dennis Rich, Richard Alan Waggoner] ▶ 1744 (4)	**2377**
I Don't Have The Heart—James Ingram (90)	3801
I Live For Your Love—Natalie Cole (87)	1072
Hold Me—Menudo (85)	198
I'm Your Man—Barry Manilow (86)	60
—Allan Dennis Rich see: Allan RICH	
Barry RICH ▶ 6176 (1)	**197**
Bongo Stomp—Little Joey And The Flips (62)	592
Charlie RICH ▶ 1498 (10)	**2900**
Lonely Weekends—Charlie Rich (60)	1117
There Won't Be Anymore—Charlie Rich (74)	987
Every Time You Touch Me (I Get High)— Charlie Rich (75)	743
Ways Of A Woman In Love— Johnny Cash And The Tennessee Two (58)	454
Break Up— Jerry Lee Lewis And His Pumping Piano (58)	98
Who Will The Next Fool Be—Bobby Bland (62)	56
Are You Still My Baby—Shirelles (64)	28
Rosanna—Capreez (66)	6.2
I Just Thought You'd Like To Know—Johnny Cash (58)	6.1
I'll Make It All Up To You— Jerry Lee Lewis And His Pumping Piano (58)	5.9
Dave RICH ▶ 8808 (1)	**39**
My Jimmie—Jeanie Johnson (58)	39
—Denise Rich see: Joy DENNY	
Don RICH [Donald Eugene Ulrich] ▶ 6443 (4)	**168**
Waitin' In Your Welfare Line—Buck Owens (66)	224
Think Of Me—Buck Owens And The Buckaroos (66)	122
Before You Go—Buck Owens (65)	61
Santa Looked A Lot Like Daddy—Buck Owens (65)	4.7
James RICH ▶ 5012 (2)	**359**
Yakety Sax—Boots Randolph (63)	*699*
Yakety Axe—Chet Atkins (65)	*19*
Cliff RICHARD [Harry Rodger Webb] ▶ 10898 (1)	**4.5**
Bachelor Boy—Cliff Richard And The Shadows (64)	9.0
Frank RICHARD ▶ 10536 (1)	**7.5**
Action Speaks Louder Than Words— Chocolate Milk (75)	67
—Little Richard see: Richard PENNIMAN	
Renald RICHARD ▶ 3684 (4)	**734**
I've Got A Woman Part 1—Jimmy McGriff (62)	*782*
I Got A Woman—Rick Nelson (63)	*361*
I Got A Woman—Freddie Scott (63)	*269*
I Gotta Woman (Part One)— Ray Charles And His Orchestra (65)	*57*
Tommy RICHARD ▶ 9123 (1)	**31**
Feel Alright—Cargoe (72)	31

Deke RICHARDS [Deke Lussier, Dennis Lussier] ▶ 333 (13)	**11066**
Love Child—Diana Ross And The Supremes (68)	*9676*
ABC—Jackson 5 (70)	8551
I Want You Back—Jackson 5 (69)	7904
The Love You Save—Jackson 5 (70)	6071
Mama's Pearl—Jackson 5 (71)	4810
Sugar Daddy—Jackson 5 (71)	2514
O.P.P.—Naughty By Nature (91)	1392
Love Child—Sweet Sensation (90)	*1079*
Maybe Tomorrow—Jackson 5 (71)	977
I Can't Dance To That Music You're Playin'— Martha Reeves & The Vandellas (68)	435
Bless You—Martha Reeves & The Vandellas (71)	298
I'm Still Waiting—Diana Ross (71)	167
I Found That Girl—Jackson 5 (70)	51
Dick RICHARDS [Richard Papazaian] ▶ 9695 (1)	**19**
Honey Hair Sugar Lips Eyes Of Blue—Crew-Cuts (56)	19
Dwight RICHARDS ▶ 10539 (1)	**7.5**
Action Speaks Louder Than Words— Chocolate Milk (75)	67
Greg RICHARDS ▶ 2040 (3)	**1970**
She Cried—Jay & The Americans (62)	*3516*
She Cried—Lettermen (70)	*222*
He Cried—Shangri-Las (66)	*202*
Jack RICHARDS ▶ 1136 (6)	**3901**
He—Al Hibbler (55)	*4351*
He—McGuire Sisters (55)	*1919*
He—Righteous Brothers (66)	*1116*
Hopelessly—Ames Brothers (54)	367
Queen Of The Senior Prom—Mills Brothers (57)	*255*
Queen Of The Senior Prom—Mills Brothers (62)	*1.4*
—Jake Hooker Richards see: Jake HOOKER	
Jay RICHARDS ▶ 10268 (1)	**11**
You're Running Out Of Kisses—Chuck Foote (61)	21
Johnny RICHARDS [Juan Ricardo Cascales] ▶ 11819 (1)	**0.0**
Young At Heart—Frank Sinatra (54)	0.0
Keith RICHARDS ▶ 23 (66) HOF	**56846**
Honky Tonk Women—Rolling Stones (69)	10430
(I Can't Get No) Satisfaction—Rolling Stones (65)	*10038*
Paint It, Black—Rolling Stones (66)	7253
Ruby Tuesday—Rolling Stones (67)	*7240*
Get Off Of My Cloud—Rolling Stones (65)	6209
Brown Sugar—Rolling Stones (71)	6055
19th Nervous Breakdown—Rolling Stones (66)	5987
Jumpin' Jack Flash—Rolling Stones (68)	*5867*
Miss You—Rolling Stones (78)	5848
Angie—Rolling Stones (73)	5117
Start Me Up—Rolling Stones (81)	4381
Emotional Rescue—Rolling Stones (80)	3524
Mother's Little Helper—Rolling Stones (66)	3076
As Tears Go By—Rolling Stones (65)	*2591*
Have You Seen Your Mother, Baby, Standing In The Shadow?—Rolling Stones (66)	2548
Tumbling Dice—Rolling Stones (72)	*2232*
Mixed Emotions—Rolling Stones (89)	1864
The Last Time—Rolling Stones (65)	*1655*
Dandelion—Rolling Stones (67)	1620
Beast Of Burden—Rolling Stones (78)	*1440*
Undercover Of The Night—Rolling Stones (83)	1367
She's A Rainbow—Rolling Stones (67)	1131
Heart Of Stone—Rolling Stones (65)	1125
Waiting On A Friend—Rolling Stones (81)	1065
Doo Doo Doo Doo Doo (Heartbreaker)— Rolling Stones (74)	973
It's Only Rock 'N Roll (But I Like It)— Rolling Stones (74)	936
As Tears Go By—Marianne Faithfull (64)	*926*
Happy—Rolling Stones (72)	891
Tell Me (You're Coming Back)—Rolling Stones (64)	793
Fool To Cry—Rolling Stones (76)	750
Rock And A Hard Place—Rolling Stones (89)	727
Wild Horses—Rolling Stones (71)	724
Satisfaction—Otis Redding (66)	*624*
She's So Cold—Rolling Stones (80)	599
Hot Stuff—Rolling Stones (76)	567
Let's Spend The Night Together—Rolling Stones (67)	*544*
Jumpin' Jack Flash—Aretha Franklin (86)	*527*
Hang Fire—Rolling Stones (82)	495
Shattered—Rolling Stones (78)	473

Keith RICHARDS ▶ 23 (66) *Continued*	**56846**
Street Fighting Man—Rolling Stones (68)	467
You Can't Always Get What You Want— Rolling Stones (73)	*462*
One Hit (To The Body)—Rolling Stones (86)	449
Lady Jane—Rolling Stones (66)	445
Ruby Tuesday—Melanie (70)	*414*
We Love You—Rolling Stones (67)	336
That Girl Belongs To Yesterday—Gene Pitney (64)	317
Tumbling Dice—Linda Ronstadt (78)	*309*
Waiting For That Day—George Michael (91)	248
You Can't Always Get What You Want— George Michael (91)	*248*
She Was Hot—Rolling Stones (84)	242
Almost Hear You Sigh—Rolling Stones (90)	209
Gimme Shelter—Grand Funk Railroad (71)	*207*
Highwire—Rolling Stones (91)	174
Gimme Shelter—Merry Clayton (70)	*105*
Out Of Time—Rolling Stones (75)	74
Beast Of Burden—Bette Midler (84)	*71*
I'm Free—Soup Dragons (90)	48
All Down The Line—Rolling Stones (72)	43
The Last Time—Buchanan Brothers (69)	*38*
Sittin' On A Fence—Twice As Much (66)	19
Jumpin' Jack Flash—Johnny Winter (71)	*15*
Let's Spend The Night Together—David Bowie (73)	*7.4*
Play With Fire—Rolling Stones (65)	2.3
Under My Thumb—Del Shannon (66)	*1.4*
Under My Thumb—Hounds (80)	*1.0*
(I Can't Get No) Satisfaction—Tight Fit (81)	*0.9*
Keni RICHARDS ▶ 6883 (1)	**131**
Turn Up The Radio—Autograph (84)	654
Nick RICHARDS ▶ 5694 (1)	**254**
I Wanna Be A Cowboy—Boys Don't Cry (86)	1016
Regina RICHARDS [Regina Marie Cuttita, Regina Marie Lee] ▶ 4468 (1)	**487**
Baby Love—Regina (86)	1461
Terry RICHARDS [Terrence Richard Marinan] ▶ 4649 (1)	**446**
Get It On—Chase (71)	891
Cindy RICHARDSON ▶ 4780 (1)	**418**
Almost Over You—Sheena Easton (83)	835
Clive RICHARDSON ▶ 6387 (3)	**176**
Earthbound—Sammy Davis Jr. (56)	*404*
Earthbound—Mario Lanza (56)	*123*
Earthbound—Roberto & His Orchestra (56)	*0.0*
David RICHARDSON ▶ 2725 (2)	**1240**
Wildflower—Skylark (73)	*2222*
Wildflower—New Birth (74)	*257*
Dwayne RICHARDSON ▶ 8363 (1)	**53**
Got A Love For You—Jomanda (91)	318
—George Baker Richardson see: George RICHEY	
Graham RICHARDSON ▶ 9614 (1)	**20**
Do Ya Do Ya (Wanna Please Me)—Samantha Fox (87)	40
Hal RICHARDSON ▶ 11781 (2)	**0.0**
Break My Heart Gently—Dorothy Collins (54)	0.0
Can This Be The End Of A Dream— Dorothy Collins (54)	0.0
Ian RICHARDSON ▶ 9636 (1)	**20**
Doctorin' The Tardis—Timelords (88)	159
J.P. RICHARDSON ▶ 248 (12)	**14015**
Running Bear—Johnny Preston (59)	*8748*
Chantilly Lace—Big Bopper (58)	*3893*
Chantilly Lace—Jerry Lee Lewis (72)	*436*
Big Bopper's Wedding—Big Bopper (58)	402
Chantilly Lace— Cat Mother And The All Night News Boys (69)	*164*
Little Red Riding Hood—Big Bopper (58)	92
Chantilly Lace—Mitch Ryder (68)	*83*
Running Bear— Sonny James The Southern Gentleman (69)	*63*
One More Chance—Rod Bernard (59)	63
White Lightning—George Jones (59)	55
Purple People Eater Meets The Witch Doctor— Joe South (58)	19
Chantilly Lace— Jive Bunny & The Mastermixers (90)	*6.7*
—Nancy Richardson see: Taja SEVELLE	
Nicholas RICHARDSON [Dick Peterson] ▶ 11132 (1)	**3.1**
Don't Say No—Kingsmen (67)	6.1

George RICHEY [George Baker Richardson] ▶ 5991 (3)	**219**
Soul Song—Joe Stampley (73)	580
'Til I Can Make It On My Own—Tammy Wynette (76)	66
Keep Me In Mind—Lynn Anderson (73)	6.5
Langston RICHEY ▶ 8245 (1)	**57**
I Need Your Loving—Human League (86)	343
Brenda RICHIE ▶ 1593 (2)	**2652**
You Are—Lionel Richie (83)	3893
Penny Lover—Lionel Richie (84)	1411
Lionel RICHIE ▶ 4 (35) HOF	**91106**
Endless Love—Diana Ross & Lionel Richie (81)	10664
Lady—Kenny Rogers (80)	8815
Three Times A Lady—Commodores (78)	8054
All Night Long (All Night)—Lionel Richie (83)	7823
Say You, Say Me—Lionel Richie (85)	6445
Hello—Lionel Richie (84)	6227
We Are The World—USA for Africa (85)	6108
Truly—Lionel Richie (82)	5536
Still—Commodores (79)	*5152*
Sail On—Commodores (79)	4188
You Are—Lionel Richie (83)	3893
Dancing On The Ceiling—Lionel Richie (86)	3417
Stuck On You—Lionel Richie (84)	3398
Oh No—Commodores (81)	2960
Easy—Commodores (77)	2936
Sweet Love—Commodores (75)	2624
Brick House—Commodores (77)	1962
Running With The Night—Lionel Richie (83)	1890
My Love—Lionel Richie (83)	1760
Just To Be Close To You—Commodores (76)	1708
Missing You—Diana Ross (84)	1594
Love Will Conquer All—Lionel Richie (86)	1538
Penny Lover—Lionel Richie (84)	1411
Ballerina Girl—Lionel Richie (86)	1411
Se La—Lionel Richie (87)	642
Too Hot Ta Trot—Commodores (77)	499
Happy People—Temptations (74)	375
Flying High—Commodores (78)	306
Fancy Dancer—Commodores (76)	271
Heroes—Commodores (80)	211
Why You Wanna Try Me—Commodores (82)	106
Deep River Woman—Lionel Richie (87)	85
I Feel Sanctified—Commodores (74)	83
Still—John Schneider (81)	*80*
This Is Your Life—Commodores (75)	28
Ernie RICHMAN ▶ 10925 (1)	**4.3**
I'll Search My Heart—Johnny Mathis (63)	13
—Jane Richman see: Jane CHILD	
—Howard S. Richmond see: Jessie CAVANAUGH	
Paul RICHMOND ▶ 2256 (3)	**1698**
Shining Star—Manhattans (80)	3368
In The Mood—Tyrone Davis (79)	31
I'll Never Find Another (Find Another Like You)— Manhattans (80)	7.4
Gary RICHRATH ▶ 1104 (5)	**4013**
Take It On The Run—REO Speedwagon (81)	3311
In Your Letter—REO Speedwagon (81)	612
Only The Strong Survive—REO Speedwagon (79)	43
Ridin' The Storm Out—REO Speedwagon (77)	29
Easy Money—REO Speedwagon (79)	19
Jascha RICHTER ▶ 9822 (1)	**16**
My Blue Angel—Michael Learns To Rock (91)	49
David RICKETTS ▶ 5055 (2)	**353**
Welcome To The Boomtown—David & David (86)	487
Ain't So Easy—David & David (87)	219
—Frederic Joseph Ricketts see: Kenneth J. ALFORD	
—Louis Rico see: Ken MOULE	
—Louis Rico see: Ted HEATH	
—Gladys Riddle see: Gladys HAMPTON	
Nelson RIDDLE ▶ 3725 (4)	**719**
Route 66 Theme— Nelson Riddle And His Orchestra (62)	644
Lolita Ya-Ya—Ventures (62)	88
That's You—Nat King Cole (60)	60
Johnny Concho Theme (Wait For Me)— Frank Sinatra (56)	23
Carlton RIDENHOUR [Chuck D.] ▶ 7708 (1)	**79**
Can't Truss It—Public Enemy (91)	238
—Margaret Jean Rider see: Maggie RYDER	

Antonia RIDGE ▶ 11782 (2)	**0.0**
The Happy Wanderer—Henri René's Musette (54)	*0.0*
The Happy Wanderer— Frank Weir & His Orchestra (54)	*0.0*
Andrew RIDGELEY ▶ 1492 (2)	**2917**
Careless Whisper— Wham! Featuring George Michael (84)	5730
Shake—Andrew Ridgeley (90)	103
Stan RIDGWAY [Stanard Funsten, Stanard Ridgway] ▶ 8381 (1)	**52**
Mexican Radio—Wall Of Voodoo (83)	209
Greg RIDLEY ▶ 7412 (1)	**97**
Hot 'N' Nasty—Humble Pie (72)	389
Teddy DeLano RIEDEL [Teddy Redell] ▶ 8659 (1)	**43**
Judy—Elvis Presley (67)	43
Otto RIEDLMAYER ▶ 5873 (1)	**234**
No One But You (In My Heart)— Ames Brothers (58)	468
Raffaele RIEFOLI ▶ 3250 (1)	**928**
Self Control—Laura Branigan (84)	2784
Jack RIELEY ▶ 7511 (3)	**91**
Sail On Sailor—Beach Boys (75)	*268*
Long Promised Road—Beach Boys (71)	56
Sail On Sailor—Beach Boys (73)	*49*
—Harlan Dale Riffe see: Dale WRIGHT	
Carlos RIGUAL ▶ 1573 (3)	**2690**
Love Me With All Your Heart (Cuando Caliente El Sol)—Ray Charles Singers (64)	*4884*
Love Me With All Of Your Heart—Bachelors (66)	*455*
Cuando Calienta El Sol (When The Sun Is Hot)— Steve Allen And His Orchestra With The Copacabana Trio (63)	*60*
Mario RIGUAL ▶ 9624 (1)	**20**
Cuando Calienta El Sol (When The Sun Is Hot)—Steve Allen And His Orchestra With The Copacabana Trio (63)	*60*
Billy Lee RILEY ▶ 9931 (1)	**15**
Shimmy, Shimmy Walk, Part 1—Megatons (62)	15
Clemon Timothy RILEY [Tim Christian, Timothy Christian Riley] ▶ 3898 (3)	**663**
Feels Good—Tony! Toni! Toné! (90)	1657
It Never Rains (In Southern California)— Tony! Toni! Toné! (90)	390
Little Walter—Tony! Toni! Toné! (88)	272
Jake RILEY ▶ 11142 (1)	**3.0**
Stranger—L.T.D. (79)	6.1
Melvin RILEY ▶ 1893 (2)	**2144**
Oh Sheila—Ready For The World (85)	2969
Love You Down—Ready For The World (86)	1154
Mike RILEY ▶ 10422 (1)	**8.6**
Music Goes 'Round And Around—Joe Pica (54)	26
Robert S. RILEY ▶ 1425 (4)	**3087**
Just Walking In The Rain—Johnnie Ray (56)	7908
Rollin' Stone— Fontane Sisters with Billy Vaughn's Orchestra (55)	*424*
B-I-N-G-O (Bingo)—Turbans (56)	28
Rollin' Stone—Eddie Fontaine with The Excels (55)	*0.0*
Steve RILEY ▶ 7213 (1)	**110**
The Ballad Of Jayne—L.A. Guns (90)	549
Teddy RILEY ▶ 1740 (11)	**2389**
I Like The Way (The Kissing Game)—Hi-Five (91)	2919
I Want Her—Keith Sweat (88)	1714
Is It Good To You—Heavy D & The Boyz (91)	404
I Wanna Get With U—Guy (90)	300
Make It Last Forever—Keith Sweat (88)	244
Let's Chill—Guy (91)	228
My Fantasy—Teddy Riley featuring Guy (89)	71
Something Just Ain't Right—Keith Sweat (88)	66
I Like—Guy (89)	56
Right And Hype—Abstrac' (89)	22
All About You—Pretty In Pink (91)	4.0
—Timothy Christian Riley see: Clemon Timothy RILEY	
Winston RILEY ▶ 5183 (1)	**329**
Double Barrel—Dave And Ansil Collins (71)	987
—Robert Rimato see: Robert HAZARD	
Nikolai RIMSKY-KORSAKOV ▶ 3259 (5)	**923**
Bumble Boogie—B. Bumble & The Stingers (61)	*975*
Flight '76—Walter Murphy Band (76)	418
Sweet Song Of India—McGuire Sisters (55)	182

Nikolai RIMSKY-KORSAKOV ▶ 3259 (5) *Continued*	**923**
Flight Of The Bumble Bee—Royal Philharmonic Orchestra (81)	*131*
Bumble Boogie—Ralph Marterie & His Orchestra (54)	*69*
—Giovanni Rota Rinaldi see: Nino ROTA	
Gary RINALDO [Gary G-Wiz] ▶ 7709 (1)	**79**
Can't Truss It—Public Enemy (91)	238
Laurin RINDER ▶ 7021 (3)	**121**
Cocomotion—El Coco (77)	261
Le Spank—Le Pamplemousse (77)	117
Dancing In Paradise—El Coco (78)	15
Al RINKER ▶ 9288 (4)	**27**
Ready Willing And Able—Doris Day (54)	*49*
Ready, Willing And Able—Gary Crosby (54)	*19*
Now Is The Time—Eileen Rodgers (55)	*4.4*
Now Is The Time—Paulette Sisters (55)	*4.4*
Chuck RIO ▶ 612 (6)	**7059**
Tequila—Champs (58)	*6762*
Tequila—Eddie Platt And His Orchestra (58)	*257*
Tequila—Hot Butter (72)	*30*
Tequila—Bill Black's Combo (64)	*9.9*
Tequila Twist—Champs (62)	*0.9*
Tequila—Stan Kenton & His Orchestra (58)	*0.0*
Jerry RIOPELLE ▶ 3258 (6)	**923**
Sunshine Girl—Parade (67)	687
All Strung Out—Nino Tempo & April Stevens (66)	*607*
All Strung Out On You—John Travolta (77)	*373*
Day After Day (It's Slippin' Away)—Shango (69)	299
Easy Driver—Kenny Loggins (78)	189
I Can't Go On Livin' Without You Baby—Nino Tempo & April Stevens (67)	19
David RIORDAN ▶ 2669 (2)	**1283**
Green-Eyed Lady—Sugarloaf (70)	3826
Mother Nature's Wine—Sugarloaf (71)	22
Carlos RIOS ▶ 2871 (1)	**1139**
Dancing On The Ceiling—Lionel Richie (86)	3417
Minnie RIPERTON ▶ 1441 (3)	**3033**
Lovin' You—Minnie Riperton (75)	6022
Inside My Love—Minnie Riperton (75)	64
Memory Lane—Minnie Riperton (79)	3.4
Artie RIPP ▶ 6140 (2)	**200**
Barbara—Temptations (2) (60)	582
Teenage Vows Of Love—Dreamers (61)	19
Louis RISBROOK ▶ 5188 (2)	**329**
Express—B.T. Express (75)	*2209*
Express—Ritchie Family (76)	*92*
William RISBROOK ▶ 5189 (2)	**329**
Express—B.T. Express (75)	*2209*
Express—Ritchie Family (76)	*92*
Paul RISER ▶ 2912 (3)	**1121**
What Becomes Of The Brokenhearted—Jimmy Ruffin (66)	2895
I Don't Know Why—Stevie Wonder (69)	*386*
I Don't Know Why—Rolling Stones (75)	*236*
Peter RISINGHAM [Peter Rizzo] ▶ 8653 (2)	**44**
Jealous—Gene Loves Jezebel (90)	164
The Motion Of Love—Gene Loves Jezebel (88)	11
Lee RITENOUR ▶ 4315 (3)	**524**
Is It You—Lee Ritenour (81)	902
Tied Up—Olivia Newton-John (83)	344
Cross My Heart—Lee Ritenour (82)	103
Claus RITTER [Gerd Thumser] ▶ 10816 (1)	**5.2**
Rosemarie—Pat Boone (64)	10
Gordon RITTER [Rick Johnson] ▶ 10364 (1)	**9.5**
Purple People Eater Meets The Witch Doctor—Joe South (58)	19
Melissa RITTER ▶ 7269 (1)	**106**
Second Chance—Tyler Collins (90)	213
David RITZ ▶ 2629 (1)	**1308**
Sexual Healing—Marvin Gaye (82)	3925
Hector RIVERA ▶ 9339 (1)	**26**
At The Party—Hector Rivera (66)	26
Jose RIVERA ▶ 8241 (1)	**57**
Going Through The Motions—Aftershock (91)	172
Pete RIVERA [Peter Hoorelbeke] ▶ 11689 (1)	**0.7**
We're Gonna Have A Good Time—Rare Earth (73)	4.3
Thomas RIVERA ▶ 11512 (1)	**1.4**
The Bells Are Ringing—Van Dykes (1) (61)	1.4
Johnny RIVERS [John Henry Ramistella] ▶ 1435 (3)	**3052**
Poor Side Of Town—Johnny Rivers (66)	*5962*
Poor Side Of Town—Al Wilson (68)	*132*
Ashes And Sand—Johnny Rivers (77)	5.1
David RIVKIN [David Z.] ▶ 6578 (1)	**154**
On The Way Up—Elisa Fiorillo (90)	617
Robert RIVKIN [Bobby Z.] ▶ 7139 (2)	**114**
Waterfall—Wendy & Lisa (87)	232
America—Prince & The Revolution (85)	220
Jerry RIX [Geertjan Lacunes] ▶ 5957 (2)	**223**
Victim Of Love—Elton John (79)	357
Who Do You Think You're Foolin'—Donna Summer (81)	312
Marco RIZO [Marco Rizo Ayala] ▶ 8087 (1)	**62**
The Charanga—Merv Griffin (61)	125
—Peter Rizzo see: Peter RISINGHAM	
Jimmy ROACH ▶ 4361 (4)	**513**
My Whole World Ended (The Moment You Left Me)—David Ruffin (69)	1875
Baby You're So Right For Me—Brenda & The Tabulations (68)	33
You And Me Together Forever—Freddie North (72)	21
Disco Sax—Houston Person (76)	6.4
Andrew ROACHFORD ▶ 4311 (1)	**525**
Cuddly Toy (Feel For Me)—Roachford (89)	525
—Roaring Lion see: Rafael DE LEON	
Dee ROBB [David R. Donaldson Jr.] ▶ 10136 (2)	**12**
Race With The Wind—Robbs (66)	7.5
Last Of The Wine—Robbs (70)	4.7
Paul ROBB ▶ 1428 (4)	**3078**
What's On Your Mind (Pure Energy)—Information Society (88)	2411
Walking Away—Information Society (88)	1283
Think—Information Society (90)	485
Repetition—Information Society (89)	105
Johnny ROBBA ▶ 8666 (1)	**43**
I'd Rather Be Here In Your Arms—Duprees (63)	86
Ayn ROBBINS ▶ 2307 (5)	**1622**
Gonna Fly Now (Theme From "Rocky")—Bill Conti (77)	*4145*
Gonna Fly Now (Theme From "Rocky")—Maynard Ferguson (77)	*595*
You Take My Heart Away—James Darren (77)	98
Rocky II Disco—Maynard Ferguson (79)	22
Theme From Rocky (Gonna Fly Now)—Rhythm Heritage (77)	*7.6*
Charles David ROBBINS ▶ 6836 (2)	**134**
All My Life—Kenny Rogers (83)	390
Dirty Looks—Juice Newton (83)	8.1
David Robert ROBBINS ▶ 8955 (1)	**35**
Stoned Cowboy—Fantasy (70)	141
Dennis ROBBINS ▶ 8698 (1)	**42**
Desire—Rockets (80)	85
Joan ROBBINS ▶ 11820 (1)	**0.0**
Pretty Baby - Oh—Austin Smiley (58)	0.0
Marty ROBBINS [Martin D. Robinson] ▶ 99 (26)	**24953**
El Paso—Marty Robbins (59)	7763
Don't Worry—Marty Robbins (61)	5511
A White Sport Coat (And A Pink Carnation)—Marty Robbins (57)	*4584*
You Don't Owe Me A Thing—Johnnie Ray (57)	*1585*
You Gave Me A Mountain—Frankie Laine (69)	1278
Devil Woman—Marty Robbins (62)	1228
Big Iron—Marty Robbins (60)	662
Is There Any Chance—Marty Robbins (60)	546
She Was Only Seventeen (He Was One Year More)—Marty Robbins (58)	469
My Woman, My Woman, My Wife—Marty Robbins (70)	*389*
Jimmy Martinez—Marty Robbins (61)	253
It's Your World—Marty Robbins (61)	197
Kate—Johnny Cash And The Tennessee Three (72)	92
Love Can't Wait—Marty Robbins (62)	78
Sugaree—Rusty York (59)	*68*
I Told The Brook—Marty Robbins (61)	59
Please Don't Blame Me—Marty Robbins (57)	53
Begging To You—Marty Robbins (63)	51
Girl From Spanish Town—Marty Robbins (64)	44
A White Sport Coat (And A Pink Carnation)—Johnny Desmond (57)	*27*
Respectfully Miss Brooks—Marty Robbins (56)	8.5
Cigarettes And Coffee Blues—Marty Robbins (63)	5.4
My Woman, My Woman, My Wife—Dean Martin (70)	*1.7*
You Don't Owe Me A Thing—Marty Robbins (57)	*0.0*
You Don't Owe Me A Thing—La Dell Sisters (57)	*0.0*
Sugaree—Hank Ballard And The Midnighters (59)	*0.0*
—Fred Allen Roberds see: Smokey ROBERDS	
Smokey ROBERDS [Fred Allen Roberds] ▶ 5010 (4)	**359**
Sunshine Girl—Parade (67)	687
Time To Get It Together—Country Coalition (70)	102
What Are We Going To Do?—David Jones (65)	71
A Woman's Way—Andy Williams (69)	4.5
Dave ROBERSON ▶ 8806 (1)	**39**
Cutie Pie—One Way (82)	273
Kevin ROBERSON [Kayo] ▶ 7493 (1)	**92**
Stone Cold Gentleman—Ralph Tresvant (91)	369
Allan ROBERTS [Mel Green] ▶ 2792 (7)	**1193**
You Always Hurt The One You Love—Clarence Henry (61)	*1553*
You Always Hurt The One You Love—Fontane Sisters (56)	*292*
Sweet Brown Eyed Baby—Ames Brothers (55)	153
Baby Has Gone Bye Bye—George Maharis (62)	151
You Always Hurt The One You Love—Somethin' Smith & The Redheads (57)	*96*
Marching Along To The Blues—Perry Como (57)	69
Into Each Life Some Rain Must Fall—Crazy Otto (56)	2.0
Art ROBERTS [Arthur Skupsky] ▶ 6036 (1)	**213**
Green Mosquito—Tune Rockers (58)	427
Austin ROBERTS [George Austin Robertson Jr.] ▶ 6607 (2)	**152**
I.O.U.—Lee Greenwood (83)	242
Don't Stop Me Baby (I'm On Fire)—Boys Band (82)	122
Billy ROBERTS ▶ 3176 (3)	**970**
Hey Joe—Leaves (66)	*549*
Hey Joe—Wilson Pickett (69)	*405*
Hey Joe—Cher (67)	*17*
Bob ROBERTS [Robert Silbert] ▶ 3271 (7)	**918**
Tall Paul—Annette With The Afterbeats (58)	1651
Tunnel Of Love—Doris Day (58)	245
King Of The Whole Wide World—Elvis Presley with the Jordanaires (62)	236
Jo Jo The Dog Faced Boy—Annette (59)	218
Girl With The Story In Her Eyes—Safaris With The Phantom's Band (60)	49
Stolen Love—Dinah Shore (56)	8.5
Where Do You Come From—Elvis Presley With The Jordanaires (62)	0.9
Brad ROBERTS ▶ 8108 (1)	**61**
Superman's Song—Crash Test Dummies (91)	61
Bruce ROBERTS ▶ 510 (29)	**8312**
No More Tears (Enough Is Enough)—Barbra Streisand/Donna Summer (79)	5346
Main Event—Barbra Streisand (79)	1784
Making Love—Roberta Flack (82)	1327
You Should Be Mine (The Woo Woo Song)—Jeffrey Osborne (86)	1213
Dynamite—Jermaine Jackson (84)	933
The Lucky One—Laura Branigan (84)	698
Anyone Can See—Irene Cara (81)	542
Stronger Than Before—Carole Bayer Sager (81)	502
Goldmine—Pointer Sisters (86)	495
Flames Of Paradise (Duet With Elton John)—Jennifer Rush (87)	441
Sugar Don't Bite—Sam Harris (84)	440
Oh, People—Patti LaBelle (86)	409
Love Always—El DeBarge (86)	328
Fool That I Am—Rita Coolidge (80)	313
I'll Make You Music—Beverly Bremers (72)	285
Secret—Heart (91)	245
I Don't Wanna Go—Joey Travolta (78)	232
You're Movin' Out Today—Bette Midler (77)	*215*
You're Moving Out Today—Carole Bayer Sager (77)	*188*
Skybird—Tony Orlando And Dawn (75)	179
You're The Only One—Dolly Parton (79)	105
Whisper In The Dark—Dionne Warwick (86)	102
Me - U = Blue—Glenn Medeiros (90)	64
Shoppin' From A To Z—Toni Basil (83)	55

Bruce ROBERTS ▶ 510 (29) ***Continued***	**8312**
Twist My Arm—Pointer Sisters (86)	47
Only My Heart Talkin'—Alice Cooper (90)	30
Our Night—Shaun Cassidy (78)	16
I Could Have Loved You—Moments (78)	10
Dream Land—Danny Bonaduce (73)	1.9
Darryl Keith ROBERTS ▶ 6332 (1)	**182**
Same Ole Love (365 Days A Year)— Anita Baker (87)	363
David Scott ROBERTS ▶ 6928 (1)	**128**
Before I Go—Starship (86)	128
Don W. ROBERTS ▶ 10614 (1)	**6.7**
Only One—Don "Red" Roberts (57)	6.7
Harriet ROBERTS ▶ 6765 (1)	**139**
Temple Of Love—Harriet (91)	278
Jack ROBERTS ▶ 9928 (1)	**15**
Here's Some Love—Tanya Tucker (76)	30
Jeanne ROBERTS [Jade Starling] ▶ 2888 (2)	**1130**
Catch Me (I'm Falling)—Pretty Poison (87)	1846
Nightime—Pretty Poison (88)	414
Jim ROBERTS ▶ 5613 (1)	**265**
13 Questions—Seatrain (71)	529
John ROBERTS ▶ 8116 (1)	**61**
Sockin' 1-2-3-4—John Roberts (67)	122
—John Godfrey Owen Roberts see: Paddy ROBERTS	
Johnnie B. ROBERTS ▶ 2817 (2)	**1175**
My Boy Lollipop—Millie Small (64)	4215
No Pity (In The Naked City)—Jackie Wilson (65)	364
Larry ROBERTS ▶ 5708 (2)	**252**
Not On The Outside—Moments (2) (68)	345
Look Over Your Shoulder—O'Jays (68)	159
Lee S. ROBERTS ▶ 4742 (1)	**426**
Smiles—Crazy Otto (55)	426
Linda ROBERTS ▶ 11821 (1)	**0.0**
Not As A Stranger—McGuire Sisters (54)	0.0
Lya ROBERTS ▶ 4372 (2)	**510**
Just Young—Andy Rose (58)	*318*
Just Young—Paul Anka (58)	*192*
Marty Dorn ROBERTS ▶ 7422 (1)	**97**
Turn Right—Kay Starr (55)	193
Mick ROBERTS ▶ 6652 (1)	**147**
Love And Pride—King (85)	295
Paddy ROBERTS [John Godfrey Owen Roberts] ▶ 4493 (6)	**479**
Lay Down Your Arms—Chordettes (56)	*814*
You Are My First Love—Nat "King" Cole (57)	209
Lay Down Your Arms—Anne Shelton (56)	*193*
Softly, Softly—Jaye P. Morgan (55)	*117*
Lay Down Your Arms— Russ Morgan & His Orchestra (56)	*0.0*
Softly, Softly— Guy Lombardo & His Royal Canadians (55)	*0.0*
Paul ROBERTS ▶ 8793 (3)	**39**
There's A Star Spangled Banner Waving #2 (The Ballad Of Francis Powers)—Red River Dave (60)	*117*
There's A Star Spangled Banner Waving Somewhere—Tommy Dee (60)	*0.0*
There's A Star Spangled Banner Waving Somewhere—Betty Johnson (60)	*0.0*
Paul N. ROBERTS ▶ 2657 (1)	**1290**
Driver's Seat—Sniff 'N' The Tears (79)	1290
Rhoda ROBERTS ▶ 4162 (6)	**577**
Put A Light In The Window—Four Lads (57)	768
Ding Dong—McGuire Sisters (58)	351
Don't Tell Me Your Troubles— Jimmy Bowen With The Rhythm Orchids (57)	31
Born To Love—Teresa Brewer (57)	14
Easy Does It—Jaye P. Morgan (58)	1.2
The Swingin' Shepherd Blues— Ella Fitzgerald & Her Shepherds (58)	*0.0*
Rick ROBERTS ▶ 658 (8)	**6642**
You Are The Woman—Firefall (76)	2171
Strange Way—Firefall (78)	1600
Just Remember I Love You—Firefall (77)	1431
Headed For A Fall—Firefall (80)	394
Livin' Ain't Livin'—Firefall (76)	390
Goodbye, I Love You—Firefall (79)	309
Love That Got Away—Firefall (80)	235
So Long—Firefall (78)	112

Ruth ROBERTS ▶ 6184 (7)	**196**
Endless—McGuire Sisters (56)	*244*
What Is A Wife—Steve Allen (55)	161
I Love Mickey—Mickey Mantle And Teresa Brewer (56)	24
The First Thing Ev'ry Morning (And The Last Thing Ev'ry Night)—Jimmy Dean (65)	19
Rock Bottom—McGuire Sisters (57)	5.5
Endless—Honey Bees (56)	*0.0*
What Is A Husband?—Jane Meadows (56)	0.0
Solomon ROBERTS ▶ 4572 (2)	**463**
Real Love—Skyy (90)	239
Give It What You Got—B.T. Express (75)	225
Brian A. ROBERTSON ▶ 1388 (6)	**3196**
The Living Years—Mike + The Mechanics (88)	3672
Silent Running (On Dangerous Ground)— Mike + The Mechanics (85)	1912
Carrie—Cliff Richard (80)	407
Nobody's Perfect—Mike + The Mechanics (88)	169
Seeing Is Believing—Mike + The Mechanics (89)	161
Wired For Sound—Cliff Richard (81)	71
Dick ROBERTSON ▶ 11411 (1)	**1.8**
Is There Somebody Else—Dream Weavers (56)	5.5
Don ROBERTSON ▶ 181 (30)	**16919**
Ringo—Lorne Greene (64)	5527
Please Help Me I'm Falling—Hank Locklin (60)	*3409*
Born To Be With You—Chordettes (56)	*2947*
Happy Whistler—Don Robertson (56)	2156
I'm Yours—Elvis Presley (65)	1788
I Love You More And More Every Day—Al Martino (64)	1787
Humming Bird—Les Paul and Mary Ford (55)	*1352*
Not One Minute More—Della Reese (59)	1216
I Really Don't Want To Know—Tommy Edwards (60)	*1085*
I Really Don't Want To Know—Ronnie Dove (66)	*753*
I Really Don't Want To Know—Elvis Presley (70)	*704*
(I Can't Help You) I'm Falling Too— Skeeter Davis (60)	*543*
Anything That's Part Of You— Elvis Presley With The Jordanaires (62)	425
Magic Fingers—Eddie Fisher (55)	359
There's Always Me— Elvis Presley With The Jordanaires (67)	294
Please Help Me I'm Falling—Rusty Draper (60)	*195*
I Really Don't Want To Know— "Little Esther" Phillips (63)	*134*
They Remind Me Too Much Of You— Elvis Presley With The Mello Men (63)	76
Born To Be With You— Sonny James The Southern Gentleman (68)	*22*
I Don't Hurt Anymore— Hank Snow The Singing Ranger And The Rainbow Ranch Boys (54)	*22*
I Really Don't Want To Know—Solomon Burke (62)	*15*
I Don't Hurt Anymore—Eddie Fisher (58)	*11*
Thank You For Loving Me—Al Martino (64)	2.2
I'm Glad That Your Falling—Betty Madigan (60)	*2.0*
Does He Mean That Much To You?—Eddy Arnold (62)	1.3
Humming Bird—Chordettes (55)	*0.0*
Humming Bird—Frankie Laine (55)	*0.0*
Born To Be With You—Lola Dee (56)	*0.0*
I Don't Hurt Anymore— Ray Anthony & His Orchestra (54)	*0.0*
I Really Don't Want To Know— Les Paul and Mary Ford (54)	*0.0*
—Ella Robertson see: Lou DINNING	
—George Austin Robertson Jr. see: Austin ROBERTS	
—Henry Macleod Robertson see: McLeod ROBERTSON	
McLeod ROBERTSON [Harry Robinson, Henry Macleod Robertson] ▶ 11091 (1)	**3.3**
Fried Onions—Lord Rockingham's XI (58)	3.3
Robbie ROBERTSON ▶ 403 (11)	**9810**
The Night They Drove Old Dixie Down—Joan Baez (71)	4530
Broken Arrow—Rod Stewart (91)	1352
The Weight—Aretha Franklin (69)	*1116*
Up On Cripple Creek—Band (69)	1059
The Weight—Jackie DeShannon (68)	*538*
The Weight—Diana Ross And The Supremes & The Temptations (69)	*334*
The Weight—Band (68)	*313*
Rag Mama Rag—Band (70)	290
Life Is A Carnival—Band (71)	216

Ophelia—Band (76)	109
Time To Kill—Band (70)	98
—Thomas Morgan Robertson see: Thomas DOLBY	
—Don D. Robey see: Deadric MALONE	
Paul ROBI [Paul Irvin Roby] ▶ 3765 (2)	**706**
You'll Never Never Know—Platters (56)	1488
He's Mine—Platters (57)	629
John ROBIE ▶ 7327 (2)	**102**
Planet Rock— Afrika Bambaataa And The Soul Sonic Force (82)	175
Remember What You Like—Jenny Burton (84)	44
Leo ROBIN ▶ 4204 (6) HOF	**564**
Prisoner Of Love— James Brown And The Famous Flames (63)	986
Wun'erful, Wun'erful! (Sides Uh-One & Uh-Two)— Stan Freberg (57)	298
Please—Frank Ifield (63)	200
It's Bigger Than You And Me—Sammy Davis Jr. (55)	125
Beyond The Blue Horizon—Lou Christie (74)	103
True Blue Lou—Tony Bennett (63)	1.3
Sid ROBIN [Sydney Rabinowitz, Sydney Robin] ▶ 3850 (7)	**678**
I Miss You So—Paul Anka (59)	*593*
I Miss You So—Chris Connor (56)	*513*
I Miss You So—Little Anthony & The Imperials With The 101 Strings (65)	*453*
No One To Cry To—Ray Charles (64)	205
Oowee, Oowee—Perry Como (65)	104
Just Because—Elvis Presley (56)	71
Sweet Lips—Jaye P. Morgan (56)	13
—Sydney Robin see: Sid ROBIN	
Charles ROBINETTE ▶ 10828 (1)	**5.1**
Monday In May—Third Condition (70)	5.1
Fran ROBINS ▶ 3071 (1)	**1025**
The House That Jack Built—Aretha Franklin (68)	2051
Jimmy ROBINS ▶ 8592 (1)	**45**
I Can't Please You—Jimmy Robins (67)	45
Alvin ROBINSON ▶ 10742 (1)	**5.6**
More And More—Carly Simon (75)	11
Bishop ROBINSON ▶ 9031 (1)	**33**
Free Me—Otis Redding (69)	131
—Bobby Robinson see: Morgan C. ROBINSON	
Chris ROBINSON ▶ 5077 (2)	**347**
She Talks To Angels—Black Crowes (91)	582
Jealous Again—Black Crowes (90)	113
Claudia ROBINSON ▶ 6960 (1)	**125**
Precious Words—Wallace Brothers (64)	125
Darren ROBINSON ▶ 11668 (1)	**0.8**
Falling In Love—Fat Boys (87)	3.9
David P. ROBINSON ▶ 9515 (1)	**22**
A Little Bit Like Magic—King Harvest (73)	67
Dawn ROBINSON ▶ 3873 (2)	**671**
Hold On—En Vogue (90)	3351
Lies—En Vogue (90)	676
Earl ROBINSON ▶ 1832 (1)	**2241**
Black And White—Three Dog Night (72)	4482
Eddie ROBINSON ▶ 8476 (2)	**49**
Shake It Well—Dramatics (77)	90
Ocean Of Thoughts And Dreams—Dramatics (78)	7.3
Eric Jay ROBINSON ▶ 4607 (1)	**452**
Dance (Disco Heat)—Sylvester (78)	904
Floyd ROBINSON ▶ 2755 (1)	**1217**
Makin' Love—Floyd Robinson (59)	1217
Frank F. ROBINSON ▶ 1455 (2)	**3002**
I've Found Someone Of My Own—Free Movement (71)	2596
The Harder I Try (The Bluer I Get)— Free Movement (71)	406
—Gerald Robinson see: Gerry ROBINSON	
Gerry ROBINSON [Jerry Reno, Gerald Robinson] ▶ 9520 (1)	**22**
Does She Do It Like She Dances— Addrisi Brothers (77)	44
—Harry Robinson see: McLeod ROBERTSON	
J. Russel ROBINSON ▶ 7017 (1)	**121**
Margie—Fats Domino (59)	364
Jack ROBINSON [Philo Jack Robinson] ▶ 11682 (1)	**0.7**
(If You Want It) Do It Yourself—Gloria Gaynor (75)	1.5
—Jay Robinson see: Sylvia ROBINSON	

Jessie Mae ROBINSON [Jessie Mae Booker] ▶ 3584 (4)	**777**
Let's Have A Party—Wanda Jackson (60)	*769*
The Other Woman—Sarah Vaughan (56)	4.9
Let's Have A Party—Rivieras (2) (64)	*1.4*
Black Night—Bobby Bland (65)	1.0
Joseph ROBINSON [R. Taylor, Robert Taylor] ▶ 10635 (3)	**6.6**
There'll Be No Backin' Out—Mickey And Sylvia (57)	7.1
Two Shadows On Your Window—Jim Reeves (57)	*3.0*
Two Shadows On Your Window—Mickey & Sylvia (57)	*3.0*
Maquet ROBINSON ▶ 11616 (1)	**1.0**
Love Me Just For Me—Special Generation (90)	6.8
—Martin D. Robinson see: Marty ROBBINS	
McEvoy ROBINSON ▶ 8575 (1)	**46**
Just One More Day—Otis Redding (65)	138
Morgan C. ROBINSON [Bobby Robinson, Morgan Clyde Robinson] ▶ 2381 (7)	**1542**
Ya Ya—Lee Dorsey (61)	2127
Warm And Tender Love—Percy Sledge (66)	*1225*
I Need Your Loving— Don Gardner And Dee Dee Ford (62)	1156
Fannie Mae—Buster Brown (60)	*717*
Don't You Worry— Don Gardner And Dee Dee Ford (62)	144
Fannie Mae—Mighty Sam (66)	*1.9*
Sugar Babe—Buster Brown (62)	1.3
Patrick ROBINSON ▶ 4623 (3)	**449**
Nothing Takes The Place Of You— Toussaint McCall (67)	*613*
Nothing Can Take The Place Of You— Brook Benton (69)	*195*
I'll Do It For You—Toussaint McCall (67)	89
Rainey ROBINSON ▶ 9951 (2)	**15**
More And More—Andy Williams (67)	32
I Look At You—Lassies (56)	12
—Ray Charles Robinson see: Ray CHARLES	
Rich ROBINSON ▶ 5078 (2)	**347**
She Talks To Angels—Black Crowes (91)	582
Jealous Again—Black Crowes (90)	113
Robert C. ROBINSON ▶ 5493 (1)	**279**
Dawn—David Rockingham Trio (63)	279
Roland ROBINSON ▶ 3824 (1)	**688**
Infatuation—Rod Stewart (84)	2065
Rudy ROBINSON ▶ 9329 (3)	**26**
Red Pepper I— Roosevelt Fountain And Pens Of Rhythm (63)	23
I'm A Practical Guy—Lee Rogers (66)	9.1
Boss Love—Lee Rogers (65)	4.2
Ruth ROBINSON ▶ 9257 (3)	**28**
I Can Make It Thru The Days (But Oh Those Lonely Nights)—Ray Charles (73)	59
Ms.—David Oliver (78)	8.6
Willie Pass The Water—Ripple (74)	7.5
Sharon ROBINSON ▶ 5157 (1)	**333**
New Attitude—Patti LaBelle (85)	999
Smokey ROBINSON [William Robinson Jr.] ▶ 9 (128) HOF	**79854**
The Tears Of A Clown— Smokey Robinson & The Miracles (70)	*7441*
My Guy—Mary Wells (64)	*7380*
My Girl—Temptations (65)	*6094*
Being With You—Smokey Robinson (81)	5255
I Second That Emotion— Smokey Robinson & The Miracles (67)	4546
Get Ready—Rare Earth (70)	*4506*
Cruisin'—Smokey Robinson (79)	4437
Shop Around— Miracles (Featuring Bill "Smokey" Robinson) (60)	*3656*
The One Who Really Loves You—Mary Wells (62)	3076
Shop Around—Captain & Tennille (76)	*3059*
Baby, Baby Don't Cry— Smokey Robinson & The Miracles (69)	2458
Ain't That Peculiar—Marvin Gaye (65)	*2266*
You've Really Got A Hold On Me—Miracles (62)	*2243*
Don't Mess With Bill—Marvelettes (66)	2112
Two Lovers—Mary Wells (62)	2082
I'll Be Doggone—Marvin Gaye (65)	2041
More Love—Kim Carnes (80)	*1898*
The Way You Do The Things You Do—UB40 (90)	*1892*
The Way You Do The Things You Do—Temptations (64)	*1796*
Ooh Baby Baby—Linda Ronstadt (78)	*1786*
You Beat Me To The Punch—Mary Wells (62)	*1687*
Going To A Go-Go—Miracles (65)	*1646*
Still Water (Love)—Four Tops (70)	1640
The Tracks Of My Tears—Johnny Rivers (67)	*1537*
If You Can Want— Smokey Robinson & The Miracles (68)	1523
The Tracks Of My Tears—Miracles (65)	*1351*
My Baby Must Be A Magician—Marvelettes (67)	1339
Ooo Baby Baby—Miracles (65)	*1254*
The Hunter Gets Captured By The Game— Marvelettes (67)	1239
Floy Joy—Supremes (72)	1145
More Love—Smokey Robinson & The Miracles (67)	*1141*
I Don't Blame You At All— Smokey Robinson & The Miracles (71)	1073
Since I Lost My Baby—Temptations (65)	1058
My Baby—Temptations (65)	1007
It's Growing—Temptations (65)	994
My Girl Has Gone—Miracles (65)	946
What's Easy For Two Is So Hard For One— Mary Wells (63)	793
Laughing Boy—Mary Wells (63)	791
When I'm Gone—Brenda Holloway (65)	773
Baby Come Close—Smokey Robinson (73)	768
The Love I Saw In You Was Just A Mirage— Smokey Robinson & The Miracles (67)	740
I'll Try Something New—Diana Ross And The Supremes & The Temptations (69)	*738*
Special Occasion— Smokey Robinson & The Miracles (68)	729
I Like It Like That—Miracles (64)	727
Tracks Of My Tears—Linda Ronstadt (75)	*724*
The Way You Do The Things You Do— Rita Coolidge (78)	*710*
Yester Love—Smokey Robinson & The Miracles (68)	664
One More Heartache—Marvin Gaye (66)	662
The Composer—Diana Ross And The Supremes (69)	637
Get Ready—Temptations (66)	*631*
Baby That's Backatcha—Smokey Robinson (75)	629
What's So Good About Good-by—Miracles (62)	627
Doggone Right— Smokey Robinson & The Miracles (69)	615
Going To A Go-Go—Rolling Stones (82)	*594*
As Long As I Know He's Mine—Marvelettes (63)	590
My Guy—Sister Sledge (82)	*585*
My Girl—Suavé (88)	*579*
Take This Heart Of Mine—Marvin Gaye (66)	568
I'll Be In Trouble—Temptations (64)	564
I'll Try Something New—Miracles (62)	*541*
Point It Out—Smokey Robinson & The Miracles (69)	525
A Love She Can Count On—Miracles (63)	500
Here I Am Baby—Marvelettes (68)	496
Automatically Sunshine—Supremes (72)	481
My Girl—Bobby Vee (68)	*476*
Let Me Be The Clock—Smokey Robinson (80)	476
The Agony And The Ecstasy—Smokey Robinson (75)	452
Your Old Stand By—Mary Wells (63)	445
That's What Love Is Made Of—Miracles (64)	416
You're My Remedy—Marvelettes (64)	376
Ain't That Peculiar—Diamond Reo (74)	*361*
Ain't It, Baby—Miracles (61)	358
You're The One—Marvelettes (66)	349
Satisfaction—Smokey Robinson & The Miracles (71)	345
Sweet Harmony—Smokey Robinson (73)	331
I'll Try Something New—A Taste Of Honey (82)	*311*
Everybody's Gotta Pay Some Dues—Miracles (61)	307
Crazy About The La La La— Smokey Robinson & The Miracles (71)	299
My Girl—Daryl Hall & John Oates Featuring David Ruffin & Eddie Kendricks (85)	*285*
The Way You Do The Things You Do— Daryl Hall & John Oates Featuring David Ruffin & Eddie Kendricks (85)	*285*
Happy—Bobby Darin (72)	282
Here I Go Again— Smokey Robinson & The Miracles (69)	281
You Threw A Lucky Punch—Gene Chandler (62)	*280*
Come On Do The Jerk—Miracles (64)	273
First I Look At The Purse—Contours (65)	267
He's A Good Guy (Yes He Is)—Marvelettes (64)	256
Malinda—Bobby Taylor & The Vancouvers (68)	254
Oooh, Baby Baby—Five Stairsteps (67)	*252*
Virgin Man—Smokey Robinson (74)	213
Your Wonderful, Sweet Sweet Love—Supremes (72)	203
Who's Lovin' You—Brenda And The Tabulations (67)	201
(You Can't Let The Boy Overpower) The Man In You— Miracles (64)	*178*
I Am I Am—Smokey Robinson (74)	172
You've Really Got A Hold On Me—Eddie Money (78)	*148*
A Breath Taking Guy—Supremes (63)	141
My Guy—Petula Clark (72)	*132*
You Are Forever—Smokey Robinson (81)	132
Quiet Storm—Smokey Robinson (76)	112
Mighty Good Lovin'—Miracles (61)	110
My Guy—Amii Stewart & Johnny Bristol (80)	*99*
My Girl—Amii Stewart & Johnny Bristol (80)	*99*
My Girl—Eddie Floyd (70)	*97*
Daylight And Darkness—Smokey Robinson (78)	97
It's Her Turn To Live—Smokey Robinson (74)	87
Tracks Of My Tears—Aretha Franklin (69)	*81*
What's Too Much—Smokey Robinson (87)	80
Going to a Go-Go—Shalamar (77)	*80*
Bad Girl—Miracles (59)	65
Operator—Brenda Holloway (65)	60
Don't Look Back—Temptations (65)	*49*
More More More Of Your Love—Bob Brady (67)	46
Open—Smokey Robinson (76)	40
Double Good Everything—Smokey Robinson (91)	39
You've Got To Earn It—Staple Singers (71)	39
Ain't That Peculiar—Fanny (72)	*29*
(You Got To Walk And) Don't Look Back— Peter Tosh (78)	*24*
Way Over There—Miracles (62)	22
(You Can't Let The Boy Overpower) The Man In You— Chuck Jackson (68)	*16*
Tears Of A Clown—Stars On 45 (81)	*12*
Don't Let Him Shop Around—Debbie Dean (61)	*10*
Ooh Baby Baby—Magnificent Men (67)	*7.6*
Your Heart Belongs To Me—Supremes (62)	5.3
You Really Got A Hold On Me— Billy Joe Royal (with Toni Wine) (81)	*3.6*
You Really Got A Hold On Me—Gayle McCormick (72)	*2.8*
I Need A Change—Miracles (60)	2.5
Broken Hearted—Miracles (61)	1.8
I Want You 'round—Marvin Gaye & Kim Weston (64)	1.3
Two Wrongs Don't Make A Right—Mary Wells (63)	0.4
Sylvia ROBINSON [J. Robinson, Jay Robinson, Sylvia Vanderpool] ▶ 564 (28)	**7658**
Pillow Talk—Sylvia (73)	4260
Love On A Two-Way Street—Moments (70)	*3309*
Love Is Strange—Mickey & Sylvia (56)	*2019*
Shame, Shame, Shame—Shirley (And Company) (75)	1375
Love Is Strange—Peaches & Herb (67)	*1374*
Sexy Mama—Moments (74)	858
Love On A Two Way Street—Stacy Lattisaw (81)	*768*
Not On The Outside—Moments (2) (68)	345
What Would I Do—Mickey And Sylvia (60)	336
All I Have—Moments (70)	247
Apache—Sugar Hill Gang (82)	*173*
I'll Erase Away Your Pain—Whatnauts (71)	140
Didn't I—Sylvia (73)	139
Baby You're So Fine—Mickey And Sylvia (61)	*100*
Sho Nuff Boogie (Part 1)—Sylvia & The Moments (74)	83
The Message— Grandmaster Flash & The Furious Five (82)	80
Sunday—Moments (2) (69)	43
Love Will Make You Fail In School— Mickey And Sylvia (57)	30
Love Is A Treasure—Mickey And Sylvia (57)	25
Freedom—Grandmaster Flash And The Furious 5 (80)	21
Lovely Way She Loves—Moments (70)	13
Lucky Me—Moments (71)	11
Love Is Strange—Buddy Holly / The Crickets (69)	*11*
Cry Cry Cry—Shirley And Company (75)	6.7
I Can't Help It—Moments (71)	6.5
Love Is Strange—Everly Brothers (65)	*3.4*
Lovedrops—Mickey And Sylvia (61)	1.8
Soul Je T'Aime—Sylvia & Ralfi Pagan (73)	*1.3*
Tom ROBINSON ▶ 6571 (1)	**155**
(Sartorial Eloquence) Don't Ya Wanna Play This Game No More?—Elton John (80)	310
—William Robinson Jr. see: Smokey ROBINSON	
Winifred ROBINSON ▶ 11441 (1)	**1.7**
I'll Be There (To Bring You Love)—Majors (64)	3.4
—Carson J. Robison see: Maggie ANDREWS	

Willard ROBISON ▶ 9356 (1)	**25**
A Cottage For Sale–Little Willie John (60)	51
Michel ROBITAILLE ▶ 6680 (1)	**145**
Clap Your Hands–Beau-Marks (60)	578
Julian ROBLEDO ▶ 4130 (2)	**584**
Three O'Clock In The Morning– Bert Kaempfert And His Orchestra (65)	*580*
Three O'Clock In The Morning–Lou Rawls (65)	*8.5*
Daniel ROBLES ▶ 3899 (1)	**663**
El Condor Pasa–Simon & Garfunkel (70)	1326
–Paul Irvin Roby see: Paul ROBI	
Len ROCCO ▶ 10171 (1)	**12**
#1 Dee Jay–Goody Goody (78)	35
Tommy ROCCO ▶ 9171 (1)	**30**
A Little Good News–Anne Murray (83)	89
Bob ROCK ▶ 7407 (2)	**98**
Dirty Water–Rock And Hyde (87)	185
You're The Only Love– Paul Hyde And The Payolas (85)	21
–Chubb Rock see: Richard SIMPSON	
Joseph ROCK ▶ 3490 (10)	**820**
Since I Don't Have You–Skyliners (59)	*2364*
This I Swear–Skyliners (59)	743
Since I Don't Have You–Don McLean (81)	*545*
I've Got Dreams To Remember–Otis Redding (68)	459
Since I Don't Have You–Chuck Jackson (64)	*403*
It Happened Today–Skyliners (59)	229
Since I Don't Have You–Art Garfunkel (79)	*180*
Since I Don't Have You–Eddie Holman (70)	*160*
Since I Don't Have You– Fred Parris & The Five Satins (82)	*4.8*
How Much–Skyliners (60)	1.5
Rikki ROCKETT [Richard Allan Ream] ▶ 1179 (10)	**3772**
Every Rose Has Its Thorn–Poison (88)	4813
Unskinny Bop–Poison (90)	2869
Something To Believe In–Poison (90)	2063
Nothin' But A Good Time–Poison (88)	1314
Talk Dirty To Me–Poison (87)	1055
I Won't Forget You–Poison (87)	1051
Fallen Angel–Poison (88)	903
Life Goes On–Poison (91)	401
Ride The Wind–Poison (91)	377
I Want Action–Poison (87)	240
–Rockwell see: Kennedy GORDY	
LeRoy W. RODDE ▶ 4228 (3)	**555**
Have You Heard–Duprees Featuring Joey Vann (63)	1071
Why Don't You Believe Me– Duprees Featuring Joey Vann (63)	*583*
Why Don't You Believe Me–Vic Damone (65)	*12*
–Vin Roddie see: Vincent RODOMISTA	
Rod RODDY ▶ 9861 (1)	**16**
Carrie's Gone–Le Roux (83)	48
Rick RODELL [Milan Radenkovich] ▶ 5101 (1)	**342**
How Many Teardrops–Lou Christie (63)	342
Jess RODEN ▶ 10065 (1)	**13**
Toyland–Alan Bown (68)	26
Curtis RODGERS ▶ 4833 (1)	**403**
Back Up Train–Al Greene & The Soul Mate's (67)	806
–Gaby Rodgers see: Jerry LEIBER	
James Frederick RODGERS ▶ 3881 (3)	**669**
It's Over–Jimmie Rodgers (66)	*473*
It's Over–Eddy Arnold (68)	*186*
Woman From Liberia–Jimmie Rodgers (60)	18
Jimmie RODGERS ▶ 2277 (4) HOF	**1662**
Mule Skinner Blues–Fendermen (60)	*3277*
California Blues–Redwing (71)	13
In The Jailhouse Now–Webb Pierce (55)	10
Mule Skinner Blues–Rusty Draper (60)	*0.0*
Nile RODGERS ▶ 140 (24) HOF	**19947**
Le Freak–Chic (78)	11074
Upside Down–Diana Ross (80)	8140
Good Times–Chic (79)	6108
We Are Family–Sister Sledge (79)	4694
Dance, Dance, Dance (Yowsah, Yowsah, Yowsah)– Chic (77)	2478
I'm Coming Out–Diana Ross (80)	2369
I Want Your Love–Chic (79)	2083
He's The Greatest Dancer–Sister Sledge (79)	1848
Rapper's Delight–Sugarhill Gang (79)	551
Backfired–Debbie Harry (81)	351
Everybody Dance–Chic (78)	267
Tick Tock–Vaughan Brothers (90)	163
Serious Kinda Girl–Christopher Max (89)	127
Rebels Are We–Chic (80)	112
Got To Love Somebody–Sister Sledge (80)	93
My Forbidden Lover–Chic (79)	91
Why–Carly Simon (82)	86
Soup For One–Chic (82)	43
Saturday–Norma Jean Wright (78)	41
Coming To America (Part One)–System (88)	25
Real People–Chic (80)	16
The Jam Was Moving–Debbie Harry (81)	11
Let's Go Out Tonight–Nile Rodgers (85)	9.9
Chip Off The Old Block–Chic (80)	0.0
Paul RODGERS ▶ 739 (15)	**5931**
All Right Now–Free (70)	*4192*
Feel Like Makin' Love–Bad Company (75)	1611
Rock 'N' Roll Fantasy–Bad Company (79)	1506
Fire And Water–Wilson Pickett (71)	960
Radioactive–Firm (85)	553
Stealer–Free (70)	359
All The Kings Horses–Firm (86)	134
All Right Now–Rod Stewart (84)	*89*
All Right Now–Pepsi & Shirlie (88)	*85*
Honey Child–Bad Company (76)	69
Satisfaction Guaranteed–Firm (85)	62
Electricland–Bad Company (82)	46
Burnin' Sky–Bad Company (77)	42
Biscuit's In The House–Biscuit (90)	34
All Right Now–Lea Roberts (75)	*18*
Richard RODGERS ▶ 314 (45) HOF	**11587**
Blue Moon–Marcels (61)	*9049*
Where Or When–Dion And The Belmonts (59)	*3185*
Some Enchanted Evening–Jay & The Americans (65)	*1354*
All At Once You Love Her–Perry Como (55)	1162
Hello Young Lovers–Paul Anka (60)	973
If I Loved You–Chad & Jeremy (65)	969
Glad To Be Unhappy–Mamas & The Papas (67)	649
Everybody's Got A Home But Me–Eddie Fisher (55)	*530*
You'll Never Walk Alone– Patti Labelle & The Blue Belles (64)	*449*
Slaughter On Tenth Avenue–Ventures (64)	411
You'll Never Walk Alone–Brooklyn Bridge (69)	*399*
My Favorite Things– Herb Alpert & The Tijuana Brass (68)	399
Everybody's Got A Home But Me–Roy Hamilton (55)	*312*
Bewitched–Betty Smith Group (58)	286
Blue Moon–Elvis Presley (56)	*266*
Do Re Mi–Mitch Miller & his Sing Along Chorus (59)	*211*
You Are Beautiful–Johnny Mathis (58)	184
You'll Never Walk Alone– Gerry And The Pacemakers (65)	*184*
Blue Moon–Ventures (61)	*139*
Blue Moon–Herb Lance & The Classics (61)	*121*
Do I Love You (Because You're Beautiful)– Vic Damone (57)	*106*
I Didn't Know What Time It Was–Ray Charles (69)	*75*
Sound Of Music–Patti Page (59)	*65*
Climb Ev'ry Mountain–Tony Bennett (59)	*64*
I Didn't Know What Time It Was– Crampton Sisters (64)	*44*
Climb Every Mountain–Hesitations (68)	*40*
Willing And Eager–Pat Boone (62)	38
March Of The Siamese Children– Kenny Ball And His Jazzmen (62)	37
Do I Love You (Because You're Beautiful)– Tony Martin (57)	*34*
You'll Never Walk Alone– Elvis Presley With The Jordanaires (68)	*25*
Do Re Mi–Anita Bryant (59)	*20*
Some Enchanted Evening–Jane Olivor (77)	*18*
Blue Moon– Jimmy Bowen With The Rhythm Orchids (58)	*12*
Love Look Away–Tony Bennett (58)	11
The Next Time It Happens–Carmen McRae (56)	9.8
Getting To Know You–Sajid Khan (68)	8.6
I Have Dreamed–Chad & Jeremy (65)	7.1
You'll Never Walk Alone–Blue Haze (73)	*7.0*
You'll Never Walk Alone–Judy Garland (54)	*5.4*
I Enjoy Being A Girl–Pat Suzuki (59)	*3.0*
Where Or When–Lettermen (63)	*1.8*
Sound Of Music–Doris Day (59)	*0.0*
I Enjoy Being A Girl–Doris Day (59)	*0.0*
Sound Of Music–David Whitfield (60)	*0.0*
Do I Love You (Because You're Beautiful)– Bob Eberly with Paul Whiteman & His Orchestra (57)	*0.0*
–Juan Raol Davis Rodiguez see: Johnny RODRIGUEZ	
Gil RODIN ▶ 11179 (1)	**2.9**
Big Noise From Winnetka–Spaghetti Head (75)	11
Vincent RODOMISTA [Vin Roddie] ▶ 4432 (4)	**495**
Bon Voyage–Janice Harper (57)	689
That's Why I Was Born–Janice Harper (57)	*301*
That's Why I Was Born–Billy Scott (57)	*0.0*
That's Why I Was Born–Margaret Whiting (57)	*0.0*
Jean RODOR ▶ 10913 (1)	**4.4**
Under The Bridges Of Paris–Dean Martin (55)	18
Frank RODRIGUEZ ▶ 6310 (1)	**183**
I Need Somebody–? & The Mysterians (66)	913
Johnny RODRIGUEZ [Juan Raol Davis Rodiguez] ▶ 7552 (2)	**89**
Ridin' My Thumb To Mexico–Johnny Rodriguez (73)	84
You Always Come Back (To Hurting Me)– Johnny Rodriguez (73)	11
Johnny D. RODRIGUEZ ▶ 9895 (1)	**15**
Got To Have Your Love– Mantronix (featuring Wondress) (90)	46
Marilyn RODRIGUEZ ▶ 5389 (1)	**296**
Bad Of The Heart–George LaMond (90)	592
–Moises Simon Rodriguez see: Moises SIMONS	
Steve RODWAY ▶ 9235 (1)	**28**
Don't Stop Trying–Rodway (82)	56
Justus G. ROE ▶ 10070 (1)	**13**
Up Your Nose–Gabriel Kaplan (77)	39
Tommy ROE ▶ 100 (17)	**24752**
Dizzy–Tommy Roe (69)	8722
Sheila–Tommy Roe (62)	6136
Everybody–Tommy Roe (63)	3895
Jam Up Jelly Tight–Tommy Roe (69)	3274
Hooray For Hazel–Tommy Roe (66)	2970
Sweet Pea–Tommy Roe (66)	2685
Heather Honey–Tommy Roe (69)	1066
Jack And Jill–Tommy Roe (69)	842
It's Now Winter's Day–Tommy Roe (66)	815
Pearl–Tommy Roe (70)	548
Stir It Up And Serve It–Tommy Roe (70)	480
Working Class Hero–Tommy Roe (73)	126
Dottie I Like It–Tommy Roe (68)	74
Sing Along With Me–Tommy Roe (67)	20
Piddle De Pat–Tommy Roe (62)	19
Little Miss Sunshine–Tommy Roe (67)	19
Gonna Take A Chance–Tommy Roe (63)	3.2
Leroy ROEBUCK ▶ 6464 (1)	**166**
About This Thing Called Love–Fabian (60)	498
Rich ROEBUCK ▶ 9217 (1)	**28**
Aiming At Your Heart–Temptations (81)	85
Heinz ROEMHELD ▶ 4115 (3)	**588**
Ruby–Ray Charles Orchestra & Chorus (60)	*781*
Ruby–Adam Wade (60)	*396*
Ruby–Bobby Milano (60)	*0.0*
Donald ROESER ▶ 2167 (3)	**1801**
(Don't Fear) The Reaper–Blue Öyster Cult (76)	1534
Burnin' For You–Blue Öyster Cult (81)	516
Shooting Shark–Blue Öyster Cult (84)	18
–K. C. Rogan see: Johnny BURKE	
Roger ROGER ▶ 7630 (1)	**84**
Back In My Arms–Nat "King" Cole (57)	168
Alex ROGERS ▶ 5599 (2)	**267**
Nobody–Perry Como (55)	*533*
Nobody–Bing Crosby (55)	*0.0*
Dann ROGERS ▶ 8618 (1)	**45**
My Merry-Go-Round–Johnny Nash (73)	134
Diane ROGERS ▶ 9061 (1)	**32**
Dancin' Holiday–Olympics (63)	96
D.J. ROGERS [Dewayne Julius Rogers] ▶ 10952 (2)	**4.1**
Love Brought Me Back–D. J. Rogers (78)	2.8
Say You Love Me–D. J. Rogers (76)	1.4
–Eugene Rogers see: Smokey ROGERS	

Evan ROGERS ▶ 763 (13)	**5744**
P.A.S.S.I.O.N.–Rythm Syndicate (91)	3002
Soldier Of Love–Donny Osmond (89)	2888
Street Of Dreams–Nia Peeples (91)	1236
Sacred Emotion–Donny Osmond (89)	1059
Hey Donna–Rythm Syndicate (91)	905
One Step Closer To You–Gavin Christopher (86)	674
The Girl I Used To Know–Brother Beyond (90)	613
My Love Is A Fire–Donny Osmond (90)	575
Facts Of Love–Jeff Lorber (86)	547
Stranger To Love–St. Paul (90)	236
Hold On–Donny Osmond (89)	96
Blinded By Love–Rythm Syndicate (91)	87
Love Will Survive–Donny Osmond (91)	27
Gerald ROGERS ▶ 10970 (1)	**4.0**
Just Between Friends–Kitty Kallen (55)	8.1
Jimmie O. ROGERS [Jimmie Ainsworth, Jimmie Otto Rogers] ▶ 3112 (1)	**1004**
Rockin' Little Angel–Ray Smith (60)	1004
Jimmy ROGERS [James A. Lane, Jay Arthur Lane] ▶ 10082 (1)	**13**
That's Alright–Little Junior Parker (58)	13
–Kay Rogers see: Eddie SNYDER	
Kenny ROGERS ▶ 2902 (6)	**1125**
Love Will Turn You Around–Kenny Rogers (82)	1322
What About Me?–Kenny Rogers (84)	866
Love Or Something Like It–Kenny Rogers (78)	424
Sweet Music Man–Kenny Rogers (77)	263
Crazy–Kenny Rogers (85)	41
Take My Hand– Kenny Rogers And The First Edition (71)	11
Larry ROGERS ▶ 11664 (1)	**0.8**
Freedom Train–James Carr (69)	2.3
Lee ROGERS [Rogers Lee Craton] ▶ 11486 (1)	**1.5**
I'm A Practical Guy–Lee Rogers (66)	9.1
Mike ROGERS ▶ 11605 (1)	**1.0**
Granny's Pad–Viceroys (63)	5.1
–Milton Shorty Rogers see: Boots BROWN	
Robert ROGERS ▶ 979 (16)	**4583**
Ain't That Peculiar–Marvin Gaye (65)	*2266*
The Way You Do The Things You Do–UB40 (90)	*1892*
The Way You Do The Things You Do–Temptations (64)	*1796*
Going To A Go-Go–Miracles (65)	*1646*
My Baby–Temptations (65)	1007
My Girl Has Gone–Miracles (65)	946
The Way You Do The Things You Do– Rita Coolidge (78)	*710*
One More Heartache–Marvin Gaye (66)	662
Going To A Go-Go–Rolling Stones (82)	*594*
That's What Love Is Made Of–Miracles (64)	416
Ain't That Peculiar–Diamond Reo (74)	*361*
The Way You Do The Things You Do– Daryl Hall & John Oates Featuring David Ruffin & Eddie Kendricks (85)	*285*
Come On Do The Jerk–Miracles (64)	273
First I Look At The Purse–Contours (65)	267
Going to a Go-Go–Shalamar (77)	*80*
Ain't That Peculiar–Fanny (72)	*29*
Ron ROGERS ▶ 2749 (2)	**1223**
Heart And Soul–T'Pau (87)	2422
Only A Heartbeat–T'Pau (91)	24
Smokey ROGERS [Eugene Rogers] ▶ 996 (4)	**4493**
Gone–Ferlin Husky (57)	*3669*
Gone–Joey Heatherton (72)	*824*
Gone–Joan Weber (57)	*0.0*
Gone–Bobby Wayne (57)	*0.0*
Stacey ROGERS ▶ 10105 (1)	**13**
Thinking Of You–Grandmaster Slice (91)	25
Gonzalo ROIG ▶ 6013 (1)	**216**
Yours (Quiereme Mucho)–Dick Contino (54)	216
Tarateno ROJAS ▶ 9657 (3)	**19**
Step Right Up (And Say You Love Me)– Nat King Cole (62)	*36*
Sucu Sucu– Ping-Ping and the Al Verlane Orchestra (61)	*7.3*
Step Right Up (And Say You Love Me)– Teresa Brewer (62)	*0.0*
Tony ROJAS [Jose A. Rojas-Miranda] ▶ 9746 (1)	**18**
The Meditation–TNT Band (69)	36

–Jose A. Rojas-Miranda see: Tony ROJAS	
Ron ROKER ▶ 4507 (3)	**474**
Up In A Puff Of Smoke–Polly Brown (74)	883
Devil's Gun–C.J. & Co. (77)	540
Dance Little Lady Dance–Danny White (77)	0.6
Wally ROKER ▶ 7550 (1)	**89**
Beach Party– King Curtis And The Noble Knights (62)	267
Gene ROLAND ▶ 8020 (1)	**65**
In This Whole Wide World–Four Preps (61)	130
Sam ROLFE ▶ 6425 (1)	**171**
The Ballad Of Paladin–Duane Eddy (62)	514
Gregg ROLIE ▶ 3987 (4)	**630**
I've Got A Lot To Learn About Love–Storm (91)	941
No One To Depend On–Santana (72)	719
Just The Same Way–Journey (79)	197
Anytime–Journey (78)	54
Don ROLLINS ▶ 2449 (2)	**1479**
The Race Is On–Jack Jones (65)	*1477*
The Race Is On–George Jones (65)	*2.4*
Jack ROLLINS ▶ 9774 (4)	**17**
I Don't Hurt Anymore–Hank Snow The Singing Ranger And The Rainbow Ranch Boys (54)	*22*
I Don't Hurt Anymore–Eddie Fisher (58)	*11*
Does He Mean That Much To You?–Eddy Arnold (62)	1.3
I Don't Hurt Anymore– Ray Anthony & His Orchestra (54)	*0.0*
–Daisy Rollocks see: Desiree ROLLOCKS	
Desiree ROLLOCKS [Daisy Dee, Daisy Rollocks] ▶ 9744 (1)	**18**
Crazy–Daisy Dee (91)	90
Wolfgang ROLOFF ▶ 11462 (1)	**1.6**
The Happy Cowboy– Billy Vaughn And His Orchestra (63)	3.2
–Del Roma see: Paul MAURIAT	
Amie ROMAN ▶ 2404 (5)	**1521**
Prove Your Love–Taylor Dayne (88)	1402
Whole Wide World–A'me Lorain (90)	1170
Nail It To The Wall–Stacy Lattisaw (86)	296
Each And Every Time–Sweet Sensation (90)	144
The Real Thing–Jellybean (87)	29
–Sam Roman see: Edgar BRONFMAN	
Davide ROMANI ▶ 6075 (3)	**209**
A Lover's Holiday–Change (80)	352
Paradise–Change (81)	92
Hold Tight–Change (81)	6.5
Ralph ROMANO ▶ 10652 (1)	**6.4**
Love Is–Maxine Starr (62)	13
Alain ROMANS ▶ 4720 (3)	**432**
Padre–Toni Arden (58)	*1727*
Padre–Valerie Carr (58)	*0.0*
Padre–Sarah Vaughan (58)	*0.0*
Sigmund ROMBERG ▶ 3076 (13) HOF	**1024**
Silver Moon–Billy Vaughn and His Orchestra (55)	*436*
Wanting You–Roger Williams (55)	369
When I Grow Too Old To Dream–Ed Townsend (58)	*219*
Drink, Drink, Drink–Mario Lanza (54)	154
Serenade–Mario Lanza (56)	*39*
Lover Come Back To Me–Cleftones (62)	17
Stout-Hearted Men–Barbra Streisand (67)	8.8
Silver Moon–Bing Crosby (55)	*0.0*
Silver Moon–Russ Morgan & His Orchestra (55)	*0.0*
When I Grow Too Old To Dream–Duke Mitchell (58)	*0.0*
Silver Moon–Ralph Marterie & His Orchestra (55)	*0.0*
Sweetheart (Will You Remember)–Hilltoppers (54)	0.0
Serenade–Eddie Calvert, his Trumpet and the Norris Paramor Orchestra (56)	*0.0*
Harold ROME ▶ 2330 (3) HOF	**1585**
(All Of A Sudden) My Heart Sings–Paul Anka (58)	*1888*
(All Of A Sudden) My Heart Sings–Mel Carter (65)	*442*
Fanny–Eddie Fisher (54)	420
–Richie Rome see: Richard V. DI CICCO	
Armando ROMEO ▶ 11330 (1)	**2.2**
One Kiss Away From Heaven (Malatia)– Tony Bennett with Percy Faith (57)	4.4
Beresford ROMEO ▶ 1845 (4)	**2204**
Back To Life–Soul II Soul (89)	2835
Keep On Movin'–Soul II Soul (89)	1385
Get A Life–Soul II Soul (90)	192
A Dream's A Dream–Soul II Soul (90)	42

Tony ROMEO ▶ 188 (10)	**16382**
I Think I Love You–Partridge Family Starring Shirley Jones & Featuring David Cassidy (70)	8857
Indian Lake–Cowsills (68)	2466
I'm Gonna Make You Mine–Lou Christie (69)	2293
It's One Of Those Nights (Yes Love)–Partridge Family Starring Shirley Jones & Featuring David Cassidy (71)	1152
Blessed Is The Rain– Brooklyn Bridge Featuring Johnny Maestro (69)	457
Welcome Me Love– Brooklyn Bridge Featuring Johnny Maestro (69)	427
Poor Baby–Cowsills (68)	380
Anthem–Wayne Newton (72)	250
Happy–Paul Anka (69)	91
Summer Days–Lou Christie (75)	8.8
Maxwell ROMER ▶ 11209 (1)	**2.7**
Shout It Out–B.T. Express (78)	8.2
Chan ROMERO ▶ 2925 (2)	**1114**
Hippy Hippy Shake–Swinging Blue Jeans (64)	*749*
Hippy Hippy Shake–Georgia Satellites (88)	*365*
Gary ROMERO [Nicholas Catsos] ▶ 6273 (1)	**187**
My True Carrie, Love–Nat King Cole (64)	374
–Romuald see: Romuald FIGUIER	
Colin RONALD ▶ 10787 (1)	**5.3**
My Faith, My Hope, My Love–Don Cornell (57)	11
Joseph RONCORONI [Milton Carson, David Greer, Dominic John, Joseph Dominic Angelo Roncoroni] ▶ 2346 (9)	**1572**
A Blossom Fell–Nat "King" Cole (55)	*4027*
Sadie's Shawl–Bob Sharples And His Music (56)	*293*
Chincherinchee–Perry Como (56)	282
Why Not Now–Matt Monro (61)	115
A Blossom Fell–Vic Barrett (55)	*0.0*
Someone Else's Roses–Doris Day (54)	0.0
A Blossom Fell–Dickie Valentine (55)	*0.0*
Sadie's Shawl–Philip Green & His Gob Music (56)	*0.0*
Sadie's Shawl–Richard Hayman And Jan August (56)	*0.0*
Ann RONELL [Ann Rosenblatt] ▶ 2636 (2)	**1303**
Willow Weep For Me–Chad & Jeremy (64)	*1303*
Willow Weep For Me– Fontane Sisters with Billy Vaughn's Orchestra (54)	*0.0*
Mick RONSON ▶ 8574 (1)	**46**
Just Another Night–Ian Hunter (79)	92
Ray ROPER ▶ 9417 (1)	**24**
Love Struck–Stonebolt (79)	48
–Brian Rosbotham see: Brian ROSSI	
Axl ROSE [William Bruce Rose Jr.] ▶ 1641 (7)	**2558**
Sweet Child O' Mine–Guns N' Roses (88)	4596
Patience–Guns N' Roses (89)	2050
Paradise City–Guns N' Roses (89)	1901
Don't Cry–Guns N' Roses (91)	1769
Welcome To The Jungle–Guns N' Roses (88)	1661
You Could Be Mine–Guns N' Roses (91)	289
Nightrain–Guns N' Roses (89)	9.3
Billy ROSE [William Samuel Rosenberg] ▶ 1226 (19) HOF	**3643**
Tonight You Belong To Me– Patience and Prudence (56)	*3814*
Does Your Chewing Gum Lose Its Flavor (On The Bedpost Over Night)–Lonnie Donegan And His Skiffle Group (61)	2524
Tonight You Belong To Me– Lawrence Welk And His Sparkling Strings (56)	*1097*
Me And My Shadow– Frank Sinatra And Sammy Davis Jr. (62)	203
Tonight You Belong To Me– Karen Chandler & Jimmy Wakely (56)	*162*
Without A Song–Roy Hamilton (55)	*145*
Happy Days And Lonely Nights– Fontane Sisters with Billy Vaughn's Orchestra (54)	*119*
Happy Days And Lonely Nights–Connie Francis (58)	*60*
I Found A Million Dollar Baby In A Five And Ten Cent Store–Mills Brothers (58)	39
I Want To Be Loved–Dinah Washington (62)	*32*
I Wanna Be Loved–Dean And Jean (64)	*28*
Without A Song (Part 1)– James Cleveland and the Cleveland Singers (66)	*18*
Clap Hands, Here Comes Charlie– Ella Fitzgerald (61)	13
You've Got To See Mamma Every Night (Or You Can't See Mamma At All)–Peggy Lee (56)	12

Billy ROSE [William Samuel Rosenberg] ▶ 1226 (19) HOF *Continued*	**3643**
More Than You Know—Platters (62)	3.2
It Happened In Monterey—Lancers (57)	3.0
Great Day—Sarah Vaughan (61)	1.9
Without A Song—Kay Starr (55)	*0.0*
Tonight You Belong To Me—Tracey Twins (56)	*0.0*
David ROSE ▶ 576 (4)	**7525**
The Stripper—David Rose And His Orchestra (62)	7507
Our Waltz—Sarah Vaughan (60)	12
Holiday For Trombones—David Rose and His Orchestra (57)	6.6
Runway—David Rose (63)	4.5
Dusty ROSE ▶ 9856 (1)	**16**
I've Got Four Big Brothers (To Look After Me)—Four Lads & Cathy Johnson (55)	32
Ed ROSE [Edward Smackels Jr.] ▶ 9780 (3)	**17**
Oh Johnny—Janie Grant (62)	*15*
Oh Johnny Oh—Kathy Linden (58)	*9.4*
Oh Johnny!—Sparkley Betty Barkley (58)	*9.4*
Fred ROSE ▶ 1699 (10) HOF	**2465**
Take These Chains From My Heart—Ray Charles With The Jack Halloran Singers And The Ray Charles Orchestra (63)	1861
Blue Eyes Crying In The Rain—Willie Nelson (75)	1083
No One Will Ever Know—Jimmie Rodgers (62)	490
Tears On My Pillow—McGuire Sisters (61)	310
Indiana Waltz—Jack Scott (60)	19
It's A Sin—Bill Haley And His Comets (58)	17
Afraid—Jimmie Rodgers (63)	15
I'll Never Stand In Your Way—Four Tophatters (56)	*11*
I'll Never Stand In Your Way—Jimmie Rodgers (63)	*7.3*
Kaw Liga—Four Preps (60)	0.5
Pam ROSE ▶ 6839 (1)	**134**
I'll Still Be Loving You—Restless Heart (87)	536
Tim ROSE ▶ 6549 (1)	**158**
Morning Dew—Lulu (68)	316
Vincent ROSE ▶ 1587 (7) HOF	**2665**
Blueberry Hill—Fats Domino (56)	*5648*
Whispering—Nino Tempo & April Stevens (63)	*1526*
Whispering—Dr. Buzzard's Original "Savannah" Band (76)	*448*
Blueberry Hill—Louis Armstrong and Gordon Jenkins and His Orchestra And Chorus (56)	*265*
Whispering—Paul Whiteman & The New Ambassador Hotel Orchestra (54)	*98*
Slowly But Surely—Gordon Jenkins And His Orchestra and Chorus (54)	8.9
Whispering—Bachelors (63)	*0.0*
—William Bruce Rose Jr. see: Axl ROSE	
John ROSELADA ▶ 7410 (1)	**97**
Kisses In The Night—Brandon (91)	97
Don ROSELAND ▶ 11821 (1)	**0.0**
Hit And Run Affair—Perry Como (54)	0.0
Manny ROSEN ▶ 6846 (1)	**133**
King Heroin—James Brown (72)	531
Enrico ROSENBAUM ▶ 5410 (1)	**292**
Gypsy Queen (Part 1)—Gypsy (70)	292
Bob ROSENBERG ▶ 3593 (3)	**774**
Dreamin'—Will To Power (87)	340
Say It's Gonna Rain—Will To Power (88)	299
Fading Away—Will To Power (89)	135
—Jerold Rosenberg see: Jerry ROSS	
—Kenneth Rosenberg see: Kenny VANCE	
Lee ROSENBERG ▶ 3018 (1)	**1063**
Too Much—Elvis Presley (57)	4251
Marvin ROSENBERG ▶ 2674 (1)	**1281**
Image Of A Girl—Safaris With The Phantom's Band (60)	2563
—William Samuel Rosenberg see: Billy ROSE	
—Ann Rosenblatt see: Ann RONELL	
Lenore ROSENBLATT ▶ 8416 (1)	**51**
Pictures In The Fire—Pat Boone (62)	102
—Richard Joel Rosenblatt see: Ritchie CORDELL	
Leonard ROSENMAN ▶ 10424 (1)	**8.6**
Theme From "East Of Eden"—Dick Jacobs And His Chorus And Orchestra (56)	8.6
Harry ROSENTHAL ▶ 10232 (1)	**11**
Georgia Rose—Tony Bennett (66)	33

Charles ROSOFF ▶ 10210 (1)	**11**
Tres Chic—Geoff Gilmore & The Sheiks (59)	34
—Adam Ross see: Irving ROTH	
Arthur ROSS ▶ 2369 (3)	**1555**
I Wanna Be Where You Are—Michael Jackson (72)	1628
I Want You—Marvin Gaye (76)	*984*
I Want You—Robert Palmer (91)	*499*
Bernice ROSS ▶ 1472 (7)	**2952**
Don't Just Stand There—Patty Duke (65)	2466
White On White—Danny Williams (64)	1727
I'll Make All Your Dreams Come True—Ronnie Dove (65)	859
Say Something Funny—Patty Duke (65)	659
Funny Little Butterflies—Patty Duke (65)	183
A Little Toy Balloon—Danny Williams (64)	56
Sad Eyes (Don't You Cry)—Echoes (61)	14
Beverly ROSS [Rachel Frank] ▶ 779 (10)	**5676**
Lollipop—Chordettes (58)	*3626*
Judy's Turn To Cry—Lesley Gore (63)	3021
Dim, Dim The Lights (I Want Some Atmosphere)—Bill Haley And His Comets (54)	*1605*
Candy Man—Roy Orbison (61)	1091
Girl Of My Best Friend—Ral Donner & The Starfires (61)	934
Remember Then—Earls (62)	822
Lollipop—Ronald And Ruby (58)	*224*
Teenage Cleopatra—Tracey Dey (63)	139
Dixieland Rock—Elvis Presley with the Jordanaires (58)	24
Dim, Dim The Lights (I Want Some Atmosphere)—Four Tophatters (54)	*0.0*
—Billy J. Ross see: Billy NESS	
Bud ROSS [Ross G. Matico] ▶ 10172 (1)	**12**
#1 Dee Jay—Goody Goody (78)	35
Dante ROSS ▶ 8514 (1)	**48**
Pop Goes The Weasel—3rd Bass (91)	333
Darryl ROSS ▶ 3510 (1)	**808**
Girls Nite Out—Tyler Collins (90)	1615
Davy ROSS ▶ 10382 (1)	**9.2**
Shape Of Things To Come—Headboys (79)	37
Diana ROSS ▶ 5977 (2)	**220**
So Close—Diana Ross (83)	383
Work That Body—Diana Ross (82)	278
Dick ROSS ▶ 8319 (1)	**54**
Groovy Summertime—Love Generation (67)	163
Herbie ROSS ▶ 8340 (1)	**54**
My Pretending Days Are Over—Dells (73)	161
Jack ROSS ▶ 5204 (1)	**328**
Cinderella—Jack Ross (62)	655
Jerry ROSS [Jerold Rosenberg] ▶ 434 (24) HOF	**9410**
Hey There—Rosemary Clooney (54)	*11126*
Whatever Lola Wants (Lola Gets)—Sarah Vaughan (55)	*2027*
Hernando's Hideaway—Archie Bleyer (54)	*1629*
Heart—Eddie Fisher (55)	*1418*
Hey There—Sammy Davis Jr. (54)	*680*
Two Lost Souls—Perry Como & Jaye P. Morgan (55)	411
Rags To Riches—Sunny & The Sunliners (63)	*343*
Heart—Four Aces (55)	*311*
Rags To Riches—Elvis Presley (71)	*223*
Whatever Lola Wants (Lola Gets)—Dinah Shore (55)	*181*
Near To You—Patti Page (55)	*149*
True Love Goes On And On—Burl Ives (63)	121
Old Shoes—Frankie Laine (54)	118
Heart—Peggy Lee (60)	*33*
Rags To Riches—Lenny Welch (66)	*29*
Steam Heat—Pointer Sisters (74)	*15*
Rags To Riches—Rays Featuring Hal Miller (58)	*6.6*
Heart—Norman Brooks (55)	*0.0*
Steam Heat—Patti Page (54)	*0.0*
Near To You—Eddie Fisher (55)	*0.0*
Hernando's Hideaway—Johnnie Ray (54)	*0.0*
Whatever Lola Wants—Carmen McRae (55)	*0.0*
Whatever Lola Wants (Lola Gets)—Ginny Gibson (55)	*0.0*
Hernando's Hideaway—Guy Lombardo & His Royal Canadians (54)	*0.0*
Jerry J. ROSS ▶ 1151 (14)	**3860**
I'm Gonna Make You Love Me—Diana Ross And The Supremes & The Temptations (68)	*6496*
Who Do You Love—Sapphires (64)	842

I'm Gonna Make You Love Me—Madeline Bell (68)	*687*
Dream Merchant—New Birth (75)	*492*
The 81—Candy And The Kisses (64)	457
Mr. Dream Merchant—Jerry Butler (67)	*434*
Everybody Monkey—Freddy Cannon (63)	338
If I Should Lose You—Dreamlovers (62)	209
Daylight Savin' Time—Keith (67)	122
Love Me—Bobby Hebb (66)	64
I'm Gonna Make You Love Me—Dee Dee Warwick (66)	*48*
Help Yourself (To All Of My Lovin')—James & Bobby Purify (68)	28
The Boy With The Beatle Hair—Swans (64)	19
When Love Slips Away—Dee Dee Warwick (67)	4.8
Lee ROSS ▶ 6551 (2)	**158**
My Shoes Keep Walking Back To You—Guy Mitchell (60)	*276*
My Shoes Keep Walking Back To You—Ray Price (57)	*39*
Lewis ROSS ▶ 5434 (1)	**290**
Keep On Smilin'—Wet Willie (74)	1449
Mark ROSS [Mark D. Ross, Marquis Ross] ▶ 4549 (4)	**466**
Me So Horny—2 Live Crew (89)	729
Banned In The U.S.A.—Luke Feat. 2 Live Crew (90)	588
Dare To Fall In Love—Brent Bourgeois (90)	505
Pop That Coochie—2 Live Crew (91)	137
—Marquis Ross see: Mark ROSS	
—Marshall Ross see: Lester POWELL	
Marv ROSS ▶ 689 (7)	**6313**
Harden My Heart—Quarterflash (81)	4036
Take Me To Heart—Quarterflash (83)	1080
Find Another Fool—Quarterflash (82)	751
Right Kind Of Love—Quarterflash (82)	247
Night Shift—Quarterflash (82)	178
Take Another Picture—Quarterflash (83)	126
Talk To Me—Quarterflash (85)	27
Merria ROSS ▶ 3916 (4)	**658**
Love Is In Control (Finger On The Trigger)—Donna Summer (82)	1455
Cocomotion—El Coco (77)	261
Lets Get It Together—El Coco (76)	81
Dancing In Paradise—El Coco (78)	15
Michael ROSS ▶ 1891 (7)	**2149**
Wild Thing—Tone Loc (88)	2613
Funky Cold Medina—Tone Loc (89)	2425
Bust A Move—Young M.C. (89)	1887
Principal's Office—Young M.C. (89)	445
I Come Off—Young M.C. (90)	147
Summer Vacation—Party (90)	*113*
Summer Vacation—Party (91)	*20*
Peter ROSS ▶ 7777 (2)	**75**
New Day For You—Basia (88)	215
Promises—Basia (89)	11
Richard H. ROSS ▶ 4981 (1)	**365**
Hum A Song (From Your Heart)—Lulu With The Dixie Flyers (70)	365
Rindy ROSS ▶ 10044 (1)	**14**
Talk To Me—Quarterflash (85)	27
Brian ROSSI [Brian Rosbotham] ▶ 10720 (1)	**5.9**
Bad Little Woman—Shadows Of Knight (66)	30
Carlo ROSSI ▶ 7585 (1)	**87**
Honestly—Kitty Kallen (55)	175
Carlo Alberto ROSSI ▶ 5236 (3)	**320**
Heavenly Lover—Teresa Brewer (59)	425
I Only Know I Love You—Four Aces (56)	*324*
I Only Know I Love You—Johnny Desmond (56)	*0.0*
Francis ROSSI ▶ 2339 (1)	**1579**
Pictures Of Matchstick Men—Status Quo (68)	1579
Pat ROSSI ▶ 11823 (1)	**0.0**
A Girl, A Girl (Zoom-Ba Di Alli Nella)—Eddie Fisher (54)	0.0
—Dale Krantz Rossington see: Dale KRANTZ	
Gary ROSSINGTON ▶ 2438 (2)	**1487**
Sweet Home Alabama—Lynyrd Skynyrd (74)	2031
What's Your Name—Lynyrd Skynyrd (77)	1619
Pietro ROSSINI ▶ 9220 (1)	**28**
Don't You Love Me—49ers (90)	85
Nini ROSSO ▶ 9778 (2)	**17**
Il Silenzio—Nini Rosso (65)	*29*
The Silence (Il Silenzio)—Al Hirt (65)	*4.5*

John ROSTILL ► 589 (3)	**7374**
Please Mr. Please—Olivia Newton-John (75)	3858
Let Me Be There—Olivia Newton-John (73)	2871
If You Love Me (Let Me Know)— Olivia Newton-John (74)	2574
Nino ROTA [Giovanni Rota Rinaldi] ► 579 (14)	**7500**
Love Theme From Romeo & Juliet— Henry Mancini, His Orchestra And Chorus (69)	*6778*
Love Theme From "The Godfather" (Speak Softly Love)—Andy Williams (72)	*619*
Love Theme From "The Godfather"— Music Of Nino Rota Conducted By Carlo Savina (72)	*204*
Speak Softly Love—Al Martino (72)	*91*
War And Peace—Vic Damone (56)	86
La Dolce Vita (The Sweet Life)— Ray Ellis And His Orchestra (61)	*80*
Love Theme From "Romeo And Juliet" (A Time For Us)—Johnny Mathis (69)	*30*
Farewell Love Scene— Romeo & Juliet Soundtrack [Nino Rota] (69)	16
Love Theme From "La Strada" (The Road)— Michel Legrand And His Orchestra (56)	*12*
Traveling Down A Lonely Road—Teddi King (56)	6.4
La Dolce Vita (The Sweet Life)— Harry Simeone Chorale (61)	*0.0*
Love Theme From "La Strada"— Jo Moutet & His Orchestra (56)	*0.0*
Love Theme From "La Strada" (The Road)— Paul Weston And His Music From Hollywood (56)	*0.0*
Theme From "War And Peace" (The Maid Of Novgorod)—Richard Maltby And His Orchestra (56)	0.0
Johnny ROTELLA ► 10641 (1)	**6.5**
Lookin' For Love—Ray Conniff And The Singers (66)	6.5
Berl ROTFELD ► 11824 (1)	**0.0**
Pretty Baby - Oh—Austin Smiley (58)	0.0
David Lee ROTH ► 1224 (12)	**3645**
Jump—Van Halen (84)	6595
Just Like Paradise—David Lee Roth (88)	1403
Panama—Van Halen (84)	1026
I'll Wait—Van Halen (84)	975
Dance The Night Away—Van Halen (79)	922
Yankee Rose—David Lee Roth (86)	691
And The Cradle Will Rock...—Van Halen (80)	183
Hot For Teacher—Van Halen (84)	182
Goin' Crazy!—David Lee Roth (86)	112
Stand Up—David Lee Roth (88)	106
Beautiful Girls—Van Halen (79)	61
Runnin' With The Devil—Van Halen (78)	12
—Eduard Roth see: Eddi ROTHÉ	
Irving ROTH [Adam Ross] ► 2715 (9)	**1248**
Sacred—Castells (61)	866
Secret—Gordon MacRae (58)	*824*
Cha Hua Hua—Pets (58)	*657*
Cha Hua Hua— Eddie Platt And His Orchestra (58)	*102*
The Willy—Willies (66)	17
Out Of The Picture—Crew-Cuts (56)	12
Make Believe Wedding—Castells (61)	1.8
Secret—Gainors (58)	*0.0*
Cha Hua Hua—Hugo & Luigi (58)	*0.0*
Michael ROTH ► 8428 (1)	**51**
Your Daddy Don't Know—Toronto (82)	101
Eddi ROTHÉ [Eduard Roth, Eddie Rothé] ► 9906 (1)	**15**
Schweizer Kanton Polka— Will Glahe And His Orchestra (57)	30
Walter ROTHENBURG ► 8074 (3)	**63**
Such A Day—Rita Raines (56)	*133*
Such A Day—Vera Lynn (56)	*55*
Your Heart - My Heart (Sehnsucht)— Frankie Laine (54)	0.0
—Cal Rotherman see: Kal MANN	
—Dean Rotherman see: David CHANDLER	
Steve ROTHERY ► 9798 (1)	**17**
Kayleigh—Marillion (85)	84
Sherman ROTHMAN ► 8649 (1)	**44**
Lovely, Lovely (Loverly, Loverly)— Chubby Checker (64)	88
Claire ROTHROCK ► 3750 (1)	**712**
Old Cape Cod—Patti Page (57)	2136

Talbot ROTHWELL [Marvin Scott] ► 10179 (4)	**12**
Friends And Neighbors—Tommy Prisco (54)	*8.7*
Friends And Neighbors—Plunkett Family (54)	*8.7*
Friends And Neighbors—Billy Cotton & Band (54)	*8.7*
Friends And Neighbors— Sammy Kaye & "Swing And Sway" Orchestra (54)	*8.7*
Martin ROTSEY ► 5859 (2)	**236**
Beds Are Burning—Midnight Oil (88)	812
Blue Sky Mine—Midnight Oil (90)	369
Fritz ROTTER ► 1398 (4)	**3181**
That's All I Want From You—Jaye P. Morgan (54)	*3173*
That's All I Want From You—Jaye P. Morgan (54)	*3173*
That's All I Want From You—Silva-Tones (57)	*7.1*
That's All I Want From You—Silva-Tones (57)	*7.1*
Bob ROUBIAN ► 3687 (2)	**733**
Popcorn Song—Cliffie Stone And His Orchestra (55)	*733*
The Popcorn Song— Russ Morgan & His Scranton Seven (55)	*0.0*
Danielle ROUBY ► 8396 (1)	**52**
When Love Has Gone Away—Richard Cocciante (76)	208
Ervin ROUSE ► 6941 (2)	**127**
Orange Blossom Special— Billy Vaughn And His Orchestra (61)	*78*
Orange Blossom Special—Johnny Cash (65)	*49*
Theda ROUSH [Theda Daffan] ► 10743 (1)	**5.6**
Rockin', Rollin' Ocean—Hank Snow (60)	11
Jean ROUSSEL ► 8119 (1)	**61**
Was Dog A Doughnut—Cat Stevens (77)	183
Guy Charles ROUTTE ► 8242 (1)	**57**
Going Through The Motions—Aftershock (91)	172
René ROUZAUD ► 11825 (1)	**0.0**
L'Homme Et L'Enfant— Eddie Constantine & Tania (56)	*0.0*
Chris ROWAN ► 8024 (1)	**64**
If I Only Could—Rowans (76)	64
Peter ROWAN ► 11421 (1)	**1.8**
Home To You—Earth Opera (69)	1.8
Dennis ROWE ► 5190 (2)	**329**
Express—B.T. Express (75)	*2209*
Express—Ritchie Family (76)	*92*
James ROWE ► 11550 (1)	**1.2**
Love Lifted Me—Kenny Rogers (76)	2.4
Kevin ROWLAND ► 2203 (2)	**1748**
Come On Eileen—Dexys Midnight Runners (83)	5225
The Celtic Soul Brothers— Dexys Midnight Runners (83)	19
Jonathan ROWLANDS ► 8504 (1)	**48**
Georgia Took Her Back—R.B. Greaves (70)	48
John ROWLES ► 7649 (1)	**83**
Cheryl Moana Marie—John Rowles (71)	166
Dave ROWNTREE ► 9677 (1)	**19**
There's No Other Way—Blur (91)	77
John ROX ► 11826 (1)	**0.0**
There Never Was A Night So Beautiful— Perry Como (54)	0.0
Tuhin ROY ► 2439 (3)	**1485**
Hold You Tight—Tara Kemp (91)	3071
Piece Of My Heart—Tara Kemp (91)	1377
Too Much—Tara Kemp (91)	4.1
Dale ROYAL ► 6456 (2)	**167**
Teddy Bear—Red Sovine (76)	478
Teddy Bear's Last Ride—Diana Williams (76)	94
—Fred Royal see: Roy ALFRED	
—Roy Be see: Roy BERMINGHAM	
Robb ROYER [Robert Wilson Royer, Robb Wilson] ► 2855 (1)	**1151**
For All We Know—Carpenters (71)	3454
Joseph ROYSTER ► 616 (10)	**7036**
Quarter To Three—U.S. Bonds (61)	8470
If You Wanna Be Happy—Jimmy Soul (63)	6827
New Orleans—U.S. Bonds (60)	*2886*
Twist, Twist Senora—Gary (U.S.) Bonds (62)	1458
High School Usa—Tommy Facenda (59)	625
New Orleans—Eddie Hodges (65)	*616*
New Orleans—Neil Diamond (68)	*383*
Treat 'Em Tough—Jimmy Soul (63)	42
Copy Cat—Gary (U.S.) Bonds (62)	9.2
New Orleans—Chartbusters (65)	*0.0*
—Dessie Rozier see: James BROWN	

Shannon RUBICAM ► 775 (5)	**5684**
I Wanna Dance With Somebody (Who Loves Me)— Whitney Houston (87)	4874
How Will I Know—Whitney Houston (85)	4102
Waiting For A Star To Fall—Boy Meets Girl (88)	3061
Oh Girl—Boy Meets Girl (85)	428
Bring Down The Moon—Boy Meets Girl (89)	270
—Lynsey Mockon Rubin see: Lynsey DePAUL	
Rick RUBIN ► 3301 (4)	**908**
(You Gotta) Fight For Your Right (To Party!)— Beastie Boys (86)	1744
Going Back To Cali—LL Cool J (88)	429
Brass Monkey—Beastie Boys (87)	278
It's Tricky—Run-D.M.C. (87)	170
David RUBINSON ► 5637 (1)	**262**
How Long (Betcha' Got A Chick On The Side)— Pointer Sisters (75)	1309
Jesús Gonzáles RUBIO ► 4488 (2)	**481**
Mexican Hat Rock—Applejacks (S) (58)	961
Mexican Hat Twist—Applejacks (S) (61)	2.8
Paul RUBIO ► 7098 (1)	**116**
Enamorado—Keith Colley (63)	232
Harry RUBY ► 2357 (2) HOF	**1566**
Who's Sorry Now—Connie Francis (58)	*4383*
Who's Sorry Now—Marie Osmond (75)	*314*
Herman RUBY ► 9318 (3)	**26**
I'll Always Be In Love With You— Jack Pleis and His Orchestra and Chorus (56)	*79*
I'll Always Be In Love With You—Stroll Kings (58)	*0.0*
I'll Always Be In Love With You—Rosemary June (58)	*0.0*
Herwig RUDISSER [Herwig Tremschnig] ► 7243 (1)	**108**
Live Is Life—Opus (86)	541
Richard RUDOLPH ► 1339 (5)	**3314**
Lovin' You—Minnie Riperton (75)	6022
Love Me All Up—Stacy Earl (91)	658
Say You Really Want Me—Kim Wilde (87)	184
Inside My Love—Minnie Riperton (75)	64
Memory Lane—Minnie Riperton (79)	3.4
Kenneth RUFFIN ► 5557 (1)	**271**
I Do—Moments (2) (69)	271
Pete RUGOLO ► 4144 (1)	**581**
Theme From Dr. Kildare (Three Stars Will Shine Tonight)—Richard Chamberlain (62)	1744
Gabriel RUIZ [Gabriel Ruiz Galindo] ► 4889 (2)	**387**
Amor—Ben E. King (61)	*1033*
Amor—Roger Williams (62)	*43*
Louis RUIZ ► 8196 (1)	**59**
The Fanatic—Felony (83)	294
Pablo Beltran RUIZ ► 3330 (2)	**897**
Sway—Bobby Rydell (60)	*1551*
Sway (Quien Sera)—Dean Martin (54)	*243*
Chris RUIZ-VELASCO ► 8758 (1)	**40**
Masquerade—Berlin (83)	40
Todd RUNDGREN ► 413 (22)	**9635**
Hello It's Me—Todd Rundgren (73)	*3393*
I Saw The Light—Todd Rundgren (72)	1424
Love Is The Answer—England Dan & John Ford Coley (79)	1383
We Gotta Get You A Woman—Runt (70)	1370
Set Me Free—Utopia (80)	641
Can We Still Be Friends—Todd Rundgren (78)	*502*
Hello It's Me—Nazz (69)	*361*
Can We Still Be Friends—Robert Palmer (79)	*282*
A Dream Goes On Forever—Todd Rundgren (74)	231
Be Nice To Me—Runt--Todd Rundgren (71)	158
Bang The Drum All Day—Todd Rundgren (83)	99
Hello It's Me—Nazz (70)	*80*
Couldn't I Just Tell You—Todd Rundgren (72)	61
The Very Last Time—Utopia (80)	51
Feet Don't Fail Me Now—Utopia (83)	42
Real Man—Todd Rundgren (75)	42
Open My Eyes—Nazz (68)	26
A Long Time, A Long Way To Go— Runt--Todd Rundgren (71)	19
You Cried Wolf—Todd Rundgren (78)	12
Piece By Piece—Tubes (85)	10
Not Wrong Long—Nazz (69)	4.3
Wolfman Jack—Todd Rundgren (75)	3.6
—Laura Lee Rundless see: Laura LEE	
—Jerome A. Rusch see: Jerry RUSH	

Billy RUSH ▶ 8549 (2)	**46**
I'm So Anxious—Southside Johnny And The Asbury Jukes (79)	42
On The Beach—Southside Johnny & Asbury Jukes (80)	4.9
Bobby RUSH [Emmitt Ellis Jr.] ▶ 7260 (1)	**107**
I' Been Watchin' You—South Side Movement (73)	214
Jennifer RUSH [Heidi Stern] ▶ 5790 (3)	**241**
Power Of Love—Laura Branigan (87)	*653*
The Power Of Love—Jennifer Rush (86)	*248*
The Power Of Love (You Are My Lady)—Air Supply (85)	*65*
Jerry RUSH [Jerome A. Rusch] ▶ 8277 (1)	**56**
Like They Say In L.A.—East L.A. Car Pool (75)	56
Mary Jo RUSH ▶ 8646 (1)	**44**
Love Never Changes—Chordettes (56)	44
Patrice RUSHEN ▶ 4985 (4)	**364**
Forget Me Nots—Patrice Rushen (82)	752
Haven't You Heard—Patrice Rushen (80)	293
Feels So Real (Won't Let Go)—Patrice Rushen (84)	69
Look Up—Patrice Rushen (80)	18
Jimmy RUSHING ▶ 11762 (1)	**0.2**
Going To Chicago Blues—Count Basie (58)	0.4
Lonnie RUSS ▶ 5998 (1)	**218**
My Wife Can't Cook—Lonnie Russ (62)	218
—Bert Russell see: Bert BERNS	
Bob RUSSELL [Sidney Keith Russell] ▶ 1635 (13) HOF	**2563**
He Ain't Heavy, He's My Brother—Hollies (69)	*2440*
He Ain't Heavy...He's My Brother—Neil Diamond (70)	*1112*
Amukiriki (The Lord Willing)—Les Paul and Mary Ford (55)	468
Ballerina—Nat "King" Cole (57)	*423*
Don't Get Around Much Anymore—Belmonts (61)	*211*
Time Was—Flamingos (61)	160
He Ain't Heavy...He's My Brother—Olivia Newton-John (75)	*141*
Don't Get Around Much Anymore—Tab Hunter (57)	*101*
It Could've Been Worse—Jesse Belvin (59)	89
Ballerina—Vaughn Monroe and his Orchestra (60)	*14*
Don't Get Around Much Anymore—Jo Stafford (55)	*13*
All The Grey Haired Men—Lettermen (68)	7.3
Ballerina—Vaughn Monroe & His Orchestra (57)	*0.0*
Bobby RUSSELL ▶ 85 (15)	**26669**
Honey—Bobby Goldsboro (68)	*9605*
Little Green Apples—O.C. Smith (68)	*5805*
The Night The Lights Went Out In Georgia—Vicki Lawrence (73)	5615
Sure Gonna Miss Her—Gary Lewis And The Playboys (66)	1553
The Joker Went Wild—Brian Hyland (66)	1079
Saturday Morning Confusion—Bobby Russell (71)	919
Popsicle—Jan & Dean (66)	820
1432 Franklin Pike Circle Hero—Bobby Russell (68)	481
Little Green Apples—Roger Miller (68)	*428*
Honey (I Miss You)—O.C. Smith (69)	*266*
Vance—Roger Miller (68)	243
Sudden Stop—Percy Sledge (68)	134
Tennessee—Jan & Dean (62)	129
Then She's A Lover—Roy Clark (70)	63
Little Green Apples—Patti Page (68)	*3.5*
Brenda RUSSELL [Brenda Gordon] ▶ 1255 (8)	**3561**
Get Here—Oleta Adams (90)	1582
Piano In The Dark—Brenda Russell (88)	1550
So Good, So Right—Brenda Russell (79)	730
Think It Over—Cheryl Ladd (78)	380
You—Earth, Wind & Fire (80)	320
Please Pardon Me (You Remind Me Of A Friend)—Rufus Featuring Chaka Khan (75)	290
Dinner With Gershwin—Donna Summer (87)	257
And Love Goes On—Earth, Wind & Fire (81)	174
Brian RUSSELL ▶ 5137 (2)	**335**
Think It Over—Cheryl Ladd (78)	380
Please Pardon Me (You Remind Me Of A Friend)—Rufus Featuring Chaka Khan (75)	290
Frank RUSSELL ▶ 7741 (1)	**77**
Why Did You Leave Me?—Vince Edwards (62)	77
Frankie RUSSELL ▶ 11096 (1)	**3.3**
Oh! My Love (Keep Your Dreams Just For Me)—June Valli (55)	6.5

Graham RUSSELL ▶ 204 (5)	**15435**
All Out Of Love—Air Supply (80)	5778
The One That You Love—Air Supply (81)	4945
Lost In Love—Air Supply (80)	4858
Sweet Dreams—Air Supply (81)	2448
Young Love—Air Supply (82)	295
Henry RUSSELL ▶ 10737 (1)	**5.6**
Yancy Derringer—Tommy Mara (59)	11
Jack RUSSELL ▶ 6139 (4)	**201**
Rock Me—Great White (87)	217
Call It Rock 'N Roll—Great White (91)	208
Save Your Love—Great White (88)	175
House Of Broken Love—Great White (90)	52
Johnny RUSSELL ▶ 5583 (1)	**269**
Act Naturally—Beatles (65)	538
Kevin RUSSELL ▶ 8972 (1)	**35**
Mega Force—707 (82)	139
Larry RUSSELL ▶ 6247 (3)	**190**
Vaya Con Dios—Drifters (64)	*412*
Vaya Con Dios—Dawn Featuring Tony Orlando (72)	*82*
Vaya Con Dios—Freddy Fender (76)	*75*
Leon RUSSELL [Claude Russell Bridges, Hank Wilson] ▶ 352 (22) HOF	**10755**
Superstar—Carpenters (71)	*6023*
She's Just My Style—Gary Lewis And The Playboys (65)	4343
Everybody Loves A Clown—Gary Lewis And The Playboys (65)	2836
This Masquerade—George Benson (76)	1880
Lady Blue—Leon Russell (75)	*1570*
Tight Rope—Leon Russell (72)	1328
(You Don't Have To) Paint Me A Picture—Gary Lewis And The Playboys (66)	967
The Loser (With A Broken Heart)—Gary Lewis And The Playboys (67)	478
Hummingbird—B.B. King (70)	455
Bluebird—Helen Reddy (75)	262
Rainbow In Your Eyes—Leon & Mary Russell (76)	235
Back To The Island—Leon Russell (75)	228
Delta Lady—Joe Cocker (69)	61
A Song For You—Andy Williams (71)	*60*
Queen Of The Roller Derby—Leon Russell (73)	35
Roll Away The Stone—Leon Russell (70)	20
Blues Power (Live)—Eric Clapton (80)	20
A Song For You—Jaye P. Morgan (71)	*10*
Superstar—Luther Vandross (84)	*7.6*
Lady Blue—George Benson (78)	*4.1*
Slipping Into Christmas—Leon Russell (72)	2.7
Tryin' To Stay 'Live—Asylum Choir (72)	2.4
Rudolph RUSSELL ▶ 11374 (1)	**2.0**
I'm A Fool For You—James Carr (67)	10
Sam RUSSELL ▶ 9129 (1)	**31**
It's So Nice—Jackie Deshannon (70)	61
—Sidney Keith Russell see: Bob RUSSELL	
Tom RUSSELL ▶ 5776 (1)	**243**
A Piece Of Paper—Gladstone (72)	485
Charley RUSSO ▶ 9593 (1)	**21**
Preacherman—Charlie Russo (63)	41
Dan RUSSO ▶ 10921 (1)	**4.4**
Toot, Toot, Tootsie—Johnston Brothers (55)	13
—Dorothy Russo see: Deena CHARLES	
Ferdinando RUSSO ▶ 8150 (1)	**60**
Ma Ma Ma Marie—Gaylords (58)	*240*
Joe RUSSO ▶ 8888 (1)	**37**
Running—Chubby Checker (82)	37
Mario RUSSO ▶ 8956 (1)	**35**
Stoned Cowboy—Fantasy (70)	141
—Harold Rustigan see: Russ REGAN	
Harold RUSTIGIAN ▶ 6402 (1)	**175**
Happy Reindeer—Dancer, Prancer And Nervous (59)	350
Mike RUTHERFORD ▶ 344 (23)	**10882**
Invisible Touch—Genesis (86)	3735
The Living Years—Mike + The Mechanics (88)	3672
In Too Deep—Genesis (87)	2454
Tonight, Tonight, Tonight—Genesis (87)	2246
Throwing It All Away—Genesis (86)	2205
Land Of Confusion—Genesis (86)	2182
No Son Of Mine—Genesis (91)	1981
Silent Running (On Dangerous Ground)—Mike + The Mechanics (85)	1912
That's All—Genesis (83)	1827

All I Need Is A Miracle—Mike + The Mechanics (86)	1677
Follow You Follow Me—Genesis (78)	761
No Reply At All—Genesis (81)	731
Taken In—Mike + The Mechanics (86)	539
Paperlate—Genesis (82)	533
Abacab—Genesis (81)	451
Taking It All Too Hard—Genesis (84)	331
Illegal Alien—Genesis (84)	277
Turn It On Again—Genesis (80)	248
Nobody's Perfect—Mike + The Mechanics (88)	169
Seeing Is Believing—Mike + The Mechanics (89)	161
Mama—Genesis (83)	137
Word Of Mouth—Mike + The Mechanics (91)	122
Your Own Special Way—Genesis (77)	56
Jim RUTLEDGE ▶ 7012 (1)	**122**
D.O.A.—Bloodrock (70)	733
Ben RYAN ▶ 9023 (1)	**33**
Heart Of My Heart—Frank Fontaine (63)	33
Charlie RYAN ▶ 2124 (4)	**1845**
Hot Rod Lincoln—Commander Cody And His Lost Planet Airmen (72)	*1950*
Hot Rod Lincoln—Charlie Ryan And The Timberline Riders (60)	*915*
Hot Rod Lincoln—Johnny Bond (60)	*790*
Side Car Cycle—Charlie Ryan And The Timberline Riders (60)	34
James E. RYAN Jr. ▶ 4168 (1)	**575**
Don't Let The Rain Fall Down On Me—Critters (67)	575
Patti RYAN ▶ 3121 (1)	**999**
Lookin' For Love—Johnny Lee (80)	2996
Paul RYAN [Paul Sapherson] ▶ 4735 (3)	**428**
The Colour Of My Love—Jefferson (69)	241
Eloise—Barry Ryan (68)	176
Love's Only Love—Engelbert (80)	11
Roma RYAN ▶ 5186 (1)	**329**
Orinoco Flow—Enya (89)	658
Tim RYAN ▶ 7498 (1)	**92**
You Can't Dance—England Dan & John Ford Coley (78)	184
—Gregory Rybarski see: Chip Z'NUFF	
Dale RYDER ▶ 10986 (1)	**4.0**
Talk About It—Boom Crash Opera (91)	20
—Jeremy Allan Ryder see: Jack HUES	
Maggie RYDER [Margaret Jean Rider] ▶ 9849 (1)	**16**
You're The Voice—John Farnham (90)	64
Mitch RYDER [William S. Levise Jr.] ▶ 6950 (1)	**126**
Joy—Mitch Ryder (67)	378
Celia RYLAND ▶ 7866 (1)	**71**
Song In Blue—Les Paul and Mary Ford (55)	214
Diane RYSER ▶ 8777 (1)	**40**
Same Old Look—Jimmy Ryser (90)	79
Jimmy RYSER ▶ 8778 (1)	**40**
Same Old Look—Jimmy Ryser (90)	79

S

Raphael SAADIQ [Charles Ray Wiggins] ▶ 3536 (4)	**793**
Feels Good—Tony! Toni! Toné! (90)	1657
It Never Rains (In Southern California)—Tony! Toni! Toné! (90)	390
Little Walter—Tony! Toni! Toné! (88)	272
The Blues—Tony! Toni! Tone! (90)	260
Jaime SABATER ▶ 4963 (3)	**370**
Bang! Bang!—Joe Cuba Sextet (66)	373
Oh Yeah!—Joe Cuba Sextet (66)	180
El Pito (I'll Never Go Back To Georgia)—Joe Cuba Sextet (66)	8.1
—Suhayla Sabir see: Djuana JOHNICAN	
Dave SABO ▶ 2201 (3)	**1751**
18 And Life—Skid Row (89)	1922
I Remember You—Skid Row (89)	1578
Youth Gone Wild—Skid Row (89)	1.6
—Antonio Adolfo Maurity Sabóia see: Antonio ADOLFO	
—Hajji Rajah Kasim Sabre see: Rodger COLLINS	

Paul SABU ▶ 9203 (1)	**29**
High On Your Love—Debbie Jacobs (80)	29
—Lugee Sacco see: Lou CHRISTIE	
—Allan Preston Sachs see: Alan MERRILL	
Norman SACHS ▶ 9969 (1)	**14**
In My Father's Footsteps—Terry Jacks (76)	29
Joseph SADDLER ▶ 11310 (1)	**2.3**
Freedom—Grandmaster Flash And The Furious 5 (80)	21
—Sade see: Helen ADU	
Barry SADLER ▶ 873 (2)	**5086**
The Ballad Of The Green Berets—SSgt. Barry Sadler (66)	9577
The "A" Team—SSgt. Barry Sadler (66)	891
Eric SADLER ▶ 7341 (1)	**101**
B.B.D. (I Thought It Was Me)?—Bell Biv DeVoe (90)	504
Michael SADLER ▶ 6288 (3)	**185**
On The Loose—Saga (82)	675
Wind Him Up—Saga (83)	200
The Flyer—Saga (83)	21
—Robert Sadoff see: Ira LEE	
Mark SAFAN ▶ 8475 (1)	**49**
I'm On My Way—Captain & Tennille (78)	49
Bob SAFFER ▶ 9057 (2)	**32**
If I Only Knew—Curt Jensen (58)	27
My Girl—Frankie Lymon (57)	11
—Sa-Fire see: Wilma COSMÉ	
Melanie SAFKA ▶ 174 (13)	**17348**
Brand New Key—Melanie (71)	8519
Lay Down (Candles In The Rain)—Melanie With The Edwin Hawkins Singers (70)	3749
Look What They've Done To My Song Ma—New Seekers Featuring Eve Graham (70)	*1607*
Ring The Living Bell—Melanie (72)	734
Bitter Bad—Melanie (73)	648
Peace Will Come (According To Plan)—Melanie (70)	638
The Nickel Song—Melanie (72)	*527*
Beautiful People—New Seekers Featuring Eve Graham (70)	256
Together Alone—Melanie (72)	235
Look What They've Done To My Song, Ma—Ray Charles (72)	*232*
The Good Book—Melanie (71)	81
Some Day I'll Be A Farmer—Melanie (72)	65
Nickel Song—New Seekers Featuring Eve Graham (71)	*55*
Bob SAGE [Robert Sage Wilber, Robert Wilber] ▶ 9756 (1)	**17**
On The Other Side—Seekers (67)	52
Carole Bayer SAGER [Carole Jean Bayer, Carole Bayer Bacharach] ▶ 102 (46) HOF	**24499**
Arthur's Theme (Best That You Can Do)—Christopher Cross (81)	6911
Nobody Does It Better—Carly Simon (77)	5897
A Groovy Kind Of Love—Mindbenders (66)	*5559*
That's What Friends Are For—Dionne & Friends (85)	5417
When I Need You—Leo Sayer (77)	5176
On My Own—Patti LaBelle & Michael McDonald (86)	5145
Groovy Kind Of Love—Phil Collins (88)	*3712*
Midnight Blue—Melissa Manchester (75)	2399
Heartlight—Neil Diamond (82)	2132
Don't Cry Out Loud—Melissa Manchester (78)	1951
It's My Turn—Diana Ross (80)	1404
Making Love—Roberta Flack (82)	1327
Love Power—Dionne Warwick & Jeffrey Osborne (87)	1032
If You Remember Me—Chris Thompson & Night (79)	961
Stronger Than Before—Carole Bayer Sager (81)	502
I'd Rather Leave While I'm In Love—Rita Coolidge (79)	461
On The Way To The Sky—Neil Diamond (82)	460
Jennifer—Bobby Sherman (71)	386
Just You And I—Melissa Manchester (76)	346
Love Always—El DeBarge (86)	328
Fool That I Am—Rita Coolidge (80)	313
Heartbreaker—Dolly Parton (78)	285
I Don't Wanna Go—Joey Travolta (78)	232
Ashes To Ashes—Mindbenders (66)	223
You're Movin' Out Today—Bette Midler (77)	*215*
You're Moving Out Today—Carole Bayer Sager (77)	*188*
Skybird—Tony Orlando And Dawn (75)	179
Night Shift—Quarterflash (82)	178
Front Page Story—Neil Diamond (83)	147
Fly Away—Peter Allen (81)	*131*
Turn Around—Neil Diamond (84)	110
Some Changes Are For Good—Dionne Warwick (81)	107
You're The Only One—Dolly Parton (79)	105
A Chance For Heaven—Christopher Cross (84)	64
Better Days—Melissa Manchester (76)	54
Come In From The Rain—Captain & Tennille (77)	54
Theme From Ice Castles (Through The Eyes Of Love)—Melissa Manchester (79)	30
Easy To Love Again—Carole Bayer Sager (81)	22
I'm Into Lookin' For Someone To Love Me—Bobby Vee (68)	20
Fly Away—Stevie Woods (82)	*19*
Our Night—Shaun Cassidy (78)	16
I'm Gonna Make You Mine—Shadows Of Knight (66)	13
I Could Have Loved You—Moments (78)	10
Break It To Me Gently—Aretha Franklin (77)	9.1
Off And Running—Lesley Gore (66)	8.1
With You—Moments (2) (76)	4.5
—Charles H. Sagle see: Carl STEVENS	
Doug SAHM ▶ 1694 (5)	**2479**
Mendocino—Sir Douglas Quintet (69)	1226
She's About A Mover—Sir Douglas Quintet (65)	*1195*
Dynamite Woman—Sir Douglas Quintet (69)	51
She's About A Mover—Otis Clay (68)	*5.9*
It Didn't Even Bring Me Down—Sir Douglas Quintet (69)	3.8
Yaso SAIJO ▶ 7106 (1)	**116**
China Nights (Shina No Yoru)—Kyu Sakamoto (63)	347
Oliver SAIN ▶ 3439 (4)	**848**
Don't Mess Up A Good Thing—Fontella Bass & Bobby McClure (65)	*791*
She's A Disco Queen—Oliver Sain (76)	33
Party Hearty—Oliver Sain (76)	19
Don't Mess Up A Good Thing—Gregg Allman (74)	*5.3*
Eddison SAINSBURY [Eddison Electrik] ▶ 11669 (1)	**0.8**
Falling In Love—Fat Boys (87)	3.9
Buffy SAINTE-MARIE ▶ 1301 (10)	**3405**
Up Where We Belong—Joe Cocker and Jennifer Warnes (82)	5012
Until It's Time For You To Go—Elvis Presley (72)	*502*
Universal Soldier—Donovan (65)	*437*
The Universal Soldier—Glen Campbell (65)	*409*
Until It's Time For You To Go—Neil Diamond (70)	*324*
I'm Gonna Be A Country Girl Again—Buffy Sainte-Marie (71)	31
Until It's Time For You To Go—Buffy Sainte-Marie (70)	*21*
He's An Indian Cowboy In The Rodeo—Buffy Sainte-Marie (72)	9.3
Until It's Time For You To Go—New Birth (73)	*2.0*
Universal Soldier—Roemans (65)	*0.0*
—Christian Sainturat see: Christian SARREL	
Ryuichi SAKAMOTO ▶ 8577 (1)	**46**
Computer Game ("Theme From The Circus")—Yellow Magic Orchestra (80)	138
Rex SALAS ▶ 6899 (2)	**130**
The Right Stuff—Vanessa Williams (88)	233
Darlin' I—Vanessa Williams (89)	27
Rudy SALAS ▶ 7503 (1)	**91**
Memories—Tierra (81)	91
Rod SALAZAR ▶ 10745 (1)	**5.6**
Tiger In The Tank—Chariots (65)	17
—Kashif Saleem see: Michael JONES	
Giuliano SALERNI ▶ 9622 (1)	**20**
Touch Me Baby—Ultimate (79)	20
Nicola SALERNO [Nisa] ▶ 4443 (5)	**493**
Torero—Renato Carosone (58)	*899*
This Is My Prayer—Ray Charles Singers (65)	124
Cappuccina—Nat King Cole (61)	11
Torero—Julius La Rosa (58)	*0.0*
Torero—Andrews Sisters (58)	*0.0*
Emily Ann SALIERS ▶ 7496 (1)	**92**
Closer To Fine—Indigo Girls (89)	185
Norman SALLITT ▶ 1569 (1)	**2697**
Here I Am (Just When I Thought I Was Over You)—Air Supply (81)	2697
Bert SALMERS-BERNSTEIN ▶ 11827 (1)	**0.0**
Joey—Betty Madigan (54)	0.0
Bert SALMIRS ▶ 5975 (1)	**220**
Come On And Get Me—Fabian (59)	440
—Salt see: Cheryl JAMES	
Charles SALTER ▶ 11617 (1)	**1.0**
Love Me Just For Me—Special Generation (90)	6.8
William SALTER ▶ 1510 (6)	**2842**
Just The Two Of Us—Grover Washington, Jr. (81)	3799
Where Is The Love—Roberta Flack & Donny Hathaway (72)	2619
I'm The One—Roberta Flack (82)	388
In The Name Of Love—Ralph MacDonald (with Bill Withers) (84)	200
Mister Magic—Grover Washington, Jr. (75)	135
Be Mine (Tonight)—Grover Washington, Jr. (82)	8.6
Sam SALTZBERG ▶ 9848 (3)	**16**
Hey, Stella! (Who Zat Down Your Cellar?)—Crew-Cuts (58)	29
Dominick The Donkey—Lou Monte with Joe Reisman's Orch. & Chorus (60)	14
First Love—Playmates (59)	12
Henri SALVADOR ▶ 8143 (1)	**60**
I Will Live My Life For You—Tony Bennett (63)	120
Senora SAM ▶ 3026 (2)	**1056**
I'll Be Good To You—Brothers Johnson (76)	*2385*
I'll Be Good To You—Quincy Jones (89)	*782*
John SAMBATARO ▶ 6733 (1)	**142**
Always—Firefall (83)	283
Richie SAMBORA ▶ 412 (11) HOF	**9645**
Livin' On A Prayer—Bon Jovi (86)	5011
You Give Love A Bad Name—Bon Jovi (86)	4318
I'll Be There For You—Bon Jovi (89)	4005
Bad Medicine—Bon Jovi (88)	3448
Born To Be My Baby—Bon Jovi (88)	3071
Wanted Dead Or Alive—Bon Jovi (87)	1804
Lay Your Hands On Me—Bon Jovi (89)	1766
We All Sleep Alone—Cher (88)	926
Does Anybody Really Fall In Love Anymore?—Kane Roberts (91)	452
Notorious—Loverboy (87)	386
Ballad Of Youth—Richie Sambora (91)	153
—Yennik Samoht see: Kenny THOMAS	
Frank SAMPEDRO ▶ 3024 (1)	**1060**
Lotta Love—Nicolette Larson (78)	2120
Joe SAMPLE ▶ 2981 (5)	**1084**
Street Life—Crusaders (79)	566
Put It Where You Want It—Crusaders (72)	*462*
Put It Where You Want It—Nino & April (73)	*53*
Don't Let It Get You Down—Crusaders (73)	28
I'm So Glad I'm Standing Here Today—Crusaders (81)	3.1
Edgar SAMPSON ▶ 9805 (1)	**17**
Don't Be That Way—Larry Elgart And His Manhattan Swing Orchestra (82)	50
—Linda Joy Sampson see: Linda SCOTT	
Phil SAMPSON ▶ 4690 (1)	**438**
I Loved 'Em Every One—T.G. Sheppard (81)	438
Warren SAMS ▶ 10989 (1)	**3.9**
Somebody Loves You—Whispers (73)	7.9
Domingo SAMUDIO [Sam Samudio, Sam the Sham] ▶ 556 (2)	**7739**
Wooly Bully—Sam The Sham And The Pharaohs (65)	7187
Ju Ju Hand—Sam The Sham And The Pharaohs (65)	553
—Sam Samudio see: Domingo SAMUDIO	
C.B. SAMUEL [Sam Kaufman] ▶ 10905 (1)	**4.4**
Dear Elvis (Page 1)—Audrey (56)	4.4
Steve SAMUEL ▶ 4983 (1)	**365**
Twist, Twist Senora—Gary (U.S.) Bonds (62)	1458
Eddy SAMUELS ▶ 10951 (1)	**4.1**
Calla Calla—Paulette Sisters (58)	12
Jerry SAMUELS [Scott David, Napoleon XIV] ▶ 768 (6)	**5719**
They're Coming To Take Me Away, Ha-Haaa!—Napoleon XIV (66)	*3925*
The Shelter Of Your Arms—Sammy Davis Jr. (63)	1200
As If I Didn't Know—Adam Wade (61)	958
They're Coming To Take Me Away, Ha-Haaa!—Napoleon XIV (73)	*60*
To Ev'ry Girl—To Ev'ry Boy (The Meaning Of Love)—Johnnie Ray (54)	44
Speaking Of Her—Adam Wade (60)	32

Keith SAMUELS ▶ 9325 (1)	**26**
I Don't Know What It Is, But It Sure Is Funky—Ripple (73)	184
Zelda SAMUELS ▶ 2543 (5)	**1400**
Lookin' For A Love—Bobby Womack (74)	*1838*
Looking For A Love—J. Geils Band (71)	*652*
Lookin' For A Love—Valentinos (62)	*169*
Dancin' Holiday—Olympics (63)	96
Furry Murray—Tradewinds (59)	76
Ian SAMWELL ▶ 4454 (1)	**491**
You Can Never Stop Me Loving You—Johnny Tillotson (63)	982
Paul SAMWELL-SMITH ▶ 3290 (2)	**909**
Shapes Of Things—Yardbirds (66)	1778
Over Under Sideways Down—Yardbirds (66)	1583
—Charles Sananes see: Charles DANVERS	
David SANBORN ▶ 8361 (1)	**53**
Sneakin' Up Behind You—Brecker Brothers (75)	265
David SANCHEZ ▶ 4748 (3)	**424**
Hooked On You—Sweet Sensation (89)	*673*
Hooked On You—Sweet Sensation (87)	*152*
She's Fly—Tony Terry (87)	49
Jose Padilla SANCHEZ ▶ 9414 (1)	**24**
The Door To Paradise—Bobby Rydell (61)	72
Ray SANCHEZ ▶ 3797 (1)	**696**
Rip Van Winkle—Devotions (64)	696
Bob SANDE ▶ 11722 (1)	**0.5**
Image - Part 1—Hank Levine And Orchestra (61)	1.4
James SANDEFUR ▶ 8950 (1)	**35**
I Can't Stop This Feelin'—Pure Prairie League (80)	71
Bobby SANDERS ▶ 9078 (1)	**32**
Baby, Is There Something On Your Mind—McKinley Travis (70)	32
David SANDERS ▶ 10898 (1)	**4.5**
(Call Me) The Traveling Man—Masqueraders (76)	23
Gerald SANDERS ▶ 10016 (1)	**14**
Bustin' Surfboards—Tornadoes (62)	56
Jesse SANDERS ▶ 10017 (1)	**14**
Bustin' Surfboards—Tornadoes (62)	56
Marty SANDERS [Marty Kupersmith] ▶ 5615 (6)	**264**
Capture The Moment—Jay And The Americans (70)	340
Words—F.R. David (83)	180
Livin' Above Your Head—Jay & The Americans (66)	115
Honey Do—Strangeloves (68)	51
Tricia Tell Your Daddy—Andy Kim (69)	44
Thank You And Goodnight—Angels (63)	21
Norman SANDERS ▶ 10018 (1)	**14**
Bustin' Surfboards—Tornadoes (62)	56
—Sonny Sanders see: William Nelson SANDERS	
William Nelson SANDERS [Sonny Sanders] ▶ 1166 (6)	**3813**
Soulful Strut—Young-Holt Unlimited (68)	*4727*
Love Makes A Woman—Barbara Acklin (68)	1694
Angel—Aretha Franklin (73)	1150
If You Need Me—Solomon Burke (63)	*786*
If You Need Me—Wilson Pickett (63)	*279*
Am I The Same Girl—Barbara Acklin (69)	*192*
Zell SANDERS [Zelma Sanders] ▶ 1894 (1)	**2143**
Sally, Go 'Round The Roses—Jaynetts (63)	4285
—Zelma Sanders see: Zell SANDERS	
David SANDERSON ▶ 2944 (2)	**1106**
Poor Boy—Royaltones (58)	*1106*
Poor Boy—Cardigans (58)	*0.0*
Chas SANDFORD [Charles Alan Sandford] ▶ 878 (4)	**5055**
Missing You—John Waite (84)	5545
Talk To Me—Stevie Nicks (85)	2585
What Kind Of Man Would I Be?—Chicago (89)	1631
Fire With Fire—Wild Blue (86)	78
—David Stuart Sandler see: Dave STUART	
Sy SANDLER ▶ 10013 (1)	**14**
Fourteen Karat Gold—Don Cherry (57)	28
Dan SANDS ▶ 8197 (1)	**59**
The Fanatic—Felony (83)	294
Evie SANDS ▶ 6144 (2)	**200**
I Love Makin' Love To You—Evie Sands (75)	367
You Can Do It—Dobie Gray (78)	234

Tommy SANDS ▶ 7203 (1)	**110**
Sing Boy Sing—Tommy Sands (58)	220
Bobby SANDSTROM ▶ 6032 (2)	**214**
Indestructible—Four Tops (88)	359
Save The Night For Me—Maureen Steele (85)	68
Vernon SANDUSKY ▶ 8413 (1)	**51**
Why (Doncha Be My Girl)—Chartbusters (64)	51
Dick SANFORD ▶ 7852 (2)	**72**
Singing Hills—Billy Vaughn and His Orchestra (58)	*216*
The Singing Hills—Don Cogan & LeRoy Holmes & His Orchestra (58)	*0.0*
Ed SANFORD ▶ 2434 (4)	**1490**
I Keep Forgettin'—Michael McDonald (82)	*3365*
Smoke From A Distant Fire—Sanford/Townsend Band (77)	1425
No Lookin' Back—Michael McDonald (85)	461
In For The Night—Dirt Band (78)	39
Gerald SANFORD ▶ 5691 (1)	**254**
If You Leave Me Tonight I'll Cry—Jerry Wallace (72)	508
William SANFORD ▶ 9725 (1)	**18**
My Anxious Heart—Four Coins (55)	36
Henry SANICOLA ▶ 5804 (3)	**240**
Mr Success—Frank Sinatra (58)	704
This Love Of Mine—5 DeMarco Sisters (55)	*14*
This Love Of Mine—Modernaires (57)	*1.9*
Anton SANKO ▶ 11533 (1)	**1.3**
Solitude Standing—Suzanne Vega (87)	6.4
Veronique SANSON ▶ 5437 (1)	**289**
Emotion—Helen Reddy (75)	579
Tony SANSONE ▶ 2291 (3)	**1645**
Walk Away Renee—Left Banke (66)	*3456*
Walk Away Renee—Four Tops (68)	*1445*
Walk Away Renee—Southside Johnny & The Jukes (86)	*32*
Nick SANTAMARIA ▶ 9001 (2)	**34**
Where I Fell In Love—Capris (61)	71
Baby Come Back To Me (The Morse Code Of Love)—Manhattan Transfer (85)	19
Carlos SANTANA ▶ 3638 (5)	**754**
Everybody's Everything—Santana (71)	1516
You Know That I Love You—Santana (79)	554
Pretty As You Feel—Jefferson Airplane (71)	512
Searchin'—Santana (81)	19
All I Ever Wanted—Santana (80)	10
Violet SANTANGELO ▶ 8191 (1)	**59**
Follow Me—Lyme & Cybelle (66)	118
Herman SANTIAGO ▶ 1868 (8)	**2184**
Why Do Fools Fall In Love—Teenagers Featuring Frankie Lymon (56)	*4057*
Why Do Fools Fall In Love—Diana Ross (81)	*2314*
Why Do Fools Fall In Love—Gale Storm (56)	*2295*
Why Do Fools Fall In Love—Diamonds (56)	*1782*
Why Do Fools Fall In Love—Happenings (67)	*389*
Why Do Fools Fall In Love—Gloria Mann (56)	*80*
Why Do Fools Fall In Love—Beach Boys (64)	*5.6*
Why Do Fools Fall In Love—Summer Wine (73)	*0.4*
—Peggy Santiglia see: Peggy FARINA	
Larry SANTOS ▶ 1205 (2)	**3691**
Candy Girl—4 Seasons (63)	3611
Knock! Knock! (Who's There?)—Orlons (64)	160
Curt SAPAUGH ▶ 4266 (1)	**540**
Try A Little Kindness—Glen Campbell (69)	1079
—Paul Sapherson see: Paul RYAN	
Joe SARACENO ▶ 4232 (3)	**553**
Surfer's Stomp—Mar-Kets (62)	524
Balboa Blue—Marketts (62)	404
The Freeze—Tony & Joe (58)	312
Tony SARAFINO ▶ 10608 (1)	**6.8**
Could Heaven Ever Be Like This (Part 1)—Idris Muhammad (77)	14
Sandi SARAYA ▶ 7578 (2)	**88**
Love Has Taken Its Toll—Saraya (89)	144
Back To The Bullet—Saraya (89)	119
Johnny SARDO ▶ 8194 (1)	**59**
Fake Out—Frankie Sardo (58)	59
—Father Guido Sarducci see: Don NOVELLO	
Christian SARREL [Christian Sainturat] ▶ 6847 (1)	**133**
There's Nothing I Can Say—Rick Nelson (64)	265

Peter SARSTEDT ▶ 5469 (2)	**282**
Where Do You Go To (My Lovely)—Peter Sarstedt (69)	258
You Are My Life—Herb Alpert & The Tijuana Brass (69)	25
—Clarence Satchell see: Andrew NOLAND	
Frank SAULINO ▶ 11236 (1)	**2.6**
Easy Way Out—Roy Orbison (79)	7.9
Joe SAULTER ▶ 9783 (1)	**17**
Electric Kingdom—Twilight 22 (83)	51
Herm SAUNDERS ▶ 11274 (1)	**2.5**
Angel Face—Percy Faith and his Orchestra (61)	2.5
Larry SAUNDERS ▶ 11751 (1)	**0.2**
We're Friends By Day (And Lovers By Night)—Whatnauts (71)	0.4
Orville SAUNDERS ▶ 11520 (1)	**1.4**
Rock Creek Park—Blackbyrds (76)	6.8
Penni SAUNDERS ▶ 9488 (1)	**23**
Rhyme Tyme People—Kool & The Gang (75)	182
Ronald SAUNDERS ▶ 8255 (1)	**57**
Sharing You—Mitty Collier (66)	57
Kevin SAUNDERSON ▶ 8688 (1)	**43**
Good Life—Inner City (89)	128
Tupper SAUSSY ▶ 2880 (2)	**1133**
Morning Girl—Neon Philharmonic (69)	1128
Heighdy-Ho Princess—Neon Philharmonic (70)	5.9
Joe SAUTER ▶ 5651 (1)	**260**
Ain't It True—Andy Williams (65)	519
Jan SAVAGE [Buck Reeder] ▶ 8662 (1)	**43**
A Thousand Shadows—Seeds (67)	130
Richard SAVAGE ▶ 7729 (1)	**77**
Moment I Saw You—Joni James (55)	154
Rick SAVAGE ▶ 1592 (12)	**2655**
Pour Some Sugar On Me—Def Leppard (88)	3871
Love Bites—Def Leppard (88)	3277
Armageddon It—Def Leppard (88)	2857
Photograph—Def Leppard (83)	1231
Hysteria—Def Leppard (88)	1083
Rocket—Def Leppard (89)	1017
Rock Of Ages—Def Leppard (83)	1009
Animal—Def Leppard (87)	796
Foolin'—Def Leppard (83)	557
Bringin' On The Heartbreak—Def Leppard (84)	157
Women—Def Leppard (87)	26
Rock Brigade—Def Leppard (80)	9.8
Paco SAVAL ▶ 10516 (2)	**7.7**
Love Songs Are Back Again—Band Of Gold (84)	*12*
Love Songs Are Back Again—Band Of Gold (84)	*12*
Joe SAVARINO ▶ 8383 (1)	**52**
Little Sandy Sleighfoot—Jimmy Dean with Ray Ellis and his Orchestra (57)	105
Phil SAVATH ▶ 11602 (1)	**1.0**
Santa Jaws (Part I)—Homemade Theatre (76)	3.1
Kevin SAVIGAR ▶ 2048 (6)	**1951**
Young Turks—Rod Stewart (81)	3203
Passion—Rod Stewart (80)	2748
Forever Young—Rod Stewart (88)	1122
Tonight I'm Yours (Don't Hurt Me)—Rod Stewart (82)	845
Every Beat Of My Heart—Rod Stewart (86)	63
Somebody Special—Rod Stewart (81)	44
Domenico SAVINO ▶ 6909 (2)	**129**
Moonlight Love—Perry Como (56)	337
Moonlight Love (Clair De Lune)—Roger Williams (57)	*34*
—Lucille Marie Raymonde Savoie see: Lucille STARR	
Tony SAVONNE ▶ 6567 (1)	**156**
The Freeze—Tony & Joe (58)	312
Nick SAVORESE ▶ 11767 (1)	**0.2**
The Puzzle—Gene McDaniels (63)	0.5
—Ronnie Savoy see: Eugene HAMILTON	
Paul SAWTELL ▶ 5507 (2)	**277**
What Have I Got Of My Own—Trini Lopez (64)	531
Texas Lady—Les Paul and Mary Ford (55)	22
Jean SAWYER [Gordon Galbraith] ▶ 2512 (5)	**1428**
Painted, Tainted Rose—Al Martino (63)	1454
Living A Lie—Al Martino (63)	963
Always Together—Al Martino (64)	533
You, No One But You—Frankie Laine (67)	151
My Cherie—Al Martino (65)	76

Mary Jane SAWYER ▶ 3868 (1)	**672**
I Feel A Song (In My Heart)—Gladys Knight & The Pips (75)	1343
Pam SAWYER ▶ 308 (30)	**11759**
Love Child—Diana Ross And The Supremes (68)	*9676*
Love Hangover—Diana Ross (76)	*5162*
If I Were Your Woman—Gladys Knight & The Pips (70)	2652
My Whole World Ended (The Moment You Left Me)—David Ruffin (69)	1875
I'm Livin' In Shame—Diana Ross And The Supremes (69)	1652
You Can't Turn Me Off (In The Middle Of Turning Me On)—High Inergy (77)	1358
Last Time I Saw Him—Diana Ross (73)	1347
Gotta Hold On To This Feeling—Jr. Walker & The All Stars (70)	1160
Love Child—Sweet Sensation (90)	*1079*
My Mistake (Was To Love You)—Diana Ross & Marvin Gaye (74)	961
Let Me Tickle Your Fancy—Jermaine Jackson (82)	820
Baby Let's Wait—Royal Guardsmen (68)	700
Just Seven Numbers (Can Straighten Out My Life)—Four Tops (71)	547
Yesterday's Dreams—Four Tops (68)	417
Take Me Girl, I'm Ready—Jr. Walker & The All Stars (71)	403
God Bless Whoever Sent You—Originals (70)	393
If I Didn't Love You—Chuck Jackson (65)	381
(It's The Way) Nature Planned It—Four Tops (72)	342
If I Ever Lose This Heaven—AWB (75)	335
I Ain't Gonna Eat Out My Heart Anymore—Young Rascals (65)	*306*
Ain't Gonna Eat Out My Heart Anymore—Angel (78)	*244*
You're My Baby (And Don't You Forget It)—Vacels (65)	232
Pops, We Love You (A Tribute To Father)—Diana Ross, Marvin Gaye, Smokey Robinson & Stevie Wonder (79)	165
Touch—Supremes (71)	156
All Or Nothing—Patti LaBelle And The Blue Belles (65)	133
I Thought It Took A Little Time (But Today I Fell In Love)—Diana Ross (76)	133
It's So Hard For Me To Say Good-Bye—Eddie Kendricks (71)	130
In These Changing Times—Four Tops (71)	105
Love Hangover—5th Dimension (76)	*40*
Sorry Doesn't Always Make It Right—Diana Ross (75)	20
Phil SAWYER ▶ 11058 (1)	**3.5**
Time Seller—Spencer Davis Group (67)	10
Ray SAWYER ▶ 8509 (1)	**48**
Life Ain't Easy—Dr. Hook And The Medicine Show (73)	95
David SAXON ▶ 4352 (4)	**514**
There Must Be A Way—Joni James (59)	*951*
There Must Be A Way—Jimmy Roselli (67)	*52*
Hocus Pocus—Patti Page (54)	23
Make A Circle—Kay Starr (63)	3.2
Grace SAXON ▶ 8623 (1)	**45**
You Were Made For Love—Dean Martin (59)	89
Sky SAXON [Richard Elvern Marsh] ▶ 2750 (4)	**1223**
Pushin' Too Hard—Seeds (66)	754
Can't Seem To Make You Mine—Seeds (67)	407
A Thousand Shadows—Seeds (67)	130
Mr. Farmer—Seeds (67)	18
Leo SAYER [Gerard Hugh Sayer] ▶ 551 (11)	**7802**
You Make Me Feel Like Dancing—Leo Sayer (76)	5541
The Show Must Go On—Three Dog Night (74)	3484
Long Tall Glasses (I Can Dance)—Leo Sayer (75)	2026
Dreaming—Cliff Richard (80)	1919
How Much Love—Leo Sayer (77)	1081
Living In A Fantasy—Leo Sayer (81)	573
Easy To Love—Leo Sayer (77)	427
Thunder In My Heart—Leo Sayer (77)	319
Giving It All Away—Roger Daltrey (73)	175
Fool For Your Love—Jimmy Hall (82)	56
One Man Band—Leo Sayer (75)	1.8
Joe SAYLES ▶ 6583 (1)	**154**
Keep It Comin'—Keith Sweat (91)	925
—Matilda Genevieve Scaduto see: Felice BRYANT	
—Giovanni Dominico Scafone Jr. see: Jack SCOTT	

Boz SCAGGS ▶ 494 (14)	**8489**
Lowdown—Boz Scaggs (76)	4316
We're All Alone—Rita Coolidge (77)	*2987*
Lido Shuffle—Boz Scaggs (77)	1677
Look What You've Done To Me—Boz Scaggs (80)	1316
Breakdown Dead Ahead—Boz Scaggs (80)	1220
Jojo—Boz Scaggs (80)	902
It's Over—Boz Scaggs (76)	402
What Can I Say—Boz Scaggs (76)	323
We Were Always Sweethearts—Boz Scaggs (71)	238
Hollywood—Boz Scaggs (78)	186
Hard Times—Boz Scaggs (77)	172
We're All Alone—Frankie Valli (76)	*37*
Dinah Flo—Boz Scaggs (72)	32
Near You—Boz Scaggs (71)	3.7
—Louis Scaglione see: Lou MONTE	
Ralph SCALA ▶ 3131 (3)	**994**
(We Ain't Got) Nothin' Yet—Blues Magoos (66)	3377
Pipe Dream—Blues Magoos (67)	242
There's A Chance We Can Make It—Blues Magoos (67)	57
Harvey SCALES ▶ 1985 (3)	**2032**
Disco Lady—Johnnie Taylor (76)	5946
Love Is Better In The A.M. (Part 1)—Johnnie Taylor (77)	96
Get Down—Harvey Scales & The 7 Sounds (67)	54
Skip SCARBOROUGH [Clarence Alexander Scarborough] ▶ 897 (8)	**4942**
Giving You The Best That I Got—Anita Baker (88)	3327
Love Or Let Me Be Lonely—Friends Of Distinction (70)	*2597*
Love Ballad—George Benson (79)	*984*
Love Ballad—L.T.D. (76)	*940*
Lovely Day—Bill Withers (77)	670
Love Or Let Me Be Lonely—Paul Davis (82)	*351*
Don't Ask My Neighbors—Emotions (77)	329
Can't Hide Love—Earth, Wind & Fire (76)	262
—Mario Scarpa see: Guy MARKS	
Greg SCELSA [Russell Caron] ▶ 5482 (1)	**280**
I'd Still Say Yes—Klymaxx (87)	841
Peter SCERRA ▶ 6822 (1)	**135**
What A Surprise—Johnny Maestro The Voice Of The Crests (61)	404
—Gene Allan Schachter see: Gene ALLAN	
Carsten SCHACK ▶ 11114 (1)	**3.2**
Wanna Dance—Yasmin (91)	16
Marilyn SCHACK [Danny Kessler] ▶ 1662 (3)	**2530**
Java—Al (He's The King) Hirt Trumpet With Chorus And Orchestra (64)	*4600*
Wear My Ring Around Your Neck—Elvis Presley (58)	3714
Java—Floyd Cramer (62)	*570*
Jack SCHAFER ▶ 6569 (1)	**155**
Wondering—Patti Page (57)	155
Milton SCHAFER ▶ 6223 (1)	**192**
He Touched Me—Barbra Streisand (65)	384
Katherine SCHAFFNER [Katherine Anderson] ▶ 5244 (1)	**319**
I Don't Want To Do Wrong—Gladys Knight & The Pips (71)	1596
—Sanford Phillip Schafler see: Ric MARLOW	
Herb SCHAPIRO ▶ 5673 (2)	**256**
This World—Staple Singers (72)	*509*
This World—Sweet Inspirations (70)	*3.4*
Stuart SCHARF ▶ 2057 (3)	**1941**
Like To Get To Know You—Spanky And Our Gang (68)	1416
Give A Damn—Spanky And Our Gang (68)	476
Anything You Choose—Spanky And Our Gang (69)	48
Walter SCHARF ▶ 1913 (1)	**2115**
Ben—Michael Jackson (72)	4231
Werner SCHARFENBERGER ▶ 3266 (2)	**920**
Sailor (Your Home Is The Sea)—Lolita (60)	2661
Cowboy Jimmy Joe (Die Sterne Der Prarie)—Lolita (61)	66
Warren SCHATZ [Ritchie Dean] ▶ 11469 (2)	**1.6**
Don't Fool With Fu Manchu—Rockin' Ramrods (65)	2.8
The Puzzle—Gene McDaniels (63)	0.5
George SCHECK ▶ 7635 (1)	**84**
Donde Esta Santa Claus? (Where Is Santa Claus?)—Augie Rios (58)	251

Jason SCHEFF ▶ 3475 (3)	**826**
What Kind Of Man Would I Be?—Chicago (89)	1631
Heart Of Mine—Boz Scaggs (88)	429
We Can Last Forever—Chicago (89)	279
Aram SCHEFRIN ▶ 6817 (2)	**135**
Morning Much Better—Ten Wheel Drive With Genya Ravan (70)	266
Cathedrals—D.C. LaRue (76)	4.0
—Gary Wayne Schelton see: Gary SHELTON	
Rudolf SCHENKER ▶ 3838 (5)	**684**
Rock You Like A Hurricane—Scorpions (84)	725
Send Me An Angel—Scorpions (91)	610
Still Loving You—Scorpions (84)	122
No One Like You—Scorpions (82)	103
Rhythm Of Love—Scorpions (88)	51
Roger SCHENZEL ▶ 9600 (1)	**21**
Sugar Plum—Ike Clanton (62)	21
Dick SCHER ▶ 10729 (1)	**5.7**
When School Starts Again—Tony Perkins (57)	11
Richard C. SCHER ▶ 8298 (2)	**55**
Hard Times For Lovers—Jennifer Holliday (85)	77
My Blue Angel—Michael Learns To Rock (91)	49
Ton SCHERPENZEEL ▶ 5877 (1)	**234**
I Want You To Be Mine—Kayak (78)	234
Victor SCHERTZINGER ▶ 2244 (3)	**1708**
I Remember You—Frank Ifield (62)	2162
Tangerine—Salsoul Orchestra (76)	*580*
Tangerine—Ahmad Jamal (59)	*47*
—Hartwig Schierbaum see: Marian GOLD	
Abe SCHIFF ▶ 10006 (2)	**14**
Time Out For Tears—Four Tunes (55)	*23*
Time Out For Tears—Chris Connor (57)	*4.7*
Steve SCHIFF ▶ 1870 (1)	**2175**
Don't You (Forget About Me)—Simple Minds (85)	4351
—Boris Claudio Schifrin see: Lalo SCHIFRIN	
Lalo SCHIFRIN [Boris Claudio Schifrin] ▶ 2693 (4)	**1269**
Mission: Impossible—Lalo Schifrin (68)	751
Burning Bridges—Mike Curb Congregation (70)	738
The Cat—Jimmy Smith (64)	106
Down Here On The Ground—Lou Rawls (68)	87
Peter SCHILLING ▶ 3549 (2)	**788**
Major Tom (Coming Home)—Peter Schilling (83)	1428
The Different Story (World Of Lust And Crime)—Peter Schilling (89)	222
Steve SCHLAKS ▶ 4191 (3)	**568**
Your Ma Said You Cried In Your Sleep Last Night—Kenny Dino (61)	795
He's Mine (I Love Him, I Love Him, I Love Him)—Alice Wonder Land (63)	290
Crazy Eyes For You—Bobby Hamilton (58)	50
—Philip Gary Schlein see: P.F. SLOAN	
Peter SCHLESS ▶ 4696 (1)	**437**
On The Wings Of Love—Jeffrey Osborne (82)	873
—Léon Schlienger see: Noel REGNEY	
Sol SCHLINGER ▶ 9282 (1)	**27**
Bikini—Bikinis (58)	54
Don SCHLITZ ▶ 2507 (1) HOF	**1431**
The Gambler—Kenny Rogers (78)	1431
Dan SCHMIDT ▶ 8345 (1)	**54**
I'm In Love Again—Pia Zadora (82)	161
Erwin R. SCHMIDT ▶ 10773 (1)	**5.4**
Drifting And Dreaming—Teddy Tyle, His Saxophone and His Orch. (58)	16
Harvey SCHMIDT ▶ 2210 (5) HOF	**1738**
My Cup Runneth Over—Ed Ames (67)	2403
Try To Remember—Gladys Knight & The Pips (75)	*957*
Try To Remember—Ed Ames (65)	*101*
Try To Remember—Brothers Four (65)	*8.3*
Try To Remember—Roger Williams (65)	*6.9*
John SCHMIDT ▶ 11828 (1)	**0.0**
Surfer's Stomp—Kay Bell and The Tuffs (62)	0.0
Timothy B. SCHMIT ▶ 2865 (3)	**1146**
I Can't Tell You Why—Eagles (80)	1924
Boys Night Out—Timothy B. Schmit (87)	539
Keep On Tryin'—Poco (75)	325
Fred SCHNEIDER ▶ 2509 (7)	**1430**
Love Shack—B-52's (89)	2771
Roam—B-52's (89)	2734
Deadbeat Club—B-52's (90)	458

Fred SCHNEIDER ► 2509 (7) *Continued*	**1430**
Rock Lobster—B-52's (80)	143
Private Idaho—B-52's (80)	70
Legal Tender—B-52's (83)	52
Monster—Fred Schneider (91)	43
Michael SCHNEIDER ► 5854 (1)	**237**
More Than Just The Two Of Us—Sneaker (81)	473
—Steven Bruce Schneider see: Steve STEVENS	
Florian SCHNEIDER-ESLEBEN ► 5067 (1)	**350**
Autobahn—Kraftwerk (75)	701
Ed SCHNUG ► 6920 (1)	**128**
A Question Of Temperature—Balloon Farm (68)	385
Harriet SCHOCK ► 1827 (1)	**2246**
Ain't No Way To Treat A Lady—Helen Reddy (75)	2246
Elmer SCHOEBEL ► 9492 (3)	**23**
Bugle Call Rag—Crazy Otto (55)	49
Nobody's Sweetheart—Johnnie Ray (55)	*13*
Nobody's Sweetheart—Jerry Cooper with The Johnny Guarnieri Swingtet (55)	*13*
Willie SCHOFIELD ► 3061 (5)	**1029**
You're So Fine—Falcons (59)	*1478*
I Found A Love - Part 1—Wilson Pickett (67)	*487*
I Found A Love— Falcons & Band (Ohio Untouchables) (62)	*276*
You're So Fine—Bunny Sigler (67)	*51*
Bring Back The Love Of Yesterday—Dells (74)	10
Tom SCHOLZ ► 276 (10)	**12593**
Amanda—Boston (86)	4040
More Than A Feeling—Boston (76)	3013
Don't Look Back—Boston (78)	2065
We're Ready—Boston (86)	1163
Long Time—Boston (77)	936
A Man I'll Never Be—Boston (78)	516
Peace Of Mind—Boston (77)	432
Still In Love—Boston (87)	270
Can'tcha Say (You Believe In Me)—Boston (87)	270
Feelin' Satisfied—Boston (79)	202
Neal SCHON ► 1431 (17)	**3067**
Don't Stop Believin'—Journey (81)	1658
I'll Be Alright Without You—Journey (86)	1156
Be Good To Yourself—Journey (86)	1150
Only The Young—Journey (85)	927
Girl Can't Help It—Journey (86)	779
Any Way You Want It—Journey (80)	771
Still They Ride—Journey (82)	754
Straight To Your Heart—Bad English (91)	390
Wheel In The Sky—Journey (78)	293
Just The Same Way—Journey (79)	197
Heaven Is A 4 Letter Word—Bad English (90)	169
Lights—Journey (78)	165
Too Late—Journey (79)	96
Stay Awhile—Journey (80)	95
Good Morning Girl—Journey (80)	95
Anytime—Journey (78)	54
Too Much Ain't Enough Love—Jimmy Barnes (88)	5.6
John SCHONBERGER ► 3815 (4)	**691**
Whispering—Nino Tempo & April Stevens (63)	*1526*
Whispering— Dr. Buzzard's Original "Savannah" Band (76)	*448*
Whispering—Paul Whiteman & The New Ambassador Hotel Orchestra (54)	*98*
Whispering—Bachelors (63)	*0.0*
Chuck SCHONING ► 11351 (2)	**2.1**
Straight Flush—Frantics (59)	9.1
Fog Cutter—Frantics (59)	3.1
Michel SCHOOTS ► 7524 (1)	**91**
Deeper Shade Of Soul—Urban Dance Squad (90)	545
—Janey Schramm see: Janey STREET	
—Solomon M. Schreiber see: Mickey Lee LANE	
—Bernard Schrieber see: Bernie LANE	
—Nook Schrier see: David CARROLL	
Artie SCHROECK ► 5706 (1)	**252**
Lovin' Things—Grassroots (69)	504
Aaron SCHROEDER [Bob Lee] ► 109 (42)	**22991**
It's Now Or Never— Elvis Presley With The Jordanaires (60)	*10781*
Stuck On You— Elvis Presley With The Jordanaires (60)	8364
Good Luck Charm— Elvis Presley With The Jordanaires (62)	6862
Big Hunk O' Love—Elvis Presley (59)	5285

I Got Stung—Elvis Presley (58)	2661
Rubber Ball—Bobby Vee (60)	2133
I'm Gonna Knock On Your Door—Eddie Hodges (61)	1994
Half Heaven - Half Heartache—Gene Pitney (62)	1463
First Name Initial— Annette With The Afterbeats (59)	1207
Twixt Twelve And Twenty—Pat Boone (59)	971
I Was The One—Elvis Presley (56)	930
Lucky Devil—Carl Dobkins, Jr. (59)	895
It's Now Or Never—John Schneider (81)	*781*
Utopia—Frank Gari (60)	774
First Anniversary—Cathy Carr (59)	736
Fools Hall Of Fame—Pat Boone (59)	646
Seein' The Right Love Go Wrong—Jack Jones (65)	553
Click Clack—Dicky Doo And The Don'ts (58)	*536*
Mandolins In The Moonlight—Perry Como (58)	464
Time And The River—Nat King Cole (60)	462
Hither And Thither And Yon—Brook Benton (60)	379
French Foreign Legion—Frank Sinatra (59)	374
It's Only The Beginning—Kalin Twins (59)	312
Anyway You Want Me (That's How I Will Be)— Elvis Presley (56)	275
Crazy With Love—Guy Mitchell (56)	*269*
Today's Teardrops—Rick Nelson (63)	261
Bandit Of My Dreams—Eddie Hodges (62)	185
Sweet Bird Of Youth—Nat "King" Cole (59)	135
Hey Little Lucy! (Don'tcha Put No Lipstick On)— Conway Twitty (59)	127
The Wang Dang Taffy-Apple Tango (Mambo Cha Cha Cha)—Pat Boone (59)	116
Sweet Stuff—Guy Mitchell (57)	105
Crazy With Love—Teresa Brewer (56)	*83*
Yesterday's Hero—Gene Pitney (64)	66
Young In Years—Diamonds (59)	33
Young Dreams—Elvis Presley with the Jordanaires (58)	24
Dixieland Rock— Elvis Presley with the Jordanaires (58)	24
You're Singing Our Love Song To Somebody Else— Jerry Wallace (60)	18
Tiger Lily—Rusty Draper (57)	7.6
Pink Sweater Angel— Johnnie Ray with Ray Conniff & His Orch. (57)	6.9
(I Have Lived, I Have Loved) I Have You— Sunny Gale (57)	4.7
Santa Bring My Baby Back To Me—Elvis Presley (57)	2.1
Click Clack—Boyd Bennett & His Rockets (58)	*0.0*
Don SCHROEDER ► 11468 (1)	**1.6**
The Searching Is Over—Joe Henderson (62)	3.1
John SCHROEDER ► 10411 (4)	**8.8**
You Don't Know—Helen Shapiro (61)	12
You Know How It Is With A Woman—Jefferson (70)	5.5
Walkin' Back To Happiness—Helen Shapiro (61)	0.5
Not As A Stranger—Tony Bennett with Percy Faith and His Orchestra (54)	0.0
Franz SCHUBERT ► 11174 (1)	**2.9**
Schubert's Serenade— Ray Conniff & His Orch. & Chorus (58)	2.9
Ralph SCHUCKETT ► 8347 (1)	**54**
Lay Down Your Arms—Graces (89)	161
—Hod David Schudson see: Hod DAVID	
Budd SCHULBERG ► 7051 (7)	**119**
Mama Guitar—Don Cornell (57)	*210*
A Face In The Crowd—Dick Lee (57)	*6.5*
A Face In The Crowd—Don Cornell (57)	*6.5*
A Face In The Crowd—Andy Griffith (57)	*6.5*
A Face In The Crowd—Art Mooney & His Orchestra (57)	*6.5*
Mama Guitar—Julius La Rosa (57)	*2.2*
Mama Guitar—Andy Griffith (57)	*0.0*
John SCHULLER ► 7363 (1)	**100**
Great Gosh A'mighty—Little Richard (86)	300
Steve SCHULMAN ► 9206 (1)	**29**
It's Unbelievable—Larks(1) (61)	58
Norbert SCHULTZE ► 8542 (1)	**47**
Lili Marlene—Al Martino (68)	140
Fritz SCHULZ-REICHEL ► 7609 (2)	**86**
It Worries Me—Frank Sinatra (54)	171
The Man With The Banjo—Ames Brothers (54)	0.0
Ira SCHUSTER [John Siras] ► 5510 (4)	**276**
In A Shanty In Old Shanty Town— Somethin' Smith & The Redheads (56)	*566*
Hold Me—Baskerville Hounds (69)	*154*
Hold Me—P.J. Proby (64)	*108*

In A Shanty In Old Shanty Town— Johnny Long & His Orchestra (56)	*0.0*
Thom SCHUYLER ► 4347 (2)	**515**
Love Will Turn You Around—Kenny Rogers (82)	1322
I Don't Know Where To Start—Eddie Rabbitt (82)	185
John SCHWAB ► 9267 (1)	**28**
Long Time Lovin' You—McGuffey Lane (81)	28
Kurt SCHWABACH ► 4487 (1)	**482**
Danke Schoen— Wayne Newton & The Newton Brothers (63)	1445
Wilbur SCHWANDT ► 3946 (1)	**645**
Dream A Little Dream Of Me— Mama Cass With The Mamas & The Papas (68)	1936
Bill SCHWARK ► 10701 (1)	**6.0**
Back To The River—Damnation Of Adam Blessing (70)	30
Arthur SCHWARTZ ► 10685 (1) HOF	**6.1**
Magic Moment—Nat King Cole (61)	12
Eddie SCHWARTZ ► 915 (6)	**4828**
Hit Me With Your Best Shot—Pat Benatar (80)	3184
Don't Shed A Tear—Paul Carrack (87)	1544
The Doctor—Doobie Brothers (89)	977
I Live By The Groove—Paul Carrack (89)	542
All Our Tomorrows—Eddie Schwartz (81)	538
Over The Line—Eddie Schwartz (82)	13
—Jacob Lewis Schwartz see: Jack LAWRENCE	
Jean SCHWARTZ ► 2327 (7) HOF	**1586**
Rock A Bye Your Baby With A Dixie Melody— Jerry Lewis (56)	*2560*
Trust In Me—Etta James (61)	*849*
Rock-A-Bye Your Baby With A Dixie Melody— Aretha Franklin (61)	*786*
Trust In Me—Patti Page (59)	*544*
Chinatown My Chinatown—Joe Pica (54)	5.4
Trust In Me—Chris Connor (57)	*1.8*
Rock A Bye Your Baby With A Dixie Melody— Judy Garland (61)	*0.0*
Melvin SCHWARTZ ► 2262 (1)	**1684**
Baby Talk—Jan & Dean (59)	1684
—Nat Schwartz see: Nat BURTON	
—Paul Schwartz see: Paul HAMPTON	
Robert SCHWARTZ ► 4440 (4)	**494**
Sweet Talkin' Guy—Chiffons (66)	1814
Out Of This World—Chiffons (66)	110
Moulty—Barbarians (66)	41
Stop, Look And Listen—Chiffons (66)	9.3
Stephen SCHWARTZ ► 2318 (5) HOF	**1603**
Day By Day—Godspell (72)	*1542*
Corner Of The Sky—Jackson 5 (72)	1050
I Guess I'll Miss The Man—Supremes (72)	37
Day By Day—Holly Sherwood (71)	*2.7*
Prepare Ye The Way Of The Lord—Holly Sherwood (71)	2.7
Andreas SCHWARZ-RUSZCZYNSKI [Andreas Schwarz] ► 6829 (2)	**134**
Holiday—Other Ones (87)	545
We Are What We Are—Other Ones (87)	261
Joe SCIACCA ► 10879 (1)	**4.7**
Last Train (Biddi-Biddi Bum-Bum)—Ray Lang (57)	9.4
Anthony SCIBETTA ► 9519 (1)	**22**
Spring In Manhattan—Tony Bennett (63)	44
Eros SCIORILLI ► 11368 (2)	**2.0**
Time Alone Will Tell—Connie Francis (67)	*3.3*
Time Alone Will Tell (Non Pensare A Me)— Jerry Vale (67)	*2.8*
Steve SCIPIO ► 6043 (2)	**213**
The Message—Cymande (73)	420
Bra—Cymande (73)	5.5
Ali SCORE ► 3704 (4)	**728**
I Ran (So Far Away)—A Flock Of Seagulls (82)	1474
Space Age Love Song—A Flock Of Seagulls (82)	637
Wishing (If I Had A Photograph Of You)— A Flock Of Seagulls (83)	612
The More You Live, The More You Love— A Flock Of Seagulls (84)	187
Mike SCORE ► 3705 (4)	**728**
I Ran (So Far Away)—A Flock Of Seagulls (82)	1474
Space Age Love Song—A Flock Of Seagulls (82)	637
Wishing (If I Had A Photograph Of You)— A Flock Of Seagulls (83)	612
The More You Live, The More You Love— A Flock Of Seagulls (84)	187

Jack SCORSONE ► 9668 (1)	**19**
Ballad Of A Girl And Boy—Graduates (59)	77
Alan Roy SCOTT ► 8318 (1)	**54**
Dancing Under A Latin Moon—Candi (88)	163
Andre SCOTT ► 8175 (1)	**60**
Miss Fine—New Yorkers (61)	60
Andrew SCOTT ► 1979 (5)	**2036**
Fox On The Run—Sweet (75)	2954
Love Is Like Oxygen—Sweet (78)	2006
Action—Sweet (76)	1094
California Nights—Sweet (78)	63
Funk It Up (David's Song)—Sweet (77)	20
Arnold SCOTT ► 10615 (1)	**6.7**
I Believe In All I Feel—G-Clefs (64)	6.7
Bertha SCOTT ► 4328 (3)	**519**
I Miss You So—Paul Anka (59)	*593*
I Miss You So—Chris Connor (56)	*513*
I Miss You So—Little Anthony & The Imperials With The 101 Strings (65)	*453*
Bobby SCOTT ► 552 (11)	**7789**
Taste Of Honey— Herb Alpert & The Tijuana Brass (65)	*5191*
He Ain't Heavy, He's My Brother—Hollies (69)	*2440*
He Ain't Heavy...He's My Brother—Neil Diamond (70)	*1112*
A Taste Of Honey— Martin Denny And His Orchestra (62)	*545*
Listen Lonely Girl—Johnny Mathis (64)	323
He Ain't Heavy...He's My Brother— Olivia Newton-John (75)	*141*
A Taste Of Honey—Tony Bennett (64)	*116*
Where Are You Going—Jerry Butler (70)	56
A Taste Of Honey—Victor Feldman Quartet (62)	*13*
A Taste Of Honey—Eddie Cano (62)	*0.0*
A Taste Of Honey—Quincy Jones (62)	*0.0*
Bon SCOTT ► 6251 (2)	**189**
Dirty Deeds—Joan Jett (90)	295
Highway To Hell—AC/DC (79)	272
Chester SCOTT ► 10434 (1)	**8.5**
I'm Sorry (I Did You Wrong)—Royal Holidays (58)	17
Clement SCOTT ► 9388 (1)	**25**
Now Is The Hour—Gale Storm (56)	74
Clifford SCOTT ► 2344 (6)	**1573**
Honky Tonk (Pts. 1 & 2)—Bill Doggett (56)	*5649*
Honky Tonk - Part 1—James Brown Soul Train (72)	*437*
Honky Tonk (Part 2)—Bill Doggett (61)	*113*
Honky Tonk '65—Lonnie Mack (65)	*77*
Hold It—Bill Doggett (58)	7.2
Honky Tonk (pt. 2)— Rusty Bryant & The Carolyn Club Band (56)	*0.0*
Clive SCOTT ► 1774 (3)	**2340**
Sky High—Jigsaw (75)	3070
Who Do You Think You Are— Bo Donaldson And The Heywoods (74)	1150
Love Fire—Jigsaw (76)	462
David SCOTT ► 3677 (1)	**740**
Whispers (Gettin' Louder)—Jackie Wilson (66)	1480
Edward SCOTT ► 10101 (2)	**13**
Funny—Jesse Belvin (58)	*15*
Funny—Gene McDaniels (62)	*10*
Frank SCOTT ► 7836 (1)	**73**
Apples And Bananas— Lawrence Welk And His Orchestra (65)	73
Freddie SCOTT ► 9136 (1)	**30**
The Door Is Open—Tommy Hunt (62)	61
—Garrett Scott see: Gary DeCARLO	
Howard SCOTT ► 1222 (22)	**3650**
Spill The Wine—Eric Burdon And War (70)	*5207*
The Cisco Kid—War (73)	4378
Why Can't We Be Friends?—War (75)	3006
Low Rider—War (75)	2369
Slippin' Into Darkness—War (71)	*2076*
The World Is A Ghetto—War (72)	1817
Gypsy Man—War (73)	1659
Summer—War (76)	1559
Me And Baby Brother—War (73)	1513
All Day Music—War (71)	704
Ballero—War (74)	472
They Can't Take Away Our Music— Eric Burdon And War Featuring Sharon Scott And The Beautiful New Born Children Of Southern California (70)	418
Spill The Wine—Isley Brothers (71)	*409*
Galaxy—War (77)	325
L.A. Sunshine—War (77)	291
Low Rider (On The Boulevard)—Latin Alliance (91)	121
Keep On Dancing—Alvin Cash (68)	114
Lonely Feelin'—War (71)	74
You Got The Power—War (82)	35
Slipping Into Darkness—Ramsey Lewis (72)	*35*
Good, Good Feelin'—War (79)	12
Outlaw—War (82)	10
Jack SCOTT [Giovanni Dominico Scafone Jr.] ► 259 (19)	**13101**
What In The World's Come Over You— Jack Scott (59)	4253
My True Love—Jack Scott (58)	3224
Goodbye Baby—Jack Scott (58)	2059
It Only Happened Yesterday—Jack Scott (60)	728
Way I Walk—Jack Scott (59)	648
Leroy—Jack Scott (58)	577
With Your Love—Jack Scott (58)	560
Oh Little One—Jack Scott (60)	294
A Little Feeling (Called Love)—Jack Scott (61)	268
There Comes A Time—Jack Scott (59)	118
Steps 1 And 2—Jack Scott (61)	105
I Never Felt Like This—Jack Scott (59)	88
Is There Something On Your Mind—Jack Scott (60)	82
Baby She's Gone—Jack Scott (57)	25
My Dream Come True—Jack Scott (61)	25
Save My Soul—Jack Scott (58)	23
Bella—Jack Scott with The Chantones (59)	20
Geraldine—Jack Scott (58)	1.9
Baby Baby—Jack Scott (59)	1.6
James SCOTT ► 2614 (2)	**1324**
You're Not Alone—Chicago (89)	1219
One Lover At A Time—Atlantic Starr (87)	210
Joe SCOTT ► 2402 (11)	**1521**
Ain't Nothing You Can Do—Bobby Bland (64)	914
Turn On Your Love Light—Bobby Bland (61)	*708*
Annie Get Your Yo-Yo—Little Junior Parker (62)	356
Blind Man—Bobby Bland (64)	*282*
Good Time Charlie—Bobby Bland (66)	227
Blind Man—Little Milton (64)	*226*
Turn On Your Love Light—Oscar Toney, Jr. (67)	*156*
Turn On Your Love Light—Human Beinz (68)	*141*
Turn On Your Love Light—Bill Black's Combo (68)	*103*
Turn On Your Love Light—Jerry Lee Lewis (72)	*4.6*
Dust Got In Daddy's Eyes—Bobby Bland (65)	0.9
Kevin SCOTT ► 6584 (1)	**154**
Keep It Comin'—Keith Sweat (91)	925
Leanne SCOTT ► 6491 (1)	**163**
L.A. International Airport—Susan Raye (71)	163
Linda SCOTT [Linda Joy Sampson] ► 1989 (2)	**2028**
Don't Bet Money Honey—Linda Scott (61)	1722
Yessiree—Linda Scott (62)	306
Marvin SCOTT ► 6815 (1)	**135**
I Kneel At Your Throne—Joe Medlin (59)	270
—Marvin Scott see: Sidney COLIN	
—Marvin Scott see: Talbot ROTHWELL	
Oliver SCOTT ► 8017 (1)	**65**
Yearning For Your Love—Gap Band (81)	130
Paul SCOTT ► 8364 (1)	**53**
Got A Love For You—Jomanda (91)	318
Paul J. SCOTT ► 11273 (1)	**2.5**
Gale Winds—Egyptian Combo (64)	5.0
—Randy L. Scott see: Shelley HAIMS	
Robin SCOTT ► 940 (1)	**4719**
Pop Muzik—M (79)	4719
Ronnie SCOTT [Jack Gellar] ► 1679 (5)	**2505**
It's A Heartache—Bonnie Tyler (78)	*3981*
Abergavenny—Shannon (69)	496
I Still Believe In Tomorrow—John & Anne Ryder (69)	300
Ice In The Sun—Status Quo (68)	217
It's A Heartache—Juice Newton (78)	*16*
Tim SCOTT [Timothy Scott McConnell] ► 7226 (1)	**109**
Swear—Sheena Easton (85)	109
Tom SCOTT ► 9597 (1)	**21**
Uptown & Country—Tom Scott (76)	21
Walter SCOTT ► 1057 (1)	**4173**
Burning Bridges—Jack Scott (60)	4173
Walter Lee SCOTT ► 9214 (1)	**28**
Keep On Dancing—Alvin Cash (68)	114
Warren SCOTT ► 9424 (1)	**24**
Stolen Angel—Scott Brothers (60)	24
Winfield SCOTT ► 195 (19)	**16134**
Return To Sender— Elvis Presley With The Jordanaires (62)	9296
Tweedle Dee—Georgia Gibbs (55)	*4176*
Many Tears Ago—Connie Francis (60)	2581
One Broken Heart For Sale— Elvis Presley With The Mello Men (63)	1777
(Such An) Easy Question— Elvis Presley With The Jordanaires (65)	1251
Burn That Candle—Bill Haley And His Comets (55)	*1091*
Yes Tonight Josephine—Johnnie Ray (57)	630
Gee Whittakers—Pat Boone (55)	*602*
Tweedlee Dee—LaVern Baker and The Gliders (55)	*597*
Long Legged Girl (With The Short Dress On)— Elvis Presley With The Jordanaires (67)	332
Candy Sweet—Pat Boone (60)	229
Tweedlee Dee—Little Jimmy Osmond (72)	*177*
Tweedlee Dee—Dave "Baby" Cortez (62)	*14*
Burn That Candle—Cues (55)	*9.4*
Sweetheart—Peggy Lee (58)	8.0
Cherry Lips—Billy Farrell (56)	6.0
Tweedlee Dee—Lancers (55)	*0.0*
Gee Whittakers—Five Keys (55)	*0.0*
Tweedlee Dee—Vicki Young (55)	*0.0*
Wini SCOTT ► 8400 (2)	**52**
My Special Prayer—Joe Simon (67)	*40*
My Special Prayer—Percy Sledge (69)	*12*
Gil SCOTT-HERON ► 6213 (3)	**193**
In The Bottle—Brother To Brother (74)	162
Home Is Where The Hatred Is—Esther Phillips (72)	28
Angel Dust—Gil Scott-Heron (78)	3.3
Vincent SCOTTO ► 6776 (3)	**138**
Vieni Vieni—Werner Müller And His Orchestra (55)	*132*
Under The Bridges Of Paris—Dean Martin (55)	18
Vieni Vieni—Terri Stevens (59)	*5.6*
Al SCRAMUZZA ► 7733 (1)	**77**
Hook And Sling-Part 1—Eddie Bo (69)	154
Charlie SCRUGGS ► 11426 (1)	**1.7**
It's A Funky Thing-Right On (Part 1)— Herbie Mann (69)	5.2
Earl SCRUGGS ► 6298 (1)	**184**
Theme from Bonnie And Clyde (Foggy Mountain Breakdown)—Flatt & Scruggs (68)	184
Joseph SCUSSA ► 10612 (1)	**6.8**
I'll Be Good—Joe Valino (57)	21
—Robin Scutt see: Mark PAUL	
Levi SEACER ► 6579 (1)	**154**
On The Way Up—Elisa Fiorillo (90)	617
Ed SEAGO ► 2258 (4)	**1694**
Early In The Morning—Vanity Fare (69)	2096
I Ain't Got Time Anymore— Glass Bottle Featuring Gary Criss (71)	697
Another Time, Another Place— Engelbert Humperdinck (71)	432
My Baby's Baby—Liquid Gold (79)	162
SEAL [Samuel Henry Olusegun Adeola] ► 3447 (1)	**845**
Crazy—Seal (91)	1689
Chuck SEALS ► 5344 (4)	**302**
Crazy Arms—Bob Beckham (60)	*584*
Crazy Arms—Ray Price (56)	*10*
Crazy Arms—Andrews Sisters (56)	*10*
Crazy Arms—Karen Chandler & Jimmy Wakely (56)	*0.0*
—Curtis Wayne Seals see: Curtis WAYNE	
Dan SEALS [Danny Wayland Seals, England Dan] ► 7144 (2)	**113**
What Can I Do With This Broken Heart— England Dan & John Ford Coley (79)	147
Late At Night—England Dan Seals (80)	129
Jim SEALS ► 822 (13)	**5346**
Get Closer— Seals & Crofts (Featuring Carolyn Willis) (76)	2732
Diamond Girl—Seals & Crofts (73)	2135
Summer Breeze—Seals & Crofts (72)	*2085*
Hummingbird—Seals & Crofts (73)	1121
We May Never Pass This Way (Again)— Seals & Crofts (73)	919

Jim SEALS ▶ 822 (13) *Continued*	**5346**
I'll Play For You—Seals & Crofts (75)	885
King Of Nothing—Seals & Crofts (74)	214
Summer Breeze (Part 1)—Isley Brothers (74)	*173*
Unborn Child—Seals & Crofts (74)	140
Baby, I'll Give It To You—Seals & Crofts (76)	65
If You See My Love—Lenny Welch (64)	6.1
Castles In The Sand—Seals & Crofts (75)	1.8
It's Never Too Late—Brenda Lee (61)	0.4
Troy SEALS ▶ 5011 (2)	**359**
I've Got A Rock N' Roll Heart—Eric Clapton (83)	988
When We Make Love—Alabama (84)	60
Steve SEAMANS ▶ 7617 (1)	**85**
Lovin' The Night Away—Dillman Band (81)	170
—Chilton Searcy see: Chilton PRICE	
Al SEARS ▶ 11294 (1)	**2.4**
Right Now, Right Now—Alan Freed (56)	4.8
Jeannette SEARS ▶ 3912 (3)	**660**
Be My Lady—Jefferson Starship (82)	704
Winds Of Change—Jefferson Starship (83)	396
Stranger—Jefferson Starship (81)	220
Pete SEARS ▶ 3630 (4)	**759**
Be My Lady—Jefferson Starship (82)	704
Winds Of Change—Jefferson Starship (83)	396
Stranger—Jefferson Starship (81)	220
Play On Love—Jefferson Starship (75)	197
Jerry SEAY ▶ 7864 (2)	**71**
Baby Love—Mother's Finest (77)	70
Fire—Mother's Finest (76)	5.1
John SEBASTIAN ▶ 71 (24) HOF	**30029**
Summer In The City—Lovin' Spoonful (66)	*7015*
Daydream—Lovin' Spoonful (66)	*5256*
Welcome Back—John Sebastian (76)	5196
Did You Ever Have To Make Up Your Mind?—Lovin' Spoonful (66)	4348
Do You Believe In Magic—Lovin' Spoonful (65)	*2340*
Rain On The Roof—Lovin' Spoonful (66)	1964
You Didn't Have To Be So Nice—Lovin' Spoonful (65)	1761
Nashville Cats—Lovin' Spoonful (66)	1684
Six O'Clock—Lovin' Spoonful (67)	1182
Darling Be Home Soon—Lovin' Spoonful (67)	*1163*
Younger Girl—Critters (66)	*855*
Younger Girl—Hondells (66)	*678*
She Is Still A Mystery—Lovin' Spoonful (67)	594
Lovin' You—Bobby Darin (67)	517
Money—Lovin' Spoonful (68)	392
Do You Believe In Magic—Shaun Cassidy (78)	*359*
She's A Lady—John Sebastian (68)	214
Good Time Music—Beau Brummels (65)	30
Full Measure—Lovin' Spoonful (67)	15
Darling Be Home Soon—Association (72)	*9.9*
Summer In The City—Quincy Jones (73)	*8.5*
Darling Be Home Soon—Bobby Darin (67)	*7.6*
Daydream—David Cassidy (73)	*6.4*
Hideaway—John Sebastian (76)	3.7
Lana SEBASTIAN [Evelyne Adrians, Lina Andrians] ▶ 7770 (2)	**76**
First...Be A Woman—Lenore O'Malley (80)	196
He—Today's People (73)	32
Mark SEBASTIAN ▶ 1772 (2)	**2341**
Summer In The City—Lovin' Spoonful (66)	*7015*
Summer In The City—Quincy Jones (73)	*8.5*
Paul SEBASTIAN [Andre Andrians] ▶ 7771 (2)	**76**
First...Be A Woman—Lenore O'Malley (80)	196
He—Today's People (73)	32
Jon SECADA [Juan Francisco Secada Ramirea] ▶ 2535 (2)	**1408**
Coming Out Of The Dark—Gloria Estefan (91)	3801
Can't Forget You—Gloria Estefan (91)	423
—Juan Francisco Secada Ramirea see: Jon SECADA	
Lucas SECON ▶ 11115 (1)	**3.2**
Wanna Dance—Yasmin (91)	16
Sholom SECUNDA ▶ 7513 (1)	**91**
Bei Mir Bist Du Schon—Louis Prima And Keely Smith (59)	365
Neil SEDAKA ▶ 50 (58) HOF	**41376**
Breaking Up Is Hard To Do—Neil Sedaka (62)	*7494*
Love Will Keep Us Together—Captain & Tennille (75)	*6699*
Lonely Night (Angel Face)—Captain & Tennille (76)	5389
Laughter In The Rain—Neil Sedaka (74)	5057
Where The Boys Are—Connie Francis (61)	4771
Bad Blood—Neil Sedaka (75)	4731
Oh Carol—Neil Sedaka (59)	2955
Happy Birthday, Sweet Sixteen—Neil Sedaka (61)	2559
Frankie—Connie Francis (59)	2530
Calendar Girl—Neil Sedaka (60)	2428
Next Door To An Angel—Neil Sedaka (62)	2255
Stairway To Heaven—Neil Sedaka (60)	2055
Breaking Up Is Hard To Do—Neil Sedaka (75)	*1889*
You Never Done It Like That—Captain & Tennille (78)	1801
Little Devil—Neil Sedaka (61)	1797
You Mean Everything To Me—Neil Sedaka (60)	1561
Diary—Neil Sedaka (58)	1436
Stupid Cupid—Connie Francis (58)	1181
Another Sleepless Night—Jimmy Clanton (60)	1057
Should've Never Let You Go—Neil Sedaka & Dara Sedaka (80)	1041
Puppet Man—Tom Jones (71)	*993*
Alice In Wonderland—Neil Sedaka (63)	979
Workin' On A Groovy Thing—5th Dimension (69)	*962*
Solitaire—Carpenters (75)	812
Love In The Shadows—Neil Sedaka (76)	796
Breaking Up Is Hard To Do—Partridge Family Starring Shirley Jones & Featuring David Cassidy (72)	*734*
Puppet Man—5th Dimension (70)	*721*
Breaking Up Is Hard To Do—Lenny Welch (70)	*683*
Run Samson Run—Neil Sedaka (60)	648
Let's Go Steady Again—Neil Sedaka (63)	640
That's When The Music Takes Me—Neil Sedaka (75)	590
Since You've Been Gone—Clyde McPhatter (59)	582
Bad Girl—Neil Sedaka (63)	575
Rainy Jane—Davy Jones (71)	562
The Immigrant—Neil Sedaka (75)	559
I Waited Too Long—LaVern Baker (59)	546
Fallin'—Connie Francis (58)	525
I Go Ape—Neil Sedaka (59)	439
King Of Clowns—Neil Sedaka (62)	422
Time Waits For No One—Friends Of Distinction (70)	407
Steppin' Out—Neil Sedaka (76)	384
Don't Hide Your Love—Cher (72)	370
Workin' On A Groovy Thing—Patti Drew (68)	*364*
Breaking Up Is Hard To Do—Happenings (68)	*309*
What Am I Gonna Do—Jimmy Clanton (61)	251
Amarillo—Neil Sedaka (77)	230
You Gotta Make Your Own Sunshine—Neil Sedaka (76)	220
Por Amor Viviremos—Captain & Tennille (75)	*204*
Time Marches On—Roy Hamilton (59)	164
We Had A Good Thing Goin'—Cyrkle (67)	162
Sunny—Neil Sedaka (64)	96
Breaking Up Is Hard On You (a/k/a Don't Take Ma Bell Away From Me)—American Comedy Network (84)	*82*
One Day Of Your Life—Andy Williams (70)	80
The Hungry Years—Wayne Newton (76)	35
Never Again—Dinah Washington (58)	9.4
Breaking Up Is Hard To Do—Heaven Bound with Tony Scotti (72)	*7.9*
Our Last Song Together—Bo Donaldson And The Heywoods (75)	6.4
Crying My Heart Out For You—Neil Sedaka (59)	5.2
Robert SEDITA ▶ 8788 (1)	**39**
Future Shock—Hello People (75)	156
Sil SEDORES [Sylvia Eisenberg, Sylvia White] ▶ 7107 (1)	**116**
China Nights (Shina No Yoru)—Kyu Sakamoto (63)	347
Pete SEEGER ▶ 262 (12) HOF	**12984**
Turn! Turn! Turn! (To Everything There Is A Season)—Byrds (65)	*6804*
If I Had A Hammer—Trini Lopez (63)	*4407*
Gotta Travel On—Billy Grammer (58)	*3674*
Kisses Sweeter Than Wine—Jimmie Rodgers (57)	2683
Guantanamera—Sandpipers (66)	2149
If I Had A Hammer (The Hammer Song)—Peter, Paul & Mary (62)	*1319*
Where Have All The Flowers Gone—Kingston Trio (62)	*1124*
Where Have All The Flowers Gone—Johnny Rivers (65)	*577*
Turn! Turn! Turn!/To Everything There Is A Season—Judy Collins (69)	*321*
Gotta Travel On—Timi Yuro (63)	*190*
We Shall Overcome—Joan Baez (63)	5.0
Gotta Travel On—Harry Belafonte (59)	*0.0*
Jerry SEELEN ▶ 4566 (1)	**465**
C'est Si Bon (It's So Good)—Conway Twitty (60)	929
Hammish SEELOCHAN ▶ 8433 (1)	**51**
Tribute (Right On)—Pasadenas (89)	304
Jeannie SEELY ▶ 8228 (1)	**58**
Anyone Who Knows What Love Is (Will Understand)—Irma Thomas (64)	231
Roxanne SEEMAN ▶ 6265 (2)	**188**
Walking On The Chinese Wall—Philip Bailey (85)	270
Night And Day—Bette Midler (91)	195
Charles SEGAL ▶ 8243 (2)	**57**
Tomboy—Ronnie Dove (68)	98
Kwela Kwela—Bill Hayes (55)	34
Jack SEGAL ▶ 844 (9)	**5227**
Hard To Get—Gisele MacKenzie (55)	3850
Scarlet Ribbons (For Her Hair)—Browns (59)	*1712*
Nothing Ever Changes My Love For You—Nat "King" Cole (56)	353
Bye Bye Barbara—Johnny Mathis (64)	302
I'm Gonna Change Him—Cathy Carr (59)	183
When Joanna Loved Me—Tony Bennett (64)	161
The Funky Gibbon—Goodies (75)	40
Keep Your Hands In Your Pockets—Playmates (62)	17
Scarlet Ribbons (For Her Hair)—Enoch Light & The Light Brigade (59)	*0.0*
Jonathan SEGAL ▶ 9164 (1)	**30**
I Feel The Magic—Belinda Carlisle (86)	60
Robert SEGARINI ▶ 8948 (1)	**36**
Day And Night—Wackers (72)	107
Bob SEGER ▶ 83 (30) HOF	**26786**
Shakedown—Bob Seger (87)	4602
Heartache Tonight—Eagles (79)	4547
Night Moves—Bob Seger (76)	2692
Still The Same—Bob Seger & The Silver Bullet Band (78)	2633
Fire Lake—Bob Seger (80)	2343
We've Got Tonight—Kenny Rogers And Sheena Easton (83)	*2255*
Against The Wind—Bob Seger (80)	2157
We've Got Tonite—Bob Seger & The Silver Bullet Band (78)	*1509*
Ramblin' Gamblin' Man—Bob Seger System (68)	1286
Even Now—Bob Seger And The Silver Bullet Band (83)	1164
You'll Accomp'ny Me—Bob Seger (80)	1094
Hollywood Nights—Bob Seger & The Silver Bullet Band (78)	1092
Like A Rock—Bob Seger & The Silver Bullet Band (86)	900
American Storm—Bob Seger & The Silver Bullet Band (86)	883
Understanding—Bob Seger & The Silver Bullet Band (84)	864
Mainstreet—Bob Seger (77)	576
Roll Me Away—Bob Seger and The Silver Bullet Band (83)	473
The Real Love—Bob Seger And The Silver Bullet Band (91)	443
Katmandu—Bob Seger (75)	384
Rock And Roll Never Forgets—Bob Seger (77)	275
The Horizontal Bop—Bob Seger (80)	274
Feel Like A Number—Bob Seger & The Silver Bullet Band (81)	224
It's You—Bob Seger & The Silver Bullet Band (86)	216
Miami—Bob Seger & The Silver Bullet Band (86)	156
Heavy Music (Part 1)—Bob Seger & The Last Heard (67)	83
Lucifer—Bob Seger System (70)	66
Get Out Of Denver—Bob Seger (74)	47
Lookin' Back—Bob Seger (71)	15
2 + 2 = ?—Bob Seger System (68)	7.3
Ivory—Bob Seger System (69)	3.2
—Frederick Segrest see: Freddie HART	
Marshall SEHORN ▶ 10724 (1)	**5.9**
One Way Out—Allman Brothers Band (72)	18
—Priscilla Seibert see: Priscilla COOLIDGE	
Rob SEIDENBERG ▶ 10555 (1)	**7.3**
Doin' The Do—Betty Boo (90)	29
Robbie SEIDMAN ▶ 5677 (2)	**256**
Summer Rain—Belinda Carlisle (90)	404
Dancing Under A Latin Moon—Candi (88)	163

Eddie SEILER ▶ 5115 (2)	**340**
Till Then—Classics (2) (63)	909
I Don't Want To Set The World On Fire—Somethin' Smith & The Redheads (58)	149
John SEITER ▶ 7421 (2)	**97**
You Don't Have To Walk In The Rain—Turtles (69)	301
Love In The City—Turtles (69)	183
Ernest SEITZ ▶ 7563 (1)	**88**
The World Is Waiting For The Sunrise—Don Gibson (61)	177
Winston SELA ▶ 2881 (1)	**1133**
Close To You—Maxi Priest (90)	3399
Ronnie SELF ▶ 335 (8)	**11035**
I'm Sorry—Brenda Lee (60)	*9449*
Sweet Nothin's—Brenda Lee (59)	4423
Everybody Loves Me But You—Brenda Lee (62)	2490
Anybody But Me—Brenda Lee (61)	806
Eventually—Brenda Lee (61)	281
Sweet Impossible You—Brenda Lee (63)	131
I'm Sorry—Joey Heatherton (72)	*61*
It Takes One To Know One—Brenda Lee (66)	4.7
Martin SELIGSON ▶ 6173 (2)	**197**
Blue Water Line—Brothers Four (62)	284
Deep Blue Sea—Jimmy Dean with Ray Ellis and his Orchestra (57)	111
Richard SELLERS ▶ 5777 (1)	**243**
A Piece Of Paper—Gladstone (72)	485
—Anthony John Selvidge see: Tony KAYE	
Danny SEMBELLO ▶ 2036 (10)	**1974**
Neutron Dance—Pointer Sisters (84)	1907
Love Me All Up—Stacy Earl (91)	658
Don't Stop—Jeffrey Osborne (84)	436
Stir It Up—Patti LaBelle (85)	378
Automatic Man—Michael Sembello (83)	371
Live My Life—Boy George (87)	323
Say You Really Want Me—Kim Wilde (87)	184
I Wanna Get Back With You—Louie Louie (90)	136
Live It Up—Gardner Cole (88)	25
When The Lights Go Out—Gerardo (91)	1.5
Michael SEMBELLO ▶ 1214 (6)	**3667**
Maniac—Michael Sembello (83)	5111
Mirror, Mirror—Diana Ross (82)	1481
Don't You Get So Mad—Jeffrey Osborne (83)	600
Automatic Man—Michael Sembello (83)	371
Eenie Meenie—Jeffrey Osborne (83)	94
When The Lights Go Out—Gerardo (91)	1.5
Murray SEMOS ▶ 9914 (1)	**15**
June July And August—Rusty Draper (58)	45
Valerio SEMPLICI ▶ 3067 (4)	**1027**
Everybody Everybody—Black Box (90)	1472
Strike It Up—Black Box (91)	1185
I Don't Know Anybody Else—Black Box (90)	395
Gonna Catch You—Lonnie Gordon (91)	30
Peggy SENDARS ▶ 6363 (3)	**179**
Over And Over—Pajama Party (89)	171
Hide And Seek—Pajama Party (90)	119
Yo No Se—Pajama Party (89)	68
Joe SENECA [Joe McGhee] ▶ 967 (5)	**4630**
Break It To Me Gently—Brenda Lee (62)	*3448*
Talk To Me—Sunny & The Sunglows (63)	*1775*
Break It To Me Gently—Juice Newton (82)	*1424*
Talk To Me, Talk To Me—Little Willie John (58)	*417*
Come A Little Closer—Romance Watson (59)	2.0
Pierre SENECAL ▶ 3166 (1)	**974**
As The Years Go By—Mashmakhan (70)	974
Jean SENN [Hubert Janssen] ▶ 9927 (1)	**15**
Watching The World Go By—Dean Martin (56)	30
Bryan SENNETT ▶ 11648 (1)	**0.9**
Down Where The Winds Blow (Chilly Winds)—Serendipity Singers (64)	2.6
Jeff SEOPARDIE ▶ 5695 (1)	**254**
I Wanna Be A Cowboy—Boys Don't Cry (86)	1016
Tony SEPE ▶ 2382 (2)	**1542**
You're The First, The Last, My Everything—Barry White (74)	4597
Good Goodby—Bob Knight Four (61)	19
—Anthony September see: Bernie LOWE	
—Anthony September see: Kal MANN	
Saverio SERACINI ▶ 6709 (6)	**142**
Chee Chee-oo Chee (Sang The Little Bird)—Perry Como & Jaye P. Morgan (55)	*570*

Chee Chee-Oo Chee—Dennis Hale (55)	*0.0*
Chee Chee-Oo Chee (Sang The Little Bird)—Gaylords (55)	*0.0*
Chee Chee-Oo Chee (Sang The Little Birds)—Mariners (55)	*0.0*
Chee Chee Oo Chee (Sang The Little Bird)—Dean Martin (55)	*0.0*
Chee Chee-Oo Chee (Sang The Little Bird)—Johnston Brothers (55)	*0.0*
Danny SERAPHINE ▶ 3402 (5)	**864**
No Tell Lover—Chicago (78)	1023
Lowdown—Chicago (71)	603
Little One—Chicago (78)	185
Take Me Back To Chicago—Chicago (78)	164
Thunder And Lightning—Chicago (80)	142
Del SERINO ▶ 4936 (1)	**378**
That's It-I Quit-I'm Movin' On—Sam Cooke (61)	756
Ronald SEROTA ▶ 4309 (1)	**527**
Three Times In Love—Tommy James (80)	1053
Eddie SERRATO ▶ 6311 (1)	**183**
I Need Somebody—? & The Mysterians (66)	913
Paul SERVICE ▶ 4907 (2)	**385**
Disco Nights (Rock-Freak)—G.Q. (79)	1528
Standing Ovation—GQ (80)	11
Glenna SESSION [Glynna Session] ▶ 6770 (1)	**138**
I'm So Glad I Fell For You—David Ruffin (69)	277
—Glynna Session see: Glenna SESSION	
Don SESSIONS ▶ 5844 (1)	**238**
Thanks A Lot—Brenda Lee (65)	475
Eddie SETSER ▶ 5179 (1)	**329**
I've Got A Rock N' Roll Heart—Eric Clapton (83)	988
Mike SETTLE ▶ 2398 (3)	**1525**
But You Know I Love You—First Edition (69)	*1122*
But You Know I Love You—Dolly Parton (81)	*248*
Settle Down (Goin' Down That Highway)—Peter, Paul & Mary (63)	156
Brian SETZER ▶ 495 (5)	**8480**
Stray Cat Strut—Stray Cats (82)	3543
(She's) Sexy + 17—Stray Cats (83)	2352
Rock This Town—Stray Cats (82)	2029
I Won't Stand In Your Way—Stray Cats (83)	492
Look At That Cadillac—Stray Cats (84)	65
Taja SEVELLE [Nancy Richardson, Taj A. Sevelle] ▶ 5973 (1)	**220**
Love Is Contagious—Taja Sevelle (87)	220
Steven SEVERIN [Steven John Bailey] ▶ 6008 (2)	**217**
Kiss Them For Me—Siouxsie And The Banshees (91)	481
Peek-A-Boo—Siouxsie & The Banshees (88)	289
Doc SEVERINSEN ▶ 3340 (1)	**892**
Stop And Smell The Roses—Mac Davis (74)	1785
David SEVILLE [Skipper Adams, Ross Bagdasarian] ▶ 154 (22)	**19074**
Witch Doctor—David Seville (58)	7033
The Chipmunk Song (Christmas Don't Be Late)—David Seville And The Chipmunks (58)	*6112*
Alvin's Harmonica—David Seville And The Chipmunks (59)	*3469*
Alvin's Orchestra—David Seville And The Chipmunks (60)	374
The Alvin Twist—Chipmunks (62)	342
Yesterday And You (Armen's Theme)—Bobby Vee (63)	*317*
Armen's Theme—David Seville (56)	*303*
The Chipmunk Song (Christmas Don't Be Late)—David Seville And The Chipmunks (59)	*254*
Armen's Theme—Joe Reisman and His Orchestra (56)	*193*
The Bird On My Head—David Seville (58)	172
The Chipmunk Song (Christmas Don't Be Late)—David Seville And The Chipmunks (62)	*148*
The Chipmunk Song (Christmas Don't Be Late)—David Seville And The Chipmunks (61)	*82*
Alvin For President—David Seville And The Chipmunks (60)	78
Judy—David Seville (59)	70
The Chipmunk Song (Christmas Don't Be Late)—David Seville And The Chipmunks (60)	*58*
Alvin's Harmonica—David Seville And The Chipmunks (61)	*20*
Gotta Get To Your House—David Seville (57)	20
Red Grapes—Sammy Davis Jr. (54)	15

Little Brass Band—David Seville (58)	13
Alvin's Harmonica—David Seville And The Chipmunks (62)	*11*
Armen's Theme—Lew Quadling & His Orchestra (56)	*0.0*
Armen's Theme—David Carroll & His Orchestra (56)	*0.0*
Ruth SEXTER ▶ 3956 (2)	**642**
Boy Without A Girl—Frankie Avalon (59)	1218
Going Nowhere—Los Bravos (66)	65
Charlie SEXTON ▶ 4724 (1)	**430**
Beat's So Lonely—Charlie Sexton (85)	860
Ken SEXTON ▶ 5956 (1)	**223**
Down The Aisle Of Love—Quin-Tones (58)	670
Kenny SEYMOUR ▶ 8057 (3)	**63**
Bring Back Your Heart—Del Vikings (61)	96
The Choice—O'Jays (68)	15
I'm Hypnotized—Anthony And The Imperials (68)	1.4
Phil SEYMOUR ▶ 4008 (1)	**624**
Precious To Me—Phil Seymour (81)	624
Rae SEYMOUR ▶ 7113 (1)	**115**
Summer Dreams—McGuire Sisters (59)	230
—Omari M. Shabazz see: Paul STEWART	
—Naomi Shackleford see: Lee HAZLEWOOD	
Terry SHADDICK ▶ 795 (1)	**5596**
Physical—Olivia Newton-John (81)	11192
Sanger SHAFER ▶ 9878 (1)	**16**
Yes Sir Ee—Dodie Stevens (59)	47
John B. SHAFFER III [Candyman] ▶ 8711 (2)	**42**
Melt In Your Mouth—Candyman (90)	115
Nightgown—Candyman (91)	10
Paul SHAFFER ▶ 5487 (2)	**279**
It's Raining Men—Weather Girls (83)	316
You Look Marvelous—Billy Crystal (85)	242
Arthur SHAFTEL ▶ 11165 (1)	**2.9**
I'm Gonna Love You—Ames Brothers (56)	5.9
—Selig Shaftel see: Sunny SKYLAR	
Fatimah SHAHEED ▶ 7232 (1)	**108**
Supersonic—J.J. Fad (88)	542
Gillian SHAKESPEARE ▶ 2861 (3)	**1148**
Beach Baby—First Class (74)	2201
Dreams Are Ten A Penny—First Class (74)	69
Funny How Love Can Be—First Class (75)	37
Joan SHAKESPEARE ▶ 10271 (1)	**11**
Your Heart Is Free Just Like The Wind—Vikki Carr (68)	21
—John Nicholas Shakespeare see: John CARTER	
Robbie SHAKESPEARE ▶ 9892 (1)	**15**
Pull Up To The Bumper—Grace Jones (81)	62
Amir SHAKIR [Spice] ▶ 2416 (2)	**1508**
Good Vibrations—Marky Mark & The Funky Bunch (91)	3166
Wildside—Marky Mark & The Funky Bunch (91)	*1432*
—Sam the Sham see: Domingo SAMUDIO	
Allen SHAMBLIN ▶ 4042 (1)	**614**
I Can't Make You Love Me—Bonnie Raitt (91)	1228
Joe SHAMWELL ▶ 11683 (1)	**0.7**
Don't Rock The Boat—Eddie Floyd (67)	1.5
Terry SHAND ▶ 2077 (4)	**1907**
You Don't Have To Be A Baby To Cry—Caravelles (63)	*3609*
Dance By The Light Of The Moon—Olympics (60)	*428*
Dance With A Dolly (With A Hole In Her Stocking)—Damita Jo (61)	*65*
You Don't Have To Be A Baby To Cry—"Tennessee" Ernie Ford (56)	*31*
Craig SHANE ▶ 7859 (2)	**72**
There's No Fool Like A Young Fool—Tab Hunter (59)	134
Things They Don't Teach You In School—Connie Freed (58)	20
Joe SHANK ▶ 6313 (3)	**182**
Unsuspecting Heart—Terri Stevens (54)	*610*
Unsuspecting Heart—Sunny Gale (54)	*120*
Unsuspecting Heart—Georgie Shaw (54)	*0.0*
Timothy Michael SHANKLIN ▶ 8920 (1)	**36**
Think His Name—Johnny Rivers (71)	181
Wayne SHANKLIN ▶ 336 (19)	**11017**
The Big Hurt—Miss Toni Fisher (59)	*4974*
Primrose Lane—Jerry Wallace with The Jewels (59)	*3631*
Chanson D'Amour (Song Of Love)—Art and Dotty Todd (58)	*2447*
West Of The Wall—Toni Fisher (62)	699
Little Coco Palm—Jerry Wallace (59)	552

Wayne SHANKLIN ► 336 (19) *Continued*	**11017**
Little Child—Eddie Albert and Sondra Lee (56)	*186*
Think His Name—Johnny Rivers (71)	181
Chanson D'Amour (Song Of Love)— Fontane Sisters (58)	*131*
Life's A Holiday—Jerry Wallace (61)	130
Primrose Lane—O.C. Smith (70)	*81*
Little Child—Lael & Cab Calloway (56)	*80*
The Big Hurt—Del Shannon (66)	*22*
Don't Tell Me Why (Pitie Senorita)—Tony Bennett with Percy Faith and His Orchestra (55)	7.1
Johnnie's Comin' Home—Johnnie Ray (55)	0.3
Little Child—Danny Kaye And Dena Kaye (56)	*0.0*
Little Child—Frankie Laine & Jimmy Boyd (56)	*0.0*
Chanson D'Amour (Song Of Love)—Ray Hartley (58)	*0.0*
L'Homme Et L'Enfant— Eddie Constantine & Tania (56)	*0.0*
Little Child—Gisele MacKenzie And Billy Quinn (56)	*0.0*
Richard SHANN ► 3220 (2)	**944**
Keep On Dancing—Gentrys (65)	3698
Don't Have To Shop Around—Mad Lads (65)	78
Del SHANNON [Charles Weeden Westover] ► 176 (19)	**17249**
Runaway—Del Shannon (61)	*10390*
Hats Off To Larry—Del Shannon (61)	4137
I Go To Pieces—Peter And Gordon (65)	*2350*
Keep Searchin' (We'll Follow The Sun)— Del Shannon (64)	2335
Little Town Flirt—Del Shannon (62)	1561
So Long Baby—Del Shannon (61)	629
Stranger In Town—Del Shannon (65)	457
Hey! Little Girl—Del Shannon (61)	416
Runaway—Charlie Kulis (75)	*327*
Two Kinds Of Teardrops—Del Shannon (63)	319
Runaway—Bonnie Raitt (77)	*294*
Sue's Gotta Be Mine—Del Shannon (63)	175
Runaway—Lawrence Welk And His Orchestra (62)	*146*
Runaway—Dawn Featuring Tony Orlando (72)	*124*
Runaway—Luis Cardenas (86)	*83*
Break Up—Del Shannon (65)	50
I Go To Pieces—Cotton, Lloyd and Christian (75)	*49*
I Won't Be There—Del Shannon (62)	28
Cry Myself To Sleep—Del Shannon (62)	0.9
Harry SHANNON ► 8672 (1)	**43**
The Other Woman—Vicki Lawrence (75)	86
Ronnie SHANNON ► 567 (4)	**7643**
Baby I Love You—Aretha Franklin (67)	4361
I Never Loved A Man (The Way I Love You)— Aretha Franklin (67)	2063
I Can't See Myself Leaving You— Aretha Franklin (69)	827
Ice Cream Song—Dynamics (69)	391
Tom SHANNON ► 2508 (4)	**1430**
Wild Weekend—Rebels (62)	2435
Rockin' Crickets— Hot-Toddys Featuring Bill Pennell (59)	*298*
Hot Shot—Buena Vistas (66)	80
Rockin' Crickets—Rockin' Rebels (63)	*75*
Hal SHAPER [John Harris] ► 5196 (3)	**328**
Softly, As I Leave You—Frank Sinatra (64)	*675*
Make Me Forget—Bobby Rydell (64)	285
Softly As I Leave You—Matt Monro (62)	*25*
Arnold SHAPIRO ► 10506 (1)	**7.8**
Snoopy For President—Royal Guardsmen (68)	23
Brad SHAPIRO ► 2417 (6)	**1505**
Don't Knock My Love - Pt. I—Wilson Pickett (71)	*2128*
Call My Name, I'll Be There—Wilson Pickett (71)	440
Don't Knock My Love— Diana Ross & Marvin Gaye (74)	*354*
Funk Factory—Wilson Pickett (72)	305
I Got To Try It One Time—Millie Jackson (74)	30
I'm Gonna Tear You A New Heart—Clarence Reid (69)	1.8
Dan SHAPIRO ► 8622 (2)	**45**
Kiss Me And Kill Me With Love—Mills Brothers (55)	*89*
Kiss Me And Kill Me With Love—McGuire Sisters (55)	*0.0*
David SHAPIRO ► 3406 (1)	**862**
Let's Live For Today—Grass Roots (67)	2587
Joe SHAPIRO ► 975 (8)	**4600**
Round And Round—Perry Como (57)	5931
Think Twice—Brook Benton (61)	2316
Treasure Of Love—Clyde McPhatter (56)	*1172*

My Little Baby—Perry Como (57)	328
Jamie Boy—Kay Starr (57)	181
Don't Destroy Me—Crash Craddock (59)	31
How Lonely Can One Be—Teresa Brewer (57)	12
Treasure Of Love—Dorothy Collins (56)	*0.0*
Joseph SHAPIRO [Mark Howard] ► 8412 (1)	**51**
Auctioneer (I'll Buy That Dream)— Les Paul & Mary Ford (54)	103
Mike SHAPIRO [Mike Sharpe] ► 2240 (3)	**1713**
Spooky—Classics IV (67)	*5516*
Spooky—Atlanta Rhythm Section (79)	*887*
Spooky—Mike Sharpe (67)	*224*
Tom SHAPIRO ► 7085 (1)	**117**
Never Give Up On A Good Thing—George Benson (82)	233
—Del Sharh see: Carl FISHER	
John SHARKEY ► 5983 (1)	**219**
Rumors—Syndicate Of Sound (66)	219
—Emanuel Sharoff see: Lanny SHORE	
Bobby SHARP [Agnes Jones] ► 2582 (4)	**1349**
Unchain My Heart— Ray Charles And His Orchestra (61)	*1906*
Don't Set Me Free—Ray Charles And His Orchestra With The Raelettes (63)	713
Unchain My Heart—Herbie Mann (68)	*73*
Hot And Cold Running Tears—Sarah Vaughan (56)	5.6
Dave SHARP ► 8385 (2)	**52**
Strength—Alarm (85)	120
Rain In The Summertime—Alarm (87)	89
—Jean Sharp see: Jean Sharp MURPHY	
Kim SHARP [Kim Anthony Guidry] ► 7697 (1)	**80**
I Love You—Vanilla Ice (91)	160
Martha SHARP ► 380 (4)	**10313**
Come Back When You Grow Up— Bobby Vee And The Strangers (67)	5983
Born A Woman—Sandy Posey (66)	2260
Single Girl—Sandy Posey (66)	1687
Maybe Just Today—Bobby Vee And The Strangers (68)	383
Martin SHARP ► 7939 (1)	**69**
Anyone For Tennis (The Savage Seven Theme)— Cream (68)	137
Randy SHARP ► 6031 (1)	**214**
Could It Be Love—Jennifer Warnes (81)	214
Todd SHARP ► 3182 (3)	**963**
Got A Hold On Me—Christine McVie (84)	1295
Love Will Show Us How—Christine McVie (84)	430
A Little Love—Juice Newton (84)	301
Jack SHARPE ► 1355 (3)	**3276**
So Rare—Jimmy Dorsey with Orchestra and Chorus (57)	*6543*
So Rare—Andy Williams (62)	*5.0*
So Rare—Mavis Rivers (60)	*3.7*
Louis SHARPE [Kayel] ► 9116 (1)	**31**
Louder Than Love—TKA (91)	92
—Mike Sharpe see: Mike SHAPIRO	
Ray SHARPE ► 4650 (1)	**445**
Linda Lu—Ray Sharpe (59)	445
Bill SHARPLEY ► 4462 (2)	**488**
Agent Double-O-Soul—Edwin Starr (65)	933
Back Street—Edwin Starr (65)	44
Marti SHARRON ► 2452 (6)	**1472**
Jump (For My Love)—Pointer Sisters (84)	3301
No One In The World—Anita Baker (87)	326
Dangerous—Natalie Cole (85)	253
Own The Night—Chaka Khan (85)	181
I Wanna Get Back With You—Louie Louie (90)	136
(Come On) Shout—Alex Brown (85)	59
Arnold SHAW ► 6256 (1)	**189**
Kiss Me Another—Georgia Gibbs (56)	566
James T. SHAW [James Timothy Shaw, Mighty Hannibal] ► 8311 (1)	**55**
Hymn No. 5—Mighty Hannibal (66)	55
Marlena SHAW ► 10355 (1)	**9.6**
Yu-Ma—Marlena Shaw (77)	9.6
Sidney SHAW ► 10251 (1)	**11**
Close—Keely Smith (60)	22
Todd SHAW [Too Short] ► 7625 (1)	**84**
The Ghetto—Too Short (90)	337
Tommy SHAW ► 621 (13)	**6960**
High Enough—Damn Yankees (90)	3426
Too Much Time On My Hands—Styx (81)	1761
Renegade—Styx (79)	994

Blue Collar Man (Long Nights)—Styx (78)	750
Fooling Yourself (The Angry Young Man)—Styx (78)	735
Sing For The Day—Styx (79)	509
Girls With Guns—Tommy Shaw (84)	431
Come Again—Damn Yankees (91)	327
Mademoiselle—Styx (76)	304
Coming Of Age—Damn Yankees (90)	237
Lonely School—Tommy Shaw (84)	213
Borrowed Time—Styx (80)	120
Remo's Theme (What If)—Tommy Shaw (85)	50
Larry SHAY ► 9383 (4)	**25**
It Takes So Long (To Say Goodbye)—Dean Martin (59)	23
When You're Smiling—Bobby Freeman (59)	*12*
When You're Smiling—Dick Hyman Trio (56)	*7.5*
Everywhere You Go—Quaker City Boys (59)	5.2
Gloria SHAYNE [Gloria Shayne Baker] ► 642 (11)	**6773**
Goodbye Cruel World—James Darren (61)	5198
The Men In My Little Girl's Life—Mike Douglas (65)	2269
Rain Rain Go Away—Bobby Vinton (62)	1134
What's The Use Of Cryin'—Eddie Fisher (58)	159
Almost There—Andy Williams (64)	131
Judy—Frankie Vaughan (58)	113
Do You Hear What I Hear— Harry Simeone Chorale (62)	*38*
Cuddly Baby—Deb-Tones (58)	27
Do You Hear What I Hear?—Bing Crosby (63)	*20*
Hail To The Conquering Hero—James Darren (62)	14
Marnie—Nat King Cole (64)	2.2
Larry SHAYNE [Ray Joseph] ► 6683 (2)	**144**
Kathy O—Diamonds (58)	*432*
Kathy O—Earl Grant (58)	*0.0*
Jules SHEAR ► 1595 (5)	**2650**
All Through The Night—Cyndi Lauper (84)	1796
If She Knew What She Wants—Bangles (86)	529
If We Never Meet Again— Tommy Conwell And The Young Rumblers (88)	251
Steady—Jules Shear (85)	142
(Believed You Were) Lucky—'Til Tuesday (89)	5.7
George SHEARING ► 4679 (6)	**439**
Lullaby Of Birdland—Blue Stars (55)	*804*
Lullaby of Birdland (54)—Ella Fitzgerald (54)	*74*
Lullaby Of Birdland—Ella Fitzgerald (56)	*0.0*
Lullaby Of Birdland—George Shearing Quintet (56)	*0.0*
Lullaby Of Birdland—Pee Wee Hunt & His Orchestra (56)	*0.0*
Lullaby Of Birdland— Ray Anthony & His Orchestra with Don Durant (56)	*0.0*
Eleanore SHEEHY ► 9202 (1)	**29**
Beat Me Daddy Eight To The Bar— Commander Cody And His Lost Planet Airmen (72)	116
Sharon SHEELEY ► 483 (9)	**8656**
Poor Little Fool—Ricky Nelson (58)	5441
Dum Dum—Brenda Lee (61)	4104
Heart In Hand—Brenda Lee (62)	1107
(He's) The Great Imposter—Fleetwoods (61)	555
So Deep—Brenda Lee (62)	233
Somethin' Else—Eddie Cochran (59)	188
Tears From An Angel—Troy Shondell (61)	128
He's So Heavenly—Brenda Lee (63)	60
Breakaway—Tracey Ullman (84)	56
Phil SHEER ► 5801 (1)	**240**
No Man Is An Island—Don Cornell (54)	480
Pat SHEERAN ► 8229 (1)	**58**
Anyone Who Knows What Love Is (Will Understand)— Irma Thomas (64)	231
Scott SHEETS ► 5108 (1)	**341**
Fire And Ice—Pat Benatar (81)	1023
SHEILA E. [Sheila Escovedo] ► 3924 (2)	**654**
A Love Bizarre—Sheila E. (85)	1233
Hold Me—Sheila E. (87)	113
Ernie SHELBY ► 7829 (2)	**73**
Nobody—Three Dog Night (68)	132
Carry Me—Joe Simon (74)	14
Thomas SHELBY ► 9019 (1)	**33**
Fantastic Voyage—Lakeside (80)	296
William SHELBY ► 2288 (5)	**1651**
The Second Time Around—Shalamar (79)	1893
And The Beat Goes On—Whispers (80)	884
It's A Love Thing—Whispers (81)	621
Make That Move—Shalamar (81)	198
I've Just Begun To Love You—Dynasty (80)	67

Ernie SHELDON ▶ 3053 (5)	**1033**
Baby The Rain Must Fall—Glenn Yarbrough (65)	1545
Seattle—Perry Como (69)	550
Baby What I Mean—Drifters (66)	*136*
Baby What I Mean—Spiral Starecase (68)	*12*
(One Of These Days) Sunday's Gonna' Come On Tuesday—New Establishment (69)	6.0
—Jon Sheldon see: Kal MANN	
Eutrice SHELL ▶ 10517 (1)	**7.7**
Walk Easy My Son—Jerry Butler (71)	15
Gladys SHELLEY ▶ 6560 (2)	**157**
Experience Unnecessary—Sarah Vaughan (55)	252
Oliver Twist—Rod McKuen (62)	188
Peter SHELLEY [Peter Alexander Southworth] ▶ 8273 (1)	**56**
Gee Baby—Peter Shelley (74)	56
Louis SHELLY ▶ 9394 (2)	**25**
Lonely Lips—Chordettes (55)	58
Frivolette—Hilltoppers (55)	16
Bob SHELTON [Bob Attlesey] ▶ 9435 (1)	**24**
Just Because—Elvis Presley (56)	71
Earl SHELTON ▶ 11754 (1)	**0.2**
One Wonderful Love—Ray Smith (60)	1.2
Gary SHELTON [Gary Wayne Schelton, Troy Shondell] ▶ 7199 (2)	**110**
Prayer And A Juke Box—Little Anthony And The Imperials (59)	104
Island In The Sky—Troy Shondell (62)	6.7
Joe SHELTON [Joe Attlesey] ▶ 9436 (1)	**24**
Just Because—Elvis Presley (56)	71
Louie SHELTON ▶ 4660 (1)	**444**
You're The Love—Seals & Crofts (78)	888
Rodney SHELTON ▶ 7201 (1)	**110**
Kissing You—Keith Washington (91)	331
Gerry SHEPHARD ▶ 10814 (1)	**5.2**
Makes You Blind—Glitter Band (76)	16
—Beresford Shepherd see: Shep SHEPHERD	
Shep SHEPHERD [Beresford Shepherd] ▶ 2349 (5)	**1569**
Honky Tonk (Pts. 1 & 2)—Bill Doggett (56)	*5649*
Honky Tonk - Part 1—James Brown Soul Train (72)	*437*
Honky Tonk (Part 2)—Bill Doggett (61)	*113*
Honky Tonk '65—Lonnie Mack (65)	*77*
Honky Tonk (pt. 2)—Rusty Bryant & The Carolyn Club Band (56)	*0.0*
Bill SHEPPARD ▶ 3376 (2)	**875**
Get On Up—Esquires (67)	1521
And Get Away—Esquires (67)	736
James SHEPPARD [James Shane Sheppard, Shane Sheppard] ▶ 1485 (14)	**2927**
Daddy's Home—Shep And The Limelites (61)	*4846*
Daddy's Home—Jermaine Jackson (72)	*2516*
Daddy's Home—Cliff Richard (82)	*659*
A Thousand Miles Away—Heartbeats (56)	*342*
Three Steps From The Altar—Shep And The Limelites (61)	307
Our Anniversary—Shep And The Limelites (62)	235
Ready For Your Love—Shep And The Limelites (61)	179
Daddy's Home—Chuck Jackson & Maxine Brown (67)	*29*
Down On My Knees—Heartbeats (58)	13
What Did Daddy Do—Shep And The Limelites (62)	5.4
A Thousand Miles Away—Fred Parris & The Five Satins (82)	*4.8*
Remember Baby—Shep And The Limelites (63)	4.5
A Thousand Miles Away—Heartbeats (60)	*2.1*
A Thousand Miles Away—Diamonds (56)	*0.0*
Neil SHEPPARD [Neil Ship] ▶ 6751 (2)	**140**
Let's Call It A Day Girl—Razor's Edge (66)	*270*
Let's Call It A Day Girl—Bobby Vee (69)	*11*
—Shane Sheppard see: James SHEPPARD	
T.G. SHEPPARD [William Neal Browder] ▶ 11169 (1)	**2.9**
Tryin' To Beat The Morning Home—T.G. Sheppard (75)	8.7
Drey SHEPPERD ▶ 5608 (1)	**265**
I Made It Through The Rain—Barry Manilow (80)	1325
Michael SHEPSTONE ▶ 8938 (2)	**36**
Shady Lady—Shepstone & Dibbens (73)	53
Please Tell Him That I Said Hello—Debbie Campbell (75)	19

—Bonnie Sheridan see: Bonnie BRAMLETT	
Sue SHERIDAN ▶ 6340 (1)	**181**
Can't Wait Another Minute—Five Star (86)	362
Tony SHERIDAN [Andrew Esmond Sheridan McGinnity] ▶ 11143 (1)	**3.0**
Why—Beatles With Tony Sheridan (64)	6.1
Lee SHERIDEN [Roger Pritchard] ▶ 6782 (2)	**138**
Save Your Kisses For Me—Brotherhood Of Man (76)	*391*
Save Your Kisses For Me—Bobby Vinton (76)	*22*
Al SHERMAN ▶ 11275 (2)	**2.5**
Don't Tell Me Why (Pitie Senorita)—Tony Bennett with Percy Faith and His Orchestra (55)	7.1
Johnnie's Comin' Home—Johnnie Ray (55)	0.3
Allan SHERMAN [Allan Copelon] ▶ 1490 (5)	**2920**
Hello Mudduh, Hello Fadduh! (A Letter From Camp)—Allan Sherman (63)	*5106*
Crazy Downtown—Allan Sherman (65)	*524*
Hello Mudduh, Hello Fadduh! (A Letter From Camp) (New 1964 Version)—Allan Sherman (64)	*202*
The Twelve Gifts Of Christmas—Allan Sherman (63)	3.4
The Drinking Man's Diet—Allan Sherman (65)	1.4
Bobby SHERMAN ▶ 6589 (1)	**154**
Waiting At The Bus Stop—Bobby Sherman (71)	308
Dwight SHERMAN ▶ 10222 (2)	**11**
So Young—Clyde Stacy (57)	*9.9*
So Young—Clyde Stacy (59)	*1.1*
Joe SHERMAN ▶ 568 (22)	**7635**
Ramblin' Rose—Nat King Cole (62)	8021
Juke Box Baby—Perry Como (56)	1713
That Sunday, That Summer—Nat King Cole (63)	1528
Graduation Day—Rover Boys (56)	*1085*
Graduation Day—Four Freshmen (56)	*995*
Eso Beso (That Kiss!)—Paul Anka (62)	769
To The Ends Of The Earth—Nat "King" Cole (56)	461
Everlovin'—Patti Page (55)	308
Graduation Day—Arbors (67)	*172*
Por Favor—Vic Damone (55)	64
Toys In The Attic—Joe Sherman, His Orchestra And Chorus (63)	*50*
Let Me Cry On Your Shoulder—Georgia Gibbs (65)	46
Let Me Tell You, Babe—Nat King Cole (66)	23
Toys In The Attic—Jack Jones (63)	*20*
As Sure As Night Must Fall—Jerry Vale (64)	14
Graduation Day—Bobby Pickett (63)	*10*
Kitty Who—Kitty Kallen (55)	5.3
Forbidden Fruit—Anita Ellis (57)	4.4
Make Like A Bunny, Honey—Jill Corey (57)	1.9
More And More Of Your Amor—Nat King Cole (64)	1.7
Toys In The Attic—Dennis Regor (63)	*0.0*
Graduation Day—Lennon Sisters & The Sparklers (56)	*0.0*
Noel SHERMAN ▶ 602 (25)	**7233**
Ramblin' Rose—Nat King Cole (62)	8021
Juke Box Baby—Perry Como (56)	1713
Graduation Day—Rover Boys (56)	*1085*
Graduation Day—Four Freshmen (56)	*995*
Eso Beso (That Kiss!)—Paul Anka (62)	769
To The Ends Of The Earth—Nat "King" Cole (56)	461
Everlovin'—Patti Page (55)	308
Beats There A Heart So True—Perry Como (58)	268
Happy Muleteer—Ivo Robic (60)	228
Graduation Day—Arbors (67)	*172*
I Must Be Dreaming—Nat "King" Cole (59)	122
It's So Easy To Say—Johnny Nash (58)	88
Por Favor—Vic Damone (55)	64
Young As We Are—Sal Mineo (59)	58
Seven Minutes In Heaven—Poni-Tails (58)	35
I Can't Sit Down—Marie & Rex (59)	34
I'll Think Of You—McGuire Sisters (58)	19
Cappuccina—Nat King Cole (61)	11
Graduation Day—Bobby Pickett (63)	*10*
Forbidden Fruit—Anita Ellis (57)	4.4
Blue Jay—LuAnn Simms (59)	2.5
Make Like A Bunny, Honey—Jill Corey (57)	1.9
Morgen (One More Sunrise)—Leslie Uggams (59)	*1.1*
Morgen (One More Sunrise)—Rex Allen (59)	*0.0*
Graduation Day—Lennon Sisters & The Sparklers (56)	*0.0*
Richard SHERMAN ▶ 650 (16) HOF	**6723**
You're Sixteen—Ringo Starr (73)	*4779*
Let's Get Together—Hayley Mills And Hayley Mills (61)	2578
You're Sixteen—Johnny Burnette (60)	*2286*
Tall Paul—Annette With The Afterbeats (58)	1651

Pineapple Princess—Annette With The Afterbeats (60)	1471
Midnight Oil—Charlie Blackwell (59)	292
Got The Feeling—Fabian (59)	230
Jo Jo The Dog Faced Boy—Annette (59)	218
Beach Time—Roger Smith (59)	126
Super-cali-fragil-istic-expi-ali-docious—Julie Andrews - Dick Van Dyke And The Pearlies (65)	114
Chitty Chitty Bang Bang—Paul Mauriat (68)	114
Chim, Chim, Cheree—New Christy Minstrels (65)	73
Dream Boy—Annette With The Afterbeats (61)	67
It's A Small Small World—Mike Curb Congregation (73)	43
My Heart Became Of Age—Annette With The Afterbeats (59)	22
Jimmy Kiss And Run—Diane Maxwell (59)	2.3
Robert SHERMAN ▶ 648 (18) HOF	**6732**
You're Sixteen—Ringo Starr (73)	*4779*
Let's Get Together—Hayley Mills And Hayley Mills (61)	2578
You're Sixteen—Johnny Burnette (60)	*2286*
Tall Paul—Annette With The Afterbeats (58)	1651
Pineapple Princess—Annette With The Afterbeats (60)	1471
Midnight Oil—Charlie Blackwell (59)	292
Got The Feeling—Fabian (59)	230
Jo Jo The Dog Faced Boy—Annette (59)	218
Beach Time—Roger Smith (59)	126
Super-cali-fragil-istic-expi-ali-docious—Julie Andrews - Dick Van Dyke And The Pearlies (65)	114
Chitty Chitty Bang Bang—Paul Mauriat (68)	114
Chim, Chim, Cheree—New Christy Minstrels (65)	73
Dream Boy—Annette With The Afterbeats (61)	67
It's A Small Small World—Mike Curb Congregation (73)	43
My Heart Became Of Age—Annette With The Afterbeats (59)	22
Don't Call Me Sweetie (Cause I'm Bitter)—Eileen Rodgers (57)	9.7
Stolen Love—Dinah Shore (56)	8.5
The Brightest Smile In Town—Ray Charles And His Orchestra (63)	6.8
Jack SHERR ▶ 6684 (2)	**144**
Kathy O—Diamonds (58)	*432*
Kathy O—Earl Grant (58)	*0.0*
Charles E. SHERRELL ▶ 7914 (1)	**70**
You Can't Play With My Yo-Yo—Yo-Yo (91)	209
Brian SHERRER ▶ 9326 (1)	**26**
I Don't Know What It Is, But It Sure Is Funky—Ripple (73)	184
Billy SHERRILL ▶ 446 (35)	**9269**
The Most Beautiful Girl—Charlie Rich (73)	5675
Sweet And Innocent—Donny Osmond (71)	2840
A Very Special Love Song—Charlie Rich (74)	1386
Almost Persuaded—David Houston (66)	*1274*
Stand By Your Man—Tammy Wynette (68)	*1181*
Stand By Your Man—Candi Staton (70)	*1135*
Southtown, U.S.A.—Dixiebelles (64)	899
Kiss Away—Ronnie Dove (65)	745
Every Time You Touch Me (I Get High)—Charlie Rich (75)	743
I Love My Friend—Charlie Rich (74)	656
Sugar Lips—Al (He's The King) Hirt Trumpet with Chorus and Orchestra (64)	642
Soul Song—Joe Stampley (73)	580
My Elusive Dreams—Bobby Vinton (70)	*548*
Almost Persuaded No. 2—Ben Colder (66)	*289*
Lullaby Of Love—Poppies (66)	241
My Elusive Dreams—Charlie Rich (75)	*205*
You Mean The World To Me—David Houston (67)	172
She's Ready—Spiral Starecase (69)	*165*
Singing My Song—Tammy Wynette (69)	92
Almost Persuaded—Etta James (69)	*77*
'Til I Can Make It On My Own—Tammy Wynette (76)	66
The Ways To Love A Man—Tammy Wynette (69)	36
My Elusive Dreams—David Houston And Tammy Wynette (67)	*33*
Kids Say The Darndest Things—Tammy Wynette (73)	24
America, The Beautiful—Charlie Rich (76)	18
Bedtime Story—Tammy Wynette (72)	17
Cry Softly—Nancy Ames (66)	16
He's Ready—Poppies (66)	*12*

Billy SHERRILL ▶ 446 (35) *Continued*	**9269**
If The World Don't End Tomorrow (I'm Comin' After You)—Carl Smith (60)	*9.8*
Have A Little Faith—David Houston (68)	8.9
Let Me Love You Goodbye—Bobby Vinton (81)	5.0
He Loves Me All The Way—Tammy Wynette (70)	2.1
I'll See Him Through—Tammy Wynette (70)	0.9
If The World Don't End Tomorrow (I'm Comin' After You)—Fairlanes (60)	*0.0*
If The World Don't End Tomorrow (I'm Comin' After You)—Doug Warren (60)	*0.0*
Mark SHERRILL ▶ 7779 (1)	**75**
I've Been Waiting For You All Of My Life—Paul Anka (81)	151
Matt SHERROD ▶ 3361 (3)	**881**
This House—Tracie Spencer (90)	2330
Tender Kisses—Tracie Spencer (91)	318
This Time Make It Funky—Tracie Spencer (91)	123
Paul SHERROD ▶ 3362 (3)	**881**
This House—Tracie Spencer (90)	2330
Tender Kisses—Tracie Spencer (91)	318
This Time Make It Funky—Tracie Spencer (91)	123
Rod SHERWOOD ▶ 7860 (2)	**72**
There's No Fool Like A Young Fool—Tab Hunter (59)	134
Things They Don't Teach You In School—Connie Freed (58)	20
Garrett Clinton SHIDER ▶ 9373 (1)	**25**
Hey Ladies—Beastie Boys (89)	302
Garry Marshall SHIDER ▶ 4749 (3)	**424**
One Nation Under A Groove - Part I—Funkadelic (78)	1189
Hey Ladies—Beastie Boys (89)	302
Do That Stuff—Parliament (76)	7.1
Harvey SHIELD ▶ 3421 (1)	**855**
The Way I Feel Tonight—Bay City Rollers (77)	855
Sue SHIFRIN [Sue Linda Shifrin-Cassidy] ▶ 4003 (9)	**625**
Lyin' To Myself—David Cassidy (90)	467
Show Some Respect—Tina Turner (85)	346
She's Trouble—Musical Youth (83)	177
How Can I Live Without Her—Christopher Atkins (82)	93
Never Say Die (Give A Little Bit More)—Cliff Richard (83)	83
Over My Head—Toni Basil (84)	61
Take No Prisoners (In The Game Of Love)—Peabo Bryson (85)	58
Don't Talk—Larry Lee (82)	16
Shy Boys—Ana (87)	6.2
—Sue Linda Shifrin-Cassidy see: Sue SHIFRIN	
Nat SHILKRET ▶ 8472 (1)	**49**
Lonesome Road—Wonder Who ? (67)	98
Carl SHILLO ▶ 11155 (1)	**3.0**
Ready For Love—Silverado (81)	6.0
Brent SHINDELL ▶ 11660 (1)	**0.8**
All I Wanna Do—Doucette (78)	2.3
Gary SHIP ▶ 9836 (1)	**16**
For Yasgur's Farm—Mountain (70)	97
—Neil Ship see: Neil SHEPPARD	
—Dannie Shipley see: Royal C. BANNON	
Ellen SHIPLEY ▶ 1298 (5)	**3412**
Heaven Is A Place On Earth—Belinda Carlisle (87)	4006
Circle In The Sand—Belinda Carlisle (88)	1402
Leave A Light On—Belinda Carlisle (89)	1186
Lay Down Your Arms—Graces (89)	161
Do You Feel Like I Feel—Belinda Carlisle (91)	124
Tom SHIPLEY ▶ 2957 (3)	**1098**
One Toke Over The Line—Brewer & Shipley (71)	1791
Tarkio Road—Brewer And Shipley (71)	404
Shake Off The Demon—Brewer And Shipley (72)	1.9
David SHIRE ▶ 988 (2)	**4537**
Washington Square—Village Stompers (63)	5892
With You I'm Born Again—Billy Preston & Syreeta (79)	3182
Jimmy SHIRL [Jack Mendelsohn] ▶ 6020 (5)	**215**
I Believe—Bachelors (64)	*702*
Sympathetic Eyes—Ames Brothers (55)	76
I Believe—Roy Hamilton (55)	*5.6*
I Believe—Elvis Presley (57)	*2.1*
My Friend—Eddie Fisher (54)	0.0
Jerry SHIRLEY ▶ 6449 (2)	**168**
Hot 'N' Nasty—Humble Pie (72)	389

Fool For A Pretty Face (Hurt By Love)—Humble Pie (80)	141
Michelle SHOCKED [Karen Michelle Johnston] ▶ 6875 (1)	**131**
Anchorage—Michelle Shocked (88)	131
—Shock G see: Gregory JACOBS	
Hank SHOCKLEE [James H. Boxley] ▶ 7710 (1)	**79**
Can't Truss It—Public Enemy (91)	238
Keith SHOCKLEE [Keith Boxley, The JBL] ▶ 7342 (1)	**101**
B.B.D. (I Thought It Was Me)?—Bell Biv DeVoe (90)	504
Stephen SHOCKLEY ▶ 5180 (3)	**329**
And The Beat Goes On—Whispers (80)	884
Fantastic Voyage—Lakeside (80)	296
Your Love Is On The One—Lakeside (81)	2.8
Don SHOEMATE ▶ 8838 (2)	**38**
Your Graduation Means Goodbye—Cardigans (58)	64
Halo Of Love—Nick Noble (57)	5.9
—Troy Shondell see: Gary SHELTON	
Lesley SHONE ▶ 10583 (1)	**7.1**
Sign Of The Times—Belle Stars (83)	49
Lanny SHORE [Emanuel Sharoff] ▶ 10669 (1)	**6.2**
To Say You're Mine—DeCastro Sisters (55)	19
Mickey SHORR [Mickey Moses] ▶ 7920 (1)	**70**
Dr. Ben Basey—Mickey Shorr And The Cutups (62)	139
Glenn SHORROCK ▶ 1285 (3)	**3455**
Cool Change—Little River Band (79)	1645
Help Is On Its Way—Little River Band (77)	1246
Man On Your Mind—Little River Band (82)	1130
Arthur SHORTER ▶ 11395 (1)	**1.9**
Peep Peep Pop Pop—Dearly Beloveds (66)	5.7
Hal SHRAGER ▶ 7505 (3)	**91**
Rebel—Carol Jarvis (57)	*269*
Snowbound For Christmas—DeCastro Sisters (55)	4.8
Rebel—Jill Whitney (57)	*0.0*
Sid SHRAGER ▶ 7506 (3)	**91**
Rebel—Carol Jarvis (57)	*269*
Snowbound For Christmas—DeCastro Sisters (55)	4.8
Rebel—Jill Whitney (57)	*0.0*
Mark SHREEVE ▶ 3764 (1)	**706**
Touch Me (I Want Your Body)—Samantha Fox (86)	2117
Michael SHRIEVE ▶ 7266 (2)	**107**
Pretty As You Feel—Jefferson Airplane (71)	512
My Pearl—Automatic Man (76)	17
—Albert Shubert see: Andy GIBSON	
Leo SHUKEN ▶ 8553 (1)	**46**
Mink Schmink—Eartha Kitt (54)	93
Eddie SHULER ▶ 8761 (2)	**40**
Sugar Bee—Cleveland Crochet And Band (60)	34
Secret Of Love—Elton Anderson With Sid Lawrence Combo (60)	13
Chester SHULL ▶ 7337 (1)	**101**
(It's No) Sin—Duprees Featuring Joey Vann (64)	*202*
Marc SHULMAN ▶ 11534 (1)	**1.3**
Solitude Standing—Suzanne Vega (87)	6.4
Alden SHUMAN ▶ 7046 (2)	**120**
Banjo's Back In Town—Teresa Brewer (55)	*359*
Banjo's Back In Town—Swing & Sway With Sammy Kaye (55)	*0.0*
Earl SHUMAN ▶ 497 (29)	**8470**
Hey There Lonely Girl—Eddie Holman (69)	*5248*
Hotel Happiness—Brook Benton (62)	2976
Left Right Out Of Your Heart (Hi-Lee Hi-Lo Hi-Lup-Up-Up)—Patti Page (58)	*1703*
Close To Cathy—Mike Clifford (62)	1504
Clinging Vine—Bobby Vinton (64)	1138
Caterina—Perry Como (62)	1019
Most People Get Married—Patti Page (62)	683
Hey There Lonely Boy—Ruby And The Romantics (63)	*635*
Hey There Lonely Girl—Robert John (80)	*523*
Banjo's Back In Town—Teresa Brewer (55)	*359*
Another Cup Of Coffee—Brook Benton (64)	317
Our Everlasting Love—Ruby And The Romantics (64)	270
Time, Time—Ed Ames (67)	216
My Shy Violet—Mills Brothers (68)	207
I Am—Tony Bennett with Ray Ellis and His Orchestra (57)	190
The Young New Mexican Puppeteer—Tom Jones (72)	177

Starry Eyed—Gary Stites (59)	94
Shoot It Again—Teresa Brewer (55)	66
I'll Be There—Eddie Holman (70)	58
Tamiami—Bill Haley And His Comets (60)	52
Things I Didn't Say—Jordan Brothers (60)	21
Buttermilk—Fontane Sisters (58)	*17*
Buttermilk—Joe Sherman, his Orchestra and Chorus (58)	*17*
High On The Hill Of Hope—Patti Page (63)	9.9
Dream Talk—Herb & Betty Warner (60)	5.2
All In Good Time—Nelson Trio (60)	4.1
One Little Kiss—Playmates (61)	1.4
Banjo's Back In Town—Swing & Sway With Sammy Kaye (55)	*0.0*
Left Right Out Of Your Heart (Hi-Lee Hi-Lo Hi-Lup-Up-Up)—Vaughn Monroe (58)	*0.0*
Frank SHUMAN ▶ 8482 (4)	**49**
Flamenco Love—Don Costa His Orchestra And Chorus (56)	*146*
Flamenco Love—Tony Martin (56)	*0.0*
Flamenco Love—Richard Hayman (56)	*0.0*
Flamenco Love—Al Caiola and his Magic Guitar (56)	*0.0*
Mort SHUMAN ▶ 65 (68) HOF	**33405**
Save The Last Dance For Me—Drifters (60)	*8918*
Surrender—Elvis Presley With The Jordanaires (61)	8380
Can't Get Used To Losing You—Andy Williams (63)	6431
Suspicion—Terry Stafford (64)	4565
This Magic Moment—Jay & The Americans (68)	*3753*
A Teenager In Love—Dion and The Belmonts (59)	*3450*
Little Sister—Elvis Presley (61)	3379
Little Children—Billy J. Kramer With The Dakotas (64)	2943
Go Jimmy Go—Jimmy Clanton (59)	2546
Turn Me Loose—Fabian (59)	2176
Hound Dog Man—Fabian (59)	1730
Marie's The Name His Latest Flame—Elvis Presley (61)	1319
I'll Save The Last Dance For You—Damita Jo (60)	1268
Sweets For My Sweet—Drifters (61)	*1182*
Hushabye—Mystics (59)	*1163*
This Magic Moment—Drifters (60)	*1087*
I Count The Tears—Drifters (60)	913
Save The Last Dance For Me—Defranco Family Featuring Tony Defranco (74)	*886*
Viva Las Vegas—Elvis Presley With The Jordanaires (64)	799
Wrong For Each Other—Andy Williams (64)	698
No One—Ray Charles With The Raeletts (63)	*684*
(If You Cry) True Love, True Love—Drifters (59)	652
I'm A Man—Fabian (58)	597
Spanish Lace—Gene McDaniels (62)	495
Plain Jane—Bobby Darin (59)	492
Kiss Me Quick—Elvis Presley With The Jordanaires (64)	450
Angel Face—James Darren (59)	443
Seven Day Weekend—Gary (U.S.) Bonds (62)	409
No One—Connie Francis (61)	*403*
Save The Last Dance For Me—Dolly Parton (83)	*379*
Hushabye—Jay & The Americans (69)	*368*
What's It Gonna Be—Dusty Springfield (67)	345
Havin' Fun—Dion (61)	329
Mess Of Blues—Elvis Presley With The Jordanaires (60)	287
Look At Granny Run, Run—Howard Tate (66)	271
(You Make Me Feel) So Good—McCoys (66)	259
Lonely Winds—Drifters (60)	241
Your Other Love—Flamingos (60)	230
I Dig Girls—Bobby Rydell (59)	218
Sweets For My Sweet—Tony Orlando (79)	*198*
A Texan And A Girl From Mexico—Anita Bryant (61)	195
Get It While You Can—Janis Joplin (71)	159
Stop—Howard Tate (68)	155
Room Full Of Tears—Drifters (61)	152
It's A Lonely Town (Lonely Without You)—Gene McDaniels (63)	136
A Teenager In Love—Four Preps (61)	*130*
Daylight Savin' Time—Keith (67)	122
Petticoat White (Summer Sky Blue)—Bobby Vinton (66)	114
Two Fools—Frankie Avalon (59)	99
If We Only Have Love—Dionne Warwicke (72)	88
Hushabye—Robert John (72)	*79*
Teenage Heartache—Ray Peterson (60)	46

Mort SHUMAN ► 65 (68) *Continued*	**33405**
White Bucks And Saddle Shoes—Bobby Pedrick, Jr. (58)	40
Strollin' In The Springtime—Fabian (60)	26
Hushabye—Beach Boys (64)	*25*
Night Rider—Elvis Presley With The Jordanaires (65)	23
Here Comes The Night—Ben E. King (61)	17
Carrying That Load—Ray Charles (63)	10
Follow Me—Drifters (65)	8.3
This Magic Moment—Richie Furay (78)	*8.2*
Wait—Jimmy Clanton (60)	7.3
Heart Of Gold—Twins (60)	6.8
No One—Brenda Lee (65)	*4.2*
Sweets For My Sweet—Central Park West (69)	*3.9*
(It's A) Long Lonely Highway—Elvis Presley (65)	2.4
Bimini Bimbo (Doin' The Limbo)—Teddy And The Twilights (62)	1.4
I Need Somebody To Lean On—Elvis Presley (64)	1.1
I Ain't Sharin' Sharon—Buddy Knox (59)	0.4
Gerry SHURY ► 4508 (3)	**474**
Up In A Puff Of Smoke—Polly Brown (74)	883
Devil's Gun—C.J. & Co. (77)	540
Dance Little Lady Dance—Danny White (77)	0.6
Leroy SIBBLIS ► 6321 (1)	**182**
Pass The Dutchie—Musical Youth (82)	1276
Jean SIBELIUS ► 6874 (1)	**131**
Karelia Suite—Royal Philharmonic Orchestra (81)	131
Karl SIBERSDORF ► 7381 (1)	**99**
Class Cutter (Yeah Yeah)—Dale Hawkins (59)	297
John SIBLEY ► 10988 (1)	**3.9**
What Goes Up (Must Come Down)—Tyrone Davis (74)	7.9
—Corby Michael John Siddons see: Mike CORBY	
—Robin Sidebotham see: Robin GEORGE	
Irving SIDERS ► 3327 (3)	**898**
Slow Walk—Sil Austin (56)	*1070*
Slow Walk—Bill Doggett (56)	*727*
Slow Walk—Ocie Smith (57)	*0.0*
Mark SIDGWICK ► 6290 (1)	**185**
Every Step Of The Way—John Waite (85)	556
George SIDNEY ► 7323 (5)	**102**
To Love Again—Four Aces (56)	*408*
To Love Again—Vic Damone (56)	*0.0*
To Love Again—Bob Manning (56)	*0.0*
To Love Again—Marc Fredericks (56)	*0.0*
To Love Again—Carmen Cavallaro (56)	*0.0*
Ben SIDRAN ► 8301 (1)	**55**
Going To The Country—Steve Miller Band (70)	110
Barry SIEGAL ► 3827 (1)	**688**
Moonflight—Vik Venus Alias: Your Main Moon Man (69)	688
Janis SIEGEL ► 11613 (1)	**1.0**
Clap Your Hands—Manhattan Transfer (75)	4.0
Jay SIEGEL ► 5732 (3)	**249**
I Hear Trumpets Blow—Tokens (66)	601
A Love So Fine—Chiffons (63)	466
Hear The Bells—Tokens (63)	148
Ralph SIEGEL ► 4387 (2)	**507**
In Heaven There Is No Beer—Clean Living (72)	580
Malaguena—Caterina Valente (55)	*434*
Florenz SIEGESMUND ► 11783 (2)	**0.0**
The Happy Wanderer—Henri René's Musette (54)	*0.0*
The Happy Wanderer—Frank Weir & His Orchestra (54)	*0.0*
William SIEVERS ► 11109 (1)	**3.2**
Walk In The Park—Claudine Longet (68)	3.2
Labi SIFFRE ► 4604 (1)	**452**
It Must Be Love—Madness (83)	452
—Georges Sigara see: Jack FISHMAN	
Davitt SIGERSON ► 9685 (1)	**19**
Lead A Double Life—Loverboy (86)	114
—Sigidi see: Sigidi ABDULLAH	
—Susanne Sigl see: Susanne MÜLLER-PI	
Bunny SIGLER ► 3147 (14)	**984**
Sweet Charlie Babe—Jackie Moore (73)	625
Don't Take Your Love—Manhattans (74)	457
Say It Again—Jermaine Stewart (88)	397
Let Me Party With You (Part 1) (Party, Party, Party)—Bunny Sigler (78)	204
Good Things Don't Last Forever—Ecstasy, Passion & Pain (74)	130
Free Man—South Shore Commission (75)	112
Let Me Make Love To You—O'Jays (75)	101
I Found My Dad—Joe Simon (72)	95
Sunshine (Part 2)—O'Jays (74)	81
Train Called Freedom—South Shore Commission (76)	17
Only You—Loleatta Holloway and Bunny Sigler (78)	16
A Mother For My Children—Whispers (74)	16
International Playboy—Wilson Pickett (73)	10
Touch And Go—Ecstasy, Passion & Pain Featuring Barbara Roy (76)	1.4
Jack SIGLER ► 759 (1)	**5778**
Love (Can Make You Happy)—Mercy (69)	5778
Carl SIGMAN ► 155 (71) HOF	**19055**
It's All In The Game—Tommy Edwards (58)	*10634*
Ebb Tide—Righteous Brothers (65)	*2977*
Losing You—Brenda Lee (63)	2471
(Where Do I Begin) Love Story—Andy Williams (71)	*2200*
The Day The Rains Came—Jane Morgan (58)	*1490*
Til—Angels (61)	*1330*
It's All In The Game—Four Tops (70)	*1294*
You're My World—Helen Reddy (77)	*1277*
Shangri La—Four Coins (57)	*1206*
What Now My Love—Sonny & Cher (66)	*986*
It's All In The Game—Cliff Richard (63)	*964*
Eleventh Hour Melody—Al Hibbler (56)	*952*
Till—Vogues (68)	*931*
World Outside—Four Coins (58)	*883*
Shangri-La—Vic Dana (64)	*878*
Ebb Tide—Lenny Welch (64)	*842*
What Now My Love—Herb Alpert & The Tijuana Brass (66)	*706*
The World We Knew (Over And Over)—Frank Sinatra (67)	690
Till—Roger Williams (57)	*656*
The Day The Rains Came—Raymond Lefevre and His Orchestra (58)	*623*
What Now My Love—Mitch Ryder (67)	*593*
You're My World—Cilla Black (64)	*591*
Eleventh Hour Melody—Lou Busch and His Orchestra (56)	*548*
Till—Tom Jones (71)	*445*
Goodbye To Rome (Arrivederci Roma)—Georgia Gibbs (55)	*439*
Just Come Home—Hugo & Luigi (59)	435
Ballerina—Nat "King" Cole (57)	*423*
Arrivederci Roma—Roger Williams (58)	*379*
My Heart Cries For You—Ray Charles (64)	*368*
Ebb Tide—Platters Featuring Tony Williams (60)	*357*
World Outside—Four Aces (58)	*327*
A Day In The Life Of A Fool—Jack Jones (66)	312
Ebb Tide—Bobby Freeman (59)	*283*
Shangri-La—Lettermen (69)	*254*
My Way Of Life—Frank Sinatra (68)	214
World Outside—Roger Williams (58)	*187*
It Worries Me—Frank Sinatra (54)	171
Till—Percy Faith And His Orchestra and Chorus (57)	*151*
Dream Along With Me (I'm On My Way To a Star)—Perry Como (56)	146
That's The Way With Love—Piero Soffici (61)	*135*
Funny Thing—Tony Bennett with Percy Faith and His Orchestra (54)	131
Six Boys And Seven Girls—Anita Bryant (59)	129
Just Yesterday—Jack Jones (65)	126
Willingly (Melodie Perdue)—Monty Kelly And His Orchestra (58)	*88*
My Heart Cries For You—Ray Stevens (59)	*40*
Music From Across The Way—James Last (72)	40
Please Don't Go So Soon (Wenn Die Liebe Will)—Jo Stafford (55)	34
That's The Way With Love—Don Costa And His Orchestra And Chorus (61)	*27*
Fool—Elvis Presley (73)	25
We All Need Love—Percy Faith And His Orchestra and Chorus (56)	18
Answer Me, My Love—Happenings (70)	*15*
Pennsylvania 6-5000—Frank Barber Orchestra (82)	14
Ballerina—Vaughn Monroe and his Orchestra (60)	*14*
Lonely Is The Name—Sammy Davis Jr. (68)	7.6
Roses Of Rio—Four Aces (58)	6.6
What Now My Love—"Groove" Holmes (66)	*5.1*
My Heart Cries For You—Connie Francis (67)	*3.3*
Arrivederci, Roma—Eddie Fisher (62)	*2.7*
Till—Tokens (68)	*1.8*
Till—Kay Armen (57)	*0.0*
Till—Dinah Shore (57)	*0.0*
Ebb Tide—Roy Hamilton (54)	*0.0*
Ebb Tide—Roy Hamilton (59)	*0.0*
11th Hour Melody—Bill Snyder (56)	*0.0*
Answer Me, My Love—Nat "King" Cole (54)	*0.0*
Arrivederci, Roma—Norman Luboff Choir (55)	*0.0*
Till—Leo Diamond His Harmonica & Orch (57)	*0.0*
Ballerina—Vaughn Monroe & His Orchestra (57)	*0.0*
Willingly (Melodie Per Due)—Johnny Desmond (58)	*0.0*
Arrivederci Roma (Goodbye To Rome)—Ralph Young (55)	*0.0*
Your Heart - My Heart (Sehnsucht)—Frankie Laine (54)	0.0
Guy SIGSWORTH ► 3448 (1)	**845**
Crazy—Seal (91)	1689
Jeff SILBAR ► 1778 (8)	**2338**
Wind Beneath My Wings—Bette Midler (89)	*3406*
Where Were You When I Was Falling In Love—Lobo (79)	848
All My Life—Kenny Rogers (83)	390
Gotta Have More Love—Climax Blues Band (80)	311
Wind Beneath My Wings—Lou Rawls (83)	*159*
Set The Night On Fire—Oak (80)	43
Secrets—Mac Davis (81)	37
You've Got A Good Love Coming—Van Stephenson (81)	16
—Robert Silbert see: Bob ROBERTS	
Sharon SILBERT ► 8528 (2)	**47**
Hey Little Lucy! (Don'tcha Put No Lipstick On)—Conway Twitty (59)	127
Things They Don't Teach You In School—Connie Freed (58)	20
Judee SILL ► 6392 (2)	**175**
Lady-O—Turtles (69)	172
Jesus Was A Crossmaker—Hollies (73)	3.5
Bob SILLER ► 6908 (1)	**130**
Powder Blue Mercedes Queen—Raiders (72)	389
Peter SILLS ► 8580 (1)	**46**
Every Face Tells A Story—Olivia Newton-John (76)	137
—François Gilbert Silly see: Gilbert BÉCAUD	
Balde SILVA ► 3645 (1)	**752**
My Angel Baby—Toby Beau (78)	1504
William SILVA ► 10441 (1)	**8.4**
Betty My Angel—Jerry Fuller (59)	17
Abner SILVER ► 1909 (15)	**2121**
There Goes My Heart—Joni James (58)	*1463*
My Love For You—Johnny Mathis (60)	679
With These Hands—Tom Jones (65)	669
Wisdom Of A Fool—Five Keys (56)	453
There Goes My Heart—Four Aces (55)	*379*
Lover Doll—Elvis Presley with the Jordanaires (58)	192
Young Abe Lincoln—Don Cornell (55)	*184*
My First Formal Gown—Patti Page (56)	126
As Long As I Have You—Don Rondo (58)	49
Young Abe Lincoln—Hugo & Luigi (55)	*16*
Rock Roll Boogie—"Tennessee" Ernie Ford (56)	16
Who's Gonna Take You To The Prom—Gaylords (56)	6.6
Bring Back Those Rockabye Baby Days—Tiny Tim (68)	5.9
Who Can Explain—Frankie Lymon and the Teenagers (56)	5.8
Not As A Stranger—Tony Bennett with Percy Faith and His Orchestra (54)	0.0
Dave SILVER [Rodd Arden] ► 8522 (1)	**47**
When You Lose The One You Love—David Whitfield with Mantovani And His Orchestra (56)	142
Lee SILVER ► 7286 (1)	**105**
Fire (I'm Keeping My Heart Away From Fire)—Les Paul and Mary Ford (57)	105
Roger SILVER ► 10252 (1)	**11**
Anytime—Journey (78)	54
—Yvonne Silver see: Donna FARGO	
—Albert Silverman see: Al STILLMAN	
Charles SILVERMAN ► 5131 (1)	**336**
Look Through Any Window—Hollies (65)	672
Dolores Vicki SILVERS ► 787 (1)	**5623**
Learnin' The Blues—Frank Sinatra (55)	5623

Shel SILVERSTEIN ▶ 182 (13)	**16892**
A Boy Named Sue—Johnny Cash (69)	6404
Sylvia's Mother— Dr. Hook And The Medicine Show (72)	3651
The Unicorn—Irish Rovers (68)	3028
The Cover Of "Rolling Stone"— Dr. Hook And The Medicine Show (72)	2776
Daddy What If—Bobby Bare (73)	299
I Got Stoned And I Missed It—Jim Stafford (75)	237
Roland The Roadie And Gertrude The Groupie— Dr. Hook And The Medicine Show (73)	179
All The Time In The World—Dr. Hook (79)	167
Carry Me, Carrie— Dr. Hook And The Medicine Show (72)	138
The New "Frankie And Johnnie" Song— Greenwood County Singers (64)	*115*
Life Ain't Easy— Dr. Hook And The Medicine Show (73)	95
The Taker—Waylon Jennings (70)	22
25 Minutes To Go—Brothers Four (62)	0.4
Tony SILVESTER ▶ 5401 (3)	**294**
Spinning Around (I Must Be Falling In Love)— Main Ingredient (71)	489
You've Been My Inspiration—Main Ingredient (70)	362
I'm Better Off Without You—Main Ingredient (70)	31
Bebu SILVETTI [Juan Fernando Silvetti Adorno] ▶ 6133 (1)	**202**
Spring Rain—Silvetti (77)	202
—Juan Fernando Silvetti Adorno see: Bebu SILVETTI	
Harry SIMEONE ▶ 3777 (10)	**703**
The Little Drummer Boy—Harry Simeone Chorale (58)	*770*
The Little Drummer Boy—Harry Simeone Chorale (59)	*542*
The Little Drummer Boy—Harry Simeone Chorale (62)	*347*
The Little Drummer Boy—Harry Simeone Chorale (60)	*220*
The Little Drummer Boy—Harry Simeone Chorale (61)	*133*
The Little Drummer Boy—Johnny Cash (59)	*69*
Little Drummer Boy—Lou Rawls (67)	*14*
The Little Drummer Boy—Moonlion (75)	*7.4*
The Little Drummer Boy—Jack Halloran Singers (62)	*2.2*
The Little Drummer Boy—Harry Simeone Chorale (63)	*2.2*
Sidney SIMIEN ▶ 5868 (1)	**235**
My Toot Toot—Jean Knight (85)	235
Lamar SIMINGTON ▶ 7603 (1)	**86**
Goodbye My Lover Goodbye—Searchers (65)	344
Joseph SIMMEL ▶ 10009 (1)	**14**
Don't Run (Come Back To Me)—KC & The Sunshine Band (Duet with Teri DeSario) (83)	28
Kim SIMMONDS ▶ 9286 (1)	**27**
Tell Mama—Savoy Brown (71)	54
Bill SIMMONS ▶ 7219 (3)	**109**
Freak-A-Zoid—Midnight Star (83)	253
Headlines—Midnight Star (86)	59
No Parking (On The Dance Floor)—Midnight Star (84)	46
Charles SIMMONS ▶ 1666 (10)	**2524**
They Just Can't Stop It the (Games People Play)— Spinners (75)	4227
Mighty Love - Pt. I—Spinners (74)	1001
Love Don't Love Nobody - Pt. I—Spinners (74)	724
Love Or Leave—Spinners (75)	438
Sadie—Spinners (75)	314
Jealousy—Major Harris (76)	97
Aiming At Your Heart—Temptations (81)	85
Brandy—O'Jays (78)	85
Once You Hit The Road—Dionne Warwick (75)	84
I Got Over Love—Major Harris (76)	15
—Chuck Simmons see: Chuck TAYLOR	
Daryl SIMMONS ▶ 649 (16)	**6725**
On Our Own—Bobby Brown (89)	3434
The Lover In Me—Sheena Easton (88)	2763
The Way You Love Me—Karyn White (88)	1851
Secret Rendezvous—Karyn White (89)	1717
Rock Wit'cha—Bobby Brown (89)	1460
Don't Be Cruel—Bobby Brown (88)	1445
Superwoman—Karyn White (89)	1259
It's No Crime—Babyface (89)	1221
My, My, My—Johnny Gill (90)	1143
Dial My Heart—Boys (88)	927
My Kinda Girl—Babyface (90)	508
Fairweather Friend—Johnny Gill (90)	468
Knocked Out—Paula Abdul (88)	378
Stone Cold Gentleman—Ralph Tresvant (91)	369
Right Down To It—Damian Dame (91)	17
Word To The Badd!!—Jermaine Jackson (91)	11
Elsie SIMMONS ▶ 10200 (1)	**11**
Wrong Again—Ames Brothers (55)	22
Gene SIMMONS [Reginald Van Helsing, Gene Klein, Chaim Witz] ▶ 1410 (9)	**3145**
Rock And Roll All Nite (Live)—Kiss (75)	*1254*
Calling Dr. Love—Kiss (77)	1219
Christine Sixteen—Kiss (77)	646
Shout It Out Loud—Kiss (76)	*563*
Radioactive—Gene Simmons (78)	314
A World Without Heroes—KISS (81)	167
Rock And Roll All Nite (Studio)—Kiss (75)	*131*
Shout It Out Loud (Live)—Kiss (77)	*104*
Flaming Youth—Kiss (76)	41
Joe SIMMONS ▶ 11240 (1)	**2.6**
Walkin' Proud—Pete Klint Quintet (67)	5.3
Joseph Ward SIMMONS ▶ 5717 (2)	**251**
You Be Illin'—Run-D.M.C. (86)	626
It's Tricky—Run-D.M.C. (87)	170
Lee SIMMONS ▶ 5158 (2)	**333**
1900 Yesterday—Liz Damon's Orient Express (70)	655
Maybe—Betty Everett (69)	10
Lonnie SIMMONS ▶ 3025 (8)	**1058**
Don't Stop The Music—Yarbrough & Peoples (81)	954
Early In The Morning—Robert Palmer (88)	*790*
Early In The Morning—Gap Band (82)	*602*
You Dropped A Bomb On Me—Gap Band (82)	529
Ooops Up—Snap! (90)	273
Burn Rubber (Why You Wanna Hurt Me)— Gap Band (81)	178
I Wouldn't Lie—Yarbrough & Peoples (86)	29
I Don't Believe You Want To Get Up And Dance (Oops, Up Side Your Head)—Gap Band (80)	14
Luther SIMMONS ▶ 5402 (3)	**294**
Spinning Around (I Must Be Falling In Love)— Main Ingredient (71)	489
You've Been My Inspiration—Main Ingredient (70)	362
I'm Better Off Without You—Main Ingredient (70)	31
Patrick SIMMONS ▶ 770 (8)	**5714**
Black Water—Doobie Brothers (74)	4848
Dependin' On You—Doobie Brothers (79)	622
So Wrong—Patrick Simmons (83)	536
Sweet Maxine—Doobie Brothers (75)	259
Echoes Of Love—Doobie Brothers (77)	101
I Cheat The Hangman—Doobie Brothers (75)	83
Dangerous—Doobie Brothers (91)	39
Wheels Of Fortune—Doobie Brothers (76)	7.7
Ron SIMMONS ▶ 8928 (1)	**36**
You Just Can't Win (By Making The Same Mistake)— Gene & Jerry (70)	108
Russell SIMMONS ▶ 9705 (1)	**19**
The Breaks (Part 1)—Kurtis Blow (80)	94
Simtec SIMMONS [Walter Simmons] ▶ 8929 (1)	**36**
You Just Can't Win (By Making The Same Mistake)— Gene & Jerry (70)	108
—Walter Simmons see: Simtec SIMMONS	
Alice D. SIMMS ▶ 6292 (5)	**185**
Foolishly Yours—Doris Day (55)	*166*
Foolishly Yours—Kay Starr (55)	*166*
I Spoke Too Soon—Crew-Cuts (54)	38
Foolishly Yours—Four Knights (55)	*0.0*
Foolishly Yours— Lee Raymond with The Costello Sisters (55)	*0.0*
Donald SIMMS ▶ 8106 (1)	**61**
Stroll Me—Kay Starr (58)	184
Earl SIMMS ▶ 3852 (2)	**677**
Funky Street—Arthur Conley (68)	1322
Aunt Dora's Love Soul Shack—Arthur Conley (68)	65
Billy SIMON ▶ 7970 (1)	**67**
Wise Up—Amy Grant (85)	134
Carly SIMON ▶ 194 (18) HOF	**16174**
You're So Vain—Carly Simon (72)	7377
Jesse—Carly Simon (80)	2247
That's The Way I've Always Heard It Should Be— Carly Simon (71)	2005
You Belong To Me—Carly Simon (78)	*1970*
Anticipation—Carly Simon (71)	1805
The Right Thing To Do—Carly Simon (73)	1273
Haven't Got Time For The Pain— Carly Simon (74)	1266
Coming Around Again—Carly Simon (86)	715
Attitude Dancing—Carly Simon (75)	564
Legend In Your Own Time—Carly Simon (72)	302
Vengeance—Carly Simon (79)	252
Let The River Run—Carly Simon (89)	217
Give Me All Night—Carly Simon (87)	174
All I Want Is You—Carly Simon (88)	154
Waterfall—Carly Simon (75)	44
You Know What To Do—Carly Simon (83)	25
You Belong To Me—Doobie Brothers (83)	*23*
Tranquillo—Carly Simon (78)	22
Dwayne SIMON ▶ 4879 (3)	**391**
I Need Love—LL Cool J (87)	765
I'm That Type Of Guy—LL Cool J (89)	696
I'm Bad—LL Cool J (87)	18
—Gus Simon see: Gus EDWARDS	
Jerry SIMON ▶ 10746 (1)	**5.6**
Tiger In The Tank—Chariots (65)	17
Joe SIMON ▶ 1225 (12)	**3644**
Power Of Love—Joe Simon (72)	*1856*
Get Down, Get Down (Get On The Floor)— Joe Simon (75)	1761
Theme From Cleopatra Jones—Joe Simon (73)	1133
Your Time To Cry—Joe Simon (70)	909
Moon Walk Part I—Joe Simon (69)	409
Trouble In My Home—Joe Simon (72)	306
You're The One For Me—Joe Simon (71)	249
Power Of Love—Martha Reeves (74)	*96*
I Need You, You Need Me—Joe Simon (76)	64
Music In My Bones—Joe Simon (75)	58
It's Hard To Get Along—Joe Simon (69)	35
Love Vibration—Joe Simon (79)	4.4
John S. SIMON ▶ 6699 (1)	**143**
My Name Is Jack—Manfred Mann (68)	143
Lowrell SIMON ▶ 4947 (1)	**376**
The Sly, Slick, And The Wicked—Lost Generation (70)	1128
Lucy SIMON ▶ 8283 (2)	**56**
Winkin', Blinkin' And Nod—Simon Sisters (64)	*60*
Wynken, Blynken And Nod—Doobie Brothers (81)	*51*
—Michael Saint Simon see: Simon SOUSSAN	
Nat SIMON ▶ 2483 (9)	**1447**
Old Lamplighter— Browns Featuring Jim Edward Brown (60)	2054
The Mama Doll Song—Patti Page (54)	*350*
Sweet Heartaches—Eddie Fisher (56)	341
Under The Sun Valley Moon—Patti Page (59)	69
It's Your Life—Bob Manning (55)	31
Oh Pain! Oh Agony! (Know What I Mean Jelly Bean)— Gisele MacKenzie (57)	17
You're Wrong All Wrong—Eileen Rodgers (56)	14
Poinciana—Ahmad Jamal Trio (58)	9.8
The Mama Doll Song— Guy Lombardo & His Royal Canadians (54)	*0.0*
Neil SIMON ▶ 11253 (1)	**2.6**
Tower Trot (And Then You Do That Step)— Dick Jacobs And His Chorus And Orchestra (57)	23
Norm SIMON ▶ 6644 (1)	**148**
I Want To Love You For What You Are— Ronnie Dove (67)	296
Paul SIMON [Jerry Landis] ▶ 5 (51) HOF	**87319**
Bridge Over Troubled Water—Simon & Garfunkel (70)	*8896*
Mrs. Robinson—Simon & Garfunkel (68)	*8641*
The Sound Of Silence—Simon & Garfunkel (65)	*7572*
50 Ways To Leave Your Lover—Paul Simon (75)	5708
Red Rubber Ball—Cyrkle (66)	4909
I Am A Rock—Simon & Garfunkel (66)	4534
Loves Me Like A Rock— Paul Simon (with The Dixie Hummingbirds) (73)	4456
Bridge Over Troubled Water—Aretha Franklin (71)	*4354*
Cecilia—Simon & Garfunkel (70)	*4069*
Kodachrome—Paul Simon (73)	3958
Mother And Child Reunion—Paul Simon (72)	3255
Homeward Bound—Simon & Garfunkel (66)	3185
The Boxer—Simon & Garfunkel (69)	3171
Hazy Shade Of Winter—Bangles (87)	*2731*
Slip Slidin' Away—Paul Simon (77)	2219
Late In The Evening—Paul Simon (80)	2033
My Little Town—Simon & Garfunkel (75)	1791
Scarborough Fair (/Canticle)— Simon & Garfunkel (68)	*1431*

Paul SIMON [Jerry Landis] ▶ 5 (51) HOF *Continued*	**87319**
Me And Julio Down By The Schoolyard—Paul Simon (72)	1387
The 59th Street Bridge Song (Feelin' Groovy)—Harpers Bizarre (67)	1359
El Condor Pasa—Simon & Garfunkel (70)	1326
A Hazy Shade Of Winter—Simon & Garfunkel (66)	*1209*
At The Zoo—Simon & Garfunkel (67)	1149
Scarborough Fair—Sergio Mendes & Brasil '66 (68)	*1088*
You Can Call Me Al—Paul Simon (86)	988
Fakin' It—Simon & Garfunkel (67)	915
The Dangling Conversation—Simon & Garfunkel (66)	875
Gone At Last—Paul Simon/Phoebe Snow (75)	728
Mrs. Robinson—Booker T. & The M.G.'s (69)	*554*
American Tune—Paul Simon (73)	525
America—Yes (72)	*394*
Hey Schoolgirl—Tom & Jerry (57)	316
Duncan—Paul Simon (72)	304
Keep The Customer Satisfied—Gary Puckett (71)	274
Allergies—Paul Simon (83)	269
Still Crazy After All These Years—Paul Simon (76)	255
One-Trick Pony—Paul Simon (80)	254
For Emily, Whenever I May Find Her—Simon & Garfunkel (72)	*203*
I Wish You Could Be Here—Cyrkle (67)	169
Bridge Over Troubled Water—Linda Clifford (79)	*159*
Graceland—Paul Simon (86)	107
For Emily—Arbors (69)	*85*
The Obvious Child—Paul Simon (90)	43
Cecilia—Times Two (88)	*31*
The Boy In The Bubble—Paul Simon (87)	29
The Lone Teen Ranger—Jerry Landis (63)	21
Sounds Of Silence—Stars On 45 (81)	*12*
The Sound Of Silence—Peaches & Herb (71)	*3.8*
America—Simon & Garfunkel (72)	*2.8*
Motorcycle—Tico And The Triumphs (62)	2.7
The Sound Of Silence—Paul Simon (74)	*2.5*

Scott SIMON ▶ 9244 (2)	**28**
Top Forty (Of The Lord)—Sha Na Na (71)	21
Only One Song—Sha Na Na (71)	6.7

Nina SIMONE [Eunice Kathleen Waymon] ▶ 8816 (1)	**39**
To Be Young, Gifted And Black—Nina Simone (69)	77

Paul SIMONON ▶ 3559 (4)	**786**
Rock The Casbah—Clash (82)	1940
Train In Vain (Stand By Me)—Clash (80)	752
Should I Stay Or Should I Go?—Clash (82)	*243*
Should I Stay Or Should I Go?—Clash (83)	*210*

Moises SIMONS [Moises Simon Rodriguez] ▶ 11255 (1)	**2.6**
Marta—Bachelors (67)	5.2

Nev SIMONS ▶ 10000 (1)	**14**
Cornbelt Symphony—Bing & Gary Crosby (54)	28

Peter SIMONS ▶ 3512 (1)	**807**
United We Stand—Brotherhood Of Man (70)	1614

Britt SIMONSON [Jack Harlen] ▶ 9579 (2)	**21**
The Alley Cat Song—David Thorne (62)	*38*
The Alley Cat Song—Peggy Lee (63)	*4.1*

Craig SIMPKINS ▶ 6640 (1)	**149**
Summertime—DJ Jazzy Jeff & The Fresh Prince (91)	1783

Mattie SIMPKINS ▶ 11318 (1)	**2.3**
It's True I'm Gonna Miss You—Carolyn Franklin (69)	4.6

Brian SIMPSON ▶ 1920 (1)	**2110**
The First Time—Surface (90)	4220

Carl SIMPSON ▶ 11158 (1)	**3.0**
Snap-Out—Interpertations (69)	8.9

Fitzroy SIMPSON ▶ 6322 (1)	**182**
Pass The Dutchie—Musical Youth (82)	1276

Hoke SIMPSON ▶ 9793 (1)	**17**
Gi Gi—Hoke Simpson (57)	17

Mike SIMPSON ▶ 9374 (1)	**25**
Hey Ladies—Beastie Boys (89)	302

Red SIMPSON ▶ 10810 (1)	**5.2**
Sam's Place—Buck Owens And The Buckaroos (67)	10

Richard SIMPSON [Chubb Rock, Richard Anthony Simpson] ▶ 11628 (1)	**0.9**
Treat 'Em Right—Chubb Rock (91)	4.7

Valerie SIMPSON ▶ 221 (50) HOF	**15121**
Ain't No Mountain High Enough—Diana Ross (70)	*6311*
Your Precious Love—Marvin Gaye & Tammi Terrell (67)	2938
Ain't Nothing Like The Real Thing—Marvin Gaye & Tammi Terrell (68)	*2127*
You're All I Need To Get By—Marvin Gaye & Tammi Terrell (68)	*2011*
Remember Me—Diana Ross (70)	1429
Solid—Ashford & Simpson (84)	1266
Ain't No Mountain High Enough—Marvin Gaye & Tammi Terrell (67)	*1259*
Reach Out And Touch (Somebody's Hand)—Diana Ross (70)	1230
I'm Every Woman—Chaka Khan (78)	989
The Boss—Diana Ross (79)	954
Let's Go Get Stoned—Ray Charles Band With The Raelets (66)	900
You're All I Need To Get By—Aretha Franklin (71)	*837*
Stuff Like That—Quincy Jones (78)	787
Ain't Nothing Like The Real Thing—Donny & Marie (76)	*755*
California Soul—5th Dimension (68)	*740*
Some Things You Never Get Used To—Diana Ross And The Supremes (68)	717
Keep On Lovin' Me Honey—Marvin Gaye & Tammi Terrell (68)	677
Found A Cure—Ashford & Simpson (79)	550
Good Lovin' Ain't Easy To Come By—Marvin Gaye & Tammi Terrell (69)	443
One Step At A Time—Maxine Brown (65)	417
Surrender—Diana Ross (71)	414
What You Gave Me—Marvin Gaye & Tammi Terrell (69)	406
Who's Gonna Take The Blame—Smokey Robinson & The Miracles (70)	316
Landlord—Gladys Knight & The Pips (80)	315
You're All I Need To Get By—Tony Orlando & Dawn (75)	*303*
Ain't Nothing Like The Real Thing—Aretha Franklin (74)	*267*
You're All I Need To Get By—Johnny Mathis/Deniece Williams (78)	*206*
Didn't You Know (You'd Have To Cry Sometime)—Gladys Knight & The Pips (69)	206
Destination: Anywhere—Marvelettes (68)	203
Don't Cost You Nothing—Ashford & Simpson (78)	201
Silly Wasn't I—Valerie Simpson (72)	184
Street Corner—Ashford & Simpson (82)	163
Onion Song—Marvin Gaye & Tammi Terrell (70)	137
I Don't Need No Doctor—Humble Pie (71)	*120*
California Soul—Marvin Gaye & Tammi Terrell (70)	*116*
Shoe Shoe Shine—Dynamic Superiors (74)	112
Don't Send Nobody Else—Ace Spectrum (74)	73
I Am Your Man—Bobby Taylor & The Vancouvers (68)	68
I Don't Need No Doctor—New Riders Of The Purple Sage (72)	*50*
I Don't Need No Doctor—Ray Charles And His Orchestra (66)	*48*
The Real Thing—Tina Britt (65)	27
Send It—Ashford & Simpson (77)	25
Love Don't Make It Right—Ashford & Simpson (80)	23
Count Your Blessings—Ashford and Simpson (86)	17
It Seems To Hang On—Ashford & Simpson (78)	14
(I'd Know You) Anywhere—Ashford & Simpson (74)	9.9
You're All I Need To Get By—Chris Christian (82)	*8.1*
Ain't Nothing Like The Real Thing—Chris Christian (82)	*8.1*
Never Had It So Good—Ronnie Milsap (65)	6.7
Clouds—Chaka Khan (80)	3.6

Gerald SIMS ▶ 2899 (8)	**1126**
Love Makes A Woman—Barbara Acklin (68)	1694
Voice Your Choice—Radiants (64)	469
Since You Showed Me How To Be Happy—Jackie Wilson (67)	461
Dear Lover—Mary Wells (66)	453
Too Hot To Hold—Major Lance (65)	46
It Ain't No Big Thing—Radiants (65)	28
(I'm Just A) Fool For You—Gene Chandler (66)	13
Here Come The Tears—Gene Chandler (65)	6.1

Larry SIMS ▶ 9506 (1)	**22**
Friends—Feather (70)	112

Frank SINATRA ▶ 5805 (3)	**240**
Mr Success—Frank Sinatra (58)	704
This Love Of Mine—5 DeMarco Sisters (55)	*14*
This Love Of Mine—Modernaires (57)	*1.9*

Gordon SINCLAIR ▶ 1208 (3)	**3680**
Americans—Byron MacGregor (73)	*3206*
The Americans (A Canadian's Opinion)—Gordon Sinclair (74)	*427*
The Americans (A Canadian's Opinion)—Tex Ritter (74)	*48*

Peter SINFIELD ▶ 3345 (5)	**888**
Peace In Our Time—Eddie Money (89)	1122
Heart Of Stone—Cher (90)	618
In The Court Of The Crimson King—King Crimson (70)	20
I Believe In Father Christmas—Greg Lake (75)	18
C'est La Vie—Greg Lake (77)	16

Artie SINGER ▶ 1426 (7)	**3086**
At The Hop—Danny & The Juniors (57)	*8260*
442 Glenwood Avenue—Pixies Three (64)	344
Wind In The Willow—Jo Stafford (57)	*335*
Dottie—Danny And The Juniors (58)	180
At The Hop—Jive Bunny And The Mastermixers (89)	*80*
At The Hop—Nick Todd (57)	*54*
Wind In The Willow—Ann Reynolds (57)	*0.0*

Bob SINGER ▶ 6314 (3)	**182**
Unsuspecting Heart—Terri Stevens (54)	*610*
Unsuspecting Heart—Sunny Gale (54)	*120*
Unsuspecting Heart—Georgie Shaw (54)	*0.0*

Guy SINGER ▶ 2739 (3)	**1230**
Whither Thou Goest—Les Paul and Mary Ford (54)	927
My Love Song—Tommy Sands (57)	295
Brass Ring—Kay Starr (57)	17

Harold SINGER ▶ 7633 (2)	**84**
Wind In The Willow—Jo Stafford (57)	*335*
Wind In The Willow—Ann Reynolds (57)	*0.0*

Lou SINGER ▶ 4676 (4)	**440**
Young And Warm And Wonderful—Tony Bennett with Frank DeVol and his Orch. (58)	*514*
Am I A Toy Or A Treasure—Kay Starr (54)	233
Dixie Danny—Laurie Sisters (55)	210
Young And Warm And Wonderful—Roger Williams (58)	*0.0*

—Singing Nun see: Jeanine DECKERS

James SINGLETARY ▶ 8253 (1)	**57**
China—Red Rockers (83)	227

Charles SINGLETON [C. Noteignis] ▶ 207 (43)	**15375**
Strangers In The Night—Frank Sinatra (66)	6342
Don't Forbid Me—Pat Boone (56)	6093
If I May—Nat "King" Cole And The Four Knights (55)	1803
Spanish Eyes—Al Martino (65)	*1721*
(Welcome) New Lovers—Pat Boone (60)	975
Just As Much As Ever—Bobby Vinton (67)	*966*
Just As Much As Ever—Bob Beckham (59)	*956*
For A Penny—Pat Boone (59)	858
Apple Green—June Valli (60)	763
Lady—Jack Jones (67)	730
The Wheel Of Hurt—Margaret Whiting (66)	*614*
My Personal Possession—Nat "King" Cole And The Four Knights (57)	*575*
The Wheel Of Hurt—Al Martino (66)	*411*
Only Those In Love—Baby Washington (65)	402
Piddily Patter Patter—Patti Page (55)	*278*
Genuine Love—Les Paul and Mary Ford (55)	271
Take A Fool's Advice—Nat King Cole (61)	183
All Of Everything—Frankie Avalon (61)	123
Light Of Love—Peggy Lee (58)	99
Remember When—Wayne Newton (65)	80
Help The Poor—B.B. King (71)	*76*
Mambo Baby—Ruth Brown And Her Rhythmakers with Orchestra (54)	*58*
Three Fools—Patti Page (62)	55
Twice As Nice—Clyde McPhatter (59)	42
One Suit—"Tennessee" Ernie Ford (57)	41
Mama (He Treats Your Daughter Mean)—Dinning Sisters Featuring Jean Dinning (55)	*31*
Mambo Baby—Georgia Gibbs (54)	*15*
I'd Better Be Careful—Bob Manning (55)	14
Slam! Bam!—Crew-Cuts (55)	12
Lover's Hymn—Fontane Sisters (59)	9.6
Hummin' And Waltzin'—Les Paul and Mary Ford (57)	7.6

Charles SINGLETON [C. Noteignis] ▶ 207 (43) *Continued*	**15375**
One Night Only—Otis Williams And His Charms (56)	7.2
Words—Pat Boone (60)	5.3
Honey Bunch—Four Knights (55)	5.0
Hep Dee Hootie (Cutie Wootie)—Tommy Sands (57)	4.7
Help The Poor—B.B. King (64)	*1.9*
Mama (He Treats Your Daughter Mean)— Ruth Brown (62)	*0.9*
Piddily Patter—Nappy Brown (55)	*0.0*
My Personal Possession—Andy Bey (57)	*0.0*
Piddily Patter Patter—Helene Dixon (55)	*0.0*
Piddily Patter Patter—Burton Sisters (55)	*0.0*
(Mama) He Treats Your Daughter Mean— Ruth Brown (55)	*0.0*
Mama (He Treats Your Daughter Mean)— Bette Anne Steele (55)	*0.0*
Charles L. SINGLETON ▶ 6939 (2)	**127**
She's Strange—Cameo (84)	325
This Time—Kiara (89)	46
Eddie SINGLETON ▶ 7775 (5)	**76**
I Believe I'll Love On—Jackie Wilson (65)	54
Think Twice—Jackie Wilson And Lavern Baker (66)	9.0
She's All Right—Jackie Wilson (64)	8.7
Spend A Little Time—Barbara Lewis (64)	3.0
Baby, That's All—Jackie Wilson (62)	2.4
Margie SINGLETON [Margaret Louis Ebey] ▶ 1830 (8)	**2242**
Lie To Me—Brook Benton (62)	1517
She Understands Me—Johnny Tillotson (64)	*808*
My True Confession—Brook Benton (63)	675
I Got What I Wanted—Brook Benton (63)	672
Dum-De-Da—Bobby Vinton (66)	*465*
Laura, What's He Got That I Ain't Got— Frankie Laine (67)	*268*
Laura (Tell Me What He's Got That I Ain't Got)— Brook Benton (67)	*55*
Tamouré—Bill Justis (63)	46
Raynoma SINGLETON [Raynoma Gordy, Raynoma Liles, Raynoma Mayberry] ▶ 10921 (1)	**4.4**
Don't Bring Back Memories—Four Tops (69)	4.4
Shelby SINGLETON ▶ 3632 (4)	**758**
Am I That Easy To Forget—Debbie Reynolds (60)	*1149*
Am I That Easy To Forget— Engelbert Humperdinck (67)	*1119*
Am I That Easy To Forget— "Little Esther" Phillips (63)	*5.3*
Am I That Easy To Forget—Skeeter Davis (60)	*0.0*
Stephen SINGLETON ▶ 3990 (3)	**629**
The Look Of Love - Part One—ABC (82)	1769
Poison Arrow—ABC (83)	732
That Was Then But This Is Now—ABC (84)	12
—Sinhô see: Jose BARBOSA DA SILVA	
Earl SINKS ▶ 5660 (1)	**258**
Two Of A Kind—Sue Thompson (62)	516
Will SINOTT ▶ 6595 (1)	**153**
Move Any Mountain—Shamen (91)	459
John SIOMOS ▶ 5337 (1)	**303**
Do You Feel Like We Do—Peter Frampton (76)	1212
—Siouxsie Sioux see: Susan BALLION	
—Leonhard Raymond Sipes see: Tommy COLLINS	
—Sirarcusa see: Ramon ARCUSA	
—John Siras see: Ira SCHUSTER	
—Sir Mix-A-Lot see: Anthony RAY	
Nikki SIXX [Frank Carlton Serafino Feranna] ▶ 1328 (12)	**3349**
Dr. Feelgood—Mötley Crüe (89)	1482
Without You—Mötley Crüe (90)	1295
Girls, Girls, Girls—Mötley Crüe (87)	1018
Don't Go Away Mad (Just Go Away)—Mötley Crüe (90)	741
Home Sweet Home '91—Mötley Crüe (91)	*651*
Kickstart My Heart—Mötley Crüe (89)	550
Looks That Kill—Mötley Crüe (84)	253
Same Ol' Situation (S.O.S.)—Mötley Crüe (90)	148
Home Sweet Home—Mötley Crüe (85)	*70*
Primal Scream—Mötley Crüe (91)	60
All I Need—Mötley Crüe (87)	52
Too Young To Fall In Love—Mötley Crüe (84)	9.3
Charlie SKARBEK ▶ 6891 (1)	**130**
Midnight Blue—Louise Tucker (83)	391

Gary SKARDINA ▶ 2761 (3)	**1214**
Jump (For My Love)—Pointer Sisters (84)	3301
Dangerous—Natalie Cole (85)	253
(Come On) Shout—Alex Brown (85)	59
—Bobby Skel see: Robert Doyle SKELTON	
Peter SKELLERN ▶ 4385 (3)	**507**
You're A Lady—Peter Skellern (72)	*289*
You're A Lady—Dawn Featuring Tony Orlando (72)	*213*
Hard Times—Peter Skellern (76)	5.4
Robert Doyle SKELTON [Bobby Skel] ▶ 9618 (1)	**20**
Sheila Ann—Bobby Skel (68)	20
Tommy SKEOCH ▶ 8286 (1)	**55**
The Way It Is—Tesla (90)	222
Mike SKILL ▶ 2805 (5)	**1187**
Talking In Your Sleep—Romantics (83)	3966
What I Like About You—Michael Morales (89)	*543*
One In A Million—Romantics (84)	404
What I Like About You—Romantics (80)	*218*
Test Of Time—Romantics (85)	115
Muzz SKILLINGS ▶ 5372 (1)	**299**
Cult Of Personality—Living Colour (89)	1195
Albert SKINNER ▶ 11192 (1)	**2.8**
Away All Boats—Al Hibbler (56)	8.5
David SKINNER ▶ 8309 (1)	**55**
River Road—Uncle Dog (73)	55
Frank SKINNER ▶ 11193 (1)	**2.8**
Away All Boats—Al Hibbler (56)	8.5
Grahame SKINNER ▶ 6527 (1)	**160**
The Honeythief—Hipsway (87)	639
Jolyon SKINNER ▶ 3944 (4)	**646**
The Colour Of Love—Billy Ocean (88)	815
Lies—Jonathan Butler (87)	534
Nice 'N' Slow—Freddie Jackson (88)	207
Have You Ever Loved Somebody— Freddie Jackson (87)	143
Terry SKINNER ▶ 2948 (3)	**1105**
Even The Nights Are Better—Air Supply (82)	2400
Touch Me When We're Dancing—Carpenters (81)	*893*
Touch Me When We're Dancing—Bama (79)	*21*
—Skip see: Clyde BATTIN	
Rodney SKIPWORTH ▶ 10248 (1)	**11**
Thinking About Your Love—Skipworth & Turner (85)	22
Josh SKLAIR ▶ 7304 (1)	**104**
All Of Me For All Of You—9.9 (85)	311
Gloria SKLEROV ▶ 3414 (4)	**857**
I Just Fall In Love Again—Anne Murray (79)	1411
He Did With Me—Vicki Lawrence (73)	360
It Could Have Been Me—Sami Jo (74)	344
I Believe I'm Gonna Love You—Frank Sinatra (75)	306
—Yani Skoradalides see: Les VANDYKE	
—Arthur Skupsky see: Art ROBERTS	
Sunny SKYLAR [Margarite Almeda, Selig Shaftel, Michael Vaughn] ▶ 828 (24) HOF	**5329**
Love Me With All Your Heart (Cuando Caliente El Sol)—Ray Charles Singers (64)	*4884*
Amor—Ben E. King (61)	*1033*
Pussy Cat—Ames Brothers (58)	956
Small Sad Sam—Phil McLean (61)	902
Nola—Billy Williams (59)	*777*
Ask Me—Nat "King" Cole (56)	*604*
Love Me With All Of Your Heart—Bachelors (66)	*455*
Nola—Morgan Brothers (59)	*360*
Don't Wait Too Long—Tony Bennett (63)	296
Besame Mucho (Part 1)—Coasters (60)	*181*
You'll Always Be The One I Love—Dean Martin (64)	136
I've Got Bells On My Heart—Don Cornell (58)	*81*
I've Got Bells On My Heart—Jane Morgan (58)	*81*
Be Mine Tonight—Andy Williams (58)	61
Don't Let The Kiddy Geddin—Kitty Kallen (54)	51
Marjolaina—Gogi Grant (58)	31
Watching The World Go By—Dean Martin (56)	30
Calla Calla—Paulette Sisters (58)	12
Besame Mucho— Steve Lawrence and Eydie Gorme (55)	*7.4*
Eso Es El Amor (This Is Love)— Morty Palitz & Orchestra with the Americanos (59)	6.2
Pennsylvania Waltz—Wayne King (57)	*2.5*
Pennsylvania Waltz—Billy Vaughn and His Orchestra (57)	*2.5*

I've Got Bells On My Heart—Don Rondo (58)	*0.0*
I've Got Bells On My Heart—Three Pennies (58)	*0.0*
SKYLARK ▶ 4914 (2)	**383**
System Of Survival—Earth, Wind & Fire (87)	220
I Can't Wait—Deniece Williams (88)	162
—Luke Skyywalker see: Luther CAMPBELL	
Freddie SLACK ▶ 3922 (2)	**656**
The House Of Blue Lights—Chuck Miller (55)	*1312*
The House Of Blue Lights—Pat Morrisey (55)	*0.0*
Paul SLADE ▶ 9596 (4)	**21**
I Need A Man—Grace Jones (77)	24
On The Beat—B. B. & Q Band (81)	12
Hold Tight—Change (81)	6.5
Searching—Change (80)	1.4
Mike SLAMER ▶ 10353 (1)	**9.7**
If Love Should Go—Streets (83)	19
—Slash see: Saul HUDSON	
Johnny SLATE ▶ 4206 (6)	**563**
Better Love Next Time—Dr. Hook (79)	1340
Don't Stop Me Baby (I'm On Fire)—Boys Band (82)	122
Blaze Of Glory—Kenny Rogers (81)	97
Holdin' On For Dear Love—Lobo (79)	74
Shotgun Rider—Delbert McClinton (81)	*45*
Shotgun Rider—Joe Sun (80)	*40*
Jean SLATER ▶ 4455 (1)	**491**
You Can Never Stop Me Loving You— Johnny Tillotson (63)	982
Terry SLATER ▶ 6142 (1)	**200**
Bowling Green—Everly Brothers (67)	400
Mark SLAUGHTER ▶ 3516 (3)	**803**
Fly To The Angels—Slaughter (90)	754
Up All Night—Slaughter (90)	547
Spend My Life—Slaughter (90)	304
Michael SLAVEN ▶ 6790 (1)	**137**
Kiss This Thing Goodbye—Del Amitri (90)	410
Frank SLAY [Frank Slay Jr.] ▶ 479 (28)	**8696**
Silhouettes—Rays (57)	*4941*
Silhouettes—Herman's Hermits (65)	*3289*
Tallahassee Lassie—Freddy Cannon (59)	2864
La Dee Dah—Billy & Lillie (57)	1426
Lucky Ladybug—Billy & Lillie (58)	900
Jump Over—Freddy Cannon (60)	624
The Push And Kick—Mark Valentino (62)	594
Buzz Buzz A-Diddle-It—Freddy Cannon (61)	526
Flying Circle—Frank Slay And His Orchestra (61)	488
Transistor Sister—Freddy Cannon (61)	471
Magic Moon (Clair De Lune)—Rays (61)	*413*
Pony Express—Danny & The Juniors (61)	344
Okefenokee—Freddy Cannon (59)	301
Bells, Bells, Bells (The Bell Song)— Billy & Lillie (59)	155
Humdinger—Freddy Cannon (60)	153
Happy Shades Of Blue—Freddie Cannon (60)	150
Silhouettes—Diamonds (57)	*130*
Teen Queen Of The Week—Freddy Cannon (62)	112
Twistin' All Night Long—Danny & The Juniors With Guest Artist Freddy Cannon (62)	86
Urge—Freddy Cannon (60)	82
Silhouettes—Steve Gibson & the Red Caps (57)	*47*
Happiness—Billy & Lillie (58)	32
Daddy Cool—Rays (57)	*21*
Daddy Cool—Diamonds (57)	*21*
(Kwa-Na-Va-Ka) Cuernavaca Choo Choo— Freddy Cannon (60)	14
I'm Comin' Home—Sammy Davis Jr. (57)	4.7
Elevator Operator—Rays (58)	3.1
Mediterranean Moon—Rays (60)	3.0
Joni SLEDGE ▶ 9854 (1)	**16**
All American Girls—Sister Sledge (81)	64
Alberto SLEZYNGER ▶ 5936 (1)	**225**
Rico Suave—Gerardo (91)	1126
Darby SLICK [Dabney R. Slick] ▶ 1463 (1)	**2975**
Somebody To Love—Jefferson Airplane (67)	2975
Grace SLICK [Grace Johnson, Grace Barnett Wing] ▶ 1619 (5)	**2607**
White Rabbit—Jefferson Airplane (67)	2405
Play On Love—Jefferson Starship (75)	197
Greasy Heart—Jefferson Airplane (68)	95
Ride The Tiger—Jefferson Starship (74)	17
Seasons—Grace Slick (80)	2.9

P.F. SLOAN [Philip Gary Schlein, Flip Sloan, Phil Sloan] ▶ 429 (25)	**9445**
Eve Of Destruction—Barry McGuire (65)	*6384*
Secret Agent Man—Johnny Rivers (66)	*3877*
A Must To Avoid—Herman's Hermits (65)	2112
You Baby—Turtles (66)	1351
Let Me Be—Turtles (65)	627
Things I Should Have Said—Grass Roots (67)	624
Where Were You When I Needed You—Grass Roots (66)	623
I Found A Girl—Jan & Dean (65)	524
Wake Up, Wake Up—Grass Roots (67)	328
(Here They Come) From All Over The World—Jan & Dean (65)	275
Another Day, Another Heartache—5th Dimension (67)	263
Kick That Little Foot Sally Ann—Round Robin (64)	254
Secret Agent Man—Ventures (66)	*212*
Take Me For What I'm Worth—Searchers (66)	212
The Sins Of A Family—P.F. Sloan (65)	79
Summer Means Fun—Bruce And Terry (64)	77
Child Of Our Times—Barry McGuire (65)	72
Can I Get To Know You Better—Turtles (66)	60
This Precious Time—Terry Knight And The Pack (67)	36
Only When You're Lonely—Grass Roots (66)	31
Unless You Care—Terry Black (64)	30
A Melody For You—Grass Roots (68)	29
One Piece Topless Bathing Suit—Rip Chords (64)	2.4
Tell 'Em I'm Surfin—Fantastic Baggys (64)	0.9
Eve Of Destruction—Turtles (70)	*0.8*
—Phil/Flip Sloan see: P.F. SLOAN	
—Edward Smackels Jr. see: Ed ROSE	
Danny SMALL ▶ 1170 (5)	**3800**
Without Love (There Is Nothing)—Tom Jones (69)	*3045*
Without Love (There Is Nothing)—Ray Charles (63)	*496*
Without Love (There Is Nothing)—Clyde McPhatter (57)	*198*
Without Love (There Is Nothing)—Oscar Toney, Jr. (68)	*60*
Without Love (There Is Nothing)—Toni Arden (57)	*0.0*
Jonathan SMALL ▶ 8083 (1)	**62**
Only Because—Platters (57)	187
Charlie SMALLS ▶ 3180 (3)	**965**
Ease On Down The Road—Diana Ross & Michael Jackson (78)	*487*
Ease On Down The Road—Consumer Rapport (75)	*432*
You Can't Win (Part 1)—Michael Jackson (79)	46
N.D. SMART II [Norman Don Smart II] ▶ 8789 (1)	**39**
Future Shock—Hello People (75)	156
—Norman Don Smart II see: N.D. SMART II	
—David Michael Smet see: David HALLYDAY	
Mick SMILEY [Mark Cipolla] ▶ 3044 (1)	**1039**
Kiss Me Deadly—Lita Ford (88)	1039
Tim SMIT ▶ 6892 (1)	**130**
Midnight Blue—Louise Tucker (83)	391
—Acacia Smith see: Stacy SMITH	
Albert B. SMITH ▶ 5102 (5)	**342**
Big Boss Man—Elvis Presley (67)	*425*
Get It From The Bottom—Steelers (69)	300
Big Boss Man—Jimmy Reed (61)	*39*
Soul Hootenanny Pt. 1—Gene Chandler (64)	*17*
I'm Your Part Time Love—Mitty Collier (63)	*3.2*
Alfred J. SMITH [Brenton Wood] ▶ 2225 (4)	**1722**
Gimme Little Sign—Brenton Wood (67)	2590
The Oogum Boogum Song—Brenton Wood (67)	696
Baby You Got It—Brenton Wood (67)	486
Lovey Dovey Kinda Lovin'—Brenton Wood (68)	1.4
Andrew SMITH ▶ 8105 (2)	**61**
I'll Be Holding On—Al Downing (75)	123
I Don't Wanna Leave You—Debbie Taylor (76)	0.4
Anthony L. SMITH ▶ 10655 (1)	**6.3**
When Love Cries—Donna Summer (91)	32
Anthony Terrell SMITH [Tone Loc] ▶ 3890 (2)	**666**
Wild Thing—Tone Loc (88)	2613
All Through The Night—Tone Loc (91)	39
Arlene SMITH ▶ 4087 (5)	**598**
Maybe—Three Degrees (70)	*895*
Maybe—Chantels (58)	*847*
He's Gone—Chantels (57)	30
The Plea—Jesters (58)	14
Maybe—Shangri-Las (64)	*8.7*
Arthur SMITH ▶ 1306 (3)	**3393**
Guitar Boogie Shuffle—Virtues (59)	*3295*
Joey Baby—Anita And Th' So-And-So's (62)	192
Guitar Boogie Shuffle Twist—Virtues (62)	*2.2*
—Barbara Ann Smith see: Barbara GEORGE	
Beasley SMITH ▶ 4415 (5)	**500**
That Lucky Old Sun—Ray Charles (63)	*950*
That Lucky Old Sun—Velvets (61)	*24*
Lonesome Lover Blues—Fontane Sisters (56)	23
That Lucky Old Sun—Floridians (61)	*2.2*
Beg Your Pardon—Billy Vaughn And His Orchestra (60)	1.5
Ben SMITH ▶ 9380 (1)	**25**
Fried Eggs—Intruders (59)	75
Bill SMITH ▶ 5438 (2)	**289**
First Quarrel—Paul & Paula (63)	680
I Wouldn't Trade You For The World—Bachelors (64)	188
Billy Dawn SMITH [Billy Dawn] ▶ 1071 (16)	**4118**
Step By Step—Crests (60)	1484
Just Born (To Be Your Baby)—Perry Como (57)	1363
Angels Listened In—Crests (59)	1087
Trouble In Paradise—Crests (60)	1055
To The Aisle—Five Satins (57)	*696*
Six Nights A Week—Crests (59)	688
Angel Smile—Nat "King" Cole (57)	553
Year Ago Tonight—Crests (59)	493
Let's Try Again—Clyde McPhatter (59)	286
Pin A Medal On Joey—James Darren (63)	277
Flower Of Love—Crests (59)	63
Little Gypsy—Ames Brothers (58)	56
Journey Of Love—Crests Featuring Johnny Maestro (60)	42
Isn't It Amazing—Crests Featuring Johnny Maestro (60)	12
This Is My Love—Passions (60)	5.8
Aisle—Roy Hamilton (57)	*0.0*
Brian SMITH ▶ 7379 (1)	**99**
Raise A Little Hell—Trooper (78)	199
Bruce A. SMITH ▶ 8123 (2)	**61**
Glide—Pleasure (79)	116
Let's Dance (Make Your Body Move)—West Street Mob (81)	30
Bud SMITH ▶ 11316 (1)	**2.3**
Cross Over—Jimmy Bowen With The Rhythm Orchids (57)	4.6
Carl M. SMITH ▶ 6127 (1)	**202**
Ten Thousand Drums—Carl Smith (59)	404
Carl William SMITH ▶ 713 (18)	**6113**
(Your Love Has Lifted Me) Higher And Higher—Rita Coolidge (77)	*5006*
Rescue Me—Fontella Bass (65)	*4146*
(Your Love Keeps Lifting Me) Higher And Higher—Jackie Wilson (67)	*2626*
Selfish One—Jackie Ross (64)	1658
We're Gonna Make It—Little Milton (65)	983
Recovery—Fontella Bass (65)	492
Who's Cheating Who?—Little Milton (65)	442
Jerk And Twine—Jackie Ross (65)	81
Because I Love You—Billy Stewart (66)	53
I've Got The Skill—Jackie Ross (64)	48
(The Story Of) Woman, Love And A Man (Part 1)—Tony Clarke (64)	35
Rescue Me—Cher (75)	*25*
Your People—Little Milton (65)	25
Rescue Me—Melissa Manchester (76)	*19*
Higher And Higher—Canada Goose (70)	*9.9*
In The Basement - Part 1—Etta James & Sugar Pie Desanto (66)	7.2
I'm Learnin'—Mary Wells (65)	2.3
Safe And Sound—Fontella Bass (66)	0.5
Chad SMITH ▶ 10605 (1)	**6.9**
Give It Away—Red Hot Chili Peppers (91)	28
Chris SMITH ▶ 7639 (1)	**83**
Ballin' The Jack—Georgia Gibbs (55)	167
Clarence SMITH ▶ 8855 (3)	**38**
Boogie Woogie—B. Bumble & The Stingers (61)	*34*
Pine Top's Boogie—Jo Stafford (59)	*3.6*
Boogie Woogie—Modernaires (57)	*1.9*
Claude SMITH ▶ 8675 (1)	**43**
In My Heart—Timetones (61)	86
Claydes SMITH ▶ 948 (33)	**4704**
Celebration—Kool & The Gang (80)	6016
Cherish—Kool & The Gang (85)	3699
Joanna—Kool & The Gang (83)	3511
Ladies Night—Kool & The Gang (79)	3414
Jungle Boogie—Kool & The Gang (73)	2506
Hollywood Swinging—Kool & The Gang (74)	2079
Summertime—DJ Jazzy Jeff & The Fresh Prince (91)	1783
Misled—Kool & The Gang (84)	1436
Get Down On It—Kool & The Gang (82)	1373
Fresh—Kool & The Gang (85)	1367
Victory—Kool & The Gang (86)	1269
Tonight—Kool & The Gang (84)	1136
Take My Heart (You Can Have It If You Want It)—Kool & The Gang (81)	1077
Stone Love—Kool & The Gang (87)	994
Emergency—Kool & The Gang (85)	915
Spirit Of The Boogie—Kool & The Gang (75)	825
Let's Go Dancin' (Ooh La, La, La)—Kool & The Gang (82)	654
Big Fun—Kool & The Gang (82)	532
Funky Stuff—Kool & The Gang (73)	473
Higher Plane—Kool & The Gang (74)	446
Kool And The Gang—Kool & The Gang (69)	329
Jones Vs. Jones—Kool & The Gang (81)	316
Caribbean Festival—Kool & The Gang (75)	268
Open Sesame - Part I—Kool & The Gang (76)	252
Rhyme Tyme People—Kool & The Gang (75)	182
Holiday—Kool & The Gang (87)	126
Let The Music Take Your Mind—Kool & The Gang (70)	85
Love And Understanding (Come Together)—Kool & The Gang (76)	48
Funky Man—Kool & The Gang (70)	41
The Gangs Back Again—Kool & The Gang (69)	37
Steppin' Out—Kool & The Gang (82)	6.6
Who's Gonna Take The Weight (Part One)—Kool & The Gang (71)	4.1
Summer Madness—Kool & The Gang (75)	0.0
Curt SMITH ▶ 1484 (2)	**2928**
Sowing The Seeds Of Love—Tears For Fears (89)	2998
Head Over Heels—Tears For Fears (85)	2858
Curtis SMITH ▶ 6196 (1)	**194**
Doctor Feel-Good—Dr. Feelgood And The Interns (62)	194
Debbie SMITH ▶ 7892 (1)	**71**
Is It Love That We're Missin'—Quincy Jones (75)	141
—Denise Katrina Smith see: Denise MATTHEWS	
Don SMITH ▶ 3741 (1)	**714**
Double Shot (Of My Baby's Love)—Swingin' Medallions (66)	1428
Eric SMITH [Free] ▶ 8169 (1)	**60**
All Nite—Entouch featuring Keith Sweat (90)	119
Ernestine SMITH ▶ 3606 (3)	**769**
Stranded In The Jungle—Cadets (56)	*810*
Stranded In The Jungle—Jayhawks (56)	*531*
Stranded In The Jungle—Gadabouts (56)	*198*
—Ethel Smith see: Elias McDANIEL	
Floyd SMITH ▶ 3936 (5)	**651**
There'll Come A Time—Betty Everett (69)	714
Since You Showed Me How To Be Happy—Jackie Wilson (67)	461
Could I Forget You—Tyrone Davis (71)	305
Love Is Funny That Way—Jackie Wilson (71)	99
Maybe—Betty Everett (69)	10
—Frances Octavia Smith see: Dale EVANS	
Frankie SMITH ▶ 4763 (1)	**422**
Double Dutch Bus—Frankie Smith (81)	843
Fred SMITH ▶ 1578 (19)	**2677**
The Duck—Jackie Lee (2) (65)	1646
Western Movies—Olympics (58)	1584
Peanut Butter—Marathons (61)	1099
Patti Ann—Johnny Crawford (62)	465
Dance By The Light Of The Moon—Olympics (60)	*428*
Spreadin' Honey—Watts 103rd Street Rhythm Band (67)	224
Hooray For The Salvation Army Band—Bill Cosby (67)	*171*
(Baby) Hully Gully—Olympics (60)	165
Baby, Do The Philly Dog—Olympics (66)	116
Your P-E-R-S-O-N-A-L-I-T-Y—Jackie Lee (2) (66)	113
Little Pedro—Olympics (61)	100
Dancin' Holiday—Olympics (63)	96
Dedicated (To The Songs I Love)—3 Friends (61)	80

Fred SMITH ▶ 1578 (19) *Continued*	**2677**
Hully Gully Again—Little Caesar And The Romans (61)	58
(I Wanna) Dance With The Teacher—Olympics (58)	26
Comic Book Crazy—Little Sammy Yates (59)	6.4
Grits 'N Corn Bread—Soul Runners (67)	3.3
Dooley—Olympics (61)	3.2
Private Eye—Olympics (59)	2.3
Frederick Dewey SMITH ▶ 8916 (1)	**36**
Kick Out The Jams—MC5 (69)	181
Gary SMITH ▶ 7099 (1)	**116**
Rockin' Into The Night—38 Special (79)	347
Gregory W. SMITH ▶ 7604 (1)	**86**
Bounce Back—Alisha (90)	172
Harry B. SMITH ▶ 7531 (2) HOF	**91**
The Sheik Of Araby (Italian Style)—Lou Monte (58)	259
Yours Is My Heart Alone—Enzo Stuarti (56)	17
Hazel SMITH ▶ 7952 (1)	**68**
(One More Year Of) Daddy's Little Girl—Ray Sawyer (76)	68
Herb SMITH ▶ 10100 (1)	**13**
The Very Best In You—Change (82)	26
Howard E. SMITH ▶ 11551 (1)	**1.2**
Love Lifted Me—Kenny Rogers (76)	2.4
Howard Russell SMITH ▶ 2348 (3)	**1571**
Third Rate Romance—Amazing Rhythm Aces (75)	1178
The End Is Not In Sight (The Cowboy Tune)—Amazing Rhythm Aces (76)	313
Amazing Grace (Used To Be Her Favorite Song)—Amazing Rhythm Aces (75)	80
Howlett SMITH ▶ 4761 (1)	**422**
Little Altar Boy—Vic Dana (61)	422
Huey P. SMITH ▶ 884 (12)	**5035**
Rockin' Pneumonia - Boogie Woogie Flu—Johnny Rivers (72)	*3059*
Sea Cruise—Frankie Ford (59)	*1598*
Don't You Just Know It—Huey (Piano) Smith And The Clowns (58)	*1140*
Birdland—Chubby Checker (63)	1076
Pop-Eye—Huey Smith (62)	394
Rockin' Pneumonia And The Boogie Woogie Flu—Huey Smith and The Clowns (57)	*112*
Don't You Just Know It—Fendermen (60)	*88*
Sea Cruise—Johnny Rivers (71)	*78*
Don't You Know Yockomo?—Huey "Piano" Smith with his Clowns (58)	67
Alimony—Frankie Ford (59)	28
Roberta—Bones (72)	27
Sea Cruise—John Fogerty (75)	*0.0*
Hurricane SMITH [Norman Arnold Smith] ▶ 1118 (1)	**3957**
Oh, Babe, What Would You Say?—Hurricane Smith (72)	3957
Jake SMITH ▶ 2445 (2)	**1483**
Hold You Tight—Tara Kemp (91)	3071
Piece Of My Heart—Tara Kemp (91)	1377
James SMITH ▶ 8532 (3)	**47**
Slippin' And Slidin' (Peepin' And Hidin')—Little Richard (56)	*180*
Slipin' And Slidin'—Sing Along With Jim And Monica (64)	*4.1*
Slippin' & Slidin'—Willie Mitchell (67)	*3.3*
—James Smith see: Jim DALE	
James Marcus SMITH [P.J. Proby] ▶ 7590 (2)	**87**
Ain't Gonna Kiss Ya—Ribbons (63)	63
Clown Shoes—Johnny Burnette (62)	24
James Milas SMITH ▶ 5496 (2)	**279**
Battle Hymn Of Lt. Calley—C Company Featuring Terry Nelson (71)	*530*
Battle Hymn Of Lt. Calley—John Deer (71)	*28*
James O. SMITH ▶ 4123 (5)	**586**
Prayer Meetin'—Willie Mitchell (68)	281
I Promise To Remember—Frankie Lymon and the Teenagers (56)	*231*
Back At The Chicken Shack, Part I—Jimmy Smith (63)	114
Midnight Special Part 1—Jimmy Smith (62)	75
I Promise—Jimmy Castor & The Juniors (56)	*0.0*
James Todd SMITH [LL Cool J] ▶ 2484 (8)	**1445**
Around The Way Girl—LL Cool J (90)	1305
I Need Love—LL Cool J (87)	765
I'm That Type Of Guy—LL Cool J (89)	696

Mama Said Knock You Out—LL Cool J (91)	473
Going Back To Cali—LL Cool J (88)	429
The Boomin' System—LL Cool J (90)	267
I'm Bad—LL Cool J (87)	18
6 Minutes Of Pleasure—LL Cool J (91)	2.6
Jerald Leroy SMITH ▶ 3335 (1)	**895**
Last Night—Mar-Keys (61)	4476
Jerry Dean SMITH ▶ 1986 (4)	**2032**
(Down At) Papa Joe's—Dixiebelles (63)	1842
Truck Stop—Jerry Smith and his Pianos (69)	173
Drivin' Home—Jerry Smith (70)	9.9
Sweet 'N' Sassy—Jerry Smith (69)	6.0
Jesse SMITH ▶ 5823 (2)	**239**
I Do (Live Version)—J. Geils Band (82)	*637*
I Do—Marvelows (65)	*556*
—Jewel Faye Smith see: Sammi SMITH	
John Robert SMITH ▶ 1286 (3)	**3455**
I Can't Wait—Nu Shooz (86)	2841
Point Of No Return—Nu Shooz (86)	764
Should I Say Yes?—Nu Shooz (88)	463
Johnny SMITH ▶ 572 (2)	**7565**
Walk Don't Run—Ventures (60)	*5836*
Walk--Don't Run '64—Ventures (64)	*1729*
Joseph SMITH III ▶ 10540 (1)	**7.5**
Action Speaks Louder Than Words—Chocolate Milk (75)	67
Keely SMITH [Dorothy Jacqueline Keely] ▶ 11665 (1)	**0.8**
When Somebody Loves You—Frank Sinatra (65)	2.3
—Kim Smith see: Kim WILDE	
Larry Edward SMITH ▶ 7264 (1)	**107**
Take It Slow (Out In The Country)—Lighthouse (71)	320
Lawrence SMITH ▶ 8632 (3)	**44**
Rappin' Rodney—Rodney Dangerfield (83)	140
The Breaks (Part 1)—Kurtis Blow (80)	94
Friends—Whodini (85)	11
Lewis SMITH ▶ 11159 (1)	**3.0**
Snap-Out—Interpertations (69)	8.9
—Linda Cheryl Smith see: Cheryl LYNN	
Lloyd SMITH ▶ 6230 (3)	**191**
Sad Girl—Intruders (69)	*367*
Sad Girl—GQ (82)	*15*
Sad Girl—Jay Wiggins (63)	*0.9*
Lloyd Ed SMITH ▶ 6887 (9)	**131**
Shake Your Rump To The Funk—Bar-Kays (76)	593
Move Your Boogie Body—Bar-Kays (79)	270
Today Is The Day—Bar-Kays (80)	150
Freakshow On The Dance Floor—Bar-Kays (84)	79
Too Hot To Stop—Bar-Kays (77)	36
Hit And Run—Bar-Kays (81)	23
Boogie Body Land—Bar-Kays (81)	23
Let's Have Some Fun—Bar-Kays (78)	8.9
Shine—Bar-Kays (79)	7.7
—Lon Christian Smith see: Chris CHRISTIAN	
Louis SMITH ▶ 7366 (1)	**100**
Get It From The Bottom—Steelers (69)	300
Lynn Marie SMITH ▶ 8700 (1)	**42**
I Just Can't Control Myself—Nature's Divine (79)	127
Marion SMITH ▶ 6207 (3)	**193**
Leave Me Alone (Let Me Cry)—Dicky Doo And The Don'ts (58)	257
Flip Top Box—Dicky Doo And The Don'ts (58)	75
Teardrops Will Fall—Dicky Doo And The Don'ts (59)	66
Marshall SMITH ▶ 5770 (1)	**244**
Street Corner Serenade—Wet Willie (77)	731
Marvin SMITH ▶ 6382 (3)	**176**
I'm Gonna Miss You—Artistics (66)	479
Time Stopped—Marvin Smith (66)	33
Remember The Rain?—21st Century (75)	0.4
Michael Larry SMITH [Michael Lovesmith] ▶ 6232 (2)	**191**
All I Do Is Think Of You—Troop (90)	198
Let's Be Young Tonight—Jermaine Jackson (76)	184
Michael Lee SMITH ▶ 6102 (6)	**206**
Cherry Baby—Starz (77)	510
Sing It, Shout It—Starz (77)	148
So Young, So Bad—Starz (78)	65
(Any Way That You Want It) I'll Be There—Starz (78)	26
Hold On To The Night—Starz (78)	18

(She's Just A) Fallen Angel—Starz (76)	6.5
Michael W. SMITH ▶ 3042 (4)	**1039**
Place In This World—Michael W. Smith (91)	2042
Find A Way—Amy Grant (85)	555
For You—Michael W. Smith (91)	241
Lead Me On—Amy Grant (88)	2.7
Mike SMITH ▶ 659 (6)	**6633**
Bits And Pieces—Dave Clark Five (64)	4088
Glad All Over—Dave Clark Five (64)	3143
Can't You See That She's Mine—Dave Clark Five (64)	2823
Try Too Hard—Dave Clark Five (66)	1282
Come Home—Dave Clark Five (65)	1101
Please Tell Me Why—Dave Clark Five (66)	830
Milton SMITH ▶ 11429 (1)	**1.7**
It's A Funky Thing-Right On (Part 1)—Herbie Mann (69)	5.2
Mira SMITH ▶ 2553 (11)	**1392**
Reconsider Me—Johnny Adams (69)	*820*
Soulshake—Peggy Scott & Jo Jo Benson (69)	*539*
The Girl Most Likely—Jeannie C. Riley (68)	427
Soul Shake—Delaney & Bonnie & Friends (70)	*392*
Oh, Singer—Jeannie C. Riley (71)	236
Buffalo Soldier—Flamingos (70)	165
There Never Was A Time—Jeannie C. Riley (69)	137
Reconsider Me—Narvel Felts (75)	*53*
I Can't Be All Bad—Johnny Adams (69)	34
The Wedding Cake—Connie Francis (69)	28
I Almost Called Your Name—Margaret Whiting (67)	8.1
Monnie SMITH ▶ 9731 (1)	**18**
Get Down—Harvey Scales & The 7 Sounds (67)	54
Nathaniel SMITH ▶ 11829 (1)	**0.0**
You Brought About A Change In Me—Jackie Wilson (68)	0.0
Neal SMITH ▶ 3005 (5)	**1072**
School's Out—Alice Cooper (72)	*2297*
Eighteen—Alice Cooper (71)	1021
Elected—Alice Cooper (72)	776
Teenage Lament '74—Alice Cooper (73)	465
School's Out—Krokus (86)	*104*
Nick SMITH ▶ 10659 (1)	**6.3**
Teenage Vows Of Love—Dreamers (61)	19
—Norman Arnold Smith see: Hurricane SMITH	
Pat SMITH ▶ 11830 (1)	**0.0**
Kewpie Doll—Jim Lowe (58)	0.0
Patti SMITH ▶ 3949 (3)	**644**
Because The Night—Patti Smith Group (78)	1235
Shooting Shark—Blue Öyster Cult (84)	18
Frederick—Patti Smith Group (79)	17
—Penny Smith see: Debbie DEAN	
Ray Anthony SMITH ▶ 11311 (1)	**2.3**
Freedom—Grandmaster Flash And The Furious 5 (80)	21
Raymond SMITH ▶ 9174 (1)	**29**
Fifteen Years Ago—Conway Twitty (70)	29
Raymond Barry SMITH ▶ 7820 (2)	**74**
Big Time Operator—Keith Hampshire (73)	145
Warmin' Up The Band—Don Everly (74)	6.6
—Reginald Leonard Smith see: Marty WILDE	
Richard B. SMITH ▶ 9867 (2)	**16**
Winter Wonderland—Andrews Sisters (54)	*16*
Winter Wonderland—Ames Brothers (55)	*16*
Richard David SMITH [Rick Smith] ▶ 7944 (2)	**68**
Stand Up—Underworld (89)	119
Underneath The Radar—Underworld (88)	85
—Rick Smith see: Richard David SMITH	
—Rickey Smith see: Ricky Darnell SMITH	
—Ricky Smith see: Ricky WILDE	
Ricky Darnell SMITH [Rickey Smith] ▶ 6810 (3)	**135**
Make That Move—Shalamar (81)	198
Save The Overtime (For Me)—Gladys Knight & The Pips (83)	179
I've Just Begun To Love You—Dynasty (80)	67
Robert James SMITH [Robert Smith] ▶ 3542 (10)	**792**
Love Song—Cure (89)	2408
Just Like Heaven—Cure (87)	604
Why Can't I Be You?—Cure (87)	279
Fascination Street—Cure (89)	194
Lullaby—Cure (89)	170

Robert James SMITH [Robert Smith] ▶ 3542 (10) *Continued*	**792**
Pictures Of You—Cure (90)	105
Close To Me—Cure (90)	101
Hot Hot Hot!!!—Cure (88)	88
Never Enough—Cure (90)	68
In Between Days—Cure (86)	0.8
Robert T. SMITH ▶ 3007 (1)	**1071**
Shimmy Shimmy Ko Ko Bop—Little Anthony And The Imperials (59)	1071
Robert William SMITH ▶ 7993 (2)	**66**
Good Old Rock 'N Roll—Cat Mother And The All Night News Boys (69)	164
Can You Dance To It?—Cat Mother And The All Night News Boys (69)	33
Robin SMITH ▶ 7826 (1)	**73**
All Fall Down—Five Star (85)	146
Roland SMITH ▶ 11547 (1)	**1.2**
Where Is Johnny Now—Sapphires (63)	1.2
Ronnie SMITH ▶ 11558 (1)	**1.2**
Strong Enough To Be Gentle—Black Oak Arkansas (76)	8.4
Sammi SMITH [Jewel Faye Smith] ▶ 9901 (1)	**15**
Kentucky—Sammi Smith (72)	15
Samuel SMITH ▶ 6367 (1)	**178**
Chop Chop Boom—Crew-Cuts (55)	356
Shanon SMITH ▶ 6637 (1)	**149**
I Want You, I Need You—Chris Christian (81)	446
Stacy SMITH [Acacia Smith] ▶ 5351 (3)	**301**
When We Kiss—Bardeux (88)	411
I Love The Bass—Bardeux (89)	168
Magic Carpet Ride—Bardeux (88)	80
Sylvia SMITH ▶ 7364 (1)	**100**
Great Gosh A'mighty—Little Richard (86)	300
Thomassina SMITH [Toni Smith, Thomassina Carrollyne Smith] ▶ 9042 (3)	**33**
Thighs High (Grip Your Hips And Move)—Tom Browne (81)	49
Funkin' For Jamaica (N.Y.)—Tom Browne (80)	35
Theme From S-Express—S-Express (88)	14
—Thomassina Carrollyne Smith see: Thomassina SMITH	
—Toni Smith see: Thomassina SMITH	
Tweed SMITH [Alice Tweed Smyth] ▶ 11526 (1)	**1.3**
Good, Good Feelin'—War (79)	12
V. Jeffrey SMITH ▶ 3434 (1)	**850**
The Promise Of A New Day—Paula Abdul (91)	3398
Victor Gabriel SMITH ▶ 4459 (1)	**491**
With Your Love—Jefferson Starship (76)	1472
Will SMITH [Fresh Prince, Willard Christopher Smith Jr.] ▶ 3432 (5)	**850**
Summertime—DJ Jazzy Jeff & The Fresh Prince (91)	1783
Parents Just Don't Understand—D.J. Jazzy Jeff & The Fresh Prince (88)	1067
A Nightmare On My Street—D.J. Jazzy Jeff & The Fresh Prince (88)	778
Girls Ain't Nothing But Trouble—D.J. Jazzy Jeff & The Fresh Prince (88)	241
I Think I Can Beat Mike Tyson—D.J. Jazzy Jeff & The Fresh Prince (89)	79
William Daniel SMITH ▶ 3646 (3)	**752**
When I Die—Motherlode (69)	1495
Saved By The Grace Of Your Love—Sons Of Champlin (77)	7.6
I Need You—Maurice White (86)	2.4
Zack SMITH ▶ 4150 (3)	**580**
Love's Got A Line On You—Scandal (83)	414
Beat Of A Heart—Scandal Featuring Patty Smyth (85)	373
Goodbye To You—Scandal (82)	248
Myrna SMITH-SCHILLING ▶ 9845 (1)	**16**
It's Gettin' Late—Beach Boys (85)	48
John SMITHSON ▶ 8638 (1)	**44**
Wait For You—Bonham (89)	221
Micheal SMOTHERMAN ▶ 4453 (3)	**492**
Can You Fool—Glen Campbell (78)	402
I Don't Want To Know Your Name—Glen Campbell (81)	89
I Just Can't Turn My Habit Into Love—Buckwheat (73)	0.4
—Alice Tweed Smyth see: Tweed SMITH	
—Carl Smyth see: Charles SMYTH	

Charles SMYTH [Cathal Joseph Patrick Smyth, Carl Smyth] ▶ 5333 (1)	**303**
Our House—Madness (83)	2122
Patty SMYTH ▶ 6467 (2)	**166**
Beat Of A Heart—Scandal Featuring Patty Smyth (85)	373
Never Enough—Patty Smyth (87)	206
Carl J. SNARE ▶ 2464 (3)	**1459**
Love Of A Lifetime—Firehouse (91)	2055
Don't Treat Me Bad—Firehouse (91)	976
All She Wrote—Firehouse (91)	374
Lester SNELL ▶ 5958 (1)	**223**
From His Woman To You—Barbara Mason (74)	446
Dee SNIDER ▶ 3364 (2)	**881**
We're Not Gonna Take It—Twisted Sister (84)	773
I Wanna Rock—Twisted Sister (84)	107
Hank SNOW ▶ 2659 (4)	**1289**
I'm Movin' On—Ray Charles And His Orchestra (59)	*492*
I'm Movin' On—Matt Lucas (63)	*472*
I'm Movin' On—John Kay (72)	*325*
I'm Movin' On—Don Gibson (59)	*0.0*
Phoebe SNOW [Phoebe Ann Laub] ▶ 1663 (2)	**2530**
Poetry Man—Phoebe Snow (75)	2518
Harpo's Blues—Phoebe Snow (75)	12
Tom SNOW ▶ 254 (22)	**13444**
Let's Hear It For The Boy—Deniece Williams (84)	5139
Don't Know Much—Linda Ronstadt (89)	*4540*
He's So Shy—Pointer Sisters (80)	4023
You Should Hear How She Talks About You—Melissa Manchester (82)	3680
Make A Move On Me—Olivia Newton-John (82)	2305
After All (Love Theme From CHANCES ARE)—Cher and Peter Cetera (89)	1696
If Ever You're In My Arms Again—Peabo Bryson (84)	1625
Deeper Than The Night—Olivia Newton-John (79)	818
You—Rita Coolidge (78)	737
Alibis—Sergio Mendes (84)	727
Gettin' Ready For Love—Diana Ross (77)	598
Somewhere Down The Road—Barry Manilow (81)	590
Livin' In Desperate Times—Olivia Newton-John (84)	440
So Far So Good—Sheena Easton (86)	377
Staying With It—Firefall (81)	320
Thunder In My Heart—Leo Sayer (77)	319
You Might Need Somebody—Turley Richards (80)	173
All I Need To Know (Don't Know Much)—Bette Midler (83)	*59*
It's Really You—Tarney/Spencer Band (78)	30
Don't Know Much—Bill Medley (81)	*22*
All The Right Moves—Jennifer Warnes/Chris Thompson (83)	22
Piece By Piece—Tubes (85)	10
George SNOWHILL ▶ 8451 (1)	**50**
Hot Potato (Mambo)—Jayne and Audrey Meadows (55)	100
Arthur SNYDER ▶ 3455 (4)	**840**
I Am Somebody Part II—Johnnie Taylor (70)	527
Toast To The Fool—Dramatics (72)	402
Stop Doggin' Me—Johnnie Taylor (72)	85
Doing My Own Thing (Part I)—Johnnie Taylor (The Soul Philosopher) (72)	84
Eddie SNYDER [Kay Rogers] ▶ 460 (30)	**9060**
A Hundred Pounds Of Clay—Gene McDaniels (61)	7256
Strangers In The Night—Frank Sinatra (66)	6342
What Will Mary Say—Johnny Mathis (63)	2198
Spanish Eyes—Al Martino (65)	*1721*
Girl With The Golden Braids—Perry Como (57)	770
Rusty Bells—Brenda Lee (65)	713
Games That Lovers Play—Eddie Fisher (66)	*696*
Talk To Me—Frank Sinatra (59)	656
The Wheel Of Hurt—Margaret Whiting (66)	*614*
Making Memories—Frankie Laine (67)	564
The Wheel Of Hurt—Al Martino (66)	*411*
Can I Trust You?—Bachelors (66)	366
Runnin' Out Of Fools—Aretha Franklin (64)	336
Mr. Songwriter—Connie Stevens (62)	335
Ten Lonely Guys—Pat Boone (62)	*317*
Come Back—Johnny Mathis (63)	286
People Like You—Eddie Fisher (67)	107
Games That Lovers Play—Wayne Newton (66)	*91*
Ten Lonely Guys—Ten Broken Hearts (62)	*81*
Remember When—Wayne Newton (65)	80

Bitter With The Sweet—Billy Eckstine (56)	69
Operator—Gladys Knight & The Pips (62)	59
It All Started With Your Kiss—Micki Marlo (57)	54
When The Snow Is On The Roses—Ed Ames (67)	52
Love Theme From "Romeo And Juliet" (A Time For Us)—Johnny Mathis (69)	*30*
Insult To Injury—Timi Yuro (63)	24
In Between Tears—Lenny Miles (61)	13
Hurry Up And Tell Me—Paul Anka (63)	5.4
Ancient History—Les Brown and His Band of Renown (56)	4.6
More Than A Miracle—Roger Williams (67)	0.5
Michael SNYDER ▶ 7996 (1)	**66**
Tip Of My Tongue—Tubes (83)	198
Ted SNYDER ▶ 2285 (3) HOF	**1652**
Who's Sorry Now—Connie Francis (58)	*4383*
Who's Sorry Now—Marie Osmond (75)	*314*
The Sheik Of Araby (Italian Style)—Lou Monte (58)	259
Brian SOARES [Brian Douglas Blanchard] ▶ 9776 (1)	**17**
Dancing In My Sleep—Secret Ties (86)	17
—Michael Anthony Sobolewski see: Michael ANTHONY	
Joe SOBOTKA ▶ 4824 (1)	**405**
Let Love Come Between Us—James & Bobby Purify (67)	809
Gino SOCCIO ▶ 6393 (1)	**175**
Dancer—Gino Soccio (79)	175
Marcy SOCKEL [Marcy Jo] ▶ 6618 (1)	**150**
Ronnie—Marcy Joe (61)	150
Bill SODEN ▶ 10455 (1)	**8.2**
Father Come On Home—Pacific Gas & Electric (70)	8.2
—Piero Soffici see: Pietro SOFFICI	
Pietro SOFFICI [Piero Soffici] ▶ 8190 (3)	**59**
That's The Way With Love—Piero Soffici (61)	*135*
That's The Way With Love—Don Costa And His Orchestra And Chorus (61)	*27*
Dear Gesu Bambino—Christian Morandi (61)	9.7
Jim SOFIA ▶ 8480 (1)	**49**
Didn't It Look So Easy—Stairsteps (71)	146
—Isadore Soifer see: Alex NORTH	
Chris SOLBERG ▶ 6325 (4)	**182**
You Know That I Love You—Santana (79)	554
Can't Keep A Good Man Down—Eddie Money (79)	106
Searchin'—Santana (81)	19
All I Ever Wanted—Santana (80)	10
Walter SOLEK ▶ 6324 (1)	**182**
Who Stole The Keeshka?—Matys Bros. (63)	364
Phil SOLEM ▶ 4028 (3)	**620**
Just The Way It Is, Baby—Rembrandts (91)	1055
Someone—Rembrandts (91)	161
Save Me—Rembrandts (91)	25
Mike SOLES ▶ 9850 (1)	**16**
Lady Love—Klowns (70)	32
Steve SOLES ▶ 9851 (1)	**16**
Lady Love—Klowns (70)	32
Joe SOLIERI ▶ 10876 (1)	**4.7**
When Your Old Wedding Ring Was New—Bruce Hayes with Mary Mayo (60)	14
Max SOLIS ▶ 10670 (1)	**6.2**
To Say You're Mine—DeCastro Sisters (55)	19
Pete SOLLEY ▶ 3537 (1)	**793**
Talking In Your Sleep—Romantics (83)	3966
Bernard SOLOMON [J. Baird] ▶ 6627 (2)	**150**
How Can I Forget—Jimmy Holiday (63)	*389*
How Can I Forget—Ben E. King (63)	*60*
—Fudgie Kae Solomon see: Fudgie KAE	
—Herbert Jay Solomon see: Herbie MANN	
James SOLOMON ▶ 5065 (3)	**351**
This Can't Be True—Eddie Holman (66)	437
Don't Stop Now—Eddie Holman (70)	260
Am I A Loser—Eddie Holman (66)	4.3
Vasilj SOLOVEV-SEDOJ ▶ 1684 (2)	**2490**
Midnight In Moscow—Kenny Ball And His Jazzmen (62)	*4981*
Midnight In Moscow—Jan Burgens & His New Orleans Syncopators (62)	*0.0*

Sy SOLOWAY ▶ 5287 (4)	**313**
Lips Of Wine—Andy Williams (57)	598
Carefree Wanderer—Bill Parsons with The All-American Boy's (59)	30
Now You Know—Little Willie John (61)	6.3
Sparkelin' Eyes—Dean Martin (61)	1.6
Belouis SOME [Neville Keighley] ▶ 7268 (2)	**106**
Some People—Belouis Some (85)	90
Imagination—Belouis Some (85)	16
Dave SOMERVILLE ▶ 10908 (1)	**4.4**
Trouble Maker—Lee Hazlewood (69)	8.9
Jimmy SOMERVILLE ▶ 6512 (1)	**161**
Smalltown Boy—Bronski Beat (84)	484
Michael SOMERVILLE ▶ 5867 (2)	**235**
Never Been Any Reason—Head East (75)	150
Love Me Tonight—Head East (76)	85
Bert SOMMER ▶ 4181 (2)	**572**
And Suddenly—Cherry People (68)	442
We're All Playing In The Same Band—Bert Sommer (70)	351
John Martin SOMMERS ▶ 962 (1)	**4659**
Thank God I'm A Country Boy—John Denver (75)	4659
Stephen SONDHEIM ▶ 1183 (11) HOF	**3752**
Tonight—Ferrante & Teicher (61)	*2067*
Small World—Johnny Mathis (59)	1090
Send In The Clowns—Judy Collins (77)	*868*
Somewhere—Len Barry (66)	*857*
Somewhere (From West Side Story)—Barbra Streisand (85)	*378*
Send In The Clowns—Judy Collins (75)	*372*
Tonight—Eddie Fisher (61)	*339*
Maria—Johnny Mathis (60)	*170*
Somewhere—P.J. Proby (65)	*94*
Maria—Johnny Mathis (61)	*30*
Tonight—Jay & The Americans (61)	*0.0*
David SONENBERG ▶ 10712 (1)	**5.9**
Love On The Phone—Suzanne Fellini (80)	24
—Frank Sorgatz see: Frank MERTENS	
Anna SOSENKO ▶ 2199 (1)	**1751**
Darling Je Vous Aime Beaucoup—Nat "King" Cole (55)	1751
Greg SOTEBEER ▶ 9997 (1)	**14**
Victory Line—Limited Warranty (86)	71
Pepe Luis SOTO ▶ 3420 (2)	**856**
Superman—Herbie Mann (79)	*654*
Superman—Celi Bee & The Buzzy Bunch (77)	*202*
George SOULE ▶ 5257 (4)	**317**
Shoes—Brook Benton With The Dixie Flyers (70)	285
I'll Be Your Everything—Percy Sledge (74)	145
After The Feeling Is Gone—Five Flights Up (70)	*50*
After The Feeling Is Gone—Lulu With The Dixie Flyers (70)	*9.9*
—Soeur Sourire see: Jeanine DECKERS	
Phil SOUSSAN ▶ 8645 (1)	**44**
Shot In The Dark—Ozzy Osbourne (86)	88
Simon SOUSSAN [Michael Saint Simon] ▶ 9482 (1)	**23**
Love And Desire (Part I)—Arpeggio (79)	69
—Joseph Alfred Souter see: Joe SOUTH	
Joe SOUTH [Joseph Alfred Souter] ▶ 78 (30)	**27967**
Yo-Yo—Osmonds (71)	5693
Rose Garden—Lynn Anderson (70)	*5684*
Hush—Deep Purple (68)	*3508*
Down In The Boondocks—Billy Joe Royal (65)	2305
Games People Play—Joe South (68)	2053
Walk A Mile In My Shoes—Joe South And The Believers (69)	1667
I Knew You When—Billy Joe Royal (65)	*1430*
Birds Of A Feather—Raiders (71)	*1026*
I Beg Your Pardon—Kon Kan (88)	849
Don't It Make You Want To Go Home—Joe South And The Believers (69)	*609*
I've Got To Be Somebody—Billy Joe Royal (65)	560
I Knew You When—Linda Ronstadt (82)	*501*
Don't It Make You Want To Go Home—Brook Benton With The Dixie Flyers (70)	*381*
Children—Joe South (70)	330
Hush—Billy Joe Royal (67)	*322*
These Are Not My People—Johnny Rivers (69)	311
How Can I Unlove You—Lynn Anderson (71)	267
Untie Me—Tams (62)	247
The Greatest Love—Dorsey Burnette (69)	221
Hush—Blue Swede (75)	*92*
Leanin' On You—Joe South (69)	65
All My Hard Times—Joe Simon (71)	65
Fool Me—Joe South (71)	52
I Knew You When—Donny Osmond (71)	*47*
Pollyanna—Classics (1) (66)	32
She's Almost You—Billy Harner (69)	27
Heart's Desire—Billy Joe Royal (66)	26
Birds Of A Feather—Joe South (68)	*10*
Silly Little Girl—Tams (64)	6.7
Rose Garden—Dobie Gray (69)	*3.3*
J.D. SOUTHER ▶ 644 (9) HOF	**6766**
Heartache Tonight—Eagles (79)	4547
Best Of My Love—Eagles (74)	4142
New Kid In Town—Eagles (76)	4051
You're Only Lonely—J.D. Souther (79)	2141
Her Town Too—James Taylor And J.D. Souther (81)	1187
The Heart Of The Matter—Don Henley (90)	820
James Dean—Eagles (74)	125
If Anybody Had A Heart—John Waite (86)	98
White Rhythm And Blues—J.D. Souther (80)	7.9
Hal SOUTHERN [Francis H. Clark, Hal Clark, Hal Sothern] ▶ 4699 (1)	**435**
I Dreamed Of A Hill-Billy Heaven—Tex Ritter (61)	870
—Peter Alexander Southworth see: Peter SHELLEY	
—Rachel Southworth see: Rachel BOLAN	
Charles SOUZA [B. Masona] ▶ 9177 (1)	**29**
Wednesday—Royal Guardsmen (67)	29
Red SOVINE [Woodrow Wilson Sovine] ▶ 3989 (3)	**629**
Missing You—Ray Peterson (61)	994
Teddy Bear—Red Sovine (76)	478
Giddyup Go—Red Sovine (66)	25
Kenny SOWDER ▶ 3064 (1)	**1027**
Lonely Street—Andy Williams (59)	3082
Rosa SOY ▶ 5937 (1)	**225**
Rico Suave—Gerardo (91)	1126
Norman SPAN [King Radio] ▶ 3736 (2)	**716**
Twistin' Matilda (and the channel)—Jimmy Soul (62)	1194
Man Smart, Woman Smarter—Robert Palmer (76)	119
Wallace SPAN ▶ 11638 (1)	**0.9**
Faith—Wallace Brothers (64)	0.9
Ernie SPANO ▶ 10357 (1)	**9.6**
Walk On With The Duke—Duke Of Earl (62)	86
Aaron SPARKS ▶ 7611 (3)	**85**
Every Day—Patti Page (55)	*134*
Every Day I Have The Blues—Billy Stewart (67)	*122*
Every Day—Count Basie And His Orchestra (55)	*0.0*
June SPARKS ▶ 10932 (1)	**4.3**
What's Happening To Me—Dale & Grace (64)	4.3
—Lloyd A. Sparks see: Randy SPARKS	
Milton SPARKS [Milton Gant] ▶ 7612 (3)	**85**
Every Day—Patti Page (55)	*134*
Every Day I Have The Blues—Billy Stewart (67)	*122*
Every Day—Count Basie And His Orchestra (55)	*0.0*
Randy SPARKS [Lloyd A. Sparks] ▶ 1797 (6)	**2296**
Green, Green—New Christy Minstrels (63)	1340
Today—New Christy Minstrels (64)	*1109*
Saturday Night—New Christy Minstrels (63)	454
Walkin' The Low Road—Randy Sparks (58)	37
Today—Jimmie Rodgers (68)	*21*
Silly Ol' Summertime—New Christy Minstrels (64)	8.6
Willie SPARKS ▶ 11771 (1)	**0.1**
Memphis Train—Buddy Miles Express (69)	0.4
Woodrow SPARROW ▶ 8162 (5)	**60**
Kool And The Gang—Kool & The Gang (69)	329
Let The Music Take Your Mind—Kool & The Gang (70)	85
Funky Man—Kool & The Gang (70)	41
The Gangs Back Again—Kool & The Gang (69)	37
Who's Gonna Take The Weight (Part One)—Kool & The Gang (71)	4.1
Anne SPEAR [Anne Spear Johnson] ▶ 10261 (1)	**11**
Only The Broken Hearted—Bob Beckham (60)	21
Abner SPECTOR ▶ 2143 (1)	**1821**
Smoky Places—Corsairs Featuring The Voice Of Jay "Bird" Uzzell (61)	1821
—Lona Spector see: Lona STEVENS	
Phil SPECTOR ▶ 61 (62) HOF	**34804**
You've Lost That Lovin' Feelin'—Righteous Brothers (64)	*9450*
To Know Him Is To Love Him—Teddy Bears (58)	*8631*
Chapel Of Love—Dixie Cups (64)	*8316*
Be My Baby—Ronettes (63)	*6059*
Spanish Harlem—Aretha Franklin (71)	*4882*
Da Doo Ron Ron—Shaun Cassidy (77)	*4512*
Da Doo Ron Ron (When He Walked Me Home)—Crystals (63)	*3838*
Baby, I Love You—Andy Kim (69)	*2808*
Then He Kissed Me—Crystals (63)	2734
Take Me Home Tonight—Eddie Money (86)	2098
Spanish Harlem—Ben E. King (60)	*2014*
Second Hand Love—Connie Francis (62)	2008
Black Pearl—Sonny Charles And The Checkmates, Ltd. (69)	1971
Just Once In My Life—Righteous Brothers (65)	1850
You've Lost That Lovin' Feeling—Daryl Hall & John Oates (80)	*1839*
Walkin' In The Rain—Jay And The Americans (69)	*1583*
You've Lost That Lovin' Feeling—Dionne Warwick (69)	*1346*
River Deep-Mountain High—Supremes & Four Tops (70)	*1281*
Be My Baby—Andy Kim (70)	*1212*
There's No Other (Like My Baby)—Crystals (61)	1172
I Can Hear Music—Beach Boys (69)	*916*
Walking In The Rain—Ronettes (64)	*887*
Baby, I Love You—Ronettes (63)	*719*
To Know You Is To Love You—Bobby Vinton (69)	*685*
Wait 'til My Bobby Gets Home—Darlene Love (63)	657
Why Do Lovers Break Each Other's Heart?—Bob B. Soxx And The Blue Jeans (63)	584
To Know You Is To Love You—Peter And Gordon (65)	*580*
Do I Love You?—Ronettes (64)	*462*
(Today I Met) The Boy I'm Gonna Marry—Darlene Love (63)	432
(The Best Part Of) Breakin' Up—Ronettes (64)	369
River Deep-Mountain High—Deep Purple (69)	*351*
Hung On You—Righteous Brothers (65)	321
Love Is All I Have To Give—Checkmates, Ltd. (69)	297
Born To Be Together—Ronettes Featuring Veronica (65)	252
Ecstasy—Ben E. King (62)	250
You've Lost That Lovin' Feelin'—Roberta Flack & Donny Hathaway (71)	*248*
Be My Boy—Paris Sisters (61)	214
Oh Why—Teddy Bears (59)	202
A Fine Fine Boy—Darlene Love (63)	184
First Taste Of Love—Ben E. King (60)	173
Not Too Young To Get Married—Bob B. Soxx And The Blue Jeans (63)	171
Young Boy Blues—Ben E. King (61)	160
Is This What I Get For Loving You?—Ronettes Featuring Veronica (65)	74
A Woman's Story—Cher (74)	60
Do I Love You?—Magic Ring (68)	*56*
Spanish Harlem—Santo & Johnny (62)	*30*
Be My Baby—Cissy Houston (71)	*24*
River Deep-Mountain High—Ike & Tina Turner (66)	*23*
Little Boy—Crystals (64)	22
You Came, You Saw, You Conquered!—Ronettes, featuring Veronica (69)	18
You've Lost That Lovin' Feelin'—Long John Baldry & Kathi MacDonald (79)	*16*
Spanish Harlem—King Curtis (65)	*15*
All Grown Up—Crystals (64)	14
Some Of Your Lovin'—Johnny Nash (61)	12
Da Doo Ron Ron (When He Walked Me Home)—Ian Matthews (72)	*7.8*
I Wonder—Butterflys (65)	7.3
I Can Hear Music—Ronettes Featuring Veronica (66)	*5.6*
I Don't Need You Anymore—Teddy Bears (59)	3.2
River Deep-Mountain High—Ike & Tina Turner (69)	*3.1*
If You Only Knew—Teddy Bears (59)	1.9
Chapel Of Love—Bette Midler (73)	*0.0*
To Know Him, Is To Love Him—Cathy Carr (58)	*0.0*
Judson SPENCE ▶ 5636 (1)	**262**
Yeah, Yeah, Yeah—Judson Spence (88)	524
Lew SPENCE ▶ 4436 (6)	**495**
Ol' Mac Donald—Frank Sinatra (60)	*604*
Nice 'N' Easy—Frank Sinatra (60)	399

Lew SPENCE ► 4436 (6) *Continued*	**495**
Half As Lovely (Twice As True)—Frank Sinatra (54)	234
Sentimental Baby—Frank Sinatra (61)	119
So Long My Love—Frank Sinatra (57)	75
Never Be Afraid— Bing Crosby with The Arthur Norman Choir (57)	50
Skip SPENCE [Alexander Spence] ► 6898 (2)	**130**
Omaha—Moby Grape (67)	75
My Best Friend—Jefferson Airplane (67)	55
Carl SPENCER ► 2678 (6)	**1278**
Let The Little Girl Dance—Billy Bland (60)	2182
Tell Me Baby—Garnet Mimms (64)	139
My Block—Four Pennies (63)	130
Deep In The Heart Of Harlem—Clyde McPhatter (64)	*112*
Yesterday's Hero—Gene Pitney (64)	66
Deep In The Heart Of Harlem—Walter Jackson (67)	*3.3*
Casey SPENCER ► 3892 (1)	**666**
I'm A Happy Man—Jive Five (65)	666
—Charles Spencer see: Randy BACHMAN	
Donnell SPENCER ► 5932 (2)	**226**
Turned Away—Chuckii Booker (89)	329
Say You Really Want Me—Kim Wilde (87)	184
Judy SPENCER ► 7911 (2)	**70**
Soft Summer Breeze—Diamonds (56)	*140*
Soft Summer Breeze— Romaine Brown & His Romaines (56)	*0.0*
Kevin SPENCER ► 6775 (2)	**138**
Make That Move—Shalamar (81)	198
Take That To The Bank—Shalamar (78)	144
Marty SPENCER ► 3363 (3)	**881**
This House—Tracie Spencer (90)	2330
Tender Kisses—Tracie Spencer (91)	318
This Time Make It Funky—Tracie Spencer (91)	123
Pete SPENCER ► 8810 (1)	**39**
Run To Me—Savoy Brown (81)	78
Richard SPENCER ► 1776 (1)	**2340**
Color Him Father—Winstons (69)	2340
Robert SPENCER ► 2883 (2)	**1133**
My Boy Lollipop—Millie Small (64)	4215
Wow Wow Wee (He's The Boy For Me)—Angels (64)	394
Sean SPENCER ► 3667 (1)	**744**
Girl You Know It's True—Milli Vanilli (88)	3721
Sheridan SPENCER ► 10193 (1)	**11**
This Is The Nite—Valiants (57)	45
Tim SPENCER ► 5632 (1)	**262**
Room Full Of Roses—Mickey Gilley (74)	262
Tracie SPENCER ► 7706 (1)	**79**
Tender Kisses—Tracie Spencer (91)	318
Trevor SPENCER ► 7059 (4)	**118**
No Time To Lose—Tarney/Spencer Band (81)	*97*
No Time To Lose—Tarney/Spencer Band (79)	*91*
It's Really You—Tarney/Spencer Band (78)	30
I'm Your Man Rock 'N' Roll— Tarney/Spencer Band (76)	29
Deedee SPERLING ► 11412 (1)	**1.8**
Where Did The Good Times Go— Dick And Deedee (63)	3.6
Anthony SPERRY ► 10157 (1)	**12**
Record Hop Blues—Quarter Notes (59)	12
Steve SPERRY ► 9934 (1)	**15**
Flame—Steve Sperry (77)	15
—Spice see: Amir SHAKIR	
Ian SPICE ► 1995 (5)	**2020**
Hands To Heaven—Breathe (88)	3472
How Can I Fall?—Breathe (88)	2861
Don't Tell Me Lies—Breathe (89)	1080
Does She Love That Man?—Breathe (90)	478
All This I Should Have Known—Breathe (89)	30
—William Spicer see: Billy STORM	
Fred SPIELMAN ► 851 (5)	**5209**
Paper Roses—Anita Bryant (60)	*3707*
Paper Roses—Marie Osmond (73)	*2674*
It Only Hurts For A Little While— Ames Brothers (56)	1919
Longest Walk—Jaye P. Morgan (55)	1916
Leave It To Your Heart—Ames Brothers (54)	201
Benjamin SPIKES ► 9679 (1)	**19**
Someday Sweetheart—Les Paul (55)	38
John C. SPIKES ► 9680 (1)	**19**
Someday Sweetheart—Les Paul (55)	38
Alan SPILTON ► 11696 (1)	**0.7**
Lover Come Back—Doris Day (62)	1.3
Hal SPINA ► 3695 (2)	**732**
Lazy Summer Night—Four Preps (58)	674
He Knows (By The Way I Live Each Day)— Gisele MacKenzie (57)	57
Joe SPINAZOLA ► 5898 (1)	**231**
Anything You Want—John Valenti (76)	463
John SPINKS ► 994 (7)	**4513**
Your Love—Outfield (86)	1674
All The Love In The World—Outfield (86)	768
For You—Outfield (90)	706
Voices Of Babylon—Outfield (89)	596
Since You've Been Gone—Outfield (87)	527
Everytime You Cry—Outfield (86)	193
My Paradise—Outfield (89)	49
Jakson SPIRES ► 4865 (2)	**397**
Highway Song—Blackfoot (79)	543
Fly Away—Blackfoot (81)	250
Harold SPIRO ► 5920 (2)	**228**
Little Games—Yardbirds (67)	412
Desdemona—Searchers (71)	45
Mark SPIRO [Markus Spiro] ► 3875 (5)	**670**
I'll See You In My Dreams—Giant (90)	782
Straight To Your Heart—Bad English (91)	390
Forget Me Not—Bad English (89)	310
I'm A Believer—Giant (89)	182
Heaven Is A 4 Letter Word—Bad English (90)	169
—Markus Spiro see: Mark SPIRO	
John SPIRT ► 3770 (2)	**704**
Martian Hop—Ran-Dells (63)	1332
Suspicions—Sidekicks (66)	519
Bill SPITALSKY ► 9009 (1)	**33**
Little Pedro—Olympics (61)	100
Sharleen SPITERI ► 9431 (1)	**24**
I Don't Want A Lover—Texas (89)	47
William SPIVERY ► 3717 (1)	**721**
Operator—Manhattan Transfer (75)	721
Gloria SPOLAN ► 4334 (1)	**518**
Hypnotized—Linda Jones (67)	1035
William SPOONER ► 7136 (3)	**114**
Don't Want To Wait Anymore—Tubes (81)	377
Tip Of My Tongue—Tubes (83)	198
Piece By Piece—Tubes (85)	10
—Murray Sporn see: Freddy FRIDAY	
Giuseppe SPOTTI ► 1412 (1)	**3142**
I Want To Be Wanted—Brenda Lee (60)	6284
Glenn SPREEN ► 11199 (1)	**2.8**
Loving You Is A Natural Thing—Ronnie Milsap (70)	8.4
Dennis SPRINGER ► 11219 (1)	**2.7**
Let's Dance (Make Your Body Move)— West Street Mob (81)	30
Philip SPRINGER ► 1489 (17)	**2920**
Moonlight Gambler—Frankie Laine (56)	*3465*
(How Little It Matters) How Little We Know— Frank Sinatra (56)	663
All Cried Out—Dusty Springfield (64)	540
Sweet William—Millie Small (64)	432
Fish—Mindy Carson (55)	248
I Want Eddie Fisher For Christmas— Betty Johnson (54)	*176*
This Is My Prayer—Ray Charles Singers (65)	124
Not One Goodbye—Jaye P. Morgan (55)	93
Dancing Chandelier—Sylvia Syms (56)	63
This Year's Santa Baby—Eartha Kitt (54)	51
Questions And Answers—In Crowd (66)	33
My Bewildered Heart—Jaye P. Morgan (56)	11
The President On The Dollar— Mitch Miller & His Orchestra (56)	7.7
Das Ist Musik—Bill Hayes (56)	6.7
Welcome Home—Shelley Fabares (63)	0.4
Moonlight Gambler— Winifred Atwell And Her Piano (57)	*0.0*
I Want Eddie Fisher For Christmas— Spike Jones with Linda Strangis (54)	*0.0*
Tony SPRINGER ► 9786 (1)	**17**
This Year's Santa Baby—Eartha Kitt (54)	51
Rick SPRINGFIELD [Richard Lewis Springthorpe] ► 108 (20)	**23005**
Jessie's Girl—Rick Springfield (81)	6373
Don't Talk To Strangers—Rick Springfield (82)	5411
Love Somebody—Rick Springfield (84)	2112
Affair Of The Heart—Rick Springfield (83)	1704
Speak To The Sky—Rick Springfield (72)	1241
Human Touch—Rick Springfield (83)	918
Love Is Alright Tonite—Rick Springfield (81)	848
What Kind Of Fool Am I—Rick Springfield (82)	749
Souls—Rick Springfield (83)	673
State Of The Heart—Rick Springfield (85)	656
Bop 'til You Drop—Rick Springfield (84)	638
Rock Of Life—Rick Springfield (88)	568
Bruce—Rick Springfield (84)	550
Don't Walk Away—Rick Springfield (84)	513
Celebrate Youth—Rick Springfield (85)	500
I Get Excited—Rick Springfield (82)	451
Take A Hand—Rick Springfield (76)	316
Taxi Dancing— Rick Springfield & Randy Crawford (84)	160
What Would The Children Think—Rick Springfield (72)	133
American Girls—Rick Springfield (74)	65
Tom SPRINGFIELD [Dionysius P. A. O'Brien] ► 520 (9)	**8182**
Georgy Girl—Seekers (66)	*6883*
I'll Never Find Another You—Seekers (65)	*3827*
A World Of Our Own—Seekers (65)	833
Losing You—Dusty Springfield (65)	75
On The Other Side—Seekers (67)	52
Island Of Dreams—Springfields (63)	22
I'll Never Find Another You— Sonny James The Southern Gentleman (67)	*2.9*
Georgy Girl—Baja Marimba Band (67)	*1.5*
The Carnival Is Over—Seekers (65)	0.5
Bruce SPRINGSTEEN ► 54 (30) HOF	**39879**
Dancing In The Dark—Bruce Springsteen (84)	5671
Fire—Pointer Sisters (78)	*5172*
Blinded By The Light— Manfred Mann's Earth Band (76)	4876
Hungry Heart—Bruce Springsteen (80)	2615
Pink Cadillac—Natalie Cole (88)	1871
Brilliant Disguise—Bruce Springsteen (87)	1871
Glory Days—Bruce Springsteen (85)	1854
I'm On Fire—Bruce Springsteen (85)	1761
Cover Me—Bruce Springsteen (84)	1715
Born In The U.S.A.—Bruce Springsteen (84)	*1691*
This Little Girl—Gary U.S. Bonds (81)	1590
My Hometown—Bruce Springsteen (85)	1436
Because The Night—Patti Smith Group (78)	1235
Tunnel Of Love—Bruce Springsteen (87)	1131
I'm Goin' Down—Bruce Springsteen (85)	1057
One Step Up—Bruce Springsteen (88)	873
Born To Run—Bruce Springsteen (75)	852
Out Of Work—Gary U.S. Bonds (82)	752
Fade Away—Bruce Springsteen (81)	626
Banned In The U.S.A.— Luke Featuring 2 Live Crew (90)	588
Light Of Day— Barbusters (Joan Jett & The Blackhearts) (87)	373
Spirit In The Night—Manfred Mann's Earth Band (77)	*346*
Prove It All Night—Bruce Springsteen (78)	317
Badlands—Bruce Springsteen (78)	257
Born In East L.A.—Cheech & Chong (85)	*256*
Fire—Bruce Springsteen & The E Street Band (87)	*242*
Tenth Avenue Freeze-Out—Bruce Springsteen (76)	75
Sandy—Hollies (75)	19
For You—Manfred Mann's Earth Band (81)	9.9
Spirit In The Night—Manfred Mann's Earth Band (76)	*2.7*
—Richard Lewis Springthorpe see: Rick SPRINGFIELD	
Craig SPROVACH ► 8633 (2)	**44**
(Call Me) When The Spirit Moves You—Touch (80)	76
Fool's Game—Michael Bolton (83)	20
Lou SPRUNG ► 7053 (2)	**119**
Ambrose (Part Five)—Linda Laurie (59)	337
Just Keep Walkin' Ambrose— Jimmy Valentine & His Orchestra (59)	21
Jeff SPRY ► 8198 (1)	**59**
The Fanatic—Felony (83)	294
Joe SPRY ► 8199 (1)	**59**
The Fanatic—Felony (83)	294
Ralph SPURLIN Jr. ► 10227 (1)	**11**
Prince Of Players— Tommy Frederick and the Hi-Notes (58)	22

Billy SQUIER ▶ 998 (11)	**4487**
The Stroke—Billy Squier (81)	1333
Rock Me Tonite—Billy Squier (84)	1134
Everybody Wants You—Billy Squier (82)	648
In The Dark—Billy Squier (81)	414
My Kinda Lover—Billy Squier (81)	334
Don't Say You Love Me—Billy Squier (89)	170
Eye On You—Billy Squier (84)	125
Emotions In Motion—Billy Squier (82)	120
Love Is The Hero—Billy Squier (86)	85
She's A Runner—Billy Squier (83)	71
All Night Long—Billy Squier (84)	52
Chris SQUIRE ▶ 1942 (6)	**2078**
Owner Of A Lonely Heart—Yes (83)	6336
Leave It—Yes (84)	669
And You And I (Part I)—Yes (72)	447
Rhythm Of Love—Yes (87)	310
It Can Happen—Yes (84)	168
Lift Me Up—Yes (91)	82
—Stacey Q see: Stacey SWAIN	
Al STAEHELY ▶ 11763 (1)	**0.2**
He Did Me Wrong, But He Did It Right—Patti Dahlstrom (74)	0.3
Jim STAFFORD ▶ 874 (7)	**5083**
Spiders And Snakes—Jim Stafford (73)	3645
Wildwood Weed—Jim Stafford (74)	2073
My Girl Bill—Jim Stafford (74)	1355
Swamp Witch—Jim Stafford (73)	614
Your Bulldog Drinks Champagne—Jim Stafford (74)	437
Jasper—Jim Stafford (76)	72
Turn Loose Of My Leg—Jim Stafford (77)	1.6
Joe STAFFORD Jr. [Joe Jeffrey] ▶ 2370 (1)	**1555**
My Pledge Of Love—Joe Jeffrey Group (69)	1555
Marge STAFFORD ▶ 11342 (1)	**2.1**
Please Please Believe Me—Cathy Carr (56)	6.4
Terry STAFFORD ▶ 11382 (1)	**2.0**
Big In Vegas—Buck Owens And The Buckaroos (69)	4.0
Jerry STAHL ▶ 9992 (1)	**14**
Right The First Time—Gamma (82)	43
Tim STAHL ▶ 5285 (1)	**313**
White Horse—Laid Back (84)	627
Chris STAINTON ▶ 3622 (4)	**764**
High Time We Went—Joe Cocker (71)	871
Woman To Woman—Joe Cocker And The Chris Stainton Band (72)	346
Pardon Me Sir—Joe Cocker (73)	308
Black-Eyed Blues—Joe Cocker (71)	1.5
Lou STALLMAN [Leizer David] ▶ 528 (26)	**8061**
Round And Round—Perry Como (57)	5931
Yogi—Ivy Three (60)	1816
Everybody's Got The Right To Love—Supremes (70)	1249
It's Gonna Take A Miracle—Deniece Williams (82)	*1178*
Treasure Of Love—Clyde McPhatter (56)	*1172*
I've Come Of Age—Billy Storm (59)	776
Don't Pity Me—Dion and The Belmonts (58)	662
Once You Understand—Think (71)	*598*
It's Gonna Take A Miracle—Royalettes (65)	*576*
If You Don't Want My Love—Robert John (68)	553
You Better Go—Derek Martin (65)	392
My Little Baby—Perry Como (57)	328
Once You Understand—Think (Featuring Lou Stallman) (74)	*279*
Warm Up To Me Baby—Jimmy Bowen With The Rhythm Orchids (57)	272
Jamie Boy—Kay Starr (57)	181
I Want To Meet Him—Royalettes (65)	172
Wonderful You—Jimmie Rodgers (59)	120
A Corner In The Sun—Walter Jackson (66)	99
I Was Meant For You (The Wah-Wah Song)—Four Knights (54)	23
Presidential Press Conference—Sickniks (61)	22
Anniversary Of Love—Caslons (61)	21
How Lonely Can One Be—Teresa Brewer (57)	12
Yen Yet Song—Gary Cane And His Friends (60)	8.2
You Don't Know Girls—Kathy Linden (59)	7.0
The Weekend—Jack Jones (66)	0.5
Treasure Of Love—Dorothy Collins (56)	*0.0*
Frank STALLONE ▶ 3806 (2)	**694**
Far From Over—Frank Stallone (83)	1363
Darlin'—Frank Stallone (84)	38

Brenard STALLWORTH [B. Fresh] ▶ 7974 (1)	**67**
Slow Love—Doc Box & B. Fresh (90)	200
Lloyd STALLWORTH ▶ 6741 (2)	**141**
Lost Someone—James Brown And The Famous Flames (61)	*417*
Lost Someone—James Brown And The Famous Flames (66)	*6.2*
Paul STALLWORTH ▶ 10992 (1)	**3.9**
Sweet Summer Music—Attitudes (76)	12
Joe STAMPLEY ▶ 7038 (2)	**120**
Not Too Long Ago—Uniques Featuring Joe Stampley (65)	240
Run And Hide—Uniques (66)	0.5
Dok STANFORD ▶ 4499 (5)	**476**
Fairy Tale—Frank Sinatra (55)	561
They Say You're Laughing At Me (While I'm Crying For You)—Al Hibbler (55)	318
You'll Get Yours—Frank Sinatra (56)	50
Johnny Concho Theme (Wait For Me)—Frank Sinatra (56)	23
Lollipop—Vince Edwards (58)	0.0
Trevor STANFORD [Russ Conway, Trevor Herbert Stanford] ▶ 10896 (2)	**4.5**
Side Saddle—Russ Conway (59)	*2.3*
Side Saddle—Freddy Morgan (59)	*2.3*
Stanislaus STANGE ▶ 10084 (1)	**13**
My Hero—Blue Notes (60)	26
Darron STANKEY ▶ 6217 (1)	**192**
Honest I Do—Innocents (60)	577
Earl STANLEY ▶ 10216 (1)	**11**
Gypsy Woman Told Me—Eddie Powers (64)	33
Hal STANLEY ▶ 6010 (6)	**216**
Fortune In Dreams—Kay Starr (54)	223
Turn Right—Kay Starr (55)	193
The Good Book—Kay Starr (56)	8.5
The Things I Never Had—Kay Starr (56)	4.4
Love Ain't Right—Kay Starr (56)	4.0
The Man Upstairs—Kay Starr (54)	0.0
Helen STANLEY ▶ 6390 (1)	**176**
Tear Drops—Lee Andrews And The Hearts (57)	703
Ian STANLEY ▶ 1032 (3)	**4265**
Everybody Wants To Rule The World—Tears For Fears (85)	4971
Shout—Tears For Fears (85)	4675
Mothers Talk—Tears For Fears (86)	541
Michael STANLEY [Michael Stanley Gee] ▶ 4230 (4)	**554**
My Town—Michael Stanley Band (83)	369
Falling In Love Again—Michael Stanley Band (81)	179
Lover—Michael Stanley Band (81)	67
Take The Time—Michael Stanley Band (82)	29
Paul STANLEY [Stanley Harvey Eisen] ▶ 799 (23)	**5542**
I Was Made For Lovin' You—Kiss (79)	1971
Forever—Kiss (90)	1355
Rock And Roll All Nite (Live)—Kiss (75)	*1254*
Hard Luck Woman—Kiss (76)	999
Detroit Rock City—Kiss (76)	870
Shout It Out Loud—Kiss (76)	*563*
Hold Me, Touch Me—Paul Stanley (78)	456
Love On A Rooftop—Desmond Child (91)	440
Sure Know Something—Kiss (79)	365
Tears Are Falling—KISS (85)	326
Shandi—Kiss (80)	273
Heaven's On Fire—KISS (84)	264
Love Gun—Kiss (77)	183
A World Without Heroes—KISS (81)	167
Reason To Live—KISS (87)	145
Rock And Roll All Nite (Studio)—Kiss (75)	*131*
Lick It Up—KISS (83)	120
Hide Your Heart—KISS (89)	110
Shout It Out Loud (Live)—Kiss (77)	*104*
Crazy Crazy Nights—KISS (87)	92
Rise To It—Kiss (90)	48
Flaming Youth—Kiss (76)	41
Let's Put The X In Sex—KISS (89)	7.3
Ray STANLEY ▶ 2394 (4)	**1530**
Glendora—Perry Como (56)	1335
Teen Age Goodnight—Chordettes (56)	90
Think Me A Kiss—Clyde McPhatter (60)	89
Come And Get It—Ray Peterson (59)	61

Steven J.C. STANLEY ▶ 6854 (1)	**132**
Genius Of Love—Tom Tom Club (82)	529
Graham STANSFIELD ▶ 10342 (1)	**9.8**
Sympathy—Rare Bird (70)	39
Lisa STANSFIELD ▶ 2155 (4)	**1811**
All Around The World—Lisa Stansfield (90)	3201
You Can't Deny It—Lisa Stansfield (90)	830
Change—Lisa Stansfield (91)	756
This Is The Right Time—Lisa Stansfield (90)	646
Vivian STANSHALL ▶ 7932 (1)	**69**
Arc Of A Diver—Steve Winwood (81)	138
Albert STANTON ▶ 1415 (3)	**3137**
The Lion Sleeps Tonight—Tokens (61)	*9030*
The Lion Sleeps Tonight—Robert John (71)	*5059*
Abilene—George Hamilton IV (63)	1276
Frank STANTON ▶ 4363 (5)	**512**
Face It Girl, It's Over—Nancy Wilson (68)	833
Tomboy—Ronnie Dove (68)	98
Heart Without A Sweetheart—Gale Storm (56)	63
June July And August—Rusty Draper (58)	45
Blue Guitar—Larry Lawrence (59)	0.9
Peggy STANZIALE ▶ 3521 (1)	**801**
Dress You Up—Madonna (85)	1602
Kevan STAPLES ▶ 7843 (1)	**72**
All Touch—Rough Trade (82)	145
Roebuck STAPLES ▶ 5749 (4)	**246**
Why? (Am I Treated So Bad)—"Cannonball" Adderley (67)	*134*
Why (Am I Treated So Bad)—Sweet Inspirations (67)	*96*
Why (Am I Treated So Bad)—Bobby Powell (67)	*13*
Why? (Am I Treated So Bad)—Staple Singers (67)	*2.9*
Cyril STAPLETON [Clyde Hamilton] ▶ 5478 (4)	**281**
Italian Theme—Cyril Stapleton And His Orchestra (56)	*563*
The Italian Theme—Dorothy Collins (56)	*0.0*
The Italian Theme—Owen Bradley & His Quintet (56)	*0.0*
The Italian Theme—Joe Reisman and His Orchestra (56)	*0.0*
Jack STAPP ▶ 5713 (1)	**251**
Chattanooga Shoe Shine Boy—Freddy Cannon (60)	503
Tommy STAR ▶ 9032 (1)	**33**
Free Me—Otis Redding (69)	131
Buddy STARCHER ▶ 4188 (2)	**569**
History Repeats Itself—Buddy Starcher (66)	*529*
History Repeats Itself—Cab Calloway (66)	*40*
—Mel Stark see: Cliff PARMAN	
—Jack Starkey see: Buddy PEPPER	
—Richard Starkey see: Ringo STARR	
John STARKS ▶ 4817 (3)	**407**
The Payback - Part I—James Brown (74)	817
Papa Don't Take No Mess - Part I—James Brown (74)	475
Pass The Peas—J.B.'s (72)	48
—Jade Starling see: Jeanne ROBERTS	
Bebe STARR ▶ 10822 (1)	**5.1**
Because Of My Pride—Fireflies (60)	15
Edwin STARR [Charles Edwin Hatcher] ▶ 1373 (14)	**3243**
Twenty-Five Miles—Edwin Starr (69)	*2304*
Oh How Happy—Shades Of Blue (66)	*1806*
Agent Double-O-Soul—Edwin Starr (65)	933
Stop Her On Sight (S.O.S.)—Edwin Starr (66)	495
Contact—Edwin Starr (79)	198
Lonely Summer—Shades Of Blue (66)	142
There You Go—Edwin Starr (73)	88
Back Street—Edwin Starr (65)	44
Headline News—Edwin Starr (66)	41
H.A.P.P.Y. Radio—Edwin Starr (79)	24
Oh How Happy—Blinky & Edwin Starr (69)	*17*
Oh How Happy—Skyliners (78)	*15*
Abyssinia Jones—Edwin Starr (76)	1.4
Twenty-Five Miles—Mongo Santamaria (69)	*0.9*
Lucille STARR [Lucille Marie Raymonde Savoie] ▶ 6905 (1)	**130**
The French Song (Quand Le Soleil Dit Bonjour Aux Montagnes)—Lucille Starr (64)	389
Maurice STARR [Larry Curtis Johnson] ▶ 142 (13)	**19905**
Step By Step—New Kids On The Block (90)	4426
Hangin' Tough—New Kids On The Block (89)	2990

Maurice STARR [Larry Curtis Johnson] ▶ 142 (13) *Continued*	**19905**
I'll Be Loving You (Forever)— New Kids On The Block (89)	2935
You Got It (The Right Stuff)— New Kids On The Block (88)	2423
Cover Girl—New Kids On The Block (89)	2256
This One's For The Children— New Kids On The Block (89)	1440
Please Don't Go Girl—New Kids On The Block (88)	1274
Tonight—New Kids On The Block (90)	1237
Ooh La La (I Can't Get Over You)— Perfect Gentlemen (90)	1039
Candy Girl—New Edition (83)	387
Let's Try It Again—New Kids On The Block (90)	175
Got To Tell Me Something—Ana (90)	124
Is This The End—New Edition (83)	20
Randy STARR [Warren Nadel] ▶ 1973 (8)	**2043**
Kissin' Cousins—Elvis Presley (64)	1612
Enchanted Sea—Islanders (59)	*1112*
After School—Randy Starr (57)	*517*
Enchanted Sea—Exotic Sounds Of Martin Denny (59)	*450*
I Know Where I'm Goin'—George Hamilton IV (58)	383
Almost In Love— Elvis Presley With The Jordanaires (68)	11
After School—Joy Layne (57)	*0.0*
After School—Teardrops (57)	*0.0*
—Ray Starr see: Ray PENNINGTON	
Ringo STARR [Richard Starkey] ▶ 364 (6)	**10583**
It Don't Come Easy—Ringo Starr (71)	5329
Photograph—Ringo Starr (73)	5208
Oh My My—Ringo Starr (74)	2014
Back Off Boogaloo—Ringo Starr (72)	1638
What Goes On—Beatles (66)	16
Oo-Wee—Ringo Starr (75)	0.0
Tony STARR ▶ 6212 (6)	**193**
Over The Weekend—Playboys (58)	302
Walk With Faith In Your Heart—Johnny Nash (59)	*121*
Walk With Faith In Your Heart—Bachelors (66)	*34*
Teen Ager's Waltz— Eddy Howard And His Orchestra (55)	17
Devil's Highway—9 LaFalce Brothers (55)	7.0
Till You're Back In My Arms—Vince Carson (56)	6.1
Paul STATHAM ▶ 7414 (1)	**97**
Cuts You Up—Peter Murphy (90)	195
Candi STATON [Canzetta Staton, Canzetta Staton-Sussewell] ▶ 7418 (2)	**97**
Sweet Feeling—Candi Staton (70)	373
When You Wake Up Tomorrow—Candi Staton (79)	16
—Canzetta Staton see: Candi STATON	
Gary ST. CLAIR ▶ 8321 (1)	**54**
Sally Had A Party—Flavor (68)	109
Arthur STEAD ▶ 3992 (2)	**629**
The Goonies 'r' Good Enough—Cyndi Lauper (85)	1031
What You See Is What You Get—Brenda K. Starr (88)	570
Russell STEAGALL ▶ 3707 (2)	**727**
Here We Go Again—Ray Charles (67)	*1452*
Here We Go Again—Nancy Sinatra (69)	*2.6*
Melvin STEALS [Mystro] ▶ 1752 (6)	**2367**
Could It Be I'm Falling In Love—Spinners (72)	4362
One Beautiful Day—Ecstasy, Passion & Pain (75)	285
Melt In Your Mouth—Candyman (90)	115
Full Time Thing (Between Dusk And Dawn)— Whirlwind (76)	9.0
Treat 'Em Right—Chubb Rock (91)	4.7
After Loving You—Major Harris (75)	0.6
Mervin STEALS [Lyric] ▶ 1753 (6)	**2367**
Could It Be I'm Falling In Love—Spinners (72)	4362
One Beautiful Day—Ecstasy, Passion & Pain (75)	285
Melt In Your Mouth—Candyman (90)	115
Full Time Thing (Between Dusk And Dawn)— Whirlwind (76)	9.0
Treat 'Em Right—Chubb Rock (91)	4.7
After Loving You—Major Harris (75)	0.6
Joseph STEC ▶ 11622 (1)	**1.0**
Just About The Same—Association (70)	4.8
Trevor STEEL ▶ 2442 (5)	**1485**
Wild, Wild West—Escape Club (88)	4224
I'll Be There—Escape Club (91)	1572
Shake For The Sheik—Escape Club (88)	509
Call It Poison—Escape Club (91)	412

Walking Through Walls—Escape Club (89)	67
Billy STEELE ▶ 6879 (1)	**131**
Strung Out—Steve Perry (84)	393
—Bob Steele see: Robert STEELE	
David STEELE ▶ 1022 (7)	**4329**
Good Thing—Fine Young Cannibals (89)	3616
She Drives Me Crazy—Fine Young Cannibals (89)	3569
Don't Look Back—Fine Young Cannibals (89)	994
It's A Shame (My Sister)—Monie Love (91)	420
I'm Not The Man I Used To Be— Fine Young Cannibals (89)	226
Johnny Come Home—Fine Young Cannibals (86)	56
I'm Not Satisfied—Fine Young Cannibals (90)	29
Greg STEELE ▶ 5361 (1)	**300**
House Of Pain—Faster Pussycat (90)	600
Larry STEELE ▶ 5523 (2)	**274**
If I'd Been The One—38 Special (83)	839
Somebody Like You—38 Special (86)	322
Lois STEELE ▶ 1007 (6)	**4416**
Ivory Tower—Cathy Carr (56)	*4201*
Ivory Tower—Gale Storm (56)	*2381*
Ivory Tower—Otis Williams And His Charms (56)	*2092*
Times Two I Love You—Three Chuckles (55)	119
Peace—McGuire Sisters (59)	39
Wanted—Perry Como (54)	0.0
Robert STEELE [Robert Miskiewicz, Bob Steele, Bobby Steele] ▶ 2276 (2)	**1663**
If Wishes Came True—Sweet Sensation (90)	3587
Thinking Of You—Sa-Fire (89)	1403
Terry STEELE ▶ 2947 (1)	**1105**
Here And Now—Luther Vandross (89)	2210
Dave STEEN ▶ 6918 (1)	**129**
Right Away—Hawks (81)	129
Roger STEEN ▶ 8495 (2)	**48**
Don't Want To Wait Anymore—Tubes (81)	377
Piece By Piece—Tubes (85)	10
Yasmin Elvira STEENHOLDT [Yasmin Jacobsen] ▶ 11116 (1)	**3.2**
Wanna Dance—Yasmin (91)	16
William STEFFE ▶ 2686 (4)	**1272**
Battle Hymn Of The Republic— Mormon Tabernacle Choir (59)	*1595*
Battle Hymn Of The Republic—Andy Williams With The St. Charles Borromeo Choir (68)	*658*
Battle Hymn Of The Republic—Mickey Newbury (71)	*222*
Battle Hymn Of The Republic—Elvis Presley (72)	*69*
Keith STEGALL ▶ 2159 (3)	**1809**
Sexy Eyes—Dr. Hook (80)	3462
We're In This Love Together—Al Jarreau (81)	1265
Simple—Johnny Mathis (84)	46
—Wanda Cleo Stegall see: Vicki YOUNG	
Bill STEGMEYER ▶ 4267 (1)	**539**
A Symphony For Susan—Arbors (66)	539
Christopher STEIN ▶ 1093 (6)	**4032**
Heart Of Glass—Blondie (79)	5717
Rapture—Blondie (81)	5100
Dreaming—Blondie (79)	716
Island Of Lost Souls—Blondie (82)	344
In Love With Love—Debbie Harry (87)	99
The Hardest Part—Blondie (80)	69
Herman STEIN ▶ 10529 (4)	**7.6**
Toy Tiger—Les Baxter & His Orchestra (55)	*3.8*
Toy Tiger—Johnny Long & His Orchestra (55)	*3.8*
Toy Tiger—Ralph Marterie & His Orchestra (55)	*3.8*
Toy Tiger— Victor Young And His Singing Strings (55)	*3.8*
Lou STEIN ▶ 8124 (6)	**61**
Soft Sands—Chordettes (57)	*122*
Soft Sands—Rover Boys (57)	*0.0*
Soft Sands—Oscar Peterson (57)	*0.0*
Soft Sands—Dorothy Collins (57)	*0.0*
Soft Sands—Ray Ellis & His Orchestra (57)	*0.0*
Soft Sands—Voices Of Walter Schumann (57)	*0.0*
Mark STEIN [Hans Herman Stein Kramer] ▶ 9538 (2)	**22**
Where Is My Mind—Vanilla Fudge (68)	71
Need Love—Vanilla Fudge (69)	16
Murray STEIN ▶ 1877 (2)	**2171**
Baby (You've Got What It Takes)— Dinah Washington & Brook Benton (60)	3840

Smooth Operator—Sarah Vaughan (59)	503
—Siegfried Alex Stein see: Alex ALSTONE	
Larry STEINBACHEK [Larry Cole, Lawrence Charles Anthony Cole,] ▶ 6513 (1)	**161**
Smalltown Boy—Bronski Beat (84)	484
Billy STEINBERG ▶ 215 (15) HOF	**15184**
Like A Virgin—Madonna (84)	*6377*
Alone—Heart (87)	4753
So Emotional—Whitney Houston (87)	3671
True Colors—Cyndi Lauper (86)	3546
Eternal Flame—Bangles (89)	3515
How Do I Make You—Linda Ronstadt (80)	2152
I Touch Myself—Divinyls (91)	2042
In Your Room—Bangles (88)	1791
I Drove All Night—Cyndi Lauper (89)	1573
Sex As A Weapon—Pat Benatar (85)	583
My Side Of The Bed—Susanna Hoffs (91)	464
Like A Surgeon— "Weird Al" Yankovic (85)	*257*
I Want You So Bad—Heart (88)	224
Jackie—Blue Zone U.K. (88)	200
My First Night Without You—Cyndi Lauper (89)	149
Lewis STEINBERG ▶ 2683 (6)	**1273**
Green Onions—Booker T. & The M.G.'s (62)	*4924*
Jellybread—Booker T. & The MGs (62)	74
Chinese Checkers—Booker T. & The MG's (63)	63
Green Onions—Dick Hyman (69)	*23*
Soul Dressing—Booker T. & The MG's (64)	4.4
Mo-Onions—Booker T. & The MG's (64)	3.7
Jacqueline STEINER ▶ 4263 (2)	**541**
M. T. A.—Kingston Trio (59)	*1082*
The M.T.A.—Gateway Singers (59)	*0.0*
Max STEINER ▶ 219 (24) HOF	**15156**
Theme From A Summer Place— Percy Faith And His Orchestra (60)	*12297*
Honey Babe—Art Mooney And His Orchestra (55)	*2294*
Theme From "A Summer Place"—Lettermen (65)	*1085*
My Own True Love—Duprees (62)	*1002*
My Own True Love—Jimmy Clanton (59)	*781*
Angel—Johnny Tillotson (65)	308
Theme from A Summer Place—Dick Roman (62)	*274*
Theme From "A Summer Place"—Ventures (69)	*218*
Theme From The Dark At The Top Of The Stairs— Ernie Freeman (60)	*93*
My Own True Love (Tara's Theme)— LeRoy Holmes And His Orchestra (54)	*61*
Tara's Theme—Meco (82)	*47*
Theme From "A Summer Place"—Lolita (61)	*5.4*
Tara's Theme—Bill Doggett (54)	*0.0*
My Own True Love—Four Coachmen (59)	*0.0*
Honey Babe—Sauter-Finegan Orchestra (55)	*0.0*
Theme From "A Summer Place"—Don Ralke (60)	*0.0*
Tara's Theme—Paul Weston & His Orchestra (54)	*0.0*
My Own True Love (Tara's Theme)— Johnny Desmond (54)	*0.0*
Theme From The Dark At The Top Of The Stairs— Chet Atkins (60)	*0.0*
(Theme From) "A Summer Place"— LeRoy Holmes & His Orchestra (60)	*0.0*
Theme From "A Summer Place"— Hugo Winterhalter And His Orchestra (60)	*0.0*
(Theme From) The Dark At The Top Of The Stairs— Bob Crosby & The Bobcats (60)	*0.0*
(Theme From) "The Dark At The Top Of The Stairs"— Percy Faith and his Orchestra (60)	*0.0*
(Theme From) "The Dark At The Top Of The Stairs"— Frank Chacksfield & His Orchestra (60)	*0.0*
—Wendy Steiner see: Wendy WALDMAN	
Robby STEINHARDT ▶ 5348 (1)	**302**
Point Of Know Return—Kansas (77)	905
Anita STEINMAN ▶ 2299 (1)	**1635**
One Night—Elvis Presley (58)	4905
Jim STEINMAN ▶ 171 (13) HOF	**17429**
Total Eclipse Of The Heart—Bonnie Tyler (83)	7599
Making Love Out Of Nothing At All—Air Supply (83)	4549
Two Out Of Three Ain't Bad—Meat Loaf (78)	2301
Read 'Em And Weep—Barry Manilow (83)	856
Rock And Roll Dreams Come Through— Jim Steinman (81)	600
Holding Out For A Hero—Bonnie Tyler (84)	489
Paradise By The Dashboard Light—Meat Loaf (78)	421
You Took The Words Right Out Of My Mouth— Meat Loaf (78)	*405*

Jim STEINMAN ▶ 171 (13) *Continued*	**17429**
Left In The Dark—Barbra Streisand (84)	335
You Took The Words Right Out Of My Mouth (Hot Summer Night)—Meat Loaf (77)	*59*
Tonight Is What It Means To Be Young—Fire Inc. (84)	30
Loving You's A Dirty Job But Somebody's Gotta Do It—Bonnie Tyler (Duet with Todd Rundgren) (86)	22
I'm Gonna Love Her For Both Of Us—Meat Loaf (81)	9.9
Albert STELLA ▶ 9879 (1)	**16**
Yes Sir Ee—Dodie Stevens (59)	47
Marcel STELLMAN [Leo Johns, Gene Martyn] ▶ 2493 (6)	**1438**
Melodie D'Amour (Melody Of Love)—Ames Brothers (57)	*2592*
Marble Breaks And Iron Bends—Drafi (66)	170
I Will Live My Life For You—Tony Bennett (63)	120
Welcome Home—Sammy Kaye & His Orchestra (61)	117
Melodie D'Amour—Marty Gold & His Orchestra (57)	*0.0*
Melodie D'Amour—Edmundo Ros & His Orchestra (57)	*0.0*
—Jerry Marvin Stembridge see: Chip YOUNG	
Douglas STENDER ▶ 10820 (1)	**5.1**
Am I Losing You—Manhattans (78)	15
Geoff STEPHENS ▶ 145 (18)	**19700**
Winchester Cathedral—New Vaudeville Band (66)	*10623*
Daddy Don't You Walk So Fast—Wayne Newton (72)	5656
There's A Kind Of Hush—Herman's Hermits (67)	*3675*
Smile A Little Smile For Me—Flying Machine (69)	3331
Doctor's Orders—Carol Douglas (74)	1742
Daughter Of Darkness—Tom Jones (70)	1619
There's A Kind Of Hush (All Over The World)—Carpenters (76)	*1207*
Sorry Suzanne—Hollies (69)	353
Silver Lady—David Soul (77)	289
My World Fell Down—Sagittarius (67)	154
Winchester Cathedral—Dana Rollin (66)	*137*
It's Like We Never Said Goodbye—Crystal Gayle (80)	118
Peek-A-Boo—New Vaudeville Band (67)	86
Sunshine Girl—Herman's Hermits (68)	80
Knock Knock Who's There—Mary Hopkin (72)	57
You Won't Find Another Fool Like Me—New Seekers Featuring Lyn Paul (74)	42
The Crying Game—Brenda Lee (65)	25
Boy—Lulu (68)	3.3
Richard STEPHENS ▶ 1697 (2)	**2475**
Wheels—String-A-Longs (60)	*4346*
Wheels—Billy Vaughn And His Orchestra (61)	*605*
Tennyson STEPHENS ▶ 9490 (1)	**23**
Party Lights—Natalie Cole (77)	23
Van STEPHENSON ▶ 3805 (7)	**695**
Modern Day Delilah—Van Stephenson (84)	823
All My Life—Kenny Rogers (83)	390
What The Big Girls Do—Van Stephenson (84)	297
It's Not You, It's Not Me—KBC Band (86)	47
Set The Night On Fire—Oak (80)	43
You've Got A Good Love Coming—Van Stephenson (81)	16
Dirty Looks—Juice Newton (83)	8.1
Willie STEPHENSON ▶ 5824 (2)	**239**
I Do (Live Version)—J. Geils Band (82)	*637*
I Do—Marvelows (65)	*556*
Charles STEPNEY ▶ 4038 (3)	**618**
That's The Way Of The World—Earth, Wind & Fire (75)	1622
Hot Dawgit—Ramsey Lewis And Earth, Wind & Fire (74)	123
What's The Name Of This Funk (Spider Man)—Ramsey Lewis (76)	47
Sam H. STEPT ▶ 9319 (3)	**26**
I'll Always Be In Love With You—Jack Pleis and His Orchestra and Chorus (56)	*79*
I'll Always Be In Love With You—Stroll Kings (58)	*0.0*
I'll Always Be In Love With You—Rosemary June (58)	*0.0*
Bruce STERLING ▶ 4546 (1)	**467**
The Way I Feel About You—Karyn White (91)	1868
Donnie Ray STERLING ▶ 11562 (1)	**1.2**
Agony of DeFeet—Parliament (81)	3.6
John STERLING ▶ 7181 (2)	**111**
The Night—Animals (83)	309
Soledad—Eric Burdon & Jimmy Witherspoon (71)	17

Lester STERLING ▶ 10696 (1)	**6.0**
Groovin'—UB40 (91)	12
—Ralph Sterling see: David CARROLL	
—Heidi Stern see: Jennifer RUSH	
Toni STERN ▶ 685 (9)	**6356**
It's Too Late—Carole King (71)	*8487*
Sweet Seasons—Carole King (72)	1709
It's Going To Take Some Time—Carpenters (72)	1120
Where You Lead—Barbra Streisand (71)	*423*
No Sad Song—Helen Reddy (71)	356
What Am I Gonna Do—Smith (70)	307
Where You Lead—Barbra Streisand (72)	*280*
It's Too Late—Bill Deal & The Rhondels (72)	*29*
As We Go Along—Monkees (68)	0.0
Liam STERNBERG ▶ 835 (1)	**5283**
Walk Like An Egyptian—Bangles (86)	5283
David STERRY ▶ 3253 (3)	**925**
Send Me An Angel—Real Life (83)	*786*
Send Me An Angel '89—Real Life (89)	*703*
Catch Me I'm Falling—Real Life (84)	360
April STEVENS [Carol Lo Tempio] ▶ 8939 (3)	**36**
A Woman's Story—Cher (74)	60
Wake Up And Love Me—April (74)	34
Teach Me Tiger—April Stevens (59)	8.6
Bobby STEVENS ▶ 6643 (1)	**148**
Love Is All I Have To Give—Checkmates, Ltd. (69)	297
—Bruce Noel Stevens see: Even STEVENS	
Carl STEVENS [Charles H. Sagle] ▶ 5271 (3)	**314**
High Sign—Diamonds (58)	560
Don't Say Goodbye—Diamonds (57)	69
Come Along With Me—Del Vikings (57)	11
Cat STEVENS [Steven Demetre Georgiou, Yusuf Islam] ▶ 249 (20)	**13800**
Peace Train—Cat Stevens (71)	2952
Here Comes My Baby—Tremeloes (67)	1586
Oh Very Young—Cat Stevens (74)	1487
Wild World—Cat Stevens (71)	*1379*
Sitting—Cat Stevens (72)	1038
Moon Shadow—Cat Stevens (71)	884
The First Cut Is The Deepest—Rod Stewart (77)	*718*
Wild World—Maxi Priest (88)	716
The Hurt—Cat Stevens (73)	710
Ready—Cat Stevens (74)	581
First Cut Is The Deepest—Keith Hampshire (73)	*432*
(Remember The Days Of The) Old Schoolyard—Cat Stevens (77)	353
Two Fine People—Cat Stevens (75)	310
Banapple Gas—Cat Stevens (76)	275
How Can I Tell You—Travis Wammack (72)	238
Was Dog A Doughnut—Cat Stevens (77)	183
Wild World—Gentrys (71)	*55*
Bad Brakes—Cat Stevens (79)	21
Matthew And Son—Cat Stevens (67)	14
Where Are You—Cat Stevens (72)	1.2
Even STEVENS [Bruce Noel Stevens] ▶ 547 (12)	**7864**
I Love A Rainy Night—Eddie Rabbitt (80)	4947
When You're In Love With A Beautiful Woman—Dr. Hook (79)	3090
Drivin' My Life Away—Eddie Rabbitt (80)	3070
Step By Step—Eddie Rabbitt (81)	2893
Love Will Turn You Around—Kenny Rogers (82)	1322
Suspicions—Eddie Rabbitt (79)	1079
Someone Could Lose A Heart Tonight—Eddie Rabbitt (81)	961
You Can't Run From Love—Eddie Rabbitt (83)	181
All The Time In The World—Dr. Hook (79)	167
Loveline—Dr. Hook (82)	132
I Can't Help Myself—Eddie Rabbitt (77)	42
Gone Too Far—Eddie Rabbitt (80)	23
—Fred Stevens see: Sol MARCUS	
Geoffrey STEVENS [Stephen Geoffrey Eisenberg] ▶ 5953 (1)	**223**
The Girl That Stood Beside Me—Bobby Darin (66)	223
Hunt STEVENS ▶ 6342 (2)	**181**
Lasting Love—Sal Mineo (57)	*362*
Lasting Love—Kitty Kallen (57)	*0.0*
Jay STEVENS ▶ 2273 (1)	**1668**
Rocky—Austin Roberts (75)	1668
Leith STEVENS ▶ 7605 (1)	**86**
Julie—Doris Day (56)	172

Lisa STEVENS ▶ 3979 (1)	**632**
Holiday—Madonna (83)	1264
Lona STEVENS [Lona Spector] ▶ 1876 (2)	**2173**
Sally, Go 'Round The Roses—Jaynetts (63)	4285
Dear Abby—Hearts (63)	31
Mark STEVENS ▶ 6202 (1)	**194**
Da' Butt—E.U. (88)	387
Mort STEVENS [Morton Aaron Suckno] ▶ 1660 (3)	**2532**
Hawaii Five-O—Ventures (69)	*2519*
Hawaii 5-0—Jive Bunny & The Mastermixers (90)	*6.7*
Hawaii 5-0—Jive Bunny & The Mastermixers (90)	*6.7*
Neil STEVENS ▶ 10662 (1)	**6.3**
Teenage Vows Of Love—Dreamers (61)	19
Perry STEVENS ▶ 6624 (1)	**150**
We Go Together—Jan & Dean (60)	300
Ray STEVENS [Harold Ray Ragsdale] ▶ 122 (25)	**21335**
The Streak—Ray Stevens (74)	5988
Everything Is Beautiful—Ray Stevens (70)	4945
Ahab, The Arab—Ray Stevens (62)	3618
Gitarzan—Ray Stevens (69)	2376
Harry The Hairy Ape—Ray Stevens (63)	850
Can't Stop Dancin'—Captain & Tennille (77)	837
Mr. Businessman—Ray Stevens (68)	817
My True Confession—Brook Benton (63)	675
Bridget The Midget (The Queen Of The Blues)—Ray Stevens (70)	490
Unwind—Ray Stevens (68)	477
America, Communicate With Me—Ray Stevens (70)	426
Jeremiah Peabody's Poly Unsaturated Quick Dissolving Fast Acting Pleasant Tasting Green And Purple Pills—Ray Stevens (61)	358
Isn't It Lonely Together—O.C. Smith (68)	*326*
Santa Claus Is Watching You—Ray Stevens (62)	231
For He's A Jolly Good Fellow—Bobby Vinton (67)	223
Moonlight Special—Ray Stevens (74)	197
Speed Ball—Ray Stevens (63)	151
Sunset Strip—Ray Stevens (70)	113
Funny Man—Ray Stevens (63)	58
Further More—Ray Stevens (62)	55
Freddie Feelgood (And His Funky Little Five Piece Band)—Ray Stevens (66)	39
The Great Escape—Ray Stevens (68)	15
Isn't It Lonely Together—Robert Knight (68)	*8.8*
Shriner's Convention—Ray Stevens (80)	3.4
Make Me Smile Again—Cathy Jean (61)	2.4
Shakin' STEVENS [Michael Barratt] ▶ 5317 (1)	**307**
Oh Julie—Barry Manilow (82)	307
Steve STEVENS [Steven Bruce Schneider] ▶ 1895 (4)	**2141**
Eyes Without A Face—Billy Idol (84)	3144
Flesh For Fantasy—Billy Idol (84)	488
Rebel Yell—Billy Idol (84)	476
You're Amazing—Robert Palmer (90)	439
Thomas M. STEVENS ▶ 8966 (1)	**35**
I Shoulda Loved Ya—Narada Michael Walden (80)	105
—Yvette Stevens see: Chaka KHAN	
—Augustus Stevenson see: Bobby STEVENSON	
Bobby STEVENSON [Augustus Stevenson] ▶ 738 (13)	**5947**
So Many Ways—Brook Benton (59)	3632
Start Movin' (In My Direction)—Sal Mineo (57)	1620
Hey Little Girl—Dee Clark (59)	*1126*
For My Good Fortune—Pat Boone (58)	*608*
Shake! Shake! Shake!—Jackie Wilson (63)	477
Rockin' Shoes—Ames Brothers (57)	227
I Don't Know—Ruth Brown (59)	179
Please Say You're Fooling—Ray Charles And His Orchestra (66)	161
You Went Back On Your Word—Clyde McPhatter (59)	43
Hey, Little Girl—Foster Sylvers (73)	*24*
I Dig You Baby—Marivn Rainwater (58)	11
No Wheels—Chordettes (59)	6.1
For My Good Fortune—Mahalia Jackson (58)	*0.0*
B.W. STEVENSON ▶ 3205 (1)	**954**
My Maria—B.W. Stevenson (73)	1909
Don STEVENSON ▶ 11264 (1)	**2.5**
Hey Grandma—Moby Grape (67)	5.1

James STEVENSON ► 8654 (2)	**44**
Jealous—Gene Loves Jezebel (90)	164
The Motion Of Love—Gene Loves Jezebel (88)	11
Joe STEVENSON ► 11160 (1)	**3.0**
Snap-Out—Interpertations (69)	8.9
John STEVENSON ► 2197 (2)	**1753**
Rock And Roll Heaven—Righteous Brothers (74)	3330
If It Feels Good, Do It—Ian Lloyd & Stories (74)	88
—Mickey Stevenson see: William STEVENSON	
William STEVENSON [Mickey Stevenson, William R. Stevenson Jr.] ► 349 (48)	**10795**
Dancing In The Street—Martha & The Vandellas (64)	*5484*
Devil With A Blue Dress On— Mitch Ryder And The Detroit Wheels (66)	*2815*
Playboy—Marvelettes (62)	2321
Pride And Joy—Marvin Gaye (63)	1884
Dancing In The Street— Mick Jagger & David Bowie (85)	*1333*
Beechwood 4-5789—Marvelettes (62)	*1082*
It Takes Two—Marvin Gaye & Kim Weston (67)	1078
My Baby Loves Me—Martha & The Vandellas (66)	*999*
What's The Matter With You Baby— Marvin Gaye & Mary Wells (64)	929
Once Upon A Time—Marvin Gaye & Mary Wells (64)	797
Nothing's Too Good For My Baby— Stevie Wonder (66)	775
Ask The Lonely—Four Tops (65)	738
Jamie—Eddie Holland (62)	637
Stubborn Kind Of Fellow—Marvin Gaye (62)	594
Hitch Hike—Marvin Gaye (63)	562
It Should Have Been Me— Gladys Knight & The Pips (68)	*557*
Twistin' Postman—Marvelettes (62)	539
Needle In A Haystack—Velvelettes (64)	477
I'll Always Love You—Spinners (65)	466
I'll Keep Holding On—Marvelettes (65)	405
Dancing In The Street—Van Halen (82)	*390*
Wild One—Martha & The Vandellas (64)	377
You've Been In Love Too Long— Martha & The Vandellas (65)	348
I Don't Want To Take A Chance—Mary Wells (61)	294
Danger Heartbreak Dead Ahead—Marvelettes (65)	246
Can You Jerk Like Me—Contours (64)	228
My Baby Loves Me—David T. Walker (69)	*174*
He Was Really Sayin' Somethin'—Velvelettes (65)	172
She Said Yes—Wilson Pickett (70)	169
What Good Am I Without You— Marvin Gaye & Kim Weston (64)	163
Loving You—Johnny Nash (74)	147
What Am I Going To Do Without Your Love— Martha & The Vandellas (66)	135
Love Me All The Way—Kim Weston (63)	130
Dancin' In The Streets—Teri DeSario with K.C. (80)	*98*
Stranded In The Middle Of Noplace— Righteous Brothers (67)	85
Dancing In The Street—Mamas & The Papas (66)	*77*
I Got What You Need—Kim Weston (67)	64
Truly Yours—Spinners (66)	63
Beechwood 4-5789—Carpenters (82)	*52*
Devil With A Blue Dress—Pratt & McClain (76)	*34*
Dancing In The Street—Ramsey Lewis (67)	*27*
I'm Crazy 'Bout My Baby—Marvin Gaye (63)	27
It Should Have Been Me—Yvonne Fair (76)	*17*
I'm Falling In Love—Hodges, James & Smith (77)	3.9
I Want You 'round—Marvin Gaye & Kim Weston (64)	1.3
Been So Nice—Righteous Brothers (67)	0.9
Dancing In The Street—Tight Fit (81)	*0.9*
Dancing In The Street—Dovells (74)	*0.3*
W.S. STEVENSON [William Aubry McCall] ► 1150 (11)	**3862**
Lonely Street—Andy Williams (59)	3082
Hot Rod Lincoln— Commander Cody And His Lost Planet Airmen (72)	*1950*
Am I That Easy To Forget—Debbie Reynolds (60)	*1149*
Am I That Easy To Forget— Engelbert Humperdinck (67)	*1119*
Hot Rod Lincoln— Charlie Ryan And The Timberline Riders (60)	*915*
Hot Rod Lincoln—Johnny Bond (60)	*790*
There She Goes—Jerry Wallace (60)	631
Three Cigarettes In An Ashtray—Patsy Cline (57)	43
Side Car Cycle— Charlie Ryan And The Timberline Riders (60)	34
Am I That Easy To Forget— "Little Esther" Phillips (63)	*5.3*
Am I That Easy To Forget—Skeeter Davis (60)	*0.0*
Rich STEVERS ► 6694 (1)	**143**
Sing A Song For Freedom—Frijid Pink (70)	430
STEVIE B [Steven Bernard Hill] ► 1899 (8)	**2138**
I'll Be By Your Side—Stevie B (91)	907
I Wanna Be The One—Stevie B (89)	535
Love Me For Life—Stevie B (90)	463
Spring Love (Come Back To Me)—Stevie B (88)	449
If You Leave Me Now—Jaya (89)	414
In My Eyes—Stevie B (89)	281
Girl I Am Searching For You—Stevie B (89)	230
Dreamin' Of Love—Stevie B (88)	87
Jimmie STEWARD ► 4374 (2)	**510**
If My Pillow Could Talk—Connie Francis (63)	984
Someone To Come Home To—Ames Brothers (59)	35
Al STEWART ► 1399 (5)	**3176**
Year Of The Cat—Al Stewart (76)	2288
Time Passages—Al Stewart (78)	1891
Midnight Rocks—Al Stewart (80)	633
Song On The Radio—Al Stewart (79)	462
On The Border—Al Stewart (77)	307
Al (2) STEWART ► 4841 (1)	**401**
Come Closer To Me (Acercate Mas)— Nat "King" Cole (58)	801
Alton STEWART ► 5367 (3)	**299**
Talk To Myself—Christopher Williams (89)	406
Another Like My Lover—Jasmine Guy (91)	122
When Will I See You Smile Again?— Bell Biv DeVoe (91)	70
Andy STEWART ► 6529 (2)	**160**
A Scottish Soldier (Green Hills Of Tyrol)— Andy Stewart (61)	150
Donald Where's Your Troosers?—Andy Stewart (61)	20
Baron STEWART ► 9669 (1)	**19**
We Been Singin' Songs—Baron Stewart (75)	19
Beverly STEWART ► 10588 (1)	**7.1**
Kathleen—Wally Lewis (58)	14
Billy STEWART ► 1439 (8)	**3034**
I Do Love You—GQ (79)	*951*
I Do Love You—Billy Stewart (65)	*899*
Sitting In The Park—Billy Stewart (65)	*713*
Reap What You Sow—Billy Stewart (62)	257
Strange Feeling—Billy Stewart (63)	110
How Nice It Is—Billy Stewart (65)	82
Sitting In The Park—GQ (80)	*14*
I Do Love You—Billy Stewart (69)	*8.2*
David A. STEWART ► 402 (20)	**9858**
Sweet Dreams (Are Made Of This)—Eurythmics (83)	6027
Here Comes The Rain Again—Eurythmics (84)	2759
Would I Lie To You?—Eurythmics (85)	2003
Lily Was Here—David A. Stewart (91)	1128
Don't Come Around Here No More— Tom Petty and The Heartbreakers (85)	1060
Missionary Man—Eurythmics (86)	989
Who's That Girl?—Eurythmics (84)	681
Sisters Are Doin' It For Themselves— Eurythmics And Aretha Franklin (85)	674
Love Is A Stranger—Eurythmics (83)	634
There Must Be An Angel (Playing With My Heart)— Eurythmics (85)	546
Right By Your Side—Eurythmics (84)	489
Don't Ask Me Why—Eurythmics (89)	350
Let's Work—Mick Jagger (87)	291
I Need A Man—Eurythmics (87)	231
Ruthless People—Mick Jagger (86)	219
Make It Better (Forget About Me)— Tom Petty and The Heartbreakers (85)	194
Thorn In My Side—Eurythmics (86)	152
You Have Placed A Chill In My Heart— Eurythmics (88)	149
It's Alright (Baby's Coming Back)—Eurythmics (86)	62
Sexcrime (Nineteen Eighty-Four)—Eurythmics (84)	23
Dorothy STEWART ► 9389 (1)	**25**
Now Is The Hour—Gale Storm (56)	74
Eric STEWART ► 861 (12)	**5171**
I'm Not In Love—10cc (75)	*4276*
The Things We Do For Love—10CC (77)	3173
I'm Not In Love—Will To Power (90)	*1398*
Neanderthal Man—Hotlegs (70)	948
Dreadlock Holiday—10 CC (78)	364
People In Love—10cc (77)	124
Good Morning Judge—10CC (77)	119
Art For Art's Sake—10CC (75)	88
For You And I—10cc (79)	60
Stranglehold—Paul McCartney (86)	60
I'm Mandy Fly Me—10cc (76)	55
The Wall Street Shuffle—10 C. C. (74)	11
—Henry Ellis Stewart see: Redd STEWART	
Jermaine STEWART ► 5255 (2)	**317**
The Word Is Out—Jermaine Stewart (85)	442
Jody—Jermaine Stewart (86)	290
John STEWART ► 216 (10)	**15180**
Daydream Believer—Monkees (67)	*9734*
Gold—John Stewart (79)	2588
Daydream Believer—Anne Murray (79)	*1419*
Midnight Wind—John Stewart (79)	505
Lost Her In The Sun—John Stewart (79)	459
Never Going Back—Lovin' Spoonful (68)	207
Armstrong—John Stewart (69)	128
Daydream Believer—Monkees (86)	*57*
One More Town—Kingston Trio (62)	56
July You're A Woman—Pat Boone (69)	26
Kit STEWART ► 6981 (1)	**124**
Won't Find Better (Than Me)—New Hope (70)	248
Michael STEWART ► 10683 (2)	**6.1**
Tower Trot (And Then You Do That Step)— Dick Jacobs And His Chorus And Orchestra (57)	23
I Love My Wife—Frank Sinatra (77)	7.0
Michael D. STEWART ► 7823 (2)	**73**
Don't You Know How Much I Love You— Ronnie Milsap (83)	138
I Love Women—Jim Hurt (80)	9.0
Morris STEWART ► 9871 (1)	**16**
What's The Name Of This Funk (Spider Man)— Ramsey Lewis (76)	47
Paul STEWART [Omari M. Shabazz] ► 7343 (1)	**101**
B.B.D. (I Thought It Was Me)?—Bell Biv DeVoe (90)	504
Peter STEWART ► 11191 (1)	**2.8**
Maybe This Day—Kissing The Pink (83)	20
Randall STEWART ► 6851 (2)	**132**
Opportunity—Jewels (64)	264
To The Other Man—Luther Ingram (70)	1.7
Redd STEWART [Henry Ellis Stewart] ► 2579 (7)	**1353**
You Belong To Me—Duprees (62)	*1989*
Tennessee Waltz—Sam Cooke (64)	*546*
Tennessee Waltz— Bobby Comstock & The Counts (59)	*385*
Bonaparte's Retreat—Billy Grammer (59)	342
Tennessee Waltz—Jerry Fuller (59)	*177*
You Belong To Me—100 Strings & Joni (60)	*46*
Soldier's Last Letter— Merle Haggard & The Strangers (71)	13
Reggie STEWART ► 8464 (1)	**50**
The Comfort Zone—Vanessa Williams (91)	99
Rod STEWART ► 103 (24)	**24451**
Da Ya Think I'm Sexy?—Rod Stewart (78)	*8390*
Tonight's The Night (Gonna Be Alright)— Rod Stewart (76)	8071
Maggie May—Rod Stewart (71)	5183
You're In My Heart (The Final Acclaim)— Rod Stewart (77)	3640
Young Turks—Rod Stewart (81)	3203
Passion—Rod Stewart (80)	2748
Infatuation—Rod Stewart (84)	2065
Stay With Me—Faces (71)	1429
Crazy About Her—Rod Stewart (89)	1149
You Wear It Well—Rod Stewart (72)	1133
Forever Young—Rod Stewart (88)	1122
Baby Jane—Rod Stewart (83)	1035
Lost In You—Rod Stewart (88)	958
Tonight I'm Yours (Don't Hurt Me)—Rod Stewart (82)	845
Ain't Love A Bitch—Rod Stewart (79)	745
I Was Only Joking—Rod Stewart (78)	675
Hot Legs—Rod Stewart (78)	516
What Am I Gonna Do (I'm So In Love With You)— Rod Stewart (83)	446
The Killing Of Georgie (Part I And II)— Rod Stewart (77)	386

Rod STEWART ► 103 (24) *Continued*	**24451**
Cindy Incidentally—Faces (73)	365
Another Heartache—Rod Stewart (86)	259
Do You Think I'm Disco?—Steve Dahl And Teenage Radiation (79)	*131*
Every Beat Of My Heart—Rod Stewart (86)	63
Somebody Special—Rod Stewart (81)	44
Sandy STEWART ► 2988 (3)	**1080**
If Anyone Falls—Stevie Nicks (83)	979
Seven Wonders—Fleetwood Mac (87)	683
Nightbird—Stevie Nicks (83)	497
—Siobhan Stewart see: Siobhan FAHEY	
Steven STEWART ► 4502 (1)	**475**
Smoke From A Distant Fire—Sanford/Townsend Band (77)	1425
Sylvester STEWART [Sly Stone] ► 51 (33)	**41047**
Everyday People—Sly & The Family Stone (68)	*9208*
Family Affair—Sly & The Family Stone (71)	8171
Thank You (Falettinme Be Mice Elf Agin)—Sly & The Family Stone (70)	5996
Hot Fun In The Summertime—Sly & The Family Stone (69)	*3717*
Dance To The Music—Sly & The Family Stone (68)	*2746*
C'mon And Swim—Bobby Freeman (64)	2736
If You Want Me To Stay—Sly & The Family Stone (73)	1552
Runnin' Away—Sly & The Family Stone (72)	1052
You're The One - Part II—Little Sister (70)	*1025*
Somebody's Watching You—Little Sister (70)	896
Stand!—Sly & The Family Stone (69)	717
I Want To Take You Higher—Ike & Tina Turner & The Ikettes (70)	*690*
Everybody Is A Star—Sly & The Family Stone (70)	663
Smilin'—Sly & The Family Stone (72)	542
Mama Said Knock You Out—LL Cool J (91)	473
Time For Livin'—Sly & The Family Stone (74)	468
I Want To Take You Higher—Sly & The Family Stone (70)	*357*
I Get High On You—Sly Stone (75)	349
Everyday People—Joan Jett and the Blackhearts (83)	*291*
Life And Death In G & A—Abaco Dream (69)	*232*
You're The One—Three Degrees (71)	*198*
I Want To Take You Higher—Sly & The Family Stone (69)	*165*
S-W-I-M—Bobby Freeman (64)	164
Life—Sly & The Family Stone (68)	132
Hot Fun In The Summertime—Dayton (82)	*117*
Hot Fun In The Summertime—David T. Walker (72)	*76*
Frisky—Sly & The Family Stone (73)	74
Loose Booty—Sly & The Family Stone (74)	30
M'lady—Sly & The Family Stone (68)	21
Sing A Simple Song—Sly & The Family Stone (69)	*21*
Sing A Simple Song—West Street Mob (82)	*16*
Dance To The Music—Stars On 45 (81)	*12*
Life And Death In G&A—Love Childs Afro Cuban Blues Band (75)	*10*
Virgil STEWART ► 2500 (2)	**1434**
Just Out Of Reach (Of My Two Open Arms)—Solomon Burke (61)	*1246*
Just Out Of Reach (Of My Two Empty Arms)—Percy Sledge (67)	*188*
Winston STEWART ► 6888 (9)	**131**
Shake Your Rump To The Funk—Bar-Kays (76)	593
Move Your Boogie Body—Bar-Kays (79)	270
Today Is The Day—Bar-Kays (80)	150
Freakshow On The Dance Floor—Bar-Kays (84)	79
Too Hot To Stop—Bar-Kays (77)	36
Hit And Run—Bar-Kays (81)	23
Boogie Body Land—Bar-Kays (81)	23
Let's Have Some Fun—Bar-Kays (78)	8.9
Shine—Bar-Kays (79)	7.7
Derek ST. HOLMES ► 7694 (1)	**80**
Hey Baby—Ted Nugent (76)	80
Curtis STIGERS ► 3925 (1)	**654**
I Wonder Why—Curtis Stigers (91)	1308
Al STILLMAN [Albert Silverman] ► 125 (50) HOF	**20848**
Moments To Remember—Four Lads (55)	*7587*
Chances Are—Johnny Mathis (57)	5455
No Not Much—Four Lads (56)	*4830*
It's Not For Me To Say—Johnny Mathis (57)	*4673*
The Way Of Love—Cher (72)	*2031*

The Breeze And I (Andalucia)—Caterina Valente (55)	*1684*
Can You Find It In Your Heart—Tony Bennett with Percy Faith and His Orchestra (56)	1683
Who Needs You—Four Lads (57)	1611
If Dreams Came True—Pat Boone (58)	1550
And That Reminds Me—Della Reese (57)	*1323*
Enchanted Island—Four Lads (58)	*1229*
There's Only One Of You—Four Lads (58)	957
I Believe—Bachelors (64)	*702*
And That Reminds Me (My Heart Reminds Me)—4 Seasons (69)	*593*
(I Love You) Don't You Forget It—Perry Como (63)	521
Every Step Of The Way—Johnny Mathis (63)	509
My Heart Reminds Me—Kay Starr (57)	*496*
Teacher Teacher—Johnny Mathis (58)	461
The Little Boy—Tony Bennett (63)	428
(There's No Place Like) Home For The Holidays—Perry Como (54)	414
Happy Anniversary—Jane Morgan (59)	*388*
Door Of Dreams—Perry Como (55)	376
No, Not Much—Vogues (69)	*361*
Moments To Remember—Vogues (69)	*335*
I Only Know I Love You—Four Aces (56)	*324*
Truly, Truly, True—Brenda Lee (65)	274
There's Nothing I Can Say—Rick Nelson (64)	265
No Not Much—Smoke Ring (69)	*215*
Eyes Of God—Four Lads (57)	179
Happy Anniversary—Four Lads (59)	*171*
Barking Dog—Crew-Cuts (54)	168
Scene Of The Crime—Dinah Shore (58)	132
That's The Way It Goes—Eddie Fisher (57)	108
Juke Box Saturday Night—Nino & the Ebb Tides (61)	88
The Way Of Love—Kathy Kirby (65)	*38*
Coming From You—Joni James (58)	27
I Saw Mommy Do The Mambo (With You Know Who)—Jimmy Boyd (54)	15
Book Of Love—Richard Maltby And His Orchestra (55)	14
Love Me Good—Jo Stafford (56)	14
Very Much In Love—Johnny Mathis (59)	13
I Believe—Roy Hamilton (55)	*5.6*
You Know How It Is—Frankie Laine (57)	5.1
I Believe—Elvis Presley (57)	*2.1*
Still Small Voice—Perry Como (59)	1.6
Romantica—Jane Morgan (60)	*0.0*
Autumn Concerto—Nick Noble (56)	*0.0*
It's Not For Me To Say—Jane Morgan (57)	*0.0*
I Only Know I Love You—Johnny Desmond (56)	*0.0*
Enchanted Island—Jane Morgan & The Troubadors (58)	*0.0*
It's Not For Me To Say—Cyril Stapleton & His Orchestra (57)	*0.0*
Christopher STILLS ► 7744 (1)	**77**
Stranger—Stephen Stills (84)	153
Stephen STILLS ► 339 (25) HOF	**10972**
For What It's Worth (Stop, Hey What's That Sound)—Buffalo Springfield (67)	*2673*
Love The One You're With—Stephen Stills (70)	*1448*
Love The One You're With—Isley Brothers (71)	*1193*
Suite: Judy Blue Eyes—Crosby, Stills & Nash (69)	1173
Southern Cross—Crosby, Stills & Nash (82)	1029
Sit Down, I Think I Love You—Mojo Men (67)	678
Marianne—Stephen Stills (71)	621
Change Partners—Stephen Stills (71)	494
Sit Yourself Down—Stephen Stills (71)	364
Rock 'N' Roll Woman—Buffalo Springfield (67)	323
It Doesn't Matter—Stephen Stills (72)	312
Fair Game—Crosby, Stills & Nash (77)	296
War Games—Crosby, Stills & Nash (83)	291
Bluebird—Buffalo Springfield (67)	236
Isn't It About Time—Stephen Stills -- Manassas (73)	235
For What It's Worth—Staple Singers (67)	*196*
Stranger—Stephen Stills (84)	153
Got It Made—Crosby, Stills, Nash & Young (89)	138
Too Much Love To Hide—Crosby, Stills & Nash (83)	94
Turn Back The Pages—Stephen Stills (75)	43
For What It's Worth—King Curtis & The Kingpins (67)	*15*
Crazies—Stephen Stills -- Manassas (72)	8.8
Jet Set (Sigh)—Stephen Stills -- Manassas (72)	8.8
Cuban Bluegrass—Stephen Stills -- Manassas (72)	8.8
For What It's Worth—Cher (69)	*5.6*
John STIMPSON ► 10339 (1)	**9.9**
La-Di-Da—Sad Café (81)	20

STING [Gordon Sumner] ► 60 (23) HOF	**35386**
Every Breath You Take—Police (83)	10116
Money For Nothing—Dire Straits (85)	5636
If You Love Somebody Set Them Free—Sting (85)	3097
King Of Pain—Police (83)	*2573*
Every Little Thing She Does Is Magic—Police (81)	2455
All This Time—Sting (91)	1694
We'll Be Together—Sting (87)	1612
De Do Do Do, De Da Da Da—Police (80)	1565
Don't Stand So Close To Me—Police (81)	*1454*
Fortress Around Your Heart—Sting (85)	1401
Wrapped Around Your Finger—Police (84)	1368
Synchronicity II—Police (83)	966
Spirits In The Material World—Police (82)	963
Russians—Sting (86)	832
Love Is The Seventh Wave—Sting (85)	823
Be Still My Beating Heart—Sting (88)	816
Roxanne—Police (79)	533
Secret Journey—Police (82)	256
Don't Stand So Close To Me '86—Police (86)	*213*
Message In A Bottle—Police (79)	136
King Of Suede—"Weird Al" Yankovic (84)	*120*
Englishman In New York—Sting (88)	40
Why Should I Cry For You?—Sting (91)	13
Dorothy STIPE ► 11009 (1)	**3.9**
Itchin'—Jimmy Jones (60)	12
Michael STIPE ► 2219 (10)	**1729**
Losing My Religion—R.E.M. (91)	2447
Stand—R.E.M. (89)	1642
Shiny Happy People—R.E.M. (91)	1294
The One I Love—R.E.M. (87)	1261
It's The End Of The World As We Know It (And I Feel Fine)—R.E.M. (88)	87
So. Central Rain (I'm Sorry)—R.E.M. (84)	50
Pop Song 89—R.E.M. (89)	43
Radio Song—R.E.M. (91)	42
Radio Free Europe—R.E.M. (83)	34
Fall On Me—R.E.M. (86)	16
Don STIRLING [Anthony Petolino] ► 7693 (1)	**80**
Too Many Rules—Connie Francis (61)	160
—Lionel Michael Stitcher see: Mitch MURRAY	
Gary STITES ► 3566 (3)	**784**
Lonely For You—Gary Stites (59)	705
Girl Like You—Gary Stites (59)	74
Hey Little Girl—Gary Stites (59)	5.6
Bill STITH ► 11699 (1)	**0.6**
Big Bruce—Steve Greenberg (69)	*3.1*
Mel STITZEL ► 11450 (2)	**1.6**
Make Love To Me—Johnny Thunder & Ruby Winters (67)	*13*
Make Love To Me!—Jo Stafford (54)	*0.0*
Jon ST. JAMES [Jon Willoughby] ► 5039 (5)	**355**
When We Kiss—Bardeux (88)	411
I Love The Bass—Bardeux (89)	168
Don't Make A Fool Of Yourself—Stacey Q (88)	125
Magic Carpet Ride—Bardeux (88)	80
Shy Girl—Stacey Q (87)	36
—Dick St. John see: Dick GOSTING	
Ray ST. JOHN ► 2989 (1)	**1079**
Smooth Operator—Sade (85)	2158
Keni ST. LEWIS ► 613 (10)	**7051**
Boogie Fever—Sylvers (76)	6020
Hot Line—Sylvers (76)	3594
Heaven Must Be Missing An Angel (Part 1)—Tavares (76)	1546
Whodunit—Tavares (77)	926
I Fooled You This Time—Gene Chandler (66)	492
Farewell My Summer Love—Michael Jackson (84)	426
Don't Take Away The Music—Tavares (76)	416
Girl Don't Care—Gene Chandler (67)	330
Cotton Candy—Sylvers (76)	95
Memory Lane—Minnie Riperton (79)	3.4
Louis ST. LOUIS ► 9289 (1)	**27**
Back To School Again—Four Tops (82)	54
Nick ST. NICHOLAS [Klaus Karl Kassbaum] ► 6248 (2)	**190**
It's Never Too Late—Steppenwolf (69)	342
America/Standing—Five Stairsteps (70)	93

Larry STOCK ▶ 1263 (15) HOF	**3539**
Blueberry Hill—Fats Domino (56)	*5648*
Morning Side Of The Mountain— Donny And Marie Osmond (74)	*1717*
You're Nobody Till Somebody Loves You— Dean Martin (64)	*699*
Morning Side Of The Mountain—Tommy Edwards (59)	*606*
Blueberry Hill— Louis Armstrong and Gordon Jenkins and His Orchestra And Chorus (56)	*265*
Hearts—Jackie Wilson (62)	211
All The Way 'round The World—Mills Brothers (56)	75
You're Nobody Till Somebody Loves You— Wonder Who ? (66)	*21*
Whispering Heart—Sherry Parsons (56)	14
You're Nobody Till Somebody Loves You— Damita Jo (62)	*10*
Slowly But Surely— Gordon Jenkins And His Orchestra and Chorus (54)	8.9
You're Nobody 'Til Somebody Loves You— Mills Brothers (54)	*6.0*
You're Nobody 'til Somebody Loves You— Dinah Washington (62)	*6.0*
Crying Roses—Kitty Kallen (57)	5.6
I'll Be Worthy Of You—Cab Calloway (56)	5.6
Mike STOCK ▶ 1063 (15)	**4156**
Never Gonna Give You Up—Rick Astley (87)	4405
Together Forever (Remix)—Rick Astley (88)	3168
I Heard A Rumour—Bananarama (87)	2288
This Time I Know It's For Real—Donna Summer (89)	1582
It Would Take A Strong Strong Man—Rick Astley (88)	1136
I Should Be So Lucky—Kylie Minogue (88)	512
It's No Secret—Kylie Minogue (88)	419
I Can't Help It—Bananarama (87)	331
Love In The First Degree—Bananarama (88)	262
More Than Physical—Bananarama (86)	74
Love, Truth And Honesty—Bananarama (88)	64
Showing Out (Get Fresh At The Weekend)— Mel & Kim (87)	51
Nothing's Gonna Stop Me Now—Samantha Fox (87)	50
Wouldn't Change A Thing—Kylie Minogue (90)	19
Love's About To Change My Heart— Donna Summer (89)	12
Wally STOCKER ▶ 9659 (2)	**19**
Head First—Babys (79)	44
If You've Got The Time—Babys (77)	18
Ron STOCKERT ▶ 9168 (1)	**30**
Slip 'N Slide—Rufus (73)	30
Jon STOCKLIN ▶ 8200 (1)	**58**
Want You To Know—Rotary Connection (69)	58
Shawn STOCKMAN ▶ 3807 (1)	**694**
Motownphilly—Boyz II Men (91)	2776
Michael Lee STOKES ▶ 4063 (7)	**607**
Gloria—Enchantment (77)	511
It's You That I Need—Enchantment (78)	430
Sunshine—Enchantment (77)	151
I Just Can't Control Myself—Nature's Divine (79)	127
Magic Man—Herb Alpert (81)	22
If You're Ready (Here It Comes)—Enchantment (78)	16
Feels Like Another One—Patti LaBelle (91)	13
—Nicholas Stokes see: Simon STOKES	
Otis STOKES ▶ 9020 (1)	**33**
Fantastic Voyage—Lakeside (80)	296
Simon STOKES [Nicholas Stokes] ▶ 6761 (2)	**139**
Captain Howdy—Simon Stokes (74)	112
Voodoo Woman— Simon Stokes & The Nighthawks (69)	55
—J. W. Stole see: Franck POURCEL	
Mike STOLLER [Elmo Glick, Jed Peters] ▶ 28 (117) HOF	**50686**
Jailhouse Rock—Elvis Presley (57)	*8238*
Kansas City—Wilbert Harrison (59)	*6968*
Charlie Brown—Coasters (59)	6481
Hound Dog—Elvis Presley (56)	*6329*
Ruby Baby—Dion (63)	*6167*
Love Potion Number Nine—Searchers (64)	*5796*
Yakety Yak—Coasters (58)	5603
There Goes My Baby—Drifters (59)	*4700*
Don't—Elvis Presley (58)	4291
Stand By Me—Ben E. King (61)	*3409*
She's Not You—Elvis Presley With The Jordanaires (62)	3394
I Keep Forgettin'—Michael McDonald (82)	*3365*

Searchin'—Coasters (57)	*3311*
Poison Ivy—Coasters (59)	2586
Drip Drop—Dion Di Muci (63)	*2250*
Reverend Mr. Black—Kingston Trio (63)	2205
Love Me—Elvis Presley (56)	*1990*
On Broadway—George Benson (78)	*1964*
Bossa Nova Baby— Elvis Presley With The Jordanaires (63)	1871
Stand By Me—Ben E. King (86)	*1763*
Along Came Jones—Coasters (59)	*1746*
Stand By Me—Spyder Turner (66)	*1730*
Black Denim Trousers And Motorcycle Boots— Cheers (55)	*1536*
Is That All There Is—Peggy Lee (69)	1534
Dance With Me—Drifters (59)	1398
On Broadway—Drifters (63)	*1347*
I (Who Have Nothing)—Tom Jones (70)	*1304*
Young Blood—Coasters (57)	*1268*
D.W. Washburn—Monkees (68)	1160
Stand By Me—Mickey Gilley (80)	*1122*
Love Potion Number Nine—Clovers (59)	*1042*
Bobbie Sue—Oak Ridge Boys (82)	1000
I'll Be There—Damita Jo (61)	897
I'm A Woman—Maria Muldaur (74)	*842*
Kansas City—Trini Lopez (63)	*840*
Little Egypt (Ying-Yang)—Coasters (61)	823
I (Who Have Nothing)—Ben E. King (63)	*810*
Only In America—Jay & The Americans (63)	804
(Bazoom) I Need Your Lovin'—Cheers (54)	*802*
Young Blood—Bad Company (76)	*795*
Loving You—Elvis Presley (57)	733
There Goes My Baby—Donna Summer (84)	*674*
Along Came Jones—Ray Stevens (69)	*668*
Stand By Me—John Lennon (75)	*647*
Lucky Lips—Ruth Brown (57)	*626*
I (Who Have Nothing)— Terry Knight And The Pack (66)	*588*
(How Bout A Little Hand For) The Boys In The Band— Boys In The Band (70)	572
What About Us—Coasters (59)	504
(When She Needs Good Lovin') She Comes To Me— Chicago Loop (66)	*428*
Run Red Run—Coasters (59)	418
I'm A Woman—Peggy Lee (62)	*394*
Framed—Cheech & Chong (76)	335
Saved—LaVern Baker (61)	327
Stand By Me—Maurice White (85)	*304*
Kansas City— James Brown And The Famous Flames (67)	*301*
Ruby, Baby—Billy "Crash" Craddock (74)	*300*
Treat Me Nice—Elvis Presley (57)	295
I Keep Forgettin'—Chuck Jackson (62)	*295*
Just Tell Her Jim Said Hello— Elvis Presley With The Jordanaires (62)	251
Stand By Me—David & Jimmy Ruffin (70)	*227*
King Creole— Elvis Presley with the Jordanaires (58)	192
(You're So Square) Baby, I Don't Care— Joni Mitchell (82)	189
Lucky Lips—Cliff Richard (63)	*180*
What To Do With Laurie—Mike Clifford (62)	165
Searching— Jack Eubanks And The Sound Of The South (61)	*149*
I (Who Have Nothing)—Sylvester (79)	*146*
I'm A Hog For You—Coasters (59)	133
Black Denim Trousers And Motorcycle Boots— Vaughn Monroe with Chorus And Orchestra (55)	*132*
Stand By Me—Earl Grant (65)	*129*
Kansas City—Hank Ballard And The Midnighters (59)	*119*
Shoppin' For Clothes—Coasters (60)	116
Rat Race—Drifters (63)	115
Love Potion Number Nine—Coasters (71)	*97*
Hound Dog—Jive Bunny And The Mastermixers (89)	*80*
Jailhouse Rock— Jive Bunny And The Mastermixers (89)	*80*
Searchin'—Jim Croce (76)	*76*
You're The Boss—Lavern Baker & Jimmy Ricks (61)	75
His Kiss—Betty Harris (64)	72
Young Blood—Bruce Willis (87)	*71*
I Who Have Nothing—Liquid Smoke (70)	*71*
My Claire De Lune—Steve Lawrence (61)	*68*
Dancin'—Perry Como (57)	61
Searchin'—Ace Cannon (64)	*59*

Blues For Me—Eddie Fisher (57)	51
Lucky Lips—Gale Storm (57)	*50*
Idol With The Golden Head—Coasters (57)	45
Kansas City—Rocky Olson (59)	*40*
Love Me—5 DeMarco Sisters (54)	*39*
One Kiss Led To Another—Coasters (56)	*37*
(When She Wants Good Lovin') My Baby Comes To Me—Coasters (57)	*29*
Fools Fall In Love—Drifters (57)	*29*
Get Him—Exciters (63)	26
Trouble—Elvis Presley with the Jordanaires (58)	24
Hound Dog—Elvis Presley (82)	*23*
Jailhouse Rock—Elvis Presley (82)	*23*
Dirty, Dirty Feeling— Elvis Presley With The Jordanaires (65)	23
Jack O' Diamonds—Ruth Brown (59)	22
Kansas City—Beatles (65)	*22*
Drip Drop—Drifters (58)	*21*
Girls Girls Girls (Part II)—Coasters (61)	21
Blueberries—Georgia Gibbs (55)	20
Stand By Me—Cassius Clay (64)	*14*
Searchin' (Medley)—Johnny Rivers (73)	*12*
Do Your Own Thing—Brook Benton (68)	8.6
Smokey Joe's Café—Robins (55)	6.4
Shadow Knows—Coasters (58)	4.6
Kansas City—Little Richard (59)	*3.8*
Santa Claus Is Back In Town—Elvis Presley (57)	2.1
Lovey—Clovers (60)	1.3
Drums—Kenny Chandler (61)	0.5
Fools Fall In Love—Elvis Presley (67)	*0.5*
Love Me—Georgia Gibbs (54)	*0.0*
Love Me—Connie Russell (54)	*0.0*
My Clair De Lune—George Feyer (61)	*0.0*
Love Me—Billy Williams Quartet (54)	*0.0*
One Kiss Led To Another—Sunny Gale (56)	*0.0*
Bazoom! (I Need Your Lovin')— Les Elgart & His Orchestra (54)	*0.0*
Morris STOLOFF ▶ 7324 (5)	**102**
To Love Again—Four Aces (56)	*408*
To Love Again—Vic Damone (56)	*0.0*
To Love Again—Bob Manning (56)	*0.0*
To Love Again—Marc Fredericks (56)	*0.0*
To Love Again—Carmen Cavallaro (56)	*0.0*
Bob STONE ▶ 615 (6)	**7038**
Gypsys, Tramps & Thieves—Cher (71)	6846
Ready, Willing And Able—American Breed (68)	92
I Can't Say No To You—Betty Everett (69)	83
We Can't Go On This Way—Unchained Mynds (69)	*14*
Don't Fool With Fu Manchu—Rockin' Ramrods (65)	2.8
We Can't Go On This Way— Teddy And The Pandas (66)	*1.4*
George STONE ▶ 4338 (3)	**517**
High Sign—Diamonds (58)	560
Shish Kebab—Ralph Marterie And His Orchestra (57)	427
Don't Say Goodbye—Diamonds (57)	69
Harry STONE ▶ 5714 (1)	**251**
Chattanooga Shoe Shine Boy—Freddy Cannon (60)	503
Henry STONE ▶ 3631 (6)	**758**
Two Hearts—Pat Boone (55)	*1486*
Have Faith—Gene Allison (58)	30
Two Hearts—Charms (55)	*0.0*
Two Hearts, Two Kisses (Make One Love)— Doris Day (55)	*0.0*
Two Hearts, Two Kisses (Make One Love)— 5 DeMarco Sisters (55)	*0.0*
Two Hearts, Two Kisses (Make One Love)— Frank Sinatra with The Nuggets (55)	*0.0*
Ivory STONE ▶ 9633 (1)	**20**
What's Too Much—Smokey Robinson (87)	80
Jesse STONE [Charles Calhoun] ▶ 496 (26) HOF	**8473**
Shake Rattle And Roll— Bill Haley And His Comets (54)	*3315*
Don't Let Go—Isaac Hayes (79)	*1196*
Don't Let Go—Roy Hamilton (57)	*1182*
Razzle-Dazzle—Bill Haley And His Comets (55)	*650*
Shake, Rattle & Roll—Arthur Conley (67)	*471*
Smack Dab In The Middle—Mills Brothers (55)	*397*
Your Cash Ain't Nothin' But Trash— Steve Miller Band (74)	341
Smack Dab In The Middle—Ray Charles And His Orchestra With The Raelettes (64)	*264*

Jesse STONE [Charles Calhoun] ▶ 496 (26) HOF *Continued*	**8473**
Don't Let Go—Commander Cody And His Lost Planet Airmen (75)	*244*
Flip Flop And Fly—Johnnie Ray (55)	*170*
Easy Lovin'—Wade Flemons (60)	114
Shake, Rattle & Roll—Jive Bunny And The Mastermixers (89)	*80*
Call Me Anytime—Frankie Avalon (61)	61
Money Honey—Elvis Presley (56)	25
Say The Words I Love To Hear—Les Paul and Mary Ford (56)	16
Baby, Baby—Billy Williams Quartet (58)	11
Why—Cues (57)	7.7
Razzle Dazzle—Jive Bunny & The Mastermixers (90)	6.7
Right Now, Right Now—Alan Freed (56)	4.8
Growin' Prettier—Johnny October (59)	3.7
Flip Flop And Fly—Goofers (55)	*0.0*
Don't Let Go—Billy Williams (57)	*0.0*
Razzle-Dazzle—Ella Mae Morse (55)	*0.0*
Smack Dab In The Middle—Ella Mae Morse (55)	*0.0*
Smack Dab In The Middle—Charlie Calhoun (55)	*0.0*
Flip Flop And Fly—Joe Turner & His Blues Kings (55)	*0.0*
—Joe Stone see: Joseph Louis STONE	
Joseph STONE ▶ 5484 (1)	**279**
I Just Don't Know—Four Lads (57)	559
Joseph Louis STONE [A. Hott, Joe Stone] ▶ 8486 (2)	**48**
Cars With The Boom—L'Trimm (88)	232
Ronnie's Rapp—Ron And The D.C. Crew (87)	8.3
Norman STONE ▶ 11559 (1)	**1.2**
Strong Enough To Be Gentle—Black Oak Arkansas (76)	8.4
—Sly Stone see: Sylvester STEWART	
Wilson STONE ▶ 8676 (1)	**43**
War And Peace—Vic Damone (56)	86
Paul STOOKEY ▶ 2012 (10)	**2002**
I Dig Rock And Roll Music—Peter, Paul & Mary (67)	1527
Wedding Song (There Is Love)—Paul Stookey (71)	*1045*
Tell It On The Mountain—Peter, Paul & Mary (64)	526
Stewball—Peter, Paul & Mary (63)	466
Wedding Song (There Is Love)—Petula Clark (72)	*152*
The Cruel War—Peter, Paul & Mary (66)	*149*
A 'Soalin'—Peter, Paul & Mary (63)	16
The Wedding Song (There Is Love)—Mary MacGregor (78)	*16*
Big Boat—Peter, Paul & Mary (62)	6.2
The Cruel War—Chad & Jill Stuart (66)	*1.0*
Marc STORACE ▶ 8539 (1)	**47**
Midnite Maniac—Krokus (84)	93
Donald STORBALL ▶ 1314 (3)	**3375**
Cool Jerk—Capitols (66)	3121
Wack Wack—Young Holt Trio (66)	470
We Got A Thing That's In The Groove—Capitols (66)	136
Axel STORDAHL ▶ 5621 (2)	**264**
Day By Day—Four Freshmen (55)	668
I Should Care—Gloria Lynne (64)	124
Carl STORIE ▶ 2228 (3)	**1720**
Dancin' Shoes—Nigel Olsson (78)	*727*
Dancin' Shoes—Faith Band (78)	*643*
Maybe The Rain Will Fall—Cascades (69)	350
Billy STORM [William Hamlin Jones, Billy Jones, William Spicer] ▶ 10194 (1)	**11**
This Is The Nite—Valiants (57)	45
Allen STORY [Shadee Hassan] ▶ 6499 (6)	**163**
I Promise To Wait My Love—Martha Reeves & The Vandellas (68)	345
The Young Folks—Diana Ross And The Supremes (69)	126
Taking My Love (And Leaving Me)—Martha Reeves & The Vandellas (69)	17
Maria (You Were The Only One)—Jimmy Ruffin (71)	14
I Truly, Truly Believe—Temptations (68)	3.6
Darling Dear—Smokey Robinson & The Miracles (70)	0.4
Erich STORZ ▶ 5994 (1)	**218**
The Little Train (Die Kleine Bimmelbahn)—Marianne Vasel & Erich Storz (58)	218
Harold STOTT [Lally Stott] ▶ 4015 (2)	**622**
Chirpy Chirpy Cheep Cheep—Mac And Katie Kissoon (71)	*1221*
Chirpy Chirpy, Cheep Cheep—Lally Stott (71)	*23*
—Lally Stott see: Harold STOTT	
Mary STOVALL ▶ 6069 (1)	**209**
First Date First Kiss First Love—Sonny James (57)	418
Elgie STOVER ▶ 5042 (1)	**355**
The Bells—Originals (70)	1418
Kenny STOVER ▶ 6271 (2)	**187**
You're The Man (Part 1)—Marvin Gaye (72)	372
Love Don't Come No Stronger (Yours And Mine)—Jeff Perry (75)	2.3
—St. Paul see: Paul PETERSON	
Jack STRACHEY ▶ 8082 (1)	**62**
These Foolish Things—James Brown And The Famous Flames (63)	187
Danny STRADELLA ▶ 4528 (2)	**470**
I Was Such A Fool (To Fall In Love With You)—Connie Francis (62)	*833*
I Was Such A Fool (To Fall In Love With You)—Flamingos (60)	*107*
Izzy STRADLIN [Jeffrey Dean Isbell] ▶ 1642 (7)	**2558**
Sweet Child O' Mine—Guns N' Roses (88)	4596
Patience—Guns N' Roses (89)	2050
Paradise City—Guns N' Roses (89)	1901
Don't Cry—Guns N' Roses (91)	1769
Welcome To The Jungle—Guns N' Roses (88)	1661
You Could Be Mine—Guns N' Roses (91)	289
Nightrain—Guns N' Roses (89)	9.3
Roy STRAIGIS ▶ 1757 (5)	**2366**
So Much In Love—Tymes (63)	*6568*
So Much In Love—Timothy B. Schmit (82)	*197*
Groovy Baby—Billy Abbott And The Jewels (63)	188
Here She Comes—Tymes (64)	39
Let's Make Love Tonight—Bobby Rydell (63)	12
Samuel STRAIN ▶ 8129 (2)	**61**
Rubber Biscuit—Blues Brothers (79)	297
I Know I Know—"Pookie" Hudson (63)	2.3
Elliot STRAITE [Dr. Freeze] ▶ 986 (2)	**4544**
I Wanna Sex You Up—Color Me Badd (91)	4560
Poison—Bell Biv DeVoe (90)	3892
Arnold STRALS ▶ 2858 (1)	**1150**
The Lord's Prayer—Sister Janet Mead (74)	2299
—Alfreda Strandberg see: Dorothy TERRISS	
Robert STRANDLUND ▶ 4753 (1)	**423**
Already Gone—Eagles (74)	846
Billy STRANGE ▶ 715 (6)	**6104**
Limbo Rock—Chubby Checker (62)	*9002*
Limbo Rock—Champs (62)	*729*
Clean Up Your Own Back Yard—Elvis Presley (69)	713
Memories—Elvis Presley (69)	*601*
Memories—Lettermen (69)	*238*
A Little Less Conversation—Elvis Presley With The Jordanaires (68)	197
Norman STRASSBERG ▶ 7636 (1)	**84**
Someone Loves You Joe—Singing Belles (60)	168
Eugene STRASSER ▶ 11242 (1)	**2.6**
The Man On Page 602—Zoot Fenster (75)	7.9
Ruth STRATCHBORNEO [Triune] ▶ 11088 (1)	**3.3**
Mojo Workout (Dance)—Larry Bright (60)	13
George E. STRATTON ▶ 5626 (1)	**263**
Misery—Dynamics (63)	525
Arthur STRAUSS ▶ 5150 (1)	**334**
St Therese Of The Roses—Billy Ward And His Dominoes (56)	668
Bob STRAUSS ▶ 4027 (1)	**620**
I Will Still Love You—Stonebolt (78)	620
Johann STRAUSS ▶ 9051 (1)	**32**
How Blue—Mills Brothers (54)	97
Oskar STRAUSS ▶ 10085 (1)	**13**
My Hero—Blue Notes (60)	26
Richard STRAUSS ▶ 1343 (3)	**3303**
Also Sprach Zarathustra (2001)—Deodato (73)	*3243*
Theme Music For The Film "2001 A Space Odyssey" (Also Sprach Zarathustra)—Berlin Philharmonic (69)	*59*
Also Sprach Zarathustra—Al Capps Band (70)	*0.8*
Billy STRAWBRIDGE ▶ 11693 (1)	**0.7**
It's Been A Long Long Time—Elgins (67)	4.3
—Jaap Streefkerk see: Steve KIRK	
Janey STREET [Janey Schramm] ▶ 8747 (1)	**40**
Say Hello To Ronnie—Janey Street (84)	81
Richard STREET ▶ 5985 (2)	**219**
Can You Do It—Contours (64)	*299*
Can You Do It—Grand Funk Railroad (76)	*139*
—Roberta Lee Streeter see: Bobbie GENTRY	
Barbra STREISAND ▶ 1421 (1)	**3109**
Love Theme From "A Star Is Born" (Evergreen)—Barbra Streisand (76)	6219
Alfred STRIANO ▶ 3225 (1)	**941**
There's A Moon Out Tonight—Capris (60)	2822
Keith STRICKLAND ▶ 2533 (6)	**1409**
Love Shack—B-52's (89)	2771
Roam—B-52's (89)	2734
Deadbeat Club—B-52's (90)	458
Rock Lobster—B-52's (80)	143
Private Idaho—B-52's (80)	70
Legal Tender—B-52's (83)	52
Harry STRIDE ▶ 7467 (2)	**94**
Bless Your Heart—Fontane Sisters with Billy Vaughn's Orchestra (54)	*282*
Bless Your Heart—Bob Dini (54)	*0.0*
Liza STRIKE [Lisa Struce] ▶ 5472 (1)	**282**
Summer Nights—Marianne Faithfull (65)	565
Claudio STRILIO ▶ 6383 (1)	**176**
Living In Oblivion—Anything Box (90)	176
Jeremy STRODE ▶ 4613 (2)	**451**
Too Shy—Kajagoogoo (83)	2226
Hang On Now—Kajagoogoo (83)	28
—Paul Julian Strohmeyer see: Green GARTSIDE	
Jon STROLL ▶ 3958 (2)	**641**
Sweet Cream Ladies, Forward March—Box Tops (68)	1153
Beat The Clock—McCoys (67)	128
Kirby ST. ROMAIN ▶ 6525 (1)	**160**
Summer's Comin'—Kirby St. Romain (63)	320
Barrett STRONG ▶ 53 (57) HOF	**40658**
I Heard It Through The Grapevine—Marvin Gaye (68)	*8871*
War—Edwin Starr (70)	*7121*
I Heard It Through The Grapevine—Gladys Knight & The Pips (67)	*6841*
Just My Imagination (Running Away With Me)—Temptations (71)	6683
I Can't Get Next To You—Temptations (69)	*6180*
Ball Of Confusion (That's What The World Is Today)—Temptations (70)	5317
I Wish It Would Rain—Temptations (68)	*5041*
Smiling Faces Sometimes—Undisputed Truth (71)	4374
Papa Was A Rollin' Stone—Temptations (72)	*4089*
Cloud Nine—Temptations (68)	*3303*
Too Busy Thinking About My Baby—Marvin Gaye (69)	3171
Psychedelic Shack—Temptations (70)	2537
Run Away Child, Running Wild—Temptations (69)	2318
That's The Way Love Is—Marvin Gaye (69)	1960
Stay In My Corner—Dells (68)	1713
I Could Never Love Another (After Loving You)—Temptations (68)	1576
The End Of Our Road—Gladys Knight & The Pips (68)	*1369*
War—Bruce Springsteen & The E Street Band (86)	*1264*
Superstar (Remember How You Got Where You Are)—Temptations (71)	1205
Friendship Train—Gladys Knight & The Pips (69)	1176
Don't Let The Joneses Get You Down—Temptations (69)	852
Please Return Your Love To Me—Temptations (68)	720
Stop The War Now—Edwin Starr (70)	685
Jamie—Eddie Holland (62)	637
Take A Look Around—Temptations (72)	601
You Need Love Like I Do (Don't You)—Gladys Knight & The Pips (70)	595
How Can I Forget—Marvin Gaye (70)	509
The End Of Our Road—Marvin Gaye (70)	*504*
Gonna Give Her All The Love I've Got—Jimmy Ruffin (67)	*474*
I Wish It Would Rain—Gladys Knight & The Pips (68)	*449*
Ungena Za Ulimwengu (Unite The World)—Temptations (70)	448
Use Your Head—Mary Wells (65)	422
It's Summer—Temptations (71)	417
Cloud Nine—Mongo Santamaria (69)	*404*
Don't Let Him Take Your Love From Me—Four Tops (69)	358
On A Sunday Afternoon—A Lighter Shade Of Brown (91)	320
Funky Music Sho Nuff Turns Me On—Edwin Starr (71)	*257*

Barrett STRONG ► 53 (57) *Continued*	**40658**
You Make Your Own Heaven And Hell Right Here On Earth—Undisputed Truth (71)	230
I Heard It Through The Grapevine—Creedence Clearwater Revival (76)	*211*
Don't You Miss Me A Little Bit Baby—Jimmy Ruffin (67)	184
I Can't Get Next To You—Al Green (70)	*178*
I Heard It Through The Grapevine (Part 1)—Roger (81)	*147*
Papa Was A Rollin' Stone—Wolf (82)	*139*
What It Is—Undisputed Truth (72)	98
Wherever I Lay My Hat (That's My Home)—Paul Young (83)	90
Gonna Give Her All The Love I've Got—Marvin Gaye (70)	*72*
Papa Was A Rollin' Stone—Undisputed Truth (72)	*68*
Hum Along And Dance—Temptations (70)	44
Can't You See (You're Losing Me)—Mary Wells (66)	28
I Heard It Thru The Grapevine—King Curtis & The Kingpins (68)	*21*
Funky Music Sho Nuff Turns Me On—Temptations (72)	*20*
I Heard It Through The Grapevine—California Raisins (88)	*18*
Such A Sweet Thing—Mary Wells (66)	14
Papa Was A Rolling Stone—Stars On 45 (81)	*12*
Take Me In Your Arms And Love Me—Gladys Knight & The Pips (67)	2.9
It's A Funny Situation—Dee Dee Sharp (66)	2.4
Message From A Black Man—Whatnauts (70)	1.7
Marcell STRONG ► 11356 (1)	**2.1**
Scratch My Back (And Mumble In My Ear)—Clarence Carter (71)	6.3
Cynthia STROTHER [Cynthia Bell] ► 7848 (1)	**72**
Bermuda—Linda Scott (62)	144
Eugene STROTHER ► 7849 (1)	**72**
Bermuda—Linda Scott (62)	144
Charles STROUSE ► 2049 (9) HOF	**1950**
Born Too Late—Poni-Tails (58)	2154
I Want To Be With You—Dee Dee Warwick (66)	*479*
We Love You Beatles—Carefrees (64)	385
Those Were The Days—Carroll O'Connor And Jean Stapleton (As The Bunkers) (71)	313
One Boy—Joanie Sommers (60)	293
I Wanna Be With You—Nancy Wilson (64)	*248*
Superman—Dino, Desi & Billy (66)	15
Kids—Kirby Stone Four (60)	6.7
One Last Kiss—Bobby Vee (60)	6.5
Gordon STROZIER ► 3138 (1)	**990**
Oh Sheila—Ready For The World (85)	2969
—Lisa Struce see: Liza STRIKE	
Dana STRUM ► 3517 (3)	**803**
Fly To The Angels—Slaughter (90)	754
Up All Night—Slaughter (90)	547
Spend My Life—Slaughter (90)	304
Joe STRUMMER [John Graham Mellor] ► 3560 (4)	**786**
Rock The Casbah—Clash (82)	1940
Train In Vain (Stand By Me)—Clash (80)	752
Should I Stay Or Should I Go?—Clash (82)	*243*
Should I Stay Or Should I Go?—Clash (83)	*210*
Jud STRUNK ► 2272 (3)	**1669**
Daisy A Day—Jud Strunk (73)	1486
The Biggest Parakeets In Town—Jud Strunk (75)	239
My Country—Jud Strunk (74)	128
Eddie STRUZICK ► 1634 (5)	**2572**
Sharing The Night Together—Dr. Hook (78)	*3646*
Falling—Le Blanc & Carr (77)	1481
Midnight Light—Le Blanc & Carr (78)	13
Sharing The Night Together—Arthur Alexander (76)	*4.4*
Sharing The Night Together—Lenny LeBlanc (76)	*0.9*
Ron STRYKERT ► 1152 (1)	**3857**
Down Under—Men At Work (82)	7714
Henry STRZELECKI ► 4700 (2)	**435**
Long Tall Texan—Murry Kellum (63)	420
Pin The Tail On The Donkey—Paul Peek (66)	29
—Barry Stuart see: Herbert NEWMAN	
Chad STUART [David Stuart] ► 2385 (6)	**1539**
A Summer Song—Chad Stuart & Jeremy Clyde (64)	2316
Yesterday's Gone—Chad Stuart & Jeremy Clyde (64)	*815*
What Do You Want With Me—Chad & Jeremy (65)	355
Yesterday's Gone—Overlanders (64)	*325*
You Are She—Chad & Jeremy (66)	38
Should I—Chad & Jeremy (65)	0.5
Dave STUART [David Stuart Sandler] ► 8727 (1)	**41**
Minnesota—Northern Light (75)	82
—David Stuart see: Chad STUART	
—Eddie Stuart see: Eddie COHEN	
Hamish STUART ► 2254 (6)	**1700**
Pick Up The Pieces—AWB (74)	5059
Cut The Cake—AWB (75)	1651
School Boy Crush—AWB (75)	485
What Cha' Gonna Do For Me—Chaka Khan (81)	255
Queen Of My Soul—Average White Band (76)	208
If Your Heart Isn't In It—Atlantic Starr (86)	165
Tommy STUART ► 6773 (1)	**138**
Hound Dog Man (Play It Again)—Lenny Le Blanc (77)	138
—Levi Stubbles see: Levi STUBBS	
Kendal STUBBS ► 9398 (1)	**24**
Special Way—Kool & The Gang (87)	122
Levi STUBBS [Levi Stubbles] ► 11022 (1)	**3.8**
Ain't That Love—Four Tops (65)	3.8
—Jim Stuberge see: Jimmy CURTISS	
Nat STUCKEY ► 7799 (1)	**75**
Waitin' In Your Welfare Line—Buck Owens (66)	224
Daryl STUERMER ► 2847 (1)	**1155**
Something Happened On The Way To Heaven—Phil Collins (90)	2309
—Jimmy Stulberger see: Jimmy CURTISS	
Sonja STURDIVANT ► 9921 (1)	**15**
Fire Of Love—Jody Reynolds (58)	30
Carl STURKEN ► 764 (13)	**5744**
P.A.S.S.I.O.N.—Rythm Syndicate (91)	3002
Soldier Of Love—Donny Osmond (89)	2888
Street Of Dreams—Nia Peeples (91)	1236
Sacred Emotion—Donny Osmond (89)	1059
Hey Donna—Rythm Syndicate (91)	905
One Step Closer To You—Gavin Christopher (86)	674
The Girl I Used To Know—Brother Beyond (90)	613
My Love Is A Fire—Donny Osmond (90)	575
Facts Of Love—Jeff Lorber (86)	547
Stranger To Love—St. Paul (90)	236
Hold On—Donny Osmond (89)	96
Blinded By Love—Rythm Syndicate (91)	87
Love Will Survive—Donny Osmond (91)	27
Andy STURMER ► 6206 (1)	**193**
Baby's Coming Back—Jellyfish (91)	193
Carl STUTZ ► 2769 (9)	**1206**
Danger! Heartbreak Ahead—Jaye P. Morgan (55)	932
I Know—Perry Como (59)	531
Little Things Mean A Lot—Joni James (59)	*461*
Kissing Tree—Billy Grammer (59)	249
Goodnight Sweet Dreams—Gordon Jenkins And His Orchestra (55)	211
Will You Willyum—Janis Martin (56)	*100*
Will You, Willyum?—Joan Hager (56)	*0.0*
Little Things Mean A Lot—John Gary (59)	*0.0*
Little Things Mean A Lot—Kitty Kallen (54)	*0.0*
Sandra ST. VICTOR ► 3435 (1)	**850**
The Promise Of A New Day—Paula Abdul (91)	3398
Viv STYGER ► 10440 (1)	**8.5**
Kwela Kwela—Bill Hayes (55)	34
Marshall James STYLER ► 5092 (2)	**344**
I'll Drink To You—Duke Jupiter (82)	209
Little Lady—Duke Jupiter (84)	135
Johnny STYLES ► 5265 (1)	**316**
Bristol Twistin' Annie—Dovells (62)	632
Jule STYNE ► 946 (35) HOF	**4711**
People—Barbra Streisand (64)	*3349*
Small World—Johnny Mathis (59)	1090
That's What I Like—Don, Dick N' Jimmy (54)	*648*
I Still Get Jealous—Louis Armstrong And The All-Stars (64)	*531*
Time After Time—Chris Montez (66)	*519*
Funny Girl—Barbra Streisand (64)	448
People—Tymes (68)	*422*
I Don't Want To Walk Without You—Barry Manilow (80)	*396*
Just In Time—Tony Bennett with Percy Faith and His Orchestra (56)	*374*
I Still Get Jealous—Joni James (59)	*247*
Time After Time—Frankie Ford (60)	*220*
Johnny Freedom—Johnny Horton (60)	211
The Things We Did Last Summer—Shelley Fabares (62)	206
Dance Only With Me—Perry Como (58)	150
It's Bigger Than You And Me—Sammy Davis Jr. (55)	125
Now!—Lena Horne (63)	110
I'll Walk Alone—Johnny Nash (57)	105
Party's Over—Doris Day (56)	*92*
People—Nat King Cole (64)	*76*
Just In Time—Dean Martin (60)	*71*
I Don't Want To Walk Without You—Phyllis McGuire (64)	*58*
Make Someone Happy—Perry Como (60)	57
It's Magic—Teddy Randazzo (58)	*51*
That's What I Like—Dean Martin (54)	*50*
Let Me Entertain You—Ray Anthony (62)	30
It's Magic—Platters (62)	*21*
Bells Are Ringing—Jo Stafford (56)	*8.2*
Bells Are Ringing—Jeri Southern (56)	*8.2*
I Am Woman—Barbra Streisand (64)	5.3
Just In Time—Jeri Southern (56)	*0.0*
The Party's Over—Carmen McRae (57)	*0.0*
The Party's Over—Lurlean Hunter (57)	*0.0*
Three Coins In The Fountain—Four Aces (54)	*0.0*
Three Coins In The Fountain—Frank Sinatra (54)	*0.0*
Money Burns A Hole In My Pocket—Dean Martin (54)	0.0
Stanley H. STYNE ► 5642 (2)	**261**
I Knew Jesus (Before He Was A Star)—Glen Campbell (73)	486
Beautiful Friendship—Ella Fitzgerald (56)	36
Jerry STYNER ► 10751 (3)	**5.5**
Frustration—Zanies (62)	6.6
You And Your Baby Blues—Solomon Burke (75)	2.6
Devil's Angels—Davie Allen And The Arrows (67)	1.9
—Subway see: Bernard ESTARDY	
—Morton Aaron Suckno see: Mort STEVENS	
Bruce SUDANO ► 1598 (10)	**2646**
Bad Girls—Donna Summer (79)	7825
Ball Of Fire—Tommy James And The Shondells (69)	1168
Starting Over Again—Dolly Parton (80)	313
Music, Harmony And Rhythm—Brooklyn Dreams (78)	156
Tell Me I'm Not Dreaming—Robert Palmer (89)	150
(Closest Thing To) Perfect—Jermaine Jackson (85)	139
Sad Eyes—Brooklyn Dreams (77)	114
Do You Remember Me?—Jermaine Jackson (86)	81
Supernatural Love—Donna Summer (84)	76
Make It Last—Brooklyn Dreams (79)	70
Harry SUKMAN ► 11141 (1)	**3.1**
Verboten! (Forbidden)—Paul Anka (58)	6.1
Cy SULACK ► 10485 (1)	**8.0**
Opposites Do Attract—All Sports Band (82)	16
Alex SULLIVAN ► 10233 (1)	**11**
Georgia Rose—Tony Bennett (66)	33
Frankie SULLIVAN ► 342 (18)	**10918**
Eye Of The Tiger—Survivor (82)	9112
Burning Heart—Survivor (85)	3695
The Search Is Over—Survivor (85)	1879
Is This Love—Survivor (86)	1596
Caught Up In You—38 Special (82)	1470
I Can't Hold Back—Survivor (84)	1376
High On You—Survivor (85)	1072
American Heartbeat—Survivor (82)	655
Poor Man's Son—Survivor (81)	418
Rockin' Into The Night—38 Special (79)	347
How Much Love—Survivor (87)	239
First Night—Survivor (85)	210
Didn't Know It Was Love—Survivor (88)	197
Summer Nights—Survivor (82)	124
Ever Since The World Began—Tommy Shaw (88)	102
Across The Miles—Survivor (89)	93
Caught In The Game—Survivor (83)	71
Man Against The World—Survivor (87)	44
Gene SULLIVAN ► 6974 (1)	**124**
When My Blue Moon Turns To Gold Again—Elvis Presley (56)	249
Larry SULLIVAN ► 3709 (3)	**727**
Cinco Robles (Five Oaks)—Russell Arms (56)	*844*
Cinco Robles (Five Oaks)—Les Paul and Mary Ford (56)	*610*
Cinco Robles (Five Oaks)—Lawrence Welk And His Sparkling Strings (57)	*0.0*

Niki SULLIVAN ▶ 6895 (3)	**130**
I'm Gonna Love You Too—Hullaballoos (64)	*366*
I'm Gonna Love You Too—Buddy Holly / The Crickets (58)	*13*
I'm Gonna Love You Too—Terry Jacks (73)	*11*
Sandra E. SULLY ▶ 10239 (1)	**11**
If You Think You're Lonely Now—Bobby Womack (81)	44
Kasim SULTON ▶ 6415 (2)	**173**
Set Me Free—Utopia (80)	641
The Very Last Time—Utopia (80)	51
Donna SUMMER [LaDonna Adrian Gaines] ▶ 185 (21)	**16671**
Bad Girls—Donna Summer (79)	7825
Love To Love You Baby—Donna Summer (75)	*4573*
Dim All The Lights—Donna Summer (79)	4457
She Works Hard For The Money—Donna Summer (83)	4225
The Wanderer—Donna Summer (80)	4199
On The Radio—Donna Summer (80)	3402
Heaven Knows—Donna Summer With Brooklyn Dreams (79)	3027
I Feel Love—Donna Summer (77)	2815
This Time I Know It's For Real—Donna Summer (89)	1582
I Love You—Donna Summer (77)	469
Starting Over Again—Dolly Parton (80)	313
Unconditional Love—Donna Summer (83)	302
Winter Melody—Donna Summer (77)	276
Rumour Has It—Donna Summer (78)	113
Love To Love You Baby—Ritchie Family (76)	*92*
Spring Affair—Donna Summer (76)	*84*
Supernatural Love—Donna Summer (84)	76
Love Has A Mind Of Its Own—Donna Summer (84)	71
Try Me, I Know We Can Make It—Donna Summer (76)	34
When Love Cries—Donna Summer (91)	32
Spring Affair—Donna Summer (77)	*0.0*
Henry Lee SUMMER [Henry Lee Swartz] ▶ 2121 (5)	**1846**
Hey Baby—Henry Lee Summer (89)	870
I Wish I Had A Girl—Henry Lee Summer (88)	675
Till Somebody Loves You—Henry Lee Summer (91)	275
Darlin' Danielle Don't—Henry Lee Summer (88)	199
Hands On The Radio—Henry Lee Summer (88)	11
Amiel SUMMERS ▶ 4989 (1)	**364**
Big John—Shirelles (61)	727
Bob SUMMERS ▶ 10243 (1)	**11**
Try Again—Patsy Cline (57)	22
—Iris Colleen Summers see: Mary FORD	
—Jerry Summers see: Jerry GROSS	
Pat SUMMERSON ▶ 9306 (1)	**27**
Night Dancin'—Taka Boom (79)	53
Bernard SUMNER ▶ 5103 (4)	**342**
True Faith—New Order (87)	637
Getting Away With It—Electronic (90)	407
Round & Round—New Order (89)	209
Blue Monday 1988—New Order (88)	105
—Gordon Sumner see: STING	
Arnold SUNDGAARD ▶ 11698 (1)	**0.6**
How Lovely Is Christmas—Bing Crosby (57)	1.3
Madeline SUNSHINE ▶ 6740 (1)	**141**
This Is Love—Paul Anka (78)	283
Richie SUPA [Richard Goodman, Richard Supa] ▶ 5025 (6)	**357**
Somethin' 'Bout You Baby I Like—Glen Campbell and Rita Coolidge (80)	*233*
Somethin' 'Bout You Baby I Like—Trini Lopez (75)	*48*
Chip Away The Stone—Aerosmith (88)	*26*
Younger Days—Joe Fagin (82)	22
Chip Away The Stone (Studio)—Aerosmith (79)	*21*
Just One Minute More—Mike Finnigan (78)	13
Robyn SUPRANER ▶ 8650 (1)	**44**
Lovely, Lovely (Loverly, Loverly)—Chubby Checker (64)	88
—Al B. Sure! see: Albert Joseph BROWN	
—Jean Surrey see: Jean DINNING	
Red SURREY [Bruno Alex Survilla] ▶ 1231 (3)	**3630**
Teen Angel—Mark Dinning (59)	*6926*
A Star Is Born (A Love Has Died)—Mark Dinning (60)	247
Teen Angel—Wednesday (74)	*88*
—Bruno Alex Survilla see: Red SURREY	
Bob SUSSER ▶ 4681 (2)	**438**
Once You Understand—Think (71)	*598*

Once You Understand—Think (Featuring Lou Stallman) (74)	*279*
Bruce SUSSMAN ▶ 3399 (3)	**867**
Copacabana (At The Copa)—Barry Manilow (78)	1800
I Made It Through The Rain—Barry Manilow (80)	1325
Hey Mambo—Barry Manilow with Kid Creole And The Coconuts (88)	6.2
Gavin SUTHERLAND ▶ 5546 (1)	**272**
Sailing—Rod Stewart (75)	272
Iain SUTHERLAND ▶ 3489 (4)	**820**
(I Don't Want To Love You But) You Got Me Anyway—Sutherland Brothers And Quiver (73)	670
Arms Of Mary—Sutherland Brothers And Quiver (76)	*94*
Arms Of Mary—Chilliwack (78)	*53*
Secrets—Sutherland Brothers & Quiver (77)	3.0
Marci SUTIN ▶ 10498 (1)	**7.8**
If I Have To Go Away—Jigsaw (77)	16
Brenda SUTTON [Brenda Turner] ▶ 6868 (2)	**132**
There Will Come A Day (I'm Gonna Happen To You)—Smokey Robinson (77)	249
Shake It Up Tonight—Cheryl Lynn (81)	97
Charles SUTTON ▶ 6784 (2)	**138**
See Saw—Moonglows (56)	*357*
See Saw—Don Cornell (56)	*56*
Glenn SUTTON ▶ 2128 (18)	**1841**
Almost Persuaded—David Houston (66)	*1274*
Kiss Away—Ronnie Dove (65)	745
Almost Persuaded No. 2—Ben Colder (66)	*289*
You're My Man—Lynn Anderson (71)	250
You Mean The World To Me—David Houston (67)	172
She's Ready—Spiral Starecase (69)	*165*
The Football Card—Glenn Sutton (78)	129
Singing My Song—Tammy Wynette (69)	92
Almost Persuaded—Etta James (69)	*77*
The Ways To Love A Man—Tammy Wynette (69)	36
Kids Say The Darndest Things—Tammy Wynette (73)	24
Bedtime Story—Tammy Wynette (72)	17
Cry Softly—Nancy Ames (66)	16
He's Ready—Poppies (66)	*12*
What's Made Milwaukee Famous (Has Made A Loser Out Of Me)—Jerry Lee Lewis (68)	10
What A Man, My Man Is—Lynn Anderson (75)	9.0
Have A Little Faith—David Houston (68)	8.9
Keep Me In Mind—Lynn Anderson (73)	6.5
Gregg SUTTON ▶ 6092 (3)	**206**
Only Time Will Tell—Nelson (91)	479
Stop—Sam Brown (89)	138
In Your Arms—Little Caesar (91)	81
Mike SUTTON ▶ 6486 (3)	**164**
There Will Come A Day (I'm Gonna Happen To You)—Smokey Robinson (77)	249
Down To Love Town—Originals (76)	99
Shake It Up Tonight—Cheryl Lynn (81)	97
Willard SVANOE ▶ 1937 (5)	**2084**
Walk Right In—Rooftop Singers (62)	*6902*
Tom Cat—Rooftop Singers (63)	829
Mama Don't Allow—Rooftop Singers (63)	296
Walk Right In—Dr. Hook (77)	*188*
Walk Right In—Moments (1) (63)	*23*
Steve SWAIM ▶ 7473 (1)	**93**
She Looks A Lot Like You—Clocks (82)	93
Stacey SWAIN [Stacey Q] ▶ 8343 (2)	**54**
Don't Make A Fool Of Yourself—Stacey Q (88)	125
Shy Girl—Stacey Q (87)	36
Tony SWAIN ▶ 4809 (6)	**409**
Cruel Summer—Bananarama (84)	1392
A Trick Of The Night—Bananarama (86)	115
The Wild Life—Bananarama (84)	104
Shy Boy (Don't It Make You Feel Good)—Bananarama (83)	74
Love Resurrection—Alison Moyet (85)	44
Robert DeNiro's Waiting—Bananarama (84)	4.7
Billy SWAN ▶ 512 (5)	**8309**
I Can Help—Billy Swan (74)	5050
Lover Please—Clyde McPhatter (62)	3075
I'm Her Fool—Billy Swan (75)	115
Everything's The Same (Ain't Nothing Changed)—Billy Swan (75)	109
Number One—Billy Swan (76)	36
—Frances Swan see: Frances FROST	
—James Dixon Swan see: Jimmy BARNES	

Marlu SWAN ▶ 9732 (1)	**18**
Number One—Billy Swan (76)	36
Don SWANDER ▶ 7452 (1)	**95**
Deep In The Heart Of Texas—Duane Eddy (62)	95
Bettye SWANN [Betty Barton, Bettye Jean Champion] ▶ 2575 (2)	**1365**
Make Me Yours—Bettye Swann (67)	1191
Fall In Love With Me—Bettye Swann (67)	174
Leon SWANSON ▶ 11426 (1)	**1.7**
Lollipop (I Like You)—Intruders (69)	6.9
Nigel SWANSTON ▶ 10850 (1)	**4.9**
Jack The Lad—3 Man Island (88)	15
—Henry Lee Swartz see: Henry Lee SUMMER	
Bobby SWAYNE ▶ 11717 (1)	**0.5**
Air Travel—Ray And Bob (62)	0.9
Patrick SWAYZE ▶ 2528 (1)	**1413**
She's Like The Wind—Patrick Swayze (87)	2825
Leroy SWEARINGEN ▶ 3713 (2)	**723**
I Really Love You—Stereos (61)	637
Goodbye My Lover Goodbye—Searchers (65)	344
Keith SWEAT ▶ 1777 (8)	**2339**
I Want Her—Keith Sweat (88)	1714
I'll Give All My Love To You—Keith Sweat (90)	1251
Make You Sweat—Keith Sweat (90)	1110
Keep It Comin'—Keith Sweat (91)	925
Make It Last Forever—Keith Sweat (88)	244
Let's Chill—Guy (91)	228
Your Love Part 2—Keith Sweat (91)	101
Something Just Ain't Right—Keith Sweat (88)	66
Mick SWEDA ▶ 9770 (1)	**17**
Smooth Up—Bulletboys (89)	68
Chuck SWEENEY ▶ 8889 (3)	**37**
How Blue—Mills Brothers (54)	97
Young Ideas—Tony Martin (55)	*4.4*
Young Ideas—Gordon Jenkins & His Orchestra (55)	*4.4*
Darrell SWEET ▶ 10284 (1)	**10**
Holiday—Nazareth (80)	63
—DeWayne Sweet see: Romeo McCALL	
Michael SWEET ▶ 3486 (3)	**821**
Honestly—Stryper (87)	680
Always There For You—Stryper (88)	126
I Believe In You—Stryper (88)	15
Rachel SWEET ▶ 9985 (1)	**14**
Voo Doo—Rachel Sweet (83)	43
—Sweet L.D. see: Djuana JOHNICAN	
Robert SWEETWATER ▶ 11642 (1)	**0.9**
Boola—Les Brown and His Band of Renown (59)	0.9
Phillip SWERN ▶ 5399 (1)	**294**
Up In A Puff Of Smoke—Polly Brown (74)	883
Pieter SWEVAL [Peter Sweval] ▶ 6641 (6)	**148**
Cherry Baby—Starz (77)	510
Sing It, Shout It—Starz (77)	148
(Any Way That You Want It) I'll Be There—Starz (78)	26
Hold On To The Night—Starz (78)	18
Rainbow Man—Looking Glass (73)	7.6
(She's Just A) Fallen Angel—Starz (76)	6.5
—DeVante Swing see: Donald DeGRATE	
Rik SWINN [Richard Charles Swinn Brewer] ▶ 9911 (1)	**15**
So Much For Love—Venetians (87)	15
Seth SWIRSKY ▶ 2280 (2)	**1659**
Tell It To My Heart—Taylor Dayne (87)	1915
Prove Your Love—Taylor Dayne (88)	1402
Bill SWOFFORD [William Oliver Swofford, Oliver] ▶ 9346 (1)	**26**
Young Birds Fly—Cryan' Shames (68)	26
—Bret Michael Sychak see: Bret MICHAELS	
John SYKES ▶ 2063 (3)	**1938**
Is This Love—Whitesnake (87)	3575
Give Me All Your Love—Whitesnake (88)	254
Still Of The Night—Whitesnake (87)	46
Keith SYKES ▶ 8410 (1)	**52**
Volcano—Jimmy Buffett (79)	155
Roosevelt SYKES ▶ 9853 (3)	**16**
Driving Wheel—Little Junior Parker (61)	14
Night Time Is The Right Time—Rufus & Carla (64)	*3.3*
Night Time Is The Right Time—Ray Charles (59)	*2.4*

Charmaine SYLVERS ▶ 6542 (2)	**159**
A Night To Remember—Shalamar (82)	260
Come Give Your Love To Me— Janet Jackson (83)	144
Edmund SYLVERS ▶ 5000 (3)	**360**
High School Dance—Sylvers (77)	1323
Any Way You Want Me—Sylvers (77)	56
Don't Stop, Get Off—Sylvers (78)	6.3
Foster SYLVERS ▶ 11545 (1)	**1.3**
Don't Stop, Get Off—Sylvers (78)	6.3
James SYLVERS ▶ 5161 (2)	**332**
High School Dance—Sylvers (77)	1323
Don't Stop, Get Off—Sylvers (78)	6.3
Leon SYLVERS ▶ 1360 (12)	**3267**
The Second Time Around—Shalamar (79)	1893
High School Dance—Sylvers (77)	1323
Dead Giveaway—Shalamar (83)	1143
Misdemeanor—Foster Sylvers (73)	916
And The Beat Goes On—Whispers (80)	884
Wish That I Could Talk To You—Sylvers (72)	247
Take That To The Bank—Shalamar (78)	144
Any Way You Want Me—Sylvers (77)	56
Action—Evelyn "Champagne" King (84)	50
Stay Away From Me—Sylvers (73)	13
Fool's Paradise—Sylvers (72)	10
Don't Stop, Get Off—Sylvers (78)	6.3
—Nidra Sylvers see: Nidra BEARD	
Ricky SYLVERS ▶ 5162 (2)	**332**
High School Dance—Sylvers (77)	1323
Don't Stop, Get Off—Sylvers (78)	6.3
—Sylvester see: Sylvester JAMES	
Terry SYLVESTER ▶ 10258 (2)	**11**
Another Night—Hollies (75)	*28*
Another Night—Wilson Brothers (79)	*3.9*
Margo SYLVIA ▶ 3050 (4)	**1035**
Happy Happy Birthday Baby—Tune Weavers (57)	*2066*
Happy Happy Birthday—Wanda Jackson (60)	*3.5*
Happy, Happy Birthday Baby—Kay Cee Jones (57)	*0.0*
Happy, Happy Birthday Baby—Dottie Ferguson (57)	*0.0*
Marty SYMES ▶ 7979 (1)	**66**
There Is No Greater Love—Wanderers (62)	133
Terry SYMMS ▶ 10633 (1)	**6.6**
What Does It Matter—Platters (59)	20
Joseph L. SYRACUSE ▶ 9932 (1)	**15**
Oh Baby—Cathy Carr (56)	44
—William Szathmary see: Bill DANA	
—Lévay Szilveszter see: Sylvester LEVAY	
Michael SZUMOWSKI ▶ 5945 (1)	**225**
Tell Me Something—Indecent Obsession (90)	449

T

Brian TABACH ▶ 10621 (1)	**6.7**
Lovin' Naturally—Sandalwood (73)	13
Ronald TABAK ▶ 9067 (1)	**32**
Flyin'—Prism (78)	159
André TABET ▶ 10994 (1)	**3.9**
Symphony—Sammy Turner (59)	16
Franklyn J. TABLEPORTER ▶ 6642 (2)	**148**
Come What May—Clyde McPhatter (58)	*145*
Come What May—Elvis Presley (66)	*3.3*
Alessandro TACCANI [Sandro Taccani] ▶ 4069 (8)	**605**
On An Evening In Roma—Dean Martin (59)	715
Come Prima—Tony Dallara (58)	*636*
Come Prima—Polly Bergen (58)	*524*
Ha! Ha! Ha! (Chella Lla)—Kay Armen (57)	*72*
Come Prima—Luciano Tajoli (58)	*0.0*
Come Prima—Domenico Modugno (58)	*0.0*
Ha! Ha! Ha! ("Che Lla La!")—Lou Monte (57)	*0.0*
HA HA HA (Chella Lla)—Sammy Kaye & His "Swing And Sway" Orchestra (57)	*0.0*
—Sandro Taccani see: Alessandro TACCANI	
Nicollet TADY ▶ 4736 (2)	**427**
You Don't Love Me Anymore (And I Can Tell)— Rick Nelson (63)	388
Hey, Mr. Sax Man—Boots Randolph (64)	118
Phyllis TAFF [Jane Harvey] ▶ 11831 (1)	**0.0**
Not As A Stranger—McGuire Sisters (54)	0.0

Eric TAGG ▶ 5059 (2)	**352**
Is It You—Lee Ritenour (81)	902
Cross My Heart—Lee Ritenour (82)	103
Larry TAGG ▶ 6738 (1)	**141**
Mutual Surrender (What A Wonderful World)— Bourgeois Tagg (86)	141
Gilles TAILLEUR ▶ 6681 (1)	**145**
Clap Your Hands—Beau-Marks (60)	578
Yukihiro TAKAHASHI ▶ 8578 (1)	**46**
Computer Game ("Theme From The Circus")— Yellow Magic Orchestra (80)	138
Nobuyuki TAKEOKA ▶ 7108 (1)	**116**
China Nights (Shina No Yoru)—Kyu Sakamoto (63)	347
Bob TALBERT ▶ 11081 (1)	**3.3**
Where Have All Our Heroes Gone—Bill Anderson (70)	6.7
Homer TALBERT ▶ 3999 (3)	**626**
Ain't Understanding Mellow— Jerry Butler And Brenda Lee Eager (71)	1077
I Wanna Do It To You—Jerry Butler (77)	203
What's Too Much—Smokey Robinson (87)	80
—Patricia Henley Talbert see: Patricia HENLEY	
Pete TALBOT ▶ 8794 (2)	**39**
Closer To The Heart—Rush (81)	*89*
Closer To The Heart—Rush (77)	*67*
—Steven Victor Tallarico see: Steven TYLER	
Lewis TALLEY ▶ 6903 (1)	**130**
Dear John—Pat Boone (60)	389
Robert TALLEY ▶ 7027 (1)	**121**
Morning After—Mar-Keys (61)	241
Don TALTY ▶ 8055 (1)	**64**
I'm Over You—Jan Bradley (65)	127
—Jascha Tambimuttu see: Tambi FERNANDO	
—Tampa Red see: Hudson WHITTAKER	
Rondalis TANDY ▶ 10426 (2)	**8.6**
No Man Is An Island—Van Dykes (2) (66)	7.6
I've Got To Go On Without You—Van Dykes (2) (66)	1.0
Norma TANEGA ▶ 3392 (2)	**869**
Walkin' My Cat Named Dog—Norma Tanega (66)	868
I'm The Sky—Eddie Rambeau (66)	2.4
Paul TANNEN ▶ 8491 (2)	**48**
(I've Got) Spring Fever—Little Willie John (61)	61
Don't Tell Me It's Raining—Johnny Tillotson (67)	17
Joe TANNER ▶ 3252 (3)	**927**
Only One Love—George Hamilton IV (57)	647
I Don't Know What It Is—Bluenotes (59)	190
My Lucky Love— Doug Franklin with The Bluenotes (58)	89
Marc TANNER ▶ 1863 (5)	**2187**
(Can't Live Without Your) Love And Affection— Nelson (90)	3603
After The Rain—Nelson (90)	1789
More Than Ever—Nelson (91)	1085
Only Time Will Tell—Nelson (91)	479
Elena—Marc Tanner Band (79)	174
June TANSEY ▶ 10708 (1)	**5.9**
Insult To Injury—Timi Yuro (63)	24
Joseph TANSINI ▶ 8328 (1)	**54**
Hold On—Badfinger (81)	108
Laverne TARDO ▶ 10217 (1)	**11**
Gypsy Woman Told Me—Eddie Powers (64)	33
—Philip Geoffrey Targett-Adams see: Phil MANZANERA	
Deborah TARIQ ▶ 8063 (1)	**63**
My Fallen Angel—Coro (91)	126
Zahid TARIQ ▶ 8064 (1)	**63**
My Fallen Angel—Coro (91)	126
Karl TARLETON ▶ 8348 (2)	**54**
I Don't Want To Lose You—Jackie Wilson (67)	60
To Be A Lover—Gene Chandler (67)	24
Alan TARNEY ▶ 864 (9)	**5143**
We Don't Talk Anymore—Cliff Richard (79)	2428
Dreaming—Cliff Richard (80)	1919
A Little In Love—Cliff Richard (80)	1316
Living In A Fantasy—Leo Sayer (81)	573
No Time To Lose—Tarney/Spencer Band (81)	*97*
No Time To Lose—Tarney/Spencer Band (79)	*91*
Wired For Sound—Cliff Richard (81)	71
It's Really You—Tarney/Spencer Band (78)	30
I'm Your Man Rock 'N' Roll— Tarney/Spencer Band (76)	29

Nat TARNOPOL ▶ 9933 (1)	**15**
Oh Baby—Cathy Carr (56)	44
Marvin TARPLIN ▶ 597 (22)	**7311**
Cruisin'—Smokey Robinson (79)	4437
Ain't That Peculiar—Marvin Gaye (65)	*2266*
I'll Be Doggone—Marvin Gaye (65)	2041
Going To A Go-Go—Miracles (65)	*1646*
The Tracks Of My Tears—Johnny Rivers (67)	*1537*
The Tracks Of My Tears—Miracles (65)	*1351*
My Girl Has Gone—Miracles (65)	946
Baby Come Close—Smokey Robinson (73)	768
The Love I Saw In You Was Just A Mirage— Smokey Robinson & The Miracles (67)	740
I Like It Like That—Miracles (64)	727
Tracks Of My Tears—Linda Ronstadt (75)	*724*
One More Heartache—Marvin Gaye (66)	662
Doggone Right—Smokey Robinson & The Miracles (69)	615
Going To A Go-Go—Rolling Stones (82)	*594*
Take This Heart Of Mine—Marvin Gaye (66)	568
Point It Out—Smokey Robinson & The Miracles (69)	525
Ain't That Peculiar—Diamond Reo (74)	*361*
It's Her Turn To Live—Smokey Robinson (74)	87
Tracks Of My Tears—Aretha Franklin (69)	*81*
Going to a Go-Go—Shalamar (77)	*80*
Open—Smokey Robinson (76)	40
Ain't That Peculiar—Fanny (72)	*29*
Mary TARVER ▶ 7910 (2)	**70**
Something Old, Something New—Paul & Paula (63)	136
Six Boys—J. Frank Wilson (65)	4.1
—Howard Tashman see: Tash HOWARD	
Laurence TASSE ▶ 8790 (1)	**39**
Future Shock—Hello People (75)	156
Terry TASSENBERG ▶ 7288 (1)	**105**
Delta Queen—Don Fardon (73)	105
—Eli Tatarsky see: Bobby ELI	
Danny TATE ▶ 4190 (1)	**568**
Affair Of The Heart—Rick Springfield (83)	1704
Geoff TATE ▶ 9607 (1)	**20**
Another Rainy Night (Without You)—Queensryche (91)	61
Joe TATE ▶ 8545 (1)	**47**
I'm So Glad—Fuzz (71)	93
Tommy TATE ▶ 8165 (2)	**60**
School Of Life—Tommy Tate (72)	100
More Power To You—Tommy Tate (72)	20
—Lawrence Taylor Tatman III see: Skip TAYLOR	
Jules TAUB [Julius Bihari] ▶ 4176 (7)	**573**
Cherry Pie—Skip & Flip (60)	1582
Beautician Blues—B.B. King (64)	62
The Girl In My Dreams—Cliques (56)	*39*
Truly—Dinning Sisters Featuring Jean Dinning (55)	9.6
Girl In My Dreams—Capris (61)	*4.0*
You're Gonna Miss Me—B.B. King (64)	2.6
The Girl In My Dreams—Four Lovers (56)	*0.0*
Doris TAUBER ▶ 5527 (2)	**274**
Fooled—Perry Como (55)	819
Livin' Dangerously—McGuire Sisters (60)	1.5
Bernie TAUPIN [Carte Blanche] ▶ 38 (51) HOF	**46642**
Crocodile Rock—Elton John (72)	6901
Philadelphia Freedom—Elton John Band (75)	6474
Don't Go Breaking My Heart— Elton John And Kiki Dee (76)	6364
Island Girl—Elton John (75)	5893
Bennie And The Jets—Elton John (74)	5459
We Built This City—Starship (85)	4638
Goodbye Yellow Brick Road—Elton John (73)	4555
These Dreams—Heart (86)	4304
Daniel—Elton John (73)	4279
Don't Let The Sun Go Down On Me—Elton John (74)	*4278*
Someone Saved My Life Tonight—Elton John (75)	3538
Don't Let The Sun Go Down On Me— George Michael (91)	*3346*
I Don't Wanna Go On With You Like That— Elton John (88)	2894
I Guess That's Why They Call It The Blues— Elton John (83)	2690
Your Song—Elton John (70)	2412
The Bitch Is Back—Elton John (74)	2289
Sorry Seems To Be The Hardest Word— Elton John (76)	2125
Rocket Man—Elton John (72)	2111

Bernie TAUPIN [Carte Blanche] ▶ 38 (51) HOF *Continued*	**46642**
Sad Songs (Say So Much)—Elton John (84)	1892
Candle In The Wind—Elton John (87)	1744
Saturday Night's Alright For Fighting—Elton John (73)	1637
Nikita—Elton John (86)	1603
I'm Still Standing—Elton John (83)	1238
How You Gonna See Me Now—Alice Cooper (78)	1236
Honky Cat—Elton John (72)	1232
Empty Garden (Hey Hey Johnny)—Elton John (82)	1190
Healing Hands—Elton John (89)	1070
Levon—Elton John (71)	875
Sacrifice—Elton John (90)	860
Wrap Her Up—Elton John (85)	852
Grow Some Funk Of Your Own—Elton John (76)	803
Friends—Elton John (71)	742
Who Wears These Shoes?—Elton John (84)	739
A Word In Spanish—Elton John (88)	673
Border Song (Holy Moses)—Aretha Franklin (70)	*643*
Kiss The Bride—Elton John (83)	583
Club At The End Of The Street—Elton John (90)	549
Tiny Dancer—Elton John (72)	461
In Neon—Elton John (84)	451
Ego—Elton John (78)	432
I Feel Like A Bullet (In The Gun Of Robert Ford)—Elton John (76)	423
You Gotta Love Someone—Elton John (90)	372
Bite Your Lip (Get Up And Dance!)—Elton John (77)	320
Heartache All Over The World—Elton John (86)	221
Lonely School Year—Hudson Brothers (75)	189
Border Song—Elton John (70)	*98*
The Rumour—Olivia Newton-John (88)	97
Step Into Christmas—Elton John (73)	40
I Engineer—Animotion (86)	39
Bad Side Of The Moon—April Wine (72)	19
Snookeroo—Ringo Starr (75)	0.0
Wally TAX ▶ 9160 (1)	**30**
Rock And Roll Star—Champagne (77)	60
Alton TAYLOR ▶ 6638 (2)	**149**
Summertime—DJ Jazzy Jeff & The Fresh Prince (91)	1783
Summer Madness—Kool & The Gang (75)	0.0
Andy TAYLOR ▶ 619 (14)	**6995**
The Reflex—Duran Duran (84)	5082
Union Of The Snake—Duran Duran (83)	4545
The Wild Boys—Duran Duran (84)	4449
A View To A Kill—Duran Duran (85)	4032
Hungry Like The Wolf—Duran Duran (82)	3924
Is There Something I Should Know—Duran Duran (83)	2395
Some Like It Hot—Power Station (85)	1943
New Moon On Monday—Duran Duran (84)	1339
Lost In You—Rod Stewart (88)	958
Rio—Duran Duran (83)	946
Save A Prayer—Duran Duran (85)	773
Take It Easy—Andy Taylor (86)	695
Communication—Power Station (85)	401
When The Rain Comes Down—Andy Taylor (86)	116
B.E. TAYLOR ▶ 10446 (2)	**8.4**
Reggae Rock 'N Roll—B. E. Taylor Group (85)	22
Karen—B. E. Taylor Group (86)	3.1
—Beloyd Taylor see: Bernard TAYLOR	
Bernard TAYLOR [Beloyd Taylor] ▶ 3591 (1)	**775**
Getaway—Earth, Wind & Fire (76)	1550
Bill TAYLOR ▶ 8079 (1)	**63**
I Wouldn't Trade You For The World—Bachelors (64)	188
Billy TAYLOR [William Edward Taylor Jr.] ▶ 7991 (1)	**66**
I Wish I Knew (How It Would Feel To Be Free)—Solomon Burke (68)	132
Billy (2) TAYLOR ▶ 8833 (1)	**38**
I Say Love—Royal Guardsmen (68)	76
Blondene TAYLOR ▶ 6027 (1)	**214**
Oop-Shoop—Crew-Cuts (54)	643
Bob TAYLOR ▶ 11290 (1)	**2.4**
Cookin'—Al Casey Combo (62)	7.2
Carmen TAYLOR ▶ 4091 (5)	**596**
Seven Days—Crew-Cuts (56)	*658*
Seven Days—Dorothy Collins (56)	*367*
Seven Days—Clyde McPhatter (56)	*142*
Love Is A Treasure—Mickey And Sylvia (57)	25
Seven Days—Snooky Lanson (56)	*0.0*

Carmol TAYLOR ▶ 11695 (1)	**0.7**
He Loves Me All The Way—Tammy Wynette (70)	2.1
Chip TAYLOR [James Wesley Voight] ▶ 119 (27) HOF	**21513**
Wild Thing—Troggs (66)	*6420*
Angel Of The Morning—Juice Newton (81)	*4537*
Angel Of The Morning—Merrilee Rush & The Turnabouts (68)	*4297*
Wild Thing—Fancy (74)	*1183*
Wild Thing—Senator Bobby (67)	*1018*
Step Out Of Your Mind—American Breed (67)	756
Any Way That You Want Me—Evie Sands (69)	*657*
I Can Make It With You—Pozo-Seco Singers (66)	*655*
I Can't Let Go—Linda Ronstadt (80)	*535*
Make Me Belong To You—Barbara Lewis (66)	516
Worry—Johnny Tillotson (64)	467
I'll Hold Out My Hand—Clique (69)	*459*
Storybook Children—Billy Vera & Judy Clay (67)	392
I Can't Let Go—Hollies (66)	*384*
Country Girl - City Man—Billy Vera & Judy Clay (68)	351
Tommy—Reparata And The Delrons (65)	251
Then I'll Count Again—Johnny Tillotson (65)	167
I Can Make It With You—Jackie de Shannon (66)	*120*
Anyway That You Want Me—American Breed (68)	*86*
Try (Just A Little Bit Harder)—Janis Joplin (70)	52
Welcome Home—Walter Jackson (65)	37
Who Are You—Stacey Cane (65)	18
I Can't Wait Until I See My Baby—Justine Washington (64)	8.0
I'll Hold Out My Hand—Wind (69)	*5.8*
Crazy Annie—Evie Sands (70)	5.3
Any Way That You Want Me—Liverpool Five (66)	*1.4*
Angel Of The Morning—Bettye Swann (69)	*0.9*
Chuck TAYLOR [Chuck Simmons] ▶ 4593 (2)	**459**
The Burning Of Atlanta—Claude King (62)	317
Save All Your Lovin' For Me—Brenda Lee (62)	284
Dallas TAYLOR ▶ 6368 (1)	**178**
Chop Chop Boom—Crew-Cuts (55)	356
Dallas W. TAYLOR ▶ 10915 (1)	**4.4**
Crazies—Stephen Stills -- Manassas (72)	8.8
Daron TAYLOR ▶ 3143 (2)	**987**
(I Wanna) Testify—Parliaments (67)	*1404*
Testify (I Wonna)—Johnnie Taylor (69)	*569*
David John TAYLOR ▶ 10663 (1)	**6.3**
Set The World On Fire—Liar (78)	6.3
Harty TAYLOR ▶ 8028 (1)	**64**
I'm Here To Get My Baby Out Of Jail—Everly Brothers (62)	128
Irving TAYLOR [Raymond Karl] ▶ 669 (9)	**6470**
Everybody Loves Somebody—Dean Martin (64)	8239
Kookie, Kookie (Lend Me Your Comb)—Edward Byrnes and Connie Stevens (59)	3430
Second Fiddle—Kay Starr (56)	353
Am I A Toy Or A Treasure—Kay Starr (54)	233
Fortune In Dreams—Kay Starr (54)	223
Brass Ring—Kay Starr (57)	17
The Good Book—Kay Starr (56)	8.5
The Things I Never Had—Kay Starr (56)	4.4
Love Ain't Right—Kay Starr (56)	4.0
Jack TAYLOR ▶ 1524 (8)	**2805**
Band Of Gold—Don Cherry (55)	*3488*
Band Of Gold—Kit Carson (55)	*1174*
Band Of Gold—Mel Carter (66)	*521*
Earthbound—Sammy Davis Jr. (56)	*404*
Earthbound—Mario Lanza (56)	*123*
Band Of Gold—Roommates (61)	*70*
Band Of Gold—Hi-Fi Four (55)	*4.8*
Earthbound—Roberto & His Orchestra (56)	*0.0*
James TAYLOR ▶ 315 (17) HOF	**11578**
Fire And Rain—James Taylor (70)	*4699*
Don't Let Me Be Lonely Tonight—James Taylor (72)	1195
Her Town Too—James Taylor And J.D. Souther (81)	1187
Steamroller Blues—Elvis Presley (73)	1079
Your Smiling Face—James Taylor (77)	971
Long Ago And Far Away—James Taylor (71)	765
Shower The People—James Taylor (76)	597
Country Road—James Taylor (71)	588
Carolina In My Mind—Crystal Mansion Featuring Johnny Caswell (70)	*314*
Mexico—James Taylor (75)	277
One Man Parade—James Taylor (73)	191

Carolina In My Mind—James Taylor (70)	*164*
Fire And Rain—R.B. Greaves (70)	*128*
Fire And Rain—Johnny Rivers & Friends (70)	*116*
Hard Times—James Taylor (81)	63
Never Die Young—James Taylor (88)	30
Tranquillo—Carly Simon (78)	22
—James Warren Taylor see: J.T. TAYLOR	
John Issac TAYLOR ▶ 2002 (2)	**2014**
Boy From New York City—Manhattan Transfer (81)	*2222*
The Boy From New York City—Ad Libs (65)	*1806*
John L. TAYLOR ▶ 3885 (9)	**667**
Since I Don't Have You—Skyliners (59)	*2364*
This I Swear—Skyliners (59)	743
Since I Don't Have You—Don McLean (81)	*545*
Since I Don't Have You—Chuck Jackson (64)	*403*
It Happened Today—Skyliners (59)	229
Since I Don't Have You—Art Garfunkel (79)	*180*
Since I Don't Have You—Eddie Holman (70)	*160*
Since I Don't Have You—Fred Parris & The Five Satins (82)	*4.8*
How Much—Skyliners (60)	1.5
Johnnie H. TAYLOR ▶ 11093 (1)	**3.3**
Disco 9000—Johnnie Taylor (77)	6.5
Johnny TAYLOR ▶ 10213 (1)	**11**
I'm Standing By—Ben E. King (62)	33
Johnny (2) TAYLOR ▶ 4389 (1)	**507**
Get On Up—Esquires (67)	1521
J.T. TAYLOR [James Warren Taylor] ▶ 1252 (18) HOF	**3571**
Celebration—Kool & The Gang (80)	6016
Cherish—Kool & The Gang (85)	3699
Joanna—Kool & The Gang (83)	3511
Ladies Night—Kool & The Gang (79)	3414
Misled—Kool & The Gang (84)	1436
Get Down On It—Kool & The Gang (82)	1373
Fresh—Kool & The Gang (85)	1367
Victory—Kool & The Gang (86)	1269
Tonight—Kool & The Gang (84)	1136
Take My Heart (You Can Have It If You Want It)—Kool & The Gang (81)	1077
Stone Love—Kool & The Gang (87)	994
Emergency—Kool & The Gang (85)	915
Let's Go Dancin' (Ooh La, La, La)—Kool & The Gang (82)	654
Big Fun—Kool & The Gang (82)	532
Jones Vs. Jones—Kool & The Gang (81)	316
Holiday—Kool & The Gang (87)	126
Special Way—Kool & The Gang (87)	122
Steppin' Out—Kool & The Gang (82)	6.6
Larry TAYLOR ▶ 8222 (1)	**58**
Time Was—Canned Heat (69)	290
Little Johnny TAYLOR [Johnny Lamont Merrett] ▶ 8516 (2)	**47**
Since I Found A New Love—Little Johnny Taylor (64)	40
Nightingale Melody—Little Johnny Taylor (64)	7.2
Livingston TAYLOR ▶ 3735 (4)	**716**
I Will Be In Love With You—Livingston Taylor (78)	635
I'll Come Running—Livingston Taylor (79)	61
Get Out Of Bed—Livingston Taylor (72)	14
Carolina Day—Livingston Taylor (71)	6.3
Lynne TAYLOR ▶ 5320 (2)	**306**
Tom Cat—Rooftop Singers (63)	829
Mama Don't Allow—Rooftop Singers (63)	296
Mary TAYLOR ▶ 4555 (1)	**466**
Queen Of The House—Jody Miller (65)	*931*
Michael C. TAYLOR ▶ 1554 (2)	**2728**
Sunshine On My Shoulders—John Denver (74)	4334
Rocky Mountain High—John Denver (72)	2566
Nick TAYLOR ▶ 7013 (1)	**122**
D.O.A.—Bloodrock (70)	733
Nigel John TAYLOR ▶ 487 (19)	**8562**
The Reflex—Duran Duran (84)	5082
Union Of The Snake—Duran Duran (83)	4545
The Wild Boys—Duran Duran (84)	4449
A View To A Kill—Duran Duran (85)	4032
Hungry Like The Wolf—Duran Duran (82)	3924
Notorious—Duran Duran (86)	3404
I Don't Want Your Love—Duran Duran (88)	2410
Is There Something I Should Know—Duran Duran (83)	2395
Some Like It Hot—Power Station (85)	1943
New Moon On Monday—Duran Duran (84)	1339

Nigel John TAYLOR ▶ 487 (19) *Continued*	**8562**
Rio—Duran Duran (83)	946
Save A Prayer—Duran Duran (85)	773
I Do What I Do—John Taylor (86)	527
All She Wants Is—Duran Duran (88)	486
Communication—Power Station (85)	401
Skin Trade—Duran Duran (87)	308
Violence Of Summer (Love's Taking Over)— Duran Duran (90)	165
Do You Believe In Shame?—Duran Duran (89)	93
Meet El Presidente—Duran Duran (87)	78
Paul TAYLOR [Paul Horowitz] ▶ 2696 (1)	**1266**
Miles Away—Winger (90)	1266
R. Dean TAYLOR ▶ 468 (11)	**8948**
Love Child—Diana Ross And The Supremes (68)	*9676*
Indiana Wants Me—R. Dean Taylor (70)	4928
All I Need—Temptations (67)	1916
I'm Livin' In Shame— Diana Ross And The Supremes (69)	1652
Love Child—Sweet Sensation (90)	*1079*
Gotta See Jane—R. Dean Taylor (71)	236
Ain't It A Sad Thing—R. Dean Taylor (71)	181
Just Look What You've Done—Brenda Holloway (67)	72
I'll Turn To Stone—Four Tops (67)	58
Taos New Mexico—R. Dean Taylor (72)	44
Candy Apple Red—R. Dean Taylor (71)	9.2
—Robert Taylor see: Joseph ROBINSON	
Robert Napoleon TAYLOR ▶ 3976 (2)	**633**
Sha La La—Manfred Mann (64)	*1755*
Sha-La-La—Shirelles (64)	*143*
Robert Percy TAYLOR ▶ 5743 (2)	**246**
Maybe I'm A Fool—Eddie Money (79)	715
You're My Everything—Lee Garrett (76)	135
Roger TAYLOR ▶ 517 (18) HOF	**8247**
The Reflex—Duran Duran (84)	5082
Union Of The Snake—Duran Duran (83)	4545
The Wild Boys—Duran Duran (84)	4449
A View To A Kill—Duran Duran (85)	4032
Hungry Like The Wolf—Duran Duran (82)	3924
Ice Ice Baby—Vanilla Ice (90)	3735
Is There Something I Should Know— Duran Duran (83)	2395
Election Day—Arcadia (85)	1950
New Moon On Monday—Duran Duran (84)	1339
Rio—Duran Duran (83)	946
Radio Ga-Ga—Queen (84)	836
Save A Prayer—Duran Duran (85)	773
Under Pressure—Queen & David Bowie (81)	689
Goodbye Is Forever—Arcadia (86)	432
A Kind Of Magic—Queen (86)	327
I Want It All—Queen (89)	251
One Vision—Queen (85)	249
Calling All Girls—Queen (82)	131
Rudy TAYLOR ▶ 3694 (6)	**733**
Early In The Morning—Robert Palmer (88)	*790*
Early In The Morning—Gap Band (82)	*602*
You Dropped A Bomb On Me—Gap Band (82)	529
Ooops Up—Snap! (90)	273
Burn Rubber (Why You Wanna Hurt Me)— Gap Band (81)	178
I Don't Believe You Want To Get Up And Dance (Oops, Up Side Your Head)—Gap Band (80)	14
Sammy TAYLOR ▶ 3594 (5)	**774**
Funny—Maxine Brown (61)	1027
Peace Pipe—B.T. Express (75)	445
Everytime (I Think About You) (Part 1)— Joey Dee & The Starliters (62)	51
Think Of Me—Maxine Brown (61)	18
Kokomo—Flamingos (61)	7.6
Skip TAYLOR [Lawrence Taylor Tatman III] ▶ 9843 (1)	**16**
Rockin' With The King—Canned Heat (72)	32
Ted TAYLOR ▶ 10924 (1)	**4.3**
Look Out—Ted Taylor (60)	4.3
Tell TAYLOR ▶ 9999 (1)	**14**
Down By The Old Mill Stream— Bruce Hayes with Mary Mayo (60)	14
—William Edward Taylor Jr. see: Billy TAYLOR	
Zola TAYLOR ▶ 5646 (2)	**261**
He's Mine—Platters (57)	629
I Wanna—Platters (57)	102

Pyotr Ilyich TCHAIKOVSKY ▶ 2901 (10)	**1125**
Nut Rocker—B. Bumble & The Stingers (62)	*861*
Where—Platters (59)	364
In Time—Steve Lawrence (61)	214
1812 Overture—Royal Philharmonic Orchestra (81)	131
Romeo And Juliet— Royal Philharmonic Orchestra (81)	131
Piano Concerto No. 1— Royal Philharmonic Orchestra (81)	131
Nutrocker—Emerson, Lake & Palmer (72)	*94*
Questions And Answers—In Crowd (66)	33
Dream Concerto—Ferrante & Teicher (59)	22
Nut Rocker—Jack B. Nimble & Quicks (62)	*0.0*
Elson TEAT ▶ 10665 (1)	**6.3**
Lonesome Whistle Blues—Freddy King (61)	19
John TEBELAK ▶ 4341 (3)	**516**
Day By Day—Godspell (72)	*1542*
Day By Day—Holly Sherwood (71)	*2.7*
Prepare Ye The Way Of The Lord—Holly Sherwood (71)	2.7
Lisa TEDESCO ▶ 5144 (1)	**334**
General Hospi-Tale—Afternoon Delights (81)	669
Richard TEE [Richard Edward Tenryk] ▶ 7163 (1)	**112**
Stuff Like That—Quincy Jones (78)	787
David TEEGARDEN ▶ 4442 (1)	**494**
God, Love And Rock & Roll—Teegarden & Van Winkle (70)	987
Towa TEI [Chung Dong-Hwa, DJ Shodai] ▶ 4103 (2)	**593**
Groove Is In The Heart—Deee-Lite (90)	2521
Power Of Love—Deee-Lite (90)	266
—Chaim Hillel Teicher see: Kenny KAREN	
Louis TEICHER ▶ 10565 (1)	**7.2**
Dream Concerto—Ferrante & Teicher (59)	22
—Phil Teitelbaum see: Terry PHILIPS	
Jay TELFER ▶ 9706 (1)	**19**
Ten Pound Note—Steel River (70)	19
Pablo TELLEZ ▶ 4786 (1)	**416**
Suavecito—Malo (72)	1249
—Gary/Harold Temkin see: Gary KNIGHT	
Jack TEMPCHIN ▶ 526 (14)	**8095**
You Belong To The City—Glenn Frey (85)	3346
Swayin' To The Music (Slow Dancin')— Johnny Rivers (77)	*2175*
The One You Love—Glenn Frey (82)	1201
Smuggler's Blues—Glenn Frey (85)	1119
True Love—Glenn Frey (88)	970
Peaceful Easy Feeling—Eagles (72)	935
Already Gone—Eagles (74)	846
Sexy Girl—Glenn Frey (84)	756
I Found Somebody—Glenn Frey (82)	570
All Those Lies—Glenn Frey (82)	403
Part Of Me, Part Of You—Glenn Frey (91)	267
The Allnighter—Glenn Frey (84)	171
Slow Dancing—Funky Kings (76)	*155*
Livin' Right—Glenn Frey (89)	11
Rod TEMPERTON ▶ 68 (18)	**32428**
Rock With You—Michael Jackson (79)	6909
Boogie Nights—Heatwave (77)	5663
Baby, Come To Me— Patti Austin (A duet with James Ingram) (82)	5139
Give Me The Night—George Benson (80)	2823
Thriller—Michael Jackson (84)	2413
The Groove Line—Heatwave (78)	1966
Sweet Freedom—Michael McDonald (86)	1812
Stomp!—Brothers Johnson (80)	1785
Off The Wall—Michael Jackson (80)	1519
Love Is In Control (Finger On The Trigger)— Donna Summer (82)	1455
Always And Forever—Heatwave (77)	*1229*
Yah Mo B There—James Ingram (83)	906
Man Size Love—Klymaxx (86)	859
Always And Forever—Whistle (90)	*449*
The Secret Garden (Sweet Seduction Suite)— Quincy Jones featuring Al B. Sure!, James Ingram, El DeBarge & Barry White (90)	416
Spice Of Life—Manhattan Transfer (83)	403
Love X Love—George Benson (80)	160
Treasure—Brothers Johnson (80)	23
Joey TEMPEST [Rolf Magnus Joakim Larson] ▶ 1292 (5)	**3444**
Carrie—Europe (87)	2479

The Final Countdown—Europe (87)	1260
Rock The Night—Europe (87)	463
Superstitious—Europe (88)	423
Cherokee—Europe (87)	59
—Bob Temple see: Bob WILSON	
Leslie TEMPLE ▶ 5259 (3)	**317**
The Watusi—Vibrations (61)	657
Feel So Bad—Ray Charles (71)	190
Continental With Me, Baby—Vibrations (61)	2.7
Van TEMPLE ▶ 9191 (1)	**29**
What She Does To Me (The Diana Song)—Producers (81)	117
Bill TEMPLETON ▶ 6688 (2)	**144**
My Treasure—Hilltoppers (55)	*288*
My Treasure—Connie Francis (55)	*0.0*
Nino TEMPO [Antonino Lo Tempio] ▶ 3659 (8)	**746**
All Strung Out—Nino Tempo & April Stevens (66)	*607*
All Strung Out On You—John Travolta (77)	*373*
Sister James—Nino Tempo And 5th Ave. Sax (73)	369
A Woman's Story—Cher (74)	60
Put It Where You Want It—Nino & April (73)	*53*
Wake Up And Love Me—April (74)	34
I Can't Go On Livin' Without You Baby— Nino Tempo & April Stevens (67)	19
Teach Me Tiger—April Stevens (59)	8.6
Benmont TENCH ▶ 4779 (3)	**418**
Sunset Grill—Don Henley (85)	675
Not Enough Love In The World—Don Henley (85)	525
Sweet, Sweet Baby (I'm Falling)—Lone Justice (85)	53
—Kathleen Wakefield Tenen see: Kathy WAKEFIELD	
Neil TENNANT ▶ 858 (11)	**5176**
West End Girls—Pet Shop Boys (86)	4375
What Have I Done To Deserve This?— Pet Shop Boys And Dusty Springfield (87)	3210
It's A Sin—Pet Shop Boys (87)	1228
Opportunities (Let's Make Lots Of Money)— Pet Shop Boys (86)	1174
Domino Dancing—Pet Shop Boys (88)	721
Getting Away With It—Electronic (90)	407
Love Comes Quickly—Pet Shop Boys (86)	188
Suburbia—Pet Shop Boys (86)	159
So Hard—Pet Shop Boys (90)	120
Left To My Own Devices—Pet Shop Boys (89)	35
How Can You Expect To Be Taken Seriously— Pet Shop Boys (91)	4.1
Jack TENNEY ▶ 10803 (1)	**5.2**
Mexicali Rose—Dick Contino (56)	5.2
Toni TENNILLE ▶ 395 (2)	**10060**
Do That To Me One More Time— Captain & Tennille (79)	6914
The Way I Want To Touch You— Captain & Tennille (75)	3145
William TENNYSON ▶ 3781 (1)	**702**
Someone—Johnny Mathis (59)	702
—Richard Edward Tenryk see: Richard TEE	
—Antoine Roberto Teppardo see: Robert TEPPER	
—Albert Tepper see: Al NEVINS	
Robert TEPPER [Antoine Roberto Teppardo, Robert M. Tepper] ▶ 1936 (6)	**2084**
Into The Night—Benny Mardones (80)	*1652*
No Easy Way Out—Robert Tepper (86)	651
Into The Night—Benny Mardones (89)	*640*
This Is Love—Paul Anka (78)	283
Le Bel Age (The Best Years)—Pat Benatar (86)	227
Don't Walk Away—Robert Tepper (86)	33
Sid TEPPER ▶ 397 (34)	**9973**
Naughty Lady Of Shady Lane—Ames Brothers (54)	*4011*
Red Roses For A Blue Lady— Bert Kaempfert And His Orchestra (65)	*2472*
When The Boy In Your Arms (Is The Boy In Your Heart)—Connie Francis (61)	2133
Red Roses For A Blue Lady—Vic Dana (65)	*1799*
Kewpie Doll—Perry Como (58)	1744
My Bonnie Lassie—Ames Brothers (55)	1315
Puppet On A String— Elvis Presley With The Jordanaires (65)	1211
If I Had A Girl—Rod Lauren (59)	752
Red Roses For A Blue Lady—Wayne Newton (65)	*706*
Nuttin' For Christmas—Art Mooney And His Orchestra, Vocal By Barry Gordon (55)	*641*

Sid TEPPER ▶ 397 (34) Continued	**9973**
All That I Am— Elvis Presley With The Jordanaires (66)	425
Summer Sounds—Robert Goulet (65)	403
On London Bridge—Jo Stafford (56)	310
Naughty Lady Of Shady Lane—Archie Bleyer (54)	*293*
Nuttin' For Christmas—Joe Ward (55)	*261*
Cap And Gown—Marty Robbins (59)	235
Comin' Down With Love—Mel Gadson (60)	206
New Orleans— Elvis Presley with the Jordanaires (58)	192
Stay Away—Elvis Presley With The Jordanaires (68)	182
Stairway Of Love—Marty Robbins (58)	162
Nuttin' For Christmas— Ricky Zahnd And The Blue Jeaners (55)	*157*
Don't Come Running Back To Me—Nancy Wilson (65)	137
Forty Nine Shades Of Green—Ames Brothers (56)	111
Nuttin' For Christmas—Fontane Sisters (55)	*102*
You're Next—Jimmy Witherspoon (65)	98
Rock Around Mother Goose—Barry Gordon (56)	89
(It Took) One Kiss—Jaye P. Morgan (59)	75
Nuttin' For Christmas—Stan Freberg (55)	*65*
Stop! And Think It Over—Perry Como (67)	48
In Love—Ames Brothers (58)	45
Stay—Ames Brothers (58)	4.0
The Wonderful World Of The Young— Andy Williams (62)	0.9
Nuttin' For Christmas—Kenny & Corky (59)	*0.8*
Nothin' For Christmas—Eartha Kitt (55)	*0.0*
Joe TERRANOVA ▶ 8883 (1)	**37**
Back To The Hop—Danny & The Juniors (61)	74
Billy TERRELL ▶ 6478 (3)	**165**
Never Gonna Let Him Know—Debbie Taylor (69)	191
Gotta Find A Way—Moments (73)	113
I've Always Had You—Benny Troy (75)	13
—Pearl White Terrell see: Pearl WHITE	
Wilbur TERRELL ▶ 2952 (3)	**1103**
Slip Away—Clarence Carter (68)	2304
Tell Mama—Etta James (67)	902
Looking For A Fox—Clarence Carter (68)	137
Dorothy TERRISS [Theodora Morse, Alfreda Strandberg] ▶ 10934 (1)	**4.2**
Three O'Clock In The Morning—Lou Rawls (65)	*8.5*
Andrew TERRY ▶ 9241 (1)	**28**
Drop By My Place—Little Carl Carlton (70)	140
Barbara TERRY ▶ 10527 (1)	**7.6**
Like Columbus Did—Reflections (64)	30
Bev TERRY ▶ 10880 (1)	**4.7**
Last Train (Biddi-Biddi Bum-Bum)—Ray Lang (57)	9.4
Dewey TERRY ▶ 636 (9)	**6818**
I'm Leaving It Up To You—Dale & Grace (63)	*7593*
The Jolly Green Giant—Kingsmen (65)	2937
I'm Leaving It (All) Up To You— Donny And Marie Osmond (74)	*2345*
Farmer John—Premiers (64)	*827*
Big Boy Pete—Olympics (60)	760
Farmer John—Tidal Waves (66)	*70*
The Letter—Sonny & Cher (65)	43
Justine—Righteous Brothers (65)	34
Surfer Street—Allisons (63)	3.7
George TERRY ▶ 2612 (1)	**1325**
Lay Down Sally—Eric Clapton (77)	3975
Johnny TERRY ▶ 9734 (2)	**18**
You've Got The Power— James Brown And The Famous Flames (60)	31
Please, Please, Please— James Brown And The Famous Flames (64)	4.6
Mike TERRY [Frances Ralston Jenkins] ▶ 11066 (1)	**3.4**
Golden Wildwood Flower—Tom & Jerry (61)	10
Tony TERRY ▶ 10134 (1)	**12**
She's Fly—Tony Terry (87)	49
William TESONE [Billy Duke] ▶ 5375 (2)	**298**
I Cried—Patti Page (54)	*582*
I Cried—Joe Damiano (59)	*14*
Al TESTA ▶ 6653 (4)	**147**
Never, Never, Never (Grande, Grande, Grande)— Shirley Bassey (73)	433
Time Alone Will Tell—Connie Francis (67)	*3.3*
Time Alone Will Tell (Non Pensare A Me)— Jerry Vale (67)	*2.8*

Quando, Quando, Quando (Tell Me When)— Pat Boone (62)	2.6
James TESTA [D.J. Kohler, Donna Kohler] ▶ 4412 (7)	**501**
Hula Hoop Song—Georgia Gibbs (58)	*395*
Your Wild Heart—Joy Layne (57)	*308*
Hula Hoop Song—Teresa Brewer (58)	*251*
Walk On With The Duke—Duke Of Earl (62)	86
Borrowed Dreams—Bobby Helms (58)	29
Your Wild Heart—Poni Tails (57)	*0.0*
Your Wild Heart—Karen Chandler (57)	*0.0*
Giancarlo TESTONI ▶ 4734 (2)	**428**
My One Sin—Four Coins (57)	*690*
My One Sin—Nat "King" Cole (55)	*594*
Peter TETTEROO ▶ 2383 (2)	**1540**
Ma Belle Amie—Tee Set (70)	2854
If You Do Believe In Love—Tee Set (70)	226
Joe TEX [Joseph Arrington Jr., Yusuf Hazziez] ▶ 144 (32)	**19779**
I Gotcha—Joe Tex (72)	6181
Hold What You've Got—Joe Tex (64)	2659
Skinny Legs And All—Joe Tex (67)	2606
I Want To (Do Everything For You)—Joe Tex (65)	*1159*
A Sweet Woman Like You—Joe Tex (65)	857
Men Are Gettin' Scarce—Joe Tex (68)	621
You Said A Bad Word—Joe Tex (72)	522
Papa Was Too—Joe Tex (66)	519
Buying A Book—Joe Tex (69)	490
The Love You Save (May Be Your Own)—Joe Tex (66)	445
Show Me—Joe Tex (67)	402
S.Y.S.L.J.F.M. (The Letter Song)—Joe Tex (66)	380
You Better Get It—Joe Tex (65)	353
Woman Like That, Yeah—Joe Tex (67)	345
I'll Never Do You Wrong—Joe Tex (68)	288
I Believe I'm Gonna Make It—Joe Tex (66)	283
A Woman Can Change A Man—Joe Tex (65)	259
Keep The One You Got—Joe Tex (68)	257
I've Got To Do A Little Bit Better—Joe Tex (66)	228
That's The Way—Joe Tex (69)	207
A Woman's Hands—Joe Tex (67)	199
You Got What It Takes—Joe Tex (65)	159
You Need Me, Baby—Joe Tex (68)	109
One Monkey Don't Stop No Show—Joe Tex (65)	71
Baby, You're Right— James Brown And The Famous Flames (61)	69
That's Your Baby—Joe Tex (69)	61
I Want To (Do Everything For You)—Raeletts (70)	*43*
I Knew Him—Joe Tex (71)	21
You're Right, Ray Charles—Joe Tex (70)	10
(When Johnny Comes Marching Home Again) I Can't See You No More—Joe Tex (69)	4.9
Give The Baby Anything The Baby Wants—Joe Tex (71)	3.7
Don't Let Your Left Hand Know—Joe Tex (65)	2.8
Gary THAIN ▶ 10509 (1)	**7.8**
Sweet Lorraine—Uriah Heep (73)	23
Glynn THAMES ▶ 4722 (1)	**431**
Daisy Petal Pickin'—Jimmy Gilmer And The Fireballs (63)	1293
Rosetta THARPE [Rosetta Nubin, Sister Rosetta Tharpe] ▶ 7804 (1)	**74**
Up Above My Head (I Hear Music In The Air)—Al (He's The King) Hirt Trumpet with Chorus and Orchestra (64)	74
Marty THAU ▶ 10245 (1)	**11**
Soul Struttin'—Jamie Lyons (67)	22
Sam THEARD ▶ 10315 (1)	**10**
Let The Good Times Roll—Ray Charles (60)	20
—Emil Theilheim see: Peppy CASTRO	
—The JBL see: Keith SHOCKLEE	
Mikis THEODORAKIS ▶ 2170 (1)	**1794**
Zorba The Greek— Herb Alpert & The Tijuana Brass (65)	1794
Mike THEODORE ▶ 11832 (1)	**0.0**
Getting It On—Dennis Coffey (72)	0.0
Sandy THEORET [Sandy Mason] ▶ 10229 (1)	**11**
When I Dream—Crystal Gayle (79)	11
—J.S. Theracon see: Walter MORRISON	
—Arthur James Theus see: Fats THEUS	
Fats THEUS [Arthur James Theus] ▶ 11200 (1)	**2.8**
The Worm—Jimmy McGriff (68)	2.8
Robert THIBODEAUX ▶ 10597 (1)	**7.0**
I'm Not A Fool Anymore—T.K. Hulin (63)	7.0

Alan THICKE ▶ 7995 (1)	**66**
Sara—Bill Champlin (82)	132
Bob THIELE [Stanley Clayton, George Douglas, Robert Thiele] ▶ 5685 (2)	**255**
What A Wonderful World—Louis Armstrong (88)	389
Sweet Song Of India—McGuire Sisters (55)	182
Doug THIELE ▶ 10080 (1)	**13**
Dancin' Like Lovers—Mary MacGregor (80)	26
Emil THIELHELM ▶ 3270 (2)	**919**
(We Ain't Got) Nothin' Yet—Blues Magoos (66)	3377
One By One—Blues Magoos (67)	150
Huey THIERRY ▶ 7458 (1)	**95**
Matilda Has Finally Come Back— Cookie & His Cupcakes (59)	189
Henderson THIGPEN ▶ 5562 (3)	**271**
Woman To Woman—Shirley Brown (74)	*767*
Don't Take My Kindness For Weakness— Soul Children (72)	46
Woman To Woman—Barbara Mandrell (78)	*12*
Alan THOMAS ▶ 5750 (2)	**245**
Going Going Gone—Brook Benton (64)	477
Lonely Life—Jackie Wilson (61)	13
Alfie THOMAS ▶ 7945 (2)	**68**
Stand Up—Underworld (89)	119
Underneath The Radar—Underworld (88)	85
Banner THOMAS ▶ 6927 (1)	**128**
Flirtin' With Disaster—Molly Hatchet (79)	383
Carla THOMAS ▶ 1446 (6)	**3025**
Gee Whiz (Look At His Eyes)—Carla Thomas (61)	*2073*
Gee Whiz—Bernadette Peters (80)	*563*
A Love Of My Own—Carla Thomas (61)	318
A Woman's Love—Carla Thomas (64)	125
I've Fallen In Love (With You)—Carla Thomas (69)	6.5
(Mama, Mama) Wish Me Good Luck— Carla Thomas (61)	1.9
Cliff THOMAS ▶ 3461 (4)	**838**
Lover's Holiday— Peggy Scott & Jo Jo Benson (68)	1147
Pickin' Wild Mountain Berries— Peggy Scott & Jo Jo Benson (68)	897
Pop-Eye—Huey Smith (62)	394
It's All Right (You're Just In Love)—Tams (64)	50
—Danny Thomas see: Danny WILDE	
Dave THOMAS ▶ 6337 (1)	**182**
Take Off—Bob & Doug McKenzie (82)	908
—Deanna Crisp Brown Thomas see: Deanna BROWN	
Dennis THOMAS ▶ 1675 (21)	**2513**
Celebration—Kool & The Gang (80)	6016
Ladies Night—Kool & The Gang (79)	3414
Jungle Boogie—Kool & The Gang (73)	2506
Hollywood Swinging—Kool & The Gang (74)	2079
Summertime—DJ Jazzy Jeff & The Fresh Prince (91)	1783
Stone Love—Kool & The Gang (87)	994
Emergency—Kool & The Gang (85)	915
Spirit Of The Boogie—Kool & The Gang (75)	825
Funky Stuff—Kool & The Gang (73)	473
Higher Plane—Kool & The Gang (74)	446
Kool And The Gang—Kool & The Gang (69)	329
Jones Vs. Jones—Kool & The Gang (81)	316
Caribbean Festival—Kool & The Gang (75)	268
Open Sesame - Part I—Kool & The Gang (76)	252
Rhyme Tyme People—Kool & The Gang (75)	182
Let The Music Take Your Mind—Kool & The Gang (70)	85
Love And Understanding (Come Together)— Kool & The Gang (76)	48
Funky Man—Kool & The Gang (70)	41
The Gangs Back Again—Kool & The Gang (69)	37
Who's Gonna Take The Weight (Part One)— Kool & The Gang (71)	4.1
Summer Madness—Kool & The Gang (75)	0.0
Don THOMAS ▶ 3673 (1)	**741**
This Door Swings Both Ways—Herman's Hermits (66)	1482
Edward S. THOMAS Jr. ▶ 3339 (6)	**893**
Lover's Holiday—Peggy Scott & Jo Jo Benson (68)	1147
Pickin' Wild Mountain Berries— Peggy Scott & Jo Jo Benson (68)	897
Pop-Eye—Huey Smith (62)	394
It's All Right (You're Just In Love)—Tams (64)	50
It's In Your Power—Joe Odom (69)	44
Look What We Have Joined Together—Sugar Blues (69)	12

Emma THOMAS ▶ 7132 (1)	**114**
I'll Be Sweeter Tomorrow (Than I Was Today)—O'Jays (67)	458
Frederick THOMAS [Frederick O'Neil Thomas] ▶ 2436 (2)	**1490**
Do Anything—Natural Selection (91)	3407
Hearts Don't Think (They Feel)—Natural Selection (91)	708
Gene THOMAS [Gene Thomasson] ▶ 1659 (4)	**2532**
Playboy—Gene & Debbe (68)	1894
Sometimes—Gene Thomas (61)	286
Lovin' Season—Gene & Debbe (68)	211
Go With Me—Gene & Debbe (67)	141
Gerald THOMAS ▶ 4010 (3)	**623**
Troglodyte (Cave Man)—Jimmy Castor Bunch (72)	3177
Spanish Hustle—Fatback Band (76)	91
Gotta Get My Hands On Some (Money)—Fatback (80)	6.0
Guy THOMAS ▶ 6668 (1)	**146**
Conviction Of The Heart—Kenny Loggins (91)	291
Harold THOMAS ▶ 8307 (1)	**55**
Ooh Baby—Deon Jackson (67)	110
Harold Larry THOMAS ▶ 10899 (1)	**4.5**
(Call Me) The Traveling Man—Masqueraders (76)	23
—Harry Thomas see: Harry BELAFONTE	
Ian THOMAS ▶ 1464 (4)	**2968**
Hold On—Santana (82)	1271
Runner—Manfred Mann's Earth Band (84)	687
Painted Ladies—Ian Thomas (73)	634
Right Before Your Eyes—America (82)	378
Irma THOMAS [Irma Lee] ▶ 2802 (1)	**1187**
Wish Someone Would Care—Irma Thomas (64)	1187
Jack Edward THOMAS ▶ 11262 (1)	**2.5**
True Love Gone (Come On Home)—Betty Madigan (57)	13
Jeff THOMAS ▶ 4169 (2)	**575**
Don't Try To Lay No Boogie Woogie On The "King Of Rock & Roll"—Crow (70)	*487*
Don't Try To Lay No Boogie-Woogie On The King Of Rock And Roll—John Baldry (71)	*88*
—Jimmie Thomas see: Leon RENÉ	
Joe THOMAS ▶ 8374 (2)	**53**
Let's Walk And Talk—Ames Brothers (54)	44
Got You On My Mind—Cookie & His Cupcakes (63)	18
Joe (2) THOMAS ▶ 6518 (1)	**161**
In Self Defense—Cornel Gunter and The Flairs (56)	161
John September THOMAS ▶ 11744 (1)	**0.2**
He'll Be Back—Players (66)	0.5
Jon THOMAS ▶ 4457 (2)	**491**
Heartbreak (It's Hurtin' Me)—Little Willie John (60)	*569*
Heartbreak (It's Hurtin' Me)—Jon Thomas And Orchestra (60)	*414*
Joseph David THOMAS Jr. ▶ 9004 (2)	**33**
Ain't Nothin' But A House Party—Show Stoppers (68)	*46*
(Ain't Nothin' But A) House Party—J. Geils Band (76)	*21*
Keith THOMAS ▶ 1800 (1)	**2294**
Baby Baby—Amy Grant (91)	4588
Kenny THOMAS [Yennik Samoht] ▶ 2234 (1)	**1715**
Stoned Love—Supremes (70)	3430
Lee THOMAS ▶ 6702 (2)	**143**
Don't Believe Him, Donna—Lenny Miles (60)	263
Eternally—Chantels (63)	22
—Leslie Thomas see: Snuff GARRETT	
Mamie THOMAS ▶ 9234 (1)	**28**
Silly Boy (She Doesn't Love You)—Lettermen (62)	56
Marvell THOMAS ▶ 8965 (1)	**35**
Pin The Tail On The Donkey—Newcomers (71)	70
Michael THOMAS [Martin Böttcher] ▶ 4157 (2)	**578**
Hawaii Tattoo—Waikikis (64)	*578*
Hawaii Tattoo—Exotic Sounds Of Martin Denny (64)	*0.0*
Mickey THOMAS ▶ 8092 (1)	**62**
Layin' It On The Line—Jefferson Starship (84)	124
Norman THOMAS ▶ 10764 (1)	**5.5**
Naughty Little Flea—Lord Flea and His Calypsonians (57)	5.5
Ron THOMAS ▶ 4941 (1)	**377**
Girl Of My Dreams—Bram Tchaikovsky (79)	377
Rufus THOMAS ▶ 935 (14)	**4751**
Walking The Dog—Rufus Thomas (63)	2025
(Do The) Push And Pull - Part 1—Rufus Thomas (70)	1096
Do The Funky Chicken—Rufus Thomas (70)	650
The Breakdown (Part 1)—Rufus Thomas (71)	588
Can Your Monkey Do The Dog—Rufus Thomas (64)	480
Jump Back—Rufus Thomas (64)	*282*
Do The Funky Penguin Part 1—Rufus Thomas (71)	256
Jump Back—King Curtis (67)	*86*
Philly Dog—Mar-Keys (66)	*45*
The Dog—Rufus Thomas (63)	41
That's Really Some Good—Rufus & Carla (64)	16
Somebody Stole My Dog—Rufus Thomas (64)	14
Philly Dog—Herbie Mann (66)	*3.7*
Memphis Train—Buddy Miles Express (69)	0.4
Susan THOMAS [Susan Marie Gallion, Susan Marie Thomas] ▶ 8992 (1)	**34**
The Woman In Me—Crystal Gayle (81)	34
—Susan Marie Thomas see: Susan THOMAS	
Terry THOMAS ▶ 2322 (8)	**1592**
If You Needed Somebody—Bad Company (90)	1041
Walk Through Fire—Bad Company (91)	687
It's Inevitable—Charlie (83)	366
She Loves To Be In Love—Charlie (78)	174
Killer Cut—Charlie (79)	151
Shake It Up—Bad Company (89)	30
Holy Water—Bad Company (90)	20
Turning To You—Charlie (77)	11
Timmy THOMAS ▶ 1061 (3)	**4159**
Why Can't We Live Together—Timmy Thomas (72)	4091
People Are Changin'—Timmy Thomas (73)	50
Gotta Give A Little Love (Ten Years After)—Timmy Thomas (84)	18
Tony THOMAS ▶ 8266 (1)	**56**
Been So Long—Pastels (58)	226
Truman THOMAS ▶ 6205 (3)	**194**
You're Welcome, Stop On By—Bobby Womack (74)	263
Free Me From My Freedom/Tie Me To A Tree (Handcuff Me)—Bonnie Pointer (78)	106
Up The Creek (Without A Paddle)—Temptations (76)	27
Vic THOMAS ▶ 9869 (1)	**16**
Stranger In Your Arms—Bobby Vee (64)	31
—Gene Thomasson see: Gene THOMAS	
Hughie THOMASSON ▶ 4920 (4)	**382**
There Goes Another Love Song—Outlaws (75)	534
Hurry Sundown—Outlaws (77)	107
Take It Any Way You Want It—Outlaws (78)	5.1
Breaker - Breaker—Outlaws (76)	4.9
—Alphonso Thompson see: Sonny THOMPSON	
—Arthur Lee Andrew Thompson see: Lee ANDREWS	
—Bonnie Thompson see: John Edward MOORE	
—Brenda L. Thompson see: Brenda JOHNSON	
Brian THOMPSON ▶ 8305 (1)	**55**
Housecall—Shabba Ranks (91)	329
Chris THOMPSON ▶ 5443 (3)	**288**
So Wrong—Patrick Simmons (83)	536
You're The Voice—John Farnham (90)	64
Love On The Airwaves—Night (81)	7.5
Clara THOMPSON ▶ 4777 (2)	**418**
Warm And Tender Love—Percy Sledge (66)	*1225*
My Adorable One—Joe Simon (64)	*20*
—Dean Kermit Thompson see: Dean KAY	
—Dennis Thompson see: Dennis TOMICH	
Denny THOMPSON ▶ 2605 (1)	**1329**
Tijuana Jail—Kingston Trio (59)	1329
Frank THOMPSON ▶ 6889 (9)	**131**
Shake Your Rump To The Funk—Bar-Kays (76)	593
Move Your Boogie Body—Bar-Kays (79)	270
Today Is The Day—Bar-Kays (80)	150
Freakshow On The Dance Floor—Bar-Kays (84)	79
Too Hot To Stop—Bar-Kays (77)	36
Hit And Run—Bar-Kays (81)	23
Boogie Body Land—Bar-Kays (81)	23
Let's Have Some Fun—Bar-Kays (78)	8.9
Shine—Bar-Kays (79)	7.7
Gary THOMPSON ▶ 6695 (1)	**143**
Sing A Song For Freedom—Frijid Pink (70)	430
Glenn THOMPSON ▶ 11359 (1)	**2.1**
We Should Be Sleeping—Eddie Money (87)	8.4
Hank THOMPSON [Orville Proctor] ▶ 7420 (5)	**97**
Six Pack To Go—Hank Thompson (60)	80
Honky Tonk Girl—Johnny Cash (60)	75
Total Strangers—Hank Thompson And His Brazos Valley Boys (59)	26
Rockin' In The Congo—Hank Thompson And His Brazos Valley Boys (57)	5.0
She's Just A Whole Lot Like You—Hank Thompson (60)	2.3
—Hilary Thompson see: Billy PEACHES	
Howard THOMPSON ▶ 3326 (2)	**899**
All 4 Love—Color Me Badd (91)	5388
Treat 'Em Right—Chubb Rock (91)	4.7
H.S. THOMPSON ▶ 5428 (2)	**290**
Clementine—Bobby Darin (60)	*1036*
Clementine—Jan & Dean (60)	*125*
James A. THOMPSON Jr. ▶ 3937 (5)	**650**
Good Guys Only Win In The Movies—Mel And Tim (70)	386
Get Down—Gene Chandler (78)	336
Simply Call It Love—Gene Chandler (70)	238
You're A Lady—Gene Chandler (71)	3.4
When You're #1—Gene Chandler (79)	1.2
—James Earl Thompson see: Jimmy JOHNSON	
Kay THOMPSON [Catherine L. Fink] ▶ 3506 (3)	**810**
Promise Me Love—Andy Williams (58)	747
Eloise—Kay Thompson (56)	109
Margarita—Chuck Rio And The Originals (59)	8.8
Lee Jay THOMPSON ▶ 5334 (1)	**303**
Our House—Madness (83)	2122
Linda THOMPSON ▶ 5354 (1)	**300**
Voices That Care—Voices That Care (91)	901
Marcus THOMPSON ▶ 4258 (1)	**544**
Rumors—Timex Social Club (86)	1633
—Paul Stephen Thompson see: Porl THOMPSON	
Porl THOMPSON [Paul Stephen Thompson] ▶ 3819 (8)	**690**
Love Song—Cure (89)	2408
Just Like Heaven—Cure (87)	604
Why Can't I Be You?—Cure (87)	279
Fascination Street—Cure (89)	194
Lullaby—Cure (89)	170
Pictures Of You—Cure (90)	105
Hot Hot Hot!!!—Cure (88)	88
Never Enough—Cure (90)	68
Richard THOMPSON ▶ 5191 (2)	**329**
Express—B.T. Express (75)	*2209*
Express—Ritchie Family (76)	*92*
Robbin THOMPSON ▶ 8021 (1)	**65**
Brite Eyes—Robbin Thompson Band (80)	65
Robert R. THOMPSON ▶ 2625 (1)	**1312**
An Open Letter To My Teenage Son—Victor Lundberg (67)	1312
Sonny THOMPSON [Alphonso Thompson] ▶ 4644 (9)	**446**
Hide Away—Freddy King (61)	460
Three Hearts In A Tangle—Roy Drusky (61)	*284*
San-Ho-Zay—Freddy King (61)	62
It Won't Be This Way (Always)—King Pins (63)	34
Have Faith—Gene Allison (58)	30
Three Hearts In A Tangle—James Brown And The Famous Flames (62)	*8.1*
You've Got To Love Her With A Feeling—Freddy King (61)	5.2
Let Them Talk—Little Willie John (59)	2.3
I'm Sorry—Bobby Bland (71)	1.7
Sylvester THOMPSON ▶ 11726 (1)	**0.4**
Just A Little Bit—Little Milton (69)	3.1
—Sylvester Thompson see: Syl JOHNSON	
Wayne Carson THOMPSON [Wayne Carson, Wayne Carson Head] ▶ 128 (19)	**20708**
The Letter—Box Tops (67)	*10569*
Always On My Mind—Willie Nelson (82)	*2961*
The Letter—Joe Cocker With Leon Russell And The Shelter People (70)	*2598*
Soul Deep—Box Tops (69)	1670
Always On My Mind—Pet Shop Boys (88)	*1512*
No Love At All—B.J. Thomas (71)	1159

Wayne Carson THOMPSON [Wayne Carson, Wayne Carson Head] ▶ 128 (19) *Continued*	**20708**
Do It Again A Little Bit Slower—Jon & Robin And The In Crowd (67)	1123
Neon Rainbow—Box Tops (67)	950
The Letter—Arbors (69)	*737*
Somebody Like Me—Eddy Arnold (66)	400
Dr. Jon (The Medicine Man)—Jon & Robin And The In Crowd (68)	201
Nine Pound Steel—Joe Simon (67)	115
You Keep Tightening Up On Me—Box Tops (70)	95
I Want Some More—Jon & Robin and The In Crowd (67)	81
Mr. Bus Driver—Bruce Channel (67)	*59*
Tulsa—Billy Joe Royal (71)	50
Drums—Jon & Robin (67)	35
Mr. Bus Driver—Neal Dover (70)	*8.5*
I'm Gonna Do All I Can (To Do Right By My Man)—Ike & Tina Turner (69)	2.2
—David Henry Thomsett see: David CLAYTON-THOMAS	
Ali THOMSON ▶ 2104 (3)	**1876**
Take A Little Rhythm—Ali Thomson (80)	1052
Really Wanna Know You—Gary Wright (81)	858
Live Every Minute—Ali Thomson (80)	394
George THORN ▶ 3863 (4)	**673**
Sweet And Gentle—Alan Dale (55)	*1346*
Sweet And Gentle—Georgia Gibbs (55)	*0.0*
Sweet And Gentle (Me Lo Dijo Adela)—Eartha Kitt & Perez Prado (55)	*0.0*
Sweet And Gentle (Me Lo Dijo Adela)—Merv Griffin & Xavier Cugat (55)	*0.0*
Blair THORNTON ▶ 6942 (3)	**127**
Take It Like A Man—Bachman-Turner Overdrive (76)	250
Down The Road—B.T.O. (78)	6.3
Free Wheelin—Bachman-Turner Overdrive (74)	0.0
John THORNTON ▶ 10406 (2)	**8.8**
Put Yourself In My Place—Elgins (66)	33
Just A Little Bit—Little Milton (69)	3.1
Kevin THORNTON ▶ 1750 (3)	**2368**
All 4 Love—Color Me Badd (91)	5388
I Wanna Sex You Up—Color Me Badd (91)	4560
I Adore Mi Amor—Color Me Badd (91)	4094
Teri THORNTON [Shirley Enid Avery] ▶ 10206 (1)	**11**
Feelin' Fruggy—Al Hirt (65)	11
Nick THORP ▶ 7965 (1)	**67**
Misfit—Curiosity Killed The Cat (87)	336
Billy THORPE ▶ 6487 (1)	**164**
Children Of The Sun—Billy Thorpe (79)	328
Pat THRALL ▶ 9423 (2)	**24**
Beg, Borrow Or Steal—Hughes/Thrall (82)	40
My Pearl—Automatic Man (76)	17
Sonny THROCKMORTON ▶ 4312 (2)	**525**
If You're Not Back In Love By Monday—Millie Jackson (77)	453
I Wish I Was Eighteen Again—George Burns (79)	299
—Gerd Thumser see: Claus RITTER	
THUNDERHAWK ▶ 10301 (1)	**10**
St. Charles—Jefferson Starship (76)	52
Henry THURSTON ▶ 11658 (1)	**0.8**
I'll Sail My Ship Alone—Jerry Lee Lewis And His Pumping Piano (59)	3.2
Scott THURSTON ▶ 5591 (2)	**267**
Remember The Nights—Motels (83)	499
Shock—Motels (85)	36
Harry TIERNEY ▶ 10377 (1) HOF	**9.3**
Alice Blue Gown—LeRoy Holmes And His Orchestra (59)	9.3
Gary TIGERMAN ▶ 8991 (1)	**34**
Seduced—Leon Redbone (81)	34
Glenn TILBROOK ▶ 3484 (3)	**822**
Hourglass—Squeeze (87)	936
853-5937—Squeeze (87)	431
Tempted—Squeeze (81)	277
Bill TILGHMAN ▶ 4151 (2)	**579**
Oh Boy—Buddy Holly / The Crickets (57)	1552
Rave On—Buddy Holly / The Crickets (58)	184
Mel TILLIS ▶ 678 (22)	**6392**
Emotions—Brenda Lee (60)	2994
Ruby, Don't Take Your Love To Town—Kenny Rogers And The First Edition (69)	*2310*
Detroit City—Bobby Bare (63)	*1484*
I Ain't Never—Webb Pierce (59)	*807*
Detroit City—Tom Jones (67)	*748*
Ten Thousand Drums—Carl Smith (59)	404
No Love Have I—Webb Pierce (59)	348
Stick With Me Baby—Everly Brothers (61)	259
Mary Don't You Weep—Stonewall Jackson (59)	197
So Wrong—Patsy Cline (62)	182
I'm Tired—Ray Peterson (61)	67
Bop-A-Lena—Ronnie Self (58)	59
In The Heart Of A Fool—Johnnie Ray (60)	17
Detroit City—Solomon Burke (67)	*17*
Curry Road—Burl Ives (63)	17
Strange—Patsy Cline (62)	10
I Ain't Never—Four Preps (59)	*8.8*
Billy, I've Got To Go To Town—Geraldine Stevens (69)	*8.1*
Detroit City No. 2—Ben Colder (63)	*4.9*
Little Miss Belong To No One—Teresa Brewer (61)	4.2
Guess I've Been Around Too Long—Carl Smith (58)	2.9
Detroit City—Dean Martin (70)	*1.3*
Roger TILLISON ▶ 5230 (1)	**322**
(You Don't Have To) Paint Me A Picture—Gary Lewis And The Playboys (66)	967
Floyd TILLMAN ▶ 7331 (1)	**101**
I Love You So Much It Hurts—Charlie Gracie (57)	101
Johnny TILLOTSON ▶ 532 (6)	**8038**
It Keeps Right On A-Hurtin'—Johnny Tillotson (62)	4800
Without You—Johnny Tillotson (61)	1590
Out Of My Mind—Johnny Tillotson (63)	896
Dreamy Eyes—Johnny Tillotson (61)	*681*
Dreamy Eyes—Johnny Tillotson (58)	*64*
Well I'm Your Man—Johnny Tillotson (58)	7.2
Abrim TILMON ▶ 1674 (9)	**2514**
Baby Let Me Take You (In My Arms)—Detroit Emeralds (72)	1285
You Want It, You Got It—Detroit Emeralds (72)	664
Do Me Right—Detroit Emeralds (71)	579
Me Myself And I—De La Soul (89)	353
Feel The Need—Leif Garrett (79)	*130*
Wear This Ring (With Love)—Detroit Emeralds (71)	78
You're Gettin' A Little Too Smart—Detroit Emeralds (73)	29
Feel The Need In Me—Detroit Emeralds (72)	*21*
Feel The Need—Detroit Emeralds (77)	*12*
Patrick TILON ▶ 7525 (1)	**91**
Deeper Shade Of Soul—Urban Dance Squad (90)	545
Ricky TIMAS ▶ 2095 (2)	**1887**
Cool It Now—New Edition (84)	3404
Count Me Out—New Edition (85)	371
Wladimir TIMM ▶ 7214 (1)	**110**
Beer Barrel Polka—Bobby Vinton (75)	329
Al TIMOTHY [Albon Timothy, King Timothy] ▶ 11697 (1)	**0.6**
(Kiss Me) Honey, Honey (Kiss Me)—Gogi Grant (59)	1.3
—Albon/King Timothy see: Al TIMOTHY	
—Michael Trevor Tinsley see: Miki DALLON	
Mike TINSLEY ▶ 8536 (1)	**47**
Make Love To Me—Helen Reddy (79)	141
Tito TINSLEY ▶ 10721 (1)	**5.9**
Bad Little Woman—Shadows Of Knight (66)	30
Peter TINTURIN ▶ 4867 (3)	**396**
I'm Sorry—Platters (57)	1021
What Will I Tell My Heart—Fats Domino (57)	*163*
What Will I Tell My Heart—Harptones (61)	*3.7*
Mario TIO ▶ 10541 (1)	**7.5**
Action Speaks Louder Than Words—Chocolate Milk (75)	67
Dimitri TIOMKIN ▶ 503 (44)	**8419**
Friendly Persuasion (Thee I Love)—Pat Boone (56)	*2555*
The High And The Mighty—Les Baxter & His Orchestra (54)	*2227*
Town Without Pity—Gene Pitney (61)	2139
Theme From "The Unforgiven" (The Need For Love)—Don Costa And His Orchestra And Chorus (60)	*982*
Hajji Baba (Persian Lament)—Nat "King" Cole (54)	923
Wild Is The Wind—Johnny Mathis (57)	*824*
Ballad Of The Alamo—Marty Robbins (60)	*694*
Sundowners—Billy Vaughn And His Orchestra (60)	*533*
Friendly Persuasion (Thee I Love)—Four Aces (56)	*389*
The Green Leaves Of Summer—Brothers Four (60)	*304*
Theme From The Sundowners—Felix Slatkin Orchestra And Chorus (60)	*254*
Ballad Of The Alamo—Bud And Travis (60)	*190*
Strange Are The Ways Of Love—Gogi Grant (58)	*178*
The Green Leaves Of Summer—Kenny Ball And His Jazzmen (62)	*142*
Strange Lady In Town—Frankie Laine (55)	*61*
Giant—Les Baxter with His Chorus and Orchestra (56)	*54*
The Guns Of Navarone—Joe Reisman And His Orchestra (61)	*49*
Theme From The High And The Mighty—Meco (82)	*47*
Giant—Art Mooney and His Orchestra and Chorus (56)	*17*
Giant—Jack Pleis and His Orchestra and Chorus (56)	*11*
Theme From The Sundowners—Mantovani And His Orchestra (60)	*9.5*
Rio Bravo—Dean Martin (59)	9.1
The Fall Of Love—Johnny Mathis (64)	5.9
Giant—Jimmy Wakely (56)	*0.0*
Giant—Rusty Draper (56)	*0.0*
The High And The Mighty—Johnny Desmond (54)	*0.0*
The Green Leaves Of Summer—Nick Perito (60)	*0.0*
Theme From The Sundowners—Eddie Calvert (60)	*0.0*
The Green Leaves Of Summer—Bud & Travis (60)	*0.0*
Strange Are The Ways Of Love—Randy Sparks (58)	*0.0*
Wild Is The Wind—Henri René & His Orchestra (57)	*0.0*
Wild Is The Wind—LeRoy Holmes & His Orchestra (57)	*0.0*
The Guns Of Navarone—Mitch Miller and The Gang (61)	*0.0*
Giant—Ray Heindorf & The Warner Bros. Orchestra (56)	*0.0*
Friendly Persuasion (Thee I Love)—Anthony Perkins (56)	*0.0*
The Unforgiven (The Need For Love)—McGuire Sisters (60)	*0.0*
Strange Lady In Town—Dimitri Tiomkin & His Orchestra (55)	*0.0*
The High And The Mighty—LeRoy Holmes & His Orchestra (54)	*0.0*
The Green Leaves Of Summer—Nelson Riddle & His Orchestra (60)	*0.0*
Friendly Persuasion (Thee I Love)—Lou Busch & His Orchestra (56)	*0.0*
The High And The Mighty—Victor Young And His Singing Strings (54)	*0.0*
Friendly Persuasion (Thee I Love)—George Cates & His Orchestra (56)	*0.0*
Friendly Persuasion (Thee I Love)—Michel Legrand & His Orchestra (56)	*0.0*
Love Theme From "Giant" (There's Never Been Anyone Else But You)—David Carroll & His Orchestra (56)	*0.0*
George TIPTON ▶ 11530 (1)	**1.3**
A Beginning From An End—Jan & Dean (66)	5.2
Glenn TIPTON ▶ 9082 (2)	**32**
You've Got Another Thing Comin'—Judas Priest (82)	89
Living After Midnight—Judas Priest (80)	5.6
Fay TISHMAN ▶ 5215 (2)	**324**
Spring Rain—Pat Boone (60)	321
The Strangest Romance—Patti Page (56)	2.7
Brent TITCOMB ▶ 7792 (1)	**75**
Sing High--Sing Low—Anne Murray (70)	75
Russ TITELMAN ▶ 8926 (1)	**36**
Sailor Boy—Chiffons (64)	72
David TITLOW ▶ 8335 (1)	**54**
I Want To Be Your Property—Blue Mercedes (88)	108
Libby TITUS ▶ 6187 (1)	**196**
Love Has No Pride—Linda Ronstadt (73)	392
Juan TIZOL ▶ 5809 (3)	**240**
Caravan—Santo & Johnny (60)	*396*
Caravan (pt. 1)—Cozy Cole (58)	*82*
Caravan (Part 2)—Cozy Cole (58)	*1.4*
Charles TOBIAS ▶ 1365 (14) HOF	**3256**
Those Lazy-Hazy-Crazy Days Of Summer—Nat King Cole (63)	2528
Old Lamplighter—Browns Featuring Jim Edward Brown (60)	2054
All Over The World—Nat King Cole (63)	603
Kathy O—Diamonds (58)	*432*
The Mama Doll Song—Patti Page (54)	*350*
Time Waits For No One—Hilltoppers (54)	253

Charles TOBIAS ▶ 1365 (14) HOF *Cont'd*	**3256**
Miss You—Jaye P. Morgan (59)	*234*
Trade Winds— Billy Vaughn And His Orchestra (59)	203
It's Your Life—Bob Manning (55)	31
It's Yours—DeCastro Sisters (56)	27
You're Wrong All Wrong— Eileen Rodgers (56)	14
Don't Sweetheart Me— Bobby Dee & Rhodie-Summers (57)	5.8
Kathy O—Earl Grant (58)	*0.0*
Fred TOBIAS [Fred Towne] ▶ 955 (15)	**4673**
Good Timin'—Jimmy Jones (60)	4490
Born Too Late—Poni-Tails (58)	2154
Little Bitty Girl—Bobby Rydell (60)	741
One Of Us (Will Weep Tonight)—Patti Page (60)	740
Johnny Will—Pat Boone (61)	608
Brigade Of Broken Hearts—Paul Evans (60)	145
I Can't Rock And Roll To Save My Soul— Pearl Bailey (56)	117
The Cheer Leader—Paul Petersen (63)	99
Banned In Boston—Merv Griffin (61)	67
Preview Of Paradise—Adam Wade (61)	41
The Water Tumbler Tune— Henri René And His Orchestra And Chorus (55)	13
Blue River—Elvis Presley (66)	5.3
Where Did I Make My Mistake— Clyde McPhatter (59)	4.8
Two Long Years—Dick Caruso (60)	3.8
Gingerbread—Gingersnaps (58)	0.0
Harry TOBIAS ▶ 2060 (4) HOF	**1939**
Sail Along Silvery Moon— Billy Vaughn and His Orchestra (57)	*3690*
Miss You—Jaye P. Morgan (59)	*234*
Sweet And Lovely—April Stevens & Nino Tempo (62)	49
Sail Along Silv'ry Moon— Karen Chandler & Her Jacks (57)	*0.0*
Henry H. TOBIAS ▶ 5986 (3)	**219**
Miss You—Jaye P. Morgan (59)	*234*
Miss You—Mulcays (56)	*141*
Miss You—Keymen (59)	*0.0*
Ken TOBIAS ▶ 1497 (1)	**2905**
Stay Awhile—Bells (71)	2905
George TOBIN ▶ 2690 (2)	**1271**
Cinnamon—Derek (68)	2256
Back Door Man—Derek (69)	286
Phil TODARO ▶ 2540 (3)	**1404**
Wild Weekend—Rebels (62)	2435
Rockin' Crickets— Hot-Toddys Featuring Bill Pennell (59)	*298*
Rockin' Crickets—Rockin' Rebels (63)	*75*
Bob TODD ▶ 8226 (3)	**58**
Quarter To Four Stomp—Stompers (62)	68
Cosmic Sea—Mystic Moods (73)	51
Honey Trippin'—Mystic Moods (75)	21
—Johnny Todd see: Sammy MASTERS	
Shunichi TOKURA ▶ 10407 (1)	**8.8**
Runaway Rita—Leif Garrett (81)	26
Israel TOLBERT ▶ 5592 (1)	**267**
Big Leg Woman (With A Short Short Mini Skirt)— Israel "Popper Stopper" Tolbert (70)	267
Michael TOLES ▶ 10182 (1)	**12**
Don't Take My Kindness For Weakness— Soul Children (72)	46
Kerryn TOLHURST ▶ 3513 (2)	**805**
Man On Your Mind—Little River Band (82)	1130
All Fired Up—Pat Benatar (88)	720
Laurence TOLHURST [Laurence Andrew Tolhurst] ▶ 3860 (7)	**674**
Love Song—Cure (89)	2408
Just Like Heaven—Cure (87)	604
Why Can't I Be You?—Cure (87)	279
Fascination Street—Cure (89)	194
Lullaby—Cure (89)	170
Pictures Of You—Cure (90)	105
Hot Hot Hot!!!—Cure (88)	88
Mel TOLKIN ▶ 11254 (1)	**2.6**
Tower Trot (And Then You Do That Step)— Dick Jacobs And His Chorus And Orchestra (57)	23
Gerry TOLMAN ▶ 8530 (1)	**47**
Too Much Love To Hide—Crosby, Stills & Nash (83)	94
Dino TOME [Chip Dale] ▶ 8657 (1)	**44**
Sub-Rosa Subway—Klaatu (77)	87
Dennis TOMICH [Dennis Thompson] ▶ 8917 (1)	**36**
Kick Out The Jams—MC5 (69)	181
Pinky TOMLIN [Truman Tomlin] ▶ 6481 (3)	**165**
What's The Reason I'm Not Pleasing You— Fats Domino (56)	*415*
What's The Reason—Bobby Edwards (62)	*225*
The Object Of My Affection— Pee Wee Hunt & His Orchestra (56)	15
Gerald TOMLINSON ▶ 11067 (1)	**3.4**
Golden Wildwood Flower—Tom & Jerry (61)	10
Amedeo TOMMASI ▶ 8101 (1)	**62**
Give Me Time (L'Amore Se Ne Va)— Dusty Springfield (67)	185
Barbara TOMSCO ▶ 3947 (2)	**645**
Say I Am (What I Am)— Tommy James And The Shondells (66)	1095
Goin' Away—Fireballs (68)	194
George TOMSCO ▶ 1761 (6)	**2361**
Say I Am (What I Am)— Tommy James And The Shondells (66)	1095
Bulldog—Fireballs (60)	772
Torquay—Fireballs (59)	634
Quite A Party—Fireballs (61)	298
Goin' Away—Fireballs (68)	194
Vaquero (Cowboy)—Fireballs (60)	24
—Tone Loc see: Anthony Terrell SMITH	
Kevin TONEY ▶ 11521 (1)	**1.4**
Rock Creek Park—Blackbyrds (76)	6.8
Norma TONEY ▶ 5466 (2)	**283**
Deeper And Deeper—Freda Payne (70)	1024
You Gave Me Something (And Everything's Alright)— Fantastic Four (67)	312
Wrightson TONGUE ▶ 10482 (1)	**8.0**
(As I Went Down To) Jerusalem—Hello People (68)	8.0
—Toni C. see: Toni COLANDREO	
Rudy TOOMBS ▶ 1223 (11)	**3648**
One Mint Julep—Ray Charles (61)	*2026*
Gum Drop—Crew-Cuts (55)	*1157*
24 Hours A Day (365 A Year)—Georgia Gibbs (55)	292
That's Your Mistake— Otis Williams And His Charms (56)	*248*
It Hurts To Be In Love—Annie Laurie (57)	47
One Mint Julep—Chet Atkins (60)	*31*
Lonesome Whistle Blues—Freddy King (61)	19
One Mint Julep—Sarah Vaughan (62)	*9.9*
Gum Drop—Mills Brothers (55)	*0.0*
That's Your Mistake—Crew-Cuts (56)	*0.0*
Gum Drop—Otis Williams & His New Group (55)	*0.0*
Earl TOON ▶ 2889 (3)	**1130**
Celebration—Kool & The Gang (80)	6016
Ladies Night—Kool & The Gang (79)	3414
Jones Vs. Jones—Kool & The Gang (81)	316
Dick TOOPS ▶ 7382 (1)	**99**
Class Cutter (Yeah Yeah)—Dale Hawkins (59)	297
—John Bernard Toorish see: Dazz JORDAN	
—Too Short see: Todd SHAW	
Sandy TORANO ▶ 6763 (1)	**139**
If You Want It—Niteflyte (79)	278
Marq TORIEN [Mark Maytorena, Mark Torien] ▶ 9771 (1)	**17**
Smooth Up—Bulletboys (89)	68
—Melvin Howard Torma see: Mel TORME	
Mel TORME [Melvin Howard Torma, Mel Tormé] ▶ 8030 (3)	**64**
The Christmas Song (Merry Christmas To You)— Nat King Cole (62)	*114*
The Christmas Song (Merry Christmas To You)— Nat King Cole (60)	*9.6*
The Christmas Song (Merry Christmas To You)— Nat "King" Cole (56)	*4.6*
—Gail Redd Torok see: Ramona REDD	
Mitchell TOROK ▶ 2859 (7)	**1148**
Caribbean—Mitchell Torok (59)	783
Pink Chiffon—Mitchell Torok (60)	347
(Open Up The Door) Let The Good Times In— Dean Martin (66)	293
Mexican Joe—Mitchell Torok (59)	*34*
Face In A Crowd—Jimmie Rodgers (63)	*15*
Mexican Joe—Pat Boone (62)	*4.9*
Face In A Crowd—Dean Martin (63)	*0.0*
Janice TORRE ▶ 1392 (2)	**3191**
Paper Roses—Anita Bryant (60)	*3707*
Paper Roses—Marie Osmond (73)	*2674*
Dean TORRENCE ▶ 7822 (1)	**73**
Bucket "T"—Ronny & The Daytonas (64)	293
George TORRENCE ▶ 10437 (1)	**8.5**
(Mama Come Quick, And Bring Your) Lickin' Stick— George Torrence & The Naturals (68)	17
Jimmy TORRES ▶ 1696 (3)	**2476**
Wheels—String-A-Longs (60)	*4346*
Wheels—Billy Vaughn And His Orchestra (61)	*605*
Take A Minute—String-A-Longs (61)	1.0
Timmy TORRES ▶ 1539 (4)	**2782**
One More Try—Timmy T (90)	5043
Time After Time—Timmy -T- (90)	238
Too Young To Love You—Timmy -T- (91)	15
What Will I Do—Timmy -T- (90)	6.8
Michael TOSTE ▶ 10132 (2)	**12**
Opposites Do Attract—All Sports Band (82)	16
I'm Your Superman—All Sports Band (81)	4.3
Blaise TOSTI ▶ 4165 (2)	**577**
Affair Of The Heart—Rick Springfield (83)	1704
Sweet Summer Lovin'—Dolly Parton (79)	17
TOTÒ [Antonio De Curtis] ▶ 9402 (3)	**24**
Always You—Betty Madigan (54)	*67*
Mala Femmena—Jimmy Roselli (63)	*5.7*
Mala Femmena—Connie Francis (63)	*5.7*
Allen TOUSSAINT [Naomi Neville] ▶ 95 (40) HOF	**25905**
Mother-In-Law—Ernie K-Doe (61)	*8663*
Southern Nights—Glen Campbell (77)	4988
Java—Al (He's The King) Hirt Trumpet With Chorus And Orchestra (64)	*4600*
I Like It Like That—Dave Clark Five (65)	*2277*
Working In The Coal Mine—Lee Dorsey (66)	*1808*
Yes We Can Can—Pointer Sisters (73)	1495
Holy Cow—Lee Dorsey (66)	*746*
Play Something Sweet (Brickyard Blues)— Three Dog Night (74)	712
Ride Your Pony—Lee Dorsey (65)	710
Get Out Of My Life, Woman—Lee Dorsey (66)	571
Java—Floyd Cramer (62)	*570*
Working In The Coal Mine—Devo (81)	*495*
Happiness—Pointer Sisters (79)	443
Freedom For The Stallion—Hues Corporation (73)	421
Fun Time—Joe Cocker (78)	348
Lipstick Traces (On A Cigarette)—O'Jays (65)	*339*
Pain In My Heart—Otis Redding (63)	332
All These Things—Uniques (66)	262
A Certain Girl—Warren Zevon (80)	*191*
Going Down Slowly—Pointer Sisters (75)	165
Go-Go Girl—Lee Dorsey (67)	161
Whipped Cream— Herb Alpert's Tijuana Brass (65)	*154*
Mother-In-Law—Clarence Carter (73)	*106*
Nearer To You—Betty Harris (67)	93
Lipstick Traces (On a Cigarette)— Benny Spellman (62)	*73*
I Cried My Last Tear—Ernie K-Doe (61)	*46*
A Certain Girl—Ernie K-Doe (61)	*40*
Everything I Do Gohn Be Funky (From Now On)— Lee Dorsey (69)	25
Greatest Love—Judy Clay (70)	23
I Like It Like That— Loggins & Messina (75)	*19*
I've Cried My Last Tear—O'Jays (65)	*15*
My Old Car—Lee Dorsey (67)	13
Real Man—Ernie K-Doe (61)	13
Java Jones—Donna Lynn (64)	*5.7*
Holy Cow—Stefan (72)	*4.2*
Girl Callin—Chocolate Milk (78)	2.9
Fortune Teller—Hardtimes (66)	2.9
Sneakin' Sally Through The Alley—Robert Palmer (75)	2.8
Work, Work, Work—Lee Dorsey (65)	0.5
Whipped Cream—Stokes (65)	*0.0*
Michel'le TOUSSANT ▶ 3189 (3)	**958**
No More Lies—Michel'le (89)	1783
Nicety—Michel'le (90)	497
Something In My Heart—Michel'le (91)	347

René TOUZET ▶ 10606 (1)	**6.9**
Mambo In The Moonlight—Gary Crosby And The Cheer Leaders (54)	21
Mike TOWERS ▶ 3902 (1)	**663**
Nobody's Fool—Kenny Loggins (88)	1325
Billy TOWNE ▶ 3282 (2)	**913**
Never On Sunday—Chordettes (61)	*1539*
Ring A Ding A Ding—Tommy Sands (57)	288
—Fred Towne see: Fred TOBIAS	
Jeff TOWNES [Jazzy Jeff] ▶ 3322 (6)	**900**
Summertime—DJ Jazzy Jeff & The Fresh Prince (91)	1783
Parents Just Don't Understand—D.J. Jazzy Jeff & The Fresh Prince (88)	1067
A Nightmare On My Street—D.J. Jazzy Jeff & The Fresh Prince (88)	778
Girls Ain't Nothing But Trouble—D.J. Jazzy Jeff & The Fresh Prince (88)	241
Deep, Deep Trouble—Simpsons (91)	100
I Think I Can Beat Mike Tyson—D.J. Jazzy Jeff & The Fresh Prince (89)	79
Chris TOWNS ▶ 8039 (3)	**64**
With All Of My Heart—Brook Benton (59)	98
The Jazz In You—Gloria Lynne (61)	26
There You Are—Johnny Mathis (61)	3.8
David TOWNSEND ▶ 4877 (4)	**392**
Happy—Surface (87)	678
Closer Than Friends—Surface (89)	207
Don't Take It Personal—Jermaine Jackson (89)	156
You Are My Everything—Surface (89)	41
Ed TOWNSEND ▶ 367 (19)	**10515**
Let's Get It On—Marvin Gaye (73)	7308
For Your Love—Ed Townsend (58)	*1775*
The Love Of My Man—Theola Kilgore (63)	1131
Finally Got Myself Together (I'm A Changed Man)—Impressions (74)	1079
For Your Love—Peaches & Herb (67)	*796*
You've Got To Take It (If You Want It)—Main Ingredient (72)	459
How Can I Forget—Jimmy Holiday (63)	*389*
For Your Love—Sam & Bill (65)	*311*
For Your Love—Wanderers (61)	*257*
What Does A Girl Do?—Shirelles (63)	256
Foolish Fool—Dee Dee Warwick (69)	250
Sooner Or Later—Impressions (75)	246
This Is My Prayer—Theola Kilgore (63)	185
I Am A Witness—Tommy Hunt (63)	138
Same Thing It Took—Impressions (75)	115
How Can I Forget—Ben E. King (63)	*60*
For Your Love—Christopher Paul & Shawn (75)	*14*
Tears Of Joy—Chuck Jackson (63)	7.5
Coming Back To You—Maxine Brown (64)	1.9
John TOWNSEND ▶ 4433 (2)	**495**
Smoke From A Distant Fire—Sanford/Townsend Band (77)	1425
In For The Night—Dirt Band (78)	39
Pete TOWNSHEND ▶ 105 (34)	**23572**
I Can See For Miles—Who (67)	2009
See Me, Feel Me—Who (70)	*1867*
Won't Get Fooled Again—Who (71)	1865
Let My Love Open The Door—Pete Townshend (80)	1506
Squeeze Box—Who (75)	1495
Who Are You—Who (78)	1459
Pinball Wizard—Who (69)	*1448*
Magic Bus—Who (68)	1283
Overture From Tommy (A Rock Opera)—Assembled Multitude (70)	1183
Happy Jack—Who (67)	1098
You Better You Bet—Who (81)	1074
Join Together—Who (72)	855
Behind Blue Eyes—Who (71)	765
Face The Face—Pete Townshend (85)	625
I'm Free—Who (69)	622
Call Me Lightning—Who (68)	615
Athena—Who (82)	541
The Relay—Who (72)	484
The Seeker—Who (70)	478
Pinball Wizard—New Seekers (73)	*409*
See Me, Feel Me—New Seekers (73)	*409*
Pictures Of Lily—Who (67)	285
After The Fire—Roger Daltrey (85)	284
5:15—Who (79)	213
I Can't Explain—Who (65)	172
Love, Reign O'er Me—Who (73)	129
Long Live Rock—Who (79)	118
Eminence Front—Who (82)	97
My Generation—Who (65)	74
Don't Let Go The Coat—Who (81)	34
A Little Is Enough—Pete Townshend (80)	31
The Real Me—Who (74)	17
The Kids Are Alright—Who (66)	14
Rough Boys—Pete Townshend (80)	12
Umberto TOZZI ▶ 2204 (2)	**1746**
Gloria—Laura Branigan (82)	4941
Ti Amo—Laura Branigan (84)	296
Terry TRABANDT ▶ 9062 (1)	**32**
Turn To Stone—Joe Walsh (75)	64
Al TRACE [Albert Trace, Clem Watts] ▶ 8570 (4)	**46**
You Call Everybody Darlin'—Mildred & Jimmie Mulcay (60)	119
Please Please Believe Me—Cathy Carr (56)	6.4
Fifty Fathoms—Jack Fascinato (56)	5.5
I Love To Sing—Jack Fascinato (56)	5.2
Ben TRACE ▶ 8710 (2)	**42**
You Call Everybody Darlin'—Mildred & Jimmie Mulcay (60)	119
Please Please Believe Me—Cathy Carr (56)	6.4
Dennis TRACY ▶ 10443 (1)	**8.4**
The Millionaire—Dr. Hook (75)	8.4
Bill TRADER ▶ 794 (2)	**5597**
(Now And Then There's) A Fool Such As I—Elvis Presley (59)	*5386*
A Fool Such As I—Bob Dylan (73)	*211*
TRADITIONAL ▶ 3 (203)	**113691**
Battle Of New Orleans—Johnny Horton (59)	*13064*
Tom Dooley—Kingston Trio (58)	*9986*
Michael—Highwaymen (61)	*9146*
The Yellow Rose Of Texas—Mitch Miller with His Orch. & Chorus (55)	*9072*
Stagger Lee—Lloyd Price (58)	*7844*
The House Of The Rising Sun—Animals (64)	*7607*
The Boll Weevil Song—Brook Benton (61)	7091
He's Got The Whole World (In His Hands)—Laurie London (58)	*5361*
Dueling Banjos—"Deliverance" Soundtrack (73)	*4998*
Banana Boat (Day-O)—Harry Belafonte (57)	*4701*
La Bamba—Los Lobos (87)	*4652*
Marianne—Terry Gilkyson And The Easy Riders (57)	*3770*
Sloop John B—Beach Boys (66)	*3647*
Don't Let The Rain Come Down (Crooked Little Man)—Serendipity Singers (64)	3454
Red River Rock—Johnny And The Hurricanes (59)	3410
House Of The Rising Sun—Frijid Pink (70)	*3040*
Children's Marching Song—Mitch Miller & his "Sing Along With Mitch" Chorus (59)	*2896*
Children's Marching Song—Cyril Stapleton And His Orchestra (59)	*2867*
The Yellow Rose Of Texas—Johnny Desmond (55)	*2853*
Marianne—Hilltoppers (57)	*2812*
Kisses Sweeter Than Wine—Jimmie Rodgers (57)	2683
Melodie D'Amour (Melody Of Love)—Ames Brothers (57)	*2592*
The Lord's Prayer—Sister Janet Mead (74)	2299
Honey Babe—Art Mooney And His Orchestra (55)	*2294*
Guantanamera—Sandpipers (66)	2149
Danny Boy—Conway Twitty (59)	*2086*
Amen—Impressions (64)	*2022*
Morning Has Broken—Cat Stevens (72)	1992
Rock Island Line—Lonnie Donegan Skiffle Group (56)	*1827*
See See Rider—Eric Burdon And The Animals (66)	*1714*
Amazing Grace—Judy Collins (70)	*1569*
Day By Day—Godspell (72)	*1542*
Beatnik Fly—Johnny And The Hurricanes (60)	1493
Abilene—George Hamilton IV (63)	1276
Midnite Special—Paul Evans (60)	*1261*
Amazing Grace—Pipes And Drums And The Military Band Of The Royal Scots Dragoon Guards (72)	*1257*
On Top Of Spaghetti—Tom Glazer And The Do-Re-Mi Children's Chorus (63)	*1194*
Wade In The Water—Ramsey Lewis (66)	*1134*
Stagger Lee—Tommy Roe (71)	*1051*
Clementine—Bobby Darin (60)	*1036*
Iko Iko—Belle Stars (89)	*940*
Iko Iko—Dixie Cups (65)	*854*
Reveille Rock—Johnny And The Hurricanes (59)	828
C C Rider—Chuck Willis (57)	*806*
Lemon Tree—Trini Lopez (65)	*795*
Stag-O-Lee—Wilson Pickett (67)	*785*
Bonnie Came Back—Duane Eddy His "Twangy" Guitar And The Rebels (59)	753
C. C. Rider—Mitch Ryder And The Detroit Wheels (65)	*728*
The Bus Stop Song (A Paper Of Pins)—Four Lads (56)	*665*
Midnight Special—Johnny Rivers (65)	*654*
La Bamba—Ritchie Valens (58)	*649*
See See Rider—LaVern Baker (62)	*629*
Dance Everyone Dance—Betty Madigan (58)	*619*
Ol' Mac Donald—Frank Sinatra (60)	*604*
Water Boy—Don Shirley Trio (61)	597
Tell It On The Mountain—Peter, Paul & Mary (64)	526
My Bonnie (My Bonnie Lies Over The Ocean)—Beatles With Tony Sheridan (64)	519
Saints Rock 'N Roll—Bill Haley And His Comets (56)	*498*
Inside-Looking Out—Animals (66)	468
Stewball—Peter, Paul & Mary (63)	466
Lemon Tree—Peter, Paul & Mary (62)	*437*
Dance By The Light Of The Moon—Olympics (60)	*428*
Just A Closer Walk With Thee—Jimmie Rodgers (60)	*427*
Michael—Trini Lopez (64)	*414*
C.C. Rider—Bobby Powell (65)	*408*
Greensleeves—Beverley Sisters (56)	*408*
Old Smokey Locomotion—Little Eva (63)	*399*
Down On Me—Big Brother And The Holding Company (68)	*395*
Wreck Of The John B—Jimmie Rodgers (60)	*386*
When The Saints Go Marching In—Fats Domino (59)	*376*
Banana Boat (Day-O)—Stan Freberg (57)	*352*
Bonaparte's Retreat—Billy Grammer (59)	342
Theme From Tunes Of Glory—Cambridge Strings & Singers (61)	*329*
Frogg—Brothers Four (61)	328
Amen—Otis Redding (68)	*318*
Kum Ba Yah—Tommy Leonetti (69)	316
Shortnin' Bread—Paul Chaplain & His Emeralds (60)	*307*
Wade In The Water—Herb Alpert & The Tijuana Brass (67)	*292*
The Pledge Of Allegiance—Red Skelton (69)	287
Danny Boy—Andy Williams (61)	*282*
National City—Joiner, Arkansas Junior High School Band (60)	282
The First Night Of The Full Moon—Jack Jones (64)	*266*
This Old Man—Purple Reign (75)	*264*
Leave Me Alone (Let Me Cry)—Dicky Doo And The Don'ts (58)	257
So High So Low—LaVern Baker (59)	234
Pop Goes The Weasel—Anthony Newley (61)	226
Iko Iko—Dr. John (72)	*226*
All My Trials—Mickey Newbury (71)	*222*
Danny Boy—Sil Austin (59)	*216*
Pearly Shells (Popo O Ewa)—Burl Ives (64)	*198*
Down In The Valley—Solomon Burke (62)	*194*
Danny Boy—Ray Price (67)	*193*
Down By The Riverside—Les Compagnons De La Chanson (60)	*175*
Rock Island Line—Don Cornell (56)	*172*
Waltzing Matilda—Jimmie Rodgers (60)	*163*
Hear The Bells—Tokens (63)	148
I'm Comin' Home—Dave Edmunds (71)	146
Baby I Do Love You—Galens (63)	141
Tom Dooley—Four Preps (61)	*130*
Home Sweet Home On The Range—Kay Starr (55)	127
Clementine—Jan & Dean (60)	*125*
The Yellow Rose Of Texas—Stan Freberg (55)	*123*
Down In The Alley—Ronnie Hawkins (70)	*110*
Off To Dublin In The Green—Abbey Tavern Singers (66)	109
Rovin' Gambler—"Tennessee" Ernie Ford (56)	106
There Is A Tavern In The Town—Four Aces (55)	106
All My Trials—Ray Stevens (71)	*104*
Muskrat—Everly Brothers (61)	98
Cindy—Teddy Vann (60)	97
I'm On My Way—Highwaymen (62)	97
He's Got The Whole World In His Hands—Mahalia Jackson (58)	*78*
Roll In My Sweet Baby's Arms—Hank Wilson (73)	72
Marianne—Lane Brothers (57)	*71*
Eh! Cumpari—Gaylord & Holiday (76)	71
All My Trials—Elvis Presley (72)	*69*

TRADITIONAL ▶ 3 (203) *Continued*	**113691**
Adeste Fideles (Oh, Come, All Ye Faithful)—Bing Crosby (60)	*67*
Dance With A Dolly (With A Hole In Her Stocking)—Damita Jo (61)	*65*
Valley To Pray—Arlo Guthrie (70)	62
La Bomba—Tokens (62)	*62*
The House Of The Rising Sun—Santa Esmeralda (78)	*57*
Man Of Constant Sorrow—Ginger Baker's Air Force (70)	52
Battle Of New Orleans—Nitty Gritty Dirt Band (74)	*51*
Down On Me—Janis Joplin (72)	*51*
Lost John—Lonnie Donegan and the Skiffle Group (56)	51
Colinda—Rod Bernard (62)	50
Pat-A-Cake—Singing Dogs (55)	48
Three Blind Mice—Singing Dogs (55)	48
Adeste Fideles (Oh, Come, All Ye Faithful)—Bing Crosby (55)	*47*
Marianne—Burl Ives (57)	*45*
Shortnin' Bread—Bell Notes (60)	*45*
Banks Of The Ohio—Olivia Newton-John (71)	39
Child Of God—Bobby Darin (60)	39
Tunes Of Glory—Mitch Miller & His Orch. And Chorus (61)	*39*
Adeste Fideles (Oh, Come, All Ye Faithful)—Bing Crosby (58)	*36*
Amen—Ovations (73)	*34*
Danny Boy—Patti Labelle And Her Blue Belles (64)	*32*
Danny Boy—Joni James (56)	*31*
Star O—Harry Belafonte (57)	30
La Bamba - Part 1—Trini Lopez (66)	*28*
Adeste Fideles (Oh, Come, All Ye Faithful)—Bing Crosby (56)	*27*
Experiments With Mice—Johnny Dankworth (56)	26
Old Slew Foot—Johnny Horton (61)	26
Adeste Fideles (Oh, Come, All Ye Faithful)—Bing Crosby (54)	*25*
Adeste Fideles (O Come All Ye Faithful)—David Whitfield (54)	*25*
Michael—Four Preps (62)	*24*
Closer Walk—Pete Fountain (60)	*24*
I Gotta Robe—Laurie London (58)	19
Marching Saints—Harry Belafonte (58)	*19*
The House Of The Rising Sun—Dolly Parton (81)	*19*
Swing Low—Floyd Cramer (62)	17
Battle Of New Orleans—Vaughn Monroe with Norman Layden, His Orchestra and Chorus (59)	*15*
All My Trials—Dick And Deedee (64)	*15*
La Bamba—Carlos Brothers (60)	*13*
Steal Away—Pat Boone (57)	12
Just A Closer Walk With Thee—Pat Boone (57)	*12*
Oh, Rock My Soul (Part I)—Peter, Paul & Mary (64)	12
Greensleeves—Mason Williams (69)	*11*
Adeste Fideles (Oh, Come, All Ye Faithful)—Bing Crosby (57)	*9.8*
Danny Boy—Jackie Wilson (65)	*9.5*
This Train—Brothers Four (62)	9.1
Soldier's Joy—Hawkshaw Hawkins (59)	8.4
Old Smokie—Johnny And The Hurricanes (61)	*6.1*
Dueling Tubas—Martin Mull and Orchestra (73)	*5.8*
Ave Maria—Lawrence Welk Glee Club (57)	5.6
Battle Of New Orleans—Harpers Bizarre (68)	*5.3*
Battle Of New Orleans—Bert Sommer (70)	*5.3*
You Can't Get To Heaven On Roller Skates—Betty Johnson (59)	*5.0*
We Shall Overcome—Joan Baez (63)	5.0
Spanish Marching Song—Joe Reisman and His Orchestra (59)	*4.7*
Every Time (I Feel His Spirit)—Patti Page (56)	4.3
Old MacDonald—Chargers (58)	*3.9*
Rock Island Line—Johnny Cash (70)	*3.5*
Miss Katy Cruel—New Christy Minstrels (64)	3.2
Day By Day—Holly Sherwood (71)	*2.7*
Rock Island Line—Lonnie Donegan Skiffle Group (61)	*2.4*
Jine The Cavalry—Mitch Miller and The Gang (59)	2.3
Ground Hog—Browns Featuring Jim Edward Brown (61)	2.3
Coming 'round the Mountain—David Seville And The Chipmunks (60)	2.2
I Heard The Voice Of Jesus—Turley Richards (70)	2.1
Revival—Johnny And The Hurricanes (60)	*1.7*
Michael - Pt. 1—Steve Alaimo (63)	*0.5*
Sweet Annie Laurie—Sammy Turner and The Twisters (59)	0.4
Mary Ann—Talbot Brothers (57)	*0.0*
Pearly Shells—Arthur Lyman (64)	*0.0*
Rock Island Line—Jimmy Gavin (56)	*0.0*
Rock Island Line—Len Dresslar (56)	*0.0*
Rock Island Line—Merrill Moore (56)	*0.0*
Dance, Everyone, Dance—Hi-Liters (58)	*0.0*
Honey Babe—Sauter-Finegan Orchestra (55)	*0.0*
Mary Ann—Edmundo Ros & His Orchestra (57)	*0.0*
The Spanish Marching Song—Ethel Smith (59)	*0.0*
Waltzing Matilda—Merrill Staton Choir (60)	*0.0*
Melodie D'Amour—Marty Gold & His Orchestra (57)	*0.0*
Just A Closer Walk With Thee—Andy Griffith (57)	*0.0*
Melodie D'Amour—Edmundo Ros & His Orchestra (57)	*0.0*
Rock Island Line—Bobby Darin & The Jaybirds (56)	*0.0*
Oh You Can't Get To Heaven—Guys And The Gals (59)	*0.0*
The Bus Stop Song (A Paper Of Pins)—Burl Ives (56)	*0.0*
Waltzing Matilda—David Carroll And His Orchestra (59)	*0.0*
He's Got The Whole World (In His Hands)—Jo March (58)	*0.0*
Dance, Everyone, Dance—Les Baxter & His Orchestra (58)	*0.0*
He's Got The Whole World In His Hands—Barbara McNair (58)	*0.0*
Down By The Riverside (Qu'l Fait Bon Vivre)—Les Barclay (60)	*0.0*
Billy TRAGESSER ▶ 9917 (1)	**15**
Love Me One More Time (Just For Old Times Sake)—Karen Nelson And Billy T (77)	30
Charles TRAHAN ▶ 6947 (1)	**126**
"B" Girls—Young & Restless (90)	253
Buck TRAIL [Ronald Killette] ▶ 2123 (1)	**1846**
Girl Watcher—O'Kaysions (68)	3691
Bobby Lee TRAMMELL ▶ 9580 (1)	**21**
You Mostest Girl—Bobby Lee Trammell (58)	21
Mike TRAMP [Michael Trempenau] ▶ 2084 (4)	**1900**
When The Children Cry—White Lion (88)	2108
Wait—White Lion (88)	1236
Tell Me—White Lion (88)	237
Little Fighter—White Lion (89)	218
Jay TRAN ▶ 6078 (1)	**209**
Only A Lonely Heart Sees—Felix Cavaliere (80)	417
—Tullo Trapani see: MANTOVANI	
Harry TRAVERS ▶ 6528 (1)	**160**
The Honeythief—Hipsway (87)	639
Mary TRAVERS ▶ 6167 (2)	**198**
Tell It On The Mountain—Peter, Paul & Mary (64)	526
Stewball—Peter, Paul & Mary (63)	466
Merle TRAVIS ▶ 375 (10)	**10405**
Sixteen Tons—"Tennessee" Ernie Ford (55)	*9525*
That's All—"Tennessee" Ernie Ford (56)	356
Sixteen Tons—Johnny Desmond (55)	*183*
Sixteen Tons—Don Harrison Band (76)	*166*
Sixteen Tons—Tom Jones (67)	*100*
Muskrat—Everly Brothers (61)	98
Smoke! Smoke! Smoke! (That Cigarette)—Commander Cody And His Lost Planet Airmen (73)	64
9 Lb. Hammer—Sanford Clark (57)	12
Loading Coal—Johnny Cash (60)	3.5
Sixteen Tons—Lou Monte (61)	*1.4*
Richard TRAVIS ▶ 8267 (1)	**56**
Been So Long—Pastels (58)	226
George TREADWELL ▶ 2578 (3)	**1354**
There Goes My Baby—Drifters (59)	*4700*
Dance With Me—Drifters (59)	1398
There Goes My Baby—Donna Summer (84)	*674*
—Angela Tremble see: Deborah HARRY	
—Michael Trempenau see: Mike TRAMP	
—Herwig Tremschnig see: Herwig RUDISSER	
Fiachra TRENCH ▶ 9967 (2)	**14**
High Energy—Evelyn Thomas (84)	20
So Many Men, So Little Time—Miquel Brown (83)	8.9
Charles TRENET ▶ 2531 (4)	**1409**
Beyond The Sea—Bobby Darin (60)	*2565*
I Wish You Love—Gloria Lynne (64)	856
La Mer (Beyond The Sea)—Roger Williams (56)	*248*
La Mer—Trade Martin (59)	*5.2*
Claude TRENIER ▶ 11034 (1)	**3.7**
Get Out Of The Car—Treniers (55)	7.4
Cliff TRENIER ▶ 11035 (1)	**3.7**
Get Out Of The Car—Treniers (55)	7.4
—Emil Trent see: Hugo PERETTI	
Jackie TRENT [Yvonne Ann Burgess] ▶ 1116 (11)	**3980**
Don't Sleep In The Subway—Petula Clark (67)	2193
I Couldn't Live Without Your Love—Petula Clark (66)	1795
Color My World—Petula Clark (66)	1085
Who Am I—Petula Clark (66)	811
Don't Give Up—Petula Clark (68)	589
The Other Man's Grass Is Always Greener—Petula Clark (67)	564
You've Got To Be Loved—Montanas (68)	408
American Boys—Petula Clark (68)	362
Look At Mine—Petula Clark (69)	144
If You Ever Leave Me—Jack Jones (68)	8.2
Run To Me—Montanas (68)	3.2
Ralph TRESVANT ▶ 7494 (1)	**92**
Stone Cold Gentleman—Ralph Tresvant (91)	369
—Van Trevor see: Robert BOULANGER	
Pete TREWAVAS ▶ 9799 (1)	**17**
Kayleigh—Marillion (85)	84
—David Tricker see: David WHITE	
—Donald Triggs see: Donald BLACKMAN	
Phil TRIM ▶ 4401 (4)	**505**
Mammy Blue—Stories (73)	*460*
Mammy Blue—Pop-Tops (71)	*355*
Oh Lord, Why Lord—Los Pop Tops (68)	125
Mammy Blue—James Darren (71)	*112*
Bobbi TRIMACHI ▶ 1996 (1)	**2020**
1, 2, 3, Red Light—1910 Fruitgum Co. (68)	4041
Sal TRIMACHI ▶ 1804 (5)	**2290**
1, 2, 3, Red Light—1910 Fruitgum Co. (68)	4041
It's Only Love—Tommy James And The Shondells (66)	725
Free As The Wind—Brooklyn Bridge (70)	72
Go Away—1910 Fruitgum Co. (70)	8.1
S.O.S. (Heart In Distress)—Christine Cooper (66)	3.4
Andy TRIPOLI ▶ 3145 (5)	**987**
We Can't Go Wrong—Cover Girls (89)	1676
Show Me—Cover Girls (87)	459
Promise Me—Cover Girls (88)	433
Inside Outside—Cover Girls (88)	204
Funk Boutique—Cover Girls (91)	202
Gregg TRIPP ▶ 3974 (2)	**634**
Heart Of Stone—Taylor Dayne (90)	1021
Cryin'—Vixen (89)	587
—Triune see: Orena D. FULMER	
—Triune see: Paula DePORES	
—Triune see: Ruth STRATCHBORNEO	
Al TRIVETTE ▶ 10313 (1)	**10**
Low Rider (On The Boulevard)—Latin Alliance (91)	121
Domenic TROIANO ▶ 5276 (3)	**314**
Dancin' Fool—Guess Who (74)	608
Seems Like I Can't Live With You, But I Can't Live Without You—Guess Who (75)	9.9
We All Need Love—Troiano (79)	5.1
Don TROTTER ▶ 4948 (1)	**376**
Love Land—Charles Wright And The Watts 103Rd Street Rhythm Band (70)	1504
Bobby TROUP ▶ 5134 (5)	**336**
Baby Baby All The Time—Superbs (64)	112
Girl Can't Help It—Little Richard (57)	106
Route 66—Depeche Mode (88)	*68*
Route 66—Manhattan Transfer (82)	*42*
Julie Is Her Name—Perez Prado and His Orchestra (61)	7.7
Larry TROUTMAN ▶ 2599 (4)	**1338**
I Want To Be Your Man—Roger (87)	1944
As We Lay—Shirley Murdock (87)	632
Hey Ladies—Beastie Boys (89)	302
Dance Floor (Part I)—Zapp (82)	51
Roger TROUTMAN ▶ 2842 (4)	**1159**
I Want To Be Your Man—Roger (87)	1944
Hey Ladies—Beastie Boys (89)	302
More Bounce To The Ounce (Part 1)—Zapp (80)	136
Dance Floor (Part I)—Zapp (82)	51

Armando TROVAIOLI [Roman Vatro] ▶ 6071 (2)	**209**
Anna—Jorgen Ingmann And His Guitar (61)	*186*
Anna—Originals (58)	*23*
Robin TROWER ▶ 9277 (1)	**27**
Caledonia—Robin Trower (76)	55
Gary TROXEL ▶ 1445 (4)	**3029**
Come Softly To Me—Fleetwoods (59)	*8460*
Graduation's Here—Fleetwoods (59)	416
Come Softly To Me—Ronnie Height (59)	*196*
Come Softly To Me— New Seekers Featuring Marty Kristian (73)	*14*
Christopher TROY ▶ 4547 (1)	**467**
The Way I Feel About You—Karyn White (91)	1868
—Doris Troy see: Doris PAYNE	
Sonny TROY ▶ 10465 (2)	**8.1**
Don't Let Love Pass Me By—Frankie Avalon (60)	10
True, True Love—Frankie Avalon (61)	9.1
Eric TROYER ▶ 9678 (1)	**19**
Mirage—Eric Troyer (80)	19
Basia TRZETRZELEWSKA ▶ 4033 (4)	**619**
Time And Tide—Basia (88)	631
Cruising For Bruising—Basia (90)	456
New Day For You—Basia (88)	215
Promises—Basia (89)	11
—Douglas Glenn Tubb see: Glenn DOUGLAS	
Ernest TUBB ▶ 3708 (4)	**727**
Walking The Floor Over You—Pat Boone (60)	*591*
I'm Walking The Floor Over You—Georgia Gibbs (57)	*104*
Tomorrow Never Comes—B.J. Thomas (66)	51
Soldier's Last Letter— Merle Haggard & The Strangers (71)	13
Glenn TUBB ▶ 4049 (1)	**612**
Skip A Rope—Henson Cargill (67)	1224
Justin TUBB ▶ 8750 (1)	**40**
Imagine That—Patsy Cline (62)	40
Hubert TUBBS ▶ 9377 (1)	**25**
You Ought To Be Havin' Fun—Tower Of Power (76)	75
Pierre TUBBS ▶ 1275 (5)	**3474**
Right Back Where We Started From— Maxine Nightingale (76)	*5350*
But It's Alright—J.J. Jackson (66)	*1049*
But It's Alright—J.J. Jackson (69)	*334*
Gotta Be The One—Maxine Nightingale (76)	99
Right Back Where We Started From—Sinitta (89)	*18*
Bob TUBERT ▶ 2864 (6)	**1146**
Satin Pillows—Bobby Vinton (65)	985
Ring Dang Doo—Sam The Sham & The Pharaohs (65)	725
When You Loved Me—Brenda Lee (64)	397
Here Comes Heaven—Eddy Arnold (67)	104
Our Winter Love—Lettermen (67)	*48*
You're The Only World I Know— Sonny James "The Southern Gentleman" (64)	33
—Joseph William Tucci see: Eric MATTHEW	
Alonzo TUCKER ▶ 1836 (14)	**2224**
Baby Workout—Jackie Wilson (63)	3553
No Pity (In The Naked City)—Jackie Wilson (65)	364
Years From Now—Jackie Wilson (61)	299
Baby Get It (And Don't Quit It)—Jackie Wilson (63)	143
I Just Can't Help It—Jackie Wilson (62)	104
There'll Be No Next Time—Jackie Wilson (62)	80
You Don't Know What It Means—Jackie Wilson (61)	71
Jim Dandy Got Married—LaVern Baker (57)	39
Big Boss Line—Jackie Wilson (64)	29
Lost—Jerry Butler with Riley Hampton's Orch. (59)	24
Squeeze Her-Tease Her (But Love Her)— Jackie Wilson (64)	9.1
Baby, That's All—Jackie Wilson (62)	2.4
I Found Love—Jackie Wilson And Linda Hopkins (62)	2.2
He's A Fool—Jackie Wilson (63)	1.4
Annette TUCKER [Annette Wiesner] ▶ 2561 (5)	**1383**
I Had Too Much To Dream (Last Night)— Electric Prunes (66)	1627
Green Light—American Breed (68)	587
Get Me To The World On Time—Electric Prunes (67)	540
High On Love—Knickerbockers (66)	14
Dr. Do-Good—Electric Prunes (67)	2.4
Ben TUCKER ▶ 5961 (1)	**223**
Comin' Home Baby—Mel Torme (62)	446

Ernest L. TUCKER ▶ 11487 (3)	**1.5**
Can She Give You Fever—Ernie Tucker (60)	*1.5*
Can She Give You Fever—Stan Robinson (60)	*1.5*
Can She Give Me Fever—Little Junior Lewis (60)	*0.0*
Ernest Monroe TUCKER ▶ 10552 (1)	**7.3**
A Cross Stands Alone—Jimmy Witter (61)	15
Handel TUCKER ▶ 5795 (1)	**241**
Just A Little Bit Longer—Maxi Priest (90)	241
Ira TUCKER Jr. ▶ 10797 (1)	**5.3**
Bad Weather—Supremes (73)	11
Johnny TUCKER ▶ 7984 (2)	**66**
A Voice In The Choir—Al Martino (67)	109
Dearest (Cara)—Al Martino (60)	35
Michael TUCKER ▶ 3056 (4)	**1033**
Fox On The Run—Sweet (75)	2954
Action—Sweet (76)	1094
California Nights—Sweet (78)	63
Funk It Up (David's Song)—Sweet (77)	20
Phil TUCKER ▶ 5940 (4)	**225**
Come Back—Jimmy Clanton (60)	264
I Can't Say Goodbye— Fireflies Featuring Ritchie Adams (59)	245
So Close To My Heart—Kathy Linden (59)	18
Because Of My Pride—Fireflies (60)	15
Rick TUCKER ▶ 11140 (2)	**3.1**
Patty Baby—Terry Noland (58)	*3.1*
Patty Baby—Rick Tucker & The Picks (58)	*3.1*
—Tommy Tucker see: Robert HIGGINBOTHAM	
—Nigel Tufnel see: Christopher GUEST	
Richard Anthony TUFO [Ritchie Tufano] ▶ 7817 (2)	**74**
Love Is Funny That Way—Jackie Wilson (71)	99
Preacher Man—Impressions (63)	41
Brett TUGGLE ▶ 3639 (2)	**754**
Just Like Paradise—David Lee Roth (88)	1403
Stand Up—David Lee Roth (88)	106
Phil TUMINELLO ▶ 3507 (2)	**809**
Can I Steal A Little Love—Frank Sinatra (57)	737
Crazy Love—Frank Sinatra (57)	145
Joseph TUNBRIDGE ▶ 10186 (1)	**11**
Got A Date With An Angel—Billy Williams (57)	46
Roberto TURATTI ▶ 7759 (1)	**76**
Boom Boom (Let's Go Back To My Room)— Paul Lekakis (87)	381
Bruce TURGON ▶ 3365 (2)	**880**
Midnight Blue—Lou Gramm (87)	1532
Ready Or Not—Lou Gramm (87)	229
John TURI ▶ 5565 (1)	**271**
No—Bulldog (72)	542
Roy TURK ▶ 637 (9) HOF	**6816**
Are You Lonesome To Night— Elvis Presley With The Jordanaires (60)	*10024*
I Don't Know Why—Linda Scott (61)	1607
Are You Lonesome Tonight—Donny Osmond (73)	*1054*
Are You Lonesome Tonight—Jaye P. Morgan (59)	*310*
I'll Get By (As Long As I Have You)— Billy Williams (58)	239
Where The Blue Of The Night—Tommy Mara (58)	193
Yes I'm Lonesome Tonight—Thelma Carpenter (60)	*149*
Yes I'm Lonesome Tonight—Dodie Stevens (60)	*116*
Love You Funny Thing—Tony Martin (56)	3.7
Jay TURNBOW ▶ 1397 (3)	**3184**
Bread And Butter—Newbeats (64)	*6160*
(The Bees Are For The Birds) The Birds Are For The Bees—Newbeats (65)	238
Bread And Butter—Robert John (83)	*50*
—Graham Morrison Turnbull see: Scott TURNER	
—Brenda Turner see: Brenda SUTTON	
C.F. TURNER ▶ 2305 (7)	**1630**
Let It Ride—Bachman-Turner Overdrive (74)	1140
Roll On Down The Highway— Bachman-Turner Overdrive (75)	1108
Take It Like A Man—Bachman-Turner Overdrive (76)	250
Blue Collar—Bachman-Turner Overdrive (73)	191
Heartaches—BTO (79)	140
Gimme Your Money Please— Bachman-Turner Overdrive (76)	47
Down The Road—B.T.O. (78)	6.3
Cile TURNER ▶ 8731 (2)	**41**
The Golden Rule—'Cile Turner (59)	*123*

The Golden Rule—Don Rondo (59)	*0.0*
Doyle TURNER ▶ 10690 (1)	**6.0**
Little Boy Blue—Huelyn Duvall (59)	12
Dwight TURNER ▶ 6823 (1)	**135**
Do Your Dance - Part I—Rose Royce (77)	269
Eric TURNER ▶ 2472 (8)	**1454**
Heaven—Warrant (89)	3557
I Saw Red—Warrant (90)	1193
Cherry Pie—Warrant (90)	992
Sometimes She Cries—Warrant (89)	824
Down Boys—Warrant (89)	567
Uncle Tom's Cabin—Warrant (91)	71
Blind Faith—Warrant (91)	40
Big Talk—Warrant (89)	23
Ike TURNER [Renrut Eki] ▶ 832 (14)	**5309**
I'm Blue (The Gong-Gong Song)—Ikettes (61)	1274
It's Gonna Work Out Fine—Ike & Tina Turner (61)	1220
Fool In Love—Ike & Tina Turner (60)	1142
Poor Fool—Ike & Tina Turner (61)	855
Bold Soul Sister—Ike & Tina Turner (69)	272
Tra La La La La—Ike & Tina Turner (62)	261
I Idolize You—Ike & Tina Turner (60)	137
Baby--Get It On—Ike & Tina Turner (75)	93
Workin' Together—Ike & Tina Turner (70)	50
You Should'a Treated Me Right— Ike & Tina Turner (62)	23
I'm Jealous—Ike & Tina Turner (61)	20
Tina's Dilemma—Ike & Tina Turner (62)	11
I Can't Believe What You Say (For Seeing What You Do)—Ike & Tina Turner (64)	6.3
Feel Good—Ike & Tina Turner (72)	4.4
Jesse Lee TURNER ▶ 3598 (1)	**773**
Little Space Girl—Jesse Lee Turner (59)	773
Joe TURNER ▶ 6915 (1)	**129**
Honey Hush—Joe Turner (59)	129
Joe Lynn TURNER [Joseph Linquito] ▶ 5933 (2)	**226**
Stone Cold—Rainbow (82)	407
Street Of Dreams—Rainbow (83)	180
John TURNER [James John Turner Phillips, James Phillips] ▶ 2422 (21)	**1499**
Little Shoemaker—Gaylords (54)	*1620*
Smile—Nat "King" Cole (54)	*828*
Chee Chee-oo Chee (Sang The Little Bird)— Perry Como & Jaye P. Morgan (55)	*570*
Smile—Timi Yuro (61)	*422*
The Bandit—Johnston Brothers (54)	*349*
Eternally—Sarah Vaughan (60)	*324*
Smile—Betty Everett & Jerry Butler (64)	*322*
Little Shoemaker— Hugo Winterhalter And His Orchestra (54)	*307*
Smile—Tony Bennett (59)	*207*
Little Serenade—Teddy Randazzo (58)	*203*
The Bandit—Tex Ritter (54)	*10*
Little Serenade—Ames Brothers (58)	*9.8*
Oh Mein Papa—Dick Lee (61)	3.1
Smile—Sunny Gale (54)	*0.0*
Chee Chee-Oo Chee—Dennis Hale (55)	*0.0*
Little Serenade—Johnston Brothers (58)	*0.0*
The Bandit—Frank Weir & His Orchestra (54)	*0.0*
Chee Chee-Oo Chee (Sang The Little Bird)— Gaylords (55)	*0.0*
Chee Chee-Oo Chee (Sang The Little Birds)— Mariners (55)	*0.0*
Chee Chee Oo Chee (Sang The Little Bird)— Dean Martin (55)	*0.0*
Chee Chee-Oo Chee (Sang The Little Bird)— Johnston Brothers (55)	*0.0*
Lee TURNER ▶ 9557 (1)	**21**
Into The Night—Dream Weavers (56)	43
Lonnie TURNER ▶ 4775 (1)	**418**
Jungle Love—Steve Miller Band (77)	837
Lou Willie TURNER ▶ 7615 (3)	**85**
Flip Flop And Fly—Johnnie Ray (55)	*170*
Flip Flop And Fly—Goofers (55)	*0.0*
Flip Flop And Fly— Joe Turner & His Blues Kings (55)	*0.0*
Phil TURNER ▶ 10249 (1)	**11**
Thinking About Your Love—Skipworth & Turner (85)	22
Priscilla TURNER ▶ 10831 (1)	**5.0**
Pony Train—Titus Turner (61)	10

Raye TURNER ▶ 9280 (2)	**27**
Watching You—Slave (80)	129
Just A Touch Of Love—Slave (80)	10
Reginald TURNER ▶ 4847 (4)	**399**
Don't Let The Green Grass Fool You—Wilson Pickett (71)	1388
I'm Gonna Love You—Intrigues (69)	115
One For The Money (Part 1)—Whispers (76)	40
Just A Little Bit More—Intrigues (70)	14
Sammy TURNER ▶ 7803 (1)	**74**
One Hurt Deserves Another—Raeletts (67)	223
Scott TURNER [Graham Morrison Turnbull] ▶ 3068 (7)	**1027**
Shutters And Boards—Jerry Wallace (62)	993
Comin' In The Back Door—Baja Marimba Band (63)	*253*
Comin' In The Back Door—Wynton Kelly (63)	*133*
The Worryin' Kind—Tommy Sands (58)	92
Blue Ribbon Baby—Tommy Sands & The Raiders (58)	90
Mexican Drummer Man—Herb Alpert's Tijuana Brass (64)	50
Silly Ol' Summertime—New Christy Minstrels (64)	8.6
Tina TURNER [Anna Mae Bullock] ▶ 2701 (6)	**1263**
Nutbush City Limits—Ike & Tina Turner (73)	*889*
Sexy Ida (Part 2)—Ike & Tina Turner (74)	222
Baby--Get It On—Ike & Tina Turner (75)	93
Nutbush City Limits—Bob Seger (76)	*72*
Up In Heah—Ike & Tina Turner (72)	65
Feel Good—Ike & Tina Turner (72)	4.4
Titus TURNER ▶ 1961 (13)	**2049**
Tell Me Why—Elvis Presley With The Jordanaires (66)	*711*
Sticks And Stones—Ray Charles & His Orchestra (60)	484
People Sure Act Funny—Arthur Conley (68)	325
Tell Me Why—Gale Storm (56)	*264*
Tell Me Why—Crew-Cuts (56)	*231*
Leave My Kitten Alone—Little Willie John (61)	*154*
Leave My Kitten Alone—Johnny Preston (61)	*113*
Leave My Kitten Alone—Little Willie John (59)	*91*
Grits Ain't Groceries (All Around The World)—Little Milton (69)	71
Soulville—Aretha Franklin (68)	*24*
Soulville—Dinah Washington (63)	*6.8*
My Soul's Got A Hole In It—Howard Tate (70)	0.4
Tell Me Why—Marie Knight (56)	*0.0*
Zeb TURNER [William Edward Grishaw] ▶ 10444 (1)	**8.4**
It's A Sin—Bill Haley And His Comets (58)	17
Ross TURNEY ▶ 7436 (2)	**96**
Fly At Night—Chilliwack (77)	185
Something Better—Chilliwack (77)	7.3
Gary TURNIER ▶ 5779 (2)	**243**
Keep On Dancin'—Gary's Gang (79)	480
Let's Lovedance Tonight—Gary's Gang (79)	4.6
Gary TUTALO ▶ 9149 (1)	**30**
Don't You Come Cryin'—Linear (90)	91
Roberta TWAIN [Lucylle Manns] ▶ 6049 (1)	**212**
Hallelujah—Sweathog (71)	635
Theodore J. TWIGGS ▶ 10494 (1)	**7.9**
Lost—Jerry Butler with Riley Hampton's Orch. (59)	24
Dwight TWILLEY ▶ 2021 (4)	**1998**
I'm On Fire—Dwight Twilley Band (75)	1021
Girls—Dwight Twilley (84)	911
Little Bit Of Love—Dwight Twilley (84)	62
Twilley Don't Mind—Dwight Twilley Band (77)	3.8
Nigel TWIST [Nigel Buckle] ▶ 8386 (2)	**52**
Strength—Alarm (85)	120
Rain In The Summertime—Alarm (87)	89
Conway TWITTY [Harold L. Jenkins] ▶ 640 (12)	**6786**
It's Only Make Believe—Conway Twitty (58)	*7964*
It's Only Make Believe—Glen Campbell (70)	*1910*
You've Never Been This Far Before—Conway Twitty (73)	829
Story Of My Love—Conway Twitty (59)	640
Don't Cry Joni—Conway Twitty (75)	257
Linda On My Mind—Conway Twitty (75)	213
Hello Darlin'—Conway Twitty (70)	186
Touch The Hand—Conway Twitty (75)	31
As Soon As I Hang Up The Phone—Loretta Lynn/Conway Twitty (74)	21
I Need Your Lovin'—Conway Twitty (57)	13
She's Mine—Conway Twitty (60)	1.2

When I'm Not With You—Conway Twitty (59)	1.2
Kay TWOMEY [Al Hill] ▶ 888 (19)	**4988**
Wooden Heart—Joe Dowell (61)	*6334*
Let Me Go Lover—Joan Weber (54)	*5883*
Hey Jealous Lover—Frank Sinatra (56)	2954
Let Me Go Lover—Teresa Brewer with The Lancers (54)	*1376*
Johnny Jingo—Hayley Mills (62)	728
Let Me Go Lover—Patti Page (54)	*216*
(I Cried at) Laura's Wedding—Barbara Lynn (63)	184
Wooden Heart—Bobby Vinton (75)	*108*
Sugar Candy—Georgia Gibbs (57)	77
In The Beginning—Frankie Laine (54)	30
Lend Me Your Comb—Carl Perkins (58)	*23*
Put The Blame On Me—Elvis Presley (65)	23
Serenade Of The Bells—Four Coins (60)	8.9
One More Time—Dean Martin (54)	*7.9*
One More Time—Ames Brothers (54)	*7.9*
Let Me Go, Lover!—Peggy Lee (55)	*0.0*
Lend Me Your Comb—Bernie Nee (58)	*0.0*
Let Me Go, Lover!—Sunny Gale (54)	*0.0*
Lend Me Your Comb—Carol Hughes (58)	*0.0*
Adele TYLER ▶ 6147 (1)	**200**
Bobbie Sue—Oak Ridge Boys (82)	1000
Alvin TYLER ▶ 2583 (6)	**1347**
Java—Al (He's The King) Hirt Trumpet With Chorus And Orchestra (64)	*4600*
Java—Floyd Cramer (62)	*570*
Baby You're So Fine—Mickey And Sylvia (61)	*100*
Forever—Sam Cooke (57)	28
Java Jones—Donna Lynn (64)	*5.7*
Gee Baby—Joe & Ann (60)	*2.4*
Dan TYLER ▶ 6148 (1)	**200**
Bobbie Sue—Oak Ridge Boys (82)	1000
Steven TYLER [Steven Victor Tallarico] ▶ 370 (17) HOF	**10466**
Angel—Aerosmith (88)	2836
Dream On—Aerosmith (76)	*2723*
Janie's Got A Gun—Aerosmith (89)	1956
Walk This Way—Aerosmith (76)	*1949*
Love In An Elevator—Aerosmith (89)	1738
Walk This Way—Run-D.M.C. (86)	*1705*
What It Takes—Aerosmith (90)	1375
Dude (Looks Like A Lady)—Aerosmith (87)	1227
Last Child—Aerosmith (76)	817
Rag Doll—Aerosmith (88)	789
The Other Side—Aerosmith (90)	642
Dream On—Aerosmith (73)	*474*
Sweet Emotion—Aerosmith (75)	464
Draw The Line—Aerosmith (77)	371
Back In The Saddle—Aerosmith (77)	195
Kings And Queens—Aerosmith (78)	73
Home Tonight—Aerosmith (76)	45
T. Texas TYLER [David Luke Myrick] ▶ 1473 (1)	**2950**
Deck Of Cards—Wink Martindale (59)	2950
Tommy TYLER ▶ 9616 (1)	**20**
Boom-A-Dip-Dip—Stan Robinson (59)	61
West TYLER ▶ 2788 (2)	**1197**
Diamonds And Pearls—Paradons (60)	*1197*
Diamonds And Pearls—Turbans (60)	*0.0*
January TYME [January Kurta] ▶ 4552 (1)	**466**
One Man Band—Three Dog Night (70)	1398
—Rob Tyner see: Robert DERMINER	
Steve TYRELL ▶ 4647 (2)	**446**
It's Only Love—B.J. Thomas (69)	*616*
It's Only Love—Elvis Presley (71)	*276*
David TYSON ▶ 1665 (5)	**2526**
Black Velvet—Alannah Myles (89)	3820
All Our Tomorrows—Eddie Schwartz (81)	538
Love Is—Alannah Myles (90)	461
Don't Hold Back Your Love—Daryl Hall & John Oates (90)	330
Over The Line—Eddie Schwartz (82)	13
Ian TYSON ▶ 3865 (4)	**673**
Someday Soon—Judy Collins (69)	328
Four Strong Winds—Bobby Bare (64)	*197*
Four Strong Winds—Neil Young (79)	*145*
Lovin' Sound—Ian & Sylvia (67)	2.3
Rick TYSON ▶ 11700 (1)	**0.6**
Big Bruce—Steve Greenberg (69)	*3.1*

Ronnie TYSON ▶ 6502 (5)	**162**
Doctor Love—First Choice (77)	236
Free Man—South Shore Commission (75)	112
Dreamin'—Loleatta Holloway (77)	46
Train Called Freedom—South Shore Commission (76)	17
This Will Be A Night To Remember—Eddie Holman (77)	6.9
—Sylvia Tyson see: Sylvia FRICKER	

U

Peter UDELL ▶ 386 (22)	**10219**
Hurting Each Other—Carpenters (72)	4895
Sealed With A Kiss—Brian Hyland (62)	*4300*
Save Your Heart For Me—Gary Lewis And The Playboys (65)	4051
Sealed With A Kiss—Gary Lewis And The Playboys (68)	*1606*
Sealed With A Kiss—Bobby Vinton (72)	*1454*
Ginny Come Lately—Brian Hyland (62)	851
Let Me Belong To You—Brian Hyland (61)	766
Warmed Over Kisses (Left Over Love)—Brian Hyland (62)	608
The Tear Of The Year—Jackie Wilson (61)	410
He Says The Same Things To Me—Skeeter Davis (64)	408
I'm Afraid To Go Home—Brian Hyland (63)	295
The Way I Am—Jackie Wilson (61)	192
I May Not Live To See Tomorrow—Brian Hyland (62)	173
I Told You So—Jimmy Jones (61)	163
If Mary's There—Brian Hyland (63)	123
It's Only The Good Times—Tommy Edwards (59)	71
Big Daddy—Jill Corey (58)	30
I Got Love—Melba Moore (70)	18
I'll Never Stop Wanting You—Brian Hyland (61)	8.8
The Night I Cried—Brian Hyland (61)	6.9
Sealed With A Kiss—Toys (68)	*6.3*
We Know—Joni James (60)	1.5
Karl Theodor UHLISCH ▶ 6698 (1)	**143**
Sweet Elizabeth—Will Glahe And His Orchestra (58)	143
Billy UHR ▶ 6201 (2)	**194**
Tears—Bobby Vinton (66)	*382*
Tears (For Souvenirs)—Ken Dodd (66)	*5.7*
Alfred UHRY ▶ 10727 (1)	**5.8**
Hootenanny Saturday Night—Brothers Four (63)	12
Rick ULFIK ▶ 9640 (1)	**20**
Fire Sign—Cory (77)	40
—Donald Eugene Ulrich see: Don RICH	
Lars ULRICH ▶ 4111 (3)	**590**
Enter Sandman—Metallica (91)	947
The Unforgiven—Metallica (91)	334
One—Metallica (89)	326
—Tracy Ulrich see: Tracii GUNS	
Björn ULVAEUS ▶ 449 (24)	**9257**
Dancing Queen—Abba (76)	4560
Take A Chance On Me—ABBA (78)	2866
One Night In Bangkok—Murray Head (85)	*2683*
Waterloo—Abba (Björn, Benny, Anna & Frida) (74)	1880
The Winner Takes It All—ABBA (80)	1780
SOS—Abba (75)	1587
Fernando—Abba (76)	1489
Knowing Me, Knowing You—Abba (77)	1220
Does Your Mother Know—ABBA (79)	1098
I Do, I Do, I Do, I Do, I Do—Abba (76)	1023
The Name Of The Game—Abba (77)	988
Mamma Mia—Abba (76)	636
Chiquitita—ABBA (79)	490
When All Is Said And Done—ABBA (82)	452
Honey, Honey—Abba (74)	*432*
Super Trouper—ABBA (81)	194
Money, Money, Money—ABBA (77)	193
Honey Honey—Sweet Dreams (74)	*108*
Lay All Your Love On Me—Information Society (89)	105
The Visitors—ABBA (82)	95
Angeleyes—ABBA (79)	95
One Night In Bangkok—Robey (85)	*55*
Voulez-Vous—ABBA (79)	29
On And On And On—ABBA (81)	12
Ivan ULZ ▶ 9715 (1)	**18**
A Letter To The Beatles—Four Preps (64)	55
Piero UMILIANI ▶ 4884 (1)	**388**
Máh-Ná-Máh-Ná—Piero Umiliani (69)	388
—Uncle Vic see: Victor BLECMAN	

Charles UNDERWOOD ▶ 4675 (1)	**441**
Monsters' Holiday—Bobby (Boris) Pickett And The Crypt-Kickers (62)	441
Henry UNDERWOOD ▶ 4632 (4)	**448**
Plaything—Nick Todd (57)	*551*
Plaything—Ted Newman (57)	*344*
Plaything—Judy Faye (57)	*0.0*
Plaything—Chuck Miller (57)	*0.0*
Samuel UNDERWOOD ▶ 4633 (4)	**448**
Plaything—Nick Todd (57)	*551*
Plaything—Ted Newman (57)	*344*
Plaything—Judy Faye (57)	*0.0*
Plaything—Chuck Miller (57)	*0.0*
John UNGER ▶ 11153 (1)	**3.0**
Help For My Waiting—Dorians (71)	9.0
Melvin UNGER ▶ 10302 (1)	**10**
Don't Tell Me Your Troubles—Jimmy Bowen With The Rhythm Orchids (57)	31
Stella UNGER ▶ 1818 (15)	**2271**
(Theme From) Around The World—Mantovani And His Orchestra (57)	*1959*
(Theme From) Around The World—Victor Young & Orchestra (57)	*1813*
Around The World—Bing Crosby (57)	*591*
Don't Cry, Baby—Etta James (61)	*323*
If It's A Dream—McGuire Sisters (55)	*76*
Around The World In Eighty Days—McGuire Sisters (57)	*45*
Where Is That Someone For Me—Joni James (55)	42
Around The World—Nat "King" Cole (57)	*15*
Don't Cry, Baby—Aretha Franklin (62)	*4.0*
If It's A Dream—Kitty Kallen (55)	*0.0*
Around The World—Jane Morgan (57)	*0.0*
Around The World—Eddie Fisher (57)	*0.0*
Around The World—Don Costa & His Orchestra (57)	*0.0*
Around The World—Manny Lopez & His Orchestra (57)	*0.0*
Around The World—Lawrence Welk & His Champagne Music (57)	*0.0*
Miriam UNIMAN [Miriam Klein, Mimi Uniman] ▶ 4246 (7)	**547**
Long Lonely Nights—Bobby Vinton (65)	*1021*
Long Lonely Nights—Clyde McPhatter (57)	*517*
Long Lonely Nights—Lee Andrews And The Hearts (57)	*429*
Long Lonely Nights—Dells (70)	*187*
Long Lonely Nights—4 Seasons (64)	*34*
Long, Lonely Nights—Kings (2) (57)	*0.0*
Long Lonely Nights—Kitty Kallen (57)	*0.0*
UNKNOWN ▶ 6119 (5)	**203**
Teardrops—Hurricanes (54)	134
You Never Miss Your Water (Till The Well Runs Dry)—"Little Esther" Phillips & "Big Al" Downing (63)	33
Green Eyes—Ravens Featuring Jimmy Ricks (55)	17
I Had A Dream—Bruce Hayes with Mary Mayo (60)	14
I Love You—Bob Stewart (57)	5.7
Mary UNOBSKY ▶ 5704 (3)	**252**
That Kind Of Woman—Merrilee Rush & The Turnabouts (68)	337
I'd Do It All Again—Sam Harris (86)	166
I Need You—Maurice White (86)	2.4
Philip UPCHURCH ▶ 2699 (2)	**1265**
You Can't Sit Down—Dovells (63)	*3787*
You Can't Sit Down (Part 2)—Phil Upchurch Combo (61)	*956*
Pat UPTON ▶ 1585 (2)	**2669**
More Today Than Yesterday—Spiral Starecase (69)	2240
No One For Me To Turn To—Spiral Starecase (69)	429
Al URBANO ▶ 11157 (1)	**3.0**
Serenade Of The Bells—Four Coins (60)	8.9
Midge URE ▶ 4461 (3)	**489**
Do They Know It's Christmas?—Band Aid (84)	865
Reap The Wild Wind—Ultravox (83)	152
Dear God—Midge Ure (89)	18
Gary USHER ▶ 1838 (8)	**2219**
Don't Give In To Him—Gary Puckett And The Union Gap (69)	1458
In My Room—Beach Boys (63)	*724*
Ten Little Indians—Beach Boys (62)	466
My Buddy Seat—Hondells (64)	142
Coming On Too Strong—Wayne Newton (65)	106

In My Room—Sagittarius (69)	*77*
409—Beach Boys (62)	*11*
409—Cantina Band (81)	*1.5*
Richard USHER ▶ 4803 (1)	**410**
Turtle Power!—Partners In Kryme (90)	820
Mike UTLEY ▶ 9249 (1)	**28**
Survive—Jimmy Buffett (80)	56
Denise UTT ▶ 11188 (1)	**2.8**
What I Wouldn't Do (For The Love Of You)—Angela Bofill (80)	5.7

V

—Emidio Vagnoni see: Shorty LONG	
Steve VAI ▶ 4835 (2)	**401**
Yankee Rose—David Lee Roth (86)	691
Goin' Crazy!—David Lee Roth (86)	112
Arthur VALANDO ▶ 10643 (1)	**6.5**
Someone On Your Mind—Champ Butler (55)	13
Kurt VALAQUEN [Kurt Harland, Kurt Larson, Kurt Harland Larson] ▶ 2771 (1)	**1205**
What's On Your Mind (Pure Energy)—Information Society (88)	2411
Marcelina VALDES ▶ 11419 (1)	**1.8**
Oh Me—Fields-Madera Orchestra (59)	5.4
Mike VALE [Michael Vucish] ▶ 1357 (6)	**3270**
Crystal Blue Persuasion—Tommy James And The Shondells (69)	6717
Ball Of Fire—Tommy James And The Shondells (69)	1168
Sugar On Sunday—Clique (69)	1154
She—Tommy James And The Shondells (69)	869
On A Sunday Afternoon—A Lighter Shade Of Brown (91)	320
Happy—Hog Heaven (71)	3.0
Peter VALE ▶ 4409 (5)	**502**
Take Me Home Tonight—Eddie Money (86)	2098
I Wouldn't Beg For Water—Sheena Easton (82)	149
Some Come Running—Jim Capaldi (88)	19
My One Temptation—Mica Paris (89)	4.6
Into My Secret—Alisha (87)	1.5
Ritchie VALENS [Richard Valenzuela, Richard Esteban Valenzuela Reyes] ▶ 450 (6)	**9238**
Donna—Ritchie Valens (58)	7188
Come On Let's Go—McCoys (66)	*965*
Come On, Let's Go—Los Lobos (87)	*586*
Come On Let's Go—Ritchie Valens (58)	*349*
That's My Little Suzie—Ritchie Valens (59)	291
Little Girl—Ritchie Valens (59)	7.8
—Dino Valenti see: Chet POWERS	
—John Valenti see: John LIVIGNI	
Billy VALENTINE ▶ 10909 (1)	**4.4**
I'm Going Home—Mickey & Sylvia (57)	4.4
Gerald VALENTINE ▶ 3139 (1)	**990**
Oh Sheila—Ready For The World (85)	2969
John VALENTINE ▶ 6106 (1)	**206**
Money$ Too Tight (To Mention)—Simply Red (86)	617
Kathy VALENTINE ▶ 2555 (2)	**1388**
Vacation—Go-Go's (82)	2046
Head Over Heels—Go-Go's (84)	1413
Kevin VALENTINE [Kevin Valentine Kosec] ▶ 7517 (1)	**91**
Love Is Like A Rock—Donnie Iris (81)	454
William VALENTINE ▶ 6107 (1)	**206**
Money$ Too Tight (To Mention)—Simply Red (86)	617
Jim VALENTINI ▶ 11237 (1)	**2.6**
Easy Way Out—Roy Orbison (79)	7.9
—Richard Valenzuela see: Ritchie VALENS	
—Ero Valladi see: Eraldo RAVIOLO	
Jim VALLANCE [R. Higgs, Rodney Higgs, James Douglas Vallance] ▶ 307 (35)	**11832**
Heaven—Bryan Adams (85)	3748
Don't Forget Me (When I'm Gone)—Glass Tiger (86)	2668
Run To You—Bryan Adams (84)	2374
Summer Of '69—Bryan Adams (85)	1803
Someday—Glass Tiger (86)	1758
Heat Of The Night—Bryan Adams (87)	1717
What About Love?—Heart (85)	1233
Somebody—Bryan Adams (85)	1191
When The Night Comes—Joe Cocker (89)	1185

It's Only Love—Bryan Adams/Tina Turner (85)	1006
One Night Love Affair—Bryan Adams (85)	925
Like No Other Night—38 Special (86)	857
There Will Never Be Another Tonight—Bryan Adams (91)	822
Rag Doll—Aerosmith (88)	789
Cuts Like A Knife—Bryan Adams (83)	762
The Other Side—Aerosmith (90)	642
This Time—Bryan Adams (83)	569
Shot Of Poison—Lita Ford (91)	520
Hearts On Fire—Bryan Adams (87)	514
Teacher, Teacher—38 Special (84)	493
Victim Of Love—Bryan Adams (87)	410
Somebody Like You—38 Special (86)	322
Back To Paradise—38 Special (87)	305
Don't Let Him Know—Prism (82)	259
Another Heartache—Rod Stewart (86)	259
Take Me To The Kaptin—Prism (77)	195
Dangerous—Loverboy (85)	173
Edge Of A Dream—Joe Cocker (84)	113
Can't Wait All Night—Juice Newton (84)	92
Jump—Loverboy (82)	67
My Song—Glass Tiger (88)	41
Spaceship Superstar—Prism (77)	25
Lonely Nights—Bryan Adams (82)	24
Now And Forever (You And Me)—Anne Murray (86)	17
Let Me Down Easy—Roger Daltrey (85)	17
Marcos VALLE ▶ 5302 (1)	**310**
Summer Samba (So Nice)—Walter Wanderley (66)	619
Paulo Sergio VALLE ▶ 5303 (1)	**310**
Summer Samba (So Nice)—Walter Wanderley (66)	619
Rudy VALLEE ▶ 5978 (2)	**220**
Talk To Me—Frank Sinatra (59)	656
Vieni Vieni—Terri Stevens (59)	*5.6*
Jim VALLEY ▶ 9453 (2)	**23**
Try, Try, Try—Jim Valley (67)	22
Granny's Pad—Viceroys (63)	5.1
John VALLINS ▶ 1760 (1)	**2364**
Too Much, Too Little, Too Late—Johnny Mathis/Deniece Williams (78)	4728
Diane VALORY ▶ 7404 (1)	**98**
Wheel In The Sky—Journey (78)	293
Ross VALORY ▶ 7748 (2)	**76**
Just The Same Way—Journey (79)	197
Anytime—Journey (78)	54
Mike VALVANO ▶ 6730 (2)	**142**
If This Is Love (I'd Rather Be Lonely)—Precisions (67)	215
What You See Is What You Get—Stoney And Meatloaf (71)	140
—Mel Van see: Don GENSON	
Lester VANADORE ▶ 9720 (1)	**18**
Alone With You—Faron Young (58)	55
Egbert VAN ALSTYNE ▶ 6590 (2) HOF	**154**
To A Sleeping Beauty—Jimmy Dean (62)	445
Drifting And Dreaming—Teddy Tyle, His Saxophone and His Orch. (58)	16
René VAN BARNEVELD ▶ 7526 (1)	**91**
Deeper Shade Of Soul—Urban Dance Squad (90)	545
Ludwig VAN BEETHOVEN ▶ 1137 (8)	**3901**
A Fifth Of Beethoven—Walter Murphy & The Big Apple Band (76)	6361
A Song Of Joy (Himno A La Alegria)—Miguel Rios (70)	1305
Midnight Blue—Louise Tucker (83)	391
Symphony No. 9—Royal Philharmonic Orchestra (81)	131
In The Arms Of My Love—Joe Valino (57)	27
Moonlight Sonata—Henry Mancini And His Orchestra (69)	26
Passion Flower—Caterina Valente (59)	2.0
For Elise—Philharmonics (77)	0.6
Albert VANCE ▶ 2020 (2)	**2000**
Disco Lady—Johnnie Taylor (76)	5946
Get Down—Harvey Scales & The 7 Sounds (67)	54
Jerry VANCE ▶ 8713 (1)	**41**
Kissin' Game—Dion (61)	83
Kenny VANCE [Kenneth Rosenberg] ▶ 6608 (2)	**152**
Capture The Moment—Jay And The Americans (70)	340
Livin' Above Your Head—Jay & The Americans (66)	115

Paul VANCE ▶ 163 (48)	**18460**
Itsy Bitsy Teenie Weenie Yellow Polkadot Bikini–Brian Hyland (60)	*7476*
Playground In My Mind–Clint Holmes (73)	5118
Catch A Falling Star–Perry Como (57)	3980
Run Joey Run–David Geddes (75)	3075
Tracy–Cuff Links (69)	2946
Gina–Johnny Mathis (62)	2333
What Will Mary Say–Johnny Mathis (63)	2198
What Is Love–Playmates (59)	1121
Leader Of The Laundromat–Detergents (64)	1105
Jennifer Tomkins–Street People (2) (69)	899
Jimmy's Girl–Johnny Tillotson (61)	894
When Julie Comes Around–Cuff Links (69)	724
Starbright–Johnny Mathis (60)	700
Wait For Me–Playmates (60)	690
Little Miss Stuck-Up–Playmates (61)	392
Can I Trust You?–Bachelors (66)	366
Run Sally Run–Cuff Links (70)	364
Tar And Cement–Verdelle Smith (66)	359
Without Your Love (Mr. Jordan)–Charlie Ross (76)	352
Hot Pants–Salvage (71)	303
Bye Bye Barbara–Johnny Mathis (64)	302
Come Back–Johnny Mathis (63)	286
She Lets Her Hair Down (Early In The Morning)–Tokens (69)	*259*
In My Room (El Amor)–Verdelle Smith (66)	234
No–Dodie Stevens (60)	202
Walk Tall–2 Of Clubs (66)	193
I'm Gonna Change Him–Cathy Carr (59)	183
Go Chase A Moonbeam–Jerry Vale (58)	109
Double-O-Seven–Detergents (65)	108
There Won't Be Any Snow (Christmas In The Jungle)–Derrik Roberts (65)	89
(The Clickity Clack Song) Four Little Heels–Brian Hyland (60)	62
Two Thousand Two Hundred Twenty Three Miles–Patti Page (60)	45
The Prettiest Girl In School–Randy Starr (58)	37
She Lets Her Hair Down (Early In The Morning)–Gene Pitney (69)	*36*
Calcutta–Four Preps (61)	*23*
Keep Your Hands In Your Pockets–Playmates (62)	17
The Chick–Lee And Paul (59)	13
There's So Much Love All Around Me–Three Degrees (71)	11
Shake Hands With A Fool–June Valli (58)	11
Oliver Cool–Oliver Cool (60)	6.5
Dommage, Dommage (Too Bad, Too Bad)–Jerry Vale (66)	*6.1*
Hurry Up And Tell Me–Paul Anka (63)	5.4
Thank You Girl–Street People (70)	4.2
Dommage, Dommage (Too Bad, Too Bad)–Paul Vance (66)	*3.7*
Mommy And Daddy Were Twistin'–Susan Summers (62)	2.7
Julie Knows–Randy Sparks (64)	0.5
She Lets Her Hair Down (Early In The Morning)–Don Young (69)	*0.0*
Itsy Bitsy Teenie Weenie Yellow Polkadot Bikini–Buddy Hackett (60)	*0.0*
Gloria VAN CLEVE [Gloria Wilson] ▶ 6470 (1)	**166**
Something Happened–Paul Anka (60)	331
Harry VANDA [Johannes Henderickus Jacob VanDenBerg] ▶ 1643 (10)	**2556**
Love Is In The Air–John Paul Young (78)	1865
Friday On My Mind–Easybeats (67)	1495
Bring A Little Lovin'–Los Bravos (68)	451
Good Times–INXS And Jimmy Barnes (87)	366
Yesterday's Hero–John Paul Young (75)	*329*
Yesterday's Hero–Bay City Rollers (76)	*265*
Lost In Your Love–John Paul Young (78)	156
St. Louis–Easybeats (69)	90
Hey, St. Peter–Flash & The Pan (79)	87
Heaven And Hell–Easybeats (67)	10
Adrian VANDENBERG [Adriaan Van Den Berg II] ▶ 3893 (3)	**665**
The Deeper The Love–Whitesnake (90)	517
Burning Heart–Vandenberg (82)	395
Now You're Gone–Whitesnake (90)	24
–Johannes Henderickus Jacob VanDenBerg see: Harry VANDA	

Lee VANDERBILT [Kenrick Des-Etages] ▶ 10530 (1)	**7.6**
Jump For Joy–Biddu Orchestra (76)	15
–Sylvia Vanderpool see: Sylvia ROBINSON	
–Donald E. Vandevelde see: Donnie VIE	
Luther VANDROSS ▶ 1184 (13)	**3749**
Don't Want To Be A Fool–Luther Vandross (91)	1159
Stop To Love–Luther Vandross (86)	1129
Power Of Love–Luther Vandross (91)	1062
Never Too Much–Luther Vandross (81)	721
Jump To It–Aretha Franklin (82)	552
Til My Baby Comes Home–Luther Vandross (85)	534
She Won't Talk To Me–Luther Vandross (89)	438
There's Nothing Better Than Love–Luther Vandross (Duet With Gregory Hines) (87)	326
Any Love–Luther Vandross (88)	306
Give Me The Reason–Luther Vandross (86)	236
Get It Right–Aretha Franklin (83)	150
Bad Boy–Luther Vandross (82)	96
The Rush–Luther Vandross (91)	71
Leroy VAN DYKE ▶ 5083 (2)	**345**
Auctioneer–Leroy Van Dyke (56)	*579*
Auctioneer–Chuck Miller (56)	*112*
Les VANDYKE [Yani Skoradalides, John Worsley, Johnny Worth] ▶ 8611 (5)	**45**
Well, I Ask Ya–Kay Starr (61)	*38*
What Do You Want?–Bobby Vee (60)	5.0
Open Up Your Heart–Rainbow (72)	2.7
Well I Ask You–Eden Kane (61)	*0.0*
La Dolce Vita (The Sweet Life)–Harry Simeone Chorale (61)	*0.0*
Nick VAN EEDE [Nicholas Eede] ▶ 859 (4)	**5175**
(I Just) Died In Your Arms–Cutting Crew (87)	3427
I've Been In Love Before–Cutting Crew (87)	1314
One For The Mockingbird–Cutting Crew (87)	395
(Between A) Rock And A Hard Place–Cutting Crew (89)	76
Hans VAN EIJCK ▶ 2384 (2)	**1540**
Ma Belle Amie–Tee Set (70)	2854
If You Do Believe In Love–Tee Set (70)	226
Daniel VANGARDE [Daniel Bangalter] ▶ 10234 (1)	**11**
Cuba–Gibson Brothers (79)	22
VANGELIS [Evangelos Papathanassiou] ▶ 730 (4)	**6013**
Chariots Of Fire - Titles–Vangelis (81)	5649
State Of Independence–Donna Summer (82)	320
I'll Find My Way Home–Jon & Vangelis (82)	250
I Hear You Now–Jon And Vangelis (80)	157
Alex VAN HALEN ▶ 931 (17)	**4760**
Jump–Van Halen (84)	6595
Why Can't This Be Love–Van Halen (86)	3498
When It's Love–Van Halen (88)	1533
Finish What Ya Started–Van Halen (88)	1115
Panama–Van Halen (84)	1026
I'll Wait–Van Halen (84)	975
Dance The Night Away–Van Halen (79)	922
Top Of The World–Van Halen (91)	819
Love Walks In–Van Halen (86)	778
Dreams–Van Halen (86)	588
Feels So Good–Van Halen (89)	435
Black And Blue–Van Halen (88)	288
And The Cradle Will Rock...–Van Halen (80)	183
Hot For Teacher–Van Halen (84)	182
Beautiful Girls–Van Halen (79)	61
Best Of Both Worlds–Van Halen (86)	29
Runnin' With The Devil–Van Halen (78)	12
Eddie VAN HALEN ▶ 932 (17)	**4760**
Jump–Van Halen (84)	6595
Why Can't This Be Love–Van Halen (86)	3498
When It's Love–Van Halen (88)	1533
Finish What Ya Started–Van Halen (88)	1115
Panama–Van Halen (84)	1026
I'll Wait–Van Halen (84)	975
Dance The Night Away–Van Halen (79)	922
Top Of The World–Van Halen (91)	819
Love Walks In–Van Halen (86)	778
Dreams–Van Halen (86)	588
Feels So Good–Van Halen (89)	435
Black And Blue–Van Halen (88)	288
And The Cradle Will Rock...–Van Halen (80)	183
Hot For Teacher–Van Halen (84)	182
Beautiful Girls–Van Halen (79)	61
Best Of Both Worlds–Van Halen (86)	29
Runnin' With The Devil–Van Halen (78)	12
Hans VAN HEMERT ▶ 2670 (2)	**1282**
How Do You Do?–Mouth & MacNeal (72)	2478
Hey, You Love–Mouth & MacNeal (72)	85
Jimmy VAN HEUSEN [Kurt Adams, Edward Chester Babcock, Arthur Williams] ▶ 710 (35)	**6130**
Love And Marriage–Frank Sinatra (55)	*3059*
All The Way–Frank Sinatra (57)	*2520*
High Hopes–Frank Sinatra "and a bunch of kids" (59)	944
(Love Is) The Tender Trap–Frank Sinatra (55)	*901*
Swinging On A Star–Big Dee Irwin (63)	789
Pocketful Of Miracles–Frank Sinatra (61)	587
The Second Time Around–Frank Sinatra (61)	491
Love And Marriage–Dinah Shore (55)	*386*
It Could Happen To You–Dinah Washington (60)	358
The Boys' Night Out–Patti Page (62)	326
Not As A Stranger–Frank Sinatra (55)	*311*
Wake Me When It's Over–Andy Williams (60)	278
Where Love Has Gone–Jack Jones (64)	235
My Dream Sonata–Nat "King" Cole (56)	*201*
Call Me Irresponsible–Frank Sinatra (63)	*187*
Somewhere Along The Way–Steve Lawrence (61)	*134*
Funny Thing–Tony Bennett with Percy Faith and His Orchestra (54)	131
How Are Ya' Fixed For Love–Frank Sinatra and Keely Smith (58)	99
Imagination–Quotations (62)	96
Call Me Irresponsible–Jack Jones (63)	*90*
You'll Get Yours–Frank Sinatra (56)	50
Come Blow Your Horn–Frank Sinatra (63)	21
It's Better In The Dark–Tony Martin (56)	21
The Same Old Song And Dance–Frank Sinatra (58)	18
Somewhere Along The Way–Roy Hamilton (59)	*8.9*
Look To Your Heart–Georgie Shaw (55)	8.7
To Love And Be Loved–Jane Morgan (58)	*7.2*
Sold To The Man With The Broken Heart–Tony Bennett with Percy Faith (57)	6.8
The Last Dance–McGuire Sisters (60)	0.8
To Love And Be Loved–Frank Sinatra (59)	*0.4*
My Dream Sonata–Roger Williams (56)	*0.0*
Love And Marriage–Helen Grayco (55)	*0.0*
(Love Is) The Tender Trap–Ella Fitzgerald (55)	*0.0*
Not As A Stranger–Henri René & His Orchestra (55)	*0.0*
All The Way–Grady Martin & The Slew Foot Five (57)	*0.0*
Harry VAN HOOF ▶ 2671 (2)	**1282**
How Do You Do?–Mouth & MacNeal (72)	2478
Hey, You Love–Mouth & MacNeal (72)	85
–René Jan van Hoogten see: Ray MAXWELL	
Rafe VAN HOY ▶ 2558 (6)	**1385**
What's Forever For–Michael Murphey (82)	989
Baby I Lied–Deborah Allen (83)	851
Late At Night–England Dan Seals (80)	129
You're Mine Tonight–Pure Prairie League (81)	29
Sail Away–Sam Neely (77)	17
Somebody's Gonna Love You–Lee Greenwood (83)	4.5
–Vanilla Ice see: Robert VAN WINKLE	
–Vanity see: Denise MATTHEWS	
–Gerald Van Kollenburg see: Jerry KOLLENBURG	
James VANLEER ▶ 7261 (1)	**107**
I' Been Watchin' You–South Side Movement (73)	214
Thijs VAN LEER ▶ 2723 (2)	**1240**
Hocus Pocus–Focus (73)	2194
Sylvia–Focus (73)	143
Robbie VAN LEEUWEN ▶ 286 (6)	**12397**
Venus–Shocking Blue (69)	*8155*
Venus–Bananarama (86)	*3151*
Mighty Joe–Shocking Blue (70)	536
Venus–Stars On 45 (81)	*442*
Long And Lonesome Road–Shocking Blue (70)	107
Never Marry A Railroad Man–Shocking Blue (71)	5.8
Koenraad VAN-LISHOUT [Kovali] ▶ 9039 (1)	**33**
Spin That Wheel–Hi Tek 3 featuring Ya Kid K (90)	98
Al VANN ▶ 11196 (1)	**2.8**
Take A Bow–Alan Dean (56)	5.6
–Harry Eugene Vann see: Van WALLS	
Maurice VANN ▶ 9351 (1)	**26**
Pushin' Your Luck–Sleepy King (61)	51

Teddy VANN [Theodore Williams] ▶ 1311 (11) 3380
Loop De Loop—Johnny Thunder (62) *2175*
Love Power—Luther Vandross (91) *1062*
Love Power—Sandpebbles (67) *988*
Forget It—Sandpebbles (67) 90
Soul Heaven—Dixie Drifter (65) 73
The Rosy Dance—Johnny Thunder (63) 42
Clap Your Hands (Part 1)—Wheels (60) 34
The Lonely Crowd—Teddy Vann (61) 34
Teenage Hayride—Tender Slim (60) 11
You—Darlene McCrea (59) 3.4
Loop De Loop—Soul Sisters (64) *1.4*

Larry VANNATA ▶ 4970 (2) 368
You—Aquatones (58) *735*
You—Gale Storm (58) *0.0*

Gino VANNELLI ▶ 1207 (9) 3682
Living Inside Myself—Gino Vannelli (81) 1843
People Gotta Move—Gino Vannelli (74) 643
Black Cars—Gino Vannelli (85) 400
Nightwalker—Gino Vannelli (81) 306
Wild Horses—Gino Vannelli (87) 292
Hurts To Be In Love—Gino Vannelli (85) 262
Love Of My Life—Gino Vannelli (76) 212
Wheels Of Life—Gino Vannelli (79) 63
The Longer You Wait—Gino Vannelli (82) 6.9

Ross VANNELLI ▶ 1158 (2) 3836
I Just Wanna Stop—Gino Vannelli (78) 3196
Surrender To Me—Ann Wilson and Robin Zander (88) 1279

Clarke VAN NESS ▶ 7128 (3) 115
Silver Dollar—Teresa Brewer (55) *205*
Silver Dollar—Barry Darvell (62) *24*
Silver Dollar—Johnny Long (55) *0.0*

Ed VANOVER ▶ 9076 (1) 32
Who Shot J.R.?—Gary Burbank with Band McNally (80) 95

Gary VAN SCYOC ▶ 7557 (1) 89
The Fife Piper—Dynatones (66) 266

Sharon VANSELOW ▶ 7427 (1) 97
The Loser—Skyliners (65) 193

Lieve VAN STEYVOORT ▶ 8786 (1) 39
Welcome Home—Sammy Kaye & His Orchestra (61) 117

—Henri Eugene Vantard see: Henri VARNA

Eric VAN TIJN ▶ 8836 (1) 38
Female Intuition—Mai Tai (86) 76

John VAN TONGEREN ▶ 5070 (1) 350
It's Not Over ('til It's Over)—Starship (87) 1049

—Harry Van Walls see: Van WALLS

Randy VANWARMER [Randy Van Wormer] ▶ 1403 (3) 3158
Just When I Needed You Most—Randy Vanwarmer (79) 2942
Suzi—Randy Vanwarmer (81) 154
Whatever You Decide—Randy Vanwarmer (80) 62

Joseph VAN WINKLE ▶ 2252 (6) 1704
Mr Custer—Larry Verne (60) 4906
Mister Livingston—Larry Verne (60) 111
Little Tin Soldier—Toy Dolls (62) 52
Johnny Willow—Fred Darian (61) 41
Roll Call Company J—Balladeers (60) 3.8
Battle Of Gettysburg—Fred Darian (61) 0.5

Robert VAN WINKLE [Vanilla Ice] ▶ 3959 (3) 640
Ice Ice Baby—Vanilla Ice (90) 3735
I Love You—Vanilla Ice (91) 160
Cool As Ice (Everybody Get Loose)—Vanilla Ice (91) 81

Steven VAN ZANDT [Miami Steve, Little Steven] ▶ 3640 (4) 754
Sun City—Artists United Against Apartheid (85) 469
Shelter—Lone Justice (87) 297
Forever—Little Steven and the Disciples Of Soul (82) 119
Sweet, Sweet Baby (I'm Falling)—Lone Justice (85) 53

Townes VAN ZANDT ▶ 5971 (1) 221
Mister Can't You See—Buffy Sainte-Marie (72) 442

Donnie VAN ZANT ▶ 4856 (4) 398
If I'd Been The One—38 Special (83) 839
Somebody Like You—38 Special (86) 322
Comin' Down Tonight—38 Special (89) 167
Rock & Roll Strategy—Thirty Eight Special (88) 163

Ronnie VAN ZANT ▶ 1394 (8) 3188
Sweet Home Alabama—Lynyrd Skynyrd (74) 2031
Free Bird—Will To Power (88) *1705*
What's Your Name—Lynyrd Skynyrd (77) 1619
Free Bird—Lynyrd Skynyrd (74) *716*
Free Bird (Live)—Lynyrd Skynyrd (76) *482*
Saturday Night Special—Lynyrd Skynyrd (75) 407
You Got That Right—Lynyrd Skynyrd (78) 61
Double Trouble—Lynyrd Skynyrd (76) 31

Emanuel VARDI ▶ 7960 (1) 67
My Daddy Is President—Little Jo Ann (62) 134

Carolyn VARGA ▶ 4678 (1) 439
When He Touches Me (Nothing Else Matters)—Peaches & Herb (69) 439

Rafael VARGAS ▶ 4531 (1) 470
Wiggle It—2 In A Room (90) 939

Henri VARNA [Henri Eugene Vantard] ▶ 11508 (1) 1.4
Vieni Vieni—Terri Stevens (59) *5.6*

Aaron VARNELL ▶ 10291 (1) 10
Trouble—Frederick Knight (72) 21

Ted VARNICK ▶ 2520 (7) 1421
In The Middle Of An Island—Tony Bennett with Ray Ellis and His Orchestra (57) *1952*
Ghost Town—Don Cherry (56) 585
In The Middle Of An Island—"Tennessee" Ernie Ford (57) *301*
Never Leave Me—Gale Storm (56) *1.9*
Never Leave Me—Bob Presto (56) *1.9*
In The Middle Of An Island—Stan Wilson (57) *0.0*
In The Middle Of An Island—Anita Kerr Quartet (57) *0.0*

Henry VARS ▶ 9330 (1) 26
It's A Cotton Candy World—Jerry Wallace (64) 52

Claude VASORI [Claude Andre Erminio Vasori, Caravelli] ▶ 9170 (1) 30
Let Me Try Again (Laisse Moi Le Temps)—Frank Sinatra (73) 148

—Claude Andre Erminio Vasori see: Claude VASORI

—Lolly Vasquez see: Lolly VEGAS

—Pat Vasquez see: Pat VEGAS

Kin VASSY ▶ 3494 (1) 818
Heed The Call—Kenny Rogers And The First Edition (70) 818

Johnny VASTANO ▶ 4811 (1) 409
Deeper Than The Night—Olivia Newton-John (79) 818

Gaetano VASTOLA ▶ 10335 (2) 9.9
You Baby You—Cleftones (56) *20*
You Baby You—Diamonds (56) *0.0*

—Roman Vatro see: Armando TROVAIOLI

Jimmie VAUGHAN ▶ 8322 (1) 54
Tick Tock—Vaughan Brothers (90) 163

Billy VAUGHN ▶ 4397 (9) 506
Just As Long As I'm With You—Pat Boone (56) 279
Do The Bop—Hilltoppers (56) 135
Searching—Hilltoppers (55) 65
Lonesome Lover Blues—Fontane Sisters (56) 23
Without My Love—Pat Boone (57) 20
Trying—Billy Vaughn and His Orchestra (58) 18
Hop Scotch Boogie—Johnny Maddox (56) 12
Little Boy Blue—Billy Vaughn and His Orchestra (56) 7.6
Faded Rose—Hilltoppers (56) 5.2

—George Vaughn see: Vaughn HORTON

Jack VAUGHN ▶ 2392 (1) 1531
Goodbye Jimmy Goodbye—Kathy Linden (59) 1531

—Michael Vaughn see: Sunny SKYLAR

Sharon VAUGHN ▶ 6061 (1) 210
My Heroes Have Always Been Cowboys—Willie Nelson (80) 210

—Wanda Vaughn see: Wanda HUTCHINSON

Wayne VAUGHN ▶ 1552 (6) 2731
Let's Groove—Earth, Wind & Fire (81) 4608
Fall In Love With Me—Earth, Wind & Fire (83) 838
Wanna Be With You—Earth, Wind & Fire (82) 150
Thinking Of You—Earth, Wind & Fire (88) 137
Side By Side—Earth, Wind & Fire (83) 65
Skat Strut—M.C. Skat Kat And The Stray Mob (91) 16

—Yvonne Vaughn see: Donna FARGO

Joe VEASEY [Joe Medwick Masters, Joe Medwick] ▶ 7187 (2) 111
Farther Up The Road—Bobby "Blue" Bland, Bill Harvey Orchestra (57) 198
If Love Ruled The World—Bobby Bland (70) 24

Bobby VEE [Robert Velline] ▶ 4930 (3) 379
I'll Make You Mine—Bobby Vee With The Eligibles (64) 356
Suzie Baby—Bobby Vee and The Shadows (59) 23
Cross My Heart—Bobby Vee (65) 0.9

—Vee Pea see: Virginia BLAND

Piet VEERMAN ▶ 9564 (1) 21
Country Woman—Magic Lantern (72) 21

Suzanne VEGA ▶ 959 (3) 4663
Tom's Diner—DNA (90) 2358
Luka—Suzanne Vega (87) 2304
Solitude Standing—Suzanne Vega (87) 6.4

—Billy Vegas see: Nuno BETTENCOURT

Lolly VEGAS [Lolly Vasquez] ▶ 972 (6) 4609
Come And Get Your Love—Redbone (74) 3137
The Witch Queen Of New Orleans—Redbone (71) 1289
Niki Hoeky—P.J. Proby (67) 781
Maggie—Redbone (70) 491
Suzie Girl—Redbone (74) 75
Number One—Eloise Laws (78) 1.8

Pat VEGAS [Pat Vasquez] ▶ 3304 (3) 906
The Witch Queen Of New Orleans—Redbone (71) 1289
Niki Hoeky—P.J. Proby (67) 781
Number One—Eloise Laws (78) 1.8

Trevor VEITCH ▶ 1466 (6) 2963
Gloria—Laura Branigan (82) 4941
Telefone (Long Distance Love Affair)—Sheena Easton (83) 1957
Steal The Night—Stevie Woods (81) 687
Just Can't Win 'Em All—Stevie Woods (82) 274
Trouble In Paradise—Al Jarreau (83) 87
Devil In A Fast Car—Sheena Easton (84) 22

Jaromir VEJVODA ▶ 7215 (1) 110
Beer Barrel Polka—Bobby Vinton (75) 329

—Freddie Vel see: Fred HENLEY

Consuelo VELAZQUEZ ▶ 7460 (2) 94
Besame Mucho (Part 1)—Coasters (60) *181*
Besame Mucho—Steve Lawrence and Eydie Gorme (55) *7.4*

Lisa VELEZ ▶ 10549 (1) 7.4
Someone To Love Me For Me—Lisa Lisa & Cult Jam (87) 52

—Ioannis Alexandres Vellotes see: Johnny OTIS

—Johnny Alexander Vellotes Jr. see: Shuggie OTIS

—Robert Velline see: Bobby VEE

Tony VELONA ▶ 2499 (5) 1435
Domani (Tomorrow)—Julius La Rosa (55) *1174*
Music To Watch Girls By—Andy Williams (67) *466*
Lollipops And Roses—Jack Jones (62) *422*
Lollipops And Roses—Paul Petersen (62) *193*
Domani (Tomorrow)—Tony Martin (55) *0.0*

Lonnie VENCENT [Lonnie Vincent Miller] ▶ 9772 (1) 17
Smooth Up—Bulletboys (89) 68

Steve VENET [Steve Venetoulis] ▶ 2679 (6) 1277
Action—Freddy Cannon (65) 1365
Peaches 'N' Cream—Ikettes (65) 487
Good Night Baby—Butterflys (64) 321
Baby Be Mine—Jelly Beans (64) 308
Poor Man's Son—Reflections (65) 257
You're My Baby (And Don't You Forget It)—Vacels (65) 232

—Steve Venetoulis see: Steve VENET

Pablo VENEZUELA ▶ 8911 (1) 36
Queen Of My Heart—René And Ray (62) 109

Jan VENNIK ▶ 11377 (1) 2.0
Grasshopper—Spin (76) 4.0

Arthur VENOSA ▶ 1193 (2) 3719
Little Star—Elegants (58) 7398
Goodnight—Elegants (58) 20

Pacifico VENTO ▶ 8161 (1) 60
Infatuation (Scapricciatiello)—Renato Carosone (56) *120*

Billy VERA [William Patrick McCord] ▶ 903 (6)	**4909**
At This Moment—Billy Vera & The Beaters (86)	*4089*
Make Me Belong To You—Barbara Lewis (66)	516
Storybook Children—Billy Vera & Judy Clay (67)	392
I Can Take Care Of Myself—Billy & The Beaters (81)	318
At This Moment—Billy & The Beaters (81)	*32*
Mean Old World—Rick Nelson (65)	16
Dino VERDE [Eduardo Verde] ▶ 9692 (5)	**19**
Romantica— Gordon Jenkins And His Orchestra and Chorus (60)	*18*
Stay Here With Me (Resta Cu 'Mme)— Domenico Modugno (58)	1.6
Ciao Ciao Bambina— Domenico Modugno (59)	*1.5*
Romantica—Jane Morgan (60)	*0.0*
La Dolce Vita (The Sweet Life)— Harry Simeone Chorale (61)	*0.0*
—Eduardo Verde see: Dino VERDE	
Giuseppe VERDI ▶ 11473 (1)	**1.6**
(Hear My Song) Violetta— Ray Adams And Orchestra (62)	6.2
Marcus VERE ▶ 5027 (2)	**357**
Living In A Box—Living In A Box (87)	694
So The Story Goes—Living In A Box (87)	20
Humberto VERGARA [Humberto Vergara Baro] ▶ 9449 (1)	**23**
Latin Active—A Lighter Shade Of Brown (91)	164
—Humberto Vergara Baro see: Humberto VERGARA	
Ed VERNON ▶ 9671 (1)	**19**
Wendegahl The Warlock—Rugbys (69)	19
Matt VERNON ▶ 5383 (2)	**298**
Steal The Night—Stevie Woods (81)	687
Just Can't Win 'Em All—Stevie Woods (82)	274
—Albert Verrecchia see: Albert WEYMAN	
—Evelyne Verrecchia see: Evelyne LENTON	
Steve VERROCA ▶ 10129 (1)	**12**
Cuore—Tony DeFranco (62)	12
Joseph VERSCHAREN ▶ 3886 (9)	**667**
Since I Don't Have You—Skyliners (59)	*2364*
This I Swear—Skyliners (59)	743
Since I Don't Have You—Don McLean (81)	*545*
Since I Don't Have You—Chuck Jackson (64)	*403*
It Happened Today—Skyliners (59)	229
Since I Don't Have You—Art Garfunkel (79)	*180*
Since I Don't Have You—Eddie Holman (70)	*160*
Since I Don't Have You— Fred Parris & The Five Satins (82)	*4.8*
How Much—Skyliners (60)	1.5
Henry VESTINE ▶ 8223 (1)	**58**
Time Was—Canned Heat (69)	290
Cyril VETTER ▶ 3742 (1)	**714**
Double Shot (Of My Baby's Love)— Swingin' Medallions (66)	1428
—Mark Ashton Vey see: Mark McVEY	
Mack VICKERY ▶ 11701 (1)	**0.6**
Big Bruce—Steve Greenberg (69)	*3.1*
Maria VIDAL [Maria Elena Fernadez-Vidal] ▶ 6129 (1)	**202**
Summer Rain—Belinda Carlisle (90)	404
Donnie VIE [Donald E. Vandevelde] ▶ 5584 (3)	**269**
Fly High Michelle—Enuff Z'Nuff (90)	228
New Thing—Enuff Z'Nuff (89)	93
Mother's Eyes—Enuff Z'Nuff (91)	19
Rafael VIGIL ▶ 3308 (3)	**906**
Bad Boy—Miami Sound Machine (86)	1668
Falling In Love (Uh-Oh)—Miami Sound Machine (86)	691
Betcha Say That— Gloria Estefan and Miami Sound Machine (87)	358
Paul VIGRASS ▶ 5648 (2)	**260**
Forever Autumn—Justin Hayward (78)	531
Men Of Learning—Vigrass & Osborne (72)	249
—Jeanne Vikki see: Rafael RENÉ	
—Hervé Vilard see: René VILLARD	
Joe VILLA [Joe Francavilla] ▶ 5312 (1)	**308**
Believe Me—Royal Teens (59)	925
Alex VILLALOBOS ▶ 9954 (1)	**15**
You Can't Get Away—Shana (90)	44
Jean VILLARD ▶ 1003 (3)	**4453**
The Three Bells—Browns (59)	*8482*
The Three Bells—Dick Flood (59)	*386*
The Three Bells—Tokens (65)	*36*
René VILLARD [Hervé Vilard] ▶ 9890 (1)	**15**
Kiss Tomorrow Goodbye—Lainie Kazan (67)	31
Edmund VILLAREAL ▶ 6055 (1)	**211**
Country Wine—Raiders (72)	422
Diana VILLEGAS ▶ 5886 (2)	**233**
You Don't Have To Go Home Tonight—Triplets (91)	1130
Sunrise—Triplets (91)	28
Sylvia VILLEGAS ▶ 5887 (2)	**233**
You Don't Have To Go Home Tonight—Triplets (91)	1130
Sunrise—Triplets (91)	28
Vicky VILLEGAS ▶ 5888 (2)	**233**
You Don't Have To Go Home Tonight—Triplets (91)	1130
Sunrise—Triplets (91)	28
Sadie VIMMERSTEDT ▶ 3541 (1)	**792**
I Wanna Be Around—Tony Bennett (63)	1585
—Vinnie Vincent see: Vince CUSANO	
Gene VINCENT [Vincent Eugene Craddock] ▶ 2564 (4)	**1375**
Be Bop A Lula—Gene Vincent and His Blue Caps (56)	*2525*
Race With The Devil— Gene Vincent and His Blue Caps (56)	116
Bluejean Bop—Gene Vincent and His Blue Caps (56)	60
Be Bop A-Lula—Everly Brothers (60)	*50*
Holly Beth VINCENT ▶ 9140 (1)	**30**
Tell That Girl To Shut Up—Transvision Vamp (88)	30
John VINCENT [John V. Imbragulio] ▶ 2028 (5)	**1991**
Rockin' Pneumonia - Boogie Woogie Flu— Johnny Rivers (72)	*3059*
Birdland—Chubby Checker (63)	1076
Rockin' Pneumonia And The Boogie Woogie Flu— Huey Smith and The Clowns (57)	*112*
Don't You Know Yockomo?— Huey "Piano" Smith with his Clowns (58)	67
Roberta—Bones (72)	27
Larry VINCENT ▶ 6906 (1)	**130**
The French Song (Quand Le Soleil Dit Bonjour Aux Montagnes)—Lucille Starr (64)	389
—Nat Vincent see: James KENDIS	
Stan VINCENT ▶ 1259 (7)	**3555**
O-o-h Child—Five Stairsteps (70)	2738
Remember Then—Earls (62)	822
Drownin' My Sorrows—Connie Francis (63)	549
Looking For Love—Connie Francis (64)	360
America/Standing—Five Stairsteps (70)	93
Indian Lady—Lou Christie (70)	56
Never—Earls (63)	41
Stevie VINCENT ▶ 5138 (2)	**335**
Dirty Cash (Money Talks)— Adventures Of Stevie V (90)	658
Jealousy—Adventures Of Stevie V (91)	12
Frankie VINCI ▶ 7267 (1)	**106**
Miles Away—Fotomaker (78)	106
Reggie VINSON ▶ 7681 (1)	**81**
Billion Dollar Babies—Alice Cooper (73)	243
Bobby VINTON ▶ 484 (8)	**8643**
Mr. Lonely—Bobby Vinton (64)	*8492*
My Melody Of Love—Bobby Vinton (74)	3485
Coming Home Soldier—Bobby Vinton (66)	2331
L-O-N-E-L-Y—Bobby Vinton (65)	843
I Love You The Way You Are—Bobby Vinton (62)	491
Mr. Lonely—Buddy Greco (62)	*274*
Red Roses For Mom—Bobby Vinton (67)	31
She Will Survive (Poland)—Bobby Vinton (82)	6.5
Michael VISCEGLIA ▶ 11535 (1)	**1.3**
Solitude Standing—Suzanne Vega (87)	6.4
Jan VISSER ▶ 3903 (1)	**663**
Little Green Bag—George Baker Selection (70)	1325
Joe VITALE ▶ 4843 (2)	**400**
Rocky Mountain Way—Joe Walsh (73)	1195
Space Age Whiz Kids—Joe Walsh (83)	203
Anna VITO [Anna Mangravito] ▶ 8597 (1)	**45**
High On A Hill—Scott English (64)	90
James VITTI ▶ 11741 (1)	**0.2**
Theme From The Black Hole—Parliament (80)	1.0
—Zoe Voeth see: Joan WHITNEY	
Janet VOGEL [Janet Vogel-Rapp] ▶ 3887 (9)	**667**
Since I Don't Have You—Skyliners (59)	*2364*
This I Swear—Skyliners (59)	743
Since I Don't Have You—Don McLean (81)	*545*
Since I Don't Have You—Chuck Jackson (64)	*403*
It Happened Today—Skyliners (59)	229
Since I Don't Have You—Art Garfunkel (79)	*180*
Since I Don't Have You—Eddie Holman (70)	*160*
Since I Don't Have You— Fred Parris & The Five Satins (82)	*4.8*
How Much—Skyliners (60)	1.5
—Janet Vogel-Rapp see: Janet VOGEL	
Steve VOICE ▶ 6355 (2)	**179**
On The Shelf—Donny & Marie (78)	265
Make Love To Me—Helen Reddy (79)	141
—James Wesley Voight see: Chip TAYLOR	
John VOLINKATY ▶ 3751 (1)	**712**
Satin Sheets—Jeanne Pruett (73)	712
Mark VOLMAN ▶ 3733 (4)	**717**
Elenore—Turtles (68)	2721
Sound Asleep—Turtles (68)	382
You Don't Have To Walk In The Rain— Turtles (69)	301
Love In The City—Turtles (69)	183
Ben VOLPELIERE-PIERROT ▶ 7966 (1)	**67**
Misfit—Curiosity Killed The Cat (87)	336
Ron VOLZ [Ron Carroll] ▶ 8457 (1)	**50**
Beat—Rockin' R's (59)	149
Fernando VON ARB ▶ 8540 (1)	**47**
Midnite Maniac—Krokus (84)	93
—Albert von Breitenbach see: Fred FISHER	
—Rudi Von der Dovenmuehle see: Rudi LINDT	
Kurt VONNEGUT ▶ 10004 (1)	**14**
Nice, Nice, Very Nice—Ambrosia (75)	71
Albert VON TILZER [Albert Gumbinsky] ▶ 3472 (6) HOF	**829**
(I'll Be With You In) Apple Blossom Time— Tab Hunter (59)	*730*
If You Don't Want My Love—Jaye P. Morgan (55)	463
Put Your Arms Around Me Honey—Fats Domino (60)	*230*
I'll Be With You In Apple Blossom Time— Wayne Newton (65)	*207*
Put Your Arms Around Me Honey—Ray Smith (60)	*15*
(I'll Be With You) In Apple Blossom Time— Four Aces (54)	*13*
Harry VON TILZER [Aaron Gumbinsky] ▶ 9412 (5) HOF	**24**
I Want A Girl—Bruce Hayes with Mary Mayo (60)	*14*
Out Of A Clear Blue Sky— Lawrence Welk And His Orchestra (61)	13
A Bird In A Gilded Cage—Crazy Otto (56)	1.5
Wait Til The Sun Shines Nellie—Crazy Otto (56)	1.5
I Want A Girl (Just Like The Girl That Married Dear Old Dad)—Crazy Otto (56)	*1.5*
Faye VOSS ▶ 830 (1)	**5316**
Sugar Shack—Jimmy Gilmer And The Fireballs (63)	10632
Paul VOUDOURIS ▶ 9959 (1)	**15**
Holding My Heart—Bang (2) (90)	44
Roger VOUDOURIS ▶ 4476 (1)	**486**
Get Used To It—Roger Voudouris (79)	971
Richard VRABCAK ▶ 11457 (1)	**1.6**
Take Your Love (And Shove It)—Kane's Cousins (69)	3.2
—Michael Vucish see: Mike VALE	
Rob VUNDERINK ▶ 5049 (1)	**354**
Sausalito Summernight—Diesel (81)	708

W

Pal WAAKTAAR ▶ 1792 (3)	**2316**
Take On Me—A-Ha (85)	4264
The Sun Always Shines On T.V.—A-Ha (85)	765
Cry Wolf—A-Ha (87)	259
Myron WACHENDORF [Myron Lee] ▶ 4289 (1)	**531**
Peter Rabbit—Dee Jay And The Runaways (66)	531
—Franz Wachsmann see: Franz WAXMAN	
Waddy WACHTEL ▶ 3895 (2)	**664**
Her Town Too—James Taylor And J.D. Souther (81)	1187
Werewolves Of London—Warren Zevon (78)	804

Tony WADDINGTON ▶ 2940 (5)	**1109**
Nothing But A Heartache—Flirtations (69)	822
Can't Stop Loving You—Tom Jones (70)	*812*
Sugar Baby Love—Rubettes (74)	*569*
Sugar Baby Love—Stars On 45 (81)	*12*
Can't Stop Lovin' You—Flirtations (70)	*2.2*
Cliff WADE ▶ 4200 (1)	**566**
Heartbreaker—Pat Benatar (79)	1131
David WADE ▶ 11765 (1)	**0.2**
Run And Hide—Uniques (66)	0.5
George WADE ▶ 11263 (1)	**2.5**
True Love Gone (Come On Home)— Betty Madigan (57)	13
Larry WADE ▶ 4937 (3)	**378**
The Love We Had (Stays On My Mind)—Dells (71)	681
It's All Up To You—Dells (72)	72
Special Memory—Jerry Butler (70)	4.2
Steve WADEY ▶ 2845 (3)	**1156**
Black Is Black—Los Bravos (66)	*3466*
Clock—Eddie Rambeau (66)	2.8
Black Is Black—Tight Fit (81)	*0.9*
Bill WADHAMS ▶ 4571 (2)	**464**
Let Him Go—Animotion (85)	435
I Want You—Animotion (86)	57
Terry WADSWORTH ▶ 10818 (1)	**5.1**
Werewolf—Frantics (60)	10
George WAGGNER ▶ 9293 (1)	**27**
Sweet Someone—Eddie And Betty (59)	54
Dave WAGGONER ▶ 3748 (2)	**712**
Evil Woman Don't Play Your Games With Me— Crow (69)	1457
Cottage Cheese—Crow (70)	453
—Richard Alan Waggoner see: Allan RICH	
—Marcy Debra Wagman see: Marci RAUER	
Dick WAGNER ▶ 1120 (9)	**3955**
I Never Cry—Alice Cooper (76)	1991
You And Me—Alice Cooper (77)	1909
Only Women—Alice Cooper (75)	*1899*
How You Gonna See Me Now—Alice Cooper (78)	1236
Just As I Am—Air Supply (85)	777
Welcome To My Nightmare—Alice Cooper (75)	301
Department Of Youth—Alice Cooper (75)	121
Only Women Bleed—Favorite Angel (90)	*108*
I Cannot Stop You—Cherry Slush (68)	9.9
Larry WAGNER ▶ 8483 (4)	**49**
Flamenco Love— Don Costa His Orchestra And Chorus (56)	*146*
Flamenco Love—Tony Martin (56)	*0.0*
Flamenco Love—Richard Hayman (56)	*0.0*
Flamenco Love—Al Caiola and his Magic Guitar (56)	*0.0*
Donnie WAHLBERG ▶ 3543 (1)	**792**
Good Vibrations— Marky Mark & The Funky Bunch (91)	3166
Mark WAHLBERG ▶ 3544 (1)	**792**
Good Vibrations— Marky Mark & The Funky Bunch (91)	3166
Dan WAHLGREN [Papa Dee, Daniel Wahlgren] ▶ 7130 (1)	**115**
My Body Says Yes—Titiyo Featuring Papa D (91)	229
—Bunny Wailer see: Neville LIVINGSTON	
Phil WAINMAN ▶ 5009 (2)	**359**
Little Games—Yardbirds (67)	412
Lady (Put The Light On Me)— Brownsville Station (77)	307
Loudon WAINWRIGHT III ▶ 2682 (1)	**1273**
Dead Skunk—Loudon Wainwright III (73)	1273
John WAITE ▶ 1015 (16)	**4378**
Missing You—John Waite (84)	5545
Price Of Love—Bad English (89)	1890
Possession—Bad English (90)	749
Back On My Feet Again—Babys (80)	576
Every Step Of The Way—John Waite (85)	556
Straight To Your Heart—Bad English (91)	390
Turn And Walk Away—Babys (80)	372
Forget Me Not—Bad English (89)	310
These Times Are Hard For Lovers—John Waite (87)	274
Silver Dreams—Babys (78)	246
Restless Heart—John Waite (85)	174
Heaven Is A 4 Letter Word—Bad English (90)	169
Midnight Rendezvous—Babys (80)	68
Head First—Babys (79)	44
Welcome To Paradise—John Waite (85)	43
If You've Got The Time—Babys (77)	18
Tom WAITS ▶ 1521 (2)	**2809**
Downtown Train—Rod Stewart (89)	*2806*
Downtown Train—Patty Smyth (87)	*3.1*
Frank WAKEFIELD ▶ 11287 (1)	**2.4**
Up To My Neck In High Muddy Water— Linda Ronstadt And The Stone Poneys (68)	7.2
Kathy WAKEFIELD [Kathleen Wakefield Tenen, Charlemagne] ▶ 1944 (10)	**2071**
Nathan Jones—Supremes (71)	1414
One Hundred Ways—Quincy Jones (81)	1012
Torture—Jacksons (84)	784
Glasshouse—Temptations (75)	499
Tell Her Love Has Felt The Need— Eddie Kendricks (74)	456
Happy—Eddie Kendricks (75)	250
There Will Come A Day (I'm Gonna Happen To You)— Smokey Robinson (77)	249
Down To Love Town—Originals (76)	99
Lonely Won't Leave Me Alone— Glenn Medeiros (87)	84
Darling Come Back Home—Eddie Kendricks (73)	61
Loucye Gordy WAKEFIELD ▶ 11060 (1)	**3.5**
Don't Let Him Shop Around—Debbie Dean (61)	*10*
Johnny WAKELIN ▶ 3021 (1)	**1061**
Black Superman - "Muhammad Ali"— Johnny Wakelin And The Kinshasa Band (75)	1061
Dave WAKELING ▶ 5832 (1)	**238**
Tenderness—General Public (84)	715
Murray WALBERG ▶ 9362 (2)	**25**
His Name Was Dean—Nathan Russell (56)	*51*
His Name Was Dean—Jimmy Wakely (56)	*0.0*
—Helen Reddy Wald see: Helen REDDY	
—Anukampa Walden see: Lisa WALDEN	
Dana WALDEN ▶ 2029 (3)	**1991**
How 'Bout Us—Champaign (81)	*1538*
Try Again—Champaign (83)	992
How 'Bout Us—Grayson Hugh and Betty Wright (90)	*122*
Lisa WALDEN [Anukampa Walden] ▶ 6953 (2)	**126**
Jimmy Lee—Aretha Franklin (86)	439
All American Girls—Sister Sledge (81)	64
Narada Michael WALDEN ▶ 377 (24)	**10358**
How Will I Know—Whitney Houston (85)	4102
I Love Your Smile—Shanice (91)	4090
I Don't Wanna Cry—Mariah Carey (91)	3692
Freeway Of Love—Aretha Franklin (85)	2925
Tell Me What You Want Me To Do— Tevin Campbell (91)	1907
We Don't Have To Take Our Clothes Off— Jermaine Stewart (86)	1796
Who's Zoomin' Who—Aretha Franklin (85)	1671
Let Me Be Your Angel—Stacy Lattisaw (80)	1019
You're A Friend Of Mine—Clarence Clemons (85)	936
Don't Make Me Wait For Love—Kenny G (87)	854
How Can I Ease The Pain—Lisa Fischer (91)	802
Jimmy Lee—Aretha Franklin (86)	439
Put Your Mouth On Me—Eddie Murphy (89)	425
I Don't Want Nobody Else (To Dance With You)— Narada Michael Walden (79)	290
Jody—Jermaine Stewart (86)	290
Baby Come To Me—Regina Belle (89)	187
I Shoulda Loved Ya—Narada Michael Walden (80)	105
Perfect Combination— Stacy Lattisaw & Johnny Gill (84)	86
Save Me—Lisa Fischer (91)	82
All American Girls—Sister Sledge (81)	64
Attack Of The Name Game—Stacy Lattisaw (82)	54
Rock-A-Lott—Aretha Franklin (87)	42
Next Time You'll Know—Sister Sledge (81)	20
Dynamite!—Stacy Lattisaw (80)	3.8
Phil WALDEN ▶ 8624 (1)	**45**
Come To Me—Otis Redding (64)	89
Wendy WALDMAN [Wendy Steiner] ▶ 2965 (4)	**1092**
Heartbeat—Don Johnson (86)	2057
Long Hot Summer Nights—Wendy Waldman (78)	44
Baby, What About You—Crystal Gayle (83)	32
Gotta Get Away—Randy Meisner (81)	12
Robert WALDROP ▶ 4226 (2)	**555**
Roam—B-52's (89)	2734
Legal Tender—B-52's (83)	52
Émile WALDTEUFEL ▶ 10196 (1)	**11**
Skaters' Waltz— Billy Vaughn And His Orchestra (60)	11
Howard WALES ▶ 11728 (1)	**0.4**
Camel Back—A.B. Skhy (69)	0.4
Kevin WALES ▶ 6135 (1)	**201**
Playground—Another Bad Creation (91)	604
Aaron WALKER [T-Bone Walker] ▶ 3783 (1)	**701**
Stormy Monday Blues—Bobby Bland (62)	701
Bee WALKER ▶ 3096 (2)	**1010**
Hey Jealous Lover—Frank Sinatra (56)	2954
You'll Always Be My Sweetheart—Bobby Van (58)	51
Brett WALKER ▶ 4465 (1)	**488**
Waiting For Love—Alias (91)	975
Cindy WALKER ▶ 438 (20)	**9369**
You Don't Know Me—Ray Charles (62)	*3379*
Dream Baby (How Long Must I Dream)— Roy Orbison (62)	*2310*
You Don't Know Me—Jerry Vale (56)	*2007*
In The Misty Moonlight—Jerry Wallace (64)	*1075*
Dream Baby (How Long Must I Dream)— Glen Campbell (71)	*667*
Lisa—Jeanne Black (60)	468
China Doll—Ames Brothers (60)	423
You Don't Know Me—Lenny Welch (60)	*401*
You Don't Know Me— Elvis Presley With The Jordanaires (67)	*383*
Distant Drums—Jim Reeves (66)	*377*
In The Misty Moonlight—Dean Martin (67)	*314*
You Don't Know Me—Mickey Gilley (81)	*297*
Give Me Love—McGuire Sisters (55)	268
Anna Marie—Jim Reeves (57)	144
Just A Little Lonesome—Bobby Helms (58)	60
Distant Drums—Vic Dana (66)	*22*
This Is It—Jim Reeves (65)	7.2
You Don't Know Me—Eddy Arnold (56)	*0.0*
You Don't Know Me—Carmen McRae (56)	*0.0*
Thank You For Calling—Jo Stafford (54)	0.0
—David Walker see: Bunker HILL	
Dennis WALKER ▶ 7197 (2)	**111**
Don't Be Afraid Of The Dark—Robert Cray Band (88)	57
Right Next Door (Because Of Me)— Robert Cray Band (87)	53
—Fred Walker see: Derf Reklaw RAHEEM	
Hysear Don WALKER ▶ 7076 (1)	**117**
Wack Wack—Young Holt Trio (66)	470
Ira WALKER ▶ 4782 (3)	**417**
I Wanna Go Back—Eddie Money (86)	*1073*
I Wanna Go Back—Billy Satellite (84)	*89*
Satisfy Me—Billy Satellite (84)	89
—James David Walker see: Jimmy McCRACKLIN	
Jerry Jeff WALKER [Ronald Clyde Crosby] ▶ 1517 (3)	**2818**
Mr. Bojangles (Prologue: Uncle Charlie And His Dog Teddy)—Nitty Gritty Dirt Band (70)	*2370*
Mr. Bojangles—Jerry Jeff Walker (68)	*286*
Mister Bo Jangles—Bobby Cole (68)	*162*
Johnny WALKER ▶ 6669 (1)	**145**
Mrs. Bluebird—Eternity's Children (68)	291
Jr. WALKER [Autry DeWalt, Autry DeWalt Mixon Jr.] ▶ 876 (7)	**5081**
Shotgun—Jr. Walker & The All Stars (65)	*3986*
Hip City - Pt. 2—Jr. Walker & The All Stars (68)	689
Shake And Fingerpop— Jr. Walker & The All Stars (65)	674
Shoot Your Shot—Jr. Walker & The All Stars (67)	405
Do The Boomerang—Jr. Walker & The All Stars (65)	379
Cleo's Mood—Jr. Walker & The All Stars (66)	215
Shotgun—Vanilla Fudge (69)	*193*
Kurt WALKER [Kurtis Blow, Kurtis Walker] ▶ 9340 (2)	**26**
The Breaks (Part 1)—Kurtis Blow (80)	94
Basketball—Kurtis Blow (85)	77
Morgan WALKER ▶ 7093 (1)	**116**
Turn On Your Radar—Prism (82)	116
Reginald WALKER ▶ 10170 (1)	**12**
Bermuda Shorts—Delroys (57)	35

Rob Roy WALKER ▶ 6210 (1)	**193**
Mind Bender—Stillwater (77)	386
Robert Eugene WALKER ▶ 10050 (1)	**13**
She's Got A Whole Number—Keith Herman (79)	27
Ron WALKER ▶ 9294 (1)	**27**
The Game Is Over (What's The Matter With You)— Brown Sugar (76)	54
Shirley WALKER ▶ 10593 (1)	**7.0**
Basketball—Kurtis Blow (85)	77
Stephen WALKER ▶ 8742 (3)	**41**
I Melt With You—Modern English (90)	*107*
I Melt With You—Modern English (83)	*88*
Hands Across The Sea—Modern English (84)	8.5
Steven WALKER [Biscuit] ▶ 10740 (1)	**5.6**
Biscuit's In The House—Biscuit (90)	34
—T-Bone Walker see: Aaron WALKER	
Wayne WALKER ▶ 1139 (13)	**3895**
Are You Sincere—Andy Williams (58)	*2058*
Little Boy Sad—Johnny Burnette (61)	1100
The Cajun Queen—Jimmy Dean (62)	610
Leavin' On Your Mind—Patsy Cline (63)	126
Igmoo (The Pride Of South Central High)— Stonewall Jackson (59)	34
In The Heart Of A Fool—Johnnie Ray (60)	17
Hello Out There—Carl Belew (62)	*13*
Hello Out There—Nick Noble (62)	*13*
Are You Sincere—Trini Lopez (65)	*11*
A Little Heartache—Eddy Arnold (62)	10
Little Miss Belong To No One—Teresa Brewer (61)	4.2
Guess I've Been Around Too Long—Carl Smith (58)	2.9
Fallen Angel—Webb Pierce (60)	0.8
Wiley WALKER ▶ 6975 (1)	**124**
When My Blue Moon Turns To Gold Again— Elvis Presley (56)	249
Bill WALLACE ▶ 4076 (2)	**602**
Clap For The Wolfman—Guess Who (74)	1703
Follow Your Daughter Home—Guess Who (73)	172
Cooky WALLACE ▶ 8436 (1)	**51**
Lover's Prayer—Wallace Brothers (64)	101
Ernest WALLACE Jr. ▶ 8437 (1)	**51**
Lover's Prayer—Wallace Brothers (64)	101
Jerry WALLACE ▶ 9006 (2)	**33**
Life's A Holiday—Jerry Wallace (61)	130
I Told The Stars—Lettermen (62)	1.7
J.L. WALLACE ▶ 2949 (3)	**1105**
Even The Nights Are Better—Air Supply (82)	2400
Touch Me When We're Dancing—Carpenters (81)	*893*
Touch Me When We're Dancing—Bama (79)	*21*
Johnny WALLACE ▶ 10274 (4)	**11**
Mama (He Treats Your Daughter Mean)— Dinning Sisters Featuring Jean Dinning (55)	*31*
Mama (He Treats Your Daughter Mean)— Ruth Brown (62)	*0.9*
(Mama) He Treats Your Daughter Mean— Ruth Brown (55)	*0.0*
Mama (He Treats Your Daughter Mean)— Bette Anne Steele (55)	*0.0*
Gordon WALLER ▶ 8981 (2)	**34**
Don't Pity Me—Peter And Gordon (65)	51
Never Ever—Peter And Gordon (68)	8.7
Jack WALLER ▶ 10187 (1)	**11**
Got A Date With An Angel—Billy Williams (57)	46
Thomas WALLER ▶ 11477 (1) HOF	**1.5**
Ain't Misbehavin'—Johnnie Ray (56)	4.6
Karl WALLINGER ▶ 4529 (1)	**470**
Ship Of Fools (Save Me From Tomorrow)— World Party (87)	470
Byron WALLS ▶ 10622 (1)	**6.7**
Lovin' Naturally—Sandalwood (73)	13
Van WALLS [Harry Van Walls, Harry Eugene Vann] ▶ 4231 (2)	**554**
Chains Of Love—Pat Boone (56)	*798*
Chains Of Love—Bobby Bland (69)	*310*
Bill WALSH ▶ 9279 (2)	**27**
How Will I Know My Love—Annette (58)	*82*
How Will I Know My Love?—Lennon Sisters (58)	*0.0*
Brock WALSH ▶ 2224 (4)	**1723**
Automatic—Pointer Sisters (84)	2321
Wot's It To Ya—Robbie Nevil (87)	988
What Love Is—Marty Balin (83)	90

Mathematics—Melissa Manchester (85)	70
Dan WALSH ▶ 1529 (13)	**2800**
Temptation Eyes—Grass Roots (70)	1969
Heaven Knows—Grass Roots (69)	1417
Glory Bound—Grass Roots (72)	745
Baby Hold On—Grass Roots (70)	728
Love Is What You Make It—Grass Roots (73)	477
Love Pains—Yvonne Elliman (79)	404
The Heartbreak Kid— Bo Donaldson And The Heywoods (74)	198
The Morning Of Our Lives—Arkade (71)	185
I Wouldn't Treat A Dog (The Way You Treated Me)— Bobby Bland (74)	39
Ain't No Love In The Heart Of The City— Bobby Bland (74)	35
Where There's Smoke There's Fire—Grass Roots (73)	16
Deeper And Deeper— Bo Donaldson And The Heywoods (74)	4.6
Sing Out The Love (In My Heart)—Arkade (70)	0.8
James Francis WALSH ▶ 6369 (1)	**178**
Cuz It's You, Girl—James Walsh Gypsy Band (78)	178
Joe WALSH ▶ 958 (11)	**4666**
Life's Been Good—Joe Walsh (78)	1720
Rocky Mountain Way—Joe Walsh (73)	1195
Life In The Fast Lane—Eagles (77)	1068
All Night Long—Joe Walsh (80)	1020
Walk Away—James Gang (71)	499
A Life Of Illusion—Joe Walsh (81)	422
Funk #49—James Gang (70)	355
Midnight Man—James Gang (71)	219
Space Age Whiz Kids—Joe Walsh (83)	203
Meadows—Joe Walsh (73)	90
Turn To Stone—Joe Walsh (75)	64
Mick WALSH ▶ 5139 (2)	**335**
Dirty Cash (Money Talks)— Adventures Of Stevie V (90)	658
Jealousy—Adventures Of Stevie V (91)	12
Steve WALSH ▶ 3059 (9)	**1030**
Point Of Know Return—Kansas (77)	905
All I Wanted—Kansas (86)	801
Portrait (He Knew)—Kansas (78)	238
Lonely Wind—Kansas (79)	118
Got To Rock On—Kansas (80)	61
Power—Kansas (87)	28
If Love Should Go—Streets (83)	19
Every Step Of The Way—Steve Walsh (80)	11
Schemer-Dreamer—Steve Walsh (80)	0.2
—Lee Walter see: Walter Lee MORRIS	
Serge WALTER ▶ 8254 (1)	**57**
All At Once—Don Cornell (54)	114
Douglas WALTERS ▶ 10575 (1)	**7.1**
Red Roses—John Laurenz (55)	14
Jim WALTERS [Walter James] ▶ 11227 (1)	**2.7**
Super Highway—Ballin' Jack (71)	5.3
—Leon S. Walton see: Leon ASHLEY	
Oscar WALTZER ▶ 3377 (1)	**875**
My True Story—Jive Five (61)	2624
Travis WAMMACK ▶ 7439 (2)	**96**
Scratchy—Travis Wammack (64)	165
Greenwood Mississippi—Little Richard (70)	81
Art WANDER ▶ 6037 (1)	**213**
Green Mosquito—Tune Rockers (58)	427
Dexter WANSEL ▶ 7102 (1)	**116**
If Only You Knew—Patti LaBelle (84)	347
Gary WANSTALL ▶ 9068 (1)	**32**
Flyin'—Prism (78)	159
Alan WARD ▶ 8159 (1)	**60**
Ca Plane Pour Moi—Plastic Bertrand (78)	179
Bill WARD ▶ 7275 (2)	**106**
Paranoid—Black Sabbath (70)	212
Iron Man—Black Sabbath (72)	211
Billy WARD [Robert L. Williams] ▶ 4746 (6)	**425**
Sixty Minute Man—Clarence Carter (73)	*349*
Bells—James Brown (60)	126
Have Mercy Baby—Bobbettes (60)	*90*
Sixty Minute Man—Rufus Thomas (70)	*53*
Have Mercy Baby— James Brown And The Famous Flames (64)	*7.2*
Sixty Minute Man—Bill Darnel (60)	*1.6*
Carlos WARD ▶ 5192 (2)	**329**
Express—B.T. Express (75)	*2209*

Express—Ritchie Family (76)	*92*
Christopher WARD ▶ 1897 (2)	**2140**
Black Velvet—Alannah Myles (89)	3820
Love Is—Alannah Myles (90)	461
Gil WARD [Giles Warde] ▶ 6421 (1)	**172**
Tell Her (You Love Her Every Day)— Frank Sinatra (65)	172
Samuel A. WARD ▶ 10919 (1) HOF	**4.4**
America, The Beautiful—Charlie Rich (76)	18
Walter WARD ▶ 5992 (2)	**219**
The Bounce—Olympics (63)	540
Baby, Do The Philly Dog—Olympics (66)	116
—Giles Warde see: Gil WARD	
Cassio WARE ▶ 8365 (1)	**53**
Got A Love For You—Jomanda (91)	318
—Dick Ware see: Roy ALFRED	
—LaVerne Ware see: Gloria JONES	
Leon WARE ▶ 2086 (10)	**1893**
I Wanna Be Where You Are—Michael Jackson (72)	1628
I Want You—Marvin Gaye (76)	*984*
I Want You—Robert Palmer (91)	*499*
If I Ever Lose This Heaven—AWB (75)	335
Lovers After All— Melissa Manchester And Peabo Bryson (81)	149
Up In Heah—Ike & Tina Turner (72)	65
Inside My Love—Minnie Riperton (75)	64
Rolling Down A Mountainside— Main Ingredient (75)	41
After The Dance—Marvin Gaye (76)	36
Got To Have You Back—Isley Brothers (67)	11
Martyn WARE ▶ 10040 (1)	**14**
Let Me Go—Heaven 17 (83)	41
William WARING ▶ 10594 (1)	**7.0**
Basketball—Kurtis Blow (85)	77
Martin WARK ▶ 6559 (1)	**157**
We Love You, Call Collect—Art Linkletter (69)	314
Johnny WARMAN [John Robert Waughman] ▶ 5489 (1)	**279**
Beat Patrol—Starship (87)	279
Pete WARNER [Peter Kessler] ▶ 11704 (1)	**0.6**
Spring Love—Cover Girls (87)	1.1
Bobby WARREN ▶ 4627 (1)	**448**
Groovy Grubworm— Harlow Wilcox And The Oakies (69)	897
Bunny WARREN ▶ 8901 (1)	**36**
Rubberneckin'—Elvis Presley (69)	73
Christian WARREN [Christian Carlos Warren, Osunlade] ▶ 5938 (1)	**225**
Rico Suave—Gerardo (91)	1126
Diane WARREN ▶ 44 (44) HOF	**43927**
Nothing's Gonna Stop Us Now—Starship (87)	4678
Look Away—Chicago (88)	4182
Blame It On The Rain—Milli Vanilli (89)	3458
Love Will Lead You Back—Taylor Dayne (90)	3389
When I See You Smile—Bad English (89)	3290
Rhythm Of The Night—DeBarge (85)	3157
If I Could Turn Back Time—Cher (89)	2821
I Get Weak—Belinda Carlisle (88)	2442
I Don't Wanna Live Without Your Love—Chicago (88)	2262
Time, Love And Tenderness—Michael Bolton (91)	2217
How Can We Be Lovers—Michael Bolton (90)	2141
I'll Be Your Shelter—Taylor Dayne (90)	2022
Just Like Jesse James—Cher (89)	2020
Set The Night To Music—Roberta Flack (91)	1968
Solitaire—Laura Branigan (83)	1808
Who Will You Run To—Heart (87)	1490
When I'm Back On My Feet Again— Michael Bolton (90)	1366
Live For Loving You—Gloria Estefan (91)	1207
When The Night Comes—Joe Cocker (89)	1185
Love And Understanding—Cher (91)	959
Your Baby Never Looked Good In Blue—Exposé (90)	825
Through The Storm— Aretha Franklin And Elton John (89)	756
Save Up All Your Tears—Cher (91)	688
Ghost Town—Cheap Trick (88)	641
I Didn't Want To Need You—Heart (90)	585
Does Anybody Really Fall In Love Anymore?— Kane Roberts (91)	452
Love On A Rooftop—Desmond Child (91)	440
Chasin' The Wind—Chicago (91)	404

Diane WARREN ► 44 (44) HOF Continued	**43927**
It Isn't, It Wasn't, It Ain't Never Gonna Be—Aretha Franklin (89)	303
Ti Amo—Laura Branigan (84)	296
Till Somebody Loves You—Henry Lee Summer (91)	275
Wherever Would I Be—Cheap Trick (90)	214
You're The Story Of My Life—Desmond Child (91)	135
Lonely Is The Night—Air Supply (86)	129
Every Road Leads Back To You—Bette Midler (91)	111
The Heart Is Not So Smart—El DeBarge with DeBarge (85)	106
What Are You Doing With A Fool Like Me—Joe Cocker (90)	59
Don't Lose Any Sleep—John Waite (87)	54
If You Asked Me To—Patti LaBelle (89)	53
And The Night Stood Still—Dion (89)	39
Take It To Heart—Michael McDonald (90)	19
The Same Love—Jets (89)	18
Wishing On The Same Star—Keedy (91)	13
Whenever You Close Your Eyes—Tommy Page (91)	11
Ed WARREN ► 2347 (11)	**1572**
Take Good Care Of Her—Adam Wade (61)	*2184*
Dearer Than Life—Brook Benton (63)	286
One Of The Lucky Ones—Anita Bryant (60)	233
Tonight I Won't Be There—Adam Wade (61)	194
My Little Marine—Jamie Horton (60)	106
Take Good Care Of Her—Mel Carter (66)	*56*
Take Good Care Of Her—Elvis Presley (74)	*41*
Adonis—Terri Stevens (59)	*35*
It's Good To Have You Back With Me—Adam Wade (62)	5.8
Raisin' Sugar Cane—Untouchables (61)	4.3
Adonis—Terri Dean (59)	*0.0*
Guy WARREN ► 6404 (1)	**174**
That Happy Feeling—Bert Kaempfert And His Orchestra (62)	174
Harry WARREN [Salvatore Antonio Guaragna] ► 571 (36) HOF	**7568**
You Must Have Been A Beautiful Baby—Bobby Darin (61)	*2364*
I Only Have Eyes For You—Flamingos (59)	*1735*
I Only Have Eyes For You—Art Garfunkel (75)	*1357*
The More I See You—Chris Montez (66)	1319
September In The Rain—Dinah Washington (61)	1242
An Affair To Remember (Our Love Affair)—Vic Damone (57)	*779*
I Love My Baby (My Baby Loves Me)—Jill Corey (56)	*752*
Innamorata (Sweetheart)—Dean Martin (56)	*695*
Innamorata (Sweetheart)—Jerry Vale (56)	*652*
At Last—Etta James (61)	*639*
Chattanooga Choo Choo—Floyd Cramer (62)	*556*
There Will Never Be Another You—Chris Montez (66)	527
You Must Have Been A Beautiful Baby—Dave Clark Five (67)	*455*
Chattanooga Choo Choo—Harpers Bizarre (67)	*339*
Chattanooga Choo Choo—Tuxedo Junction (78)	*307*
The Rose Tattoo—Perry Como (55)	*286*
Chattanooga Choo Choo—Ernie Fields Orch. (60)	*228*
I Only Have Eyes For You—Lettermen (66)	*122*
I Only Have Eyes For You—Jerry Butler (72)	*113*
Separate Tables—Vic Damone (59)	*18*
You'll Never Know—Shirley Bassey with the Rita Williams Singers (61)	16
An Affair To Remember (Our Love Affair)—Nat "King" Cole (57)	*15*
At Last—Frank Barber Orchestra (82)	*14*
Chattanooga Choo Choo—Frank Barber Orchestra (82)	*14*
I've Got A Gal In Kalamazoo—Frank Barber Orchestra (82)	14
Dormi Dormi Dormi—Eydie Gorme (58)	6.7
I Only Have Eyes For You—Cliff Richard (64)	*5.3*
At Last—Percy Faith and his Orchestra (61)	*2.5*
Innamorata—Frank Verna (56)	*0.0*
Separate Tables—Eydie Gorme (58)	*0.0*
An Affair To Remember—ViVienne (57)	*0.0*
The Rose Tattoo—Percy Faith & His Orchestra (55)	*0.0*
An Affair To Remember—Pete King & His Orchestra (57)	*0.0*
An Affair To Remember (Our Love Affair)—Angela Drake (57)	*0.0*
An Affair To Remember (Our Love Affair)—Carmen Cavallaro (57)	*0.0*

I Love My Baby (My Baby Loves Me)—Benny Strong & His Orchestra (57)	*0.0*
James Edward WARREN ► 3286 (1)	**911**
Everybody's Got To Learn Sometime—Korgis (80)	911
Norman WARREN ► 8723 (1)	**41**
Martinique—Exotic Sounds Of Martin Denny (59)	41
David WAS [David Jay Weiss] ► 3148 (4)	**984**
Walk The Dinosaur—Was (Not Was) (89)	1386
Spy In The House Of Love—Was (Not Was) (88)	745
Where Did Your Heart Go?—Wham! (86)	232
Anything Can Happen—Was (Not Was) (89)	100
Don WAS [Don Edward Fagenson] ► 3149 (4)	**984**
Walk The Dinosaur—Was (Not Was) (89)	1386
Spy In The House Of Love—Was (Not Was) (88)	745
Where Did Your Heart Go?—Wham! (86)	232
Anything Can Happen—Was (Not Was) (89)	100
Lalomie WASHBURN ► 5440 (1)	**289**
At Midnight (My Love Will Lift You Up)—Rufus Featuring Chaka Khan (77)	577
—Baby Washington see: Jeanette WASHINGTON	
Carrol WASHINGTON ► 1968 (2)	**2044**
Mr. Big Stuff—Jean Knight (71)	5978
You Think You're Hot Stuff—Jean Knight (71)	154
Dinah WASHINGTON [Ruth Lee Jones] ► 7492 (4)	**92**
We Have Love—Dinah Washington (60)	152
It's A Mean Old Man's World—Dinah Washington (62)	26
Soulville—Aretha Franklin (68)	*24*
Soulville—Dinah Washington (63)	*6.8*
Earl WASHINGTON ► 11727 (1)	**0.4**
Just A Little Bit—Little Milton (69)	3.1
Ferdinand WASHINGTON ► 1612 (14)	**2623**
I'll Be Home—Pat Boone (56)	*3005*
Pledging My Love—Johnny Ace (55)	*1021*
Pledging My Love—Roy Hamilton (58)	*609*
Pledging My Love—Johnny Tillotson (60)	*221*
Pledging My Love—Teresa Brewer (55)	*160*
Get Off My Back Woman—B.B. King (69)	144
Black Nights—Lowell Fulsom (65)	38
I'll Be Home—Platters (66)	*10*
I'll Be Home—Flamingos (56)	*0.0*
Pledging My Love—Four Lads (55)	*0.0*
Pledging My Love—Tommy Mara (55)	*0.0*
Pledging My Love—Jesse Belvin (58)	*0.0*
Pledging My Love—Sanford Clark (60)	*0.0*
Pledging My Love—Ronnie Gaylord (55)	*0.0*
Freddie WASHINGTON ► 5019 (3)	**358**
Forget Me Nots—Patrice Rushen (82)	752
Haven't You Heard—Patrice Rushen (80)	293
Feels So Real (Won't Let Go)—Patrice Rushen (84)	69
Jeanette WASHINGTON [Baby Washington, Justine Washington] ► 6299 (4)	**184**
Nobody Cares (About Me)—Jeanette (Baby) Washington (61)	170
Who's Going To Take Care Of Me—Justine Washington (64)	9.2
Let Love Go By—Jeanette (Baby) Washington (61)	4.3
The Clock—Baby Washington (64)	0.9
Joel WASHINGTON ► 8366 (1)	**53**
Got A Love For You—Jomanda (91)	318
—Joyce Washington see: Joyce KENNEDY	
—Justine Washington see: Jeanette WASHINGTON	
Keith WASHINGTON ► 7202 (1)	**110**
Kissing You—Keith Washington (91)	331
Kendrick WASHINGTON ► 11618 (1)	**1.0**
Love Me Just For Me—Special Generation (90)	6.8
Ned WASHINGTON ► 1646 (30) HOF	**2551**
Town Without Pity—Gene Pitney (61)	2139
Hajji Baba (Persian Lament)—Nat "King" Cole (54)	923
Wild Is The Wind—Johnny Mathis (57)	*824*
When You Wish Upon A Star—Dion And The Belmonts (60)	*609*
To Love Again—Four Aces (56)	*408*
Strange Are The Ways Of Love—Gogi Grant (58)	*178*
Strange Lady In Town—Frankie Laine (55)	*61*
Man From Laramie—Voices Of Walter Schumann (55)	*47*
When You Wish Upon A Star—Joni James (55)	*33*
My Foolish Heart—Demensions (63)	29
I'm Gettin' Sentimental Over You—Nelson Riddle and His Orchestra (58)	*18*

Make Me A Child Again—Frankie Laine (56)	12
Fire Down Below—Jeri Southern (57)	*8.4*
Fire Down Below—Roger King Mozian (57)	*8.4*
The Fall Of Love—Johnny Mathis (64)	5.9
I'm Gettin' Sentimental Over You—Modernaires (57)	*1.9*
Love Me—Billy Eckstine (54)	0.0
To Love Again—Vic Damone (56)	*0.0*
To Love Again—Bob Manning (56)	*0.0*
To Love Again—Marc Fredericks (56)	*0.0*
To Love Again—Carmen Cavallaro (56)	*0.0*
The Man From Laramie—Al Martino (55)	*0.0*
The Man From Laramie—Ralph Young (55)	*0.0*
The High And The Mighty—Johnny Desmond (54)	*0.0*
When You Wish Upon A Star—Cliff Edwards (55)	*0.0*
Strange Are The Ways Of Love—Randy Sparks (58)	*0.0*
The Man From Laramie—Eddy Howard & His Orchestra (55)	*0.0*
The Unforgiven (The Need For Love)—McGuire Sisters (60)	*0.0*
When You Wish Upon A Star—Rosemary Clooney & Harry James (55)	*0.0*
When You Wish Upon A Star—Jack Pleis and His Orchestra and Chorus (55)	*0.0*
Patti WASHINGTON ► 5494 (2)	**279**
Gidget—James Darren (59)	*542*
Gidget—Four Preps (58)	*15*
Stephen C. WASHINGTON ► 6997 (3)	**123**
Slide—Slave (77)	640
Watching You—Slave (80)	129
Make Up Your Mind—Aurra (82)	78
Tom WASHINGTON ► 10502 (1)	**7.8**
Funky Chicken—Willie Henderson And The Soul Explosions (70)	23
Pete WATERMAN ► 1064 (15)	**4156**
Never Gonna Give You Up—Rick Astley (87)	4405
Together Forever (Remix)—Rick Astley (88)	3168
I Heard A Rumour—Bananarama (87)	2288
This Time I Know It's For Real—Donna Summer (89)	1582
It Would Take A Strong Strong Man—Rick Astley (88)	1136
I Should Be So Lucky—Kylie Minogue (88)	512
It's No Secret—Kylie Minogue (88)	419
I Can't Help It—Bananarama (87)	331
Love In The First Degree—Bananarama (88)	262
More Than Physical—Bananarama (86)	74
Love, Truth And Honesty—Bananarama (88)	64
Showing Out (Get Fresh At The Weekend)—Mel & Kim (87)	51
Nothing's Gonna Stop Me Now—Samantha Fox (87)	50
Wouldn't Change A Thing—Kylie Minogue (90)	19
Love's About To Change My Heart—Donna Summer (89)	12
Chris WATERS [Christopher Waters Dunn, Chris Dunn] ► 2850 (1)	**1154**
Sexy Eyes—Dr. Hook (80)	3462
Crystal WATERS ► 4711 (1)	**433**
Gypsy Woman (She's Homeless)—Crystal Waters (91)	867
Ervan WATERS ► 10458 (1)	**8.2**
Here's A Heart—Diplomats (64)	25
Miles WATERS ► 10503 (2)	**7.8**
Some Come Running—Jim Capaldi (88)	19
My One Temptation—Mica Paris (89)	4.6
Roger WATERS ► 341 (4)	**10931**
Another Brick In The Wall (Part 2)—Pink Floyd (80)	9336
Money—Pink Floyd (73)	1535
Run Like Hell—Pink Floyd (80)	96
Us And Them—Pink Floyd (74)	23
Alton WATKINS ► 11777(1)	**0.1**
Bad, Bold And Beautiful Girl—Persuaders (73)	0.4
Tom WATKINS ► 10323 (1)	**10**
When Will I Be Famous—Bros (88)	20
Viola WATKINS ► 9003 (2)	**33**
Gee—Pixies Three (64)	*90*
Gee—Jan & Dean (60)	*44*
Wanda WATKINS ► 6056 (1)	**211**
Country Wine—Raiders (72)	422
Nicholas WATKINSON ► 9409 (1)	**24**
Back Of My Hand (I've Got Your Number)—Jags (80)	48
Jody WATLEY ► 756 (9)	**5798**
Looking For A New Love—Jody Watley (87)	4041
Real Love—Jody Watley (89)	3609
Don't You Want Me—Jody Watley (87)	2205

Jody WATLEY ▶ 756 (9) *Continued*	**5798**
Friends—Jody Watley (89)	1337
Some Kind Of Lover—Jody Watley (88)	1295
I Want You—Jody Watley (91)	205
Still A Thrill—Jody Watley (87)	148
Full Of Fire—Shalamar (80)	136
Precious Love—Jody Watley (90)	70
Bo WATSON [Boaz Watson] ▶ 3089 (6)	**1015**
Rock Steady—Whispers (87)	1571
Operator—Midnight Star (84)	854
Midas Touch—Midnight Star (86)	347
Meeting In The Ladies Room—Klymaxx (85)	193
Body Talk—Deele (84)	140
Scientific Love—Midnight Star (85)	60
—Boaz Watson see: Bo WATSON	
Bruce William WATSON ▶ 5171 (3)	**332**
In A Big Country—Big Country (83)	1155
Fields Of Fire—Big Country (84)	159
Wonderland—Big Country (84)	12
Deek WATSON ▶ 5481 (3)	**280**
(I Love You) For Sentimental Reasons—Sam Cooke (57)	*396*
For Sentimental Reasons—Cleftones (61)	*165*
For Sentimental Reasons—Spaniels (61)	*0.0*
Doc WATSON ▶ 9882 (1)	**16**
Valley To Pray—Arlo Guthrie (70)	62
Jeff WATSON ▶ 4814 (1)	**408**
Goodbye—Night Ranger (85)	815
Johnny WATSON [Johnny Guitar Watson, John Jacob Watson] ▶ 4444 (3)	**493**
A Real Mother For Ya—Johnny "Guitar" Watson (77)	349
Don't Change Horses (In The Middle Of A Stream)—Tower Of Power (74)	284
I Don't Want To Be A Lone Ranger—Johnny "Guitar" Watson (75)	2.2
—June Watson see: June Watson WILLIAMS	
Martyn WATSON ▶ 10784 (1)	**5.3**
Make Out Alright—Divinyls (91)	16
Maybelle WATSON ▶ 5253 (3)	**318**
My Melancholy Baby—Tommy Edwards (59)	*830*
My Melancholy Baby—Marcels (62)	*123*
My Melancholy Baby—Willie Gibson & The Boys (55)	*0.0*
Robert WATSON ▶ 11025 (1)	**3.8**
Love On The Airwaves—Night (81)	7.5
Stan WATSON ▶ 10311 (1)	**10**
He Don't Really Love You—Delfonics (68)	30
Wilbert WATSON ▶ 10001 (1)	**14**
I Still Love You—Fats Domino (57)	57
Sam WATTERS ▶ 1751 (3)	**2368**
All 4 Love—Color Me Badd (91)	5388
I Wanna Sex You Up—Color Me Badd (91)	4560
I Adore Mi Amor—Color Me Badd (91)	4094
Garth WATT-ROY ▶ 6716 (1)	**142**
Magic Woman Touch—Hollies (73)	284
Charlie WATTS ▶ 11715 (1)	**0.5**
Play With Fire—Rolling Stones (65)	2.3
—Clem Watts see: Al TRACE	
Erskin WATTS ▶ 9413 (1)	**24**
It's Better To Have (And Don't Need)—Don Covay (74)	48
Glenn WATTS ▶ 9089 (1)	**32**
Is It Because I'm Black—Syl Johnson (69)	95
Mayme WATTS ▶ 4608 (8)	**451**
Midnight Flyer—Nat "King" Cole (59)	597
Alright Okay You Win—Peggy Lee (59)	145
Give Me Your Love—Nat "King" Cole (59)	74
Ooh What A Day—Sarah Vaughan (60)	28
Truly Love—Johnny Nash (58)	22
Point Of No Return—Adam Wade (61)	21
So Will I—Ames Brothers (55)	8.1
Since I Made You Cry—Rivieras (1) (60)	6.2
Nathan WATTS ▶ 5598 (1)	**267**
Free—Deniece Williams (76)	1067
Noble WATTS ▶ 7730 (1)	**77**
Hard Times (The Slop)—Noble "Thin Man" Watts & His Rhythm Sparks (57)	77
Robert WATZ ▶ 8099 (1)	**62**
Got To Get—Leila K with Rob 'N' Raz (90)	248
—John Robert Waughman see: Johnny WARMAN	

Franz WAXMAN [Franz Wachsmann] ▶ 10464 (3)	**8.1**
Theme From Taras Bulba (The Wishing Star)—Jerry Butler (62)	*16*
Theme From Taras Bulba (The Wishing Star)—Maxine Starr (62)	*0.0*
Theme From Taras Bulba (The Wishing Star)—Ferrante & Teicher (62)	*0.0*
Jeff WAXMAN ▶ 10713 (1)	**5.9**
Love On The Phone—Suzanne Fellini (80)	24
Dave WAY ▶ 3167 (1)	**973**
I Like The Way (The Kissing Game)—Hi-Five (91)	2919
Pete WAY ▶ 11459 (1)	**1.6**
Too Hot To Handle—UFO (77)	3.2
Fee WAYBILL [John Waldo Waybill] ▶ 2588 (5)	**1346**
She's A Beauty—Tubes (83)	1661
Too Late To Say Goodbye—Richard Marx (90)	919
Edge Of A Broken Heart—Vixen (88)	570
Don't Want To Wait Anymore—Tubes (81)	377
Piece By Piece—Tubes (85)	10
—John Waldo Waybill see: Fee WAYBILL	
—Eunice Kathleen Waymon see: Nina SIMONE	
Artie WAYNE [Wayne Douglas Kent] ▶ 3094 (5)	**1012**
Midnight Mary—Joey Powers (63)	1854
3000 Miles—Brian Hyland (66)	56
Flashback—5th Dimension (73)	*55*
Mommy And Daddy Were Twistin'—Susan Summers (62)	2.7
Flashback—Paul Anka (73)	*0.3*
Bernie WAYNE [Bernard Weitzner] ▶ 789 (9)	**5622**
Blue Velvet—Bobby Vinton (63)	*8754*
Little Red Rented Rowboat—Joe Dowell (62)	637
I Don't Want To See Tomorrow—Nat King Cole (64)	637
Port Au Prince—Nelson Riddle And His Orchestra (56)	*489*
Dum Dum Dee Dum—Johnny Cymbal (63)	100
You Forgot All The Words—Frank Sinatra (56)	79
Blue Velvet—Statues (60)	*46*
Where Were You When I Needed You—Jerry Vale (65)	11
Port-Au-Prince—Winifred Atwell with Frank Chacksfield & His Orchestra (56)	*0.0*
Curtis WAYNE [Curtis Wayne Seals] ▶ 6748 (1)	**141**
Love Bug—Jack Jones (65)	281
Dig WAYNE [Timothy Wayne Ball] ▶ 5880 (1)	**233**
Just Got Lucky—JoBoxers (83)	467
Don WAYNE ▶ 9315 (1)	**26**
Saginaw, Michigan—Lefty Frizzell (64)	53
Dottie WAYNE ▶ 2551 (2)	**1392**
The Night Has A Thousand Eyes—Bobby Vee (62)	4114
(There'll Come A Day When) Ev'ry Little Bit Hurts—Bobby Vee (64)	63
—Edith Wayne see: Brian HOLLAND	
—Edith Wayne see: Eddie HOLLAND	
—Edith Wayne see: Lamont DOZIER	
Jeff WAYNE ▶ 5649 (2)	**260**
Forever Autumn—Justin Hayward (78)	531
Men Of Learning—Vigrass & Osborne (72)	249
Mabel WAYNE ▶ 4541 (11) HOF	**468**
In A Little Spanish Town ('twas On A Night Like This)—Bing Crosby And The Buddy Cole Trio (56)	*365*
In A Little Spanish Town—Russ Carlyle And His Orchestra (54)	*247*
Ramona—Blue Diamonds (60)	*152*
In A Little Spanish Town—Smith Brothers (54)	*30*
In A Little Spanish Town—Blue Diamonds (61)	*23*
Ramona—Lancers (57)	*3.0*
It Happened In Monterey—Lancers (57)	3.0
In A Little Spanish Town Cha Cha—Sy Oliver (58)	*3.0*
In A Little Spanish Town—Al Lombardy (54)	*0.0*
In A Little Spanish Town—David Carroll & His Orchestra (54)	*0.0*
In A Little Spanish Town ('Twas On A Night Like This)—Lawrence Welk & His Sparklers (54)	*0.0*
Randy WAYNE ▶ 8023 (1)	**65**
Another Heartache—Rod Stewart (86)	259
Sid WAYNE [Sidney Weinberg] ▶ 338 (32)	**10993**
See You In September—Happenings (66)	*5461*
I Need Your Love Tonight—Elvis Presley (59)	2712

It's Impossible—Perry Como (70)	*2155*
I'm Gonna Knock On Your Door—Eddie Hodges (61)	1994
Two Different Worlds—Don Rondo (56)	*1457*
Do The Clam—Elvis Presley With The Jordanaires Jubilee Four & Carole Lombard Trio (65)	929
See You In September—Tempos (59)	*829*
Flaming Star—Elvis Presley With The Jordanaires (61)	770
First Anniversary—Cathy Carr (59)	736
My Love For You—Johnny Mathis (60)	679
Mangos—Rosemary Clooney (57)	*654*
Ninety Nine Years (Dead Or Alive)—Guy Mitchell (56)	635
Winner Take All—Platters (56)	*635*
Spinout—Elvis Presley With The Jordanaires (66)	614
Two Different Worlds—Roger Williams And Jane Morgan (56)	*427*
Two Different Worlds—Lenny Welch (65)	*403*
It's Impossible—New Birth (71)	*400*
It's Only The Beginning—Kalin Twins (59)	312
Fish—Mindy Carson (55)	248
Lover Doll—Elvis Presley with the Jordanaires (58)	192
Biology—Danny Valentino (60)	*106*
If I'm Elected—Eddie Fisher (56)	54
As Long As I Have You—Don Rondo (58)	49
Slowly But Surely—Elvis Presley With The Jordanaires (65)	23
Two Different Worlds—Dick Haymes (56)	*11*
Das Ist Musik—Bill Hayes (56)	6.7
Language Of Love—Cindy And Lindy (57)	6.4
Crossroads Of Love—Tempos Featuring Mike Lazo (59)	1.2
Biology—Sue Raney (60)	*0.0*
Winner Take All—Sunny Gale (56)	*0.0*
Two Different Worlds—Dick Kallman (56)	*0.0*
Mangos—Buddy Morrow & His Orchestra (57)	*0.0*
Vincent WAYNE ▶ 9693 (1)	**19**
Live Your Life Before You Die—Pointer Sisters (75)	57
Fred WEATHERLY ▶ 2619 (7)	**1318**
Danny Boy—Conway Twitty (59)	*2086*
Danny Boy—Andy Williams (61)	*282*
Danny Boy—Ray Price (67)	*193*
Danny Boy—Patti LaBelle And Her Blue Belles (64)	*32*
Danny Boy—Joni James (56)	*31*
Danny Boy—Jackie Wilson (65)	*9.5*
Roses Of Picardy—Buddy Greco (61)	3.3
Jim WEATHERLY ▶ 191 (13) HOF	**16277**
Midnight Train To Georgia—Gladys Knight & The Pips (73)	5397
Neither One Of Us (Wants To Be The First To Say Goodbye)—Gladys Knight & The Pips (73)	4554
Best Thing That Ever Happened To Me—Gladys Knight & The Pips (74)	*3746*
The Need To Be—Jim Weatherly (74)	1131
Where Peaceful Waters Flow—Gladys Knight & The Pips (73)	697
Love Finds Its Own Way—Gladys Knight & The Pips (75)	324
Between Her Goodbye And My Hello—Gladys Knight & The Pips (74)	131
You're The Best Thing That Ever Happened To Me—Ray Price (73)	*81*
Best Thing That Ever Happened To Me—Persuaders (74)	*79*
I'll Still Love You—Jim Weatherly (75)	64
You Are A Song—Batdorf & Rodney (75)	48
Loving You Is Just An Old Habit—Jim Weatherly (72)	13
My First Day Without Her—Dennis Yost And The Classics IV (75)	13
William WEATHERSPOON ▶ 1682 (9)	**2497**
What Becomes Of The Brokenhearted—Jimmy Ruffin (66)	2895
I've Passed This Way Before—Jimmy Ruffin (66)	1244
I'm Not My Brother's Keeper—Flaming Ember (70)	894
Women's Love Rights—Laura Lee (71)	705
Rip Off—Laura Lee (72)	327
I'll Say Forever My Love—Jimmy Ruffin (68)	136
It's So Hard Being A Loser—Contours (67)	136
I Am The Man For You Baby—Edwin Starr (68)	13
Love And Liberty—Laura Lee (72)	2.7
Blue WEAVER [Derek John Weaver] ▶ 2054 (3)	**1942**
(Our Love) Don't Throw It All Away—Andy Gibb (78)	2401
Hold On To My Love—Jimmy Ruffin (80)	1303
Help Me!—Marcy Levy & Robin Gibb (80)	180
—Derek John Weaver see: Blue WEAVER	

Jerry WEAVER ▶ 4319 (1)	**523**
I've Been Lonely For So Long—Frederick Knight (72)	1046
—Bernard Webb see: Paul McCARTNEY	
Danny WEBB ▶ 1930 (3)	**2094**
One Summer Night—Danleers (58)	*1599*
One Summer Night—Diamonds (61)	*448*
I Really Love You—Danleers (58)	47
—Gary Anthony James Webb see: Gary NUMAN	
—Harry Rodger Webb see: Cliff RICHARD	
Jay WEBB ▶ 10432 (1)	**8.6**
Old Slew Foot—Johnny Horton (61)	26
Jimmy WEBB ▶ 56 (37) HOF	**37215**
Mac Arthur Park—Donna Summer (78)	*6578*
Wichita Lineman—Glen Campbell (68)	*5760*
MacArthur Park—Richard Harris (68)	*5285*
Worst That Could Happen—Brooklyn Bridge (68)	4091
Galveston—Glen Campbell (69)	*3812*
Up-Up And Away—5th Dimension (67)	*2856*
All I Know—Garfunkel (73)	1911
Honey Come Back—Glen Campbell (70)	1317
Where's The Playground Susie—Glen Campbell (69)	971
By The Time I Get To Phoenix—Glen Campbell (67)	*811*
Carpet Man—5th Dimension (68)	662
Paper Cup—5th Dimension (67)	501
Mac Arthur Park (Part II)—Four Tops (71)	*486*
The Girls' Song—5th Dimension (70)	376
By The Time I Get To Phoenix—Isaac Hayes (69)	*341*
The Yard Went On Forever—Richard Harris (68)	302
Easy For You To Say—Linda Ronstadt (83)	192
Up-Up And Away—Hugh Masekela (67)	*169*
Do What You Gotta Do—Bobby Vee (68)	*145*
Didn't We—Richard Harris (69)	*141*
Didn't We—Barbra Streisand (72)	*131*
Mixed Up Guy—Joey Scarbury (71)	66
Do What You Gotta Do—Nina Simone (68)	*55*
By The Time I Get To Phoenix—Mad Lads (69)	*43*
First Hymn From Grand Terrace—Mark Lindsay (69)	39
By The Time I Get To Phoenix—Glen Campbell (71)	*38*
Montage From How Sweet It Is (I Know That You Know)—Love Generation (68)	*37*
Song Seller—Raiders (72)	24
Montage—Picardy (68)	*16*
Up-Up And Away—Johnny Mann Singers (67)	*13*
You're So Young—Shane Martin (68)	13
Do What You Gotta Do—Al Wilson (68)	*12*
MacArthur Park—Waylon Jennings And The Kimberlys (69)	*9.8*
Galveston—Roger Williams (69)	*6.0*
Wichita Lineman—Sergio Mendes & Brasil '66 (69)	*3.5*
MacArthur Park—Al Capps Band (70)	*0.8*
It's A Sin When You Love Somebody—Joe Cocker (75)	0.0
Laura WEBB [Laura Webb Childress] ▶ 4358 (2)	**514**
Mr Lee—Bobbettes (57)	*2273*
I Shot Mr Lee—Bobbettes (60)	*297*
William WEBB ▶ 6276 (1)	**187**
Competition Ain't Nothin'—Little Carl Carlton (68)	374
Andrew Lloyd WEBBER ▶ 1544 (15) HOF	**2754**
Superstar—Murray Head With The Trinidad Singers (69)	*1860*
I Don't Know How To Love Him—Helen Reddy (71)	*1613*
I Don't Know How To Love Him—Yvonne Elliman (71)	*783*
Superstar - Jesus Christ Superstar—Murray Head (71)	*656*
Memory—Barry Manilow (82)	*493*
Memory - The Theme From Andrew Lloyd Webber's Musical ''Cats''—Barbra Streisand (82)	*228*
Don't Cry For Me Argentina—Festival (80)	63
Everything's Alright—Yvonne Elliman (71)	*28*
Christmas Dream—Perry Como (74)	13
Superstar—Assembled Multitude (71)	*4.1*
The Temple—Assembled Multitude (71)	4.1
Simon Zealotes—Assembled Multitude (71)	4.1
Everything's Alright—Assembled Multitude (71)	*4.1*
Everything's Alright—Kimberlys (71)	*0.4*
I Don't Know How To Love Him—Kimberlys (71)	*0.4*
Lloyd WEBBER ▶ 8114 (2)	**61**
Hold On—Radiants (68)	92
Wanted: Lover, No Experience Necessary—Laura Lee (67)	30
Felix WEBER ▶ 5739 (1)	**247**
Symptoms Of True Love—Tracie Spencer (88)	494

—Allen Webster see: Lew DOUGLAS	
Danny WEBSTER ▶ 7398 (3)	**98**
Slide—Slave (77)	640
Watching You—Slave (80)	129
Just A Touch Of Love—Slave (80)	10
Greg WEBSTER ▶ 5453 (4)	**285**
Funky Worm—Ohio Players (73)	1438
Ecstasy—Ohio Players (73)	621
Pain (Part 1)—Ohio Players (71)	208
Got Pleasure—Ohio Players (72)	14
Paul Francis WEBSTER ▶ 211 (66) HOF	**15327**
Love Is A Many Splendored Thing—Four Aces (55)	*8585*
April Love—Pat Boone (57)	5035
Friendly Persuasion (Thee I Love)—Pat Boone (56)	*2555*
Honey Babe—Art Mooney And His Orchestra (55)	*2294*
The Twelfth Of Never—Donny Osmond (73)	*2152*
Somewhere, My Love—Ray Conniff And The Singers (66)	*1994*
Padre—Toni Arden (58)	*1727*
A Certain Smile—Johnny Mathis (58)	*1228*
I'll Remember Tonight—Pat Boone (58)	749
Secret Love—Freddy Fender (75)	*697*
Ballad Of The Alamo—Marty Robbins (60)	*694*
Anastasia—Pat Boone (56)	*671*
Secret Love—Billy Stewart (66)	*556*
The Twelfth Of Never—Johnny Mathis (57)	*421*
Friendly Persuasion (Thee I Love)—Four Aces (56)	*389*
Love Is A Many-Splendored Thing—Don Cornell (55)	*365*
The Green Leaves Of Summer—Brothers Four (60)	*304*
A Very Precious Love—Ames Brothers (58)	*280*
Veni-Vidi-Vici (I Came, I Saw, I Conquered)—Gaylords (54)	256
Shenandoah Rose—Hugo & Luigi (57)	*197*
Ballad Of The Alamo—Bud And Travis (60)	*190*
A Little Love Can Go A Long Long Way—Dream Weavers Featuring Wade Buff (56)	*184*
(The Song Of) Raintree County—Nat "King" Cole (57)	154
If You Wanna See Mamie Tonight—Ames Brothers (56)	97
Sweet Thursday—Johnny Mathis (62)	90
Too Beautiful To Last—Engelbert Humperdinck (72)	85
Who Are We—Gogi Grant (56)	64
Giant—Les Baxter with His Chorus and Orchestra (56)	*54*
The Shadow Of Your Smile—Boots Randolph (66)	*39*
The Fountain Of Youth—Four Lads (59)	37
Love Is A Many-Splendored Thing—Four Preps (62)	*24*
Marianna—Johnny Mathis (62)	20
Secret Love—Jimmy Ricks (59)	*19*
Giant—Art Mooney and His Orchestra and Chorus (56)	*17*
Laurie, My Love—Johnny Mathis (61)	17
Giant—Jack Pleis and His Orchestra and Chorus (56)	*11*
Love Theme From "The Sandpiper" (The Shadow Of Your Smile)—Tony Bennett (65)	*10*
Rio Bravo—Dean Martin (59)	9.1
Bluebell—Mitch Miller and His Orchestra and Chorus (58)	*5.9*
A Farewell To Arms—Gale Storm (58)	*3.1*
A Farewell To Arms—Marty Gold & His Orchestra (58)	*3.1*
Love Is A Many Splendored Thing—Don, Dick N' Jimmy (55)	*2.3*
Padre—Valerie Carr (58)	*0.0*
Giant—Jimmy Wakely (56)	*0.0*
Giant—Rusty Draper (56)	*0.0*
Padre—Sarah Vaughan (58)	*0.0*
Blue Bell—Scott Engel (58)	*0.0*
Secret Love—Doris Day (54)	*0.0*
A Certain Smile—Sunny Gale (58)	*0.0*
Shenandoah Rose—Peter Hanley (57)	*0.0*
A Certain Smile—Jerry Fuller (58)	*0.0*
A Certain Smile—Andy Russell (58)	*0.0*
A Certain Smile—Milton Sparks (58)	*0.0*
A Very Precious Love—Doris Day (58)	*0.0*
Shenandoah Rose—Johnny Desmond (57)	*0.0*
A Very Precious Love—Jack Jones (58)	*0.0*
A Very Precious Love—Bonnie Guitar (58)	*0.0*
Honey Babe—Sauter-Finegan Orchestra (55)	*0.0*
Shenandoah Rose—Jack Halloran Singers (57)	*0.0*
A Very Precious Love—Johnston Brothers (58)	*0.0*
The Green Leaves Of Summer—Bud & Travis (60)	*0.0*
The Guns Of Navarone—Mitch Miller and The Gang (61)	*0.0*

Giant—Ray Heindorf & The Warner Bros. Orchestra (56)	*0.0*
Friendly Persuasion (Thee I Love)—Anthony Perkins (56)	*0.0*
A Little Love Can Go A Long, Long Way—Johnny Desmond (56)	*0.0*
Love Theme From "Giant" (There's Never Been Anyone Else But You)—David Carroll & His Orchestra (56)	*0.0*
Ron WEBSTER ▶ 4082 (1)	**599**
The Last Farewell—Roger Whittaker (75)	1198
Warwick WEBSTER ▶ 2727 (4)	**1239**
Man In The Raincoat—Priscilla Wright (55)	*1239*
Man In The Raincoat—Marion Marlowe (55)	*0.0*
The Man In The Raincoat—Karen Chandler (55)	*0.0*
The Man In The Raincoat—Lita Roza with Bob Sharples & His Music (55)	*0.0*
—Paul Wechselmann see: Paul MANN	
Murray WECHT [Morris C. Wecht] ▶ 5578 (5)	**269**
Wind In The Willow—Jo Stafford (57)	*335*
If I Should Lose You—Dreamlovers (62)	209
Inky Dinky Spider (The Spider Song)—Kids Next Door (65)	111
Drummer Man—Nancy Sinatra (69)	4.9
Wind In The Willow—Ann Reynolds (57)	*0.0*
Julius WECHTER ▶ 3604 (1)	**771**
Spanish Flea—Herb Alpert & The Tijuana Brass (66)	771
—David L. Weck see: Henry WECK	
Henry WECK [David L. Weck] ▶ 6122 (2)	**203**
Kings Of The Party—Brownsville Station (74)	474
The Martian Boogie—Brownsville Station (77)	180
Sam WEEDMAN ▶ 6228 (1)	**191**
Baby Makes Her Blue Jeans Talk—Dr. Hook (82)	574
Gary WEEKS ▶ 9815 (1)	**16**
Could You Ever Love Me Again—Gary & Dave (73)	33
Ralph WEEKS ▶ 6137 (1)	**201**
Something I Want To Tell You—Johnny and The Expressions (66)	201
Ricardo WEEKS ▶ 4837 (1)	**401**
I Wonder Why—Dion and The Belmonts (58)	802
Hermon WEEMS ▶ 4039 (3)	**617**
You've Got To Pay The Price—Al Kent (67)	*605*
You Got To Pay The Price—Gloria Taylor (69)	*591*
Show Time—Detroit Emeralds (68)	57
Ted WEEMS ▶ 9553 (1)	**21**
Why Do I—Lee Andrews And The Hearts (58)	43
Eric WEIDEMAN ▶ 11756 (1)	**0.2**
That's When I Think Of You—1927 (89)	0.4
John WEIDER ▶ 2916 (5)	**1119**
San Franciscan Nights—Eric Burdon And The Animals (67)	1697
Sky Pilot (Part One)—Eric Burdon & The Animals (68)	1609
When I Was Young—Eric Burdon & The Animals (67)	1085
Monterey—Eric Burdon & The Animals (67)	1017
Anything—Eric Burdon & The Animals (68)	187
—George William Weidler see: George WILDER	
—Walter Wolfgang Weidler see: Walter WILDER	
—Warren Weidler see: Warner WILDER	
Dick WEIGAND ▶ 3749 (2)	**712**
Evil Woman Don't Play Your Games With Me—Crow (69)	1457
Cottage Cheese—Crow (70)	453
Larry WEIGAND ▶ 4475 (1)	**486**
Evil Woman Don't Play Your Games With Me—Crow (69)	1457
Cynthia WEIL ▶ 49 (89) HOF	**41510**
You've Lost That Lovin' Feelin'—Righteous Brothers (64)	*9450*
(You're My) Soul And Inspiration—Righteous Brothers (66)	*7442*
Don't Know Much—Linda Ronstadt (89)	*4540*
Kicks—Paul Revere And The Raiders Featuring Mark Lindsay (66)	4107
He's So Shy—Pointer Sisters (80)	4023
Never Gonna Let You Go—Sergio Mendes (83)	3746
Blame It On The Bossa Nova—Eydie Gorme (63)	3142
Here You Come Again—Dolly Parton (77)	2755
Somewhere Out There—Linda Ronstadt And James Ingram (86)	2590
My Dad—Paul Petersen (62)	2461
On Broadway—George Benson (78)	*1964*

Cynthia WEIL ▶ 49 (89) HOF *Continued*	**41510**
Hungry—Paul Revere And The Raiders Featuring Mark Lindsay (66)	1931
Running With The Night—Lionel Richie (83)	1890
I'm Gonna Be Strong—Gene Pitney (64)	1883
You've Lost That Lovin' Feeling— Daryl Hall & John Oates (80)	*1839*
I Just Can't Help Believing—B.J. Thomas (70)	1786
Uptown—Crystals (62)	1673
If Ever You're In My Arms Again—Peabo Bryson (84)	1625
Walkin' In The Rain—Jay And The Americans (69)	*1583*
Love Will Conquer All—Lionel Richie (86)	1538
Just Once— Quincy Jones Featuring James Ingram (81)	1525
Rock And Roll Lullaby—B.J. Thomas (72)	1491
We Gotta Get Out Of This Place—Animals (65)	1474
On Broadway—Drifters (63)	*1347*
You've Lost That Lovin' Feeling— Dionne Warwick (69)	*1346*
Bless You—Tony Orlando (61)	1332
He's Sure The Boy I Love—Crystals (62)	1298
Shape Of Things To Come— Max Frost And The Troopers (68)	1289
Conscience—James Darren (62)	1112
It's Getting Better—Mama Cass (69)	1101
Magic Town—Vogues (66)	1013
Saturday Night At The Movies—Drifters (64)	974
All Of You—Julio Iglesias & Diana Ross (84)	919
Walking In The Rain—Ronettes (64)	*887*
Only In America—Jay & The Americans (63)	804
I'll Take You Home—Drifters (63)	758
Make Your Own Kind Of Music— Mama Cass Elliot (69)	*735*
Don't Be Afraid, Little Darlin'— Steve Lawrence (63)	735
Brown Eyed Woman—Bill Medley (68)	662
Looking Through The Eyes Of Love—Gene Pitney (65)	*646*
Johnny Loves Me—Shelley Fabares (62)	624
Looking Through The Eyes Of Love—Partridge Family Starring Shirley Jones & Featuring David Cassidy (72)	*611*
Somewhere Down The Road—Barry Manilow (81)	590
New World Coming—Mama Cass Elliot (70)	562
Proud—Johnny Crawford (62)	547
If A Woman Answers (Hang Up The Phone)— Leroy Van Dyke (62)	496
Home Of The Brave—Jody Miller (65)	*446*
(You're My) Soul And Inspiration— Donny & Marie (77)	*407*
I Want You To Meet My Baby—Eydie Gorme (64)	389
So Far So Good—Sheena Easton (86)	377
The Last Time I Made Love— Joyce Kennedy & Jeffrey Osborne (84)	369
So Long Dixie—Blood, Sweat & Tears (72)	360
Heart—Kenny Chandler (63)	*340*
Mary's Little Lamb—James Darren (62)	330
We're Going All The Way—Jeffrey Osborne (84)	325
Baby Come And Get It—Pointer Sisters (85)	323
One To One—Carole King (82)	319
Peace Brother Peace—Bill Medley (68)	316
Don't Make My Baby Blue—Frankie Laine (63)	305
Through The Fire—Chaka Khan (85)	257
Born To Be Together— Ronettes Featuring Veronica (65)	252
You've Lost That Lovin' Feelin'— Roberta Flack & Donny Hathaway (71)	*248*
It's Gonna Be Fine—Glenn Yarbrough (65)	234
A Girl Has To Know—G-Clefs (62)	174
Amy—Paul Petersen (63)	164
Right Here And Now—Bill Medley (82)	158
Olympia—Sergio Mendes (84)	145
Come On Over To My Place—Drifters (65)	144
Where Have You Been (All My Life)— Arthur Alexander (62)	130
Happy Times (Are Here To Stay)—Tony Orlando (61)	129
Heart! (I Hear You Beating)—Wayne Newton (63)	*116*
Mamacita—Grass Roots (75)	101
It's A Happening World—Tokens (67)	96
Cindy's Gonna Cry—Johnny Crawford (63)	77
Angelica—Oliver (70)	*76*
Home Of The Brave—Bonnie And The Treasures (65)	*67*
Little Miss U.S.A.—Barry Mann (61)	61
All I Need To Know (Don't Know Much)— Bette Midler (83)	*59*

Heart To Heart—Errol Sober (79)	56
Feelings—Barry Mann (70)	53
The Princess And The Punk—Barry Mann (76)	43
It's Not Easy—Will-O-Bees (68)	33
Don't Know Much—Bill Medley (81)	*22*
Help Me—Andy Williams (62)	19
You've Lost That Lovin' Feelin'— Long John Baldry & Kathi MacDonald (79)	*16*
Let Me In—Derringer (76)	10
Talk To Me Baby—Barry Mann (64)	6.2
Make Your Own Kind Of Music—Barbra Streisand (72)	*5.7*
Angelica—Barry Mann (66)	*3.4*
Kurt WEILL ▶ 357 (12) HOF	**10679**
Mack The Knife—Bobby Darin (59)	*14687*
Moritat (A Theme From "The Three Penny Opera")— Dick Hyman Trio (56)	*2349*
A Theme From "The Three Penny Opera" (Moritat)— Richard Hayman And Jan August (56)	*1429*
The Bilbao Song—Andy Williams (61)	936
Mack The Knife—Ella Fitzgerald (60)	*743*
A Theme From Threepenny Opera (Mack The Knife)— Louis Armstrong And His All-Stars (56)	*570*
A Theme From (The Three Penny Opera) 'Moritat'— Billy Vaughn and His Orchestra (56)	*375*
Moritat (A Theme From "The Three Penny Opera")— Lawrence Welk And His Sparkling Strings (56)	*354*
September Song—Jimmy Durante (63)	*333*
Moritat (Theme From "Three Penny Opera")— Les Paul (56)	*310*
September Song—Roy Clark (69)	*98*
Moritat (A Theme From "Three Penny Opera")— Owen Bradley & His Orchestra (56)	*0.0*
—Sidney Weinberg see: Sid WAYNE	
Herb WEINER [Steve Donroy] ▶ 1964 (5)	**2047**
It's My Party—Lesley Gore (63)	*7824*
I'm Just A Dancing Partner—Platters (56)	118
It's My Party— Dave Stewart With Barbara Gaskin (81)	*64*
What Does It Matter—Platters (59)	20
Sometimes I Wish I Were A Boy—Lesley Gore (64)	19
—Matthew Weiner see: Matthew WILDER	
Bernard WEINMAN ▶ 3019 (1)	**1063**
Too Much—Elvis Presley (57)	4251
—Gary Lee Weinrib see: Geddy LEE	
Bobby WEINSTEIN [Bobby Wilding, Robert Wilding] ▶ 513 (24) HOF	**8303**
Goin' Out Of My Head— Little Anthony And The Imperials (64)	*3749*
Pretty Blue Eyes—Steve Lawrence (59)	2838
Hurt So Bad—Lettermen (69)	*2180*
Hurt So Bad—Linda Ronstadt (80)	*1686*
Hurt So Bad—Little Anthony And The Imperials (65)	*1409*
Goin' Out Of My Head—Lettermen (67)	*1323*
I'm On The Outside (Looking In)— Little Anthony And The Imperials (64)	1253
It's Gonna Take A Miracle—Deniece Williams (82)	*1178*
Sweet Cream Ladies, Forward March—Box Tops (68)	1153
Have You Looked Into Your Heart—Jerry Vale (64)	860
It's Gonna Take A Miracle—Royalettes (65)	*576*
Big Wide World—Teddy Randazzo (63)	423
You Better Go—Derek Martin (65)	392
Sinner Man—Trini Lopez (65)	335
In Time—Steve Lawrence (61)	214
I Want To Meet Him—Royalettes (65)	172
A Miracle—Frankie Avalon (62)	65
Around The Corner—Duprees (65)	56
Goin' Out Of My Head—Frank Sinatra (69)	*36*
Dear Heart—Teddy Randazzo (63)	13
I Was A Boy (When You Needed A Man)— Billy Shields (69)	11
Poor Boy—Royalettes (65)	7.8
Hurt So Bad—Jackie DeShannon (70)	*1.0*
The Weekend—Jack Jones (66)	0.5
—Leslie Weinstein see: Leslie WEST	
Bob WEIR ▶ 6912 (4)	**129**
Truckin'—Grateful Dead (71)	237
Bombs Away—Bob Weir (78)	85
The Music Never Stopped—Grateful Dead (75)	49
Sugar Magnolia—Grateful Dead (73)	6.1
Graham WEIR ▶ 5741 (1)	**247**
(Forever) Live And Die— Orchestral Manoeuvres In The Dark (86)	740

Larry WEIR ▶ 7031 (1)	**121**
Cover Of Love—Michael Damian (89)	482
—Michael Damian Weir see: Michael DAMIAN	
Neil WEIR ▶ 5742 (1)	**247**
(Forever) Live And Die— Orchestral Manoeuvres In The Dark (86)	740
Danny WEIS ▶ 6805 (1)	**136**
Apricot Brandy—Rhinoceros (69)	272
—Bernard Weisbaum see: Bernie BAUM	
Steve WEISBERG ▶ 7734 (1)	**77**
Christmas For Cowboys—John Denver (75)	77
Harvey WEISENFELD ▶ 6852 (1)	**132**
Somebody Cares— Tommy James And The Shondells (68)	397
Al WEISMAN ▶ 9601 (2)	**21**
Confession Of A Sinner—Stylers (56)	26
Baby, Baby You—Coney Island Kids (55)	15
Ben WEISMAN [Al Hill] ▶ 414 (47)	**9626**
Wooden Heart—Joe Dowell (61)	*6334*
Let Me Go Lover—Joan Weber (54)	*5883*
The Night Has A Thousand Eyes—Bobby Vee (62)	4114
Lonely Blue Boy—Conway Twitty (59)	2068
Let Me Go Lover— Teresa Brewer with The Lancers (54)	*1376*
Follow That Dream—Elvis Presley (62)	1103
Do The Clam—Elvis Presley With The Jordanaires Jubilee Four & Carole Lombard Trio (65)	929
Rock-A-Hula Baby ("Twist" Special)— Elvis Presley With The Jordanaires (61)	854
All I See Is You—Dusty Springfield (66)	818
Fame And Fortune— Elvis Presley With The Jordanaires (60)	751
I'll Touch A Star—Terry Stafford (64)	745
Spinout—Elvis Presley With The Jordanaires (66)	614
The Bridge Of Love—Joe Dowell (61)	386
Don't Ask Me Why—Elvis Presley (58)	373
I Love Makin' Love To You—Evie Sands (75)	367
Moon Light Swim—Tony Perkins (57)	*335*
Moonlight Swim—Nick Noble (57)	*285*
You Can Do It—Dobie Gray (78)	234
Let Me Go Lover—Patti Page (54)	*216*
It Feels So Right— Elvis Presley With The Jordanaires (65)	216
As Long As I Have You— Elvis Presley with the Jordanaires (58)	192
Wooden Heart—Bobby Vinton (75)	*108*
Sweet Stuff—Guy Mitchell (57)	105
(There'll Come A Day When) Ev'ry Little Bit Hurts— Bobby Vee (64)	63
I Got Lucky—Elvis Presley with the Jordanaires (62)	62
This Is Living—Elvis Presley with the Jordanaires (62)	62
Riding The Rainbow— Elvis Presley with the Jordanaires (62)	62
A Kiss For Christmas (O Tannenbaum)— Joe Dowell (61)	32
In The Beginning—Frankie Laine (54)	30
Coming From You—Joni James (58)	27
Confession Of A Sinner—Stylers (56)	26
Crawfish—Elvis Presley with the Jordanaires (58)	24
Lend Me Your Comb—Carl Perkins (58)	*23*
Slowly But Surely— Elvis Presley With The Jordanaires (65)	23
Baby, Baby You—Coney Island Kids (55)	15
Third Finger - Left Hand—Eileen Rodgers (57)	8.2
One More Time—Dean Martin (54)	*7.9*
One More Time—Ames Brothers (54)	*7.9*
Tiger Lily—Rusty Draper (57)	7.6
I Like Girls—Johnny Restivo (59)	6.5
Pocketful Of Rainbows—Deane Hawley (61)	6.4
Still Small Voice—Perry Como (59)	1.6
Moonlight Swim—Joel Grey (57)	*0.0*
Let Me Go, Lover!—Peggy Lee (55)	*0.0*
Lend Me Your Comb—Bernie Nee (58)	*0.0*
Let Me Go, Lover!—Sunny Gale (54)	*0.0*
Lend Me Your Comb—Carol Hughes (58)	*0.0*
Fred WEISMANTEL ▶ 3237 (2)	**934**
Lovely One—Four Voices (56)	683
That Stranger Used To Be My Girl—Trade Martin (62)	503
Charles WEISS ▶ 6671 (1)	**145**
He's Mine (I Love Him, I Love Him, I Love Him)— Alice Wonder Land (63)	290
—David Jay Weiss see: David WAS	

Donna WEISS ▶ 908 (5)	**4870**
Bette Davis Eyes—Kim Carnes (81)	8923
Sugar Don't Bite—Sam Harris (84)	440
That Kind Of Woman—Merrilee Rush & The Turnabouts (68)	337
Divided Hearts—Kim Carnes (86)	70
Turn Around And Love You—Rita Coolidge (69)	2.2
George David WEISS [B.Y. Forster] ▶ 306 (71) HOF	**11832**
The Lion Sleeps Tonight—Tokens (61)	*9030*
Can't Help Falling In Love—Elvis Presley With The Jordanaires (61)	*5450*
The Lion Sleeps Tonight—Robert John (71)	*5059*
How Important Can It Be—Joni James (55)	*2495*
That Sunday, That Summer—Nat King Cole (63)	1528
A Walkin' Miracle—Essex Featuring Anita Humes (63)	1442
Let's Put It All Together—Stylistics (74)	*1045*
Mr. Wonderful—Peggy Lee (56)	*899*
Lullaby Of Birdland—Blue Stars (55)	*804*
Mr. Wonderful—Sarah Vaughan (56)	*674*
Hello Heartache, Goodbye Love—Little Peggy March (63)	666
Heavy Fallin' Out—Stylistics (74)	552
Can't Help Falling In Love—Corey Hart (86)	*544*
I Wish I Were A Princess—Little Peggy March (63)	501
Wild In The Country—Elvis Presley With The Jordanaires (61)	471
Mandolins In The Moonlight—Perry Como (58)	464
Mr. Wonderful—Teddi King (56)	*459*
Snoopy's Christmas—Royal Guardsmen (67)	431
How Important Can It Be—Sarah Vaughan (55)	*429*
And Now—Della Reese (60)	398
What A Wonderful World—Louis Armstrong (88)	389
Starlight, Starbright—Linda Scott (61)	384
Too Close For Comfort—Eydie Gorme (56)	*381*
Can't Help Falling In Love—Al Martino (70)	*308*
I Don't See Me In Your Eyes Anymore—Charlie Rich (74)	298
B'wa Nina (Pretty Girl)—Tokens (62)	269
Stay With Me—Lorraine Ellison (66)	261
The Impossible Happened—Little Peggy March (63)	258
I'll Take You Home—Corsairs Featuring Jay "Bird" Uzzell (62)	240
Can't Give You Anything (But My Love)—Stylistics (75)	227
Johnny Freedom—Johnny Horton (60)	211
Star On A TV Show—Stylistics (75)	165
Hey Little Lucy! (Don'tcha Put No Lipstick On)—Conway Twitty (59)	127
I'll Never Be Free—Kay Starr (61)	118
Thank You Baby—Stylistics (75)	111
Jacques D'Iraque—Sammy Davis Jr. (56)	80
Lullaby of Birdland (54)—Ella Fitzgerald (54)	*74*
Funky Weekend—Stylistics (75)	61
You Are Beautiful—Stylistics (76)	58
A Far Far Better Thing—Della Reese (61)	53
Toys In The Attic—Joe Sherman, His Orchestra And Chorus (63)	*50*
Let Me Cry On Your Shoulder—Georgia Gibbs (65)	46
Can't Help Falling In Love—Andy Williams (70)	*26*
Let Me Tell You, Babe—Nat King Cole (66)	23
I'll Step Aside—Georgie Shaw (55)	22
Toys In The Attic—Jack Jones (63)	*20*
Wheel Of Fortune—LaVern Baker (60)	*15*
As Sure As Night Must Fall—Jerry Vale (64)	14
Love Is The Answer—Van Mc Coy & The Soul City Symphony (74)	13
Let's Put It All Together—Band Of Gold (84)	*12*
Wheel Of Fortune—Knightsbridge Strings (59)	*10*
Oh! What It Seemed To Be—Castells (62)	7.9
Summer Love—Joni James (57)	6.5
These Things I Offer You (For A Lifetime)—Playmates (60)	5.7
Big Boat—Tokens (62)	1.8
Can't Help Falling In Love With You—Jimmy Castor (80)	*1.8*
More And More Of Your Amor—Nat King Cole (64)	1.7
Mr. Wonderful—Mello-Larks (56)	*0.0*
Toys In The Attic—Dennis Regor (63)	*0.0*
Mr. Wonderful—Bette Anne Steele (56)	*0.0*
Cross Over The Bridge—Patti Page (54)	0.0
How Important Can It Be—Lou Monte (55)	*0.0*
Lullaby Of Birdland—Ella Fitzgerald (56)	*0.0*
Too Close For Comfort—Lillian Briggs (56)	*0.0*
Too Close For Comfort—Sammy Davis Jr. (56)	*0.0*
How Important Can It Be?—Teresa Brewer (55)	*0.0*
Can't Help Falling In Love—Keely Smith (61)	*0.0*
How Important Can It Be?—Connee Boswell (55)	*0.0*
Can't Help Falling In Love—Four Esquires (61)	*0.0*
A Girl, A Girl (Zoom-Ba Di Alli Nella)—Eddie Fisher (54)	0.0
Lullaby Of Birdland—Ray Anthony & His Orchestra with Don Durant (56)	*0.0*
Hy WEISS ▶ 5142 (7)	**334**
Walking Along—Diamonds (58)	*783*
We Belong Together—Robert & Johnny (58)	*339*
We Belong Together—Jimmy Velvet (63)	*151*
Life Is But A Dream—Earls (61)	118
Walking Along—Solitaires (58)	*0.0*
We Belong Together—Belmonts (61)	*0.0*
We Belong Together—Robert & Johnny (61)	*0.0*
Larry WEISS ▶ 324 (19)	**11367**
Rhinestone Cowboy—Glen Campbell (75)	6322
Bend Me, Shape Me—American Breed (67)	*6075*
Help Me Girl—Eric Burdon And The Animals (66)	*651*
Help Me Girl—Outsiders (66)	*588*
Dream Merchant—New Birth (75)	*492*
Mr. Dream Merchant—Jerry Butler (67)	*434*
More Than The Eye Can See—Al Martino (67)	434
Darling Take Me Back—Lenny Welch (65)	317
Ten Lonely Guys—Pat Boone (62)	*317*
Leave Me Alone—Baby Washington (63)	233
Together Again—Bobby Sherman (72)	152
Mr. Wishing Well—Nat King Cole (63)	110
Ten Lonely Guys—Ten Broken Hearts (62)	*81*
Does He Really Care For Me—Ruby And The Romantics (65)	62
(In The) Cold Light Of Day—Gene Pitney (66)	28
Insult To Injury—Timi Yuro (63)	24
Getting Ready For The Heartbreak—Chuck Jackson (62)	18
Bend Me, Shape Me—Storm (71)	*13*
Bend Me, Shape Me—Tight Fit (81)	*0.9*
—Marilyn Weiss see: Marilyn Weiss ALLEN	
Marion WEISS ▶ 4086 (1)	**598**
I Wish That We Were Married—Ronnie And The Hi-Lites (62)	1197
Sam WEISS ▶ 7147 (3)	**113**
Walking Along—Diamonds (58)	*783*
I Believe In You—Robert & Johnny (58)	4.3
Walking Along—Solitaires (58)	*0.0*
Stephan WEISS ▶ 7148 (5)	**113**
Music, Music, Music—Sensations Featuring Yvonne Baker (61)	*138*
Music, Music, Music—Crazy Otto (55)	*49*
Music Music Music—Happenings (68)	*30*
Music, Music, Music—Teresa Brewer (73)	*9.4*
Your Heart - My Heart (Sehnsucht)—Frankie Laine (54)	0.0
Mark WEITZ ▶ 3586 (3)	**776**
Tomorrow—Strawberry Alarm Clock (67)	1241
Sit With The Guru—Strawberry Alarm Clock (68)	242
Barefoot In Baltimore—Strawberry Alarm Clock (68)	224
—Bernard Weltzner see: Bernie WAYNE	
—Alvin Welch see: Alvin CASH	
Bob WELCH ▶ 980 (6)	**4568**
Sentimental Lady—Bob Welch (77)	2038
Ebony Eyes—Bob Welch (78)	1288
Precious Love—Bob Welch (79)	985
Hot Love, Cold World—Bob Welch (78)	344
Church—Bob Welch (79)	66
Silver Heels—Blaze (76)	19
Bruce WELCH ▶ 2065 (3)	**1936**
Please Mr. Please—Olivia Newton-John (75)	3858
Bachelor Boy—Cliff Richard And The Shadows (64)	9.0
Don't It Make You Feel Good—Overlanders (64)	5.0
Dan WELCH ▶ 6070 (1)	**209**
First Date First Kiss First Love—Sonny James (57)	418
Patrick WELCH ▶ 5324 (3)	**305**
Fibbin'—Patti Page (58)	569
My Empty Room—Little Anthony And The Imperials (60)	39
Nine O'Clock—McGuire Sisters (60)	2.5
Frank WELDON ▶ 7561 (1)	**88**
Second Fiddle—Kay Starr (56)	353
William WELDON ▶ 8215 (1)	**58**
I'm Gonna Move To The Outskirts Of Town—Ray Charles (61)	116
Lawrence WELK ▶ 8881 (1)	**37**
Wun'erful, Wun'erful! (Sides Uh-One & Uh-Two)—Stan Freberg (57)	298
Freddy WELLER ▶ 566 (8)	**7650**
Dizzy—Tommy Roe (69)	8722
Jam Up Jelly Tight—Tommy Roe (69)	3274
Jack And Jill—Tommy Roe (69)	842
We Gotta All Get Together—Paul Revere And The Raiders Featuring Mark Lindsay (69)	554
Pearl—Tommy Roe (70)	548
Stir It Up And Serve It—Tommy Roe (70)	480
She Drives Me Out Of My Mind—Swingin' Medallions (66)	136
Campfire Girls—Billy Joe Royal (66)	28
Paul WELLER ▶ 4145 (2)	**581**
My Ever Changing Moods—Style Council (84)	545
You're The Best Thing—Style Council (84)	36
Larry WELLINGTON ▶ 11075 (1)	**3.4**
Dream World—Four Coins (58)	6.8
Alma WELLS ▶ 5775 (1)	**243**
Age For Love—Jimmy Charles (60)	486
Bryan WELLS ▶ 1708 (4)	**2454**
Yester-Me, Yester-You, Yesterday—Stevie Wonder (69)	*2495*
A Place In The Sun—Stevie Wonder (66)	1928
Travlin' Man—Stevie Wonder (67)	458
Yester-Me, Yester-You, Yesterday—Stars On 45 (82)	*27*
Carl WELLS ▶ 8674 (3)	**43**
Let Me Be Good To You—Carla Thomas (66)	119
The Hunter—Ike & Tina Turner (69)	12
Freedom Train—James Carr (69)	2.3
Ed WELLS ▶ 5528 (3)	**274**
A Casual Look—Six Teens (56)	*260*
Arrow Of Love—Six Teens (57)	14
Casual Look—Lorry Raine (56)	*0.0*
Josephine WELLS ▶ 11192 (1)	**2.8**
Maybe This Day—Kissing The Pink (83)	20
Kevin WELLS ▶ 4911 (1)	**384**
Walking On A Thin Line—Huey Lewis and the News (84)	768
Mary WELLS [L.R. Peques, Mary Womack] ▶ 3991 (3)	**629**
Bye Bye Baby—Mary Wells (61)	501
The Doctor—Mary Wells (68)	233
Dig The Way I Feel—Mary Wells (70)	24
Robert WELLS ▶ 4526 (7)	**470**
Mobile—Julius La Rosa (54)	534
When Joanna Loved Me—Tony Bennett (64)	161
The Christmas Song (Merry Christmas To You)—Nat King Cole (62)	*114*
Eloise—Kay Thompson (56)	109
The Christmas Song (Merry Christmas To You)—Nat King Cole (60)	*9.6*
The Ballad Of Waterhole #3 (Code Of The West)—Roger Miller (67)	7.9
The Christmas Song (Merry Christmas To You)—Nat "King" Cole (56)	*4.6*
Sonny WELLS ▶ 9534 (1)	**22**
One Heart—George Hamilton IV (58)	44
Tom WELLS ▶ 7714 (1)	**79**
WKRP In Cincinnati—Steve Carlisle (81)	158
Wes WELLS ▶ 7367 (1)	**100**
Get It From The Bottom—Steelers (69)	300
Vince WELNICK ▶ 8496 (2)	**48**
Don't Want To Wait Anymore—Tubes (81)	377
Piece By Piece—Tubes (85)	10
Señor WENCES [Wenceslao Moreno] ▶ 10815 (1)	**5.2**
S'-All Right? S'-All Right!—Senor Wences (59)	16
Percy WENRICH ▶ 1841 (6) HOF	**2211**
Sail Along Silvery Moon—Billy Vaughn and His Orchestra (57)	*3690*
Hula Love—Buddy Knox with The Rhythm Orchids (57)	1598
Moonlight Bay—Drifters (58)	*199*
Moonlight Bay—Joe Leahy & His Orchestra (58)	*0.0*
Moonlight Bay—Jimmie Haskell & His Orchestra (58)	*0.0*
Sail Along Silv'ry Moon—Karen Chandler & Her Jacks (57)	*0.0*

Jack V. WENZEL ▶ 10472 (1)	**8.1**
Boss—Rumblers (63)	48
Erwin WENZLAFF ▶ 3442 (4)	**847**
I Got A Wife—Mark IV (59)	1423
My Wife, The Dancer—Eddie & Dutch (70)	195
(Make With) The Shake—Mark IV (58)	71
Move Over Rover—Mark IV (59)	5.1
Carel WERBER ▶ 7018 (2)	**121**
Cast Your Fate To The Wind—Shelby Flint (66)	*231*
Cast Your Fate To The Wind—Steve Alaimo (65)	*12*
Steve WERFEL ▶ 4899 (3)	**385**
I Live For Your Love—Natalie Cole (87)	1072
I'm Gonna Miss You—Kenny Loggins (88)	60
If You're Serious—Riff (91)	15
David WERNER ▶ 2185 (1)	**1769**
Cradle Of Love—Billy Idol (90)	3538
Fred H. WERNER ▶ 3719 (1)	**721**
Desiderata—Les Crane (71)	1441
Harald WERNER ▶ 8596 (1)	**45**
Now I Know—Jack Jones (67)	181
Kay WERNER ▶ 3896 (2)	**664**
The Clapping Song (Clap Pat Clap Slap)—Shirley Ellis (65)	*1719*
The Clapping Song—Pia Zadora (82)	*271*
Sue WERNER ▶ 3897 (2)	**664**
The Clapping Song (Clap Pat Clap Slap)—Shirley Ellis (65)	*1719*
The Clapping Song—Pia Zadora (82)	*271*
Ron WERNSMAN ▶ 8458 (1)	**50**
Beat—Rockin' R's (59)	149
Howard WERTH ▶ 8035 (1)	**64**
Indian Summer—Audience (71)	128
Fred WESLEY ▶ 2308 (7)	**1621**
Get On The Good Foot - Part 1—James Brown (72)	1605
Hot Pants Pt. 1 (She Got To Use What She Got To Get What She Wants)—James Brown (71)	1325
The Payback - Part I—James Brown (74)	817
Papa Don't Take No Mess - Part I—James Brown (74)	475
Reality—James Brown (75)	56
Keep On Doin' What You're Doin'—Bobby Byrd (72)	39
Me And My Baby Got A Good Thing Going—Lyn Collins (72)	17
Gertie WESLEY ▶ 9704 (1)	**19**
Reality—James Brown (75)	56
Arthur WEST ▶ 11427 (1)	**1.7**
Lollipop (I Like You)—Intruders (69)	6.9
Bill WEST ▶ 10812 (1)	**5.2**
Is This Me?—Jim Reeves (63)	10
Bob WEST ▶ 1703 (1)	**2460**
I'll Be There—Jackson 5 (70)	9838
—David West see: Norman NEWELL	
Dottie WEST ▶ 6870 (2)	**131**
Country Sunshine—Dottie West (73)	379
Is This Me?—Jim Reeves (63)	10
Gary WEST [Gary Eldon Hodgden, Gary Hodgden] ▶ 7772 (2)	**76**
You've Got What I Need—Shooting Star (80)	87
Hollywood—Shooting Star (82)	65
Hedy WEST ▶ 4353 (3)	**514**
500 Miles Away From Home—Bobby Bare (63)	*1427*
Five Hundred Miles—Heaven Bound With Tony Scotti (71)	*109*
500 Miles—Hooters (89)	*6.5*
James WEST ▶ 6218 (1)	**192**
Honest I Do—Innocents (60)	577
Jerry WEST [J. D. Miller, Joseph D. Miller] ▶ 3080 (2)	**1023**
This Should Go On Forever—Rod Bernard (59)	1411
Rainin' In My Heart—Slim Harpo (61)	634
—Joe West see: Sonny WEST	
Kyle WEST ▶ 3257 (3)	**923**
Nite And Day—Al B. Sure! (88)	1529
Off On Your Own (Girl)—Al B. Sure! (88)	288
Just Ask Me To—Tevin Campbell (91)	29
Leslie WEST [Leslie Weinstein] ▶ 5256 (2)	**317**
Mississippi Queen—Mountain (70)	1100
The Animal Trainer And The Toad—Mountain (71)	85
Norman WEST ▶ 5519 (1)	**275**
Hearsay—Soul Children (72)	550

Red WEST ▶ 2052 (9)	**1947**
I'm A Fool—Dino, Desi & Billy (65)	1193
Separate Ways—Elvis Presley (72)	1102
If You Talk In Your Sleep—Elvis Presley (74)	810
Big Big World—Johnny Burnette (61)	460
Let's Give Adam And Eve Another Chance—Gary Puckett And The Union Gap (70)	446
Hey Hey Woman—Joe Jeffrey (69)	30
That's Someone You Never Forget—Elvis Presley With The Jordanaires (67)	4.3
If You Think I Don't Need You—Elvis Presley (64)	1.1
If Every Day Was Like Christmas—Elvis Presley (66)	0.9
Richard WEST ▶ 6596 (1)	**153**
Move Any Mountain—Shamen (91)	459
—Rick West see: Richard WESTFIELD	
Robert WEST ▶ 5687 (2)	**255**
I Found A Love - Part 1—Wilson Pickett (67)	*487*
I Found A Love—Falcons & Band (Ohio Untouchables) (62)	*276*
Sonny WEST [Joe West] ▶ 4152 (2)	**579**
Oh Boy—Buddy Holly / The Crickets (57)	1552
Rave On—Buddy Holly / The Crickets (58)	184
Steve WEST ▶ 6701 (1)	**143**
Bang Bang—Danger Danger (90)	286
Tommy WEST [Thomas R. Picardo, T.P. West] ▶ 2742 (12)	**1229**
Medicine Man (Part 1)—Buchanan Brothers (69)	1162
American City Suite—Cashman & West (72)	696
Son Of A Lovin' Man—Buchanan Brothers (69)	336
Songman—Cashman & West (72)	264
But For Love—Jerry Naylor (70)	252
Sausalito—Al Martino (69)	231
He'd Rather Have The Rain—Heaven Bound With Tony Scotti (71)	86
The King Of Rock 'N' Roll—Cashman & West (73)	31
Baby, Baby I Love You—Terry Cashman (76)	30
California On My Mind—Morning Mist (71)	26
Richard And Me—Gene & Tommy (67)	2.8
A Song That Never Comes—Mama Cass Elliot (70)	2.1
—T.P. West see: Tommy WEST	
Kent WESTBERRY ▶ 3849 (4)	**678**
I Just Don't Understand—Ann-Margret (61)	1253
Cherry Berry Wine—Charlie McCoy (61)	116
Hello Out There—Carl Belew (62)	*13*
Hello Out There—Nick Noble (62)	*13*
WEST COAST RAP ALL-STARS ▶ 4408 (1)	**503**
We're All In The Same Gang—West Coast Rap All-Stars (90)	503
Neil WESTEN ▶ 10926 (1)	**4.3**
I'll Search My Heart—Johnny Mathis (63)	13
Thomas P. WESTENDORF ▶ 10826 (1)	**5.1**
I'll Take You Home Again Kathleen—Slim Whitman (57)	5.1
Paul WESTERBERG ▶ 6098 (1)	**206**
I'll Be You—Replacements (89)	206
—Johnny Westerlund see: Johnny WESTERN	
Johnny WESTERN [Johnny Westerlund] ▶ 6426 (1)	**171**
The Ballad Of Paladin—Duane Eddy (62)	514
Floyd WESTFALL ▶ 8769 (2)	**40**
Summer Kisses—Floyd & Jerry With The Counterpoints (66)	69
Believe In Things—Floyd and Jerry With The Counterpoints (66)	10
Jerry WESTFALL ▶ 8770 (2)	**40**
Summer Kisses—Floyd & Jerry With The Counterpoints (66)	69
Believe In Things—Floyd and Jerry With The Counterpoints (66)	10
Richard WESTFIELD [Rick West, Richard Allen Westfield] ▶ 2958 (14)	**1098**
Jungle Boogie—Kool & The Gang (73)	2506
Hollywood Swinging—Kool & The Gang (74)	2079
Summertime—DJ Jazzy Jeff & The Fresh Prince (91)	1783
Spirit Of The Boogie—Kool & The Gang (75)	825
Funky Stuff—Kool & The Gang (73)	473
Higher Plane—Kool & The Gang (74)	446
Kool And The Gang—Kool & The Gang (69)	329
Caribbean Festival—Kool & The Gang (75)	268
Rhyme Tyme People—Kool & The Gang (75)	182
Let The Music Take Your Mind—Kool & The Gang (70)	85

Funky Man—Kool & The Gang (70)	41
The Gangs Back Again—Kool & The Gang (69)	37
Who's Gonna Take The Weight (Part One)—Kool & The Gang (71)	4.1
Summer Madness—Kool & The Gang (75)	0.0
Clive WESTLAKE ▶ 2900 (5)	**1125**
All I See Is You—Dusty Springfield (66)	818
A Minute Of Your Time—Tom Jones (68)	610
It's Gotta Last Forever—Billy J. Kramer With The Dakotas (65)	109
Losing You—Dusty Springfield (65)	75
No One Better Than You—Petula Clark (69)	34
—Frank Weston see: Len BEADLE	
—Gary Weston see: Gary KNIGHT	
Paul WESTON [Paul Wetstein] ▶ 5576 (3)	**270**
Day By Day—Four Freshmen (55)	668
I Should Care—Gloria Lynne (64)	124
Make Me A Child Again—Frankie Laine (56)	12
Robert Patrick WESTON [Robert Harris] ▶ 1273 (1)	**3481**
I'm Henry VIII, I Am—Herman's Hermits (65)	6962
—Ruth Alston Weston see: Ruth BROWN	
Jamie WEST-ORAM ▶ 2875 (8)	**1137**
One Thing Leads To Another—Fixx (83)	2676
Saved By Zero—Fixx (83)	900
Are We Ourselves?—Fixx (84)	811
Secret Separation—Fixx (86)	629
The Sign Of Fire—Fixx (83)	523
Driven Out—Fixx (89)	236
Sunshine In The Shade—Fixx (84)	96
Stand Or Fall—Fixx (82)	67
—Charles Weeden Westover see: Del SHANNON	
Frank C. WESTPHAL ▶ 10613 (1)	**6.7**
When You Come To The End Of The Day—Red Foley (55)	13
Paul WESTWOOD ▶ 6720 (1)	**142**
Wrap Her Up—Elton John (85)	852
—Paul Wetstein see: Paul WESTON	
—Marvin Wetter see: Marvin MONTGOMERY	
John WETTON ▶ 1422 (5)	**3109**
Heat Of The Moment—Asia (82)	2585
Don't Cry—Asia (83)	1413
Only Time Will Tell—Asia (82)	916
The Smile Has Left Your Eyes—Asia (83)	479
Go—Asia (85)	345
Ray WETZEL ▶ 8705 (1)	**42**
Intermission Riff—Bernie Lowe Orchestra (58)	42
Ned WEVER ▶ 4563 (3)	**465**
Trust In Me—Etta James (61)	*849*
Trust In Me—Patti Page (59)	*544*
Trust In Me—Chris Connor (57)	*1.8*
Jerry WEXLER ▶ 2138 (14)	**1827**
Twenty-Five Miles—Edwin Starr (69)	*2304*
A Natural Woman (You Make Me Feel Like)—Aretha Franklin (67)	1752
Everybody Needs Somebody To Love—Wilson Pickett (67)	*511*
Minimum Love—Mac McAnally (83)	435
Everybody Needs Somebody To Love—Solomon Burke (64)	*302*
That's When It Hurts—Ben E. King (64)	261
Honey Love—Bunny Paul with The Harptones (54)	*177*
Soul Dance Number Three—Wilson Pickett (67)	117
I'm Standing By—Ben E. King (62)	33
Honey Love—Four Lovers (56)	*5.6*
Honey Love—Narvel Felts (60)	*4.8*
Twenty-Five Miles—Mongo Santamaria (69)	*0.9*
Honey Love—Vicki Young (54)	*0.0*
Honey Love—Drifters Featuring Clyde McPhatter (54)	*0.0*
François WEYER ▶ 11644 (1)	**0.9**
Tonight's The Night—S.S.O. (76)	1.8
Albert WEYMAN [Albert Verrecchia] ▶ 11069 (1)	**3.4**
Miss Broadway—Belle Epoque (78)	6.8
Tina WEYMOUTH ▶ 3487 (8)	**821**
Burning Down The House—Talking Heads (83)	1439
Wild Wild Life—Talking Heads (86)	742
Genius Of Love—Tom Tom Club (82)	529
And She Was—Talking Heads (85)	350
This Must Be The Place (Naïve Melody)—Talking Heads (83)	156

Tina WEYMOUTH ▶ 3487 (8) *Continued*	**821**
Once In A Lifetime—Talking Heads (86)	39
Life During Wartime (This Ain't No Party.. This Aint No Disco.. This Ain't No Foolin' Around)—Talking Heads (79)	25
Psycho Killer—Talking Heads (78)	8.0
—Vincent Neil Wharton see: Vince NEIL	
David WHEAT ▶ 7521 (1)	**91**
Coocoo U—Kingston Trio (59)	182
Billy Edd WHEELER ▶ 842 (7)	**5246**
Coward Of The County—Kenny Rogers (79)	5361
Reverend Mr. Black—Kingston Trio (63)	2205
Jackson—Nancy Sinatra & Lee Hazlewood (67)	1499
Desert Pete—Kingston Trio (63)	561
Ode To The Little Brown Shack Out Back—Billy Edd Wheeler (64)	334
What To Do With Laurie—Mike Clifford (62)	165
Blistered—Johnny Cash (69)	130
Buddy WHEELER ▶ 3367 (2)	**878**
Need You—Donnie Owens (58)	856
Tomorrow—Donnie Owens (58)	22
Carl WHEELER ▶ 4474 (2)	**486**
Feels Good—Tony! Toni! Toné! (90)	1657
Whatever You Want—Tony! Toni! Toné! (91)	143
Caron WHEELER ▶ 3485 (2)	**821**
Back To Life—Soul II Soul (89)	2835
Livin' In The Light—Caron Wheeler (90)	225
Francis WHEELER ▶ 7602 (1)	**86**
The Sheik Of Araby (Italian Style)—Lou Monte (58)	259
William WHEELER ▶ 9060 (1)	**32**
Song For The Lonely—Platters (61)	64
Ekko WHELAN ▶ 8819 (1)	**39**
There's A New Moon Over My Shoulder—Bonnie Guitar (57)	116
James WHELAN ▶ 3396 (1)	**868**
Mad About You—Belinda Carlisle (86)	2603
Dianne WHILES ▶ 6948 (1)	**126**
Country Sunshine—Dottie West (73)	379
Sterling WHIPPLE ▶ 3698 (3)	**730**
The Last Game Of The Season (A Blind Man In The Bleachers)—David Geddes (75)	*615*
The Blind Man In The Bleachers—Kenny Starr (75)	*83*
Forever Lovers—Mac Davis (76)	33
David WHITAKER ▶ 11072 (1)	**3.4**
Lonely One—Kai Winding (63)	6.8
Yolanda WHITAKER [Yo-Yo] ▶ 7915 (1)	**70**
You Can't Play With My Yo-Yo—Yo-Yo (91)	209
Ian WHITCOMB ▶ 1717 (3)	**2443**
You Turn Me On (Turn On Song)—Ian Whitcomb And Bluesville (65)	2187
N-E-R-V-O-U-S!—Ian Whitcomb (65)	304
This Sporting Life—Ian Whitcomb & Bluesville (65)	104
Leonard WHITCUP ▶ 3730 (4)	**718**
The "A" Team—SSgt. Barry Sadler (66)	891
Kissin' On The Phone—Paul Anka (61)	449
Bewildered—Mickey & Sylvia (58)	*205*
Bewildered—James Brown And The Famous Flames (61)	*187*
Alan WHITE ▶ 4598 (2)	**455**
After The Lights Go Down Low—Al Hibbler (56)	*1362*
After The Lights Go Down Low—George Maharis (62)	*3.1*
Alan (2) WHITE ▶ 8094 (1)	**62**
Rhythm Of Love—Yes (87)	310
—Aretha White see: Aretha FRANKLIN	
Barry WHITE [Barry Eugene Carter, Barry Eugene White] ▶ 113 (21)	**22379**
Love's Theme—Love Unlimited Orchestra (73)	4839
You're The First, The Last, My Everything—Barry White (74)	4597
Can't Get Enough Of Your Love, Babe—Barry White (74)	3529
I'm Gonna Love You Just A Little More Baby—Barry White (73)	3118
Never, Never Gonna Give Ya Up—Barry White (73)	2036
Walkin' In The Rain With The One I Love—Love Unlimited (72)	1754
What Am I Gonna Do With You—Barry White (75)	1342
I Belong To You—Love Unlimited (74)	707
Satin Soul—Love Unlimited Orchestra (75)	665
Oh What A Night For Dancing—Barry White (78)	552
Let The Music Play—Barry White (75)	512

I've Got So Much To Give—Barry White (73)	481
Honey Please, Can't Ya See—Barry White (74)	460
Your Sweetness Is My Weakness—Barry White (78)	346
I'll Do For You Anything You Want Me To—Barry White (75)	338
It May Be Winter Outside (But In My Heart It's Spring)—Felice Taylor (67)	*308*
Rhapsody In White—Love Unlimited Orchestra (74)	125
My Sweet Summer Suite—Love Unlimited Orchestra (76)	114
Under The Influence Of Love—Love Unlimited (74)	53
It May Be Winter Outside (But In My Heart It's Spring)—Love Unlimited (73)	*36*
Baby, We Better Try To Get It Together—Barry White (76)	6.1
—Barry White see: Robert KINGSTON	
—Barry Eugene White see: Barry WHITE	
Calvin WHITE ▶ 8607 (1)	**45**
Forget It—Sandpebbles (67)	90
Carl WHITE ▶ 2894 (4)	**1129**
Papa Oom Mow Mow—Trashmen (63)	*1861*
Bird Is The Word—Trashmen (63)	*1861*
Papa-Oom-Mow-Mow—Rivingtons (62)	*480*
The Bird's The Word—Rivingtons (63)	*315*
Chris WHITE ▶ 1448 (5)	**3016**
Hold Your Head Up—Argent (72)	2531
I Love You—People (68)	1700
Keep On Running Away—Lazy Racer (79)	50
Imagine The Swan—Zombies (69)	45
Spanish Wine—Lou Christie (77)	3.2
Danny WHITE ▶ 4034 (4)	**619**
Time And Tide—Basia (88)	631
Cruising For Bruising—Basia (90)	456
New Day For You—Basia (88)	215
Promises—Basia (89)	11
David WHITE [David Tricker, David Ernest White] ▶ 378 (25)	**10350**
At The Hop—Danny & The Juniors (57)	*8260*
You Don't Own Me—Lesley Gore (63)	5712
1-2-3—Len Barry (65)	*5700*
The Fly—Chubby Checker (61)	2626
Like A Baby—Len Barry (65)	1065
The Boy Next Door—Secrets (63)	798
Rock And Roll Is Here To Stay—Danny And The Juniors (58)	650
The Dawn Of Correction—Spokesmen (65)	608
Birthday Party—Pixies Three (63)	455
Pop Pop Pop-Pie—Sherrys (62)	435
442 Glenwood Avenue—Pixies Three (64)	344
Hey You! Little Boo-Ga-Loo—Chubby Checker (66)	187
One, Two, Three—Ramsey Lewis (67)	*131*
The Thought Of Loving You—Crystal Mansion (68)	83
At The Hop—Jive Bunny And The Mastermixers (89)	*80*
Back To The Hop—Danny & The Juniors (61)	74
It's That Time Of The Year—Len Barry (66)	64
At The Hop—Nick Todd (57)	*54*
Cold Cold Winter—Pixies Three (63)	45
Lip Sync (To The Tongue Twisters)—Len Barry (65)	36
Dancin' The Strand—Maureen Gray (62)	33
Oo-La-La-Limbo—Danny & The Juniors (63)	16
Doin' The Continental Walk—Danny & The Juniors (62)	3.6
At The Shore—Johnny Caswell (63)	3.1
Slop Time—Sherrys (63)	1.8
—David Ernest White see: David WHITE	
Dennis WHITE ▶ 10526 (1)	**7.6**
You Got To Keep On Bumpin'—Kay-Gees (74)	61
Edward WHITE ▶ 2734 (12)	**1234**
C'est La Vie—Sarah Vaughan (55)	*771*
Happiness Street—Georgia Gibbs (56)	*689*
Flowers Mean Forgiveness—Frank Sinatra (56)	582
Happiness Street—Tony Bennett with Percy Faith and His Orchestra (56)	*510*
C'est La Vie—Sunny Gale (55)	*57*
Crazy Otto Rag—Hugo & Luigi (55)	*24*
Star Love—Playmates (59)	23
Mashuga—Louis Prima & Keely Smith (60)	15
Bring Back My Baby To Me—Ella Mae Morse (54)	6.5
C'est La Vie—DeJohn Sisters (55)	*2.9*
Crazy Otto Rag—Crazy Otto (55)	*0.0*
The Crazy Otto Rag—Happy Hoagy Carmichael (55)	*0.0*

Eric Foster WHITE ▶ 2139 (3)	**1827**
I Can't Wait Another Minute—Hi-Five (91)	1339
My Name Is Not Susan—Whitney Houston (91)	470
Just Another Girlfriend—Hi-Five (91)	18
Gary B. WHITE ▶ 3471 (1)	**830**
Long Long Time—Linda Ronstadt (70)	830
Joan WHITE [Josephine Herrmann] ▶ 10383 (2)	**9.2**
Get Up! Get Up! (You Sleepyhead)—Jaye P. Morgan (56)	*18*
Get Up Get Up (You Sleepy Head)—LaVern Baker with The Gliders (56)	*0.0*
Karyn WHITE ▶ 2136 (2)	**1829**
Romantic—Karyn White (91)	4086
The Way I Feel About You—Karyn White (91)	1868
Ken WHITE ▶ 9142 (1)	**30**
The Devil Came Up To Michigan—K.M.C. Kru (91)	*243*
—L. White see: Murray COHEN	
Larry WHITE ▶ 7956 (1)	**67**
Girlfriend—Bobby Brown (86)	202
L.E. WHITE ▶ 7442 (1)	**95**
After The Fire Is Gone—Conway Twitty Loretta Lynn (71)	95
Leann WHITE ▶ 8735 (1)	**41**
I Get Off On It—Tony Joe White (80)	82
Lenny WHITE ▶ 8438 (2)	**51**
Peanut Butter—Twennynine Featuring Lenny White (79)	91
Kid Stuff—Lenny White (80)	21
Mark WHITE ▶ 1589 (7)	**2661**
The Look Of Love - Part One—ABC (82)	1769
When Smokey Sings—ABC (87)	1756
Be Near Me—ABC (85)	1562
Poison Arrow—ABC (83)	732
(How To Be A) Millionaire—ABC (86)	711
Vanity Kills—ABC (86)	36
That Was Then But This Is Now—ABC (84)	12
Maurice WHITE ▶ 251 (31) HOF	**13560**
Best Of My Love—Emotions (77)	7303
Shining Star—Earth, Wind & Fire (75)	4991
Let's Groove—Earth, Wind & Fire (81)	4608
September—Earth, Wind & Fire (78)	2728
Sing A Song—Earth, Wind & Fire (75)	2498
That's The Way Of The World—Earth, Wind & Fire (75)	1622
Serpentine Fire—Earth, Wind & Fire (77)	1513
Saturday Nite—Earth, Wind & Fire (76)	856
Fall In Love With Me—Earth, Wind & Fire (83)	838
Fantasy—Earth, Wind & Fire (78)	662
Mighty Mighty—Earth, Wind & Fire (74)	583
Keep Your Head To The Sky—Earth, Wind & Fire (73)	409
Evil—Earth, Wind & Fire (73)	340
I Am Love—Jennifer Holliday (83)	334
You—Earth, Wind & Fire (80)	320
Let Me Talk—Earth, Wind & Fire (80)	319
Kalimba Story—Earth, Wind & Fire (74)	290
Tip Of My Tongue—Tubes (83)	198
Devotion—Earth, Wind & Fire (74)	186
And Love Goes On—Earth, Wind & Fire (81)	174
Sun Goddess—Ramsey Lewis And Earth, Wind & Fire (75)	162
In The Stone—Earth, Wind & Fire (79)	161
Wanna Be With You—Earth, Wind & Fire (82)	150
Thinking Of You—Earth, Wind & Fire (88)	137
Hot Dawgit—Ramsey Lewis And Earth, Wind & Fire (74)	123
Star—Earth, Wind & Fire (79)	121
Flowers—Emotions (76)	93
Love Is Life—Earth, Wind & Fire (71)	72
Side By Side—Earth, Wind & Fire (83)	65
Smile—Emotions (78)	33
Skat Strut—M.C. Skat Kat And The Stray Mob (91)	16
Pearl WHITE [Pearl White Terrell] ▶ 10098 (1)	**13**
Tears From My Heart—Thurston Harris (58)	26
Peter WHITE ▶ 2703 (2)	**1262**
Time Passages—Al Stewart (78)	1891
Midnight Rocks—Al Stewart (80)	633
Ray WHITE ▶ 6077 (1)	**209**
You Be Illin'—Run-D.M.C. (86)	626
Reggie WHITE [Blitz] ▶ 6726 (1)	**142**
Serious—Donna Allen (87)	852

Robert WHITE ▶ 9721 (1)	**18**
The Topical Song—Barron Knights (79)	*55*
Roger WHITE ▶ 9507 (1)	**22**
Friends—Feather (70)	112
Ronnie WHITE ▶ 826 (14)	**5332**
My Girl—Temptations (65)	*6094*
You Beat Me To The Punch—Mary Wells (62)	*1687*
My Girl Has Gone—Miracles (65)	946
One More Heartache—Marvin Gaye (66)	662
My Girl—Suavé (88)	*579*
My Girl—Bobby Vee (68)	*476*
Everybody's Gotta Pay Some Dues—Miracles (61)	307
My Girl—Daryl Hall & John Oates Featuring David Ruffin & Eddie Kendricks (85)	*285*
You Threw A Lucky Punch—Gene Chandler (62)	*280*
Come On Do The Jerk—Miracles (64)	273
My Girl—Amii Stewart & Johnny Bristol (80)	*99*
My Girl—Eddie Floyd (70)	*97*
Don't Look Back—Temptations (65)	*49*
(You Got To Walk And) Don't Look Back—Peter Tosh (78)	*24*
—Sylvia White see: Sil SEDORES	
Ted WHITE ▶ 1495 (3)	**2907**
(Sweet Sweet Baby) Since You've Been Gone—Aretha Franklin (68)	*3603*
Think—Aretha Franklin (68)	2204
Since You've Been Gone—Ramsey Lewis (68)	*7.3*
Tony Joe WHITE ▶ 540 (10)	**7922**
Rainy Night In Georgia—Brook Benton (70)	4458
Polk Salad Annie—Tony Joe White (69)	1983
I've Got A Thing About You Baby—Elvis Presley (74)	*573*
Roosevelt And Ira Lee (Night Of The Mossacin)—Tony Joe White (69)	360
Steamy Windows—Tina Turner (89)	325
Willie & Laura Mae Jones—Dusty Springfield (69)	168
I Get Off On It—Tony Joe White (80)	82
Save Your Sugar For Me—Tony Joe White (70)	8.1
I Got A Thing About You Baby—Billy Lee Riley (72)	*6.9*
For Ol' Times Sake—Elvis Presley (73)	0.0
Verdine WHITE ▶ 2152 (9) HOF	**1812**
That's The Way Of The World—Earth, Wind & Fire (75)	1622
Serpentine Fire—Earth, Wind & Fire (77)	1513
Fantasy—Earth, Wind & Fire (78)	662
Mighty Mighty—Earth, Wind & Fire (74)	583
Let Me Talk—Earth, Wind & Fire (80)	319
Kalimba Story—Earth, Wind & Fire (74)	290
And Love Goes On—Earth, Wind & Fire (81)	174
Come Go With Me—Pockets (77)	49
Baby, Baby My Love's All For You—Deniece Williams (78)	11
Wayne WHITE ▶ 9193 (1)	**29**
Amerikan Music—Steve Alaimo (72)	58
William WHITE ▶ 5116 (1)	**340**
I'm Sorry—Platters (57)	1021
Nick WHITECROSS ▶ 11003 (2)	**3.9**
Maybe This Day—Kissing The Pink (83)	20
Certain Things Are Likely—K.T.P./Kissing The Pink (87)	4.3
—Beaurls Whitehead see: Peter WHITEHEAD	
Charlie WHITEHEAD ▶ 5498 (2)	**279**
(Shu-Doo-Pa-Poo-Poop) Love Being Your Fool—Travis Wammack (75)	352
She Didn't Know (She Kept On Talking)—Dee Dee Warwick (70)	308
Don WHITEHEAD ▶ 9421 (1)	**24**
Love Is Life—Earth, Wind & Fire (71)	72
John WHITEHEAD ▶ 1303 (10)	**3401**
Back Stabbers—O'Jays (72)	4999
Wake Up Everybody (Part 1)—Harold Melvin And The Blue Notes (75)	1592
Ain't No Stoppin' Us Now—McFadden & Whitehead (79)	1423
Bad Luck (Part 1)—Harold Melvin And The Blue Notes (75)	*1407*
I'll Always Love My Mama (Part I)—Intruders (73)	618
Where Are All My Friends—Harold Melvin And The Blue Notes (74)	117
Bad Luck—Ritchie Family (76)	*92*
Tell The World How I Feel About 'Cha Baby—Harold Melvin And The Blue Notes (76)	66
Let's Groove—Archie Bell & The Drells (76)	38
Bad Luck—Atlanta Disco Band (76)	*14*
Peter WHITEHEAD [Beaurls Whitehead] ▶ 5966 (3)	**222**
Macho Man—Village People (78)	679
Ready For The '80s—Village People (79)	147
I Want To Dance With You (Dance With Me)—Ritchie Family (75)	45
Fred WHITEHOUSE ▶ 10772 (1)	**5.4**
Sam, You Made The Pants Too Long—Barbra Streisand (66)	21
Reid WHITELAW ▶ 6379 (3)	**177**
Goody Goody Gumdrops—1910 Fruitgum Co. (68)	638
(We'll Meet In The) "Yellow Forest"—Jay & The Americans (67)	32
Diane—Golden Gate (70)	4.4
Bobby WHITESIDE ▶ 3787 (1)	**699**
Comin' In And Out Of Your Life—Barbra Streisand (81)	1398
Norman WHITFIELD ▶ 21 (92) HOF	**60883**
I Heard It Through The Grapevine—Marvin Gaye (68)	*8871*
War—Edwin Starr (70)	*7121*
I Heard It Through The Grapevine—Gladys Knight & The Pips (67)	*6841*
Just My Imagination (Running Away With Me)—Temptations (71)	6683
I Can't Get Next To You—Temptations (69)	*6180*
Ball Of Confusion (That's What The World Is Today)—Temptations (70)	5317
Car Wash—Rose Royce (76)	5173
I Wish It Would Rain—Temptations (68)	*5041*
Smiling Faces Sometimes—Undisputed Truth (71)	4374
Papa Was A Rollin' Stone—Temptations (72)	*4089*
Cloud Nine—Temptations (68)	*3303*
Too Busy Thinking About My Baby—Marvin Gaye (69)	3171
Beauty Is Only Skin Deep—Temptations (66)	2987
You're My Everything—Temptations (67)	2625
Psychedelic Shack—Temptations (70)	2537
(I Know) I'm Losing You—Rare Earth (70)	*2495*
Run Away Child, Running Wild—Temptations (69)	2318
Ain't Too Proud To Beg—Temptations (66)	*2123*
That's The Way Love Is—Marvin Gaye (69)	1960
Pride And Joy—Marvin Gaye (63)	1884
(I Know) I'm Losing You—Temptations (66)	*1880*
Masterpiece—Temptations (73)	1870
I Could Never Love Another (After Loving You)—Temptations (68)	1576
(Loneliness Made Me Realize) It's You That I Need—Temptations (67)	1525
I Wanna Get Next To You—Rose Royce (77)	1486
The End Of Our Road—Gladys Knight & The Pips (68)	*1369*
War—Bruce Springsteen & The E Street Band (86)	*1264*
Knockin' Boots—Candyman (90)	1245
Superstar (Remember How You Got Where You Are)—Temptations (71)	1205
Friendship Train—Gladys Knight & The Pips (69)	1176
Too Many Fish In The Sea—Marvelettes (64)	*1040*
(I Know) I'm Losing You—Rod Stewart With Faces (71)	*942*
Don't Let The Joneses Get You Down—Temptations (69)	852
Ain't Too Proud To Beg—Rolling Stones (74)	*829*
Please Return Your Love To Me—Temptations (68)	720
Stop The War Now—Edwin Starr (70)	685
Girl (Why You Wanna Make Me Blue)—Temptations (64)	667
Theme Song From "Which Way Is Up"—Stargard (78)	662
Take A Look Around—Temptations (72)	601
You Need Love Like I Do (Don't You)—Gladys Knight & The Pips (70)	595
It Should Have Been Me—Gladys Knight & The Pips (68)	*557*
Hey Girl (I Like Your Style)—Temptations (73)	541
Let Your Hair Down—Temptations (73)	538
How Can I Forget—Marvin Gaye (70)	509
The End Of Our Road—Marvin Gaye (70)	*504*
Needle In A Haystack—Velvelettes (64)	477
Gonna Give Her All The Love I've Got—Jimmy Ruffin (67)	*474*
I Wish It Would Rain—Gladys Knight & The Pips (68)	*449*
Ungena Za Ulimwengu (Unite The World)—Temptations (70)	448
The Plastic Man—Temptations (73)	437
It's Summer—Temptations (71)	417
Cloud Nine—Mongo Santamaria (69)	*404*
Everybody Needs Love—Gladys Knight & The Pips (67)	383
Don't Let Him Take Your Love From Me—Four Tops (69)	358
Heavenly—Temptations (74)	356
On A Sunday Afternoon—A Lighter Shade Of Brown (91)	320
Too Many Fish In The Sea—Mitch Ryder And The Detroit Wheels (67)	*300*
Do Your Dance - Part I—Rose Royce (77)	269
Ooh Boy—Rose Royce (77)	265
Funky Music Sho Nuff Turns Me On—Edwin Starr (71)	*257*
You Make Your Own Heaven And Hell Right Here On Earth—Undisputed Truth (71)	230
You + Me = Love—Undisputed Truth (77)	217
I Heard It Through The Grapevine—Creedence Clearwater Revival (76)	*211*
Don't You Miss Me A Little Bit Baby—Jimmy Ruffin (67)	184
I Can't Get Next To You—Al Green (70)	*178*
He Was Really Sayin' Somethin'—Velvelettes (65)	172
I'm Going Down—Rose Royce (77)	172
You've Got My Soul On Fire—Temptations (74)	167
Sail Away—Temptations (84)	152
I Heard It Through The Grapevine (Part 1)—Roger (81)	*147*
Papa Was A Rollin' Stone—Wolf (82)	*139*
What It Is—Undisputed Truth (72)	98
Help Yourself—Undisputed Truth (74)	91
Wherever I Lay My Hat (That's My Home)—Paul Young (83)	90
Gonna Give Her All The Love I've Got—Marvin Gaye (70)	*72*
Papa Was A Rollin' Stone—Undisputed Truth (72)	*68*
(I Know) I'm Losing You—Uptown (86)	*55*
Hum Along And Dance—Temptations (70)	44
I'm In Love (And I Love The Feeling)—Rose Royce (78)	44
I Gotta Let You Go—Martha Reeves & The Vandellas (70)	34
The Girl's Alright With Me—Temptations (64)	23
I Heard It Thru The Grapevine—King Curtis & The Kingpins (68)	*21*
Funky Music Sho Nuff Turns Me On—Temptations (72)	*20*
I Heard It Through The Grapevine—California Raisins (88)	*18*
It Should Have Been Me—Yvonne Fair (76)	*17*
Papa Was A Rolling Stone—Stars On 45 (81)	*12*
Ain't Too Proud To Beg—Rick Astley (89)	*8.7*
Ain't Too Proud To Beg—Magnificent Men (67)	*7.6*
What You Waitin' For—Stargard (78)	3.7
Lonely Lonely Girl Am I—Velvelettes (65)	2.8
Message From A Black Man—Whatnauts (70)	1.7
Let's Go Down To The Disco—Undisputed Truth (77)	0.0
Brad WHITFORD ▶ 4752 (2)	**423**
Last Child—Aerosmith (76)	817
Kings And Queens—Aerosmith (78)	73
Mike WHITFORD ▶ 10851 (1)	**4.9**
Jack The Lad—3 Man Island (88)	15
Art WHITING ▶ 10405 (1)	**8.8**
Woman From Liberia—Jimmie Rodgers (60)	18
George WHITING ▶ 4567 (2)	**465**
My Blue Heaven—Fats Domino (56)	*919*
My Blue Heaven—Bobby Day (60)	*10*
Richard WHITING ▶ 7637 (5) HOF	**84**
Wun'erful, Wun'erful! (Sides Uh-One & Uh-Two)—Stan Freberg (57)	298
Beyond The Blue Horizon—Lou Christie (74)	103
On The Good Ship Lollipop—Wonder Who ? (66)	16
Guilty—Crests (62)	9.8
True Blue Lou—Tony Bennett (63)	1.3
Ray WHITLEY ▶ 997 (9)	**4490**
What Kind Of Fool (Do You Think I Am)—Tams (63)	*1800*
What Kind Of Fool Do You Think I Am—Bill Deal & The Rhondels (69)	*862*
I've Been Hurt—Bill Deal & The Rhondels (69)	726
Run, Run, Look And See—Brian Hyland (66)	537
Hey Girl Don't Bother Me—Tams (64)	470
Be Young, Be Foolish, Be Happy—Tams (68)	375
You Lied To Your Daddy—Tams (64)	130
Backwards And Forwards—December's Children (68)	41
I Found A Rainbow—Swingin' Medallions (67)	4.6

Bobby WHITLOCK ► 8775 (3)	**40**
Bell Bottom Blues–Eric Clapton (73)	*45*
Bell Bottom Blues–Derek And The Dominos (71)	*34*
Where There's A Will There's A Way–Delaney & Bonnie (72)	1.1
Tom WHITLOCK ► 1026 (5)	**4312**
Take My Breath Away (Love Theme From TOP GUN)–Berlin (86)	4143
Danger Zone–Kenny Loggins (86)	2682
Meet Me Half Way–Kenny Loggins (87)	1448
Winner Takes It All–Sammy Hagar (87)	250
Crazy World–Big Trouble (87)	102
–Jerry Whitman see: June WINTERS	
Joan WHITNEY [Zoe Parentau, Zoe Voeth] ► 3906 (9)	**662**
No Other Arms No Other Lips–Chordettes (59)	*741*
Cool Shake–Del Vikings (57)	461
Pupalina–Gaylords (54)	*213*
How Lonely Can I Get–Kitty Kallen (55)	*182*
No Other Arms No Other Lips–Four Aces (59)	*119*
Candy Cha Cha–Jan August-Richard Hayman (58)	32
How Lonely Can I Get?–Lancers (55)	*0.0*
Pupalina (My Little Doll)–Jimmy Durante (54)	*0.0*
Pupalina (My Little Doll)–Guy Lombardo & His Royal Canadians (54)	*0.0*
Marva WHITNEY ► 8275 (1)	**56**
It's My Thing (You Can't Tell Me Who To Sock It To)–Marva Whitney (69)	112
Carson WHITSETT ► 5034 (2)	**357**
Why Not Me–Fred Knoblock (80)	637
Don't Girls Get Lonely–Glenn Shorrock (83)	76
Beth Slater WHITSON ► 8332 (2)	**54**
Let Me Call You Sweetheart–Timi Yuro (62)	*94*
Let Me Call You Sweetheart–Bruce Hayes with Mary Mayo (60)	*14*
Ray WHITT ► 6752 (2)	**140**
Little Pigeon–Sal Mineo (58)	*140*
Little Pigeon–Chuck Sims (58)	*0.0*
Hudson WHITTAKER [Tampa Red] ► 11303 (1)	**2.3**
It Hurts Me Too–Elmore James (65)	4.6
Roger WHITTAKER ► 4083 (1)	**599**
The Last Farewell–Roger Whittaker (75)	1198
Danny WHITTEN ► 5024 (2)	**358**
I Don't Want To Talk About It–Rod Stewart (79)	297
Hole In My Pocket–Barry Goldberg Reunion (68)	60
Peggy WHITTINGTON ► 3315 (1)	**902**
Think–Brenda Lee (64)	902
Vicki WICKHAM ► 2112 (3)	**1862**
You Don't Have To Say You Love Me–Dusty Springfield (66)	*4119*
You Don't Have To Say You Love Me–Elvis Presley (70)	*1432*
You Don't Have To Say You Love Me–Four Sonics (68)	*36*
John WICKS ► 8173 (1)	**60**
Starry Eyes–Records (79)	119
Stacey WIDELITZ ► 2529 (1)	**1413**
She's Like The Wind–Patrick Swayze (87)	2825
Fred WIEDER ► 7938 (1)	**69**
Batman–Jan & Dean (66)	206
Judy WIEDER ► 5212 (2)	**325**
It Must Be Love–Alton McClain & Destiny (79)	469
Star Love–Cheryl Lynn (79)	181
Jane WIEDLIN ► 1656 (8)	**2539**
Vacation–Go-Go's (82)	2046
Our Lips Are Sealed–Go-Go's (81)	1438
Rush Hour–Jane Wiedlin (88)	1247
Turn To You–Go-Go's (84)	530
Get Up And Go–Go-Go's (82)	260
Inside A Dream–Jane Wiedlin (88)	148
Blue Kiss–Jane Wiedlin (85)	80
Yes Or No–Go-Go's (84)	16
–Jeffrey Phillip Wielandt see: Zakk WYLDE	
Herb WIENER ► 9719 (2)	**18**
I Hear Those Bells–Dinah Washington (55)	55
Joey–Betty Madigan (54)	0.0
Jean WIENER ► 6613 (2)	**151**
The Touch (Le Grisbi)–Three Suns (54)	*148*
The Touch–Betty Johnson (54)	*5.6*

Stuart WIENER ► 5075 (2)	**348**
To The Aisle–Five Satins (57)	*696*
Aisle–Roy Hamilton (57)	*0.0*
Rusty WIER ► 9650 (1)	**20**
Don't It Make You Wanna Dance?–Rusty Wier (75)	20
Rick WIESEND ► 8717 (1)	**41**
Wait A Minute–Tim Tam And The Turn-Ons (66)	82
–Annette Wiesner see: Annette TUCKER	
Caroline WIGGINS ► 6108 (1)	**206**
Money$ Too Tight (To Mention)–Simply Red (86)	617
–Charles Ray Wiggins see: Raphael SAADIQ	
Dwayne WIGGINS ► 3876 (4)	**670**
Feels Good–Tony! Toni! Toné! (90)	1657
Little Walter–Tony! Toni! Toné! (88)	272
The Blues–Tony! Toni! Tone! (90)	260
Whatever You Want–Tony! Toni! Toné! (91)	143
Jay WIGGINS ► 6231 (3)	**191**
Sad Girl–Intruders (69)	*367*
Sad Girl–GQ (82)	*15*
Sad Girl–Jay Wiggins (63)	*0.9*
Keith WIGGINS ► 11312 (1)	**2.3**
Freedom–Grandmaster Flash And The Furious 5 (80)	21
Steve WIGHTMAN ► 10667 (1)	**6.3**
You Know The Feelin'–Steve Wightman (76)	6.3
Anders WIKSTRÖM ► 10894 (1)	**4.5**
Rev It Up–Newcity Rockers (87)	14
–Robert Wilber see: Bob SAGE	
Sandy WILBURN ► 7486 (1)	**93**
I Like Your Lovin' (Do You Like Mine)–Chi-Lites (70)	185
–Nelson Wilbury see: George HARRISON	
–Otis Wilbury see: Jeff LYNNE	
Harlow WILCOX ► 4628 (1)	**448**
Groovy Grubworm–Harlow Wilcox And The Oakies (69)	897
John Griffitt WILCOX ► 3727 (4)	**719**
Set Me Free–Utopia (80)	641
We Connect–Stacey Q (86)	535
The Very Last Time–Utopia (80)	51
Feet Don't Fail Me Now–Utopia (83)	42
Christian WILDE ► 6955 (1)	**126**
Grover Henson Feels Forgotten–Bill Cosby (70)	126
Danny WILDE [Danny Thomas, Danny C. Wilde] ► 4029 (3)	**620**
Just The Way It Is, Baby–Rembrandts (91)	1055
Someone–Rembrandts (91)	161
Save Me–Rembrandts (91)	25
–Eugene Wilde see: Ronnie E. BROOMFIELD	
Kim WILDE [Kim Fowler, Kim Smith] ► 6593 (1)	**153**
You Came–Kim Wilde (88)	307
Marty WILDE [Frere Manston, Reginald Leonard Smith] ► 2634 (7)	**1304**
Kids In America–Kim Wilde (82)	850
Abergavenny–Shannon (69)	496
Bad Boy–Marty Wilde (60)	*307*
I Still Believe In Tomorrow–John & Anne Ryder (69)	300
Ice In The Sun–Status Quo (68)	217
Go For It–Kim Wilde (85)	131
Bad Boy–Robin Luke (60)	*0.0*
Ricky WILDE [Richard James Reginald Steven Smith, Ricky Steven Reginald Smith, Ricky Smith, Ricki Wilde] ► 3948 (3)	**644**
Kids In America–Kim Wilde (82)	850
You Came–Kim Wilde (88)	307
Go For It–Kim Wilde (85)	131
Alec WILDER ► 7863 (4) HOF	**72**
If She Should Come To You (La Montana)–Anthony Newley (60)	*120*
Ain'tcha Cha Comin' Out T Tonight–Jo Stafford (55)	48
I'll Be Around–Don Cherry (56)	7.0
How Lovely Is Christmas–Bing Crosby (57)	1.3
George WILDER [George William Weidler] ► 11223 (1)	**2.7**
Down In The Bottom Of The Well–Wilder Brothers (54)	8.1
Matthew WILDER [Matthew Weiner] ► 1599 (4)	**2646**
Break My Stride–Matthew Wilder (83)	3738

The Kid's American–Matthew Wilder (84)	437
Wild Women Do–Natalie Cole (90)	292
Bouncin' Off The Walls–Matthew Wilder (84)	243
–P.G. Wilder see: P.G. WYLDER	
Walter WILDER [Walter Wolfgang Weidler] ► 11224 (1)	**2.7**
Down In The Bottom Of The Well–Wilder Brothers (54)	8.1
Warner WILDER [Warner Alfred Weidler, Werther Alfred Weidler, Warren Weidler] ► 4032 (3)	**619**
Love Means (You Never Have To Say You're Sorry)–Sounds Of Sunshine (71)	594
Sack Dress–Beavers (58)	22
Down In The Bottom Of The Well–Wilder Brothers (54)	8.1
Frank WILDHORN ► 2030 (3)	**1991**
Where Do Broken Hearts Go–Whitney Houston (88)	3452
Miracles–Stacy Lattisaw (83)	523
Shy Boys–Ana (87)	6.2
–Bobby Wilding see: Bobby WEINSTEIN	
Charles WILDMAN [Willy Mattes] ► 11063 (1)	**3.4**
Riviera Concerto–Roger Williams (60)	3.4
–Raven Wildroot see: Gene BARGE	
–Donald MacRae Wilhoite see: Don RAYE	
Orion WILHOITE ► 7879 (1)	**71**
Slide–Slave (77)	640
Crawford WILKERSON [HI-C] ► 8830 (1)	**38**
I'm Not Your Puppet–Hi-C (91)	115
–Bucky Wilkin see: John Buck WILKIN	
John Buck WILKIN [Bucky Wilkin] ► 1129 (5)	**3930**
G.T.O.–Ronny & The Daytonas (64)	3310
Sandy–Ronny & The Daytonas (65)	636
Apartment 21–Bobbie Gentry (70)	134
Dianne, Dianne–Ronny & The Daytonas (66)	118
California Bound–Ronny & The Daytonas (64)	109
Marijohn WILKIN ► 1043 (7)	**4225**
Waterloo–Stonewall Jackson (59)	4628
P.T. 109–Jimmy Dean (62)	2113
I Just Don't Understand–Ann-Margret (61)	1253
One Day At A Time–Marilyn Sellars (74)	224
Mary Don't You Weep–Stonewall Jackson (59)	197
Igmoo (The Pride Of South Central High)–Stonewall Jackson (59)	34
Fallen Angel–Webb Pierce (60)	0.8
David WILKINS ► 2315 (1)	**1606**
Coming On Strong–Brenda Lee (66)	1606
Geoff WILKINS ► 9571 (1)	**21**
Light Up The World With Sunshine–Hamilton, Joe Frank & Dennison (76)	42
Ronnie WILKINS ► 1917 (9)	**2112**
Son-Of-A Preacher Man–Dusty Springfield (68)	*2224*
The Land Of Milk And Honey–Vogues (66)	626
Spread It On Thick–Gentrys (65)	447
Love Of The Common People–Winstons (69)	*407*
Growin'–Loggins & Messina (75)	341
Love Of The Common People–Paul Young (84)	*288*
Poor Little Cupid–Joe Dowell (62)	18
A Woman Of The World–Gentrys (66)	5.6
Son Of A Preacher Man–Aretha Franklin (70)	*0.0*
Dudley WILKINSON ► 5667 (3)	**257**
Because Of You–Sammy Davis Jr. (54)	*241*
Because Of You–Chris Montez (67)	*218*
Because Of You–Rome & Paris (66)	*55*
William WILLDRIDGE ► 10651 (1)	**6.3**
Secret Of Love–Elton Anderson With Sid Lawrence Combo (60)	13
Albert WILLEMETZ ► 6801 (2)	**136**
My Man–Peggy Lee (59)	*340*
My Man–Barbra Streisand (65)	*204*
Elliot WILLENSKY ► 860 (2)	**5172**
Got To Be There–Michael Jackson (71)	*5083*
Got To Be There–Chaka Khan (83)	*89*
Allen WILLIAMS ► 11210 (1)	**2.7**
Shout It Out–B.T. Express (78)	8.2
Alonzo WILLIAMS ► 8664 (1)	**43**
Turn Off The Lights–World Class Wreckin' Cru (88)	43

Alvin WILLIAMS ► 6532 (3)	**160**
Rang Tang Ding Dong (I Am The Japanese Sandman)—Cellos (57)	*160*
Rang Tang Ding Dong—Chuck Miller (57)	*0.0*
Rang Tang Ding Dong (I'm The Japanese Sandman)—Ray Stevens (57)	*0.0*
Andre WILLIAMS [Zephire Andre Williams] ► 2268 (8)	**1672**
Twine Time—Alvin Cash & The Crawlers (65)	1567
What's The Matter With You Baby—Marvin Gaye & Mary Wells (64)	929
Shake A Tail Feather—James & Bobby Purify (67)	*829*
Shake A Tail Feather—Five Du-Tones (63)	*412*
The Funky Judge—Bull & The Matadors (68)	370
Rib Tip's (Part 1)—Andre Williams & His Orch. (66)	26
Gotta Get To Know You—Bobby Bland (69)	25
Pearl Time—Andre Williams (67)	19
—Anna Delores Williams see: Anna KING	
—Arthur Williams see: Jimmy VAN HEUSEN	
—Barney Williams see: Luther DIXON	
Bernice WILLIAMS ► 1106 (9)	**4005**
Duke Of Earl—Gene Chandler (62)	*9144*
Better Tell Him No—Starlets (61)	433
The Barracuda—Alvin Cash & The Crawlers (65)	238
The Girl's A Devil—Dukays (61)	165
Nite Owl—Dukays (62)	*89*
Walk On With The Duke—Duke Of Earl (62)	86
Duchess Of Earl—Pearlettes (62)	*50*
Nite Owl—Dukays (62)	*5.7*
Duchess Of Earl—Bobbie Smith & The Dreamgirls (62)	*0.0*
Bert A. WILLIAMS ► 5600 (2)	**267**
Nobody—Perry Como (55)	*533*
Nobody—Bing Crosby (55)	*0.0*
Bobby WILLIAMS ► 9820 (2)	**16**
The Wedding—Solitaires (55)	*36*
The Wedding—Chordettes (55)	*13*
Boris WILLIAMS [Boris Peter Bransby-Williams] ► 3820 (8)	**690**
Love Song—Cure (89)	2408
Just Like Heaven—Cure (87)	604
Why Can't I Be You?—Cure (87)	279
Fascination Street—Cure (89)	194
Lullaby—Cure (89)	170
Pictures Of You—Cure (90)	105
Hot Hot Hot!!!—Cure (88)	88
Never Enough—Cure (90)	68
Charles WILLIAMS [Isaac Cozerbreit] ► 1266 (2)	**3522**
Theme From The Apartment—Ferrante & Teicher With Their Orch. & Chrous (60)	*3475*
Theme From The Apartment—Meco (82)	*47*
Charlie WILLIAMS ► 3811 (7)	**693**
500 Miles Away From Home—Bobby Bare (63)	*1427*
I Got Stripes—Johnny Cash (59)	321
Five Hundred Miles—Heaven Bound With Tony Scotti (71)	*109*
Application For Love—Roy Clark (63)	24
Listen, They're Playing My Song—Ray Charles (68)	8.0
500 Miles—Hooters (89)	*6.5*
Right Or Left At Oak Street—Roy Clark (69)	4.0
Cheri WILLIAMS ► 8367 (1)	**53**
Got A Love For You—Jomanda (91)	318
—Clara Bell Williams see: Cara BELL	
Clarence WILLIAMS ► 4189 (3) HOF	**568**
My Bucket's Got A Hole In It—Ricky Nelson (58)	557
Sugar Blues—Don Costa (62)	*6.7*
Sugar Blues—Ace Cannon (62)	*4.5*
—Curly Williams see: Dave WILLIAMS	
Curtis Edward WILLIAMS ► 2164 (10)	**1805**
Earth Angel (Will You Be Mine)—Penguins (54)	*2284*
Earth Angel (Will You Be Mine)—Crew-Cuts (55)	*1777*
Earth Angel—New Edition (86)	*545*
Earth Angel (Will You Be Mine)—Vogues (69)	*486*
Earth Angel—Johnny Tillotson (60)	*230*
Earth Angel (Will You Be Mine)—Gloria Mann (55)	*74*
Elizabeth—Dave Ford And The Hollywood Flames (62)	14
Earth Angel—Fred Parris & The Five Satins (82)	*4.8*
Earth Angel—Cleftones (61)	*2.3*
Earth Angel—Les Baxter & The Bombers (54)	*0.0*

Curtis Fitzgerald WILLIAMS ► 1975 (11)	**2040**
Cherish—Kool & The Gang (85)	3699
Joanna—Kool & The Gang (83)	3511
Misled—Kool & The Gang (84)	1436
Fresh—Kool & The Gang (85)	1367
Victory—Kool & The Gang (86)	1269
Tonight—Kool & The Gang (84)	1136
Stone Love—Kool & The Gang (87)	994
Emergency—Kool & The Gang (85)	915
Let's Go Dancin' (Ooh La, La, La)—Kool & The Gang (82)	654
Big Fun—Kool & The Gang (82)	532
Holiday—Kool & The Gang (87)	126
Dan Edward WILLIAMS ► 7824 (2)	**73**
Don't You Know How Much I Love You—Ronnie Milsap (83)	138
I Love Women—Jim Hurt (80)	9.0
Danny WILLIAMS ► 8246 (1)	**57**
I Need Your Loving—Human League (86)	343
Dave WILLIAMS [Curly Williams, Doc Williams] ► 1000 (5)	**4483**
Whole Lot Of Shakin' Going On—Jerry Lee Lewis (57)	*3567*
Whole Lotta Shakin' Goin' On—Chubby Checker (60)	*484*
Whole Lot Of Shakin' Going On—Conway Twitty (60)	*265*
Whole Lotta Shakin' Goin' On—Cat Mother And The All Night News Boys (69)	*164*
Pitty Pat Band—Dori Anne Gray (56)	3.4
David Charles WILLIAMS ► 5913 (1)	**229**
You've Got To Take It (If You Want It)—Main Ingredient (72)	459
David Larry WILLIAMS ► 9186 (1)	**29**
Le Spank—Le Pamplemousse (77)	117
David Z. WILLIAMS ► 4672 (1)	**442**
Don't Hold Back—Chanson (78)	884
—Delores Williams see: LaVern BAKER	
Deniece WILLIAMS [June Deniece Chandler] ► 4798 (4)	**412**
Free—Deniece Williams (76)	1067
Silly—Deniece Williams (81)	347
Next Love—Deniece Williams (84)	42
I've Got The Next Dance—Deniece Williams (79)	26
—Doc Williams see: Dave WILLIAMS	
Dub WILLIAMS [James William Pebworth] ► 1764 (6)	**2360**
Release Me (And Let Me Love Again)—Engelbert Humperdinck (67)	*4487*
Release Me—Esther Phillips "Little Esther" (62)	*2523*
I'll Release You—Joann Bon And The Coquettes (67)	*33*
Release Me—Johnny Adams (68)	*29*
Release Me—Jivin' Gene (60)	*13*
Release Me—Esther Phillips (67)	*7.2*
Eddie WILLIAMS ► 11306 (1)	**2.3**
Driftin' Blues—Bobby Bland (68)	6.9
Eugene WILLIAMS ► 2031 (2)	**1990**
Tryin' To Live My Life Without You—Bob Seger (81)	*1918*
Trying To Live My Life Without You—Otis Clay (72)	*72*
Frederick WILLIAMS ► 6956 (1)	**126**
Bad Motorcycle—Storey Sisters (58)	251
Frederick B. WILLIAMS ► 866 (5)	**5123**
Gonna Make You Sweat—C & C Music Factory (Featuring Freedom Williams) (90)	4586
Here We Go—C & C Music Factory (Featuring Freedom Williams And Zelma Davis) (91)	3090
Things That Make You Go Hmmmm—C & C Music Factory (Featuring Freedom Williams) (91)	2086
You're My One And Only (True Love)—Seduction (89)	682
Breakdown—Seduction (90)	46
—Freedom Williams see: Frederick B. WILLIAMS	
—Gary Williams see: Gerry GRANAHAN	
George R. WILLIAMS ► 1824 (3)	**2259**
So Much In Love—Tymes (63)	*6568*
So Much In Love—Timothy B. Schmit (82)	*197*
Let's Make Love Tonight—Bobby Rydell (63)	12
Greg WILLIAMS ► 8426 (1)	**51**
I Call Your Name—Switch (79)	102
Guy T. WILLIAMS ► 11313 (1)	**2.3**
Freedom—Grandmaster Flash And The Furious 5 (80)	21
Hank WILLIAMS [Hiram King Williams] ► 530 (26) HOF	**8058**
I'm So Lonesome I Could Cry—B.J. Thomas And The Triumphs (66)	*2630*

Jambalaya (On The Bayou)—Blue Ridge Rangers (72)	*1499*
I Can't Help It (If I'm Still In Love With You)—Johnny Tillotson (62)	*792*
You Win Again—Fats Domino (62)	*623*
Jambalaya (On The Bayou)—Fats Domino (61)	*553*
Your Cheating Heart—Ray Charles With The Jack Halloran Singers And The Ray Charles Orchestra (62)	*492*
I Can't Help It—Adam Wade (60)	*398*
My Heart Would Know—Al Martino (65)	318
Long Gone Lonesome Blues—Hank Williams, Jr. (64)	206
Your Cheatin' Heart—George Hamilton IV (58)	*156*
Your Cheatin' Heart—Billy Vaughn And His Orchestra (59)	*144*
Jambalaya (On The Bayou)—Little Brenda Lee (9 Years Old) (56)	*76*
Jambalaya (On The Bayou)—Nitty Gritty Dirt Band (72)	*53*
I Can't Help It (If I'm Still In Love With You)—Al Martino (68)	*28*
I Can't Help It (If I'm Still In Love With You)—Margaret Whiting (58)	*28*
I Can't Help It (If I'm Still In Love With You)—B.J. Thomas (67)	*13*
You Win Again—Paulette Sisters (55)	*12*
Jambalaya—Bobby Comstock & The Counts (60)	*11*
I'm So Lonesome I Could Cry—Terry Bradshaw (76)	*11*
I'm So Lonesome I Could Cry—Johnny Tillotson (62)	*8.2*
There'll Be No Teardrops Tonight—Adam Wade (62)	*3.2*
Cold, Cold Heart—Dinah Washington (62)	2.2
You Win Again—Jerry Lee Lewis (58)	*1.9*
Kaw Liga—Four Preps (60)	0.5
I'm So Lonesome I Could Cry—Hank Wilson (73)	*0.0*
There'll Be No Teardrops Tonight—Tony Bennett (54)	*0.0*
Harry WILLIAMS Jr. ► 2600 (2)	**1334**
Never Let You Go—Bloodstone (73)	697
Outside Woman—Bloodstone (74)	637
Henry WILLIAMS ► 4832 (1)	**403**
Give Your Baby A Standing Ovation—Dells (73)	807
—Hiram King Williams see: Hank WILLIAMS	
Hugh WILLIAMS [Wilhelm Grosz] ► 2099 (9)	**1881**
Harbor Lights—Platters (60)	*2551*
Red Sails In The Sunset—Platters Featuring Tony Williams (60)	*574*
Red Sails In The Sunset—Fats Domino (63)	*526*
Red Sails In The Sunset—Tab Hunter (57)	*70*
Tomorrow Night—Damita Jo (65)	27
Harbor Lights—Mulcays (55)	*13*
Harbor Lights—Seymour & His Heartbeat Trumpet (59)	*1.6*
Isle Of Capri—Gaylords (54)	*0.0*
Isle Of Capri—Jackie Lee & His Orchestra (54)	*0.0*
J. Mayo WILLIAMS ► 3128 (4)	**995**
Corinna Corinna—Ray Peterson (60)	*1744*
Drinking Wine Spo-Dee O'dee—Jerry Lee Lewis (73)	599
Corrine Corrina—Joe Turner (56)	*342*
Corrine, Corrina—Swingin' Sam (56)	*0.0*
James L. WILLIAMS ► 5299 (3)	**310**
Look At Me Girl—Bobby Vee And The Strangers (66)	272
When I Think Of You—Leif Garrett (79)	*26*
When I Think Of You—James & Michael (77)	*12*
James N. WILLIAMS ► 9566 (2)	**21**
Something's On Your Mind—D Train (84)	37
You're The One For Me—"D" Train (82)	5.8
James Rodger WILLIAMS ► 2093 (11)	**1888**
Love Rollercoaster—Ohio Players (75)	5251
Fire—Ohio Players (74)	4114
Skin Tight—Ohio Players (74)	1151
Who'd She Coo?—Ohio Players (76)	885
Sweet Sticky Thing—Ohio Players (75)	411
Fopp—Ohio Players (76)	398
I Want To Be Free—Ohio Players (75)	335
Jive Turkey (Part 1)—Ohio Players (74)	245
O-H-I-O—Ohio Players (77)	144
Feel The Beat (Everybody Disco)—Ohio Players (77)	42
It's Been A Long Long Time—Elgins (67)	4.3
Jerry WILLIAMS Jr. ► 2297 (9)	**1641**
She's A Heartbreaker—Gene Pitney (68)	1367
She's All I Got—Freddie North (71)	*694*
To The Other Woman (I'm The Other Woman)—Doris Duke (70)	369
(Shu-Doo-Pa-Poo-Poop) Love Being Your Fool—Travis Wammack (75)	352

Jerry WILLIAMS Jr. ▶ 2297 (9) ***Continued***	**1641**
Seems Like I Gotta Do Wrong—Whispers (70)	340
She Didn't Know (She Kept On Talking)—Dee Dee Warwick (70)	308
Feet Start Walking—Doris Duke (70)	45
She's All I Got—Johnny Paycheck (71)	*8.0*
God Bless—Arthur Conley (70)	6.8
Jerry L. WILLIAMS ▶ 10556 (1)	**7.2**
Big Party—Barbara And The Browns (64)	14
Jerry Lynn WILLIAMS ▶ 1839 (5)	**2215**
Giving It Up For Your Love—Delbert McClinton (80)	1582
Forever Man—Eric Clapton (85)	573
Pretending—Eric Clapton (89)	283
Tick Tock—Vaughan Brothers (90)	163
See What Love Can Do—Eric Clapton (85)	9.0
—Jerry Anthony Williams see: Leon HUFF	
Jill WILLIAMS ▶ 11438 (1)	**1.7**
All I Want To Be Is Your Woman—Carolyn Franklin (70)	1.7
Jim WILLIAMS ▶ 5246 (1)	**319**
You're Making A Mistake—Platters (58)	319
Jimmy WILLIAMS ▶ 1279 (12)	**3466**
A Lover's Question—Clyde McPhatter (58)	*2994*
Think Twice—Brook Benton (61)	2316
(You Don't Know) How Glad I Am—Nancy Wilson (64)	*1420*
A Lover's Question—Otis Redding (69)	*429*
I Told Myself A Lie—Clyde McPhatter (59)	285
Only Love (Can Save Me Now)—Solomon Burke (65)	58
How Glad I Am—Kiki Dee Band (75)	*55*
A Lover's Question—Jacky Ward (78)	*49*
Someone To Come Home To—Ames Brothers (59)	35
A Lover's Question—Ernestine Anderson (61)	*34*
Nothing Goes Up (Without Coming Down)—Nat King Cole (63)	26
A Lover's Question—Loggins & Messina (75)	*12*
Joe WILLIAMS ▶ 8839 (3)	**38**
Party Blues—Count Basie Small Band with Ella Fitzgerald and Joe Williams (57)	66
Baby, Please Don't Go—Them (65)	*13*
Baby Please Don't Go—Amboy Dukes (68)	*3.3*
John WILLIAMS ▶ 400 (12) HOF	**9867**
Cantina Band—Meco (77)	2487
Star Wars Theme—Meco (77)	*2487*
Theme From "Close Encounters Of The Third Kind"—John Williams (77)	1186
Empire Strikes Back (Medley)—Meco (80)	1005
Star Wars (Main Title)—John Williams/London Symphony Orchestra (77)	*985*
Theme From Close Encounters—Meco (77)	598
Main Title (Theme From "Jaws")—John Williams (75)	556
Themes From E.T. (The Extra-Terrestrial)—Walter Murphy (82)	319
Ewok Celebration—Meco (83)	218
Can You Read My Mind—Maureen McGovern (79)	157
Theme From Superman (Main Title)—John Williams/London Symphony Orchestra (79)	91
Nice To Be Around—Maureen McGovern (74)	4.9
—John David Williams see: John DAVID	
Jonathan WILLIAMS ▶ 10870 (1)	**4.7**
Girls (Part I)—Moments And Whatnauts (75)	24
Joseph Amos WILLIAMS ▶ 10007 (1)	**14**
What You're Missing—Chicago (83)	28
Joseph Stanley WILLIAMS ▶ 4844 (2)	**400**
Pamela—Toto (88)	655
Ewok Celebration—Meco (83)	218
June Watson WILLIAMS [June Watson, June Williams Kerenhappuch] ▶ 6409 (1)	**174**
Midas Touch—Midnight Star (86)	347
Ken WILLIAMS ▶ 1878 (9)	**2171**
Everybody Plays The Fool—Main Ingredient (72)	*4562*
Everybody Plays The Fool—Aaron Neville (91)	*1326*
Love, Love, Love—Donny Hathaway (73)	309
Seven Lonely Nights—Four Tops (75)	54
Put On Your Shoes And Walk—Clarence Carter (73)	45
You Can Call Me Rover—Main Ingredient (73)	28
Three Steps From True Love—Reflections (75)	15
It's True I'm Gonna Miss You—Carolyn Franklin (69)	4.6
Help Me (Get Myself Back Together Again)—Spellbinders (66)	0.9

Kenneth J. WILLIAMS ▶ 10542 (1)	**7.5**
Action Speaks Louder Than Words—Chocolate Milk (75)	67
Larry WILLIAMS ▶ 490 (9)	**8511**
Let Your Love Flow—Bellamy Brothers (76)	4564
Short Fat Fannie—Larry Williams (57)	1892
Bony Moronie—Larry Williams (57)	*1046*
Slow Down—Beatles (64)	*568*
You Bug Me Baby—Larry Williams (57)	322
Bony Moronie—Appalachians (63)	*194*
Slow Down—Crow (70)	*34*
Dizzy Miss Lizzy—Larry Williams (58)	31
Boney Moronie—Cheeks (80)	*22*
Lawton WILLIAMS ▶ 2580 (7)	**1352**
Shame On Me—Bobby Bare (62)	*1068*
Fraulein—Bobby Helms (57)	*552*
Fraulein—Steve Lawrence (57)	*154*
Shame On Me—Chuck Jackson (67)	*106*
Geisha Girl—Hank Locklin (57)	59
Fraulein—Don Estes (57)	*0.0*
Fraulein—Vic Sabrino (57)	*0.0*
Lenny WILLIAMS ▶ 6717 (1)	**142**
Don't Change Horses (In The Middle Of A Stream)—Tower Of Power (74)	284
Leslie WILLIAMS ▶ 10418 (1)	**8.7**
Experiments With Mice—Johnny Dankworth (56)	26
Linda WILLIAMS [Linda Bookout] ▶ 8002 (1)	**66**
Mr. Penguin - Pt. 1—Lunar Funk (72)	197
Louis WILLIAMS ▶ 7895 (1)	**71**
It's Wonderful To Be In Love—Ovations (Featuring Louis Wiliams) (65)	212
Marlon WILLIAMS [Marley Marl] ▶ 3456 (4)	**840**
Around The Way Girl—LL Cool J (90)	1305
Mama Said Knock You Out—LL Cool J (91)	473
The Boomin' System—LL Cool J (90)	267
6 Minutes Of Pleasure—LL Cool J (91)	2.6
Mason WILLIAMS ▶ 971 (4)	**4617**
Classical Gas—Mason Williams (68)	4525
Cinderella Rockafella—Esther & Abi Ofarim (68)	138
Baroque-A-Nova—Mason Williams (68)	44
Saturday Night At The World—Mason Williams (69)	0.9
Matt WILLIAMS ▶ 5321 (2)	**306**
I Gotta Know—Elvis Presley With The Jordanaires (60)	607
Hushabye Little Guitar—Paul Evans (60)	4.5
Maurice WILLIAMS ▶ 226 (8)	**14970**
Little Darlin'—Diamonds (57)	*7547*
Stay—Maurice Williams & The Zodiacs (60)	*4312*
Stay—4 Seasons (64)	*1296*
Stay—Jackson Browne (78)	*797*
May I—Bill Deal & The Rhondels (68)	711
Little Darlin'—Gladiolas (57)	*241*
I Remember—Maurice Williams & The Zodiacs (61)	51
Come Along—Maurice Williams & The Zodiacs (61)	15
Mentor WILLIAMS ▶ 1349 (4)	**3290**
Drift Away—Dobie Gray (73)	3233
When We Make Love—Alabama (84)	60
So High (Rock Me Baby And Roll Me Away)—Dave Mason (77)	52
We Can't Dance To Your Music—Grass Roots (73)	1.4
Milan WILLIAMS ▶ 1486 (7)	**2925**
Brick House—Commodores (77)	1962
Machine Gun—Commodores (74)	912
Old-Fashion Love—Commodores (80)	874
Too Hot Ta Trot—Commodores (77)	499
Wonderland—Commodores (79)	384
Only You—Commodores (83)	332
I Feel Sanctified—Commodores (74)	83
Otis WILLIAMS ▶ 3663 (6)	**744**
Two Hearts—Pat Boone (55)	*1486*
Little Turtle Dove—Otis Williams And His Charms (61)	4.9
Two Hearts—Charms (55)	*0.0*
Two Hearts, Two Kisses (Make One Love)—Doris Day (55)	*0.0*
Two Hearts, Two Kisses (Make One Love)—5 DeMarco Sisters (55)	*0.0*
Two Hearts, Two Kisses (Make One Love)—Frank Sinatra with The Nuggets (55)	*0.0*

Otis Clayburne WILLIAMS [Otis Miles Jr.] ▶ 6357 (1)	**179**
Treat Her Like A Lady—Temptations (84)	358
Paul WILLIAMS ▶ 166 (24) HOF	**17658**
We've Only Just Begun—Carpenters (70)	7395
Love Theme From "A Star Is Born" (Evergreen)—Barbra Streisand (76)	6219
Rainy Days And Mondays—Carpenters (71)	5070
An Old Fashioned Love Song—Three Dog Night (71)	3275
You And Me Against The World—Helen Reddy (74)	1819
I Won't Last A Day Without You—Carpenters (74)	*1455*
The Family Of Man—Three Dog Night (72)	1414
Out In The Country—Three Dog Night (70)	1391
Cried Like A Baby—Bobby Sherman (71)	1369
My Fair Share—Seals & Crofts (77)	600
Rainbow Connection—Kermit (Jim Henson) (79)	539
Waking Up Alone—Paul Williams (72)	269
Talk It Over In The Morning—Anne Murray (71)	172
Watch Closely Now—Kris Kristofferson (77)	164
So Many People—Chase (71)	118
That's What Friends Are For—B.J. Thomas (72)	79
I Won't Last A Day Without You—Maureen McGovern (73)	*68*
Let Me Be The One—Al Wilson (75)	65
I Won't Last A Day Without You—Al Wilson (75)	*65*
Inspiration—Paul Williams (73)	56
Someday Man—Monkees (69)	44
Traveling Boy—Garfunkel (74)	28
Only Me—First Edition (68)	15
Nice To Be Around—Maureen McGovern (74)	4.9
Paul Hucklebuck WILLIAMS ▶ 11576 (1)	**1.2**
Here's My Confession—Wyatt (Earp) McPherson (61)	2.3
Ralph WILLIAMS ▶ 1969 (2)	**2044**
Mr. Big Stuff—Jean Knight (71)	5978
You Think You're Hot Stuff—Jean Knight (71)	154
—Ralph Thomas Williams see: Tony CLARKE	
Red WILLIAMS [Willis J. Williams] ▶ 11170 (1)	**2.9**
Tryin' To Beat The Morning Home—T.G. Sheppard (75)	8.7
Ricardo WILLIAMS ▶ 4197 (2)	**566**
Me So Horny—2 Live Crew (89)	729
Firecracker—Mass Production (79)	421
Richard B. WILLIAMS ▶ 6517 (1)	**161**
The Ballad Of Irving—Frank Gallop (66)	483
Richard John WILLIAMS ▶ 6493 (1)	**163**
Play The Game Tonight—Kansas (82)	814
Robert Earl WILLIAMS ▶ 5543 (1)	**273**
Guilty—Al Green (72)	273
—Robert L. Williams see: Billy WARD	
Ronnie Lee WILLIAMS ▶ 9737 (1)	**18**
Mellow Lovin'—Judy Cheeks (78)	54
—Sibelius Williams see: Malcolm DODDS	
Spencer WILLIAMS ▶ 5860 (3) HOF	**236**
I Ain't Got Nobody—David Lee Roth (85)	461
Everybody Loves My Baby—Dinah Washington with Eddie Chamblee & His Orch. (57)	5.9
I Found A New Baby—Bobby Darin (62)	4.9
Stephan WILLIAMS ▶ 7574 (1)	**88**
Save Your Love—Great White (88)	175
Steven Richard WILLIAMS ▶ 8846 (1)	**38**
Crazy—Manhattans (83)	76
Tex WILLIAMS ▶ 9055 (1)	**32**
Smoke! Smoke! Smoke! (That Cigarette)—Commander Cody And His Lost Planet Airmen (73)	64
—Theodore Williams see: Teddy VANN	
Theodore WILLIAMS Jr. ▶ 6553 (5)	**157**
Soldier Boy—Ella Fitzgerald (55)	*315*
Soldier Boy—Pat O'Day (55)	*0.0*
Soldier Boy—Sunny Gale (55)	*0.0*
Soldier Boy—Eydie Gorme (55)	*0.0*
Soldier Boy—Four Fellows (55)	*0.0*
Thomas WILLIAMS ▶ 6312 (1)	**182**
Pretty Girls Everywhere—Eugene Church and The Fellows (58)	365
Tony WILLIAMS ▶ 3769 (2)	**704**
You'll Never Never Know—Platters (56)	1488
One In A Million—Platters (56)	416
Trevor WILLIAMS ▶ 8036 (1)	**64**
Indian Summer—Audience (71)	128

Tyrone WILLIAMS ▶ 9058 (1)	**32**
Welcome To Our World (Of Merry Music)—Mass Production (77)	32
Vernon WILLIAMS ▶ 10435 (1)	**8.5**
I'm Sorry (I Did You Wrong)—Royal Holidays (58)	17
Vesta WILLIAMS ▶ 7868 (1)	**71**
Congratulations—Vesta (89)	214
Walter WILLIAMS ▶ 6270 (2)	**187**
Lonely Drifter—Pieces Of Eight (67)	*357*
Lonely Drifter—O'Jays (63)	*18*
—Willis J. Williams see: Red WILLIAMS	
Yvonne WILLIAMS ▶ 8440 (1)	**50**
(1-2-3-4-5-6-7) Count The Days—Inez & Charlie Foxx (67)	151
—Zephire Andre Williams see: Andre WILLIAMS	
Billy WILLIAMSON ▶ 6371 (2)	**178**
Birth Of The Boogie—Bill Haley And His Comets (55)	432
Week End—Kingsmen (58)	102
Catherine WILLIAMSON ▶ 10057 (1)	**13**
All The Way Down—Etta James (73)	40
—Catherine Williamson see: Catherine CAFRA	
Sonny Boy WILLIAMSON II [Aleck Ford, Alex Miller] ▶ 10403 (2)	**8.8**
One Way Out—Allman Brothers Band (72)	18
Eyesight To The Blind—Richie Havens (73)	3.0
Wade WILLIAMSTON ▶ 3971 (1)	**634**
Movin'—Brass Construction (76)	1268
Foy WILLING ▶ 7315 (1)	**103**
No One To Cry To—Ray Charles (64)	205
James WILLINGHAM ▶ 8130 (2)	**61**
Been So Long—Pastels (58)	226
I'm Down To My Last Heartbreak—Wilson Pickett (63)	8.2
Allee WILLIS [Alta Sherral Willis] ▶ 641 (21) HOF	**6776**
What Have I Done To Deserve This?—Pet Shop Boys And Dusty Springfield (87)	3210
Lead Me On—Maxine Nightingale (79)	3179
September—Earth, Wind & Fire (78)	2728
Boogie Wonderland—Earth, Wind & Fire With The Emotions (79)	2219
Neutron Dance—Pointer Sisters (84)	1907
I Want You Tonight—Pablo Cruise (79)	841
Stir It Up—Patti LaBelle (85)	378
I Am Love—Jennifer Holliday (83)	334
Live My Life—Boy George (87)	323
Be There—Pointer Sisters (87)	211
In The Stone—Earth, Wind & Fire (79)	161
Star—Earth, Wind & Fire (79)	121
I Shoulda Loved Ya—Narada Michael Walden (80)	105
Can't Let Go—Stephen Stills Featuring Michael Finnigan (84)	88
Love Me Again—Rita Coolidge (78)	73
All American Girls—Sister Sledge (81)	64
Shoppin' From A To Z—Toni Basil (83)	55
The Blue Side—Crystal Gayle (80)	44
God Knows—Debby Boone (78)	44
Next Time You'll Know—Sister Sledge (81)	20
Where's Your Angel?—Lani Hall (81)	11
Alonzo WILLIS ▶ 6703 (3)	**143**
Puddin N' Tain (Ask Me Again I'll Tell You The Same)—Alley Cats (63)	343
Gator Tails And Monkey Ribs—Spats Featuring Dick Johnson (64)	20
Peppermint Man—Dick Dale And His Del-Tones (63)	8.5
—Alta Sherral Willis see: Allee WILLIS	
Bobby WILLIS ▶ 10901 (1)	**4.5**
He Won't Ask Me—Cilla Black (64)	4.5
Chuck WILLIS [Harold Willis] ▶ 492 (15)	**8500**
I Feel So Bad—Elvis Presley (61)	2474
The Door Is Still Open To My Heart—Dean Martin (64)	*2167*
Close Your Eyes—Peaches & Herb (67)	*1934*
C C Rider—Chuck Willis (57)	*806*
The Door Is Still Open To My Heart—Don Cornell (55)	*459*
What A Dream—Patti Page (54)	*452*
Don't Deceive Me—Ruth Brown (60)	212
Hang Up My Rock And Roll Shoes—Chuck Willis (58)	183
Betty And Dupree—Chuck Willis (58)	121
Close Your Eyes—Five Keys (55)	*83*
My Life—Chuck Willis (58)	68
The Door Is Still Open—Hilltoppers (55)	*50*
What A Dream—Conway Twitty (60)	*29*
The Door Is Still Open—Cardinals (55)	*0.0*
[Oh] What A Dream—Ruth Brown & Rhythmakers (54)	*0.0*
Eddie WILLIS ▶ 7808 (1)	**74**
Home Cookin—Jr. Walker & The All Stars (69)	223
Ginger WILLIS [Dorothy Jean Heppel] ▶ 9527 (1)	**22**
Lumberjack—Hal Willis (64)	44
Hal WILLIS [Leonard François Joseph Guy Gauthier] ▶ 9528 (1)	**22**
Lumberjack—Hal Willis (64)	44
—Harold Willis see: Chuck WILLIS	
Luvenia WILLIS ▶ 8274 (1)	**56**
You're My Baby—Sarah Vaughan (60)	112
Marvin WILLIS ▶ 2986 (2)	**1082**
Float On—Floaters (77)	*3048*
Bloat On Featuring The Bloaters—Cheech & Chong (77)	*328*
Pete WILLIS ▶ 4417 (5)	**499**
Photograph—Def Leppard (83)	1231
Rock Of Ages—Def Leppard (83)	1009
Foolin'—Def Leppard (83)	557
Bringin' On The Heartbreak—Def Leppard (84)	157
Rock Brigade—Def Leppard (80)	9.8
Victor WILLIS ▶ 1131 (4)	**3924**
Y.M.C.A.—Village People (78)	7239
In The Navy—Village People (79)	3766
Macho Man—Village People (78)	679
Go West—Village People (79)	259
Wallace WILLIS ▶ 10725 (1)	**5.8**
Steal Away—Pat Boone (57)	12
Winston WILLIS ▶ 7171 (2)	**112**
Walking Along—Diamonds (58)	*783*
Walking Along—Solitaires (58)	*0.0*
—Jon Willoughby see: Jon ST. JAMES	
Tanyayette WILLOUGHBY ▶ 6090 (2)	**207**
A Lover's Holiday—Change (80)	352
Paradise—Change (81)	92
Bob WILLS ▶ 2208 (6)	**1739**
San Antonio Rose—Floyd Cramer (61)	*1569*
My Shoes Keep Walking Back To You—Guy Mitchell (60)	*276*
My Shoes Keep Walking Back To You—Ray Price (57)	*39*
San Antonio Rose—Johnny Maddox And The Rhythmasters (55)	*7.5*
Faded Love—Patsy Cline (63)	*5.4*
Faded Love—Jackie de Shannon (63)	*4.5*
Dave WILLS ▶ 9418 (1)	**24**
Love Struck—Stonebolt (79)	48
Johnnie Lee WILLS ▶ 10847 (2)	**4.9**
Faded Love—Patsy Cline (63)	*5.4*
Faded Love—Jackie de Shannon (63)	*4.5*
Rick WILLS ▶ 5338 (1)	**303**
Do You Feel Like We Do—Peter Frampton (76)	1212
Meredith WILLSON ▶ 2617 (10) HOF	**1321**
Till There Was You—Anita Bryant (59)	*1101*
Seventy Six Trombones—Hugo & Luigi (58)	*100*
Seventy Six Trombones—Billy May and His Orchestra (58)	*100*
If I Knew—Nat King Cole (60)	11
Till There Was You—Valjean (At The Piano) (62)	*8.7*
Seventy-Six Trombones—Vera Lynn (58)	*0.0*
Seventy Six Trombones—King Sisters (58)	*0.0*
Seventy Six Trombones—Jonah Jones Quartet (58)	*0.0*
Seventy Six Trombones—Jimmy McPartland's All-Stars (58)	*0.0*
Seventy Six Trombones—Arthur Godfrey with Norman Leyden & His Orchestra (58)	*0.0*
Alan C. WILSON ▶ 1624 (4)	**2601**
Going Up The Country—Canned Heat (68)	2036
On The Road Again—Canned Heat (68)	1500
Time Was—Canned Heat (69)	290
Poor Moon—Canned Heat (69)	6.9
Ann WILSON ▶ 1089 (15)	**4051**
Never—Heart (85)	2388
Magic Man—Heart (76)	2291
Barracuda—Heart (77)	1624
Straight On—Heart (78)	1064
Heartless—Heart (78)	789
Even It Up—Heart (80)	530
Crazy On You—Heart (76)	*521*
Dog & Butterfly—Heart (79)	515
This Man Is Mine—Heart (82)	497
Dreamboat Annie—Heart (76)	455
The Best Man In The World—Ann Wilson (86)	298
How Can I Refuse—Heart (83)	279
Little Queen—Heart (77)	164
Crazy On You—Heart (77)	*110*
Kick It Out—Heart (77)	53
Anthony WILSON ▶ 5627 (1)	**263**
Misery—Dynamics (63)	525
Belinda WILSON ▶ 5581 (2)	**269**
If It Ain't One Thing...It's Another—Richard "Dimples" Fields (82)	331
All Of Me For All Of You—9.9 (85)	311
Bob WILSON [Bob Temple] ▶ 6471 (1)	**166**
Something Happened—Paul Anka (60)	331
Brian WILSON ▶ 45 (80) HOF	**42455**
I Get Around—Beach Boys (64)	*8633*
Good Vibrations—Beach Boys (66)	*8071*
Surf City—Jan & Dean (63)	6644
Help Me, Rhonda—Beach Boys (65)	*6345*
Surfin' U.S.A.—Beach Boys (63)	*4923*
California Girls—Beach Boys (65)	*3984*
Surfer Girl—Beach Boys (63)	*3040*
Fun, Fun, Fun—Beach Boys (64)	*2657*
California Girls—David Lee Roth (85)	*2548*
Be True To Your School—Beach Boys (63)	2214
Little Honda—Hondells (64)	*2173*
Wouldn't It Be Nice—Beach Boys (66)	*2149*
Dead Man's Curve—Jan & Dean (64)	2112
Do It Again—Beach Boys (68)	2041
Surfin' Safari—Beach Boys (62)	*2024*
When I Grow Up (To Be A Man)—Beach Boys (64)	1865
Dance, Dance, Dance—Beach Boys (64)	*1784*
Drag City—Jan & Dean (63)	1652
Heroes And Villains—Beach Boys (67)	1373
Darlin'—Beach Boys (67)	*1159*
Don't Worry Baby—B.J. Thomas (77)	*1157*
Shut Down—Beach Boys (63)	*1051*
Little Deuce Coupe—Beach Boys (63)	1016
The Little Girl I Once Knew—Beach Boys (65)	913
Don't Worry Baby—Beach Boys (64)	*903*
Ride The Wild Surf—Jan & Dean (64)	823
In My Room—Beach Boys (63)	*724*
Wild Honey—Beach Boys (67)	622
Sidewalk Surfin'—Jan & Dean (64)	605
The New Girl In School—Jan & Dean (64)	600
Help Me Rhonda—Johnny Rivers (75)	*596*
Surfin' USA—Leif Garrett (77)	*569*
Caroline, No—Brian Wilson (66)	518
Almost Summer—Celebration Featuring Mike Love (78)	501
God Only Knows—Beach Boys (66)	*484*
Ten Little Indians—Beach Boys (62)	466
It's O.K.—Beach Boys (76)	446
Friends—Beach Boys (68)	422
Good Vibrations—Todd Rundgren (76)	*391*
Good Timin'—Beach Boys (79)	372
Break Away—Beach Boys (69)	368
Wendy—Beach Boys (64)	286
Add Some Music To Your Day—Beach Boys (70)	274
Sail On Sailor—Beach Boys (75)	*268*
Shut Down—Beach Boys (81)	*240*
Surfin' USA—Beach Boys (81)	*240*
I Get Around—Beach Boys (81)	*240*
Fun, Fun, Fun—Beach Boys (81)	*240*
Surfin' Safari—Beach Boys (81)	*240*
Help Me Rhonda—Beach Boys (81)	*240*
Good Vibrations—Beach Boys (81)	*240*
Surfin' U.S.A.—Beach Boys (74)	*230*
Darlin'—Paul Davis Featuring Susan Collins (78)	*215*
Here Comes The Night—Beach Boys (79)	195
Please Let Me Wonder—Beach Boys (65)	178
My Buddy Seat—Hondells (64)	142
God Only Knows—Marilyn Scott (77)	*97*
Little Honda—Beach Boys (64)	*90*
Don't Worry Baby—Tokens (70)	*89*
Darlin'—Yipes!! (80)	*80*
In My Room—Sagittarius (69)	*77*
Surfin'—Beach Boys (62)	65
Sail On Sailor—Beach Boys (73)	*49*

Brian WILSON ▶ 45 (80) *Continued*	**42455**
God Only Knows—Vogues (70)	*26*
Don't Back Down—Beach Boys (64)	25
Little Saint Nick—Beach Boys (63)	23
Good Vibrations— Hugo Montenegro, His Orchestra And Chorus (69)	*23*
Custom Machine—Bruce And Terry (64)	14
Goin' On—Beach Boys (80)	12
409—Beach Boys (62)	*11*
She Knows Me Too Well—Beach Boys (64)	5.0
409—Cantina Band (81)	*1.5*
Surfer Girl—Cantina Band (81)	*1.5*
I Get Around—Cantina Band (81)	*1.5*
Fun, Fun, Fun—Cantina Band (81)	*1.5*
Help Me Rhonda—Cantina Band (81)	*1.5*
Good Vibrations—Cantina Band (81)	*1.5*
California Girls—Cantina Band (81)	*1.5*
Wouldn't It Be Nice—Cantina Band (81)	*1.5*
Dance, Dance, Dance—Cantina Band (81)	*1.5*
Bryce WILSON ▶ 9896 (1)	**15**
Got To Have Your Love— Mantronix (featuring Wondress) (90)	46
Carl WILSON ▶ 3232 (7)	**938**
Dance, Dance, Dance—Beach Boys (64)	*1784*
Friends—Beach Boys (68)	422
Good Timin'—Beach Boys (79)	372
Long Promised Road—Beach Boys (71)	56
It's Gettin' Late—Beach Boys (85)	48
What's Your Hurry Darlin'—Ironhorse (80)	15
Dance, Dance, Dance—Cantina Band (81)	*1.5*
Carlos WILSON ▶ 6742 (3)	**141**
Fencewalk—Mandrill (73)	406
Mandrill—Mandrill (71)	40
I Refuse To Smile—Mandrill (72)	0.4
Carnie WILSON ▶ 1182 (4)	**3759**
Hold On—Wilson Phillips (90)	4433
Release Me—Wilson Phillips (90)	3701
You're In Love—Wilson Phillips (91)	3185
The Dream Is Still Alive—Wilson Phillips (91)	1006
Charles K. WILSON ▶ 3680 (7)	**737**
Early In The Morning—Robert Palmer (88)	*790*
Early In The Morning—Gap Band (82)	*602*
You Dropped A Bomb On Me—Gap Band (82)	529
Ooops Up—Snap! (90)	273
Burn Rubber (Why You Wanna Hurt Me)—Gap Band (81)	178
I Don't Believe You Want To Get Up And Dance (Oops, Up Side Your Head)—Gap Band (80)	14
Shake—Gap Band (79)	4.3
Cindy WILSON ▶ 2534 (6)	**1409**
Love Shack—B-52's (89)	2771
Roam—B-52's (89)	2734
Deadbeat Club—B-52's (90)	458
Rock Lobster—B-52's (80)	143
Private Idaho—B-52's (80)	70
Legal Tender—B-52's (83)	52
Clyde WILSON [Steve Mancha, Clyde Darnell Wilson] ▶ 3000 (2)	**1073**
She's Not Just Another Woman—8th Day (71)	2012
Keep On Loving Me (You'll See The Change)— Bobby Bland (70)	67
—Clyde Darnell Wilson see: Clyde WILSON	
Dennis WILSON ▶ 7282 (1)	**105**
Friends—Beach Boys (68)	422
Don WILSON ▶ 9416 (2)	**24**
The 2,000 Pound Bee (Part 2)—Ventures (62)	19
Skip To M'Limbo—Ventures (63)	5.5
Earl WILSON ▶ 5946 (1)	**224**
Kissin' On The Phone—Paul Anka (61)	449
Floyd WILSON ▶ 7927 (1)	**69**
Do You Love Me— Jaye P. Morgan and Eddy Arnold (57)	69
—Forest Gene Wilson see: Forrest WILSON	
Forrest WILSON ▶ 2351 (7)	**1569**
Ko Ko Mo (I Love You So)—Perry Como (55)	*3070*
Ko Ko Mo (I Love You So)—Crew-Cuts (55)	*1319*
Poco Loco—Gene & Eunice (59)	211
This Is My Story—Mickey And Sylvia (60)	0.4
Ko Ko Mo—Dooley Sisters (55)	*0.0*
Ko Ko Mo (I Love You So)—Hutton Sisters (55)	*0.0*
Ko Ko Mo (I Love You So)— Bill Darnel & Betty Clooney (55)	*0.0*

Frank Edward WILSON ▶ 234 (27)	**14481**
Love Child—Diana Ross And The Supremes (68)	*9676*
Keep On Truckin' (Part 1)—Eddie Kendricks (73)	5698
You've Made Me So Very Happy— Blood, Sweat & Tears (69)	*5673*
Boogie Down—Eddie Kendricks (73)	4614
Stoned Love—Supremes (70)	3430
All I Need—Temptations (67)	1916
Up The Ladder To The Roof—Supremes (70)	1815
I'm Livin' In Shame— Diana Ross And The Supremes (69)	1652
Still Water (Love)—Four Tops (70)	1640
Love Child—Sweet Sensation (90)	*1079*
Son Of Sagittarius—Eddie Kendricks (74)	630
Chained—Marvin Gaye (68)	611
Whole Lot Of Shakin' In My Heart (Since I Met You)— Miracles (66)	403
You've Made Me So Very Happy— Brenda Holloway (67)	*353*
(It's The Way) Nature Planned It—Four Tops (72)	342
Somebody (Somewhere) Needs You— Darrell Banks (66)	334
Castles In The Sand—Little Stevie Wonder (64)	304
If You Let Me—Eddie Kendricks (72)	277
I'm So Thankful—Ikettes (65)	222
Look What You've Done To My Heart— Marilyn McCoo & Billy Davis Jr. (77)	199
I'm Gonna Hold On Long As I Can—Marvelettes (69)	183
Touch—Supremes (71)	156
It's So Hard For Me To Say Good-Bye— Eddie Kendricks (71)	130
In These Changing Times—Four Tops (71)	105
Just Look What You've Done—Brenda Holloway (67)	72
Darling Come Back Home—Eddie Kendricks (73)	61
You've Made Me So Very Happy—Lou Rawls (70)	*5.5*
Gerald WILSON ▶ 3701 (2)	**728**
Viva Tirado - Part 1—El Chicano (70)	595
La Raza—Kid Frost (90)	399
—Gloria Wilson see: Gloria VAN CLEVE	
—Gloria Mia Wilson see: Gloria LYNNE	
—Hank Wilson see: Leon RUSSELL	
—Harry "Rocky" Wilson see: Maggie ANDREWS	
Herbert WILSON ▶ 7538 (1)	**90**
I Walk Alone—Marty Robbins (68)	90
Hugh WILSON ▶ 7715 (1)	**79**
WKRP In Cincinnati—Steve Carlisle (81)	158
Ian WILSON ▶ 8336 (1)	**54**
Run Home Girl—Sad Café (79)	108
Jackie WILSON ▶ 1317 (12)	**3366**
Baby Workout—Jackie Wilson (63)	3553
(You Were Made For) All My Love—Jackie Wilson (60)	1762
You Better Know It—Jackie Wilson (59)	489
No Pity (In The Naked City)—Jackie Wilson (65)	364
Your One And Only Love—Jackie Wilson (61)	350
Baby Get It (And Don't Quit It)—Jackie Wilson (63)	143
I Just Can't Help It—Jackie Wilson (62)	104
You Don't Know What It Means—Jackie Wilson (61)	71
Big Boss Line—Jackie Wilson (64)	29
Squeeze Her-Tease Her (But Love Her)— Jackie Wilson (64)	9.1
I Found Love—Jackie Wilson And Linda Hopkins (62)	2.2
He's A Fool—Jackie Wilson (63)	1.4
James WILSON ▶ 5768 (1)	**244**
Jody's Got Your Girl And Gone—Johnnie Taylor (71)	731
Jeff WILSON ▶ 3568 (2)	**784**
Let Me Love You Tonight—Pure Prairie League (80)	1568
Still Right Here In My Heart—Pure Prairie League (81)	523
Joe WILSON ▶ 10848 (1)	**4.9**
Funky Fever—Clarence Carter (68)	20
Johnny WILSON ▶ 3780 (3)	**702**
Love The World Away—Kenny Rogers (80)	1217
Easy As Pie—Billy "Crash" Craddock (75)	179
Make Believe It's Your First Time— Bobby Vinton (79)	68
Julian WILSON ▶ 5497 (2)	**279**
Battle Hymn Of Lt. Calley— C Company Featuring Terry Nelson (71)	*530*
Battle Hymn Of Lt. Calley—John Deer (71)	*28*
Kim WILSON ▶ 2691 (3)	**1270**
Tuff Enuff—Fabulous Thunderbirds (86)	1158
Powerful Stuff—Fabulous Thunderbirds (88)	139

Stand Back—Fabulous Thunderbirds (87)	65
—Lee Wilson see: Albert BEACH	
Louis WILSON ▶ 6743 (3)	**141**
Fencewalk—Mandrill (73)	406
Mandrill—Mandrill (71)	40
I Refuse To Smile—Mandrill (72)	0.4
Margaret WILSON ▶ 10496 (1)	**7.8**
Think About Your Children—Mary Hopkin (70)	24
Marie WILSON ▶ 4665 (3)	**443**
Anymore—Teresa Brewer (60)	1292
Before This Day Ends—Eddy Arnold (60)	*38*
Before This Day Ends—George Hamilton IV (60)	*0.0*
Melvin WILSON ▶ 7470 (2)	**93**
It's Been A Long Time—New Birth (74)	176
Granddaddy (Part 1)—New Birth (75)	17
Meri WILSON ▶ 3275 (1)	**915**
Telephone Man—Meri Wilson (77)	915
Mike WILSON ▶ 9222 (1)	**28**
Another Sleepless Night—Shawn Christopher (91)	57
Murry WILSON [Reggie Dunbar] ▶ 6301 (1)	**184**
Break Away—Beach Boys (69)	368
Nancy WILSON ▶ 993 (15)	**4520**
Never—Heart (85)	2388
Magic Man—Heart (76)	2291
Barracuda—Heart (77)	1624
Straight On—Heart (78)	1064
There's The Girl—Heart (87)	1044
Heartless—Heart (78)	789
Even It Up—Heart (80)	530
Crazy On You—Heart (76)	*521*
Dog & Butterfly—Heart (79)	515
This Man Is Mine—Heart (82)	497
Dreamboat Annie—Heart (76)	455
The Best Man In The World—Ann Wilson (86)	298
How Can I Refuse—Heart (83)	279
Little Queen—Heart (77)	164
Crazy On You—Heart (77)	*110*
Norro WILSON ▶ 1385 (7)	**3209**
The Most Beautiful Girl—Charlie Rich (73)	5675
A Very Special Love Song—Charlie Rich (74)	1386
I Love My Friend—Charlie Rich (74)	656
Soul Song—Joe Stampley (73)	580
July 12, 1939—Charlie Rich (70)	102
He Loves Me All The Way—Tammy Wynette (70)	2.1
I'll See Him Through—Tammy Wynette (70)	0.9
Paul WILSON ▶ 6657 (2)	**147**
Lovers Never Say Goodbye—Flamingos (58)	228
Mio Amore—Flamingos (60)	196
Paul David WILSON ▶ 5052 (1)	**354**
Notice Me—Nikki (90)	707
Phill WILSON ▶ 10562 (1)	**7.2**
Wishin' On A Rainbow—Phill Wilson (61)	7.2
Ric WILSON ▶ 4114 (4)	**588**
After The Rain—Nelson (90)	1789
Fencewalk—Mandrill (73)	406
Mandrill—Mandrill (71)	40
I Refuse To Smile—Mandrill (72)	0.4
Ricky WILSON ▶ 8882 (2)	**37**
Rock Lobster—B-52's (80)	143
Legal Tender—B-52's (83)	52
—Robb Wilson see: Robb ROYER	
Robert WILSON ▶ 9011 (2)	**33**
Ooops Up—Snap! (90)	273
I Don't Believe You Want To Get Up And Dance (Oops, Up Side Your Head)—Gap Band (80)	14
Ron WILSON ▶ 2019 (7)	**2000**
Wipe Out—Surfaris (63)	*4648*
Wipe Out—Surfaris (66)	*1843*
Wipeout—Fat Boys (87)	*961*
Point Panic—Surfaris (63)	378
Surfer Joe—Surfaris (63)	236
Wipe Out—Jive Bunny & The Mastermixers (90)	*6.7*
Wipe Out—Surfaris (70)	*4.6*
Ronnie WILSON ▶ 7403 (3)	**98**
Ooops Up—Snap! (90)	273
Yearning For Your Love—Gap Band (81)	130
I Don't Believe You Want To Get Up And Dance (Oops, Up Side Your Head)—Gap Band (80)	14
Ross WILSON ▶ 8455 (1)	**50**
Primitive Love Rites—Mondo Rock (87)	100

Shanice WILSON [Shanice Knox] ▶ 3083 (1)	**1022**
I Love Your Smile–Shanice (91)	4090
–Simone Wilson see: Simone Antoinette JOHNSON	
Stanley C. WILSON ▶ 11054 (1)	**3.5**
Jane, Jane, Jane–Kingston Trio (62)	3.5
Tony WILSON ▶ 645 (6)	**6766**
Brother Louie–Stories (73)	5338
You Sexy Thing–Hot Chocolate (75)	4632
Emma–Hot Chocolate (75)	2191
You Could Have Been A Lady–April Wine (72)	695
Disco Queen–Hot Chocolate (75)	659
Think About Your Children–Mary Hopkin (70)	24
Turner WILSON ▶ 2895 (4)	**1129**
Papa Oom Mow Mow–Trashmen (63)	*1861*
Bird Is The Word–Trashmen (63)	*1861*
Papa-Oom-Mow-Mow–Rivingtons (62)	*480*
The Bird's The Word–Rivingtons (63)	*315*
Vance WILSON ▶ 5511 (1)	**276**
Oh What A Night For Dancing–Barry White (78)	552
Wendy WILSON ▶ 1811 (3)	**2281**
Release Me–Wilson Phillips (90)	3701
You're In Love–Wilson Phillips (91)	3185
The Dream Is Still Alive–Wilson Phillips (91)	1006
Willie WILSON ▶ 5847 (1)	**237**
Substitute–Clout (78)	237
Woody WILSON ▶ 5746 (2)	**246**
Ball Of Fire–Tommy James And The Shondells (69)	1168
Crazy Legs–Donald Austin (73)	25
Damon WIMBLEY ▶ 11670 (1)	**0.8**
Falling In Love–Fat Boys (87)	3.9
Carvin WINANS [Carvin Lawrence Winans] ▶ 5353 (1)	**301**
Make It Like It Was–Regina Belle (90)	301
Angela WINBUSH ▶ 5656 (6)	**259**
I'll Be Good–René and Angela (85)	253
Young Love–Janet Jackson (82)	110
You Don't Have To Cry–René and Angela (86)	66
Your Smile–René and Angela (86)	60
I Have Learned To Respect The Power Of Love–Stephanie Mills (86)	11
I Love You More–René & Angela (81)	6.6
Jesse WINCHESTER [Jesse James Winchester, Jesse Ridout Winchester] ▶ 3532 (4)	**797**
Say What–Jesse Winchester (81)	410
Rhumba Girl–Nicolette Larson (79)	320
Nothing But A Breeze–Jesse Winchester (77)	61
Yankee Lady–Brewer And Shipley (72)	5.5
Jai WINDING ▶ 7081 (1)	**117**
New York Minute–Don Henley (90)	351
Toni WINE ▶ 478 (14)	**8733**
A Groovy Kind Of Love–Mindbenders (66)	*5559*
Candida–Dawn (70)	4981
Groovy Kind Of Love–Phil Collins (88)	*3712*
Black Pearl–Sonny Charles And The Checkmates, Ltd. (69)	1971
What Are You Doing Sunday–Dawn Featuring Tony Orlando (71)	683
Your Husband - My Wife–Brooklyn Bridge (69)	462
Tonight You're Gonna Fall In Love With Me–Shirelles (64)	296
Ashes To Ashes–Mindbenders (66)	223
Mr. And Mrs. Untrue–Candi Staton (71)	150
I Think I Love You Again–Brenda Lee (70)	40
I'm Into Lookin' For Someone To Love Me–Bobby Vee (68)	20
You Came, You Saw, You Conquered!–Ronettes, featuring Veronica (69)	18
Off And Running–Lesley Gore (66)	8.1
Holly Go Softly–Cornerstone (70)	7.3
–Grace Barnett Wing see: Grace SLICK	
Ed WINGATE ▶ 7118 (1)	**115**
The Whole World Is A Stage–Fantastic Four (67)	345
Kip WINGER ▶ 2248 (6)	**1707**
Headed For A Heartbreak–Winger (89)	884
Seventeen–Winger (89)	595
Can't Get Enuff–Winger (90)	464
Easy Come, Easy Go–Winger (91)	364
Hungry–Winger (89)	31
Madalaine–Winger (88)	27

Pete WINGFIELD ▶ 2556 (3)	**1387**
Eighteen With A Bullet–Pete Wingfield (75)	1322
Tribute (Right On)–Pasadenas (89)	304
Making A Good Thing Better–Olivia Newton-John (77)	14
Gerhard WINKLER ▶ 10553 (2)	**7.3**
Answer Me, My Love–Happenings (70)	*15*
Answer Me, My Love–Nat "King" Cole (54)	*0.0*
Ray WINKLER ▶ 11466 (1)	**1.6**
Welcome To My World–Jim Reeves (64)	3.2
Sol WINKLER ▶ 8037 (2)	**64**
Broken Promise–Four Coins (57)	90
Lonely Lips–Chordettes (55)	58
Paul WINLEY ▶ 3297 (3)	**909**
Rinky Dink–Baby Cortez (62)	1807
Let It Roll (Let The Good Times Roll)–Earl Knight & George Kelley (59)	5.5
So Strange–Jesters (57)	0.3
Hal WINN [Jerry Winn] ▶ 1565 (10)	**2705**
Gimme Little Sign–Brenton Wood (67)	2590
Theme From Dr. Kildare (Three Stars Will Shine Tonight)–Richard Chamberlain (62)	1744
Cindy's Birthday–Johnny Crawford (62)	1448
Your Nose Is Gonna Grow–Johnny Crawford (62)	695
Baby You Got It–Brenton Wood (67)	486
Cosmic Sea–Mystic Moods (73)	51
Honey Trippin'–Mystic Moods (75)	21
Love Like A Fool–Georgettes (58)	*2.9*
Love Like A Fool–Fontane Sisters (58)	*2.9*
Lovey Dovey Kinda Lovin'–Brenton Wood (68)	1.4
–Jerry Winn see: Hal WINN	
Joseph WINNER ▶ 8042 (2)	**64**
Little Brown Jug–Frank Barber Orchestra (82)	*50*
Little Brown Jug–Frank Barber Orchestra (82)	*14*
Barry WINSLOW ▶ 8834 (1)	**38**
I Say Love–Royal Guardsmen (68)	76
Jerry WINSTON ▶ 10394 (2)	**9.0**
Can I Come Over Tonight–Velours (57)	12
Remember–Velours (58)	8.7
Edgar WINTER ▶ 748 (3)	**5871**
Frankenstein–Edgar Winter Group (73)	5532
Keep Playin' That Rock 'N' Roll–Edgar Winter's White Trash (71)	233
Hangin' Around–Edgar Winter Group (73)	214
Gregg WINTER ▶ 10895 (1)	**4.5**
Rev It Up–Newcity Rockers (87)	14
Kurt WINTER ▶ 1427 (8)	**3081**
Clap For The Wolfman–Guess Who (74)	1703
Rain Dance–Guess Who (71)	1323
Hand Me Down World–Guess Who (70)	1302
Hang On To Your Life–Guess Who (71)	496
Heartbroken Bopper–Guess Who (72)	448
Follow Your Daughter Home–Guess Who (73)	172
Runnin' Back To Saskatoon–Guess Who (72)	45
Broken–Guess Who (71)	42
George Dodson WINTERS ▶ 11243 (1)	**2.6**
The Man On Page 602–Zoot Fenster (75)	7.9
June WINTERS [June Peretti, Jerry Whitman] ▶ 7949 (2)	**68**
Experience Unnecessary–Sarah Vaughan (55)	252
Bad Girl–Valerie Carr (58)	15
Robert L. WINTERS ▶ 10199 (1)	**11**
Magic Man–Robert Winters & Fall (81)	45
Muff WINWOOD [Mervyn Winwood] ▶ 2797 (4)	**1190**
Gimme Some Lovin'–Spencer Davis Group (66)	*2448*
Gimme Some Lovin'–Blues Brothers (80)	*890*
Gimme Some Lovin' Part One–Traffic, Etc. (71)	*217*
Gimme Some Lovin'–Kongas (78)	*15*
Steve WINWOOD ▶ 347 (23)	**10830**
Higher Love–Steve Winwood (86)	4547
Roll With It–Steve Winwood (88)	4539
Gimme Some Lovin'–Spencer Davis Group (66)	*2448*
The Finer Things–Steve Winwood (87)	1736
I'm A Man–Spencer Davis Group (67)	*1717*
Don't You Know What The Night Can Do?–Steve Winwood (88)	1713
While You See A Chance–Steve Winwood (81)	1658
Valerie–Steve Winwood (87)	1522
Holding On–Steve Winwood (88)	1174
Back In The High Life Again–Steve Winwood (87)	1076

Gimme Some Lovin'–Blues Brothers (80)	*890*
One And Only Man–Steve Winwood (90)	737
Freedom Overspill–Steve Winwood (86)	661
Still In The Game–Steve Winwood (82)	300
Talking Back To The Night–Steve Winwood (88)	228
Gimme Some Lovin' Part One–Traffic, Etc. (71)	*217*
Hearts On Fire–Steve Winwood (89)	205
Empty Pages–Traffic (70)	166
Arc Of A Diver–Steve Winwood (81)	138
Paper Sun–Traffic Featuring Stevie Winwood (67)	108
Valerie–Steve Winwood (82)	86
I'm A Man–Chicago (71)	*78*
Gimme Some Lovin'–Kongas (78)	*15*
James WIRRICK ▶ 6446 (2)	**168**
You Make Me Feel (Mighty Real)–Sylvester (78)	*305*
You Make Me Feel (Mighty Real)–Jimmy Somerville (90)	*32*
–Joseph Harold Wirtshafter see: Bobby WORTH	
Fred WISE [Al Hill] ▶ 578 (30)	**7504**
Wooden Heart–Joe Dowell (61)	*6334*
Let Me Go Lover–Joan Weber (54)	*5883*
Lonely Blue Boy–Conway Twitty (59)	2068
Kissin' Cousins–Elvis Presley (64)	1612
Let Me Go Lover–Teresa Brewer with The Lancers (54)	*1376*
Follow That Dream–Elvis Presley (62)	1103
Rock-A-Hula Baby ("Twist" Special)–Elvis Presley With The Jordanaires (61)	854
Fame And Fortune–Elvis Presley With The Jordanaires (60)	751
I'll Touch A Star–Terry Stafford (64)	745
The Bridge Of Love–Joe Dowell (61)	386
Don't Ask Me Why–Elvis Presley (58)	373
Let Me Go Lover–Patti Page (54)	*216*
It Feels So Right–Elvis Presley With The Jordanaires (65)	216
As Long As I Have You–Elvis Presley with the Jordanaires (58)	192
Wooden Heart–Bobby Vinton (75)	*108*
I Got Lucky–Elvis Presley with the Jordanaires (62)	62
This Is Living–Elvis Presley with the Jordanaires (62)	62
Riding The Rainbow–Elvis Presley with the Jordanaires (62)	62
A Kiss For Christmas (O Tannenbaum)–Joe Dowell (61)	32
In The Beginning–Frankie Laine (54)	30
Crawfish–Elvis Presley with the Jordanaires (58)	24
Lend Me Your Comb–Carl Perkins (58)	*23*
Put The Blame On Me–Elvis Presley (65)	23
One More Time–Dean Martin (54)	*7.9*
One More Time–Ames Brothers (54)	*7.9*
Pocketful Of Rainbows–Deane Hawley (61)	6.4
Let Me Go, Lover!–Peggy Lee (55)	*0.0*
Lend Me Your Comb–Bernie Nee (58)	*0.0*
Let Me Go, Lover!–Sunny Gale (54)	*0.0*
Lend Me Your Comb–Carol Hughes (58)	*0.0*
Richie WISE ▶ 9122 (1)	**31**
He's My Girl–David Hallyday (87)	92
Scott WISEMAN ▶ 4227 (3)	**555**
Have I Told You Lately That I Love You–Ricky Nelson (57)	*433*
Remember Me–Willie Nelson (76)	120
Have I Told You Lately That I Love You?–Crazy Otto (56)	*2.0*
Jimmy WISNER ▶ 1945 (8)	**2070**
Asia Minor–Kokomo (61)	1962
Don't Throw Your Love Away–Searchers (64)	1264
Somewhere–Tymes (63)	1065
Perfect Love–Frankie Avalon (60)	244
Here She Comes–Tymes (64)	39
Rosie–Chubby Checker (62)	9.6
Leroy–Norma Tracey And The Cinderella Kids (65)	4.6
The Magic Of Our Summer Love–Tymes (64)	0.9
Alain WISNIAK ▶ 10392 (1)	**9.0**
Supernature–Cerrone (78)	27
Bill WITHERS ▶ 131 (16) HOF	**20536**
Lean On Me–Bill Withers (72)	5558
Ain't No Sunshine–Bill Withers (71)	4461
Lean On Me–Club Nouveau (87)	3944
Just The Two Of Us–Grover Washington, Jr. (81)	3799

Bill WITHERS ▶ 131 (16) HOF *Continued*	**20536**
Use Me–Bill Withers (72)	2729
Lovely Day–Bill Withers (77)	670
Kissing My Love–Bill Withers (73)	627
Grandma's Hands–Bill Withers (71)	471
The Same Love That Made Me Laugh– Bill Withers (74)	411
Let Us Love–Bill Withers (72)	406
In The Name Of Love– Ralph MacDonald (with Bill Withers) (84)	200
Who Is He And What Is He To You– Creative Source (74)	171
Make Love To Your Mind–Bill Withers (75)	121
Friend Of Mine–Bill Withers (73)	35
Heartbreak Road–Bill Withers (74)	14
Harlem–5th Dimension (74)	6.9
Ken WITHROW ▶ 4895 (2)	**387**
What I Am–Edie Brickell & The New Bohemians (88)	1562
Circle–Edie Brickell & The New Bohemians (89)	371
Debbie WITKOWSKI [Deborah Kucan, Deborah Witkowski] ▶ 7909 (1)	**70**
Vitamin L–B. E. Taylor Group (84)	140
Rick WITKOWSKI ▶ 7725 (3)	**78**
Vitamin L–B. E. Taylor Group (84)	140
Reggae Rock 'N Roll–B. E. Taylor Group (85)	22
Karen–B. E. Taylor Group (86)	3.1
–Ramona Marie Witry see: Mona DONATO	
Steve WITTMACK ▶ 7644 (1)	**83**
When The Rain Begins To Fall– Jermaine Jackson And Pia Zadora (85)	250
Hans WITTSTATT ▶ 3779 (1)	**702**
Pepe–Duane Eddy His "Twangy" Guitar And The Rebels (60)	702
–Chaim Witz see: Gene SIMMONS	
Murray WIZELL ▶ 11750 (1)	**0.2**
I May Never Pass This Way Again–Perry Como (59)	0.4
Anka WOLBERT [Anke Wolert] ▶ 9828 (1)	**16**
Imagination–Xymox (90)	33
Charles WOLCOTT ▶ 3206 (3)	**954**
Ruby Duby Du–Tobin Matthews & Co. (60)	*607*
Ruby Duby Du From Key Witness– Charles Wolcott (60)	*346*
Ruby Duby Du–Pepper Pots (60)	*0.0*
Richard Lee WOLD [Richard Parker] ▶ 3788 (1)	**699**
Comin' In And Out Of Your Life– Barbra Streisand (81)	1398
–Anke Wolert see: Anka WOLBERT	
Dick WOLF [Richard Wolfe] ▶ 3132 (12)	**993**
After School–Randy Starr (57)	*517*
I Know Where I'm Goin'–George Hamilton IV (58)	383
Got A Match–Daddy-O's (58)	*379*
True True Happiness–Johnny Tillotson (59)	221
Got A Match–Frank Gallop (58)	*215*
When Will I Know–George Hamilton IV (58)	142
I Must Be Dreaming–Nat "King" Cole (59)	122
Blonde Bombshell–Don Rondo (58)	5.0
Blue Jay–LuAnn Simms (59)	2.5
Got A Match–Lou Stein (58)	*0.0*
After School–Joy Layne (57)	*0.0*
After School–Teardrops (57)	*0.0*
Don WOLF ▶ 2569 (10)	**1370**
Love Is All We Need–Tommy Edwards (58)	*1872*
Love Is All We Need–Mel Carter (66)	*369*
Love Is All We Need–Vic Dana (64)	*201*
Exclusively Yours–Carl Dobkins, Jr. (60)	121
Let's Be Lovers–Playmates (58)	103
Mary Ann Thomas–Bobby Freeman (59)	*31*
Majesty Of Love– Marvin Rainwater and Connie Francis (57)	22
Love Is A Sacred Thing–Kitty Kallen (58)	18
How Do You Know It's Love–Teresa Brewer (60)	2.1
Mary Ann Thomas–Buddy Heart (59)	*0.0*
Ina WOLF [Christina Ganahl] ▶ 1320 (4)	**3361**
Sara–Starship (85)	3794
Who's Johnny (Short Circuit Theme)–El DeBarge (86)	2021
No Way Out–Jefferson Starship (84)	771
Playing With The Boys–Kenny Loggins (86)	204
Jack WOLF ▶ 6901 (4)	**130**
Keep Me In Mind–Patti Page (55)	213
My Boyfriend Got A Beatle Haircut–Donna Lynn (64)	62

Java Jones–Donna Lynn (64)	*5.7*
(These Are) The Closing Credits–Robert Goulet (63)	2.7
Karin WOLF ▶ 11372 (1)	**2.0**
Ya Mama–Wuf Ticket (83)	8.1
Lenny WOLF ▶ 9522 (1)	**22**
Get It On–Kingdom Come (88)	44
Peter WOLF [Peter Blankfield] ▶ 927 (17)	**4773**
Freeze-Frame–J. Geils Band (82)	3225
Lights Out–Peter Wolf (84)	1089
Must Of Got Lost–J. Geils Band (74)	1063
Give It To Me–J. Geils Band (73)	1008
Come As You Are–Peter Wolf (87)	875
Come Back–J. Geils Band (80)	540
One Last Kiss–J. Geils Band (78)	468
Love Stinks–J. Geils Band (80)	428
I Need You Tonight–Peter Wolf (84)	363
Oo-Ee-Diddley-Bop!–Peter Wolf (85)	107
99 Worlds–Peter Wolf (90)	104
Take It Back–J. Geils Band (79)	82
Can't Get Started–Peter Wolf (87)	74
Just Can't Wait–J. Geils Band (80)	52
Make Up Your Mind–J. Geils Band (73)	39
You're The Only One–Geils (77)	15
Givin' It All Up–J. Geils Band (75)	11
Peter F. WOLF ▶ 711 (7)	**6125**
We Built This City–Starship (85)	4638
Everybody Have Fun Tonight–Wang Chung (86)	4287
Sara–Starship (85)	3794
Who's Johnny (Short Circuit Theme)–El DeBarge (86)	2021
No Way Out–Jefferson Starship (84)	771
True Blue Love–Lou Gramm (90)	351
Playing With The Boys–Kenny Loggins (86)	204
Danny WOLFE ▶ 2080 (3)	**1901**
Sugar Moon–Pat Boone (58)	1763
Hey Shirley (This Is Squirrely)–Shirley & Squirrely (76)	138
Gonna Back Up Baby– Gene Vincent and His Blue Caps (56)	69
–Randy Craig Wolfe see: Randy CALIFORNIA	
–Richard Wolfe see: Dick WOLF	
Shirley WOLFE ▶ 5288 (4)	**313**
Lips Of Wine–Andy Williams (57)	598
Carefree Wanderer– Bill Parsons with The All-American Boy's (59)	30
Now You Know–Little Willie John (61)	6.3
Sparkelin' Eyes–Dean Martin (61)	1.6
Steve WOLFE [Victor William Batty] ▶ 2003 (3)	**2013**
It's A Heartache–Bonnie Tyler (78)	*3981*
Beg, Steal Or Borrow–New Seekers (72)	45
It's A Heartache–Juice Newton (78)	*16*
Bill WOLFER ▶ 4192 (3)	**567**
Dancing In The Sheets–Shalamar (84)	1023
Pretty Mess–Vanity (84)	108
One Sunny Day/Dueling Bikes From Quicksilver– Ray Parker Jr. (86)	4.3
David WOLFERT ▶ 4858 (3)	**398**
Songbird–Barbra Streisand (78)	480
Heartbreaker–Dolly Parton (78)	285
Party Music–Pat Lundi (75)	30
Elliot WOLFF ▶ 420 (5)	**9566**
Straight Up–Paula Abdul (88)	4509
Cold Hearted–Paula Abdul (89)	3992
Whole Wide World–A'me Lorain (90)	1170
Heart Of Stone–Taylor Dayne (90)	1021
Follow My Heartbeat–A'me Lorain (90)	139
Martin WOLFF ▶ 9523 (1)	**22**
Get It On–Kingdom Come (88)	44
Helmut WOLFGRUBER ▶ 7194 (1)	**111**
How To Dance–Bingoboys (91)	554
Carl WOLFOLK ▶ 2118 (2)	**1850**
Can I Change My Mind–Tyrone Davis (68)	3123
Is It Something You've Got–Tyrone Davis (69)	577
Mack WOLFSON ▶ 2730 (14)	**1236**
C'est La Vie–Sarah Vaughan (55)	*771*
Happiness Street–Georgia Gibbs (56)	*689*
Flowers Mean Forgiveness–Frank Sinatra (56)	582
Happiness Street–Tony Bennett with Percy Faith and His Orchestra (56)	*510*
C'est La Vie–Sunny Gale (55)	*57*
Crazy Otto Rag–Hugo & Luigi (55)	*24*
Star Love–Playmates (59)	23

Mashuga–Louis Prima & Keely Smith (60)	15
Bring Back My Baby To Me–Ella Mae Morse (54)	6.5
Salt Water Taffy–Morty Jay & The Surferin' Cats (63)	3.6
C'est La Vie–DeJohn Sisters (55)	*2.9*
Ev'rybody's Cryin'–Jimmie Beaumont (61)	0.4
Crazy Otto Rag–Crazy Otto (55)	*0.0*
The Crazy Otto Rag–Happy Hoagy Carmichael (55)	*0.0*
David WOLINSKI ▶ 1856 (8)	**2194**
Ain't Nobody–Rufus And Chaka Khan (83)	869
Do You Love What You Feel–Rufus and Chaka (79)	625
Hollywood–Rufus Featuring Chaka Khan (77)	427
I Really Don't Need No Light–Jeffrey Osborne (82)	334
Little One–Chicago (78)	185
Take Me Back To Chicago–Chicago (78)	164
The Medicine Song–Stephanie Mills (84)	139
Strange–Jellyroll (70)	6.7
John WOLOSCHUK [Chip Dale] ▶ 4868 (3)	**396**
Calling Occupants Of Interplanetary Craft– Carpenters (77)	*660*
Sub-Rosa Subway–Klaatu (77)	87
Calling Occupants–Klaatu (77)	*45*
Sid WOLOSHIN ▶ 9111 (2)	**31**
We're Together–Hillside Singers (72)	55
Take Life A Little Easier–Rodney Allen Rippy (73)	34
Bobby WOMACK ▶ 1045 (21)	**4220**
I'm In Love–Aretha Franklin (74)	*998*
That's The Way I Feel About Cha– (The Preacher) Bobby Womack (& Peace) (71)	969
I'm A Midnight Mover–Wilson Pickett (68)	706
I Can Understand It–New Birth (73)	606
I'm In Love–Wilson Pickett (67)	*571*
It's All Over Now–Rolling Stones (64)	*474*
Woman's Gotta Have It– (The Preacher) Bobby Womack (72)	468
I Found A True Love–Wilson Pickett (68)	360
Jealous Love–Wilson Pickett (68)	266
You're Welcome, Stop On By–Bobby Womack (74)	263
Across 110th Street– (Performed By Bobby Womack & Peace) (73)	243
It's All Over Now–Valentinos (64)	*225*
Check It Out–Bobby Womack (75)	72
Breezin'–George Benson (76)	61
More Than I Can Stand–Bobby Womack (70)	56
Daylight–Vicki Sue Robinson (76)	*54*
How I Miss You Baby–Bobby Womack (69)	47
Love Has Finally Come At Last– Bobby Womack and Patti LaBelle (84)	46
Baby, Help Me–Percy Sledge (67)	44
If You Think You're Lonely Now–Bobby Womack (81)	44
Daylight–Bobby Womack (76)	*16*
Cecil WOMACK [Zekkariyas] ▶ 5305 (4)	**309**
Love T.K.O.–Teddy Pendergrass (80)	533
The Doctor–Mary Wells (68)	233
Dig The Way I Feel–Mary Wells (70)	24
I Can't Live Without Your Love– Teddy Pendergrass (81)	6.2
Curtis WOMACK ▶ 11231 (1)	**2.6**
I'll Make It Alright–Valentinos (The Lovers) (63)	2.6
Linda WOMACK [Linda Marie Campbell, Linda Cooke, Zeriya Zekkariyas] ▶ 5148 (2)	**334**
Love T.K.O.–Teddy Pendergrass (80)	533
Woman's Gotta Have It– (The Preacher) Bobby Womack (72)	468
–Mary Womack see: Mary WELLS	
Shirley WOMACK ▶ 5071 (2)	**350**
It's All Over Now–Rolling Stones (64)	*474*
It's All Over Now–Valentinos (64)	*225*
Tranita WOMACK ▶ 10289 (1)	**10**
Lovin' Is Really My Game–Brainstorm (77)	21
Chris Wong WON ▶ 5380 (3)	**298**
Me So Horny–2 Live Crew (89)	729
Banned In The U.S.A.– Luke Featuring 2 Live Crew (90)	588
Pop That Coochie–2 Live Crew (91)	137
Stevie WONDER [Steven Judkins, Steviand Hardaway Morris, Eivets Rednow] ▶ 7 (82) HOF	**83858**
The Tears Of A Clown– Smokey Robinson & The Miracles (70)	*7441*
I Just Called To Say I Love You–Stevie Wonder (84)	5885
I Was Made To Love Her–Stevie Wonder (67)	*5544*

Stevie WONDER [Steven Judkins, Stevland Hardaway Morris, Eivets Rednow] ▶ 7 (82) HOF *Continued*	**83858**
Superstition—Stevie Wonder (72)	*5509*
You Haven't Done Nothin'—Stevie Wonder (74)	5230
Signed, Sealed, Delivered I'm Yours— Stevie Wonder (70)	*5081*
I Wish—Stevie Wonder (76)	*4484*
You Are The Sunshine Of My Life—Stevie Wonder (73)	*4440*
Sir Duke—Stevie Wonder (77)	*4420*
Boogie On Reggae Woman—Stevie Wonder (74)	4369
Uptight (Everything's Alright)—Stevie Wonder (65)	*4256*
That Girl—Stevie Wonder (82)	4208
Part-Time Lover—Stevie Wonder (85)	3997
Higher Ground—Stevie Wonder (73)	3798
My Cherie Amour—Stevie Wonder (69)	*3557*
Tell Me Something Good—Rufus (74)	3531
Master Blaster (Jammin')—Stevie Wonder (80)	*3419*
Until You Come Back To Me (That's What I'm Gonna Do)—Aretha Franklin (73)	*3181*
Send One Your Love—Stevie Wonder (79)	2835
Little Ole Man (Uptight - Everything's Alright)— Bill Cosby (67)	*2587*
Living For The City—Stevie Wonder (73)	*2487*
If You Really Love Me—Stevie Wonder (71)	2411
Shoo-Be-Doo-Be-Doo-Da-Day—Stevie Wonder (68)	1997
Let's Get Serious—Jermaine Jackson (80)	1855
It's A Shame—Spinners (70)	1453
Don't You Worry 'Bout A Thing—Stevie Wonder (74)	1340
I Ain't Gonna Stand For It—Stevie Wonder (80)	1272
I'm Wondering—Stevie Wonder (67)	1268
Go Home—Stevie Wonder (85)	1239
Do I Do—Stevie Wonder (82)	1124
Signed, Sealed, Delivered (I'm Yours)— Peter Frampton (77)	*1028*
I Think It's Love—Jermaine Jackson (86)	892
Love Light In Flight—Stevie Wonder (84)	888
Never Had A Dream Come True—Stevie Wonder (70)	728
Superwoman (Where Were You When I Needed You)— Stevie Wonder (72)	686
You Met Your Match—Stevie Wonder (68)	659
Skeletons—Stevie Wonder (87)	633
To Know You Is To Love You—B.B. King (73)	549
Overjoyed—Stevie Wonder (86)	530
Loving You Is Sweeter Than Ever—Four Tops (66)	435
It's A Shame (My Sister)—Monie Love (91)	420
As—Stevie Wonder (77)	391
I Don't Know Why—Stevie Wonder (69)	*386*
Another Star—Stevie Wonder (77)	366
Pop Goes The Weasel—3rd Bass (91)	333
You're Supposed To Keep Your Love For Me— Jermaine Jackson (80)	323
Up Tight—Ramsey Lewis (66)	*275*
I Don't Know Why—Rolling Stones (75)	*236*
You Are My Heaven— Roberta Flack With Donny Hathaway (80)	216
Ribbon In The Sky—Stevie Wonder (82)	201
All In Love Is Fair—Barbra Streisand (74)	185
Outside My Window—Stevie Wonder (80)	160
I Was Made To Love Her— King Curtis & The Kingpins (67)	*88*
Lately—Stevie Wonder (81)	86
Uptight—Shalamar (77)	*80*
Keep On Running—Stevie Wonder (72)	61
My Love—Julio Iglesias Featuring Stevie Wonder (88)	56
Hey Love—Stevie Wonder (67)	53
We'll Have It Made—Spinners (71)	52
Living For The City—Ray Charles (75)	*50*
You Will Know—Stevie Wonder (88)	47
Get It—Stevie Wonder & Michael Jackson (88)	44
Never Dreamed You'd Leave In Summer— Stevie Wonder (71)	43
Land Of La La—Stevie Wonder (86)	34
Gotta Have You—Stevie Wonder (91)	33
Uptight (Everything's Alright)—Nancy Wilson (66)	*28*
I Wish—Stars On 45 (82)	*27*
Sir Duke—Stars On 45 (82)	*27*
Superstition—Stars On 45 (82)	*27*
Master Blaster—Stars On 45 (82)	*27*
My Cherie Amour—Stars On 45 (82)	*27*
Isn't She Lovely—Stars On 45 (82)	27
I Was Made To Love Her—Stars On 45 (82)	*27*
Uptight Everything's All Right—Stars On 45 (82)	*27*

You Are The Sunshine Of My Life—Stars On 45 (82)	*27*
Just A Little Misunderstanding—Contours (66)	26
Happier Than The Morning Sun—B.J. Thomas (72)	13
Tears Of A Clown—Stars On 45 (81)	*12*
Bad Weather—Supremes (73)	11
My Cherie Amour—Soul Train Gang (77)	*8.1*
Until You Come Back To Me (That's What I'm Gonna Do) (Medley)—Luther Vandross (84)	*7.6*
Uptight (Everything's Alright)—Jazz Crusaders (66)	*2.8*
Albert S. WOOD ▶ 7978 (1)	**67**
(The Bad Donkey) Pum-Pa-Lum—Steve Lawrence (57)	67
Bobby WOOD ▶ 2839 (4)	**1162**
Talking In Your Sleep—Crystal Gayle (78)	1069
Half The Way—Crystal Gayle (79)	1014
He Got You—Ronnie Milsap (82)	178
What's Your Name, What's Your Number— Andrea True Connection (78)	63
—Brenton Wood see: Alfred J. SMITH	
—Charles Osgood Wood see: Charles OSGOOD	
Chris WOOD ▶ 9295 (1)	**27**
Paper Sun—Traffic Featuring Stevie Winwood (67)	108
Danny WOOD ▶ 3108 (1)	**1006**
I'll Be Your Everything—Tommy Page (90)	3017
George WOOD ▶ 8680 (1)	**43**
Jenny Brown—Smothers Brothers (63)	43
Guy WOOD ▶ 2803 (8)	**1187**
Till Then—Classics (2) (63)	909
Wedding—June Valli (58)	829
The Little Boy—Tony Bennett (63)	428
French Foreign Legion—Frank Sinatra (59)	374
Haunted Guitar—Three Suns (56)	61
Pink Sweater Angel— Johnnie Ray with Ray Conniff & His Orch. (57)	6.9
Did You Ever Get The Roses—Ames Brothers (57)	5.3
My One And Only Love—Roy Hamilton (58)	1.1
Haydn WOOD ▶ 11444 (1)	**1.7**
Roses Of Picardy—Buddy Greco (61)	3.3
Johnny WOOD ▶ 10306 (1)	**10**
Without My Love—Pat Boone (57)	20
Ken WOOD [Walter R. Moody] ▶ 1912 (6)	**2117**
Happy Organ—Dave "Baby" Cortez (59)	5914
Whistling Organ—Dave "Baby" Cortez (59)	293
Cat Nip—Dave "Baby" Cortez (60)	89
Fiesta—Dave "Baby" Cortez (62)	3.5
Hurricane—Dave "Baby" Cortez (60)	3.0
Piano Shuffle—Dave "Baby" Cortez (59)	0.8
Lauren WOOD ▶ 3942 (1)	**649**
Please Don't Leave—Lauren Wood (79)	649
Leo WOOD ▶ 9753 (2)	**18**
Runnin' Wild—Les Paul and Mary Ford (56)	13
Somebody Stole My Gal—Johnston Brothers (55)	13
Mark WOOD ▶ 9021 (1)	**33**
Fantastic Voyage—Lakeside (80)	296
Peter John WOOD ▶ 2834 (3)	**1163**
Year Of The Cat—Al Stewart (76)	2288
Square Rooms—Al Corley (85)	39
You Know What To Do—Carly Simon (83)	25
Randy WOOD ▶ 9043 (1)	**32**
Searching—Hilltoppers (55)	65
Ron WOOD ▶ 3039 (3)	**1046**
Stay With Me—Faces (71)	1429
One Hit (To The Body)—Rolling Stones (86)	449
Cindy Incidentally—Faces (73)	365
Stuart John WOOD ▶ 3214 (1)	**948**
Money Honey—Bay City Rollers (76)	1897
Terrell WOOD [Orlando Terrell Woods, Terrell Woods] ▶ 5193 (2)	**329**
Express—B.T. Express (75)	*2209*
Express—Ritchie Family (76)	*92*
Woody WOODALL ▶ 11694 (1)	**0.7**
It's Been A Long Long Time—Elgins (67)	4.3
—Lily Pearl Woodard see: Pearl WOODS	
Steve WOODARD ▶ 4253 (2)	**545**
Let Me Love You Tonight—Pure Prairie League (80)	1568
Friends—Feather (70)	112
Terry WOODFORD ▶ 3244 (3)	**930**
Angel In Your Arms—Hot (77)	2701
After The Feeling Is Gone—Five Flights Up (70)	*50*
After The Feeling Is Gone— Lulu With The Dixie Flyers (70)	*9.9*

Daniel WOODGATE ▶ 5335 (1)	**303**
Our House—Madness (83)	2122
—Bobby Woodlen see: Bobby MADERA	
Bruce WOODLEY ▶ 1655 (2)	**2539**
Red Rubber Ball—Cyrkle (66)	4909
I Wish You Could Be Here—Cyrkle (67)	169
James WOODLEY ▶ 6103 (1)	**206**
Mystery Lady—Billy Ocean (85)	617
Jezz WOODROFFE ▶ 4346 (3)	**515**
Big Log—Robert Plant (83)	830
Little By Little—Robert Plant (85)	418
Burning Down One Side—Robert Plant (82)	89
Adam WOODS ▶ 2876 (8)	**1137**
One Thing Leads To Another—Fixx (83)	2676
Saved By Zero—Fixx (83)	900
Are We Ourselves?—Fixx (84)	811
Secret Separation—Fixx (86)	629
The Sign Of Fire—Fixx (83)	523
Driven Out—Fixx (89)	236
Sunshine In The Shade—Fixx (84)	96
Stand Or Fall—Fixx (82)	67
Belita WOODS ▶ 10290 (1)	**10**
Lovin' Is Really My Game—Brainstorm (77)	21
Betty WOODS ▶ 7967 (1)	**67**
Too Bad—Ben E. King (62)	67
Donald WOODS ▶ 5987 (1)	**219**
Death Of An Angel—Kingsmen (64)	438
Doris WOODS ▶ 5988 (1)	**219**
Death Of An Angel—Kingsmen (64)	438
Ellen WOODS ▶ 10214 (1)	**11**
I'm Standing By—Ben E. King (62)	33
Harry WOODS ▶ 3711 (5) HOF	**726**
Try A Little Tenderness—Otis Redding (66)	*946*
Try A Little Tenderness—Three Dog Night (69)	*803*
River Stay 'Way From My Door—Frank Sinatra (60)	201
Try A Little Tenderness—Commitments (91)	*127*
Try A Little Tenderness—Aretha Franklin (62)	*0.4*
Hosea WOODS ▶ 2182 (3)	**1778**
Walk Right In—Rooftop Singers (62)	*6902*
Walk Right In—Dr. Hook (77)	*188*
Walk Right In—Moments (1) (63)	*23*
J.J. WOODS ▶ 7312 (4)	**103**
Pinch Me (Baby, Convince Me)—Ohio Express (69)	144
Sunshine, Red Wine—Crazy Elephant (69)	64
When We Get Married—1910 Fruitgum Co. (69)	56
Gimme Some More—Crazy Elephant (69)	42
—Millard Delbert Woods see: Nick WOODS	
Nick WOODS [Millard Delbert Woods] ▶ 5473 (2)	**282**
Peace Of Mind—Nancy Wilson (68)	281
Miss Katy Cruel—New Christy Minstrels (64)	3.2
Paul WOODS ▶ 6353 (1)	**180**
Motortown—Kane Gang (87)	540
—Paul Phillip Woods see: Pye DUBOIS	
Pearl WOODS [Lily Pearl Woodard] ▶ 3712 (10)	**726**
Something's Got A Hold On Me—Etta James (62)	899
Stop The Wedding—Etta James (62)	706
Next Door To The Blues—Etta James (62)	219
Poverty—Bobby Bland (66)	50
It's A Mean Old Man's World— Dinah Washington (62)	26
You're All I Need—Bobby Bland (67)	25
That Did It—Bobby Bland (67)	13
Don't Stop The Wedding—Ann Cole (62)	10
There's Nothing Like Love— Jackie Wilson And Linda Hopkins (62)	4.3
Every Time My Heart Sings—Jimmie Rodgers (61)	4.2
Peter WOODS ▶ 7089 (1)	**116**
A Girl In Trouble (Is A Temporary Thing)— Romeo Void (84)	466
Sonny WOODS ▶ 6894 (3)	**130**
I Need Your Lovin'—Roy Hamilton (59)	*299*
Seven Day Fool—Etta James (61)	92
I Need Your Lovin'—Clarence Paul (59)	*0.0*
Willie WOODS ▶ 3241 (4)	**932**
Shake And Fingerpop—Jr. Walker & The All Stars (65)	674
Cleo's Back—Jr. Walker & The All Stars (65)	510
Do The Boomerang—Jr. Walker & The All Stars (65)	379
Cleo's Mood—Jr. Walker & The All Stars (66)	215

Ollie WOODSON ▶ 6358 (1)	**179**
Treat Her Like A Lady—Temptations (84)	358
Keren WOODWARD ▶ 3515 (8)	**803**
I Heard A Rumour—Bananarama (87)	2288
Cruel Summer—Bananarama (84)	1392
I Can't Help It—Bananarama (87)	331
Love In The First Degree—Bananarama (88)	262
The Wild Life—Bananarama (84)	104
More Than Physical—Bananarama (86)	74
Love, Truth And Honesty—Bananarama (88)	64
Robert DeNiro's Waiting—Bananarama (84)	4.7
Chuck WOOLERY ▶ 3915 (2)	**658**
Naturally Stoned—Avant-Garde (68)	603
Fly With Me—Avant-Garde (68)	55
Sheb WOOLEY [Shelby Fredrick Wooley] ▶ 500 (14)	**8447**
Purple People Eater—Sheb Wooley (58)	6880
Are You Satisfied—Rusty Draper (55)	*1239*
That's My Pa—Sheb Wooley (61)	606
Don't Go Near The Eskimos—Ben Colder (62)	*235*
Sweet Chile—Sheb Wooley (59)	135
Harper Valley P.T.A. (Later That Same Day)—Ben Colder (68)	*111*
Still No. 2—Ben Colder (63)	*36*
Hello Wall No. 2—Ben Colder (63)	*16*
Are You Satisfied—Toni Arden (55)	*14*
Skin Tight, Pin Striped, Purple Pedal Pushers—Sheb Wooley (61)	11
Detroit City No. 2—Ben Colder (63)	*4.9*
Are You Satisfied—Sheb Wooley (55)	*4.8*
Santa And The Purple People Eater—Sheb Wooley (58)	3.1
Are You Satisfied?—Jimmy Wakely with Gloria Wood (55)	*0.0*
—Shelby Fredrick Wooley see: Sheb WOOLEY	
Andrew WOOLFOLK ▶ 9083 (1)	**32**
Proud—Joe Chemay Band (81)	63
—Gwendolyn Hines Woolfolk see: Vinnie BARRETT	
Eric WOOLFSON ▶ 818 (18)	**5373**
Eye In The Sky—Alan Parsons Project (82)	3993
Time—Alan Parsons Project (81)	1286
Games People Play—Alan Parsons Project (80)	1174
Don't Answer Me—Alan Parsons Project (84)	875
Damned If I Do—Alan Parsons Project (79)	718
I Wouldn't Want To Be Like You—Alan Parsons (77)	546
Prime Time—Alan Parsons Project (84)	415
(The System Of) Doctor Tarr And Professor Fether—Alan Parsons Project (76)	292
Let's Talk About Me—Alan Parsons Project (85)	260
Psychobabble—Alan Parsons Project (82)	257
You Don't Believe—Alan Parsons Project (83)	240
Sunshine Games—Music Explosion (67)	176
Don't Let It Show—Alan Parsons Project (77)	136
Stereotomy—Alan Parsons Project (86)	65
Days Are Numbers (The Traveller)—Alan Parsons Project (85)	63
Snake Eyes—Alan Parsons Project (81)	44
Raven—Alan Parsons (76)	22
What Goes Up—Alan Parsons Project (78)	8.2
Bruce WOOLLEY ▶ 6261 (2)	**188**
Video Killed The Radio Star—Buggles (79)	312
I'm Not Perfect (But I'm Perfect For You)—Grace Jones (86)	168
Bobby WOOTEN ▶ 3127 (2)	**995**
I'll Give All My Love To You—Keith Sweat (90)	1251
Make You Sweat—Keith Sweat (90)	1110
Jimmy WORK ▶ 8465 (1)	**49**
Making Believe—Ray Charles (63)	49
Lyle WORKMAN ▶ 5575 (1)	**270**
I Don't Mind At All—Bourgeois Tagg (87)	540
—Randy Van Wormer see: Randy VANWARMER	
Bernie WORRELL ▶ 4754 (6)	**423**
Flash Light—Parliament (78)	1115
Aqua Boogie (A Psychoalphadiscobetabioaquadoloop)—Parliament (78)	62
Up For The Down Stroke—Parliament (74)	57
You And Your Folks, Me And My Folks—Funkadelic (71)	34
Chocolate City—Parliament (75)	16
Do That Stuff—Parliament (76)	7.1
Bobby WORTH [Joseph Harold Wirtshafter] ▶ 1058 (4)	**4168**
Don't You Know—Della Reese (59)	7675
Is This The End Of The Line—Joni James (55)	397
Your Teenage Dreams—Johnny Mathis (63)	126
The Same Old Song And Dance—Frank Sinatra (58)	18
—Johnny Worth/Worsley see: Les VANDYKE	
Ted WORTHAM ▶ 7774 (2)	**76**
You're Throwing A Good Love Away—Spinners (77)	144
The Whole Town's Laughing At Me—Teddy Pendergrass (77)	7.2
—Paul Clayton Worthington see: Paul CLAYTON	
Gordon WORTHY ▶ 8949 (1)	**36**
Oo-Ee-Diddley-Bop!—Peter Wolf (85)	107
Bill WRAY ▶ 4336 (6)	**517**
This Could Be The Night—Loverboy (86)	1219
So Close—Diana Ross (83)	383
Lead A Double Life—Loverboy (86)	114
Surrender—Trixter (91)	104
One In A Million—Trixter (91)	84
Pinball, That's All—Bill Wray (79)	2.8
Jim WRAY ▶ 8077 (2)	**63**
Surrender—Trixter (91)	104
One In A Million—Trixter (91)	84
Link WRAY ▶ 3243 (4)	**931**
Rumble—Link Wray & His Ray Men (58)	*1033*
Raw Hide—Link Wray & His Ray Men (59)	629
Jack The Ripper—Link Wray & His Ray Men (63)	191
Rumble—Jack Nitzsche (63)	*9.0*
—Adrian Wright see: Philip WRIGHT	
Andrew WRIGHT ▶ 814 (4)	**5401**
When A Man Loves A Woman—Percy Sledge (66)	*6157*
When A Man Loves A Woman—Michael Bolton (91)	*4080*
When A Man Loves A Woman—Bette Midler (80)	*398*
When A Woman Loves A Man—Esther Phillips (66)	*166*
Ben WRIGHT ▶ 5128 (1)	**337**
One Hundred Ways—Quincy Jones (81)	1012
Betty WRIGHT [Bessie Regina Norris, Bessie Norris] ▶ 2954 (7)	**1101**
I Wanna Sex You Up—Color Me Badd (91)	4560
Knockin' Boots—Candyman (90)	1245
Baby Sitter—Betty Wright (72)	470
It's Hard To Stop (Doing Something When It's Good To You)—Betty Wright (73)	116
Let Me Be Your Lovemaker—Betty Wright (73)	85
Where Is The Love—Betty Wright (75)	37
Tonight Is The Night Pt. 2—Betty Wright (78)	18
Charles WRIGHT ▶ 1626 (7)	**2595**
Express Yourself—Charles Wright And The Watts 103rd Street Rhythm Band (70)	1587
Love Land—Charles Wright And The Watts 103rd Street Rhythm Band (70)	1504
Do Your Thing—Watts 103rd Street Rhythm Band (69)	1496
Your Love (Means Everything To Me)—Charles Wright And The Watts 103rd Street Band (71)	207
Till You Get Enough—Watts 103rd Street Rhythm Band (69)	200
Solution For Pollution—Charles Wright And The Watts 103rd Street Rhythm Band (71)	77
Nobody (Tellin' Me 'Bout My Baby)—Charles Wright And The Watts 103rd Street Rhythm Band (71)	18
Dale WRIGHT [Harlan Dale Riffe] ▶ 4714 (2)	**433**
She's Neat—Dale Wright With The Rock-Its (58)	387
Please Don't Do It—Dale Wright (58)	46
Dorothy WRIGHT ▶ 3710 (3)	**727**
Cinco Robles (Five Oaks)—Russell Arms (56)	*844*
Cinco Robles (Five Oaks)—Les Paul and Mary Ford (56)	*610*
Cinco Robles (Five Oaks)—Lawrence Welk And His Sparkling Strings (57)	*0.0*
Gary WRIGHT ▶ 398 (7)	**9928**
Dream Weaver—Gary Wright (76)	5406
Love Is Alive—Gary Wright (76)	3819
Really Wanna Know You—Gary Wright (81)	858
Phantom Writer—Gary Wright (77)	209
Sing A Song—David Clayton-Thomas (72)	31
Made To Love You—Gary Wright (76)	25
Touch And Gone—Gary Wright (78)	19
—Gavin Christopher Wright see: Gavin CHRISTOPHER	
Greg WRIGHT ▶ 4929 (1)	**379**
You're A Special Part Of Me—Diana Ross & Marvin Gaye (73)	1138
Kenneth WRIGHT ▶ 9014 (1)	**33**
I'll Be There—Joyce "Fenderella" Irby (90)	99
Lawrence WRIGHT ▶ 2646 (1)	**1297**
Among My Souvenirs—Connie Francis (59)	2593
Michael WRIGHT ▶ 8975 (1)	**35**
Apache—Sugar Hill Gang (82)	*173*
Othie WRIGHT ▶ 10960 (1)	**4.1**
Just Be Sincere—Jackie Wilson (67)	12
Philip WRIGHT [Philip Adrian Wright, Adrian Wright] ▶ 1722 (1)	**2429**
Don't You Want Me—Human League (82)	7286
Ray WRIGHT ▶ 10527 (1)	**7.6**
You Got To Keep On Bumpin'—Kay-Gees (74)	61
Rick WRIGHT ▶ 10183 (1)	**11**
Us And Them—Pink Floyd (74)	23
Robert Byron WRIGHT [Robert Bruce] ▶ 9540 (2)	**22**
Come Go With Me—Pockets (77)	49
Baby, Baby My Love's All For You—Deniece Williams (78)	11
Robert Craig WRIGHT ▶ 6850 (2)	**133**
Baubles Bangles And Beads—Kirby Stone Four (58)	*398*
Baubles Bangles And Beads—Jonah Jones Quartet (58)	*0.0*
Ruben WRIGHT ▶ 10916 (1)	**4.4**
I'm Walking Out On You—Ruben Wright (66)	4.4
Stanley WRIGHT ▶ 11833 (1)	**0.0**
I Love My Girl—Metronomes (57)	0.0
Steve WRIGHT ▶ 1698 (7)	**2467**
Jeopardy—Greg Kihn Band (83)	*3516*
The Breakup Song (They Don't Write 'Em)—Greg Kihn Band (81)	1125
Lucky—Greg Kihn (85)	449
Love Never Fails—Greg Kihn Band (83)	168
Happy Man—Greg Kihn Band (82)	135
I Lost On Jeopardy—"Weird Al" Yankovic (84)	*18*
Every Love Song—Greg Kihn Band (82)	15
Syreeta WRIGHT ▶ 1220 (9)	**3653**
Signed, Sealed, Delivered I'm Yours—Stevie Wonder (70)	*5081*
If You Really Love Me—Stevie Wonder (71)	2411
It's A Shame—Spinners (70)	1453
Signed, Sealed, Delivered (I'm Yours)—Peter Frampton (77)	*1028*
To Know You Is To Love You—B.B. King (73)	549
It's A Shame (My Sister)—Monie Love (91)	420
Fancy Lady—Billy Preston (75)	60
We'll Have It Made—Spinners (71)	52
Never Dreamed You'd Leave In Summer—Stevie Wonder (71)	43
Ted WRIGHT ▶ 3370 (1)	**877**
Out Of Sight—James Brown And His Orchestra (64)	877
Robert WRIGHTSIL ▶ 8069 (2)	**63**
I Ain't Got To Love Nobody Else—Masqueraders (68)	175
(Call Me) The Traveling Man—Masqueraders (76)	23
Allie WRUBEL ▶ 3169 (2) HOF	**972**
Zip-A-Dee Doo-Dah—Bob B. Soxx And The Blue Jeans (62)	1913
Gone With The Wind—Duprees Featuring Joey Vann (63)	31
Carl WURTZ ▶ 6162 (1)	**198**
With You All The Way—New Edition (86)	198
Joseph WYANT ▶ 11010 (1)	**3.9**
Itchin'—Jimmy Jones (60)	12
Dwight WYATT ▶ 6585 (1)	**154**
Keep It Comin'—Keith Sweat (91)	925
Johnny WYATT ▶ 4646 (1)	**446**
Once Upon A Time—Rochell And The Candles With Johnny Wyatt (61)	892
Paul WYATT ▶ 10682 (1)	**6.1**
Taste Of Tears—Johnny Mathis (64)	12
Richard WYATT ▶ 6257 (1)	**188**
A Little Bit Of Love (Is All It Takes)—New Edition (86)	377

Sid WYCHE [Sid Jaxon, Sidney Jackson Wyche] ▶ 870 (6)	**5101**
Big Hunk O' Love—Elvis Presley (59)	5285
Woman A Lover A Friend—Jackie Wilson (60)	1407
Talk That Talk—Jackie Wilson (59)	691
Love Love Love—Clovers (56)	*546*
Love Love Love—Diamonds (56)	*315*
Alright Okay You Win—Peggy Lee (59)	145
John WYKER ▶ 2286 (2)	**1651**
Motorcycle Mama—Sailcat (72)	1246
Let Love Come Between Us—James & Bobby Purify (67)	809
Zakk WYLDE [Jeffrey Phillip Wielandt] ▶ 9396 (1)	**25**
No More Tears—Ozzy Osbourne (91)	74
P.G. WYLDER [Harald Baierl, P.G. Wilder] ▶ 4745 (1)	**425**
All Or Nothing—Milli Vanilli (89)	1700
Richard WYLIE ▶ 3354 (6)	**885**
Knockin' Boots—Candyman (90)	1245
With This Ring—Platters (67)	1217
Washed Ashore (On A Lonely Island In The Sea)—Platters (67)	333
Hijackin' Love—Johnnie Taylor (71)	191
Don't Sign The Paper Baby (I Want You Back)—Jimmy Delphs (68)	14
I Spy (For The FBI)—Jamo Thomas & His Party Brothers Orchestra (66)	5.2
Bill WYMAN ▶ 6094 (2)	**206**
In Another Land—Bill Wyman (67)	206
Play With Fire—Rolling Stones (65)	2.3
Tammy WYNETTE [Virginia Wynette Pugh] ▶ 2751 (5)	**1223**
Stand By Your Man—Tammy Wynette (68)	*1181*
Stand By Your Man—Candi Staton (70)	*1135*
Singing My Song—Tammy Wynette (69)	92
'til I Can Make It On My Own—Tammy Wynette (76)	66
The Ways To Love A Man—Tammy Wynette (69)	36
Dony WYNN ▶ 11493 (1)	**1.5**
Sweet Lies—Robert Palmer (88)	4.4
Philippe WYNN [Philippe Wynne] ▶ 6018 (3)	**215**
Me Myself And I—De La Soul (89)	353
Kiss You Back—Digital Underground (91)	322
(Not Just) Knee Deep - Part 1—Funkadelic (79)	182
Tommy WYNN ▶ 9487 (1)	**23**
Ann-Marie—Belmonts (63)	46
Tony WYNN ▶ 11404 (1)	**1.9**
Trade Winds, Trade Winds—Aki Aleong (61)	5.6
Kevin WYNNE ▶ 9646 (1)	**20**
Puss N Boots—Kon Kan (89)	78
Barbara WYRICK ▶ 4255 (3)	**545**
Tell Me A Lie—Sami Jo (74)	844
Lovin' You, Lovin' Me—Candi Staton (72)	104
Right Feeling At The Wrong Time—Hot (77)	37

X

—Joseph Ximenes see: Travis FAIRCHILD	
—Lorraine Ximenes see: Coventry FAIRCHILD	

Y

Louis YAGUDA ▶ 8148 (1)	**60**
Words—F.R. David (83)	180
—Ya Kid K see: Manuela KAMOSI	
—Yakov Yakubovitsh see: Jacob JACOBS	
Herb YAKUS ▶ 4108 (4)	**591**
Chain Gang—Bobby Scott (55)	*1174*
Chain Gang—Len Dresslar (56)	*7.2*
Chain Gang—Johnny Oliver (56)	*0.0*
Chain Gang—Lawrence Welk & His Champagne Music (56)	*0.0*
Milton YAKUS ▶ 3062 (4)	**1028**
Old Cape Cod—Patti Page (57)	2136
Go On With The Wedding—Patti Page (55)	*976*
Go On With The Wedding—Kitty Kallen & Georgie Shaw (55)	*288*
Go On With The Wedding—Modernaires (56)	*0.0*
William YANCEY ▶ 11755 (1)	**0.2**
One Wonderful Love—Ray Smith (60)	1.2
Marvin YANCY ▶ 929 (15)	**4772**
I've Got Love On My Mind—Natalie Cole (77)	3003
This Will Be—Natalie Cole (75)	2336
Our Love—Natalie Cole (77)	1689
Inseparable—Natalie Cole (75)	745
Sophisticated Lady (She's A Different Lady)—Natalie Cole (76)	730
Baby I've Been Missing You—Independents (73)	372
Mr. Melody—Natalie Cole (76)	277
The More You Do It (The More I Like It Done To Me)—Ronnie Dyson (76)	243
Same Thing It Took—Impressions (75)	115
Let This Be A Lesson To You—Independents (74)	97
It's All Over—Independents (73)	79
Just As Long As You Need Me, Part I—Independents (72)	74
It's Cool—Tymes (76)	55
Loving Power—Impressions (76)	31
You—Aretha Franklin (76)	7.1
Al YANKOVIC ▶ 3267 (7)	**920**
Eat It—"Weird Al" Yankovic (84)	*1414*
Like A Surgeon—"Weird Al" Yankovic (85)	*257*
Ricky—"Weird Al" Yankovic (83)	*188*
King Of Suede—"Weird Al" Yankovic (84)	*120*
I Love Rocky Road—"Weird Al" Yankovic (83)	*26*
I Lost On Jeopardy—"Weird Al" Yankovic (84)	*18*
Fat—"Weird Al" Yankovic (88)	*12*
Steve YANO ▶ 8831 (1)	**38**
I'm Not Your Puppet—Hi-C (91)	115
—William Yarborough see: William BELL	
—Alisa Peoples Yarbrough see: Alisa PEOPLES	
—Ben Yardley see: Estelle LEVITT	
Christine YARIAN [Christine Perrin] ▶ 1135 (8)	**3904**
It's So Hard To Say Goodbye To Yesterday—Boyz II Men (91)	4853
Do It Baby—Miracles (74)	1443
Hallelujah Day—Jackson 5 (73)	582
Don't Take Away The Music—Tavares (76)	416
A Little Bit Of Love (Is All It Takes)—New Edition (86)	377
Don't Cha Love It—Miracles (74)	108
Don't Let It End ('til You Let It Begin)—Miracles (73)	105
Cotton Candy—Sylvers (76)	95
Peter YARROW ▶ 586 (10)	**7416**
Torn Between Two Lovers—Mary MacGregor (76)	6718
Puff (The Magic Dragon)—Peter, Paul & Mary (63)	5656
Day Is Done—Peter, Paul & Mary (69)	*938*
Tell It On The Mountain—Peter, Paul & Mary (64)	526
This Girl (Has Turned Into A Woman)—Mary MacGregor (77)	164
The Cruel War—Peter, Paul & Mary (66)	*149*
Day Is Done—Brooklyn Bridge (70)	*19*
For A While—Mary MacGregor (77)	18
The Cruel War—Chad & Jill Stuart (66)	*1.0*
Don't Ever Take Away My Freedom—Peter Yarrow (72)	0.7
Carolyn Jean YATES ▶ 5815 (1)	**239**
I Won't Mention It Again—Ray Price (71)	479
Ralph YATES ▶ 8084 (1)	**62**
Only Because—Platters (57)	187
Steven YATES [Tom Drake] ▶ 7109 (1)	**116**
Ally Ally Oxen Free—Kingston Trio (63)	231
Adam YAUCH ▶ 3854 (3)	**676**
(You Gotta) Fight For Your Right (To Party!)—Beastie Boys (86)	1744
Hey Ladies—Beastie Boys (89)	302
Brass Monkey—Beastie Boys (87)	278
Robert YEAZEL ▶ 4768 (1)	**419**
Tongue In Cheek—Sugarloaf (71)	419
Jack YELLEN [Jacek Jelen', Jack Selig Yellen] ▶ 2815 (10) HOF	**1178**
Ain't She Sweet—Beatles (64)	*1085*
Alabama Jubilee—Ferko String Band (55)	*975*
Hardhearted Hannah—Ray Charles Orchestra & Chorus (60)	179
Forgive Me—Al Martino (65)	177
Ain't She Sweet—Johnston Brothers (55)	*13*
Are You Havin' Any Fun—Crew-Cuts (55)	12
Ain't She Sweet—Modernaires (56)	*4.4*
Alabama Jubilee—Art Mooney & His Orchestra (55)	*0.0*
Alabama Jubilee—David Carroll & His Orchestra (55)	*0.0*
Alabama Jubilee—Cliff Steward & The San Francisco Boys (55)	*0.0*
—Jack Selig Yellen see: Jack YELLEN	
Robert YELLIN ▶ 11288 (1)	**2.4**
Up To My Neck In High Muddy Water—Linda Ronstadt And The Stone Poneys (68)	7.2
Peter YELLOWSTONE [Peter Papini] ▶ 6356 (2)	**179**
On The Shelf—Donny & Marie (78)	265
Make Love To Me—Helen Reddy (79)	141
Bob YEOMANS ▶ 7499 (1)	**92**
You Can't Dance—England Dan & John Ford Coley (78)	184
Jim YESTER ▶ 4618 (2)	**450**
No Fair At All—Association (67)	327
Goodbye Columbus—Association (69)	123
Maury YESTON ▶ 4085 (2)	**598**
Till I Loved You (The Love Theme From Goya)—Barbra Streisand And Don Johnson (88)	514
What Can You Get A Wookiee For Christmas (When He Already Owns A Comb?)—Star Wars Intergalactic Droid Choir & Chorale (80)	84
Monte YOHO ▶ 5594 (1)	**267**
There Goes Another Love Song—Outlaws (75)	534
Yutaka YOKOKURA [Carlos Del Rosario] ▶ 10149 (1)	**12**
Love Light—Yutaka (81)	24
—Yonah see: Wyn JACKSON	
—Dave York see: David KINZIE	
Bob YOSCO [Rocco Giuseppe Iosco] ▶ 11030 (1)	**3.7**
Spaghetti Rag—Johnny Maddox And The Rhythmasters (55)	7.5
—Hasegawa Yoshida see: Freddy MORGAN	
—Andrew Youakim see: Andy KIM	
Chris YOULDEN ▶ 5495 (1)	**279**
I'm Tired—Savoy Brown (69)	279
Vincent YOUMANS ▶ 798 (10) HOF	**5546**
Tea For Two Cha Cha—Tommy Dorsey Orchestra Starring Warren Covington (58)	*4704*
I Want To Be Happy Cha Cha—Enoch Light & The Light Brigade (58)	*661*
I Want To Be Happy Cha Cha—Tommy Dorsey Orchestra starring Warren Covington (58)	*153*
Without A Song—Roy Hamilton (55)	*145*
Tea For Two—Nino Tempo & April Stevens (64)	*99*
Without A Song (Part 1)—James Cleveland and the Cleveland Singers (66)	*18*
More Than You Know—Platters (62)	3.2
Great Day—Sarah Vaughan (61)	1.9
Without A Song—Kay Starr (55)	*0.0*
Tea For Two Cha Cha—Bill Ador & His Orchestra (58)	*0.0*
—Alexander Young see: George ALEXANDER	
Andre Romell YOUNG [Andre Young, Dr. Dre] ▶ 3190 (3)	**958**
No More Lies—Michel'le (89)	1783
Nicety—Michel'le (90)	497
Something In My Heart—Michel'le (91)	347
Angus YOUNG ▶ 3332 (7)	**896**
Moneytalks—AC/DC (90)	607
You Shook Me All Night Long—AC/DC (80)	530
Back In Black—AC/DC (80)	471
Dirty Deeds—Joan Jett (90)	295
Highway To Hell—AC/DC (79)	272
Let's Get It Up—AC/DC (82)	184
Guns For Hire—AC/DC (83)	25
Chip YOUNG [Jerry Marvin Stembridge] ▶ 11120 (1)	**3.1**
My Back Scratcher—Frank Frost (66)	6.3
Earl YOUNG ▶ 6935 (2)	**127**
Hold Back The Night—Trammps (76)	*426*
Hold Back The Night—Graham Parker And The Rumour (77)	*83*
Eldee YOUNG ▶ 7077 (1)	**117**
Wack Wack—Young Holt Trio (66)	470

Faron YOUNG ▶ 4098 (3)	**594**
Goin' Steady—Tommy Sands (57)	571
Alone With You—Faron Young (58)	55
Backtrack—Faron Young (61)	10
Gary YOUNG ▶ 7479 (1)	**93**
Wizard Of Love—Ly-Dells (61)	279
George YOUNG ▶ 1644 (10)	**2556**
Love Is In The Air—John Paul Young (78)	1865
Friday On My Mind—Easybeats (67)	1495
Bring A Little Lovin'—Los Bravos (68)	451
Good Times—INXS And Jimmy Barnes (87)	366
Yesterday's Hero—John Paul Young (75)	*329*
Yesterday's Hero—Bay City Rollers (76)	*265*
Lost In Your Love—John Paul Young (78)	156
St. Louis—Easybeats (69)	90
Hey, St. Peter—Flash & The Pan (79)	87
Heaven And Hell—Easybeats (67)	10
James YOUNG ▶ 4126 (3)	**585**
Love At First Sight—Styx (91)	751
Lorelei—Styx (76)	614
Best Thing—Styx (72)	57
Jesse Colin YOUNG [Perry Miller] ▶ 7798 (2)	**75**
Darkness, Darkness—Youngbloods (70)	40
Sunlight—Youngbloods (69)	35
Joe YOUNG ▶ 1072 (17)	**4117**
I'm Gonna Sit Right Down And Write Myself A Letter—Billy Williams (57)	*4377*
Rock A Bye Your Baby With A Dixie Melody—Jerry Lewis (56)	*2560*
My Mammy—Happenings (67)	1237
Rock-A-Bye Your Baby With A Dixie Melody—Aretha Franklin (61)	*786*
In A Shanty In Old Shanty Town—Somethin' Smith & The Redheads (56)	*566*
In A Little Spanish Town ('twas On A Night Like This)—Bing Crosby And The Buddy Cole Trio (56)	*365*
Five Foot Two—Don Johnson (60)	194
In A Little Spanish Town—Smith Brothers (54)	*30*
In A Little Spanish Town—Blue Diamonds (61)	*23*
I'm Gonna Sit Right Down And Write Myself A Letter—Fabian (60)	*12*
Sittin' On Top Of The World—Jerry Mar (57)	6.0
Rock A Bye Your Baby With A Dixie Melody—Judy Garland (61)	*0.0*
In A Shanty In Old Shanty Town—Johnny Long & His Orchestra (56)	*0.0*
I'm Gonna Sit Right Down And Write Myself A Letter—Larry Storch (57)	*0.0*
I'm Gonna Sit Right Down And Write Myself A Letter—Hop A Long Wong (57)	*0.0*
I'm Gonna Sit Right Down And Write Myself A Letter—Harry The Hipster (57)	*0.0*
In A Little Spanish Town ('Twas On A Night Like This)—Lawrence Welk & His Sparklers (54)	*0.0*
John YOUNG ▶ 1244 (7)	**3611**
Seventeen—Boyd Bennett And His Rockets (55)	*4540*
Seventeen—Fontane Sisters with Billy Vaughn's Orchestra (55)	*3907*
My Boy Flat Top—Dorothy Collins (55)	*859*
Seventeen—Rusty Draper (55)	*534*
My Boy Flat Top—Boyd Bennett And His Rockets (55)	*350*
Seventeen—Frankie Ford (61)	*37*
Seventeen—Ella Mae Morse (55)	*0.0*
Kenny YOUNG ▶ 322 (18)	**11390**
Under The Boardwalk—Drifters (64)	*4327*
Arizona—Mark Lindsay (69)	2236
Just A Little Bit Better—Herman's Hermits (65)	2038
One Kiss For Old Times' Sake—Ronnie Dove (65)	1675
A Little Bit Of Heaven—Ronnie Dove (65)	1532
When Liking Turns To Loving—Ronnie Dove (66)	1089
Don't Go Out Into The Rain (You're Going To Melt)—Herman's Hermits (67)	951
Silver Bird—Mark Lindsay (70)	852
I've Got Sand In My Shoes—Drifters (64)	540
Ai No Corrida (I-No-Ko-ree-da)—Quincy Jones (81)	489
Only You Can—Fox (75)	234
Please Don't Kiss Me Again—Charmettes (63)	137
Under The Boardwalk—Bruce Willis (87)	*110*
Under The Boardwalk—Billy Joe Royal (78)	*71*
Doin' The Do—Betty Boo (90)	29
The Record (Baby, I Love You)—Ben E. King (65)	22

I Found A Daisy In The City—Barry Darvell (65)	11
Captain Of Your Ship—Reparata And The Delrons (68)	1.9
Malcolm YOUNG ▶ 3333 (7)	**896**
Moneytalks—AC/DC (90)	607
You Shook Me All Night Long—AC/DC (80)	530
Back In Black—AC/DC (80)	471
Dirty Deeds—Joan Jett (90)	295
Highway To Hell—AC/DC (79)	272
Let's Get It Up—AC/DC (82)	184
Guns For Hire—AC/DC (83)	25
Marvin YOUNG [Young MC] ▶ 1806 (7)	**2286**
Wild Thing—Tone Loc (88)	2613
Funky Cold Medina—Tone Loc (89)	2425
Bust A Move—Young M.C. (89)	1887
Principal's Office—Young M.C. (89)	445
I Come Off—Young M.C. (90)	147
That's The Way Love Goes—Young M.C. (91)	139
Pick Up The Pace 1990—Young M.C. (90)	32
Neil YOUNG ▶ 235 (25)	**14454**
Heart Of Gold—Neil Young (72)	6394
Lotta Love—Nicolette Larson (78)	2120
Ohio—Crosby, Stills, Nash & Young (70)	1314
Love Is A Rose—Linda Ronstadt (75)	1129
After The Goldrush—Prelude (74)	1014
Only Love Can Break Your Heart—Neil Young (70)	*874*
Old Man—Neil Young (72)	559
Cinnamon Girl—Gentrys (70)	*494*
Cinnamon Girl—Neil Young With Crazy Horse (70)	*373*
War Song—Neil Young And Graham Nash With The Stray Gators (72)	251
Down By The River—Buddy Miles (70)	*201*
Walk On—Neil Young (74)	180
Got It Made—Crosby, Stills, Nash & Young (89)	138
American Dream—Crosby, Stills, Nash & Young (88)	103
When You Dance I Can Really Love—Neil Young (71)	94
Little Thing Called Love—Neil Young (83)	88
Rust Never Sleeps (Hey Hey, My My [Into The Black])—Neil Young & Crazy Horse (79)	67
Southern Pacific—Neil Young & Crazy Horse (81)	59
Dance, Dance, Dance—New Seekers (72)	46
Music Is Love—David Crosby (71)	43
On The Way Home—Buffalo Springfield (68)	30
Expecting To Fly—Buffalo Springfield (67)	19
Down By The River—Brooklyn Bridge (70)	*8.5*
Only Love Can Break A Heart—Jackie Deshannon (72)	*5.3*
Tell Me Why—Matthews' Southern Comfort (71)	5.0
Otha YOUNG ▶ 1728 (2)	**2411**
The Sweetest Thing (I've Ever Known)—Juice Newton (81)	2196
Sweet, Sweet Smile—Carpenters (78)	430
Paul YOUNG ▶ 5223 (4)	**323**
Everything Must Change—Paul Young (85)	305
Some People—Paul Young (86)	214
Run Home Girl—Sad Café (79)	108
La-Di-Da—Sad Café (81)	20
Reggie YOUNG ▶ 6278 (2)	**187**
I Found A True Love—Wilson Pickett (68)	360
Buster Browne—Willie Mitchell (65)	13
Rida Johnson YOUNG ▶ 11834 (1)	**0.0**
Sweetheart (Will You Remember)—Hilltoppers (54)	0.0
Rolande YOUNG ▶ 9302 (2)	**27**
Sunshine And Rain—Teddy Bart (57)	*53*
Sunshine And Rain—Bob Whalen (57)	*0.0*
Ron YOUNG ▶ 8737 (1)	**41**
In Your Arms—Little Caesar (91)	81
Rusty YOUNG ▶ 2431 (3)	**1492**
Crazy Love—Poco (79)	1153
Shoot For The Moon—Poco (82)	336
Rose Of Cimarron—Poco (76)	2.4
Sheila YOUNG ▶ 2102 (3)	**1881**
I Love You For All Seasons—Fuzz (71)	1579
Like An Open Door—Fuzz (71)	255
I'm So Glad—Fuzz (71)	93
Starleana YOUNG ▶ 9268 (2)	**27**
Make Up Your Mind—Aurra (82)	78
Just A Touch Of Love—Slave (80)	10
Steve YOUNG ▶ 4004 (1)	**625**
Seven Bridges Road—Eagles (80)	625
Vicki YOUNG [Wanda Cleo Stegall] ▶ 9817 (1)	**16**
Let There Be You—Five Keys (57)	33

Victor YOUNG ▶ 777 (30)	**5679**
Love Letters—Ketty Lester (62)	*2808*
When I Fall In Love—Lettermen (61)	*2046*
(Theme From) Around The World—Mantovani And His Orchestra (57)	*1959*
(Theme From) Around The World—Victor Young & Orchestra (57)	*1813*
Love Letters—Elvis Presley (66)	*886*
Around The World—Bing Crosby (57)	*591*
Blue Star (The "Medic" Theme)—Felicia Sanders (55)	*541*
Written On The Wind—Four Aces (56)	261
Theme From The Medic—Victor Young And His Singing Strings (55)	*98*
When I Fall In Love—Etta Jones (61)	*98*
When I Fall In Love—Donny Osmond (73)	*77*
If It's A Dream—McGuire Sisters (55)	*76*
Around The World In Eighty Days—McGuire Sisters (57)	*45*
Where Is That Someone For Me—Joni James (55)	42
Blue Star—Ventures (66)	*33*
My Foolish Heart—Demensions (63)	29
Sam, You Made The Pants Too Long—Barbra Streisand (66)	21
Around The World—Nat "King" Cole (57)	*15*
Love Letters—Joni James (56)	*10*
Golden Earrings—Five Satins (61)	3.2
When I Fall In Love—Natalie Cole (88)	*2.4*
Love Me—Billy Eckstine (54)	0.0
If It's A Dream—Kitty Kallen (55)	*0.0*
Around The World—Jane Morgan (57)	*0.0*
Around The World—Eddie Fisher (57)	*0.0*
Around The World—Don Costa & His Orchestra (57)	*0.0*
Around The World—Manny Lopez & His Orchestra (57)	*0.0*
Around The World—Lawrence Welk & His Champagne Music (57)	*0.0*
Theme From "Medic"—Les Baxter His Chorus And Orchestra (55)	*0.0*
Blue Star (The "Medic" Theme)—Charlie Applewhite with Victor Young & His Orchestra (55)	*0.0*
Welton YOUNG ▶ 4105 (2)	**591**
Tra La La La Suzy—Dean And Jean (63)	718
The Majestic—Dion (61)	465
Willie David YOUNG ▶ 3221 (2)	**944**
Keep On Dancing—Gentrys (65)	3698
Don't Have To Shop Around—Mad Lads (65)	78
—Young MC see: Marvin YOUNG	
Robert Gene YOUNT ▶ 1765 (6)	**2360**
Release Me (And Let Me Love Again)—Engelbert Humperdinck (67)	*4487*
Release Me—Esther Phillips "Little Esther" (62)	*2523*
I'll Release You—Joann Bon And The Coquettes (67)	*33*
Release Me—Johnny Adams (68)	*29*
Release Me—Jivin' Gene (60)	*13*
Release Me—Esther Phillips (67)	*7.2*
—Yo-Yo see: Yolanda WHITAKER	
Sebastian YRADIER ▶ 3106 (2)	**1008**
La Paloma—Billy Vaughn And His Orchestra (58)	997
La Paloma Twist—Chubby Checker (62)	23
Byong YU ▶ 10731 (1)	**5.7**
Ride The Tiger—Jefferson Starship (74)	17
Adam YURMAN ▶ 9702 (1)	**19**
Playing With Lightning—Shot In The Dark (81)	38
Timi YURO [Rosemary Timotea Aurro] ▶ 11280 (1)	**2.5**
She Really Loves You—Timi Yuro (61)	5.0
—Roy Yustrom see: Bill NORVAS	
Maurice YVAIN ▶ 6802 (2)	**136**
My Man—Peggy Lee (59)	*340*
My Man—Barbra Streisand (65)	*204*

Z

ZACAR [Ciro Dammicco] ▶ 6296 (1)	**185**
When A Child Is Born—Michael Holm (74)	369
John ZACHARY ▶ 10936 (1)	**4.2**
Different Strokes—Syl Johnson (67)	8.5
Eddie ZACK ▶ 10014 (1)	**14**
Fourteen Karat Gold—Don Cherry (57)	28
Randall ZACUTO ▶ 10857 (1)	**4.9**
Joker—Snail (78)	4.9

Michael ZAGER ▶ 949 (6)	**4701**
Forgive Me, Girl—Spinners (79)	2453
I've Loved You For A Long Time—Spinners (80)	1698
Let's All Chant—Michael Zager Band (78)	662
Morning Much Better— Ten Wheel Drive With Genya Ravan (70)	266
Nothing Remains The Same—Spinners (81)	84
Do It With Feeling—Michael Zager's Moon Band Featuring Peabo Bryson (76)	5.8
—Benjamin Zamberg see: Benny BELL	
—Francis Zambon see: Mark JAMES	
Robin ZANDER ▶ 3822 (4)	**689**
Can't Stop Falling Into Love—Cheap Trick (90)	1076
Tonight It's You—Cheap Trick (85)	422
Stop This Game—Cheap Trick (80)	334
Never Had A Lot To Lose—Cheap Trick (89)	116
Herb ZANE ▶ 10907 (1)	**4.4**
Man In The Phone Booth—Wanderer (57)	8.9
Dan ZANES ▶ 9792 (1)	**17**
I Still Want You—Del Fuegos (86)	34
Alex ZANETIS ▶ 1211 (7)	**3672**
Snap Your Fingers—Joe Henderson (62)	*2221*
As Usual—Brenda Lee (63)	1975
I'm Saving My Love—Skeeter Davis (63)	500
Snap Your Fingers—Barbara Lewis (63)	*120*
I'm Gonna Change Everything—Jim Reeves (62)	11
Guilty—Jim Reeves (63)	10
Backtrack—Faron Young (61)	10
Laura ZANIN ▶ 7536 (1)	**90**
Sole Sole Sole— Siw Malmkvist - Umberto Marcato (64)	180
Frank ZAPPA ▶ 4057 (4)	**609**
Valley Girl—Frank Zappa (82)	471
Dancin' Fool—Frank Zappa (79)	247
Don't Eat The Yellow Snow—Frank Zappa (74)	124
I Don't Wanna Get Drafted—Frank Zappa (80)	2.2
Moon Unit ZAPPA ▶ 5862 (1)	**235**
Valley Girl—Frank Zappa (82)	471
Abel ZARATE ▶ 4787 (1)	**416**
Suavecito—Malo (72)	1249
Hy ZARET ▶ 340 (14)	**10969**
Unchained Melody— Les Baxter His Chorus And Orchestra (55)	*8661*
Unchained Melody—Al Hibbler (55)	*4376*
Unchained Melody—Righteous Brothers (65)	*3432*
Unchained Melody—Roy Hamilton (55)	*2241*
Unchained Melody—Righteous Brothers (90)	*1154*
No Other Arms No Other Lips—Chordettes (59)	*741*
Young And Warm And Wonderful— Tony Bennett with Frank DeVol and his Orch. (58)	*514*
Unchained Melody (1990)—Righteous Brothers (90)	*502*
Unchained Melody—Vito & The Salutations (63)	*312*
No Other Arms No Other Lips—Four Aces (59)	*119*
Unchained Melody—Sweet Inspirations (68)	*70*
Unchained Melody—Blackwells (60)	*47*
Unchained Melody—June Valli (55)	*44*
Unchained Melody (Live)—Heart (81)	*10*
Richard ZATORSKI ▶ 3254 (3)	**925**
Send Me An Angel—Real Life (83)	*786*
Send Me An Angel '89—Real Life (89)	*703*
Catch Me I'm Falling—Real Life (84)	360
Joe ZAWINUL ▶ 1671 (5)	**2516**
Mercy, Mercy, Mercy—Buckinghams (67)	*2966*
Mercy, Mercy, Mercy— "Cannonball" Adderley (66)	*1426*
Mercy, Mercy, Mercy—Marlena Shaw (67)	*209*
Mercy, Mercy, Mercy— Larry Williams & Johnny Watson (67)	*34*
Country Preacher—Cannonball Adderley Quintet (70)	21
Vincent ZECCOLA ▶ 10347 (1)	**9.7**
Good Goodby—Bob Knight Four (61)	19
Hans ZEEMAN ▶ 11021 (1)	**3.8**
My Bewildered Heart—Jaye P. Morgan (56)	11
Randy ZEHRINGER ▶ 10376 (1)	**9.3**
Jesse Brady—McCoys (68)	9.3
—Rick Zehringer see: Rick DERRINGER	
Milan ZEKAVICA ▶ 2443 (5)	**1485**
Wild, Wild West—Escape Club (88)	4224
I'll Be There—Escape Club (91)	1572
Shake For The Sheik—Escape Club (88)	509
Call It Poison—Escape Club (91)	412
Walking Through Walls—Escape Club (89)	67
—Zekkariyas see: Cecil WOMACK	
—Zeriya Zekkariyas see: Linda WOMACK	
Gary ZEKLEY [Brandon Chase, Yodar Critch, Alan Gary Zekley] ▶ 1919 (7)	**2111**
I'd Wait A Million Years—Grass Roots (69)	2231
Sooner Or Later—Grass Roots (71)	1771
Yellow Balloon—Yellow Balloon (67)	647
Hallelujah—Sweathog (71)	635
Breakaway—Big Pig (88)	207
The Grooviest Girl In The World—Fun And Games (69)	190
Good Feelin' Time—Yellow Balloon (67)	30
Danny ZELLA ▶ 8333 (1)	**54**
Wicked Ruby—Danny Zella & his Zell Rocks (58)	54
Phil ZELLER ▶ 5050 (2)	**354**
I'm Comin' Home, Cindy—Trini Lopez (66)	431
I Can't Believe I'm Losing You—Frank Sinatra (68)	277
Linda Kay ZERATO ▶ 10709 (1)	**5.9**
The Lights Of Tucson—Jim Campbell (70)	5.9
Lou ZERATO ▶ 3280 (5)	**913**
Beg, Borrow And Steal—Ohio Express (67)	957
Party Girl—Bernadette Carroll (64)	432
Hey Jean, Hey Dean—Dean And Jean (64)	362
They're Here—Boots Walker (67)	27
Frisco Bay—Navajo (72)	11
Aryan ZERO [John Campbell Picard] ▶ 5526 (2)	**274**
Switchin' To Glide—Kings (80)	548
This Beat Goes On—Kings (80)	0.0
—Eve Jay Zeserson see: Eve JAY	
—Maurice Zeserson see: Lee MORRIS	
Nick ZESSES ▶ 2301 (4)	**1634**
I Just Want To Celebrate—Rare Earth (71)	2092
Hey Big Brother—Rare Earth (71)	928
You Gotta Have Love In Your Heart— Supremes & Four Tops (71)	210
Mother Nature—Temptations (72)	38
Fred ZEUFELD ▶ 11606 (1)	**1.0**
Granny's Pad—Viceroys (63)	5.1
Warren ZEVON ▶ 3620 (3)	**764**
Werewolves Of London—Warren Zevon (78)	804
Poor Poor Pitiful Me—Linda Ronstadt (78)	437
Follow Me—Lyme & Cybelle (66)	118
—Edward James Zgorecki see: Ed GRAY	
—Richard Adam Ziegler see: Ritchie ADAMS	
Aaron ZIGMAN ▶ 2630 (4)	**1308**
Crush On You—Jets (86)	2253
Private Number—Jets (86)	291
Anything Can Happen—Was (Not Was) (89)	100
I Wasn't The One (Who Said Goodbye)— Agnetha Faltskog (88)	6.1
—Bill Zimmerman see: Bill GIANT	
Charles ZIMMERMAN ▶ 9682 (1)	**19**
Young Dove's Calling—Couplings (58)	38
—Bill/Harvey Zimmerman see: Bill GIANT	
Charles A. ZIMMERMANN ▶ 10479 (1)	**8.0**
Anchors Aweigh—Four Preps (62)	24
Frank ZINCAVAGE ▶ 7090 (1)	**116**
A Girl In Trouble (Is A Temporary Thing)— Romeo Void (84)	466
Tom ZINSER ▶ 8139 (1)	**60**
Mississippi Mama—Owen B. (70)	60
Dan ZIPFEL ▶ 10887 (1)	**4.6**
Joanie—Bay Bops (58)	14
Richie ZITO ▶ 6033 (2)	**214**
Love You Like I Never Loved Before— John O'Banion (81)	588
Reach Out—Giorgio Moroder (84)	53
—Alex Zivojinovich see: Alex LIFESON	
Peter ZIZZO ▶ 5369 (1)	**299**
Whispers—Corina (91)	299
Chip Z'NUFF [Gregory Rybarski] ▶ 9104 (1)	**31**
New Thing—Enuff Z'Nuff (89)	93
Wally ZOBER ▶ 5976 (1)	**220**
Come On And Get Me—Fabian (59)	440
Pete ZORN ▶ 9984 (1)	**14**
I've Been Lovin' You—Easy Street (76)	57
Irwin Elliott ZUCKER [Jack Elliott] ▶ 7972 (2)	**67**
Theme from Charlie's Angels— Henry Mancini And His Orchestra (77)	118
Fat Albert (Hey, Hey, Hey)— Fat Albert Orchestra and Chorus (68)	32
Artie ZWIRN ▶ 1538 (3)	**2785**
Sorry (I Ran All The Way Home)—Impalas (59)	4846
(It's Been A Long Time) Pretty Baby— Gino & Gina (58)	680
Oh What A Fool—Impalas (59)	43
Walter ZWOL [Walter Zwolinski] ▶ 7177 (2)	**111**
New York City—Zwol (78)	86
Call Out My Name—Zwol (79)	25

Top 1000 Writers By Score

1	Paul McCARTNEY
2	John LENNON
3	TRADITIONAL
4	Lionel RICHIE
5	Paul SIMON
6	Neil DIAMOND
7	Stevie WONDER
8	PRINCE
9	Smokey ROBINSON
10	Barry GIBB
11	Burt BACHARACH
12	Eddie HOLLAND
13	Carole KING
14	Brian HOLLAND
15	Lamont DOZIER
16	Paul ANKA
17	Hal DAVID
18	Michael JACKSON
19	Gerry GOFFIN
20	Curtis MAYFIELD
21	Norman WHITFIELD
22	Mick JAGGER
23	Keith RICHARDS
24	Jerry LEIBER
25	Sam COOKE
26	Kal MANN
27	Billy JOEL
28	Mike STOLLER
29	Robin GIBB
30	Barry MANN
31	Bob DYLAN
32	Leon HUFF
33	Jeff BARRY
34	Kenneth GAMBLE
35	George MICHAEL
36	John FOGERTY
37	Elton JOHN
38	Bernie TAUPIN
39	John D. LOUDERMILK
40	Bob CREWE
41	Howard GREENFIELD
42	Phil COLLINS
43	Bob GAUDIO
44	Diane WARREN
45	Brian WILSON
46	Chuck BERRY
47	Boudleaux BRYANT
48	Daryl HALL
49	Cynthia WEIL
50	Neil SEDAKA
51	Sylvester STEWART
52	James BROWN
53	Barrett STRONG
54	Bruce SPRINGSTEEN
55	Maurice GIBB
56	Jimmy WEBB
57	Jerry FULLER
58	Tony HATCH
59	David GATES
60	STING
61	Phil SPECTOR
62	George HARRISON
63	Doc POMUS
64	Berry GORDY
65	Mort SHUMAN
66	John DENVER
67	Hank BALLARD
68	Rod TEMPERTON
69	John FARRAR
70	Jeff LYNNE
71	John SEBASTIAN
72	Buck RAM
73	Otis BLACKWELL
74	John MELLENCAMP
75	Sonny BONO
76	Roy ORBISON
77	Freddie PERREN
78	Joe SOUTH
79	James Samuel HARRIS
80	Terry LEWIS
81	Ellie GREENWICH
82	Mike LOVE
83	Bob SEGER
84	John PHILLIPS
85	Bobby RUSSELL
86	Dave APPELL
87	Mac DAVIS
88	Lee HAZLEWOOD
89	Linda McCARTNEY
90	Dennis DeYOUNG
91	Laura NYRO
92	Fats DOMINO
93	Madonna L. CICCONE
94	Donovan LEITCH
95	Allen TOUSSAINT
96	Marvin GAYE
97	Michael Leslie JONES
98	Bert BERNS
99	Marty ROBBINS
100	Tommy ROE
101	Ray PARKER Jr.
102	Carole Bayer SAGER
103	Rod STEWART
104	Richard MARX
105	Pete TOWNSHEND
106	Felix CAVALIERE
107	Robert ALLEN
108	Rick SPRINGFIELD
109	Aaron SCHROEDER
110	Ray DAVIES
111	Clyde OTIS
112	Irwin LEVINE
113	Barry WHITE
114	Lee POCKRISS
115	Steve MILLER
116	Dave BARTHOLOMEW
117	Bob MERRILL
118	Freddie MERCURY
119	Chip TAYLOR
120	Giorgio MORODER
121	Bobby DARIN
122	Ray STEVENS
123	Kenny LOGGINS
124	Luther DIXON
125	Al STILLMAN
126	Per GESSLE
127	Harlan HOWARD
128	Wayne Carson THOMPSON
129	Isaac HAYES
130	Eric CARMEN
131	Bill WITHERS
132	Thom BELL
133	Otis REDDING
134	Peter CETERA
135	David BOWIE
136	Mark JAMES
137	Harry Wayne CASEY
138	Tony MACAULAY
139	Kenneth EDMONDS
140	Nile RODGERS
141	David PAICH
142	Maurice STARR
143	Bernard EDWARDS
144	Joe TEX
145	Geoff STEPHENS
146	Gilbert O'SULLIVAN
147	Don HENLEY
148	David FOSTER
149	Rick FINCH
150	Ric OCASEK
151	Bernie LOWE
152	Jack KELLER
153	Don GIBSON
154	David SEVILLE
155	Carl SIGMAN
156	Tommy JAMES
157	Roger MILLER
158	Eddie BRIGATI
159	Elvis PRESLEY
160	L. Russell BROWN
161	Glenn FREY
162	Graham GOULDMAN
163	Paul VANCE
164	Mutt LANGE
165	Eugene RECORD
166	Paul WILLIAMS
167	Johnny MERCER
168	Mike CHAPMAN
169	Baker KNIGHT
170	Debbie GIBSON
171	Jim STEINMAN
172	Ernie MARESCA
173	Jon BON JOVI
174	Melanie SAFKA
175	Christopher CROSS
176	Del SHANNON
177	Ritchie CORDELL
178	Al GREEN
179	Jim CROCE
180	Gloria ESTEFAN
181	Don ROBERTSON
182	Shel SILVERSTEIN
183	Will JENNINGS
184	Hoyt AXTON
185	Donna SUMMER
186	Kevin CRONIN
187	Dallas FRAZIER
188	Tony ROMEO
189	Steve CROPPER
190	Dean PITCHFORD
191	Jim WEATHERLY
192	Joe MELSON
193	Dick MANNING
194	Carly SIMON
195	Winfield SCOTT
196	Stevie NICKS
197	Burton CUMMINGS
198	Randy BACHMAN
199	Dennis LAMBERT
200	Jim PETERIK
201	Michael MASSER
202	Bobby HART
203	Rudy CLARK
204	Graham RUSSELL
205	Rod ARGENT
206	Dan FOGELBERG
207	Charles SINGLETON
208	Mitch MURRAY
209	Gordon LIGHTFOOT
210	Albert HAMMOND
211	Paul Francis WEBSTER
212	Andy KIM
213	Don COVAY
214	Melvin ENDSLEY
215	Billy STEINBERG
216	John STEWART
217	Don McLEAN
218	John BETTIS
219	Max STEINER

220 Nick ASHFORD
221 Valerie SIMPSON
222 Sandy LINZER
223 Linda CREED
224 Van McCOY
225 Clint BALLARD Jr.
226 Maurice WILLIAMS
227 Robert LAMM
228 Colin James HAY
229 Bob HILLIARD
230 Dave CLARK
231 Randy GOODRUM
232 Tommy BOYCE
233 Christine McVIE
234 Frank Edward WILSON
235 Neil YOUNG
236 Brook BENTON
237 Nicky CHINN
238 John DEACON
239 Al HOFFMAN
240 Ivory Joe HUNTER
241 Henry COSBY
242 Lou GRAMM
243 Antonio REID
244 Alan O'DAY
245 John OATES
246 Norman GIMBEL
247 Lloyd PRICE
248 J.P. RICHARDSON
249 Cat STEVENS
250 Rupert HOLMES
251 Maurice WHITE
252 Desmond CHILD
253 Steve PERRY
254 Tom SNOW
255 Bryan ADAMS
256 Wes FARRELL
257 Thomas F. KELLY
258 Jerry HERMAN
259 Jack SCOTT
260 Terry KIRKMAN
261 Dino FEKARIS
262 Pete SEEGER
263 Steve KIPNER
264 Hank COCHRAN
265 Keith FORSEY
266 Wally GOLD
267 Alan GORDON
268 Brian POTTER
269 Kenny NOLAN
270 Graham GOBLE
271 Kent LaVOIE
272 Floyd CRAMER
273 Sammy CAHN
274 Randy NEWMAN
275 Henry MANCINI
276 Tom SCHOLZ
277 Joe BROOKS
278 Harold LOGAN
279 Ray EVANS
280 Jay LIVINGSTON
281 Irving BERLIN
282 Felice BRYANT
283 Lewis MARTINÉE
284 Jimmy DEAN
285 Billy PRESTON
286 Robbie VAN LEEUWEN
287 Seth JUSTMAN
288 Mariah CAREY
289 James PANKOW
290 André POPP
291 Rick JAMES
292 Harry NILSSON
293 Jonathan CAIN
294 Justin HAYWARD
295 Gerry RAFFERTY
296 Phil EVERLY
297 George Henry JACKSON
298 Don EVERLY
299 Bobbie GENTRY
300 Denny RANDELL
301 Bobby GOLDSBORO
302 Leon RENÉ
303 Van MORRISON
304 Kris KRISTOFFERSON
305 Ronald Norman MILLER
306 George David WEISS
307 Jim VALLANCE
308 Pam SAWYER
309 Peter CALLANDER
310 Don BLACK
311 Buddy BUIE
312 Eddie CORNELIUS
313 Ben RALEIGH
314 Richard RODGERS
315 James TAYLOR
316 Dewey BUNNELL
317 Johnny BRISTOL
318 Russ BALLARD
319 Pete HAM
320 Herbert NEWMAN
321 Richard ADLER
322 Kenny YOUNG
323 Peter FRAMPTON
324 Larry WEISS
325 Jackie DeSHANNON
326 Aretha FRANKLIN
327 Dick HOLLER
328 Holly KNIGHT
329 Bobby DAY
330 Graham NASH
331 Oliver LEIBER
332 Acker BILK
333 Deke RICHARDS
334 Chris KENNER
335 Ronnie SELF
336 Wayne SHANKLIN
337 Eddie HEYWOOD
338 Sid WAYNE
339 Stephen STILLS
340 Hy ZARET
341 Roger WATERS
342 Frankie SULLIVAN
343 Joni MITCHELL
344 Mike RUTHERFORD
345 Dion DiMUCCI
346 Artie RESNICK
347 Steve WINWOOD
348 Al JACKSON
349 William STEVENSON
350 Hans ENGELMANN
351 Harvey FUQUA
352 Leon RUSSELL
353 Frank GUIDA
354 David PACK
355 Rod McKUEN
356 Bruce HORNSBY
357 Kurt WEILL
358 Deadric MALONE
359 Mack DAVID
360 Alex NORTH
361 Jackson BROWNE
362 Paul DAVIS
363 Danny JANSSEN
364 Ringo STARR
365 Cole PORTER
366 Lincoln CHASE
367 Ed TOWNSEND
368 Michael McDONALD
369 Ed MARSHALL
370 Steven TYLER
371 Galt MacDERMOT
372 Joseph KOSMA
373 Tom PETTY
374 Patrick Raymond LEONARD
375 Merle TRAVIS
376 Billy OCEAN
377 Narada Michael WALDEN
378 David WHITE
379 Garry BONNER
380 Martha SHARP
381 Johnny NASH
382 Tom T. HALL
383 Dewayne BLACKWELL
384 Willie MITCHELL
385 C. Carson PARKS
386 Peter UDELL
387 Luigi CREATORE
388 Hugo PERETTI
389 Gary GELD
390 Clifton DAVIS
391 Ray HILDEBRAND
392 James RADO
393 Gerome RAGNI
394 Willie NELSON
395 Toni TENNILLE
396 Roy C. BENNETT
397 Sid TEPPER
398 Gary WRIGHT
399 Mark LINDSAY
400 John WILLIAMS
401 Jimmie CRANE
402 David A. STEWART
403 Robbie ROBERTSON
404 Richard BERRY
405 Roger COOK
406 Jeanine DECKERS
407 Robert PARISSI
408 Shadow MORTON
409 Bill DANOFF
410 Luis GUGLIELMI
411 John MADARA
412 Richie SAMBORA
413 Todd RUNDGREN
414 Ben WEISMAN
415 Ned MILLER
416 Huey LEWIS
417 Gene PITNEY
418 Warren MOORE
419 Al JACOBS
420 Elliot WOLFF
421 Sylvia MOY
422 Klaus-Günter NEUMANN
423 Sammy FAIN
424 Barry De VORZON
425 Sonny CURTIS
426 Norman PETTY
427 Mark KNOPFLER
428 Paul EVANS
429 P.F. SLOAN
430 Mitchell PARISH
431 Sherman EDWARDS
432 David PORTER
433 Roger GREENAWAY
434 Jerry ROSS
435 Pat BALLARD
436 Howard JONES
437 Steve GREENBERG
438 Cindy WALKER
439 Errol BROWN
440 Steve BARRI
441 James HOLVAY
442 Ewan MacCOLL
443 General JOHNSON
444 Terry BRITTEN
445 Ronnie MACK
446 Billy SHERRILL
447 Marguerite MONNOT
448 Benny ANDERSSON
449 Björn ULVAEUS
450 Ritchie VALENS
451 Teddy RANDAZZO
452 Phil MEDLEY
453 Robby KRIEGER
454 Harold FALTERMEYER

455 Rick EVANS
456 Ruthann FRIEDMAN
457 Carl PERKINS
458 Peter DeANGELIS
459 Peter LORD
460 Eddie SNYDER
461 Sara ALLEN
462 Perez PRADO
463 J.R. COBB
464 Jerome KERN
465 Joe MEEK
466 Barbara MASON
467 Henry GLOVER
468 R. Dean TAYLOR
469 Jerry REED
470 Jerry BUTLER
471 Michael HUTCHENCE
472 Dee CLARK
473 Domenico MODUGNO
474 Jerry RAGOVOY
475 Robert PALMER
476 Jan BERRY
477 Roger NICHOLS
478 Toni WINE
479 Frank SLAY
480 Jesse JAMES
481 Jim MORRISON
482 Frank LOESSER
483 Sharon SHEELEY
484 Bobby VINTON
485 Ray CHARLES
486 Ernest GOLD
487 Nigel John TAYLOR
488 Ronald BLACKWELL
489 Percy MAYFIELD
490 Larry WILLIAMS
491 Stephen BISHOP
492 Chuck WILLIS
493 John CARTER
494 Boz SCAGGS
495 Brian SETZER
496 Jesse STONE
497 Earl SHUMAN
498 Les REED
499 Ollie JONES
500 Sheb WOOLEY
501 Simon Le BON
502 Nick RHODES
503 Dimitri TIOMKIN
504 Norman GREENBAUM
505 Charles FOX
506 Ray MANZAREK
507 Trevor PEACOCK
508 Tim HARDIN
509 Johnny OTIS
510 Bruce ROBERTS
511 Dolly PARTON
512 Billy SWAN
513 Bobby WEINSTEIN

514 Paul JABARA
515 Gilbert BÉCAUD
516 John DENSMORE
517 Roger TAYLOR
518 Bert KAEMPFERT
519 Wayne COCHRAN
520 Tom SPRINGFIELD
521 Andy FARRISS
522 Robert CLIVILLÉS
523 Heino GAZE
524 Janet JACKSON
525 Peter GABRIEL
526 Jack TEMPCHIN
527 Gene MacLELLAN
528 Lou STALLMAN
529 Dan PENN
530 Hank WILLIAMS
531 William DEES
532 Johnny TILLOTSON
533 Corey HART
534 Stephen BRAY
535 Fonce MIZELL
536 Graham LYLE
537 Barry MASON
538 Donald FAGEN
539 Ronald DUNBAR
540 Tony Joe WHITE
541 Stuart HAMBLEN
542 Roy ALFRED
543 Rudy MARTINEZ
544 Audrey ALLISON
545 Joe ALLISON
546 Annie LENNOX
547 Even STEVENS
548 Lindsey BUCKINGHAM
549 Eddy GRANT
550 Jimmy DRIFTWOOD
551 Leo SAYER
552 Bobby SCOTT
553 Hugh MASEKELA
554 Deborah HARRY
555 Marvin MOORE
556 Domingo SAMUDIO
557 Roland ORZABAL
558 Clement A. BOZEWSKI
559 Elliot LURIE
560 Ritchie ADAMS
561 O'Kelly ISLEY
562 Ric CARTEY
563 Carole JOYNER
564 Sylvia ROBINSON
565 Richard KERR
566 Freddy WELLER
567 Ronnie SHANNON
568 Joe SHERMAN
569 Dan HARTMAN
570 Bob MARCUCCI
571 Harry WARREN
572 Johnny SMITH

573 Ronald ISLEY
574 Rudolph ISLEY
575 Chips MOMAN
576 David ROSE
577 Bruce JOHNSTON
578 Fred WISE
579 Nino ROTA
580 Sammy HAGAR
581 David CLAYTON-THOMAS
582 Frederick KNIGHT
583 Pete BELLOTTE
584 Jerry GOLDSTEIN
585 John BARRY
586 Peter YARROW
587 Don DAVIS
588 Marvin HAMLISCH
589 John ROSTILL
590 Leon CARR
591 George M. BROWN
592 Phil CODY
593 Artie KORNFELD
594 Bill ANDERSON
595 Irving GORDON
596 Michael BOLTON
597 Marvin TARPLIN
598 Richard DEHR
599 Terry GILKYSON
600 Frank MILLER
601 Franco MIGLIACCI
602 Noel SHERMAN
603 David COLE
604 Billy DAVIS
605 Claude DeMETRIUS
606 Richard CARPENTER
607 Walter BECKER
608 Johnny CASH
609 Jerry CAPEHART
610 Tony HESTER
611 Parker McGEE
612 Chuck RIO
613 Keni ST. LEWIS
614 David ESSEX
615 Bob STONE
616 Joseph ROYSTER
617 Spooner OLDHAM
618 Eric CLAPTON
619 Andy TAYLOR
620 Clarence PAUL
621 Tommy SHAW
622 Ken HAWKER
623 Gerry BECKLEY
624 Tom JOHNSTON
625 Leslie BRICUSSE
626 Mars BONFIRE
627 Dick ADDRISI
628 Don ADDRISI
629 Mark FARNER
630 Alvertis ISBELL
631 Robert JOHN

632 Rick DEES
633 Hal BLAIR
634 Tom BAHLER
635 Don HARRIS
636 Dewey TERRY
637 Roy TURK
638 Ben MARGULIES
639 Chrissie HYNDE
640 Conway TWITTY
641 Allee WILLIS
642 Gloria SHAYNE
643 Charlotte CAFFEY
644 J.D. SOUTHER
645 Tony WILSON
646 Charles Henry JACKSON Jr.
647 Benny DAVIS
648 Robert SHERMAN
649 Daryl SIMMONS
650 Richard SHERMAN
651 Morris LEVY
652 George DUNING
653 Lorenz HART
654 Tony BANKS
655 Buddy HOLLY
656 Ed COBB
657 Joey LEVINE
658 Rick ROBERTS
659 Mike SMITH
660 Les EMMERSON
661 Dub ALLBRITTEN
662 Albert Philip McKAY
663 Malou RENÉ
664 Winfred LOVETT
665 Buddy KILLEN
666 Bobby FREEMAN
667 Jack LAWRENCE
668 Paul LEKA
669 Irving TAYLOR
670 Billy IDOL
671 Jimmy KENNEDY
672 Charles DAWES
673 Alan BERGMAN
674 Marilyn BERGMAN
675 Al CLEVELAND
676 Clarence QUICK
677 Fred FASSERT
678 Mel TILLIS
679 Bob MARLEY
680 Kerry LIVGREN
681 J. Leslie McFARLAND
682 Chris HAYES
683 Janis IAN
684 Sylvia FRICKER
685 Toni STERN
686 Glen BALLARD
687 Duane EDDY
688 Danny KORTCHMAR
689 Marv ROSS

690 Terry JACKS
691 Steve DUBOFF
692 Doug FIEGER
693 John KAY
694 Roger CHRISTIAN
695 Hoagy CARMICHAEL
696 Al BYRON
697 Gary KEMP
698 Daniel MOORE
699 Bruce FISHER
700 Robert L. KING
701 Jerry ALLISON
702 George BRUNS
703 Sylvester LEVAY
704 Billy PAGE
705 Robert GUIDRY
706 Joe JACKSON
707 Scott ENGLISH
708 Glen HARDIN
709 Andy GIBB
710 Jimmy VAN HEUSEN
711 Peter F. WOLF
712 John GUMMOE
713 Carl William SMITH
714 Hank HUNTER
715 Billy STRANGE
716 Rodney CROWELL
717 Elliot CHIPRUT
718 Bill JUSTIS
719 Don GEORGE
720 Lou CHRISTIE
721 Twyla HERBERT
722 Vini PONCIA
723 Peter ALLEN
724 Bobby HEBB
725 Richard LEIGH
726 John DURRILL
727 Florrie PALMER
728 Alex HARVEY
729 Amanda McBROOM
730 VANGELIS
731 Raynard MINER
732 Warren BROOKS
733 Mort GARSON
734 Otto HARBACH
735 Greg PERRY
736 Larry KOLBER
737 Stan LEBOWSKY
738 Bobby STEVENSON
739 Paul RODGERS
740 Dick GOSTING
741 Reggie LUCAS
742 Rick NIELSEN
743 Bo GENTRY
744 Homer BANKS
745 Manos HADJIDAKIS
746 Gale GARNETT
747 Gary BRUCE
748 Edgar WINTER

749 August MSARURGWA
750 Rick DAVIES
751 Oscar HAMMERSTEIN
752 Tom BLACKBURN
753 Lou HANDMAN
754 Helen MILLER
755 Stephan PRAGER
756 Jody WATLEY
757 Mark BARKAN
758 Roger HODGSON
759 Jack SIGLER
760 Willie DIXON
761 Mike HAZLEWOOD
762 Keith McCORMACK
763 Evan ROGERS
764 Carl STURKEN
765 Donnie IRIS
766 Alice COOPER
767 Mickie GRANT
768 Jerry SAMUELS
769 Donna FARGO
770 Patrick SIMMONS
771 Eddie FLOYD
772 Mike LEANDER
773 Don BREWER
774 George MERRILL
775 Shannon RUBICAM
776 Max CROOK
777 Victor YOUNG
778 Carl DOUGLAS
779 Beverly ROSS
780 Michael CRAIG
781 Roy HAY
782 Jon MOSS
783 George O'DOWD
784 Gene ALLAN
785 Berthold BRECHT
786 Jerry LIVINGSTON
787 Dolores Vicki SILVERS
788 Jimmy DUNCAN
789 Bernie WAYNE
790 Kendall L. HAYES
791 Elmer BERNSTEIN
792 Ivan DOROSCHUK
793 Earl King JOHNSON
794 Bill TRADER
795 Terry SHADDICK
796 Terry MELCHER
797 Mark LONDON
798 Vincent YOUMANS
799 Paul STANLEY
800 Hank DeVITO
801 Dennis W. MORGAN
802 Bob MONTGOMERY
803 Lou ADLER
804 George GERSHWIN
805 Peter BECKETT
806 Anita POREE
807 Lowman PAULING

808 Bob DAVIE
809 Peter LUCIA
810 Bobby BLOOM
811 John MARASCALCO
812 Al KASHA
813 Calvin LEWIS
814 Andrew WRIGHT
815 Willis Alan RAMSEY
816 Wally HOLMES
817 Johnny LEHMANN
818 Eric WOOLFSON
819 Barbara LEWIS
820 King FLOYD
821 Carol CONNORS
822 Jim SEALS
823 Gary ANDERSON
824 Marc BLITZSTEIN
825 Artie GLENN
826 Ronnie WHITE
827 Amy GRANT
828 Sunny SKYLAR
829 Keith DIAMOND
830 Faye VOSS
831 Allen REYNOLDS
832 Ike TURNER
833 Janna ALLEN
834 André CYMONE
835 Liam STERNBERG
836 Michael James EDWARDS
837 Leonard CASTON
838 Michael NESMITH
839 Jack NANCE
840 Anthony NEWLEY
841 Gene BARGE
842 Billy Edd WHEELER
843 Martin L. GORE
844 Jack SEGAL
845 Freddie GORMAN
846 Martin PAGE
847 Alan FREED
848 Ahmet ERTEGUN
849 Leon PAYNE
850 Mike POST
851 Fred SPIELMAN
852 Kennedy GORDY
853 Allan CLARKE
854 Ralph BASS
855 Alan PARSONS
856 Tom GLAZER
857 Robert HAZARD
858 Neil TENNANT
859 Nick VAN EEDE
860 Elliot WILLENSKY
861 Eric STEWART
862 Larry EVOY
863 Robert BATEMAN
864 Alan TARNEY
865 Ennio MORRICONE
866 Frederick B. WILLIAMS

867 Walter NIMS
868 Hachidai NAKAMURA
869 Sascha BURLAND
870 Sid WYCHE
871 Arthur ALTMAN
872 Martha DAVIS
873 Barry SADLER
874 Jim STAFFORD
875 Richard PENNIMAN
876 Jr. WALKER
877 William HART
878 Chas SANDFORD
879 Duane HITCHINGS
880 Raymond Earl JACKSON
881 Chris LOWE
882 Eddie RABBITT
883 Peter GREEN
884 Huey P. SMITH
885 Dash CROFTS
886 Dennis LINDE
887 Mick RALPHS
888 Kay TWOMEY
889 Nick GILDER
890 Frank MILLS
891 Dickey BETTS
892 Eugene PEARSON
893 Arthur KENT
894 Harry CHAPIN
895 Ivy Jo HUNTER
896 Barbara GEORGE
897 Skip SCARBOROUGH
898 Woodrow Buddy JOHNSON
899 Chet POWERS
900 Bruce BLACKMAN
901 Ira GERSHWIN
902 Eddy RAY
903 Billy VERA
904 Berton AVERRE
905 Billy HILL
906 Peter DeROSE
907 Sylvia DEE
908 Donna WEISS
909 Chuck BARRIS
910 Robert PLANT
911 Cyndi LAUPER
912 Neil FINN
913 Gregg DIAMOND
914 Jerry LORDAN
915 Eddie SCHWARTZ
916 Bernard Leon JACKSON
917 Barry EASTMOND
918 Ben E. KING
919 Barbara ACKLIN
920 Gene McDANIELS
921 Terence Trent D'ARBY
922 Robin MOORE
923 James Anthony DEAN
924 Ken DARBY

925 Ray DORSET
926 Paul CARRACK
927 Peter WOLF
928 John Bobby BERRY
929 Marvin YANCY
930 Michael ANTHONY
931 Alex VAN HALEN
932 Eddie VAN HALEN
933 Hughie CANNON
934 Gregory ABBOTT
935 Rufus THOMAS
936 Robert MAXWELL
937 Ronald BELL
938 Redd EVANS
939 Joey DEE
940 Robin SCOTT
941 Lee MORRIS
942 Bruce CHANNEL
943 Margaret COBB
944 Stanley KAHAN
945 John S. CARTER
946 Jule STYNE
947 Robert BELL
948 Claydes SMITH
949 Michael ZAGER
950 Reggie CALLOWAY
951 Dennis COFFEY
952 Mike CAMPBELL
953 Lou JOSIE
954 David MALLOY
955 Fred TOBIAS
956 Mike ANTHONY
957 George GREEN
958 Joe WALSH
959 Suzanne VEGA
960 George KHOURY
961 Dave MANN
962 John Martin SOMMERS
963 Judy PARKER
964 Maurice IRBY
965 Stig ANDERSON
966 David COVERDALE
967 Joe SENECA
968 Leonard L. CAPIZZI
969 Bobby PICKETT
970 R.B. GREAVES
971 Mason WILLIAMS
972 Lolly VEGAS
973 Eddie CURTIS
974 Dick GLASSER
975 Joe SHAPIRO
976 Dorsey BURNETTE
977 Ben PETERS
978 Bert REISFELD
979 Robert ROGERS
980 Bob WELCH
981 Phil BAPTISTE
982 Alberto CURCI
983 Charles CHAPLIN
984 Irene CARA
985 James LEE
986 Elliot STRAITE
987 Lois Ann BLAISCH
988 David SHIRE
989 Erik DARLING
990 Michael GORE
991 Marty BALIN
992 Ellas McDANIEL
993 Nancy WILSON
994 John SPINKS
995 Bickley REICHNER
996 Smokey ROGERS
997 Ray WHITLEY
998 Billy SQUIER
999 Jimmy CLANTON
1000 Dave WILLIAMS

Top 100 Writers and Their Collaborators

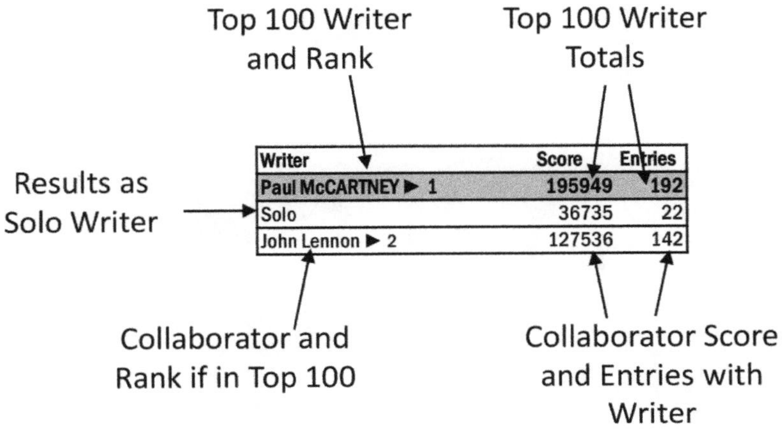

Note that the columns are not additive. For example, one song with a writer and four collaborators appears as five entries, not one.

Paul McCARTNEY ▶ 1	**195949**	**192**
Solo	36735	22
John Lennon ▶ 2	127536	142
Linda McCartney ▶ 89	26192	21
Michael Jackson ▶ 18	4450	1
Elvis Costello	629	2
Denny Laine	377	3
Eric Stewart	30	1
Sean Ono Lennon	12	1
Yoko Ono	12	1
Ringo Starr	5.3	1
J. Nicolas Felgen	0.5	1
Otto Demmlar	0.5	1
John LENNON ▶ 2	**166587**	**163**
Solo	37009	18
Paul McCartney ▶ 1	127536	142
Carlos Alomar	1910	1
David Bowie	1910	1
Yoko Ono	143	3
Sean Ono Lennon	12	1
Ringo Starr	5.3	1
J. Nicolas Felgen	0.5	1
Otto Demmlar	0.5	1
TRADITIONAL ▶ 3	**113691**	**203**
Lionel RICHIE ▶ 4	**91106**	**35**
Solo	81488	20
Michael Jackson ▶ 18	3054	1
Brenda Richie	2652	2
Cynthia Weil ▶ 49	1458	2
Carlos Rios	1139	1
Michael Frenchik	1139	1
Greg Phillinganes	834	2
Thomas McClary	575	4
Ronald LaPread	557	4
Milan Williams	422	3
Walter Orange	422	3
William King	410	2
Jeff Bowen	137	2
Donald Baldwin	125	1
Darrell Jones	105	1
David Cochrane	53	1
William Roderick Miller	12	1
Paul SIMON ▶ 5	**87319**	**51**
Solo	82685	44
Bruce Woodley	2539	2
Art Garfunkel	1417	3
Daniel Robles	663	1
Forere Motloheloa	15	1
Neil DIAMOND ▶ 6	**86693**	**68**
Solo	78789	55
Gilbert Bécaud	3014	2
Alan Bergman	2179	1
Marilyn Bergman	2179	1
Carole Bayer Sager	1026	4
Alan Lindgren	940	2
Burt Bacharach ▶ 11	796	3
Richard Winchell Bennett	460	1
David Foster	245	1
Tom Hensley	87	1
Bob Feldman	40	2
Cliff Adams	40	2
Eddie Snyder	40	2
Jerry Goldstein	40	2
Larry Weiss	40	2
Lockie Edwards	40	2
Richard Gottehrer	40	2
Stanley Kahan	40	2
Wes Farrell	40	2

Stevie WONDER ▶ 7	**83858**	**82**
Solo	68537	43
Henry Cosby	8630	18
Sylvia Moy	6146	16
Syreeta Wright	3623	8
Lula Mae Hardaway	3317	8
Lee Garrett	3023	5
Smokey Robinson ▶ 9	2484	2
Clarence Paul	1090	4
Morris Broadnax	1090	4
Bill Cosby	647	1
Don Hunter	375	3
Jermaine Jackson	297	1
Michael Omartian	297	1
Ivy Jo Hunter	217	1
Paul Riser	155	2
Eric Mercury	108	1
David Steele	84	1
Simone Antoinette Johnson	84	1
Dante Ross	48	1
John Dajani	48	1
John Gamble	48	1
Michael Berrin	48	1
Pete Nash	48	1
Peter Gabriel	48	1
Ira Tucker Jr.	5.3	1
PRINCE ▶ 8	**82519**	**60**
Solo	77629	46
Stevie Nicks	1119	1
Stanley Burrell	1073	1
Morris Day	880	3
Sheila E.	617	1
Martika	533	1
James Samuel Harris ▶ 79	356	1
Terry Lewis ▶ 80	356	1
Jesse Woods Johnson	304	1
Sheena Easton	242	1
Lisa Coleman	225	2
Wendy Melvoin	225	2
David Rivkin	154	1
Elisa Fiorillo	154	1
Levi Seacer	154	1
Mark Alton Brown	37	1
Matt Fink	37	1
Robert Rivkin	37	1
Christopher Moon	26	1
Dez Dickerson	17	1
John B. Shaffer III	3	1
Seth Justman	3	1
Smokey ROBINSON ▶ 9	**79854**	**128**
Solo	50651	57
Marvin Tarplin	7311	22
Warren Moore	6955	24
Ronnie White	5332	14
Robert Rogers	4583	16
Al Cleveland	4323	8
Berry Gordy ▶ 64	3396	7
Henry Cosby	2484	2
Stevie Wonder ▶ 7	2484	2
Terry Johnson	974	3
Frank Edward Wilson	820	1
Pamela Moffett	269	2
Janie Bradford	222	1
Rose Ella Jones	211	3
Michel Legrand	141	1
Don Covay	93	1
Homer Talbert	20	1
Ivory Stone	20	1

Lonnie Kirtz	20	1
Cornelius Grant	19	1
Loucye Gordy Wakefield	3	1
William Stevenson	1	1
Barry GIBB ▶ 10	**75961**	**79**
Solo	19543	6
Robin Gibb ▶ 29	49563	58
Maurice Gibb ▶ 55	37130	54
Andy Gibb	5916	3
Blue Weaver	1200	1
Albhy Galuten	1152	3
George Bitzer	113	1
Michael Jackson ▶ 18	25	1
Burt BACHARACH ▶ 11	**72248**	**139**
Solo	1014	2
Hal David ▶ 17	56217	105
Carole Bayer Sager	9131	13
Bob Hilliard	3434	12
Mack David	2323	4
Luther Dixon	2157	2
Christopher Cross	1749	2
Peter Allen	1728	1
Neil Diamond ▶ 6	796	3
Bruce Roberts	719	3
Jack Wolf	106	1
Marv Ross	59	1
Paul Anka ▶ 16	12	1
Sidney Shaw	11	1
Eddie HOLLAND ▶ 12	**72158**	**163**
Solo	0	0
Brian Holland ▶ 14	64427	142
Lamont Dozier ▶ 15	63606	136
Norman Whitfield ▶ 21	6796	17
Ronald Dunbar	3401	16
Cornelius Grant	1791	4
Frank DeVol	1542	1
David White	972	2
John Madara	972	2
Len Barry	972	2
Steve Winwood	908	1
Will Jennings	908	1
R. Dean Taylor	731	3
Sylvia Moy	653	4
Frank Edward Wilson	639	1
Daphne Dumas	324	2
Norma Toney	205	1
General Johnson	181	1
Ivy Jo Hunter	136	1
Jack Goga	136	1
Jeff Bowen	136	1
Jim Vallance	128	1
Steven Tyler	128	1
Harold Beatty	128	1
James Anthony Dean	82	1
Ronald Alonzo Miller	79	1
William Stevenson	57	1
Scherrie Payne	56	1
John Thornton	8.4	1
Art Posey	4.0	1
Josef Powell	4.0	1
Melvin Ragin	4.0	1
Reggie Burke	4.0	1
Angelo Bond	1.0	2
Eddie Kendricks	0.9	1
Frederick Long	0.5	1
Janie Bradford	0.1	1
Carole KING ▶ 13	**71479**	**127**
Solo	12245	12

Carole KING ▶ 13 *Cont'd*	**71479**	**127**
Gerry Goffin ▶ 19	48978	101
Toni Stern	6356	9
David Palmer	2531	2
Howard Greenfield ▶ 41	1202	2
Phil Spector ▶ 61	749	3
Jerry Wexler	584	1
Cynthia Weil ▶ 49	212	3
Traditional ▶ 3	133	1
Brian HOLLAND ▶ 14	**70184**	**164**
Solo	0	0
Lamont Dozier ▶ 15	64509	145
Eddie Holland ▶ 12	64427	142
Robert Bateman	4685	10
Freddie Gorman	3946	7
Georgia Dobbins	3729	5
William Garrett	3729	5
Ronald Dunbar	3444	19
Frank DeVol	1542	1
Bernie Lowe	1253	1
Kal Mann ▶ 26	1253	1
David White	972	2
John Madara	972	2
Len Barry	972	2
William Stevenson	953	2
Steve Winwood	908	1
Will Jennings	908	1
Sylvia Moy	653	4
Daphne Dumas	343	3
Norma Toney	205	1
General Johnson	181	1
Angelo Bond	159	3
Harold Beatty	134	2
Jim Vallance	128	1
Steven Tyler	128	1
Michael Larry Smith	99	1
Janie Bradford	64	2
Berry Gordy ▶ 64	64	1
Scherrie Payne	56	1
R. Dean Taylor	14	1
John Thornton	8.4	1
Reggie Brown	5.3	1
Stafford Floyd	5.3	1
Art Posey	4.0	1
Josef Powell	4.0	1
Melvin Ragin	4.0	1
Reggie Burke	4.0	1
Art Glasser	2.1	2
Jerry Light	2.1	2
Martin Coleman	2.1	2
Stuart Avig	2.1	2
George Fowler	1.1	1
Frederick Long	0.5	1
Lamont DOZIER ▶ 15	**67349**	**151**
Solo	653	3
Brian Holland ▶ 14	64509	145
Eddie Holland ▶ 12	63606	136
Ronald Dunbar	3442	17
Phil Collins ▶ 42	1928	1
Frank DeVol	1542	1
David White	972	2
John Madara	972	2
Len Barry	972	2
Steve Winwood	908	1
Will Jennings	908	1
Sylvia Moy	653	4
Daphne Dumas	343	3
Debbie Gibson	257	1

Freddie Gorman	217	2
Norma Toney	205	1
General Johnson	181	1
Angelo Bond	159	3
Jim Vallance	128	1
Steven Tyler	128	1
Scherrie Payne	56	1
R. Dean Taylor	14	1
John Thornton	8.4	1
McKinley Jackson	1.3	1
Frederick Long	0.5	1
Janie Bradford	0.1	1
Paul ANKA ▶ 16	**67142**	**72**
Solo	61526	57
Alberto Curci	4567	2
Claude François	501	3
Jacques Revaux	501	3
David Foster	238	1
Johnny Harris	141	2
Alain Le Govic	90	2
Maxime Piolot	90	2
Michel Pelay	90	2
Yves-Jacques Lavot	90	2
Claude Vasori	30	1
Michel Jourdan	30	1
Romuald Figuier	30	1
Sammy Cahn	30	1
Howard Greenfield ▶ 41	20	1
René Villard	15	1
Burt Bacharach ▶ 11	12	1
Douglas McCormick	2.7	1
Hal DAVID ▶ 17	**64969**	**131**
Solo	0	0
Burt Bacharach ▶ 11	56217	105
Lee Pockriss	2838	2
Sherman Edwards	2763	8
Albert Hammond	1413	2
Paul Hampton	650	2
Archie Jordan	634	2
Carlo Alberto Rossi	212	1
Alfred Kealoha Perry	89	1
Traditional ▶ 3	89	1
Marco Rizo	62	1
Leon Carr	36	2
Henry Mancini	33	1
Giorgio Calabrese	13	3
Umberto Bindi	13	3
Sid Lippman	8.3	1
Michael JACKSON ▶ 18	**63846**	**27**
Solo	51588	16
Paul McCartney ▶ 1	4450	1
Lionel Richie ▶ 4	3054	1
Steven Randall Jackson	2406	3
Randy Hansen	1500	1
Al Yankovic	713	2
Bryan Loren	69	1
Jackie Jackson	64	2
Barry Gibb ▶ 10	25	1
Maurice Gibb ▶ 55	25	1
Gerry GOFFIN ▶ 19	**63481**	**125**
Solo	0	0
Carole King ▶ 13	48978	101
Michael Masser	6645	9
Jack Keller	3848	9
Barry Goldberg	1320	1
Barry Mann ▶ 30	1291	2
Wes Farrell	1208	1
Phil Spector ▶ 61	749	3

Jerry Wexler	584	1
Preston Glass	527	1
Herbert Cox	237	1
Morris Levy	237	1
Scott Cutler	156	1
Traditional ▶ 3	133	1
Cynthia Weil ▶ 49	43	1
Russ Titelman	36	1
Howard Greenfield ▶ 41	0.9	1
Curtis MAYFIELD ▶ 20	**62945**	**101**
Solo	59415	91
Jerry Butler	3348	6
Calvin Carter	2645	4
Oscar Brown Jr.	87	1
Clarence Burke Jr.	52	1
Gregory Keith Fowler	52	1
Dino Fekaris	38	1
Donny Hathaway	4.4	1
Norman WHITFIELD ▶ 21	**60883**	**92**
Solo	12058	17
Barrett Strong ▶ 53	39582	50
Eddie Holland ▶ 12	6796	17
Rodger Penzabene	3916	7
Cornelius Grant	2666	5
William Stevenson	1211	5
Janie Bradford	1057	1
Marvin Gaye ▶ 96	658	2
Al Hamilton	208	1
Betty Wright	208	1
Eugene Hamilton	208	1
Richard Wylie	208	1
Willie Clarke	208	1
Dwight Turner	135	1
Angelo Bond	76	1
Ed Gray	46	1
Eddie Brigati	46	1
Felix Cavaliere	46	1
Mike Vale	46	1
Tommy James	46	1
Eddie Kendricks	1	1
Mick JAGGER ▶ 22	**58528**	**71**
Solo	1274	2
Keith Richards ▶ 23	56846	66
Andrew Loog Oldham	1172	2
Bill Wyman	0	1
Brian Jones	0	1
Charlie Watts	0	1
Ron Wood	150	1
David A. Stewart	219	2
Steve Jordan	70	1
George Michael ▶ 35	83	1
Daryl Hall ▶ 48	73	1
Carlos Alomar	188	1
Keith RICHARDS ▶ 23	**56846**	**66**
Solo	0	0
Mick Jagger ▶ 22	56846	66
Andrew Loog Oldham	1172	2
Ron Wood	150	1
George Michael ▶ 35	83	1
Steve Jordan	70	1
Bill Wyman	0	1
Brian Jones	0	1
Charlie Watts	0	1
Jerry LEIBER ▶ 24	**54926**	**122**
Solo	0	0
Mike Stoller ▶ 28	50650	116
Ben E. King	4414	12
Phil Spector ▶ 61	3471	4

Jerry LEIBER ▶ 24 *Cont'd*	**54926**	**122**
Doc Pomus ▶ 63	1842	4
Billy Edd Wheeler	1540	3
George Treadwell	1354	3
Lover Patterson	1075	2
Barry Mann ▶ 30	1029	3
Cynthia Weil ▶ 49	1029	3
Ed Sanford	841	1
Michael McDonald	841	1
Carlo Donida	730	5
Giulio Rapetti	730	5
Irving Nahan	280	1
Lewis Lebish	280	1
Ollie Jones	224	1
Adele Tyler	200	1
Dan Tyler	200	1
Wood Newton	200	1
Artie Butler	56	1
Shadow Morton	56	1
Kent Harris	39	1
Van McCoy	38	1
Claude Debussy	23	2
Bert Berns ▶ 98	6.4	1
Ray Passman	6.4	1
Sam COOKE ▶ 25	**52616**	**70**
Solo	48388	60
Herb Alpert	1945	5
Lou Adler	1945	5
Arthur Conley	1825	2
Otis Redding	1825	2
Clint Lavert	390	2
James W. Alexander	68	1
Kal MANN ▶ 26	**52570**	**89**
Solo	6392	7
Dave Appell ▶ 86	25973	47
Bernie Lowe	17822	39
Billy Strange	4501	1
Brian Holland ▶ 14	1253	1
Freddie Gorman	1253	1
Georgia Dobbins	1253	1
Robert Bateman	1253	1
William Garrett	1253	1
Cornell Muldrow	947	1
Dee Clark	947	1
Philip Upchurch	947	1
Jesús Gonzáles Rubio	481	2
Huey P. Smith	359	1
John Vincent	359	1
Rose Marie Chivetti	115	1
Bob Horn	108	1
Bickley Reichner	57	1
Jose Padilla Sanchez	24	1
Sebastian Yradier	11	1
James Lord Pierpont	1.1	1
Billy JOEL ▶ 27	**52367**	**37**
Solo	52367	37
Mike STOLLER ▶ 28	**50686**	**117**
Solo	0	0
Jerry Leiber ▶ 24	50650	116
Ben E. King	4414	12
Doc Pomus ▶ 63	1842	4
George Treadwell	1354	3
Lover Patterson	1075	2
Barry Mann ▶ 30	1029	3
Cynthia Weil ▶ 49	1029	3
Ed Sanford	841	1
Michael McDonald	841	1
Billy Edd Wheeler	790	2

Carlo Donida	730	5
Giulio Rapetti	730	5
Irving Nahan	280	1
Lewis Lebish	280	1
Ollie Jones	224	1
Adele Tyler	200	1
Dan Tyler	200	1
Wood Newton	200	1
Bert Berns ▶ 98	42	2
Kent Harris	39	1
Van McCoy	38	1
Claude Debussy	23	2
Ray Passman	6.4	1
Robin GIBB ▶ 29	**50528**	**62**
Solo	11	1
Barry Gibb ▶ 10	49563	58
Maurice Gibb ▶ 55	36231	46
Andy Gibb	2525	1
Blue Weaver	742	2
Barry MANN ▶ 30	**50481**	**104**
Solo	1730	5
Cynthia Weil ▶ 49	36406	77
Larry Kolber	5410	6
Phil Spector ▶ 61	5207	8
Dan Hill	2129	2
Mike Anthony	1701	3
Tom Snow	1540	3
Gerry Goffin ▶ 19	1291	2
Jerry Leiber ▶ 24	1029	3
Mike Stoller ▶ 28	1029	3
James Horner	863	1
Hank Hunter	842	1
Leo Sayer	540	1
Howard Greenfield ▶ 41	368	4
Jeff Barry ▶ 33	123	1
James Ingram	108	1
Noel Sherman	29	1
Marc Phillips	19	1
Joe Shapiro	16	1
Bob DYLAN ▶ 31	**50201**	**55**
Solo	49250	49
Jacques Levy	370	2
Tom Petty	301	3
Jim Cregan	280	1
Kevin Savigar	280	1
Rod Stewart	280	1
Mike Campbell	178	1
George Harrison ▶ 62	123	2
Jeff Lynne ▶ 70	123	2
Roy Orbison ▶ 76	123	2
Leon HUFF ▶ 32	**49284**	**128**
Solo	1584	4
Kenneth Gamble ▶ 34	45567	116
Cary Gilbert	4179	8
Jerry Butler	3368	14
Jerry J. Ross	2432	4
Gene McFadden	1831	3
John Whitehead	1831	3
Joe Simon	650	2
Anthony Jackson	634	2
Ralston McGriff	302	1
Jerry Akines	66	1
Len Barry	64	3
David White	63	2
John Madara	63	2
Roland Chambers	19	1
Victor Carstarphen	9.6	1
Linda Creed	9.5	1

Thom Bell	9.5	1
Cecil Womack	3.1	1
Jeff BARRY ▶ 33	**47971**	**95**
Solo	3451	4
Ellie Greenwich ▶ 81	26594	52
Phil Spector ▶ 61	11708	24
Andy Kim	10546	16
Peter Allen	2682	2
Shadow Morton	2185	2
Bobby Bloom	1735	7
Ben Raleigh	1289	2
Jim Cretecos	672	1
Robin McNamara	672	1
Artie Resnick	488	2
Cliff Crofford	421	1
Mike Leeson	420	1
Peter Vale	420	1
Hank Medress	216	1
Steve Venet	210	2
Nino Tempo	196	2
Bert Berns ▶ 98	135	2
Barry Mann ▶ 30	123	1
Cynthia Weil ▶ 49	123	1
Marty Sanders	47	2
April Stevens	11	1
Mike Maniscalco	10	1
Richie Cerniglia	10	1
Neil Brian Goldberg	3.1	1
Mentor Williams	0.7	1
Kenneth GAMBLE ▶ 34	**47761**	**129**
Solo	313	2
Leon Huff ▶ 32	45567	116
Cary Gilbert	4156	7
Jerry Butler	3368	14
Jerry J. Ross	3255	8
Thom Bell	861	5
Linda Creed	687	3
Joe Simon	650	2
Anthony Jackson	634	2
Gene McFadden	155	1
John Whitehead	155	1
Cynthia Biggs	116	1
Dexter Wansel	116	1
Archie Bell	111	1
James A. Bishop	91	2
Mikki Farrow	63	1
Roland Chambers	19	1
Joe Renzetti	4.8	1
William E. Jackson III	4.8	1
Len Barry	0.6	1
George MICHAEL ▶ 35	**47568**	**19**
Solo	43698	16
Andrew Ridgeley	2865	1
Deon Estus	923	1
Keith Richards ▶ 23	83	1
Mick Jagger ▶ 22	83	1
John FOGERTY ▶ 36	**47537**	**30**
Solo	47537	30
Elton JOHN ▶ 37	**46707**	**51**
Solo	0	0
Bernie Taupin ▶ 38	42867	46
Gary Osborne	3685	4
Davey Johnstone	1306	3
Tom Robinson	155	1
Charlie Morgan	142	1
Fred Mandel	142	1
Paul Westwood	142	1

Bernie TAUPIN ▶ 38	**46642**	**51**
Solo	0	0
Elton John ▶ 37	42867	46
Martin Page	3311	2
Davey Johnstone	1306	3
Dennis Lambert	1159	1
Peter F. Wolf	1159	1
Alice Cooper	412	1
Dick Wagner	412	1
Charlie Morgan	142	1
Fred Mandel	142	1
Paul Westwood	142	1
Bill Hudson	38	1
Brett Hudson	38	1
Mark Hudson	38	1
Michael Parker	38	1
Holly Knight	13	1
Mike Chapman	13	1
John D. LOUDERMILK ▶ 39	**46403**	**47**
Solo	43823	43
Marijohn Wilkin	2314	1
Murrey Harman	190	1
Gwen Loudermilk	73	1
Orville B. Campbell	2.6	1
Bob CREWE ▶ 40	**45527**	**86**
Solo	0	0
Bob Gaudio ▶ 43	24162	29
Frank Slay	7774	25
Kenny Nolan	6134	6
Denny Randell	3875	9
Sandy Linzer	2449	6
L. Russell Brown	1683	4
Freddy Cannon	955	1
Bud Rehak	911	1
Eddie Rambeau	911	1
Charlie Calello	482	3
Larry Weiss	217	1
Claude Debussy	138	1
Cindy Bullens	107	2
Raymond Bloodworth	92	2
Larry Santos	80	1
Jerry Corbetta	75	1
Charles Fox	70	1
Valmond Harris	26	1
Robert Boulanger	26	1
Bob Davie	6.0	1
Sid Bass	0.7	1
Gary Knight	0.2	1
Howard GREENFIELD ▶ 41	**45400**	**74**
Solo	0	0
Neil Sedaka ▶ 50	28039	46
Jack Keller	11728	10
Helen Miller	3675	6
Carole King ▶ 13	1202	2
Barry Mann ▶ 30	368	4
Ken Hirsch	297	1
Armando Martinez	68	1
Kenny Karen	27	1
Louis St. Louis	27	1
Paul Anka ▶ 16	20	1
Michael Lloyd	11	1
Gloria Shayne	6.9	1
Gerry Goffin ▶ 19	0.9	1
Keely Smith	0.8	1
Phil COLLINS ▶ 42	**44814**	**34**
Solo	33504	16
Mike Rutherford	6700	15
Tony Banks	6700	15

Lamont Dozier ▶ 15	1928	1
Nathan East	1526	1
Philip Bailey	1526	1
Daryl Stuermer	1155	1
Bob GAUDIO ▶ 43	**44746**	**53**
Solo	11359	6
Bob Crewe ▶ 40	24162	29
Judy Parker	4657	6
Sandy Linzer	2815	2
Tom Austin	1016	5
Bill Dalton	707	4
Bill Crandall	704	3
Peggy Farina	617	1
Joe Villa	308	1
Jake Holmes	120	4
Jerry Corbetta	75	1
Lenny Lee Goldsmith	4.0	1
Larry Qualiano	3.4	1
Diane WARREN ▶ 44	**43927**	**44**
Solo	35241	25
Albert Hammond	4064	5
Desmond Child	2395	6
Martine Clémenceau	904	1
Michael Bolton	811	3
Emilio Estefan	402	1
Gloria Estefan	402	1
Bryan Adams	395	1
Jim Vallance	395	1
Rick Nielsen	321	1
Paul Stanley	147	1
Jon Bon Jovi	113	1
Richie Sambora	113	1
Giancarlo Bigazzi	99	1
Umberto Tozzi	99	1
Henry Lee Summer	92	1
Michael McDonald	9.7	1
Brian WILSON ▶ 45	**42455**	**80**
Solo	3955	3
Mike Love ▶ 82	25670	47
Jan Berry	4825	5
Roger Christian	4034	11
Chuck Berry ▶ 46	2982	4
Tony Asher	1279	6
Carl Wilson	887	4
Van Dyke Parks	750	3
Gary Usher	708	6
Artie Kornfeld	528	1
Alan Jardine	272	2
Murry Wilson	184	1
Bob Norman	150	1
Dennis Wilson	105	1
Joe Knott	91	1
Jack Rieley	63	2
Ray Kennedy	63	2
Tandyn Almer	63	2
Chuck BERRY ▶ 46	**42354**	**59**
Solo	38128	50
Brian Wilson ▶ 45	2982	4
Alan Freed	1244	5
Russ Fratto	1244	5
Boudleaux BRYANT ▶ 47	**41708**	**52**
Solo	30079	23
Felice Bryant	11413	27
Floyd Cramer	216	2
Skeeter Davis	216	2
Daryl HALL ▶ 48	**41531**	**37**
Solo	22360	12
John Oates	12237	16

Sara Allen	9051	11
Janna Allen	5294	4
Warren Pash	1577	1
John Beeby	964	1
Danny Kortchmar	200	1
George Green	200	1
Jon Bon Jovi	200	1
Rick Giles	200	1
Rick Iantosca	81	1
David A. Stewart	73	1
Mick Jagger ▶ 22	73	1
Cynthia WEIL ▶ 49	**41510**	**89**
Solo	0	0
Barry Mann ▶ 30	36406	77
Phil Spector ▶ 61	5207	8
Tom Snow	4577	7
Lionel Richie ▶ 4	1458	2
Jerry Leiber ▶ 24	1029	3
Mike Stoller ▶ 28	1029	3
James Horner	863	1
Michael Masser	542	1
Greg Phillinganes	513	1
Julio Iglesias	306	1
Tony Renis	306	1
Carole King ▶ 13	212	3
Jeff Barry ▶ 33	123	1
James Ingram	108	1
David Foster	86	1
Tom Keane	86	1
Gerry Goffin ▶ 19	43	1
Rick Derringer	5.0	1
Neil SEDAKA ▶ 50	**41376**	**58**
Solo	5979	2
Howard Greenfield ▶ 41	28039	46
Phil Cody	6690	7
Roger Atkins	663	2
Armando Martinez	68	1
Edward Grossman	4.7	1
Sylvester STEWART ▶ 51	**41047**	**33**
Solo	39545	30
Thomas Coman	1450	2
George Clinton	53	1
Gregory Jacobs	53	1
James McCants	53	1
James Todd Smith	53	1
Leroy McCants	53	1
Marlon Williams	53	1
Walter Morrison	53	1
William Earl Collins	53	1
James BROWN ▶ 52	**40809**	**99**
Solo	28939	46
Alfred James Ellis	3970	6
Bobby Byrd	1773	12
Fred Wesley	1621	7
Betty Jean Newsome	1396	1
Charles Bobbit	1176	9
Nat Jones	1091	7
Bud Hobgood	788	6
Ron Lenhoff	787	4
Joe Mims	535	1
David Matthews	418	3
John Starks	407	3
Jo Bogaert	295	1
Manuela Kamosi	295	1
Steven James Brown	213	3
Robert Ginyard	176	1
Lloyd Stallworth	141	2
Manny Rosen	133	1

James BROWN ▶ 52 *Cont'd*	**40809**	**99**
Hayward Moore	114	1
Lyn Collins	101	2
Charles E. Sherrell	70	1
Yolanda Whitaker	70	1
Andy Gibson	65	1
Bill Wray	63	2
Jim Wray	63	2
Marva Whitney	56	1
Joe Tex	34	1
Gertie Wesley	19	1
Johnny Terry	18	2
Hearlon Martin	9.8	1
Gladys Knochelman	1.1	1
Barrett STRONG ▶ 53	**40658**	**57**
Solo	44	3
Norman Whitfield ▶ 21	39582	50
Rodger Penzabene	3042	7
Janie Bradford	1057	1
Wade Flemons	712	2
Robert Eugene Miller	571	1
William Stevenson	318	1
Chuck Barksdale	141	1
Ed Gray	46	1
Eddie Brigati	46	1
Felix Cavaliere	46	1
Mike Vale	46	1
Tommy James	46	1
Marvin Gaye ▶ 96	30	1
Cornelius Grant	1.0	1
Bruce SPRINGSTEEN ▶ 54	**39879**	**30**
Solo	39059	27
Patti Smith	618	1
Chris Wong Won	118	1
David Hobbs	118	1
Luther Campbell	118	1
Mark Ross	118	1
Cheech Marin	85	1
Tommy Chong	85	1
Maurice GIBB ▶ 55	**37342**	**55**
Solo	0	0
Barry Gibb ▶ 10	37130	54
Robin Gibb ▶ 29	36231	46
Andy Gibb	2525	1
George Bitzer	113	1
Michael Jackson ▶ 18	25	1
Jimmy WEBB ▶ 56	**37215**	**37**
Solo	37215	37
Jerry FULLER ▶ 57	**36872**	**18**
Solo	36638	14
John Hobbs	188	2
Dave Burgess	38	1
William Silva	8.4	1
Tony HATCH ▶ 58	**36867**	**33**
Solo	31273	20
Jackie Trent	3980	11
Petula Clark	1353	1
Allan Sherman	262	1
David GATES ▶ 59	**36656**	**30**
Solo	36386	29
Larry Knechtel	270	1
STING ▶ 60	**35386**	**23**
Solo	32092	20
Mark Knopfler	2818	1
Sergei Prokofiev	416	1
Al Yankovic	60	1
Phil SPECTOR ▶ 61	**34804**	**62**
Solo	10318	8

Ellie Greenwich ▶ 81	12046	26
Jeff Barry ▶ 33	11708	24
Barry Mann ▶ 30	5207	8
Cynthia Weil ▶ 49	5207	8
Jerry Leiber ▶ 24	3471	4
Hank Hunter	1004	1
Carole King ▶ 13	749	3
Gerry Goffin ▶ 19	749	3
Irwin Levine	663	2
Toni Wine	663	2
Leroy R. Bates	586	1
Mike Leeson	420	1
Peter Vale	420	1
Tony Powers	339	2
Pete Andreoli	295	3
Vini Poncia	295	3
Doc Pomus ▶ 63	291	3
Bobby Stevens	148	1
April Stevens	20	1
Nino Tempo	20	1
Terry Philips	5.8	1
George HARRISON ▶ 62	**34690**	**36**
Solo	31637	31
Ringo Starr	2604	1
Jeff Lynne ▶ 70	334	3
Bob Dylan ▶ 31	123	2
Roy Orbison ▶ 76	123	2
Tom Petty	123	2
Eric Clapton	115	1
Doc POMUS ▶ 63	**34552**	**73**
Solo	139	1
Mort Shuman ▶ 65	31373	60
Jerry Leiber ▶ 24	1842	4
Mike Stoller ▶ 28	1842	4
Alan Jeffreys	667	2
Phil Spector ▶ 61	291	3
Dave Appell ▶ 86	237	1
Bob Feldman	52	1
Jerry Goldstein	52	1
Richard Gottehrer	52	1
Reginald Ashby	1.5	1
Ken Hirsch	1.3	1
Berry GORDY ▶ 64	**34098**	**64**
Solo	10688	13
Deke Richards	7992	9
Fonce Mizell	7992	9
Freddie Perren ▶ 77	7992	9
Billy Davis	4216	13
Gwen Gordy	3956	11
Smokey Robinson ▶ 9	3396	7
Hal Davis	2605	2
Bob West	2460	1
Willie Hutch	2460	1
Frank Edward Wilson	1838	4
Janie Bradford	1610	5
Brenda Holloway	1508	3
Patrice Holloway	1508	3
Henry Cosby	607	2
Marv Johnson	507	3
Al Abrams	462	1
John O'Den	462	1
Stanley Ossman	462	1
Pam Sawyer	330	1
R. Dean Taylor	330	1
Anthony Criss	199	1
Keir Gist	199	1
Vincent Brown	199	1
Alma McKnight	150	1

William Stevenson	147	1
Donald Fletcher	146	1
Jerry Marcellino	146	1
Mel Larson	146	1
James Carmichael	125	1
Kathy Wakefield	125	1
Ronald Norman Miller	125	1
Angelo Bond	77	1
Jean Mayer	77	1
Brian Holland ▶ 14	64	1
Sonny Woods	31	1
Chris Clark	4.7	1
Loucye Gordy Wakefield	3.5	1
Robert Gordy	2.4	1
Mort SHUMAN ▶ 65	**33405**	**68**
Solo	0	0
Doc Pomus ▶ 63	31373	60
J. Leslie McFarland	1471	1
Jerry Ragovoy	466	4
Jerry J. Ross	61	1
Bob Feldman	52	1
Jerry Goldstein	52	1
Richard Gottehrer	52	1
Eric Blau	29	1
Jacques Brel	29	1
Kenny Lynch	4.1	1
John DENVER ▶ 66	**32965**	**29**
Solo	28116	26
Michael C. Taylor	2728	2
Bill Danoff	2121	1
Taffy Danoff	2121	1
Dick Kniss	1445	1
Hank BALLARD ▶ 67	**32756**	**20**
Solo	30489	10
Etta James	1696	6
Johnny Otis	1696	6
Billy Myles	528	2
Nathaniel Nathan	43	2
Gene Redd Sr.	7.5	1
Rod TEMPERTON ▶ 68	**32428**	**18**
Solo	30965	13
Derek Bramble	202	1
Merria Ross	485	1
Quincy Jones	816	3
El DeBarge	104	1
Siedah Garrett	104	1
James Ingram	226	1
Michael McDonald	226	1
George Johnson	446	1
Louis E. Johnson	446	1
Valerie Johnson	446	1
John FARRAR ▶ 69	**30604**	**13**
Solo	29067	10
Tom Snow	1153	1
Don Black	213	1
Hank Marvin	213	1
Lee Ritenour	172	1
Jeff LYNNE ▶ 70	**30101**	**39**
Solo	27441	29
Tom Petty	2449	9
Roy Orbison ▶ 76	491	3
George Harrison ▶ 62	334	3
Mike Campbell	196	1
Bob Dylan ▶ 31	123	2
John SEBASTIAN ▶ 71	**30029**	**24**
Solo	26800	20
Steve Boone	3229	4
Mark Sebastian	2341	2

Buck RAM ▶ 72	**29842**	**43**
Solo	25545	25
Al Nevins	1708	3
Artie Dunn	1708	3
Morty Nevins	1708	3
Paul Robi	706	2
Tony Williams	704	2
Claude Baum	398	1
Peter Tinturin	340	1
William White	340	1
Mickey Addy	312	1
Zola Taylor	261	2
Tito Madi	198	3
Pyotr Ilyich Tchaikovsky	182	1
Alessandro Taccani	131	1
Mario Panzeri	131	1
Vincenzo Di Paola	131	1
Jonathan Small	62	1
Ralph Yates	62	1
Kim Gannon	0.7	1
Walter Kent	0.7	1
Aaron Collins	0.7	1
Otis BLACKWELL ▶ 73	**29549**	**46**
Solo	2605	12
Elvis Presley	12027	9
Winfield Scott	6162	3
Eddie Cooley	2981	8
Andrew Barksdale	2447	3
Charles Merenstein	2447	3
Jimmy Jones	2447	3
Jack Hammer	2194	4
Bobby Stevenson	873	4
Jimmy Williams	142	1
Lee Cathy	111	1
Jacqueline Burks	7.2	1
Dorian Burton	6.1	1
Eugene Randolph	6.1	1
John MELLENCAMP ▶ 74	**29412**	**22**
Solo	24943	19
George Green	4469	3
Sonny BONO ▶ 75	**29202**	**27**
Solo	27972	22
Solo	5134	5
Jack Nitzsche	1069	4
Larry Williams	161	1
Roy ORBISON ▶ 76	**29154**	**40**
Joe Melson	15144	17
William Dees	8041	11
Jeff Lynne ▶ 70	491	3
Tom Petty	491	3
Johnny Cash	206	1
Bob Dylan ▶ 31	123	2
George Harrison ▶ 62	123	2
Chris Price	87	1
Bobby Goldsboro	45	1
Sam Phillips	5.9	1
Freddie PERREN ▶ 77	**29120**	**33**
Solo	0	0
Dino Fekaris	11370	13
Berry Gordy ▶ 64	7992	9
Deke Richards	7992	9
Fonce Mizell	7992	9
Keni St. Lewis	6213	6
Christine Yarian	3715	7
Anthony Criss	199	1
Keir Gist	199	1
Vincent Brown	199	1
Joe SOUTH ▶ 78	**27967**	**30**

Solo	27543	29
Barry Harris	424	1
James Samuel HARRIS ▶ 79	**27420**	**41**
Solo	0	0
Terry Lewis ▶ 80	27420	41
Janet Jackson	5172	6
Karyn White	1362	1
Melanie Andrews	695	1
Morris Day	511	2
Prince ▶ 8	356	1
Danny Williams	57	1
Dave Eiland	57	1
Herman R. Davis	57	1
Langston Richey	57	1
Terry LEWIS ▶ 80	**27420**	**41**
Solo	0	0
James Samuel Harris ▶ 79	27420	41
Janet Jackson	5172	6
Karyn White	1362	1
Melanie Andrews	695	1
Morris Day	511	2
Prince ▶ 8	356	1
Danny Williams	57	1
Dave Eiland	57	1
Herman R. Davis	57	1
Langston Richey	57	1
Ellie GREENWICH ▶ 81	**27087**	**59**
Solo	0	0
Jeff Barry ▶ 33	26594	52
Phil Spector ▶ 61	12046	26
Shadow Morton	2185	2
Tony Powers	487	5
Mike Leeson	420	1
Peter Vale	420	1
Hank Medress	216	1
Steve Venet	210	2
Mike Lendell	3.6	1
Ellen Foley	2.5	1
Jeff Kent	2.5	1
Mike LOVE ▶ 82	**26865**	**51**
Solo	0	0
Brian Wilson ▶ 45	25670	47
Terry Melcher	1195	4
John Phillips ▶ 84	878	1
Scott McKenzie	878	1
Tony Asher	717	2
Carl Wilson	595	2
Alan Jardine	167	1
Joe Knott	91	1
Gary Usher	4.2	2
Bob SEGER ▶ 83	**26786**	**30**
Solo	24115	28
Harold Faltermeyer	1534	1
Keith Forsey	1534	1
Don Henley	1137	1
Glenn Frey	1137	1
J.D. Souther	1137	1
John PHILLIPS ▶ 84	**26672**	**22**
Solo	20307	14
Michelle Phillips	4072	5
Dennis Doherty	1415	2
Mike Love ▶ 82	878	1
Scott McKenzie	878	1
Terry Melcher	878	1
Bobby RUSSELL ▶ 85	**26669**	**15**
Solo	26194	13
Buzz Cason	475	2
Dave APPELL ▶ 86	**26665**	**50**

Solo	0	0
Kal Mann ▶ 26	25973	47
Bernie Lowe	3915	9
Sandy Linzer	455	2
Doc Pomus ▶ 63	237	1
Rose Marie Chivetti	115	1
James Lord Pierpont	1.1	1
Jesús Gonzáles Rubio	0.9	1
Mac DAVIS ▶ 87	**26634**	**29**
Solo	24068	21
Doc Severinsen	892	1
Billy Strange	874	4
Mark James	790	1
Larry Collins	7.6	1
Delaney Bramlett	2.3	1
Lee HAZLEWOOD ▶ 88	**26589**	**43**
Solo	21631	26
Duane Eddy	4880	16
Marty Cooper	78	1
Linda McCARTNEY ▶ 89	**26327**	**22**
Solo	135	1
Paul McCartney ▶ 1	26192	21
Dennis DeYOUNG ▶ 90	**26261**	**21**
Solo	25463	16
James Young	585	3
Glen Burtnick	250	1
Tommy Shaw	212	2
Laura NYRO ▶ 91	**26210**	**13**
Solo	26210	13
Fats DOMINO ▶ 92	**26166**	**71**
Solo	5097	9
Dave Bartholomew	19673	54
Earl King Johnson	2869	4
Robert Guidry	980	3
John Marascalco	615	1
Tommy Boyce	615	1
Al Lewis	343	1
Sylvester Bradford	343	1
Roy Hayes	300	1
Jack Jessup	265	3
Pee Wee Maddux	265	3
Earl Palmer	184	2
Reginald Hall	16	1
Wilbert Watson	14	1
Al Downing	1.0	1
Marion Carpenter	0.9	1
Tim Gillis	0.9	1
Madonna L. CICCONE ▶ 93	**25991**	**19**
Solo	3028	2
Patrick Raymond Leonard	9312	7
Stephen Bray	5894	5
Shep Pettibone	2914	2
Brian Elliot	2121	1
Gardner Cole	1425	1
Peter Rafelson	1425	1
Ingrid Chavez	1298	1
Lenny Kravitz	1298	1
Bruce Gaitsch	743	1
Donovan LEITCH ▶ 94	**25987**	**20**
Solo	25987	20
Allen TOUSSAINT ▶ 95	**25905**	**40**
Solo	23464	35
Alvin Tyler	1294	3
Freddy Friday	1294	3
Marilyn Schack	1292	2
Chris Kenner	1148	2
Bugs Bower	1.1	1
Jack Wolf	1.1	1

Marvin GAYE ▶ 96	**25616**	**35**
Solo	11889	7
William Stevenson	3862	13
Ed Townsend	3654	1
Ivy Jo Hunter	2470	8
Al Cleveland	2085	4
Renaldo Benson	2085	4
Anna Gordy	1334	2
David Ritz	1308	1
Odell Brown	1308	1
James Nyx	858	2
Norman Whitfield ▶ 21	658	2
George Gordy	576	3
Clarence Paul	435	2
Elgie Stover	355	1
Iris Gordy	355	1
Dave Hamilton	248	1
Kenny Stover	186	1
Gwen Gordy	146	1
Sandra Greene	146	1

Barrett Strong ▶ 53	30	1
Leon Ware	18	1
Michael Leslie JONES ▶ 97	**25188**	**23**
Solo	13056	7
Lou Gramm	12113	15
Ian McDonald	226	1
Eric Clapton	19	1
Bert BERNS ▶ 98	**24981**	**59**
Solo	9564	17
Phil Medley	5078	7
Wes Farrell	5047	8
Jerry Ragovoy	3640	11
Jerry Wexler	863	5
Edwin Starr	461	2
Harvey Fuqua	461	2
Johnny Bristol	461	2
Bob Feldman	451	2
Jerry Goldstein	451	2
Richard Gottehrer	451	2
Stanley Kahan	436	2

Solomon Burke	332	4
Jeff Barry ▶ 33	135	2
Babe Chivian	61	2
Joseph C. Martin	61	2
Traditional ▶ 3	61	2
Mike Leander	50	1
Carl Spencer	43	1
Jimmy Radcliffe	43	1
Mike Stoller ▶ 28	42	2
Jerry Leiber ▶ 24	6.4	1
Ray Passman	6.4	1
Van Morrison	6.1	1
Marty ROBBINS ▶ 99	**24953**	**26**
Solo	24953	26
Tommy ROE ▶ 100	**24752**	**17**
Solo	17810	11
Freddy Weller	6933	5
Felton Jarvis	9.3	1

Top 200 Writers: First and Biggest

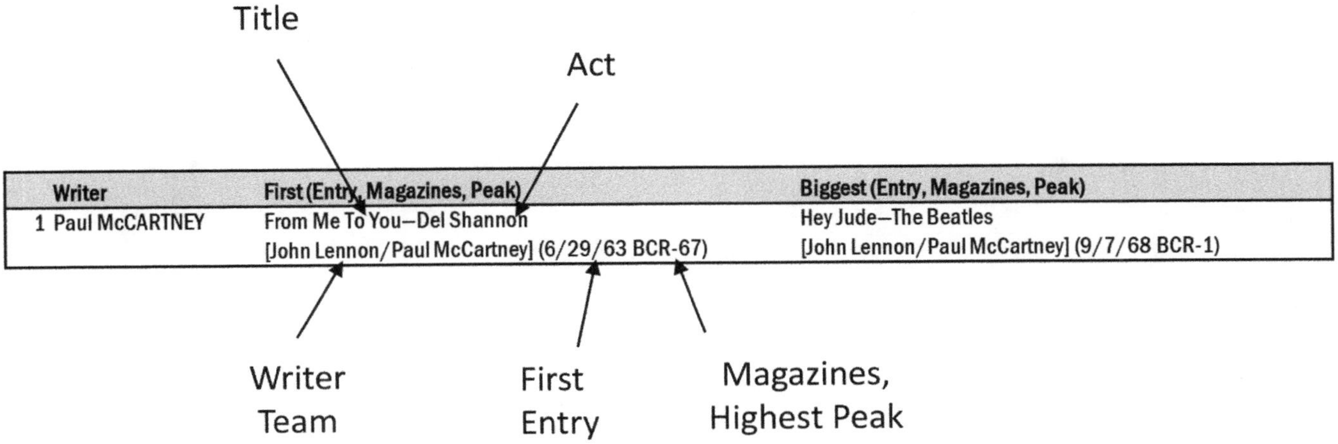

Italics: Multiple First Entries in the same week

This section is for first and biggest in this era. For some writers those career milestones may fall before or after this era.

Writer	First (Entry, Magazines, Peak)	Biggest (Entry, Magazines, Peak)
1 Paul McCARTNEY	From Me To You—Del Shannon [John Lennon/Paul McCartney] (6/29/63 BCR-67)	Hey Jude—The Beatles [John Lennon/Paul McCartney] (9/7/68 BCR-1)
2 John LENNON	From Me To You—Del Shannon [John Lennon/Paul McCartney] (6/29/63 BCR-67)	Hey Jude—The Beatles [John Lennon/Paul McCartney] (9/7/68 BCR-1)
3 TRADITIONAL	*Adeste Fideles (O Come All Ye Faithful)—David Whitfield; Adeste Fideles—Bing Crosby [Traditional] (12/6/54 Rt-50)*	Battle Of New Orleans—Johnny Horton [Jimmy Driftwood/Traditional] (4/25/59 BCRt-1)
4 Lionel RICHIE	I Feel Sanctified—Commodores [Jeff Bowen/Ronald LaPread/Thomas McClary/ William Roderick Miller/Walter Orange/Lionel Richie/ Milan Williams] (11/16/74 BC-75)	Endless Love—Diana Ross & Lionel Richie [Lionel Richie] (7/4/81 BCR-1)
5 Paul SIMON	Hey Schoolgirl—Tom & Jerry [Art Garfunkel/Paul Simon] (12/2/57 BCR-41)	Bridge Over Troubled Water—Simon & Garfunkel [Paul Simon] (1/31/70 BCR-1)
6 Neil DIAMOND	Ten Lonely Guys—Pat Boone [Cliff Adams/Neil Diamond/Lockie Edwards/ Wes Farrell/Bob Feldman/Jerry Goldstein/ Richard Gottehrer/Stanley Kahan/Eddie Snyder/ Larry Weiss] (9/15/62 BCR-43)	I'm A Believer—The Monkees [Neil Diamond] (12/3/66 BCR-1)
7 Stevie WONDER	Uptight (Everything's Alright)—Stevie Wonder [Henry Cosby/Sylvia Moy/Stevie Wonder] (12/11/65 BCR-3)	The Tears Of A Clown—Smokey Robinson & The Miracles [Henry Cosby/Smokey Robinson/Stevie Wonder] (10/10/70 BCR-1)
8 PRINCE	Soft And Wet—Prince [Christopher Moon/Prince] (9/30/78 BCR-74)	When Doves Cry—Prince [Prince] (6/2/84 BC-1)
9 Smokey ROBINSON	Bad Girl—The Miracles [Berry Gordy/Smokey Robinson] (10/3/59 BC-62)	The Tears Of A Clown—Smokey Robinson & The Miracles [Henry Cosby/Smokey Robinson/Stevie Wonder] (10/10/70 BCR-1)
10 Barry GIBB	New York Mining Disaster 1941 (Have You Seen My Wife, Mr. Jones)—The Bee Gees [Barry Gibb/Robin Gibb] (5/27/67 BCR-14)	Shadow Dancing—Andy Gibb [Andy Gibb/Barry Gibb/Maurice Gibb/Robin Gibb] (4/15/78 BCR-1)
11 Burt BACHARACH	Keep Me In Mind—Patti Page [Burt Bacharach/Jack Wolf] (3/28/55 CR-26)	Raindrops Keep Fallin' On My Head—B.J. Thomas [Burt Bacharach/Hal David] (10/25/69 BCR-1)
12 Eddie HOLLAND	Locking Up My Heart—The Marvelettes [Lamont Dozier/Brian Holland/Eddie Holland] (3/9/63 BCR-44)	Where Did Our Love Go—The Supremes [Lamont Dozier/Brian Holland/Eddie Holland] (7/11/64 BCR-1)
13 Carole KING	Will You Love Me Tomorrow—The Shirelles [Gerry Goffin/Carole King] (11/21/60 BCR-1)	It's Too Late—Carole King [Carole King/Toni Stern] (6/12/71 BCR-1)
14 Brian HOLLAND	All The Love I've Got—Marv Johnson [Janie Bradford/Berry Gordy/Brian Holland] (6/13/60 BCR-58)	Where Did Our Love Go—The Supremes [Lamont Dozier/Brian Holland/Eddie Holland] (7/11/64 BCR-1)
15 Lamont DOZIER	Strange I Know—The Marvelettes [Lamont Dozier/Freddie Gorman/Brian Holland] (11/24/62 BCR-49)	Where Did Our Love Go—The Supremes [Lamont Dozier/Brian Holland/Eddie Holland] (7/11/64 BCR-1)
16 Paul ANKA	Diana—Paul Anka [Paul Anka] (6/29/57 BCR-1)	Lonely Boy—Paul Anka [Paul Anka/Alberto Curci] (5/23/59 BCR-1)
17 Hal DAVID	My Baby's Got Such Lovin' Ways—The McGuire Sisters [Leon Carr/Hal David] (1/7/56 CR-40)	Raindrops Keep Fallin' On My Head—B.J. Thomas [Burt Bacharach/Hal David] (10/25/69 BCR-1)
18 Michael JACKSON	Shake Your Body (Down To The Ground)—Jacksons [Michael Jackson/Steven Randall Jackson] (1/20/79 BCR-3)	Say Say Say—Paul McCartney and Michael Jackson [Michael Jackson/Paul McCartney] (10/15/83 BC-1)
19 Gerry GOFFIN	Lovin' Touch—Mark Dinning [Gerry Goffin/Jack Keller] (8/22/60 BCR-64)	Go Away Little Girl—Steve Lawrence [Gerry Goffin/Carole King] (11/10/62 BCR-1)
20 Curtis MAYFIELD	He Will Break Your Heart—Jerry Butler [Jerry Butler/Calvin Carter/Curtis Mayfield] (10/15/60 BCR-3)	He Don't Love You (Like I Love You)—Tony Orlando & Dawn [Jerry Butler/Calvin Carter/Curtis Mayfield] (3/8/75 BCR-1)
21 Norman WHITFIELD	Pride And Joy—Marvin Gaye [Marvin Gaye/William Stevenson/Norman Whitfield] (5/18/63 BCR-9)	I Heard It Through The Grapevine—Marvin Gaye [Barrett Strong/Norman Whitfield] (11/16/68 BCR-1)
22 Mick JAGGER	That Girl Belongs To Yesterday—Gene Pitney [Mick Jagger/Keith Richards] (1/18/64 BCR-49)	Honky Tonk Women—The Rolling Stones [Mick Jagger/Keith Richards] (7/19/69 BCR-1)
23 Keith RICHARDS	That Girl Belongs To Yesterday—Gene Pitney [Mick Jagger/Keith Richards] (1/18/64 BCR-49)	Honky Tonk Women—The Rolling Stones [Mick Jagger/Keith Richards] (7/19/69 BCR-1)
24 Jerry LEIBER	(Bazoom) I Need Your Lovin'—The Cheers [Jerry Leiber/Mike Stoller] (10/11/54 BCRt-15)	Jailhouse Rock—Elvis Presley [Jerry Leiber/Mike Stoller] (9/30/57 BCR-1)
25 Sam COOKE	You Send Me—Teresa Brewer; You Send Me—Sam Cooke [Sam Cooke] (10/14/57 BCtRt-1)	You Send Me—Sam Cooke [Sam Cooke] (10/14/57 BCtRt-1)

Writer	First (Entry, Magazines, Peak)	Biggest (Entry, Magazines, Peak)
26 Kal MANN	Take Me Back To Toyland—Nat "King" Cole [Bob Horn/Bernie Lowe/Kal Mann] (12/23/55 BCR-32)	Limbo Rock—Chubby Checker [Kal Mann/Billy Strange] (9/8/62 BCR-1)
27 Billy JOEL	Piano Man—Billy Joel [Billy Joel] (2/9/74 BCR-16)	It's Still Rock And Roll To Me—Billy Joel [Billy Joel] (5/24/80 BCR-1)
28 Mike STOLLER	(Bazoom) I Need Your Lovin'—The Cheers [Jerry Leiber/Mike Stoller] (10/11/54 BCRt-15)	Jailhouse Rock—Elvis Presley [Jerry Leiber/Mike Stoller] (9/30/57 BCR-1)
29 Robin GIBB	New York Mining Disaster 1941 (Have You Seen My Wife, Mr. Jones)—The Bee Gees [Barry Gibb/Robin Gibb] (5/27/67 BCR-14)	Shadow Dancing—Andy Gibb [Andy Gibb/Barry Gibb/Maurice Gibb/Robin Gibb] (4/15/78 BCR-1)
30 Barry MANN	She Say (Oom Dooby Doom)—The Diamonds [Mike Anthony/Barry Mann] (1/19/59 BCR-12)	You've Lost That Lovin' Feelin'—The Righteous Brothers [Barry Mann/Phil Spector/Cynthia Weil] (12/12/64 BCR-1)
31 Bob DYLAN	Blowin' In The Wind—Peter, Paul & Mary [Bob Dylan] (6/29/63 BCR-2)	Mr. Tambourine Man—The Byrds [Bob Dylan] (5/8/65 BCR-1)
32 Leon HUFF	Mixed-Up, Shook-Up, Girl—Patty & The Emblems [Leon Huff/Ralston McGriff] (6/20/64 BCR-28)	Me And Mrs. Jones—Billy Paul [Kenneth Gamble/Cary Gilbert/Leon Huff] (10/21/72 BCR-1)
33 Jeff BARRY	Teenage Sonata—Sam Cooke [Jeff Barry] (2/29/60 BCR-40)	Sugar, Sugar—The Archies [Jeff Barry/Andy Kim] (7/19/69 BCR-1)
34 Kenneth GAMBLE	Everybody Monkey—Freddy Cannon [Kenneth Gamble/Jerry J. Ross] (7/27/63 BCR-51)	Me And Mrs. Jones—Billy Paul [Kenneth Gamble/Cary Gilbert/Leon Huff] (10/21/72 BCR-1)
35 George MICHAEL	Bad Boys—Wham! U.K. [George Michael] (8/6/83 BC-50)	Careless Whisper—Wham! Featuring George Michael [George Michael/Andrew Ridgeley] (12/22/84 BC-1)
36 John FOGERTY	Proud Mary—Creedence Clearwater Revival [John Fogerty] (1/18/69 BCR-1)	Proud Mary—Creedence Clearwater Revival [John Fogerty] (1/18/69 BCR-1)
37 Elton JOHN	Border Song—Elton John [Elton John/Bernie Taupin] (8/15/70 BCR-69)	Crocodile Rock—Elton John [Elton John/Bernie Taupin] (12/9/72 BCR-1)
38 Bernie TAUPIN	Border Song—Elton John [Elton John/Bernie Taupin] (8/15/70 BCR-69)	Crocodile Rock—Elton John [Elton John/Bernie Taupin] (12/9/72 BCR-1)
39 John D. LOUDERMILK	*A Rose And A Baby Ruth—Eddie Fontaine; A Rose And A Baby Ruth—George Hamilton IV [John D. Loudermilk] (10/27/56 BCRt-6)*	Indian Reservation (The Lament Of The Cherokee)—Raiders [John D. Loudermilk] (4/10/71 BCR-1)
40 Bob CREWE	*Silhouettes—Steve Gibson & the Red Caps; Silhouettes—The Diamonds; Silhouettes—The Rays [Bob Crewe/Frank Slay] (10/7/57 BCRt-2)*	Big Girls Don't Cry—The 4 Seasons [Bob Crewe/Bob Gaudio] (10/20/62 BCR-1)
41 Howard GREENFIELD	Stupid Cupid—Connie Francis [Howard Greenfield/Neil Sedaka] (7/28/58 BCR-16)	My Heart Has A Mind Of Its Own—Connie Francis [Howard Greenfield/Jack Keller] (8/15/60 BCR-1)
42 Phil COLLINS	Follow You Follow Me—Genesis [Tony Banks/Phil Collins/Mike Rutherford] (4/22/78 BCR-22)	Against All Odds (Take A Look At Me Now)—Phil Collins [Phil Collins] (2/25/84 BC-1)
43 Bob GAUDIO	Short Shorts—Royal Teens [Tom Austin/Bill Crandall/Bill Dalton/Bob Gaudio] (1/13/58 BCRt-3)	Big Girls Don't Cry—The 4 Seasons [Bob Crewe/Bob Gaudio] (10/20/62 BCR-1)
44 Diane WARREN	Solitaire—Laura Branigan [Martine Clémenceau/Diane Warren] (3/19/83 BC-7)	Nothing's Gonna Stop Us Now—Starship [Albert Hammond/Diane Warren] (1/31/87 BC-1)
45 Brian WILSON	Surfin'—The Beach Boys [Mike Love/Brian Wilson] (2/10/62 BC-75)	I Get Around—The Beach Boys [Mike Love/Brian Wilson] (5/23/64 BCR-1)
46 Chuck BERRY	*Maybellene—Johnny Long & His Orchestra; Maybellene—Jim Lowe; Maybellene—Chuck Berry [Chuck Berry/Russ Fratto/Alan Freed] (8/8/55 BCRt-4)*	My Ding-A-Ling—Chuck Berry [Chuck Berry] (7/29/72 BCR-1)
47 Boudleaux BRYANT	I've Been Thinking—The Four Lads [Boudleaux Bryant] (3/5/55 CRt-33)	All I Have To Do Is Dream—The Everly Brothers [Boudleaux Bryant] (4/14/58 BCR-1)
48 Daryl HALL	She's Gone—Daryl Hall & John Oates [Daryl Hall/John Oates] (1/26/74 BCR-48)	Maneater—Daryl Hall & John Oates [Sara Allen/Daryl Hall/John Oates] (10/16/82 BC-1)
49 Cynthia WEIL	Bless You—Tony Orlando [Barry Mann/Cynthia Weil] (7/31/61 BCR-11)	You've Lost That Lovin' Feelin'—The Righteous Brothers [Barry Mann/Phil Spector/Cynthia Weil] (12/12/64 BCR-1)
50 Neil SEDAKA	Stupid Cupid—Connie Francis [Howard Greenfield/Neil Sedaka] (7/28/58 BCR-16)	Breaking Up Is Hard To Do—Neil Sedaka [Howard Greenfield/Neil Sedaka] (6/23/62 BCR-1)
51 Sylvester STEWART	C'mon And Swim—Bobby Freeman [Thomas Coman/Sylvester Stewart] (7/4/64 BCR-5)	Everyday People—Sly & The Family Stone [Sylvester Stewart] (11/30/68 BCR-1)
52 James BROWN	Try Me—James Brown And The Famous Flames [James Brown] (12/15/58 BC-48)	I Got You (I Feel Good)—James Brown And The Famous Flames [James Brown] (11/6/65 BCR-1)

Writer	First (Entry, Magazines, Peak)	Biggest (Entry, Magazines, Peak)
53 Barrett STRONG	Jamie—Eddie Holland [William Stevenson/Barrett Strong] (1/15/62 BCR-30)	I Heard It Through The Grapevine—Marvin Gaye [Barrett Strong/Norman Whitfield] (11/16/68 BCR-1)
54 Bruce SPRINGSTEEN	Sandy—The Hollies [Bruce Springsteen] (4/12/75 BC-85)	Dancing In The Dark—Bruce Springsteen [Bruce Springsteen] (5/26/84 BC-1)
55 Maurice GIBB	(The Lights Went Out In) Massachusetts—The Bee Gees [Barry Gibb/Maurice Gibb/Robin Gibb] (11/11/67 BCR-11)	Shadow Dancing—Andy Gibb [Andy Gibb/Barry Gibb/Maurice Gibb/Robin Gibb] (4/15/78 BCR-1)
56 Jimmy WEBB	Up-Up And Away—The 5th Dimension [Jimmy Webb] (6/3/67 BCR-4)	Mac Arthur Park—Donna Summer [Jimmy Webb] (9/9/78 BCR-1)
57 Jerry FULLER	Betty My Angel—Jerry Fuller [Jerry Fuller/William Silva] (8/22/59 BCR-90)	Travelin' Man—Ricky Nelson [Jerry Fuller] (4/22/61 BCR-1)
58 Tony HATCH	*Look For A Star—Deane Hawley; Look For A Star—Garry Miles; Look For A Star—Billy Vaughn And His Orchestra; Look For A Star—Nicky Como; Look For A Star Part One—Garry Mills [Tony Hatch] (6/20/60 BCtRt-13)*	Downtown—Petula Clark [Tony Hatch] (12/19/64 BCR-1)
59 David GATES	Popsicles And Icicles—The Murmaids [David Gates] (11/16/63 BCR-1)	Make It With You—Bread [David Gates] (6/13/70 BCR-1)
60 STING	Roxanne—The Police [Sting] (2/10/79 BCR-31)	Every Breath You Take—The Police [Sting] (6/4/83 BC-1)
61 Phil SPECTOR	To Know Him Is To Love Him—The Teddy Bears [Phil Spector] (9/22/58 BCRt-1)	You've Lost That Lovin' Feelin'—The Righteous Brothers [Barry Mann/Phil Spector/Cynthia Weil] (12/12/64 BCR-1)
62 George HARRISON	The Inner Light—The Beatles [George Harrison] (3/30/68 B-96)	My Sweet Lord—George Harrison [George Harrison] (11/28/70 BCR-1)
63 Doc POMUS	Yum Yum—The Fontane Sisters [Doc Pomus] (3/2/56 R-45)	Save The Last Dance For Me—The Drifters [Doc Pomus/Mort Shuman] (9/5/60 BCR-1)
64 Berry GORDY	Reet Petite (The Finest Girl You Ever Want To Meet)—Jackie Wilson [Billy Davis/Berry Gordy] (9/23/57 BCR-23)	I'll Be There—The Jackson 5 [Hal Davis/Berry Gordy/Willie Hutch/Bob West] (9/19/70 BCR-1)
65 Mort SHUMAN	White Bucks And Saddle Shoes—Bobby Pedrick, Jr. [Doc Pomus/Mort Shuman] (11/1/58 BC-74)	Save The Last Dance For Me—The Drifters [Doc Pomus/Mort Shuman] (9/5/60 BCR-1)
66 John DENVER	Leaving On A Jet Plane—Gloria Loring [John Denver] (10/11/69 R-98)	Leaving On A Jet Plane—Peter, Paul & Mary [John Denver] (10/25/69 BCR-1)
67 Hank BALLARD	Dance With Me Henry (Wallflower)—Georgia Gibbs [Hank Ballard/Etta James/Johnny Otis] (3/7/55 BCRt-1)	The Twist—Chubby Checker [Hank Ballard] (11/13/61 BCR-1)
68 Rod TEMPERTON	Boogie Nights—Heatwave [Rod Temperton] (7/9/77 BCR-2)	Rock With You—Michael Jackson [Rod Temperton] (11/3/79 BCR-1)
69 John FARRAR	Have You Never Been Mellow—Olivia Newton-John [John Farrar] (1/25/75 BCR-1)	You're The One That I Want—John Travolta And Olivia Newton-John [John Farrar] (4/1/78 BCR-1)
70 Jeff LYNNE	Do Ya—The Move [Jeff Lynne] (10/28/72 BCR-88)	Don't Bring Me Down—Electric Light Orchestra [Jeff Lynne] (7/28/79 BCR-3)
71 John SEBASTIAN	Do You Believe In Magic—The Lovin' Spoonful [John Sebastian] (8/21/65 BCR-4)	Summer In The City—The Lovin' Spoonful [Steve Boone/John Sebastian/Mark Sebastian] (7/9/66 BCR-1)
72 Buck RAM	Only You (And You Alone)—The Platters [Buck Ram] (8/1/55 BCtRt-3)	The Great Pretender—The Platters [Buck Ram] (12/9/55 BCRt-1)
73 Otis BLACKWELL	You're The Apple Of My Eye—The Four Lovers [Otis Blackwell] (5/4/56 BR-62)	Don't Be Cruel—Elvis Presley [Otis Blackwell/Elvis Presley] (7/27/56 BCR-1)
74 John MELLENCAMP	I Need A Lover—John Cougar [John Mellencamp] (9/15/79 BCR-28)	Jack & Diane—John Cougar [John Mellencamp] (7/24/82 BC-1)
75 Sonny BONO	You Bug Me Baby—Larry Williams [Sonny Bono/Larry Williams] (10/14/57 BCR-37)	I Got You Babe—Sonny & Cher [Sonny Bono] (7/10/65 BCR-1)
76 Roy ORBISON	So Long I'm Gone—Warren Smith [Roy Orbison/Sam Phillips] (6/10/57 B-72)	Oh, Pretty Woman—Roy Orbison And The Candy Men [William Dees/Roy Orbison] (8/29/64 BCR-1)
77 Freddie PERREN	I Want You Back—The Jackson 5 [Berry Gordy/Fonce Mizell/Freddie Perren/Deke Richards] (11/15/69 BCR-1)	ABC—The Jackson 5 [Berry Gordy/Fonce Mizell/Freddie Perren/Deke Richards] (3/14/70 BCR-1)
78 Joe SOUTH	Untie Me—The Tams [Joe South] (10/13/62 BCR-60)	Yo-Yo—The Osmonds [Joe South] (9/11/71 BCR-1)
79 James Samuel HARRIS	Just Be Good To Me—The S.O.S. Band [James Samuel Harris/Terry Lewis] (8/27/83 BC-42)	Escapade—Janet Jackson [James Samuel Harris/Janet Jackson/Terry Lewis] (1/20/90 BC-1)

Writer	First (Entry, Magazines, Peak)	Biggest (Entry, Magazines, Peak)
80 Terry LEWIS	Just Be Good To Me—The S.O.S. Band [James Samuel Harris/Terry Lewis] (8/27/83 BC-42)	Escapade—Janet Jackson [James Samuel Harris/Janet Jackson/Terry Lewis] (1/20/90 BC-1)
81 Ellie GREENWICH	This Is It—Jay & The Americans [Ellie Greenwich/Tony Powers] (7/14/62 CR-83)	Chapel Of Love—The Dixie Cups [Jeff Barry/Ellie Greenwich/Phil Spector] (5/2/64 BCR-1)
82 Mike LOVE	Surfin'—The Beach Boys [Mike Love/Brian Wilson] (2/10/62 BC-75)	I Get Around—The Beach Boys [Mike Love/Brian Wilson] (5/23/64 BCR-1)
83 Bob SEGER	Heavy Music (Part 1)—Bob Seger & The Last Heard [Bob Seger] (9/9/67 CR-70)	Shakedown—Bob Seger [Harold Faltermeyer/Keith Forsey/Bob Seger] (5/23/87 BC-1)
84 John PHILLIPS	California Dreamin'—The Mama's & The Papa's [John Phillips/Michelle Phillips] (1/1/66 BCR-2)	Monday, Monday—The Mama's & The Papa's [John Phillips] (4/9/66 BCR-1)
85 Bobby RUSSELL	Tennessee—Jan & Dean [Buzz Cason/Bobby Russell] (5/26/62 BCR-69)	Honey—Bobby Goldsboro [Bobby Russell] (3/23/68 BCR-1)
86 Dave APPELL	Rocka Conga—The Applejacks [Dave Appell/Kal Mann] (12/20/58 BCR-31)	Bristol Stomp—The Dovells [Dave Appell/Kal Mann] (9/4/61 BCR-2)
87 Mac DAVIS	You're Good For Me—Lou Rawls [Larry Collins/Mac Davis] (5/11/68 CR-88)	Baby Don't Get Hooked On Me—Mac Davis [Mac Davis] (7/1/72 BCR-1)
88 Lee HAZLEWOOD	Fool—Sanford Clark [Lee Hazlewood] (7/20/56 BCtRt-7)	These Boots Are Made For Walkin'—Nancy Sinatra [Lee Hazlewood] (1/22/66 BCR-1)
89 Linda McCARTNEY	Another Day—Paul McCartney [Linda McCartney/Paul McCartney] (2/27/71 BCR-5)	Silly Love Songs—Wings [Linda McCartney/Paul McCartney] (4/10/76 BCR-1)
90 Dennis DeYOUNG	Best Thing—Styx [Dennis DeYoung/James Young] (9/16/72 BR-82)	Babe—Styx [Dennis DeYoung] (10/6/79 BCR-1)
91 Laura NYRO	Wedding Bell Blues—Laura Nyro [Laura Nyro] (12/3/66 C-96)	Wedding Bell Blues—The 5th Dimension [Laura Nyro] (9/20/69 BCR-1)
92 Fats DOMINO	*Ain't It A Shame—Fats Domino; Ain't That A Shame—Pat Boone [Dave Bartholomew/Fats Domino] (6/18/55 BCtRt-1)*	Ain't That A Shame—Pat Boone [Dave Bartholomew/Fats Domino] (6/18/55 BCtRt-1)
93 Madonna L. CICCONE	Lucky Star—Madonna [Madonna L. Ciccone] (8/18/84 BC-4)	Vogue—Madonna [Madonna L. Ciccone/Shep Pettibone] (4/14/90 BC-1)
94 Donovan LEITCH	Catch The Wind—Donovan [Donovan Leitch] (5/8/65 BCR-22)	Sunshine Superman—Donovan [Donovan Leitch] (7/23/66 BCR-1)
95 Allen TOUSSAINT	Mother-In-Law—Ernie K-Doe [Allen Toussaint] (3/13/61 BCR-1)	Mother-In-Law—Ernie K-Doe [Allen Toussaint] (3/13/61 BCR-1)
96 Marvin GAYE	Beechwood 4-5789—The Marvelettes [Marvin Gaye/George Gordy/William Stevenson] (8/4/62 BCR-17)	Let's Get It On—Marvin Gaye [Marvin Gaye/Ed Townsend] (7/7/73 BCR-1)
97 Michael Leslie JONES	Feels Like The First Time—Foreigner [Michael Leslie Jones] (3/26/77 BCR-4)	Waiting For A Girl Like You—Foreigner [Lou Gramm/Michael Leslie Jones] (10/10/81 BCR-2)
98 Bert BERNS	Push Push—Austin Taylor [Bert Berns/Phil Medley] (11/14/60 BC-90)	Hang On Sloopy—The McCoys [Bert Berns/Wes Farrell] (8/14/65 BCRt-1)
99 Marty ROBBINS	Respectfully Miss Brooks—Marty Robbins [Marty Robbins] (6/29/56 R-72)	El Paso—Marty Robbins [Marty Robbins] (11/9/59 BCR-1)
100 Tommy ROE	Sheila—Tommy Roe [Tommy Roe] (7/14/62 BCR-1)	Dizzy—Tommy Roe [Tommy Roe/Freddy Weller] (1/18/69 BCR-1)
101 Ray PARKER Jr.	You Got The Love—Rufus Featuring Chaka Khan [Chaka Khan/Ray Parker Jr.] (10/12/74 BCR-9)	Ghostbusters—Ray Parker Jr. [Ray Parker Jr.] (6/16/84 BC-1)
102 Carole Bayer SAGER	A Groovy Kind Of Love—The Mindbenders [Carole Bayer Sager/Toni Wine] (4/2/66 BCR-1)	Arthur's Theme (Best That You Can Do)—Christopher Cross [Peter Allen/Burt Bacharach/Christopher Cross/ Carole Bayer Sager] (8/15/81 BCR-1)
103 Rod STEWART	Maggie May—Rod Stewart [Martin Quittenton/Rod Stewart] (8/14/71 BCR-1)	Da Ya Think I'm Sexy?—Rod Stewart [Carmine Appice/Duane Hitchings/Rod Stewart] (12/16/78 BCR-1)
104 Richard MARX	What About Me?—Kenny Rogers [David Foster/Richard Marx/Kenny Rogers] (9/15/84 BC-15)	Right Here Waiting—Richard Marx [Richard Marx] (7/8/89 BC-1)
105 Pete TOWNSHEND	I Can't Explain—The Who [Pete Townshend] (2/20/65 BCR-57)	I Can See For Miles—The Who [Pete Townshend] (10/7/67 BCR-8)
106 Felix CAVALIERE	You Better Run—The Young Rascals [Eddie Brigati/Felix Cavaliere] (6/11/66 BCR-20)	Groovin'—The Young Rascals [Eddie Brigati/Felix Cavaliere] (4/22/67 BCR-1)
107 Robert ALLEN	(There's No Place Like) Home For The Holidays—Perry Como [Robert Allen/Al Stillman] (11/22/54 BCR-12)	Moments To Remember—The Four Lads [Robert Allen/Al Stillman] (8/27/55 BCR-2)

Writer	First (Entry, Magazines, Peak)	Biggest (Entry, Magazines, Peak)
108 Rick SPRINGFIELD	Speak To The Sky—Rick Springfield [Rick Springfield] (7/29/72 BCR-14)	Jessie's Girl—Rick Springfield [Rick Springfield] (3/28/81 BCR-1)
109 Aaron SCHROEDER	I Was The One—Elvis Presley [Hal Blair/Claude DeMetrius/Bill Peppers/ Aaron Schroeder] (3/10/56 BCR-16)	It's Now Or Never—Elvis Presley With The Jordanaires [Eduardo di Capua/Wally Gold/Aaron Schroeder] (7/18/60 BCR-1)
110 Ray DAVIES	You Really Got Me—The Kinks [Ray Davies] (9/26/64 BCR-5)	You Really Got Me—The Kinks [Ray Davies] (9/26/64 BCR-5)
111 Clyde OTIS	No Other One—Eddie Fisher [Ivory Joe Hunter/Clyde Otis] (3/23/56 BCR-29)	The Boll Weevil Song—Brook Benton [Brook Benton/Clyde Otis/Traditional] (5/15/61 BCR-2)
112 Irwin LEVINE	You're Gonna Need Magic—Roy Hamilton [Bob Brass/Irwin Levine] (4/29/61 BCR-66)	Knock Three Times—Dawn [L. Russell Brown/Irwin Levine] (11/14/70 BCR-1)
113 Barry WHITE	It May Be Winter Outside (But In My Heart It's Spring)—Felice Taylor [Paul Politi/Barry White] (1/14/67 BCR-39)	Love's Theme—Love Unlimited Orchestra [Barry White] (12/1/73 BCR-1)
114 Lee POCKRISS	Catch A Falling Star—Perry Como [Lee Pockriss/Paul Vance] (12/30/57 BCR-1)	Itsy Bitsy Teenie Weenie Yellow Polkadot Bikini—Brian Hyland [Lee Pockriss/Paul Vance] (6/27/60 BCRt-1)
115 Steve MILLER	Living In The U.S.A.—Steve Miller Band [Steve Miller] (11/9/68 BCR-72)	Abracadabra—Steve Miller Band [Steve Miller] (5/29/82 BC-1)
116 Dave BARTHOLOMEW	*Ain't It A Shame—Fats Domino; Ain't That A Shame—Pat Boone [Dave Bartholomew/Fats Domino] (6/18/55 BCtRt-1)*	Ain't That A Shame—Pat Boone [Dave Bartholomew/Fats Domino] (6/18/55 BCtRt-1)
117 Bob MERRILL	Tell Me Tell Me—June Valli [Bob Merrill] (9/4/54 CR-23)	Honeycomb—Jimmie Rodgers [Bob Merrill] (8/3/57 BCRt-1)
118 Freddie MERCURY	Killer Queen—Queen [Freddie Mercury] (2/8/75 BCR-11)	Crazy Little Thing Called Love—Queen [Freddie Mercury] (12/22/79 BCR-1)
119 Chip TAYLOR	I Can't Wait Until I See My Baby—Justine Washington [Jerry Ragovoy/Chip Taylor] (3/21/64 B-93)	Wild Thing—The Troggs [Chip Taylor] (6/18/66 BCR-1)
120 Giorgio MORODER	Son Of My Father—Giorgio [Pete Bellotte/Giorgio Moroder] (2/19/72 BCR-34)	Call Me—Blondie [Clement A. Bozewski/Deborah Harry/Giorgio Moroder] (2/16/80 BCR-1)
121 Bobby DARIN	Splish Splash—Bobby Darin [Bobby Darin/Murray Kaufman/Jean Murray] (6/16/58 BCR-2)	Dream Lover—Bobby Darin [Bobby Darin] (4/18/59 BCR-2)
122 Ray STEVENS	Make Me Smile Again—Cathy Jean [Ray Stevens] (6/12/61 R-98)	The Streak—Ray Stevens [Ray Stevens] (4/13/74 BCR-1)
123 Kenny LOGGINS	House At Pooh Corner—Nitty Gritty Dirt Band [Kenny Loggins] (4/24/71 BCR-38)	Footloose—Kenny Loggins [Kenny Loggins/Dean Pitchford] (1/28/84 BC-1)
124 Luther DIXON	Why Baby Why—Pat Boone [Luther Dixon/Larry Harrison] (3/9/57 BCRt*-6)	Soldier Boy—The Shirelles [Luther Dixon/Florence Green] (3/17/62 BCR-1)
125 Al STILLMAN	(There's No Place Like) Home For The Holidays—Perry Como [Robert Allen/Al Stillman] (11/22/54 BCR-12)	Moments To Remember—The Four Lads [Robert Allen/Al Stillman] (8/27/55 BCR-2)
126 Per GESSLE	The Look—Roxette [Per Gessle] (2/11/89 BC-1)	It Must Have Been Love—Roxette [Per Gessle] (4/7/90 BC-1)
127 Harlan HOWARD	Heartaches By The Number—Guy Mitchell [Harlan Howard] (10/5/59 BCR-1)	Heartaches By The Number—Guy Mitchell [Harlan Howard] (10/5/59 BCR-1)
128 Wayne Carson THOMPSON	Somebody Like Me—Eddy Arnold [Wayne Carson Thompson] (10/8/66 BCR-36)	The Letter—The Box Tops [Wayne Carson Thompson] (8/12/67 BCR-1)
129 Isaac HAYES	How Do You Quit (Someone You Love)—Carla Thomas [Isaac Hayes/Raymond Moore/David Porter] (2/13/65 R-85)	Theme From Shaft—Isaac Hayes [Isaac Hayes] (10/16/71 BCR-1)
130 Eric CARMEN	Don't Want To Say Goodbye—Raspberries [Wally Bryson/Eric Carmen] (4/29/72 BCR-86)	All By Myself—Eric Carmen [Eric Carmen/Sergei Rachmaninoff] (12/13/75 BCR-1)
131 Bill WITHERS	Ain't No Sunshine—Bill Withers [Bill Withers] (7/3/71 BCR-3)	Lean On Me—Bill Withers [Bill Withers] (4/15/72 BCR-1)
132 Thom BELL	La - La - Means I Love You—The Delfonics [Thom Bell/William Hart] (2/3/68 BCR-3)	You Make Me Feel Brand New—The Stylistics Featurng Airrion Love & Russell Thompkins, Jr. [Thom Bell/Linda Creed] (3/16/74 BCR-1)
133 Otis REDDING	These Arms Of Mine—Otis Redding [Otis Redding] (5/4/63 BCR-80)	Respect—Aretha Franklin [Otis Redding] (4/29/67 BCR-1)
134 Peter CETERA	Lowdown—Chicago [Peter Cetera/Danny Seraphine] (5/8/71 BCR-25)	Hard To Say I'm Sorry—Chicago [Peter Cetera/David Foster] (6/5/82 BC-1)
135 David BOWIE	Changes—David Bowie [David Bowie] (4/8/72 BCR-59)	Let's Dance—David Bowie [David Bowie] (3/26/83 BC-1)

Writer	First (Entry, Magazines, Peak)	Biggest (Entry, Magazines, Peak)
136 Mark JAMES	The Eyes Of A New York Woman—B.J. Thomas [Mark James] (6/8/68 BCR-28)	Suspicious Minds—Elvis Presley [Mark James] (9/13/69 BCR-1)
137 Harry Wayne CASEY	Rock Your Baby—George McCrae [Harry Wayne Casey/Rick Finch] (5/25/74 BCR-1)	That's The Way (I Like It)—K.C. & The Sunshine Band [Harry Wayne Casey/Rick Finch] (10/18/75 BCR-1)
138 Tony MACAULAY	Baby, Now That I've Found You—The Foundations [Tony Macaulay/John Macleod] (12/16/67 BCR-8)	Build Me Up Buttercup—The Foundations [Michael D'Abo/Tony Macaulay] (12/21/68 BCR-1)
139 Kenneth EDMONDS	I'd Still Say Yes—Klymaxx [Kenneth Edmonds/Joyce Irby/Greg Scelsa] (5/2/87 BC-18)	I'm Your Baby Tonight—Whitney Houston [Kenneth Edmonds/Antonio Reid] (10/20/90 BC-1)
140 Nile RODGERS	Dance, Dance, Dance (Yowsah, Yowsah, Yowsah)—Chic [Bernard Edwards/Kenny Lehman/Nile Rodgers] (10/22/77 BCR-6)	Le Freak—Chic [Bernard Edwards/Nile Rodgers] (10/28/78 BCR-1)
141 David PAICH	Houston (I'm Comin' To See You)—Glen Campbell [David Paich] (2/2/74 BCR-54)	Rosanna—Toto [David Paich] (4/17/82 BC-2)
142 Maurice STARR	Candy Girl—New Edition [Michael Jonzun/Maurice Starr] (4/30/83 BC-46)	Step By Step—New Kids On The Block [Maurice Starr] (5/26/90 BC-1)
143 Bernard EDWARDS	Dance, Dance, Dance (Yowsah, Yowsah, Yowsah)—Chic [Bernard Edwards/Kenny Lehman/Nile Rodgers] (10/22/77 BCR-6)	Le Freak—Chic [Bernard Edwards/Nile Rodgers] (10/28/78 BCR-1)
144 Joe TEX	Baby, You're Right—James Brown And The Famous Flames [James Brown/Joe Tex] (8/21/61 BR-49)	I Gotcha—Joe Tex [Joe Tex] (1/22/72 BCR-2)
145 Geoff STEPHENS	The Crying Game—Brenda Lee [Geoff Stephens] (1/9/65 BC-87)	Winchester Cathedral—The New Vaudeville Band [Geoff Stephens] (10/29/66 BCR-1)
146 Gilbert O'SULLIVAN	Alone Again (Naturally)—Gilbert O'Sullivan [Gilbert O'Sullivan] (6/17/72 BCR-1)	Alone Again (Naturally)—Gilbert O'Sullivan [Gilbert O'Sullivan] (6/17/72 BCR-1)
147 Don HENLEY	Witchy Woman—Eagles [Don Henley/Bernie Leadon] (8/26/72 BCR-8)	One Of These Nights—Eagles [Glenn Frey/Don Henley] (5/31/75 BCR-1)
148 David FOSTER	Got To Be Real—Cheryl Lynn [David Foster/Cheryl Lynn/David Paich] (11/11/78 BCR-9)	Hard To Say I'm Sorry—Chicago [Peter Cetera/David Foster] (6/5/82 BC-1)
149 Rick FINCH	Rock Your Baby—George McCrae [Harry Wayne Casey/Rick Finch] (5/25/74 BCR-1)	That's The Way (I Like It)—K.C. & The Sunshine Band [Harry Wayne Casey/Rick Finch] (10/18/75 BCR-1)
150 Ric OCASEK	Just What I Needed—The Cars [Ric Ocasek] (6/17/78 BCR-24)	Shake It Up—The Cars [Ric Ocasek] (7/11/81 BCR-3)
151 Bernie LOWE	Put Me In The Mood— The Fontane Sisters with Billy Vaughn's Orchestra [Bernie Lowe/Al Lubar] (4/4/55 R-23)	Mashed Potato Time—Dee Dee Sharp [Robert Bateman/Georgia Dobbins/William Garrett/ Freddie Gorman/Brian Holland/Bernie Lowe/Kal Mann] (2/19/62 BCR-1)
152 Jack KELLER	Just Between You And Me—The Chordettes [Lee Cathy/Jack Keller] (8/3/57 BCR-12)	My Heart Has A Mind Of Its Own—Connie Francis [Howard Greenfield/Jack Keller] (8/15/60 BCR-1)
153 Don GIBSON	Oh Lonesome Me—Don Gibson [Don Gibson] (2/22/58 BCRt-3)	I Can't Stop Loving You—Ray Charles [Don Gibson] (4/30/62 BCRt-1)
154 David SEVILLE	Red Grapes—Sammy Davis Jr. [Frank Cady/David Seville] (11/29/54 R-73)	Witch Doctor—David Seville [David Seville] (4/7/58 BCR-1)
155 Carl SIGMAN	Answer Me, My Love—Nat "King" Cole [Carl Sigman/Gerhard Winkler] (5/29/54 BC-PRE)	It's All In The Game—Tommy Edwards [Charles Dawes/Carl Sigman] (8/11/58 BCR-1)
156 Tommy JAMES	Mony Mony—Tommy James And The Shondells [Bobby Bloom/Ritchie Cordell/Bo Gentry/Tommy James] (3/30/68 BCR-3)	Crimson And Clover—Tommy James And The Shondells [Tommy James/Peter Lucia] (12/14/68 BCR-1)
157 Roger MILLER	Invitation To The Blues—Ray Price [Roger Miller] (9/8/58 B-92)	King Of The Road—Roger Miller [Roger Miller] (1/30/65 BCR-3)
158 Eddie BRIGATI	You Better Run—The Young Rascals [Eddie Brigati/Felix Cavaliere] (6/11/66 BCR-20)	Groovin'—The Young Rascals [Eddie Brigati/Felix Cavaliere] (4/22/67 BCR-1)
159 Elvis PRESLEY	Heartbreak Hotel—Elvis Presley [Mae Boren Axton/Thomas Durden/Elvis Presley] (3/3/56 BCRt-1)	Don't Be Cruel—Elvis Presley [Otis Blackwell/Elvis Presley] (7/27/56 BCR-1)
160 L. Russell BROWN	She Ain't Lovin' You—The Distant Cousins [Raymond Bloodworth/L. Russell Brown/Bob Crewe] (8/27/66 C-90)	Knock Three Times—Dawn [L. Russell Brown/Irwin Levine] (11/14/70 BCR-1)
161 Glenn FREY	Take It Easy—Eagles [Jackson Browne/Glenn Frey] (5/20/72 BCR-6)	One Of These Nights—Eagles [Glenn Frey/Don Henley] (5/31/75 BCR-1)
162 Graham GOULDMAN	For Your Love—The Yardbirds [Graham Gouldman] (5/8/65 BCR-4)	I'm Not In Love—10cc [Graham Gouldman/Eric Stewart] (5/10/75 BCR-2)

Writer	First (Entry, Magazines, Peak)	Biggest (Entry, Magazines, Peak)
163 Paul VANCE	Catch A Falling Star—Perry Como [Lee Pockriss/Paul Vance] (12/30/57 BCR-1)	Itsy Bitsy Teenie Weenie Yellow Polkadot Bikini—Brian Hyland [Lee Pockriss/Paul Vance] (6/27/60 BCRt-1)
164 Mutt LANGE	Do You Believe In Love—Huey Lewis And The News [Mutt Lange] (2/6/82 BCR-7)	(Everything I Do) I Do It For You—Bryan Adams [Bryan Adams/Michael Kamen/Mutt Lange] (6/29/91 BC-1)
165 Eugene RECORD	Two Little Kids—Peaches & Herb [Barbara Acklin/Carl Davis/Eugene Record] (12/16/67 BCR-31)	Oh Girl—The Chi-Lites [Eugene Record] (4/1/72 BCR-1)
166 Paul WILLIAMS	Only Me—The First Edition [Roger Nichols/Paul Williams] (5/11/68 R-81)	We've Only Just Begun—Carpenters [Roger Nichols/Paul Williams] (9/12/70 BCR-1)
167 Johnny MERCER	Dream—Four Aces [Johnny Mercer] (8/7/54 CR-13)	Moon River—Henry Mancini, His Orchestra And Chorus [Henry Mancini/Johnny Mercer] (9/30/61 BCtRt-5)
168 Mike CHAPMAN	Co-Co—The Sweet [Mike Chapman/Nicky Chinn] (9/25/71 BCR-85)	Kiss You All Over—Exile [Mike Chapman/Nicky Chinn] (7/8/78 BCR-1)
169 Baker KNIGHT	I Got A Feeling, Lonesome Town—Ricky Nelson [Baker Knight] (10/6/58 BCR-7)	Lonesome Town—Ricky Nelson [Baker Knight] (10/6/58 BCR-7)
170 Debbie GIBSON	Only In My Dreams—Debbie Gibson [Debbie Gibson] (5/9/87 BC-4)	Lost In Your Eyes—Debbie Gibson [Debbie Gibson] (1/21/89 BC-1)
171 Jim STEINMAN	You Took The Words Right Out Of My Mouth (Hot Summer Night)—Meat Loaf [Jim Steinman] (11/5/77 CR-73)	Total Eclipse Of The Heart—Bonnie Tyler [Jim Steinman] (7/16/83 BC-1)
172 Ernie MARESCA	No One Knows—Dion and The Belmonts [Ken Hecht/Ernie Maresca] (8/11/58 BCR-15)	Runaround Sue—Dion [Dion DiMucci/Ernie Maresca] (9/18/61 BCR-1)
173 Jon BON JOVI	Runaway—Bon Jovi [Jon Bon Jovi/George Karak] (2/25/84 BC-37)	Livin' On A Prayer—Bon Jovi [Jon Bon Jovi/Desmond Child/Richie Sambora] (12/13/86 BC-1)
174 Melanie SAFKA	Lay Down (Candles In The Rain)—Melanie With The Edwin Hawkins Singers [Melanie Safka] (4/18/70 BCR-3)	Brand New Key—Melanie [Melanie Safka] (10/23/71 BCR-1)
175 Christopher CROSS	Ride Like The Wind—Christopher Cross [Christopher Cross] (2/9/80 BCR-2)	Arthur's Theme (Best That You Can Do)—Christopher Cross [Peter Allen/Burt Bacharach/Christopher Cross/Carole Bayer Sager] (8/15/81 BCR-1)
176 Del SHANNON	Runaway—Del Shannon [Max Crook/Del Shannon] (3/6/61 BCR-1)	Runaway—Del Shannon [Max Crook/Del Shannon] (3/6/61 BCR-1)
177 Ritchie CORDELL	S.O.S. (Heart In Distress)—Christine Cooper [Ritchie Cordell/Sal Trimachi] (2/5/66 CR-98)	Mony Mony—Tommy James And The Shondells [Bobby Bloom/Ritchie Cordell/Bo Gentry/Tommy James] (3/30/68 BCR-3)
178 Al GREEN	Tired Of Being Alone—Al Green [Al Green] (7/24/71 BCR-6)	Let's Stay Together—Al Green [Al Green/Al Jackson/Willie Mitchell] (11/27/71 BCR-1)
179 Jim CROCE	Age (Where I Started Again)—Horatio [Ingrid Croce/Jim Croce] (7/26/69 R-95)	Bad, Bad Leroy Brown—Jim Croce [Jim Croce] (4/14/73 BCR-1)
180 Gloria ESTEFAN	Words Get In The Way—Miami Sound Machine [Gloria Estefan] (6/14/86 BC-5)	Anything For You—Gloria Estefan and Miami Sound Machine [Gloria Estefan] (3/12/88 BC-1)
181 Don ROBERTSON	I Really Don't Want To Know—Les Paul and Mary Ford [Howard Lee Barnes/Don Robertson] (5/29/54 B-PRE)	Ringo—Lorne Greene [Hal Blair/Don Robertson] (10/31/64 BCR-1)
182 Shel SILVERSTEIN	25 Minutes To Go—The Brothers Four [Shel Silverstein] (11/10/62 R-100)	A Boy Named Sue—Johnny Cash [Shel Silverstein] (7/26/69 BCR-1)
183 Will JENNINGS	*Somewhere In The Night—Helen Reddy; Somewhere In The Night—Batdorf & Rodney [Will Jennings/Richard Kerr] (11/29/75 BCR-69)*	Up Where We Belong—Joe Cocker and Jennifer Warnes [Will Jennings/Jack Nitzsche/Buffy Sainte-Marie] (8/21/82 BC-1)
184 Hoyt AXTON	Greenback Dollar—The Kingston Trio [Hoyt Axton/Ken Ramsey] (1/19/63 BCRt-17)	Joy To The World—Three Dog Night [Hoyt Axton] (3/6/71 BCR-1)
185 Donna SUMMER	Love To Love You Baby—Donna Summer [Pete Bellotte/Giorgio Moroder/Donna Summer] (11/8/75 BCR-1)	Bad Girls—Donna Summer [Joe Esposito/Eddie Hokenson/Bruce Sudano/Donna Summer] (5/26/79 BCR-1)
186 Kevin CRONIN	Roll With The Changes—REO Speedwagon [Kevin Cronin] (5/13/78 BCR-42)	Keep On Loving You—REO Speedwagon [Kevin Cronin] (11/29/80 BCR-1)
187 Dallas FRAZIER	*Alley Oop—The Hollywood Argyles; Alley Oop—Danté And The Evergreens [Dallas Frazier] (5/23/60 BCtRt-1)*	Alley Oop—The Hollywood Argyles [Dallas Frazier] (5/23/60 BCtRt-1)
188 Tony ROMEO	Indian Lake—The Cowsills [Tony Romeo] (5/25/68 BCR-6)	I Think I Love You—The Partridge Family Starring Shirley Jones & Featuring David Cassidy [Tony Romeo] (9/26/70 BCR-1)

Writer	First (Entry, Magazines, Peak)	Biggest (Entry, Magazines, Peak)
189 Steve CROPPER	Pop-Eye Stroll—The Mar-Keys [Steve Cropper/Booker T. Jones Jr.] (3/31/62 B-94)	(Sittin' On) The Dock Of The Bay—Otis Redding [Steve Cropper/Otis Redding] (1/27/68 BCR-1)
190 Dean PITCHFORD	Fame—Irene Cara [Michael Gore/Dean Pitchford] (6/14/80 BCR-3)	Footloose—Kenny Loggins [Kenny Loggins/Dean Pitchford] (1/28/84 BC-1)
191 Jim WEATHERLY	Loving You Is Just An Old Habit—Jim Weatherly [Jim Weatherly] (12/23/72 CR-90)	Midnight Train To Georgia—Gladys Knight & The Pips [Jim Weatherly] (8/25/73 BCR-1)
192 Joe MELSON	Up Town—Roy Orbison [Joe Melson/Roy Orbison] (12/28/59 BCR-70)	Crying—Roy Orbison [Joe Melson/Roy Orbison] (8/7/61 BCR-1)
193 Dick MANNING	Jilted—Teresa Brewer [Robert Colby/Dick Manning] (5/29/54 B-PRE)	Hot Diggity (Dog Ziggity Boom)—Perry Como [Al Hoffman/Dick Manning] (3/2/56 BCR-2)
194 Carly SIMON	That's The Way I've Always Heard It Should Be—Carly Simon [Jacob Brackman/Carly Simon] (4/17/71 BCR-7)	You're So Vain—Carly Simon [Carly Simon] (12/2/72 BCR-1)
195 Winfield SCOTT	*Tweedle Dee—Georgia Gibbs; Tweedlee Dee—Vicki Young; Tweedlee Dee—LaVern Baker and The Gliders [Winfield Scott] (1/3/55 BCtRt-3)*	Return To Sender—Elvis Presley With The Jordanaires [Otis Blackwell/Winfield Scott] (10/13/62 BCR-1)
196 Stevie NICKS	Rhiannon (Will You Ever Win)—Fleetwood Mac [Stevie Nicks] (3/6/76 BCR-9)	Dreams—Fleetwood Mac [Stevie Nicks] (4/16/77 BCR-1)
197 Burton CUMMINGS	These Eyes—The Guess Who [Randy Bachman/Burton Cummings] (4/5/69 BCR-3)	American Woman—The Guess Who [Randy Bachman/Burton Cummings/Jim Kale/Garry Peterson] (3/21/70 BCR-1)
198 Randy BACHMAN	These Eyes—The Guess Who [Randy Bachman/Burton Cummings] (4/5/69 BCR-3)	American Woman—The Guess Who [Randy Bachman/Burton Cummings/Jim Kale/Garry Peterson] (3/21/70 BCR-1)
199 Dennis LAMBERT	Find My Way Back Home—The Nashville Teens [Lou Courtney/Dennis Lambert] (3/13/65 B-98)	Don't Pull Your Love—Hamilton, Joe Frank & Reynolds [Dennis Lambert/Brian Potter] (5/15/71 BCR-1)
200 Jim PETERIK	You Wouldn't Listen—The I'des Of March [Michael Borch/Larry Millas/Jim Peterik] (6/11/66 BCR-41)	Eye Of The Tiger—Survivor [Jim Peterik/Frankie Sullivan] (6/5/82 BC-1)

Top 100 One Hit Wonders as Solo Writers

Writer	Song—Act	Score
1 Ewan MacCOLL	The First Time Ever I Saw Your Face—Roberta Flack	9289
2 Trevor PEACOCK	Mrs. Brown You've Got A Lovely Daughter—Herman's Hermits	8352
3 Amanda McBROOM	The Rose—Bette Midler	6013
4 Gary BRUCE	Moody River—Pat Boone	5879
5 Jack SIGLER	Love (Can Make You Happy)—Mercy	5778
6 Mickie GRANT	Pink Shoe Laces—Dodie Stevens	5720
7 Dolores Vicki SILVERS	Learnin' The Blues—Frank Sinatra	5623
8 Kendall L. HAYES	Walk On By—Leroy Van Dyke	5609
9 Hank DeVITO	Queen Of Hearts—Juice Newton	5541
10 Liam STERNBERG	Walk Like An Egyptian—Bangles	5283
11 Walter NIMS	Precious And Few—Climax	5122
12 Eugene PEARSON	A Thousand Stars—Kathy Young With The Innocents	4973
13 Chuck BARRIS	Palisades Park—Freddy Cannon	4864
14 Ray DORSET	In The Summertime—Mungo Jerry	4780
15 Robin SCOTT	Pop Muzik—M	4719
16 John Martin SOMMERS	Thank God I'm A Country Boy—John Denver	4659
17 R.B. GREAVES	Take A Letter Maria—R.B. Greaves	4621
18 Lois Ann BLAISCH	Could've Been—Tiffany	4537
19 Walter SCOTT	Burning Bridges—Jack Scott	4173
20 Kathryn FULTON	Fool #1—Brenda Lee	4110
21 Jim GOLD	Nice To Be With You—Gallery	4081
22 Jan HAMMER	Miami Vice Theme—Jan Hammer	4048
23 Scott JOPLIN	The Entertainer—Marvin Hamlisch	4001
24 Hurricane SMITH	Oh, Babe, What Would You Say?—Hurricane Smith	3957
25 Julie GOLD	From A Distance—Bette Midler	3697
26 William DeVAUGHN	Be Thankful For What You Got—William Devaughn	3624
27 Brian CARMAN	Pipeline—Chantay's	3580
28 Bobby McFERRIN	Don't Worry Be Happy (Edit)—Bobby McFerrin	3324
29 Ricky Lynn CHRISTIAN	I Don't Need You—Kenny Rogers	2988
30 Darby SLICK	Somebody To Love—Jefferson Airplane	2975
31 T. Texas TYLER	Deck Of Cards—Wink Martindale	2950
32 LaForrest COPE	You Give Good Love—Whitney Houston	2931
33 Ken TOBIAS	Stay Awhile—The Bells	2905
34 David NICHTERN	Midnight At The Oasis—Maria Muldaur	2877
35 Claudine CLARK	Party Lights—Claudine Clark	2853
36 Don JULIAN	The Jerk—The Larks (2)	2839
37 Steve GIBB	She Believes In Me—Kenny Rogers	2715
38 Norman SALLITT	Here I Am (Just When I Thought I Was Over You)—Air Supply	2697
39 Dan BAIRD	Keep Your Hands To Yourself—Georgia Satellites	2532
40 Ron HOLDEN	Love You So—Ron Holden With The Thunderbirds	2451
41 Pearl LENDHURST	Be Bop Baby—Ricky Nelson	2445
42 Lynn MALSBY	I Miss You—Klymaxx	2434
43 Paul PENA	Jet Airliner—Steve Miller Band	2374
44 Richard SPENCER	Color Him Father—The Winstons	2340
45 Gary BURR	Love's Been A Little Bit Hard On Me—Juice Newton	2319
46 Lewis DeWITT	Flowers On The Wall—The Statler Brothers	2283
47 Gershon KINGSLEY	Popcorn—Hot Butter	2281
48 Walter Earl BROWN	If I Can Dream—Elvis Presley	2264
49 Harriet SCHOCK	Ain't No Way To Treat A Lady—Helen Reddy	2246
50 Walter MARKS	I've Gotta Be Me—Sammy Davis Jr.	2244
51 Frank MYERS	You And I—Eddie Rabbitt with Crystal Gayle	2189

Writer	Song—Act	Score
52 Harry NOBLE	Hold Me, Thrill Me, Kiss Me—Mel Carter	2107
53 Barney PERRY	Walking In Rhythm—The Blackbyrds	2039
54 Bobby GOSH	A Little Bit More—Dr. Hook	2035
55 Robert W. COBERT	Quentin's Theme—Charles Randolph Grean Sounde	1940
56 Ace CANNON	Tuff—Ace Cannon	1940
57 Jack LEWIS	Teen Age Idol—Rick Nelson	1936
58 Shuggie OTIS	Strawberry Letter 23—The Brothers Johnson	1933
59 Randall McNEILL	If I Could Reach You—The 5th Dimension	1920
60 Abner SPECTOR	Smoky Places—Corsairs Featuring The Voice Of Jay "Bird" Uzzell	1821
61 Gary Lee COOPER	Let's Go All The Way—Sly Fox	1813
62 Shirley EIKHARD	Something To Talk About—Bonnie Raitt	1803
63 Mikis THEODORAKIS	Zorba The Greek—Herb Alpert & The Tijuana Brass	1794
64 Bobby NUNN	Rocket 2 U—The Jets	1786
65 Anna SOSENKO	Darling Je Vous Aime Beaucoup—Nat "King" Cole	1751
66 Len BOONE	You Made Me Believe In Magic—Bay City Rollers	1735
67 Noel GAY	Leaning On The Lamp Post—Herman's Hermits	1730
68 Lee Roy ABERNATHY	Wonderful Time Up There—Pat Boone	1725
69 Jesse HARMS	Walk On Water—Eddie Money	1722
70 Freddie HART	Easy Loving—Freddie Hart	1696
71 Melvin SCHWARTZ	Baby Talk—Jan & Dean	1684
72 Jay STEVENS	Rocky—Austin Roberts	1668
73 Danny O'KEEFE	Good Time Charlie's Got The Blues—Danny O'Keefe	1633
74 David WILKINS	Coming On Strong—Brenda Lee	1606
75 Joe PASQUALE	I Remember Holding You—Boys Club	1604
76 Francis ROSSI	Pictures Of Matchstick Men—The Status Quo	1579
77 Joe STAFFORD Jr.	My Pledge Of Love—Joe Jeffrey Group	1555
78 Bernice BEDWELL	Lotta Lovin'—Gene Vincent and His Blue Caps	1533
79 Jack VAUGHN	Goodbye Jimmy Goodbye—Kathy Linden	1531
80 Robert ASCHER	Tracy's Theme—Spencer Ross	1499
81 Kirsty MacCOLL	They Don't Know—Tracey Ullman	1490
82 Keith CARRADINE	I'm Easy—Keith Carradine	1467
83 David GILLAM	Teenager's Romance—Ricky Nelson	1450
84 Don SCHLITZ	The Gambler—Kenny Rogers	1431
85 Alberto DOMINGUEZ	Perfidia—The Ventures	1405
86 Denny THOMPSON	Tijuana Jail—The Kingston Trio	1329
87 Dorothea JOYCE	Love's Lines, Angles And Rhymes—The 5th Dimension	1315
88 Robert R. THOMPSON	An Open Letter To My Teenage Son—Victor Lundberg	1312
89 Vincent BELL	The Rain—Oran "Juice" Jones	1291
90 Paul N. ROBERTS	Driver's Seat—Sniff 'N' The Tears	1290
91 Patrick HERNANDEZ	Born To Be Alive—Patrick Hernandez	1277
92 Loudon WAINWRIGHT III	Dead Skunk—Loudon Wainwright III	1273
93 Steve GOODMAN	The City Of New Orleans—Arlo Guthrie	1272
94 Paul TAYLOR	Miles Away—Winger	1266
95 David Leigh BYRON	Shadows Of The Night—Pat Benatar	1261
96 Lea MAALFRID	You Could Have Been With Me—Sheena Easton	1230
97 Tito PUENTE	Oye Como Va—Santana	1218
98 Floyd ROBINSON	Makin' Love—Floyd Robinson	1217
99 Larry GROCE	Junk Food Junkie—Larry Groce	1193
100 Irma THOMAS	Wish Someone Would Care—Irma Thomas	1187

Decades: Top Writers for the '50s, '60s, '70s and '80s by Score and Entries

In this section, decade is determined by earliest entry on any chart.
Ties for numbers of entries are broken by score for those writers.

'50s: Top Writers by Score

1	TRADITIONAL	53772
2	Jerry LEIBER	28924
3	Mike STOLLER	28924
4	Boudleaux BRYANT	28626
5	Buck RAM	27765
6	Paul ANKA	26048
7	Robert ALLEN	21317
8	Otis BLACKWELL	18679
9	Fats DOMINO	18065
10	Al STILLMAN	17889
11	David SEVILLE	17645
12	Bob MERRILL	17227
13	Dave BARTHOLOMEW	16184
14	Elvis PRESLEY	15757
15	Melvin ENDSLEY	15190
16	Marty ROBBINS	14558
17	Kal MANN	14108
18	Dick MANNING	14072
19	Bernie LOWE	13509
20	J.P. RICHARDSON	13262
21	Chuck BERRY	13095
22	Ivory Joe HUNTER	12870
23	Al HOFFMAN	12628
24	Baker KNIGHT	12327
25	Paul Francis WEBSTER	11891
26	Jack SCOTT	11599
27	Lloyd PRICE	11040
28	Eddie HEYWOOD	10867
29	Hans ENGELMANN	10780
30	Richard ADLER	10490
31	Joseph KOSMA	10440
32	Felice BRYANT	10312
33	Sammy CAHN	10193
34	Wayne SHANKLIN	10187
35	Harold LOGAN	10148
36	Merle TRAVIS	10077
37	Sam COOKE	10021
38	Ed MARSHALL	9996
39	Kurt WEILL	9903
40	Ray EVANS	9669
41	Jay LIVINGSTON	9669
42	Carl SIGMAN	9568
43	Dewayne BLACKWELL	9403
44	Luis GUGLIELMI	9354
45	Charles SINGLETON	9136
46	Jerry ROSS	9028
47	Clyde OTIS	9018
48	Pat BALLARD	8989
49	Perez PRADO	8966
50	Marguerite MONNOT	8906

51	Phil SPECTOR	8838
52	Sammy FAIN	8647
53	Hy ZARET	8205
54	Bobby DARIN	8027
55	Maurice WILLIAMS	7788
56	Aaron SCHROEDER	7769
57	Jimmy DRIFTWOOD	7742
58	Alex NORTH	7729
59	Ritchie VALENS	7687
60	Sheb WOOLEY	7647
61	Stuart HAMBLEN	7439
62	Doc POMUS	7365
63	Harlan HOWARD	7361
64	Marvin MOORE	7357
65	Frank LOESSER	7335
66	Ric CARTEY	7241
67	Carole JOYNER	7241
68	Don ROBERTSON	7236
69	Cole PORTER	7116
70	Jimmie CRANE	7053
71	Chuck RIO	7019
72	Domenico MODUGNO	6933
73	Carl PERKINS	6912
74	Al JACOBS	6902
75	Winfield SCOTT	6805
76	Mort SHUMAN	6803
77	Irving BERLIN	6776
78	Lee POCKRISS	6717
79	Audrey ALLISON	6691
80	Joe ALLISON	6691
81	George DUNING	6680
82	John D. LOUDERMILK	6648
83	Ollie JONES	6505
84	Johnny MERCER	6401
85	Norman PETTY	6200
86	George BRUNS	6200
87	Peter DeANGELIS	6154
88	Bob MARCUCCI	6154
89	Don GEORGE	6075
90	Brook BENTON	6059
91	Ned MILLER	5894
92	Tom BLACKBURN	5836
93	Franco MIGLIACCI	5814
94	August MSARURGWA	5777
95	Mickie GRANT	5720
96	Jesse STONE	5695
97	Dolores Vicki SILVERS	5623
98	Bob HILLIARD	5570
99	Jerome KERN	5566
100	Bobby STEVENSON	5542

101	Sharon SHEELEY	5534
102	Stan LEBOWSKY	5502
103	Vincent YOUMANS	5489
104	Lee HAZLEWOOD	5460
105	Clarence QUICK	5451
106	Bill TRADER	5386
107	Hal DAVID	5361
108	Otto HARBACH	5343
109	Charles DAWES	5317
110	Roy ALFRED	5313
111	Neil SEDAKA	5186
112	Johnny OTIS	5184
113	Howard GREENFIELD	5181
114	Leon RENÉ	5115
115	Bob DAVIE	5097
116	Berthold BRECHT	5086
117	Marc BLITZSTEIN	5086
118	Roy C. BENNETT	5063
119	Sid TEPPER	5063
120	Herbert NEWMAN	5037
121	Jack SEGAL	4974
122	Bob CREWE	4945
123	Frank SLAY	4945
124	Luther DIXON	4943
125	Bill JUSTIS	4883
126	Richard DEHR	4861
127	Terry GILKYSON	4861
128	Frank MILLER	4861
129	Lou STALLMAN	4741
130	Dimitri TIOMKIN	4737
131	Alan FREED	4650
132	Irving GORDON	4605
133	Don GIBSON	4596
134	Bert REISFELD	4569
135	Alberto CURCI	4567
136	Tom GLAZER	4523
137	Bickley REICHNER	4503
138	Jimmy CLANTON	4486
139	Sid WAYNE	4483
140	Jimmy KENNEDY	4475
141	Jean VILLARD	4434
142	Ronnie SELF	4423
143	Ken DARBY	4422
144	Jack FULTON	4416
145	Lois STEELE	4416
146	Al LEWIS	4386
147	Sid MANKER	4375
148	Jimmy VAN HEUSEN	4334
149	Conway TWITTY	4309
150	Jack NANCE	4303

'50s: Top Writers by Entries

1	TRADITIONAL	82
2	Sammy CAHN	58
3	Paul Francis WEBSTER	50
4	Al HOFFMAN	49
5	Jerry LEIBER	47
6	Mike STOLLER	47
7	Dick MANNING	46
8	Irving BERLIN	45
9	Robert ALLEN	42
10	Fats DOMINO	41
11	Bob MERRILL	39
12	Dave BARTHOLOMEW	38
13	Carl SIGMAN	37
14	Al STILLMAN	36
15	Johnny MERCER	36
16	Buck RAM	35
17	Kal MANN	29
18	Sammy FAIN	29
19	Bernie LOWE	28
20	Clyde OTIS	28
21	Aaron SCHROEDER	27
22	Otis BLACKWELL	26
23	Charles SINGLETON	26
24	Bob HILLIARD	26
25	Dimitri TIOMKIN	26
26	Ben WEISMAN	26
27	Jerry LIVINGSTON	26
28	George David WEISS	25
29	Ned WASHINGTON	25
30	Boudleaux BRYANT	24
31	Chuck BERRY	24
32	Frederick LOEWE	24
33	Buddy KAYE	23
34	Ray EVANS	22
35	Jay LIVINGSTON	22
36	Jimmy VAN HEUSEN	22
37	Oscar HAMMERSTEIN	22
38	Roy C. BENNETT	21
39	Sid TEPPER	21
40	Richard RODGERS	21
41	Rose Marie McCOY	21
42	Alan Jay LERNER	21
43	Harold ADAMSON	21
44	Richard ADLER	20
45	Cole PORTER	20
46	Sid WAYNE	20
47	Mack DAVID	20
48	Luigi CREATORE	20
49	Hugo PERETTI	20
50	Victor YOUNG	20

51	Norman PETTY	19
52	Noel SHERMAN	19
53	Jerry ROSS	18
54	Frank LOESSER	18
55	John MARASCALCO	18
56	Jule STYNE	18
57	Brook BENTON	17
58	Jesse STONE	17
59	Johnny CASH	17
60	Robert MELLIN	17
61	Harry WARREN	17
62	Gene DePAUL	17
63	Mitchell PARISH	17
64	Sunny SKYLAR	17
65	John TURNER	17
66	Geoffrey PARSONS	17
67	Ivory Joe HUNTER	16
68	Tom GLAZER	16
69	Fred EBB	16
70	Stuart HAMBLEN	15
71	Doc POMUS	15
72	Peter DeANGELIS	15
73	Bob MARCUCCI	15
74	Roy ALFRED	15
75	Milt GABLER	15
76	Fred WISE	15
77	Morris LEVY	15
78	Nicholas BRODSZKY	15
79	Wayne SHANKLIN	14
80	Jimmie CRANE	14
81	George BRUNS	14
82	Sammy GALLOP	14
83	George GOLDNER	14
84	Buddy KNOX	14
85	Al FRISCH	14
86	Henry GLOVER	14
87	Paul KLEIN	14
88	Paul ANKA	13
89	David SEVILLE	13
90	Jack SCOTT	13
91	Felice BRYANT	13
92	Marvin MOORE	13
93	Al JACOBS	13
94	Mort SHUMAN	13
95	John D. LOUDERMILK	13
96	Bob CREWE	13
97	Frank SLAY	13
98	Jimmy KENNEDY	13
99	Al LEWIS	13
100	Richard PENNIMAN	13

101	Jack LAWRENCE	13
102	Kay TWOMEY	13
103	Dave ALLDRED	13
104	Stella UNGER	13
105	Gus KAHN	13
106	Teddy POWELL	13
107	Johnny MARKS	13
108	Don ROBERTSON	12
109	Domenico MODUGNO	12
110	Lee HAZLEWOOD	12
111	Lou STALLMAN	12
112	Berry GORDY	12
113	Donnie LANIER	12
114	Jimmy BOWEN	12
115	Philip SPRINGER	12
116	Joe LUBIN	12
117	Bennie BENJAMIN	12
118	Abner SILVER	12
119	Billy MURE	12
120	Dick WOLF	12
121	Larry COLEMAN	12
122	Jerry BOCK	12
123	Marty ROBBINS	11
124	Carl PERKINS	11
125	Winfield SCOTT	11
126	Lee POCKRISS	11
127	Ollie JONES	11
128	Neil SEDAKA	11
129	Richard DEHR	11
130	Terry GILKYSON	11
131	Frank MILLER	11
132	Alan FREED	11
133	Irving GORDON	11
134	Bickley REICHNER	11
135	Buddy HOLLY	11
136	Julius DIXON	11
137	Joe YOUNG	11
138	Billy ROSE	11
139	Sylvia FINE	11
140	Bill HALEY	11
141	Hoagy CARMICHAEL	11
142	Mack WOLFSON	11
143	Edward WHITE	11
144	Sigmund ROMBERG	11
145	Freddy MORGAN	11
146	Lotar OLIAS	11
147	Charles TOBIAS	11
148	Jimmy McHUGH	11
149	George MOTOLA	11

23 writers tied with 10 entries.

'60s: Top Writers by Score

1	Paul McCARTNEY	111303
2	John LENNON	110649
3	Eddie HOLLAND	58516
4	Brian HOLLAND	56586
5	Lamont DOZIER	52745
6	Smokey ROBINSON	49963
7	Burt BACHARACH	48664
8	Hal DAVID	44827
9	Gerry GOFFIN	43909
10	Bob DYLAN	42832
11	Neil DIAMOND	41257
12	TRADITIONAL	40788
13	Carole KING	39945
14	Kal MANN	38379
15	Jeff BARRY	38371
16	Bob GAUDIO	38342
17	Curtis MAYFIELD	38303
18	Brian WILSON	37773
19	Paul SIMON	37072
20	Tony HATCH	36842
21	Barry MANN	35470
22	Mick JAGGER	35056
23	Keith RICHARDS	35056
24	Sam COOKE	34569
25	Bob CREWE	32135
26	Howard GREENFIELD	32024
27	John D. LOUDERMILK	31153
28	Jerry FULLER	30980
29	Hank BALLARD	30329
30	James BROWN	28782
31	Norman WHITFIELD	27902
32	Doc POMUS	26121
33	Jimmy WEBB	26096
34	Dave APPELL	25955
35	Sonny BONO	25941
36	Mort SHUMAN	25718
37	Cynthia WEIL	25530
38	Donovan LEITCH	25210
39	John PHILLIPS	24818
40	John SEBASTIAN	24452
41	Ellie GREENWICH	24213
42	Roy ORBISON	24187
43	Tommy ROE	24112
44	Bert BERNS	23165
45	Mike LOVE	22564
46	John FOGERTY	22479
47	Felix CAVALIERE	22042
48	Barrett STRONG	21744
49	Laura NYRO	21536
50	Lee HAZLEWOOD	21051
51	Bobby RUSSELL	20072
52	Phil SPECTOR	20039
53	Otis REDDING	19252
54	Berry GORDY	18886
55	Roger MILLER	18707
56	Jerry LEIBER	18558
57	Sylvester STEWART	18410
58	Paul ANKA	18180
59	Eddie BRIGATI	17975
60	Chuck BERRY	17617
61	Jack KELLER	17141
62	Del SHANNON	16785
63	Mike STOLLER	16758
64	Allen TOUSSAINT	16499
65	Ernie MARESCA	16041
66	Wayne Carson THOMPSON	15886
67	Neil SEDAKA	15693
68	Ray DAVIES	15574
69	Luther DIXON	15570
70	Chip TAYLOR	15497
71	Aaron SCHROEDER	14962
72	Dave CLARK	14742
73	Geoff STEPHENS	14626
74	Don GIBSON	14510
75	Tommy BOYCE	14096
76	Max STEINER	13893
77	Don COVAY	13856
78	Joe SOUTH	13404
79	Kenneth GAMBLE	13381
80	Graham GOULDMAN	13380
81	Jerry HERMAN	13261
82	Bobby DARIN	13252
83	Clyde OTIS	13187
84	Rod ARGENT	13009
85	Joe TEX	12999
86	Bobby HART	12935
87	Joe MELSON	12713
88	Hank COCHRAN	12678
89	Floyd CRAMER	12671
90	Lee POCKRISS	12661
91	Steve CROPPER	12611
92	Leon HUFF	12422
93	Harlan HOWARD	12351
94	Jimmy DEAN	12298
95	Pete SEEGER	12076
96	Bobbie GENTRY	11937
97	Dallas FRAZIER	11613
98	Ritchie CORDELL	11597
99	Sandy LINZER	11582
100	André POPP	11475
101	Henry COSBY	11316
102	Mark JAMES	11278
103	Johnny MERCER	11241
104	Wally GOLD	11120
105	Paul VANCE	11120
106	Acker BILK	11094
107	Chris KENNER	10782
108	Artie RESNICK	10756
109	Bobby GOLDSBORO	10648
110	Frank GUIDA	10442
111	Galt MacDERMOT	10432
112	Dion DiMUCCI	10334
113	Martha SHARP	10313
114	C. Carson PARKS	10263
115	Dick HOLLER	10190
116	Mac DAVIS	10177
117	Wes FARRELL	10170
118	John STEWART	10151
119	Ray HILDEBRAND	10128
120	Tommy JAMES	10055
121	James RADO	10043
122	Gerome RAGNI	10043
123	Kenny YOUNG	9961
124	William STEVENSON	9952
125	Marty ROBBINS	9912
126	Jeanine DECKERS	9739
127	Richard BERRY	9728
128	Mark LINDSAY	9644
129	Henry MANCINI	9587
130	Clint BALLARD Jr.	9560
131	Gene PITNEY	9558
132	Klaus-Günter NEUMANN	9519
133	Terry KIRKMAN	9503
134	Shel SILVERSTEIN	9471
135	P.F. SLOAN	9445
136	Alan GORDON	9417
137	Garry BONNER	9417
138	Don ROBERTSON	9332
139	James HOLVAY	9237
140	Andy KIM	9237
141	Rick EVANS	9175
142	Shadow MORTON	9173
143	Winfield SCOTT	9151
144	Ruthann FRIEDMAN	9149
145	Don BLACK	9050
146	Rudy CLARK	8936
147	Steve BARRI	8936
148	Otis BLACKWELL	8887
149	Sylvia MOY	8831
150	Ray STEVENS	8755

'60s: Top Writers by Entries

1	Eddie HOLLAND	97
2	Paul McCARTNEY	96
3	John LENNON	96
4	Brian HOLLAND	94
5	Burt BACHARACH	90
6	Gerry GOFFIN	89
7	TRADITIONAL	89
8	Hal DAVID	88
9	Lamont DOZIER	85
10	Carole KING	80
11	Smokey ROBINSON	76
12	Curtis MAYFIELD	68
13	Barry MANN	65
14	Jeff BARRY	62
15	Kal MANN	56
16	James BROWN	56
17	Bob CREWE	52
18	Cynthia WEIL	51
19	Doc POMUS	49
20	Bert BERNS	49
21	Mort SHUMAN	48
22	Jerry LEIBER	48
23	Ellie GREENWICH	47
24	Kenneth GAMBLE	46
25	Steve CROPPER	46
26	Brian WILSON	45
27	Dave APPELL	45
28	Phil SPECTOR	45
29	Mike STOLLER	44
30	Sam COOKE	43
31	Howard GREENFIELD	42
32	Leon HUFF	41
33	Deadric MALONE	41
34	William STEVENSON	37
35	Norman WHITFIELD	35
36	Bob DYLAN	34
37	Paul VANCE	34
38	Berry GORDY	33
39	Henry MANCINI	33
40	Tony HATCH	32
41	Paul ANKA	32
42	Luther DIXON	32
43	Clyde OTIS	32
44	Bob GAUDIO	31
45	Johnny MERCER	31
46	John D. LOUDERMILK	30
47	Lee HAZLEWOOD	30
48	George David WEISS	30

49	Roy ORBISON	29
50	Otis REDDING	28
51	Jack KELLER	28
52	Jerry RAGOVOY	28
53	Fats DOMINO	28
54	Isaac HAYES	27
55	Teddy RANDAZZO	27
56	Booker T. JONES Jr.	27
57	Mick JAGGER	26
58	Keith RICHARDS	26
59	Barrett STRONG	26
60	Joe TEX	26
61	David PORTER	26
62	Carl SIGMAN	26
63	Jimmy WEBB	25
64	Allen TOUSSAINT	25
65	Don COVAY	25
66	Lee POCKRISS	25
67	Sandy LINZER	25
68	Eddie SNYDER	25
69	Billy DAVIS	25
70	Mike LOVE	24
71	Harlan HOWARD	24
72	P.F. SLOAN	24
73	Jerry GOLDSTEIN	24
74	Chuck BERRY	23
75	Bobby DARIN	23
76	Sylvia MOY	23
77	Denny RANDELL	23
78	Van McCOY	23
79	Morris LEVY	23
80	Chip TAYLOR	22
81	Richard RODGERS	22
82	Jerry BUTLER	22
83	Neil DIAMOND	21
84	Sonny BONO	21
85	Steve BARRI	21
86	David WHITE	21
87	Bob FELDMAN	21
88	Richard GOTTEHRER	21
89	Roger MILLER	20
90	Neil SEDAKA	20
91	Bobby GOLDSBORO	20
92	Wes FARRELL	20
93	Brook BENTON	20
94	Bob HILLIARD	20
95	Bill ANDERSON	20
96	Bobby WEINSTEIN	20

97	Dave BARTHOLOMEW	20
98	Ray CHARLES	20
99	Tommy BOYCE	19
100	Ben RALEIGH	19
101	John MADARA	19
102	Billy SHERRILL	19
103	Sammy CAHN	19
104	Paul SIMON	18
105	John SEBASTIAN	18
106	Joe SOUTH	18
107	Henry COSBY	18
108	Bert KAEMPFERT	18
109	Harvey FUQUA	18
110	Ben WEISMAN	18
111	Mark BARKAN	18
112	Warren MOORE	18
113	Luigi CREATORE	18
114	Hugo PERETTI	18
115	Eddie FLOYD	18
116	Donovan LEITCH	17
117	Ritchie CORDELL	17
118	Don ROBERTSON	17
119	Ray STEVENS	17
120	Boudleaux BRYANT	17
121	Dan PENN	17
122	Peter UDELL	17
123	Leon CARR	17
124	Earl SHUMAN	17
125	Joey LEVINE	17
126	Nick ASHFORD	17
127	Valerie SIMPSON	17
128	Ivy Jo HUNTER	17
129	Dimitri TIOMKIN	17
130	John PHILLIPS	16
131	Bobby HART	16
132	Artie RESNICK	16
133	Galt MacDERMOT	16
134	Henry GLOVER	16
135	Mack DAVID	16
136	Gary GELD	16
137	Charles SINGLETON	16
138	Oscar HAMMERSTEIN	16
139	Leslie BRICUSSE	16
140	Jule STYNE	16
141	Larry KUSIK	16
142	Carl DAVIS	16
143	B.B. KING	16

Eighteen writers tied with 15 entries.

'70s: Top Writers by Score

1	Barry GIBB	58778
2	Paul McCARTNEY	54616
3	Stevie WONDER	51611
4	Paul SIMON	43606
5	John LENNON	36290
6	Robin GIBB	35598
7	Neil DIAMOND	33806
8	Leon HUFF	33644
9	Bernie TAUPIN	32518
10	Elton JOHN	32478
11	Norman WHITFIELD	31810
12	David GATES	31067
13	Kenneth GAMBLE	31034
14	Carole KING	29141
15	Maurice GIBB	28024
16	Linda McCARTNEY	26074
17	Lionel RICHIE	25525
18	George HARRISON	25273
19	John DENVER	24384
20	Curtis MAYFIELD	24228
21	Freddie PERREN	23955
22	John FOGERTY	22690
23	Paul ANKA	22664
24	Barry WHITE	22225
25	Sylvester STEWART	22149
26	John FARRAR	21379
27	Rod STEWART	20219
28	Neil SEDAKA	19935
29	Gilbert O'SULLIVAN	19552
30	Harry Wayne CASEY	19376
31	Rick FINCH	19376
32	Smokey ROBINSON	19319
33	Freddie MERCURY	19271
34	Jeff LYNNE	18933
35	Marvin GAYE	18257
36	Barrett STRONG	18048
37	Eric CARMEN	18040
38	Paul WILLIAMS	17628
39	Irwin LEVINE	17583
40	Melanie SAFKA	17348
41	Jim CROCE	16966
42	Thom BELL	16647
43	Jim WEATHERLY	16277
44	Hoyt AXTON	16187
45	Al GREEN	16002
46	Rod TEMPERTON	15767
47	Mac DAVIS	15618
48	Bill WITHERS	15258
49	L. Russell BROWN	15030
50	Billy JOEL	14909
51	Don McLEAN	14668
52	Gordon LIGHTFOOT	14626
53	Robert LAMM	14534
54	TRADITIONAL	14273
55	Nile RODGERS	14197
56	Bernard EDWARDS	14197
57	Alan O'DAY	14111
58	Neil YOUNG	14085
59	Carly SIMON	13963
60	Mick JAGGER	13822
61	Keith RICHARDS	13822
62	Joe SOUTH	13637
63	Glenn FREY	13490
64	Gerry GOFFIN	13467
65	Don HENLEY	13412
66	Kent LaVOIE	12684
67	Linda CREED	12592
68	Ray STEVENS	12577
69	Joe BROOKS	12550
70	Bruce SPRINGSTEEN	12535
71	Dennis DeYOUNG	12445
72	Dino FEKARIS	12440
73	James PANKOW	12336
74	Dennis LAMBERT	12239
75	Brian POTTER	12239
76	Billy PRESTON	12209
77	Steve MILLER	12087
78	Gerry RAFFERTY	11989
79	Hal DAVID	11949
80	Randy NEWMAN	11883
81	Tony MACAULAY	11864
82	Kris KRISTOFFERSON	11857
83	Pete TOWNSHEND	11746
84	Eddie CORNELIUS	11613
85	Eugene RECORD	11594
86	Kenny LOGGINS	11567
87	Cat STEVENS	11484
88	Pete HAM	11477
89	Chuck BERRY	11472
90	Dewey BUNNELL	11292
91	Kenny NOLAN	11287
92	Burt BACHARACH	11243
93	James BROWN	11229
94	Isaac HAYES	11175
95	James TAYLOR	11089
96	Jimmy WEBB	10927
97	Peter CETERA	10780
98	Daryl HALL	10611
99	Ringo STARR	10577
100	George Henry JACKSON	10485
101	Maurice WHITE	10458
102	Bob SEGER	10425
103	Berry GORDY	10396
104	Tony ROMEO	10268
105	Eddie HOLLAND	10263
106	Burton CUMMINGS	10257
107	Brian HOLLAND	10134
108	Toni TENNILLE	10060
109	Donna SUMMER	9988
110	Randy GOODRUM	9979
111	Clifton DAVIS	9941
112	Randy BACHMAN	9858
113	Mike CHAPMAN	9733
114	Nicky CHINN	9733
115	Bill DANOFF	9700
116	Peter CALLANDER	9628
117	Peter FRAMPTON	9578
118	Gary WRIGHT	9499
119	Carole Bayer SAGER	9411
120	Ewan MacCOLL	9289
121	Errol BROWN	9259
122	Willie MITCHELL	9206
123	David PAICH	8979
124	Todd RUNDGREN	8960
125	General JOHNSON	8850
126	Jeff BARRY	8722
127	Allen TOUSSAINT	8721
128	Roger NICHOLS	8704
129	Joni MITCHELL	8671
130	John D. LOUDERMILK	8602
131	Michael Leslie JONES	8494
132	John WILLIAMS	8471
133	Lamont DOZIER	8457
134	Stevie NICKS	8374
135	Charles FOX	8227
136	Norman GIMBEL	8137
137	Rupert HOLMES	8110
138	Gene MacLELLAN	8090
139	Leon RUSSELL	8090
140	Albert HAMMOND	8059
141	Paul JABARA	8046
142	Bob CREWE	7996
143	Barry MANN	7929
144	Al JACKSON	7926
145	Norman GREENBAUM	7897
146	David BOWIE	7893
147	Christine McVIE	7867
148	Nick ASHFORD	7854
149	Valerie SIMPSON	7854
150	Frank Edward WILSON	7821

'70s: Top Writers by Entries

1	Leon HUFF	76
2	Kenneth GAMBLE	71
3	Brian HOLLAND	58
4	Paul McCARTNEY	56
5	Eddie HOLLAND	54
6	Lamont DOZIER	52
7	Norman WHITFIELD	46
8	Barry GIBB	43
9	Carole KING	43
10	James BROWN	39
11	Dennis LAMBERT	38
12	Brian POTTER	38
13	John LENNON	37
14	Smokey ROBINSON	34
15	Neil DIAMOND	33
16	Stevie WONDER	32
17	Robin GIBB	32
18	Curtis MAYFIELD	30
19	Bernie TAUPIN	29
20	Maurice GIBB	29
21	TRADITIONAL	29
22	Elton JOHN	28
23	Hal DAVID	28
24	Freddie PERREN	27
25	Thom BELL	26
26	Gerry GOFFIN	26
27	Jeff BARRY	26
28	Paul ANKA	25
29	Neil SEDAKA	25
30	Nick ASHFORD	25
31	Valerie SIMPSON	25
32	David GATES	24
33	Barrett STRONG	24
34	Eugene RECORD	24
35	Burt BACHARACH	24
36	Barry MANN	23
37	Van McCOY	23
38	Paul SIMON	22
39	George HARRISON	22
40	Harry Wayne CASEY	22
41	Rick FINCH	22
42	Paul WILLIAMS	22
43	Irwin LEVINE	22
44	Mick JAGGER	22
45	Keith RICHARDS	22
46	Buddy BUIE	22
47	O'Kelly ISLEY	22
48	Ronald ISLEY	22
49	Rudolph ISLEY	22
50	Linda McCARTNEY	21
51	John DENVER	21
52	L. Russell BROWN	21
53	Carole Bayer SAGER	21
54	Albert HAMMOND	21
55	Barry WHITE	20
56	Al GREEN	20
57	Linda CREED	20
58	Kris KRISTOFFERSON	20
59	Maurice WHITE	20
60	Burton CUMMINGS	20
61	Jeff LYNNE	19
62	Neil YOUNG	19
63	Ronald DUNBAR	19
64	Pam SAWYER	19
65	Lee OSKAR	19
66	Tony MACAULAY	18
67	Johnny BRISTOL	18
68	Howard SCOTT	18
69	Thomas ALLEN	18
70	Harold BROWN	18
71	Lonnie JORDAN	18
72	Charles MILLER	18
73	Allan FELDER	18
74	Sylvester STEWART	17
75	Cat STEVENS	17
76	General JOHNSON	17
77	Howard GREENFIELD	17
78	Roger GREENAWAY	17
79	Roger COOK	17
80	Tommy JAMES	17
81	Charles Henry JACKSON Jr.	17
82	Cynthia WEIL	17
83	Morris DICKERSON	17
84	Marvin GAYE	16
85	Eric CARMEN	16
86	Mac DAVIS	16
87	Benny ANDERSSON	16
88	Björn ULVAEUS	16
89	Bob DYLAN	16
90	Mike HAZLEWOOD	16
91	Brian WILSON	16
92	Andrew NOLAND	16
93	John FOGERTY	15
94	Pete TOWNSHEND	15
95	Isaac HAYES	15
96	Berry GORDY	15
97	Mike CHAPMAN	15
98	Nicky CHINN	15
99	Leon RUSSELL	15
100	Pete BELLOTTE	15
101	Van MORRISON	15
102	Sam COOKE	15
103	Billy SHERRILL	15
104	Jerry LEIBER	15
105	Marvin YANCY	15
106	Homer BANKS	15
107	Leroy BONNER	15
108	Marshall JONES	15
109	Ralph MIDDLEBROOKS	15
110	Marvin PIERCE	15
111	Ronald BELL	15
112	Dino FEKARIS	14
113	James TAYLOR	14
114	George Henry JACKSON	14
115	Todd RUNDGREN	14
116	Frank Edward WILSON	14
117	Robert L. KING	14
118	Donald FAGEN	14
119	Walter BECKER	14
120	Giorgio MORODER	14
121	Angelo BOND	14
122	Mike STOLLER	14
123	George CLINTON	14
124	George M. BROWN	14
125	Robert BELL	14
126	Claydes SMITH	14
127	Dennis THOMAS	14
128	Ernie ISLEY	14
129	Lionel RICHIE	13
130	Melanie SAFKA	13
131	Jim WEATHERLY	13
132	Bill WITHERS	13
133	Kenny NOLAN	13
134	Daryl HALL	13
135	Willie MITCHELL	13
136	Allen TOUSSAINT	13
137	Joni MITCHELL	13
138	Bob CREWE	13
139	David BOWIE	13
140	Greg PERRY	13
141	Sylvia ROBINSON	13
142	Don DAVIS	13
143	Alice COOPER	13
144	Norman HARRIS	13
145	Marvin ISLEY	13
146	Chris JASPER	13
147	Bunny SIGLER	13

Fourteen writers tied with 12 entries.

'80s: Top Writers by Score

1	Lionel RICHIE	65581
2	PRINCE	62160
3	Michael JACKSON	51959
4	George MICHAEL	42847
5	Phil COLLINS	37327
6	Billy JOEL	35352
7	STING	33010
8	Daryl HALL	30721
9	Paul McCARTNEY	29753
10	John MELLENCAMP	27930
11	Diane WARREN	27902
12	Bruce SPRINGSTEEN	27226
13	Stevie WONDER	25673
14	Rick SPRINGFIELD	21251
15	Madonna L. CICCONE	20843
16	Richard MARX	20577
17	John LENNON	19636
18	Ray PARKER Jr.	18715
19	James Samuel HARRIS	17502
20	Terry LEWIS	17502
21	Debbie GIBSON	17301
22	Christopher CROSS	17283
23	David FOSTER	17225
24	Giorgio MORODER	17057
25	Michael Leslie JONES	16210
26	Rod TEMPERTON	16108
27	Ric OCASEK	16103
28	Kevin CRONIN	16035
29	Graham RUSSELL	15435
30	Colin James HAY	14865
31	Gloria ESTEFAN	14623
32	Bob SEGER	14537
33	Billy STEINBERG	14519
34	Jim STEINMAN	14244
35	Dean PITCHFORD	14105
36	Maurice STARR	13522
37	Thomas F. KELLY	13225
38	Lewis MARTINÉE	12407
39	John DEACON	12383
40	Carole Bayer SAGER	12179
41	Will JENNINGS	12102
42	Barry GIBB	12100
43	Tom SNOW	11830
44	Steve PERRY	11790
45	David BOWIE	11757
46	Elton JOHN	11665
47	Neil DIAMOND	11629
48	Dennis DeYOUNG	11569
49	Bernie TAUPIN	11561
50	Jonathan CAIN	11492
51	Steve KIPNER	11491
52	Jim PETERIK	11438
53	Jon BON JOVI	11432
54	Cynthia WEIL	11243
55	Oliver LEIBER	11097
56	Burt BACHARACH	11087
57	Seth JUSTMAN	11043
58	Jim VALLANCE	11036
59	Holly KNIGHT	10893
60	David PAICH	10821
61	Frankie SULLIVAN	10802
62	Jeff LYNNE	10782
63	Kenneth EDMONDS	10736
64	Desmond CHILD	10706
65	Bruce HORNSBY	10292
66	Robin GIBB	10163
67	Billy OCEAN	10032
68	Patrick Raymond LEONARD	10023
69	Keith FORSEY	9883
70	John OATES	9853
71	Mike RUTHERFORD	9851
72	Rick JAMES	9842
73	Steve MILLER	9830
74	Per GESSLE	9706
75	Michael MASSER	9673
76	Kenny LOGGINS	9575
77	Smokey ROBINSON	9555
78	Mutt LANGE	9549
79	Richie SAMBORA	9456
80	Howard JONES	9405
81	Steve GREENBERG	9395
82	Roger WATERS	9385
83	Dan FOGELBERG	9346
84	Peter CETERA	9332
85	Bryan ADAMS	9267
86	Mick JAGGER	9263
87	John FARRAR	9225
88	Sara ALLEN	9015
89	Huey LEWIS	8863
90	David A. STEWART	8730
91	Steve WINWOOD	8560
92	Nigel John TAYLOR	8529
93	Elliot WOLFF	8501
94	Brian SETZER	8480
95	Robert PALMER	8442
96	Simon Le BON	8399
97	Nick RHODES	8399
98	Antonio REID	8334
99	Peter GABRIEL	7967
100	John BETTIS	7929
101	Lou GRAMM	7890
102	Annie LENNOX	7885
103	Mike CHAPMAN	7801
104	Corey HART	7749
105	Roger TAYLOR	7713
106	Terry BRITTEN	7708
107	Roland ORZABAL	7698
108	Stevie NICKS	7654
109	Keith RICHARDS	7581
110	Stephen BRAY	7337
111	Andy FARRISS	7292
112	Graham LYLE	7288
113	Tom PETTY	7235
114	Michael HUTCHENCE	7230
115	Sammy HAGAR	7119
116	Eddy GRANT	7049
117	Dolly PARTON	7002
118	Andy TAYLOR	6995
119	Mark KNOPFLER	6984
120	Russ BALLARD	6848
121	Chrissie HYNDE	6808
122	Charlotte CAFFEY	6771
123	Graham GOBLE	6695
124	Donna SUMMER	6676
125	Paul SIMON	6440
126	Christine McVIE	6427
127	Barry MANN	6392
128	David PACK	6354
129	Harold FALTERMEYER	6328
130	Marv ROSS	6313
131	Albert HAMMOND	6270
132	Narada Michael WALDEN	6122
133	Gerry GOFFIN	6105
134	Florrie PALMER	6022
135	Amanda McBROOM	6013
136	VANGELIS	6013
137	Chris HAYES	5965
138	Peter F. WOLF	5949
139	Danny KORTCHMAR	5822
140	Maurice GIBB	5817
141	Tony BANKS	5786
142	George M. BROWN	5761
143	Daryl SIMMONS	5728
144	Nile RODGERS	5695
145	George MERRILL	5684
146	Shannon RUBICAM	5684
147	Michael CRAIG	5663
148	Roy HAY	5663
149	Jon MOSS	5663
150	George O'DOWD	5663

'80s: Top Writers by Entries

1	PRINCE	43
2	David FOSTER	38
3	Paul McCARTNEY	37
4	Stevie WONDER	32
5	Jim VALLANCE	30
6	John LENNON	29
7	James Samuel HARRIS	28
8	Terry LEWIS	28
9	Phil COLLINS	27
10	Jonathan CAIN	26
11	Steve PERRY	24
12	Holly KNIGHT	24
13	Michael JACKSON	23
14	Daryl HALL	23
15	Jim PETERIK	23
16	Bryan ADAMS	23
17	Lionel RICHIE	22
18	Billy JOEL	22
19	Diane WARREN	22
20	Barry GIBB	22
21	Giorgio MORODER	21
22	Cynthia WEIL	21
23	John MELLENCAMP	20
24	Carole Bayer SAGER	20
25	Mutt LANGE	20
26	Mike LOVE	20
27	STING	19
28	Bruce SPRINGSTEEN	19
29	Elton JOHN	19
30	Kenneth EDMONDS	19
31	Desmond CHILD	19
32	Mike RUTHERFORD	19
33	David A. STEWART	19
34	Brian WILSON	19
35	Bernie TAUPIN	18
36	Mick JAGGER	18
37	Nigel John TAYLOR	18
38	Tom PETTY	18
39	Narada Michael WALDEN	18
40	George M. BROWN	18
41	Will JENNINGS	17
42	Tom SNOW	17
43	Burt BACHARACH	17
44	Frankie SULLIVAN	17
45	Jeff LYNNE	17
46	Robin GIBB	17
47	Simon Le BON	17
48	Nick RHODES	17
49	Roger TAYLOR	17
50	Ronald BELL	17
51	J.T. TAYLOR	17
52	Rick SPRINGFIELD	16
53	Ric OCASEK	16
54	Dean PITCHFORD	16
55	Antonio REID	16
56	Maurice GIBB	16
57	Robert BELL	16
58	Claydes SMITH	16
59	George MICHAEL	15
60	Thomas F. KELLY	15
61	Kenny LOGGINS	15
62	Smokey ROBINSON	15
63	Steve WINWOOD	15
64	Annie LENNOX	15
65	Mike CHAPMAN	15
66	Sammy HAGAR	15
67	Bruce ROBERTS	15
68	Madonna L. CICCONE	14
69	Bob SEGER	14
70	David BOWIE	14
71	Neil DIAMOND	14
72	Andy TAYLOR	14
73	Matt AITKEN	14
74	Mike STOCK	14
75	Pete WATERMAN	14
76	Franne GOLDE	14
77	Richard MARX	13
78	Michael Leslie JONES	13
79	Billy STEINBERG	13
80	Jon BON JOVI	13
81	Michael MASSER	13
82	Stevie NICKS	13
83	Keith RICHARDS	13
84	Barry MANN	13
85	Tony BANKS	13
86	Nile RODGERS	13
87	Randy GOODRUM	13
88	Michael ANTHONY	13
89	Alex VAN HALEN	13
90	Eddie VAN HALEN	13
91	Allee WILLIS	13
92	Curtis BEDEAU	13
93	Gerard CHARLES	13
94	Hugh CLARKE	13
95	Brian GEORGE	13
96	Paul GEORGE	13
97	Ray PARKER Jr.	12
98	Rod TEMPERTON	12
99	Billy OCEAN	12
100	Terry BRITTEN	12
101	Andy FARRISS	12
102	Rod STEWART	12
103	Steve CLARK	12
104	Joe ELLIOTT	12
105	Rick SAVAGE	12
106	Lucien GEORGE	12
107	Paul DEAN	12
108	Jerry LEIBER	12
109	Mike STOLLER	12
110	Kevin CRONIN	11
111	Dennis DeYOUNG	11
112	Rick JAMES	11
113	Huey LEWIS	11
114	John BETTIS	11
115	Lou GRAMM	11
116	Michael HUTCHENCE	11
117	Lamont DOZIER	11
118	Martin PAGE	11
119	Billy SQUIER	11
120	Eric WOOLFSON	11
121	Alan PARSONS	11
122	George HARRISON	11
123	Tom BAILEY	11
124	Alannah CURRIE	11
125	Kim CARNES	11
126	Adam CLAYTON	11
127	Dave EVANS	11
128	Paul HEWSON	11
129	Larry MULLEN	11
130	Michael OMARTIAN	11
131	Rick ALLEN	11
132	Andy GOLDMARK	11
133	Curtis Fitzgerald WILLIAMS	11
134	Jay GRAYDON	11
135	Sandy LINZER	11

Twenty-five writers tied with 10 entries.

Writer Alias and Alternate Name Index

Official writer names used in the indices have last names shown in upper case. Alternate names are all shown in regular upper and lower case.

Writers in Index With Alternate Names

A

Sigidi ABDULLAH
Al ABRAMS
Andy ACKERS
Billy ADAMS
Kevin ADAMS
Ritchie ADAMS
Marvin Lee ADAY
Antonio ADOLFO
Bill ADOR
Helen ADU
Walter AFANASIEFF
Marcel AGERON
Morris ALBERT
George ALEXANDER
Jules ALEXANDER
Tracy Lee ALEXANDER
Kenneth J. ALFORD
Roy ALFRED
Gene ALLAN
Laurie ALLEN
Marilyn Weiss ALLEN
Na ALLEN
Georgio ALLENTINI
Michele ALLER
Bob ALLISON
John ALLISON
Alex ALSTONE
John ALTWERGER
Alan ALY
Bill AMESBURY
Tracey AMOS
Tobias ANDERSEN
Gary ANDERSON
John W. ANDERSON
Jon ANDERSON
Keith ANDERSON
Liz ANDERSON
Melvin ANDERSON
Sonny ANDERSON
Mike ANDRE
Ronald ANDRE
Pete ANDREOLI
Lee ANDREWS
Maggie ANDREWS
Maya ANGELOU
Ron ANIELLO
Paul ANKA
Tex ANN
Bill ANSON
Adam ANT
Pete ANTEL
Malcolm ANTHONY
Michael ANTHONY
Mike ANTHONY
Ray ANTHONY
Dave APPELL
Mary APPLEGATE
Ramon ARCUSA
Harold ARLEN
Lillian Hardin ARMSTRONG
Kokomo ARNOLD
Sidney ARODIN
Brooks ARTHUR
Bobby ARVON
Leon ASHLEY
Jan ASHTON
Bobby AUSTIN
David AUSTIN
Gene AUSTIN
Frankie AVALON
Johnny AVERAGE
Stuart AVIG
Corina AYALA
Charles AZNAVOUR

B

Randy BACHMAN
Don BACKY
Andy BADALE
John BADANJEK
Wally BADAROU
Randy BADAZZ
Ralph BAILEY
Razzy BAILEY
George BAKER
LaVern BAKER
Lefty BAKER
Mickey BAKER
Yvonne BAKER
Marty BALIN
Hank BALLARD
Pat BALLARD
Susan BALLION
Michael BALZARY
Afrika BAMBAATAA
Jon BANFIELD
Peter Douglas Cameron BANKS
Peter W. BANKS
Sidney BANKS
Royal C. BANNON
Phil BAPTISTE
Dave BARBAROSSA
Jose BARBOSA DA SILVA
Gene BARGE
Howard Ellington Riddiford BARNES
Jimmy BARNES
Addy BARON
Sandy BARON
Richard BARRETT
Vinnie BARRETT
Steve BARRI
Eric BARRIER
Jeff BARRY
John BARRY
Len BARRY
Lionel BART
Dave BARTHOLOMEW
Joss BASELLI
Toni BASIL
Ralph BASS
Robert BATEMAN
Clyde BATTIN
Bernie BAUM
Claude BAUM
Nora BAYES
T.D. BAYLESS
Amir BAYYAN
Albert BEACH
Reb BEACH
Len BEADLE
Nidra BEARD
Jackey BEAVERS
Gilbert BÉCAUD
Hank BEDUCCI
Bernice BEDWELL
Harry BELAFONTE
Adrian BELEW
Andy BELL
Benny BELL
Cara BELL
Larry BELL
Louise BELL
Marcus BELL
Ronald BELL
Tony BELL
William BELL
Dan BELLOC
Tony BELLUS
Phil BELMONTE
Jorge BEN
Pat BENATAR
Benito BENITES
Bennie BENJAMIN
Dale BENNETT
Headley BENNETT
Roy C. BENNETT
Gary BENSON
Brook BENTON
Borney BERGANTINE
Marilyn BERGMAN
Milton BERLE
Irving BERLIN
Roy BERMINGHAM
Ben BERNIE
Bert BERNS
Alan BERNSTEIN
Leonard BERNSTEIN
Chuck BERRY
John Bobby BERRY
Harmon BETHEA
Nuno BETTENCOURT
Henri BETTI
Dickey BETTS
Frankie BEVERLY
Wayne BICKERTON
Lou BIDEU
Acker BILK
Bob BILYK
Beeb BIRTLES
Bill BLACK
Don BLACK
Edward C. BLACK
Gene BLACK
Jay BLACK
Donald BLACKMAN
Larry BLACKMON
Otis BLACKWELL
Alan BLAIKLEY
David Marvin BLAKE
Eubie BLAKE
Virginia BLAND
Ralph BLANE
Victor BLECMAN
Philippe Gerard BLOCH
Conny BLOMQVIST
Amanda BLUE
Barry BLUE
David BLUE
Robbie BLUNT
Edwin BOCAGE
Walfried BÖCKER
Jo BOGAERT
Marc BOLAN
Rachel BOLAN
James BOLDEN
Andre BOLTON
Michael BOLTON
Jon BON JOVI
Johnny BOND
Mars BONFIRE
Garry BONNER
Sonny BONO
Betty BOO
Chuckii BOOKER
Daniel BOONE
Pat BOONE
Chris BOSTOCK
Roddy BOTTUM
Georges BOULANGER
Robert BOULANGER
Gene BOURGEOIS
Steve BOWDEN
David BOWIE
Tommy BOYCE
Clement A. BOZEWSKI
Dale BOZZIO
Bonnie BRAMLETT
Delaney BRAMLETT
Erik BRANN
Richard BRANNAN
Joanne BRATTON
Eric BREED
Peter BREGANTE
Beverly BREMERS
Teresa BREWER
Larry BRIGHT
Tim BRINKHURST
Darnell BRISTOL
Johnny BRISTOL
Bruce BROADUS
Bruce BROMBERG
Edgar BRONFMAN
Steve BRONSKI
Chuck BROOKS
Dianne BROOKS
Harvey BROOKS
Mel BROOKS
Ronnie E. BROOMFIELD
Albert Joseph BROWN
Alex BROWN
Bobby BROWN
Boots BROWN
Buster (2) BROWN
Deanna BROWN
Deidra BROWN
Douglas Fontaine BROWN
Errol BROWN
Floyd BROWN
George BROWN
James BROWN
James B. BROWN
L. Russell BROWN
Larry BROWN
Lew BROWN
Mark Alton BROWN
Nappy BROWN
Piney BROWN
Ruth BROWN
Sheree BROWN
Timothy BROWN
Yamma BROWN
Ed BRUCE
Anthony Michael BRUNO
Radcliffe BRYAN
Felice BRYANT
Marty BRYANT
Tracey BRYN
Peabo BRYSON
Chico BUARQUE DE HOLLANDA
Jan BUCKINGHAM
Dominic BUGATTI
Buddy BUIE
Allen BUNN
Dewey BUNNELL
Gary BURBANK
John BURCH
Leroy BURGESS

Lord BURGESS
Johnny BURKE
Joseph Francis BURKE
Selassie BURKE
Solomon BURKE
Sascha BURLAND
Billy BURNETTE
Rocky BURNETTE
Dick BURNS
Juana BURNS
Kenneth BURNS
Marvin Louis BURNS
Richard BURNS
Stanley BURRELL
Glen BURTNICK
Dorian BURTON
Nat BURTON
Ray BURTON
Fini BUSCH
Louis F. BUSH
Harry BUTLER
Terry BUTLER
William Earl BUTLER
Max BYGRAVES
Donald BYRD
David John BYRON

C

Catherine CAFRA
Elana CAGER
Joseph CAGLE
Sammy CAHN
Jonathan CAIN
J.J. CALE
Kevin CALHOUN
Roy CALHOUN
Randy CALIFORNIA
Allen CALLAIS
Peter CALLANDER
Paul CALLIRIS
John William CALLIS
Buster CAMPBELL
Junior CAMPBELL
Luther CAMPBELL
Milton CAMPBELL
Freddy CANNON
Anna CANTÙ
Irene CARA
Frank CARI
Max CARL
Russ CARLYLE
James CARMICHAEL
Pete CARPENTER
Michael CARR
Bert CARROLL
David CARROLL
Jenny Lou CARSON
Hans CARSTE
Chip CARTER
Deborah CARTER
Joe CARTER
John CARTER
June CARTER
Alvin CASH
Terry CASHMAN
Buzz CASON
Francesco CASSANO
Boomer CASTLEMAN
Peppy CASTRO
Demetrius CATES
Lee CATHY
Jessie CAVANAUGH
Marc CERRONE
David CHANDLER
Gene CHANDLER
Bruce CHANNEL
Jean CHAPEL
Blondie CHAPLIN
Saul CHAPLIN
Moose CHARLAP
Deena CHARLES
Dick CHARLES
Ray CHARLES
Sonny CHARLES
Clifton CHASE
Ellison CHASE
Armetia CHATMAN
Peter CHATMAN
Chubby CHECKER
Vincent CHEESMAN
Neneh CHERRY
Bruno CHERUBINI
Jane CHILD
Toni CHILDS
Babe CHIVIAN
Chris CHRISTIAN
Lou CHRISTIE
Johnnie CHRISTO
Gavin CHRISTOPHER
Madonna L. CICCONE
Angelo M. CIFELLI
Dee CLARK
Gene CLARK
Michael CLARK
Allan CLARKE
Tony CLARKE
Vince CLARKE
Paul CLAYTON
David CLAYTON-THOMAS
Martine CLÉMENCEAU
Clem CLEMPSON
N.J. CLESI
Jimmy CLIFF
Buzz CLIFFORD
David CLOWNEY
J.R. COBB
Cy COBEN
Ray COBURN
Richard COBURN
Hank COCHRAN
Todd COCHRAN
Joe COCKER
Thomas J. COE
Eddie COHEN
Lisa COHEN
Murray COHEN
James M. COHN
Toni COLANDREO
Nat "King" COLE
Tony COLE
Bud COLEMAN
Cy COLEMAN
Duke COLEMAN
John Ford COLEY
Sidney COLIN
Gail COLLINS
Lyn COLLINS
Rodger COLLINS
Tommy COLLINS
William Earl COLLINS
Ornella Ferrari COLOMBI
Jessi COLTER
Tony COLTON
Russ COLUMBO
Thomas COMAN
Betty COMDEN
Chester CONN
Andy CONNELL
Jane CONNELL
Carol CONNORS
Con CONRAD
Connie CONWAY
Norma CONWAY
Norman COOK
Sam COOKE
Priscilla COOLIDGE
Alice COOPER
Dick COOPER
Cowboy COPAS
Peter COR
Mike CORBY
Ritchie CORDELL
Attrell CORDES
Vincent COREA
John COREY
Wilma COSMÉ
Fran COSMO
Don COSTA
Alec R. COSTANDINOS
Elvis COSTELLO
Bobby COTTER
Charles Cane COURTNEY
David COURTNEY
Lou COURTNEY
Don COVAY
Joey COVINGTON
Art CRAFER
Bill CRANDALL
Cy CRANE
Jimmie CRANE
Luigi CREATORE
Linda CREED
Walt CREMONINI
Bob CREWE
Peter CRISS
G.L. CROCKETT
Cliff CROFFORD
Dash CROFTS
David CROOKS
Chris CROSS
Christopher CROSS
J.C. CROWLEY
Bettye CRUTCHER
Gene CRYSLER
Joe CUBA
Fabrice CUITAD
John CUMMINGS
Charles H. CUPPETT
Barry CURTIS
Chris CURTIS
Eddie CURTIS
King CURTIS
Mann CURTIS
Jimmy CURTISS
Vince CUSANO
Johnny CYMBAL
André CYMONE

D

Donnie DACUS
Robert DADE
Ted DAFFAN
Pierre-Alain DAHAN
E.G. DAILY
Sally Jo DAKOTA
Dick DALE
Jim DALE
Bobby DALL
Dick DALLAS
Miki DALLON
Michael DAMIAN
Bill DANA
Vic DANA
Walter DANA
Rodney DANGERFIELD
Charles N. DANIELS
Taffy DANOFF
Ron DANTE
Charles DANVERS
Evelyn DANZIG
Ken DARBY
Terence Trent D'ARBY
Marcus DARE
Bobby DARIN
August DARNELL
Shelby DARNELL
Chris DARWAY
Ted DARYLL
Doc DAUGHERTY
Hod DAVID
John DAVID
Sunny DAVID
Bill DAVIDSON
Eduardo DAVIDSON
Bob DAVIE
Iva DAVIES
Mike DAVIES
Billy DAVIS
Chip DAVIS
Janice DAVIS
Larry DAVIS
Mac DAVIS
Pepper DAVIS
Rainy DAVIS
Skeeter DAVIS
Arlan DAY
Bobby DAY
Joey DAY
Jon DAY
Daddio DAYLIE
Chris DE BURGH
Rafael DE LEON
Waldo DE LOS RIOS
Anton DE WAAL
Debbie DEAN
Eddie DEAN
Mary DEAN
Bunny DeBARGE
Gary DeCARLO
Jeanine DECKERS
Joey DEE
Johnnie DEE
Lenny DEE
Sylvia DEE
Tommy DEE
Rick DEES
Donald DeGRATE
Dux DeJOHN
Julie DeJOHN
Leo DeJOHN
Desmond DEKKER
Jimmy DeKNIGHT
Prentice DeLANEY
Pierre DELANOË
Claude DeMETRIUS
Tony DeMEUR
Joy DENNY
John DENVER
Suzanne DePASSE
Lynsey DePAUL
Paula DePORES
Robert DERMINER
Candy DeROUGE
Rick DERRINGER
Sugar Pie DeSANTO
Jackie DeSHANNON
Johnny DESMOND
Paul DESMOND
Alice DeSOTO
Buddy DeSYLVA
Yvonne DEVANEY
C.C. DeVILLE
Willy DeVILLE
Mohandas DeWESE
Al DEXTER
Guy D'HARDELOT
Richard V. Di CICCO
Keith DIAMOND
Max DIAMOND
Manu DIBANGO
Dez DICKERSON
Morris DICKERSON
Danny DILL
Jean DINNING
Lou DINNING
Ralph DINO
Joe DIXIE
Julius DIXON
Luther DIXON
Jimmie DODD
Malcolm DODDS
Thomas DOLBY
Morris DOLLISON
John Grayton DOLPHIN
Fats DOMINO
Bonita DONATO
Mona DONATO

Lonnie DONEGAN
Carlo DONIDA
William DOUCHETTE
Chip DOUGLAS
Glenn DOUGLAS
Lew DOUGLAS
Saxie DOWELL
Taime DOWNE
Gene DOZIER
Lamont DOZIER
Jimmy DRAKE
Clarence DRAYTON
Jean-Paul DREAU
Jimmy DRIFTWOOD
Matt DUBEY
Pye DUBOIS
Vernon DUKE
Sly DUNBAR
Johnny DUNCAN
Don DUNN
Donald "Duck" DUNN
Lorenzo DUNN
Jack DUPREE
Robbie DUPREE

E

Dennis EAST
Sheena EASTON
Billy ECKSTINE
George EDDY
Harry EDELSTEIN
Kenneth EDMONDS
Jerry EDMONTON
Bobby EDWARDS
Gus EDWARDS
Webley EDWARDS
Arthur EGNOIAN
Rohusuke EI
Kurtis EL KHALEEL
Leila EL KHALIFI
Bobby ELI
Joey B. ELLIS
Shirley ELLIS
Ted ELLIS
Lorraine ELLISON
Ziggy ELMAN
Vince ELY
Lee EMERSON
Leroy EMMANUEL
ENYA
Tom ERDELYI
Roky ERICKSON
Ahmet ERTEGUN
Jacqueline ERTEL
Dee ERVIN
Jesus ESCAMILLA
Jose Augusto ESQUIBEL
David ESSEX
Bernard ESTARDY
Gloria ESTEFAN
Steve ETTINGER
Darrell EUBANKS
Chris EVANS
Dale EVANS
Jean EVANS
Paul EVANS
Redd EVANS
David Franklin EWER

F

Bent FABRICIUS-BJERRE
Siobhan FAHEY
Sammy FAIN
Dede FAIRBANKS
Herman FAIRBANKS
Coventry FAIRCHILD
Travis FAIRCHILD
FALCO
Billy FALCON
Georgie FAME
Wayne FAMOUS
Kamaal FAREED
Donna FARGO
Frank FARIAN
Mimi FARINA
Peggy FARINA
Wes FARRELL
Cee FARROW
Eric FAULKNER
Buzz FEITEN
J. Nicolas FELGEN
Kurt FELTZ
Freddy FENDER
Shiller Shaun FEQUIERE
Iris FERNANDO
Tambi FERNANDO
Louis FERRARI
Edward FERRELL
Buddy FEYNE
Harold FIELDS
Romuald FIGUIER
Bob FINIZ
John L. FINNERAN
Lance FINNEY
Elisa FIORILLO
Carl T. FISCHER
Carl FISHER
Fred FISHER
Jack FISHMAN
Jay FISHMAN
Robert FITOUSSI
Daniel FLEISHOUR
Kye FLEMING
B.F. FLIP
Mike FLOREALE
Gerard FLORIO
Red FOLEY
Eddie FONTAINE
Frankie FORD
Mary FORD
Perry FORD
Jimmy Dee FORE
George FORREST
Larry FOTINE
Pete FOUNTAIN
Gloria FOWLES
Robin FOX
Paula FRANCES
Connie FRANCIS
Aretha FRANKLIN
Carolyn FRANKLIN
John FRED
Fergie FREDERIKSEN
Alan FREED
Arthur FREED
Ruth FREED
Max C. FREEDMAN
Roy FREELAND
Ernie FREEMAN
Paul FREES
Ace FREHLEY
James FREUD
Sylvia FRICKER
Freddy FRIDAY
Stephen FRIEDLAND
Bill FRIES
Max FRITH
Lefty FRIZZELL
Frances FROST
Richard FROST
Thomas FROST
Giuseppe FUCILLI
Dolores FULLER
Orena D. FULMER
Lowell FULSOM
Harvey FUQUA

G

Milt GABLER
Serge GAINSBOURG
Lee GALLO
Simon GALLUP
Albhy GALUTEN
Chris GANTRY
John Virgo GARRETT III
Snuff GARRETT
Green GARTSIDE
Bob GAUDIO
Noel GAY
Ronnie GAYLORD
Don GENSON
Bobbie GENTRY
Barbara GEORGE
Gil GEORGE
Jimmy GEORGE
Kenny GEORGE
Robin GEORGE
Raeford GERALD
Danyel GÉRARD
Greg GERARD
Paul GIACALONE
Bill GIANT
Andy GIBSON
Bob GIBSON
Damita Jo GIBSON
Sal GIGLIO Jr.
V.C. GILBERT
Dizzy GILLESPIE
Robert GINYARD
Harry GIOSASI
Hubert GIRAUD
Junior GISCOMBE
Charles Andre GLENN
Gary GLITTER
Henry GLOVER
Jean GLOVER
Ann GODWIN
Ernest GOLD
Ernie GOLD
Marian GOLD
Al GOODMAN
Larry GOODMAN
Alan GORDON
Jon GORDON
Mack GORDON
Rexton GORDON
Anna GORDY
Berry GORDY
George GORDY
Gwen GORDY
Iris GORDY
Kennedy GORDY
Robert GORDY
Thelma GORDY
Lesley GORE
Michael GORE
Eydie GORME
Dick GOSTING
Boon GOULD
Don GRADY
Charles GRAHAM
Lou GRAMM
Gerry GRANAHAN
Harold GRANT
Milton GRANT
Ed GRAY
Jerry GRAY
Von GRAY
Jerry GRAZIANO
Al GREEN
Florence GREEN
Peter GREEN
Tony GREEN
Peter John GREENALL
Earl GREENE
Jeanie GREENE
Bobby GREGG
C. Delyle GREGORY
Edwin GREINES
Maria GREVER
Paris GREY
Curly GRIFFIN
James GRIFFIN
William GRIFFIN
Jeffrey Warren GROB
Jerry GROSS
Carl GROSSMAN
Michael GUERRA
Christopher GUEST
Luis GUGLIELMI
Robert GUIDRY
Bonnie GUITAR
Tracii GUNS
Billy GUY
Ronnie GUY

H

Buddy HACKETT
Skip HAHN
Shelley HAIMS
Arsenio HALL
Graeme HALL
Jon Kingsley HALL
Rick HALL
David HALLYDAY
Christopher HAMILL
Al HAMILTON
Bob HAMILTON
Eugene HAMILTON
Russ HAMILTON
Jack HAMMER
Albert HAMMOND
Gladys HAMPTON
Paul HAMPTON
James S. HANCOCK
W.C. HANDY
Isabel HANSEN
Mich HANSEN
Otto HARBACH
E.Y. HARBURG
Regi HARGIS
Ron HARGRAVE
Steve HARLEY
W. Franke HARLING
Murrey HARMAN
Slim HARPO
Don HARRIS
James Samuel HARRIS
Ted HARRIS
George HARRISON
Deborah HARRY
Bobby HART
Freddie HART
Roger HART
David HASKINS
Kevin HASKINS
Tony HATCH
Donny HATHAWAY
Howard HAUSEY
Allen HAWIRKO
Ken HAWKER
Isaac HAYES
Michael Peter HAYES
Peter Lind HAYES
Henry HAYNES
Robert HAZARD
Eddie HAZEL
Lee HAZLEWOOD
Mike HAZLEWOOD
Nicky HEADON
Ted HEATH
HEAVY D
Fred HELLERMAN
Levon HELM
Ray HENDERSON
Jimi HENDRIX
Fred HENLEY
Patricia HENLEY
Kent HENRY
Keith HERMAN
Richie HERNANDEZ
Bernard HERRMANN
David HESS
Paul HEWSON
Ersel HICKEY
Robert HIGGINBOTHAM
Bertie HIGGINS
Monk HIGGINS
Diane HILDERBRAND

Billy HILL
Bunker HILL
Dusty HILL
Z.Z. HILL
Tony HILLER
Bob HILLIARD
Earl HINES
Nevelle HODGE
Christine HODGSON
Martin Lee HOENES
Noddy HOLDER
Brian HOLLAND
Eddie HOLLAND
Brenda HOLLOWAY
Wrecia HOLLOWAY
Buddy HOLLY
Carolyn HOLMES
Rupert HOLMES
Wally HOLMES
Per HOLM-PETERSEN
Isaac HOLT
Jake HOOKER
James HOOKER
Nellee HOOPER
Joseph HOOVEN
Marilyn HOOVEN
Jamie HORTON
McKinley HORTON
Vaughn HORTON
Ollie HOSKINS
Bart HOWARD
Bruce Robert HOWARD
Chesley HOWARD
Ken HOWARD
Tash HOWARD
Dayton HOWE
Brad HOWELL
Bob HUDSON
Glenda HUDSON
Saul HUDSON
Jack HUES
Leon HUFF
Brian HUGG
Mike HUGG
Bill HUGHES
Bunny HULL
Geraldine HUNT
Tommy HUNT
Ian HUNTER
Ivy Jo HUNTER
Mike HURST
Willie HUTCH
Wanda HUTCHINSON
Frankie L. HUTCHISON
Paul HYDE
Jeff HYMAN

I

Janis IAN
Charles IBGUI
Bobby ICON
Billy IDOL
Jorgen INGMANN
Joyce IRBY
Donnie IRIS
Jesse Eric ITZLER

J

Charles Henry JACKSON Jr.
Dave JACKSON
Dimple M. JACKSON
Fred JACKSON
George Harold JACKSON
J.J. JACKSON
Jackie JACKSON
Jermaine JACKSON
Joe JACKSON
Michael JACKSON
Mick JACKSON
Stonewall JACKSON
Wyn JACKSON
Gregory JACOBS
Jacob JACOBS
Cheryl JAMES
Doug JAMES
Elmore JAMES
Etta JAMES
Jimmy JAMES
Mark JAMES
Rick JAMES
Sonny JAMES
Sylvester JAMES
Tim JAMES
Tommy JAMES
Herbert JARCZYK
Michael JARY
Eve JAY
Fred JAY
Michael JAY
William JEFFERY
Frances JEFFORDS
Henry JEROME
Joan JETT
Elton JOHN
Robert JOHN
Djuana JOHNICAN
Brenda JOHNSON
Charles Icarus JOHNSON
Earl King JOHNSON
Errison JOHNSON
Garry JOHNSON
General JOHNSON
Jimmy JOHNSON
Jimmy Ray JOHNSON
Keg JOHNSON
Margaret JOHNSON
Robert Bubber JOHNSON
Robert White JOHNSON
Sid JOHNSON
Simone Antoinette JOHNSON
Syl JOHNSON
Joy Byers JOHNSTON
Pete JOLLY
George Wydell JONES Jr.
Eddie JONES
Emridge JONES
George JONES
George Curtis JONES
Gloria JONES
John Paul JONES
Kevin JONES
Michael JONES
Rick JONES
Stephen Charles JONES
Michael JONZUN
Dazz JORDAN
Joe JORDAN
Lonnie JORDAN
Joe JOSEA
Jeannie JOY
Udo JÜRGENS
Bill JUSTIS

K

Fudgie KAE
Bert KAEMPFERT
Stanley KAHAN
Marvin KAHN
Maewa KAIHAN
Wayne KAMBES
Manuela KAMOSI
Murray KANE
George KARAK
Kenny KAREN
Jerry KASENETZ
Ed KASSNER
Jeff KATZ
Charles E. KAUFMAN
Murray KAUFMAN
Dean KAY
John KAY
Buddy KAYE
Florence KAYE
Norman KAYE
Tony KAYE
Ernie K-DOE
Ramsey KEARNEY
Arrett KEEFER
Speedy KEEN
Brian KEITH
Lisa KEITH
Milton KELLEM
Ted KELLEM
Casey KELLY
James KENDIS
Eddie KENDRICKS
Joyce KENNEDY
Gilbert E. KENNINGTON
KENNY G
Walter KENT
Jo KERR
Wesaline Hopson KERR
Bernard KESSLAIR
Chaka KHAN
Perry KIBBLE
Johnny KIDD
Buddy KILLEN
Andy KIM
Tom KIMMEL
Albert KING
Anna KING
Anthony KING
B.B. KING
Ben E. KING
Carole KING
Gary KING
Harry J. KING
Jonathan KING
Pee Wee KING
Tom KING
Gershon KINGSLEY
Robert KINGSTON
David KINZIE
Jim KIRK
Steve KIRK
Denny KLAWSON
Paul (2) KLEIN
Jayney KLIMEK
Gary KNIGHT
Holly KNIGHT
Richard KNIGHT
Terry KNIGHT
Fred KNOBLOCK
Frank KOCIAN
Géo KOGER
Alan KOHAN
Jerry KOLLENBURG
Otto KOLLMAN
Dale KRANTZ
Joern Volsgaard KRISTENSEN
Leah KUNKEL

L

Patti LaBELLE
Yves LACOMBLEZ
David LAFLAMME
Linda LAFLAMME
Denny LAINE
Frankie LAINE
Corky LAING
Sol LAKE
Leon LANDGREN
Phyllis LANDSBERG
Bernie LANE
Burton LANE
Grace LANE
Ken LANE
Mickey Lee LANE
Red LANE
Mutt LANGE
Jens Kjaer LARSEN
Åke Gerhard LARSSON
D.C. LaRUE
Denise LaSALLE
James LAST
Paul LAURENCE
Linda LAURIE
Stijn LAUWERS
Kent LaVOIE
Yves-Jacques LAVOT
Eddie LAWRENCE
Jack LAWRENCE
Rhett LAWRENCE
Steve LAWRENCE
R.W. LAWS
Ricky LAYNE
Mickey LEADER
Mike LEANDER
Huddie LEDBETTER
Ish LEDESMA
Les LEDO
Dickey LEE
Geddy LEE
Ira LEE
Jack LEE
Laura LEE
Martin LEE
Nikki LEE
Peggy LEE
Tommy LEE
Sonny LeGLAIRE
Jerry LEIBER
Mitch LEIGH
Prince LELEIOHOKU
Pierre LeMAIRE
Francis LEMARQUE
Mike LENDELL
Evelyne LENTON
Anita LEONARD
Sylvester LEVAY
Cy LEVITAN
Estelle LEVITT
Eunice LEVY
Gail LEVY
Marcy LEVY
Bunny LEWIS
Furry LEWIS
Huey LEWIS
Sam LEWIS
Ted LIFE
Alex LIFESON
Philamore LINCOLN
Rudi LINDT
Sam LING
Harry LINK
Horace LINSLEY
Jack LITTLE
John LiVIGNI
Jerry LIVINGSTON
Neville LIVINGSTON
Bernhard LLOYD
Ian LLOYD
Nick LOCKWOOD
E. Ein LOGGINS
Barbara LOMAS
Burt LONG
Frederick LONG
Shorty LONG
Michael David LOOKOFSKY
Peter LORD
Bryan LOREN
John D. LOUDERMILK
Charlie LOUVIN
Ira LOUVIN
Bernie LOWE
Eric LOWEN
Joe LUBIN
Stephen LUNT
Annabella LWIN
Gene LYND
Barbara LYNN
Cheryl LYNN
Gloria LYNNE
Jeff LYNNE
Ruth LYONS

M
Tony MACAULAY
Ewan MacCOLL
Iain MacFADYEN
Cecil MACK
Geoff MACK
Ira MACK
Lonnie MACK
Fred Aylor MacRAE
John MADARA
Pee Wee MADDUX
Bobby MADERA
Tito MADI
Guy MAGENTA
Taj MAHAL
Deadric MALONE
Kurt MALOO
Henry MANCINI
James MANGRUM
Barry MANILOW
Andrew MANN
Barry MANN
Dave MANN
Herbie MANN
Jeff MANN
Kal MANN
Lois MANN
Paul MANN
Dick MANNING
MANTOVANI
Phil MANZANERA
Rolf MARBOT
Peggy MARCH
Sol MARCUS
Teena MARIE
Jon MARK
Pigmeat MARKHAM
Biz MARKIE
Guy MARKS
Spiro MARKS
Bob MARLEY
Ziggy MARLEY
Ric MARLOW
Johnny MARR
Tracy MARROW
Mick MARS
Celia MARSHALL
Guy MARSHALL
Michael MARSHALL
Allen MARTANCIK
Vince MARTELL
MARTIKA
Dean MARTIN Jr.
Hearlon MARTIN
Lennie MARTIN
Marilyn MARTIN
Moon MARTIN
Trade MARTIN
Lewis MARTINÉE
Rudy MARTINEZ
Holt MARVELL
Hank MARVIN
Hugh MASEKELA
Sammy MASTERS
John MASTRANGELO

Louis MATHIS
Eric MATTHEW
Denise MATTHEWS
Kaiya MATTHEWS
Theresa MATTHIAS
Paul MAURIAT
Christopher MAX
Ray MAXWELL
Iris MAY
Hans-Jörg MAYER
Henry MAYER
Thomas McALEESE
Smokey McALLISTER
Romeo McCALL
Linda McCARTNEY
Paul McCARTNEY
O.B. McCLINTON
Jimmy McCRACKLIN
Junie McCREE
Ellas McDANIEL
Jack McDUFF
Dave McENERY
Mike McGEAR
Ralston McGRIFF
Roger McGUINN
Anne McIAN
Goldy McJOHN
Scotty McKAY
Scott McKENZIE
Van McLAIN
Shamus M'COOL
Warner McPHERSON
Wyatt McPHERSON
Rod McQUEEN
Ted McRAE
Mark McVEY
Christine McVIE
Punky MEADOWS
Joe MEEK
Terry MELCHER
Robert MELLIN
Lord MELODY
Fred MENDELSOHN
Norma MENDOZA
Freddie MERCURY
Michael MERLO
Wandra MERRELL
Alan MERRILL
Bob MERRILL
Frank MERTENS
Wilbur MESHEL
Helmut MEYERS
Marcus MEYN
George MICHAEL
Michele MICHAELE
Bret MICHAELS
Lee Eugene MICHAELS
Roy MICHAELS
Stephen MICHAELS
John MILES
Bubber MILEY
Francis Philip MILITARY
John A. MILLER
Nathan MILLER
Ronald Norman MILLER

Lucky MILLINDER
Hank MILLS
Argentry MITCHELL
Bobby MITCHELL
Ronny MITCHELL
Jason MIZELL
Essra MOHAWK
Arturo MOLINA Jr.
Larry MOLLIN
Chips MOMAN
Dick MONDA
Jeff MONDAY
Eddie MONEY
Bob MONROE
Martin MONTAGUE
Tony MONTANA
Lou MONTE
Chris MONTEZ
Lisa MONTGOMERY
Marvin MONTGOMERY
Debra Mae MOORE
John Edward MOORE
Mark Anthony MORALES
Mike MORE
Marianito MORES
Rushton MOREVE
Freddy MORGAN
Lee MORRIS
Walter Lee MORRIS
Walter MORRISON
Shadow MORTON
Ken MOULE
James MTUME
Hakim Rashad MUHAMMAD
Richard MULLAN
Susanne MÜLLER-PI
Moon MULLICAN
Mark MUNIZ
Michael MURPHEY
Jean Sharp MURPHY
Henry MURRAY
Lyn MURRAY
Mitch MURRAY
Ted MURRY
Valerie MURTAGH
Giuseppe MUSTACCHI
Billy MYLES
N
Vinny NACCARATO
Otha NASH
Pete NASH
Nathaniel NATHAN
Kim NAZEL
Jimmy NEBB
Joe NEGRO
Al NEIBURG
Vince NEIL
Earl NELSON
Neil NEPHEW
Billy NESS
Loz NETTO
Al NEVINS
Norman NEWELL
Anthony NEWLEY

Herbert NEWMAN
Kelly NICKELS
Charly NIESSEN
Andrew NOLAND
Terry NOLAND
Bob NORMAN
Alex NORTH
Daniel NORTON
Bill NORVAS
Aldo NOVA
Don NOVELLO
Gary NUMAN
Laura NYRO
O
Ric OCASEK
Billy OCEAN
Brooks O'DELL
Kenny O'DELL
John O'DEN
George O'DOWD
Charles Raymond OFFENBERG
Spooner OLDHAM
Fred OLDÖRP
Chico De OLIVEIRA
Tony ORLANDO
Benjamin ORR
Roland ORZABAL
Robert Eugene OSBORN
Ozzy OSBOURNE
Charles OSGOOD
Lee OSKAR
Stanley OSSMAN
Gilbert O'SULLIVAN
John OSWALD
Clyde OTIS
Johnny OTIS
Shuggie OTIS
Bonnie OWENS
Shirley OWENS
P
Rickie PAGE
Jeffrey Robert PAIN
Bobby PAINE
Larson PAINE
Wally PALMAR
Florrie PALMER
King PALMER
Sandy PALMER
Peter PAN
Jean-Pierre PAQUIN
Harry PARESS
Jeff PARIS
Barry PARKER
Junior PARKER
Ross PARKER
Willia Dean PARKER
Robert PARLEE
Cliff PARMAN
Clarence PAUL
Les PAUL
Mark PAUL
Doris PAYNE
Leon PAYNE
Billy PEACHES

Charlie PEACOCK
Marti PELLOW
Mike PENDER
Dan PENN
Richard PENNIMAN
Ray PENNINGTON
Alisa PEOPLES
Buddy PEPPER
Danny PEPPERMINT
Hugo PERETTI
Nils PERNE
Jean-Jacques PERREY
Jack PERRICONE
Willie PERRYMAN
Betty PETERSON
Frank PETERSON
Paul PETERSON
Thomas John PETERSON
Peter PFAB
Gary PHILIPPET
Terry PHILIPS
Michelle PHILLIPS
Jim PHOTOGLO
Edith PIAF
Angelo PICCIONI
Irwin PINCUS
Gene PITNEY
John POCISK
Bonnie POINTER
Edward POLA
Peter POLL
Lew POLLACK
Doc POMUS
Jack PONTI
Iggy POP
W. Albert POSER
Mike POST
Franck POURCEL
Lester POWELL
Teddy POWELL
Chet POWERS
Tony POWERS
Chano POZO
Stephan PRAGER
Lili PREMILOVICH
Reg PRESLEY
Johnny PRESTON
André PREVIN
Dory PREVIN
Chilton PRICE
Harvey PRICE
Ronn PRICE
Maxi PRIEST
PRINCE
Spencer PROFFER
Skip PROKOP
Curly PUTMAN
Q
Suzi QUATRO
Eddy QUINTELA
Fizzy QWICK
R
Buzz RABIN
Trevor RABIN
Bobby RACKEP

James RADO
Jerry RAGOVOY
Derf Reklaw RAHEEM
Ma RAINEY
Ralph RAINGER
Marvin RAINWATER
Buck RAM
Phil RAMACON
Bill RAMAL
Eddie RAMBEAU
Giulio RAPETTI
Herman RAREBELL
Renato RASCEL
Lisa RATNER
Marci RAUER
Bruno RAVEL
Eraldo RAVIOLO
Anthony RAY
Bob RAY
Don RAY
Don RAYE
Joe RAYE
Andy RAZAF
Mac REBENNACK
Gene REDD Jr.
Gene REDD Sr.
Ramona REDD
Helen REDDY
Gino REDI
Jerry REED
Eskew REEDER
Gordon REES
Russ REGAN
Domenico REGIACORTE
Noel REGNEY
Bud REHAK
Antonio REID
Perri Arlette REID
Johnny REINE
Gladys REINHARDT
Joe REISMAN
Leon RENÉ
Rafael RENÉ
Tony RENIS
Jacques REVAUX
Paul REVERE
Al REX
Sergio REYES
Eugene REYNOLDS
Jody REYNOLDS
Malvina REYNOLDS
Nick RHODES
Bonny RICE
Eddie RICE
Josh RICE
Allan RICH
Don RICH
Cliff RICHARD
Deke RICHARDS
Dick RICHARDS
Johnny RICHARDS
Regina RICHARDS
Terry RICHARDS
Nicholas RICHARDSON
George RICHEY

Carlton RIDENHOUR
Stan RIDGWAY
Teddy DeLano RIEDEL
Clemon Timothy RILEY
Gary RINALDO
Peter RISINGHAM
Claus RITTER
Gordon RITTER
Pete RIVERA
Johnny RIVERS
David RIVKIN
Robert RIVKIN
Jerry RIX
Marco RIZO
Dee ROBB
Marty ROBBINS
Smokey ROBERDS
Kevin ROBERSON
Allan ROBERTS
Art ROBERTS
Austin ROBERTS
Bob ROBERTS
Jeanne ROBERTS
Paddy ROBERTS
McLeod ROBERTSON
Paul ROBI
Sid ROBIN
Gerry ROBINSON
Jack ROBINSON
Jessie Mae ROBINSON
Joseph ROBINSON
Morgan C. ROBINSON
Smokey ROBINSON
Sylvia ROBINSON
Rikki ROCKETT
Rick RODELL
Vincent RODOMISTA
Johnny RODRIGUEZ
D.J. ROGERS
Jimmie O. ROGERS
Jimmy ROGERS
Lee ROGERS
Smokey ROGERS
Tony ROJAS
Desiree ROLLOCKS
Gary ROMERO
Joseph RONCORONI
Ann RONELL
Axl ROSE
Billy ROSE
Ed ROSE
Beverly ROSS
Bud ROSS
Jerry ROSS
Mark ROSS
Brian ROSSI
Nino ROTA
Irving ROTH
Eddi ROTHÉ
Talbot ROTHWELL
Theda ROUSH
Robb ROYER
Herwig RUDISSER
Gabriel RUIZ
Bobby RUSH

Jennifer RUSH
Jerry RUSH
Bob RUSSELL
Brenda RUSSELL
Leon RUSSELL
Paul RYAN
Maggie RYDER
Mitch RYDER
S
Raphael SAADIQ
Bob SAGE
Carole Bayer SAGER
Eddison SAINSBURY
Nicola SALERNO
Domingo SAMUDIO
C.B. SAMUEL
Jerry SAMUELS
Marty SANDERS
William Nelson SANDERS
Zell SANDERS
Chas SANDFORD
Christian SARREL
Jan SAVAGE
Jean SAWYER
Sky SAXON
Leo SAYER
Skip SCARBOROUGH
Greg SCELSA
Marilyn SCHACK
Katherine SCHAFFNER
Warren SCHATZ
Lalo SCHIFRIN
Aaron SCHROEDER
Ira SCHUSTER
Andreas SCHWARZ-RUSZCZYNSKI
Jack SCOTT
Linda SCOTT
Ronnie SCOTT
Tim SCOTT
SEAL
Dan SEALS
Lana SEBASTIAN
Paul SEBASTIAN
Jon SECADA
Sil SEDORES
Joe SENECA
Jean SENN
Glenna SESSION
Taja SEVELLE
Steven SEVERIN
David SEVILLE
John B. SHAFFER III
Amir SHAKIR
Del SHANNON
Hal SHAPER
Joseph SHAPIRO
Mike SHAPIRO
Bobby SHARP
Kim SHARP
Louis SHARPE
James T. SHAW
Todd SHAW
Gloria SHAYNE
Larry SHAYNE

SHEILA E.
Peter SHELLEY
Bob SHELTON
Gary SHELTON
Joe SHELTON
Shep SHEPHERD
James SHEPPARD
Neil SHEPPARD
T.G. SHEPPARD
Tony SHERIDAN
Lee SHERIDEN
Allan SHERMAN
Sue SHIFRIN
Jimmy SHIRL
Michelle SHOCKED
Hank SHOCKLEE
Keith SHOCKLEE
Lanny SHORE
Mickey SHORR
Dave SILVER
Bebu SILVETTI
Gene SIMMONS
Simtec SIMMONS
Paul SIMON
Nina SIMONE
Moises SIMONS
Britt SIMONSON
Richard SIMPSON
Charles SINGLETON
Margie SINGLETON
Raynoma SINGLETON
Nikki SIXX
Robert Doyle SKELTON
Sunny SKYLAR
Frank SLAY
Darby SLICK
Grace SLICK
P.F. SLOAN
N.D. SMART II
Mick SMILEY
Alfred J. SMITH
Anthony Terrell SMITH
Billy Dawn SMITH
Eric SMITH
Hurricane SMITH
James Marcus SMITH
James Todd SMITH
Keely SMITH
Michael Larry SMITH
Richard David SMITH
Ricky Darnell SMITH
Robert James SMITH
Sammi SMITH
Stacy SMITH
Thomassina SMITH
Tweed SMITH
Will SMITH
Charles SMYTH
Phoebe SNOW
Eddie SNYDER
Brian SOARES
Marcy SOCKEL
Pietro SOFFICI
Bernard SOLOMON
Belouis SOME

Simon SOUSSAN
Joe SOUTH
Hal SOUTHERN
Charles SOUZA
Red SOVINE
Norman SPAN
Milton SPARKS
Randy SPARKS
Anne SPEAR
Skip SPENCE
Mark SPIRO
Rick SPRINGFIELD
Tom SPRINGFIELD
Craig SPROVACH
Jon ST. JAMES
Nick ST. NICHOLAS
Joe STAFFORD Jr.
Lou STALLMAN
Brenard STALLWORTH
Trevor STANFORD
Michael STANLEY
Paul STANLEY
Cyril STAPLETON
Edwin STARR
Lucille STARR
Maurice STARR
Randy STARR
Ringo STARR
Candi STATON
Melvin STEALS
Mervin STEALS
Robert STEELE
Yasmin Elvira STEENHOLDT
Mark STEIN
Larry STEINBACHEK
Marcel STELLMAN
April STEVENS
Carl STEVENS
Cat STEVENS
Even STEVENS
Geoffrey STEVENS
Lona STEVENS
Mort STEVENS
Ray STEVENS
Shakin' STEVENS
Steve STEVENS
Bobby STEVENSON
W.S. STEVENSON
William STEVENSON
STEVIE B
Paul STEWART
Redd STEWART
Sylvester STEWART
Al STILLMAN
STING
Don STIRLING
Simon STOKES
Mike STOLLER
Jesse STONE
Joseph Louis STONE
Billy STORM
Allen STORY
Harold STOTT
Izzy STRADLIN
Elliot STRAITE

Ruth STRATCHBORNEO
Janey STREET
Liza STRIKE
Cynthia STROTHER
Joe STRUMMER
Chad STUART
Dave STUART
Levi STUBBS
Donna SUMMER
Henry Lee SUMMER
Richie SUPA
Red SURREY
Brenda SUTTON
Stacey SWAIN
Bettye SWANN
Pieter SWEVAL
Rik SWINN
Bill SWOFFORD

T

Alessandro TACCANI
Phyllis TAFF
Jules TAUB
Bernie TAUPIN
Bernard TAYLOR
Billy TAYLOR
Chip TAYLOR
Chuck TAYLOR
Irving TAYLOR
J.T. TAYLOR
Little Johnny TAYLOR
Paul TAYLOR
Skip TAYLOR
Richard TEE
Towa TEI
Joey TEMPEST
Nino TEMPO
Robert TEPPER
Dorothy TERRISS
Mike TERRY
William TESONE
James TESTA
Joe TEX
Rosetta THARPE
Sandy THEORET
Fats THEUS
Bob THIELE
Frederick THOMAS
Gene THOMAS
Irma THOMAS
Kenny THOMAS
Michael THOMAS
Susan THOMAS
Hank THOMPSON
Kay THOMPSON
Porl THOMPSON
Sonny THOMPSON
Wayne Carson THOMPSON
Teri THORNTON
Al TIMOTHY
Fred TOBIAS
Laurence TOLHURST
Dino TOME
Dennis TOMICH
Pinky TOMLIN
Marq TORIEN
Mel TORME
TOTÒ
Allen TOUSSAINT
Jeff TOWNES
Al TRACE
Buck TRAIL
Mike TRAMP
Jackie TRENT
Armando TROVAIOLI
Annette TUCKER
Richard Anthony TUFO
Ike TURNER
Joe Lynn TURNER
John TURNER
Scott TURNER
Tina TURNER
Zeb TURNER
Roberta TWAIN
Nigel TWIST
Conway TWITTY
Kay TWOMEY
Steven TYLER
T. Texas TYLER
January TYME

U

Miriam UNIMAN

V

Kurt VALAQUEN
Mike VALE
Ritchie VALENS
Kevin VALENTINE
Jim VALLANCE
Gloria VAN CLEVE
Nick VAN EEDE
Jimmy VAN HEUSEN
Robert VAN WINKLE
Steven VAN ZANDT
Kenny VANCE
Harry VANDA
Adrian VANDENBERG
Lee VANDERBILT
Les VANDYKE
Daniel VANGARDE
VANGELIS
Koenraad VAN-LISHOUT
Teddy VANN
Randy VANWARMER
Henri VARNA
Claude VASORI
Joe VEASEY
Bobby VEE
Lolly VEGAS
Pat VEGAS
Lonnie VENCENT
Steve VENET
Billy VERA
Dino VERDE
Humberto VERGARA
Maria VIDAL
Donnie VIE
Joe VILLA
René VILLARD
Gene VINCENT
John VINCENT
Anna VITO
Janet VOGEL
Ron VOLZ
Albert VON TILZER
Harry VON TILZER

W

Myron WACHENDORF
Dan WAHLGREN
Kathy WAKEFIELD
Lisa WALDEN
Wendy WALDMAN
Aaron WALKER
Jerry Jeff WALKER
Jr. WALKER
Kurt WALKER
Steven WALKER
Van WALLS
Jim WALTERS
Billy WARD
Gil WARD
Johnny WARMAN
Pete WARNER
Christian WARREN
Harry WARREN
David WAS
Don WAS
Dinah WASHINGTON
Jeanette WASHINGTON
Chris WATERS
Bo WATSON
Johnny WATSON
Franz WAXMAN
Fee WAYBILL
Artie WAYNE
Bernie WAYNE
Curtis WAYNE
Dig WAYNE
Sid WAYNE
Blue WEAVER
Laura WEBB
Murray WECHT
Henry WECK
Herb WEINER
Bobby WEINSTEIN
Ben WEISMAN
George David WEISS
Mary WELLS
Señor WENCES
Gary WEST
Jerry WEST
Leslie WEST
Sonny WEST
Tommy WEST
Johnny WESTERN
Richard WESTFIELD
Paul WESTON
Robert Patrick WESTON
Albert WEYMAN
Yolanda WHITAKER
Barry WHITE
David WHITE
Joan WHITE
Pearl WHITE
Reggie WHITE
Peter WHITEHEAD
Joan WHITNEY
Hudson WHITTAKER
Danny WILDE
Kim WILDE
Marty WILDE
Ricky WILDE
George WILDER
Matthew WILDER
Walter WILDER
Warner WILDER
Charles WILDMAN
Crawford WILKERSON
John Buck WILKIN
Andre WILLIAMS
Boris WILLIAMS
Charles WILLIAMS
Dave WILLIAMS
Deniece WILLIAMS
Dub WILLIAMS
Frederick B. WILLIAMS
Hank WILLIAMS
Hugh WILLIAMS
June Watson WILLIAMS
Linda WILLIAMS
Marlon WILLIAMS
Otis Clayburne WILLIAMS
Red WILLIAMS
Sonny Boy WILLIAMSON II
Allee WILLIS
Chuck WILLIS
Ginger WILLIS
Hal WILLIS
Bob WILSON
Clyde WILSON
Forrest WILSON
Murry WILSON
Shanice WILSON
Carvin WINANS
Jesse WINCHESTER
Hal WINN
June WINTERS
Muff WINWOOD
Fred WISE
Debbie WITKOWSKI
Anka WOLBERT
Richard Lee WOLD
Dick WOLF
Ina WOLF
Peter WOLF
Steve WOLFE
John WOLOSCHUK
Cecil WOMACK
Linda WOMACK
Stevie WONDER
Ken WOOD
Terrell WOOD
Nick WOODS
Pearl WOODS
Sheb WOOLEY
Bobby WORTH
Betty WRIGHT
Dale WRIGHT
Philip WRIGHT
Robert Byron WRIGHT
Sid WYCHE
Zakk WYLDE
P.G. WYLDER
Tammy WYNETTE
Philippe WYNN

Y

Christine YARIAN
Steven YATES
Jack YELLEN
Peter YELLOWSTONE
Yutaka YOKOKURA
Bob YOSCO
Andre Romell YOUNG
Chip YOUNG
Jesse Colin YOUNG
Marvin YOUNG
Vicki YOUNG
Timi YURO

Z

ZACAR
Gary ZEKLEY
Aryan ZERO
Chip Z'NUFF
Irwin Elliott ZUCKER
Walter ZWOL

Alternate Names for Writers in Indices

A	
Lee Abbott	Jack LEE
Joseph Abend	Hank BEDUCCI
Andrew A. Acuarulo	Andy ACKERS
Frances Adair	Frances JEFFORDS
Billy Adams	Kevin ADAMS
Kurt Adams	Jimmy VAN HEUSEN
Skipper Adams	David SEVILLE
Michael Lee Aday	Marvin Lee ADAY
Joel Adelberg	Jeff BARRY
Keith Chagall Adelsohn	Keith HERMAN
Keith Herman Adelsohn	Keith HERMAN
Evelyne Adrians	Lana SEBASTIAN
Helen Folasade Adu	Helen ADU
Vladimir Nikitich Afanasieff	Walter AFANASIEFF
Don Louis Agreti	Don GRADY
Zyah Ahmonue	Malcolm ANTHONY
Jimmie Ainsworth	Jimmie O. ROGERS
Mike Akapoff	Ernie FREEMAN
Al B. Sure!	Albert Joseph BROWN
Louis Al	Louis MATHIS
Ramon Arcusa Alcón	Ramon ARCUSA
Fitzroy Alexander	Lord MELODY
Gary Alexander	Jules ALEXANDER
Jules Gary Alexander	Jules ALEXANDER
Keith Vincent Constantine Alexander	Keith DIAMOND
John Alford	John ALLISON
Kenneth Alford	Kenneth J. ALFORD
Nathaniel A. Allen Jr.	Na ALLEN
Christopher Thomas Allen	Chris CROSS
George Allen	Georgio ALLENTINI
Joey Allen	Joseph CAGLE
Margarite Almeda	Sunny SKYLAR
Almo	Alan GORDON
Randy Alpert	Randy BADAZZ
Gerhard Altstedt	Otto KOLLMAN
Jack Altwerger	John ALTWERGER
Brandon Aly	Alan ALY
Opal Jean Amburgey	Jean CHAPEL
Stuart Ames	Stuart AVIG
Barbara Amesbury	Bill AMESBURY
David Amy	Bruce BROMBERG
Peter Anders	Pete ANDREOLI
Tobias William Andersen	Tobias ANDERSEN
André Cymone Anderson	André CYMONE
Andre Simon Anderson	André CYMONE
E. Anderson	Chuck BERRY
John Roy Anderson	Jon ANDERSON
John William Anderson	John W. ANDERSON
Katherine Anderson	Katherine SCHAFFNER
Toby Anderson	Tobias ANDERSEN
Walter B. Anderson	Sonny ANDERSON
Bonita Ann Andre	Bonita DONATO
Ronald Lawrence Andre	Ronald ANDRE
Andre Andrians	Paul SEBASTIAN
Lina Andrians	Lana SEBASTIAN
Patricia Andrzejewski	Pat BENATAR
Bob Andy	Keith ANDERSON
Ish Angel	Ish LEDESMA
Robert Anson	Philamore LINCOLN
Pete Antell	Pete ANTEL
Marc Anthony	Mark MUNIZ
Mark Anthony	Mark MUNIZ
Mark Anthony	Tony HATCH
Raymond Antonini	Ray ANTHONY
Peter Blaise Antonio	Pete ANTEL
Benjamin Anzelevitz	Ben BERNIE
Luca Anzilotti	John Virgo GARRETT III
David Leon Appell	Dave APPELL
Mary Susan Applegate	Mary APPLEGATE
Michael Joseph Apruzzese	Mike ANDRE
Rodd Arden	Dave SILVER
Hyman Arluck	Harold ARLEN
George Armand	Joe REISMAN
Reginald Moxon Armitage	Noel GAY
Chris Armstrong	Lester POWELL
James Arnold	Kokomo ARNOLD
Sidney Arnondin	Sidney ARODIN
Victor Aronson	Ted KELLEM
Peter Arpadys	Pierre-Alain DAHAN
Joseph Arrington Jr.	Joe TEX
Robert Anthony Arvonio	Bobby ARVON
Charles William Ashworth	Charlie PEACOCK
David Asner	Pepper DAVIS
Bambaataa Khayan Assim	Afrika BAMBAATAA
Bob Astor	Robert DADE
Bob Attlesey	Bob SHELTON
Joe Attlesey	Joe SHELTON
Georgie Auld	John ALTWERGER
Timothy James Auringer	Tim JAMES
Rosemary Timotea Aurro	Timi YURO
Christine Authors	Christine HODGSON
Francis Thomas Avallone	Frankie AVALON
Shirley Enid Avery	Teri THORNTON
Valerie Avon	Valerie MURTAGH
Aida Ayala	Corina AYALA
Marco Rizo Ayala	Marco RIZO
Myint Myint Aye	Annabella LWIN
Muhammad Abdul Aziz	Jermaine JACKSON
Charles Aznaourian	Charles AZNAVOUR
Shanour Varenagh Aznavurjian	Charles AZNAVOUR
B	
B. Fresh	Brenard STALLWORTH
B. Junior	Richard BARRETT
Edward Chester Babcock	Jimmy VAN HEUSEN
Babyface	Kenneth EDMONDS
Carole Bayer Bacharach	Carole Bayer SAGER
Randolph Charles Bachman	Randy BACHMAN
Johnny Backbeat	John BADANJEK
Angelo Badalamenti	Andy BADALE
Angelo Badale	Andy BADALE
Waliou Jacques Daniel Badarou	Wally BADAROU
Margarita Mimi Baez	Mimi FARINA
Ross Bagdasarian	David SEVILLE
Harald Baierl	P.G. WYLDER
J. R. Bailey	Ralph BAILEY
James Ralph Bailey	Ralph BAILEY
Raisie Michael Bailey	Razzy BAILEY
Steven John Bailey	Steven SEVERIN
J. Baird	Bernard SOLOMON
Gloria Shayne Baker	Gloria SHAYNE
John Baker	Jon DAY
Jonathan Charles Baker	Jon DAY
Linda Baker	Linda LAFLAMME
McHouston Baker	Mickey BAKER
John Baldwin	John Paul JONES
John Paul Baldwin	John Paul JONES
David William Balfe	Rod McQUEEN
Umpeylia Marema Balinton	Sugar Pie DeSANTO
Harry Balk	Tom KING
Reginald Maurice Ball	Reg PRESLEY
Timothy Wayne Ball	Dig WAYNE
Francis Drake Ballard	Pat BALLARD
John Andrew Banfield	Jon BANFIELD
Daniel Bangalter	Daniel VANGARDE
Darrell Banks	Darrell EUBANKS
Peter Banks	Peter W. BANKS
Peter Memory Banks	Peter Douglas Cameron BANKS
R.C. Bannon	Royal C. BANNON
Philip Baptiste	Phil BAPTISTE
David Barbe	Dave BARBAROSSA
Mary Ann Barcaro	Dux DeJOHN
Annette Bard	Toni CHILDS
Dave Barker	David CROOKS
Lawrence Barnard	Larson PAINE
Robert Barnard	Bobby PAINE
Bettye Jean Crutcher Barnes	Bettye CRUTCHER
Martin Barnes	Martin LEE
Charlie Barnet	Dale BENNETT
Robin Barnetti	Robin FOX

Michael Barratt	Shakin' STEVENS
Jonny Bartels	Kurt FELTZ
Curt Bartholomew	Barry CURTIS
Betty Barton	Bettye SWANN
Dave Barton	Dave BARTHOLOMEW
Rob Base	Robert GINYARD
Giuseppe Ottavia Basile	Joss BASELLI
Joseph Octave Basile	Joss BASELLI
Antonia Basilotta	Toni BASIL
Thomas Lee Bass	Tommy LEE
Ralph Basso Jr.	Ralph BASS
Ellas Otha Bates	Ellas McDANIEL
Nicholas James Bates	Nick RHODES
Margaret Annemarie Battavio	Peggy MARCH
Victor William Batty	Steve WOLFE
Carole Jean Bayer	Carole Bayer SAGER
Bayété	Todd COCHRAN
Theodore Debs Bayless	T.D. BAYLESS
Khalis Bayyan	Ronald BELL
Richard Earl Beach Jr.	Reb BEACH
Trevor Beacham	Chris EVANS
Leonard Stanley Beadle	Len BEADLE
Teddy Bear	Ted McRAE
Robert L. Beavers	Jackey BEAVERS
Lew Bedell	Lou BIDEU
Lewis Joseph Bedinsky	Lou BIDEU
Tommy Bedwell	Bernice BEDWELL
Lionel Begleiter	Lionel BART
Israel Isidore Beilin	Irving BERLIN
Peter Jan Cor Belenky	Peter COR
Robert Steven Belew	Adrian BELEW
Andrew Ivan Bell	Andy BELL
Anthony Bell	Tony BELL
Anthony Salvatore Bell	Tony BELL
Cynthia Bell	Cynthia STROTHER
Kevin Bell	Amir BAYYAN
Larry Vernard Bell	Larry BELL
Mark Thomas Bell	Marcus BELL
Raymond Bell	Harry BELAFONTE
Ronald Nathan Bell	Ronald BELL
Theresa Bell	Leon HUFF
Sammy Bella	Wilbur MESHEL
Daniel Edward Bellack	Dan BELLOC
Emerson Lee Bellamy	Lee EMERSON
Tracey Bryn Belland	Tracey BRYN
Jenny Bellestar	Theresa MATTHIAS
Mary L. Belline	Louise BELL
Anthony Bellusci	Tony BELLUS
Jean-Paul Benchetrit	Jean-Paul DREAU
Norma Bender	Norma MENDOZA
Frank Bendinelli	Ralston McGRIFF
Claude A. Benjamin	Bennie BENJAMIN
Tim Benjamin	Helmut MEYERS
Deadly Headley Bennett	Headley BENNETT
Felix Headley Bennett	Headley BENNETT
Headley George Bennett	Headley BENNETT
Jane Sperry Bennett	Jane CONNELL
Sanford Irving Bereofsky	Sandy BARON
Biagio Bergantino	Borney BERGANTINE

Max Berlin	Marc CERRONE
Mendel Berlinger	Milton BERLE
Friedel Berlipp	Peter POLL
Henry Bernard	Henry GLOVER
Lisa Bernard	Lisa KEITH
Bertrand Russell Berns	Bert BERNS
Alan Kenneth Bernstein	Alan BERNSTEIN
Louis Bernstein	Leonard BERNSTEIN
Neil Bernstein	Neil NEPHEW
Charles Edward Anderson Berry	Chuck BERRY
John Berry	John Bobby BERRY
Gerard Bertelkamp	Beeb BIRTLES
Bernd Bertie	Bert KAEMPFERT
Ange Eugene Betti	Henri BETTI
Forrest Richard Betts	Dickey BETTS
Howard Beverly	Frankie BEVERLY
Eithne Ni Bhraonain	ENYA
Arthur Ronald Bickerton	Wayne BICKERTON
Jan Bidewell	Jan BUCKINGHAM
Joe Bihari	Joe JOSEA
Julius Bihari	Jules TAUB
Saul Samuel Bihari	Sam LING
Bernard Stanley Bilk	Acker BILK
Birdlegs	Sidney BANKS
Biri	Ornella Ferrari COLOMBI
Bud Birmingham	Maggie ANDREWS
Biscuit	Steven WALKER
Frank Bjorn	Bent FABRICIUS-BJERRE
William Patton Black Jr.	Bill BLACK
Lawrence Ernest Black	Larry BLACKMON
Larry Ernest Blackmon	Larry BLACKMON
Donald Blackstone	Don BLACK
Howard Blaikley	Alan BLAIKLEY
Howard Blaikley	Ken HOWARD
John Hendry Blair	Johnny CYMBAL
James Hubert Blake	Eubie BLAKE
Brian Douglas Blanchard	Brian SOARES
Carte Blanche	Bernie TAUPIN
Milton Bland	Monk HIGGINS
Virginia P. Bland	Virginia BLAND
Peter Blankfield	Peter WOLF
Betty Blasco	Betty PETERSON
David Blatt	Jay BLACK
Blitz	Emridge JONES
Blitz	Gary KING
Blitz	Harry J. KING
Blitz	Reggie WHITE
Gene Bloch	Gene BLACK
Walter Bloch	Gene BLACK
Walter Eugene Bloch	Gene BLACK
Ulf Conny Blomquest	Conny BLOMQVIST
Philip Wallach Blondheim	Scott McKENZIE
Conny Bloom	Conny BLOMQVIST
Kurtis Blow	Kurt WALKER
Barry Ian Blue	Barry BLUE
Ray Blum	Ramon ARCUSA

Elisa Blumberg	Lisa RATNER
Dede Blythe	Dede FAIRBANKS
Eddie Bo	Edwin BOCAGE
Bobby Z.	Robert RIVKIN
Eddie Bocage	Edwin BOCAGE
Joseph R. Bochenek	Joe RAYE
Joseph Raye Bochenek	Joe RAYE
Peter William Bockbanks	Peter W. BANKS
Udo Jürgen Bockelman	Udo JÜRGENS
Chet Bolins	Chris DARWAY
Michael Bolotin	Michael BOLTON
Cyrus Whitfield Bond	Johnny BOND
Gary "U. S." Bonds	Gary ANDERSON
Mark Bones	Bert KAEMPFERT
John F. Bongiovi	Jon BON JOVI
Bono	Paul HEWSON
Salvatore Phillip Bono	Sonny BONO
Eugene Booker	Chuckii BOOKER
Jessie Mae Booker	Jessie Mae ROBINSON
Robert Nesta Marley Booker	Bob MARLEY
Linda Bookout	Linda WILLIAMS
Charles E. Boone	Pat BOONE
Bootsy	Andy CONNELL
Leonard W. Borisoff	Len BARRY
William Paul Borsey Jr.	Willy DeVILLE
Ted Ellis Botkin	Ted ELLIS
Martin Böttcher	Michael THOMAS
Roswell Christopher Bottum	Roddy BOTTUM
Bob Boulanger	Robert BOULANGER
Hans Bouwens	George BAKER
Joseph Steven Bowden	Steve BOWDEN
Johannes Bowens	George BAKER
Doc Box	Jon GORDON
James H. Boxley	Hank SHOCKLEE
Keith Boxley	Keith SHOCKLEE
Sidney Thomas Boyce	Tommy BOYCE
Delaine Alvin Bramlett	Delaney BRAMLETT
Pierre Brancourt	Yves-Jacques LAVOT
Richard Martin Brannan	Richard BRANNAN
Spady Brannan	Richard BRANNAN
Boris Peter Bransby-Williams	Boris WILLIAMS
Joanne Jackson Bratton	Joanne BRATTON
Erik Braun	Erik BRANN
Eric T. Breed	Eric BREED
Lionel Breeze	Lyn MURRAY
Merel Peter Bregante	Peter BREGANTE
Paul Emil Breitenfield	Paul DESMOND
Theresa Veronica Breuer	Teresa BREWER
Richard Charles Swinn Brewer	Rik SWINN
Jimmy Brewster	Milt GABLER
Brianbert	Brian HOLLAND
Brianbert	Robert BATEMAN
Claude Russell Bridges	Leon RUSSELL
Julian Ferebree Bright	Larry BRIGHT
Dee Bristol	Darnell BRISTOL
Iris Bristol	Iris GORDY
John William Bristol	Johnny BRISTOL

Eustace Britchforth	Lefty BAKER
William M. A. Broad	Billy IDOL
Mary Christine Brockert	Teena MARIE
James Brockman	James KENDIS
Arnold Brodsky	Brooks ARTHUR
Israel Brodsky	Roy C. BENNETT
Roy Brodsky	Roy C. BENNETT
Charles Brooks	Chuck BROOKS
Charles Lee Brooks	Chuck BROOKS
Craig Brooks	Craig SPROVACH
Elmore Brooks	Elmore JAMES
Fred Brooks	Fred HELLERMAN
Gwendolyn Dianne Brooks	Dianne BROOKS
Harvey Goldstein Brooks	Harvey BROOKS
Ronald Broomfield	Ronnie E. BROOMFIELD
Raymond Brost	Ray HENDERSON
Stephen Broughton	Stephen LUNT
Steve Broughton	Stephen LUNT
Thomas August Darnell Browder	August DARNELL
William Neal Browder	T.G. SHEPPARD
James Hooker Brown Jr.	James HOOKER
James Joseph Brown Jr.	James BROWN
Alexandra Louise Brown	Alex BROWN
Deanna Crisp Brown	Deanna BROWN
Doug Brown	Douglas Fontaine BROWN
Ed Brown	Edward C. BLACK
Fontaine Brown	Douglas Fontaine BROWN
Frankie Brown	Ted DAFFAN
George Brown	Billy HILL
Jimmy Brown	James B. BROWN
Lawrence Russell Brown	L. Russell BROWN
Lester Errol Brown	Errol BROWN
Mark Brown	Mark Alton BROWN
Michael D. Brown	Michael David LOOKOFSKY
Mike Brown	Michael David LOOKOFSKY
Napoleon Brown	Nappy BROWN
Robert Barrisford Brown	Bobby BROWN
Shereelynn Sarah Brown	Sheree BROWN
Wandra Merrell Brown	Wandra MERRELL
Brownmark	Mark Alton BROWN
Louis Brownstein	Lew BROWN
Robert Bruce	Robert Byron WRIGHT
William Edwin Bruce	Ed BRUCE
C. Bruno	Bruno CHERUBINI
Tony Bruno	Anthony Michael BRUNO
Dougie Bryan	Radcliffe BRYAN
Lamar C. Bryant	Marty BRYANT
Robert L. Bryson	Peabo BRYSON

Francisco Buarque de Hollanda	Chico BUARQUE DE HOLLANDA
Chico Buarque	Chico BUARQUE DE HOLLANDA
Martyn Jeryl Buchwald	Marty BALIN
Bonnie Buckingham	Bonnie GUITAR
Nigel Buckle	Nigel TWIST
Dominique Bugatti	Dominic BUGATTI
Perry Carlton Buie	Buddy BUIE
Anna Mae Bullock	Tina TURNER
Farrokh Bulsara	Freddie MERCURY
Alden Bunn	Allen BUNN
Lee Martin Bunnell	Dewey BUNNELL
Bunny D.	Elana CAGER
Ian Buonconsiglio	Ian LLOYD
Charles Burbank	Charles IBGUI
John Alexander Burchell	John BURCH
Jon Mark Burchell	Jon MARK
Jon Michael Burchell	Jon MARK
Yvonne Ann Burgess	Jackie TRENT
Irving Burgie	Lord BURGESS
Irving Louis Burgie	Lord BURGESS
Lord Burgie	Lord BURGESS
Clem Burke	Clement A. BOZEWSKI
J. Francis Burke	Joseph Francis BURKE
John Francis Burke	Johnny BURKE
K.S.H.S. Burke	Selassie BURKE
Sonny Burke	Joseph Francis BURKE
Granville A. Burland	Sascha BURLAND
Dorsey William Burnette	Billy BURNETTE
Jonathan Burnette	Rocky BURNETTE
Dick Burns	Richard BURNS
Morry Burns	Moon MULLICAN
Richard "Dick" Warren Burns	Dick BURNS
Richard Brian Burns	Richard BURNS
Juana Burns-Sperling	Juana BURNS
Kirk Burrell	Stanley BURRELL
Earl Solomon Burroughs	Jack HAMMER
Glenn Burtnick	Glen BURTNICK
George Burton	Dorian BURTON
Raybon Owen Busby	Buzz RABIN
Lou Busch	Louis F. BUSH
Louis Ferdinand Busch	Louis F. BUSH
Billy Butler	William Earl BUTLER
Geezer Butler	Terry BUTLER
Terence Butler	Terry BUTLER
Terence Michael Butler	Terry BUTLER
William E.M. Butler	William Earl BUTLER
William Henry Butler	Harry BUTLER
Joy Byers	Joy Byers JOHNSTON
Walter William Bygraves	Max BYGRAVES
Donaldson Toussaint L'Ouverture Byrd	Donald BYRD
Robert James Byrd	Bobby DAY
David Byron	David John BYRON
C	
Toni C.	Toni COLANDREO
Joseph Alan Cagle	Joseph CAGLE

Gilberto Miguel Calderón	Joe CUBA
John W. Cale	J.J. CALE
John Weldon Cale	J.J. CALE
Charles Calhoun	Jesse STONE
Royalston Calhoun	Roy CALHOUN
Peter Robin Callander	Peter CALLANDER
Jo Callis	John William CALLIS
E. Camino	Isabel HANSEN
James Milton Campbell Jr.	Milton CAMPBELL
Barbara Campbell	Sam COOKE
Bonnie Maureen Campbell	Bonnie OWENS
Cecil Eustace Bustamente Campbell	Buster CAMPBELL
Linda Marie Campbell	Linda WOMACK
William Campbell	Junior CAMPBELL
Candyman	John B. SHAFFER III
Aldo Caponi	Don BACKY
Aldo Caporuscio	Aldo NOVA
Caravelli	Claude VASORI
Anthony E. Cardenas	Tony MONTANA
Frank Cariola	Frank CARI
Tyran Carlo	Billy DAVIS
Lisa Keith Carlson	Lisa KEITH
Delyle Gregory Carmichael	C. Delyle GREGORY
Greg Carmichael	C. Delyle GREGORY
James Anthony Carmichael	James CARMICHAEL
Russell Caron	Greg SCELSA
Clarence E. Carpenter	Pete CARPENTER
Joe "Fingers" Carr	Louis F. BUSH
Candy Carroll	Carolyn FRANKLIN
Ron Carroll	Ron VOLZ
Roy Carroll	Milt GABLER
Milton Carson	Harold FIELDS
Milton Carson	Howard Ellington Riddiford BARNES
Milton Carson	Joseph RONCORONI
Wayne Carson	Wayne Carson THOMPSON
Barry Eugene Carter	Barry WHITE
Bo Carter	Armetia CHATMAN
Bobby Carter	Bobby COTTER
Fernando Alan Carter	Chip CARTER
Jake Carter	Joe CARTER
Juan Ricardo Cascales	Johnny RICHARDS
June Carter Cash	June CARTER
James E. Cason	Buzz CASON
Franco Cassano	Francesco CASSANO
Michael Anthony Orlando Cassavitis	Tony ORLANDO
Michael O. Cassavitis	Tony ORLANDO
Eddie Cassen	Ed KASSNER
Walden Robert Cassotto	Bobby DARIN
Owens Boomer Castleman	Boomer CASTLEMAN
Demetrius Emery Cates	Demetrius CATES
Demo Cates	Demetrius CATES
Nicholas Catsos	Gary ROMERO
Christopher Cedzich	Chris GANTRY

Peter A. Ceragioli Jr.	Pete JOLLY
Jean-Marc Cerrone	Marc CERRONE
Jean-Pierre Cerrone	Marc CERRONE
Elio Cesare	Tony RENIS
Anthony George Chalk	Tony COLTON
James E. Chambers	Jimmy CLIFF
Rick Chambers	Ritchie ADAMS
Bettye Jean Champion	Bettye SWANN
June Deniece Chandler	Deniece WILLIAMS
Terence William Chaplin	Blondie CHAPLIN
William Terence Chaplin	Blondie CHAPLIN
Martine Chapot	Martine CLÉMENCEAU
Morris I. Charlap	Moose CHARLAP
Charlemagne	Berry GORDY
Charlemagne	James CARMICHAEL
Charlemagne	Kathy WAKEFIELD
Charlemagne	Ronald Norman MILLER
Bobby Charles	Robert GUIDRY
Edwin Charles	Larry BROWN
Leslie Charles	Billy OCEAN
R.B. Charles	Randy BACHMAN
Ray (2) Charles	Charles Raymond OFFENBERG
Brandon Chase	Gary ZEKLEY
Clifton Nathaniel Chase	Clifton CHASE
Jiggs Chase	Clifton CHASE
Bo Chatman	Armetia CHATMAN
John Len Chatman	Peter CHATMAN
Armenter Chatmon	Armetia CHATMAN
Cheese	Hearlon MARTIN
Vincent Rodney Cheesman	Vincent CHEESMAN
Neneh Mariann Cherry	Neneh CHERRY
George Forrest Chichester Jr.	George FORREST
Laura Webb Childress	Laura WEBB
Marvin Leonard Chivian	Babe CHIVIAN
Tim Christian	Clemon Timothy RILEY
John Christoforou	Johnnie CHRISTO
Chuck D.	Carlton RIDENHOUR
Chung Dong-Hwa	Towa TEI
Chunky A	Arsenio HALL
Terry Noland Church	Terry NOLAND
Cinthy Churchill	Marilyn Weiss ALLEN
Chubby Cifelli	Angelo M. CIFELLI
Mark Cipolla	Mick SMILEY
Delectus Clark	Dee CLARK
Francis H. Clark	Hal SOUTHERN
Hal Clark	Hal SOUTHERN
Harold Eugene Clark	Gene CLARK
Lee Clark	Lee GALLO
Michael George Jackson Clark	Mick JACKSON
Michael James Bruce Clark	Michael CLARK
Alan Clarke	Allan CLARKE
Boomer Clarke	Boomer CASTLEMAN
Harold Allan Clarke	Allan CLARKE
Alison Clarkson	Betty BOO
Stanley Clayton	Bob THIELE

Clémentine	Martine CLÉMENCEAU
David Clempson	Clem CLEMPSON
Nick Jeannine Clesi	N.J. CLESI
Reese Francis Clifford	Buzz CLIFFORD
Christopher Cloud	Tommy BOYCE
James B. Cobb Jr.	J.R. COBB
Seymour Coben	Cy COBEN
Garland Petty Cochran	Hank COCHRAN
Todd Thomas Cochran	Todd COCHRAN
Raymond Alfred Cockburn	Ray COBURN
John R. Cocker	Joe COCKER
Thomas Coe	Thomas J. COE
Alice Cohen	Alice DeSOTO
Daniel Cohen	Casey KELLY
David Alexander Cohen	David COURTNEY
Edwin Greines Cohen	Edwin GREINES
Elizabeth Cohen	Betty COMDEN
Jacob Cohen	Rodney DANGERFIELD
Jean Cohen	Bernard KESSLAIR
Kalman Cohen	Kal MANN
Leah Cohen	Leah KUNKEL
Lisa Catherine Cohen	Lisa COHEN
Maurice Alfred Cohen	Michael CARR
Samuel Cohen	Sammy CAHN
Stuart David Cohen	David BLUE
Chester Cohn	Chester CONN
Jim "Chopper" Cohn	James M. COHN
Antoinette Colandreo	Toni COLANDREO
Larry Cole	Larry STEINBACHEK
Lawrence Charles Anthony Cole	Larry STEINBACHEK
Ervan Coleman	Bud COLEMAN
Morris Lee Coleman	Duke COLEMAN
Thelma Louise Coleman	Thelma GORDY
Nathaniel Adams Coles	Nat "King" COLE
Allen Collay	Allen CALLAIS
John Edward Colley	John Ford COLEY
Bootsy Collins	William Earl COLLINS
Gloria Lavern Collins	Lyn COLLINS
William Collins	William Earl COLLINS
Thomas F. Coman III	Thomas COMAN
Perry Cone	Jack PERRICONE
Andrew John Connell	Andy CONNELL
Robin Conrad	Peter CALLANDER
Dale Frances Consalvi	Dale BOZZIO
Bob Conte	Bob GAUDIO
Russ Conway	Trevor STANFORD
Dale Cook	Sam COOKE
David Albert Cook	David ESSEX
Grace Cook	Eddie HAZEL
Norman Quentin Cook	Norman COOK
Quentin Leo Cook	Norman COOK
Samuel Cook	Sam COOKE
Charles Cooke	Sam COOKE
Linda Cooke	Linda WOMACK
Whey Cooler	Vincent COREA
Mark Cooper	Milton GRANT
Willie A. Cooper	Dick COOPER
Lloyd Copas	Cowboy COPAS
Allan Copelon	Allan SHERMAN
Sam Corgliano	Ricky LAYNE
Corina	Corina AYALA

Harold Cornelius	Harold FIELDS
Harry Cornelius	Harold FIELDS
Dave "Baby" Cortez	David CLOWNEY
Domenick Costa	Don COSTA
Suzanne Coston	Suzanne DePASSE
Robert L. Cotter	Bobby COTTER
Pierre Cour	Pierre LeMAIRE
C.C. Courtney	Charles Cane COURTNEY
John Preston Courville	Johnny PRESTON
John Coury	John COREY
Julian Covey	Philamore LINCOLN
Isaac Cozerbreit	Charles WILLIAMS
Vincent Eugene Craddock	Gene VINCENT
Arthur S. Crafa	Art CRAFER
Denise Ora Craig	Denise LaSALLE
Jimmy Craig	Milton KELLEM
Edyth Craighead	Brian HOLLAND
Edyth Craighead	Eddie HOLLAND
Edyth Craighead	Lamont DOZIER
Vincent Crane	Vincent CHEESMAN
Rogers Lee Craton	Lee ROGERS
Cliff Crawford	Cliff CROFFORD
Hugh Anthony Cregg	Huey LEWIS
Valter Cremonini	Walt CREMONINI
Walter Cremonini	Walt CREMONINI
Robert Stanley Crewe Jr.	Bob CREWE
Peter George Criscoula	Peter CRISS
Yodar Critch	Gary ZEKLEY
George Crockett	G.L. CROCKETT
Howard Crockett	Howard HAUSEY
Clifton Thomas Crofford	Cliff CROFFORD
Darrell G. Crofts	Dash CROFTS
Ronald Clyde Crosby	Jerry Jeff WALKER
John Charles Crowley II	J.C. CROWLEY
Christopher Crummy	Chris CURTIS
Connie Crunk	Connie CONWAY
Norma Crunk	Norma CONWAY
Bettye Jean Crutcher	Bettye CRUTCHER
Napoleon Brown Goodson Culp	Nappy BROWN
Barbara Lynn Cumby	Barbara LYNN
John William Cummings	John CUMMINGS
Antonio De Curtis	TOTÒ
Memphis Curtis	Eddie CURTIS
Memphis Eddie Curtis	Eddie CURTIS
Vincent John Cusano	Vince CUSANO
Cutfather	Mich HANSEN
Regina Marie Cuttita	Regina RICHARDS
Claudio Cuza	Eduardo DAVIDSON
D	
D J Pogo	Simone Antoinette JOHNSON
D J Quik	David Marvin BLAKE
Desmond Dacres	Desmond DEKKER
James O. Dacus	Donnie DACUS
Daddy G	Gene BARGE
Robert Ernest Dade	Robert DADE
Theda Daffan	Theda ROUSH
Theron Eugene Daffan	Ted DAFFAN
Sharon Lee Dain	Jackie DeSHANNON

Marquis Dair	Marcus DARE
Soleil Dakota	Sally Jo DAKOTA
Chip Dale	Dino TOME
Chip Dale	John WOLOSCHUK
Ciro Dammicco	ZACAR
Russ Damon	Les LEDO
Jim Dandy	James MANGRUM
Bob Dane	Hugo PERETTI
Damian Dane	Bruce BROADUS
Danilov	Walter DANA
Wladyslaw Danilowski	Walter DANA
Mary Catherine Danoff	Taffy DANOFF
David Dante	David HESS
Ralph Edward Daugherty	Doc DAUGHERTY
John Davenport	Otis BLACKWELL
Vincent Paul Davey	Vince ELY
David J.	David HASKINS
David Z.	David RIVKIN
F. R. David	Robert FITOUSSI
Janice David	Janice DAVIS
Leizer David	Lou STALLMAN
Scott David	Jerry SAMUELS
William Frederick Davidson	Bill DAVIDSON
Robert Bunyan Davie II	Bob DAVIE
Hutch Davie	Bob DAVIE
Ivor Arthur Davies	Iva DAVIES
Michael Philip Leslie Davies	Mike DAVIES
Bill Davis	William DOUCHETTE
Brenda Holloway Davis	Brenda HOLLOWAY
Charles Neil Davis	Charles N. DANIELS
Denise L. Davis	Rainy DAVIS
Jeffery Davis	Joseph HOOVEN
Jonathan Davis	Kamaal FAREED
Lawrence Davis	Larry DAVIS
Louis F. Davis	Chip DAVIS
Mavis Vegas Davis	Michele ALLER
Morris Davis	Mac DAVIS
Rick Davis	Erik BRANN
Robert Michael Davis	Bob MONROE
Roquel Davis	Billy DAVIS
Scott Davis	Mac DAVIS
Sheriff Tex Davis	William DOUCHETTE
Christopher John Davison	Chris DE BURGH
Billy Dawn	Billy Dawn SMITH
Bernard Colin Day	Bob ALLISON
Billy Day	Bill DAVIDSON
Daddy-O Daylie	Daddio DAYLIE
Holmes Daylie	Daddio DAYLIE
Maria Joaquia de la Portilla Torres	Maria GREVER
Eddy Quintela de Mendonça	Eddy QUINTELA
Willy de Moor	Bill ADOR
Willy Noël De Moor	Bill ADOR
Giovanni Alfredo De Simone	Johnny DESMOND
Robert Allen Deal	Mick MARS
Ritchie Dean	Warren SCHATZ
Elisa Dease	Elisa FIORILLO
Etterlene DeBarge	Bunny DeBARGE
Chris DeBurgh	Chris DE BURGH
Jeanne-Paule Marie Deckers	Jeanine DECKERS
Daisy Dee	Desiree ROLLOCKS
Jackie Dee	Jackie DeSHANNON
Jean Dee	Yvonne DEVANEY
Johnny Dee	John D. LOUDERMILK
Kool Moe Dee	Mohandas DeWESE
Papa Dee	Dan WAHLGREN
Prince Markie Dee	Mark Anthony MORALES
Johnny Deerfield	Ron HARGRAVE
Rigdon Osmond Dees III	Rick DEES
Michaele DeFerraro	Michele MICHAELE
James DeFore	Jimmy Dee FORE
John Richard DeGiuli	Johnnie DEE
Jean Ann Del Grosso	Laurie ALLEN
Carlos Del Rosario	Yutaka YOKOKURA
Prentice John Delaney Jr.	Prentice DeLANEY
Sean Delaney	Prentice DeLANEY
Hollis Rudolph DeLaughter	Red LANE
Reginald DeLong	Richard COBURN
Paul DeMaya	Paul GIACALONE
Claude Demetrius	Claude DeMETRIUS
Marcias DeNegri	Kenny GEORGE
Thomas DeQuincey	Jo BOGAERT
Derek	Johnny CYMBAL
Vassilis Dertilis	Billy ADAMS
Kenrick Des-Etages	Lee VANDERBILT
Yves Dessca	Yves-Jacques LAVOT
Leonard George DeStoppelaire	Lenny DEE
George Gard DeSylva	Buddy DeSYLVA
Wolfgang Detmann	Candy DeROUGE
Marcella Detroit	Marcy LEVY
Henry John Deutschendorf Jr.	John DENVER
Antonio DeVerdis-Mazzone	Tony GREEN
Autry DeWalt	Jr. WALKER
Allison Dewar	Scott TURNER
Sidney DeWayne	Sid JOHNSON
Daddy Dewdrop	Dick MONDA
Ruggiero Eugenio di Rodolpho Colombo	Russ COLUMBO
Janey Diamond	Jayney KLIMEK
Emmanuel N'Djoke Dibango	Manu DIBANGO
Odilien Dibango	Manu DIBANGO
Bruno Ravel DiCecco	Bruno RAVEL
Paul Revere Dick	Paul REVERE
Dicken	Jeffrey Robert PAIN
B.B. Dickerson	Morris DICKERSON
Desmond D'Andrea Dickerson	Dez DICKERSON
Morris Dewayne Dickerson	Morris DICKERSON
Bo Diddley	Ellas McDANIEL
Joseph DiFrancesco	Joey DAY
Julie DiGiovanni	Julie DeJOHN
Leo DiGiovanni	Leo DeJOHN
Mary Ann DiGiovanni	Dux DeJOHN
Horace Eldred Dill	Danny DILL
Joseph DiNicola	Joey DEE
Ella Lucille Dinning	Lou DINNING
Eugenia Joy Dinning	Jean DINNING
Eugene Dixon	Gene CHANDLER
Julius E. Dixson Sr.	Julius DIXON
DJ Eddie F	Edward FERRELL
DJ Shodai	Towa TEI
Burton D'Lugoff	Burt LONG
Conrad K. Dober	Con CONRAD
Ivan Wesley Dodd	Jimmie DODD
Maurice Dollison	Morris DOLLISON
Antoine Dominique Domino Jr.	Fats DOMINO
Kevin Michael Dompe	Kevin HASKINS
Tom Donahue	Thomas COMAN
David R. Donaldson Jr.	Dee ROBB
Tommy Donaldson	Tommy DEE
Anthony James Donegan	Lonnie DONEGAN
Philip Donnely	Robbie BLUNT
Raymond Donnez	Don RAY
Steve Donroy	Cy CRANE
Steve Donroy	Herb WEINER
Dicky Doo	Gerry GRANAHAN
Raymond Doughty	Ray BURTON
George Douglas	Bob THIELE
Horace Kirby Dowell	Saxie DOWELL
Richard Doyle	Shamus M'COOL
Ugene Lloyd Dozier	Gene DOZIER
Dr. Dre	Andre Romell YOUNG
Dr. Freeze	Elliot STRAITE
Dr. John	Mac REBENNACK
Dr. Robert	Bruce Robert HOWARD
Tom Drake	Steven YATES
Clarence R. Drayton	Clarence DRAYTON
Clay Drayton	Clarence DRAYTON
L. A. Dre	Andre BOLTON
Hans Drechsler	Joe DIXIE
Marilyn Marie Droman	Marilyn MARTIN
Joe Dube	Jeffrey Warren GROB
Matthew D. Dubinsky	Matt DUBEY
Damita Jo DuBlanc	Damita Jo GIBSON
Eric Duhn	Fred OLDÖRP
Billy Duke	William TESONE
Robert Duke	Joe MEEK
Vladimir Dukelsky	Vernon DUKE
William Dumaresq	Max FRITH
Lowell Fillmore Dunbar	Sly DUNBAR
Reggie Dunbar	Murry WILSON
Richard Dunbar	Richard KNIGHT
John Richard Duncan	Johnny DUNCAN
Chris Dunn	Chris WATERS
Christopher Waters Dunn	Chris WATERS
Donald Lewis Dunn	Don DUNN
Donald V. Dunn	Donald "Duck" DUNN
Larry Dunn	Lorenzo DUNN
Champion Jack Dupree	Jack DUPREE
William Thomas Dupree	Jack DUPREE
Robert H. Dupuis	Robbie DUPREE
Reginald Kenneth Dwight	Elton JOHN
E	
Earthquake	Floyd BROWN

Linda Louise Eastman	Linda McCARTNEY
Tim Eaton	Buster (2) BROWN
Ebb Tide	Ted HARRIS
Margaret Louis Ebey	Margie SINGLETON
Dolores Eble	Dolores FULLER
William Eckstein	Billy ECKSTINE
William Clarence Eckstein	Billy ECKSTINE
Hal Eddy	Harry EDELSTEIN
Mirriam Eddy	Jessi COLTER
Kenneth Brian Edmonds	Kenneth EDMONDS
Dennis Edmonton	Mars BONFIRE
Patricia Louise Edwards	Patti LaBELLE
Nicholas Eede	Nick VAN EEDE
Norma Deloris Egstrom	Peggy LEE
Rokusuke Ei	Rohusuke EI
Takeo Ei	Rohusuke EI
Robert Charles Eichorn	Bobby ICON
Eva Ein	E. Ein LOGGINS
Stanley Harvey Eisen	Paul STANLEY
Denise Eisenberg	Joy DENNY
Stephen Geoffrey Eisenberg	Geoffrey STEVENS
Sylvia Eisenberg	Sil SEDORES
Lawrence Eisler	Eddie LAWRENCE
Renrut Eki	Ike TURNER
El Sati	Stijn LAUWERS
Eddison Electrik	Eddison SAINSBURY
Bob Elgin	Stanley KAHAN
Tracey Elizondo	Tracey AMOS
Jack Elliott	Irwin Elliott ZUCKER
Max Elliott	Maxi PRIEST
Emmitt Ellis Jr.	Bobby RUSH
Joseph Ellis	Joey B. ELLIS
Marybelle Luraine Ellison	Lorraine ELLISON
Shirley Elliston	Shirley ELLIS
Elmo	Garry BONNER
England Dan	Dan SEALS
Linda Epstein	Linda CREED
Hermann Erbel	Herman RAREBELL
Tomas Erdélyi	Tom ERDELYI
Edward Marshall Erenberg	Celia MARSHALL
Eric B.	Eric BARRIER
Roger Kynard Erickson	Roky ERICKSON
Holly Erlanger	Holly KNIGHT
Janet Ann Errico	Jan ASHTON
John Errington	John MILES
King Errison	Errison JOHNSON
DeFosco T. Ervin Jr.	Dee ERVIN
Roy Erwin	Max BYGRAVES
Irene Cara Escalera	Irene CARA
Sheila Escovedo	SHEILA E.
Esquerita	Eskew REEDER
Zecca Esquibel	Jose Augusto ESQUIBEL
Steve Ett	Steve ETTINGER
James Etta	Etta JAMES
Bill Eustrom	Bill NORVAS
Bill Roy Eustrom	Bill NORVAS
Christopher Robin Evans	Chris EVANS

Ernest Evans	Chubby CHECKER
Glenda Joyce Evans	Glenda HUDSON
Judy Evans	Marilyn HOOVEN
Louis Evans	Redd EVANS
Jean Evens	Jean EVANS
Bill Everette	Bill JUSTIS
Jacqueline Everly	Jacqueline ERTEL
Dave Ewer	David Franklin EWER
F	
Bent Fabric	Bent FABRICIUS-BJERRE
Peter Fadden	Joseph Francis BURKE
Don Edward Fagenson	Don WAS
Phyllis Fairbanks	Phyllis LANDSBERG
David Fairstein	Fabrice CUITAD
Gloria Fajardo	Gloria ESTEFAN
William Falcone	Billy FALCON
Eric Falconer	Eric FAULKNER
Jake Falsworth	Jake HOOKER
Giuseppe Fanciulli	Giuseppe FUCILLI
Melville Farley	Gordon REES
Michael George Farr	Mike LEANDER
Jesse Oris Farrow	Chet POWERS
Fatboy Slim	Norman COOK
Father MC	Timothy BROWN
Sid Faust	Lee CATHY
Samuel E. Feinberg	Sammy FAIN
Bernard Feinstein	Buddy FEYNE
Howard R. Feiten	Buzz FEITEN
Marc Feld	Marc BOLAN
Jerome Solon Felder	Doc POMUS
Jeff Feldman	Jeff MANN
Camillo Jean Nicolas Felgen	J. Nicolas FELGEN
Fenderella	Joyce IRBY
Jack Fenton	Jay FISHMAN
Frank Carlton Serafino Feranna	Nikki SIXX
Maria Elena Fernadez-Vidal	Maria VIDAL
Osvaldo Nicolas Ferraro Gutierrez	Waldo DE LOS RIOS
Eddie Ferrell	Edward FERRELL
Roger Garfield Ferrier	Roger HART
Addy Fieger	Addy BARON
Harold C. Fields	Harold FIELDS
Robert J. Finizio	Bob FINIZ
Catherine L. Fink	Kay THOMPSON
Janis Eddy Fink	Janis IAN
Harry Finkelman	Ziggy ELMAN
Larry Finnegan	John L. FINNERAN
John Lawrence Finneran	John L. FINNERAN
Lance Finnie	Lance FINNEY
Carlton James Fisher	Carl FISHER
Gail Fisher	Gail LEVY
Patty Fisher	Ruth FREED
James Eugene Fitzwater Jr.	Gene CRYSLER
Louisa Flavell	Maewa KAIHAN
Flea	Michael BALZARY
Daniel Dale Fleishour	Daniel FLEISHOUR
Rhonda Kye Fleming	Kye FLEMING
Gerald Florio	Gerard FLORIO
Danny Flower	Daniel FLEISHOUR

Edward Fluri	Eddie RAMBEAU
Wesley Donald Fogel	Wes FARRELL
Clyde Julian Foley	Red FOLEY
Fern Foley	Bobby AUSTIN
Iris Ann Folwell	Iris FERNANDO
Alan Bernard Forbes	Eugene REYNOLDS
Brute Force	Stephen FRIEDLAND
Aleck Ford	Sonny Boy WILLIAMSON II
Dean Ford	Thomas McALEESE
Dee Dee Ford	Wrecia HOLLOWAY
Naomi Ford	Lee HAZLEWOOD
James Foreman	James MTUME
Gene Forrest	Forrest WILSON
Steven William Forrest	Steve BRONSKI
B.Y. Forster	George David WEISS
Lawrence Constantine Fotinakis	Larry FOTINE
Kim Fowler	Kim WILDE
Loreto Domenico Fraieli	Jimmie CRANE
Joe Francavilla	Joe VILLA
Concetta Rosa Maria Franconero	Connie FRANCIS
Rachel Frank	Beverly ROSS
Sy Franklin	Herman FAIRBANKS
Henry St. Claire Fredericks	Taj MAHAL
Dennis Hardy Frederiksen	Fergie FREDERIKSEN
Ronald L. Fredianelli	Ronnie GAYLORD
Free	Eric SMITH
Albert James Freed	Alan FREED
David Freedman	Dave MANN
Ray Freeman	Max C. FREEDMAN
Solomon Hersh Frees	Paul FREES
Paul Daniel Frehley	Ace FREHLEY
Guy Freidline	Guy MAGENTA
Roy Freirich	Roy FREELAND
Bernie Friedman	B.F. FLIP
John L. Friga	Jonathan CAIN
William Orville Frizzell	Lefty FRIZZELL
Eunice Frost	Eunice LEVY
Frances Claire Frost	Frances FROST
Darrell Fuller	Dolores FULLER
Orena D. Fullmer	Orena D. FULMER
Lowell Fulson	Lowell FULSOM
Stanard Funsten	Stan RIDGWAY
Gwen Fuqua	Gwen GORDY
Vincent Damon Furnier	Alice COOPER
G	
Paul Francis Gadd	Gary GLITTER
Guy Mitchell Gaglio	Guy MARSHALL
LaDonna Adrian Gaines	Donna SUMMER
Gordon Galbraith	Jean SAWYER
Gabriel Ruiz Galindo	Gabriel RUIZ
Grace Lane Gallico	Grace LANE
Susan Marie Gallion	Susan THOMAS
Lee A.C. Gallo	Lee GALLO
Simon Johnathan Gallup	Simon GALLUP
Alan Bruce Galuten	Albhy GALUTEN
Christina Ganahl	Ina WOLF
Milton Gant	Milton SPARKS

Phillip Gantose	Russ CARLYLE
George Garoufis	George BROWN
Samuel Garrett	Hank MILLS
Thomas Leslie Garrett	Snuff GARRETT
David Garrick	David John BYRON
Ted Gary	Milton KELLEM
Édith Giovanna Gassion	Edith PIAF
Leonard François Joseph Guy Gauthier	Hal WILLIS
Anna Gaye	Anna GORDY
Gloria Gaynor	Gloria FOWLES
Michael Stanley Gee	Michael STANLEY
Jack Gellar	Ronnie SCOTT
Art Gentry	Argentry MITCHELL
Will Gentry	Ramsey KEARNEY
Jimmy Pete Georgantones	Jimmy GEORGE
Boy George	George O'DOWD
Hazel Gilman George	Gil GEORGE
Keni St. George	Kenny GEORGE
Steven Demetre Georgiou	Cat STEVENS
Christopher Charles Geppert	Christopher CROSS
Raymond Godfrey Gerald	Raeford GERALD
Philippe Gerard	Philippe Gerard BLOCH
Åke Gerhard	Åke Gerhard LARSSON
Linda Gertz	Linda LAURIE
Albert Andrew Gibson	Andy GIBSON
S. Gibson	Mickey BAKER
Samuel Robert Gibson	Bob GIBSON
Iris May Giebler	Iris MAY
Plinky Giglio	Sal GIGLIO Jr.
Jack V.C. Gilbert	V.C. GILBERT
Vivian Clark Gilbert	V.C. GILBERT
Rhonda Fleming Gill	Kye FLEMING
John Birks Gillespie	Dizzy GILLESPIE
Michelle Gilliam	Michelle PHILLIPS
Gino	Harry GIOSASI
Lucien Ginsburg	Serge GAINSBOURG
Giorgio	Georgio ALLENTINI
Aristides Michael Giosasi	Harry GIOSASI
Pat Giraldo	Pat BENATAR
Norman Washington Giscombe	Junior GISCOMBE
Kenny Gist Jr.	Kenny O'DELL
Morris Gittler	Mack GORDON
Elmo Glick	Jerry LEIBER
Elmo Glick	Mike STOLLER
Edgar Dean Glosup	Eddie DEAN
Henry Bernard Glover	Henry GLOVER
John Raymond Goadsby	Goldy McJOHN
Stuart Leslie Goddard	Adam ANT
Ray Godfrey	Raeford GERALD
Eleanor Goldberg	Nora BAYES
Ernest Goldberg	Ernie GOLD
Ronnie Golden	Tony DeMEUR
Ernst Siegmund Goldner	Ernest GOLD
Hilliard Goldsmith	Bob HILLIARD
David Goldstein	Rupert HOLMES

Harvey Goldstein	Harvey BROOKS
Lesley Sue Goldstein	Lesley GORE
Michael Goldstein	Michael GORE
Jose Gomera	Louis FERRARI
Jesse Gonzales	Jesus ESCAMILLA
Luciano Gonzales	Chano POZO
Richard Goodman	Richie SUPA
Willie Albert Goodman	Al GOODMAN
Jon D. Gordon III	Jon GORDON
Brenda Gordon	Brenda RUSSELL
Rexton Ralston Fernando Gordon	Rexton GORDON
George Weldon Gordy	George GORDY
Horgay Gordy	George GORDY
Margaret Gordy	Margaret JOHNSON
Raynoma Gordy	Raynoma SINGLETON
Thelma Louise Gordy	Thelma GORDY
Kenneth Bruce Gorelick	KENNY G
Eydie Gormé	Eydie GORME
Edith Gormezano	Eydie GORME
Bernhard Gössling	Bernhard LLOYD
Richard St. John Gosting	Dick GOSTING
Seymour Gottlieb	Cy CRANE
Ronald Norman Gould	Ronald Norman MILLER
Rowland Charles Gould	Boon GOULD
John Fred Gourrier	John FRED
Jerry Grace	Jerry GRAZIANO
Louis A. Grammatico	Lou GRAMM
Carmine Granito	Ron DANTE
Jerry Grant	Gerry GRANAHAN
Mark Grant	Milton GRANT
Neil Grant	Iain MacFADYEN
Sandy Grassi	Sandy PALMER
Eddie Gray	Ed GRAY
John Gray	John Grayton DOLPHIN
Juliet Gray	Lyn COLLINS
Yvonne Gray	Von GRAY
Generoso Graziano	Jerry GRAY
Robert Greco	Bobby GREGG
Alan Green	Arlan DAY
Barry Ian Green	Barry BLUE
Earl Green	Earl GREENE
Mel Green	Allan ROBERTS
Peter Charles Green	Daniel BOONE
Rupert Greenall	Peter John GREENALL
Peter Alan Greenbaum	Peter GREEN
Florence Greenberg	Florence GREEN
Albert L. Greene	Al GREEN
David Greer	Harold FIELDS
David Greer	Joseph RONCORONI
Gregorian	Frank PETERSON
F. Gregorian	Frank PETERSON
William Michael Griffin Jr.	William GRIFFIN
Curley Griffin	Curly GRIFFIN
Howard Griffin	Curly GRIFFIN
William Edward Grishaw	Zeb TURNER
Max C. Gronenthal	Max CARL
Jerome David Gross	Jerry GROSS
Arthur Grossman	Arthur FREED

Wilhelm Grosz	Hugh WILLIAMS
Will Grosz	Hugh WILLIAMS
Carl Groszman	Carl GROSSMAN
Salvatore Antonio Guaragna	Harry WARREN
Kim Anthony Guidry	Kim SHARP
Robert Charles Guidry	Robert GUIDRY
Guitar Slim	Eddie JONES
Aaron Gumbinsky	Harry VON TILZER
Albert Gumbinsky	Albert VON TILZER
George Charles Gunn	Anton DE WAAL
Gregory Gerard Guralski	Greg GERARD
Howard J. Gustafson	Bart HOWARD
Elizabeth Ann Guttman	E.G. DAILY
Helen Guy	Guy D'HARDELOT
Frank V. Guzzo	Frankie FORD
Gary G-Wiz	Gary RINALDO
H	
Elizabeth Jane Haaby	Liz ANDERSON
Leonard Hacker	Buddy HACKETT
George Hackney	Anthony NEWLEY
Christopher Haden-Guest	Christopher GUEST
Gary Loren Hahn	Skip HAHN
Shelley G. Haims	Shelley HAIMS
Marquis X. Hair	Marcus DARE
Deborah Carter Hall	Deborah CARTER
Graeme Anthony Hall	Graeme HALL
James Faye Hall	Sunny DAVID
John Kingsley Hall	Jon Kingsley HALL
Marcel Theo Hall	Biz MARKIE
Roe E. Hall	Rick HALL
Bobby Godfrey Mitchell Halstead	Bobby MITCHELL
Robert Harston Hamilton Jr.	Bob HAMILTON
Albert Prentis Hamilton	Al HAMILTON
Clyde Hamilton	Cyril STAPLETON
Hammer	Stanley BURRELL
Osman Handani	Otha NASH
William Christopher Handy	W.C. HANDY
Mich Hedin Hansen	Mich HANSEN
Edgar Yipsel Harburg	E.Y. HARBURG
Charles Hardin	Buddy HOLLY
Lillian Hardin	Lillian Hardin ARMSTRONG
Reginald J. Hargis	Regi HARGIS
Hans Haring	Hans CARSTE
Kurt Harland	Kurt VALAQUEN
Jack Harlen	Britt SIMONSON
William Franke Harling	W. Franke HARLING
Allen Harlow	Allen HAWIRKO
Murrey Mizell Harman Jr.	Murrey HARMAN
Buddy Harman	Murrey HARMAN
Terry Harmon	Carl T. FISCHER
Charles Harold	Charles H. CUPPETT
Jimmy Harper	James S. HANCOCK
Don "Sugarcane" Harris	Don HARRIS
Don Francis Bowman Harris	Don HARRIS
Jimmy Jam Harris	James Samuel HARRIS

John Harris	Hal SHAPER
Marcene Harris	Dimple M. JACKSON
Robert Harris	Robert Patrick WESTON
Katherine Harrison	Claude BAUM
Robert L. Harshman	Bobby HART
Gladys Hart	Gladys REINHARDT
Jane Harvey	Phyllis TAFF
David John Haskins	David HASKINS
A.G. Hassan	Ann GODWIN
Shadee Hassan	Allen STORY
Charles Edwin Hatcher	Edwin STARR
Douglas Farthing Hatlelid	Chip DOUGLAS
Otto Abels Hauerbach	Otto HARBACH
Howard Elton Hausey	Howard HAUSEY
Kenneth Alan James Hawker	Ken HAWKER
Jamesetta Hawkins	Etta JAMES
Judy Hayden	Tex ANN
Kevin Calhoun Hazlett	Kevin CALHOUN
Hammond Hazlewood	Albert HAMMOND
Hammond Hazlewood	Mike HAZLEWOOD
Yusuf Hazziez	Joe TEX
Wayne Carson Head	Wayne Carson THOMPSON
Nicholas Bowen Headon	Nicky HEADON
Topper Headon	Nicky HEADON
Frederick Heath	Johnny KIDD
Frederick Albert Heath	Johnny KIDD
Mark Lavon Helm	Levon HELM
Reginald Van Helsing	Gene SIMMONS
Charles Hemphill	Sonny CHARLES
Gayla Henderson	Jamie HORTON
James Marshall Hendrix	Jimi HENDRIX
Johnny Allen Hendrix	Jimi HENDRIX
Robert Raymond Henson	Bob RAY
Dorothy Jean Heppel	Ginger WILLIS
Piet Herbert	Marcus MEYN
Bernard Hermann	Bernard HERRMANN
Josephine Herrmann	Joan WHITE
Paul David Hewson	Paul HEWSON
Hi-C	Crawford WILKERSON
Regi Hargis Hickman	Regi HARGIS
Elbert Joseph Higgins	Bertie HIGGINS
Doris Elaine Higginson	Doris PAYNE
R. Higgs	Jim VALLANCE
Rodney Higgs	Jim VALLANCE
Diane Hildebrand	Diane HILDERBRAND
Al Hill	Ben WEISMAN
Al Hill	Fred WISE
Al Hill	Kay TWOMEY
Arzell Hill	Z.Z. HILL
Bob Hill	Fred HELLERMAN
David Hill	David HESS
Joe Michael Hill	Dusty HILL
Stanley Hill	Noel GAY
Steven Bernard Hill	STEVIE B
William Joseph Hill	Billy HILL
Anthony Toby Hiller	Tony HILLER
Brian Frederick Hines	Denny LAINE
Earl Kenneth Hines	Earl HINES
Fatha Hines	Earl HINES
Thomas Eugene Hobbs II	Tom KIMMEL
Isadore Hochberg	E.Y. HARBURG
Gary Hodgden	Gary WEST
Gary Eldon Hodgden	Gary WEST
Maurice Hodge	Nevelle HODGE
Michael Hodgkinson	Johnny AVERAGE
Marty Lee Hoenes	Martin Lee HOENES
Alan Hold	Mickey LEADER
Neville Holder	Noddy HOLDER
Charles Hardin Holley	Buddy HOLLY
Jesse Hollis	Brook BENTON
Per Holm	Per HOLM-PETERSEN
Carol E. Holmes	Carolyn HOLMES
Christine Holmes	Christine HODGSON
Robert Howard Holmes	Bob HUDSON
Waldo T. Holmes	Wally HOLMES
Patricia Louise Holt	Patti LaBELLE
Redd Holt	Isaac HOLT
Johann Holzel	FALCO
Homer	Henry HAYNES
Paul Andrew Hooper	Nellee HOOPER
Peter Hoorelbeke	Pete RIVERA
Wesaline Hopson	Wesaline Hopson KERR
Paul Horowitz	Paul TAYLOR
George Vaughn Horton	Vaughn HORTON
James McKinley Horton	McKinley HORTON
Lisa Horton	Lisa MONTGOMERY
A. Hott	Joseph Louis STONE
A. Hott	Paul (2) KLEIN
Philemon Hou	Hugh MASEKELA
Mark Howard	Joseph SHAPIRO
Robert Bruce Howard	Bruce Robert HOWARD
Steven Howard	Herbert NEWMAN
Bones Howe	Dayton HOWE
Ronald Guy Hruska	Ronnie GUY
Jerry Reed Hubbard	Jerry REED
Jerry Reid Hubbard	Jerry REED
Josefine Huber-Busch	Fini BUSCH
Bryan Hudson	Bryan LOREN
Bryan Loren Hudson	Bryan LOREN
Baldemar Huerta	Freddy FENDER
Brian John Hug	Brian HUGG
Michael John Hug	Mike HUGG
Bill Keith Hughes	Bill HUGHES
Billie Hughes	Bill HUGHES
Jeri K. Hull	Bunny HULL
Ronald Hulme	Russ HAMILTON
Eddie Humphrey	Gregory JACOBS
Humpty Hump	Gregory JACOBS
Ralph Uriah Hunsecker	Ralph BLANE
Charles James Hunt	Tommy HUNT
Billy Joe Hunter	Lou BIDEU
George Ivy Hunter	Ivy Jo HUNTER
Ivy George Hunter	Ivy Jo HUNTER
Sandra Elayne Hurvitz	Essra MOHAWK
F. Hutch	Frankie L. HUTCHISON
Frank Hutch	Frankie L. HUTCHISON
William McKinley Hutchinson	Willie HUTCH
Willie M. Hutchison	Willie HUTCH
Tammy Hutson	Lisa COHEN
Harry Hyams	Gary BENSON
I	
Paula Ianello	Paula FRANCES
Ice-T	Tracy MARROW
Dominic Ierace	Donnie IRIS
Roy Ilene	Milt GABLER
Barry Imberman	Barry MANN
John V. Imbragulio	John VINCENT
Susan Bridget Inskip	Florrie PALMER
Anthony Gordon Instone	Tony MACAULAY
Rocco Giuseppe Iosco	Bob YOSCO
Big Dee Irwin	Dee ERVIN
Roy Irwin	Max BYGRAVES
Jeffrey Dean Isbell	Izzy STRADLIN
Afrika Islam	Charles Andre GLENN
Yusuf Islam	Cat STEVENS
J	
Leroy O'Niel Jackson Jr.	Leroy BURGESS
Billy Jackson	Gene DOZIER
Chuck Jackson	Charles Henry JACKSON Jr.
David Ian Jackson	Joe JACKSON
David Waymond Jackson	Stonewall JACKSON
Harold Jackson	George Harold JACKSON
J. L. Jackson	J.J. JACKSON
Jerome Louis Jackson	J.J. JACKSON
Joanne Jackson	Joanne BRATTON
Michael Joe Jackson	Michael JACKSON
Shanna V. Jackson	Paris GREY
Sigmund Esco Jackson	Jackie JACKSON
Thomas Gregory Jackson	Tommy JAMES
David-John Jackson-Rich	Dave JACKSON
Gregory Edward Jacobs	Gregory JACOBS
Fred Jacobsen	Fred JAY
Yasmin Jacobsen	Yasmin Elvira STEENHOLDT
Friedrich Alex Jacobson	Fred JAY
Jam Master Jay	Jason MIZELL
Jim Jam	James BROWN
Jimmy Jam	James Samuel HARRIS
Arthur James	James GRIFFIN
Chris D. James	Chris BOSTOCK
Douglas Thomas James	Doug JAMES
Freddy James	Teddy POWELL
Marguerite James	Teddy POWELL
Michael Francis James	Jimmy JAMES
Walter James	Jim WALTERS
Lu Janis	Dick MONDA
Hubert Janssen	Jean SENN
Max Jarczyk	Michael JARY
Maximilian Jarczyk	Michael JARY
Tommy Jarrett	Thomas J. COE
Sid Jaxon	Sid WYCHE
Jesse Jaymes	Jesse Eric ITZLER
Jazzy Jeff	Jeff TOWNES
Allan Jeffrey	Irwin PINCUS
Joe Jeffrey	Joe STAFFORD Jr.

William Jeffrey	William JEFFERY
Jacek Jelen'	Jack YELLEN
Deidre Yvonne Jenkins	Deidra BROWN
Frances Ralston Jenkins	Mike TERRY
Harold L. Jenkins	Conway TWITTY
Joe Jenkins	Herbert JARCZYK
John Jerome	Harold FIELDS
John Jerome	Howard Ellington Riddiford BARNES
Nick Jesson	Nick LOCKWOOD
Jethro	Kenneth BURNS
José Jimenez	Bill DANA
Jivin' Gene	Gene BOURGEOIS
Bruce Anthony Johannesson	C.C. DeVILLE
Dominic John	Joseph RONCORONI
Leo Johns	Marcel STELLMAN
Earl Silas Johnson IV	Earl King JOHNSON
Frederic Homer Johnson Jr.	Keg JOHNSON
Anne Spear Johnson	Anne SPEAR
Bob Johnson	Robert White JOHNSON
Brooks O'Dell Johnson	Brooks O'DELL
Bubber Johnson	Robert Bubber JOHNSON
Charles Foster Johnson	Charles Icarus JOHNSON
Dr. Marguerite Ann Johnson	Maya ANGELOU
Errison Pallman Johnson	Errison JOHNSON
Grace Johnson	Grace SLICK
James A. Johnson	Rick JAMES
Jellybean Johnson	Garry JOHNSON
Jimmy Johnson	Jimmy Ray JOHNSON
Larry Curtis Johnson	Maurice STARR
Michael Edwin Johnson	Michael JONZUN
Mirriam Johnson	Jessi COLTER
Norman Earl Johnson	General JOHNSON
Rick Johnson	Gordon RITTER
Robert Johnson	Robert Bubber JOHNSON
Robert Albin Johnson	Robert White JOHNSON
Sidney DeWayne Johnson	Sid JOHNSON
Sylvester Johnson	Syl JOHNSON
John Harold Johnston	Johnny REINE
Karen Michelle Johnston	Michelle SHOCKED
Jokern	Nils PERNE
George Jones Jr.	George Wydell JONES Jr.
Agnes Jones	Bobby SHARP
Billy Jones	Billy STORM
Brian Keith Jones	Hakim Rashad MUHAMMAD
Charlie Jones	Stephen Charles JONES
Curt Jones	George Curtis JONES
David Robert Jones	David BOWIE
Frederick Joseph Jones	Rick JONES
Gale Jones	Ramona REDD
George Glenn Jones	George JONES
Juggy Jones	Henry MURRAY
Kevin T. Jones	Kevin JONES
Kipper Jones	Kevin JONES
Ora Denise Jones	Denise LaSALLE
Paul Laurence Jones	Paul LAURENCE
Priscilla Jones	Priscilla COOLIDGE
Ruth Lee Jones	Dinah WASHINGTON
William Hamlin Jones	Billy STORM
Danny Jordan	Gerard FLORIO
Etterlene Jordan	Bunny DeBARGE
Leroy Jordan	Lonnie JORDAN
Robert Joseph Jordan	Joe JORDAN
Ronnie Jordan	Joe JORDAN
Terrence P. Jordan	Terry MELCHER
Jörn K	Joern Volsgaard KRISTENSEN
Ray Joseph	Larry SHAYNE
Barbara Joyce	Barbara LOMAS
Steven Judkins	Stevie WONDER
Larry Julian	Larry DAVIS
Lorin Julian	Larry DAVIS
William Everett Justis	Bill JUSTIS
K	
Norman Kaaihue	Norman KAYE
Ernest Kador	Ernie K-DOE
Berthold Kaempfert	Bert KAEMPFERT
Dave Kaffinetti	David Franklin EWER
Stanley J. Kahan	Stanley KAHAN
Murl Kahn	Marvin KAHN
Mauricio Alberto Kaiserman	Morris ALBERT
John Kalapana	Webley EDWARDS
Thanos Kalliris	Paul CALLIRIS
Alan Kallman	Chesley HOWARD
Melvin Kaminsky	Mel BROOKS
Manuela Barbra Monasco Kamosi	Manuela KAMOSI
Peter T. Kane	King PALMER
Peter T. Kane	Richard MULLAN
Sandra Kane	Jeff KATZ
Sandra Kane	Jerry KASENETZ
Kangol Kid	Shiller Shaun FEQUIERE
Gilbert Edward Kaplan	Gilbert E. KENNINGTON
Moses Simon Kaplan	Murray KANE
Saul Kaplan	Saul CHAPLIN
David Kapp	Mickey LEADER
George Nick Karakoglou	George KARAK
Raymond Karl	Irving TAYLOR
Florence Karlen	Florence KAYE
Neneh Mariann Karlsson	Neneh CHERRY
John Kasandra	John W. ANDERSON
Kashif	Michael JONES
Klaus Karl Kassbaum	Nick ST. NICHOLAS
Edward Kassner	Ed KASSNER
Charlie Kaufman	Charles E. KAUFMAN
Sam Kaufman	C.B. SAMUEL
Seymour Kaufman	Cy COLEMAN
Walter Maurice Kaufman	Walter KENT
Jules Leonard Kaye	Buddy KAYE
Kayel	Louis SHARPE
Bob Kayli	Robert GORDY
Kayo	Kevin ROBERSON
Carl Keats	Carl GROSSMAN
Rusty Keefer	Arrett KEEFER
Dorothy Jacqueline Keely	Keely SMITH
John David Keen	Speedy KEEN
Neville Keighley	Belouis SOME
Marilyn Keith	Marilyn BERGMAN
Jaan Kenbrovin	James KENDIS
Edward James Kendrick	Eddie KENDRICKS
John Henry Kendricks	Hank BALLARD
Tracey Bryn Kennedy	Tracey BRYN
Alan Kenneth	Alan BERNSTEIN
Al Kent	Al HAMILTON
Wayne Douglas Kent	Artie WAYNE
June Williams Kerenhappuch	June Watson WILLIAMS
Jonathan Michael Kerr	Jo KERR
Wesaline Kerr	Wesaline Hopson KERR
Danny Kessler	Marilyn SCHACK
Denise Kessler	Rainy DAVIS
Peter Kessler	Pete WARNER
Gérard Daniel Kherlakian	Danyel GÉRARD
Kid Creole	August DARNELL
Kid Frost	Arturo MOLINA Jr.
William D. Killen	Buddy KILLEN
Ronald Killette	Buck TRAIL
King Radio	Norman SPAN
Dominic Roy King	Dominic BUGATTI
Earl King	Earl King JOHNSON
Kenneth George King	Jonathan KING
Pearl King	Earl King JOHNSON
Riley B. King	B.B. KING
Philip Kinorra	Philamore LINCOLN
Harold Kirchstein	Harold GRANT
Bert Klamkin	Bert CARROLL
Daniel Robert Klawon	Denny KLAWSON
Carol Klein	Carole KING
Gene Klein	Gene SIMMONS
Miriam Klein	Miriam UNIMAN
Annette Kleinbard	Carol CONNORS
Mary Klopprogge	Mary APPLEGATE
Richard Terrance Knapp	Terry KNIGHT
Etterlene Knight	Bunny DeBARGE
James Frederick Knobloch	Fred KNOBLOCK
Shanice Knox	Shanice WILSON
Buz Kohan	Alan KOHAN
D.J. Kohler	James TESTA
Donna Kohler	James TESTA
Otto Kollmann	Otto KOLLMAN
Georges Konyn	Géo KOGER
Jean A. Koons	Jeannie JOY
Nathan Korb	Francis LEMARQUE
Kevin Valentine Kosec	Kevin VALENTINE

Alexandre Kouyoumdjian	Alec R. COSTANDINOS
Kovali	Koenraad VAN-LISHOUT
Hans Herman Stein Kramer	Mark STEIN
Wayne Kramer	Wayne KAMBES
Joachim Fritz Krauledat	John KAY
Peter Kreuder	Peter PAN
Richard Charles Krieg	Dick CHARLES
Christian F. Kruzinski	Cee FARROW
Götz Gustav Ksinski	Gershon KINGSLEY
Deborah Kucan	Debbie WITKOWSKI
Julius Frank Anthony Kuczynski	Pee Wee KING
Michael Kunze	Stephan PRAGER
Marty Kupersmith	Marty SANDERS
January Kurta	January TYME
Emanuel Kurtz	Mann CURTIS
Manny Kurtz	Mann CURTIS
June Evelyn Kuykendall	Rickie PAGE
Robert Harry Kuykendall	Bobby DALL
L	
Carlo Donida Labati	Carlo DONIDA
Art Laboe	Arthur EGNOIAN
Solomon Lachoff	Sol LAKE
Geertjan Lacunes	Jerry RIX
Pierre Dewey LaFontaine Jr.	Pete FOUNTAIN
Laurence Gordon Laing	Corky LAING
Richard Carroll Lamb	Dick DALLAS
Danny Lamego	Danny PEPPERMINT
Olivier René Marie Lamotte d'Incamps	Chico De OLIVEIRA
Harry Land	Bernie LOWE
Leon Land	Leon LANDGREN
Jerry Landis	Paul SIMON
James A. Lane	Jimmy ROGERS
Jani Lane	John OSWALD
Jay Arthur Lane	Jimmy ROGERS
Kermit Lane	Ken LANE
Dorothy Veronica Langan	Dory PREVIN
Dory Langdon	Dory PREVIN
Lee Lange	Bunny LEWIS
Robert John Lange	Mutt LANGE
Joseph LaPollo	Ellison CHASE
Joan Marie Larkin	Joan JETT
Kurt Larson	Kurt VALAQUEN
Kurt Harland Larson	Kurt VALAQUEN
Rolf Magnus Joakim Larson	Joey TEMPEST
Jacques Larue	Marcel AGERON
Hans Last	James LAST
Phoebe Ann Laub	Phoebe SNOW
Mary Dean Lauria	Mary DEAN
Stijn Willem Jozef Lauwers	Stijn LAUWERS
Jean-Pierre Lauzon	Jean-Pierre PAQUIN
Roland Kent LaVoie	Kent LaVOIE
Yves Lavot	Yves-Jacques LAVOT
Yves Lavot-Dessca	Yves-Jacques LAVOT

Samuel T. Lawmaster	Sammy MASTERS
Fred Lawrence	Luigi CREATORE
James Everett Lawrence	Rhett LAWRENCE
Ronald Lawrence	Ronald ANDRE
Richard W. Laws	R.W. LAWS
LayLaw	Larry GOODMAN
Leadbelly	Huddie LEDBETTER
Louis Leazer	Lew POLLACK
Richie Lecea	Richie HERNANDEZ
Ismael Angel Ledesma	Ish LEDESMA
Bob Lee	Aaron SCHROEDER
Ed Lee	Isaac HAYES
Irma Lee	Irma THOMAS
Jack Nathan Lee	Jack LEE
Jackie Lee	Earl NELSON
Marty Lee	Martin Lee HOENES
Mary Elizabeth Johnson Lee	Jeanie GREENE
Myron Lee	Myron WACHENDORF
Regina Marie Lee	Regina RICHARDS
Sophie LeGlaire	Sonny LeGLAIRE
Sydney Leibowitz	Steve LAWRENCE
Amanda Blue Leigh	Amanda BLUE
Leila K	Leila EL KHALIFI
William Pitt Leleiohoku II Kalaho'olewa	Prince LELEIOHOKU
Pierre Louis Lemaire	Pierre LeMAIRE
Jules Lemare	Charles N. DANIELS
Dave Leon	Dave APPELL
Jack Leonard	Jack LITTLE
Jean Marcel Leroy	Jean-Jacques PERREY
Pierre Leroyer	Pierre DELANOË
Mike Leslie	Mike DAVIES
Tom Leslie	Snuff GARRETT
Lesslie	Snuff GARRETT
Henry Robert Merrill Levan	Bob MERRILL
Evelyn Levine	Evelyn DANZIG
Samuel M. Levine	Sam LEWIS
Gerald Levinson	Jerry LIVINGSTON
William S. Levise Jr.	Mitch RYDER
Lee Oskar Levitin	Lee OSKAR
Seymour Levittan	Cy LEVITAN
Burton Levy	Burton LANE
Marcella Levy	Marcy LEVY
Bridges George McGibbon Lewis	Bunny LEWIS
Debravon Lewis	Fizzy QWICK
Ken Lewis	Ken HAWKER
Travis Lewis	Michael MURPHEY
Walter Lewis	Furry LEWIS
Mik Lezan	Kim NAZEL
David Charles L'Heureux	D.C. LaRUE
Geoffrey Brillhart Lieb	Jeff PARIS
Theodore Life Jr.	Ted LIFE
Lil' Louis	Marvin Louis BURNS
Raynoma Liles	Raynoma SINGLETON
Anthony Frederick Lilly	Anthony KING
Jorge Lima Menezes	Jorge BEN
Limahl	Christopher HAMILL
Jack Limber	Luigi CREATORE
Joseph Conrad Lind	Peter Lind HAYES
Bryan Eugene Lindsay	Gene LYND

John Henry Linkey	Harry LINK
Joseph Linquito	Joe Lynn TURNER
Horace Linsky	Horace LINSLEY
John Lione	Trade MARTIN
Steven Barry Lipkin	Steve BARRI
Dickey Lee Lipscomb	Dickey LEE
Max K. Lipscomb	Scotty McKAY
Beverly Bremers Lipton	Beverly BREMERS
Little Steven	Steven VAN ZANDT
Little Jack Little	Jack LITTLE
Bunny Livingstone	Neville LIVINGSTON
LL Cool J	James Todd SMITH
Antonino Lo Tempio	Nino TEMPO
Carol Lo Tempio	April STEVENS
Lobo	Kent LaVOIE
James Hugh Loden	Sonny JAMES
Michael Logiudice	Mike ANTHONY
Timothy London	Tim BRINKHURST
Frederick Earl Long	Frederick LONG
Shorty Long	Frederick LONG
Lester Lopez	Les LEDO
Estelle Loring	Estelle LEVITT
Sam Lorraine	Harold FIELDS
Charles Elzer Loudermilk	Charlie LOUVIN
Ira Lonnie Loudermilk	Ira LOUVIN
Louiguy	Luis GUGLIELMI
Monie Love	Simone Antoinette JOHNSON
Francesco Paolo LoVecchio	Frankie LAINE
Michael Lovesmith	Michael Larry SMITH
Lene Lovich	Lili PREMILOVICH
David Eric Lowen	Eric LOWEN
Bernard Lowenthal	Bernie LOWE
Joe Lubinsky	Joe LUBIN
Lemeul Eugene Lucas	Gene AUSTIN
Yamma Brown Lumar	Yamma BROWN
Stephen Broughton Lunt	Stephen LUNT
Deke Lussier	Deke RICHARDS
Dennis Lussier	Deke RICHARDS
Cathy Lynn	Lee CATHY
Lyric	Mervin STEALS
M	
M.C. Hammer	Stanley BURRELL
M.C. Zipp	Jens Kjaer LARSEN
Warner Mack	Warner McPHERSON
Declan Patrick Aloysius MacManus	Elvis COSTELLO
Warner MacPherson	Warner McPHERSON
Johnny MacRae	Fred Aylor MacRAE
Gonzalvo Macrillo	Junie McCREE
Chauki Maddi	Tito MADI
Murphy Monroe Maddux Jr.	Pee Wee MADDUX
Fred Madison	Fred MENDELSOHN
Madonna	Madonna L. CICCONE
John L. Madora	John MADARA
Richard Maes	Tracy Lee ALEXANDER
Johnny Maestro	John MASTRANGELO
John Martin Maher	Johnny MARR
Edward J. Mahoney	Eddie MONEY
Sananda Maitreya	Terence Trent D'ARBY
Mamared	Anna CANTÙ

Jerry Mamberg	Jake HOOKER
Steve Mancha	Clyde WILSON
Enrico Nicola Mancini	Henry MANCINI
Anna Mangravito	Anna VITO
Pedro Manilla	Angelo PICCIONI
Pedro Manilla	MANTOVANI
David A. Mann	Dave MANN
John R. Mann	Jim KIRK
Gerry Manners	Bill ANSON
Lucylle Manns	Roberta TWAIN
Leroy Mannuel	Leroy EMMANUEL
Frere Manston	Marty WILDE
Annunzio Paolo Mantovani	MANTOVANI
Kurtis Mantronik	Kurtis EL KHALEEL
Dee Marak	Paul ANKA
Little Peggy March	Peggy MARCH
Friedel Albrecht Marcuse	Rolf MARBOT
Marcy Jo	Marcy SOCKEL
Guy Marfontaine	Yves-Jacques LAVOT
Michael Jay Margules	Michael JAY
Norman Margulies	Jerry RAGOVOY
Terrence Richard Marinan	Terry RICHARDS
Rinaldo R. Marino	Lennie MARTIN
Spiros D. Markantonatos	Spiro MARKS
Dewey Markham	Pigmeat MARKHAM
David Marks	Spiro MARKS
Mark Markwell	Hugo PERETTI
Mark Markwell	Luigi CREATORE
Marley Marl	Marlon WILLIAMS
David Nesta Marley	Ziggy MARLEY
Thomas Marlowe	Fred JACKSON
Thomas Marlowe	W. Albert POSER
Marta Marrero	MARTIKA
Richard Elvern Marsh	Sky SAXON
Vincent James Martemucci	Vince MARTELL
Allen Martin	Allen MARTANCIK
Dino Martin	Dean MARTIN Jr.
John David Martin	Moon MARTIN
Lenny Martin	Lennie MARTIN
Raymond Stuart Martin	Lester POWELL
Rich Martin	Richard FROST
T. Martin	Martin MONTAGUE
Tom Martin	Thomas FROST
Vincent John Martin	Vince CLARKE
Yvonne Martin	Yvonne BAKER
Luiz Antonio Martinez	Lewis MARTINÉE
Mariano Martinez	Marianito MORES
Robert Martinez	Rudy MARTINEZ
Gene Martyn	Marcel STELLMAN
Babe Marvin	Babe CHIVIAN
Hank Brian Marvin	Hank MARVIN
Albert Eric Maschwitz	Holt MARVELL
Eric Maschwitz	Holt MARVELL
Maskman	Harmon BETHEA
Sandy Mason	Sandy THEORET
B. Masona	Charles SOUZA
Joe Medwick Masters	Joe VEASEY
Louis Aldine Mathis	Louis MATHIS
Ross G. Matico	Bud ROSS
Vera Matson	Ken DARBY

Willy Mattes	Charles WILDMAN
Audrey Matthews	Kaiya MATTHEWS
Eugenie Theresa Matthias	Theresa MATTHIAS
Raynoma Mayberry	Raynoma SINGLETON
Mark Maytorena	Marq TORIEN
MC Blowfish	Gregory JACOBS
MC Bones	Walfried BÖCKER
MC Breed	Eric BREED
MC Breeze	Joey B. ELLIS
James McAllister	Smokey McALLISTER
Perry McBride	Perry KIBBLE
C.W. McCall	Bill FRIES
Cash McCall	Morris DOLLISON
Romeo "Breath" McCall	Romeo McCALL
William Aubry McCall	W.S. STEVENSON
Peter Michael McCartney	Mike McGEAR
Obie McClinton	O.B. McCLINTON
Osbie Burnett McClinton	O.B. McCLINTON
Timothy Scott McConnell	Tim SCOTT
William Patrick McCord	Billy VERA
Dennis McCrohan	Mars BONFIRE
Gerald McCrohan	Jerry EDMONTON
Christopher McDaniels	Christopher MAX
James Solomon McDonald	Solomon BURKE
Brother Jack McDuff	Jack McDUFF
Eugene McDuffy	Jack McDUFF
Albert Geoffrey McElhinney	Geoff MACK
Van McElvain	Van McLAIN
Joe McGhee	Joe SENECA
Andrew Esmond Sheridan McGinnity	Tony SHERIDAN
Colin McGlinchy	James FREUD
Yvonne McGowan	Yvonne DEVANEY
James Joseph McGuinn III	Roger McGUINN
James Roger McGuinn	Roger McGUINN
Jim McGuinn	Roger McGUINN
Lonnie McIntosh	Lonnie MACK
Jenny McKeown	Theresa MATTHIAS
James Horton McKinley	McKinley HORTON
Perri McKissack	Perri Arlette REID
Mark McLaughlin	Marti PELLOW
Bruce McMeans	Bruce CHANNEL
Wayne McNatt	Wayne FAMOUS
Donna McPherson	Wyatt McPHERSON
Richard Cecil McPherson	Cecil MACK
Teddy McRae	Ted McRAE
Theodore McRae	Ted McRAE
Norman Meade	Jerry RAGOVOY
Edwin Lionel Meadows	Punky MEADOWS
Meat Loaf	Marvin Lee ADAY
Samuel Medoff	Dick MANNING
Joe Medwick	Joe VEASEY
Robert George Meek	Joe MEEK
Mike Meezy	Michael MARSHALL

Heinz Meier	Henry MAYER
Kurt Meier	Kurt MALOO
Theodore Meister	Ted DARYLL
John Graham Mellor	Joe STRUMMER
Mellow Man Ace	Sergio REYES
Israel Melnikoff	Robert MELLIN
Memphis Slim	Peter CHATMAN
Murray Mencher	Ted MURRY
Jack Mendelsohn	Jimmy SHIRL
Samuel Mendola	Vic DANA
Michel Merlo	Michael MERLO
Billy Merman	Bill GIANT
Johnny Lamont Merrett	Little Johnny TAYLOR
Billy Meshel	Wilbur MESHEL
Sol H. Meshel	Wilbur MESHEL
Edward Mesner	Billy NESS
Dwight Meyers	HEAVY D
Miami Steve	Steven VAN ZANDT
Irving Micahnik	Ira MACK
Stephen Michael	Stephen MICHAELS
Irwin Michnick	Mitch LEIGH
Joey Edward Michno	Joey COVINGTON
Charlie Midnight	Charles E. KAUFMAN
Mighty Hannibal	James T. SHAW
Francis Cosmo Migliaccio	Fran COSMO
Mikaljon	Al ABRAMS
Mikaljon	John O'DEN
Mikaljon	Stanley OSSMAN
Malvina Milder	Malvina REYNOLDS
Otis Miles Jr.	Otis Clayburne WILLIAMS
Garry Miles	Buzz CASON
Jean Miles	Buck RAM
Junior Miles	Edgar BRONFMAN
James Wesley Miley	Bubber MILEY
Frank Military	Francis Philip MILITARY
Alex Miller	Sonny Boy WILLIAMSON II
Bob Miller	Shelby DARNELL
Branko Bernard Miller	Tony COLE
J. D. Miller	Jerry WEST
James Henry Miller	Ewan MacCOLL
Joseph D. Miller	Jerry WEST
Lonnie Vincent Miller	Lonnie VENCENT
Lost John Miller	John A. MILLER
Ned Miller	Nathan MILLER
Perry Miller	Jesse Colin YOUNG
Shorty Miller	Roy MICHAELS
Geraldine Milligan	Geraldine HUNT
Lucius Venable Millinder	Lucky MILLINDER
Yvonne Mills	Yvonne BAKER
Little Milton	Milton CAMPBELL
Dennis Minogue	Terry CASHMAN
Robert Miskiewicz	Robert STEELE
Jacqueline Misrahi	Michele MICHAELE
Art Mitchell	Argentry MITCHELL
Bobby Mitchell	Michael GUERRA
James Mitchell	Ronny MITCHELL
Ronnie Mitchell	Ronny MITCHELL
Autry DeWalt Mixon Jr.	Jr. WALKER
Mogol	Giulio RAPETTI
Ivan Mogull	Phil BELMONTE

Lawrence Molomoflavich	Larry MOLLIN
Gustav Molvik	Taime DOWNE
Lincoln Wayne Moman	Chips MOMAN
Robert E. Moncrief	Bobby EDWARDS
Richard Anthony Monsour	Dick DALE
Magnificent Montague	Nathaniel NATHAN
Nathaniel Montague	Nathaniel NATHAN
Ezekiel Christopher Montanez	Chris MONTEZ
Anne Black Montgomery	Anne McIAN
Walter R. Moody	Ken WOOD
Deborah Mae Moore	Debra Mae MOORE
James H. Moore	Slim HARPO
James Isaac Moore	Slim HARPO
Johnny Moore	John Edward MOORE
Mae Moore	Debra Mae MOORE
Peter Lord Moreland	Peter LORD
Wenceslao Moreno	Señor WENCES
Mariano Mores	Marianito MORES
Neil Moret	Charles N. DANIELS
John Russell Morgan	Rushton MOREVE
James Corbitt Morris	Jimmy DRIFTWOOD
Stevland Hardaway Morris	Stevie WONDER
Theodora Morse	Dorothy TERRISS
Al Mortimer	Henry JEROME
David Mortimer	David AUSTIN
David Michael Mortimer	David AUSTIN
George Morton	Shadow MORTON
Mickey Moses	Mickey SHORR
Mickie Most	Michael Peter HAYES
Georges Moustaki	Giuseppe MUSTACCHI
Michael Mozart	Nikki LEE
A. Muller	Warner WILDER
Aubrey Wilson Mullican	Moon MULLICAN
Jeffrey Steven Mundy	Jeff MONDAY
Marco Antonio Muniz	Mark MUNIZ
Mark Anthony Muniz	Mark MUNIZ
Michael David Munves	Mike MORE
Michael Münzing	Benito BENITES
Michael Martin Murphey	Michael MURPHEY
Murray the K	Murray KAUFMAN
James E. Myers	Jimmy DeKNIGHT
Sharon Lee Myers	Jackie DeSHANNON
David Luke Myrick	T. Texas TYLER
Mystro	Melvin STEALS
Vince Nacardo	Vinny NACCARATO
Warren Nadel	Randy STARR
Brad Nail	Brad HOWELL
Dolores Nance	Jody REYNOLDS
Napoleon XIV	Jerry SAMUELS
Peter Nash	Pete NASH
N. Nathan	Nathaniel NATHAN
Sydney Nathan	Lois MANN
N	
Kim Renard Nazel	Kim NAZEL
James H. Nebbergall	Jimmy NEBB
Allen J. Neiburg	Al NEIBURG
Albert Nelson	Albert KING

Benjamin Earl Nelson	Ben E. KING
Paul Reginald Nelson	Paul HYDE
Prince Rogers Nelson	PRINCE
Nervous Norvus	Jimmy DRAKE
Lawrence Thomas Netto	Loz NETTO
Nevelle	Nevelle HODGE
Naomi Neville	Allen TOUSSAINT
Laura Lee Newton	Laura LEE
Prime Minister Pete Nice	Pete NASH
Stephen Nice	Steve HARLEY
Jean Nicolas	J. Nicolas FELGEN
Carl Niessen	Charly NIESSEN
Carl Niessen-Reisfeld	Charly NIESSEN
Fred Nightingale	Tony HATCH
Ollie Nightingale	Ollie HOSKINS
Joe Nigro	Joe NEGRO
Laura Nigro	Laura NYRO
Nisa	Nicola SALERNO
Mary Catherine Nivert	Taffy DANOFF
Taffy Nivert	Taffy DANOFF
William Myles Nobles	Billy MYLES
Bob Norberg	Bob NORMAN
Bessie Norris	Betty WRIGHT
Bessie Regina Norris	Betty WRIGHT
Sonny Norton	Daniel NORTON
William H. Norvas	Bill NORVAS
C. Notelgnis	Charles SINGLETON
Rosetta Nubin	Rosetta THARPE
A. Nugetre	Ahmet ERTEGUN
Nuggy	Ahmet ERTEGUN
Michael Nuttall	Mike FLOREALE
Anita Leonard Nye	Anita LEONARD
O	
Enya Patricia O'Brennan	ENYA
Dionysius P. A. O'Brien	Tom SPRINGFIELD
Bonnie Lynn O'Farrell	Bonnie BRAMLETT
Shirley Marie O'Garra	Shirley ELLIS
Ersel O'Hickey	Ersel HICKEY
Ade Olayinka	Melvin ANDERSON
Dewey Lindon Oldham Jr.	Spooner OLDHAM
Oliver	Bill SWOFFORD
Michael Olsen	Lee Eugene MICHAELS
Samuel Henry Olusegun Adeola	SEAL
Dennis Thomas Oosthuis	Dennis EAST
Johnny Orlando	Hugo PERETTI
Anne Orlowski	Gene PITNEY
Sheena Shirley Orr	Sheena EASTON
Ann Orson	Elton JOHN
Roland Jaime Orzabal de la Quintana	Roland ORZABAL
Benjamin Orzechowski	Benjamin ORR
Robert Eugene Osborne	Robert Eugene OSBORN
Bobby Van Osbourne	Robert Eugene OSBORN
John Michael Osbourne	Ozzy OSBOURNE
Bob Osburn	Robert Eugene OSBORN

Brian O'Shea	Brian KEITH
Mike Ossman	Stanley OSSMAN
James Newell Osterberg Jr.	Iggy POP
Raymond O'Sullivan	Gilbert O'SULLIVAN
Raymond Edward O'Sullivan	Gilbert O'SULLIVAN
Osunlade	Christian WARREN
John Kennedy Oswald	John OSWALD
Richard T. Otcasek	Ric OCASEK
Johnny Otis Jr.	Shuggie OTIS
Clive Otis	Clyde OTIS
Clyde Lovern Otis	Clyde OTIS
Phyliss Otis	Johnny OTIS
Curtis Ousley	King CURTIS
Virginia Lucille Overstake	Jenny Lou CARSON
Cliff Owens	Clyde OTIS
Barbara Linda Ozen	Barbara LYNN
Barbara Lynn Ozen	Barbara LYNN
P	
P. Red	Willie PERRYMAN
June Page	Rickie PAGE
Wally Palamarchuk	Wally PALMAR
Ralph Palladino	Ralph DINO
Cedric King Palmer	King PALMER
Sandra L. Palmer	Sandy PALMER
Georgios Kyriacos Panayiotou	George MICHAEL
George Pantazi	Georges BOULANGER
Teodoro Paoletta	Teddy POWELL
Evangelos Papathanassiou	VANGELIS
Richard Papazaian	Dick RICHARDS
Peter Papini	Peter YELLOWSTONE
Gail Collins Pappalardi	Gail COLLINS
Zoe Parentau	Joan WHITNEY
Peylia Parham	Sugar Pie DeSANTO
Johnny Paris	John POCISK
Noel Paris	Noel REGNEY
Clarke Ross Parker	Ross PARKER
Deanie Parker	Willia Dean PARKER
Gordon Rod Parker	Hubert GIRAUD
Herman Parker	Junior PARKER
Richard Parker	Richard Lee WOLD
Sol Parker	Barry PARKER
Willa Dean Parker	Willia Dean PARKER
Robere Parlez	Robert PARLEE
Ian Hunter Patterson	Ian HUNTER
Pat Patterson	Leon PAYNE
Lynn Paul	Buck RAM
Victor Paul	Luigi CREATORE
Clarence Pauling	Clarence PAUL
Pavel	Frank KOCIAN
George Paxton	George EDDY
Leon Roger Payne	Leon PAYNE
William Peaches	Billy PEACHES
Charles Graham Peate	Charles GRAHAM
Benjamin Franklin Peay	Brook BENTON
Pebbles	Perri Arlette REID
James William Pebworth	Dub WILLIAMS
Herman Peckar	Bobby RACKEP

Jorgen Ingmann Pedersen	Jorgen INGMANN
Robert John Pedrick	Robert JOHN
Gayla Peevey	Jamie HORTON
Louis Russell Pegues	Lou COURTNEY
Mary Frances Penick	Skeeter DAVIS
Daniel Pennington	Dan PENN
Ramon Daniel Pennington	Ray PENNINGTON
Wallace Daniel Pennington	Dan PENN
Jacques Pépino	James BOLDEN
L.R. Peques	Mary WELLS
Marvin Karlton Percy	Marvin RAINWATER
June Peretti	June WINTERS
Christine Anne Perfect	Christine McVIE
Henri Perret	Kelly NICKELS
Christine Perrin	Christine YARIAN
Columbus Perry	Piney BROWN
Al Perton	Max DIAMOND
Harry Perzigian	Harry PARESS
Frank Peter	Frank PETERSON
Jed Peters	Jerry LEIBER
Jed Peters	Mike STOLLER
Dick Peterson	Nicholas RICHARDSON
Tom Petersson	Thomas John PETERSON
Anthony Petolino	Don STIRLING
Paul Pfab	Peter PFAB
Francis Philip	Francis Philip MILITARY
Gary Edmund Philippet	Gary PHILIPPET
Frank Phillips	Billy GUY
Gary Phillips	Gary PHILIPPET
James Phillips	John TURNER
James John Turner Phillips	John TURNER
Phil Phillips	Phil BAPTISTE
James G. Photoglo	Jim PHOTOGLO
Jim Photoglou	Jim PHOTOGLO
Piano Red	Willie PERRYMAN
John Campbell Picard	Aryan ZERO
Thomas R. Picardo	Tommy WEST
Frederick Picariello	Freddy CANNON
Angelo Ferdinando Piccioni	Angelo PICCIONI
Albert Piccirilli	Al REX
Michael John Hurst Pickworth	Mike HURST
Mike Pickworth	Mike HURST
Barry Alan Pincus	Barry MANILOW
Pipou Pipokas	Yves LACOMBLEZ
Donny Pitts	Donny HATHAWAY
Plinky	Sal GIGLIO Jr.
Sal Plinky	Sal GIGLIO Jr.
Henry Plischke	Kent HENRY
Clarence Albert Poindexter	Al DEXTER
Patricia Eva Pointer	Bonnie POINTER
Eddie Pola	Edward POLA
Sidney Edward Pollacsek	Edward POLA
Lester William Polsfuss	Les PAUL
Jerome Pomus	Doc POMUS
Giacomo Pontoriero	Jack PONTI

Coe Porter	Thomas J. COE
Gary Posie	David LAFLAMME
Michael Postil	Mike POST
Clive Powell	Georgie FAME
Chester William Powers Jr.	Chet POWERS
Harry Pratt	Harvey FUQUA
Lili Marlene Premilovich	Lili PREMILOVICH
John Barry Prendergast	John BARRY
Michael John Prendergast	Mike PENDER
Dory V. Shannon Previn	Dory PREVIN
Michael Price	Harvey PRICE
Ronald K. Price	Ronn PRICE
Gertrude Pridgett	Ma RAINEY
Prince Be	Attrell CORDES
Prince Buster	Buster CAMPBELL
Arabian Prince	Kim NAZEL
Fresh Prince	Will SMITH
Roger Pritchard	Lee SHERIDEN
Andreas Ludwig Priwin	André PREVIN
P.J. Proby	James Marcus SMITH
Orville Proctor	Hank THOMPSON
Salek Profesorski	Spencer PROFFER
Josephine Moore Proffitt	Sylvia DEE
Ronald Harry Prokop	Skip PROKOP
Ronn Prokop	Skip PROKOP
Bryan Pugh	Perry FORD
Virginia Wynette Pugh	Tammy WYNETTE
Luigi Pulci	Gino REDI
Howard Stanley Puris	Tony POWERS
Billy Purser	Gary BURBANK
Claude Putman Jr.	Curly PUTMAN
Q	
Susan Kay Quattrochio	Suzi QUATRO
Eddy Quintela Mendonca	Eddy QUINTELA
R	
Trevor Charles Rabin	Trevor RABIN
Sydney Rabinowitz	Sid ROBIN
Trevor Charles Rabinowitz	Trevor RABIN
Andrew Racheck	Bud REHAK
Milan Radenkovich	Rick RODELL
James Radomski	James RADO
Jordan Ragovoy	Jerry RAGOVOY
Harold Ray Ragsdale	Ray STEVENS
Milton Rajonsky	Boots BROWN
Rakim	William GRIFFIN
Samuel Ram	Buck RAM
Bellino Ramaglia	Bill RAMAL
John Henry Ramistella	Johnny RIVERS
Phil Ramocon	Phil RAMACON
Joey Ramone	Jeff HYMAN
Johnny Ramone	John CUMMINGS
Tommy Ramone	Tom ERDELYI
Andrew Ramsbottom	Andrew MANN
Ande Rand	Buck RAM
Buddy Randell	Bill CRANDALL
Donald James Randolph	Don COVAY
Brian Robson Rankin	Hank MARVIN
Shabba Ranks	Rexton GORDON

Renato Ranucci	Renato RASCEL
Paul Rapport	Paul EVANS
Michael Charles Rashkow	Mike LENDELL
Marcy Rauer	Marci RAUER
Raun	Ron ANIELLO
Jean Monte Ray	Jean GLOVER
Adreamentania Paul Razafkeriefo	Andy RAZAF
Richard Allan Ream	Rikki ROCKETT
Edward Henry Reardon	Eddie FONTAINE
Malcolm John Rebennack	Mac REBENNACK
Red River Dave	Dave McENERY
Clarence Eugene Redd III	Gene REDD Jr.
Clarence Eugene Redd Jr.	Gene REDD Sr.
Gail Redd	Ramona REDD
Teddy Redell	Teddy DeLano RIEDEL
P. G. Redi	Gino REDI
Eivets Rednow	Stevie WONDER
Rob Reeco	Bob HAMILTON
Buck Reeder	Jan SAVAGE
Steven Quincy Reeder	Eskew REEDER
Ruth Evelyn Reeves	Ruth LYONS
Shirley Reeves	Shirley OWENS
Dominique Regia-Corte	Domenico REGIACORTE
Ralph Reichenthal	Ralph RAINGER
Antonio M. Reid	Antonio REID
L.A. Reid	Antonio REID
Derf Reklaw	Derf Reklaw RAHEEM
Paul Remy	MANTOVANI
Googie René	Rafael RENÉ
Rafael L. "Googie" René	Rafael RENÉ
Rafael Leon René	Rafael RENÉ
Jerry Renewych	Bob BILYK
Jerry Reno	Gerry ROBINSON
Franz Reuter	Frank FARIAN
Franz Reuther	Frank FARIAN
Jacques Revaud	Jacques REVAUX
Tony Rey	Anthony Michael BRUNO
George Reyam	Hans-Jörg MAYER
Helen Rhodes	Guy D'HARDELOT
David Rice	Josh RICE
Mack Rice	Bonny RICE
Sir Mack Rice	Bonny RICE
Stephen Rice	Eddie RICE
Allan Dennis Rich	Allan RICH
Denise Rich	Joy DENNY
Little Richard	Richard PENNIMAN
Jake Hooker Richards	Jake HOOKER
George Baker Richardson	George RICHEY
Nancy Richardson	Taja SEVELLE
Jane Richman	Jane CHILD
Howard S. Richmond	Jessie CAVANAUGH
Frederic Joseph Ricketts	Kenneth J. ALFORD
Louis Rico	Ken MOULE
Louis Rico	Ted HEATH
Gladys Riddle	Gladys HAMPTON

Margaret Jean Rider	Maggie RYDER
Stanard Ridgway	Stan RIDGWAY
Harlan Dale Riffe	Dale WRIGHT
Timothy Christian Riley	Clemon Timothy RILEY
Robert Rimato	Robert HAZARD
Giovanni Rota Rinaldi	Nino ROTA
Peter Rizzo	Peter RISINGHAM
Roaring Lion	Rafael DE LEON
Fred Allen Roberds	Smokey ROBERDS
John Godfrey Owen Roberts	Paddy ROBERTS
George Austin Robertson Jr.	Austin ROBERTS
Ella Robertson	Lou DINNING
Henry Macleod Robertson	McLeod ROBERTSON
Thomas Morgan Robertson	Thomas DOLBY
Don D. Robey	Deadric MALONE
Sydney Robin	Sid ROBIN
William Robinson Jr.	Smokey ROBINSON
Bobby Robinson	Morgan C. ROBINSON
Gerald Robinson	Gerry ROBINSON
Harry Robinson	McLeod ROBERTSON
J. Robinson	Sylvia ROBINSON
Jay Robinson	Sylvia ROBINSON
Martin D. Robinson	Marty ROBBINS
Morgan Clyde Robinson	Morgan C. ROBINSON
Philo Jack Robinson	Jack ROBINSON
Ray Charles Robinson	Ray CHARLES
Carson J. Robison	Maggie ANDREWS
Paul Irvin Roby	Paul ROBI
Chubb Rock	Richard SIMPSON
Rockwell	Kennedy GORDY
Vin Roddie	Vincent RODOMISTA
Gaby Rodgers	Jerry LEIBER
Juan Raol Davis Rodiguez	Johnny RODRIGUEZ
Moises Simon Rodriguez	Moises SIMONS
K. C. Rogan	Johnny BURKE
Dewayne Julius Rogers	D.J. ROGERS
Eugene Rogers	Smokey ROGERS
Jimmie Otto Rogers	Jimmie O. ROGERS
Kay Rogers	Eddie SNYDER
Milton Shorty Rogers	Boots BROWN
Jose A. Rojas-Miranda	Tony ROJAS
Daisy Rollocks	Desiree ROLLOCKS
Del Roma	Paul MAURIAT
Sam Roman	Edgar BRONFMAN
Richie Rome	Richard V. Di CICCO
Romuald	Romuald FIGUIER
Joseph Dominic Angelo Roncoroni	Joseph RONCORONI
Brian Rosbotham	Brian ROSSI
William Bruce Rose Jr.	Axl ROSE
Jerold Rosenberg	Jerry ROSS
Kenneth Rosenberg	Kenny VANCE
William Samuel Rosenberg	Billy ROSE
Ann Rosenblatt	Ann RONELL
Richard Joel Rosenblatt	Ritchie CORDELL
Adam Ross	Irving ROTH

Billy J. Ross	Billy NESS
Mark D. Ross	Mark ROSS
Marquis Ross	Mark ROSS
Marshall Ross	Lester POWELL
Dale Krantz Rossington	Dale KRANTZ
Eduard Roth	Eddi ROTHÉ
Eddie Rothé	Eddi ROTHÉ
Cal Rotherman	Kal MANN
Dean Rotherman	David CHANDLER
Roy Be	Roy BERMINGHAM
Fred Royal	Roy ALFRED
Robert Wilson Royer	Robb ROYER
Dessie Rozier	James BROWN
Lynsey Mockon Rubin	Lynsey DePAUL
Laura Lee Rundless	Laura LEE
Jerome A. Rusch	Jerry RUSH
Bert Russell	Bert BERNS
Sidney Keith Russell	Bob RUSSELL
Dorothy Russo	Deena CHARLES
Harold Rustigan	Russ REGAN
Gregory Rybarski	Chip Z'NUFF
Jeremy Allan Ryder	Jack HUES
S	
Suhayla Sabir	Djuana JOHNICAN
Antonio Adolfo Maurity Sabóia	Antonio ADOLFO
Hajji Rajah Kasim Sabre	Rodger COLLINS
Lugee Sacco	Lou CHRISTIE
Allan Preston Sachs	Alan MERRILL
Sade	Helen ADU
Robert Sadoff	Ira LEE
Sa-Fire	Wilma COSMÉ
Charles H. Sagle	Carl STEVENS
Christian Sainturat	Christian SARREL
Kashif Saleem	Michael JONES
Salt	Cheryl JAMES
Yennik Samoht	Kenny THOMAS
Linda Joy Sampson	Linda SCOTT
Sam Samudio	Domingo SAMUDIO
Charles Sananes	Charles DANVERS
Sonny Sanders	William Nelson SANDERS
Zelma Sanders	Zell SANDERS
Charles Alan Sandford	Chas SANDFORD
David Stuart Sandler	Dave STUART
Peggy Santiglia	Peggy FARINA
Paul Sapherson	Paul RYAN
Father Guido Sarducci	Don NOVELLO
Clarence Satchell	Andrew NOLAND
Lucille Marie Raymonde Savoie	Lucille STARR
Ronnie Savoy	Eugene HAMILTON
Gerard Hugh Sayer	Leo SAYER
Matilda Genevieve Scaduto	Felice BRYANT
Giovanni Dominico Scafone Jr.	Jack SCOTT
Louis Scaglione	Lou MONTE
Clarence Alexander Scarborough	Skip SCARBOROUGH
Mario Scarpa	Guy MARKS
Gene Allan Schachter	Gene ALLAN
Sanford Phillip Schafler	Ric MARLOW

Gary Wayne Schelton	Gary SHELTON
Hartwig Schierbaum	Marian GOLD
Boris Claudio Schifrin	Lalo SCHIFRIN
Philip Gary Schlein	P.F. SLOAN
Léon Schlienger	Noel REGNEY
Steven Bruce Schneider	Steve STEVENS
Janey Schramm	Janey STREET
Sholom Schreiber	Mickey Lee LANE
Solomon M Schreiber	Mickey Lee LANE
Bernard Schrieber	Bernie LANE
Nook Schrier	David CARROLL
Hod David Schudson	Hod DAVID
Jacob Lewis Schwartz	Jack LAWRENCE
Nat Schwartz	Nat BURTON
Paul Schwartz	Paul HAMPTON
Andreas Schwarz	Andreas SCHWARZ-RUSZCZYNSKI
Garrett Scott	Gary DeCARLO
Marvin Scott	Sidney COLIN
Marvin Scott	Talbot ROTHWELL
Randy L. Scott	Shelley HAIMS
Robin Scutt	Mark PAUL
Curtis Wayne Seals	Curtis WAYNE
Danny Wayland Seals	Dan SEALS
Chilton Searcy	Chilton PRICE
Juan Francisco Secada Ramirea	Jon SECADA
Frederick Segrest	Freddie HART
Priscilla Seibert	Priscilla COOLIDGE
Anthony John Selvidge	Tony KAYE
Anthony September	Bernie LOWE
Anthony September	Kal MANN
Glynna Session	Glenna SESSION
Taj A. Sevelle	Taja SEVELLE
Omari M. Shabazz	Paul STEWART
Naomi Shackleford	Lee HAZLEWOOD
Selig Shaftel	Sunny SKYLAR
John Nicholas Shakespeare	John CARTER
Sam the Sham	Domingo SAMUDIO
Del Sharh	Carl FISHER
Emanuel Sharoff	Lanny SHORE
Jean Sharp	Jean Sharp MURPHY
Mike Sharpe	Mike SHAPIRO
James Timothy Shaw	James T. SHAW
Jon Sheldon	Kal MANN
Beresford Shepherd	Shep SHEPHERD
James Shane Sheppard	James SHEPPARD
Shane Sheppard	James SHEPPARD
Bonnie Sheridan	Bonnie BRAMLETT
Sue Linda Shifrin-Cassidy	Sue SHIFRIN
Neil Ship	Neil SHEPPARD
Dannie Shipley	Royal C. BANNON
Shock G	Gregory JACOBS
Troy Shondell	Gary SHELTON
Albert Shubert	Andy GIBSON
Corby Michael John Siddons	Mike CORBY
Robin Sidebotham	Robin GEORGE
Georges Sigara	Jack FISHMAN
Sigidi	Sigidi ABDULLAH
Susanne Sigl	Susanne MÜLLER-PI

Robert Silbert	Bob ROBERTS
François Gilbert Silly	Gilbert BÉCAUD
Yvonne Silver	Donna FARGO
Albert Silverman	Al STILLMAN
Juan Fernando Silvetti Adorno	Bebu SILVETTI
Chuck Simmons	Chuck TAYLOR
Walter Simmons	Simtec SIMMONS
Gus Simon	Gus EDWARDS
Michael Saint Simon	Simon SOUSSAN
Richard Anthony Simpson	Richard SIMPSON
Singing Nun	Jeanine DECKERS
Sinhô	Jose BARBOSA DA SILVA
Siouxsie Sioux	Susan BALLION
Leonhard Raymond Sipes	Tommy COLLINS
Sir Mix-A-Lot	Anthony RAY
Sirarcusa	Ramon ARCUSA
John Siras	Ira SCHUSTER
Bobby Skel	Robert Doyle SKELTON
Skip	Clyde BATTIN
Yani Skoradalides	Les VANDYKE
Arthur Skupsky	Art ROBERTS
Luke Skyywalker	Luther CAMPBELL
Slash	Saul HUDSON
Frank Slay Jr.	Frank SLAY
Dabney R. Slick	Darby SLICK
Flip Sloan	P.F. SLOAN
Phil Sloan	P.F. SLOAN
Edward Smackels Jr.	Ed ROSE
Norman Don Smart II	N.D. SMART II
David Michael Smet	David HALLYDAY
Willard Christopher Smith Jr.	Will SMITH
Acacia Smith	Stacy SMITH
Barbara Ann Smith	Barbara GEORGE
Denise Katrina Smith	Denise MATTHEWS
Ethel Smith	Ellas McDANIEL
Frances Octavia Smith	Dale EVANS
James Smith	Jim DALE
Jewel Faye Smith	Sammi SMITH
Kim Smith	Kim WILDE
Linda Cheryl Smith	Cheryl LYNN
Lon Christian Smith	Chris CHRISTIAN
Norman Arnold Smith	Hurricane SMITH
Penny Smith	Debbie DEAN
Reba Jeanette Smith	Debbie DEAN
Reginald Leonard Smith	Marty WILDE
Richard James Reginald Steven Smith	Ricky WILDE
Rick Smith	Richard David SMITH
Rickey Smith	Ricky Darnell SMITH
Ricky Smith	Ricky WILDE
Ricky Steven Reginald Smith	Ricky WILDE
Robert Smith	Robert James SMITH
Thomassina Carrollyne Smith	Thomassina SMITH
Toni Smith	Thomassina SMITH
Alice Tweed Smyth	Tweed SMITH
Carl Smyth	Charles SMYTH

Cathal Joseph Patrick Smyth	Charles SMYTH
Michael Anthony Sobolewski	Michael ANTHONY
Piero Soffici	Pietro SOFFICI
Isadore Soifer	Alex NORTH
Fudgie Kae Solomon	Fudgie KAE
Herbert Jay Solomon	Herbie MANN
Frank Sorgatz	Frank MERTENS
Hal Sothern	Hal SOUTHERN
Soeur Sourire	Jeanine DECKERS
Joseph Alfred Souter	Joe SOUTH
Peter Alexander Southworth	Peter SHELLEY
Rachel Southworth	Rachel BOLAN
Woodrow Wilson Sovine	Red SOVINE
Lloyd A. Sparks	Randy SPARKS
Lona Spector	Lona STEVENS
Alexander Spence	Skip SPENCE
Charles Spencer	Randy BACHMAN
Spice	Amir SHAKIR
William Spicer	Billy STORM
Markus Spiro	Mark SPIRO
Murray Sporn	Freddy FRIDAY
Richard Lewis Springthorpe	Rick SPRINGFIELD
Dick St. John	Dick GOSTING
St. Paul	Paul PETERSON
Stacey Q	Stacey SWAIN
Trevor Herbert Stanford	Trevor STANFORD
Mel Stark	Cliff PARMAN
Jack Starkey	Buddy PEPPER
Jack Retherford Starkey	Buddy PEPPER
Richard Starkey	Ringo STARR
Jade Starling	Jeanne ROBERTS
Ray Starr	Ray PENNINGTON
Canzetta Staton	Candi STATON
Canzetta Staton-Sussewell	Candi STATON
Bob Steele	Robert STEELE
Bobby Steele	Robert STEELE
Wanda Cleo Stegall	Vicki YOUNG
Siegfried Alex Stein	Alex ALSTONE
Wendy Steiner	Wendy WALDMAN
Jerry Marvin Stembridge	Chip YOUNG
Ralph Sterling	David CARROLL
Heidi Stern	Jennifer RUSH
Bruce Noel Stevens	Even STEVENS
Carole Yvette Marie Stevens	Chaka KHAN
Fred Stevens	Sol MARCUS
Yvette Stevens	Chaka KHAN
William R. Stevenson Jr.	William STEVENSON
Augustus Stevenson	Bobby STEVENSON
Mickey Stevenson	William STEVENSON
Henry Ellis Stewart	Redd STEWART
Siobhan Stewart	Siobhan FAHEY
Lionel Michael Stitcher	Mitch MURRAY
Nicholas Stokes	Simon STOKES
J. W. Stole	Franck POURCEL
Joe Stone	Joseph Louis STONE

Sly Stone	Sylvester STEWART
Lally Stott	Harold STOTT
Alfreda Strandberg	Dorothy TERRISS
Jaap Streefkerk	Steve KIRK
Roberta Lee Streeter	Bobbie GENTRY
Gartside Paul Strohmeyer	Green GARTSIDE
Paul Julian Strohmeyer	Green GARTSIDE
Lisa Struce	Liza STRIKE
Barry Stuart	Herbert NEWMAN
David Stuart	Chad STUART
Eddie Stuart	Eddie COHEN
Levi Stubbles	Levi STUBBS
Jim Stuberge	Jimmy CURTISS
Jimmy Stulberger	Jimmy CURTISS
Subway	Bernard ESTARDY
Morton Aaron Suckno	Mort STEVENS
Iris Colleen Summers	Mary FORD
Jerry Summers	Jerry GROSS
Gordon Sumner	STING
Richard Supa	Richie SUPA
Jean Surrey	Jean DINNING
Bruno Alex Survilla	Red SURREY
Frances Swan	Frances FROST
James Dixon Swan	Jimmy BARNES
Henry Lee Swartz	Henry Lee SUMMER
Sweet L.D.	Djuana JOHNICAN
DeWayne Sweet	Romeo McCALL
Peter Sweval	Pieter SWEVAL
DeVante Swing	Donald DeGRATE
William Oliver Swofford	Bill SWOFFORD
Bret Michael Sychak	Bret MICHAELS
Nidra Sylvers	Nidra BEARD
Sylvester	Sylvester JAMES
William Szathmary	Bill DANA
Lévay Szilveszter	Sylvester LEVAY
T	
Sandro Taccani	Alessandro TACCANI
Patricia Henley Talbert	Patricia HENLEY
Steven Victor Tallarico	Steven TYLER
Jascha Tambimuttu	Tambi FERNANDO
Tampa Red	Hudson WHITTAKER
Philip Geoffrey Targett-Adams	Phil MANZANERA
Howard Tashman	Tash HOWARD
Eli Tatarsky	Bobby ELI
Lawrence Taylor Tatman III	Skip TAYLOR
William Edward Taylor Jr.	Billy TAYLOR
Beloyd Taylor	Bernard TAYLOR
James Warren Taylor	J.T. TAYLOR
R. Taylor	Joseph ROBINSON
Robert Taylor	Joseph ROBINSON
Chaim Hillel Teicher	Kenny KAREN
Phil Teitelbaum	Terry PHILIPS
Gary Temkin	Gary KNIGHT
Harold Temkin	Gary KNIGHT
Bob Temple	Bob WILSON
Kathleen Wakefield Tenen	Kathy WAKEFIELD
Richard Edward Tenryk	Richard TEE
Antoine Roberto Teppardo	Robert TEPPER
Albert Tepper	Al NEVINS

Robert M. Tepper	Robert TEPPER
Pearl White Terrell	Pearl WHITE
Sister Rosetta Tharpe	Rosetta THARPE
The JBL	Keith SHOCKLEE
Emil Theilheim	Peppy CASTRO
J.S. Theracon	Walter MORRISON
Arthur James Theus	Fats THEUS
Robert Thiele	Bob THIELE
Danny Thomas	Danny WILDE
Deanna Crisp Brown Thomas	Deanna BROWN
Frederick O'Neil Thomas	Frederick THOMAS
Harry Thomas	Harry BELAFONTE
Jimmie Thomas	Leon RENÉ
Leslie Thomas	Snuff GARRETT
Susan Marie Thomas	Susan THOMAS
Gene Thomasson	Gene THOMAS
Alphonso Thompson	Sonny THOMPSON
Arthur Lee Andrew Thompson	Lee ANDREWS
Bonnie Thompson	John Edward MOORE
Brenda L. Thompson	Brenda JOHNSON
Dean Thompson	Dean KAY
Dean Kermit Thompson	Dean KAY
Dennis Thompson	Dennis TOMICH
Hilary Thompson	Billy PEACHES
James Earl Thompson	Jimmy JOHNSON
Paul Stephen Thompson	Porl THOMPSON
Sylvester Thompson	Syl JOHNSON
David Henry Thomsett	David CLAYTON-THOMAS
Gerd Thumser	Claus RITTER
Albon Timothy	Al TIMOTHY
King Timothy	Al TIMOTHY
Michael Trevor Tinsley	Miki DALLON
Johnny Todd	Sammy MASTERS
Laurence Andrew Tolhurst	Laurence TOLHURST
Truman Tomlin	Pinky TOMLIN
Tone Loc	Anthony Terrell SMITH
Too Short	Todd SHAW
John Bernard Toorish	Dazz JORDAN
Mark Torien	Marq TORIEN
Melvin Howard Torma	Mel TORME
Mel Tormé	Mel TORME
Gail Redd Torok	Ramona REDD
Fred Towne	Fred TOBIAS
Albert Trace	Al TRACE
Tulio Trapani	MANTOVANI
Angela Tremble	Deborah HARRY
Michael Trempenau	Mike TRAMP
Herwig Tremschnig	Herwig RUDISSER
Emil Trent	Hugo PERETTI
Van Trevor	Robert BOULANGER
David Tricker	David WHITE
Donald Triggs	Donald BLACKMAN
Triune	Orena D. FULMER
Triune	Paula DePORES
Triune	Ruth STRATCHBORNEO
Doris Troy	Doris PAYNE
Douglas Glenn Tubb	Glenn DOUGLAS

Joseph William Tucci	Eric MATTHEW
Tommy Tucker	Robert HIGGINBOTHAM
Ritchie Tufano	Richard Anthony TUFO
Nigel Tufnel	Christopher GUEST
Graham Morrison Turnbull	Scott TURNER
Brenda Turner	Brenda SUTTON
Rob Tyner	Robert DERMINER
Sylvia Tyson	Sylvia FRICKER
U	
Donald Eugene Ulrich	Don RICH
Tracy Ulrich	Tracii GUNS
Uncle Vic	Victor BLECMAN
Mimi Uniman	Miriam UNIMAN
V	
Emidio Vagnoni	Shorty LONG
Dino Valenti	Chet POWERS
John Valenti	John LiVIGNI
Richard Esteban Valenzuela Reyes	Ritchie VALENS
Richard Valenzuela	Ritchie VALENS
Ero Valladi	Eraldo RAVIOLO
James Douglas Vallance	Jim VALLANCE
Adriaan Van Den Berg II	Adrian VANDENBERG
René Jan van Hoogten	Ray MAXWELL
Gerald Van Kollenburg	Jerry KOLLENBURG
Harry Van Walls	Van WALLS
Mel Van	Don GENSON
Johannes Henderickus Jacob VanDenBerg	Harry VANDA
Sylvia Vanderpool	Sylvia ROBINSON
Donald E. Vandevelde	Donnie VIE
Vanilla Ice	Robert VAN WINKLE
Vanity	Denise MATTHEWS
Harry Eugene Vann	Van WALLS
Henri Eugene Vantard	Henri VARNA
Claude Andre Erminio Vasori	Claude VASORI
Lolly Vasquez	Lolly VEGAS
Pat Vasquez	Pat VEGAS
Roman Vatro	Armando TROVAIOLI
George Vaughn	Vaughn HORTON
Michael Vaughn	Sunny SKYLAR
Wanda Vaughn	Wanda HUTCHINSON
Yvonne Vaughn	Donna FARGO
Vee Pea	Virginia BLAND
Billy Vegas	Nuno BETTENCOURT
Freddie Vel	Fred HENLEY
Johnny Alexander Veliotes Jr.	Shuggie OTIS
Ioannis Alexandres Veliotes	Johnny OTIS
Robert Velline	Bobby VEE
Steve Venetoulis	Steve VENET
Eduardo Verde	Dino VERDE
Humberto Vergara Baro	Humberto VERGARA
Albert Verrecchia	Albert WEYMAN
Evelyne Verrecchia	Evelyne LENTON
Mark Ashton Vey	Mark McVEY
Jeanne Vikki	Rafael RENÉ

Hervé Vilard	René VILLARD
Nat Vincent	James KENDIS
Vinnie Vincent	Vince CUSANO
Zoe Voeth	Joan WHITNEY
Janet Vogel-Rapp	Janet VOGEL
James Wesley Voight	Chip TAYLOR
Albert von Breitenbach	Fred FISHER
Rudi Von der Dovenmuehle	Rudi LINDT
Michael Vucish	Mike VALE
W	
Franz Wachsmann	Franz WAXMAN
Richard Alan Waggoner	Allan RICH
Marcy Debra Wagman	Marci RAUER
Daniel Wahlgren	Dan WAHLGREN
Bunny Wailer	Neville LIVINGSTON
Helen Reddy Wald	Helen REDDY
Anukampa Walden	Lisa WALDEN
David Walker	Bunker HILL
Fred Walker	Derf Reklaw RAHEEM
James David Walker	Jimmy McCRACKLIN
Kurtis Walker	Kurt WALKER
T-Bone Walker	Aaron WALKER
Lee Walter	Walter Lee MORRIS
Leon S. Walton	Leon ASHLEY
Giles Warde	Gil WARD
Dick Ware	Roy ALFRED
LaVerne Ware	Gloria JONES
Christian Carlos Warren	Christian WARREN
Baby Washington	Jeanette WASHINGTON
Joyce Washington	Joyce KENNEDY
Justine Washington	Jeanette WASHINGTON
Boaz Watson	Bo WATSON
John Jacob Watson	Johnny WATSON
Johnny Guitar Watson	Johnny WATSON
June Watson	June Watson WILLIAMS
Clem Watts	Al TRACE
John Robert Waughman	Johnny WARMAN
John Waldo Waybill	Fee WAYBILL
Eunice Kathleen Waymon	Nina SIMONE
Edith Wayne	Brian HOLLAND
Edith Wayne	Eddie HOLLAND
Edith Wayne	Lamont DOZIER
Derek John Weaver	Blue WEAVER
Bernard Webb	Paul McCARTNEY
Gary Anthony James Webb	Gary NUMAN
Harry Rodger Webb	Cliff RICHARD
Allen Webster	Lew DOUGLAS
Paul Wechselmann	Paul MANN
Morris C. Wecht	Murray WECHT
David L. Weck	Henry WECK
George William Weidler	George WILDER
Walter Wolfgang Weidler	Walter WILDER
Warner Alfred Weidler	Warner WILDER
Warren Weidler	Warner WILDER
Werther Alfred Weidler	Warner WILDER
Sidney Weinberg	Sid WAYNE

Matthew Weiner	Matthew WILDER
Gary Lee Weinrib	Geddy LEE
Leslie Weinstein	Leslie WEST
Michael Damian Weir	Michael DAMIAN
Bernard Weisbaum	Bernie BAUM
David Jay Weiss	David WAS
Marilyn Weiss	Marilyn Weiss ALLEN
Bernard Weitzner	Bernie WAYNE
Alvin Welch	Alvin CASH
David West	Norman NEWELL
Joe West	Sonny WEST
Rick West	Richard WESTFIELD
T.P. West	Tommy WEST
Johnny Westerlund	Johnny WESTERN
Richard Allen Westfield	Richard WESTFIELD
Frank Weston	Len BEADLE
Gary Weston	Gary KNIGHT
Ruth Alston Weston	Ruth BROWN
Charles Weeden Westover	Del SHANNON
Paul Wetstein	Paul WESTON
Marvin Wetter	Marvin MONTGOMERY
Vincent Neil Wharton	Vince NEIL
Aretha White	Aretha FRANKLIN
Barry White	Robert KINGSTON
Barry Eugene White	Barry WHITE
David Ernest White	David WHITE
L. White	Murray COHEN
Sylvia White	Sil SEDORES
Beauris Whitehead	Peter WHITEHEAD
Jerry Whitman	June WINTERS
Jeffrey Phillip Wielandt	Zakk WYLDE
Annette Wiesner	Annette TUCKER
Charles Ray Wiggins	Raphael SAADIQ
Robert Wilber	Bob SAGE
Robert Sage Wilber	Bob SAGE
Nelson Wilbury	George HARRISON
Otis Wilbury	Jeff LYNNE
Danny C. Wilde	Danny WILDE
Eugene Wilde	Ronnie E. BROOMFIELD
Ricki Wilde	Ricky WILDE
P.G. Wilder	P.G. WYLDER
Bobby Wilding	Bobby WEINSTEIN
Robert Wilding	Bobby WEINSTEIN
Raven Wildroot	Gene BARGE
Donald MacRae Wilhoite	Don RAYE
Bucky Wilkin	John Buck WILKIN
Anna Delores Williams	Anna KING
Arthur Williams	Jimmy VAN HEUSEN
Barney Williams	Luther DIXON
Clara Bell Williams	Cara BELL
Curly Williams	Dave WILLIAMS

Delores Williams	LaVern BAKER
Doc Williams	Dave WILLIAMS
Freedom Williams	Frederick B. WILLIAMS
Gary Williams	Gerry GRANAHAN
Hiram King Williams	Hank WILLIAMS
Jerry Anthony Williams	Leon HUFF
John David Williams	John DAVID
Ralph Thomas Williams	Tony CLARKE
Robert L. Williams	Billy WARD
Sibelius Williams	Malcolm DODDS
Theodore Williams	Teddy VANN
Willis J. Williams	Red WILLIAMS
Zephire Andre Williams	Andre WILLIAMS
Catherine Williamson	Catherine CAFRA
Alta Sherral Willis	Allee WILLIS
Harold Willis	Chuck WILLIS
Jon Willoughby	Jon ST. JAMES
Clyde Darnell Wilson	Clyde WILSON
Forest Gene Wilson	Forrest WILSON
Gloria Wilson	Gloria VAN CLEVE
Gloria Mia Wilson	Gloria LYNNE
Hank Wilson	Leon RUSSELL
Harry "Rocky" Wilson	Maggie ANDREWS
Lee Wilson	Albert BEACH
Robb Wilson	Robb ROYER
Simone Wilson	Simone Antoinette JOHNSON
Carvin Lawrence Winans	Carvin WINANS
Jesse James Winchester	Jesse WINCHESTER
Jesse Ridout Winchester	Jesse WINCHESTER
Grace Barnett Wing	Grace SLICK
Jerry Winn	Hal WINN
Mervyn Winwood	Muff WINWOOD
Joseph Harold Wirtshafter	Bobby WORTH
Deborah Witkowski	Debbie WITKOWSKI
Ramona Marie Witry	Mona DONATO
Chaim Witz	Gene SIMMONS
Anke Wolert	Anka WOLBERT
Randy Craig Wolfe	Randy CALIFORNIA
Richard Wolfe	Dick WOLF
Mary Womack	Mary WELLS
Brenton Wood	Alfred J. SMITH
Charles Osgood Wood	Charles OSGOOD
Lily Pearl Woodard	Pearl WOODS
Bobby Woodlen	Bobby MADERA
Millard Delbert Woods	Nick WOODS
Orlando Terrell Woods	Terrell WOOD
Paul Phillip Woods	Pye DUBOIS
Terrell Woods	Terrell WOOD

Shelby Fredrick Wooley	Sheb WOOLEY
Gwendolyn Hines Woolfolk	Vinnie BARRETT
Randy Van Wormer	Randy VANWARMER
John Worsley	Les VANDYKE
Johnny Worth	Les VANDYKE
Paul Clayton Worthington	Paul CLAYTON
Adrian Wright	Philip WRIGHT
Gavin Christopher Wright	Gavin CHRISTOPHER
Philip Adrian Wright	Philip WRIGHT
Sidney Jackson Wyche	Sid WYCHE
Philippe Wynne	Philippe WYNN
X	
Joseph Ximenes	Travis FAIRCHILD
Lorraine Ximenes	Coventry FAIRCHILD
Y	
Ya Kid K	Manuela KAMOSI
Yakov Yakubovitsh	Jacob JACOBS
William Yarborough	William BELL
Alisa Peoples Yarbrough	Alisa PEOPLES
Ben Yardley	Estelle LEVITT
Jack Selig Yellen	Jack YELLEN
Yonah	Wyn JACKSON
Dave York	David KINZIE
Hasegawa Yoshida	Freddy MORGAN
Andrew Youakim	Andy KIM
Young MC	Marvin YOUNG
Alexander Young	George ALEXANDER
Andre Young	Andre Romell YOUNG
Yo-Yo	Yolanda WHITAKER
Roy Yustrom	Bill NORVAS
Z	
Benjamn Zamberg	Benny BELL
Francis Zambon	Mark JAMES
Richard Zehringer	Rick DERRINGER
Rick Zehringer	Rick DERRINGER
Rick Dean Zehringer	Rick DERRINGER
Zekkariyas	Cecil WOMACK
Zeriya Zekkariyas	Linda WOMACK
Alan Gary Zekley	Gary ZEKLEY
Eve Jay Zeserson	Eve JAY
Maurice Zeserson	Lee MORRIS
Edward James Zgorecki	Ed GRAY
Richard Adam Ziegler	Ritchie ADAMS
Bill Zimmerman	Bill GIANT
Harvey Zimmerman	Bill GIANT
Alex Zivojinovich	Alex LIFESON
Walter Zwolinski	Walter ZWOL

The Writer Teams

Top 2000 Writer Teams and Their Songs

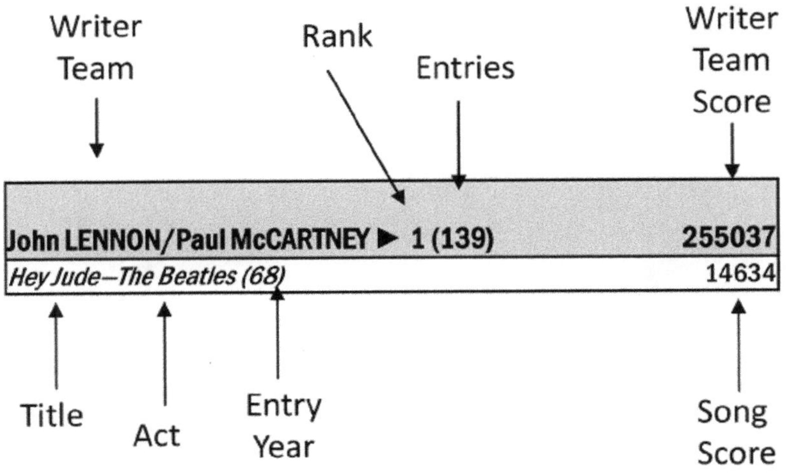

Italics: Multiple Recordings

There are 10,773 writer teams. Members of writer teams are listed in alphabetical order by last name. Song scores are shown and the writer team score is the simple sum of those scores.

Writer Teams are scored by awarding the full song credit to the entity to which it is attributed, regardless of the number of writers on the team rather than dividing it, as is done in the Writers section. In Writer Teams scoring "Paul Simon" as a single-member team is treated in the same way as two-member team "Mick Jagger/Keith Richards" because credit is not allocated to individual writers.

Each writer team's attributed songs are shown in order of chart strength, beginning with the strongest. The song catalog is shown only for multi-writer teams in this section. While single writers are listed for rank, their song catalogs are found in the Writer Index.

John LENNON/Paul McCARTNEY ▶ 1 (139)	**255037**
Hey Jude—The Beatles (68)	14634
I Want To Hold Your Hand—The Beatles (64)	14194
She Loves You—The Beatles (64)	10567
Get Back—The Beatles With Billy Preston (69)	8698
Let It Be—The Beatles (70)	8679
We Can Work It Out—The Beatles (65)	8664
A Hard Day's Night—The Beatles (64)	8359
Can't Buy Me Love—The Beatles (64)	8269
I Feel Fine—The Beatles (64)	8162
Hello Goodbye—The Beatles (67)	8134
Yesterday—The Beatles (65)	7927
Help!—The Beatles (65)	7847
Love Me Do—The Beatles (64)	7070
All You Need Is Love—The Beatles (67)	6800
Ticket To Ride—The Beatles (65)	6556
Paperback Writer—The Beatles (66)	6493
A World Without Love—Peter And Gordon (64)	6461
Come Together—The Beatles (69)	6145
Eight Days A Week—The Beatles (65)	6070
Yellow Submarine—The Beatles (66)	5464
The Long And Winding Road—The Beatles (70)	5434
Penny Lane—The Beatles (67)	5144
Lady Madonna—The Beatles (68)	5119
Nowhere Man—The Beatles (66)	5024
Please Please Me—The Beatles (64)	4866
Do You Want To Know A Secret—The Beatles (64)	4830
Lucy In The Sky With Diamonds—Elton John (74)	4586
Got To Get You Into My Life—The Beatles (76)	2422
The Fool On The Hill—Sergio Mendes & Brasil '66 (68)	2327
She's A Woman—The Beatles (64)	2317
You Won't See Me—Anne Murray (74)	1945
Day Tripper—The Beatles (65)	1881
Revolution—The Beatles (68)	1855
The Ballad Of John And Yoko—The Beatles (69)	1848
Strawberry Fields Forever—The Beatles (67)	1798
We Can Work It Out—Stevie Wonder (71)	1496
Bad To Me—Billy J. Kramer With The Dakotas (64)	1411
You've Got To Hide Your Love Away—The Silkie (65)	1392
Give Peace A Chance—Plastic Ono Band (69)	1367
P.S. I Love You—The Beatles (64)	1327
Goodbye—Mary Hopkin (69)	1267
Nobody I Know—Peter And Gordon (64)	1242
Got To Get You Into My Life—Earth, Wind & Fire (78)	1210
Eleanor Rigby—The Beatles (66)	1186
I Saw Him Standing There—Tiffany (88)	1114
Michelle—David & Jonathan (66)	1048
Birthday—Underground Sunshine (69)	1006
Hey Jude—Wilson Pickett (68)	933
I Don't Want To See You Again—Peter And Gordon (64)	871
And I Love Her—The Beatles (64)	866
Eleanor Rigby—Aretha Franklin (69)	807
Yesterday—Ray Charles (67)	797
She Came In Through The Bathroom Window—Joe Cocker (69)	697
From A Window—Billy J. Kramer With The Dakotas (64)	694
Eleanor Rigby—Ray Charles (68)	673
Come Together—Aerosmith (78)	659
I Saw Her Standing There—The Beatles (64)	638
I'll Cry Instead—The Beatles (64)	638
Oh! Darling—Robin Gibb (78)	626
A Hard Day's Night—Ramsey Lewis Trio (66)	532
Rain—The Beatles (66)	508
All My Loving—The Beatles (64)	480
Thank You Girl—The Beatles (64)	466
You're Going To Lose That Girl—Stars On 45 (81)	442
Do You Want To Know A Secret—Stars On 45 (81)	442
I Should Have Known Better—Stars On 45 (81)	442
We Can Work It Out—Stars On 45 (81)	442
Drive My Car—Stars On 45 (81)	442
I'll Be Back—Stars On 45 (81)	442
Nowhere Man—Stars On 45 (81)	442
No Reply—Stars On 45 (81)	442
Let It Be—Joan Baez (71)	435
And I Love Him—Esther Phillips (65)	406
Ringo's Theme (This Boy)—George Martin And His Orch. (64)	389
I'll Keep You Satisfied—Billy J. Kramer With The Dakotas (64)	373
And I Love Her—George Martin And His Orch. (64)	352
Come Together—Ike & Tina Turner & The Ikettes (70)	348
From Me To You—The Beatles (64)	345
It's For You—Springwell (71)	334
I Am The Walrus—The Beatles (67)	317
Ob-La-Di, Ob-La-Da—Arthur Conley (68)	282
If I Fell—The Beatles (64)	277
With A Little Help From My Friends—Joe Cocker (68)	272
Magical Mystery Tour—Ambrosia (77)	262
Baby You're A Rich Man—The Beatles (67)	258
Ob-La-Di, Ob-La-Da—The Beatles (76)	224
I Don't Want To Spoil The Party—The Beatles (65)	221
Ticket To Ride—Carpenters (70)	196
Don't Let Me Down—The Beatles With Billy Preston (69)	194
Michelle—Billy Vaughn His Orchestra & Chorus (66)	188
Dear Prudence—Katfish (75)	186
I Want To Hold Your Hand—Boston Pops Orchestra Arthur Fiedler Conductor (64)	184
Day Tripper—Anne Murray (74)	181
I Should Have Known Better—The Beatles (64)	172
Julia—Ramsey Lewis (69)	145
Yes It Is—The Beatles (65)	137
You've Got To Hide Your Love Away—The Beatles (82)	134
I Should Have Known Better—The Beatles (82)	134
All You Need Is Love—The Beatles (82)	134
Magical Mystery Tour—The Beatles (82)	134
A Hard Day's Night—The Beatles (82)	134
Ticket To Ride—The Beatles (82)	134
Get Back—The Beatles (82)	134
Got To Get You Into My Life—Blood, Sweat & Tears (75)	128
You Can't Do That—The Beatles (64)	126
Michelle—Bud Shank (66)	116
Dear Prudence—The Five Stairsteps (70)	110
From Me To You—Del Shannon (63)	110
A World Without Love—Bobby Rydell (64)	99
Back In The U.S.S.R.—Chubby Checker (69)	70
Day Tripper—Ramsey Lewis (66)	70
I'm Happy Just To Dance With You—Anne Murray (80)	59
Here, There And Everywhere—Emmylou Harris (76)	55
Drive My Car—Gary Toms Empire (75)	52
From A Window—Chad & Jeremy (65)	45
I'm A Loser—The Beatles (65)	37
It's For You—Cilla Black (64)	34
Sgt. Pepper's Lonely Hearts Club Band—The Beatles (78)	24
With A Little Help From My Friends—The Beatles (78)	24
You Can't Do That—Nilsson (67)	23
Lady Madonna—Fats Domino (68)	16
There's A Place—The Beatles (64)	13
Here, There And Everywhere—The Fourmost (66)	12
I'm Happy Just To Dance With You—The Beatles (64)	12
Step Inside Love—Cilla Black (68)	11
Drive My Car—Bob Kuban And The In-Men (66)	11
She's A Woman—José Feliciano (69)	9.6
Get Back—Billy Preston (78)	9.4
I Want To Hold Your Hand—Stars On 45 (81)	8.0
A Hard Day's Night—Stars On 45 (81)	8.0
Good Day Sunshine—Stars On 45 (81)	8.0
Please Please Me—Stars On 45 (81)	8.0
From Me To You—Stars On 45 (81)	8.0
All My Loving—The Beatles (64)	6.4
This Boy—The Beatles (64)	6.4
Rocky Raccoon—Richie Havens (69)	4.0
All My Loving—The Hollyridge Strings (64)	3.8
Day Tripper—The Vontastics (66)	2.4
Good Day Sunshine—Claudine Longet (67)	0.9
Lamont DOZIER/Brian HOLLAND/Eddie HOLLAND ▶ 2 (107)	**167934**
Where Did Our Love Go—The Supremes (64)	9056
I Can't Help Myself—Four Tops (65)	8859
Come See About Me—The Supremes (64)	8772
Baby Love—The Supremes (64)	8476
Stop! In The Name Of Love—The Supremes (65)	7776
You Can't Hurry Love—The Supremes (66)	7615
I Hear A Symphony—The Supremes (65)	6983
Reach Out I'll Be There—Four Tops (66)	6413
You Keep Me Hangin' On—The Supremes (66)	6251
Love Is Here And Now You're Gone—The Supremes (67)	5783
Reflections—Diana Ross And The Supremes (67)	5395
Back In My Arms Again—The Supremes (65)	4991
Heat Wave—Martha & The Vandellas (63)	4013
You Keep Me Hangin' On—Kim Wilde (87)	3516
Baby I Need Your Lovin'—Johnny Rivers (67)	3362
My World Is Empty Without You—The Supremes (66)	3008
It's The Same Old Song—Four Tops (65)	2864
Standing In The Shadows Of Love—Four Tops (66)	2566
Bernadette—Four Tops (67)	2554
Jimmy Mack—Martha & The Vandellas (67)	2552
How Sweet It Is To Be Loved By You—Marvin Gaye (64)	2463
How Sweet It Is (To Be Loved By You)—James Taylor (75)	2292
You Keep Me Hangin' On—The Vanilla Fudge (68)	2110
Nowhere To Run—Martha & The Vandellas (65)	1982
Mickey's Monkey—The Miracles (63)	1976
Heaven Must Have Sent You—Bonnie Pointer (79)	1857
You Can't Hurry Love—Phil Collins (82)	1813
Love Is Like An Itching In My Heart—The Supremes (66)	1721
I'm Ready For Love—Martha & The Vandellas (66)	1702
Quicksand—Martha & The Vandellas (63)	1686
In And Out Of Love—Diana Ross And The Supremes (67)	1650
Baby I Need Your Loving—Four Tops (64)	1637
Take Me In Your Arms (Rock Me)—The Doobie Brothers (75)	1636
Nothing But Heartaches—The Supremes (65)	1633
Can I Get A Witness—Marvin Gaye (63)	1429
You're A Wonderful One—Marvin Gaye (64)	1385
7-Rooms Of Gloom—Four Tops (67)	1376
Heat Wave—Linda Ronstadt (75)	1210
Forever Came Today—Diana Ross And The Supremes (68)	1145
Something About You—Four Tops (65)	1109
Come And Get These Memories—Martha & The Vandellas (63)	1109
How Sweet It Is (To Be Loved By You)—Jr. Walker & The All Stars (66)	1081
Shake Me, Wake Me (When It's Over)—Four Tops (66)	1067
(I'm A) Road Runner—Jr. Walker & The All Stars (66)	1035
Where Did Our Love Go—Donnie Elbert (71)	1001
When The Lovelight Starts Shining Through His Eyes—The Supremes (63)	958
(Come 'round Here) I'm The One You Need—The Miracles (66)	943
You Keep Running Away—Four Tops (67)	912
I Can't Help Myself (Sugar Pie, Honey Bunch)—Donnie Elbert (72)	858
You Lost The Sweetest Boy—Mary Wells (63)	855
Come See About Me—Jr. Walker & The All Stars (67)	794
Baby Don't You Do It—Marvin Gaye (64)	737
Don't Do It—The Band (72)	698
Reach Out I'll Be There—Diana Ross (71)	619
I Gotta Dance To Keep From Crying—The Miracles (63)	546
Stop In The Name Of Love—The Hollies (83)	525
Can I Get A Witness—Lee Michaels (71)	522
Your Unchanging Love—Marvin Gaye (67)	484
Take Me In Your Arms (Rock Me A Little While)—Kim Weston (65)	440
Locking Up My Heart—The Marvelettes (63)	428
Live Wire—Martha & The Vandellas (64)	418
I Can't Help Myself (Sugar Pie, Honey Bunch)—Bonnie Pointer (79)	407
It's The Same Old Song—KC & The Sunshine Band (78)	395
Little Darling (I Need You)—The Doobie Brothers (77)	392
I'm In A Different World—Four Tops (68)	381
Little Darling, I Need You—Marvin Gaye (66)	372
In My Lonely Room—Martha & The Vandellas (64)	348
Heaven Must Have Sent You—The Elgins (66)	326
Helpless—Kim Weston (66)	316
Why Can't We Be Lovers—Holland-Dozier (72)	313
Without The One You Love (Life's Not Worth While)—Four Tops (64)	306
Forever Came Today—The Jackson 5 (75)	305
Don't Leave Me Starvin' For Your Love (Part 1)—Holland-Dozier (73)	273
I Guess I'll Always Love You—The Isley Brothers (66)	243

Lamont DOZIER/Brian HOLLAND/ Eddie HOLLAND ▶ 2 (107) *Continued*	**167934**
Baby, I Need Your Loving—O.C. Smith (70)	239
Where Did Our Love Go—The J. Geils Band (76)	205
Darling Baby—The Elgins (66)	197
Something About You—Le Blanc & Carr (77)	183
You Keep Me Hangin' On—The Vanilla Fudge (67)	165
Just Ain't Enough Love—Eddie Holland (64)	160
Love (Makes Me Do Foolish Things)— Martha & The Vandellas (65)	154
Candy To Me—Eddie Holland (64)	141
Baby, I Need Your Lovin'—Eric Carmen (79)	135
You Keep Me Hanging On—Wilson Pickett (69)	133
I Just Can't Walk Away—Four Tops (83)	124
Reach Out, I'll Be There—Gloria Gaynor (75)	119
Jimmy Mack—Sheena Easton (86)	115
Leaving Here—Eddie Holland (64)	114
Reach Out, I'll Be There—The Ritchie Family (76)	92
Come See About Me—Nella Dodds (64)	92
I Can't Help Myself (Sugar Pie, Honey Bunch)— Shalamar (77)	80
Stop! In the Name of Love—Shalamar (77)	80
It's The Same Old Song—Shalamar (77)	80
Reach Out—Merrilee Rush (68)	70
Stop! In The Name Of Love—Margie Joseph (71)	64
My World Is Empty Without You—Jose Feliciano (69)	46
Back In My Arms Again—Genya Ravan (78)	41
Run, Run, Run—The Supremes (64)	24
Stop In The Name Of Love—Stars On 45 (81)	12
Reach Out I'll Be There—Stars On 45 (81)	12
I Think You Need Love—Dionne Warwicke (73)	10
If It's Good To You (It's Good For You)— Flaming Ember (71)	9.0
I Can't Help Myself—The Magnificent Men (67)	7.6
Darling Baby—Jackie Moore (72)	3.5
Take Me In Your Arms (Rock Me A Little While)— The Isley Brothers (68)	1.8
You Keep Me Hangin' On—Jackie DeShannon (70)	1.0
Reach Out I'll Be There—The New Seekers (74)	0.7
Burt BACHARACH/Hal DAVID ▶ 3 (105)	**112434**
Raindrops Keep Fallin' On My Head— B.J. Thomas (69)	10203
This Guy's In Love With You—Herb Alpert (68)	9073
(They Long To Be) Close To You—Carpenters (70)	7620
One Less Bell To Answer—The 5th Dimension (70)	7509
What's New Pussycat?—Tom Jones (65)	4965
Blue On Blue—Bobby Vinton (63)	4326
Only Love Can Break A Heart—Gene Pitney (62)	3874
Wishin' And Hopin'—Dusty Springfield (64)	3504
I Say A Little Prayer—Dionne Warwick (67)	3302
The Look Of Love— Sergio Mendes & Brasil '66 (68)	3151
Walk On By—Dionne Warwick (64)	2790
What The World Needs Now Is Love— Jackie deShannon (65)	2689
(The Man Who Shot) Liberty Valance— Gene Pitney (62)	2442
I'll Never Fall In Love Again—Dionne Warwick (69)	2372
Anyone Who Had A Heart—Dionne Warwick (63)	2092
This Girl's In Love With You—Dionne Warwick (69)	2079
Message To Michael—Dionne Warwick (66)	2078
Always Something There To Remind Me— Naked Eyes (83)	1983
Do You Know The Way To San José— Dionne Warwick (68)	1893
Alfie—Dionne Warwick (67)	1730
Wives And Lovers—Jack Jones (63)	1677
I Say A Little Prayer—Aretha Franklin (68)	1449
Don't Make Me Over—Dionne Warwick (62)	1150
Promises, Promises—Dionne Warwick (68)	1078
Twenty Four Hours From Tulsa—Gene Pitney (63)	977
You'll Never Get To Heaven (If You Break My Heart)— The Stylistics (73)	836
What The World Needs Now Is Love—Tom Clay (71)	836
Don't Make Me Over—Sybil (89)	835
Magic Moments—Perry Como (57)	834
I Just Don't Know What To Do With Myself— Dionne Warwick (66)	827
Everybody's Out Of Town—B.J. Thomas (70)	796
Reach Out For Me—Dionne Warwick (64)	794
Always Something There To Remind Me— R.B. Greaves (70)	784
Make It Easy On Yourself—The Walker Bros. (65)	781

True Love Never Runs Smooth—Gene Pitney (63)	775
The Look Of Love—Dusty Springfield (67)	749
Make It Easy On Yourself—Jerry Butler (62)	738
Who Is Gonna Love Me?—Dionne Warwick (68)	727
Story Of My Life—Marty Robbins (57)	692
Are You There (With Another Girl)— Dionne Warwick (65)	683
Trains And Boats And Planes—Dionne Warwick (66)	662
You'll Never Get To Heaven (If You Break My Heart)— Dionne Warwick (64)	651
Living Together, Growing Together— The 5th Dimension (73)	623
Make It Easy On Yourself—Dionne Warwick (70)	617
Alfie—Cher (66)	533
I'm A Better Man—Engelbert Humperdinck (69)	523
Windows Of The World—Dionne Warwick (67)	510
Let Me Go To Him—Dionne Warwick (70)	506
The Green Grass Starts To Grow— Dionne Warwick (70)	502
Paper Mache—Dionne Warwick (70)	479
The April Fools—Dionne Warwick (69)	474
Be True To Yourself—Bobby Vee (63)	466
The Love Of A Boy—Timi Yuro (62)	465
My Little Red Book—Love (66)	458
Odds And Ends—Dionne Warwick (69)	427
I Wake Up Crying—Chuck Jackson (61)	415
Blue Guitar—Richard Chamberlain (63)	413
Another Night—Dionne Warwick (66)	396
Walk On By—Isaac Hayes (69)	367
To Wait For Love—Herb Alpert (68)	365
(There's) Always Something There To Remind Me— Lou Johnson (64)	363
Trains And Boats And Planes— Billy J. Kramer & The Dakotas (65)	357
(There's) Always Something There To Remind Me— Sandie Shaw (64)	337
With Open Arms—Jane Morgan (59)	319
I Just Don't Know What To Do With Myself— Gary Puckett (70)	315
A House Is Not A Home—Dionne Warwick (64)	286
A House Is Not A Home—Brook Benton (64)	260
Reach Out For Me—Lou Johnson (63)	247
Long Ago Tomorrow—B.J. Thomas (71)	224
Here I Am—Dionne Warwick (65)	188
Lost Horizon—Shawn Phillips (73)	159
A Lifetime Of Loneliness—Jackie De Shannon (65)	158
Who Gets The Guy—Dionne Warwick (71)	147
(There's) Always Something There To Remind Me— Dionne Warwick (68)	141
Looking With My Eyes—Dionne Warwick (65)	139
(They Long To Be) Close To You— Jerry Butler Featuring Brenda Lee Eager (72)	133
Promise Her Anything—Tom Jones (66)	131
Don't Make Me Over—Jennifer Warnes (79)	131
Let Me Be Lonely—Dionne Warwick (68)	112
Me Japanese Boy I Love You—Bobby Goldsboro (64)	104
Walk On By—Sybil (90)	95
Don't Make Me Over—Brenda & The Tabulations (70)	95
The Look Of Love—Isaac Hayes (71)	94
The Breaking Point—Chuck Jackson (61)	46
I Say A Little Prayer—Glen Campbell (71)	38
This Empty Place—Dionne Warwick (63)	38
Come And Get Me—Jackie deShannon (66)	34
Close To You—B.T. Express (76)	31
The Beginning Of Loneliness—Dionne Warwick (67)	30
Wendy Wendy—The Four Coins (58)	26
Make The Music Play—Dionne Warwick (63)	22
Saturday Sunshine—Burt Bacharach (63)	19
I Just Don't Know What To Do With Myself— Tommy Hunt (62)	13
Only Love Can Break A Heart—Margaret Whiting (67)	13
From Rocking Horse To Rocking Chair— Paul Anka (64)	11
Walk On By—AWB (79)	7.4
Alfie—Cilla Black (66)	6.1
I'll Never Fall In Love Again—Burt Bacharach (69)	4.9
Forgive Me (For Giving You Such A Bad Time)— Babs Tino (62)	3.5
Somebody Else's Sweetheart—The Wanderers (61)	1.8
It's The Love That Really Counts (In The Long Run)— The Shirelles (62)	1.8
Who's Been Sleeping In My Bed?—Linda Scott (64)	1.3
Walk On By—Gloria Gaynor (75)	1.1

Rome Will Never Leave You— Richard Chamberlain (64)	1.0
Only Love Can Break A Heart—Bobby Vinton (77)	0.9
Mick JAGGER/Keith RICHARDS ▶ 4 (60)	**110743**
Honky Tonk Women—The Rolling Stones (69)	10430
(I Can't Get No) Satisfaction— The Rolling Stones (65)	10038
Paint It, Black—The Rolling Stones (66)	7253
Ruby Tuesday—The Rolling Stones (67)	7240
Get Off Of My Cloud—The Rolling Stones (65)	6209
Brown Sugar—The Rolling Stones (71)	6055
19th Nervous Breakdown—The Rolling Stones (66)	5987
Jumpin' Jack Flash—The Rolling Stones (68)	5867
Miss You—The Rolling Stones (78)	5848
Angie—The Rolling Stones (73)	5117
Start Me Up—The Rolling Stones (81)	4381
Emotional Rescue—The Rolling Stones (80)	3524
Mother's Little Helper—The Rolling Stones (66)	3076
Have You Seen Your Mother, Baby, Standing In The Shadow?— The Rolling Stones (66)	2548
Tumbling Dice—The Rolling Stones (72)	2232
Mixed Emotions—The Rolling Stones (89)	1864
The Last Time—The Rolling Stones (65)	1655
Dandelion—The Rolling Stones (67)	1620
Beast Of Burden—The Rolling Stones (78)	1440
Undercover Of The Night—The Rolling Stones (83)	1367
She's A Rainbow—The Rolling Stones (67)	1131
Heart Of Stone—The Rolling Stones (65)	1125
Waiting On A Friend—The Rolling Stones (81)	1065
Doo Doo Doo Doo Doo (Heartbreaker)— The Rolling Stones (74)	973
It's Only Rock 'N Roll (But I Like It)— The Rolling Stones (74)	936
Happy—The Rolling Stones (72)	891
Tell Me (You're Coming Back)— The Rolling Stones (64)	793
Fool To Cry—The Rolling Stones (76)	750
Rock And A Hard Place—The Rolling Stones (89)	727
Wild Horses—The Rolling Stones (71)	724
Satisfaction—Otis Redding (66)	624
She's So Cold—The Rolling Stones (80)	599
Hot Stuff—The Rolling Stones (76)	567
Let's Spend The Night Together— The Rolling Stones (67)	544
Jumpin' Jack Flash—Aretha Franklin (86)	527
Hang Fire—The Rolling Stones (82)	495
Shattered—The Rolling Stones (78)	473
Street Fighting Man—The Rolling Stones (68)	467
You Can't Always Get What You Want— The Rolling Stones (73)	462
Lady Jane—The Rolling Stones (66)	445
Ruby Tuesday—Melanie (70)	414
We Love You—The Rolling Stones (67)	336
That Girl Belongs To Yesterday—Gene Pitney (64)	317
Tumbling Dice—Linda Ronstadt (78)	309
You Can't Always Get What You Want— George Michael (91)	248
She Was Hot—The Rolling Stones (84)	242
Gimme Shelter—Grand Funk Railroad (71)	207
Highwire—The Rolling Stones (91)	174
Gimme Shelter—Merry Clayton (70)	105
Out Of Time—The Rolling Stones (75)	74
Beast Of Burden—Bette Midler (84)	71
I'm Free—The Soup Dragons (90)	48
All Down The Line—The Rolling Stones (72)	43
The Last Time—The Buchanan Brothers (69)	38
Sittin' On A Fence—Twice As Much (66)	19
Jumpin' Jack Flash—Johnny Winter (71)	15
Let's Spend The Night Together—David Bowie (73)	7.4
Under My Thumb—Del Shannon (66)	1.4
Under My Thumb—Hounds (80)	1.0
(I Can't Get No) Satisfaction—Tight Fit (81)	0.9
Barry GIBB/Maurice GIBB/Robin GIBB ▶ 5 (44)	**100483**
Stayin' Alive—Bee Gees (77)	9872
Night Fever—Bee Gees (78)	9237
How Deep Is Your Love—Bee Gees (77)	7757
Too Much Heaven—Bee Gees (78)	6865
Islands In The Stream— Kenny Rogers Duet with Dolly Parton (83)	6346
Tragedy—Bee Gees (79)	6069
Jive Talkin'—Bee Gees (75)	5841

Barry GIBB/Maurice GIBB/Robin GIBB ► 5 (44) *Continued*	**100483**
If I Can't Have You—Yvonne Elliman (78)	4924
Lonely Days—Bee Gees (70)	4559
You Should Be Dancing—Bee Gees (76)	4461
Love So Right—Bee Gees (76)	3669
Love You Inside Out—Bee Gees (79)	3185
I've Gotta Get A Message To You—The Bee Gees (68)	3087
Guilty—Barbra Streisand & Barry Gibb (80)	2811
I Started A Joke—The Bee Gees (68)	2767
Desire—Andy Gibb (80)	2687
Nights On Broadway—Bee Gees (75)	2655
Fanny (Be Tender With My Love)—Bee Gees (75)	1717
Heartbreaker—Dionne Warwick (82)	1606
Run To Me—Bee Gees (72)	1396
(The Lights Went Out In) Massachusetts—The Bee Gees (67)	1232
One—Bee Gees (89)	1162
Words—The Bee Gees (68)	1127
Boogie Child—Bee Gees (77)	1054
First Of May—The Bee Gees (69)	706
The Woman In You—Bee Gees (83)	642
More Than A Woman—Tavares (77)	508
Jumbo—The Bee Gees (68)	397
You Stepped Into My Life—Melba Moore (78)	350
He's A Liar—Bee Gees (81)	336
Warm Ride—Rare Earth (78)	335
Living Eyes—Bee Gees (81)	310
Someone Belonging To Someone—Bee Gees (83)	242
Marley Purt Drive—Jose Feliciano (69)	193
Chain Reaction—Diana Ross (86)	114
You Win Again—Bee Gees (87)	82
Saw A New Morning—Bee Gees (73)	82
You Stepped Into My Life—Wayne Newton (79)	32
Only One Woman—Nigel Olsson (75)	31
When He's Gone—Bee Gees (91)	11
Fanny (Be Tender With My Love)—Gino Cunico (75)	9.9
Nights On Broadway—Candi Staton (77)	8.1
Chain Reaction—Diana Ross (85)	5.0
Wouldn't I Be Someone—Bee Gees (73)	0.7

Gerry GOFFIN/Carole KING ► 6 (94)	**94936**
Go Away Little Girl—Steve Lawrence (62)	8171
Take Good Care Of My Baby—Bobby Vee (61)	7900
The Loco-Motion—Little Eva (62)	7718
Go Away Little Girl—Donny Osmond (71)	6840
Will You Love Me Tomorrow—The Shirelles (60)	5738
The Loco-Motion—Grand Funk (74)	4636
Pleasant Valley Sunday—The Monkees (67)	3972
Up On The Roof—The Drifters (62)	2924
I Can't Stay Mad At You—Skeeter Davis (63)	2616
The Loco-Motion—Kylie Minogue (88)	2519
One Fine Day—The Chiffons (63)	2130
Don't Say Nothin' Bad (About My Baby)—The Cookies (63)	2050
I'm Into Something Good—Herman's Hermits (64)	1902
Hey, Girl—Freddie Scott (63)	1793
Hey Girl—Donny Osmond (71)	1748
Don't Bring Me Down—The Animals (66)	1719
Keep Your Hands Off My Baby—Little Eva (62)	1642
Her Royal Majesty—James Darren (62)	1551
Go Away Little Girl—The Happenings (66)	1386
Hi-De-Ho—Blood, Sweat & Tears (70)	1305
Some Kind Of Wonderful—The Drifters (61)	1244
Chains—The Cookies (62)	1234
Sharing You—Bobby Vee (62)	1134
One Fine Day—Carole King (80)	1089
I've Got Bonnie—Bobby Rydell (62)	1069
Will You Love Me Tomorrow—The 4 Seasons Featuring The "Sound" Of Frankie Valli (68)	1009
Oh No Not My Baby—Maxine Brown (64)	960
Halfway To Paradise—Bobby Vinton (68)	936
Halfway To Paradise—Tony Orlando (61)	897
Walking Proud—Steve Lawrence (63)	764
This Little Girl—Dion (63)	761
I Want To Stay Here—Steve And Eydie (63)	735
Take Good Care Of My Baby—Bobby Vinton (68)	690
When My Little Girl Is Smiling—The Drifters (62)	674
Point Of No Return—Gene McDaniels (62)	648
It Might As Well Rain Until September—Carole King (62)	646
Every Breath I Take—Gene Pitney (61)	623
I Can't Stop Talking About You—Steve And Eydie (63)	559
Up On The Roof—James Taylor (79)	522
Poor Little Rich Girl—Steve Lawrence (63)	492
What A Sweet Thing That Was—The Shirelles (61)	486
Hey Girl—Bobby Vee (68)	476
He Knows I Love Him Too Much—The Paris Sisters (62)	453
He's In Town—The Tokens (64)	438
Will You Still Love Me Tomorrow—Dave Mason (78)	431
I'm Into Somethin' Good—Earl-Jean (64)	425
How Many Tears—Bobby Vee (61)	395
Porpoise Song—The Monkees (68)	391
At The Club—The Drifters (65)	386
I Can't Hear You No More—Helen Reddy (76)	382
On This Side Of Goodbye—The Righteous Brothers (66)	344
Why'd You Wanna Make Me Cry—Connie Stevens (62)	297
Don't Forget About Me—Dusty Springfield (69)	270
Oh! No Not My Baby—Rod Stewart (73)	197
Oh No, Not My Baby—Merry Clayton (72)	194
Will You Still Love Me Tomorrow—Roberta Flack (72)	184
Up On The Roof—The Cryan' Shames (68)	174
Walkin' With My Angel—Bobby Vee (61)	166
Will Power—The Cookies (63)	156
Will You Love Me Tomorrow?—Melanie (73)	152
It's Gonna Be Alright—Maxine Brown (65)	146
Keep Your Love Locked (Deep In Your Heart)—Paul Petersen (62)	141
Goin' Back—The Byrds (67)	125
One Fine Day—Rita Coolidge (79)	116
I Can't Hear You—Betty Everett (64)	106
Everybody Go Home—Eydie Gorme (63)	104
So Much Love—Ben E. King (66)	102
I Can't Make It Alone—Lou Rawls (69)	99
I Can't Make It Alone—Bill Medley (68)	87
I Need You—Chuck Jackson (65)	72
When My Little Girl Is Smiling—Steve Alaimo (71)	71
So Much Love—Steve Alaimo (66)	67
Where Does Love Go—Freddie Scott (64)	50
Don't Forget About Me—The American Breed (67)	48
Wasn't Born To Follow—The Byrds (69)	45
Dreamin' About You—Annette And The Vonnair Sisters (61)	37
High Out Of Time—Carole King (76)	23
One Fine Day—Julie (76)	19
Sweet Sweetheart—Bobby Vee (70)	17
I Don't Think You Know Me—The American Breed (67)	15
Hey Girl—The Lettermen (70)	14
He's A Bad Boy—Carole King (63)	13
I Can't Say Goodbye—Bobby Vee (62)	10
Go Away Little Boy—Marlena Shaw (77)	9.6
Will You Love Me Tomorrow—Dana Valery (76)	9.4
Yours Until Tomorrow—Vivian Reed (68)	8.2
I Need You—The Rationals (68)	7.7
Up On The Roof—Laura Nyro (70)	7.4
Don't Forget About Me—Barbara Lewis (66)	7.0
What I Gotta Do (To Make You Jealous)—Little Eva (63)	7.0
Down Home—Rick Nelson (63)	5.1
I Just Can't Say Goodbye—Bobby Rydell (64)	3.3
Will You Love Me Tomorrow?—Linda Ronstadt (70)	1.7
Smackwater Jack—Carole King (71)	0.0

Elton JOHN/Bernie TAUPIN ► 7 (43)	**83123**
Crocodile Rock—Elton John (72)	6901
Philadelphia Freedom—The Elton John Band (75)	6474
Don't Go Breaking My Heart—Elton John And Kiki Dee (76)	6364
Island Girl—Elton John (75)	5893
Bennie And The Jets—Elton John (74)	5459
Goodbye Yellow Brick Road—Elton John (73)	4555
Daniel—Elton John (73)	4279
Don't Let The Sun Go Down On Me—Elton John (74)	4278
Someone Saved My Life Tonight—Elton John (75)	3538
Don't Let The Sun Go Down On Me—George Michael (91)	3346
I Don't Wanna Go On With You Like That—Elton John (88)	2894
Your Song—Elton John (70)	2412
The Bitch Is Back—Elton John (74)	2289
Sorry Seems To Be The Hardest Word—Elton John (76)	2125
Rocket Man—Elton John (72)	2111
Sad Songs (Say So Much)—Elton John (84)	1892
Candle In The Wind—Elton John (87)	1744
Saturday Night's Alright For Fighting—Elton John (73)	1637
Nikita—Elton John (86)	1603
I'm Still Standing—Elton John (83)	1238
Honky Cat—Elton John (72)	1232
Empty Garden (Hey Hey Johnny)—Elton John (82)	1190
Healing Hands—Elton John (89)	1070
Levon—Elton John (71)	875
Sacrifice—Elton John (90)	860
Friends—Elton John (71)	742
Who Wears These Shoes?—Elton John (84)	739
A Word In Spanish—Elton John (88)	673
Border Song (Holy Moses)—Aretha Franklin (70)	643
Kiss The Bride—Elton John (83)	583
Club At The End Of The Street—Elton John (90)	549
Tiny Dancer—Elton John (72)	461
In Neon—Elton John (84)	451
Ego—Elton John (78)	432
I Feel Like A Bullet (In The Gun Of Robert Ford)—Elton John (76)	423
You Gotta Love Someone—Elton John (90)	372
Bite Your Lip (Get Up And Dance!)—Elton John (77)	320
Heartache All Over The World—Elton John (86)	221
Border Song—Elton John (70)	98
The Rumour—Olivia Newton-John (88)	97
Step Into Christmas—Elton John (73)	40
Bad Side Of The Moon—April Wine (72)	19
Snookeroo—Ringo Starr (75)	0.0

Paul SIMON ► 8 (44)	**82685**
Lionel RICHIE ► 9 (20)	**81488**

Jerry LEIBER/Mike STOLLER ► 10 (82)	**80838**
Jailhouse Rock—Elvis Presley (57)	8238
Kansas City—Wilbert Harrison (59)	6968
Charlie Brown—The Coasters (59)	6481
Hound Dog—Elvis Presley (56)	6329
Ruby Baby—Dion (63)	6167
Love Potion Number Nine—The Searchers (64)	5796
Yakety Yak—The Coasters (58)	5603
Don't—Elvis Presley (58)	4291
Searchin'—The Coasters (57)	3311
Poison Ivy—The Coasters (59)	2586
Drip Drop—Dion Di Muci (63)	2250
Love Me—Elvis Presley (56)	1990
Bossa Nova Baby—Elvis Presley With The Jordanaires (63)	1871
Along Came Jones—The Coasters (59)	1746
Black Denim Trousers And Motorcycle Boots—The Cheers (55)	1536
Is That All There Is—Peggy Lee (69)	1534
D.W. Washburn—The Monkees (68)	1160
Love Potion Number Nine—The Clovers (59)	1042
I'm A Woman—Maria Muldaur (74)	842
Kansas City—Trini Lopez (63)	840
Little Egypt (Ying-Yang)—The Coasters (61)	823
(Bazoom) I Need Your Lovin'—The Cheers (54)	802
Loving You—Elvis Presley (57)	733
Along Came Jones—Ray Stevens (69)	668
Lucky Lips—Ruth Brown (57)	626
(How Bout A Little Hand For) The Boys In The Band—The Boys In The Band (70)	572
What About Us—The Coasters (59)	504
(When She Needs Good Lovin') She Comes To Me—The Chicago Loop (66)	428
Run Red Run—The Coasters (59)	418
I'm A Woman—Peggy Lee (62)	394
Framed—Cheech & Chong (76)	335
Saved—LaVern Baker (61)	327
Kansas City—James Brown And The Famous Flames (67)	301
Ruby, Baby—Billy "Crash" Craddock (74)	300
Treat Me Nice—Elvis Presley (57)	295
I Keep Forgettin'—Chuck Jackson (62)	295
Just Tell Her Jim Said Hello—Elvis Presley With The Jordanaires (62)	251
King Creole—Elvis Presley with the Jordanaires (58)	192
(You're So Square) Baby, I Don't Care—Joni Mitchell (82)	189
Lucky Lips—Cliff Richard (63)	180
Searching—Jack Eubanks And The Sound Of The South (61)	149
I'm A Hog For You—The Coasters (59)	133

Jerry LEIBER/Mike STOLLER ▶ 10 (82) *Continued*	**80838**
Black Denim Trousers And Motorcycle Boots—Vaughn Monroe with Chorus And Orchestra (55)	132
Kansas City—Hank Ballard And The Midnighters (59)	119
Love Potion Number Nine—The Coasters (71)	97
Jailhouse Rock—Jive Bunny And The Mastermixers (89)	80
Hound Dog—Jive Bunny And The Mastermixers (89)	80
Searchin'—Jim Croce (76)	76
You're The Boss—Lavern Baker & Jimmy Ricks (61)	75
Dancin'—Perry Como (57)	61
Searchin'—Ace Cannon (64)	59
Blues For Me—Eddie Fisher (57)	51
Lucky Lips—Gale Storm (57)	50
Idol With The Golden Head—The Coasters (57)	45
Kansas City—Rocky Olson (59)	40
Love Me—5 DeMarco Sisters (54)	39
One Kiss Led To Another—The Coasters (56)	37
(When She Wants Good Lovin') My Baby Comes To Me—The Coasters (57)	29
Fools Fall In Love—The Drifters (57)	29
Trouble—Elvis Presley with the Jordanaires (58)	24
Jailhouse Rock—Elvis Presley (82)	23
Hound Dog—Elvis Presley (82)	23
Dirty, Dirty Feeling—Elvis Presley With The Jordanaires (65)	23
Jack O' Diamonds—Ruth Brown (59)	22
Kansas City—The Beatles (65)	22
Drip Drop—The Drifters (58)	21
Girls Girls Girls (Part II)—The Coasters (61)	21
Blueberries—Georgia Gibbs (55)	20
Searchin'—Johnny Rivers (73)	12
Do Your Own Thing—Brook Benton (68)	8.6
Smokey Joe's Café—The Robins (55)	6.4
Shadow Knows—The Coasters (58)	4.6
Kansas City—Little Richard (59)	3.8
Santa Claus Is Back In Town—Elvis Presley (57)	2.1
Lovey—The Clovers (60)	1.3
Drums—Kenny Chandler (61)	0.5
Fools Fall In Love—Elvis Presley (67)	0.5
Bazoom! (I Need Your Lovin')—Les Elgart & His Orchestra (54)	0.0
One Kiss Led To Another—Sunny Gale (56)	0.0
Love Me—The Billy Williams Quartet (54)	0.0
Love Me—Connie Russell (54)	0.0
Love Me—Georgia Gibbs (54)	0.0
Neil DIAMOND ▶ 11 (55)	**78789**
PRINCE ▶ 12 (46)	**77629**
TRADITIONAL ▶ 13 (99)	**77319**
Barrett STRONG/Norman WHITFIELD ▶ 14 (41)	**70818**
I Heard It Through The Grapevine—Marvin Gaye (68)	8871
War—Edwin Starr (70)	7121
I Heard It Through The Grapevine—Gladys Knight & The Pips (67)	6841
Just My Imagination (Running Away With Me)—The Temptations (71)	6683
I Can't Get Next To You—The Temptations (69)	6180
Ball Of Confusion (That's What The World Is Today)—The Temptations (70)	5317
Smiling Faces Sometimes—Undisputed Truth (71)	4374
Papa Was A Rollin' Stone—The Temptations (72)	4089
Cloud Nine—The Temptations (68)	3303
Psychedelic Shack—The Temptations (70)	2537
Run Away Child, Running Wild—The Temptations (69)	2318
That's The Way Love Is—Marvin Gaye (69)	1960
War—Bruce Springsteen & The E Street Band (86)	1264
Superstar (Remember How You Got Where You Are)—The Temptations (71)	1205
Friendship Train—Gladys Knight & The Pips (69)	1176
Don't Let The Joneses Get You Down—The Temptations (69)	852
Please Return Your Love To Me—The Temptations (68)	720
Stop The War Now—Edwin Starr (70)	685
Take A Look Around—The Temptations (72)	601
You Need Love Like I Do (Don't You)—Gladys Knight & The Pips (70)	595
How Can I Forget—Marvin Gaye (70)	509
Gonna Give Her All The Love I've Got—Jimmy Ruffin (67)	474
Ungena Za Ulimwengu (Unite The World)—The Temptations (70)	448
It's Summer—The Temptations (71)	417
Cloud Nine—Mongo Santamaria (69)	404
Don't Let Him Take Your Love From Me—Four Tops (69)	358
Funky Music Sho Nuff Turns Me On—Edwin Starr (71)	257
You Make Your Own Heaven And Hell Right Here On Earth—The Undisputed Truth (71)	230
I Heard It Through The Grapevine—Creedence Clearwater Revival (76)	211
I Can't Get Next To You—Al Green (70)	178
I Heard It Through The Grapevine (Part 1)—Roger (81)	147
Papa Was A Rollin' Stone—Wolf (82)	139
What It Is—The Undisputed Truth (72)	98
Gonna Give Her All The Love I've Got—Marvin Gaye (70)	72
Papa Was A Rollin' Stone—The Undisputed Truth (72)	68
Hum Along And Dance—The Temptations (70)	44
I Heard It Thru The Grapevine—King Curtis & The Kingpins (68)	21
Funky Music Sho Nuff Turns Me On—The Temptations (72)	20
I Heard It Through The Grapevine—The California Raisins (88)	18
Papa Was A Rolling Stone—Stars On 45 (81)	12
Message From A Black Man—The Whatnauts (70)	1.7
Stevie WONDER ▶ 15 (43)	**68537**
Kenneth GAMBLE/Leon HUFF ▶ 16 (83)	**68287**
Love Train—The O'Jays (73)	5733
TSOP (The Sound Of Philadelphia)—MFSB Featuring The Three Degrees (74)	5419
You'll Never Find Another Love Like Mine—Lou Rawls (76)	4173
When Will I See You Again—The Three Degrees (74)	4029
If You Don't Know Me By Now—Harold Melvin And The Blue Notes (72)	3604
Use Ta Be My Girl—The O'Jays (78)	3380
If You Don't Know Me By Now—Simply Red (89)	3293
Cowboys To Girls—The Intruders (68)	3286
Expressway To Your Heart—Soul Survivors (67)	3264
I Love Music (Part 1)—The O'Jays (75)	2798
Enjoy Yourself—The Jacksons (76)	2647
Drowning In The Sea Of Love—Joe Simon (71)	2257
The Love I Lost (Part 1)—Harold Melvin And The Blue Notes (73)	2070
I Can't Stop Dancing—Archie Bell & The Drells (68)	1681
Put Your Hands Together—The O'Jays (73)	1517
Engine Number 9—Wilson Pickett (70)	1414
Together—Tierra (80)	1181
Now That We Found Love—Heavy D & The Boyz (91)	1100
"There's Gonna Be A" Showdown—Archie Bell & The Drells (68)	1090
Close The Door—Teddy Pendergrass (78)	805
Thanks For Saving My Life—Billy Paul (74)	709
Forever Mine—The O'Jays (79)	688
(Love Is Like A) Baseball Game—The Intruders (68)	650
Time To Get Down—The O'Jays (73)	578
Hope That We Can Be Together Soon—Sharon Paige And Harold Melvin And The Blue Notes (75)	548
United—Peaches & Herb (68)	534
Explosion In Your Soul—Soul Survivors (67)	511
Give The People What They Want—The O'Jays (75)	505
You Gonna Make Me Love Somebody Else—The Jones Girls (79)	469
I Don't Love You Anymore—Teddy Pendergrass (77)	428
I Miss You (Part I)—Harold Melvin And The Blue Notes (72)	423
Pool Of Bad Luck—Joe Simon (72)	415
Show You The Way To Go—The Jacksons (77)	412
Do The Choo Choo—Archie Bell & The Drells (68)	386
992 Arguments—The O'Jays (72)	356
Now That We Found Love—Third World (78)	333
Sexy—MFSB (75)	317
Girl, Don't Let It Get You Down—The O'Jays (80)	309
You're The Reason Why—The Ebonys (71)	293
Slow Drag—The Intruders (68)	291
Deeper (In Love With You)—O'Jays (70)	279
Together—The Intruders (67)	266
You're My Latest, My Greatest Inspiration—Teddy Pendergrass (81)	265
One Night Affair—Jerry Butler (72)	239
Goin' Places—The Jacksons (77)	234
Message In Our Music—The O'Jays (76)	231
Turn Off The Lights—Teddy Pendergrass (79)	225
Yesterday I Had The Blues—Harold Melvin And The Blue Notes (73)	224
Silly, Silly, Fool—Dusty Springfield (70)	203
See You When I Git There—Lou Rawls (77)	175
When Love Is New—Arthur Prysock (76)	167
Baby I'm Lonely—The Intruders (67)	143
I Wanna Know Your Name—The Intruders (73)	140
Love Is The Message—MFSB Featuring The Three Degrees (74)	126
Impossible Mission (Mission Impossible)—Soul Survivors (68)	125
Satisfaction Guaranteed (Or Take Your Love Back)—Harold Melvin And The Blue Notes (74)	120
One Night Affair—The O'Jays (69)	97
I Love Music—The Ritchie Family (76)	92
T.S.O.P.—The Ritchie Family (76)	92
Darlin' Darlin' Baby (Sweet, Tender, Love)—The O'Jays (76)	90
My Balloon's Going Up—Archie Bell & The Drells (69)	82
United (Part 1)—The Music Makers (67)	78
This Is My Love Song—The Intruders (70)	73
I'm Girl Scoutin'—The Intruders (71)	71
Slow Motion (Part 1)—Johnny Williams (73)	70
I Bet He Don't Love You (Like I Love You)—The Intruders (71)	58
Groovy People—Lou Rawls (76)	57
Let's Make A Baby—Billy Paul (76)	53
(We'll Be) United—The Intruders (66)	51
I Just Love The Man—The Jones Girls (81)	47
I Love My Baby—Archie Bell & The Drells (69)	43
Am I Black Enough For You—Billy Paul (73)	29
Let Me Be Good To You—Lou Rawls (79)	28
A Love That's Real—The Intruders (67)	26
Work On Me—The O'Jays (77)	25
The Zip—MFSB (75)	20
You're My Blessing—Lou Rawls (80)	19
Pray For Me—The Intruders (71)	13
Looky Looky (Look At Me Girl)—The O'Jays (70)	6.3
Now I'm A Woman—Nancy Wilson (71)	5.8
Check Yourself—Italian Asphalt & Pavement Company (70)	2.6
Sing A Happy Song—The O'Jays (79)	2.4
A World Without Music—Archie Bell & The Drells (70)	0.4
Doc POMUS/Mort SHUMAN ▶ 17 (59)	**62642**
Save The Last Dance For Me—The Drifters (60)	8918
Surrender—Elvis Presley With The Jordanaires (61)	8380
Can't Get Used To Losing You—Andy Williams (63)	6431
Suspicion—Terry Stafford (64)	4565
This Magic Moment—Jay & The Americans (68)	3753
A Teenager In Love—Dion and The Belmonts (59)	3450
Little Sister—Elvis Presley (61)	3379
Go Jimmy Go—Jimmy Clanton (59)	2546
Turn Me Loose—Fabian (59)	2176
Hound Dog Man—Fabian (59)	1730
Marie's The Name His Latest Flame—Elvis Presley (61)	1319
I'll Save The Last Dance For You—Damita Jo (60)	1268
Sweets For My Sweet—The Drifters (61)	1182
Hushabye—The Mystics (59)	1163
This Magic Moment—The Drifters (60)	1087
I Count The Tears—The Drifters (60)	913
Save The Last Dance For Me—The Defranco Family Featuring Tony Defranco (74)	886
Viva Las Vegas—Elvis Presley With The Jordanaires (64)	799
Wrong For Each Other—Andy Williams (64)	698
No One—Ray Charles With The Raeletts (63)	684
(If You Cry) True Love, True Love—The Drifters (59)	652
I'm A Man—Fabian (58)	597
Spanish Lace—Gene McDaniels (62)	495
Plain Jane—Bobby Darin (59)	492
Kiss Me Quick—Elvis Presley With The Jordanaires (64)	450
Angel Face—James Darren (59)	443
Seven Day Weekend—Gary (U.S.) Bonds (62)	409
No One—Connie Francis (61)	403
Save The Last Dance For Me—Dolly Parton (83)	379
Hushabye—Jay & The Americans (69)	368
Havin' Fun—Dion (61)	329

Doc POMUS/Mort SHUMAN ► 17 (59) — 62642
Continued

Mess Of Blues— Elvis Presley With The Jordanaires (60)	287
Lonely Winds—The Drifters (60)	241
Your Other Love—The Flamingos (60)	230
I Dig Girls—Bobby Rydell (59)	218
Sweets For My Sweet—Tony Orlando (79)	198
A Texan And A Girl From Mexico—Anita Bryant (61)	195
Room Full Of Tears—The Drifters (61)	152
It's A Lonely Town (Lonely Without You)— Gene McDaniels (63)	136
A Teenager In Love—The Four Preps (61)	130
Petticoat White (Summer Sky Blue)— Bobby Vinton (66)	114
Two Fools—Frankie Avalon (59)	99
Hushabye—Robert John (72)	79
Teenage Heartache—Ray Peterson (60)	46
White Bucks And Saddle Shoes— Bobby Pedrick, Jr. (58)	40
Strollin' In The Springtime—Fabian (60)	26
Hushabye—The Beach Boys (64)	25
Night Rider— Elvis Presley With The Jordanaires (65)	23
Here Comes The Night—Ben E. King (61)	17
Carrying That Load—Ray Charles (63)	10
This Magic Moment—Richie Furay (78)	8.2
Wait—Jimmy Clanton (60)	7.3
Heart Of Gold—The Twins (60)	6.8
No One—Brenda Lee (65)	4.2
Sweets For My Sweet—Central Park West (69)	3.9
(It's A) Long Lonely Highway—Elvis Presley (65)	2.4
Bimini Bimbo (Doin' The Limbo)— Teddy And The Twilights (62)	1.4
I Need Somebody To Lean On—Elvis Presley (64)	1.1
I Ain't Sharin' Sharon—Buddy Knox (59)	0.4

Paul ANKA ► 18 (57) — 61526

Curtis MAYFIELD ► 19 (91) — 59415

Howard GREENFIELD/Neil SEDAKA ► 20 (45) — 55941

Breaking Up Is Hard To Do—Neil Sedaka (62)	7494
Love Will Keep Us Together— The Captain & Tennille (75)	6699
Where The Boys Are—Connie Francis (61)	4771
Oh Carol—Neil Sedaka (59)	2955
Happy Birthday, Sweet Sixteen—Neil Sedaka (61)	2559
Frankie—Connie Francis (59)	2530
Calendar Girl—Neil Sedaka (60)	2428
Next Door To An Angel—Neil Sedaka (62)	2255
Stairway To Heaven—Neil Sedaka (60)	2055
Breaking Up Is Hard To Do—Neil Sedaka (75)	1889
You Never Done It Like That— Captain & Tennille (78)	1801
Little Devil—Neil Sedaka (61)	1797
You Mean Everything To Me—Neil Sedaka (60)	1561
Diary—Neil Sedaka (58)	1436
Stupid Cupid—Connie Francis (58)	1181
Another Sleepless Night—Jimmy Clanton (60)	1057
Puppet Man—Tom Jones (71)	993
Alice In Wonderland—Neil Sedaka (63)	979
Breaking Up Is Hard To Do— The Partridge Family Starring Shirley Jones & Featuring David Cassidy (72)	734
Puppet Man—The 5th Dimension (70)	721
Breaking Up Is Hard To Do—Lenny Welch (70)	683
Run Samson Run—Neil Sedaka (60)	648
Let's Go Steady Again—Neil Sedaka (63)	640
Since You've Been Gone—Clyde McPhatter (59)	582
Bad Girl—Neil Sedaka (63)	575
Rainy Jane—Davy Jones (71)	562
I Waited Too Long—LaVern Baker (59)	546
Fallin'—Connie Francis (58)	525
I Go Ape—Neil Sedaka (59)	439
King Of Clowns—Neil Sedaka (62)	422
Time Waits For No One— The Friends Of Distinction (70)	407
Don't Hide Your Love—Cher (72)	370
Breaking Up Is Hard To Do—The Happenings (68)	309
What Am I Gonna Do—Jimmy Clanton (61)	251
Amarillo—Neil Sedaka (77)	230
You Gotta Make Your Own Sunshine— Neil Sedaka (76)	220
Time Marches On—Roy Hamilton (59)	164
We Had A Good Thing Goin'—The Cyrkle (67)	162
Sunny—Neil Sedaka (64)	96
Breaking Up Is Hard On You (a/k/a Don't Take Ma Bell Away From Me)— The American Comedy Network (84)	82
One Day Of Your Life—Andy Williams (70)	80
The Hungry Years—Wayne Newton (76)	35
Breaking Up Is Hard To Do— Heaven Bound with Tony Scotti (72)	7.9
Our Last Song Together— Bo Donaldson And The Heywoods (75)	6.4
Crying My Heart Out For You—Neil Sedaka (59)	5.2

Barry MANN/Cynthia WEIL ► 21 (60) — 55073

(You're My) Soul And Inspiration— The Righteous Brothers (66)	7442
Kicks—Paul Revere And The Raiders Featuring Mark Lindsay (66)	4107
Never Gonna Let You Go—Sergio Mendes (83)	3746
Blame It On The Bossa Nova—Eydie Gorme (63)	3142
Here You Come Again—Dolly Parton (77)	2755
My Dad—Paul Petersen (62)	2461
Hungry—Paul Revere And The Raiders Featuring Mark Lindsay (66)	1931
I'm Gonna Be Strong—Gene Pitney (64)	1883
I Just Can't Help Believing—B.J. Thomas (70)	1786
Uptown—The Crystals (62)	1673
Just Once— Quincy Jones Featuring James Ingram (81)	1525
Rock And Roll Lullaby—B.J. Thomas (72)	1491
We Gotta Get Out Of This Place—The Animals (65)	1474
Bless You—Tony Orlando (61)	1332
He's Sure The Boy I Love—The Crystals (62)	1298
Shape Of Things To Come— Max Frost And The Troopers (68)	1289
Conscience—James Darren (62)	1112
It's Getting Better—Mama Cass (69)	1101
Magic Town—The Vogues (66)	1013
Saturday Night At The Movies—The Drifters (64)	974
I'll Take You Home—The Drifters (63)	758
Make Your Own Kind Of Music— Mama Cass Elliot (69)	735
Don't Be Afraid, Little Darlin'— Steve Lawrence (63)	735
Brown Eyed Woman—Bill Medley (68)	662
Looking Through The Eyes Of Love—Gene Pitney (65)	646
Johnny Loves Me—Shelley Fabares (62)	624
Looking Through The Eyes Of Love— The Partridge Family Starring Shirley Jones & Featuring David Cassidy (72)	611
New World Coming—Mama Cass Elliot (70)	562
Proud—Johnny Crawford (62)	547
If A Woman Answers (Hang Up The Phone)— Leroy Van Dyke (62)	496
Home Of The Brave—Jody Miller (65)	446
(You're My) Soul And Inspiration— Donny & Marie (77)	407
I Want You To Meet My Baby—Eydie Gorme (64)	389
So Long Dixie—Blood, Sweat & Tears (72)	360
Heart—Kenny Chandler (63)	340
Mary's Little Lamb—James Darren (62)	330
We're Going All The Way—Jeffrey Osborne (84)	325
Peace Brother Peace—Bill Medley (68)	316
Don't Make My Baby Blue—Frankie Laine (63)	305
It's Gonna Be Fine—Glenn Yarbrough (65)	234
A Girl Has To Know—The G-Clefs (62)	174
Amy—Paul Petersen (63)	164
Right Here And Now—Bill Medley (82)	158
Olympia—Sergio Mendes (84)	145
Come On Over To My Place—The Drifters (65)	144
Where Have You Been (All My Life)— Arthur Alexander (62)	130
Heart! (I Hear You Beating)—Wayne Newton (63)	116
Mamacita—The Grass Roots (75)	101
It's A Happening World—The Tokens (67)	96
Cindy's Gonna Cry—Johnny Crawford (63)	77
Angelica—Oliver (70)	76
Home Of The Brave—Bonnie And The Treasures (65)	67
Little Miss U.S.A.—Barry Mann (61)	61
Heart To Heart—Errol Sober (79)	56
Feelings—Barry Mann (70)	53
The Princess And The Punk—Barry Mann (76)	43
It's Not Easy—The Will-O-Bees (68)	33
Talk To Me Baby—Barry Mann (64)	6.2
Make Your Own Kind Of Music—Barbra Streisand (72)	5.7
Angelica—Barry Mann (66)	3.4

Linda McCARTNEY/Paul McCARTNEY ► 22 (21) — 52385

Silly Love Songs—Wings (76)	7833
My Love—Paul McCartney & Wings (73)	7686
Listen To What The Man Said—Wings (75)	5030
Live And Let Die—Wings (73)	4780
Band On The Run—Paul McCartney & Wings (74)	4486
Uncle Albert/Admiral Halsey— Paul & Linda McCartney (71)	4182
Let 'Em In—Wings (76)	3857
Junior's Farm—Paul McCartney & Wings (74)	3216
Another Day—Paul McCartney (71)	2814
Jet—Paul McCartney & Wings (74)	2272
Helen Wheels—Paul McCartney & Wings (73)	2098
Hi, Hi, Hi—Wings (72)	1491
Venus And Mars Rock Show—Wings (75)	748
Give Ireland Back To The Irish—Wings (72)	518
Live And Let Die—Guns N' Roses (91)	506
Mary Had A Little Lamb—Wings (72)	378
Letting Go—Wings (75)	234
Sally G—Paul McCartney & Wings (74)	133
My Love—Margie Joseph (74)	114
Mine For Me—Rod Stewart (74)	6.2
Little Woman Love—Wings (72)	4.6

Billy JOEL ► 23 (37) — 52367

Michael JACKSON ► 24 (16) — 51588

Smokey ROBINSON ► 25 (57) — 50651

Bob DYLAN ► 26 (49) — 49250

Sam COOKE ► 27 (60) — 48388

Mike LOVE/Brian WILSON ► 28 (39) — 48191

I Get Around—The Beach Boys (64)	8633
Good Vibrations—The Beach Boys (66)	8071
Help Me, Rhonda—The Beach Boys (65)	6345
California Girls—The Beach Boys (65)	3984
Fun, Fun, Fun—The Beach Boys (64)	2657
California Girls—David Lee Roth (85)	2548
Be True To Your School—The Beach Boys (63)	2214
Little Honda—The Hondells (64)	2173
Do It Again—The Beach Boys (68)	2041
Surfin' Safari—The Beach Boys (62)	2024
When I Grow Up (To Be A Man)—The Beach Boys (64)	1865
Darlin'—The Beach Boys (67)	1159
Wild Honey—The Beach Boys (67)	622
Help Me Rhonda—Johnny Rivers (75)	596
It's O.K.—The Beach Boys (76)	446
Good Vibrations—Todd Rundgren (76)	391
Wendy—The Beach Boys (64)	286
Good Vibrations—The Beach Boys (81)	240
Surfin' Safari—The Beach Boys (81)	240
Help Me Rhonda—The Beach Boys (81)	240
Fun, Fun, Fun—The Beach Boys (81)	240
I Get Around—The Beach Boys (81)	240
Darlin'—Paul Davis Featuring Susan Collins (78)	215
Here Comes The Night—The Beach Boys (79)	195
Please Let Me Wonder—The Beach Boys (65)	178
Little Honda—The Beach Boys (64)	90
Darlin'—Yipes!! (80)	80
Surfin'—The Beach Boys (62)	65
Don't Back Down—The Beach Boys (64)	25
Little Saint Nick—The Beach Boys (63)	23
Good Vibrations— Hugo Montenegro, His Orchestra And Chorus (69)	23
Custom Machine—Bruce And Terry (64)	14
Goin' On—The Beach Boys (80)	12
She Knows Me Too Well—The Beach Boys (64)	5.0
California Girls—The Cantina Band (81)	1.5
Good Vibrations—The Cantina Band (81)	1.5
Help Me Rhonda—The Cantina Band (81)	1.5
Fun, Fun, Fun—The Cantina Band (81)	1.5
I Get Around—The Cantina Band (81)	1.5

Bob CREWE/Bob GAUDIO ► 29 (28) — 48175

Big Girls Don't Cry—The 4 Seasons (62)	10012
Walk Like A Man—The 4 Seasons (63)	8138
Rag Doll—The 4 Seasons Featuring The "Sound" Of Frankie Valli (64)	7976
Can't Take My Eyes Off You—Frankie Valli (67)	7410
Ronnie—The 4 Seasons Featuring The "Sound" Of Frankie Valli (64)	2454
Silence Is Golden—The Tremeloes (67)	2043
Save It For Me—The 4 Seasons Featuring The "Sound" Of Frankie Valli (64)	1587

Bob CREWE/Bob GAUDIO ▶ 29 (28) *Continued*	**48175**
Bye, Bye, Baby (Baby, Goodbye)—The 4 Seasons Featuring The "Sound" Of Frankie Valli (65)	1453
Can't Take My Eyes Off You—The Lettermen (67)	1323
The Sun Ain't Gonna Shine (Anymore)—The Walker Bros. (66)	1271
To Give (The Reason I Live)—Frankie Valli (67)	836
I Make A Fool Of Myself—Frankie Valli (67)	799
The Proud One—The Osmonds (75)	633
Girl Come Running—The 4 Seasons Featuring The "Sound" Of Frankie Valli (65)	604
Walk Like A Man—Mary Jane Girls (86)	290
Can't Take My Eyes Off You—Nancy Wilson (69)	255
Soon (I'll Be Home Again)—The 4 Seasons Featuring Frankie Valli (63)	214
The Proud One—Frankie Valli (66)	211
Toy Soldier—The 4 Seasons Featuring The "Sound" Of Frankie Valli (65)	204
The Sun Ain't Gonna Shine Anymore—Nielsen/Pearson (81)	168
Little Boy (In Grown Up Clothes)—The 4 Seasons (65)	113
Whatever You Want—Jerry Butler (63)	65
Don't Mention My Name—Shepherd Sisters (63)	58
I Can't Take My Eyes Off You—Pet Shop Boys (91)	37
You're Ready Now—Frankie Valli (66)	8.3
The Sun Ain't Gonna Shine Anymore—Fuzzy Bunnies (68)	6.0
Big Girls Don't Cry—Gidea Park (81)	3.7
Walk Like A Man—Gidea Park (81)	3.7
John FOGERTY ▶ 30 (30)	**47537**
Dave APPELL/Kal MANN ▶ 31 (35)	**43882**
Bristol Stomp—The Dovells (61)	6389
The Wah-Watusi—The Orlons (62)	5536
Let's Twist Again—Chubby Checker (61)	3771
South Street—The Orlons (63)	3753
Don't Hang Up—The Orlons (62)	3423
Ride!—Dee Dee Sharp (62)	2161
Popeye The Hitchhiker—Chubby Checker (62)	1843
Gravy (For My Mashed Potatoes)—Dee Dee Sharp (62)	1715
Loddy Lo—Chubby Checker (63)	1447
Do The Bird—Dee Dee Sharp (63)	1407
The Cha-Cha-Cha—Bobby Rydell (62)	1405
Dancin' Party—Chubby Checker (62)	1242
Let's Limbo Some More—Chubby Checker (63)	1110
Dance The Mess Around—Chubby Checker (61)	912
Hey, Bobba Needle—Chubby Checker (64)	888
Hully Gully Baby—The Dovells (62)	838
Crossfire!—The Orlons (63)	821
Butterfly Baby—Bobby Rydell (63)	757
Wildwood Days—Bobby Rydell (63)	674
Twist It Up—Chubby Checker (63)	596
Wild!—Dee Dee Sharp (63)	555
Do The New Continental—The Dovells (62)	542
Rocka Conga—The Applejacks (S) (58)	423
Rock Me In The Cradle Of Love—Dee Dee Sharp (63)	350
Bon-Doo-Wah—The Orlons (63)	289
Surf Party—Chubby Checker (63)	241
She Wants T' Swim—Chubby Checker (64)	241
The Popeye Waddle—Don Covay (62)	223
Rules Of Love—The Orlons (64)	97
Teach Me To Twist—Bobby Rydell - Chubby Checker (62)	84
Let's Twist Again—Jive Bunny And The Mastermixers (89)	80
Where Did I Go Wrong—Dee Dee Sharp (64)	39
Mother, Please!—Jo Ann Campbell (63)	20
Lets Twist Again—Jive Bunny & The Mastermixers (90)	6.7
Stop Monkeyin' Aroun'—The Dovells (63)	6.3
John D. LOUDERMILK ▶ 32 (43)	**43823**
George MICHAEL ▶ 33 (16)	**43698**
James Samuel HARRIS/Terry LEWIS ▶ 34 (31)	**40635**
Miss You Much—Janet Jackson (89)	4522
Human—The Human League (86)	4223
When I Think Of You—Janet Jackson (86)	3710
Love Will Never Do (Without You)—Janet Jackson (90)	3500
Sensitivity—Ralph Tresvant (90)	2969

Rub You The Right Way—Johnny Gill (90)	2737
I Didn't Mean To Turn You On—Robert Palmer (86)	2661
Control—Janet Jackson (86)	2464
Nasty—Janet Jackson (86)	2409
What Have You Done For Me Lately—Janet Jackson (86)	2231
If It Isn't Love—New Edition (88)	1864
Diamonds—Herb Alpert (87)	1768
Tender Love—Force M.D.'s (86)	1303
Saturday Love—Cherrelle (86)	565
Fake—Alexander O'Neal (87)	534
Never Knew Love Like This—Alexander O'Neal (88)	468
Making Love In The Rain—Herb Alpert (87)	379
Just Be Good To Me—The S.O.S. Band (83)	354
The Finest—The S.O.S. Band (86)	326
All True Man—Alexander O'Neal (91)	291
Keep Your Eye On Me—Herb Alpert (87)	239
Can You Stand The Rain—New Edition (89)	227
The Heat Of Heat—Patti Austin (86)	211
Tell Me If You Still Care—The S.O.S. Band (83)	173
Just The Way You Like It—The S.O.S. Band (84)	155
Encore—Cheryl Lynn (84)	117
I Didn't Mean To Turn You On—Cherrelle (84)	91
Dub Be Good To Me—Beats International (90)	72
Borrowed Love—Bingoboys (91)	35
Wrap My Body Tight—Johnny Gill (91)	30
You're Not My Kind Of Girl—New Edition (88)	5.3
Sylvester STEWART ▶ 35 (30)	**39545**
Bruce SPRINGSTEEN ▶ 36 (27)	**39059**
Harry Wayne CASEY/Rick FINCH ▶ 37 (21)	**38687**
That's The Way (I Like It)—K.C. & The Sunshine Band (75)	6457
Please Don't Go—K.C. & The Sunshine Band (79)	6091
(Shake, Shake, Shake) Shake Your Booty—K C & The Sunshine Band (76)	4899
I'm Your Boogie Man—K C & The Sunshine Band (77)	4680
Get Down Tonight—K.C. & The Sunshine Band (75)	4656
Keep It Comin' Love—KC & The Sunshine Band (77)	4615
Rock Your Baby—George McCrae (74)	4499
Dance Across The Floor—Jimmy "Bo" Horne (78)	502
Boogie Shoes—KC & The Sunshine Band (78)	501
I Like To Do It—KC & The Sunshine Band (76)	385
I Get Lifted—George McCrae (75)	352
Do You Wanna Go Party—KC & The Sunshine Band (79)	238
Wrap Your Arms Around Me—K C & The Sunshine Band (77)	210
I Can't Leave You Alone—George McCrae (74)	161
Who Do Ya Love—KC & The Sunshine Band (78)	115
Honey I—George McCrae (76)	106
That's The Way I Like It—The Ritchie Family (76)	92
Do You Feel All Right—KC & The Sunshine Band (78)	64
Shotgun Shuffle—The Sunshine Band (75)	29
Look At You—George McCrae (75)	24
Let's Go Rock And Roll—K.C. & The Sunshine Band (80)	11
Chuck BERRY ▶ 38 (50)	**38128**
Bernard EDWARDS/Nile RODGERS ▶ 39 (18)	**37934**
Le Freak—Chic (78)	11074
Upside Down—Diana Ross (80)	8140
Good Times—Chic (79)	6108
We Are Family—Sister Sledge (79)	4694
I'm Coming Out—Diana Ross (80)	2369
I Want Your Love—Chic (79)	2083
He's The Greatest Dancer—Sister Sledge (79)	1848
Rapper's Delight—Sugarhill Gang (79)	551
Backfired—Debbie Harry (81)	351
Everybody Dance—Chic (78)	267
Rebels Are We—Chic (80)	112
Got To Love Somebody—Sister Sledge (80)	93
My Forbidden Lover—Chic (79)	91
Why—Carly Simon (82)	86
Soup For One—Chic (82)	43
Real People—Chic (80)	16
The Jam Was Moving—Debbie Harry (81)	11
Chip Off The Old Block—Chic (80)	0.0
Eddie BRIGATI/Felix CAVALIERE ▶ 40 (13)	**37250**
Groovin'—The Young Rascals (67)	9580
People Got To Be Free—The Rascals (68)	9189
A Beautiful Morning—The Young Rascals (68)	5558
How Can I Be Sure—The Young Rascals (67)	4109
A Girl Like You—The Young Rascals (67)	2139

I've Been Lonely Too Long—The Young Rascals (67)	1562
It's Wonderful—The Young Rascals (67)	1044
A Ray Of Hope—The Rascals (68)	981
Groovin'—Booker T. & The M.G.'s (67)	957
How Can I Be Sure—David Cassidy (72)	939
You Better Run—The Young Rascals (66)	833
You Better Run—Pat Benatar (80)	350
People Gotta Be Free—The 5th Dimension (70)	11
Jimmy WEBB ▶ 41 (37)	**37215**
John LENNON ▶ 42 (18)	**37009**
Paul McCARTNEY ▶ 43 (22)	**36735**
Jerry FULLER ▶ 44 (14)	**36638**
David GATES ▶ 45 (29)	**36386**
Diane WARREN ▶ 46 (25)	**35241**
Jeff BARRY/Ellie GREENWICH/Phil SPECTOR ▶ 47 (23)	**33864**
Chapel Of Love—The Dixie Cups (64)	8316
Be My Baby—The Ronettes (63)	6059
Da Doo Ron Ron—Shaun Cassidy (77)	4512
Da Doo Ron Ron (When He Walked Me Home)—The Crystals (63)	3838
Baby, I Love You—Andy Kim (69)	2808
Then He Kissed Me—The Crystals (63)	2734
River Deep-Mountain High—The Supremes & Four Tops (70)	1281
Be My Baby—Andy Kim (70)	1212
I Can Hear Music—The Beach Boys (69)	916
Baby, I Love You—The Ronettes (63)	719
Wait 'til My Bobby Gets Home—Darlene Love (63)	657
River Deep-Mountain High—Deep Purple (69)	351
A Fine Fine Boy—Darlene Love (63)	184
Not Too Young To Get Married—Bob B. Soxx And The Blue Jeans (63)	171
Be My Baby—Cissy Houston (71)	24
River Deep-Mountain High—Ike & Tina Turner (66)	23
Little Boy—The Crystals (64)	22
All Grown Up—The Crystals (64)	14
Da Doo Ron Ron (When He Walked Me Home)—Ian Matthews (72)	7.8
I Wonder—The Butterflys (65)	7.3
I Can Hear Music—The Ronettes Featuring Veronica (66)	5.6
River Deep-Mountain High—Ike & Tina Turner (69)	3.1
Chapel Of Love—Bette Midler (73)	0.0
Phil COLLINS ▶ 48 (16)	**33504**
Robert ALLEN/Al STILLMAN ▶ 49 (26)	**33148**
Moments To Remember—The Four Lads (55)	7587
Chances Are—Johnny Mathis (57)	5455
No Not Much—The Four Lads (56)	4830
It's Not For Me To Say—Johnny Mathis (57)	4673
Can You Find It In Your Heart—Tony Bennett with Percy Faith and His Orchestra (56)	1683
Who Needs You—The Four Lads (57)	1611
If Dreams Came True—Pat Boone (58)	1550
Enchanted Island—The Four Lads (58)	1229
There's Only One Of You—The Four Lads (58)	957
Every Step Of The Way—Johnny Mathis (63)	509
Teacher Teacher—Johnny Mathis (58)	461
(There's No Place Like) Home For The Holidays—Perry Como (54)	414
Happy Anniversary—Jane Morgan (59)	388
Door Of Dreams—Perry Como (55)	376
No, Not Much—The Vogues (69)	361
Moments To Remember—The Vogues (69)	335
No Not Much—The Smoke Ring (69)	215
Eyes Of God—The Four Lads (57)	179
Happy Anniversary—The Four Lads (59)	171
Scene Of The Crime—Dinah Shore (58)	132
Book Of Love—Richard Maltby And His Orchestra (55)	14
Love Me Good—Jo Stafford (56)	14
You Know How It Is—Frankie Laine (57)	5.1
It's Not For Me To Say—Cyril Stapleton & His Orchestra (57)	0.0
Enchanted Island—Jane Morgan & The Troubadors (58)	0.0
It's Not For Me To Say—Jane Morgan (57)	0.0
John DENSMORE/Robby KRIEGER/Ray MANZAREK/Jim MORRISON ▶ 50 (16)	**33087**
Light My Fire—The Doors (67)	8461
Hello, I Love You—The Doors (68)	6496
Touch Me—The Doors (68)	5980

John DENSMORE/Robby KRIEGER/ Ray MANZAREK/Jim MORRISON ► 50 (16) *Continued*	**33087**
Light My Fire–Jose Feliciano (68)	4958
Love Her Madly–The Doors (71)	1978
People Are Strange–The Doors (67)	1529
Riders On The Storm–The Doors (71)	1436
Love Me Two Times–The Doors (67)	731
The Unknown Soldier–The Doors (68)	682
Wishful Sinful–The Doors (69)	464
L.A. Woman–Billy Idol (90)	208
Light My Fire–Amii Stewart (79)	51
Roadhouse Blues–The Doors (70)	38
Light My Fire–Rhetta Hughes (69)	33
Light My Fire–The Doors (68)	32
Love Street–The Doors (68)	9.0
STING ► 51 (20)	**32092**
George HARRISON ► 52 (31)	**31637**
Tony HATCH ► 53 (20)	**31273**
Berry GORDY/Fonce MIZELL/ Freddie PERREN/Deke RICHARDS ► 54 (8)	**31174**
ABC–The Jackson 5 (70)	8551
I Want You Back–The Jackson 5 (69)	7904
The Love You Save–The Jackson 5 (70)	6071
Mama's Pearl–The Jackson 5 (71)	4810
Sugar Daddy–The Jackson 5 (71)	2514
Maybe Tomorrow–The Jackson 5 (71)	977
Bless You–Martha Reeves & The Vandellas (71)	298
I Found That Girl–The Jackson 5 (70)	51
Dave BARTHOLOMEW/Fats DOMINO ► 55 (44)	**30995**
Ain't That A Shame–Pat Boone (55)	6966
I'm In Love Again–Fats Domino (56)	3481
I'm Walkin'–Fats Domino (57)	2846
Whole Lotta Loving–Fats Domino (58)	2302
Blue Monday–Fats Domino (56)	2195
My Girl Josephine–Fats Domino (60)	1293
Let The Four Winds Blow–Fats Domino (61)	1081
Valley Of Tears–Fats Domino (57)	1025
I'm Walkin'–Ricky Nelson (57)	939
Bo Weevil–Teresa Brewer (56)	908
Ain't That A Shame!–The 4 Seasons Featuring Frankie Valli (63)	760
My Girl Josephine–Jerry Jaye (67)	721
Ain't It A Shame–Fats Domino (55)	665
Country Boy–Fats Domino (60)	600
Shu Rah–Fats Domino (61)	516
It's You I Love–Fats Domino (57)	423
Ain't That A Shame–Cheap Trick (79)	411
Wait And See–Fats Domino (57)	406
Natural Born Lover–Fats Domino (60)	381
I'm In Love Again–The Fontane Sisters (56)	355
When I See You–Fats Domino (57)	328
I Want You To Know–Fats Domino (57)	295
Let The Four Winds Blow–Roy Brown (57)	280
Tell Me That You Love Me–Fats Domino (60)	274
Big Beat–Fats Domino (57)	269
So Long–Fats Domino (56)	245
Bo Weevil–Fats Domino (56)	220
I'm In Love Again–Rick Nelson (63)	189
Poor Me–Fats Domino (55)	184
Yes My Darling–Fats Domino (58)	141
Honey Chile–Fats Domino (56)	105
Little Mary–Fats Domino (58)	72
No, No–Fats Domino (58)	60
The Rooster Song–Fats Domino (57)	19
Don't You Know I Love You–Fats Domino (58)	18
Don't Blame It On Me–Fats Domino (56)	10
I Just Cry–Fats Domino (61)	7.0
Young School Girl–Fats Domino (58)	3.3
Dance With Mr. Domino–Fats Domino (62)	1.3
If You Need Me–Fats Domino (60)	1.1
Ain't That A Shame–Ronnie Gaylord (55)	0.0
I'm Walkin'–Larry Storch (57)	0.0
Bo Weevil–Bonnie Lou (56)	0.0
Poor Me–Bill Carey (55)	0.0
Rod TEMPERTON ► 56 (13)	**30965**
Hank BALLARD ► 57 (10)	**30489**
Joe MELSON/Roy ORBISON ► 58 (17)	**30289**
Crying–Roy Orbison (61)	6223
Running Scared–Roy Orbison (61)	6095
Only The Lonely (Know How I Feel)– Roy Orbison (60)	5979
Blue Bayou–Linda Ronstadt (77)	4470
Crying–Don McLean (81)	2185
Blue Angel–Roy Orbison (60)	1636
Blue Bayou–Roy Orbison (63)	1151
The Crowd–Roy Orbison (62)	908
Crying–Jay & The Americans (66)	569
I'm Hurtin'–Roy Orbison (60)	410
Memories Of Maria–The Music Of Jerry Byrd (62)	244
Running Scared–The Fools (81)	170
Up Town–Roy Orbison (59)	161
Laugh–The Velvets (61)	55
Only The Lonely– Sonny James (The Southern Gentleman) (69)	23
Actress–Roy Orbison (62)	9.5
Lana–Gene McCannon (63)	0.5
Galt MacDERMOT/James RADO/ Gerome RAGNI ► 59 (12)	**30206**
Hair–The Cowsills (69)	8011
Let The Sunshine In (The Flesh Failures)– The 5th Dimension (69)	5902
Aquarius–The 5th Dimension (69)	5902
Easy To Be Hard–Three Dog Night (69)	5385
Good Morning Starshine–Oliver (69)	4408
Be-In (Hare Krishna)–The Happenings (69)	209
Where Do I Go–The Happenings (69)	209
Easy To Be Hard– Hair (Original Soundtrack)/Cheryl Barnes (79)	76
Where Do I Go–Carla Thomas (68)	45
Good Morning Starshine– Strawberry Alarm Clock (69)	45
Ain't Got No–Nina Simone (69)	6.9
I Got Life–Nina Simone (69)	6.9
Boudleaux BRYANT ► 60 (23)	**30079**
L. Russell BROWN/Irwin LEVINE ► 61 (17)	**29304**
Knock Three Times–Dawn (70)	9840
Tie A Yellow Ribbon Round The Ole Oak Tree– Dawn Featuring Tony Orlando (73)	8042
Say, Has Anybody Seen My Sweet Gypsy Rose– Dawn Featuring Tony Orlando (73)	3651
I Woke Up In Love This Morning– The Partridge Family Starring Shirley Jones & Featuring David Cassidy (71)	1847
Steppin' Out (Gonna Boogie Tonight)– Tony Orlando And Dawn (74)	1391
Who's In The Strawberry Patch With Sally– Tony Orlando And Dawn (73)	839
Summer Sand–Dawn (71)	744
I Play And Sing–Dawn (71)	724
We're Free–Beverly Bremers (72)	654
I Hear Those Church Bells Ringing–Dusk (71)	494
Am I Losing You– The Partridge Family Starring Shirley Jones & Featuring David Cassidy (72)	417
Angel Baby–Dusk (71)	311
Number Wonderful–Rock Flowers (71)	143
It Only Hurts When I Try To Smile– Dawn Featuring Tony Orlando (74)	135
Treat Me Like A Good Piece Of Candy–Dusk (71)	65
Is There Anyone Home?–Jimmy Druiett (72)	5.2
Should I Tie A Yellow Ribbon Round The Ole Oak Tree? The Answer–Connie Francis (73)	0.7
John FARRAR ► 62 (10)	**29067**
James BROWN ► 63 (46)	**28939**
Nick ASHFORD/Valerie SIMPSON ► 64 (41)	**28849**
Ain't No Mountain High Enough–Diana Ross (70)	6311
Your Precious Love– Marvin Gaye & Tammi Terrell (67)	2938
Ain't Nothing Like The Real Thing– Marvin Gaye & Tammi Terrell (68)	2127
You're All I Need To Get By– Marvin Gaye & Tammi Terrell (68)	2011
Remember Me–Diana Ross (70)	1429
Solid–Ashford & Simpson (84)	1266
Ain't No Mountain High Enough– Marvin Gaye & Tammi Terrell (67)	1259
Reach Out And Touch (Somebody's Hand)– Diana Ross (70)	1230
I'm Every Woman–Chaka Khan (78)	989
The Boss–Diana Ross (79)	954
You're All I Need To Get By–Aretha Franklin (71)	837
Ain't Nothing Like The Real Thing– Donny & Marie (76)	755
California Soul–The 5th Dimension (68)	740
Some Things You Never Get Used To– Diana Ross And The Supremes (68)	717
Keep On Lovin' Me Honey– Marvin Gaye & Tammi Terrell (68)	677
Found A Cure–Ashford & Simpson (79)	550
Good Lovin' Ain't Easy To Come By– Marvin Gaye & Tammi Terrell (69)	443
Surrender–Diana Ross (71)	414
What You Gave Me– Marvin Gaye & Tammi Terrell (69)	406
Who's Gonna Take The Blame– Smokey Robinson & The Miracles (70)	316
Landlord–Gladys Knight & The Pips (80)	315
You're All I Need To Get By– Tony Orlando & Dawn (75)	303
Ain't Nothing Like The Real Thing– Aretha Franklin (74)	267
You're All I Need To Get By– Johnny Mathis/Deniece Williams (78)	206
Didn't You Know (You'd Have To Cry Sometime)– Gladys Knight & The Pips (69)	206
Destination: Anywhere– The Marvelettes (68)	203
Don't Cost You Nothing–Ashford & Simpson (78)	201
Street Corner–Ashford & Simpson (82)	163
Onion Song–Marvin Gaye & Tammi Terrell (70)	137
California Soul–Marvin Gaye & Tammi Terrell (70)	116
Shoe Shoe Shine–Dynamic Superiors (74)	112
Don't Send Nobody Else–Ace Spectrum (74)	73
I Am Your Man–Bobby Taylor & The Vancouvers (68)	68
Send It–Ashford & Simpson (77)	25
Love Don't Make It Right–Ashford & Simpson (80)	23
Count Your Blessings–Ashford and Simpson (86)	17
It Seems To Hang On–Ashford & Simpson (78)	14
(I'd Know You) Anywhere–Ashford & Simpson (74)	9.9
Ain't Nothing Like The Real Thing– Chris Christian (82)	8.1
You're All I Need To Get By–Chris Christian (82)	8.1
Clouds–Chaka Khan (80)	3.6
John DENVER ► 65 (26)	**28116**
Sonny BONO ► 66 (22)	**27972**
Joe SOUTH ► 67 (29)	**27543**
Jeff LYNNE ► 68 (29)	**27441**
Mike CHAPMAN/Nicky CHINN ► 69 (18)	**27210**
Kiss You All Over–Exile (78)	7882
Mickey–Toni Basil (82)	5959
Little Willy–The Sweet (73)	3958
Stumblin' In–Suzi Quatro And Chris Norman (79)	2721
Ballroom Blitz–The Sweet (75)	2550
Heart And Soul–Huey Lewis and the News (83)	1620
Living Next Door To Alice–Smokie (76)	937
You Thrill Me–Exile (78)	360
She's In Love With You–Suzi Quatro (79)	354
Blockbuster–The Sweet (73)	280
If You Can't Give Me Love–Suzi Quatro (79)	216
Can The Can–Suzi Quatro (76)	167
Lipstick–Suzi Quatro (81)	166
Co-Co–The Sweet (71)	22
48 Crash–Suzi Quatro (74)	7.6
If You Think You Know How To Love Me– Smokey (75)	4.8
Try It On–Exile (77)	3.4
Part Of Me That Needs You Most–Jay Black (80)	2.9
Barry GIBB/Robin GIBB ► 70 (13)	**27089**
Woman In Love–Barbra Streisand (80)	7247
How Can You Mend A Broken Heart–Bee Gees (71)	6914
Emotion–Samantha Sang (77)	5831
Love Me–Yvonne Elliman (76)	1469
Holiday–The Bee Gees (67)	1119
To Love Somebody–The Bee Gees (67)	1006
My World–Bee Gees (72)	995
New York Mining Disaster 1941 Have You Seen My Wife, Mr. Jones–The Bee Gees (67)	983
Come On Over–Olivia Newton-John (76)	650
Edge Of The Universe–Bee Gees (77)	520
Promises–Barbra Streisand (81)	276
To Love Somebody–The Sweet Inspirations (68)	56
Mr. Natural–Bee Gees (74)	22
John SEBASTIAN ► 71 (20)	**26800**

Lee POCKRISS/Paul VANCE ▶ 72 (26)	**26655**
Itsy Bitsy Teenie Weenie Yellow Polkadot Bikini–Brian Hyland (60)	7476
Playground In My Mind–Clint Holmes (73)	5118
Catch A Falling Star–Perry Como (57)	3980
Tracy–The Cuff Links (69)	2946
What Is Love–The Playmates (59)	1121
Leader Of The Laundromat–The Detergents (64)	1105
Jimmy's Girl–Johnny Tillotson (61)	894
When Julie Comes Around–The Cuff Links (69)	724
Starbright–Johnny Mathis (60)	700
Wait For Me–The Playmates (60)	690
Little Miss Stuck-Up–The Playmates (61)	392
Run Sally Run–The Cuff Links (70)	364
Hot Pants–Salvage (71)	303
No–Dodie Stevens (60)	202
Walk Tall–2 Of Clubs (66)	193
Go Chase A Moonbeam–Jerry Vale (58)	109
Double-O-Seven–The Detergents (65)	108
There Won't Be Any Snow (Christmas In The Jungle)–Derrik Roberts (65)	89
(The Clickity Clack Song) Four Little Heels–Brian Hyland (60)	62
The Prettiest Girl In School–Randy Starr (58)	37
The Chick–Lee And Paul (59)	13
Shake Hands With A Fool–June Valli (58)	11
Oliver Cool–Oliver Cool (60)	6.5
Dommage, Dommage (Too Bad, Too Bad)–Jerry Vale (66)	6.1
Dommage, Dommage (Too Bad, Too Bad)–Paul Vance (66)	3.7
Itsy Bitsy Teenie Weenie Yellow Polkadot Bikini–Buddy Hackett (60)	0.0
Laura NYRO ▶ 73 (13)	**26210**
Bobby RUSSELL ▶ 74 (13)	**26194**
Donovan LEITCH ▶ 75 (20)	**25987**
Buck RAM ▶ 76 (25)	**25545**
Dennis DeYOUNG ▶ 77 (16)	**25463**
Marty ROBBINS ▶ 78 (26)	**24953**
John MELLENCAMP ▶ 79 (19)	**24943**
Bernie LOWE/Kal MANN ▶ 80 (26)	**24931**
(Let Me Be Your) Teddy Bear–Elvis Presley (57)	7775
Butterfly–Andy Williams (57)	4791
We Got Love–Bobby Rydell (59)	3621
Butterfly–Charlie Gracie (57)	2197
Kissin' Time–Bobby Rydell (59)	1393
Remember You're Mine–Pat Boone (57)	1255
Twenty Miles–Chubby Checker (63)	929
Ninety Nine Ways–Tab Hunter (57)	920
Fabulous–Charlie Gracie (57)	709
Back To School Again–Timmie "Oh Yeah" Rogers (57)	476
You're The Greatest–Billy Scott (57)	181
Party Time–Sal Mineo (57)	112
Just Like In The Movies–The Upbeats (58)	102
Follow Your Heart–The Four Coins (57)	94
The Greatest Thing–Georgia Gibbs (56)	85
Butterfly–Bob Carroll (57)	81
Fabulous–Steve Lawrence (57)	80
Kissin' Time–Kiss (74)	56
Groovy Tonight–Bobby Rydell (60)	23
(Let Me Be Your) Teddy Bear–Elvis Presley (82)	23
I'm Still A King To You–Don Cherry (56)	17
Wanderin' Eyes–Charlie Gracie (57)	5.7
Beat–Billy May And His Orchestra (56)	5.0
You're The Greatest–Valerie Carr (57)	0.0
Ninety-Nine Ways–Charlie Gracie (57)	0.0
Butterfly–Billy Williams (57)	0.0
Jeff BARRY/Ellie GREENWICH ▶ 81 (23)	**24554**
Do Wah Diddy Diddy–Manfred Mann (64)	8308
Hanky Panky–Tommy James And The Shondells (66)	6771
I Wanna Love Him So Bad–The Jelly Beans (64)	1628
People Say–The Dixie Cups (64)	1548
Maybe I Know–Lesley Gore (64)	1454
The Kind Of Boy You Can't Forget–The Raindrops (63)	1132
Look Of Love–Lesley Gore (64)	848
Give Us Your Blessings–The Shangri-Las (65)	554
What A Guy–The Raindrops (63)	549
Don't Ever Leave Me–Connie Francis (64)	442
Little Bell–The Dixie Cups (64)	276

You Should Have Seen The Way He Looked At Me–The Dixie Cups (64)	270
That Boy John–The Raindrops (63)	228
Out In The Streets–The Shangri-Las (65)	175
Give Us Your Blessing–Ray Peterson (63)	149
I'll Take You Where The Music's Playing–The Drifters (65)	146
Do-Wah-Diddy–The Exciters (64)	55
Do Wah Diddy Diddy–Stars On 45 (81)	12
Hickory Dickery Dock–Baby Jane And The Rock-A-Byes (63)	3.2
When The Boy's Happy (The Girl's Happy Too)–The Four Pennies (63)	2.7
One More Tear–The Raindrops (64)	1.9
Doo Wah Diddy Diddy–Tight Fit (81)	0.9
He Ain't No Angel–The Ad Libs (65)	0.5
Dennis LAMBERT/Brian POTTER ▶ 82 (38)	**24258**
Don't Pull Your Love–Hamilton, Joe Frank & Reynolds (71)	4833
Ain't No Woman (Like The One I've Got)–Four Tops (73)	3986
It Only Takes A Minute–Tavares (75)	1975
Keeper Of The Castle–Four Tops (72)	1655
Country Boy (You Got Your Feet In L.A.)–Glen Campbell (75)	1187
Are You Man Enough–Four Tops (73)	1185
Look In My Eyes Pretty Woman–Tony Orlando And Dawn (74)	930
One Tin Soldier The Legend Of Billy Jack–Coven (71)	917
This Heart–Gene Redding (74)	878
One Tin Soldier–The Original Caste (69)	801
Remember What I Told You To Forget–Tavares (75)	694
It's A Cryin' Shame–Gayle McCormick (71)	608
Daisy Mae–Hamilton, Joe Frank & Reynolds (71)	605
The Runway–The Grass Roots (72)	555
Give It To The People–The Righteous Brothers (74)	537
Dream On–The Righteous Brothers (74)	479
One Chain Don't Make No Prison–Four Tops (74)	371
Ashes To Ashes–The 5th Dimension (73)	307
I Just Can't Get You Out Of My Mind–Four Tops (74)	288
You Brought The Woman Out Of Me–Evie Sands (75)	254
Don't Pull Your Love–Glen Campbell (76)	228
Too Late–Tavares (74)	193
One Tin Soldier (The Legend Of Billy Jack)–Coven (73)	143
Love Music–Raiders (73)	131
One Chain (Don't Make No Prison)–Santana (79)	117
One Tin Soldier The Legend Of Billy Jack–Coven (73)	111
Put A Little Love Away–The Emotions (74)	91
Gonna Be Alright Now–Gayle McCormick (71)	65
You Brought The Woman Out Of Me–Hot (78)	52
Once A Fool–Kiki Dee (76)	37
To Love You–Country Store (70)	16
Don't Pull Your Love–Sam & Dave (71)	11
The House On Telegraph Hill–Bo Donaldson And The Heywoods (75)	7.0
Who Gets Your Love–Dusty Springfield (73)	6.5
If That's The Way You Want It–Diamond Head (73)	2.2
One Good Woman–Hamilton, Joe Frank & Reynolds (72)	1.6
Love Music–Sergio Mendes & Brasil '77 (73)	0.7
My Ship–Tavares (75)	0.0
Al GREEN/Al JACKSON/Willie MITCHELL ▶ 83 (7)	**24197**
Let's Stay Together–Al Green (71)	7842
I'm Still In Love With You–Al Green (72)	5102
You Ought To Be With Me–Al Green (72)	4701
Look What You Done For Me–Al Green (72)	3798
Call Me (Come Back Home)–Al Green (73)	1660
Let's Stay Together–Tina Turner (84)	755
Let's Stay Together–Isaac Hayes (72)	340
Bob SEGER ▶ 84 (28)	**24115**
Mac DAVIS ▶ 85 (21)	**24068**
Otis BLACKWELL/Elvis PRESLEY ▶ 86 (9)	**24053**
Don't Be Cruel–Elvis Presley (56)	10167
All Shook Up–Elvis Presley (57)	9084
Don't Be Cruel–Bill Black's Combo (60)	2335
Don't Be Cruel–Cheap Trick (88)	2074
All Shook Up–Suzi Quatro (74)	154
All Shook Up–Jive Bunny And The Mastermixers (89)	80

Don't Be Cruel–Barbara Lynn (63)	74
Paralyzed–Elvis Presley (56)	62
Don't Be Cruel (To A Heart That's True)–Elvis Presley (82)	23
Lou GRAMM/Michael Leslie JONES ▶ 87 (14)	**23773**
Waiting For A Girl Like You–Foreigner (81)	8009
Hot Blooded–Foreigner (78)	3751
Double Vision–Foreigner (78)	2677
Cold As Ice–Foreigner (77)	2348
Say You Will–Foreigner (87)	1610
That Was Yesterday–Foreigner (85)	1231
Head Games–Foreigner (79)	1218
Dirty White Boy–Foreigner (79)	979
Blue Morning, Blue Day–Foreigner (78)	838
Juke Box Hero–Foreigner (82)	447
Reaction To Action–Foreigner (85)	214
Heart Turns To Stone–Foreigner (88)	209
Down On Love–Foreigner (85)	198
Luanne–Foreigner (82)	44
Ray PARKER Jr. ▶ 88 (15)	**23646**
Pete TOWNSHEND ▶ 89 (34)	**23572**
Allen TOUSSAINT ▶ 90 (35)	**23464**
Howard GREENFIELD/Jack KELLER ▶ 91 (9)	**23454**
My Heart Has A Mind Of Its Own–Connie Francis (60)	8856
Everybody's Somebody's Fool–Connie Francis (60)	8043
Breakin' In A Brand New Broken Heart–Connie Francis (61)	3470
Venus In Blue Jeans–Jimmy Clanton (62)	2008
Your Used To Be–Brenda Lee (63)	676
I Wish I'd Never Been Born–Patti Page (60)	257
Don't Read The Letter–Patti Page (60)	123
Poor Little Puppet–Cathy Carroll (62)	21
What's Come Over This World?–Billy Carr (65)	0.5
Simon Le BON/Nick RHODES/Andy TAYLOR/Nigel John TAYLOR/Roger TAYLOR ▶ 92 (8)	**23454**
The Reflex–Duran Duran (84)	5082
Union Of The Snake–Duran Duran (83)	4545
The Wild Boys–Duran Duran (84)	4449
Hungry Like The Wolf–Duran Duran (82)	3924
Is There Something I Should Know–Duran Duran (83)	2395
New Moon On Monday–Duran Duran (84)	1339
Rio–Duran Duran (83)	946
Save A Prayer–Duran Duran (85)	773
Boudleaux BRYANT/Felice BRYANT ▶ 93 (27)	**22826**
Bye Bye Love–The Everly Brothers (57)	7746
Wake Up Little Susie–The Everly Brothers (57)	6983
Problems–The Everly Brothers (58)	3453
Take A Message To Mary–The Everly Brothers (59)	1270
Poor Jenny–The Everly Brothers (59)	784
Have A Good Time–Sue Thompson (62)	761
Wake Up Little Susie–Simon and Garfunkel (82)	477
Raining In My Heart–Leo Sayer (78)	267
Love Of My Life–The Everly Brothers (58)	258
Come Live With Me–Ray Charles (73)	156
Willie Can–Sue Thompson (63)	147
Teen Ex–The Browns Featuring Jim Edward Brown (60)	126
Bye Bye Love–Webb Pierce (57)	109
Wake Up Little Suzie–Jive Bunny And The Mastermixers (89)	80
Always It's You–The Everly Brothers (60)	78
Come Live With Me–Roy Clark (73)	48
Auf Wiedersehen Marlene–Bob Moore (62)	33
Raining In My Heart–Buddy Holly / The Crickets (59)	13
Brand New Heartache–The Everly Brothers (60)	9.6
She Wears My Ring–Solomon King (68)	7.8
Fall Away–Eddie Albert (65)	6.0
Bye Bye Love–Will Jordan (59)	5.6
My Hero (That's What You Are)–Sue Thompson (62)	4.9
Tina–The Easy Riders (57)	2.4
Sweet Sugar Lips–The Kalin Twins (59)	1.5
Bye, Bye, Love–Chuck Miller (57)	0.0
Bye Bye Love–T. Tommy (57)	0.0
Dino FEKARIS/Freddie PERREN ▶ 94 (13)	**22740**
Reunited–Peaches & Herb (79)	7690
I Will Survive–Gloria Gaynor (78)	7179
Shake Your Groove Thing–Peaches & Herb (78)	2986
Makin' It–David Naughton (79)	2897
I Pledge My Love–Peaches & Herb (80)	870
I Will Survive–Sa-Fire (89)	247

Dino FEKARIS/Freddie PERREN ► 94 (13) *Continued*	**22740**
We've Got Love—Peaches & Herb (79)	221
Let Me Know (I Have A Right)—Gloria Gaynor (79)	220
A Little Lovin' (Keeps The Doctor Away)—The Raes (78)	209
That Once In A Lifetime—Demis Roussos (78)	173
Roller-Skatin' Mate (Part 1)—Peaches & Herb (79)	32
Reunited—Band Of Gold (84)	12
Anybody Wanna Party?—Gloria Gaynor (79)	4.6
Ray EVANS/Jay LIVINGSTON ► 95 (31)	**22683**
Tammy—Debbie Reynolds (57)	9194
Whatever Will Be, Will Be (Que Sera, Sera)—Doris Day (56)	6972
To Each His Own—The Platters (60)	1235
Mona Lisa—Carl Mann (59)	948
Bonanza—Al Caiola And His Orchestra (61)	895
Tammy—The Ames Brothers (57)	793
Mona Lisa—Conway Twitty (59)	581
Que Sera, Sera (Whatever Will Be, Will Be)—The High Keys (63)	355
Wish Me A Rainbow—Gunter Kallmann Chorus (66)	327
All The Time—Johnny Mathis (58)	327
Que Sera, Sera (Whatever Will Be, Will Be)—Mary Hopkin (70)	259
To Each His Own—Frankie Laine (68)	170
Almost In Your Arms—Johnny Nash (58)	153
Let Me Be Loved—Mantovani And His Orchestra (57)	109
To Each His Own—The Tymes (64)	100
Another Time, Another Place—Patti Page (58)	82
You're So Right For Me—Tony Bennett with Ralph Sharon and his Orch. (58)	70
Silver Bells—Bing Crosby and Carol Richards (54)	39
Love Song From "Houseboat" (Almost In Your Arms)—Sam Cooke (58)	36
Never Let Me Go—Nat "King" Cole (56)	20
Silver Bells—Bing Crosby and Carol Richards (57)	14
Bonanza!—Johnny Cash (62)	3.2
Buttons And Bows—Don Robertson (61)	0.5
Love Song From "Houseboat" (Almost In Your Arms)—Les Baxter & His Orchestra (58)	0.0
Love Song From "Houseboat" (Almost In Your Arms)—Don Costa & His Orchestra (58)	0.0
Main Title/Tammy—Joseph Gershenson & The Universal-International Orchestra (57)	0.0
Whatever Will Be Will Be (Que Será Será)—Eddy Howard (56)	0.0
Tammy—Richard Hayman, His Orchestra And Chorus (57)	0.0
Tammy—Bill Snyder & His Orchestra (57)	0.0
Let Me Be Loved—Eydie Gorme (57)	0.0
Tammy—Pat Kirby (57)	0.0
Daryl HALL ► 96 (12)	**22360**
Ray DAVIES ► 97 (28)	**22236**
Rick SPRINGFIELD ► 98 (18)	**22219**
Thom BELL/Linda CREED ► 99 (17)	**22156**
You Make Me Feel Brand New—The Stylistics Featurng Airrion Love & Russell Thompkins, Jr. (74)	5023
The Rubberband Man—The Spinners (76)	4975
Betcha By Golly, Wow—The Stylistics Featurng Airrion Love & Russell Thompkins, Jr. (72)	3608
You Are Everything—The Stylistics (71)	2438
Rockin' Roll Baby—The Stylistics (73)	1272
People Make The World Go Round—The Stylistics (72)	969
I'm Coming Home—The Spinners (74)	864
Stop, Look, Listen (To Your Heart)—The Stylistics (71)	803
One Man Band (Plays All Alone)—Ronnie Dyson (73)	768
Ghetto Child—The Spinners (73)	517
Living A Little, Laughing A Little—The Spinners (75)	291
Life Is A Song Worth Singing—Johnny Mathis (73)	226
I'm Coming Home—Johnny Mathis (73)	198
Help Me Find A Way (To Say I Love You)—Little Anthony And The Imperials (70)	106
Quick, Fast, In A Hurry—New York City (74)	75
You Make Me Feel Brand New—Band Of Gold (84)	12
Betcha By Golly Wow—Band Of Gold (84)	12
Lee HAZLEWOOD ► 100 (26)	**21631**
Richard MARX ► 101 (8)	**21097**
Jeff BARRY/Andy KIM ► 102 (16)	**21092**
Sugar, Sugar—The Archies (69)	12247
Jingle Jangle—The Archies (69)	2684
How'd We Ever Get This Way—Andy Kim (68)	1172
Sugar Sugar—Wilson Pickett (70)	1116
So Good Together—Andy Kim (69)	785
Shoot 'em Up, Baby—Andy Kim (68)	590
Feelin' So Good (S.k.o.o.b.y.-D.o.o.)—The Archies (68)	552
Who's Your Baby?—The Archies (70)	546
Sugar Sugar—Stars On 45 (81)	442
Rainbow Ride—Andy Kim (68)	351
I Wish I Were—Andy Kim (71)	219
A Friend In The City—Andy Kim (70)	140
It's Your Life—Andy Kim (70)	116
You Got Style—Jon & Robin (68)	92
I Been Moved—Andy Kim (71)	32
Oh My My—The Monkees (70)	7.4
Thomas F. KELLY/Billy STEINBERG ► 103 (8)	**20928**
Like A Virgin—Madonna (84)	6377
Alone—Heart (87)	4753
So Emotional—Whitney Houston (87)	3671
True Colors—Cyndi Lauper (86)	3546
I Drove All Night—Cyndi Lauper (89)	1573
Sex As A Weapon—Pat Benatar (85)	583
I Want You So Bad—Heart (88)	224
Jackie—Blue Zone U.K. (88)	200
Alex NORTH/Hy ZARET ► 104 (11)	**20850**
Unchained Melody—Les Baxter His Chorus And Orchestra (55)	8661
Unchained Melody—Al Hibbler (55)	4376
Unchained Melody—The Righteous Brothers (65)	3432
Unchained Melody—Roy Hamilton (55)	2241
Unchained Melody—The Righteous Brothers (90)	1154
Unchained Melody (1990)—The Righteous Brothers (90)	502
Unchained Melody—Vito & The Salutations (63)	312
Unchained Melody—The Sweet Inspirations (68)	70
Unchained Melody—The Blackwells (60)	47
Unchained Melody—June Valli (55)	44
Unchained Melody (Live)—Heart (81)	10
Jim PETERIK/Frankie SULLIVAN ► 105 (15)	**20839**
Eye Of The Tiger—Survivor (82)	9112
Burning Heart—Survivor (85)	3695
The Search Is Over—Survivor (85)	1879
Is This Love—Survivor (86)	1596
I Can't Hold Back—Survivor (84)	1376
High On You—Survivor (85)	1072
American Heartbeat—Survivor (82)	655
Poor Man's Son—Survivor (81)	418
How Much Love—Survivor (87)	239
First Night—Survivor (85)	210
Didn't Know It Was Love—Survivor (88)	197
Summer Nights—Survivor (82)	124
Ever Since The World Began—Tommy Shaw (88)	102
Across The Miles—Survivor (89)	93
Caught In The Game—Survivor (83)	71
Freddie MERCURY ► 106 (11)	**20821**
Garry BONNER/Alan GORDON ► 107 (20)	**20646**
Happy Together—The Turtles (67)	9222
She'd Rather Be With Me—The Turtles (67)	4329
You Know What I Mean—The Turtles (67)	1570
Celebrate—Three Dog Night (70)	1496
She's My Girl—The Turtles (67)	1458
The Cat In The Window (The Bird In The Sky)—Petula Clark (67)	667
Jill—Gary Lewis And The Playboys (67)	512
Girls In Love—Gary Lewis And The Playboys (67)	472
Melancholy Music Man—The Righteous Brothers (67)	338
As Long As You're Here—Zalman Yanovsky (67)	137
Happy Together (A Fantasy)—Captain & Tennille (80)	131
Happy Together—Dawn Featuring Tony Orlando (72)	124
Happy Together—The Nylons (87)	56
Me About You—The Lovin' Spoonful (69)	53
Me About You—The Mojo Men (67)	43
The Dance At St. Francis—The Barracuda (68)	26
Me About You—The Turtles (70)	3.8
When The Good Sun Shines—Elmo & Almo (67)	1.9
Kitty Doyle—Dino, Desi & Billy (67)	1.9
Two In The Afternoon—Dino, Desi & Billy (67)	1.4
Barry WHITE ► 108 (16)	**20372**
Gary GELD/Peter UDELL ► 109 (19)	**20336**
Hurting Each Other—Carpenters (72)	4895
Sealed With A Kiss—Brian Hyland (62)	4300
Save Your Heart For Me—Gary Lewis And The Playboys (65)	4051
Sealed With A Kiss—Gary Lewis And The Playboys (68)	1606
Sealed With A Kiss—Bobby Vinton (72)	1454
Ginny Come Lately—Brian Hyland (62)	851
Let Me Belong To You—Brian Hyland (61)	766
Warmed Over Kisses (Left Over Love)—Brian Hyland (62)	608
The Tear Of The Year—Jackie Wilson (61)	410
He Says The Same Things To Me—Skeeter Davis (64)	408
I'm Afraid To Go Home—Brian Hyland (63)	295
The Way I Am—Jackie Wilson (61)	192
I May Not Live To See Tomorrow—Brian Hyland (62)	173
I Told You So—Jimmy Jones (61)	163
If Mary's There—Brian Hyland (63)	123
I Got Love—Melba Moore (70)	18
I'll Never Stop Wanting You—Brian Hyland (61)	8.8
The Night I Cried—Brian Hyland (61)	6.9
Sealed With A Kiss—The Toys (68)	6.3
John PHILLIPS ► 110 (14)	**20307**
Tommy BOYCE/Bobby HART ► 111 (10)	**20195**
Last Train To Clarksville—The Monkees (66)	8046
Valleri—The Monkees (68)	5053
I Wonder What She's Doing Tonite—Tommy Boyce & Bobby Hart (67)	2377
Words—The Monkees (67)	1659
Alice Long (You're Still My Favorite Girlfriend)—Tommy Boyce & Bobby Hart (68)	1025
(I'm Not Your) Steppin' Stone—The Monkees (66)	668
Out And About—Tommy Boyce & Bobby Hart (67)	489
Tear Drop City—The Monkees (69)	461
Goodbye Baby (I Don't Want To See You Cry)—Tommy Boyce & Bobby Hart (68)	373
Sometimes She's A Little Girl—Tommy Boyce & Bobby Hart (67)	44
Tony BANKS/Phil COLLINS/ Mike RUTHERFORD ► 112 (15)	**20101**
Invisible Touch—Genesis (86)	3735
In Too Deep—Genesis (87)	2454
Tonight, Tonight, Tonight—Genesis (87)	2246
Throwing It All Away—Genesis (86)	2205
Land Of Confusion—Genesis (86)	2182
No Son Of Mine—Genesis (91)	1981
That's All—Genesis (83)	1827
Follow You Follow Me—Genesis (78)	761
No Reply At All—Genesis (81)	731
Paperlate—Genesis (82)	533
Abacab—Genesis (81)	451
Taking It All Too Hard—Genesis (84)	331
Illegal Alien—Genesis (84)	277
Turn It On Again—Genesis (80)	248
Mama—Genesis (83)	137
Joe TEX ► 113 (31)	**19745**
Chip TAYLOR ► 114 (14)	**19647**
Steve MILLER ► 115 (10)	**19553**
Gilbert O'SULLIVAN ► 116 (9)	**19552**
Sara ALLEN/Daryl HALL/John OATES ► 117 (6)	**19552**
Maneater—Daryl Hall & John Oates (82)	7727
I Can't Go For That (No Can Do)—Daryl Hall & John Oates (81)	7283
You Make My Dreams—Daryl Hall & John Oates (81)	2226
Adult Education—Daryl Hall & John Oates (84)	1464
Possession Obsession—Daryl Hall & John Oates (85)	431
Missed Opportunity—Daryl Hall & John Oates (88)	421
Barry GIBB ► 118 (6)	**19543**
Ray STEVENS ► 119 (22)	**19391**
Ric OCASEK ► 120 (22)	**19289**
Harlan HOWARD ► 121 (27)	**19204**
O'Kelly ISLEY/Ronald ISLEY/ Rudolph ISLEY ► 122 (21)	**19194**
It's Your Thing—The Isley Brothers (69)	6205
That Lady (Part 1)—The Isley Brothers (73)	3068
Nobody But Me—The Human Beinz (67)	3029
Shout - Part 1—Joey Dee & The Starliters (62)	2111
Respectable—The Outsiders (66)	1172
I Turned You On—The Isley Brothers (69)	1108
Shout Part One—The Isley Brothers (59)	544
Lay-Away—The Isley Brothers (72)	409
Work To Do—The Isley Brothers (72)	364

O'Kelly ISLEY/Ronald ISLEY/ Rudolph ISLEY ▶ 122 (21) *Continued*	**19194**
Twistin' With Linda—The Isley Brothers (62)	320
Keep On Doin'—The Isley Brothers (70)	232
Freedom—The Isley Brothers (71)	215
Was It Good To You—The Isley Brothers (69)	169
Girls Will Be Girls, Boys Will Be Boys— The Isley Brothers (70)	116
Shout—Lulu And The Luvers (64)	42
Respectable—The Chants (61)	24
Shout! - Part 1—The Chambers Brothers (68)	21
Get Into Something—The Isley Brothers (70)	18
Respectable—The Isley Brothers (60)	14
Shout - Part 1—The Isley Brothers (62)	8.8
Shout—Lulu (67)	6.1
Don GIBSON ▶ 123 (24)	**19106**
Maurice STARR ▶ 124 (10)	**19082**
Roy C. BENNETT/Sid TEPPER ▶ 125 (33)	**19069**
Naughty Lady Of Shady Lane— The Ames Brothers (54)	4011
Red Roses For A Blue Lady— Bert Kaempfert And His Orchestra (65)	2472
When The Boy In Your Arms (Is The Boy In Your Heart)—Connie Francis (61)	2133
Red Roses For A Blue Lady—Vic Dana (65)	1799
Kewpie Doll—Perry Como (58)	1744
Puppet On A String— Elvis Presley With The Jordanaires (65)	1211
If I Had A Girl—Rod Lauren (59)	752
Red Roses For A Blue Lady—Wayne Newton (65)	706
Nuttin' For Christmas—Art Mooney And His Orchestra, Vocal By Barry Gordon (55)	641
All That I Am— Elvis Presley With The Jordanaires (66)	425
Summer Sounds—Robert Goulet (65)	403
On London Bridge—Jo Stafford (56)	310
Naughty Lady Of Shady Lane—Archie Bleyer (54)	293
Nuttin' For Christmas—Joe Ward (55)	261
Cap And Gown—Marty Robbins (59)	235
Comin' Down With Love—Mel Gadson (60)	206
New Orleans— Elvis Presley with the Jordanaires (58)	192
Stay Away—Elvis Presley With The Jordanaires (68)	182
Stairway Of Love—Marty Robbins (58)	162
Nuttin' For Christmas— Ricky Zahnd And The Blue Jeaners (55)	157
Don't Come Running Back To Me—Nancy Wilson (65)	137
Forty Nine Shades Of Green—The Ames Brothers (56)	111
Nuttin' For Christmas—The Fontane Sisters (55)	102
You're Next—Jimmy Witherspoon (65)	98
Rock Around Mother Goose—Barry Gordon (56)	89
(It Took) One Kiss—Jaye P. Morgan (59)	75
Nuttin' For Christmas—Stan Freberg (55)	65
Stop! And Think It Over—Perry Como (67)	48
In Love—The Ames Brothers (58)	45
Stay—The Ames Brothers (58)	4.0
The Wonderful World Of The Young— Andy Williams (62)	0.9
Nuttin' For Christmas—Kenny & Corky (59)	0.8
Nothin' For Christmas—Eartha Kitt (55)	0.0
David SEVILLE ▶ 126 (21)	**19066**
Richard ADLER/Jerry ROSS ▶ 127 (24)	**18821**
Hey There—Rosemary Clooney (54)	11126
Whatever Lola Wants (Lola Gets)— Sarah Vaughan (55)	2027
Hernando's Hideaway—Archie Bleyer (54)	1629
Heart—Eddie Fisher (55)	1418
Hey There—Sammy Davis Jr. (54)	680
Two Lost Souls—Perry Como & Jaye P. Morgan (55)	411
Rags To Riches—Sunny & The Sunliners (63)	343
Heart—Four Aces (55)	311
Rags To Riches—Elvis Presley (71)	223
Whatever Lola Wants (Lola Gets)—Dinah Shore (55)	181
Near To You—Patti Page (55)	149
True Love Goes On And On—Burl Ives (63)	121
Old Shoes—Frankie Laine (54)	118
Heart—Peggy Lee (60)	33
Rags To Riches—Lenny Welch (66)	29
Steam Heat—Pointer Sisters (74)	15
Rags To Riches—The Rays Featuring Hal Miller (58)	6.6
Hernando's Hideaway— Guy Lombardo & His Royal Canadians (54)	0.0
Whatever Lola Wants (Lola Gets)—Ginny Gibson (55)	0.0
Whatever Lola Wants—Carmen McRae (55)	0.0
Hernando's Hideaway—Johnnie Ray (54)	0.0
Near To You—Eddie Fisher (55)	0.0
Steam Heat—Patti Page (54)	0.0
Heart—Norman Brooks (55)	0.0
Bill WITHERS ▶ 128 (12)	**18782**
Bobby DARIN ▶ 129 (23)	**18779**
Wayne Carson THOMPSON ▶ 130 (15)	**18580**
Isaac HAYES/David PORTER ▶ 131 (31)	**18570**
Soul Man—Sam & Dave (67)	6911
I Thank You—Sam & Dave (68)	1993
B-A-B-Y—Carla Thomas (66)	1648
Soul Man—Blues Brothers (78)	1370
Hold On! I'm A Comin'—Sam & Dave (66)	1302
Your Good Thing (Is About To End)—Lou Rawls (69)	1274
When Something Is Wrong With My Baby— Sam & Dave (67)	545
Show Me How—The Emotions (71)	508
Soul Sister, Brown Sugar—Sam & Dave (68)	501
I Thank You—ZZ Top (80)	446
Wrap It Up—The Fabulous Thunderbirds (86)	313
You Got Me Hummin—Cold Blood (70)	299
You Got Me Hummin'—Sam & Dave (66)	235
The Sweeter He Is Part I—The Soul Children (69)	232
Soul Man—Ramsey Lewis (67)	207
Something Good (Is Going To Happen To You)— Carla Thomas (67)	156
Said I Wasn't Gonna Tell Nobody—Sam & Dave (66)	118
Hold On I'm Coming— Chuck Jackson & Maxine Brown (67)	90
Born Again—Sam & Dave (69)	70
You've Got Me Hummin'—Hassles (67)	64
Everybody Got To Believe In Somebody— Sam & Dave (68)	60
When Something Is Wrong With My Baby— Linda Ronstadt (featuring Aaron Neville) (90)	57
Your Good Thing (Is About To End)—Mable John (66)	57
You Don't Know Like I Know—Sam & Dave (66)	44
When Something Is Wrong With My Baby— Otis & Carla (69)	26
Wrap It Up—Archie Bell & The Drells (70)	25
Baby-Baby Don't Stop Now—Sam & Dave (70)	14
How Can You Mistreat The One You Love— Jean & The Darlings (67)	2.4
When Tomorrow Comes—Carla Thomas (67)	1.0
A Dime A Dozen—Carla Thomas (68)	0.9
Stealing Love—The Emotions (70)	0.4
Per GESSLE ▶ 132 (6)	**18476**
Roger MILLER ▶ 133 (21)	**18247**
Harold LOGAN/Lloyd PRICE ▶ 134 (15)	**17938**
Personality—Lloyd Price (59)	7779
I'm Gonna Get Married—Lloyd Price (59)	4720
Lady Luck—Lloyd Price And His Orchestra (60)	1501
Come Into My Heart—Lloyd Price (59)	1300
Question—Lloyd Price And His Orchestra (60)	887
Wont'Cha Come Home—Lloyd Price (59)	615
No If's No And's— Lloyd Price And His Orchestra (60)	337
For Love—Lloyd Price And His Orchestra (60)	335
(You Better) Know What You're Doin'— Lloyd Price And His Orchestra (60)	180
Just Call Me (And I'll Understand)— Lloyd Price And His Orchestra (60)	137
(You've Got) Personality—Mitch Ryder (68)	83
Three Little Pigs—Lloyd Price (59)	31
Billie Baby—Lloyd Price (64)	26
Who Coulda' Told You (They Lied)—Lloyd Price (60)	6.1
Mary And Man-O— Lloyd Price And His Great Orchestra (61)	1.5
Sammy FAIN/Paul Francis WEBSTER ▶ 135 (23)	**17821**
Love Is A Many Splendored Thing—Four Aces (55)	8585
April Love—Pat Boone (57)	5035
A Certain Smile—Johnny Mathis (58)	1228
I'll Remember Tonight—Pat Boone (58)	749
Secret Love—Freddy Fender (75)	697
Secret Love—Billy Stewart (66)	556
Love Is A Many-Splendored Thing—Don Cornell (55)	365
A Very Precious Love—The Ames Brothers (58)	280
A Little Love Can Go A Long Long Way— The Dream Weavers Featuring Wade Buff (56)	184
If You Wanna See Mamie Tonight— The Ames Brothers (56)	97
Love Is A Many-Splendored Thing— The Four Preps (62)	24
Secret Love—Jimmy Ricks (59)	19
Love Is A Many Splendored Thing— Don, Dick N' Jimmy (55)	2.3
A Little Love Can Go A Long, Long Way— Johnny Desmond (56)	0.0
A Very Precious Love—The Johnston Brothers (58)	0.0
A Very Precious Love—Bonnie Guitar (58)	0.0
A Very Precious Love—Jack Jones (58)	0.0
A Very Precious Love—Doris Day (58)	0.0
A Certain Smile—Milton Sparks (58)	0.0
A Certain Smile—Jerry Fuller (58)	0.0
A Certain Smile—Andy Russell (58)	0.0
A Certain Smile—Sunny Gale (58)	0.0
Secret Love—Doris Day (54)	0.0
Tommy ROE ▶ 136 (11)	**17810**
Richard DEHR/Terry GILKYSON/ Frank MILLER ▶ 137 (9)	**17766**
Memories Are Made Of This—Dean Martin (55)	8655
Greenfields—The Brothers Four (60)	6907
Love Is A Golden Ring— Frankie Laine with The Easy Riders (57)	891
Memories Are Made Of This—Gale Storm (55)	785
Memories Are Made Of This—The Drifters (66)	271
Memories Are Made Of This—Mindy Carson (55)	217
Green Fields—The Vogues (69)	25
Memories Are Made Of This—Roger Williams (59)	14
Greenfields—Julius La Rosa (60)	0.0
Thomas ALLEN/Harold BROWN/ Morris DICKERSON/Lonnie JORDAN/ Charles MILLER/Lee OSKAR/Howard SCOTT ▶ 138 (10)	**17638**
Spill The Wine—Eric Burdon And War (70)	5207
The Cisco Kid—War (73)	4378
Slippin' Into Darkness—War (71)	2076
The World Is A Ghetto—War (72)	1817
Gypsy Man—War (73)	1659
Me And Baby Brother—War (73)	1513
Ballero—War (74)	472
Spill The Wine—The Isley Brothers (71)	409
Lonely Feelin'—War (71)	74
Slipping Into Darkness—Ramsey Lewis (72)	35
Bob MERRILL ▶ 139 (41)	**17616**
Baker KNIGHT ▶ 140 (20)	**17593**
Peter CALLANDER/Mitch MURRAY ▶ 141 (7)	**17398**
Billy, Don't Be A Hero— Bo Donaldson And The Heywoods (74)	4779
The Night Chicago Died—Paper Lace (74)	4648
Hitchin' A Ride—Vanity Fare (70)	3768
The Ballad Of Bonnie And Clyde—Georgie Fame (68)	3288
Even The Bad Times Are Good—The Tremeloes (67)	509
The Black-Eyed Boys—Paper Lace (74)	343
Billy--Don't Be A Hero—Paper Lace (74)	63
Melanie SAFKA ▶ 142 (13)	**17348**
Debbie GIBSON ▶ 143 (9)	**17301**
Steve BARRI/P.F. SLOAN ▶ 144 (20)	**17275**
Eve Of Destruction—Barry McGuire (65)	6384
Secret Agent Man—Johnny Rivers (66)	3877
A Must To Avoid—Herman's Hermits (65)	2112
You Baby—The Turtles (66)	1351
Things I Should Have Said—The Grass Roots (67)	624
Where Were You When I Needed You— The Grass Roots (66)	623
I Found A Girl—Jan & Dean (65)	524
Wake Up, Wake Up—The Grass Roots (67)	328
(Here They Come) From All Over The World— Jan & Dean (65)	275
Another Day, Another Heartache— The 5th Dimension (67)	263
Kick That Little Foot Sally Ann—Round Robin (64)	254
Secret Agent Man—The Ventures (66)	212
Take Me For What I'm Worth—The Searchers (66)	212
Summer Means Fun—Bruce And Terry (64)	77
Can I Get To Know You Better—The Turtles (66)	60
This Precious Time—Terry Knight And The Pack (67)	36
Only When You're Lonely—The Grass Roots (66)	31
Unless You Care—Terry Black (64)	30
Tell 'Em I'm Surfin—Fantastic Baggys (64)	0.9
Eve Of Destruction—The Turtles (70)	0.8

Jim STEINMAN ▶ 145 (12)	**17185**
Madonna L. CICCONE/ Patrick Raymond LEONARD ▶ 146 (6)	**17138**
Live To Tell—Madonna (86)	4537
Like A Prayer—Madonna (89)	4495
Who's That Girl—Madonna (87)	3738
Cherish—Madonna (89)	2774
Oh Father—Madonna (89)	816
Hanky Panky—Madonna (90)	778
Mark JAMES ▶ 147 (11)	**17119**
Jim CROCE ▶ 148 (10)	**16966**
Jon BON JOVI/Desmond CHILD/ Richie SAMBORA ▶ 149 (5)	**16774**
Livin' On A Prayer—Bon Jovi (86)	5011
You Give Love A Bad Name—Bon Jovi (86)	4318
Bad Medicine—Bon Jovi (88)	3448
Born To Be My Baby—Bon Jovi (88)	3071
We All Sleep Alone—Cher (88)	926
Shel SILVERSTEIN ▶ 150 (9)	**16712**
Al HOFFMAN/Dick MANNING ▶ 151 (21)	**16414**
Hot Diggity (Dog Ziggity Boom)—Perry Como (56)	5854
Allegheny Moon—Patti Page (56)	5270
O Dio Mio—Annette (60)	1390
Moon Talk—Perry Como (58)	697
Mama Teach Me To Dance—Eydie Gorme (56)	687
Ivy Rose—Perry Como (57)	559
Don't Stay Away Too Long—Eddie Fisher (55)	490
Belonging To Someone—Patti Page (58)	482
La Plume De Ma Tante—Hugo & Luigi (59)	398
You're Cheatin' Yourself (If You're Cheatin' On Me)— Frank Sinatra (57)	135
Mi Casa, Su Casa (My House Is Your House)— Perry Como (57)	115
I Was Hoping You'd Ask Me—Janice Harper (58)	111
Daydreams—Art Mooney And His Orchestra (56)	68
Gotta Lotta Love—Steve Alaimo (63)	57
I Can't Tell A Waltz From A Tango—Patti Page (54)	57
Thirteen Going On Fourteen—The Crew-Cuts (56)	23
Addio—The Ames Brothers (54)	15
Forget Her—Tony Bennett with Percy Faith and His Orchestra (56)	5.5
Gilly Gilly Ossenfeffer Katzenellen Bogen By The Sea—The Four Lads (54)	0.0
Mama, Teach Me To Dance— Bobby Madera & His Orchestra (56)	0.0
Allegheny Moon— Grady Martin & His Slew Foot Five (56)	0.0
Tony ROMEO ▶ 152 (10)	**16382**
Michael CRAIG/Roy HAY/ Jon MOSS/George O'DOWD ▶ 153 (7)	**16352**
Do You Really Want To Hurt Me—Culture Club (82)	5783
Time (Clock Of The Heart)—Culture Club (83)	4056
Miss Me Blind—Culture Club (84)	2167
I'll Tumble 4 Ya—Culture Club (83)	1624
Church Of The Poison Mind—Culture Club (83)	1501
The War Song—Culture Club (84)	766
Mistake No. 3—Culture Club (84)	455
Jim WEATHERLY ▶ 154 (13)	**16277**
David BOWIE ▶ 155 (20)	**16183**
Bryan ADAMS/Jim VALLANCE ▶ 156 (17)	**16097**
Heaven—Bryan Adams (85)	3748
Run To You—Bryan Adams (84)	2374
Summer Of '69—Bryan Adams (85)	1803
Heat Of The Night—Bryan Adams (87)	1717
Somebody—Bryan Adams (85)	1191
It's Only Love— Bryan Adams/Tina Turner (85)	1006
One Night Love Affair—Bryan Adams (85)	925
Cuts Like A Knife—Bryan Adams (83)	762
This Time—Bryan Adams (83)	569
Hearts On Fire—Bryan Adams (87)	514
Teacher, Teacher—38 Special (84)	493
Victim Of Love—Bryan Adams (87)	410
Don't Let Him Know—Prism (82)	259
Dangerous—Loverboy (85)	173
Edge Of A Dream—Joe Cocker (84)	113
Lonely Nights—Bryan Adams (82)	24
Let Me Down Easy—Roger Daltrey (85)	17
William DEES/Roy ORBISON ▶ 157 (11)	**16083**
Oh, Pretty Woman— Roy Orbison And The Candy Men (64)	8819
It's Over—Roy Orbison (64)	2050
(Oh) Pretty Woman—Van Halen (82)	1208
Ride Away—Roy Orbison (65)	995
Goodnight—Roy Orbison (65)	873
Breakin' Up Is Breakin' My Heart—Roy Orbison (66)	686
Twinkle Toes—Roy Orbison (66)	450
Crawling Back—Roy Orbison (65)	429
(Say) You're My Girl—Roy Orbison (65)	335
Communication Breakdown—Roy Orbison (66)	230
Walk On—Roy Orbison (68)	7.9
Adam CLAYTON/Dave EVANS/ Paul HEWSON/Larry MULLEN ▶ 158 (14)	**16059**
With Or Without You—U2 (87)	4346
I Still Haven't Found What I'm Looking For— U2 (87)	3862
Desire—U2 (88)	2667
Mysterious Ways—U2 (91)	2021
Angel Of Harlem—U2 (88)	876
Where The Streets Have No Name—U2 (87)	803
Pride (In The Name Of Love)—U2 (84)	535
In God's Country—U2 (87)	300
New Year's Day—U2 (83)	295
When Love Comes To Town—U2 With B. B. King (89)	105
The Fly—U2 (91)	78
All I Want Is You—U2 (89)	76
I Will Follow—U2 (84)	57
Where The Streets Have No Name— Pet Shop Boys (91)	37
Marc BLITZSTEIN/Berthold BRECHT/ Kurt WEILL ▶ 159 (3)	**16000**
Mack The Knife—Bobby Darin (59)	14687
Mack The Knife—Ella Fitzgerald (60)	743
A Theme From Threepenny Opera (Mack The Knife)— Louis Armstrong And His All-Stars (56)	570
Kenneth EDMONDS/Antonio REID/ Daryl SIMMONS ▶ 160 (12)	**15988**
On Our Own—Bobby Brown (89)	3434
The Lover In Me—Sheena Easton (88)	2763
The Way You Love Me—Karyn White (88)	1851
Secret Rendezvous—Karyn White (89)	1717
Don't Be Cruel—Bobby Brown (88)	1445
Superwoman—Karyn White (89)	1259
It's No Crime—Babyface (89)	1221
Dial My Heart—The Boys (88)	927
My Kinda Girl—Babyface (90)	508
Fairweather Friend—Johnny Gill (90)	468
Knocked Out—Paula Abdul (88)	378
Right Down To It—Damian Dame (91)	17
Dion DiMUCCI/Ernie MARESCA ▶ 161 (6)	**15980**
Runaround Sue—Dion (61)	10242
Lovers Who Wander—Dion (62)	2550
Donna The Prima Donna—Dion (Di Muci) (63)	2208
Runaround Sue—Leif Garrett (77)	949
Runaround Sue—The Four Preps (62)	24
Runaround Sue—Jive Bunny & The Mastermixers (90)	6.7
Charles FOX/Norman GIMBEL ▶ 162 (8)	**15941**
Killing Me Softly With His Song—Roberta Flack (73)	7658
I Got A Name—Jim Croce (73)	2549
Happy Days—Pratt & McClain (76)	2197
Ready To Take A Chance Again—Barry Manilow (78)	1827
Different Worlds—Maureen McGovern (79)	886
Making Our Dreams Come True—Cyndi Grecco (76)	709
Killing Me Softly—Al B. Sure! (88)	86
Deeply—Anson Williams (77)	30
Andy FARRISS/Michael HUTCHENCE ▶ 163 (11)	**15939**
Need You Tonight—INXS (87)	4241
Devil Inside—INXS (88)	2910
What You Need—INXS (86)	2667
New Sensation—INXS (88)	2229
Never Tear Us Apart—INXS (88)	1469
Suicide Blonde—INXS (90)	1317
The One Thing—INXS (83)	545
Bitter Tears—INXS (91)	337
Original Sin—INXS (84)	162
I Send A Message—INXS (84)	50
Kiss The Dirt (Falling Down The Mountain)—INXS (86)	11
Roger NICHOLS/ Paul WILLIAMS ▶ 164 (12)	**15886**
We've Only Just Begun—Carpenters (70)	7395
Rainy Days And Mondays—Carpenters (71)	5070
I Won't Last A Day Without You—Carpenters (74)	1455
Out In The Country—Three Dog Night (70)	1391
Talk It Over In The Morning—Anne Murray (71)	172
So Many People—Chase (71)	118
I Won't Last A Day Without You—Maureen McGovern (73)	68
I Won't Last A Day Without You—Al Wilson (75)	65
Let Me Be The One—Al Wilson (75)	65
Someday Man—The Monkees (69)	44
Traveling Boy—Garfunkel (74)	28
Only Me—The First Edition (68)	15
Dallas FRAZIER ▶ 165 (11)	**15777**
Annie LENNOX/ David A. STEWART ▶ 166 (15)	**15769**
Sweet Dreams (Are Made Of This)—Eurythmics (83)	6027
Here Comes The Rain Again—Eurythmics (84)	2759
Would I Lie To You?—Eurythmics (85)	2003
Missionary Man—Eurythmics (86)	989
Who's That Girl?—Eurythmics (84)	681
Sisters Are Doin' It For Themselves— Eurythmics And Aretha Franklin (85)	674
Love Is A Stranger—Eurythmics (83)	634
There Must Be An Angel (Playing With My Heart)— Eurythmics (85)	546
Right By Your Side—Eurythmics (84)	489
Don't Ask Me Why—Eurythmics (89)	350
I Need A Man—Eurythmics (87)	231
Thorn In My Side—Eurythmics (86)	152
You Have Placed A Chill In My Heart— Eurythmics (88)	149
It's Alright (Baby's Coming Back)—Eurythmics (86)	62
Sexcrime (Nineteen Eighty-Four)—Eurythmics (84)	23
Kevin CRONIN ▶ 167 (12)	**15707**
Barry MANN/Phil SPECTOR/Cynthia WEIL ▶ 168 (8)	**15621**
You've Lost That Lovin' Feelin'— The Righteous Brothers (64)	9450
You've Lost That Lovin' Feeling— Daryl Hall & John Oates (80)	1839
Walkin' In The Rain—Jay And The Americans (69)	1583
You've Lost That Lovin' Feeling— Dionne Warwick (69)	1346
Walking In The Rain—The Ronettes (64)	887
Born To Be Together— The Ronettes Featuring Veronica (65)	252
You've Lost That Lovin' Feelin'— Roberta Flack & Donny Hathaway (71)	248
You've Lost That Lovin' Feelin'— Long John Baldry & Kathi MacDonald (79)	16
Kenneth EDMONDS/Antonio REID ▶ 169 (10)	**15604**
I'm Your Baby Tonight—Whitney Houston (90)	3804
Every Little Step—Bobby Brown (89)	2865
Giving You The Benefit—Pebbles (90)	2301
Girlfriend—Pebbles (88)	1891
Can't Stop—After 7 (90)	1836
Miracle—Whitney Houston (91)	1127
Love Makes Things Happen—Pebbles (90)	846
Heat Of The Moment—After 7 (90)	780
Nothin (that compares 2 U)—Jacksons (89)	78
Heat Of The Moment—After 7 (89)	76
Peter CETERA/David FOSTER ▶ 170 (5)	**15531**
Hard To Say I'm Sorry—Chicago (82)	6596
Glory Of Love (Theme From The Karate Kid Part II)— Peter Cetera (86)	4132
You're The Inspiration—Chicago (84)	3035
Stay The Night—Chicago (84)	981
Love Me Tomorrow—Chicago (82)	788
Christopher CROSS ▶ 171 (7)	**15488**
Dan FOGELBERG ▶ 172 (14)	**15422**
Gordon LIGHTFOOT ▶ 173 (16)	**15368**
Ric CARTEY/Carole JOYNER ▶ 174 (7)	**15361**
Young Love—Tab Hunter (57)	8452
Young Love—Sonny James (56)	5688
Young Love—Donny Osmond (73)	531
Young Love—The Crew-Cuts (56)	343
Young Love—Lesley Gore (66)	334
Young Love—Ray Stevens (76)	13
Young Love—Ric Cartey with The Jiva-Tones (56)	0.0
Melvin ENDSLEY ▶ 175 (6)	**15190**
John STEWART ▶ 176 (10)	**15180**
Don McLEAN ▶ 177 (10)	**15165**

Curtis BEDEAU/Gerard CHARLES/ Hugh CLARKE/Brian GEORGE/ Lucien GEORGE/Paul GEORGE ▶ 178 (11)	**15161**
Head To Toe–Lisa Lisa And Cult Jam (87)	4435
Lost In Emotion–Lisa Lisa And Cult Jam (87)	3486
Naughty Girls (Need Love Too)–Samantha Fox (88)	2531
All Cried Out– Lisa Lisa And Cult Jam With Full Force Featuring Paul Anthony And Bow Legged Lou (86)	1667
I Wanna Have Some Fun–Samantha Fox (88)	1135
I Wonder If I Take You Home– Lisa Lisa and Cult Jam with Full Force (85)	656
Thanks For My Child–Cheryl "Pepsii" Riley (88)	509
Little Jackie Wants To Be A Star– Lisa Lisa And Cult Jam (89)	441
Can You Feel The Beat–Lisa Lisa And Cult Jam (85)	231
Why Can't You Come Home–Ex-Girlfriend (91)	48
Go For Yours–Lisa Lisa & Cult Jam with Full Force (88)	22
Bobby DALL/C.C. DeVILLE/ Bret MICHAELS/Rikki ROCKETT ▶ 179 (10)	**15088**
Every Rose Has Its Thorn–Poison (88)	4813
Unskinny Bop–Poison (90)	2869
Something To Believe In–Poison (90)	2063
Nothin' But A Good Time–Poison (88)	1314
Talk Dirty To Me–Poison (87)	1055
I Won't Forget You–Poison (87)	1051
Fallen Angel–Poison (88)	903
Life Goes On–Poison (91)	401
Ride The Wind–Poison (91)	377
I Want Action–Poison (87)	240
Peter DeANGELIS/Bob MARCUCCI ▶ 180 (20)	**14981**
Why–Frankie Avalon (59)	7611
Dede Dinah–Frankie Avalon (57)	1252
I'll Wait For You–Frankie Avalon (58)	1197
With All My Heart–Jodie Sands (57)	1183
Why–Donny Osmond (72)	1103
Where Are You–Frankie Avalon (60)	784
You Are Mine–Frankie Avalon (62)	616
You Excite Me–Frankie Avalon (58)	296
I Love My Girl–The Hilltoppers (57)	217
What Happens Now–Mona Carol (56)	202
I Love My Girl–Cozy Morley (57)	185
The Puppet Song–Frankie Avalon (60)	167
Swingin' On A Rainbow–Frankie Avalon (59)	84
Will I Always Be Your Sweetheart–Mona Carol (56)	41
With All My Heart–Judy Scott (57)	23
Calypso Parakeet–Patty Brandon (57)	12
I'm Happy–The Four Dates (58)	4.9
With All My Heart–Al Martino (65)	2.8
Will I Always Be Your Sweetheart–Kitty Kallen (56)	0.0
With All My Heart–Buddy Greco (57)	0.0
Maurice WILLIAMS ▶ 181 (8)	**14970**
Eric CARMEN ▶ 182 (16)	**14873**
Robert LAMM ▶ 183 (11)	**14838**
Hoyt AXTON ▶ 184 (5)	**14490**
Terry BRITTEN/Graham LYLE ▶ 185 (6)	**14449**
What's Love Got To Do With It–Tina Turner (84)	6553
We Don't Need Another Hero (Thunderdome)– Tina Turner (85)	3300
Typical Male–Tina Turner (86)	3200
What You Get Is What You See–Tina Turner (87)	776
Two People–Tina Turner (86)	493
Soul Inspiration–Anita Baker (90)	129
Rod ARGENT ▶ 186 (8)	**14147**
Walter BECKER/Donald FAGEN ▶ 187 (17)	**14130**
Rikki Don't Lose That Number–Steely Dan (74)	2950
Do It Again–Steely Dan (72)	2218
Reeling In The Years–Steely Dan (73)	2111
Hey Nineteen–Steely Dan (80)	1601
Peg–Steely Dan (77)	1459
Deacon Blues–Steely Dan (78)	825
Josie–Steely Dan (78)	619
FM (No Static At All)–Steely Dan (78)	561
Time Out Of Mind–Steely Dan (81)	531
Black Friday–Steely Dan (75)	400
Show Biz Kids–Steely Dan (73)	342
My Old School–Steely Dan (73)	211
Pretzel Logic–Steely Dan (74)	153
Don't Let Me In–Sneaker (82)	80
Do It Again–Club House (83)	40
Kid Charlemagne–Steely Dan (76)	16
Bad Sneakers–Steely Dan (75)	13
Luigi CREATORE/Solomon LINDA/ Hugo PERETTI/Albert STANTON/ George David WEISS ▶ 188 (2)	**14090**
The Lion Sleeps Tonight–The Tokens (61)	9030
The Lion Sleeps Tonight–Robert John (71)	5059
Spooner OLDHAM/Dan PENN ▶ 189 (12)	**14044**
Cry Like A Baby–The Box Tops (68)	6020
I'm Your Puppet–James & Bobby Purify (66)	2932
It Tears Me Up–Percy Sledge (66)	1461
Sweet Inspiration–The Sweet Inspirations (68)	1368
I Met Her In Church–The Box Tops (68)	462
Wish You Didn't Have To Go– James & Bobby Purify (67)	428
Out Of Left Field–Percy Sledge (67)	342
Sweet Inspiration–Barbra Streisand (72)	280
Take Me (Just As I Am)–Solomon Burke (67)	265
Cry Like A Baby–Kim Carnes (80)	249
Are You Never Coming Home–Sandy Posey (67)	214
Toys Are Made For Children–The Uniques (69)	22
Will JENNINGS/Steve WINWOOD ▶ 190 (10)	**14039**
Higher Love–Steve Winwood (86)	4547
The Finer Things–Steve Winwood (87)	1736
Don't You Know What The Night Can Do?– Steve Winwood (88)	1713
While You See A Chance–Steve Winwood (81)	1658
Valerie–Steve Winwood (87)	1522
Holding On–Steve Winwood (88)	1174
Back In The High Life Again–Steve Winwood (87)	1076
Still In The Game–Steve Winwood (82)	300
Talking Back To The Night–Steve Winwood (88)	228
Valerie–Steve Winwood (82)	86
J.P. RICHARDSON ▶ 191 (11)	**14005**
Stig ANDERSON/Benny ANDERSSON/ Björn ULVAEUS ▶ 192 (10)	**13921**
Dancing Queen–Abba (76)	4560
Waterloo–Abba (Björn, Benny, Anna & Frida) (74)	1880
SOS–Abba (75)	1587
Fernando–Abba (76)	1489
Knowing Me, Knowing You–Abba (77)	1220
I Do, I Do, I Do, I Do, I Do–Abba (76)	1023
The Name Of The Game–Abba (77)	988
Mamma Mia–Abba (76)	636
Honey, Honey–Abba (74)	432
Honey Honey–Sweet Dreams (74)	108
Tommy ROE/Freddy WELLER ▶ 193 (5)	**13866**
Dizzy–Tommy Roe (69)	8722
Jam Up Jelly Tight–Tommy Roe (69)	3274
Jack And Jill–Tommy Roe (69)	842
Pearl–Tommy Roe (70)	548
Stir It Up And Serve It–Tommy Roe (70)	480
Dick ADDRISI/Don ADDRISI ▶ 194 (15)	**13803**
Never My Love–The Association (67)	6833
Never My Love–The 5th Dimension (71)	1564
Never My Love–Blue Swede (74)	1499
We've Got To Get It On Again– The Addrisi Brothers (72)	1040
Slow Dancin' Don't Turn Me On– The Addrisi Brothers (77)	881
Time For Livin'–The Association (68)	639
I Believe You–Dorothy Moore (77)	596
Little Miss Sad–The Five Emprees (65)	187
Ghost Dancer–The Addrisi Brothers (79)	162
Cherrystone–The Addrisi Brothers (59)	110
I Believe You–Carpenters (78)	99
One Last Time–Glen Campbell (72)	98
Never My Love–The Addrisi Brothers (77)	82
I Can Feel You–The Addrisi Brothers (72)	7.9
Never My Love–The Sandpebbles (68)	3.2
John BETTIS/Richard CARPENTER ▶ 195 (7)	**13778**
Top Of The World–Carpenters (73)	5097
Yesterday Once More–Carpenters (73)	4231
Only Yesterday–Carpenters (75)	2333
Goodbye To Love–Carpenters (72)	1867
Those Good Old Dreams–Carpenters (81)	93
Yesterday Once More–The Spinners (81)	84
Top Of The World–Lynn Anderson (73)	74
John CARTER/Ken HAWKER ▶ 196 (6)	**13744**
Little Bit O' Soul–The Music Explosion (67)	6710
Can't You Hear My Heartbeat– Herman's Hermits (65)	5330
Is It True–Brenda Lee (64)	1118
Sunday For Tea–Peter And Gordon (67)	525
Little Bit O' Soul–Bullet (72)	50
Let's Go To San Francisco–Stars On 45 (81)	12
Cat STEVENS ▶ 197 (18)	**13729**
Audrey ALLISON/Joe ALLISON ▶ 198 (3)	**13689**
He'll Have To Go–Jim Reeves (59)	10202
Teen Age Crush–Tommy Sands (57)	3179
He'll Have To Go–Solomon Burke (64)	308
Mariah CAREY/Ben MARGULIES ▶ 199 (3)	**13623**
Love Takes Time–Mariah Carey (90)	4682
Vision Of Love–Mariah Carey (90)	4507
Someday–Mariah Carey (91)	4433
Joe SHERMAN/Noel SHERMAN ▶ 200 (13)	**13605**
Ramblin' Rose–Nat King Cole (62)	8021
Juke Box Baby–Perry Como (56)	1713
Graduation Day–The Rover Boys (56)	1085
Graduation Day–The Four Freshmen (56)	995
Eso Beso (That Kiss!)–Paul Anka (62)	769
To The Ends Of The Earth–Nat "King" Cole (56)	461
Everlovin'–Patti Page (55)	308
Graduation Day–The Arbors (67)	172
Por Favor–Vic Damone (55)	64
Graduation Day–Bobby Pickett (63)	10
Forbidden Fruit–Anita Ellis (57)	4.4
Make Like A Bunny, Honey–Jill Corey (57)	1.9
Graduation Day– The Lennon Sisters & The Sparklers (56)	0.0
John DEACON ▶ 201 (4)	**13584**
Errol BROWN/Tony WILSON ▶ 202 (5)	**13516**
Brother Louie–Stories (73)	5338
You Sexy Thing–Hot Chocolate (75)	4632
Emma–Hot Chocolate (75)	2191
You Could Have Been A Lady–April Wine (72)	695
Disco Queen–Hot Chocolate (75)	659
James Samuel HARRIS/ Janet JACKSON/Terry LEWIS ▶ 203 (5)	**13433**
Escapade–Janet Jackson (90)	4680
Rhythm Nation–Janet Jackson (89)	3288
Come Back To Me–Janet Jackson (90)	2853
Alright–Janet Jackson (90)	2323
State Of The World–Janet Jackson (91)	290
Lorenz HART/Richard RODGERS ▶ 204 (9)	**13403**
Blue Moon–The Marcels (61)	9049
Where Or When–Dion And The Belmonts (59)	3185
Glad To Be Unhappy–The Mamas & The Papas (67)	649
Blue Moon–Elvis Presley (56)	266
Blue Moon–Herb Lance & The Classics (61)	121
I Didn't Know What Time It Was–Ray Charles (69)	75
I Didn't Know What Time It Was– The Crampton Sisters (64)	44
Blue Moon– Jimmy Bowen With The Rhythm Orchids (58)	12
Where Or When–The Lettermen (63)	1.8
Phil CODY/Neil SEDAKA ▶ 205 (7)	**13380**
Laughter In The Rain–Neil Sedaka (74)	5057
Bad Blood–Neil Sedaka (75)	4731
Should've Never Let You Go– Neil Sedaka & Dara Sedaka (80)	1041
Solitaire–Carpenters (75)	812
Love In The Shadows–Neil Sedaka (76)	796
The Immigrant–Neil Sedaka (75)	559
Steppin' Out–Neil Sedaka (76)	384
Bob CREWE/Frank SLAY ▶ 206 (23)	**13364**
Silhouettes–The Rays (57)	4941
Silhouettes–Herman's Hermits (65)	3289
La Dee Dah–Billy & Lillie (57)	1426
Lucky Ladybug–Billy & Lillie (58)	900
Jump Over–Freddy Cannon (60)	624
Buzz Buzz A-Diddle-It–Freddy Cannon (61)	526
Pony Express–Danny & The Juniors (61)	344
Okefenokee–Freddy Cannon (59)	301
Bells, Bells, Bells (The Bell Song)– Billy & Lillie (59)	155
Humdinger–Freddy Cannon (60)	153
Happy Shades Of Blue–Freddie Cannon (60)	150
Silhouettes–The Diamonds (57)	130
Teen Queen Of The Week–Freddy Cannon (62)	112
Twistin' All Night Long–Danny & The Juniors With Guest Artist Freddy Cannon (62)	86
Urge–Freddy Cannon (60)	82
Silhouettes–Steve Gibson & the Red Caps (57)	47

Bob CREWE/Frank SLAY ▶ 206 (23) *Cont'd*	**13364**
Happiness—Billy & Lillie (58)	32
Daddy Cool—The Diamonds (57)	21
Daddy Cool—The Rays (57)	21
(Kwa-Na-Va-Ka) Cuernavaca Choo Choo—Freddy Cannon (60)	14
I'm Comin' Home—Sammy Davis Jr. (57)	4.7
Elevator Operator—The Rays (58)	3.1
Mediterranean Moon—The Rays (60)	3.0
Neil YOUNG ▶ 207 (22)	**13311**
Jerry HERMAN ▶ 208 (11)	**13299**
Rupert HOLMES ▶ 209 (9)	**13294**
Dave CLARK/Mike SMITH ▶ 210 (6)	**13266**
Bits And Pieces—The Dave Clark Five (64)	4088
Glad All Over—The Dave Clark Five (64)	3143
Can't You See That She's Mine—The Dave Clark Five (64)	2823
Try Too Hard—The Dave Clark Five (66)	1282
Come Home—The Dave Clark Five (65)	1101
Please Tell Me Why—The Dave Clark Five (66)	830
Jimmie CRANE/Al JACOBS ▶ 211 (12)	**13225**
I Need You Now—Eddie Fisher (54)	6888
Hurt—Timi Yuro (61)	3272
Every Day Of My Life—Bobby Vinton (72)	1257
Hurt—Elvis Presley (76)	517
Ev'ry Day Of My Life—The McGuire Sisters (56)	516
My Believing Heart—Joni James (55)	411
Hurt—Little Anthony And The Imperials (66)	222
Hurt—Roy Hamilton (54)	63
Hurt—The Manhattans (75)	58
I Need You Now—Ronnie Dove (69)	21
I Need You Now—100 Strings And Joni (60)	1.1
Ev'ry Day Of My Life—Vera Lynn (56)	0.0
Dub ALLBRITTEN/Ronnie SELF ▶ 212 (7)	**13223**
I'm Sorry—Brenda Lee (60)	9449
Everybody Loves Me But You—Brenda Lee (62)	2490
Anybody But Me—Brenda Lee (61)	806
Eventually—Brenda Lee (61)	281
Sweet Impossible You—Brenda Lee (63)	131
I'm Sorry—Joey Heatherton (72)	61
It Takes One To Know One—Brenda Lee (66)	4.7
Gloria ESTEFAN ▶ 213 (7)	**13172**
Jimmy DRIFTWOOD/TRADITIONAL ▶ 214 (5)	**13142**
Battle Of New Orleans—Johnny Horton (59)	13064
Battle Of New Orleans—Nitty Gritty Dirt Band (74)	51
Battle Of New Orleans—Vaughn Monroe with Norman Layden, His Orchestra and Chorus (59)	15
Battle Of New Orleans—Harpers Bizarre (68)	5.3
Battle Of New Orleans—Bert Sommer (70)	5.3
Jack SCOTT ▶ 215 (19)	**13101**
Terry KIRKMAN ▶ 216 (5)	**13075**
Stevie NICKS ▶ 217 (9)	**13067**
Michael Leslie JONES ▶ 218 (7)	**13056**
Graham GOULDMAN ▶ 219 (8)	**13044**
Van McCOY ▶ 220 (33)	**12959**
Rick ALLEN/Steve CLARK/Phil COLLEN/Joe ELLIOTT/Mutt LANGE/Rick SAVAGE ▶ 221 (6)	**12900**
Pour Some Sugar On Me—Def Leppard (88)	3871
Love Bites—Def Leppard (88)	3277
Armageddon It—Def Leppard (88)	2857
Hysteria—Def Leppard (88)	1083
Rocket—Def Leppard (89)	1017
Animal—Def Leppard (87)	796
Charles DAWES/Carl SIGMAN ▶ 222 (3)	**12893**
It's All In The Game—Tommy Edwards (58)	10634
It's All In The Game—Four Tops (70)	1294
It's All In The Game—Cliff Richard (63)	964
David PAICH ▶ 223 (9)	**12855**
Ivory Joe HUNTER ▶ 224 (19)	**12753**
Max STEINER ▶ 225 (14)	**12715**
Carole KING/Toni STERN ▶ 226 (9)	**12712**
It's Too Late—Carole King (71)	8487
Sweet Seasons—Carole King (72)	1709
It's Going To Take Some Time—Carpenters (72)	1120
Where You Lead—Barbra Streisand (71)	423
No Sad Song—Helen Reddy (71)	356
What Am I Gonna Do—Smith (70)	307
Where You Lead—Barbra Streisand (72)	280
It's Too Late—Bill Deal & The Rhondels (72)	29

As We Go Along—The Monkees (68)	0.0
Kent LaVOIE ▶ 227 (12)	**12684**
Rod STEWART ▶ 228 (4)	**12613**
Randy NEWMAN ▶ 229 (10)	**12554**
Joe BROOKS ▶ 230 (4)	**12550**
Graham RUSSELL ▶ 231 (4)	**12546**
Al BYRON/Paul EVANS ▶ 232 (3)	**12503**
Roses Are Red (My Love)—Bobby Vinton (62)	10687
Happy Go Lucky Me—Paul Evans (60)	1584
Long As The Rose Is Red—Florraine Darlin (62)	231
Jonathan CAIN/Steve PERRY ▶ 233 (7)	**12483**
Open Arms—Journey (82)	4821
Who's Crying Now—Journey (81)	3618
Separate Ways (Worlds Apart)—Journey (83)	1982
Suzanne—Journey (86)	673
After The Fall—Journey (83)	628
Send Her My Love—Journey (83)	590
Why Can't This Night Go On Forever—Journey (87)	171
Irving BERLIN ▶ 234 (54)	**12480**
Bruce FISHER/Billy PRESTON ▶ 235 (4)	**12478**
Will It Go Round In Circles—Billy Preston (73)	5175
Nothing From Nothing—Billy Preston (74)	5114
You Are So Beautiful—Joe Cocker (75)	2189
You Are So Beautiful—Billy Preston (74)	0.0
Graham GOBLE ▶ 236 (8)	**12470**
Kenneth GAMBLE/Cary GILBERT/Leon HUFF ▶ 237 (7)	**12468**
Me And Mrs. Jones—Billy Paul (72)	6926
Don't Leave Me This Way—Thelma Houston (76)	4138
Livin' For The Weekend—The O'Jays (76)	736
Me And Mrs. Jones—Ron Banks And The Dramatics (75)	371
Don't Leave Me This Way—Communards (86)	261
Let's Clean Up The Ghetto—Philadelphia International All Stars (77)	27
Don't Let The Music Slip Away—Archie Bell & The Drells (69)	8.6
Floyd CRAMER ▶ 238 (8)	**12462**
Alan O'DAY ▶ 239 (8)	**12418**
Lewis MARTINÉE ▶ 240 (7)	**12407**
Robbie VAN LEEUWEN ▶ 241 (6)	**12397**
Robert BATEMAN/Georgia DOBBINS/William GARRETT/Freddie GORMAN/Brian HOLLAND ▶ 242 (4)	**12383**
Please Mr. Postman—The Marvelettes (61)	7831
Please Mr. Postman—Carpenters (74)	4500
Please Mr. Postman—Gentle Persuasion (83)	45
Please Mr. Postman—The Beatles (64)	6.4
Tommy JAMES/Robert L. KING ▶ 243 (13)	**12371**
Draggin' The Line—Tommy James (71)	5158
Tighter, Tighter—Alive And Kicking (70)	3353
Nothing To Hide—Tommy James (71)	663
Gotta Get Back To You—Tommy James And The Shondells (70)	636
I'm Comin' Home—Tommy James (71)	603
Come To Me—Tommy James And The Shondells (70)	437
Love Song—Tommy James (72)	331
Ball And Chain—Tommy James (70)	327
Cat's Eye In The Window—Tommy James (72)	327
Boo, Boo, Don't 'Cha Be Blue—Tommy James (73)	288
Tell 'Em Willie Boy 's A'Comin'—Tommy James (72)	159
Celebration—Tommy James (72)	68
Adrienne—Tommy James (71)	21
Tom SCHOLZ ▶ 244 (8)	**12368**
Otis BLACKWELL/Winfield SCOTT ▶ 245 (3)	**12324**
Return To Sender—Elvis Presley With The Jordanaires (62)	9296
One Broken Heart For Sale—Elvis Presley With The Mello Men (63)	1777
(Such An) Easy Question—Elvis Presley With The Jordanaires (65)	1251
Jimmy DEAN ▶ 246 (4)	**12288**
Bob CREWE/Kenny NOLAN ▶ 247 (6)	**12269**
My Eyes Adored You—Frankie Valli (74)	5362
Lady Marmalade—Labelle (75)	5277
Get Dancin'—Disco Tex & The Sex-O-Lettes Featuring Sir Monti Rock III (74)	1522
Lady Marmalade—The Ritchie Family (76)	92
Hickory—Frankie Valli And The 4 Seasons (74)	12
So Good—The Eleventh Hour (74)	3.0

Henry COSBY/Sylvia MOY/Stevie WONDER ▶ 248 (12)	**12253**
Uptight (Everything's Alright)—Stevie Wonder (65)	4256
My Cherie Amour—Stevie Wonder (69)	3557
Shoo-Be-Doo-Be-Doo-Da-Day—Stevie Wonder (68)	1997
I'm Wondering—Stevie Wonder (67)	1268
Never Had A Dream Come True—Stevie Wonder (70)	728
Up Tight—Ramsey Lewis (66)	275
Uptight—Shalamar (77)	80
Uptight (Everything's Alright)—Nancy Wilson (66)	28
Uptight Everything's All Right—Stars On 45 (82)	27
My Cherie Amour—Stars On 45 (82)	27
My Cherie Amour—Soul Train Gang (77)	8.1
Uptight (Everything's Alright)—The Jazz Crusaders (66)	2.8
Carole KING ▶ 249 (12)	**12245**
Gerry GOFFIN/Michael MASSER ▶ 250 (8)	**12236**
Theme From Mahogany (Do You Know Where You're Going To)—Diana Ross (75)	4699
Saving All My Love For You—Whitney Houston (85)	3224
Tonight, I Celebrate My Love—Peabo Bryson/Roberta Flack (83)	1798
Nothing's Gonna Change My Love For You—Glenn Medeiros (87)	1315
Someone That I Used To Love—Natalie Cole (80)	768
So Sad The Song—Gladys Knight & The Pips (76)	300
Long And Lasting Love (Once In A Lifetime)—Glenn Medeiros (88)	113
One More Chance—Diana Ross (81)	18
Harry NILSSON ▶ 251 (12)	**12220**
David MALLOY/Eddie RABBITT/Even STEVENS ▶ 252 (7)	**12208**
I Love A Rainy Night—Eddie Rabbitt (80)	4947
Drivin' My Life Away—Eddie Rabbitt (80)	3070
Step By Step—Eddie Rabbitt (81)	2893
Someone Could Lose A Heart Tonight—Eddie Rabbitt (81)	961
You Can't Run From Love—Eddie Rabbitt (83)	181
Loveline—Dr. Hook (82)	132
Gone Too Far—Eddie Rabbitt (80)	23
Richard SHERMAN/Robert SHERMAN ▶ 253 (13)	**12195**
You're Sixteen—Ringo Starr (73)	4779
Let's Get Together—Hayley Mills And Hayley Mills (61)	2578
You're Sixteen—Johnny Burnette (60)	2286
Pineapple Princess—Annette With The Afterbeats (60)	1471
Midnight Oil—Charlie Blackwell (59)	292
Got The Feeling—Fabian (59)	230
Beach Time—Roger Smith (59)	126
Super-cali-fragil-istic-expi-ali-docious—Julie Andrews - Dick Van Dyke And The Pearlies (65)	114
Chitty Chitty Bang Bang—Paul Mauriat (68)	114
Chim, Chim, Cheree—The New Christy Minstrels (65)	73
Dream Boy—Annette With The Afterbeats (61)	67
It's A Small Small World—The Mike Curb Congregation (73)	43
My Heart Became Of Age—Annette With The Afterbeats (59)	22
Lou CHRISTIE/Twyla HERBERT ▶ 254 (10)	**12144**
Lightnin' Strikes—Lou Christie (65)	6323
Two Faces Have I—Lou Christie (63)	3221
The Gypsy Cried—Lou Christie (63)	1196
Rhapsody In The Rain—Lou Christie (66)	860
Outside The Gates Of Heaven—Lou Christie (66)	290
Are You Getting Any Sunshine?—Lou Christie (69)	154
Painter—Lou Christie (66)	93
Shake Hands And Walk Away Cryin'—Lou Christie(67)	5.4
Big Time—Lou Christie (66)	2.8
Glory River—Lou Christie (70)	0.0
Bobbie GENTRY ▶ 255 (8)	**12119**
Ritchie ADAMS/Malou RENÉ ▶ 256 (3)	**12115**
Tossin' And Turnin'—Bobby Lewis (61)	12039
What A Walk—Bobby Lewis (61)	73
Tossin' And Turnin'—Bunny Sigler (73)	2.2
Steve DUBOFF/Artie KORNFELD ▶ 257 (5)	**12095**
The Rain, The Park & Other Things—The Cowsills (67)	7643
The Pied Piper—Crispian St. Peters (66)	4251
Pied Piper—The Changin' Times (65)	131
Did You Ever—The Hullaballoos (65)	68
Another Page—Connie Francis (67)	2.3

Freddie PERREN/Keni ST. LEWIS ▶ 258 (4)	**12086**
Boogie Fever–The Sylvers (76)	6020
Hot Line–The Sylvers (76)	3594
Heaven Must Be Missing An Angel (Part 1)–Tavares (76)	1546
Whodunit–Tavares (77)	926
Norman WHITFIELD ▶ 259 (17)	**12058**
Don GEORGE/TRADITIONAL ▶ 260 (3)	**12048**
The Yellow Rose Of Texas–Mitch Miller with His Orch. & Chorus (55)	9072
The Yellow Rose Of Texas–Johnny Desmond (55)	2853
The Yellow Rose Of Texas–Stan Freberg (55)	123
Carly SIMON ▶ 261 (8)	**11985**
Bobby GOLDSBORO ▶ 262 (25)	**11971**
André POPP ▶ 263 (5)	**11966**
Van MORRISON ▶ 264 (23)	**11950**
Clement A. BOZEWSKI/Deborah HARRY/Christopher STEIN ▶ 265 (5)	**11947**
Heart Of Glass–Blondie (79)	5717
Rapture–Blondie (81)	5100
Dreaming–Blondie (79)	716
Island Of Lost Souls–Blondie (82)	344
The Hardest Part–Blondie (80)	69
Marvin GAYE ▶ 266 (7)	**11889**
Hank COCHRAN ▶ 267 (14)	**11878**
Billy DAVIS/Berry GORDY/Gwen GORDY ▶ 268 (11)	**11869**
Lonely Teardrops–Jackie Wilson (58)	3299
You Got What It Takes–Marv Johnson (59)	2631
You Got What It Takes–The Dave Clark Five (67)	1890
That's Why (I Love You So)–Jackie Wilson (59)	1212
All I Could Do Was Cry–Etta James (60)	949
I'll Be Satisfied–Jackie Wilson (59)	851
To Be Loved–Jackie Wilson (58)	522
Lonely Teardrops–Brian Hyland (71)	402
Lonely Teardrops–Narvel Felts (76)	77
We Have Love–Jackie Wilson (58)	23
All I Could Do Was Cry–Joe Tex (60)	14
Otto HARBACH/Jerome KERN ▶ 269 (4)	**11863**
Smoke Gets In Your Eyes–The Platters (58)	10667
Smoke Gets In Your Eyes–Blue Haze (72)	1048
Smoke Gets In Your Eyes–The Four Preps (61)	130
(When Your Heart's On Fire) Smoke Gets In Your Eyes–Richard Barrett (58)	18
Luigi CREATORE/Hugo PERETTI/George David WEISS ▶ 270 (26)	**11863**
Can't Help Falling In Love–Elvis Presley With The Jordanaires (61)	5450
Let's Put It All Together–The Stylistics (74)	1045
Hello Heartache, Goodbye Love–Little Peggy March (63)	666
Heavy Fallin' Out–The Stylistics (74)	552
Can't Help Falling In Love–Corey Hart (86)	544
I Wish I Were A Princess–Little Peggy March (63)	501
Wild In The Country–Elvis Presley With The Jordanaires (61)	471
Snoopy's Christmas–The Royal Guardsmen (67)	431
And Now–Della Reese (60)	398
Can't Help Falling In Love–Al Martino (70)	308
B'wa Nina (Pretty Girl)–The Tokens (62)	269
The Impossible Happened–Little Peggy March (63)	258
I'll Take You Home–Corsairs Featuring Jay "Bird" Uzzell (62)	240
Can't Give You Anything (But My Love)–The Stylistics (75)	227
Star On A TV Show–The Stylistics (75)	165
Thank You Baby–The Stylistics (75)	111
Funky Weekend–The Stylistics (75)	61
You Are Beautiful–The Stylistics (76)	58
A Far Far Better Thing–Della Reese (61)	53
Can't Help Falling In Love–Andy Williams (70)	26
Love Is The Answer–Van Mc Coy & The Soul City Symphony (74)	13
Let's Put It All Together–Band Of Gold (84)	12
Big Boat–The Tokens (62)	1.8
Can't Help Falling In Love With You–Jimmy Castor (80)	1.8
Can't Help Falling In Love–The Four Esquires (61)	0.0
Can't Help Falling In Love–Keely Smith (61)	0.0
Sandy LINZER/Denny RANDELL ▶ 271 (22)	**11793**
Working My Way Back To You–The Spinners (79)	2453
Keep The Ball Rolling–Jay And The Techniques (67)	1852
Working My Way Back To You–The 4 Seasons Featuring The "Sound" Of Frankie Valli (66)	1672
Opus 17 (Don't You Worry 'Bout Me)–The 4 Seasons Featuring The "Sound" Of Frankie Valli (66)	1584
Native New Yorker–Odyssey (77)	1155
Attack–The Toys (65)	1083
Goodnight My Love–The Happenings (66)	397
The Mouse–Soupy Sales (65)	379
Can't Get Enough Of You, Baby–? And The Mysterians (67)	355
Baby Make Your Own Sweet Music–Jay And The Techniques (68)	333
You Keep Me Dancing–Samantha Sang (78)	168
Penny Arcade–The Cyrkle (67)	149
Weekend Lover–Odyssey (78)	124
Goodnight My Love–The Duprees (68)	54
May My Heart Be Cast Into Stone–The Toys (66)	18
Betrayed–The 4 Seasons (65)	4.6
Working My Way Back To You–Gidea Park (81)	3.7
Opus 17–Gidea Park (81)	3.7
Hallelujah–The Invitations (65)	3.7
Can I Carry Your Balloon–The Swampseeds (68)	0.5
Breakin' Down The Walls Of Heartache–The Bandwagon (68)	0.5
Keep The Ball Rollin'–Al Hirt (68)	0.5
Stephen BRAY/Madonna L. CICCONE ▶ 272 (5)	**11788**
Express Yourself–Madonna (89)	3109
True Blue–Madonna (86)	2906
Causing A Commotion–Madonna (87)	2831
Angel–Madonna (85)	1848
Keep It Together–Madonna (90)	1095
Otis REDDING ▶ 273 (13)	**11787**
Dave APPELL/Bernie LOWE/Kal MANN ▶ 274 (9)	**11745**
Wild One–Bobby Rydell (60)	4945
Swingin' School–Bobby Rydell (60)	2224
Good Time Baby–Bobby Rydell (61)	1828
Ding A Ling–Bobby Rydell (60)	936
The Fish–Bobby Rydell (61)	799
I Wanna Thank You–Bobby Rydell (61)	781
Lose Her–Bobby Rydell (62)	140
Cherié–Bobby Rydell (61)	89
Gee, It's Wonderful–Bobby Rydell (62)	2.2
Justin HAYWARD ▶ 275 (14)	**11677**
Don HARRIS/Dewey TERRY ▶ 276 (8)	**11677**
I'm Leaving It Up To You–Dale & Grace (63)	7593
I'm Leaving It (All) Up To You–Donny And Marie Osmond (74)	2345
Farmer John–The Premiers (64)	827
Big Boy Pete–The Olympics (60)	760
Farmer John–Tidal Waves (66)	70
The Letter–Sonny & Cher (65)	43
Justine–The Righteous Brothers (65)	34
Surfer Street–The Allisons (63)	3.7
Lou HANDMAN/Roy TURK ▶ 277 (5)	**11652**
Are You Lonesome To-Night–Elvis Presley With The Jordanaires (60)	10024
Are You Lonesome Tonight–Donny Osmond (73)	1054
Are You Lonesome Tonight–Jaye P. Morgan (59)	310
Yes I'm Lonesome Tonight–Thelma Carpenter (60)	149
Yes I'm Lonesome Tonight–Dodie Stevens (60)	116
Sylvester LEVAY/Stephan PRAGER ▶ 278 (7)	**11618**
Fly, Robin, Fly–Silver Convention (75)	5615
Get Up And Boogie (That's Right)–Silver Convention (76)	5492
Lady Bump–Penny McLean (76)	216
No, No, Joe–Silver Convention (76)	96
Fly, Robin, Fly–The Ritchie Family (76)	92
Lady Bump–The Ritchie Family (76)	92
Save Me–Silver Convention (75)	14
Burt BACHARACH/Carole Bayer SAGER ▶ 279 (4)	**11616**
That's What Friends Are For–Dionne & Friends (85)	5417
On My Own–Patti LaBelle And Michael McDonald (86)	5145
Love Power–Dionne Warwick & Jeffrey Osborne (87)	1032
Easy To Love Again–Carole Bayer Sager (81)	22
William BECK/Leroy BONNER/Marshall JONES/Ralph MIDDLEBROOKS/Andrew NOLAND/Marvin PIERCE/James Rodger WILLIAMS ▶ 280 (8)	**11580**
Love Rollercoaster–Ohio Players (75)	5251
Fire–Ohio Players (74)	4114
Who'd She Coo?–Ohio Players (76)	885
Sweet Sticky Thing–Ohio Players (75)	411
Fopp–Ohio Players (76)	398
I Want To Be Free–Ohio Players (75)	335
O-H-I-O–Ohio Players (77)	144
Feel The Beat (Everybody Disco)–Ohio Players (77)	42
Eduardo Di CAPUA/Wally GOLD/Aaron SCHROEDER ▶ 281 (2)	**11562**
It's Now Or Never–Elvis Presley With The Jordanaires (60)	10781
It's Now Or Never–John Schneider (81)	781
Tom BLACKBURN/George BRUNS ▶ 282 (7)	**11488**
The Ballad Of Davy Crockett–Bill Hayes (55)	6567
Ballad Of Davy Crockett–Fess Parker (55)	2764
Ballad Of Davy Crockett–"Tennessee" Ernie Ford (55)	2107
The Ballad Of Davy Crockett–Walter Schumann (55)	45
Johnny Tremain–Billy Vaughn and His Orchestra (57)	6.0
The Ballad Of Davy Crockett–Rusty Draper (55)	0.0
The Ballad Of Davy Crockett–Steve Allen (55)	0.0
Hal BLAIR/Don ROBERTSON ▶ 283 (6)	**11464**
Ringo–Lorne Greene (64)	5527
Please Help Me I'm Falling–Hank Locklin (60)	3409
I'm Yours–Elvis Presley (65)	1788
(I Can't Help You) I'm Falling Too–Skeeter Davis (60)	543
Please Help Me I'm Falling–Rusty Draper (60)	195
I'm Glad That Your Falling–Betty Madigan (60)	2.0
Glenn FREY/Don HENLEY ▶ 284 (4)	**11440**
One Of These Nights–Eagles (75)	5146
Lyin' Eyes–Eagles (75)	3949
The Long Run–Eagles (79)	2002
Tequila Sunrise–Eagles (73)	344
James PANKOW ▶ 285 (8)	**11432**
Albert HAMMOND/Mike HAZLEWOOD ▶ 286 (13)	**11410**
It Never Rains In Southern California–Albert Hammond (72)	3547
The Air That I Breathe–The Hollies (74)	2405
Gimme Dat Ding–The Pipkins (70)	2051
Little Arrows–Leapy Lee (68)	1529
I'm A Train–Albert Hammond (74)	607
The Free Electric Band–Albert Hammond (73)	474
If You Gotta Break Another Heart–Albert Hammond (73)	218
One Night Stand–The Magic Lanterns (70)	165
Down By The River–Albert Hammond (72)	164
The Peacemaker–Albert Hammond (73)	70
Air Disaster–Albert Hammond (74)	69
Names, Tags, Numbers & Labels–The Association (73)	56
Half A Million Miles From Home–Albert Hammond (73)	54
Max CROOK/Del SHANNON ▶ 287 (6)	**11365**
Runaway–Del Shannon (61)	10390
Runaway–Charlie Kulis (75)	327
Runaway–Bonnie Raitt (77)	294
Runaway–Lawrence Welk And His Orchestra (62)	146
Runaway–Dawn Featuring Tony Orlando (72)	124
Runaway–Luis Cardenas (86)	83
Bob GAUDIO ▶ 288 (6)	**11359**
Eddie CORNELIUS ▶ 289 (5)	**11345**
Dewey BUNNELL ▶ 290 (5)	**11304**
Daryl HALL/John OATES ▶ 291 (9)	**11277**
Out Of Touch–Daryl Hall & John Oates (84)	4068
Sara Smile–Daryl Hall & John Oates (76)	3191
She's Gone–Daryl Hall & John Oates (76)	2526
Do What You Want, Be What You Are–Daryl Hall & John Oates (76)	504
I Don't Wanna Lose You–Daryl Hall & John Oates (78)	356
She's Gone–Daryl Hall & John Oates (74)	306
She's Gone–Tavares (74)	299
Good Night & Good Morning–Jim Capaldi (76)	22
Goodnight And Goodmorning–Cecilio & Kapono (76)	4.8

Russ BALLARD ▶ 292 (16)	**11266**
Henri BELOLO/Jacques MORALI/ Victor WILLIS ▶ 293 (3)	**11264**
Y.M.C.A.–Village People (78)	7239
In The Navy–Village People (79)	3766
Go West–Village People (79)	259
Steve KIPNER/Terry SHADDICK ▶ 294 (1)	**11192**
Physical–Olivia Newton-John (81)	11192
James TAYLOR ▶ 295 (15)	**11175**
Randy GOODRUM ▶ 296 (6)	**11157**
Steve CROPPER/Otis REDDING ▶ 297 (10)	**11137**
(Sittin' On) The Dock Of The Bay–Otis Redding (68)	7420
(Sittin' On) The Dock Of The Bay– Michael Bolton (88)	1137
The Happy Song (Dum-Dum)–Otis Redding (68)	722
Fa-Fa-Fa-Fa-Fa (Sad Song)–Otis Redding (66)	553
On The Dock Of The Bay–The Dells (69)	452
Mr. Pitiful–Otis Redding (65)	416
(Sittin' On) The Dock Of The Bay–The Reddings (82)	200
(Sittin' On) The Dock Of The Bay– Sergio Mendes & Brasil '66 (69)	101
(Sittin' On) The Dock Of The Bay–Sammy Hagar (79)	92
(Sittin' On) The Dock Of The Bay– King Curtis & The Kingpins (68)	45
Gene ALLAN/Bobby VINTON ▶ 298 (4)	**11128**
Mr. Lonely–Bobby Vinton (64)	8492
Coming Home Soldier–Bobby Vinton (66)	2331
Mr. Lonely–Buddy Greco (62)	274
Red Roses For Mom–Bobby Vinton (67)	31
Don BLACK/Mark LONDON ▶ 299 (2)	**11124**
To Sir With Love–Lulu (67)	10546
Best Of Both Worlds–Lulu (67)	579
Oliver LEIBER ▶ 300 (4)	**11097**
Peter FRAMPTON ▶ 301 (7)	**11081**
Leon CARR/Earl SHUMAN ▶ 302 (10)	**11047**
Hey There Lonely Girl–Eddie Holman (69)	5248
Hotel Happiness–Brook Benton (62)	2976
Most People Get Married–Patti Page (62)	683
Hey There Lonely Boy–Ruby And The Romantics (63)	635
Hey There Lonely Girl–Robert John (80)	523
Another Cup Of Coffee–Brook Benton (64)	317
Our Everlasting Love–Ruby And The Romantics (64)	270
My Shy Violet–The Mills Brothers (68)	207
The Young New Mexican Puppeteer–Tom Jones (72)	177
High On The Hill Of Hope–Patti Page (63)	9.9
Colin James HAY ▶ 303 (6)	**11008**
Leon RENÉ ▶ 304 (6)	**11003**
Leonard CASTON/Anita POREE/ Frank Edward WILSON ▶ 305 (3)	**10942**
Keep On Truckin' (Part 1)–Eddie Kendricks (73)	5698
Boogie Down–Eddie Kendricks (73)	4614
Son Of Sagittarius–Eddie Kendricks (74)	630
Tommy JAMES/Peter LUCIA ▶ 306 (3)	**10940**
Crimson And Clover– Tommy James And The Shondells (68)	9176
Crimson And Clover– Joan Jett & The Blackhearts (82)	1672
I'm Alive–Blue Swede (75)	92
George GOLDNER/Morris LEVY/ Frankie LYMON/Jimmy MERCHANT/ Herman SANTIAGO ▶ 307 (8)	**10922**
Why Do Fools Fall In Love– The Teenagers Featuring Frankie Lymon (56)	4057
Why Do Fools Fall In Love–Diana Ross (81)	2314
Why Do Fools Fall In Love–Gale Storm (56)	2295
Why Do Fools Fall In Love–The Diamonds (56)	1782
Why Do Fools Fall In Love–The Happenings (67)	389
Why Do Fools Fall In Love–Gloria Mann (56)	80
Why Do Fools Fall In Love–The Beach Boys (64)	5.6
Why Do Fools Fall In Love–Summer Wine (73)	0.4
Joni MITCHELL ▶ 308 (19)	**10915**
Evan ROGERS/Carl STURKEN ▶ 309 (9)	**10912**
P.A.S.S.I.O.N.–Rythm Syndicate (91)	3002
Soldier Of Love–Donny Osmond (89)	2888
Street Of Dreams–Nia Peeples (91)	1236
Sacred Emotion–Donny Osmond (89)	1059
Hey Donna–Rythm Syndicate (91)	905
The Girl I Used To Know–Brother Beyond (90)	613
My Love Is A Fire–Donny Osmond (90)	575
Facts Of Love–Jeff Lorber (86)	547
Blinded By Love–Rythm Syndicate (91)	87
Roger WATERS ▶ 310 (2)	**10871**
Clint BALLARD Jr. ▶ 311 (10)	**10826**
Larry KOLBER/Barry MANN ▶ 312 (6)	**10820**
Patches–Dickey Lee (62)	4183
I Love How You Love Me–Bobby Vinton (68)	3635
I Love How You Love Me–The Paris Sisters (61)	2552
Sweet Little You–Neil Sedaka (61)	354
Let Me Be The One–Peaches & Herb (69)	68
Let Me Be The One–The Paris Sisters (62)	26
Rick JAMES ▶ 313 (15)	**10808**
Calvin LEWIS/Andrew WRIGHT ▶ 314 (4)	**10801**
When A Man Loves A Woman–Percy Sledge (66)	6157
When A Man Loves A Woman–Michael Bolton (91)	4080
When A Man Loves A Woman–Bette Midler (80)	398
When A Woman Loves A Man–Esther Phillips (66)	166
Geoff STEPHENS ▶ 315 (3)	**10785**
Franco MIGLIACCI/Domenico MODUGNO ▶ 316 (3)	**10773**
Nel Blu Dipinto Di Blu (Volare)– Domenico Modugno (58)	10773
(Nel Blu Dipinto Di Blu) Volare– Umberto Marcato (58)	0.0
Nel Blu Dipinto Di Blu–Rosa Linda (58)	0.0
Deke RICHARDS/Pam SAWYER/ R. Dean TAYLOR/Frank Edward WILSON ▶ 317 (2)	**10755**
Love Child–Diana Ross And The Supremes (68)	9676
Love Child–Sweet Sensation (90)	1079
Rick DAVIES/Roger HODGSON ▶ 318 (9)	**10743**
The Logical Song–Supertramp (79)	2915
It's Raining Again–Supertramp (82)	1898
Take The Long Way Home–Supertramp (79)	1451
Give A Little Bit–Supertramp (77)	1217
Goodbye Stranger–Supertramp (79)	1209
Dreamer–Supertramp (80)	1034
My Kind Of Lady–Supertramp (83)	550
Bloody Well Right–Supertramp (75)	348
Breakfast In America–Supertramp (80)	120
Irene CARA/Keith FORSEY/Giorgio MORODER ▶ 319 (2)	**10725**
Flashdance...What A Feeling–Irene Cara (83)	9574
Why Me?–Irene Cara (83)	1151
Berry GORDY ▶ 320 (13)	**10688**
Bobby DAY ▶ 321 (10)	**10684**
Jerry ALLISON/Buddy HOLLY/Norman PETTY ▶ 322 (9)	**10674**
Peggy Sue–Buddy Holly / The Crickets (57)	4478
That'll Be The Day–Buddy Holly / The Crickets (57)	4320
That'll Be The Day–Linda Ronstadt (76)	1413
Think It Over–Buddy Holly / The Crickets (58)	325
Peggy Sue–The Beach Boys (78)	133
That'll Be The Day–The Everly Brothers (65)	5.0
That'll Be The Day– Buddy Holly & The Three Tunes (57)	0.0
That'll Be The Day–Jeff Allen (57)	0.0
Peggy Sue–Jackie Walker (57)	0.0
Keith McCORMACK/Faye VOSS ▶ 323 (1)	**10632**
Sugar Shack–Jimmy Gilmer And The Fireballs (63)	10632
Del SHANNON ▶ 324 (11)	**10627**
Buddy BUIE/J.R. COBB ▶ 325 (14)	**10549**
Stormy–Classics IV Featuring Dennis Yost (68)	4909
I Take It Back–Sandy Posey (67)	1475
Everyday With You Girl– Classics IV Featuring Dennis Yost (69)	1298
Most Of All–B.J. Thomas (70)	718
What Am I Crying For?– Dennis Yost And The Classics IV (72)	559
Stormy–Santana (78)	450
Change Of Heart– Dennis Yost And The Classics IV (69)	360
The Funniest Thing– Dennis Yost And The Classics IV (70)	282
Where Did All The Good Times Go– Dennis Yost And The Classics IV (70)	190
Soul Train–Classics IV (68)	176
Something I'll Remember–Sandy Posey (68)	57
Rosanna–Dennis Yost And The Classics IV (73)	30
I Ain't Much–Atlanta Rhythm Section (80)	29
Back Up Against The Wall– Atlanta Rhythm Section (79)	18
Lamont DOZIER/Ronald DUNBAR/ Brian HOLLAND/Eddie HOLLAND ▶ 326 (9)	**10536**
Band Of Gold–Freda Payne (70)	6004
Give Me Just A Little More Time– Chairmen Of The Board (70)	2390
Mind, Body And Soul–The Flaming Ember (69)	1044
(You've Got Me) Dangling On A String– Chairmen Of The Board (70)	558
While You're Out Looking For Sugar?– The Honey Cone (69)	183
Shades Of Green–The Flaming Ember (70)	173
Girls It Ain't Easy–The Honey Cone (69)	149
Take Me With You–The Honey Cone (70)	28
You've Got Me Dangling On A String– Donny Osmond (77)	8.4
Jack NANCE/Conway TWITTY ▶ 327 (5)	**10516**
It's Only Make Believe–Conway Twitty (58)	7964
It's Only Make Believe–Glen Campbell (70)	1910
Story Of My Love–Conway Twitty (59)	640
She's Mine–Conway Twitty (60)	1.2
When I'm Not With You–Conway Twitty (59)	1.2
Dean PITCHFORD/Tom SNOW ▶ 328 (3)	**10514**
Let's Hear It For The Boy–Deniece Williams (84)	5139
You Should Hear How She Talks About You– Melissa Manchester (82)	3680
After All (Love Theme From "Chances Are")– Cher and Peter Cetera (89)	1696
Randy BACHMAN/Burton CUMMINGS ▶ 329 (4)	**10485**
These Eyes–The Guess Who (69)	3940
No Time–The Guess Who (69)	3320
Laughing–The Guess Who (69)	2066
These Eyes–Jr. Walker & The All Stars (69)	1159
Gerry RAFFERTY ▶ 330 (6)	**10483**
Ed MARSHALL ▶ 331 (3)	**10465**
Ralph BASS/Lowman PAULING ▶ 332 (6)	**10400**
Dedicated To The One I Love– The Mamas & The Papas (67)	5052
Dedicated To The One I Love–The Shirelles (61)	5044
Dedicated To The One I Love–The Shirelles (59)	96
Dedicated To The One I Love–Bernadette Peters (81)	90
Dedicated To The One I Love–The Temprees (72)	59
Dedicated To The One I Love–The "5" Royales (61)	58
Bob FELDMAN/Jerry GOLDSTEIN/ Richard GOTTEHRER ▶ 333 (14)	**10400**
My Boyfriend's Back–The Angels (63)	8148
Night Time–The Strangeloves (66)	764
Cara-Lin–The Strangeloves (65)	565
Let's Stomp–Bobby Comstock (63)	288
Giving Up On Love–Jerry Butler (64)	257
What's Gonna Happen When Summer's Done– Freddy Cannon (62)	143
What Time Is It?–The Jive Five (62)	103
Out In The Sun (Hey-O)–The Beach Nuts (65)	63
Sorrow–David Bowie (73)	53
A Letter From Betty–Bobby Vee (63)	11
I'm On Fire–Jerry Lee Lewis (64)	2.7
I'm Tossin' And Turnin' Again–Bobby Lewis (62)	1.3
Your Boyfriend's Back– Bobby Comstock & The Counts (63)	0.4
Broadway–Freddy Cannon (62)	0.4
Alan PARSONS/Eric WOOLFSON ▶ 334 (17)	**10394**
Eye In The Sky–Alan Parsons Project (82)	3993
Time–Alan Parsons Project (81)	1286
Games People Play–Alan Parsons Project (80)	1174
Don't Answer Me–Alan Parsons Project (84)	875
Damned If I Do–Alan Parsons Project (79)	718
I Wouldn't Want To Be Like You– Alan Parsons (77)	546
Prime Time–Alan Parsons Project (84)	415
(The System Of) Doctor Tarr And Professor Fether– Alan Parsons Project (76)	292
Let's Talk About Me–Alan Parsons Project (85)	260
Psychobabble–Alan Parsons Project (82)	257
You Don't Believe–Alan Parsons Project (83)	240
Don't Let It Show–Alan Parsons Project (77)	136
Stereotomy–Alan Parsons Project (86)	65
Days Are Numbers (The Traveller)– Alan Parsons Project (85)	63
Snake Eyes–Alan Parsons Project (81)	44
Raven–Alan Parsons (76)	22
What Goes Up–Alan Parsons Project (78)	8.2

Cole PORTER ▶ 335 (27)	**10389**
Joseph KOSMA ▶ 336 (5)	**10383**
Merle TRAVIS ▶ 337 (8)	**10349**
Phil SPECTOR ▶ 338 (8)	**10318**
Martha SHARP ▶ 339 (4)	**10313**
C. Carson PARKS ▶ 340 (2)	**10263**
Stephen STILLS ▶ 341 (17)	**10249**
Tom T. HALL ▶ 342 (8)	**10242**
Dewayne BLACKWELL ▶ 343 (9)	**10229**
Steven ADLER/Saul HUDSON/ Duff McKAGAN/Axl ROSE/Izzy STRADLIN ▶ 344 (5)	**10217**
Sweet Child O' Mine—Guns N' Roses (88)	4596
Patience—Guns N' Roses (89)	2050
Paradise City—Guns N' Roses (89)	1901
Welcome To The Jungle—Guns N' Roses (88)	1661
Nightrain—Guns N' Roses (89)	9.3
Johnny NASH ▶ 345 (5)	**10211**
Ritchie CORDELL ▶ 346 (4)	**10183**
Acker BILK ▶ 347 (1)	**10177**
Sammy CAHN/Jimmy VAN HEUSEN ▶ 348 (22)	**10168**
Love And Marriage—Frank Sinatra (55)	3059
All The Way—Frank Sinatra (57)	2520
High Hopes— Frank Sinatra "and a bunch of kids" (59)	944
(Love Is) The Tender Trap—Frank Sinatra (55)	901
Pocketful Of Miracles—Frank Sinatra (61)	587
The Second Time Around—Frank Sinatra (61)	491
Love And Marriage—Dinah Shore (55)	386
The Boys' Night Out—Patti Page (62)	326
Wake Me When It's Over—Andy Williams (60)	278
Where Love Has Gone—Jack Jones (64)	235
Call Me Irresponsible—Frank Sinatra (63)	187
How Are Ya' Fixed For Love— Frank Sinatra and Keely Smith (58)	99
Call Me Irresponsible—Jack Jones (63)	90
Come Blow Your Horn—Frank Sinatra (63)	21
It's Better In The Dark—Tony Martin (56)	21
Look To Your Heart—Georgie Shaw (55)	8.7
To Love And Be Loved—Jane Morgan (58)	7.2
Sold To The Man With The Broken Heart— Tony Bennett with Percy Faith (57)	6.8
The Last Dance—The McGuire Sisters (60)	0.8
To Love And Be Loved—Frank Sinatra (59)	0.4
(Love Is) The Tender Trap—Ella Fitzgerald (55)	0.0
Love And Marriage—Helen Grayco (55)	0.0
Clement A. BOZEWSKI/Deborah HARRY/ Giorgio MORODER ▶ 349 (1)	**10151**
Call Me—Blondie (80)	10151
Clifton DAVIS ▶ 350 (5)	**10150**
John MADARA/David WHITE ▶ 351 (11)	**10127**
You Don't Own Me—Lesley Gore (63)	5712
The Fly—Chubby Checker (61)	2626
The Boy Next Door—The Secrets (63)	798
Birthday Party—The Pixies Three (63)	455
Pop Pop Pop-Pie—The Sherrys (62)	435
Cold Cold Winter—The Pixies Three (63)	45
Dancin' The Strand—Maureen Gray (62)	33
Oo-La-La-Limbo—Danny & The Juniors (63)	16
Doin' The Continental Walk— Danny & The Juniors (62)	3.6
At The Shore—Johnny Caswell (63)	3.1
Slop Time—The Sherrys (63)	1.8
Bob DAVIE/Marvin MOORE ▶ 352 (6)	**10123**
Green Door—Jim Lowe (56)	9717
By You By You By You—Jim Lowe (57)	197
I Feel The Beat—Jim Lowe (56)	148
Rock And Roll Rhapsody—Four Aces (58)	56
Green Door—The Jerms (69)	4.7
Just Love Me—Jaye P. Morgan (56)	1.3
Andy GIBB/Barry GIBB/ Maurice GIBB/Robin GIBB ▶ 353 (1)	**10099**
Shadow Dancing—Andy Gibb (78)	10099
Bert BERNS/Wes FARRELL ▶ 354 (8)	**10093**
Hang On Sloopy—The McCoys (65)	6827
Hang On Sloopy—Ramsey Lewis Trio (65)	1400
My Girl Sloopy—The Vibrations (64)	637
Goodbye Baby (Baby Goodbye)— Solomon Burke (64)	588

(My Girl) Sloopy— Little Caesar And The Consuls (65)	340
Everybody Do The Sloopy—Johnny Thunder (65)	163
Hang On Sloopy—Rick Derringer (75)	96
Hang On Sloopy—The Lettermen (70)	42
Jerry BUTLER/Kenneth GAMBLE/Leon HUFF ▶ 355 (13)	**10079**
Only The Strong Survive—Jerry Butler (69)	3213
Never Give You Up—Jerry Butler (68)	1243
Hey, Western Union Man—Jerry Butler (68)	1108
A Brand New Me—Dusty Springfield (69)	1011
What's The Use Of Breaking Up—Jerry Butler (69)	960
Moody Woman—Jerry Butler (69)	921
Are You Happy—Jerry Butler (68)	543
Don't Let Love Hang You Up—Jerry Butler (69)	360
Lost—Jerry Butler (67)	297
I Could Write A Book—Jerry Butler (70)	294
Brand New Me—Aretha Franklin (71)	115
A Brand New Me—Jerry Butler (69)	12
Been A Long Time—Betty Everett (69)	4.3
Stan LEBOWSKY/Herbert NEWMAN ▶ 356 (3)	**10077**
The Wayward Wind—Gogi Grant (56)	9460
The Wayward Wind—Tex Ritter (56)	406
The Wayward Wind—Gogi Grant (61)	211
Toni TENNILLE ▶ 357 (2)	**10060**
Dash CROFTS/Jim SEALS ▶ 358 (9)	**10057**
Get Closer— Seals & Crofts (Featuring Carolyn Willis) (76)	2732
Diamond Girl—Seals & Crofts (73)	2135
Summer Breeze—Seals & Crofts (72)	2085
Hummingbird—Seals & Crofts (73)	1121
We May Never Pass This Way (Again)— Seals & Crofts (73)	919
I'll Play For You—Seals & Crofts (75)	885
Summer Breeze (Part 1)— The Isley Brothers (74)	173
If You See My Love—Lenny Welch (64)	6.1
Castles In The Sand—Seals & Crofts (75)	1.8
Don EVERLY/Phil EVERLY ▶ 359 (4)	**10038**
Cathy's Clown—The Everly Brothers (60)	9441
Gone, Gone, Gone—The Everly Brothers (64)	522
Should We Tell Him—The Everly Brothers (58)	71
Maybe Tomorrow—The Everly Brothers (57)	5.0
Mae Boren AXTON/Thomas DURDEN/ Elvis PRESLEY ▶ 360 (4)	**9967**
Heartbreak Hotel—Elvis Presley (56)	9660
Heartbreak Hotel—Frijid Pink (70)	236
Heartbreak Hotel—Roger Miller (66)	53
Heartbreak Hotel—Stan Freberg (56)	17
Michael ANTHONY/David Lee ROTH/ Alex VAN HALEN/Eddie VAN HALEN ▶ 361 (8)	**9957**
Jump—Van Halen (84)	6595
Panama—Van Halen (84)	1026
I'll Wait—Van Halen (84)	975
Dance The Night Away—Van Halen (79)	922
And The Cradle Will Rock...—Van Halen (80)	183
Hot For Teacher—Van Halen (84)	182
Beautiful Girls—Van Halen (79)	61
Runnin' With The Devil—Van Halen (78)	12
Albert Philip McKAY/Maurice WHITE ▶ 362 (4)	**9928**
Best Of My Love—The Emotions (77)	7303
Sing A Song—Earth, Wind & Fire (75)	2498
Flowers—The Emotions (76)	93
Smile—The Emotions (78)	33
Rudy CLARK ▶ 363 (11)	**9921**
Steve GEORGE/John LANG/Richard PAGE ▶ 364 (4)	**9907**
Broken Wings—Mr. Mister (85)	5158
Kyrie—Mr. Mister (85)	4320
Something Real (Inside Me/Inside You)— Mr. Mister (87)	420
The Border—Mr. Mister (87)	8.7
Eddie HOLLAND/Norman WHITFIELD ▶ 365 (11)	**9894**
Beauty Is Only Skin Deep—The Temptations (66)	2987
Ain't Too Proud To Beg—The Temptations (66)	2123
(Loneliness Made Me Realize) It's You That I Need— The Temptations (67)	1525

Too Many Fish In The Sea—The Marvelettes (64)	1040
Ain't Too Proud To Beg—The Rolling Stones (74)	829
Girl (Why You Wanna Make Me Blue)— The Temptations (64)	667
Everybody Needs Love— Gladys Knight & The Pips (67)	383
Too Many Fish In The Sea— Mitch Ryder And The Detroit Wheels (67)	300
The Girl's Alright With Me—The Temptations (64)	23
Ain't Too Proud To Beg—Rick Astley (89)	8.7
Ain't Too Proud To Beg—The Magnificent Men (67)	7.6
J. Fred COOTS/Charles KENNY/Nick KENNY ▶ 366 (1)	**9892**
Love Letters In The Sand—Pat Boone (57)	9892
Will JENNINGS/Richard KERR ▶ 367 (6)	**9859**
I'll Never Love This Way Again—Dionne Warwick (79)	3458
Looks Like We Made It—Barry Manilow (77)	3436
Somewhere In The Night—Barry Manilow (78)	1230
Somewhere In The Night—Helen Reddy (75)	918
No Night So Long—Dionne Warwick (80)	723
Somewhere In The Night—Batdorf & Rodney (75)	94
Hal DAVIS/Berry GORDY/ Willie HUTCH/Bob WEST ▶ 368 (1)	**9838**
I'll Be There—The Jackson 5 (70)	9838
Thom BELL/William HART ▶ 369 (12)	**9827**
La - La - Means I Love You—The Delfonics (68)	3448
Didn't I (Blow Your Mind This Time)— The Delfonics (70)	1925
Didn't I (Blow Your Mind)— New Kids On The Block (89)	1171
Ready Or Not Here I Come (Can't Hide From Love)— The Delfonics (68)	642
You Got Yours And I'll Get Mine— The Delfonics (69)	584
Break Your Promise—The Delfonics (68)	575
Trying To Make A Fool Of Me— The Delfonics (70)	497
I'm Sorry—The Delfonics (68)	413
Over And Over—The Delfonics (71)	325
La La Means I Love You—Tierra (81)	142
Somebody Loves You—The Delfonics (69)	83
Funny Feeling—The Delfonics (69)	24
Andrew BARKSDALE/Otis BLACKWELL/ Jimmy JONES/Charles MERENSTEIN ▶ 370 (3)	**9788**
Handy Man—Jimmy Jones (59)	5670
Handy Man—James Taylor (77)	3089
Handy Man—Del Shannon (64)	1029
Chris KENNER ▶ 371 (13)	**9780**
Matt AITKEN/Mike STOCK/Pete WATERMAN ▶ 372 (9)	**9772**
Never Gonna Give You Up—Rick Astley (87)	4405
Together Forever (Remix)—Rick Astley (88)	3168
It Would Take A Strong Strong Man— Rick Astley (88)	1136
I Should Be So Lucky—Kylie Minogue (88)	512
It's No Secret—Kylie Minogue (88)	419
Showing Out (Get Fresh At The Weekend)— Mel & Kim (87)	51
Nothing's Gonna Stop Me Now—Samantha Fox (87)	50
Wouldn't Change A Thing—Kylie Minogue (90)	19
Love's About To Change My Heart— Donna Summer (89)	12
Henry MANCINI/Johnny MERCER ▶ 373 (13)	**9769**
Moon River— Henry Mancini, His Orchestra And Chorus (61)	3649
Moon River—Jerry Butler (61)	3029
Days of Wine And Roses— Henry Mancini His Orchestra & Chorus (63)	1363
Days Of Wine And Roses—Andy Williams (63)	942
Charade— Henry Mancini And His Orchestra and Chorus (63)	631
Sweetheart Tree—Johnny Mathis (65)	111
Sweetheart Tree— Henry Mancini And His Orchestra (65)	43
Charade—Andy Williams (64)	0.5
Days Of Wine And Roses—Pat Boone (63)	0.0
Moon River—The Fuller Brothers (61)	0.0
Charade—The Four Freshmen (63)	0.0
Moon River—Jean Thomas (62)	0.0
Charade—Adam Wade (63)	0.0

Robert CLIVILLÉS/Frederick B. WILLIAMS ► 374 (3)	**9762**
Gonna Make You Sweat—C & C Music Factory (Featuring Freedom Williams) (90)	4586
Here We Go—C & C Music Factory (Featuring Freedom Williams And Zelma Davis) (91)	3090
Things That Make You Go Hmmmm—C & C Music Factory (Featuring Freedom Williams) (91)	2086
Duane EDDY/Lee HAZLEWOOD ► 375 (16)	**9759**
Rebel 'rouser—Duane Eddy (58)	2375
(Dance With The) Guitar Man—Duane Eddy And The Rebelettes (62)	2041
Cannonball—Duane Eddy His "Twangy" guitar and The Rebels (58)	1147
Lonely One—Duane Eddy His "Twangy" guitar and The Rebels (59)	881
Boss Guitar—Duane Eddy And The Rebelettes (63)	722
Yep—Duane Eddy His "Twangy" guitar and The Rebels (59)	522
Some Kind A Earthquake—Duane Eddy His "Twangy" guitar and The Rebels (59)	513
Shazam—Duane Eddy His "Twangy" Guitar And The Rebels (60)	362
Kommotion—Duane Eddy (60)	345
First Love First Tears—Duane Eddy His "Twangy" guitar and The Rebels (59)	256
Quiet Three—Duane Eddy His "Twangy" guitar and The Rebels (59)	255
Your Baby's Gone Surfin'—Duane Eddy (63)	161
Lonely Boy, Lonely Guitar—Duane Eddy (63)	134
Moovin' N' Groovin'—Duane Eddy (58)	31
The Battle—Duane Eddy and The Rebels (62)	13
Stretchin' Out—Duane Eddy and The Rebelettes (62)	0.4
Jeanine DECKERS ► 376 (2)	**9739**
Robbie ROBERTSON ► 377 (10)	**9738**
Robert PARISSI ► 378 (7)	**9733**
John WILLIAMS ► 379 (9)	**9714**
Smokey ROBINSON/Ronnie WHITE ► 380 (10)	**9697**
My Girl—The Temptations (65)	6094
You Beat Me To The Punch—Mary Wells (62)	1687
My Girl—Suavé (88)	579
My Girl—Bobby Vee (68)	476
Everybody's Gotta Pay Some Dues—The Miracles (61)	307
My Girl—Daryl Hall & John Oates Featuring David Ruffin & Eddie Kendricks (85)	285
My Girl—Amii Stewart & Johnny Bristol (80)	99
My Girl—Eddie Floyd (70)	97
Don't Look Back—The Temptations (65)	49
(You Got To Walk And) Don't Look Back—Peter Tosh (78)	24
Christine McVIE ► 381 (6)	**9683**
Harold LOGAN/Lloyd PRICE/TRADITIONAL ► 382 (3)	**9680**
Stagger Lee—Lloyd Price (58)	7844
Stagger Lee—Tommy Roe (71)	1051
Stag-O-Lee—Wilson Pickett (67)	785
Homer BANKS/Carl HAMPTON/ Raymond Earl JACKSON ► 383 (8)	**9671**
(If Loving You Is Wrong) I Don't Want To Be Right—Luther Ingram (72)	5399
If You're Ready (Come Go With Me)—The Staple Singers (73)	1796
(If Loving You Is Wrong) I Don't Want To Be Right—Barbara Mandrell (79)	775
Touch A Hand, Make A Friend—The Staple Singers (74)	770
I'll Be Your Shelter (In Time Of Storm)—Luther Ingram (72)	584
If Loving You Is Wrong I Don't Want To Be Right—Millie Jackson (75)	204
Be What You Are—The Staple Singers (73)	122
I Could Never Be Happy—The Emotions (72)	21
Hans ENGELMANN ► 384 (5)	**9649**
Berton AVERRE/Doug FIEGER ► 385 (3)	**9637**
My Sharona—The Knack (79)	9055
Baby Talks Dirty—The Knack (80)	422
Can't Put A Price On Love—The Knack (80)	160
Willie NELSON ► 386 (10)	**9629**
Graham GOULDMAN/Eric STEWART ► 387 (9)	**9614**
I'm Not In Love—10cc (75)	4276
The Things We Do For Love—10CC (77)	3173
I'm Not In Love—Will To Power (90)	1398
Dreadlock Holiday—10 CC (78)	364
People In Love—10cc (77)	124
Good Morning Judge—10CC (77)	119
Art For Art's Sake—10CC (75)	88
For You And I—10cc (79)	60
The Wall Street Shuffle—10 C. C. (74)	11
Luis GUGLIELMI ► 388 (4)	**9598**
Robin MOORE/Barry SADLER ► 389 (1)	**9577**
The Ballad Of The Green Berets—SSgt. Barry Sadler (66)	9577
Richard BERRY ► 390 (8)	**9570**
Bert BERNS ► 391 (17)	**9564**
Paul DAVIS ► 392 (12)	**9530**
Mort GARSON/Bob HILLIARD ► 393 (7)	**9524**
Our Day Will Come—Ruby And The Romantics (63)	6254
Our Day Will Come—Frankie Valli (75)	1249
My Summer Love—Ruby And The Romantics (63)	1134
Young Wings Can Fly (Higher Than You Know)—Ruby And The Romantics (63)	499
Jacqueline—Bobby Helms (58)	228
Baby Come Home—Ruby And The Romantics (64)	106
Take A Chance—Jaye P. Morgan (57)	53
Carole Bayer SAGER/Toni WINE ► 394 (5)	**9522**
A Groovy Kind Of Love—The Mindbenders (66)	5559
Groovy Kind Of Love—Phil Collins (88)	3712
Ashes To Ashes—The Mindbenders (66)	223
I'm Into Lookin' For Someone To Love Me—Bobby Vee (68)	20
Off And Running—Lesley Gore (66)	8.1
Steve CROPPER/Eddie FLOYD ► 395 (8)	**9516**
Knock On Wood—Amii Stewart (79)	4967
634-5789 (Soulsville, U.S.A)—Wilson Pickett (66)	2078
Knock On Wood—Eddie Floyd (66)	1439
You Don't Know What You Mean To Me—Sam & Dave (68)	453
Knock On Wood—Otis & Carla (67)	443
I've Got To Have Your Love—Eddie Floyd (69)	120
On A Saturday Night—Eddie Floyd (67)	14
Love Is A Doggone Good Thing—Eddie Floyd (67)	1.9
John Bobby BERRY/Don COVAY ► 396 (8)	**9503**
Pony Time—Chubby Checker (61)	8332
The Continental Walk—Hank Ballard And The Midnighters (61)	672
Pony Time—Don Covay and The Goodtimers (61)	281
The Continental Walk—The Rollers (61)	81
Gilee—Sonny Spencer (59)	64
Hey Lover—Debbie Dovale (63)	61
I'm Hanging Up My Heart For You—Solomon Burke (62)	8.1
Your Memory—The Five Satins (60)	3.0
Winfield SCOTT ► 397 (14)	**9491**
Gary WRIGHT ► 398 (5)	**9490**
Peter DeROSE/Mitchell PARISH ► 399 (3)	**9450**
Deep Purple—Nino Tempo & April Stevens (63)	7500
Deep Purple—Donny And Marie Osmond (75)	1422
Deep Purple—Billy Ward And His Dominoes (57)	528
Todd RUNDGREN ► 400 (18)	**9450**
Lee MORRIS/Bernie WAYNE ► 401 (3)	**9437**
Blue Velvet—Bobby Vinton (63)	8754
I Don't Want To See Tomorrow—Nat King Cole (64)	637
Blue Velvet—The Statues (60)	46
Ken DARBY/George R. POULTON/ Elvis PRESLEY ► 402 (4)	**9428**
Love Me Tender—Elvis Presley (56)	8241
Love Me Tender—Richard Chamberlain (62)	673
Love Me Tender—Percy Sledge (67)	405
Love Me Tender—Henri René (56)	108
Don ROBERTSON ► 403 (13)	**9420**
Pat BALLARD ► 404 (9)	**9410**
Steve GREENBERG ► 405 (3)	**9395**
Wally GOLD/Aaron SCHROEDER ► 406 (6)	**9379**
Good Luck Charm—Elvis Presley With The Jordanaires (62)	6862
Lucky Devil—Carl Dobkins, Jr. (59)	895
Fools Hall Of Fame—Pat Boone (59)	646
Time And The River—Nat King Cole (60)	462
Hither And Thither And Yon—Brook Benton (60)	379
Sweet Bird Of Youth—Nat "King" Cole (59)	135
Isaac HAYES ► 407 (8)	**9376**
André CYMONE/Jody WATLEY ► 408 (6)	**9368**
Looking For A New Love—Jody Watley (87)	4041
Real Love—Jody Watley (89)	3609
Some Kind Of Lover—Jody Watley (88)	1295
I Want You—Jody Watley (91)	205
Still A Thrill—Jody Watley (87)	148
Precious Love—Jody Watley (90)	70
Eugene RECORD ► 409 (13)	**9348**
Ben E. KING/Jerry LEIBER/Mike STOLLER ► 410 (9)	**9344**
Stand By Me—Ben E. King (61)	3409
Stand By Me—Ben E. King (86)	1763
Stand By Me—Spyder Turner (66)	1730
Stand By Me—Mickey Gilley (80)	1122
Stand By Me—John Lennon (75)	647
Stand By Me—Maurice White (85)	304
Stand By Me—David & Jimmy Ruffin (70)	227
Stand By Me—Earl Grant (65)	129
Stand By Me—Cassius Clay (64)	14
Tom BAILEY/Alannah CURRIE/Joe LEEWAY ► 411 (8)	**9323**
Hold Me Now—Thompson Twins (84)	3557
Lay Your Hands On Me—Thompson Twins (85)	1742
King For A Day—Thompson Twins (86)	1479
Doctor! Doctor!—Thompson Twins (84)	1247
Lies—Thompson Twins (83)	612
You Take Me Up—Thompson Twins (84)	304
Love On Your Side—Thompson Twins (83)	286
The Gap—Thompson Twins (84)	95
Bob GAUDIO/Judy PARKER ► 412 (5)	**9306**
December, 1963 (Oh, What A Night)—The Four Seasons (75)	5913
Who Loves You—Four Seasons (75)	3116
Silver Star—The Four Seasons (76)	172
Down The Hall—The Four Seasons (77)	102
Who Loves You—Gidea Park (81)	3.7
Ewan MacCOLL ► 413 (1)	**9289**
Bert BERNS/Phil MEDLEY ► 414 (5)	**9284**
Twist And Shout—The Beatles (64)	6394
Twist And Shout—The Isley Brothers (62)	2072
Twist And Shout—The Beatles (86)	529
If I Didn't Have A Dime (To Play The Jukebox)—Gene Pitney (62)	279
Push Push—Austin Taylor (60)	9.6
Ned MILLER ► 415 (6)	**9284**
Eddie HEYWOOD ► 416 (4)	**9272**
Ronnie MACK ► 417 (4)	**9271**
Leonard L. CAPIZZI/Bobby PICKETT ► 418 (3)	**9247**
Monster Mash—Bobby (Boris) Pickett And The Crypt-Kickers (62)	7305
Monster Mash—Bobby (Boris) Pickett And The Crypt-Kickers (73)	1895
Monster Mash—Bobby (Boris) Pickett And The Crypt-Kickers (70)	47
Peter CETERA ► 419 (4)	**9233**
Charles SINGLETON ► 420 (11)	**9224**
Teddy RANDAZZO/Bobby WEINSTEIN ► 421 (6)	**9206**
Goin' Out Of My Head—Little Anthony And The Imperials (64)	3749
Pretty Blue Eyes—Steve Lawrence (59)	2838
Goin' Out Of My Head—The Lettermen (67)	1323
I'm On The Outside (Looking In)—Little Anthony And The Imperials (64)	1253
Goin' Out Of My Head—Frank Sinatra (69)	36
Poor Boy—The Royalettes (65)	7.8
Gene CHANDLER/Earl EDWARDS/ Bernice WILLIAMS ► 422 (3)	**9193**
Duke Of Earl—Gene Chandler (62)	9144
Duchess Of Earl—The Pearlettes (62)	50
Duchess Of Earl—Bobbie Smith & The Dreamgirls (62)	0.0
David PACK ► 423 (5)	**9181**

Dave ALLDRED/Jimmy BOWEN/ Buddy KNOX/Donnie LANIER ▶ 424 (11)	**9181**
Party Doll—Buddy Knox with The Rhythm Orchids (57)	4735
Party Doll—Steve Lawrence (57)	1892
I'm Stickin' With You— Jimmy Bowen With The Rhythm Orchids (57)	1396
Rock Your Little Baby To Sleep— Buddy Knox with The Rhythm Orchids (57)	698
Party Doll— Cat Mother And The All Night News Boys (69)	164
Party Doll—Wingy Manone And His Orchestra (57)	133
I Trusted You— Jimmy Bowen With The Rhythm Orchids (57)	76
Ever Lovin' Fingers— Jimmy Bowen With The Rhythm Orchids (57)	44
I'm Stickin' With You—The Fontane Sisters (57)	36
Party Doll—Roy Brown (57)	7.0
I'm Stickin' With You—Roy Brown (57)	0.0
Rick EVANS ▶ 425 (3)	**9175**
Bruce CHANNEL/Margaret COBB ▶ 426 (3)	**9160**
Hey! Baby—Bruce Channel (62)	8663
Hey! Baby—Jose Feliciano (69)	381
Hey Baby—Ringo Starr (76)	116
Howard JONES ▶ 427 (9)	**9152**
Ruthann FRIEDMAN ▶ 428 (2)	**9149**
Phil BAPTISTE/George KHOURY ▶ 429 (4)	**9135**
Sea Of Love—Phil Phillips with The Twilights (59)	5548
Sea Of Love—The Honeydrippers (84)	3169
Sea Of Love—Del Shannon (81)	406
Verdie Mae—Phil Phillips (59)	11
Paul ANKA/Alberto CURCI ▶ 430 (2)	**9133**
Lonely Boy—Paul Anka (59)	9133
Lonely Boy—Donny Osmond (72)	0.0
Klaus-Günter NEUMANN ▶ 431 (2)	**9123**
Rodger PENZABENE/Barrett STRONG/ Norman WHITFIELD ▶ 432 (6)	**9122**
I Wish It Would Rain—The Temptations (68)	5041
I Could Never Love Another (After Loving You)— The Temptations (68)	1576
The End Of Our Road—Gladys Knight & The Pips (68)	1369
The End Of Our Road—Marvin Gaye (70)	504
I Wish It Would Rain—Gladys Knight & The Pips (68)	449
Don't You Miss Me A Little Bit Baby— Jimmy Ruffin (67)	184
Wayne SHANKLIN ▶ 433 (12)	**9090**
Ritchie VALENS ▶ 434 (4)	**9088**
Brook BENTON/Clyde OTIS ▶ 435 (11)	**9088**
Kiddio—Brook Benton (60)	3969
Thank You Pretty Baby—Brook Benton (59)	1669
Endlessly—Brook Benton (59)	1535
Same One—Brook Benton (60)	1295
Mother Nature, Father Time—Brook Benton (65)	375
This Time Of The Year—Brook Benton (59)	185
This Time Of The Year—Brook Benton (60)	22
Endlessly—Mavis Staples (72)	14
I Ain't Giving Up Nothing—Ben Hewitt (59)	13
Endlessly—Sonny James (70)	5.1
I Just Want To Love You—Clyde McPhatter (60)	5.0
Gretchen CHRISTOPHER/ Barbara ELLIS/Gary TROXEL ▶ 436 (4)	**9087**
Come Softly To Me—The Fleetwoods (59)	8460
Graduation's Here—The Fleetwoods (59)	416
Come Softly To Me—Ronnie Height (59)	196
Come Softly To Me— The New Seekers Featuring Marty Kristian (73)	14
Michael ANTHONY/Sammy HAGAR/ Alex VAN HALEN/Eddie VAN HALEN ▶ 437 (9)	**9084**
Why Can't This Be Love—Van Halen (86)	3498
When It's Love—Van Halen (88)	1533
Finish What Ya Started—Van Halen (88)	1115
Top Of The World—Van Halen (91)	819
Love Walks In—Van Halen (86)	778
Dreams—Van Halen (86)	588
Feels So Good—Van Halen (89)	435
Black And Blue—Van Halen (88)	288
Best Of Both Worlds—Van Halen (86)	29
Perez PRADO ▶ 438 (8)	**9047**
Joey DEE/Henry GLOVER ▶ 439 (1)	**9044**
Peppermint Twist - Part 1— Joey Dee & The Starliters (61)	9044

Ray HILDEBRAND ▶ 440 (1)	**9041**
Boyd BENNETT/Chuck GORMAN/John YOUNG ▶ 441 (5)	**9018**
Seventeen— Boyd Bennett And His Rockets (55)	4540
Seventeen—The Fontane Sisters with Billy Vaughn's Orchestra (55)	3907
Seventeen—Rusty Draper (55)	534
Seventeen—Frankie Ford (61)	37
Seventeen—Ella Mae Morse (55)	0.0
Kal MANN/Billy STRANGE ▶ 442 (1)	**9002**
Limbo Rock—Chubby Checker (62)	9002
Joe MEEK ▶ 443 (3)	**8993**
Pete BELLOTTE/Harold FALTERMEYER/ Keith FORSEY ▶ 444 (2)	**8949**
Hot Stuff—Donna Summer (79)	8596
Cold Love—Donna Summer (80)	353
George GREEN/John MELLENCAMP ▶ 445 (3)	**8937**
Hurts So Good—John Cougar (82)	6837
Crumblin' Down—John Cougar Mellencamp (83)	1614
Rain On The Scarecrow— John Cougar Mellencamp (86)	486
Charles Henry JACKSON Jr./Marvin YANCY ▶ 446 (11)	**8925**
I've Got Love On My Mind—Natalie Cole (77)	3003
This Will Be—Natalie Cole (75)	2336
Our Love—Natalie Cole (77)	1689
Inseparable—Natalie Cole (75)	745
Baby I've Been Missing You—The Independents (73)	372
Mr. Melody—Natalie Cole (76)	277
The More You Do It (The More I Like It Done To Me)— Ronnie Dyson (76)	243
Let This Be A Lesson To You— The Independents (74)	97
It's All Over—The Independents (73)	79
It's Cool—The Tymes (76)	55
Loving Power—The Impressions (76)	31
Jackie DeSHANNON/Donna WEISS ▶ 447 (1)	**8923**
Bette Davis Eyes—Kim Carnes (81)	8923
Redd EVANS/Dave MANN ▶ 448 (2)	**8908**
There! I've Said It Again—Bobby Vinton (63)	8758
There I've Said It Again—Sam Cooke (59)	149
Bert REISFELD/Jean VILLARD ▶ 449 (3)	**8905**
The Three Bells—The Browns (59)	8482
The Three Bells—Dick Flood (59)	386
The Three Bells—The Tokens (65)	36
Michael JACKSON/Paul McCARTNEY ▶ 450 (1)	**8900**
Say Say Say— Paul McCartney and Michael Jackson (83)	8900
Carl PERKINS ▶ 451 (15)	**8883**
Seth JUSTMAN ▶ 452 (3)	**8854**
Jack FULTON/Lois STEELE ▶ 453 (6)	**8832**
Ivory Tower—Cathy Carr (56)	4201
Ivory Tower—Gale Storm (56)	2381
Ivory Tower—Otis Williams And His Charms (56)	2092
Times Two I Love You—The Three Chuckles (55)	119
Peace—The McGuire Sisters (59)	39
Wanted—Perry Como (54)	0.0
Pete SEEGER ▶ 454 (4)	**8827**
Henry COSBY/Clarence PAUL ▶ 455 (3)	**8827**
Fingertips - Pt 2—Little Stevie Wonder (63)	8343
Workout Stevie, Workout— Little Stevie Wonder (63)	457
Fingertips—Stars On 45 (82)	27
Glenn FREY/Jack TEMPCHIN ▶ 456 (10)	**8814**
You Belong To The City—Glenn Frey (85)	3346
The One You Love—Glenn Frey (82)	1201
Smuggler's Blues—Glenn Frey (85)	1119
True Love—Glenn Frey (88)	970
Sexy Girl—Glenn Frey (84)	756
I Found Somebody—Glenn Frey (82)	570
All Those Lies—Glenn Frey (82)	403
Part Of Me, Part Of You—Glenn Frey (91)	267
The Allnighter—Glenn Frey (84)	171
Livin' Right—Glenn Frey (89)	11
Barbara MASON ▶ 457 (6)	**8798**
Jerry REED ▶ 458 (12)	**8790**
Kris KRISTOFFERSON ▶ 459 (17)	**8781**

Robert BATEMAN/Georgia DOBBINS/ William GARRETT/Freddie GORMAN/ Brian HOLLAND/Bernie LOWE/Kal MANN ▶ 460 (1)	**8768**
Mashed Potato Time—Dee Dee Sharp (62)	8768
Jimmy DeKNIGHT/Max C. FREEDMAN ▶ 461 (4)	**8764**
(We're Gonna) Rock Around The Clock— Bill Haley And His Comets (55)	8240
(We're Gonna) Rock Around The Clock— Bill Haley And His Comets (74)	381
Rock Around The Clock— Jive Bunny And The Mastermixers (89)	80
(We're Gonna) Rock Around The Clock— Bill Haley and His Comets (54)	64
Bill JUSTIS/Sid MANKER ▶ 462 (4)	**8749**
Raunchy—Bill Justis (57)	5369
Raunchy—Ernie Freeman (57)	2380
Raunchy—Billy Vaughn and His Orchestra (57)	999
Raunchy—Muvva "Guitar" Hubbard (57)	0.0
Chris HAYES/Huey LEWIS ▶ 463 (4)	**8743**
Stuck With You—Huey Lewis and the News (86)	4661
I Want A New Drug— Huey Lewis and the News (84)	2380
I Know What I Like— Huey Lewis and the News (87)	1139
Small World—Huey Lewis and the News (88)	563
John MADARA/Artie SINGER/David WHITE ▶ 464 (4)	**8738**
At The Hop—Danny & The Juniors (57)	8260
442 Glenwood Avenue—The Pixies Three (64)	344
At The Hop— Jive Bunny And The Mastermixers (89)	80
At The Hop—Nick Todd (57)	54
Bruce HORNSBY/John HORNSBY ▶ 465 (5)	**8735**
Jacob's Ladder—Huey Lewis and the News (87)	3640
Mandolin Rain—Bruce Hornsby And The Range (87)	2210
The Valley Road—Bruce Hornsby & The Range (88)	1734
Across The River—Bruce Hornsby & The Range (90)	765
Look Out Any Window— Bruce Hornsby & The Range (88)	387
Leslie BRICUSSE/Anthony NEWLEY ▶ 466 (14)	**8720**
The Candy Man—Sammy Davis, Jr. With The Mike Curb Congregation (72)	5982
What Kind Of Fool Am I—Sammy Davis Jr. (62)	1653
Who Can I Turn To (When Nobody Needs Me)— Tony Bennett (64)	814
Who Can I Turn To—Dionne Warwick (65)	151
What Kind Of Fool Am I—Anthony Newley (62)	57
The People Tree—Sammy Davis, Jr. With The Mike Curb Congregation (72)	32
What Kind Of Fool Am I—Robert Goulet (62)	31
What Kind Of Fool Am I— Mantovani And His Orchestra (62)	0.0
What Kind Of Fool Am I—Billy Eckstine (62)	0.0
What Kind Of Fool Am I—Ronnie Aldrich (62)	0.0
What Kind Of Fool Am I—Billy Daniels (62)	0.0
What Kind Of Fool Am I—The Cordials (62)	0.0
What Kind Of Fool Am I—Burt Farber (62)	0.0
What Kind Of Fool Am I—Vic Damone (62)	0.0
Marguerite MONNOT ▶ 467 (6)	**8690**
Jesse JAMES ▶ 468 (8)	**8686**
Thomas ALLEN/Harold BROWN/ Morris DICKERSON/Jerry GOLDSTEIN/ Lonnie JORDAN/Charles MILLER/ Lee OSKAR/Howard SCOTT ▶ 469 (7)	**8672**
Why Can't We Be Friends?—War (75)	3006
Low Rider—War (75)	2369
Summer—War (76)	1559
All Day Music—War (71)	704
They Can't Take Away Our Music— Eric Burdon And War Featuring Sharon Scott And The Beautiful New Born Children Of Southern California (70)	418
Galaxy—War (77)	325
L.A. Sunshine—War (77)	291
Arthur ALTMAN/Norman GIMBEL/ Paul MAURIAT/Franck POURCEL ▶ 470 (1)	**8660**
I Will Follow Him—Little Peggy March (63)	8660
Elliot WOLFF ▶ 471 (3)	**8640**

George MERRILL/Shannon RUBICAM ▶ 472 (4)	**8634**
I Wanna Dance With Somebody (Who Loves Me)—Whitney Houston (87)	4874
Waiting For A Star To Fall—Boy Meets Girl (88)	3061
Oh Girl—Boy Meets Girl (85)	428
Bring Down The Moon—Boy Meets Girl (89)	270
Giorgio MORODER/Tom WHITLOCK ▶ 473 (5)	**8625**
Take My Breath Away (Love Theme From TOP GUN)—Berlin (86)	4143
Danger Zone—Kenny Loggins (86)	2682
Meet Me Half Way—Kenny Loggins (87)	1448
Winner Takes It All—Sammy Hagar (87)	250
Crazy World—Big Trouble (87)	102
Luther DIXON/Florence GREEN ▶ 474 (1)	**8622**
Soldier Boy—The Shirelles (62)	8622
Dave BARTHOLOMEW/Fats DOMINO/Earl King JOHNSON ▶ 475 (4)	**8606**
I Hear You Knocking—Gale Storm (55)	5135
I Hear You Knocking—Dave Edmunds (70)	3442
I Hear You Knocking—Fats Domino (61)	29
I Hear You Knocking—Smiley Lewis (55)	0.0
George Henry JACKSON ▶ 476 (3)	**8594**
Andrew BERNARD/John FRED ▶ 477 (2)	**8523**
Judy In Disguise (With Glasses)—John Fred & His Playboy Band (67)	8168
Hey Hey Bunny—John Fred & His Playboy Band (68)	355
Stephen BISHOP ▶ 478 (6)	**8509**
Georges BOULANGER/Jimmy KENNEDY ▶ 479 (4)	**8502**
My Prayer—The Platters (56)	8202
My Prayer—Ray, Goodman & Brown (80)	266
My Prayer—Johnny Thunder (66)	34
My Prayer—The Ink Spots (56)	0.0
Ronald BLACKWELL ▶ 480 (3)	**8496**
Roland GIFT/David STEELE ▶ 481 (6)	**8491**
Good Thing—Fine Young Cannibals (89)	3616
She Drives Me Crazy—Fine Young Cannibals (89)	3569
Don't Look Back—Fine Young Cannibals (89)	994
I'm Not The Man I Used To Be—Fine Young Cannibals (89)	226
Johnny Come Home—Fine Young Cannibals (86)	56
I'm Not Satisfied—Fine Young Cannibals (90)	29
J. Leslie McFARLAND/Aaron SCHROEDER ▶ 482 (2)	**8480**
Stuck On You—Elvis Presley With The Jordanaires (60)	8364
The Wang Dang Taffy-Apple Tango (Mambo Cha Cha Cha)—Pat Boone (59)	116
Brian SETZER ▶ 483 (5)	**8480**
Ernest GOLD ▶ 484 (5)	**8472**
Gary ANDERSON/Gene BARGE/Frank GUIDA/Joseph ROYSTER ▶ 485 (1)	**8470**
Quarter To Three—U.S. Bonds (61)	8470
Pete BELLOTTE/Giorgio MORODER/Donna SUMMER ▶ 486 (9)	**8455**
Love To Love You Baby—Donna Summer (75)	4573
I Feel Love—Donna Summer (77)	2815
I Love You—Donna Summer (77)	469
Winter Melody—Donna Summer (77)	276
Rumour Has It—Donna Summer (78)	113
Love To Love You Baby—The Ritchie Family (76)	92
Spring Affair—Donna Summer (76)	84
Try Me, I Know We Can Make It—Donna Summer (76)	34
Spring Affair—Donna Summer (77)	0.0
Bobby BLOOM/Ritchie CORDELL/Bo GENTRY/Tommy JAMES ▶ 487 (4)	**8423**
Mony Mony—Tommy James And The Shondells (68)	4671
Mony Mony "Live"—Billy Idol (87)	3728
Mony Mony—Billy Idol (81)	23
Mony Mony—Tight Fit (81)	0.9
Boris FOMIN/Gene RASKIN ▶ 488 (1)	**8414**
Those Were The Days—Mary Hopkin (68)	8414
Carmine APPICE/Duane HITCHINGS/Rod STEWART ▶ 489 (1)	**8390**
Da Ya Think I'm Sexy?—Rod Stewart (78)	8390
Jesse STONE ▶ 490 (22)	**8385**
Norman GREENBAUM ▶ 491 (6)	**8379**
Trevor PEACOCK ▶ 492 (1)	**8352**

Bob BRASS/Al KOOPER/Irwin LEVINE ▶ 493 (2)	**8350**
This Diamond Ring—Gary Lewis And The Playboys (65)	7757
I Must Be Seeing Things—Gene Pitney (65)	593
Larry WILLIAMS ▶ 494 (8)	**8350**
Tim HARDIN ▶ 495 (7)	**8333**
Dolly PARTON ▶ 496 (7)	**8312**
Artie RESNICK/Kenny YOUNG ▶ 497 (8)	**8288**
Under The Boardwalk—The Drifters (64)	4327
One Kiss For Old Times' Sake—Ronnie Dove (65)	1675
A Little Bit Of Heaven—Ronnie Dove (65)	1532
I've Got Sand In My Shoes—The Drifters (64)	540
Under The Boardwalk—Bruce Willis (87)	110
Under The Boardwalk—Billy Joe Royal (78)	71
The Record (Baby, I Love You)—Ben E. King (65)	22
I Found A Daisy In The City—Barry Darvell (65)	11
Allan CLARKE/Tony HICKS/Graham NASH ▶ 498 (11)	**8287**
On A Carousel—The Hollies (67)	2080
Carrie-Anne—The Hollies (67)	2018
Stop Stop Stop—The Hollies (66)	2003
Pay You Back With Interest—The Hollies (67)	585
Tell Me To My Face—Keith (67)	500
Dear Eloise—The Hollies (67)	416
King Midas In Reverse—The Hollies (67)	292
On A Carousel—Glass Moon (82)	180
Have You Ever Loved Somebody—The Searchers (66)	165
Pay You Back With Interest—Gary O' (81)	45
Do The Best You Can—The Hollies (68)	3.5
Sam COSLOW/Ken LANE/Irving TAYLOR ▶ 499 (1)	**8239**
Everybody Loves Somebody—Dean Martin (64)	8239
Billy SWAN ▶ 500 (3)	**8234**
Percy MAYFIELD ▶ 501 (7)	**8232**
Chuck WILLIS ▶ 502 (14)	**8231**
Ann FARINA/Johnny FARINA/Santo FARINA ▶ 503 (6)	**8222**
Sleep Walk—Santo & Johnny (59)	6980
Tear Drop—Santo & Johnny (59)	945
Love Lost—Santo & Johnny (60)	105
Hop Scotch—Santo & Johnny (61)	92
Sleepwalk—Larry Carlton (82)	82
Bullseye—Santo & Johnny (60)	18
Wayne COCHRAN ▶ 504 (3)	**8216**
James EDWARDS/Carl FEASTER/Claude FEASTER/James C. KEYES/Floyd F. McRAE ▶ 505 (2)	**8209**
Sh-Boom—The Crew-Cuts (54)	7040
Sh-Boom—The Chords (54)	1169
Randy BACHMAN ▶ 506 (9)	**8196**
Glenn FREY/Don HENLEY/J.D. SOUTHER ▶ 507 (2)	**8193**
Best Of My Love—Eagles (74)	4142
New Kid In Town—Eagles (76)	4051
Peter LORD ▶ 508 (2)	**8192**
Luigi CREATORE/Al HOFFMAN/Dick MANNING/Hugo PERETTI ▶ 509 (9)	**8182**
Secretly—Jimmie Rodgers (58)	4105
Are You Really Mine—Jimmie Rodgers (58)	1540
Oh Oh I'm Falling In Love Again—Jimmie Rodgers (58)	1234
I'm Never Gonna Tell—Jimmie Rodgers (59)	568
Make Me A Miracle—Jimmie Rodgers (58)	387
Secretly—The Lettermen (65)	243
You Understand Me—Sam Cooke (60)	99
Lulu Had A Baby—Chico Holiday (59)	3.7
You Understand Me—Jimmie Rodgers (58)	1.6
Rohusuke EI/Hachidai NAKAMURA ▶ 510 (1)	**8172**
Sukiyaki—Kyu Sakamoto (63)	8172
Danny JANSSEN ▶ 511 (3)	**8172**
Jimmie CRANE/Milt GABLER/Al JACOBS ▶ 512 (5)	**8166**
If I Give My Heart To You—Doris Day (54)	4238
If I Give My Heart To You—Denise Lor (54)	1609
If I Give My Heart To You—Dinah Shore (54)	1206
If I Give My Heart To You—Kitty Kallen (59)	711
If I Give My Heart To You—Connee Boswell (54)	402

Paul LEKA/Shelley PINZ ▶ 513 (3)	**8163**
Green Tambourine—The Lemon Pipers (67)	7211
Rice Is Nice—The Lemon Pipers (68)	521
Jelly Jungle (Of Orange Marmalade)—The Lemon Pipers (68)	431
Tony MACAULAY ▶ 514 (7)	**8154**
John PHILLIPS/Michelle PHILLIPS ▶ 515 (5)	**8144**
California Dreamin'—The Mama's & The Papa's (66)	4824
Creeque Alley—The Mamas & The Papas (67)	2486
California Dreamin'—Bobby Womack (68)	442
California Dreamin'—The Beach Boys (86)	249
California Dreamin'—America (79)	142
Albert HAMMOND/Diane WARREN ▶ 516 (5)	**8128**
Nothing's Gonna Stop Us Now—Starship (87)	4678
I Don't Wanna Live Without Your Love—Chicago (88)	2262
Through The Storm—Aretha Franklin And Elton John (89)	756
It Isn't, It Wasn't, It Ain't Never Gonna Be—Aretha Franklin (89)	303
Lonely Is The Night—Air Supply (86)	129
Gene MacLELLAN ▶ 517 (3)	**8090**
Phil GERNHARD/Dick HOLLER ▶ 518 (1)	**8083**
Snoopy Vs. The Red Baron—The Royal Guardsmen (66)	8083
Graham NASH ▶ 519 (9)	**8080**
Mark LINDSAY/Terry MELCHER ▶ 520 (6)	**8068**
Good Thing—Paul Revere And The Raiders Featuring Mark Lindsay (66)	3322
Him Or Me - What's It Gonna Be?—Paul Revere And The Raiders Featuring Mark Lindsay (67)	2110
I Had A Dream—Paul Revere And The Raiders Featuring Mark Lindsay (67)	1319
Ups And Downs—Paul Revere And The Raiders (67)	879
Peace Of Mind—Paul Revere And The Raiders Featuring Mark Lindsay (67)	433
Gone Movin' On—Raiders (70)	4.0
Bert KAEMPFERT/Charles SINGLETON/Eddie SNYDER ▶ 521 (2)	**8063**
Strangers In The Night—Frank Sinatra (66)	6342
Spanish Eyes—Al Martino (65)	1721
Hank WILLIAMS ▶ 522 (25)	**8058**
Peter GABRIEL ▶ 523 (9)	**8051**
Charles BASKERVILLE/Clarence BASSETT/William Henry MILLER/James SHEPPARD ▶ 524 (4)	**8050**
Daddy's Home—Shep And The Limelites (61)	4846
Daddy's Home—Jermaine Jackson (72)	2516
Daddy's Home—Cliff Richard (82)	659
Daddy's Home—Chuck Jackson & Maxine Brown (67)	29
Johnny TILLOTSON ▶ 525 (6)	**8038**
Corey HART ▶ 526 (9)	**8035**
Benny DAVIS/Ted MURRY ▶ 527 (5)	**8001**
Don't Break The Heart That Loves You—Connie Francis (62)	6052
Follow The Boys—Connie Francis (63)	1325
Whose Heart Are You Breaking Tonight—Connie Francis (65)	358
Baby's First Christmas—Connie Francis (61)	257
The Biggest Sin Of All—Connie Francis (62)	9.5
Tony HATCH/Jackie TRENT ▶ 528 (11)	**7960**
Don't Sleep In The Subway—Petula Clark (67)	2193
I Couldn't Live Without Your Love—Petula Clark (66)	1795
Color My World—Petula Clark (66)	1085
Who Am I—Petula Clark (66)	811
Don't Give Up—Petula Clark (68)	589
The Other Man's Grass Is Always Greener—Petula Clark (67)	564
You've Got To Be Loved—The Montanas (68)	408
American Boys—Petula Clark (68)	362
Look At Mine—Petula Clark (69)	144
If You Ever Leave Me—Jack Jones (68)	8.2
Run To Me—The Montanas (68)	3.2
Bruce BELLAND/Glen LARSON ▶ 529 (7)	**7951**
26 Miles (Santa Catalina) —The Four Preps (58)	2990
Big Man—The Four Preps (58)	2564
Down By The Station—The Four Preps (59)	1665
Got A Girl—The Four Preps (60)	514
More Money For You And Me—The Four Preps (61)	130
Cinderella—The Four Preps (58)	64
The Big Draft—The Four Preps (62)	24

Jerry BUTLER/Calvin CARTER/ Curtis MAYFIELD ▶ 530 (4)	**7934**
He Don't Love You (Like I Love You)– Tony Orlando & Dawn (75)	4607
He Will Break Your Heart–Jerry Butler (60)	3246
He Don't Love You–Jim Croce (76)	76
He Will Break Your Heart– The Righteous Brothers (66)	4.8
Alan FREED/Harvey FUQUA ▶ 531 (8)	**7934**
Sincerely–The McGuire Sisters (54)	6576
Most Of All–Don Cornell (55)	1147
Sincerely–The 4 Seasons (64)	115
Sincerely–Paul Anka (69)	86
Sincerely–The Tokens (61)	11
Most Of All–The Fontane Sisters with Billy Vaughn's Orchestra (55)	0.0
Most Of All–The Moonglows (55)	0.0
Sincerely–The Moonglows (55)	0.0
Stuart HAMBLEN ▶ 532 (16)	**7911**
Johnny BRAGG/Buddy KILLEN/ Robert S. RILEY ▶ 533 (1)	**7908**
Just Walking In The Rain–Johnnie Ray (56)	7908
Frank BEARD/Billy GIBBONS/Dusty HILL ▶ 534 (16)	**7894**
Legs–ZZ Top (84)	1701
Sleeping Bag–ZZ Top (85)	1591
Tush–ZZ Top (75)	835
La Grange–ZZ Top (74)	740
Stages–ZZ Top (86)	629
Rough Boy–ZZ Top (86)	621
Velcro Fly–ZZ Top (86)	451
Gimme All Your Lovin'–ZZ Top (83)	417
It's Only Love–ZZ Top (76)	308
Doubleback–ZZ Top (90)	295
Sharp Dressed Man–ZZ Top (83)	150
Leila–ZZ Top (81)	45
Arrested For Driving While Blind–ZZ Top (77)	43
Cheap Sunglasses–ZZ Top (80)	32
Give It Up–ZZ Top (91)	23
Enjoy And Get It On–ZZ Top (77)	14
Cy CRANE/John GLUCK/ Wally GOLD/Herb WEINER ▶ 535 (2)	**7887**
It's My Party–Lesley Gore (63)	7824
It's My Party– Dave Stewart With Barbara Gaskin (81)	64
Tony Joe WHITE ▶ 536 (9)	**7881**
Rudy JACKSON/Eddy RAY ▶ 537 (5)	**7876**
Hearts Of Stone–The Fontane Sisters with Billy Vaughn's Orchestra (54)	5978
Hearts Of Stone–The Charms (54)	1329
Hearts Of Stone–The Blue Ridge Rangers (73)	570
Hearts Of Stone–The McGuire Sisters (55)	0.0
Hearts Of Stone–Vicki Young (54)	0.0
Michael CRAIG/Roy HAY/Jon MOSS/ George O'DOWD/Phil PICKETT ▶ 538 (3)	**7875**
Karma Chameleon–Culture Club (83)	5903
Move Away–Culture Club (86)	1007
It's A Miracle–Culture Club (84)	965
Jake HOOKER/Alan MERRILL ▶ 539 (1)	**7869**
I Love Rock 'N Roll– Joan Jett & The Blackhearts (82)	7869
Kenny LOGGINS/Michael McDONALD ▶ 540 (3)	**7869**
What A Fool Believes–The Doobie Brothers (79)	5311
This Is It–Kenny Loggins (79)	2064
I Gotta Try–Michael McDonald (82)	495
Alan BERGMAN/Marilyn BERGMAN/ Marvin HAMLISCH ▶ 541 (2)	**7859**
The Way We Were–Barbra Streisand (73)	6902
The Way We Were–Gladys Knight & The Pips (75)	957
Lindsey BUCKINGHAM ▶ 542 (6)	**7843**
Reggie LUCAS/James MTUME ▶ 543 (7)	**7827**
The Closer I Get To You– Roberta Flack With Donny Hathaway (78)	4396
Never Knew Love Like This Before– Stephanie Mills (80)	2443
What Cha Gonna Do With My Lovin'– Stephanie Mills (79)	611
Sweet Sensation–Stephanie Mills (80)	171
Back Together Again– Roberta Flack with Donny Hathaway (80)	111

Whatcha Gonna Do With My Lovin'–Inner City (90)	82
You Know How To Love Me–Phyllis Hyman (79)	12
Eddy GRANT ▶ 544 (5)	**7826**
Joe ESPOSITO/Eddie HOKENSON/ Bruce SUDANO/Donna SUMMER ▶ 545 (1)	**7825**
Bad Girls–Donna Summer (79)	7825
Chris LOWE/Neil TENNANT ▶ 546 (8)	**7815**
West End Girls–Pet Shop Boys (86)	4375
It's A Sin–Pet Shop Boys (87)	1228
Opportunities (Let's Make Lots Of Money)– Pet Shop Boys (86)	1174
Domino Dancing–Pet Shop Boys (88)	721
Suburbia–Pet Shop Boys (86)	159
So Hard–Pet Shop Boys (90)	120
Left To My Own Devices–Pet Shop Boys (89)	35
How Can You Expect To Be Taken Seriously– Pet Shop Boys (91)	4.1
Amadeu Do VALE/Jose GALHARDO/ Raul PORTELA ▶ 547 (3)	**7805**
Lisbon Antigua– Nelson Riddle And His Orchestra (55)	7507
Lisbon Antigua (In Old Lisbon)– Mitch Miller & His Orchestra (56)	298
Lisbon Antigua– Lawrence Welk & His Champagne Music (56)	0.0
Michael GORE/Dean PITCHFORD ▶ 548 (3)	**7804**
All The Man That I Need–Whitney Houston (90)	4418
Fame–Irene Cara (80)	3098
Red Light–Linda Clifford (80)	288
Jackson BROWNE ▶ 549 (13)	**7774**
Nick GILDER/James McCULLOCH ▶ 550 (5)	**7768**
Hot Child In The City–Nick Gilder (78)	7241
Here Comes The Night–Nick Gilder (78)	320
Rock Me–Nick Gilder (79)	193
Roxy Roller–Sweeney Todd (76)	13
Roxy Roller (Bryan Adams)–Sweeney Todd (76)	0.7
George Richard DAVIS Jr./Lee DIAMOND ▶ 551 (4)	**7760**
Tell It Like It Is–Aaron Neville (66)	6327
Tell It Like It Is–Heart (80)	1344
Tell It Like It Is–Andy Williams (76)	63
She Took You For A Ride–Aaron Neville (67)	25
Robert PALMER ▶ 552 (5)	**7754**
Janice JOHNSON/Perry KIBBLE ▶ 553 (2)	**7752**
Boogie Oogie Oogie–A Taste Of Honey (78)	7729
Do It Good–Taste Of Honey (79)	23
Domingo SAMUDIO ▶ 554 (2)	**7739**
Heino GAZE ▶ 555 (6)	**7739**
Barry MASON/Les REED ▶ 556 (10)	**7730**
Kiss Me Goodbye–Petula Clark (68)	1753
Winter World Of Love–Engelbert Humperdinck (69)	1474
Delilah–Tom Jones (68)	1459
The Last Waltz–Engelbert Humperdinck (67)	892
Les Bicyclettes De Belsize– Engelbert Humperdinck (68)	766
Here It Comes Again–The Fortunes (65)	517
Everybody Knows–The Dave Clark Five (67)	437
I'm Coming Home–Tom Jones (67)	237
I Never Said Goodbye–Engelbert Humperdinck (72)	187
Love Is All–Engelbert Humperdinck (73)	9.8
Elliot LURIE ▶ 557 (4)	**7725**
Colin James HAY/Ron STRYKERT ▶ 558 (1)	**7714**
Down Under–Men At Work (82)	7714
Rudy MARTINEZ ▶ 559 (3)	**7712**
Bob BERRYHILL/Pat CONNOLLY/ Jim FULLER/Ron WILSON ▶ 560 (6)	**7698**
Wipe Out–The Surfaris (63)	4648
Wipe Out–The Surfaris (66)	1843
Wipeout–Fat Boys (87)	961
Surfer Joe–The Surfaris (63)	236
Wipe Out–Jive Bunny & The Mastermixers (90)	6.7
Wipe Out–The Surfaris (70)	4.6
Archie BELL/Billy BUTTIER ▶ 561 (1)	**7682**
Tighten Up–Archie Bell & The Drells (68)	7682
Tom EVANS/Pete HAM ▶ 562 (2)	**7676**
Without You–Nilsson (71)	7670
Without You–Heart (78)	6.6
Roy ALFRED/Shorty ALLEN ▶ 563 (2)	**7675**
Rock And Roll Waltz–Kay Starr (55)	7669
Blue Bolero–Richard Hayes (56)	6.4

Giacomo PUCCINI/Bobby WORTH ▶ 564 (1)	**7675**
Don't You Know–Della Reese (59)	7675
Roger COOK/Roger GREENAWAY ▶ 565 (9)	**7668**
You've Got Your Troubles–The Fortunes (65)	2028
Green Grass– Gary Lewis And The Playboys (66)	1953
My Baby Loves Lovin'–White Plains (70)	1636
I Was Kaiser Bill's Batman– Whistling Jack Smith (67)	1009
Softly Whispering I Love You– The English Congregation (72)	708
Lovin' You Baby–White Plains (70)	121
Melting Pot– Blue Mink Featuring Madeleine Bell (70)	110
This Golden Ring–The Fortunes (66)	59
We Got A Dream–Ocean (71)	44
Ronnie SHANNON ▶ 566 (4)	**7643**
Gary JACKSON/Raynard MINER/ Carl William SMITH ▶ 567 (3)	**7642**
(Your Love Has Lifted Me) Higher And Higher– Rita Coolidge (77)	5006
(Your Love Keeps Lifting Me) Higher And Higher– Jackie Wilson (67)	2626
Higher And Higher–Canada Goose (70)	9.9
Pete HAM ▶ 568 (4)	**7639**
John S. CARTER/Tim GILBERT ▶ 569 (3)	**7636**
Incense And Peppermints– Strawberry Alarm Clock (67)	7462
That Acapulco Gold–The Rainy Daze (67)	169
Sea Shell–Strawberry Alarm Clock (68)	5.2
Sheb WOOLEY ▶ 570 (5)	**7636**
Joe SHAPIRO/Lou STALLMAN ▶ 571 (6)	**7624**
Round And Round–Perry Como (57)	5931
Treasure Of Love–Clyde McPhatter (56)	1172
My Little Baby–Perry Como (57)	328
Jamie Boy–Kay Starr (57)	181
How Lonely Can One Be–Teresa Brewer (57)	12
Treasure Of Love–Dorothy Collins (56)	0.0
George GERSHWIN/Ira GERSHWIN ▶ 572 (9)	**7618**
I Got Rhythm–The Happenings (67)	5952
Love Walked In–Dinah Washington (60)	884
But Not For Me–Ketty Lester (62)	383
Our Love Is Here To Stay–Dinah Washington (61)	179
Love Walked In–The Flamingos (59)	152
Someone To Watch Over Me–Frank Sinatra (54)	60
But Not For Me–Johnny Nash (59)	3.7
Love Is Here To Stay–Chris Montez (68)	2.7
Blah-Blah-Blah–Steve Lawrence (59)	0.0
Brook BENTON/Belford HENDRICKS/ Clyde OTIS ▶ 573 (6)	**7602**
It's Just A Matter Of Time–Brook Benton (59)	5155
Looking Back–Nat "King" Cole (58)	2318
Looking Back–Joe Simon (68)	62
Nothing In The World–Nat "King" Cole (58)	31
It's Just A Matter Of Time– Sonny James, The Southern Gentleman (70)	31
Looking Back–Dinah Washington (60)	5.1
Giorgio MORODER/Donna SUMMER ▶ 574 (2)	**7601**
The Wanderer–Donna Summer (80)	4199
On The Radio–Donna Summer (80)	3402
Jon BON JOVI/Richie SAMBORA ▶ 575 (3)	**7575**
I'll Be There For You–Bon Jovi (89)	4005
Wanted Dead Or Alive–Bon Jovi (87)	1804
Lay Your Hands On Me–Bon Jovi (89)	1766
Johnny SMITH ▶ 576 (2)	**7565**
Aretha FRANKLIN ▶ 577 (7)	**7534**
David ROSE ▶ 578 (3)	**7518**
Jackey BEAVERS/Johnny BRISTOL/ Harvey FUQUA ▶ 579 (1)	**7492**
Someday We'll Be Together– Diana Ross And The Supremes (69)	7492
Jenny Lou CARSON/Kay TWOMEY/ Ben WEISMAN/Fred WISE ▶ 580 (5)	**7476**
Let Me Go Lover–Joan Weber (54)	5883
Let Me Go Lover– Teresa Brewer with The Lancers (54)	1376
Let Me Go Lover–Patti Page (54)	216
Let Me Go, Lover!–Sunny Gale (54)	0.0
Let Me Go, Lover!–Peggy Lee (55)	0.0

Frederick KNIGHT ► 581 (4)	**7470**
Shadow MORTON ► 582 (5)	**7468**
Henry COSBY/Smokey ROBINSON/ Stevie WONDER ► 583 (2)	**7453**
The Tears Of A Clown— Smokey Robinson & The Miracles (70)	7441
Tears Of A Clown—Stars On 45 (81)	12
Michael DELAHUNTY/David GLASPER/ Marcus LILLINGTON/Ian SPICE ► 584 (4)	**7444**
Hands To Heaven—Breathe (88)	3472
How Can I Fall?—Breathe (88)	2861
Don't Tell Me Lies—Breathe (89)	1080
All This I Should Have Known—Breathe (89)	30
Dominic BUGATTI/Frank MUSKER ► 585 (9)	**7438**
Every Woman In The World—Air Supply (80)	3052
Heaven On The 7th Floor—Paul Nicholas (77)	2721
Modern Girl—Sheena Easton (81)	1013
Married Men—Bette Midler (79)	261
Every Home Should Have One—Patti Austin (83)	166
Every Home Should Have One—Patti Austin (81)	133
On The Strip—Paul Nicholas (78)	69
Heaven On The Seventh Floor—The Mighty Pope (77)	15
Mystery Girl—The Dukes (82)	6.7
Marvin GAYE/Ivy Jo HUNTER/ William STEVENSON ► 586 (8)	**7411**
Dancing In The Street—Martha & The Vandellas (64)	5484
Dancing In The Street— Mick Jagger & David Bowie (85)	1333
Dancing In The Street—Van Halen (82)	390
Dancin' In The Streets—Teri DeSario with K.C. (80)	98
Dancing In The Street—The Mamas & The Papas (66)	77
Dancing In The Street—Ramsey Lewis (67)	27
Dancing In The Street—Tight Fit (81)	0.9
Dancing In The Street—The Dovells (74)	0.3
Benny ANDERSSON/Björn ULVAEUS ► 587 (12)	**7408**
Take A Chance On Me—ABBA (78)	2866
The Winner Takes It All—ABBA (80)	1780
Does Your Mother Know—ABBA (79)	1098
Chiquitita—ABBA (79)	490
When All Is Said And Done—ABBA (82)	452
Super Trouper—ABBA (81)	194
Money, Money, Money—ABBA (77)	193
Lay All Your Love On Me—Information Society (89)	105
The Visitors—ABBA (82)	95
Angeleyes—ABBA (79)	95
Voulez-Vous—ABBA (79)	29
On And On And On—ABBA (81)	12
Vito PICONE/Arthur VENOSA ► 588 (1)	**7398**
Little Star—The Elegants (58)	7398
Michael D'ABO/Tony MACAULAY ► 589 (1)	**7390**
Build Me Up Buttercup—The Foundations (68)	7390
Richard MULLAN/Jack RICHARDS ► 590 (3)	**7387**
He—Al Hibbler (55)	4351
He—The McGuire Sisters (55)	1919
He—The Righteous Brothers (66)	1116
Elton JOHN/Gary OSBORNE ► 591 (4)	**7370**
Little Jeannie—Elton John (80)	4655
Blue Eyes—Elton John (82)	1448
Part-Time Love—Elton John (78)	822
Chloe—Elton John (81)	446
Scott ENGLISH/Larry WEISS ► 592 (6)	**7356**
Bend Me, Shape Me—The American Breed (67)	6075
Help Me Girl—Eric Burdon And The Animals (66)	651
Help Me Girl—The Outsiders (66)	588
(In The) Cold Light Of Day—Gene Pitney (66)	28
Bend Me, Shape Me—Storm (71)	13
Bend Me, Shape Me—Tight Fit (81)	0.9
Frank LOESSER ► 593 (22)	**7353**
Howard GREENFIELD/Helen MILLER ► 594 (6)	**7351**
Foolish Little Girl—The Shirelles (63)	2718
It Hurts To Be In Love—Gene Pitney (64)	2451
Charms—Bobby Vee (63)	1117
Rumors—Johnny Crawford (62)	912
I'll Make Him Love Me—Barbara Lewis (67)	89
It Hurts To Be In Love—Dan Hartman (81)	64
Don COVAY ► 595 (7)	**7348**
Bob CREWE/Sandy LINZER/Denny RANDELL ► 596 (6)	**7346**

Let's Hang On!—The 4 Seasons Featuring The "Sound" Of Frankie Valli (65)	6625
Let's Hang On—Barry Manilow (82)	370
Dusty—The Rag Dolls (65)	323
Society Girl—The Rag Dolls (64)	20
Watch Out, Sally!—Diane Renay (64)	4.9
Let's Hang On—Gidea Park (81)	3.7
Alan ARKIN/Bob CAREY/Erik DARLING ► 597 (4)	**7343**
Banana Boat Song—The Tarriers (56)	4406
Banana Boat Song—The Fontane Sisters (56)	1239
Banana Boat Song—Steve Lawrence (56)	939
Banana Boat Song—Sarah Vaughan (56)	758
Henry HOFFMAN/Gary KLEIN ► 598 (2)	**7321**
Bobby's Girl—Marcie Blane (62)	7201
What Does A Girl Do?—Marcie Blane (63)	120
Marvin GAYE/Ed TOWNSEND ► 599 (1)	**7308**
Let's Get It On—Marvin Gaye (73)	7308
Kenneth GAMBLE/Leon HUFF/Jerry J. ROSS ► 600 (4)	**7295**
I'm Gonna Make You Love Me—Diana Ross And The Supremes & The Temptations (68)	6496
I'm Gonna Make You Love Me—Madeline Bell (68)	687
Love Me—Bobby Hebb (66)	64
I'm Gonna Make You Love Me— Dee Dee Warwick (66)	48
Dee CLARK ► 601 (3)	**7292**
Bruce JOHNSTON ► 602 (2)	**7290**
John William CALLIS/ Philip OAKEY/Philip WRIGHT ► 603 (1)	**7286**
Don't You Want Me—The Human League (82)	7286
Bert BERNS/Jerry RAGOVOY ► 604 (11)	**7281**
Cry Baby—Garnet Mimms & The Enchanters (63)	3220
Piece Of My Heart— Big Brother And The Holding Company (68)	1544
Cry Baby—Janis Joplin (71)	651
I'll Take Good Care Of You—Garnet Mimms (66)	619
Baby Don't You Weep— Garnet Mimms & The Enchanters (63)	567
Piece Of My Heart—Erma Franklin (67)	223
One Way Love—The Drifters (64)	169
Look Away—Garnet Mimms (64)	127
One Girl—Garnet Mimms (64)	120
Piece Of My Heart—Sammy Hagar (82)	31
Heart Be Still—Lorraine Ellison (67)	11
Luther DIXON/Stanley KAHAN/Eddie SNYDER ► 605 (2)	**7269**
A Hundred Pounds Of Clay—Gene McDaniels (61)	7256
In Between Tears—Lenny Miles (61)	13
Joseph CAGLE/Steven CHAMBERLIN/ Jerry DIXON/John OSWALD/Eric TURNER ► 606 (8)	**7268**
Heaven—Warrant (89)	3557
I Saw Red—Warrant (90)	1193
Cherry Pie—Warrant (90)	992
Sometimes She Cries—Warrant (89)	824
Down Boys—Warrant (89)	567
Uncle Tom's Cabin—Warrant (91)	71
Blind Faith—Warrant (91)	40
Big Talk—Warrant (89)	23
Jean DINNING/Red SURREY ► 607 (3)	**7260**
Teen Angel—Mark Dinning (59)	6926
A Star Is Born (A Love Has Died)—Mark Dinning (60)	247
Teen Angel—Wednesday (74)	88
Jon BON JOVI ► 608 (4)	**7232**
Gerry GOFFIN/Jack KELLER ► 609 (8)	**7222**
Run To Him—Bobby Vee (61)	5173
Girls Grow Up Faster Than Boys—The Cookies (63)	591
It Started All Over Again—Brenda Lee (62)	546
Don't Try To Fight It, Baby—Eydie Gorme (63)	311
Don't Ask Me To Be Friends— The Everly Brothers (62)	259
Lovin' Touch—Mark Dinning (60)	170
How Can I Meet Her?—The Everly Brothers (62)	127
No One Can Make My Sunshine Smile— The Everly Brothers (62)	44
Gary DeCARLO/Dale FRASHUER/Paul LEKA ► 610 (3)	**7209**
Na Na Hey Hey Kiss Him Goodbye—Steam (69)	5814
Kiss Him Goodbye—The Nylons (87)	977
I've Gotta Make You Love Me—Steam (70)	418

Angelo BOND/General JOHNSON/Greg PERRY ► 611 (5)	**7184**
Somebody's Been Sleeping— 100 Proof Aged In Soul (70)	2587
Bring The Boys Home—Freda Payne (71)	2168
Stick-Up—The Honey Cone (71)	2010
Everything Good Is Bad—100 Proof Aged In Soul (72)	364
One Man's Leftovers (Is Another Man's Feast)— 100 Proof Aged In Soul (71)	54
Sherman EDWARDS/Sid WAYNE ► 612 (6)	**7166**
See You In September—The Happenings (66)	5461
See You In September—The Tempos (59)	829
Flaming Star— Elvis Presley With The Jordanaires (61)	770
Biology—Danny Valentino (60)	106
Crossroads Of Love— The Tempos Featuring Mike Lazo (59)	1.2
Biology—Sue Raney (60)	0.0
Bill DANOFF ► 613 (3)	**7155**
Oscar HAMMERSTEIN/Richard RODGERS ► 614 (30)	**7152**
Some Enchanted Evening—Jay & The Americans (65)	1354
All At Once You Love Her—Perry Como (55)	1162
Hello Young Lovers—Paul Anka (60)	973
If I Loved You—Chad & Jeremy (65)	969
Everybody's Got A Home But Me—Eddie Fisher (55)	530
You'll Never Walk Alone— Patti Labelle & The Blue Belles (64)	449
You'll Never Walk Alone—Brooklyn Bridge (69)	399
Everybody's Got A Home But Me—Roy Hamilton (55)	312
Do Re Mi—Mitch Miller & his Sing Along Chorus (59)	211
You Are Beautiful—Johnny Mathis (58)	184
You'll Never Walk Alone— Gerry And The Pacemakers (65)	184
Do I Love You (Because You're Beautiful)— Vic Damone (57)	106
Sound Of Music—Patti Page (59)	65
Climb Ev'ry Mountain—Tony Bennett (59)	64
Climb Every Mountain—The Hesitations (68)	40
Do I Love You (Because You're Beautiful)— Tony Martin (57)	34
You'll Never Walk Alone— Elvis Presley With The Jordanaires (68)	25
Do Re Mi—Anita Bryant (59)	20
Some Enchanted Evening—Jane Olivor (77)	18
Love Look Away—Tony Bennett (58)	11
The Next Time It Happens—Carmen McRae (56)	9.8
Getting To Know You—Sajid Khan (68)	8.6
I Have Dreamed—Chad & Jeremy (65)	7.1
You'll Never Walk Alone—Blue Haze (73)	7.0
You'll Never Walk Alone—Judy Garland (54)	5.4
I Enjoy Being A Girl—Pat Suzuki (59)	3.0
Do I Love You (Because You're Beautiful)— Bob Eberly with Paul Whiteman & His Orchestra (57)	0.0
I Enjoy Being A Girl—Doris Day (59)	0.0
Sound Of Music—David Whitfield (60)	0.0
Sound Of Music—Doris Day (59)	0.0
Phil EVERLY ► 615 (4)	**7151**
Paul JABARA/Bruce ROBERTS ► 616 (2)	**7130**
No More Tears (Enough Is Enough)— Barbra Streisand/Donna Summer (79)	5346
Main Event—Barbra Streisand (79)	1784
Dick HOLLER ► 617 (5)	**7119**
Nuno BETTENCOURT/Gary CHERONE ► 618 (2)	**7116**
More Than Words—Extreme (91)	4589
Hole Hearted—Extreme (91)	2526
Gus CANNON/Erik DARLING/ Willard SVANOE/Hosea WOODS ► 619 (3)	**7113**
Walk Right In—The Rooftop Singers (62)	6902
Walk Right In—Dr. Hook (77)	188
Walk Right In—The Moments (1) (63)	23
Lincoln CHASE ► 620 (11)	**7107**
Don EVERLY ► 621 (6)	**7103**
Brook BENTON/Clyde OTIS/TRADITIONAL ► 622 (1)	**7091**
The Boll Weevil Song—Brook Benton (61)	7091
Nino ROTA ► 623 (8)	**7090**
Freddie PERREN/Christine YARIAN ► 624 (5)	**7090**
It's So Hard To Say Goodbye To Yesterday— Boyz II Men (91)	4853

Freddie PERREN/Christine YARIAN ► 624 (5) *Continued*	**7090**
Do It Baby–The Miracles (74)	1443
Hallelujah Day–The Jackson 5 (73)	582
Don't Cha Love It–The Miracles (74)	108
Don't Let It End ('Til You Let It Begin)–The Miracles (73)	105
Lyn DUDDY/Lee POCKRISS ► 625 (1)	**7079**
Johnny Angel–Shelley Fabares (62)	7079
Gene PITNEY ► 626 (8)	**7074**
Irving GORDON ► 627 (13)	**7063**
Eddie MILLER/Dub WILLIAMS/Robert Gene YOUNT ► 628 (5)	**7060**
Release Me (And Let Me Love Again)–Engelbert Humperdinck (67)	4487
Release Me–Esther Phillips "Little Esther" (62)	2523
Release Me–Johnny Adams (68)	29
Release Me–Jivin' Gene (60)	13
Release Me–Esther Phillips (67)	7.2
Chuck RIO ► 629 (6)	**7059**
David ESSEX ► 630 (3)	**7048**
Randy BACHMAN/Burton CUMMINGS/Jim KALE/Garry PETERSON ► 631 (1)	**7040**
American Woman–The Guess Who (70)	7040
Bob STONE ► 632 (5)	**7037**
Ollie JONES ► 633 (6)	**7034**
Peter BECKETT/J.C. CROWLEY ► 634 (2)	**7028**
Baby Come Back–Player (77)	6598
Prisoner Of Your Love–Player (78)	430
Steve BOONE/John SEBASTIAN/Mark SEBASTIAN ► 635 (2)	**7024**
Summer In The City–The Lovin' Spoonful (66)	7015
Summer In The City–Quincy Jones (73)	8.5
John BONHAM/John Paul JONES/Jimmy PAGE/Robert PLANT ► 636 (7)	**7022**
Whole Lotta Love–Led Zeppelin (69)	4704
D'yer Mak'er–Led Zeppelin (73)	1260
Rock And Roll–Led Zeppelin (72)	411
Whole Lotta Love–C.C.S. (71)	247
Whole Lotta Love–King Curtis & The Kingpins (71)	230
Good Times Bad Times–Led Zeppelin (69)	160
Whole Lotta Love–The Wonder Band (79)	8.7
Ringo STARR ► 637 (2)	**6966**
Fred MURRAY/Robert Patrick WESTON ► 638 (1)	**6962**
I'm Henry VIII, I Am–Herman's Hermits (65)	6962
Gerry BECKLEY ► 639 (4)	**6951**
Ray CHARLES ► 640 (20)	**6950**
Rudy CLARK/Artie RESNICK ► 641 (3)	**6949**
Good Lovin'–The Young Rascals (66)	6878
Good Lovin'–The Olympics (65)	51
Good Lovin'–Grateful Dead (78)	19
Charles G. MATTHEWS/Gladys REINHARDT ► 642 (6)	**6948**
White Silver Sands–Don Rondo (57)	2977
White Silver Sands–Bill Black's Combo (60)	2957
White Silver Sands–Dave Gardner (57)	795
-twistin'-White Silver Sands–Bill Black's Combo (62)	118
White Silver Sands–Owen Bradley Quintet (57)	101
White Silver Sands–The Lennon Sisters (57)	0.0
Jerry LEIBER/Phil SPECTOR ► 643 (4)	**6941**
Spanish Harlem–Aretha Franklin (71)	4882
Spanish Harlem–Ben E. King (60)	2014
Spanish Harlem–Santo & Johnny (62)	30
Spanish Harlem–King Curtis (65)	15
Parker McGEE ► 644 (4)	**6935**
Seth JUSTMAN/Peter WOLF ► 645 (11)	**6931**
Freeze-Frame–The J. Geils Band (82)	3225
Must Of Got Lost–The J. Geils Band (74)	1063
Give It To Me–The J. Geils Band (73)	1008
Come Back–The J. Geils Band (80)	540
One Last Kiss–The J. Geils Band (78)	468
Love Stinks–The J. Geils Band (80)	428
Take It Back–The J. Geils Band (79)	82
Just Can't Wait–The J. Geils Band (80)	52
Make Up Your Mind–The J. Geils Band (73)	39
You're The Only One–Geils (77)	15
Givin' It All Up–The J. Geils Band (75)	11

Bill BERRY/Peter BUCK/Mike MILLS/Michael STIPE ► 646 (10)	**6917**
Losing My Religion–R.E.M. (91)	2447
Stand–R.E.M. (89)	1642
Shiny Happy People–R.E.M. (91)	1294
The One I Love–R.E.M. (87)	1261
It's The End Of The World As We Know It (And I Feel Fine)–R.E.M. (88)	87
So. Central Rain (I'm Sorry)–R.E.M. (84)	50
Pop Song 89–R.E.M. (89)	43
Radio Song–R.E.M. (91)	42
Radio Free Europe–R.E.M. (83)	34
Fall On Me–R.E.M. (86)	16
Peter ALLEN/Burt BACHARACH/Christopher CROSS/Carole Bayer SAGER ► 647 (1)	**6911**
Arthur's Theme (Best That You Can Do)–Christopher Cross (81)	6911
Mars BONFIRE ► 648 (3)	**6904**
Kenny LOGGINS/Dean PITCHFORD ► 649 (2)	**6900**
Footloose–Kenny Loggins (84)	6174
I'm Free (Heaven Helps The Man)–Kenny Loggins (84)	726
Marvin HAMLISCH/Carole Bayer SAGER ► 650 (4)	**6896**
Nobody Does It Better–Carly Simon (77)	5897
If You Remember Me–Chris Thompson & Night (79)	961
Theme From Ice Castles (Through The Eyes Of Love)–Melissa Manchester (79)	30
Break It To Me Gently–Aretha Franklin (77)	9.1
Johann Sebastian BACH/Sandy LINZER/Denny RANDELL ► 651 (4)	**6891**
A Lover's Concerto–The Toys (65)	6662
A Lover's Concerto–Sarah Vaughan (66)	208
A Lover's Concerto–Stars On 45 (81)	12
A Lover's Concerto–Mrs. Miller (66)	9.1
Jim DALE/Tom SPRINGFIELD ► 652 (1)	**6883**
Georgy Girl–The Seekers (66)	6883
Burt BACHARACH/Bob HILLIARD ► 653 (12)	**6868**
Tower Of Strength–Gene McDaniels (61)	2388
Any Day Now (My Wild Beautiful Bird)–Chuck Jackson (62)	1371
Please Stay–The Drifters (61)	1293
Any Day Now–Ronnie Milsap (82)	1068
Don't You Believe It–Andy Williams (62)	496
Any Day Now–Percy Sledge (69)	91
You're Following Me–Perry Como (61)	83
You Don't Have To Be A Tower Of Strength–Gloria Lynne (61)	44
Please Stay–The Dave Clark Five (68)	19
Waiting For Charlie–Etta James (62)	10
Waiting For Charlie To Come Home–Marlena Shaw (67)	3.3
Mexican Divorce–The Drifters (62)	0.5
Jacques BREL/Rod McKUEN ► 654 (3)	**6838**
Seasons In The Sun–Terry Jacks (74)	6335
If You Go Away–Damita Jo (66)	275
If You Go Away–Terry Jacks (74)	227
Artie DUNN/Al NEVINS/Morty NEVINS/Buck RAM ► 655 (3)	**6830**
Twilight Time–The Platters (58)	6653
Twilight Time–Dick Contino (56)	149
Twilight Time–Andy Williams (62)	28
Carmela GUIDA/Frank GUIDA/Joseph ROYSTER ► 656 (1)	**6827**
If You Wanna Be Happy–Jimmy Soul (63)	6827
Burton CUMMINGS ► 657 (11)	**6822**
Bill ANDERSON ► 658 (21)	**6815**
Keith DIAMOND/Billy OCEAN ► 659 (2)	**6805**
Caribbean Queen (No More Love On The Run)–Billy Ocean (84)	4341
Suddenly–Billy Ocean (85)	2464
Larry WEISS ► 660 (3)	**6791**
Rod McKUEN ► 661 (5)	**6790**
Berry GORDY/Smokey ROBINSON ► 662 (6)	**6784**
Shop Around–The Miracles (Featuring Bill "Smokey" Robinson) (60)	3656
Shop Around–Captain & Tennille (76)	3059
Bad Girl–The Miracles (59)	65
I Need A Change–The Miracles (60)	2.5

Broken Hearted–The Miracles (61)	1.8
Two Wrongs Don't Make A Right–Mary Wells (63)	0.4
Andy GIBB/Barry GIBB ► 663 (2)	**6782**
(Love Is) Thicker Than Water–Andy Gibb (77)	5791
Time Is Time–Andy Gibb (80)	991
William E. JACKSON III/Roy STRAIGIS/George R. WILLIAMS ► 664 (3)	**6778**
So Much In Love–The Tymes (63)	6568
So Much In Love–Timothy B. Schmit (82)	197
Let's Make Love Tonight–Bobby Rydell (63)	12
Ernie MARESCA ► 665 (6)	**6775**
Rick DEES ► 666 (1)	**6774**
Larry HUFF/William LINTON ► 667 (1)	**6758**
Easier Said Than Done–The Essex (63)	6758
Tom BAHLER ► 668 (4)	**6728**
Marilyn McLEOD/Pam SAWYER ► 669 (4)	**6725**
Love Hangover–Diana Ross (76)	5162
You Can't Turn Me Off (In The Middle Of Turning Me On)–High Inergy (77)	1358
Pops, We Love You (A Tribute To Father)–Diana Ross, Marvin Gaye, Smokey Robinson & Stevie Wonder (79)	165
Love Hangover–The 5th Dimension (76)	40
Phil JARRELL/Peter YARROW ► 670 (1)	**6718**
Torn Between Two Lovers–Mary MacGregor (76)	6718
David PAICH/Boz SCAGGS ► 671 (4)	**6718**
Lowdown–Boz Scaggs (76)	4316
Lido Shuffle–Boz Scaggs (77)	1677
It's Over–Boz Scaggs (76)	402
What Can I Say–Boz Scaggs (76)	323
Rick NOWELS/Ellen SHIPLEY ► 672 (4)	**6717**
Heaven Is A Place On Earth–Belinda Carlisle (87)	4006
Circle In The Sand–Belinda Carlisle (88)	1402
Leave A Light On–Belinda Carlisle (89)	1186
Do You Feel Like I Feel–Belinda Carlisle (91)	124
Ed GRAY/Tommy JAMES/Mike VALE ► 673 (1)	**6717**
Crystal Blue Persuasion–Tommy James And The Shondells (69)	6717
David CLAYTON-THOMAS ► 674 (3)	**6711**
Roger BALL/Malcolm DUNCAN/Alan GORRIE/Robbie McINTOSH/Onnie McINTYRE/Hamish STUART ► 675 (2)	**6710**
Pick Up The Pieces–AWB (74)	5059
Cut The Cake–AWB (75)	1651
Vinnie BARRETT/Bobby ELI ► 676 (4)	**6702**
Love Won't Let Me Wait–Major Harris (75)	3713
Sideshow–Blue Magic (74)	2571
Three Ring Circus–Blue Magic (74)	407
Sideshow–Band Of Gold (84)	12
Rafael DE LEON/Richard DEHR/Terry GILKYSON/Frank MILLER/TRADITIONAL ► 677 (6)	**6698**
Marianne–Terry Gilkyson And The Easy Riders (57)	3770
Marianne–The Hilltoppers (57)	2812
Marianne–The Lane Brothers (57)	71
Marianne–Burl Ives (57)	45
Mary Ann–Edmundo Ros & His Orchestra (57)	0.0
Mary Ann–The Talbot Brothers (57)	0.0
Simon Le BON/Nick RHODES/Nigel John TAYLOR ► 678 (5)	**6687**
Notorious–Duran Duran (86)	3404
I Don't Want Your Love–Duran Duran (88)	2410
All She Wants Is–Duran Duran (88)	486
Skin Trade–Duran Duran (87)	308
Meet El Presidente–Duran Duran (87)	78
James BROWN/Alfred James ELLIS ► 679 (4)	**6681**
Cold Sweat - Part 1–James Brown And The Famous Flames (67)	2719
Mother Popcorn (You Got To Have A Mother For Me) Part 1–James Brown (69)	2396
Say It Loud - I'm Black And I'm Proud (Part 1)–James Brown (68)	1559
Soul Pride (Part 1)–James Brown (69)	7.3
Mark KNOPFLER ► 680 (7)	**6645**
Jan BERRY/Brian WILSON ► 681 (1)	**6644**
Surf City–Jan & Dean (63)	6644

Rick ROBERTS ▶ 682 (8)	**6642**
Johnny OTIS ▶ 683 (13)	**6633**
Ed COBB ▶ 684 (7)	**6622**
Les EMMERSON ▶ 685 (9)	**6616**
Peter H. BROWN/Robert RANS ▶ 686 (5)	**6606**
Material Girl—Madonna (85)	3543
Dance With Me—Peter Brown Special Background Vocals: Betty Wright (78)	2150
Do Ya Wanna Get Funky With Me—Peter Brown (77)	660
You Should Do It—Peter Brown (78)	214
Crank It Up (Funk Town) Pt. 1—Peter Brown (79)	39
Claude DeMETRIUS ▶ 687 (5)	**6604**
Joel HIRSCHHORN/Al KASHA ▶ 688 (8)	**6601**
The Morning After—Maureen McGovern (73)	3712
Will You Be Staying After Sunday—The Peppermint Rainbow (68)	1080
Let's Start All Over Again—Ronnie Dove (66)	941
One More Mountain To Climb—Ronnie Dove (67)	408
Your Time Hasn't Come Yet, Baby—Elvis Presley With The Jordanaires (68)	203
Stay And Love Me All Summer—Brian Hyland (69)	147
For A Friend—The Bugaloos (70)	54
We May Never Love Like This Again—Maureen McGovern (75)	54
Eric CARMEN/Sergei RACHMANINOFF ▶ 689 (2)	**6592**
All By Myself—Eric Carmen (75)	5141
Never Gonna Fall In Love Again—Eric Carmen (76)	1451
Dennis MATKOSKY/Michael SEMBELLO ▶ 690 (2)	**6592**
Maniac—Michael Sembello (83)	5111
Mirror, Mirror—Diana Ross (82)	1481
Wayne BRATHWAITE/Barry EASTMOND/ Billy OCEAN ▶ 691 (3)	**6590**
There'll Be Sad Songs (To Make You Cry)—Billy Ocean (86)	4280
Love Zone—Billy Ocean (86)	1312
Love Is Forever—Billy Ocean (86)	997
Ina WOLF/Peter F. WOLF ▶ 692 (3)	**6586**
Sara—Starship (85)	3794
Who's Johnny (Short Circuit Theme)—El DeBarge (86)	2021
No Way Out—Jefferson Starship (84)	771
Mutt LANGE ▶ 693 (5)	**6582**
Kenny NOLAN ▶ 694 (10)	**6565**
Jeff BARRY/Ellie GREENWICH/ Shadow MORTON ▶ 695 (2)	**6554**
Leader Of The Pack—The Shangri-Las (64)	6265
Leader Of The Pack—Twisted Sister (85)	289
Jerry HERST/Jack SHARPE ▶ 696 (3)	**6552**
So Rare—Jimmy Dorsey with Orchestra and Chorus (57)	6543
So Rare—Andy Williams (62)	5.0
So Rare—Mavis Rivers (60)	3.7
Alan Jay LERNER/Frederick LOEWE ▶ 697 (24)	**6544**
On The Street Where You Live—Vic Damone (56)	2704
I Could Have Danced All Night—Sylvia Syms (56)	921
On The Street Where You Live—Andy Williams (64)	563
I Could Have Danced All Night—Rosemary Clooney (56)	544
On The Street Where You Live—Eddie Fisher (56)	487
Almost Like Being In Love—Michael Johnson (78)	477
I've Grown Accustomed To Your Face—Rosemary Clooney (56)	394
Gigi—Vic Damone (58)	216
How To Handle A Woman—Johnny Mathis (60)	85
I Could Have Danced All Night—Ben E. King (63)	38
I've Grown Accustomed To Your Face—Gordon MacRae (56)	37
I Could Have Danced All Night—Dinah Shore (56)	36
With A Little Bit Of Luck—Jo Stafford (56)	28
Get Me To The Church On Time—Julius La Rosa (56)	11
On The Street Where You Live—Lawrence Welk And His Champagne Music (56)	3.3
I've Grown Accustomed To Your Face—Bob Eberly with Enoch Light & His Orchestra (56)	0.0
I've Grown Accustomed To Her Face—Sammy Kaye & His "Swing And Sway" Orchestra (56)	0.0
I've Grown Accustomed To Her Face—Lawrence Welk & His Champagne Music (56)	0.0
I Could Have Danced All Night—Lawrence Welk & His Champagne Music (56)	0.0
I've Grown Accustomed To Her Face—Sid Feller & His Orchestra (56)	0.0
Gigi—The Strollers Featuring Artie Malvin (58)	0.0
Gigi—Billy Eckstine (58)	0.0
Gigi—Bing Crosby (58)	0.0
Gigi—Tony Martin (58)	0.0
Winfred LOVETT ▶ 698 (5)	**6543**
Alan BERGMAN/Marilyn BERGMAN/ Neil DIAMOND ▶ 699 (1)	**6538**
You Don't Bring Me Flowers—Barbra & Neil (78)	6538
Robert JOHN ▶ 700 (1)	**6529**
John BETTIS/Michael CLARK ▶ 701 (4)	**6529**
Slow Hand—Pointer Sisters (81)	4979
Heart Of The Night—Juice Newton (82)	780
The Woman In Me—Donna Summer (82)	667
Wild Again—Starship (88)	102
Chip DAVIS/Bill FRIES ▶ 702 (4)	**6506**
Convoy—C.W. McCall (75)	5960
Wolf Creek Pass—C.W. McCall (75)	215
Old Home Filler-Up An' Keep On-A-Truckin' Cafe—C.W. McCall (74)	198
There Won't Be No Country Music (There Won't Be No Rock 'N' Roll)—C.W. McCall (76)	133
Bobby FREEMAN ▶ 703 (8)	**6505**
Bryan ADAMS/Michael KAMEN/Mutt LANGE ▶ 704 (1)	**6505**
(Everything I Do) I Do It For You—Bryan Adams (91)	6505
Les REED/Geoff STEPHENS ▶ 705 (3)	**6500**
There's A Kind Of Hush—Herman's Hermits (67)	3675
Daughter Of Darkness—Tom Jones (70)	1619
There's A Kind Of Hush (All Over The World)—Carpenters (76)	1207
Janna ALLEN/Daryl HALL ▶ 706 (2)	**6490**
Kiss On My List—Daryl Hall & John Oates (81)	4868
Method Of Modern Love—Daryl Hall & John Oates (84)	1622
Ray BURTON/Helen REDDY ▶ 707 (1)	**6487**
I Am Woman—Helen Reddy (72)	6487
Freddie GARRITY/Mitch MURRAY ▶ 708 (1)	**6476**
I'm Telling You Now—Freddie And The Dreamers (65)	6476
Burt BACHARACH/Mack DAVID/Luther DIXON ▶ 709 (2)	**6471**
Baby It's You—Smith (69)	4062
Baby It's You—The Shirelles (61)	2409
Tom JOHNSTON ▶ 710 (7)	**6469**
Edward HEYMAN/Victor YOUNG ▶ 711 (9)	**6468**
Love Letters—Ketty Lester (62)	2808
When I Fall In Love—The Lettermen (61)	2046
Love Letters—Elvis Presley (66)	886
Blue Star (The "Medic" Theme)—Felicia Sanders (55)	541
When I Fall In Love—Etta Jones (61)	98
When I Fall In Love—Donny Osmond (73)	77
Love Letters—Joni James (56)	10
When I Fall In Love—Natalie Cole (88)	2.4
Blue Star (The "Medic" Theme)—Charlie Applewhite with Victor Young & His Orchestra (55)	0.0
Eddy ARNOLD/Cindy WALKER ▶ 712 (7)	**6467**
You Don't Know Me—Ray Charles (62)	3379
You Don't Know Me—Jerry Vale (56)	2007
You Don't Know Me—Lenny Welch (60)	401
You Don't Know Me—Elvis Presley With The Jordanaires (67)	383
You Don't Know Me—Mickey Gilley (81)	297
You Don't Know Me—Carmen McRae (56)	0.0
You Don't Know Me—Eddy Arnold (56)	0.0
Sylvia DEE/Arthur KENT ▶ 713 (2)	**6450**
The End Of The World—Skeeter Davis (63)	6448
Wait For Me—Rita Pavone (64)	1.8
Kenny YOUNG ▶ 714 (6)	**6449**
Bert KAEMPFERT/Kay TWOMEY/ Ben WEISMAN/Fred WISE ▶ 715 (2)	**6442**
Wooden Heart—Joe Dowell (61)	6334
Wooden Heart—Bobby Vinton (75)	108
Ed TOWNSEND ▶ 716 (12)	**6438**
Jonathan CAIN/Steve PERRY/Neal SCHON ▶ 717 (6)	**6424**
Don't Stop Believin'—Journey (81)	1658
I'll Be Alright Without You—Journey (86)	1156
Be Good To Yourself—Journey (86)	1150
Only The Young—Journey (85)	927
Girl Can't Help It—Journey (86)	779
Still They Ride—Journey (82)	754
Clarence QUICK ▶ 718 (6)	**6419**
Henry MANCINI ▶ 719 (20)	**6413**
Buddy BUIE/J.R. COBB/ Harry MIDDLEBROOKS/Mike SHAPIRO ▶ 720 (2)	**6403**
Spooky—Classics IV (67)	5516
Spooky—Atlanta Rhythm Section (79)	887
Fred FASSERT ▶ 721 (3)	**6403**
General JOHNSON/Barney PERKINS/ Greg PERRY ▶ 722 (1)	**6401**
Want Ads—The Honey Cone (71)	6401
Kal MANN ▶ 723 (7)	**6392**
Bob MARLEY ▶ 724 (5)	**6391**
Tony HESTER ▶ 725 (10)	**6384**
Fred SPIELMAN/Janice TORRE ▶ 726 (2)	**6381**
Paper Roses—Anita Bryant (60)	3707
Paper Roses—Marie Osmond (73)	2674
Johnny CASH ▶ 727 (21)	**6375**
Edgar BATTLE/Eddie DURHAM ▶ 728 (2)	**6369**
Topsy II—Cozy Cole (58)	6164
Topsy I—Cozy Cole (58)	205
Bill DANOFF/Taffy DANOFF/John DENVER ▶ 729 (1)	**6363**
Take Me Home, Country Roads—John Denver (71)	6363
Janis IAN ▶ 730 (6)	**6361**
Walter MURPHY/Ludwig VAN BEETHOVEN ▶ 731 (1)	**6361**
A Fifth Of Beethoven—Walter Murphy & The Big Apple Band (76)	6361
Sylvia FRICKER ▶ 732 (2)	**6359**
Jon ANDERSON/Trevor HORN/ Trevor RABIN/Chris SQUIRE ▶ 733 (1)	**6336**
Owner Of A Lonely Heart—Yes (83)	6336
Kenny LOGGINS ▶ 734 (4)	**6332**
Robert BELL/Ronald BELL/ George M. BROWN/Eumir DEODATO/ Robert MICKENS/Claydes SMITH/ J.T. TAYLOR/Dennis THOMAS/Earl TOON ▶ 735 (2)	**6332**
Celebration—Kool & The Gang (80)	6016
Jones Vs. Jones—Kool & The Gang (81)	316
Irwin LEVINE/Toni WINE ▶ 736 (6)	**6324**
Candida—Dawn (70)	4981
What Are You Doing Sunday—Dawn Featuring Tony Orlando (71)	683
Your Husband - My Wife—Brooklyn Bridge (69)	462
Mr. And Mrs. Untrue—Candi Staton (71)	150
I Think I Love You Again—Brenda Lee (70)	40
Holly Go Softly—Cornerstone (70)	7.3
Martin QUITTENTON/Rod STEWART ▶ 737 (2)	**6316**
Maggie May—Rod Stewart (71)	5183
You Wear It Well—Rod Stewart (72)	1133
Sonny CURTIS ▶ 738 (7)	**6309**
Janna ALLEN/Sara ALLEN/ Daryl HALL/Warren PASH ▶ 739 (1)	**6308**
Private Eyes—Daryl Hall & John Oates (81)	6308
Warren MOORE/Smokey ROBINSON/ Marvin TARPLIN ▶ 740 (6)	**6303**
I'll Be Doggone—Marvin Gaye (65)	2041
The Tracks Of My Tears—Johnny Rivers (67)	1537
The Tracks Of My Tears—The Miracles (65)	1351
Tracks Of My Tears—Linda Ronstadt (75)	724
Take This Heart Of Mine—Marvin Gaye (66)	568
Tracks Of My Tears—Aretha Franklin (69)	81
Terry JACKS ▶ 741 (6)	**6293**
Herbert NEWMAN ▶ 742 (4)	**6290**
Chris ARNOLD/David MARTIN/ Geoff MORROW ▶ 743 (4)	**6289**
Can't Smile Without You—Barry Manilow (78)	5240
Annabella—Hamilton, Joe Frank & Reynolds (71)	460
Can't You Hear The Song?—Wayne Newton (72)	435
It's Up To You Petula—Edison Lighthouse (71)	153
Kim GANNON/Giuseppe SPOTTI ▶ 744 (1)	**6284**
I Want To Be Wanted—Brenda Lee (60)	6284

Billy BUTLER/Bill DOGGETT/ Clifford SCOTT/Shep SHEPHERD ▶ 745 (5)	**6276**
Honky Tonk (Pts. 1 & 2)—Bill Doggett (56)	5649
Honky Tonk - Part 1— The James Brown Soul Train (72)	437
Honky Tonk (Part 2)—Bill Doggett (61)	113
Honky Tonk '65—Lonnie Mack (65)	77
Honky Tonk (pt. 2)— Rusty Bryant & The Carolyn Club Band (56)	0.0
Renaldo BENSON/Al CLEVELAND/ Marvin GAYE ▶ 746 (4)	**6254**
What's Going On—Marvin Gaye (71)	5213
What's Going On—Cyndi Lauper (87)	885
Wholy Holy—Aretha Franklin (72)	151
What's Going On—Quincy Jones (71)	4.6
Jackie DeSHANNON/Sharon SHEELEY ▶ 747 (7)	**6243**
Dum Dum—Brenda Lee (61)	4104
Heart In Hand—Brenda Lee (62)	1107
(He's) The Great Imposter—The Fleetwoods (61)	555
So Deep—Brenda Lee (62)	233
Tears From An Angel—Troy Shondell (61)	128
He's So Heavenly—Brenda Lee (63)	60
Breakaway—Tracey Ullman (84)	56
Marv ROSS ▶ 748 (5)	**6241**
David JENKINS/Cory LERIOS ▶ 749 (4)	**6234**
Whatcha Gonna Do?—Pablo Cruise (77)	2803
Love Will Find A Way—Pablo Cruise (78)	2597
Don't Want To Live Without It—Pablo Cruise (78)	793
Never Had A Love—Pablo Cruise (78)	42
Clint BALLARD Jr./Fred TOBIAS ▶ 750 (8)	**6233**
Good Timin'—Jimmy Jones (60)	4490
Little Bitty Girl—Bobby Rydell (60)	741
One Of Us (Will Weep Tonight)—Patti Page (60)	740
Brigade Of Broken Hearts—Paul Evans (60)	145
Banned In Boston—Merv Griffin (61)	67
Preview Of Paradise—Adam Wade (61)	41
Where Did I Make My Mistake—Clyde McPhatter (59)	4.8
Two Long Years—Dick Caruso (60)	3.8
Barbra STREISAND/Paul WILLIAMS ▶ 751 (1)	**6219**
Love Theme From "A Star Is Born" (Evergreen)— Barbra Streisand (76)	6219
Larry PARKS/Jay TURNBOW ▶ 752 (2)	**6210**
Bread And Butter—The Newbeats (64)	6160
Bread And Butter—Robert John (83)	50
Alice COOPER/Dick WAGNER ▶ 753 (5)	**6207**
I Never Cry—Alice Cooper (76)	1991
You And Me—Alice Cooper (77)	1909
Only Women—Alice Cooper (75)	1899
Welcome To My Nightmare—Alice Cooper (75)	301
Only Women Bleed—Favorite Angel (90)	108
David CLOWNEY/Jim KRIEGSMANN/ Ken WOOD ▶ 754 (2)	**6207**
Happy Organ—Dave "Baby" Cortez (59)	5914
Whistling Organ—Dave "Baby" Cortez (59)	293
Joe JACKSON ▶ 755 (6)	**6167**
Frank DeVOL/Lamont DOZIER/ Brian HOLLAND/Eddie HOLLAND ▶ 756 (1)	**6167**
The Happening—The Supremes (67)	6167
James HOLVAY ▶ 757 (1)	**6157**
Cindy WALKER ▶ 758 (13)	**6136**
Al CAPPS/Mary DEAN ▶ 759 (1)	**6135**
Half-Breed—Cher (73)	6135
Willie CLARKE/Clarence REID ▶ 760 (8)	**6134**
Clean Up Woman—Betty Wright (71)	3048
Rockin' Chair—Gwen McCrae (75)	1685
Nobody But You Babe—Clarence Reid (69)	692
Girls Can't Do What The Guys Do—Betty Wright (68)	428
Secretary—Betty Wright (74)	230
If You Love Me Like You Say You Love Me— Betty Wright (72)	41
Oola La—Betty Wright (75)	8.1
You Got Your Thing On A String—J.P. Robinson (69)	3.1
Joe BROUSSARD/Carrol WASHINGTON/ Ralph WILLIAMS ▶ 761 (2)	**6132**
Mr. Big Stuff—Jean Knight (71)	5978
You Think You're Hot Stuff—Jean Knight (71)	154
Leon RUSSELL ▶ 762 (13)	**6131**
Billy PAGE ▶ 763 (5)	**6128**
Simon CLIMIE/Dennis W. MORGAN ▶ 764 (2)	**6116**
I Knew You Were Waiting (For Me)— Aretha Franklin & George Michael (87)	3691
My Heart Can't Tell You No—Rod Stewart (88)	2425
John GUMMOE ▶ 765 (2)	**6116**
Lee GARRETT/Lula Mae HARDAWAY/ Stevie WONDER/Syreeta WRIGHT ▶ 766 (2)	**6109**
Signed, Sealed, Delivered I'm Yours— Stevie Wonder (70)	5081
Signed, Sealed, Delivered (I'm Yours)— Peter Frampton (77)	1028
Ronald Norman MILLER/Orlando MURDEN ▶ 767 (4)	**6108**
For Once In My Life—Stevie Wonder (68)	5883
For Once In My Life—Jackie Wilson (68)	148
For Once In My Life—Tony Bennett (67)	50
For Once In My Life—Stars On 45 (82)	27
Michael JACKSON/Lionel RICHIE ▶ 768 (1)	**6108**
We Are The World—USA for Africa (85)	6108
Lou ADLER/Johnny RIVERS ▶ 769 (2)	**6094**
Poor Side Of Town—Johnny Rivers (66)	5962
Poor Side Of Town—Al Wilson (68)	132
Rodney CROWELL ▶ 770 (3)	**6093**
Elliot CHIPRUT ▶ 771 (2)	**6092**
Kerry LIVGREN ▶ 772 (6)	**6089**
George DUNING ▶ 773 (4)	**6046**
Arthur Wilton BROWN/Vincent CHEESMAN/ Michael FINESILVER/Peter KER ▶ 774 (1)	**6038**
Fire—The Crazy World Of Arthur Brown (68)	6038
Berry GORDY/Brenda HOLLOWAY/ Patrice HOLLOWAY/Frank Edward WILSON ▶ 775 (3)	**6032**
You've Made Me So Very Happy— Blood, Sweat & Tears (69)	5673
You've Made Me So Very Happy— Brenda Holloway (67)	353
You've Made Me So Very Happy—Lou Rawls (70)	5.5
Bonnie BRAMLETT/Delaney BRAMLETT/ Leon RUSSELL ▶ 776 (2)	**6031**
Superstar—Carpenters (71)	6023
Superstar—Luther Vandross (84)	7.6
Gilbert BÉCAUD/Neil DIAMOND ▶ 777 (2)	**6027**
Love On The Rocks—Neil Diamond (80)	4576
September Morn'—Neil Diamond (79)	1451
Minnie RIPERTON/Richard RUDOLPH ▶ 778 (1)	**6022**
Lovin' You—Minnie Riperton (75)	6022
Fred FOSTER/Kris KRISTOFFERSON ▶ 779 (2)	**6017**
Me And Bobby McGee—Janis Joplin (71)	5615
Me And Bobby McGee—Jerry Lee Lewis (71)	402
Hugh MASEKELA ▶ 780 (3)	**6017**
Amanda McBROOM ▶ 781 (1)	**6013**
Will HUDSON/Irving MILLS ▶ 782 (2)	**6012**
Moonglow—Morris Stoloff Conducting The Columbia Pictures Orchestra (56)	4036
Moonglow—George Cates & His Orchestra (56)	1975
Warren BROOKS ▶ 783 (3)	**6000**
Larry COLLINS/Alex HARVEY ▶ 784 (2)	**5995**
Delta Dawn—Helen Reddy (73)	5954
Delta Dawn—Tanya Tucker (72)	41
Smokey ROBINSON/Marvin TARPLIN ▶ 785 (4)	**5991**
Cruisin'—Smokey Robinson (79)	4437
The Love I Saw In You Was Just A Mirage— Smokey Robinson & The Miracles (67)	740
I Like It Like That—The Miracles (64)	727
It's Her Turn To Live—Smokey Robinson (74)	87
Ralph BAILEY/Rudy CLARK/Ken WILLIAMS ▶ 786 (4)	**5988**
Everybody Plays The Fool—The Main Ingredient (72)	4562
Everybody Plays The Fool—Aaron Neville (91)	1326
Seven Lonely Nights—Four Tops (75)	54
Put On Your Shoes And Walk—Clarence Carter (73)	45
Chrissie HYNDE ▶ 787 (5)	**5988**
Bruce HAWES/Joseph JEFFERSON/ Charles SIMMONS ▶ 788 (4)	**5980**
They Just Can't Stop It the (Games People Play)— The Spinners (75)	4227
Mighty Love - Pt. I—The Spinners (74)	1001
Love Or Leave—The Spinners (75)	438
Sadie—The Spinners (75)	314
Alvertis ISBELL ▶ 789 (1)	**5980**
Borney BERGANTINE/Betty PETERSON ▶ 790 (2)	**5979**
My Happiness—Connie Francis (58)	5960
My Happiness—Fats Domino (57)	19
Neil SEDAKA ▶ 791 (2)	**5979**
Sherman EDWARDS/Ben RALEIGH ▶ 792 (5)	**5969**
Dungaree Doll—Eddie Fisher (55)	2143
Wonderful Wonderful—Johnny Mathis (57)	1803
Wonderful! Wonderful!—The Tymes (63)	1667
Rock Right—Georgia Gibbs (56)	355
Wonderful! Wonderful!— Jan Peerce with Joe Reisman & His Orchestra (57)	0.0
Mark FARNER ▶ 793 (10)	**5964**
Chuck BERRY/Brian WILSON ▶ 794 (4)	**5963**
Surfin' U.S.A.—The Beach Boys (63)	4923
Surfin' USA—Leif Garrett (77)	569
Surfin' USA—The Beach Boys (81)	240
Surfin' U.S.A.—The Beach Boys (74)	230
Otis BLACKWELL/Eddie COOLEY ▶ 795 (8)	**5962**
Fever—Peggy Lee (58)	2762
Fever—The McCoys (65)	2289
Fever—Little Willie John (56)	793
Fever—Rita Coolidge (73)	72
Fever—Earl Grant (57)	38
Fever—Pete Bennett & The Embers (61)	7.2
Fever—Little Willie John (58)	0.0
Fever—Ray Peterson (57)	0.0
Joe PERRY/Steven TYLER ▶ 796 (5)	**5958**
Walk This Way—Aerosmith (76)	1949
Love In An Elevator—Aerosmith (89)	1738
Walk This Way—Run-D.M.C. (86)	1705
Draw The Line—Aerosmith (77)	371
Back In The Saddle—Aerosmith (77)	195
Mike CAMPBELL/Tom PETTY ▶ 797 (6)	**5957**
Stop Draggin' My Heart Around—Stevie Nicks (with Tom Petty And The Heartbreakers) (81)	3309
Refugee—Tom Petty And The Heartbreakers (80)	1188
You Got Lucky—Tom Petty and The Heartbreakers (82)	1111
Here Comes My Girl— Tom Petty And The Heartbreakers (80)	131
Ways To Be Wicked—Lone Justice (85)	115
A Woman In Love (It's Not Me)— Tom Petty and the Heartbreakers (81)	104
Richard LEIGH ▶ 798 (2)	**5953**
Robert BLACKWELL/John MARASCALCO ▶ 799 (8)	**5947**
Good Golly Miss Molly— Mitch Ryder And The Detroit Wheels (66)	2815
Rip It Up—Little Richard (56)	1068
Good Golly Miss Molly—Little Richard (58)	791
Rip It Up—Bill Haley And His Comets (56)	751
Good Golly Miss Molly—The Swinging Blue Jeans (64)	269
Ready Teddy—Little Richard (56)	244
Good Golly Miss Molly— Jive Bunny & The Mastermixers (90)	6.7
Good Golly Miss Molly—The Valiants (58)	0.0
Don DAVIS/Harvey SCALES/Albert VANCE ▶ 800 (1)	**5946**
Disco Lady—Johnnie Taylor (76)	5946
Charlie FOXX/Inez FOXX ▶ 801 (5)	**5940**
Mockingbird—Carly Simon & James Taylor (74)	3070
Mockingbird—Inez Foxx (63)	2534
Hurt By Love—Inez Foxx (64)	312
Mockingbird—Aretha Franklin (67)	20
He's The One You Love—Inez Foxx (63)	3.6
Al CLEVELAND/Smokey ROBINSON ▶ 802 (3)	**5938**
I Second That Emotion— Smokey Robinson & The Miracles (67)	4546
Special Occasion—Smokey Robinson & The Miracles (68)	729
Yester Love—Smokey Robinson & The Miracles (68)	664
Al LEWIS/Vincent ROSE/Larry STOCK ▶ 803 (3)	**5922**
Blueberry Hill—Fats Domino (56)	5648
Blueberry Hill—Louis Armstrong and Gordon Jenkins and His Orchestra And Chorus (56)	265
Slowly But Surely— Gordon Jenkins And His Orchestra and Chorus (54)	8.9

Brian A. ROBERTSON/Mike RUTHERFORD ► 804 (4)	**5914**
The Living Years—Mike + The Mechanics (88)	3672
Silent Running (On Dangerous Ground)—Mike + The Mechanics (85)	1912
Nobody's Perfect—Mike + The Mechanics (88)	169
Seeing Is Believing—Mike + The Mechanics (89)	161
Jackie DeSHANNON/Jimmy HOLIDAY/Randy MYERS ► 805 (5)	**5905**
Put A Little Love In Your Heart—Jackie DeShannon (69)	3577
Put A Little Love In Your Heart—Annie Lennox & Al Green (88)	1389
Love Will Find A Way—Jackie De Shannon (69)	529
Brighton Hill—Jackie Deshannon (70)	207
Bad Water—The Raeletts (71)	202
Bob GOLDSTEIN/David SHIRE ► 806 (1)	**5892**
Washington Square—The Village Stompers (63)	5892
Andy ARMER/Randy BADAZZ ► 807 (2)	**5886**
Rise—Herb Alpert (79)	5495
Rotation—Herb Alpert (79)	391
Gary BRUCE ► 808 (1)	**5879**
Gilbert BÉCAUD/Mann CURTIS/Pierre DELANOË ► 809 (6)	**5878**
Let It Be Me—Betty Everett & Jerry Butler (64)	2995
Let It Be Me—The Everly Brothers (60)	2197
Let It Be Me—Willie Nelson (82)	368
Let It Be Me—Glen Campbell And Bobbie Gentry (69)	224
Let It Be Me—Jill Corey (57)	87
Let It Be Me—The Sweet Inspirations (67)	6.2
Roland ORZABAL/Curt SMITH ► 810 (2)	**5857**
Sowing The Seeds Of Love—Tears For Fears (89)	2998
Head Over Heels—Tears For Fears (85)	2858
Barbara ACKLIN/Eugene RECORD ► 811 (6)	**5847**
Have You Seen Her—The Chi-Lites (71)	5172
Stoned Out Of My Mind—The Chi-Lites (73)	514
There Will Never Be Any Peace (Until God Is Seated At The Conference Table)—The Chi-Lites (74)	94
Toby—The Chi-Lites (75)	48
Have You Seen Her—Band Of Gold (84)	12
Let Me Be The Man My Daddy Was—The Chi-Lites (69)	7.6
Gale GARNETT ► 812 (2)	**5846**
Lou ADLER/Herb ALPERT/Sam COOKE ► 813 (5)	**5834**
Wonderful World—Herman's Hermits (65)	3144
Wonderful World—Sam Cooke (60)	1801
(What A) Wonderful World—Art Garfunkel With James Taylor & Paul Simon (78)	839
Wonderful World—The Ovations (73)	34
(What A) Wonderful World—Johnny Nash (76)	17
Len BARRY/Lamont DOZIER/Brian HOLLAND/Eddie HOLLAND/John MADARA/David WHITE ► 814 (2)	**5831**
1-2-3—Len Barry (65)	5700
One, Two, Three—Ramsey Lewis (67)	131
Deadric MALONE ► 815 (26)	**5830**
Madonna L. CICCONE/Shep PETTIBONE ► 816 (2)	**5827**
Vogue—Madonna (90)	5025
Rescue Me—Madonna (91)	803
Aretha FRANKLIN/Ted WHITE ► 817 (3)	**5814**
(Sweet Sweet Baby) Since You've Been Gone—Aretha Franklin (68)	3603
Think—Aretha Franklin (68)	2204
Since You've Been Gone—Ramsey Lewis (68)	7.3
James Anthony DEAN/John Henry GLOVER ► 818 (2)	**5797**
You Don't Have To Be A Star (To Be In My Show)—Marilyn McCoo & Billy Davis Jr. (76)	5716
I Hope We Get To Love In Time—Marilyn McCoo & Billy Davis Jr. (76)	81
Clive DAVIS/Graham RUSSELL ► 819 (1)	**5778**
All Out Of Love—Air Supply (80)	5778
Jack SIGLER ► 820 (1)	**5778**
Susanna HOFFS/Thomas F. KELLY/Billy STEINBERG ► 821 (3)	**5770**
Eternal Flame—Bangles (89)	3515
In Your Room—Bangles (88)	1791
My Side Of The Bed—Susanna Hoffs (91)	464

Edgar WINTER ► 822 (2)	**5764**
André PREVIN/Dory PREVIN ► 823 (1)	**5758**
(Theme From) Valley Of The Dolls—Dionne Warwick (68)	5758
Ernie ISLEY/Marvin ISLEY/O'Kelly ISLEY/Ronald ISLEY/Rudolph ISLEY/Chris JASPER ► 824 (17)	**5753**
Fight The Power Part 1—The Isley Brothers (75)	2590
For The Love Of You (Part 1 & 2)—The Isley Brothers (75)	696
Don't Say Goodnight (It's Time For Love) (Parts 1 & 2)—The Isley Brothers (80)	378
What It Comes Down To—The Isley Brothers (73)	311
Live It Up Part 1—The Isley Brothers (74)	287
Livin' In The Life—The Isley Brothers (77)	278
Need A Little Taste Of Love—The Doobie Brothers (89)	273
Harvest For The World—The Isley Brothers (76)	239
Who Loves You Better - Part 1—The Isley Brothers (76)	186
Hurry Up And Wait—The Isley Brothers (81)	171
The Pride (Part 1)—The Isley Brothers (77)	104
Take Me To The Next Phase—The Isley Brothers (78)	92
Midnight Sky (Part 1)—The Isley Brothers (75)	81
I Wanna Be With You (Part I)—The Isley Brothers (79)	40
Inside You (Part 1)—The Isley Brothers (81)	14
For The Love Of You—Houston Person (76)	6.4
It's A Disco Night (Rock Don't Stop)—The Isley Brothers (79)	5.8
Allan CLARKE/Roger COOK/Roger GREENAWAY ► 825 (1)	**5749**
Long Cool Woman (In A Black Dress)—The Hollies (72)	5749
Bobby SCOTT ► 826 (5)	**5748**
Carlos ALOMAR/David BOWIE/John LENNON ► 827 (1)	**5730**
Fame—David Bowie (75)	5730
George MICHAEL/Andrew RIDGELEY ► 828 (1)	**5730**
Careless Whisper—Wham! Featuring George Michael (84)	5730
Lee HAYS/Pete SEEGER ► 829 (2)	**5726**
If I Had A Hammer—Trini Lopez (63)	4407
If I Had A Hammer (The Hammer Song)—Peter, Paul & Mary (62)	1319
Florrie PALMER ► 830 (1)	**5721**
Mickie GRANT ► 831 (1)	**5720**
Donna FARGO ► 832 (7)	**5716**
Dick GOSTING ► 833 (5)	**5714**
James W. GLASER/Jimmy PAYNE ► 834 (1)	**5707**
Woman, Woman—The Union Gap Featuring Gary Puckett (67)	5707
David COURTNEY/Leo SAYER ► 835 (4)	**5687**
The Show Must Go On—Three Dog Night (74)	3484
Long Tall Glasses (I Can Dance)—Leo Sayer (75)	2026
Giving It All Away—Roger Daltrey (73)	175
One Man Band—Leo Sayer (75)	1.8
Hal DAVID/Lee POCKRISS ► 836 (2)	**5676**
My Heart Is An Open Book—Carl Dobkins, Jr. (59)	5285
(New In) The Ways Of Love—Tommy Edwards (59)	391
Rory BOURKE/Billy SHERRILL/Norro WILSON ► 837 (1)	**5675**
The Most Beautiful Girl—Charlie Rich (73)	5675
Henry COSBY/Lula Mae HARDAWAY/Sylvia MOY/Stevie WONDER ► 838 (3)	**5659**
I Was Made To Love Her—Stevie Wonder (67)	5544
I Was Made To Love Her—King Curtis & The Kingpins (67)	88
I Was Made To Love Her—Stars On 45 (82)	27
Peter CALLANDER/Geoff STEPHENS ► 839 (1)	**5656**
Daddy Don't You Walk So Fast—Wayne Newton (72)	5656
Leonard LIPTON/Peter YARROW ► 840 (1)	**5656**
Puff (The Magic Dragon)—Peter, Paul & Mary (63)	5656
VANGELIS ► 841 (1)	**5649**
Mark KNOPFLER/STING ► 842 (1)	**5636**
Money For Nothing—Dire Straits (85)	5636
Bob GAUDIO/Sandy LINZER ► 843 (2)	**5631**

Dawn (Go Away)—The 4 Seasons Featuring The "Sound" Of Frankie Valli (64)	5627
Dawn—Gidea Park (81)	3.7
Dolores Vicki SILVERS ► 844 (1)	**5623**
Ann Marie HAMILTON/Danny HAMILTON ► 845 (2)	**5622**
Fallin' In Love—Hamilton, Joe Frank & Reynolds (75)	4594
Winners And Losers—Hamilton, Joe Frank And Reynolds (75)	1028
Glen HARDIN ► 846 (3)	**5616**
Kendall L. HAYES ► 847 (1)	**5609**
Ivan DOROSCHUK ► 848 (4)	**5598**
Bill TRADER ► 849 (2)	**5597**
Vic BRIGGS/Eric BURDON/Barry JENKINS/Danny McCULLOCH/John WEIDER ► 850 (5)	**5595**
San Franciscan Nights—Eric Burdon And The Animals (67)	1697
Sky Pilot (Part One)—Eric Burdon & The Animals (68)	1609
When I Was Young—Eric Burdon & The Animals (67)	1085
Monterey—Eric Burdon & The Animals (67)	1017
Anything—Eric Burdon & The Animals (68)	187
Pino DONAGGIO/Simon NAPIER-BELL/Vicki WICKHAM ► 851 (3)	**5587**
You Don't Have To Say You Love Me—Dusty Springfield (66)	4119
You Don't Have To Say You Love Me—Elvis Presley (70)	1432
You Don't Have To Say You Love Me—The Four Sonics (68)	36
Mark BARKAN/Ben RALEIGH ► 852 (5)	**5584**
She's A Fool—Lesley Gore (63)	3745
That's The Way Boys Are—Lesley Gore (64)	1325
I Don't Wanna Be A Loser—Lesley Gore (64)	327
Bring A Little Sunshine (To My Heart)—Vic Dana (65)	185
Just Let Me Cry—Lesley Gore (63)	3.2
Franco MIGLIACCI/Domenico MODUGNO/Mitchell PARISH ► 853 (6)	**5576**
Volare—Bobby Rydell (60)	3928
Volare (Nel Blu Dipinto Di Blu)—Dean Martin (58)	1266
Volare—Al Martino (75)	365
Volare (Nel Blu Di Pinto Di Blu)—The McGuire Sisters (58)	17
Volare (Nel Blu Dipinto Di Blu)—Jesse Belvin (58)	0.0
Volare (Nel Blu, Dipinto Di Blu)—Alan Dale (58)	0.0
Harry GIOSASI/Artie ZWIRN ► 854 (3)	**5570**
Sorry (I Ran All The Way Home)—The Impalas (59)	4846
(It's Been A Long Time) Pretty Baby—Gino & Gina (58)	680
Oh What A Fool—The Impalas (59)	43
Carl DOUGLAS ► 855 (1)	**5556**
Mark LEONARD/Chas SANDFORD/John WAITE ► 856 (1)	**5545**
Missing You—John Waite (84)	5545
Hank DeVITO ► 857 (1)	**5541**
Vini PONCIA/Leo SAYER ► 858 (1)	**5541**
You Make Me Feel Like Dancing—Leo Sayer (76)	5541
Jerry LEIBER/Doc POMUS/Mike STOLLER ► 859 (4)	**5527**
She's Not You—Elvis Presley With The Jordanaires (62)	3394
Young Blood—The Coasters (57)	1268
Young Blood—Bad Company (76)	795
Young Blood—Bruce Willis (87)	71
Linda CREED/Michael MASSER ► 860 (3)	**5526**
Greatest Love Of All—Whitney Houston (86)	4409
The Greatest Love Of All—George Benson (77)	660
Hold Me—Teddy Pendergrass (84)	457
Hal DAVID/Sherman EDWARDS ► 861 (8)	**5526**
Broken Hearted Melody—Sarah Vaughan (59)	2677
Johnny Get Angry—Joanie Sommers (62)	1932
Outside My Window—The Fleetwoods (60)	556
You'll Answer To Me—Patti Page (61)	226
Home Is Where The Heart Is—Elvis Presley with the Jordanaires (62)	62
A Whistling Tune—Elvis Presley with the Jordanaires (62)	62
When The Boys Get Together—Joanie Sommers (62)	5.7
Don't Let It Happen To Us—The Shirelles (63)	3.3

Bernie BAUM/Bill GIANT/Florence KAYE ▶ 862 (4)	**5525**
(You're the) Devil In Disguise—Elvis Presley With The Jordanaires (63)	3964
That's Old Fashioned (That's The Way Love Should Be)—The Everly Brothers (62)	1204
Young And In Love—Chris Crosby (64)	357
Today, Tomorrow And Forever—Elvis Presley (64)	1.1
Stephen GEYER/Mike POST ▶ 863 (1)	**5521**
The Theme From "The Greatest American Hero" (Believe It Or Not)—Joey Scarbury (81)	5521
Johanna HALL/John HALL ▶ 864 (5)	**5510**
Dance With Me—Orleans (75)	2736
Still The One—Orleans (76)	2374
Reach—Orleans (77)	298
What You Do To Me—Carl Wilson (83)	92
Ms. Grace—The Tymes (74)	8.6
John HOLT/Duke REID ▶ 865 (1)	**5506**
The Tide Is High—Blondie (80)	5506
Arthur ALTMAN/Manos HADJIDAKIS ▶ 866 (1)	**5503**
All Alone Am I—Brenda Lee (62)	5503
Charles BURCHILL/Jim KERR/ Michael MacNEIL ▶ 867 (3)	**5492**
Alive And Kicking—Simple Minds (85)	3897
Sanctify Yourself—Simple Minds (86)	1088
All The Things She Said—Simple Minds (86)	507
Arthur CONLEY/Sam COOKE/Otis REDDING ▶ 868 (2)	**5475**
Sweet Soul Music—Arthur Conley (67)	5467
Sweet Soul Music—The Magnificent Men (67)	7.6
Bruce HORNSBY ▶ 869 (4)	**5465**
Julius DIXON/Beverly ROSS ▶ 870 (4)	**5456**
Lollipop—The Chordettes (58)	3626
Dim, Dim The Lights (I Want Some Atmosphere)—Bill Haley And His Comets (54)	1605
Lollipop—Ronald And Ruby (58)	224
Dim, Dim The Lights (I Want Some Atmosphere)—The Four Tophatters (54)	0.0
Dave CLARK/Lenny DAVIDSON ▶ 871 (5)	**5454**
Catch Us If You Can—The Dave Clark Five (65)	2966
At The Scene—The Dave Clark Five (66)	1146
Everybody Knows (I Still Love You)—The Dave Clark Five (64)	926
I've Got To Have A Reason—The Dave Clark Five (67)	311
Red And Blue—The Dave Clark Five (67)	106
Luther DIXON/Allyson KHENT ▶ 872 (3)	**5453**
Sixteen Candles—Crests (58)	5437
Lovin' Up A Storm—Jerry Lee Lewis (59)	12
16 Candles—Fred Parris & The Five Satins (82)	4.8
Jack DANIELS/John Edward MOORE ▶ 873 (5)	**5453**
Turn Back The Hands Of Time—Tyrone Davis (70)	4386
I'll Be Right Here—Tyrone Davis (70)	540
(I Can Feel Those Vibrations) This Love Is Real—Jackie Wilson (70)	323
One-Way Ticket—Tyrone Davis (71)	167
You Keep Me Holding On—Tyrone Davis (71)	36
Mike ANTHONY/Paul KAUFMAN ▶ 874 (1)	**5448**
Poetry In Motion—Johnny Tillotson (60)	5448
John ROSTILL ▶ 875 (2)	**5445**
Sharon SHEELEY ▶ 876 (1)	**5441**
Ollie BLANCHARD/Johnnie MALONE ▶ 877 (3)	**5434**
Please Love Me Forever—Bobby Vinton (67)	3277
Please Love Me Forever—Cathy Jean And The Roommates (61)	2128
Please Love Me Forever—Tommy Edwards (58)	29
Ian DEVANEY/Andy MORRIS/Lisa STANSFIELD ▶ 878 (4)	**5433**
All Around The World—Lisa Stansfield (90)	3201
You Can't Deny It—Lisa Stansfield (90)	830
Change—Lisa Stansfield (91)	756
This Is The Right Time—Lisa Stansfield (90)	646
Bobby HEBB ▶ 879 (1)	**5422**
Mary Hadler GILBERT/V.C. GILBERT ▶ 880 (2)	**5421**
Shifting Whispering Sands—Billy Vaughn and His Orchestra (55)	2970
Shifting Whispering Sands—Rusty Draper (55)	2452
Barry DE VORZON ▶ 881 (3)	**5415**
Michael BOLTON/Doug JAMES ▶ 882 (2)	**5408**
How Am I Supposed To Live Without You—Michael Bolton (89)	4042
How Am I Supposed To Live Without You—Laura Branigan (83)	1366
Jesse BELVIN/Gaynel HODGE/ Curtis Edward WILLIAMS ▶ 883 (9)	**5403**
Earth Angel (Will You Be Mine)—The Penguins (54)	2284
Earth Angel (Will You Be Mine)—The Crew-Cuts (55)	1777
Earth Angel—New Edition (86)	545
Earth Angel (Will You Be Mine)—The Vogues (69)	486
Earth Angel—Johnny Tillotson (60)	230
Earth Angel (Will You Be Mine)—Gloria Mann (55)	74
Earth Angel—Fred Parris & The Five Satins (82)	4.8
Earth Angel—The Cleftones (61)	2.3
Earth Angel—Les Baxter & The Bombers (54)	0.0
Willis Alan RAMSEY ▶ 884 (3)	**5400**
Wally HOLMES ▶ 885 (4)	**5393**
Tommy SHAW ▶ 886 (7)	**5393**
John BARRY/Don BLACK ▶ 887 (4)	**5392**
Born Free—Roger Williams (66)	3587
Thunderball—Tom Jones (65)	923
Born Free—The Hesitations (68)	597
Diamonds Are Forever—Shirley Bassey (72)	284
Bryan ABRAMS/Mark CALDERON/ Isaac HAYES/Howard THOMPSON/ Kevin THORNTON/Sam WATTERS ▶ 888 (1)	**5388**
All 4 Love—Color Me Badd (91)	5388
Al GREEN ▶ 889 (3)	**5384**
Ben E. KING/Jerry LEIBER/ Lover PATTERSON/Mike STOLLER/ George TREADWELL ▶ 890 (2)	**5373**
There Goes My Baby—The Drifters (59)	4700
There Goes My Baby—Donna Summer (84)	674
Cornelius GRANT/Eddie HOLLAND/ Norman WHITFIELD ▶ 891 (4)	**5372**
(I Know) I'm Losing You—Rare Earth (70)	2495
(I Know) I'm Losing You—The Temptations (66)	1880
(I Know) I'm Losing You—Rod Stewart With Faces (71)	942
(I Know) I'm Losing You—Uptown (86)	55
J. Vincent EDWARDS/Pierre TUBBS ▶ 892 (2)	**5368**
Right Back Where We Started From—Maxine Nightingale (76)	5350
Right Back Where We Started From—Sinitta (89)	18
Vincent YOUMANS ▶ 893 (3)	**5364**
Barbara LEWIS ▶ 894 (4)	**5364**
Peter ALLEN/Jeff BARRY ▶ 895 (2)	**5363**
I Honestly Love You—Olivia Newton-John (74)	5140
I Honestly Love You—Olivia Newton-John (77)	223
Roger BOWLING/Billy Edd WHEELER ▶ 896 (1)	**5361**
Coward Of The County—Kenny Rogers (79)	5361
King FLOYD ▶ 897 (4)	**5354**
Warren MOORE/Smokey ROBINSON ▶ 898 (6)	**5351**
Ooh Baby Baby—Linda Ronstadt (78)	1786
Ooo Baby Baby—The Miracles (65)	1254
Since I Lost My Baby—The Temptations (65)	1058
It's Growing—The Temptations (65)	994
Oooh, Baby Baby—The Five Stairsteps (67)	252
Ooh Baby Baby—The Magnificent Men (67)	7.6
Andy FRASER/Paul RODGERS ▶ 899 (5)	**5343**
All Right Now—Free (70)	4192
Fire And Water—Wilson Pickett (71)	960
All Right Now—Rod Stewart (84)	89
All Right Now—Pepsi & Shirlie (88)	85
All Right Now—Lea Roberts (75)	18
Carlos RIGUAL/Sunny SKYLAR ▶ 900 (2)	**5339**
Love Me With All Your Heart (Cuando Caliente El Sol)—Ray Charles Singers (64)	4884
Love Me With All Of Your Heart—The Bachelors (66)	455
Artie GLENN ▶ 901 (4)	**5332**
Willie DIXON ▶ 902 (11)	**5324**
Kenny LOGGINS/Jim MESSINA ▶ 903 (4)	**5322**
Your Mama Don't Dance—Kenny Loggins With Jim Messina (72)	3088
Your Mama Don't Dance—Poison (89)	1055
My Music—Loggins & Messina (73)	1015
Watching The River Run—Loggins & Messina (74)	164
Buddy HOLLY/Norman PETTY ▶ 904 (11)	**5315**
It's So Easy—Linda Ronstadt (77)	1953
True Love Ways—Peter And Gordon (65)	1390
Maybe Baby—Buddy Holly / The Crickets (58)	997
Not Fade Away—The Rolling Stones (64)	417
Everyday—James Taylor (85)	250
True Love Ways—Mickey Gilley (80)	74
Everyday—John Denver (72)	64
Not Fade Away—Tanya Tucker (78)	54
Everyday—Buddy Holly / The Crickets (57)	53
Not Fade Away—Eric Hine (81)	40
Listen To Me—Buddy Holly / The Crickets (58)	23
Earl BEAL/Ray EDWARDS/ William HORTON/Richard LEWIS ▶ 905 (3)	**5311**
Get A Job—The Silhouettes (58)	5224
Get A Job—Nino & the Ebb Tides (61)	88
Get A Job—The Mills Brothers (58)	0.0
Louis F. BUSH/Allan SHERMAN ▶ 906 (2)	**5308**
Hello Mudduh, Hello Fadduh! (A Letter From Camp)—Allan Sherman (63)	5106
Hello Mudduh, Hello Fadduh! (A Letter From Camp) (New 1964 Version)—Allan Sherman (64)	202
Brenda RICHIE/Lionel RICHIE ▶ 907 (2)	**5305**
You Are—Lionel Richie (83)	3893
Penny Lover—Lionel Richie (84)	1411
Daniel MOORE ▶ 908 (4)	**5291**
Eddie CURTIS/Ahmet ERTEGUN/Steve MILLER ▶ 909 (1)	**5290**
The Joker—Steve Miller Band (73)	5290
Stanley ADAMS/Maria GREVER ▶ 910 (4)	**5286**
What A Diff'rence A Day Makes—Dinah Washington (59)	4151
What A Diff'rence A Day Makes—Esther Phillips (75)	1007
What A Diff'rence A Day Made—Jerry Martin (55)	128
What A Diff'rence A Day Made—Vaughn Monroe & His Orchestra (55)	0.0
Aaron SCHROEDER/Sid WYCHE ▶ 911 (1)	**5285**
Big Hunk O' Love—Elvis Presley (59)	5285
Liam STERNBERG ▶ 912 (1)	**5283**
Michael James EDWARDS ▶ 913 (2)	**5282**
David GRAHAME/Eric MARTIN ▶ 914 (1)	**5278**
To Be With You—Mr. Big (91)	5278
Bobby HART/Teddy RANDAZZO/ Bobby WEINSTEIN ▶ 915 (4)	**5276**
Hurt So Bad—The Lettermen (69)	2180
Hurt So Bad—Linda Ronstadt (80)	1686
Hurt So Bad—Little Anthony And The Imperials (65)	1409
Hurt So Bad—Jackie DeShannon (70)	1.0
Ben WEISMAN/Fred WISE ▶ 916 (12)	**5275**
Lonely Blue Boy—Conway Twitty (59)	2068
Follow That Dream—Elvis Presley (62)	1103
Fame And Fortune—Elvis Presley With The Jordanaires (60)	751
The Bridge Of Love—Joe Dowell (61)	386
Don't Ask Me Why—Elvis Presley (58)	373
It Feels So Right—Elvis Presley With The Jordanaires (65)	216
As Long As I Have You—Elvis Presley with the Jordanaires (58)	192
Riding The Rainbow—Elvis Presley with the Jordanaires (62)	62
This Is Living—Elvis Presley with the Jordanaires (62)	62
A Kiss For Christmas (O Tannenbaum)—Joe Dowell (61)	32
Crawfish—Elvis Presley with the Jordanaires (58)	24
Pocketful Of Rainbows—Deane Hawley (61)	6.4
Billy GRIFFIN/Warren MOORE ▶ 917 (1)	**5274**
Love Machine (Part 1)—The Miracles (75)	5274
Tom CRAIN/Charlie DANIELS/ Joel DIGREGORIO/Fred EDWARDS/ Charles HAYWARD/James W. MARSHALL ▶ 918 (3)	**5272**
The Devil Went Down To Georgia—Charlie Daniels Band (79)	3303
In America—Charlie Daniels Band (80)	1335
The Legend Of Wooley Swamp—Charlie Daniels Band (80)	633

Jerry ALLISON/Sonny CURTIS ▶ 919 (2)	**5272**
More Than I Can Say—Leo Sayer (80)	5089
More Than I Can Say—Bobby Vee (61)	183
Michael NESMITH ▶ 920 (12)	**5261**
Geoffrey DOWNES/John WETTON ▶ 921 (4)	**5259**
Heat Of The Moment—Asia (82)	2585
Don't Cry—Asia (83)	1413
Only Time Will Tell—Asia (82)	916
Go—Asia (85)	345
Bob MUSEL/Jack TAYLOR ▶ 922 (5)	**5258**
Band Of Gold—Don Cherry (55)	3488
Band Of Gold—Kit Carson (55)	1174
Band Of Gold—Mel Carter (66)	521
Band Of Gold—The Roommates (61)	70
Band Of Gold—The Hi-Fi Four (55)	4.8
Ike TURNER ▶ 923 (11)	**5252**
Bunny LEWIS/MANTOVANI ▶ 924 (2)	**5241**
Cara, Mia—Jay & The Americans (65)	3711
Cara Mia—David Whitfield with Mantovani And His Orchestra (54)	1531
Martin L. GORE ▶ 925 (11)	**5240**
Joey LEVINE/Artie RESNICK ▶ 926 (4)	**5227**
Yummy Yummy Yummy—Ohio Express (68)	4175
Quick Joey Small (Run Joey Run)—Kasenetz-Katz Singing Orchestral Circus (68)	1017
All's Quiet On West 23rd—Julie Budd (68)	31
That's The Tune—The Vogues (66)	2.9
Kevin ADAMS/Jimmy PATERSON/ Kevin ROWLAND ▶ 927 (1)	**5225**
Come On Eileen—Dexys Midnight Runners (83)	5225
Sammy HAGAR ▶ 928 (9)	**5224**
Jerry SAMUELS ▶ 929 (4)	**5217**
John BETTIS/Jon LIND ▶ 930 (1)	**5216**
Crazy For You—Madonna (85)	5216
Roland ORZABAL/Ian STANLEY ▶ 931 (2)	**5216**
Shout—Tears For Fears (85)	4675
Mothers Talk—Tears For Fears (86)	541
George HARRISON/Ringo STARR ▶ 932 (1)	**5208**
Photograph—Ringo Starr (73)	5208
Kennedy GORDY ▶ 933 (2)	**5207**
Leon PAYNE ▶ 934 (5)	**5207**
Dan HARTMAN ▶ 935 (9)	**5201**
Gloria SHAYNE ▶ 936 (1)	**5198**
Buddy BUIE/Dean DAUGHTRY/Robert NIX ▶ 937 (4)	**5186**
So In To You—Atlanta Rhythm Section (77)	2327
Imaginary Lover—Atlanta Rhythm Section (78)	1818
I'm Not Gonna Let It Bother Me Tonight—Atlanta Rhythm Section (78)	932
Dog Days—Atlanta Rhythm Section (77)	109
Robert HAZARD ▶ 938 (2)	**5184**
Tony MACAULAY/John MacLEOD ▶ 939 (8)	**5177**
Baby, Now That I've Found You—The Foundations (67)	2250
Baby Take Me In Your Arms—Jefferson (69)	1242
In The Bad, Bad Old Days (Before You Loved Me)—The Foundations (69)	510
That Same Old Feeling—Pickettywitch (70)	493
That Same Old Feeling—The Fortunes (70)	298
Back On My Feet Again—The Foundations (68)	278
My Little Chickadee—The Foundations (69)	79
Let The Heartaches Begin—Long John Baldry (68)	28
Albert HAMMOND/Carole Bayer SAGER ▶ 940 (1)	**5176**
When I Need You—Leo Sayer (77)	5176
Jerry CAPEHART/Eddie COCHRAN ▶ 941 (7)	**5176**
Summertime Blues—Blue Cheer (68)	2126
Summertime Blues—Eddie Cochran (58)	1493
Summertime Blues—The Who (70)	976
C'mon Everybody—Eddie Cochran (58)	493
C'mon Everybody—Jive Bunny And The Mastermixers (89)	80
Summertime Blues—Jive Bunny & The Mastermixers (90)	6.7
Teenage Heaven—Eddie Cochran (59)	0.8
Elliot WILLENSKY ▶ 942 (2)	**5172**
Johnny BRISTOL/Vernon BULLOCK/ Harvey FUQUA ▶ 943 (2)	**5172**

What Does It Take (To Win Your Love)—Jr. Walker & The All Stars (69)	3648
If I Could Build My Whole World Around You—Marvin Gaye & Tammi Terrell (67)	1524
Freddy FRIDAY/Marilyn SCHACK/ Allen TOUSSAINT/Alvin TYLER ▶ 944 (2)	**5169**
Java—Al (He's The King) Hirt Trumpet With Chorus And Orchestra (64)	4600
Java—Floyd Cramer (62)	570
R. Dean TAYLOR ▶ 945 (4)	**5161**
Larry EVOY ▶ 946 (3)	**5159**
Mark LINDSAY ▶ 947 (6)	**5153**
Joe GREENE/Billy PRESTON ▶ 948 (3)	**5148**
Outa-Space—Billy Preston (72)	4684
You're So Unique—Billy Preston (73)	405
I Wrote A Simple Song—Billy Preston (72)	59
Nick VAN EEDE ▶ 949 (3)	**5137**
Robert BELL/Ronald BELL/ James BONNEFORD/ George M. BROWN/Claydes SMITH/ J.T. TAYLOR/Curtis Fitzgerald WILLIAMS ▶ 950 (2)	**5134**
Cherish—Kool & The Gang (85)	3699
Misled—Kool & The Gang (84)	1436
Roy ORBISON ▶ 951 (5)	**5134**
Danny DIMINNO/Carmen LOMBARDO ▶ 952 (1)	**5132**
Return To Me—Dean Martin (58)	5132
Ennio MORRICONE ▶ 953 (2)	**5125**
Walter NIMS ▶ 954 (1)	**5122**
Tony MACAULAY/Barry MASON ▶ 955 (4)	**5118**
Love Grows (Where My Rosemary Goes)—Edison Lighthouse (70)	4513
My Marie—Engelbert Humperdinck (70)	564
Melanie Makes Me Smile—Tony Burrows (70)	31
Melanie Makes Me Smile—Terry Williams (72)	10
Harry VANDA/George YOUNG ▶ 956 (10)	**5113**
Love Is In The Air—John Paul Young (78)	1865
Friday On My Mind—The Easybeats (67)	1495
Bring A Little Lovin'—Los Bravos (68)	451
Good Times—INXS And Jimmy Barnes (87)	366
Yesterday's Hero—John Paul Young (75)	329
Yesterday's Hero—Bay City Rollers (76)	265
Lost In Your Love—John Paul Young (78)	156
St. Louis—The Easybeats (69)	90
Hey, St. Peter—Flash & The Pan (79)	87
Heaven And Hell—The Easybeats (67)	10
Ronald DUNBAR/General JOHNSON ▶ 957 (1)	**5109**
Patches—Clarence Carter (70)	5109
Fats DOMINO ▶ 958 (9)	**5097**
Steve CROPPER/Al JACKSON/ Booker T. JONES Jr./Lewis STEINBERG ▶ 959 (6)	**5092**
Green Onions—Booker T. & The M.G.'s (62)	4924
Jellybread—Booker T. & The MGs (62)	74
Chinese Checkers—Booker T. & The MG's (63)	63
Green Onions—Dick Hyman (69)	23
Soul Dressing—Booker T. & The MG's (64)	4.4
Mo-Onions—Booker T. & The MG's (64)	3.7
Hank BALLARD/Etta JAMES/Johnny OTIS ▶ 960 (6)	**5089**
Dance With Me Henry (Wallflower)—Georgia Gibbs (55)	5087
Dance With Me Georgie—The Bobbettes (60)	2.5
The Italian Wallflower (I'll Dance With Her Henry)—Lou Monte (55)	0.0
The Wallflower (Dance With Me Henry)—Lee Winters (55)	0.0
The Wallflower—Etta James & The Peaches (55)	0.0
The Wallflower—The Three Rays (55)	0.0
Mike CHAPMAN/Holly KNIGHT ▶ 961 (6)	**5079**
Love Is A Battlefield—Pat Benatar (83)	3131
The Best—Tina Turner (89)	940
Hanging On A Heart Attack—Device (86)	505
Hands Tied—Scandal Featuring Patty Smyth (84)	338
Pleasure And Pain—Divinyls (86)	84
Who Says—Device (86)	81

Paul SIMON/Bruce WOODLEY ▶ 962 (2)	**5078**
Red Rubber Ball—The Cyrkle (66)	4909
I Wish You Could Be Here—The Cyrkle (67)	169
Lee DAVID/Billy ROSE ▶ 963 (4)	**5074**
Tonight You Belong To Me—Patience and Prudence (56)	3814
Tonight You Belong To Me—Lawrence Welk And His Sparkling Strings (56)	1097
Tonight You Belong To Me—Karen Chandler & Jimmy Wakely (56)	162
Tonight You Belong To Me—The Tracey Twins (56)	0.0
Roger CHRISTIAN/Brian WILSON ▶ 964 (7)	**5062**
Don't Worry Baby—B.J. Thomas (77)	1157
Shut Down—The Beach Boys (63)	1051
Little Deuce Coupe—The Beach Boys (63)	1016
Don't Worry Baby—The Beach Boys (64)	903
Sidewalk Surfin'—Jan & Dean (64)	605
Shut Down—The Beach Boys (81)	240
Don't Worry Baby—The Tokens (70)	89
Carole KING/David PALMER ▶ 965 (2)	**5062**
Jazzman—Carole King (74)	4084
Nightingale—Carole King (74)	978
James ATKIN/Derry BROWNSON/ Mark DECLOEDT/Ian DENCH/Zac FOLEY ▶ 966 (2)	**5049**
Unbelievable—EMF (91)	4783
Lies—EMF (91)	266
Russell HILDRETH/Timmy TORRES ▶ 967 (1)	**5043**
One More Try—Timmy T (90)	5043
Peter GREEN ▶ 968 (4)	**5037**
Tim RICE/Andrew Lloyd WEBBER ▶ 969 (12)	**5020**
Superstar—Murray Head With The Trinidad Singers (69)	1860
I Don't Know How To Love Him—Helen Reddy (71)	1613
I Don't Know How To Love Him—Yvonne Elliman (71)	783
Superstar - Jesus Christ Superstar—Murray Head (71)	656
Don't Cry For Me Argentina—Festival (80)	63
Everything's Alright—Yvonne Elliman (71)	28
Everything's Alright—The Assembled Multitude (71)	4.1
Simon Zealotes—The Assembled Multitude (71)	4.1
The Temple—The Assembled Multitude (71)	4.1
Superstar—The Assembled Multitude (71)	4.1
I Don't Know How To Love Him—The Kimberlys (71)	0.4
Everything's Alright—The Kimberlys (71)	0.4
Will JENNINGS/Jack NITZSCHE/ Buffy SAINTE-MARIE ▶ 970 (1)	**5012**
Up Where We Belong—Joe Cocker and Jennifer Warnes (82)	5012
Vivian KEITH/Ben PETERS ▶ 971 (1)	**5010**
Before The Next Teardrop Falls—Freddy Fender (75)	5010
Dave CLARK ▶ 972 (2)	**5004**
Leon HUFF/Gene McFADDEN/ John WHITEHEAD ▶ 973 (1)	**4999**
Back Stabbers—The O'Jays (72)	4999
Philip BAILEY/Lorenzo DUNN/ Maurice WHITE ▶ 974 (1)	**4991**
Shining Star—Earth, Wind & Fire (75)	4991
Tom SNOW/Cynthia WEIL ▶ 975 (3)	**4990**
He's So Shy—Pointer Sisters (80)	4023
Somewhere Down The Road—Barry Manilow (81)	590
So Far So Good—Sheena Easton (86)	377
Mikhail MATUSOVSKIJ/ Vasilj SOLOVEV-SEDOJ ▶ 976 (2)	**4981**
Midnight In Moscow—Kenny Ball And His Jazzmen (62)	4981
Midnight In Moscow—Jan Burgens & His New Orleans Syncopators (62)	0.0
Frank MILLS ▶ 977 (3)	**4978**
Warren MOORE/Smokey ROBINSON/ Robert ROGERS/Marvin TARPLIN ▶ 978 (6)	**4975**
Ain't That Peculiar—Marvin Gaye (65)	2266
Going To A Go-Go—The Miracles (65)	1646
Going To A Go-Go—The Rolling Stones (82)	594
Ain't That Peculiar—Diamond Reo (74)	361
Going to a Go-Go—Shalamar (77)	80
Ain't That Peculiar—Fanny (72)	29

Eugene PEARSON ► 979 (1)	**4973**
Ferdi BOLLAND/Rob BOLLAND/FALCO ► 980 (2)	**4973**
Rock Me Amadeus—Falco (86)	4222
Vienna Calling—Falco (86)	751
Chris HUGHES/Roland ORZABAL/ Ian STANLEY ► 981 (1)	**4971**
Everybody Wants To Rule The World—Tears For Fears (85)	4971
Patrick SIMMONS ► 982 (3)	**4969**
Dennis LINDE ► 983 (5)	**4965**
Bob MONTGOMERY ► 984 (4)	**4959**
Fred DARIAN/Al DeLORY/Joseph VAN WINKLE ► 985 (4)	**4951**
Mr. Custer—Larry Verne (60)	4906
Johnny Willow—Fred Darian (61)	41
Roll Call Company J—The Balladeers (60)	3.8
Battle Of Gettysburg—Fred Darian (61)	0.5
Richard STEPHENS/Jimmy TORRES ► 986 (2)	**4951**
Wheels—The String-A-Longs (60)	4346
Wheels—Billy Vaughn And His Orchestra (61)	605
Smokey ROBINSON/Robert ROGERS ► 987 (5)	**4950**
The Way You Do The Things You Do—UB40 (90)	1892
The Way You Do The Things You Do—The Temptations (64)	1796
The Way You Do The Things You Do—Rita Coolidge (78)	710
The Way You Do The Things You Do—Daryl Hall & John Oates Featuring David Ruffin & Eddie Kendricks (85)	285
First I Look At The Purse—The Contours (65)	267
Rick NIELSEN ► 988 (7)	**4949**
Barbara GEORGE ► 989 (3)	**4943**
Giancarlo BIGAZZI/Umberto TOZZI/ Trevor VEITCH ► 990 (1)	**4941**
Gloria—Laura Branigan (82)	4941
Woodrow Buddy JOHNSON ► 991 (8)	**4934**
Bob CALILLI/Michael David LOOKOFSKY/ Tony SANSONE ► 992 (3)	**4934**
Walk Away Renee—The Left Banke (66)	3456
Walk Away Renee—Four Tops (68)	1445
Walk Away Renee—Southside Johnny & The Jukes (86)	32
Johnny LEHMANN/Herbert L. MILLER ► 993 (1)	**4933**
Night—Jackie Wilson (60)	4933
Gene ADKINSON/Wade BUFF ► 994 (8)	**4927**
It's Almost Tomorrow—The Dream Weavers (55)	2855
It's Almost Tomorrow—Jo Stafford (55)	1089
It's Almost Tomorrow—Snooky Lanson (55)	494
It's Almost Tomorrow—David Carroll And His Orchestra (55)	371
It's Almost Tomorrow—Jimmy Velvet (65)	117
You're Mine—The Dream Weavers (56)	0.3
It's Almost Tomorrow—Ray Anthony & His Orchestra with Don Durant (56)	0.0
It's Almost Tomorrow—Lawrence Welk & His Champagne Music (55)	0.0
Chet POWERS ► 995 (5)	**4922**
Eugene RECORD/William Nelson SANDERS ► 996 (2)	**4919**
Soulful Strut—Young-Holt Unlimited (68)	4727
Am I The Same Girl—Barbara Acklin (69)	192
Lor CRANE/Bernice ROSS ► 997 (4)	**4908**
Don't Just Stand There—Patty Duke (65)	2466
White On White—Danny Williams (64)	1727
Say Something Funny—Patty Duke (65)	659
A Little Toy Balloon—Danny Williams (64)	56
Ronald Norman MILLER/Bryan WELLS ► 998 (4)	**4908**
Yester-Me, Yester-You, Yesterday—Stevie Wonder (69)	2495
A Place In The Sun—Stevie Wonder (66)	1928
Travlin' Man—Stevie Wonder (67)	458
Yester-Me, Yester-You, Yesterday—Stars On 45 (82)	27
Dave BARTHOLOMEW/Earl King JOHNSON/ Anita STEINMAN ► 999 (1)	**4905**
One Night—Elvis Presley (58)	4905

Charlotte CAFFEY ► 1000 (1)	**4904**
Diane LAMPERT/Joe SENECA ► 1001 (2)	**4872**
Break It To Me Gently—Brenda Lee (62)	3448
Break It To Me Gently—Juice Newton (82)	1424
Carol CONNORS/Bill CONTI/Ayn ROBBINS ► 1002 (5)	**4867**
Gonna Fly Now (Theme From "Rocky")—Bill Conti (77)	4145
Gonna Fly Now (Theme From "Rocky")—Maynard Ferguson (77)	595
You Take My Heart Away—James Darren (77)	98
Rocky II Disco—Maynard Ferguson (79)	22
Theme From Rocky (Gonna Fly Now)—Rhythm Heritage (77)	7.6
Phil COULTER/ William Wylie MacPherson MARTIN ► 1003 (5)	**4866**
Saturday Night—Bay City Rollers (75)	4835
Hi Hi Hazel—Gary And The Hornets (66)	16
Julie Ann—Ginger (76)	11
Congratulations—Cliff Richard (68)	3.7
Forever And Ever—Slik (76)	1.2
Fred BURCH/Gerald NELSON ► 1004 (4)	**4865**
Tragedy—Thomas Wayne with The DeLons (59)	2908
Tragedy—The Fleetwoods (61)	1366
Tragedy—Brian Hyland (68)	561
Eternally—Thomas Wayne with The DeLons (59)	30
Larry Lee BUTLER/Chips MOMAN ► 1005 (1)	**4865**
(Hey Won't You Play) Another Somebody Done Somebody Wrong Song—B.J. Thomas (75)	4865
Chuck BARRIS ► 1006 (1)	**4864**
August MSARURGWA ► 1007 (4)	**4863**
Donnie IRIS ► 1008 (3)	**4851**
Harvey PRICE/Dan WALSH ► 1009 (9)	**4847**
Temptation Eyes—The Grass Roots (70)	1969
Heaven Knows—The Grass Roots (69)	1417
Baby Hold On—The Grass Roots (70)	728
Love Is What You Make It—The Grass Roots (73)	477
The Heartbreak Kid—Bo Donaldson And The Heywoods (74)	198
Ain't No Love In The Heart Of The City—Bobby Bland (74)	35
Where There's Smoke There's Fire—The Grass Roots (73)	16
Deeper And Deeper—Bo Donaldson And The Heywoods (74)	4.6
Sing Out The Love (In My Heart)—Arkade (70)	0.8
Scott ENGLISH/Richard KERR ► 1010 (3)	**4843**
Mandy—Barry Manilow (74)	4532
I Am What I Am—Lois Fletcher (74)	263
Brandy—Scott English (72)	48
Gregg DIAMOND ► 1011 (3)	**4840**
John KAY/Rushton MOREVE ► 1012 (1)	**4838**
Magic Carpet Ride—Steppenwolf (68)	4838
Rob HYMAN/Cyndi LAUPER ► 1013 (1)	**4828**
Time After Time—Cyndi Lauper (84)	4828
David FOSTER/John PARR ► 1014 (1)	**4824**
St. Elmo's Fire (Man In Motion)—John Parr (85)	4824
Kurt WEILL ► 1015 (6)	**4818**
Jimmy DUNCAN ► 1016 (5)	**4818**
Noddy HOLDER/Jim LEA ► 1017 (9)	**4813**
Cum On Feel The Noize—Quiet Riot (83)	2756
Run Runaway—Slade (84)	816
My Oh My—Slade (84)	396
Mama Weer All Crazee Now—Quiet Riot (84)	324
Mama Weer All Crazee Now—Slade (72)	194
Gudbuy T' Jane—Slade (73)	186
Cum On Feel The Noize—Slade (73)	87
Take Me Bak 'Ome—Slade (72)	40
Little Sheila—Slade (85)	15
Eric CARMEN/Dean PITCHFORD ► 1018 (3)	**4812**
Make Me Lose Control—Eric Carmen (88)	2490
Almost Paradise...Love Theme From Footloose—Mike Reno And Ann Wilson (84)	1939
I Wanna Hear It From Your Lips—Eric Carmen (85)	384
Sammy CAHN/Gene DePAUL ► 1019 (9)	**4801**
Teach Me Tonight—The DeCastro Sisters (54)	3787
Teach Me Tonight—George Maharis (62)	774

Teach Me Tonight Cha Cha—The DeCastro Sisters (58)	179
Teach Me Tonight—Al Jarreau (82)	60
Teach Me Tonight—The Big Three: Sarah Vaughan/Joe Williams/Count Basie (60)	1.5
Who Are They To Say—The DeCastro Sisters (58)	0.7
Teach Me Tonight—The Modernaires Featuring Paula Kelly & George Auld (54)	0.0
Teach Me Tonight—Jo Stafford (54)	0.0
Teach Me Tonight—Janet Brace (54)	0.0
Jerry LORDAN ► 1020 (7)	**4794**
Gene McDANIELS ► 1021 (6)	**4791**
Michael MASSER/Ronald Norman MILLER ► 1022 (1)	**4788**
Touch Me In The Morning—Diana Ross (73)	4788
David COLE ► 1023 (5)	**4781**
David PAICH/Jeff PORCARO ► 1024 (3)	**4781**
Africa—Toto (82)	4097
Stranger In Town—Toto (84)	580
Holyanna—Toto (85)	104
Ray DORSET ► 1025 (1)	**4780**
Michael JACKSON/Steven Randall JACKSON ► 1026 (2)	**4765**
Shake Your Body (Down To The Ground)—Jacksons (79)	3398
Lovely One—Jacksons (80)	1367
Wayne VAUGHN/Maurice WHITE ► 1027 (2)	**4758**
Let's Groove—Earth, Wind & Fire (81)	4608
Wanna Be With You—Earth, Wind & Fire (82)	150
John DURRILL/Norman EZELL/ Michael RABON ► 1028 (5)	**4755**
Western Union—The Five Americans (67)	2583
I See The Light—The Five Americans (65)	795
Sound Of Love—The Five Americans (67)	657
Zip Code—The Five Americans (67)	404
Evol-Not Love—The Five Americans (66)	315
Gary BEISBIER/James HOLVAY ► 1029 (4)	**4754**
Don't You Care—The Buckinghams (67)	2879
Hey Baby (They're Playing Our Song)—The Buckinghams (67)	1754
Give It To Me—The Mob (71)	71
I Dig Everything About You—The Mob (70)	50
Gregory ABBOTT ► 1030 (2)	**4752**
Martha DAVIS ► 1031 (5)	**4744**
Johnny MERCER ► 1032 (13)	**4743**
Dickey BETTS ► 1033 (6)	**4738**
Don HENLEY/Danny KORTCHMAR ► 1034 (3)	**4735**
Dirty Laundry—Don Henley (82)	4004
Johnny Can't Read—Don Henley (82)	392
I Can't Stand Still—Don Henley (83)	339
Nat KIPNER/John VALLINS ► 1035 (1)	**4728**
Too Much, Too Little, Too Late—Johnny Mathis/Deniece Williams (78)	4728
Buddy BUIE/J.R. COBB/Emory GORDY ► 1036 (3)	**4726**
Traces—Classics IV Featuring Dennis Yost (69)	4007
Midnight—Dennis Yost And The Classics IV (69)	481
Traces—The Lettermen (69)	238
Andy KIM ► 1037 (2)	**4719**
Robin SCOTT ► 1038 (1)	**4719**
Hughie CANNON ► 1039 (10)	**4718**
Don BREWER ► 1040 (1)	**4703**
Hal DAVIS/Donald FLETCHER/Dean PARKS ► 1041 (1)	**4702**
Dancing Machine—The Jackson 5 (74)	4702
Bert KALMAR/Harry RUBY/Ted SNYDER ► 1042 (2)	**4697**
Who's Sorry Now—Connie Francis (58)	4383
Who's Sorry Now—Marie Osmond (75)	314
Billy HILL ► 1043 (9)	**4696**
Dennis COFFEY ► 1044 (3)	**4688**
Gunnar NELSON/Matthew NELSON/ Marc TANNER ► 1045 (2)	**4688**
(Can't Live Without Your) Love And Affection—Nelson (90)	3603
More Than Ever—Nelson (91)	1085
Tom SPRINGFIELD ► 1046 (6)	**4686**

Hoagy CARMICHAEL/Stuart GORRELL ▶ 1047 (4)	**4685**
Georgia On My Mind—Ray Charles (60)	4142
Georgia On My Mind—Michael Bolton (90)	390
Georgia On My Mind—The Righteous Brothers (66)	112
Georgia On My Mind—Willie Nelson (78)	41
Des DYER/Clive SCOTT ▶ 1048 (3)	**4681**
Sky High—Jigsaw (75)	3070
Who Do You Think You Are— Bo Donaldson And The Heywoods (74)	1150
Love Fire—Jigsaw (76)	462
Roy HEAD/Gene KURTZ ▶ 1049 (1)	**4680**
Treat Her Right—Roy Head And The Traits (65)	4680
Steve CROPPER/Donald "Duck" DUNN/ Al JACKSON/Booker T. JONES Jr. ▶ 1050 (5)	**4678**
Time Is Tight—Booker T. & The M.G.'s (69)	2035
Soul-Limbo—Booker T. & The M.G.'s (68)	1495
Hip Hug-Her—Booker T. & The M.G.'s (67)	719
Melting Pot—Booker T. & The M.G.'s (71)	365
Slim Jenkin's Place—Booker T. & The M.G.'s (67)	64
Suzanne VEGA ▶ 1051 (2)	**4662**
William HUDSPETH/Michael KENNEDY ▶ 1052 (1)	**4662**
Heartbeat - It's A Lovebeat— The Defranco Family Featuring Tony Defranco (73)	4662
John Martin SOMMERS ▶ 1053 (1)	**4659**
Don FELDER/Glenn FREY/Don HENLEY ▶ 1054 (1)	**4658**
Hotel California—Eagles (77)	4658
Melvin STEALS/Mervin STEALS ▶ 1055 (4)	**4657**
Could It Be I'm Falling In Love— The Spinners (72)	4362
One Beautiful Day—Ecstasy, Passion & Pain (75)	285
Full Time Thing (Between Dusk And Dawn)— Whirlwind (76)	9.0
After Loving You—Major Harris (75)	0.6
Bruce BLACKMAN ▶ 1056 (5)	**4656**
Maurice IRBY ▶ 1057 (2)	**4654**
Dennis LAMBERT/Martin PAGE/ Bernie TAUPIN/Peter F. WOLF ▶ 1058 (1)	**4638**
We Built This City—Starship (85)	4638
John D. LOUDERMILK/Marijohn WILKIN ▶ 1059 (1)	**4628**
Waterloo—Stonewall Jackson (59)	4628
Johnny COLLA/Chris HAYES/Huey LEWIS ▶ 1060 (1)	**4627**
The Power Of Love—Huey Lewis and the News (85)	4627
Barry MANN/Tom SNOW/Cynthia WEIL ▶ 1061 (3)	**4621**
Don't Know Much—Linda Ronstadt (89)	4540
All I Need To Know (Don't Know Much)— Bette Midler (83)	59
Don't Know Much—Bill Medley (81)	22
R.B. GREAVES ▶ 1062 (1)	**4621**
Mariah CAREY/Robert CLIVILLÉS/ David COLE ▶ 1063 (1)	**4618**
Emotions—Mariah Carey (91)	4618
Bob HILLIARD/Lee POCKRISS ▶ 1064 (4)	**4617**
(Seven Little Girls) Sitting In The Back Seat— Paul Evans and The Curls (59)	2385
In My Little Corner Of The World— Anita Bryant (60)	1752
Kookie Little Paradise—Jo Ann Campbell (60)	323
Kookie Little Paradise—The Tree Swingers (60)	157
Harold FALTERMEYER/Keith FORSEY/ Bob SEGER ▶ 1065 (1)	**4602**
Shakedown—Bob Seger (87)	4602
Michael OMARTIAN/Donna SUMMER ▶ 1066 (3)	**4597**
She Works Hard For The Money—Donna Summer (83)	4225
Unconditional Love—Donna Summer (83)	302
Love Has A Mind Of Its Own—Donna Summer (84)	71
Peter RADCLIFFE/Tony SEPE/Barry WHITE ▶ 1067 (1)	**4597**
You're The First, The Last, My Everything— Barry White (74)	4597
Sherman MARSHALL/Phil PUGH ▶ 1068 (1)	**4589**
Then Came You—Dionne Warwicke And Spinners (74)	4589

Amy GRANT/Keith THOMAS ▶ 1069 (1)	**4588**
Baby Baby—Amy Grant (91)	4588
Per GESSLE/Mats PERSSON ▶ 1070 (2)	**4581**
Listen To Your Heart—Roxette (89)	3652
Spending My Time—Roxette (91)	929
Philip BAILEY/Phil COLLINS/Nathan EAST ▶ 1071 (1)	**4579**
Easy Lover—Philip Bailey (84)	4579
Lincoln CHASE/Shirley ELLIS ▶ 1072 (1)	**4579**
The Name Game—Shirley Ellis (64)	4579
Al DUBIN/Harry WARREN ▶ 1073 (6)	**4574**
I Only Have Eyes For You—The Flamingos (59)	1735
I Only Have Eyes For You—Art Garfunkel (75)	1357
September In The Rain—Dinah Washington (61)	1242
I Only Have Eyes For You—The Lettermen (66)	122
I Only Have Eyes For You—Jerry Butler (72)	113
I Only Have Eyes For You—Cliff Richard (64)	5.3
Mike APPEL/Jim CRETECOS/Wes FARRELL ▶ 1074 (1)	**4568**
Doesn't Somebody Want To Be Wanted— The Partridge Family Starring Shirley Jones & Featuring David Cassidy (71)	4568
George FISCHOFF/Tony POWERS ▶ 1075 (4)	**4561**
98.6—Keith (66)	2675
Lazy Day—Spanky And Our Gang (67)	1247
Ain't Gonna Lie—Keith (66)	601
Run To My Lovin' Arms—Lenny Welch (65)	38
Bryan ABRAMS/Mark CALDERON/ Willie CLARKE/Elliot STRAITE/ Kevin THORNTON/Sam WATTERS/ Betty WRIGHT ▶ 1076 (1)	**4560**
I Wanna Sex You Up—Color Me Badd (91)	4560
Dick GLASSER ▶ 1077 (8)	**4555**
Frank GUIDA/Joseph ROYSTER ▶ 1078 (6)	**4553**
New Orleans—U.S. Bonds (60)	2886
High School Usa—Tommy Facenda (59)	625
New Orleans—Eddie Hodges (65)	616
New Orleans—Neil Diamond (68)	383
Treat 'Em Tough—Jimmy Soul (63)	42
New Orleans—The Chartbusters (65)	0.0
Glenn FREY/Don HENLEY/ Bob SEGER/J.D. SOUTHER ▶ 1079 (1)	**4547**
Heartache Tonight—Eagles (79)	4547
Lamont DOZIER/Brian HOLLAND/ Eddie HOLLAND/Will JENNINGS/ Steve WINWOOD ▶ 1080 (1)	**4539**
Roll With It—Steve Winwood (88)	4539
Homer BANKS/Bettye CRUTCHER/ Don DAVIS/Raymond Earl JACKSON ▶ 1081 (3)	**4537**
Who's Making Love—Johnnie Taylor (68)	3954
Who's Making Love—Blues Brothers (80)	342
Who's Making Love—Young-Holt Unlimited (69)	241
Lois Ann BLAISCH ▶ 1082 (1)	**4537**
Al GREEN/Mabon HODGES ▶ 1083 (5)	**4534**
Here I Am (Come And Take Me)—Al Green (73)	1801
Here I Am (Come And Take Me)—UB40 (91)	1696
Take Me To The River—Talking Heads (78)	717
Take Me To The River—Syl Johnson (75)	193
Love And Happiness—Earnest Jackson (73)	125
Mason WILLIAMS ▶ 1084 (2)	**4526**
Al FRAZIER/John Earl (Sonny) HARRIS/ Carl WHITE/Turner WILSON ▶ 1085 (4)	**4517**
Papa Oom Mow Mow—The Trashmen (63)	1861
Bird Is The Word—The Trashmen (63)	1861
Papa-Oom-Mow-Mow—The Rivingtons (62)	480
The Bird's The Word—The Rivingtons (63)	315
John SPINKS ▶ 1086 (7)	**4513**
Felix CAVALIERE ▶ 1087 (9)	**4495**
Smokey ROGERS ▶ 1088 (4)	**4493**
Billy SQUIER ▶ 1089 (11)	**4487**
Jerry CAPEHART ▶ 1090 (4)	**4485**
Dave WILLIAMS ▶ 1091 (5)	**4483**
David ARKIN/Earl ROBINSON ▶ 1092 (1)	**4482**
Black And White—Three Dog Night (72)	4482
Kelly GORDON/Dean KAY ▶ 1093 (2)	**4478**
That's Life—Frank Sinatra (66)	4437
That's Life—David Lee Roth (86)	40

Charles AXTON/Gilbert CAPLE/ Chips MOMAN/Floyd NEWMAN/ Jerald Leroy SMITH ▶ 1094 (1)	**4476**
Last Night—Mar-Keys (61)	4476
Johnny CHRISTOPHER/Mark JAMES/ Wayne Carson THOMPSON ▶ 1095 (2)	**4472**
Always On My Mind—Willie Nelson (82)	2961
Always On My Mind—Pet Shop Boys (88)	1512
Robert MAXWELL/Carl SIGMAN ▶ 1096 (6)	**4459**
Ebb Tide—The Righteous Brothers (65)	2977
Ebb Tide—Lenny Welch (64)	842
Ebb Tide— The Platters Featuring Tony Williams (60)	357
Ebb Tide—Bobby Freeman (59)	283
Ebb Tide—Roy Hamilton (54)	0.0
Ebb Tide—Roy Hamilton (59)	0.0
Donna SUMMER ▶ 1097 (1)	**4457**
Billy VERA ▶ 1098 (4)	**4455**
Bobby DARIN/Murray KAUFMAN/ Jean MURRAY ▶ 1099 (1)	**4440**
Splish Splash—Bobby Darin (58)	4440
Gary KEMP ▶ 1100 (4)	**4440**
John DURRILL ▶ 1101 (2)	**4437**
Glen BALLARD/Chynna PHILLIPS/ Carnie WILSON ▶ 1102 (1)	**4433**
Hold On—Wilson Phillips (90)	4433
Arthur EGNOIAN/Sandy NELSON ▶ 1103 (2)	**4431**
Teen Beat—Sandy Nelson (59)	3896
Teen Beat '65—Sandy Nelson (64)	535
Christine McVIE/Robbie PATTON ▶ 1104 (1)	**4430**
Hold Me—Fleetwood Mac (82)	4430
Mutt LANGE/Billy OCEAN ▶ 1105 (2)	**4427**
Get Outta My Dreams, Get Into My Car— Billy Ocean (88)	4022
Licence To Chill—Billy Ocean (89)	405
Ronnie SELF ▶ 1106 (1)	**4423**
Lou JOSIE ▶ 1107 (3)	**4403**
Gilbert BÉCAUD/Pierre DELANOË/ Carl SIGMAN ▶ 1108 (6)	**4403**
The Day The Rains Came—Jane Morgan (58)	1490
What Now My Love—Sonny & Cher (66)	986
What Now My Love— Herb Alpert & The Tijuana Brass (66)	706
The Day The Rains Came— Raymond LeFevre and His Orchestra (58)	623
What Now My Love—Mitch Ryder (67)	593
What Now My Love—"Groove" Holmes (66)	5.1
James BEAUMONT/Walter LESTER/ Lennie MARTIN/Joseph ROCK/ John L. TAYLOR/Joseph VERSCHAREN/ Janet VOGEL ▶ 1109 (7)	**4400**
Since I Don't Have You—The Skyliners (59)	2364
This I Swear—The Skyliners (59)	743
Since I Don't Have You—Don McLean (81)	545
Since I Don't Have You—Chuck Jackson (64)	403
Since I Don't Have You—Art Garfunkel (79)	180
Since I Don't Have You—Eddie Holman (70)	160
Since I Don't Have You— Fred Parris & The Five Satins (82)	4.8
Bob WELCH ▶ 1110 (5)	**4396**
Eunice LEVY/Jake PORTER/Forrest WILSON ▶ 1111 (5)	**4389**
Ko Ko Mo (I Love You So)—Perry Como (55)	3070
Ko Ko Mo (I Love You So)—The Crew-Cuts (55)	1319
Ko Ko Mo (I Love You So)— Bill Darnel & Betty Clooney (55)	0.0
Ko Ko Mo (I Love You So)—The Hutton Sisters (55)	0.0
Ko Ko Mo—The Dooley Sisters (55)	0.0
Fred AHLERT/Joe YOUNG ▶ 1112 (5)	**4388**
I'm Gonna Sit Right Down And Write Myself A Letter— Billy Williams (57)	4377
I'm Gonna Sit Right Down And Write Myself A Letter— Fabian (60)	12
I'm Gonna Sit Right Down And Write Myself A Letter— Harry The Hipster (57)	0.0
I'm Gonna Sit Right Down And Write Myself A Letter— Hop A Long Wong (57)	0.0
I'm Gonna Sit Right Down And Write Myself A Letter— Larry Storch (57)	0.0

Otis BLACKWELL/Jack HAMMER ▶ 1113 (4)	**4388**
Great Balls Of Fire—Jerry Lee Lewis (57)	4298
Great Balls Of Fire—Tiny Tim (69)	83
Great Balls Of Fire— Jive Bunny & The Mastermixers (90)	6.7
Great Balls Of Fire—Georgia Gibbs (57)	0.0
David COVERDALE/Bernie MARSDEN ▶ 1114 (1)	**4367**
Here I Go Again—Whitesnake (87)	4367
Keith FORSEY/Steve SCHIFF ▶ 1115 (1)	**4351**
Don't You (Forget About Me)—Simple Minds (85)	4351
Walter AFANASIEFF/Mariah CAREY ▶ 1116 (1)	**4348**
Can't Let Go—Mariah Carey (91)	4348
Clyde OTIS/Murray STEIN ▶ 1117 (2)	**4343**
Baby (You've Got What It Takes)— Dinah Washington & Brook Benton (60)	3840
Smooth Operator—Sarah Vaughan (59)	503
Al CAPPS/Snuff GARRETT/ Gary LEWIS/Leon RUSSELL ▶ 1118 (1)	**4343**
She's Just My Style— Gary Lewis And The Playboys (65)	4343
Yvonne BAKER/Alphonso HOWELL/ George MINOR ▶ 1119 (1)	**4334**
Let Me In—The Sensations (62)	4334
John DENVER/Dick KNISS/ Michael C. TAYLOR ▶ 1120 (1)	**4334**
Sunshine On My Shoulders—John Denver (74)	4334
Cub KODA/Michael LUTZ ▶ 1121 (3)	**4323**
Smokin' In The Boy's Room—Brownsville Station (73)	3499
Smokin' In The Boys Room—Mötley Crüe (85)	773
Mama Don't Allow No Parkin'— Brownsville Station (74)	50
Allen REYNOLDS ▶ 1122 (2)	**4317**
Peter McCANN ▶ 1123 (2)	**4315**
Howard Ellington Riddiford BARNES/ Harold FIELDS/Joseph RONCORONI ▶ 1124 (5)	**4310**
A Blossom Fell—Nat "King" Cole (55)	4027
Chincherinchee—Perry Como (56)	282
A Blossom Fell—Dickie Valentine (55)	0.0
Someone Else's Roses—Doris Day (54)	0.0
A Blossom Fell—Vic Barrett (55)	0.0
Martin PAGE/Bernie TAUPIN ▶ 1125 (1)	**4304**
These Dreams—Heart (86)	4304
David E. LEWIS/Jonathan LEWIS/ Wayne I. LEWIS ▶ 1126 (1)	**4301**
Always—Atlantic Starr (87)	4301
Bob MERRILL/Jule STYNE ▶ 1127 (5)	**4301**
People—Barbra Streisand (64)	3349
Funny Girl—Barbra Streisand (64)	448
People—The Tymes (68)	422
People—Nat King Cole (64)	76
I Am Woman—Barbra Streisand (64)	5.3
Nick FELDMAN/Jack HUES/Peter F. WOLF ▶ 1128 (1)	**4287**
Everybody Have Fun Tonight—Wang Chung (86)	4287
Steve CASH/Larry Michael LEE ▶ 1129 (2)	**4286**
Jackie Blue—The Ozark Mountain Daredevils (75)	4157
If I Only Knew—The Ozark Mountain Daredevils (76)	128
Zell SANDERS/Lona STEVENS ▶ 1130 (1)	**4285**
Sally, Go 'Round The Roses—The Jaynetts (63)	4285
Thom BELL/Phil HURTT ▶ 1131 (2)	**4281**
I'll Be Around—The Spinners (72)	4157
I'll Be Around—What Is This (85)	124
David TYSON/Christopher WARD ▶ 1132 (2)	**4281**
Black Velvet—Alannah Myles (89)	3820
Love Is—Alannah Myles (90)	461
Carol CONNORS/Marshall CONNORS ▶ 1133 (1)	**4281**
Hey Little Cobra—The Rip Chords (63)	4281
Tommy BOYCE/Wes FARRELL/Bobby HART ▶ 1134 (1)	**4277**
Come A Little Bit Closer—Jay & The Americans (64)	4277
Al HOFFMAN/Dick MANNING/ Bickley REICHNER ▶ 1135 (1)	**4276**
Papa Loves Mambo—Perry Como (54)	4276
Madonna L. CICCONE/Gardner COLE/ Peter RAFELSON ▶ 1136 (1)	**4274**
Open Your Heart—Madonna (86)	4274
Magne FURUHOLMEN/Morten HARKET/ Pal WAAKTAAR ▶ 1137 (1)	**4264**
Take On Me—A-Ha (85)	4264
Michael BURTON/Sylvia ROBINSON ▶ 1138 (1)	**4260**
Pillow Talk—Sylvia (73)	4260
Dan HILL/Barry MANN ▶ 1139 (2)	**4258**
Sometimes When We Touch—Dan Hill (77)	4251
Let The Song Last Forever—Dan Hill (78)	7.4
Chris DE BURGH ▶ 1140 (4)	**4254**
Bill BEASLEY/Joan NORRIS/ Lee ROSENBERG/Bernard WEINMAN ▶ 1141 (1)	**4251**
Too Much—Elvis Presley (57)	4251
Rufus THOMAS ▶ 1142 (9)	**4244**
Dimitri TIOMKIN ▶ 1143 (19)	**4243**
Madonna L. CICCONE/Brian ELLIOT ▶ 1144 (1)	**4241**
Papa Don't Preach—Madonna (86)	4241
Michael ZAGER ▶ 1145 (3)	**4235**
Don BLACK/Walter SCHARF ▶ 1146 (1)	**4231**
Ben—Michael Jackson (72)	4231
Larry CANSLER/Michael MURPHEY ▶ 1147 (2)	**4229**
Wildfire—Michael Murphey (75)	4221
School Teacher— Kenny Rogers And The First Edition (72)	7.9
Johnnie CHRISTO/John HOLLIDAY/ Amos PIZZEY/Trevor STEEL/Milan ZEKAVICA ▶ 1148 (1)	**4224**
Wild, Wild West—The Escape Club (88)	4224
Dimitri TIOMKIN/Paul Francis WEBSTER ▶ 1149 (16)	**4222**
Friendly Persuasion (Thee I Love)—Pat Boone (56)	2555
Ballad Of The Alamo—Marty Robbins (60)	694
Friendly Persuasion (Thee I Love)—Four Aces (56)	389
The Green Leaves Of Summer— The Brothers Four (60)	304
Ballad Of The Alamo—Bud And Travis (60)	190
Giant— Les Baxter with His Chorus and Orchestra (56)	54
Giant— Art Mooney and His Orchestra and Chorus (56)	17
Giant—Jack Pleis and His Orchestra and Chorus (56)	11
Rio Bravo—Dean Martin (59)	9.1
Love Theme From "Giant" (There's Never Been Anyone Else But You)— David Carroll & His Orchestra (56)	0.0
Friendly Persuasion (Thee I Love)— Anthony Perkins (56)	0.0
Giant— Ray Heindorf & The Warner Bros. Orchestra (56)	0.0
The Guns Of Navarone— Mitch Miller and The Gang (61)	0.0
The Green Leaves Of Summer—Bud & Travis (60)	0.0
Giant—Jimmy Wakely (56)	0.0
Giant—Rusty Draper (56)	0.0
James Richard HENDRICKS ▶ 1150 (4)	**4221**
Bernard Leon JACKSON/Brian SIMPSON ▶ 1151 (1)	**4220**
The First Time—Surface (90)	4220
Harry CHAPIN/Sandra CHAPIN ▶ 1152 (1)	**4219**
Cat's In The Cradle—Harry Chapin (74)	4219
Barbie GAYE/Morris LEVY/ Johnnie B. ROBERTS/Robert SPENCER ▶ 1153 (1)	**4215**
My Boy Lollipop—Millie Small (64)	4215
Paul GAYTEN/Robert GUIDRY ▶ 1154 (2)	**4207**
But I Do—Clarence Henry (61)	4122
But I Do—Bobby Vinton (72)	85
Michael BRUCE/Glen BUXTON/ Alice COOPER/Dennis DUNAWAY/ Neal SMITH ▶ 1155 (4)	**4198**
School's Out—Alice Cooper (72)	2297
Eighteen—Alice Cooper (71)	1021
Elected—Alice Cooper (72)	776
School's Out—Krokus (86)	104
Raynard MINER/Carl William SMITH ▶ 1156 (4)	**4192**
Rescue Me—Fontella Bass (65)	4146
Rescue Me—Cher (75)	25
Rescue Me—Melissa Manchester (76)	19
I'm Learnin'—Mary Wells (65)	2.3
Mick RALPHS ▶ 1157 (3)	**4191**
Tom PETTY ▶ 1158 (7)	**4191**
Glen BALLARD/Chynna PHILLIPS/ Carnie WILSON/Wendy WILSON ▶ 1159 (2)	**4191**
You're In Love—Wilson Phillips (91)	3185
The Dream Is Still Alive—Wilson Phillips (91)	1006
Jr. WALKER ▶ 1160 (2)	**4179**
Marilyn GARRETT/Dottie WAYNE/ Ben WEISMAN ▶ 1161 (2)	**4177**
The Night Has A Thousand Eyes—Bobby Vee (62)	4114
(There'll Come A Day When) Ev'ry Little Bit Hurts— Bobby Vee (64)	63
Walter SCOTT ▶ 1162 (1)	**4173**
Sigidi ABDULLAH/Harold CLAYTON ▶ 1163 (1)	**4167**
Take Your Time (Do It Right) (Part 1)— The S.O.S. Band (80)	4167
Timmy THOMAS ▶ 1164 (3)	**4159**
Johnny COLLA/Huey LEWIS ▶ 1165 (2)	**4144**
The Heart Of Rock & Roll— Huey Lewis and the News (84)	2167
If This Is It—Huey Lewis and the News (84)	1977
Robin LUKE ▶ 1166 (3)	**4143**
Phil MEDLEY ▶ 1167 (5)	**4142**
Bobby BROWN/Gene GRIFFIN ▶ 1168 (1)	**4142**
My Prerogative—Bobby Brown (88)	4142
Bob BARRON/Burt LONG ▶ 1169 (2)	**4139**
Cindy Oh Cindy—Eddie Fisher (56)	2225
Cindy Oh Cindy—Vince Martin with The Tarriers (56)	1914
Brian CONNOLLY/Stephen PRIEST/ Andrew SCOTT/Michael TUCKER ▶ 1170 (4)	**4131**
Fox On The Run—The Sweet (75)	2954
Action—The Sweet (76)	1094
California Nights—The Sweet (78)	63
Funk It Up (David's Song)—The Sweet (77)	20
Dimitri TIOMKIN/Ned WASHINGTON ▶ 1171 (9)	**4131**
Town Without Pity—Gene Pitney (61)	2139
Hajji Baba (Persian Lament)— Nat "King" Cole (54)	923
Wild Is The Wind—Johnny Mathis (57)	824
Strange Are The Ways Of Love—Gogi Grant (58)	178
Strange Lady In Town—Frankie Laine (55)	61
The Fall Of Love—Johnny Mathis (64)	5.9
The Unforgiven (The Need For Love)— The McGuire Sisters (60)	0.0
Strange Are The Ways Of Love—Randy Sparks (58)	0.0
The High And The Mighty—Johnny Desmond (54)	0.0
Glen BALLARD/Siedah GARRETT ▶ 1172 (1)	**4127**
Man In The Mirror—Michael Jackson (88)	4127
Bert KEYES/Sylvia ROBINSON ▶ 1173 (3)	**4120**
Love On A Two-Way Street—Moments (70)	3309
Love On A Two Way Street—Stacy Lattisaw (81)	768
Sunday—The Moments (2) (69)	43
Jerry LEIBER/Barry MANN/ Mike STOLLER/Cynthia WEIL ▶ 1174 (3)	**4114**
On Broadway—George Benson (78)	1964
On Broadway—The Drifters (63)	1347
Only In America—Jay & The Americans (63)	804
Kathryn FULTON ▶ 1175 (1)	**4110**
Carl CICCHETTI/Donald CLAPS ▶ 1176 (1)	**4109**
Beep Beep—The Playmates (58)	4109
Billy IDOL/Steve STEVENS ▶ 1177 (3)	**4107**
Eyes Without A Face—Billy Idol (84)	3144
Flesh For Fantasy—Billy Idol (84)	488
Rebel Yell—Billy Idol (84)	476
John CAFFERTY ▶ 1178 (9)	**4105**
Tom KEIFER ▶ 1179 (8)	**4103**
George MERRILL/Shannon RUBICAM/ Narada Michael WALDEN ▶ 1180 (1)	**4102**
How Will I Know—Whitney Houston (85)	4102

Greg KIHN/Steve WRIGHT ▶ 1181 (3)	**4100**
Jeopardy—Greg Kihn Band (83)	3516
Lucky—Greg Kihn (85)	449
Happy Man—Greg Kihn Band (82)	135
Jörn FAHRENKROG-PETERSEN/Carlo KARGES ▶ 1182 (1)	**4100**
99 Luftballons—Nena (83)	4100
Alfie AGIUS/Cy CURNIN/ Peter John GREENALL/ Jamie WEST-ORAM/Adam WOODS ▶ 1183 (3)	**4098**
One Thing Leads To Another—The Fixx (83)	2676
Saved By Zero—The Fixx (83)	900
The Sign Of Fire—The Fixx (83)	523
Oscar HAMMERSTEIN/Jerome KERN ▶ 1184 (5)	**4096**
I've Told Every Little Star—Linda Scott (61)	3657
Ol' Man River— Bing Crosby And The Buddy Cole Trio (56)	345
Ol' Man River—Earl Grant (58)	94
Can't Help Lovin' That Girl Of Mine— The Excels (61)	0.5
Ol' Man River—Johnny Nash (62)	0.0
Bryan ABRAMS/Mark CALDERON/ Hamza LEE/Kevin THORNTON/Sam WATTERS ▶ 1185 (1)	**4094**
I Adore Mi Amor—Color Me Badd (91)	4094
Paul CARRACK ▶ 1186 (2)	**4093**
Mike HAWKER/Ivor RAYMONDE ▶ 1187 (7)	**4092**
I Only Want To Be With You—Bay City Rollers (76)	1517
I Only Want To Be With You—Dusty Springfield (64)	1347
Stay Awhile—Dusty Springfield (64)	460
I Only Wanna Be With You—Samantha Fox (89)	438
I Only Want To Be With You—Nicolette Larson (82)	267
Stay Awhile—The Continental Miniatures (78)	42
I Only Want To Be With You—The Tourists (80)	20
Jarvis BAKER/Sylvester JACKSON/ Narada Michael WALDEN/Shanice WILSON ▶ 1188 (1)	**4090**
I Love Your Smile—Shanice (91)	4090
James Samuel HARRIS/ Terry LEWIS/Karyn WHITE ▶ 1189 (1)	**4086**
Romantic—Karyn White (91)	4086
Mike PHILLIPS ▶ 1190 (2)	**4083**
David BELLAMY/Jim STAFFORD ▶ 1191 (2)	**4082**
Spiders And Snakes—Jim Stafford (73)	3645
Your Bulldog Drinks Champagne—Jim Stafford (74)	437
Jim GOLD ▶ 1192 (1)	**4081**
Elmer BERNSTEIN/Sylvia FINE ▶ 1193 (9)	**4080**
Themes From The Man With The Golden Arm— Richard Maltby And His Orchestra (56)	1358
Main Title And Molly O From The Man With The Golden Arm— Dick Jacobs And His Chorus And Orchestra (56)	962
Main Title From The Man With The Golden Arm— Elmer Bernstein And Orchestra (56)	817
Themes From The Man With The Golden Arm— Billy May And His Orchestra (56)	547
Delilah Jones—The McGuire Sisters (56)	191
Main Title Golden Arm—Les Elgart and Orchestra (56)	187
Main Title From "The Man With The Golden Arm"— Buddy Morrow And His Orchestra (56)	18
Delilah Jones—Danny Kaye (56)	0.0
Molly-O—Ralph Young (56)	0.0
Edwin HAWKINS ▶ 1194 (3)	**4078**
Adrienne ANDERSON/Barry MANILOW ▶ 1195 (5)	**4071**
Could It Be Magic—Barry Manilow (75)	2240
Some Kind Of Friend—Barry Manilow (83)	602
Daybreak—Barry Manilow (77)	595
Street Singin'—Lady Flash (76)	532
Could It Be Magic—Donna Summer (76)	102
Jonathan EDWARDS ▶ 1196 (3)	**4069**
Alan BLAIKLEY/Ken HOWARD ▶ 1197 (3)	**4069**
Have I The Right?—The Honeycombs (64)	3306
I've Lost You—Elvis Presley (70)	400
I Can't Stop—The Honeycombs (64)	362
Martin FRY/Mark WHITE ▶ 1198 (4)	**4065**
When Smokey Sings—ABC (87)	1756
Be Near Me—ABC (85)	1562
(How To Be A) Millionaire—ABC (86)	711
Vanity Kills—ABC (86)	36
Paul EVANS/Jack REARDON ▶ 1199 (3)	**4064**
When—The Kalin Twins (58)	3515
Worried Guy—Johnny Tillotson (64)	523
I Think About You All The Time—Paul Evans (58)	26
Alan Nicholas GRAHAM/Bobby MITCHELL ▶ 1200 (2)	**4061**
The Flame—Cheap Trick (88)	3887
Remember My Name—House Of Lords (90)	174
Jan HAMMER ▶ 1201 (1)	**4048**
Jeffrey E. COHEN/Narada Michael WALDEN ▶ 1202 (3)	**4047**
Freeway Of Love—Aretha Franklin (85)	2925
You're A Friend Of Mine—Clarence Clemons (85)	936
Baby Come To Me—Regina Belle (89)	187
Neil FINN ▶ 1203 (5)	**4046**
Bobbi TRIMACHI/Sal TRIMACHI ▶ 1204 (1)	**4041**
1, 2, 3, Red Light—1910 Fruitgum Co. (68)	4041
Linda LAURIE ▶ 1205 (1)	**4039**
Ray WHITLEY ▶ 1206 (7)	**4034**
Richard ADLER/Robert ALLEN ▶ 1207 (4)	**4033**
Everybody Loves A Lover—Doris Day (58)	2433
Everybody Loves A Lover—The Shirelles (62)	1101
Girl On Page 44—The Four Lads (59)	489
Everybody Loves A Lover—The Angels (62)	9.1
Jim PETERIK ▶ 1208 (6)	**4032**
John BARRY/Simon Le BON/Nick RHODES/ Andy TAYLOR/Nigel John TAYLOR/ Roger TAYLOR ▶ 1209 (1)	**4032**
A View To A Kill—Duran Duran (85)	4032
Gary GLITTER/Mike LEANDER ▶ 1210 (4)	**4031**
Rock And Roll Part 2—Gary Glitter (72)	2384
Do You Wanna Touch Me (Oh Yeah)— Joan Jett & The Blackhearts (82)	693
I Didn't Know I Loved You (Till I Saw You Rock And Roll)—Gary Glitter (72)	533
I'm The Leader Of The Gang—Brownsville Station (74)	422
Chuck MANGIONE ▶ 1211 (5)	**4031**
Henry CREAMER/J. Turner LAYTON ▶ 1212 (2)	**4030**
Way Down Yonder In New Orleans— Freddie Cannon (59)	4029
After You've Gone—Frankie Avalon (62)	0.5
George DAVIS/John Issac TAYLOR ▶ 1213 (2)	**4028**
Boy From New York City—The Manhattan Transfer (81)	2222
The Boy From New York City—The Ad Libs (65)	1806
Terry Lynn ELLIS/Denzil FOSTER/ Cindy HERRON/Maxine JONES/ Thomas McELROY/Dawn ROBINSON ▶ 1214 (2)	**4028**
Hold On—En Vogue (90)	3351
Lies—En Vogue (90)	676
Gloria ESTEFAN/Enrique GARCIA ▶ 1215 (2)	**4022**
1-2-3— Gloria Estefan and Miami Sound Machine (88)	2190
Rhythm Is Gonna Get You— Gloria Estefan and Miami Sound Machine (87)	1833
Alan OSMOND/Merrill OSMOND ▶ 1216 (1)	**4017**
Down By The Lazy River—The Osmonds (72)	4017
Tony MACAULAY/Geoff STEPHENS ▶ 1217 (4)	**4014**
Smile A Little Smile For Me—The Flying Machine (69)	3331
Sorry Suzanne—The Hollies (69)	353
Silver Lady—David Soul (77)	289
You Won't Find Another Fool Like Me— The New Seekers Featuring Lyn Paul (74)	42
Gary RICHRATH ▶ 1218 (5)	**4013**
Dave LOGGINS ▶ 1219 (5)	**4008**
Scott JOPLIN ▶ 1220 (1)	**4001**
Sascha BURLAND ▶ 1221 (2)	**4001**
Ralph MacDONALD/William SALTER/ Bill WITHERS ▶ 1222 (2)	**3999**
Just The Two Of Us—Grover Washington, Jr. (81)	3799
In The Name Of Love— Ralph MacDonald (with Bill Withers) (84)	200
Ronnie SCOTT/Steve WOLFE ▶ 1223 (2)	**3997**
It's A Heartache—Bonnie Tyler (78)	3981
It's A Heartache—Juice Newton (78)	16
Kenny O'DELL ▶ 1224 (6)	**3995**
Odis ECHOLS/Charlie PHILLIPS ▶ 1225 (2)	**3995**
Sugartime—The McGuire Sisters (57)	3995
Sugartime—Charlie Phillips (57)	0.0
Mike LEANDER/Charles MILLS ▶ 1226 (3)	**3994**
Lady Godiva—Peter And Gordon (66)	2817
Knight In Rusty Armour—Peter And Gordon (66)	1175
The Jokers—Peter And Gordon (67)	2.4
Terence Trent D'ARBY/Sean OLIVER ▶ 1227 (1)	**3992**
Wishing Well—Terence Trent D'Arby (88)	3992
Jack BLADES/Ted NUGENT/Tommy SHAW ▶ 1228 (3)	**3990**
High Enough—Damn Yankees (90)	3426
Come Again—Damn Yankees (91)	327
Coming Of Age—Damn Yankees (90)	237
Buzz CASON/Mac GAYDEN ▶ 1229 (4)	**3986**
Everlasting Love—Carl Carlton (74)	1789
Everlasting Love—Robert Knight (67)	1702
Everlasting Love—Rex Smith/Rachel Sweet (81)	474
Blessed Are The Lonely—Robert Knight (68)	21
Ken HIRSCH/Ronald Norman MILLER ▶ 1230 (6)	**3984**
I've Never Been To Me—Charlene (82)	3262
Used To Be—Charlene & Stevie Wonder (82)	379
Can't We Try—Teddy Pendergrass (80)	333
It Ain't Easy Comin' Down—Charlene (77)	4.6
I've Never Been To Me—Charlene (77)	3.0
Freddie—Charlene (77)	2.4
Johnny BURKE/Erroll GARNER ▶ 1231 (5)	**3981**
Misty—Johnny Mathis (59)	1736
Misty—Ray Stevens (75)	1222
Misty—Lloyd Price (63)	848
Misty—The Vibrations (65)	153
Misty—Sarah Vaughan (59)	22
Jesse BARISH ▶ 1232 (4)	**3980**
Jimmy CLANTON ▶ 1233 (2)	**3976**
Eric CLAPTON/Marcy LEVY/George TERRY ▶ 1234 (1)	**3975**
Lay Down Sally—Eric Clapton (77)	3975
Coz CANLER/Jimmy MARINOS/ Wally PALMAR/Mike SKILL/Pete SOLLEY ▶ 1235 (1)	**3966**
Talking In Your Sleep— The Romantics (83)	3966
Andrew GOLD ▶ 1236 (3)	**3960**
Hurricane SMITH ▶ 1237 (1)	**3957**
Brian WILSON ▶ 1238 (3)	**3955**
Ted DARYLL/Greg RICHARDS ▶ 1239 (3)	**3940**
She Cried—Jay & The Americans (62)	3516
She Cried—The Lettermen (70)	222
He Cried—The Shangri-Las (66)	202
Leonard BERNSTEIN/Stephen SONDHEIM ▶ 1240 (8)	**3934**
Tonight—Ferrante & Teicher (61)	2067
Somewhere—Len Barry (66)	857
Somewhere (From West Side Story)— Barbra Streisand (85)	378
Tonight—Eddie Fisher (61)	339
Maria—Johnny Mathis (60)	170
Somewhere—P.J. Proby (65)	94
Maria—Johnny Mathis (61)	30
Tonight—Jay & The Americans (61)	0.0
Marcus MILLER/Luther VANDROSS ▶ 1241 (8)	**3928**
Don't Want To Be A Fool—Luther Vandross (91)	1159
Power Of Love—Luther Vandross (91)	1062
Jump To It—Aretha Franklin (82)	552
Til My Baby Comes Home— Luther Vandross (85)	534
Any Love—Luther Vandross (88)	306
Get It Right—Aretha Franklin (83)	150
Bad Boy—Luther Vandross (82)	96
The Rush—Luther Vandross (91)	71
Odell BROWN/Marvin GAYE/David RITZ ▶ 1242 (1)	**3925**
Sexual Healing—Marvin Gaye (82)	3925
Don COSTA ▶ 1243 (1)	**3920**

John DeNICOLA/Donald MARKOWITZ/ Franke PREVITE ▶ 1244 (1)	**3918**
(I've Had) The Time Of My Life— Bill Medley And Jennifer Warnes (87)	3918
Reginald HALL/Joe JONES ▶ 1245 (2)	**3915**
You Talk Too Much—Joe Jones & His Orchestra (60)	3885
You Talk Too Much—Frankie Ford (60)	29
Elvin BISHOP ▶ 1246 (4)	**3912**
Raymond BLOODWORTH/L. Russell BROWN ▶ 1247 (6)	**3908**
C'mon Marianne—The 4 Seasons Featuring The "Sound" Of Frankie Valli (67)	1901
Watch The Flowers Grow—The 4 Seasons Featuring The "Sound" Of Frankie Valli (67)	765
The Girl I'll Never Know (Angels Never Fly This Low)— Frankie Valli (69)	525
C'mon Marianne—Donny Osmond (76)	435
Nothing Succeeds Like Success— Bill Deal & The Rhondels (70)	277
Singles Game—Jay And The Techniques (68)	4.6
Tillman FRANKS/Johnny HORTON ▶ 1248 (2)	**3903**
Sink The Bismarck—Johnny Horton (60)	3896
When It's Springtime In Alaska (It's Forty Below)— Johnny Horton (59)	6.6
Kim CARNES/Dave ELLINGSON ▶ 1249 (2)	**3900**
Don't Fall In Love With A Dreamer— Kenny Rogers with Kim Carnes (80)	3393
Does It Make You Remember—Kim Carnes (82)	507
Fred FAIRBRASS/Richard FAIRBRASS/ Rob MANZOLI ▶ 1250 (1)	**3898**
I'm Too Sexy—Right Said Fred (91)	3898
Ingrid CHAVEZ/Madonna L. CICCONE/ Lenny KRAVITZ ▶ 1251 (1)	**3894**
Justify My Love—Madonna (90)	3894
Elliot STRAITE ▶ 1252 (1)	**3892**
Paul Steven BLISS/Steve KIPNER ▶ 1253 (1)	**3891**
Heart Attack—Olivia Newton-John (82)	3891
Stella UNGER/Victor YOUNG ▶ 1254 (7)	**3890**
(Theme From) Around The World— Mantovani And His Orchestra (57)	1959
(Theme From) Around The World— Victor Young & Orchestra (57)	1813
If It's A Dream—The McGuire Sisters (55)	76
Where Is That Someone For Me—Joni James (55)	42
Around The World— Lawrence Welk & His Champagne Music (57)	0.0
Around The World—Manny Lopez & His Orchestra (57)	0.0
If It's A Dream—Kitty Kallen (55)	0.0
Bill CHAMPLIN/David FOSTER/Jay GRAYDON ▶ 1255 (2)	**3881**
After The Love Has Gone—Earth, Wind & Fire (79)	3559
Friends In Love— Dionne Warwick And Johnny Mathis (82)	322
Merle KILGORE/Claude KING ▶ 1256 (2)	**3878**
Wolverton Mountain—Claude King (62)	3425
(I'm The Girl From) Wolverton Mountain— Jo Ann Campbell (62)	453
Nancy LEE/Clyde OTIS ▶ 1257 (2)	**3877**
The Stroll—The Diamonds (57)	3877
The Stroll—The Lancers (57)	0.0
David COVERDALE/John SYKES ▶ 1258 (3)	**3875**
Is This Love—Whitesnake (87)	3575
Give Me All Your Love—Whitesnake (88)	254
Still Of The Night—Whitesnake (87)	46
Paul CLAYTON/Larry EHRLICH/ Ronnie GILBERT/Lee HAYS/ Fred HELLERMAN/Dave LAZAR/Pete SEEGER ▶ 1259 (3)	**3865**
Gotta Travel On—Billy Grammer (58)	3674
Gotta Travel On—Timi Yuro (63)	190
Gotta Travel On—Harry Belafonte (59)	0.0
Jimmy CURRIE/Lonnie DONEGAN ▶ 1260 (2)	**3863**
I'll Never Fall In Love Again—Tom Jones (69)	3450
I'll Never Fall In Love Again—Tom Jones (67)	413
John ROSTILL/Bruce WELCH ▶ 1261 (1)	**3858**
Please Mr. Please—Olivia Newton-John (75)	3858
Charles CHAPLIN ▶ 1262 (3)	**3858**
Antonina ARMATO/Bobby BROWN/ Ian PRINCE ▶ 1263 (1)	**3857**
She Ain't Worth It— Glenn Medeiros featuring Bobby Brown (90)	3857
Phil COLLINS/Lamont DOZIER ▶ 1264 (1)	**3857**
Two Hearts—Phil Collins (88)	3857
Marty BALIN ▶ 1265 (1)	**3853**
Jack SEGAL ▶ 1266 (1)	**3850**
Jerry CORBETTA/John C. PHILLIPS/ David RIORDAN ▶ 1267 (2)	**3848**
Green-Eyed Lady—Sugarloaf (70)	3826
Mother Nature's Wine—Sugarloaf (71)	22
Alonzo TUCKER/Jackie WILSON ▶ 1268 (6)	**3840**
Baby Workout—Jackie Wilson (63)	3553
Baby Get It (And Don't Quit It)—Jackie Wilson (63)	143
I Just Can't Help It—Jackie Wilson (62)	104
Big Boss Line—Jackie Wilson (64)	29
Squeeze Her-Tease Her (But Love Her)— Jackie Wilson (64)	9.1
I Found Love—Jackie Wilson And Linda Hopkins (62)	2.2
Jacob BRACKMAN/Carly SIMON ▶ 1269 (3)	**3836**
That's The Way I've Always Heard It Should Be— Carly Simon (71)	2005
Haven't Got Time For The Pain—Carly Simon (74)	1266
Attitude Dancing—Carly Simon (75)	564
Ira KOSLOFF/Maurice MYSELS ▶ 1270 (1)	**3831**
I Want You I Need You I Love You—Elvis Presley (56)	3831
Les BAXTER ▶ 1271 (2)	**3819**
Gary ANDERSON/Gene BARGE ▶ 1272 (2)	**3805**
School Is Out—Gary (U.S.) Bonds (61)	3371
School Is In—Gary (U.S.) Bonds (61)	434
Emilio ESTEFAN/Gloria ESTEFAN/ Jon SECADA ▶ 1273 (1)	**3801**
Coming Out Of The Dark—Gloria Estefan (91)	3801
Jud FRIEDMAN/Allan RICH ▶ 1274 (1)	**3801**
I Don't Have The Heart—James Ingram (90)	3801
Danny SMALL ▶ 1275 (5)	**3800**
Vito BRATTA/Mike TRAMP ▶ 1276 (4)	**3799**
When The Children Cry—White Lion (88)	2108
Wait—White Lion (88)	1236
Tell Me—White Lion (88)	237
Little Fighter—White Lion (89)	218
Bobby STEVENSON ▶ 1277 (2)	**3793**
Jimmy BUFFETT ▶ 1278 (7)	**3789**
Wayne WALKER ▶ 1279 (5)	**3789**
Dee CLARK/Kal MANN/Cornell MULDROW/ Philip UPCHURCH ▶ 1280 (1)	**3787**
You Can't Sit Down—The Dovells (63)	3787
Allen Alvoid JONES Jr./Andrew LOVE/ Richard SHANN/Willie David YOUNG ▶ 1281 (2)	**3776**
Keep On Dancing—The Gentrys (65)	3698
Don't Have To Shop Around—The Mad Lads (65)	78
Vincent BRANTLEY/Ricky TIMAS ▶ 1282 (2)	**3774**
Cool It Now—New Edition (84)	3404
Count Me Out—New Edition (85)	371
Bill POST/Doree POST ▶ 1283 (3)	**3763**
Sixteen Reasons—Connie Stevens (60)	3679
Sixteen Reasons—Laverne & Shirley (76)	84
Rawhide—Bill & Doree Post (59)	0.0
James LEE ▶ 1284 (5)	**3761**
Layng MARTINE Jr. ▶ 1285 (6)	**3761**
Jimmy CHAMBERS/George CHANDLER/ Jimmy HELMS/William HENSHALL ▶ 1286 (1)	**3755**
I've Been Thinking About You—Londonbeat (91)	3755
Jo BOGAERT/Manuela KAMOSI ▶ 1287 (2)	**3752**
Pump Up The Jam—Technotronic (89)	3746
Rockin' Over The Beat—Technotronic (90)	5.2
Alan TARNEY ▶ 1288 (2)	**3743**
Greg PRESTOPINO/Matthew WILDER ▶ 1289 (1)	**3738**
Break My Stride—Matthew Wilder (83)	3738
Jimmy KENNEDY/Hugh WILLIAMS ▶ 1290 (7)	**3736**
Harbor Lights—The Platters (60)	2551
Red Sails In The Sunset— The Platters Featuring Tony Williams (60)	574
Red Sails In The Sunset—Fats Domino (63)	526
Red Sails In The Sunset—Tab Hunter (57)	70
Harbor Lights—The Mulcays (55)	13
Harbor Lights— Seymour & His Heartbeat Trumpet (59)	1.6
Isle Of Capri—The Gaylords (54)	0.0
David BOWIE/Floyd BROWN/John DEACON/ Brian MAY/Freddie MERCURY/ Roger TAYLOR/Robert VAN WINKLE ▶ 1291 (1)	**3735**
Ice Ice Baby—Vanilla Ice (90)	3735
Joe GARLAND ▶ 1292 (8)	**3732**
Chuck BERRY/Russ FRATTO/Alan FREED ▶ 1293 (5)	**3731**
Maybellene—Chuck Berry (55)	2343
Maybelline—Johnny Rivers (64)	1388
Maybellene—Ralph Marterie & His Orchestra (55)	0.0
Maybellene—Johnny Long & His Orchestra (55)	0.0
Maybellene—Jim Lowe (55)	0.0
Harold ARLEN/Johnny MERCER ▶ 1294 (9)	**3730**
That Old Black Magic— Louis Prima And Keely Smith (58)	1560
That Old Black Magic—Bobby Rydell (61)	886
That Old Black Magic—Sammy Davis Jr. (55)	614
One For My Baby (And One More For The Road)— Tony Bennett with Ray Conniff (57)	254
Come Rain Or Come Shine—Ray Charles (60)	160
Come Rain Or Come Shine—Rosemary Clooney (56)	124
Come Rain Or Come Shine—Jerry Lewis (56)	124
Old Black Magic—The Clovers (59)	4.4
Come Rain Or Come Shine—Ray Charles (68)	1.8
Kayode ADEYEMO/Rodney HOLLAMAN/ Kevin LYLES/William PETTAWAY/ Sean SPENCER ▶ 1295 (1)	**3721**
Girl You Know It's True—Milli Vanilli (88)	3721
Henry GROSS ▶ 1296 (6)	**3720**
Bert CARROLL/Russell MOODY/ Marilyn SCHACK ▶ 1297 (1)	**3714**
Wear My Ring Around Your Neck—Elvis Presley (58)	3714
Arlester CHRISTIAN ▶ 1298 (7)	**3712**
George CALLENDER/Wayne SHANKLIN ▶ 1299 (2)	**3712**
Primrose Lane—Jerry Wallace with The Jewels (59)	3631
Primrose Lane—O.C. Smith (70)	81
Lolly VEGAS ▶ 1300 (3)	**3703**
Marc BOLAN ▶ 1301 (6)	**3701**
Chynna PHILLIPS/Carnie WILSON/ Wendy WILSON ▶ 1302 (1)	**3701**
Release Me—Wilson Phillips (90)	3701
Clark DATCHLER ▶ 1303 (2)	**3700**
Barry DESPENZA/Carl WOLFOLK ▶ 1304 (2)	**3700**
Can I Change My Mind—Tyrone Davis (68)	3123
Is It Something You've Got—Tyrone Davis (69)	577
Julie GOLD ▶ 1305 (1)	**3697**
Gene CLARK/Roger McGUINN ▶ 1306 (1)	**3696**
You Showed Me—The Turtles (68)	3696
Bob RUSSELL/Bobby SCOTT ▶ 1307 (3)	**3693**
He Ain't Heavy, He's My Brother—Hollies (69)	2440
He Ain't Heavy...He's My Brother—Neil Diamond (70)	1112
He Ain't Heavy...He's My Brother— Olivia Newton-John (75)	141
Gilbert BÉCAUD/Mack DAVID ▶ 1308 (1)	**3693**
It Must Be Him—Vikki Carr (67)	3693
Mariah CAREY/Narada Michael WALDEN ▶ 1309 (1)	**3692**
I Don't Wanna Cry—Mariah Carey (91)	3692
Joey LEVINE/Kris RESNICK ▶ 1310 (7)	**3691**
Chewy Chewy—Ohio Express (68)	2224
Down At Lulu's—Ohio Express (68)	793
Shake—The Shadows Of Knight (68)	446
You Got The Love— Professor Morrison's Lollipop (68)	178
I'm In Love With You— Kasenetz-Katz Super Cirkus (69)	46
Yes Sir—The Music Explosion (68)	2.3
Down In Tennessee— Kasenetz-Katz Singing Orchestral Circus (68)	1.3
Wayne PITTMAN/Buck TRAIL ▶ 1311 (1)	**3691**
Girl Watcher—The O'Kaysions (68)	3691
KENNY G ▶ 1312 (2)	**3691**

Harry TOBIAS/Percy WENRICH ▶ 1313 (2)	**3690**
Sail Along Silvery Moon—Billy Vaughn and His Orchestra (57)	3690
Sail Along Silv'ry Moon—Karen Chandler & Her Jacks (57)	0.0
Charlie RYAN/W.S. STEVENSON ▶ 1314 (4)	**3690**
Hot Rod Lincoln—Commander Cody And His Lost Planet Airmen (72)	1950
Hot Rod Lincoln—Charlie Ryan And The Timberline Riders (60)	915
Hot Rod Lincoln—Johnny Bond (60)	790
Side Car Cycle—Charlie Ryan And The Timberline Riders (60)	34
Eliot DANIEL/Larry MOREY ▶ 1315 (1)	**3681**
Lavender Blue—Sammy Turner (59)	3681
Gordon SINCLAIR ▶ 1316 (3)	**3680**
Ian HUNTER ▶ 1317 (3)	**3676**
Bill CONTI/Mike LEESON ▶ 1318 (1)	**3674**
For Your Eyes Only—Sheena Easton (81)	3674
Aaron COLLINS/Maxwell DAVIS/Sam LING ▶ 1319 (4)	**3666**
Eddie My Love—The Fontane Sisters with Billy Vaughn's Orchestra (56)	1670
Eddie My Love—The Chordettes (56)	1068
Eddie My Love—The Teen Queens (56)	856
So All Alone—The Teen Queens (56)	72
Mickey NEWBURY ▶ 1320 (6)	**3663**
Michael BOLTON/Andy GOLDMARK ▶ 1321 (2)	**3657**
Love Is A Wonderful Thing—Michael Bolton (91)	2873
Soul Provider—Michael Bolton (89)	784
Ava ALDRIDGE/Eddie STRUZICK ▶ 1322 (3)	**3651**
Sharing The Night Together—Dr. Hook (78)	3646
Sharing The Night Together—Arthur Alexander (76)	4.4
Sharing The Night Together—Lenny LeBlanc (76)	0.9
George GOEHRING/Edna LEWIS ▶ 1323 (1)	**3650**
Lipstick On Your Collar—Connie Francis (59)	3650
Gary BROOKER/Matthew FISHER/Keith REID ▶ 1324 (6)	**3648**
A Whiter Shade Of Pale—Procol Harum (67)	3537
A Whiter Shade Of Pale—R.B. Greaves (70)	62
A Whiter Shade Of Pale—The Hesitations (68)	29
A Whiter Shade Of Pale—Procol Harum (72)	14
Whiter Shade Of Pale—Hagar, Schon, Aaronson, Shrieve (84)	5.6
A Whiter Shade Of Pale—Shorty Long (69)	0.4
Morris ALBERT/Louis GASTÉ ▶ 1325 (2)	**3645**
Feelings—Morris Albert (75)	3636
Feelings—Walter Jackson (76)	9.1
Bob MERRILL/Terry SHAND ▶ 1326 (2)	**3640**
You Don't Have To Be A Baby To Cry—The Caravelles (63)	3609
You Don't Have To Be A Baby To Cry—"Tennessee" Ernie Ford (56)	31
Biff JONES/Chuck MEYER ▶ 1327 (5)	**3637**
Suddenly There's A Valley—Gogi Grant (55)	1757
Suddenly There's A Valley—Jo Stafford (55)	1118
Suddenly There's A Valley—Julius La Rosa (55)	522
Suddenly There's A Valley—The Mills Brothers (55)	194
Suddenly There's A Valley—Patty Andrews (55)	47
Amy GRANT/Wayne KIRKPATRICK/Charlie PEACOCK ▶ 1328 (1)	**3631**
Every Heartbeat—Amy Grant (91)	3631
Arnold LANNI ▶ 1329 (3)	**3630**
Chips MOMAN ▶ 1330 (3)	**3626**
William DeVAUGHN ▶ 1331 (1)	**3624**
Paul WILLIAMS ▶ 1332 (3)	**3623**
Willie DENSON/Luther DIXON ▶ 1333 (2)	**3622**
Mama Said—The Shirelles (61)	2972
A Tear—Gene McDaniels (61)	650
Jane CHILD ▶ 1334 (2)	**3621**
Chet KELLEY/Thomas R. KING ▶ 1335 (2)	**3619**
Time Won't Let Me—The Outsiders (66)	2793
Girl In Love—The Outsiders (66)	826
Attrell CORDES/Gary KEMP ▶ 1336 (1)	**3619**
Set Adrift On Memory Bliss—PM Dawn (91)	3619
John LODGE ▶ 1337 (6)	**3619**
Ritchie BLACKMORE/Ian GILLAN/Roger GLOVER/Jon LORD/Ian PAICE ▶ 1338 (3)	**3615**
Smoke On The Water—Deep Purple (73)	3242
Woman From Tokyo—Deep Purple (73)	226
Black Night—Deep Purple (70)	148
Larry SANTOS ▶ 1339 (1)	**3611**
William S. COOK ▶ 1340 (8)	**3609**
Peter Ronald BROWN/Jack BRUCE/Eric CLAPTON ▶ 1341 (1)	**3604**
Sunshine Of Your Love—Cream (68)	3604
Gerry MARSDEN ▶ 1342 (5)	**3601**
David E. LEWIS/Wayne I. LEWIS ▶ 1343 (5)	**3599**
Secret Lovers—Atlantic Starr (85)	3103
Circles—Atlantic Starr (82)	338
When Love Calls—Atlantic Starr (81)	69
Love Crazy—Atlantic Starr (91)	54
Touch A Four Leaf Clover—Atlantic Starr (83)	34
Will JENNINGS/Michael MASSER ▶ 1344 (1)	**3593**
Didn't We Almost Have It All—Whitney Houston (87)	3593
Steve KIPNER/John Lewis PARKER ▶ 1345 (1)	**3593**
Hard Habit To Break—Chicago (84)	3593
Paul JABARA ▶ 1346 (1)	**3589**
Deena CHARLES/Russ DeSALVO/Robert STEELE ▶ 1347 (1)	**3587**
If Wishes Came True—Sweet Sensation (90)	3587
Bobby HART/Danny JANSSEN ▶ 1348 (3)	**3581**
Something's Wrong With Me—Austin Roberts (72)	1783
Keep On Singing—Helen Reddy (74)	1390
Keep On Singing—Austin Roberts (73)	409
Brian CARMAN ▶ 1349 (1)	**3580**
Spencer DAVIS/Muff WINWOOD/Steve WINWOOD ▶ 1350 (4)	**3571**
Gimme Some Lovin'—Spencer Davis Group (66)	2448
Gimme Some Lovin'—Blues Brothers (80)	890
Gimme Some Lovin' Part One—Traffic, Etc. (71)	217
Gimme Some Lovin'—Kongas (78)	15
Mark HOLDING/Robbie NEVIL/Duncan PAIN ▶ 1351 (1)	**3569**
C'est La Vie—Robbie Nevil (86)	3569
Ted DAFFAN ▶ 1352 (7)	**3568**
Don ALTFELD/Jan BERRY/Roger CHRISTIAN ▶ 1353 (2)	**3567**
The Little Old Lady (From Pasadena)—Jan & Dean (64)	3373
The Anaheim, Azusa & Cucamonga Sewing Circle, Book Review And Timing Association—Jan & Dean (64)	194
Harold DORMAN ▶ 1354 (3)	**3566**
Larry HENLEY/Jeff SILBAR ▶ 1355 (2)	**3565**
Wind Beneath My Wings—Bette Midler (89)	3406
Wind Beneath My Wings—Lou Rawls (83)	159
Rick NELSON ▶ 1356 (4)	**3564**
Stephen MITCHELL/Marti SHARRON/Gary SKARDINA ▶ 1357 (2)	**3554**
Jump (For My Love)—Pointer Sisters (84)	3301
Dangerous—Natalie Cole (85)	253
John Buck WILKIN ▶ 1358 (3)	**3553**
John HURLEY/Ronnie WILKINS ▶ 1359 (6)	**3551**
Son-Of-A Preacher Man—Dusty Springfield (68)	2224
The Land Of Milk And Honey—The Vogues (66)	626
Love Of The Common People—The Winstons (69)	407
Love Of The Common People—Paul Young (84)	288
A Woman Of The World—The Gentrys (66)	5.6
Son Of A Preacher Man—Aretha Franklin (70)	0.0
Joe WALSH ▶ 1360 (5)	**3549**
Michael GORDON ▶ 1361 (2)	**3542**
Harry ELSTON/Hugh MASEKELA ▶ 1362 (1)	**3539**
Grazing In The Grass—The Friends Of Distinction (69)	3539
Andy GOLDMARK/Bruce ROBERTS ▶ 1363 (6)	**3538**
You Should Be Mine (The Woo Woo Song)—Jeffrey Osborne (86)	1213
Dynamite—Jermaine Jackson (84)	933
Goldmine—Pointer Sisters (86)	495
Flames Of Paradise (Duet With Elton John)—Jennifer Rush (87)	441
Oh, People—Patti LaBelle (86)	409
Twist My Arm—Pointer Sisters (86)	47
Billy IDOL/David WERNER ▶ 1364 (1)	**3538**
Cradle Of Love—Billy Idol (90)	3538
Sylvester BRADFORD/Al LEWIS ▶ 1365 (6)	**3538**
Tears On My Pillow—Little Anthony And The Imperials (58)	3214
Wishful Thinking—Little Anthony And The Imperials (59)	138
Uh Huh Mm—Sonny James (57)	100
Walkin' Home From School—Gene Vincent and His Blue Caps (58)	73
Tears On My Pillow—Johnny Tillotson (69)	7.6
Tears On My Pillow—Fred Parris & The Five Satins (82)	4.8
Frank KONTE/Mike PINERA ▶ 1366 (1)	**3535**
Ride Captain Ride—Blues Image (70)	3535
Bob HILLIARD/Philip SPRINGER ▶ 1367 (3)	**3535**
Moonlight Gambler—Frankie Laine (56)	3465
Dancing Chandelier—Sylvia Syms (56)	63
The President On The Dollar—Mitch Miller & His Orchestra (56)	7.7
Ann WILSON/Nancy WILSON ▶ 1368 (3)	**3535**
Magic Man—Heart (76)	2291
Heartless—Heart (78)	789
Dreamboat Annie—Heart (76)	455
Regi HARGIS/Eddie IRONS/Ray RANSOM ▶ 1369 (1)	**3530**
Dazz—Brick (76)	3530
Jeff LYNNE/Tom PETTY ▶ 1370 (5)	**3524**
Free Fallin'—Tom Petty (89)	1714
I Won't Back Down—Tom Petty (89)	1038
Learning To Fly—Tom Petty and the Heartbreakers (91)	469
A Face In The Crowd—Tom Petty (90)	225
Into The Great Wide Open—Tom Petty and the Heartbreakers (91)	79
Charles WILLIAMS ▶ 1371 (2)	**3522**
Mick MARS/Nikki SIXX ▶ 1372 (3)	**3518**
Dr. Feelgood—Mötley Crüe (89)	1482
Without You—Mötley Crüe (90)	1295
Don't Go Away Mad (Just Go Away)—Mötley Crüe (90)	741
Brook BENTON/Jimmy WILLIAMS ▶ 1373 (5)	**3517**
A Lover's Question—Clyde McPhatter (58)	2994
A Lover's Question—Otis Redding (69)	429
A Lover's Question—Jacky Ward (78)	49
A Lover's Question—Ernestine Anderson (61)	34
A Lover's Question—Loggins & Messina (75)	12
Mick JAGGER/Andrew Loog OLDHAM/Keith RICHARDS ▶ 1374 (2)	**3517**
As Tears Go By—The Rolling Stones (65)	2591
As Tears Go By—Marianne Faithfull (64)	926
Charles DANVERS/Carl SIGMAN ▶ 1375 (9)	**3516**
'Til—The Angels (61)	1330
Till—The Vogues (68)	931
Till—Roger Williams (57)	656
Till—Tom Jones (71)	445
Till—Percy Faith And His Orchestra and Chorus (57)	151
Till—The Tokens (68)	1.8
Till—Leo Diamond His Harmonica & Orch (57)	0.0
Till—Dinah Shore (57)	0.0
Till—Kay Armen (57)	0.0
Mike LOVE/Scott McKENZIE/Terry MELCHER/John PHILLIPS ▶ 1376 (1)	**3513**
Kokomo—The Beach Boys (88)	3513
Harold ARLEN/E.Y. HARBURG ▶ 1377 (5)	**3512**
Ding Dong! The Witch Is Dead—The Fifth Estate (67)	1521
Over The Rainbow—The Demensions (60)	1404
Themes From The Wizard Of Oz—Meco (78)	477
Over The Rainbow—Gary Tanner (78)	109
Over The Rainbow—The Baysiders (60)	0.0
Clifford ADAMS/Robert BELL/Ronald BELL/James BONNEFORD/George M. BROWN/Claydes SMITH/J.T. TAYLOR/Curtis Fitzgerald WILLIAMS ▶ 1378 (1)	**3511**
Joanna—Kool & The Gang (83)	3511
Thomas DOLBY/Jo KERR ▶ 1379 (1)	**3507**
She Blinded Me With Science—Thomas Dolby (83)	3507
Huddie LEDBETTER ▶ 1380 (4)	**3504**

Rachel BOLAN/Dave SABO ▶ 1381 (3)	**3501**
18 And Life—Skid Row (89)	1922
I Remember You—Skid Row (89)	1578
Youth Gone Wild—Skid Row (89)	1.6
Tom PAXTON ▶ 1382 (4)	**3494**
Elton JOHN/Davey JOHNSTONE/ Bernie TAUPIN ▶ 1383 (2)	**3493**
I Guess That's Why They Call It The Blues— Elton John (83)	2690
Grow Some Funk Of Your Own—Elton John (76)	803
Henry MAYER/Bobby VINTON ▶ 1384 (1)	**3485**
My Melody Of Love—Bobby Vinton (74)	3485
Ma RAINEY/TRADITIONAL ▶ 1385 (4)	**3479**
See See Rider—Eric Burdon And The Animals (66)	1714
C. C. Rider—Mitch Ryder And The Detroit Wheels (65)	728
See See Rider—LaVern Baker (62)	629
C.C. Rider—Bobby Powell (65)	408
Tom JONES/Harvey SCHMIDT ▶ 1386 (5)	**3477**
My Cup Runneth Over—Ed Ames (67)	2403
Try To Remember—Gladys Knight & The Pips (75)	957
Try To Remember—Ed Ames (65)	101
Try To Remember—The Brothers Four (65)	8.3
Try To Remember—Roger Williams (65)	6.9
Rudy TOOMBS ▶ 1387 (8)	**3472**
Michelle GRAINGER/Tony HAYES/ Steve WADEY ▶ 1388 (3)	**3469**
Black Is Black—Los Bravos (66)	3466
Clock—Eddie Rambeau (66)	2.8
Black Is Black—Tight Fit (81)	0.9
Boz SCAGGS ▶ 1389 (6)	**3469**
Jeff BARRY/Bobby BLOOM ▶ 1390 (6)	**3464**
Montego Bay—Bobby Bloom (70)	1958
Heavy Makes You Happy (Sha-Na-Boom Boom)— The Staple Singers (71)	754
Sunshine—The Archies (70)	589
Make Me Happy—Bobby Bloom (71)	141
Montego Bay—Amazulu (87)	22
Sha La Boom Boom—Bobby Bloom (73)	0.4
Fred EBB/John KANDER ▶ 1391 (5)	**3464**
My Coloring Book—Kitty Kallen (62)	1467
My Coloring Book—Sandy Stewart (62)	1420
Theme From New York, New York—Frank Sinatra (80)	577
My Coloring Book—Barbra Streisand (62)	0.0
My Coloring Book—George Chakiris (62)	0.0
Robert MATHER/Keith STEGALL/ Chris WATERS ▶ 1392 (1)	**3462**
Sexy Eyes—Dr. Hook (80)	3462
John CAPEK/Marc JORDAN ▶ 1393 (2)	**3457**
Rhythm Of My Heart—Rod Stewart (91)	3022
Pieces Of Ice—Diana Ross (83)	434
Bryan ADAMS/Mutt LANGE ▶ 1394 (1)	**3455**
Can't Stop This Thing We Started—Bryan Adams (91)	3455
Ersel HICKEY/Ed E. MILLER/TRADITIONAL ▶ 1395 (1)	**3454**
Don't Let The Rain Come Down (Crooked Little Man)—The Serendipity Singers (64)	3454
James GRIFFIN/Fred KARLIN/Robb ROYER ▶ 1396 (1)	**3454**
For All We Know—Carpenters (71)	3454
Charles Henry JACKSON Jr./ Frank WILDHORN ▶ 1397 (1)	**3452**
Where Do Broken Hearts Go—Whitney Houston (88)	3452
Al HOFFMAN/Charles KING/Dick MANNING ▶ 1398 (1)	**3451**
Hawaiian Wedding Song—Andy Williams (58)	3451
Jeff BARRY ▶ 1399 (4)	**3451**
Alan OSMOND/Merrill OSMOND/ Wayne OSMOND ▶ 1400 (5)	**3449**
Hold Her Tight—The Osmonds (72)	1163
Crazy Horses—The Osmonds (72)	882
Let Me In—The Osmonds (73)	668
Goin' Home—The Osmonds (73)	522
We Can Make It Together— Steve & Eydie Featuring The Osmonds (72)	215
Ian ANDERSON ▶ 1401 (7)	**3443**
Mitch MURRAY ▶ 1402 (4)	**3437**
Bobby BLOOM/Ritchie CORDELL/Bo GENTRY ▶ 1403 (1)	**3435**
Indian Giver—1910 Fruitgum Co. (69)	3435

Rick CHERTOFF/Gary CORBETT/ Cyndi LAUPER/Stephen LUNT ▶ 1404 (1)	**3432**
She Bop—Cyndi Lauper (84)	3432
Kenny THOMAS/Frank Edward WILSON ▶ 1405 (1)	**3430**
Stoned Love—The Supremes (70)	3430
Irving TAYLOR ▶ 1406 (1)	**3430**
Alicia BRIDGES/Susan HUTCHESON ▶ 1407 (2)	**3427**
I Love The Nightlife (Disco 'Round)— Alicia Bridges (78)	3417
Body Heat—Alicia Bridges (79)	9.2
Johnny COWELL ▶ 1408 (5)	**3426**
Jack PERRICONE/Paul VANCE ▶ 1409 (2)	**3426**
Run Joey Run—David Geddes (75)	3075
Without Your Love (Mr. Jordan)—Charlie Ross (76)	352
Michael FRENCHIK/Lionel RICHIE/ Carlos RIOS ▶ 1410 (1)	**3417**
Dancing On The Ceiling—Lionel Richie (86)	3417
Robert BELL/Ronald BELL/ George M. BROWN/ Meekaaeel MUHAMMED/Claydes SMITH/ J.T. TAYLOR/Dennis THOMAS/Earl TOON ▶ 1411 (1)	**3414**
Ladies Night—Kool & The Gang (79)	3414
Dickie GOODMAN/Bill RAMAL ▶ 1412 (2)	**3412**
Mr. Jaws—Dickie Goodman (75)	3166
Kong—Dickie Goodman (77)	246
Tom KING/Ira MACK/Fred MENDELSOHN/ John POCISK/TRADITIONAL ▶ 1413 (1)	**3410**
Red River Rock—Johnny And The Hurricanes (59)	3410
Ingrid CHAVEZ/Elliot ERICKSON/ Frederick THOMAS ▶ 1414 (1)	**3407**
Do Anything—Natural Selection (91)	3407
Mickey BAKER/Ellas McDANIEL/ Sylvia ROBINSON ▶ 1415 (4)	**3407**
Love Is Strange—Mickey & Sylvia (56)	2019
Love Is Strange—Peaches & Herb (67)	1374
Love Is Strange—Buddy Holly / The Crickets (69)	11
Love Is Strange—The Everly Brothers (65)	3.4
Hoyt AXTON/David P. JACKSON ▶ 1416 (1)	**3406**
No No Song—Ringo Starr (75)	3406
Vince GUARALDI ▶ 1417 (3)	**3402**
Mike ANTHONY/Barry MANN ▶ 1418 (3)	**3402**
She Say (Oom Dooby Doom)—The Diamonds (59)	1292
I'll Never Dance Again—Bobby Rydell (62)	1211
The Grass Is Greener—Brenda Lee (63)	899
Gary BENSON/Maxi PRIEST/Winston SELA ▶ 1419 (1)	**3399**
Close To You—Maxi Priest (90)	3399
Paula ABDUL/Peter LORD/V. Jeffrey SMITH/ Sandra ST. VICTOR ▶ 1420 (1)	**3398**
The Promise Of A New Day—Paula Abdul (91)	3398
Joe EGAN/Gerry RAFFERTY ▶ 1421 (2)	**3387**
Stuck In The Middle With You—Stealers Wheel (73)	2928
Everyone's Agreed That Everything Will Turn Out Fine—Stealers Wheel (73)	459
Bennie BENJAMIN/George David WEISS ▶ 1422 (11)	**3386**
How Important Can It Be—Joni James (55)	2495
How Important Can It Be—Sarah Vaughan (55)	429
I Don't See Me In Your Eyes Anymore— Charlie Rich (74)	298
I'll Never Be Free—Kay Starr (61)	118
I'll Step Aside—Georgie Shaw (55)	22
Wheel Of Fortune—LaVern Baker (60)	15
Wheel Of Fortune—The Knightsbridge Strings (59)	10
How Important Can It Be?—Connee Boswell (55)	0.0
How Important Can It Be?—Teresa Brewer (55)	0.0
How Important Can It Be—Lou Monte (55)	0.0
Cross Over The Bridge—Patti Page (54)	0.0
Joe RAPOSO ▶ 1423 (2)	**3384**
Blanche CARTER ▶ 1424 (2)	**3382**
Sammy GALLOP/Jerry LIVINGSTON ▶ 1425 (2)	**3377**
Wake The Town And Tell The People— Les Baxter His Chorus And Orchestra (55)	2302
Wake The Town And Tell The People— Mindy Carson (55)	1076

Michael ESPOSITO/Ronald GILBERT/ Ralph SCALA/Emil THIELHELM ▶ 1426 (1)	**3377**
(We Ain't Got) Nothin' Yet—Blues Magoos (66)	3377
Leo GRAHAM/Paul RICHMOND ▶ 1427 (2)	**3376**
Shining Star—The Manhattans (80)	3368
I'll Never Find Another (Find Another Like You)— The Manhattans (80)	7.4
Billy PRESTON ▶ 1428 (4)	**3375**
Dino ESPOSITO ▶ 1429 (5)	**3375**
Norman LUBOFF ▶ 1430 (2)	**3374**
Robert BLACKWELL/Enotris JOHNSON/ Richard PENNIMAN ▶ 1431 (3)	**3368**
Long Tall Sally—Little Richard (56)	1982
Long Tall Sally—Pat Boone (56)	1222
Long Tall Sally— Cat Mother And The All Night News Boys (69)	164
Jerry LEIBER/Michael McDONALD/ Ed SANFORD/Mike STOLLER ▶ 1432 (1)	**3365**
I Keep Forgettin'—Michael McDonald (82)	3365
Ritchie CORDELL/Bo GENTRY ▶ 1433 (5)	**3349**
Mirage—Tommy James And The Shondells (67)	1826
I Like The Way—Tommy James And The Shondells (67)	664
Out Of The Blue— Tommy James And The Shondells (67)	415
Get Out Now—Tommy James And The Shondells (68)	403
We Gotta Go Home—The Music Explosion (67)	41
Sam LEWIS/Jean SCHWARTZ/Joe YOUNG ▶ 1434 (3)	**3346**
Rock A Bye Your Baby With A Dixie Melody— Jerry Lewis (56)	2560
Rock-A-Bye Your Baby With A Dixie Melody— Aretha Franklin (61)	786
Rock A Bye Your Baby With A Dixie Melody— Judy Garland (61)	0.0
Ellas McDANIEL ▶ 1435 (15)	**3342**
Art CRAFER/Jimmy NEBB ▶ 1436 (6)	**3341**
No Arms Can Ever Hold You (Like These Arms Of Mine)—Georgie Shaw (55)	1126
No Other Arms—Pat Boone (55)	1053
No Arms Can Ever Hold You— The Bachelors (64)	791
No Arms Can Ever Hold You (Like These Arms Of Mine)—The Gaylords (55)	187
No Arms Can Ever Hold You— Bobby Vinton (70)	184
No Arms Can Ever Hold You— Jimmy Young with Bob Sharples & His Music (55)	0.0
Robert HIGGINBOTHAM ▶ 1437 (6)	**3338**
Gino VANNELLI ▶ 1438 (7)	**3336**
Alan O'DAY/John STEVENSON ▶ 1439 (1)	**3330**
Rock And Roll Heaven— The Righteous Brothers (74)	3330
Anita BAKER/Randy HOLLAND/ Skip SCARBOROUGH ▶ 1440 (1)	**3327**
Giving You The Best That I Got—Anita Baker (88)	3327
Leroy BELL/Casey JAMES ▶ 1441 (3)	**3326**
Mama Can't Buy You Love—Elton John (79)	2115
Livin' It Up (Friday Night)—Bell & James (79)	1206
This Time Baby—Jackie Moore (79)	6.1
Bobby McFERRIN ▶ 1442 (1)	**3324**
Arthur HAMILTON ▶ 1443 (9)	**3321**
Norman GIMBEL/Eddie HEYWOOD ▶ 1444 (3)	**3317**
Canadian Sunset—Andy Williams (56)	2711
Land Of Dreams— Hugo Winterhalter's Orchestra And Chorus (54)	552
Canadian Sunset—Etta Jones (61)	54
Kenneth Edward BELL/ Terry SKINNER/J.L. WALLACE ▶ 1445 (3)	**3314**
Even The Nights Are Better—Air Supply (82)	2400
Touch Me When We're Dancing—Carpenters (81)	893
Touch Me When We're Dancing—Bama (79)	21
Wes FARRELL/Jerry GOLDSTEIN ▶ 1446 (2)	**3312**
Come On Down To My Boat— Every Mothers' Son (67)	3309
I Can't Stop—The Osmond Brothers (71)	2.1
Rickie Lee JONES ▶ 1447 (5)	**3305**
Richard STRAUSS ▶ 1448 (3)	**3303**
Walter EGAN ▶ 1449 (6)	**3302**

Kate PIERSON/Fred SCHNEIDER/ Keith STRICKLAND/Cindy WILSON ▶ 1450 (3)	**3299**
Love Shack—The B-52's (89)	2771
Deadbeat Club—The B-52's (90)	458
Private Idaho—The B-52's (80)	70
Buck OWENS ▶ 1451 (4)	**3297**
Arthur SMITH ▶ 1452 (2)	**3297**
David LASLEY/Allee WILLIS ▶ 1453 (3)	**3296**
Lead Me On—Maxine Nightingale (79)	3179
Love Me Again—Rita Coolidge (78)	73
The Blue Side—Crystal Gayle (80)	44
Lee Eugene MICHAELS ▶ 1454 (2)	**3295**
Jack LAWRENCE ▶ 1455 (6)	**3293**
Phillip MITCHELL ▶ 1456 (6)	**3291**
Victor CARSTARPHEN/Gene McFADDEN/ John WHITEHEAD ▶ 1457 (6)	**3288**
Wake Up Everybody (Part 1)— Harold Melvin And The Blue Notes (75)	1592
Bad Luck (Part 1)— Harold Melvin And The Blue Notes (75)	1407
Where Are All My Friends— Harold Melvin And The Blue Notes (74)	117
Bad Luck—The Ritchie Family (76)	92
Tell The World How I Feel About 'Cha Baby— Harold Melvin And The Blue Notes (76)	66
Bad Luck—The Atlanta Disco Band (76)	14
Stan JONES ▶ 1458 (9)	**3284**
Reggie CALLOWAY/Vincent CALLOWAY/ Melvin GENTRY/Belinda LIPSCOMB ▶ 1459 (1)	**3279**
I Wanna Be Rich—Calloway (90)	3279
Vaughn HORTON/Jimmie RODGERS ▶ 1460 (2)	**3277**
Mule Skinner Blues—The Fendermen (60)	3277
Mule Skinner Blues—Rusty Draper (60)	0.0
Peter BISCHOF-FALLENSTEIN/ Frank FARIAN/Dietmar KAWOHL ▶ 1461 (1)	**3277**
Girl I'm Gonna Miss You—Milli Vanilli (89)	3277
Morris BROADNAX/Clarence PAUL/ Stevie WONDER ▶ 1462 (4)	**3269**
Until You Come Back To Me (That's What I'm Gonna Do)—Aretha Franklin (73)	3181
Hey Love—Stevie Wonder (67)	53
Just A Little Misunderstanding—The Contours (66)	26
Until You Come Back To Me (That's What I'm Gonna Do) (Medley)— Luther Vandross (84)	7.6
Dick MANNING/Dante MARCHETTI ▶ 1463 (4)	**3268**
Fascination— Jane Morgan with the Troubadors (57)	2924
Fascination— Dick Jacobs And His Chorus And Orchestra (57)	327
Fascination—Nat "King" Cole (57)	15
Fascination—Dinah Shore (57)	1.9
Dino FEKARIS/Nick ZESSES ▶ 1464 (4)	**3267**
I Just Want To Celebrate—Rare Earth (71)	2092
Hey Big Brother—Rare Earth (71)	928
You Gotta Have Love In Your Heart— The Supremes & Four Tops (71)	210
Mother Nature—The Temptations (72)	38
Sidney BECHET ▶ 1465 (4)	**3265**
Jack TEMPCHIN ▶ 1466 (3)	**3265**
Bill BACKER/Roger COOK/ Billy DAVIS/Roger GREENAWAY ▶ 1467 (2)	**3265**
I'd Like To Teach The World To Sing (In Perfect Harmony)—The New Seekers (71)	1791
I'd Like To Teach The World To Sing (In Perfect Harmony)—The Hillside Singers (71)	1474
Huey P. SMITH/John VINCENT ▶ 1468 (4)	**3265**
Rockin' Pneumonia - Boogie Woogie Flu— Johnny Rivers (72)	3059
Rockin' Pneumonia And The Boogie Woogie Flu— Huey Smith and The Clowns (57)	112
Don't You Know Yockomo?— Huey "Piano" Smith with his Clowns (58)	67
Roberta—Bones (72)	27
Donald STORBALL ▶ 1469 (2)	**3257**

George GERSHWIN/Ira GERSHWIN/ DuBose HEYWARD ▶ 1470 (7)	**3247**
Summertime—Billy Stewart (66)	1685
I Loves You Porgy—Nina Simone (59)	1423
Summertime—The Marcels (61)	107
Summertime—Sam Cooke (57)	20
Summertime—Rick Nelson (62)	7.8
Summertime (Part 2)—Sam Cooke (59)	4.4
Summertime—Will Sanders (61)	0.0
Bobby CALDWELL/Paul GORDON ▶ 1471 (1)	**3246**
The Next Time I Fall—Peter Cetera (86)	3246
Reg PRESLEY ▶ 1472 (4)	**3244**
Steven TYLER ▶ 1473 (3)	**3243**
Jerry LIVINGSTON/Paul Francis WEBSTER ▶ 1474 (13)	**3239**
The Twelfth Of Never—Donny Osmond (73)	2152
The Twelfth Of Never—Johnny Mathis (57)	421
Veni-Vidi-Vici (I Came, I Saw, I Conquered)— The Gaylords (54)	256
Shenandoah Rose—Hugo & Luigi (57)	197
Sweet Thursday—Johnny Mathis (62)	90
Who Are We—Gogi Grant (56)	64
The Fountain Of Youth—The Four Lads (59)	37
Laurie, My Love—Johnny Mathis (61)	17
Bluebell— Mitch Miller and His Orchestra and Chorus (58)	5.9
Shenandoah Rose—The Jack Halloran Singers (57)	0.0
Shenandoah Rose—Johnny Desmond (57)	0.0
Shenandoah Rose—Peter Hanley (57)	0.0
Blue Bell—Scott Engel (58)	0.0
Ahmet ERTEGUN/Betty NELSON ▶ 1475 (2)	**3238**
Don't Play That Song— Aretha Franklin With The Dixie Flyers (70)	1651
Don't Play That Song (You Lied)—Ben E. King (62)	1588
Mentor WILLIAMS ▶ 1476 (1)	**3233**
Bill CUOMO/Randy GOODRUM/ Craig KRAMPF/Steve PERRY ▶ 1477 (1)	**3231**
Oh Sherrie—Steve Perry (84)	3231
Mike LEANDER/Ed SEAGO ▶ 1478 (3)	**3225**
Early In The Morning—Vanity Fare (69)	2096
I Ain't Got Time Anymore— The Glass Bottle Featuring Gary Criss (71)	697
Another Time, Another Place— Engelbert Humperdinck (71)	432
Billy NICHOLS ▶ 1479 (2)	**3222**
Harold FALTERMEYER/Keith FORSEY ▶ 1480 (1)	**3215**
The Heat Is On—Glenn Frey (84)	3215
Chris LOWE/Neil TENNANT/Allee WILLIS ▶ 1481 (1)	**3210**
What Have I Done To Deserve This?— Pet Shop Boys And Dusty Springfield (87)	3210
Gail LEVY/Vincent LEVY/Joe ZAWINUL ▶ 1482 (3)	**3210**
Mercy, Mercy, Mercy—The Buckinghams (67)	2966
Mercy, Mercy, Mercy—Marlena Shaw (67)	209
Mercy, Mercy, Mercy— Larry Williams & Johnny Watson (67)	34
Jimmy HOLIDAY/Eddie REEVES ▶ 1483 (2)	**3204**
All I Ever Need Is You—Sonny & Cher (71)	2452
Don't Change On Me—Ray Charles (71)	751
Carmine APPICE/Duane HITCHINGS/ Kevin SAVIGAR/Rod STEWART ▶ 1484 (1)	**3203**
Young Turks—Rod Stewart (81)	3203
Peter Ronald BROWN/Jack BRUCE ▶ 1485 (2)	**3202**
White Room—Cream (68)	3165
I Feel Free—Belinda Carlisle (88)	37
Ross VANNELLI ▶ 1486 (1)	**3196**
Luther INGRAM/Bonny RICE ▶ 1487 (2)	**3195**
Respect Yourself—The Staple Singers (71)	1800
Respect Yourself—Bruce Willis (87)	1395
Bernd BERWANGER/Roger DALTON/ Frank FARIAN/Brad HOWELL ▶ 1488 (1)	**3187**
Baby Don't Forget My Number—Milli Vanilli (89)	3187
Eddie SCHWARTZ ▶ 1489 (1)	**3184**
Carol CONNORS/David SHIRE ▶ 1490 (1)	**3182**
With You I'm Born Again— Billy Preston & Syreeta (79)	3182

L. Russell BROWN/Bob CREWE ▶ 1491 (2)	**3181**
Sock It To Me-Baby!— Mitch Ryder And The Detroit Wheels (67)	3156
Fancy Dancer—Frankie Valli (79)	25
Fritz ROTTER/Fritz ROTTER ▶ 1492 (2)	**3181**
That's All I Want From You—Jaye P. Morgan (54)	3173
That's All I Want From You—The Silva-Tones (57)	7.1
Al BRAGGS/Deadric MALONE ▶ 1493 (4)	**3178**
Share Your Love With Me—Aretha Franklin (69)	1587
Share Your Love With Me—Kenny Rogers (81)	993
Share Your Love With Me—Bobby Bland (64)	534
To Share Your Love—Fantastic Four (67)	63
Jimmy CASTOR/Langdon FRIDIE/ Douglas GIBSON/Harry JENSEN/ Robert MANIGAULT/Gerald THOMAS ▶ 1494 (1)	**3177**
Troglodyte (Cave Man)— The Jimmy Castor Bunch (72)	3177
Glen BALLARD/Clif MAGNESS/David PACK ▶ 1495 (1)	**3171**
All I Need—Jack Wagner (84)	3171
Janie BRADFORD/Barrett STRONG/ Norman WHITFIELD ▶ 1496 (1)	**3171**
Too Busy Thinking About My Baby—Marvin Gaye (69)	3171
George JOHNSON/Louis E. JOHNSON/ Senora SAM ▶ 1497 (2)	**3167**
I'll Be Good To You—The Brothers Johnson (76)	2385
I'll Be Good To You—Quincy Jones (89)	782
Dan HARTMAN/Amir SHAKIR/ Donnie WAHLBERG/Mark WAHLBERG ▶ 1498 (1)	**3166**
Good Vibrations— Marky Mark & The Funky Bunch (91)	3166
Alexandra FORBES/Jeffrey FRANZEL ▶ 1499 (1)	**3164**
Don't Rush Me—Taylor Dayne (88)	3164
Wayne BRATHWAITE/Barry EASTMOND/ Mutt LANGE/Billy OCEAN ▶ 1500 (1)	**3161**
When The Going Gets Tough, The Tough Get Going— Billy Ocean (85)	3161
Randy VANWARMER ▶ 1501 (3)	**3158**
Mack GORDON/Harry WARREN ▶ 1502 (6)	**3148**
The More I See You—Chris Montez (66)	1319
At Last—Etta James (61)	639
There Will Never Be Another You— Chris Montez (66)	527
Chattanooga Choo Choo—Harpers Bizarre (67)	339
Chattanooga Choo Choo—Tuxedo Junction (78)	307
You'll Never Know— Shirley Bassey with the Rita Williams Singers (61)	16
Dave PEVERETT ▶ 1503 (5)	**3148**
Nicky HEADON/Michael Geoffrey JONES/ Paul SIMONON/Joe STRUMMER ▶ 1504 (4)	**3145**
Rock The Casbah—The Clash (82)	1940
Train In Vain (Stand By Me)—The Clash (80)	752
Should I Stay Or Should I Go?—The Clash (82)	243
Should I Stay Or Should I Go?—The Clash (83)	210
Rosie HAMLIN ▶ 1505 (3)	**3135**
John GLUCK/Neval NADER ▶ 1506 (4)	**3126**
Mecca—Gene Pitney (63)	1433
Lovers By Night, Strangers By Day— The Fleetwoods (62)	581
Punish Her—Bobby Vee (62)	567
Trouble Is My Middle Name—Bobby Vinton (62)	546
Jack H. CLEMENT ▶ 1507 (11)	**3121**
Audrey ALLISON/Joe ALLISON/ Charles GREAN ▶ 1508 (2)	**3119**
He'll Have To Stay—Jeanne Black (60)	3119
He'll Have To Stay—Corina Minette (60)	0.0
Noel BALL/Ken MOFFITT ▶ 1509 (4)	**3111**
Oh Julie—The Crescendos (57)	2335
Letter From Sherry—Dale Ward (63)	749
Oh Julie—Sammy Salvo (57)	27
Oh Julie—Otis Williams & His Charms (58)	0.0
Arthur ROSS/Leon WARE ▶ 1510 (3)	**3111**
I Wanna Be Where You Are—Michael Jackson (72)	1628
I Want You—Marvin Gaye (76)	984
I Want You—Robert Palmer (91)	499
Robert ALLEN ▶ 1511 (10)	**3107**

John BARBATA/Howard KAYLAN/ Al NICHOL/Jim PONS/Mark VOLMAN ▶ 1512 (2)	**3103**
Elenore—The Turtles (68)	2721
Sound Asleep—The Turtles (68)	382
Janie BRADFORD/Berry GORDY ▶ 1513 (4)	**3093**
Money (That's what I want)—Barrett Strong (60)	1212
Money—The Kingsmen (64)	1174
Money (That's What I Want) Part 1— Jr. Walker & The All Stars (66)	391
Money—The Flying Lizards (79)	317
Even STEVENS ▶ 1514 (1)	**3090**
Buzz CASON/Snuff GARRETT/ Hachidai NAKAMURA ▶ 1515 (1)	**3090**
Sukiyaki—A Taste Of Honey (81)	3090
Jimmy NORMAN/Jerry RAGOVOY ▶ 1516 (1)	**3088**
Time Is On My Side—The Rolling Stones (64)	3088
Carl BELEW/Kenny SOWDER/W.S. STEVENSON ▶ 1517 (1)	**3082**
Lonely Street—Andy Williams (59)	3082
Daniele DAVOLI/Mirko LIMONI/ Valerio SEMPLICI ▶ 1518 (4)	**3082**
Everybody Everybody—Black Box (90)	1472
Strike It Up—Black Box (91)	1185
I Don't Know Anybody Else—Black Box (90)	395
Gonna Catch You—Lonnie Gordon (91)	30
Glenn FREY/Don HENLEY/Randy MEISNER ▶ 1519 (1)	**3081**
Take It To The Limit—Eagles (75)	3081
Peter TETTEROO/Hans VAN EIJCK ▶ 1520 (2)	**3080**
Ma Belle Amie—The Tee Set (70)	2854
If You Do Believe In Love—The Tee Set (70)	226
Paul GORDON/Jay GRUSKA ▶ 1521 (1)	**3079**
Friends And Lovers— Gloria Loring & Carl Anderson (86)	3079
Joseph HOOVEN/Alfred J. SMITH/Hal WINN ▶ 1522 (3)	**3078**
Gimme Little Sign—Brenton Wood (67)	2590
Baby You Got It—Brenton Wood (67)	486
Lovey Dovey Kinda Lovin'—Brenton Wood (68)	1.4
Will HAMMOND Jr./Tuhin ROY/Jake SMITH ▶ 1523 (1)	**3071**
Hold You Tight—Tara Kemp (91)	3071
Dorsey BURNETTE ▶ 1524 (2)	**3070**
Lew BROWN/Buddy DeSYLVA/ Ray HENDERSON ▶ 1525 (5)	**3065**
Together—Connie Francis (61)	2968
The Birth Of The Blues—Sammy Davis Jr. (55)	58
Best Things In Life Are Free—Richard Cannon (58)	20
It All Depends On You—Jerry Lewis (57)	19
The Birth Of The Blues—Lenny Dee (55)	0.0
Alan BERNSTEIN/Vic MILLROSE ▶ 1526 (1)	**3064**
This Girl Is A Woman Now— Gary Puckett And The Union Gap (69)	3064
Gary NUMAN ▶ 1527 (2)	**3061**
Russ HAMILTON ▶ 1528 (4)	**3059**
Warren CASEY/Jim JACOBS ▶ 1529 (2)	**3057**
Summer Nights— John Travolta, Olivia Newton-John & Cast (78)	2789
Greased Lightnin'—John Travolta (78)	268
Stevie WONDER/Syreeta WRIGHT ▶ 1530 (4)	**3055**
If You Really Love Me—Stevie Wonder (71)	2411
To Know You Is To Love You—B.B. King (73)	549
We'll Have It Made—The Spinners (71)	52
Never Dreamed You'd Leave In Summer— Stevie Wonder (71)	43
Rolf HARRIS ▶ 1531 (2)	**3053**
Alex CALL/Jim KELLER ▶ 1532 (1)	**3051**
867-5309/Jenny—Tommy Tutone (82)	3051
Arnold INGRAM/James MITCHELL Jr./ Marvin WILLIS ▶ 1533 (1)	**3048**
Float On—The Floaters (77)	3048
Ivory Joe HUNTER/Clyde OTIS ▶ 1534 (6)	**3047**
Ain't That Loving You Baby— Elvis Presley With The Jordanaires (64)	1406
Out Of Sight Out Of Mind—The Five Keys (56)	860
Out Of Sight, Out Of Mind— Little Anthony And The Imperials (69)	410
No Other One—Eddie Fisher (56)	315

Out Of Sight - Out Of Mind—Sunny & The Sunliners (64)	54
Out Of Sight, Out Of Mind—The Essex (63)	1.7
Aaron SCHROEDER/Sid WAYNE ▶ 1535 (3)	**3042**
I'm Gonna Knock On Your Door—Eddie Hodges (61)	1994
First Anniversary—Cathy Carr (59)	736
It's Only The Beginning—The Kalin Twins (59)	312
Chaka KHAN/Tony MAIDEN ▶ 1536 (1)	**3041**
Sweet Thing—Rufus Featuring Chaka Khan (75)	3041
Rose Marie McCOY/Charles SINGLETON ▶ 1537 (14)	**3039**
If I May—Nat "King" Cole And The Four Knights (55)	1803
My Personal Possession— Nat "King" Cole And The Four Knights (57)	575
Piddily Patter Patter—Patti Page (55)	278
Genuine Love—Les Paul and Mary Ford (55)	271
Mambo Baby—Ruth Brown And Her Rhythmakers with Orchestra (54)	58
Mambo Baby—Georgia Gibbs (54)	15
I'd Better Be Careful—Bob Manning (55)	14
Slam! Bam!—The Crew-Cuts (55)	12
One Night Only—Otis Williams And His Charms (56)	7.2
Honey Bunch—The Four Knights (55)	5.0
Piddily Patter Patter—The Burton Sisters (55)	0.0
Piddily Patter Patter—Helene Dixon (55)	0.0
My Personal Possession—Andy Bey (57)	0.0
Piddily Patter—Nappy Brown (55)	0.0
Robert GUIDRY ▶ 1538 (3)	**3038**
Billy STEWART ▶ 1539 (8)	**3034**
Madonna L. CICCONE ▶ 1540 (2)	**3028**
Pete BELLOTTE/Greg MATHIESON/ Giorgio MORODER/Donna SUMMER ▶ 1541 (1)	**3027**
Heaven Knows— Donna Summer With Brooklyn Dreams (79)	3027
Joe BURKE/Al DUBIN ▶ 1542 (2)	**3024**
For You—Rick Nelson (63)	2166
Tip-Toe Thru' The Tulips With Me—Tiny Tim (68)	858
Dan HARTMAN/Charles E. KAUFMAN ▶ 1543 (4)	**3022**
Living In America—James Brown (85)	1992
We Are The Young—Dan Hartman (84)	641
Second Nature—Dan Hartman (85)	384
Gravity—James Brown (86)	4.8
Edna LEWIS/Beverly ROSS ▶ 1544 (1)	**3021**
Judy's Turn To Cry—Lesley Gore (63)	3021
Jordan KNIGHT/Tommy PAGE/Danny WOOD ▶ 1545 (1)	**3017**
I'll Be Your Everything—Tommy Page (90)	3017
Matt DIKE/Michael ROSS/Marvin YOUNG ▶ 1546 (3)	**3017**
Funky Cold Medina—Tone Loc (89)	2425
Principal's Office—Young M.C. (89)	445
I Come Off—Young M.C. (90)	147
Stanley J. LEWIS/Ferdinand WASHINGTON ▶ 1547 (3)	**3016**
I'll Be Home—Pat Boone (56)	3005
I'll Be Home—The Platters (66)	10
I'll Be Home—The Flamingos (56)	0.0
Rube BLOOM/Johnny MERCER ▶ 1548 (3)	**3015**
Fools Rush In—Rick Nelson (63)	1909
Fools Rush In (Where Angels Fear To Tread)— Brook Benton (60)	1092
Fools Rush In—Etta James (62)	14
Kye FLEMING/Dennis W. MORGAN ▶ 1549 (5)	**3014**
Nobody—Sylvia (2) (82)	1577
Smoky Mountain Rain—Ronnie Milsap (80)	1012
Years—Wayne Newton (80)	408
Fooled By A Feeling—Barbara Mandrell (79)	14
I Was Country When Country Wasn't Cool— Barbara Mandrell (81)	3.9
Frank F. ROBINSON ▶ 1550 (2)	**3002**
Randy HANSEN/Michael JACKSON ▶ 1551 (1)	**3000**
State Of Shock—Jacksons (84)	3000
Robert BELL/Ronald BELL/ George M. BROWN/Robert MICKENS/ Claydes SMITH/Dennis THOMAS/ Richard WESTFIELD ▶ 1552 (3)	**2998**

Hollywood Swinging—Kool & The Gang (74)	2079
Funky Stuff—Kool & The Gang (73)	473
Higher Plane—Kool & The Gang (74)	446
Terry BRITTEN/Christine HODGSON ▶ 1553 (1)	**2996**
Devil Woman—Cliff Richard (76)	2996
Wanda MALLETTE/Bob MORRISON/ Patti RYAN ▶ 1554 (1)	**2996**
Lookin' For Love—Johnny Lee (80)	2996
Keith DIAMOND/Mutt LANGE/Billy OCEAN ▶ 1555 (1)	**2995**
Loverboy—Billy Ocean (84)	2995
Ramsey KEARNEY/Mel TILLIS ▶ 1556 (1)	**2994**
Emotions—Brenda Lee (60)	2994
Al FRISCH/Sid WAYNE ▶ 1557 (9)	**2994**
Two Different Worlds—Don Rondo (56)	1457
Winner Take All—The Platters (56)	635
Two Different Worlds— Roger Williams And Jane Morgan (56)	427
Two Different Worlds—Lenny Welch (65)	403
If I'm Elected—Eddie Fisher (56)	54
Two Different Worlds—Dick Haymes (56)	11
Language Of Love—Cindy And Lindy (57)	6.4
Two Different Worlds—Dick Kallman (56)	0.0
Winner Take All—Sunny Gale (56)	0.0
Ricky Lynn CHRISTIAN ▶ 1558 (1)	**2988**
Mick HUCKNALL/Neil MOSS ▶ 1559 (1)	**2985**
Holding Back The Years—Simply Red (86)	2985
Benito BENITES/Toni COLANDREO/ John Virgo GARRETT III ▶ 1560 (1)	**2984**
The Power—Snap! (90)	2984
Darby SLICK ▶ 1561 (1)	**2975**
Les KUMMEL/Ronnie RICE ▶ 1562 (2)	**2973**
Things I'd Like To Say—The New Colony Six (68)	1717
I Will Always Think About You— The New Colony Six (68)	1256
Arthur BROOKS/Richard BROOKS/ Jerry BUTLER ▶ 1563 (6)	**2972**
For Your Precious Love— Jerry Butler & The Impressions (58)	1045
For Your Precious Love—Oscar Toney, Jr. (67)	778
For Your Precious Love— Garnet Mimms & The Enchanters (63)	662
For Your Precious Love— Jackie Wilson And Count Basie (68)	411
Your Precious Love—Linda Jones (72)	74
For Your Precious Love—Jerry Butler (66)	1.4
Ray EVANS/Jay LIVINGSTON/Henry MANCINI ▶ 1564 (4)	**2970**
Dear Heart—Andy Williams (64)	1324
Dear Heart—Jack Jones (64)	1154
In The Arms Of Love—Andy Williams (66)	249
Dear Heart— Henry Mancini's Orchestra And Chorus (64)	243
Melvin RILEY/Gordon STROZIER/ Gerald VALENTINE ▶ 1565 (1)	**2969**
Oh Sheila—Ready For The World (85)	2969
Ian THOMAS ▶ 1566 (4)	**2968**
Carla THOMAS ▶ 1567 (5)	**2963**
Teena MARIE ▶ 1568 (3)	**2961**
Jessi COLTER ▶ 1569 (3)	**2956**
Matt AITKEN/Sarah DALLIN/ Siobhan FAHEY/Mike STOCK/ Pete WATERMAN/Keren WOODWARD ▶ 1570 (4)	**2955**
I Heard A Rumour—Bananarama (87)	2288
I Can't Help It—Bananarama (87)	331
Love In The First Degree—Bananarama (88)	262
More Than Physical—Bananarama (86)	74
Sammy CAHN/Kay TWOMEY/Bee WALKER ▶ 1571 (1)	**2954**
Hey Jealous Lover—Frank Sinatra (56)	2954
T. Texas TYLER ▶ 1572 (1)	**2950**
Jerry PETERS/Anita POREE/ Skip SCARBOROUGH ▶ 1573 (2)	**2948**
Love Or Let Me Be Lonely— The Friends Of Distinction (70)	2597
Love Or Let Me Be Lonely— Paul Davis (82)	351

Bobby BARE/Orville LUNSFORD/ Bill PARSONS ▶ 1574 (1)	**2944**
All American Boy— Bill Parsons And His Orchestra (58)	2944
J. Leslie McFARLAND/Mort SHUMAN ▶ 1575 (1)	**2943**
Little Children— Billy J. Kramer With The Dakotas (64)	2943
Bill GIANT/David HESS/Buddy KAYE ▶ 1576 (3)	**2943**
Speedy Gonzales—Pat Boone (62)	2754
The Next Kiss (Is The Last Goodbye)— Conway Twitty (61)	170
Speedy Gonzales—David Dante (61)	19
Leon HAYWOOD ▶ 1577 (8)	**2942**
Dave BARTHOLOMEW/Fats DOMINO/ Robert GUIDRY ▶ 1578 (3)	**2939**
Walking To New Orleans—Fats Domino (60)	2113
It Keeps Rainin'—Fats Domino (61)	735
Before I Grow Too Old—Fats Domino (60)	92
Lynn EASTON/Don HARRIS/Dewey TERRY ▶ 1579 (1)	**2937**
The Jolly Green Giant—The Kingsmen (65)	2937
Charles CARPENTER/Louis DUNLAP/ Earl HINES ▶ 1580 (1)	**2935**
You Can Depend On Me—Brenda Lee (61)	2935
Allen COLLINS/Ronnie VAN ZANT ▶ 1581 (4)	**2934**
Free Bird—Will To Power (88)	1705
Free Bird—Lynyrd Skynyrd (74)	716
Free Bird (Live)—Lynyrd Skynyrd (76)	482
Double Trouble—Lynyrd Skynyrd (76)	31
LaForrest COPE ▶ 1582 (1)	**2931**
Ricky BELL/Michael BIVINS/ Carl BOURELLY/Ronnie DeVOE ▶ 1583 (1)	**2931**
Do Me!—Bell Biv DeVoe (90)	2931
Bob LIND ▶ 1584 (3)	**2929**
Janet JACKSON ▶ 1585 (1)	**2927**
Bernard BELLE/Teddy RILEY/Dave WAY ▶ 1586 (1)	**2919**
I Like The Way (The Kissing Game)—Hi-Five (91)	2919
Carlo DONIDA/Jerry LEIBER/ Giulio RAPETTI/Mike STOLLER ▶ 1587 (5)	**2919**
I (Who Have Nothing)—Tom Jones (70)	1304
I (Who Have Nothing)—Ben E. King (63)	810
I (Who Have Nothing)— Terry Knight And The Pack (66)	588
I (Who Have Nothing)—Sylvester (79)	146
I Who Have Nothing—Liquid Smoke (70)	71
Mel TILLIS ▶ 1588 (3)	**2917**
J.J. CALE ▶ 1589 (8)	**2914**
Jack CONRAD/Ray KENNEDY ▶ 1590 (3)	**2914**
Every Time I Think Of You—The Babys (78)	1477
Isn't It Time—The Babys (77)	1422
Just For The Moment—Ray Kennedy (80)	15
Reggie CALLOWAY ▶ 1591 (3)	**2911**
Frank MAUDSLEY/Paul REYNOLDS/ Ali SCORE/Mike SCORE ▶ 1592 (4)	**2911**
I Ran (So Far Away)—A Flock Of Seagulls (82)	1474
Space Age Love Song—A Flock Of Seagulls (82)	637
Wishing (If I Had A Photograph Of You)— A Flock Of Seagulls (83)	612
The More You Live, The More You Love— A Flock Of Seagulls (84)	187
Johnny BRISTOL ▶ 1593 (4)	**2910**
Julian LENNON ▶ 1594 (3)	**2905**
Ken TOBIAS ▶ 1595 (1)	**2905**
Huey P. SMITH ▶ 1596 (5)	**2904**
Thomas COMAN/Sylvester STEWART ▶ 1597 (2)	**2900**
C'mon And Swim—Bobby Freeman (64)	2736
S-W-I-M—Bobby Freeman (64)	164
Kenny LOGGINS/Melissa MANCHESTER ▶ 1598 (1)	**2897**
Whenever I Call You "Friend"—Kenny Loggins (78)	2897
James Anthony DEAN/Paul RISER/ William WEATHERSPOON ▶ 1599 (1)	**2895**
What Becomes Of The Brokenhearted— Jimmy Ruffin (66)	2895
Dave MASON ▶ 1600 (8)	**2894**
Deadric MALONE/Joe SCOTT ▶ 1601 (10)	**2892**
Ain't Nothing You Can Do—Bobby Bland (64)	914
Turn On Your Love Light—Bobby Bland (61)	708
Annie Get Your Yo-Yo—Little Junior Parker (62)	356
Blind Man—Bobby Bland (64)	282
Blind Man—Little Milton (64)	226
Turn On Your Love Light—Oscar Toney, Jr. (67)	156
Turn On Your Love Light—The Human Beinz (68)	141
Turn On Your Love Light—Bill Black's Combo (68)	103
Turn On Your Love Light—Jerry Lee Lewis (72)	4.6
Dust Got In Daddy's Eyes—Bobby Bland (65)	0.9
Glenn SHORROCK ▶ 1602 (2)	**2890**
Dorian BURTON/Eugene RANDOLPH ▶ 1603 (3)	**2887**
A Tear Fell—Teresa Brewer (56)	2559
A Tear Fell—Ray Charles (64)	328
A Tear Fell—Ivory Joe Hunter (56)	0.0
Rick CHUDACOFF/Robbie DUPREE ▶ 1604 (1)	**2883**
Steal Away—Robbie Dupree (80)	2883
Norman NEWELL/Cyril ORNADEL ▶ 1605 (2)	**2880**
Portrait Of My Love—Steve Lawrence (61)	2254
Portrait Of My Love—The Tokens (67)	626
Sid JACOBSON/Jimmy KRONDES ▶ 1606 (1)	**2879**
(At) The End (Of A Rainbow)—Earl Grant (58)	2879
Sammy JOHNS ▶ 1607 (2)	**2877**
David NICHTERN ▶ 1608 (1)	**2877**
Simon GALLUP/Roger O'DONNELL/ Robert James SMITH/Porl THOMPSON/ Laurence TOLHURST/Boris WILLIAMS ▶ 1609 (4)	**2876**
Love Song—The Cure (89)	2408
Fascination Street—The Cure (89)	194
Lullaby—The Cure (89)	170
Pictures Of You—The Cure (90)	105
Junior CAMPBELL/Thomas McALEESE ▶ 1610 (2)	**2874**
Reflections Of My Life—The Marmalade (70)	2469
Rainbow—The Marmalade (70)	405
David John BRIGGS ▶ 1611 (1)	**2874**
Al GOODMAN/Walter Lee MORRIS/Harry RAY ▶ 1612 (2)	**2869**
Special Lady—Ray, Goodman & Brown (80)	2439
Look At Me (I'm In Love)—The Moments (75)	430
Patrick ADAMS/Cathy DENNIS/ C. Delyle GREGORY ▶ 1613 (1)	**2867**
Touch Me (All Night Long)—Cathy Dennis (91)	2867
Freddy CANNON/Bob CREWE/Frank SLAY ▶ 1614 (1)	**2864**
Tallahassee Lassie—Freddy Cannon (59)	2864
Ewart ABNER/John C. MOORE ▶ 1615 (4)	**2863**
At My Front Door (Crazy Little Mama)— Pat Boone (55)	1950
At My Front Door (Crazy Little Mama)— El Dorados And Magnificents (55)	653
At My Front Door—Dee Clark (60)	260
(Crazy Little Mama Song) At My Front Door— The Modernaires (55)	0.0
Sol LAKE ▶ 1616 (3)	**2862**
Robert BATEMAN/Brian HOLLAND/ William STEVENSON ▶ 1617 (2)	**2859**
Playboy—The Marvelettes (62)	2321
Twistin' Postman—The Marvelettes (62)	539
Melissa MANCHESTER/Carole Bayer SAGER ▶ 1618 (4)	**2853**
Midnight Blue—Melissa Manchester (75)	2399
Just You And I—Melissa Manchester (76)	346
Better Days—Melissa Manchester (76)	54
Come In From The Rain—Captain & Tennille (77)	54
Bob CREWE/Denny RANDELL ▶ 1619 (3)	**2853**
Swearin' To God—Frankie Valli (75)	2151
I Wanna Dance Wit' Choo (Doo Dat Dance)— Disco Tex & The Sex-O-Lettes Featuring Sir Monti Rock III (75)	676
Jam Band—Disco Tex & The Sex-O-Lettes (75)	26
Claudine CLARK ▶ 1620 (1)	**2853**
Harry CHAPIN ▶ 1621 (9)	**2851**
Billy LYALL/David PATON ▶ 1622 (2)	**2851**
Magic—Pilot (75)	2804
Just A Smile—Pilot (75)	47
Frederick LONG/William STEVENSON ▶ 1623 (2)	**2850**
Devil With A Blue Dress On— Mitch Ryder And The Detroit Wheels (66)	2815
Devil With A Blue Dress—Pratt & McClain (76)	34
Harold FALTERMEYER ▶ 1624 (1)	**2849**
Jim POST ▶ 1625 (2)	**2848**
Desmond CHILD/Diane WARREN ▶ 1626 (3)	**2843**
Just Like Jesse James—Cher (89)	2020
Save Up All Your Tears—Cher (91)	688
You're The Story Of My Life—Desmond Child (91)	135
Nick ACQUAVIVA/Ted VARNICK ▶ 1627 (7)	**2842**
In The Middle Of An Island— Tony Bennett with Ray Ellis and His Orchestra (57)	1952
Ghost Town—Don Cherry (56)	585
In The Middle Of An Island— "Tennessee" Ernie Ford (57)	301
Never Leave Me—Gale Storm (56)	1.9
Never Leave Me—Bob Presto (56)	1.9
In The Middle Of An Island— The Anita Kerr Quartet (57)	0.0
In The Middle Of An Island—Stan Wilson (57)	0.0
Richard BASKIN/David FOSTER/Tom KEANE ▶ 1628 (1)	**2842**
Will You Still Love Me?—Chicago (86)	2842
John Robert SMITH ▶ 1629 (1)	**2841**
Rick HALL/Billy SHERRILL ▶ 1630 (1)	**2840**
Sweet And Innocent—Donny Osmond (71)	2840
Don JULIAN ▶ 1631 (1)	**2839**
Bent FABRICIUS-BJERRE ▶ 1632 (1)	**2839**
Desmond CHILD/Steven TYLER ▶ 1633 (1)	**2836**
Angel—Aerosmith (88)	2836
Snuff GARRETT/Gary LEWIS/Leon RUSSELL ▶ 1634 (1)	**2836**
Everybody Loves A Clown— Gary Lewis And The Playboys (65)	2836
Nellee HOOPER/Simon LAW/ Beresford ROMEO/Caron WHEELER ▶ 1635 (1)	**2835**
Back To Life—Soul II Soul (89)	2835
Art GARFUNKEL/Paul SIMON ▶ 1636 (3)	**2834**
Scarborough Fair (/Canticle)— Simon & Garfunkel (68)	1431
Scarborough Fair—Sergio Mendes & Brasil '66 (68)	1088
Hey Schoolgirl—Tom & Jerry (57)	316
Alex CALL ▶ 1637 (2)	**2834**
Dennis DOHERTY/John PHILLIPS ▶ 1638 (2)	**2829**
I Saw Her Again—The Mamas & The Papas (66)	2615
For The Love Of Ivy—The Mamas & The Papas (68)	214
Hal DAVID/Albert HAMMOND ▶ 1639 (2)	**2827**
To All The Girls I've Loved Before— Julio Iglesias & Willie Nelson (84)	2750
99 Miles From L.A.—Albert Hammond (75)	77
Patrick SWAYZE/Stacey WIDELITZ ▶ 1640 (1)	**2825**
She's Like The Wind—Patrick Swayze (87)	2825
Alfonso GENTILE/Joseph LUCCISANO/ Alfred STRIANO ▶ 1641 (1)	**2822**
There's A Moon Out Tonight—The Capris (60)	2822
Eric CLAPTON ▶ 1642 (5)	**2822**
Johnny MERCER/Harry WARREN ▶ 1643 (2)	**2818**
You Must Have Been A Beautiful Baby— Bobby Darin (61)	2364
You Must Have Been A Beautiful Baby— The Dave Clark Five (67)	455
Jerry Jeff WALKER ▶ 1644 (3)	**2818**
Tom AUSTIN/Bill CRANDALL/ Bill DALTON/Bob GAUDIO ▶ 1645 (3)	**2815**
Short Shorts—Royal Teens (58)	2815
Short Shorts— Tiny Bradshaw & His Orchestra (58)	0.0
Short Shorts—The Four Winds (58)	0.0
Thomas BOGDANY/Ernie MARESCA ▶ 1646 (2)	**2811**
Shout! Shout! (Knock Yourself Out)— Ernie Maresca (62)	1995
Come On Little Angel—The Belmonts (62)	817
Tom WAITS ▶ 1647 (2)	**2809**

Tom SHANNON/Phil TODARO ▶ 1648 (3)	**2808**
Wild Weekend—The Rebels (62)	2435
Rockin' Crickets— The Hot-Toddys Featuring Bill Pennell (59)	298
Rockin' Crickets—Rockin' Rebels (63)	75
Jimmy GEORGE ▶ 1649 (1)	**2802**
Terence Trent D'ARBY ▶ 1650 (4)	**2802**
Dale EVANS ▶ 1651 (3)	**2800**
Peter ALLEN/Carole Bayer SAGER ▶ 1652 (3)	**2799**
Don't Cry Out Loud—Melissa Manchester (78)	1951
I'd Rather Leave While I'm In Love—Rita Coolidge (79)	461
Jennifer—Bobby Sherman (71)	386
Rick ALLEN/Steve CLARK/Joe ELLIOTT/ Mutt LANGE/Rick SAVAGE/Pete WILLIS ▶ 1653 (3)	**2797**
Photograph—Def Leppard (83)	1231
Rock Of Ages—Def Leppard (83)	1009
Foolin'—Def Leppard (83)	557
Denise LaSALLE ▶ 1654 (5)	**2797**
George CAMPBELL/Marvin MOORE ▶ 1655 (4)	**2796**
Four Walls—Jim Reeves (57)	1889
Four Walls—Jim Lowe (57)	881
Four Walls—Kay Starr (62)	26
Four Walls—Dorothy Collins (57)	0.0
Stan VINCENT ▶ 1656 (2)	**2794**
James BROWN/Betty Jean NEWSOME ▶ 1657 (1)	**2793**
It's A Man's Man's Man's World— James Brown And The Famous Flames (66)	2793
Les CHADWICK/Leo MAGUIRE/ Fred MARSDEN/Gerry MARSDEN ▶ 1658 (1)	**2786**
Don't Let The Sun Catch You Crying— Gerry And The Pacemakers (64)	2786
Giancarlo BIGAZZI/Steve PICCOLO/ Raffaele RIEFOLI ▶ 1659 (1)	**2784**
Self Control—Laura Branigan (84)	2784
Billy SHERRILL/Glenn SUTTON ▶ 1660 (10)	**2783**
Almost Persuaded—David Houston (66)	1274
Kiss Away—Ronnie Dove (65)	745
Almost Persuaded No. 2—Ben Colder (66)	289
You Mean The World To Me—David Houston (67)	172
She's Ready—The Spiral Starecase (69)	165
Almost Persuaded—Etta James (69)	77
Kids Say The Darndest Things—Tammy Wynette (73)	24
Bedtime Story—Tammy Wynette (72)	17
He's Ready—The Poppies (66)	12
Have A Little Faith—David Houston (68)	8.9
Barry MANILOW/Marty PANZER ▶ 1661 (3)	**2783**
It's A Miracle—Barry Manilow (75)	1361
Even Now—Barry Manilow (78)	813
This One's For You—Barry Manilow (76)	608
Christine McVIE/Eddy QUINTELA ▶ 1662 (3)	**2779**
Little Lies—Fleetwood Mac (87)	1985
As Long As You Follow—Fleetwood Mac (88)	414
Save Me—Fleetwood Mac (90)	380
Melanie ANDREWS/James Samuel HARRIS/ Janet JACKSON/Terry LEWIS ▶ 1663 (1)	**2779**
Let's Wait Awhile—Janet Jackson (87)	2779
Dallas AUSTIN/Michael BIVINS/ Nathan MORRIS/Shawn STOCKMAN ▶ 1664 (1)	**2776**
Motownphilly—Boyz II Men (91)	2776
Bill BLACK ▶ 1665 (8)	**2773**
Peter BECKETT/Steve KIPNER ▶ 1666 (1)	**2773**
Twist Of Fate—Olivia Newton-John (83)	2773
Arthur KENT/Ed WARREN ▶ 1667 (6)	**2766**
Take Good Care Of Her—Adam Wade (61)	2184
Dearer Than Life—Brook Benton (63)	286
Tonight I Won't Be There—Adam Wade (61)	194
Take Good Care Of Her—Mel Carter (66)	56
Take Good Care Of Her—Elvis Presley (74)	41
It's Good To Have You Back With Me— Adam Wade (62)	5.8
Ralph MacDONALD/William SALTER ▶ 1668 (2)	**2754**
Where Is The Love—Roberta Flack & Donny Hathaway (72)	2619
Mister Magic—Grover Washington, Jr. (75)	135

Phil CHEN/Jim CREGAN/Gary GRAINGER/ Kevin SAVIGAR/Rod STEWART ▶ 1669 (1)	**2748**
Passion—Rod Stewart (80)	2748
Ben RALEIGH/Don WOLF ▶ 1670 (10)	**2740**
Love Is All We Need—Tommy Edwards (58)	1872
Love Is All We Need—Mel Carter (66)	369
Love Is All We Need—Vic Dana (64)	201
Exclusively Yours—Carl Dobkins, Jr. (60)	121
Let's Be Lovers—The Playmates (58)	103
Mary Ann Thomas—Bobby Freeman (59)	31
Majesty Of Love— Marvin Rainwater and Connie Francis (57)	22
Love Is A Sacred Thing—Kitty Kallen (58)	18
How Do You Know It's Love— Teresa Brewer (60)	2.1
Mary Ann Thomas—Buddy Heart (59)	0.0
Benny ANDERSSON/Tim RICE/Björn ULVAEUS ▶ 1671 (2)	**2738**
One Night In Bangkok—Murray Head (85)	2683
One Night In Bangkok—Robey (85)	55
Kate PIERSON/Fred SCHNEIDER/ Keith STRICKLAND/Robert WALDROP/ Cindy WILSON ▶ 1672 (1)	**2734**
Roam—The B-52's (89)	2734
Pat BEST ▶ 1673 (5)	**2734**
Jackie FAUTHEREE/Wayne GRAY ▶ 1674 (2)	**2732**
Cradle Of Love—Johnny Preston (60)	2731
Cradle Of Love—Ronnie & Robyn (66)	0.5
Bob CREWE/Eddie RAMBEAU/Bud REHAK ▶ 1675 (1)	**2732**
Navy Blue—Diane Renay (64)	2732
Richard MORRIS/Sylvia MOY ▶ 1676 (4)	**2730**
Honey Chile—Martha Reeves & The Vandellas (67)	1767
Love Bug Leave My Heart Alone— Martha & The Vandellas (67)	707
(We've Got) Honey Love— Martha Reeves & The Vandellas (69)	249
Forget Me Not—Martha Reeves & The Vandellas (68)	6.2
Albert Philip McKAY/ Maurice WHITE/Allee WILLIS ▶ 1677 (1)	**2728**
September—Earth, Wind & Fire (78)	2728
Fred NEIL ▶ 1678 (3)	**2722**
Larry DERMER/Joe GALDO/Rafael VIGIL ▶ 1679 (3)	**2717**
Bad Boy—Miami Sound Machine (86)	1668
Falling In Love (Uh-Oh)—Miami Sound Machine (86)	691
Betcha Say That— Gloria Estefan and Miami Sound Machine (87)	358
Ritchie ADAMS/Alan BERNSTEIN ▶ 1680 (5)	**2716**
After The Lovin'—Engelbert Humperdinck (76)	2368
The Next Hundred Years—Al Martino (77)	283
This Moment In Time—Engelbert Humperdinck (78)	59
Goodbye My Friend—Engelbert Humperdinck (77)	3.4
Kentucky Mornin'—Al Martino (77)	2.4
Steve GIBB ▶ 1681 (1)	**2715**
Bickley REICHNER/Sid WAYNE ▶ 1682 (1)	**2712**
I Need Your Love Tonight—Elvis Presley (59)	2712
Al CLEVELAND/Terry JOHNSON/ Smokey ROBINSON ▶ 1683 (2)	**2712**
Baby, Baby Don't Cry— Smokey Robinson & The Miracles (69)	2458
Malinda—Bobby Taylor & The Vancouvers (68)	254
David BYRNE/Chris FRANTZ/ Jerry HARRISON/Tina WEYMOUTH ▶ 1684 (5)	**2711**
Burning Down The House—Talking Heads (83)	1439
Wild Wild Life—Talking Heads (86)	742
And She Was—Talking Heads (85)	350
This Must Be The Place (Naïve Melody)— Talking Heads (83)	156
Life During Wartime (This Ain't No Party.. This Aint No Disco.. This Ain't No Foolin' Around)— Talking Heads (79)	25
FALCO/Andrew PIERCY/Robert PONGER ▶ 1685 (1)	**2710**
Der Kommissar—After The Fire (83)	2710
Alan FREW/Sam REID/Jim VALLANCE ▶ 1686 (2)	**2710**
Don't Forget Me (When I'm Gone)—Glass Tiger (86)	2668
My Song—Glass Tiger (88)	41

Petula CLARK/Tony HATCH ▶ 1687 (1)	**2706**
You're The One—The Vogues (65)	2706
Buddy KILLEN ▶ 1688 (4)	**2706**
Tom BRASFIELD/Clayton IVEY/ Terry WOODFORD ▶ 1689 (1)	**2701**
Angel In Your Arms—Hot (77)	2701
Norman SALLITT ▶ 1690 (1)	**2697**
Teddy POWELL/Bobby SHARP ▶ 1691 (4)	**2697**
Unchain My Heart— Ray Charles And His Orchestra (61)	1906
Don't Set Me Free—Ray Charles And His Orchestra With The Raelettes (63)	713
Unchain My Heart—Herbie Mann (68)	73
Hot And Cold Running Tears—Sarah Vaughan (56)	5.6
Johnny PARKER ▶ 1692 (3)	**2695**
Charles E. McCORMICK ▶ 1693 (2)	**2692**
Wayne DUNCAN/Freddy FENDER ▶ 1694 (2)	**2691**
Wasted Days And Wasted Nights—Freddy Fender (75)	2670
Wasted Days And Wasted Nights—Freddy Fender (60)	21
William DOUCHETTE/Gene VINCENT ▶ 1695 (3)	**2691**
Be Bop A Lula—Gene Vincent and His Blue Caps (56)	2525
Race With The Devil— Gene Vincent and His Blue Caps (56)	116
Be Bop A-Lula—The Everly Brothers (60)	50
Neneh CHERRY/Cameron McVEY/ Jamie MORGAN/Phil RAMACON ▶ 1696 (1)	**2690**
Buffalo Stance—Neneh Cherry (89)	2690
Howard Lee BARNES/Don ROBERTSON ▶ 1697 (6)	**2689**
I Really Don't Want To Know—Tommy Edwards (60)	1085
I Really Don't Want To Know—Ronnie Dove (66)	753
I Really Don't Want To Know—Elvis Presley (70)	704
I Really Don't Want To Know— "Little Esther" Phillips (63)	134
I Really Don't Want To Know—Solomon Burke (62)	15
I Really Don't Want To Know— Les Paul and Mary Ford (54)	0.0
Ronnie GILBERT/Lee HAYS/ Fred HELLERMAN/Sam KENNEDY/ Huddie LEDBETTER/Pete SEEGER/ TRADITIONAL ▶ 1698 (1)	**2683**
Kisses Sweeter Than Wine—Jimmie Rodgers (57)	2683
Barbara LYNN/Huey P. MEAUX ▶ 1699 (2)	**2682**
You'll Lose A Good Thing—Barbara Lynn (62)	2239
You'll Lose A Good Thing—Freddy Fender (76)	443
David HESS/Aaron SCHROEDER ▶ 1700 (2)	**2679**
I Got Stung—Elvis Presley (58)	2661
You're Singing Our Love Song To Somebody Else— Jerry Wallace (60)	18
John BARRY ▶ 1701 (7)	**2678**
Margaret LEWIS/Mira SMITH ▶ 1702 (10)	**2674**
Reconsider Me—Johnny Adams (69)	820
Soulshake—Peggy Scott & Jo Jo Benson (69)	539
The Girl Most Likely—Jeannie C. Riley (68)	427
Soul Shake—Delaney & Bonnie & Friends (70)	392
Oh, Singer—Jeannie C. Riley (71)	236
There Never Was A Time—Jeannie C. Riley (69)	137
Reconsider Me—Narvel Felts (75)	53
I Can't Be All Bad—Johnny Adams (69)	34
The Wedding Cake—Connie Francis (69)	28
I Almost Called Your Name—Margaret Whiting (67)	8.1
Leon CARR/Paul VANCE ▶ 1703 (6)	**2674**
Gina—Johnny Mathis (62)	2333
She Lets Her Hair Down (Early In The Morning)— The Tokens (69)	259
Two Thousand Two Hundred Twenty Three Miles— Patti Page (60)	45
She Lets Her Hair Down (Early In The Morning)— Gene Pitney (69)	36
Julie Knows—Randy Sparks (64)	0.5
She Lets Her Hair Down (Early In The Morning)— Don Young (69)	0.0
Lorenzo BARCELATA ▶ 1704 (2)	**2672**
Pat UPTON ▶ 1705 (2)	**2669**
Bertie HIGGINS/Sonny LIMBO ▶ 1706 (1)	**2665**
Key Largo—Bertie Higgins (81)	2665
Chas SANDFORD ▶ 1707 (2)	**2663**
Michael JAY/MARTIKA ▶ 1708 (1)	**2662**
Toy Soldiers—Martika (89)	2662

Fini BUSCH/Mickey LEADER/ Werner SCHARFENBERGER ▶ 1709 (1)	**2661**
Sailor (Your Home Is The Sea)—Lolita (60)	2661
Sandy NELSON/Richard PODOLOR ▶ 1710 (4)	**2660**
Let There Be Drums—Sandy Nelson (61)	2590
...And Then There Were Drums—Sandy Nelson (62)	52
Drum Stomp—Sandy Nelson (62)	13
Let There Be Drums—The Incredible Bongo Band (73)	4.3
James W. ALEXANDER/Zelda SAMUELS ▶ 1711 (3)	**2659**
Lookin' For A Love—Bobby Womack (74)	1838
Looking For A Love—The J. Geils Band (71)	652
Lookin' For A Love—The Valentinos (62)	169
Vinicius De MORAES/Norman GIMBEL/ Antonio Carlos JOBIM ▶ 1712 (1)	**2656**
The Girl From Ipanema—Getz/Gilberto (64)	2656
John Paul JONES/Jimmy PAGE/ Robert PLANT ▶ 1713 (4)	**2653**
Black Dog—Led Zeppelin (71)	1455
Fool In The Rain—Led Zeppelin (79)	673
Trampled Under Foot—Led Zeppelin (75)	436
Black Dog—Newcity Rockers (87)	89
Gloria JONES/Clay McMURRAY/Pam SAWYER ▶ 1714 (1)	**2652**
If I Were Your Woman—Gladys Knight & The Pips (70)	2652
Marvin HAMLISCH/Howard LIEBLING ▶ 1715 (3)	**2652**
California Nights—Lesley Gore (67)	1534
Sunshine, Lollipops And Rainbows—Lesley Gore (65)	1112
Too Little Time—Brenda Lee (66)	5.1
Craig ATKINSON/John BYRNE/ Roy CHANEY/Kenn ELLNER/John MICHALSKI ▶ 1716 (1)	**2651**
Psychotic Reaction—Count Five (66)	2651
John BARRY/Leslie BRICUSSE/ Anthony NEWLEY ▶ 1717 (1)	**2651**
Goldfinger—Shirley Bassey (65)	2651
Franne GOLDE/Dennis LAMBERT/ Walter ORANGE ▶ 1718 (1)	**2649**
Nightshift—Commodores (85)	2649
Arthur BAKER/Tommy FARAGHER/ Lotti GOLDEN ▶ 1719 (2)	**2649**
With Every Beat Of My Heart—Taylor Dayne (89)	2568
Undeniable—Ms. Adventures (90)	81
Gerry GOFFIN/Barry GOLDBERG ▶ 1720 (1)	**2639**
I've Got To Use My Imagination— Gladys Knight & The Pips (73)	2639
Billy IDOL ▶ 1721 (6)	**2639**
John DeNICOLA/Franke PREVITE ▶ 1722 (1)	**2638**
Hungry Eyes—Eric Carmen (87)	2638
Zane GREY/Len HANKS ▶ 1723 (2)	**2636**
(Every Time I Turn Around) Back In Love Again— L.T.D. (77)	2620
Dancin'—Grey and Hanks (79)	16
TRADITIONAL/Fred WEATHERLY ▶ 1724 (6)	**2632**
Danny Boy—Conway Twitty (59)	2086
Danny Boy—Andy Williams (61)	282
Danny Boy—Ray Price (67)	193
Danny Boy—Patti Labelle And Her Blue Belles (64)	32
Danny Boy—Joni James (56)	31
Danny Boy—Jackie Wilson (65)	9.5
Cy COLEMAN/Carolyn LEIGH ▶ 1725 (7)	**2629**
Witchcraft—Frank Sinatra (57)	1455
Firefly—Tony Bennett (58)	1081
Real Live Girl—Steve Alaimo (65)	47
Pass Me By—Peggy Lee (65)	29
Hey, Look Me Over— Pete King Chorale and Orchestra (61)	11
My How The Time Goes By—Patti Page (57)	5.7
Pass Me By—Mike Douglas (65)	0.0
Mitch BOTTLER/Gary ZEKLEY ▶ 1726 (3)	**2628**
I'd Wait A Million Years—The Grass Roots (69)	2231
Breakaway—Big Pig (88)	207
The Grooviest Girl In The World— The Fun And Games (69)	190
Desmond CHILD/Joan JETT ▶ 1727 (3)	**2627**
I Hate Myself For Loving You— Joan Jett and the Blackhearts (88)	1501
Little Liar—Joan Jett and the Blackhearts (88)	911
House Of Fire—Alice Cooper (90)	215
Larry BLACKMON/Tomi JENKINS ▶ 1728 (3)	**2626**
Word Up—Cameo (86)	1982
Candy—Cameo (86)	604
Freaky Dancin'—Cameo (81)	40
Cornelius GRANT/Rodger PENZABENE/ Norman WHITFIELD ▶ 1729 (1)	**2625**
You're My Everything—The Temptations (67)	2625
Phil BELMONTE/Eugene PITT/ Oscar WALTZER ▶ 1730 (1)	**2624**
My True Story—The Jive Five (61)	2624
Freddy CURCI/Steve DEMARCHI ▶ 1731 (1)	**2619**
More Than Words Can Say—Alias (90)	2619
George M. BROWN ▶ 1732 (1)	**2617**
Steve KIPNER/Cliff MAGNESS ▶ 1733 (1)	**2616**
Impulsive—Wilson Phillips (90)	2616
Lamont DOZIER/Brian HOLLAND/ Eddie HOLLAND/Sylvia MOY ▶ 1734 (4)	**2614**
This Old Heart Of Mine (Is Weak For You)— The Isley Brothers (66)	1339
This Old Heart Of Mine— Rod Stewart (with Ronald Isley) (90)	1125
This Old Heart Of Mine (Is Weak For You)— Tammi Terrell (69)	96
This Old Heart Of Mine—Rod Stewart (76)	53
Matt DIKE/Michael ROSS/ Anthony Terrell SMITH/Marvin YOUNG ▶ 1735 (1)	**2613**
Wild Thing—Tone Loc (88)	2613
Jesse D. HODGES/William MICHAEL ▶ 1736 (1)	**2611**
Mission Bell—Donnie Brooks (60)	2611
Danny SEMBELLO/Allee WILLIS ▶ 1737 (3)	**2608**
Neutron Dance—Pointer Sisters (84)	1907
Stir It Up—Patti LaBelle (85)	378
Live My Life—Boy George (87)	323
Henry GLOVER/Morris LEVY ▶ 1738 (2)	**2606**
California Sun—The Rivieras (2) (64)	2473
California Sun—Joe Jones (61)	133
Sue ENNIS/Ann WILSON/Nancy WILSON ▶ 1739 (4)	**2605**
Straight On—Heart (78)	1064
Even It Up—Heart (80)	530
Dog & Butterfly—Heart (79)	515
This Man Is Mine—Heart (82)	497
Otis BLACKWELL ▶ 1740 (12)	**2605**
Paula BROWN/Mitchel EVANS/ James WHELAN ▶ 1741 (1)	**2603**
Mad About You—Belinda Carlisle (86)	2603
Kenneth EDMONDS/Daryl SIMMONS ▶ 1742 (2)	**2603**
Rock Wit'cha—Bobby Brown (89)	1460
My, My, My—Johnny Gill (90)	1143
Desmond CHILD/Joe PERRY/Steven TYLER ▶ 1743 (2)	**2602**
What It Takes—Aerosmith (90)	1375
Dude (Looks Like A Lady)—Aerosmith (87)	1227
Amy GRANT/Mark MUELLER/ Michael OMARTIAN ▶ 1744 (1)	**2600**
That's What Love Is For—Amy Grant (91)	2600
Bobby EDWARDS/Terry FELL/ Fred HENLEY/Mildred IMES ▶ 1745 (4)	**2598**
You're The Reason—Bobby Edwards (61)	2462
You're The Reason—Joe South (61)	136
You're The Reason—Gerry And The Pacemakers (65)	0.0
You're The Reason—Hank Locklin (61)	0.0
Nick FELDMAN/Jack HUES ▶ 1746 (4)	**2598**
Let's Go—Wang Chung (87)	1295
To Live And Die In L.A.—Wang Chung (85)	566
Hypnotize Me—Wang Chung (87)	403
Don't Let Go—Wang Chung (84)	335
Jay FERGUSON ▶ 1747 (4)	**2595**
Edgar LESLIE/Lawrence WRIGHT ▶ 1748 (1)	**2593**
Among My Souvenirs—Connie Francis (59)	2593
Marcel STELLMAN/TRADITIONAL ▶ 1749 (3)	**2592**
Melodie D'Amour (Melody Of Love)— The Ames Brothers (57)	2592
Melodie D'Amour— Edmundo Ros & His Orchestra (57)	0.0
Melodie D'Amour—Marty Gold & His Orchestra (57)	0.0
James HORNER/Barry MANN/Cynthia WEIL ▶ 1750 (1)	**2590**
Somewhere Out There— Linda Ronstadt And James Ingram (86)	2590
Fred JAY/Al JULIA ▶ 1751 (1)	**2588**
I Cried A Tear—LaVern Baker (58)	2588
Michael JULIEN/Giulio RAPETTI/ David SHAPIRO ▶ 1752 (1)	**2587**
Let's Live For Today—The Grass Roots (67)	2587
Bill COSBY/Henry COSBY/ Sylvia MOY/Stevie WONDER ▶ 1753 (1)	**2587**
Little Ole Man (Uptight - Everything's Alright)— Bill Cosby (67)	2587
Robert DURAND/Ron ELLIOTT ▶ 1754 (2)	**2583**
Just A Little—The Beau Brummels (65)	2227
Don't Talk To Strangers—The Beau Brummels (65)	357
Robert Eugene MILLER ▶ 1755 (8)	**2581**
Gerry GOFFIN/Barry MANN ▶ 1756 (2)	**2581**
Who Put The Bomp (In The Bomp, Bomp, Bomp)— Barry Mann (61)	2389
I Could Have Loved You So Well—Ray Peterson (61)	192
Gene PITNEY/Aaron SCHROEDER ▶ 1757 (3)	**2580**
Rubber Ball—Bobby Vee (60)	2133
Today's Teardrops—Rick Nelson (63)	261
Bandit Of My Dreams—Eddie Hodges (62)	185
Jeff BARRY/Ben RALEIGH ▶ 1758 (2)	**2579**
Tell Laura I Love Her—Ray Peterson (60)	2552
Tell Laura I Love Her—Johnny T. Angel (74)	27
Ken ASCHER/Paul WILLIAMS ▶ 1759 (4)	**2578**
You And Me Against The World—Helen Reddy (74)	1819
Rainbow Connection—Kermit (Jim Henson) (79)	539
Watch Closely Now—Kris Kristofferson (77)	164
Inspiration—Paul Williams (73)	56
Errol BROWN ▶ 1760 (4)	**2577**
Rod ARGENT/Chris WHITE ▶ 1761 (2)	**2576**
Hold Your Head Up—Argent (72)	2531
Imagine The Swan—The Zombies (69)	45
Jules SHEAR ▶ 1762 (3)	**2576**
Tommy BOYCE/Curtis LEE ▶ 1763 (2)	**2575**
Pretty Little Angel Eyes—Curtis Lee (61)	2252
Under The Moon Of Love—Curtis Lee (61)	323
Jackson BROWNE/Danny KORTCHMAR ▶ 1764 (1)	**2571**
Somebody's Baby—Jackson Browne (82)	2571
Reather DIXON/Helen GATHERS/ Emma POUGHT/Jannie POUGHT/ Laura WEBB ▶ 1765 (2)	**2571**
Mr. Lee—The Bobbettes (57)	2273
I Shot Mr. Lee—The Bobbettes (60)	297
Felipe DELGADO/Elbert LINNEAR/ Ce Ce PENISTON ▶ 1766 (1)	**2569**
Finally—Ce Ce Peniston (91)	2569
Brenda RUSSELL ▶ 1767 (3)	**2568**
John DENVER/Michael C. TAYLOR ▶ 1768 (1)	**2566**
Rocky Mountain High—John Denver (72)	2566
Albert LASRY/Jack LAWRENCE/ Charles TRENET ▶ 1769 (1)	**2565**
Beyond The Sea—Bobby Darin (60)	2565
Robert White JOHNSON/Taylor RHODES ▶ 1770 (1)	**2564**
Where Does My Heart Beat Now—Celine Dion (90)	2564
Hans VAN HEMERT/Harry VAN HOOF ▶ 1771 (2)	**2564**
How Do You Do?—Mouth & MacNeal (72)	2478
Hey, You Love—Mouth & MacNeal (72)	85
Richard CLASKY/Marvin ROSENBERG ▶ 1772 (1)	**2563**
Image Of A Girl— The Safaris With The Phantom's Band (60)	2563
Johnnie CHRISTO/John HOLLIDAY/ Trevor STEEL/Milan ZEKAVICA ▶ 1773 (4)	**2560**
I'll Be There—The Escape Club (91)	1572
Shake For The Sheik—The Escape Club (88)	509
Call It Poison—The Escape Club (91)	412
Walking Through Walls—The Escape Club (89)	67

Armando MANZANERO/Sid WAYNE ▶ 1774 (2)	**2555**
It's Impossible—Perry Como (70)	2155
It's Impossible—The New Birth (71)	400
Ray ALLEN/Wandra MERRELL ▶ 1775 (4)	**2549**
Pepino The Italian Mouse—Lou Monte (62)	2271
Pepino's Friend Pasqual (The Italian Pussy-cat)—Lou Monte (63)	202
That's How It Goes—George Maharis (63)	48
Spanish Nights And You—Connie Francis (66)	28
Barry DE VORZON/Ted ELLIS ▶ 1776 (2)	**2545**
Dreamin'—Johnny Burnette (60)	2376
Dreamin'—John Schneider (82)	169
Billy MYLES ▶ 1777 (7)	**2545**
Julia Ward HOWE/William STEFFE ▶ 1778 (4)	**2544**
Battle Hymn Of The Republic—The Mormon Tabernacle Choir (59)	1595
Battle Hymn Of The Republic—Andy Williams With The St. Charles Borromeo Choir (68)	658
Battle Hymn Of The Republic—Mickey Newbury (71)	222
Battle Hymn Of The Republic—Elvis Presley (72)	69
Jerry KNIGHT/Aaron ZIGMAN ▶ 1779 (2)	**2544**
Crush On You—The Jets (86)	2253
Private Number—The Jets (86)	291
Carl BONURA/Raymond CERONI ▶ 1780 (2)	**2543**
I've Had It—The Bell Notes (59)	2423
I've Had It—Fanny (74)	121
Johnny CYMBAL/George TOBIN ▶ 1781 (2)	**2543**
Cinnamon—Derek (68)	2256
Back Door Man—Derek (69)	286
David FOSTER/Boz SCAGGS ▶ 1782 (2)	**2536**
Look What You've Done To Me—Boz Scaggs (80)	1316
Breakdown Dead Ahead—Boz Scaggs (80)	1220
Freddie GORMAN/Bob HAMILTON ▶ 1783 (2)	**2535**
(Just Like) Romeo & Juliet—The Reflections (64)	2234
(Just Like) Romeo And Juliet—Sha Na Na (75)	301
Gene THOMAS ▶ 1784 (4)	**2532**
Mort STEVENS ▶ 1785 (3)	**2532**
Dan BAIRD ▶ 1786 (1)	**2532**
Janis Lee GWIN/Linda MARTIN ▶ 1787 (1)	**2531**
Chick-A-Boom (Don't Ya Jes' Love It)—Daddy Dewdrop (71)	2531
Phoebe SNOW ▶ 1788 (2)	**2530**
Perry BOTKIN Jr./Barry DE VORZON ▶ 1789 (3)	**2528**
Nadia's Theme (The Young And The Restless)—Barry De Vorzon and Perry Botkin, Jr. (76)	2470
Bless The Beasts And Children—Carpenters (71)	39
Bless The Beasts And Children—Barry De Vorzon & Perry Botkin, Jr. (77)	20
Jack LAWRENCE/Richard MYERS ▶ 1790 (2)	**2528**
Hold My Hand—Don Cornell (54)	2528
Hold My Hand—Guy Lombardo & His Royal Canadians (54)	0.0
Hans CARSTE/Charles TOBIAS ▶ 1791 (1)	**2528**
Those Lazy-Hazy-Crazy Days Of Summer—Nat King Cole (63)	2528
Marty BLOOM/Ernest BREUER/Billy ROSE ▶ 1792 (1)	**2524**
Does Your Chewing Gum Lose Its Flavor (On The Bedpost Over Night)—Lonnie Donegan And His Skiffle Group (61)	2524
Al STEWART/Peter WHITE ▶ 1793 (2)	**2524**
Time Passages—Al Stewart (78)	1891
Midnight Rocks—Al Stewart (80)	633
Dmitry BRILL/Kamaal FAREED/Herbie HANCOCK/Kier KIRBY/Towa TEI ▶ 1794 (1)	**2521**
Groove Is In The Heart—Deee-Lite (90)	2521
Lenny KRAVITZ ▶ 1795 (2)	**2519**
Steve PERRY ▶ 1796 (3)	**2515**
Skip SCARBOROUGH ▶ 1797 (4)	**2515**
John ELLISON ▶ 1798 (3)	**2514**
Benny DAVIS/Abner SILVER ▶ 1799 (3)	**2511**
There Goes My Heart—Joni James (58)	1463
With These Hands—Tom Jones (65)	669
There Goes My Heart—Four Aces (55)	379
Steve CROPPER/Wilson PICKETT ▶ 1800 (7)	**2509**
In The Midnight Hour—Wilson Pickett (65)	1036
In The Midnight Hour—Cross Country (73)	725
In The Midnight Hour—The Mirettes (68)	421
Don't Fight It—Wilson Pickett (65)	293
In The Midnight Hour—The Wanted (67)	25
In The Midnight Hour—Samantha Sang (79)	7.5
It's All Over—Wilson Pickett (65)	1.4
Robert BELL/Ronald BELL/Donald BOYCE/George M. BROWN/Robert MICKENS/Claydes SMITH/Dennis THOMAS/Richard WESTFIELD ▶ 1801 (1)	**2506**
Jungle Boogie—Kool & The Gang (73)	2506
Brook BENTON/Luchi DeJESUS/Clyde OTIS ▶ 1802 (2)	**2504**
A Rockin' Good Way (To Mess Around And Fall In Love)—Dinah Washington & Brook Benton (60)	2398
I Want You Forever—Brook Benton (59)	106
Milan WILLIAMS ▶ 1803 (4)	**2503**
Nino OLIVIERO/Riz ORTOLANI ▶ 1804 (2)	**2503**
More—Kai Winding & Orchestra (63)	2503
More Theme From Mondo Cane—Martin Denny (63)	0.0
Grace SLICK ▶ 1805 (3)	**2503**
Bill ADOR ▶ 1806 (1)	**2503**
Alex ZANETIS ▶ 1807 (4)	**2496**
Jerry BOCK/Lawrence HOLOFCENER/George David WEISS ▶ 1808 (9)	**2492**
Mr. Wonderful—Peggy Lee (56)	899
Mr. Wonderful—Sarah Vaughan (56)	674
Mr. Wonderful—Teddi King (56)	459
Too Close For Comfort—Eydie Gorme (56)	381
Jacques D'Iraque—Sammy Davis Jr. (56)	80
Too Close For Comfort—Sammy Davis Jr. (56)	0.0
Too Close For Comfort—Lillian Briggs (56)	0.0
Mr. Wonderful—Bette Anne Steele (56)	0.0
Mr. Wonderful—The Mello-Larks (56)	0.0
Leo SAYER/Alan TARNEY ▶ 1809 (2)	**2492**
Dreaming—Cliff Richard (80)	1919
Living In A Fantasy—Leo Sayer (81)	573
Eddie SNYDER/Paul VANCE ▶ 1810 (3)	**2489**
What Will Mary Say—Johnny Mathis (63)	2198
Come Back—Johnny Mathis (63)	286
Hurry Up And Tell Me—Paul Anka (63)	5.4
Charlie DANIELS ▶ 1811 (6)	**2488**
Wilson PICKETT/Brad SHAPIRO ▶ 1812 (2)	**2482**
Don't Knock My Love - Pt. I—Wilson Pickett (71)	2128
Don't Knock My Love—Diana Ross & Marvin Gaye (74)	354
Mac REBENNACK ▶ 1813 (3)	**2480**
Mack DAVID/Jerry LIVINGSTON ▶ 1814 (4)	**2480**
Young Emotions—Ricky Nelson (60)	1584
Hanging Tree—Marty Robbins (59)	599
Seventy Seven Sunset Strip—The Big Sound of Don Ralke (59)	298
Seventy Seven Sunset Strip—Frank Ortega Trio (59)	0.0
Norman PETTY ▶ 1815 (5)	**2480**
Doug EDWARDS/David RICHARDSON ▶ 1816 (2)	**2479**
Wildflower—Skylark (73)	2222
Wildflower—The New Birth (74)	257
Mic MICHAELI/Joey TEMPEST ▶ 1817 (1)	**2479**
Carrie—Europe (87)	2479
Doug SAHM ▶ 1818 (4)	**2478**
Bernard EDWARDS/Kenny LEHMAN/Nile RODGERS ▶ 1819 (1)	**2478**
Dance, Dance, Dance (Yowsah, Yowsah, Yowsah)—Chic (77)	2478
Jan BERRY/Roger CHRISTIAN/Brian WILSON ▶ 1820 (2)	**2475**
Drag City—Jan & Dean (63)	1652
Ride The Wild Surf—Jan & Dean (64)	823
Diane HILDERBRAND/Jack KELLER ▶ 1821 (1)	**2475**
Easy Come, Easy Go—Bobby Sherman (70)	2475
Cayet MANGIARACINA/Gene PITNEY ▶ 1822 (1)	**2471**
Hello Mary Lou—Ricky Nelson (61)	2471
Jean RENARD/Carl SIGMAN ▶ 1823 (1)	**2471**
Losing You—Brenda Lee (63)	2471
Bernie LOWE/Bickley REICHNER ▶ 1824 (3)	**2468**
Teen Age Prayer—Gale Storm (55)	1780
Teen Age Prayer—Gloria Mann (55)	625
Teen Age Prayer—Kitty White (55)	63
Oliver HOOD ▶ 1825 (8)	**2462**
William KING/Ronald LaPREAD/Thomas McCLARY/Walter ORANGE/Lionel RICHIE/Milan WILLIAMS ▶ 1826 (2)	**2461**
Brick House—Commodores (77)	1962
Too Hot Ta Trot—Commodores (77)	499
Frank GUIDA ▶ 1827 (1)	**2461**
Johnny BRISTOL/Wade BROWN/David H. JONES ▶ 1828 (4)	**2453**
Love Me For A Reason—The Osmonds (74)	1275
That's How Love Goes—Jermaine Jackson (72)	467
We've Come Too Far To End It Now—Smokey Robinson & The Miracles (72)	421
I Can't Stand To See You Cry—Smokey Robinson & The Miracles (72)	290
Greg CARROLL/Doris PAYNE ▶ 1829 (5)	**2453**
Just One Look—Doris Troy (63)	1890
Just One Look—Linda Ronstadt (79)	260
Just One Look—The Hollies (67)	251
Just One Look—The Hollies (64)	38
Just One Look—Anne Murray (74)	13
Ron HOLDEN ▶ 1830 (1)	**2451**
Bill CHAMPLIN/Jay GRAYDON/Steve LUKATHER ▶ 1831 (1)	**2450**
Turn Your Love Around—George Benson (81)	2450
Nat SIMON/Charles TOBIAS ▶ 1832 (5)	**2448**
Old Lamplighter—The Browns Featuring Jim Edward Brown (60)	2054
The Mama Doll Song—Patti Page (54)	350
It's Your Life—Bob Manning (55)	31
You're Wrong All Wrong—Eileen Rodgers (56)	14
The Mama Doll Song—Guy Lombardo & His Royal Canadians (54)	0.0
Bert KAEMPFERT ▶ 1833 (3)	**2446**
Carol DECKER/Ron ROGERS ▶ 1834 (2)	**2446**
Heart And Soul—T'Pau (87)	2422
Only A Heartbeat—T'Pau (91)	24
Pearl LENDHURST ▶ 1835 (1)	**2445**
Pete BYRNE/Rob FISHER ▶ 1836 (3)	**2434**
Promises, Promises—Naked Eyes (83)	1540
When The Lights Go Out—Naked Eyes (83)	509
(What) In The Name Of Love—Naked Eyes (84)	385
Lynn MALSBY ▶ 1837 (1)	**2434**
Bill LEVERTY/Carl J. SNARE ▶ 1838 (2)	**2429**
Love Of A Lifetime—Firehouse (91)	2055
All She Wrote—Firehouse (91)	374
John KAY ▶ 1839 (2)	**2420**
Eddie CURTIS ▶ 1840 (8)	**2420**
Tom HAMILTON/Steven TYLER ▶ 1841 (2)	**2420**
Janie's Got A Gun—Aerosmith (89)	1956
Sweet Emotion—Aerosmith (75)	464
Angelo BOND/Ronald DUNBAR/General JOHNSON/Greg PERRY ▶ 1842 (2)	**2419**
Pay To The Piper—Chairmen Of The Board (70)	1695
You've Got To Crawl (Before You Walk)—The 8th Day (71)	724
Wes FARRELL/Gerry GOFFIN ▶ 1843 (1)	**2417**
I'll Meet You Halfway—The Partridge Family Starring Shirley Jones & Featuring David Cassidy (71)	2417
Walt ALDRIDGE/Tom BRASFIELD ▶ 1844 (1)	**2415**
(There's) No Gettin' Over Me—Ronnie Milsap (81)	2415
Camillo BARGONI/Al STILLMAN ▶ 1845 (4)	**2412**
And That Reminds Me—Della Reese (57)	1323
And That Reminds Me (My Heart Reminds Me)—The 4 Seasons (69)	593
My Heart Reminds Me—Kay Starr (57)	496
Autumn Concerto—Nick Noble (56)	0.0
Paul ROBB/Kurt VALAQUEN ▶ 1846 (1)	**2411**
What's On Your Mind (Pure Energy)—Information Society (88)	2411
Alan GORDON ▶ 1847 (3)	**2405**
Howard GREENFIELD/Carole KING ▶ 1848 (1)	**2402**
Crying In The Rain—The Everly Brothers (62)	2402

Barry GIBB/Blue WEAVER ▶ 1849 (1)	**2401**
(Our Love) Don't Throw It All Away–Andy Gibb (78)	2401
William BELL/Booker T. JONES Jr. ▶ 1850 (7)	**2396**
To Be A Lover–Billy Idol (86)	1625
I Forgot To Be Your Lover–William Bell (69)	558
Private Number–Judy Clay & William Bell (68)	99
A Tribute To A King–William Bell (68)	66
Everybody Loves A Winner–William Bell (67)	39
All God's Children Got Soul–Dorothy Morrison (69)	8.0
Born Under A Bad Sign–William Bell (69)	0.5
Warren DAVIS/George MALONE/ Charles PATRICK ▶ 1851 (3)	**2392**
Book Of Love–The Monotones (58)	2045
Book Of Love–The Raindrops (64)	259
Book of Love–Nino & the Ebb Tides (61)	88
Cliff GOLDSMITH/Fred SMITH ▶ 1852 (9)	**2391**
Western Movies–The Olympics (58)	1584
Patti Ann–Johnny Crawford (62)	465
(Baby) Hully Gully–The Olympics (60)	165
Dedicated (To The Songs I Love)– The 3 Friends (61)	80
Hully Gully Again– Little Caesar And The Romans (61)	58
(I Wanna) Dance With The Teacher– The Olympics (58)	26
Comic Book Crazy–Little Sammy Yates (59)	6.4
Dooley–The Olympics (61)	3.2
Private Eye–The Olympics (59)	2.3
Burt BACHARACH/Neil DIAMOND/ Carole Bayer SAGER ▶ 1853 (3)	**2388**
Heartlight–Neil Diamond (82)	2132
Front Page Story–Neil Diamond (83)	147
Turn Around–Neil Diamond (84)	110
Gene BLACK/Holly KNIGHT/ Ann WILSON/Nancy WILSON ▶ 1854 (1)	**2388**
Never–Heart (85)	2388
Bernard Leon JACKSON ▶ 1855 (2)	**2386**
Hoagy CARMICHAEL/Mitchell PARISH ▶ 1856 (6)	**2385**
Star Dust–Billy Ward And His Dominoes (57)	1814
Stardust–Nino Tempo & April Stevens (64)	465
Stardust–Frank Sinatra (62)	34
Star Dust–Connee Boswell (56)	32
Stardust–Nat "King" Cole (57)	31
Star Dust– Jaye P. Morgan And The Morgan Brothers (58)	8.5
Jan BERRY/Arnie GINSBURG ▶ 1857 (2)	**2383**
Jennie Lee–Jan & Arnie (58)	2196
Jennie Lee–Billy Ward And His Dominoes (58)	187
Joe COBB/Van McCOY ▶ 1858 (8)	**2383**
Right On The Tip Of My Tongue– Brenda & The Tabulations (71)	1092
So Much Love–Faith, Hope & Charity (70)	552
Triangle Of Love (Hey Diddle Diddle)– The Presidents (71)	293
And My Heart Sang (Tra La La)– Brenda & The Tabulations (70)	229
Heavy Love–David Ruffin (76)	155
A Part Of You–Brenda & The Tabulations (71)	32
The Language Of Love–The Intrigues (71)	21
Baby Don't Take Your Love– Faith, Hope & Charity (70)	10
Simon Le BON/Nick RHODES/Roger TAYLOR ▶ 1859 (2)	**2382**
Election Day–Arcadia (85)	1950
Goodbye Is Forever–Arcadia (86)	432
Al CASEY/Duane EDDY ▶ 1860 (1)	**2380**
Forty Miles Of Bad Road–Duane Eddy His "Twangy" guitar and The Rebels (59)	2380
Bill JUSTIS/Ray STEVENS ▶ 1861 (1)	**2376**
Gitarzan–Ray Stevens (69)	2376
Paul PENA ▶ 1862 (1)	**2374**
Jerry LEIBER/Mike STOLLER/ Billy Edd WHEELER ▶ 1863 (2)	**2370**
Reverend Mr. Black–The Kingston Trio (63)	2205
What To Do With Laurie–Mike Clifford (62)	165
Manos HADJIDAKIS ▶ 1864 (5)	**2364**
Rick KELLY/Linda MALLAH/Don POWELL ▶ 1865 (1)	**2361**
Make It Real–The Jets (88)	2361
Burton CUMMINGS/Kurt WINTER ▶ 1866 (5)	**2354**
Rain Dance–The Guess Who (71)	1323
Hang On To Your Life–The Guess Who (71)	496
Heartbroken Bopper–The Guess Who (72)	448
Runnin' Back To Saskatoon–The Guess Who (72)	45
Broken–The Guess Who (71)	42
Bobby WOMACK ▶ 1867 (6)	**2352**
Vinnie BARRETT/Bobby ELI/John FREEMAN ▶ 1868 (2)	**2351**
Just Don't Want To Be Lonely– The Main Ingredient (74)	2140
Just Don't Want To Be Lonely–Ronnie Dyson (73)	210
Claude JOHNSON ▶ 1869 (3)	**2348**
Rich DODSON ▶ 1870 (2)	**2345**
Carlo DONIDA/Giulio RAPETTI ▶ 1871 (1)	**2344**
Al Di La'–Emilio Pericoli (62)	2344
Andy CONNELL/Corinne DREWERY/ Martin JACKSON ▶ 1872 (2)	**2344**
Breakout–Swing Out Sister (87)	1952
Twilight World–Swing Out Sister (87)	393
Perri Arlette REID ▶ 1873 (1)	**2344**
Leonard LEE ▶ 1874 (4)	**2343**
Grady MARTIN/Alex ZANETIS ▶ 1875 (2)	**2341**
Snap Your Fingers–Joe Henderson (62)	2221
Snap Your Fingers–Barbara Lewis (63)	120
Richard SPENCER ▶ 1876 (1)	**2340**
Walter DONALDSON/Gus KAHN ▶ 1877 (8)	**2340**
Love Me Or Leave Me–Sammy Davis Jr. (55)	1367
Makin' Whoopee–Ray Charles (64)	469
Yes Sir That's My Baby–Ricky Nelson (60)	465
Yes Sir That's My Baby–Four Aces (57)	20
Yes Sir, That's My Baby– Julius Wechter & The Baja Marimba Band (68)	15
Carolina In The Morning–Mitch Miller & his "Sing Along With Mitch" Chorus (59)	3.9
Love Me Or Leave Me–Billy Eckstine (55)	0.0
Love Me Or Leave Me–Lena Horne (55)	0.0
Eric LOWEN/Dan NAVARRO ▶ 1878 (1)	**2339**
We Belong–Pat Benatar (84)	2339
Debbie HUPP/Bob MORRISON ▶ 1879 (1)	**2338**
You Decorated My Life–Kenny Rogers (79)	2338
Christopher NEIL/Mike RUTHERFORD ▶ 1880 (3)	**2338**
All I Need Is A Miracle–Mike + The Mechanics (86)	1677
Taken In–Mike + The Mechanics (86)	539
Word Of Mouth–Mike + The Mechanics (91)	122
Matt MALNECK/Robert MAXWELL/ Carl SIGMAN ▶ 1881 (3)	**2338**
Shangri La–The Four Coins (57)	1206
Shangri-La–Vic Dana (64)	878
Shangri-La–The Lettermen (69)	254
Mark BARKAN/Sandy BARON/George EDDY ▶ 1882 (4)	**2338**
The Writing On The Wall–Adam Wade (61)	2168
Let True Love Begin–Nat King Cole (61)	104
Mr. Happiness–Johnny Maestro With The Coeds (61)	61
Flying Blue Angels– George, Johnny And The Pilots (62)	3.6
Barbara ACKLIN/Stanley BURRELL/ Eugene RECORD ▶ 1883 (1)	**2337**
Have You Seen Her–M.C. Hammer (90)	2337
Bill MEDLEY ▶ 1884 (4)	**2337**
Earl NELSON/Bob RELF ▶ 1885 (4)	**2336**
Harlem Shuffle–The Rolling Stones (86)	1790
Harlem Shuffle–Bob & Earl (63)	494
Harlem Shuffle–The Traits (66)	32
Don't Ever Leave Me–Bob & Earl (62)	20
Matt SHERROD/Paul SHERROD/ Marty SPENCER ▶ 1886 (1)	**2330**
This House–Tracie Spencer (90)	2330
Jonathan CAIN/John WAITE ▶ 1887 (3)	**2330**
Price Of Love–Bad English (89)	1890
Turn And Walk Away–The Babys (80)	372
Midnight Rendezvous–The Babys (80)	68
Henri HERPIN/Harold ROME ▶ 1888 (2)	**2330**
(All Of A Sudden) My Heart Sings–Paul Anka (58)	1888
(All Of A Sudden) My Heart Sings–Mel Carter (65)	442
Franz DOELLE ▶ 1889 (5)	**2329**
Moon MARTIN ▶ 1890 (4)	**2329**
Pete BURNS/Steve COY/ Wayne HUSSEY/Tim LEVER/Mike PERCY ▶ 1891 (5)	**2327**
You Spin Me Round (Like A Record)– Dead Or Alive (85)	1071
Brand New Lover–Dead Or Alive (86)	1017
Come Home With Me Baby–Dead Or Alive (89)	117
Lover Come Back To Me–Dead Or Alive (85)	84
Something In My House–Dead Or Alive (87)	38
Tracy CHAPMAN ▶ 1892 (4)	**2326**
Bruce HART/Stephen LAWRENCE ▶ 1893 (1)	**2326**
You Take My Breath Away–Rex Smith (79)	2326
Tolga KATAS/Charlie PENNACHIO ▶ 1894 (1)	**2325**
Sending All My Love–Linear (90)	2325
Dick MANNING/Larry STOCK ▶ 1895 (2)	**2323**
Morning Side Of The Mountain– Donny And Marie Osmond (74)	1717
Morning Side Of The Mountain– Tommy Edwards (59)	606
Chris BARBOSA/Ed CHISOLM ▶ 1896 (2)	**2322**
Let The Music Play–Shannon (83)	1909
Give Me Tonight–Shannon (84)	413
Mark GOLDENBERG/Brock WALSH ▶ 1897 (1)	**2321**
Automatic–Pointer Sisters (84)	2321
Teddy RANDAZZO/Lou STALLMAN/ Bobby WEINSTEIN ▶ 1898 (5)	**2320**
It's Gonna Take A Miracle– Deniece Williams (82)	1178
It's Gonna Take A Miracle– The Royalettes (65)	576
You Better Go–Derek Martin (65)	392
I Want To Meet Him–The Royalettes (65)	172
The Weekend–Jack Jones (66)	0.5
Gary BURR ▶ 1899 (1)	**2319**
Skip PROKOP ▶ 1900 (3)	**2318**
Clive METCALFE/Keith NOBLE/Chad STUART ▶ 1901 (1)	**2316**
A Summer Song–Chad Stuart & Jeremy Clyde (64)	2316
Clyde OTIS/Joe SHAPIRO/Jimmy WILLIAMS ▶ 1902 (1)	**2316**
Think Twice–Brook Benton (61)	2316
Billy SHERRILL/Tammy WYNETTE ▶ 1903 (2)	**2316**
Stand By Your Man–Tammy Wynette (68)	1181
Stand By Your Man–Candi Staton (70)	1135
Phil COLLINS/Daryl STUERMER ▶ 1904 (1)	**2309**
Something Happened On The Way To Heaven– Phil Collins (90)	2309
Alex ALSTONE/Tom GLAZER ▶ 1905 (1)	**2307**
More–Perry Como (56)	2307
John FARRAR/Tom SNOW ▶ 1906 (1)	**2305**
Make A Move On Me–Olivia Newton-John (82)	2305
Bert BERNS/Johnny BRISTOL/ Harvey FUQUA/Edwin STARR/Jerry WEXLER ▶ 1907 (2)	**2305**
Twenty-Five Miles–Edwin Starr (69)	2304
Twenty-Five Miles–Mongo Santamaria (69)	0.9
Albhy GALUTEN/Barry GIBB ▶ 1908 (3)	**2305**
What Kind Of Fool– Barbra Streisand & Barry Gibb (81)	1271
This Woman–Kenny Rogers (84)	574
Take The Short Way Home–Dionne Warwick (83)	460
William ARMSTRONG/Marcus DANIEL/ Wilbur TERRELL ▶ 1909 (1)	**2304**
Slip Away–Clarence Carter (68)	2304
Charlie DORE/Julian LITTMAN ▶ 1910 (1)	**2303**
Strut–Sheena Easton (84)	2303
Barbara LOMAS/Louis RISBROOK/ William RISBROOK/Dennis ROWE/ Richard THOMPSON/Carlos WARD/ Terrell WOOD ▶ 1911 (2)	**2302**
Express–B.T. Express (75)	2209
Express–The Ritchie Family (76)	92
Arnold STRALS/TRADITIONAL ▶ 1912 (1)	**2299**
The Lord's Prayer–Sister Janet Mead (74)	2299
Charlie RICH ▶ 1913 (7)	**2298**
Chris KENNER/Allen TOUSSAINT ▶ 1914 (2)	**2295**
I Like It Like That–The Dave Clark Five (65)	2277
I Like It Like That–Loggins & Messina (75)	19

Daniel ASH/David HASKINS/Kevin HASKINS ▶ 1915 (2)	**2295**
So Alive—Love and Rockets (89)	2251
No Big Deal—Love and Rockets (89)	44
Max STEINER/TRADITIONAL/ Paul Francis WEBSTER ▶ 1916 (2)	**2294**
Honey Babe—Art Mooney And His Orchestra (55)	2294
Honey Babe—The Sauter-Finegan Orchestra (55)	0.0
Gary BEISBIER/James William GUERCIO/ James HOLVAY ▶ 1917 (1)	**2292**
Susan—The Buckinghams (67)	2292
Benny MARDONES/Robert TEPPER ▶ 1918 (2)	**2291**
Into The Night—Benny Mardones (80)	1652
Into The Night—Benny Mardones (89)	640
Don DAVIS ▶ 1919 (1)	**2291**
Ian WHITCOMB ▶ 1920 (2)	**2291**
Bruce GAITSCH/Richard MARX ▶ 1921 (2)	**2290**
Don't Mean Nothing—Richard Marx (87)	2111
Nothin' To Hide—Poco (89)	179
Jimmy PAGE/Robert PLANT ▶ 1922 (4)	**2289**
Immigrant Song—Led Zeppelin (70)	1706
Over The Hills And Far Away—Led Zeppelin (73)	487
Livin' Lovin' Maid—Led Zeppelin (70)	58
Stairway To Heaven—Far Corporation (86)	38
Al STEWART/Peter John WOOD ▶ 1923 (1)	**2288**
Year Of The Cat—Al Stewart (76)	2288
Milton KELLEM ▶ 1924 (5)	**2284**
Lewis DeWITT ▶ 1925 (1)	**2283**
Mark CHARRON ▶ 1926 (4)	**2283**
Bill BUCHANAN/Dickie GOODMAN ▶ 1927 (4)	**2282**
The Flying Saucer (Pts. 1 & 2)— Buchanan And Goodman (56)	1700
Flying Saucer The Second— Buchanan And Goodman (57)	410
Santa And The Satellite— Buchanan And Goodman (57)	116
Buchanan And Goodman On Trial— Buchanan And Goodman (56)	55
Leroy BONNER/Marshall JONES/ Ralph MIDDLEBROOKS/ Walter MORRISON/Bruce NAPIER/ Andrew NOLAND/Marvin PIERCE/ Greg WEBSTER ▶ 1928 (4)	**2282**
Funky Worm—Ohio Players (73)	1438
Ecstasy—Ohio Players (73)	621
Pain (Part 1)—Ohio Players (71)	208
Got Pleasure—Ohio Players (72)	14
Gershon KINGSLEY ▶ 1929 (1)	**2281**
Paul RODGERS ▶ 1930 (5)	**2281**
Ivy Jo HUNTER/William STEVENSON ▶ 1931 (6)	**2276**
Ask The Lonely—Four Tops (65)	738
I'll Always Love You—The Spinners (65)	466
I'll Keep Holding On—The Marvelettes (65)	405
Wild One—Martha & The Vandellas (64)	377
Can You Jerk Like Me—The Contours (64)	228
Truly Yours—The Spinners (66)	63
Carl BELEW/Shelby SINGLETON/ W.S. STEVENSON ▶ 1932 (4)	**2273**
Am I That Easy To Forget—Debbie Reynolds (60)	1149
Am I That Easy To Forget— Engelbert Humperdinck (67)	1119
Am I That Easy To Forget— "Little Esther" Phillips (63)	5.3
Am I That Easy To Forget—Skeeter Davis (60)	0.0
John CARTER/Gillian SHAKESPEARE ▶ 1933 (2)	**2271**
Beach Baby—First Class (74)	2201
Dreams Are Ten A Penny—First Class (74)	69
Dorian BURTON/Paul HAMPTON ▶ 1934 (1)	**2270**
You Don't Know What You've Got (Until You Lose It)— Ral Donner (61)	2270
Mary CANDY/Eddie V. DEANE/ Gloria SHAYNE ▶ 1935 (1)	**2269**
The Men In My Little Girl's Life—Mike Douglas (65)	2269
Billy MAYHEW ▶ 1936 (4)	**2269**
Walter Earl BROWN ▶ 1937 (1)	**2264**
Hans ENGELMANN/Tom GLAZER ▶ 1938 (2)	**2262**
Melody Of Love—Four Aces (54)	2262
Melody Of Love— Tony Martin & Dinah Shore (55)	0.0
Vincent COREA/Jeanne ROBERTS ▶ 1939 (2)	**2261**
Catch Me (I'm Falling)— Pretty Poison (87)	1846
Nightime—Pretty Poison (88)	414
Steven ASKEW/Nick BEGGS/ Christopher HAMILL/Stuart NEALE/ Jeremy STRODE ▶ 1940 (2)	**2254**
Too Shy—Kajagoogoo (83)	2226
Hang On Now—Kajagoogoo (83)	28
Danny DILL/Mel TILLIS ▶ 1941 (4)	**2250**
Detroit City—Bobby Bare (63)	1484
Detroit City—Tom Jones (67)	748
Detroit City—Solomon Burke (67)	17
Detroit City—Dean Martin (70)	1.3
Kelly KEAGY ▶ 1942 (1)	**2250**
Henry JEROME/Bobbi MARTIN ▶ 1943 (2)	**2247**
For The Love Of Him—Bobbi Martin (70)	2119
Give A Woman Love—Bobbi Martin (70)	128
Teddy VANN ▶ 1944 (8)	**2247**
Mike MAINIERI/Carly SIMON ▶ 1945 (1)	**2247**
Jesse—Carly Simon (80)	2247
Harriet SCHOCK ▶ 1946 (1)	**2246**
Ekundayo PARIS/Nelson PIGFORD ▶ 1947 (1)	**2246**
It's Ecstasy When You Lay Down Next To Me— Barry White (77)	2246
Gerry GOFFIN/Carole KING/Phil SPECTOR ▶ 1948 (3)	**2246**
Just Once In My Life—The Righteous Brothers (65)	1850
Hung On You—The Righteous Brothers (65)	321
Is This What I Get For Loving You?— The Ronettes Featuring Veronica (65)	74
Gilbert GABRIEL/Nick LAIRD-CLOWES ▶ 1949 (2)	**2245**
Life In A Northern Town—The Dream Academy (85)	1832
The Love Parade—The Dream Academy (86)	413
Walter MARKS ▶ 1950 (1)	**2244**
Dorothy LaBOSTRIE/Joe LUBIN/ Richard PENNIMAN ▶ 1951 (5)	**2243**
Tutti Frutti—Pat Boone (56)	1434
Tutti Frutti—Little Richard (56)	649
Tutti-Frutti—Jive Bunny And The Mastermixers (89)	80
Tutti Frutti—Jive Bunny And The Mastermixers (89)	80
Tutti-Frutti—Art Mooney & His Orchestra (56)	0.0
Bennie BENJAMIN/Gloria CALDWELL/ Sol MARCUS ▶ 1952 (3)	**2242**
Don't Let Me Be Misunderstood— Santa Esmeralda Starring Larry Gomez (77)	1226
Don't Let Me Be Misunderstood—The Animals (65)	1016
Don't Let Me Be Misunderstood—Nina Simone (65)	0.0
Stevie NICKS/PRINCE ▶ 1953 (1)	**2238**
Stand Back—Stevie Nicks (83)	2238
Rocky BURNETTE/Ron COLEMAN ▶ 1954 (1)	**2237**
Tired Of Toein' The Line—Rocky Burnette (80)	2237
Cliff CROFFORD ▶ 1955 (2)	**2231**
Eleanor BROADWATER/Robert CHAISSON/ Dale HAWKINS/Stanley J. LEWIS ▶ 1956 (4)	**2231**
Suzie Q (Part One)— Creedence Clearwater Revival (68)	1687
Susie Q—Dale Hawkins (57)	544
Susie-Q—José Feliciano (70)	0.0
Susie-Q—The Crew-Cuts (57)	0.0
Madonna L. CICCONE/Bruce GAITSCH/ Patrick Raymond LEONARD ▶ 1957 (1)	**2230**
La Isla Bonita—Madonna (87)	2230
Pete CARPENTER/Mike POST ▶ 1958 (3)	**2229**
The Rockford Files—Mike Post (75)	1507
Theme From Magnum P.I.—Mike Post (82)	718
Theme From "Baa Baa Black Sheep"— Mike Post (77)	3.3
Jon HENDRICKS ▶ 1959 (3)	**2227**
Bill GIBSON/Sean HOPPER/Huey LEWIS ▶ 1960 (1)	**2226**
Hip To Be Square—Huey Lewis and the News (86)	2226
Hank LOCKLIN ▶ 1961 (4)	**2222**
Joseph MODELISTE/Art NEVILLE/ Leo NOCENTELLI/George PORTER ▶ 1962 (6)	**2220**
Cissy Strut—The Meters (69)	731
Sophisticated Cissy—The Meters (69)	475
Chicken Strut—The Meters (70)	361
Look-Ka Py Py—The Meters (69)	346
Ease Back—The Meters (69)	213
Hand Clapping Song—The Meters (70)	94
Sascha BURLAND/Don ELLIOT ▶ 1963 (2)	**2220**
Uh! Oh! (Part 2)—The Nutty Squirrels (59)	2146
Uh! Oh! (Part 1)—The Nutty Squirrels (59)	74
Jon LIND/Allee WILLIS ▶ 1964 (1)	**2219**
Boogie Wonderland— Earth, Wind & Fire With The Emotions (79)	2219
Colin COOPER/John CUFFLEY/ Peter HAYCOCK/Derek HOLT/Rick JONES ▶ 1965 (1)	**2219**
Couldn't Get It Right—Climax Blues Band (77)	2219
Wayne BICKERTON/Tony WADDINGTON ▶ 1966 (5)	**2218**
Nothing But A Heartache—The Flirtations (69)	822
Can't Stop Loving You—Tom Jones (70)	812
Sugar Baby Love—The Rubettes (74)	569
Sugar Baby Love—Stars On 45 (81)	12
Can't Stop Lovin' You—The Flirtations (70)	2.2
Nancie MANTZ/Annette TUCKER ▶ 1967 (3)	**2216**
I Had Too Much To Dream (Last Night)— The Electric Prunes (66)	1627
Green Light—The American Breed (68)	587
Dr. Do-Good—The Electric Prunes (67)	2.4
Peter DeANGELIS/Jean SAWYER ▶ 1968 (4)	**2214**
Painted, Tainted Rose—Al Martino (63)	1454
Always Together—Al Martino (64)	533
You, No One But You—Frankie Laine (67)	151
My Cherie—Al Martino (65)	76
David Leland ELLIOTT/Terry STEELE ▶ 1969 (1)	**2210**
Here And Now—Luther Vandross (89)	2210
Juan Carlos CALDERÓN ▶ 1970 (2)	**2208**
David Paul BRYANT/Franne GOLDE/ Jody WATLEY ▶ 1971 (1)	**2205**
Don't You Want Me—Jody Watley (87)	2205
Joey TEMPEST ▶ 1972 (4)	**2204**
Don BURCH ▶ 1973 (3)	**2201**
Nick GILDER/Holly KNIGHT ▶ 1974 (1)	**2200**
The Warrior—Scandal Featuring Patty Smyth (84)	2200
Francis LAI/Carl SIGMAN ▶ 1975 (1)	**2200**
(Where Do I Begin) Love Story—Andy Williams (71)	2200
Jimmy HUGHES ▶ 1976 (2)	**2199**
Michael BREWER/Tom SHIPLEY ▶ 1977 (3)	**2197**
One Toke Over The Line— Brewer & Shipley (71)	1791
Tarkio Road—Brewer And Shipley (71)	404
Shake Off The Demon—Brewer And Shipley (72)	1.9
Otha YOUNG ▶ 1978 (1)	**2196**
Joe SENECA ▶ 1979 (3)	**2194**
Jan AKKERMAN/Thijs VAN LEER ▶ 1980 (1)	**2194**
Hocus Pocus—Focus (73)	2194
Richard V. DI CICCO/ Russell FAITH/Clarence KEHNER ▶ 1981 (1)	**2192**
Bobby Sox To Stockings—Frankie Avalon (59)	2192
Frank MYERS ▶ 1982 (1)	**2189**
Larry BANKS/Milton BENNETT ▶ 1983 (1)	**2189**
Go Now!—The Moody Blues (65)	2189
Brook BENTON/Margie SINGLETON ▶ 1984 (2)	**2188**
Lie To Me—Brook Benton (62)	1517
I Got What I Wanted—Brook Benton (63)	672
Lee ANDREWS/Bernice DAVIS/ Douglas HENDERSON/Miriam UNIMAN ▶ 1985 (7)	**2187**
Long Lonely Nights—Bobby Vinton (65)	1021
Long Lonely Nights—Clyde McPhatter (57)	517
Long Lonely Nights—Lee Andrews And The Hearts (57)	429
Long Lonely Nights—The Dells (70)	187
Long Lonely Nights—The 4 Seasons (64)	34
Long, Lonely Nights—The Kings (2) (57)	0.0
Long Lonely Nights—Kitty Kallen (57)	0.0

James BROWN/Nat JONES ▶ 1986 (7)	**2182**
Bring It Up— James Brown And The Famous Flames (67)	556
Ain't That A Groove Part 1— James Brown And The Famous Flames (66)	496
Money Won't Change You Part 1— James Brown And The Famous Flames (66)	493
Don't Be A Drop-Out— James Brown And The Famous Flames (66)	443
Tit For Tat (Ain't No Taking Back)— James Brown (68)	189
Sweet Little Baby Boy— James Brown And The Famous Flames (66)	4.6
New Breed (Part 1) (The Boo-Ga-Loo)— James Brown (66)	0.5
Cyndi LAUPER/Essra MOHAWK ▶ 1987 (1)	**2182**
Change Of Heart—Cyndi Lauper (86)	2182
Henry GLOVER/Carl SPENCER ▶ 1988 (1)	**2182**
Let The Little Girl Dance—Billy Bland (60)	2182
Gene SIMMONS ▶ 1989 (3)	**2178**
David FRANK/Mic MURPHY ▶ 1990 (4)	**2178**
Don't Disturb This Groove—The System (87)	1797
You Are In My System—The System (83)	182
This Is My Night—Chaka Khan (85)	157
You Are In My System—Robert Palmer (83)	42
Joe DONG/Teddy VANN ▶ 1991 (2)	**2176**
Loop De Loop—Johnny Thunder (62)	2175
Loop De Loop—Soul Sisters (64)	1.4
Johnny LEHMANN ▶ 1992 (2)	**2175**
Ray HILDEBRAND/Jill JACKSON ▶ 1993 (2)	**2174**
Young Lovers—Paul & Paula (63)	2050
First Day Back At School—Paul & Paula (63)	125
Ritchie CORDELL/Joey LEVINE ▶ 1994 (1)	**2168**
Gimme Gimme Good Lovin'—Crazy Elephant (69)	2168
Johnny MERCER/Victor SCHERTZINGER ▶ 1995 (1)	**2162**
I Remember You—Frank Ifield (62)	2162
Stevie NICKS/Sandy STEWART ▶ 1996 (3)	**2159**
If Anyone Falls—Stevie Nicks (83)	979
Seven Wonders—Fleetwood Mac (87)	683
Nightbird—Stevie Nicks (83)	497
Helen ADU/Ray ST. JOHN ▶ 1997 (1)	**2158**
Smooth Operator—Sade (85)	2158
Burt BACHARACH/Bruce ROBERTS/ Carole Bayer SAGER ▶ 1998 (3)	**2156**
Making Love—Roberta Flack (82)	1327
Stronger Than Before—Carole Bayer Sager (81)	502
Love Always—El DeBarge (86)	328
Harold BARLOW/Cesare BIXIO/ Phil BRITO/Bixio CHERUBINI ▶ 1999 (1)	**2155**
Mama—Connie Francis (60)	2155
Jimi HENDRIX ▶ 2000 (9)	**2154**

Writer Index to Top 2000 Writer Teams

Top 30 Writer Teams in Words, Charts and Graphs: Stories and Analytics

Writer Rank — Writer Team Rank — Writer Team Entries, Score

John LENNON *(2)*/Paul McCARTNEY*(1)* ► 1 (139) 255037

In this section, the records charted by the Top 30 writer teams are shown on a timeline graph to illustrate the team's rise and its longevity of popularity. In some cases an individual writer constitutes a writing "team;" that is, a solo writer accrues all the points for that recording. A writer's ranking as an individual writer may differ from his or her ranking as a writing team if the writer also accrues points from a share of those collaborations.

"Transcendent" songs are those scoring over 10,000 points—10 times the average score for their time—which places them in the top 50 records of the era, the top 0.2% Those scoring over 7500 points are in the top 1% of the records, approximately the top 250.

NOTE: Time and points scales differ in each chart.

John LENNON *(2)*/Paul McCARTNEY*(1)* ▶ 1 (139) 255037

Can there possibly be anything significant left unsaid about this duo after 55 years of biographies, interviews and analysis? Probably not, but this is my chance to make a few observations.

No surprise to enthusiasts, although it was to me--their first nationally charted record as a writing team was Del Shannon's "From Me To You" which appeared about the same time as the Beatles' own "Please Please Me" was on air at WLS in Chicago. Neither charted strongly, even though it was only a few months before the Invasion.

For all their prowess as songwriters, the record charts say their strongest work was as a writing *and* performing unit. Prior to the breakup only one cover song showed exceptional popularity. Peter and Gordon's "A World Without Love" did not have a Beatles equivalent, so effectively it was a Beatle record. Nearly 83% of Lennon/McCartney's writer points were earned by the Beatles.

After the Beatles broke up, neither their legacy records nor others' covers made much of a dent. Only Elton John's "Lucy in the Sky...," Anne Murray's "You Won't See Me" and their own "Got To Get You Into My Life" are notable. But with that said, the legacy they created is remarkable. Three of their records, including two of the top three of the era were transcendent in their time placing them in the top 0.2% of the charted songs. Nine more exceeded 7.5 times the average popularity, placing them in the top 1% of the charted songs. As a team, Lennon & McCartney ranks 68th in efficiency averaging over 1500 points for their 139 entries. The team-act combination of Lennon-McCartney and the Beatles, placed 8th, averaging 3345 points over 63 entries.

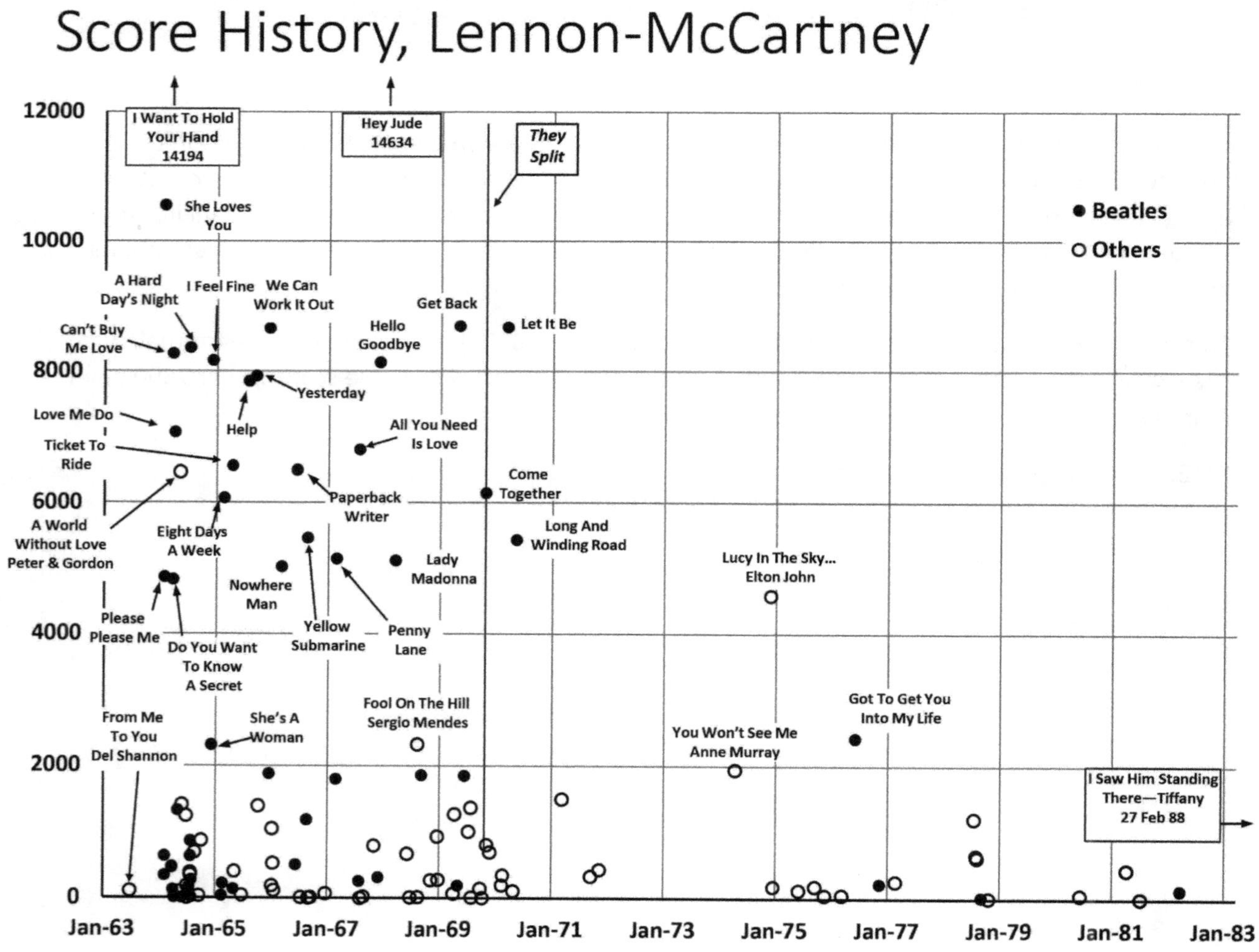

Triopoly: Paul McCartney, John Lennon, Linda McCartney

	Paul McCARTNEY ▶ 1	John LENNON ▶ 2	Linda McCARTNEY ▶ 89	Writer Total
Paul McCARTNEY ▶ 1	22	142	21	192
John LENNON ▶ 2	142	18	0	163
Linda McCARTNEY ▶ 89	21	0	1	22
Writer Total	192	163	22	

In numbers, Paul and John had similar sized solo chart careers—about 20 songs. By far the majority of their charted songs and writer points were from the partnership, augmented in McCartney's case by the songs of Paul and Linda and collaborations with Michael Jackson.

The first solo effort by one of them was Peter & Gordon's "Woman", written by Paul as Bernard Webb; the first after the breakup was John's ominous "Cold Turkey." While the McCartneys, via Wings, had improving circumstances through the '70s, Lennon was mostly absent from the charts after 1975 until his death when, ironically, "Just Like Starting Over" became his strongest solo effort.

Paul's two biggest post-Beatles records were duets with Motown alumni, Stevie Wonder and Michael Jackson; both placed in the top 1% of the era as did "My Love," "Silly Love Songs" and Lennon's "Just Like Starting Over." Linda and Paul are the 22nd-ranked writer team, and their combination with Wings averaged 2798 points over 16 entries, placing them 18th. Only about 1% of their chart points were scored by groups with no McCartney.

Score History, John, Yoko, Paul & Linda

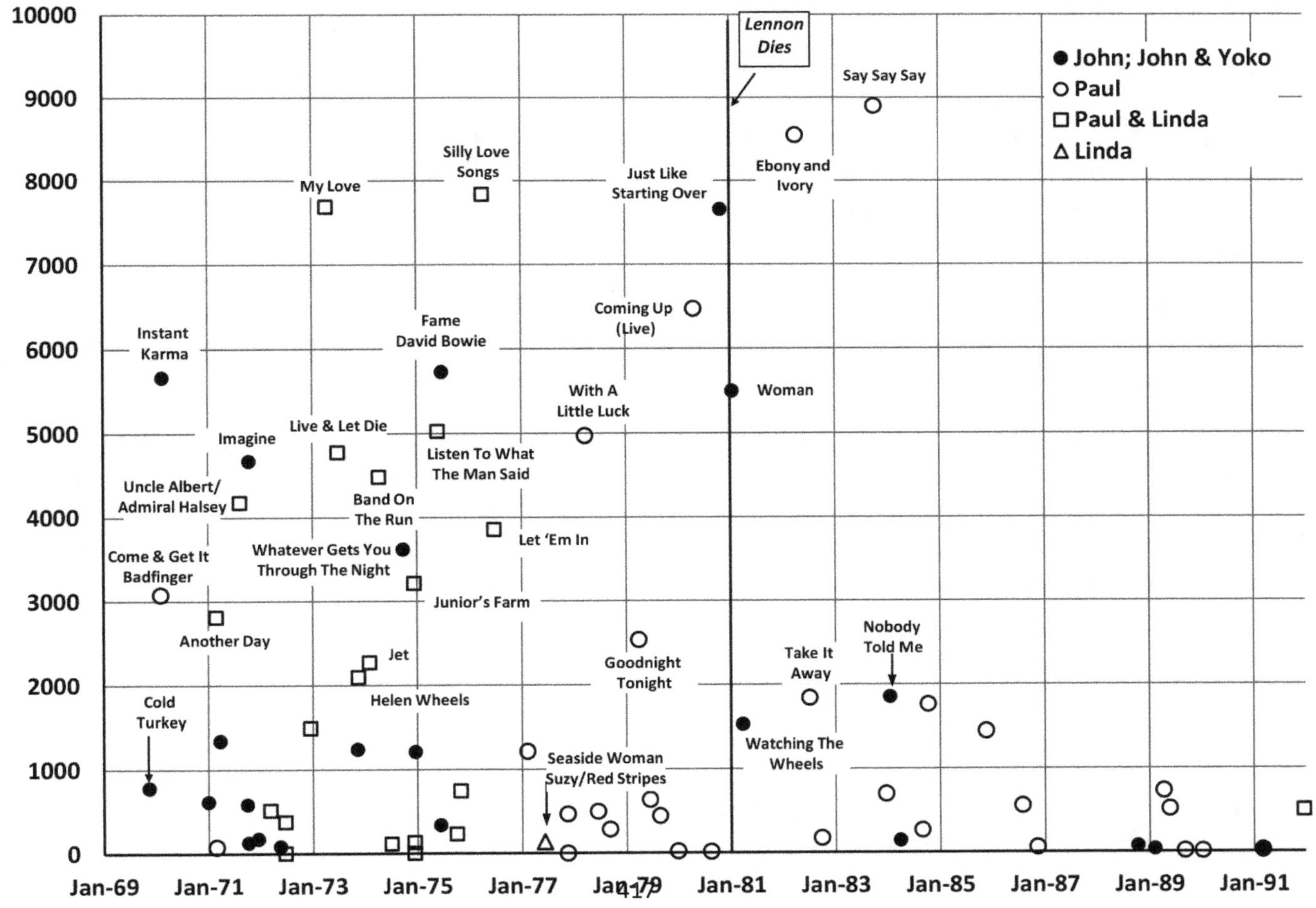

Lamont DOZIER *(15)*/Brian HOLLAND *(14)*/Eddie HOLLAND *(12)* ► 2 (107) 167934

The years 1960-1962 could be considered the pre-history of Holland-Dozier-Holland (HDH). Brian Holland was the first of the three to chart in 1960 with a song for Marv Johnson. In the next year he teamed with Robert Bateman, and the two became known as Brianbert. Brianbert were part of an important inflection point for Motown, the Marvelettes' "Please Mr. Postman."

How that song was written is a highly non-linear story; particularly when it also emerged as the very similar "Mashed Potato Time." Per Wikipedia, William Garrett offered "Please Mr. Postman" to the Marvelettes' Georgia Dobbins as a blues song. Dobbins rewrote it, but left the group. Brianbert (Brian Holland and Robert Bateman) polished it and Freddie Gorman--a postman, curiously enough—as well as a songwriter also helped the Marvelettes made it a hit. Brianbert and Gorman are credited in BMI and on the label. Berry Gordy was also on the copyright but it's hard to see his involvement. Most attributions these days, including that of EMI, the current publisher, are to Robert Bateman/Georgia Dobbins/William Garrett/Freddie Gorman/Brian Holland, which I've accepted. This is a slight variance from the generally inclusive methodology described in the Appendix.

Holland was joined by Lamont Dozier in 1962 for another Marvelettes song, "Strange I Know." Soon after, in early 1963, Eddie Holland joined Brian and Dozier for the first time for the Marvelettes' "Tie A String Around Your Finger." Janie Bradford is also credited. The timeline begins with the assembly of HDH.

The first year or so started slowly, and then, BOOM. There really is no warning on the timeline that "Where Did Our Love Go" was about to happen, but in the course of ten months HDH was responsible for writing five songs that ended up in the Top 1% of this era: four for the Supremes and one for The Four Tops. Ultimately they would add one more.

Of their 107 chart entries in this era, 43 were covers or alternate releases. The best charting cover in the '60s was Johnny Rivers' "Baby I Need Your Lovin." That was surpassed by Kim Wilde's "You Keep Me Hanging On" in 1987.

Even though they wrote nearly exclusively with one another, individual writers occasionally paired with others. Perhaps the most consequential pairing was between Eddie Holland and Norman Whitfield, who created "Ain't Too Proud To Beg" (with Cornelius Grant), "(I Know) I'm Losing You" and "Too Many Fish In The Sea." Sylvia Moy joined them for "This Old Heart Of Mine" originally by the Isley Brothers, which was covered three more times. HDH was credited post-recording on Len Barry's 1-2-3 for its similarity to "Ask Any Girl"—an inadvertent collaboration.

After the split with Berry Gordy, HDH continued to write together under the alias Edith Wayne or Edyth Craighead, generally with others. The most notable HDH+ entries after the breakup were collaborations with Ronald Dunbar supporting Freda Payne, Honey Cone, Chairmen Of The Board, and Flaming Ember.

HDH songs charted for 49 acts, the three highest scoring of which were The Supremes (81238, 17 entries), Four Tops (30169, 13 entries), and Martha And The Vandellas (13963, 9 entries). Their entries with the Supremes *averaged* 4779 points; nearly 5 times the popularity of the average song of their time, the highest average for any writer team/act combination with more than five entries.[1] Moreover, three-quarters of their points were scored by those three acts, which accounted for less than a third of their chart entries.

[1] Strangely, HDH did not write The Supremes' biggest hit. That was "Love Child," 9676 points, by Deke Richards/Pam Sawyer/R. Dean Taylor/Frank Edward Wilson.

Score History, Holland-Dozier-Holland

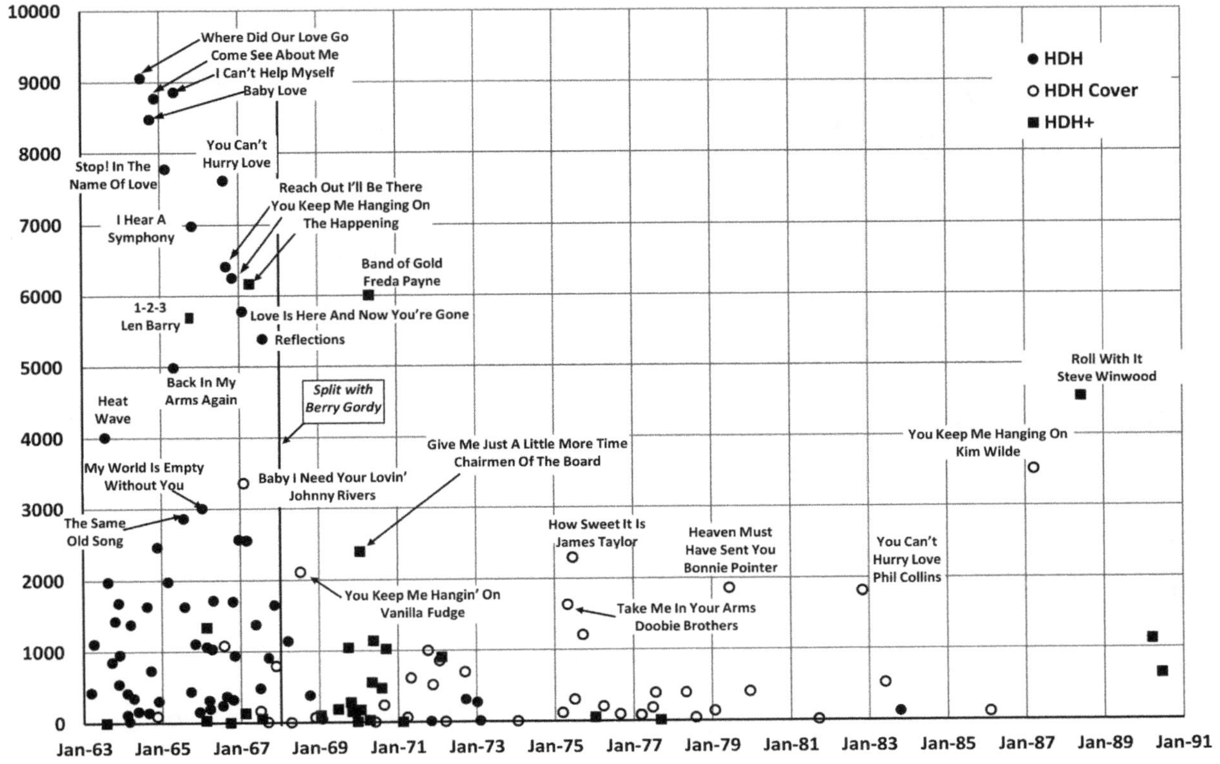

HDH At Motown: The Glory Years

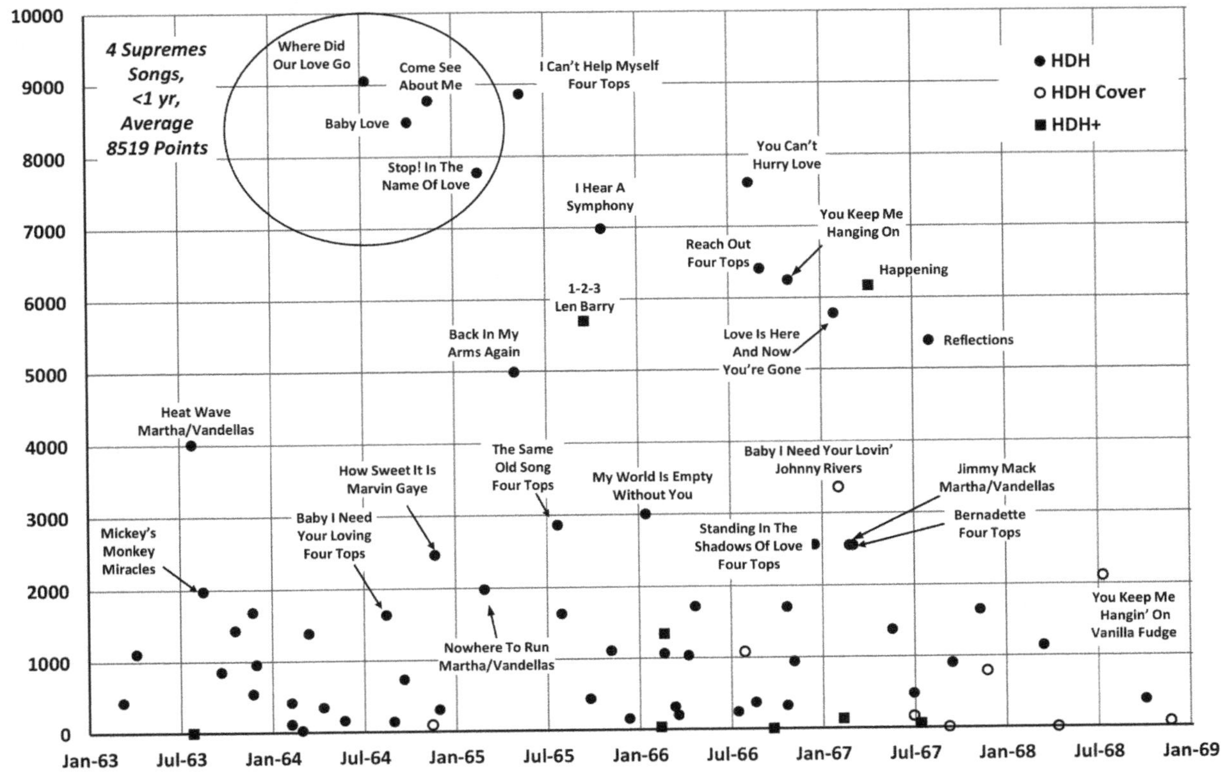

Sidebar: How the major Motown writers collaborated

	Stevie WONDER ▶ 7	Smokey ROBINSON ▶ 9	Eddie HOLLAND ▶ 12	Brian HOLLAND ▶ 14	Lamont DOZIER ▶ 15	Norman WHITFIELD ▶ 21	Barrett STRONG ▶ 53	Berry GORDY ▶ 64	Marvin GAYE ▶ 96	Writer Total	Notes
Stevie WONDER ▶ 7	43	2								**82**	Henry Cosby, 18; Sylvia Moy,16
Smokey ROBINSON ▶ 9	2	57						7		**128**	Marvin Tarplin, 22; Warren Moore, 24; Robert Rogers, 16; Ronnie White, 14
Eddie HOLLAND ▶ 12			*0*	*142*	*136*	17				**163**	
Brian HOLLAND ▶ 14			*142*	*0*	*145*			1		**164**	
Lamont DOZIER ▶ 15			*136*	*145*	*3*					**151**	
Norman WHITFIELD ▶ 21			17			17	50		2	**92**	
Barrett STRONG ▶ 53						50	3		1	**57**	
Berry GORDY ▶ 64		7		1				13		**64**	Freddie Perren, 9
Marvin GAYE ▶ 96						2	1		7	**35**	
Writer Total	**82**	**128**	**163**	**164**	**151**	**92**	**57**	**64**	**35**		

Motown writers are a study in different collaboration styles. About half of Stevie Wonder and Smokey Robinson's songs were written as solo efforts. Norman Whitfield and Barrett Strong wrote extensively together; Strong has very few credits that don't involve Whitfield; as noted, Whitfield worked to great effect with Eddie Holland.

HDH occupies the middle box in this chart. Virtually all of their credits were with one another in some fashion, and they were virtually never credited as solo writers. This is nearly the "Brill Building" mode of having one main collaborator and virtually no solo work.

Burt BACHARACH *(11)*/Hal DAVID *(17)* ▶ 3 (105) 112434

Burt Bacharach and Hal David first charted together with Marty Robbins' "Story Of My Life" in 1957. It would be 1962 before they had a hit of substance: "(The Man Who Shot) Liberty Valance" with Gene Pitney. But 1962 was a good year in that it also marked their first of 33 charted songs with Dionne Warwick, "Don't Make Me Over."

The apex of the Bacharach-David era came between 1968 and 1971 with four huge hits, and other smaller gems. "Raindrops Keep Fallin' On My Head," was a transcendent hit, recorded by B.J. Thomas. "This Guy's In Love With You" was sung by Herb Alpert, the only act to have number one hits both as a vocalist and an instrumentalist. "Close To You" was a B-side for Richard Chamberlain and Dionne Warwick before The Carpenters' success. "One Less Bell To Answer" by the 5th Dimension was originally done by Keely Smith and Rosemary Clooney. The latter three songs score in the top 1%.

Their personal fame was asymmetric with Bacharach the more visible and celebrated. This eventually led to a split in 1973 over the score for a movie failure, "The Lost Horizon," and a fall from the charts. Bacharach found a second wave of popularity in the 1980s, working with his third wife, Carole Bayer Sager. "That's What Friends Are For" even involved Dionne Warwick. David had one remaining moderate success in 1984, "To All The Girls I've Loved Before," written with Albert Hammond and recorded by Julio Iglesias and Willie Nelson.

Their charted collaborations comprised 105 of Bacharach's 139 total entries and David's 131. Their 56217 collaboration points was a large majority for both writers. Thirty-three acts charted their songs, with the most points scored by Dionne Warwick, although as an act-writer team combination they only averaged 907 points. As a team overall, Bacharach and David averaged 1071 points, their average lifted by the big hits mentioned above.

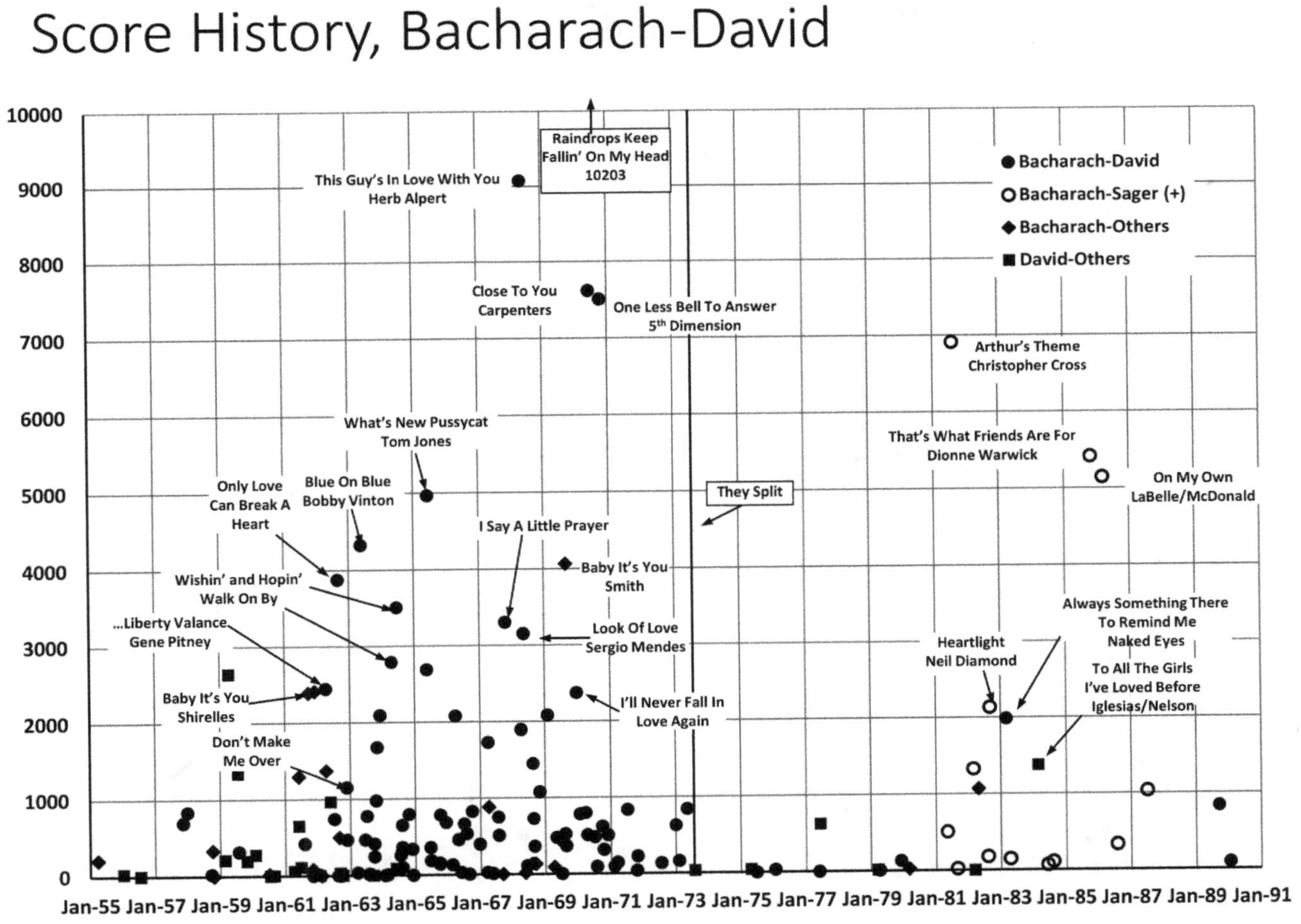

Mick JAGGER *(22)*/Keith RICHARDS *(23)* ► 4 (60) 110743

The story of Jagger and Richards is the story of the Rolling Stones and vice versa. The Stones charted 54 times; 47 were compositions by Jagger/Richards or Jagger/Richards and others. The two writers charted 60 songs together; in combination with others, only six more. Keith Richards had no solo credits and none without Jagger. Jagger had only two solo credits and five without Keith.

In his biography *Life*, Keith discussed when, as a teen-ager, he re-met Mick, "a guy I knew at primary school," at the train station at Dartford in 1961. Mick had "every record Chuck Berry ever made" and a collection of discs by other R&B acts. He added at the time, "Mick is the greatest R&B singer this side of the Atlantic and I don't mean maybe."

They did not come to writing easily. The old story that Andrew Loog Oldham locked the two of them in a kitchen in Willesden and forced them to write a song is confirmed by Keith in "Life." They eventually had the first two lines and some interesting chords. "Once you've got that idea, the rest will come," he noted. The result was "As Tears Go By," Oldham is also credited on the song, and Marianne Faithfull recorded it first. The Stones' version appeared later and was somewhat bigger.

There was not much warning that "Satisfaction" would explode the way it did; it and "Honky Tonk Women" were the two Jagger-Richards transcendent songs, each residing in the top 50 of the era. The duo ranked 5th in score in the '60s and 14th in the '70s. Jagger-Richards and the Stones are the 26th-ranked writer-act pair of the era, averaging 2507 points over 43 entries. As a team, Jagger-Richards' 60 entries ranks 66th, averaging 1846 points, and the Rolling Stones were the number 3 act for the era.

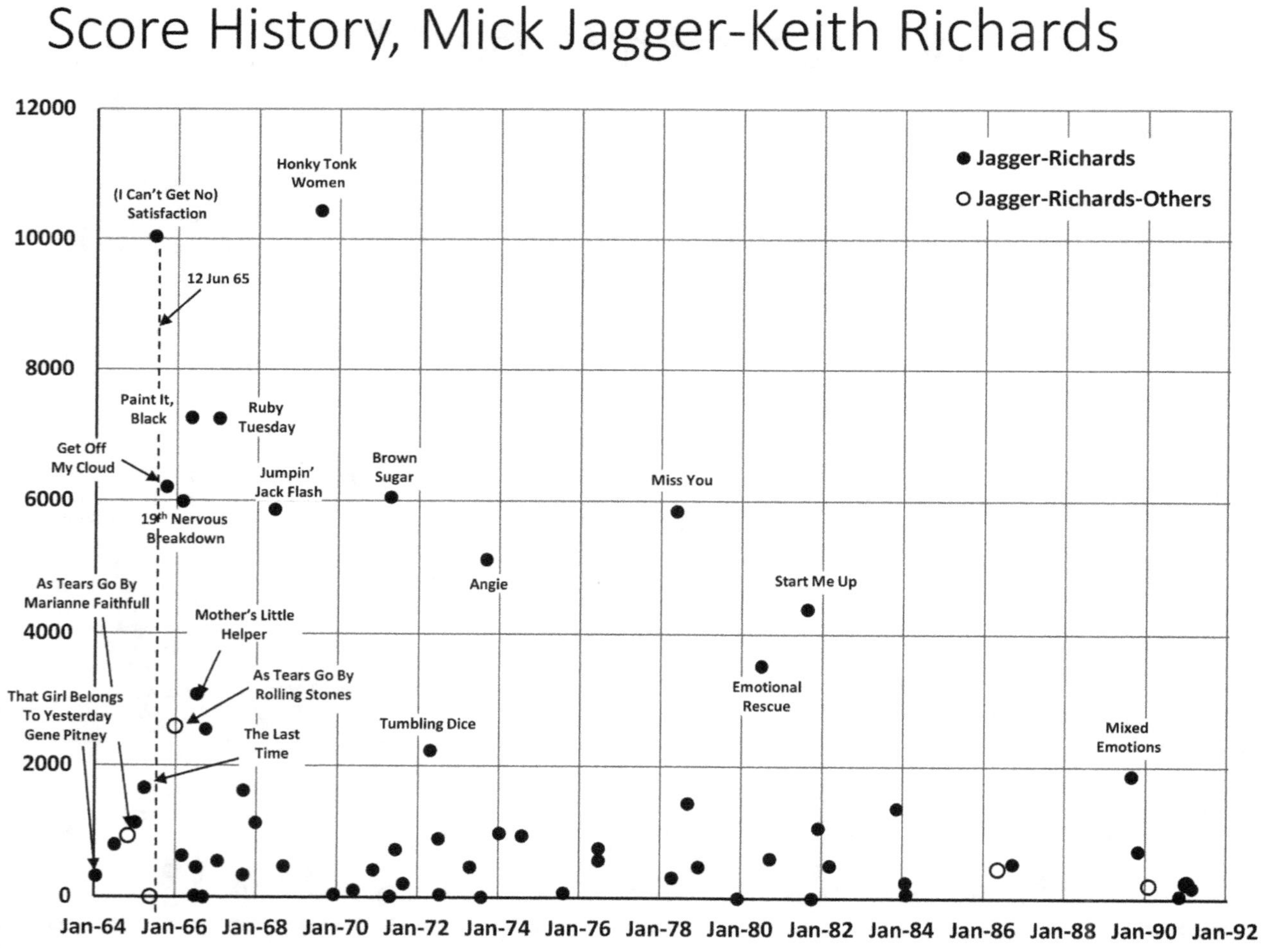

Barry GIBB *(10)*/Maurice GIBB *(29)*/Robin GIBB *(55)* ► 5 (44) 100483

There are four distinct Bee Gees periods. Their chart history started in the late days of the British Invasion, and right before the psychedelic era with an almost folky sound. Surprisingly, as memorable as their first four songs were ("New York Mining Disaster 1941," "To Love Somebody," "Holiday," and "Massachusetts") they had only average chart performance.

The early '70s, their second phase, was a slow period for them as writers and the Bee Gees as an act, as only "Lonely Days" and "How Can You Mend A Broken Heart" made much of a mark. But Barry, Maurice and Robin Gibb as writers were masters of reinvention. By 1975, disco was just starting to happen and "Jive Talking" became their biggest record to date. "Nights On Broadway" and "Fanny (Be Tender With My Love)" were solid follow-ups that had a different sound from their previous work. This started phase 3.

The Bee Gees were on RSO records and Robert Stigwood was the producer of what became "Saturday Night Fever." As they were recording an album in a studio in France, he contacted them to ask if they had any songs they might be able to contribute. Eventually, they wrote songs for the soundtrack, virtually all in one weekend. However, they did not participate in the making of the movie. The music was only added in post-production, and it became a sensation. The Brothers Gibb owned the charts in 1977 and 1978 largely due to two factors: the "Saturday Night Fever" soundtrack and the success of Andy Gibb.

On the chart, Andy Gibb's history can be seen as a skyrocket in the middle of the Bee Gees disco era: he spent 95 consecutive weeks on the chart, including three #1 songs. But both he and disco as a craze had largely burned out by 1980, and the Bee Gees lost chart presence, although in the '80s the Gibb brothers wrote huge hits for others including Barbra Streisand, Dionne Warwick and the Kenny Rogers/Dolly Parton duo. Curiously, as successful as they were as writers, there were only three cover versions of Bee Gees songs that charted, none of consequence.

As writers, the Gibbs were pretty much a closed shop. Barry had 79 writer credits, 73 with his brothers, and 6 solo. Three of the 73 included Albhy Galutin, and one each with Michael Jackson, Blue Weaver and George Bitzer. Robin's record was similar, with only two credits with Blue Weaver. Maurice had one collaboration with George Bitzer and one with Michael Jackson, but Barry was also a co-writer on both.

	Barry GIBB ► 10	Robin GIBB ► 29	Maurice GIBB ► 55	Writer Total	Notes
Barry GIBB ► 10	6	58	54	79	Andy Gibb, 3
Robin GIBB ► 29	58	1	46	62	Andy Gibb, 1
Maurice GIBB ► 55	54	46	0	55	Andy Gibb, 1
Writer Total	79	62	55		

Barry Gibb's solo work ranks him as the fifth most efficient writer team averaging 3257 points over his six solo entries. Barry, Maurice and Robin rank 28th averaging 2284 points over 44 entries. As an act-writer team combination, the Bee Gees-Barry, Maurice and Robin rank 19th with an average of 2277 points over 29 entries. They produced one transcendent song in the Top 50 for the era—Shadow Dancing—and one that just missed—Stayin' Alive. Three more—"I Just Want To Be Your Everything," "Night Fever," and "How Deep Is Your Love" make the top 1%. As acts, The Bee Gees rank sixth and Andy Gibb 103rd.

Score History, Barry, Maurice & Robin Gibb

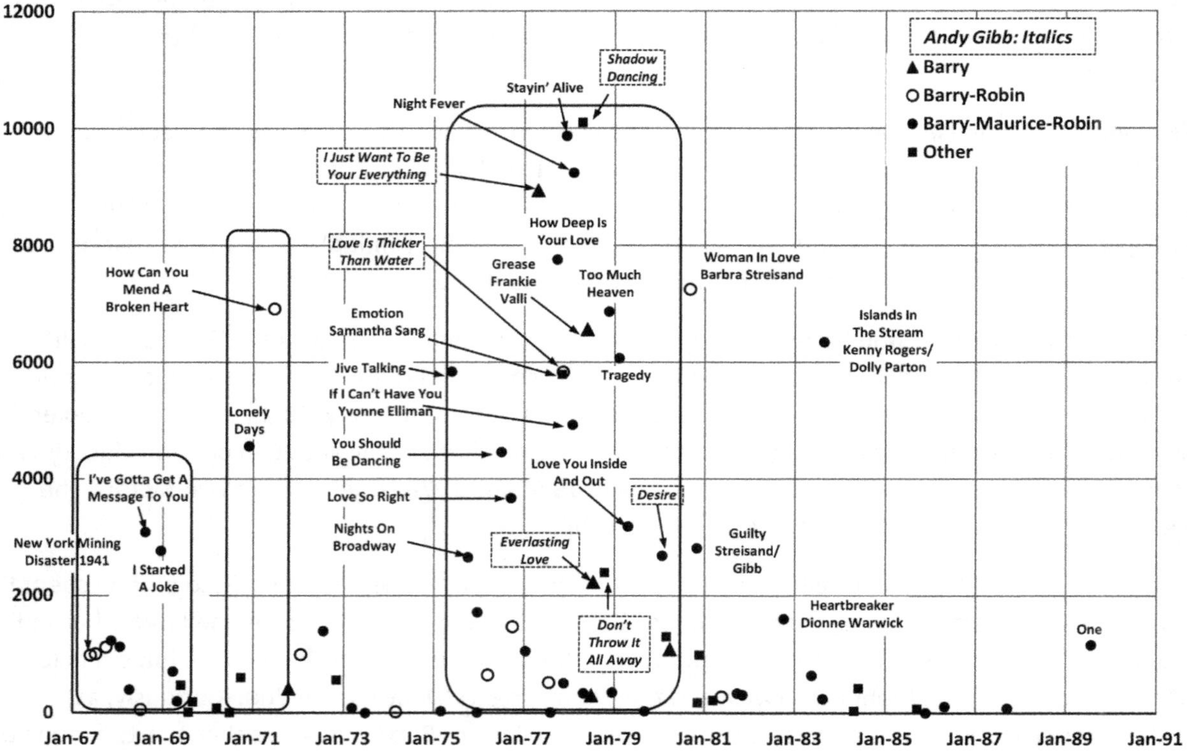

Closeup: Sat. Night Fever/Andy Gibb Era

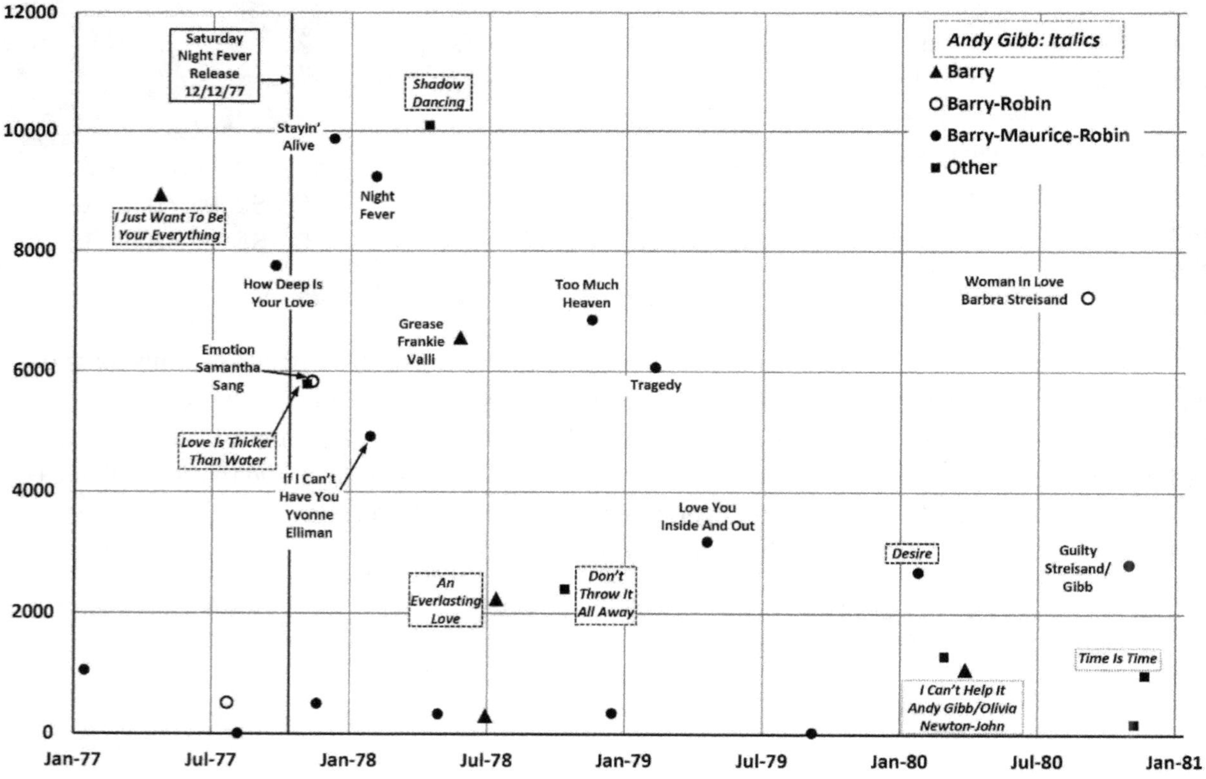

Gerry GOFFIN *(19)*/Carole KING *(13)* ► 6 (94) 94936

The story of Gerry Goffin and Carol Jean Klein AKA Carole King with the backdrop of their lives as songwriters has been made mainstream by the musical "Beautiful." At Queens College, Carole was a classmate of Paul Simon. During her freshman year she was introduced to an older chemistry major—Gerry. He was writing lyrics for a musical, but Carole was not interested in writing show tunes. Eventually, they started writing pop songs together, and were married in anticipation of their first child, Louise. Carole worked as a secretary, Gerry in a polymer testing lab. They wrote songs at night, and sold some to Aldon Music—Al Nevins and Don Kirshner.

One evening, returning home from bowling with friends, Gerry found a note on the tape recorder that Kirshner needed a lyric by the next day for the Shirelles. Carole had left music on the tape and gone to play mah-jongg with her mother. Goffin said "The lyric came out easy." The song, "Will You Love Me Tomorrow," was finished by 2 AM. It went to #1 for the Shirelles, the first #1 by an African-American female group and Goffin-King's first charted song as a writer team.

Eva Boyd worked as a baby sitter for Gerry and Carole, and she sang the demo version of "Loco-motion," which the writers had intended for Dee Dee Sharp. Don Kirshner liked the demo and released it as the first single on a new record label he created, Dimension. It went to #1 for "Little Eva."

Clearly they had been successful writers, but following the timeline it's easy to see their chart status was in decline as they reached the mid-'60s. "Pleasant Valley Sunday" was their last high point for new compositions. They divorced in 1968; The decline in their marriage might be taken as a metaphor for the changing role of songwriters in the music business, as more acts began to write and record their own songs, eschewing the new Tin Pan Alley.

Of their 94 charted songs, 48 were multiple entries: 32 covers of 16 original recordings. "Will You Love Me Tomorrow" charted seven times; "Up On The Roof," "Go Away Little Girl/Boy" and "One Fine Day" four times each. They placed three songs in the top 1% for the era—"Go Away Little Girl" by Steve Lawrence (their biggest), The Loco-Motion, and "Take Good Care Of My Baby" by Bobby Vee. The duo also charted with Cynthia Weil, Jerry Wexler ("Natural Woman"), Howard Greenfield and three times with Phil Spector, including "Just Once In My Life" for the Righteous Brothers.

Separately, Gerry Goffin wrote eight songs with Brill/1650 stalwarts Jack Keller ("Run To Him") and Barry Mann ("Who Put The Bomp"); he also wrote with Wes Farrell, Russ Titelman and Scott Cutler. Carole and Howard Greenfield collaborated on "Crying In The Rain" for the Everly Brothers.

Sixty-four acts charted with their songs but only one recorded more than five of them—Bobby Vee—and his seven recordings averaged 1443 points, placing the Act-Team combination 103rd. However, despite their elevated place in the lore, and perhaps because of the assembly line nature of the work they did, their entire catalog only averaged 1010 points for 279th place.

Goffin and King ranked as the number four team for the '60s by points and number three by entries. For the '70s, Carole ranked 14th for score and ninth for entries.

Obviously, Carole King went on to have an important career as an artist, writing solo and together with Toni Stern, Cynthia Weil and David Palmer, and placing "It's Too Late" in the Top 1%. Gerry Goffin's most productive collaboration after working with Carole was with Michael Masser, charting nine songs including "Saving All My Love For You" for Whitney Houston and "Theme From Mahogany" by Diana Ross.

Score History, Gerry Goffin-Carole King

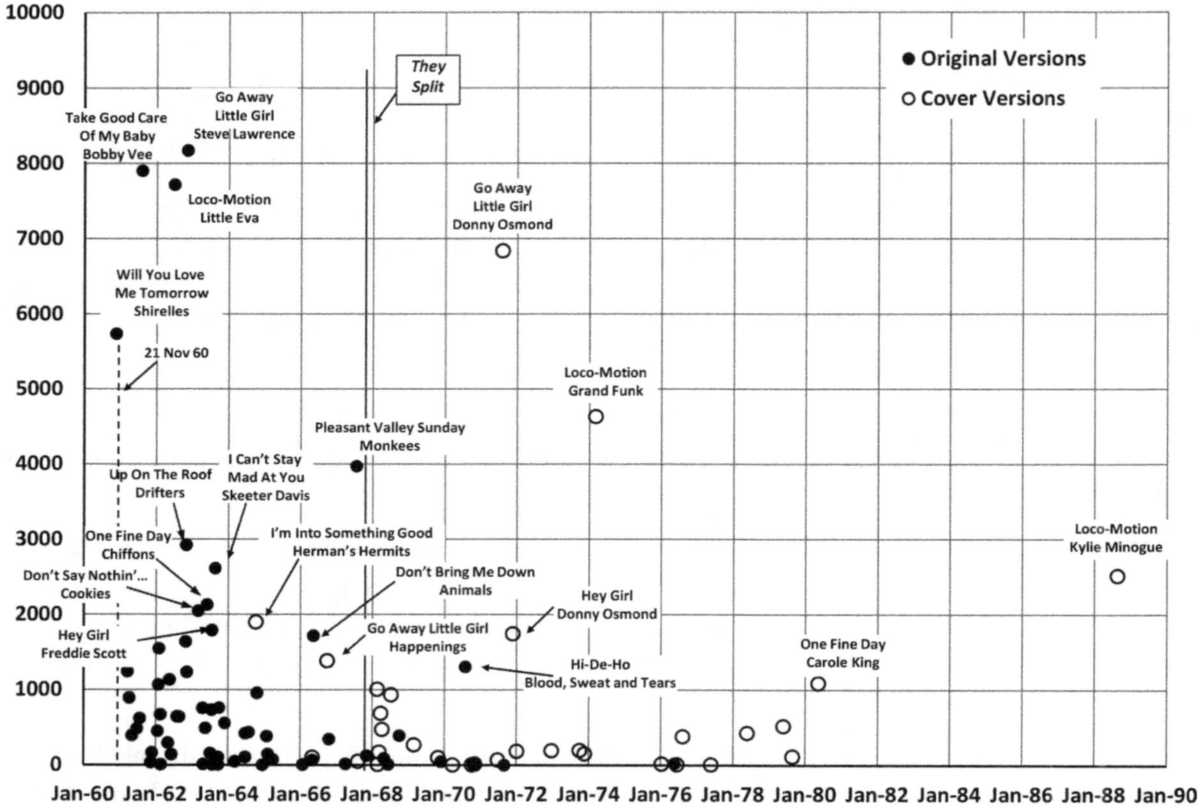

Score History, King, Goffin & Others

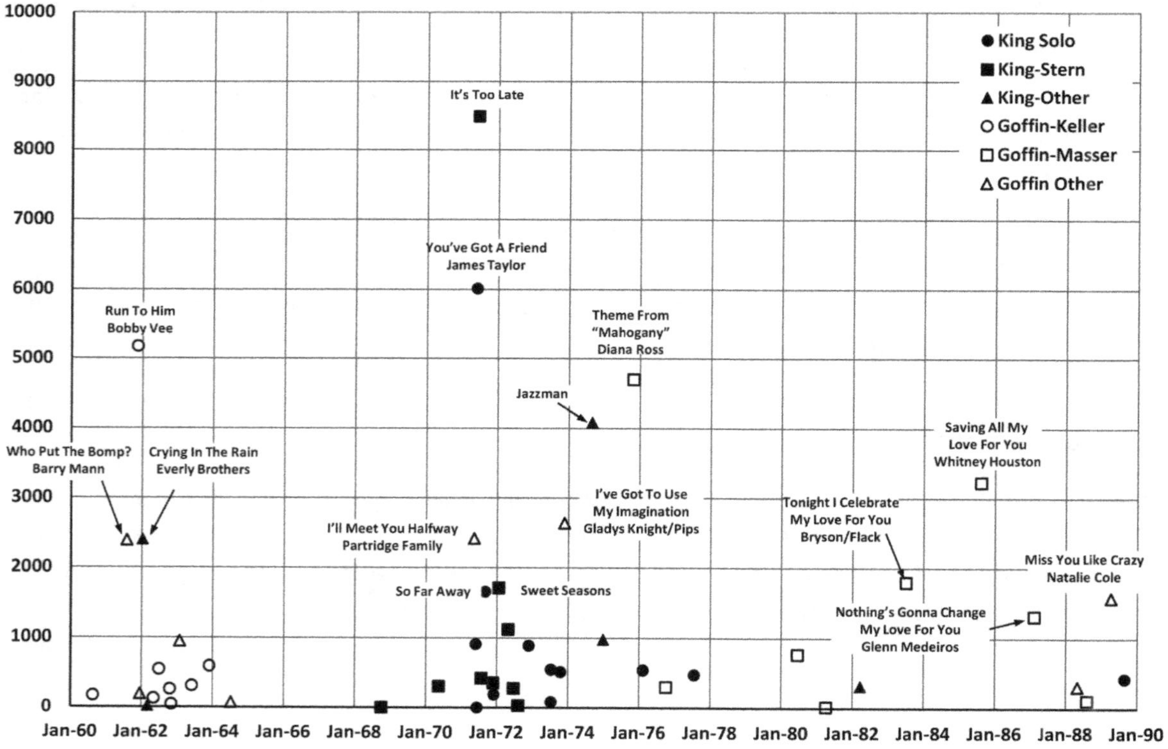

Sidebar: "Brill Building" Pop[2]

Before there were recordings, there was still popular music. New music was demonstrated in the store by a song plugger, bought as sheet music and taken home for the family pianist to learn. The song was everything.

From before the turn of the twentieth century there were the song mills in New York on West 28th Street between 5th and 6th, collectively known as Tin Pan Alley. Songs that survive today—and that includes a large number of songs in this database--were written by the denizens of Tin Pan Alley: Vincent Youmans, Harry von Tilzer, Irving Berlin and George Gershwin to name a few.

But as recordings became more available, the performance—a combination of act and song—became what people bought. No longer did they have to buy sheet music: they could buy records.

The successor to Tin Pan Alley in the 1950s and 1960s was centered in two buildings: 1650 Broadway and the Brill Building at 1619 Broadway. There were hundreds of music businesses crammed into these buildings, including some of the most memorable publishers and writing teams of the era.

Looking back at what they became, it's incredible that all these great writers were not just contemporaries but classmates. The new Tin Pan Alley was primarily a team rather than solo environment. In some cases, the teams were married couples—Gerry Goffin and Carole King; Barry Mann and Cynthia Weil; Jeff Barry and Ellie Greenwich. In other cases they just worked well together: Jerry Leiber and Mike Stoller; Doc Pomus and Mort Shuman, Burt Bacharach and Hal David. And in one case, their families lived in the same building and they went to high school together: Howard Greenfield and Neil Sedaka. And occasionally, the teams cross-fertilized.

Shown on the next page is a grid of the number of charted records by the most productive 1650/Brill writers, and the number of times each collaborated with another of those writers. The shaded boxes are solo writer credits. Note that virtually all the songs were collaborations of two or three; each writer was primarily either a musician or a lyricist. Carole King who had the most solo credits accumulated those after she became a performer. Even though Phil Spector doesn't neatly fit the Brill Building cohort—he was a bicoastal producer and label owner—he is listed in collaborations with so many of these writers it seemed necessary to include him.

Pop music in the '50s and early '60s was driven by singers and singing groups. Those groups needed songs, and the writers produced them. The groups needed instrumental backing, and the studio musicians provided it. The story played out in geographical centers across the country—Detroit, New York, Philadelphia, Memphis, Los Angeles, Chicago; among official and unofficial bands of studio players--The Funk Brothers, The Wrecking Crew, Booker T & the MGs and The Mob among them.

Even for band members who could play their instruments or write some songs, studio time was too precious to leave to the amateurs and recording too expensive to leave to chancy material. And this model—professional writers and musicians backing young rock and pop faces and voices—operated well until the British Invasion. As time passed, it became expected that bands would write their own songs and play their own instruments. There became less need for writers and less work for studio musicians. The singer-songwriter emerged—some of them even writing-mill alumni like Carole King and Neil Diamond. By 1970, the model had changed.

[2] The best reference for history and stories about Brill Building Pop is "Always Magic In The Air" by Ken Emerson.

	Burt BACHARACH ▶ 11	Carole KING ▶ 13	Hal DAVID ▶ 17	Gerry GOFFIN ▶ 19	Jerry LEIBER ▶ 24	Mike STOLLER ▶ 28	Barry MANN ▶ 30	Jeff BARRY ▶ 33	Howard GREENFIELD ▶ 41	Cynthia WEIL ▶ 49	Neil SEDAKA ▶ 50	Phil SPECTOR ▶ 61	Doc POMUS ▶ 63	Mort SHUMAN ▶ 65	Ellie GREENWICH ▶ 81	Writer Total	Notes
Burt BACHARACH ▶ 11	2		105													**139**	Bob Hilliard, 12
Carole KING ▶ 13		12		101					2	3		3				**127**	
Hal DAVID ▶ 17	105		0													**131**	
Gerry GOFFIN ▶ 19		101		0			2		1	1		3				**125**	Jack Keller, 9
Jerry LEIBER ▶ 24					0	116	3			3		4	4			**122**	
Mike STOLLER ▶ 28					116	0	3			3			4			**117**	
Barry MANN ▶ 30				2	3	3	5	1	4	77		8				**104**	
Jeff BARRY ▶ 33							1	4		1		24			52	**95**	
Howard GREENFIELD ▶ 41		2		1			4		0		46					**74**	Jack Keller, 10
Cynthia WEIL ▶ 49		3		1	3	3	77	1		0		8				**89**	
Neil SEDAKA ▶ 50									46		2					**58**	
Phil SPECTOR ▶ 61		3		3	4		8	24		8		8	3		26	**62**	
Doc POMUS ▶ 63					4	4						3	1	60		**73**	
Mort SHUMAN ▶ 65													60	0		**68**	
Ellie GREENWICH ▶ 81								52				26			0	**59**	
Writer Total	**139**	**127**	**131**	**125**	**122**	**117**	**104**	**95**	**74**	**89**	**58**	**62**	**73**	**68**	**59**		

Elton JOHN *(37)*/Bernie TAUPIN *(38)* ► 7 (43) 83123

And speaking of the singer-songwriter era, Elton John is a prime example, although his early history with Bernie Taupin is a bit reminiscent of the songwriting duos of the Brill Building and 1650 Broadway. In 1967, both writers responded to an ad placed by Liberty Records and were paired up by an executive there. They wrote for Dick James Music, with Elton cutting demos at night.

After a short induction period, they hit big. By 1973, they were fixtures at least on FM until 1976. As a team, Elton the flashy one, Bernie the shy one. The name for the album "Captain Fantastic And The Brown Dirt Cowboy" did not come from nowhere. As writers, they always shared copyright credit from music and lyrics as Lennon and McCartney did, even if the true story was division of labor. Taupin recounts, "My lyrics always came before Elton's music" and the idea that they worked separately in "two rooms" seems to be an accurate story.

One might think that people who worked in such an independent fashion would find it easy to work with others in the same way. That was largely not true, at least for charted records; their history was perfectly symmetric. Each charted 51 songs. Forty-six were collaborations of the two of them, and five were with other writers.

Elton wrote four of those songs with Gary Osborne during a hiatus with Bernie—a hiatus apparent from the empty space on the graph between 1978 and 1982. Bernie, without Elton, collaborated on "We Built This City" for Starship and one song each for Heart, Animotion, Alice Cooper and the Hudson Brothers.

They placed no songs in the top 1%. Elton John singing John/Taupin songs as an act/writer team averaged 1838 points to rank 63rd, although that rank would be higher if the Elton John Band (Philadelphia Freedom) and Elton John/Kiki Dee (Don't Go Breakin' My Heart) were included. Only 5 non-Elton related acts charted their songs.

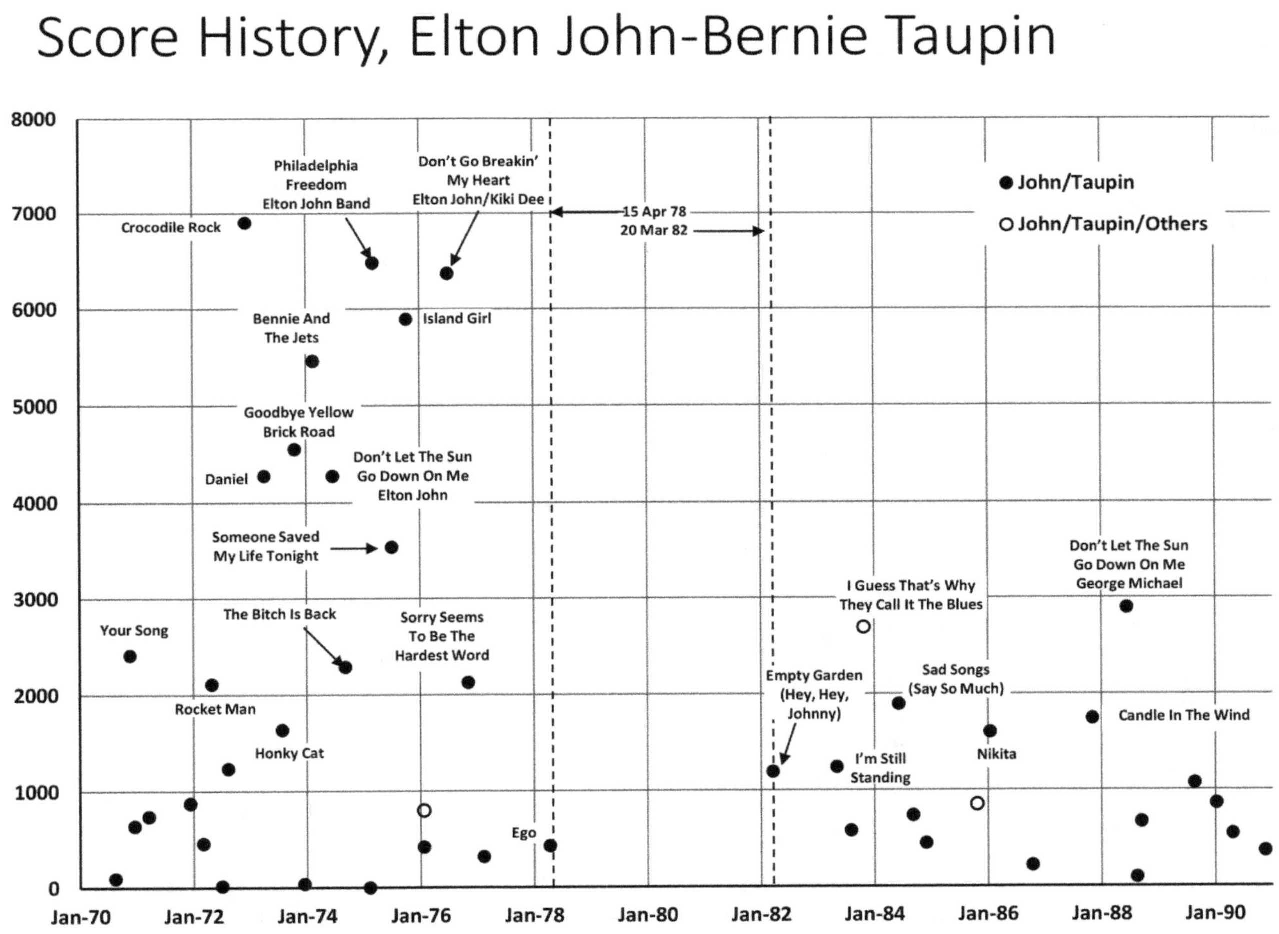

Paul SIMON *(5)* ► 8 (44) 82685

Paul Simon and Art Garfunkel have known each other since grade school, and had their first charted record as Tom and Jerry in 1957, "Hey Schoolgirl." After a hiatus, they recorded a folk album in 1964, "Wednesday Morning, 3 AM," which contained an acoustic version of "Sound of Silence." The album was not a success.

The rise of Motown was largely coincident with the British Invasion in 1964. The American counter-revolution really only came in 1965 with folk-rock, and "Mr. Tambourine Man" by the Byrds was the first telling shot. "Like A Rolling Stone" followed, and the genre took hold. In June, 1965, Columbia producer Tom Wilson, hoping to play into the genre, decided to overdub an electric guitar track onto the acoustic version of "Sound of Silence." At that time, Paul and Artie had split; Paul was in England, where he wrote "Red Rubber Ball" with Bruce Woodley, and "Homeward Bound." He was unaware of the overdub when the new track took off.

Simon and Garfunkel became instantly recognizable voices of the '60s. The "off-again" part of their "on-again, off-again" relationship kicked in after recording the classic album "Bridge Over Troubled Water." Artie went off to do movies and Paul went out on his own, yet another singer-songwriter. Artie had a reasonable solo recording career as well, fueled by songs of some of the best writers, most notably, Jimmy Webb. Over the years they would occasionally reunite for a recording or a tour.

Ten cover versions charted; most importantly Aretha Franklin's "Bridge Over Troubled Water" and the Bangles' "Hazy Shade Of Winter." Simon & Garfunkel singing Paul Simon averaged 3345 points, (10th place); Paul Simon singing his own songs averaged 1610 points (82nd place); he was the number 19 writer of the '60s by score. Performing, Simon & Garfunkel ranks as the 45th act, and Simon solo as 143rd. Paul had three top 1% songs: "Sound Of Silence," "Bridge Over Troubled Water," and "Mrs. Robinson."

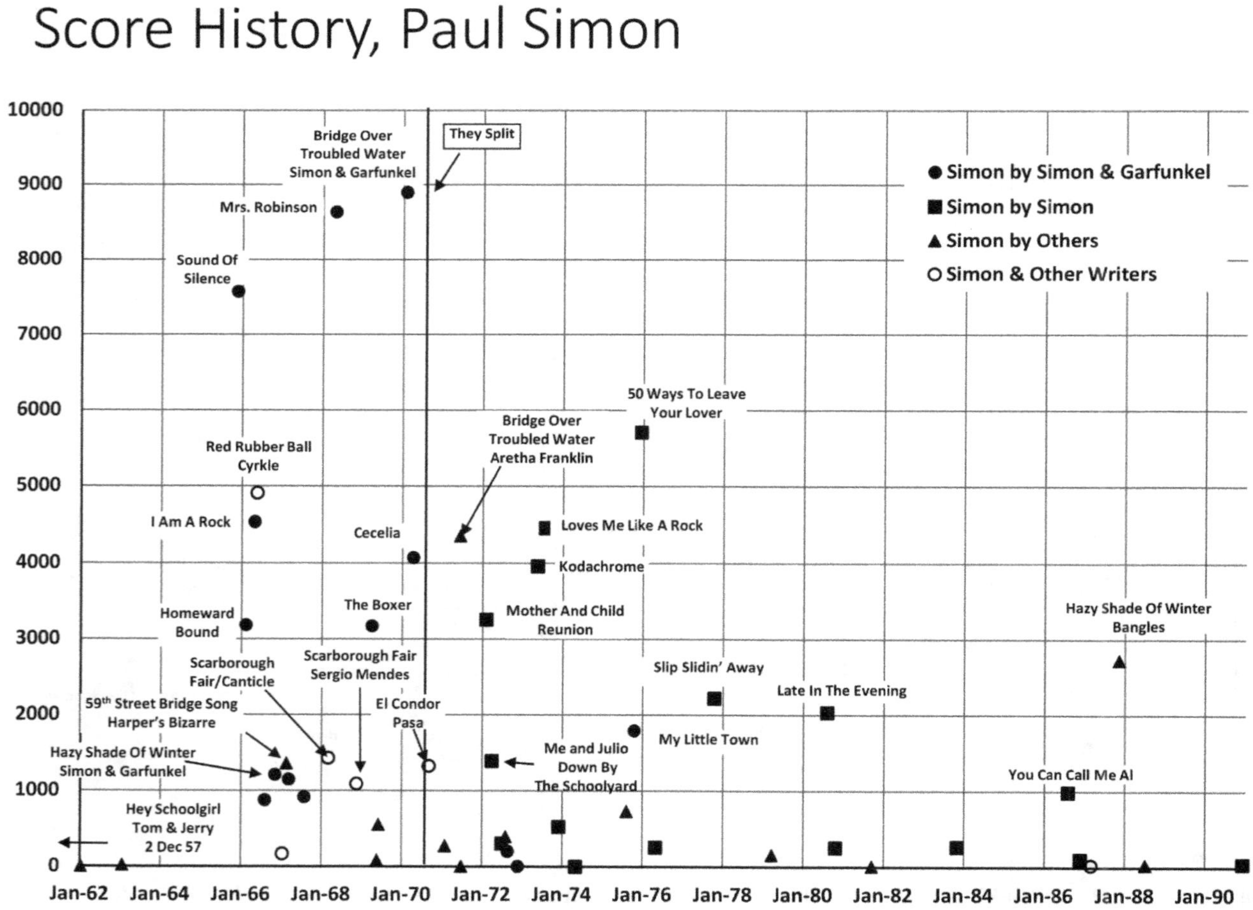

Lionel RICHIE *(4)* ► 9 (20) 81488

Lionel Richie is something of an enigma. In writer credits, he ranks number 4; as a writing team—solo—he ranks number 9. By every measure, he had a productive career in front of him, but he chose to walk away in 1987.

The Commodores formed at Tuskeegee Institute in 1968 with Lionel as singer and saxophonist. Over the next decade they prospered as an act. But after his success as a vocalist with Diana Ross on the theme song for the movie "Endless Love" he decided to pursue a solo career, which met with even larger success.

After "Se La," however, he took a hiatus from recording and, as Wikipedia puts it, maintained a leisurely recording schedule that was not impactful. But there is no argument that he was a force on the charts in the 1980s, ranking as the number two writer team in that decade.

Lionel Richie was one of the most efficient artists of all time. As a solo act-writer team combination, his songs averaged over 4000 points, good for third place in the era; Richie with the Commodores placed seventh. Lionel Richie's writing team average of 4074 points ranks as number 1 for the era. He was the 51st-ranked act; the Commodores were 68th. Surprisingly, he only had 20 songs as a solo writer, but some very intense hits.

Lionel Richie had one transcendent hit, "Endless Love." He had three more that rank in the top 1%: "Lady," "Three Times A Lady" and "All Night Long."

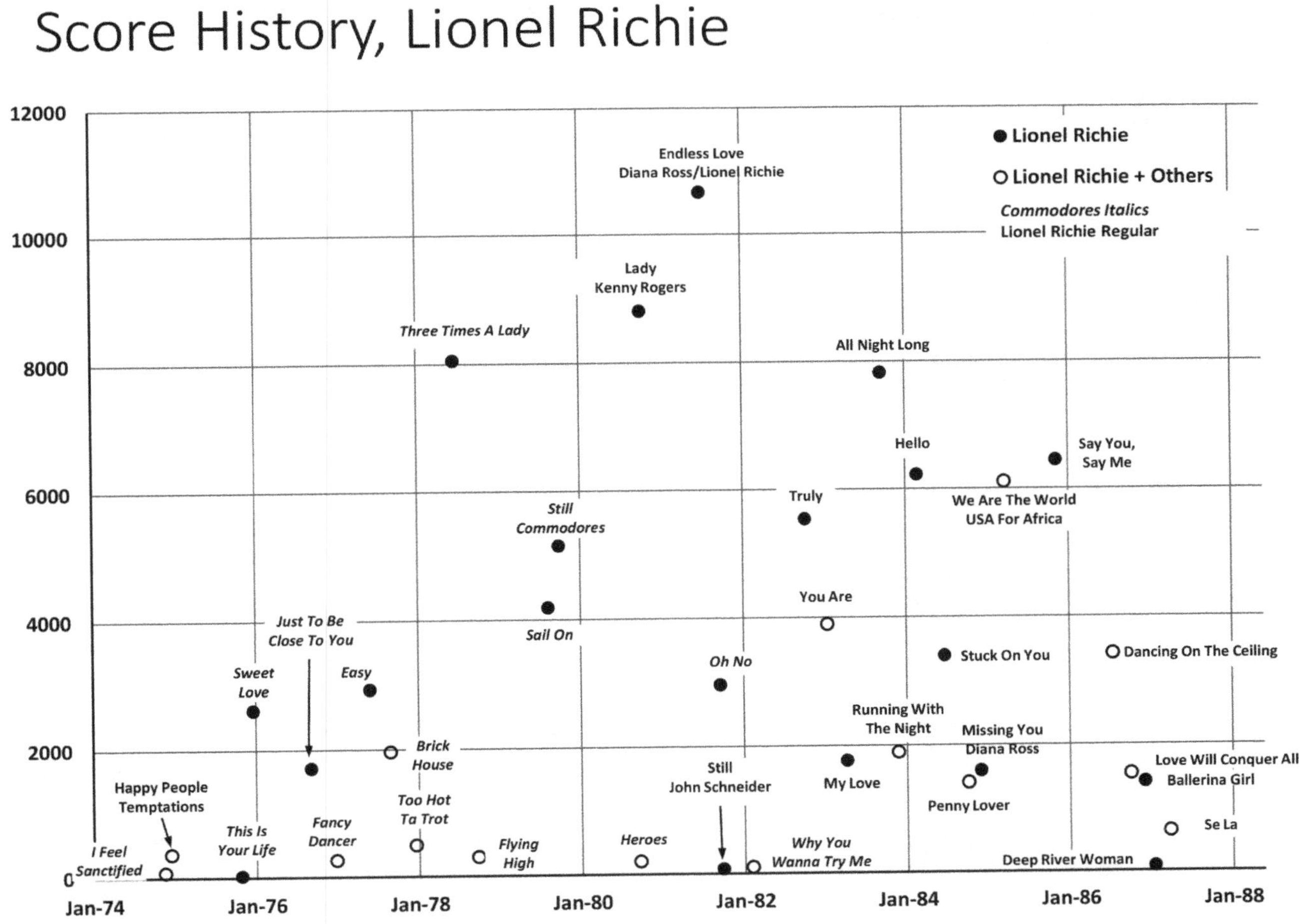

Jerry LEIBER *(24)*/Mike STOLLER *(28)*► 10 (82) 80838

When Leiber and Stoller come up in the conversation, three things come immediately to mind for me: Elvis, The Coasters and "Stand By Me." And if I think about it for a minute after that, The Drifters. Leiber and Stoller were a Brill Building pair, but their history goes back way before the Aldon era.

Although both were born on the East coast, they met in 1950 after their families moved to Los Angeles. They were foils as personalities but they shared a love for what they called "alley music," and their first songs appeared almost immediately after they first got together. Their big break came in 1952 when Big Mama Thornton recorded "Hound Dog." Her recording sold 500,000 copies; Elvis' later version sold over 10 million worldwide. "Kansas City," another of their standards, was also written during 1952.

The earliest part of their career is not scored here because it occurred well before the era; however, for the '50s period they were the highest pointing team by a wide margin. Between 1955 and 1991, the duo charted 116 records together and with others. Forty-six acts charted with their songs, and 23 of their songs charted more than once, including "I Who Have Nothing" five times, "Kansas City" seven times and "Stand By Me" nine times. Perhaps because of the size of their catalog, their average scores were not so high. Their 15 hits each for Elvis and the Coasters averaged 1619 and 1456 points respectively. Overall, however, their 82 songs as Leiber and Stoller only averaged 986 points.

But to dwell on that average is to miss their importance in creating the musical fusion that became rock and roll.

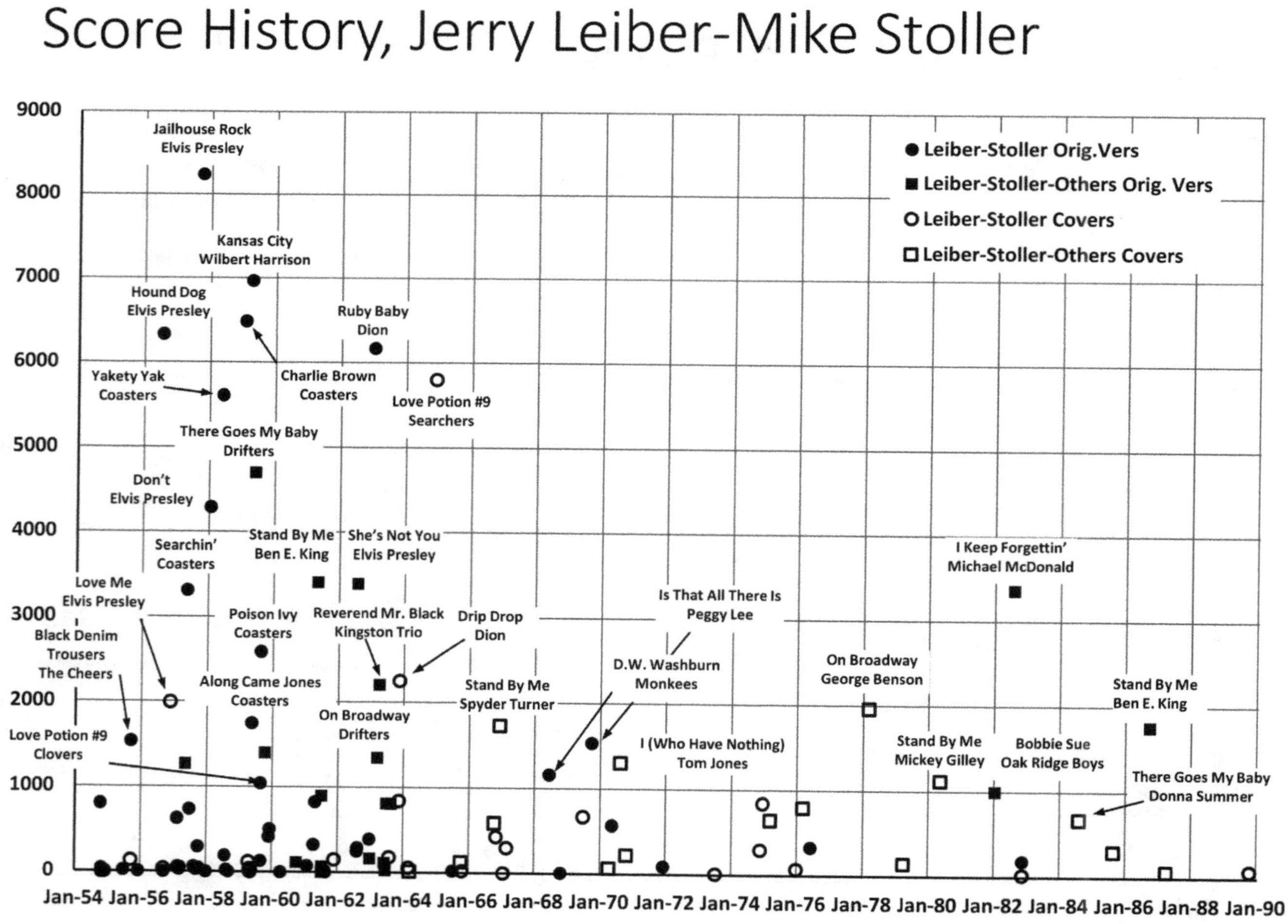

Neil DIAMOND *(6)* ▶ 11 (55) 78789

Neil Diamond started writing songs at age 16. He attended Erasmus Hall High School in Brooklyn, classmates with Barbra Streisand, and eventually Abraham Lincoln High School, classmates with Neil Sedaka. In 1962, at the age of 21 he was one of ten writers on a country-sounding quasi-novelty record called "Ten Lonely Guys." The names of all the writers are mentioned in the song, which was recorded by Pat Boone as well as the Ten Broken Hearts.

In the mid-'60s, Ellie Greenwich heard him and was impressed, played some of his material for her husband Jeff Barry, and together they convinced Leiber and Stoller to give him a short writing contract. According to Ken Emerson, Diamond requested a raise, Leiber and Stoller balked and Barry, Greenwich and Diamond formed Tallyrand Music. They eventually wound up with a deal with Bert Berns, one of the principals of Bang Records, where Diamond first appeared as a recording artist.

Neil Diamond had one transcendent hit, "I'm A Believer" by the Monkees, one of the top 5 of the era by this methodology, and that record constituted 20% of his score as a writing team. The bulk of his charted records—40 of them--were Neil Diamond singing his own songs, and those records averaged 1282 points. He was the 23rd-ranked act. Ironically, none of his top 3 hits features him as a solo writer and singer. Only six of his songs that he originally recorded were covered; "Red Red Wine" charted four times. As a writer, his record was somewhat stronger, as he ranks sixth overall, and was the seventh-ranked writer in the '70s.

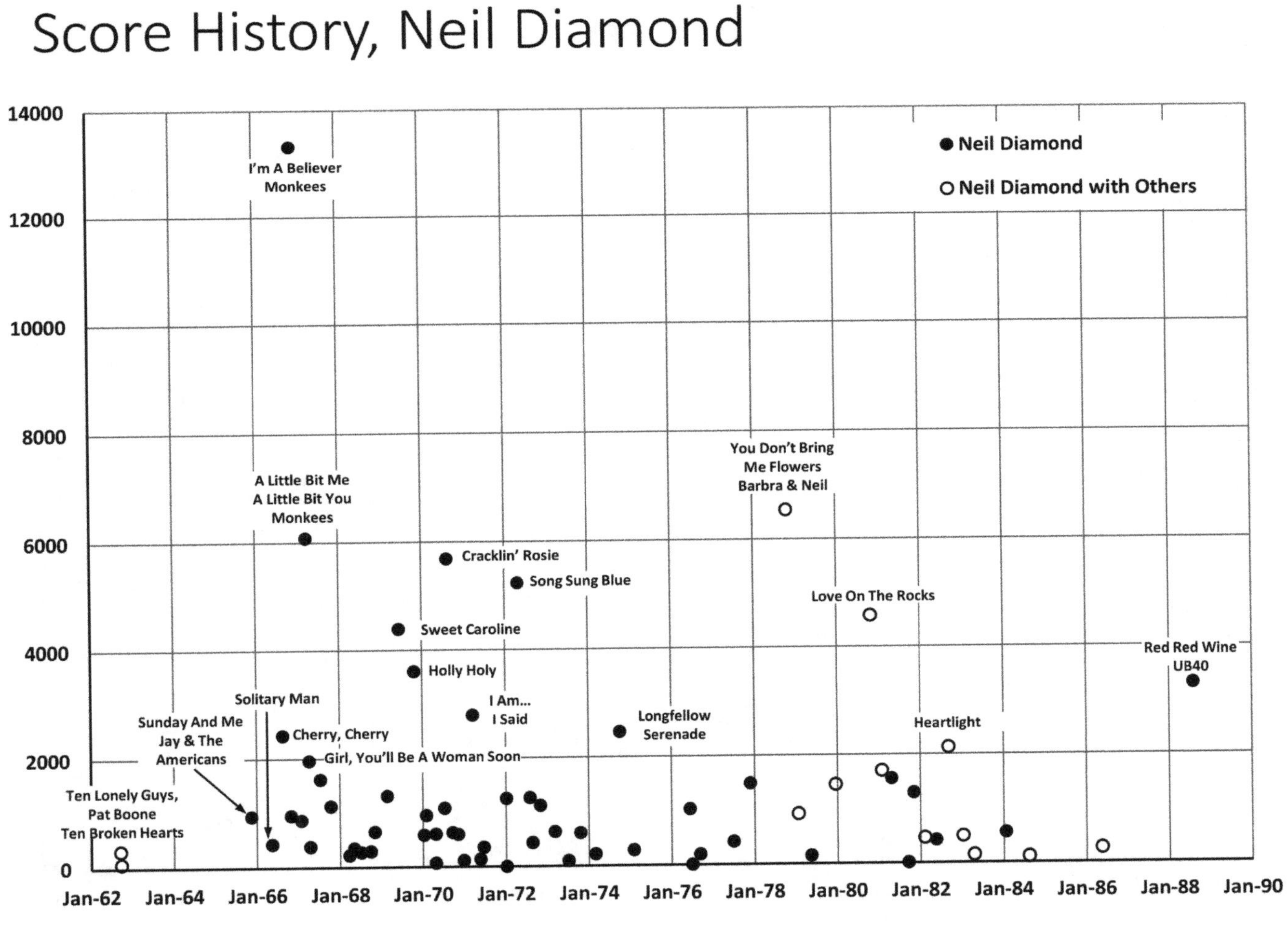

PRINCE ***(8)*** **► 12 (46) 77629**

Prince Rogers Nelson started writing songs at the age of seven. As with many writers, his first recorded work seems early in retrospect because we think of him as an act of the '80s and beyond; however, his first album "For You" was released in 1978. The iconic "1999" didn't appear until 1982, and "Purple Rain" was two years further down the road.

Prince created an entire ecosystem of acts around him, from Wendy & Lisa to Vanity 6 to The Time to Sheila E. His Paisley Park Studios nurtured that ecosystem and became his home. Analogous to Elvis Presley's Graceland, he wanted it to become a public venue.

Lionel Richie and Prince owned the '80s points list as writers, standing well above Michael Jackson in third place. Prince had the most charted songs of the decade with 43. As an act and writer combination, he averaged 1699 points, but his eight charted records as Prince And The Revolution averaged 2609, good for 23rd place.

For the era, Prince placed eighth as a writer and 76th as an act. Despite this, however, he placed no songs in the top 1%.

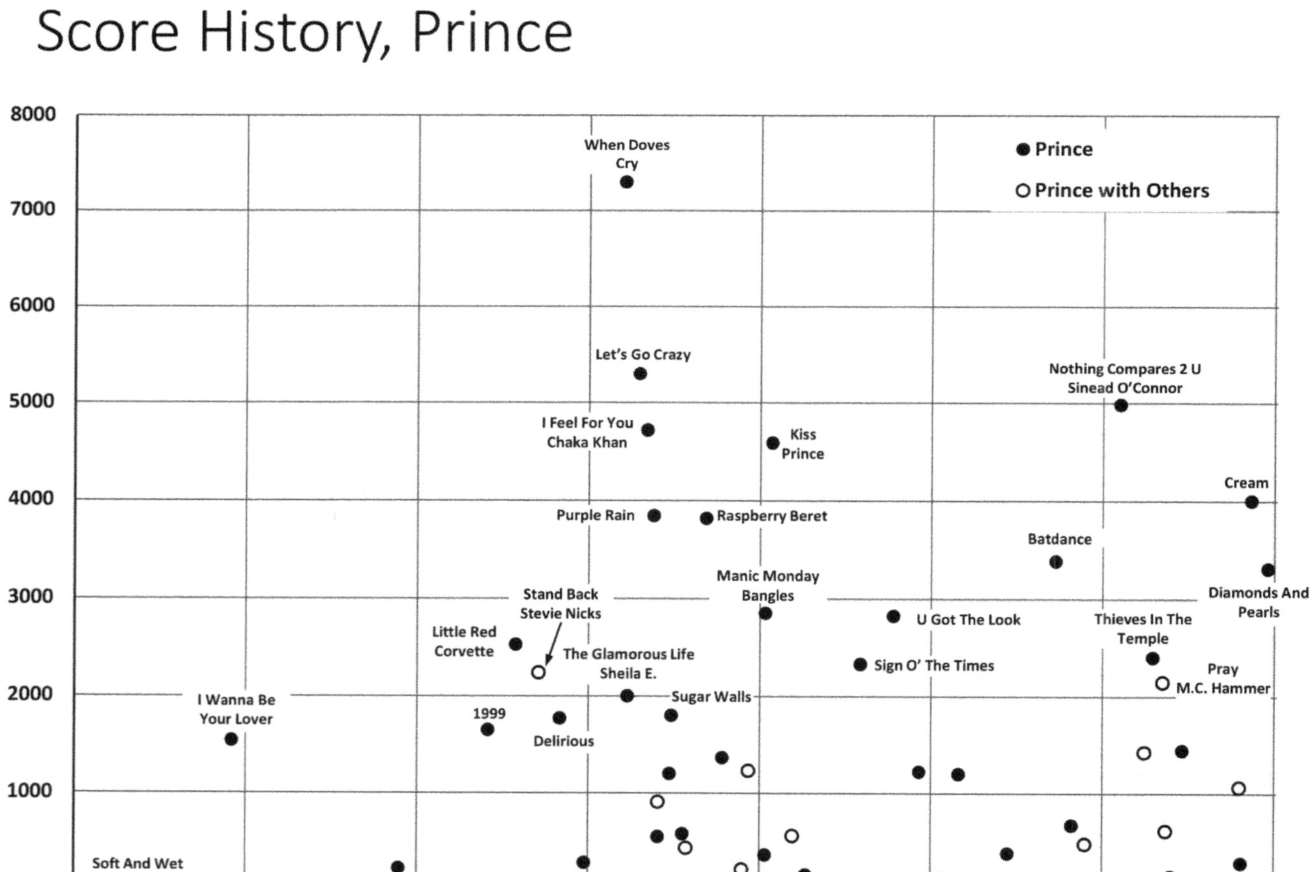

TRADITIONAL *(3)* ► 13 (99) 77319

It's worth mentioning that for this study, either partial or full credit could be allocated to traditional sources. In many cases it involved judgment: a significant reworking of a traditional tune for me constituted enough originality to qualify for credit as an adaptation. Simply rewriting new words for an old song generally meant apportioning credit between the new writer and Traditional.

Perhaps the most controversial call in this area is designating "House Of The Rising Sun" by the Animals as Traditional. The song surely is; however, ASCAP attributes Nicholas Bacon, Libby Holmes, Josh White; BMI attributes Alan Price. But Price's copyright lists it as an arrangement, not original. Even though the Animals treatment has become the standard, I've called it Traditional.

With that said, 203 entries qualified for total or partial credit to Traditional. Over half of those entries occurred prior to 1961, and so Traditional was the number 3 writer and number 12 solo writer in the '50s.

It should come as no surprise that popular tunes charted multiple times. In fact, 45 songs comprised 143 of the 203 entries, notably: "Battle Of New Orleans," "La Bamba," and "C. C. Rider" five times, "Mary Ann/Marianne" six times, "Adeste Fideles" and "Danny Boy" seven times and "Rock Island Line" eight times.

Ninety-nine entries were deemed fully Traditional, and they are shown on the timeline. Three of these songs finished in the Top 1%: "Tom Dooley" by the Kingston Trio which was nearly transcendent at 9985 points; "Michael" by The Highwaymen and "House Of The Rising Sun" by The Animals.

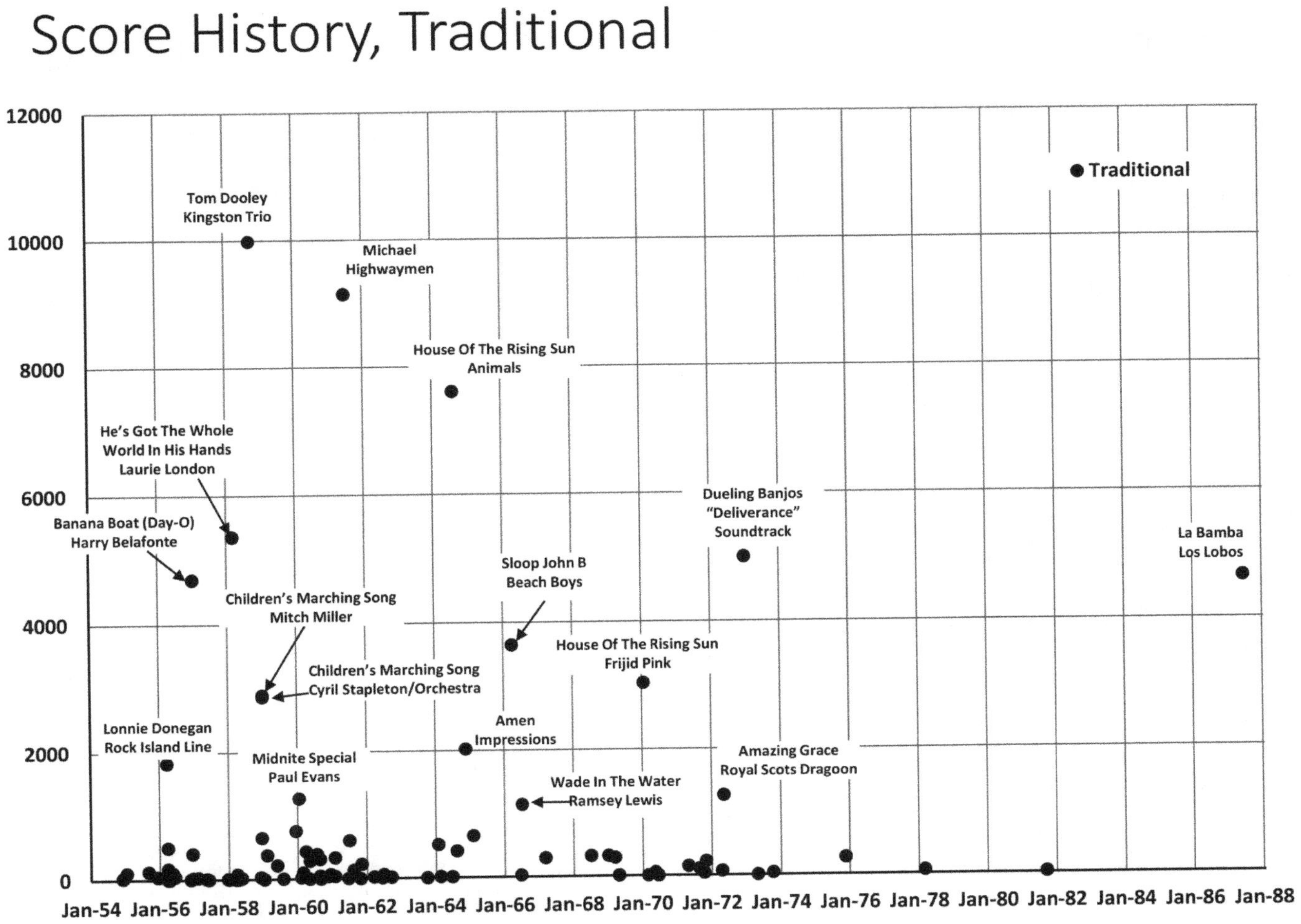

Barrett STRONG *(53)*/Norman WHITFIELD *(21)*► 14 (41) 70818

The Barrett Strong and Norman Whitfield collaboration began with Jimmy Ruffin's "Gonna Give Her All The Love I Got." Next was Gladys Knight and the Pips version of "I Heard It Through The Grapevine." The duo powered the Temptations' middle years in the psychedelic soul genre. Writing at the beginning of the '70s, their songs had a strong protest and distrust vibe. Consider: "War" by Edwin Starr and "Smiling Faces Sometimes" by Undisputed Truth. Their heyday was 1967 to 1973. The chart is stark, demonstrating that it ended as sharply as it began, about the time Motown moved to Los Angeles, and both writers moved on to other things.

For some of their songs, they collaborated with Rodger Penzabene, an interesting and tragic character. Penzabene was a childhood friend of Cornelius Grant, musical director for the Temptations, and through him contributed to a number of Motown songs. There are various stories that Rodger's wife was cheating on him and he could not bear to leave her. Whether true or not, he committed suicide New Year's Eve, 1967.

A number of their songs were recorded multiple times. "(I Know) I'm Losing You" and "Papa Was A Rolling Stone" charted four times each, and "I Heard It Through The Grapevine" made the charts seven times.

The latter song is an example of the occasional extreme variability among the charts. Marvin Gaye's version scored near the top for the era in *Billboard*, with seven weeks at #1. In *Cash Box*, it spent five weeks at #1. On the other hand, its chart life in *Record World* was good but not spectacular; three weeks less on the chart and only one at #1. Even so, it scores as a top 1% record under this methodology which combines the chart histories.

Strong and Whitfield contributed 15 songs to the Temptations, averaging 2316 points with them, good for 39th place. Their average would also be high with Marvin Gaye, but they only had four songs together.

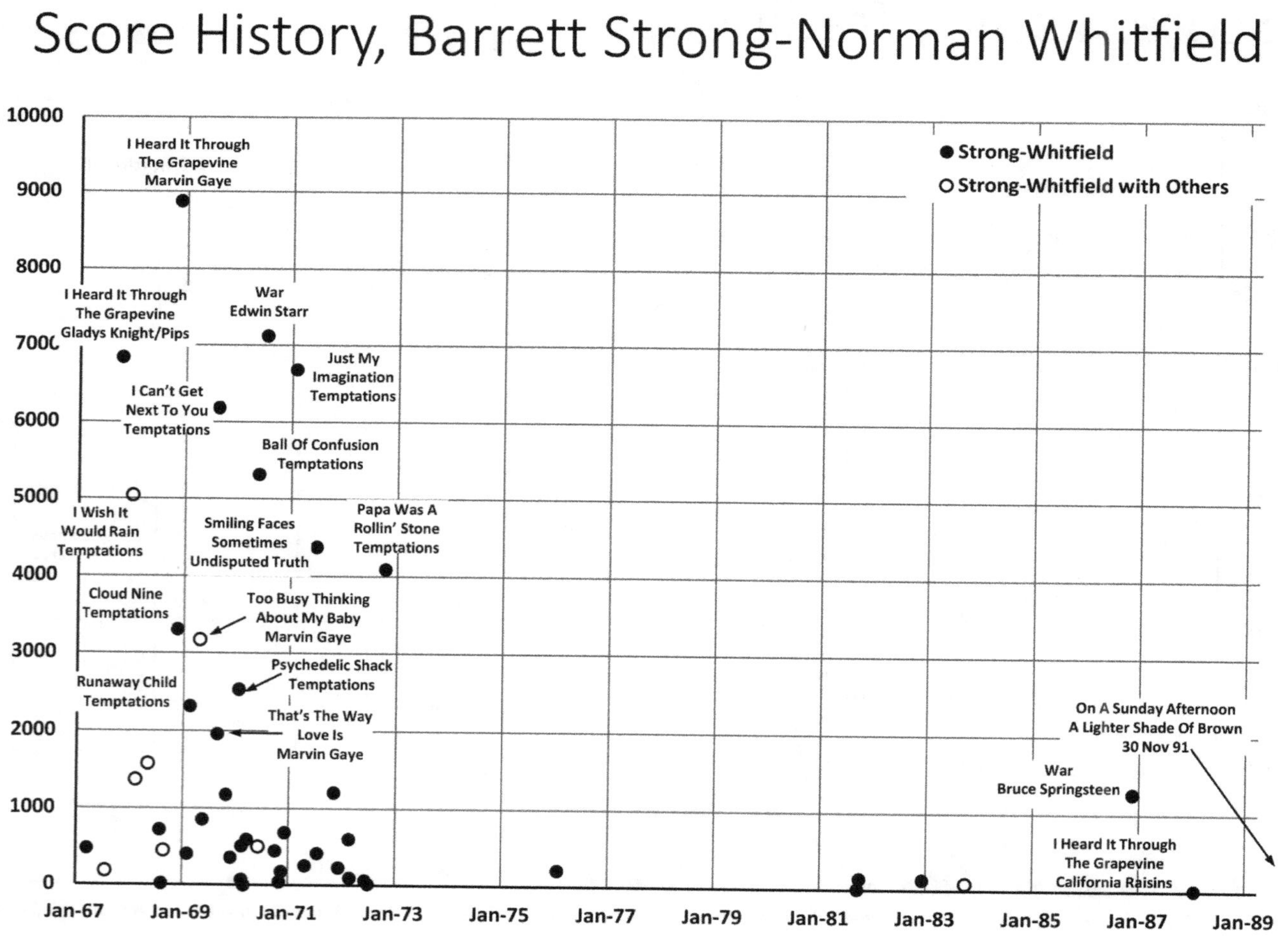

Stevie WONDER *(7)* ► 15 (43) 68537

Stevie Wonder was born in Saginaw, Michigan to Calvin Judkins and Lula Mae Hardaway. Six weeks premature, he contracted retinopathy of prematurity, which caused both retinas to detach, leaving him blind. At age 11, he was discovered by Ronnie White of the Miracles, and signed by Berry Gordy.

Although he was the youngest person to have a #1 record (Fingertips Pt 2), his first charted writing credit was "Uptight" which entered in December, 1965. "Uptight" charted seven times, including as Bill Cosby's "Little Ole Man," the only important cover of any of his recordings in the era.

All of his charted songs, which included things he did not perform such as "It's A Shame" by The Spinners and "Tears of A Clown" by Smokey Robinson and the Miracles, were collaborations until Superwoman in 1972. From that point on, virtually all of his charted songs were solo compositions. Ironically, his highest charting writer credit was "Tears Of A Clown."

Perhaps because of his blindness, and that they were easier to feel, he had a fondness for writing for the black keys on the piano. The black keys themselves form a pentatonic scale, and largely comprise the standard scale for G-flat major or E-flat minor, which he used often. The funky intro to "Superstition" consists only of black keys.

Stevie Wonder placed no songs in the top 1%. His high career score results from an uncommon consistency at 2-5 times the average song, which is apparent from the timeline. In fact, for the 30 songs he charted as act and sole writer, he averaged 2139 points for 48th place, and placed 4th as an act. He was the number 3 writer for the '70s and number 13 for the '80s by score.

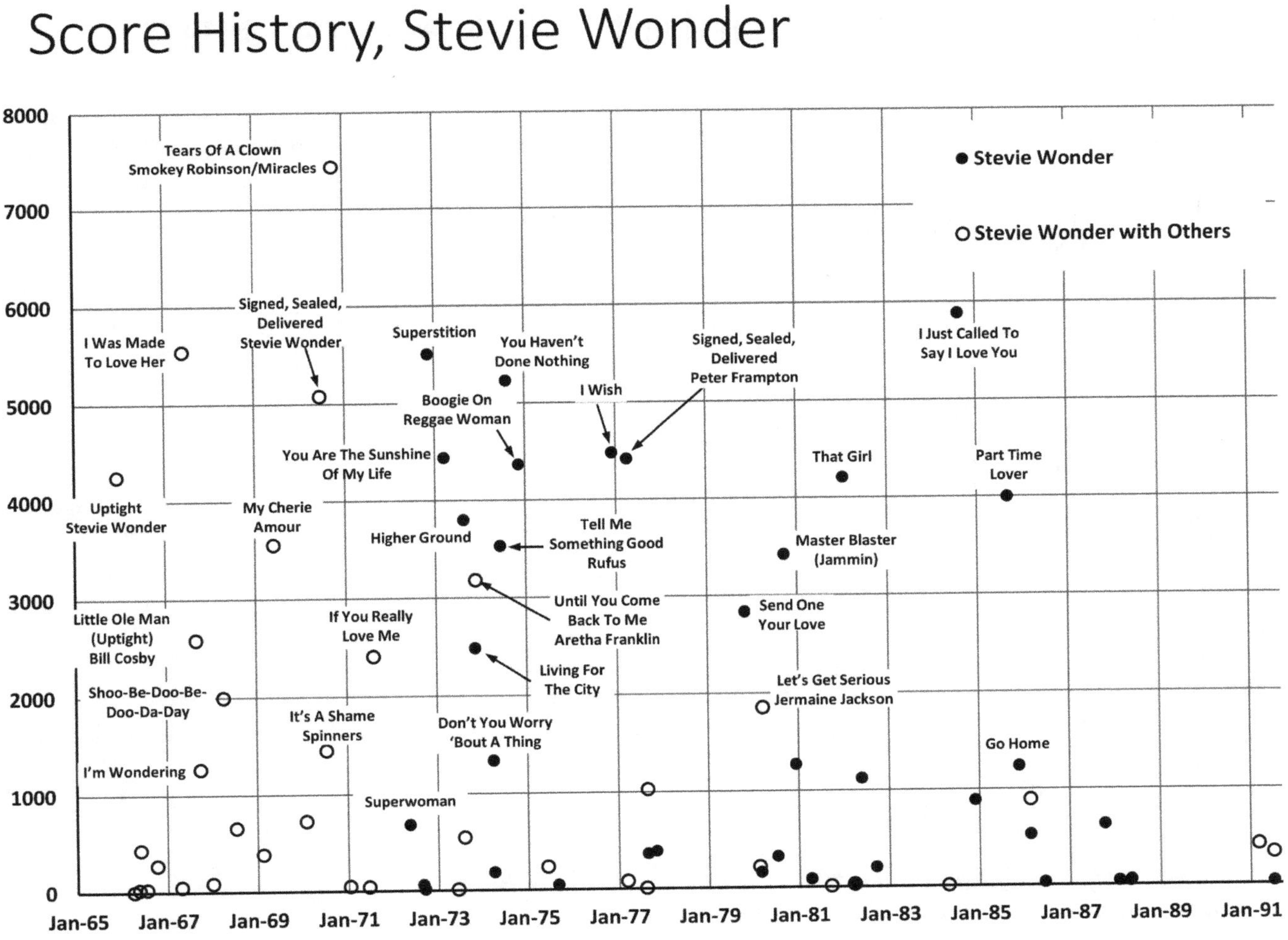

Kenneth GAMBLE *(34)*/Leon HUFF *(32)*► 16 (83) 68287

Kenny Gamble and Leon Huff were to Philadelphia in the early '70s what Berry Gordy was to Detroit in the '60s. As writers and producers, they had separate chart history until mid-1966 when they first collaborated (prophetically) on (We'll Be) United by the Intruders. There were interesting points in their pre-history: Gamble co-wrote "Who Do You Love" by the Sapphires and the uncharacteristic "The Boy With The Beatle Haircut;" Huff collaborated on "Mixed-Up Shook-Up Girl" by Patty And The Emblems.

Huff started as a studio pianist, playing on the Ronettes "Baby I Love You" and the Ad Libs "Boy From New York City." Gamble had a singing group, The Romeos, and Leon Huff eventually joined.

Twenty-nine acts brought to the pop charts 83 of the over 3000 songs Gamble-Huff wrote. The O'Jays and Harold Melvin And The Blue Notes, both staple Philadelphia acts, charted their songs 22 times, comprising 30% of Gamble and Huff's total score. They also worked extensively with Jerry Butler during the sessions leading to "The Ice Man Cometh," one of the most acclaimed soul albums ever.

They rank number 4 in scoring and number 1 in entries in the 1970s. Curiously, none of their songs appear in the top 1%.

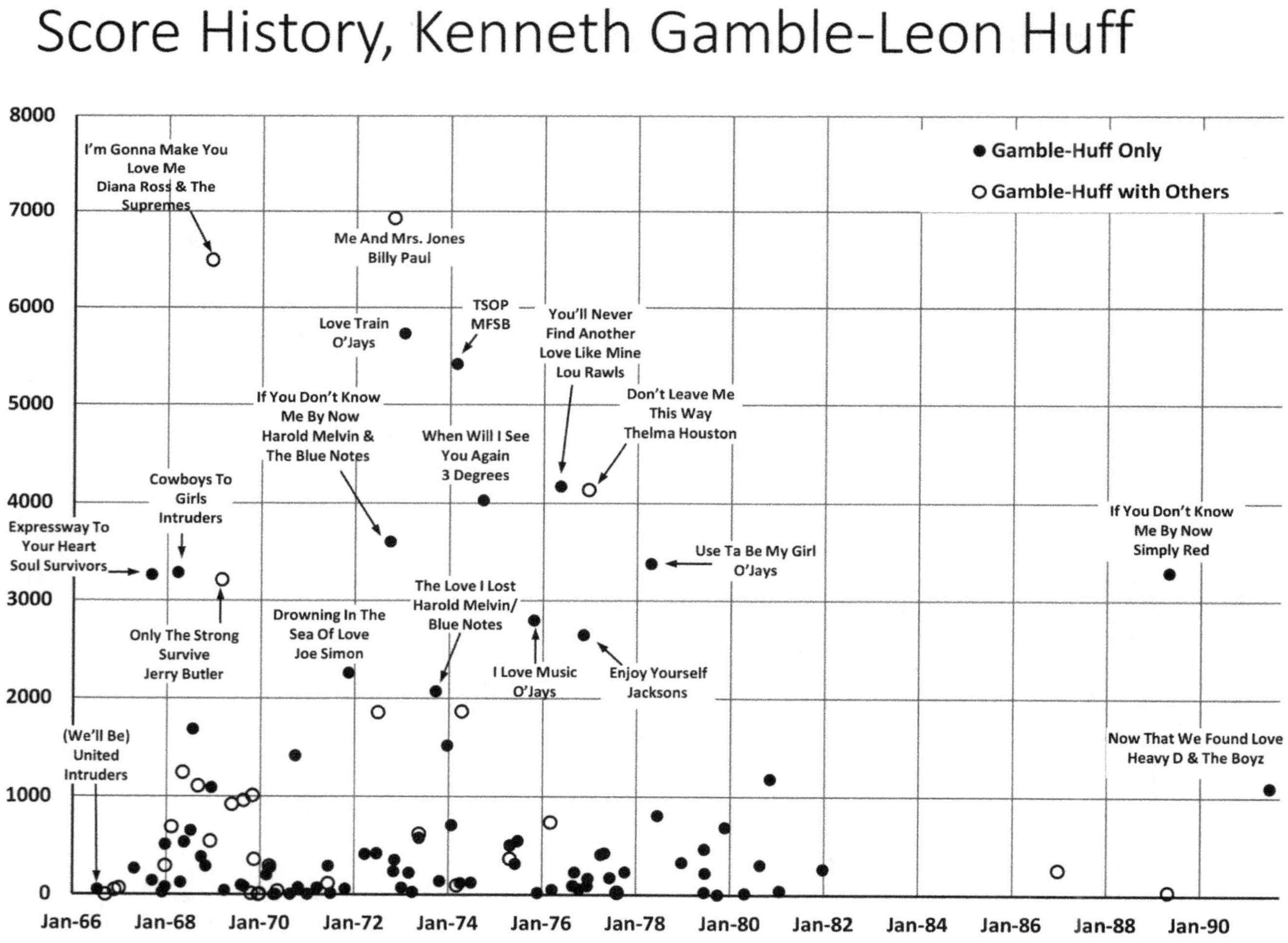

Sidebar: The Other Side Of Philadelphia Soul

Thom BELL *(132)*/Linda CREED *(223)* ▶ 99 (17) 22156

Even though they didn't score as highly as Gamble-Huff, the story of Philadelphia soul in the early 1970s would be incomplete without Thom Bell and Linda Creed. Bell's first impact was as writer and producer for The Delfonics, mostly with William Hart, and in the early '70s he also arranged for Gamble-Huff. At about the same time he began writing with Linda Creed.

The records the two of them created for The Stylistics are classics; listening to The Delfonics and Stylistics together it's easy to hear the similarities in approach. The two also wrote for The Spinners—originally known as The Detroit Spinners—after they moved from Motown to Atlantic. As a writing team, virtually all their points were scored with The Spinners and The Stylistics even though seven different acts charted their 17 songs.

Each went on to have other impact. After The Spinners, most of Bell's work was production, including albums for Dionne Warwick, Deniece Williams and Elton John. Linda Creed wrote with Michael Masser and created, among other songs, "The Greatest Love Of All" which was recorded by George Benson and Whitney Houston. That song was written during her battle with breast cancer, a battle she lost just before Whitney Houston's version topped the charts.

Honorable mention in this category also goes to the team of Gene McFadden and John Whitehead. This duo, with Victor Carstarphen, was the other engine behind Harold Melvin and the Blue Notes and the O'Jays, among others. As performers, McFadden & Whitehead's "Ain't No Stoppin' Us Now" became an anthem for the Philadelphia sports teams, for which they did custom versions.

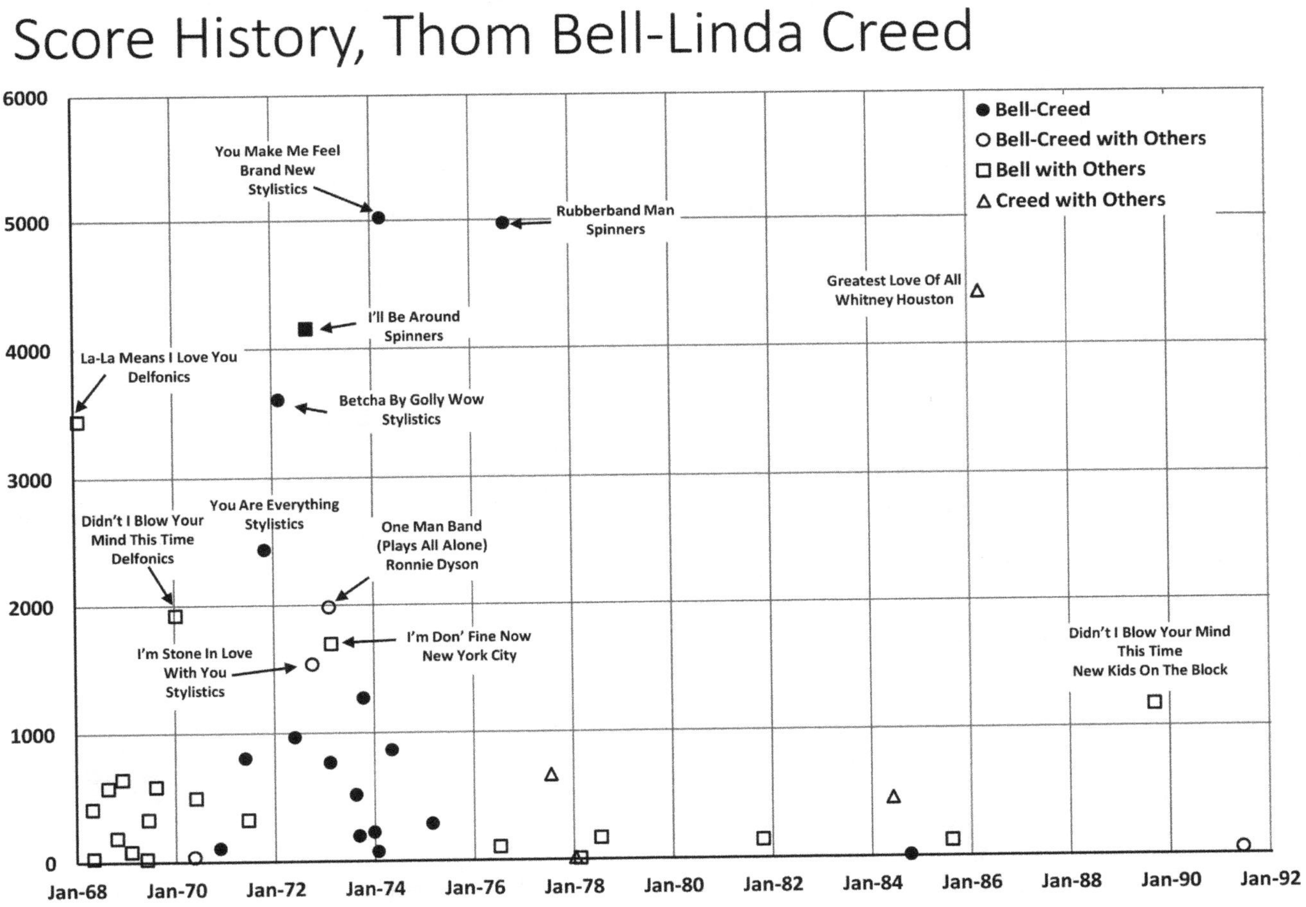

And one more Sidebar: Philadelphia Blue-Eyed Soul in the Late '70s

Daryl HALL *(49)*► 96 (12)

Daryl Hohl grew up in Pottstown, PA and John Oates in New York, but they met at a band competition when trying to dodge gunfire from rival gangs, ending up in the same elevator. Shared musical interest and school at Temple got them working together; their first album was "Whole Oats"—corrupting both names—containing the tasty but unsuccessful "Fall In Philadelphia." Their place in blue-eyed soul was assured with "She's Gone" from their next album "Abandoned Luncheonette" although it did not become a big hit until they left Atlantic for RCA Victor and released "Daryl Hall And John Oates," remembered as the silver album.

"Sara Smile," "Rich Girl," "Do What You Want…Be What You Are" all sit firmly in the soul mode, and helped round out the Philadelphia sound at the end of the '70s. The advent of disco relegated that sound to history, and pushed Hall and Oates to New York in the early '80s. But Philadelphia remains home, and soul remains their base.

As a writer team, Hall & Oates ranks 291st—mostly their '70s work--but their collaboration with Sara Allen—mostly from the early '80s--ranks 117th. Combining all those efforts, Daryl Hall ranks 49th as a writer. Hall & Oates ranks 20th as an act, virtually totally on the writer credits of Hall, Oates, Sara Allen and her sister Janna Allen. Hall & Oates with the writer team Hall/Oates/Sara Allen ranks 11th, averaging 3259 points over 6 entries; the writer team itself ranks fourth with the same average. There were very few cover versions of their songs, the most successful being John Paul Young's version of "Everytime You Go Away."

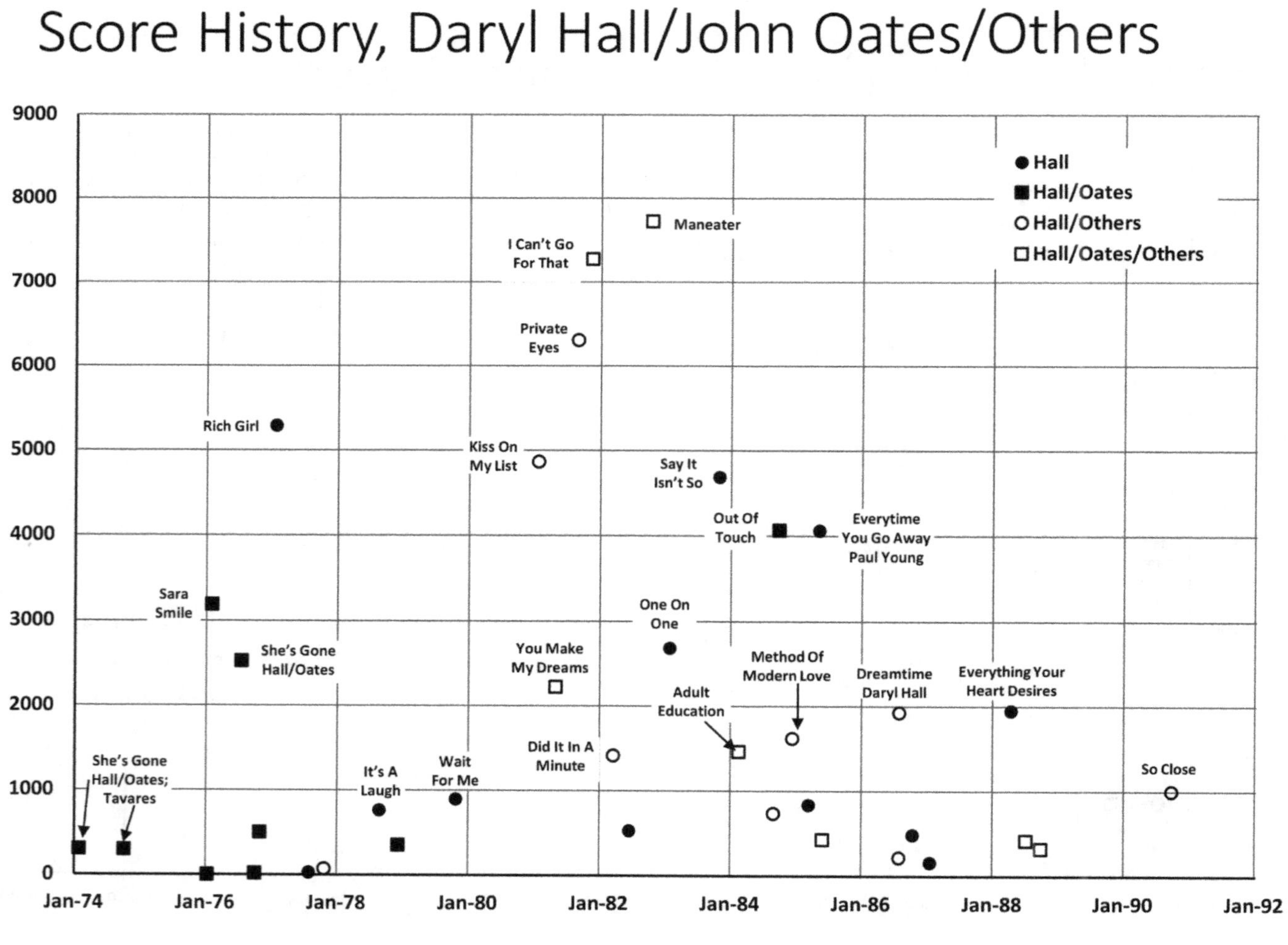

Doc POMUS *(63)*/Mort SHUMAN (66) ► 17 (59) 62642

Jerome Felder, a nice middle-class boy who had been paralyzed by polio at the age of six gave himself the name Doc Pomus to keep his parents from knowing he was singing the blues in African-American clubs. In the 40s, he worked with Otis Blackwell, Mickey Baker and King Curtis. He wrote on his own in the early '50s, eventually meeting the much younger songwriting pair, Jerry Leiber and Mike Stoller.

Mort Shuman went to Abraham Lincoln High, was a year older than Neil Sedaka, and was dating Pomus' cousin. After the two met, Pomus encouraged Shuman to write songs, and over a couple of years taught him the craft. Because Shuman was 11 years younger than Pomus, he had more of an ear for the music of the time. Eventually the two became effective collaborators.

Their big break came when Otis Blackwell introduced them to Paul Case who managed Hill and Range music, and a writing contract ensued. While they may have had Elvis as a goal, their first real singer was Fabian Forte, kind of an Elvis knock-off. Fabian recorded five of their songs, as did other heartthrobs like James Darren and Frankie Avalon. And eventually so did Elvis.

The duo broke up in 1965, after 60 charted songs; Pomus leaving the business after a debilitating fall, Shuman moving to France. Shuman had one outside chart hit of significance, "Little Children," written with J. Leslie McFarland for Billy J. Kramer in 1964. They had two transcendent hits—"Save The Last Dance For Me" by the Drifters and "Surrender" by Elvis that accounted for over a quarter of their career points. They averaged 1878 points over seven hits for the Drifters and 1627 over nine hits for Elvis, ranking 24th in points in the '50s and sixth in the '60s.

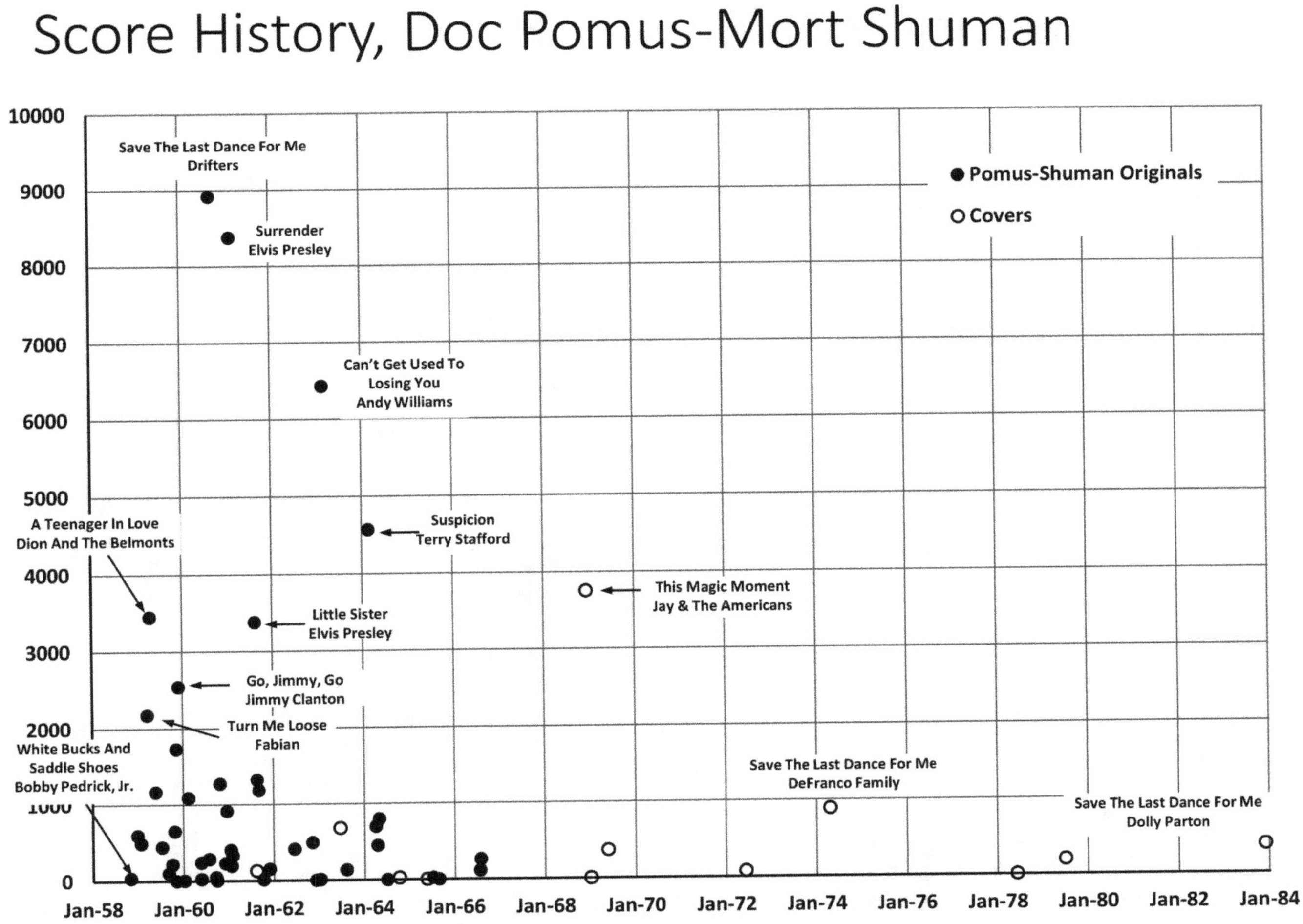

Paul ANKA *(16)* ► 18 (57) 61526

Paul Anka's "Diana" was his first charted song, and it went to #1; he was 16 at the time. A number of hits followed in the next three years including "Lonely Boy," "Put Your Head On My Shoulder," and "Puppy Love." The copyright for "Lonely Boy," his biggest and only transcendent hit, lists him as the sole writer; however, in BMI, Alberto Curci is also credited. Curci was a violinist early in the 20th century and may have been awarded rights due to a similarity in melody between "Lonely Boy" and one of his compositions.

Anka's career, both writing and performing, went on hiatus about the time of the British Invasion. But being a writer as well as a performer there were other ways to stay in the public arena. He wrote the Tonight Show theme for Johnny Carson, and wrote songs for and acted in "The Longest Day." In the late '60s he became something of a master at adapting new words to melodies from songs with non-English lyrics.

"My Way" was originally a song by Claude Francois and Jacques Revaux. One night at dinner with Frank Sinatra and some colleagues, Sinatra told him he intended to quit the business, which inspired Anka to write a valedictory for him. It had only moderate chart success then but lives on as a standard. Anka's big comeback as a writer was "She's A Lady," for Tom Jones in 1971. As a performer, he had to wait three more years for "(You're) Having My Baby" to start a new chart run.

By far, Paul Anka performed the songs he wrote. Of his 57 solo writing efforts, he charted 40, comprising three-quarters of his career score, averaging 1146 points. Solo, as an act, he ranks 25th. No one else recorded more than one of his songs, except Annette, who recorded two. The only major chart success for a cover was Donny Osmond's version of "Puppy Love," nearly as big as the original.

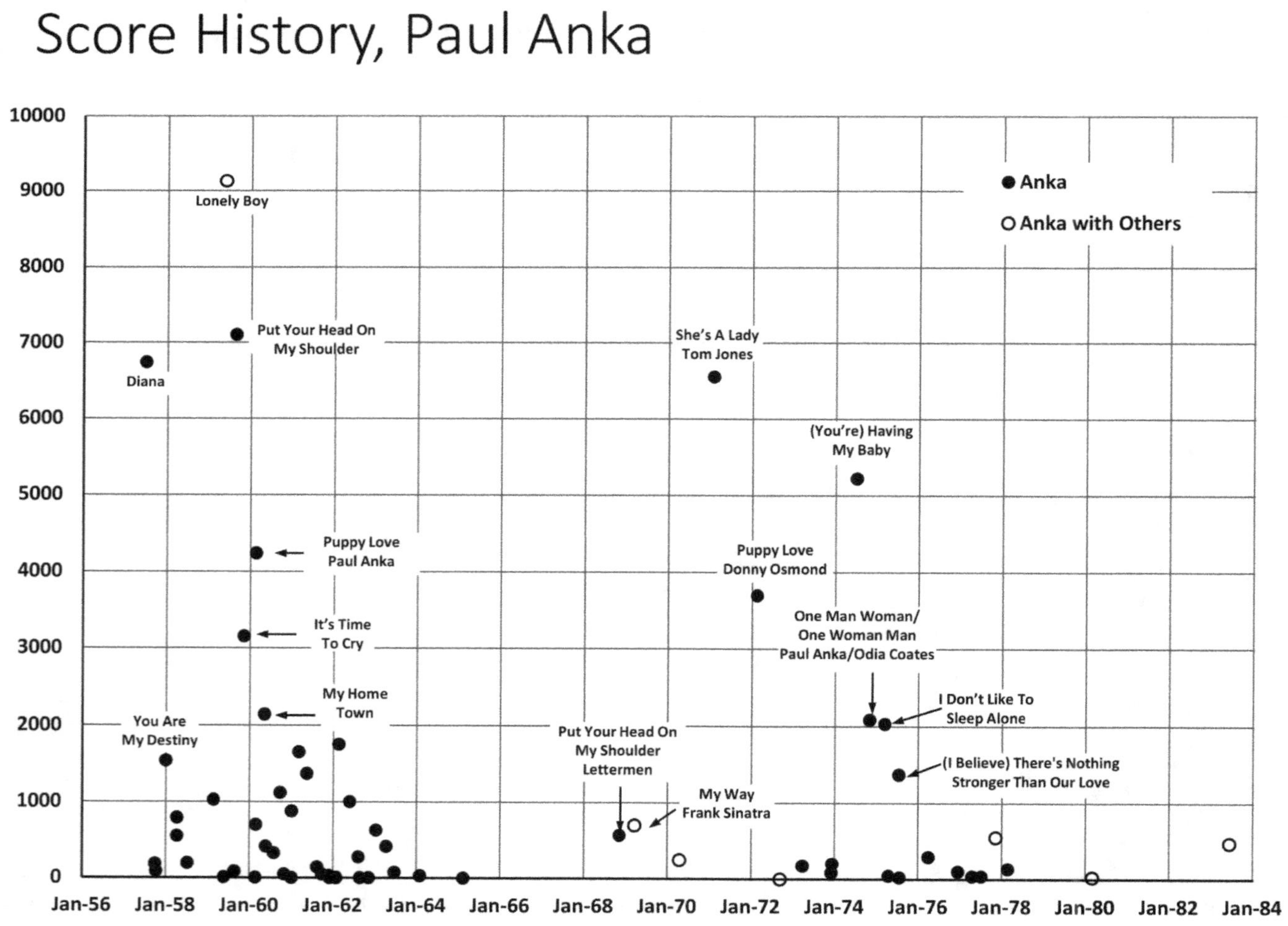

Curtis MAYFIELD *(20)* ▶ 19 (91) 59415

Curtis Mayfield joined The Roosters, a band led by Jerry Butler, in 1958. When the band evolved into Jerry Butler and the Impressions and had a hit with "For Your Precious Love," Butler went solo. Mayfield's first charted song was "He Will Break Your Heart," co-written with Butler and Vee-Jay record exec Calvin Carter.

Mayfield's first charted solo writing effort was "Gypsy Woman," recorded by The Impressions. He also wrote for a number of other Chicago acts, including Major Lance, who went to the same high school as he and Jerry Butler. Lance charted 11 times with Mayfield songs, including "Um Um Um Um Um" and "Monkey Time." Jan Bradley peaked at 13 with "Mama Didn't Lie."

Mayfield had a hugely successful 1963-64 with the Major Lance songs and five Impressions hits in a year's time, starting with "It's All Right" and ending with "You Must Believe Me." At the same time, Mayfield's lyrical message was subtly changing from love songs to songs embodying more social justice themes, a progression that lasted through the '60s. Not long after leaving the Impressions at the end of the decade, he took up the challenge of writing movie music for the blaxploitation film "Superfly." Even his songs for the movie had a message—and it was counter to that of the movie itself. He also did the music for the 1975 movie "Let's Do It Again."

Curtis Mayfield was prolific. He charted 91 records as a solo writer, by 22 acts. Over 60% of those entries were recorded by The Impressions, Major Lance or Mayfield himself. But with that said, only a few charted strongly and his average score as a writer was about 650 with no songs in the top 1%. Seven of his solo writing efforts charted as covers, the strongest, "Gypsy Woman" by Brian Hyland. Ironically, the biggest cover was of his first hit, the collaboration with Butler and Carter: Tony Orlando And Dawn's version of "He Will Break Your Heart" called "He Don't Love You." He was the number 10 writer team of the '60s and number 21 in the '70s.

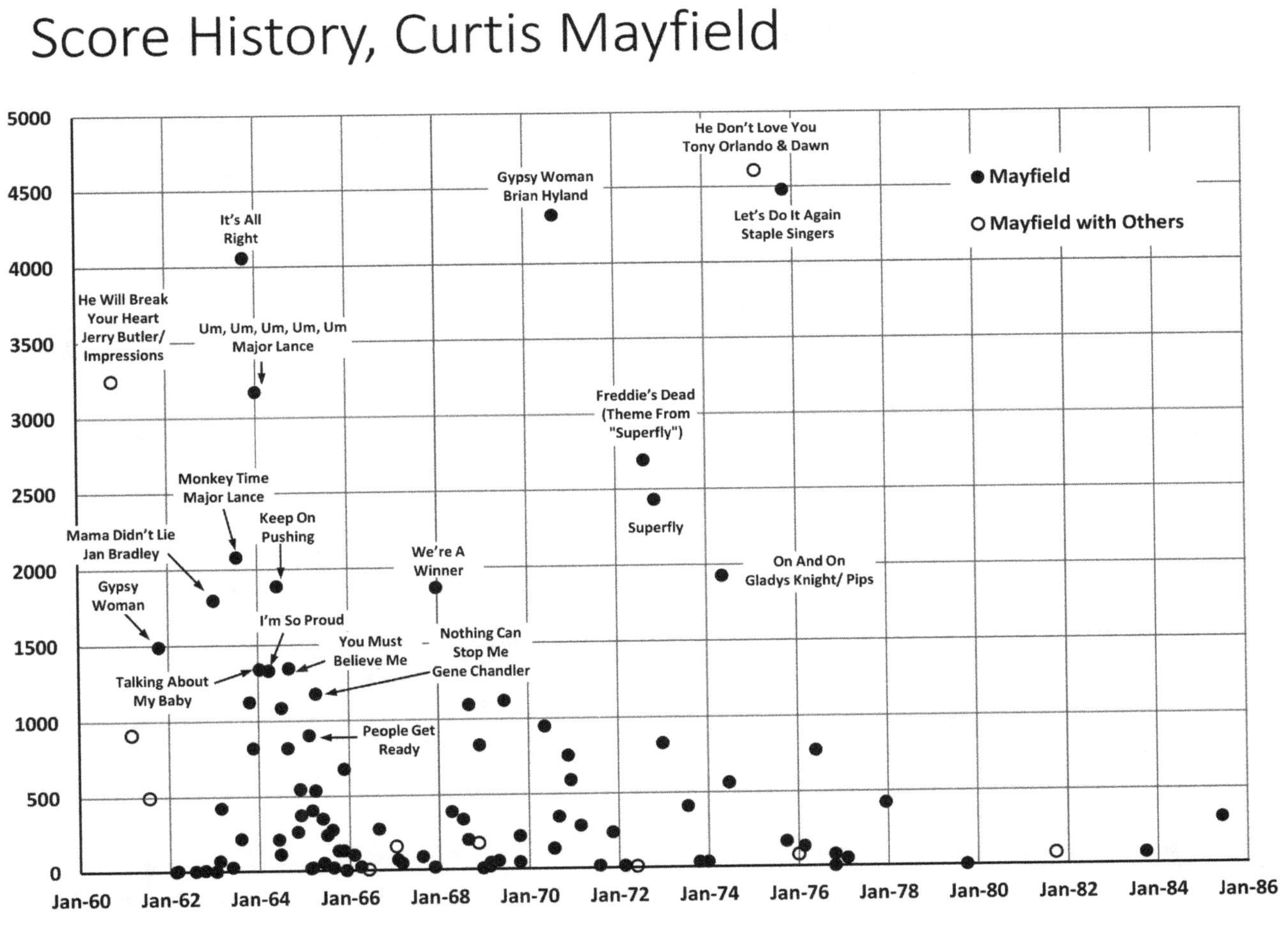

Howard GREENFIELD *(41)*/Neil SEDAKA *(50)* ▶ 20 (45) 55941

Neil Sedaka and Howie Greenfield's families lived in the same building. Neil took Saturday classes at Julliard with the goal of becoming a classical pianist. Howie's mother introduced herself to him and suggested he and her son—"a poet"—should get together. A chance meeting with Doc Pomus and Mort Shuman sent them to the office door of Aldon Records, where they met Don Kirshner who was not much older than they were. After much drama, the three of them sold Connie Francis on "Stupid Cupid" in 1958. She followed it with "Fallen" which was not so successful, and "Frankie," which was. Greenfield/Sedaka's biggest hit for her was "Where The Boys Are."

As a performer, Sedaka started a slow rise: "Diary" in 1958 and "Oh! Carol" in 1959. Things took off in 1960 with "Stairway To Heaven" and "Calendar Girl," reaching an apex in 1962 with "Breaking Up Is Hard To Do" which finished just outside the era top 1%. As successful as this pair was, Greenfield had two hits with Jack Keller for Connie Francis that surpassed any with Sedaka: "My Heart Has A Mind Of Its Own" and "Everybody's Somebody's Fool." Both were transcendent hits, and Greenfield actually outranks Sedaka as an individual writer.

After "Alice In Wonderland" it's difficult not to notice the gap on the chart. Certainly, the British Invasion had something to do with it. Additionally, the business situation changed with Aldon Music and Sedaka personally. During the mid-'60's he still wrote a bit with Greenfield: "Puppet Man" was copyrighted 1970. Mainly, he plotted his comeback as a performer, which started in 1972 and blossomed in 1974.

His last hurrahs with Howie were written in 1973: "Love Will Keep Us Together," made famous by The Captain & Tennille two years later, and the prophetic "Our Last Song Together" which barely charted for Bo Donaldson And The Heywoods. Ironically, these two songs were copyrighted the same day with consecutive registration numbers. Sedaka's later hits were written with Phil Cody. Howie never again matched his previous success.

Score History, Howie Greenfield-Neil Sedaka

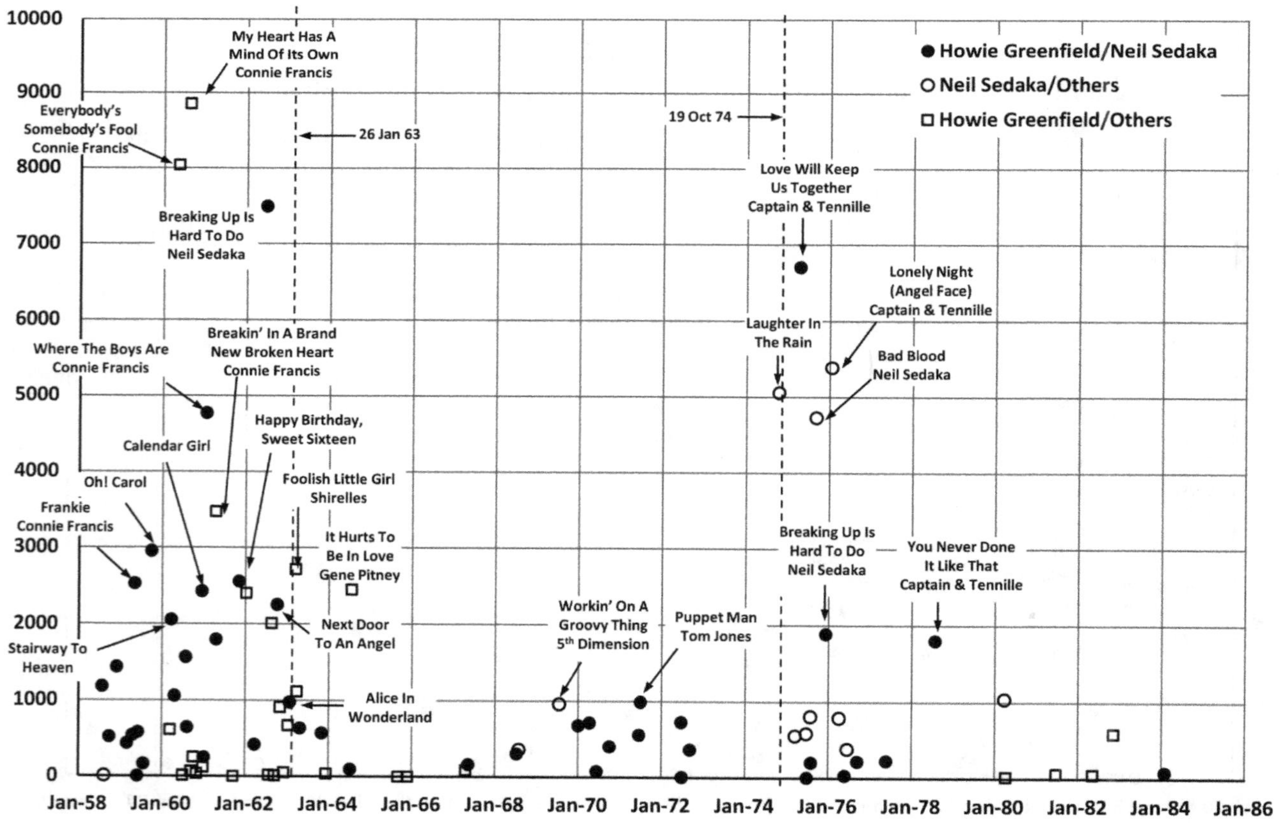

Barry MANN *(30)*/Cynthia WEIL *(49)*▶ 21 (60) 55073

Barry Mann and Cynthia Weil were the most durable of the early '60s writer teams. Barry Mann found his way into Aldon music a few months before Carole King and Gerry Goffin, and worked with whoever was available, including Jack Keller, Howie Greenfield and Larry Kolber. Cynthia Weil met him in Teddy Randazzo's manager's office when Greenfield and Mann walked in. Weil was smitten—later she jokingly said she stalked him at Aldon--writing with King and Goffin until Mann noticed her and they started to work together—on many levels.

"Bless You" was their first writing adventure, a follow up for Tony Orlando to Goffin-King's "Halfway To Paradise." They were married the month "Bless You" peaked, October 1961. "On Broadway" was written from Weil's love for the theatre. Leiber and Stoller liked it for The Drifters, but weren't satisfied with what they'd heard. Leiber and Stoller offered to help rewrite it, and it became a hit. All four—Mann, Weil, Leiber and Stoller--are credited.

They did not suffer the impact of the British Invasion in quite the same way that the other Brillers did. They adapted to changing musical tastes, writing against type for The Animals, Paul Revere And the Raiders and (gasp) Max Frost And The Troopers. Their catalog of charted songs continued to contain new material, even though there is a chart gap in the mid-'70s.

Forty-one acts charted 60 Mann-Weil songs, no act with more than 3. Not so different than Goffin-King: 64 acts, no more than 7 for any act. As a team they averaged 918 points over those 60 songs and placed 11th in score in the '60s. Twenty-four of their chart entries were repeat recordings of 10 songs. The Righteous Brothers' "You've Lost That Lovin' Feeling," (which also credited Phil Spector) was BMI's most played song of the 20th century, and a top 1% hit. All in all, the song charted five times and had above average to great performance in three of them.

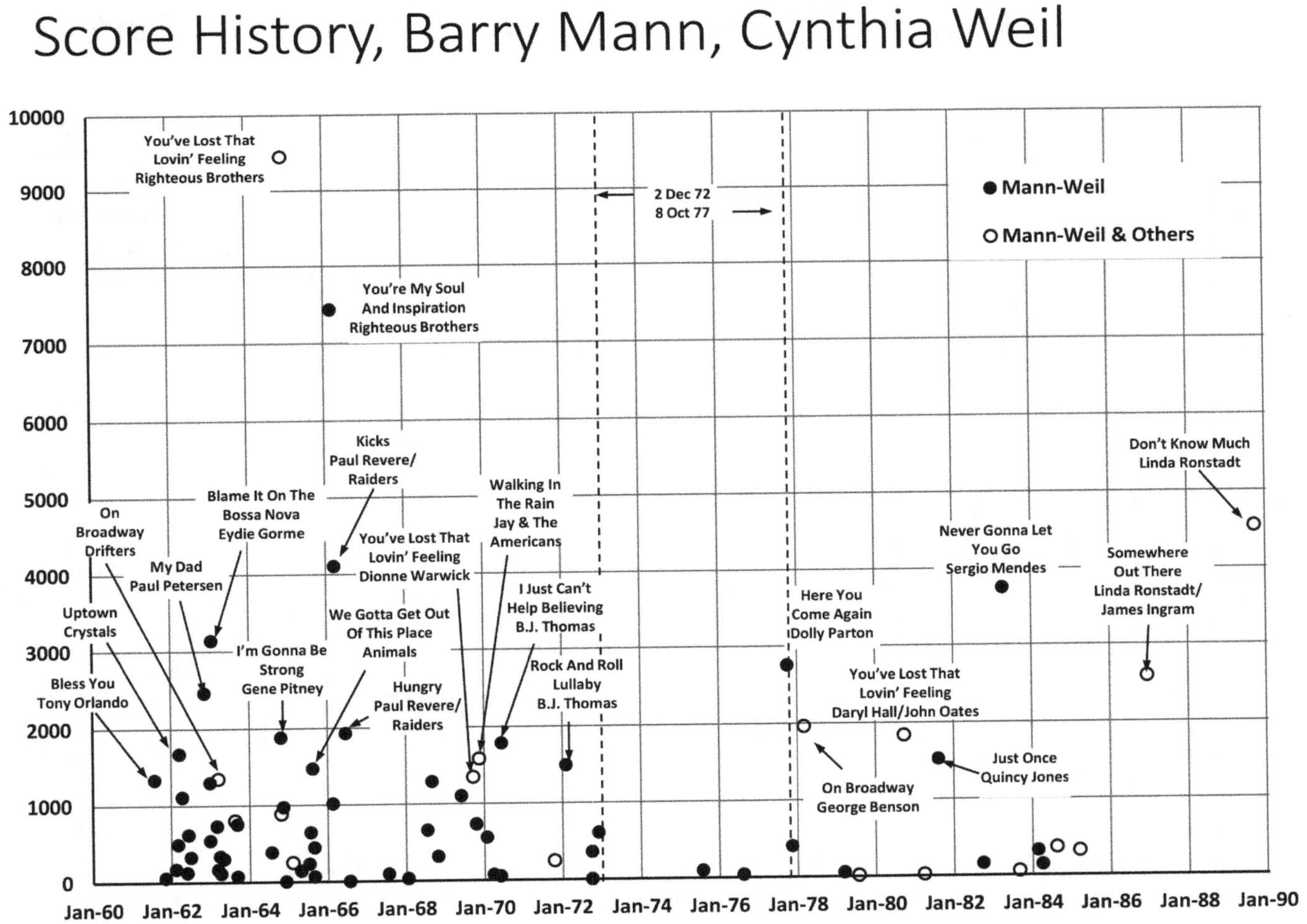

Sidebar: Mann Without Weil and Vice Versa

Both before they became a team and after, Mann and Weil wrote with other collaborators, many of which were outside the Brill Building circle. This was obviously the case in the '70s and beyond.

Barry Mann worked with a number of writers before Weil. He and Mike Anthony wrote "She Say (Oom Dooby Doom)," a doo-wop parody for the Diamonds and "Footsteps" with Hank Hunter for Steve Lawrence. He and Howie Greenfield charted four times. He was not done with parody, writing "Who Put The Bomp (In The Bomp Bomp Bomp)" with Gerry Goffin.

He had two very big hits with Larry Kolber: "I Love How You Love Me" for the Paris Sisters in 1961, and the musically similar but thematically orthogonal "Patches" for Dickey Lee in 1962. He pretty much settled in, literally and figuratively, with Cynthia Weil after that.

The period between about 1972 and 1975 has them mostly off the charts, and starting in about 1976, each collaborated with other writers even though they also re-emerged with songs to which they both contributed. Mann wrote by himself and with Dan Hill and Marc Phillips. Weil wrote with Rick Derringer, Tom Snow and Lionel Richie, among others.

While it's not easy to find the story, they were divorced in the early 80s, but remarried. Some of their work in the late '80s also included other writers.

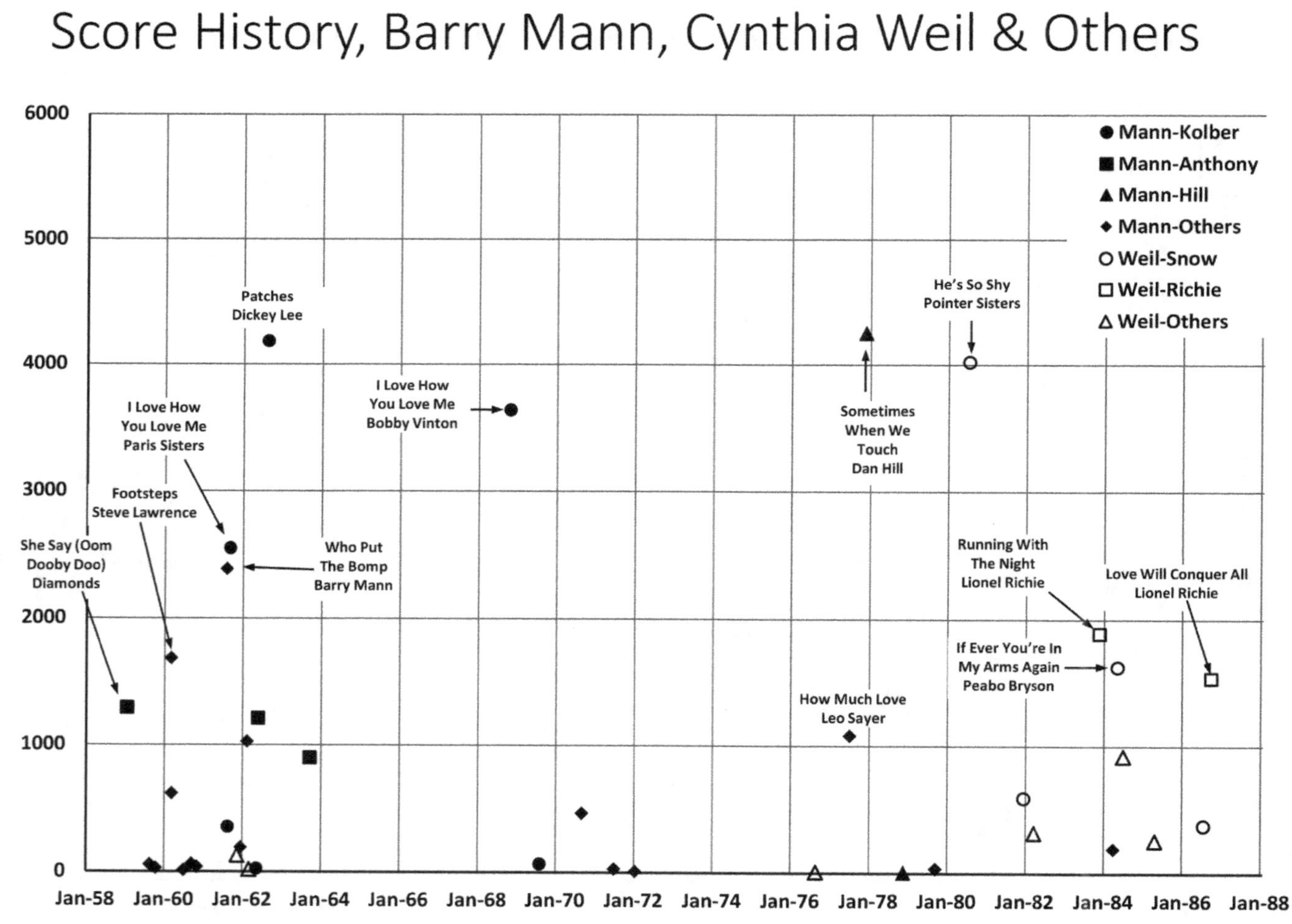

Billy JOEL *(27)*▶ 23 (37) 52367

Billy Joel is the ultimate closed shop. Ranking 27th as an individual writer and 23rd as a writer team, he charted 37 songs—all of which he wrote solo—and only one act charted with his songs: Billy Joel.

While in his early years he hated comparisons to Elton John—"I can't escape him. We're even next to each other in the record bin."—there are fair similarities. Both are classically trained pianists and at least in early years wrote some songs of similar style: compare the piano breaks in "Funeral For A Friend" or "Burn Down The Mission" and "The Ballad Of Billy The Kid." Eventually Billy got over it, I think, and saw the comparison as a compliment to two all-time greats.

Two observations about his music. While it's clear that characters, names, places and bits of his history show up as snippets in his songs, the lyrics are not necessarily as literally true or autobiographical as some people have implied with interview questions (including me). It simply illustrates that people tend to write what they know even if they're writing what they imagine. Second, reinvention was nearly a survival instinct for him, particularly noticing the differences in genre among his early albums—"Nylon Curtain's" Beatle-esque flavor and the Four Seasons sound on "An Innocent Man" as two examples.

Perhaps it's also notable that after his album "River of Dreams," like Lionel Richie, he adopted a more leisurely recording schedule. His album "Fantasies and Delusions" was a return to his classical roots, something he expressed the desire to do from the beginning of his career. For his 37 entries he averaged 1415 points, well above the average song, and placed sixth among writer teams in points in the '80s. As an act he ranks 39th. Although none of his entries made the top 1%, "It's Still Rock And Roll To Me" came close.

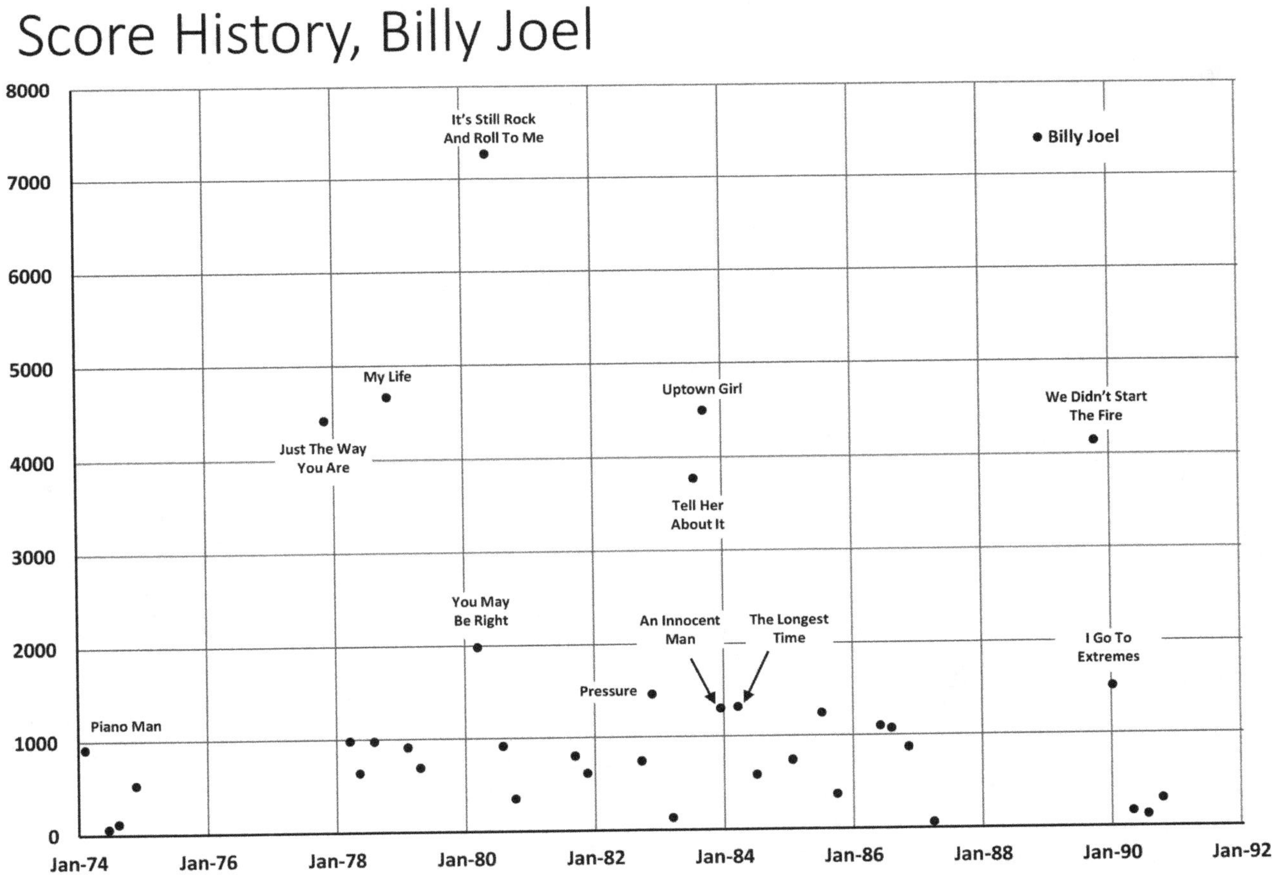

Michael JACKSON *(18)* ► 24 (16)

It's not surprising that he is remembered more for his contributions as a performer than as a writer, because his emergence as a solo performer on "Off The Wall" occurred about the same time as his first writer credit, 1979.

His writing style was unique. He heard the songs and arrangements in his head and built them up track by track as he sang them for others to notate.[3] He said, "The lyrics, the strings, the chords, everything comes at the moment like a gift that is put right into your head and that's how I hear it." In a way, this explains why his writing credits are nearly all solo credits, and why every song sounded like a performance.

Two of his few collaborations are noteworthy. "Say Say Say" with Paul McCartney came after Michael released "Thriller" and after Wings broke up; it placed in the top 1% for the era. "We Are The World" was written with Lionel Richie and performed as a benefit by "USA For Africa," a collage of US artists including the writers, Stevie Wonder, Diana Ross and many others. These are two of Michael's four highest scoring writing credits.

As a solo writer, Michael Jackson ranks 24th, on the basis of only 16 solo writer credits, and as the number 3 writer of the '80s. As an act he ranks 12th; as a writer-act combination, his average of 3901 points for 11 entries places him fourth in the era. As a writer, he placed two songs in the top 1%. His whole solo writing catalog averages 3324 points.

The most notable covers of Michael Jackson songs are parodies. "Weird Al" Yankovic charted with "Fat" (parody of "Bad") and "Eat It" (parody of "Beat It") which got to number 4 in 1984.

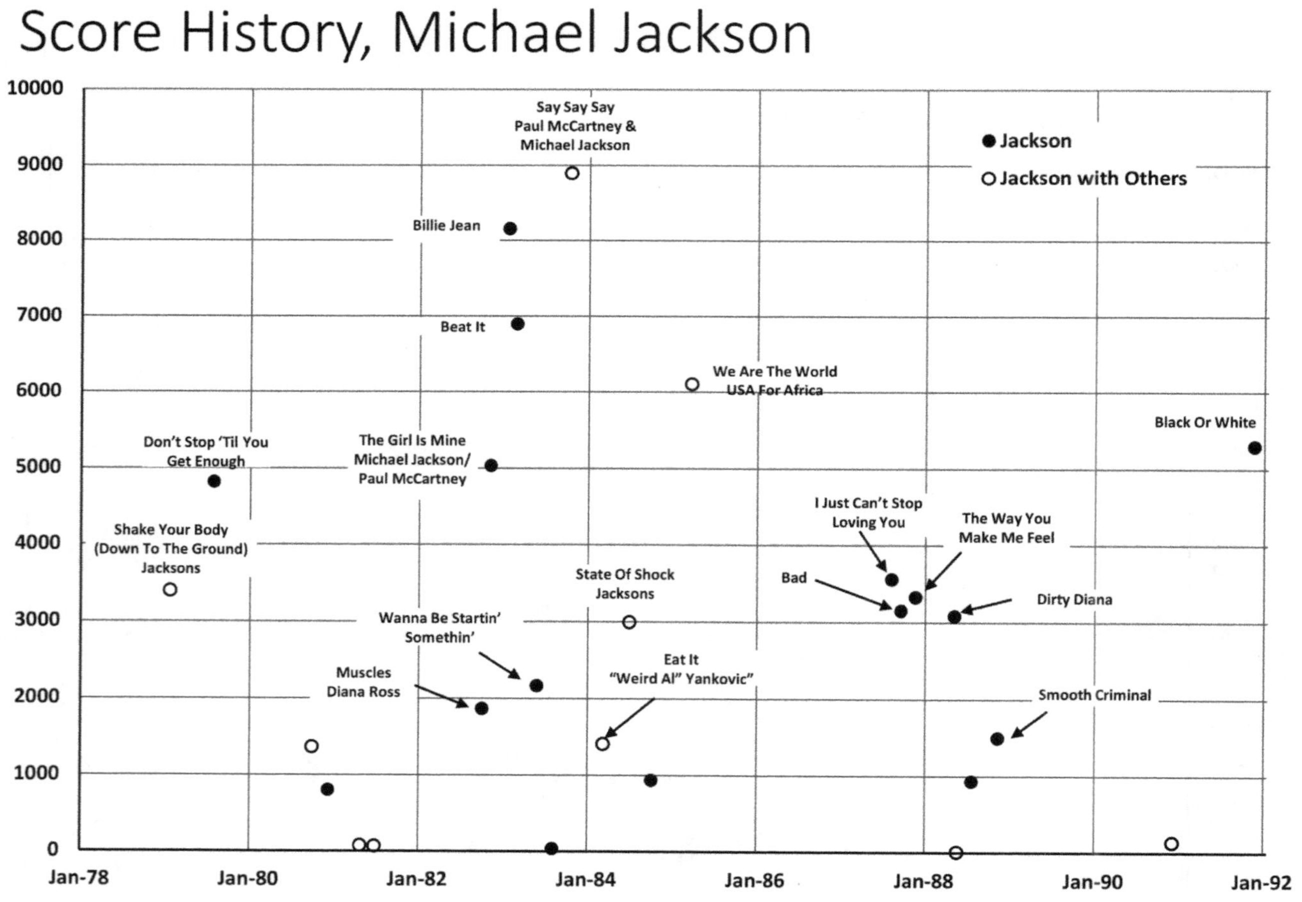

[3] Per Lucy Jones in New Music Express, Apr 2, 2014.

Smokey ROBINSON *(9)* ► 25 (57) 50651

Smokey Robinson had 128 writer credits in this era, 57 of which were solo efforts; those solo efforts—less than half his total canon--comprised nearly 2/3 of his 79,854 total writer points. He collaborated with 22 other writers on his charted songs. Teaming up with Marvin Tarplin, Warren Moore, Ronnie White, Robert Rogers, Al Cleveland and Berry Gordy produced many classic hits, but his highest ranking configuration was as sole writer.

Smokey met Berry Gordy in 1957 at the age of 17. Gordy helped the Miracles get their first recording, "Got A Job," on End Records, and they were one of the first acts Gordy signed to Tamla records. Even though he had written over 100 songs in high school, his early charted songs as a writer were collaborations with Gordy. The first, in 1959, "Bad Girl" didn't do much, but "Shop Around" was only about a year in the future. It would be Motown's first million seller.

Two of his five #1 writer credits came as a solo writer: "My Guy" for Mary Wells and "Being With You" as a solo performer. With the Miracles he had only one #1, "Tears Of A Clown," a collaboration with Stevie Wonder and Henry Cosby. Of 57 solo credits, 17 songs charted more than once, including "My Guy" and "You Really Got A Hold On Me," each four times. Twenty-one acts charted with his songs but only The Marvelettes, The Miracles, and Smokey as a solo artist more than five times. He averaged 888 points over his 57 credits and ranks as act number 275. He was the number six writer team by points in the '60s.

His highest ranking collaboration was with Ronnie White, which produced only three different charted songs; however, two of them were "Don't Look Back" recorded by The Temptations and Peter Tosh, and "My Girl" which charted six times, including The Temptations trip to #1 with it.

Score History, Smokey Robinson

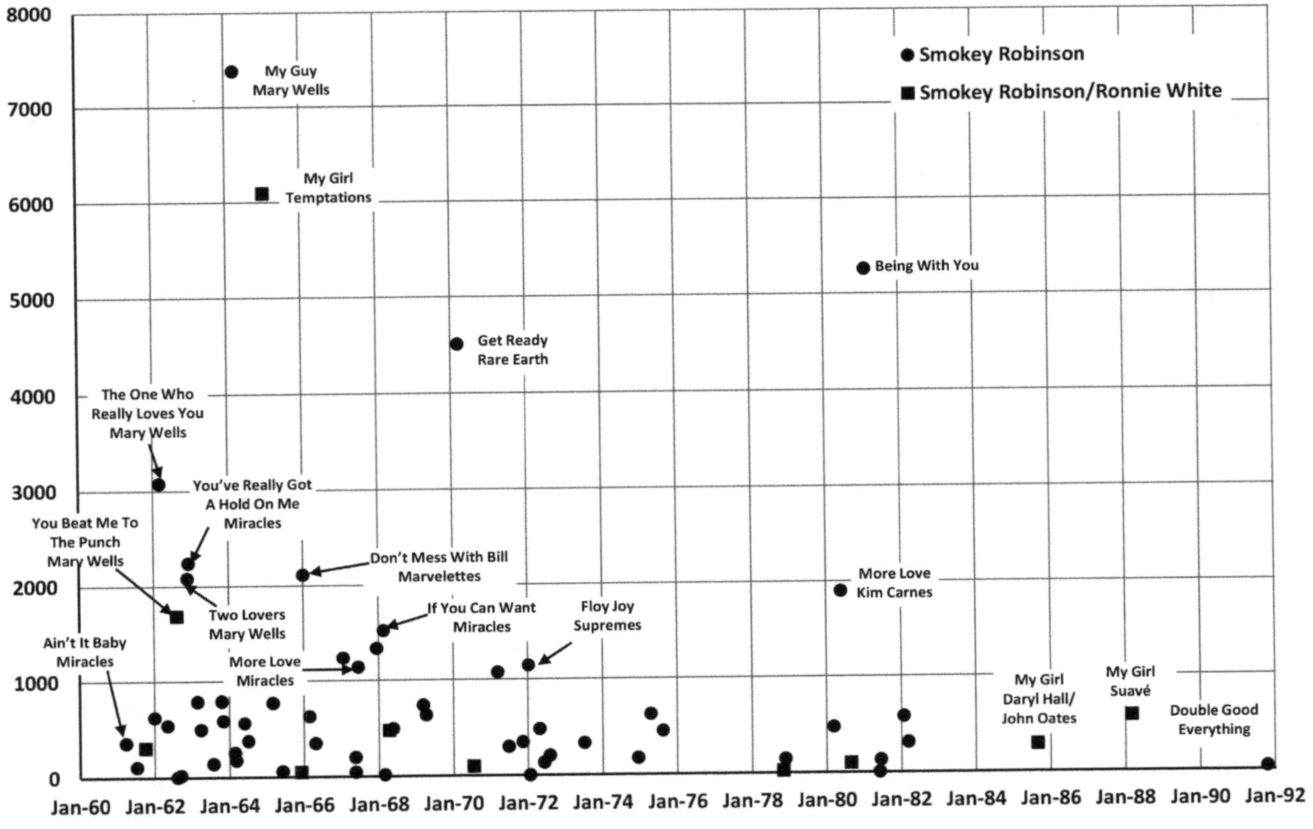

Bob DYLAN *(31)* ► 26 (49) 49250

As a writer, Bob Dylan first appeared on the singles charts via Peter, Paul and Mary. Albert Grossman, who managed both Dylan and PP&M brought them "Blowin' In The Wind," and it was a major success at a time when folk music was peaking on the American music scene. It was followed quickly by "Don't Think Twice, It's All Right," which did not score as well as "Blowin' In The Wind."[4]

The British Invasion elbowed a lot of folk music—and other genres--off the charts. By 1965 for Dylan the times were changing as well, as he incorporated his early rock roots with his folk virtuosity on the album "Bringing It All Back Home." His first charted single as an artist, "Subterranean Homesick Blues," was more of a line in the sand than a commercial success, but suggested what was to come the next month when the Byrds released Dylan's "Mr. Tambourine Man" as the first telling American rock response to the British Invasion. Dylan reinforced this change in his style later that year at the Newport Folk Festival by showing up with an electric band, a move that was roundly booed in folk circles, and led to the angry lyrics of the song "Positively 4th Street."

Dylan charted 49 songs as a writer, 20 also as the performer, averaging 1032 points (162nd for the act-writer team combination). Ninety-eight percent of his score came as a solo writer. A total of 22 acts charted his songs, accounting for nearly 60 percent of his writer credit. Fifteen of the entries were multiple recordings and by far the most successful was the first, "Blowin' In The Wind. The '60s were his biggest writer decade: he placed tenth.

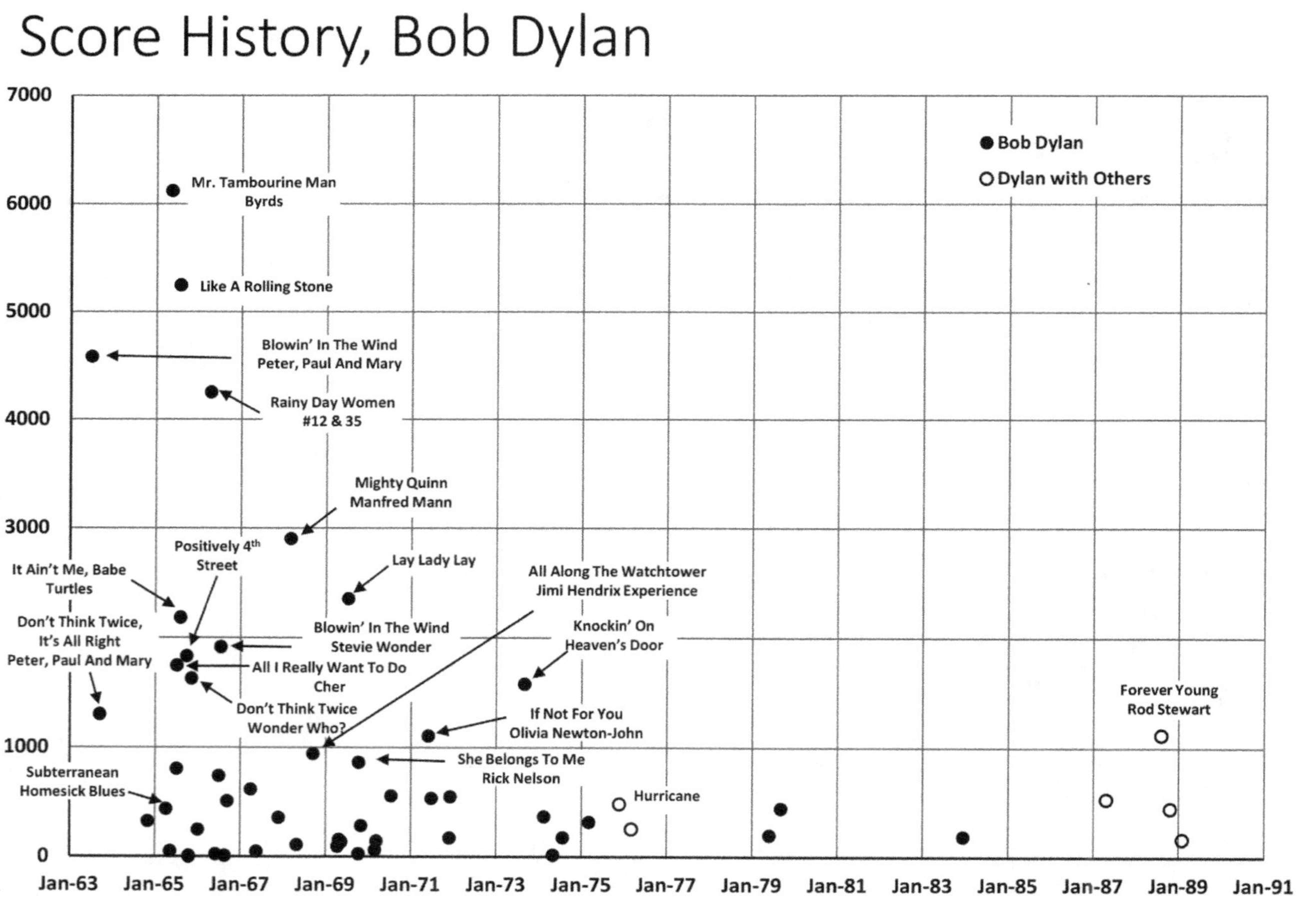

[4] According to Dylan, "Blowin' In The Wind" borrows the tune from a spiritual called "No More Auction Block." For purposes of this book, I've credited him with the music as an adaptation; an argument can be made for sharing credit with Traditional.

Sam COOKE *(25)* ► 27 (60)

Sam Cooke, born Samuel Cook in Clarksdale, Mississippi, moved to Chicago at an early age. He sang in gospel groups until 1957, the beginning of his solo career. His first chart appearance both as a performer and as a writer was "You Send Me," which was also his highest scoring song, barely outpointing "Chain Gang." However, neither song qualified for the top 1%.

Perhaps his most moving song is "A Change Is Gonna Come." It was written in late 1963, but only released as a single as a B side after his death. In retrospect, it fits in with the tenor of the times and the times to come in the mid to late 1960s.

Over 90% of his writer points were scored as a solo writer, and 73% as a solo writer-act combination. He had only one significant writer collaboration: with Herb Alpert and Lou Adler on "Wonderful World." The label of that record said "Barbara Campbell," Sam's high school girlfriend and later wife, but Cooke, Alpert and Adler are credited by BMI. Some of his records gave label credit to "L. C. Cooke," his brother, but again Sam Cooke was listed in BMI. "Sweet Soul Music," his third biggest credit, was attributed to him posthumously as Arthur Conley "borrowed" his song "Yeah, Man."

Of his 71 chart entries as a writer, 49 were of songs that charted more than once. Among them, "Bring It On Home To Me" four times, "Cupid" and "Wonderful World" five times, and "You Send Me" six times. Thirty-one acts recorded his songs, only one more than once. As a combination of act and writer, he averaged 1254 points for 28 chart entries. He ranks as the 54th act for the era and the 21st writer team of the '60s.

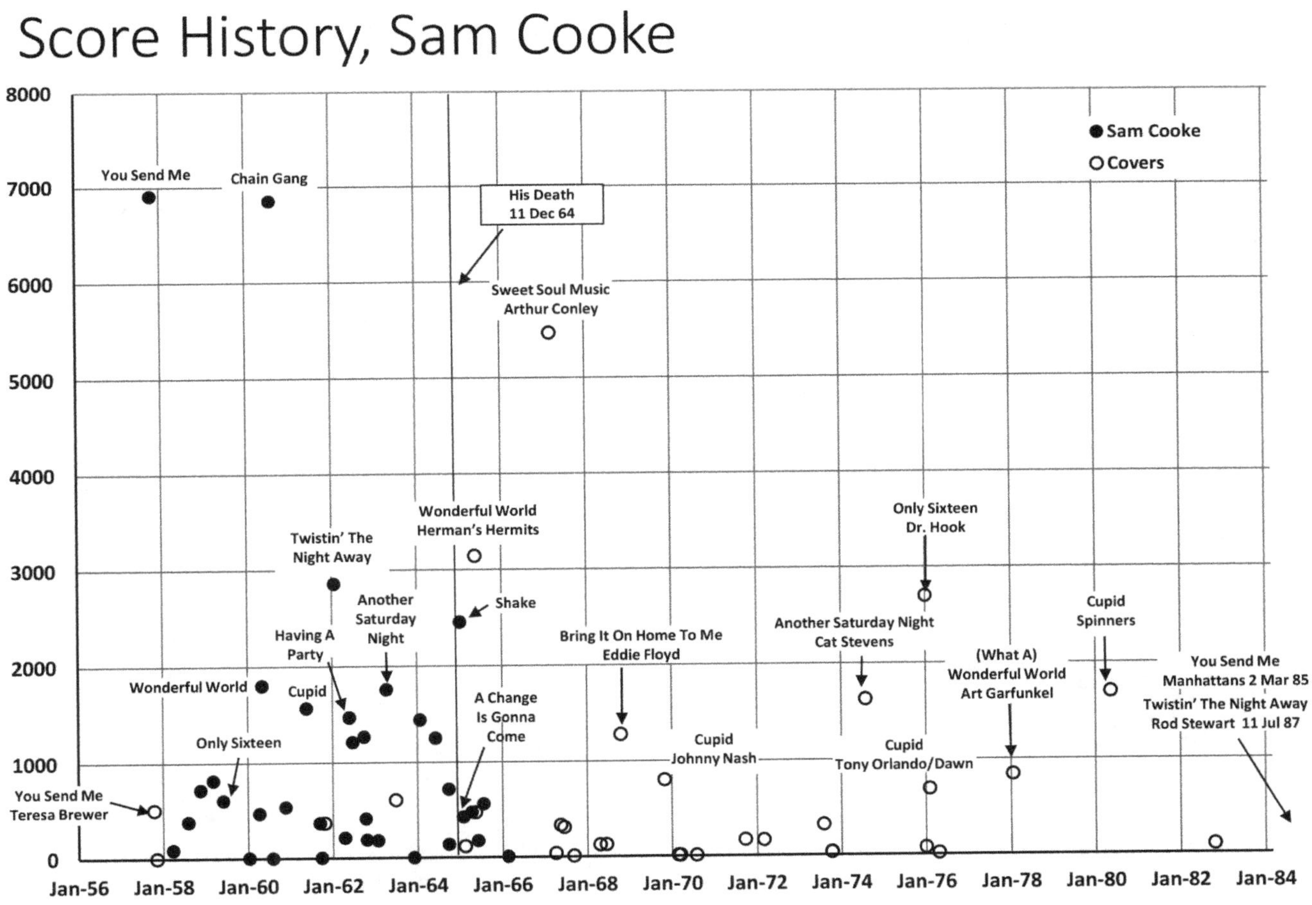

Mike LOVE *(82)*/Brian WILSON *(46)* ► 28 (39) 48191

If this book had been written in the 1980s, the writer team of Mike Love and Brian Wilson would not have scored so high; however, in the early nineties, Love sued for writer credit on a number of songs that initially credited only Wilson and was compensated by the courts.

The crowded chart below shows how much activity and popularity these writers had in the 1963-1966 period, more or less bounded by "Surfin' USA" and "Good Vibrations." It may be that Wilson's music in Pet Sounds and after was more mature and better, but the charts loved surf and cars. Love-Wilson had six songs scoring twice the average chart strength or above; Brian Wilson with others had four more. Things slowed markedly by the end of the decade, and never recovered the early glory, with only "Kokomo" flashing back.

Famously, Brian Wilson repurposed the music from Chuck Berry's "Sweet Little Sixteen" with a new set of lyrics he called "Surfin' USA." Wilson argued that imitation is the sincerest form of flattery; Berry argued plagiarism is a copyright violation. The disagreement was settled out of court, awarding publishing rights to Berry. There are a number of versions of the label of this record: some credit Brian Wilson only and some credit Chuck Berry only. BMI now awards the rights to Chuck Berry; the most recent copyright credits lyrics to Brian Wilson and music to Chuck Berry, which is also how I have credited it.

Of the 84 chart entries that featured one or both of them, 49 were recorded more than once. Brian Wilson had 18 collaborators and Mike Love 10, but by far the bulk of their individual writer points came as a result of this team. The act- writer team combination with the Beach Boys averaged 1621 points for 28 entries, ranking 77th. The Love-Wilson collaboration ranks 41st in points and 26th in entries in the '60s. Their two biggest songs, "I Get Around" and "Good Vibrations" placed in the top 1%.

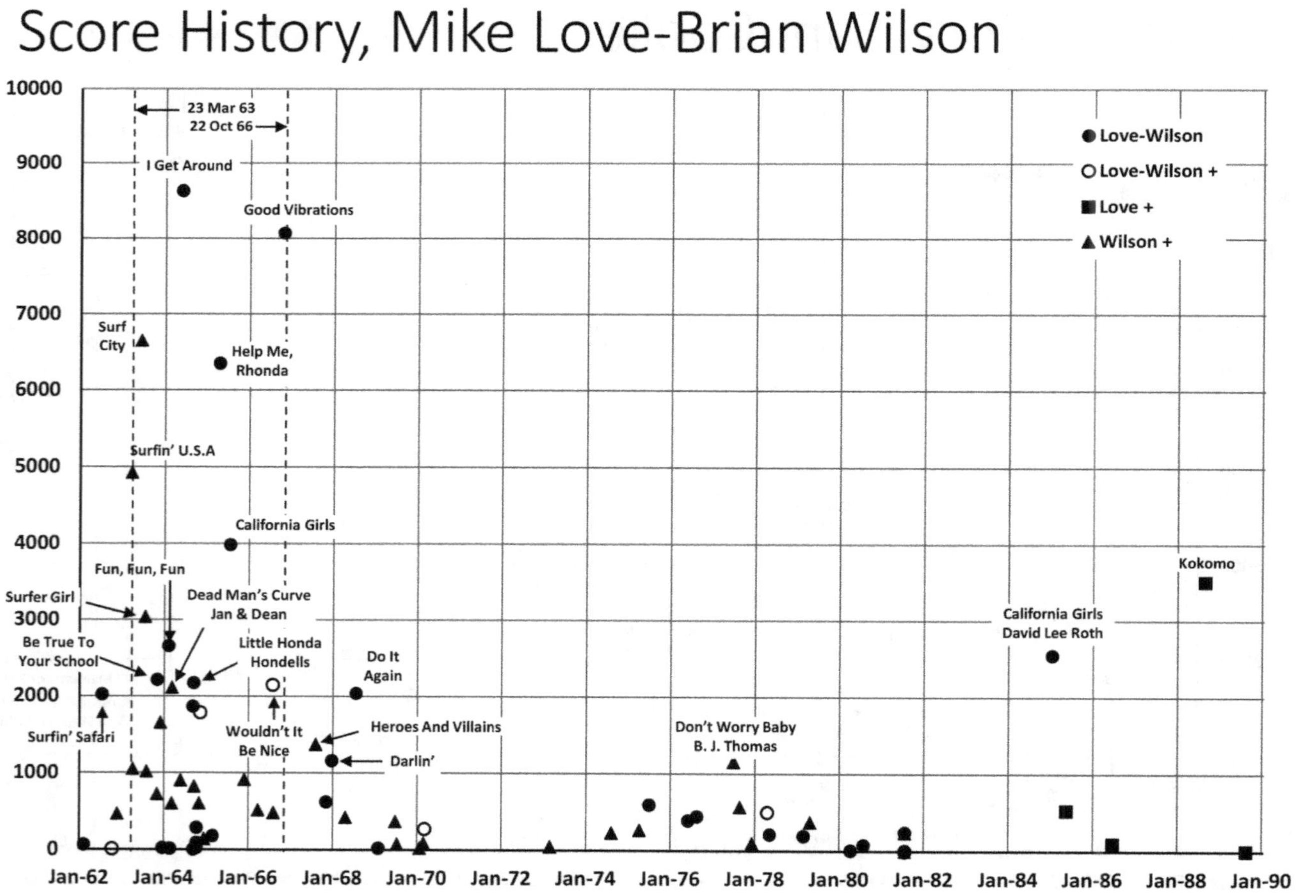

Bob CREWE *(40)*/Bob GAUDIO *(43)* ▶ 29 (28) 48175

In 1962, Bob Gaudio's solo writer career broke through with "Sherry," for his group, The 4 Seasons, which scored high in the top 1% of the era. The partnership of Crewe and Gaudio produced a string of hits for The 4 Seasons, but also for Frankie Valli, The Tremeloes and the Walker Brothers. But that string, the writing collaboration and for that matter, The 4 Seasons had played themselves out by 1968.

There are four important regions in this timeline. In the years 1957-60, both writers had success in other venues. Gaudio with the Royal Teens and Crewe writing with Frank Slay for The Rays and Freddy Cannon. The years 1962-68 are the aforementioned good years. Then there is the 1970-74 period where neither writer had chart success. Finally, there is a return to popularity for both—although separately—in 1975-76. Gaudio wrote with Judy Parker for the new-sound 4 Seasons and Crewe wrote with Kenny Nolan and others, most notably to support Labelle, Disco-Tex And The Sex-O-Lettes and Frankie Valli.

As a writer team they only had 28 entries of 19 different songs. Five charted multiple times including "Can't Take My Eyes Off You," four times, and "The Sun Ain't Gonna Shine (Any More)" and "Walk Like A Man" three times each. Fourteen acts charted with their songs: the ten entries by The 4 Seasons averaged 3276 points, the tenth best act-writer team combination. They were the seventh-ranked writer team by points in the '60s, with one transcendent hit, "Big Girls Don't Cry" and two more in the top 1%, "Walk Like A Man" and "Rag Doll. Bob Crewe had 21 other collaborators over his career, and Gaudio had 11 but each was the highest charting collaborator with the other.

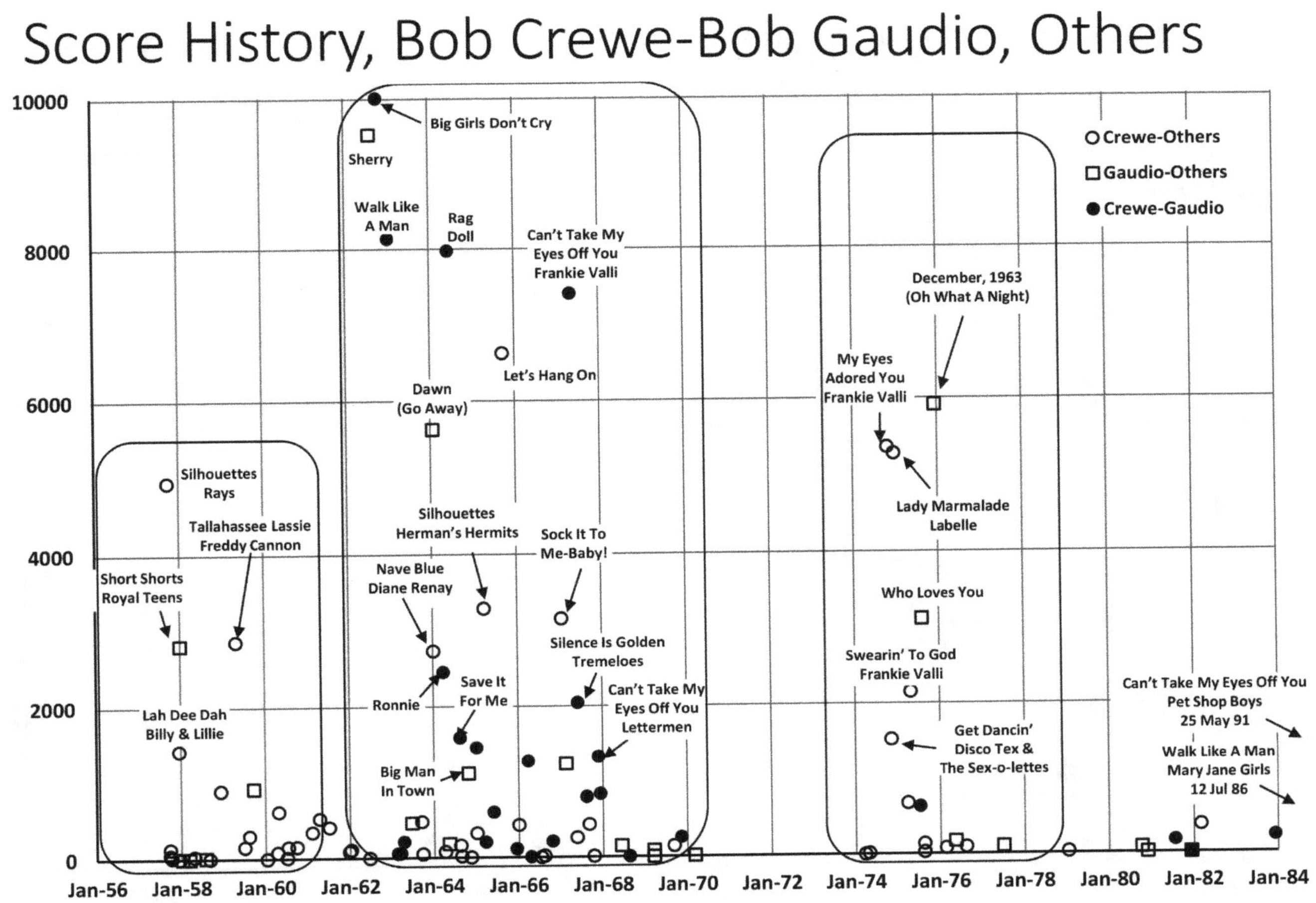

John FOGERTY *(36)* ► 30 (30) 47537

Regardless of how the music sounds, John Fogerty's roots were in California, not Louisiana. He started writing while he was in the National Guard in 1966-67, and "Proud Mary" was his first copyrighted single, December 27, 1968. According to Songfacts.com, Fogerty wrote the song from three proto-titles for songs: Proud Mary, Riverboat and Rolling On The River.

Between 1969 and 1972 Fogerty and Creedence Clearwater Revival had a consistent run of successful singles. Many of them were two-sided hits, although the sides were generally not of equal popularity. As with many writers, his first chart entry—"Proud Mary" was the most successful of the bunch.

The timeline is pretty empty between 1972 and 1976, apparently caused by difficulties within the band, and simply running out of gas. In addition, Fogerty had legal difficulties with his record company. In one case, he was sued for self-plagiarism; in essence, sounding too much like John Fogerty. Much as Tommy James did, he left the industry for a number of years to let the dust settle, until resurfacing in the mid-'80s, as can be seen on the timeline.

Fogerty has no shared writer credits on his singles. Similarly, the only significant cover version of one of his singles was Ike & Tina Turner's reinvention of "Proud Mary." Creedence and Fogerty comprise nearly 95% of the performance of Fogerty's writer credits. Fogerty averaged 1585 points as a writer, good for 101st place. As a combination, Creedence and Fogerty averaged 2411 points per entry, ranking 29th. Creedence was the 60th-ranked act.

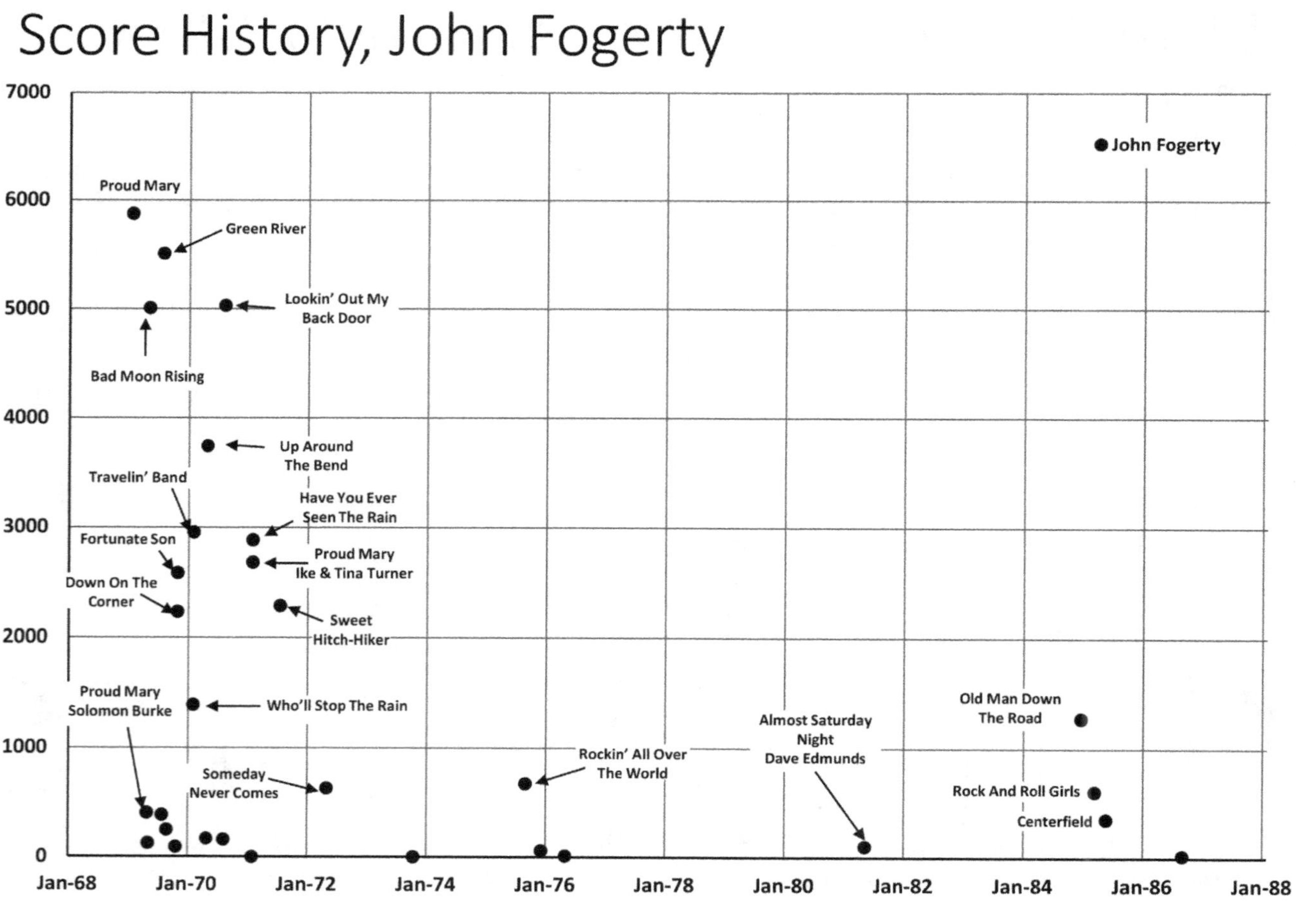

And a couple of author's choice extras to round out the section:

Dave APPELL *(86)*/Kal MANN *(26)* ▶ 31 (35)

Dave Appell's core competency was as an arranger, work he did dating to the 1940s. His earliest work as a recording artist was with his band, The Applejacks (née Dave Appell Four). Kal Mann was a comedy writer who became a lyricist at the urging of Bernie Lowe (see sidebar). The three of them, Mann, Lowe and Appell were responsible for getting Cameo-Parkway records off the ground in Philadelphia in the late 1950s.

Integral to the growth of Cameo-Parkway was the presence of American Bandstand in Philadelphia. Local acts were always the bullpen for American Bandstand if other acts did not show up. Many of those were in the Cameo-Parkway stable.

Their first major act was Bobby Rydell who had 12 charted records for Appell-Mann (and Appell-Mann-Lowe). Duets with Chubby Checker added two more. Chubby Checker, Dee Dee Sharp, The Dovells and The Orlons were also important consumers of their work.

"The Bristol Stomp", their strongest charting record, was derived from a dance done by local teenagers to a song called "Every Day Of The Week" by The Students. Mann and Appell hammered out their song to capitalize on the local craze. It had a slow start but with local support, a breakout in Chicago, and an appearance on American Bandstand by The Dovells, it took off.

Appell and Mann had 35 entries with 10 acts. The act-writer team combination with the Orlons averaged 2320 points over six entries to rank 38th. There were virtually no covers of any of their charted songs except in two Jive Bunny medleys in 1989 and 1990. For the '60s they ranked eighth in points and 12th in entries.

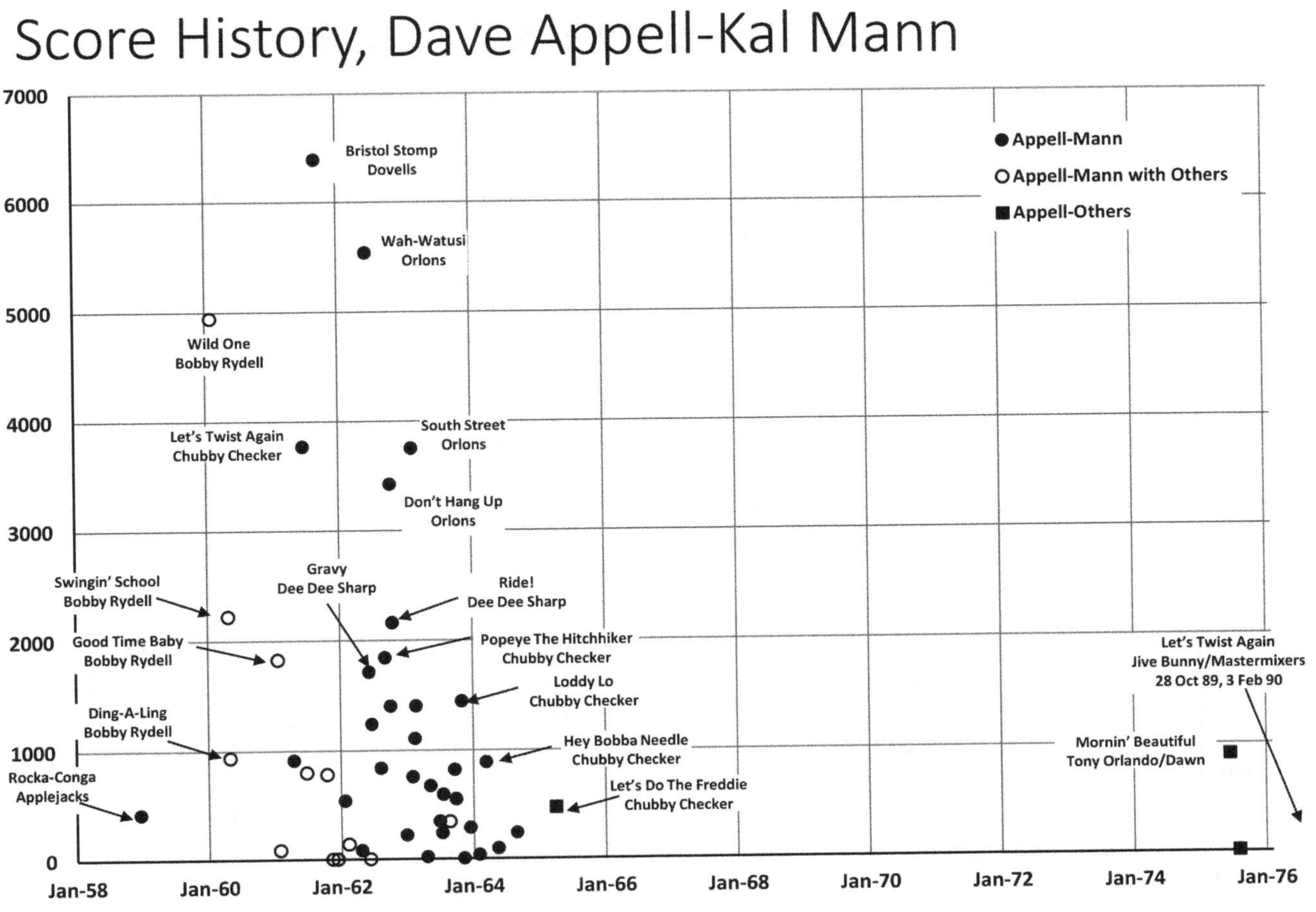

Bernie LOWE *(151)*/Kal MANN *(26)* ► 80 (26) 24931

Although not so highly ranked, Lowe and Mann fill out more of the history of Cameo-Parkway, and obviously overlap with Appell and Mann. After Lowe coaxed Mann into the music business, the pair wrote "Teddy Bear," which was eventually published by Hill and Range, and recorded by Elvis Presley. It was their biggest hit as a duo. Their next hit, "Butterfly" was eventually attributed to "Anthony September" a collective alias they used to avoid existing legal encumbrances.

"Mashed Potato Time" was their biggest hit together, but it is credited more broadly to the writers of "Please Mr. Postman" as well. Most attributions these days are to Robert Bateman/Georgia Dobbins/William Garrett/Freddie Gorman/Brian Holland for that song, and Lowe and Mann are added to "Mashed Potato Time." "Limbo Rock" is shown here although only Mann and Billy Strange are officially credited. Strange alone is on the instrumental version by The Champs. Mann added lyrics for Chubby Checker.

Cameo-Parkway had a good run between 1958 and 1964, but fell on hard times for three reasons. First, the British Invasion, which remade the pop music scene in the first half of 1964; second, the move of American Bandstand from Philadelphia to Los Angeles, and finally the three principals were either ill, retired or lost interest before selling to Allen Klein. Nothing but a couple of covers or medley reissues dents the timeline for Lowe and Mann after "Birdland" in 1963.

They charted 26 entries with 20 acts. Charlie Gracie claims the most at four, Bobby Rydell had three and Elvis two. As a team they ranked number four in points and number seven in entries in the '50s.

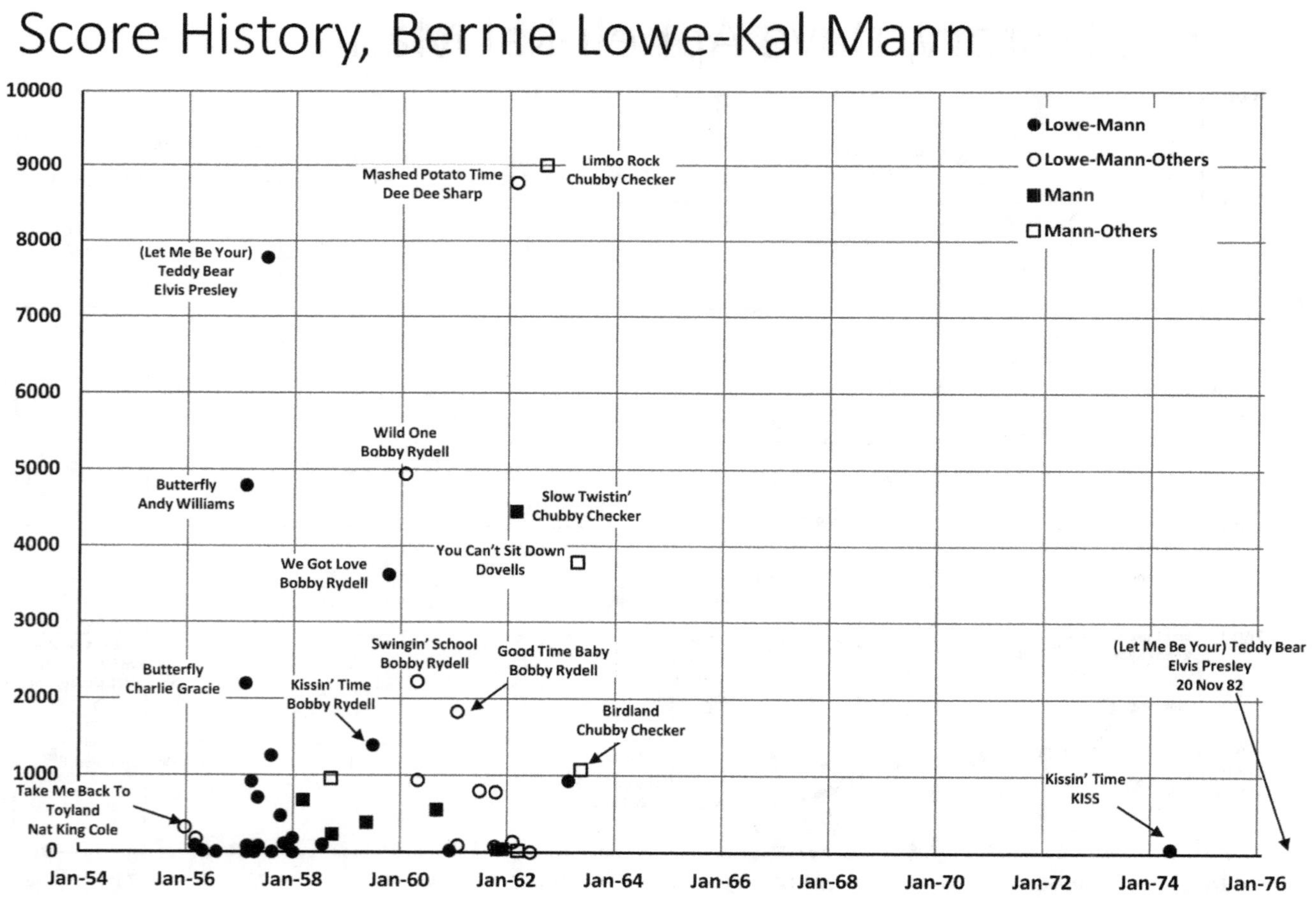

Bonus: Jeff Barry's Collaborations

In retrospect it's difficult to connect the style of the writers of "Tell Laura I Love Her," "Chip Chip," "Sugar Sugar," and "Montego Bay," and yet they were all Jeff Barry collaborations. As seen in the Brill Building sidebar, Barry's main writing partner was his wife Ellie Greenwich who shared 52 of his 95 writing credits. But Phil Spector was also an important collaborator with both of them, overlapping with 24 of Barry's credits and 26 of Greenwich's. In fact, Greenwich introduced Barry to Spector.

There are two distinct lumps on the timeline. The first lump peaks in the 1963-64 time frame, which corresponds with the Greenwich marriage and Greenwich-Spector collaborations. Barry and Greenwich divorced by the end of 1965. Their own chart presence virtually ceased except for Tommy James' "Hanky Panky" which had been written three years prior. They continued to work together, but mainly on publishing Neil Diamond's songs.

The Monkees led to the Archies which led to the next phase of his career. Don Kirshner liked Diamond's "I'm A Believer" and got Jeff Barry to produce it as well as the Diamond-penned follow-up, "A Little Bit Me, A Little Bit You" for the Monkees. And then Kirshner's relationship with the band blew up. Kirshner, deciding that an animated cartoon could not rebel the way a human one had, developed Monkees II: The Archies, and Barry was the main songwriter and producer. Around the same time, Andy Kim traveled from Toronto to New York, pitched a song to Barry, who helped revise it, then recorded him and mentored him. They collaborated after for three years, including writing the transcendent hit "Sugar Sugar." This was the second lump on the timeline.

Jeff Barry had 25 collaborators and as a writer ranks 33rd. His collaboration with Greenwich ranks 81st and with Greenwich and Spector, 47th. Fourteen songs charted multiple times including "Do Wah Diddy Diddy" and "River Deep—Mountain High" four times each. In addition to "Sugar Sugar," "Do Wah Diddy Diddy" and "Chapel of Love" are in the top 1%.

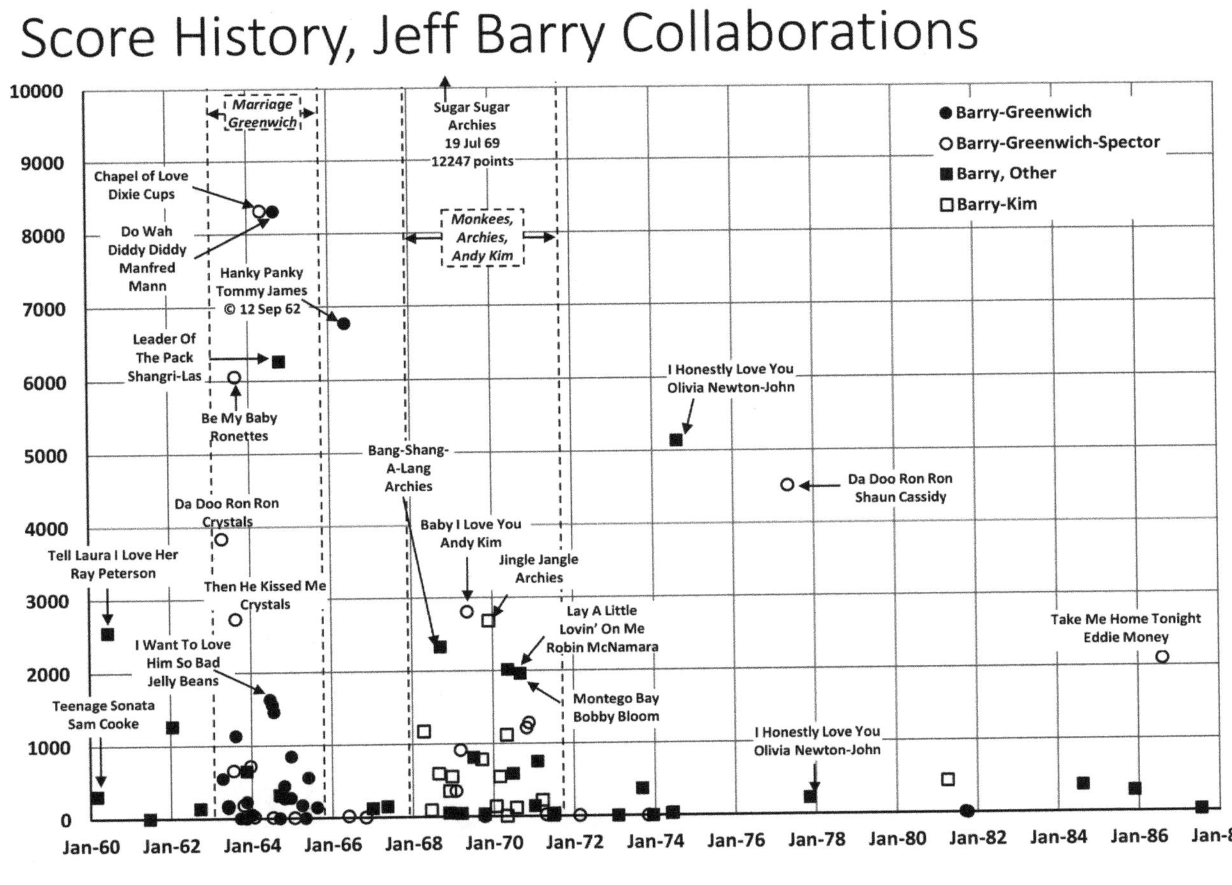

The Top 200 Writer Teams, and the Acts Who Recorded Their Songs

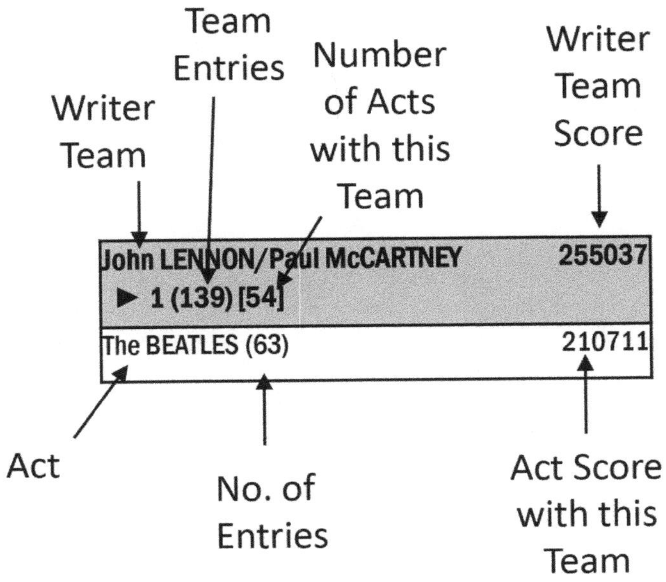

John LENNON/Paul McCARTNEY ► 1 (139) [54]	**255037**
The BEATLES (63)	210711
PETER And GORDON (3)	8574
Elton JOHN (1)	4586
STARS ON 45 (13)	3578
Billy J. KRAMER with The DAKOTAS (3)	2478
Sergio MENDES & BRASIL '66 (1)	2327
Anne MURRAY (3)	2186
Stevie WONDER (1)	1496
Ray CHARLES (2)	1470
The SILKIE (1)	1392
PLASTIC ONO BAND (1)	1367
Mary HOPKIN (1)	1267
EARTH, WIND & FIRE (1)	1210
TIFFFANY (1)	1114
DAVID & JONATHAN (1)	1048
UNDERGROUND SUNSHINE (1)	1006
Joe COCKER (2)	969
Wilson PICKETT (1)	933
Aretha FRANKLIN (1)	807
George MARTIN And His Orchestra (2)	741
AEROSMITH (1)	659
Robin GIBB (1)	626
Ramsey LEWIS Trio (1)	532
Joan BAEZ (1)	435
Esther PHILLIPS (1)	406
Ike & Tina TURNER (1)	348
SPRINGWELL (1)	334
Arthur CONLEY (1)	282
AMBROSIA (1)	262
Ramsey LEWIS (2)	214
CARPENTERS (1)	196
Billy VAUGHN and His Orchestra (1)	188
KATFISH (1)	186
BOSTON POPS Orchestra (1)	184
BLOOD, SWEAT & TEARS (1)	128
Bud SHANK (1)	116
FIVE STAIRSTEPS (1)	110
Del SHANNON (1)	110
Bobby RYDELL (1)	99
Chubby CHECKER (1)	70
Emmylou HARRIS (1)	55
Gary TOMS Empire (1)	52
CHAD & JEREMY (1)	45
Cilla BLACK (2)	45
NILSSON (1)	23
Fats DOMINO (1)	16
The FOURMOST (1)	12
Bob KUBAN And The IN-MEN (1)	11
José FELICIANO (1)	9.6
Billy PRESTON (1)	9.4
Richie HAVENS (1)	4.0
HOLLYRIDGE STRINGS (1)	3.8
The VONTASTICS (1)	2.4
Claudine LONGET (1)	0.9
Lamont DOZIER/ Brian HOLLAND/ Eddie HOLLAND ► 2 (107) [49]	**167934**
The SUPREMES/Diana ROSS And The SUPREMES (17)	81238
FOUR TOPS (13)	30169
MARTHA & The VANDELLAS (9)	13963
Marvin GAYE (6)	6869
Kim WILDE (1)	3516
The MIRACLES/ Smokey ROBINSON & The MIRACLES (3)	3465
Johnny RIVERS (1)	3362
Jr. WALKER & The ALL STARS (3)	2911
James TAYLOR (1)	2292
VANILLA FUDGE (2)	2275
Bonnie POINTER (2)	2265
DOOBIE BROTHERS (2)	2027
Donnie ELBERT (2)	1860
Phil COLLINS (1)	1813
Linda RONSTADT (1)	1210
Mary WELLS (1)	855
Kim WESTON (2)	756
The BAND (1)	698
Diana ROSS (1)	619
HOLLAND-DOZIER (2)	586
The HOLLIES (1)	525
The ELGINS (2)	523
Lee MICHAELS (1)	522
The MARVELETTES (1)	428
Eddie HOLLAND (3)	416
KC & The SUNSHINE BAND (1)	395
JACKSON 5 (1)	305
ISLEY BROTHERS (2)	244
O.C. SMITH (1)	239
SHALAMAR (3)	239
J. GEILS Band (1)	205
Le BLANC & CARR (1)	183
Eric CARMEN (1)	135
Wilson PICKETT (1)	133
Gloria GAYNOR (1)	119
Sheena EASTON (1)	115
RITCHIE FAMILY (1)	92
Nella DODDS (1)	92
Merrilee RUSH (1)	70
Margie JOSEPH (1)	64
José FELICIANO (1)	46
Genya RAVAN (1)	41
STARS ON 45 (2)	24
Dionne WARWICK (1)	10
FLAMING EMBER (1)	9.0
MAGNIFICENT MEN (1)	7.6
Jackie MOORE (1)	3.5
Jackie DeSHANNON (1)	1.0
NEW SEEKERS (1)	0.7
Burt BACHARACH/Hal DAVID ► 3 (105) [54]	**112434**
Dionne WARWICK (33)	29923
B.J. THOMAS (3)	11223
Herb ALPERT (2)	9438
5TH DIMENSION (2)	8132
Gene PITNEY (4)	8068
CARPENTERS (1)	7620
Tom JONES (2)	5096
Bobby VINTON (2)	4326
Dusty SPRINGFIELD (2)	4253
Sergio MENDES & BRASIL '66 (1)	3151
Jackie DeSHANNON (3)	2880
NAKED EYES (1)	1983
Jack JONES (1)	1677
Aretha FRANKLIN (1)	1449
SYBIL (2)	930
Jerry BUTLER (2)	872
The STYLISTICS (1)	836
Tom CLAY (1)	836
Perry COMO (1)	834
R.B. GREAVES (1)	784
WALKER BROS. (1)	781
Marty ROBBINS (1)	692
Lou JOHNSON (2)	610
CHER (1)	533
Engelbert HUMPERDINCK (1)	523
Bobby VEE (1)	466
Timi YURO (1)	465
Chuck JACKSON (2)	462
Isaac HAYES (2)	461
LOVE (1)	458
Richard CHAMBERLAIN (2)	414
Billy J. KRAMER with The DAKOTAS (1)	357
Sandie SHAW (1)	337
Jane MORGAN (1)	319
Gary PUCKETT (1)	315
Brook BENTON (1)	260
Shawn PHILLIPS (1)	159
Jennifer WARNES (1)	131
Bobby GOLDSBORO (1)	104
BRENDA & The TABULATIONS (1)	95
Glen CAMPBELL/ Anne MURRAY (1)	38
B.T. EXPRESS (1)	31
FOUR COINS (1)	26
Burt BACHARACH (2)	24
Tommy HUNT (1)	13
Margaret WHITING (1)	13
Paul ANKA (1)	11
AVERAGE WHITE BAND/AWB (1)	7.4
Cilla BLACK (1)	6.1
Babs TINO (1)	3.5
The WANDERERS (1)	1.8
The SHIRELLES (1)	1.8
Linda SCOTT (1)	1.3
Gloria GAYNOR (1)	1.1
Mick JAGGER/Keith RICHARDS ► 4 (60) [18]	**110743**
ROLLING STONES (43)	107789
Otis REDDING (1)	624
Aretha FRANKLIN (1)	527
MELANIE (1)	414
Gene PITNEY (1)	317
Linda RONSTADT (1)	309
George MICHAEL (1)	248
GRAND FUNK RAILROAD (1)	207
Merry CLAYTON (1)	105
Bette MIDLER (1)	71
SOUP DRAGONS (1)	48
BUCHANAN BROTHERS (1)	38
TWICE AS MUCH (1)	19
Johnny WINTER (1)	15
David BOWIE (1)	7.4
Del SHANNON (1)	1.4
The HOUNDS (1)	1.0
TIGHT FIT (1)	0.9
Barry GIBB/ Maurice GIBB/ Robin GIBB ► 5 (44) [15]	**100483**
BEE GEES (29)	80521
Kenny ROGERS & Dolly PARTON (1)	6346
Yvonne ELLIMAN (1)	4924
Barbra STREISAND & Barry GIBB (1)	2811
Andy GIBB (1)	2687
Dionne WARWICK (1)	1606
TAVARES (1)	508
Melba MOORE (1)	350
RARE EARTH (1)	335
José FELICIANO (1)	193
Diana ROSS (2)	119
Wayne NEWTON (1)	32
Nigel OLSSON (1)	31
Gino CUNICO (1)	9.9
Candi STATON (1)	8.1
Gerry GOFFIN/Carole KING ► 6 (94) [64]	**94936**
Bobby VEE (7)	10100
Steve LAWRENCE (3)	9427
LITTLE EVA (3)	9367
Donny OSMOND (2)	8588
The SHIRELLES (2)	6224
The DRIFTERS (4)	5228
GRAND FUNK RAILROAD (1)	4636
The MONKEES (2)	4363
The COOKIES (3)	3440
Skeeter DAVIS (1)	2616
Kylie MINOGUE (1)	2519
The CHIFFONS (1)	2130
HERMAN'S HERMITS (1)	1902
Freddie SCOTT (2)	1843
Carole KING (5)	1771
The ANIMALS/ Eric BURDON & The ANIMALS (1)	1719
Bobby VINTON (2)	1625
James DARREN (1)	1551
The HAPPENINGS (1)	1386
BLOOD, SWEAT & TEARS (1)	1305
STEVE And EYDIE (2)	1295
Maxine BROWN (2)	1106
Bobby RYDELL (2)	1072
4 SEASONS (1)	1009
Tony ORLANDO (1)	897
DION (1)	761
Gene McDANIELS (1)	648
Gene PITNEY (1)	623
James TAYLOR (1)	522
PARIS SISTERS (1)	453
The TOKENS (1)	438
Dave MASON (1)	431
EARL-JEAN (1)	425
Helen REDDY (1)	382
RIGHTEOUS BROTHERS (1)	344
Connie STEVENS (1)	297
Dusty SPRINGFIELD (1)	270
Rod STEWART (1)	197
Merry CLAYTON (1)	194
Roberta FLACK (1)	184
CRYAN' SHAMES (1)	174
The BYRDS (2)	170
MELANIE (1)	152
Paul PETERSEN (1)	141
Steve ALAIMO (2)	138
Rita COOLIDGE (1)	116
Betty EVERETT (1)	106
Eydie GORME (1)	104
Ben E. KING (1)	102
Lou RAWLS (1)	99
Bill MEDLEY (1)	87
Chuck JACKSON (1)	72
AMERICAN BREED (2)	62
ANNETTE (1)	37
JULIE (1)	19
The LETTERMEN (1)	14
Marlena SHAW (1)	9.6
Dana VALERY (1)	9.4
Vivian REED (1)	8.2
The RATIONALS (1)	7.7
Laura NYRO (1)	7.4
Barbara LEWIS (1)	7.0
Rick NELSON (1)	5.1
Linda RONSTADT (1)	1.7
Elton JOHN/Bernie TAUPIN ► 7 (43) [8]	**83123**
Elton JOHN (36)	66179
Elton JOHN Band (1)	6474
Elton JOHN and Kiki DEE (1)	6364
George MICHAEL (1)	3346
Aretha FRANKLIN (1)	643
Olivia NEWTON-JOHN (1)	97

Elton JOHN/Bernie TAUPIN ► 7 (43) [8] ***Cont'd***	**83123**
APRIL WINE (1)	19
Ringo STARR (1)	0.0
Paul SIMON ► 8 (44) [16]	**82685**
SIMON & GARFUNKEL (14)	46214
Paul SIMON (16)	25764
Aretha FRANKLIN (1)	4354
The BANGLES (1)	2731
HARPERS BIZARRE (1)	1359
Paul SIMON/Phoebe SNOW (1)	728
BOOKER T. & The M.G.'s (1)	554
YES (1)	394
Gary PUCKETT (1)	274
Linda CLIFFORD (1)	159
The ARBORS (1)	85
TIMES TWO (1)	31
Jerry LANDIS (1)	21
STARS ON 45 (1)	12
PEACHES & HERB (1)	3.8
TICO And The TRIUMPHS (1)	2.7
Lionel RICHIE ► 9 (20) [6]	**81488**
Lionel RICHIE (8)	32685
The COMMODORES (8)	27650
Diana ROSS & Lionel RICHIE (1)	10664
Kenny ROGERS (1)	8815
Diana ROSS (1)	1594
John SCHNEIDER (1)	80
Jerry LEIBER/Mike STOLLER ► 10 (82) [46]	**80838**
Elvis PRESLEY (15)	24285
The COASTERS (15)	21841
DION (2)	8417
Wilbert HARRISON (1)	6968
The SEARCHERS (1)	5796
The CHEERS (2)	2338
Peggy LEE (2)	1928
The MONKEES (1)	1160
The CLOVERS (2)	1044
Maria MULDAUR (1)	842
Trini LOPEZ (1)	840
Ray STEVENS (1)	668
Ruth BROWN (2)	648
BOYS IN THE BAND (1)	572
CHICAGO LOOP (1)	428
CHEECH & CHONG (1)	335
LaVern BAKER (1)	327
James BROWN (1)	301
Billy "Crash" CRADDOCK (1)	300
Chuck JACKSON (1)	295
Joni MITCHELL (1)	189
Cliff RICHARD (1)	180
JIVE BUNNY & THE MASTERMIXERS (2)	159
Jack EUBANKS (1)	149
Vaughn MONROE (1)	132
Hank BALLARD And The MIDNIGHTERS (1)	119
Jim CROCE (1)	76
LaVern BAKER & Jimmy RICKS (1)	75
Perry COMO (1)	61
Ace CANNON (1)	59
Eddie FISHER (1)	51
The DRIFTERS (2)	50
Gale STORM (1)	50
Rocky OLSON (1)	40
FIVE DeMARCO SISTERS (1)	39
The BEATLES (1)	22
Georgia GIBBS (2)	20
Johnny RIVERS (1)	12
Brook BENTON (1)	8.6
The ROBINS (1)	6.4

LITTLE RICHARD (1)	3.8
Kenny CHANDLER (1)	0.5
Sunny GALE (1)	0.0
Billy WILLIAMS Quartet (1)	0.0
Connie RUSSELL (1)	0.0
Les ELGART and His Orchestra (1)	0.0
Neil DIAMOND ► 11 (55) [13]	**78789**
Neil DIAMOND (40)	51292
The MONKEES (2)	19409
UB40 (2)	3855
JAY & The AMERICANS (1)	942
Vic DANA (2)	653
DEEP PURPLE (1)	648
Mark LINDSAY (1)	626
Bobby WOMACK (1)	430
Glen CAMPBELL (1)	418
Ronnie DOVE (1)	385
Jr. WALKER & The ALL STARS (1)	114
STARS ON 45 (1)	12
T.G. SHEPPARD (1)	5.7
PRINCE ► 12 (46) [16]	**77629**
PRINCE (22)	37375
PRINCE And The REVOLUTION (8)	20869
Sinead O'CONNOR (1)	4985
Chaka KHAN (1)	4722
The BANGLES (1)	2853
SHEILA E. (2)	2557
Sheena EASTON (1)	1802
Tevin CAMPBELL (1)	1444
ART OF NOISE (1)	387
Meli'sa MORGAN (1)	370
The FAMILY (1)	105
The TIME (2)	61
MARTIKA (1)	40
APOLLONIA 6 (1)	33
Mitch RYDER (1)	15
Elisa FIORILLO (1)	9.0
TRADITIONAL ► 13 (99) [83]	**77319**
KINGSTON TRIO (1)	9986
The HIGHWAYMEN (1)	9146
The ANIMALS/Eric BURDON & The ANIMALS (1)	7607
Laurie LONDON (2)	5381
"DELIVERANCE" Soundtrack (1)	4998
Harry BELAFONTE (3)	4751
LOS LOBOS (1)	4652
BEACH BOYS (1)	3647
FRIJID PINK (1)	3040
Mitch MILLER (2)	2935
Cyril STAPLETON And His Orchestra (1)	2867
The IMPRESSIONS (1)	2022
Lonnie DONEGAN And His SKIFFLE GROUP (3)	1880
Paul EVANS (1)	1261
PIPES And DRUMS And The MILITARY BAND Of The ROYAL SCOTS DRAGOON GUARDS (1)	1257
Ramsey LEWIS (1)	1134
Jimmie RODGERS (2)	813
Duane EDDY (1)	753
Johnny RIVERS (1)	654
Ritchie VALENS (1)	649
Don SHIRLEY/Trio (1)	597
The BEATLES (1)	519
Bill HALEY And His COMETS (1)	498
Trini LOPEZ (2)	442
BEVERLY SISTERS (1)	408
Fats DOMINO (1)	376
CAMBRIDGE STRINGS & SINGERS (1)	329

Otis REDDING (1)	318
Tommy LEONETTI (1)	316
Paul CHAPLAIN & His EMERALDS (1)	307
Herb ALPERT & The TIJUANA BRASS (1)	292
Red SKELTON (1)	287
JOINER, ARKANSAS JUNIOR HIGH SCHOOL BAND (1)	282
PURPLE REIGN (1)	264
Anthony NEWLEY (1)	226
Mickey NEWBURY (1)	222
Sil AUSTIN (1)	216
Bing CROSBY (6)	211
Don CORNELL (1)	172
FOUR PREPS (2)	154
Dave EDMUNDS (1)	146
Kay STARR (1)	127
"Tennessee" Ernie FORD (1)	106
FOUR ACES (1)	106
Ray STEVENS (1)	104
Teddy VANN (1)	97
SINGING DOGS (2)	95
Mahalia JACKSON (1)	78
Elvis PRESLEY (1)	69
The TOKENS (1)	62
SANTA ESMERALDA (1)	57
Ginger BAKER's Air Force (1)	52
BELL NOTES (1)	45
Olivia NEWTON-JOHN (1)	39
Bobby DARIN (1)	39
The OVATIONS (1)	34
David WHITFIELD (1)	25
Pete FOUNTAIN (1)	24
Dolly PARTON (1)	19
Floyd CRAMER (1)	17
DICK And DEEDEE (1)	15
CARLOS BROTHERS (1)	13
Pat BOONE (1)	12
PETER, PAUL & MARY (1)	12
Mason WILLIAMS (1)	11
BROTHERS FOUR (1)	9.1
Hawkshaw HAWKINS (1)	8.4
JOHNNY And The HURRICANES (2)	7.8
Martin MULL And Orchestra (1)	5.8
Lawrence WELK/Orchestra (1)	5.6
Patti PAGE (1)	4.3
Johnny CASH (1)	3.5
David SEVILLE And The CHIPMUNKS (1)	2.2
Turley RICHARDS (1)	2.1
Steve ALAIMO (1)	0.5
GUYS and The GALS (1)	0.0
Barbara McNAIR (1)	0.0
Jo MARCH (1)	0.0
Len DRESSLAR (1)	0.0
Bobby DARIN & The JAYBIRDS (1)	0.0
Jimmy GAVIN (1)	0.0
Merrill MOORE (1)	0.0
Andy GRIFFITH (1)	0.0
Barrett STRONG/ Norman WHITFIELD ► 14 (41) [17]	**70818**
The TEMPTATIONS (15)	34734
Marvin GAYE (4)	11412
Gladys KNIGHT & The PIPS (3)	8612
Edwin STARR (3)	8063
UNDISPUTED TRUTH (4)	4769
Bruce SPRINGSTEEN And The E STREET Band (1)	1264
Jimmy RUFFIN (1)	474

Mongo SANTAMARIA (1)	404
FOUR TOPS (1)	358
CREEDENCE CLEARWATER REVIVAL (1)	211
Al GREEN (1)	178
ROGER (1)	147
WOLF (1)	139
KING CURTIS & The KINGPINS (1)	21
CALIFORNIA RAISINS (1)	18
STARS ON 45 (1)	12
The WHATNAUTS (1)	1.7
Stevie WONDER ► 15 (43) [9]	**68537**
Stevie WONDER (30)	64171
RUFUS Featuring Chaka KHAN (1)	3531
Jermaine JACKSON (1)	323
Barbra STREISAND (1)	185
STARS ON 45 (6)	164
Julio IGLESIAS (1)	56
Ray CHARLES (1)	50
Stevie WONDER & Michael JACKSON (1)	44
B.J. THOMAS (1)	13
Kenneth GAMBLE/Leon HUFF ► 16 (83) [29]	**68287**
The O'JAYS (16)	16593
Harold MELVIN And The BLUE NOTES (5)	6441
MFSB (4)	5882
The INTRUDERS (2) (12)	5069
Lou RAWLS (5)	4452
3° DEGREES (1)	4029
SOUL SURVIVORS (3)	3900
JACKSON 5 (3)	3293
SIMPLY RED (1)	3293
Archie BELL & The DRELLS (6)	3283
Joe SIMON (2)	2672
Teddy PENDERGRASS (4)	1723
Wilson PICKETT (1)	1414
TIERRA (1)	1181
HEAVY D & The BOYZ (1)	1100
Billy PAUL (3)	790
Sharon PAIGE (1)	548
PEACHES & HERB (1)	534
JONES GIRLS (2)	516
THIRD WORLD (1)	333
The EBONYS (1)	293
Jerry BUTLER (1)	239
Dusty SPRINGFIELD (1)	203
RITCHIE FAMILY (2)	184
Arthur PRYSOCK (1)	167
MUSIC MAKERS (1)	78
Johnny WILLIAMS (1)	70
Nancy WILSON (1)	5.8
The DUPREES (1)	2.6
Doc POMUS/Mort SHUMAN ► 17 (59) [36]	**62642**
Elvis PRESLEY (9)	14639
The DRIFTERS (7)	13144
Andy WILLIAMS (2)	7128
Terry STAFFORD (1)	4565
FABIAN (4)	4530
JAY & The AMERICANS (2)	4120
DION And The BELMONTS (1)	3450
Jimmy CLANTON (2)	2553
DAMITA JO (1)	1268
The MYSTICS (1)	1163
DEFRANCO FAMILY (1)	886
Ray CHARLES (2)	695
Gene McDANIELS (2)	631
Bobby DARIN (1)	492
James DARREN (1)	443

Doc POMUS/Mort SHUMAN ▶ 17 (59) [36] *Cont'd*	**62642**
Gary (U.S.) BONDS (1)	409
Connie FRANCIS (1)	403
Dolly PARTON (1)	379
DION (1)	329
The FLAMINGOS (1)	230
Bobby RYDELL (1)	218
Tony ORLANDO (1)	198
Anita BRYANT (1)	195
FOUR PREPS (1)	130
Robert JOHN (2)	118
Bobby VINTON (1)	114
Frankie AVALON (1)	99
Ray PETERSON (1)	46
BEACH BOYS (1)	25
Ben E. KING (1)	17
Richie FURAY (1)	8.2
The TWINS (1)	6.8
Brenda LEE (1)	4.2
CENTRAL PARK WEST (1)	3.9
TEDDY And The TWILIGHTS (1)	1.4
Buddy KNOX (1)	0.4
Paul ANKA ▶ 18 (57) [17]	**61526**
Paul ANKA (40)	45848
Tom JONES (1)	6556
Donny OSMOND (1)	3699
Paul ANKA with Odia COATES (1)	2087
Buddy HOLLY/The CRICKETS (1)	1028
Connie FRANCIS (1)	701
The LETTERMEN (1)	571
ANNETTE (2)	468
5TH DIMENSION (1)	178
Leif GARRETT (1)	137
Don GOODWIN (1)	89
Patti PAGE (1)	52
Frank SINATRA (1)	48
Little Peggy MARCH (1)	33
Linda RONSTADT (1)	25
Mitch MILLER (1)	5.8
Bobby RYDELL (1)	1.9
Curtis MAYFIELD ▶ 19 (91) [22]	**59415**
The IMPRESSIONS (36)	22529
Major LANCE (11)	8482
Curtis MAYFIELD (10)	7335
STAPLE SINGERS (2)	4609
Brian HYLAND (1)	4320
Gene CHANDLER (8)	3624
Gladys KNIGHT & The PIPS (1)	1927
Jan BRADLEY (1)	1796
Aretha FRANKLIN (4)	898
Barbara MASON (1)	827
Jerry BUTLER (2)	826
MAIN INGREDIENT (1)	589
Johnny RIVERS (1)	422
Jeff BECK And Rod STEWART (1)	304
FIVE STAIRSTEPS (4)	269
Walter JACKSON (1)	261
Billy BUTLER & The CHANTERS (1)	236
The TUBES (1)	72
The FASCINATIONS (1)	69
The BARDS (1)	17
Curtis MAYFIELD & Linda CLIFFORD (1)	3.9
The FASINATIONS (1)	0.0
Howard GREENFIELD/ Neil SEDAKA ▶ 20 (45) [21]	**55941**
Neil SEDAKA (20)	30683
Connie FRANCIS (4)	9007
CAPTAIN & TENNILLE (2)	8500

Jimmy CLANTON (2)	1308
Tom JONES (1)	993
PARTRIDGE FAMILY (1)	734
5TH DIMENSION (1)	721
Lenny WELCH (1)	683
Clyde McPHATTER (1)	582
David JONES (1)	562
LaVern BAKER (1)	546
FRIENDS OF DISTINCTION (1)	407
CHER (1)	370
The HAPPENINGS (1)	309
Roy HAMILTON (1)	164
The CYRKLE (1)	162
AMERICAN COMEDY NETWORK (1)	82
Andy WILLIAMS (1)	80
Wayne NEWTON (1)	35
HEAVEN BOUND (1)	7.9
Bo DONALDSON And The HEYWOODS (1)	6.4
Barry MANN/Cynthia WEIL ▶ 21 (60) [41]	**55073**
RIGHTEOUS BROTHERS (1)	7442
Paul REVERE And The RAIDERS/RAIDERS (2)	6038
Sergio MENDES (2)	3891
Eydie GORME (2)	3531
B.J. THOMAS (2)	3277
The CRYSTALS (2)	2971
Dolly PARTON (1)	2755
Paul PETERSEN (2)	2625
Gene PITNEY (2)	2528
MAMA CASS (3)	2399
The DRIFTERS (3)	1877
Quincy JONES (1)	1525
The ANIMALS/Eric BURDON & The ANIMALS (1)	1474
James DARREN (2)	1441
Tony ORLANDO (1)	1332
Max FROST & The TROOPERS (1)	1289
Bill MEDLEY (3)	1136
The VOGUES (1)	1013
Steve LAWRENCE (1)	735
Shelley FABARES (1)	624
Johnny CRAWFORD (2)	624
PARTRIDGE FAMILY (1)	611
Leroy VAN DYKE (1)	496
Jody MILLER (1)	446
Donny And Marie OSMOND (1)	407
BLOOD, SWEAT & TEARS (1)	360
Kenny CHANDLER (1)	340
Jeffrey OSBORNE (1)	325
Frankie LAINE (1)	305
Glenn YARBROUGH (1)	234
The G-CLEFS (1)	174
Barry MANN (5)	166
Arthur ALEXANDER (1)	130
Wayne NEWTON (1)	116
GRASS ROOTS (1)	101
The TOKENS (1)	96
OLIVER (1)	76
BONNIE and The TREASURES (1)	67
Errol SOBER (1)	56
The WILL-O-BEES (1)	33
Barbra STREISAND (1)	5.7
Linda McCARTNEY/ Paul McCARTNEY ▶ 22 (21) [6]	**52385**
Paul McCARTNEY & WINGS/WINGS (16)	44763
Paul & Linda McCARTNEY (1)	4182
Paul McCARTNEY (1)	2814

GUNS N' ROSES (1)	506
Margie JOSEPH (1)	114
Rod STEWART (1)	6.2
Billy JOEL ▶ 23 (37) [1]	**52367**
Billy JOEL (37)	52367
Michael JACKSON ▶ 24 (16) [6]	**51588**
Michael JACKSON (11)	42906
Michael JACKSON/ Paul McCARTNEY (1)	5033
Diana ROSS (1)	1868
Rebbie JACKSON (1)	937
JACKSON 5 (1)	803
CLUB HOUSE (1)	40
Smokey ROBINSON ▶ 25 (57) [21]	**50651**
Mary WELLS (5)	14121
The MIRACLES/ Smokey ROBINSON & The MIRACLES (13)	8960
Smokey ROBINSON (8)	7485
The MARVELETTES (8)	6757
RARE EARTH (1)	4506
Kim CARNES (1)	1898
The SUPREMES (3)	1829
The TEMPTATIONS (2)	1195
Brenda HOLLOWAY (2)	833
The SUPREMES/ Diana ROSS And The SUPREMES (3)	783
Diana ROSS And The SUPREMES & The TEMPTATIONS (1)	738
SISTER SLEDGE (1)	585
A TASTE OF HONEY (1)	311
BRENDA & The TABULATIONS (1)	201
Eddie MONEY (1)	148
Petula CLARK (1)	132
Amii STEWART & Johnny BRISTOL (1)	99
Bob BRADY (1)	46
Chuck JACKSON (1)	16
Billy Joe ROYAL (1)	3.6
Gayle McCORMICK (1)	2.8
Bob DYLAN ▶ 26 (49) [22]	**49250**
Bob DYLAN (20)	20630
The BYRDS (4)	7655
PETER, PAUL & MARY (4)	6287
MANFRED MANN (3)	2910
The TURTLES (1)	2181
Stevie WONDER (1)	1913
CHER (1)	1745
WONDER WHO? (1)	1628
Olivia NEWTON-JOHN (1)	1107
Jimi HENDRIX Experience (1)	944
Rick NELSON And The STONE CANYON BAND (1)	865
Johnny CASH (1)	326
MANFRED MANN'S EARTH BAND (1)	199
Bob DYLAN/The BAND (1)	177
ISLEY BROTHERS (1)	173
BOX TOPS (1)	156
Turley RICHARDS (1)	144
Joan BAEZ (1)	93
FERRANTE & TEICHER (1)	60
Phil FLOWERS & The FLOWER SHOP (1)	27
BEAU BRUMMELS (1)	21
GRASS ROOTS (1)	7.4
Sam COOKE ▶ 27 (60) [31]	**48388**
Sam COOKE (28)	35105

DR. HOOK (1)	2695
The SPINNERS (1)	1698
Cat STEVENS (1)	1628
Eddie FLOYD (1)	1280
Johnny NASH (1)	801
Tony ORLANDO And DAWN (1)	689
Teresa BREWER (1)	505
The ANIMALS/Eric BURDON & The ANIMALS (1)	470
The FLAMINGOS (1)	468
Carla THOMAS (1)	412
Rod STEWART (2)	394
SIMS TWINS (1)	365
Otis REDDING (1)	331
SAM & DAVE (1)	309
Johnnie MORISETTE (1)	212
PONDEROSA TWINS + ONE (1)	168
Luther INGRAM (1)	163
Aretha FRANKLIN (1)	126
Jackie WILSON And COUNT BASIE (1)	123
Johnny RIVERS (1)	115
Luther VANDROSS (1)	96
Jim CROCE (1)	76
The OVATIONS (2)	67
BRITISH WALKERS (1)	35
The MANHATTANS (1)	22
Ray CHARLES (1)	12
5TH DIMENSION (1)	11
Lou RAWLS (1)	9.8
Johnnie TAYLOR (1)	1.4
Plas JOHNSON & His Orchestra (1)	0.0
Mike LOVE/Brian WILSON ▶ 28 (39) [10]	**48191**
BEACH BOYS (26)	42144
David Lee ROTH (1)	2548
The HONDELLS (1)	2173
Johnny RIVERS (1)	596
Todd RUNDGREN (1)	391
Paul DAVIS (1)	215
YIPES!! (1)	80
Hugo MONTENEGRO (1)	23
BRUCE And TERRY (1)	14
MECO (5)	7.7
Bob CREWE/Bob GAUDIO ▶ 29 (28) [14]	**48175**
4 SEASONS (10)	32755
Frankie VALLI (5)	9264
The TREMELOES/Brian POOLE And The TREMELOES (1)	2043
The LETTERMEN (1)	1323
WALKER BROS. (1)	1271
The OSMONDS (1)	633
MARY JANE GIRLS (1)	290
Nancy WILSON (1)	255
NIELSEN/PEARSON (1)	168
Jerry BUTLER (1)	65
SHEPHERD SISTERS (1)	58
PET SHOP BOYS (1)	37
GIDEA PARK (2)	7.4
FUZZY BUNNIES (1)	6.0
John FOGERTY ▶ 30 (30) [8]	**47537**
CREEDENCE CLEARWATER REVIVAL (17)	40983
John FOGERTY (7)	3015
Ike & Tina TURNER (1)	2683
Solomon BURKE (1)	406
Al WILSON (1)	250
Dave EDMUNDS (1)	103
CHECKMATES, LTD. (1)	93
BLUE RIDGE RANGERS (1)	2.9

Dave APPELL/Kal MANN ► 31 (35) [10]	**43882**
The ORLONS (6)	13917
Chubby CHECKER (10)	12290
The DOVELLS (4)	7775
Dee Dee SHARP (6)	6227
Bobby RYDELL (3)	2836
The APPLEJACKS (1)	423
Don COVAY (1)	223
JIVE BUNNY & THE MASTERMIXERS (2)	86
Bobby RYDELL - Chubby CHECKER (1)	84
Jo Ann CAMPBELL (1)	20
John D. LOUDERMILK ► 32 (43) [34]	**43823**
Sue THOMPSON (4)	9785
Paul REVERE And The RAIDERS/RAIDERS (1)	8111
The CASINOS (1)	3592
George HAMILTON IV (1)	2627
EVERLY BROTHERS (1)	2520
Johnny TILLOTSON (1)	2470
Connie FRANCIS (2)	1727
NASHVILLE TEENS (1)	1529
DICK And DEEDEE (1)	1357
Kris JENSEN (1)	1250
John D. LOUDERMILK (5)	1233
The NEWBEATS (1)	1158
Glen CAMPBELL (2)	1032
Don FARDON (1)	1027
Eddie COCHRAN (1)	856
Bobby VEE (1)	743
Johnny FERGUSON (1)	718
Sandy POSEY (1)	513
Marianne FAITHFULL (1)	498
LENNON SISTERS (1)	303
TOBY BEAU (1)	257
Mark DINNING (1)	160
Eddy ARNOLD (1)	137
Billy GRAVES (1)	78
Marvin RAINWATER (1)	72
Cecelia BATTEN (1)	53
JAMUL (1)	6.9
Bob LUMAN (1)	4.5
Bobby WOOD (1)	3.3
Boots RANDOLPH (1)	2.2
Eddie FONTAINE (1)	0.0
Carol HUGHES (1)	0.0
Don CORNELL (1)	0.0
Ernest ASHWORTH (1)	0.0
George MICHAEL ► 33 (16) [2]	**43698**
George MICHAEL (10)	28845
WHAM! (6)	14853
James Samuel HARRIS/ Terry LEWIS ► 34 (31) [15]	**40635**
Janet JACKSON (6)	18836
HUMAN LEAGUE (1)	4223
Ralph TRESVANT (1)	2969
Johnny GILL (2)	2767
Robert PALMER (1)	2661
Herb ALPERT (3)	2387
NEW EDITION (3)	2096
FORCE M.D.'S (1)	1303
Alexander O'NEAL (3)	1294
S.O.S. BAND (4)	1008
CHERRELLE (2)	655
Patti AUSTIN (1)	211
Cheryl LYNN (1)	117
BEATS INTERNATIONAL (1)	72
BINGOBOYS (1)	35
Sylvester STEWART ► 35 (30) [12]	**39545**

SLY & THE FAMILY STONE (18)	35633
LITTLE SISTER (2)	1921
Ike & Tina TURNER (1)	690
Sly STONE (1)	349
Joan JETT & The BLACKHEARTS (1)	291
ABACO DREAM (1)	232
3° DEGREES (1)	198
DAYTON (1)	117
David T. WALKER (1)	76
WEST STREET MOB (1)	16
STARS ON 45 (1)	12
LOVE CHILDS AFRO CUBAN BLUES BAND (1)	10
Bruce SPRINGSTEEN ► 36 (27) [8]	**39059**
Bruce SPRINGSTEEN (16)	23804
MANFRED MANN'S EARTH BAND (4)	5235
POINTER SISTERS (1)	5172
Gary (U.S.) BONDS (2)	2342
Natalie COLE (1)	1871
Joan JETT & The BLACKHEARTS (1)	373
Bruce SPRINGSTEEN And The E STREET Band (1)	242
The HOLLIES (1)	19
Harry Wayne CASEY/Rick FINCH ► 37 (21) [4]	**38687**
KC & The SUNSHINE BAND (14)	32951
George McCRAE (5)	5142
Jimmy "Bo" HORNE (1)	502
RITCHIE FAMILY (1)	92
Chuck BERRY ► 38 (50) [23]	**38128**
Chuck BERRY (27)	23006
Johnny RIVERS (1)	5249
Lonnie MACK (1)	2755
BEACH BOYS (1)	2213
Linda RONSTADT (1)	1061
Dave CLARK Five (1)	935
Elvis PRESLEY (1)	900
ELECTRIC LIGHT ORCHESTRA (1)	593
The BEATLES (2)	315
Ronnie HAWKINS (1)	276
Tommy ROE (1)	218
The VELAIRES (1)	171
CAT MOTHER and the ALL NIGHT NEWS BOYS (1)	164
DION (1)	147
Peter TOSH (1)	43
Bill BLACK'S Combo (1)	42
The CORONADOS (1)	17
Johnny WINTER (1)	11
Jerry Lee LEWIS (1)	7.2
JIVE BUNNY & The MASTERMIXERS (1)	6.7
Ernest TUBB (1)	0.0
"Big" Tiny LITTLE (1)	0.0
Helene DIXON (1)	0.0
Bernard EDWARDS/ Nile RODGERS ► 39 (18) [6]	**37934**
CHIC (9)	19792
Diana ROSS (2)	10508
SISTER SLEDGE (3)	6636
SUGARHILL GANG (1)	551
Debbie HARRY (2)	362
Carly SIMON (1)	86
Eddie BRIGATI/Felix CAVALIERE ► 40 (13) [5]	**37250**
YOUNG RASCALS/RASCALS (9)	34993
BOOKER T. & The M.G.'s (1)	957
David CASSIDY (1)	939
Pat BENATAR (1)	350

5TH DIMENSION (1)	11
Jimmy WEBB ► 41 (37) [28]	**37215**
Glen CAMPBELL (5)	12672
Donna SUMMER (1)	6578
Richard HARRIS (3)	5728
5TH DIMENSION (4)	4394
BROOKLYN BRIDGE (1)	4091
Art GARFUNKEL (1)	1911
FOUR TOPS (1)	486
Isaac HAYES (1)	341
Linda RONSTADT (1)	192
Hugh MASEKELA (1)	169
Bobby VEE (1)	145
Barbra STREISAND (1)	131
Joey SCARBURY (1)	66
Nina SIMONE (1)	55
MAD LADS (1)	43
Mark LINDSAY (1)	39
Glen CAMPBELL/ Anne MURRAY (1)	38
LOVE GENERATION (1)	37
Paul REVERE And The RAIDERS/RAIDERS (1)	24
PICARDY (1)	16
Johnny MANN Singers (1)	13
Shane MARTIN (1)	13
Al WILSON (1)	12
Waylon JENNINGS And The KIMBERLYS (1)	9.8
Roger WILLIAMS (1)	6.0
Sergio MENDES & BRASIL '66 (1)	3.5
AL CAPPS Band (1)	0.8
Joe COCKER (1)	0.0
John LENNON ► 42 (18) [6]	**37009**
John LENNON (9)	24874
John LENNON/ PLASTIC ONO BAND (5)	11042
The LETTERMEN (1)	589
Ringo STARR (1)	340
Barbra STREISAND (1)	130
Tracie SPENCER (1)	35
Paul McCARTNEY ► 43 (22) [5]	**36735**
Paul McCARTNEY & WINGS/WINGS (7)	16780
Paul McCARTNEY (12)	15170
BADFINGER (1)	3078
PETER And GORDON (1)	1438
EVERLY BROTHERS (1)	269
Jerry FULLER ► 44 (14) [7]	**36638**
Gary PUCKETT And The UNION GAP (3)	16148
Rick NELSON (5)	14521
Al WILSON (2)	5696
DINO, DESI & BILLY (1)	226
The CASCADES (1)	27
Jerry FULLER (1)	11
O.C. SMITH (1)	9.1
David GATES ► 45 (29) [11]	**36386**
BREAD (13)	26935
The MURMAIDS (2)	4908
David GATES (6)	3257
Gladys KNIGHT & The PIPS (1)	706
The GIRLFRIENDS (1)	305
Mark LINDSAY (1)	106
Brenda LEE (1)	82
Vicki Sue ROBINSON (1)	50
The WHISPERS (1)	16
Telly SAVALAS (1)	14
Ralfi PAGAN (1)	7.4
Diane WARREN ► 46 (25) [20]	**35241**
Taylor DAYNE (2)	5411
CHICAGO (2)	4587

CHER (2)	3780
Michael BOLTON (2)	3583
MILLI VANILLI (1)	3458
BAD ENGLISH (1)	3290
DeBARGE (1)	3157
Belinda CARLISLE (1)	2442
HEART (2)	2074
Roberta FLACK (1)	1968
EXPOSÉ (1)	825
CHEAP TRICK (1)	214
Bette MIDLER (1)	111
El DeBARGE With DeBARGE (1)	106
Joe COCKER (1)	59
John WAITE (1)	54
Patti LaBELLE (1)	53
DION (1)	39
The JETS (1)	18
KEEDY (1)	13
Jeff BARRY/Ellie GREENWICH/ Phil SPECTOR ► 47 (23) [15]	**33864**
DIXIE CUPS (1)	8316
The RONETTES (3)	6784
The CRYSTALS (4)	6608
Shaun CASSIDY (1)	4512
Andy KIM (2)	4019
SUPREMES & FOUR TOPS (1)	1281
BEACH BOYS (1)	916
Darlene LOVE (2)	841
DEEP PURPLE (1)	351
BOB B. SOXX And The BLUE JEANS (1)	171
Ike & Tina TURNER (2)	26
Cissy HOUSTON (1)	24
Ian MATTHEWS (1)	7.8
The BUTTERFLYS (1)	7.3
Bette MIDLER (1)	0.0
Phil COLLINS ► 48 (16) [2]	**33504**
Phil COLLINS (14)	31772
GENESIS (2)	1732
Robert ALLEN/Al STILLMAN ► 49 (26) [13]	**33148**
FOUR LADS (7)	16563
Johnny MATHIS (4)	11098
Tony BENNETT (1)	1683
Pat BOONE (1)	1550
Perry COMO (2)	790
The VOGUES (2)	696
Jane MORGAN (3)	388
SMOKE RING (1)	215
Dinah SHORE (1)	132
Richard MALTBY And His Orchestra (1)	14
Jo STAFFORD (1)	14
Frankie LAINE (1)	5.1
Cyril STAPLETON And His Orchestra (1)	0.0
John DENSMORE/ Robby KRIEGER/ Ray MANZAREK/ Jim MORRISON ► 50 (16) [5]	**33087**
The DOORS (12)	27837
José FELICIANO (1)	4958
Billy IDOL (1)	208
Amii STEWART (1)	51
Rhetta HUGHES (1)	33
STING ► 51 (20) [2]	**32092**
The POLICE (12)	22597
STING (8)	9495
George HARRISON ► 52 (31) [11]	**31637**
George HARRISON (16)	24231
The BEATLES (3)	5251
Richie HAVENS (1)	1210

George HARRISON ► 52 (31) [11] *Cont'd*	**31637**
Ringo STARR (1)	380
Shirley BASSEY (1)	247
Ronnie SPECTOR (1)	173
BOOKER T. & The M.G.'s (1)	66
STARS ON 45 (4)	32
Billy PRESTON (1)	28
Johnny RODRIGUEZ (1)	14
SILVER HAWK (1)	3.4
Tony HATCH ► 53 (20) [14]	**31273**
Petula CLARK (6)	21587
Bobby RYDELL (1)	3638
Garry MILES (1)	1432
Billy VAUGHN and His Orchestra (1)	1083
Chris MONTEZ (1)	891
Deane HAWLEY (1)	777
Garry MILLS (1)	739
CRYAN' SHAMES (1)	491
The SEARCHERS (1)	320
Connie FRANCIS (2)	249
Mrs. MILLER (1)	27
Dolly PARTON (1)	25
PETER And GORDON (1)	11
Nicky COMO (1)	0.0
Berry GORDY/ Fonce MIZELL/ Freddie PERREN/ Deke RICHARDS ► 54 (8) [2]	**31174**
JACKSON 5 (7)	30877
MARTHA & The VANDELLAS (1)	298
Dave BARTHOLOMEW/ Fats DOMINO ► 55 (44) [13]	**30995**
Fats DOMINO (31)	19467
Pat BOONE (1)	6966
Rick NELSON (2)	1128
Teresa BREWER (1)	908
4 SEASONS (1)	760
Jerry JAYE (1)	721
CHEAP TRICK (1)	411
FONTANE SISTERS (1)	355
Roy BROWN (1)	280
Bill CAREY (1)	0.0
Larry STORCH (1)	0.0
BONNIE LOU (1)	0.0
Ronnie GAYLORD (1)	0.0
Rod TEMPERTON ► 56 (13) [8]	**30965**
Michael JACKSON (3)	10841
HEATWAVE (3)	8859
Patti AUSTIN (1)	5139
George BENSON (2)	2983
Michael McDONALD (1)	1812
KLYMAXX (1)	859
WHISTLE (1)	449
BROTHERS JOHNSON (1)	23
Hank BALLARD ► 57 (10) [5]	**30489**
Chubby CHECKER (2)	22920
Hank BALLARD And The MIDNIGHTERS (5)	6833
FAT BOYS (1)	725
JIVE BUNNY & The MASTERMIXERS (1)	6.7
Ernie FREEMAN (1)	3.6
Joe MELSON/Roy ORBISON ► 58 (17) [9]	**30289**
Roy ORBISON (9)	22572
Linda RONSTADT (1)	4470
Don McLEAN (1)	2185
JAY & The AMERICANS (1)	569
Jerry BYRD (1)	244
The FOOLS (1)	170
The VELVETS (1)	55
Sonny JAMES (1)	23
Gene McCANNON (1)	0.5
Galt MacDERMOT/ James RADO/ Gerome RAGNI ► 59 (12) [9]	**30206**
5TH DIMENSION (2)	11805
The COWSILLS (1)	8011
THREE DOG NIGHT (1)	5385
OLIVER (1)	4408
The HAPPENINGS (2)	418
HAIR (Original Soundtrack)/ Cheryl BARNES (1)	76
Carla THOMAS (1)	45
STRAWBERRY ALARM CLOCK (1)	45
Nina SIMONE (2)	14
Boudleaux BRYANT ► 60 (23) [18]	**30079**
EVERLY BROTHERS (5)	18218
Bob MOORE and His Orchestra (1)	2888
Bob LUMAN (1)	2859
NAZARETH (1)	2521
Richard CHAMBERLAIN (1)	1309
Bobbie GENTRY & Glen CAMPBELL (1)	694
Frankie LAINE (1)	482
Carly SIMON & James TAYLOR (1)	345
Jim REEVES (1)	298
Andy GIBB And Victoria PRINCIPAL (1)	206
NITTY GRITTY DIRT BAND (1)	161
FOUR LADS (1)	63
Eddy ARNOLD (2)	25
Jim CAPALDI (1)	6.4
The BROWNS (1)	4.7
Rusty DRAPER (1)	0.0
Chuck MILLER (1)	0.0
Bobby LORD (1)	0.0
L. Russell BROWN/Irwin LEVINE ► 61 (17) [7]	**29304**
Tony ORLANDO And DAWN (8)	25367
PARTRIDGE FAMILY (2)	2264
DUSK (3)	870
Beverly BREMERS (1)	654
ROCK FLOWERS (1)	143
Jimmy DRUIETT (1)	5.2
Connie FRANCIS (1)	0.7
John FARRAR ► 62 (10) [3]	**29067**
Olivia NEWTON-JOHN (8)	21203
John TRAVOLTA And Olivia NEWTON-JOHN (1)	6783
Olivia NEWTON-JOHN & Cliff RICHARD (1)	1080
James BROWN ► 63 (46) [12]	**28939**
James BROWN (35)	24503
The DARTELLS (1)	1481
Otis REDDING (1)	821
The J.B.'s (1)	658
Joey DEE & The STARLITERS (1)	476
Lyn COLLINS (1)	362
Anna KING (1)	183
Nat KENDRICK And The SWANS (1)	170
Jimmy HUGHES (1)	134
Bobby BYRD (1)	97
MACEO And The MACKS (1)	45
Steve ALAIMO (1)	9.3
Nick ASHFORD/ Valerie SIMPSON ► 64 (41) [17]	**28849**
Diana ROSS (5)	10338
Marvin GAYE & Tammi TERRELL (9)	10116
ASHFORD & SIMPSON (9)	2269
Aretha FRANKLIN (2)	1104
Chaka KHAN (2)	992
Donny And Marie OSMOND (1)	755
5TH DIMENSION (1)	740
The SUPREMES/ Diana ROSS And The SUPREMES (1)	717
Gladys KNIGHT & The PIPS (2)	521
The MIRACLES/ Smokey ROBINSON & The MIRACLES (1)	316
Tony ORLANDO And DAWN (1)	303
Johnny MATHIS/Deniece WILLIAMS (1)	206
The MARVELETTES (1)	203
DYNAMIC SUPERIORS (1)	112
ACE SPECTRUM (1)	73
Bobby TAYLOR & The VANCOUVERS (1)	68
Chris CHRISTIAN (2)	16
John DENVER ► 65 (26) [6]	**28116**
John DENVER (21)	19130
PETER, PAUL & MARY (1)	7725
Cliff DeYOUNG (1)	929
Mary TRAVERS (1)	260
Placido DOMINGO & John DENVER (1)	70
Gloria LORING (1)	2.2
Sonny BONO ► 66 (22) [6]	**27972**
SONNY & CHER (13)	17898
CHER (4)	7362
SONNY (2)	1976
UB40 (1)	480
Etta JAMES (1)	239
Lawrence WELK/Orchestra (1)	16
Joe SOUTH ► 67 (29) [17]	**27543**
Lynn ANDERSON (2)	5951
The OSMONDS (1)	5693
Joe SOUTH (7)	4786
Billy Joe ROYAL (5)	4643
DEEP PURPLE (1)	3508
Paul REVERE And The RAIDERS/RAIDERS (1)	1026
Linda RONSTADT (1)	501
Brook BENTON (1)	381
Johnny RIVERS (1)	311
The TAMS (2)	254
Dorsey BURNETTE (1)	221
BLUE SWEDE (1)	92
Joe SIMON (1)	65
Donny OSMOND (1)	47
The CLASSICS (1) (1)	32
Billy HARNER (1)	27
Dobie GRAY (1)	3.3
Jeff LYNNE ► 68 (29) [6]	**27441**
ELECTRIC LIGHT ORCHESTRA (24)	24720
Olivia NEWTON-JOHN/ ELECTRIC LIGHT ORCHESTRA (1)	1996
Dave EDMUNDS (1)	521
Odia COATES (1)	152
The MOVE (1)	36
Jeff LYNNE (1)	17
Mike CHAPMAN/Nicky CHINN ► 69 (18) [8]	**27210**
EXILE (3)	8245
The SWEET (4)	6809
Toni BASIL (1)	5959
Suzi QUATRO And Chris NORMAN (1)	2721
Huey LEWIS and the NEWS (1)	1620
SMOKIE (2)	942
Suzi QUATRO (5)	910
Jay BLACK (1)	2.9
Barry GIBB/Robin GIBB ► 70 (13) [6]	**27089**
BEE GEES (7)	11559
Barbra STREISAND (2)	7523
Samantha SANG (1)	5831
Yvonne ELLIMAN (1)	1469
Olivia NEWTON-JOHN (1)	650
SWEET INSPIRATIONS (1)	56
John SEBASTIAN ► 71 (20) [9]	**26800**
LOVIN' SPOONFUL (9)	18924
John SEBASTIAN (3)	5413
The CRITTERS (1)	855
The HONDELLS (1)	678
Bobby DARIN (2)	524
Shaun CASSIDY (1)	359
BEAU BRUMMELS (1)	30
The ASSOCIATION (1)	9.9
David CASSIDY (1)	6.4
Lee POCKRISS/Paul VANCE ► 72 (26) [19]	**26655**
Brian HYLAND (2)	7538
Clint HOLMES (1)	5118
CUFF LINKS (3)	4034
Perry COMO (1)	3980
The PLAYMATES (3)	2203
The DETERGENTS (2)	1213
Johnny TILLOTSON (1)	894
Johnny MATHIS (1)	700
SALVAGE (1)	303
Dodie STEVENS (1)	202
2 OF CLUBS (1)	193
Jerry VALE (2)	115
Derrik ROBERTS (1)	89
Randy STARR (1)	37
LEE And PAUL (1)	13
June VALLI (1)	11
Oliver COOL (1)	6.5
Paul VANCE (1)	3.7
Buddy HACKETT (1)	0.0
Laura NYRO ► 73 (13) [7]	**26210**
5TH DIMENSION (5)	15106
BLOOD, SWEAT & TEARS (1)	5381
THREE DOG NIGHT (1)	2845
Barbra STREISAND (3)	2666
Thelma HOUSTON (1)	131
Peggy LIPTON (1)	76
Laura NYRO (1)	5.1
Bobby RUSSELL ► 74 (13) [10]	**26194**
Bobby GOLDSBORO (1)	9605
O.C. SMITH (2)	6072
Vicki LAWRENCE (1)	5615
Gary LEWIS And The PLAYBOYS (1)	1553
Bobby RUSSELL (2)	1400
Brian HYLAND (1)	1079
Roger MILLER (2)	671
Percy SLEDGE (1)	134
Roy CLARK (1)	63
Patti PAGE (1)	3.5
Donovan LEITCH ► 75 (20) [5]	**25987**
DONOVAN (16)	25329
HERMAN'S HERMITS (1)	523
VANILLA FUDGE (1)	133
Willie BOBO (1)	1.4
SENATOR BOBBY And SENATOR McKINLEY (1)	1.0

Buck RAM ► 76 (25) [17]	**25545**
The PLATTERS (9)	18208
Franck POURCEL (1)	2646
The HILLTOPPERS (1)	2041
Ringo STARR (1)	1985
FONTANE SISTERS (1)	444
Cornel GUNTER and The FLAIRS (1)	75
Tony MARTIN (1)	61
Tony WILLIAMS (1)	27
Mr. Acker BILK (1)	27
Bobby HATFIELD (1)	14
Wayne NEWTON (1)	12
FIVE SATINS (1)	4.8
Stan FREBERG (1)	0.0
Jackie RIGGS (1)	0.0
The DRIFTERS (1)	0.0
The COLTS (1)	0.0
Lola DEE (1)	0.0
Dennis DeYOUNG ► 77 (16) [2]	**25463**
STYX (12)	23771
Dennis DeYOUNG (4)	1692
Marty ROBBINS ► 78 (26) [9]	**24953**
Marty ROBBINS (18)	21900
Johnnie RAY (1)	1585
Frankie LAINE (1)	1278
Johnny CASH And The TENNESSEE TWO/THREE (1)	92
Rusty YORK (1)	68
Johnny DESMOND (1)	27
Dean MARTIN (1)	1.7
LA DELL SISTERS (1)	0.0
Hank BALLARD And The MIDNIGHTERS (1)	0.0
John MELLENCAMP ► 79 (19) [1]	**24943**
John MELLENCAMP (19)	24943
Bernie LOWE/Kal MANN ► 80 (26) [20]	**24931**
Elvis PRESLEY (2)	7797
Bobby RYDELL (3)	5037
Andy WILLIAMS (1)	4791
Charlie GRACIE (4)	2911
Pat BOONE (1)	1255
Chubby CHECKER (1)	929
Tab HUNTER (1)	920
Timmie ROGERS (1)	476
Billy SCOTT (1)	181
Sal MINEO (1)	112
The UPBEATS (1)	102
FOUR COINS (1)	94
Georgia GIBBS (1)	85
Bob CARROLL (1)	81
Steve LAWRENCE (1)	80
KISS (1)	56
Don CHERRY (1)	17
Billy MAY And His Orchestra (1)	5.0
Valerie CARR (1)	0.0
Billy WILLIAMS (1)	0.0
Jeff BARRY/Ellie GREENWICH ► 81 (23) [16]	**24554**
MANFRED MANN (1)	8308
Tommy JAMES And The SHONDELLS (1)	6771
Lesley GORE (2)	2302
DIXIE CUPS (3)	2094
The RAINDROPS (4)	1910
JELLY BEANS (1)	1628
The SHANGRI-LAS (2)	729
Connie FRANCIS (1)	442
Ray PETERSON (1)	149
The DRIFTERS (1)	146
The EXCITERS (1)	55
STARS ON 45 (1)	12
BABY JANE & The ROCKABYES (1)	3.2
FOUR PENNIES (1)	2.7
TIGHT FIT (1)	0.9
AD LIBS (1)	0.5
Dennis LAMBERT/Brian POTTER ► 82 (38) [24]	**24258**
FOUR TOPS (5)	7486
HAMILTON, JOE FRANK & REYNOLDS (3)	5440
TAVARES (4)	2862
Glen CAMPBELL (2)	1415
COVEN (3)	1170
RIGHTEOUS BROTHERS (2)	1016
Tony ORLANDO And DAWN (1)	930
Gene REDDING (1)	878
ORIGINAL CASTE (1)	801
Gayle McCORMICK (2)	674
GRASS ROOTS (1)	555
5TH DIMENSION (1)	307
Evie SANDS (1)	254
Paul REVERE And The RAIDERS/RAIDERS (1)	131
SANTANA (1)	117
The EMOTIONS (1)	91
HOT (1)	52
Kiki DEE (1)	37
COUNTRY STORE (1)	16
SAM & DAVE (1)	11
Bo DONALDSON And The HEYWOODS (1)	7.0
Dusty SPRINGFIELD (1)	6.5
DIAMOND HEAD (1)	2.2
Sergio MENDES & BRASIL '66 (1)	0.7
Al GREEN/Al JACKSON/ Willie MITCHELL ► 83 (7) [3]	**24197**
Al GREEN (5)	23103
Tina TURNER (1)	755
Isaac HAYES (1)	340
Bob SEGER ► 84 (28) [4]	**24115**
Bob SEGER & The SILVER BULLET BAND (12)	10558
Bob SEGER (10)	9856
Kenny ROGERS & Sheena EASTON (1)	2255
Bob SEGER System (5)	1446
Mac DAVIS ► 85 (21) [11]	**24068**
Elvis PRESLEY (2)	8294
Mac DAVIS (9)	7456
Kenny ROGERS And The FIRST EDITION (1)	2846
Bobby GOLDSBORO (1)	1958
GALLERY (1)	1440
O.C. SMITH (2)	943
Candi STATON (1)	603
Glen CAMPBELL (1)	358
Mark LINDSAY (1)	105
Nancy SINATRA (1)	56
Marian LOVE (1)	10
Otis BLACKWELL/Elvis PRESLEY ► 86 (9) [6]	**24053**
Elvis PRESLEY (4)	19336
Bill BLACK'S Combo (1)	2335
CHEAP TRICK (1)	2074
Suzi QUATRO (1)	154
JIVE BUNNY & THE MASTERMIXERS (1)	80
Barbara LYNN (1)	74
Lou GRAMM/ Michael Leslie JONES ► 87 (14) [1]	**23773**
FOREIGNER (14)	23773
Ray PARKER Jr. ► 88 (15) [3]	**23646**
Ray PARKER Jr./RAYDIO (13)	22453
NEW EDITION (1)	1152
Maxine NIGHTINGALE (1)	42
Pete TOWNSHEND ► 89 (34) [5]	**23572**
The WHO (26)	19112
Pete TOWNSHEND (4)	2175
ASSEMBLED MULTITUDE (1)	1183
NEW SEEKERS (2)	819
Roger DALTREY (1)	284
Allen TOUSSAINT ► 90 (35) [22]	**23464**
Ernie K-DOE (4)	8761
Glen CAMPBELL (1)	4988
Lee DORSEY (8)	4036
POINTER SISTERS (3)	2103
THREE DOG NIGHT (1)	712
DEVO (1)	495
HUES CORPORATION (1)	421
The O'JAYS (2)	354
Joe COCKER (1)	348
Otis REDDING (1)	332
The UNIQUES (1)	262
Warren ZEVON (1)	191
Herb ALPERT & The TIJUANA BRASS (1)	154
Clarence CARTER (1)	106
Betty HARRIS (1)	93
Benny SPELLMAN (1)	73
Judy CLAY (1)	23
STEFAN (1)	4.2
CHOCOLATE MILK (1)	2.9
The HARDTIMES (1)	2.9
Robert PALMER (1)	2.8
The STOKES (1)	0.0
Howard GREENFIELD/ Jack KELLER ► 91 (9) [6]	**23454**
Connie FRANCIS (3)	20370
Jimmy CLANTON (1)	2008
Brenda LEE (1)	676
Patti PAGE (2)	380
Cathy CARROLL (1)	21
Billy CARR (1)	0.5
Simon Le BON/Nick RHODES/ Andy TAYLOR/ Nigel John TAYLOR/ Roger TAYLOR ► 92 (8) [1]	**23454**
DURAN DURAN (8)	23454
Boudleaux BRYANT/ Felice BRYANT ► 93 (27) [18]	**22826**
EVERLY BROTHERS (8)	20581
Sue THOMPSON (3)	913
SIMON & GARFUNKEL (1)	477
Leo SAYER (1)	267
Ray CHARLES (1)	156
The BROWNS (1)	126
Webb PIERCE (1)	109
JIVE BUNNY & THE MASTERMIXERS (1)	80
Roy CLARK (1)	48
Bob MOORE and His Orchestra (1)	33
Buddy HOLLY/ The CRICKETS (1)	13
Solomon KING (1)	7.8
Eddie ALBERT (1)	6.0
Will JORDAN (1)	5.6
EASY RIDERS (1)	2.4
KALIN TWINS (1)	1.5
Chuck MILLER (1)	0.0
T. TOMMY (1)	0.0
Dino FEKARIS/Freddie PERREN ► 94 (13) [7]	**22740**
PEACHES & HERB (5)	11798
Gloria GAYNOR (3)	7404
David NAUGHTON (1)	2897
SA-FIRE (1)	247
The RAES (1)	209
Demis ROUSSOS (1)	173
BAND OF GOLD (1)	12
Ray EVANS/Jay LIVINGSTON ► 95 (31) [30]	**22683**
Debbie REYNOLDS (1)	9194
Doris DAY (1)	6972
The PLATTERS (1)	1235
Carl MANN (1)	948
Al CAIOLA And His Orchestra (1)	895
AMES BROTHERS (1)	793
Conway TWITTY (1)	581
HIGH KEYES (1)	355
Gunter KALLMANN Chorus (1)	327
Johnny MATHIS (1)	327
Mary HOPKIN (1)	259
Frankie LAINE (1)	170
Johnny NASH (1)	153
MANTOVANI And His Orchestra (1)	109
The TYMES (1)	100
Patti PAGE (1)	82
Tony BENNETT (1)	70
Bing CROSBY and Carol RICHARDS (2)	53
Sam COOKE (1)	36
Nat King COLE (1)	20
Johnny CASH (1)	3.2
Don ROBERTSON (1)	0.5
Les BAXTER (1)	0.0
Don COSTA And His Orchestra (1)	0.0
Eydie GORME (1)	0.0
Richard HAYMAN And His Orchestra (1)	0.0
Pat KIRBY (1)	0.0
Bill SNYDER (1)	0.0
Joseph GERSHENSON & The UNIVERSAL-INTERNATIONAL Orchestra (1)	0.0
Eddy HOWARD (1)	0.0
Daryl HALL ► 96 (12) [3]	**22360**
Daryl HALL & John OATES (9)	17652
Paul YOUNG (1)	4062
Daryl HALL (2)	646
Ray DAVIES ► 97 (28) [5]	**22236**
The KINKS (24)	19524
HERMAN'S HERMITS (1)	2256
VAN HALEN (1)	352
The PRETENDERS (1)	103
TIGHT FIT (1)	0.9
Rick SPRINGFIELD ► 98 (18) [2]	**22219**
Rick SPRINGFIELD (17)	22058
Rick SPRINGFIELD & Randy CRAWFORD (1)	160
Thom BELL/Linda CREED ► 99 (17) [7]	**22156**
The STYLISTICS (6)	14113
The SPINNERS (4)	6646
Ronnie DYSON (1)	768
Johnny MATHIS (2)	425
LITTLE ANTHONY And The IMPERIALS (1)	106
NEW YORK CITY (1)	75
BAND OF GOLD (2)	23

Lee HAZLEWOOD ▶ 100 (26) [12]	**21631**
Nancy SINATRA (12)	15584
Sanford CLARK (3)	2261
Nancy SINATRA & Lee HAZLEWOOD (2)	1113
Dean MARTIN (1)	935
DINO, DESI & BILLY (1)	671
Al CASEY (1)	402
Frank SINATRA (1)	336
The GALLAHADS (1)	209
KON KAN (1)	78
VANILLA FUDGE (1)	16
The ASTRONAUTS (1)	15
Ronnie DOVE (1)	12
Richard MARX ▶ 101 (8) [1]	**21097**
Richard MARX (8)	21097
Jeff BARRY/Andy KIM ▶ 102 (16) [6]	**21092**
The ARCHIES (4)	16029
Andy KIM (8)	3405
Wilson PICKETT (1)	1116
STARS ON 45 (1)	442
JON & ROBIN (1)	92
The MONKEES (1)	7.4
Thomas F. KELLY/ Billy STEINBERG ▶ 103 (8) [6]	**20928**
MADONNA (1)	6377
Cyndi LAUPER (2)	5119
HEART (2)	4977
Whitney HOUSTON (1)	3671
Pat BENATAR (1)	583
BLUE ZONE U.K. (1)	200
Alex NORTH/Hy ZARET ▶ 104 (11) [9]	**20850**
Les BAXTER (1)	8661
RIGHTEOUS BROTHERS (3)	5088
Al HIBBLER (1)	4376
Roy HAMILTON (1)	2241
VITO & The SALUTATIONS (1)	312
SWEET INSPIRATIONS (1)	70
The BLACKWELLS (1)	47
June VALLI (1)	44
HEART (1)	10
Jim PETERIK/Frankie SULLIVAN ▶ 105 (15) [2]	**20839**
SURVIVOR (14)	20737
Tommy SHAW (1)	102
Freddie MERCURY ▶ 106 (11) [2]	**20821**
QUEEN (10)	20758
Freddie MERCURY (1)	64
Garry BONNER/Alan GORDON ▶ 107 (20) [14]	**20646**
The TURTLES (5)	16584
THREE DOG NIGHT (1)	1496
Gary LEWIS And The PLAYBOYS (2)	985
Petula CLARK (1)	667
RIGHTEOUS BROTHERS (1)	338
Zalman YANOVSKY (1)	137
CAPTAIN & TENNILLE (1)	131
Tony ORLANDO And DAWN (1)	124
The NYLONS (1)	56
LOVIN' SPOONFUL (1)	53
MOJO MEN (1)	43
The BARRACUDA (1)	26
DINO, DESI & BILLY (2)	3.3
ELMO & ALMO (1)	1.9
Barry WHITE ▶ 108 (16) [3]	**20372**
Barry WHITE (10)	12168

LOVE UNLIMITED ORCHESTRA (4)	5743
LOVE UNLIMITED (2)	2461
Gary GELD/Peter UDELL ▶ 109 (19) [9]	**20336**
Brian HYLAND (9)	7133
Gary LEWIS And The PLAYBOYS (2)	5657
CARPENTERS (1)	4895
Bobby VINTON (1)	1454
Jackie WILSON (2)	602
Skeeter DAVIS (1)	408
Jimmy JONES (1)	163
Melba MOORE (1)	18
The TOYS (1)	6.3
John PHILLIPS ▶ 110 (14) [6]	**20307**
MAMAS & The PAPAS (7)	13581
Scott McKENZIE (3)	4820
5TH DIMENSION (1)	1133
John PHILLIPS (1)	744
Paul MAURIAT And His Orchestra (1)	17
STARS ON 45 (1)	12
Tommy BOYCE/Bobby HART ▶ 111 (10) [2]	**20195**
The MONKEES (5)	15887
Tommy BOYCE & Bobby HART (5)	4308
Tony BANKS/Phil COLLINS/ Mike RUTHERFORD ▶ 112 (15) [1]	**20101**
GENESIS (15)	20101
Joe TEX ▶ 113 (31) [2]	**19745**
Joe TEX (30)	19702
The RAELETTS (1)	43
Chip TAYLOR ▶ 114 (14) [13]	**19647**
The TROGGS (1)	6420
Juice NEWTON (1)	4537
Merrilee RUSH & The TURNABOUTS (1)	4297
FANCY (1)	1183
SENATOR BOBBY (1)	1018
Evie SANDS (1)	657
POZO-SECO SINGERS (1)	655
Johnny TILLOTSON (2)	634
Jackie DeSHANNON (1)	120
AMERICAN BREED (1)	86
Walter JACKSON (1)	37
LIVERPOOL FIVE (1)	1.4
Bettye SWANN (1)	0.9
Steve MILLER ▶ 115 (10) [2]	**19553**
Steve MILLER Band (7)	10097
Steve MILLER (3)	9456
Gilbert O'SULLIVAN ▶ 116 (9) [2]	**19552**
Gilbert O'SULLIVAN (8)	19184
Hurricane SMITH (1)	368
Sara ALLEN/Daryl HALL/ John OATES ▶ 117 (6) [1]	**19552**
Daryl HALL & John OATES (6)	19552
Barry GIBB ▶ 118 (6) [5]	**19543**
Andy GIBB (2)	11174
Frankie VALLI (1)	6566
Andy GIBB & Olivia NEWTON-JOHN (1)	1086
BEE GEES (1)	414
Teri DeSARIO (1)	304
Ray STEVENS ▶ 119 (22) [5]	**19391**
Ray STEVENS (18)	18832
O.C. SMITH (1)	326
Bobby VINTON (1)	223
Robert KNIGHT (1)	8.8
CATHY JEAN (1)	2.4

Ric OCASEK ▶ 120 (22) [3]	**19289**
The CARS (18)	17898
Ric OCASEK (3)	1225
Ian LLOYD (1)	166
Harlan HOWARD ▶ 121 (27) [20]	**19204**
Guy MITCHELL (1)	7361
Ray CHARLES (1)	4303
Joe SIMON (3)	1916
Burl IVES (4)	1573
Brenda LEE (1)	1517
Johnny TILLOTSON (1)	537
Candi STATON (1)	469
Patsy CLINE (1)	383
Melba MONTGOMERY (1)	284
Jim REEVES (2)	235
Wanda JACKSON (1)	220
KINGSTON TRIO (1)	190
Charlie RICH (1)	104
Ella WASHINGTON (1)	34
Pat ZILL (2)	26
Bobby BARE (1)	18
Z.Z. HILL (1)	18
Shirley CAESAR (1)	13
Fats DOMINO (1)	1.9
Trini LOPEZ (1)	1.8
O'Kelly ISLEY/Ronald ISLEY/ Rudolph ISLEY ▶ 122 (21) [8]	**19194**
ISLEY BROTHERS (14)	12788
HUMAN BEINZ (1)	3029
Joey DEE & The STARLITERS (1)	2111
The OUTSIDERS (1)	1172
LULU And The LUVERS (1)	42
The CHANTS (1)	24
CHAMBERS BROTHERS (1)	21
LULU (1)	6.1
Don GIBSON ▶ 123 (24) [12]	**19106**
Ray CHARLES (1)	11133
Don GIBSON (13)	5777
Tommy McLAIN (1)	1307
Patsy CLINE (1)	392
Roy ORBISON (1)	195
Fats DOMINO (1)	185
Count BASIE (1)	71
Bob LUMAN (1)	32
Johnny CASH (1)	14
The SWALLOWS (1)	0.0
Jackie WALKER (1)	0.0
Gene AMMONS (1)	0.0
Maurice STARR ▶ 124 (10) [3]	**19082**
NEW KIDS ON THE BLOCK (8)	17919
PERFECT GENTLEMEN (1)	1039
ANA (1)	124
Roy C. BENNETT/Sid TEPPER ▶ 125 (33) [25]	**19069**
AMES BROTHERS (4)	4171
Bert KAEMPFERT And His Orchestra (1)	2472
Connie FRANCIS (1)	2133
Elvis PRESLEY (4)	2011
Vic DANA (1)	1799
Perry COMO (2)	1793
Rod LAUREN (1)	752
Wayne NEWTON (1)	706
Art MOONEY and His Orchestra (1)	641
Robert GOULET (1)	403
Marty ROBBINS (2)	397
Jo STAFFORD (1)	310
Archie BLEYER (1)	293
Joe WARD (1)	261
Mel GADSON (1)	206

Ricky ZAHND And The BLUE JEANERS (1)	157
Nancy WILSON (1)	137
FONTANE SISTERS (1)	102
Jimmy WITHERSPOON (1)	98
Barry GORDON (1)	89
Jaye P. MORGAN (1)	75
Stan FREBERG (1)	65
Andy WILLIAMS (1)	0.9
KENNY And CORKY (1)	0.8
Eartha KITT (1)	0.0
David SEVILLE ▶ 126 (21) [6]	**19066**
David SEVILLE And The CHIPMUNKS (11)	10945
David SEVILLE (6)	7610
Bobby VEE (1)	317
Joe REISMAN and His Orchestra (1)	193
David CARROLL And His Orchestra (1)	0.0
Lew QUADLING & His Orchestra (1)	0.0
Richard ADLER/Jerry ROSS ▶ 127 (24) [22]	**18821**
Rosemary CLOONEY (1)	11126
Sarah VAUGHAN (1)	2027
Archie BLEYER (1)	1629
Eddie FISHER (2)	1418
Sammy DAVIS Jr. (1)	680
Perry COMO & Jaye P. MORGAN (1)	411
SUNNY & The SUNGLOWS (1)	343
FOUR ACES (1)	311
Elvis PRESLEY (1)	223
Dinah SHORE (1)	181
Patti PAGE (2)	149
Burl IVES (1)	121
Frankie LAINE (1)	118
Peggy LEE (1)	33
Lenny WELCH (1)	29
POINTER SISTERS (1)	15
The RAYS (1)	6.6
Johnnie RAY (1)	0.0
Guy LOMBARDO And His ROYAL CANADIANS (1)	0.0
Ginny GIBSON (1)	0.0
Carmen McRAE (1)	0.0
Norman BROOKS (1)	0.0
Bill WITHERS ▶ 128 (12) [3]	**18782**
Bill WITHERS (10)	14831
CLUB NOUVEAU (1)	3944
5TH DIMENSION (1)	6.9
Bobby DARIN ▶ 129 (23) [10]	**18779**
Bobby DARIN (14)	17042
GERRY And The PACEMAKERS (1)	977
Tim HARDIN (1)	399
Billy VAUGHN and His Orchestra (1)	190
BUCKWHEAT (1)	85
Trini LOPEZ (1)	36
Bobby DARIN & Orchestra (1)	23
PARIS SISTERS (1)	15
Anne MURRAY (1)	11
Dick JACOBS And His Orchestra/Chorus (1)	0.0
Wayne Carson THOMPSON ▶ 130 (15) [9]	**18580**
BOX TOPS (4)	13284
Joe COCKER (1)	2598
JON & ROBIN (4)	1441
The ARBORS (1)	737
Eddy ARNOLD (1)	400

Wayne Carson THOMPSON ► 130 (15) [9] ***Cont'd***	**18580**
Bruce CHANNEL (1)	59
Billy Joe ROYAL (1)	50
Neal DOVER (1)	8.5
Ike & Tina TURNER (1)	2.2
Isaac HAYES/David PORTER ► 131 (31) [17]	**18570**
SAM & DAVE (11)	11792
Carla THOMAS (4)	1806
BLUES BROTHERS (1)	1370
Lou RAWLS (1)	1274
The EMOTIONS (2)	508
ZZ TOP (1)	446
FABULOUS THUNDERBIRDS (1)	313
COLD BLOOD (1)	299
SOUL CHILDREN (1)	232
Ramsey LEWIS (1)	207
Chuck JACKSON & Maxine BROWN (1)	90
The HASSLES (1)	64
Linda RONSTADT (1)	57
Mable JOHN (1)	57
OTIS & CARLA (1)	26
Archie BELL & The DRELLS (1)	25
JEAN & The DARLINGS (1)	2.4
Per GESSLE ► 132 (6) [1]	**18476**
ROXETTE (6)	18476
Roger MILLER ► 133 (21) [7]	**18247**
Roger MILLER (15)	17329
Eddy ARNOLD (1)	457
Andy WILLIAMS (1)	317
Del SHANNON (1)	136
Ray PRICE (1)	3.3
Jim REEVES (1)	2.3
Wayne NEWTON (1)	1.9
Harold LOGAN/Lloyd PRICE ► 134 (15) [2]	**17938**
Lloyd PRICE (14)	17855
Mitch RYDER (1)	83
Sammy FAIN/ Paul Francis WEBSTER ► 135 (23) [20]	**17821**
FOUR ACES (1)	8585
Pat BOONE (2)	5784
Johnny MATHIS (1)	1228
Freddy FENDER (1)	697
Billy STEWART (1)	556
AMES BROTHERS (2)	377
Don CORNELL (1)	365
DREAM WEAVERS (1)	184
FOUR PREPS (1)	24
Jimmy RICKS (1)	19
DON, DICK N' JIMMY (1)	2.3
Doris DAY (2)	0.0
Jack JONES (1)	0.0
Bonnie GUITAR (1)	0.0
JOHNSTON BROTHERS (1)	0.0
Johnny DESMOND (1)	0.0
Jerry FULLER (1)	0.0
Sunny GALE (1)	0.0
Andy RUSSELL (1)	0.0
Milton SPARKS (1)	0.0
Tommy ROE ► 136 (11) [1]	**17810**
Tommy ROE (11)	17810
Richard DEHR/Terry GILKYSON/ Frank MILLER ► 137 (9) [9]	**17766**
Dean MARTIN (1)	8655
BROTHERS FOUR (1)	6907
Frankie LAINE (1)	891

Gale STORM (1)	785
The DRIFTERS (1)	271
Mindy CARSON (1)	217
The VOGUES (1)	25
Roger WILLIAMS (1)	14
Julius La ROSA (1)	0.0
Thomas ALLEN/ Harold BROWN/ Morris DICKERSON/ Lonnie JORDAN/ Charles MILLER/Lee OSKAR/ Howard SCOTT ► 138 (10) [3]	**17638**
WAR (8)	17195
ISLEY BROTHERS (1)	409
Ramsey LEWIS (1)	35
Bob MERRILL ► 139 (41) [37]	**17616**
Jimmie RODGERS (1)	5979
Perry COMO (1)	2680
Sarah VAUGHAN (1)	2261
Teresa BREWER (2)	2058
Rosemary CLOONEY (2)	1538
Eileen RODGERS (2)	969
Valerie CARR (1)	394
Mr. Acker BILK (1)	363
June VALLI (1)	252
Tony BENNETT (2)	200
BABY JANE & The ROCKABYES (1)	168
Mahalia JACKSON (1)	144
Ginny GIBSON (1)	85
MILLS BROTHERS (1)	84
Frankie LAINE (1)	69
Johnnie RAY (1)	50
Roy HAMILTON (1)	50
The GAYLORDS (1)	47
AMES BROTHERS (1)	45
Lonnie SATTIN/Orchestra (1)	45
Peggy KING (1)	44
Andy GRIFFITH (1)	32
Anita BRYANT (1)	21
Doris DAY (1)	12
Guy MITCHELL (1)	8.2
Jane MORGAN (1)	4.0
Somethin' SMITH & The REDHEADS (1)	3.1
Eddie FISHER (1)	2.1
Tony MARTIN (1)	2.0
Tommy LEONETTI (1)	2.0
Ralph YOUNG (1)	2.0
David ROSE And His Orchestra (1)	0.4
Pat O'DAY (1)	0.0
Georgie SHAW (1)	0.0
Josephine PREMICE (1)	0.0
Bonnie LAKE & Her BEAUS (1)	0.0
Eydie GORME & Steve LAWRENCE (1)	0.0
Baker KNIGHT ► 140 (20) [8]	**17593**
Rick NELSON (9)	11799
Elvis PRESLEY (1)	2415
Dean MARTIN (4)	1283
Ray PETERSON (2)	1146
SUGAR BEARS (1)	453
Frank SINATRA (1)	324
Sonny KNIGHT (1)	129
Dave DUDLEY (1)	43
Peter CALLANDER/ Mitch MURRAY ► 141 (7) [5]	**17398**
PAPER LACE (3)	5053
Bo DONALDSON And The HEYWOODS (1)	4779
VANITY FARE (1)	3768
Georgie FAME (1)	3288

The TREMELOES/Brian POOLE And The TREMELOES (1)	509
Melanie SAFKA ► 142 (13) [3]	**17348**
MELANIE (9)	15197
NEW SEEKERS (3)	1918
Ray CHARLES (1)	232
Debbie GIBSON ► 143 (9) [1]	**17301**
Debbie GIBSON (9)	17301
Steve BARRI/P.F. SLOAN ► 144 (20) [14]	**17275**
Barry McGUIRE (1)	6384
Johnny RIVERS (1)	3877
HERMAN'S HERMITS (1)	2112
GRASS ROOTS (4)	1606
The TURTLES (3)	1413
JAN & DEAN (2)	799
5TH DIMENSION (1)	263
ROUND ROBIN (1)	254
The VENTURES (1)	212
The SEARCHERS (1)	212
BRUCE And TERRY (1)	77
Terry KNIGHT And The PACK (1)	36
Terry BLACK (1)	30
FANTASTIC BAGGYS (1)	0.9
Jim STEINMAN ► 145 (12) [7]	**17185**
Bonnie TYLER (2)	7621
AIR SUPPLY (1)	4549
MEAT LOAF (5)	3195
Barry MANILOW (1)	856
Jim STEINMAN (1)	600
Barbra STREISAND (1)	335
FIRE INC. (1)	30
Madonna L. CICCONE/ Patrick Raymond LEONARD ► 146 (6) [1]	**17138**
MADONNA (6)	17138
Mark JAMES ► 147 (11) [7]	**17119**
Elvis PRESLEY (4)	7289
BLUE SWEDE (1)	5017
B.J. THOMAS (2)	4227
BOX TOPS (1)	449
Dee Dee WARWICK (1)	123
Anne MURRAY (1)	8.0
BLOOD, SWEAT & TEARS (1)	5.7
Jim CROCE ► 148 (10) [3]	**16966**
Jim CROCE (8)	16847
MELANIE (1)	102
Frank SINATRA (1)	18
Jon BON JOVI/Desmond CHILD/ Richie SAMBORA ► 149 (5) [2]	**16774**
BON JOVI (4)	15848
CHER (1)	926
Shel SILVERSTEIN ► 150 (9) [6]	**16712**
DR. HOOK (4)	6744
Johnny CASH (1)	6404
IRISH ROVERS (1)	3028
Bobby BARE (1)	299
Jim STAFFORD (1)	237
BROTHERS FOUR (1)	0.4
Al HOFFMAN/Dick MANNING ► 151 (21) [16]	**16414**
Perry COMO (4)	7225
Patti PAGE (3)	5809
ANNETTE (1)	1390
Eydie GORME (1)	687
Eddie FISHER (1)	490
HUGO & LUIGI (1)	398
Frank SINATRA (1)	135
Janice HARPER (1)	111
Art MOONEY and His Orchestra (1)	68

Steve ALAIMO (1)	57
The CREW-CUTS (1)	23
AMES BROTHERS (1)	15
Tony BENNETT (1)	5.5
Bobby MADERA & His Orchestra (1)	0.0
Grady MARTIN And The SLEW FOOT FIVE (1)	0.0
FOUR LADS (1)	0.0
Tony ROMEO ► 152 (10) [6]	**16382**
PARTRIDGE FAMILY (2)	10009
The COWSILLS (2)	2845
Lou CHRISTIE (2)	2302
BROOKLYN BRIDGE (2)	884
Wayne NEWTON (1)	250
Paul ANKA (1)	91
Michael CRAIG/Roy HAY/ Jon MOSS/George O'DOWD ► 153 (7) [1]	**16352**
CULTURE CLUB (7)	16352
Jim WEATHERLY ► 154 (13) [6]	**16277**
Gladys KNIGHT & The PIPS (6)	14848
Jim WEATHERLY (3)	1209
Ray PRICE (1)	81
The PERSUADERS (1)	79
BATDORF & RODNEY (1)	48
CLASSICS IV (1)	13
David BOWIE ► 155 (20) [2]	**16183**
David BOWIE (19)	15617
MOTT THE HOOPLE (1)	566
Bryan ADAMS/Jim VALLANCE ► 156 (17) [7]	**16097**
Bryan ADAMS (11)	14036
Bryan ADAMS/Tina TURNER (1)	1006
.38 SPECIAL (1)	493
PRISM (1)	259
LOVERBOY (1)	173
Joe COCKER (1)	113
Roger DALTREY (1)	17
William DEES/Roy ORBISON ► 157 (11) [2]	**16083**
Roy ORBISON (10)	14875
VAN HALEN (1)	1208
Adam CLAYTON/Dave EVANS/ Paul HEWSON/Larry MULLEN ► 158 (14) [2]	**16059**
U2 (13)	16023
PET SHOP BOYS (1)	37
Marc BLITZSTEIN/ Berthold BRECHT/Kurt WEILL ► 159 (3) [3]	**16000**
Bobby DARIN (1)	14687
Ella FITZGERALD (1)	743
Louis ARMSTRONG And His All-Stars (1)	570
Kenneth EDMONDS/ Antonio REID/Daryl SIMMONS ► 160 (12) [8]	**15988**
Bobby BROWN (2)	4878
Karyn WHITE (3)	4827
Sheena EASTON (1)	2763
BABYFACE (2)	1730
The BOYS (1)	927
Johnny GILL (1)	468
Paula ABDUL (1)	378
DAMIAN DAME (1)	17
Dion DIMUCCI/Ernie MARESCA ► 161 (6) [4]	**15980**
DION (3)	15000
Leif GARRETT (1)	949
FOUR PREPS (1)	24
JIVE BUNNY & The MASTERMIXERS (1)	6.7

Charles FOX/Norman GIMBEL ► 162 (8) [8]	**15941**
Roberta FLACK (1)	7658
Jim CROCE (1)	2549
PRATT & McCLAIN (1)	2197
Barry MANILOW (1)	1827
Charles FOX/Norman GIMBEL ► 162 (8) [8] Cont'd	**15941**
Maureen McGOVERN (1)	886
Cyndi GRECCO (1)	709
AL B. SURE! (1)	86
Anson WILLIAMS (1)	30
Andy FARRISS/ Michael HUTCHENCE ► 163 (11) [1]	**15939**
INXS (11)	15939
Roger NICHOLS/Paul WILLIAMS ► 164 (12) [9]	**15886**
CARPENTERS (3)	13920
THREE DOG NIGHT (1)	1391
Anne MURRAY (1)	172
Al WILSON (2)	131
CHASE (1)	118
Maureen McGOVERN (1)	68
The MONKEES (1)	44
Art GARFUNKEL (1)	28
Kenny ROGERS And The FIRST EDITION (1)	15
Dallas FRAZIER ► 165 (11) [11]	**15777**
HOLLYWOOD ARGYLES (1)	6926
OAK RIDGE BOYS (1)	4183
DANTE and the EVERGREENS (1)	1398
Charlie RICH (1)	1150
O.C. SMITH (1)	711
Engelbert HUMPERDINCK (1)	658
Elvis PRESLEY (1)	390
FOUR PREPS (1)	130
Jack GREENE (1)	89
Dallas FRAZIER (1)	73
The DYNA-SORES (1)	71
Annie LENNOX/ David A. STEWART ► 166 (15) [1]	**15769**
EURYTHMICS (15)	15769
Kevin CRONIN ► 167 (12) [1]	**15707**
REO SPEEDWAGON (12)	15707
Barry MANN/Phil SPECTOR/ Cynthia WEIL ► 168 (8) [7]	**15621**
RIGHTEOUS BROTHERS (1)	9450
Daryl HALL & John OATES (1)	1839
JAY & The AMERICANS (1)	1583
Dionne WARWICK (1)	1346
The RONETTES (2)	1139
Roberta FLACK & Donny HATHAWAY (1)	248
Long John BALDRY (1)	16
Kenneth EDMONDS/ Antonio REID ► 169 (10) [5]	**15604**
PEBBLES (3)	5039
Whitney HOUSTON (2)	4931
Bobby BROWN (1)	2865
AFTER 7 (3)	2692
The JACKSONS (1)	78
Peter CETERA/David FOSTER ► 170 (5) [2]	**15531**
CHICAGO (4)	11399
Peter CETERA (1)	4132
Christopher CROSS ► 171 (7) [1]	**15488**

Christopher CROSS (7)	15488
Dan FOGELBERG ► 172 (14) [2]	**15422**
Dan FOGELBERG (13)	14732
Dan FOGELBERG/ Tim WEISBERG (1)	690
Gordon LIGHTFOOT ► 173 (16) [5]	**15368**
Gordon LIGHTFOOT (11)	14440
PETER, PAUL & MARY (2)	632
Glen CAMPBELL (1)	240
Anne MURRAY (1)	45
Spyder TURNER (1)	11
Ric CARTEY/Carole JOYNER ► 174 (7) [7]	**15361**
Tab HUNTER (1)	8452
Sonny JAMES (1)	5688
Donny OSMOND (1)	531
The CREW-CUTS (1)	343
Lesley GORE (1)	334
Ray STEVENS (1)	13
Ric CARTEY with The JIVA-TONES (1)	0.0
Melvin ENDSLEY ► 175 (6) [5]	**15190**
Guy MITCHELL (2)	11975
Andy WILLIAMS (1)	1619
Jill COREY (1)	893
Marty ROBBINS (1)	702
Melvin ENDSLEY (1)	0.0
John STEWART ► 176 (10) [6]	**15180**
The MONKEES (2)	9791
John STEWART (4)	3681
Anne MURRAY (1)	1419
LOVIN' SPOONFUL (1)	207
KINGSTON TRIO (1)	56
Pat BOONE (1)	26
Don McLEAN ► 177 (10) [3]	**15165**
Don MCLEAN (8)	14040
Perry COMO (1)	1090
Bobby GOLDSBORO (1)	36
Curtis BEDEAU/ Gerard CHARLES/ Hugh CLARKE/Brian GEORGE/ Lucien GEORGE/Paul GEORGE ► 178 (11) [4]	**15161**
LISA LISA And CULT JAM (7)	10938
Samantha FOX (2)	3666
Cheryl "Pepsii" RILEY (1)	509
EX-GIRLFRIEND (1)	48
Bobby DALL/C.C. DeVILLE/ Bret MICHAELS/ Rikki ROCKETT ► 179 (10) [1]	**15088**
POISON (10)	15088
Peter DeANGELIS/ Bob MARCUCCI ► 180 (20) [12]	**14981**
Frankie AVALON (8)	12007
Jodie SANDS (1)	1183
Donny OSMOND (1)	1103
Mona CAROL (2)	243
The HILLTOPPERS (1)	217
Cozy MORLEY (1)	185
Judy SCOTT (1)	23
Patty BRANDON (1)	12
FOUR DATES (1)	4.9
Al MARTINO (1)	2.8
Kitty KALLEN (1)	0.0
Buddy GRECO (1)	0.0
Maurice WILLIAMS ► 181 (8) [6]	**14970**

The DIAMONDS (1)	7547
Maurice WILLIAMS & The ZODIACS (3)	4378
4 SEASONS (1)	1296
Jackson BROWNE (1)	797
Bill DEAL & The RHONDELS (1)	711
The GLADIOLAS (1)	241
Eric CARMEN ► 182 (16) [5]	**14873**
RASPBERRIES (6)	7366
Shaun CASSIDY (2)	5011
Eric CARMEN (6)	2427
Michael DAMIAN (1)	42
EUCLID BEACH BAND (1)	27
Robert LAMM ► 183 (11) [1]	**14838**
CHICAGO (11)	14838
Hoyt AXTON ► 184 (5) [4]	**14490**
THREE DOG NIGHT (2)	14025
STEPPENWOLF (1)	326
Hoyt AXTON (1)	132
SUNSHINE COMPANY (1)	5.8
Terry BRITTEN/Graham LYLE ► 185 (6) [2]	**14449**
Tina TURNER (5)	14321
Anita BAKER (1)	129
Rod ARGENT ► 186 (8) [4]	**14147**
The ZOMBIES (5)	12952
SANTANA (1)	677
Juice NEWTON (1)	483
The ROAD (1)	35
Walter BECKER/Donald FAGEN ► 187 (17) [3]	**14130**
STEELY DAN (15)	14010
SNEAKER (1)	80
CLUB HOUSE (1)	40
Luigi CREATORE/ Solomon LINDA/ Hugo PERETTI/ Albert STANTON/ George David WEISS ► 188 (2) [2]	**14090**
The TOKENS (1)	9030
Robert JOHN (1)	5059
Spooner OLDHAM/Dan PENN ► 189 (12) [9]	**14044**
BOX TOPS (2)	6483
James & Bobby PURIFY (2)	3361
Percy SLEDGE (2)	1803
SWEET INSPIRATIONS (1)	1368
Barbra STREISAND (1)	280
Solomon BURKE (1)	265
Kim CARNES (1)	249
Sandy POSEY (1)	214
The UNIQUES (1)	22
Will JENNINGS/ Steve WINWOOD ► 190 (10) [1]	**14039**
Steve WINWOOD (10)	14039
J.P. RICHARDSON ► 191 (11) [9]	**14005**
Johnny PRESTON (1)	8748
BIG BOPPER (3)	4387
Jerry Lee LEWIS (1)	436
CAT MOTHER and the ALL NIGHT NEWS BOYS (1)	164
Mitch RYDER (1)	83
Sonny JAMES (1)	63
Rod BERNARD (1)	63
George JONES (1)	55
JIVE BUNNY & The MASTERMIXERS (1)	6.7

Stig ANDERSON/ Benny ANDERSSON/ Björn ULVAEUS ► 192 (10) [2]	**13921**
ABBA (9)	13813
SWEET DREAMS (1)	108
Tommy ROE/Freddy WELLER ► 193 (5) [1]	**13866**
Tommy ROE (5)	13866
Dick ADDRISI/Don ADDRISI ► 194 (15) [9]	**13803**
The ASSOCIATION (2)	7473
ADDRISI BROTHERS (6)	2283
5TH DIMENSION (1)	1564
BLUE SWEDE (1)	1499
Dorothy MOORE (1)	596
FIVE EMPREES (1)	187
CARPENTERS (1)	99
Glen CAMPBELL (1)	98
The SANDPEBBLES (1)	3.2
John BETTIS/ Richard CARPENTER ► 195 (7) [3]	**13778**
CARPENTERS (5)	13621
The SPINNERS (1)	84
Lynn ANDERSON (1)	74
John CARTER/Ken HAWKER ► 196 (6) [6]	**13744**
MUSIC EXPLOSION (1)	6710
HERMAN'S HERMITS (1)	5330
Brenda LEE (1)	1118
PETER And GORDON (1)	525
BULLET (1)	50
STARS ON 45 (1)	12
Cat STEVENS ► 197 (18) [7]	**13729**
Cat STEVENS (12)	9985
The TREMELOES/Brian POOLE And The TREMELOES (1)	1586
Rod STEWART (1)	718
Maxi PRIEST (1)	716
Keith HAMPSHIRE (1)	432
Travis WAMMACK (1)	238
The GENTRYS (1)	55
Audrey ALLISON/Joe ALLISON ► 198 (3) [3]	**13689**
Jim REEVES (1)	10202
Tommy SANDS (1)	3179
Solomon BURKE (1)	308
Mariah CAREY/Ben MARGULIES ► 199 (3) [1]	**13623**
Mariah CAREY (3)	13623
Joe SHERMAN/Noel SHERMAN ► 200 (13) [12]	**13605**
Nat King COLE (2)	8482
Perry COMO (1)	1713
ROVER BOYS (1)	1085
FOUR FRESHMEN (1)	995
Paul ANKA (1)	769
Patti PAGE (1)	308
The ARBORS (1)	172
Vic DAMONE (1)	64
Bobby "Boris" PICKETT (1)	10
Anita Ellis (1)	4.4
Jill COREY (1)	1.9
LENNON SISTERS & The SPARKLERS (1)	0.0

Top 200 Writer Teams: First and Biggest

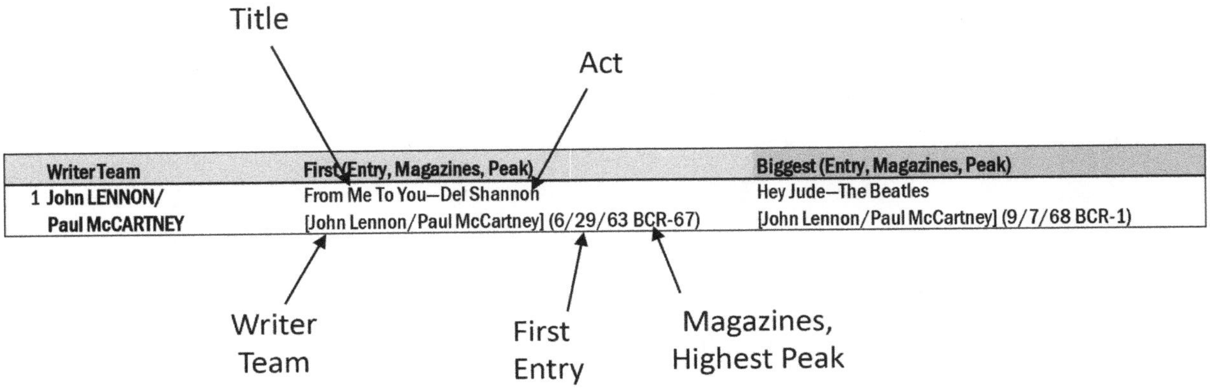

Italics: Multiple First Entries in the same week

This section is for first and biggest in this era. For some writer teams those career milestones may fall before or after this era.

Writer	First (Entry, Magazines, Peak)	Biggest (Entry, Magazines, Peak)
1 John LENNON/Paul McCARTNEY	From Me To You—Del Shannon [John Lennon/Paul McCartney] (6/29/63 BCR-67)	Hey Jude—The Beatles [John Lennon/Paul McCartney] (9/7/68 BCR-1)
2 Lamont DOZIER/ Brian HOLLAND/Eddie HOLLAND	Locking Up My Heart—The Marvelettes [Lamont Dozier/Brian Holland/Eddie Holland] (3/9/63 BCR-44)	Where Did Our Love Go—The Supremes [Lamont Dozier/Brian Holland/Eddie Holland] (7/11/64 BCR-1)
3 Burt BACHARACH/Hal DAVID	Story Of My Life—Marty Robbins [Burt Bacharach/Hal David] (11/11/57 BCR-26)	Raindrops Keep Fallin' On My Head—B.J. Thomas [Burt Bacharach/Hal David] (10/25/69 BCR-1)
4 Mick JAGGER/Keith RICHARDS	That Girl Belongs To Yesterday—Gene Pitney [Mick Jagger/Keith Richards] (1/18/64 BCR-49)	Honky Tonk Women—The Rolling Stones [Mick Jagger/Keith Richards] (7/19/69 BCR-1)
5 Barry GIBB/Maurice GIBB/ Robin GIBB	(The Lights Went Out In) Massachusetts— The Bee Gees [Barry Gibb/Maurice Gibb/Robin Gibb] (11/11/67 BCR-11)	Stayin' Alive—Bee Gees [Barry Gibb/Maurice Gibb/Robin Gibb] (12/10/77 BCR-1)
6 Gerry GOFFIN/Carole KING	Will You Love Me Tomorrow—The Shirelles [Gerry Goffin/Carole King] (11/21/60 BCR-1)	Go Away Little Girl—Steve Lawrence [Gerry Goffin/Carole King] (11/10/62 BCR-1)
7 Elton JOHN/Bernie TAUPIN	Border Song—Elton John [Elton John/Bernie Taupin] (8/15/70 BCR-69)	Crocodile Rock—Elton John [Elton John/Bernie Taupin] (12/9/72 BCR-1)
8 Paul SIMON	Motorcycle—Tico And The Triumphs [Paul Simon] (1/6/62 BR-97)	Bridge Over Troubled Water—Simon & Garfunkel [Paul Simon] (1/31/70 BCR-1)
9 Lionel RICHIE	This Is Your Life—Commodores [Lionel Richie] (10/25/75 CR-77)	Endless Love—Diana Ross & Lionel Richie [Lionel Richie] (7/4/81 BCR-1)
10 Jerry LEIBER/Mike STOLLER	(Bazoom) I Need Your Lovin'—The Cheers [Jerry Leiber/Mike Stoller] (10/11/54 BCRt-15)	Jailhouse Rock—Elvis Presley [Jerry Leiber/Mike Stoller] (9/30/57 BCR-1)
11 Neil DIAMOND	Sunday And Me—Jay & The Americans [Neil Diamond] (11/13/65 BCR-18)	I'm A Believer—The Monkees [Neil Diamond] (12/3/66 BCR-1)
12 PRINCE	I Wanna Be Your Lover—Prince [Prince] (11/3/79 BCR-11)	When Doves Cry—Prince [Prince] (6/2/84 BC-1)
13 TRADITIONAL	*Adeste Fideles (O Come All Ye Faithful)— David Whitfield; Adeste Fideles—Bing Crosby [Traditional] (12/6/54 Rt-50)*	Tom Dooley—The Kingston Trio [Traditional] (9/27/58 BCR-1)
14 Barrett STRONG/Norman WHITFIELD	Gonna Give Her All The Love I've Got—Jimmy Ruffin [Barrett Strong/Norman Whitfield] (3/18/67 BCR-29)	I Heard It Through The Grapevine—Marvin Gaye [Barrett Strong/Norman Whitfield] (11/16/68 BCR-1)
15 Stevie WONDER	Superwoman (Where Were You When I Needed You)— Stevie Wonder [Stevie Wonder] (5/20/72 BCR-32)	I Just Called To Say I Love You—Stevie Wonder [Stevie Wonder] (8/18/84 BC-1)
16 Kenneth GAMBLE/Leon HUFF	(We'll Be) United—The Intruders [Kenneth Gamble/Leon Huff] (7/16/66 BCR-78)	Love Train—The O'Jays [Kenneth Gamble/Leon Huff] (1/13/73 BCR-1)
17 Doc POMUS/Mort SHUMAN	White Bucks And Saddle Shoes—Bobby Pedrick, Jr. [Doc Pomus/Mort Shuman] (11/1/58 BC-74)	Save The Last Dance For Me—The Drifters [Doc Pomus/Mort Shuman] (9/5/60 BCR-1)
18 Paul ANKA	Diana—Paul Anka [Paul Anka] (6/29/57 BCR-1)	Put Your Head On My Shoulder—Paul Anka [Paul Anka] (8/24/59 BCR-2)
19 Curtis MAYFIELD	Gypsy Woman—The Impressions [Curtis Mayfield] (10/16/61 BCR-13)	Let's Do It Again—The Staple Singers [Curtis Mayfield] (10/18/75 BCR-1)
20 Howard GREENFIELD/Neil SEDAKA	Stupid Cupid—Connie Francis [Howard Greenfield/Neil Sedaka] (7/28/58 BCR-16)	Breaking Up Is Hard To Do—Neil Sedaka [Howard Greenfield/Neil Sedaka] (6/23/62 BCR-1)
21 Barry MANN/Cynthia WEIL	Bless You—Tony Orlando [Barry Mann/Cynthia Weil] (7/31/61 BCR-11)	(You're My) Soul And Inspiration— The Righteous Brothers [Barry Mann/Cynthia Weil] (3/5/66 BCR-1)
22 Linda McCARTNEY/Paul McCARTNEY	Another Day—Paul McCartney [Linda McCartney/Paul McCartney] (2/27/71 BCR-5)	Silly Love Songs—Wings [Linda McCartney/Paul McCartney] (4/10/76 BCR-1)
23 Billy JOEL	Piano Man—Billy Joel [Billy Joel] (2/9/74 BCR-16)	It's Still Rock And Roll To Me—Billy Joel [Billy Joel] (5/24/80 BCR-1)
24 Michael JACKSON	Don't Stop 'til You Get Enough—Michael Jackson [Michael Jackson] (7/28/79 BCR-1)	Billie Jean—Michael Jackson [Michael Jackson] (1/22/83 BC-1)
25 Smokey ROBINSON	Ain't It, Baby—The Miracles [Smokey Robinson] (3/27/61 BCR-40)	My Guy—Mary Wells [Smokey Robinson] (3/28/64 BCR-1)
26 Bob DYLAN	Blowin' In The Wind—Peter, Paul & Mary [Bob Dylan] (6/29/63 BCR-2)	Mr. Tambourine Man—The Byrds [Bob Dylan] (5/8/65 BCR-1)
27 Sam COOKE	*You Send Me—Teresa Brewer; You Send Me—Sam Cooke [Sam Cooke] (10/14/57 BCtRt-1)*	You Send Me—Sam Cooke [Sam Cooke] (10/14/57 BCtRt-1)

Writer	First (Entry, Magazines, Peak)	Biggest (Entry, Magazines, Peak)
28 Mike LOVE/Brian WILSON	Surfin'—The Beach Boys [Mike Love/Brian Wilson] (2/10/62 BC-75)	I Get Around—The Beach Boys [Mike Love/Brian Wilson] (5/23/64 BCR-1)
29 Bob CREWE/Bob GAUDIO	Big Girls Don't Cry—The 4 Seasons [Bob Crewe/Bob Gaudio] (10/20/62 BCR-1)	Big Girls Don't Cry—The 4 Seasons [Bob Crewe/Bob Gaudio] (10/20/62 BCR-1)
30 John FOGERTY	Proud Mary—Creedence Clearwater Revival [John Fogerty] (1/18/69 BCR-1)	Proud Mary—Creedence Clearwater Revival [John Fogerty] (1/18/69 BCR-1)
31 Dave APPELL/Kal MANN	Rocka Conga—The Applejacks [Dave Appell/Kal Mann] (12/20/58 BCR-31)	Bristol Stomp—The Dovells [Dave Appell/Kal Mann] (9/4/61 BCR-2)
32 John D. LOUDERMILK	*A Rose And A Baby Ruth—Eddie Fontaine;* *A Rose And A Baby Ruth—George Hamilton IV* *[John D. Loudermilk] (10/27/56 BCRt-6)*	Indian Reservation (The Lament Of The Cherokee)— Raiders [John D. Loudermilk] (4/10/71 BCR-1)
33 George MICHAEL	Bad Boys—Wham! U.K. [George Michael] (8/6/83 BC-50)	Faith—George Michael [George Michael] (10/24/87 BC-1)
34 James Samuel HARRIS/Terry LEWIS	Just Be Good To Me—The S.O.S. Band [James Samuel Harris/Terry Lewis] (8/27/83 BC-42)	Miss You Much—Janet Jackson [James Samuel Harris/Terry Lewis] (9/2/89 BC-1)
35 Sylvester STEWART	Dance To The Music—Sly & The Family Stone [Sylvester Stewart] (2/10/68 BCR-5)	Everyday People—Sly & The Family Stone [Sylvester Stewart] (11/30/68 BCR-1)
36 Bruce SPRINGSTEEN	Sandy—The Hollies [Bruce Springsteen] (4/12/75 BC-85)	Dancing In The Dark—Bruce Springsteen [Bruce Springsteen] (5/26/84 BC-1)
37 Harry Wayne CASEY/Rick FINCH	Rock Your Baby—George McCrae [Harry Wayne Casey/Rick Finch] (5/25/74 BCR-1)	That's The Way (I Like It)—K.C. & The Sunshine Band [Harry Wayne Casey/Rick Finch] (10/18/75 BCR-1)
38 Chuck BERRY	Thirty Days (To Come Back Home)—Chuck Berry [Chuck Berry] (10/29/55 CRt-42)	My Ding-A-Ling—Chuck Berry [Chuck Berry] (7/29/72 BCR-1)
39 Bernard EDWARDS/Nile RODGERS	Everybody Dance—Chic [Bernard Edwards/Nile Rodgers] (4/22/78 BCR-38)	Le Freak—Chic [Bernard Edwards/Nile Rodgers] (10/28/78 BCR-1)
40 Eddie BRIGATI/Felix CAVALIERE	You Better Run—The Young Rascals [Eddie Brigati/Felix Cavaliere] (6/11/66 BCR-20)	Groovin'—The Young Rascals [Eddie Brigati/Felix Cavaliere] (4/22/67 BCR-1)
41 Jimmy WEBB	Up-Up And Away—The 5th Dimension [Jimmy Webb] (6/3/67 BCR-4)	Mac Arthur Park—Donna Summer [Jimmy Webb] (9/9/78 BCR-1)
42 John LENNON	Cold Turkey—Plastic Ono Band [John Lennon] (11/15/69 BCR-26)	(Just Like) Starting Over—John Lennon [John Lennon] (11/1/80 BCR-1)
43 Paul McCARTNEY	Woman—Peter And Gordon [Paul McCartney] (2/12/66 BCR-12)	Ebony And Ivory—Paul McCartney [Paul McCartney] (4/10/82 BCR-1)
44 Jerry FULLER	Travelin' Man—Ricky Nelson [Jerry Fuller] (4/22/61 BCR-1)	Travelin' Man—Ricky Nelson [Jerry Fuller] (4/22/61 BCR-1)
45 David GATES	Popsicles And Icicles—The Murmaids [David Gates] (11/16/63 BCR-1)	Make It With You—Bread [David Gates] (6/13/70 BCR-1)
46 Diane WARREN	Rhythm Of The Night—DeBarge [Diane Warren] (2/16/85 BC-3)	Look Away—Chicago [Diane Warren] (9/24/88 BC-1)
47 Jeff BARRY/Ellie GREENWICH/ Phil SPECTOR	Da Doo Ron Ron (When He Walked Me Home)— The Crystals [Jeff Barry/Ellie Greenwich/Phil Spector] (4/20/63 BCR-3)	Chapel Of Love—The Dixie Cups [Jeff Barry/Ellie Greenwich/Phil Spector] (5/2/64 BCR-1)
48 Phil COLLINS	Misunderstanding—Genesis [Phil Collins] (5/17/80 BCR-9)	Against All Odds (Take A Look At Me Now)— Phil Collins [Phil Collins] (2/25/84 BC-1)
49 Robert ALLEN/Al STILLMAN	(There's No Place Like) Home For The Holidays— Perry Como [Robert Allen/Al Stillman] (11/22/54 BCR-12)	Moments To Remember—The Four Lads [Robert Allen/Al Stillman] (8/27/55 BCR-2)
50 John DENSMORE/ Robby KRIEGER/Ray MANZAREK/ Jim MORRISON	Light My Fire—The Doors [John Densmore/Robby Krieger/Ray Manzarek/ Jim Morrison] (5/27/67 BCR-1)	Light My Fire—The Doors [John Densmore/Robby Krieger/Ray Manzarek/Jim Morrison] (5/27/67 BCR-1)
51 STING	Roxanne—The Police [Sting] (2/10/79 BCR-31)	Every Breath You Take—The Police [Sting] (6/4/83 BC-1)
52 George HARRISON	The Inner Light—The Beatles [George Harrison] (3/30/68 B-96)	My Sweet Lord—George Harrison [George Harrison] (11/28/70 BCR-1)
53 Tony HATCH	*Look For A Star—Deane Hawley;* *Look For A Star—Garry Miles;* *Look For A Star—Billy Vaughn And His Orchestra;* *Look For A Star—Nicky Como;.* *Look For A Star Part One—Garry Mills* *[Tony Hatch] (6/20/60 BCtRt-13)*	Downtown—Petula Clark [Tony Hatch] (12/19/64 BCR-1)
54 Berry GORDY/Fonce MIZELL/ Freddie PERREN/Deke RICHARDS	I Want You Back—The Jackson 5 [Berry Gordy/Fonce Mizell/Freddie Perren/Deke Richards] (11/15/69 BCR-1)	ABC—The Jackson 5 [Berry Gordy/Fonce Mizell/Freddie Perren/Deke Richards] (3/14/70 BCR-1)

Writer	First (Entry, Magazines, Peak)	Biggest (Entry, Magazines, Peak)
55 Dave BARTHOLOMEW/Fats DOMINO	*Ain't It A Shame—Fats Domino; Ain't That A Shame—Pat Boone [Dave Bartholomew/Fats Domino] (6/18/55 BCtRt-1)*	Ain't That A Shame—Pat Boone [Dave Bartholomew/Fats Domino] (6/18/55 BCtRt-1)
56 Rod TEMPERTON	Boogie Nights—Heatwave [Rod Temperton] (7/9/77 BCR-2)	Rock With You—Michael Jackson [Rod Temperton] (11/3/79 BCR-1)
57 Hank BALLARD	Finger Poppin' Time—Hank Ballard And The Midnighters [Hank Ballard] (5/16/60 BCR-6)	The Twist—Chubby Checker [Hank Ballard] (11/13/61 BCR-1)
58 Joe MELSON/Roy ORBISON	Up Town—Roy Orbison [Joe Melson/Roy Orbison] (12/28/59 BCR-70)	Crying—Roy Orbison [Joe Melson/Roy Orbison] (8/7/61 BCR-1)
59 Galt MacDERMOT/ James RADO/Gerome RAGNI	Where Do I Go—Carla Thomas [Galt MacDermot/James Rado/Gerome Ragni] (10/19/68 BR-75)	Hair—The Cowsills [Galt MacDermot/James Rado/Gerome Ragni] (3/15/69 BCR-1)
60 Boudleaux BRYANT	I've Been Thinking—The Four Lads [Boudleaux Bryant] (3/5/55 CRt-33)	All I Have To Do Is Dream—The Everly Brothers [Boudleaux Bryant] (4/14/58 BCR-1)
61 L. Russell BROWN/Irwin LEVINE	Knock Three Times—Dawn [L. Russell Brown/Irwin Levine] (11/14/70 BCR-1)	Knock Three Times—Dawn [L. Russell Brown/Irwin Levine] (11/14/70 BCR-1)
62 John FARRAR	Have You Never Been Mellow—Olivia Newton-John [John Farrar] (1/25/75 BCR-1)	You're The One That I Want—John Travolta And Olivia Newton-John [John Farrar] (4/1/78 BCR-1)
63 James BROWN	Try Me—James Brown And The Famous Flames [James Brown] (12/15/58 BC-48)	I Got You (I Feel Good)—James Brown And The Famous Flames [James Brown] (11/6/65 BCR-1)
64 Nick ASHFORD/Valerie SIMPSON	Ain't No Mountain High Enough—Marvin Gaye & Tammi Terrell [Nick Ashford/Valerie Simpson] (5/13/67 BCR-19)	Ain't No Mountain High Enough—Diana Ross [Nick Ashford/Valerie Simpson] (8/8/70 BCR-1)
65 John DENVER	Leaving On A Jet Plane—Gloria Loring [John Denver] (10/11/69 R-98)	Leaving On A Jet Plane—Peter, Paul & Mary [John Denver] (10/25/69 BCR-1)
66 Sonny BONO	I Got You Babe—Sonny & Cher [Sonny Bono] (7/10/65 BCR-1)	I Got You Babe—Sonny & Cher [Sonny Bono] (7/10/65 BCR-1)
67 Joe SOUTH	Untie Me—The Tams [Joe South] (10/13/62 BCR-60)	Yo-Yo—The Osmonds [Joe South] (9/11/71 BCR-1)
68 Jeff LYNNE	Do Ya—The Move [Jeff Lynne] (10/28/72 BCR-88)	Don't Bring Me Down—Electric Light Orchestra [Jeff Lynne] (7/28/79 BCR-3)
69 Mike CHAPMAN/Nicky CHINN	Co-Co—The Sweet [Mike Chapman/Nicky Chinn] (9/25/71 BCR-85)	Kiss You All Over—Exile [Mike Chapman/Nicky Chinn] (7/8/78 BCR-1)
70 Barry GIBB/Robin GIBB	New York Mining Disaster 1941 (Have You Seen My Wife, Mr. Jones)—The Bee Gees [Barry Gibb/Robin Gibb] (5/27/67 BCR-14)	Woman In Love—Barbra Streisand [Barry Gibb/Robin Gibb] (9/6/80 BCR-1)
71 John SEBASTIAN	Do You Believe In Magic—The Lovin' Spoonful [John Sebastian] (8/21/65 BCR-4)	Daydream—The Lovin' Spoonful [John Sebastian] (2/26/66 BCR-1)
72 Lee POCKRISS/Paul VANCE	Catch A Falling Star—Perry Como [Lee Pockriss/Paul Vance] (12/30/57 BCR-1)	Itsy Bitsy Teenie Weenie Yellow Polkadot Bikini—Brian Hyland [Lee Pockriss/Paul Vance] (6/27/60 BCRt-1)
73 Laura NYRO	Wedding Bell Blues—Laura Nyro [Laura Nyro] (12/3/66 C-96)	Wedding Bell Blues—The 5th Dimension [Laura Nyro] (9/20/69 BCR-1)
74 Bobby RUSSELL	Sure Gonna Miss Her—Gary Lewis And The Playboys [Bobby Russell] (3/5/66 BCR-8)	Honey—Bobby Goldsboro [Bobby Russell] (3/23/68 BCR-1)
75 Donovan LEITCH	Catch The Wind—Donovan [Donovan Leitch] (5/8/65 BCR-22)	Sunshine Superman—Donovan [Donovan Leitch] (7/23/66 BCR-1)
76 Buck RAM	Only You (And You Alone)—The Platters [Buck Ram] (8/1/55 BCtRt-3)	The Great Pretender—The Platters [Buck Ram] (12/9/55 BCRt-1)
77 Dennis DeYOUNG	Lady—Styx [Dennis DeYoung] (12/7/74 BCR-6)	Babe—Styx [Dennis DeYoung] (10/6/79 BCR-1)
78 Marty ROBBINS	Respectfully Miss Brooks—Marty Robbins [Marty Robbins] (6/29/56 R-72)	El Paso—Marty Robbins [Marty Robbins] (11/9/59 BCR-1)
79 John MELLENCAMP	I Need A Lover—John Cougar [John Mellencamp] (9/15/79 BCR-28)	Jack & Diane—John Cougar [John Mellencamp] (7/24/82 BC-1)
80 Bernie LOWE/Kal MANN	The Greatest Thing—Georgia Gibbs [Bernie Lowe/Kal Mann] (3/2/56 R-54)	(Let Me Be Your) Teddy Bear—Elvis Presley [Bernie Lowe/Kal Mann] (6/24/57 BCR-1)
81 Jeff BARRY/Ellie GREENWICH	What A Guy—The Raindrops [Jeff Barry/Ellie Greenwich] (4/13/63 BCR-34)	Do Wah Diddy Diddy—Manfred Mann [Jeff Barry/Ellie Greenwich] (8/29/64 BCR-1)
82 Dennis LAMBERT/Brian POTTER	One Tin Soldier—The Original Caste [Dennis Lambert/Brian Potter] (10/18/69 BCR-34)	Don't Pull Your Love—Hamilton, Joe Frank & Reynolds [Dennis Lambert/Brian Potter] (5/15/71 BCR-1)

Writer	First (Entry, Magazines, Peak)	Biggest (Entry, Magazines, Peak)
83 Al GREEN/Al JACKSON/Willie MITCHELL	Let's Stay Together—Al Green [Al Green/Al Jackson/Willie Mitchell] (11/27/71 BCR-1)	Let's Stay Together—Al Green [Al Green/Al Jackson/Willie Mitchell] (11/27/71 BCR-1)
84 Bob SEGER	Heavy Music (Part 1)—Bob Seger & The Last Heard [Bob Seger] (9/9/67 CR-70)	Night Moves—Bob Seger [Bob Seger] (12/4/76 BCR-4)
85 Mac DAVIS	Good Time Girl—Nancy Sinatra [Mac Davis] (11/30/68 BCR-65)	Baby Don't Get Hooked On Me—Mac Davis [Mac Davis] (7/1/72 BCR-1)
86 Otis BLACKWELL/Elvis PRESLEY	Don't Be Cruel—Elvis Presley [Otis Blackwell/Elvis Presley] (7/27/56 BCR-1)	Don't Be Cruel—Elvis Presley [Otis Blackwell/Elvis Presley] (7/27/56 BCR-1)
87 Lou GRAMM/Michael Leslie JONES	Cold As Ice—Foreigner [Lou Gramm/Michael Leslie Jones] (7/23/77 BCR-6)	Waiting For A Girl Like You—Foreigner [Lou Gramm/Michael Leslie Jones] (10/10/81 BCR-2)
88 Ray PARKER Jr.	Jack And Jill—Raydio [Ray Parker Jr.] (12/17/77 BCR-6)	Ghostbusters—Ray Parker Jr. [Ray Parker Jr.] (6/16/84 BC-1)
89 Pete TOWNSHEND	I Can't Explain—The Who [Pete Townshend] (2/20/65 BCR-57)	I Can See For Miles—The Who [Pete Townshend] (10/7/67 BCR-8)
90 Allen TOUSSAINT	Mother-In-Law—Ernie K-Doe [Allen Toussaint] (3/13/61 BCR-1)	Mother-In-Law—Ernie K-Doe [Allen Toussaint] (3/13/61 BCR-1)
91 Howard GREENFIELD/Jack KELLER	Everybody's Somebody's Fool—Connie Francis [Howard Greenfield/Jack Keller] (5/9/60 BCR-1)	My Heart Has A Mind Of Its Own—Connie Francis [Howard Greenfield/Jack Keller] (8/15/60 BCR-1)
92 Simon Le BON/Nick RHODES/ Andy TAYLOR/ Nigel John TAYLOR/Roger TAYLOR	Hungry Like The Wolf—Duran Duran [Simon Le Bon/Nick Rhodes/Andy Taylor/ Nigel John Taylor/Roger Taylor] (12/25/82 BC-3)	The Reflex—Duran Duran [Simon Le Bon/Nick Rhodes/Andy Taylor/ Nigel John Taylor/Roger Taylor] (4/21/84 BC-1)
93 Boudleaux BRYANT/Felice BRYANT	Bye Bye Love—The Everly Brothers [Boudleaux Bryant/Felice Bryant] (5/20/57 BCRt-1)	Bye Bye Love—The Everly Brothers [Boudleaux Bryant/Felice Bryant] (5/20/57 BCRt-1)
94 Dino FEKARIS/Freddie PERREN	That Once In A Lifetime—Demis Roussos [Dino Fekaris/Freddie Perren] (5/27/78 BCR-47)	Reunited—Peaches & Herb [Dino Fekaris/Freddie Perren] (3/17/79 BCR-1)
95 Ray EVANS/Jay LIVINGSTON	Silver Bells—Bing Crosby and Carol Richards [Ray Evans/Jay Livingston] (12/20/54 R-43)	Tammy—Debbie Reynolds [Ray Evans/Jay Livingston] (7/6/57 BCtRt-1)
96 Daryl HALL	Rich Girl—Daryl Hall & John Oates [Daryl Hall] (1/22/77 BCR-1)	Rich Girl—Daryl Hall & John Oates [Daryl Hall] (1/22/77 BCR-1)
97 Ray DAVIES	You Really Got Me—The Kinks [Ray Davies] (9/26/64 BCR-5)	You Really Got Me—The Kinks [Ray Davies] (9/26/64 BCR-5)
98 Rick SPRINGFIELD	Speak To The Sky—Rick Springfield [Rick Springfield] (7/29/72 BCR-14)	Jessie's Girl—Rick Springfield [Rick Springfield] (3/28/81 BCR-1)
99 Thom BELL/Linda CREED	Help Me Find A Way (To Say I Love You)— Little Anthony And The Imperials [Thom Bell/Linda Creed] (11/21/70 BCR-65)	You Make Me Feel Brand New—The Stylistics Featurng Airrion Love & Russell Thompkins, Jr. [Thom Bell/Linda Creed] (3/16/74 BCR-1)
100 Lee HAZLEWOOD	Fool—Sanford Clark [Lee Hazlewood] (7/20/56 BCtRt-7)	These Boots Are Made For Walkin'—Nancy Sinatra [Lee Hazlewood] (1/22/66 BCR-1)
101 Richard MARX	Should've Known Better—Richard Marx [Richard Marx] (9/26/87 BC-3)	Right Here Waiting—Richard Marx [Richard Marx] (7/8/89 BC-1)
102 Jeff BARRY/Andy KIM	How'd We Ever Get This Way—Andy Kim [Jeff Barry/Andy Kim] (4/13/68 BCR-16)	Sugar, Sugar—The Archies [Jeff Barry/Andy Kim] (7/19/69 BCR-1)
103 Thomas F. KELLY/Billy STEINBERG	Like A Virgin—Madonna [Thomas F. Kelly/Billy Steinberg] (11/17/84 BC-1)	Like A Virgin—Madonna [Thomas F. Kelly/Billy Steinberg] (11/17/84 BC-1)
104 Alex NORTH/Hy ZARET	Unchained Melody—Al Hibbler [Alex North/Hy Zaret] (3/21/55 BCtRt-1)	Unchained Melody— Les Baxter His Chorus And Orchestra [Alex North/Hy Zaret] (4/30/55 BCtRt-1)
105 Jim PETERIK/Frankie SULLIVAN	Poor Man's Son—Survivor [Jim Peterik/Frankie Sullivan] (10/17/81 BCR-33)	Eye Of The Tiger—Survivor [Jim Peterik/Frankie Sullivan] (6/5/82 BC-1)
106 Freddie MERCURY	Killer Queen—Queen [Freddie Mercury] (2/8/75 BCR-11)	Crazy Little Thing Called Love—Queen [Freddie Mercury] (12/22/79 BCR-1)
107 Garry BONNER/Alan GORDON	Happy Together—The Turtles [Garry Bonner/Alan Gordon] (2/11/67 BCR-1)	Happy Together—The Turtles [Garry Bonner/Alan Gordon] (2/11/67 BCR-1)
108 Barry WHITE	Walkin' In The Rain With The One I Love— Love Unlimited [Barry White] (3/18/72 BCR-7)	Love's Theme—Love Unlimited Orchestra [Barry White] (12/1/73 BCR-1)
109 Gary GELD/Peter UDELL	The Tear Of The Year—Jackie Wilson [Gary Geld/Peter Udell] (1/14/61 BCR-40)	Hurting Each Other—Carpenters [Gary Geld/Peter Udell] (1/15/72 BCR-1)
110 John PHILLIPS	Monday, Monday—The Mama's & The Papa's [John Phillips] (4/9/66 BCR-1)	Monday, Monday—The Mama's & The Papa's [John Phillips] (4/9/66 BCR-1)
111 Tommy BOYCE/Bobby HART	Last Train To Clarksville—The Monkees [Tommy Boyce/Bobby Hart] (9/3/66 BCR-1)	Last Train To Clarksville—The Monkees [Tommy Boyce/Bobby Hart] (9/3/66 BCR-1)

Writer	First (Entry, Magazines, Peak)	Biggest (Entry, Magazines, Peak)
112 Tony BANKS/Phil COLLINS/ Mike RUTHERFORD	Follow You Follow Me—Genesis [Tony Banks/Phil Collins/Mike Rutherford] (4/22/78 BCR-22)	Invisible Touch—Genesis [Tony Banks/Phil Collins/Mike Rutherford] (5/31/86 BC-1)
113 Joe TEX	Hold What You've Got—Joe Tex [Joe Tex] (12/19/64 BCR-5)	I Gotcha—Joe Tex [Joe Tex] (1/22/72 BCR-2)
114 Chip TAYLOR	Worry—Johnny Tillotson [Chip Taylor] (7/18/64 BCR-45)	Wild Thing—The Troggs [Chip Taylor] (6/18/66 BCR-1)
115 Steve MILLER	Living In The U.S.A.—Steve Miller Band [Steve Miller] (11/9/68 BCR-72)	Abracadabra—Steve Miller Band [Steve Miller] (5/29/82 BC-1)
116 Gilbert O'SULLIVAN	Alone Again (Naturally)—Gilbert O'Sullivan [Gilbert O'Sullivan] (6/17/72 BCR-1)	Alone Again (Naturally)—Gilbert O'Sullivan [Gilbert O'Sullivan] (6/17/72 BCR-1)
117 Sara ALLEN/Daryl HALL/ John OATES	You Make My Dreams—Daryl Hall & John Oates [Sara Allen/Daryl Hall/John Oates] (5/2/81 BCR-5)	Maneater—Daryl Hall & John Oates [Sara Allen/Daryl Hall/John Oates] (10/16/82 BC-1)
118 Barry GIBB	Don't Wanna Live Inside Myself—Bee Gees [Barry Gibb] (10/16/71 BCR-30)	I Just Want To Be Your Everything—Andy Gibb [Barry Gibb] (4/23/77 BCR-1)
119 Ray STEVENS	Make Me Smile Again—Cathy Jean [Ray Stevens] (6/12/61 R-98)	The Streak—Ray Stevens [Ray Stevens] (4/13/74 BCR-1)
120 Ric OCASEK	Just What I Needed—The Cars [Ric Ocasek] (6/17/78 BCR-24)	Shake It Up—The Cars [Ric Ocasek] (7/11/81 BCR-3)
121 Harlan HOWARD	Heartaches By The Number—Guy Mitchell [Harlan Howard] (10/5/59 BCR-1)	Heartaches By The Number—Guy Mitchell [Harlan Howard] (10/5/59 BCR-1)
122 O'Kelly ISLEY/Ronald ISLEY/ Rudolph ISLEY	Shout Part One—The Isley Brothers [O'Kelly Isley/Ronald Isley/Rudolph Isley] (9/7/59 BCR-28)	It's Your Thing—The Isley Brothers [O'Kelly Isley/Ronald Isley/Rudolph Isley] (3/15/69 BCR-2)
123 Don GIBSON	Oh Lonesome Me—Don Gibson [Don Gibson] (2/22/58 BCRt-3)	I Can't Stop Loving You—Ray Charles [Don Gibson] (4/30/62 BCRt-1)
124 Maurice STARR	Please Don't Go Girl—New Kids On The Block [Maurice Starr] (6/25/88 BC-10)	Step By Step—New Kids On The Block [Maurice Starr] (5/26/90 BC-1)
125 Roy C. BENNETT/Sid TEPPER	Naughty Lady Of Shady Lane—The Ames Brothers [Roy C. Bennett/Sid Tepper] (7/10/54 BCtRt-3)	Naughty Lady Of Shady Lane—The Ames Brothers [Roy C. Bennett/Sid Tepper] (7/10/54 BCtRt-3)
126 David SEVILLE	*Armen's Theme—David Carroll & His Orchestra; Armen's Theme—Joe Reisman and His Orchestra; Armen's Theme—David Seville; Armen's Theme—Lew Quadling & His Orchestra [David Seville] (12/8/56 Rt-36)*	Witch Doctor—David Seville [David Seville] (4/7/58 BCR-1)
127 Richard ADLER/Jerry ROSS	Hernando's Hideaway—Archie Bleyer [Richard Adler/Jerry Ross] (5/29/54 BCR-PRE)	Hey There—Rosemary Clooney [Richard Adler/Jerry Ross] (7/3/54 BCtR-1)
128 Bill WITHERS	Ain't No Sunshine—Bill Withers [Bill Withers] (7/3/71 BCR-3)	Lean On Me—Bill Withers [Bill Withers] (4/15/72 BCR-1)
129 Bobby DARIN	Dream Lover—Bobby Darin [Bobby Darin] (4/18/59 BCR-2)	Dream Lover—Bobby Darin [Bobby Darin] (4/18/59 BCR-2)
130 Wayne Carson THOMPSON	Somebody Like Me—Eddy Arnold [Wayne Carson Thompson] (10/8/66 BCR-36)	The Letter—The Box Tops [Wayne Carson Thompson] (8/12/67 BCR-1)
131 Isaac HAYES/David PORTER	You Don't Know Like I Know—Sam & Dave [Isaac Hayes/David Porter] (1/8/66 BCR-80)	Soul Man—Sam & Dave [Isaac Hayes/David Porter] (9/9/67 BCR-1)
132 Per GESSLE	The Look—Roxette [Per Gessle] (2/11/89 BC-1)	It Must Have Been Love—Roxette [Per Gessle] (4/7/90 BC-1)
133 Roger MILLER	Invitation To The Blues—Ray Price [Roger Miller] (9/8/58 B-92)	King Of The Road—Roger Miller [Roger Miller] (1/30/65 BCR-3)
134 Harold LOGAN/Lloyd PRICE	Personality—Lloyd Price [Harold Logan/Lloyd Price] (4/27/59 BCR-2)	Personality—Lloyd Price [Harold Logan/Lloyd Price] (4/27/59 BCR-2)
135 Sammy FAIN/Paul Francis WEBSTER	Secret Love—Doris Day [Sammy Fain/Paul Francis Webster] (5/29/54 B-PRE)	Love Is A Many Splendored Thing—Four Aces [Sammy Fain/Paul Francis Webster] (8/1/55 BCtRt-1)
136 Tommy ROE	Sheila—Tommy Roe [Tommy Roe] (7/14/62 BCR-1)	Sheila—Tommy Roe [Tommy Roe] (7/14/62 BCR-1)
137 Richard DEHR/Terry GILKYSON/ Frank MILLER	*Memories Are Made Of This—Mindy Carson; Memories Are Made Of This—Dean Martin; Memories Are Made Of This—Gale Storm [Richard Dehr/Terry Gilkyson/Frank Miller] (12/9/55 BCtRt-1)*	Memories Are Made Of This—Dean Martin [Richard Dehr/Terry Gilkyson/Frank Miller] (11/21/55 BCtRt-1)

Writer	First (Entry, Magazines, Peak)	Biggest (Entry, Magazines, Peak)
138 Thomas ALLEN/ Harold BROWN/ Morris DICKERSON/ Lonnie JORDAN/Charles MILLER/ Lee OSKAR/Howard SCOTT	Spill The Wine—Eric Burdon And War [Thomas Allen/Harold Brown/ Morris Dickerson/Lonnie Jordan/Charles Miller/ Lee Oskar/Howard Scott] (5/23/70 BCR-1)	Spill The Wine—Eric Burdon And War [Thomas Allen/Harold Brown/ Morris Dickerson/Lonnie Jordan/Charles Miller/ Lee Oskar/Howard Scott] (5/23/70 BCR-1)
139 Bob MERRILL	Tell Me Tell Me—June Valli [Bob Merrill] (9/4/54 CR-23)	Honeycomb—Jimmie Rodgers [Bob Merrill] (8/3/57 BCRt-1)
140 Baker KNIGHT	*I Got A Feeling—Ricky Nelson; Lonesome Town—Ricky Nelson [Baker Knight] (10/6/58 BCR-7)*	Lonesome Town—Ricky Nelson [Baker Knight] (10/6/58 BCR-7)
141 Peter CALLANDER/Mitch MURRAY	Even The Bad Times Are Good—The Tremeloes [Peter Callander/Mitch Murray] (9/30/67 BCR-28)	Billy, Don't Be A Hero— Bo Donaldson And The Heywoods [Peter Callander/Mitch Murray] (4/13/74 BCR-1)
142 Melanie SAFKA	Lay Down (Candles In The Rain)— Melanie With The Edwin Hawkins Singers [Melanie Safka] (4/18/70 BCR-3)	Brand New Key—Melanie [Melanie Safka] (10/23/71 BCR-1)
143 Debbie GIBSON	Only In My Dreams—Debbie Gibson [Debbie Gibson] (5/9/87 BC-4)	Lost In Your Eyes—Debbie Gibson [Debbie Gibson] (1/21/89 BC-1)
144 Steve BARRI/P.F. SLOAN	Kick That Little Foot Sally Ann—Round Robin [Steve Barri/P.F. Sloan] (5/23/64 BCR-61)	Eve Of Destruction—Barry McGuire [Steve Barri/P.F. Sloan] (8/14/65 BCR-1)
145 Jim STEINMAN	You Took The Words Right Out Of My Mouth (Hot Summer Night)—Meat Loaf [Jim Steinman] (11/5/77 CR-73)	Total Eclipse Of The Heart—Bonnie Tyler [Jim Steinman] (7/16/83 BC-1)
146 Madonna L. CICCONE/ Patrick Raymond LEONARD	Live To Tell—Madonna [Madonna L. Ciccone/Patrick Raymond Leonard] (4/12/86 BC-1)	Live To Tell—Madonna [Madonna L. Ciccone/Patrick Raymond Leonard] (4/12/86 BC-1)
147 Mark JAMES	The Eyes Of A New York Woman—B.J. Thomas [Mark James] (6/8/68 BCR-28)	Suspicious Minds—Elvis Presley [Mark James] (9/13/69 BCR-1)
148 Jim CROCE	You Don't Mess Around With Jim—Jim Croce [Jim Croce] (6/24/72 BCR-7)	Bad, Bad Leroy Brown—Jim Croce [Jim Croce] (4/14/73 BCR-1)
149 Jon BON JOVI/Desmond CHILD/ Richie SAMBORA	You Give Love A Bad Name—Bon Jovi [Jon Bon Jovi/Desmond Child/Richie Sambora] (9/6/86 BC-1)	Livin' On A Prayer—Bon Jovi [Jon Bon Jovi/Desmond Child/Richie Sambora] (12/13/86 BC-1)
150 Shel SILVERSTEIN	25 Minutes To Go—The Brothers Four [Shel Silverstein] (11/10/62 R-100)	A Boy Named Sue—Johnny Cash [Shel Silverstein] (7/26/69 BCR-1)
151 Al HOFFMAN/Dick MANNING	Gilly Gilly Ossenfeffer Katzenellen Bogen By The Sea— The Four Lads [Al Hoffman/Dick Manning] (7/3/54 C-PRE)	Hot Diggity (Dog Ziggity Boom)—Perry Como [Al Hoffman/Dick Manning] (3/2/56 BCR-2)
152 Tony ROMEO	Indian Lake—The Cowsills [Tony Romeo] (5/25/68 BCR-6)	I Think I Love You—The Partridge Family Starring Shirley Jones & Featuring David Cassidy [Tony Romeo] (9/26/70 BCR-1)
153 Michael CRAIG/Roy HAY/ Jon MOSS/George O'DOWD	Do You Really Want To Hurt Me—Culture Club [Michael Craig/Roy Hay/Jon Moss/George O'Dowd] (12/4/82 BC-1)	Do You Really Want To Hurt Me—Culture Club [Michael Craig/Roy Hay/Jon Moss/George O'Dowd] (12/4/82 BC-1)
154 Jim WEATHERLY	Loving You Is Just An Old Habit—Jim Weatherly [Jim Weatherly] (12/23/72 CR-90)	Midnight Train To Georgia—Gladys Knight & The Pips [Jim Weatherly] (8/25/73 BCR-1)
155 David BOWIE	Changes—David Bowie [David Bowie] (4/8/72 BCR-59)	Let's Dance—David Bowie [David Bowie] (3/26/83 BC-1)
156 Bryan ADAMS/Jim VALLANCE	Don't Let Him Know—Prism [Bryan Adams/Jim Vallance] (1/30/82 BCR-39)	Heaven—Bryan Adams [Bryan Adams/Jim Vallance] (4/20/85 BC-1)
157 William DEES/Roy ORBISON	It's Over—Roy Orbison [William Dees/Roy Orbison] (4/11/64 BCR-8)	Oh, Pretty Woman—Roy Orbison And The Candy Men [William Dees/Roy Orbison] (8/29/64 BCR-1)
158 Adam CLAYTON/Dave EVANS/ Paul HEWSON/Larry MULLEN	New Year's Day—U2 [Adam Clayton/Dave Evans/Paul Hewson/ Larry Mullen] (4/2/83 BC-50)	With Or Without You—U2 [Adam Clayton/Dave Evans/Paul Hewson/Larry Mullen] (3/21/87 BC-1)
159 Marc BLITZSTEIN/Berthold BRECHT/Kurt WEILL	A Theme From Threepenny Opera (Mack The Knife)— Louis Armstrong And His All-Stars [Marc Blitzstein/Berthold Brecht/Kurt Weill] (1/13/56 BRt-6)	Mack The Knife—Bobby Darin [Marc Blitzstein/Berthold Brecht/Kurt Weill] (8/24/59 BCR-1)
160 Kenneth EDMONDS/ Antonio REID/Daryl SIMMONS	Knocked Out—Paula Abdul [Kenneth Edmonds/Antonio Reid/Daryl Simmons] (6/18/88 BC-41)	On Our Own—Bobby Brown [Kenneth Edmonds/Antonio Reid/Daryl Simmons] (6/10/89 BC-2)
161 Dion DiMUCCI/Ernie MARESCA	Runaround Sue—Dion [Dion DiMucci/Ernie Maresca] (9/18/61 BCR-1)	Runaround Sue—Dion [Dion DiMucci/Ernie Maresca] (9/18/61 BCR-1)

Writer	First (Entry, Magazines, Peak)	Biggest (Entry, Magazines, Peak)
162 Charles FOX/Norman GIMBEL	Killing Me Softly With His Song—Roberta Flack [Charles Fox/Norman Gimbel] (1/20/73 BCR-1)	Killing Me Softly With His Song—Roberta Flack [Charles Fox/Norman Gimbel] (1/20/73 BCR-1)
163 Andy FARRISS/Michael HUTCHENCE	The One Thing—INXS [Andy Farriss/Michael Hutchence] (3/26/83 BC-30)	Need You Tonight—INXS [Andy Farriss/Michael Hutchence] (10/24/87 BC-1)
164 Roger NICHOLS/Paul WILLIAMS	Only Me—The First Edition [Roger Nichols/Paul Williams] (5/11/68 R-81)	We've Only Just Begun—Carpenters [Roger Nichols/Paul Williams] (9/12/70 BCR-1)
165 Dallas FRAZIER	*Alley Oop—The Hollywood Argyles; Alley Oop—Danté And The Evergreens [Dallas Frazier] (5/23/60 BCtRt-1)*	Alley Oop—The Hollywood Argyles [Dallas Frazier] (5/23/60 BCtRt-1)
166 Annie LENNOX/David A. STEWART	Sweet Dreams (Are Made Of This)—Eurythmics [Annie Lennox/David A. Stewart] (5/14/83 BC-1)	Sweet Dreams (Are Made Of This)—Eurythmics [Annie Lennox/David A. Stewart] (5/14/83 BC-1)
167 Kevin CRONIN	Roll With The Changes—REO Speedwagon [Kevin Cronin] (5/13/78 BCR-42)	Keep On Loving You—REO Speedwagon [Kevin Cronin] (11/29/80 BCR-1)
168 Barry MANN/Phil SPECTOR/ Cynthia WEIL	Walking In The Rain—The Ronettes [Barry Mann/Phil Spector/Cynthia Weil] (10/24/64 BCR-20)	You've Lost That Lovin' Feelin'— The Righteous Brothers [Barry Mann/Phil Spector/Cynthia Weil] (12/12/64 BCR-1)
169 Kenneth EDMONDS/Antonio REID	Girlfriend—Pebbles [Kenneth Edmonds/Antonio Reid] (1/30/88 BC-5)	I'm Your Baby Tonight—Whitney Houston [Kenneth Edmonds/Antonio Reid] (10/20/90 BC-1)
170 Peter CETERA/David FOSTER	Hard To Say I'm Sorry—Chicago [Peter Cetera/David Foster] (6/5/82 BC-1)	Hard To Say I'm Sorry—Chicago [Peter Cetera/David Foster] (6/5/82 BC-1)
171 Christopher CROSS	Ride Like The Wind—Christopher Cross [Christopher Cross] (2/9/80 BCR-2)	Ride Like The Wind—Christopher Cross [Christopher Cross] (2/9/80 BCR-2)
172 Dan FOGELBERG	Part Of The Plan—Dan Fogelberg [Dan Fogelberg] (12/28/74 BCR-24)	Longer—Dan Fogelberg [Dan Fogelberg] (12/15/79 BCR-1)
173 Gordon LIGHTFOOT	For Lovin' Me—Peter, Paul & Mary [Gordon Lightfoot] (1/23/65 BCR-24)	Sundown—Gordon Lightfoot [Gordon Lightfoot] (4/6/74 BCR-1)
174 Ric CARTEY/Carole JOYNER	*Young Love—The Crew-Cuts; Young Love—Sonny James [Ric Cartey/Carole Joyner] (12/22/56 BCtRt-1)*	Young Love—Tab Hunter [Ric Cartey/Carole Joyner] (1/12/57 BCtRt-1)
175 Melvin ENDSLEY	Singing The Blues—Guy Mitchell [Melvin Endsley] (10/20/56 BCtRt-1)	Singing The Blues—Guy Mitchell [Melvin Endsley] (10/20/56 BCtRt-1)
176 John STEWART	One More Town—The Kingston Trio [John Stewart] (9/29/62 BCR-81)	Daydream Believer—The Monkees [John Stewart] (11/11/67 BCR-1)
177 Don McLEAN	And I Love You So—Bobby Goldsboro [Don McLean] (5/8/71 BC-83)	American Pie—Don McLean [Don McLean] (11/27/71 BCR-1)
178 Curtis BEDEAU/ Gerard CHARLES/ Hugh CLARKE/Brian GEORGE/ Lucien GEORGE/Paul GEORGE	I Wonder If I Take You Home— Lisa Lisa and Cult Jam with Full Force [Curtis Bedeau/Gerard Charles/Hugh Clarke/ Brian George/Lucien George/Paul George] (6/8/85 BC-33)	Head To Toe—Lisa Lisa And Cult Jam [Curtis Bedeau/Gerard Charles/Hugh Clarke/ Brian George/Lucien George/Paul George] (4/11/87 BC-1)
179 Bobby DALL/C.C. DeVILLE/ Bret MICHAELS/Rikki ROCKETT	Talk Dirty To Me—Poison [Bobby Dall/C.C. DeVille/Bret Michaels/Rikki Rockett] (3/14/87 BC-9)	Every Rose Has Its Thorn—Poison [Bobby Dall/C.C. DeVille/Bret Michaels/ Rikki Rockett] (10/29/88 BC-1)
180 Peter DeANGELIS/Bob MARCUCCI	Will I Always Be Your Sweetheart—Mona Carol [Peter DeAngelis/Bob Marcucci] (5/11/56 Rt-71)	Why—Frankie Avalon [Peter DeAngelis/Bob Marcucci] (11/16/59 BCR-1)
181 Maurice WILLIAMS	Little Darlin'—The Diamonds [Maurice Williams] (3/2/57 BCRt-1)	Little Darlin'—The Diamonds [Maurice Williams] (3/2/57 BCRt-1)
182 Eric CARMEN	Go All The Way—Raspberries [Eric Carmen] (7/1/72 BCR-3)	That's Rock 'N' Roll—Shaun Cassidy [Eric Carmen] (7/23/77 BCR-3)
183 Robert LAMM	Questions 67 And 68—Chicago [Robert Lamm] (8/9/69 BCR-71)	Saturday In The Park—Chicago [Robert Lamm] (7/29/72 BCR-3)
184 Hoyt AXTON	Willie Jean—The Sunshine Company [Hoyt Axton] (10/19/68 R-95)	Joy To The World—Three Dog Night [Hoyt Axton] (3/6/71 BCR-1)
185 Terry BRITTEN/Graham LYLE	What's Love Got To Do With It—Tina Turner [Terry Britten/Graham Lyle] (5/19/84 BC-1)	What's Love Got To Do With It—Tina Turner [Terry Britten/Graham Lyle] (5/19/84 BC-1)
186 Rod ARGENT	She's Not There—The Zombies [Rod Argent] (10/3/64 BCR-1)	She's Not There—The Zombies [Rod Argent] (10/3/64 BCR-1)
187 Walter BECKER/Donald FAGEN	Do It Again—Steely Dan [Walter Becker/Donald Fagen] (11/18/72 BCR-6)	Rikki Don't Lose That Number—Steely Dan [Walter Becker/Donald Fagen] (5/4/74 BCR-3)
188 Luigi CREATORE/ Solomon LINDA/Hugo PERETTI/ Albert STANTON/George David WEISS	The Lion Sleeps Tonight—The Tokens [Luigi Creatore/Solomon Linda/Hugo Peretti/ Albert Stanton/George David Weiss] (11/13/61 BCR-1)	The Lion Sleeps Tonight—The Tokens [Luigi Creatore/Solomon Linda/Hugo Peretti/ Albert Stanton/George David Weiss] (11/13/61 BCR-1)

Writer	First (Entry, Magazines, Peak)	Biggest (Entry, Magazines, Peak)
189 Spooner OLDHAM/Dan PENN	I'm Your Puppet—James & Bobby Purify [Spooner Oldham/Dan Penn] (9/24/66 BCR-5)	Cry Like A Baby—The Box Tops [Spooner Oldham/Dan Penn] (2/24/68 BCR-2)
190 Will JENNINGS/Steve WINWOOD	While You See A Chance—Steve Winwood [Will Jennings/Steve Winwood] (2/7/81 BCR-7)	Higher Love—Steve Winwood [Will Jennings/Steve Winwood] (6/14/86 BC-1)
191 J.P. RICHARDSON	Chantilly Lace—Big Bopper [J.P. Richardson] (8/4/58 BCR-4)	Running Bear—Johnny Preston [J.P. Richardson] (10/12/59 BCR-1)
192 Stig ANDERSON/ Benny ANDERSSON/Björn ULVAEUS	Waterloo—Abba (Björn, Benny, Anna & Frida) [Stig Anderson/Benny Andersson/Björn Ulvaeus] (5/25/74 BCR-6)	Dancing Queen—Abba [Stig Anderson/Benny Andersson/Björn Ulvaeus] (12/11/76 BCR-1)
193 Tommy ROE/Freddy WELLER	Dizzy—Tommy Roe [Tommy Roe/Freddy Weller] (1/18/69 BCR-1)	Dizzy—Tommy Roe [Tommy Roe/Freddy Weller] (1/18/69 BCR-1)
194 Dick ADDRISI/Don ADDRISI	Cherrystone—The Addrisi Brothers [Dick Addrisi/Don Addrisi] (6/1/59 BCR-62)	Never My Love—The Association [Dick Addrisi/Don Addrisi] (8/26/67 BCR-1)
195 John BETTIS/Richard CARPENTER	Goodbye To Love—Carpenters [John Bettis/Richard Carpenter] (7/8/72 BCR-6)	Top Of The World—Carpenters [John Bettis/Richard Carpenter] (9/29/73 BCR-1)
196 John CARTER/Ken HAWKER	Is It True—Brenda Lee [John Carter/Ken Hawker] (10/10/64 BCR-14)	Little Bit O' Soul—The Music Explosion [John Carter/Ken Hawker] (5/6/67 BCR-1)
197 Cat STEVENS	Matthew And Son—Cat Stevens [Cat Stevens] (3/25/67 CR-92)	Peace Train—Cat Stevens [Cat Stevens] (9/25/71 BCR-4)
198 Audrey ALLISON/Joe ALLISON	Teen Age Crush—Tommy Sands [Audrey Allison/Joe Allison] (2/16/57 BCR-1)	He'll Have To Go—Jim Reeves [Audrey Allison/Joe Allison] (12/21/59 BCR-1)
199 Mariah CAREY/Ben MARGULIES	Vision Of Love—Mariah Carey [Mariah Carey/Ben Margulies] (6/2/90 BC-1)	Love Takes Time—Mariah Carey [Mariah Carey/Ben Margulies] (9/15/90 BC-1)
200 Joe SHERMAN/Noel SHERMAN	Everlovin'—Patti Page [Joe Sherman/Noel Sherman] (1/24/55 CR-17)	Ramblin' Rose—Nat King Cole [Joe Sherman/Noel Sherman] (7/28/62 BCR-1)

Top 100 One-Writer Teams

1 Paul SIMON ▶ 8	35 John DENVER ▶ 65	69 Maurice STARR ▶ 124
2 Lionel RICHIE ▶ 9	36 Sonny BONO ▶ 66	70 David SEVILLE ▶ 126
3 Neil DIAMOND ▶ 11	37 Joe SOUTH ▶ 67	71 Bill WITHERS ▶ 128
4 PRINCE ▶ 12	38 Jeff LYNNE ▶ 68	72 Bobby DARIN ▶ 129
5 TRADITIONAL ▶ 13	39 John SEBASTIAN ▶ 71	73 Wayne Carson THOMPSON ▶ 130
6 Stevie WONDER ▶ 15	40 Laura NYRO ▶ 73	74 Per GESSLE ▶ 132
7 Paul ANKA ▶ 18	41 Bobby RUSSELL ▶ 74	75 Roger MILLER ▶ 133
8 Curtis MAYFIELD ▶ 19	42 Donovan LEITCH ▶ 75	76 Tommy ROE ▶ 136
9 Billy JOEL ▶ 23	43 Buck RAM ▶ 76	77 Bob MERRILL ▶ 139
10 Michael JACKSON ▶ 24	44 Dennis DeYOUNG ▶ 77	78 Baker KNIGHT ▶ 140
11 Smokey ROBINSON ▶ 25	45 Marty ROBBINS ▶ 78	79 Melanie SAFKA ▶ 142
12 Bob DYLAN ▶ 26	46 John MELLENCAMP ▶ 79	80 Debbie GIBSON ▶ 143
13 Sam COOKE ▶ 27	47 Bob SEGER ▶ 84	81 Jim STEINMAN ▶ 145
14 John FOGERTY ▶ 30	48 Mac DAVIS ▶ 85	82 Mark JAMES ▶ 147
15 John D. LOUDERMILK ▶ 32	49 Ray PARKER Jr. ▶ 88	83 Jim CROCE ▶ 148
16 George MICHAEL ▶ 33	50 Pete TOWNSHEND ▶ 89	84 Shel SILVERSTEIN ▶ 150
17 Sylvester STEWART ▶ 35	51 Allen TOUSSAINT ▶ 90	85 Tony ROMEO ▶ 152
18 Bruce SPRINGSTEEN ▶ 36	52 Daryl HALL ▶ 96	86 Jim WEATHERLY ▶ 154
19 Chuck BERRY ▶ 38	53 Ray DAVIES ▶ 97	87 David BOWIE ▶ 155
20 Jimmy WEBB ▶ 41	54 Rick SPRINGFIELD ▶ 98	88 Dallas FRAZIER ▶ 165
21 John LENNON ▶ 42	55 Lee HAZLEWOOD ▶ 100	89 Kevin CRONIN ▶ 167
22 Paul McCARTNEY ▶ 43	56 Richard MARX ▶ 101	90 Christopher CROSS ▶ 171
23 Jerry FULLER ▶ 44	57 Freddie MERCURY ▶ 106	91 Dan FOGELBERG ▶ 172
24 David GATES ▶ 45	58 Barry WHITE ▶ 108	92 Gordon LIGHTFOOT ▶ 173
25 Diane WARREN ▶ 46	59 John PHILLIPS ▶ 110	93 Melvin ENDSLEY ▶ 175
26 Phil COLLINS ▶ 48	60 Joe TEX ▶ 113	94 John STEWART ▶ 176
27 STING ▶ 51	61 Chip TAYLOR ▶ 114	95 Don McLEAN ▶ 177
28 George HARRISON ▶ 52	62 Steve MILLER ▶ 115	96 Maurice WILLIAMS ▶ 181
29 Tony HATCH ▶ 53	63 Gilbert O'SULLIVAN ▶ 116	97 Eric CARMEN ▶ 182
30 Rod TEMPERTON ▶ 56	64 Barry GIBB ▶ 118	98 Robert LAMM ▶ 183
31 Hank BALLARD ▶ 57	65 Ray STEVENS ▶ 119	99 Hoyt AXTON ▶ 184
32 Boudleaux BRYANT ▶ 60	66 Ric OCASEK ▶ 120	100 Rod ARGENT ▶ 186
33 John FARRAR ▶ 62	67 Harlan HOWARD ▶ 121	
34 James BROWN ▶ 63	68 Don GIBSON ▶ 123	

Top 100 Two-Writer Teams

1 John LENNON/Paul McCARTNEY ▶ 1	51 Steve BARRI/P.F. SLOAN ▶ 144
2 Burt BACHARACH/Hal DAVID ▶ 3	52 Madonna L. CICCONE/Patrick Raymond LEONARD ▶ 146
3 Mick JAGGER/Keith RICHARDS ▶ 4	53 Al HOFFMAN/Dick MANNING ▶ 151
4 Gerry GOFFIN/Carole KING ▶ 6	54 Bryan ADAMS/Jim VALLANCE ▶ 156
5 Elton JOHN/Bernie TAUPIN ▶ 7	55 William DEES/Roy ORBISON ▶ 157
6 Jerry LEIBER/Mike STOLLER ▶ 10	56 Dion DiMUCCI/Ernie MARESCA ▶ 161
7 Barrett STRONG/Norman WHITFIELD ▶ 14	57 Charles FOX/Norman GIMBEL ▶ 162
8 Kenneth GAMBLE/Leon HUFF ▶ 16	58 Andy FARRISS/Michael HUTCHENCE ▶ 163
9 Doc POMUS/Mort SHUMAN ▶ 17	59 Roger NICHOLS/Paul WILLIAMS ▶ 164
10 Howard GREENFIELD/Neil SEDAKA ▶ 20	60 Annie LENNOX/David A. STEWART ▶ 166
11 Barry MANN/Cynthia WEIL ▶ 21	61 Kenneth EDMONDS/Antonio REID ▶ 169
12 Linda McCARTNEY/Paul McCARTNEY ▶ 22	62 Peter CETERA/David FOSTER ▶ 170
13 Mike LOVE/Brian WILSON ▶ 28	63 Ric CARTEY/Carole JOYNER ▶ 174
14 Bob CREWE/Bob GAUDIO ▶ 29	64 Peter DeANGELIS/Bob MARCUCCI ▶ 180
15 Dave APPELL/Kal MANN ▶ 31	65 Terry BRITTEN/Graham LYLE ▶ 185
16 James Samuel HARRIS/Terry LEWIS ▶ 34	66 Walter BECKER/Donald FAGEN ▶ 187
17 Harry Wayne CASEY/Rick FINCH ▶ 37	67 Spooner OLDHAM/Dan PENN ▶ 189
18 Bernard EDWARDS/Nile RODGERS ▶ 39	68 Will JENNINGS/Steve WINWOOD ▶ 190
19 Eddie BRIGATI/Felix CAVALIERE ▶ 40	69 Tommy ROE/Freddy WELLER ▶ 193
20 Robert ALLEN/Al STILLMAN ▶ 49	70 Dick ADDRISI/Don ADDRISI ▶ 194
21 Dave BARTHOLOMEW/Fats DOMINO ▶ 55	71 John BETTIS/Richard CARPENTER ▶ 195
22 Joe MELSON/Roy ORBISON ▶ 58	72 John CARTER/Ken HAWKER ▶ 196
23 L. Russell BROWN/Irwin LEVINE ▶ 61	73 Audrey ALLISON/Joe ALLISON ▶ 198
24 Nick ASHFORD/Valerie SIMPSON ▶ 64	74 Mariah CAREY/Ben MARGULIES ▶ 199
25 Mike CHAPMAN/Nicky CHINN ▶ 69	75 Joe SHERMAN/Noel SHERMAN ▶ 200
26 Barry GIBB/Robin GIBB ▶ 70	76 Errol BROWN/Tony WILSON ▶ 202
27 Lee POCKRISS/Paul VANCE ▶ 72	77 Lorenz HART/Richard RODGERS ▶ 204
28 Bernie LOWE/Kal MANN ▶ 80	78 Phil CODY/Neil SEDAKA ▶ 205
29 Jeff BARRY/Ellie GREENWICH ▶ 81	79 Bob CREWE/Frank SLAY ▶ 206
30 Dennis LAMBERT/Brian POTTER ▶ 82	80 Dave CLARK/Mike SMITH ▶ 210
31 Otis BLACKWELL/Elvis PRESLEY ▶ 86	81 Jimmie CRANE/Al JACOBS ▶ 211
32 Lou GRAMM/Michael Leslie JONES ▶ 87	82 Dub ALLBRITTEN/Ronnie SELF ▶ 212
33 Howard GREENFIELD/Jack KELLER ▶ 91	83 Jimmy DRIFTWOOD/TRADITIONAL ▶ 214
34 Boudleaux BRYANT/Felice BRYANT ▶ 93	84 Charles DAWES/Carl SIGMAN ▶ 222
35 Dino FEKARIS/Freddie PERREN ▶ 94	85 Carole KING/Toni STERN ▶ 226
36 Ray EVANS/Jay LIVINGSTON ▶ 95	86 Al BYRON/Paul EVANS ▶ 232
37 Thom BELL/Linda CREED ▶ 99	87 Jonathan CAIN/Steve PERRY ▶ 233
38 Jeff BARRY/Andy KIM ▶ 102	88 Bruce FISHER/Billy PRESTON ▶ 235
39 Thomas F. KELLY/Billy STEINBERG ▶ 103	89 Tommy JAMES/Robert L. KING ▶ 243
40 Alex NORTH/Hy ZARET ▶ 104	90 Otis BLACKWELL/Winfield SCOTT ▶ 245
41 Jim PETERIK/Frankie SULLIVAN ▶ 105	91 Bob CREWE/Kenny NOLAN ▶ 247
42 Garry BONNER/Alan GORDON ▶ 107	92 Gerry GOFFIN/Michael MASSER ▶ 250
43 Gary GELD/Peter UDELL ▶ 109	93 Richard SHERMAN/Robert SHERMAN ▶ 253
44 Tommy BOYCE/Bobby HART ▶ 111	94 Lou CHRISTIE/Twyla HERBERT ▶ 254
45 Roy C. BENNETT/Sid TEPPER ▶ 125	95 Ritchie ADAMS/Malou RENÉ ▶ 256
46 Richard ADLER/Jerry ROSS ▶ 127	96 Steve DUBOFF/Artie KORNFELD ▶ 257
47 Isaac HAYES/David PORTER ▶ 131	97 Freddie PERREN/Keni ST. LEWIS ▶ 258
48 Harold LOGAN/Lloyd PRICE ▶ 134	98 Don GEORGE/TRADITIONAL ▶ 260
49 Sammy FAIN/Paul Francis WEBSTER ▶ 135	99 Otto HARBACH/Jerome KERN ▶ 269
50 Peter CALLANDER/Mitch MURRAY ▶ 141	100 Sandy LINZER/Denny RANDELL ▶ 271

Top 100 Three-Writer Teams

1	Lamont DOZIER/Brian HOLLAND/Eddie HOLLAND ▶ 2
2	Barry GIBB/Maurice GIBB/Robin GIBB ▶ 5
3	Jeff BARRY/Ellie GREENWICH/Phil SPECTOR ▶ 47
4	Galt MacDERMOT/James RADO/Gerome RAGNI ▶ 59
5	Al GREEN/Al JACKSON/Willie MITCHELL ▶ 83
6	Tony BANKS/Phil COLLINS/Mike RUTHERFORD ▶ 112
7	Sara ALLEN/Daryl HALL/John OATES ▶ 117
8	O'Kelly ISLEY/Ronald ISLEY/Rudolph ISLEY ▶ 122
9	Richard DEHR/Terry GILKYSON/Frank MILLER ▶ 137
10	Jon BON JOVI/Desmond CHILD/Richie SAMBORA ▶ 149
11	Marc BLITZSTEIN/Berthold BRECHT/Kurt WEILL ▶ 159
12	Kenneth EDMONDS/Antonio REID/Daryl SIMMONS ▶ 160
13	Barry MANN/Phil SPECTOR/Cynthia WEIL ▶ 168
14	Stig ANDERSON/Benny ANDERSSON/Björn ULVAEUS ▶ 192
15	James Samuel HARRIS/Janet JACKSON/Terry LEWIS ▶ 203
16	Kenneth GAMBLE/Cary GILBERT/Leon HUFF ▶ 237
17	Henry COSBY/Sylvia MOY/Stevie WONDER ▶ 248
18	David MALLOY/Eddie RABBITT/Even STEVENS ▶ 252
19	Clement A. BOZEWSKI/Deborah HARRY/ Christopher STEIN ▶ 265
20	Billy DAVIS/Berry GORDY/Gwen GORDY ▶ 268
21	Luigi CREATORE/Hugo PERETTI/George David WEISS ▶ 270
22	Dave APPELL/Bernie LOWE/Kal MANN ▶ 274
23	Eduardo Di CAPUA/Wally GOLD/Aaron SCHROEDER ▶ 281
24	Henri BELOLO/Jacques MORALI/Victor WILLIS ▶ 293
25	Leonard CASTON/Anita POREE/Frank Edward WILSON ▶ 305
26	Irene CARA/Keith FORSEY/Giorgio MORODER ▶ 319
27	Jerry ALLISON/Buddy HOLLY/Norman PETTY ▶ 322
28	Bob FELDMAN/Jerry GOLDSTEIN/Richard GOTTEHRER ▶ 333
29	Clement A. BOZEWSKI/Deborah HARRY/ Giorgio MORODER ▶ 349
30	Jerry BUTLER/Kenneth GAMBLE/Leon HUFF ▶ 355
31	Mae Boren AXTON/Thomas DURDEN/Elvis PRESLEY ▶ 360
32	Steve GEORGE/John LANG/Richard PAGE ▶ 364
33	J. Fred COOTS/Charles KENNY/Nick KENNY ▶ 366
34	Matt AITKEN/Mike STOCK/Pete WATERMAN ▶ 372
35	Harold LOGAN/Lloyd PRICE/TRADITIONAL ▶ 382
36	Homer BANKS/Carl HAMPTON/Raymond Earl JACKSON ▶ 383
37	Ken DARBY/George R. POULTON/Elvis PRESLEY ▶ 402
38	Ben E. KING/Jerry LEIBER/Mike STOLLER ▶ 410
39	Tom BAILEY/Alannah CURRIE/Joe LEEWAY ▶ 411
40	Gene CHANDLER/Earl EDWARDS/Bernice WILLIAMS ▶ 422
41	Rodger PENZABENE/Barrett STRONG/Norman WHITFIELD ▶ 432
42	Gretchen CHRISTOPHER/Barbara ELLIS/Gary TROXEL ▶ 436
43	Boyd BENNETT/Chuck GORMAN/John YOUNG ▶ 441
44	Pete BELLOTTE/Harold FALTERMEYER/Keith FORSEY ▶ 444
45	John MADARA/Artie SINGER/David WHITE ▶ 464
46	Dave BARTHOLOMEW/Fats DOMINO/Earl King JOHNSON ▶ 475
47	Pete BELLOTTE/Giorgio MORODER/Donna SUMMER ▶ 486
48	Carmine APPICE/Duane HITCHINGS/Rod STEWART ▶ 489
49	Bob BRASS/Al KOOPER/Irwin LEVINE ▶ 493
50	Allan CLARKE/Tony HICKS/Graham NASH ▶ 498
51	Sam COSLOW/Ken LANE/Irving TAYLOR ▶ 499
52	Ann FARINA/Johnny FARINA/Santo FARINA ▶ 503
53	Glenn FREY/Don HENLEY/J.D. SOUTHER ▶ 507
54	Jimmie CRANE/Milt GABLER/Al JACOBS ▶ 512
55	Bert KAEMPFERT/Charles SINGLETON/Eddie SNYDER ▶ 521
56	Jerry BUTLER/Calvin CARTER/Curtis MAYFIELD ▶ 530
57	Johnny BRAGG/Buddy KILLEN/Robert S. RILEY ▶ 533
58	Frank BEARD/Billy GIBBONS/Dusty HILL ▶ 534
59	Alan BERGMAN/Marilyn BERGMAN/Marvin HAMLISCH ▶ 541
60	Amadeu Do VALE/Jose GALHARDO/Raul PORTELA ▶ 547
61	Gary JACKSON/Raynard MINER/Carl William SMITH ▶ 567
62	Brook BENTON/Belford HENDRICKS/Clyde OTIS ▶ 573
63	Jackey BEAVERS/Johnny BRISTOL/Harvey FUQUA ▶ 579
64	Henry COSBY/Smokey ROBINSON/Stevie WONDER ▶ 583
65	Marvin GAYE/Ivy Jo HUNTER/William STEVENSON ▶ 586
66	Bob CREWE/Sandy LINZER/Denny RANDELL ▶ 596
67	Alan ARKIN/Bob CAREY/Erik DARLING ▶ 597
68	Kenneth GAMBLE/Leon HUFF/Jerry J. ROSS ▶ 600
69	John William CALLIS/Philip OAKEY/Philip WRIGHT ▶ 603
70	Luther DIXON/Stanley KAHAN/Eddie SNYDER ▶ 605
71	Gary DeCARLO/Dale FRASHUER/Paul LEKA ▶ 610
72	Angelo BOND/General JOHNSON/Greg PERRY ▶ 611
73	Brook BENTON/Clyde OTIS/TRADITIONAL ▶ 622
74	Eddie MILLER/Dub WILLIAMS/Robert Gene YOUNT ▶ 628
75	Steve BOONE/John SEBASTIAN/Mark SEBASTIAN ▶ 635
76	Johann Sebastian BACH/Sandy LINZER/Denny RANDELL ▶ 651
77	Carmela GUIDA/Frank GUIDA/Joseph ROYSTER ▶ 656
78	William E. JACKSON III/Roy STRAIGIS/ George R. WILLIAMS ▶ 664
79	Ed GRAY/Tommy JAMES/Mike VALE ▶ 673
80	Simon Le BON/Nick RHODES/Nigel John TAYLOR ▶ 678

81	Wayne BRATHWAITE/Barry EASTMOND/Billy OCEAN ► 691
82	Jeff BARRY/Ellie GREENWICH/Shadow MORTON ► 695
83	Alan BERGMAN/Marilyn BERGMAN/Neil DIAMOND ► 699
84	Bryan ADAMS/Michael KAMEN/Mutt LANGE ► 704
85	Burt BACHARACH/Mack DAVID/Luther DIXON ► 709
86	Jonathan CAIN/Steve PERRY/Neal SCHON ► 717
87	General JOHNSON/Barney PERKINS/Greg PERRY ► 722
88	Bill DANOFF/Taffy DANOFF/John DENVER ► 729
89	Warren MOORE/Smokey ROBINSON/Marvin TARPLIN ► 740
90	Chris ARNOLD/David MARTIN/Geoff MORROW ► 743
91	Renaldo BENSON/Al CLEVELAND/Marvin GAYE ► 746
92	David CLOWNEY/Jim KRIEGSMANN/Ken WOOD ► 754
93	Joe BROUSSARD/Carrol WASHINGTON/Ralph WILLIAMS ► 761
94	Bonnie BRAMLETT/Delaney BRAMLETT/Leon RUSSELL ► 776
95	Ralph BAILEY/Rudy CLARK/Ken WILLIAMS ► 786
96	Bruce HAWES/Joseph JEFFERSON/Charles SIMMONS ► 788
97	Don DAVIS/Harvey SCALES/Albert VANCE ► 800
98	Al LEWIS/Vincent ROSE/Larry STOCK ► 803
99	Jackie DeSHANNON/Jimmy HOLIDAY/Randy MYERS ► 805
100	Gilbert BÉCAUD/Mann CURTIS/Pierre DELANOË ► 809

Top 100 Most Efficient Writer Team-Act Combinations
(Average Score/Entry, Greater Than 5 Entries)

	Writer Team	Act Grouping	Avg Score/ Entries
1	Lamont DOZIER/ Brian HOLLAND/ Eddie HOLLAND	The SUPREMES/ Diana ROSS And The SUPREMES	4779/17
2	Berry GORDY/Fonce MIZELL/ Freddie PERREN/ Deke RICHARDS	JACKSON 5	4411/7
3	Lionel RICHIE	Lionel RICHIE	4086/8
4	Michael JACKSON	Michael JACKSON	3901/11
5	Eddie BRIGATI/Felix CAVALIERE	YOUNG RASCALS/ RASCALS	3888/9
6	Tony HATCH	Petula CLARK	3598/6
7	Lionel RICHIE	The COMMODORES	3456/8
8	John LENNON/Paul McCARTNEY	The BEATLES	3345/63
9	Paul SIMON	SIMON & GARFUNKEL	3301/14
10	Bob CREWE/Bob GAUDIO	4 SEASONS	3276/10
11	Sara ALLEN/Daryl HALL/ John OATES	Daryl HALL & John OATES	3259/6
12	L. Russell BROWN/Irwin LEVINE	Tony ORLANDO And DAWN	3171/8
13	James Samuel HARRIS/ Terry LEWIS	Janet JACKSON	3139/6
14	Per GESSLE	ROXETTE	3079/6
15	Simon Le BON/Nick RHODES/ Andy TAYLOR/ Nigel John TAYLOR/ Roger TAYLOR	DURAN DURAN	2932/8
16	George MICHAEL	George MICHAEL	2885/10
17	Madonna L. CICCONE/ Patrick Raymond LEONARD	MADONNA	2856/6
18	Linda McCARTNEY/ Paul McCARTNEY	Paul McCARTNEY & WINGS/WINGS	2798/16
19	Barry GIBB/Maurice GIBB/ Robin GIBB	BEE GEES	2777/29
20	John LENNON	John LENNON	2764/9
21	John FARRAR	Olivia NEWTON-JOHN	2650/8
22	Richard MARX	Richard MARX	2637/8
23	PRINCE	PRINCE And The REVOLUTION	2609/8
24	Boudleaux BRYANT/ Felice BRYANT	EVERLY BROTHERS	2573/8
25	Joe MELSON/Roy ORBISON	Roy ORBISON	2508/9
26	Mick JAGGER/Keith RICHARDS	ROLLING STONES	2507/43
27	George MICHAEL	WHAM!	2475/6
28	Jim WEATHERLY	Gladys KNIGHT & The PIPS	2475/6
29	John FOGERTY	CREEDENCE CLEARWATER REVIVAL	2411/17
30	Gilbert O'SULLIVAN	Gilbert O'SULLIVAN	2398/8
31	Paul McCARTNEY	Paul McCARTNEY & WINGS/WINGS	2397/7
32	Robert ALLEN/Al STILLMAN	FOUR LADS	2366/7
33	Harry Wayne CASEY/Rick FINCH	KC & The SUNSHINE BAND	2354/14
34	Thom BELL/Linda CREED	The STYLISTICS	2352/6
35	Michael CRAIG/Roy HAY/ Jon MOSS/George O'DOWD	CULTURE CLUB	2336/7

	Writer Team	Act Grouping	Avg Score/ Entries
36	Lamont DOZIER/Brian HOLLAND/Eddie HOLLAND	FOUR TOPS	2321/13
37	John DENSMORE/ Robby KRIEGER/ Ray MANZAREK/ Jim MORRISON	The DOORS	2320/12
38	Dave APPELL/Kal MANN	The ORLONS	2320/6
39	Barrett STRONG/ Norman WHITFIELD	The TEMPTATIONS	2316/15
40	Phil COLLINS	Phil COLLINS	2269/14
41	Maurice STARR	NEW KIDS ON THE BLOCK	2240/8
42	Christopher CROSS	Christopher CROSS	2213/7
43	Dave CLARK/Mike SMITH	Dave CLARK Five	2211/6
44	Bernard EDWARDS/Nile RODGERS	CHIC	2199/9
45	Dub ALLBRITTEN/Ronnie SELF	Brenda LEE	2194/6
46	Rick ALLEN/Steve CLARK/ Phil COLLEN/Joe ELLIOTT/ Mutt LANGE/Rick SAVAGE	DEF LEPPARD	2150/6
47	Thomas ALLEN/ Harold BROWN/ Morris DICKERSON/ Lonnie JORDAN/ Charles MILLER/ Lee OSKAR/Howard SCOTT	WAR	2149/8
48	Stevie WONDER	Stevie WONDER	2139/30
49	Jim CROCE	Jim CROCE	2106/8
50	John SEBASTIAN	LOVIN' SPOONFUL	2103/9
51	Michael Leslie JONES	FOREIGNER	2099/6
52	Freddie MERCURY	QUEEN	2076/10
53	David GATES	BREAD	2072/13
54	Buck RAM	The PLATTERS	2023/9
55	David MALLOY/ Eddie RABBITT/Even STEVENS	Eddie RABBITT	2013/6
56	Dennis DeYOUNG	STYX	1981/12
57	Sylvester STEWART	SLY & THE FAMILY STONE	1980/18
58	Daryl HALL	Daryl HALL & John OATES	1961/9
59	John PHILLIPS	MAMAS & The PAPAS	1940/7
60	Floyd CRAMER	Floyd CRAMER	1929/6
61	Debbie GIBSON	Debbie GIBSON	1922/9
62	STING	The POLICE	1883/12
63	Doc POMUS/Mort SHUMAN	The DRIFTERS	1878/7
64	Elton JOHN/Bernie TAUPIN	Elton JOHN	1838/36
65	Daryl HALL/John OATES	Daryl HALL & John OATES	1825/6
66	Jonathan CAIN/Steve PERRY	JOURNEY	1783/7
67	Lewis MARTINÉE	EXPOSÉ	1772/7
68	Don McLEAN	Don MCLEAN	1755/8
69	Gerry RAFFERTY	Gerry RAFFERTY	1747/6
70	Ray PARKER Jr.	Ray PARKER Jr./ RAYDIO	1727/13
71	PRINCE	PRINCE	1699/22
72	Lou GRAMM/Michael Leslie JONES	FOREIGNER	1698/14

	Writer Team	Act Grouping	Avg Score/ Entries
73	Melanie SAFKA	MELANIE	1689/9
74	David PAICH	TOTO	1665/7
75	Barry GIBB/Robin GIBB	BEE GEES	1651/7
76	Doc POMUS/Mort SHUMAN	Elvis PRESLEY	1627/9
77	Mike LOVE/Brian WILSON	BEACH BOYS	1621/26
78	Tommy ROE	Tommy ROE	1619/11
79	Jerry LEIBER/Mike STOLLER	Elvis PRESLEY	1619/15
80	Christine McVIE	FLEETWOOD MAC	1614/6
81	Paul SIMON	Paul SIMON	1610/16
82	Stevie NICKS	FLEETWOOD MAC	1590/6
83	Donovan LEITCH	DONOVAN	1583/16
84	Peter FRAMPTON	Peter FRAMPTON	1563/6
85	Curtis BEDEAU/ Gerard CHARLES/ Hugh CLARKE/Brian GEORGE/ Lucien GEORGE/Paul GEORGE	LISA LISA And CULT JAM	1563/7
86	André CYMONE/Jody WATLEY	Jody WATLEY	1561/6
87	Graham GOBLE	LITTLE RIVER BAND	1559/8
88	Lamont DOZIER/Brian HOLLAND/Eddie HOLLAND	MARTHA & The VANDELLAS	1551/9
89	Tom SCHOLZ	BOSTON	1546/8
90	Stig ANDERSON/ Benny ANDERSSON/ Björn ULVAEUS	ABBA	1535/9
91	Howard GREENFIELD/ Neil SEDAKA	Neil SEDAKA	1534/20
92	George HARRISON	George HARRISON	1514/16
93	Bobby DALL/C.C. DeVILLE/ Bret MICHAELS/Rikki ROCKETT	POISON	1509/10
94	Peter DeANGELIS/Bob MARCUCCI	Frankie AVALON	1501/8
95	Carly SIMON	Carly SIMON	1498/8
96	Bruce SPRINGSTEEN	Bruce SPRINGSTEEN	1488/16
97	William DEES/Roy ORBISON	Roy ORBISON	1487/10
98	Bill WITHERS	Bill WITHERS	1483/10
99	Jim PETERIK/Frankie SULLIVAN	SURVIVOR	1481/14
100	Jerry LEIBER/Mike STOLLER	The COASTERS	1456/15

Top 100 Most Efficient Writer Teams
(Average Score/Entry, Greater Than 5 Entries)

Writer Team ▶ Rank	Avg Score/ Entries
1 Lionel RICHIE ▶ 9	4074/20
2 Berry GORDY/Fonce MIZELL/Freddie PERREN/ Deke RICHARDS ▶ 54	3897/8
3 Al GREEN/Al JACKSON/Willie MITCHELL ▶ 83	3457/7
4 Sara ALLEN/Daryl HALL/John OATES ▶ 117	3259/6
5 Barry GIBB ▶ 118	3257/6
6 Michael JACKSON ▶ 24	3224/16
7 Per GESSLE ▶ 132	3079/6
8 Hank BALLARD ▶ 57	3049/10
9 Simon Le BON/Nick RHODES/Andy TAYLOR/ Nigel John TAYLOR/Roger TAYLOR ▶ 92	2932/8
10 John FARRAR ▶ 62	2907/10
11 Eddie BRIGATI/Felix CAVALIERE ▶ 40	2865/13
12 Madonna L. CICCONE/Patrick Raymond LEONARD ▶ 146	2856/6
13 George MICHAEL ▶ 33	2731/16
14 Otis BLACKWELL/Elvis PRESLEY ▶ 86	2673/9
15 Dion DiMUCCI/Ernie MARESCA ▶ 161	2663/6
16 Richard MARX ▶ 101	2637/8
17 Jerry FULLER ▶ 44	2617/14
18 Thomas F. KELLY/Billy STEINBERG ▶ 103	2616/8
19 Howard GREENFIELD/Jack KELLER ▶ 91	2606/9
20 Melvin ENDSLEY ▶ 175	2532/6
21 Galt MacDERMOT/James RADO/Gerome RAGNI ▶ 59	2517/12
22 Linda McCARTNEY/Paul McCARTNEY ▶ 22	2495/21
23 Peter CALLANDER/Mitch MURRAY ▶ 141	2485/7
24 Terry BRITTEN/Graham LYLE ▶ 185	2408/6
25 Rod TEMPERTON ▶ 56	2382/13
26 Michael CRAIG/Roy HAY/Jon MOSS/ George O'DOWD ▶ 153	2336/7
27 John CARTER/Ken HAWKER ▶ 196	2291/6
28 Barry GIBB/Maurice GIBB/Robin GIBB ▶ 5	2284/44
29 Christopher CROSS ▶ 171	2213/7
30 Dave CLARK/Mike SMITH ▶ 210	2211/6
31 Ric CARTEY/Carole JOYNER ▶ 174	2194/7
32 Gilbert O'SULLIVAN ▶ 116	2172/9
33 Rick ALLEN/Steve CLARK/Phil COLLEN/Joe ELLIOTT/ Mutt LANGE/Rick SAVAGE ▶ 221	2150/6
34 Bernard EDWARDS/Nile RODGERS ▶ 39	2107/18
35 Phil COLLINS ▶ 48	2094/16
36 Barry GIBB/Robin GIBB ▶ 70	2084/13
37 John DENSMORE/Robby KRIEGER/Ray MANZAREK/ Jim MORRISON ▶ 50	2068/16
38 Robbie VAN LEEUWEN ▶ 241	2066/6
39 John LENNON ▶ 42	2056/18
40 Bob CREWE/Kenny NOLAN ▶ 247	2045/6
41 Tommy BOYCE/Bobby HART ▶ 111	2019/10
42 Laura NYRO ▶ 73	2016/13
43 Bobby RUSSELL ▶ 74	2015/13
44 Charles FOX/Norman GIMBEL ▶ 162	1993/8
45 Richard DEHR/Terry GILKYSON/Frank MILLER ▶ 137	1974/9
46 John BETTIS/Richard CARPENTER ▶ 195	1968/7
47 Steve MILLER ▶ 115	1955/10
48 Barry MANN/Phil SPECTOR/Cynthia WEIL ▶ 168	1953/8

Writer Team ▶ Rank	Avg Score/ Entries
49 Elton JOHN/Bernie TAUPIN ▶ 7	1933/43
50 Debbie GIBSON ▶ 143	1922/9
51 Phil CODY/Neil SEDAKA ▶ 205	1911/7
52 Hal BLAIR/Don ROBERTSON ▶ 283	1911/6
53 Maurice STARR ▶ 124	1908/10
54 Alex NORTH/Hy ZARET ▶ 104	1895/11
55 Max CROOK/Del SHANNON ▶ 287	1894/6
56 Bob GAUDIO ▶ 288	1893/6
57 Freddie MERCURY ▶ 106	1893/11
58 Dub ALLBRITTEN/Ronnie SELF ▶ 212	1889/7
59 Gloria ESTEFAN ▶ 213	1882/7
60 Paul SIMON ▶ 8	1879/44
61 Maurice WILLIAMS ▶ 181	1871/8
62 Michael Leslie JONES ▶ 218	1865/7
63 Daryl HALL ▶ 96	1863/12
64 Randy GOODRUM ▶ 296	1860/6
65 Shel SILVERSTEIN ▶ 150	1857/9
66 Mick JAGGER/Keith RICHARDS ▶ 4	1846/60
67 Harry Wayne CASEY/Rick FINCH ▶ 37	1842/21
68 John LENNON/Paul McCARTNEY ▶ 1	1835/139
69 Colin James HAY ▶ 303	1835/6
70 Leon RENÉ ▶ 304	1834/6
71 Larry KOLBER/Barry MANN ▶ 312	1803/6
72 Jonathan CAIN/Steve PERRY ▶ 233	1783/7
73 Joe MELSON/Roy ORBISON ▶ 58	1782/17
74 Kenneth GAMBLE/Cary GILBERT/Leon HUFF ▶ 237	1781/7
75 Lewis MARTINÉE ▶ 240	1772/7
76 Rod ARGENT ▶ 186	1768/8
77 Thomas ALLEN/Harold BROWN/Morris DICKERSON/ Lonnie JORDAN/Charles MILLER/Lee OSKAR/ Howard SCOTT ▶ 138	1764/10
78 Dino FEKARIS/Freddie PERREN ▶ 94	1749/13
79 Gerry RAFFERTY ▶ 330	1747/6
80 David MALLOY/Eddie RABBITT/Even STEVENS ▶ 252	1744/7
81 Ralph BASS/Lowman PAULING ▶ 332	1733/6
82 Barrett STRONG/Norman WHITFIELD ▶ 14	1727/41
83 L. Russell BROWN/Irwin LEVINE ▶ 61	1724/17
84 Bob CREWE/Bob GAUDIO ▶ 29	1721/28
85 Marvin GAYE ▶ 266	1698/7
86 Lou GRAMM/Michael Leslie JONES ▶ 87	1698/14
87 Jim CROCE ▶ 148	1697/10
88 PRINCE ▶ 12	1688/46
89 Bob DAVIE/Marvin MOORE ▶ 352	1687/6
90 Paul McCARTNEY ▶ 43	1670/22
91 Sylvester LEVAY/Stephan PRAGER ▶ 278	1660/7
92 Will JENNINGS/Richard KERR ▶ 367	1643/6
93 Tom BLACKBURN/George BRUNS ▶ 282	1641/7
94 Tony ROMEO ▶ 152	1638/10
95 Graham GOULDMAN ▶ 219	1631/8
96 Tommy ROE ▶ 136	1619/11
97 Christine McVIE ▶ 381	1614/6
98 STING ▶ 51	1605/20
99 Stevie WONDER ▶ 15	1594/43
100 Dennis DeYOUNG ▶ 77	1591/16

Decades: Top Writer Teams for the '50s, '60s, '70s and '80s by Score and Entries

In this section, decade is determined by earliest entry on any chart.
Ties for numbers of entries are broken by score for those writers.

'50s: Top Writer Teams by Score

1	Jerry LEIBER/Mike STOLLER	54564
2	Robert ALLEN/Al STILLMAN	31728
3	TRADITIONAL	31541
4	Bernie LOWE/Kal MANN	23896
5	Buck RAM	23475
6	Dave BARTHOLOMEW/Fats DOMINO	22565
7	Paul ANKA	21482
8	Boudleaux BRYANT/Felice BRYANT	20625
9	Ray EVANS/Jay LIVINGSTON	19338
10	Otis BLACKWELL/Elvis PRESLEY	19313
11	Boudleaux BRYANT	18313
12	Richard ADLER/Jerry ROSS	18057
13	David SEVILLE	17638
14	Bob MERRILL	17081
15	Sammy FAIN/Paul Francis WEBSTER	16544
16	Alex NORTH/Hy ZARET	15323
17	Marc BLITZSTEIN/Berthold BRECHT/Kurt WEILL	15257
18	Melvin ENDSLEY	15190
19	Al HOFFMAN/Dick MANNING	14967
20	Marty ROBBINS	14558
21	Ric CARTEY/Carole JOYNER	14483
22	Harold LOGAN/Lloyd PRICE	14445
23	Doc POMUS/Mort SHUMAN	13607
24	Audrey ALLISON/Joe ALLISON	13381
25	J.P. RICHARDSON	13252
26	Jimmy DRIFTWOOD/TRADITIONAL	13080
27	Baker KNIGHT	12327
28	Chuck BERRY	12314
29	Peter DeANGELIS/Bob MARCUCCI	12308
30	Ivory Joe HUNTER	12279
31	Don GEORGE/TRADITIONAL	12048
32	Jack SCOTT	11599
33	Tom BLACKBURN/George BRUNS	11488
34	Franco MIGLIACCI/Domenico MODUGNO	10773
35	Otto HARBACH/Jerome KERN	10685
36	Charles DAWES/Carl SIGMAN	10634
37	Richard DEHR/Terry GILKYSON/Frank MILLER	10563
38	Joseph KOSMA	10374
39	Howard GREENFIELD/Neil SEDAKA	10363
40	Bob DAVIE/Marvin MOORE	10118
41	Merle TRAVIS	10077
42	Sam COOKE	10021
43	Ed MARSHALL	9989
44	J. Fred COOTS/Charles KENNY/Nick KENNY	9892
45	Stan LEBOWSKY/Herbert NEWMAN	9866
46	Mae Boren AXTON/Thomas DURDEN/Elvis PRESLEY	9678
47	Hans ENGELMANN	9649
48	Dewayne BLACKWELL	9403
49	Luis GUGLIELMI	9278
50	Roy C. BENNETT/Sid TEPPER	9248
51	Eddie HEYWOOD	9166
52	Gretchen CHRISTOPHER/Barbara ELLIS/Gary TROXEL	9073
53	Pat BALLARD	8989
54	Perez PRADO	8966
55	Bert REISFELD/Jean VILLARD	8869
56	Phil SPECTOR	8838
57	Jack FULTON/Lois STEELE	8832
58	Bill JUSTIS/Sid MANKER	8749
59	Marguerite MONNOT	8685
60	Jack NANCE/Conway TWITTY	8605
61	Wayne SHANKLIN	8369
62	Ken DARBY/George R. POULTON/Elvis PRESLEY	8350
63	John MADARA/Artie SINGER/David WHITE	8315
64	Jimmy DeKNIGHT/Max C. FREEDMAN	8304
65	James EDWARDS/Carl FEASTER/ Claude FEASTER/James C. KEYES/Floyd F. McRAE	8209
66	Georges BOULANGER/Jimmy KENNEDY	8202
67	Jimmie CRANE/Milt GABLER/Al JACOBS	8166
68	Bob CREWE/Frank SLAY	7981
69	Sammy CAHN/Jimmy VAN HEUSEN	7953
70	Ann FARINA/Johnny FARINA/Santo FARINA	7925
71	Jimmie CRANE/Al JACOBS	7878
72	Harold LOGAN/Lloyd PRICE/TRADITIONAL	7844
73	Luigi CREATORE/Al HOFFMAN/Dick MANNING/ Hugo PERETTI	7839
74	Amadeu Do VALE/Jose GALHARDO/Raul PORTELA	7805
75	Maurice WILLIAMS	7788
76	Roy ALFRED/Shorty ALLEN	7675
77	Giacomo PUCCINI/Bobby WORTH	7675
78	Joe SHAPIRO/Lou STALLMAN	7624
79	Ritchie VALENS	7537
80	Brook BENTON/Belford HENDRICKS/Clyde OTIS	7504
81	Jenny Lou CARSON/Kay TWOMEY/ Ben WEISMAN/Fred WISE	7476
82	Stuart HAMBLEN	7439
83	Vito PICONE/Arthur VENOSA	7398
84	Harlan HOWARD	7361
85	Alan ARKIN/Bob CAREY/Erik DARLING	7343
86	Rudy JACKSON/Eddy RAY	7307
87	Frank LOESSER	7298
88	Bruce BELLAND/Glen LARSON	7283
89	Cole PORTER	7116
90	Charles SINGLETON	7102
91	Chuck RIO	7019
92	Sheb WOOLEY	7018
93	Don ROBERTSON	6814
94	Artie DUNN/Al NEVINS/Morty NEVINS/ Buck RAM	6802
95	Irving BERLIN	6776
96	Carl PERKINS	6717
97	Alan FREED/Harvey FUQUA	6576
98	Jerry HERST/Jack SHARPE	6543
99	Winfield SCOTT	6490
100	Ollie JONES	6467

'50s: Top Writer Teams by Entries

1	Irving BERLIN	45
2	Jerry LEIBER/Mike STOLLER	44
3	TRADITIONAL	41
4	Bob MERRILL	37
5	Dave BARTHOLOMEW/Fats DOMINO	31
6	Ray EVANS/Jay LIVINGSTON	22
7	Bernie LOWE/Kal MANN	22
8	Robert ALLEN/Al STILLMAN	22
9	Alan Jay LERNER/Frederick LOEWE	20
10	Cole PORTER	20
11	Roy C. BENNETT/Sid TEPPER	20
12	Chuck BERRY	20
13	Sammy FAIN/Paul Francis WEBSTER	20
14	Al HOFFMAN/Dick MANNING	19
15	Buck RAM	19
16	Richard ADLER/Jerry ROSS	18
17	Oscar HAMMERSTEIN/Richard RODGERS	17
18	Frank LOESSER	17
19	Stuart HAMBLEN	15
20	Peter DeANGELIS/Bob MARCUCCI	15
21	Rose Marie McCOY/Charles SINGLETON	14
22	Nicholas BRODSZKY/Sammy CAHN	13
23	Jesse STONE	13
24	Sammy CAHN/Jimmy VAN HEUSEN	13
25	Jack SCOTT	13
26	Ivory Joe HUNTER	13
27	Doc POMUS/Mort SHUMAN	13
28	Boudleaux BRYANT/Felice BRYANT	13
29	Johnny CASH	12
30	Bob CREWE/Frank SLAY	12
31	David SEVILLE	12
32	Paul ANKA	12
33	Dimitri TIOMKIN/Paul Francis WEBSTER	11
34	Johnny MERCER	11
35	Marty ROBBINS	11
36	Boudleaux BRYANT	11
37	Dave ALLDRED/Jimmy BOWEN/Buddy KNOX/ Donnie LANIER	10
38	Gene DePAUL/Johnny MERCER	10
39	Gordon JENKINS	10
40	Jerry LIVINGSTON/Paul Francis WEBSTER	10
41	John D. LOUDERMILK	10
42	Don GIBSON	10
43	Winfield SCOTT	10
44	Wayne SHANKLIN	10
45	Howard GREENFIELD/Neil SEDAKA	10
46	Johnny MARKS	9
47	Franz GRUBER/Josef MOHR	9
48	W.C. HANDY	9
49	Chuck WILLIS	9
50	Dimitri TIOMKIN	9
51	Jerry BOCK/Lawrence HOLOFCENER/ George David WEISS	9
52	Otis BLACKWELL	9
53	Elmer BERNSTEIN/Sylvia FINE	9
54	Irving GORDON	9
55	Joe SHERMAN/Noel SHERMAN	9
56	Carl PERKINS	9
57	Betty COMDEN/Adolph GREEN/Jule STYNE	8
58	Henry GLOVER	8
59	Meredith WILLSON	8
60	Al FRISCH/Sid WAYNE	8
61	Robert ALLEN	8
62	Bennie BENJAMIN/George David WEISS	8
63	Ray CHARLES	8
64	Duane EDDY/Lee HAZLEWOOD	8
65	Pat BALLARD	8
66	Sam COOKE	8
67	Tom GLAZER/Budd SCHULBERG	7
68	Hank WILLIAMS	7
69	Malcolm ARNOLD	7
70	Roy ALFRED/Abner SILVER	7
71	Deadric MALONE/Ferdinand WASHINGTON	7
72	Stella UNGER/Victor YOUNG	7
73	Eddie CURTIS	7
74	Nick ACQUAVIVA/Ted VARNICK	7
75	Gene ADKINSON/Wade BUFF	7
76	Don ROBERTSON	7
77	Luigi CREATORE/Al HOFFMAN/Dick MANNING/ Hugo PERETTI	7
78	Perez PRADO	7
79	Tom BLACKBURN/George BRUNS	7
80	Baker KNIGHT	7
81	Jerry ALLISON/Buddy HOLLY/Norman PETTY	6
82	Rafael DE LEON/Richard DEHR/Terry GILKYSON/ Frank MILLER/TRADITIONAL	6
83	Harold ADAMSON/Stella UNGER/Victor YOUNG	6
84	Camillo BARGONI	6
85	Lester LEE/Ned WASHINGTON	6
86	James Lord PIERPONT	6
87	Sunny SKYLAR	6
88	Lionel NEWMAN	6
89	Wally GOLD	6
90	Ettore MIONORETTI/Geoffrey PARSONS/ Saverio SERACINI/John TURNER	6
91	Larry COLEMAN/Fred EBB/Paul KLEIN	6
92	Billy MURE	6
93	Harold ADAMSON/Leo McCAREY/Harry WARREN	6
94	Matt DUBEY/Harold KARR	6
95	Fred EBB/Paul KLEIN	6
96	Elias McDANIEL	6
97	Bob HILLIARD	6
98	Joe LUBIN/Irving ROTH	6
99	Dimitri TIOMKIN/Ned WASHINGTON	6
100	Ben RALEIGH/Don WOLF	6
101	Edward WHITE/Mack WOLFSON	6
102	Bobby DAY	6
103	Harold ARLEN/Johnny MERCER	6
104	Billy DAVIS/Berry GORDY/Gwen GORDY	6
105	Sammy CAHN/Gene DePAUL	6
106	Kurt WEILL	6
107	Lee POCKRISS/Paul VANCE	6
108	Joe SHAPIRO/Lou STALLMAN	6
109	Jack FULTON/Lois STEELE	6
110	J.P. RICHARDSON	6
111	Melvin ENDSLEY	6

'60s: Top Writer Teams by Score

1	John LENNON/Paul McCARTNEY	219720
2	Lamont DOZIER/Brian HOLLAND/Eddie HOLLAND	147699
3	Burt BACHARACH/Hal DAVID	85164
4	Gerry GOFFIN/Carole KING	74450
5	Mick JAGGER/Keith RICHARDS	67767
6	Doc POMUS/Mort SHUMAN	47486
7	Bob CREWE/Bob GAUDIO	47040
8	Dave APPELL/Kal MANN	43372
9	Bob DYLAN	42832
10	Neil DIAMOND	41217
11	Barry MANN/Cynthia WEIL	40867
12	Curtis MAYFIELD	36376
13	Eddie BRIGATI/Felix CAVALIERE	35951
14	Barrett STRONG/Norman WHITFIELD	33479
15	Paul SIMON	33273
16	Smokey ROBINSON	31934
17	Tony HATCH	31247
18	John D. LOUDERMILK	31080
19	Jerry FULLER	30942
20	TRADITIONAL	30814
21	Sam COOKE	30638
22	Galt MacDERMOT/James RADO/Gerome RAGNI	30130
23	Howard GREENFIELD/Neil SEDAKA	30059
24	Hank BALLARD	29757
25	John DENSMORE/Robby KRIEGER/ Ray MANZAREK/Jim MORRISON	28913
26	Jeff BARRY/Ellie GREENWICH/Phil SPECTOR	26828
27	Jimmy WEBB	26096
28	Donovan LEITCH	25210
29	Sonny BONO	25054
30	Jeff BARRY/Ellie GREENWICH	24541
31	Jerry LEIBER/Mike STOLLER	23647
32	Joe MELSON/Roy ORBISON	23304
33	Howard GREENFIELD/Jack KELLER	22778
34	John FOGERTY	22479
35	Laura NYRO	21536
36	James BROWN	21295
37	John SEBASTIAN	21225
38	Tommy BOYCE/Bobby HART	20195
39	Bobby RUSSELL	19598
40	John PHILLIPS	19527
41	Mike LOVE/Brian WILSON	19104
42	Lee HAZLEWOOD	19083
43	Garry BONNER/Alan GORDON	18835
44	Jeff BARRY/Andy KIM	18474
45	Roger MILLER	18241
46	Paul ANKA	17911
47	Tommy ROE	17684
48	Sylvester STEWART	16960
49	Wayne Carson THOMPSON	15828
50	Lee POCKRISS/Paul VANCE	15598
51	Ray DAVIES	15574
52	Isaac HAYES/David PORTER	15537
53	Steve BARRI/P.F. SLOAN	15161
54	Dion DiMUCCI/Ernie MARESCA	15024
55	William DEES/Roy ORBISON	14875
56	Chuck BERRY	14693
57	Don GIBSON	14510
58	O'Kelly ISLEY/Ronald ISLEY/Rudolph ISLEY	14229
59	Allen TOUSSAINT	14067
60	Gary GELD/Peter UDELL	13969
61	Chip TAYLOR	13927
62	John CARTER/Ken HAWKER	13683
63	Barry MANN/Phil SPECTOR/Cynthia WEIL	13518
64	Spooner OLDHAM/Dan PENN	13515
65	Joe SOUTH	13404
66	Dave CLARK/Mike SMITH	13266
67	Jerry HERMAN	13261
68	Graham GOULDMAN	13044
69	Rod ARGENT	12987
70	Joe TEX	12964
71	Bobby DARIN	12911
72	Tommy ROE/Freddy WELLER	12838
73	Max STEINER	12608
74	Kenneth GAMBLE/Leon HUFF	12605
75	Al BYRON/Paul EVANS	12503
76	Floyd CRAMER	12455
77	Otis BLACKWELL/Winfield SCOTT	12324
78	Jimmy DEAN	12288
79	Lou CHRISTIE/Twyla HERBERT	12144
80	Ritchie ADAMS/Malou RENÉ	12112
81	Steve DUBOFF/Artie KORNFELD	12095
82	Bobbie GENTRY	11937
83	Nick ASHFORD/Valerie SIMPSON	11796
84	Dave APPELL/Bernie LOWE/Kal MANN	11745
85	Hank COCHRAN	11651
86	Otis REDDING	11604
87	Hal BLAIR/Don ROBERTSON	11464
88	Henry COSBY/Sylvia MOY/Stevie WONDER	11383
89	Bob GAUDIO	11278
90	Dallas FRAZIER	11204
91	André POPP	11161
92	Gene ALLAN/Bobby VINTON	11128
93	Don BLACK/Mark LONDON	11124
94	Mark JAMES	10945
95	Larry KOLBER/Barry MANN	10820
96	Harlan HOWARD	10789
97	Geoff STEPHENS	10785
98	Eduardo Di CAPUA/Wally GOLD/Aaron SCHROEDER	10781
99	Keith McCORMACK/Faye VOSS	10632
100	Bobby GOLDSBORO	10603

'60s: Top Writer Teams by Entries

1	John LENNON/Paul McCARTNEY	93
2	Burt BACHARACH/Hal DAVID	74
3	Gerry GOFFIN/Carole KING	70
4	Lamont DOZIER/Brian HOLLAND/Eddie HOLLAND	69
5	Curtis MAYFIELD	62
6	Barry MANN/Cynthia WEIL	42
7	TRADITIONAL	41
8	Doc POMUS/Mort SHUMAN	41
9	Sam COOKE	36
10	Smokey ROBINSON	34
11	Bob DYLAN	34
12	Dave APPELL/Kal MANN	32
13	Paul ANKA	29
14	John D. LOUDERMILK	29
15	James BROWN	27
16	Jerry LEIBER/Mike STOLLER	26
17	Joe TEX	25
18	Jimmy WEBB	25
19	Mick JAGGER/Keith RICHARDS	23
20	Deadric MALONE	22
21	Isaac HAYES/David PORTER	22
22	Bob CREWE/Bob GAUDIO	22
23	Allen TOUSSAINT	21
24	Chuck BERRY	21
25	Lee HAZLEWOOD	21
26	Mike LOVE/Brian WILSON	21
27	Jeff BARRY/Ellie GREENWICH	21
28	Harlan HOWARD	20
29	Bobby DARIN	20
30	Bobby GOLDSBORO	19
31	Steve BARRI/P.F. SLOAN	19
32	Roger MILLER	19
33	Sonny BONO	19
34	Tony HATCH	19
35	Neil DIAMOND	19
36	Van McCOY	18
37	Kenneth GAMBLE/Leon HUFF	18
38	Joe SOUTH	18
39	Howard GREENFIELD/Neil SEDAKA	18
40	Lee POCKRISS/Paul VANCE	17
41	Donovan LEITCH	17
42	Jeff BARRY/Ellie GREENWICH/Phil SPECTOR	17
43	Sandy LINZER/Denny RANDELL	16
44	Gary GELD/Peter UDELL	16
45	Bill ANDERSON	15
46	Ray STEVENS	15
47	Garry BONNER/Alan GORDON	15
48	John SEBASTIAN	15
49	Henry MANCINI	14

50	Hank WILLIAMS	14
51	Bert BERNS	14
52	Don GIBSON	14
53	Paul SIMON	14
54	Luigi CREATORE/Hugo PERETTI/George David WEISS	13
55	Henry MANCINI/Johnny MERCER	13
56	Roy C. BENNETT/Sid TEPPER	13
57	Bob FELDMAN/Jerry GOLDSTEIN/ Richard GOTTEHRER	13
58	Hank COCHRAN	13
59	O'Kelly ISLEY/Ronald ISLEY/Rudolph ISLEY	13
60	Joe MELSON/Roy ORBISON	13
61	Barrett STRONG/Norman WHITFIELD	13
62	Leslie BRICUSSE/Anthony NEWLEY	12
63	Dave BARTHOLOMEW/Fats DOMINO	12
64	Chris KENNER	12
65	Marty ROBBINS	12
66	Nick ASHFORD/Valerie SIMPSON	12
67	Chip TAYLOR	12
68	Ray DAVIES	12
69	Jerry FULLER	12
70	Jimmy REED	11
71	Baker KNIGHT	11
72	Oscar HAMMERSTEIN/Richard RODGERS	11
73	Bob CREWE/Frank SLAY	11
74	Burt BACHARACH/Bob HILLIARD	11
75	Tony HATCH/Jackie TRENT	11
76	Jerry BUTLER/Kenneth GAMBLE/Leon HUFF	11
77	John MADARA/David WHITE	11
78	Otis REDDING	11
79	Wayne Carson THOMPSON	11
80	John PHILLIPS	11
81	John DENSMORE/Robby KRIEGER/ Ray MANZAREK/Jim MORRISON	11
82	Galt MacDERMOT/James RADO/Gerome RAGNI	11
83	Harold LOGAN/Lloyd PRICE	10
84	Ike TURNER	10
85	Pete TOWNSHEND	10
86	Berry GORDY	10
87	Del SHANNON	10
88	Max STEINER	10
89	Jerry HERMAN	10
90	Spooner OLDHAM/Dan PENN	10
91	William DEES/Roy ORBISON	10
92	Tommy ROE	10
93	Bobby RUSSELL	10
94	Tommy BOYCE/Bobby HART	10
95	John FOGERTY	10
96	Eddie BRIGATI/Felix CAVALIERE	10

Fourteen writer teams tied with 9.

'70s: Top Writer Teams by Score

1	Barry GIBB/Maurice GIBB/Robin GIBB	74618
2	Elton JOHN/Bernie TAUPIN	63600
3	Linda McCARTNEY/Paul McCARTNEY	51878
4	Kenneth GAMBLE/Leon HUFF	49469
5	Stevie WONDER	44195
6	Paul SIMON	42943
7	Harry Wayne CASEY/Rick FINCH	38676
8	Barrett STRONG/Norman WHITFIELD	35761
9	David GATES	30797
10	Neil DIAMOND	30441
11	John LENNON/Paul McCARTNEY	29629
12	L. Russell BROWN/Irwin LEVINE	29304
13	Mick JAGGER/Keith RICHARDS	27643
14	Bernard EDWARDS/Nile RODGERS	26715
15	Lionel RICHIE	24690
16	Dennis LAMBERT/Brian POTTER	23457
17	Al GREEN/Al JACKSON/Willie MITCHELL	23443
18	Berry GORDY/Fonce MIZELL/Freddie PERREN/ Deke RICHARDS	23270
19	John FOGERTY	22690
20	George HARRISON	22669
21	Curtis MAYFIELD	22663
22	Burt BACHARACH/Hal DAVID	22485
23	Sylvester STEWART	22149
24	Paul ANKA	22134
25	Thom BELL/Linda CREED	22132
26	Dino FEKARIS/Freddie PERREN	21612
27	John FARRAR	21167
28	Barry WHITE	20372
29	Gilbert O'SULLIVAN	19552
30	John DENVER	19535
31	Mike CHAPMAN/Nicky CHINN	19462
32	John LENNON	19434
33	Freddie MERCURY	19271
34	Jeff LYNNE	18933
35	Barry GIBB	18457
36	Thomas ALLEN/Harold BROWN/ Morris DICKERSON/Lonnie JORDAN/ Charles MILLER/Lee OSKAR/Howard SCOTT	17638
37	Melanie SAFKA	17348
38	Jim CROCE	16966
39	Gerry GOFFIN/Carole KING	16878
40	Barry GIBB/Robin GIBB	16400
41	Jim WEATHERLY	16277
42	Charles FOX/Norman GIMBEL	15855
43	Roger NICHOLS/Paul WILLIAMS	15827
44	Rod TEMPERTON	15767
45	Howard GREENFIELD/Neil SEDAKA	15437
46	Nick ASHFORD/Valerie SIMPSON	15247
47	Billy JOEL	14909
48	Bill WITHERS	14838
49	Eric CARMEN	14731
50	Don McLEAN	14668
51	Gordon LIGHTFOOT	14626
52	Robert LAMM	14534
53	Hoyt AXTON	14484
54	Lamont DOZIER/Brian HOLLAND/Eddie HOLLAND	14120
55	Mac DAVIS	13936
56	Stig ANDERSON/Benny ANDERSSON/ Björn ULVAEUS	13921
57	Joe SOUTH	13637
58	John BETTIS/Richard CARPENTER	13601
59	Peter CALLANDER/Mitch MURRAY	13601
60	Paul McCARTNEY	13486
61	Neil YOUNG	13011
62	Carole KING/Toni STERN	12712
63	Kent LaVOIE	12684
64	Rod STEWART	12613
65	Joe BROOKS	12550
66	Bruce FISHER/Billy PRESTON	12478
67	Alan O'DAY	12418
68	Tommy JAMES/Robert L. KING	12371
69	Phil CODY/Neil SEDAKA	12339
70	Bob CREWE/Kenny NOLAN	12269
71	Kenneth GAMBLE/Cary GILBERT/Leon HUFF	12198
72	Ray STEVENS	12159
73	Freddie PERREN/Keni ST. LEWIS	12086
74	Norman WHITFIELD	12058
75	Dennis DeYOUNG	11958
76	Bruce SPRINGSTEEN	11917
77	Randy NEWMAN	11883
78	Walter BECKER/Donald FAGEN	11879
79	Carole KING	11815
80	Lou GRAMM/Michael Leslie JONES	11812
81	Pete TOWNSHEND	11746
82	Sylvester LEVAY/Stephan PRAGER	11618
83	William BECK/Leroy BONNER/ Marshall JONES/Ralph MIDDLEBROOKS/ Andrew NOLAND/Marvin PIERCE/ James Rodger WILLIAMS	11580
84	Glenn FREY/Don HENLEY	11440
85	James PANKOW	11432
86	Cat STEVENS	11413
87	Eddie CORNELIUS	11345
88	Dewey BUNNELL	11292
89	Henri BELOLO/Jacques MORALI/Victor WILLIS	11264
90	Marvin GAYE	11251
91	James TAYLOR	11082
92	Chuck BERRY	11072
93	Carly SIMON	11053
94	Leonard CASTON/Anita POREE/Frank Edward WILSON	10942
95	Jimmy WEBB	10927
96	Gerry RAFFERTY	10295
97	TRADITIONAL	10294
98	Tony ROMEO	10268
99	Andy GIBB/Barry GIBB/Maurice GIBB/Robin GIBB	10099
100	Toni TENNILLE	10060

'70s: Top Writer Teams by Entries

1	Kenneth GAMBLE/Leon HUFF	58
2	Dennis LAMBERT/Brian POTTER	37
3	Lamont DOZIER/Brian HOLLAND/Eddie HOLLAND	31
4	Neil DIAMOND	30
5	Curtis MAYFIELD	27
6	Elton JOHN/Bernie TAUPIN	26
7	Burt BACHARACH/Hal DAVID	24
8	John LENNON/Paul McCARTNEY	24
9	Barry GIBB/Maurice GIBB/Robin GIBB	24
10	David GATES	23
11	Barrett STRONG/Norman WHITFIELD	23
12	Gerry GOFFIN/Carole KING	22
13	Mick JAGGER/Keith RICHARDS	22
14	Nick ASHFORD/Valerie SIMPSON	21
15	George HARRISON	21
16	Paul SIMON	21
17	Harry Wayne CASEY/Rick FINCH	20
18	Linda McCARTNEY/Paul McCARTNEY	20
19	Jeff LYNNE	19
20	James BROWN	18
21	John DENVER	18
22	Stevie WONDER	18
23	Norman WHITFIELD	17
24	Neil YOUNG	17
25	Sylvester STEWART	17
26	L. Russell BROWN/Irwin LEVINE	17
27	Kris KRISTOFFERSON	16
28	Howard GREENFIELD/Neil SEDAKA	16
29	Barry WHITE	16
30	Paul ANKA	16
31	Van McCOY	15
32	Van MORRISON	15
33	TRADITIONAL	15
34	Cat STEVENS	15
35	Pete TOWNSHEND	15
36	Thom BELL/Linda CREED	15
37	John FOGERTY	15
38	Bob DYLAN	14
39	Todd RUNDGREN	14
40	Smokey ROBINSON	14
41	Mac DAVIS	14
42	Mike CHAPMAN/Nicky CHINN	14
43	Ernie ISLEY/Marvin ISLEY/O'Kelly ISLEY/ Ronald ISLEY/Rudolph ISLEY/Chris JASPER	13
44	Barry MANN/Cynthia WEIL	13
45	Joni MITCHELL	13
46	James TAYLOR	13
47	Walter BECKER/Donald FAGEN	13
48	Tommy JAMES/Robert L. KING	13
49	Eric CARMEN	13
50	Jim WEATHERLY	13
51	Melanie SAFKA	13
52	Sam COOKE	12
53	David BOWIE	12
54	Leon RUSSELL	12
55	Allen TOUSSAINT	12
56	Albert HAMMOND/Mike HAZLEWOOD	12
57	Kent LaVOIE	12
58	Gordon LIGHTFOOT	12
59	Eugene RECORD	11
60	Charles Henry JACKSON Jr./Marvin YANCY	11
61	Jimmy WEBB	11
62	Carole KING	11
63	Bill WITHERS	11
64	Billy JOEL	11
65	Luigi CREATORE/Hugo PERETTI/George David WEISS	10
66	Tim RICE/Andrew Lloyd WEBBER	10
67	Dick ADDRISI/Don ADDRISI	10
68	Tony HESTER	10
69	Burton CUMMINGS	10
70	Bob SEGER	10
71	Joe SOUTH	10
72	Stig ANDERSON/Benny ANDERSSON/Björn ULVAEUS	10
73	Roger NICHOLS/Paul WILLIAMS	10
74	Jim CROCE	10
75	Thomas ALLEN/Harold BROWN/ Morris DICKERSON/Lonnie JORDAN/ Charles MILLER/Lee OSKAR/Howard SCOTT	10
76	John LENNON	10
77	Dino FEKARIS/Freddie PERREN	10
78	Pete BELLOTTE/Giorgio MORODER/Donna SUMMER	9
79	Bruce SPRINGSTEEN	9
80	Paul McCARTNEY	9
81	Robert LAMM	9
82	Gilbert O'SULLIVAN	9
83	Harry CHAPIN	8
84	Joe COBB/Van McCOY	8
85	Harvey PRICE/Dan WALSH	8
86	Ray DAVIES	8
87	Russ BALLARD	8
88	Stephen STILLS	8
89	Les EMMERSON	8
90	Mark FARNER	8
91	Daryl HALL/John OATES	8
92	Graham GOULDMAN/Eric STEWART	8
93	Isaac HAYES	8
94	Homer BANKS/Carl HAMPTON/ Raymond Earl JACKSON	8
95	Dash CROFTS/Jim SEALS	8
96	James PANKOW	8
97	William BECK/Leroy BONNER/Marshall JONES/ Ralph MIDDLEBROOKS/Andrew NOLAND/ Marvin PIERCE/James Rodger WILLIAMS	8
98	Alan O'DAY	8
99	Carole KING/Toni STERN	8
100	Don McLEAN	8
101	Bernard EDWARDS/Nile RODGERS	8

'80s: Top Writer Teams by Score

1	PRINCE	59416
2	Lionel RICHIE	56799
3	Michael JACKSON	41469
4	George MICHAEL	39059
5	Billy JOEL	35352
6	James Samuel HARRIS/Terry LEWIS	31000
7	STING	29716
8	Phil COLLINS	28086
9	Bruce SPRINGSTEEN	27141
10	Stevie WONDER	24309
11	John MELLENCAMP	23462
12	Simon Le BON/Nick RHODES/Andy TAYLOR/ Nigel John TAYLOR/Roger TAYLOR	23454
13	Paul McCARTNEY	21801
14	Diane WARREN	21109
15	Thomas F. KELLY/Billy STEINBERG	20928
16	Jim PETERIK/Frankie SULLIVAN	20839
17	Rick SPRINGFIELD	20464
18	Sara ALLEN/Daryl HALL/John OATES	19552
19	Ray PARKER Jr.	18715
20	Richard MARX	18175
21	Tony BANKS/Phil COLLINS/Mike RUTHERFORD	17358
22	Debbie GIBSON	17301
23	John LENNON	16791
24	Jon BON JOVI/Desmond CHILD/Richie SAMBORA	16774
25	Madonna L. CICCONE/Patrick Raymond LEONARD	16359
26	Michael CRAIG/Roy HAY/Jon MOSS/ George O'DOWD	16352
27	Barry GIBB/Maurice GIBB/Robin GIBB	16343
28	Ric OCASEK	16103
29	Bryan ADAMS/Jim VALLANCE	16097
30	Annie LENNOX/David A. STEWART	15769
31	Peter CETERA/David FOSTER	15531
32	Christopher CROSS	15488
33	Daryl HALL	15390
34	Kevin CRONIN	15132
35	Curtis BEDEAU/Gerard CHARLES/ Hugh CLARKE/Brian GEORGE/ Lucien GEORGE/Paul GEORGE	15113
36	Kenneth EDMONDS/Antonio REID/ Daryl SIMMONS	14995
37	Mick JAGGER/Keith RICHARDS	14864
38	Rod TEMPERTON	14748
39	Elton JOHN/Bernie TAUPIN	14395
40	Terry BRITTEN/Graham LYLE	14321
41	Andy FARRISS/Michael HUTCHENCE	14285
42	Will JENNINGS/Steve WINWOOD	14039
43	Jim STEINMAN	14000
44	Adam CLAYTON/Dave EVANS/Paul HEWSON/ Larry MULLEN	13923
45	Maurice STARR	13319
46	Bob SEGER	13003
47	Gloria ESTEFAN	12612
48	Graham RUSSELL	12546
49	Jonathan CAIN/Steve PERRY	12483
50	Lewis MARTINÉE	12407
51	David MALLOY/Eddie RABBITT/Even STEVENS	12208
52	John DEACON	12120
53	Lou GRAMM/Michael Leslie JONES	11962
54	Burt BACHARACH/Carole Bayer SAGER	11616
55	Dennis DeYOUNG	11509
56	Bernard EDWARDS/Nile RODGERS	11219
57	Steve KIPNER/Terry SHADDICK	11192
58	Oliver LEIBER	11097
59	Colin James HAY	11008
60	Irene CARA/Keith FORSEY/Giorgio MORODER	10725
61	Stephen BRAY/Madonna L. CICCONE	10693
62	Dean PITCHFORD/Tom SNOW	10514
63	Michael Leslie JONES	10230
64	Steven ADLER/Saul HUDSON/Duff McKAGAN/ Axl ROSE/Izzy STRADLIN	10217
65	David BOWIE	10200
66	Steve GEORGE/John LANG/Richard PAGE	9907
67	Matt AITKEN/Mike STOCK/Pete WATERMAN	9753
68	Steve MILLER	9716
69	Steve GREENBERG	9395
70	Bobby DALL/C.C. DeVILLE/Bret MICHAELS/ Rikki ROCKETT	9378
71	Dan FOGELBERG	9346
72	Roger WATERS	9336
73	Tom BAILEY/Alannah CURRIE/Joe LEEWAY	9323
74	Howard JONES	9152
75	André CYMONE/Jody WATLEY	9094
76	Rick JAMES	9042
77	George GREEN/John MELLENCAMP	8937
78	Jackie DeSHANNON/Donna WEISS	8923
79	Michael JACKSON/Paul McCARTNEY	8900
80	Seth JUSTMAN	8854
81	Smokey ROBINSON	8759
82	Chris HAYES/Huey LEWIS	8743
83	Alan PARSONS/Eric WOOLFSON	8672
84	George MERRILL/Shannon RUBICAM	8634
85	Giorgio MORODER/Tom WHITLOCK	8625
86	Jeff LYNNE	8508
87	Elliot WOLFF	8501
88	Brian SETZER	8480
89	Roland GIFT/David STEELE	8462
90	Michael ANTHONY/Sammy HAGAR/ Alex VAN HALEN/Eddie VAN HALEN	8265
91	Glenn FREY/Jack TEMPCHIN	8144
92	Albert HAMMOND/Diane WARREN	8128
93	Bruce HORNSBY/John HORNSBY	7970
94	Peter GABRIEL	7967
95	John FARRAR	7900
96	Per GESSLE	7880
97	Michael CRAIG/Roy HAY/Jon MOSS/ George O'DOWD/Phil PICKETT	7875
98	Jake HOOKER/Alan MERRILL	7869
99	David PAICH	7813
100	Corey HART	7749

'80s: Top Writer Teams by Entries

1	PRINCE	35
2	Stevie WONDER	24
3	James Samuel HARRIS/Terry LEWIS	24
4	John LENNON/Paul McCARTNEY	22
5	Billy JOEL	22
6	Bruce SPRINGSTEEN	18
7	Bryan ADAMS/Jim VALLANCE	17
8	John MELLENCAMP	17
9	Ric OCASEK	16
10	STING	16
11	Annie LENNOX/David A. STEWART	15
12	Jim PETERIK/Frankie SULLIVAN	15
13	Rick SPRINGFIELD	14
14	Michael JACKSON	14
15	Mike LOVE/Brian WILSON	13
16	Bob SEGER	13
17	Elton JOHN/Bernie TAUPIN	13
18	Tony BANKS/Phil COLLINS/Mike RUTHERFORD	13
19	George MICHAEL	13
20	Lionel RICHIE	13
21	Mick JAGGER/Keith RICHARDS	12
22	Barry GIBB/Maurice GIBB/Robin GIBB	12
23	Ray PARKER Jr.	12
24	Diane WARREN	12
25	Phil COLLINS	12
26	Billy SQUIER	11
27	Alan PARSONS/Eric WOOLFSON	11
28	Adam CLAYTON/Dave EVANS/Paul HEWSON/ Larry MULLEN	11
29	Paul McCARTNEY	11
30	Jeff LYNNE	10
31	Dan FOGELBERG	10
32	Bernard EDWARDS/Nile RODGERS	10
33	Dennis DeYOUNG	10
34	Will JENNINGS/Steve WINWOOD	10
35	Curtis BEDEAU/Gerard CHARLES/ Hugh CLARKE/Brian GEORGE/Lucien GEORGE/ Paul GEORGE	10
36	John CAFFERTY	9
37	Pete TOWNSHEND	9
38	Frank BEARD/Billy GIBBONS/Dusty HILL	9
39	Glenn FREY/Jack TEMPCHIN	9
40	Rick JAMES	9
41	Howard JONES	9
42	Andy FARRISS/Michael HUTCHENCE	9
43	Kenneth EDMONDS/Antonio REID/Daryl SIMMONS	9
44	Kevin CRONIN	9
45	Debbie GIBSON	9
46	Nick ASHFORD/Valerie SIMPSON	8
47	Martin L. GORE	8
48	Ray DAVIES	8
49	George HARRISON	8
50	Paul SIMON	8
51	Russ BALLARD	8
52	Corey HART	8
53	Peter GABRIEL	8
54	Michael ANTHONY/Sammy HAGAR/ Alex VAN HALEN/Eddie VAN HALEN	8
55	Smokey ROBINSON	8
56	Tom BAILEY/Alannah CURRIE/Joe LEEWAY	8
57	Matt AITKEN/Mike STOCK/Pete WATERMAN	8
58	David BOWIE	8
59	Lou GRAMM/Michael Leslie JONES	8
60	Jim STEINMAN	8
61	Rod TEMPERTON	8
62	Daryl HALL	8
63	Thomas F. KELLY/Billy STEINBERG	8
64	Simon Le BON/Nick RHODES/Andy TAYLOR/ Nigel John TAYLOR/Roger TAYLOR	8
65	Bill BERRY/Peter BUCK/Mike MILLS/ Michael STIPE	7
66	Sammy HAGAR	7
67	Lamont DOZIER/Brian HOLLAND/Eddie HOLLAND	7
68	David MALLOY/Eddie RABBITT/Even STEVENS	7
69	Lewis MARTINÉE	7
70	Jonathan CAIN/Steve PERRY	7
71	Christopher CROSS	7
72	Michael CRAIG/Roy HAY/Jon MOSS/George O'DOWD	7
73	John LENNON	7
74	Rick ALLEN/Steve CLARK/Phil COLLEN/ Joe ELLIOTT/Mutt LANGE/Rick SAVAGE	6
75	John DENVER	6
76	Martin DUISER/Jaap EGGERMONT	6
77	Benny ANDERSSON/Björn ULVAEUS	6
78	Billy IDOL	6
79	Tom KEIFER	6
80	Andy GOLDMARK/Bruce ROBERTS	6
81	John SPINKS	6
82	Jackson BROWNE	6
83	Stevie NICKS	6
84	Mike CHAPMAN/Holly KNIGHT	6
85	Kenneth GAMBLE/Leon HUFF	6
86	Rupert HOLMES	6
87	Mike CAMPBELL/Tom PETTY	6
88	Jonathan CAIN/Steve PERRY/Neal SCHON	6
89	Neil DIAMOND	6
90	Gerry GOFFIN/Michael MASSER	6
91	Chris LOWE/Neil TENNANT	6
92	Bobby DALL/C.C. DeVILLE/Bret MICHAELS/ Rikki ROCKETT	6
93	Colin James HAY	6
94	Maurice STARR	6
95	Richard MARX	6
96	Sara ALLEN/Daryl HALL/John OATES	6

Thirty-seven writer teams tied with 5.

The Songs And Acts

Index of Charted Songs
Alphabetical Order

Data for the 24,426 songs are listed in alphabetical order by title then by entry date. A number of attributes for each are presented. The title, act, label/number, magazines, earliest entry and highest chart position are shown for all. If applicable, it is noted that the cut is from an EP, Medley or Two-Sided Winner (TSW), whether the cut is instrumental and whether words and music can be attributed separately. Additionally, if applicable, there are notes regarding foreign origin of lyrics and whether they have been translated or English lyrics substituted *de novo*. Parodies and response songs are also flagged.

Song Title—Act—Label

No effort has been made to record all the variations in wording or spelling of titles of the same record and the listing should be considered adequate to identify the cut but not necessarily exact. Songs that charted multiple times are shown in italics, and equivalent songs are grouped together. Where titles differ significantly I have added a parenthetical to make it clear they are associated. The label/number citation is generally that listed in the original magazines.

Medleys, Two-Sided Winners (TSW) and EPs

Because this work is primarily about writers, these agglomerated units have been broken down into their components; thus, each song in a medley is listed and scored individually (example: Aquarius and Let The Sunshine In) but the medley (Aquarius/Let The Sunshine In) is not scored. In the same way, credit for Two-Sided Winners (TSW) and EPs is divided up to attribute to the component songs; the underlying EP, Medley or TSW itself is not listed or scored. In the index, these are designated as (EP), (Med) or (TSW). In some cases a cut will appear twice because it appeared twice in a medley.

Entry Date - Magazines - Peak

This data is taken from all three magazines of record: Billboard (B), Cash Box (C) and Music Vendor/Record World (R) for the years 1955-1991. Additionally, some cuts from 1954 have been listed, but not scored. The magazines' chart methodologies varied over the years covered, sometimes even to the number of records on the chart. By the summer of 1958, all three had settled on charts of 1-100 weekly, generally with no ties at rank.

Entry Date (m/d/yy) is the earliest entry of the record in any of the magazines. Peak is the highest peak achieved in any of the magazines. For EP and Medley cuts the peak is that of the Medley or EP itself, with the exception of three EP cuts that charted separately. These are noted along with the peak of the EP. For TSW sides, data refer to the highest rank of all magazine appearances either as a separately charting side or as part of the TSW.

Tagalongs

The latter two magazines would occasionally list multiple versions of a song in the same chart rank, and distinguish which was the strongest version that week. These groupings are called tagalongs. Cases where multiple recordings are shown entering the chart in the same month and year and achieving the same chart peak are recognizable as tagalongs in at least one magazine. As an example see "What Kind Of Fool Am I?"

In this section, records treated as tagalongs are designated as either Ct or Rt. In some cases, different songs with similar titles and different writers were erroneously grouped by the magazine as tagalongs. An asterisk is added in these cases.

Foreign Language or Origin

[F]=Foreign Language; [FET]=Foreign origin translated to English; [FDE]=Foreign Origin, de novo English lyrics

Songs recorded in a non-English language are attributed to the original writers; however, it was common for such tunes to be repurposed with English lyrics. If the lyrics or the essential idea of the song was carried forward into English words, the original lyricist is credited along with the English lyricist. If new, unrelated lyrics have been written and added to the original melody, the composer and the English lyricist only are credited. The foreign language lyricist does not receive credit if the lyrics are de novo English.

Instrumental

[I]=Instrumental; [IM]=Instrumental, lyrics attribution separable from music; [IWM]=Instrumental, musical score and lyrics have same writers

Some records are written as instrumentals without lyrics and lyrics were never added. These, and cuts attributed to only one writer are designated [I]. In many cases, songs with lyrics were recorded as instrumentals. If credit for words and music is separable and attributable to two different people—information that is usually found in the copyright--the cut is designated [IM]. If credit is for "words and music" and composer and lyricist credit is inseparable the cut is designated [IWM]. The lyricist on an instrumental version of a song written with lyrics does not receive credit unless that lyricist also has a music credit.

Parody

This indicates a derivative song involving new lyrics for an existing, recognizable song, such as those written by "Weird Al" Yankovic or by Sheb Wooley as Ben Colder. In many cases, however, the parody lyricist is not credited as such by rights, copyright or label. Parodies are indexed with the underlying record and represented by [P].

Response

Some songs are written as a response to an original, as "Son-In-Law" relative to "Mother-In-Law." Response songs do not always use the same music but are also generally indexed with the original record because of the close relationship. Response songs are represented by [R].

Italics: Multiple Recordings

LOVE IS BLUE (L'AMOUR EST BLEU) *Paul Mauriat And His Orchestra—Philips 40495 [André Popp] [ASC] (12/30/67 BCR-1) [IM]*

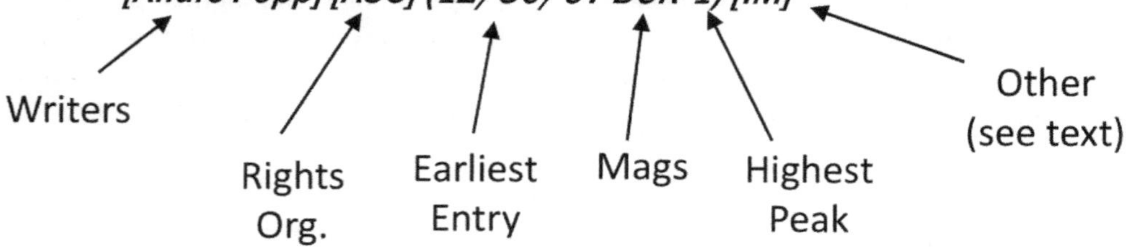

A

A BANDA (AH BAHN-DA) Herb Alpert & The Tijuana Brass—A&M 870 [Chico Buarque De Hollanda] [ASC] (9/9/67 BCR-31) [I]

A 'SOALIN' Peter, Paul & Mary—Warner Bros. 5402 [Tracy Batteast/Elena Mezzetti/Paul Stookey] [ASC] (12/21/63 C-79)

THE "A" TEAM SSgt. Barry Sadler—RCA Victor 47-8804 [Phyllis Landsberg*/Barry Sadler/Leonard Whitcup] [ASC] (4/23/66 BCR-16)

ABACAB Genesis—Atlantic 3891 [Tony Banks/Phil Collins/Mike Rutherford] [ASC] (12/19/81 BCR-26)

ABADABADANGO Kim Carnes—EMI America 8281 [Kim Carnes/Dave Ellingson/Duane Hitchings] [ASC] (8/3/85 BC-67)

ABC The Jackson 5—Motown 1163 [Berry Gordy/Fonce Mizell/Freddie Perren/Deke Richards] [ASC] (3/14/70 BCR-1)

ABC'S OF LOVE Frankie Lymon and the Teenagers—Gee 1022 [Richard Barrett/George Goldner*/Morris Levy‡] [BMI] (9/29/56 BCR-37)

ABERGAVENNY Shannon—Heritage 814 [Ronnie Scott/Marty Wilde] [ASC] (6/28/69 BCR-32)

ABIGAIL BEECHER Freddy Cannon—Warner Bros. 5409 [Robert Boulanger/Dick Heard] [ASC] (2/1/64 BCR-16)

ABILENE George Hamilton IV—RCA Victor 47-8181 [Lester L. Brown/Bob Gibson/Albert Stanton*/Traditional] [BMI] (6/15/63 BCR-15)

ABOUT THIS THING CALLED LOVE Fabian—Chancellor 1047 [Clyde Norris/Jerry Ragovoy/Leroy Roebuck] [BMI] (2/20/60 BCR-31)

ABOVE THE STARS Mr. Acker Bilk—Atco 6230 [Bob Merrill] [ASC] (6/30/62 BCR-40) [I]

ABRA-CA-DABRA The Defranco Family Featuring Tony Defranco—20th Century 2070 [Timothy D. Martin/Walt Meskell] [BMI] (12/29/73 BCR-22)

ABRACADABRA Steve Miller Band—Capitol 5126 [Steve Miller] [ASC] (5/29/82 BC-1)

ABRAHAM, MARTIN AND JOHN *Dion—Laurie 3464 [Dick Holler] [BMI] (10/19/68 BCR-2)*

ABRAHAM, MARTIN AND JOHN *Moms Mabley—Mercury 72935 [Dick Holler] [BMI] (6/21/69 BCR-35)*

ABRAHAM, MARTIN AND JOHN *Smokey Robinson & The Miracles—Tamla 54184 [Dick Holler] [BMI] (6/28/69 BCR-31)*

COLE, COOKE AND REDDING *(based on Abraham, Martin And John) Wilson Pickett—Atlantic 2722 [Dick Holler] (TSW) [NA] (5/2/70 BCR-52) [P]*

ABRAHAM, MARTIN AND JOHN *Tom Clay—Mowest 5002 [Dick Holler] (Med) [BMI] (7/10/71 BCR-7)*

ABSOLUTE BEGINNERS David Bowie—EMI America 8308 [David Bowie] [ASC] (3/29/86 BC-53)

ABSOLUTELY RIGHT Five Man Electrical Band—Lionel 3220 [Les Emmerson] [BMI] (10/9/71 BCR-19)

ABYSSINIA JONES Edwin Starr—Granite 532 [Edwin Starr] [BMI] (2/7/76 B-98)

ACE IN THE HOLE *Somethin' Smith & The Redheads—Epic 9106 [James Dempsey/George Mitchell] [NA] (6/6/55 CR-41)*

ACE IN THE HOLE *Roberta Sherwood with The Singing Waiters—Decca 31091 [James Dempsey/George Mitchell] [NA] (5/30/60 R-78)*

ACE OF SPADE O.V. Wright—Back Beat 615 [Deadric Malone] [BMI] (10/24/70 BCR-41)

—ACERCATE MAS see: COME CLOSER TO ME

ACROSS 110TH STREET (Performed By Bobby Womack & Peace)—United Artists 196 [J.J. Johnson/Bobby Womack] [BMI] (3/17/73 BCR-49)

ACROSS THE MILES Survivor—Scotti Brothers 68526 [Jim Peterik/Frankie Sullivan] [ASC] (1/21/89 BC-67)

ACROSS THE RIVER Bruce Hornsby & The Range—RCA 2621 [Bruce Hornsby/John Hornsby] [ASC] (6/23/90 BC-16)

ACROSS THE STREET Lenny O'Henry—Atco 6291 [Charlie Calello/Bob Crewe/Valmond Harris] [ASC] (4/18/64 BCR-73)

ACROSS THE STREET (IS A MILLION MILES AWAY) Ray Peterson—MGM 13299 [Gene Pitney] [BMI] (1/16/65 C-99)

ACT NATURALLY The Beatles—Capitol 5498 [Voni Morrison/Johnny Russell] [BMI] (9/18/65 BCR-21)

ACTION Freddy Cannon—Warner Bros. 5645 [Tommy Boyce/Steve Venet] [BMI] (8/14/65 BCR-10)

ACTION The Sweet—Capitol 4220 [Brian Connolly/Stephen Priest/Andrew Scott/Michael Tucker] [ASC] (2/14/76 BCR-10)

ACTION Evelyn "Champagne" King—RCA 13682 [Dana Meyers/Leon Sylvers] [ASC] (1/7/84 B-75)

ACTION SPEAKS LOUDER THAN WORDS Chocolate Milk—RCA Victor 10290 [Amadee Castenell/Ernest Dabon/Robert Dabon/Lloyd Harris/Frank Richard/Dwight Richards/Joseph Smith III/Mario Tio/Kenneth J. Williams] [BMI] (7/12/75 BCR-69)

ACTRESS Roy Orbison—Monument 456 [Joe Melson/Roy Orbison] [BMI] (2/19/62 R-87)

ADAM AND EVE Paul Anka—ABC-Paramount 10082 [Paul Anka] [BMI] (2/22/60 BR-90)

ADD SOME MUSIC TO YOUR DAY The Beach Boys—Brother/Reprise 0894 [Joe Knott/Mike Love/Brian Wilson] [BMI] (3/7/70 BCR-39)

ADDAMS GROOVE M.C. Hammer—Capitol 44794 [Stanley Burrell/Vic Mizzy/Felton Pilate] [BMI] (12/7/91 BC-7)

ADDICTED TO LOVE Robert Palmer—Island 99570 [Robert Palmer] [ASC] (2/8/86 BC-1)

ADDIO The Ames Brothers—RCA Victor 47-5897 [Al Hoffman/Dick Manning] [ASC] (12/18/54 C-40)

ADESTE FIDELES (O COME ALL YE FAITHFUL) *David Whitfield—London 1508 [Traditional] [NA] (12/6/54 Rt-PRE)*

ADESTE FIDELES (OH, COME, ALL YE FAITHFUL) *Bing Crosby—Decca 23777 [Traditional] [NA] (12/6/54 Rt-PRE)*

ADESTE FIDELES (OH, COME, ALL YE FAITHFUL) *Bing Crosby—Decca 23777 [Traditional] [NA] (12/16/55 R-56)*

ADESTE FIDELES (OH, COME, ALL YE FAITHFUL) *Bing Crosby—Decca 23777 [Traditional] [NA] (12/22/56 R-61)*

ADESTE FIDELES (OH, COME, ALL YE FAITHFUL) *Bing Crosby—Decca 23777 [Traditional] [NA] (12/23/57 R-67)*

ADESTE FIDELES (OH, COME, ALL YE FAITHFUL) *Bing Crosby—Decca 23777 [Traditional] [NA] (12/8/58 R-72)*

ADESTE FIDELES (OH, COME, ALL YE FAITHFUL) *Bing Crosby—Decca 23777 [Traditional] [NA] (12/12/60 BR-45)*

ADIOS AMIGO Jim Reeves—RCA Victor 47-8019 [Ralph Freed/Jerry Livingston] [BMI] (5/5/62 BCR-72)

ADONIS *Terri Stevens—Felsted 8586 [George Goehring/Ed Warren] [ASC] (8/17/59 CtR-79)*

ADONIS *Terri Dean—Laurie 3032 [George Goehring/Ed Warren] [ASC] (8/22/59 Ct-79)*

ADORABLE *The Fontane Sisters with Billy Vaughn's Orchestra—Dot 15428 [Buck Ram] [ASC] (10/24/55 BCtRt-20)*

ADORABLE *The Colts—Vita 112 [Buck Ram] [ASC] (10/24/55 Rt-29)*

ADORABLE *The Drifters—Atlantic 1078 [Buck Ram] [ASC] (10/31/55 CtRt-20)*

ADRIENNE Tommy James—Roulette 7100 [Tommy James/Robert L. King] [BMI] (3/20/71 BCR-90)

ADULT EDUCATION Daryl Hall & John Oates—RCA 13714 [Sara Allen/Daryl Hall/John Oates] [BMI] (2/18/84 BC-8)

ADVICE FOR THE YOUNG AT HEART Tears For Fears—Fontana 876 894 [Nicky Holland/Roland Orzabal] [BMI] (3/3/90 BC-62)

AFFAIR OF THE HEART Rick Springfield—RCA 13497 [Rick Springfield/Danny Tate/Blaise Tosti] [BMI] (4/16/83 BC-9)

AN AFFAIR TO REMEMBER (OUR LOVE AFFAIR) *Vic Damone—Columbia 40945 [Harold Adamson/Leo McCarey/Harry Warren] [ASC] (7/6/57 BCRt-25)*

AN AFFAIR TO REMEMBER (OUR LOVE AFFAIR) *Carmen Cavallaro—Decca 30362 [Harold Adamson/Leo McCarey/Harry Warren] [ASC] (7/6/57 Rt-25)*

AN AFFAIR TO REMEMBER *Pete King & His Orchestra—Liberty 55075 [Harold Adamson/Leo McCarey/Harry Warren] [ASC] (8/12/57 Rt-40)*

AN AFFAIR TO REMEMBER *ViVienne—VIP 1007 [Harold Adamson/Leo McCarey/Harry Warren] [ASC] (8/26/57 Rt-25)*

AN AFFAIR TO REMEMBER (OUR LOVE AFFAIR) *Angela Drake—MGM 12499 [Harold Adamson/Leo McCarey/Harry Warren] [ASC] (9/2/57 Rt-40)*

AN AFFAIR TO REMEMBER (OUR LOVE AFFAIR) *Nat "King" Cole—Capitol EAP 1-813 [Harold Adamson/Leo McCarey/Harry Warren] (EP) [ASC] (9/9/57 R-55)*

AFRAID Jimmie Rodgers—Dot 16428 [Fred Rose] [ASC] (2/9/63 R-82)

AFRICA Thundermug—Big Tree 154 [Arthur Joseph DeAngelis/William Arthur Durst] [BMI] (12/16/72 R-93)

AFRICA Toto—Columbia 03335 [David Paich/Jeff Porcaro] [ASC] (10/30/82 BC-1)

AFRICAN WALTZ *Cannonball Adderley Orchestra—Riverside 45457 [Galt MacDermot] [BMI] (4/3/61 BCtRt-41) [IM]*

AFRICAN WALTZ *Johnny Dankworth and His Orchestra—Roulette 4353 [Galt MacDermot] [BMI] (4/8/61 CtRt-41) [IM]*

AFRICAN WALTZ *Ian Fraser—London 1976 [Galt MacDermot] [BMI] (4/10/61 Rt-61) [IM]*

AFRICANISM Kongas—Polydor 14461 [Marc Cerrone/Don Ray] (Med) [BMI] (4/8/78 BC-84)

AFRIKAAN BEAT Bert Kaempfert And His Orchestra—Decca 31350 [Bert Kaempfert] [BMI] (1/15/62 BCR-27) [I]

AFRO-STRUT The Nite-Liters—RCA Victor 74-0591 [Harvey Fuqua/Charles Hearndon] [BMI] (2/26/72 BCR-39) [I]

AFTER ALL Al Jarreau—Warner Bros. 29262 [David Foster/Jay Graydon/Al Jarreau] [BMI] (10/13/84 BC-69)

AFTER ALL (LOVE THEME FROM CHANCES ARE) Cher and Peter Cetera—Geffen 27529 [Dean Pitchford/Tom Snow] [BMI] (3/11/89 BC-6)

AFTER ALL THIS TIME Merry Clayton—Ode 66018/66020 [Carole King] [ASC] (12/4/71 BCR-62)

AFTER HOURS Lew Douglas & His Orchestra—Todd 1029 [Avery Parrish] [ASC] (6/29/59 R-85) [IM]

AFTER I CRY TONIGHT Lanier and Co.—Larc 81010 [Phillip Mitchell] [BMI] (12/4/82 B-48)

AFTER LOVING YOU Della Reese—ABC-Paramount 10691 [John William Lantz/Eddie Miller] [BMI] (7/10/65 BC-81)

AFTER LOVING YOU Major Harris—Atlantic 3248 [Melvin Steals/Mervin Steals] [BMI] (3/22/75 R-99)

AFTER MIDNIGHT *Eric Clapton—Atco 6784 [J.J. Cale] [BMI] (10/10/70 BCR-13)*

AFTER MIDNIGHT *J.J. Cale—Shelter 7321 [J.J. Cale] [BMI] (5/20/72 BCR-42)*

AFTER MIDNIGHT *Maggie Bell—Atlantic 3018 [J.J. Cale] [BMI] (4/20/74 BCR-76)*

AFTER SCHOOL Tommy Charles—Decca 29946 [Harry Edelstein/Cliff Parman] [ASC] (7/21/56 B-92)

AFTER SCHOOL *Randy Starr–Dale 100 [Randy Starr/Dick Wolf] [ASC] (4/6/57 BCtRt-22)*
AFTER SCHOOL *Joy Layne–Mercury 71080 [Randy Starr/Dick Wolf] [ASC] (4/6/57 CtRt-22)*
AFTER SCHOOL *The Teardrops–King 5037 [Randy Starr/Dick Wolf] [ASC] (5/18/57 Rt-22)*
AFTER THE DANCE Marvin Gaye–Tamla 54273 [Marvin Gaye/Leon Ware] [ASC] (8/14/76 BR-74)
AFTER THE FALL Journey–Columbia 04004 [Jonathan Cain/Steve Perry] [ASC] (7/9/83 BC-23)
AFTER THE FEELING IS GONE *Lulu With The Dixie Flyers–Atco 6761 [George Soule/Terry Woodford] [BMI] (7/4/70 CR-94)*
AFTER THE FEELING IS GONE *Five Flights Up–T-A 207 [George Soule/Terry Woodford] [BMI] (12/5/70 BCR-84)*
AFTER THE FIRE Roger Daltrey–Atlantic 89491 [Pete Townshend] [GL] (9/14/85 BC-48)
AFTER THE FIRE IS GONE Conway Twitty Loretta Lynn–Decca 32776 [L.E. White] [BMI] (2/6/71 BC-56)
AFTER THE FIRST ONE Yonah–Free Flight 11696 [Wyn Jackson] [ASC] (9/1/79 C-97)
AFTER THE GLITTER FADES Stevie Nicks–Modern 7405 [Stevie Nicks] [BMI] (5/15/82 BC-31)
AFTER THE GOLDRUSH Prelude–Island 002 [Neil Young] [BMI] (9/14/74 BCR-12)
AFTER THE LIGHTS GO DOWN LOW *Al Hibbler–Decca 29982 [Phil Belmonte*/Leroy Lovett/Alan White] [BMI] (8/3/56 BCR-15)*
AFTER THE LIGHTS GO DOWN LOW *George Maharis–Epic 9504 [Phil Belmonte*/Leroy Lovett/Alan White] [BMI] (5/5/62 C-94)*
AFTER THE LOVE HAS GONE Earth, Wind & Fire–ARC 11033 [Bill Champlin/David Foster/Jay Graydon] [ASC] (7/7/79 BCR-2)
AFTER THE LOVIN' Engelbert Humperdinck–Epic 50270 [Ritchie Adams/Alan Bernstein] [BMI] (10/16/76 BCR-5)
AFTER THE RAIN Nelson–DGC 19667 [Gunnar Nelson/Matthew Nelson/Marc Tanner/Ric Wilson] [ASC] (11/3/90 BC-6)
AFTER THE SUMMER'S GONE PC Quest–Headliner/RCA 62051 [Tim James/Mike Piccirillo] [BMI] (8/17/91 BC-41)
AFTER YOU Dionne Warwick–Arista 0498 [Doug Frank/Doug James] [BMI] (3/29/80 BCR-65)
AFTER YOU'VE GONE Frankie Avalon–Chancellor 1101 [Henry Creamer/J. Turner Layton] [ASC] (1/29/62 R-100)
AFTERNOON DELIGHT Starland Vocal Band–Windsong 10588 [Bill Danoff] [ASC] (5/1/76 BCR-1)
AGAIN The Lettermen–Capitol 4851 [Dorcas Cochran/Lionel Newman] [BMI] (10/27/62 CR-82)
AGAINST ALL ODDS (TAKE A LOOK AT ME NOW) Phil Collins–Atlantic 89700 A [Phil Collins] [ASC] (2/25/84 BC-1)
AGAINST THE WIND Bob Seger–Capitol 4863 [Bob Seger] [ASC] (5/3/80 BCR-5)
AGE FOR LOVE Jimmy Charles–Promo 1003 [Marie Latimer/Alma Wells] [BMI] (11/14/60 BCR-42)
AGE (WHERE I STARTED AGAIN) Horatio–Event 3304 [Ingrid Croce/Jim Croce] [ASC] (8/2/69 R-95)
AGENT DOUBLE-O-SOUL Edwin Starr–Ric-Tic 103 [Bill Sharpley/Edwin Starr] [BMI] (7/24/65 BCR-20)
THE AGONY AND THE ECSTASY Smokey Robinson–Tamla 54261 [Smokey Robinson] [ASC] (8/16/75 BCR-36)
AGONY OF DEFEET Parliament–Casablanca 2317 [Donna Lynn Clinton/Ronald Dunbar/Donnie Ray Sterling] [BMI] (1/17/81 R-96)
AH! LEAH! Donnie Iris–MCA/Carousel 51025 [Mark Avsec/Donnie Iris] [ASC] (12/13/80 BCR-22)
AHAB, THE ARAB Ray Stevens–Mercury 71966 [Ray Stevens] [BMI] (6/23/62 BCR-2)
AI NO CORRIDA (I-NO-KO-REE-DA) Quincy Jones–A&M 2309 [Chaz Jankel/Kenny Young] [ASC] (4/11/81 BCR-26)
AIMING AT YOUR HEART The Temptations–Gordy 7208 [Joseph Jefferson/Rich Roebuck/Charles Simmons] [BMI] (9/12/81 BCR-67)
AIN'T DOING TOO BAD (PART 1) Bobby Bland–Duke 383 [Deadric Malone] [BMI] (10/10/64 BCR-26)
AIN'T EVEN DONE WITH THE NIGHT John Cougar–Riva 207 [John Mellencamp] [ASC] (1/31/81 BCR-15)
AIN'T GONNA BE THAT WAY Marv Johnson–United Artists 226 [Berry Gordy/Marv Johnson] [ASC] (5/23/60 BCR-49)
AIN'T GONNA BUMP NO MORE (WITH NO BIG FAT WOMAN) Joe Tex–Epic 50313 [Buddy Killen/Bennie McGinty] [BMI] (3/19/77 BCR-10)
AIN'T GONNA CRY NO MORE Brenda Lee–Decca 31970 [David Gates] [BMI] (6/25/66 BCR-77)
—AIN'T GONNA EAT OUT MY HEART ANY MORE see: I AIN'T GONNA..
AIN'T GONNA' HURT NOBODY *Brick–Bang 735 [Regi Hargis] [ASC] (12/31/77 BCR-76)*
AIN'T GONNA HURT NOBODY *Kid 'N Play–Select 64847 [Regi Hargis/Eric Johnson/Christopher Reid] [ASC] (11/16/91 B-51)*
AIN'T GONNA KISS YA The Ribbons–Marsh 202 [James Marcus Smith] [BMI] (1/26/63 BCR-76)
AIN'T GONNA LIE Keith–Mercury 72596 [George Fischoff/Tony Powers] [BMI] (8/27/66 BCR-27)
AIN'T GONNA REST (TILL I GET YOU) The Five Stairsteps–Windy C 605 [Clarence Burke Jr./Clarence Burke Sr.] [BMI] (4/1/67 BCR-82)
AIN'T GONNA TELL ANYBODY Jimmy Gilmer and The Fireballs–Dot 16583 [Ken Davis/Juanita Jordan] [BMI] (3/14/64 BCR-46)
AIN'T GOT NO Nina Simone–RCA Victor 47-9686 [Galt MacDermot/James Rado/Gerome Ragni] (Med) [ASC] (1/4/69 BR-94)
AIN'T GOT NO HOME *Clarence Henry "Frog Man"–Argo 5259 [Clarence "Frogman" Henry] [BMI] (11/24/56 BCR-28)*
AIN'T GOT NO HOME *The Band–Capitol 3758 [Clarence "Frogman" Henry] [BMI] (11/24/73 BCR-53)*
AIN'T GOT TIME The Impressions–Curtom 1957 [Curtis Mayfield] [BMI] (2/27/71 BCR-49)
AIN'T IT A SAD THING R. Dean Taylor–Rare Earth 5023 [R. Dean Taylor] [BMI] (2/6/71 BCR-58)
AIN'T IT A SHAME Major Lance–Okeh 7223 [Curtis Mayfield] [BMI] (6/5/65 BCR-77)
AIN'T IT, BABY The Miracles–Tamla 54036 [Smokey Robinson] [ASC] (3/27/61 BCR-40)
AIN'T IT FUNKY NOW (PART 1) James Brown–King 6280 [James Brown] [BMI] (11/15/69 BCR-24) [I]
AIN'T IT LIKE HIM Edwin Hawkins Singers–Pavillion 20002 [Edwin Hawkins] [ASC] (8/2/69 R-86)
AIN'T IT THE TRUTH Mary Wells–20th Century 544 [Lou Courtney] [BMI] (10/31/64 BCR-28)
AIN'T IT TRUE Andy Williams–Columbia 43358 [Mike Lewis/Joe Sauter] [BMI] (9/4/65 BCR-31)
AIN'T LOVE A BITCH Rod Stewart–Warner Bros. 8810 [Gary Grainger/Rod Stewart] [ASC] (4/21/79 BCR-14)
AIN'T MISBEHAVIN' Johnnie Ray–Columbia 40649 [Harry Brooks/Andy Razaf/Thomas Waller] [ASC] (3/23/56 R-86)
AIN'T NO FUTURE IN YO' FRONTIN' M.C. Breed–SDEG 91-062 [Eric Breed/Schzelle Harris/Herman Lang] [BMI] (9/14/91 B-66)
AIN'T NO LOVE IN THE HEART OF THE CITY Bobby Bland–Dunhill/ABC 15003 [Harvey Price/Dan Walsh] [ASC] (8/10/74 BCR-90)
AIN'T NO MOUNTAIN HIGH ENOUGH *Marvin Gaye & Tammi Terrell–Tamla 54149 [Nick Ashford/Valerie Simpson] [ASC] (5/13/67 BCR-19)*
AIN'T NO MOUNTAIN HIGH ENOUGH *Diana Ross–Motown 1169 [Nick Ashford/Valerie Simpson] [ASC] (8/8/70 BCR-1)*
AIN'T NO STOPPIN' US NOW McFadden & Whitehead–Philadelphia Int'l 3681 [Jerry Allen Cohen/Gene McFadden/John Whitehead] [BMI] (4/21/79 BCR-12)
AIN'T NO SUNSHINE Bill Withers–Sussex 219 [Bill Withers] [BMI] (7/3/71 BCR-3)
AIN'T NO TELLING Bobby Bland–Duke 390 [Deadric Malone] [BMI] (4/24/65 BR-93)
AIN'T NO WAY Aretha Franklin–Atlantic 2486 [Carolyn Franklin] [BMI] (4/6/68 BCR-16)
AIN'T NO WAY TO TREAT A LADY Helen Reddy–Capitol 4128 [Harriet Schock] [ASC] (8/9/75 BCR-5)
AIN'T NO WOMAN (LIKE THE ONE I'VE GOT) Four Tops–Dunhill 4339 [Dennis Lambert/Brian Potter] [BMI] (2/3/73 BCR-1)
AIN'T NOBODY Rufus And Chaka Khan–Warner Bros. 29555 [David Wolinski] [ASC] (10/1/83 BC-22)
AIN'T NOBODY HOME *Howard Tate–Verve 10420 [Jerry Ragovoy] [ASC] (8/6/66 BCR-57)*
AIN'T NOBODY HOME *B.B. King–ABC 11316 [Jerry Ragovoy] [ASC] (10/30/71 BCR-46)*
AIN'T NOTHIN' BUT A HOUSE PARTY *The Show Stoppers–Heritage 800 [Carl Fisher/Joseph David Thomas Jr.] [BMI] (5/18/68 BCR-87)*
(AIN'T NOTHIN' BUT A) HOUSE PARTY *The J. Geils Band–Atlantic 3350 [Carl Fisher/Joseph David Thomas Jr.] [BMI] (7/31/76 C-77)*
AIN'T NOTHIN' GOIN' ON BUT THE RENT Gwen Guthrie–Polydor 885106 [Gwen Guthrie] [ASC] (8/2/86 BC-42)
AIN'T NOTHING GONNA KEEP ME FROM YOU Teri Desario–Casablanca 929 [Barry Gibb] [BMI] (7/1/78 BCR-42)
AIN'T NOTHING LIKE THE REAL THING *Marvin Gaye & Tammi Terrell–Tamla 54163 [Nick Ashford/Valerie Simpson] [ASC] (4/13/68 BCR-7)*
AIN'T NOTHING LIKE THE REAL THING *Aretha Franklin–Atlantic 3200 [Nick Ashford/Valerie Simpson] [ASC] (8/31/74 BCR-44)*
AIN'T NOTHING LIKE THE REAL THING *Donny & Marie–Polydor/Kolob 14363 [Nick Ashford/Valerie Simpson] [ASC] (11/20/76 BCR-21)*
AIN'T NOTHING LIKE THE REAL THING *Chris Christian–Boardwalk 7-11-149 [Nick Ashford/Valerie Simpson] (Med) [ASC] (8/28/82 B-88)*
AIN'T NOTHING YOU CAN DO Bobby Bland–Duke 375 [Deadric Malone/Joe Scott] [BMI] (3/7/64 BCR-16)
AIN'T SHE SWEET *The Johnston Brothers–London 1526 [Milton Ager/Jack Yellen] (Med) [ASC] (7/11/55 R-61)*
AIN'T SHE SWEET *The Modernaires–Coral 61555 [Milton Ager/Jack Yellen] [ASC] (1/20/56 R-86)*
AIN'T SHE SWEET *The Beatles–Atco 6308 [Milton Ager/Jack Yellen] [ASC] (7/18/64 BCR-13)*
AIN'T SO EASY David & David–A&M 2905 [David Baerwald/David Ricketts] [ASC] (1/24/87 BC-51)
AIN'T THAT A GROOVE PART 1 James Brown And The Famous Flames–King 6025 [James Brown/Nat Jones] [BMI] (3/5/66 BCR-36)
AIN'T IT A SHAME *Fats Domino–Imperial 5348 [Dave Bartholomew/Fats Domino] [BMI] (6/18/55 BCtRt-1)*
AIN'T THAT A SHAME *Pat Boone–Dot 15377 [Dave Bartholomew/Fats Domino] [BMI] (6/18/55 BCtRt-1)*

AIN'T THAT A SHAME *Ronnie Gaylord—Wing 90000*
[Dave Bartholomew/Fats Domino] [BMI] (7/4/55 Rt-39)

AIN'T THAT A SHAME! *The 4 Seasons Featuring Frankie Valli—Vee-Jay 512*
[Dave Bartholomew/Fats Domino] [BMI] (4/20/63 BCR-20)

AIN'T THAT A SHAME *Cheap Trick—Epic 50743*
[Dave Bartholomew/Fats Domino] [BMI] (8/4/79 BCR-35)

AIN'T THAT ENOUGH FOR YOU John Davis And The Monster Orchestra—Sam 5011
[John E. Davis] [ASC] (12/23/78 B-89)

AIN'T THAT JUST LIKE A WOMAN Fats Domino—Imperial 5723
[Claude DeMetrius/Fleecie Moore] [BMI] (1/23/61 BCR-26)

AIN'T THAT JUST LIKE ME The Searchers—Kapp 584
[Earl Carroll/Billy Guy] [BMI] (4/4/64 BCR-50)

AIN'T THAT LOVE *Micki Marlo—ABC-Paramount 9807*
[Ray Charles] [BMI] (3/23/57 R-81)

AIN'T THAT LOVE *Harry Belafonte—RCA Victor 47-7289*
[Ray Charles] [BMI] (7/26/58 C-70)

AIN'T THAT LOVE Four Tops—Columbia 43356 [Levi Stubbs] [NA] (7/31/65 B-93)

AIN'T THAT LOVING YOU Bobby Bland—Duke 338
[Deadric Malone] [BMI] (3/31/62 BC-86)

AIN'T THAT LOVING YOU BABY Betty Everett & Jerry Butler—Vee-Jay 613
[Jimmy Reed] [BMI] (9/5/64 C-91)

AIN'T THAT LOVING YOU BABY Elvis Presley With The Jordanaires—
RCA Victor 47-8440 [Ivory Joe Hunter/Clyde Otis] [BMI] (10/10/64 BCR-12)

AIN'T THAT LOVING YOU (FOR MORE REASONS THAN ONE) *Luther Ingram—KoKo 2105*
[Homer Banks/Allen Alvoid Jones Jr.] [BMI] (5/23/70 BCR-45)

AIN'T THAT LOVING YOU (FOR MORE REASONS THAN ONE)
Isaac Hayes & David Porter—Enterprise 9049
[Homer Banks/Allen Alvoid Jones Jr.] [BMI] (4/29/72 BCR-67)

AIN'T THAT PECULIAR *Marvin Gaye—Tamla 54122*
[Warren Moore/Smokey Robinson/Robert Rogers/Marvin Tarplin]
[ASC] (10/2/65 BCR-7)

AIN'T THAT PECULIAR *Fanny—Reprise 1080*
[Warren Moore/Smokey Robinson/Robert Rogers/Marvin Tarplin]
[ASC] (4/29/72 BCR-85)

AIN'T THAT PECULIAR *Diamond Reo—Big Tree 16030*
[Warren Moore/Smokey Robinson/Robert Rogers/Marvin Tarplin]
[ASC] (12/28/74 BCR-36)

AIN'T TOO PROUD TO BEG *The Temptations—Gordy 7054*
[Eddie Holland/Norman Whitfield] [BMI] (5/21/66 BCR-8)

AIN'T TOO PROUD TO BEG *The Magnificent Men—Capitol 5976*
[Eddie Holland/Norman Whitfield] (Med) [BMI] (9/9/67 BCR-90)

AIN'T TOO PROUD TO BEG *The Rolling Stones—Rolling Stones 19302*
[Eddie Holland/Norman Whitfield] [BMI] (11/9/74 BCR-15)

AIN'T TOO PROUD TO BEG *Rick Astley—RCA 9030*
[Eddie Holland/Norman Whitfield] [BMI] (8/19/89 B-89)

AIN'T UNDERSTANDING MELLOW Jerry Butler And Brenda Lee Eager—Mercury 73255
[Herscholt Polk/Homer Talbert] [BMI] (12/11/71 BCR-21)

AIN'T WASTIN' TIME NO MORE The Allman Brothers Band—Capricorn 0003
[Gregg Allman] [BMI] (4/29/72 BCR-72)

AIN'TCHA CHA COMIN' OUT TONIGHT Jo Stafford—Columbia 40538
[Norman Gimbel/Alec Wilder] [BMI] (8/27/55 CR-43)

AIR DISASTER Albert Hammond—Mums 6030
[Albert Hammond/Mike Hazlewood] [ASC] (6/29/74 BCR-68)

THE AIR THAT I BREATHE The Hollies—Epic 11100
[Albert Hammond/Mike Hazlewood] [ASC] (4/20/74 BCR-5)

AIR TRAVEL Ray And Bob—Ledo 1151
[Bobby Ray Appleberry/Bobby Swayne] [BMI] (6/23/62 B-99)

AIRPLANE SONG (MY AIRPLANE) The Royal Guardsmen—Laurie 3391
[Boomer Castleman/Michael Murphey] [BMI] (6/17/67 BCR-46)

AIRPORT LOVE THEME (GWEN AND VERN) Vincent Bell—Decca 32659
[Alfred Newman] [ASC] (3/28/70 BCR-27) [IM]

—AISLE see: TO THE AISLE

AJAX AIRLINES Hudson And Landry—Dore 868
[Bob Hudson/Ron Landry] [ASC] (12/25/71 BC-68)

AJAX LIQUOR STORE Hudson and Landry—Dore 855
[Bob Hudson/Ron Landry] [ASC] (4/24/71 BCR-43)

AL DI LA' *Emilio Pericoli—Warner Bros. 5259*
[Carlo Donida/Giulio Rapetti] [ASC] (5/14/62 BCR-6) [F]

AL DI LA *Connie Francis—MGM 13116*
[Carlo Donida/Ervin Drake/Giulio Rapetti] [ASC] (12/22/62 BCR-59) [F,FDE]

AL-DI-LA *Ray Charles Singers—Command 4049*
[Carlo Donida/Ervin Drake/Giulio Rapetti] [ASC] (7/11/64 BCR-25) [FDE]

ALABAM *Cowboy Copas—Starday 501 [Cowboy Copas] [BMI] (9/26/60 BCtRt-42)*

ALABAM *Pat Boone—Dot 16152 [Cowboy Copas] [BMI] (10/24/60 BCtRt-42)*

ALABAMA GETAWAY Grateful Dead—Arista 0519
[Jerry Garcia/Robert Hunter] [ASC] (6/14/80 BCR-66)

ALABAMA JUBILEE *Ferko String Band—Media 1010*
[George L. Cobb/Jack Yellen] [ASC] (5/30/55 BCRt-11)

ALABAMA JUBILEE *Art Mooney & His Orchestra—MGM 12000*
[George L. Cobb/Jack Yellen] [ASC] (5/30/55 Rt-11)

ALABAMA JUBILEE *Cliff Steward & The San Francisco Boys—Coral 61446*
[George L. Cobb/Jack Yellen] [ASC] (6/13/55 Rt-22)

ALABAMA JUBILEE *David Carroll & His Orchestra—Mercury 70642*
[George L. Cobb/Jack Yellen] [ASC] (6/13/55 Rt-22)

ALABAMA WILD MAN Jerry Reed—RCA Victor 74-0738
[Jerry Reed] [BMI] (7/15/72 BCR-62)

ALABAMY BOUND *Les Paul and Mary Ford—Capitol 3301*
[Buddy DeSylva/Bud Green/Ray Henderson] [ASC] (12/1/55 Rt-56)

ALABAMY BOUND *The Mulcays—Cardinal 1014*
[Buddy DeSylva/Bud Green/Ray Henderson] [ASC] (12/16/55 Rt-56)

ALADDIN Bobby Curtola—Del-Fi 4185
[Basil Hurdon/Dyer Hurdon] [BMI] (10/27/62 BC-92)

ALBATROSS Fleetwood Mac—Epic 10436 [Peter Green] [BMI] (3/15/69 CR-98) [I]

ALBERT FLASHER The Guess Who—RCA Victor 74-0458
[Burton Cummings] (TSW) [BMI] (4/10/71 BCR-22)

ALEXANDER'S RAGTIME BAND Crazy Otto—Polydor 22009A
[Irving Berlin] (Med) [NA] (1/10/55 R-30) [IWM]

ALFIE *Cher—Imperial 66192 [Burt Bacharach/Hal David] [ASC] (7/30/66 BCR-31)*

ALFIE *Cilla Black—Capitol 5674 [Burt Bacharach/Hal David] [ASC] (8/27/66 B-95)*

ALFIE *Dionne Warwick—Scepter 12187*
[Burt Bacharach/Hal David] [ASC] (4/1/67 BCR-15)

ALFIE *Eivets Rednow—Gordy 7076 [Burt Bacharach] [ASC] (9/14/68 BCR-66) [IM]*

ALIBIS Sergio Mendes—A&M 2639 [Tony Macaulay/Tom Snow] [ASC] (5/26/84 BC-29)

ALICE BLUE GOWN LeRoy Holmes And His Orchestra—MGM 12833
[Harry Tierney] [NA] (10/19/59 R-85) [IM]

ALICE EVERYDAY Book Of Love—Sire 19550 [Ted Ottaviano] [BMI] (3/9/91 C-85)

ALICE IN WONDERLAND Neil Sedaka—RCA Victor 47-8137
[Howard Greenfield/Neil Sedaka] [BMI] (1/26/63 BCR-17)

ALICE LONG (YOU'RE STILL MY FAVORITE GIRLFRIEND)
Tommy Boyce & Bobby Hart—A&M 948 [Tommy Boyce/Bobby Hart] [BMI]
(6/29/68 BCR-16)

ALICE'S ROCK & ROLL RESTAURANT Arlo Guthrie—Reprise 0877
[Arlo Guthrie] [ASC] (12/13/69 B-97)

ALIEN Atlanta Rhythm Section—Columbia 02471
[Buddy Buie/Randy Lewis/Steve McRay] [BMI] (8/29/81 BCR-27)

ALIMONY Frankie Ford—Ace 566
[Joe Caronna/Frankie Ford/Huey P. Smith] [BMI] (7/11/59 BCR-71)

ALISON Elvis Costello—Columbia 10705 [Elvis Costello] (TSW) [ASC] (3/11/78 C-61)

ALIVE Bee Gees—Atco 6909 [Barry Gibb/Maurice Gibb] [BMI] (11/4/72 BCR-26)

ALIVE AGAIN Chicago—Columbia 10845 [James Pankow] [ASC] (10/21/78 BCR-12)

ALIVE AND KICKING Simple Minds—A&M 2783
[Charles Burchill/Jim Kerr/Michael MacNeil] [ASC] (10/19/85 BC-3)

ALL James Darren—Warner Bros. 5874[Domenico Colarossi*/Marian Grudeff/
Ray Jessel/Nino Oliviero] [BMI] (1/14/67 BCR-33) [FDE]

ALL ABOUT LOVE Eddie Fisher—RCA Victor 47-6746
[Mack Gordon/Josef Myrow] [ASC] (1/19/57 R-85)

ALL ABOUT MY GIRL Jimmy McGriff—Sue 777 [Jimmy McGriff] [BMI] (1/5/63 BCR-50) [I]

ALL ABOUT YOU Pretty In Pink—Motown 2087
[Tammy Lucas/Teddy Riley] [ASC] (9/21/91 B-96)

ALL ALONE Terri Stevens—Felsted 8538 [Irving Berlin] [ASC] (10/27/58 CR-69)

ALL ALONE AM I Brenda Lee—Decca 31424
[Arthur Altman/Manos Hadjidakis] [BMI] (9/22/62 BCR-3) [FDE]

ALL ALONG THE WATCHTOWER The Jimi Hendrix Experience—Reprise 0767
[Bob Dylan] [SE] (9/14/68 BCR-18)

ALL AMERICAN BOY Bill Parsons And His Orchestra—Fraternity 835
[Bobby Bare*/Orville Lunsford*/Bill Parsons*] [BMI] (12/13/58 BCR-2)

ALL AMERICAN GIRLS Sister Sledge—Cotillion 46007
[Joni Sledge/Lisa Walden/Narada Michael Walden/Allee Willis] [BMI] (2/21/81 BR-67)

ALL AROUND America—Capitol 4817 [Gerry Beckley/Dewey Bunnell] [ASC] (2/9/80 R-93)

ALL AROUND THE WORLD Lisa Stansfield—Arista 1-9928
[Ian Devaney/Andy Morris/Lisa Stansfield] [ASC] (2/3/90 BC-3)

ALL AT ONCE Don Cornell—Coral 61253
[Leroy Lovett/Serge Walter] [ASC] (11/22/54 R-50)

ALL AT ONCE YOU LOVE HER Perry Como—RCA Victor 47-6294
[Oscar Hammerstein/Richard Rodgers] [ASC] (10/24/55 BCR-10)

ALL BY MYSELF Eric Carmen—Arista 0165
[Eric Carmen/Sergei Rachmaninoff*] [BMI] (12/13/75 BCR-1)

ALL CRIED OUT Dusty Springfield—Philips 40229
[Buddy Kaye/Philip Springer] [ASC] (9/26/64 BCR-31)

ALL CRIED OUT
Lisa Lisa And Cult Jam With Full Force Featuring Paul Anthony And Bow Legged Lou—
Columbia 05844
[Curtis Bedeau/Gerard Charles/Hugh Clarke/Brian George/Lucien George/Paul George]
[BMI] (7/26/86 BC-8)

ALL DAY AND ALL OF THE NIGHT The Kinks—Reprise 0334
[Ray Davies] [BMI] (12/26/64 BCR-6)

ALL DAY MUSIC War—United Artists 50815
[Thomas Allen/Harold Brown/Morris Dickerson/Jerry Goldstein/Lonnie Jordan/Charles Miller/Lee Oskar/Howard Scott] [ASC] (8/7/71 BCR-28)

ALL DOWN THE LINE The Rolling Stones—Rolling Stones 19104
[Mick Jagger/Keith Richards] [BMI] (7/22/72 CR-74)

ALL FALL DOWN Five Star—RCA 14108 [Barry Blue/Robin Smith] [ASC] (9/14/85 BC-65)

ALL FIRED UP Pat Benatar—Chrysalis 43268
[Pat Benatar/Myron Grombacher/Kerryn Tolhurst] [ASC] (7/2/88 BC-19)

ALL 4 LOVE Color Me Badd—Giant 19236
[Bryan Abrams/Mark Calderon/Isaac Hayes*/Howard Thompson/Kevin Thornton/Sam Watters*] [ASC] (11/2/91 BC-1)

ALL GOD'S CHILDREN GOT SOUL Dorothy Morrison—Elektra 45671
[William Bell/Booker T. Jones Jr.] [BMI] (8/30/69 BR-95)

ALL GROWN UP The Crystals—Philles 122
[Jeff Barry/Ellie Greenwich/Phil Spector] [BMI] (7/11/64 BC-85)

ALL HIS CHILDREN Charley Pride/Henry Mancini—RCA Victor 74-0624
[Alan Bergman/Marilyn Bergman/Henry Mancini] [ASC] (3/4/72 BC-92)

ALL I COULD DO WAS CRY *Etta James—Argo 5359*
[Billy Davis/Berry Gordy/Gwen Gordy] [BMI] (4/23/60 BCR-23)

ALL I COULD DO WAS CRY *Joe Tex—Anna 1119*
[Billy Davis/Berry Gordy/Gwen Gordy] [ASC] (8/22/60 R-89)

ALL I DO IS THINK OF YOU Troop—Atlantic 87952
[Brian Holland/Michael Larry Smith] [BMI] (7/7/90 B-47)

ALL I EVER NEED IS YOU Sonny & Cher—Kapp 2151
[Jimmy Holiday/Eddie Reeves] [ASC] (10/16/71 BCR-6)

ALL I EVER WANTED Santana—Columbia 11218
[Alex Ligertwood/Carlos Santana/Chris Solberg] [BMI] (3/15/80 R-86)

ALL I HAVE The Moments—Stang 5017
[George Kerr/Sylvia Robinson] [BMI] (11/21/70 BCR-56)

ALL I HAVE TO DO IS DREAM *The Everly Brothers—Cadence 1348*
[Boudleaux Bryant] [BMI] (4/14/58 BCR-1)

ALL I HAVE TO DO IS DREAM *The Everly Brothers—Cadence 1348*
[Boudleaux Bryant] [BMI] (7/24/61 B-96)

ALL I HAVE TO DO IS DREAM *Richard Chamberlain—MGM 13121*
[Boudleaux Bryant] [BMI] (2/2/63 BCR-13)

ALL I HAVE TO DO IS DREAM *Bobbie Gentry & Glen Campbell—Capitol 2745*
[Boudleaux Bryant] [BMI] (2/14/70 BCR-27)

(ALL I HAVE TO DO IS) DREAM *Nitty Gritty Dirt Band—United Artists 655*
[Boudleaux Bryant] [BMI] (8/2/75 BCR-57)

ALL I HAVE TO DO IS DREAM *Andy Gibb And Victoria Principal—RSO 1065*
[Boudleaux Bryant] [BMI] (8/15/81 BCR-51)

ALL I HAVE TO OFFER YOU (IS ME) Charley Pride—RCA Victor 74-0167
[Dallas Frazier/A.L. "Doodle" Owens] [BMI] (8/23/69 BCR-86)

ALL I KNOW Garfunkel—Columbia 45926 [Jimmy Webb] [ASC] (9/8/73 BCR-6)

ALL I KNOW IS THE WAY I FEEL Pointer Sisters—RCA 5112
[Estelle Levitt/Jerry Ragovoy] [ASC] (2/21/87 B-93)

ALL I NEED The Temptations—Gordy 7061
[Eddie Holland/R. Dean Taylor/Frank Edward Wilson] [BMI] (4/29/67 BCR-8)

ALL I NEED Jack Wagner—Qwest 29238
[Glen Ballard/Clif Magness/David Pack] [ASC] (10/20/84 BC-2)

ALL I NEED Mötley Crüe—Elektra 69429 [Tommy Lee/Nikki Sixx] [ASC] (11/28/87 BC-83)

ALL I NEED IS A MIRACLE Mike + The Mechanics—Atlantic 89450
[Christopher Neil/Mike Rutherford] [ASC] (3/22/86 BC-5)

ALL I NEED IS TIME Gladys Knight & The Pips—Soul 35107
[Bud Reneau] [ASC] (8/11/73 BCR-61)

ALL I NEED IS YOU Les Paul and Mary Ford—Columbia 41350
[William Engvick/Les Paul] [ASC] (2/16/59 R-83)

ALL I NEED IS YOU Blue Train—Zoo 14018
[Paul Betts/Alan Fearn/Simon Husbands/Anthony C. Osborne] [BMI] (10/5/91 BC-46)

—ALL I NEED TO KNOW see: DON'T KNOW MUCH

ALL I REALLY WANT TO DO *The Byrds—Columbia 43332 [Bob Dylan] [SE] (7/3/65 BCtRt-9)*

ALL I REALLY WANT TO DO *Cher—Imperial 66114 [Bob Dylan] [SE] (7/3/65 BCtRt-9)*

ALL I SEE IS YOU Dusty Springfield—Philips 40396
[Ben Weisman/Clive Westlake] [ASC] (9/10/66 BCR-19)

ALL I SEE IS YOUR FACE Dan Hill—20th Century Fox 2378
[Dan Hill] [ASC] (8/12/78 BCR-35)

ALL I WANNA DO Doucette—Mushroom 7036
[Jerry Doucette/Arlyn Eric Olson/Brent Shindell] [ASC] (10/14/78 C-97)

ALL I WANNA DO IS MAKE LOVE TO YOU Heart—Capitol 44507
[Mutt Lange] [ASC] (3/31/90 BC-1)

ALL I WANT Howard Jones—Elektra 69494 [Howard Jones] [BMI] (1/17/87 BC-69)

ALL I WANT IS YOU Carly Simon—Arista 1-9653
[Jacob Brackman/Andy Goldmark/Carly Simon] [ASC] (1/23/88 BC-54)

ALL I WANT IS YOU U2—Island 99199
[Adam Clayton/Dave Evans/Paul Hewson/Larry Mullen] [ASC] (7/1/89 BC-64)

ALL I WANT TO BE IS YOUR WOMAN Carolyn Franklin—RCA Victor 74-0373
[Jill Williams] [BMI] (9/12/70 R-99)

ALL I WANTED Kansas—MCA 52958 [Steve Morse/Steve Walsh] [BMI] (11/1/86 BC-19)

ALL I'M MISSING IS YOU Glenn Medeiros—MCA 53886
[Antonina Armato/Ray Parker Jr.] [ASC] (8/11/90 BC-32)

ALL IN GOOD TIME Nelson Trio—Guaranteed 203
[Mort Garson/Earl Shuman] [ASC] (1/16/60 C-94)

ALL IN LOVE IS FAIR Barbra Streisand—Columbia 46024
[Stevie Wonder] [ASC] (3/30/74 BCR-57)

ALL IN MY MIND *Maxine Brown—Nomar 103*
[Maxine M. Brown/Fred Johnson/Leroy Kirkland] [BMI] (12/31/60 BCRt-15)

ALL IN MY MIND *Dakota Staton—Capitol 4512*
[Maxine M. Brown/Fred Johnson/Leroy Kirkland] [BMI] (1/30/61 Rt-16)

ALL LIPS N' HIPS Electric Boys—Atco 98973 [Conny Blomqvist] [ASC] (7/14/90 B-76)

ALL MAMA'S CHILDREN Carl Perkins—Sun 243
[Johnny Cash/Carl Perkins] [BMI] (6/22/56 R-21)

ALL MY HARD TIMES Joe Simon—Spring 118 [Joe South] [BMI] (9/4/71 BCR-75)

ALL MY LIFE Kenny Rogers—Liberty 1495
[Charles David Robbins/Jeff Silbar/Van Stephenson] [BMI] (4/30/83 BC-37)

ALL MY LIFE Linda Ronstadt (featuring Aaron Neville)—Elektra 64987
[Karla Bonoff] [BMI] (1/27/90 BC-11)

ALL MY LOVING *The Beatles—Capitol of Canada 72144*
[John Lennon/Paul McCartney] [ASC] (3/28/64 BCR-31)

ALL MY LOVING *The Beatles—Capitol EAP-2121*
[John Lennon/Paul McCartney] (EP) [ASC] (5/30/64 BCR-86)

ALL MY LOVING *The Hollyridge Strings—Capitol 5207*
[John Lennon/Paul McCartney] [ASC] (7/4/64 B-93) [IWM]

ALL MY TRIALS *Dick And Deedee—Warner Bros. 5411 [Traditional] [NA] (2/22/64 B-89)*

ALL MY TRIALS *Ray Stevens—Barnaby 2039 [Traditional] [NA] (8/28/71 BCR-70)*

ALL MY TRIALS *Mickey Newbury—Elektra 45750*
[Traditional] (Med) [BMI] (11/6/71 BCR-24)

ALL MY TRIALS *Elvis Presley—RCA Victor 74-0672*
[Traditional] (Med) [BMI] (4/22/72 BCR-59)

ALL NIGHT LONG Jo Stafford—Columbia 40640 [Chilton Price] [BMI] (3/10/56 B-99)

ALL NIGHT LONG Sandy Nelson—Imperial 5860
[John Grayton Dolphin] [BMI] (7/14/62 B-75) [I]

ALL NIGHT LONG Joe Walsh—Full Moon/Asylum 46639
[Joe Walsh] [ASC] (5/17/80 BCR-17)

ALL NIGHT LONG (ALL NIGHT) Lionel Richie—Motown 1698
[Lionel Richie] [ASC] (9/17/83 BC-1)

ALL NIGHT LONG Billy Squier—Capitol 5422 [Billy Squier] [NA] (10/20/84 BC-75)

ALL NIGHT THING The Invisible Man's Band—Mango 103
[Clarence Burke Jr./Dean Gant/Alex Masucci] [BMI] (5/3/80 BCR-45)

ALL NIGHT WITH ME Laura Branigan—Atlantic 4023 [Chris Montan] [ASC] (3/20/82 B-69)

ALL NITE Entouch featuring Keith Sweat—Vintertainment 69260
[Eric McCaine/Eric Smith] [ASC] (1/13/90 BC-65)

—ALL NITE LONG see: NIGHT TRAIN

(ALL OF A SUDDEN) MY HEART SINGS *Paul Anka—ABC-Paramount 9987*
[Henri Herpin/Harold Rome] [ASC] (12/1/58 BCR-8) [FDE]

(ALL OF A SUDDEN) MY HEART SINGS *Mel Carter—Imperial 66138*
[Henri Herpin/Harold Rome] [ASC] (10/30/65 BCR-35) [FDE]

ALL OF EVERYTHING Frankie Avalon—Chancellor 1071
[Charles Singleton] [BMI] (2/13/61 BCR-70)

ALL OF ME FOR ALL OF YOU 9.9—RCA 14082
[Richard "Dimples" Fields/Josh Sklair/Belinda Wilson] [ASC] (8/24/85 BC-48)

ALL OF MY LIFE Sam Cooke—Keen 3-2005 [Lou Adler/Herb Alpert] [BMI] (6/2/58 R-55)

ALL OF MY LIFE Lesley Gore—Mercury 72412
[Helen Miller/Tony Powers] [BMI] (3/20/65 BCR-71)

ALL OF MY LOVE Bobby Caldwell—Polydor 2212 [Bobby Caldwell] [BMI] (9/11/82 BC-70)

ALL OF YOU *Sammy Davis Jr.—Decca 29402 [Cole Porter] [ASC] (1/29/55 CtRt-37)*

ALL OF YOU *Tony Martin—RCA Victor 47-5946 [Cole Porter] [ASC] (1/29/55 CtRt-25)*

ALL OF YOU *Mel Torme—Coral 61294 [Cole Porter] [ASC] (2/14/55 Rt-61)*

ALL OF YOU Julio Iglesias & Diana Ross—Columbia 04507
[Julio Iglesias/Tony Renis/Cynthia Weil] [ASC] (7/7/84 BC-12)

ALL OR NOTHING Patti LaBelle And The Blue Belles—Atlantic 2311
[Lori Burton/Pam Sawyer] [BMI] (11/27/65 BCR-68)

ALL OR NOTHING Milli Vanilli—Arista 1-9923
[David Clayton-Thomas/Frank Farian/Brad Howell/P.G. Wylder] [BMI] (12/30/89 BC-4)

ALL OUR TOMORROWS Eddie Schwartz—Atco 7342
[Eddie Schwartz/David Tyson] [ASC] (12/12/81 BCR-28)

ALL OUT OF LOVE Air Supply—Arista 0520
[Clive Davis/Graham Russell] [BMI] (6/7/80 BCR-1)

ALL OVER AGAIN Johnny Cash—Columbia 41251 [Johnny Cash] [ASC] (9/29/58 BCR-38)

ALL OVER ME Charlie Rich—Epic 50142 [Ben Peters] [BMI] (9/20/75 C-90)

ALL OVER THE WORLD Nat King Cole—Capitol 4919
[Al Frisch/Charles Tobias] [ASC] (2/23/63 BCR-32)

ALL OVER THE WORLD Electric Light Orchestra—MCA 41289
[Jeff Lynne] [BMI] (8/2/80 BCR-8)

ALL RIGHT Christopher Cross—Warner Bros. 29843
[Christopher Cross] [ASC] (1/22/83 BC-9)

ALL RIGHT NOW *Free—A&M 1206 [Andy Fraser/Paul Rodgers] [BMI] (8/15/70 BCR-3)*

ALL RIGHT NOW *Lea Roberts—United Artists 626*
[Andy Fraser/Paul Rodgers] [BMI] (4/12/75 BR-85)

ALL RIGHT NOW *Rod Stewart—Warner Bros. 29122*
[Andy Fraser/Paul Rodgers] [BMI] (12/15/84 BC-72)

ALL RIGHT NOW *Pepsi & Shirlie—Polydor 887277*
[Andy Fraser/Paul Rodgers] [BMI] (2/20/88 BC-66)

ALL ROADS (LEAD BACK TO YOU) Donny Most—United Artists 871
[Jeff Marmelzat/Spencer Proffer] [BMI] (12/4/76 B-97)

ALL SHE WANTS IS Duran Duran—Capitol 44287
[Simon Le Bon/Nick Rhodes/Nigel John Taylor] [ASC] (12/24/88 BC-22)

ALL SHE WANTS TO DO IS DANCE Don Henley—Geffen 29065
[Danny Kortchmar] [ASC] (2/23/85 BC-9)

ALL SHE WROTE Firehouse—Epic 73984
[Bill Leverty/Carl J. Snare] [ASC] (11/16/91 BC-37)

ALL SHOOK UP *Elvis Presley—RCA Victor 47-6870*
[Otis Blackwell/Elvis Presley] [BMI] (3/30/57 BCR-1)

ALL SHOOK UP *Suzi Quatro—Bell 45,477*
[Otis Blackwell/Elvis Presley] [BMI] (7/13/74 BCR-53)

ALL SHOOK UP *Jive Bunny And The Mastermixers—Music Factory 99140*
[Otis Blackwell/Elvis Presley] (Med) [BMI] (10/28/89 BC-11)

ALL STRUNG OUT *Nino Tempo & April Stevens—White Whale 236*
[Jerry Riopelle/Nino Tempo] [BMI] (9/10/66 BCR-26)

ALL STRUNG OUT ON YOU *John Travolta—Midland Int'l 10907*
[Jerry Riopelle/Nino Tempo] [BMI] (2/19/77 BCR-28)

ALL THAT GLITTERS ISN'T GOLD The Cover Girls—Capitol 44545
[David Cole] [ASC] (4/7/90 BC-47)

ALL THAT I AM Elvis Presley With The Jordanaires—RCA Victor 47-8941
[Roy C. Bennett/Sid Tepper] [ASC] (10/1/66 BCR-39)

(ALL THAT I'M ASKING IS) SYMPATHY Johnny Maddox—Dot 15730
[Joe Burke/Benny Davis] [ASC] (4/14/58 R-81)

ALL THE GREY HAIRED MEN The Lettermen—Capitol 2196
[Jack Keller/Bob Russell] [ASC] (6/8/68 R-92)

ALL THE KIDS ON THE STREET The Hollywood Stars—Arista 0241
[C. Mark Anthony/Kim Fowley] [BMI] (5/14/77 B-94)

ALL THE KING'S HORSES Aretha Franklin—Atlantic 2883
[Aretha Franklin] [BMI] (6/3/72 BCR-17)

ALL THE KINGS HORSES The Firm—Atlantic 89458
[Paul Rodgers] [ASC] (2/15/86 BC-61)

ALL THE LOVE IN THE WORLD The Outfield—Columbia 05894
[John Spinks] [ASC] (6/7/86 BC-19)

ALL THE LOVE I'VE GOT Marv Johnson—United Artists 226
[Janie Bradford/Berry Gordy/Brian Holland] [BMI] (6/13/60 BCR-58)

ALL THE MAN THAT I NEED Whitney Houston—Arista 2156
[Michael Gore/Dean Pitchford] [BMI] (12/22/90 BC-1)

ALL THE RIGHT MOVES Jennifer Warnes/Chris Thompson—Casablanca 814603
[Barry Alfonso/Tom Snow] [ASC] (11/12/83 B-85)

—ALL THE ROADS see: TOUS LES CHEMINS

ALL THE THINGS SHE SAID Simple Minds—A&M 2828
[Charles Burchill/Jim Kerr/Michael MacNeil] [ASC] (4/5/86 BC-28)

ALL THE TIME Johnny Mathis—Columbia 41152
[Ray Evans/Jay Livingston] [ASC] (4/7/58 BCR-35)

ALL THE TIME IN THE WORLD Dr. Hook—Capitol 4677
[Shel Silverstein/Even Stevens] [BMI] (2/3/79 BCR-54)

ALL THE WAITING IS NOT IN VAIN Tyrone Davis—Dakar 609
[Carl Davis/Eugene Record] [BMI] (8/2/69 CR-83)

ALL THE WAY *Frank Sinatra—Capitol 3793*
[Sammy Cahn/Jimmy Van Heusen] [ASC] (9/23/57 BCRt-3)

ALL THE WAY *Grady Martin & The Slew Foot Five—Decca 30453*
[Jimmy Van Heusen] [ASC] (10/14/57 Rt-12) [IM]

ALL THE WAY Brick—Bang 4810 [Paul Davis] [BMI] (6/7/80 C-93)

ALL THE WAY Calloway—Solar 74516
[Reggie Calloway/Vincent Calloway] [BMI] (7/21/90 BC-59)

ALL THE WAY DOWN Etta James—Chess 2144
[Trevor Lawrence/Gabriel Mekler/Catherine Williamson] [BMI] (10/6/73 C-70)

ALL THE WAY LOVER Millie Jackson—Spring 179 [Benny Latimore] [BMI] (4/8/78 C-88)

ALL THE WAY 'ROUND THE WORLD The Mills Brothers—Decca 29781
[Jack Meskill/Larry Stock] [ASC] (1/20/56 BR-63)

ALL THE YOUNG DUDES Mott The Hoople—Columbia 45673
[David Bowie] [BMI] (9/23/72 BCR-32)

ALL THESE THINGS The Uniques—Paula 238 [Allen Toussaint] [BMI] (4/30/66 BCR-44)

ALL THINGS ARE POSSIBLE Dan Peek—MCA/Songbird 41123
[Chris Christian/Dan Peek] [ASC] (9/15/79 BC-78)

ALL THIS I SHOULD HAVE KNOWN Breathe—A&M 1401
[Michael Delahunty/David Glasper/Marcus Lillington/Ian Spice] [ASC] (4/22/89 C-76)

ALL THIS LOVE DeBarge—Gordy 1660 [El DeBarge] [ASC] (4/16/83 BC-9)

ALL THIS TIME Tiffany—MCA 53371 [Tim James/Steve McClintock] [BMI] (11/5/88 BC-6)

ALL THIS TIME Sting—A&M 1541 [Sting] [BMI] (1/19/91 BC-5)

ALL THOSE LIES Glenn Frey—Asylum 69857
[Glenn Frey/Jack Tempchin*] [ASC] (12/11/82 BC-37)

ALL THOSE YEARS AGO George Harrison—Dark Horse 49725
[George Harrison] [ASC] (5/23/81 BCR-2)

ALL THROUGH THE NIGHT Cyndi Lauper—Portrait 37-04639
[Jules Shear] [BMI] (10/6/84 BC-5)

ALL THROUGH THE NIGHT Tone Loc—Delicious Vinyl 866 104-4
[Eric Johnson/Tony Joseph/Anthony Terrell Smith] [ASC] (12/14/91 B-80)

ALL TIME HIGH Rita Coolidge—A&M 2551 [John Barry/Tim Rice] [BMI] (7/2/83 BC-33)

ALL TOUCH Rough Trade—Boardwalk 167
[Carole Pope/Kevan Staples] [ASC] (12/18/82 BC-58)

ALL TRUE MAN Alexander O'Neal—Tabu/Epic Associated 73627
[James Samuel Harris/Terry Lewis] [ASC] (2/23/91 BC-43)

ALL YOU GET FROM LOVE IS A LOVE SONG Carpenters—A&M 1940
[Steve Eaton] [ASC] (5/21/77 BCR-35)

ALL YOU NEED IS LOVE *The Beatles—Capitol 5964*
[John Lennon/Paul McCartney] [ASC] (7/22/67 BCR-1)

ALL YOU NEED IS LOVE *The Beatles—Capitol 5107*
[John Lennon/Paul McCartney] (Med) [ASC] (3/27/82 BCR-12)

ALL YOU ZOMBIES Hooters—Columbia 04854
[Eric Bazilian/Rob Hyman] [ASC] (5/18/85 BC-53)

ALL YOUR GOODIES ARE GONE (THE LOSER'S SEAT) The Parliaments—Revilot 211
[George Clinton/Clarence Haskins/Billy Nelson] [BMI] (10/14/67 BCR-62)

—ALLE PORTE DEL SOLE see: TO THE DOOR OF THE SUN

ALLEGHENY MOON *Patti Page—Mercury 70878*
[Al Hoffman/Dick Manning] [ASC] (6/1/56 BCRt-2)

ALLEGHENY MOON *Grady Martin & His Slew Foot Five—Decca 30022*
[Al Hoffman/Dick Manning] [ASC] (9/8/56 Rt-6) [IWM]

ALLENTOWN Billy Joel—Columbia 03413 [Billy Joel] [ASC] (11/27/82 BC-14)

ALLERGIES Paul Simon—Warner Bros. 29453 [Paul Simon] [BMI] (11/5/83 BC-44)

ALLEY CAT *Bent Fabric And His Piano—Atco 6226*
[Bent Fabricius-Bjerre] [BMI] (7/14/62 BCR-6) [IM]

THE ALLEY CAT SONG *David Thorne—Riverside 4530*
[Bent Fabricius-Bjerre/Britt Simonson] [BMI] (10/20/62 BR-76)

THE ALLEY CAT SONG *Peggy Lee—Capitol 4942*
[Bent Fabricius-Bjerre/Britt Simonson] [BMI] (4/13/63 R-92)

ALLEY OOP *The Hollywood Argyles*
[Gary Paxton]—Lute 5905 [Dallas Frazier] [BMI] (5/23/60 BCtRt-1)

ALLEY OOP *Danté And The Evergreens—Madison 130*
[Dallas Frazier] [BMI] (5/23/60 BCtRt-1)

ALLEY OOP *The Dyna-Sores—Rendezvous 120 [Dallas Frazier] [BMI] (5/30/60 BRt-49)*

ALLEY OOP *(parody of Alley Oop) The Four Preps—Capitol 4599*
[Dallas Frazier] (Med) [BMI] (8/14/61 BCR-14) [P]

ALLIES Heart—Epic 04184 [Jonathan Cain] [ASC] (10/29/83 B-83)

ALLIGATOR BOGALOO Lou Donaldson—Blue Note 1934
[Lou Donaldson] [BMI] (10/28/67 BC-93) [I]

THE ALLNIGHTER Glenn Frey—MCA 52461
[Glenn Frey/Jack Tempchin] [ASC] (9/29/84 BC-53)

ALL'S QUIET ON WEST 23RD Julie Budd—MGM 13925
[Joey Levine/Artie Resnick] [BMI] (8/10/68 CR-87)

ALLY ALLY OXEN FREE The Kingston Trio—Capitol 5078
[Rod McKuen/Steven Yates] [ASC] (11/16/63 BCR-60)

ALMOST GROWN Chuck Berry—Chess 1722 [Chuck Berry] [BMI] (3/30/59 BCR-31)

ALMOST HEAR YOU SIGH The Rolling Stones—Rolling Stones 73093
[Mick Jagger/Steve Jordan/Keith Richards] [ASC] (2/10/90 BC-50)

ALMOST IN LOVE Elvis Presley With The Jordanaires—RCA Victor 47-9610
[Luiz Bonfá/Randy Starr] [ASC] (9/28/68 BC-91)

ALMOST IN YOUR ARMS Johnny Nash—ABC-Paramount 9960
[Ray Evans/Jay Livingston] [ASC] (10/13/58 BCR-49)

—ALMOST IN YOUR ARMS see: LOVE SONG FROM HOUSEBOAT

ALMOST LIKE BEING IN LOVE Michael Johnson—EMI America 8004
[Alan Jay Lerner/Frederick Loewe] [ASC] (8/12/78 BCR-32)

ALMOST OVER YOU Sheena Easton—EMI America 8186
[Jennifer Kimball/Cindy Richardson] [BMI] (12/10/83 BC-23)

ALMOST PARADISE *The Norman Petty Trio—ABC-Paramount 9787*
[Norman Petty] [BMI] (2/16/57 BCtRt-17) [IWM]

ALMOST PARADISE *Roger Williams—Kapp 175*
[Norman Petty] [BMI] (2/16/57 BCtRt-16) [IWM]

ALMOST PARADISE *Lou Stein—RKO Unique 385*
[Norman Petty] [BMI] (2/23/57 BCtRt-16) [IWM]

ALMOST PARADISE...LOVE THEME FROM FOOTLOOSE
Mike Reno And Ann Wilson—Columbia 04418
[Eric Carmen/Dean Pitchford] [BMI] (5/12/84 BC-7)

ALMOST PERSUADED *David Houston—Epic 10025*
[Billy Sherrill/Glenn Sutton] [BMI] (7/16/66 BCR-21)

ALMOST PERSUADED NO. 2 *(parody of Almost Persuaded) Ben Colder—MGM 13590*
[Billy Sherrill/Glenn Sutton] [BMI] (10/1/66 BCR-51) [P]

ALMOST PERSUADED *Etta James—Cadet 5630*
[Billy Sherrill/Glenn Sutton] [BMI] (1/18/69 BCR-79)

ALMOST SATURDAY NIGHT *John Fogerty—Asylum 45291*
[John Fogerty] (TSW) [ASC] (12/6/75 BCR-78)

ALMOST SATURDAY NIGHT *Dave Edmunds—Swan Song 72000*
[John Fogerty] [ASC] (5/9/81 BC-54)

ALMOST SUMMER Celebration Featuring Mike Love—MCA 40891
[Alan Jardine/Mike Love/Brian Wilson] [BMI] (4/22/78 BCR-28)

ALMOST THERE Andy Williams—Columbia 43128
[Jerry Keller/Gloria Shayne] [ASC] (10/17/64 BCR-67)

ALONE (WHY MUST I BE ALONE) *Shepherd Sisters—Lance 125*
[Morty Craft/Selma Craft] [BMI] (9/16/57 BCRt-18)

ALONE (WHY MUST I BE ALONE) *The Brother Sisters—Mercury 71195*
[Morty Craft/Selma Craft] [BMI] (10/21/57 Rt-18)

ALONE *The 4 Seasons—Vee-Jay 597 [Morty Craft/Selma Craft] [BMI] (6/6/64 BCR-24)*

ALONE Heart—Capitol 44002 [Thomas F. Kelly/Billy Steinberg] [ASC] (5/16/87 BC-1)

ALONE AGAIN Dokken—Elektra 69650
[Mick Brown/Don Dokken/George Lynch/Jeff Pilson] [ASC] (5/4/85 BC-64)

ALONE AGAIN (NATURALLY) Gilbert O'Sullivan—MAM 3619
[Gilbert O'Sullivan] [BMI] (6/17/72 BCR-1)

ALONE AGAIN OR Love—Elektra 45700 [Bryan MacLean] [BMI] (9/12/70 BR-96)

ALONE AT LAST Jackie Wilson—Brunswick 55170
[Johnny Lehmann] [BMI] (10/10/60 BCR-7)

ALONE WITH YOU Faron Young—Capitol 3982
[Roy Drusky/Lester Vanadore/Faron Young] [BMI] (8/11/58 B-51)

ALONE WITH YOU Brenda Lee—Decca 31628
[Jackie DeShannon] [ASC] (5/30/64 BCR-27)

ALONG CAME JONES *The Coasters—Atco 6141*
[Jerry Leiber/Mike Stoller] [BMI] (5/18/59 BCR-8)

ALONG CAME JONES *Ray Stevens—Monument 1150*
[Jerry Leiber/Mike Stoller] [BMI] (6/28/69 BCR-21)

ALONG COMES A WOMAN Chicago—Warner/Full Moon 29082
[Peter Cetera/Mark Goldenberg] [ASC] (2/23/85 BC-14)

ALONG COMES MARY *The Association—Valiant 741*
[Tandyn Almer] [BMI] (5/21/66 BCR-7)

ALONG COMES MARY *Baja Marimba Band—A&M 862*
[Tandyn Almer] [BMI] (8/5/67 BCR-96) [I]

ALPHABET ST. Prince—Paisley Park 7-27900 [Prince] [ASC] (4/30/88 BC-8)

ALREADY GONE Eagles—Asylum 11036
[Robert Strandlund/Jack Tempchin] [ASC] (5/4/74 BCR-17)

ALRIGHT Janet Jackson—A&M 1479
[James Samuel Harris/Janet Jackson/Terry Lewis] [BMI] (4/7/90 BC-4)

ALRIGHT IN THE CITY Dunn & McCashen—Capitol 2935
[Don Dunn/Tony McCashen] [ASC] (11/7/70 B-91)

ALRIGHT OKAY YOU WIN Peggy Lee—Capitol 4115
[Mayme Watts*/Sid Wyche] [BMI] (1/17/59 BCR-62)

AL'S PLACE Al (He's The King) Hirt Trumpet with Chorus and Orchestra—
RCA Victor 47-8542 [Robert Allen] [ASC] (4/17/65 BCR-49) [I]

THEME MUSIC FOR THE FILM "2001 A SPACE ODYSSEY" (ALSO SPRACH ZARATHUSTRA)
Berlin Philharmonic—Polydor 15009
[Richard Strauss] [NA] (12/13/69 BR-78) [I]

ALSO SPRACH ZARATHUSTRA *Al Capps Band—Columbia 45219*
[Richard Strauss] (Med) [ASC] (10/10/70 C-97) [I]

ALSO SPRACH ZARATHUSTRA (2001) *Deodato—CTI 12*
[Richard Strauss] [NA] (2/3/73 BCR-2) [I]

ALVIN FOR PRESIDENT David Seville And The Chipmunks—Liberty 55277
[David Seville] [ASC] (9/5/60 BCR-71)

ALVIN STONE (THE BIRTH & DEATH OF A GANGSTER) Fantastic Four—Westbound 5009
[Calvin Colbert/Al Hamilton] [BMI] (7/19/75 BCR-56)

THE ALVIN TWIST The Chipmunks—Liberty 55424
[David Seville] [ASC] (2/26/62 BCR-40)

ALVIN'S BOO-GA-LOO Alvin Cash & The Registers—Mar-V-Lus 6014
[James Leonard Jones] [BMI] (11/26/66 BCR-69)

ALVIN'S HARMONICA *David Seville And The Chipmunks—Liberty 55179*
[David Seville] [ASC] (2/14/59 BCR-3)

ALVIN'S HARMONICA *David Seville And The Chipmunks—Liberty 55250*
[David Seville] [ASC] (12/25/61 B-73)

ALVIN'S HARMONICA *David Seville And The Chipmunks—Liberty 55250*
[David Seville] [ASC] (12/22/62 BR-87)

ALVIN'S ORCHESTRA David Seville And The Chipmunks—Liberty 55233
[David Seville] [ASC] (2/8/60 BCR-32)

ALWAYS Sammy Turner—Big Top 3029 [Irving Berlin] [ASC] (10/19/59 BCR-17)

ALWAYS Luther Ingram—KoKo 2115
[Johnny Baylor/Luther Ingram] [BMI] (3/24/73 BC-64)

ALWAYS Firefall—Atlantic 89916 [Paul Crosta/John Sambataro] [BMI] (1/15/83 BC-51)

ALWAYS Atlantic Starr—Warner Bros. 28455
[David E. Lewis/Jonathan Lewis/Wayne I. Lewis] [ASC] (3/28/87 BC-1)

ALWAYS AND FOREVER *Heatwave—Epic 50490*
[Rod Temperton] [ASC] (12/24/77 BCR-12)

ALWAYS AND FOREVER *Whistle—Select 2014 [Rod Temperton] [ASC] (4/7/90 BC-35)*

ALWAYS DAVID Ruby Winters—Diamond 265
[Eddie Hinton/Wayne Jackson/Dan Penn] [BMI] (9/27/69 CR-85)

ALWAYS IN MY HEART Los Indios Tabajaras—RCA Victor 47-8313
[Ernesto Lecuona] [ASC] (2/8/64 BCR-66) [IM]

ALWAYS IT'S YOU The Everly Brothers—Warner Bros. 5151
[Boudleaux Bryant/Felice Bryant] [BMI] (4/23/60 BC-56)

ALWAYS KEEP ME IN YOUR HEART Four Aces—Radnor 301
[Russell Faith/Clarence Kehner] [ASC] (4/26/69 R-98)

ALWAYS ON MY MIND *Willie Nelson—Columbia 02741*
[Johnny Christopher/Mark James/Wayne Carson Thompson] [BMI] (3/6/82 BCR-4)

ALWAYS ON MY MIND *Pet Shop Boys—EMI-Manhattan 50123*
[Johnny Christopher/Mark James/Wayne Carson Thompson] [BMI] (3/26/88 BC-4)

ALWAYS THERE FOR YOU Stryper—Enigma 75019
[Michael Sweet] [BMI] (7/23/88 BC-71)

ALWAYS TOGETHER Al Martino—Capitol 5239
[Peter DeAngelis/Jean Sawyer] [ASC] (8/15/64 BCR-32)

ALWAYS TOGETHER The Dells—Cadet 5621
[Robert Eugene Miller] [BMI] (10/12/68 BCR-18)

—ALWAYS YOU see: MALA FEMMENA

AM I A LOSER Eddie Holman—Parkway 106
[Eddie Holman/James Solomon] [BMI] (11/12/66 R-97)

AM I A TOY OR A TREASURE Kay Starr—Capitol 2887
[Arthur Altman/Lou Singer/Irving Taylor] [ASC] (9/11/54 CR-22)

AM I BLACK ENOUGH FOR YOU Billy Paul—Philadelphia Int'l 3526
[Kenneth Gamble/Leon Huff] [BMI] (3/31/73 BCR-79)

AM I BLUE *Ray Charles—Atlantic 2106 [Harry Akst/Grant Clarke] [ASC] (7/24/61 R-95)*

AM I BLUE *Cher—MCA 40039 [Harry Akst/Grant Clarke] [ASC] (4/28/73 CR-79)*

AM I FORGIVEN Isle Of Man—Pasha 05900
[Ron Aniello/Robert Parlee] [BMI] (8/9/86 B-90)

AM I GROOVING YOU Freddie Scott—Shout 212
[Jeff Barry/Bert Berns] [BMI] (5/13/67 BCR-71)

AM I LOSING YOU Jim Reeves—RCA Victor 47-7800
[Jim Reeves] [BMI] (10/24/60 BCR-22)

AM I LOSING YOU
The Partridge Family Starring Shirley Jones & Featuring David Cassidy—Bell 45,200
[L. Russell Brown/Irwin Levine] [BMI] (3/25/72 BCR-31)

AM I LOSING YOU The Manhattans—Columbia 10674
[Alvin Fields/Barbara Morr/Douglas Stender] [BMI] (3/4/78 CR-89)

AM I THAT EASY TO FORGET *Debbie Reynolds—Dot 15985*
[Carl Belew/Shelby Singleton/W.S. Stevenson‡] [BMI] (1/18/60 BCRt-18)*

AM I THAT EASY TO FORGET *Skeeter Davis—RCA Victor 47-7671*
[Carl Belew/Shelby Singleton/W.S. Stevenson‡] [BMI] (2/1/60 Rt-18)*

AM I THAT EASY TO FORGET *"Little Esther" Phillips—Lenox 5560*
[Carl Belew/Shelby Singleton/W.S. Stevenson‡] [BMI] (2/2/63 CR-95)*

AM I THAT EASY TO FORGET *Engelbert Humperdinck—Parrot 40023*
[Carl Belew/Shelby Singleton/W.S. Stevenson‡] [BMI] (12/16/67 BCR-11)*

AM I THE MAN Jackie Wilson—Brunswick 55170
[Bob Hamilton/Tom King] [BMI] (10/24/60 BCR-23)

—AM I THE SAME GIRL see: SOULFUL STRUT

AMANDA Dionne Warwicke—Scepter 12326
[Artie Butler/Mark Lindsay] [BMI] (8/7/71 BR-83)

AMANDA Waylon—RCA 11596 [Bob McDill] [ASC] (6/2/79 BCR-54)

AMANDA Boston—MCA 52756 [Tom Scholz] [ASC] (9/27/86 BC-1)

AMAPOLA Jacky Noguez And His Orchestra—Jamie 1148
[Joseph M. LaCalle] [ASC] (1/11/60 BCR-36) [I]

AMARILLO Neil Sedaka—Elektra 45406
[Howard Greenfield/Neil Sedaka] [BMI] (5/28/77 BCR-44)

AMAZING GRACE *Judy Collins—Elektra 45709*
[John Newton/Traditional] [NA] (12/12/70 BCR-12)

AMAZING GRACE
The Pipes And Drums And The Military Band Of The Royal Scots Dragoon Guards—
RCA Victor 74-0709
[Traditional] [NA] (5/13/72 BCR-10) [IM]

AMAZING GRACE (USED TO BE HER FAVORITE SONG) The Amazing Rhythm Aces—
ABC 12142 [Howard Russell Smith] [ASC] (12/20/75 BC-72)

AMBER CASCADES America—Warner Bros. 8238 [Dewey Bunnell] [ASC] (8/21/76 BC-75)

AMBROSE (PART FIVE) Linda Laurie—Glory 290
[Linda Laurie/Wes McWain/Lou Sprung] [BMI] (1/10/59 BCR-46)

—AME CALINE see: SOUL COAXING

AMEN *The Impressions—ABC-Paramount 10602 [Traditional] [NA] (11/21/64 BCR-6)*

AMEN *Otis Redding—Atco 6592 [Traditional] [NA] (7/6/68 BCR-34)*

AMEN *The Ovations—MGM 14623 [Traditional] (Med) [NA] (10/13/73 BCR-56)*

AMERICA *Yes—Atlantic 2899 [Paul Simon] [BMI] (8/5/72 BCR-38)*

AMERICA *Simon & Garfunkel—Columbia 45663 [Paul Simon] [BMI] (11/25/72 B-97)*

AMERICA Neil Diamond—Capitol 4994 [Neil Diamond] [SE] (4/25/81 BCR-8)

AMERICA Prince & The Revolution—Paisley Park 7-28999
[Mark Alton Brown/Lisa Coleman/Matt Fink/Wendy Melvoin/Prince/Robert Rivkin] [ASC]
(10/19/85 BC-46)

AMERICA, COMMUNICATE WITH ME Ray Stevens—Barnaby 2016
[Ray Stevens] [BMI] (7/18/70 BCR-27)

AMERICA IS MY HOME - PT. 1 James Brown And The Famous Flames—King 6112 [James Brown/Hayward Moore] [BMI] (5/25/68 BCR-52)

AMERICA/STANDING The Five Stairsteps—Buddah 188 [Larry Byrom/Jerry Edmonton/John Kay/Nick St. Nicholas/Stan Vincent] (TSW) [BMI] (10/10/70 BCR-66)

AMERICA, THE BEAUTIFUL Charlie Rich—Epic 50222 [Katharine Lee Bates/Kermit Goell/Billy Sherrill/Samuel A. Ward] [BMI] (5/8/76 C-78)

AMERICAN BOYS Petula Clark—Warner Bros.-Seven Arts 7244 [Tony Hatch/Jackie Trent] [BMI] (11/23/68 BCR-49)

AMERICAN CITY SUITE Cashman & West—Dunhill 4324 [Terry Cashman/Tommy West] [ASC] (9/16/72 BCR-19)

AN AMERICAN DREAM The Dirt Band—United Artists 1330 [Rodney Crowell] [BMI] (12/1/79 BCR-11)

AMERICAN DREAM Simon F.—Reprise 28237 [Simon Fellowes] [BMI] (10/10/87 BC-83)

AMERICAN DREAM Crosby, Stills, Nash & Young—Atlantic 89003 [Neil Young] [ASC] (11/12/88 C-59)

AMERICAN GIRLS Rick Springfield—Columbia 46057 [Rick Springfield] [ASC] (7/6/74 BCR-64)

AMERICAN HEARTBEAT Survivor—Scotti Brothers 03213 [Jim Peterik/Frankie Sullivan] [ASC] (9/25/82 BC-17)

AMERICAN MADE Oak Ridge Boys—MCA 52179 [Bob DiPiero/Patrick J. McManus] [BMI] (3/19/83 B-72)

AMERICAN MEMORIES Shamus M'Cool—Perspective 107 [Shamus M'Cool] [BMI] (7/4/81 BC-80)

AMERICAN MUSIC Pointer Sisters—Planet 13254 [Parker McGee] [BMI] (6/26/82 BC-15)

AMERICAN PATROL *Frank Barber Orchestra—Victory 1001 [Frank W. Meacham] (Med) [NA] (5/8/82 B-61) [IM]*

AMERICAN PATROL *Larry Elgart And His Manhattan Swing Orchestra—RCA 13219 [Frank W. Meacham] (Med) [NA] (6/5/82 BC-31) [IM]*

AMERICAN PIE Don McLean—United Artists 50856 [Don McLean] [BMI] (11/27/71 BCR-1)

AMERICAN STORM Bob Seger & The Silver Bullet Band—Capitol 5532 [Bob Seger] [ASC] (3/15/86 BC-13)

AMERICAN TUNE Paul Simon—Columbia 45900 [Paul Simon] [BMI] (12/1/73 BCR-27)

AMERICAN WOMAN The Guess Who—RCA Victor 74-0325 [Randy Bachman/Burton Cummings/Jim Kale/Garry Peterson] (TSW) [BMI] (3/21/70 BCR-1)

AMERICANS *Byron MacGregor—Westbound 222 [Gordon Sinclair] [BMI] (12/29/73 BCR-1)*

THE AMERICANS (A CANADIAN'S OPINION) *Gordon Sinclair—Avco 4628 [Gordon Sinclair] [BMI] (1/5/74 BCR-20)*

THE AMERICANS (A CANADIAN'S OPINION) *Tex Ritter—Capitol 3814 [Gordon Sinclair] [BMI] (2/2/74 BR-65)*

AMERIKAN MUSIC Steve Alaimo—Entrance 7507 [John Carlton/Wayne White] [BMI] (4/15/72 BCR-78)

AMIE Pure Prairie League—RCA Victor 10184 [Craig Fuller] [BMI] (3/1/75 BCR-27)

AMNESIA Shalamar—Solar 69682 [George Duke/Howard Hewett] [ASC] (11/17/84 BC-71)

AMONG MY SOUVENIRS Connie Francis—MGM 12841 [Edgar Leslie/Lawrence Wright] [ASC] (11/9/59 BCR-5)

AMOR *Ben E. King—Atco 6203 [Ricardo Lopez Mendez*/Gabriel Ruiz/Sunny Skylar] [BMI] (7/31/61 BCR-14)*

AMOR *Roger Williams—Kapp 447 [Gabriel Ruiz] [BMI] (3/5/62 BCR-87) [IM]*

—AMORE SCUSAMI see: MY LOVE FORGIVE ME

—AMOS & ANDY SONG see: LIKE A SUNDAY IN SALEM

AMOS MOSES Jerry Reed—RCA Victor 47-9904 [Jerry Reed] [BMI] (10/17/70 BCR-5)

AMUKIRIKI (THE LORD WILLING) Les Paul and Mary Ford—Capitol 3248 [Jerry Livingston/Bob Russell] [ASC] (9/19/55 BCR-24)

AMY Paul Petersen—Colpix 676 [Barry Mann/Cynthia Weil] [BMI] (3/9/63 BCR-65)

THE ANAHEIM, AZUSA & CUCAMONGA SEWING CIRCLE, BOOK REVIEW AND TIMING ASSOCIATION Jan & Dean—Liberty 55724 [Don Altfeld/Jan Berry/Roger Christian] [BMI] (9/19/64 BCR-50)

ANASTASIA *Pat Boone—Dot 15521 [Alfred Newman/Paul Francis Webster] [ASC] (12/8/56 BCRt-22)*

ANASTASIA *Guy Lombardo & His Royal Canadians—Capitol 3601 [Alfred Newman] [ASC] (12/22/56 Rt-22) [IM]*

ANASTASIA *Roger Williams—Kapp 169 [Alfred Newman] [ASC] (12/22/56 Rt-22) [IM]*

ANASTASIA *LeRoy Holmes & His Orchestra—MGM 12392 [Alfred Newman] [ASC] (12/22/56 Rt-22) [IM]*

ANASTASIA *The Victor Young Singing Strings—Decca 30164 [Alfred Newman] [ASC] (12/29/56 Rt-22) [IM]*

ANCHORAGE Michelle Shocked—Mercury 870611 [Michelle Shocked] [ASC] (12/10/88 BC-66)

ANCHORS AWEIGH The Four Preps—Capitol 4716 [Royal Lovell/Alfred Hart Miles/Charles A. Zimmermann] (Med) [ASC] (3/17/62 BCR-61)

ANCIENT HISTORY Les Brown and His Band of Renown—Capitol 3517 [Stanley Kahan/Eddie Snyder] [ASC] (10/6/56 R-85)

AND GET AWAY The Esquires—Bunky 7752 [Gilbert Moorer/Bill Sheppard] [BMI] (11/25/67 BCR-22)

AND I AM TELLING YOU I'M NOT GOING Jennifer Holliday—Geffen 29983 [Tom Eyen/Henry Krieger] [BMI] (7/3/82 BC-22)

AND I LOVE HER *The Beatles—Capitol 5235 [John Lennon/Paul McCartney] [ASC] (7/25/64 BC-12)*

AND I LOVE HER *George Martin And His Orch.—United Artists 745 [John Lennon/Paul McCartney] [ASC] (7/25/64 CR-16) [IWM]*

AND I LOVE HIM *Esther Phillips—Atlantic 2281 [John Lennon/Paul McCartney] [ASC] (5/8/65 BCR-51)*

AND I LOVE YOU SO *Bobby Goldsboro—United Artists 50776 [Don McLean] [BMI] (5/8/71 BC-83)*

AND I LOVE YOU SO *Perry Como—RCA Victor 74-0906 [Don McLean] [BMI] (4/7/73 BCR-18)*

AND LOVE GOES ON Earth, Wind & Fire—ARC 11434 [Lorenzo Dunn/David Foster/Brenda Russell/Maurice White/Verdine White] [ASC] (2/7/81 BCR-54)

AND MY HEART SANG (TRA LA LA) Brenda & The Tabulations—Top & Bottom 403 [Joe Cobb/Van McCoy] [BMI] (5/2/70 BCR-58)

AND NOW Della Reese—RCA Victor 47-7784 [Luigi Creatore/Hugo Peretti/George David Weiss] [ASC] (8/15/60 BCR-31)

...AND ROSES AND ROSES Andy Williams—Columbia 43257 [Dorival Caymmi/Ray Gilbert] [ASC] (3/27/65 BCR-31)

AND SHE WAS Talking Heads—Sire 28917 [David Byrne/Chris Frantz*/Jerry Harrison*/Tina Weymouth*] [ASC] (9/7/85 BC-48)

AND SHE'S MINE Spanky And Our Gang—Mercury 72926 [Kenny Hodges] [BMI] (6/7/69 BC-97)

AND SO IT GOES Billy Joel—Columbia 73602 [Billy Joel] [ASC] (10/20/90 BC-37)

AND SUDDENLY The Cherry People—Heritage 801 [Michael David Lookofsky/Bert Sommer] [BMI] (7/6/68 BCR-43)

AUTUMN CONCERTO *Billy Vaughn & His Orchestra—Dot 15466 [Camillo Bargoni] [ASC] (6/22/56 Rt-74) [IM]*

AUTUMN CONCERTO *Richard Hayman His Harmonica and Orchestra—Mercury 70884 [Camillo Bargoni] [ASC] (6/22/56 Rt-74) [IM]*

AUTUMN CONCERTO *Nick Noble—Mercury 70959 [Camillo Bargoni/Al Stillman] [ASC] (10/6/56 Rt-77) [FDE]*

AUTUMN CONCERTO *Carmen Cavallaro And His Orchestra—Decca 30076 [Camillo Bargoni] [ASC] (10/6/56 Rt-77) [IM]*

AND THAT REMINDS ME *Della Reese—Jubilee 5292 [Camillo Bargoni/Al Stillman] [ASC] (8/5/57 BCtRt-10) [FDE]*

MY HEART REMINDS ME *Kay Starr—RCA Victor 47-6981 [Camillo Bargoni/Al Stillman] [ASC] (8/5/57 BCtRt-10) [FDE]*

MY HEART REMINDS ME *Ambrose & His Orchestra—MGM 12542 [Camillo Bargoni] [ASC] (9/2/57 Rt-17) [IM]*

MY HEART REMINDS ME *Richard Hayman—Mercury 71178 [Camillo Bargoni] [ASC] (9/9/57 Rt-17) [IM]*

MY HEART REMINDS ME *Carmen Cavallaro—Decca 30448 [Camillo Bargoni] [ASC] (9/30/57 Rt-10) [IM]*

AND THAT REMINDS ME (MY HEART REMINDS ME) *The 4 Seasons—Crewe 333 [Camillo Bargoni/Al Stillman] [ASC] (9/6/69 BCR-27) [FDE]*

AND THE ANGELS SING *The Three Chuckles—Vik 0194 [Ziggy Elman/Johnny Mercer] [ASC] (3/17/56 B-70)*

AND THE ANGELS SING *Johnny Nash—ABC-Paramount 10026 [Ziggy Elman/Johnny Mercer] [ASC] (6/22/59 R-80)*

AND THE BEAT GOES ON The Whispers—Solar 11894 [William Shelby/Stephen Shockley/Leon Sylvers] [ASC] (2/2/80 BCR-19)

AND THE CRADLE WILL ROCK... Van Halen—Warner Bros. 49501 [Michael Anthony/David Lee Roth/Alex Van Halen/Eddie Van Halen] [ASC] (5/24/80 BCR-55)

AND THE GRASS WON'T PAY NO MIND Mark Lindsay—Columbia 45229 [Neil Diamond] [SE] (9/19/70 BCR-36)

AND THE HEAVENS CRIED Ronnie Savoy—MGM 12950 [Gwynn Elias/Irving Reid] [BMI] (11/28/60 BCR-84)

AND THE NIGHT STOOD STILL Dion—Arista 1-9797 [Diane Warren] [ASC] (8/5/89 BC-75)

...AND THEN THERE WERE DRUMS Sandy Nelson—Imperial 5870 [Sandy Nelson/Richard Podolor] [BMI] (9/22/62 BC-65) [I]

AND WE DANCED Hooters—Columbia 05568 [Eric Bazilian/Rob Hyman] [ASC] (8/10/85 BC-21)

AND WHEN I DIE Blood, Sweat & Tears—Columbia 45008 [Laura Nyro] [BMI] (10/18/69 BCR-1)

AND WHEN SHE SMILES The Wildweeds—Vanguard 35134 [Al Anderson] [BMI] (6/12/71 R-71)

AND YOU AND I (PART I) Yes—Atlantic 2920 [Jon Anderson/Bill Bruford*/Steve Howe*/Chris Squire*] [ASC] (10/28/72 BCR-32)

—ANDALUCIA see: BREEZE AND I

ANDREA The Sunrays—Tower 191 [Rick Henn] [BMI] (1/15/66 BCR-29)

ANGEL Johnny Tillotson—MGM 13316 [Ray Evans/Jay Livingston/Max Steiner] [ASC] (2/13/65 BCR-51)

ANGEL Rod Stewart—Mercury 73344 [Jimi Hendrix] [ASC] (11/18/72 BCR-37)

ANGEL Aretha Franklin—Atlantic 2969 [Carolyn Franklin/William Nelson Sanders] [BMI] (6/30/73 BCR-13)

ANGEL (WHAT IN THE WORLD'S COME OVER US) Atlanta Rhythm Section—Polydor 14262 [Barry Bailey/Buddy Buie/Robert Nix] [BMI] (2/22/75 BCR-74)

ANGEL Madonna—Sire 29008 [Stephen Bray/Madonna L. Ciccone] [ASC] (4/27/85 BC-5)

ANGEL Aerosmith—Geffen 28249 [Desmond Child/Steven Tyler] [ASC] (1/30/88 BC-3)

ANGEL BABY Dean Martin—Capitol 3988 [John Michael/Charly Niessen] [BMI] (6/23/58 BCR-27) [FDE]

ANGEL BABY *Rosie And The Originals—Highland 1011 [Rosie Hamlin] [BMI] (12/5/60 BCR-5)*

ANGEL BABY *Angelica—Quality/Ultra 15171 [Rosie Hamlin] [BMI] (10/19/91 BC-29)*

ANGEL BABY Dusk—Bell 961 [L. Russell Brown/Irwin Levine] [BMI] (1/23/71 BCR-52)

ANGEL DUST Gil Scott-Heron—Arista 0366 [Gil Scott-Heron] [ASC] (12/16/78 R-97)

ANGEL EYES The Jeff Healey Band—Arista 1-9808 [John Hiatt/Fred Koller] [BMI] (6/3/89 BC-5)

ANGEL FACE James Darren—Colpix 119 [Doc Pomus/Mort Shuman] [BMI] (7/13/59 BCR-43)

ANGEL FACE Percy Faith and his Orchestra—Columbia 42011 [Herm Saunders] (Med) [ASC] (5/29/61 R-91) [IM]

ANGEL IN BLUE The J. Geils Band—EMI America 8100 [Seth Justman] [ASC] (5/22/82 BC-32)

ANGEL IN MY POCKET One To One—Warner Bros. 28739 [Leslie Howe/Louise Reny] [ASC] (8/23/86 BC-79)

ANGEL IN YOUR ARMS Hot—Big Tree 16085 [Tom Brasfield/Clayton Ivey/Terry Woodford] [ASC] (2/12/77 BCR-6)

ANGEL OF HARLEM U2—Island 99254 [Adam Clayton/Dave Evans/Paul Hewson/Larry Mullen] [ASC] (12/17/88 BC-14)

ANGEL OF THE MORNING *Merrilee Rush & The Turnabouts—Bell 705 [Chip Taylor] [BMI] (4/27/68 BCR-3)*

ANGEL OF THE MORNING *Bettye Swann—Capitol 2515 [Chip Taylor] [BMI] (6/21/69 CR-100)*

ANGEL OF THE MORNING *Juice Newton—Capitol 4976 [Chip Taylor] [BMI] (2/21/81 BCR-1)*

ANGEL ON MY SHOULDER *Shelby Flint—Valiant 6001 [Shelby Flint] [BMI] (12/26/60 BCRt-22)*

ANGEL ON MY SHOULDER *Jerry Wallace—Apex 76733 [Shelby Flint] [BMI] (1/2/61 Rt-88)*

ANGEL PIE (POSTILLION) Peggy King—Columbia 40638 [Don George/Gerhard Jussenhoven] [ASC] (4/7/56 B-81) [FDE]

ANGEL SAY NO Tommy Tutone—Columbia 11278 [Tommy Heath/Jim Keller] [BMI] (5/17/80 BCR-38)

ANGEL SMILE Nat "King" Cole—Capitol 3860 [Luther Dixon/Bert Keyes/Billy Dawn Smith] [BMI] (12/30/57 BCR-28)

THE ANGEL SONG Great White—Capitol 44449 [Mark Kendall/Alan Niven] [ASC] (9/23/89 BC-30)

ANGELA JONES Johnny Ferguson—MGM 12855 [John D. Loudermilk] [BMI] (2/6/60 BCR-27)

—ANGELA see: THEME FROM TAXI

ANGELEYES ABBA—Atlantic 3609 [Benny Andersson/Björn Ulvaeus] (TSW) [BMI] (9/8/79 BCR-64)

ANGELIA Richard Marx—EMI 50218 [Richard Marx] [ASC] (10/7/89 BC-2)

ANGELICA *Barry Mann—Capitol 5695 [Barry Mann/Cynthia Weil] [BMI] (7/23/66 C-96)*

ANGELICA *Oliver—Crewe 341 [Barry Mann/Cynthia Weil] [BMI] (3/28/70 BCR-73)*

ANGELINE The Allman Brothers Band—Arista 0555 [Dickey Betts/Johnny Cobb/Mike Lawler] [BMI] (9/13/80 BCR-58)

ANGELITO René & René—Columbia 43045 [René Herrera/René Ornelas] [BMI] (6/13/64 BCR-38) [F]

ANGELS IN THE SKY (54) *Tony Martin—RCA Victor 47-5757 [Dick Glasser] [BMI] (8/14/54 C-19)*

ANGELS IN THE SKY *The Crew-Cuts—Mercury 70741 [Dick Glasser] [BMI] (11/14/55 BCRt-10)*

ANGELS IN THE SKY *Tony Martin—RCA Victor 47-5757 [Dick Glasser] [BMI] (2/10/56 Rt-17)*

ANGELS LISTENED IN The Crests—Coed 515 [Lee Cathy/Billy Dawn Smith] [BMI] (8/15/59 BCR-15)

ANGIE The Rolling Stones—Rolling Stones 19105 [Mick Jagger/Keith Richards] [ASC] (9/8/73 BCR-1)

ANGIE BABY Helen Reddy—Capitol 3972 [Alan O'Day] [ASC] (10/19/74 BCR-1)

ANGRY Frank Pizani—Bally 1040 [Henry Brunies/Merritt Brunies/Jules Cassard/Dudley Mecum] [ASC] (9/16/57 B-70)

ANIMAL Def Leppard—Mercury 888832 [Rick Allen*/Steve Clark/Phil Collen/Joe Elliott/Mutt Lange/Rick Savage] [ASC] (10/10/87 BC-19)

ANIMAL HOUSE Stephen Bishop—ABC 12435 [Stephen Bishop] [BMI] (12/16/78 BCR-57)

ANIMAL INSTINCT Commodores—Motown 1788 [Martin Page] [ASC] (5/25/85 BC-43)

THE ANIMAL TRAINER AND THE TOAD Mountain—Windfall 534 [Sandy Palmer/Leslie West] [ASC] (3/27/71 BC-71)

ANIMAL ZOO Spirit—Epic 10648 [Jay Ferguson] [BMI] (9/12/70 BCR-97)

ANN-MARIE The Belmonts—Sabrina 509 [Danny Jordan/Tommy Wynn] [BMI] (4/13/63 BC-81)

ANNA *The Originals—Jackpot 48012 [Armando Trovaioli] [BMI] (11/8/58 CR-79) [IM]*

ANNA *Jorgen Ingmann And His Guitar—Atco 6195 [Armando Trovaioli] [BMI] (5/15/61 BCR-54) [IM]*

ANNA (GO TO HIM) Arthur Alexander—Dot 16387 [Arthur Alexander] [BMI] (10/20/62 BCR-67)

ANNA MARIE Jim Reeves—RCA Victor 47-7070 [Cindy Walker] [BMI] (11/18/57 BR-29)

ANNABELLA Hamilton, Joe Frank & Reynolds—Dunhill 4287 [Chris Arnold/David Martin/Geoff Morrow] [BMI] (8/21/71 BCR-35)

ANNABELLE Daniel Boone—Mercury 73339 [Daniel Boone/Rod McQueen] [ASC] (10/28/72 BCR-60)

ANNIE FANNY The Kingsmen—Wand 189 [Lynn Easton] [BMI] (8/7/65 BCR-29)

ANNIE GET YOUR YO-YO Little Junior Parker—Duke 345 [Deadric Malone/Joe Scott] [BMI] (2/5/62 BCR-51)

ANNIE MAE Natalie Cole—Capitol 4572 [Natalie Cole] [BMI] (6/24/78 R-93)

ANNIE'S SONG John Denver—RCA Victor 0295 [John Denver] [ASC] (5/25/74 BCR-1)

ANNIVERSARY OF LOVE The Caslons—Seeco 6078 [Sid Jacobson/Lou Stallman] [BMI] (9/9/61 BCR-89)

ANNIVERSARY SONG The Mulcays—Cardinal 1050 [Saul Chaplin/Iosef Ivanovici/Al Jolson] [ASC] (6/1/56 R-78) [IWM]

ANOTHER BRICK IN THE WALL (PART 2) Pink Floyd—Columbia 11187 [Roger Waters] [BMI] (1/19/80 BCR-1)

ANOTHER CUP OF COFFEE Brook Benton—Mercury 72266 [Leon Carr/Earl Shuman] [ASC] (5/16/64 BCR-40)

ANOTHER DAY Paul McCartney—Apple 1829 [Linda McCartney/Paul McCartney] (TSW) [ASC] (2/27/71 BCR-5)

ANOTHER DAY, ANOTHER HEARTACHE The 5th Dimension—Soul City 755 [Steve Barri/P.F. Sloan] [ASC] (4/29/67 BCR-43)

ANOTHER DAY IN PARADISE Phil Collins—Atlantic 88774 [Phil Collins] [ASC] (11/4/89 BC-1)

ANOTHER HEARTACHE Rod Stewart—Warner Bros. 28631 [Bryan Adams/Rod Stewart/Jim Vallance/Randy Wayne] [BMI] (8/30/86 BC-46)

ANOTHER LIKE MY LOVER Jasmine Guy—Warner Bros. 19486 [Timmy Gatling/Alton Stewart] [ASC] (3/23/91 BC-66)

ANOTHER LOVE Ian Lloyd & Stories—Kama Sutra 594 [Bobby Flax/Lanny Lambert] [ASC] (8/17/74 C-98)

ANOTHER LOVER Giant Steps—A&M 1226 [Colin Campsie/Gardner Cole/George McFarlane] [BMI] (8/20/88 BC-12)

ANOTHER NIGHT Dionne Warwick—Scepter 12181 [Burt Bacharach/Hal David] [ASC] (12/24/66 BCR-35)

ANOTHER NIGHT *The Hollies—Epic 50110 [Allan Clarke/Tony Hicks/Terry Sylvester] [BMI] (6/28/75 B-71)*

ANOTHER NIGHT *Wilson Brothers—Atco 7205 [Allan Clarke/Tony Hicks/Terry Sylvester] [BMI] (10/6/79 B-94)*

ANOTHER NIGHT Aretha Franklin—Arista 1-9453 [Giuseppe Cantarelli/Roy Freeland] [BMI] (1/18/86 BC-22)

ANOTHER ONE BITES THE DUST Queen—Elektra 47031 [John Deacon] [BMI] (8/16/80 BCR-1)

ANOTHER PAGE Connie Francis—MGM 13665 [Steve Duboff/Artie Kornfeld] [BMI] (2/11/67 C-98)

ANOTHER PARK, ANOTHER SUNDAY The Doobie Brothers—Warner Bros. 7795 [Tom Johnston] [BMI] (4/6/74 BCR-30)

ANOTHER PART OF ME Michael Jackson—Epic 07962 [Michael Jackson] [BMI] (7/23/88 BC-11)

ANOTHER PLACE ANOTHER TIME Jerry Lee Lewis—Smash 2146 [Jerry Chesnut] [BMI] (3/30/68 B-97)

ANOTHER PUFF Jerry Reed—RCA Victor 74-0613 [Earl Jarrett/Jerry Reed] [BMI] (1/8/72 BCR-65)

ANOTHER RAINY DAY IN NEW YORK CITY Chicago—Columbia 10360 [Robert Lamm] [ASC] (6/26/76 BCR-31)

ANOTHER RAINY NIGHT (WITHOUT YOU) Queensryche—EMI 50372 [Chris DeGarmo/Eddie Jackson/Geoff Tate] [BMI] (11/23/91 C-73)

ANOTHER SATURDAY NIGHT *Sam Cooke—RCA Victor 47-8164 [Sam Cooke] [BMI] (4/13/63 BCR-10)*

ANOTHER SATURDAY NIGHT *Cat Stevens—A&M 1602 [Sam Cooke] [BMI] (8/3/74 BCR-6)*

ANOTHER SLEEPLESS NIGHT Jimmy Clanton—Ace 585 [Howard Greenfield/Neil Sedaka] [BMI] (4/18/60 BCR-17)

ANOTHER SLEEPLESS NIGHT Anne Murray—Capitol 5083 [Charlie Black/Rory Bourke] [ASC] (1/30/82 BCR-44)

ANOTHER SLEEPLESS NIGHT Shawn Christopher—Arista 2148 [Tracey Amos/Mike Wilson] [ASC] (2/16/91 B-67)

ANOTHER STAR Stevie Wonder—Tamla 54286 [Stevie Wonder] [ASC] (8/27/77 BCR-32)

ANOTHER TICKET Eric Clapton And His Band—RSO 1064 [Eric Clapton] [BMI] (6/13/81 BC-78)

ANOTHER TIME, ANOTHER PLACE Patti Page—Mercury 71294 [Ray Evans/Jay Livingston] [ASC] (4/12/58 BC-38)

ANOTHER TIME, ANOTHER PLACE Engelbert Humperdinck—Parrot 40065 [Mike Leander/Ed Seago] [BMI] (8/21/71 BCR-40)

ANOTHERLOVERHOLENYOHEAD Prince And The Revolution—Paisley Park 7-28620 [Prince] [ASC] (7/19/86 BC-63)

ANSWER ME, MY LOVE *Nat "King" Cole—Capitol 2687*
[Carl Sigman/Gerhard Winkler] [ASC] (5/29/54 BC-PRE) [FDE]

ANSWER ME, MY LOVE *The Happenings—Jubilee 5686*
[Carl Sigman/Gerhard Winkler] [ASC] (1/17/70 CR-93) [FDE]

THE ANSWER TO A MAIDEN'S PRAYER June Valli—Mercury 71422
[Chuck Darwin/Lawrence Jefferson] [BMI] (3/2/59 BC-71)

THE ANSWER TO MY PRAYER Neil Sedaka—RCA Victor 47-8737
[Chris Allen/Peter Allen*/Dick Everitt] [ASC] (2/5/66 BCR-76)

ANSWERING MACHINE Rupert Holmes—MCA 41235
[Rupert Holmes] [ASC] (5/3/80 BCR-32)

ANTHEM Wayne Newton—Chelsea 0109
[Tony Romeo] [BMI] (12/9/72 BCR-45)

ANTHONY BOY Chuck Berry—Chess 1716
[Chuck Berry] [BMI] (2/2/59 BCR-60)

—ANTHONY'S SONG see: MOVIN' OUT

ANTICIPATION Carly Simon—Elektra 45759 [Carly Simon] [ASC] (12/4/71 BCR-10)

ANTHONY AND CLEOPATRA THEME *Alex North—20th Fox 408*
[Alex North] [ASC] (6/8/63 R-95) [I]

ANTONY AND CLEOPATRA THEME *Ferrante & Teicher—United Artists 607*
[Alex North] [ASC] (6/29/63 B-83) [I]

ANY DAY NOW (MY WILD BEAUTIFUL BIRD) *Chuck Jackson—Wand 122*
[Burt Bacharach/Bob Hilliard] [ASC] (4/9/62 BCR-12)

ANY DAY NOW *Percy Sledge—Atlantic 2616*
[Burt Bacharach/Bob Hilliard] [ASC] (4/12/69 BCR-77)

ANY DAY NOW *Ronnie Milsap—RCA 13216*
[Burt Bacharach/Bob Hilliard] [ASC] (5/1/82 BC-14)

ANY LOVE Luther Vandross—Epic 08047
[Marcus Miller/Luther Vandross] [ASC] (10/8/88 BC-44)

ANY OTHER WAY Chuck Jackson—Wand 141 [William Bell] [BMI] (10/19/63 BCR-60)

(ANY WAY THAT YOU WANT IT) I'LL BE THERE Starz—Capitol 4546
[Brendan Harkin/Michael Lee Smith/Pieter Sweval] [ASC] (3/11/78 BC-79)

ANY WAY THAT YOU WANT ME *Liverpool Five—RCA Victor 8968*
[Chip Taylor] [BMI] (12/24/66 B-98)

ANYWAY THAT YOU WANT ME *The American Breed—Acta 827*
[Chip Taylor] [BMI] (7/27/68 BCR-75)

ANY WAY THAT YOU WANT ME *Evie Sands—A&M 1090*
[Chip Taylor] [BMI] (8/16/69 BCR-34)

ANY WAY YOU WANT IT The Dave Clark Five—Epic 9739
[Dave Clark] [BMI] (11/14/64 BCR-9)

ANY WAY YOU WANT IT Journey—Columbia 11213
[Steve Perry/Neal Schon] [BMI] (3/1/80 BCR-21)

ANY WAY YOU WANT ME The Sylvers—Capitol 4493
[Edmund Sylvers/Leon Sylvers] [ASC] (10/29/77 BC-72)

ANYBODY BUT ME Brenda Lee—Decca 31309
[Dub Allbritten/Ronnie Self] [BMI] (9/25/61 BCR-22)

ANYBODY WANNA PARTY? Gloria Gaynor—Polydor 14558
[Dino Fekaris/Freddie Perren] [ASC] (6/30/79 C-94)

ANYMORE Teresa Brewer—Coral 62219
[Roy Drusky/Vic McAlpin/Marie Wilson] [BMI] (7/25/60 BCR-17)

ANYONE CAN FALL IN LOVE Doris Day—Columbia 40300
[Sammy Cahn/David Holt] [ASC] (9/18/54 CR-41)

ANYONE CAN MOVE A MOUNTAIN Don Anthony—Ford 159
[Johnny Marks] [ASC] (4/11/70 R-55)

ANYONE CAN SEE Irene Cara—Network 47950
[Irene Cara/Bruce Roberts] [ASC] (11/28/81 BCR-41)

ANYONE FOR TENNIS (THE SAVAGE SEVEN THEME) Cream—Atco 6575
[Eric Clapton/Martin Sharp] [BMI] (5/11/68 BCR-59)

ANYONE WHO HAD A HEART Dionne Warwick—Scepter 1262
[Burt Bacharach/Hal David] [ASC] (12/7/63 BCR-7)

ANYONE WHO KNOWS WHAT LOVE IS (WILL UNDERSTAND) Irma Thomas—Imperial 66041
[Judith Arbuckle/Randy Newman/Jeannie Seely/Pat Sheeran] [BMI] (6/27/64 BCR-52)

ANYTHING Eric Burdon & The Animals—MGM 13917
[Vic Briggs/Eric Burdon/Barry Jenkins/Danny McCulloch/John Weider] [BMI] (4/6/68 BCR-54)

ANYTHING CAN HAPPEN Was (Not Was)—Chrysalis 43365
[David Was/Don Was/Aaron Zigman] [ASC] (4/29/89 BC-72)

ANYTHING FOR YOU Gloria Estefan and Miami Sound Machine—Epic 07759
[Gloria Estefan] [BMI] (3/12/88 BC-1)

ANYTHING GOES Harpers Bizarre—Warner Bros. 7063
[Cole Porter] [ASC] (8/19/67 BCR-43)

ANYTHING I WANT Kevin Paige—Chrysalis 23444 [Kevin Paige] [BMI] (1/20/90 BC-29)

ANYTHING IS POSSIBLE Debbie Gibson—Atlantic 87793
[Lamont Dozier/Debbie Gibson] [BMI] (11/17/90 BC-26)

ANYTHING THAT'S PART OF YOU Elvis Presley With The Jordanaires—
RCA Victor 47-7992 [Don Robertson] [ASC] (3/12/62 BCR-31)

ANYTHING YOU CHOOSE Spanky And Our Gang—Mercury 72890
[Stuart Scharf] [ASC] (2/15/69 BCR-85)

ANYTHING YOU WANT John Valenti—Ariola America 7625
[John LiVigni/Joe Spinazola] [BMI] (8/14/76 BCR-37)

ANYTIME Journey—Columbia 10757
[Robert Fleischman/Gregg Rolie/Neal Schon/Roger Silver/Ross Valory] [BMI] (6/10/78 BR-75)

ANYTIME McAuley Schenker Group—Capitol 44471
[Steve Mann/Robin McAuley] [ASC] (2/17/90 BC-68)

ANYTIME AT ALL Frank Sinatra—Reprise 0350 [Baker Knight] [BMI] (2/27/65 BCR-46)

ANYTIME (I'LL BE THERE) *Frank Sinatra—Reprise 1327*
[Paul Anka] [BMI] (4/19/75 BC-75)

ANYTIME (I'LL BE THERE) *Paul Anka—United Artists 789*
[Paul Anka] [BMI] (4/3/76 BCR-33)

ANYTIME YOU WANT ME Garnet Mimms—United Artists 694
[Garnet Mimms/Jerry Ragovoy] [BMI] (2/22/64 R-83)

ANYWAY THE WIND BLOWS Doris Day—Columbia 41569
[By Dunham/Joseph Hooven/Marilyn Hooven] [ASC] (2/22/60 BR-50)

ANYWAY YOU WANT ME (THAT'S HOW I WILL BE) Elvis Presley—RCA Victor 47-6643
[Clyde Otis/Aaron Schroeder] [ASC] (10/27/56 BR-27)

ANYWHERE WITH YOU Rubber Rodeo—Mercury 880175
[Bob Holmes/Trish Milliken] [BMI] (8/25/84 B-86)

APACHE *Jorgen Ingmann And His Guitar—Atco 6184*
[Jerry Lordan] [BMI] (1/21/61 BCR-2) [I]

APACHE *Sonny James—RCA Victor 7858*
[Jerry Lordan] [BMI] (3/6/61 BR-87)

APACHE '65 *The Arrows Featuring Davie Allan—Tower 116*
[Jerry Lordan] [BMI] (2/13/65 BCR-64) [I]

APACHE *Sugar Hill Gang—Sugar Hill 774*
[Clifton Chase/Cheryl Cook/Jerry Lordan/Sylvia Robinson/Michael Wright] [BMI] (2/13/82 BCR-53)*

APARTMENT 21 Bobbie Gentry—Capitol 2849 [John Buck Wilkin] [BMI] (7/4/70 BCR-69)

APE CALL Nervous Norvus—Dot 15485 [Jimmy Drake] [ASC] (7/28/56 BCR-28)

APEMAN The Kinks—Reprise 0979 [Ray Davies] [BMI] (1/2/71 BCR-33)

APOLOGIZE Ed Ames—RCA Victor 47-9517
[Michael Gordon/James Griffin] [BMI] (5/4/68 BCR-64)

APPLE CIDER Five By Five—Paula 319 [Dennis Fridkin] [BMI] (3/8/69 R-89)

APPLE GREEN June Valli—Mercury 71588 [Charles Singleton] [BMI] (3/7/60 BCR-20)

APPLE OF MY EYE Roy Head And The Traits—Back Beat 555
[Roy Head] [BMI] (11/20/65 BCR-23)

APPLE OF MY EYE Badfinger—Apple 1864 [Pete Ham] [ASC] (1/26/74 C-88)

APPLE SCRUFFS George Harrison—Apple 1828
[George Harrison] (TSW) [ASC] (2/27/71 R-10)

APPLES AND BANANAS Lawrence Welk And His Orchestra—Dot 16697
[Frank Scott] [ASC] (4/3/65 BCR-75) [I]

APPLES, PEACHES, PUMPKIN PIE Jay And The Techniques—Smash 2086
[Maurice Irby] [BMI] (7/15/67 BCR-3)

APPLICATION FOR LOVE Roy Clark—Capitol 5047
[Bobby Bare/Charlie Williams] [BMI] (10/5/63 R-86)

APRICOT BRANDY Rhinoceros—Elektra 45647
[Michael Fonfara/Danny Weis] [BMI] (2/22/69 BC-46) [I]

APRIL AGAIN Dean Martin—Reprise 0761 [Glen Hardin] [BMI] (8/10/68 CR-64)

THE APRIL FOOLS Dionne Warwick—Scepter 12249
[Burt Bacharach/Hal David] [ASC] (5/10/69 BCR-33)

APRIL IN PARIS *Count Basie And His Orchestra—Clef 89162*
[Vernon Duke] [ASC] (1/6/56 BCRt-28) [IM]

APRIL IN PARIS *The Modernaires—Coral 61599*
[Vernon Duke/E.Y. Harburg] [ASC] (3/23/56 BRt-51)

APRIL IN PARIS *Count Basie Big Band with Ella Fitzgerald—Clef 89172*
[Vernon Duke/E.Y. Harburg] [ASC] (12/22/56 Rt-50)

APRIL LOVE Pat Boone—Dot 15660
[Sammy Fain/Paul Francis Webster] [ASC] (10/26/57 BCR-1)

AQUA BOOGIE (A PSYCHOALPHADISCOBETABIOAQUADOLOOP)
Parliament—Casablanca 950
[George Clinton/William Earl Collins/Bernie Worrell] [BMI] (12/30/78 BR-67)

AQUARIUS *The 5th Dimension—Soul City 772*
[Galt MacDermot/James Rado/Gerome Ragni] (Med) [ASC] (3/8/69 BCR-1)

AQUARIUS *Dick Hyman—Command 4129 [Galt MacDermot] [ASC] (8/16/69 R-95) [IM]*

ARC OF A DIVER Steve Winwood—Island 49726
[Vivian Stanshall/Steve Winwood] [BMI] (5/9/81 BCR-48)

ARCHIE'S MELODY The By-Liners—Felsted 8631
[Jan Crutchfield/Gerald Nelson] [BMI] (1/15/62 R-63)

ARE 'FRIENDS' ELECTRIC? Gary Numan & Tubeway Army—Atco 7206
[Gary Numan] [BMI] (6/28/80 CR-96)

ARE WE OURSELVES? The Fixx—MCA 52444
[Alfie Agius/Dan Brown*/Cy Curnin/Peter John Greenall/Jamie West-Oram/Adam Woods] [ASC] (8/18/84 BC-15)

ARE YOU A BOY OR ARE YOU A GIRL The Barbarians—Laurie 3308
[Douglas Morris/Ron Morris] [BMI] (9/18/65 BCR-55)

ARE YOU GETTING ANY SUNSHINE? Lou Christie—Buddah 149
[Lou Christie/Twyla Herbert] [BMI] (12/6/69 BCR-57)

ARE YOU GETTING ENOUGH HAPPINESS Hot Chocolate—EMI America 8143
[Errol Brown] [ASC] (12/18/82 BC-65)

ARE YOU HAPPY Jerry Butler—Mercury 72876
[Jerry Butler/Kenneth Gamble/Leon Huff] [BMI] (12/7/68 BCR-33)

ARE YOU HAVIN' ANY FUN The Crew-Cuts—Mercury 70710
[Sammy Fain/Jack Yellen] [ASC] (10/29/55 C-49)

ARE YOU LONELY FOR ME Freddie Scott—Shout 207
[Bert Berns] [BMI] (12/17/66 BCR-23)

ARE YOU LONESOME TONIGHT *Jaye P. Morgan—MGM 12752*
[Lou Handman/Roy Turk] [ASC] (2/2/59 BCR-40)

ARE YOU LONESOME TO NIGHT *Elvis Presley With The Jordanaires—RCA Victor 47-7810*
[Lou Handman/Roy Turk] [ASC] (11/7/60 BCR-1)

YES I'M LONESOME TONIGHT *(response to Are You Lonesome Tonight)*
Thelma Carpenter—Coral 62241
[Lou Handman/Roy Turk] [NA] (12/19/60 BCtRt-47) [R]

YES I'M LONESOME TONIGHT *(response to Are You Lonesome Tonight)*
Dodie Stevens—Dot 16167
[Lou Handman/Roy Turk] [NA] (12/19/60 BCtRt-47) [R]

ARE YOU LONESOME TONIGHT *Donny Osmond—MGM 14677*
[Lou Handman/Roy Turk] (TSW) [ASC] (11/24/73 BCR-14)

ARE YOU MAN ENOUGH Four Tops—Dunhill 4354
[Dennis Lambert/Brian Potter] [BMI] (6/23/73 BCR-14)

ARE YOU MY WOMAN? (TELL ME SO) The Chi-Lites—Brunswick 55442
[Eugene Record] [BMI] (12/19/70 BR-67)

ARE YOU NERVOUS? The Instrumentals—Hanover 4502
[Albert R. Levy] [BMI] (7/12/58 C-64) [I]

ARE YOU NEVER COMING HOME Sandy Posey—MGM 13824
[Spooner Oldham/Dan Penn] [BMI] (10/14/67 BCR-59)

ARE YOU OLD ENOUGH Mark Lindsay—Columbia 45462
[Alan O'Day] [BMI] (10/2/71 BCR-69)

ARE YOU READY? Pacific Gas & Electric With The Blackberries—Columbia 45158
[Charles Edward Allen/John Michael Hill] [BMI] (5/23/70 BCR-10)

ARE YOU REALLY MINE Jimmie Rodgers—Roulette 4090
[Luigi Creatore/Al Hoffman/Dick Manning/Hugo Peretti] [ASC] (7/21/58 BCR-10)

ARE YOU SATISFIED *Rusty Draper—Mercury 70757*
[Homer Escamilla/Sheb Wooley] [BMI] (12/9/55 BCtRt-12)

ARE YOU SATISFIED *Sheb Wooley—MGM 12114*
[Homer Escamilla/Sheb Wooley] [BMI] (12/9/55 BCtRt-14)

ARE YOU SATISFIED *Toni Arden—RCA Victor 47-6346*
[Homer Escamilla/Sheb Wooley] [BMI] (12/9/55 BRt-22)

ARE YOU SATISFIED? *Jimmy Wakely with Gloria Wood—Decca 29756*
[Homer Escamilla/Sheb Wooley] [BMI] (12/23/55 Rt-14)

ARE YOU SERIOUS Tyrone Davis—Highrise 2005
[L.V. Johnson/Roger Miner] [BMI] (12/25/82 B-57)

ARE YOU SINCERE *Andy Williams—Cadence 1340 [Wayne Walker] [BMI] (1/20/58 BCR-5)*

ARE YOU SINCERE *Trini Lopez—Reprise 0376 [Wayne Walker] [BMI] (6/12/65 B-85)*

ARE YOU SORRY Joni James—MGM 12828
[Milton Ager/Benny Davis] [ASC] (9/14/59 R-48)

ARE YOU STILL MY BABY The Shirelles—Scepter 1292
[Charlie Rich] [BMI] (12/26/64 BCR-91)

ARE YOU SURE The Allisons—London 1977
[Bob Allison/John Allison] [ASC] (3/27/61 CR-72)

ARE YOU SURE So—EMI 50109 [Marcus Bell/Mark Long] [BMI] (2/20/88 BC-41)

ARE YOU SURE HANK DONE IT THIS WAY Waylon Jennings—RCA Victor 10379
[Waylon Jennings] [BMI] (9/20/75 BCR-60)

ARE YOU THERE (WITH ANOTHER GIRL) Dionne Warwick—Scepter 12122
[Burt Bacharach/Hal David] [ASC] (12/11/65 BCR-35)

ARIA FROM THE MARRIAGE OF FIGARO The Royal Philharmonic Orchestra—RCA 12304
[Wolfgang Amadeus Mozart] (Med) [NA] (10/31/81 BCR-9) [I]

ARIEL Dean Friedman—Lifesong 45022
[Dean Friedman] [ASC] (4/9/77 BCR-17)

ARIZONA Mark Lindsay—Columbia 45037 [Kenny Young] [ASC] (11/29/69 BCR-9)

ARMAGEDDON IT Def Leppard—Mercury 870692 [Rick Allen*/Steve Clark/Phil Collen/
Joe Elliott/Mutt Lange/Rick Savage] [ASC] (11/19/88 BC-2)

ARMED AND EXTREMELY DANGEROUS First Choice—Philly Groove 175
[Allan Felder/Norman Harris] [BMI] (2/24/73 BCR-19)

ARMEN'S THEME *David Seville—Liberty 55041*
[David Seville] [ASC] (12/1/56 BCRt-34) [IWM]

ARMEN'S THEME *Joe Reisman and His Orchestra—RCA Victor 47-6740*
[David Seville] [ASC] (12/1/56 BRt-36) [IWM]

ARMEN'S THEME *David Carroll & His Orchestra—Mercury 71000*
[David Seville] [ASC] (12/1/56 Rt-36) [IWM]

ARMEN'S THEME *Lew Quadling & His Orchestra—Coral 61754*
[David Seville] [ASC] (12/8/56 Rt-36) [IWM]

YESTERDAY AND YOU (ARMEN'S THEME) *Bobby Vee—Liberty 55636*
[David Seville] [ASC] (10/26/63 BCR-53)

ARMS OF MARY *Sutherland Brothers And Quiver—Columbia 10284*
[Iain Sutherland] [BMI] (4/3/76 BCR-71)

ARMS OF MARY *Chilliwack—Mushroom 7033 [Iain Sutherland] [BMI] (8/5/78 BC-67)*

THE ARMS OF ORION Prince With Sheena Easton—Warner Bros. 22757
[Sheena Easton/Prince] [BMI] (10/21/89 BC-33)

ARMSTRONG John Stewart—Capitol 2605 [John Stewart] [BMI] (8/23/69 BCR-65)

AROUND THE CORNER The Duprees—Columbia 43336
[Billy Barberis/Bobby Hart/Wilbur Meshel/Teddy Randazzo/Bobby Weinstein] [ASC]
(7/10/65 BCR-81)

AROUND THE WAY GIRL LL Cool J—Def Jam 73609
[James Todd Smith/Marlon Williams] [NA] (12/1/90 BC-9)

—AROUND THE WORLD see: THEME FROM AROUND...

ARRESTED FOR DRIVING WHILE BLIND ZZ Top—London 251
[Frank Beard/Billy Gibbons/Dusty Hill] [BMI] (3/5/77 BC-74)

ARRIVEDERCI ROMA (GOODBYE TO ROME) *The Three Suns—RCA Victor 47-6273*
[Pietro Garinei/Alessandro Giovannini/Renato Rascel] [ASC] (10/17/55 Rt-16) [F]

GOODBYE TO ROME (ARRIVEDERCI ROMA) *Georgia Gibbs—Mercury 70743*
*[Pietro Garinei/Alessandro Giovannini/Renato Rascel/Carl Sigman] [ASC] (11/7/55
BCRt-16) [FDE]*

ARRIVEDERCI, ROMA *The Norman Luboff Choir—Columbia 40604*
*[Pietro Garinei/Alessandro Giovannini/Renato Rascel/Carl Sigman] [ASC]
(11/21/55 Rt-17) [FDE]*

ARRIVEDERCI ROMA (GOODBYE TO ROME) *Ralph Young—Decca 29741*
*[Pietro Garinei/Alessandro Giovannini/Renato Rascel/Carl Sigman] [ASC]
(12/1/55 Rt-17) [FDE]*

ARRIVEDERCI ROMA *Mario Lanza—RCA Victor 47-7164*
[Pietro Garinei/Alessandro Giovannini/Renato Rascel] [ASC] (2/24/58 BCtRt-14) [F]

ARRIVEDERCI ROMA *Roger Williams—Kapp 210*
*[Pietro Garinei/Alessandro Giovannini/Renato Rascel/Carl Sigman] [ASC] (2/24/58
BCtRt-14) [FDE]*

ARRIVEDERCI ROMA *Frank Chacksfield & His Orchestra—London 1797*
[Renato Rascel] [ASC] (4/7/58 Rt-14) [IM]

ARRIVEDERCI ROMA (GOODBYE TO ROME) *The Three Suns—RCA Victor 47-6273*
[Pietro Garinei/Alessandro Giovannini/Renato Rascel] [ASC] (4/14/58 Rt-14) [F]

ARRIVEDERCI, ROMA *Eddie Fisher—ABC-Paramount 10326*
*[Pietro Garinei/Alessandro Giovannini/Renato Rascel/Carl Sigman] [ASC]
(5/26/62 R-95) [F,FDE]*

ARROW OF LOVE The Six Teens—Flip 322 [Ed Wells] [BMI] (7/29/57 B-80)

ARROW THROUGH ME Wings—Columbia 11070
[Paul McCartney] [ASC] (8/25/79 BCR-27)

ART FOR ART'S SAKE 10CC—Mercury 73725
[Graham Gouldman/Eric Stewart] [BMI] (11/29/75 BCR-63)

ARTHUR'S THEME (BEST THAT YOU CAN DO) Christopher Cross—Warner Bros. 49787
[Peter Allen/Burt Bacharach/Christopher Cross/Carole Bayer Sager] [BMI]
(8/15/81 BCR-1)

ARTIFICIAL FLOWERS *Bobby Darin—Atco 6179*
[Jerry Bock/Sheldon Harnick] [BMI] (9/26/60 BCtR-14)

ARTIFICIAL FLOWERS *Phil Napoleon—Capitol 4485*
[Jerry Bock/Sheldon Harnick] [BMI] (12/10/60 Ct-42)

AS Stevie Wonder—Tamla 54291 [Stevie Wonder] [ASC] (11/5/77 BCR-36)

(AS I WENT DOWN TO) JERUSALEM Hello People—Philips 40531
[Wrightson Tongue] [BMI] (8/17/68 CR-92)

AS IF I DIDN'T KNOW Adam Wade—Coed 553
[Larry Kusik/Jerry Samuels] [BMI] (7/24/61 BCR-10)

AS LONG AS HE TAKES CARE OF HOME Candi Staton—Warner Bros. 8038
[Phillip Mitchell] [BMI] (12/14/74 BCR-42)

AS LONG AS I GOT YOU Laura Lee—Chess 2041
[Gene Barge/Laura Lee] [BMI] (4/6/68 C-80)

AS LONG AS I HAVE YOU Elvis Presley with the Jordanaires—RCA Victor EPA-4319
[Ben Weisman/Fred Wise] (EP) [ASC] (7/26/58 CR-14)

AS LONG AS I HAVE YOU Don Rondo—Jubilee 5334
[Abner Silver/Sid Wayne] [ASC] (8/16/58 CR-65)

AS LONG AS I KNOW HE'S MINE The Marvelettes—Tamla 54088
[Smokey Robinson] [ASC] (11/2/63 BCR-43)

AS LONG AS SHE NEEDS ME Sammy Davis Jr.—Reprise 20,138
[Lionel Bart] [BMI] (1/19/63 BCR-57)

AS LONG AS YOU FOLLOW Fleetwood Mac—Warner Bros. 27644
[Christine McVie/Eddy Quintela] [BMI] (11/26/88 BC-40)

AS LONG AS YOU'RE HERE Zalman Yanovsky—Buddah 12
[Garry Bonner/Alan Gordon] [BMI] (10/7/67 CR-51)

AS SOON AS I HANG UP THE PHONE Loretta Lynn/Conway Twitty—MCA 40251
[Conway Twitty] [BMI] (8/17/74 C-81)

AS SURE AS NIGHT MUST FALL Jerry Vale—Columbia 42994
[Joe Sherman/George David Weiss] [ASC] (3/21/64 R-87)

AS TEARS GO BY *Marianne Faithfull—London 9697*
[Mick Jagger/Andrew Loog Oldham/Keith Richards] [BMI] (10/31/64 BCR-22)

AS TEARS GO BY *The Rolling Stones—London 9808*
[Mick Jagger/Andrew Loog Oldham/Keith Richards] [BMI] (12/25/65 BCR-3)

AS THE YEARS GO BY Mashmakhan—Epic 10634
[Pierre Senecal] [BMI] (8/22/70 BCR-26)

AS THE YEARS GO PASSING BY Albert King—Atlantic 2604
[Deadric Malone] [BMI] (3/1/69 R-96)

AS TIME GOES BY *Johnnie Ray—Columbia 40392 [Herman Hupfeld] [ASC] (1/8/55 C-35)*

AS TIME GOES BY *Bill Snyder—Decca 29827 [Herman Hupfeld] [ASC] (6/29/56 R-82)*

AS TIME GOES BY *Fats Domino—Imperial IMP-147 [Herman Hupfeld] (EP) [ASC] (5/11/57 R-53)*

AS TIME GOES BY *Johnny Nash—ABC-Paramount 9996 [Herman Hupfeld] [ASC] (3/9/59 BCR-34)*

AS TIME GOES BY *Nilsson—RCA Victor 0039 [Herman Hupfeld] [ASC] (8/25/73 BC-64)*

AS USUAL Brenda Lee—Decca 31570 [Alex Zanetis] [BMI] (11/30/63 BCR-6)

AS WE GO ALONG The Monkees—Colgems 1031 [Carole King/Toni Stern] (TSW) [ASC] (10/5/68 R-63)

AS WE LAY Shirley Murdock—Elektra 69518 [William Beck/Larry Troutman] [BMI] (1/17/87 BC-23)

ASHES AND SAND Johnny Rivers—Soul City 007 [Johnny Rivers] [ASC] (2/5/77 B-96)

ASHES BY NOW Rodney Crowell—Warner Bros. 49224 [Rodney Crowell] [ASC] (5/3/80 BCR-33)

ASHES TO ASHES The Mindbenders—Fontana 1555 [Carole Bayer Sager/Toni Wine] [BMI] (8/13/66 BCR-55)

ASHES TO ASHES The 5th Dimension—Bell 45,380 [Dennis Lambert/Brian Potter] [BMI] (8/4/73 BCR-50)

ASHES TO ASHES David Bowie—RCA 12078 [David Bowie] [BMI] (10/4/80 C-79)

ASIA MINOR Kokomo—Felsted 8612 [Edvard Grieg/Jimmy Wisner] [ASC] (1/30/61 BCR-8) [I]

ASK ME *Nat "King" Cole—Capitol 3328 [Heino Gaze/Sunny Skylar] [ASC] (1/27/56 BCRt-21) [FDE]*

ASK ME (DEINE ERSTE LIEBE) *Alice Babs—Decca 29804 [Heino Gaze/Charly Niessen] [ASC] (3/2/56 Rt-21) [F]*

ASK ME Maxine Brown—Wand 135 [Brenda Bruno/Tony Bruno] [BMI] (3/30/63 BC-75)

ASK ME Inez Foxx—Symbol 926 [Windsor King] [BMI] (1/11/64 BCR-78)

ASK ME Elvis Presley With The Jordanaires—RCA Victor 47-8440 [Bernie Baum/Bill Giant/Florence Kaye/Domenico Modugno] [BMI] (10/10/64 BCR-10) [FDE]

ASK ME Ecstasy, Passion & Pain—Roulette 7159 [Barbara Jean Gaskins] [BMI] (10/12/74 BCR-52)

ASK ME NO QUESTIONS B.B. King—ABC 11290 [B.B. King] [BMI] (2/13/71 BCR-39)

ASK ME WHAT YOU WANT Millie Jackson—Spring 123 [Millie Jackson/Billy Nichols] [BMI] (3/25/72 BCR-17)

ASK THE LONELY Four Tops—Motown 1073 [Ivy Jo Hunter/William Stevenson] [ASC] (2/6/65 BCR-24)

ASTRAL MAN Nektar—Passport 7904 [Roye Albrighton/Allan Freeman/Ron Howden/Derek Moore] [BMI] (5/10/75 B-91)

THE ASTRONAUT (PARTS 1 & 2) Jose Jimenez—Kapp 409 [Bill Dana/Don Hinkley] [ASC] (6/26/61 BCR-19)

AT LAST *Etta James—Argo 5380 [Mack Gordon/Harry Warren] [ASC] (1/9/61 BCR-30)*

AT LAST *Percy Faith and his Orchestra—Columbia 42011 [Harry Warren] (Med) [ASC] (5/29/61 R-91) [IM]*

AT LAST *Frank Barber Orchestra—Victory 1001 [Harry Warren] (Med) [ASC] (5/8/82 B-61) [IM]*

AT MIDNIGHT (MY LOVE WILL LIFT YOU UP) Rufus Featuring Chaka Khan—ABC 12239 [Tony Maiden/Lalomie Washburn] [ASC] (2/5/77 BCR-30)

AT MIDNIGHT T-Connection—Dash 5048 [Theophilus Coakley/David Mackey] [BMI] (3/10/79 B-56)

AT MY FRONT DOOR (CRAZY LITTLE MAMA) *Pat Boone—Dot 15422 [Ewart Abner/John C. Moore] [BMI] (10/3/55 BCtRt-7)*

AT MY FRONT DOOR (CRAZY LITTLE MAMA) *El Dorados And Magnificents—Vee-Jay 147 [Ewart Abner/John C. Moore] [BMI] (10/3/55 BCtRt-7)*

(CRAZY LITTLE MAMA SONG) AT MY FRONT DOOR *The Modernaires—Coral 61513 [Ewart Abner/John C. Moore] [BMI] (10/17/55 Rt-14)*

AT MY FRONT DOOR *Dee Clark—Abner 1037 [Ewart Abner/John C. Moore] [BMI] (3/7/60 BCR-56)*

AT SEVENTEEN Janis Ian—Columbia 10154 [Janis Ian] [BMI] (6/14/75 BCR-1)

AT THE CLUB Ray Charles And His Orchestra—ABC-Paramount 10314 [Percy Mayfield] [BMI] (3/19/62 BCR-40)

AT THE CLUB The Drifters—Atlantic 2268 [Gerry Goffin/Carole King] [BMI] (1/30/65 BCR-32)

—AT THE COPA see: COPACABANA

(AT) THE END (OF A RAINBOW) Earl Grant—Decca 30719 [Sid Jacobson/Jimmy Krondes] [ASC] (8/25/58 BCR-7)

AT THE HOP *Danny & The Juniors—ABC-Paramount 9871 [John Madara/Artie Singer/David White] [BMI] (11/18/57 BCRt-1)*

AT THE HOP *Nick Todd—Dot 15675 [John Madara/Artie Singer/David White] [BMI] (12/2/57 BRt-1)*

AT THE HOP *Jive Bunny And The Mastermixers—Music Factory 99140 [John Madara/Artie Singer/David White] (Med) [BMI] (10/28/89 BC-11)*

AT THE PARTY Hector Rivera—Barry! 1011 [Hector Rivera] [BMI] (12/31/66 CR-83)

AT THE SCENE The Dave Clark Five—Epic 9882 [Dave Clark/Lenny Davidson] [BMI] (1/29/66 BCR-12)

AT THE SHORE Johnny Caswell—Smash 1833 [John Madara/David White] [BMI] (8/3/63 BR-97)

AT THE TOP OF THE STAIRS The Formations—MGM 13899 [Jerry Akines/Leon Huff] [BMI] (2/17/68 BCR-64)

AT THE ZOO Simon & Garfunkel—Columbia 44046 [Paul Simon] [BMI] (3/11/67 BCR-13)

AT THIS MOMENT *Billy & The Beaters—Alfa 7005 [Billy Vera] [ASC] (9/5/81 BC-77)*

AT THIS MOMENT *Billy Vera & The Beaters—Rhino 74403 [Billy Vera] [ASC] (11/8/86 BC-1)*

ATHENA The Who—Warner Bros. 29905 [Pete Townshend] [GL] (9/4/82 BC-28)

ATLANTA LADY (SOMETHING ABOUT YOUR LOVE) Marty Balin—EMI America 8093 [Jesse Barish] [BMI] (9/12/81 BCR-26)

ATLANTIS Donovan—Epic 10434 [Donovan Leitch] [BMI] (4/5/69 BCR-7)

ATOMIC Blondie—Chrysalis 2410 [Clement A. Bozewski*/Jimmy Destri/Deborah Harry] [ASC] (5/17/80 BCR-39)

ATTACK The Toys—DynoVoice 214 [Sandy Linzer/Denny Randell] [BMI] (12/11/65 BCR-14)

ATTACK OF THE NAME GAME Stacy Lattisaw—Cotillion 7-99968 [Lincoln Chase*/Jeffrey E. Cohen/Shirley Ellis*/Narada Michael Walden] [ASC] (10/16/82 BC-70)

ATTITUDE DANCING Carly Simon—Elektra 45246 [Jacob Brackman/Carly Simon] [ASC] (5/10/75 BCR-21)

AU REVOIR Teresa Brewer—Coral 61225 [By Dunham/Joseph Hooven/Marilyn Hooven] [ASC] (8/28/54 C-31)

AUBREY Bread—Elektra 45832 [David Gates] [ASC] (2/3/73 BCR-11)

AUCTIONEER *Leroy Van Dyke—Dot 15503 [Buddy Black/Leroy Van Dyke] [ASC] (11/24/56 BCRt-22)*

AUCTIONEER *Chuck Miller—Mercury 71001 [Buddy Black/Leroy Van Dyke] [ASC] (12/1/56 BRt-34)*

AUCTIONEER (I'LL BUY THAT DREAM) Les Paul & Mary Ford—Capitol 2839 [Hayward Morris/Joseph Shapiro] [ASC] (7/3/54 C-28)

AUF WIEDERSEHEN MARLENE Bob Moore—Monument 457 [Boudleaux Bryant/Felice Bryant*] [BMI] (3/19/62 R-75) [I]

AUNT DORA'S LOVE SOUL SHACK Arthur Conley—Atco 6622 [Jackie Avery/Arthur Conley/Ronald Grier/Earl Simms] [BMI] (10/19/68 BCR-75)

AUTHORITY SONG John Cougar Mellencamp—Riva 216 [John Mellencamp] [ASC] (3/17/84 BC-12)

AUTOBAHN Kraftwerk—Vertigo 203 [Ralf Hutter/Florian Schneider-Esleben] [ASC] (3/15/75 BCR-19) [I]

AUTOGRAPH John Denver—RCA 11915 [John Denver] [ASC] (2/23/80 BCR-52)

AUTOMATIC Pointer Sisters—Planet 13730 [Mark Goldenberg/Brock Walsh] [BMI] (1/28/84 BC-5)

AUTOMATIC MAN Michael Sembello—Warner Bros. 29485 [David Batteau/Danny Sembello/Michael Sembello] [ASC] (9/24/83 BC-34)

AUTOMATICALLY SUNSHINE The Supremes—Motown 1200 [Smokey Robinson] [ASC] (4/29/72 BCR-37)

—AUTUMN CONCERTO see: AND THAT REMINDS ME

AUTUMN LEAVES *Roger Williams—Kapp 116 [Joseph Kosma] [ASC] (8/1/55 BCRt-1) [IM]*

AUTUMN LEAVES *Jackie Gleason—Capitol 3223 [Joseph Kosma] [ASC] (9/19/55 BRt-2) [IM]*

AUTUMN LEAVES *Victor Young And His Singing Strings—Decca 29653 [Joseph Kosma] [ASC] (10/3/55 BRt-2) [IM]*

AUTUMN LEAVES *Mitch Miller & His Orchestra—Columbia 50033 [Joseph Kosma/Johnny Mercer/Jacques Prevert] [ASC] (11/12/55 B-41) [FET]*

AUTUMN LEAVES *The Ray Charles Singers—MGM 12068 [Joseph Kosma/Johnny Mercer/Jacques Prevert] [ASC] (11/12/55 B-55) [FET]*

AUTUMN LEAVES *Steve Allen—Coral 61485 [Joseph Kosma] [ASC] (11/12/55 B-35) [IM]*

AUTUMN LEAVES *Bette McLaurin with Ray Ellis' Orch. And Chorus—Atco 6099 [Joseph Kosma/Johnny Mercer/Jacques Prevert] [ASC] (10/28/57 Rt-79) [FET]*

AUTUMN LEAVES *Keely Smith—Capitol 3820 [Joseph Kosma/Johnny Mercer/Jacques Prevert] [ASC] (10/28/57 Rt-79) [FET]*

AUTUMN LEAVES - 1965 *Roger Williams—Kapp 707 [Joseph Kosma] [ASC] (10/16/65 B-92) [IM]*

AUTUMN OF MY LIFE Bobby Goldsboro—United Artists 50318 [Bobby Goldsboro] [BMI] (6/29/68 BCR-12)

AUTUMN WALTZ Tony Bennett with Percy Faith and His Orchestra and Chorus—Columbia 40770 [Cy Coleman/Bob Hilliard] [ASC] (11/10/56 BR-41)

AVE MARIA Lawrence Welk Glee Club—Coral 65523 [Traditional] [NA] (12/30/57 R-82)

THE AVENGER Duane Eddy And The Rebels—Jamie 1206 [Duane Eddy] [BMI] (11/27/61 R-93) [I]

AVENGING ANNIE *Andy Pratt—Columbia 45804 [Andy Pratt] [ASC] (4/28/73 BCR-54)*

AVENGING ANNIE *Roger Daltrey—MCA 40800 [Andy Pratt] [ASC] (10/1/77 BCR-83)*

AW SHUCKS, HUSH YOUR MOUTH Jimmy Reed—Vee-Jay 425 [Jimmy Reed] [BMI] (1/27/62 BC-93)

AWAITING ON YOU ALL Silver Hawk—Westbound 178 [George Harrison] [ASC] (5/22/71 C-94)

AWAY ALL BOATS Al Hibbler—Decca 29950 [Lenny Adelson/Albert Skinner/Frank Skinner] [ASC] (8/18/56 B-77)

AXEL F Harold Faltermeyer—MCA 52536 [Harold Faltermeyer] [ASC] (3/30/85 BC-3) [I]

B

B-A-B-Y Carla Thomas—Stax 195 [Isaac Hayes/David Porter] [BMI] (8/20/66 BCR-11)

THE B.B. JONES B.B. King—BluesWay 61019
[Maya Angelou/Quincy Jones] (TSW) [ASC] (9/21/68 BCR-74)

"B" GIRLS Young & Restless—Pandisc 056
[Leonerist Johnson/Charles Trahan] [BMI] (5/5/90 BC-54)

B-I-N-G-O (BINGO) The Turbans—Herald 478 [Robert S. Riley] [BMI] (5/25/56 R-76)

B'WA NINA (PRETTY GIRL) The Tokens—RCA Victor 47-7991
[Luigi Creatore/Hugo Peretti/George David Weiss] [ASC] (2/5/62 BCR-46)

BABE Styx—A&M 2188 [Dennis DeYoung] [ASC] (10/6/79 BCR-1)

BABY, BABY Billy Williams Quartet—Coral 61932 [Jesse Stone] [BMI] (3/17/58 B-78)

BABY BABY Jack Scott—Top Rank 2028 [Jack Scott] [BMI] (12/21/59 R-97)

BABY BABY Eighth Wonder—WTG 31-68610
[Sam Domingo/John Forte] [ASC] (4/1/89 BC-81)

BABY BABY Amy Grant—A&M 1549 [Amy Grant/Keith Thomas] [ASC] (2/23/91 BC-1)

BABY BABY ALL THE TIME The Superbs—Dore 715 [Bobby Troup] [ASC] (9/5/64 BCR-76)

BABY, BABY, BABY Sam Cooke—RCA Victor 47-8129
[Sam Cooke] [BMI] (1/26/63 BCR-60)

BABY BABY BABY Anna King-Bobby Byrd—Smash 1884
[Bobby Byrd/Anna King] [BMI] (3/28/64 BCR-52)

(BABY, BABY) BE GOOD TO ME The McGuire Sisters—Coral 61532
[Lillian Barco/Buddy Kaye] [ASC] (1/7/56 CR-46)

BABY, BABY DON'T CRY Smokey Robinson & The Miracles—Tamla 54178
[Al Cleveland/Terry Johnson/Smokey Robinson] [ASC] (1/4/69 BCR-7)

BABY-BABY DON'T STOP NOW Sam & Dave—Atlantic 2714
[Isaac Hayes/David Porter] [ASC] (3/7/70 R-86)

BABY, BABY I LOVE YOU Terry Cashman—Lifesong 45015
[Terry Cashman/Tommy West] [ASC] (11/13/76 BC-79)

BABY, BABY MY LOVE'S ALL FOR YOU Deniece Williams—Columbia 10648
[Verdine White/Robert Byron Wright*] [ASC] (1/28/78 CR-91)

BABY, BABY YOU The Coney Island Kids—Jubilee 5215
[Al Weisman/Ben Weisman] [ASC] (10/24/55 R-73)

BABY BE MINE The Jelly Beans—Red Bird 10-011
[Jeff Barry/Ellie Greenwich/Steve Venet] [BMI] (9/26/64 BCR-49)

BABY BLUE The Echoes—Seg-Way 103
[Sam Gulino/Valerien Lagueux] [BMI] (2/27/61 BCR-12)

BABY BLUE Badfinger—Apple 1844 [Pete Ham] [ASC] (3/18/72 BCR-9)

BABY BOY Mary Kay Place as Loretta Haggers—Columbia 10422
[Mary Kay Place] [ASC] (10/23/76 BCR-60)

BABY CAN I HOLD YOU Tracy Chapman—Elektra 69356
[Tracy Chapman] [ASC] (11/5/88 BC-39)

BABY COME AND GET IT Pointer Sisters—Planet 14041
[James Ingram/Barry Mann/Cynthia Weil] [BMI] (3/23/85 BC-41)

BABY, COME BACK The Equals—RCA Victor 47-9583
[Eddy Grant] [ASC] (8/17/68 BCR-26)

BABY COME BACK Player—RSO 879 [Peter Beckett/J.C. Crowley] [BMI] (10/1/77 BCR-1)

BABY COME BACK Billy Rankin—A&M 2613 [Billy Rankin] [BMI] (3/10/84 BC-52)

BABY COME BACK TO ME (THE MORSE CODE OF LOVE) The Manhattan Transfer—
Atlantic 89594 [Nick Santamaria] [ASC] (2/2/85 B-83)

BABY COME CLOSE Smokey Robinson—Tamla 54239
[Pamela Moffett/Smokey Robinson/Marvin Tarplin] [ASC] (11/3/73 BCR-27)

BABY COME HOME Ruby And The Romantics—Kapp 601
[Mort Garson/Bob Hilliard] [ASC] (7/11/64 BCR-70)

BABY COME HOME TO ME Burl Ives—Decca 31479 [Harlan Howard] [BMI] (3/23/63 R-79)

BABY COME ON HOME Solomon Burke—Atlantic 2314
[Bert Berns] [BMI] (1/8/66 BCR-73)

BABY, COME TO ME Patti Austin (A duet with James Ingram)—Qwest 50036
[Rod Temperton] [ASC] (4/24/82 BC-1)

BABY COME TO ME Regina Belle—Columbia 68969
[Jeffrey E. Cohen/Narada Michael Walden] [ASC] (10/14/89 BC-60)

BABY, DO THE PHILLY DOG The Olympics—Mirwood 5523
[Sherlie Mae Matthews/Fred Smith/Walter Ward] [BMI] (10/1/66 BCR-63)

BABY DOLL *Andy Williams—Cadence 1303*
[Bernie Hanighen/Kenyon Hopkins] [ASC] (12/1/56 BCRt-26)

BABY DOLL *Ralph Young—Epic 9194*
[Bernie Hanighen/Kenyon Hopkins] [ASC] (12/8/56 Rt-26)

BABY DOLL *Chuck Miller—Mercury 71001*
[Bernie Hanighen/Kenyon Hopkins] [ASC] (12/8/56 Rt-26)

BABY DOLL *Percy Faith & His Orchestra—Columbia 40764*
[Kenyon Hopkins] [ASC] (12/8/56 Rt-26) [IM]

BABY, DON'T BE LOOKING IN MY MIND Joe Simon—Sound Stage 7 2634
[Harlan Howard] [BMI] (6/21/69 BCR-51)

BABY DON'T CHANGE YOUR MIND Gladys Knight & The Pips—Buddah 569
[Van McCoy] [BMI] (6/11/77 BCR-51)

BABY DON'T FORGET MY NUMBER Milli Vanilli—Arista 1-9832
[Bernd Berwanger*/Roger Dalton/Frank Farian/Brad Howell] [SA] (4/29/89 BC-1)

BABY DON'T GET HOOKED ON ME Mac Davis—Columbia 45618
[Mac Davis] [BMI] (7/1/72 BCR-1)

BABY DON'T GO Sonny & Cher—Reprise 0392 [Sonny Bono] [BMI] (8/21/65 BCR-8)

BABY DON'T GO Karla Bonoff—Columbia 11206
[Karla Bonoff/Kenny Edwards] [BMI] (2/23/80 BCR-64)

BABY DON'T TAKE YOUR LOVE Faith, Hope & Charity—Maxwell 808
[Joe Cobb/Van McCoy] [BMI] (9/26/70 BR-92)

BABY, DON'T YOU CRY (THE NEW SWINGOVA RHYTHM)
Ray Charles And His Orchestra—ABC-Paramount 10530
[Woodrow Buddy Johnson] [ASC] (2/22/64 BCR-39)

BABY DON'T YOU DO IT *Marvin Gaye—Tamla 54101*
[Lamont Dozier/Brian Holland/Eddie Holland] [BMI] (9/19/64 BCR-27)

DON'T DO IT *The Band—Capitol 3433*
[Lamont Dozier/Brian Holland/Eddie Holland] [BMI] (9/16/72 BCR-23)

BABY DON'T YOU KNOW Wild Cherry—Epic/Sweet City 50306
[Robert Parissi] [ASC] (1/8/77 BCR-43)

BABY DON'T YOU WEEP Garnet Mimms & The Enchanters—United Artists 658
[Bert Berns/Jerry Ragovoy] [BMI] (11/9/63 BCR-30)

BABY ELEPHANT WALK *Lawrence Welk And His Orchestra—Dot 16364*
[Henry Mancini] [ASC] (6/2/62 BCRt-39) [I]

BABY ELEPHANT WALK *The Miniature Men—Dolton 57*
[Henry Mancini] [ASC] (6/9/62 BRt-39) [I]

BABY ELEPHANT WALK *Kai Winding—Verve 10258*
[Henry Mancini] [ASC] (7/21/62 Rt-39) [I]

BABY FACE *Little Richard—Specialty 645*
[Harry Akst/Benny Davis] [ASC] (9/15/58 BCR-41)

BABY FACE *Bobby Vee—Liberty 55325 [Harry Akst/Benny Davis] [ASC] (5/13/61 C-97)*

BABY FACE *Bobby Darin—Atco 6236 [Harry Akst/Benny Davis] [ASC] (9/29/62 BCR-38)*

BABY FACE *The Wing And A Prayer Fife And Drum Corps.—Wing & A Prayer 103*
[Harry Akst/Benny Davis] [ASC] (11/15/75 BCR-14)

BABY FAT Robert Byrne—Mercury 74070
[Tom Brasfield/Robert Byrne] [ASC] (6/9/79 C-93)

BABY GET IT (AND DON'T QUIT IT) Jackie Wilson—Brunswick 55250
[Alonzo Tucker/Jackie Wilson] [BMI] (9/21/63 BCR-57)

BABY—GET IT ON Ike & Tina Turner—United Artists 598
[Ike Turner/Tina Turner*] [BMI] (5/31/75 BCR-64)

BABY GRAND Billy Joel—Columbia 06994 [Billy Joel] [ASC] (4/4/87 BC-75)

BABY, HANG UP THE PHONE Carl Graves—A&M 1620
[Patrick J. McManus/Lefty Pedroski] [ASC] (11/30/74 BCR-50)

BABY HAS GONE BYE BYE George Maharis—Epic 9555
[Robert Allen/Allan Roberts] [ASC] (11/10/62 BCR-60)

BABY, HELP ME Percy Sledge—Atlantic 2383 [Bobby Womack] [BMI] (2/18/67 BCR-87)

BABY HOLD ON The Grass Roots—Dunhill 4237
[Harvey Price/Dan Walsh] [ASC] (5/2/70 BCR-25)

BABY HOLD ON Eddie Money—Columbia 10663
[Jimmy Lyon/Eddie Money] [BMI] (1/28/78 BCR-5)

(BABY) HULLY GULLY The Olympics—Arvee 562
[Cliff Goldsmith/Fred Smith] [BMI] (2/1/60 BCR-57)

BABY I DO LOVE YOU The Galens—Challenge 9212
[Pepper Davis/Leonard Grainger/Traditional] [BMI] (11/9/63 BCR-68)

BABY I LIED Deborah Allen—RCA 13600
[Deborah Allen/Rory Bourke/Rafe Van Hoy] [BMI] (10/15/83 BC-23)

BABY, I LOVE YOU *The Ronettes—Philles 118*
[Jeff Barry/Ellie Greenwich/Phil Spector] [BMI] (12/21/63 BCR-24)

BABY, I LOVE YOU *Andy Kim—Steed 716*
[Jeff Barry/Ellie Greenwich/Phil Spector] [BMI] (5/17/69 BCR-5)

BABY I LOVE YOU *Jimmy Holiday—Minit 32002 [Jimmy Holiday] [BMI] (9/3/66 B-98)*

BABY I LOVE YOU *Little Milton—Checker 1227 [Jimmy Holiday] [BMI] (4/25/70 BCR-82)*

BABY I LOVE YOU Aretha Franklin—Atlantic 2427
[Ronnie Shannon] [BMI] (7/22/67 BCR-3)

BABY, I LOVE YOUR WAY *Peter Frampton—A&M 1832*
[Peter Frampton] [ASC] (6/19/76 BCR-12)

BABY, I LOVE YOUR WAY *Will To Power—Epic 08034*
[Peter Frampton] (Med) [ASC] (9/10/88 BC-1)

BABY I NEED YOU The Manhattans—Carnival 514
[Edward Bivins/Joe Evans] [BMI] (3/19/66 BC-96)

BABY I NEED YOUR LOVING *Four Tops—Motown 1062*
[Lamont Dozier/Brian Holland/Eddie Holland] [BMI] (8/15/64 BCR-11)

BABY I NEED YOUR LOVIN' *Johnny Rivers—Imperial 66227*
[Lamont Dozier/Brian Holland/Eddie Holland] [BMI] (2/4/67 BCR-3)

BABY, I NEED YOUR LOVING *O.C. Smith—Columbia 45206*
[Lamont Dozier/Brian Holland/Eddie Holland] [BMI] (8/22/70 BCR-52)

BABY, I NEED YOUR LOVIN' *Eric Carmen—Arista 0384*
[Lamont Dozier/Brian Holland/Eddie Holland] [BMI] (1/27/79 BCR-60)

BABY I WANT YOU Funky Communication Committee—Free Flight 11595
[Dennis Clifton/John Ingram] [BMI] (7/7/79 BCR-47)

BABY, I'LL GIVE IT TO YOU Seals & Crofts—Warner Bros. 8277
[Lana Bogan/Jim Seals] [BMI] (11/20/76 BC-58)

BABY I'M-A WANT YOU Bread—Elektra 45751 [David Gates] [ASC] (10/16/71 BCR-3)

BABY I'M BURNIN' Dolly Parton—RCA 11420 [Dolly Parton] [BMI] (12/9/78 BCR-25)

BABY, I'M FOR REAL The Originals—Soul 35066
[Marvin Gaye/Anna Gordy] [ASC] (9/6/69 BCR-13)

BABY I'M HOOKED Con Funk Shun—Mercury 814581
[Cedric Martin/Van Ross Redding] [BMI] (1/7/84 B-76)

BABY I'M LONELY The Intruders—Gamble 209 [Kenneth Gamble/Leon Huff] [BMI] (9/16/67 BCR-65)

***BABY, I'M YOURS** Barbara Lewis—Atlantic 2283 [Van McCoy] [BMI] (6/5/65 BCR-10)*

***BABY, I'M YOURS** Jody Miller—Epic 10785 [Van McCoy] [BMI] (9/25/71 BCR-83)*

***BABY, I'M YOURS** Debby Boone—Warner/Curb 8554 [Van McCoy] (TSW) [BMI] (5/27/78 B-79)*

BABY, IS THERE SOMETHING ON YOUR MIND McKinley Travis—Pride 2 [Bobby Sanders] [BMI] (7/18/70 BCR-88)

BABY IT'S COLD OUTSIDE Ray Charles And Betty Carter—ABC-Paramount 10298 [Frank Loesser] [ASC] (2/19/62 BR-91)

BABY, IT'S TONIGHT Jude Cole—Reprise 19869 [Jude Cole] [BMI] (4/14/90 BC-11)

***BABY IT'S YOU** The Shirelles—Scepter 1227 [Burt Bacharach/Mack David/Luther Dixon] [ASC] (12/4/61 BCR-8)*

***BABY IT'S YOU** Smith—Dunhill 4206 [Burt Bacharach/Mack David/Luther Dixon] [ASC] (9/6/69 BCR-3)*

BABY I'VE BEEN MISSING YOU The Independents—Wand 11258 [Charles Henry Jackson Jr./Marvin Yancy] [ASC] (7/14/73 BCR-36)

—BABY I'VE BEEN THINKING see: SOCIETY'S CHILD

BABY JANE Rod Stewart—Warner Bros. 29608 [Jay Davis/Rod Stewart] [ASC] (5/28/83 BC-14)

BABY LET ME KISS YOU King Floyd—Chimneyville 437 [King Floyd] [BMI] (3/6/71 BCR-19)

BABY LET ME TAKE YOU (IN MY ARMS) Detroit Emeralds—Westbound 203 [Abrim Tilmon] [BMI] (5/27/72 BCR-17)

BABY LET'S WAIT The Royal Guardsmen—Laurie 3461 [Lori Burton/Pam Sawyer] [BMI] (11/9/68 BCR-33)

BABY LOVE The Supremes—Motown 1066 [Lamont Dozier/Brian Holland/Eddie Holland] [BMI] (10/3/64 BCR-1)

BABY LOVE Mother's Finest—Epic 50407 [Jerry Seay] [ASC] (9/10/77 BCR-58)

BABY LOVE Regina—Atlantic 89417 [Stephen Bray/Mary E. Kessler/Regina Richards] [ASC] (6/21/86 BC-10)

BABY MAKE IT SOON The Flying Machine—Congress 6012 [Tony Macaulay] [ASC] (2/21/70 BCR-87)

BABY MAKE ME FEEL SO GOOD The Five Stairsteps & Cubie—Curtom 1936 [Curtis Mayfield] [BMI] (2/15/69 CR-89)

BABY MAKE YOUR OWN SWEET MUSIC Jay And The Techniques—Smash 2154 [Sandy Linzer/Denny Randell] [BMI] (4/13/68 BCR-53)

BABY MAKES HER BLUE JEANS TALK Dr. Hook—Casablanca 2347 [Ron Haffkine/Dennis Locorriere/Sam Weedman] [BMI] (2/27/82 BCR-25)

BABY, NOW THAT I'VE FOUND YOU The Foundations—Uni 55038 [Tony Macaulay/John Macleod] [ASC] (12/16/67 BCR-8)

BABY OH BABY The Shells—Johnson 104 [Nathaniel Bouknight/Walter Coleman/Hiram Johnson] [BMI] (12/5/60 BCR-16)

BABY PLEASE COME BACK HOME J.J. Barnes—Groovesville 1006 [J.J. Barnes/Don Davis] [BMI] (5/20/67 BCR-50)

***BABY, PLEASE DON'T GO** Them—Parrot 9727 [Joe Williams] [ASC] (4/3/65 CR-92)*

***BABY PLEASE DON'T GO** The Amboy Dukes—Mainstream 676 [Joe Williams] [BMI] (3/23/68 CR-97)*

BABY SCRATCH MY BACK Slim Harpo—Excello 2273 [Slim Harpo] [BMI] (1/22/66 BCR-13) [I]

BABY SHE'S GONE Jack Scott—ABC-Paramount 9818 [Jack Scott] [BMI] (5/4/57 R-80)

BABY SITTER Betty Wright—Alston 4614 [Willie Clarke/Clarence Reid/Betty Wright] [BMI] (9/9/72 BCR-41)

BABY SITTIN' BOOGIE Buzz Clifford—Columbia 41876 [Johnny Parker] [ASC] (1/7/61 BCR-6)

BABY STEP BACK Gordon Lightfoot—Warner Bros. 50012 [Gordon Lightfoot] [ASC] (4/3/82 BC-50)

BABY TAKE ME IN YOUR ARMS Jefferson—Janus 106 [Tony Macaulay/John Macleod] [ASC] (12/6/69 BCR-19)

BABY TALK Jan & Dean—Dore 522 [Melvin Schwartz] [BMI] (7/6/59 BCR-7)

BABY TALK Alisha—Vanguard 35262 [Greg Brown/Logankoya*] [ASC] (12/21/85 BC-68)

BABY TALKS DIRTY The Knack—Capitol 4822 [Berton Averre/Doug Fieger] [ASC] (2/9/80 BCR-30)

(BABY TELL ME) CAN YOU DANCE Shanice Wilson—A&M 2939 [Bryan Loren] [BMI] (11/7/87 BC-50)

BABY, THAT'S ALL Jackie Wilson—Brunswick 55233 [Eddie Singleton/Alonzo Tucker] [BMI] (9/29/62 C-98)

BABY THAT'S BACKATCHA Smokey Robinson—Tamla 54258 [Smokey Robinson] [ASC] (4/19/75 BCR-26)

BABY THE RAIN MUST FALL Glenn Yarbrough—RCA Victor 47-8498 [Elmer Bernstein/Ernie Sheldon] [ASC] (3/13/65 BCR-12)

BABY TOYS The Toys—DynoVoice 222 [Tom DeCillis/Richard Layton] [BMI] (9/3/66 BCR-76)

(BABY) TURN ON TO ME The Impressions—Curtom 1954 [Curtis Mayfield] [BMI] (9/5/70 BCR-47)

BABY, WE BETTER TRY TO GET IT TOGETHER Barry White—20th Century 2298 [Barry White] [BMI] (7/24/76 B-92)

BABY, WE'VE GOT LOVE Johnnie Taylor—Derby 1006 [Sam Cooke] [BMI] (11/30/63 B-98)

BABY, WHAT A BIG SURPRISE Chicago—Columbia 10620 [Peter Cetera] [ASC] (9/24/77 BCR-4)

BABY, WHAT ABOUT YOU Crystal Gayle—Warner Bros. 29582 [Josh Leo/Wendy Waldman] [BMI] (9/10/83 B-83)

BABY WHAT DO YOU WANT ME TO DO Barbara Lewis—Atlantic 2361 [Grant Higgins] [BMI] (10/29/66 BCR-74)

***BABY WHAT I MEAN** The Drifters—Atlantic 2366 [Frank S. Hamilton/Ernie Sheldon] [BMI] (12/3/66 BCR-62)*

***BABY WHAT I MEAN** The Spiral Starecase—Columbia 44442 [Frank S. Hamilton/Ernie Sheldon] [BMI] (3/30/68 R-91)*

***BABY WHAT YOU WANT ME TO DO** Jimmy Reed—Vee-Jay 333 [Jimmy Reed] [BMI] (1/30/60 BCR-37)*

***BABY WHAT YOU WANT ME TO DO** Etta James—Argo 5459 [Jimmy Reed] [BMI] (1/25/64 BR-82)*

BABY, WHAT'S WRONG Lonnie Mack—Fraternity 918 [Jimmy Reed] [BMI] (11/30/63 B-93)

BABY WON'T YOU LET ME ROCK 'N ROLL YOU Ten Years After—Columbia 45530 [Alvin Lee] [ASC] (1/15/72 BCR-61)

BABY WORKOUT Jackie Wilson—Brunswick 55239 [Alonzo Tucker/Jackie Wilson] [BMI] (3/2/63 BCR-4)

BABY YOU COME ROLLIN' ACROSS MY MIND The Peppermint Trolley Company—Acta 815 [Jesse Lee Kincaid] [BMI] (6/8/68 BCR-38)

BABY YOU GOT IT Brenton Wood—Double Shot 121 [Joseph Hooven/Alfred J. Smith/Hal Winn] [ASC] (11/18/67 BCR-34)

BABY, YOU LOOK GOOD TO ME TONIGHT John Denver—RCA 10854 [Bill Danoff] [ASC] (12/25/76 BC-65)

BABY YOU'RE A RICH MAN The Beatles—Capitol 5964 [John Lennon/Paul McCartney] [ASC] (7/29/67 BCR-34)

BABY, YOU'RE DRIVING ME CRAZY Joey Dee—Roulette 4467 [Joey Dee/Henry Glover/Morris Levy‡] [BMI] (1/12/63 BR-89)

BABY, YOU'RE RIGHT James Brown And The Famous Flames—King 5524 [James Brown/Joe Tex] [BMI] (8/21/61 BR-49)

—BABY YOU'RE SO FINE see: GEE BABY

BABY YOU'RE SO RIGHT FOR ME Brenda & The Tabulations—Dionn 507 [Gary Klein/Jimmy Roach] [BMI] (3/16/68 BCR-83)

BABY (YOU'VE GOT WHAT IT TAKES) Dinah Washington & Brook Benton—Mercury 71565 [Clyde Otis/Murray Stein] [BMI] (1/25/60 BCR-2)

BABY'S COMING BACK Jellyfish—Charisma 98837 [Andy Sturmer] [BMI] (3/9/91 BC-46)

BABY'S FIRST CHRISTMAS Connie Francis—MGM 13051 [Benny Davis/Ted Murry] [ASC] (12/11/61 BCR-22)

BABY'S GONE Gene Thomas—United Artists 640 [Bobby Goldsboro/Roy Orbison] [BMI] (11/16/63 BCR-77)

BACARDI Ralph Marterie—United Artists 315 [Johnny Pate] [BMI] (6/12/61 R-92) [I]

BACHELOR BOY Cliff Richard And The Shadows—Epic 9691 [Cliff Richard/Bruce Welch] [ASC] (7/4/64 BR-90)

***BACIARE BACIARE (KISSING KISSING)** Dorothy Collins—Top Rank 2024 [Willy Dehmel/Joe Niessen/Bert Reisfeld] [NA] (11/23/59 BCRt-43) [FET]*

***BACIARE BACIARE (KISSING KISSING)** Ilse Werner—Top Rank 2023 [Willy Dehmel/Joe Niessen] [NA] (11/30/59 Rt-59) [F]*

BACK AND FORTH Cameo—Atlanta Artists 888385 [Larry Blackmon/Tomi Jenkins/Kevin Kendrick/Nathan Leftenant] [BMI] (4/25/87 BC-50)

BACK AT THE CHICKEN SHACK, PART I Jimmy Smith—Blue Note 1877 [James O. Smith] [BMI] (3/9/63 BCR-63) [I]

BACK BEAT NO. 1 The Rondels—Amy 825 [Leonard Collins/James Petze/Leonard Petze/Ray Pizzi] [BMI] (7/10/61 BCR-66) [I]

BACK DOOR MAN Derek—Bang 566 [Johnny Cymbal/George Tobin] [BMI] (2/22/69 BCR-47)

BACK FOR A TASTE OF YOUR LOVE Syl Johnson—Hi 2250 [Darryl Carter/Brenda Johnson/Syl Johnson] [BMI] (10/20/73 BCR-72)

BACK HOME AGAIN John Denver—RCA Victor 10065 [John Denver] [ASC] (9/21/74 BCR-5)

BACK IN BABY'S ARMS Patsy Cline—Decca 31483 [Bob Montgomery] [BMI] (4/20/63 R-98)

BACK IN BLACK AC/DC—Atlantic 3787 [Brian Johnson/Angus Young/Malcolm Young] [ASC] (12/13/80 BCR-37)

BACK IN LOVE AGAIN The Buckinghams—Columbia 44533 [Martin Grebb] [BMI] (6/1/68 BCR-45)

BACK IN MY ARMS Nat "King" Cole—Capitol 3860 [Julie Mandel/Roger Roger] [BMI] (12/30/57 CR-32)

***BACK IN MY ARMS AGAIN** The Supremes—Motown 1075 [Lamont Dozier/Brian Holland/Eddie Holland] [BMI] (5/1/65 BCR-1)*

***BACK IN MY ARMS AGAIN** Genya Ravan—20th Century Fox 2374 [Lamont Dozier/Brian Holland/Eddie Holland] [BMI] (8/5/78 BCR-76)*

BACK IN STRIDE Maze Featuring Frankie Beverly—Capitol 5431 [Frankie Beverly] [BMI] (3/16/85 BC-81)

BACK IN THE HIGH LIFE AGAIN Steve Winwood—Island 28472 [Will Jennings/Steve Winwood] [BMI] (5/30/87 BC-13)

BACK IN THE SADDLE Aerosmith—Columbia 10516 [Joe Perry/Steven Tyler] [ASC] (4/9/77 BCR-38)

BACK IN THE USA *Chuck Berry—Chess 1729 [Chuck Berry] [BMI] (6/20/59 BCR-37)*
BACK IN THE U.S.A. *Linda Ronstadt—Asylum 45519*
[Chuck Berry] [BMI] (8/19/78 BCR-11)
BACK IN THE U.S.S.R. Chubby Checker—Buddah 100
[John Lennon/Paul McCartney] [ASC] (4/5/69 BCR-82)
BACK OF MY HAND (I'VE GOT YOUR NUMBER) The Jags—Island 49202
[John Alder/Nicholas Watkinson] [ASC] (5/10/80 BCR-78)
BACK OFF BOOGALOO Ringo Starr—Apple 1849 [Ringo Starr] [BMI] (3/25/72 BCR-8)
BACK ON HOLIDAY Robbie Nevil—EMI 50152
[David Paul Bryant/Steven Dubin/Robbie Nevil] [ASC] (11/12/88 BC-30)
BACK ON MY FEET AGAIN The Foundations—Uni 55058
[Tony Macaulay/John Macleod] [ASC] (3/9/68 BCR-41)
BACK ON MY FEET AGAIN The Babys—Chrysalis 2398
[Dominic Bugatti/Frank Musker/John Waite] [BMI] (1/19/80 BCR-26)
BACK ON THE CHAIN GANG The Pretenders—Sire 29840
[Chrissie Hynde] [ASC] (12/11/82 BC-5)
BACK ON THE STREET AGAIN The Sunshine Company—Imperial 66260
[Steve Gillette] [ASC] (10/21/67 BCR-36)
BACK STABBERS The O'Jays—Philadelphia Int'l 3517
[Leon Huff/Gene McFadden/John Whitehead] [BMI] (7/8/72 BCR-1)
BACK STREET Edwin Starr—Ric-Tic 107
[Bill Sharpley/Edwin Starr] [BMI] (11/20/65 BCR-81)
BACK TO DREAMIN' AGAIN Pat Shannon—Uni 55191
[Kenny Nolan] [ASC] (1/17/70 CR-76)
BACK TO LIFE Soul II Soul—Virgin 99171
[Nellee Hooper/Simon Law/Beresford Romeo/Caron Wheeler] [BMI] (9/23/89 BC-3)
BACK TO PARADISE 38 Special—A&M 2955
[Bryan Adams/Pat Benatar/Jim Vallance] [BMI] (7/25/87 BC-41)
BACK TO SCHOOL AGAIN Timmie "Oh Yeah" Rogers—Cameo 116
[Bernie Lowe/Kal Mann] [BMI] (10/7/57 BCR-30)
BACK TO SCHOOL AGAIN Four Tops—RSO 1069
[Howard Greenfield/Louis St. Louis] [BMI] (5/15/82 B-71)
—BACK TO THE BASICS OF LOVE see: LUCKENBACH, TEXAS
BACK TO THE BULLET Saraya—Polydor 889976
[Sandy Linzer/Gregg Munier/Sandi Saraya] [BMI] (11/11/89 BC-63)
BACK TO THE HOP Danny & The Juniors—Swan 4082
[Joe Terranova/David White] [BMI] (9/11/61 BCR-80)
BACK TO THE ISLAND Leon Russell—Shelter 40483
[Leon Russell] [BMI] (12/27/75 BCR-53)
BACK TO THE RIVER Damnation Of Adam Blessing—United Artists 50726
[Ray Benich/Adam Blessing/Bob Kalamasz/Jim Quinn/Bill Schwark] [ASC]
(12/19/70 CR-85)
BACK TOGETHER AGAIN Daryl Hall & John Oates—RCA 10970
[John Oates] [BMI] (5/7/77 BCR-25)
BACK TOGETHER AGAIN Roberta Flack with Donny Hathaway—Atlantic 3661
[Reggie Lucas/James Mtume] [BMI] (5/17/80 BCR-56)
BACK UP AGAINST THE WALL Atlanta Rhythm Section—Polydor/BGO 2039
[Buddy Buie/J.R. Cobb] [BMI] (12/8/79 R-81)
BACK UP TRAIN Al Greene & The Soul Mate's—Hot Line 15000
[Palmer James/Curtis Rodgers] [BMI] (11/25/67 BCR-31)
BACK WHEN MY HAIR WAS SHORT Gunhill Road—Kama Sutra 569
[Glenn Leopold] [ASC] (3/31/73 BCR-25)
BACK WHERE YOU BELONG 38 Special—A&M 2615
[Gary O'Connor] [ASC] (2/4/84 BC-20)
BACKFIELD IN MOTION Mel And Tim—Bamboo 107
[Mel Harden/Tim McPherson] [BMI] (10/18/69 BCR-10)
BACKFIRED Debbie Harry—Chrysalis 2526
[Bernard Edwards/Nile Rodgers] [BMI] (8/15/81 BCR-39)
BACKSTAGE Gene Pitney—Musicor 1171
[Fred Anisfield/Willie Denson] [BMI] (4/16/66 BCR-24)
BACKSTROKIN' Fatback—Spring 3012 [Bill Curtis/Johnny Flippin] [BMI] (7/26/80 R-94)
BACKTRACK Faron Young—Capitol 4616
[Faron Young/Alex Zanetis] [BMI] (9/30/61 BC-89)
BACKWARDS AND FORWARDS December's Children—World Pacific 77887
[Ray Whitley] [BMI] (5/18/68 CR-80)
BACKYARD Pebbles—MCA 53982
[Kenneth Edmonds/Cheryl James/Antonio Reid] [BMI] (4/13/91 BC-73)
BAD *Michael Jackson—Epic 07418 [Michael Jackson] [BMI] (9/19/87 BC-1)*
FAT *(parody of Bad) "Weird Al" Yankovic—Rock 'n' Roll 07769*
[Michael Jackson/Al Yankovic] [NA] (5/21/88 BC-89) [P]
BAD, BAD BILLY Snuff—Warner/Curb 29615
[Jim Bowling/Robbie House/Chuck Larson] [ASC] (8/20/83 B-88)
BAD, BAD LEROY BROWN *Jim Croce—ABC 11359 [Jim Croce] [ASC] (4/14/73 BCR-1)*
BAD, BAD LEROY BROWN *Frank Sinatra—Reprise 1196 [Jim Croce] [ASC] (4/6/74 B-83)*
BAD BLOOD Neil Sedaka—Rocket/MCA 40460
[Phil Cody/Neil Sedaka] [BMI] (9/13/75 BCR-1)
BAD, BOLD AND BEAUTIFUL GIRL The Persuaders—Atco 6919
[Nelson Daniels/Robert Holloman/Jackie Members/Richard Poindexter/Robert Poindexter/Alton Watkins] [BMI] (6/2/73 C-100)

BAD BOY The Jive Bombers—Savoy 1508
[Lillian Hardin Armstrong] [ASC] (2/2/57 BCR-22)
BAD BOY *Marty Wilde—Epic 9356 [Marty Wilde] [BMI] (2/1/60 BCRt-42)*
BAD BOY *Robin Luke—Dot 16040 [Marty Wilde] [BMI] (2/1/60 Rt-42)*
BAD BOY Luther Vandross—Epic 03205
[Marcus Miller/Luther Vandross] (Med) [ASC] (10/30/82 BC-55)
BAD BOY Ray Parker Jr.—Arista 1030 [Ray Parker Jr.] [ASC] (11/27/82 BC-28)
BAD BOY Miami Sound Machine—Epic 05805
[Larry Dermer/Joe Galdo/Rafael Vigil] [BMI] (3/8/86 BC-8)
BAD BOYS Wham! U.K.—Columbia 03932 [George Michael] [ASC] (8/6/83 BC-50)
BAD BRAKES Cat Stevens—A&M 2109 [Alun Davies/Cat Stevens] [ASC] (1/27/79 B-83)
BAD CASE OF LOVING YOU (DOCTOR, DOCTOR) Robert Palmer—Island 49016
[Moon Martin] [BMI] (7/21/79 BCR-9)
(THE BAD DONKEY) PUM-PA-LUM Steve Lawrence—Coral 61792
[Albert S. Wood] [ASC] (3/16/57 B-45)
BAD EYE Willie Mitchell—Hi 2103 [Willie Mitchell] [BMI] (5/7/66 BCR-68) [I]
BAD GIRL Valerie Carr—Roulette 4092
[Luigi Creatore/Hugo Peretti/June Winters] [NA] (10/13/58 R-82)
BAD GIRL The Miracles—Chess 1734
[Berry Gordy/Smokey Robinson] [ASC] (10/3/59 BC-62)
BAD GIRL Neil Sedaka—RCA Victor 47-8254
[Howard Greenfield/Neil Sedaka] [BMI] (11/2/63 BCR-31)
BAD GIRLS Donna Summer—Casablanca 988
[Joe Esposito/Eddie Hokenson/Bruce Sudano/Donna Summer] [BMI] (5/26/79 BCR-1)
BAD LITTLE WOMAN The Shadows Of Knight—Dunwich 128
[Herbie Armstrong/Victor Catling/Rod Demick/Brian Rossi/Tito Tinsley] [BMI]
(9/3/66 BCR-88)
BAD LOVE Eric Clapton—Duck/Reprise 19980
[Eric Clapton/Michael Leslie Jones] [BMI] (3/10/90 BC-73)
BAD LUCK (PART 1) *Harold Melvin And The Blue Notes—Philadelphia Int'l 3562*
[Victor Carstarphen/Gene McFadden/John Whitehead] [BMI] (3/22/75 BCR-13)
BAD LUCK *The Atlanta Disco Band—Ariola America 7611*
[Victor Carstarphen/Gene McFadden/John Whitehead] [BMI] (1/10/76 BCR-91) [IWM]
BAD LUCK *The Ritchie Family—Marlin 3306*
[Victor Carstarphen/Gene McFadden/John Whitehead] (Med) [BMI]
(8/28/76 BCR-17) [IWM]
BAD MAN BLUNDER The Kingston Trio—Capitol 4379
[Lee Hays/Cisco Houston] [BMI] (5/30/60 BCR-37)
BAD MEDICINE Bon Jovi—Mercury 870657
[Jon Bon Jovi/Desmond Child/Richie Sambora] [ASC] (9/24/88 BC-1)
BAD MISUNDERSTANDING The Critters—Kapp 793
[Pete Andreoli/Vini Poncia] [BMI] (11/26/66 BCR-48)
BAD MOON RISING Creedence Clearwater Revival—Fantasy 622
[John Fogerty] (TSW) [BMI] (5/3/69 BCR-1)
BAD MOTORCYCLE The Storey Sisters—Cameo 126
[Al Browne/Frederick Williams] [BMI] (2/22/58 BCR-41)
BAD OF THE HEART George LaMond—Columbia 73339
[Phillip Andreula/Marilyn Rodriguez] [ASC] (5/12/90 BC-25)
BAD SIDE OF THE MOON April Wine—Big Tree 142
[Elton John/Bernie Taupin] [BMI] (7/29/72 CR-89)
BAD SNEAKERS Steely Dan—ABC 12128
[Walter Becker/Donald Fagen] [ASC] (8/30/75 C-90)
BAD TIME Grand Funk—Capitol 4046 [Mark Farner] [BMI] (4/5/75 BCR-4)
BAD TIMES Tavares—Capitol 4811 [Gerard McMahon] [ASC] (1/5/80 BCR-47)
BAD TO ME Billy J. Kramer With The Dakotas—Imperial 66027
[John Lennon/Paul McCartney] [ASC] (5/30/64 BCR-9)
BAD WATER The Raeletts—Tangerine 1014
[Jackie DeShannon/Jimmy Holiday/Randy Myers] [BMI] (2/27/71 BCR-58)
BAD WEATHER The Supremes—Motown 1225
[Ira Tucker Jr./Stevie Wonder] [ASC] (6/9/73 BC-87)
BADGE Cream—Atco 6668 [Eric Clapton/George Harrison] [BMI] (3/29/69 BCR-56)
BADLANDS Bruce Springsteen—Columbia 10801
[Bruce Springsteen] [ASC] (8/19/78 BCR-42)
BAHAMA MAMA Four Aces—Decca 30242 [Luther Dixon] [BMI] (3/16/57 BCR-28)
BAJA The Astronauts—RCA Victor 47-8194 [Lee Hazlewood] [BMI] (7/20/63 BR-92) [I]
BAKER STREET Gerry Rafferty—United Artists 1192
[Gerry Rafferty] [BMI] (4/15/78 BCR-1)
BALANCO NO SAMBA Stan Getz—Verve 10279 [Gary McFarland] [BMI] (2/23/63 R-95) [I]
BALBOA BLUE The Marketts—Liberty 55443
[Alexander Goldstein*/Jean Sharp Murphy/Joe Saraceno] [ASC] (4/21/62 BCR-48) [I]
BALL AND CHAIN Tommy James—Roulette 7084
[Tommy James/Robert L. King] [BMI] (7/25/70 BCR-44)
BALL OF CONFUSION (THAT'S WHAT THE WORLD IS TODAY) The Temptations—Gordy 7099
[Barrett Strong/Norman Whitfield] [BMI] (5/23/70 BCR-1)
BALL OF FIRE Tommy James And The Shondells—Roulette 7060
[Tommy James/Paul Naumann/Bruce Sudano/Mike Vale/Woody Wilson] [BMI]
(10/4/69 BCR-10)
BALLAD OF A GIRL AND BOY Graduates—Shan-Todd 0055
[John Cappello/Bruce Hammond/Tony Mancuso/Jack Scorsone] [BMI] (3/9/59 BCR-74)

BALLAD OF A TEENAGE QUEEN Johnny Cash and the Tennessee Two—Sun 283
[Jack H. Clement] [BMI] (1/20/58 BCR-16)

THE BALLAD OF BONNIE AND CLYDE Georgie Fame—Epic 10283
[Peter Callander/Mitch Murray] [BMI] (2/10/68 BCR-6)

THE BALLAD OF DAVY CROCKETT *Bill Hayes—Cadence 1256*
[Tom Blackburn/George Bruns] [BMI] (2/14/55 BCtRt-1)

BALLAD OF DAVY CROCKETT *"Tennessee" Ernie Ford—Capitol 3058*
[Tom Blackburn/George Bruns] [BMI] (2/21/55 BCtRt-1)

BALLAD OF DAVY CROCKETT *Fess Parker—Columbia 40449*
[Tom Blackburn/George Bruns] [BMI] (2/21/55 BCtRt-1)

THE BALLAD OF DAVY CROCKETT *Rusty Draper—Mercury 70555*
[Tom Blackburn/George Bruns] [BMI] (2/21/55 Rt-24)

THE BALLAD OF DAVY CROCKETT *Steve Allen—Coral 61368*
[Tom Blackburn/George Bruns] [BMI] (2/28/55 Rt-24)

THE BALLAD OF DAVY CROCKETT *Walter Schumann—RCA Victor 47-6041*
[Tom Blackburn/George Bruns] [BMI] (4/11/55 BRt-1)

PANCHO LOPEZ (DAVY CROCKETT) *(parody of The Ballad Of Davy Crockett)*
Lalo Guerrero—Real 1301
[Tom Blackburn/George Bruns/Lalo Guerrero] [BMI] (8/8/55 CR-26) [P]

BALLAD OF EASY RIDER The Byrds—Columbia 44990
[Roger McGuinn] [BMI] (11/1/69 BCR-65)

THE BALLAD OF EVEL KNIEVEL John Culliton Mahoney—Amherst 701
[Ron Kramer/Dean Kay] [ASC] (9/14/74 CR-85)

—BALLAD OF FRANCIS POWERS see:
THERE'S A STAR SPANGLED BANNER WAVING SOMEWHERE

THE BALLAD OF IRVING Frank Gallop—Kapp 745
[John Aylesworth/Frank Peppiatt/Richard B. Williams] [ASC] (4/16/66 BCR-34)

THE BALLAD OF JAYNE L.A. Guns—Vertigo 876 984
[Mick Cripps/Tracii Guns/Philip F. Lewis/Kelly Nickels/Steve Riley] [BMI]
(4/7/90 BC-31)

THE BALLAD OF JED CLAMPETT
Lester Flatt, Earl Scruggs & The Foggy Mountain Boys—Columbia 42606
[Paul Henning] [BMI] (12/1/62 BCR-44)

THE BALLAD OF JOHN AND YOKO The Beatles—Apple 2531
[John Lennon/Paul McCartney] [ASC] (6/14/69 BCR-7)

THE BALLAD OF PALADIN Duane Eddy—RCA Victor 47-8047
[Richard Boone/Sam Rolfe/Johnny Western] [BMI] (6/30/62 BCR-33) [IWM]

BALLAD OF THE ALAMO *Marty Robbins—Columbia 41809*
[Dimitri Tiomkin/Paul Francis Webster] [ASC] (10/17/60 BCtRt-34)

BALLAD OF THE ALAMO *Bud And Travis—Liberty 55284*
[Dimitri Tiomkin/Paul Francis Webster] [ASC] (10/17/60 BCtRt-35)

THE BALLAD OF THE GREEN BERETS SSgt. Barry Sadler—RCA Victor 47-8739
[Robin Moore/Barry Sadler] [ASC] (1/29/66 BCR-1)

BALLAD OF THUNDER ROAD *Robert Mitchum—Capitol 3986*
[Robert Mitchum/Don Raye] [ASC] (9/8/58 BR-62)

THE BALLAD OF THUNDER ROAD *Robert Mitchum—Capitol 3986*
[Robert Mitchum/Don Raye] [ASC] (2/24/62 BCR-52)

BALLAD OF TWO BROTHERS Autry Inman—Epic 10389
[Bobby Braddock/Buddy Killen/Curly Putman] [BMI] (11/16/68 BCR-48)

THE BALLAD OF WATERHOLE #3 (CODE OF THE WEST) Roger Miller—Smash 2121
[Dave Grusin/Robert Wells] [ASC] (10/14/67 C-91)

BALLAD OF YOU & ME & POONEIL Jefferson Airplane—RCA Victor 47-9297
[Paul Kantner] [BMI] (9/2/67 BCR-24)

BALLAD OF YOUTH Richie Sambora—Mercury 868 790
[Tom Morolda/Richie Sambora] [ASC] (9/21/91 BC-53)

BALLERINA *Nat "King" Cole—Capitol 3619*
[Bob Russell/Carl Sigman] [ASC] (2/9/57 BCRt-29)

BALLERINA *Vaughn Monroe & His Orchestra—RCA Victor 47-3257*
[Bob Russell/Carl Sigman] [ASC] (2/23/57 Rt-39)

BALLERINA *Vaughn Monroe and his Orchestra—United Artists 214*
[Bob Russell/Carl Sigman] [ASC] (4/11/60 R-85)

BALLERINA GIRL Lionel Richie—Motown 1873
[Lionel Richie] [ASC] (12/6/86 BC-7)

BALLERO War—United Artists 432
[Thomas Allen/Harold Brown/Morris Dickerson/Lonnie Jordan/Charles Miller/
Lee Oskar/Howard Scott] [ASC]
(6/1/74 BCR-29) [I]

BALLIN' THE JACK Georgia Gibbs—Mercury 70572
[Jim Burris/Chris Smith] [NA] (3/14/55 R-42)

BALLROOM BLITZ The Sweet—Capitol 4055
[Mike Chapman/Nicky Chinn] [ASC] (6/14/75 BCR-5)

BAMA LAMA BAMA LOO Little Richard—Specialty 692
[Richard Penniman] [BMI] (7/18/64 B-82)

BANANA BOAT (DAY-O) *Harry Belafonte—RCA Victor 47-6771*
[Traditional] [ASC] (1/5/57 BCRt-2)

BANANA BOAT (DAY-O) *(parody of Banana Boat-Day O) Stan Freberg—Capitol 3687*
[Stan Freberg/Traditional] [ASC] (3/30/57 BCRt-11) [P]

BANANA BOAT SONG *The Fontane Sisters—Dot 15527*
[Alan Arkin/Bob Carey/Erik Darling] [BMI] (12/15/56 BCtRt-2)

BANANA BOAT SONG *The Tarriers—Glory 249*
[Alan Arkin/Bob Carey/Erik Darling] [BMI] (12/15/56 BCtRt-2)

BANANA BOAT SONG *Sarah Vaughan—Mercury 71020*
[Alan Arkin/Bob Carey/Erik Darling] [BMI] (12/15/56 BCtRt-2)

BANANA BOAT SONG *Steve Lawrence—Coral 61761*
[Alan Arkin/Bob Carey/Erik Darling] [BMI] (12/22/56 BCtRt-2)

BANAPPLE GAS Cat Stevens—A&M 1785 [Cat Stevens] [ASC] (1/31/76 BCR-41)

BAND OF GOLD *Kit Carson—Capitol 3283*
[Bob Musel/Jack Taylor] [BMI] (11/19/55 BCtRt-4)

BAND OF GOLD *Don Cherry—Columbia 40597*
[Bob Musel/Jack Taylor] [BMI] (11/21/55 BCtRt-4)

BAND OF GOLD *The Hi-Fi Four—King 4856*
[Bob Musel/Jack Taylor] [BMI] (12/9/55 BRt-31)

BAND OF GOLD *The Roommates—Valmor 010*
[Bob Musel/Jack Taylor] [BMI] (8/28/61 CR-79)

BAND OF GOLD *Mel Carter—Imperial 66165*
[Bob Musel/Jack Taylor] [BMI] (4/9/66 BCR-31)

BAND OF GOLD Freda Payne—Invictus 9075
[Lamont Dozier/Ronald Dunbar/Brian Holland/Eddie Holland] [BMI] (4/25/70 BCR-1)

BAND ON THE RUN Paul McCartney & Wings—Apple 1873
[Linda McCartney/Paul McCartney] [ASC] (4/13/74 BCR-1)

THE BANDIT *Johnston Brothers—London 1470*
[Michael Carr/Alfredo do Nascimento/John Turner] [ASC] (10/9/54 CRt-17)

THE BANDIT *Tex Ritter—Capitol 2916*
[Michael Carr/Alfredo do Nascimento/John Turner] [ASC] (10/9/54 CtRt-PRE)

THE BANDIT *Percy Faith & His Orchestra—Columbia 40323*
[Alfredo do Nascimento] [ASC] (10/9/54 CtRt-PRE) [IM]

THE BANDIT *Frank Weir & His Orchestra—London 1464*
[Michael Carr/Alfredo do Nascimento/John Turner] [ASC] (10/18/54 Rt-PRE)

THE BANDIT *Ronald Chesney—RCA Victor 47-5875*
[Alfredo do Nascimento] [ASC] (10/25/54 Rt-PRE) [IM]

THE BANDIT (O' CANGACIERO) *Eddie Barclay and His Orch.—Tico 249*
[Alfredo do Nascimento] [ASC] (6/20/55 R-30) [IM]

BANDIT OF MY DREAMS Eddie Hodges—Cadence 1410
[Gene Pitney/Aaron Schroeder] [BMI] (1/20/62 BCR-65)

BANG A GONG (GET IT ON) *T. Rex—Reprise 1032 [Marc Bolan] [ASC] (12/18/71 BCR-10)*

BANG A GONG *Witch Queen—Roadshow 11551 [Marc Bolan] [ASC] (4/28/79 B-68)*

GET IT ON *The Power Station—Capitol 5479 [Marc Bolan] [ASC] (6/8/85 BC-9)*

BANG! BANG! The Joe Cuba Sextet—Tico 475
[Joe Cuba/Jaime Sabater] [BMI] (10/22/66 BCR-45) [F]

BANG BANG Danger Danger—Imagine/Epic 73380
[Bruno Ravel/Steve West] [BMI] (6/2/90 BC-47)

BANG BANG (MY BABY SHOT ME DOWN) Cher—Imperial 66160
[Sonny Bono] [BMI] (3/5/66 BCR-2)

BANG-SHANG-A-LANG The Archies—Calendar 1006 [Jeff Barry] [BMI] (9/14/68 BCR-6)

BANG THE DRUM ALL DAY Todd Rundgren—Bearsville 29686
[Todd Rundgren] [BMI] (4/30/83 BC-63)

BANG YOUR HEAD (METAL HEALTH) Quiet Riot—Pasha 04267
[Frankie Banali/Carlos Cavazo/Tony Cavazo/Kevin Dubrow] [BMI] (1/7/84 BC-24)

BANGLA-DESH George Harrison—Apple 1836
[George Harrison] (TSW) [ASC] (9/11/71 BCR-13)

BANJO BOY *Jan And Kjeld—Kapp 335 [Charly Niessen] [ASC] (6/6/60 BCtRt-35) [F]*

BANJO BOY *Dorothy Collins—Top Rank 2052*
[Buddy Kaye/Charly Niessen] [ASC] (6/6/60 BCtRt-35) [FET]

BANJO BOY *Art Mooney And His Orchestra—MGM 12908*
[Buddy Kaye/Charly Niessen] [ASC] (6/13/60 BCtRt-43) [FET]

BANJO WOOGIE *The Ban-Joes—Columbia 40536*
[Norman Malkin/Freddy Morgan/Jad Paul] [ASC] (7/18/55 Rt-72)

BANJO WOOGIE *Georgie Shaw—Decca 29595*
[Norman Malkin/Freddy Morgan/Jad Paul] [ASC] (7/18/55 Rt-72)

BANJO WOOGIE *The Sunnysiders—Kapp 114*
[Norman Malkin/Freddy Morgan/Jad Paul] [ASC] (7/18/55 Rt-72)

BANJO'S BACK IN TOWN *Teresa Brewer—Coral 61448*
[Marshall Brown/Alden Shuman/Earl Shuman] [ASC] (7/2/55 CRt-20)

BANJO'S BACK IN TOWN *Swing & Sway With Sammy Kaye—Columbia 40517*
[Marshall Brown/Alden Shuman/Earl Shuman] [ASC] (7/4/55 Rt-20)

BANKS OF THE OHIO Olivia Newton-John—Uni 55304
[Traditional] [NA] (10/16/71 BCR-82)

BANNED IN BOSTON Merv Griffin—Carlton 540
[Clint Ballard Jr./Fred Tobias] [ASC] (2/20/61 CR-77)

BANNED IN THE U.S.A. Luke Featuring 2 Live Crew—Luke 98915
[Luther Campbell/David Hobbs/Mark Ross/Bruce Springsteen/Chris Wong Won] [BMI]
(7/21/90 BC-18)

BANZAI PIPELINE Henry Mancini And His Orchestra—RCA Victor 47-8184
[Henry Mancini] [ASC] (6/15/63 BCR-93) [I]

BARBARA The Temptations (2)—Goldisc 3001
[Neil Kleinhandler/Neil Lapidus/Artie Ripp] [BMI] (3/28/60 BCR-26)

BARBARA-ANN *The Regents—Gee 1065 [Fred Fassert] [BMI] (5/1/61 BCR-8)*

BARBARA ANN *The Beach Boys—Capitol 5561 [Fred Fassert] [BMI] (12/25/65 BCR-1)*

***BARBARA ANN** The Beach Boys—Capitol 5030 [Fred Fassert] (Med) [BMI] (7/25/81 BCR-5)*

BARBARA, I LOVE YOU The New Colony Six—Mercury 73004 [Billy Herman/Chuck Jobes/Les Kummel] [BMI] (12/27/69 BCR-78)

BAREFOOT IN BALTIMORE Strawberry Alarm Clock—Uni 55076 [Roy Freeman/Ed King/Mark Weitz] [ASC] (8/10/68 BCR-46)

BAREFOOTIN' Robert Parker—Nola 721 [Robert Parker] [BMI] (4/23/66 BCR-7)

***KEEP YOUR EYE ON THE SPARROW** Merry Clayton—Ode 66110 [Morgan Ames/Dave Grusin] [BMI] (7/26/75 BCR-45)*

***BARETTA'S THEME ("KEEP YOUR EYE ON THE SPARROW")** Rhythm Heritage—ABC 12177 [Morgan Ames/Dave Grusin] [BMI] (4/10/76 BCR-16)*

—BARKING AT AIRPLANES see: CRAZY IN THE NIGHT

BARKING DOG The Crew-Cuts—Mercury 70490 [Robert Chabrier/Al Stillman] [ASC] (11/27/54 CR-19)

BAROQUE-A-NOVA Mason Williams—Warner Bros.-Seven Arts 7235 [Allan Blye/Mason Williams] [BMI] (10/12/68 BCR-79) [I]

THE BARRACUDA Alvin Cash & The Crawlers—Mar-V-Lus 6005 [Bernice Williams] [BMI] (3/27/65 BCR-56)

BARRACUDA Heart—Portrait 70004 [Michael Derosier/Roger Fisher/Ann Wilson/Nancy Wilson] [ASC] (5/28/77 BCR-10)

THE BASIE TWIST Count Basie and His Orchestra—Roulette 4403 [Benny Carter] [ASC] (12/25/61 BR-82) [I]

BASKETBALL Kurtis Blow—Polydor 881529 [Curtis Bedeau/James Bralower/Gerard Charles/Hugh Clarke/ Robert Arthur Ford Jr./Brian George/Paul George/James B. Moore/Kurt Walker/ Shirley Walker/William Waring] [BMI] (4/13/85 BC-71)

—BASKETBALL JONES see: LOVE JONES

BATDANCE Prince—Warner Bros. 22924 [Prince] [ASC] (6/17/89 BC-1)

BATMAN Jan & Dean—Liberty 55860 [Don Altfeld/Jan Berry/Fred Wieder] [BMI] (2/12/66 BCR-52)

BATMAN & HIS GRANDMOTHER Dickie Goodman—Red Bird 10-058 [George Goldner*/Dickie Goodman] [BMI] (5/21/66 BCR-69)

***BATMAN THEME** Neal Hefti—RCA Victor 47-8755 [Neal Hefti] [ASC] (2/5/66 BCR-28) [I]*

***BATMAN THEME** The Marketts—Warner Bros. 5696 [Neal Hefti] [ASC] (2/5/66 BCR-10) [I]*

THE BATTLE Duane Eddy and The Rebels—Jamie 1209 [Duane Eddy/Lee Hazlewood] [BMI] (1/22/62 CR-90)

***BATTLE HYMN OF LT. CALLEY** C Company Featuring Terry Nelson—Plantation 73 [James Milas Smith/Julian Wilson] [BMI] (4/17/71 BCR-11)*

***BATTLE HYMN OF LT. CALLEY** John Deer—Royal American 34 [James Milas Smith/Julian Wilson] [BMI] (4/17/71 R-72)*

***BATTLE HYMN OF THE REPUBLIC** The Mormon Tabernacle Choir—Columbia 41459 [Julia Ward Howe/William Steffe] [BMI] (9/7/59 BCR-11)*

***BATTLE HYMN OF THE REPUBLIC** Andy Williams With The St. Charles Borromeo Choir—Columbia 44650 [Julia Ward Howe/William Steffe] [BMI] (10/19/68 BCR-33)*

***BATTLE HYMN OF THE REPUBLIC** Mickey Newbury—Elektra 45750 [Julia Ward Howe/William Steffe] (Med) [BMI] (11/6/71 BCR-24)*

***BATTLE HYMN OF THE REPUBLIC** Elvis Presley—RCA Victor 74-0672 [Julia Ward Howe/William Steffe] (Med) [BMI] (4/22/72 BCR-59)*

BATTLE OF GETTYSBURG Fred Darian—JAF 2020 [Fred Darian/Al DeLory/Joseph Van Winkle] [ASC] (2/27/61 B-100)

BATTLE OF KOOKAMONGA Homer & Jethro—RCA Victor 47-7585 [Jimmy Driftwood/J.J. Reynolds] [BMI] (8/31/59 BCR-14)

***BATTLE OF NEW ORLEANS** Johnny Horton—Columbia 41339 [Jimmy Driftwood/Traditional] [BMI] (4/25/59 BCRt-1)*

***BATTLE OF NEW ORLEANS** Vaughn Monroe with Norman Layden, His Orchestra and Chorus—RCA Victor 7495 [Jimmy Driftwood/Traditional] [BMI] (5/25/59 BRt-1)*

***BATTLE OF NEW ORLEANS** Harpers Bizarre—Warner Bros.-Seven Arts 7223 [Jimmy Driftwood/Traditional] [BMI] (9/21/68 B-95)*

***BATTLE OF NEW ORLEANS** Bert Sommer—Eleuthera 472 [Jimmy Driftwood/Traditional] [BMI] (12/12/70 C-93)*

***BATTLE OF NEW ORLEANS** Nitty Gritty Dirt Band—United Artists 544 [Jimmy Driftwood/Traditional] [BMI] (10/12/74 BC-72)*

BATTLESHIP CHAINS Georgia Satellites—Elektra 69497 [Terry Anderson] [ASC] (3/28/87 B-86)

***BAUBLES BANGLES AND BEADS** Jonah Jones Quartet—Capitol 3893 [Aleksandr Borodin/George Forrest/Robert Craig Wright] [ASC] (3/24/58 Rt-25) [IWM]*

***BAUBLES BANGLES AND BEADS** The Kirby Stone Four—Columbia 41183 [Aleksandr Borodin/George Forrest/Robert Craig Wright] [ASC] (6/16/58 BCRt-25)*

***(BAZOOM) I NEED YOUR LOVIN'** The Cheers—Capitol 2921 [Jerry Leiber/Mike Stoller] [BMI] (10/11/54 BCRt-15)*

***BAZOOM! (I NEED YOUR LOVIN')** Les Elgart & His Orchestra—Columbia 40388 [Jerry Leiber/Mike Stoller] [BMI] (11/29/54 Rt-PRE)*

B.B.D. (I THOUGHT IT WAS ME)? Bell Biv DeVoe—MCA 53897 [Darrol Durant/Roney Hooks/Eric Sadler/Keith Shocklee/Paul Stewart] [ASC] (10/13/90 BC-23)

BE Neil Diamond—Columbia 45942 [Neil Diamond] [SE] (10/20/73 BCR-19)

***BE ANYTHING (BUT BE MINE)** Gloria Lynne—Fontana 1890 [Irving Gordon] [ASC] (4/4/64 BC-88)*

***BE ANYTHING (BUT BE MINE)** Connie Francis—MGM 13237 [Irving Gordon] [ASC] (4/11/64 BCR-20)*

***BE BOP A LULA** Gene Vincent and His Blue Caps—Capitol 3450 [William Douchette/Gene Vincent] [BMI] (6/15/56 BCR-5)*

***BE BOP A-LULA** The Everly Brothers—Cadence 1380 [William Douchette/Gene Vincent] [BMI] (7/2/60 BC-74)*

BE BOP BABY Ricky Nelson—Imperial 5463 [Pearl Lendhurst] [BMI] (10/5/57 BCR-5)

BE CAREFUL OF STONES THAT YOU THROW Dion—Columbia 42810 [Bonnie Dodd] [BMI] (6/29/63 BCR-30)

BE CAREFUL WITH A FOOL B.B. "Blues Boy" King and His Orchestra—RPM 494 [Joe Josea‡/B.B. King] [BMI] (7/22/57 B-95)

BE GOOD TO ME BABY Luther Ingram—KoKo 2107 [Johnny Baylor] [BMI] (5/1/71 BCR-88)

BE GOOD TO YOURSELF Journey—Columbia 05869 [Jonathan Cain/Steve Perry/Neal Schon] [ASC] (4/12/86 BC-9)

BE-IN (HARE KRISHNA) The Happenings—Jubilee 5666 [Galt MacDermot/James Rado/Gerome Ragni] (Med) [ASC] (6/28/69 BCR-29)

BE MAD LITTLE GIRL Bobby Darin—Capitol 5079 [Bobby Darin] [BMI] (11/23/63 BCR-59)

BE MINE TONIGHT Andy Williams—Cadence 1340 [Maria Teresa Lara/Sunny Skylar] [BMI] (1/20/58 R-64)

BE MINE (TONIGHT) Grover Washington, Jr.—Elektra 47246 [William Eaton/Ralph MacDonald/William Salter] [ASC] (2/6/82 B-92)

BE MINE TONIGHT Neil Diamond—Columbia 02928 [Neil Diamond] [SE] (5/22/82 BC-35)

***BE MY BABY** The Ronettes—Philles 116 [Jeff Barry/Ellie Greenwich/Phil Spector] [BMI] (8/31/63 BCR-1)*

***BE MY BABY** Andy Kim—Steed 729 [Jeff Barry/Ellie Greenwich/Phil Spector] [BMI] (10/31/70 BCR-11)*

***BE MY BABY** Cissy Houston—Janus 145 [Jeff Barry/Ellie Greenwich/Phil Spector] [BMI] (4/24/71 BC-86)*

BE MY BABY Dick And Deedee—Warner Bros. 5608 [Dick Gosting] [BMI] (3/6/65 BCR-87)

BE MY BOY The Paris Sisters—Gregmark 2 [Phil Spector] [BMI] (4/24/61 BCR-56)

BE MY GIRL The Four-Evers—Smash 1887 [Bob Gaudio] [ASC] (5/23/64 BCR-49)

BE MY GIRL The Dramatics—ABC 12235 [Michael E. Henderson] [ASC] (12/25/76 BCR-53)

BE MY GUEST Fats Domino—Imperial 5629 [Tommy Boyce/Fats Domino/John Marascalco] [BMI] (10/19/59 BCR-8)

BE MY LADY The Meters—Warner Bros. 8434 [Joseph Modeliste/Art Neville/Cyril Neville/Leo Nocentelli/George Porter] [BMI] (9/17/77 BC-78)

BE MY LADY Jefferson Starship—Grunt 13350 [Jeannette Sears/Pete Sears] [BMI] (10/9/82 BC-26)

***BE MY LOVE** Joni James—MGM 12948 [Nicholas Brodszky/Sammy Cahn] [ASC] (10/17/60 Rt-89)*

***BE MY LOVE** Joanie Sommers—Warner Bros. 5177 [Nicholas Brodszky/Sammy Cahn] [ASC] (10/24/60 Rt-89)*

BE MY LOVER Alice Cooper—Warner Bros. 7568 [Michael Bruce] [BMI] (3/11/72 BCR-36)

BE NEAR ME ABC—Mercury 880626 [Martin Fry/Mark White] [BMI] (8/24/85 BC-9)

BE NICE TO ME Runt--Todd Rundgren—Bearsville 31002 [Todd Rundgren] [BMI] (4/10/71 BCR-59)

BE STILL MY BEATING HEART Sting—A&M 2992 [Sting] [BMI] (1/16/88 BC-15)

BE THANKFUL FOR WHAT YOU GOT William Devaughn—Roxbury 0236 [William DeVaughn] [BMI] (4/13/74 BCR-1)

BE THERE Pointer Sisters—MCA 53120 [Franne Golde/Allee Willis] [BMI] (8/8/87 BC-42)

BE TRUE TO YOUR SCHOOL The Beach Boys—Capitol 5069 [Mike Love*/Brian Wilson] [BMI] (11/2/63 BCR-6)

BE TRUE TO YOURSELF Bobby Vee—Liberty 55581 [Burt Bacharach/Hal David] [ASC] (6/15/63 BCR-33)

BE WHAT YOU ARE The Staple Singers—Stax 0164 [Homer Banks/Carl Hampton/Raymond Earl Jackson] [BMI] (6/16/73 BCR-66)

BE WITH YOU Bangles—Columbia 68744 [Walker Igleheart/Debbi Peterson] [ASC] (5/6/89 BC-19)

BE YOUNG, BE FOOLISH, BE HAPPY The Tams—ABC 11066 [J.R. Cobb/Ray Whitley] [BMI] (6/8/68 BCR-38)

BE YOUR MAN Jesse Johnson's Revue—A&M 2702 [Jesse Woods Johnson] [ASC] (3/16/85 BC-51)

BEACH BABY First Class—UK 49022 [John Carter/Gillian Shakespeare] [BMI] (7/20/74 BCR-3)

BEACH GIRL Pat Boone—Dot 16658 [Bruce Johnston/Terry Melcher] [BMI] (9/26/64 BCR-67)

BEACH PARTY King Curtis And The Noble Knights—Capitol 4788 [King Curtis/Luther Dixon*/Wally Roker*] [BMI] (6/30/62 BCR-56) [I]

BEACH PARTY Dave York And The Beachcombers—P-K-M 6700 [David Kinzie/Fred Mikesell] [BMI] (8/18/62 BR-63)

BEACH TIME Roger Smith—Warner Bros. 5068 [Richard Sherman/Robert Sherman] [BMI] (6/13/59 BCR-59)

BEACHCOMBER Bobby Darin At The Piano—Atco 6173 [Bobby Darin] [BMI] (8/29/60 BCR-50) [I]

BEANS IN MY EARS The Serendipity Singers—Philips 40198
[Len Chandler] [BMI] (5/23/64 BCR-25)

***BEAST OF BURDEN** The Rolling Stones—Rolling Stones 19309*
[Mick Jagger/Keith Richards] [ASC] (9/9/78 BCR-7)

***BEAST OF BURDEN** Bette Midler—Atlantic 89712*
[Mick Jagger/Keith Richards] [ASC] (2/11/84 BC-71)

BEAT Billy May And His Orchestra—Capitol 3486
[Bernie Lowe*/Kal Mann] [ASC] (7/27/56 R-84)

BEAT Rockin' R's—Tempus 7541
[Ted Minar*/Ron Volz/Ron Wernsman] [BMI] (3/21/59 BCR-57) [I]

***THE BEAT GOES ON** Sonny & Cher—Atco 6461 [Sonny Bono] [BMI] (1/14/67 BCR-3)*

***THE BEAT GOES ON** Lawrence Welk And His Orchestra—Dot 17001*
[Sonny Bono] [BMI] (4/15/67 CR-91) [IWM]

***BEAT IT** Michael Jackson—Epic 03759 [Michael Jackson] [BMI] (2/26/83 BC-1)*

***EAT IT** (parody of Beat It) "Weird Al" Yankovic—Rock 'n' Roll 04374*
[Michael Jackson/Al Yankovic] [NA] (3/10/84 BC-4) [P]

BEAT ME DADDY EIGHT TO THE BAR
Commander Cody And His Lost Planet Airmen—Paramount 0169
[Ray McKinley*/Hughie Prince/Don Raye/Eleanore Sheehy‡] [ASC] (7/22/72 BCR-75)

BEAT OF A HEART Scandal Featuring Patty Smyth—Columbia 04750
[Keith Mack/Zack Smith/Patty Smyth] [BMI] (1/26/85 BC-40)

BEAT PATROL Starship—RCA 5308
[Johnny Warman] [ASC] (9/26/87 BC-46)

BEAT STREET BREAKDOWN PART I
Grandmaster Melle Mel & the Furious Five With Mr. Ness & Cowboy—Atlantic 89659
[Melvin Glover/Reggie Griffin] [BMI] (8/4/84 B-86)

BEAT THE CLOCK The McCoys—Bang 543
[Richard Gottehrer/Jon Stroll] [BMI] (5/6/67 BCR-58)

BEATNIK FLY Johnny And The Hurricanes—Warwick 520
[Tom King/Ira Mack‡/John Pocisk/Traditional] [BMI] (1/25/60 BCR-10) [IM]

BEAT'S SO LONELY Charlie Sexton—MCA 52715
[Keith Forsey/Charlie Sexton] [ASC] (12/14/85 BC-17)

BEATS THERE A HEART SO TRUE Perry Como—RCA Victor 47-7274
[Jack Keller/Noel Sherman] [ASC] (7/21/58 CR-31)

BEAUCOUPS OF BLUES Ringo Starr—Apple 2969 [Buzz Rabin] [BMI] (10/31/70 BCR-69)

BEAUTICIAN BLUES B.B. King—Kent 403
[B.B. King/Jules Taub‡] [BMI] (10/24/64 BCR-80)

BEAUTIFUL Gordon Lightfoot—Reprise 1088 [Gordon Lightfoot] [ASC] (5/20/72 BCR-58)

BEAUTIFUL DELILAH Chuck Berry—Chess 1697 [Chuck Berry] [BMI] (7/28/58 B-81)

BEAUTIFUL FRIENDSHIP Ella Fitzgerald—Verve 2012
[Donald Kahn/Stanley H. Styne] [ASC] (7/28/56 BR-74)

BEAUTIFUL GIRLS Van Halen—Warner Bros. 49035
[Michael Anthony/David Lee Roth/Alex Van Halen/Eddie Van Halen] [ASC]
(9/1/79 BCR-80)

A BEAUTIFUL MORNING The Young Rascals—Atlantic 2493
[Eddie Brigati/Felix Cavaliere] [ASC] (4/6/68 BCR-2)

BEAUTIFUL OBSESSION Sir Chauncey And His Exciting Strings—Warner Bros. 5150
[Ernie Freeman] [ASC] (4/25/60 BCR-70) [IM]

***BEAUTIFUL PEOPLE** Kenny O'Dell—Vegas 718 [Kenny O'Dell] [BMI] (11/11/67 BCR-31)*

***BEAUTIFUL PEOPLE** Bobby Vee And The Strangers—Liberty 56009*
[Kenny O'Dell] [BMI] (11/11/67 BCR-22)

BEAUTIFUL PEOPLE The New Seekers Featuring Eve Graham—Elektra 45710
[Melanie Safka] (TSW) [ASC] (12/12/70 BCR-53)

A BEAUTIFUL STORY Sonny & Cher—Atco 6480 [Sonny Bono] [BMI] (4/29/67 BCR-53)

BEAUTIFUL SUNDAY Daniel Boone—Mercury 73281
[Daniel Boone/Rod McQueen] [ASC] (6/3/72 BCR-15)

***BEAUTIFUL WEEKEND** Googie René—Class 212 [Rafael René] [ASC] (8/26/57 Rt-47) [I]*

***BEAUTIFUL WEEKEND** Ernie Freeman—Imperial 5461*
[Rafael René] [ASC] (8/26/57 Rt-47) [I]

***BEAUTIFUL WEEKEND** Andy Anderson—Kapp 193 [Rafael René] [ASC] (8/26/57 Rt-54) [I]*

BEAUTY IS ONLY SKIN DEEP The Temptations—Gordy 7055
[Eddie Holland/Norman Whitfield] [BMI] (8/20/66 BCR-3)

BECAUSE The Dave Clark Five—Epic 9704 [Dave Clark] [ASC] (8/1/64 BCR-3)

BECAUSE I LOVE YOU Billy Stewart—Chess 1948
[Billy Davis/Raynard Miner/Carl William Smith] [BMI] (1/8/66 BCR-76)

BECAUSE I LOVE YOU The Five Stairsteps—Buddah 188
[Clarence Burke Jr.] (TSW) [BMI] (10/10/70 BCR-68)

BECAUSE I LOVE YOU (THE POSTMAN SONG) Stevie B—LMR/RCA 2724
[Warren Brooks] [BMI] (10/6/90 BC-1)

BECAUSE IT'S TIME McKendree Spring—Decca 32773
[Fran McKendree] [BMI] (1/23/71 R-82)

—BECAUSE OF ME see: RIGHT NEXT DOOR

BECAUSE OF MY PRIDE The Fireflies—Ribbon 6906
[Bernard Kahn/Bebe Starr/Phil Tucker*] [ASC] (4/9/60 C-86)

***BECAUSE OF YOU** Sammy Davis Jr.—Decca 29200*
[Arthur Hammerstein/Dudley Wilkinson] [ASC] (10/9/54 CR-38)

***BECAUSE OF YOU** Rome & Paris—Roulette 4681*
[Arthur Hammerstein/Dudley Wilkinson] [ASC] (6/18/66 CR-69)

***BECAUSE OF YOU** Chris Montez—A&M 839*
[Arthur Hammerstein/Dudley Wilkinson] [ASC] (3/4/67 BCR-55)

BECAUSE OF YOU Kracker—Dunhill 4329
[Victor Angulo/Art Casado/Carl Driggs/Chuck Francour/Carlos Garcia] [ASC]
(12/9/72 R-72)

BECAUSE OF YOU The Cover Girls—Fever 1914 [David Cole] [ASC] (11/28/87 BC-27)

BECAUSE THE NIGHT Patti Smith Group—Arista 0318
[Patti Smith/Bruce Springsteen] [ASC] (4/8/78 BCR-10)

BECAUSE THEY'RE YOUNG Duane Eddy And The Rebels—Jamie 1156
[Don Costa] [ASC] (5/9/60 BCR-3) [IM]

BECAUSE YOU'RE YOUNG Jimmie Rodgers—Roulette 4129
[Luigi Creatore/Hugo Peretti] [ASC] (2/9/59 BCR-41)

BED AND BOARD Barbara Mason—Buddah 296
[Bobby Flax/Lanny Lambert] [BMI] (6/10/72 BCR-66)

BED OF ROSE'S The Statler Brothers—Mercury 73141
[Harold Reid] [BMI] (1/16/71 BCR-41)

BEDS ARE BURNING Midnight Oil—Columbia 07433
[Peter Garrett/Peter Gifford*/Rob Hirst/James Moginie/Martin Rotsey*] [BMI]
(4/2/88 BC-17)

BEDTIME STORY Tammy Wynette—Epic 10818
[Billy Sherrill/Glenn Sutton] [BMI] (1/29/72 B-86)

***BEECHWOOD 4-5789** The Marvelettes—Tamla 54065*
[Marvin Gaye/George Gordy/William Stevenson] [ASC] (8/4/62 BCR-17)

***BEECHWOOD 4-5789** Carpenters—A&M 2405*
[Marvin Gaye/George Gordy/William Stevenson] [ASC] (4/24/82 BC-74)

BEEN A LONG TIME Betty Everett—Uni 55174
[Jerry Butler/Kenneth Gamble/Leon Huff] [BMI] (12/20/69 B-96)

BEEN SO LONG The Pastels—Argo 5287
[Dee Ervin/Tony Thomas/Richard Travis/James Willingham] [BMI] (3/3/58 BC-24)

BEEN SO NICE The Righteous Brothers—Verve 10551
[Douglas Fontaine Brown/William Stevenson] [BMI] (10/14/67 C-99)

BEEN TO CANAAN Carole King—Ode 66031 [Carole King] [ASC] (11/25/72 BCR-17)

BEEN TOO LONG ON THE ROAD Mark Lindsay—Columbia 45385
[David Gates] [ASC] (5/29/71 BCR-63)

BEEP BEEP The Playmates—Roulette 4115
[Carl Cicchetti/Donald Claps] [BMI] (10/27/58 BCR-3)

BEER BARREL POLKA Bobby Vinton—ABC 12056
[Lew Brown/Wladimir Timm/Jaromir Vejvoda] (TSW) [ASC] (3/15/75 BCR-33) [FDE]

(THE BEES ARE FOR THE BIRDS) THE BIRDS ARE FOR THE BEES The Newbeats—
Hickory 1305 [Bob Finnicum/Larry Parks/Jay Turnbow] [BMI] (4/3/65 BCR-50)

BEFORE AND AFTER Chad & Jeremy—Columbia 43277
[Van McCoy] [BMI] (5/15/65 BCR-15)

BEFORE I GO Starship—Grunt 14393 [David Scott Roberts] [BMI] (7/5/86 BC-61)

BEFORE I GROW TOO OLD Fats Domino—Imperial 5660
[Dave Bartholomew/Fats Domino/Robert Guidry] [BMI] (4/23/60 BCR-74)

BEFORE MY HEART FINDS OUT Gene Cotton—Ariola America 7675
[Randy Goodrum] [ASC] (1/21/78 BCR-16)

BEFORE THE NEXT TEARDROP FALLS Freddy Fender—ABC/Dot 17540
[Vivian Keith/Ben Peters] [BMI] (2/1/75 BCR-1)

***BEFORE THIS DAY ENDS** Eddy Arnold—RCA Victor 47-7794*
[Roy Drusky/Vic McAlpin/Marie Wilson] [BMI] (10/10/60 Rt-80)

***BEFORE THIS DAY ENDS** George Hamilton IV—ABC-Paramount 10125*
[Roy Drusky/Vic McAlpin/Marie Wilson] [BMI] (10/31/60 Rt-80)

BEFORE YOU GO Buck Owens—Capitol 5410
[Buck Owens/Don Rich] [BMI] (5/8/65 BCR-78)

BEG, BORROW AND STEAL Ohio Express—Cameo 483
[Joey Day/Lou Zerato] [ASC] (9/30/67 BCR-23)

BEG, BORROW OR STEAL Hughes/Thrall—Boulevard
[Glenn Hughes/Pat Thrall] [ASC] (12/18/82 B-79)

BEG ME Chuck Jackson—Wand 154 [Rudy Clark] [BMI] (5/16/64 BCR-45)

BEG, STEAL OR BORROW The New Seekers—Elektra 45780
[Tony Cole/Graeme Hall/Steve Wolfe] [ASC] (4/22/72 BCR-81)

BEG YOUR PARDON Billy Vaughn And His Orchestra—Dot 16064
[Francis Craig/Beasley Smith] [ASC] (4/30/60 C-98) [I]

BEGGIN' The 4 Seasons Featuring The "Sound" Of Frankie Valli—Philips 40433
[Peggy Farina/Bob Gaudio] [BMI] (3/4/67 BCR-12)

BEGGING TO YOU Marty Robbins—Columbia 42890
[Marty Robbins] [BMI] (11/30/63 BC-74)

BEGIN TO LOVE (COMINCIAMO AD AMARCI) Robert Goulet—Columbia 43224
[Sydney Lee/Gino Mescoli/Vito Pallavicini] [BMI] (3/6/65 CR-79)

A BEGINNING FROM AN END Jan & Dean—Liberty 55849
[Jan Berry/Roger Christian/Cleve Herman/George Tipton] [BMI] (1/22/66 R-94)

THE BEGINNING OF LONELINESS Dionne Warwick—Scepter 12187
[Burt Bacharach/Hal David] [ASC] (3/18/67 BCR-79)

THE BEGINNING OF MY END The Unifics—Kapp 957
[Guy Draper] [BMI] (12/14/68 BCR-26)

BEGINNING TO FEEL THE PAIN Mac Davis—Columbia 45302
[Mac Davis] [BMI] (2/27/71 B-92)

BEGINNINGS Chicago—Columbia 45417
[Robert Lamm] (TSW) [ASC] (6/26/71 BCR-7)

BEHIND BLUE EYES The Who—Decca 32888 [Pete Townshend] [BMI] (10/30/71 BCR-24)

BEHIND CLOSED DOORS Charlie Rich—Epic 10950
[Kenny O'Dell] [BMI] (4/28/73 BCR-13)

BEHIND THE DOOR Cher—Imperial 66217 [Graham Gouldman] [BMI] (11/12/66 BCR-76)

BEHIND THE WHEEL Depeche Mode—Sire 27991
[Martin L. Gore] (Med) [ASC] (5/7/88 BC-61)

BEI MIR BIST DU SCHON Louis Prima And Keely Smith—Dot 15956
[Sammy Cahn/Saul Chaplin/Jacob Jacobs/Sholom Secunda] [ASC]
(6/22/59 BCR-25) [FDE]

BEIN' HERE WITH YOU TONIGHT Gene Cotton & American Ace—Knoll 5001
[Gene Cotton] [ASC] (10/10/81 C-93)

BEING TRUE TO ONE ANOTHER Tony Bennett—Columbia 41341
[Robert Allen/Bob Hilliard] [ASC] (3/28/59 CR-56)

BEING WITH YOU Smokey Robinson—Tamla 54321
[Smokey Robinson] [ASC] (2/14/81 BCR-1)

BEL SANTE Mitch Miller with His Orch. & Chorus—Columbia 40575
[Charlotte Chait/Mack Discant] [ASC] (10/17/55 R-65)

BELIEVE HALF OF WHAT YOU SEE (AND NONE OF WHAT YOU HEAR)
Leon Haywood—20th Century 2146
[Leon Haywood] [BMI] (2/8/75 B-94)

BELIEVE IN HUMANITY Carole King—Ode 66035
[Carole King] (TSW) [ASC] (7/14/73 BCR-24)

BELIEVE IN ME Dan Fogelberg—Full Moon 04447 [Dan Fogelberg] [ASC] (4/28/84 BC-48)

BELIEVE IN ME BABY - PART 1 Jesse James—20th Century Fox 6684
[Jesse Anderson/Shena DeMell/Sugar Pie DeSanto] [BMI] (10/21/67 B-92)

BELIEVE IN THINGS Floyd and Jerry With The Counterpoints—Presta 1003
[Floyd Westfall/Jerry Westfall] [BMI] (5/7/66 R-92)

—BELIEVE IT OR NOT see: THEME FROM THE GREATEST AMERICAN HERO

BELIEVE ME Royal Teens—Capitol 4261
[Tom Austin/Bob Gaudio/Joe Villa] [BMI] (10/3/59 BCR-24)

BELIEVE WHAT YOU SAY Ricky Nelson—Imperial 5503
[Dorsey Burnette/Johnny Burnette] [BMI] (3/29/58 BCR-8)

(BELIEVED YOU WERE) LUCKY 'Til Tuesday—Epic 08059
[Aimee Mann/Jules Shear] [ASC] (1/21/89 B-95)

BELL BOTTOM BLUES *Derek And The Dominos—Atco 6803*
[Eric Clapton/Bobby Whitlock] [BMI] (2/13/71 BCR-81)*

BELL BOTTOM BLUES *Eric Clapton—Polydor 15056*
[Eric Clapton/Bobby Whitlock] [BMI] (2/17/73 BCR-78)*

—BELL SONG see: BELLS, BELLS, BELLS

BELLA Jack Scott with The Chantones—Carlton 504 [Jack Scott] [BMI] (3/16/59 CR-82)

BELLA LINDA The Grassroots—Dunhill 4162
[Steve Barri/Lucio Battisti/Barry Gross] [ASC] (11/23/68 BCR-19) [FDE]

BELLE Al Green—Hi 77505
[Reuben Fairfax/Al Green/Fred Jordan] [BMI] (12/24/77 BCR-69)

THE BELLE OF ST. MARK Sheila E.—Warner Bros. 29180 [Prince] [ASC] (10/27/84 BC-30)

BELLS James Brown—King 5423 [Billy Ward] [BMI] (11/14/60 BCR-68)

THE BELLS The Originals—Soul 35069
[Marvin Gaye/Anna Gordy/Iris Gordy/Elgie Stover] [ASC] (1/31/70 BCR-12)

BELLS ARE RINGING *Jo Stafford—Columbia 40782*
[Betty Comden/Adolph Green/Jule Styne] [ASC] (11/17/56 Rt-73)

BELLS ARE RINGING *Jeri Southern—Decca 30114*
[Betty Comden/Adolph Green/Jule Styne] [ASC] (11/17/56 Rt-73)

THE BELLS ARE RINGING The Van Dykes (1)—DeLuxe 6193
[Thomas Rivera] [BMI] (7/31/61 B-99)

THE BELLS AT MY WEDDING Paul Anka—ABC-Paramount 10279
[Paul Anka] [BMI] (12/16/61 C-98)

BELLS, BELLS, BELLS (THE BELL SONG) Billy & Lillie—Swan 4036
[Bob Crewe/Frank Slay] [BMI] (7/13/59 BCR-38)

BELLS OF ST MARY'S *Terry & The Mellos featuring Terry Corin—Amy 812*
[A. Emmett Adams/Douglas Furber] [ASC] (12/5/60 Rt-80)

THE BELLS OF ST. MARY'S *Lynn Taylor & The Peachettes—Clock 1033*
[A. Emmett Adams/Douglas Furber] [ASC] (12/5/60 Rt-94)

THE BELLS OF ST. MARY'S *The Baysiders—Everest 19393*
[A. Emmett Adams/Douglas Furber] [ASC] (12/5/60 Rt-82)

BELONGING TO SOMEONE Patti Page—Mercury 71247
[Al Hoffman/Dick Manning] [ASC] (1/6/58 BCR-28)

BEN Michael Jackson—Motown 1207 [Don Black/Walter Scharf] [ASC] (8/5/72 BCR-1)

BEN CRAZY Dickie Goodman & Dr. I.M. Ill—Diamond 119
[Dickie Goodman/Vera Hodes*] [BMI] (7/14/62 BCR-44)

BEND IT Dave Dee, Dozy, Beaky, Mick And Tich—Fontana 1559
[Alan Blaikley] [BMI] (1/7/67 C-100)

BEND ME, SHAPE ME *The American Breed—Acta 811*
[Scott English/Larry Weiss] [BMI] (11/18/67 BCR-1)

BEND ME, SHAPE ME *Storm—Sunflower 113*
[Scott English/Larry Weiss] [BMI] (9/18/71 CR-89)

BEND ME, SHAPE ME *Tight Fit—Arista 0638*
[Scott English/Larry Weiss] (Med) [BMI] (10/10/81 B-89)

BENNIE AND THE JETS Elton John—MCA 40198
[Elton John/Bernie Taupin] [BMI] (2/16/74 BCR-1)

BERLIN MELODY *Billy Vaughn And His Orchestra—Dot 16262*
[Heino Gaze] [ASC] (9/11/61 BCRt-39) [IM]

BERLIN MELODY *Kurt Edelhagen—Decca 31303 [Heino Gaze] [ASC] (10/9/61 Rt-39) [IM]*

BERMUDA Linda Scott—Canadian-American 134
[Cynthia Strother/Eugene Strother*] [BMI] (2/10/62 BCR-66)

BERMUDA SHORTS The Delroys—Apollo 514
[Milton Holder/Ernest Kelley*/Reginald Walker] [BMI] (8/31/57 C-56)

BERNADETTE Four Tops—Motown 1104
[Lamont Dozier/Brian Holland/Eddie Holland] [BMI] (3/4/67 BCR-4)

BERNARDINE Pat Boone—Dot 15570 [Johnny Mercer] [ASC] (5/4/57 BCR-13)

BERRY TREE Bill Hayes—Cadence 1261 [Saul Chaplin] [ASC] (4/30/55 CR-39)

THE BERTHA BUTT BOOGIE - PART I The Jimmy Castor Bunch—Atlantic 3232
[Jimmy Castor/Johnny Pruitt] [BMI] (2/8/75 BCR-16)

BERTHA LOU *Clint Miller—ABC-Paramount 9878*
[John Marascalco] [BMI] (12/30/57 BCRt-49)

BERTHA LOU *Johnny Faire—Surf 5019 [John Marascalco] [BMI] (12/30/57 Rt-55)*

BESAME MUCHO *Steve Lawrence and Eydie Gorme—Coral 61411*
[Sunny Skylar/Consuelo Velazquez] [ASC] (5/23/55 R-76)

BESAME MUCHO (PART 1) *The Coasters—Atco 6163*
[Sunny Skylar/Consuelo Velazquez] [BMI] (4/9/60 BCR-53)

THE BEST Tina Turner—Capitol 44442 [Mike Chapman/Holly Knight] [ASC]
(9/2/89 BC-12)

BEST BEAT IN TOWN Switch—Gordy 7168 [Bobby DeBarge] [ASC] (6/30/79 BCR-69)

THE BEST DISCO IN TOWN *The Ritchie Family—Marlin 3306*
[Henri Belolo/Richard V. Di Cicco/Phil Hurtt/Jacques Morali] (Med) [BMI]
(8/28/76 BCR-17)

THE BEST DISCO IN TOWN *The Ritchie Family—Marlin 3306*
[Henri Belolo/Richard V. Di Cicco/Phil Hurtt/Jacques Morali] (Med) [BMI]
(8/28/76 BCR-17)

THE BEST MAN IN THE WORLD Ann Wilson—Capitol 5654
[John Barry/Sue Ennis/Ann Wilson/Nancy Wilson] [BMI] (11/29/86 BC-52)

BEST OF BOTH WORLDS Lulu—Epic 10260
[Don Black/Mark London] [BMI] (12/9/67 BCR-32)

BEST OF BOTH WORLDS Van Halen—Warner Bros. 28505
[Michael Anthony/Sammy Hagar/Alex Van Halen/Eddie Van Halen] [ASC]
(11/22/86 C-83)

BEST OF EVERYTHING Johnny Mathis—Columbia 41491
[Sammy Cahn/Alfred Newman] [ASC] (10/24/59 BCR-62)

BEST OF LUCK TO YOU Earl Gains—HBR 481
[Lawrence H. Lee Jr.] [BMI] (7/23/66 R-85)

THE BEST OF ME David Foster And Olivia Newton-John—Atlantic 89420
[David Foster/Jeremy Lubbock/Richard Marx] [BMI] (6/7/86 BC-80)

BEST OF MY LOVE Eagles—Asylum 45218
[Glenn Frey/Don Henley/J.D. Souther] [BMI] (11/30/74 BCR-1)

BEST OF MY LOVE The Emotions—Columbia 10544
[Albert Philip McKay/Maurice White] [ASC] (6/11/77 BCR-1)

THE BEST OF TIMES Styx—A&M 2300 [Dennis DeYoung] [ASC] (1/24/81 BCR-3)

BEST OF TIMES Peter Cetera—Full Moon 27712
[Peter Cetera/Patrick Raymond Leonard] [ASC] (10/29/88 BC-50)

(THE BEST PART OF) BREAKIN' UP The Ronettes—Philles 120
[Pete Andreoli/Vini Poncia/Phil Spector] [BMI] (4/4/64 BCR-39)

BEST THING Styx—Wooden Nickel 73-0106
[Dennis DeYoung/James Young] [ASC] (9/16/72 BR-82)

YOU'RE THE BEST THING THAT EVER HAPPENED TO ME *Ray Price—Columbia 45889*
[Jim Weatherly] [ASC] (8/25/73 BCR-75)

BEST THING THAT EVER HAPPENED TO ME *Gladys Knight & The Pips—Buddah 403*
[Jim Weatherly] [ASC] (2/9/74 BCR-2)

BEST THING THAT EVER HAPPENED TO ME *The Persuaders—Atco 6956*
[Jim Weatherly] [ASC] (2/16/74 BCR-64)

BEST THINGS IN LIFE ARE FREE Richard Cannon—Capitol 4093
[Lew Brown/Buddy DeSylva/Ray Henderson] [ASC] (12/1/58 R-83)

—BEST YEARS see: LE BEL AGE

BET YOUR HEART ON ME Johnny Lee—Full Moon/Asylum
[Jimmy Ray McBride] [ASC] (10/10/81 BCR-54)

BETCHA BY GOLLY, WOW
The Stylistics Featumg Airrion Love & Russell Thompkins, Jr.—Avco 4591
[Thom Bell/Linda Creed] [BMI] (2/19/72 BCR-3)

BETCHA BY GOLLY WOW *Band Of Gold—RCA 13866*
[Thom Bell/Linda Creed] (Med) [BMI] (10/13/84 BC-64)

BETCHA SAY THAT Gloria Estefan and Miami Sound Machine—Epic 07371
[Larry Dermer/Joe Galdo/Rafael Vigil] [BMI] (9/5/87 BC-36)

BETCHA SHE DON'T LOVE YOU Evelyn King—RCA 13380
[Michael Jones] [BMI] (1/15/83 BC-36)

BETH Kiss—Casablanca 863
[Peter Criss/Bob Ezrin/Stan Penridge] (TSW) [ASC] (9/4/76 BCR-7)

BETRAYED The 4 Seasons—Philips 40278
[Sandy Linzer/Denny Randell] [BMI] (4/24/65 C-91)

BETTE DAVIS EYES Kim Carnes—EMI America 8077
[Jackie DeShannon/Donna Weiss] [BMI] (3/28/81 BCR-1)

BETTER BE GOOD TO ME Tina Turner—Capitol 5387
[Mike Chapman/Nicky Chinn/Holly Knight] [ASC] (9/15/84 BC-5)

BETTER BE HOME SOON Crowded House—Capitol 44164
[Neil Finn] [BMI] (7/9/88 BC-42)

BETTER BY THE POUND Funkadelic—Westbound 5014
[George Clinton/Eddie Hazel] [BMI] (11/1/75 B-99)

BETTER DAYS Melissa Manchester—Arista 0183
[Melissa Manchester/Carole Bayer Sager] [BMI] (5/1/76 BC-71)

A BETTER LOVE Londonbeat—Radioactive 54101
[Jimmy Chambers/George Chandler/Ian Edward Green/Jimmy Helms/William Henshall] [BMI] (5/11/91 BC-12)

BETTER LOVE NEXT TIME Dr. Hook—Capitol 4785
[Larry Keith/Steve Pippin/Johnny Slate] [BMI] (10/13/79 BCR-12)

BETTER MAN THAN I Terry Knight And The Pack—Lucky Eleven 226
[Brian Hugg/Mike Hugg] [BMI] (5/7/66 C-96)

BETTER PLACE TO BE (PARTS 1 & 2) Harry Chapin—Elektra 45327
[Harry Chapin] [ASC] (6/12/76 BCR-76)

BETTER TELL HIM NO The Starlets—PAM 1003 [Bernice Williams] [BMI] (4/24/61 BCR-38)

BETTER THINGS The Kinks—Arista 0649 [Ray Davies] [ASC] (11/28/81 BR-91)

BETTER TO GIVE THAN RECEIVE Joe Hinton—Back Beat 539
[Deadric Malone] [BMI] (10/12/63 BR-89)

BETTER USE YOUR HEAD Little Anthony And The Imperials—Veep 1228
[Victoria Pike/Teddy Randazzo] [BMI] (5/7/66 BCR-46)

BETTY AND DUPREE Chuck Willis—Atlantic 1168 [Chuck Willis] [BMI] (2/3/58 B-33)

BETTY IN BERMUDAS The Dovells—Parkway 882
[Dave Appell/Rose Marie Chivetti*/Kal Mann] [BMI] (8/24/63 BCR-39)

BETTY LOU GOT A NEW PAIR OF SHOES Bobby Freeman—Josie 841
[Bobby Freeman] [BMI] (8/2/58 BCR-31)

BETTY MY ANGEL Jerry Fuller—Challenge 59052
[Jerry Fuller/William Silva] [BMI] (8/22/59 BCR-90)

(BETWEEN A) ROCK AND A HARD PLACE Cutting Crew—Virgin 99215
[Kevin MacMichael/Nick Van Eede] [BMI] (5/13/89 BC-75)

BETWEEN HER GOODBYE AND MY HELLO Gladys Knight & The Pips—Soul 35111
[Jim Weatherly] [ASC] (6/29/74 BCR-57)

BETWEEN YOU BABY AND ME LOVE Curtis Mayfield & Linda Clifford—Curtom 941
[Curtis Mayfield] [BMI] (10/6/79 R-96)

BEWILDERED *Mickey & Sylvia—Vik 0324*
[Teddy Powell/Leonard Whitcup] [ASC] (5/5/58 BCR-49)

BEWILDERED *James Brown And The Famous Flames—King 5442*
[Teddy Powell/Leonard Whitcup] [ASC] (2/18/61 BCR-40)

BEWITCHED The Betty Smith Group—London 1787
[Richard Rodgers] [ASC] (5/12/58 BCR-40) [IM]

BEYOND Herb Alpert—A&M 2246 [Richard Hewson] [ASC] (6/21/80 BCR-50) [I]

BEYOND THE BLUE HORIZON Lou Christie—Three Brothers 402
[W. Franke Harling/Leo Robin/Richard Whiting] [ASC] (2/16/74 BCR-72)

LA MER (BEYOND THE SEA) *Roger Williams—Kapp 138*
[Albert Lasry/Charles Trenet] [ASC] (3/3/56 BCR-37) [IM]

LA MER *Trade Martin—Gee 1053*
[Albert Lasry/Charles Trenet] [ASC] (12/28/59 R-95) [IM]

BEYOND THE SEA *Bobby Darin—Atco 6158*
[Albert Lasry/Jack Lawrence/Charles Trenet] [ASC] (1/18/60 BCR-6) [FDE]

BEYOND THE SUNSET Pat Boone—Dot 16006
[Blanche Brock/Virgil Brock] [ASC] (11/23/59 BCR-51)

THE BIBLE TELLS ME SO *Nick Noble—Wing 90003 [Dale Evans] [ASC] (7/11/55 BCtRt-7)*

THE BIBLE TELLS ME SO *Ralph Young—Decca 29615 [Dale Evans] [ASC] (8/15/55 Rt-21)*

THE BIBLE TELLS ME SO *Don Cornell—Coral 61467*
[Dale Evans] (TSW) [ASC] (9/24/55 BCtRt-7)

BICYCLE MORNING Billy Sans—Atco 6945 [Paschal Cusimano] [BMI] (1/19/74 CR-91)

BICYCLE RACE Queen—Elektra 45541 [Freddie Mercury] (TSW) [BMI] (11/11/78 BCR-18)

—BICYCLETTES DE BELSIZE see: LES BICYCLETTES DE BELSIZE

—BIDDI BIDDI BUM BUM see: LAST TRAIN

BIFF THE FRIENDLY PURPLE BEAR Dick Feller—United Artists XW316-W
[Dick Feller] [BMI] (12/8/73 R-93)

BIG BAD JOHN *Jimmy Dean—Columbia 42175 [Jimmy Dean] [BMI] (10/2/61 BCR-1)*

BIG BRUCE *(parody of Big John) Steve Greenberg—Trip 3000*
[Jimmy Dean/Bud Reneau/Bill Stith*/Rick Tyson*/Mack Vickery*] [BMI] (7/26/69 B-97) [P]*

THE BIG BEAT Dick Jacobs And His Chorus And Orchestra—Coral 61794
[Ann DeLugg/Milton DeLugg] [ASC] (3/16/57 B-87) [I]

BIG BEAT Fats Domino—Imperial 5477
[Dave Bartholomew/Fats Domino] [BMI] (12/21/57 BCR-36)

BIG BIG WORLD Johnny Burnette—Liberty 55318
[Fred Burch/Gerald Nelson/Red West] [BMI] (4/17/61 BCR-43)

BIG BOAT The Tokens—RCA Victor 47-8018
[Luigi Creatore/Hugo Peretti/George David Weiss] [ASC] (4/16/62 R-97)

BIG BOAT Peter, Paul & Mary—Warner Bros. 5325
[Peter Lane*/Elena Mezzetti/Milton Okun*/Paul Stookey] [ASC] (12/15/62 BC-93)

BIG BOPPER'S WEDDING Big Bopper—Mercury 71375
[J.P. Richardson] [BMI] (11/29/58 BCR-34)

BIG BOSS LINE Jackie Wilson—Brunswick 55266
[Alonzo Tucker/Jackie Wilson] [BMI] (5/23/64 BR-75)

BIG BOSS MAN *Jimmy Reed—Vee-Jay 380*
[Luther Dixon/Albert B. Smith] [BMI] (5/29/61 BC-78)

SOUL HOOTENANNY PT. 1 *Gene Chandler—Constellation 114*
[Luther Dixon/Albert B. Smith] [BMI] (4/25/64 BC-90)

BIG BOSS MAN *Elvis Presley—RCA Victor 47-9341*
[Luther Dixon/Albert B. Smith] [BMI] (10/14/67 BCR-36)

BIG BOY PETE The Olympics—Arvee 595
[Don Harris/Dewey Terry] [BMI] (5/23/60 BCR-20)

BIG BROTHER Dickey Lee—Hall 1924
[Jack H. Clement/Dickey Lee/Allen Reynolds] [BMI] (12/12/64 CR-73)

BIG BROWN EYES The Redjacks—Apt 25006 [Lou Bartel] [BMI] (8/18/58 BR-84)

—BIG BRUCE see: BIG BAD JOHN

BIG CITY MISS RUTH ANN Gallery—Sussex 248 [Tom Lazaros] [BMI] (12/23/72 BCR-12)

BIG COLD WIND Pat Boone—Dot 16244
[Stanley Kahan/Robert Mosely] [BMI] (8/14/61 BCR-19)

THE BIG CRASH Eddie Money—Columbia 04199
[Duane Hitchings/Eddie Money] [ASC] (11/19/83 BC-54)

BIG D *Jo Stafford—Columbia 40697 [Frank Loesser] [ASC] (6/22/56 Rt-76)*

BIG D *The DeJohn Sisters—Epic 9172 [Frank Loesser] [ASC] (6/22/56 Rt-76)*

BIG DADDY Jill Corey—Columbia 41202
[Lee Pockriss/Peter Udell] [ASC] (9/1/58 BCR-79)

THE BIG DRAFT The Four Preps—Capitol 4716
[Bruce Belland/Glen Larson] (Med) [BMI] (3/17/62 BCR-61)

BIG FUN Kool & The Gang—De-Lite 822
[Clifford Adams/Robert Bell/Ronald Bell/George M. Brown/Eumir Deodato/Robert Mickens/Michael Ray/Claydes Smith/J.T. Taylor/Curtis Fitzgerald Williams] [BMI] (8/28/82 BC-21)

BIG GIRLS DON'T CRY *The 4 Seasons—Vee-Jay 465*
[Bob Crewe/Bob Gaudio] [BMI] (10/20/62 BCR-1)

BIG GIRLS DON'T CRY *Gidea Park—Profile 5003*
[Bob Crewe/Bob Gaudio] (Med) [BMI] (12/26/81 BC-82)

BIG GUITAR *Owen Bradley Quintet—Decca 30564*
[Frank DeRosa/Robert Genovese] [BMI] (1/27/58 BCtRt-24) [IM]

BIG GUITAR *Sam (The Man) Taylor And His Orchestra—MGM 12613*
[Frank DeRosa/Robert Genovese] [BMI] (1/27/58 CtRt-24) [IM]

BIG GUITAR *Frank DeRosa & His D Men—Dot 15696*
[Frank DeRosa/Robert Genovese] [BMI] (1/27/58 Rt-24) [IM]

BIG GUITAR *Irving Ashby—Imperial 5485*
[Frank DeRosa/Robert Genovese] [BMI] (1/27/58 Rt-24) [IM]

BIG GUITAR *David Hill—RCA Victor 47-7181*
[Larry Coleman/Frank DeRosa/Robert Genovese] [BMI] (3/24/58 Rt-44)

BIG HUNK O' LOVE Elvis Presley—RCA Victor 47-7600
[Aaron Schroeder/Sid Wyche] [BMI] (6/29/59 BCR-1)

THE BIG HURT *Miss Toni Fisher—Signet 275 [Wayne Shanklin] [ASC] (11/16/59 BCR-2)*

THE BIG HURT *Del Shannon—Liberty 55866 [Wayne Shanklin] [ASC] (4/23/66 BCR-91)*

BIG IN JAPAN Alphaville—Atlantic 89665
[Marian Gold/Bernhard Lloyd/Frank Mertens] [BMI] (11/24/84 BC-66)

BIG IN VEGAS Buck Owens And The Buckaroos—Capitol 2646
[Buck Owens/Terry Stafford] [BMI] (11/29/69 BC-97)

BIG IRON Marty Robbins—Columbia 41589 [Marty Robbins] [BMI] (3/14/60 BCR-22)

BIG JOHN The Shirelles—Scepter 1223
[John Patton/Amiel Summers] [BMI] (9/18/61 BCR-21)

BIG LEG WOMAN (WITH A SHORT SHORT MINI SKIRT) Israel "Popper Stopper" Tolbert—Warren 106 [Israel Tolbert] [BMI] (10/31/70 BCR-58)

BIG LOG Robert Plant—Atlantic 99844
[Robbie Blunt/Robert Plant/Jezz Woodroffe*] [ASC] (8/6/83 BC-20)

BIG LOVE Joe Henderson—Todd 1077 [Louis Innis] [BMI] (9/8/62 BCR-68)

BIG LOVE Fleetwood Mac—Warner Bros. 28398
[Lindsey Buckingham] [ASC] (3/28/87 BC-5)

BIG MAN The Four Preps—Capitol 3960
[Bruce Belland/Glen Larson] [BMI] (4/28/58 BCR-5)

BIG MAN IN TOWN
The 4 Seasons Featuring The "Sound" Of Frankie Valli—Philips 40238
[Bob Gaudio] [ASC] (11/7/64 BCR-14)

BIG MISTAKE Peter Cetera—Full Moon 28507
[Peter Cetera/Amos Galpin] [ASC] (1/24/87 BC-55)

THE BIG MONEY Rush—Mercury 884191
[Geddy Lee/Alex Lifeson/Neil Peart] [CA] (11/9/85 BC-45)

BIG NAME BUTTON Royal Teens—ABC-Paramount 9918
[Leon Carr/Buddy Kaye] [ASC] (5/24/58 CR-59)

BIG NOISE FROM WINNETKA Spaghetti Head—Private Stock 45,014
[Ray Bauduc/Bob Crosby/Bob Haggart/Gil Rodin] [ASC] (5/10/75 C-90) [I]

BIG PARTY Barbara And The Browns—Stax 150
[Chips Moman/Jerry L. Williams‡] [BMI] (5/2/64 BR-89)

BIG RIVER Buddy Brennan Quartet—Warwick 517 [Martin Manning] [ASC] (12/14/59 CR-62)

BIG RIVER, BIG MAN Claude King—Columbia 42043 [Mike Phillips] [ASC] (7/17/61 B-82)

BIG SHOT Billy Joel—Columbia 10913 [Billy Joel] [ASC] (2/10/79 BCR-13)

BIG TALK Warrant—Columbia 73035 [Joseph Cagle*/Steven Chamberlin*/Jerry Dixon*/John Oswald/Eric Turner*] [BMI] (11/4/89 BC-86)

BIG TIME Lou Christie—Colpix 799 [Lou Christie/Twyla Herbert] [BMI] (3/19/66 B-95)

BIG TIME Peter Gabriel—Geffen 28503 [Peter Gabriel] [BMI] (11/29/86 BC-8)

BIG TIME OPERATOR Keith Hampshire—A&M 1486 [Tony Colton/Raymond Barry Smith] [ASC] (11/24/73 BCR-58)

THE BIG TIME SPENDER (PART I) Cornbread & Biscuits—Maske 102 [Larry Kerrin/Lea Lendon] [NA] (11/14/60 B-75)

BIG-TOWN BOY Shirley Matthews & The Big Town Girls—Atlantic 2210 [Eddie Rambeau/Bud Rehak] [BMI] (1/18/64 CR-77)

BIG WIDE WORLD Teddy Randazzo—Colpix 662 [Billy Barberis/Teddy Randazzo/Bobby Weinstein] [BMI] (1/26/63 BCR-34)

BIG YELLOW TAXI *The Neighborhood—Big Tree 102 [Joni Mitchell] [ASC] (6/27/70 BCR-24)*

BIG YELLOW TAXI *Joni Mitchell—Reprise 0906 [Joni Mitchell] [ASC] (7/11/70 BC-67)*

BIG YELLOW TAXI *Joni Mitchell—Asylum 45221 [Joni Mitchell] [ASC] (12/21/74 BCR-24)*

BIGFOOT Bro Smith—Big Tree 16061 [Jonas Cash] [BMI] (4/24/76 BCR-53)

THE BIGGEST PARAKEETS IN TOWN Jud Strunk—Melodyland 6015 [Charlie Drew/Jud Strunk] [ASC] (6/28/75 BCR-50)

BIGGEST PART OF ME Ambrosia—Warner Bros. 49225 [David Pack] [BMI] (4/5/80 BCR-2)

THE BIGGEST SIN OF ALL Connie Francis—MGM 13087 [Benny Davis/Ted Murry] [ASC] (8/11/62 CR-89)

BIKINI The Bikinis—Roulette 4073 [John Altwerger/Sol Schlinger] [BMI] (5/31/58 CR-57)

THE BILBAO SONG Andy Williams—Cadence 1398 [Berthold Brecht/Johnny Mercer/Kurt Weill] [ASC] (4/17/61 BCR-19) [FET]

BILL BAILEY, WON'T YOU PLEASE COME HOME *Maria Marshall—Beech 712 [Hughie Cannon] [NA] (9/8/56 R-75)*

BILL BAILEY WON'T YOU PLEASE COME HOME *Brenda Lee—Decca 30806 [Hughie Cannon] [NA] (2/2/59 R-78)*

WON'T YOU COME HOME BILL BAILEY *Bobby Darin—Atco 6167 [Hughie Cannon] [NA] (5/23/60 BCR-16)*

WON'CHA COME HOME, BILL BAILEY *Della Reese—RCA Victor 47-7867 [Hughie Cannon] [NA] (4/3/61 BR-74)*

BILL BAILEY, WON'T YOU PLEASE COME HOME *Ella Fitzgerald—Verve 10288 [Hughie Cannon] [NA] (4/6/63 BR-75)*

BILLIE BABY Lloyd Price—Double-L 729 [Harold Logan/Lloyd Price] [BMI] (1/11/64 BR-84)

BILLIE JEAN *Michael Jackson—Epic 03509 [Michael Jackson] [BMI] (1/22/83 BC-1)*

BILLIE JEAN *Club House—Atlantic 89795 [Michael Jackson] (Med) [BMI] (8/6/83 BC-75)*

BILLION DOLLAR BABIES Alice Cooper—Warner Bros. 7724 [Michael Bruce/Alice Cooper/Reggie Vinson] [BMI] (8/4/73 BCR-36)

BILLY Kathy Linden—Felsted 8510 [Joe Goodwin/James Kendis/Herman Paley] [ASC] (3/3/58 BCR-5)

BILLY AND SUE B.J. Thomas And The Triumphs—Hickory 1395 [Mark Charron] [BMI] (6/18/66 BCR-23)

BILLY BAYOU Jim Reeves—RCA Victor 47-7380 [Roger Miller] [BMI] (12/8/58 B-95)

BILLY BOY'S TUNE The Three Graces—Golden Crest 528 [Jack Evans/Cy Levitan] [ASC] (8/29/59 C-100)

—BILLY, I'VE GOT TO GO TO TOWN see: RUBY, DON'T TAKE YOUR LOVE TO TOWN

BILLY, DON'T BE A HERO *Bo Donaldson And The Heywoods—ABC 11435 [Peter Callander/Mitch Murray] [BMI] (4/13/74 BCR-1)*

BILLY—DON'T BE A HERO *Paper Lace—Mercury 73479 [Peter Callander/Mitch Murray] [BMI] (4/20/74 BCR-68)*

BILLY YOU'RE MY FRIEND Gene Pitney—Musicor 1331 [Ed Goldman] [BMI] (11/2/68 BCR-90)

BIMBOMBEY Jimmie Rodgers—Roulette 4116 [Luigi Creatore/Mack David/Hugo Peretti] [ASC] (11/10/58 BCR-11)

BIMINI BIMBO (DOIN' THE LIMBO) Teddy And The Twilights—Swan 4126 [Doc Pomus/Mort Shuman] [BMI] (12/8/62 R-99)

BIOLOGY *Danny Valentino—MGM 12881 [Sherman Edwards/Sid Wayne] [ASC] (5/7/60 BCtRt-65)*

BIOLOGY *Sue Raney—Capitol 4360 [Sherman Edwards/Sid Wayne] [ASC] (5/21/60 CtRt-76)*

THE BIPLANE, EVER MORE The Irish Rovers—Decca 32371 [Marty Cooper] [BMI] (9/14/68 BCR-78)

THE BIRD The Time—Warner Bros. 29094 [Morris Day/Prince] [ASC] (2/23/85 BC-36)

BIRD DANCE BEAT The Trashmen—Garrett 4003 [George Garrett] [BMI] (2/8/64 BCR-26)

BIRD DOG The Everly Brothers—Cadence 1350 [Boudleaux Bryant] [BMI] (8/4/58 BCR-2)

THE BIRD HAS FLOWN Deep Purple—Tetragrammaton 1519 [Ritchie Blackmore/Rod Evans/Jon Lord] [ASC] (3/22/69 C-99)

A BIRD IN A GILDED CAGE Crazy Otto—Decca 29753A [Harry Von Tilzer] (Med) [ASC] (2/3/56 R-90) [IM]

THE BIRD MAN The Highwaymen—United Artists 475 [Elmer Bernstein/Mack David] [ASC] (7/7/62 BCR-64)

THE BIRD ON MY HEAD David Seville—Liberty 55140 [David Seville] [ASC] (6/21/58 BC-36)

BIRDLAND Chubby Checker—Parkway 873 [Kal Mann/Huey P. Smith/John Vincent*] [BMI] (5/18/63 BCR-12)

BIRDMAN PART ONE (TITLE NO. 1 AGAIN) Rare Bird—Polydor 15079 [Andrew Curtis/David Franklin Ewer/Steve Gould/Paul Karas/Fred Kelly] [BMI] (9/1/73 R-96)

THE BIRDS AND THE BEES Jewel Akens—Era 3141 [Herbert Newman] [ASC] (1/23/65 BCR-2)

—BIRDS ARE FOR THE BEES see: BEES ARE FOR THE BIRDS

BIRDS OF A FEATHER *Joe South—Capitol 2060 [Joe South] [BMI] (1/27/68 BCR-94)*

BIRDS OF A FEATHER *Raiders—Columbia 45453 [Joe South] [BMI] (9/4/71 BCR-13)*

BIRDS OF ALL NATIONS George McCannon III—Amos 135 [Ray Buzzeo] [BMI] (5/9/70 C-97)

BIRDS OF BRITAIN The Bob Crewe Generation—DynoVoice 902 [Bob Crewe/Bob Davie] [BMI] (10/28/67 BR-89) [I]

THE BIRD'S THE WORD *The Rivingtons—Liberty 55553 [Al Frazier/John Earl (Sonny) Harris/Carl White/Turner Wilson] [BMI] (3/30/63 BCR-43)*

THE BIRD IS THE WORD *(as part of Surfin' Bird) The Trashmen—Garrett 4002 [Al Frazier/John Earl (Sonny) Harris/Carl White/Turner Wilson] (Med) [BMI] (12/7/63 BCR-2)*

BIRMINGHAM BLUES Charlie Daniels Band—Kama Sutra 606 [Charlie Daniels] [BMI] (11/29/75 C-79)

—BIRTH AND DEATH OF A GANGSTER see: ALVIN STONE

THE BIRTH OF THE BEAT Sandy Nelson—Imperial 5809 [Sandy Nelson] [BMI] (2/24/62 B-75) [I]

THE BIRTH OF THE BLUES *Sammy Davis Jr.—Decca 29393 [Lew Brown/Buddy DeSylva/Ray Henderson] [ASC] (1/17/55 Rt-74)*

THE BIRTH OF THE BLUES *Lenny Dee—Decca 29360 [Lew Brown/Buddy DeSylva/Ray Henderson] [ASC] (1/17/55 Rt-74)*

BIRTH OF THE BOOGIE Bill Haley And His Comets—Decca 29418 [Johnny Grande/Bill Haley/Billy Williamson] (TSW) [BMI] (4/16/55 BCR-18)

BIRTHDAY Underground Sunshine—Intrepid 75002 [John Lennon/Paul McCartney] [ASC] (7/12/69 BCR-19)

BIRTHDAY PARTY Sil Austin—Mercury 71027 [Sil Austin] [BMI] (2/2/57 BR-74) [I]

BIRTHDAY PARTY The Pixies Three—Mercury 72130 [John Madara/David White] [BMI] (8/17/63 BCR-40)

BIRTHDAY SUIT Johnny Kemp—Columbia 68569 [Rhett Lawrence/Dean Pitchford] [BMI] (2/18/89 BC-31)

BISCUIT'S IN THE HOUSE Biscuit—Columbia 73585 [Steve Arcand*/Andy Fraser/Rob Hathcock/Joseph E. Malloy/Paul Rodgers/Steven Walker] [ASC] (10/27/90 BC-75)

BIT BY BIT Stephanie Mills—MCA 52617 [Harold Faltermeyer/Franne Golde] [ASC] (7/6/85 BC-76)

THE BITCH IS BACK Elton John—MCA 40297 [Elton John/Bernie Taupin] [BMI] (9/7/74 BCR-4)

BITE YOUR LIP (GET UP AND DANCE!) Elton John—MCA/Rocket 40677 [Elton John/Bernie Taupin] [BMI] (2/12/77 BCR-28)

BITS AND PIECES The Dave Clark Five—Epic 9671 [Dave Clark/Mike Smith] [BMI] (3/28/64 BCR-3)

BITTER BAD Melanie—Neighborhood 4210 [Melanie Safka] [ASC] (2/10/73 BCR-30)

BITTER TEARS INXS—Atlantic 87760 [Andy Farriss/Michael Hutchence] [ASC] (4/6/91 BC-36)

BITTER WITH THE SWEET Billy Eckstine—RCA Victor 47-6436 [Stanley Kahan/Eddie Snyder] [ASC] (3/2/56 BR-55)

BLACK AND BLUE Van Halen—Warner Bros. 27891 [Michael Anthony/Sammy Hagar/Alex Van Halen/Eddie Van Halen] [ASC] (5/21/88 BC-34)

BLACK AND TAN FANTASY David Rose And His Orchestra—MGM 13086 [Duke Ellington/Bubber Miley] [ASC] (8/11/62 R-96) [I]

BLACK AND WHITE Three Dog Night—Dunhill 4317 [David Arkin/Earl Robinson] [ASC] (7/29/72 BCR-1)

BLACK BERRIES - PT. 1 The Isley Brothers—T-Neck 906 [O'Kelly Isley] [ASC] (8/30/69 BCR-43)

BLACK BETTY Ram Jam—Epic 50357 [Huddie Ledbetter] [BMI] (6/4/77 BCR-13)

BLACK BYRD Donald Byrd—Blue Note 212 [Larry Mizell] [ASC] (5/26/73 BCR-71)

BLACK CARS Gino Vannelli—HME 04889 [Roy Freeland/Gino Vannelli] [BMI] (5/4/85 BC-42)

BLACK CAT Janet Jackson—A&M 1477 [Janet Jackson] [BMI] (9/8/90 BC-1)

BLACK CLOUD Chubby Checker—Parkway 873 [Bill Brock] [BMI] (6/1/63 BC-89)

BLACK DENIM TROUSERS AND MOTORCYCLE BOOTS *The Cheers—Capitol 3219 [Jerry Leiber/Mike Stoller] [BMI] (9/12/55 BCtRt-6)*

BLACK DENIM TROUSERS AND MOTORCYCLE BOOTS *Vaughn Monroe with Chorus And Orchestra—RCA Victor 47-6260 [Jerry Leiber/Mike Stoller] [BMI] (9/19/55 BCtRt-6)*

BLACK DOG *Led Zeppelin—Atlantic 2849*
[John Paul Jones/Jimmy Page/Robert Plant] [ASC] (12/18/71 BCR-9)

BLACK DOG *Newcity Rockers—Critique 728*
[John Paul Jones/Jimmy Page/Robert Plant] [ASC] (4/18/87 BC-66)

BLACK-EYED BLUES Joe Cocker—A&M 1258
[Joe Cocker/Chris Stainton] (TSW) [ASC] (6/12/71 BC-22)

THE BLACK-EYED BOYS Paper Lace—Mercury 73620
[Peter Callander/Mitch Murray] [ASC] (10/5/74 BCR-41)

BLACK FOX Freddy Robinson—World Pacific 88155
[Monk Higgins] [BMI] (7/25/70 BCR-45) [I]

BLACK FRIDAY Steely Dan—ABC 12101
[Walter Becker/Donald Fagen] [ASC] (5/17/75 BCR-31)

BLACK HANDS WHITE COTTON The Caboose—Enterprise 9015
[David Bell/Kenneth Edward Bell/C.P. Reeves] [BMI] (7/18/70 BCR-67)

BLACK IS BLACK *Los Bravos—Press 60002*
[Michelle Grainger/Tony Hayes/Steve Wadey] [BMI] (8/13/66 BCR-2)

BLACK IS BLACK *Tight Fit—Arista 0638*
[Michelle Grainger/Tony Hayes/Steve Wadey] (Med) [BMI] (10/10/81 B-89)

BLACK KISSES (NEVER MAKE YOU BLUE) Curtie And The Boombox—RCA 14103
[Peter Koelewijn] [ASC] (7/27/85 BC-81)

BLACK LAND FARMER *Frankie Miller—Starday 424*
[Frankie Miller] [BMI] (7/10/61 BCtRt-78)

BLACK LAND FARMER *Wink Martindale—Dot 16243*
[Frankie Miller] [BMI] (7/31/61 BCtRt-77)

BLACK LASSIE (FEATURING JOHNNY STASH) Cheech & Chong—Ode 66104
[Tommy Chong/Cheech Marin/Billy Page/Gene Page] [ASC] (11/2/74 BCR-47) [P]

BLACK LEATHER Kings Of The Sun—RCA 8646
[Cliff Hoad/Jeff Hoad] [BMI] (7/30/88 B-98)

BLACK MAGIC WOMAN Santana—Columbia 45270 [Peter Green] [BMI] (11/7/70 BCR-3)

BLACK NIGHT Bobby Bland—Duke 386 [Jessie Mae Robinson] [ASC] (1/2/65 B-99)

BLACK NIGHT Deep Purple—Warner Bros. 7405
[Ritchie Blackmore/Ian Gillan/Roger Glover/Jon Lord/Ian Paice] [ASC]
(12/5/70 BCR-61)

BLACK NIGHTS Lowell Fulsom—Kent 431
[Ferdinand Washington] [BMI] (12/25/65 BCR-87)

BLACK OR WHITE Michael Jackson—Epic 74100
[Michael Jackson] [BMI] (11/23/91 BC-1)

BLACK PEARL Sonny Charles And The Checkmates, Ltd.—A&M 1053
[Irwin Levine/Phil Spector/Toni Wine] [BMI] (4/26/69 BCR-10)

BLACK SEEDS KEEP ON GROWING The Main Ingredient—RCA Victor 74-0517
[Donald McPherson] [BMI] (9/4/71 BCR-74)

BLACK SHEEP Sam The Sham And The Pharaohs—MGM 13747
[Bob McDill] [ASC] (6/10/67 BCR-61)

BLACK SLACKS Joe Bennett And The Sparkletones—ABC-Paramount 9837
[Joe Bennett/Jimmy Denton] [BMI] (7/20/57 BCR-16)

BLACK STATIONS/WHITE STATIONS M+M—RCA 13802
[Mark Gane/Martha Johnson] [ASC] (6/30/84 BC-63)

BLACK SUPERMAN - "MUHAMMAD ALI"
Johnny Wakelin And The Kinshasa Band—Pye 71012
[Johnny Wakelin] [ASC] (3/8/75 BCR-18)

BLACK VELVET Alannah Myles—Atlantic 88742
[David Tyson/Christopher Ward] [BMI] (12/30/89 BC-1)

BLACK WATER The Doobie Brothers—Warner Bros. 8062
[Patrick Simmons] [ASC] (12/21/74 BCR-1)

BLACKJACK Rupert Holmes—MCA 51045 [Rupert Holmes] [ASC] (2/14/81 C-92)

BLAH BLAH BLAH Nicola Paone—ABC-Paramount 9993
[Nicola Paone] [ASC] (1/31/59 BCRt*-36)

BLAH-BLAH-BLAH Steve Lawrence—Coral 62080
[George Gershwin/Ira Gershwin] [ASC] (2/9/59 Rt*-76)

BLAME IT ON LOVE Smokey Robinson & Barbara Mitchell—Tamla 1684
[Dave DeLuca/Ted Munda] [BMI] (7/2/83 BC-48)

BLAME IT ON THE BOOGIE *Mick Jackson—Atco 7091*
[Dave Jackson/Mick Jackson/Elmar Krohn] [ASC] (8/12/78 BCR-61)

BLAME IT ON THE BOOGIE *The Jacksons—Epic 50595*
[Dave Jackson/Mick Jackson/Elmar Krohn] [ASC] (9/30/78 BCR-54)

BLAME IT ON THE BOSSA NOVA Eydie Gorme—Columbia 42661
[Barry Mann/Cynthia Weil] [BMI] (1/19/63 BCR-6)

BLAME IT ON THE RADIO John Parr—Atlantic 89333 [John Parr] [ASC] (12/13/86 B-88)

BLAME IT ON THE RAIN Milli Vanilli—Arista 1-9904
[Diane Warren] [ASC] (10/7/89 BC-1)

BLANKET ON THE GROUND Billie Jo Spears—United Artists 584
[Roger Bowling] [BMI] (5/3/75 BCR-69)

BLAZE OF GLORY Kenny Rogers—Liberty 1441
[Larry Keith/Danny Morrison/Johnny Slate] [BMI] (11/21/81 BCR-66)

BLAZE OF GLORY Jon Bon Jovi—Mercury 875 896 [Jon Bon Jovi] [ASC] (7/21/90 BC-1)

BLESS OUR LOVE *Gene Chandler—Constellation 136*
[William Earl Butler] [BMI] (9/26/64 BCR-39)

GOD BLESS OUR LOVE *The Ballads—Venture 615*
[William Earl Butler] [BMI] (7/20/68 BCR-41)

BLESS THE BEASTS AND CHILDREN *Carpenters—A&M 1289*
[Perry Botkin Jr./Barry De Vorzon] (TSW) [BMI] (11/20/71 B-16)

BLESS THE BEASTS AND CHILDREN *Barry De Vorzon & Perry Botkin, Jr.—A&M 1890*
[Perry Botkin Jr./Barry De Vorzon] [BMI] (1/22/77 B-82) [IWM]

BLESS YOU Tony Orlando—Epic 9452 [Barry Mann/Cynthia Weil] [BMI] (7/31/61 BCR-11)

BLESS YOU Martha Reeves & The Vandellas—Gordy 7110
[Berry Gordy/Fonce Mizell/Freddie Perren/Deke Richards] [ASC] (10/9/71 BCR-43)

BLESS YOUR HEART *Bob Dini—Coral 61307*
[Milton Drake/Duke Enston/Harry Stride] [NA] (12/6/54 Rt-PRE)

BLESS YOUR HEART *The Fontane Sisters with Billy Vaughn's Orchestra—Dot 15265*
[Milton Drake/Duke Enston/Harry Stride] [NA] (12/6/54 Rt-24)

BLESSED ARE THE BELIEVERS Anne Murray—Capitol 4987
[Charlie Black/Rory Bourke/Sandy Pinkard] [ASC] (3/28/81 BCR-34)

BLESSED ARE THE LONELY Robert Knight—Rising Sons 707
[Buzz Cason/Mac Gayden] [BMI] (1/20/68 BR-90)

BLESSED IS THE RAIN The Brooklyn Bridge Featuring Johnny Maestro—Buddah 95
[Tony Romeo] [BMI] (3/8/69 BCR-36)

BLIND EYE Uriah Heep—Mercury 73349 [Ken Hensley] (TSW) [ASC] (1/20/73 BR-87)

BLIND FAITH Warrant—Columbia 73598
[Joseph Cagle*/Steven Chamberlin*/Jerry Dixon*/John Oswald/Eric Turner*] [BMI]
(6/29/91 BC-84)

BLIND MAN *Little Milton—Checker 1096*
[Deadric Malone/Joe Scott] [BMI] (12/26/64 BCtRt-47)

BLIND MAN *Bobby Bland—Duke 386*
[Deadric Malone/Joe Scott] [BMI] (12/26/64 BCtRt-47)

—BLIND MAN IN THE BLEACHERS see: LAST GAME OF THE SEASON

BLINDED BY LOVE Rythm Syndicate—Impact 54275
[Evan Rogers/Carl Sturken] [BMI] (12/28/91 C-58)

BLINDED BY THE LIGHT Manfred Mann's Earth Band—Warner Bros. 8252
[Bruce Springsteen] [ASC] (11/13/76 BCR-1)

BLIP BLOP Bill Doggett—King 5138 [Candy Johnson] [BMI] (8/4/58 B-82) [I]

BLISTERED Johnny Cash—Columbia 45020
[Billy Edd Wheeler] (TSW) [ASC] (11/29/69 BC-50)

THE BLIZZARD Jim Reeves—RCA Victor 47-7855 [Harlan Howard] [BMI] (3/13/61 BCR-47)

—BLOAT ON see: FLOAT ON

THE BLOB *The Five Blobs—Columbia 41250*
[Burt Bacharach/Mack David] [ASC] (10/6/58 BCRt-33)

THE BLOB *The Zanies—Era 1080*
[Burt Bacharach/Mack David] [ASC] (10/20/58 Rt-77)

BLOCKBUSTER The Sweet—Bell 45,361
[Mike Chapman/Nicky Chinn] [ASC] (6/9/73 BCR-43)

BLONDE BOMBSHELL Don Rondo—Jubilee 5319
[Billy Mure/Dick Wolf] [BMI] (3/17/58 R-85)

BLOOD IS THICKER THAN WATER William Devaughn—Roxbury 2001
[Russell Faith/Palmer C. Rakes] [ASC] (9/7/74 BCR-43)

BLOOD RED AND GOIN' DOWN Tanya Tucker—Columbia 45892
[Curly Putman] [BMI] (8/25/73 BC-74)

BLOODY WELL RIGHT Supertramp—A&M 1660
[Rick Davies/Roger Hodgson] [ASC] (4/5/75 BCR-35)

A BLOSSOM FELL *Dickie Valentine—London 1554*
[Howard Ellington Riddiford Barnes/Harold Fields/Joseph Roncoroni] [ASC]
(4/25/55 Rt-3)

A BLOSSOM FELL *Vic Barrett—London 1566*
[Howard Ellington Riddiford Barnes/Harold Fields/Joseph Roncoroni] [ASC]
(5/2/55 Rt-14)

A BLOSSOM FELL *Nat "King" Cole—Capitol 3095*
[Howard Ellington Riddiford Barnes/Harold Fields/Joseph Roncoroni] (TSW) [ASC]
(5/21/55 BCRt-2)

BLOW AWAY George Harrison—Dark Horse 8763
[George Harrison] [ASC] (2/24/79 BCR-12)

BLOWIN' IN THE WIND *Peter, Paul & Mary—Warner Bros. 5368*
[Bob Dylan] [SE] (6/29/63 BCR-2)

BLOWIN' IN THE WIND *Stevie Wonder—Tamla 54136 [Bob Dylan] [SE] (7/16/66 BCR-8)*

BLOWING AWAY The 5th Dimension—Soul City 780 [Laura Nyro] [BMI] (1/3/70 BCR-12)

BLOWING KISSES IN THE WIND Paula Abdul—Captive/Virgin 98683
[Peter Lord] [ASC] (10/19/91 BC-3)

BLT Lee Oskar—United Artists 807 [Greg Errico/Lee Oskar] [ASC] (6/26/76 BCR-59) [I]

BLUE ANGEL Roy Orbison—Monument 425
[Joe Melson/Roy Orbison] [BMI] (9/5/60 BCR-9)

BLUE AUTUMN Bobby Goldsboro—United Artists 50087
[Bobby Goldsboro] [BMI] (11/26/66 BCR-30)

BLUE BAYOU *Roy Orbison—Monument 824*
[Joe Melson/Roy Orbison] [BMI] (9/7/63 BCR-10)

BLUE BAYOU *Linda Ronstadt—Asylum 45431*
[Joe Melson/Roy Orbison] [BMI] (9/10/77 BCR-2)

BLUE BLUE DAY Don Gibson—RCA Victor 47-7010 [Don Gibson] [BMI] (6/9/58 BCR-16)

BLUE BOLERO Richard Hayes—ABC-Paramount 9706
[Roy Alfred/Shorty Allen] [ASC] (6/8/56 R-80)

BLUE BOY Jim Reeves—RCA Victor 47-7266 [Boudleaux Bryant] [BMI] (7/19/58 BCR-45)

BLUE CHRISTMAS *Elvis Presley—RCA Victor LOC-1035 [Billy Hayes/Jay Johnson] (EP) [ASC] (12/30/57 R-49)*

BLUE CHRISTMAS *The Browns Featuring Jim Edward Brown—RCA Victor 47-7866 [Billy Hayes/Jay Johnson] [ASC] (12/19/60 B-97)*

BLUE COLLAR Bachman-Turner Overdrive—Mercury 73417 [C.F. Turner] [BMI] (11/24/73 BCR-58)

BLUE COLLAR MAN (LONG NIGHTS) Styx—A&M 2087 [Tommy Shaw] [ASC] (9/9/78 BCR-20)

BLUE COMET BLUES Bill Haley And His Comets—Decca 30085 [Franny Beecher/Al Rex] [BMI] (11/3/56 R-71) [I]

BLUE EYES Elton John—Geffen 29954 [Elton John/Gary Osborne] [BMI] (7/10/82 BC-10)

BLUE EYES CRYING IN THE RAIN Willie Nelson—Columbia 10176 [Fred Rose] [ASC] (8/23/75 BCR-21)

BLUE FLAME Billy Vaughn And His Orchestra—Dot 16397 [Joe Bishop/James Noble] [ASC] (10/13/62 R-85) [IM]

BLUE GUITAR Larry Lawrence—King 5183 [Larry Fotine/Frank Stanton] [ASC] (3/9/59 R-100)

BLUE GUITAR Richard Chamberlain—MGM 13170 [Burt Bacharach/Hal David] [ASC] (9/28/63 BCR-41)

BLUE GUITAR Justin Hayward And John Lodge—Threshold 67021 [Justin Hayward] [ASC] (12/6/75 BC-82)

BLUE HAWAII Billy Vaughn And His Orchestra—Dot 15879 [Ralph Rainger] [ASC] (12/22/58 BCR-20) [IM]

BLUE HEARTACHES Tommy Edwards—MGM 12916 [Gene Pitney] [BMI] (10/17/60 R-96)

BLUE JAY LuAnn Simms—Jubilee 5370 [Noel Sherman/Dick Wolf] [BMI] (5/11/59 R-95)

BLUE JEAN David Bowie—EMI America 8231 [David Bowie] [ASC] (9/15/84 BC-5)

BLUE JEANS Chocolate Milk—RCA Victor 12335 [Lee Hayes/Howard Redmon] [BMI] (12/12/81 R-93)

BLUE KISS Jane Wiedlin—I.R.S. 52674 [Randell Kirsch/Jane Wiedlin] [ASC] (9/28/85 BC-74)

BLUE LIGHT David Gilmour—Columbia 04378 [David Gilmour] [BMI] (4/7/84 BC-62)

BLUE MIRAGE *Monty Kelly & His Orchestra with Dr. Samuel Hoffman—Essex 386 [Lotar Olias] [ASC] (1/31/55 Rt-65) [IM]*

BLUE MIRAGE (DON'T GO) *Les Baxter & His Orchestra—Capitol 3040 [Sam Coslow/Lotar Olias] [ASC] (1/31/55 Rt-13)*

BLUE MIRAGE (DON'T GO) *Guy Lombardo And His Royal Canadians—Decca 29377 [Lotar Olias] [ASC] (1/31/55 CtRt-11) [IM]*

BLUE MIRAGE (DON'T GO) *Ralph Marterie And His Orchestra—Mercury 70535 [Lotar Olias] [ASC] (1/31/55 CtRt-11) [IM]*

BLUE MIRAGE (DON'T GO) *Percy Faith & His Orchestra—Columbia 40428 [Sam Coslow/Lotar Olias] [ASC] (2/7/55 Rt-39)*

BLUE MIRAGE *Frank Chacksfield & His Orchestra—London 1535 [Sam Coslow/Lotar Olias] [ASC] (3/14/55 Rt-13)*

BLUE MONDAY Fats Domino—Imperial 5417 [Dave Bartholomew/Fats Domino*] [BMI] (12/22/56 BCR-5)

BLUE MONDAY 1988 New Order—Qwest 27979 [Gillian Gilbert/Peter Hook/Stephen Morris/Bernard Sumner] [ASC] (4/30/88 BC-68)

BLUE MONEY Van Morrison—Warner Bros. 7462 [Van Morrison] [BMI] (2/6/71 BCR-14)

BLUE MOON *Elvis Presley—RCA Victor 47-6640 [Lorenz Hart/Richard Rodgers] [ASC] (9/29/56 BCR-36)*

BLUE MOON *Jimmy Bowen With The Rhythm Orchids—Roulette 4102 [Lorenz Hart/Richard Rodgers] [ASC] (10/11/58 C-92)*

BLUE MOON *The Marcels—Colpix 186 [Lorenz Hart/Richard Rodgers] [ASC] (2/27/61 BCR-1)*

BLUE MOON *Herb Lance & The Classics—Promo 1010 [Lorenz Hart/Richard Rodgers] [ASC] (3/6/61 BR-50)*

BLUE MOON *The Ventures—Dolton 47 [Richard Rodgers] [ASC] (10/16/61 BCR-54) [IM]*

BLUE MOON OF KENTUCKY Dick Haiman And the Dial Tones—Horizon 1596 [Bill Monroe] [BMI] (10/9/61 R-99)

BLUE MORNING, BLUE DAY Foreigner—Atlantic 3543 [Lou Gramm/Michael Leslie Jones] [ASC] (12/23/78 BCR-15)

BLUE ON BLUE Bobby Vinton—Epic 9593 [Burt Bacharach/Hal David] [ASC] (5/18/63 BCR-1)

BLUE RIBBON BABY Tommy Sands And The Raiders—Capitol 4036 [Diane Lampert/Scott Turner] [BMI] (9/1/58 BC-50)

BLUE RIVER Elvis Presley—RCA Victor 47-8740 [Paul Evans/Fred Tobias] [ASC] (1/1/66 BC-95)

BLUE SHADOWS B.B. King—Kent 426 [Lowell Fulsom] [BMI] (6/12/65 BC-97)

THE BLUE SIDE Crystal Gayle—Columbia 11270 [David Lasley/Allee Willis] [ASC] (6/7/80 BC-81)

BLUE SIDE OF LONESOME Jim Reeves—RCA Victor 47-8902 [Leon Payne] [BMI] (8/27/66 BCR-59)

BLUE SKIRT WALTZ Luther Brandon And His All American Boys—Fraternity 852 [Vaclav Blaha/Mitchell Parish] [ASC] (8/10/59 R-85)

BLUE SKY Joan Baez—A&M 1703 [Dickey Betts] [BMI] (7/12/75 BCR-57)

BLUE SKY MINE Midnight Oil—Columbia 73250 [Peter Garrett/Peter Gifford*/Rob Hirst/James Moginie/Martin Rotsey*] [BMI] (2/17/90 BC-27)

—BLUE STAR see: THEME FROM "MEDIC"

BLUE STRINGS Hugo Winterhalter and his Orchestra—RCA Victor 47-7599 [Mort Garson] [ASC] (10/12/59 R-91) [I]

BLUE SUEDE SHOES *Carl Perkins—Sun 234 [Carl Perkins] [BMI] (3/3/56 BCRt-1)*

BLUE SUEDE SHOES *Boyd Bennett And His Rockets—King 4903 [Carl Perkins] [BMI] (3/23/56 BRt-1)*

BLUE SUEDE SHOES *Bob Roubian—Capitol 3373 [Carl Perkins] [BMI] (3/23/56 Rt-1)*

BLUE SUEDE SHOES *Elvis Presley—RCA Victor EPA-747 [Carl Perkins] [BMI] (4/7/56 BRt-2)*

BLUE SUEDE SHOES *Jim Lowe—Dot 15456 [Carl Perkins] [BMI] (4/13/56 Rt-1)*

BLUE SUEDE SHOES *Cat Mother And The All Night News Boys—Polydor 14002 [Carl Perkins] (Med) [BMI] (6/21/69 BCR-12)*

BLUE SUEDE SHOES *Johnny Rivers—United Artists 198 [Carl Perkins] [BMI] (3/3/73 BCR-27)*

BLUE TANGO Bill Black's Combo—Hi 2027 [Leroy Anderson] [ASC] (11/21/60 BCR-11) [I]

BLUE TOMORROW Billy Vaughn And His Orchestra—Dot 16220 [Tommy Griffin/Freddie Morris] [BMI] (5/29/61 BCR-50) [I]

BLUE VELVET *The Statues—Liberty 55245 [Lee Morris/Bernie Wayne] [ASC] (8/8/60 BCR-80)*

BLUE VELVET *Bobby Vinton—Epic 9614 [Lee Morris/Bernie Wayne] [ASC] (8/10/63 BCR-1)*

BLUE WATER LINE The Brothers Four—Columbia 42256 [Dora Graf/Martin Seligson] [BMI] (1/20/62 BCR-56)

BLUE WINTER Connie Francis—MGM 13214 [John Gluck/Ben Raleigh] [BMI] (2/8/64 BCR-13)

BLUE WORLD The Moody Blues—Threshold 6054 [Justin Hayward] [ASC] (11/12/83 BC-62)

BLUEBELL *Mitch Miller and His Orchestra and Chorus—Columbia 41235 [Jerry Livingston/Paul Francis Webster] [ASC] (10/13/58 BRt-94)*

BLUE BELL *Scott Engel—Orbit 512 [Jerry Livingston/Paul Francis Webster] [ASC] (10/20/58 Rt-95)*

BLUEBERRIES Georgia Gibbs—Mercury 70647 [Jerry Leiber/Mike Stoller] [BMI] (6/27/55 CR-45)

BLUEBERRY HILL *Fats Domino—Imperial 5407 [Al Lewis/Vincent Rose/Larry Stock] [ASC] (9/29/56 BCRt-3)*

BLUEBERRY HILL *Louis Armstrong and Gordon Jenkins and His Orchestra And Chorus—Decca 30091 [Al Lewis/Vincent Rose/Larry Stock] [ASC] (10/20/56 BRt-3)*

BLUEBIRD The Buffalo Springfield—Atco 6499 [Stephen Stills] [BMI] (7/8/67 BCR-58)

BLUEBIRD Helen Reddy—Capitol 4108 [Leon Russell] [BMI] (6/28/75 BCR-34)

BLUEBIRD THE BUZZARD AND THE ORIOLE Bobby Day—Class 241 [Leon René] [BMI] (12/20/58 BCR-54)

BLUEBIRDS OVER THE MOUNTAIN *Ersel Hickey—Epic 9263 [Ersel Hickey] [BMI] (3/29/58 BCR-39)*

BLUEBIRDS OVER THE MOUNTAIN *The Echoes—Smash 1766 [Ersel Hickey] [BMI] (11/10/62 C-86)*

BLUEBIRDS OVER THE MOUNTAIN *The Beach Boys—Capitol 2360 [Ersel Hickey] [BMI] (11/30/68 BCR-36)*

BLUEJEAN BOP Gene Vincent and His Blue Caps—Capitol 3558 [Hal Levy/Gene Vincent] [NA] (10/20/56 R-59)

BLUER THAN BLUE Michael Johnson—EMI America 8001 [Randy Goodrum] [ASC] (4/22/78 BCR-10)

THE BLUES Randy Newman and Paul Simon—Warner Bros. 29803 [Randy Newman] [ASC] (1/15/83 BC-51)

THE BLUES Tony! Toni! Tone!—Wing 873 994 [Raphael Saadiq/Dwayne Wiggins] [ASC] (6/2/90 BC-46)

BLUES BEFORE AND AFTER The Smithereens—Enigma/Capitol 44516 [Pat DiNizio] [BMI] (5/5/90 BC-87)

BLUES FOR ME Eddie Fisher—RCA Victor 47-6849 [Jerry Leiber/Mike Stoller] [BMI] (3/16/57 R-58)

THE BLUES FROM KISS ME DEADLY (I'D RATHER HAVE THE BLUES) Nat "King" Cole—Capitol 3136 [Frank DeVol] [ASC] (6/6/55 CR-46)

BLUES POWER (LIVE) Eric Clapton—RSO 1051 [Eric Clapton/Leon Russell] [BMI] (11/8/80 B-76)

BLUES STAY AWAY FROM ME *Billy Vaughn And His Orchestra—Dot 15960 [Alton Delmore/Rabon Delmore/Henry Glover/Wayne Raney] [BMI] (7/25/59 C-82) [IWM]*

BLUES (STAY AWAY FROM ME) *Ace Cannon—Hi 2051 [Alton Delmore/Rabon Delmore/Henry Glover/Wayne Raney] [BMI] (4/2/62 BCR-33) [IWM]*

BLUE'S THEME The Arrows Featuring Davie Allen—Tower 295 [Davie Allan*/Mike Curb] [BMI] (4/15/67 BCR-27) [IWM]

BO DIDDLEY *Joe Reisman and His Orchestra And Chorus—RCA Victor 47-6121 [Ellas McDaniel] [BMI] (5/2/55 CtRt-29)*

BO DIDDLEY *Bo Diddley—Checker 814 [Ellas McDaniel] [BMI] (5/9/55 CtRt-29)*

BO DIDDLEY *Jerry Murad's Harmonicats—Mercury 70629 [Ellas McDaniel] [BMI] (5/23/55 Rt-40)*

BO WEEVIL *Teresa Brewer—Coral 61590 [Dave Bartholomew/Fats Domino] [BMI] (2/25/56 BCtRt-15)*

***BO WEEVIL** Fats Domino—Imperial 5375*
[Dave Bartholomew/Fats Domino] [BMI] (2/25/56 BCtRt-15)
***BO WEEVIL** Bonnie Lou—King 4900*
Dave Bartholomew/Fats Domino] [BMI] (4/6/56 Rt-15)
BOATS AGAINST THE CURRENT Eric Carmen—Arista 0295
[Eric Carmen] [BMI] (12/24/77 BC-88)
BOBBIE SUE Oak Ridge Boys—MCA 52006
[Jerry Leiber*/Wood Newton/Mike Stoller*/Adele Tyler/Dan Tyler] [BMI] (1/16/82 BCR-12)
BOBBY Neil Scott—Portrait P-102 [Jo Davis/B.L. Porter] [BMI] (6/12/61 BCR-52)
BOBBY SOX TO STOCKINGS Frankie Avalon—Chancellor 1036
[Richard V. Di Cicco/Russell Faith/Clarence Kehner] [ASC] (5/18/59 BCR-6)
BOBBY'S GIRL Marcie Blane—Seville 120
[Henry Hoffman/Gary Klein] [BMI] (10/6/62 BCR-2)
BODY Jacksons—Epic 04673 [Marlon Jackson] [BMI] (10/27/84 BC-46)
BODY HEAT Alicia Bridges—Polydor 14539
[Alicia Bridges/Susan Hutcheson] [BMI] (4/7/79 B-86)
BODY LANGUAGE Queen—Elektra 47452 [Freddie Mercury] [BMI] (5/1/82 BC-11)
BODY ROCK Maria Vidal—EMI America 8233
[John Bettis/Sylvester Levay] [ASC] (9/8/84 BC-43)
BODY TALK The Deele—Solar 69785
[Stanley Burke/Melvin Gentry/Carl Greene/Antonio Reid/Bo Watson*] [BMI] (1/21/84 BC-63)
BODYHEAT (PART 1) James Brown—Polydor 14360
[Deanna Brown/Deidra Brown/Yamma Brown] [BMI] (2/5/77 BR-88)
BOHEMIAN RHAPSODY Queen—Elektra 45297 [Freddie Mercury] [ASC] (12/27/75 BCR-4)
BOLD SOUL SISTER Ike & Tina Turner—Blue Thumb 104
[Ike Turner] [BMI] (12/20/69 BCR-54)
THE BOLL WEEVIL SONG Brook Benton—Mercury 71820
[Brook Benton/Clyde Otis/Traditional] [BMI] (5/15/61 BCR-2)
BOMBS AWAY Bob Weir—Arista 0315
[John Perry Barlow/Bob Weir] [ASC] (3/18/78 BC-63)
BON BON VIE (GIMME THE GOOD LIFE) T.S. Monk—Mirage 3790
[L. Russell Brown/Sandy Linzer] [BMI] (2/21/81 BCR-63)
BON-DOO-WAH The Orlons—Cameo 287
[Dave Appell/Kal Mann] [ASC] (12/14/63 BCR-35)
BON VOYAGE Janice Harper—Prep 111
[Oliver Merritt/Vincent Rodomista] [ASC] (7/20/57 BCR-13)
***BONANZA** Al Caiola And His Orchestra—United Artists 302*
[Ray Evans/Jay Livingston] [ASC] (3/27/61 BCR-19) [IWM]
***BONANZA!** Johnny Cash—Columbia 42512*
[Ray Evans/Jay Livingston] [ASC] (9/15/62 B-94)
BONAPARTE'S RETREAT Billy Grammer—Monument 403
[Pee Wee King/Redd Stewart/Traditional] [BMI] (4/11/59 BCR-49)
BONG BONG (I LOVE YOU MADLY) Vince Castro—Apt 25007
[Vince Castro Jr./Charles Merenstein] [BMI] (8/11/58 R-81)
BONGO BONGO Steve Miller Band—Capitol 5442
[Chris McCarty/Steve Miller] [ASC] (2/16/85 BC-80)
BONGO BONGO BONGO Preston Epps—Original Sound 9
[Arthur Egnoian/Jack Nitzsche] [BMI] (7/2/60 BCR-41) [I]
BONGO GUITAR (OYE NEGRA) Ralph Marterie & His Orchestra—Mercury 70482
[Johnnie Camacho/Noro Morales] [NA] (11/27/54 C-37) [I]
***BONGO ROCK** Preston Epps—Original Sound 4*
[Arthur Egnoian/Preston Epps] [BMI] (5/16/59 BCR-13) [I]
***BONGO ROCK** The Incredible Bongo Band—Pride 1015/MGM 14588*
[Arthur Egnoian/Preston Epps] [BMI] (6/9/73 BCR-51) [I]
BONGO STOMP Little Joey And The Flips—Joy 262
[Sy Kaplan/Marc Levin/Barry Rich] [BMI] (6/9/62 BCR-30)
BONGOLA Preston Epps—Top Rank 2067 [Milton DeLugg] [BMI] (9/26/60 R-85) [I]
***BONNIE BLUE GAL** Mitch Miller with His Orch. & Chorus—Columbia 40575*
[Jessie Cavanaugh/William Engvick] [BMI] (10/17/55 BCtRt-27)
BONNIE BLUE GAL
Lawrence Welk And His Champagne Music And The McGuire Sisters—Coral 61515
[Jessie Cavanaugh/William Engvick] [BMI] (10/24/55 CtRt-27)
BONNIE CAME BACK Duane Eddy His "Twangy" Guitar And The Rebels—Jamie 1144
[Traditional] [NA] (12/14/59 BCR-20) [I]
***BONY MORONIE** Larry Williams—Specialty 615 [Larry Williams] [BMI] (10/21/57 BCR-17)*
***BONY MORONIE** The Appalachians—ABC-Paramount 10419*
[Larry Williams] [BMI] (3/30/63 BCR-61)
***BONEY MORONIE** Cheeks—Capitol 4883 [Larry Williams] [BMI] (6/28/80 CR-90)*
BOO, BOO, DON'T 'CHA BE BLUE Tommy James—Roulette 7140
[Tommy James/Robert L. King] [BMI] (2/10/73 BCR-39)
—BOO BOO MAN see: MAMA LOOK A BOO BOO
BOO BOO STICK BEAT Chet Atkins—RCA Victor 47-7589
[Murrey Harman/John D. Loudermilk] [BMI] (9/14/59 BCR-43) [I]
BOO-GA-LOO Tom & Jerrio—ABC-Paramount 10638
[Sammy Kaplan*/Jerry Murray] [BMI] (4/17/65 BCR-43)
(BOO HOO) I'M GONNA CRY Lloyd Price—ABC-Paramount 10177
[John Bobby Berry/Don Covay/Lloyd Price*] [BMI] (1/9/61 CR-76)
BOOGALOO DOWN BROADWAY The Fantastic Johnny C—Phil-L.A. Of Soul 305
[Jesse James] [BMI] (10/7/67 BCR-7)
THE BOOGALOO PARTY The Flamingos—Philips 40347
[Zeke Carey/Willie Clarke/Doug McClure] [BMI] (3/19/66 BCR-91)
BOOGIE BANDS AND ONE NIGHT STANDS Kathy Dalton—DiscReet 1210
[Greg Dempsey] [BMI] (8/10/74 BCR-56)
BOOGIE BEAR Boyd Bennett—Mercury 71479 [Boyd Bennett] [BMI] (8/24/59 BCR-63)
BOOGIE BODY LAND Bar-Kays—Mercury 76088
[James Edward Alexander/Charles Leonard Allen/Michael Beard/Mark Bynum/ Larry Dodson/Sherman Guy/Harvey Henderson/Allen Alvoid Jones Jr./ Lloyd Ed Smith/Winston Stewart/Frank Thompson] [BMI] (1/17/81 R-83)
BOOGIE CHILD Bee Gees—RSO 867
[Barry Gibb/Maurice Gibb/Robin Gibb] [BMI] (1/15/77 BCR-12)
BOOGIE DOWN Eddie Kendricks—Tamla 54243
[Leonard Caston/Anita Poree/Frank Edward Wilson] [BMI] (12/29/73 BCR-1)
BOOGIE DOWN Al Jarreau—Warner Bros. 29624
[Al Jarreau/Michael Omartian] [BMI] (6/18/83 BC-68)
BOOGIE FEVER The Sylvers—Capitol 4179
[Freddie Perren/Keni St. Lewis] [ASC] (1/24/76 BCR-1)
BOOGIE NIGHTS Heatwave—Epic 50370 [Rod Temperton] [ASC] (7/9/77 BCR-2)
BOOGIE ON REGGAE WOMAN Stevie Wonder—Tamla 54254
[Stevie Wonder] [ASC] (11/9/74 BCR-1)
BOOGIE OOGIE OOGIE A Taste Of Honey—Capitol 4565
[Janice Johnson/Perry Kibble] [BMI] (6/17/78 BCR-1)
BOOGIE SHOES KC & The Sunshine Band—TK 1025
[Harry Wayne Casey/Rick Finch] [BMI] (2/4/78 BCR-33)
BOOGIE WONDERLAND Earth, Wind & Fire With The Emotions—ARC 10956
[Jon Lind/Allee Willis] [ASC] (5/12/79 BCR-5)
***BOOGIE WOOGIE** The Modernaires—Coral 61779*
[Clarence Smith] (Med) [NA] (2/16/57 R-72)
***PINE TOP'S BOOGIE** Jo Stafford—Columbia 41413*
[Norman Gimbel/Clarence Smith] [ASC] (8/17/59 R-95)
***BOOGIE WOOGIE** B. Bumble & The Stingers—Rendezvous 151*
[Clarence Smith] [NA] (6/26/61 BR-82) [IM]
BOOGIE WOOGIE BUGLE BOY Bette Midler—Atlantic 2964
[Hughie Prince/Don Raye] [ASC] (5/5/73 BCR-5)
BOOGIE WOOGIE COUNTRY GIRL Southwind—Blue Thumb 111
[Reginald Ashby/Doc Pomus] [BMI] (5/23/70 R-97)
BOOGIE WOOGIE DANCIN' SHOES Claudja Barry—Chrysalis 2313
[Claudja Barry*/Matz Björklund/Jörg Evers/Keith Forsey/Jürgen Korduletsch] [BMI] (4/7/79 BCR-56)
BOOGIE WOOGIE MAN Paul Davis—Bang 599 [Paul Davis] [BMI] (12/23/72 BCR-67)
BOOK OF LOVE Richard Maltby And His Orchestra—"X" 0158
[Robert Allen/Al Stillman] [NA] (9/26/55 R-75)
***BOOK OF LOVE** The Monotones—Argo 5290*
[Warren Davis/George Malone/Charles Patrick] [BMI] (3/22/58 BCR-5)
***BOOK OF LOVE** Nino & the Ebb Tides—Madison 166*
[Warren Davis/George Malone/Charles Patrick] (Med) [BMI] (8/26/61 BCR-57)
***BOOK OF LOVE** The Raindrops—Jubilee 5469*
[Warren Davis/George Malone/Charles Patrick] [BMI] (3/14/64 BCR-51)
BOOLA Les Brown and His Band of Renown—Coral 62085
[Robert Sweetwater] [BMI] (2/16/59 R-99) [IWM]
BOOM-A-DIP-DIP Stan Robinson—Monument 402
[Nonne Coan/William Douchette/Tommy Tyler] [BMI] (3/14/59 BC-75)
***BOOM BOOM** John Lee Hooker—Vee-Jay 438 [John Lee Hooker] [BMI] (5/26/62 BCR-60)*
***BOOM BOOM** The Animals—MGM 13298 [John Lee Hooker] [BMI] (12/5/64 BCR-35)*
BOOM BOOM BOOMERANG The DeCastro Sisters—Abbott 3003
[Lonnie Coleman] [BMI] (4/11/55 BCR-24)
BOOM BOOM (LET'S GO BACK TO MY ROOM) Paul Lekakis—ZYX 1266
[Riccardo Ballerini/Michele Chieregato/Thomas Hooker/Stefano Montin/ Roberto Turatti] [BMI] (2/21/87 BC-43)
BOOM BOOM (OUT GO THE LIGHTS) Pat Travers—Polydor 2003
[Stanley J. Lewis] [BMI] (9/1/79 BCR-56)
BOOM! THERE SHE WAS Scritti Politti Featuring Roger—Warner Bros. 27976
[David Gamson/Green Gartside] [ASC] (6/18/88 BC-53)
BOOMERANG Frankie Valli—Private Stock 45,109
[Victoria Pike/Teddy Randazzo] [BMI] (10/16/76 C-90)
THE BOOMIN' SYSTEM LL Cool J—Def Jam 73457
[James Todd Smith/Marlon Williams] [ASC] (9/29/90 BC-37)
BOOT-LEG Booker T. & The MG's—Stax 169
[Charles Axton/Donald "Duck" Dunn/Isaac Hayes/Wayne Jackson] [BMI] (5/29/65 BCR-50) [I]
BOOTY BUTT The Ray Charles Orchestra—Tangerine 1015
[Ray Charles] [BMI] (3/20/71 BCR-24) [I]
BOOTZILLA Bootsy's Rubber Band—Warner Bros. 8512
[George Clinton/William Earl Collins] [BMI] (3/4/78 CR-59)
BOP Dan Seals—EMI America 8289 [Paul Davis/Jennifer Kimball] [BMI] (1/25/86 BC-42)
BOP-A-LENA Ronnie Self—Columbia 41101
[Webb Pierce/Mel Tillis] [BMI] (3/8/58 BC-60)

BOP 'TIL YOU DROP Rick Springfield—RCA 13861 [Rick Springfield] [BMI] (8/18/84 BC-20)

BOPPIN' IN A SACK The Lane Brothers—RCA Victor 47-7220 [Cy Coben/Bob Farris] [ASC] (5/10/58 CR-53)

BOPPIN' THE BLUES Carl Perkins—Sun 243 [Curly Griffin/Carl Perkins] [BMI] (6/22/56 BCR-19)

THE BORDER America—Capitol 5236 [Russ Ballard/Dewey Bunnell] [ASC] (6/18/83 BC-33)

THE BORDER Mr. Mister—RCA 5325 [Steve George/John Lang/Richard Page] [ASC] (11/14/87 C-88)

BORDER SONG *Elton John—Uni 55246 [Elton John/Bernie Taupin] [BMI] (8/15/70 BCR-69)*

BORDER SONG (HOLY MOSES) *Aretha Franklin—Atlantic 2772 [Elton John/Bernie Taupin] (TSW) [BMI] (12/19/70 BCR-23)*

BORDERLINE Madonna—Sire 29354 [Reggie Lucas] [BMI] (3/10/84 BC-9)

THE BORDERLINES Jeffrey Osborne—A&M 2695 [Raymond C. Jones] [ASC] (1/19/85 BC-38)

BORN A WOMAN Sandy Posey—MGM 13501 [Martha Sharp] [BMI] (7/23/66 BCR-9)

BORN AGAIN Sam & Dave—Atlantic 2608 [Isaac Hayes/David Porter] [ASC] (3/15/69 BCR-72)

BORN FREE *Roger Williams—Kapp 767 [John Barry/Don Black] [BMI] (8/27/66 BCR-7)*

BORN FREE *The Hesitations—Kapp 878 [John Barry/Don Black] [BMI] (1/6/68 BCR-27)*

BORN IN THE U.S.A. *Bruce Springsteen—Columbia 04680 [Bruce Springsteen] [ASC] (11/10/84 BC-8)*

BORN IN EAST L.A. *(parody of Born In The USA) Cheech & Chong—MCA 52655 [Tommy Chong*/Cheech Marin/Bruce Springsteen] [ASC] (9/21/85 BC-48) [P]*

BORN TO BE ALIVE Patrick Hernandez—Columbia 10986 [Patrick Hernandez] [ASC] (6/9/79 BCR-16)

BORN TO BE BY YOUR SIDE Brenda Lee—Decca 32119 [Jerry Reed] [BMI] (4/8/67 C-93)

BORN TO BE MY BABY Bon Jovi—Mercury 872156 [Jon Bon Jovi/Desmond Child/Richie Sambora] [ASC] (11/26/88 BC-2)

BORN TO BE TOGETHER The Ronettes Featuring Veronica—Philles 126 [Barry Mann/Phil Spector/Cynthia Weil] [BMI] (2/6/65 BCR-52)

BORN TO BE WILD *Steppenwolf—Dunhill 4138 [Mars Bonfire] [BMI] (7/13/68 BCR-2)*

BORN TO BE WILD *Wilson Pickett—Atlantic 2631 [Mars Bonfire] [BMI] (5/10/69 BCR-44)*

BORN TO BE WITH YOU *The Chordettes—Cadence 1291 [Don Robertson] [ASC] (5/25/56 BCRt-4)*

BORN TO BE WITH YOU *Lola Dee—Mercury 70870 [Don Robertson] [ASC] (5/25/56 Rt-5)*

BORN TO BE WITH YOU *Sonny James The Southern Gentleman—Capitol 2271 [Don Robertson] [ASC] (11/23/68 B-81)*

—BORN TO GET AROUND see: BORN TO GET DOWN

BORN TO GET DOWN (BORN TO GET AROUND) Muscle Shoals Horns—Bang 721 [David William Huff/Clarence Jones] [BMI] (5/15/76 R-98)

BORN TO LOSE Ray Charles—ABC-Paramount 10330 [Ted Daffan] [BMI] (5/12/62 BCR-39)

BORN TO LOVE Teresa Brewer—Coral 61878 [Kenny Jacobson/Rhoda Roberts] [ASC] (9/9/57 R-72)

BORN TO RUN Bruce Springsteen—Columbia 10209 [Bruce Springsteen] [ASC] (9/13/75 BCR-17)

BORN TO WANDER Rare Earth—Rare Earth 5021 [Tom Baird] [ASC] (12/12/70 BCR-13)

BORN TOO LATE Poni-Tails—ABC-Paramount 9934 [Charles Strouse/Fred Tobias] [ASC] (7/7/58 BCR-7)

BORN UNDER A BAD SIGN William Bell—Stax 0054 [William Bell/Booker T. Jones Jr.] [BMI] (11/22/69 C-100)

BORROWED DREAMS Bobby Helms—Decca 30682 [Vlad Maleckar/James Testa] [BMI] (7/14/58 BR-60)

BORROWED LOVE Bingoboys—Atlantic 87676 [James Samuel Harris/Terry Lewis] [ASC] (6/29/91 B-71)

BORROWED TIME Styx—A&M 2228 [Dennis DeYoung/Tommy Shaw] [ASC] (3/22/80 BCR-63)

BOSS The Rumblers—Dot 16421 [Bob Jones*/Michael Kelishes*/John Kirkland*/George Lloyd*/Wayne Matteson*/ Jack V. Wenzel] [BMI] (2/16/63 BCR-82) [I]

THE BOSS Diana Ross—Motown 1462 [Nick Ashford/Valerie Simpson] [ASC] (7/7/79 BCR-19)

BOSS GUITAR Duane Eddy And The Rebelettes—RCA Victor 47-8131 [Duane Eddy/Lee Hazlewood] [BMI] (2/9/63 BCR-21)

BOSS LOVE Lee Rogers—D-Town 1050 [Cara Bell/Mike Hanks/Rudy Robinson] [BMI] (7/31/65 R-98)

BOSSA NOVA BABY Elvis Presley With The Jordanaires—RCA Victor 47-8243 [Jerry Leiber/Mike Stoller] [BMI] (10/12/63 BCR-7)

THE (BOSSA NOVA) BIRD The Dells—Argo 5428 [Billy Davis/Shirley Hall] [BMI] (12/22/62 BR-97)

BOSSA NOVA U.S.A. Dave Brubeck Quartet—Columbia 42651 [Dave Brubeck] [BMI] (1/5/63 BCR-69) [I]

THE BOSTON FANCY *Gisele MacKenzie—"X" 0137 [David E. Coleman] [BMI] (8/8/55 Rt-46)*

THE BOSTON FANCY *Marian Caruso—Decca 29565 [David E. Coleman] [BMI] (8/8/55 Rt-49)*

BOTH SIDES NOW *Judy Collins—Elektra 45639 [Joni Mitchell] [ASC] (11/2/68 BCRt-8)*

BOTH SIDES NOW *The Johnstons—Tetragrammaton 1507 [Joni Mitchell] [ASC] (11/2/68 Rt-71)*

FROM BOTH SIDES NOW *Dion—Laurie 3495 [Joni Mitchell] [ASC] (4/26/69 B-91)*

BOTTLE OF WINE The Fireballs—Atco 6491 [Tom Paxton] [ASC] (12/30/67 BCR-7)

BOULEVARD Jackson Browne—Asylum 47003 [Jackson Browne] [ASC] (7/5/80 BCR-13)

BOULEVARD OF NIGHTINGALES Tony Martin—RCA Victor 47-5757 [Sammy Gallop/Al Hoffman] [ASC] (7/17/54 C-37)

THE BOUNCE The Olympics—Tri Disc 106 [Charles Fizer/Eddie Lewis/Walter Ward] [BMI] (4/20/63 BCR-40)

BOUNCE BACK Alisha—MCA 53802 [Michael Jay/Gregory W. Smith] [BMI] (5/26/90 BC-54)

BOUNCE, ROCK, SKATE, ROLL (PART 1) Vaughan Mason And Crew—Brunswick 211 [Jerome Bell/Gregory Bufford/Vaughan Mason] [BMI] (3/1/80 BCR-81)

BOUNCIN' OFF THE WALLS Matthew Wilder—Private I 4-04617 [Matthew Wilder] [ASC] (9/22/84 BC-46)

BOWLING GREEN The Everly Brothers—Warner Bros. 7020 [Jacqueline Ertel/Terry Slater] [BMI] (5/13/67 BCR-40)

THE BOXER Simon & Garfunkel—Columbia 44785 [Paul Simon] [BMI] (4/5/69 BCR-3)

BOY Lulu—Epic 10346 [Alan Blaikley/Ken Howard/Geoff Stephens] [ASC] (6/29/68 R-94)

BOY BLUE Cyndi Lauper—Portrait 37-07181 [Jeff Bova/Cyndi Lauper/Stephen Lunt] [BMI] (6/6/87 BC-71)

THE BOY FROM NEW YORK CITY *The Ad Libs—Blue Cat 102 [George Davis*/John Issac Taylor] [BMI] (1/16/65 BCR-7)*

BOY FROM NEW YORK CITY *The Manhattan Transfer—Atlantic 3816 [George Davis/John Issac Taylor] [BMI] (5/23/81 BCR-7)*

BOY IN THE BOX Corey Hart—EMI America 8287 [Corey Hart] [ASC] (9/14/85 BC-25)

THE BOY IN THE BUBBLE Paul Simon—Warner Bros. 28460 [Forere Motloheloa/Paul Simon] [BMI] (3/7/87 BC-84)

BOY, I'VE BEEN TOLD Sa-Fire—Cutting 870 514-7 [Mark Muniz] [ASC] (9/24/88 BC-48)

A BOY NAMED SUE Johnny Cash—Columbia 44944 [Shel Silverstein] [BMI] (7/26/69 BCR-1)

THE BOY NEXT DOOR The Secrets—Philips 40146 [John Madara/David White] [BMI] (11/9/63 BCR-18)

BOY ON PAGE THIRTY FIVE Cathy Carr—Fraternity 743 [Leon Carr/Hal David] [ASC] (7/20/56 R-80)

BOY TOY Tia—RCA 5107 [Roy Bermingham/James M. Cohn/Charles Ibgui] [ASC] (3/7/87 B-97)

THE BOY WITH THE BEATLE HAIR The Swans—Cameo 302 [Kenneth Gamble/William E. Jackson III/Joe Renzetti/Jerry J. Ross] [BMI] (2/29/64 BR-85)

BOY WITHOUT A GIRL Frankie Avalon—Chancellor 1036 [Sid Jacobson/Ruth Sexter] [ASC] (5/25/59 BCR-10)

BOYS The Beatles—Capitol 6066 [Luther Dixon/Wes Farrell] [BMI] (10/23/65 C-73)

THE BOYS ARE BACK IN TOWN Thin Lizzy—Mercury 73786 [Phil Lynott] [ASC] (5/15/76 BCR-10)

BOYS DO CRY Joe Bennett And The Sparkletones—Paris 537 [Wayne Arthur/Joe Bennett] [BMI] (10/31/59 C-95)

BOYS DO FALL IN LOVE Robin Gibb—Mirage 99743 [Maurice Gibb/Robin Gibb] [BMI] (6/2/84 BC-37)

THE BOYS' NIGHT OUT Patti Page—Mercury 72013 [Sammy Cahn/Jimmy Van Heusen] [ASC] (8/4/62 BCR-46)

BOYS NIGHT OUT Timothy B. Schmit—MCA 53137 [Bruce Gaitsch/Will Jennings/Timothy B. Schmit] [ASC] (9/19/87 BC-25)

THE BOYS OF SUMMER Don Henley—Geffen 29141 [Mike Campbell/Don Henley] [ASC] (11/10/84 BC-5)

BRA Cymande—Janus 215 [Patrick Patterson/Steve Scipio] [BMI] (6/2/73 C-93)

BRAND NEW HEARTACHE The Everly Brothers—Cadence 1388 [Boudleaux Bryant/Felice Bryant] [BMI] (11/12/60 C-84)

BRAND NEW KEY Melanie—Neighborhood 4201 [Melanie Safka] [ASC] (10/23/71 BCR-1)

BRAND NEW LOVE AFFAIR PART I & II Chicago—Columbia 10200 [James Pankow] [ASC] (8/30/75 BCR-43)

BRAND NEW LOVE AFFAIR Jigsaw—Chelsea 3043 [Charles Graham/Iris May] [ASC] (8/21/76 BCR-66)

BRAND NEW LOVER Dead Or Alive—Epic 06374 [Pete Burns/Steve Coy/Wayne Hussey/Tim Lever/Mike Percy] [ASC] (11/29/86 BC-15)

A BRAND NEW ME *Jerry Butler—Mercury 72960 [Jerry Butler/Kenneth Gamble/Leon Huff] [BMI] (10/25/69 R-74)*

A BRAND NEW ME *Dusty Springfield—Atlantic 2685 [Jerry Butler/Kenneth Gamble/Leon Huff] [BMI] (11/1/69 BCR-22)*

BRAND NEW ME *Aretha Franklin—Atlantic 2796 [Jerry Butler/Kenneth Gamble/Leon Huff] (TSW) [BMI] (6/12/71 BCR-10)*

BRANDY The O'Jays—Philadelphia Int'l 3652 [Joseph Jefferson/Charles Simmons] [BMI] (8/12/78 BCR-71)

—BRANDY see: MANDY

BRANDY (YOU'RE A FINE GIRL) Looking Glass—Epic 10874 [Elliot Lurie] [ASC] (6/10/72 BCR-1)

BRASS BUTTONS The String-A-Longs—Warwick 625 [Norman Petty] [BMI] (3/20/61 BCR-34) [I]

BRASS IN POCKET (I'M SPECIAL) The Pretenders—Sire 49181
[James Honeyman-Scott/Chrissie Hynde] [ASC] (2/16/80 BCR-13)

BRASS MONKEY Beastie Boys—Def Jam 07020
[Mike Diamond/Adam Horovitz/Rick Rubin/Adam Yauch] [ASC] (3/21/87 BC-48)

BRASS RING Kay Starr—RCA Victor 47-6748
[Guy Singer/Irving Taylor] [ASC] (1/12/57 R-78)

BRAZIL *The Ritchie Family—20th Century 2218*
[Ary Barroso] [BMI] (8/2/75 BCR-10) [IM]

BRAZIL *The Ritchie Family—Marlin 3306*
[Ary Barroso] (Med) [BMI] (8/28/76 BCR-17) [IM]

BRAZILIAN RHAPSODY PART 2 Caesar Giovannini & His Orchestra—Bally 1026
[Caesar Giovannini] [ASC] (2/16/57 R-78) [I]

BREAD AND BUTTER *The Newbeats—Hickory 1269*
[Larry Parks/Jay Turnbow] [BMI] (8/8/64 BCR-1)

BREAD AND BUTTER *Robert John—Motown 1664*
[Larry Parks/Jay Turnbow] [BMI] (2/12/83 B-68)

BREAK AWAY The Beach Boys—Capitol 2530
[Brian Wilson/Murry Wilson] [BMI] (6/28/69 BCR-35)

BREAK AWAY Art Garfunkel—Columbia 10273
[Benny Gallagher/Graham Lyle] [BMI] (12/27/75 BCR-38)

BREAK AWAY (FROM THAT BOY) The Newbeats—Hickory 1290
[Louis Mathis/Marc Mathis] [BMI] (1/23/65 BCR-34)

BREAK EVERY RULE Tina Turner—Capitol 44003
[Rupert Hine/Jeannette Obstoj] [ASC] (5/9/87 BC-74)

BREAK IT TO ME GENTLY *Brenda Lee—Decca 31348*
[Diane Lampert/Joe Seneca] [ASC] (1/8/62 BCR-4)

BREAK IT TO ME GENTLY *Juice Newton—Capitol 5148*
[Diane Lampert/Joe Seneca] [ASC] (8/21/82 BC-9)

BREAK IT TO ME GENTLY Aretha Franklin—Atlantic 3393
[Marvin Hamlisch/Carole Bayer Sager] [ASC] (6/18/77 B-85)

BREAK IT TO THEM GENTLY Burton Cummings—Portrait 70016
[Burton Cummings] [BMI] (7/8/78 BCR-81)

BREAK IT UP Foreigner—Atlantic 4044 [Michael Leslie Jones] [ASC] (5/15/82 BC-26)

BREAK MY HEART David Ruffin—Warner Bros. 49030 [David Garner] [BMI] (9/29/79 R-93)

BREAK MY HEART GENTLY Dorothy Collins—Audiovox 108
[John M. Klein/Hal Richardson] [ASC] (10/4/54 R-PRE)

BREAK MY MIND Bobby Wood—MGM 13797 [John D. Loudermilk] [BMI] (12/9/67 C-96)

BREAK MY STRIDE Matthew Wilder—Private I 4-04113
[Greg Prestopino/Matthew Wilder] [ASC] (9/17/83 BC-2)

BREAK OUT Mitch Ryder And The Detroit Wheels—New Voice 811
[Herbert Bernstein/Gary Knight] [BMI] (5/28/66 BCR-62)

BREAK UP Jerry Lee Lewis And His Pumping Piano—Sun 303
[Charlie Rich] [BMI] (9/8/58 BCR-52)

BREAK UP Del Shannon—Amy 925 [Del Shannon] [BMI] (5/22/65 BCR-83)

BREAK UP TO MAKE UP *The Stylistics—Avco 4611*
[Thom Bell/Linda Creed/Kenneth Gamble] [BMI] (2/10/73 BCR-5)

BREAK UP TO MAKE UP *Cynthia—MicMac 3558*
[Thom Bell/Linda Creed/Kenneth Gamble] [BMI] (6/22/91 B-70)

BREAK YOUR PROMISE The Delfonics—Philly Groove 152
[Thom Bell/William Hart] [BMI] (8/24/68 BCR-35)

BREAKAWAY Millie Jackson—Spring 134 [Raeford Gerald] [BMI] (4/7/73 C-80)

BREAKAWAY Tracey Ullman—MCA/Stiff 52385
[Jackie DeShannon/Sharon Sheeley] [BMI] (6/16/84 BC-70)

BREAKAWAY Big Pig—A&M 3014 [Mitch Bottler/Gary Zekley] [ASC] (3/19/88 BC-55)

BREAKDANCE Irene Cara—Geffen 29328
[Irene Cara/Bunny Hull/Giorgio Moroder] [ASC] (3/24/84 BC-8)

THE BREAKDOWN (PART 1) Rufus Thomas—Stax 0098
[Eddie Floyd/Bonny Rice/Rufus Thomas] [BMI] (8/7/71 BCR-31)

BREAKDOWN Tom Petty And The Heartbreakers—Shelter 62008
[Tom Petty] [ASC] (11/5/77 BCR-33)

BREAKDOWN Seduction—Vendetta 1503
[Robert Clivillés/David Cole/Frederick B. Williams] [ASC] (10/6/90 BC-76)

BREAKDOWN DEAD AHEAD Boz Scaggs—Columbia 11241
[David Foster/Boz Scaggs] [ASC] (3/29/80 BCR-11)

BREAKER - BREAKER The Outlaws—Arista 0188 [Hughie Thomasson] [BMI] (7/3/76 B-94)

BREAKFAST FOR TWO Country Joe McDonald—Fantasy 758
[Joe McDonald] [BMI] (11/29/75 B-92)

BREAKFAST IN AMERICA Supertramp—A&M 2292
[Rick Davies/Roger Hodgson] [ASC] (12/13/80 BCR-62)

BREAKFAST IN BED Dusty Springfield—Atlantic 2606
[Donnie Fritts/Eddie Hinton] [BMI] (4/12/69 B-91)

BREAKIN' AWAY Al Jarreau—Warner Bros. 49842
[Tom Canning/Jay Graydon/Al Jarreau] [BMI] (11/28/81 BCR-43)

BREAKIN' DOWN THE WALLS OF HEARTACHE The Bandwagon—Epic 10352
[Sandy Linzer/Denny Randell] [BMI] (8/17/68 C-100)

BREAKIN' IN A BRAND NEW BROKEN HEART Connie Francis—MGM 12995
[Howard Greenfield/Jack Keller] [BMI] (4/10/61 BCR-3)

BREAKIN'.. THERE'S NO STOPPIN' US Ollie And Jerry—Polydor 821708
[Ollie Brown/Jerry Knight] [ASC] (6/2/84 BC-8)

BREAKIN' UP IS BREAKIN' MY HEART Roy Orbison—MGM 13446
[William Dees/Roy Orbison] [BMI] (1/22/66 BCR-24)

BREAKING AWAY Balance—Portrait 24-02177
[Peppy Castro] [BMI] (7/11/81 BCR-22)

THE BREAKING POINT Chuck Jackson—Wand 115
[Burt Bacharach/Hal David] [ASC] (10/30/61 R-64)

BREAKING UP IS HARD TO DO Jivin' Gene And The Jokers—Mercury 71485
[Gene Bourgeois/Huey P. Meaux] [BMI] (9/5/59 BCR-31)

BREAKING UP IS HARD TO DO *Neil Sedaka—RCA Victor 47-8046*
[Howard Greenfield/Neil Sedaka] [BMI] (6/23/62 BCR-1)

BREAKING UP IS HARD TO DO *The Happenings—B.T. Puppy 543*
[Howard Greenfield/Neil Sedaka] [BMI] (7/13/68 BCR-43)

BREAKING UP IS HARD TO DO *Lenny Welch—Commonwealth United 3004*
[Howard Greenfield/Neil Sedaka] [BMI] (1/3/70 BCR-29)

BREAKING UP IS HARD TO DO
The Partridge Family Starring Shirley Jones & Featuring David Cassidy—Bell 45,235
[Howard Greenfield/Neil Sedaka] [BMI] (6/24/72 BCR-24)

BREAKING UP IS HARD TO DO *Heaven Bound with Tony Scotti—MGM 14412*
[Howard Greenfield/Neil Sedaka] [BMI] (7/8/72 R-94)

BREAKING UP IS HARD TO DO *Neil Sedaka—Rocket/MCA 40500*
[Howard Greenfield/Neil Sedaka] [BMI] (12/13/75 BCR-7)

BREAKING UP IS HARD ON YOU (A/K/A DON'T TAKE MA BELL AWAY FROM ME)
(parody of Breaking Up Is Hard To Do) The American Comedy Network—Critique 704
[Howard Greenfield/Neil Sedaka] [BMI] (2/4/84 BC-70) [P]

BREAKING UP SOMEBODY'S HOME *Ann Peebles—Hi 2205*
[Al Jackson/Timothy Matthews] [BMI] (2/12/72 CR-83)

BREAKING UP SOMEBODY'S HOME *Albert King—Stax 0147*
[Al Jackson/Timothy Matthews] [BMI] (1/27/73 BC-91)

BREAKING US IN TWO Joe Jackson—A&M 2510 [Joe Jackson] [ASC] (1/15/83 BC-17)

BREAKOUT Swing Out Sister—Mercury 888016
[Andy Connell/Corinne Drewery/Martin Jackson] [BMI] (8/15/87 BC-5)

THE BREAKS (PART 1) Kurtis Blow—Mercury 76075
[Robert Arthur Ford Jr./James B. Moore/Russell Simmons/Lawrence Smith/Kurt Walker]
[ASC] (7/26/80 BCR-58)

THE BREAKUP SONG (THEY DON'T WRITE 'EM) Greg Kihn Band—Beserkley 47149
[Greg Kihn/Gary Philippet/Steve Wright] [ASC] (5/23/81 BCR-15)

BREAKWATER Lawrence Welk And His Orchestra—Dot 16488
[Larry Gordon/Margaret Gordon*] [ASC] (6/22/63 B-100) [IM]

A BREATH TAKING GUY The Supremes—Motown 1044
[Smokey Robinson] [BMI] (7/27/63 BCR-69)

BREATHLESS Jerry Lee Lewis—Sun 288 [Otis Blackwell] [BMI] (3/1/58 BCR-7)

THE BREEZE AND I (ANDALUCIA) *Caterina Valente—Decca 29467*
[Ernesto Lecuona/Al Stillman] [BMI] (3/28/55 BCR-6)

THE BREEZE AND I *Santo & Johnny—Canadian American 115*
[Ernesto Lecuona] [BMI] (5/23/60 R-79) [IM]

BREEZE (BLOW MY BABY BACK TO ME) Al Hibbler—Decca 29660
[Joe Goodwin/James Hanley/Ballard MacDonald] [NA] (8/29/55 R-46)

BREEZIN' George Benson—Warner Bros. 8268
[Bobby Womack] [BMI] (10/16/76 B-63) [I]

BRENDA The Cupids—KC 115 [Joe Norman] [BMI] (6/8/63 BCR-45)

BRIAN'S SONG Michel LeGrand—Bell 45,171
[Michel Legrand] [ASC] (1/22/72 BCR-51) [I]

BRICK HOUSE Commodores—Motown 1425
[William King/Ronald LaPread/Thomas McClary/Walter Orange/Lionel Richie/
Milan Williams] [ASC] (8/27/77 BCR-5)

—BRICKYARD BLUES see: PLAY SOMETHING SWEET

THE BRIDGE OF LOVE Joe Dowell—Smash 1717
[Ben Weisman/Fred Wise] [ASC] (10/9/61 BCR-40)

BRIDGE OVER TROUBLED WATER *Simon & Garfunkel—Columbia 45079*
[Paul Simon] [BMI] (1/31/70 BCR-1)

BRIDGE OVER TROUBLED WATER *Aretha Franklin—Atlantic 2796*
[Paul Simon] (TSW) [BMI] (6/12/71 BCR-2)

BRIDGE OVER TROUBLED WATER *Linda Clifford—RSO/Curtom 921*
[Paul Simon] [BMI] (3/24/79 BCR-41)

BRIDGET THE MIDGET (THE QUEEN OF THE BLUES) Ray Stevens—Barnaby 2024
[Ray Stevens] [BMI] (12/19/70 BCR-43)

BRIGADE OF BROKEN HEARTS Paul Evans—Guaranteed 210
[Clint Ballard Jr./Fred Tobias] [ASC] (8/1/60 BCR-57)

BRIGHT LIGHTS AND BLONDE HAIRED WOMEN "Tennessee" Ernie Ford—Capitol 3343
[Eddie Kirk] [NA] (2/10/56 R-40)

BRIGHT LIGHTS BIG CITY *Jimmy Reed—Vee-Jay 398*
[Jimmy Reed] [BMI] (9/16/61 BCR-58)

BRIGHT LIGHTS, BIG CITY *Sonny James—Capitol 3114*
[Jimmy Reed] [BMI] (7/17/71 BC-91)

BRIGHTEN THE CORNER WHERE YOU ARE
The Browns Featuring Jim Edward Brown—RCA Victor 47-7780
[Charles Hutchison Gabriel/Ina Duley Ogdon] [ASC] (8/29/60 R-61)

THE BRIGHTEST SMILE IN TOWN Ray Charles And His Orchestra—ABC-Paramount 10405
[Ray Charles/Barry De Vorzon/Robert Sherman] [BMI] (3/9/63 B-92)

BRIGHTON HILL Jackie Deshannon—Imperial 66438
[Jackie DeShannon/Jimmy Holiday/Randy Myers] [BMI] (2/21/70 BCR-52)

BRILLIANT DISGUISE Bruce Springsteen—Columbia 07595
[Bruce Springsteen] [ASC] (10/3/87 BC-4)

BRING A LITTLE LOVIN' Los Bravos—Parrot 3020
[Harry Vanda/George Young] [ASC] (5/18/68 BCR-34)

BRING A LITTLE SUNSHINE (TO MY HEART) Vic Dana—Dolton 305
[Mark Barkan/Ben Raleigh] [BMI] (5/22/65 BCR-64)

BRING BACK MY BABY TO ME Ella Mae Morse—Capitol 2992
[Ira Kosloff/Edward White/Mack Wolfson] [ASC] (11/29/54 R-79)

BRING BACK MY LOVE June Valli—RCA Victor 47-7149
[Lincoln Chase] [BMI] (2/3/58 R-79)

BRING BACK THE LOVE OF YESTERDAY The Dells—Cadet 5703
[Willie Schofield] [BMI] (10/26/74 B-87)

BRING BACK THE TIME B.J. Thomas—Scepter 12154
[Mark Charron] [BMI] (7/23/66 BCR-71)

BRING BACK THOSE ROCKABYE BABY DAYS Tiny Tim—Reprise 0760
[Saul Bernie*/Harold Christy*/Abner Silver] [BMI] (8/24/68 BC-95)

BRING BACK YOUR HEART The Del Vikings—ABC-Paramount 10208
[Edward Ellen/Kenny Seymour] [BMI] (5/27/61 CR-66)

BRING DOWN THE MOON Boy Meets Girl—RCA 8807
[George Merrill/Shannon Rubicam] [BMI] (1/28/89 BC-49)

BRING IT ALL BACK Grayson Hugh—RCA 9093 [Grayson Hugh] [ASC] (10/28/89 B-87)

BRING IT HOME (AND GIVE IT TO ME) Hot Sauce—Volt 4076
[Na Allen] [BMI] (5/20/72 BR-93)

BRING IT ON HOME TO ME *Sam Cooke—RCA Victor 47-8036*
[Sam Cooke] [BMI] (6/23/62 BCR-9)

BRING IT ON HOME TO ME *The Animals—MGM 13339*
[Sam Cooke] [BMI] (5/15/65 BCR-23)

BRING IT ON HOME TO ME *Eddie Floyd—Stax 0012*
[Sam Cooke] [BMI] (10/19/68 BCR-12)

BRING IT ON HOME *Lou Rawls—Capitol 2856 [Sam Cooke] [BMI] (8/1/70 BCR-95)*

BRING IT UP James Brown And The Famous Flames—King 6071
[James Brown/Nat Jones] [BMI] (1/7/67 BCR-28)

BRING THE BOYS HOME Freda Payne—Invictus 9092
[Angelo Bond/General Johnson/Greg Perry] [BMI] (5/22/71 BCR-5)

BRING US TOGETHER Patti Page—Mercury 71247 [Harold Beebe] [BMI] (1/6/58 R-85)

BRING YOUR LOVE TO ME The Righteous Brothers—Moonglow 238
[Bobby Hatfield/Bill Medley] [BMI] (1/30/65 B-83)

BRINGIN' ON THE HEARTBREAK Def Leppard—Mercury 818779
[Rick Allen/Steve Clark/Joe Elliott/Rick Savage/Pete Willis] [ASC] (6/9/84 BC-61)

BRINGING IT BACK Elvis Presley—RCA Victor 10401
[Greg Gordon] [BMI] (10/25/75 BC-65)

(BRINGING OUT) THE GIRL IN ME Maxine Nightingale—Windsong 11729
[Ray Parker Jr.] [ASC] (11/3/79 BC-73)

BRINK OF DISASTER Lesley Gore—Mercury 72726
[Michael Gordon/James Griffin] [BMI] (10/7/67 BCR-82)

BRISTOL STOMP The Dovells—Parkway 827
[Dave Appell/Kal Mann] [ASC] (9/4/61 BCR-2)

BRISTOL TWISTIN' ANNIE The Dovells—Parkway 838
[Robert Lewis/Johnny Styles] [BMI] (5/7/62 BCR-27)

BRITE EYES Robbin Thompson Band—Ovation 1157
[Robbin Thompson] [ASC] (10/18/80 BC-66)

BROADWAY Freddy Cannon—Swan 4117
[Bob Feldman/Jerry Goldstein/Richard Gottehrer] [BMI] (9/1/62 C-100)

BROKEN The Guess Who—RCA Victor 74-0458
[Burton Cummings/Kurt Winter] (TSW) [BMI] (4/10/71 BCR-29)

BROKEN ARROW Rod Stewart—Warner Bros. 19274
[Robbie Robertson] [ASC] (10/19/91 BC-9)

BROKEN HEART The Fiestas—Old Town 1122
[Ronald Moseley/Gene Redd Sr.] [BMI] (8/18/62 BCR-53)

BROKEN HEART AND A PILLOW FILLED WITH TEARS Patti Page—Mercury 71870
[Paul Anka] [BMI] (9/25/61 BR-80)

BROKEN HEARTED The Miracles—Tamla 54044
[Berry Gordy/Smokey Robinson] [ASC] (7/3/61 B-97)

BROKEN HEARTED ME Anne Murray—Capitol 4773
[Randy Goodrum] [ASC] (9/22/79 BCR-12)

BROKEN HEARTED MELODY Sarah Vaughan—Mercury 71477
[Hal David/Sherman Edwards] [ASC] (7/18/59 BCR-6)

BROKEN LAND The Adventures—Elektra 69414 [Pat Gribben] [ASC] (4/30/88 BC-83)

A BROKEN MAN The Malibu's—White Whale 289
[Thomas Allbert/Tommy Amato/Quitman Dennis] [BMI] (1/25/69 R-87)

BROKEN PROMISE The Four Coins—Epic 9253
[James Goldsborough/Sol Winkler] [ASC] (12/16/57 CR-48)

BROKEN VOW The Chordettes—Cadence 1382 [Bob Bush] [BMI] (7/11/60 R-86)

BROKEN WINGS Mr. Mister—RCA 14136
[Steve George/John Lang/Richard Page] [ASC] (9/21/85 BC-1)

BRONTOSAURUS STOMP The Piltdown Men—Capitol 4414
[Ed Cobb/Lincoln Mayorga] [BMI] (8/22/60 BCR-72) [I]

BROOKLYN Cody Jameson—Atco 7073 [Lefty Pedroski] [ASC] (3/19/77 BCR-71)

BROOKLYN GIRLS Robbie Dupree—Elektra 47145
[Roy Freeland/Bill LaBounty] [BMI] (5/23/81 BCR-54)

BROOKLYN ROADS Neil Diamond—Uni 55065
[Neil Diamond] [SE] (5/4/68 BCR-34)

BROOMSTICK COWBOY Bobby Goldsboro—United Artists 952
[Bobby Goldsboro] [BMI] (12/11/65 BCR-52)

BROTHER, DON'T YOU WALK AWAY Hooters—Columbia album cut
[Eric Bazilian/Rick Chertoff/Rob Hyman] [ASC] (2/17/90 C-85)

BROTHER-IN-LAW (HE'S A MOOCHER) Paul Peek—Fairlane 702
[Paul Peek] [BMI] (5/15/61 B-84)

BROTHER LOUIE Stories—Kama Sutra 577
[Errol Brown/Tony Wilson] [ASC] (6/2/73 BCR-1)

BROTHER LOVE'S TRAVELLING SALVATION SHOW Neil Diamond—Uni 55109
[Neil Diamond] [SE] (2/22/69 BCR-12)

BROTHER RAPP (PART 1) & (PART 2) James Brown—King 6310
[James Brown] [BMI] (5/2/70 BCR-24)

BROTHER'S GONNA WORK IT OUT Willie Hutch—Motown 1222
[Willie Hutch] [ASC] (4/28/73 BCR-60)

BROUGHT UP IN NEW YORK (BROUGHT DOWN IN L.A.) Paul Anka—RCA Victor 11351
[Paul Anka/Douglas McCormick] [BMI] (9/16/78 R-92)

BROWN ARMS IN HOUSTON Orpheus—MGM 14022
[Joe Henry/Lesley Miller] [BMI] (5/24/69 BCR-88)

BROWN EYED GIRL *Van Morrison—Bang 545 [Van Morrison] [BMI] (6/24/67 BCR-7)*

BROWN EYED GIRL *El Chicano—Kapp 2173 [Van Morrison] [BMI] (6/17/72 BCR-42)*

BROWN EYED WOMAN Bill Medley—MGM 13959
[Barry Mann/Cynthia Weil] [BMI] (7/20/68 BCR-35)

BROWN PAPER BAG Syndicate Of Sound—Buddah 156
[Steve Jenkins] [BMI] (3/28/70 BCR-73)

BROWN SUGAR The Rolling Stones—Rolling Stones 19100
[Mick Jagger/Keith Richards] [BMI] (4/24/71 BCR-1)

BROWNSVILLE Joy Of Cooking—Capitol 3075
[Toni Brown/Terry Garthwaite/Furry Lewis] [BMI] (4/24/71 BCR-66)

BRUCE Rick Springfield—Mercury 880405 [Rick Springfield] [BMI] (11/17/84 BC-26)

BRUSH A LITTLE SUNSHINE Tommy Roe—ABC 11281
[Stan Gelber] [ASC] (11/21/70 R-63)

BRUSH CREEK RAG Johnny Maddox And The Rhythmasters—Dot 15365
[Eleanora Beauchamp] (Med) [ASC] (5/28/55 C-43) [I]

BUBBLE GUM MUSIC
The Rock And Roll Dubble Bubble Trading Card Co. Of Philadelphia-19141—Buddah 78
[Bob Feldman/Jerry Goldstein] [BMI] (1/11/69 BCR-64)

BUBBLES *Frankie Laine—Columbia 40433 [Bob Merrill] [ASC] (3/5/55 CRt-47)*

BUBBLES *Josephine Premice—Coral 61354 [Bob Merrill] [ASC] (3/14/55 Rt-70)*

BUCHANAN AND GOODMAN ON TRIAL Buchanan And Goodman—Luniverse 102
[Bill Buchanan*/Dickie Goodman] [BMI] (10/27/56 BC-42)

BUCKAROO Buck Owens & His Buckaroos—Capitol 5517
[Bob Morris] [BMI] (11/13/65 BCR-55) [I]

BUCKET "T" Ronny & The Daytonas—Mala 492
[Don Altfeld/Jan Berry*/Roger Christian/Dean Torrence*] [BMI] (12/19/64 BCR-54)

BUFFALO SOLDIER The Flamingos—Polydor 14019
[David Barnes/Margaret Lewis/Mira Smith] [BMI] (3/14/70 BCR-56)

BUFFALO STANCE Neneh Cherry—Virgin 99231
[Neneh Cherry/Cameron McVey/Jamie Morgan/Phil Ramacon] [BMI] (4/1/89 BC-3)

BUGLE CALL RAG Crazy Otto—Polydor 22009A
[Billy Meyers/Jack Pettis/Elmer Schoebel] (Med) [ASC] (1/10/55 R-30) [I]

BUILD ME UP BUTTERCUP The Foundations—Uni 55101
[Michael D'Abo/Tony Macaulay] [BMI] (12/21/68 BCR-1)

BUILD YOUR LOVE (ON A STRONG FOUNDATION) Johnnie Ray—Columbia 40942
[Ollie Jones] [BMI] (7/6/57 BCR-27)

BULLDOG The Fireballs—Top Rank 2026 [George Tomsco] [BMI] (1/11/60 BCR-21) [I]

BULLISH Herb Alpert/Tijuana Brass—A&M 2655
[John Barnes*/Jimmie Cameron] [BMI] (9/15/84 B-90) [I]

BULLSEYE Santo & Johnny—Canadian American 120
[Ann Farina/Johnny Farina/Santo Farina] [BMI] (11/21/60 R-74) [I]

BULLWHIP ROCK The Cyclones—Trophy 500 [Wayne Brooks] [BMI] (9/29/58 BR-83) [I]

BUMBLE BEE *LaVern Baker—Atlantic 2077 [Leroy Fullylove] [BMI] (11/14/60 BCR-36)*

BUMBLE BEE *The Searchers—Kapp 49 [Leroy Fullylove] [BMI] (3/20/65 BCR-18)*

BUMBLE BOOGIE *Ralph Marterie & His Orchestra—Mercury 70406*
[Jack Fina/Nikolai Rimsky-Korsakov] [NA] (7/31/54 C-36) [I]

BUMBLE BOOGIE *B. Bumble & The Stingers—Rendezvous 140*
[Jack Fina/Nikolai Rimsky-Korsakov] [ASC] (3/4/61 BCR-18) [I]

FLIGHT OF THE BUMBLE BEE *The Royal Philharmonic Orchestra—RCA 12304*
[Nikolai Rimsky-Korsakov] (Med) [NA] (10/31/81 BCR-9) [I]

BUMP ME BABY PT. 1 Dooley Silverspoon—Cotton 636
[Sonny Casella] [ASC] (2/15/75 BCR-80)

BUNGLE IN THE JUNGLE Jethro Tull—Chrysalis 2101
[Ian Anderson] [ASC] (10/26/74 BCR-10)

BUNNY HOP The Applejacks (S)—Cameo 158
[Ray Anthony/Leonard Auletti] [BMI] (2/23/59 BCR-70) [IWM]

BURN RUBBER (WHY YOU WANNA HURT ME) The Gap Band—Mercury 76091 [Lonnie Simmons/Rudy Taylor/Charles K. Wilson] [BMI] (1/24/81 BCR-47)

BURN THAT CANDLE Bill Haley And His Comets—Decca 29713 [Winfield Scott] [BMI] (10/24/55 BCRt-13)

BURN THAT CANDLE The Cues—Capitol 3245 [Winfield Scott] [BMI] (10/31/55 BRt-23)

BURNIN' FOR YOU Blue Öyster Cult—Columbia 02415 [Rich Meltzer/Donald Roeser] [ASC] (8/8/81 BCR-34)

BURNIN' SKY Bad Company—Swan Song 70112 [Paul Rodgers] [ASC] (5/14/77 BCR-78)

BURNIN' THING Mac Davis—Columbia 10148 [Mac Davis] [BMI] (5/31/75 BCR-52)

BURNING BRIDGES Jack Scott—Top Rank 2041 [Walter Scott] [SE] (4/18/60 BCR-2)

BURNING BRIDGES The Mike Curb Congregation—MGM 14151 [Mike Curb/Lalo Schifrin] [BMI] (11/7/70 BCR-29)

BURNING DOWN ONE SIDE Robert Plant—Swan Song 99979 [Robbie Blunt/Robert Plant/Jezz Woodroffe] [ASC] (9/11/82 BC-64)

BURNING DOWN THE HOUSE Talking Heads—Sire 29565 [David Byrne/Chris Frantz/Jerry Harrison/Tina Weymouth] [ASC] (7/30/83 BC-9)

BURNING FLAME Vitamin Z—Geffen 29039 [Geoff Barradale/Philip Jesson/Nick Lockwood] [ASC] (6/15/85 BC-70)

BURNING HEART Vandenberg—Atco 99947 [Adrian Vandenberg] [ASC] (12/25/82 BC-39)

BURNING HEART Survivor—Scotti Brothers 05663 [Jim Peterik/Frankie Sullivan] [ASC] (11/2/85 BC-2)

BURNING LIKE A FLAME Dokken—Elektra 69435 [Mick Brown/Don Dokken/George Lynch/Jeff Pilson] [ASC] (12/19/87 BC-72)

BURNING LOVE Elvis Presley—RCA Victor 74-0769 [Dennis Linde] [BMI] (8/19/72 BCR-1)

BURNING LOVE Elvis Presley—RCA 13351 [Dennis Linde] (Med) [BMI] (11/20/82 BC-71)

THE BURNING OF ATLANTA Claude King—Columbia 42581 [Chuck Taylor] [BMI] (9/29/62 BCR-45)

BURNING SPEAR The Soulful Strings—Cadet 5576 [Richard L. Evans] [BMI] (2/3/68 BCR-64) [I]

BUS STOP The Hollies—Imperial 66186 [Graham Gouldman] [BMI] (7/23/66 BCR-3)

THE BUS STOP SONG (A PAPER OF PINS) The Four Lads—Columbia 40736 [Ken Darby/Traditional] [ASC] (8/17/56 BCRt-18)

THE BUS STOP SONG (A PAPER OF PINS) Burl Ives—Decca 30046 [Ken Darby/Traditional] [ASC] (9/8/56 Rt-26)

BUST A MOVE Young M.C.—Delicious Vinyl 105 [Matt Dike/Luther Rabb*/Michael Ross/Marvin Young] [ASC] (7/29/89 BC-7)

BUST OUT The Busters—Arlen 735 [Dave Benjamin] [BMI] (8/31/63 BCR-25) [I]

BUSTED Ray Charles And His Orchestra—ABC-Paramount 10481 [Harlan Howard] [BMI] (9/7/63 BCR-2)

BUSTER BROWNE Willie Mitchell—Hi 2091 [Willie Mitchell/Reggie Young] [BMI] (7/3/65 BC-91) [I]

BUSTIN' LOOSE (PART 1) Chuck Brown & The Soul Searchers—Source 40967 [Charles L. Brown] [BMI] (1/13/79 BCR-29)

BUSTIN' OUT Rick James—Gordy 7167 [Rick James] [ASC] (5/12/79 BCR-71)

BUSTIN' SURFBOARDS The Tornadoes—Aertaun 100 [Leonard Delaney/Gerald Sanders/Jesse Sanders/Norman Sanders] [BMI] (10/27/62 CR-71) [I]

(BUT AS THEY SAY) THAT'S LIFE Jack Pleis And His Orchestra—Decca 30303 [Moose Charlap/Jack Pleis] [ASC] (6/17/57 B-69) [I]

BUT FOR LOVE Jerry Naylor—Columbia 45106 [Terry Cashman/Eugene Pistilli/Tommy West] [ASC] (3/21/70 BCR-42)

BUT I DO Clarence Henry—Argo 5378 [Paul Gayten/Robert Guidry] [BMI] (2/6/61 BCR-3)

BUT I DO Bobby Vinton—Epic 10936 [Paul Gayten/Robert Guidry] [BMI] (12/30/72 BCR-71)

BUT IT'S ALRIGHT J.J. Jackson—Calla 119 [J.J. Jackson/Pierre Tubbs] [BMI] (10/1/66 BCR-19)

BUT IT'S ALRIGHT J.J. Jackson—Warner Bros.-Seven Arts 7276 [J.J. Jackson/Pierre Tubbs] [BMI] (5/24/69 BCR-45)

BUT NOT FOR ME Johnny Nash—ABC-Paramount 10046 [George Gershwin/Ira Gershwin] [ASC] (9/28/59 R-96)

BUT NOT FOR ME Ketty Lester—Era 3080 [George Gershwin/Ira Gershwin] [ASC] (6/16/62 BCR-41)

BUT ON THE OTHER HAND BABY Ray Charles And His Orchestra—ABC-Paramount 10266 [Ray Charles/Percy Mayfield] [BMI] (12/11/61 BC-72)

BUT YOU KNOW I LOVE YOU The First Edition—Reprise 0799 [Mike Settle] [BMI] (1/11/69 BCR-15)

BUT YOU KNOW I LOVE YOU Dolly Parton—RCA 12200 [Mike Settle] [BMI] (4/4/81 BCR-41)

BUT YOU'RE MINE Sonny & Cher—Atco 6381 [Sonny Bono] [BMI] (10/9/65 BCR-15)

BUTTER BOY Fanny—Casablanca 814 [Jean Millington] [BMI] (1/25/75 BCR-27)

BUTTERFLY Andy Williams—Cadence 1308 [Bernie Lowe/Kal Mann] [ASC] (2/9/57 BCtRt-1)

BUTTERFLY Charlie Gracie—Cameo 105 [Bernie Lowe/Kal Mann] [ASC] (2/9/57 BCtRt-1)

BUTTERFLY Bob Carroll—Bally 1028 [Bernie Lowe/Kal Mann] [ASC] (2/23/57 BRt-1)

BUTTERFLY Billy Williams—Coral 61795 [Bernie Lowe/Kal Mann] [ASC] (2/23/57 Rt-1)

BUTTERFLY Danyel Gérard—MGM/Verve 10670 [Howard Ellington Riddiford Barnes/Ralph Bernet/Mike Curb/Mack David/Danyel Gérard] [ASC] (6/10/72 BCR-75)

BUTTERFLY BABY Bobby Rydell—Cameo 242 [Dave Appell/Kal Mann] [ASC] (2/2/63 BCR-22)

BUTTERMILK The Fontane Sisters—Dot 15782 [Mort Garson/Earl Shuman] [ASC] (6/30/58 Rt-76)

BUTTERMILK Joe Sherman, his Orchestra and Chorus—Epic 9277 [Mort Garson/Earl Shuman] [ASC] (6/30/58 Rt-76)

BUTTERNUT Jimmy Heap—Capitol 3333 [Cecil Harris/George (2) Harrison] [BMI] (3/10/56 B-93) [I]

BUTTON OFF MY SHIRT Paul Carrack—Chrysalis 43288 [Billy Livsey/Graham Lyle] [BMI] (9/10/88 B-91)

BUTTONS AND BOWS Don Robertson—RCA Victor 47-7862 [Ray Evans/Jay Livingston] [ASC] (4/24/61 R-100) [IWM]

BUY FOR ME THE RAIN Nitty Gritty Dirt Band—Liberty 55948 [Greg Copeland/Steve Noonan] [BMI] (4/1/67 BCR-45)

BUYING A BOOK Joe Tex—Dial 4090 [Joe Tex] [BMI] (4/5/69 BCR-33)

BUZZ BUZZ A-DIDDLE-IT Freddy Cannon—Swan 4071 [Bob Crewe/Frank Slay] [BMI] (4/24/61 BCR-35)

BUZZ BUZZ BUZZ Hollywood Flames—Ebb 119 [Bobby Day/John Grayton Dolphin] [BMI] (11/11/57 BCtRt-11)

BUZZ BUZZ BUZZ Rusty Draper—Mercury 71221 [Bobby Day/John Grayton Dolphin] [BMI] (11/18/57 CtRt-19)

BUZZY BROWN Tim Davis—Metromedia 253 [James Cooke] [ASC] (9/2/72 BCR-78)

BY THE BEND OF THE RIVER Joe Leahy & His Orchestra—RKO Unique 397 [Clara Edwards] [ASC] (7/20/57 C-57)

BY THE LIGHT OF THE SILVERY MOON Jimmy Bowen With The Rhythm Orchids—Roulette 4083 [Gus Edwards/Edward Madden] [NA] (7/7/58 BCR-46)

BY THE TIME I GET TO PHOENIX Glen Campbell—Capitol 2015 [Jimmy Webb] [BMI] (10/21/67 BCR-26)

BY THE TIME I GET TO PHOENIX The Mad Lads—Volt 4016 [Jimmy Webb] [BMI] (7/19/69 BCR-84)

BY THE TIME I GET TO PHOENIX Isaac Hayes—Enterprise 9003 [Jimmy Webb] [BMI] (8/23/69 BCR-37)

BY THE TIME I GET TO PHOENIX Glen Campbell—Capitol 3200 [Jimmy Webb] (Med) [BMI] (10/23/71 BCR-72)

BY YOU BY YOU BY YOU Jim Lowe—Dot 15525 [Bob Davie/Marvin Moore] [BMI] (1/5/57 BR-43)

BYE BYE BABY Mary Wells—Motown 1003 [Mary Wells] [BMI] (1/21/61 BCR-41)

BYE BYE BABY U.S. 1—Private Stock 45,045 [Marc Bellack/Joey Levine] [BMI] (11/15/75 BCR-90)

BYE, BYE, BABY (BABY, GOODBYE) The 4 Seasons Featuring The "Sound" Of Frankie Valli—Philips 40260 [Bob Crewe/Bob Gaudio] [BMI] (1/16/65 BCR-6)

BYE BYE BABY GOODBYE Teresa Brewer—Coral 62126 [Frank McNulty] [ASC] (7/6/59 CR-95)

BYE BYE BARBARA Johnny Mathis—Mercury 72229 [Jack Segal/Paul Vance] [ASC] (1/18/64 BCR-46)

BYE BYE BLACKBIRD Art Mooney And His Orchestra—MGM 12744 [Mort Dixon/Ray Henderson] [ASC] (1/24/59 C-95)

BYE BYE BLUES Bert Kaempfert And His Orchestra—Decca 31882 [Dave Bennett/Chauncey Gray/Fred Hamm/Bert Lown*] [ASC] (1/15/66 BCR-41) [IWM]

BYE BYE JOHNNY Chuck Berry—Chess 1754 [Chuck Berry] [BMI] (5/30/60 CR-64)

BYE BYE LOVE The Everly Brothers—Cadence 1315 [Boudleaux Bryant/Felice Bryant] [BMI] (5/20/57 BCRt-1)

BYE BYE LOVE Webb Pierce—Decca 30321 [Boudleaux Bryant/Felice Bryant] [BMI] (5/25/57 BRt-1)

BYE BYE LOVE T. Tommy—Dot 15576 [Boudleaux Bryant/Felice Bryant] [BMI] (6/1/57 Rt-1)

BYE, BYE, LOVE Chuck Miller—Mercury 71118 [Boudleaux Bryant/Felice Bryant] [BMI] (6/1/57 Rt-1)

BYE BYE LOVE Will Jordan—Hanover 4529 [Boudleaux Bryant/Felice Bryant] [BMI] (8/3/59 R-91)

C

C-I-T-Y John Cafferty And The Beaver Brown Band—Scotti Brothers 05452 [John Cafferty] [BMI] (8/10/85 BC-18)

CA C'EST L'AMOUR Tony Bennett with Neal Hefti and his Orch.—Columbia 41032 [Cole Porter] [ASC] (10/14/57 BCRt-36)

CA C'EST L'AMOUR Freddy Martin & His Orchestra—Capitol 3795 [Cole Porter] [ASC] (10/14/57 Rt-75)

CA C'EST L'AMOUR Tina Robin—Coral 61889 [Cole Porter] [ASC] (10/14/57 Rt-36)

CA PLANE POUR MOI Plastic Bertrand—Sire 1020 [Francis Jean Deprijck/Yves Lacomblez/Alan Ward*] [ASC] (4/29/78 BC-47) [F]

CAB DRIVER The Mills Brothers—Dot 17041 [C. Carson Parks] [BMI] (1/27/68 BCR-19)

CABARET King Richard's Fluegel Knights—MTA 115 [John Kander] [BMI] (1/28/67 R-98) [IM]

CABARET Herb Alpert & The Tijuana Brass—A&M 925 [John Kander] [BMI] (4/20/68 BCR-69) [IM]

—CACAHUATA see: PEANUTS

CAFE AMORE Spyro Gyra—MCA 51035 [Chet Catallo] [BMI] (1/31/81 BC-77) [I]

THE CAJUN QUEEN Jimmy Dean—Columbia 42282
[Wayne Walker] [BMI] (1/27/62 BCR-22)

CALCUTTA *Lawrence Welk And His Orchestra—Dot 16161*
[Heino Gaze] [ASC] (12/12/60 BCRt-1) [IM]

CALCUTTA *Werner Muller—Decca 31189 [Heino Gaze] [ASC] (12/19/60 Rt-66) [IM]*

CALCUTTA *The Four Preps—Capitol 4508*
[Heino Gaze/Lee Pockriss/Paul Vance] [ASC] (1/30/61 BR-90) [FDE]

CALDONIA James Brown—Smash 1898 [Fleecie Moore] [BMI] (4/25/64 BR-84)

CALEDONIA Robin Trower—Chrysalis 2122
[James Dewar/Robin Trower] [ASC] (12/4/76 BC-81)

CALENDAR GIRL Neil Sedaka—RCA Victor 47-7829
[Howard Greenfield/Neil Sedaka] [BMI] (12/12/60 BCR-4)

CALICO Tommy James—Roulette 7147
[John Andaloro/Joel Diamond/Tommy James/Peter Lucia] [BMI] (10/20/73 C-94)

CALIFORNIA Debby Boone—Warner/Curb 8511 [Joe Brooks] [ASC] (2/11/78 BCR-50)

CALIFORNIA BLUES Redwing—Fantasy 657 [Jimmie Rodgers] [BMI] (4/24/71 C-83)

CALIFORNIA BOUND Ronny & The Daytonas—Mala 490
[John Buck Wilkin] [BMI] (11/7/64 BCR-72)

CALIFORNIA DAY Starland Vocal Band—Windsong 10785
[Bill Danoff] [ASC] (10/16/76 B-66)

CALIFORNIA DREAMIN' *The Mama's & The Papa's—Dunhill 4020*
[John Phillips/Michelle Phillips] [ASC] (1/1/66 BCR-2)

CALIFORNIA DREAMIN' *Bobby Womack—Minit 32055*
[John Phillips/Michelle Phillips] [ASC] (11/23/68 BCR-42)

CALIFORNIA DREAMIN' *America—American Int'l 700*
[John Phillips/Michelle Phillips] [ASC] (3/24/79 BCR-56)

CALIFORNIA DREAMIN' The Beach Boys—Capitol 5630
[John Phillips/Michelle Phillips] [ASC] (9/20/86 BC-49)

CALIFORNIA EARTHQUAKE Mama Cass—Dunhill 4166
[John Hartford] [BMI] (10/26/68 BCR-65)

CALIFORNIA EARTHQUAKE Norman Greenbaum—Reprise 1008
[Norman Greenbaum] [BMI] (5/15/71 B-93)

CALIFORNIA GIRL Eddie Floyd—Stax 0060
[Eddie Floyd/Booker T. Jones Jr.] [BMI] (2/21/70 BCR-40)

CALIFORNIA GIRL (AND THE TENNESSEE SQUARE)
Tompall & The Glaser Brothers—MGM 14036
[Jack H. Clement] [BMI] (4/5/69 BR-88)

CALIFORNIA GIRLS *The Beach Boys—Capitol 5464*
[Mike Love/Brian Wilson] [BMI] (7/24/65 BCR-3)*

CALIFORNIA GIRLS *The Cantina Band—Millennium 11818*
[Mike Love/Brian Wilson] (Med) [BMI] (7/25/81 B-81)*

CALIFORNIA GIRLS *David Lee Roth—Warner Bros. 29102*
[Mike Love/Brian Wilson] [BMI] (1/19/85 BC-3)*

CALIFORNIA KID AND REEMO Lobo—Big Tree 119
[Michael Gately/Robert John] [BMI] (9/4/71 BCR-66)

CALIFORNIA MY WAY The Main Ingredient—RCA Victor 10095
[Willie Hutch] [BMI] (11/16/74 B-75)

CALIFORNIA NIGHTS Lesley Gore—Mercury 72649
[Marvin Hamlisch/Howard Liebling] [ASC] (1/28/67 BCR-11)

CALIFORNIA NIGHTS The Sweet—Capitol 4610
[Brian Connolly/Stephen Priest/Andrew Scott/Michael Tucker] [ASC] (8/12/78 BCR-76)

CALIFORNIA ON MY MIND Morning Mist—Event 206
[Terry Cashman/Tommy West] [ASC] (8/7/71 BR-81)

CALIFORNIA SAGA (ON MY WAY TO SUNNY CALIFORN-I-A) The Beach Boys—Brother/Reprise 1156 [Alan Jardine] [BMI] (5/12/73 BR-84)

CALIFORNIA SOUL *The 5th Dimension—Soul City 770*
[Nick Ashford/Valerie Simpson] [ASC] (12/21/68 BCR-21)

CALIFORNIA SOUL *Marvin Gaye & Tammi Terrell—Tamla 54192*
[Nick Ashford/Valerie Simpson] (TSW) [ASC] (4/25/70 BCR-50)

CALIFORNIA SUN *Joe Jones—Roulette 4344*
[Henry Glover/Morris Levy‡] [BMI] (3/20/61 BCR-67)

CALIFORNIA SUN *The Rivieras (2)—Riviera 1401*
[Henry Glover/Morris Levy‡] [BMI] (1/18/64 BCR-5)

THE CALL Anne Murray—Capitol 4207 [Gene MacLellan] [BMI] (2/21/76 BC-91)

CALL IT LOVE Poco—RCA 9038
[Billy Crain/Ronnie Guilbeau/Richard Lonow] [ASC] (8/26/89 BC-18)

CALL IT POISON The Escape Club—Atlantic 87759
[Johnnie Christo/John Holliday/Trevor Steel/Milan Zekavica] [BMI] (2/23/91 BC-28)

CALL IT ROCK 'N ROLL Great White—Capitol 44676
[Mark Kendall/Michael Lardie/Tony Montana/Alan Niven/Jack Russell] [ASC] (3/2/91 BC-49)

CALL ME Johnny Mathis—Columbia 41253
[Belford Hendricks/Clyde Otis] [BMI] (9/29/58 BCR-12)

CALL ME Chris Montez—A&M 780 [Tony Hatch] [BMI] (1/8/66 BCR-22)

CALL ME Aretha Franklin—Atlantic 2706
[Aretha Franklin] (TSW) [BMI] (2/14/70 BCR-13)

CALL ME Blondie—Chrysalis 2414
[Clement A. Bozewski*/Deborah Harry/Giorgio Moroder] [ASC] (2/16/80 BCR-1)

CALL ME Skyy—Salsoul 2152 [Randy Muller] [ASC] (12/12/81 BCR-24)

CALL ME Go West—Chrysalis 42865 [Peter Cox/Richard Drummie] [ASC] (6/1/85 BC-48)

CALL ME Dennis DeYoung—A&M 2816 [Dennis DeYoung] [ASC] (3/15/86 BC-54)

CALL ME ANYTIME Frankie Avalon—Chancellor 1071 [Jesse Stone] [BMI] (2/20/61 R-53)

CALL ME (COME BACK HOME) Al Green—Hi 2235
[Al Green/Al Jackson/Willie Mitchell] [BMI] (2/17/73 BCR-8)

CALL ME IRRESPONSIBLE *Frank Sinatra—Reprise 20,151*
[Sammy Cahn/Jimmy Van Heusen] [ASC] (3/2/63 BCtRt-62)

CALL ME IRRESPONSIBLE *Jack Jones—Kapp 516*
[Sammy Cahn/Jimmy Van Heusen] [ASC] (4/13/63 BCtRt-62)

CALL ME LIGHTNING The Who—Decca 32288 [Pete Townshend] [BMI] (3/23/68 BCR-24)

CALL ME MR. IN-BETWEEN Burl Ives—Decca 31405
[Harlan Howard] [BMI] (7/7/62 BCR-15)

(CALL ME) THE TRAVELING MAN The Masqueraders—HBS/ABC-Paramount 12157
[Sammie Hutchins/Lee Jones/David Sanders/Harold Larry Thomas/Robert Wrightsil] [BMI] (2/14/76 CR-86)

CALL ME UP IN DREAMLAND Van Morrison—Warner Bros. 7488
[Van Morrison] [BMI] (6/5/71 B-95)

(CALL ME) WHEN THE SPIRIT MOVES YOU Touch—Atco 7222
[Mark Mangold/Craig Sprovach*] [ASC] (7/26/80 BCR-65)

(CALL ME YOUR) ANYTHING MAN Bobby Moore—Scepter 12405
[Harold Beatty] [ASC] (8/9/75 B-99)

CALL MY NAME, I'LL BE THERE Wilson Pickett—Atlantic 2824
[Dave Crawford/Willie Martin/Brad Shapiro] [ASC] (8/21/71 BCR-41)

THE CALL OF THE SOUTH Bing & Gary Crosby—Decca 29147
[Irving Berlin] [ASC] (7/24/54 C-46)

CALL ON ME Bobby Bland—Duke 360 [Deadric Malone] [BMI] (1/5/63 BCR-22)

CALL ON ME Chicago—Columbia 46062 [Lee Loughnane] [ASC] (6/22/74 BCR-6)

CALL OUT MY NAME Zwol—EMI America 8009 [Walter Zwol] [ASC] (1/27/79 BC-75)

CALL TO THE HEART Giuffria—MCA 52497
[David Glen Eisley/Gregg Giuffria] [ASC] (11/10/84 BC-15)

CALLA CALLA The Paulette Sisters—Aamco 101
[Lenny Adelson/Eddy Samuels/Sunny Skylar] [BMI] (10/25/58 C-87)

CALLIN' DOCTOR CASEY John D. Loudermilk—RCA Victor 47-8054
[John D. Loudermilk] [BMI] (7/28/62 BR-83)

CALLING ALL GIRLS Queen—Elektra 69981 [Roger Taylor] [BMI] (7/31/82 BC-60)

CALLING AMERICA Electric Light Orchestra—CBS Associated 05766
[Jeff Lynne] [ASC] (2/1/86 BC-18)

CALLING DR. LOVE Kiss—Casablanca 880 [Gene Simmons] [ASC] (3/12/77 BCR-10)

CALLING IT LOVE Animotion—Polydor 889054
[Desmond Child/Anton Fig] [ASC] (6/10/89 BC-53)

CALLING OCCUPANTS *Klaatu—Capitol 4412*
[Terry Draper/John Woloschuk] (TSW) [ASC] (4/2/77 BCR-62)

CALLING OCCUPANTS OF INTERPLANETARY CRAFT *Carpenters—A&M 1978*
[Terry Draper/John Woloschuk] [ASC] (9/24/77 BCR-24)

CALYPSO John Denver—RCA Victor 10353 [John Denver] (TSW) [ASC] (9/27/75 BCR-1)

CALYPSO ITALIANO Lou Monte—RCA Victor 47-6848
[Wandra Merrell/Lou Monte] [BMI] (3/23/57 R-49)

CALYPSO MELODY *David Rose And His Orchestra—MGM 12430*
[Larry Clinton] [ASC] (3/2/57 BCRt-25) [IWM]

CALYPSO MELODY *Danny Welton—Dot 15559 [Larry Clinton] [ASC] (5/11/57 Rt-43) [IWM]*

CALYPSO PARAKEET Patty Brandon—Chancellor 1002
[Peter DeAngelis/Bob Marcucci] [ASC] (4/6/57 R-79)

CAMEL BACK A.B. Skhy—MGM 14086 [Howard Wales] [ASC] (12/6/69 B-100) [I]

CAMPFIRE GIRLS Billy Joe Royal—Columbia 43740
[Freddy Weller] [BMI] (8/27/66 BCR-90)

CAN I Eddie Kendricks—Tamla 54210
[Hal Davis/Herman Griffith] [ASC] (11/20/71 CR-92)

CAN I CALL YOU MY GIRL PC Quest—RCA 62018
[Monty Brinkley/John Duarte/Tim James/Steve McClintock] [BMI] (5/4/91 B-58)

CAN I CARRY YOUR BALLOON The Swampseeds—Epic 10281
[Sandy Linzer/Denny Randell] [BMI] (4/20/68 C-100)

CAN I CHANGE MY MIND Tyrone Davis—Dakar 602
[Barry Despenza/Carl Wolfolk] [BMI] (12/21/68 BCR-5)

CAN I COME OVER TONIGHT The Velours—Onyx 512
[Don Haywoode/Jerry Winston] [BMI] (7/8/57 B-83)

CAN I GET A WITNESS *Marvin Gaye—Tamla 54087*
[Lamont Dozier/Brian Holland/Eddie Holland] [BMI] (10/19/63 BCR-18)

CAN I GET A WITNESS *Lee Michaels—A&M 1303*
[Lamont Dozier/Brian Holland/Eddie Holland] [BMI] (11/20/71 BCR-34)

CAN I GET TO KNOW YOU BETTER The Turtles—White Whale 238
[Steve Barri/P.F. Sloan] [ASC] (10/29/66 BCR-78)

CAN I STEAL A LITTLE LOVE Frank Sinatra—Capitol 3608
[Phil Tuminello] [ASC] (1/12/57 BCR-20)

CAN I TRUST YOU? The Bachelors—London 20010
[Emidio Remigi/Eddie Snyder/Paul Vance] [ASC] (6/25/66 BCR-37) [FDE]

CAN SHE GIVE YOU FEVER *Stan Robinson—Amy 810*
[Ersel Hickey/Ernest L. Tucker] [BMI] (10/24/60 Rt-95)

CAN SHE GIVE YOU FEVER *Ernie Tucker—Earth 501*
[Ersel Hickey/Ernest L. Tucker] [BMI] (10/24/60 Rt-95)

CAN SHE GIVE ME FEVER *Little Junior Lewis—Fury 1040*
[Ersel Hickey/Ernest L. Tucker] [BMI] (10/31/60 Rt-95)

CAN THE CAN Suzi Quatro—Big Tree 16053
[Mike Chapman/Nicky Chinn] [ASC] (1/24/76 BCR-56)

CAN THIS BE REAL Natural Four—Curtom 1990
[Michael J. Hawkins/Janice Hutson/Leroy Hutson] [ASC] (12/22/73 BCR-25)

CAN THIS BE THE END OF A DREAM Dorothy Collins—Audiovox 108
[John M. Klein/Hal Richardson] [ASC] (10/4/54 R-PRE)

CAN WE STILL BE FRIENDS *Todd Rundgren—Bearsville 0324*
[Todd Rundgren] [BMI] (5/27/78 BCR-29)

CAN WE STILL BE FRIENDS *Robert Palmer—Island 49137*
[Todd Rundgren] [BMI] (12/15/79 BCR-50)

CAN YOU DANCE TO IT? Cat Mother And The All Night News Boys—Polydor 14007
[Robert William Smith] [BMI] (9/27/69 CR-78)

CAN YOU DO IT *The Contours—Gordy 7029*
[Thelma Gordy/Richard Street] [ASC] (4/4/64 BCR-41)

CAN YOU DO IT *Grand Funk Railroad—MCA 40590*
[Thelma Gordy/Richard Street] [ASC] (8/7/76 BC-45)

CAN YOU FEEL IT Bobby Goldsboro—United Artists 50650
[Bobby Goldsboro] [BMI] (4/4/70 BCR-67)

CAN YOU FEEL IT Jacksons—Epic 01032
[Jackie Jackson/Michael Jackson] [BMI] (4/25/81 BCR-68)

CAN YOU FEEL THE BEAT Lisa Lisa And Cult Jam—Columbia 05669
[Curtis Bedeau/Gerard Charles/Hugh Clarke/Brian George/Lucien George/Paul George] [BMI] (11/16/85 BC-69)

CAN YOU FIND IT IN YOUR HEART
Tony Bennett with Percy Faith and His Orchestra—Columbia 40667
[Robert Allen/Al Stillman] [ASC] (4/6/56 BCR-6)

CAN YOU FOOL Glen Campbell—Capitol 4584
[Micheal Smotherman] [ASC] (10/21/78 BCR-38)

CAN YOU GET TO THAT Funkadelic—Westbound 185
[George Clinton/Ernie Harris] [BMI] (9/4/71 BCR-61)

CAN YOU HANDLE IT? Graham Central Station—Warner Bros. 7782
[Larry Graham] [BMI] (4/13/74 BCR-49)

CAN YOU JERK LIKE ME The Contours—Gordy 7037
[Ivy Jo Hunter/William Stevenson] [ASC] (12/12/64 BCR-47)

CAN YOU PLEASE CRAWL OUT YOUR WINDOW? Bob Dylan—Columbia 43477
[Bob Dylan] [SE] (1/1/66 BCR-55)

CAN YOU READ MY MIND Maureen McGovern—Warner/Curb 8750
[Leslie Bricusse/John Williams] [BMI] (2/24/79 BCR-52)

CAN YOU STAND THE RAIN New Edition—MCA 53464
[James Samuel Harris/Terry Lewis] [ASC] (2/11/89 BC-44)

CAN YOU STOP THE RAIN Peabo Bryson—Columbia 73745
[Walter Afanasieff/John Bettis] [ASC] (6/22/91 BC-52)

CAN YOUR MONKEY DO THE DOG Rufus Thomas—Stax 144
[Steve Cropper/Rufus Thomas] [BMI] (2/1/64 BCR-35)

CANADIAN SUNSET *Hugo Winterhalter And His Orchestra—RCA Victor 47-6537*
[Eddie Heywood] [BMI] (6/23/56 BCtRt-1) [IM]

CANADIAN SUNSET *Andy Williams—Cadence 1297*
[Norman Gimbel/Eddie Heywood] [BMI] (8/10/56 BCtRt-1)

CANADIAN SUNSET *Etta Jones—Prestige 191*
[Norman Gimbel/Eddie Heywood] [BMI] (2/27/61 BCR-74)

CANADIAN SUNSET *Sounds Orchestral—Parkway 958*
[Eddie Heywood] [BMI] (7/24/65 BCR-71) [IM]

CANDIDA Dawn—Bell 903 [Irwin Levine/Toni Wine] [BMI] (7/25/70 BCR-1)

CANDLE IN THE WIND Elton John—MCA 53196
[Elton John/Bernie Taupin] [BMI] (11/7/87 BC-6)

CANDY The Astors—Stax 170 [Steve Cropper/Isaac Hayes] [BMI] (7/10/65 BCR-54)

CANDY Cameo—Atlanta Artists 888193
[Larry Blackmon/Tomi Jenkins] [BMI] (12/27/86 BC-21)

CANDY Iggy Pop—Virgin 98900 [Iggy Pop] [BMI] (11/24/90 BC-28)

CANDY APPLE RED Bonnie Guitar—Dolton 10 [Bonnie Guitar] [BMI] (11/30/59 BR-78)

CANDY APPLE RED R. Dean Taylor—Rare Earth 5030
[R. Dean Taylor] [BMI] (8/7/71 CR-92)

CANDY CHA CHA Jan August-Richard Hayman—Mercury 71371
[Mack David/Alex Kramer/Joan Whitney] [ASC] (10/27/58 R-82) [IWM]

CANDY GIRL The 4 Seasons—Vee-Jay 539 [Larry Santos] [ASC] (6/29/63 BCR-3)

CANDY GIRL New Edition—Streetwise 1108
[Michael Jonzun/Maurice Starr] [ASC] (4/30/83 BC-46)

CANDY MAN Roy Orbison—Monument 447
[Fred Neil/Beverly Ross] [BMI] (8/7/61 BCR-25)

THE CANDY MAN Sammy Davis, Jr. With The Mike Curb Congregation—MGM 14320
[Leslie Bricusse/Anthony Newley] [BMI] (3/11/72 BCR-1)

CANDY SWEET Pat Boone—Dot 16122 [Winfield Scott] [BMI] (8/8/60 BCR-35)

CANDY TO ME Eddie Holland—Motown 1063
[Lamont Dozier/Brian Holland/Eddie Holland] [BMI] (8/29/64 BCR-58)

CANDY'S GOING BAD Golden Earring—Track/MCA 40309
[Barry Hay/George Kooymans] [ASC] (10/5/74 BCR-78)

CANNED HAM Norman Greenbaum—Reprise 0919
[Norman Greenbaum] [BMI] (6/6/70 BCR-30)

CANNONBALL Duane Eddy His "Twangy" guitar and The Rebels—Jamie 1111
[Duane Eddy/Lee Hazlewood] [BMI] (10/27/58 BCR-15) [I]

CANNONBALL Supertramp—A&M 2731 [Rick Davies] [ASC] (5/25/85 BC-28)

CAN'T BUY ME LOVE The Beatles—Capitol 5150
[John Lennon/Paul McCartney] [ASC] (3/21/64 BCR-1)

CAN'T CHANGE MY HEART Cate Brothers—Asylum 45326
[Earl Cate/Ernie Cate] [BMI] (7/17/76 BCR-73)

CAN'T FIGHT THIS FEELING REO Speedwagon—Epic 04713
[Kevin Cronin] [ASC] (1/19/85 BC-1)

CAN'T FIND THE TIME *Orpheus—MGM 13882 [Bruce Arnold] [BMI] (3/2/68 C-88)*

CAN'T FIND THE TIME *Orpheus—MGM 13882 [Bruce Arnold] [BMI] (8/23/69 BCR-72)*

CAN'T FIND THE TIME *Rose Colored Glass—Bang 584*
[Bruce Arnold] [BMI] (4/10/71 BCR-51)

CAN'T FORGET YOU Gloria Estefan—Epic 73864
[Jorge Casas/Clay Ostwald/Jon Secada] [BMI] (6/8/91 BC-35)

CAN'T GET ENOUGH Bad Company—Swan Song 70015
[Mick Ralphs] [ASC] (8/3/74 BCR-1)

CAN'T GET ENOUGH OF YOU, BABY ? And The Mysterians—Cameo 467
[Sandy Linzer/Denny Randell] [BMI] (3/25/67 BCR-47)

CAN'T GET ENOUGH OF YOUR LOVE, BABE Barry White—20th Century 2120
[Barry White] [BMI] (7/27/74 BCR-1)

CAN'T GET ENUFF Winger—Atlantic 87884
[Reb Beach/Kip Winger] [BMI] (7/28/90 BC-28)

CAN'T GET IT OUT OF MY HEAD Electric Light Orchestra—United Artists 573
[Jeff Lynne] [ASC] (12/7/74 BCR-9)

CAN'T GET OVER LOSING YOU Donnie Elbert—Rare Bullet 101
[Donnie Elbert] [BMI] (11/14/70 BCR-91)

CAN'T GET OVER (THE BOSSA NOVA) Eydie Gorme—Columbia 43082
[Marilyn Gins/Eydie Gorme/Steve Lawrence] [BMI] (8/29/64 B-87)

CAN'T GET STARTED Peter Wolf—EMI 43012
[Peter Wolf] [ASC] (5/23/87 BC-75)

CAN'T GET USED TO LOSING YOU Andy Williams—Columbia 42674
[Doc Pomus/Mort Shuman] [BMI] (2/23/63 BCR-1)

CAN'T GIVE YOU ANYTHING (BUT MY LOVE) The Stylistics—Avco 4656
[Luigi Creatore/Hugo Peretti/George David Weiss] [ASC] (7/5/75 BCR-51)

CAN'T HELP BUT LOVE YOU The Standells—Tower 348
[Don Bennett/Ethon McElroy] [BMI] (11/25/67 BCR-72)

CAN'T HELP FALLING IN LOVE *The Four Esquires—Terrace 5502*
[Luigi Creatore/Hugo Peretti/George David Weiss] [ASC] (11/27/61 Rt-6)

CAN'T HELP FALLING IN LOVE *Elvis Presley With The Jordanaires—*
RCA Victor 47-7968 [Luigi Creatore/Hugo Peretti/George David Weiss] [ASC] (12/4/61 BCRt-2)

CAN'T HELP FALLING IN LOVE *Keely Smith—Dot 16298*
[Luigi Creatore/Hugo Peretti/George David Weiss] [ASC] (12/18/61 Rt-6)

CAN'T HELP FALLING IN LOVE *Al Martino—Capitol 2746*
[Luigi Creatore/Hugo Peretti/George David Weiss] [ASC] (2/7/70 BCR-51)

CAN'T HELP FALLING IN LOVE *Andy Williams—Columbia 45094*
[Luigi Creatore/Hugo Peretti/George David Weiss] [ASC] (2/21/70 BC-85)

CAN'T HELP FALLING IN LOVE WITH YOU *Jimmy Castor—Long Distance 702*
[Luigi Creatore/Hugo Peretti/George David Weiss] [ASC] (4/26/80 C-98)

CAN'T HELP FALLING IN LOVE *Corey Hart—EMI America 8368*
[Luigi Creatore/Hugo Peretti/George David Weiss] [ASC] (12/6/86 BC-24)

CAN'T HELP LOVIN' THAT GIRL OF MINE The Excels—RSVP 111
[Oscar Hammerstein/Jerome Kern] [ASC] (6/5/61 B-100)

—CAN'T HIDE FROM LOVE see: READY OR NOT HERE I COME

CAN'T HIDE LOVE Earth, Wind & Fire—Columbia 10309
[Skip Scarborough] [BMI] (3/27/76 BCR-39)

CAN'T HOLD BACK (YOUR LOVING) Kano—Mirage 3878
[Barbara Addoms/Anna Cantù/Luciano Ninzatti/Stefano Pulga] [ASC] (12/26/81 B-89)

CAN'T IT ALL BE LOVE Randy Edelman—Arista 0268
[Randy Edelman] [BMI] (10/22/77 CR-80)

CAN'T KEEP A GOOD MAN DOWN Eddie Money—Columbia 10981
[Dan Alexander/Eddie Money/Chris Solberg] [BMI] (5/12/79 BCR-63)

CAN'T LET A WOMAN Ambrosia—20th Century 2310 [David Pack] [BMI] (12/4/76 CR-88)

CAN'T LET GO Stephen Stills Featuring Michael Finnigan—Atlantic 89611
[Joe Esposito/Allee Willis] [BMI] (10/6/84 BC-67)

CAN'T LET GO Mariah Carey—Columbia 74088
[Walter Afanasieff/Mariah Carey] [ASC] (11/16/91 BC-1)

CAN'T LET YOU OUT OF MY SIGHT Chuck Jackson & Maxine Brown—Wand 191
[Roger Atkins/Helen Miller] [BMI] (8/21/65 BCR-85)

(CAN'T LIVE WITHOUT YOUR) LOVE AND AFFECTION Nelson—DGC 19689
[Gunnar Nelson/Matthew Nelson/Marc Tanner] [ASC] (7/7/90 BC-1)

CAN'T NOBODY LOVE YOU Solomon Burke—Atlantic 2196
[James Mitchell] [BMI] (7/20/63 BC-66)
CAN'T PUT A PRICE ON LOVE The Knack—Capitol 4853
[Berton Averre/Doug Fieger] [ASC] (4/5/80 BCR-59)
CAN'T SATISFY The Impressions—ABC 10831 [Curtis Mayfield] [BMI] (8/27/66 BCR-59)
CAN'T SAY NOTHIN' Curtis Mayfield—Curtom 1993
[Curtis Mayfield] [BMI] (12/29/73 BCR-83)
CAN'T SEEM TO MAKE YOU MINE The Seeds—GNP Crescendo 354
[Sky Saxon] [BMI] (4/15/67 BCR-41)
CAN'T SHAKE LOOSE Agnetha Faltskog—Polydor 815230
[Russ Ballard] [ASC] (8/27/83 BC-29)
CAN'T SLEEP The Rockets—RSO 926 [John Badanjek] [ASC] (4/21/79 BCR-51)
CAN'T SMILE WITHOUT YOU Barry Manilow—Arista 0305
[Chris Arnold/David Martin/Geoff Morrow] [BMI] (2/4/78 BCR-2)
CAN'T STAY AWAY FROM YOU Gloria Estefan and Miami Sound Machine—Epic 07641
[Gloria Estefan] [BMI] (11/21/87 BC-6)
CAN'T STOP Rick James—Gordy 1776 [Rick James] [ASC] (3/30/85 BC-50)
CAN'T STOP After 7—Virgin 98961
[Kenneth Edmonds/Antonio Reid] [BMI] (7/28/90 BC-6)
CAN'T STOP DANCIN' Captain & Tennille—A&M 1912
[John Pritchard/Ray Stevens] [BMI] (3/19/77 BCR-13)
CAN'T STOP FALLING INTO LOVE Cheap Trick—Epic 73444
[Rick Nielsen/Thomas John Peterson/Robin Zander] [BMI] (7/21/90 BC-7)
CAN'T STOP GROOVIN' NOW, WANNA DO IT SOME MORE B.T. Express—Columbia 10346
[Billy Nichols] [BMI] (6/5/76 BCR-52)
CAN'T STOP LOVING YOU The Last Word—Atco 6498
[Michael Byrnes/John Lombardo] [BMI] (10/7/67 BCR-76)
CAN'T STOP LOVIN' YOU *The Flirtations—Deram 85062*
[Wayne Bickerton/Tony Waddington] [ASC] (7/11/70 C-96)
CAN'T STOP LOVING YOU *Tom Jones—Parrot 40056*
[Wayne Bickerton/Tony Waddington] [ASC] (11/14/70 BCR-15)
—CAN'T STOP LOVING YOU see also: I CAN'T STOP LOVING YOU
CAN'T STOP THIS THING WE STARTED Bryan Adams—A&M 1576
[Bryan Adams/Mutt Lange] [ASC] (9/14/91 BC-1)
CAN'T TAKE MY EYES OFF YOU *Frankie Valli—Philips 40446*
[Bob Crewe/Bob Gaudio] [BMI] (5/13/67 BCR-1)
CAN'T TAKE MY EYES OFF YOU *The Lettermen—Capitol 2054*
[Bob Crewe/Bob Gaudio] (Med) [BMI] (12/9/67 BCR-6)
CAN'T TAKE MY EYES OFF YOU *Nancy Wilson—Capitol 2644*
[Bob Crewe/Bob Gaudio] [BMI] (11/22/69 BCR-52)
I CAN'T TAKE MY EYES OFF YOU *Pet Shop Boys—EMI 50351*
[Bob Crewe/Bob Gaudio] (Med) [BMI] (5/25/91 BC-72)
CAN'T TRUSS IT Public Enemy—Def Jam 73870
[Carlton Ridenhour/Gary Rinaldo/Hank Shocklee] [BMI] (10/19/91 B-50)
CAN'T WAIT ALL NIGHT Juice Newton—RCA 13863
[Bryan Adams/Eric Kagna/Jim Vallance] [BMI] (8/11/84 BC-66)
CAN'T WAIT ANOTHER MINUTE Five Star—RCA 14421
[Paul Chiten/Sue Sheridan] [BMI] (9/13/86 BC-41)
CAN'T WAIT FOR SUMMER Steve Lawrence—Coral 61834
[John Gluck/Diane Lampert] [ASC] (5/27/57 BCR-38)
CAN'T WE BE SWEETHEARTS The Cleftones—Gee 1016
[Herbert Cox/George Goldner*/Morris Levy‡] [BMI] (7/21/56 CR-43)
CAN'T WE TRY Teddy Pendergrass—Philadelphia Int'l 3107
[Ken Hirsch/Ronald Norman Miller] [BMI] (8/16/80 BCR-39)
CAN'T WE TRY Dan Hill—Columbia 07050 [Beverly Hill/Dan Hill] [SO] (6/6/87 BC-6)
CAN'T YOU FIND ANOTHER WAY (OF DOING IT) Sam & Dave—Atlantic 2540
[Homer Banks/Raymond Earl Jackson] [BMI] (8/3/68 BCR-42)
CAN'T YOU HEAR MY HEARTBEAT Herman's Hermits—MGM 13310
[John Carter/Ken Hawker] [ASC] (1/30/65 BCR-1)
CAN'T YOU HEAR THE SONG? Wayne Newton—Chelsea 0105
[Chris Arnold/David Martin/Geoff Morrow] [BMI] (9/23/72 BCR-27)
CAN'T YOU JUST SEE ME Aretha Franklin—Columbia 43203
[Belford Hendricks/Clyde Otis] [BMI] (1/30/65 BR-93)
CAN'T YOU SEE *Waylon Jennings—RCA Victor 10721 [Toy Caldwell] [BMI] (10/9/76 B-97)*
CAN'T YOU SEE *The Marshall Tucker Band—Capricorn 0278*
[Toy Caldwell] [BMI] (8/20/77 BC-70)
CAN'T YOU SEE ME CRY The New Colony Six—Mercury 72817
[Ray Graffia/Jerry Kollenburg] [BMI] (6/15/68 BCR-52)
CAN'T YOU SEE THAT SHE'S MINE The Dave Clark Five—Epic 9692
[Dave Clark/Mike Smith] [ASC] (6/13/64 BCR-4)
CAN'T YOU SEE (YOU'RE LOSING ME) Mary Wells—Atco 6392
[Barrett Strong] [BMI] (1/22/66 BCR-85)
CAN'TCHA SAY (YOU BELIEVE IN ME) Boston—MCA 53029
[Brad Delp/Gerald Green/Tom Scholz] (Med) [ASC] (3/7/87 BC-20)
CANTINA BAND Meco—Millennium 604 [John Williams] (Med) [BMI] (7/30/77 BCR-1) [I]
CANVAS OF LIFE Minor Detail—Polydor 815 329
[John Hughes/Willie Hughes] [ASC] (9/24/83 B-92)
CAP AND GOWN Marty Robbins—Columbia 41408
[Roy C. Bennett/Sid Tepper] [ASC] (6/15/59 BCR-44)
CAPPUCCINA Nat King Cole—Capitol 4623
[Giuseppe Massara/Vito Pallavicini/Nicola Salerno/Noel Sherman] [ASC]
(9/25/61 R-78) [F,FDE]
CAPTAIN HOWDY Simon Stokes—Casablanca 0007
[Simon Stokes] [ASC] (6/8/74 BCR-64)
THE CAPTAIN OF HER HEART Double—A&M 2838
[Felix Haug/Kurt Maloo] [ASC] (6/28/86 BC-16)
CAPTAIN OF YOUR SHIP Reparata And The Delrons—Mala 589
[Estelle Levitt/Kenny Young] [BMI] (2/17/68 R-97)
CAPTURE THE MOMENT Jay And The Americans—United Artists 50654
[Richard Reicheg/Marty Sanders/Kenny Vance] [BMI] (3/14/70 BCR-42)
CAPTURE YOUR HEART Blue—Rocket/MCA 40706
[Hugh Nicholson] [BMI] (5/7/77 BC-88)
CAR WASH Rose Royce—MCA 40615 [Norman Whitfield] [BMI] (10/23/76 BCR-1)
CARA-LIN The Strangeloves—Bang 508
[Bob Feldman/Jerry Goldstein/Richard Gottehrer] [BMI] (9/11/65 BCR-32)
CARA MIA *David Whitfield with Mantovani And His Orchestra—London 1486*
[Bunny Lewis/Mantovani] [ASC] (8/14/54 BCR-9)
CARA, MIA *Jay & The Americans—United Artists 881*
[Bunny Lewis/Mantovani] [ASC] (5/29/65 BCR-3)
CARAMBA The Champs—Challenge 59043
[Dave Burgess] [BMI] (4/6/59 CR-94) [I]
CARAVAN (PART 2) *Cozy Cole—Grand Award 1023*
[Duke Ellington/Juan Tizol] [ASC] (11/24/58 C-97) [I]
CARAVAN (PT. 1) *Cozy Cole—Grand Award 1023*
[Duke Ellington/Juan Tizol] [ASC] (11/24/58 R-56) [I]
CARAVAN *Santo & Johnny—Canadian-American 111*
[Duke Ellington/Juan Tizol] [ASC] (2/29/60 BCR-39) [I]
CARAVAN OF LOVE Isley Jasper Isley—CBS Associated 05611
[Ernie Isley/Marvin Isley/Chris Jasper] [ASC] (12/7/85 BC-51)
CAREFREE HIGHWAY Gordon Lightfoot—Reprise 1309
[Gordon Lightfoot] [ASC] (8/31/74 BCR-10)
CAREFREE WANDERER Bill Parsons with The All-American Boy's—Fraternity 838
[John Howard/Sy Soloway/Shirley Wolfe] [BMI] (3/30/59 CR-80)
CAREFUL MAN John Edwards—Aware 043 [James E. Lewis] [BMI] (11/16/74 C-86)
CARELESS Bobby Vinton—Epic 9869
[Eddy Howard/Dick Jurgens/Lew Quadling] [ASC] (12/18/65 C-82)
CARELESS LOVE Ray Charles—ABC-Paramount 10345
[Ray Charles] [BMI] (7/28/62 BCR-46)
CARELESS WHISPER Wham! Featuring George Michael—Columbia 04691
[George Michael/Andrew Ridgeley] [ASC] (12/22/84 BC-1)
THE CARELESS YEARS *Sue Raney—Capitol 3745 [Joe Lubin] [BMI] (7/13/57 Rt-83)*
THE CARELESS YEARS *Duke Mitchell—Liberty 55086 [Joe Lubin] [BMI] (7/20/57 Rt-84)*
CAREY Joni Mitchell—Reprise 1029 [Joni Mitchell] [ASC] (8/21/71 BCR-92)
CARIBBEAN Mitchell Torok—Guyden 2018 [Mitchell Torok] [BMI] (7/27/59 BCR-27)
CARIBBEAN FESTIVAL Kool & The Gang—De-Lite 1573
[Robert Bell/Ronald Bell/George M. Brown/Robert Mickens/Otha Nash/
Claydes Smith/Dennis Thomas/Richard Westfield] [BMI] (10/25/75 BCR-45) [I]
CARIBBEAN QUEEN (NO MORE LOVE ON THE RUN) Billy Ocean—Jive 9199
[Keith Diamond/Billy Ocean] [BMI] (8/11/84 BC-1)
CARMEN Herb Alpert & The Tijuana Brass—A&M 890
[Georges Bizet] [BMI] (1/6/68 BCR-50) [I]
CARMEN'S BOOGIE The Crew-Cuts—Mercury 70634
[George Cates/Mel Leven] [BMI] (6/11/55 CR-42)
A CARNIVAL IN VENICE The Mills Brothers—Decca 29115
[Buddy Kaye/Dick Manning] [ASC] (7/10/54 C-PRE)
THE CARNIVAL IS OVER The Seekers—Capitol 5531
[Tom Springfield] [ASC] (11/20/65 C-100)
CAROL *Chuck Berry—Chess 1700 [Chuck Berry] [BMI] (8/25/58 BCR-18)*
CAROL *Tommy Roe—ABC-Paramount 10543 [Chuck Berry] [BMI] (4/25/64 BCR-52)*
CAROLINA DAY Livingston Taylor—Capricorn 8012
[Livingston Taylor] [ASC] (2/6/71 B-93)
CAROLINA IN MY MIND *Crystal Mansion Featuring Johnny Caswell—Colossus 128*
[James Taylor] [ASC] (10/17/70 BCR-47)
CAROLINA IN MY MIND *James Taylor—Apple 1805*
[James Taylor] [ASC] (11/7/70 BCR-67)
CAROLINA IN THE MORNING
Mitch Miller & his "Sing Along With Mitch" Chorus—Columbia 41317
[Walter Donaldson/Gus Kahn] [ASC] (1/12/59 R-92)
CAROLINA IN THE PINES Michael Murphey—Epic 50131
[Michael Murphey] [BMI] (8/16/75 BCR-21)
CAROLINA MOON *The Melody Makers—Hollis 1001*
[Joe Burke/Benny Davis] [ASC] (9/2/57 R-72)
CAROLINA MOON *Connie Francis—MGM 12683*
[Joe Burke/Benny Davis] [ASC] (7/14/58 R-32)
CAROLINE Concrete Blonde—I.R.S. 10217
[Johnette Lin Napolitano] [BMI] (12/29/90 C-84)
CAROLINE, NO Brian Wilson—Capitol 5610
[Tony Asher/Brian Wilson] [BMI] (3/26/66 BCR-31)

CAROLYN Merle Haggard And The Strangers—Capitol 3222
[Tommy Collins] [BMI] (12/4/71 BCR-58)

CARPET MAN The 5th Dimension—Soul City 762 [Jimmy Webb] [BMI] (1/27/68 BCR-22)

CARRIE Cliff Richard—EMI America 8035
[Terry Britten/Brian A. Robertson] [BMI] (2/23/80 BCR-34)

CARRIE Europe—Epic 07282 [Mic Michaeli/Joey Tempest] [BMI] (8/1/87 BC-3)

CARRIE-ANNE The Hollies—Epic 10180
[Allan Clarke/Tony Hicks/Graham Nash] [BMI] (6/17/67 BCR-9)

CARRIE'S GONE J.C. Stone—Private Stock 45,002
[Robert L. Johnston] [BMI] (10/5/74 C-92)

CARRIE'S GONE Le Roux—RCA 13456
[Fergie Frederiksen/Jim Odom/Rod Roddy] [BMI] (3/19/83 BC-80)

THE CARROLL COUNTY ACCIDENT Porter Wagoner—RCA Victor 47-9651
[Bob Ferguson] [BMI] (1/25/69 BCR-92)

CARRY ME Joe Simon—Spring 145 [Phillip Mitchell/Ernie Shelby] [BMI] (4/6/74 R-87)

CARRY ME David Crosby / Graham Nash—ABC 12140
[David Crosby] [BMI] (11/8/75 BCR-44)

CARRY ME BACK The Rascals—Atlantic 2664 [Felix Cavaliere] [ASC] (8/30/69 BCR-10)

CARRY ME, CARRIE Dr. Hook And The Medicine Show—Columbia 45667
[Shel Silverstein] [BMI] (9/9/72 BCR-68)

CARRY ON WAYWARD SON Kansas—Kirshner 4267
[Kerry Livgren] [BMI] (12/11/76 BCR-7)

CARRYING THAT LOAD Ray Charles—Atlantic 2174
[Doc Pomus/Mort Shuman] [BMI] (1/12/63 R-88)

CARS Gary Numan—Atco 7211 [Gary Numan] [BMI] (2/16/80 BCR-4)

CARS WITH THE BOOM L'Trimm—Atlantic 89005
[Elana Cager/Larry Davis/Rachel De Rougemont/Paul (2) Klein*/Joseph Louis Stone] [BMI] (9/24/88 BC-54)

CASANOVA Levert—Atlantic 89217 [Reggie Calloway] [BMI] (8/15/87 BC-5)

CASANOVA BROWN The Young Sisters—Twirl 2001
[Tom King/Ira Mack‡/Maron McKenzie/John Pocisk] [BMI] (9/29/62 C-93)

CASE OF YOU Frank Stallone—Scotti Brothers 603
[Joni Mitchell] [ASC] (9/27/80 BR-67)

CASINO ROYALE Herb Alpert & The Tijuana Brass—A&M 850
[Burt Bacharach] [ASC] (4/8/67 BCR-21) [IM]

CASONOVA (YOUR PLAYING DAYS ARE OVER) Ruby Andrews—Zodiac 1004
[Jo Armstead/Milton Middlebrook] [BMI] (8/5/67 BCR-33)

CAST YOUR FATE TO THE WIND *Martin Denny, and His Orchestra—Liberty 55514*
[Vince Guaraldi] [BMI] (12/15/62 Ct-40) [IM]

CAST YOUR FATE TO THE WIND *Vince Guaraldi Trio—Fantasy 563*
[Vince Guaraldi] [BMI] (12/8/62 BCtR-22) [IM]

CAST YOUR FATE TO THE WIND *Sounds Orchestral—Parkway 942*
[Vince Guaraldi] [BMI] (3/20/65 BCR-7) [IM]

CAST YOUR FATE TO THE WIND *Steve Alaimo—ABC-Paramount 10680*
[Vince Guaraldi/Carel Werber] [BMI] (6/12/65 BR-89)

CAST YOUR FATE TO THE WIND *Shelby Flint—Valiant 743*
[Vince Guaraldi/Carel Werber] [BMI] (8/13/66 BCR-59)

CASTIN' MY SPELL Johnny Otis Show—Capitol 4168
[Alvin Johnson/Edwin Johnson] [BMI] (4/25/59 BCR-52)

CASTLES IN THE AIR *Don McLean—United Artists 50887*
[Don McLean] (TSW) [BMI] (4/22/72 B-12)

CASTLES IN THE AIR *Don McLean—Millennium 11819*
[Don McLean] [BMI] (10/24/81 BCR-31)

CASTLES IN THE SAND Little Stevie Wonder—Tamla 54090
[Hal Davis/Marc Gordon/Mary O'Brien/Frank Edward Wilson] [ASC] (2/29/64 BCR-52)

CASTLES IN THE SAND Seals & Crofts—Warner Bros. 8130
[Dash Crofts/Jim Seals] [BMI] (9/13/75 C-97)

A CASUAL LOOK *The Six Teens—Flip 315 [Ed Wells] [BMI] (7/14/56 BCRt-35)*

CASUAL LOOK *Lorry Raine—Dot 15493 [Ed Wells] [BMI] (9/8/56 Rt-80)*

THE CAT Jimmy Smith—Verve 10330 [Lalo Schifrin] [BMI] (8/29/64 BCR-67) [I]

THE CAT IN THE WINDOW (THE BIRD IN THE SKY) Petula Clark—Warner Bros. 7073
[Garry Bonner/Alan Gordon] [BMI] (9/2/67 BCR-24)

CAT NIP Dave "Baby" Cortez—Clock 1024
[David Clowney/Ken Wood] [BMI] (6/13/60 CR-75) [I]

CAT PEOPLE (PUTTING OUT FIRE) David Bowie—Backstreet 52024
[David Bowie/Giorgio Moroder] [BMI] (4/17/82 BC-61)

CAT SCRATCH FEVER Ted Nugent—Epic 50425 [Ted Nugent] [ASC] (7/23/77 BCR-20)

THE CAT WALK The Village Soul Choir—Abbott 2010
[Charles Ezra Matthews] [BMI] (2/14/70 BCR-55)

CATCH A FALLING STAR Perry Como—RCA Victor 47-7128
[Lee Pockriss/Paul Vance] [ASC] (12/30/57 BCR-1)

CATCH A LITTLE MOONBEAM *The Rinky Dinks—Capitol 4146*
[Doc Burch] [BMI] (2/9/59 CtR-57)

CATCH A LITTLE MOONBEAM *Doc Burch—Challenge 59038*
[Doc Burch] [BMI] (3/7/59 Ct-75)

CATCH ME I'M FALLING Real Life—Curb/MCA 52362
[David Sterry/Richard Zatorski] [BMI] (3/24/84 BC-40)

CATCH ME (I'M FALLING) Pretty Poison—Virgin 99416
[Vincent Corea/Jeanne Roberts] [ASC] (9/26/87 BC-8)

CATCH MY FALL Billy Idol—Chrysalis 42840 [Billy Idol] [ASC] (11/3/84 BC-50)

CATCH THE WIND Donovan—Hickory 1309 [Donovan Leitch] [ASC] (5/8/65 BCR-22)

CATCH US IF YOU CAN The Dave Clark Five—Epic 9833
[Dave Clark/Lenny Davidson] [BMI] (8/21/65 BCR-4)

CATCHING THE SUN Spyro Gyra—MCA 41180
[Jay Beckenstein] [BMI] (4/12/80 BCR-68) [I]

CATERINA Perry Como—RCA Victor 47-8004
[Bugs Bower/Earl Shuman] [ASC] (3/19/62 BCR-17)

CATERPILLAR CRAWL The Strangers—Titan 1701
[John Callard/Joel Scott Hill/Harold Kirby/Ron Lynch] [NA] (8/10/59 BR-49) [I]

CATFISH Four Tops—ABC 12214
[Fred Bridges/Mikki Farrow/Lawrence Payton] [BMI] (10/23/76 BCR-71)

CATHEDAL IN THE PINES Pat Boone—Dot DEP-1057
[Charles Kenny/Nick Kenny] (EP) [ASC] (9/9/57 R-61)

CATHEDRALS D.C. LaRue—Pyramid 8007
[D.C. LaRue/Aram Schefrin] [BMI] (11/6/76 B-94)

CATHY'S CLOWN The Everly Brothers—Warner Bros. 5151
[Don Everly/Phil Everly*] [BMI] (4/18/60 BCR-1)

CAT'S EYE IN THE WINDOW Tommy James—Roulette 7126
[Tommy James/Robert L. King] [BMI] (5/13/72 BCR-48)

CAT'S IN THE CRADLE Harry Chapin—Elektra 45203
[Harry Chapin/Sandra Chapin] [ASC] (9/21/74 BCR-1)

THE CATTLE CALL
Eddy Arnold with Hugo Winterhalter's Orch. And Chorus—RCA Victor 47-6139
[Tex Owens] [ASC] (6/11/55 BCR-20)

THE CATTLE CALL *Dinah Shore—RCA Victor 47-6897 [Tex Owens] [ASC] (6/17/57 B-92)*

CAUGHT IN A DREAM Alice Cooper—Warner Bros. 7490
[Michael Bruce] [BMI] (6/12/71 BCR-83)

CAUGHT IN THE GAME Survivor—Scotti Brothers 04074
[Jim Peterik/Frankie Sullivan] [ASC] (10/22/83 BC-77)

CAUGHT UP IN THE RAPTURE Anita Baker—Elektra 69511
[Garry Glenn/Diane Quander] [ASC] (11/29/86 BC-37)

CAUGHT UP IN YOU 38 Special—A&M 2412
[Don Barnes/Jeff Carlisi/Jim Peterik/Frankie Sullivan] [ASC] (5/1/82 BC-9)

CAUSING A COMMOTION Madonna—Sire 28224
[Stephen Bray/Madonna L. Ciccone] [ASC] (9/12/87 BC-2)

—CAVALLERIA RUSTICANA see: THEME FROM RAGING BULL

C.B. SAVAGE Rod Hart—Plantation 144 [Rod Hart] [BMI] (12/11/76 BCR-59)

—C.C. RIDER see: SEE SEE RIDER

CE SOIR Golden Earring—Track/MCA 40369
[John Fenton/Barry Hay/George Kooymans] [ASC] (3/22/75 C-90)

CECILIA *Simon & Garfunkel—Columbia 45133 [Paul Simon] [BMI] (4/11/70 BCR-1)*

CECILIA *Times Two—Reprise 27871 [Paul Simon] [BMI] (7/9/88 B-79)*

CELEBRATE Three Dog Night—Dunhill 4229
[Garry Bonner/Alan Gordon] [BMI] (2/21/70 BCR-11)

CELEBRATE ME HOME Kenny Loggins—Columbia 10652
[Bob James/Kenny Loggins] [ASC] (4/1/78 R-64)

CELEBRATE YOUTH Rick Springfield—RCA 14047 [Rick Springfield] [ASC] (4/6/85 BC-26)

CELEBRATION Tommy James—Roulette 7135
[Tommy James/Robert L. King] [BMI] (10/21/72 BCR-73)

CELEBRATION Kool & The Gang—De-Lite 807
[Robert Bell/Ronald Bell/George M. Brown/Eumir Deodato/Robert Mickens/Claydes Smith/J.T. Taylor/Dennis Thomas/Earl Toon] [BMI] (10/25/80 BCR-1)

CELIA OF THE SEALS Donovan—Epic 10694 [Donovan Leitch] [BMI] (2/6/71 BCR-62)

THE CELTIC SOUL BROTHERS Dexys Midnight Runners—Mercury 811142
[Micky Billingham/Jimmy Paterson/Kevin Rowland] [ASC] (5/28/83 B-86)

CENTERFIELD John Fogerty—Warner Bros. 29053 [John Fogerty] [ASC] (5/25/85 BC-44)

CENTERFOLD The J. Geils Band—EMI America 8102
[Seth Justman] [ASC] (11/7/81 BCR-1)

CENTIPEDE Rebbie Jackson—Columbia 04547 [Michael Jackson] [BMI] (10/6/84 BC-15)

CENTURY'S END Donald Fagen—Warner Bros. 27972
[Donald Fagen/Tim Meher] [ASC] (4/2/88 BC-77)

A CERTAIN GIRL *Ernie K-Doe—Minit 634 [Allen Toussaint] [BMI] (11/13/61 B-71)*

A CERTAIN GIRL *Warren Zevon—Asylum 46610 [Allen Toussaint] [BMI] (3/8/80 BCR-57)*

A CERTAIN SMILE *Johnny Mathis—Columbia 41193*
[Sammy Fain/Paul Francis Webster] [ASC] (6/21/58 BCRt-11)

A CERTAIN SMILE *Sunny Gale—Decca 30670*
[Sammy Fain/Paul Francis Webster] [ASC] (6/23/58 Rt-11)

A CERTAIN SMILE *Milton Sparks—Hunt 320*
[Sammy Fain/Paul Francis Webster] [ASC] (7/14/58 Rt-11)

A CERTAIN SMILE *Jerry Fuller—Lin 5015*
[Sammy Fain/Paul Francis Webster] [ASC] (7/21/58 Rt-11)

A CERTAIN SMILE *Andy Russell—RCA Victor 47-7299*
[Sammy Fain/Paul Francis Webster] [ASC] (7/21/58 Rt-11)

CERTAIN THINGS ARE LIKELY K.T.P./Kissing The Pink—Mercury 885727
[Simon Aldridge/Stephen Cusack/Jon Kingsley Hall/Nick Whitecross] [BMI] (6/13/87 B-97)

CERVEZA *Boots Brown & His Blockbusters—RCA Victor 47-7269*
[Boots Brown] [ASC] (8/11/58 BCR-53) [I]

CERVEZA Bert Kaempfert And His Orchestra—Decca 30866 [Boots Brown] [ASC] (1/16/61 BCR-58) [I]
C'EST LA VIE Sarah Vaughan—Mercury 70727 [Edward White/Mack Wolfson] [ASC] (11/7/55 BCRt-16)
C'EST LA VIE The DeJohn Sisters—Epic 9131 [Edward White/Mack Wolfson] [ASC] (11/7/55 BRt-16)
C'EST LA VIE Sunny Gale—RCA Victor 47-6286 [Edward White/Mack Wolfson] [ASC] (11/7/55 BRt-16)
C'EST LA VIE Greg Lake—Atlantic 3405 [Greg Lake/Peter Sinfield] [ASC] (8/27/77 BC-87)
C'EST LA VIE Robbie Nevil—EMI 50047 [Mark Holding/Robbie Nevil/Duncan Pain] [BMI] (10/11/86 BC-2)
C'EST SI BON (IT'S SO GOOD) Conway Twitty—MGM 12969 [Henri Betti/Jerry Seelen] [ASC] (12/26/60 BCR-10) [FDE]
CH CH CHERIE Johnny Average Band—Bearsville 49671 [Johnny Average/Griffith McRee] [ASC] (2/21/81 BCR-53)
CHA CHA BABY Ted Heath and His Orchestra—London 1809 [Ted Heath/Carroll Levis/Ken Moule] [BMI] (6/16/58 R-82) [I]
THE CHA-CHA-CHA Bobby Rydell—Cameo 228 [Dave Appell/Kal Mann] [ASC] (10/6/62 BCR-10)
CHA HUA HUA Hugo & Luigi—Roulette 4074 [Joe Lubin/Irving Roth] [BMI] (5/19/58 CtRt-16) [I]
CHA HUA HUA The Pets—Arwin 109 [Joe Lubin/Irving Roth] [BMI] (5/24/58 BCtRt-16) [I]
CHA HUA HUA Eddie Platt And His Orchestra—Gone 5031 [Joe Lubin/Irving Roth] [BMI] (5/24/58 BCtRt-16) [I]
CHAIN GANG Bobby Scott—ABC-Paramount 9658 [Sol Quasha/Herb Yakus] [ASC] (12/30/55 BCRt-10)
CHAIN GANG Johnny Oliver—MGM 12164 [Sol Quasha/Herb Yakus] [ASC] (2/3/56 Rt-11)
CHAIN GANG Len Dresslar—Mercury 70774 [Sol Quasha/Herb Yakus] [ASC] (2/18/56 B-78)
CHAIN GANG Lawrence Welk & His Champagne Music—Coral 61595 [Sol Quasha/Herb Yakus] [ASC] (3/2/56 Rt-15)
CHAIN GANG Sam Cooke—RCA Victor 47-7783 [Sam Cooke] [BMI] (8/8/60 BCR-2)
CHAIN GANG Jackie Wilson And Count Basie—Brunswick 55373 [Sam Cooke] [BMI] (4/20/68 BCR-58)
CHAIN GANG Jim Croce—Lifesong 45001 [Sam Cooke] (Med) [BMI] (1/3/76 BCR-56)
CHAIN OF FOOLS Aretha Franklin—Atlantic 2464 [Don Covay] [BMI] (12/9/67 BCR-1)
CHAIN OF FOOLS (PART 1) Jimmy Smith—Verve 10583 [Don Covay] [BMI] (4/6/68 B-100)
CHAIN OF FOOLS Little Caesar—DGC 19693 [Don Covay] [BMI] (6/16/90 BC-78)
CHAIN REACTION Diana Ross—RCA 14244 [Barry Gibb/Maurice Gibb/Robin Gibb] [BMI] (11/30/85 B-95)
CHAIN REACTION Diana Ross—RCA 14244 [Barry Gibb/Maurice Gibb/Robin Gibb] [BMI] (5/3/86 BC-66)
CHAINED Marvin Gaye—Tamla 54170 [Frank Edward Wilson] [BMI] (9/14/68 BCR-32)
CHAINED AND BOUND Otis Redding—Volt 121 [Otis Redding] [BMI] (10/10/64 BCR-41)
CHAINS The Cookies—Dimension 1002 [Gerry Goffin/Carole King] [BMI] (11/10/62 BCR-12)
CHAINS AND THINGS B.B. King—ABC 11280 [Dave (2) Clark/B.B. King] [BMI] (10/24/70 BCR-39)
CHAINS OF LOVE Pat Boone—Dot 15490 [Ahmet Ertegun/Van Walls*] [BMI] (9/8/56 BCR-15)*
CHAINS OF LOVE Bobby Bland—Duke 449 [Ahmet Ertegun/Van Walls*] [BMI] (9/13/69 BCR-51)*
CHAINS OF LOVE The Drifters—Atlantic 2285 [James A. Bishop/Kenneth Gamble] [BMI] (4/24/65 BR-90)
CHAINS OF LOVE Erasure—Sire 27844 [Andy Bell/Vince Clarke] [ASC] (7/30/88 BC-12)
CHAIRMAN OF THE BOARD Chairmen Of The Board—Invictus 9086 [Lamont Dozier/Brian Holland] [BMI] (2/13/71 BCR-33)
CHAMELEON Herbie Hancock—Columbia 46002 [Herbie Hancock/Paul J. Jackson*/Harvey Mason*/Bennie Maupin*] [BMI] (3/16/74 BCR-41) [I]
CHAMPAGNE JAM Atlanta Rhythm Section—Polydor 14504 [Buddy Buie/J.R. Cobb/Robert Nix] [BMI] (9/16/78 BCR-43)
A CHANCE FOR HEAVEN Christopher Cross—Columbia 04492 [Burt Bacharach/Christopher Cross/Carole Bayer Sager] [ASC] (6/16/84 BC-76)
CHANCES ARE Johnny Mathis—Columbia 40993 [Robert Allen/Al Stillman] [ASC] (9/2/57 BCR-1)
CHANGE Tears For Fears—Mercury 812677 [Roland Orzabal] [BMI] (8/6/83 BC-73)
CHANGE John Waite—Chrysalis 42606 [Holly Knight] [ASC] (3/2/85 BC-54)
CHANGE Lisa Stansfield—Arista 12363 [Ian Devaney/Andy Morris/Lisa Stansfield] [BMI] (11/2/91 BC-20)
A CHANGE IS GONNA COME Sam Cooke—RCA Victor 47-8486 [Sam Cooke] [BMI] (1/30/65 BCR-31)
A CHANGE IS GONNA COME The 5th Dimension—Bell 860 [Sam Cooke] (Med/TSW) [BMI] (2/28/70 BR-54)
CHANGE OF HEART Dennis Yost And The Classics IV—Imperial 66393 [Buddy Buie/J.R. Cobb] [BMI] (7/26/69 BCR-47)
CHANGE OF HEART Eric Carmen—Arista 0354 [Eric Carmen] [BMI] (9/16/78 BCR-19)
CHANGE OF HEART Tom Petty and The Heartbreakers—Backstreet 52181 [Tom Petty] [ASC] (2/26/83 BC-21)
CHANGE OF HEART Cyndi Lauper—Portrait 37-06431 [Cyndi Lauper*/Essra Mohawk] [BMI] (11/29/86 BC-3)
A CHANGE ON THE WAY Terry Knight And The Pack—Lucky Eleven 229 [Terry Knight] [BMI] (8/27/66 CR-74)
CHANGE PARTNERS Stephen Stills—Atlantic 2806 [Stephen Stills] [BMI] (6/5/71 BCR-38)
CHANGE WITH THE TIMES Van McCoy—Avco 4660 [Van McCoy] [BMI] (10/4/75 BCR-46)
CHANGES Crispian St. Peters—Jamie 1324 [Phil Ochs] [ASC] (9/17/66 BCR-57)
CHANGES David Bowie—RCA Victor 74-0605 [David Bowie] [BMI] (4/8/72 BCR-59)
CHANGES David Bowie—RCA Victor 74-0605 [David Bowie] [BMI] (11/23/74 BCR-28)
CHANGES Loggins & Messina—Columbia 10077 [Jim Messina] [ASC] (1/25/75 BCR-62)
CHANGES IN LATITUDES, CHANGES IN ATTITUDES Jimmy Buffett—ABC 12305 [Jimmy Buffett] [BMI] (9/17/77 BCR-34)
CHANSON D'AMOUR (SONG OF LOVE) Art and Dotty Todd—Era 1064 [Wayne Shanklin] [ASC] (3/31/58 BCRt-5)
CHANSON D'AMOUR (SONG OF LOVE) The Fontane Sisters—Dot 15736 [Wayne Shanklin] [ASC] (4/7/58 BRt-5)
CHANSON D'AMOUR (SONG OF LOVE) Ray Hartley—RCA Victor 47-7228 [Wayne Shanklin] [ASC] (5/26/58 Rt-5)
CHANTEZ-CHANTEZ (SHAN-TAY, "SING") Dinah Shore—RCA Victor 47-6792 [Irving Fields/Albert Gamse] [BMI] (2/2/57 BCR-27)
CHANTILLY LACE Big Bopper—Mercury 71343 [J.P. Richardson] [BMI] (8/4/58 BCR-4)
CHANTILLY LACE Mitch Ryder—DynoVoice 905 [J.P. Richardson] (Med) [BMI] (1/27/68 BCR-58)
CHANTILLY LACE Cat Mother And The All Night News Boys—Polydor 14002 [J.P. Richardson] (Med) [BMI] (6/21/69 BCR-12)
CHANTILLY LACE Jerry Lee Lewis—Mercury 73273 [J.P. Richardson] [BMI] (3/4/72 BCR-42)
CHANTILLY LACE Jive Bunny & The Mastermixers—Music Factory/Atco 99122 [J.P. Richardson] (Med) [BMI] (2/3/90 BC-67)
CHAPEL BY THE SEA Billy Vaughn And His Orchestra—Dot 16329 [V.C. Gilbert] [BMI] (3/5/62 BR-69) [IM]
—CHAPEL IN THE MOONLIGHT see: IN THE CHAPEL...
CHAPEL OF DREAMS The Dubs—Gone 5069 [Billy Myles] [BMI] (8/24/59 BC-74)
CHAPEL OF LOVE The Dixie Cups—Red Bird 10-001 [Jeff Barry/Ellie Greenwich/Phil Spector] [BMI] (5/2/64 BCR-1)
CHAPEL OF LOVE Bette Midler—Atlantic 2980 [Jeff Barry/Ellie Greenwich/Phil Spector] (TSW) [BMI] (11/3/73 BR-47)
CHARADE Henry Mancini And His Orchestra and Chorus—RCA Victor 47-8256 [Henry Mancini/Johnny Mercer] [ASC] (11/23/63 BCRt-36)
CHARADE The Four Freshmen—Capitol 5083 [Henry Mancini/Johnny Mercer] [ASC] (11/23/63 Rt-53)
CHARADE Adam Wade—Epic 9639 [Henry Mancini/Johnny Mercer] [ASC] (11/30/63 Rt-53)
CHARADE Andy Williams—Columbia 42950 [Henry Mancini/Johnny Mercer] [ASC] (1/18/64 B-100)
CHARADE Sammy Kaye And His Orchestra—Decca 31589 [Henry Mancini] [ASC] (4/4/64 BCR-31) [IM]
THE CHARANGA Merv Griffin—Carlton 545 [Hal David/Marco Rizo] [ASC] (4/10/61 BCR-69)
CHARIOT ROCK The Champs—Challenge 59018 [Dave Burgess] [BMI] (8/4/58 BCR-49) [I]
CHARIOTS OF FIRE - TITLES Vangelis—Polydor 2189 [Vangelis] [ASC] (12/12/81 BCR-1) [I]
CHARITY BALL Fanny—Reprise 1033 [Alice DeBuhr/Jean Millington/June Millington] [BMI] (9/18/71 BCR-32)
CHARLENA The Sevilles—J.C. 116 [Herman Chaney/Manuel Chavez] [BMI] (1/23/61 BCR-84)
THE CHARLESTON Ernie Fields Orch.—Rendezvous 150 [James P. Johnson/Cecil Mack] [NA] (6/19/61 BCRt-44) [IWM]
CHARLESTON Cozy Cole—Artistique 2194 [James P. Johnson/Cecil Mack] [NA] (7/24/61 Rt-44) [IWM]
CHARLESTON PARISIEN Guy Lombardo & His Royal Canadians—Capitol 3411 [Jean-Pierre Moulin] [BMI] (6/22/56 Rt-78) [IM]
CHARLESTON PARISIEN Leo Clarens & His Orchestra—Columbia 40702 [Jean-Pierre Moulin] [BMI] (6/22/56 Rt-78) [IM]
CHARLEY MY BOY Somethin' Smith & The Redheads—Epic 9106 [Ted Fiorito/Gus Kahn] [ASC] (7/18/55 R-78)
CHARLIE BROWN The Coasters—Atco 6132 [Jerry Leiber/Mike Stoller] [BMI] (2/2/59 BCR-2)
CHARM THE SNAKE Christopher Cross—Warner Bros. 28864 [Christopher Cross/Michael Omartian] [ASC] (10/26/85 BC-68)
CHARMAINE The Four Freshmen—Capitol 3292 [Lew Pollack/Erno Rapeé] [ASC] (12/10/55 BR-69)
CHARMAINE The Bachelors—London 9584 [Lew Pollack/Erno Rapeé] [ASC] (6/15/63 R-82)
CHARMAINE The Four Preps—Capitol 4974 [Lew Pollack/Erno Rapeé] [ASC] (6/15/63 R-79)
CHARMER Tim Moore—Asylum 45214 [Tim Moore] [NA] (2/1/75 BCR-69)

CHARMING BILLY Johnny Preston—Mercury 71691
[Johnny Preston] [BMI] (10/15/60 CR-51)

CHARMS Bobby Vee—Liberty 55530
[Howard Greenfield/Helen Miller] [BMI] (3/30/63 BCR-13)

CHASE Giorgio Moroder—Casablanca 956 [Giorgio Moroder] [BMI] (1/20/79 BCR-33) [I]

CHASE ME Con Funk Shun—Mercury 74059
[Michael V. Cooper/Felton Pilate] [BMI] (6/9/79 CR-65)

CHASE THE CLOUDS AWAY Chuck Mangione—A&M 1707
[Chuck Mangione] [BMI] (7/19/75 B-96) [I]

CHASIN' THE WIND Chicago—Reprise 19466 [Diane Warren] [ASC] (1/19/91 BC-31)

***CHATTANOOGA CHOO CHOO** Ernie Fields Orch.—Rendezvous 117*
[Harry Warren] [ASC] (2/15/60 BCR-54) [IM]

***CHATTANOOGA CHOO CHOO** Floyd Cramer—RCA Victor 47-7978*
[Harry Warren] [ASC] (1/8/62 BCR-29) [IM]

***CHATTANOOGA CHOO CHOO** Harpers Bizarre—Warner Bros. 7090*
[Mack Gordon/Harry Warren] [ASC] (11/11/67 BCR-45)

***CHATTANOOGA CHOO CHOO** Tuxedo Junction—Butterfly 1205*
[Mack Gordon/Harry Warren] [ASC] (4/22/78 BCR-32)

***CHATTANOOGA CHOO CHOO** Frank Barber Orchestra—Victory 1001*
[Harry Warren] (Med) [ASC] (5/8/82 B-61) [IM]

CHATTANOOGA SHOE SHINE BOY Freddy Cannon—Swan 4050
[Jack Stapp/Harry Stone] [BMI] (2/1/60 BCR-27)

CHEAP SUNGLASSES ZZ Top—Warner Bros. 49220
[Frank Beard/Billy Gibbons/Dusty Hill] [BMI] (6/28/80 BCR-80)

CHEAPER TO KEEP HER Johnnie Taylor—Stax 0176 [Bonny Rice] [BMI] (10/6/73 BCR-15)

A CHEAT Sanford Clark—Dot 15516 [Lee Hazlewood] [ASC] (12/8/56 B-74)

THE CHEATER Bob Kuban And The In-Men—Musicland U.S.A. 20,001
[John Krenski] [BMI] (1/29/66 BCR-12)

CHECK IT OUT Tavares—Capitol 3674
[Floyd Butler/Billy Osborne] [ASC] (9/22/73 BCR-34)

CHECK IT OUT Bobby Womack—United Artists 621
[Bobby Womack] [BMI] (4/12/75 BCR-74)

CHECK IT OUT John Cougar Mellencamp—Mercury 870 126
[John Mellencamp] [ASC] (2/6/88 BC-14)

CHECK OUT YOUR MIND The Impressions—Curtom 1951
[Curtis Mayfield] [BMI] (5/16/70 BCR-21)

CHECK YOURSELF Italian Asphalt & Pavement Company—Colossus 110
[Kenneth Gamble/Leon Huff] [BMI] (5/2/70 B-97)

***CHEE CHEE OO CHEE (SANG THE LITTLE BIRD)** Dean Martin—Capitol 3133*
[Ettore Mionoretti/Geoffrey Parsons/Saverio Seracini/John Turner] [BMI]
(5/30/55 Rt-41) [FET]

***CHEE CHEE-OO CHEE** Dennis Hale—London 1575*
[Ettore Mionoretti/Geoffrey Parsons/Saverio Seracini/John Turner] [BMI]
(5/30/55 Rt-64) [FET]

***CHEE CHEE-OO CHEE (SANG THE LITTLE BIRD)** The Johnston Brothers—London 1565*
[Ettore Mionoretti/Geoffrey Parsons/Saverio Seracini/John Turner] [BMI]
(5/30/55 Rt-16) [FET]

***CHEE CHEE-OO CHEE (SANG THE LITTLE BIRD)** The Gaylords—Mercury 70630*
[Ettore Mionoretti/Geoffrey Parsons/Saverio Seracini/John Turner] [BMI]
(5/30/55 Rt-16) [FET]

***CHEE CHEE-OO CHEE (SANG THE LITTLE BIRDS)** The Mariners—Columbia 40514*
[Ettore Mionoretti/Geoffrey Parsons/Saverio Seracini/John Turner] [BMI]
(5/30/55 Rt-64) [FET]

CHEE CHEE-OO CHEE (SANG THE LITTLE BIRD)
Perry Como & Jaye P. Morgan—RCA Victor 47-6137
[Ettore Mionoretti/Geoffrey Parsons/Saverio Seracini/John Turner] (TSW) [BMI]
(6/25/55 BCRt-16) [FET]

CHEER Potliquor—Janus 179 [George Ratzlaff] [BMI] (2/5/72 BCR-58)

THE CHEER LEADER Paul Petersen—Colpix 707
[Lee Pockriss/Fred Tobias] [ASC] (11/30/63 BCR-75)

CHEESEBURGER IN PARADISE Jimmy Buffett—ABC 12358
[Jimmy Buffett] [BMI] (4/22/78 BCR-29)

—CHELLA LLA see: HA HA HA

CHELSEA MORNING Judy Collins—Elektra 45657 [Joni Mitchell] [ASC] (8/2/69 BC-78)

CHERCHEZ LA FEMME/SE SI BON Dr. Buzzard's Original "Savannah" Band—RCA 10827
[Stony Browder/August Darnell] (Med) [BMI] (11/6/76 BCR-23)

CHERIÉ Bobby Rydell—Cameo 186
[Dave Appell/Bernie Lowe/Kal Mann] [ASC] (1/28/61 BCR-54)

CHERIE I LOVE YOU Pat Boone—Dot 15750 [Lillian Goodman] [ASC] (4/28/58 BCR-33)

***CHERISH** The Association—Valiant 747 [Terry Kirkman] [BMI] (8/27/66 BCR-1)*

***CHERISH** David Cassidy—Bell 45,150 [Terry Kirkman] [BMI] (10/30/71 BCR-3)*

CHERISH Kool & The Gang—De-Lite 880869
[Robert Bell/Ronald Bell/James Bonneford/George M. Brown/Claydes Smith/J.T. Taylor/Curtis Fitzgerald Williams] [BMI] (7/6/85 BC-2)

CHERISH Madonna—Sire 22883
[Madonna L. Ciccone/Patrick Raymond Leonard] [BMI] (8/19/89 BC-1)

CHERISH WHAT IS DEAR TO YOU (WHILE IT'S NEAR TO YOU) Freda Payne—Invictus 9085
[Angelo Bond/Lamont Dozier/Brian Holland] [BMI] (2/6/71 BCR-27)

CHEROKEE Larry Elgart And His Manhattan Swing Orchestra—RCA 13219
[Ray Noble] (Med) [ASC] (6/5/82 BC-31) [IWM]

CHEROKEE Europe—Epic 07638 [Joey Tempest] [BMI] (11/28/87 B-72)

CHERRY BABY Starz—Capitol 4399
[Jeffrey Warren Grob/Brendan Harkin/Richie Ranno/Michael Lee Smith/Pieter Sweval] [ASC] (3/19/77 BCR-27)

CHERRY BERRY WINE Charlie McCoy—Cadence 1390
[Charlie McCoy/Gilbert Metters/Kent Westberry] [BMI] (2/13/61 BR-61)

CHERRY BOMB John Cougar Mellencamp—Mercury 888 934
[John Mellencamp] [ASC] (10/24/87 BC-8)

***CHERRY, CHERRY** Neil Diamond—Bang 528 [Neil Diamond] [SE] (8/20/66 BCR-5)*

***"CHERRY CHERRY" FROM HOT AUGUST NIGHT** Neil Diamond—MCA 40017*
[Neil Diamond] [SE] (3/10/73 BCR-24)

CHERRY HILL PARK Billy Joe Royal—Columbia 44902
[William Gilmore/Robert Nix] [BMI] (9/27/69 BCR-15)

CHERRY LIPS Billy Farrell—Imperial 7001 [Winfield Scott] [BMI] (4/13/56 R-81)

CHERRY PIE Skip & Flip—Brent 7010
[Joe Josea‡/Marvin Phillips*/Jules Taub*‡] [BMI] (3/26/60 BCR-11)

CHERRY PIE Warrant—Columbia 73510
[Joseph Cagle*/Steven Chamberlin*/Jerry Dixon*/John Oswald/Eric Turner*] [BMI] (9/8/90 BC-10)

***CHERRY PINK AND APPLE BLOSSOM WHITE** Perez Prado And His Orchestra—*
RCA Victor 47-5965 [Luis Guglielmi] [ASC] (1/31/55 BCtRt-1) [IM]

***CHERRY PINK AND APPLE BLOSSOM WHITE** Alan Dale—Coral 61373*
[Marcel Ageron/Mack David/Luis Guglielmi] [ASC] (3/7/55 BCtRt-1) [FET]

***CHERRY PINK (AND APPLE BLOSSOM WHITE)** Georgie Auld & His Auld-Stars—Coral 61381*
[Luis Guglielmi] [ASC] (3/21/55 Rt-11) [IM]

CHERRY PINK AND APPLE BLOSSOM WHITE
Xavier Cugat & His Orchestra—Columbia 40472
[Luis Guglielmi] [ASC] (4/4/55 Rt-11) [IM]

***CHERRY PINK AND APPLE BLOSSOM WHITE** Jerry Murad's Harmonicats—Columbia 41816*
[Luis Guglielmi] [ASC] (11/14/60 BCR-22) [IM]

CHERRYSTONE The Addrisi Brothers—Del-Fi 4116
[Dick Addrisi/Don Addrisi] [BMI] (6/1/59 BCR-62)

CHERYL MOANA MARIE John Rowles—Kapp 2102
[Nat Kipner/John Rowles] [ASC] (1/2/71 BCR-64)

CHESTNUT MARE Byrds—Columbia 45259
[Jacques Levy/Roger McGuinn] [BMI] (11/28/70 C-95)

CHEVY VAN Sammy Johns—GRC 2046 [Sammy Johns] [BMI] (2/1/75 BCR-5)

CHEWY CHEWY Ohio Express—Buddah 70
[Joey Levine/Kris Resnick] [BMI] (10/19/68 BCR-8)

CHI CHI MERENGUE The Eloise Trio—Decca 31047 [Eloise Lewis] [ASC] (4/11/60 CR-79)

***CHICAGO** Frank Sinatra—Capitol 3793 [Fred Fisher] [ASC] (9/23/57 BCRt-45)*

***CHICAGO** Grady Martin & The Slew Foot Five—Decca 30453*
[Fred Fisher] [ASC] (11/11/57 Rt-54) [IWM]

CHICAGO Graham Nash—Atlantic 2804 [Graham Nash] [BMI] (5/29/71 BCR-29)

THE CHICAGO THEME (LOVE LOOP) Hubert Laws—CTI 27
[Bob James] [ASC] (9/13/75 R-96) [I]

THE CHICK Lee And Paul—Columbia 41337
[Lee Pockriss/Paul Vance] [ASC] (3/14/59 BC-84)

CHICK-A-BOOM Van Morrison—Bang 552
[Bert Berns/Van Morrison] [BMI] (11/11/67 R-91)

CHICK-A-BOOM (DON'T YA JES' LOVE IT) Daddy Dewdrop—Sunflower 105
[Janis Lee Gwin/Linda Martin] [ASC] (3/6/71 BCR-5)

CHICKA CHICKA HONEY Robin Luke with The Jolly Drifters—Dot 15839
[Robin Luke] [ASC] (10/20/58 R-91)

CHICKEN, BABY, CHICKEN Tony Harris—Ebb 104 [Oscar Harris] [BMI] (9/2/57 B-89)

CHICKEN FEED Bent Fabric And His Piano—Atco 6245
[Bent Fabricius-Bjerre/Jorgen Ingmann] [ASC] (12/22/62 BCR-46) [IM]

CHICKEN STRUT The Meters—Josie 1018
[Joseph Modeliste/Art Neville/Leo Nocentelli/George Porter] [BMI] (3/21/70 BCR-49) [I]

CHICO AND THE MAN (MAIN THEME) José Feliciano—RCA Victor 10145
[Jose Feliciano] [ASC] (1/25/75 B-96)

CHILD OF CLAY Jimmie Rodgers—A&M 871
[Jimmy Curtiss/Ernie Maresca] [BMI] (9/9/67 BCR-30)

CHILD OF GOD Bobby Darin—Atco 6183 [Traditional] [NA] (11/21/60 BCR-72)

A CHILD OF GOD (IT'S HARD TO BELIEVE) Millie Jackson—Spring 119
[Don French/Millie Jackson] [BMI] (11/6/71 R-75)

CHILD OF OUR TIMES Barry McGuire—Dunhill 4014 [P.F. Sloan] [ASC] (11/6/65 BCR-72)

CHILDREN Joe South—Capitol 2755 [Joe South] [BMI] (3/14/70 BCR-48)

CHILDREN OF THE NIGHT Richard Marx—EMI 50288
[Richard Marx] [ASC] (4/28/90 BC-12)

CHILDREN OF THE SUN Billy Thorpe—Capricorn 0321/Polydor 2018
[Spencer Proffer/Billy Thorpe] [BMI] (7/21/79 BCR-41)

CHILDREN'S CHRISTMAS SONG The Supremes—Motown 1085
[Isabelle Freeman] [ASC] (12/18/65 R-90)

***CHILDREN'S MARCHING SONG** Mitch Miller & his "Sing Along With Mitch" Chorus—*
Columbia 41317 [Traditional] [ASC] (1/5/59 BCtRt-3)

CHILDREN'S MARCHING SONG *Cyril Stapleton And His Orchestra—London 1851 [Traditional] [ASC] (1/5/59 BCtRt-3)*

THIS OLD MAN *Purple Reign—Private Stock 45,052 [Traditional] [ASC] (11/22/75 BCR-48)*

CHILLS AND FEVER Ronnie Love And His Orchestra—Dot 16144 [Billy Ness/Bobby Rackep] [BMI] (1/9/61 BCR-72)

—CHILLY WINDS see: DOWN WHERE THE WINDS BLOW

CHIM, CHIM, CHEREE The New Christy Minstrels—Columbia 43215 [Richard Sherman/Robert Sherman] [BMI] (3/13/65 BCR-78)

CHINA Red Rockers—Columbia 03786 [John Griffith/Darren Hill/David Kahne/James Singletary] [BMI] (6/4/83 BC-53)

CHINA DOLL The Ames Brothers—RCA Victor 47-7655 [Cindy Walker] [BMI] (1/18/60 BCR-38)

CHINA GIRL David Bowie—EMI America 8165 [David Bowie/Iggy Pop] [BMI] (6/4/83 BC-9)

CHINA GROVE The Doobie Brothers—Warner Bros. 7728 [Tom Johnston] [BMI] (8/18/73 BCR-8)

CHINA NIGHTS (SHINA NO YORU) Kyu Sakamoto—Capitol 5016 [Yaso Saijo/Sil Sedores/Nobuyuki Takeoka] [ASC] (8/10/63 BCR-37) [F]

CHINATOWN MY CHINATOWN Joe Pica—Original 512 [Jean Schwartz] [ASC] (11/1/54 R-82) [IM]

CHINCHERINCHEE Perry Como—RCA Victor 47-6670 [Howard Ellington Riddiford Barnes/Harold Fields/Joseph Roncoroni] [ASC] (10/20/56 BCR-33)

CHINESE CHECKERS Booker T. & The MG's—Stax 137 [Steve Cropper/Al Jackson/Booker T. Jones Jr./Lewis Steinberg] [BMI] (7/27/63 BCR-78) [I]

CHINESE KUNG FU Banzaii—Scepter 12407 [Bernard Estardy] [BMI] (10/11/75 B-98) [I]

CHINESE ROCK AND EGG ROLL Buddy Hackett—Coral 61594 [Buddy Hackett] [ASC] (3/16/56 BCR-44)

—CHING-CHING see: HAPPY JOSE

CHIP AWAY THE STONE (STUDIO) *Aerosmith—Columbia 10890 [Richie Supa] [ASC] (1/20/79 B-77)*

CHIP AWAY THE STONE *Aerosmith—Columbia 08536 [Richie Supa] [ASC] (12/31/88 C-82)*

CHIP CHIP Gene McDaniels—Liberty 55405 [Jeff Barry/Cliff Crofford/Artie Resnick] [BMI] (1/15/62 BCR-10)

CHIP OFF THE OLD BLOCK Eddy Arnold—RCA Victor 47-7435 [James (2) Lee] [ASC] (2/23/59 BR-82)

CHIP OFF THE OLD BLOCK Chic—Atlantic 3768 [Bernard Edwards/Nile Rodgers] (TSW) [BMI] (11/22/80 B-79)

THE CHIPMUNK SONG (CHRISTMAS DON'T BE LATE) *David Seville And The Chipmunks—Liberty 55168 [David Seville] [ASC] (12/1/58 BCR-1)*

THE CHIPMUNK SONG (CHRISTMAS DON'T BE LATE) *David Seville And The Chipmunks—Liberty 55250 [David Seville] [ASC] (11/23/59 BCR-37)*

THE CHIPMUNK SONG (CHRISTMAS DON'T BE LATE) *David Seville And The Chipmunks—Liberty 55250 [David Seville] [ASC] (12/12/60 B-45)*

THE CHIPMUNK SONG (CHRISTMAS DON'T BE LATE) *David Seville And The Chipmunks—Liberty 55250 [David Seville] [ASC] (12/18/61 BCR-39)*

THE CHIPMUNK SONG (CHRISTMAS DON'T BE LATE) *David Seville And The Chipmunks—Liberty 55250 [David Seville] [ASC] (12/8/62 BCR-40)*

CHIQUITITA ABBA—Atlantic 3629 [Benny Andersson/Björn Ulvaeus] [ASC] (11/10/79 BCR-29)

CHIRPY CHIRPY, CHEEP CHEEP *Lally Stott—Philips 40695 [Giuseppe Cassia*/Harold Stott] [ASC] (4/3/71 BR-85)*

CHIRPY CHIRPY CHEEP CHEEP *Mac And Katie Kissoon—ABC 11306 [Giuseppe Cassia*/Harold Stott] [ASC] (7/24/71 BCR-17)*

—CHITARRA ROMANA see: ROMAN GUITAR

CHITTLINS Gus Jenkins—Tower 107 [Gus Jenkins] [BMI] (11/14/64 R-90) [I]

CHITTY CHITTY BANG BANG Paul Mauriat—Philips 40574 [Richard Sherman/Robert Sherman] [BMI] (11/16/68 BCR-76) [IWM]

CHLOE Elton John—Geffen 49788 [Elton John/Gary Osborne] [BMI] (7/25/81 BCR-31)

CHOCOLATE CHIP Isaac Hayes—HBS/ABC 12118 [Isaac Hayes] [BMI] (8/9/75 BCR-65)

CHOCOLATE CITY Parliament—Casablanca 831 [George Clinton/William Earl Collins/Bernie Worrell] [BMI] (6/14/75 BC-86)

THE CHOICE The O'Jays—Bell 737 [Kenny Seymour] [BMI] (9/21/68 BR-93)

CHOICE OF COLORS The Impressions—Curtom 1943 [Curtis Mayfield] [BMI] (6/21/69 BCR-18)

THE CHOKIN' KIND *Joe Simon—Sound Stage 7 2628 [Harlan Howard] [BMI] (3/15/69 BCR-11)*

CHOKIN' KIND *Z.Z. Hill—Mankind 12017 [Harlan Howard] [BMI] (10/9/71 CR-83)*

CHOO CHOO CH'BOOGIE Bill Haley And His Comets—Decca 30148 [Denver Darling/Milt Gabler/Vaughn Horton] [ASC] (12/15/56 R-59)

CHOO CHOO MAMA Ten Years After—Columbia 45736 [Alvin Lee] [ASC] (12/16/72 B-89)

CHOO CHOO TRAIN The Box Tops—Mala 12,005 [Donnie Fritts/Eddie Hinton] [BMI] (5/25/68 BCR-17)

CHOP CHOP BOOM The Crew-Cuts—Mercury 70597 [Samuel Smith*/Dallas Taylor] (TSW) [BMI] (4/30/55 BCR-14)

CHOPPIN' CHA CHA Marty Ames—Dot 15876 [Frederic Chopin*/Robert Marzell] [BMI] (1/12/59 R-98)

CHORUS Erasure—Sire 4-19202 [Andy Bell/Vince Clarke] [ASC] (8/10/91 B-83)

—CHOVE CHUVA see: CONSTANT RAIN

CHOW MEIN The Gaylords—Mercury 70543 [Bob Merrill] [ASC] (3/12/55 C-28)

CHRISTINA Terry Jacks—Private Stock 45,023 [Terry Jacks] [BMI] (5/31/75 C-83)

CHRISTINE SIXTEEN Kiss—Casablanca 889 [Gene Simmons] [ASC] (7/16/77 BCR-20)

CHRISTMAS ALPHABET The McGuire Sisters—Coral 61303 [Buddy Kaye/Jules Loman] [ASC] (12/18/54 CR-34)

CHRISTMAS AULD LANG SYNE Bobby Darin—Atco 6183 [Mann Curtis/Francis Philip Military] [ASC] (11/14/60 BCR-32)

CHRISTMAS DREAM Perry Como—RCA Victor 10122 [André Heller*/Tim Rice/Andrew Lloyd Webber] [ASC] (12/21/74 BC-88) [F]

CHRISTMAS FOR COWBOYS John Denver—RCA Victor 10464 [Steve Weisberg] [ASC] (12/13/75 BCR-58)

CHRISTMAS SONG Gilbert O'Sullivan—MAM 3645 [Gilbert O'Sullivan] [ASC] (12/27/75 R-92)

THE CHRISTMAS SONG (MERRY CHRISTMAS TO YOU) *Nat "King" Cole—Capitol 3561 [Mel Torme/Robert Wells] [ASC] (12/29/56 R-85)*

THE CHRISTMAS SONG (MERRY CHRISTMAS TO YOU) *Nat King Cole—Capitol 3561 [Mel Torme/Robert Wells] [ASC] (12/12/60 B-80)*

THE CHRISTMAS SONG (MERRY CHRISTMAS TO YOU) *Nat King Cole—Capitol 3561 [Mel Torme/Robert Wells] [ASC] (12/15/62 BR-45)*

CHUCK E.'S IN LOVE Rickie Lee Jones—Warner Bros. 8825 [Rickie Lee Jones] [ASC] (4/28/79 BCR-4)

CHUG-A-LUG Roger Miller—Smash 1926 [Roger Miller] [BMI] (9/5/64 BCR-5)

CHURCH Bob Welch—Capitol 4719 [Bob Welch] [ASC] (5/26/79 BCR-73)

CHURCH BELLS MAY RING *The Willows—Melba 102 [Morty Craft/Richard Davis*/Joseph Martin*/Ralph Martin*/Anthony Middleton*] [BMI] (3/30/56 BCtRt-17)*

CHURCH BELLS MAY RING *The Diamonds—Mercury 70835 [Morty Craft/Richard Davis*/Joseph Martin*/Ralph Martin*/Anthony Middleton*] [BMI] (4/6/56 BCtRt-17)*

CHURCH OF THE POISON MIND Culture Club—Virgin/Epic 04144 [Michael Craig/Roy Hay/Jon Moss/George O'Dowd] [ASC] (10/22/83 BC-10)

CHURCH STREET SOUL REVIVAL Tommy James—Roulette 7093 [Ritchie Cordell/Tommy James] [BMI] (12/5/70 BCR-44)

CIAO CIAO BAMBINA *Domenico Modugno—Decca 30845 [Domenico Modugno/Dino Verde] [ASC] (3/9/59 B-97) [F]*

CIAO CIAO BAMBINA *Jacky Noguez And His Orchestra—Jamie 1127 [Domenico Modugno] [ASC] (6/15/59 BCRt-12) [IM]*

CIAO CIAO BAMBINA *Jos Cleber & His Orchestra—Columbia 41422 [Domenico Modugno] [ASC] (7/6/59 Rt-34) [IM]*

CIGARETTES AND COFFEE BLUES Marty Robbins—Columbia 42701 [Marty Robbins] [BMI] (3/16/63 B-93)

CIMARRON (ROLL ON) *Les Paul and Mary Ford—Capitol 3444 [Johnny Bond] [BMI] (6/1/56 CR-48)*

CIMARRON (ROLL ON) *Billy Vaughn And His Orchestra—Dot 15836 [Johnny Bond] [BMI] (10/6/58 BCR-27) [I]*

CINCO ROBLES (FIVE OAKS) *Russell Arms—Era 1026 [Larry Sullivan/Dorothy Wright] [BMI] (12/22/56 BCtRt-14)*

CINCO ROBLES (FIVE OAKS) *Les Paul and Mary Ford—Capitol 3612 [Larry Sullivan/Dorothy Wright] [BMI] (12/29/56 BCtRt-14)*

CINCO ROBLES (FIVE OAKS) *Lawrence Welk And His Sparkling Strings—Coral 61765 [Larry Sullivan/Dorothy Wright] [BMI] (1/12/57 CtRt-14)*

CINDERELLA The Four Preps—Capitol 4078 [Bruce Belland/Glen Larson] [BMI] (11/3/58 BR-69)

CINDERELLA Paul Anka—ABC-Paramount 10239 [Paul Anka] [BMI] (8/14/61 BCR-51)

CINDERELLA Jack Ross—Dot 16333 [Elmer Nemeth/Jack Ross] [ASC] (3/17/62 BCR-16)

CINDERELLA Firefall—Atlantic 3392 [Larry Burnett] [ASC] (3/26/77 BCR-30)

CINDERELLA ROCKAFELLA Esther & Abi Ofarim—Philips 40526 [Nancy Ames/Mason Williams] [BMI] (3/16/68 BCR-67)

CINDERELLA SUNSHINE Paul Revere And The Raiders Featuring Mark Lindsay—Columbia 44655 [Mark Lindsay] [BMI] (10/12/68 BCR-42)

CINDY Teddy Vann—Triple-X 101 [Traditional] [BMI] (2/27/60 CR-59)

CINDY INCIDENTALLY Faces—Warner Bros. 7681 [Rod Stewart/Ron Wood] [ASC] (3/10/73 BCR-43)

CINDY OH CINDY *Eddie Fisher—RCA Victor 47-6677 [Bob Barron/Burt Long] [BMI] (10/6/56 BCtRt-9)*

CINDY OH CINDY *Vince Martin with The Tarriers—Glory 247 [Bob Barron/Burt Long] [BMI] (10/6/56 BCtRt-9)*

CINDY'S BIRTHDAY Johnny Crawford—Del-Fi 4178 [Jeff Hooven/Hal Winn] [BMI] (5/7/62 BCR-8)

CINDY'S GONNA CRY Johnny Crawford—Del-Fi 4221 [Barry Mann/Cynthia Weil] [BMI] (9/7/63 BCR-72)

CINNAMON Derek—Bang 558 [Johnny Cymbal/George Tobin] [ASC] (9/14/68 BCR-9)

THE CINNAMON CINDER (IT'S A VERY NICE DANCE) The Pastel Six–Zen 102
[Russ Regan] [BMI] (12/22/62 BCR-21)
***CINNAMON GIRL** The Gentrys–Sun 1114 [Neil Young] [BMI] (4/4/70 BCR-45)*
***CINNAMON GIRL** Neil Young With Crazy Horse–Reprise 0911*
[Neil Young] [BMI] (6/20/70 BCR-52)
CINNAMON SINNER Tony Bennett with Percy Faith and His Orchestra–Columbia 40272
[Lincoln Chase] [BMI] (7/17/54 BCR-16)
CIRCLE Edie Brickell & The New Bohemians–Geffen 27580
[Alan Aly/Edie Brickell/John Bush/John Houser/Ken Withrow] [ASC] (4/8/89 BC-32)
CIRCLE GAME Buffy Sainte-Marie–Vanguard 35108 [Joni Mitchell] [ASC] (8/15/70 R-95)
CIRCLE IN THE SAND Belinda Carlisle–MCA 53308
[Rick Nowels/Ellen Shipley] [ASC] (4/16/88 BC-7)
THE CIRCLE IS SMALL (I CAN SEE IT IN YOUR EYES) Gordon Lightfoot–Warner Bros. 8518
[Gordon Lightfoot] [ASC] (2/11/78 BCR-31)
CIRCLE OF LOVE Steve Miller Band–Capitol 5086 [Steve Miller] [ASC] (1/23/82 BC-55)
CIRCLES The New Seekers–Elektra 45787 [Harry Chapin] [ASC] (7/15/72 BC-87)
CIRCLES Atlantic Starr–A&M 2392
[David E. Lewis/Wayne I. Lewis] [ASC] (3/27/82 BCR-38)
CIRCUS Mike Quatro Jam Band–Evolution 1062
[John Finley*/Mike Quatro/Suzi Quatro] [BMI] (7/1/72 CR-74)
THE CISCO KID War–United Artists 163
[Thomas Allen/Harold Brown/Morris Dickerson/Lonnie Jordan/Charles Miller/
Lee Oskar/Howard Scott] [ASC] (3/3/73 BCR-1)
CISSY STRUT The Meters–Josie 1005
[Joseph Modeliste/Art Neville/Leo Nocentelli/George Porter] [BMI] (4/12/69 BCR-23) [I]
A CITY GIRL STOLE MY COUNTRY BOY Patti Page–Mercury 71792
[Yvette Ball/Robert Mosely/Russell Murray] [BMI] (4/10/61 B-90)
CITY IN THE SKY The Staple Singers–Stax 0215
[Charlie Chalmers/Donna Rhodes/Sandra Rhodes] [BMI] (7/13/74 BCR-58)
***CITY LIGHTS** Don Rondo–Jubilee 5334 [Bill Anderson] [BMI] (8/9/58 CR-74)*
***CITY LIGHTS** Ray Price–Columbia 41191 [Bill Anderson] [BMI] (8/25/58 B-71)*
***CITY LIGHTS** Ivory Joe Hunter–Dot 15880 [Bill Anderson] [BMI] (3/2/59 B-92)*
***CITY LIGHTS** Debbie Reynolds–Dot 16071 [Bill Anderson] [BMI] (5/2/60 BCR-55)*
CITY OF ANGELS The Highlights–Bally 1016
[Bev Dusham/Nick Jovan] [BMI] (10/20/56 BCR-24)
THE CITY OF NEW ORLEANS Arlo Guthrie–Reprise 1103
[Steve Goodman] [ASC] (7/29/72 BCR-17)
CITY OF WINDOWS Stephen Monahan–Kapp 835
[Tom Lazaros/Stephen Monahan] [BMI] (7/8/67 CR-71)
CIU CIU BELLA Danny Kaye–Capitol 3603 [Sylvia Fine] [ASC] (12/22/56 R-76)
CLAIR Gilbert O'Sullivan–MAM 3626 [Gilbert O'Sullivan] [ASC] (10/21/72 BCR-2)
***MOONLIGHT LOVE (CLAIR DE LUNE)** Roger Williams–Kapp 186*
[Claude Debussy/Domenico Savino] [ASC] (7/13/57 CR-54) [IM]
***MY CLAIR DE LUNE** George Feyer–Cadence 1403*
[Claude Debussy/Jerry Leiber/Mike Stoller] [ASC] (7/10/61 Rt-89)
***MY CLAIRE DE LUNE** Steve Lawrence–United Artists 335*
[Claude Debussy/Jerry Leiber/Mike Stoller] [ASC] (7/10/61 BCRt-68)
***MAGIC MOON (CLAIR DE LUNE)** The Rays–XYZ 607*
[Bob Crewe/Claude Debussy/Frank Slay] [BMI] (7/17/61 BCR-45)
CLAP FOR THE WOLFMAN The Guess Who–RCA Victor 0324
[Burton Cummings/Bill Wallace/Kurt Winter] [BMI] (7/13/74 BCR-6)
CLAP HANDS, HERE COMES CHARLIE Ella Fitzgerald–Verve 10241
[Ballard MacDonald/Joseph Meyer/Billy Rose] [ASC] (12/4/61 R-86)
CLAP YOUR HANDS (PART 1) The Wheels–Folly 800 [Teddy Vann] [BMI] (1/23/60 C-79)
CLAP YOUR HANDS The Beau-Marks–Shad 5017
[Joey Frechette/Ray Hutchinson/Michel Robitaille/Gilles Tailleur] [BMI]
(5/16/60 BCR-38)
CLAP YOUR HANDS The Manhattan Transfer–Atlantic 3277
[Tim Hauser/Laurel Masse/Ira Newborn/Janis Siegel] [ASC] (8/2/75 C-95)
***THE CLAPPING SONG (CLAP PAT CLAP SLAP)** Shirley Ellis–Congress 234*
[Lincoln Chase/Kay Werner/Sue Werner] [BMI] (3/20/65 BCR-7)
***THE CLAPPING SONG** Pia Zadora–Elektra/Curb 69889*
[Lincoln Chase/Kay Werner/Sue Werner] [BMI] (12/11/82 BC-36)
CLASS Chubby Checker–Parkway 804 [Kal Mann] [ASC] (5/18/59 BCR-33)
CLASS CUTTER (YEAH YEAH) Dale Hawkins–Checker 916
[Nick Jovan/Karl Sibersdorf/Dick Toops] [BMI] (3/14/59 BCR-43)
CLASSICAL GAS Mason Williams–Warner Bros.-Seven Arts 7190
[Mason Williams] [BMI] (6/22/68 BCR-1) [I]
CLAUDETTE The Everly Brothers–Cadence 1348 [Roy Orbison] [BMI] (4/14/58 BCR-30)
CLAY IDOL Betty Johnson–Bally 1013
[Lew Douglas/Glory M. Fox/Luther King Laney] [ASC] (8/3/56 BR-72)
CLEAN UP WOMAN Betty Wright–Alston 4601
[Willie Clarke/Clarence Reid] [BMI] (11/20/71 BCR-4)
CLEAN UP YOUR OWN BACK YARD Elvis Presley–RCA Victor 47-9747
[Mac Davis/Billy Strange] [BMI] (7/5/69 BCR-18)
CLEANIN' UP THE TOWN The Bus Boys–Arista 1-9229
[Brian O'Neal/Kevin O'Neal] [ASC] (8/4/84 BC-68)
***CLEMENTINE** Jan & Dean–Dore 539*
[Barker Bradford/Percy Montrose/H.S. Thompson/Traditional] [NA] (2/8/60 BCRt-45)
***CLEMENTINE** Bobby Darin–Atco 6161*
[Barker Bradford/Percy Montrose/H.S. Thompson/Traditional] [NA] (3/14/60 BCRt-11)
CLEO'S BACK Jr. Walker & The All Stars–Soul 35013
[Willie Woods] [BMI] (10/9/65 BCR-34) [I]
CLEO'S MOOD Jr. Walker & The All Stars–Soul 35017
[Harvey Fuqua/Jr. Walker/Willie Woods] [BMI] (1/15/66 BCR-49) [I]
***CLICK CLACK** Dicky Doo And The Don'ts–Swan 4001*
[Dave Alldred/Gerry Granahan/Aaron Schroeder] [ASC] (1/27/58 BCRt-28)
***CLICK CLACK** Boyd Bennett & His Rockets–King 5115*
[Dave Alldred/Gerry Granahan/Aaron Schroeder] [ASC] (2/10/58 Rt-29)
THE CLICK SONG NUMBER ONE Cher–Imperial 66282
[Miriam Makeba] [ASC] (2/10/68 CR-78)
THE CLIMB The Kingsmen–Wand 183 [Lynn Easton] [BMI] (5/1/65 BCR-39)
***CLIMB EV'RY MOUNTAIN** Tony Bennett–Columbia 41520*
[Oscar Hammerstein/Richard Rodgers] [ASC] (12/21/59 BCR-74)
***CLIMB EVERY MOUNTAIN** The Hesitations–Kapp 911*
[Oscar Hammerstein/Richard Rodgers] [ASC] (5/25/68 BCR-84)
CLINGING VINE Bobby Vinton–Epic 9705
[Leon Carr/Grace Lane/Earl Shuman] [ASC] (8/8/64 BCR-11)
THE CLOCK Baby Washington–Sue 104 [Jeanette Washington] [BMI] (9/19/64 BC-100)
CLOCK Eddie Rambeau–DynoVoice 225
[Michelle Grainger/Tony Hayes/Steve Wadey] [BMI] (10/15/66 C-95)
–CLOCK OF THE HEART see: TIME
CLONES (WE'RE ALL) Alice Cooper–Warner Bros. 49204
[David Carron] [ASC] (5/10/80 BCR-40)
CLOSE Keely Smith–Dot 16089 [Burt Bacharach/Sidney Shaw] [ASC] (7/4/60 R-80)
CLOSE ENOUGH TO PERFECT Alabama–RCA 13294
[Carl Chambers] [BMI] (9/4/82 BC-65)
CLOSE MY EYES FOREVER Lita Ford–RCA 8899
[Lita Ford/Ozzy Osbourne] [ASC] (3/4/89 BC-8)
CLOSE THE DOOR Jim Lowe–Dot 15381 [Fred Ebb/Paul Klein] [BMI] (7/9/55 CR-27)
CLOSE THE DOOR Teddy Pendergrass–Philadelphia Int'l 3648
[Kenneth Gamble/Leon Huff] [BMI] (6/17/78 BCR-16)
CLOSE TO CATHY Mike Clifford–United Artists 489
[Bob Goodman/Earl Shuman] [ASC] (9/8/62 BCR-11)
CLOSE TO ME The Cure–Fiction/Elektra 64911
[Robert James Smith] [ASC] (12/22/90 BC-64)
***(THEY LONG TO BE) CLOSE TO YOU** Carpenters–A&M 1183*
[Burt Bacharach/Hal David] [ASC] (6/13/70 BCR-1)
(THEY LONG TO BE) CLOSE TO YOU
Jerry Butler Featuring Brenda Lee Eager–Mercury 73301
[Burt Bacharach/Hal David] [ASC] (7/22/72 BCR-66)
***CLOSE TO YOU** B.T. Express–Roadshow 7005*
[Burt Bacharach/Hal David] [ASC] (1/24/76 BC-82)
CLOSE TO YOU Maxi Priest–Charisma 98951
[Gary Benson/Maxi Priest/Winston Sela] [BMI] (6/30/90 BC-1)
CLOSE TOGETHER Jimmy Reed–Vee-Jay 373 [Jimmy Reed] [BMI] (1/23/61 BCR-68)
CLOSE YOUR EYES Tony Bennett–Columbia 40427
[Bernice Petkere] [ASC] (1/31/55 CRt*-18)
***CLOSE YOUR EYES** The Five Keys–Capitol 3032 [Chuck Willis] [BMI] (2/21/55 CRt-33)*
***CLOSE YOUR EYES** Peaches & Herb–Date 1549 [Chuck Willis] [BMI] (3/25/67 BCR-8)*
CLOSE YOUR EYES Edward Bear–Capitol 3581 [Larry Evoy] [ASC] (4/14/73 BCR-24)
THE CLOSER I GET TO YOU Roberta Flack With Donny Hathaway–Atlantic 3463
[Reggie Lucas/James Mtume] [BMI] (2/11/78 BCR-2)
CLOSER THAN FRIENDS Surface–Columbia 08537
[Bernard Leon Jackson/David Townsend] [ASC] (4/15/89 BC-57)
CLOSER TO FINE Indigo Girls–Epic 68912
[Amy Ray*/Emily Ann Saliers] [BMI] (7/22/89 BC-52)
CLOSER TO HOME Grand Funk Railroad–Capitol 2877
[Mark Farner] [BMI] (8/8/70 BCR-22)
***CLOSER TO THE HEART** Rush–Mercury 73958*
[Geddy Lee/Alex Lifeson/Neil Peart/Pete Talbot] [ASC] (10/29/77 BCR-76)
***CLOSER TO THE HEART** Rush–Mercury 76124*
[Geddy Lee/Alex Lifeson/Neil Peart/Pete Talbot] [ASC] (12/5/81 BCR-69)
–CLOSER WALK see: JUST A CLOSER WALK...
THE CLOSER YOU GET Alabama–RCA 13524
[Mark Eugene Gray/James P. Pennington] [BMI] (5/7/83 BC-38)
(CLOSEST THING TO) PERFECT Jermaine Jackson–Arista 1-9356
[Jermaine Jackson/Michael Omartian/Bruce Sudano] [BMI] (6/8/85 BC-60)
***CLOUD NINE** The Temptations–Gordy 7081*
[Barrett Strong/Norman Whitfield] [BMI] (11/16/68 BCR-4)
***CLOUD NINE** Mongo Santamaria–Columbia 44740*
[Barrett Strong/Norman Whitfield] [BMI] (2/1/69 BCR-29) [IWM]
CLOUDS The Spacemen–Alton 254 [Julius Dixon] [BMI] (10/12/59 BCR-36) [I]
CLOUDS David Gates–Elektra 45857 [David Gates] [ASC] (6/30/73 BCR-33)
CLOUDS Chaka Khan–Warner Bros. 49216
[Nick Ashford/Valerie Simpson] [ASC] (5/31/80 R-95)
CLOUDY SUMMER AFTERNOON (RAINDROPS) Barry McGuire–Dunhill 4028
[Travis Edmonson] [BMI] (5/21/66 BCR-62)

CLOWN SHOES Johnny Burnette—Liberty 55416
[James Marcus Smith] [BMI] (3/3/62 CR-86)

CLUB AT THE END OF THE STREET Elton John—MCA 53818
[Elton John/Bernie Taupin] [BMI] (4/28/90 BC-24)

CLUB MICHELLE Eddie Money—Columbia 04376
[Ray Burton/Ralph Carter/Mitchell Froom/Eddie Money] [BMI] (2/25/84 BC-66)

C'MON Poco—Epic 10714 [Richie Furay] [NA] (3/20/71 BCR-63)

C'MON AND GET MY LOVE D Mob Introducing Cathy Dennis—FFRR 886 798-4
[Danny Poku] [BMI] (12/16/89 BC-7)

C'MON AND SWIM Bobby Freeman—Autumn 2
[Thomas Coman/Sylvester Stewart] [BMI] (7/4/64 BCR-5)

C'MON BABY Buddy Knox with The Rhythm Orchids—Roulette 4082
[Buddy Knox] [BMI] (7/12/58 C-63)

C'MON EVERYBODY *Eddie Cochran—Liberty 55166*
[Jerry Capehart/Eddie Cochran] [BMI] (11/10/58 BCR-35)

C'MON EVERYBODY *Jive Bunny And The Mastermixers—Music Factory 99140*
[Jerry Capehart/Eddie Cochran] (Med) [BMI] (10/28/89 BC-11)

C'MON EVERYBODY Elvis Presley—RCA Victor EPA-4382
[Joy Byers Johnston] (EP) [ASC] (7/4/64 B-92)

C'MON MARIANNE *The 4 Seasons Featuring The "Sound" Of Frankie Valli—*
Philips 40460 [Raymond Bloodworth/L. Russell Brown] [BMI] (6/10/67 BCR-9)

C'MON MARIANNE *Donny Osmond—Polydor/Kolob 14320*
[Raymond Bloodworth/L. Russell Brown] [BMI] (5/29/76 BCR-38)

CO-CO The Sweet—Bell 45,126 [Mike Chapman/Nicky Chinn] [ASC] (9/25/71 BCR-85)

COAL MINER'S DAUGHTER Loretta Lynn—Decca 32749
[Loretta Lynn] [BMI] (12/5/70 B-83)

COCAINE Eric Clapton And His Band—RSO 1039 [J.J. Cale] (TSW) [BMI] (6/14/80 BCR-30)

COCOANUT WOMAN Harry Belafonte—RCA Victor 47-6885
[Harry Belafonte/Lord Burgess] [ASC] (5/18/57 BCR-26)

COCOMOTION El Coco—AVI 147
[W. Michael Lewis/Laurin Rinder/Merria Ross] [BMI] (11/26/77 BCR-44) [IWM]

COCONUT Nilsson—RCA Victor 74-0718 [Harry Nilsson] [BMI] (6/3/72 BCR-8)

—CODE OF THE WEST see: BATTLE OF WATERHOLE #3

COLD AS ICE Foreigner—Atlantic 3410
[Lou Gramm/Michael Leslie Jones] [ASC] (7/23/77 BCR-6)

COLD BLOODED Rick James—Gordy 1687 [Rick James] [ASC] (7/23/83 BC-38)

COLD, COLD HEART Dinah Washington—Mercury 72040
[Hank Williams] [BMI] (11/17/62 B-96)

COLD COLD WINTER The Pixies Three—Mercury 72208
[John Madara/David White] [BMI] (12/14/63 BR-79)

COLD FEET Albert King—Stax 241
[Al Jackson/Albert King] [BMI] (1/20/68 BCR-65) [IWM]

COLD HEARTED Paula Abdul—Virgin 99196 [Elliot Wolff] [ASC] (6/24/89 BC-1)

COLD LOVE Donna Summer—Geffen 49634
[Pete Bellotte/Harold Faltermeyer/Keith Forsey] [BMI] (11/29/80 BCR-33)

COLD SWEAT - PART 1 James Brown And The Famous Flames—King 6110
[James Brown/Alfred James Ellis] [BMI] (7/15/67 BCR-4)

COLD TURKEY Plastic Ono Band—Apple 1813 [John Lennon] [GL] (11/15/69 BCR-26)

COLDBLOODED James Brown—Polydor 14258
[James Brown] (TSW) [BMI] (12/7/74 BC-44)

THE COLDEST DAYS OF MY LIFE (PART 1) The Chi-Lites—Brunswick 55478
[Carl Davis/Eugene Record] [BMI] (7/8/72 BCR-40)

—COLE, COOKE AND REDDING see: ABRAHAM, MARTIN AND JOHN

COLINDA Rod Bernard—Hall-Way 1902 [Rod Bernard/Traditional] [BMI] (4/7/62 CR-76)

COLLEGE MAN *Bill Justis—Phillips Int'l 3522*
[Bill Justis] [BMI] (3/1/58 BCRt-37) [IWM]

COLLEGE MAN *Ralph Marterie & His Orchestra—Mercury 71279*
[Bill Justis] [BMI] (3/17/58 Rt-46) [IWM]

COLONEL BOGEY *Mitch Miller And His Orchestra—Columbia 41066*
[Kenneth J. Alford] (Med) [NA] (12/30/57 BCR-15) [I]

COLONEL BOGEY *Art Mooney And His Orchestra—MGM 12590*
[Kenneth J. Alford] (Med) [NA] (12/30/57 BCR-16) [I]

COLONEL BOGEY *Carlson's Raiders—Capitol 3857*
[Kenneth J. Alford] (Med) [NA] (12/30/57 R-16) [I]

COLONEL BOGEY *Edmundo Ros And His Orchestra—London 1779*
[Kenneth J. Alford] [NA] (1/4/58 BCtRt-15) [I]

COLONEL BOGEY *David Terry & His Orchestra—RCA Victor 47-7153*
[Kenneth J. Alford] (Med) [NA] (2/24/58 R-20) [I]

COLOR HIM FATHER The Winstons—Metromedia 117
[Richard Spencer] [BMI] (5/24/69 BCR-6)

COLOR MY WORLD Petula Clark—Warner Bros. 5882
[Tony Hatch/Jackie Trent] [ASC] (12/24/66 BCR-15)

COLORADO Danny Holien—Tumbleweed 1004 [Danny Holien] [ASC] (9/9/72 BCR-66)

COLORADO CALL Shad O'Shea & The 18 Wheelers—Private Stock 45,071
[Shad O'Shea] [BMI] (2/28/76 C-79)

COLORS Ice-T—Sire/Warner 27902
[Charles Andre Glenn/Tracy Marrow] [ASC] (6/11/88 B-70)

COLOUR MY WORLD Chicago—Columbia 45417
[James Pankow] (TSW) [ASC] (6/26/71 BCR-7)

THE COLOUR OF LOVE Billy Ocean—Jive 9707
[Wayne Brathwaite/Barry Eastmond/Billy Ocean/Jolyon Skinner] [ASC] (5/28/88 BC-17)

THE COLOUR OF MY LOVE Jefferson—Decca 32501
[Paul Ryan] [BMI] (8/16/69 BCR-65)

COLOURS Donovan—Hickory 1324 [Donovan Leitch] [ASC] (8/7/65 BCR-40)

THE COMANCHEROS Claude King—Columbia 42196
[Tillman Franks] [ASC] (11/6/61 BCR-63)

COME A LITTLE BIT CLOSER Jay & The Americans—United Artists 759
[Tommy Boyce/Wes Farrell/Bobby Hart] [BMI] (9/12/64 BCR-3)

COME A LITTLE CLOSER Romance Watson—Coral 62133
[Joe Seneca] [ASC] (8/3/59 R-96)

COME AGAIN Damn Yankees—Warner Bros. 19408
[Jack Blades/Ted Nugent/Tommy Shaw] [BMI] (4/13/91 BC-41)

COME ALONG Maurice Williams & The Zodiacs—Herald 559
[Maurice Williams] [BMI] (4/10/61 B-83)

COME ALONG WITH ME The Del Vikings—Mercury 71180
[Carl Stevens] [BMI] (10/12/57 C-60)

COME AN' GET YOURSELF SOME Leon Haywood—20th Century 2191
[Charles Richard Cason] [ASC] (7/12/75 BC-82)

COME AND GET IT Ray Peterson—RCA Victor 47-7578
[Ray Stanley] [BMI] (8/31/59 CR-80)

COME AND GET IT Badfinger—Apple 1815 [Paul McCartney] [ASC] (2/7/70 BCR-3)

COME AND GET ME Jackie deShannon—Imperial 66171
[Burt Bacharach/Hal David] [ASC] (5/28/66 BCR-83)

COME AND GET THESE MEMORIES Martha & The Vandellas—Gordy 7014
[Lamont Dozier/Brian Holland/Eddie Holland] [BMI] (4/6/63 BCR-20)

COME AND GET YOUR LOVE Redbone—Epic 11035 [Lolly Vegas] [BMI] (1/5/74 BCR-5)

COME AND GET YOUR LOVE Roger Daltrey—MCA 40453
[Russ Ballard] [ASC] (9/13/75 BCR-61)

COME AND STAY WITH ME Marianne Faithfull—London 9731
[Jackie DeShannon] [BMI] (2/27/65 BCR-26)

COME AS YOU ARE Peter Wolf—EMI America 8350
[Tim Mayer/Peter Wolf] [ASC] (2/28/87 BC-14)

COME BACK Jimmy Clanton—Ace 600
[Jimmie Crane/Phil Tucker] [ASC] (8/22/60 BCR-60)

COME BACK Johnny Mathis—Mercury 72184
[Eddie Snyder/Paul Vance] [ASC] (9/28/63 BCR-47)

COME BACK The Five Stairsteps—Windy C 603
[Clarence Burke Sr./Gregory Keith Fowler] [BMI] (10/29/66 BCR-61)

COME BACK The J. Geils Band—EMI America 8032
[Seth Justman/Peter Wolf] [ASC] (2/2/80 BCR-32)

COME BACK AND STAY Paul Young—Columbia 04313 [Jack Lee] [BMI] (2/4/84 BC-22)

COME BACK BABY Roddie Joy—Red Bird 10-021
[Mike Lewis/Ricky Lisi] [BMI] (3/20/65 BCR-75)

COME BACK HOME Bobby Goldsboro—United Artists 50807
[Bobby Goldsboro] [BMI] (7/17/71 BCR-69)

COME BACK MY LOVE Jerry Butler—Abner 1017
[Roy Hamilton/Clyde Otis] [BMI] (10/11/58 C-94)

COME BACK SILLY GIRL The Lettermen—Capitol 4699
[Barry Mann] [BMI] (2/12/62 BCR-17)

COME BACK TO ME Janet Jackson—A&M 1475
[James Samuel Harris/Janet Jackson/Terry Lewis] [BMI] (6/30/90 BC-1)

COME BACK WHEN YOU GROW UP Bobby Vee And The Strangers—Liberty 55964
[Martha Sharp] [BMI] (7/8/67 BCR-2)

COME BLOW YOUR HORN Frank Sinatra—Reprise 20,184
[Sammy Cahn/Jimmy Van Heusen] [ASC] (6/15/63 CR-83)

COME CLOSER TO ME (ACERCATE MAS) Nat "King" Cole—Capitol 4004
[Osvaldo Farres/Al (2) Stewart] [BMI] (7/7/58 BCR-17) [FET]

COME DANCE WITH ME Eddie Quinteros—Brent 7009
[Eddie Quinteros] [BMI] (3/7/60 CR-76)

COME DANCE WITH ME Jay & The Americans—United Artists 669
[Mat Maurer/Tony Powers] [BMI] (11/23/63 BCR-76)

COME DANCING The Kinks—Arista 1054 [Ray Davies] [ASC] (5/7/83 BC-6)

COME GET TO THIS Marvin Gaye—Tamla 54241 [Marvin Gaye] [ASC] (11/3/73 BCR-18)

COME GIVE YOUR LOVE TO ME Janet Jackson—A&M 2552
[Glen Barbee/Charmaine Sylvers] [ASC] (2/5/83 BC-58)

COME GO WITH ME *The Dell-Vikings—Dot 15538*
[Clarence Quick] [BMI] (2/16/57 BCRt-3)

COME GO WITH ME *Sunny Gale—Decca 30231 [Clarence Quick] [BMI] (3/2/57 Rt-5)*

COME GO WITH ME *Dion—Laurie 3171 [Clarence Quick] [BMI] (6/15/63 BCR-48)*

COME GO WITH ME *The Del Vikings—Scepter 12367*
[Clarence Quick] [BMI] (1/20/73 R-80)

COME GO WITH ME *The Beach Boys—Caribou 02633*
[Clarence Quick] [BMI] (11/21/81 BCR-18)

COME GO WITH ME Pockets—Columbia 10632
[Al McKinney/Verdine White/Robert Byron Wright] [ASC] (12/31/77 BCR-75)

COME GO WITH ME Exposé—Arista 1-9555 [Lewis Martinée] [ASC] (1/24/87 BC-5)

COME HOME *Bubber Johnson—King 4822*
[Robert Bubber Johnson] [BMI] (11/12/55 BRt-78)

COME HOME *Eydie Gorme—ABC-Paramount 9655 [Robert Bubber Johnson] [BMI] (1/13/56 Rt-78)*

COME HOME *Arthur Prysock—Wing 90016 [Robert Bubber Johnson] [BMI] (1/13/56 Rt-78)*

COME HOME Eileen Barton—Coral 61530 [Grace E. Burt] [NA] (1/13/56 Rt*-78)

COME HOME The Dave Clark Five—Epic 9763 [Dave Clark/Mike Smith] [BMI] (2/6/65 BCR-13)

COME HOME WITH ME BABY Dead Or Alive—Epic 68885 [Pete Burns/Steve Coy/Wayne Hussey/Tim Lever/Mike Percy] [ASC] (7/1/89 BC-64)

COME IN FROM THE RAIN Captain & Tennille—A&M 1944 [Melissa Manchester/Carole Bayer Sager] [BMI] (6/11/77 B-61)

COME IN STRANGER Johnny Cash—Sun 295 [Johnny Cash] [BMI] (6/9/58 B-66)

COME INTO MY HEART Lloyd Price—ABC-Paramount 10062 [Harold Logan/Lloyd Price] [BMI] (10/19/59 BCR-16)

COME INTO MY LIFE Jimmy Cliff—A&M 1167 [Jimmy Cliff] [BMI] (3/14/70 BCR-89)

COME INTO MY LIFE Al Martino—Capitol 3056 [Michael Berardi/Richard Berardi/Kurt Hertha/Henry Mayer] [BMI] (4/10/71 R-97) [FDE]

COME LIVE WITH ME *Roy Clark—Dot 17449 [Boudleaux Bryant/Felice Bryant] [BMI] (5/12/73 BCR-79)*

COME LIVE WITH ME *Ray Charles—Crossover 973 [Boudleaux Bryant/Felice Bryant] [BMI] (11/3/73 BCR-52)*

COME MONDAY Jimmy Buffett—Dunhill 4385 [Jimmy Buffett] [BMI] (4/27/74 BCR-26)

COME ON Tommy Roe—ABC-Paramount 10515 [Rick Hall/Dan Penn] [BMI] (1/18/64 BCR-27)

COME ON AND GET ME Fabian—Chancellor 1041 [Bert Salmirs/Wally Zober] [BMI] (9/7/59 BCR-29)

COME ON AND SAY IT The Grass Roots—Dunhill 4249 [Warren Entner/Rob Grill/Dennis Provisor] [BMI] (9/19/70 BCR-37)

COME ON AND SEE ME Tammi Terrell—Motown 1095 [Johnny Bristol/Harvey Fuqua] [ASC] (5/28/66 BC-80)

COME ON BABY Bruce Channel—Smash 1769 [Bruce Channel/Margaret Cobb*/Marvin Montgomery] [BMI] (7/14/62 BR-95)

COME ON DO THE JERK The Miracles—Tamla 54109 [Warren Moore/Smokey Robinson/Robert Rogers/Ronnie White] [ASC] (12/12/64 BCR-50)

COME ON DOWN Savage Grace—Reprise 0924 [Ron Koss] [BMI] (7/18/70 C-92)

COME ON DOWN (FROM THE TOP OF THAT HILL) Jackie deShannon—Imperial 66224 [John Bromley/David Cleminson/Paula Cooper] [BMI] (2/18/67 R-99)

COME ON DOWN TO MY BOAT Every Mothers' Son—MGM 13733 [Wes Farrell/Jerry Goldstein] [BMI] (5/6/67 BCR-5)

COME ON EILEEN Dexys Midnight Runners—Mercury 76189 [Kevin Adams/Jimmy Paterson/Kevin Rowland] [ASC] (1/22/83 BC-1)

COME ON LET'S GO *Ritchie Valens—Del-Fi 4106 [Ritchie Valens] [BMI] (9/22/58 BCR-42)*

COME ON LET'S GO *The McCoys—Bang 522 [Ritchie Valens] [BMI] (4/23/66 BCR-17)*

COME ON, LET'S GO *Los Lobos—Slash 28186 [Ritchie Valens] [BMI] (9/12/87 BC-21)*

COME ON LITTLE ANGEL The Belmonts—Sabrina 505 [Thomas Bogdany/Ernie Maresca] [BMI] (7/21/62 BCR-26)

COME ON OVER The Strollers—Carlton 546 [Evans/Larry Kerrin] [BMI] (4/10/61 B-91)

COME ON OVER Olivia Newton-John—MCA 40525 [Barry Gibb/Robin Gibb] [BMI] (3/13/76 BCR-23)

COME ON OVER TO MY HOUSE Layng Martine—Barnaby 2053 [Layng Martine Jr.] [BMI] (12/25/71 CR-88)

COME ON OVER TO MY PLACE The Drifters—Atlantic 2285 [Barry Mann/Cynthia Weil] [BMI] (4/24/65 BCR-60)

COME ON, REACT! The Fireballs—Atco 6614 [Steve Dodge] [BMI] (11/2/68 BCR-58)

COME ON SAY IT Henry Gross—A&M 1534 [Henry Gross] [ASC] (7/6/74 CR-70)

(COME ON) SHOUT Alex Brown—Mercury 880694 [Marti Sharron/Gary Skardina] [ASC] (5/4/85 BC-76)

COME ON SOCK IT TO ME Syl Johnson—Twilight 100 [Jesse Anderson/Jo Armstead/Syl Johnson] [BMI] (8/12/67 BC-92)

COME ON UP The Young Rascals—Atlantic 2353 [Felix Cavaliere] [ASC] (9/24/66 BCR-37)

COME OUT FIGHTING Easterhouse—Columbia 68552 [Andy Perry] [ASC] (4/1/89 BC-69)

COME PRIMA *Tony Dallara—Mercury 71327 [Vincenzo Di Paola/Mario Panzeri/Alessandro Taccani] [ASC] (11/10/58 BCRt-21) [F]*

COME PRIMA *Domenico Modugno—Decca 30777 [Vincenzo Di Paola/Mario Panzeri/Alessandro Taccani] [ASC] (11/10/58 CtRt-21) [F]*

COME PRIMA *Luciano Tajoli—Capitol 4086 [Vincenzo Di Paola/Mario Panzeri/Alessandro Taccani] [ASC] (11/10/58 Rt-72) [F]*

COME PRIMA *Polly Bergen—Columbia 41275 [Vincenzo Di Paola/Mario Panzeri/Buck Ram/Alessandro Taccani] [ASC] (11/15/58 BCtRt-24) [F,FDE]*

COME RAIN OR COME SHINE *Rosemary Clooney—Columbia 40774 [Harold Arlen/Johnny Mercer] [ASC] (11/10/56 Rt-23)*

COME RAIN OR COME SHINE *Jerry Lewis—Decca 30124 [Harold Arlen/Johnny Mercer] [ASC] (11/10/56 Rt-23)*

COME RAIN OR COME SHINE *Ray Charles—Atlantic 2084 [Harold Arlen/Johnny Mercer] [ASC] (11/26/60 BCR-47)*

COME RAIN OR COME SHINE *Ray Charles—Atlantic 2084 [Harold Arlen/Johnny Mercer] [ASC] (1/20/68 B-98)*

(COME 'ROUND HERE) I'M THE ONE YOU NEED The Miracles—Tamla 54140 [Lamont Dozier/Brian Holland/Eddie Holland] [BMI] (11/5/66 BCR-17)

COME RUNNING Van Morrison—Warner Bros. 7383 [Van Morrison] [BMI] (3/28/70 BCR-30)

COME RUNNING BACK Dean Martin—Reprise 0466 [Dick Glasser] [BMI] (5/7/66 BCR-35)

COME SAIL AWAY Styx—A&M 1977 [Dennis DeYoung] [ASC] (9/10/77 BCR-8)

COME SATURDAY MORNING The Sandpipers—A&M 1134 [Fred Karlin/Dory Previn] [ASC] (12/20/69 BCR-13)

COME SEE Major Lance—Okeh 7216 [Curtis Mayfield] [BMI] (3/6/65 BCR-40)

COME SEE ABOUT ME *The Supremes—Motown 1068 [Lamont Dozier/Brian Holland/Eddie Holland] [BMI] (11/14/64 BCtR-1)*

COME SEE ABOUT ME *Nella Dodds—Wand 187 [Lamont Dozier/Brian Holland/Eddie Holland] [BMI] (11/14/64 BCtR-39)*

COME SEE ABOUT ME *Jr. Walker & The All Stars—Soul 35041 [Lamont Dozier/Brian Holland/Eddie Holland] [BMI] (11/25/67 BCR-24)*

—COME SEPTEMBER see: THEME FROM COME SEPTEMBER

COME SHARE THE GOOD TIMES WITH ME Julie Monday—Rainbow 100 [Joe Brooks*/Gilbert E. Kennington] [ASC] (7/23/66 BCR-92)

COME SOFTLY TO ME *The Fleetwoods—Dolphin 1 [Gretchen Christopher/Barbara Ellis/Gary Troxel] [BMI] (3/2/59 BCRt-1)*

COME SOFTLY TO ME *Ronnie Height—Dore 516 [Gretchen Christopher/Barbara Ellis/Gary Troxel] [BMI] (3/9/59 BRt-1)*

COME SOFTLY TO ME *The New Seekers Featuring Marty Kristian—MGM/Verve 10698 [Gretchen Christopher/Barbara Ellis/Gary Troxel] [BMI] (1/20/73 BCR-92)*

COME TO ME *Johnny Mathis—Columbia 41082 [Robert Allen/Peter Lind Hayes] [ASC] (1/13/58 BCRt-23)*

COME TO ME *Julie Wilson—Vik 0312 [Robert Allen/Peter Lind Hayes] [ASC] (1/13/58 Rt-27)*

COME TO ME *Marv Johnson—United Artists 160 [Berry Gordy/Marv Johnson] [ASC] (3/14/59 BCRt-25)*

COME TO ME *Frances Burnett—Coral 62092 [Berry Gordy/Marv Johnson] [ASC] (3/30/59 Rt-71)*

COME TO ME Otis Redding—Volt 116 [Otis Redding/Phil Walden] [BMI] (3/21/64 BCR-69)

COME TO ME Tommy James And The Shondells—Roulette 7076 [Tommy James/Robert L. King] [BMI] (5/16/70 BCR-34)

COME TO ME France Joli—Prelude 8001 [Tony Green] [BMI] (9/1/79 BCR-15)

COME TO ME Aretha Franklin—Arista 0600 [Willard Price] [BMI] (5/30/81 BCR-76)

COME TO ME SOFTLY Jimmy James & The Vagabonds—Atco 6551 [Jimmy James] [BMI] (3/23/68 BR-76)

COME TO THE SUNSHINE Harpers Bizarre—Warner Bros. 7028 [Van Dyke Parks] [BMI] (5/20/67 BCR-36)

COME TOGETHER *The Beatles—Apple 2654 [John Lennon/Paul McCartney] (TSW) [ASC] (10/25/69 BCR-1)*

COME TOGETHER *Ike & Tina Turner & The Ikettes—Minit 32087 [John Lennon/Paul McCartney] [ASC] (2/21/70 BCR-49)*

COME TOGETHER *Aerosmith—Columbia 10802 [John Lennon/Paul McCartney] [ASC] (8/5/78 BCR-20)*

—COME TOGETHER see: LOVE AND UNDERSTANDING

COME TOMORROW Manfred Mann—Ascot 2170 [Frank Augustus/Stanley Kahan/Dolores Phillips] [BMI] (2/20/65 BCR-42)

COME WHAT MAY *Clyde McPhatter—Atlantic 1185 [Franklyn J. Tableporter] [BMI] (5/12/58 B-43)*

COME WHAT MAY *Elvis Presley—RCA Victor 47-8870 [Franklyn J. Tableporter] [BMI] (6/25/66 C-94)*

THE COMFORT ZONE Vanessa Williams—Wing 865 072 [Kevin Jones/Reggie Stewart] [ASC] (12/7/91 B-62)

COMIC BOOK CRAZY Little Sammy Yates—Genie 103/4 [Cliff Goldsmith/Fred Smith] [NA] (3/2/59 R-86)

COMIN' BACK TO ME (OOH BABY) Smith—Dunhill 4246 [Alan Parker] [BMI] (8/8/70 CR-66)

COMIN' DOWN TONIGHT 38 Special—A&M 1424 [Max Carl/Jeff Carlisi/Robert White Johnson/Donnie Van Zant] [BMI] (6/24/89 BC-50)

COMIN' DOWN WITH LOVE Mel Gadson—Big Top 3034 [Roy C. Bennett/Sid Tepper] [NA] (5/14/60 BCR-50)

COMIN' HOME Delaney & Bonnie And Friends Featuring Eric Clapton—Atco 6725 [Bonnie Bramlett/Delaney Bramlett*/Eric Clapton] [BMI] (2/14/70 BCR-73)

COMIN' HOME BABY Mel Torme—Atlantic 2165 [Bob Dorough/Ben Tucker] [BMI] (11/3/62 BCR-36)

COMIN' IN AND OUT OF YOUR LIFE Barbra Streisand—Columbia 02621 [Bobby Whiteside/Richard Lee Wold] [BMI] (11/14/81 BCR-9)

COMIN' IN THE BACK DOOR *Baja Marimba Band—Almo 201 [Scott Turner] [BMI] (12/21/63 BC-41) [I]*

COMIN' IN THE BACK DOOR *Wynton Kelly—Verve 10310 [Scott Turner] [BMI] (12/28/63 R-50) [I]*

COMIN' ON Bill Black's Combo—Hi 2072 [Willie Mitchell] [BMI] (1/25/64 BCR-67) [I]

COMING AROUND AGAIN Carly Simon—Arista 1-9525 [Carly Simon] [ASC] (11/1/86 BC-18)

COMING BACK TO YOU Maxine Brown—Wand 142 [James W. Alexander/Ed Townsend] [BMI] (1/4/64 B-99)

COMING DOWN FROM LOVE Bobby Caldwell—Clouds 21 [Bobby Caldwell] [BMI] (4/19/80 BCR-42)

COMING FROM YOU Joni James—MGM 12660 [Al Stillman/Ben Weisman] [ASC] (6/9/58 R-81)

COMING HOME Cinderella—Mercury 872982 [Tom Keifer] [ASC] (4/8/89 BC-20)

COMING HOME SOLDIER Bobby Vinton—Epic 10090 [Gene Allan/Bobby Vinton] [BMI] (11/12/66 BCR-6)

COMING OF AGE Damn Yankees—Warner Bros. 19838 [Jack Blades/Ted Nugent/Tommy Shaw] [BMI] (4/21/90 BC-50)

COMING ON STRONG Brenda Lee—Decca 32018 [David Wilkins] [BMI] (10/1/66 BCR-9)

COMING ON TOO STRONG Wayne Newton—Capitol 5338 [Raul Abeyta/Gary Usher] [BMI] (1/30/65 BR-65)

COMING OUT OF THE DARK Gloria Estefan—Epic 73666 [Emilio Estefan/Gloria Estefan/Jon Secada] [BMI] (1/26/91 BC-1)

COMING 'ROUND THE MOUNTAIN David Seville And The Chipmunks—Liberty 55246 [Traditional] [NA] (5/7/60 C-96)

COMING TO AMERICA (PART ONE) The System—Atco 99320 [Nancy Huang/Nile Rodgers] [BMI] (7/9/88 BC-85)

COMING UP (LIVE AT GLASGOW) Paul McCartney & Wings—Columbia 11263 [Paul McCartney] [ASC] (4/26/80 BCR-1)

COMING UP CLOSE 'Til Tuesday—Epic 06571 [Aimee Mann] [ASC] (1/10/87 BC-59)

COMING UP YOU The Cars—Elektra 69432 [Ric Ocasek] [ASC] (1/23/88 BC-74)

COMMOTION Creedence Clearwater Revival—Fantasy 625 [John Fogerty] (TSW) [BMI] (7/26/69 BCR-14)

COMMUNICATION David McCallum—Capitol 5571 [Billie Barnum/David McCallum] [ASC] (3/5/66 CR-95)

COMMUNICATION Spandau Ballet—Chrysalis 42770 [Gary Kemp] [BMI] (3/31/84 BC-59)

COMMUNICATION The Power Station—Capitol 5511 [Derek Bramble/Robert Palmer/Andy Taylor/Nigel John Taylor] [ASC] (9/7/85 BC-32)

COMMUNICATION BREAKDOWN Roy Orbison—MGM 13634 [William Dees/Roy Orbison] [BMI] (12/10/66 BCR-60)

COMPARED TO WHAT Les McCann & Eddie Harris—Atlantic 2694 [Gene McDaniels] [BMI] (1/10/70 BC-85)

COMPETITION AIN'T NOTHIN' Little Carl Carlton—Back Beat 588 [Louise Hiram/William Webb] [BMI] (6/8/68 BCR-51)

THE COMPOSER Diana Ross And The Supremes—Motown 1146 [Smokey Robinson] [ASC] (4/12/69 BCR-21)

COMPROMISE The McGuire Sisters—Coral 62135 [Edwin Greines/Murray Kane] [ASC] (8/10/59 R-91)

COMPUTER GAME ("THEME FROM THE CIRCUS") Yellow Magic Orchestra—Horizon 127 [Haruomi Hosono/Ryuichi Sakamoto/Yukihiro Takahashi] [ASC] (2/2/80 BCR-60) [I]

CONCEALED WEAPONS The J. Geils Band—EMI America 8242 [Paul Justman/Seth Justman] [ASC] (11/3/84 BC-63)

***CONCRETE AND CLAY** Eddie Rambeau—DynoVoice 204 [Tommy Moeller/Brian Parker] [BMI] (4/24/65 BCtRt-11)*

***CONCRETE AND CLAY** Unit Four Plus Two—London 9751 [Tommy Moeller/Brian Parker] [BMI] (4/24/65 BCtRt-11)*

CONDITION RED The Goodees—Hip 8005 [Fred Briggs/Don Davis] [BMI] (12/21/68 BCR-38)

CONEY ISLAND BABY The Excellents—Blast 205 [Peter Alonzo/Vincent Catalano] [BMI] (11/24/62 BCR-51)

CONFESSIN' THE BLUES Dakota Staton—Capitol 4012 [Walter Brown/Jay McShann] [ASC] (7/21/58 R-85)

CONFESSION OF A SINNER The Stylers—Jubilee 5253 [Al Weisman/Ben Weisman] [BMI] (11/24/56 B-72)

***CONFIDENTIAL** Sonny Knight—Dot 15507 [Dorinda Morgan] [ASC] (11/3/56 BCRt-20)*

***CONFIDENTIAL** Charles Brown—Aladdin 3342 [Dorinda Morgan] [ASC] (11/3/56 Rt-26)*

***CONFIDENTIAL** Bubber Johnson—King 4988 [Dorinda Morgan] [ASC] (11/3/56 Rt-26)*

***CONFIDENTIAL** Rusty Draper—Mercury 70989 [Dorinda Morgan] [ASC] (11/10/56 Rt-26)*

CONFUSION Electric Light Orchestra—Jet 5064 [Jeff Lynne] [BMI] (10/13/79 BCR-37)

CONGA Miami Sound Machine—Epic 05457 [Enrique Garcia] [BMI] (10/19/85 BC-10)

CONGRATULATIONS Rick Nelson—Imperial 66017 [Jerry Fuller] [BMI] (3/14/64 BR-63)

CONGRATULATIONS Cliff Richard—Uni 55069 [Phil Coulter/William Wylie MacPherson Martin] [BMI] (6/8/68 BR-98)

CONGRATULATIONS Vesta—A&M 1407 [Tena Clark/Gary Prim/Vesta Williams] [ASC] (9/9/89 BC-55)

CONQUISTADOR Procol Harum—A&M 1347 [Gary Brooker/Keith Reid] [ASC] (5/27/72 BCR-16)

CONSCIENCE James Darren—Colpix 630 [Barry Mann/Cynthia Weil] [BMI] (4/14/62 BCR-11)

CONSTANT RAIN (CHOVE CHUVA) Sergio Mendes & Brasil '66—A&M 825 [Jorge Ben/Norman Gimbel] [BMI] (12/24/66 BCR-71) [FDE]

CONTACT Edwin Starr—20th Century Fox 2396 [Robert Dickerson/Arthur Pullam/Edwin Starr] [BMI] (1/27/79 BCR-56)

CONTINENTAL MELODY Billy Vaughn And His Orchestra—Dot 16359 [Hans Carste] [ASC] (5/26/62 R-95) [I]

***THE CONTINENTAL WALK** Hank Ballard And The Midnighters—King 5491 [John Bobby Berry/Don Covay] [BMI] (4/3/61 BCtRt-24)*

***THE CONTINENTAL WALK** The Rollers—Liberty 55320 [John Bobby Berry/Don Covay] [BMI] (4/10/61 BCtRt-24)*

CONTINENTAL WITH ME, BABY The Vibrations—Checker 974 [Leslie Temple] [BMI] (4/24/61 R-96)

—CONTINUING STORY OF HARPER VALLEY PTA see: HARPER VALLEY PTA

CONTROL Janet Jackson—A&M 2877 [James Samuel Harris/Terry Lewis] [ASC] (11/1/86 BC-5)

CONTROL OF ME Les Emmerson—Lion 141 [Les Emmerson] [BMI] (12/30/72 BCR-37)

CONTROVERSY Prince—Warner Bros. 49808 [Prince] [ASC] (10/17/81 BCR-49)

CONVENTION '72 The Delegates—Mainstream 5525 [Nick Cenci/Nick Kousaleous] [ASC] (10/21/72 BCR-8)

CONVICTION OF THE HEART Kenny Loggins—Columbia 74029 [Kenny Loggins/Guy Thomas] [BMI] (10/19/91 BC-45)

CONVOY C.W. McCall—MGM 14839 [Chip Davis/Bill Fries] [SE] (11/22/75 BCR-1)

COO COO Big Brother And The Holding Company—Mainstream 678 [Peter Albin] [ASC] (11/23/68 B-84)

COOCHIE COOCHIE COO Hudson Brothers—Casablanca 816 [Bill Hudson/Brett Hudson/Mark Hudson] [BMI] (2/1/75 R-87)

COOCOO U The Kingston Trio—Capitol 4303 [Bill Loughborough/David Wheat] [BMI] (11/16/59 BCR-59)

COOK WITH HONEY Judy Collins—Elektra 45831 [Valerie Carter] [ASC] (2/10/73 BCR-29)

COOKIN' Al Casey Combo—Stacy 925 [Brad Bauder/Al Casey/Bob Taylor] [BMI] (4/7/62 BR-92) [I]

COOL (PART 1) The Time—Warner Bros. 49864 [Dez Dickerson/Prince] [ASC] (1/23/82 BR-84)

COOL AID Paul Humphrey & His Cool Aid Chemists—Lizard 21006 [Gabriel Mekler] [ASC] (3/13/71 BCR-22) [I]

COOL AS ICE (EVERYBODY GET LOOSE) Vanilla Ice—SBK 07369 [Gail "Sky" King/Jennece Moore/Robert Van Winkle] [BMI] (10/5/91 BC-67)

COOL CHANGE Little River Band—Capitol 4789 [Glenn Shorrock] [BMI] (10/20/79 BCR-10)

COOL IT NOW New Edition—MCA 52455 [Vincent Brantley/Ricky Timas] [ASC] (9/22/84 BC-2)

COOL JERK The Capitols—Karen 1524 [Donald Storball] [BMI] (4/16/66 BCR-4)

COOL LOVE Pablo Cruise—A&M 2349 [David Jenkins/Cory Lerios/John Pierce] [ASC] (7/4/81 BCR-13)

COOL MAGIC Steve Miller Band—Capitol 5162 [Kenny Lee Lewis/Gary Mallaber] [BMI] (10/9/82 BC-53)

COOL NIGHT Paul Davis—Arista 0645 [Paul Davis] [BMI] (11/7/81 BCR-11)

COOL PLACES Sparks And Jane Wiedlin—Atlantic 89866 [Ron Mael/Russell Mael] [ASC] (4/9/83 BC-44)

COOL SHAKE The Del Vikings—Mercury 71132 [Alex Kramer/Joan Whitney] [ASC] (7/6/57 BCR-39)

***COOL WATER** Frankie Laine—Columbia 40457 [Bob Nolan] [BMI] (4/2/55 C-32)*

***COOL WATER** Jack Scott—Top Rank 2055 [Bob Nolan] [BMI] (7/11/60 BCR-52)*

***COOL WATER** The Blue Belles—New Town 5009 [Bob Nolan] [BMI] (1/26/63 R-83)*

COPACABANA (AT THE COPA) Barry Manilow—Arista 0339 [Jack Feldman/Barry Manilow/Bruce Sussman] [BMI] (6/10/78 BCR-6)

COPY CAT Gary (U.S.) Bonds—Legrand 1020 [Gene Barge/Frank Guida/Patricia Matthews/Joseph Royster] [BMI] (8/25/62 B-92)

COQUETTE Fats Domino—Imperial 5553 [Johnny Green/Gus Kahn/Carmen Lombardo] [ASC] (11/3/58 BCR-61)

CORAZON Carole King—Ode 66039 [Carole King] [ASC] (10/20/73 BCR-27) [F]

***CORRINE CORRINA** Joe Turner—Atlantic 1088 [Armetia Chatman/Mitchell Parish/J. Mayo Williams] [ASC] (4/28/56 BCRt-34)*

***CORRINE, CORRINA** Swingin' Sam—Coral 61628 [Armetia Chatman/Mitchell Parish/J. Mayo Williams] [ASC] (5/4/56 Rt-71)*

***CORINNA CORINNA** Ray Peterson—Dunes 2002 [Armetia Chatman/Mitchell Parish/J. Mayo Williams] [ASC] (11/21/60 BCR-6)*

CORNBELT SYMPHONY Bing & Gary Crosby—Decca 29147 [Robert Mellin/Nev Simons] [BMI] (7/3/54 C-44)

A CORNER IN THE SUN Walter Jackson—Okeh 7260 [Layng Martine Jr./Lou Stallman] [BMI] (10/29/66 BCR-76)

CORNER OF THE SKY The Jackson 5—Motown 1214 [Stephen Schwartz] [ASC] (10/21/72 BCR-12)

***CORRIDO ROCK (PT. 1)** "Handsome" Jim Balcom—Dot 15711 [Jim Balcom/Arthur Egnoian] [BMI] (3/15/58 CRt-56) [I]*

***CORRIDO ROCK** Jimmy Church's Magicians—Verve 10126 [Jim Balcom/Arthur Egnoian] [BMI] (3/31/58 Rt-73) [IM]*

COSMIC SEA The Mystic Moods—Warner Bros. 7686 [Don McGinnis/Bob Todd/Hal Winn] [ASC] (4/21/73 BCR-78) [I]

COSTAFINE TOWN Splinter—Dark Horse 10002 [Bill Elliot/Bob Purvis] [BMI] (12/14/74 BCR-69)

COTTAGE CHEESE Crow—Amaret 119 [Dave Waggoner/Dick Weigand] [BMI] (5/16/70 BCR-55)

A COTTAGE FOR SALE Little Willie John—King 5342 [Larry Conley/Willard Robison] [ASC] (5/9/60 B-63)

COTTON CANDY Al Hirt—RCA Victor 47-8346 [Les Ledo] [BMI] (4/4/64 BCR-12) [I]

COTTON CANDY The Sylvers—Capitol 4255
[Freddie Perren/Keni St. Lewis/Christine Yarian] [ASC] (6/26/76 BC-59)

COTTON JENNY Anne Murray—Capitol 3260 [Gordon Lightfoot] [ASC] (4/1/72 B-71)

COTTON FIELDS *The Highwaymen—United Artists 370*
[Huddie Ledbetter] [BMI] (11/27/61 BCR-10)

COTTONFIELDS *Ace Cannon—Hi 2065 [Huddie Ledbetter] [BMI] (6/22/63 BCR-67) [IWM]*

COTTONFIELDS *The Beach Boys—Capitol 2765 [Huddie Ledbetter] [BMI] (5/23/70 R-95)*

COULD HEAVEN EVER BE LIKE THIS (PART 1) Idris Muhammad—Kudu 939
[David Matthews/Tony Sarafino] [BMI] (10/1/77 B-76)

COULD I BE DREAMING Pointer Sisters—Planet 47920
[Marlo Henderson/Trevor Lawrence/Anita Pointer] [BMI] (11/8/80 BCR-52)

COULD I FORGET YOU Tyrone Davis—Dakar 623
[Leo Graham/Raymond Haley/Floyd Smith] [BMI] (3/6/71 BCR-52)

COULD I HAVE THIS DANCE Anne Murray—Capitol 4920
[Wayland Holyfield/Bob House] [ASC] (9/6/80 BCR-33)

COULD IT BE FOREVER David Cassidy—Bell 45,187
[Wes Farrell/Danny Janssen] [BMI] (2/12/72 BCR-15)

COULD IT BE I'M FALLING IN LOVE The Spinners—Atlantic 2927
[Melvin Steals/Mervin Steals] [BMI] (12/30/72 BCR-1)

COULD IT BE LOVE Jennifer Warnes—Arista 0611 [Randy Sharp] [BMI] (12/5/81 BCR-47)

COULD IT BE MAGIC *Barry Manilow—Arista 0126*
[Adrienne Anderson/Barry Manilow] [BMI] (6/21/75 BCR-6)

COULD IT BE MAGIC *Donna Summer—Oasis 405*
[Adrienne Anderson/Barry Manilow] [BMI] (5/1/76 BC-52)

COULD THIS BE LOVE Seduction—Vendetta 1509 [Robert Clivillés] [ASC] (6/9/90 BC-11)

COULD THIS BE MAGIC The Dubs—Gone 5011
[Richard Blandon/Hiram Johnson*] [BMI] (11/4/57 BCR-24)

COULD YOU EVER LOVE ME AGAIN Gary & Dave—London 200
[Dave Beckett/Gary Weeks] [ASC] (11/17/73 BCR-91)

COULD YOU PUT YOUR LIGHT ON, PLEASE Harry Chapin—Elektra 45792
[Harry Chapin] [ASC] (7/29/72 CR-81)

COULDN'T GET IT RIGHT Climax Blues Band—Sire 736
[Colin Cooper/John Cuffley/Peter Haycock/Derek Holt/Rick Jones] [ASC]
(2/12/77 BCR-3)

COULDN'T I JUST TELL YOU Todd Rundgren—Bearsville 0007
[Todd Rundgren] [BMI] (7/8/72 BR-71)

COULD'VE BEEN Tiffany—MCA 53231 [Lois Ann Blaisch] [BMI] (11/28/87 BC-1)

COUNT DOWN Dave "Baby" Cortez—Roulette 4679
[David Clowney/Henry Glover/Morris Levy‡] [BMI] (5/21/66 BCR-60) [IWM]

COUNT EVERY STAR *The Rivieras (1)—Coed 503*
[Bruno Coquatrix/Sammy Gallop] [ASC] (8/25/58 BCR-62) [FDE]

COUNT EVERY STAR *Donnie And The Dreamers—Whale 500*
[Bruno Coquatrix/Sammy Gallop] [ASC] (5/1/61 BCR-35) [FDE]

COUNT EVERY STAR *Linda Scott—Canadian-American 133*
[Bruno Coquatrix/Sammy Gallop] [ASC] (4/7/62 BCR-41) [FDE]

COUNT ME IN Gary Lewis And The Playboys—Liberty 55778
[Glen Hardin] [BMI] (4/3/65 BCR-2)

COUNT ME OUT New Edition—MCA 52703
[Vincent Brantley/Ricky Timas] [ASC] (11/2/85 BC-51)

COUNT ON ME Jefferson Starship—Grunt 11196 [Jesse Barish] [BMI] (3/11/78 BCR-8)

COUNT ON ME Gerard McMahon—Full Moon 29699
[Gerard McMahon] [BMI] (4/9/83 B-85)

COUNT YOUR BLESSINGS Ashford and Simpson—Capitol 5598
[Nick Ashford/Valerie Simpson] [ASC] (9/27/86 B-84)

COUNT YOUR BLESSINGS (INSTEAD OF SHEEP) *Eddie Fisher—RCA Victor 47-5871*
[Irving Berlin] [ASC] (10/4/54 BCR-5)

COUNT YOUR BLESSINGS (INSTEAD OF SHEEP) *Bing Crosby—Decca 29251*
[Irving Berlin] [ASC] (10/4/54 R-PRE)

COUNT YOUR BLESSINGS INSTEAD OF SHEEP *Arthur Godfrey—Columbia 40321*
[Irving Berlin] [ASC] (10/4/54 R-PRE)

COUNT YOUR BLESSINGS INSTEAD OF SHEEP *Rosemary Clooney—Columbia 40370*
[Irving Berlin] [ASC] (12/13/54 Rt-PRE)

COUNTING THE DAYS Joey Kid—Atlantic 87898 [Craig Bevan] [BMI] (5/5/90 B-70)

COUNTRY BOY Fats Domino—Imperial 5645
[Dave Bartholomew/Fats Domino] [BMI] (1/25/60 BCR-25)

COUNTRY BOY (YOU GOT YOUR FEET IN L.A.) Glen Campbell—Capitol 4155
[Dennis Lambert/Brian Potter] [BMI] (11/8/75 BCR-11)

COUNTRY GIRL - CITY MAN Billy Vera & Judy Clay—Atlantic 2480
[Ted Daryll/Chip Taylor] [BMI] (2/17/68 BCR-36)

COUNTRY PREACHER Cannonball Adderley Quintet—Capitol 2698
[Joe Zawinul] [BMI] (1/17/70 BC-86) [I]

COUNTRY ROAD James Taylor—Warner Bros. 7460 [James Taylor] [ASC] (2/6/71 BCR-25)

COUNTRY SIDE OF LIFE Wet Willie—Capricorn 0212
[Rick Hirsch] [BMI] (10/19/74 BCR-62)

COUNTRY SUNSHINE Dottie West—RCA Victor 0072
[Billy Davis/Dottie West/Dianne Whiles*] [ASC] (9/15/73 BCR-45)

COUNTRY WINE The Raiders—Columbia 45535
[Edmund Villareal/Wanda Watkins] [ASC] (1/22/72 BCR-28)

COUNTRY WOMAN The Magic Lantern—Charisma 100
[Piet Veerman] [BMI] (7/8/72 BCR-88)

COUPLE DAYS OFF Huey Lewis & The News—EMI 50346
[Chris Hayes/Huey Lewis/Geoffrey Palmer] [ASC] (4/27/91 BC-8)

COURT OF LOVE The Unifics—Kapp 935 [Guy Draper] [BMI] (9/21/68 BCR-15)

THE COURT ROOM Clarence Carter—Atlantic 2801 [Red Lane] [BMI] (5/8/71 BCR-42)

COUSIN OF MINE Sam Cooke—RCA Victor 47-8426 [Sam Cooke] [BMI] (9/26/64 BCR-24)

COVER GIRL New Kids On The Block—Columbia 69088
[Maurice Starr] [ASC] (9/16/89 BC-2)

COVER ME Percy Sledge—Atlantic 2453
[Marlin Greene/Eddie Hinton] [BMI] (11/18/67 BCR-42)

COVER ME Bruce Springsteen—Columbia 04561
[Bruce Springsteen] [ASC] (8/11/84 BC-7)

COVER OF LOVE Michael Damian—Cypress 1430
[Janine Best/Michael Damian/Troy Johnson/Larry Weir] [BMI] (6/17/89 BC-30)

THE COVER OF "ROLLING STONE" Dr. Hook And The Medicine Show—Columbia 45732
[Shel Silverstein] [BMI] (11/25/72 BCR-4)

COWARD OF THE COUNTY Kenny Rogers—United Artists 1327
[Roger Bowling/Billy Edd Wheeler] [BMI] (11/17/79 BCR-1)

THE COWBOY AND THE LADY John Denver—RCA 12345
[Bobby Goldsboro] [BMI] (10/31/81 BCR-66)

COWBOY BOOTS Dave Dudley—Golden Ring 3030 [Baker Knight] [BMI] (9/21/63 BR-74)

COWBOY CONVENTION Ohio Express—Buddah 147
[Peter Barnfather/John Carter] [BMI] (11/22/69 CR-52)

COWBOY JIMMY JOE (DIE STERNE DER PRARIE) Lolita—Kapp 370
[Fini Busch/Werner Scharfenberger] [BMI] (2/6/61 BCR-76) [F]

COWBOY SONG Thin Lizzy—Mercury 73841
[Brian Downey/Phil Lynott] [ASC] (9/18/76 B-77)

—COWBOY TUNE see: END IS NOT IN SIGHT

COWBOYS TO GIRLS The Intruders—Gamble 214
[Kenneth Gamble/Leon Huff] [BMI] (3/23/68 BCR-5)

A COWBOY'S WORK IS NEVER DONE Sonny & Cher—Kapp 2163
[Sonny Bono] [BMI] (2/19/72 BCR-6)

CRACKERBOX PALACE George Harrison—Dark Horse 8313
[George Harrison] [ASC] (1/29/77 BCR-17)

CRACKIN' UP Bo Diddley—Checker 924 [Ellas McDaniel] [BMI] (7/6/59 BC-62)

CRACKLIN' ROSIE *Neil Diamond—Uni 55250 [Neil Diamond] [SE] (8/15/70 BCR-1)*

CRACKLIN' ROSIE *Stars On 45—Radio 3863*
[Neil Diamond] (Med) [SE] (9/19/81 BCR-55)

CRADLE OF LOVE *Johnny Preston—Mercury 71598*
[Jackie Fautheree/Wayne Gray] [BMI] (3/19/60 BCR-5)

CRADLE OF LOVE *Ronnie & Robyn—HBR 489*
[Jackie Fautheree/Wayne Gray] [BMI] (7/23/66 C-100)

CRADLE OF LOVE Billy Idol—Chrysalis 23509
[Billy Idol/David Werner] [ASC] (5/5/90 BC-2)

CRANK IT UP (FUNK TOWN) PT. 1 Peter Brown—Drive 6278
[Peter H. Brown/Robert Rans] [BMI] (7/14/79 BCR-86)

CRASH (HAVE SOME FUN) TKA—Tommy Boy 19527
[Frank De Wulf/Paul Lannoy] [ASC] (12/1/90 BC-69)

CRAWFISH Elvis Presley with the Jordanaires—RCA Victor EPA-4321
[Ben Weisman/Fred Wise] (EP) [ASC] (8/18/58 R-56)

CRAWLING BACK Roy Orbison—MGM 13410
[William Dees/Roy Orbison] [BMI] (11/6/65 BCR-29)

CRAZAY Jesse Johnson—A&M 2878 [Jesse Woods Johnson] [ASC] (10/25/86 BC-53)

CRAZIES Stephen Stills -- Manassas—Atlantic 2888
[Stephen Stills/Dallas W. Taylor] (Med) [BMI] (7/15/72 BR-86)

CRAZY Patsy Cline—Decca 31317 [Willie Nelson] [BMI] (10/9/61 BCR-9)

CRAZY (KEEP ON FALLING) The John Hall Band—EMI America 8096
[Johanna Hall/John Hall/Bob Leinbach/Eric Parker] [BMI] (12/26/81 BCR-42)

CRAZY The Manhattans—Columbia 44-03940
[John Vernon Anderson/Steven Richard Williams] [ASC] (7/30/83 BC-72)

CRAZY Kenny Rogers—RCA 13975 [Richard Marx/Kenny Rogers] [ASC] (1/26/85 B-79)

CRAZY Icehouse—Chrysalis 43156
[Iva Davies/Robert Kretschmer/Andy Qunta] [ASC] (10/17/87 BC-14)

CRAZY The Boys—ZTT/Sire 19298
[Hakeem Abdulsamad/Khiry Abdulsamad/Tajh Abdulsamad] [BMI] (8/25/90 BC-29)

CRAZY Daisy Dee—RCA 2812
[Olivier Abbeloos/Walfried Böcker/Patrick De Meyer/Helmut Meyers/Desiree Rollocks]
[BMI] (3/30/91 B-73)

CRAZY Seal—Motown 2053 [Seal/Guy Sigsworth] [BMI] (6/22/91 BC-6)

CRAZY ABOUT HER Rod Stewart—Warner Bros. 27657
[Jim Cregan/Duane Hitchings/Rod Stewart] [ASC] (5/6/89 BC-11)

CRAZY ABOUT THE LA LA LA Smokey Robinson & The Miracles—Tamla 54206
[Smokey Robinson] [ASC] (6/26/71 BCR-49)

CRAZY ANNIE Evie Sands—A&M 1157 [Al Gorgoni/Chip Taylor] [BMI] (2/7/70 R-92)

CRAZY ARMS *The Andrews Sisters—Capitol 3567*
[Ralph Mooney/Chuck Seals] [BMI] (12/8/56 Rt-82)

CRAZY ARMS *Ray Price—Columbia 21510*
[Ralph Mooney/Chuck Seals] [BMI] (12/8/56 Rt-82)

CRAZY ARMS *Karen Chandler & Jimmy Wakely—Decca 30040 [Ralph Mooney/Chuck Seals] [BMI] (12/29/56 Rt-82)*

CRAZY ARMS *Bob Beckham—Decca 31029 [Ralph Mooney/Chuck Seals] [BMI] (1/4/60 BCR-34)*

CRAZY 'BOUT YA BABY The Crew-Cuts—Mercury 70341 [Pat Barrett/Rudi Maugeri] [BMI] (5/29/54 BCR-PRE)

CRAZY COUNTRY HOP Johnny Otis Show—Capitol 4060 [Johnny Otis] [BMI] (11/10/58 B-87)

CRAZY CRAZY NIGHTS KISS—Mercury 888796 [Adam Mitchell/Paul Stanley] [BMI] (9/26/87 BC-65)

—CRAZY DOWNTOWN see: DOWNTOWN

CRAZY EYES FOR YOU Bobby Hamilton—Apt 25002 [Bobby Hamilton/Steve Schlaks] [BMI] (8/4/58 B-40)

CRAZY FEELIN' Jefferson Starship—Grunt 11374 [Jesse Barish] [BMI] (9/9/78 BCR-54)

CRAZY FOR YOU Madonna—Geffen 29051 [John Bettis/Jon Lind] [ASC] (3/2/85 BC-1)

CRAZY HORSES The Osmonds—MGM 14450 [Alan Osmond/Merrill Osmond/Wayne Osmond] [BMI] (10/21/72 BCR-14)

CRAZY IN THE NIGHT (BARKING AT AIRPLANES) Kim Carnes—EMI America 8267 [Kim Carnes] [ASC] (5/11/85 BC-15)

CRAZY LEGS Donald Austin—Eastbound 603 [Donald Austin/Woody Wilson] [BMI] (2/17/73 CR-87) [I]

—CRAZY LITLE MAMA see: AT MY FRONT DOOR

A CRAZY LITTLE PALACE (THAT'S MY HOME) Billy Williams Quartet—Coral 61576 [Bernie Lowe/Kal Mann/Bickley Reichner] [ASC] (3/9/56 BCR-49)

CRAZY LITTLE THING CALLED LOVE Queen—Elektra 46579 [Freddie Mercury] [BMI] (12/22/79 BCR-1)

CRAZY LOVE Frank Sinatra—Capitol 3703 [Sammy Cahn/Phil Tuminello] [ASC] (4/20/57 BCR-34)

CRAZY LOVE Paul Anka—ABC-Paramount 9907 [Paul Anka] [BMI] (4/7/58 BCR-19)

CRAZY LOVE Helen Reddy—Capitol 3138 [Van Morrison] [BMI] (7/24/71 BCR-27)

CRAZY LOVE Poco—ABC 12439 [Rusty Young] [ASC] (1/13/79 BCR-14)

CRAZY LOVE The Allman Brothers Band—Capricorn 0320 [Dickey Betts] [BMI] (3/24/79 BCR-29)

CRAZY MAMA J.J. Cale—Shelter 7314 [J.J. Cale] [BMI] (1/29/72 BCR-22)

CRAZY ON YOU *Heart—Mushroom 7021 [Roger Fisher/Ann Wilson/Nancy Wilson] [ASC] (4/10/76 BCR-35)*

CRAZY ON YOU *Heart—Mushroom 7021 [Roger Fisher/Ann Wilson/Nancy Wilson] [ASC] (12/31/77 BCR-62)*

THE CRAZY OTTO RAG *Hugo & Luigi—Mercury 70563 [Luigi Creatore/Hugo Peretti/Edward White/Mack Wolfson] [ASC] (3/28/55 Rt-68) [IWM]*

THE CRAZY OTTO RAG *Crazy Otto—Decca 29503 [Luigi Creatore/Hugo Peretti/Edward White/Mack Wolfson] [ASC] (5/2/55 Rt-74) [IWM]*

THE CRAZY OTTO RAG *Happy Hoagy Carmichael—Coral 61384 [Luigi Creatore/Hugo Peretti/Edward White/Mack Wolfson] [ASC] (5/2/55 Rt-74)*

CRAZY TALK Chilliwack—Sire 716 [William A. Henderson] [BMI] (12/28/74 BC-90)

CRAZY WITH LOVE *Guy Mitchell—Columbia 40769 [Josephine Peoples/Aaron Schroeder] [ASC] (10/20/56 BRt-40)*

CRAZY WITH LOVE *Teresa Brewer—Coral 61737 [Josephine Peoples/Aaron Schroeder] [ASC] (10/20/56 BRt-40)*

CRAZY WORLD Big Trouble—Epic 07432 [Giorgio Moroder/Tom Whitlock] [ASC] (10/17/87 BC-71)

CREAM Prince—Paisley Park 19175 [Prince] [ASC] (9/28/91 BC-1)

THE CREATURE (FROM A SCIENCE FICTION MOVIE) Buchanan & Ancell—Flying Saucer 501 [Bob Ancell/Bill Buchanan] [BMI] (12/9/57 B-85)

CREEQUE ALLEY The Mamas & The Papas—Dunhill 4083 [John Phillips/Michelle Phillips] [ASC] (4/29/67 BCR-4)

CRIED LIKE A BABY Bobby Sherman—Metromedia 206 [Craig Doerge/Paul Williams] [ASC] (2/6/71 BCR-10)

CRIMSON AND CLOVER *Tommy James And The Shondells—Roulette 7028 [Tommy James/Peter Lucia] [BMI] (12/14/68 BCR-1)*

CRIMSON AND CLOVER *Joan Jett & The Blackhearts—Boardwalk 7-11-144 [Tommy James/Peter Lucia] [BMI] (5/1/82 BC-6)*

CRITICIZE Alexander O'Neal—Tabu 4-07600 [Garry Johnson/Alexander O'Neal] [ASC] (11/14/87 BC-70)

CROCE DI ORO (CROSS OF GOLD) *Patti Page—Mercury 70713 [Kim Gannon] [ASC] (10/3/55 BCtRt-15)*

CROCE DI ORO (CROSS OF GOLD) *Joan Regan—London 1605 [Kim Gannon] [ASC] (10/10/55 BCtRt-15)*

CROCE DI ORO (CROSS OF GOLD) *Red Foley & Betty Foley—Decca 29704 [Kim Gannon] [ASC] (11/7/55 Rt-21)*

CROCODILE ROCK Elton John—MCA 40000 [Elton John/Bernie Taupin] [BMI] (12/9/72 BCR-1)

—CROOKED LITTLE MAN see: DON'T LET THE RAIN COME DOWN

CROSS MY BROKEN HEART The Jets—MCA 53123 [Stephen Bray/Tony Pierce] [ASC] (6/6/87 BC-7)

CROSS MY HEART Bobby Vee—Liberty 55761 [Sonny Curtis/Snuff Garrett/Bobby Vee] [BMI] (2/6/65 B-99)

CROSS MY HEART Billy Stewart—Chess 2002 [Warren Hagood/Dave Henderson/Sid Pinchback] [BMI] (12/2/67 BCR-77)

CROSS MY HEART Lee Ritenour—Elektra 69892 [Lee Ritenour/Eric Tagg] [BMI] (12/4/82 BC-69)

CROSS MY HEART Eighth Wonder—WTG 31-08036 [Michael Jay] [BMI] (11/19/88 BC-52)

—CROSS OF GOLD see: CROCE DI ORO

CROSS OVER Jimmy Bowen With The Rhythm Orchids—Roulette 4023 [Ollie Jones/Bud Smith] [BMI] (10/7/57 R-85)

CROSS OVER THE BRIDGE Patti Page—Mercury 70302 [Bennie Benjamin/George David Weiss] [ASC] (5/29/54 BC-PRE)

A CROSS STANDS ALONE Jimmy Witter—United Artists 301 [Joe DeAngelis/Ernest Monroe Tucker] [BMI] (5/1/61 B-89)

CROSSFIRE Johnny And The Hurricanes—Warwick 502 [T.J. Fowler/Tom King] [BMI] (4/27/59 BCR-21) [I]

CROSSFIRE! The Orlons—Cameo 273 [Dave Appell/Kal Mann] [ASC] (9/21/63 BCR-19)

CROSSFIRE TIME Dee Clark—Constellation 108 [Don Covay/Horace Ott] [BMI] (11/2/63 BCR-78)

CROSSROADS Cream—Atco 6646 [Robert Johnson] [BMI] (1/25/69 BCR-17)

CROSSROADS Tracy Chapman—Elektra 69273 [Tracy Chapman] [ASC] (10/28/89 BC-88)

CROSSROADS OF LOVE The Tempos Featuring Mike Lazo—Climax 105 [Sherman Edwards/Sid Wayne] [ASC] (10/19/59 R-98)

CROSSTOWN TRAFFIC The Jimi Hendrix Experience—Reprise 0792 [Jimi Hendrix] [ASC] (11/30/68 BCR-36)

THE CROWD Roy Orbison—Monument 461 [Joe Melson/Roy Orbison] [BMI] (5/26/62 BCR-19)

CROWN OF CREATION Jefferson Airplane—RCA Victor 47-9644 [Paul Kantner] [BMI] (11/2/68 BR-64)

THE CRUDE OIL BLUES Jerry Reed—RCA Victor 0224 [Jerry Reed] [BMI] (2/9/74 BC-91)

CRUEL SHOES Steve Martin—Warner Bros. 49122 [Steve Martin] [ASC] (11/17/79 BR-90)

CRUEL SUMMER Bananarama—London 810127 [Sarah Dallin/Siobhan Fahey/Steve Jolley/Tony Swain/Keren Woodward] [BMI] (7/21/84 BC-9)

CRUEL TO BE KIND Nick Lowe—Columbia 11018 [Ian Gomm/Nick Lowe] [BMI] (7/21/79 BCR-12)

THE CRUEL WAR *Chad & Jill Stuart—Columbia 43467 [Paul Stookey/Peter Yarrow] [ASC] (4/16/66 C-99)*

THE CRUEL WAR *Peter, Paul & Mary—Warner Bros. 5809 [Paul Stookey/Peter Yarrow] [ASC] (4/23/66 BCR-52)*

CRUISIN' Smokey Robinson—Tamla 54306 [Smokey Robinson/Marvin Tarplin] [ASC] (10/6/79 BCR-1)

CRUISING FOR BRUISING Basia—Epic 73239 [Basia Trzetrzelewska/Danny White] [BMI] (4/7/90 BC-27)

CRUMBLIN' DOWN John Cougar Mellencamp—Riva 214 [George Green/John Mellencamp] [ASC] (10/15/83 BC-8)

CRUMBS OFF THE TABLE The Glass House—Invictus 9071 [Lamont Dozier/Ronald Dunbar/Brian Holland/Eddie Holland/Scherrie Payne] [BMI] (10/18/69 BCR-54)

CRUNCHY GRANOLA SUITE Neil Diamond—Uni 55310 [Neil Diamond] (TSW) [SE] (1/8/72 B-36)

CRUSH ON YOU The Jets—MCA 52774 [Jerry Knight/Aaron Zigman] [BMI] (4/12/86 BC-3)

THE CRUSHER The Novas—Parrot 45005 [Bobby Nolan] [BMI] (1/9/65 BCR-62)

CRY *The Knightsbridge Strings—Top Rank 2006 [Churchill Kohlman] [ASC] (7/6/59 BCR-16) [IWM]*

CRY *Paul Anka—ABC-Paramount 10338 [Churchill Kohlman] [ASC] (8/4/62 R-100)*

CRY *Ray Charles—ABC-Paramount 10615 [Churchill Kohlman] [ASC] (2/6/65 BCRt-58)*

CRY *Cavril Payne—Pulse 1002 [Churchill Kohlman] [ASC] (2/27/65 Rt-78)*

CRY *Ronnie Dove—Diamond 214 [Churchill Kohlman] [ASC] (11/19/66 BCR-13)*

CRY *Lynn Anderson—Columbia 45529 [Churchill Kohlman] [ASC] (1/29/72 BCR-71)*

CRY Godley & Creme—Polydor 881786 [Lol Crème/Kevin Godley] [BMI] (7/20/85 BC-16)

CRY Waterfront—Polydor 871110 [Phil Cilia/Chris Duffy] [BMI] (4/8/89 BC-10)

CRY BABY *Bonnie Sisters—Rainbow 328 [Sylvester Hopkins/Fred Parris] [NA] (2/17/56 BCRt-25)*

CRY BABY *The Billy Williams Quartet—Coral 61576 [Sylvester Hopkins/Fred Parris] [NA] (2/17/56 Rt-25)*

CRY BABY *Garnet Mimms & The Enchanters—United Artists 629 [Bert Berns/Jerry Ragovoy] [BMI] (8/17/63 BCR-4)*

CRY BABY *Janis Joplin—Columbia 45379 [Bert Berns/Jerry Ragovoy] [BMI] (5/8/71 BCR-20)*

CRY BABY CRY The Angels—Caprice 112 [Morris Bailey] [BMI] (2/5/62 BCR-35)

CRY CRY CRY Bobby Bland—Duke 327 [Deadric Malone] [BMI] (10/15/60 BCR-53)

CRY CRY CRY Shirley And Company—Vibration 535 [Sylvia Robinson] [BMI] (6/14/75 B-91)

CRY FOR HELP Rick Astley—RCA 2774 [Rick Astley/Rob Fisher] [BMI] (2/16/91 BC-7)

CRY JUST A LITTLE Paul Davis—Bang 4811 [Paul Davis] [BMI] (7/19/80 BR-78)

CRY JUST A LITTLE BIT Shakin' Stevens—Epic 04338 [Bob Heatlie] [ASC] (4/21/84 BC-67)

CRY LIKE A BABY *The Box Tops—Mala 593 [Spooner Oldham/Dan Penn] [BMI] (2/24/68 BCR-2)*

CRY LIKE A BABY *Kim Carnes—EMI America 8058 [Spooner Oldham/Dan Penn] [BMI] (10/4/80 BCR-44)*

CRY ME A RIVER *Julie London—Liberty 55006 [Arthur Hamilton] [ASC] (10/31/55 BCRt-13)*

CRY ME A RIVER *Eileen Barton—Coral 61530 [Arthur Hamilton] [ASC] (11/7/55 Rt-15)*

CRY ME A RIVER *Kitty White—Mercury 70722 [Arthur Hamilton] [ASC] (11/7/55 Rt-15)*

CRY ME A RIVER *Jill Corey—Columbia 40596 [Arthur Hamilton] [ASC] (12/30/55 Rt-24)*

CRY ME A RIVER *Janice Harper—Capitol 4324 [Arthur Hamilton] [ASC] (1/4/60 BCRt-41)*

CRY ME A RIVER *Julie London—Liberty 55227 [Arthur Hamilton] [ASC] (1/4/60 Rt-41)*

CRY ME A RIVER *Joe Cocker—A&M 1200 [Arthur Hamilton] [ASC] (10/3/70 BCR-7)*

CRY MYSELF TO SLEEP Del Shannon—Big Top 3112 [Del Shannon] [BMI] (6/30/62 B-99)

CRY ON MY SHOULDER Johnny Crawford—Del-Fi 4203 [Bill Buchanan/Jack Keller] [ASC] (4/27/63 C-100)

CRY SOFTLY Nancy Ames—Epic 10056 [Buddy Killen/Billy Sherrill*/Glenn Sutton*] [BMI] (10/8/66 BCR-95)

CRY SOFTLY LONELY ONE Roy Orbison—MGM 13764 [Don Gant/Joe Melson] [BMI] (7/22/67 BCR-45)

CRY TO ME *Solomon Burke—Atlantic 2131 [Bert Berns] [BMI] (1/22/62 BCR-38)*

CRY TO ME *Betty Harris—Jubilee 5456 [Bert Berns] [BMI] (9/21/63 BCR-23)*

CRY TO ME *Freddie Scott—Shout 211 [Bert Berns] [BMI] (3/25/67 BCR-58)*

CRY TO ME Loleatta Holloway—Aware 047 [David Camon/Sam Dees] [BMI] (3/15/75 BC-66)

CRY WOLF A-Ha—Warner Bros. 28500 [Magne Furuholmen/Pal Waaktaar] [BMI] (1/24/87 BC-50)

CRYIN' Vixen—EMI 50167 [Jeff Paris/Gregg Tripp] [BMI] (1/28/89 BC-22)

CRYIN' IN THE STREETS (PART I) George Perkins & The Silver Stars—Silver Fox 18 [Ted Harris/Sam A. Matter/Kerry Porter] [ASC] (3/21/70 BCR-47)

CRYING *Roy Orbison—Monument 447 [Joe Melson/Roy Orbison] [BMI] (8/7/61 BCR-1)*

CRYING *Jay & The Americans—United Artists 50016 [Joe Melson/Roy Orbison] [BMI] (5/28/66 BCR-25)*

CRYING *Don McLean—Millennium 11799 [Joe Melson/Roy Orbison] [BMI] (1/24/81 BCR-5)*

THE CRYING GAME Brenda Lee—Decca 31728 [Geoff Stephens] [ASC] (1/9/65 BC-87)

CRYING IN THE CHAPEL *Sonny Til & The Orioles—Jubilee 6001 [Artie Glenn] [BMI] (10/3/59 CR-53)*

CRYING IN THE CHAPEL *Adam Wade—Epic 9752 [Artie Glenn] [BMI] (1/30/65 B-88)*

CRYING IN THE CHAPEL *Elvis Presley With The Jordanaires—RCA Victor 447-0643 [Artie Glenn] [BMI] (4/24/65 BCR-3)*

CRYING IN THE CHAPEL *Carol Fran—Port 3000 [Artie Glenn] [BMI] (5/29/65 R-6)*

CRYING IN THE RAIN The Everly Brothers—Warner Bros. 5250 [Howard Greenfield/Carole King] [BMI] (1/8/62 BCR-6)

CRYING LIKE A BABY The Jive Five—Musicor 1250 [General Johnson] [BMI] (7/29/67 C-94)

CRYING MY HEART OUT FOR YOU Neil Sedaka—RCA Victor 47-7530 [Howard Greenfield/Neil Sedaka] [BMI] (6/27/59 C-89)

CRYING ROSES Kitty Kallen—Decca 30516 [Mann Curtis/Larry Stock] [ASC] (12/9/57 R-82)

CRYING TIME Ray Charles With The Jack Halloran Singers And The Ray Charles Orchestra With The Raelettes—ABC-Paramount 10739 [Buck Owens] [BMI] (12/11/65 BCR-5)

CRYSTAL BLUE PERSUASION Tommy James And The Shondells—Roulette 7050 [Ed Gray/Tommy James/Mike Vale] [BMI] (6/7/69 BCR-1)

CRYSTAL CHANDELIER Vic Dana—Dolton 313 [Theodore C. Harris] [SE] (11/27/65 BCR-45)

—CUANDO CALIENTE EL SOL see: LOVE ME WITH ALL YOUR HEART

CUBA Gibson Brothers—Island 8832 [Jean Joseph Kluger/Daniel Vangarde] [ASC] (6/23/79 B-81)

CUBAN BLUEGRASS Stephen Stills -- Manassas—Atlantic 2888 [Joe Lala/Stephen Stills] (Med) [BMI] (7/15/72 BR-86)

CUDDLE ME Ronnie Gaylord—Mercury 70285 [Ronnie Gaylord] [BMI] (5/29/54 BC-PRE)

CUDDLY BABY The Deb-Tones—RCA Victor 47-7242 [Noel Regney/Gloria Shayne] [BMI] (6/21/58 C-73)

CUDDLY TOY (FEEL FOR ME) Roachford—Epic 68549 [Andrew Roachford] [ASC] (4/15/89 BC-25)

—CUERNAVACA CHOO CHOO see: KWA-NA-VA-KA

CULT OF PERSONALITY Living Colour—Epic 68611 [William Calhoun/Corey Glover/Vernon Reid/Muzz Skillings] [ASC] (3/11/89 BC-8)

CUM ON FEEL THE NOIZE *Slade—Polydor 15069 [Noddy Holder/Jim Lea] [ASC] (4/28/73 BCR-63)*

CUM ON FEEL THE NOIZE *Quiet Riot—Pasha 04005 [Noddy Holder/Jim Lea] [ASC] (9/17/83 BC-5)*

CUORE Tony DeFranco—Valmor 18 [Steve Verroca] [BMI] (6/23/62 R-91)

CUPID *Sam Cooke—RCA Victor 47-7883 [Sam Cooke] [BMI] (5/22/61 BCR-13)*

CUPID *Johnny Rivers—Imperial 66087 [Sam Cooke] [BMI] (2/13/65 BCR-45)*

CUPID *Johnny Nash—JAD 220 [Sam Cooke] [BMI] (11/1/69 BCR-35)*

CUPID *Tony Orlando & Dawn—Elektra 45302 [Sam Cooke] [BMI] (2/7/76 BCR-21)*

CUPID *The Spinners—Atlantic 3664 [Sam Cooke] (Med) [BMI] (5/17/80 BCR-4)*

—CURIOUS MIND see: UM UM UM UM UM

CURLY Jimmy Clanton—Laurie 3508 [Gary Osborne] [BMI] (11/15/69 B-97)

THE CURLY SHUFFLE Jump 'N the Saddle—Atlantic 89718 [Peter Quinn] [ASC] (12/3/83 BC-9)

CURRY ROAD Burl Ives—Decca 31453 [Burl Ives/Mel Tillis] [BMI] (1/12/63 R-80)

CUSTOM MACHINE Bruce And Terry—Columbia 42956 [Mike Love*/Brian Wilson] [BMI] (2/22/64 B-85)

CUT THE CAKE AWB—Atlantic 3261 [Roger Ball/Malcolm Duncan/Alan Gorrie/Robbie McIntosh/Onnie McIntyre/Hamish Stuart] [ASC] (4/5/75 BCR-10)

CUTIE PIE One Way—MCA 52049 [Theodore Dudley/Greg Green/Al Hudson/Glenda Hudson/Jon Meadows/Terry Morgan/Dave Roberson] [BMI] (5/29/82 BC-45)

CUTS BOTH WAYS Gloria Estefan—Epic 73395 [Gloria Estefan] [BMI] (6/30/90 BC-44)

CUTS LIKE A KNIFE Bryan Adams—A&M 2553 [Bryan Adams/Jim Vallance] [BMI] (6/11/83 BC-15)

CUTS YOU UP Peter Murphy—Beggars Banquet 9140 [Peter Murphy/Paul Statham] [BMI] (3/24/90 BC-55)

CUZ IT'S YOU, GIRL James Walsh Gypsy Band—RCA 11403 [James Francis Walsh] [BMI] (10/21/78 BCR-58)

CYCLES Frank Sinatra—Reprise 0764 [Gayle Caldwell] [BMI] (9/21/68 BCR-23)

D

DARLIN' The Hilltoppers—Dot 15318 [Jim Cassin/Duke Enston/Teddy Powell*] [ASC] (1/17/55 CR-16)

D-I-V-O-R-C-E Tammy Wynette—Epic 10315 [Bobby Braddock/Curly Putman] [BMI] (6/22/68 BCR-63)

D.O.A. Bloodrock—Capitol 3009 [Rick Cobb/Eddie Grundy/Stevie Hill/Lee Pickens/Jim Rutledge/Nick Taylor] [BMI] (12/26/70 BCR-21)

D.W. WASHBURN The Monkees—Colgems 1023 [Jerry Leiber/Mike Stoller] [BMI] (6/15/68 BCR-10)

DA' BUTT E.U.—EMI 50115 [Marcus Miller/Mark Stevens] [ASC] (4/9/88 BC-35)

DA DOO RON RON (WHEN HE WALKED ME HOME) *The Crystals—Philles 112 [Jeff Barry/Ellie Greenwich/Phil Spector] [BMI] (4/20/63 BCR-3)*

DA DOO RON RON (WHEN HE WALKED ME HOME) *Ian Matthews—Vertigo 103 [Jeff Barry/Ellie Greenwich/Phil Spector] [BMI] (2/19/72 BR-96)*

DA DOO RON RON *Shaun Cassidy—Warner/Curb 8365 [Jeff Barry/Ellie Greenwich/Phil Spector] [BMI] (5/14/77 BCR-1)*

DA YA THINK I'M SEXY? *Rod Stewart—Warner Bros. 8724 [Carmine Appice/Duane Hitchings*/Rod Stewart] [ASC] (12/16/78 BCR-1)*

DO YOU THINK I'M DISCO? *Steve Dahl And Teenage Radiation—Ovation 1132 [Carmine Appice/Steve Dahl/Rod Stewart] [ASC] (9/15/79 BCR-58) [P]*

DADDY COOL *The Rays—Cameo 117 [Bob Crewe/Frank Slay] [BMI] (10/21/57 Rt-59)*

DADDY COOL *The Diamonds—Mercury 71197 [Bob Crewe/Frank Slay] [BMI] (10/21/57 Rt-59)*

DADDY COOL Boney M—Atco 7063 [Frank Farian/Hans-Jörg Mayer] [ASC] (12/25/76 BC-65)

DADDY COULD SWEAR, I DECLARE Gladys Knight & The Pips—Soul 35105 [Johnny Bristol/Gladys Knight/Merald Knight] [ASC] (4/28/73 BCR-15)

DADDY DON'T YOU WALK SO FAST Wayne Newton—Chelsea 0100 [Peter Callander/Geoff Stephens] [BMI] (4/15/72 BCR-1)

DADDY-O *The Fontane Sisters with Billy Vaughn's Orchestra—Dot 15428 [Buford Abner/Charlie Gore/Louis Innis] [BMI] (10/24/55 BCtRt-11)*

DADDY-O *Bonnie Lou—King 4835 [Buford Abner/Charlie Gore/Louis Innis] [BMI] (10/24/55 BCtRt-13)*

DADDY SANG BASS Johnny Cash—Columbia 44689 [Carl Perkins] [BMI] (12/28/68 BCR-42)

DADDY WHAT IF Bobby Bare—RCA Victor 0197 [Shel Silverstein] [BMI] (12/29/73 BCR-41)

DADDY'S HOME *Shep And The Limelites—Hull 740 [Charles Baskerville*/Clarence Bassett*/William Henry Miller/James Sheppard] [BMI] (3/27/61 BCR-2)*

DADDY'S HOME *Chuck Jackson & Maxine Brown—Wand 1155 [Charles Baskerville*/Clarence Bassett*/William Henry Miller/James Sheppard] [BMI] (4/29/67 BCR-87)*

DADDY'S HOME *Jermaine Jackson—Motown 1216 [Charles Baskerville*/Clarence Bassett*/William Henry Miller/James Sheppard] [BMI] (12/9/72 BCR-6)*

DADDY'S HOME *Cliff Richard—EMI America 8103 [Charles Baskerville*/Clarence Bassett*/William Henry Miller/James Sheppard] [BMI] (1/16/82 BCR-22)*

DADDY'S LITTLE GIRL Al Martino—Capitol 5825 [Bobby Burke/Horace Gerlach] [ASC] (1/28/67 BCR-40)

DADDY'S LITTLE MAN O.C. Smith—Columbia 44948 [Mac Davis] [BMI] (8/23/69 BCR-28)

DAISY A DAY Jud Strunk—MGM 14463 [Jud Strunk] [ASC] (2/10/73 BCR-10)

DAISY JANE America—Warner Bros. 8118 [Gerry Beckley] [ASC] (7/19/75 BCR-20)

DAISY MAE Hamilton, Joe Frank & Reynolds—Dunhill 4296
[Dennis Lambert/Brian Potter] [BMI] (11/27/71 BCR-32)

DAISY PETAL PICKIN' Jimmy Gilmer And The Fireballs—Dot 16539
[Juanita Jordan/Keith McCormack/Glynn Thames] [BMI] (12/14/63 BCR-11)

—DAMMI DAMMI DAMMI see: FROM THE BOTTOM OF MY HEART

DAMMIT ISN'T GOD'S LAST NAME Frankie Laine—ABC 11224
[Dick Monda] [BMI] (6/14/69 BCR-80)

DAMN IT ALL Gene Cotton—ABC 12087 [Rob Galbraith] [BMI] (5/17/75 BC-73)

DAMNED IF I DO Alan Parsons Project—Arista 0454
[Alan Parsons/Eric Woolfson] [BMI] (9/29/79 BCR-27)

DANCE Ratt—Atlantic 89354
[Robbin Crosby/Warren DeMartini/Beau Hill/Stephen Pearcy] [BMI] (2/21/87 BC-53)

DANCE ACROSS THE FLOOR Jimmy "Bo" Horne—Sunshine Sound 1003
[Harry Wayne Casey/Rick Finch] [BMI] (3/18/78 BCR-38)

DANCE AND SHAKE YOUR TAMBOURINE Universal Robot Band—Red Greg 207
[Patrick Adams] [ASC] (4/9/77 BCR-86)

THE DANCE AT ST. FRANCIS The Barracuda—RCA Victor 47-9660
[Garry Bonner/Alan Gordon] [BMI] (12/7/68 CR-86)

DANCE AWAY Roxy Music—Atco 7100 [Bryan Ferry] [BMI] (4/21/79 BCR-44)

DANCE BY THE LIGHT OF THE MOON *The Olympics—Arvee 5020*
[Jimmy Eaton/Cliff Goldsmith/Mickey Leader*/Terry Shand*/Fred Smith/Traditional] [BMI] (12/5/60 BCR-25)*

DANCE WITH A DOLLY (WITH A HOLE IN HER STOCKING) *Damita Jo—Mercury 71871*
[Jimmy Eaton/Mickey Leader/Terry Shand/Traditional] [ASC] (10/2/61 R-68)

DANCE, DANCE, DANCE Joey Dee—Roulette 4503
[Windsor King/Morris Levy‡] [BMI] (7/13/63 BCR-89)

DANCE, DANCE, DANCE *The Beach Boys—Capitol 5306*
[Mike Love/Brian Wilson/Carl Wilson] [BMI] (11/7/64 BCR-8)*

DANCE, DANCE, DANCE *The Cantina Band—Millennium 11818*
[Mike Love/Brian Wilson/Carl Wilson] (Med) [BMI] (7/25/81 B-81)*

DANCE, DANCE, DANCE The New Seekers—Elektra 45805
[Neil Young] [BMI] (9/23/72 BR-84)

DANCE, DANCE, DANCE (YOWSAH, YOWSAH, YOWSAH) Chic—Atlantic 3435
[Bernard Edwards/Kenny Lehman/Nile Rodgers] [BMI] (10/22/77 BCR-6)

DANCE (DISCO HEAT) Sylvester—Fantasy 827
[Victor Orsborn/Eric Jay Robinson] [ASC] (8/19/78 BCR-17)

DANCE, EVERYBODY, DANCE The Dartells—Dot 16502 [Randy Ray] [BMI] (8/24/63 B-99)

DANCE EVERYONE DANCE *Betty Madigan—Coral 62007*
[Sid Danoff/Abraham Zevi Idelsohn/Traditional] [ASC] (7/28/58 BCRt-27) [FDE]

DANCE, EVERYONE, DANCE *The Hi-Liters—Hanover 4506*
[Sid Danoff/Abraham Zevi Idelsohn/Traditional] [ASC] (8/11/58 Rt-30) [FDE]

DANCE, EVERYONE, DANCE *Les Baxter & His Orchestra—Capitol 4032*
[Sid Danoff/Abraham Zevi Idelsohn/Traditional] [ASC] (8/25/58 Rt-29) [FDE]

DANCE FLOOR (PART I) Zapp—Warner Bros. 29961
[Larry Troutman/Roger Troutman] [BMI] (8/7/82 C-68)

DANCE HALL DAYS Wang Chung—Geffen 29310
[Darren Costin/Nick Feldman/Jack Hues] [BMI] (4/21/84 BC-16)

DANCE LITTLE LADY DANCE Danny White—RCR 19765
[Biddu Appaiah/Ron Roker/Gerry Shury] [BMI] (2/26/77 B-100)

DANCE LITTLE SISTER (PART ONE) Terence Trent D'Arby—Columbia 08023
[Terence Trent D'Arby] [BMI] (9/10/88 BC-28)

DANCE MASTER PT. 1 Willie Henderson—Playboy 50057
[Willie Henderson/Quinton Joseph] [BMI] (6/22/74 BCR-56)

DANCE MR. SNOWMAN DANCE The Crew-Cuts—Mercury 70491
[Luigi Creatore/Hugo Peretti] [ASC] (12/6/54 R-81)

DANCE ON LITTLE GIRL Paul Anka—ABC-Paramount 10220
[Paul Anka] [BMI] (5/15/61 BCR-10)

DANCE ONLY WITH ME Perry Como—RCA Victor 47-7202
[Betty Comden/Adolph Green/Jule Styne] [ASC] (4/7/58 R-33)

DANCE THE KUNG FU Carl Douglas—20th Century 2168
[Biddu Appaiah/Carl Douglas] [BMI] (2/8/75 BCR-46)

DANCE THE MESS AROUND Chubby Checker—Parkway 822
[Dave Appell/Kal Mann] [ASC] (4/17/61 BCR-16)

DANCE THE NIGHT AWAY Van Halen—Warner Bros. 8823
[Michael Anthony/David Lee Roth/Alex Van Halen/Eddie Van Halen] [ASC] (4/28/79 BCR-15)

DANCE TO THE BOP Gene Vincent and His Blue Caps—Capitol 3839
[Floyd Edge] [BMI] (11/18/57 BCR-28)

DANCE TO THE MUSIC *Sly & The Family Stone—Epic 10256*
[Sylvester Stewart] [BMI] (2/10/68 BCR-5)

DANCE TO THE MUSIC *Stars On 45—Radio 3863*
[Sylvester Stewart] (Med) [BMI] (9/19/81 BCR-55)

DANCE WIT ME Rufus Featuring Chaka Khan—ABC 12179
[Gavin Christopher] [ASC] (4/24/76 BCR-37)

DANCE WIT' ME - PART 1 Rick James—Gordy 1619 [Rick James] [ASC] (5/29/82 BC-56)

—DANCE WITH A DOLLY... see: DANCE BY THE LIGHT OF THE MOON

DANCE WITH ME The Drifters—Atlantic 2040
[Lewis Lebish/Jerry Leiber*/Irving Nahan*/Mike Stoller*/George Treadwell*] [BMI] (10/12/59 BCR-10)

DANCE WITH ME The Mojo Men—Autumn 19
[Jimmy Alaimo/Paul Curcio] [BMI] (10/30/65 BCR-61)

DANCE WITH ME Orleans—Asylum 45261
[Johanna Hall/John Hall] [BMI] (7/19/75 BCR-4)

DANCE WITH ME Peter Brown Special Background Vocals: Betty Wright—Drive 6269
[Peter H. Brown/Robert Rans] [BMI] (3/4/78 BCR-8)

—DANCE WITH ME GEORGIE (HENRY) see: WALLFLOWER

DANCE WITH MR. DOMINO Fats Domino—Imperial 5863
[Dave Bartholomew/Fats Domino] [BMI] (7/21/62 B-98)

DANCE WITH THE DEVIL Cozy Powell—Chrysalis 2029
[Philip Dennys/Michael Peter Hayes] [ASC] (3/16/74 BCR-43) [I]

(DANCE WITH THE) GUITAR MAN Duane Eddy And The Rebelettes—RCA Victor 47-8087
[Duane Eddy/Lee Hazlewood] [BMI] (9/29/62 BCR-9)

DANCE WITH YOU Carrie Lucas—Solar 11482
[Kossi Gardner] [ASC] (5/12/79 B-70)

DANCER Gino Soccio—Warner Bros./RFC 8757 [Gino Soccio] [ASC] (4/7/79 BCR-48)

DANCIN' Perry Como—RCA Victor 47-6991
[Jerry Leiber/Mike Stoller] [BMI] (8/17/57 BC-51)

DANCIN' Crown Heights Affair—De-Lite 1588
[William Anderson] [BMI] (2/19/77 BCR-42) [I]

DANCIN' Grey and Hanks—RCA 11460 [Zane Grey/Len Hanks] [BMI] (3/10/79 BR-83)

DANCIN' FEVER Claudja Barry—Salsoul 2058
[Claudja Barry*/Jörg Evers/Jürgen Korduletsch] [ASC] (2/25/78 B-72)

DANCIN' FOOL The Guess Who—RCA Victor 10075
[Burton Cummings/Domenic Troiano] [BMI] (11/16/74 BCR-24)

DANCIN' FOOL Frank Zappa—Zappa 10 [Frank Zappa] [ASC] (4/14/79 BCR-45)

DANCIN' HOLIDAY The Olympics—Tri Disc 107
[Diane Rogers/Zelda Samuels/Fred Smith] [BMI] (7/6/63 BCR-71)

—DANCIN' IN THE FUNKSHINE see: FUNK 'N' ROLL

DANCIN' IN THE KEY OF LIFE Steve Arrington—Atlantic 89535
[India Arrington/Steve Arrington] [BMI] (8/17/85 BC-68)

DANCIN' IN THE STREETS The Ames Brothers—RCA Victor 47-7474
[Stan Lebowsky/Johnny Lehmann] [BMI] (3/9/59 R-97)

DANCIN' KID
Disco Tex & The Sex-O-Lettes Featuring Sir Monti Rock III—Chelsea 3045
[Kenny Nolan] [ASC] (7/3/76 BCR-60)

DANCIN' LIKE LOVERS Mary MacGregor—RSO 1025
[Larry Herbstritt/Doug Thiele] [ASC] (5/17/80 B-72)

DANCIN' MAN Q—Epic 50335 [Robert Peckman] [BMI] (3/12/77 BCR-20)

DANCIN' (ON A SATURDAY NIGHT) Flash Cadillac & The Continental Kids—Epic 11102
[Barry Blue/Lynsey DePaul] [BMI] (5/25/74 BCR-79)

DANCIN' OUT OF MY HEART Ronnie Dove—Diamond 233
[Andy Badale/Charmaine Harma] [ASC] (12/2/67 BCR-64)

DANCIN' PARTY Chubby Checker—Parkway 842
[Dave Appell/Kal Mann] [ASC] (6/23/62 BCR-12)

DANCIN' ROUND AND ROUND Olivia Newton-John—MCA 41074
[Adam Mitchell] [BMI] (9/22/79 B-82)

DANCIN' SHOES *Nigel Olsson—Bang 740 [Carl Storie] [BMI] (12/9/78 BC-13)*

DANCIN' SHOES *Faith Band—Mercury 74037 [Carl Storie] [BMI] (12/16/78 BCR-13)*

DANCIN' THE STRAND Maureen Gray—Landa 689
[John Madara/David White] [BMI] (5/26/62 BR-83)

DANCIN' THRU THE NIGHT L.A. Jets—RCA Victor 10668
[John Desautels] [BMI] (6/19/76 C-91)

DANCIN' WITH MY MIRROR Corey Hart—EMI America 8385
[Corey Hart] [ASC] (3/28/87 B-88)

DANCING BEAR The Mamas & The Papas—Dunhill 4113
[John Phillips] [ASC] (12/9/67 BCR-36)

DANCING CHANDELIER Sylvia Syms—Decca 30143
[Bob Hilliard/Philip Springer] [ASC] (12/22/56 BR-68)

DANCING IN HEAVEN (ORBITAL BE-BOP) Q-Feel—Jive 1220
[Brian Fairweather/Martin Page] [ASC] (6/17/89 B-75)

DANCING IN MY SLEEP Secret Ties—Night Wave 9201
[Brian Soares] [ASC] (12/13/86 B-91)

DANCING IN PARADISE El Coco—AVI 203
[W. Michael Lewis/Laurin Rinder/Merria Ross] [BMI] (10/28/78 B-91)

DANCING IN THE CITY Marshall Hain—Harvest 4648
[Kit Hain/Julian Marshall] [ASC] (12/9/78 BCR-39)

DANCING IN THE DARK Bruce Springsteen—Columbia 04463
[Bruce Springsteen] [ASC] (5/26/84 BC-1)

DANCING IN THE MOONLIGHT King Harvest—Perception 515
[Sherman Kelly] [ASC] (10/28/72 BCR-10)

DANCING IN THE MOONLIGHT (IT'S CAUGHT ME IN ITS SPOTLIGHT) Thin Lizzy—Mercury 73945 [Phil Lynott] [ASC] (10/1/77 C-92)

DANCING IN THE SHADOWS After The Fire—Epic 03908
[Peter Douglas Cameron Banks/Andrew Piercy] [ASC] (5/28/83 B-85)

DANCING IN THE SHEETS Shalamar—Columbia 04372
[Dean Pitchford/Bill Wolfer] [BMI] (3/10/84 BC-17)

DANCING IN THE STREET *Martha & The Vandellas—Gordy 7033*
[Marvin Gaye/Ivy Jo Hunter/William Stevenson] [ASC] (8/22/64 BCR-2)*

DANCING IN THE STREET *The Mamas & The Papas—Dunhill 4057*
[Marvin Gaye/Ivy Jo Hunter/William Stevenson] [ASC] (12/3/66 BC-73)*
DANCING IN THE STREET *Ramsey Lewis—Cadet 5573*
[Marvin Gaye/Ivy Jo Hunter/William Stevenson] [ASC] (9/23/67 B-84) [IWM]*
DANCING IN THE STREET *The Dovells—Event 216*
[Marvin Gaye/Ivy Jo Hunter/William Stevenson] [ASC] (8/10/74 C-100)*
DANCIN' IN THE STREETS *Teri DeSario with K.C.—Casablanca 2278*
[Marvin Gaye/Ivy Jo Hunter/William Stevenson] [ASC] (6/21/80 BCR-66)*
DANCING IN THE STREET *Tight Fit—Arista 0638*
[Marvin Gaye/Ivy Jo Hunter/William Stevenson] (Med) [ASC] (10/10/81 B-89)*
DANCING IN THE STREET *Van Halen—Warner Bros. 29986*
[Marvin Gaye/Ivy Jo Hunter/William Stevenson] [ASC] (5/22/82 BC-38)*
DANCING IN THE STREET *Mick Jagger & David Bowie—EMI America 8288*
[Marvin Gaye/Ivy Jo Hunter/William Stevenson] [ASC] (8/31/85 BC-7)*
DANCING MACHINE The Jackson 5—Motown 1286
[Hal Davis/Donald Fletcher/Dean Parks] [ASC] (3/9/74 BCR-1)
DANCING ON THE CEILING Lionel Richie—Motown 1843
[Michael Frenchik/Lionel Richie/Carlos Rios] [ASC] (7/19/86 BC-2)
DANCING QUEEN Abba—Atlantic 3372
[Stig Anderson/Benny Andersson/Björn Ulvaeus] [BMI] (12/11/76 BCR-1)
DANCING TO YOUR MUSIC Archie Bell & The Drells—Glades 1707
[Eddie Haynes/Phillip Mitchell] [BMI] (3/17/73 BCR-61)
DANCING UNDER A LATIN MOON Candi—I.R.S. 53436
[Michael Jay/Alan Roy Scott/Robbie Seidman] [BMI] (10/15/88 BC-61)
DANCING WITH MY SHADOW The Four Voices—Columbia 41076
[Lenny Adelson/Lyn Murray] [ASC] (1/25/58 BCR-46)
DANCING WITH THE MOUNTAINS John Denver—RCA 12017
[John Denver] [ASC] (6/21/80 B-97)
DANDELION The Rolling Stones—London 905
[Mick Jagger/Keith Richards] [BMI] (9/9/67 BCR-6)
DANDY Herman's Hermits—MGM 13603 [Ray Davies] [BMI] (10/1/66 BCR-5)
DANG ME Roger Miller—Smash 1881 [Roger Miller] [BMI] (6/6/64 BCR-5)
DANGER Vic Dana—Dolton 73 [Bob Beckham/Buzz Cason] [BMI] (5/18/63 BCR-76)
DANGER! HEARTBREAK AHEAD Jaye P. Morgan—RCA Victor 47-6016
[Carl Barefoot/Carl Stutz] (TSW) [ASC] (4/9/55 BCR-10)
DANGER HEARTBREAK DEAD AHEAD The Marvelettes—Tamla 54120
[Ivy Jo Hunter/Clarence Paul/William Stevenson] [ASC] (8/14/65 BCR-57)
DANGER! SHE'S A STRANGER The Five Stairsteps—Windy C 604
[Clarence Burke Jr./Gregory Keith Fowler/Curtis Mayfield] [BMI] (1/14/67 BCR-67)
DANGER ZONE Kenny Loggins—Columbia 05893
[Giorgio Moroder/Tom Whitlock] [ASC] (5/10/86 BC-2)
DANGEROUS Natalie Cole—Modern 99648
[Stephen Mitchell/Marti Sharron/Gary Skardina] [ASC] (5/4/85 BC-55)
DANGEROUS Loverboy—Columbia 05711
[Bryan Adams/Jim Vallance] [BMI] (11/16/85 BC-65)
DANGEROUS Roxette—EMI 50233 [Per Gessle] [BMI] (12/16/89 BC-1)
DANGEROUS The Doobie Brothers—Capitol 44700
[Patrick Simmons] [ASC] (5/25/91 C-75)
THE DANGLING CONVERSATION Simon & Garfunkel—Columbia 43728
[Paul Simon] [BMI] (8/6/66 BCR-15)
DANIEL Elton John—MCA 40046 [Elton John/Bernie Taupin] [BMI] (4/7/73 BCR-2)
(THE SONG OF) DANIEL BOONE (THE DADDY OF THEM ALL)
Loren Becker With Enoch Light Orch. & Chorus—Waldorf Music-Hall 217
[Lew Davies/Enoch Light] [ASC] (7/2/55 CRt-48)*
DANIEL BOONE (THE DADDY OF THEM ALL) *Dick Lee—"X" 0145*
[Lew Davies/Enoch Light] [ASC] (7/4/55 Rt-72)*
DANIEL BOONE (THE DADDY OF THEM ALL) *Ken Carson—Media 1011*
[Lew Davies/Enoch Light] [ASC] (7/4/55 Rt-72)*
DANKE SCHOEN Wayne Newton & The Newton Brothers —Capitol 4989
[Milt Gabler/Bert Kaempfert/Kurt Schwabach] [BMI] (7/13/63 BCR-10) [FET]
DANNY BOY *Joni James—MGM 12369 [Traditional/Fred Weatherly] [NA] (11/17/56 R-78)*
DANNY BOY *Sil Austin—Mercury 71442 [Traditional] [NA] (5/30/59 BCR-54) [IM]*
DANNY BOY *Conway Twitty—MGM 12826*
[Traditional/Fred Weatherly] [NA] (9/21/59 BCR-7)
DANNY BOY *Andy Williams—Columbia 42199*
[Traditional/Fred Weatherly] [NA] (10/28/61 BCR-39)
DANNY BOY *Patti Labelle And Her Blue Belles—Parkway 935*
[Traditional/Fred Weatherly] [NA] (12/19/64 B-76)
DANNY BOY *Jackie Wilson—Brunswick 55277*
[Traditional/Fred Weatherly] [NA] (2/27/65 B-94)
DANNY BOY *Ray Price—Columbia 44042*
[Traditional/Fred Weatherly] [NA] (3/25/67 BCR-60)
DANNY'S ALL-STAR JOINT Rickie Lee Jones—Warner Bros. 49100
[Rickie Lee Jones] [ASC] (11/17/79 R-93)
DANNY'S SONG Anne Murray—Capitol 3481 [Kenny Loggins] [ASC] (12/23/72 BCR-5)
DANSERO Joni James—MGM 12607
[Lee Daniels/Richard Hayman/Barry Parker] [ASC] (1/27/58 R-85)
DARE ME Pointer Sisters—Planet 14126
[David Innis/Sam Lorber] [ASC] (7/13/85 BC-11)
DARE TO FALL IN LOVE Brent Bourgeois—Charisma 98971
[Peter Beckett/Brent Bourgeois/Mark Ross] [BMI] (4/28/90 BC-25)
THE DARK END OF THE STREET James Carr—Goldwax 317
[Chips Moman/Dan Penn] [BMI] (2/4/67 BCR-77)
DARK HORSE George Harrison—Apple 1877 [George Harrison] [ASC] (11/23/74 BCR-15)
DARK LADY Cher—MCA 40161 [John Durrill] [ASC] (1/12/74 BCR-1)
DARK MOON *Bonnie Guitar—Dot 15550 [Ned Miller] [BMI] (4/13/57 BCtRt-2)*
DARK MOON *Gale Storm—Dot 15558 [Ned Miller] [BMI] (4/20/57 BCtRt-2)*
DARKEST STREET IN TOWN Jimmy Clanton—Ace 8005
[Howard Greenfield/Kenny Karen] [BMI] (12/8/62 BCR-77)
DARKNESS, DARKNESS The Youngbloods—RCA Victor 74-0342
[Jesse Colin Young] [ASC] (5/2/70 BCR-83)
DARLIN' *The Beach Boys—Capitol 2068*
[Mike Love/Brian Wilson] [BMI] (12/23/67 BCR-10)
DARLIN' *Paul Davis Featuring Susan Collins—Bang 736*
[Mike Love/Brian Wilson] [BMI] (5/13/78 BCR-45)
DARLIN' *Yipes!!—Millennium 11791 [Mike Love/Brian Wilson] [BMI] (8/2/80 BCR-68)*
DARLIN' Frank Stallone—Polydor 821382
[Vince DiCola/Mark Hudson/Frank Stallone] [ASC] (5/5/84 BC-81)
DARLIN' DANIELLE DON'T Henry Lee Summer—CBS Associated 07909
[Henry Lee Summer] [BMI] (5/28/88 BC-57)
DARLIN' DARLIN' BABY (SWEET, TENDER, LOVE) The O'Jays—Philadelphia Int'l 3610
[Kenneth Gamble/Leon Huff] [BMI] (12/18/76 BCR-72)
DARLIN' I Vanessa Williams—Wing 871 936
[Kenny Harris/Rex Salas] [BMI] (6/3/89 BC-82)
DARLING BABY *The Elgins—V.I.P. 25029*
[Lamont Dozier/Brian Holland/Eddie Holland] [BMI] (3/19/66 BCR-55)
DARLING BABY *Jackie Moore—Atlantic 2861*
[Lamont Dozier/Brian Holland/Eddie Holland] [BMI] (3/18/72 C-97)
DARLING BE HOME SOON *The Lovin' Spoonful—Kama Sutra 220*
[John Sebastian] [BMI] (2/11/67 BCR-11)
DARLING BE HOME SOON *Bobby Darin—Atlantic 2420*
[John Sebastian] [BMI] (7/29/67 B-93)
DARLING BE HOME SOON *The Association—Columbia 45602*
[John Sebastian] [BMI] (5/27/72 CR-90)
DARLING COME BACK HOME Eddie Kendricks—Tamla 54236
[Errison Johnson/Kathy Wakefield/Frank Edward Wilson] [BMI] (6/30/73 BCR-67)
DARLING! DARLING! DARLING! Jo Stafford—Columbia 40406
[Allan Copeland/Jack Lloyd] [ASC] (2/12/55 C-44)
DARLING DEAR Smokey Robinson & The Miracles—Tamla 54189
[George Gordy/Rosemary Gordy/Allen Story] [BMI] (5/2/70 B-100)
DARLING I LOVE YOU Al Martino—20th Fox 153
[Aldo Provenzano] [BMI] (8/15/59 BCR-52)
DARLING IT'S WONDERFUL *The Lovers—Lamp 2005 [Allen Bunn] [BMI] (8/19/57 B-48)*
DARLING IT'S WONDERFUL *Dale & Grace—Montel 930*
[Allen Bunn] [BMI] (7/25/64 CR-91)
DARLING JE VOUS AIME BEAUCOUP Nat "King" Cole—Capitol 3027
[Anna Sosenko] (TSW) [ASC] (4/9/55 BCR-6)
DARLING LORRAINE The Knockouts—Shad 5013
[Rosemary Gallagher*/Edward Parente] [BMI] (12/19/59 BCR-35)
DARLING TAKE ME BACK Lenny Welch—Kapp 662 [Larry Weiss] [BMI] (5/29/65 BCR-39)
THE DARTELL STOMP The Mustangs—Providence 401
[Dick Burns] [NA] (10/3/64 BC-92) [I]
DAS IST MUSIK Bill Hayes—Cadence 1294
[Philip Springer/Sid Wayne] [ASC] (6/22/56 R-79) [FET]
DAS MACHEN NUR DIE BEINE VON DOLORES *Crazy Otto—Polydor 22009B*
[Michael Jary] (Med) [ASC] (1/17/55 R-1) [IM]
DAS MACHEN NUR DIE BEINE VON DOLORES
Johnny Maddox And The Rhythmasters—Dot 15325
[Michael Jary] (Med) [ASC] (1/24/55 BCR-1) [IM]
DAUGHTER The Blenders—Witch 114 [Hilliard Jones] [BMI] (7/6/63 BCR-55)
DAUGHTER OF DARKNESS Tom Jones—Parrot 40048
[Les Reed/Geoff Stephens] [BMI] (4/25/70 BCR-10)
DAWN David Rockingham Trio—Josie 913
[Robert C. Robinson] [BMI] (11/9/63 BCR-52) [I]
DAWN (GO AWAY)
The 4 Seasons Featuring The "Sound" Of Frankie Valli—Philips 40166
[Bob Gaudio/Sandy Linzer] [BMI] (2/1/64 BCR-3)
DAWN *Gidea Park—Profile 5003*
[Bob Gaudio/Sandy Linzer] (Med) [BMI] (12/26/81 BC-82)
THE DAWN OF CORRECTION The Spokesmen—Decca 31844
[Ray Gilmore/John Madara/David White] [BMI] (9/18/65 BCR-22)
DAWNING Winifred Atwell—London 1843
[Charles Gounod] [NA] (12/15/58 R-95)
DAY AFTER DAY Bill Cecere—Anchor 143
[Bud Green/Richard Himber] [ASC] (1/27/58 R-84)
DAY AFTER DAY Badfinger—Apple 1841 [Pete Ham] [ASC] (11/27/71 BCR-1)
DAY AFTER DAY (IT'S SLIPPIN' AWAY) Shango—A&M 1014
[Stuart Margolin/Thomas Reynolds/Jerry Riopelle] [BMI] (3/1/69 BCR-57)

DAY AND NIGHT The Wackers—Elektra 45816
[Randy Bishop/Jean-Pierre Paquin/Robert Segarini] [BMI] (11/18/72 BCR-65)

DAY BY DAY The Four Freshmen—Capitol 3154
[Sammy Cahn/Axel Stordahl/Paul Weston] [ASC] (7/9/55 BCR-21)

DAY BY DAY (EVERY MINUTE OF THE HOUR) The Continental 4—Jay Walking 011
[Eugene Lemon/Bobby Martin] [BMI] (5/29/71 BCR-60)

DAY BY DAY *Holly Sherwood—Carousel 30,057*
[Stephen Schwartz/John Tebelak/Traditional] (Med) [ASC] (10/2/71 CR-91)

DAY BY DAY *Godspell—Bell 45,210*
[Stephen Schwartz/John Tebelak/Traditional] [ASC] (5/13/72 BCR-9)

DAY BY DAY Hooters—Columbia 05730
[Eric Bazilian/Rick Chertoff/Rob Hyman] [ASC] (12/14/85 BC-18)

DAY DREAMING Aretha Franklin—Atlantic 2866 [Aretha Franklin] [BMI] (3/11/72 BCR-5)

DAY FOR DECISION Johnny Sea—Warner Bros. 5820
[Allen Peltier] [BMI] (6/11/66 BCR-20)

DAY I DIED, THE The Playmates—Roulette 4100 [Sherman Edwards] [ASC] (9/29/58 B-81)

THE DAY I FOUND MYSELF The Honey Cone—Hot Wax 7113
[Lamont Dozier/Ronald Dunbar/Brian Holland/Eddie Holland/General Johnson] [BMI] (2/12/72 BCR-15)

DAY-IN DAY-OUT David Bowie—EMI America 8380 [David Bowie] [ASC] (4/4/87 BC-21)

A DAY IN MY LIFE (WITHOUT YOU) Lisette Melendez—Fever 38-73787
[Carlos Berrios/Lisette Melendez/Franc Reyes] [ASC] (9/28/91 B-49)

A DAY IN THE LIFE OF A FOOL Jack Jones—Kapp 781
[Luiz Bonfá/Carl Sigman] [ASC] (10/22/66 BCR-55) [FDE]

DAY IS DONE *Peter, Paul & Mary—Warner Bros.-Seven Arts 7279*
[Peter Yarrow] [ASC] (4/19/69 BCR-20)

DAY IS DONE *Brooklyn Bridge—Buddah 193 [Peter Yarrow] [ASC] (10/3/70 BCR-89)*

THE DAY THAT CURLY BILLY SHOT DOWN CRAZY SAM MCGEE The Hollies—Epic 11051
[Allan Clarke] [NA] (11/3/73 C-86)

THE DAY THE RAINS CAME *Jane Morgan—Kapp 235*
[Gilbert Bécaud/Pierre Delanoë/Carl Sigman] [ASC] (9/13/58 BCtRt-14) [FET]

THE DAY THE RAINS CAME *Raymond Lefevre and His Orchestra—Kapp 231*
[Gilbert Bécaud/Pierre Delanoë/Carl Sigman*] [ASC] (9/13/58 BCtRt-14) [IWM]*

DAY TRIPPER *The Beatles—Capitol 5555*
[John Lennon/Paul McCartney] [ASC] (12/18/65 BCR-5)

DAY TRIPPER *The Vontastics—St. Lawrence 1014*
[John Lennon/Paul McCartney] [ASC] (9/3/66 BC-98)

DAY TRIPPER *Ramsey Lewis—Cadet 5553*
[John Lennon/Paul McCartney] [ASC] (12/24/66 BR-74) [IWM]

DAY TRIPPER *Anne Murray—Capitol 4000*
[John Lennon/Paul McCartney] [ASC] (12/21/74 BCR-44)

DAYBREAK Al Hibbler—Decca 29441 [Harold Adamson/Ferde Grofe] [ASC] (5/2/55 R-76)

DAYBREAK Nilsson—RCA Victor 0246 [Harry Nilsson] [BMI] (4/6/74 BCR-23)

DAYBREAK Barry Manilow—Arista 0273
[Adrienne Anderson/Barry Manilow] [BMI] (10/1/77 BCR-21)

—DAYBREAK see: STORYBOOK CHILDREN

DAYBREAKER Electric Light Orchestra—United Artists 405
[Jeff Lynne] [ASC] (4/20/74 BCR-61) [I]

DAYDREAM *The Lovin' Spoonful—Kama Sutra 208*
[John Sebastian] [BMI] (2/26/66 BCR-1)

DAYDREAM *David Cassidy—Bell 45,386 [John Sebastian] [BMI] (8/18/73 C-91)*

DAYDREAM BELIEVER *The Monkees—Colgems 1012*
[John Stewart] [BMI] (11/11/67 BCR-1)

DAYDREAM BELIEVER *Anne Murray—Capitol 4813*
[John Stewart] [BMI] (12/22/79 BCR-10)

DAYDREAM BELIEVER *The Monkees—Arista 1-9532*
[John Stewart] [BMI] (10/25/86 BC-78)

DAYDREAMER C.C. & Company—Westbound 5016 [Terry Dempsey] [ASC] (1/3/76 B-91)

DAYDREAMS Art Mooney And His Orchestra—MGM 12277
[Al Hoffman/Dick Manning] [ASC] (7/7/56 BCR-42)

DAYDREAMS Johnny Crawford—Del-Fi 4162 [Al Hazan] [BMI] (6/12/61 BC-70)

DAYLIGHT *Bobby Womack—United Artists 763*
[Harold Payne/Bobby Womack] [BMI] (3/20/76 CR-88)

DAYLIGHT *Vicki Sue Robinson—RCA 10775*
[Harold Payne/Bobby Womack] [BMI] (10/2/76 BC-63)

DAYLIGHT AND DARKNESS Smokey Robinson—Tamla 54293
[Rose Ella Jones/Smokey Robinson] [ASC] (5/27/78 BCR-70)

DAYLIGHT SAVIN' TIME Keith—Mercury 72695
[Jerry J. Ross/Mort Shuman] [BMI] (6/10/67 BCR-59)

DAYS ARE NUMBERS (THE TRAVELLER) Alan Parsons Project—Arista 1-9349
[Alan Parsons/Eric Woolfson] [BMI] (4/27/85 BC-71)

DAYS GONE BY Poco—Atlantic 89674 [Paul Cotton] [ASC] (4/28/84 B-80)

DAYS GONE DOWN (STILL GOT THE LIGHT IN YOUR EYES) Gerry Rafferty—
United Artists 1298 [Gerry Rafferty] [BMI] (6/2/79 BCR-17)

DAYS LIKE THESE Asia—Geffen 19677 [Steven Leslie Jones] [ASC] (9/22/90 BC-55)

THE DAYS OF SAND AND SHOVELS Bobby Vinton—Epic 10485
[Doyle Marsh/Bud Reneau] [ASC] (6/7/69 BCR-21)

DAYS OF WINE AND ROSES *Henry Mancini His Orchestra & Chorus—RCA Victor 47-8120*
[Henry Mancini/Johnny Mercer] [ASC] (1/19/63 BCtRt-29)

DAYS OF WINE AND ROSES *Pat Boone—Dot 16439*
[Henry Mancini/Johnny Mercer] [ASC] (2/16/63 Rt-30)

DAYS OF WINE AND ROSES *Andy Williams—Columbia 42674*
[Henry Mancini/Johnny Mercer] [ASC] (2/23/63 BCtRt-26)

DAYTIME FRIENDS Kenny Rogers—United Artists 1027
[Ben Peters] [BMI] (7/30/77 BCR-28)

DAYTIME NIGHT-TIME Keith Hampshire—A&M 1403
[Mike Hugg] [BMI] (12/16/72 BCR-32)

DAZZ Brick—Bang 727 [Regi Hargis/Eddie Irons/Ray Ransom] [ASC] (10/23/76 BCR-3)

DE DO DO DO, DE DA DA DA The Police—A&M 2275 [Sting] [BMI] (10/25/80 BCR-10)

DEACON BLUES Steely Dan—ABC 12355
[Walter Becker/Donald Fagen] [ASC] (4/1/78 BCR-17)

DEAD END STREET Lou Rawls—Capitol 5869
[David Axelrod/Ben Raleigh] (Med) [BMI] (3/25/67 BCR-29)

DEAD END STREET MONOLOGUE Lou Rawls—Capitol 5869
[Lou Rawls] (Med) [BMI] (3/25/67 BCR-29)

DEAD GIVEAWAY Shalamar—Solar 69819
[Marcus Dare/Joey Gallo/Leon Sylvers] [ASC] (6/25/83 BC-16)

THE DEAD HEART Midnight Oil—Columbia 07964
[Peter Garrett/Rob Hirst/James Moginie] [BMI] (7/30/88 BC-49)

DEAD MAN'S CURVE Jan & Dean—Liberty 55672
[Jan Berry/Roger Christian/Artie Kornfeld/Brian Wilson] [BMI] (3/7/64 BCR-8)

DEAD SKUNK Loudon Wainwright III—Columbia 45726
[Loudon Wainwright III] [ASC] (1/20/73 BCR-12)

DEADBEAT CLUB The B-52's—Reprise 19938
[Kate Pierson/Fred Schneider/Keith Strickland/Cindy Wilson] [ASC] (4/21/90 BC-27)

DEADEND STREET The Kinks—Reprise 0540 [Ray Davies] [BMI] (12/31/66 BCR-72)

DEALER IN DREAMS Bobby Darin—Decca 30737
[Bobby Darin/Don Kirshner] [ASC] (10/13/58 R-95)

DEAR ABBY The Hearts—Tuff 370 [Lona Stevens] [BMI] (10/19/63 BCR-84)

DEAR ANN George Baker Selection—Colossus 117
[George Baker] [ASC] (6/13/70 BCR-82) [FET]

DEAR DAD Chuck Berry—Chess 1926 [Chuck Berry] [BMI] (4/3/65 BCR-82)

DEAR DELILAH Grapefruit—Equinox 70000 [George Alexander] [ASC] (3/2/68 BR-98)

DEAR ELOISE The Hollies—Epic 10251
[Allan Clarke/Tony Hicks*/Graham Nash] [BMI] (12/2/67 BCR-40)

DEAR ELVIS (PAGE 1) Audrey—Plus 104 [C.B. Samuel] [BMI] (9/22/56 B-87)

DEAR GESU BAMBINO Christian Morandi—Decca 31343
[Pier Quinto Cariaggi/Pietro Soffici] [ASC] (12/25/61 R-89) [F]

DEAR GOD Midge Ure—Chrysalis 43319 [Midge Ure] [ASC] (3/11/89 BC-90)

DEAR HEART Teddy Randazzo—Colpix 684
[Billy Barberis/Teddy Randazzo/Bobby Weinstein] [BMI] (4/27/63 R-92)

DEAR HEART *Andy Williams—Columbia 43180*
[Ray Evans/Jay Livingston/Henry Mancini] [ASC] (11/28/64 BCtRt-15)

DEAR HEART *Jack Jones—Kapp 635*
[Ray Evans/Jay Livingston/Henry Mancini] [ASC] (11/28/64 BCtRt-15)

DEAR HEART *Henry Mancini's Orchestra And Chorus—RCA Victor 8458*
[Ray Evans/Jay Livingston/Henry Mancini] [ASC] (11/28/64 BCtRt-15)

DEAR HEARTS AND GENTLE PEOPLE The Springfields—Philips 40072
[Sammy Fain/Bob Hilliard] [ASC] (10/27/62 BCR-78)

DEAR IVAN Jimmy Dean—Columbia 42259 [Jimmy Dean] [BMI] (1/1/62 BCR-15)

DEAR JOHN Pat Boone—Dot 16152
[Billy Barton*/Fuzzy Owen/Lewis Talley] [BMI] (10/24/60 BCR-44)

DEAR LADY TWIST Gary (U.S.) Bonds—Legrand 1015
[Frank Guida] [BMI] (12/11/61 BCR-6)

DEAR LONELY HEARTS Nat King Cole—Capitol 4870
[Emil Anton/Bob Halley] [BMI] (11/10/62 BCR-10)

DEAR LOVE Sonny James—Capitol 3734 [Dub Dickerson] [BMI] (6/29/57 R-73)

DEAR LOVER Mary Wells—Atco 6392 [Carl Davis/Gerald Sims] [BMI] (2/12/66 BCR-40)

DEAR MR. D.J. PLAY IT AGAIN Tina Robin—Mercury 71852
[Gerry Goffin/Howard Greenfield/Carole King] [BMI] (9/18/61 B-95)

DEAR MR. JESUS Powersource—PowerVision 8603
[Richard Klender] [ASC] (12/19/87 BC-61)

DEAR MRS. APPLEBEE Flip Cartridge—Parrot 306
[Philip Barr/Wilbur Meshel] [BMI] (8/6/66 BCR-85)

DEAR ONE Larry Finnegan—Old Town 1113
[John L. Finneran/Vincent Finneran] [BMI] (2/24/62 BCR-10)

DEAR PRUDENCE *The Five Stairsteps—Buddah 165*
[John Lennon/Paul McCartney] (TSW) [ASC] (5/2/70 BC-66)

DEAR PRUDENCE *Katfish—Big Tree 16045*
[John Lennon/Paul McCartney] [ASC] (9/20/75 BCR-57)

DEARER THAN LIFE Brook Benton—Mercury 72099
[Arthur Kent/Ed Warren] [ASC] (3/9/63 BCR-50)

DEAREST Mickey & Sylvia—Vik 0267
[Mickey Baker/Ellas McDaniel/Prentice Herman Polk Jr.] [BMI] (4/6/57 BCR-39)

DEAREST (CARA) Al Martino—20th Fox 184
[Danny DiMinno/Giacomo Puccini/Johnny Tucker] [ASC] (3/14/60 R-81) [FDE]

DEATH OF AN ANGEL The Kingsmen—Wand 164
[Donald Woods/Doris Woods] [BMI] (9/12/64 BCR-33)

DECEMBER, 1963 (OH, WHAT A NIGHT) The Four Seasons—Warner/Curb 8168 [Bob Gaudio/Judy Parker] [ASC] (12/27/75 BCR-1)

DECK OF CARDS Wink Martindale—Dot 15968 [T. Texas Tyler] [BMI] (9/12/59 BCR-4)

THE DECLARATION The 5th Dimension—Bell 860 [René DeKnight/Thomas Jefferson/Julius Johnsen] (TSW) [BMI] (2/28/70 BCR-54)

DEDE DINAH Frankie Avalon—Chancellor 1011 [Peter DeAngelis/Bob Marcucci] [ASC] (12/30/57 BCR-7)

DEDICATED FOLLOWER OF FASHION The Kinks—Reprise 0471 [Ray Davies] [BMI] (5/14/66 BCR-36)

***DEDICATED TO THE ONE I LOVE** The Shirelles—Scepter 1203 [Ralph Bass/Lowman Pauling] [BMI] (5/16/59 BC-67)*

***DEDICATED TO THE ONE I LOVE** The Shirelles—Scepter 1203 [Ralph Bass/Lowman Pauling] [BMI] (1/23/61 BCRt-3)*

***DEDICATED TO THE ONE I LOVE** The "5" Royales—King 5453 [Ralph Bass/Lowman Pauling] [BMI] (1/23/61 BRt-8)*

***DEDICATED TO THE ONE I LOVE** The Mamas & The Papas—Dunhill 4077 [Ralph Bass/Lowman Pauling] [BMI] (2/25/67 BCR-2)*

***DEDICATED TO THE ONE I LOVE** The Temprees—We Produce 1808 [Ralph Bass/Lowman Pauling] [BMI] (8/26/72 BCR-74)*

***DEDICATED TO THE ONE I LOVE** Bernadette Peters—MCA 51152 [Ralph Bass/Lowman Pauling] [BMI] (8/8/81 BC-65)*

DEDICATED (TO THE SONGS I LOVE) The 3 Friends—Imperial 5763 [Cliff Goldsmith/Fred Smith] [BMI] (7/17/61 BCR-72)

DEDICATION Bay City Rollers—Arista 0233 [Guy Fletcher/Doug Flett] [ASC] (2/12/77 BCR-60)

THE DEDICATION SONG Freddy Cannon—Warner Bros. 5693 [Russ Regan] [BMI] (2/19/66 BCR-41)

DEEP BLUE George Harrison—Apple 1836 [George Harrison] (TSW) [ASC] (9/11/71 B-23)

DEEP BLUE SEA Jimmy Dean with Ray Ellis and his Orchestra—Columbia 40995 [Steven Harvey/Martin Seligson] [BMI] (9/30/57 BCR-57)

DEEP, DEEP TROUBLE The Simpsons—Geffen 19007 [Matt Groening/Jeff Townes] [BMI] (3/9/91 BC-66)

DEEP ENOUGH FOR ME Ocean—Kama Sutra 525 [Richard Erbe/Rich Gael] [ASC] (6/19/71 BCR-67)

***DEEP IN THE HEART OF HARLEM** Clyde McPhatter—Mercury 72220 [Jimmy Radcliffe/Carl Spencer] [BMI] (1/4/64 BCR-68)*

***DEEP IN THE HEART OF HARLEM** Walter Jackson—Okeh 7285 [Jimmy Radcliffe/Carl Spencer] [BMI] (7/1/67 C-96)*

DEEP IN THE HEART OF TEXAS Duane Eddy—RCA Victor 47-7999 [Don Swander] [BMI] (4/21/62 BCR-71) [IM]

DEEP IN THE NIGHT The Candymen—ABC-Paramount 11023 [John Adkins/Buddy Buie/Robert Nix] [BMI] (1/6/68 R-79)

DEEP INSIDE MY HEART Randy Meisner—Epic 50939 [Eric Kaz/Randy Meisner] [ASC] (10/18/80 BCR-22)

***DEEP PURPLE** Billy Ward And His Dominoes—Liberty 55099 [Peter DeRose/Mitchell Parish] [ASC] (9/9/57 BCR-22)*

***DEEP PURPLE** Nino Tempo & April Stevens—Atco 6273 [Peter DeRose/Mitchell Parish] [ASC] (9/14/63 BCR-1)*

***DEEP PURPLE** Donny And Marie Osmond—MGM/Kolob 14840 [Peter DeRose/Mitchell Parish] [ASC] (12/13/75 BCR-14)*

DEEP RIVER WOMAN Lionel Richie—Motown 1873 TSW [Lionel Richie] [ASC] (1/17/87 BC-71)

DEEPER AND DEEPER Freda Payne—Invictus 9080 [Lamont Dozier/Ronald Dunbar/Brian Holland/Eddie Holland/Norma Toney] [BMI] (9/12/70 BCR-18)

DEEPER AND DEEPER Bo Donaldson And The Heywoods—ABC 11402 [Harvey Price/Dan Walsh] [ASC] (1/19/74 R-93)

DEEPER (IN LOVE WITH YOU) O'Jays—Neptune 22 [Kenneth Gamble/Leon Huff] [BMI] (3/21/70 BCR-58)

DEEPER SHADE OF SOUL Urban Dance Squad—Arista 2026 [Ernest Adrian/Ray Barretto/Silvano Matadin/Michel Schoots/Patrick Tilon/René Van Barneveld] [BMI] (12/15/90 BC-21)

DEEPER THAN THE NIGHT Olivia Newton-John—MCA 41009 [Tom Snow/Johnny Vastano] [BMI] (4/14/79 BCR-11)

THE DEEPER THE LOVE Whitesnake—Geffen 19951 [David Coverdale/Adrian Vandenberg] [ASC] (1/20/90 BC-26)

DEEPLY Anson Williams—Chelsea 3061 [Charles Fox/Norman Gimbel] [BMI] (3/19/77 BCR-84)

—DEEPNESS OF YOUR EYES see: MASTER OF EYES

—DEINE ERSTE LIEBE see: ASK ME

DEJA VU Dionne Warwick—Arista 0459 [Adrienne Anderson/Isaac Hayes] [BMI] (11/10/79 BCR-11)

DELAWARE Perry Como—RCA Victor 47-7670 [Irving Gordon] [ASC] (1/18/60 BCR-16)

DELIA GONE Pat Boone—Dot 16122 [Caperton Henley] [BMI] (8/22/60 BCR-66)

DELICIOUS Jim Backus & Friend—Jubilee 5330 [Mort Garson/Buddy Kaye] [ASC] (7/7/58 BCR-36)

DELILAH Tom Jones—Parrot 40025 [Barry Mason/Les Reed] [ASC] (3/16/68 BCR-15)

***DELILAH JONES** The McGuire Sisters—Coral 61627 [Elmer Bernstein/Sylvia Fine] [ASC] (5/5/56 BCRt-36)*

***DELILAH JONES** Danny Kaye—Decca 29904 [Elmer Bernstein/Sylvia Fine] [ASC] (6/8/56 Rt-78)*

DELIRIOUS Prince—Warner Bros. 29503 [Prince] [ASC] (9/3/83 BC-8)

***DELTA DAWN** Tanya Tucker—Columbia 45588 [Larry Collins/Alex Harvey] [ASC] (7/1/72 B-72)*

***DELTA DAWN** Helen Reddy—Capitol 3645 [Larry Collins/Alex Harvey] [ASC] (6/23/73 BCR-1)*

DELTA DIRT Larry Gatlin—Monument 8622 [Larry Gatlin] [BMI] (9/14/74 B-84)

DELTA LADY Joe Cocker—A&M 1112 [Leon Russell] [BMI] (10/4/69 BCR-69)

DELTA QUEEN Don Fardon—Chelsea 0115 [Terry Tassenberg] [ASC] (3/10/73 BCR-68)

DEMONSTRATION Otis Redding—Atco 6742 [Don Covay/Otis Redding] [BMI] (4/4/70 CR-75)

DENISE Randy And The Rainbows—Rust 5059 [Neil Levenson] [BMI] (6/8/63 BCR-10)

DEPARTMENT OF YOUTH Alice Cooper—Atlantic 3280 [Alice Cooper/Bob Ezrin/Dick Wagner] [BMI] (8/9/75 BCR-58)

DEPENDIN' ON YOU The Doobie Brothers—Warner Bros. 49029 [Michael McDonald/Patrick Simmons] [ASC] (8/11/79 BCR-25)

***DER KOMMISSAR** After The Fire—Epic 03559 [Falco/Andrew Piercy/Robert Ponger] [ASC] (2/12/83 BC-5) [FET]*

***DER KOMMISSAR (THE COMMISSIONER)** Falco—A&M 2532 [Falco/Robert Ponger] [ASC] (4/2/83 C-74) [F]*

***DESAFINADO** Stan Getz/Charlie Byrd—Verve 10260 [Antonio Carlos Jobim] [BMI] (8/18/62 BCRt-10) [IM]*

***DESAFINADO** Si Zentner And His Orchestra—Liberty 55499 [Antonio Carlos Jobim] [BMI] (9/29/62 Rt-56) [IM]*

***DESAFINADO (SLIGHTLY OUT OF TUNE)** Pat Thomas—MGM 13102 [Jessie Cavanaugh/Jon Hendricks/Antonio Carlos Jobim/Newton Mendonça] [BMI] (10/20/62 BRt-10)*

***DESAFINADO (SLIGHTLY OUT OF TUNE)** Ella Fitzgerald—Verve 10274 [Jessie Cavanaugh/Jon Hendricks/Antonio Carlos Jobim/Newton Mendonça] [BMI] (10/27/62 Rt-10)*

DESDEMONA The Searchers—RCA Victor 74-0484 [Valerie Murtagh/Harold Spiro] [ASC] (8/14/71 BCR-79)

DESERIE The Charts—Everlast 5001 [Les Cooper/Clarence Johnson] [BMI] (7/15/57 B-88)

DESERT MOON Dennis DeYoung—A&M 2666 [Dennis DeYoung] [ASC] (9/8/84 BC-10)

DESERT PETE The Kingston Trio—Capitol 5005 [Billy Edd Wheeler] [ASC] (7/20/63 BCR-30)

DESIDERATA Les Crane—Warner Bros. 7520 [Max Ehrmann/Fred H. Werner] [ASC] (10/9/71 BCR-8)

DESIRE Andy Gibb—RSO 1019 [Barry Gibb/Maurice Gibb/Robin Gibb] [BMI] (1/26/80 BCR-4)

DESIRE Rockets—RSO 1022 [John Badanjek/Dennis Robbins] [ASC] (2/16/80 BCR-70)

DESIRE U2—Island 99250 [Adam Clayton/Dave Evans/Paul Hewson/Larry Mullen] [ASC] (10/1/88 BC-2)

DESIRE ME Sam Cooke—Keen 34002 [Bruce Culver] [BMI] (12/21/57 BC-47)

DESIREE' The Left Banke—Smash 2119 [Tom Feher/Michael David Lookofsky] [BMI] (10/28/67 B-98)

DESIREE Neil Diamond—Columbia 10657 [Neil Diamond] [SE] (11/26/77 BCR-9)

DESPERATE BUT NOT SERIOUS Adam Ant—Epic 03688 [Adam Ant/Marco Pirroni] [ASC] (3/12/83 BC-66)

DESTINATION: ANYWHERE The Marvelettes—Tamla 54171 [Nick Ashford/Valerie Simpson] [ASC] (10/5/68 BCR-51)

DESTINATION UNKNOWN Missing Persons—Capitol 5161 [Dale Bozzio/Terry Bozzio/Warren Cuccurullo] [BMI] (10/2/82 BC-40)

DESTINY Jose Feliciano—RCA Victor 74-0358 [Jose Feliciano] (TSW) [BMI] (7/4/70 BCR-73)

DESTROYER The Kinks—Arista 0619 [Ray Davies] [ASC] (10/31/81 B-85)

DETERIORATA National Lampoon—Banana 218 [Christopher Guest/Tony Hendra*] [ASC] (10/14/72 BCR-88)

***DETROIT CITY** Bobby Bare—RCA Victor 47-8183 [Danny Dill/Mel Tillis] [BMI] (6/8/63 BCR-12)*

***DETROIT CITY** Tom Jones—Parrot 40012 [Danny Dill/Mel Tillis] [BMI] (3/11/67 BCR-19)*

***DETROIT CITY** Solomon Burke—Atlantic 2459 [Danny Dill/Mel Tillis] [BMI] (12/2/67 C-86)*

***DETROIT CITY** Dean Martin—Reprise 0955 [Danny Dill/Mel Tillis] [BMI] (10/24/70 C-99)*

***DETROIT CITY NO. 2** (parody of Detroit City) Ben Colder—MGM 13167 [Danny Dill/Mel Tillis/Sheb Wooley] [BMI] (10/12/63 B-90) [P]*

DETROIT ROCK CITY Kiss—Casablanca 863 [Bob Ezrin/Paul Stanley] (TSW) [BMI] (9/4/76 BCR-7)

DEVIL IN A FAST CAR Sheena Easton—EMI America 8201 [Greg Mathieson/Trevor Veitch] [BMI] (4/14/84 B-79)

DEVIL IN THE BOTTLE T.G. Sheppard—Melodyland 6002 [Bobby David] [ASC] (1/25/75 BCR-54)

DEVIL INSIDE INXS—Atlantic 89144 [Andy Farriss/Michael Hutchence] [ASC] (2/13/88 BC-2)

THE DEVIL MADE ME DO IT Golden Earring—21 Records 108 [Barry Hay/George Kooymans] [ASC] (4/23/83 BC-79)

***DEVIL OR ANGEL** Bobby Vee—Liberty 55270 [Blanche Carter] [BMI] (8/1/60 BCtR-4)*

DEVIL OR ANGEL *The Hollywood Flames—Atco 6171*
[Blanche Carter] [BMI] (9/17/60 Ct-18)
THE DEVIL CAME UP TO MICHIGAN *K.M.C. Kru—Curb 76884*
[Tom Crain/Charlie Daniels/Joel DiGregorio/Tracy Edmond/Fred Edwards/ Charles Hayward/James W. Marshall/Ken White] [BMI] (8/31/91 BC-46) [P]
THE DEVIL WENT DOWN TO GEORGIA *Charlie Daniels Band—Epic 50700*
[Tom Crain/Charlie Daniels/Joel DiGregorio/Fred Edwards/Charles Hayward/ James W. Marshall] [BMI] (6/23/79 BCR-3)
DEVIL WITH A BLUE DRESS ON *Mitch Ryder And The Detroit Wheels—New Voice 817*
[Frederick Long/William Stevenson] (Med) [BMI] (10/8/66 BCR-3)
DEVIL WITH A BLUE DRESS *Pratt & McClain—Reprise 1361*
[Frederick Long/William Stevenson] [BMI] (7/17/76 B-71)
DEVIL WOMAN Marty Robbins—Columbia 42486
[Marty Robbins] [BMI] (7/28/62 BCR-14)
DEVIL WOMAN Cliff Richard—Rocket/MCA 40574
[Terry Britten/Christine Hodgson] [BMI] (6/26/76 BCR-5)
DEVIL YOU Stampeders—Bell 45,154 [Rich Dodson] [ASC] (12/4/71 BCR-47)
DEVIL'S ANGELS Davie Allen And The Arrows—Tower 341
[Mike Curb/Jerry Styner] [BMI] (7/29/67 B-97) [IM]
DEVIL'S GUN C.J. & Co.—Westbound 55400
[Barry Blue/Ron Roker/Gerry Shury] [BMI] (5/21/77 BCR-36)
DEVIL'S HIGHWAY The 9 LaFalce Brothers—RCA Victor 47-5981
[Sammy Gallop/Tony Starr] [ASC] (1/24/55 R-78)
DEVOTED TO YOU *The Everly Brothers—Cadence 1350*
[Boudleaux Bryant] [BMI] (8/4/58 BCR-9)
DEVOTED TO YOU *Carly Simon and James Taylor—Elektra 45506*
[Boudleaux Bryant] [BMI] (8/19/78 BCR-34)
DEVOTION Janice Harper—Capitol 3984 [Otto Cesana] [ASC] (6/23/58 BCR-67)
DEVOTION Earth, Wind & Fire—Columbia 10026
[Philip Bailey/Maurice White] [ASC] (9/28/74 BCR-33)
DIAL MY HEART The Boys—Motown 53301
[Kenneth Edmonds/Antonio Reid/Daryl Simmons] [BMI] (12/10/88 BC-13)
DIALOGUE (PARTS I & II) Chicago—Columbia 45717
[Robert Lamm] [ASC] (10/21/72 BCR-17)
DIAMOND GIRL Seals & Crofts—Warner Bros. 7708
[Dash Crofts/Jim Seals] [BMI] (5/12/73 BCR-6)
DIAMOND HEAD The Ventures—Dolton 303 [Danny Hamilton] [BMI] (1/30/65 BCR-70) [I]
DIAMOND RING Jerry Wallace—Challenge 59027
[Jimmy Isle/Ronnie Isle] [BMI] (12/8/58 B-78)
DIAMONDS Chris Rea—United Artists/Magnet 1285 [Chris Rea] [ASC] (3/31/79 BCR-44)
DIAMONDS Herb Alpert—A&M 2929
[James Samuel Harris/Terry Lewis] [ASC] (4/11/87 BC-5)
DIAMONDS AND PEARLS *The Paradons—Milestone 2003*
[West Tyler] [BMI] (8/22/60 BCRt-15)
DIAMONDS AND PEARLS *The Turbans—Roulette 4281 [West Tyler] [BMI] (9/5/60 Rt-36)*
DIAMONDS AND PEARLS Prince—Paisley Park 19083 [Prince] [ASC] (12/7/91 BC-1)
DIAMONDS AND RUST Joan Baez—A&M 1737 [Joan Báez] [ASC] (9/20/75 BCR-35)
DIAMONDS ARE FOREVER Shirley Bassey—United Artists 50845
[John Barry/Don Black] [BMI] (1/15/72 BCR-54)
DIANA *Paul Anka—ABC-Paramount 9831 [Paul Anka] [BMI] (6/29/57 BCR-1)*
DIANA *Bobby Rydell—Capitol 5352 [Paul Anka] [BMI] (2/13/65 BR-98)*
—DIANA SONG see: WHAT SHE DOES TO ME
DIANE *Joe Harnell And His Orchestra—Kapp 521*
[Lew Pollack/Erno Rapeé] [ASC] (4/6/63 BCR-66) [IWM]
DIANE *The Bachelors—London 9639 [Lew Pollack/Erno Rapeé] [ASC] (4/4/64 BCR-10)*
DIANE The Golden Gate—Audio Fidelity 161
[Richard Bell/Billy Carl/Reid Whitelaw] [BMI] (3/7/70 R-97)
DIANNE, DIANNE Ronny & The Daytonas—RCA Victor 47-8896
[Merle Kilgore/John Buck Wilkin] [BMI] (9/3/66 BCR-69)
DIARY Neil Sedaka—RCA Victor 47-7408
[Howard Greenfield/Neil Sedaka] [BMI] (12/1/58 BCR-8)
DIARY Bread—Elektra 45784 [David Gates] [ASC] (4/15/72 BCR-11)
DICK AND JANE Bobby Vinton—ABC 12056
[Dewayne Blackwell] (TSW) [BMI] (3/15/75 BC-33)
DID IT IN A MINUTE Daryl Hall & John Oates—RCA 13065
[Janna Allen/Sara Allen/Daryl Hall] [BMI] (3/20/82 BCR-9)
DID YOU BOOGIE (WITH YOUR BABY) Flash Cadillac & The Continental Kids—
Private Stock 45,079 [Rod McQueen] [ASC] (7/24/76 BCR-25)
DID YOU EVER The Hullaballoos—Roulette 4593
[Steve Duboff/Artie Kornfeld] [BMI] (2/13/65 BR-72)
DID YOU EVER GET THE ROSES The Ames Brothers—RCA Victor 47-6821
[Jimmy Kennedy/Guy Wood] [ASC] (3/9/57 R-82)
DID YOU EVER HAVE TO MAKE UP YOUR MIND? The Lovin' Spoonful—Kama Sutra 209
[John Sebastian] [BMI] (5/7/66 BCR-2)
DID YOU EVER SEE A DREAM WALKING Fats Domino—Imperial 5875
[Mack Gordon/Harry Revel] [ASC] (9/29/62 BCR-72)
DID YOU HAVE A HAPPY BIRTHDAY? Paul Anka—ABC-Paramount 9956
[Paul Anka/Howard Greenfield] [BMI] (12/14/63 BR-86)
DID YOU SEE HER EYES The Illusion—Steed 718 [Jeff Barry] [BMI] (7/5/69 BCR-24)

DIDDLE-DEE-DUM (WHAT HAPPENS WHEN YOUR LOVE HAS GONE)
The Belmonts—Sabrina 507
[Angelo D'Aleo/Fred Milano] [ASC] (11/10/62 BCR-51)
DIDN'T I Sylvia—Vibration 524
[William A. Brown/Michael Burton/Al Goodman/Sylvia Robinson*] [BMI] (7/7/73 BCR-65)
DIDN'T I (BLOW YOUR MIND THIS TIME) *The Delfonics—Philly Groove 161*
[Thom Bell/William Hart] [BMI] (1/10/70 BCR-9)
DIDN'T I (BLOW YOUR MIND) *New Kids On The Block—Columbia 68960*
[Thom Bell/William Hart] [BMI] (9/16/89 BC-8)
DIDN'T IT LOOK SO EASY The Stairsteps—Buddah 213
[Fred Goodman/Allen Martancik/Jim Sofia] [BMI] (2/6/71 BCR-60)
DIDN'T KNOW IT WAS LOVE Survivor—Scotti Brothers 08067
[Jim Peterik/Frankie Sullivan] [ASC] (10/8/88 BC-53)
DIDN'T WE *Richard Harris—Dunhill 4194 [Jimmy Webb] [ASC] (6/7/69 BCR-63)*
DIDN'T WE *Barbra Streisand—Columbia 45739 [Jimmy Webb] [ASC] (12/9/72 BCR-65)*
DIDN'T WE ALMOST HAVE IT ALL Whitney Houston—Arista 1-9616
[Will Jennings/Michael Masser] [BMI] (8/1/87 BC-1)
DIDN'T YOU KNOW (YOU'D HAVE TO CRY SOMETIME) Gladys Knight & The Pips—
Soul 35057 [Nick Ashford/Valerie Simpson] [ASC] (3/8/69 BCR-57)
A DIFFERENT CORNER George Michael—Columbia 05888
[George Michael] [ASC] (4/26/86 BC-7)
DIFFERENT DRUM Stone Poneys Featuring Linda Ronstadt—Capitol 2004
[Michael Nesmith] [BMI] (11/4/67 BCR-12)
THE DIFFERENT STORY (WORLD OF LUST AND CRIME) Peter Schilling—Elektra 69307
[Hubert Kemmler/Susanne Müller-Pi/Peter Schilling] [ASC] (3/25/89 BC-53)
DIFFERENT STROKES Syl Johnson—Twilight 103
[John Cameron/John Zachary] [BMI] (10/14/67 BC-95)
DIFFERENT WORLDS Maureen McGovern—Warner/Curb 8835
[Charles Fox/Norman Gimbel] [BMI] (6/30/79 BCR-18)
DIG THE GOLD Joyce Cobb—Cream 7939
[Joyce Cobb/Lynn Lewis] [ASC] (11/24/79 BCR-42)
DIG THE WAY I FEEL Mary Wells—Jubilee 5684
[Mary Wells/Cecil Womack] [BMI] (1/24/70 C-80)
DIGGING YOUR SCENE The Blow Monkeys—RCA 14325
[Bruce Robert Howard] [ASC] (5/3/86 BC-14)
DIGITAL DISPLAY Ready For The World—MCA 52734 [Greg Potts] [BMI] (12/7/85 BC-21)
DIM ALL THE LIGHTS Donna Summer—Casablanca 2201
[Donna Summer] [ASC] (8/25/79 BCR-2)
DIM, DIM THE LIGHTS (I WANT SOME ATMOSPHERE) *Bill Haley And His Comets—*
Decca 29317 [Julius Dixon/Beverly Ross] [BMI] (11/1/54 BCRt-11)
DIM, DIM THE LIGHTS (I WANT SOME ATMOSPHERE) *The Four Tophatters—Cadence 1243*
[Julius Dixon/Beverly Ross] [BMI] (11/1/54 Rt-PRE)
A DIME A DOZEN Carla Thomas—Stax 251
[Isaac Hayes/David Porter] [BMI] (4/27/68 C-99)
DINAH FLO Boz Scaggs—Columbia 45670 [Boz Scaggs] [ASC] (9/30/72 BR-86)
DING A LING Bobby Rydell—Cameo 175
[Dave Appell/Bernie Lowe/Kal Mann] [ASC] (4/30/60 BCR-17)
DING DONG The McGuire Sisters—Coral 61991
[Kenny Jacobson/Rhoda Roberts] [ASC] (5/31/58 BCR-36)
DING DONG; DING DONG George Harrison—Apple 1879
[George Harrison] [ASC] (1/11/75 BCR-36)
DING DONG! THE WITCH IS DEAD The Fifth Estate—Jubilee 5573
[Harold Arlen/E.Y. Harburg] [ASC] (5/13/67 BCR-11)
DINNER WITH DRAC (PT. 1) John Zacherle—Cameo 130
[Kal Mann] [ASC] (3/10/58 BCR-6)
DINNER WITH GERSHWIN Donna Summer—Geffen 28418
[Brenda Russell] [ASC] (8/22/87 BC-48)
DIRTY CASH (MONEY TALKS) Adventures Of Stevie V—Mercury 875 802
[Stevie Vincent/Mick Walsh] [BMI] (7/21/90 BC-23)
DIRTY DEEDS Joan Jett—Blackheart/CBS 73267
[Bon Scott/Angus Young/Malcolm Young] [ASC] (1/27/90 BC-36)
DIRTY DIANA Michael Jackson—Epic 07739 [Michael Jackson] [BMI] (5/7/88 BC-1)
DIRTY, DIRTY FEELING Elvis Presley With The Jordanaires—RCA Victor EPA-4383
[Jerry Leiber/Mike Stoller] (EP) [BMI] (7/10/65 BCR-70)
DIRTY LAUNDRY Don Henley—Asylum 69894
[Don Henley/Danny Kortchmar] [ASC] (10/30/82 BC-3)
DIRTY LOOKS Juice Newton—Capitol 5289
[Charles David Robbins/Van Stephenson] [BMI] (11/5/83 B-90)
DIRTY LOVE Thunder—Geffen 19026 [Luke Morley] [BMI] (6/1/91 BC-55)
DIRTY MAN Laura Lee—Chess 2013 [Robert Eugene Miller] [BMI] (9/9/67 BCR-52)
DIRTY WATER *The Standells—Tower 185 [Ed Cobb] [BMI] (4/16/66 BCR-7)*
DIRTY WATER *The Inmates—Polydor 2032 [Ed Cobb] [BMI] (12/8/79 BCR-47)*
DIRTY WATER Rock And Hyde—Capitol 5691
[Paul Hyde/Bob Rock] [BMI] (4/25/87 BC-61)
DIRTY WHITE BOY Foreigner—Atlantic 3618
[Lou Gramm/Michael Leslie Jones] [ASC] (9/8/79 BCR-12)
THE DIS-ADVANTAGES OF YOU Brass Ring Featuring Phil Bodner—Dunhill 4065
[Mitch Leigh] [ASC] (2/4/67 BCR-36) [I]

DIS-GORILLA (PART 1) Rick Dees And His Cast Of Idiots—RSO 866
[Shelley Fisher/Willie Hall/Bobby Manuel] [BMI] (1/15/77 BCR-56)

DISAPPEAR INXS—Atlantic 87784
[Jon Farriss/Michael Hutchence] [ASC] (11/24/90 BC-7)

DISCIPLINE OF LOVE (WHY DID YOU DO IT) Robert Palmer—Island 99597
[David Batteau/Don Freeman] [ASC] (11/16/85 BC-79)

DISCO DUCK (PART I) Rick Dees And His Cast Of Idiots—RSO 857
[Rick Dees] [BMI] (8/14/76 BCR-1)

DISCO INFERNO The Trammps—Atlantic 3389
[Leroy Green/Tyrone G. Kersey] [BMI] (3/5/77 BCR-8)

DISCO LADY Johnnie Taylor—Columbia 10281
[Don Davis/Harvey Scales/Albert Vance] [BMI] (2/7/76 BCR-1)

DISCO LUCY (I LOVE LUCY THEME) Wilton Place Street Band—Island 078
[Eliot Daniel] [BMI] (1/8/77 BCR-19) [IM]

DISCO NIGHTS (ROCK-FREAK) G.Q.—Arista 0388
[Keith Crier/Herb Lane/Emanuel Rahiem LeBlanc/Paul Service] [BMI] (3/17/79 BCR-10)

DISCO 9000 Johnnie Taylor—Columbia 10610
[Jackie Avery/Johnnie H. Taylor] [BMI] (10/1/77 B-86)

DISCO QUEEN Hot Chocolate—Big Tree 16038
[Errol Brown/Tony Wilson] [ASC] (5/24/75 BCR-21)

DISCO RUFUS Stargard—MCA 40825
[Mark Davis/Michael Nash] [BMI] (3/4/78 B-88) [I]

DISCO SAX Houston Person—Westbound 5015
[Jimmy Roach] (TSW) [BMI] (1/17/76 B-91) [I]

DISCO TO GO The Brides Of Funkenstein—Atlantic 3498
[George Clinton/William Earl Collins] [BMI] (11/11/78 R-88)

DISCOMANIA The Lovers—Lamp 2005
[Henri Belolo/Phil Hurtt/Jacques Morali] [BMI] (5/14/77 B-100)

***DISTANT DRUMS** Jim Reeves—RCA Victor 47-8789 [Cindy Walker] [BMI] (4/9/66 BCR-43)*

***DISTANT DRUMS** Vic Dana—Dolton 324 [Cindy Walker] [BMI] (10/29/66 CR-84)*

DISTANT LOVER Marvin Gaye—Tamla 54253
[Marvin Gaye/Gwen Gordy/Sandra Greene] [ASC] (9/21/74 BCR-28)

DISTANT SHORES Chad & Jeremy—Columbia 43682
[James William Guercio] [ASC] (7/9/66 BCR-30)

DIVIDED HEARTS Kim Carnes—EMI America 8322
[Kim Carnes/Collin Ellingson/Kathy Kurasch/Donna Weiss] [ASC] (5/24/86 BC-72)

***THEME FROM DIXIE** Duane Eddy—Jamie 1183*
[Daniel Decatur Emmett] [NA] (3/20/61 BCR-36) [IWM]

***DIXIE** Mickey Newbury—Elektra 45750*
[Daniel Decatur Emmett] (Med) [NA] (11/6/71 BCR-24)

***DIXIE** Elvis Presley—RCA Victor 74-0672*
[Daniel Decatur Emmett] (Med) [NA] (4/22/72 BCR-59)

DIXIE DANNY The Laurie Sisters—Mercury 70548
[Bickley Reichner/Lou Singer] [ASC] (3/28/55 BCR-30)

DIXIE ROCK Wet Willie—Capricorn 0231
[Jack Hall/Jimmy Hall/Rick Hirsch] [BMI] (5/31/75 B-96)

DIXIELAND ROCK Elvis Presley with the Jordanaires—RCA Victor EPA-4321
[Beverly Ross/Aaron Schroeder] (EP) [ASC] (8/18/58 R-56)

DIZZY Tommy Roe—ABC 11164 [Tommy Roe/Freddy Weller] [BMI] (1/18/69 BCR-1)

DIZZY MISS LIZZY Larry Williams—Specialty 626
[Larry Williams] [BMI] (3/31/58 BR-69)

DO ANYTHING Natural Selection—EastWest 98724
[Ingrid Chavez/Elliot Erickson/Frederick Thomas] [ASC] (8/10/91 BC-2)

DO ANYTHING YOU WANNA (PART 1) Harold Betters—Gateway 747
[Harold Betters/Daddio Daylie‡/George Henry Green‡/Chuck Ramsey] [BMI] (11/14/64 BCR-74) [I]

DO, DO, DO (WHAT YOUR HEART SAYS) Tony Martin—RCA Victor 47-6039
[Jack Lawrence/Joe Pasternak] [ASC] (4/2/55 C-35)

DO I DO Stevie Wonder—Tamla 1612 [Stevie Wonder] [ASC] (5/29/82 BC-13)

DO I LIKE IT Nat "King" Cole—Capitol 3939
[James DeLeston/Jack Hammer] [BMI] (3/24/58 BR-27)

***DO I LOVE YOU?** The Ronettes—Philles 121*
[Pete Andreoli/Vini Poncia/Phil Spector] [BMI] (6/20/64 BCR-34)

***DO I LOVE YOU?** The Magic Ring—Music Factory 404*
[Pete Andreoli/Vini Poncia/Phil Spector] [BMI] (5/18/68 R-72)

***DO I LOVE YOU** Paul Anka—Buddah 252*
[Paul Anka/Yves-Jacques Lavot/Alain Le Govic/Michel Pelay/Maxime Piolot] [BMI] (9/25/71 BCR-38) [FET]

***DO I LOVE YOU (YES IN EVERY WAY)** Donna Fargo—Warner Bros. 8509*
[Paul Anka/Yves-Jacques Lavot/Alain Le Govic/Michel Pelay/Maxime Piolot] [BMI] (3/18/78 C-94) [FET]

***DO I LOVE YOU (BECAUSE YOU'RE BEAUTIFUL)** Vic Damone—Columbia 40858*
[Oscar Hammerstein/Richard Rodgers] [ASC] (4/6/57 BRt-58)

***DO I LOVE YOU (BECAUSE YOU'RE BEAUTIFUL)** Tony Martin—RCA Victor 47-6863*
[Oscar Hammerstein/Richard Rodgers] [ASC] (4/20/57 BRt-58)

DO I LOVE YOU (BECAUSE YOU'RE BEAUTIFUL)
Bob Eberly with Paul Whiteman & His Orchestra—Grand Award 1013
[Oscar Hammerstein/Richard Rodgers] [ASC] (5/4/57 Rt-58)

DO I MAKE MYSELF CLEAR Etta James & Sugar Pie Desanto—Cadet 5519
[Shena DeMell/Sugar Pie DeSanto] [BMI] (12/4/65 BC-94)

DO IT Neil Diamond—Bang 580 [Neil Diamond] [SE] (11/7/70 BCR-30)

DO IT AGAIN The Beach Boys—Capitol 2239
[Mike Love/Brian Wilson] [BMI] (7/20/68 BCR-7)

***DO IT AGAIN** Steely Dan—ABC 11338*
[Walter Becker/Donald Fagen] [ASC] (11/18/72 BCR-6)

***DO IT AGAIN** Club House—Atlantic 89795*
[Walter Becker/Donald Fagen] (Med) [ASC] (8/6/83 BC-75)

DO IT AGAIN The Kinks—Arista 1-9309 [Ray Davies] [ASC] (12/22/84 BC-41)

DO IT AGAIN A LITTLE BIT SLOWER Jon & Robin And The In Crowd—Abnak 119
[Wayne Carson Thompson] [BMI] (4/22/67 BCR-17)

DO IT ANY WAY YOU WANNA People's Choice—TSOP 4769
[Leon Huff] [BMI] (8/9/75 BCR-11)

DO IT BABY The Miracles—Tamla 54248
[Freddie Perren/Christine Yarian] [ASC] (8/3/74 BCR-9)

DO IT, FLUID The Blackbyrds—Fantasy 729 [Donald Byrd] [BMI] (9/7/74 BCR-69)

DO IT FOR LOVE Sheena Easton—EMI America 8295
[Adele Bertei/Mary Alice Kessler] [SA] (10/26/85 BC-28)

DO IT GOOD Taste Of Honey—Capitol 4744
[Janice Johnson/Perry Kibble] [BMI] (8/11/79 B-79)

DO IT IN THE NAME OF LOVE Candi Staton—Fame 91009
[Bobby Bloom/Neil Brian Goldberg] [BMI] (2/3/73 BCR-61)

DO IT IN THE NAME OF LOVE Ben E. King—Atlantic 3274
[Patrick Grant/Gwen Guthrie] [BMI] (6/7/75 BCR-60)

DO IT OR DIE Atlanta Rhythm Section—Polydor/BGO 14568
[Buddy Buie/J.R. Cobb/Ronnie W. Hammond] [BMI] (5/26/79 BCR-19)

DO IT - RAT NOW Bill Black's Combo—Hi 2064 [Carl McVoy] [BMI] (4/20/63 BCR-37) [I]

DO IT RIGHT Brook Benton—Mercury 72365 [Rudy Clark] [BMI] (12/12/64 BCR-56)

DO IT ('TIL YOU'RE SATISFIED) B.T. Express—Roadshow 12395
[Billy Nichols] [BMI] (9/21/74 BCR-2)

DO IT TO MY MIND Johnny Bristol—Atlantic 3360
[Johnny Bristol] [ASC] (11/20/76 BCR-42)

DO IT WITH FEELING Michael Zager's Moon Band Featuring Peabo Bryson—Bang 720
[Paul Davis/Michael Zager] [BMI] (3/20/76 B-94)

DO ME! Bell Biv DeVoe—MCA 53848
[Ricky Bell/Michael Bivins/Carl Bourelly/Ronnie DeVoe] [ASC] (6/30/90 BC-3)

DO ME BABY Meli'sa Morgan—Capitol 5523 [Prince] [ASC] (1/25/86 BC-46)

DO ME RIGHT Detroit Emeralds—Westbound 172
[James Mitchell Jr./Abrim Tilmon] [BMI] (1/23/71 BCR-42)

***DO RE MI** Mitch Miller & his Sing Along Chorus—Columbia 41499*
[Oscar Hammerstein/Richard Rodgers] [ASC] (11/7/59 BCtRt-48)

***DO RE MI** Anita Bryant—Carlton 523*
[Oscar Hammerstein/Richard Rodgers] [ASC] (12/21/59 BCtRt-48)

DO-RE-MI Lee Dorsey—Fury 1056 [Earl King Johnson] [BMI] (12/18/61 BCR-27)

DO RIGHT Paul Davis—Bang 4808 [Paul Davis] [BMI] (3/8/80 BCR-17)

***DO SOMETHING TO ME** ? And The Mysterians—Cameo 496*
[Jim Calvert/Norman Marzano/Paul Naumann] [BMI] (9/9/67 R-97)

***DO SOMETHING TO ME** Tommy James And The Shondells—Roulette 7024*
[Jim Calvert/Norman Marzano/Paul Naumann] [BMI] (10/5/68 BCR-24)

DO THAT STUFF Parliament—Casablanca 871
[George Clinton/Garry Marshall Shider/Bernie Worrell] [BMI] (11/27/76 R-90)

DO THAT TO ME ONE MORE TIME The Captain & Tennille—Casablanca 2215
[Toni Tennille] [BMI] (10/20/79 BCR-1)

DO THE BARTMAN The Simpsons—Geffen 5439-19004-7
[Michael Jackson/Bryan Loren] [BMI] (12/8/90 C-22)

DO THE BEST YOU CAN The Hollies—Epic 10361
[Allan Clarke/Tony Hicks/Graham Nash] [BMI] (9/14/68 B-93)

DO THE BIRD Dee Dee Sharp—Cameo 244
[Dave Appell/Kal Mann] [ASC] (2/23/63 BCR-10)

DO THE BOOMERANG Jr. Walker & The All Stars—Soul 35012
[Henry Cosby/Jr. Walker/Willie Woods] [ASC] (6/5/65 BCR-35)

DO THE BOP The Hilltoppers—Dot 15451 [Billy Vaughn] [ASC] (3/9/56 R-37)

DO THE CHOO CHOO Archie Bell & The Drells—Atlantic 2559
[Kenneth Gamble/Leon Huff] [BMI] (9/28/68 BCR-43)

DO THE CLAM
Elvis Presley With The Jordanaires Jubilee Four & Carole Lombard Trio —
RCA Victor 47-8500
[Dolores Fuller/Sid Wayne/Ben Weisman] [ASC] (2/27/65 BCR-15)

DO THE FREDDIE Freddie And The Dreamers—Mercury 72428
[Lou Courtney/Dennis Lambert] [BMI] (4/24/65 BCR-14)

DO THE FUNKY CHICKEN Rufus Thomas—Stax 0059
[Rufus Thomas] [ASC] (1/31/70 BCR-28)

DO THE FUNKY PENGUIN PART 1 Rufus Thomas—Stax 0112
[Jo Bridges/Tom Nixon/Bonny Rice/Rufus Thomas] [BMI] (12/18/71 BCR-44)

DO THE MONKEY King Curtis—Capitol 4998
[Rudy Clark/Bobby Darin] [BMI] (8/24/63 B-92) [IWM]

DO THE NEW CONTINENTAL The Dovells—Parkway 833
[Dave Appell/Kal Mann] [ASC] (1/22/62 BCR-32)

(DO THE) PUSH AND PULL - PART 1 Rufus Thomas—Stax 0079 [Rufus Thomas] [ASC] (12/12/70 BCR-20)

DO THE THING Lou Courtney—Riverside 4589 [Lou Courtney] [BMI] (4/8/67 BCR-62)

DO THEY KNOW IT'S CHRISTMAS? Band Aid—Columbia 04749 [Bob Geldof/Midge Ure] [ASC] (12/22/84 BC-7)

DO UNTO ME James & Bobby Purify—Bell 700 [Richie Grasso/Gary Illingworth/Morris Levy‡] [BMI] (1/13/68 BCR-50)

DO-WACKA-DO Roger Miller—Smash 1947 [Roger Miller] [BMI] (11/28/64 BCR-31)

DO WHAT YOU DID Thurston Harris—Aladdin 3399 [Thurston Harris] [BMI] (1/13/58 B-57)

DO WHAT YOU DO Jermaine Jackson—Arista 1-9279 [Ralph Dino/Larry Di Tomaso] [ASC] (10/27/84 BC-12)

DO WHAT YOU DO DO WELL Ned Miller—Fabor 137 [Ned Miller] [BMI] (12/26/64 BCR-52)

DO WHAT YOU GOTTA DO *Al Wilson—Soul City 761 [Jimmy Webb] [BMI] (1/20/68 CR-93)*

DO WHAT YOU GOTTA DO *Bobby Vee—Liberty 56057 [Jimmy Webb] [BMI] (8/17/68 BCR-62)*

DO WHAT YOU GOTTA DO *Nina Simone—RCA Victor 47-9602 [Jimmy Webb] [BMI] (10/19/68 BR-78)*

DO WHAT YOU SET OUT TO DO Bobby Bland—Duke 472 [Deadric Malone] [BMI] (2/19/72 BCR-55)

DO WHAT YOU WANNA DO Five Flights Up—T-A 202 [J.B. Bingham] [ASC] (8/22/70 BCR-25)

DO WHAT YOU WANNA DO T-Connection—Dash 5032 [Theophilus Coakley] [BMI] (3/12/77 BC-46)

DO WHAT YOU WANT, BE WHAT YOU ARE Daryl Hall & John Oates—RCA 10808 [Daryl Hall/John Oates] [BMI] (10/30/76 BCR-39)

DO YA *The Move—United Artists 50928 [Jeff Lynne] [ASC] (10/28/72 BCR-88)*

DO YA *Electric Light Orchestra—United Artists 939 [Jeff Lynne] [ASC] (2/5/77 BCR-16)*

DO YA DO YA (WANNA PLEASE ME) Samantha Fox—Jive 1031 [Michael Bissell/Graham Richardson] [ASC] (3/14/87 BC-81)

DO YA WANNA GET FUNKY WITH ME Peter Brown—Drive 6258 [Peter H. Brown/Robert Rans] [BMI] (9/3/77 BCR-18)

DO YOU BELIEVE IN LOVE Huey Lewis and the News—Chrysalis 2589 [Mutt Lange] [ASC] (2/6/82 BCR-7)

DO YOU BELIEVE IN MAGIC *The Lovin' Spoonful—Kama Sutra 201 [John Sebastian] [BMI] (8/21/65 BCR-4)*

DO YOU BELIEVE IN MAGIC *Shaun Cassidy—Warner/Curb 8533 [John Sebastian] [BMI] (3/25/78 BCR-31)*

DO YOU BELIEVE IN SHAME? Duran Duran—Capitol 44337 [Eleanor Broadwater‡/Robert Chaisson*/Dale Hawkins/Simon Le Bon/ Stanley J. Lewis/Nick Rhodes/Nigel John Taylor] [ASC] (3/18/89 BC-63)

DO YOU COMPUTE? Donnie Iris—MCA 52230 [Mark Avsec/Donnie Iris] [ASC] (7/2/83 BC-64)

DO YOU FEEL ALL RIGHT KC & The Sunshine Band—TK 1030 [Harry Wayne Casey/Rick Finch] [BMI] (10/7/78 BCR-63)

DO YOU FEEL LIKE I FEEL Belinda Carlisle—MCA 54183 [Rick Nowels/Ellen Shipley] [ASC] (10/19/91 BC-60)

DO YOU FEEL LIKE WE DO Peter Frampton—A&M 1867 [Peter Frampton/Mick Gallagher/John Siomos/Rick Wills] [ASC] (9/18/76 BCR-10)

DO YOU HEAR WHAT I HEAR *Harry Simeone Chorale—Mercury 72065 [Noel Regney/Gloria Shayne] [ASC] (12/22/62 R-66)*

DO YOU HEAR WHAT I HEAR? *Bing Crosby—Capitol 5088 [Noel Regney/Gloria Shayne] [ASC] (12/21/63 C-66)*

DO YOU KNOW HOW TO TWIST Hank Ballard—King 5593 [Hank Ballard/Nathaniel Nathan/Gene Redd Sr.] [BMI] (2/10/62 BR-87)

DO YOU KNOW THE WAY TO SAN JOSÉ Dionne Warwick—Scepter 12216 [Burt Bacharach/Hal David] [ASC] (4/6/68 BCR-8)

DO YOU KNOW WHAT I MEAN Lee Michaels—A&M 1262 [Lee Eugene Michaels] [ASC] (7/31/71 BCR-4)

DO YOU KNOW WHAT TIME IT IS? P-Nut Gallery—Buddah 239 [Bobby Flax/Lanny Lambert] [BMI] (6/5/71 BCR-54)

—DO YOU KNOW WHERE YOU'RE GOING TO see: THEME FROM MAHOGANY

DO YOU LOVE ME Jaye P. Morgan and Eddy Arnold—RCA Victor 47-6842 [Floyd Wilson] [BMI] (3/23/57 R-60)

DO YOU LOVE ME *The Contours—Gordy 7005 [Berry Gordy] [ASC] (8/11/62 BCR-2)*

DO YOU LOVE ME *The Dave Clark Five—Epic 9678 [Berry Gordy] [ASC] (5/2/64 BCR-8)*

DO YOU LOVE ME *Andy Fraser—Island 99784 [Berry Gordy] [ASC] (3/3/84 BC-82)*

DO YOU LOVE ME *The Contours—Motown Yesteryear 448 [Berry Gordy] [ASC] (6/4/88 BC-11)*

DO YOU LOVE ME LIKE YOU KISS ME (SCAPRICCIATIELLO) The McGuire Sisters—Coral 62021 [Fernando Albano/Al Hoffman/Dick Manning] [ASC] (8/11/58 R-81) [FDE]

DO YOU LOVE SOMEBODY Luther Ingram—KoKo 728 [Johnny Baylor] [BMI] (4/8/78 R-97)

DO YOU LOVE WHAT YOU FEEL Rufus and Chaka—MCA 41131 [David Wolinski] [ASC] (11/17/79 BCR-22)

DO YOU MIND *Andy Williams—Cadence 1381 [Lionel Bart] [ASC] (6/13/60 BCtRt-45)*

DO YOU MIND *Anthony Newley—London 1918 [Lionel Bart] [ASC] (6/13/60 BCtRt-45)*

DO YOU REALLY WANT TO HURT ME Culture Club—Virgin/Epic 03368 [Michael Craig/Roy Hay/Jon Moss/George O'Dowd] [ASC] (12/4/82 BC-1)

DO YOU REMEMBER? Phil Collins—Atlantic 87955 [Phil Collins] [BMI] (4/28/90 BC-3)

DO YOU REMEMBER ME? Jermaine Jackson—Arista 1-9502 [Jermaine Jackson/Michael Omartian/Bruce Sudano] [BMI] (7/5/86 BC-66)

DO YOU SEE MY LOVE (FOR YOU GROWING) Jr. Walker & The All Stars—Soul 35073 [Jackey Beavers/Johnny Bristol] [BMI] (7/4/70 BCR-25)

—DO YOU THINK I'M DISCO see: DA YA THINK I'M SEXY

DO YOU WANNA GET AWAY Shannon—Mirage 99655 [Chris Barbosa/Ann Godwin] [ASC] (4/6/85 BC-49)

DO YOU WANNA GO PARTY KC & The Sunshine Band—TK 1033 [Harry Wayne Casey/Rick Finch] [BMI] (5/19/79 BCR-43)

DO YOU WANNA HOLD ME? Bow Wow Wow—RCA 13467 [Matthew Ashman/Dave Barbarossa/Leigh Gorman/Annabella Lwin*/Malcolm McLaren] [ASC] (4/23/83 BC-66)

DO YOU WANNA MAKE LOVE Peter McCann—20th Century 2335 [Peter McCann] [ASC] (4/23/77 BCR-5)

DO YOU WANNA TOUCH ME (OH YEAH) Joan Jett & The Blackhearts—Boardwalk 11-150-7 [Gary Glitter/Mike Leander] [BMI] (7/31/82 BC-20)

DO YOU WANT CRYING Katrina And The Waves—Capitol 5450 [Vince De La Cruz] [BMI] (7/27/85 BC-31)

DO YOU WANT ME Salt-N-Pepa—Next Plateau 331 [Hurby Azor] [ASC] (3/23/91 BC-21)

DO YOU WANT TO DANCE *Bobby Freeman—Josie 835 [Bobby Freeman] [BMI] (4/12/58 BCR-5)*

DO YOU WANT TO DANCE *Del Shannon—Amy 911 [Bobby Freeman] [BMI] (9/19/64 BCR-43)*

DO YOU WANNA DANCE? *The Beach Boys—Capitol 5372 [Bobby Freeman] [BMI] (2/27/65 BCR-12)*

DO YOU WANNA DANCE *The Mamas & The Papas—Dunhill 4171 [Bobby Freeman] [BMI] (11/23/68 BCR-43)*

DO YOU WANT TO DANCE? *Bette Midler—Atlantic 2928 [Bobby Freeman] [BMI] (12/23/72 BCR-13)*

DO YOU WANNA DANCE *The Ramones—Sire 1017 [Bobby Freeman] [BMI] (4/15/78 BC-86)*

DO YOU WANT TO KNOW A SECRET *The Beatles—Vee-Jay 587 [John Lennon/Paul McCartney] [ASC] (3/28/64 BCR-2)*

DO YOU WANT TO KNOW A SECRET *Stars On 45—Radio 3810 [John Lennon/Paul McCartney] (Med) [ASC] (4/11/81 BCR-1)*

DO YOUR DANCE - PART I Rose Royce—Whitfield 8440 [Dwight Turner/Norman Whitfield] [BMI] (9/17/77 BCR-39)

DO YOUR OWN THING Brook Benton—Cotillion 44007 [Jerry Leiber/Mike Stoller] [BMI] (10/26/68 BR-94)

DO YOUR THING The Watts 103rd Street Rhythm Band—Warner Bros.-Seven Arts 7250 [Melvin Dunlap*/James Gadson*/Albert Philip McKay*/John Rayford*/Charles Wright] [BMI] (2/1/69 BCR-11)

DO YOUR THING *Isaac Hayes—Enterprise 9042 [Isaac Hayes] [BMI] (2/19/72 BCR-23)*

DO YOUR THING *James & Bobby Purify—Casablanca 812 [Isaac Hayes] [BMI] (12/7/74 CR-71)*

THE DOCTOR Mary Wells—Jubilee 5621 [Mary Wells/Cecil Womack] [BMI] (5/11/68 BCR-54)

THE DOCTOR The Doobie Brothers—Capitol 44376 [Tom Johnston/Charles E. Kaufman/Eddie Schwartz] [BMI] (5/20/89 BC-9)

DOCTOR! DOCTOR! Thompson Twins—Arista 1-9209 [Tom Bailey/Alannah Currie/Joe Leeway] [ASC] (5/26/84 BC-10)

DOCTOR FEEL-GOOD Dr. Feelgood And The Interns—Okeh 7144 [Curtis Smith] [BMI] (4/7/62 BCR-66)

DOCTOR LOVE First Choice—Gold Mind 4004 [Allan Felder/Norman Harris/Ronnie Tyson] [BMI] (9/10/77 BCR-41)

DOCTOR MY EYES Jackson Browne—Asylum 11004 [Jackson Browne] [ASC] (3/11/72 BCR-8)

DOCTORIN' THE TARDIS The Timelords—TVT 4025 [James Cauty/Mike Chapman/Nicky Chinn/William Ernest Drummond/Gary Glitter/ Ron Granier/Mike Leander/Ian Richardson] [ASC] (12/17/88 BC-66)

DOCTOR'S ORDERS Carol Douglas—Midland Int'l 10113 [Roger Cook/Roger Greenaway/Geoff Stephens] [ASC] (11/23/74 BCR-10)

THE DODO Jumpin' Gene Simmons—Hi 2080 [Milton Addington/Dickey Lee/Allen Reynolds] [BMI] (11/7/64 BCR-73)

DOES ANYBODY KNOW I'M HERE The Dells—Cadet 5631 [Robert Eugene Miller] [BMI] (12/28/68 BCR-36)

DOES ANYBODY REALLY FALL IN LOVE ANYMORE? Kane Roberts—DGC 19009 [Jon Bon Jovi/Desmond Child/Richie Sambora/Diane Warren] [ASC] (4/27/91 BC-33)

DOES ANYBODY REALLY KNOW WHAT TIME IT IS? Chicago—Columbia 45264 [Robert Lamm] [ASC] (11/7/70 BCR-5)

DOES HE MEAN THAT MUCH TO YOU? Eddy Arnold—RCA Victor 47-8102 [Don Robertson/Jack Rollins] [ASC] (12/22/62 B-98)

DOES HE REALLY CARE FOR ME Ruby And The Romantics—Kapp 646 [Fred Anisfield/Larry Weiss] [BMI] (2/13/65 BCR-82)

DOES IT MAKE YOU REMEMBER Kim Carnes—EMI America 8147 [Kim Carnes/Dave Ellingson] [ASC] (11/6/82 BC-36)

DOES SHE DO IT LIKE SHE DANCES The Addrisi Brothers—Buddah 579 [Steve Duboff/Gerry Robinson] [ASC] (8/27/77 BC-74)

DOES SHE LOVE THAT MAN? Breathe—A&M 1535
[David Glasper/Marcus Lillington/Ian Spice*] [ASC] (11/10/90 BC-33)

DOES YOUR CHEWING GUM LOSE ITS FLAVOR (ON THE BEDPOST OVER NIGHT)
Lonnie Donegan And His Skiffle Group—Dot 15911
[Marty Bloom/Ernest Breuer/Billy Rose] [ASC] (7/24/61 BCR-5)

DOES YOUR HEART BEAT FOR ME Betty Johnson—Atlantic 2019
[Arnold Johnson/Russ Morgan/Mitchell Parish] [ASC] (4/18/59 C-91)

DOES YOUR MAMA KNOW ABOUT ME Bobby Taylor & The Vancouvers—Gordy 7069
[Tom Baird/Tommy Chong] [ASC] (4/6/68 BCR-29)

DOES YOUR MOTHER KNOW ABBA—Atlantic 3574
[Benny Andersson/Björn Ulvaeus] [BMI] (5/19/79 BCR-16)

DOESN'T SOMEBODY WANT TO BE WANTED
The Partridge Family Starring Shirley Jones & Featuring David Cassidy—Bell 963
[Mike Appel/Jim Cretecos/Wes Farrell] [BMI] (2/6/71 BCR-1)

THE DOG Rufus Thomas—Stax 130 [Rufus Thomas] [ASC] (2/9/63 BCR-87)

DOG & BUTTERFLY Heart—Portrait 70025
[Sue Ennis/Ann Wilson/Nancy Wilson] [ASC] (2/3/79 BCR-30)

DOG DAYS Atlanta Rhythm Section—Polydor 14411
[Buddy Buie/Dean Daughtry/Robert Nix] [BMI] (8/20/77 BCR-63)

DOG EAT DOG Ted Nugent—Epic 50301 [Ted Nugent] [ASC] (11/20/76 BC-82)

DOGFACE SOLDIER *Russ Morgan And His Orchestra—Decca 29703*
[Bert Gold/Ken Hart] [ASC] (10/22/55 BCRt-24)

DOG FACE SOLDIER *Joe Lipman—MGM 12102*
[Bert Gold/Ken Hart] [ASC] (10/24/55 Rt-24)

DOGFACE SOLDIER *Stephen Make—Original 523*
[Bert Gold/Ken Hart] [ASC] (11/7/55 Rt-34)

DOGGIN' AROUND *Jackie Wilson—Brunswick 55166 [Lena Agree] [NA] (4/4/60 BCR-15)*

STOP DOGGIN' ME AROUND *Klique—MCA 52250 [Lena Agree] [NA] (10/8/83 BC-50)*

DOGGONE RIGHT Smokey Robinson & The Miracles—Tamla 54183
[Al Cleveland/Smokey Robinson/Marvin Tarplin] [ASC] (6/14/69 BCR-32)

DOIN' OUR THING Clarence Carter—Atlantic 2660
[Clarence Carter/Allyn Lee/Clemmi McCants] [BMI] (9/27/69 BCR-46)

DOIN' THE CONTINENTAL WALK Danny & The Juniors—Swan 4100
[John Madara/David White] [BMI] (4/14/62 B-93)

DOIN' THE DO Betty Boo—Sire 19570
[Betty Boo/Estelle Levitt/Rob Seidenberg*/Kenny Young] [ASC] (11/3/90 BC-82)

(DOIN' THE) LOVERS LEAP Webb Pierce—Decca 31058
[Lee Emerson] [BMI] (3/21/60 BR-70)

DOING IT ALL FOR MY BABY Huey Lewis and the News—Chrysalis 43143
[Phil Cody/Mike Duke] [BMI] (7/18/87 BC-6)

DOING IT TO DEATH Fred Wesley & The J.B.'s—People 621
[James Brown] [BMI] (5/26/73 BCR-21)

DOING MY OWN THING (PART I) Johnnie Taylor (The Soul Philosopher)—Stax 0122
[Arthur Snyder] [ASC] (4/1/72 CR-63)

DOLL HOUSE Donnie Brooks—Era 3028
[Ruby Berry/Louis Duhig] [BMI] (11/7/60 BCR-31)

A DOLLAR A NICKEL AND A DIME Danny Machin—Derby 859
[Richard Mullan/King Palmer] [BMI] (10/11/54 R-72)

A DOLLAR DOWN The Limeliters—RCA Victor 47-7859
[Cisco Houston] [BMI] (3/27/61 BCR-44)

DOLLY Craig Brown—20th Fox 109 [Johnny Guy] [BMI] (8/18/58 R-90)

DOLLY DAGGER Jimi Hendrix—Reprise 1044 [Jimi Hendrix] [ASC] (10/23/71 BCR-74)

DOMANI (TOMORROW) *Julius La Rosa—Cadence 1265*
[Ulpio Minucci/Tony Velona] [ASC] (6/20/55 BCRt-7) [FET]

DOMANI (TOMORROW) *Tony Martin—RCA Victor 47-6167*
[Ulpio Minucci/Tony Velona] [ASC] (6/20/55 Rt-7) [FET]

DOMINICK THE DONKEY Lou Monte with Joe Reisman's Orch. & Chorus—Roulette 4308
[Ray Allen/Wandra Merrell/Sam Saltzberg] [BMI] (12/26/60 R-86)

DOMINIQUE The Singing Nun—Philips 40152
[Jeanine Deckers] [ASC] (11/2/63 BCR-1) [F]

DOMINO Van Morrison—Warner Bros. 7434 [Van Morrison] [BMI] (11/7/70 BCR-6)

DOMINO DANCING Pet Shop Boys—EMI-Manhattan 50161
[Chris Lowe/Neil Tennant] [ASC] (10/8/88 BC-18)

DOMINOES Robbie Nevil—EMI 50053
[Richard Eastman/Bobby Hart/Robbie Nevil] [ASC] (2/14/87 BC-13)

DOMMAGE, DOMMAGE (TOO BAD, TOO BAD) *Jerry Vale—Columbia 43774*
[Lee Pockriss/Paul Vance] [ASC] (10/8/66 B-93)

DOMMAGE, DOMMAGE (TOO BAD, TOO BAD) *Paul Vance—Scepter 12164*
[Lee Pockriss/Paul Vance] [ASC] (10/8/66 B-97)

DON QUICHOTTE Magazine 60—Baja 001
[Jean-Luc Drion/Domenico Regiacorte] [ASC] (5/10/86 BC-56) [F]

DONALD WHERE'S YOUR TROOSERS? Andy Stewart—Warwick 665
[Iain MacFadyen/Andy Stewart] [ASC] (8/21/61 B-77)

DONCHA' THINK IT'S TIME Elvis Presley—RCA Victor 47-7240
[Brook Benton*/Willie Dixon/Clyde Otis] [BMI] (4/14/58 BR-21)

DONDE ESTA SANTA CLAUS? (WHERE IS SANTA CLAUS?) Augie Rios—Metro 20010
[Hubert Giraud/Alvin Greiner/George Scheck] [ASC] (12/1/58 BCR-36)

DONE TOO SOON Neil Diamond—Uni 55278 [Neil Diamond] [SE] (5/22/71 BCR-65)

DONG DONG DIKI DI-KI DONG Super Cirkus—Super K 9
[Marinus Gerritsen*/George Kooymans] [ASC] (9/27/69 R-89)

DONNA Ritchie Valens—Del-Fi 4110 [Ritchie Valens] [BMI] (11/24/58 BCR-1)

DONNA THE PRIMA DONNA Dion (Di Muci)—Columbia 42852
[Dion DiMucci/Ernie Maresca] [ASC] (9/7/63 BCR-6)

DONNIE The Bermudas—Era 3125 [George Motola/Rickie Page] [BMI] (4/18/64 BCR-44)

DON'T Elvis Presley—RCA Victor 47-7150
[Jerry Leiber/Mike Stoller] [BMI] (1/20/58 BCR-1)

DON'T ANSWER ME Alan Parsons Project—Arista 1-9160
[Alan Parsons/Eric Woolfson] [BMI] (3/3/84 BC-15)

DON'T ANSWER THE DOOR PART 1 B.B. King—ABC 10856
[Jimmy Johnson*/B.B. King*] [BMI] (10/15/66 BCR-45)

DON'T ASK ME TO BE FRIENDS The Everly Brothers—Warner Bros. 5297
[Gerry Goffin/Jack Keller] [BMI] (10/20/62 BCR-48)

DON'T ASK ME (TO BE LONELY) The Dubs—Gone 5002
[Richard Blandon/Hiram Johnson] [BMI] (7/15/57 B-72)

DON'T ASK ME WHY Elvis Presley—RCA Victor 47-7280
[Ben Weisman/Fred Wise] [ASC] (6/23/58 BCR-28)

DON'T ASK ME WHY Billy Joel—Columbia 11331 [Billy Joel] [ASC] (8/2/80 BCR-17)

DON'T ASK ME WHY Eurythmics—Arista 1-9880
[Annie Lennox/David A. Stewart] [BMI] (9/30/89 BC-37)

DON'T ASK MY NEIGHBORS The Emotions—Columbia 10622
[Skip Scarborough] [BMI] (10/22/77 BCR-44)

DON'T BACK DOWN The Beach Boys—Capitol R-5267
[Mike Love*/Brian Wilson] (EP) [BMI] (10/10/64 C-57)

DON'T BE A DROP-OUT James Brown And The Famous Flames—King 6056
[James Brown/Nat Jones] [BMI] (10/8/66 BCR-32)

DON'T BE AFRAID (DO AS I SAY) Frankie Karl & The Dreams—D.C. 180
[William Jackson] [BMI] (12/14/68 B-93)

DON'T BE AFRAID, LITTLE DARLIN' Steve Lawrence—Columbia 42699
[Barry Mann/Cynthia Weil] [BMI] (3/2/63 BCR-19)

DON'T BE AFRAID OF THE DARK The Robert Cray Band—Mercury 870596
[Dennis Walker] [BMI] (9/24/88 BC-74)

DON'T BE ANGRY *Nappy Brown—Savoy 1155*
[Nappy Brown/Rose Marie McCoy/Fred Mendelsohn] [BMI] (4/11/55 BCtRt-9)

DON'T BE ANGRY *The Crew-Cuts—Mercury 70597*
[Nappy Brown/Rose Marie McCoy/Fred Mendelsohn] (TSW) [BMI] (4/30/55 BCtRt-9)

DON'T BE CRUEL *Elvis Presley—RCA Victor 47-6604*
[Otis Blackwell/Elvis Presley] [BMI] (7/27/56 BCR-1)

DON'T BE CRUEL *Bill Black's Combo—Hi 2026*
[Otis Blackwell/Elvis Presley] [BMI] (9/10/60 BCR-7) [IWM]

DON'T BE CRUEL *Barbara Lynn—Jamie 1244*
[Otis Blackwell/Elvis Presley] [BMI] (2/23/63 BCR-74)

DON'T BE CRUEL (TO A HEART THAT'S TRUE) *Elvis Presley—RCA 13351*
[Otis Blackwell/Elvis Presley] (Med) [BMI] (11/20/82 BC-71)

DON'T BE CRUEL *Cheap Trick—Epic 07965*
[Otis Blackwell/Elvis Presley] [BMI] (7/30/88 BC-3)

DON'T BE CRUEL Bobby Brown—MCA 53327
[Kenneth Edmonds/Antonio Reid/Daryl Simmons] [BMI] (7/23/88 BC-7)

DON'T BE MY ENEMY Wang Chung—Geffen 29193
[Darren Costin/Nick Feldman/Jack Hues] [BMI] (9/22/84 B-86)

DON'T BE THAT WAY Larry Elgart And His Manhattan Swing Orchestra—RCA 13219
[Benny Goodman/Mitchell Parish/Edgar Sampson] (Med) [NA] (6/5/82 BC-31) [IWM]

DON'T BELIEVE HIM, DONNA Lenny Miles—Scepter 1212
[Luther Dixon/Lee Thomas] [BMI] (12/31/60 BCR-41)

DON'T BET MONEY HONEY Linda Scott—Canadian-American 127
[Linda Scott] [BMI] (6/26/61 BCR-9)

DON'T BLAME IT ON ME Fats Domino—Imperial 5375
[Dave Bartholomew/Fats Domino] [BMI] (3/30/56 R-82)

DON'T BLAME ME The Everly Brothers—Warner Bros. 5501
[Dorothy Fields/Jimmy McHugh] [ASC] (9/18/61 BCR-20)

DON'T BLAME THE CHILDREN Sammy Davis Jr.—Reprise 0566
[H.B. Barnum/Ivan Reeve] [BMI] (5/27/67 BCR-37)

DON'T BREAK MY HEART Romeo's Daughter—Jive 1140
[Craig Joiner/Mutt Lange] [ASC] (10/15/88 BC-68)

DON'T BREAK THE HEART THAT LOVES YOU Connie Francis—MGM 13059
[Benny Davis/Ted Murry] [ASC] (2/5/62 BCR-1)

DON'T BRING BACK MEMORIES Four Tops—Motown 1147
[Raynoma Singleton] [BMI] (5/3/69 R-92)

DON'T BRING ME DOWN The Animals—MGM 13514
[Gerry Goffin/Carole King] [BMI] (5/14/66 BCR-11)

DON'T BRING ME DOWN Electric Light Orchestra—Jet 5060
[Jeff Lynne] [BMI] (7/28/79 BCR-3)

DON'T BURN DOWN THE BRIDGE Gladys Knight & The Pips—Buddah 433
[Ronald Alonzo Miller] (TSW) [BMI] (1/25/75 B-45)

DON'T BURN ME Paul Kelly—Warner Bros. 7657 [Paul Kelly] [BMI] (1/27/73 B-79)

DON'T CALL ME SWEETIE (CAUSE I'M BITTER) Eileen Rodgers—Columbia 40908
[Mel Leven/Robert Sherman] [ASC] (6/3/57 B-83)

DON'T CALL US, WE'LL CALL YOU Sugarloaf/Jerry Corbetta—Claridge 402
[John S. Carter/Jerry Corbetta] [ASC] (12/7/74 BCR-9)
DON'T CHA LOVE IT The Miracles—Tamla 54256
[Freddie Perren/Christine Yarian] [ASC] (12/14/74 BCR-63)
DON'T CHANGE INXS—Atco 99874
[Garry Beers/Andy Farriss/Jon Farriss/Tim Farriss/Michael Hutchence/Kirk Pengilly] [ASC] (7/16/83 B-80)
DON'T CHANGE HORSES (IN THE MIDDLE OF A STREAM)
Tower Of Power—Warner Bros. 7828
[Johnny Watson/Lenny Williams] [BMI] (7/20/74 BCR-26)
DON'T CHANGE ON ME Ray Charles—ABC/TRC 11291
[Jimmy Holiday/Eddie Reeves] [ASC] (3/6/71 BCR-27)
DON'T CHANGE YOUR LOVE The Five Stairsteps & Cubie—Curtom 1931
[Curtis Mayfield] [BMI] (8/24/68 BCR-59)
DON'T CLOSE YOUR EYES Kix—Atlantic 88902
[Bob Halligan/John Palumbo/Donnie Purnell] [BMI] (9/9/89 BC-9)
DON'T COME AROUND HERE NO MORE Tom Petty and The Heartbreakers—MCA 52496
[Tom Petty/David A. Stewart] [ASC] (3/16/85 BC-13)
DON'T COME KNOCKIN' Fats Domino—Imperial 5675
[Fats Domino] [BMI] (6/25/60 BCR-21)
DON'T COME RUNNING BACK TO ME Nancy Wilson—Capitol 5340
[Roy C. Bennett/Sid Tepper] [ASC] (1/30/65 BCR-58)
DON'T COST YOU NOTHING Ashford & Simpson—Warner Bros. 8514
[Nick Ashford/Valerie Simpson] [ASC] (2/25/78 BCR-53)
DON'T CROSS THE RIVER America—Warner Bros. 7670
[Dan Peek] [ASC] (1/27/73 BCR-20)
DON'T CRY Frankie Laine—Columbia 40693 [Frank Loesser] [ASC] (7/7/56 B-83)
DON'T CRY Asia—Geffen 29571 [Geoffrey Downes/John Wetton] [BMI] (7/30/83 BC-9)
DON'T CRY Guns N' Roses—Geffen 19027
[Saul Hudson/Duff McKagan/Axl Rose/Izzy Stradlin] [ASC] (9/21/91 BC-7)
DON'T CRY, BABY *Etta James—Argo 5393*
[Saul Bernie/James P. Johnson/Stella Unger] [ASC] (8/7/61 BCR-39)
DON'T CRY, BABY *Aretha Franklin—Columbia 42456*
[Saul Bernie/James P. Johnson/Stella Unger] [ASC] (7/21/62 B-92)
DON'T CRY DADDY Elvis Presley—RCA Victor 47-9768
[Mac Davis] (TSW) [BMI] (11/29/69 BCR-5)
DON'T CRY FOR ME ARGENTINA Festival—RSO 1020
[Tim Rice/Andrew Lloyd Webber] [ASC] (3/8/80 BCR-72)
DON'T CRY JONI Conway Twitty—MCA 40407 [Conway Twitty] [BMI] (12/13/75 BCR-45)
DON'T CRY MY LOVE The Impressions—ABC 11135
[Oscar Brown Jr./Curtis Mayfield] [BMI] (11/16/68 BCR-55)
—DON'T CRY MY LOVE see: FAITHFUL HUSSAR
DON'T CRY NO MORE Bobby Bland—Duke 340 [Deadric Malone] [BMI] (7/22/61 BCR-49)
DON'T CRY OUT LOUD Melissa Manchester—Arista 0373
[Peter Allen/Carole Bayer Sager] [BMI] (11/11/78 BCR-10)
DON'T DECEIVE ME Ruth Brown—Atlantic 2052 [Chuck Willis] [BMI] (3/14/60 BCR-58)
DON'T DESTROY ME Crash Craddock—Columbia 41470
[Barry Mann/Joe Shapiro] [BMI] (10/17/59 BC-77)
DON'T DISTURB THIS GROOVE The System—Atlantic 89320
[David Frank/Mic Murphy] [ASC] (4/11/87 BC-4)
DON'T DO IT Micky Dolenz—Challenge 59353 [Micky Dolenz] [BMI] (3/4/67 BCR-75)
—DON'T DO IT see: BABY DON'T YOU DO IT
DON'T DO ME Randy Bell—Epic 04497 [Randy Bell] [NA] (7/7/84 B-90)
DON'T DO ME LIKE THAT Tom Petty And The Heartbreakers—Backstreet 41138
[Tom Petty] [ASC] (11/17/79 BCR-7)
DON'T DREAM IT'S OVER Crowded House—Capitol 5614 [Neil Finn] [BMI] (1/17/87 BC-2)
DON'T DROP MY LOVE Anita Ward—Juana 3425 [Frederick Knight] [BMI] (11/3/79 B-87)
DON'T EAT THE YELLOW SNOW Frank Zappa—DiscReet 1312
[Frank Zappa] [ASC] (10/12/74 BCR-62)
DON'T EVER BE LONELY (A POOR LITTLE FOOL LIKE ME)
Cornelius Brothers & Sister Rose—United Artists 50954
[Eddie Cornelius] [BMI] (9/2/72 BCR-19)
DON'T EVER LEAVE ME Paul Anka—ABC-Paramount 10040
[Paul Anka] [BMI] (8/24/59 CR-60)
DON'T EVER LEAVE ME Bob & Earl—Tempe 102
[Earl Nelson/Bob Relf] [BMI] (10/20/62 B-85)
DON'T EVER LEAVE ME Connie Francis—MGM 13287
[Jeff Barry/Ellie Greenwich] [BMI] (10/24/64 BCR-37)
DON'T EVER LOVE ME Harry Belafonte—RCA Victor 47-6830
[Harry Belafonte/Lord Burgess*] [ASC] (3/16/57 BR-51)
DON'T EVER SAY GOODBYE Rick Derringer—Blue Sky 9 2788
[Rick Derringer] [BMI] (2/23/80 R-93)
DON'T EVER TAKE AWAY MY FREEDOM Peter Yarrow—Warner Bros. 7567
[Peter Yarrow] [ASC] (4/8/72 B-100)
DON'T EVER WANNA LOSE YA New England—Infinity 50,013
[John Fannon] [ASC] (5/5/79 BCR-40)
DON'T EXPECT ME TO BE YOUR FRIEND Lobo—Big Tree 158
[Kent LaVoie] [ASC] (12/30/72 BCR-4)
DON'T FALL IN LOVE WITH A DREAMER Kenny Rogers with Kim Carnes—
United Artists 1345 [Kim Carnes/Dave Ellingson] [ASC] (3/29/80 BCR-4)
(DON'T FEAR) THE REAPER Blue Öyster Cult—Columbia 10384
[Donald Roeser] [ASC] (7/31/76 BCR-7)
DON'T FENCE ME IN *Tommy Edwards—MGM 12871*
[Robert Fletcher/Cole Porter] [ASC] (2/15/60 BCR-45)
DON'T FENCE ME IN *George Maharis—Epic 9569*
[Robert Fletcher/Cole Porter] [ASC] (2/23/63 B-93)
DON'T FIGHT IT Wilson Pickett—Atlantic 2306
[Steve Cropper/Wilson Pickett] [BMI] (11/6/65 BCR-53)
DON'T FIGHT IT Kenny Loggins with Steve Perry—Columbia 03192
[Kenny Loggins/Steve Perry/Dean Pitchford] [BMI] (8/28/82 BC-15)
DON'T FIGHT THE HANDS (THAT NEED YOU) Hamilton, Joe Frank & Dennison—
Playboy 6088 [Bobby Caldwell/Jimmy George] [ASC] (10/30/76 B-72)
DON'T FOOL WITH FU MANCHU Rockin' Ramrods—Claridge 301
[Warren Schatz/Bob Stone] [NA] (11/27/65 R-97)
DON'T FORBID ME Pat Boone—Dot 15521 [Charles Singleton] [BMI] (12/8/56 BCR-1)
DON'T FORGET ABOUT ME *Barbara Lewis—Atlantic 2316*
[Gerry Goffin/Carole King] [BMI] (1/29/66 B-91)
DON'T FORGET ABOUT ME *The American Breed—Acta 808*
[Gerry Goffin/Carole King] [BMI] (8/19/67 CR-74)
DON'T FORGET ABOUT ME *Dusty Springfield—Atlantic 2606*
[Gerry Goffin/Carole King] [BMI] (3/1/69 BCR-52)
DON'T FORGET I LOVE YOU The Butanes—Enrica 1007
[James "Petey" Martin] [NA] (7/31/61 B-96)
DON'T FORGET I STILL LOVE YOU Bobbi Martin—Coral 62426
[Guy Louis] [BMI] (11/28/64 BCR-18)
DON'T FORGET ME (WHEN I'M GONE) Glass Tiger—Manhattan 50037
[Alan Frew/Sam Reid/Jim Vallance] [ASC] (7/12/86 BC-2)
DON'T FORGET TO DANCE The Kinks—Arista 1-9075
[Ray Davies] [ASC] (8/20/83 BC-29)
DON'T FORGET TO REMEMBER
Bee Gees Featuring Barry Gibb, Maurice Gibb & Colin Peterson—Atco 6702
[Barry Gibb/Maurice Gibb] [BMI] (8/30/69 BCR-46)
DON'T GET AROUND MUCH ANYMORE *Jo Stafford—Columbia 40406*
[Duke Ellington/Bob Russell] [ASC] (1/29/55 C-47)
DON'T GET AROUND MUCH ANYMORE *Tab Hunter—Dot 15548*
[Duke Ellington/Bob Russell] [ASC] (3/23/57 BCR-48)
DON'T GET AROUND MUCH ANYMORE *The Belmonts—Sabrina 501*
[Duke Ellington/Bob Russell] [ASC] (9/4/61 BCR-57)
DON'T GET CLOSE Little Anthony & The Imperials—United Artists 50625
[Jerry Akines/Johnnie Bellmon] [BMI] (2/28/70 C-98)
DON'T GET ME WRONG The Pretenders—Sire 28630
[Chrissie Hynde] [ASC] (10/11/86 BC-10)
DON'T GIRLS GET LONELY Glenn Shorrock—Capitol 5267
[Stephen Allen Davis/Carson Whitsett] [BMI] (9/24/83 BC-69)
DON'T GIVE IN TO HIM Gary Puckett And The Union Gap—Columbia 44788
[Gary Usher] [BMI] (3/15/69 BCR-11)
DON'T GIVE IT UP Robbie Patton—Liberty 1420
[David Adelstein/Buzz Cason*/Mac Gayden*/Robbie Patton] [ASC] (7/11/81 BCR-26)
DON'T GIVE UP Petula Clark—Warner Bros.-Seven Arts 7216
[Tony Hatch/Jackie Trent] [BMI] (7/20/68 BCR-23)
DON'T GIVE UP Peter Gabriel/Kate Bush—Geffen 28463
[Peter Gabriel] [BMI] (4/4/87 BC-69)
DON'T GIVE UP ON US David Soul—Private Stock 45,129
[Tony Macaulay] [ASC] (1/29/77 BCR-1)
DON'T GO AWAY MAD (JUST GO AWAY) Mötley Crüe—Elektra 64962
[Mick Mars/Nikki Sixx] [ASC] (5/26/90 BC-15)
DON'T GO BREAKING MY HEART Elton John And Kiki Dee—Rocket/MCA 40585
[Elton John/Bernie Taupin] [BMI] (7/3/76 BCR-1)
DON'T GO HOME *The Playmates—Roulette 4072*
[Stan Lebowsky/Johnny Lehmann] [ASC] (5/19/58 BCR-23)
DON'T GO HOME (MY LITTLE DARLIN') *The Shirelles—Scepter 12185*
[Stan Lebowsky/Johnny Lehmann] [ASC] (2/4/67 C-87)
DON'T GO NEAR THE INDIANS *Rex Allen—Mercury 71997*
[Lorene Mann] [BMI] (9/15/62 BCR-16)
DON'T GO NEAR THE ESKIMOS *(parody of Don't Go Near The Indians)*
Ben Colder—MGM 13104
[Lorene Mann/Sheb Wooley] [BMI] (11/24/62 BCR-46) [P]
DON'T GO OUT INTO THE RAIN (YOU'RE GOING TO MELT) Herman's Hermits—MGM 13761
[Kenny Young] [BMI] (6/24/67 BCR-13)
—DON'T GO see: BLUE MIRAGE
DON'T GO TO STRANGERS *Vaughn Monroe with Orchestra And Chorus—*
RCA Victor 47-6358 [Redd Evans/Arthur Kent/Dave Mann] [ASC] (1/21/56 BR-38)
DON'T GO TO STRANGERS *Etta Jones—Prestige 180*
[Redd Evans/Arthur Kent/Dave Mann] [ASC] (10/15/60 BCRt-36)
DON'T GO TO STRANGERS *Andy Williams—Cadence 1389*
[Redd Evans/Arthur Kent/Dave Mann] [ASC] (11/14/60 Rt-46)

DON'T HANG UP The Orlons—Cameo 231
[Dave Appell/Kal Mann] [ASC] (10/13/62 BCR-4)

DON'T HAVE TO SHOP AROUND The Mad Lads—Volt 127
[Allen Alvoid Jones Jr./Andrew Love/Richard Shann/Willie David Young] [BMI] (10/23/65 BCR-73)

DON'T HIDE YOUR LOVE Cher—Kapp 2184
[Howard Greenfield/Neil Sedaka] [BMI] (9/9/72 BCR-45)

DON'T HOLD BACK Chanson—Ariola America 7717
[James Jamerson Jr./David Z. Williams] [ASC] (11/4/78 BCR-20)

DON'T HOLD BACK YOUR LOVE Daryl Hall & John Oates—Arista 2157
[Gerald O'Brien/Richard Page/David Tyson] [BMI] (12/29/90 BC-33)

DON'T IT MAKE MY BROWN EYES BLUE Crystal Gayle—United Artists 1016
[Richard Leigh] [ASC] (7/30/77 BCR-1)

DON'T IT MAKE YOU FEEL GOOD The Overlanders—Hickory 1275
[Hank Marvin/Bruce Welch] [BMI] (11/21/64 R-95)

DON'T IT MAKE YOU WANNA DANCE? Rusty Wier—20th Century 2219
[Rusty Wier] [ASC] (9/6/75 B-82)

DON'T IT MAKE YOU WANT TO GO HOME *Joe South And The Believers—Capitol 2592*
[Joe South] [BMI] (8/16/69 BCR-41)

DON'T IT MAKE YOU WANT TO GO HOME *Brook Benton With The Dixie Flyers—Cotillion 44078 [Joe South] [BMI] (5/23/70 BCR-34)*

DON'T JUST STAND THERE Patty Duke—United Artists 875
[Lor Crane/Bernice Ross] [BMI] (6/19/65 BCR-5)

DON'T KNOCK MY LOVE - PT. I *Wilson Pickett—Atlantic 2797*
[Wilson Pickett/Brad Shapiro] [BMI] (4/24/71 BCR-7)

DON'T KNOCK MY LOVE *Diana Ross & Marvin Gaye—Motown 1296*
[Wilson Pickett/Brad Shapiro] [BMI] (7/13/74 BCR-38)

DON'T KNOCK THE ROCK Bill Haley And His Comets—Decca 30148
[Fred Karger/Robert E. Kent] [ASC] (12/15/56 R-49)

DON'T KNOW MUCH *Bill Medley—Liberty 1402*
[Barry Mann/Tom Snow/Cynthia Weil] [BMI] (3/28/81 BC-88)

ALL I NEED TO KNOW (DON'T KNOW MUCH) *Bette Midler—Atlantic 89789*
[Barry Mann/Tom Snow/Cynthia Weil] [BMI] (9/3/83 BC-77)

DON'T KNOW MUCH *Linda Ronstadt—Elektra 69261*
[Barry Mann/Tom Snow/Cynthia Weil] [BMI] (9/30/89 BC-2)

DON'T KNOW WHAT YOU GOT (TILL IT'S GONE) Cinderella—Mercury 870644
[Tom Keifer] [ASC] (8/27/88 BC-12)

DON'T LEAVE ME IN THE MORNING Odia Coates—United Artists 601
[Paul Anka/Johnny Harris] [BMI] (4/19/75 BCR-80)

DON'T LEAVE ME STARVIN' FOR YOUR LOVE (PART 1) Holland-Dozier—Invictus 9133
[Lamont Dozier/Brian Holland/Eddie Holland] [BMI] (1/6/73 BCR-42)

DON'T LEAVE ME THIS WAY *Thelma Houston—Tamla 54278*
[Kenneth Gamble/Cary Gilbert/Leon Huff] [BMI] (12/18/76 BCR-1)

DON'T LEAVE ME THIS WAY *Communards—MCA/London 52928*
[Kenneth Gamble/Cary Gilbert/Leon Huff] [BMI] (12/27/86 BC-40)

DON'T LET GO *Roy Hamilton—Epic 9257 [Jesse Stone] [BMI] (12/23/57 BCRt-11)*

DON'T LET GO *Billy Williams—Coral 61932 [Jesse Stone] [BMI] (12/23/57 Rt-11)*

DON'T LET GO *Commander Cody And His Lost Planet Airmen—Warner Bros. 8073*
[Jesse Stone] [BMI] (2/22/75 BCR-43)

DON'T LET GO *Isaac Hayes—Polydor 2011 [Jesse Stone] [BMI] (10/27/79 BCR-17)*

DON'T LET GO Wang Chung—Geffen 29377
[Nick Feldman/Jack Hues] [BMI] (2/4/84 BC-38)

DON'T LET GO THE COAT The Who—Warner Bros. 49743
[Pete Townshend] [GL] (6/27/81 BC-77)

DON'T LET HER BE YOUR BABY The Contours—Gordy 7016
[Berry Gordy] [ASC] (4/6/63 BCR-64)

DON'T LET HIM GO REO Speedwagon—Epic 02127
[Kevin Cronin] [ASC] (6/13/81 BCR-22)

DON'T LET HIM KNOW Prism—Capitol 5082
[Bryan Adams/Jim Vallance] [BMI] (1/30/82 BCR-39)

—DON'T LET HIM SHOP AROUND see: SHOP AROUND

DON'T LET HIM TAKE YOUR LOVE FROM ME Four Tops—Motown 1159
[Barrett Strong/Norman Whitfield] [BMI] (11/29/69 BCR-42)

DON'T LET IT END Styx—A&M 2543 [Dennis DeYoung] [ASC] (4/30/83 BC-6)

DON'T LET IT END ('TIL YOU LET IT BEGIN) The Miracles—Tamla 54237
[Freddie Perren/Christine Yarian] [ASC] (8/4/73 BCR-56)

DON'T LET IT GET YOU DOWN The Crusaders—Blue Thumb 225
[Joe Sample] [BMI] (5/12/73 BCR-86) [I]

DON'T LET IT HAPPEN TO US The Shirelles—Scepter 1259
[Hal David/Sherman Edwards] [ASC] (9/14/63 C-93)

DON'T LET IT SHOW Alan Parsons Project—Arista 0288
[Alan Parsons/Eric Woolfson] [BMI] (11/26/77 BCR-58)

DON'T LET LOVE HANG YOU UP Jerry Butler—Mercury 72991
[Jerry Butler/Kenneth Gamble/Leon Huff] [BMI] (11/15/69 BCR-38)

DON'T LET LOVE PASS ME BY Frankie Avalon—Chancellor 1056
[Rick Petrone/Sonny Troy] [BMI] (10/10/60 B-85)

DON'T LET ME BE LONELY TONIGHT James Taylor—Warner Bros. 7655
[James Taylor] [ASC] (11/25/72 BCR-12)

DON'T LET ME BE MISUNDERSTOOD *Nina Simone—Phillips 40232*
[Bennie Benjamin/Gloria Caldwell/Sol Marcus] [ASC] (2/27/65 Rt-20)

DON'T LET ME BE MISUNDERSTOOD *The Animals—MGM 13311*
[Bennie Benjamin/Gloria Caldwell/Sol Marcus] [ASC] (2/6/65 BCRt-15)

DON'T LET ME BE MISUNDERSTOOD
Santa Esmeralda Starring Larry Gomez—Casablanca 902
[Bennie Benjamin/Gloria Caldwell/Sol Marcus] [ASC] (11/5/77 BCR-14)

DON'T LET ME CROSS OVER Carl Butler—Columbia 42593
[Penny Jay] [BMI] (2/9/63 BCR-88)

DON'T LET ME DOWN The Beatles With Billy Preston—Apple 2490
[John Lennon/Paul McCartney] (TSW) [ASC] (5/3/69 BCR-33)

DON'T LET ME IN Sneaker—Handshake 02714
[Walter Becker/Donald Fagen] [ASC] (2/27/82 BCR-63)

DON'T LET THE FLAME BURN OUT Jackie Deshannon—Amherst 725
[Jackie DeShannon] [ASC] (10/29/77 BCR-68)

DON'T LET THE GREEN GRASS FOOL YOU Wilson Pickett—Atlantic 2781
[Jerry Akines/Johnnie Bellmon/Victor Drayton/Reginald Turner] [BMI] (1/16/71 BCR-10)

DON'T LET THE JONESES GET YOU DOWN The Temptations—Gordy 7086
[Barrett Strong/Norman Whitfield] [BMI] (5/17/69 BCR-17)

DON'T LET THE KIDDY GEDDIN Kitty Kallen—Decca 29268
[Andy Ackers/Hal Dickinson/Sunny Skylar] [NA] (10/4/54 CR-26)

DON'T LET THE MUSIC SLIP AWAY Archie Bell & The Drells—Atlantic 2721
[Kenneth Gamble/Cary Gilbert*/Leon Huff] [BMI] (12/27/69 B-90)

DON'T LET THE RAIN COME DOWN (CROOKED LITTLE MAN) The Serendipity Singers—Philips 40175 [Ersel Hickey/Ed E. Miller/Traditional] [BMI] (2/29/64 BCR-5)

DON'T LET THE RAIN FALL DOWN ON ME The Critters—Kapp 838
[James E. Ryan Jr.] [BMI] (7/8/67 BCR-32)

DON'T LET THE SUN CATCH YOU CRYIN' Ray Charles—Atlantic 2047
[Joseph Perkins Greene] [ASC] (2/8/60 B-95)

DON'T LET THE SUN CATCH YOU CRYING Gerry And The Pacemakers—Laurie 3251
[Les Chadwick*/Leo Maguire*/Fred Marsden*/Gerry Marsden] [BMI] (5/23/64 BCR-4)

DON'T LET THE SUN GO DOWN ON ME *Elton John—MCA 40259*
[Elton John/Bernie Taupin] [BMI] (6/22/74 BCR-1)

DON'T LET THE SUN GO DOWN ON ME *George Michael—Columbia 74086*
[Elton John/Bernie Taupin] [BMI] (12/7/91 BC-1)

DON'T LET YOUR LEFT HAND KNOW Joe Tex—Dial 4006 [Joe Tex] [BMI] (4/10/65 B-95)

DON'T LOOK ANY FURTHER *Dennis Edwards—Gordy 1715*
[Franne Golde/Duane Hitchings/Dennis Lambert] [BMI] (4/28/84 B-72)

DON'T LOOK ANY FURTHER *The Kane Gang—Capitol 44115*
[Franne Golde/Duane Hitchings/Dennis Lambert] [BMI] (2/6/88 BC-64)

DON'T LOOK BACK *The Temptations—Gordy 7047*
[Smokey Robinson/Ronnie White] [ASC] (12/4/65 BC-78)

(YOU GOT TO WALK AND) DON'T LOOK BACK *Peter Tosh—Rolling Stones 19308*
[Smokey Robinson/Ronnie White] [ASC] (11/4/78 B-81)

DON'T LOOK BACK Boston—Epic 50590 [Tom Scholz] [ASC] (8/19/78 BCR-4)

DON'T LOOK BACK Fine Young Cannibals—MCA 53695
[Roland Gift/David Steele] [ASC] (8/12/89 BC-10)

DON'T LOOK DOWN - THE SEQUEL Go West—Chrysalis 43141
[Peter Cox/Richard Drummie] [ASC] (8/1/87 BC-39)

DON'T LOSE ANY SLEEP John Waite—EMI America 43040
[Diane Warren] [ASC] (9/26/87 BC-79)

DON'T LOSE MY NUMBER Phil Collins—Atlantic 89536
[Phil Collins] [ASC] (7/20/85 BC-4)

DON'T MAKE A FOOL OF YOURSELF Stacey Q—Atlantic 89135
[Skip Hahn/Jon St. James/Stacey Swain] [BMI] (2/27/88 BC-66)

DON'T MAKE ME DO IT Patrick Simmons—Elektra 69817
[Mario Cipollina/Johnny Colla/Bill Gibson/Chris Hayes/Sean Hopper/Huey Lewis] [ASC] (6/18/83 B-75)

DON'T MAKE ME DREAM ABOUT YOU Chris Isaak—Reprise 19357
[Chris Isaak] [ASC] (4/13/91 C-79)

DON'T MAKE ME OVER *Dionne Warwick—Scepter 1239*
[Burt Bacharach/Hal David] [ASC] (11/24/62 BCR-17)

DON'T MAKE ME OVER *Brenda & The Tabulations—Top & Bottom 404*
[Burt Bacharach/Hal David] [ASC] (8/1/70 BCR-76)

DON'T MAKE ME OVER *Jennifer Warnes—Arista 0455*
[Burt Bacharach/Hal David] [ASC] (12/8/79 BCR-67)

DON'T MAKE ME OVER *Sybil—Next Plateau 325*
[Burt Bacharach/Hal David] [ASC] (9/23/89 BC-20)

DON'T MAKE ME PAY FOR HIS MISTAKES Z.Z. Hill—Hill 222
[Miles Grayson/Bobby Lexing] [BMI] (2/27/71 BCR-62)

DON'T MAKE ME WAIT FOR LOVE Kenny G—Arista 1-9625
[Walter Afanasieff/Preston Glass/Narada Michael Walden] [ASC] (8/29/87 BC-15)

DON'T MAKE MY BABY BLUE Frankie Laine—Columbia 42767
[Barry Mann/Cynthia Weil] [BMI] (5/4/63 BCR-51)

DON'T MAKE THE GOOD GIRLS GO BAD Della Humphrey—Arctic 144
[Jack Corbitt/Clarence Reid] [BMI] (11/30/68 B-79)

DON'T MEAN NOTHING Richard Marx—Manhattan 50079
[Bruce Gaitsch/Richard Marx] [ASC] (6/13/87 BC-3)

DON'T MENTION MY NAME Shepherd Sisters—Atlantic 2176
[Bob Crewe/Bob Gaudio] [BMI] (3/2/63 BC-76)

DON'T MESS UP A GOOD THING *Fontella Bass & Bobby McClure—Checker 1097*
[Oliver Sain] [BMI] (2/6/65 BCR-29)

DON'T MESS UP A GOOD THING *Gregg Allman—Capricorn 0042*
[Oliver Sain] [BMI] (4/20/74 C-91)

DON'T MESS WITH BILL The Marvelettes—Tamla 54126
[Smokey Robinson] [ASC] (1/1/66 BCR-7)

DON'T MISUNDERSTAND ME Rossington Collins Band—MCA 41284
[Allen Collins/Barry Harwood/Dale Krantz] [BMI] (7/26/80 BCR-55)

DON'T NEED A GUN Billy Idol—Chrysalis 43087 [Billy Idol] [ASC] (1/24/87 BC-37)

DON'T PAT ME ON THE BACK AND CALL ME BROTHER
John W. Anderson Presents KaSandra—Capitol 2342
[John W. Anderson] [BMI] (12/14/68 B-91)

DON'T PAY THE FERRYMAN Chris DeBurgh—A&M 2511
[Chris de Burgh] [BMI] (4/30/83 BC-32)

DON'T PITY ME Dion and The Belmonts—Laurie 3021
[Sid Jacobson/Lou Stallman] [BMI] (12/8/58 BCR-35)

DON'T PITY ME Peter And Gordon—Capitol 5532
[Peter Asher/Gordon Waller] [BMI] (11/6/65 BCR-80)

DON'T PITY ME Faith, Hope & Charity—20th Century Fox 2370
[Van McCoy] [BMI] (7/22/78 R-84)

DON'T PLAY THAT SONG (YOU LIED) *Ben E. King—Atco 6222*
[Ahmet Ertegun/Betty Nelson] [BMI] (4/21/62 BCR-11)

DON'T PLAY THAT SONG *Aretha Franklin With The Dixie Flyers—Atlantic 2751*
[Ahmet Ertegun/Betty Nelson] [BMI] (8/8/70 BCR-7)

DON'T PULL YOUR LOVE *Hamilton, Joe Frank & Reynolds—Dunhill 4276*
[Dennis Lambert/Brian Potter] [BMI] (5/15/71 BCR-1)

DON'T PULL YOUR LOVE *Sam & Dave—Atlantic 2839*
[Dennis Lambert/Brian Potter] [BMI] (11/6/71 CR-93)

DON'T PULL YOUR LOVE *Glen Campbell—Capitol 4245*
[Dennis Lambert/Brian Potter] (Med) [BMI] (3/27/76 BCR-27)

DON'T PUSH IT DON'T FORCE IT Leon Haywood—20th Century Fox 2443
[Leon Haywood] [BMI] (4/5/80 BCR-49)

DON'T PUSH ME Hedgehoppers Anonymous—Parrot 9817
[Jonathan King] [BMI] (4/9/66 R-96)

DON'T READ THE LETTER Patti Page—Mercury 71745
[Howard Greenfield/Jack Keller] [BMI] (12/26/60 BCR-65)

DON'T ROCK THE BOAT Eddie Floyd—Stax 219
[Eddie Floyd/Joe Shamwell] [BMI] (7/1/67 B-98)

DON'T RUN (COME BACK TO ME)
KC & The Sunshine Band (Duet with Teri DeSario)—Epic 03556
[Harry Wayne Casey/Joseph Simmel] [BMI] (3/19/83 C-79)

DON'T RUN MY LIFE Spys—EMI America 8124
[John Blanco/John DiGaudio/Ed Gagliardi/Al Greenwood/Billy Milne] [BMI]
(8/14/82 BC-72)

DON'T RUSH ME Taylor Dayne—Arista 1-9722
[Alexandra Forbes/Jeffrey Franzel] [ASC] (11/5/88 BC-1)

DON'T SAY GOODBYE The Diamonds—Mercury 71128
[Nat Goodman/Carl Stevens/George Stone] [NA] (6/15/57 R-56)

DON'T SAY GOODNIGHT AND MEAN GOODBYE The Shirelles—Scepter 1255
[Joe DeAngelis/Charles Partee] [BMI] (6/15/63 BCR-26)

DON'T SAY GOODNIGHT (IT'S TIME FOR LOVE) (PARTS 1 & 2)
The Isley Brothers—T-Neck 2290
[Ernie Isley/Marvin Isley/O'Kelly Isley/Ronald Isley/Rudolph Isley/Chris Jasper] [ASC]
(3/29/80 BCR-39)

DON'T SAY NO The Kingsmen—Wand 1157
[Barry Curtis/Nicholas Richardson] [BMI] (6/10/67 R-95)

DON'T SAY NO Billy Burnette—Columbia 11380 [Billy Burnette] [ASC] (11/1/80 BCR-68)

DON'T SAY NO TONIGHT Eugene Wilde—Philly World 7-99608
[Ronnie E. Broomfield/McKinley Horton] [BMI] (12/7/85 BC-76)

DON'T SAY NOTHIN' BAD (ABOUT MY BABY) The Cookies—Dimension 1008
[Gerry Goffin/Carole King] [BMI] (3/2/63 BCR-7)

DON'T SAY YOU DON'T REMEMBER Beverly Bremers—Scepter 12315
[Estelle Levitt/Helen Miller] [BMI] (5/29/71 BCR-13)

DON'T SAY YOU LOVE ME Billy Squier—Capitol 44420
[Billy Squier] [ASC] (6/24/89 BC-58)

DON'T SAY YOU'RE SORRY Paul Anka—ABC-Paramount 10168
[Paul Anka] [BMI] (1/2/61 R-95)

DON'T SEND NOBODY ELSE Ace Spectrum—Atlantic 3012
[Nick Ashford/Valerie Simpson] [ASC] (9/28/74 BCR-57)

DON'T SET ME FREE Ray Charles And His Orchestra With The Raelettes—
ABC-Paramount 10405 [Teddy Powell/Bobby Sharp] [ASC] (2/23/63 BCR-20)

DON'T SHED A TEAR Paul Carrack—Chrysalis 43164
[Rob Friedman/Eddie Schwartz] [ASC] (11/14/87 BC-9)

DON'T SHUT ME OUT Kevin Paige—Chrysalis 23389 [Kevin Paige] [BMI] (8/19/89 BC-17)

DON'T SIGN THE PAPER BABY (I WANT YOU BACK) Jimmy Delphs—Karen 1538
[Tony Hester/Richard Wylie] [BMI] (5/18/68 BCR-94)

DON'T SLEEP IN THE SUBWAY Petula Clark—Warner Bros. 7049
[Tony Hatch/Jackie Trent] [BMI] (6/3/67 BCR-5)

DON'T SPREAD IT AROUND Barbara Lynn—Jamie 1286
[Bobby O'Neil/Leo O'Neil] [BMI] (10/3/64 BR-93)

DON'T STAND SO CLOSE TO ME *The Police—A&M 2301 [Sting] [BMI] (2/7/81 BCR-9)*

DON'T STAND SO CLOSE TO ME '86 *The Police—A&M 2879*
[Sting] [BMI] (10/25/86 BC-46)

DON'T STAY AWAY TOO LONG Eddie Fisher—RCA Victor 47-6196
[Al Hoffman/Dick Manning] (TSW) [ASC] (9/3/55 BCR-16)

DON'T STOP Fleetwood Mac—Warner Bros. 8413 [Christine McVie] [BMI] (7/9/77 BCR-1)

DON'T STOP Jeffrey Osborne—A&M 2687
[David Batteau/Danny Sembello] [ASC] (10/13/84 BC-41)

DON'T STOP BELIEVIN' Olivia Newton-John—MCA 40600
[John Farrar] [BMI] (8/7/76 BCR-33)

DON'T STOP BELIEVIN' Journey—Columbia 02567
[Jonathan Cain/Steve Perry/Neal Schon] [BMI] (10/31/81 BCR-8)

DON'T STOP, GET OFF The Sylvers—Casablanca 938
[Edmund Sylvers/Foster Sylvers/James Sylvers/Leon Sylvers/Ricky Sylvers] [ASC]
(10/14/78 R-94)

DON'T STOP IT NOW Hot Chocolate—Big Tree 16060 [Errol Brown] [ASC] (4/3/76 BCR-42)

DON'T STOP ME BABY (I'M ON FIRE) The Boys Band—Elektra 47406
[Larry Keith/Steve Pippin/Austin Roberts/Johnny Slate] [BMI] (3/6/82 BCR-61)

DON'T STOP ME NOW Queen—Elektra 46008 [Freddie Mercury] [BMI] (2/10/79 BCR-77)

DON'T STOP NOW Eddie Holman—ABC 11261
[Eddie Holman/James Solomon] (TSW) [BMI] (5/2/70 BCR-32)

DON'T STOP THE MUSIC Yarbrough & Peoples—Mercury 76085
[Jonah Ellis/Alisa Peoples/Lonnie Simmons] [BMI] (1/24/81 BCR-17)

DON'T STOP THE WEDDING Ann Cole—Roulette 4452
[Fred Johnson/Leroy Kirkland/Pearl Woods] [BMI] (11/3/62 BR-90)

DON'T STOP 'TIL YOU GET ENOUGH Michael Jackson—Epic 50742
[Michael Jackson] [BMI] (7/28/79 BCR-1)

DON'T STOP TRYING Rodway—Millennium 13111
[Norman Dolph/Steve Rodway] [BMI] (12/11/82 BC-78)

DON'T SWEETHEART ME Bobby Dee & Rhodie-Summers—Anchor 31
[Cliff Friend/Charles Tobias] [ASC] (2/2/57 R-80)

DON'T TAKE AWAY THE MUSIC Tavares—Capitol 4348
[Freddie Perren/Keni St. Lewis/Christine Yarian] [BMI] (10/30/76 BCR-34)

DON'T TAKE IT OUT ON ME Bobbi Martin—Coral 62475
[Ritchie Adams/Larry Kusik] [BMI] (2/12/66 C-91)

DON'T TAKE IT PERSONAL Jermaine Jackson—Arista 1-9875
[Dave Conley/Derrick Culler/David Townsend] [ASC] (11/18/89 BC-64)

DON'T TAKE IT SO HARD
Paul Revere And The Raiders Featuring Mark Lindsay—Columbia 44553
[Mark Lindsay] [BMI] (6/22/68 BCR-18)

DON'T TAKE MY KINDNESS FOR WEAKNESS The Soul Children—Stax 0132
[James Banks/Eddie Marion/Henderson Thigpen/Michael Toles*] [BMI] (7/22/72 C-73)

DON'T TAKE MY MIND ON A TRIP Boy George—Virgin 99272
[Gene Griffin] [BMI] (4/8/89 C-86)

DON'T TAKE THE STARS The Mystics—Laurie 3038
[Mark L. Harris/Ruth Harris] [BMI] (10/10/59 BCR-75)

DON'T TAKE YOUR GUNS TO TOWN Johnny Cash—Columbia 41313
[Johnny Cash] [ASC] (1/17/59 BCR-23)

DON'T TAKE YOUR LOVE The Manhattans—Columbia 10045
[Allan Felder/Ron Kersey/Bunny Sigler] [BMI] (12/28/74 BCR-37)

DON'T TAKE YOUR LOVE FROM ME *Grady Martin And The Slew Foot Five—Decca 29691*
[Henry Nemo] [ASC] (2/17/56 R-81) [IWM]

DON'T TAKE YOUR LOVE FROM ME *Joni James—MGM 12353*
[Henry Nemo] [ASC] (11/3/56 R-82)

DON'T TAKE YOUR LOVE FROM ME *Gloria Lynne—Everest 2044*
[Henry Nemo] [ASC] (7/4/64 B-76)

DON'T TALK Larry Lee—Columbia 02740
[Terry Britten/Sue Shifrin] [ASC] (6/26/82 B-81)

DON'T TALK TO STRANGERS The Beau Brummels—Autumn 20
[Robert Durand/Ron Elliott] [BMI] (10/9/65 BCR-51)

DON'T TALK TO STRANGERS Rick Springfield—RCA 13070
[Rick Springfield] [BMI] (3/6/82 BCR-2)

DON'T TELL ME GOODNIGHT Lobo—Big Tree 16033
[Kent LaVoie] [ASC] (3/22/75 BCR-27)

DON'T TELL ME IT'S RAINING Johnny Tillotson—MGM 13738
[Paul Tannen] [BMI] (6/10/67 R-86)

DON'T TELL ME LIES Breathe—A&M 1267
[Michael Delahunty/David Glasper/Marcus Lillington/Ian Spice] [ASC] (1/14/89 BC-10)

DON'T TELL ME NOT TO LOVE YOU *Joni James—MGM 12175*
[Russell Faith/Clarence Kehner] [ASC] (2/17/56 BRt-73)

DON'T TELL ME NOT TO LOVE YOU *June Valli—RCA Victor 47-6331*
[Russell Faith/Clarence Kehner] [ASC] (2/24/56 Rt-73)

DON'T TELL ME THE TIME Martha Davis—Capitol 44057
[Martha Davis] [BMI] (11/21/87 B-80)

DON'T TELL ME WHY (PITIE SENORITA)
Tony Bennett with Percy Faith and His Orchestra–Columbia 40523
[Guy Magenta/Wayne Shanklin/Al Sherman] [ASC] (6/13/55 R-77)

DON'T TELL ME YOU LOVE ME Night Ranger–Boardwalk
[Jack Blades] [BMI] (1/15/83 BC-40)

DON'T TELL ME YOUR TROUBLES Jimmy Bowen With The Rhythm Orchids–Roulette 4017
[Kenny Jacobson/Rhoda Roberts/Melvin Unger] [ASC] (8/26/57 R-60)

DON'T TELL ME YOUR TROUBLES Don Gibson–RCA Victor 47-7566
[Don Gibson] [BMI] (8/10/59 BCR-53)

DON'T TELL YOUR MAMA (WHERE YOU'VE BEEN) Eddie Floyd–Stax 0036
[Eddie Floyd/Booker T. Jones Jr.] [BMI] (6/14/69 BCR-73)

DON'T THINK...FEEL Neil Diamond–Columbia 10405
[Neil Diamond] [SE] (9/11/76 BCR-43)

DON'T THINK TWICE, IT'S ALL RIGHT *Peter, Paul & Mary–Warner Bros. 5385*
[Bob Dylan] [SE] (9/14/63 BCR-9)

DON'T THINK TWICE *The Wonder Who ?–Philips 40324 [Bob Dylan] [SE] (11/6/65 BCR-9)*

DON'T THROW AWAY ALL THOSE TEARDROPS Frankie Avalon–Chancellor 1048
[Diane DeNota] [BMI] (3/7/60 BCR-19)

DON'T THROW OUR LOVE AWAY Orleans–Infinity 50,017
[Larry Hoppen/Bob Leinbach/Marilyn Mason] [BMI] (8/4/79 C-92)

DON'T THROW YOUR LOVE AWAY The Searchers–Kapp 593
[William E. Jackson III/Jimmy Wisner] [BMI] (5/30/64 BCR-13)

DON'T TIE ME DOWN Anthony & The Imperials–Veep 1225
[Ritchie Adams/Victoria Pike/Teddy Randazzo] [BMI] (3/18/67 R-97)

DON'T TOUCH ME *Jeannie Seely–Monument 933*
[Hank Cochran] [BMI] (5/28/66 BCR-74)

DON'T TOUCH ME *Bettye Swann–Capitol 2382 [Hank Cochran] [BMI] (3/8/69 BCR-32)*

DON'T TOUCH ME THERE The Tubes–A&M 1826
[Jane Dornacker/Ron Nagle] [BMI] (6/26/76 BC-61)

DON'T TREAT ME BAD Firehouse–Epic 73676
[William Cosby Ellis/Michael Foster/Bill Leverty/Carl J. Snare] [ASC] (3/2/91 BC-19)

DON'T TRY TO FIGHT IT, BABY Eydie Gorme–Columbia 42790
[Gerry Goffin/Jack Keller] [BMI] (6/1/63 BCR-50)

DON'T TRY TO LAY NO BOOGIE WOOGIE ON THE "KING OF ROCK & ROLL"
Crow–Amaret 125
[Jeff Thomas] [BMI] (10/10/70 BCR-35)

DON'T TRY TO LAY NO BOOGIE-WOOGIE ON THE KING OF ROCK AND ROLL
John Baldry–Warner Bros. 7506
[Jeff Thomas] [BMI] (8/21/71 BCR-73)

DON'T TRY TO STOP IT Roman Holliday–Jive 9092
[Brian Bonhomme] [ASC] (10/1/83 BC-66)

DON'T TURN THE LIGHT OUT Cliff Richard–Rocket/MCA 40724
[Guy Fletcher/Doug Flett] [ASC] (6/4/77 BC-57)

DON'T WAIT FOR HEROES Dennis DeYoung–A&M 2692
[Dennis DeYoung] [ASC] (12/8/84 BC-81)

DON'T WAIT TOO LONG Tony Bennett–Columbia 42886
[Sunny Skylar] [ASC] (10/12/63 BCR-49)

DON'T WAKE ME UP IN THE MORNING, MICHAEL
The Peppermint Rainbow–Decca 732498
[Al Kasha] [BMI] (6/7/69 BCR-43)

DON'T WALK AWAY Rick Springfield–RCA 13813
[Rick Springfield] [BMI] (5/26/84 BC-26)

DON'T WALK AWAY Robert Tepper–Scotti Brothers 05879
[Robert Tepper] [ASC] (5/3/86 BC-80)

DON'T WALK AWAY Toni Childs–A&M 1237
[Toni Childs/Phil Ramacon] [ASC] (8/6/88 BC-72)

DON'T WALK AWAY FROM ME Dee Clark–Vee-Jay 409
[Calvin Carter/Horace Ott] [BMI] (11/13/61 R-90)

DON'T WANNA FALL IN LOVE Jane Child–Warner Bros. 19933
[Jane Child] [BMI] (2/10/90 BC-2)

DON'T WANNA LIVE INSIDE MYSELF Bee Gees–Atco 6847
[Barry Gibb] [BMI] (10/16/71 BCR-30)

DON'T WANNA LOSE YOU Gloria Estefan–Epic 68959
[Gloria Estefan] [BMI] (7/8/89 BC-1)

DON'T WANNA THINK ABOUT PAULA Dickey Lee–Smash 1808
[Dickey Lee/Allen Reynolds] [BMI] (3/9/63 BCR-68)

DON'T WANT NO-BODY J.D. Drews–Unicorn 95000
[Paul Delph/Daphna Edwards] [BMI] (12/27/80 B-79)

DON'T WANT TO BE A FOOL Luther Vandross–Epic 73879
[Marcus Miller/Luther Vandross] [ASC] (8/3/91 BC-9)

DON'T WANT TO LIVE WITHOUT IT Pablo Cruise–A&M 2076
[David Jenkins/Cory Lerios] [ASC] (9/16/78 BCR-18)

DON'T WANT TO SAY GOODBYE Raspberries–Capitol 3280
[Wally Bryson/Eric Carmen] [BMI] (4/29/72 BCR-86)

DON'T WANT TO WAIT ANYMORE The Tubes–Capitol 5007
[Rick Anderson/Michael Cotten/David Foster/Charles Prince/William Spooner/
Roger Steen/Fee Waybill/Vince Welnick] [BMI] (6/20/81 BCR-35)

DON'T WASTE MY TIME John Mayall–Polydor 14004
[John Mayall] [BMI] (9/27/69 BCR-56)

DON'T WASTE YOUR TIME Yarbrough & Peoples–Total Experience 2400
[Jonah Ellis] [BMI] (4/14/84 BC-45)

DON'T WORRY Marty Robbins–Columbia 41922 [Marty Robbins] [BMI] (1/21/61 BCR-2)

DON'T WORRY ABOUT ME Frank Sinatra–Capitol 2787
[Rube Bloom/Ted Koehler] [ASC] (5/29/54 B-PRE)

DON'T WORRY BABY *The Beach Boys–Capitol 5174*
[Roger Christian/Brian Wilson] [BMI] (5/23/64 BCR-22)

DON'T WORRY BABY *The Tokens–Buddah 159*
[Roger Christian/Brian Wilson] [BMI] (2/28/70 BCR-71)

DON'T WORRY BABY *B.J. Thomas–MCA 40735*
[Roger Christian/Brian Wilson] [BMI] (7/2/77 BCR-13)

DON'T WORRY BE HAPPY (EDIT) Bobby McFerrin–EMI-Manhattan 50146
[Bobby McFerrin] [BMI] (7/30/88 BC-1)

DON'T WORRY 'BOUT ME Vincent Edwards–Decca 31413
[Rube Bloom/Ted Koehler] [ASC] (8/4/62 BR-72)

(DON'T WORRY) IF THERE'S A HELL BELOW WE'RE ALL GOING TO GO
Curtis Mayfield–Curtom 1955
[Curtis Mayfield] [BMI] (11/21/70 BCR-24)

DON'T WORRY MOTHER, YOUR SON'S HEART IS PURE The McCoys–Bang 532
[Rick Derringer] [BMI] (9/24/66 BCR-51)

–DON'T YA JES' LOVE IT see: CHICK-A-BOOM

–DON'T YA WANNA PLAY THIS GAME NO MORE see: SARTORIAL ELOQUENCE

DON'T YOU BELIEVE IT Andy Williams–Columbia 42523
[Burt Bacharach/Bob Hilliard] [ASC] (9/1/62 BCR-39)

DON'T YOU CARE The Buckinghams–Columbia 44053
[Gary Beisbier/James Holvay] [BMI] (3/11/67 BCR-5)

DON'T YOU COME CRYIN' Linear–Atlantic 87877
[Tolga Katas/Charlie Pennachio/Gary Tutalo] [BMI] (7/14/90 BC-70)

DON'T YOU (FORGET ABOUT ME) Simple Minds–A&M 2703
[Keith Forsey/Steve Schiff] [ASC] (2/23/85 BC-1)

DON'T YOU GET SO MAD Jeffrey Osborne–A&M 2561
[Don Freeman/Jeffrey Osborne/Michael Sembello] [BMI] (7/16/83 BC-25)

DON'T YOU JUST KNOW IT *Huey (Piano) Smith And The Clowns–Ace 545*
[Huey P. Smith] [BMI] (3/15/58 BCR-9)

DON'T YOU JUST KNOW IT *The Fendermen–Soma 1142*
[Huey P. Smith] [BMI] (8/29/60 CR-76)

DON'T YOU KNOW Della Reese–RCA Victor 47-7591
[Giacomo Puccini/Bobby Worth] [ASC] (9/7/59 BCR-1)

DON'T YOU KNOW Keith Everett–TMP-Ting 118
[Keith Gravenhorst] [BMI] (5/7/66 R-96)

DON'T YOU KNOW HOW MUCH I LOVE YOU Ronnie Milsap–RCA 13564
[Michael D. Stewart/Dan Edward Williams] [BMI] (8/13/83 BC-58)

DON'T YOU KNOW I LOVE YOU Fats Domino–Imperial 5492
[Dave Bartholomew/Fats Domino] [BMI] (3/8/58 CR-54)

DON'T YOU KNOW WHAT LOVE IS Touch–Atco 7311
[Mark Mangold] [ASC] (1/31/81 BC-69)

DON'T YOU KNOW WHAT THE NIGHT CAN DO? Steve Winwood–Virgin 99290
[Will Jennings/Steve Winwood] [BMI] (8/20/88 BC-5)

DON'T YOU KNOW YOCKOMO? Huey "Piano" Smith with his Clowns–Ace 553
[Huey P. Smith/John Vincent‡] [BMI] (12/8/58 B-56)

DON'T YOU LET ME DOWN Peter Criss–Casablanca 952
[Peter Criss/Stan Penridge] [ASC] (12/30/78 R-97)

DON'T YOU LOVE ME 49ers–4th & Broadway 447 506-0
[Gianfranco Bortolotti/Diego Maria Leoni/Pietro Rossini] [ASC] (6/16/90 BC-77)

DON'T YOU MISS ME A LITTLE BIT BABY Jimmy Ruffin–Soul 35035
[Rodger Penzabene/Barrett Strong/Norman Whitfield] [BMI] (7/22/67 BCR-55)

DON'T YOU WANNA BE MINE Denise Lopez–A&M 75021 1526
[Ted Jacobs/Michael Jay] [BMI] (11/3/90 BC-84)

DON'T YOU WANT ME The Human League–A&M/Virgin 2397
[John William Callis/Philip Oakey/Philip Wright] [ASC] (3/6/82 BCR-1)

DON'T YOU WANT ME Jody Watley–MCA 53162
[David Paul Bryant/Franne Golde/Jody Watley] [BMI] (10/3/87 BC-5)

DON'T YOU WORRY Don Gardner And Dee Dee Ford–Fire 513
[Don Gardner/Morgan C. Robinson] [BMI] (8/25/62 BCR-66)

DON'T YOU WORRY 'BOUT A THING Stevie Wonder–Tamla 54245
[Stevie Wonder] [ASC] (3/30/74 BCR-10)

–DON'T YOU WORRY 'BOUT ME see: OPUS 17

DON'T YOU WRITE HER OFF McGuinn, Clark & Hillman–Capitol 4693
[Robert Hippard/Roger McGuinn] [BMI] (3/17/79 BCR-33)

DOO DOO DOO DOO DOO (HEARTBREAKER) The Rolling Stones–Rolling Stones 19109
[Mick Jagger/Keith Richards] [ASC] (1/12/74 BCR-10)

DO-WAH-DIDDY *The Exciters–United Artists 662*
[Jeff Barry/Ellie Greenwich] [BMI] (1/4/64 BR-78)

DO WAH DIDDY DIDDY *Manfred Mann–Ascot 2157*
[Jeff Barry/Ellie Greenwich] [BMI] (8/29/64 BCR-1)

DO WAH DIDDY DIDDY *Stars On 45–Radio 3863*
[Jeff Barry/Ellie Greenwich] (Med) [BMI] (9/19/81 BCR-55)

DOO WAH DIDDY DIDDY *Tight Fit–Arista 0638*
[Jeff Barry/Ellie Greenwich] (Med) [BMI] (10/10/81 B-89)

THE DOODLE SONG Frankie Miller—Chrysalis 2145 [Francis John Miller] [ASC] (6/25/77 BCR-69)

DOOLEY The Olympics—Arvee 5031 [Cliff Goldsmith/Fred Smith] [BMI] (6/19/61 B-94)

THE DOOR IS OPEN Tommy Hunt—Scepter 1226 [Helen Miller/Freddie Scott] [BMI] (1/1/62 BCR-78)

THE DOOR IS STILL OPEN *The Hilltoppers—Dot 15351 [Chuck Willis] [BMI] (4/4/55 CtRt-16)*

THE DOOR IS STILL OPEN *The Cardinals—Atlantic 1054 [Chuck Willis] [BMI] (4/4/55 Rt-16)*

THE DOOR IS STILL OPEN TO MY HEART *Don Cornell—Coral 61393 [Chuck Willis] (TSW) [BMI] (5/21/55 BCtRt-16)*

THE DOOR IS STILL OPEN TO MY HEART *Dean Martin—Reprise 0307 [Chuck Willis] [BMI] (9/26/64 BCR-6)*

DOOR OF DREAMS Perry Como—RCA Victor 47-6059 [Robert Allen/Al Stillman] [ASC] (3/7/55 CR-23)

THE DOOR TO PARADISE Bobby Rydell—Cameo 201 [Bernie Lowe/Kal Mann/Jose Padilla Sanchez*] [ASC] (10/9/61 BCR-81)

DOOR TO YOUR HEART The Dramatics—Cadet 5704 [Tony Hester] [BMI] (7/27/74 BCR-50)

DORAVILLE Atlanta Rhythm Section—Polydor 14248 [Barry Bailey/Buddy Buie/Robert Nix] [BMI] (9/21/74 BCR-35)

DORMI DORMI DORMI Eydie Gorme—ABC-Paramount 9925 [Sammy Cahn/Harry Warren] [ASC] (5/12/58 R-82)

A DOSE OF ROCK 'N' ROLL Ringo Starr—Atlantic 3361 [Carl Grossman] [BMI] (10/2/76 BCR-26)

DOTTIE Danny And The Juniors—ABC-Paramount 9926 [John Madara/Artie Singer] [BMI] (6/9/58 BCR-41)

DOTTIE I LIKE IT Tommy Roe—ABC 11039 [Tommy Roe] [BMI] (2/10/68 CR-69)

DOUBLE BARREL Dave And Ansil Collins—Big Tree 115 [Ansel Collins*/David Crooks*/Winston Riley] [ASC] (5/29/71 BCR-14)

DOUBLE DUTCH BUS Frankie Smith—WMOT 5356 [William A. Bloom/Frankie Smith] [BMI] (5/16/81 BCR-15)

DOUBLE GOOD EVERYTHING Smokey Robinson—SBK 07370 [Smokey Robinson] [ASC] (10/26/91 BC-84)

DOUBLE LOVIN' The Osmonds—MGM 14259 [Mickey Buckins/George Henry Jackson] [BMI] (5/15/71 BCR-9)

DOUBLE-O-SEVEN The Detergents—Roulette 4603 [Lee Pockriss/Paul Vance] [ASC] (3/20/65 BCR-59)

DOUBLE SHOT (OF MY BABY'S LOVE) Swingin' Medallions—Smash 2033 [Don Smith/Cyril Vetter] [BMI] (4/23/66 BCR-13)

DOUBLE TROUBLE Lynyrd Skynyrd—MCA 40532 [Allen Collins/Ronnie Van Zant] [BMI] (3/20/76 BC-80)

DOUBLE VISION Foreigner—Atlantic 3514 [Lou Gramm/Michael Leslie Jones] [ASC] (9/23/78 BCR-2)

DOUBLE YELLOW LINE The Music Machine—Original Sound 71 [Sean Bonniwell] [BMI] (5/20/67 C-100)

DOUBLEBACK ZZ Top—Warner Bros. 19812 [Frank Beard/Billy Gibbons/Dusty Hill] [BMI] (5/19/90 BC-42)

DOWN AND OUT IN NEW YORK CITY James Brown—Polydor 14168 [Bodie Chandler/Barry De Vorzon] [BMI] (3/10/73 BCR-50)

DOWN AT LULU'S Ohio Express—Buddah 56 [Joey Levine/Kris Resnick] [BMI] (7/27/68 BCR-19)

(DOWN AT) PAPA JOE'S The Dixiebelles—Sound Stage 7 2507 [Jerry Dean Smith] [ASC] (9/28/63 BCR-9)

DOWN BOYS Warrant—Columbia 68606 [Joseph Cagle*/Steven Chamberlin*/Jerry Dixon*/John Oswald/Eric Turner*] [BMI] (4/29/89 BC-27)

DOWN BY THE LAZY RIVER The Osmonds—MGM 14324 [Alan Osmond/Merrill Osmond] [BMI] (1/22/72 BCR-3)

DOWN BY THE OLD MILL STREAM Bruce Hayes with Mary Mayo—Dwain 812 [Tell Taylor] (EP) [NA] (2/15/60 R-63)

DOWN BY THE RIVER *Brooklyn Bridge—Buddah 179 [Neil Young] [BMI] (7/11/70 B-91)*

DOWN BY THE RIVER *Buddy Miles—Mercury 73086 [Neil Young] [BMI] (7/18/70 BCR-68)*

DOWN BY THE RIVER Albert Hammond—Mums 6009 [Albert Hammond/Mike Hazlewood] [ASC] (7/22/72 BCR-64)

DOWN BY THE RIVERSIDE *Les Compagnons De La Chanson—Capitol 4342 [Georges Aber/Pierre Delanoë/Rolf Marbot/Traditional] [NA] (3/7/60 BRt-60) [F]*

DOWN BY THE RIVERSIDE (QU'L FAIT BON VIVRE) *Les Barclay—Mercury 71596 [Georges Aber/Pierre Delanoë/Rolf Marbot/Traditional] [NA] (3/21/60 Rt-78) [F]*

DOWN BY THE STATION The Four Preps—Capitol 4312 [Bruce Belland/Glen Larson] [BMI] (12/14/59 BCR-13)

DOWN HERE ON THE GROUND Lou Rawls—Capitol 2252 [Gale Garnett/Lalo Schifrin] [BMI] (8/31/68 BCR-69)

DOWN HOME Rick Nelson—Decca 31533 [Gerry Goffin/Carole King] [BMI] (9/28/63 R-90)

DOWN IN TENNESSEE Kasenetz-Katz Singing Orchestral Circus—Buddah 52 [Joey Levine/Kris Resnick] [BMI] (7/27/68 C-98)

—DOWN IN THE ALLEY see: DOWN IN THE VALLEY

DOWN IN THE BOONDOCKS Billy Joe Royal—Columbia 43305 [Joe South] [BMI] (7/3/65 BCR-6)

DOWN IN THE BOTTOM OF THE WELL The Wilder Brothers—"X" 0053 [George Wilder/Walter Wilder/Warner Wilder] [ASC] (11/22/54 R-73)

DOWN IN THE VALLEY *Solomon Burke—Atlantic 2147 [Bert Berns/Solomon Burke/Babe Chivian*/Joseph C. Martin*/Traditional] [BMI] (5/26/62 BCR-59)*

DOWN IN THE ALLEY *Ronnie Hawkins—Cotillion 44060 [Bert Berns/Solomon Burke/Babe Chivian*/Joseph C. Martin*/Traditional] [BMI] (1/31/70 BCR-75)*

DOWN IN VIRGINIA Jimmy Reed—Vee-Jay 287 [Ewart Abner*/Jimmy Reed/Mary Lee Reed*] [BMI] (8/11/58 B-93)

DOWN ON LOVE Foreigner—Atlantic 89493 [Lou Gramm/Michael Leslie Jones] [ASC] (8/17/85 BC-54)

DOWN ON ME *Big Brother And The Holding Company—Mainstream 662 [Janis Joplin/Traditional] [ASC] (8/31/68 BCR-43)*

DOWN ON ME *Janis Joplin—Columbia 45630 [Janis Joplin/Traditional] [ASC] (7/8/72 BCR-79)*

DOWN ON MY KNEES The Heartbeats—Roulette 4054 [James Sheppard] [BMI] (4/19/58 C-60)

DOWN ON THE CORNER Creedence Clearwater Revival—Fantasy 634 [John Fogerty] (TSW) [BMI] (10/25/69 BCR-3)

DOWN THE AISLE Ike Clanton—Ace 583 [Rose Brandel/Cynthia Norwood] [BMI] (5/23/60 B-91)

DOWN THE AISLE (WEDDING SONG) Patti Labelle And The Blue Belles—Newtown 5777 [Anthony Levinson] [BMI] (9/7/63 BCR-29)

DOWN THE AISLE OF LOVE The Quin-Tones—Hunt 321 [Phyllis Carr/Carolyn Holmes/Ken Sexton] [BMI] (8/18/58 BCR-20)

DOWN THE HALL The Four Seasons—Warner/Curb 8407 [Bob Gaudio/Judy Parker] [ASC] (7/16/77 BCR-65)

DOWN THE ROAD B.T.O.—Mercury 73987 [Robbie Bachman/James Clench/Blair Thornton/C.F. Turner] [SO] (4/1/78 C-92)

DOWN THE STREET TO 301 Johnny Cash—Sun 343 [Jack H. Clement] [BMI] (7/11/60 B-85)

DOWN TO LOVE TOWN The Originals—Soul 35119 [Don Daniels/Mike Sutton/Kathy Wakefield] [BMI] (10/23/76 BC-47)

DOWN TO THE LINE Bachman-Turner Overdrive—Mercury 73724 [C. Mark Anthony*/Randy Bachman/Alice Cooper*/Kim Fowley*] [BMI] (11/22/75 BCR-38)

DOWN TO THE NIGHTCLUB Tower Of Power—Warner Bros. 7635 [Emilio Castillo/David Garibaldi/Steve Kupka] [ASC] (10/21/72 BCR-66)

DOWN TO THE STATION B.W. Stevenson—Warner Bros. 8343 [Dennis Linde] [BMI] (4/2/77 BCR-76)

DOWN UNDER Men At Work—Columbia 03303 [Colin James Hay/Ron Strykert] [BMI] (11/6/82 BC-1)

DOWN WHERE THE WINDS BLOW (CHILLY WINDS) The Serendipity Singers—Philips 40215 [Bob Bowers/John Madden/Bryan Sennett] [BMI] (8/1/64 C-96)

DOWN YONDER Johnny And The Hurricanes—Big Top 3036 [L. Wolfe Gilbert] [BMI] (5/23/60 BCR-27) [I]

THE DOWNEASTER "ALEXA" Billy Joel—Columbia 73333 [Billy Joel] [ASC] (5/5/90 BC-57)

DOWNTOWN *Petula Clark—Warner Bros. 5494 [Tony Hatch] [ASC] (12/19/64 BCR-1)*

CRAZY DOWNTOWN *(parody of Downtown) Allan Sherman—Warner Bros. 5614 [Tony Hatch/Allan Sherman] [ASC] (3/27/65 BCR-25) [P]*

DOWNTOWN *Mrs. Miller—Capitol 5640 [Tony Hatch] [ASC] (4/30/66 BC-82)*

DOWNTOWN *Dolly Parton—RCA 13756 [Tony Hatch] [ASC] (4/14/84 B-80)*

DOWNTOWN One 2 Many—A&M 1272 [Don Black/Dag Kolsrud/Jan Ovland] [BMI] (3/25/89 BC-37)

DOWNTOWN LIFE Daryl Hall & John Oates—Arista 1-9753 [Sara Allen/Daryl Hall/Rick Iantosca/John Oates] [BMI] (10/1/88 BC-31)

DOWNTOWN TRAIN *Patty Smyth—Columbia 07112 [Tom Waits] [NA] (6/13/87 B-95)*

DOWNTOWN TRAIN *Rod Stewart—Warner Bros. 22685 [Tom Waits] [NA] (11/25/89 BC-1)*

DR. BEN BASEY Mickey Shorr And The Cutups—Tuba 8001 [Dickie Goodman/Mickey Shorr] [NA] (6/16/62 BCR-60)

DR. DO-GOOD The Electric Prunes—Reprise 0594 [Nancie Mantz/Annette Tucker] [BMI] (7/1/67 R-99)

DR. FEELGOOD Mötley Crüe—Elektra 69271 [Mick Mars/Nikki Sixx] [ASC] (9/2/89 BC-5)

DR. HECKYLL & MR. JIVE Men At Work—Columbia 04111 [Colin James Hay] [ASC] (9/17/83 BC-26)

DR. JON (THE MEDICINE MAN) Jon & Robin And The In Crowd—Abnak 127 [Wayne Carson Thompson] [BMI] (2/17/68 BCR-52)

DRAG CITY Jan & Dean—Liberty 55641 [Jan Berry/Roger Christian/Brian Wilson] [BMI] (11/30/63 BCR-10)

DRAG MY BAD NAME DOWN The 4 Of Us—Columbia 73243 [Steven Christopher Mallon/Brendan Philip Murphy/Declan Joseph Murphy/Paul Gerard Murphy] [BMI] (4/21/90 BC-55)

DRAGGIN' THE LINE Tommy James—Roulette 7103 [Tommy James/Robert L. King] [BMI] (6/5/71 BCR-1)

DRAW OF THE CARDS Kim Carnes—EMI America 8087 [Kim Carnes/Bill Cuomo/Dave Ellingson/Val Garay] [ASC] (8/8/81 BCR-25)

DRAW THE LINE Aerosmith—Columbia 10637 [Joe Perry/Steven Tyler] [BMI] (10/15/77 BCR-37)

DREADLOCK HOLIDAY 10 CC—Polydor 14511
[Graham Gouldman/Eric Stewart] [BMI] (9/30/78 BCR-36)

DREAM *Four Aces—Decca 29217 [Johnny Mercer] [ASC] (8/7/54 CR-13)*

DREAM *The Mulcays—Cardinal 1023 [Johnny Mercer] [ASC] (10/4/54 R-PRE)*

DREAM *Betty Johnson—Atlantic 1186 [Johnny Mercer] [ASC] (5/26/58 BCR-45)*

DREAM *Etta James—Argo 5390 [Johnny Mercer] [ASC] (5/22/61 BCR-42)*

DREAM *Dinah Washington—Mercury 71958 [Johnny Mercer] [ASC] (4/23/62 BCR-77)*

DREAM A LITTLE DREAM OF ME Mama Cass With The Mamas & The Papas—Dunhill 4145
[Fabian Andre/Gus Kahn/Wilbur Schwandt] [ASC] (7/6/68 BCR-8)

DREAM ALONG WITH ME (I'M ON MY WAY TO A STAR) Perry Como—RCA Victor 47-6590
[Carl Sigman] [ASC] (7/28/56 BR-47)

DREAM BABY (HOW LONG MUST I DREAM) *Roy Orbison—Monument 456*
[Cindy Walker] [BMI] (2/5/62 BCR-4)

DREAM BABY (HOW LONG MUST I DREAM) *Glen Campbell—Capitol 3062*
[Cindy Walker] [BMI] (3/6/71 BCR-21)

DREAM BOY Annette With The Afterbeats—Buena Vista 374
[Richard Sherman/Robert Sherman] [BMI] (1/30/61 BR-67)

DREAM BOY-DREAM GIRL Cynthia & Johnny O.—MicMac 2539
[Charlie Jimenez] [BMI] (9/1/90 B-53)

DREAM CONCERTO Ferrante & Teicher—United Artists 196
[Arthur Ferrante/Pyotr Ilyich Tchaikovsky/Louis Teicher] [ASC] (12/7/59 R-86) [IWM]

A DREAM GOES ON FOREVER Todd Rundgren—Bearsville 0020
[Todd Rundgren] [BMI] (3/23/74 BCR-46)

THE DREAM (HOLD ON TO YOUR DREAM) Irene Cara—Geffen/Network 29396
[Pete Bellotte/Irene Cara/Giorgio Moroder] [ASC] (12/10/83 BC-37)

THE DREAM IS STILL ALIVE Wilson Phillips—SBK 07356
[Glen Ballard/Chynna Phillips/Carnie Wilson/Wendy Wilson] [ASC] (6/1/91 BC-11)

DREAM LAND Danny Bonaduce—Lion 145 [Bruce Roberts] [BMI] (3/3/73 R-97)

DREAM LOVER *Bobby Darin—Atco 6140 [Bobby Darin] [BMI] (4/18/59 BCR-2)*

DREAM LOVER *The Paris Sisters—MGM 13236 [Bobby Darin] [BMI] (6/13/64 BCR-91)*

DREAM LOVER The Marshall Tucker Band—Capricorn 0300
[Jerry Eubanks/George McCorkle] [BMI] (6/24/78 BCR-75)

DREAM LOVER The Rebel Pebbles—I.R.S. 13821
[Robin Fox/Ashley Hall/Rachel Murray] [BMI] (4/20/91 BC-42)

DREAM ME HOME Mac Davis—Columbia 45773 [Mac Davis] [BMI] (2/10/73 BCR-66)

MR. DREAM MERCHANT *Jerry Butler—Mercury 72721*
[Jerry J. Ross/Larry Weiss] [BMI] (10/21/67 BCR-38)

DREAM MERCHANT *The New Birth—Buddah 470*
[Jerry J. Ross/Larry Weiss] [BMI] (7/5/75 BCR-31)

THE DREAM NEVER DIES Cooper Brothers—Capricorn 0308
[Richard Cooper] [ASC] (10/14/78 BCR-44)

DREAM ON *Aerosmith—Columbia 45894 [Steven Tyler] [BMI] (10/6/73 BCR-32)*

DREAM ON *Aerosmith—Columbia 10278 [Steven Tyler] [BMI] (1/3/76 BCR-6)*

DREAM ON The Righteous Brothers—Haven 7006
[Dennis Lambert/Brian Potter] [BMI] (11/9/74 BCR-32)

DREAM ON LITTLE DREAMER Perry Como—RCA Victor 47-8533
[Fred Burch/Jan Crutchfield] [BMI] (4/10/65 BCR-24)

DREAM POLICE Cheap Trick—Epic 50774 [Rick Nielsen] [BMI] (10/6/79 BCR-26)

DREAM TALK Herb & Betty Warner—Jubilee 5380
[Bugs Bower/Earl Shuman] [ASC] (3/5/60 C-94)

DREAM WEAVER Gary Wright—Warner Bros. 8167 [Gary Wright] [ASC] (1/3/76 BCR-1)

DREAM WORLD The Four Coins—Epic 9276
[Fred Ebb/Larry Wellington] [BMI] (7/21/58 R-83)

DREAM BOAT *The Paulette Sisters—Capitol 3068 [Jack Hoffman] [ASC] (4/11/55 Rt-74)*

DREAMBOAT *5 DeMarco Sisters—Decca 29470 [Jack Hoffman] [ASC] (4/11/55 Rt-74)*

DREAMBOAT *Lou Monte—RCA Victor 47-6072 [Jack Hoffman] [ASC] (4/11/55 Rt-79)*

DREAMBOAT ANNIE Heart—Mushroom 7023
[Ann Wilson/Nancy Wilson] [ASC] (12/11/76 BCR-32)

DREAMER Four Aces—Decca 29989
[Edward Alperson/Michael Carr] [ASC] (6/29/56 BCR-43)

THE DREAMER Neil Sedaka—RCA Victor 47-8209
[Ronnie Grossman] [BMI] (7/27/63 BCR-37)

DREAMER Supertramp—A&M 2269
[Rick Davies/Roger Hodgson] [ASC] (9/20/80 BCR-15)

DREAMER The Association—Elektra 47094 [Moon Martin] [BMI] (1/31/81 BCR-66)

DREAMIN' *Johnny Burnette—Liberty 55258*
[Barry De Vorzon/Ted Ellis] [BMI] (7/9/60 BCR-5)

DREAMIN' *John Schneider—Scotti Brothers 02889*
[Barry De Vorzon/Ted Ellis] [BMI] (5/15/82 BC-45)

DREAMIN' Loleatta Holloway—Gold Mind 4000
[Allan Felder/Norman Harris/Ronnie Tyson] [BMI] (2/5/77 B-72)

DREAMIN' Will To Power—Epic 07199 [Bob Rosenberg] [BMI] (6/27/87 BC-50)

DREAMIN' Vanessa Williams—Wing 871 078
[Michael Forte/Lisa Montgomery/Geneva Paschal] [ASC] (1/7/89 BC-8)

DREAMIN' ABOUT YOU Annette And The Vonnair Sisters—Vista 388
[Gerry Goffin/Carole King] [BMI] (11/27/61 R-85)

DREAMIN' IS EASY Steel Breeze—RCA 13427 [Ken Goorabian] [BMI] (1/15/83 BC-30)

DREAMIN' OF LOVE Stevie B—LMR 74001 [Stevie B] [BMI] (4/16/88 BC-78)

DREAMING Blondie—Chrysalis 2379
[Clement A. Bozewski*/Deborah Harry/Christopher Stein] [ASC] (9/29/79 BCR-20)

DREAMING Cliff Richard—EMI America 8057
[Leo Sayer/Alan Tarney] [ASC] (9/13/80 BCR-7)

DREAMING Orchestral Manoeuvres In The Dark—A&M 3002
[Paul Humphreys/Andrew McCluskey] [ASC] (3/12/88 BC-16)

DREAMING A DREAM Crown Heights Affair—De-Lite 1570
[Britt Britton/Freida Nerangis] [BMI] (8/2/75 BCR-34)

DREAMS Buddy Miles—Mercury 73119 [Gregg Allman] [BMI] (10/10/70 BR-85)

DREAMS Fleetwood Mac—Warner Bros. 8371 [Stevie Nicks] [BMI] (4/16/77 BCR-1)

DREAMS Van Halen—Warner Bros. 28702
[Michael Anthony/Sammy Hagar/Alex Van Halen/Eddie Van Halen] [ASC]
(5/24/86 BC-22)

A DREAM'S A DREAM Soul II Soul—Virgin 98955
[Billie Rae Calvin*/Nellee Hooper/Beresford Romeo] [NA] (6/30/90 BC-81)

DREAMS ARE TEN A PENNY First Class—UK 49028
[John Carter/Gillian Shakespeare] [BMI] (11/9/74 BC-71)

DREAMS OF THE EVERYDAY HOUSEWIFE *Glen Campbell—Capitol 2224*
[Chris Gantry] [BMI] (6/22/68 BCR-32)

DREAMS OF THE EVERYDAY HOUSEWIFE *Wayne Newton—MGM 13955*
[Chris Gantry] [BMI] (6/29/68 BCR-43)

DREAMTIME Daryl Hall—RCA 14387 [John Beeby/Daryl Hall] [BMI] (8/2/86 BC-5)

DREAMY EYES The Four Preps—Capitol 3576
[Bebe Blake/Jack Hoffman] [ASC] (12/22/56 B-56)

DREAMY EYES *Johnny Tillotson—Cadence 1353 [Johnny Tillotson] [BMI] (11/3/58 BR-63)*

DREAMY EYES *Johnny Tillotson—Cadence 1409*
[Johnny Tillotson] [BMI] (11/20/61 BCR-35)

DREIDEL Don McLean—United Artists 51100 [Don McLean] [BMI] (12/23/72 BCR-19)

DRESS YOU UP Madonna—Sire 28919
[Andrea LaRusso/Peggy Stanziale] [ASC] (8/17/85 BC-5)

DRESSED FOR SUCCESS Roxette—EMI 50204 [Per Gessle] [BMI] (5/27/89 BC-14)

DRIFT AWAY Dobie Gray—Decca 33057 [Mentor Williams] [ASC] (2/17/73 BCR-4)

DRIFTIN' BLUES Bobby Bland—Duke 432
[Charles Mose Brown/Johnny Dudley Moore/Eddie Williams] [BMI] (3/9/68 B-96)

DRIFTING AND DREAMING Teddy Tyle, His Saxophone and His Orch.—Golden Crest 500
[Loyal Curtis/Erwin R. Schmidt/Egbert Van Alstyne] [ASC] (5/5/58 R-77) [IM]

DRIFTWOOD The Moody Blues—London 273 [Justin Hayward] [ASC] (11/4/78 BCR-59)

DRINK, DRINK, DRINK Mario Lanza—RCA Victor 447-0775
[Dorothy Donnelly/Sigmund Romberg] [ASC] (10/16/54 CR-29)

THE DRINKING MAN'S DIET Allan Sherman—Warner Bros. 5672
[Neal Hefti/Allan Sherman] [ASC] (12/18/65 B-98)

DRINKING WINE SPO-DEE O'DEE Jerry Lee Lewis—Mercury 73374
[Granville McGhee/J. Mayo Williams*] [ASC] (3/31/73 BCR-25)

DRIP DROP *The Drifters—Atlantic 1187*
[Jerry Leiber/Mike Stoller] [BMI] (8/11/58 B-58)

DRIP DROP *Dion Di Muci—Columbia 42917*
[Jerry Leiber/Mike Stoller] [BMI] (11/16/63 BCR-5)

DRIVE The Cars—Elektra 69706 [Ric Ocasek] [ASC] (8/4/84 BC-3)

DRIVE IN SHOW Eddie Cochran—Liberty 55087 [Fred Dexter] [BMI] (9/16/57 B-82)

DRIVE MY CAR *Bob Kuban And The In-Men—Musicland U.S.A. 20,007*
[John Lennon/Paul McCartney] [ASC] (7/16/66 BC-93)

DRIVE MY CAR *Gary Toms Empire—Pickwick Int'l 6509*
[John Lennon/Paul McCartney] [ASC] (11/22/75 BC-69)

DRIVE MY CAR *Stars On 45—Radio 3810*
[John Lennon/Paul McCartney] (Med) [ASC] (4/11/81 BCR-1)

DRIVEN OUT The Fixx—RCA 8837
[Dan Brown/Cy Curnin/Peter John Greenall/Jamie West-Oram/Adam Woods] [ASC]
(2/18/89 BC-47)

DRIVER'S SEAT Sniff 'N' The Tears—Atlantic 3604
[Paul N. Roberts] [BMI] (7/21/79 BCR-10)

DRIVIN' HOME Duane Eddy And The Rebels—Jamie 1195
[Duane Eddy/Larry Knechtel] [BMI] (7/17/61 BCR-65) [I]

DRIVIN' HOME Jerry Smith—Decca 32679 [Jerry Dean Smith] [ASC] (6/27/70 CR-94) [I]

DRIVIN' MY LIFE AWAY Eddie Rabbitt—Elektra 46656
[David Malloy/Eddie Rabbitt/Even Stevens] [BMI] (6/21/80 BCR-5)

DRIVIN' WHEEL Foghat—Bearsville 0313
[Dave Peverett/Roderick Price] [ASC] (11/20/76 BCR-34)

DRIVING WHEEL Little Junior Parker—Duke 335
[Roosevelt Sykes] [BMI] (4/24/61 BCR-85)

DROP BY MY PLACE Little Carl Carlton—Back Beat 613
[Jo Armstead/Fred Bridges*/Bobby Eaton*/Richard Knight*/Andrew Terry*] [BMI]
(7/11/70 BCR-64)

DROP THE PILOT Joan Armatrading—A&M 2538
[Joan Armatrading] [BMI] (5/28/83 BC-78)

DROWN IN MY OWN TEARS Don Shirley—Cadence 1408
[Henry Glover] [BMI] (1/6/62 BR-98) [I]

DROWNIN' MY SORROWS Connie Francis—MGM 13160
[Hank Hunter/Stan Vincent] [BMI] (7/27/63 BCR-26)

DROWNING IN THE SEA OF LOVE Joe Simon—Spring 120 [Kenneth Gamble/Leon Huff] [BMI] (11/13/71 BCR-6)

THE DRUM Bobby Sherman—Metromedia 217 [Alan O'Day] [BMI] (5/1/71 BCR-16)

DRUM STOMP Sandy Nelson—Imperial 5829 [Sandy Nelson/Richard Podolor] [BMI] (5/26/62 BC-86) [I]

DRUMMER MAN Nancy Sinatra—Reprise 0851 [Murray Wecht] [BMI] (9/13/69 BC-96)

DRUMMIN' UP A STORM Sandy Nelson—Imperial 5829 [Richard Podolor] [BMI] (4/28/62 B-67) [I]

DRUMS Kenny Chandler—United Artists 342 [Jerry Leiber/Mike Stoller] [BMI] (8/21/61 R-100)

DRUMS Jon & Robin—Abnak 122 [Wayne Carson Thompson] [BMI] (8/12/67 BR-80)

DRUMS ARE MY BEAT Sandy Nelson—Imperial 5809 [Sandy Nelson] [BMI] (2/5/62 BCR-29) [I]

DRY YOUR EYES Brenda & The Tabulations—Dionn 500 [Maurice Coates/Brenda J. Payton] [BMI] (2/25/67 BCR-16)

—DUB BE GOOD TO ME see: JUST BE GOOD TO ME

DUBUQUE BLUES The Association—Warner Bros.-Seven Arts 7349 [Jules Alexander] [BMI] (11/22/69 CR-81)

—DUCHESS OF EARL see: DUKE OF EARL

THE DUCK Jackie Lee (2)—Mirwood 5502 [Earl Nelson/Fred Smith] [BMI] (11/13/65 BCR-12)

DUDE (LOOKS LIKE A LADY) Aerosmith—Geffen 28240 [Desmond Child/Joe Perry/Steven Tyler] [ASC] (10/3/87 BC-14)

THE DUDELSACK SONG (PLAY TO ME MY DARLING) The Chordettes—Cadence 1259 [Archie Bleyer/Klaus-Günter Neumann] [NA] (3/28/55 R-73)

DUELING BANJOS *"Deliverance" Soundtrack—Warner Bros. 7659 [Traditional] [BMI] (1/6/73 BCR-1) [I]*

DUELING TUBAS *(parody of Dueling Banjos) Martin Mull and Orchestra—Capricorn 0019 [Traditional] [NA] (5/5/73 BR-92) [P, I]*

—DUELING TUBAS see: DUELING BANJOS

DUKE OF EARL *Gene Chandler—Vee-Jay 416 [Gene Chandler/Earl Edwards/Bernice Williams] [BMI] (1/6/62 BCR-1)*

DUCHESS OF EARL *(response to Duke Of Earl) Bobbie Smith & The Dreamgirls—Big Top 3100 [Gene Chandler/Earl Edwards/Bernice Williams] [BMI] (3/5/62 Rt*-72) [R]*

DUCHESS OF EARL *(response to Duke Of Earl) The Pearlettes—Vee-Jay 435 [Gene Chandler/Earl Edwards/Bernice Williams] [BMI] (3/5/62 BCRt-72) [R]*

DUKEY STICK (PT. 2) George Duke—Epic 50531 [George Duke] [ASC] (5/27/78 R-91)

—DUM-DE-DA see: SHE UNDERSTANDS ME

DUM DUM Brenda Lee—Decca 31272 [Jackie DeShannon/Sharon Sheeley] [BMI] (6/19/61 BCR-3)

DUM DUM DEE DUM Johnny Cymbal—Kapp 539 [Marvin Moore/Bernie Wayne] [BMI] (7/27/63 BCR-74)

—DUM-DUM see: HAPPY SONG

DUMB HEAD Ginny Arnell—MGM 13177 [David Hess/Camille Monte] [ASC] (11/16/63 BCR-49)

DUMPLIN'S *Doc Bagby—Okeh 7089 [Harry Bagby/Irving Nahan*] [NA] (9/2/57 BCRt-47) [I]*

DUMPLIN'S *Ernie Freeman—Imperial 5461 [Harry Bagby/Irving Nahan*] [NA] (9/2/57 BRt-60) [I]*

DUNCAN Paul Simon—Columbia 45638 [Paul Simon] [BMI] (7/1/72 BCR-50)

DUNGAREE DOLL Eddie Fisher—RCA Victor 47-6337 [Sherman Edwards/Ben Raleigh] [ASC] (12/1/55 BCR-7)

DUSIC Brick—Bang 734 [James B. Brown/Regi Hargis/Ray Ransom] [ASC] (9/3/77 BCR-18)

DUST GOT IN DADDY'S EYES Bobby Bland—Duke 390 [Deadric Malone/Joe Scott] [BMI] (5/1/65 C-99)

DUST IN THE WIND Kansas—Kirshner 4274 [Kerry Livgren] [BMI] (1/28/78 BCR-3)

DUSTY The Rag Dolls—Mala 493 [Bob Crewe/Sandy Linzer/Denny Randell] [BMI] (1/16/65 BCR-48)

DUTCHMAN'S GOLD Walter Brennan With Billy Vaughn And His Orchestra—Dot 16066 [Jerry Capehart] [BMI] (4/18/60 BCR-27)

DUVID CROCKETT (THE BALLAD OF DAVY CROCKETT) (parody similar to Big Bad John and Ringo) Mickey Katz And His Orchestra—Capitol 3144 [Tom Blackburn/George Bruns/Mickey Katz] [BMI] (7/2/55 C-44) [P]

D'YER MAK'ER Led Zeppelin—Atlantic 2986 [John Bonham/John Paul Jones/Jimmy Page*/Robert Plant] [ASC] (10/13/73 BCR-15)

DYNAMITE Brenda Lee—Decca 30333 [Mort Garson/Tom Glazer] [ASC] (6/15/57 BCR-54)

DYNAMITE! Stacy Lattisaw—Cotillion 45015 [Bunny Hull/Narada Michael Walden] [BMI] (7/12/80 R-94)

DYNAMITE Jermaine Jackson—Arista 1-9190 [Andy Goldmark/Bruce Roberts] [ASC] (7/21/84 BC-15)

DYNAMITE WOMAN Sir Douglas Quintet—Smash 2233 [Doug Sahm] [BMI] (7/26/69 BCR-78)

DYNOMITE - PART I Tony Camillo's Bazuka—A&M 1666 [Tony Camillo] [BMI] (4/12/75 BCR-10) [I]

E

EACH AND EVERY TIME Sweet Sensation—Atco 98906 [Ken Cedar/Arnie Roman] [ASC] (10/20/90 BC-59)

EACH WORD'S A BEAT OF MY HEART Mink DeVille—Atlantic 89750 [Willy DeVille] [BMI] (2/11/84 B-89)

EAGLES FLY Sammy Hagar—Geffen 28185 [Sammy Hagar] [ASC] (10/24/87 BC-81)

EARACHE MY EYE (FEATURING ALICE BOWIE) Cheech & Chong—Ode 66102 [Tommy Chong/Gaye Delorme/Cheech Marin] [ASC] (8/10/74 BCR-4)

EARLY EVERY MORNING (EARLY EVERY EVENING TOO) Dinah Washington—Mercury 71778 [Belford Hendricks/Clyde Otis] [BMI] (2/27/61 BCR-60)

EARLY IN THE MORNIN' Ray Charles—Atlantic 2094 [Dallas Bartley/Leo Hickman/Louis Jordan] [BMI] (3/18/61 CR-83)

EARLY IN THE MORNING *The Rinky-Dinks (Dash is important)—Atco 6121 [Bobby Darin/Woody Harris] [BMI] (7/14/58 BCtRt-23)*

EARLY IN THE MORNING *Buddy Holly / The Crickets—Coral 62006 [Bobby Darin/Woody Harris] [BMI] (7/14/58 BCtRt-23)*

EARLY IN THE MORNING Vanity Fare—Page One 21,027 [Mike Leander/Ed Seago] [BMI] (11/8/69 BCR-9)

EARLY IN THE MORNING *The Gap Band—Total Experience 8201 [Lonnie Simmons/Rudy Taylor/Charles K. Wilson] [BMI] (5/22/82 BC-24)*

EARLY IN THE MORNING *Robert Palmer—EMI-Manhattan 50157 [Lonnie Simmons/Rudy Taylor/Charles K. Wilson] [BMI] (10/22/88 BC-19)*

—EARLY IN THE MORNING see: SHE LETS HER HAIR DOWN

EARLY MORNING LOVE Sammy Johns—GRC 2021 [Sammy Johns] [BMI] (9/14/74 BCR-41)

EARLY MORNING RAIN Peter, Paul & Mary—Warner Bros. 5659 [Gordon Lightfoot] [ASC] (10/9/65 BCR-91)

EARTH ANGEL (WILL YOU BE MINE) *The Penguins—DooTone 348 [Jesse Belvin/Gaynel Hodge/Curtis Edward Williams] [BMI] (12/25/54 BCtRt-2)*

EARTH ANGEL *Les Baxter & The Bombers—Capitol 3002 [Jesse Belvin/Gaynel Hodge/Curtis Edward Williams] [BMI] (12/27/54 Rt-PRE)*

EARTH ANGEL (WILL YOU BE MINE) *Gloria Mann—Sound 109 [Jesse Belvin/Gaynel Hodge/Curtis Edward Williams] [BMI] (1/10/55 BRt-9)*

EARTH ANGEL (WILL YOU BE MINE) *The Crew-Cuts—Mercury 70529 [Jesse Belvin/Gaynel Hodge/Curtis Edward Williams] (TSW) [BMI] (4/9/55 BCtRt-2)*

EARTH ANGEL *Johnny Tillotson—Cadence 1377 [Jesse Belvin/Gaynel Hodge/Curtis Edward Williams] [BMI] (4/9/60 BCR-57)*

EARTH ANGEL *The Cleftones—Gee 1074 [Jesse Belvin/Gaynel Hodge/Curtis Edward Williams] [BMI] (11/13/61 R-96)*

EARTH ANGEL (WILL YOU BE MINE) *The Vogues—Reprise 0820 [Jesse Belvin/Gaynel Hodge/Curtis Edward Williams] [BMI] (4/12/69 BCR-24)*

EARTH ANGEL *Fred Parris & The Five Satins—Elektra 47411 [Jesse Belvin/Gaynel Hodge/Curtis Edward Williams] (Med) [BMI] (2/27/82 BC-71)*

EARTH ANGEL *New Edition—MCA 52905 [Jesse Belvin/Gaynel Hodge/Curtis Edward Williams] [BMI] (8/16/86 BC-21)*

EARTHBOUND *Sammy Davis Jr.—Decca 30035 [Bob Musel/Clive Richardson/Jack Taylor] [BMI] (8/18/56 BCtRt-30)*

EARTHBOUND *Mario Lanza—RCA Victor 47-6644 [Bob Musel/Clive Richardson/Jack Taylor] [BMI] (9/15/56 BCtRt-30)*

EARTHBOUND *Roberto & His Orchestra—Coral 61673 [Bob Musel/Clive Richardson/Jack Taylor] [BMI] (9/15/56 Rt-30) [IWM]*

EASE BACK The Meters—Josie 1008 [Joseph Modeliste/Art Neville/Leo Nocentelli/George Porter] [BMI] (7/19/69 BCR-55) [I]

EASE ON DOWN THE ROAD *Consumer Rapport—Wing & A Prayer 101 [Charlie Smalls] [BMI] (4/12/75 BCR-41)*

EASE ON DOWN THE ROAD *Diana Ross & Michael Jackson—MCA 40947 [Charlie Smalls] [BMI] (9/2/78 BCR-36)*

EASIER SAID THAN DONE The Essex—Roulette 4494 [Larry Huff/William Linton] [BMI] (6/1/63 BCR-1)

EAST WEST Herman's Hermits—MGM 13639 [Graham Gouldman] [BMI] (12/3/66 BCR-12)

EASTER PARADE *Rosemary Clooney—Columbia J-234 [Irving Berlin] [ASC] (4/11/55 Rt-75)*

EASTER PARADE *Guy Lombardo And His Royal Canadians—Decca 23817 [Irving Berlin] [ASC] (4/11/55 Rt-75)*

EASTER PARADE *Bing Crosby—Decca 23819 [Irving Berlin] [ASC] (4/11/55 Rt-75)*

EASTER PARADE *Harry James & His Orchestra—Columbia 36545 [Irving Berlin] [ASC] (4/11/55 Rt-75) [IWM]*

EASY Commodores—Motown 1418 [Lionel Richie] [ASC] (5/28/77 BCR-4)

EASY AS PIE Billy "Crash" Craddock—ABC/Dot 17584 [Rory Bourke/Gene Dobbins/Johnny Wilson] [ASC] (12/13/75 BC-52)

EASY COME, EASY GO Bobby Sherman—Metromedia 177 [Diane Hilderbrand/Jack Keller] [ASC] (2/7/70 BCR-5)

EASY COME, EASY GO The Spinners—Atlantic 3462 [Leroy Bell/Thom Bell/Casey James] [BMI] (2/18/78 R-89)

EASY COME, EASY GO Winger—Atlantic 87773 [Kip Winger] [BMI] (2/9/91 BC-35)

EASY DOES IT Jaye P. Morgan—RCA Victor 47-7326
[Kenny Jacobson/Rhoda Roberts] [ASC] (9/15/58 R-98)

EASY DRIVER Kenny Loggins—Columbia 10866
[David Plehn/Jerry Riopelle] [BMI] (12/2/78 BCR-54)

***EASY EVIL** John Kay—Dunhill 4360 [Alan O'Day] [ASC] (9/8/73 CR-92)*

***EASY EVIL** Travis Wammack—Capricorn 0242 [Alan O'Day] [ASC] (9/27/75 BCR-72)*

EASY FOR YOU TO SAY Linda Ronstadt—Asylum 69838
[Jimmy Webb] [ASC] (4/23/83 BC-54)

EASY LIVIN' Uriah Heep—Mercury 73307 [Ken Hensley] [ASC] (7/22/72 BCR-32)

EASY LOVE Dionne Warwick—Arista 0572
[Randy Cate/Steve Dorff/Larry Herbstritt] [BMI] (11/22/80 BCR-62)

EASY LOVER Philip Bailey—Columbia 04679
[Philip Bailey/Phil Collins/Nathan East] [ASC] (11/24/84 BC-1)

EASY LOVIN' Wade Flemons—Vee-Jay 344 [Jesse Stone] [BMI] (4/16/60 BCR-70)

EASY LOVING Freddie Hart—Capitol 3115 [Freddie Hart] [BMI] (8/21/71 BCR-12)

EASY MONEY REO Speedwagon—Epic 50764 [Gary Richrath] [ASC] (9/29/79 R-88)

EASY RIDER (LET THE WIND PAY THE WAY) Iron Butterfly—Atco 6782
[Ron Bushy/Lee Dorman/Robert Edmondson/Doug Ingle] [BMI] (10/17/70 BCR-64)

EASY STREET The Edgar Winter Group—Epic 50034
[Dan Hartman] [BMI] (10/5/74 BCR-83)

EASY TO BE FREE Rick Nelson—Decca 732635 [Rick Nelson] [BMI] (3/7/70 BCR-44)

***EASY TO BE HARD** Three Dog Night—Dunhill 4203
[Galt MacDermot/James Rado/Gerome Ragni] [ASC] (8/2/69 BCR-1)*

***EASY TO BE HARD** Hair (Original Soundtrack)/Cheryl Barnes—RCA 11548
[Galt MacDermot/James Rado/Gerome Ragni] [ASC] (4/28/79 BC-64)*

EASY TO LOVE Leo Sayer—Warner Bros. 8502
[Albert Hammond/Leo Sayer] [ASC] (12/3/77 BCR-31)

EASY TO LOVE AGAIN Carole Bayer Sager—Boardwalk 118
[Burt Bacharach/Carole Bayer Sager] [ASC] (9/5/81 C-76)

EASY WAY OUT Roy Orbison—Asylum 46048
[Richard Brannan/Frank Saulino/Jim Valentini] [ASC] (6/16/79 C-92)

—EAT IT see: BEAT IT

EAT MY SHORTS Rick Dees—Atlantic 89601
[Rick Dees/Mondo Fax] [NA] (12/1/84 BC-66)

EATEN ALIVE Diana Ross—RCA 14181
[Barry Gibb/Maurice Gibb/Michael Jackson] [BMI] (9/21/85 BC-77)

***EBB TIDE** Roy Hamilton—Epic 9068
[Robert Maxwell/Carl Sigman] [ASC] (10/4/54 R-PRE)*

***EBB TIDE** Bobby Freeman—Josie 872
[Robert Maxwell/Carl Sigman] [ASC] (11/21/59 BCtRt-46)*

***EBB TIDE** Roy Hamilton—Epic 9068
[Robert Maxwell/Carl Sigman] [ASC] (11/30/59 CtRt-46)*

***EBB TIDE** The Platters Featuring Tony Williams—Mercury 71624
[Robert Maxwell/Carl Sigman] [ASC] (5/9/60 BCR-37)*

***EBB TIDE** Lenny Welch—Cadence 1422
[Robert Maxwell/Carl Sigman] [ASC] (3/21/64 BCR-20)*

***EBB TIDE** The Righteous Brothers—Philles 130
[Robert Maxwell/Carl Sigman] [ASC] (11/27/65 BCR-4)*

EBONY AND IVORY Paul McCartney—Columbia 02860
[Paul McCartney] [ASC] (4/10/82 BCR-1)

EBONY EYES The Everly Brothers—Warner Bros. 5199
[John D. Loudermilk] [BMI] (1/23/61 BCR-6)

EBONY EYES Bob Welch—Capitol 4543 [Bob Welch] [ASC] (1/28/78 BCR-10)

EBONY EYES Rick James featuring Smokey Robinson—Gordy 1714
[Rick James] [ASC] (12/10/83 BC-43)

ECHO The Emotions (1)—Kapp 490
[Henry Boye/Dom Collura*/Larry Cusimano*/Joe Favale/Tony Maltese*/Joe Negro*] [BMI] (11/17/62 BCR-55)

ECHO PARK Keith Barbour—Epic 10486 [Buzz Clifford] [BMI] (9/20/69 BCR-33)

ECHOES OF LOVE The Doobie Brothers—Warner Bros. 8471
[Willie Mitchell/Earl Randle/Patrick Simmons] [BMI] (10/8/77 BCR-66)

ECSTASY Ben E. King—Atco 6215 [Doc Pomus/Phil Spector] [BMI] (1/29/62 BCR-50)

ECSTASY Ohio Players—Westbound 216
[Leroy Bonner/Marshall Jones/Ralph Middlebrooks/Walter Morrison/ Bruce Napier*/Andrew Noland/Marvin Pierce*/Greg Webster] [BMI] (8/4/73 BCR-31)

***EDDIE MY LOVE** The Teen Queens—RPM 453
[Aaron Collins/Maxwell Davis/Sam Ling‡] [BMI] (2/17/56 BCtRt-4)*

***EDDIE MY LOVE** The Fontane Sisters with Billy Vaughn's Orchestra—Dot 15450
[Aaron Collins/Maxwell Davis/Sam Ling‡] [BMI] (3/2/56 BCtRt-4)*

***EDDIE MY LOVE** The Chordettes—Cadence 1284
[Aaron Collins/Maxwell Davis/Sam Ling‡] [BMI] (3/3/56 BCtRt-4)*

EDDIE'S LOVE Eddie Kendricks—Tamla 54218
[Leonard Caston/Anita Poree] [BMI] (6/10/72 BC-77)

EDGE OF A BROKEN HEART Vixen—EMI 50141
[Richard Marx/Fee Waybill] [ASC] (9/17/88 BC-26)

EDGE OF A DREAM Joe Cocker—Capitol 5412
[Bryan Adams/Jim Vallance] [BMI] (10/20/84 BC-63)

THE EDGE OF HEAVEN Wham!—Columbia 06182 [George Michael] [ASC] (7/5/86 BC-10)

EDGE OF SEVENTEEN (JUST LIKE THE WHITE WINGED DOVE) Stevie Nicks—Modern 7401
[Stevie Nicks] [BMI] (2/20/82 BCR-11)

EDGE OF THE UNIVERSE Bee Gees—RSO 880
[Barry Gibb/Robin Gibb] [BMI] (7/23/77 BCR-26)

EDIE (CIAO BABY) The Cult—Sire 22873 [Ian Astbury/Billy Duffy] [ASC] (9/30/89 B-93)

EEFANANNY The Ardells—Epic 9621 [Jerry Reed] [BMI] (9/28/63 CR-85)

EENIE MEENIE Jeffrey Osborne—A&M 2530
[Raymond Pounds/Michael Sembello] [ASC] (3/12/83 BC-68)

THE EGGPLANT THAT ATE CHICAGO Dr. West's Medicine Show And Junk Band—Go Go 100
[Norman Greenbaum] [BMI] (11/12/66 BCR-52)

EGO Elton John—MCA 40892 [Elton John/Bernie Taupin] [BMI] (4/15/78 BCR-22)

EH! CUMPARI Gaylord & Holiday—Prodigal 0622
[Archie Bleyer/Julius La Rosa/Traditional] [BMI] (2/21/76 BCR-72)

EH MARIE EH MARIE Lou Monte—RCA Victor 47-7265
[Wandra Merrell] [BMI] (6/14/58 CR-58)

8 X 10 Bill Anderson—Decca 31521
[Bill Anderson/Walter Haynes] [BMI] (8/10/63 BCR-53)

EIGHT DAYS A WEEK The Beatles—Capitol 5371
[John Lennon/Paul McCartney] [ASC] (2/20/65 BCR-1)

853-5937 Squeeze—A&M 2994 [Chris Difford/Glenn Tilbrook] [ASC] (12/19/87 BC-32)

EIGHT MEN, FOUR WOMEN O.V. Wright—Back Beat 580
[Deadric Malone] [BMI] (4/15/67 BCR-60)

EIGHT MILES HIGH The Byrds—Columbia 43578
[Gene Clark/David Crosby/Roger McGuinn] [BMI] (4/2/66 BCR-12)

867-5309/JENNY Tommy Tutone—Columbia 02646
[Alex Call/Jim Keller] [BMI] (1/23/82 BCR-4)

EIGHTEEN Connie Francis—MGM 12490
[Bradford Boobis/Neil Nephew] [NA] (6/15/57 R-54)

EIGHTEEN Alice Cooper—Warner Bros. 7449
[Michael Bruce/Glen Buxton/Alice Cooper/Dennis Dunaway/Neal Smith] [BMI] (2/20/71 BCR-18)

18 AND LIFE Skid Row—Atlantic 88883 [Rachel Bolan/Dave Sabo] [ASC] (7/8/89 BC-4)

1812 OVERTURE The Royal Philharmonic Orchestra—RCA 12304
[Pyotr Ilyich Tchaikovsky] (Med) [NA] (10/31/81 BCR-9) [I]

EIGHTEEN WITH A BULLET Pete Wingfield—Island 026
[Pete Wingfield] [ASC] (8/23/75 BCR-14)

18 YELLOW ROSES Bobby Darin—Capitol 4970 [Bobby Darin] [BMI] (5/4/63 BCR-10)

8TH WONDER Sugarhill Gang—Sugar Hill 553
[Cheryl Cook/Ronald LaPread] [BMI] (2/7/81 BC-82)

THE 81 Candy And The Kisses—Cameo 336
[Kenneth Gamble/Jerry J. Ross] [BMI] (11/14/64 BCR-39)

—EL AMOR see: IN MY ROOM

EL BIMBO Bimbo Jet—Scepter 12406 [Claude Ganem] [ASC] (5/24/75 BC-43) [I]

EL CONDOR PASA Simon & Garfunkel—Columbia 45237
[Daniel Robles/Paul Simon] [BMI] (9/5/70 BCR-11)

EL MATADOR The Kingston Trio—Capitol 4338
[Jane Bowers/Lord Burgess] [BMI] (2/15/60 BCR-32)

EL PASO Marty Robbins—Columbia 41511 [Marty Robbins] [BMI] (11/9/59 BCR-1)

EL PITO (I'LL NEVER GO BACK TO GEORGIA) The Joe Cuba Sextet—Tico 470
[Joe Cuba*/Jaime Sabater] [BMI] (7/30/66 CR-96)

EL PUSSY CAT Mongo Santamaria—Columbia 43171
[Bobby Capers] [BMI] (3/6/65 B-97) [I]

EL RANCHO ROCK The Champs—Challenge 59007
[Silvano R. Ramos] [NA] (5/5/58 BCR-15) [IM]

—EL SOLO TORRO see: LONELY BULL

EL WATUSI Ray Barretto y su Charanga Moderna—Tico 419
[Ray Barretto] [BMI] (4/6/63 BCR-17) [F]

***ELEANOR RIGBY** The Beatles—Capitol 5715
[John Lennon/Paul McCartney] [ASC] (8/20/66 BCR-11)*

***ELEANOR RIGBY** Ray Charles—ABC/TRC 11090
[John Lennon/Paul McCartney] [ASC] (6/8/68 BCR-26)*

***ELEANOR RIGBY** Aretha Franklin—Atlantic 2683
[John Lennon/Paul McCartney] [ASC] (11/8/69 BCR-17)*

ELECTED Alice Cooper—Warner Bros. 7631
[Michael Bruce/Glen Buxton/Alice Cooper/Dennis Dunaway/Neal Smith] [BMI] (9/30/72 BCR-16)

ELECTION DAY Arcadia—Capitol 5501
[Simon Le Bon/Nick Rhodes/Roger Taylor] [ASC] (10/26/85 BC-6)

ELECTRIC AVENUE Eddy Grant—Portrait 37-03793 [Eddy Grant] [ASC] (4/16/83 BC-1)

ELECTRIC BLUE Icehouse—Chrysalis 43201
[Iva Davies/John Oates] [ASC] (2/13/88 BC-7)

ELECTRIC BOOGIE Marcia Griffiths—Mango 126
[Neville Livingston] [ASC] (12/9/89 BC-47)

ELECTRIC KINGDOM Twilight 22—Vanguard 35241
[Gordon Bahary/Errol Moore/Joe Saulter] [ASC] (12/17/83 BC-79)

ELECTRIC STORIES
The 4 Seasons Featuring The "Sound" Of Frankie Valli—Philips 40577
[Sandy Linzer/Mike Petrillo] [BMI] (12/14/68 BCR-38)

ELECTRIC YOUTH Debbie Gibson—Atlantic 88919
[Debbie Gibson] [ASC] (4/1/89 BC-9)

ELECTRICLAND Bad Company—Swan Song 99966 [Paul Rodgers] [ASC] (10/2/82 BC-74)

THE ELECTRONIC MAGNETISM (THAT'S HEAVY, BABY) Solomon Burke—MGM 14221
[Bernadine Burke/Melanie Burke/Solomon Burke Jr.] [BMI] (3/13/71 BC-95)

ELENA Marc Tanner Band—Elektra 46003
[Nat Jeffrey/Jeff Monday/Marc Tanner] [ASC] (3/3/79 BCR-45)

ELENORE The Turtles—White Whale 276
[John Barbata/Howard Kaylan/Al Nichol/Jim Pons/Mark Volman] [BMI]
(9/21/68 BCR-5)

ELEPHANT WALK *The Kings (2)—RCA Victor 47-7419 [Jack Gale] [BMI] (12/22/58 Rt-80)*

ELEPHANT WALK *The Chords—Metro 20015 [Jack Gale] [BMI] (3/9/59 Rt-91)*

ELEPHANTS TANGO The Commanders With Eddie Grady—Decca 29323
[Bernie Landes] [BMI] (2/5/55 CR-36)

ELEVATE MY MIND Stereo MC's—4th & Broadway 447 519-1
[Robert Birch/Nick Hallam] [BMI] (6/1/91 B-39)

ELEVATOR OPERATOR The Rays—XYZ 2001 [Bob Crewe/Frank Slay] [BMI] (9/15/58 R-93)

ELEVENTH HOUR MELODY *Al Hibbler—Decca 29789*
[King Palmer/Carl Sigman] [ASC] (1/20/56 BCtRt-11)*

ELEVENTH HOUR MELODY *Lou Busch and His Orchestra—Capitol 3349*
[King Palmer/Carl Sigman] [ASC] (2/10/56 BCtRt-11)*

11TH HOUR MELODY *Bill Snyder—Decca 29827*
[King Palmer/Carl Sigman*] [ASC] (3/2/56 Rt-11) [IWM]*

ELI'S COMING Three Dog Night—Dunhill 4215 [Laura Nyro] [BMI] (10/18/69 BCR-7)

ELIZABETH Dave Ford And The Hollywood Flames—Goldie 1101
[John Bobby Berry/Don Covay/Dave Ford/Curtis Edward Williams] [BMI] (8/25/62 R-84)

ELOISE Kay Thompson—Cadence 1286
[Kay Thompson/Robert Wells] [ASC] (3/10/56 B-39)

ELOISE Barry Ryan—MGM 14010 [Paul Ryan] [BMI] (12/21/68 BCR-50)

ELUSIVE BUTTERFLY Bob Lind—World Pacific 77808 [Bob Lind] [BMI] (1/22/66 BCR-5)

ELVIRA *Dallas Frazier—Capitol 5560 [Dallas Frazier] [BMI] (4/30/66 BCR-72)*

ELVIRA *The Oak Ridge Boys—MCA 51084 [Dallas Frazier] [BMI] (5/9/81 BCR-1)*

EMERGENCY Kool & The Gang—De-Lite 884199
[Clifford Adams/Robert Bell/Ronald Bell/James Bonneford/George M. Brown/
Robert Mickens/Michael Ray/Claydes Smith/J.T. Taylor/Dennis Thomas/
Curtis Fitzgerald Williams] [BMI] (10/26/85 BC-18)

EMINENCE FRONT The Who—Warner Bros. 29814
[Pete Townshend] [GL] (12/25/82 BC-68)

EMMA Hot Chocolate—Big Tree 16031 [Errol Brown/Tony Wilson] [ASC] (1/25/75 BCR-4)

EMMARETTA Deep Purple—Tetragrammaton 1519
[Ritchie Blackmore/Rod Evans/Jon Lord] [ASC] (3/15/69 CR-93)

EMOTION Helen Reddy—Capitol 4021
[Patti Dahlstrom/Veronique Sanson] [ASC] (2/1/75 BCR-22) [FDE]

EMOTION Samantha Sang—Private Stock 45,178
[Barry Gibb/Robin Gibb] [BMI] (11/12/77 BCR-1)

EMOTION Barbra Streisand—Columbia 04707 [Peter S. Bliss] [ASC] (3/9/85 BC-79)

EMOTION IN MOTION Ric Ocasek—Geffen 28617 [Ric Ocasek] [ASC] (9/6/86 BC-15)

EMOTIONAL RESCUE The Rolling Stones—Rolling Stones 20001
[Mick Jagger/Keith Richards] [ASC] (7/5/80 BCR-3)

EMOTIONS Brenda Lee—Decca 31195
[Ramsey Kearney/Mel Tillis] [BMI] (12/31/60 BCR-3)

EMOTIONS Mariah Carey—Columbia 73977
[Mariah Carey/Robert Clivillés/David Cole] [ASC] (8/31/91 BC-1)

EMOTIONS IN MOTION Billy Squier—Capitol 5135 [Billy Squier] [ASC] (7/31/82 BC-61)

THE EMPEROR'S NEW CLOTHES Sinead O'Connor—Ensign/Chrysalis 23528
[Sinead O'Connor] [BMI] (6/23/90 BC-57)

EMPIRE STRIKES BACK (MEDLEY) Meco—RSO 1038
[John Williams] [BMI] (6/14/80 BCR-9) [I]

EMPTY ARMS *Ivory Joe Hunter—Atlantic 1128*
[Ivory Joe Hunter] [BMI] (3/30/57 BCtRt-15)

EMPTY ARMS *Teresa Brewer—Coral 61805 [Ivory Joe Hunter] [BMI] (3/30/57 BCtRt-15)*

EMPTY ARMS *Sonny James—Capitol 3015 [Ivory Joe Hunter] [BMI] (4/10/71 B-93)*

EMPTY BEACH Tricia Leigh Fisher—Atco 98932 [Dennis East] [ASC] (8/25/90 BC-69)

EMPTY GARDEN (HEY HEY JOHNNY) Elton John—Geffen 50049
[Elton John/Bernie Taupin] [BMI] (3/20/82 BCR-12)

EMPTY PAGES Traffic—United Artists 50692
[Jim Capaldi*/Steve Winwood] [BMI] (9/5/70 BCR-57)

ENAMORADO Keith Colley—Unical 3006
[Keith Colley/Paul Rubio] [BMI] (9/7/63 BCR-66) [F]

ENCHANTED The Platters—Mercury 71427 [Buck Ram] [ASC] (3/21/59 BCR-12)

ENCHANTED ISLAND *The Four Lads—Columbia 41194*
[Robert Allen/Al Stillman] [ASC] (6/14/58 BCRt-9)

ENCHANTED ISLAND *Jane Morgan & The Troubadors—Kapp 221*
[Robert Allen/Al Stillman] [ASC] (6/16/58 Rt-27)

ENCHANTED SEA *The Exotic Sounds Of Martin Denny—Liberty 55212*
[Frank Metis/Randy Starr] [ASC] (9/28/59 BCtRt-20) [IWM]

ENCHANTED SEA *The Islanders—Mayflower 16*
[Frank Metis/Randy Starr] [ASC] (9/28/59 BCtRt-15) [IWM]

ENCORE Cheryl Lynn—Columbia 04256
[James Samuel Harris/Terry Lewis] [ASC] (2/11/84 BC-69)

THE END IS NOT IN SIGHT (THE COWBOY TUNE) The Amazing Rhythm Aces—ABC 12202
[Howard Russell Smith] [ASC] (9/11/76 BCR-42)

THE END OF OUR ROAD *Gladys Knight & The Pips—Soul 35042*
[Rodger Penzabene/Barrett Strong/Norman Whitfield] [BMI] (2/10/68 BCR-11)

THE END OF OUR ROAD *Marvin Gaye—Tamla 54195*
[Rodger Penzabene/Barrett Strong/Norman Whitfield] [BMI] (6/6/70 BCR-28)

THE END OF THE INNOCENCE Don Henley—Geffen 22925
[Don Henley/Bruce Hornsby] [ASC] (6/24/89 BC-5)

END OF THE LINE Traveling Wilburys—Wilbury 7-27637
[Bob Dylan/George Harrison/Jeff Lynne/Roy Orbison/Tom Petty] [SE] (2/4/89 BC-53)

THE END OF THE WORLD Skeeter Davis—RCA Victor 47-8098
[Sylvia Dee/Arthur Kent] [ASC] (1/12/63 BCR-1)

ENDLESS *The McGuire Sisters—Coral 61703*
[Bill Katz/Ruth Roberts] [ASC] (9/8/56 BCRt-36)

ENDLESS *The Honey Bees—Imperial 5400 [Bill Katz/Ruth Roberts] [ASC] (9/29/56 Rt-42)*

ENDLESS LOVE Diana Ross & Lionel Richie—Motown 1519
[Lionel Richie] [ASC] (7/4/81 BCR-1)

ENDLESS NIGHTS Eddie Money—Columbia 07035
[John Cesario/Michele Collyer/Steve Mullen] [ASC] (4/11/87 BC-21)

ENDLESS SLEEP *Gene Ross—Herald 517 [Jody Reynolds] [BMI] (5/3/58 CtRt-11)*

ENDLESS SLEEP *Jody Reynolds—Demon 1507 [Jody Reynolds] [BMI] (5/17/58 BCtRt-5)*

ENDLESS SLEEP *Hank Williams, Jr.—MGM 13278*
[Jody Reynolds] [BMI] (10/31/64 BCR-81)

ENDLESS SUMMER NIGHTS Richard Marx—EMI 50113
[Richard Marx] [ASC] (1/23/88 BC-2)

ENDLESSLY *Brook Benton—Mercury 71443*
[Brook Benton/Clyde Otis] [BMI] (4/13/59 BCR-11)

ENDLESSLY *Sonny James—Capitol 2914*
[Brook Benton/Clyde Otis] [BMI] (10/17/70 C-91)

ENDLESSLY *Mavis Staples—Volt 4086 [Brook Benton/Clyde Otis] [BMI] (10/7/72 C-85)*

ENERGY CRISIS '74 Dickie Goodman—Rainy Wednesday 206
[Dickie Goodman] [BMI] (1/26/74 BCR-29)

ENERGY CRISIS '79 Dickie Goodman—Hotline 1017
[Dickie Goodman/Susan Goodman] [BMI] (6/30/79 CR-75)

ENGINE ENGINE #9 Roger Miller—Smash 1983 [Roger Miller] [BMI] (5/8/65 BCR-7)

ENGINE NUMBER 9 Wilson Pickett—Atlantic 2765
[Kenneth Gamble/Leon Huff] [BMI] (9/26/70 BCR-13)

ENGLAND SWINGS Roger Miller—Smash 2010 [Roger Miller] [BMI] (10/30/65 BCR-6)

ENGLISH MUFFINS AND IRISH STEW Sylvia Syms—Decca 29969
[Moose Charlap/Bob Hilliard] [ASC] (8/3/56 BR-37)

ENGLISHMAN IN NEW YORK Sting—A&M 1200 [Sting] [BMI] (4/16/88 BC-80)

ENJOY AND GET IT ON ZZ Top—London 252
[Frank Beard/Billy Gibbons/Dusty Hill] [BMI] (5/21/77 C-82)

ENJOY THE SILENCE Depeche Mode—Sire 19885 [Martin L. Gore] [BMI] (4/14/90 BC-2)

ENJOY YOURSELF The Jacksons—Epic 50289
[Kenneth Gamble/Leon Huff] [BMI] (11/13/76 BCR-4)

ENOUGH IS ENOUGH April Wine—Capitol 5133 [Myles Goodwyn] [ASC] (7/3/82 BC-50)

ENTER SANDMAN Metallica—Elektra 64857
[Kirk Hammett/James Hetfield/Lars Ulrich] [ASC] (8/24/91 BC-16)

THE ENTERTAINER Tony Clarke—Chess 1924 [Tony Clarke] [BMI] (3/27/65 BCR-26)

THE ENTERTAINER Marvin Hamlisch—MCA 40174 [Scott Joplin] [BMI] (3/16/74 BCR-1) [I]

THE ENTERTAINER Billy Joel—Columbia 10064 [Billy Joel] [ASC] (11/23/74 BCR-34)

EPIC Faith No More—Slash 19813
[Mike Bordin/Roddy Bottum/Billy Gould/Jim Martin/Michael Patton] [ASC]
(6/9/90 BC-7)

EPISTLE TO DIPPY Donovan—Epic 10127 [Donovan Leitch] [BMI] (2/4/67 BCR-10)

ERES TU (TOUCH THE WIND) Mocedades—Tara 100
[Juan Carlos Calderón] [ASC] (12/29/73 BCR-9) [F]

ESCALATOR OF LIFE Robert Hazard—RCA 13449 [Robert Hazard] [ASC] (3/5/83 BC-52)

ESCAPADE Janet Jackson—A&M 1490
[James Samuel Harris/Janet Jackson/Terry Lewis] [ASC] (1/20/90 BC-1)

ESCAPE-ISM (PART 1) James Brown—People 2500
[James Brown/David Matthews*] [BMI] (6/5/71 BCR-35)

ESCAPE (THE PINA COLADA SONG) Rupert Holmes—Infinity 50,035
[Rupert Holmes] [ASC] (10/20/79 BCR-1)

ESO BESO (THAT KISS!) Paul Anka—RCA Victor 47-8097
[Joe Sherman/Noel Sherman] [ASC] (10/27/62 BCR-19)

ESO ES EL AMOR (THIS IS LOVE) Morty Palitz & Orchestra with the Americanos—Josie 850
[Pepe Iglesias/Sunny Skylar] [ASC] (1/24/59 C-92)

—ET POURTANT see: YET I KNOW

ETERNAL FLAME Bangles—Columbia 68533
[Susanna Hoffs/Thomas F. Kelly/Billy Steinberg] [ASC] (2/4/89 BC-1)

ETERNALLY Thomas Wayne with The DeLons—Fernwood 111
[Fred Burch/Gerald Nelson] [BMI] (5/11/59 BCR-85)

ETERNALLY *Sarah Vaughan—Mercury 71562*
[Charles Chaplin/Geoffrey Parsons/John Turner] [ASC] (1/25/60 BCR-41)*

***LIMELIGHT** (Music of "Eternally") Mr. Acker Bilk—Atco 6238*
[Charles Chaplin] [ASC] (10/27/62 BCR-66) [IM]

ETERNALLY The Chantels—Ludix 101 [Luther Dixon/Lee Thomas] [BMI] (3/2/63 BCR-77)

ETERNITY Vikki Carr—Liberty 56132 [Bob Crewe/Charles Fox] [BMI] (9/20/69 BCR-66)

EUROPA AND THE PIRATE TWINS Thomas Dolby—Capitol 5238
[Thomas Dolby] [ASC] (6/18/83 BC-65)

A EUROPEAN (SPEAKS UP FOR THE U. S.) Guido Sarducci—A&M 1504
[Matt Neuman/Don Novello] [BMI] (2/23/74 R-96)

EVE Jim Capaldi—Island 1204 [Jim Capaldi] [ASC] (4/8/72 B-91)

***EVE OF DESTRUCTION** Barry McGuire—Dunhill 4009*
[Steve Barri/P.F. Sloan] [ASC] (8/14/65 BCR-1)

***EVE OF DESTRUCTION** The Turtles—White Whale 355*
[Steve Barri/P.F. Sloan] [ASC] (6/27/70 B-100)

EVEN IT UP Heart—Epic 50847
[Sue Ennis/Ann Wilson/Nancy Wilson] [ASC] (2/9/80 BCR-30)

EVEN NOW Barry Manilow—Arista 0330
[Barry Manilow/Marty Panzer] [BMI] (5/6/78 BCR-17)

EVEN NOW Bob Seger And The Silver Bullet Band—Capitol 5213
[Bob Seger] [ASC] (3/12/83 BC-9)

EVEN THE BAD TIMES ARE GOOD Jerry Wallace—Challenge 59265
[Carl Belew/Clyde Pitts] [BMI] (10/10/64 R-89)

EVEN THE BAD TIMES ARE GOOD The Tremeloes—Epic 10233
[Peter Callander/Mitch Murray] [BMI] (9/30/67 BCR-28)

EVEN THE NIGHTS ARE BETTER Air Supply—Arista 0692
[Kenneth Edward Bell/Terry Skinner/J.L. Wallace] [BMI] (6/12/82 BC-5)

EVENING RAIN Earl Grant—Decca 30819 [Leon Pober] [ASC] (1/19/59 BCR-48)

EVENTUALLY Brenda Lee—Decca 31272
[Dub Allbritten/Ronnie Self] [BMI] (6/19/61 BCR-41)

EVER LOVIN' FINGERS Jimmy Bowen With The Rhythm Orchids—Roulette 4001
[Dave Alldred*/Jimmy Bowen/Buddy Knox*/Donnie Lanier] [BMI] (3/9/57 B-63)

EVER SINCE THE WORLD BEGAN Tommy Shaw—Atlantic 89138
[Jim Peterik/Frankie Sullivan] [ASC] (2/13/88 BC-75)

EVER SINCE YOU WENT AWAY
Les Elgart and His Orch. With Don Forbes—Columbia 40414
[Angelo Gallucci] [BMI] (2/5/55 CR-38)

EVERGLADES The Kingston Trio—Capitol 4441 [Harlan Howard] [BMI] (9/12/60 BCR-60)

EVERGREEN Booker T.—Epic 50031 [Booker T. Jones Jr.] [BMI] (11/30/74 R-90) [I]

***EVERLASTING LOVE** Robert Knight—Rising Sons 705*
[Buzz Cason/Mac Gayden] [BMI] (9/23/67 BCR-11)

***EVERLASTING LOVE** Carl Carlton—Back Beat 27001*
[Buzz Cason/Mac Gayden] [BMI] (9/21/74 BCR-6)

***EVERLASTING LOVE** Rex Smith/Rachel Sweet—Columbia 02169*
[Buzz Cason/Mac Gayden] [BMI] (6/27/81 BCR-32)

AN EVERLASTING LOVE Andy Gibb—RSO 904 [Barry Gibb] [BMI] (7/15/78 BCR-5)

EVERLASTING LOVE Howard Jones—Elektra 69308 [Howard Jones] [ASC] (3/18/89 BC-12)

EVERLOVIN' Patti Page—Mercury 70528
[Joe Sherman/Noel Sherman] [ASC] (1/24/55 CR-17)

EVERLOVIN' Rick Nelson—Imperial 5770 [Dave Burgess] [BMI] (9/25/61 BCR-16)

***EVERY BEAT OF MY HEART** Pips—Vee-Jay 386 [Johnny Otis] [BMI] (5/8/61 BCtRt-6)*

***EVERY BEAT OF MY HEART** Gladys Knight & The Pips—Fury 1050*
[Johnny Otis] [BMI] (5/15/61 BCtRt-13)

***EVERY BEAT OF MY HEART** James Brown And The Famous Flames—King 5710*
[Johnny Otis] [BMI] (2/9/63 B-99) [IWM]

EVERY BEAT OF MY HEART Crown Heights Affair—De-Lite 1575
[Britt Britton/Freida Nerangis] [BMI] (12/6/75 BC-83)

EVERY BEAT OF MY HEART Rod Stewart—Warner Bros. 28625
[Kevin Savigar/Rod Stewart] [ASC] (11/22/86 BC-80)

EVERY BREATH I TAKE Gene Pitney—Musicor 1011
[Gerry Goffin/Carole King] [BMI] (7/24/61 BCR-27)

EVERY BREATH YOU TAKE The Police—A&M 2542 [Sting] [BMI] (6/4/83 BC-1)

EVERY DAY Joni James—M-G-M 11753 [Kenny Jacobson] [ASC] (7/3/54 C-48)

EVERY DAY AND EVERY NIGHT The Trolls—ABC 10823
[Richard Clark/Max Jordan] [BMI] (10/22/66 BR-96)

***EVERY DAY** Patti Page—Mercury 70657*
[Peter Chatman/Aaron Sparks/Milton Sparks] [BMI] (7/18/55 CRt-43)

***EVERY DAY** Count Basie And His Orchestra—Clef 89149*
[Peter Chatman/Aaron Sparks/Milton Sparks] [BMI] (8/8/55 Rt-50)

***EVERY DAY I HAVE THE BLUES** Billy Stewart—Chess 1991*
[Peter Chatman/Aaron Sparks/Milton Sparks] [BMI] (2/11/67 BCR-71)

—EVERY DAY I HAVE THE BLUES see: EVERY DAY

***EVERY DAY I HAVE TO CRY** Steve Alaimo—Checker 1032*
[Arthur Alexander] [BMI] (1/5/63 BCR-36)

***EVERYDAY I HAVE TO CRY** The Gentrys—MGM 13495*
[Arthur Alexander] [BMI] (5/14/66 BR-77)

***EVERY DAY I HAVE TO CRY SOME** Arthur Alexander—Buddah 492*
[Arthur Alexander] [BMI] (8/30/75 BCR-45)

EVERY FACE TELLS A STORY Olivia Newton-John—MCA 40642
[Michael Allison/Don Black/Peter Sills] [BMI] (11/6/76 BC-55)

EVERY GENERATION Ronnie Laws—United Artists 1334
Ronnie Laws] [ASC] (3/22/80 R-97)

EVERY HEARTBEAT Amy Grant—A&M 1557
[Amy Grant/Wayne Kirkpatrick/Charlie Peacock] [ASC] (6/15/91 BC-2)

***EVERY HOME SHOULD HAVE ONE** Patti Austin—Qwest 49854*
[Dominic Bugatti/Frank Musker] [BMI] (12/12/81 BCR-62)

***EVERY HOME SHOULD HAVE ONE** Patti Austin—Qwest 29727*
[Dominic Bugatti/Frank Musker] [BMI] (3/19/83 BC-51)

EVERY KINDA PEOPLE Robert Palmer—Island 100 [Andy Fraser] [BMI] (3/25/78 BCR-13)

EVERY LITTLE BIT HURTS Brenda Holloway—Tamla 54094
[Ed Cobb] [BMI] (5/2/64 BCR-13)

***EVERY LITTLE KISS** Bruce Hornsby And The Range—RCA 5165*
[Bruce Hornsby] [ASC] (7/26/86 BC-62)

***EVERY LITTLE KISS** Bruce Hornsby And The Range—RCA 5165*
[Bruce Hornsby] [ASC] (5/16/87 BC-14)

EVERY LITTLE STEP Bobby Brown—MCA 53618
[Kenneth Edmonds/Antonio Reid] [BMI] (3/25/89 BC-2)

EVERY LITTLE TEARDROP Gallagher And Lyle—A&M 1904
[Benny Gallagher/Graham Lyle] [BMI] (4/2/77 C-92)

EVERY LITTLE THING I DO Dion and The Belmonts—Laurie 3035
[Mike Anthony/Stan Lebowsky] [BMI] (9/7/59 BCR-39)

EVERY LITTLE THING SHE DOES IS MAGIC The Police—A&M 2371
[Sting] [BMI] (9/26/81 BCR-3)

EVERY LOVE SONG Greg Kihn Band—Beserkley 47441
[Dave Carpender*/Greg Kihn/Larry Lynch*/Gary Philippet*/Steve Wright] [ASC]
(7/17/82 B-82)

EVERY MAN OUGHTA HAVE A WOMAN William Bell—Stax 248
[William Bell*/Alvertis Isbell*/Booker T. Jones Jr.] [BMI] (3/30/68 CR-83)

—EVERY MINUTE OF THE HOUR see: DAY BY DAY

EVERY NIGHT, EVERY DAY Jimmy McCracklin—Imperial 66094
[Jimmy McCracklin] [BMI] (3/20/65 BCR-86)

EVERY NIGHT (I PRAY) The Chantels—End 1015
[Richard Barrett*/George Goldner*] [BMI] (3/24/58 BCR-32)

EVERY NIGHT (WITHOUT YOU) Paul Anka—RCA Victor 47-8068
[Paul Anka] [BMI] (8/11/62 BCR-46)

EVERY ROAD LEADS BACK TO YOU Bette Midler—Atlantic 87572
[Diane Warren] [ASC] (11/30/91 BC-70)

EVERY ROSE HAS ITS THORN Poison—Enigma 44203
[Bobby Dall/C.C. DeVille/Bret Michaels/Rikki Rockett] [BMI] (10/29/88 BC-1)

EVERY STEP OF THE WAY Johnny Mathis—Columbia 42799
[Robert Allen/Al Stillman] [ASC] (5/18/63 BCR-30)

EVERY STEP OF THE WAY Steve Walsh—Kirshner 4288 [Steve Walsh] [BMI] (5/3/80 CR-85)

EVERY STEP OF THE WAY John Waite—EMI America 8282
[Ivan Kral/Mark Sidgwick/John Waite*] [ASC] (8/10/85 BC-24)

EVERY TIME (I FEEL HIS SPIRIT) Patti Page—Mercury 70971
[Traditional] [NA] (11/24/56 B-87)

EVERY TIME I HEAR YOUR NAME Patti Page—Mercury 72044
[George Motola/Rickie Page] [BMI] (10/27/62 R-87)

EVERY TIME I THINK OF YOU The Babys—Chrysalis 2279
[Jack Conrad/Ray Kennedy] [BMI] (12/30/78 BCR-8)

(EVERY TIME I TURN AROUND) BACK IN LOVE AGAIN L.T.D.—A&M 1974
[Zane Grey/Len Hanks] [BMI] (9/17/77 BCR-4)

EVERY TIME MY HEART SINGS Jimmie Rodgers—Roulette 4349
[Pearl Woods] [BMI] (3/27/61 R-96)

EVERY TIME YOU TOUCH ME (I GET HIGH) Charlie Rich—Epic 50103
[Charlie Rich/Billy Sherrill] [BMI] (5/24/75 BCR-19)

EVERY WHICH WAY BUT LOOSE Eddie Rabbitt—Elektra 45554
[Milton L. Brown/Steve Dorff/Snuff Garrett] [BMI] (1/20/79 BCR-30)

EVERY WOMAN IN THE WORLD Air Supply—Arista 0564
[Dominic Bugatti/Frank Musker] [BMI] (10/25/80 BCR-3)

EVERYBODY Tommy Roe—ABC-Paramount 10478 [Tommy Roe] [BMI] (10/5/63 BCR-3)

EVERYBODY BE DANCIN' Starbuck—Private Stock 45,144
[Bruce Blackman] [ASC] (4/9/77 BCR-38)

EVERYBODY BUT ME G.W. Kenny—Kama Sutra 581 [Gerard Kenny] [BMI] (8/25/73 C-89)

EVERYBODY DANCE Chic—Atlantic 3469
[Bernard Edwards/Nile Rodgers] [BMI] (4/22/78 BCR-38)

EVERYBODY DANCE Ta Mara & The Seen—A&M 2768
[Jesse Woods Johnson] [ASC] (10/12/85 BC-24)

EVERYBODY DO THE SLOOPY Johnny Thunder—Diamond 192
[Bert Berns/Wes Farrell] [BMI] (11/27/65 BCR-67)

EVERYBODY EVERYBODY Black Box—RCA 2628
[Daniele Davoli/Mirko Limoni/Valerio Semplici] [ASC] (8/4/90 BC-7)

EVERYBODY GO HOME Eydie Gorme—Columbia 42854
[Gerry Goffin/Carole King] [BMI] (9/28/63 BCR-70)

EVERYBODY GOT TO BELIEVE IN SOMEBODY Sam & Dave—Atlantic 2568
[Isaac Hayes/David Porter] [ASC] (11/2/68 BCR-73)

EVERYBODY HAVE FUN TONIGHT Wang Chung—Geffen 28562
[Nick Feldman/Jack Hues/Peter F. Wolf] [BMI] (10/4/86 BC-1)

EVERYBODY IS A STAR Sly & The Family Stone—Epic 10555 [Sylvester Stewart] (TSW) [BMI] (1/3/70 BCR-1)

EVERYBODY KNOWS Steve Lawrence—Columbia 43047 [Jimmy Duncan/Les Reed] [BMI] (5/23/64 BCR-57)

EVERYBODY KNOWS The Dave Clark Five—Epic 10265 [Barry Mason/Les Reed] [ASC] (12/9/67 BCR-41)

EVERYBODY KNOWS ABOUT MY GOOD THING (PT. 1) Little Johnny Taylor—Ronn 55 [Miles Grayson/Lermon Horton] [BMI] (12/11/71 BCR-43)

EVERYBODY KNOWS HER Jonathan Edwards—Atco 6881 [Jonathan Edwards] [ASC] (4/1/72 R-87)

EVERYBODY KNOWS (I STILL LOVE YOU) The Dave Clark Five—Epic 9722 [Dave Clark/Lenny Davidson] [BMI] (10/3/64 BCR-14)

EVERYBODY KNOWS MATILDA Duke Baxter—VMC 740 [Duke Baxter] [BMI] (7/12/69 BCR-52)

EVERYBODY LIKES TO CHA CHA CHA Sam Cooke—Keen 3-2018 [Sam Cooke] [BMI] (3/7/59 BCR-28)

EVERYBODY LOVES A CLOWN Gary Lewis And The Playboys—Liberty 55818 [Snuff Garrett/Gary Lewis/Leon Russell] [BMI] (9/25/65 BCR-4)

EVERYBODY LOVES A GOOD TIME Major Lance—Okeh 7233 [Van McCoy] [BMI] (12/11/65 R-98)

EVERYBODY LOVES A LOVE SONG Mac Davis—Columbia 45727 [Mac Davis] [BMI] (11/11/72 BCR-39)

EVERYBODY LOVES A LOVER *Doris Day—Columbia 41195 [Richard Adler/Robert Allen] [ASC] (7/7/58 BCR-6)*

EVERYBODY LOVES A LOVER *The Angels—Caprice 116 [Richard Adler/Robert Allen] [ASC] (6/16/62 R-93)*

EVERYBODY LOVES A LOVER *The Shirelles—Scepter 1243 [Richard Adler/Robert Allen] [ASC] (12/1/62 BCR-17)*

EVERYBODY LOVES A NUT Johnny Cash—Columbia 43673 [Jack H. Clement] [BMI] (6/18/66 BCR-67)

EVERYBODY LOVES A RAIN SONG B.J. Thomas—MCA 40854 [Mark James/Chips Moman] [BMI] (1/21/78 BCR-43)

EVERYBODY LOVES A WINNER William Bell—Stax 212 [William Bell/Booker T. Jones Jr.] [BMI] (4/15/67 BCR-78)

EVERYBODY LOVES ME BUT YOU Brenda Lee—Decca 31379 [Dub Allbritten*/Ronnie Self] [BMI] (4/9/62 BCR-5)

EVERYBODY LOVES MY BABY Dinah Washington with Eddie Chamblee & His Orch.—Mercury 71220 [Jack Palmer/Spencer Williams] [ASC] (12/2/57 R-81)

EVERYBODY LOVES SOMEBODY Dean Martin—Reprise 0281 [Sam Coslow*/Ken Lane/Irving Taylor] [ASC] (6/27/64 BCR-1)

EVERYBODY MONKEY Freddy Cannon—Swan 4149 [Kenneth Gamble/Jerry J. Ross] [BMI] (7/27/63 BCR-51)

EVERYBODY MOVE Cathy Dennis—Polydor 867 988 [Terry Britten/Cathy Dennis/Mike Leeson] [ASC] (12/14/91 B-90)

EVERYBODY NEEDS A RAINBOW Ray Stevens—Barnaby 610 [Layng Martine Jr.] [BMI] (11/30/74 C-83)

EVERYBODY NEEDS LOVE Gladys Knight & The Pips—Soul 35034 [Eddie Holland/Norman Whitfield] [BMI] (7/8/67 BCR-39)

EVERYBODY NEEDS LOVE Stephen Bishop—ABC 12406 [Stephen Bishop] [ASC] (9/9/78 BCR-29)

EVERYBODY NEEDS SOMEBODY TO LOVE *Solomon Burke—Atlantic 2241 [Bert Berns/Solomon Burke/Jerry Wexler] [BMI] (7/18/64 BCR-58)*

EVERYBODY NEEDS SOMEBODY TO LOVE *Wilson Pickett—Atlantic 2381 [Bert Berns/Solomon Burke/Jerry Wexler] [BMI] (2/4/67 BCR-29)*

EVERYBODY OUGHT TO BE IN LOVE Paul Anka—United Artists 1018 [Paul Anka] [BMI] (7/9/77 BCR-75)

EVERYBODY OUT'TA THE POOL The Lifeguards—ABC-Paramount 10021 [Frank Pingatore] [ASC] (5/11/59 CR-87)

EVERYBODY PLAYS THE FOOL *The Main Ingredient—RCA Victor 74-0731 [Ralph Bailey/Rudy Clark/Ken Williams] [BMI] (7/8/72 BCR-1)*

EVERYBODY PLAYS THE FOOL *Aaron Neville—A&M 1563 [Ralph Bailey/Rudy Clark/Ken Williams] [BMI] (7/13/91 BC-8)*

(EVERYBODY WANNA GET RICH) RITE AWAY Dr. John—Atco 6957 [Mac Rebennack] [BMI] (5/4/74 BCR-72)

EVERYBODY WANTS TO FIND A BLUEBIRD Randy Edelman—20th Century 2155 [Randy Edelman] [BMI] (2/15/75 BCR-75)

EVERYBODY WANTS TO RULE THE WORLD Tears For Fears—Mercury 880659 [Chris Hughes/Roland Orzabal/Ian Stanley] [BMI] (3/16/85 BC-1)

EVERYBODY WANTS YOU Billy Squier—Capitol 5163 [Billy Squier] [ASC] (10/2/82 BC-31)

EVERYBODY'S EVERYTHING Santana—Columbia 45472 [Milton S. Brown Jr./Tyrone Moss/Carlos Santana] [BMI] (10/9/71 BCR-9)

EVERYBODY'S GOT A HOME BUT ME *Eddie Fisher—RCA Victor 47-6337 [Oscar Hammerstein/Richard Rodgers] [ASC] (12/1/55 BCtRt-25)*

EVERYBODY'S GOT A HOME BUT ME *Roy Hamilton—Epic 9132 [Oscar Hammerstein/Richard Rodgers] [ASC] (12/9/55 BCtRt-25)*

EVERYBODY'S GOT THE RIGHT TO LOVE The Supremes—Motown 1167 [Lou Stallman] [BMI] (7/11/70 BCR-13)

EVERYBODY'S GOT TO LEARN SOMETIME The Korgis—Asylum 47055 [James Edward Warren] [ASC] (10/11/80 BCR-18)

EVERYBODY'S GOTTA PAY SOME DUES The Miracles—Tamla 54048 [Smokey Robinson/Ronnie White] [ASC] (10/2/61 BCR-52)

EVERYBODY'S HAD THE BLUES Merle Haggard And The Strangers—Capitol 3641 [Merle Haggard] [BMI] (9/1/73 BCR-62)

EVERYBODY'S OUT OF TOWN B.J. Thomas—Scepter 12277 [Burt Bacharach/Hal David] [ASC] (3/28/70 BCR-15)

EVERYBODY'S SOMEBODY'S FOOL The Heartbeats—Rama 231 [Ace Adams/Regina Adams/Gladys Hampton*] [BMI] (7/15/57 B-78)

EVERYBODY'S SOMEBODY'S FOOL Connie Francis—MGM 12899 [Howard Greenfield/Jack Keller] [BMI] (5/9/60 BCR-1)

EVERYBODY'S TALKIN' *Nilsson—RCA Victor 47-9544 [Fred Neil] [BMI] (8/3/68 CR-51)*

EVERYBODY'S TALKIN' *Nilsson—RCA Victor 74-0161 [Fred Neil] [BMI] (8/2/69 BCR-6)*

EVERYBODY'S TRYING TO BE MY BABY The Beatles—Capitol R-5365 [Carl Perkins] (EP) [BMI] (2/13/65 BCR-67)

EVERYBODY'S TWISTING DOWN IN MEXICO Billy Vaughn And His Orchestra—Dot 16295 [Jerry Kennedy/Buddy Killen] [BMI] (11/27/61 R-73) [I]

EVERYDAY *Buddy Holly / The Crickets—Coral 61885 [Buddy Holly/Norman Petty] [BMI] (11/30/57 CR-51)*

EVERYDAY *John Denver—RCA Victor 74-0647 [Buddy Holly/Norman Petty] [BMI] (3/11/72 BCR-76)*

EVERYDAY *James Taylor—Columbia 05681 [Buddy Holly/Norman Petty] [BMI] (11/9/85 BC-61)*

EVERYDAY Della Reese—RCA Victor 47-7750 [Luigi Creatore/Marguerite Monnot/Hugo Peretti] [ASC] (5/9/60 CR-51)

EVERYDAY I WRITE THE BOOK Elvis Costello And The Attractions—Columbia 04045 [Elvis Costello] [ASC] (8/20/83 BC-36)

EVERYDAY PEOPLE *Sly & The Family Stone—Epic 10407 [Sylvester Stewart] [BMI] (11/30/68 BCR-1)*

EVERYDAY PEOPLE *Joan Jett and the Blackhearts—Blackheart 52272 [Sylvester Stewart] [BMI] (9/10/83 BC-37)*

EVERYDAY WITH YOU GIRL Classics IV Featuring Dennis Yost—Imperial 66378 [Buddy Buie/J.R. Cobb] [BMI] (4/26/69 BCR-15)

EVERYDAY WITHOUT YOU Hamilton, Joe Frank & Reynolds—Playboy 6068 [Danny Hamilton] [BMI] (4/3/76 BC-62)

EVERYONE WAS THERE Bob Kayli—Carlton 482 [Berry Gordy/Robert Gordy] [BMI] (10/4/58 BC-96)

EVERY 1'S A WINNER Hot Chocolate—Infinity 50002 [Errol Brown] [ASC] (11/11/78 BCR-6)

EVERYONE'S AGREED THAT EVERYTHING WILL TURN OUT FINE Stealers Wheel—A&M 1450 [Joe Egan/Gerry Rafferty] [BMI] (6/30/73 BCR-31)

EVERYONE'S GONE TO THE MOON Jonathan King—Parrot 9774 [Jonathan King] [BMI] (9/11/65 BCR-10)

EVERYONE'S LAUGHING The Spaniels—Vee-Jay 246 [Calvin Carter] [BMI] (7/1/57 B-69)

EVERYOTHERDAY Or-N-More—EMI 50359 [Mike More/Orfeh] [ASC] (8/31/91 BC-46)

EVERYTHING Jody Watley—MCA 53714 [Gardner Cole/James Newton Howard] [BMI] (10/14/89 BC-4)

EVERYTHING A MAN COULD EVER NEED Glen Campbell—Capitol 2843 [Mac Davis] [BMI] (7/4/70 BCR-43)

EVERYTHING COUNTS Depeche Mode—Sire 22993 [Martin L. Gore] [BMI] (5/27/89 C-76)

EVERYTHING GOOD IS BAD 100 Proof Aged In Soul—Hot Wax 7202 [Angelo Bond/General Johnson/Greg Perry] [BMI] (4/1/72 BCR-45)

EVERYTHING I DO GOHN BE FUNKY (FROM NOW ON) Lee Dorsey—Amy 11,055 [Allen Toussaint] [BMI] (6/28/69 BCR-91)

(EVERYTHING I DO) I DO IT FOR YOU Bryan Adams—A&M 1567 [Bryan Adams/Michael Kamen/Mutt Lange] [BMI] (6/29/91 BC-1)

EVERYTHING I HAVE IS YOURS Dorothy Collins—Top Rank 2013 [Harold Adamson/Burton Lane] [ASC] (9/28/59 R-93)

EVERYTHING I NEED Men At Work—Columbia 04929 [Colin James Hay] [BMI] (5/25/85 BC-41)

EVERYTHING I OWN Bread—Elektra 45765 [David Gates] [ASC] (1/22/72 BCR-5)

EVERYTHING IN MY HEART Corey Hart—EMI America 8300 [Corey Hart] [ASC] (11/30/85 BC-30)

EVERYTHING IS ALRIGHT Spider—Dreamland 103 [Holly Knight] [ASC] (8/2/80 B-86)

EVERYTHING IS BEAUTIFUL Ray Stevens—Barnaby 2011 [Ray Stevens] [BMI] (3/28/70 BCR-1)

EVERYTHING IS GOING TO BE ALRIGHT Teegarden & Van Winkle—Westbound 171 [Bill Moss] [BMI] (12/5/70 BCR-56)

EVERYTHING IS GOOD ABOUT YOU The Lettermen—Capitol 3020 [James Anthony Dean/Eddie Holland] [BMI] (1/23/71 BCR-73)

EVERYTHING MUST CHANGE Paul Young—Columbia 05712 [Ian Kewley/Paul Young] [BMI] (11/23/85 BC-47)

EVERYTHING SHE WANTS Wham!—Columbia 04840 [George Michael] [ASC] (3/23/85 BC-1)

EVERYTHING THAT 'CHA DO (WILL COME BACK TO YOU) Wet Willie—Capricorn 0254 [Rick Hirsch] [BMI] (5/22/76 BC-66)

EVERYTHING THAT TOUCHES YOU The Association—Warner Bros. 7163/Warner Bros.-Seven Arts 7163 [Terry Kirkman] [BMI] (1/27/68 BCR-9)

EVERYTHING WORKS IF YOU LET IT Cheap Trick—Epic 50887 [Rick Nielsen] [BMI] (5/24/80 BCR-44)

EVERYTHING YOU DO (YOU'RE SEXING ME) Fiona (Duet With Kip Winger)—Atlantic 88823 [Lance Cosgrove/Fiona Flanagan/Beau Hill] [ASC] (11/25/89 BC-52)

EVERYTHING YOUR HEART DESIRES Daryl Hall & John Oates—Arista 1-9684 [Daryl Hall] [BMI] (4/16/88 BC-3)

EVERYTHING'S ALRIGHT The Newbeats—Hickory 1282 [John D. Loudermilk] [BMI] (10/24/64 BCR-15)

***EVERYTHING'S ALRIGHT** The Assembled Multitude—Atlantic 2780 [Tim Rice/Andrew Lloyd Webber] (Med) [ASC] (2/6/71 BR-87) [IWM]*

***EVERYTHING'S ALRIGHT** The Kimberlys—Happy Tiger 572 [Tim Rice/Andrew Lloyd Webber] (Med) [ASC] (3/20/71 B-99)*

***EVERYTHING'S ALRIGHT** Yvonne Elliman—Decca 32870 [Tim Rice/Andrew Lloyd Webber] [ASC] (9/25/71 BCR-92)*

EVERYTHING'S BEEN CHANGED The 5th Dimension—Bell 45,338 [Paul Anka] [BMI] (3/31/73 BCR-55)

EVERYTHING'S COMING UP LOVE David Ruffin—Motown 1393 [Van McCoy] [BMI] (6/12/76 BCR-49)

EVERYTHING'S THE SAME (AIN'T NOTHING CHANGED) Billy Swan—Monument 8661 [Billy Swan] [BMI] (9/27/75 BCR-67)

EVERYTHING'S TUESDAY Chairmen Of The Board—Invictus 9079 [Lamont Dozier/Daphne Dumas/Ronald Dunbar/Brian Holland/Eddie Holland] [BMI] (8/1/70 BCR-38)

EVERYTIME (I THINK ABOUT YOU) (PART 1) Joey Dee & The Starliters—Roulette 4431 [Joey Dee/Henry Glover/Morris Levy‡/Sammy Taylor] [BMI] (6/16/62 CR-77)

EVERYTIME YOU CRY The Outfield—Columbia 06295 [John Spinks] [ASC] (9/20/86 BC-57)

EVERYTIME YOU GO AWAY Paul Young—Columbia 04867 [Daryl Hall] [BMI] (5/11/85 BC-1)

EVERYWHERE Fleetwood Mac—Warner Bros. 28143 [Christine McVie] [BMI] (11/28/87 BC-13)

EVERYWHERE YOU GO Quaker City Boys—Swan 4026 [Mark Fisher/Joe Goodwin/Larry Shay] [ASC] (3/21/59 C-93)

EVIL Earth, Wind & Fire—Columbia 45888 [Philip Bailey/Maurice White] [ASC] (8/4/73 BCR-50)

EVIL BOLL-WEEVIL Grand Canyon—Bang 713 [Edward C. Black/Jeffrey Markus McKee] [BMI] (10/19/74 BCR-61)

***EVIL WAYS** Santana—Columbia 45069 [Clarence "Sonny" Henry] [BMI] (1/24/70 BCR-7)*

***EVIL WAYS** Carlos Santana & Buddy Miles—Columbia 45666 [Clarence "Sonny" Henry] (TSW) [BMI] (9/16/72 BCR-67)*

EVIL WOMAN Electric Light Orchestra—United Artists 729 [Jeff Lynne] [BMI] (11/15/75 BCR-9)

EVIL WOMAN DON'T PLAY YOUR GAMES WITH ME Crow—Amaret 112 [Dave Waggoner/Dick Weigand/Larry Weigand] [BMI] (10/4/69 BCR-16)

EVOL-NOT LOVE The Five Americans—HBR 468 [John Durrill/Norman Ezell/Michael Rabon] [BMI] (4/16/66 BCR-51)

***EV'RY DAY OF MY LIFE** The McGuire Sisters—Coral 61703 [Jimmie Crane/Al Jacobs] [ASC] (9/8/56 BCRt-26)*

***EV'RY DAY OF MY LIFE** Vera Lynn—London 1688 [Jimmie Crane/Al Jacobs] [ASC] (10/20/56 Rt-26)*

***EVERY DAY OF MY LIFE** Bobby Vinton—Epic 10822 [Jimmie Crane/Al Jacobs] [ASC] (1/29/72 BCR-13)*

EV'RY NIGHT ABOUT THIS TIME The Diamonds—Mercury 70889 [Ted Koehler/James V. Monaco] [ASC] (6/22/56 R-83)

EV'RY NIGHT AT NINE O'CLOCK Somethin' Smith & The Redheads—Epic 9247 [Al Hoffman] [ASC] (12/9/57 R-73)

EV'RYBODY'S CRYIN' Jimmie Beaumont—May 112 [Waldense Hall/Mack Wolfson] [BMI] (12/25/61 B-100)

EV'RYBODY'S TWISTIN' Frank Sinatra—Reprise 20,063 [Rube Bloom/Ted Koehler] [ASC] (3/26/62 BCR-67)

EWOK CELEBRATION Meco—Arista 1-9045 [Ben Burtt*/John Williams/Joseph Stanley Williams] [BMI] (7/2/83 BC-60) [F]

EXCLUSIVELY YOURS Carl Dobkins, Jr.—Decca 31088 [Ben Raleigh/Don Wolf] [ASC] (5/9/60 BCR-62)

EXCLUSIVITY Damian Dame—LaFace 2-4000 [Bruce Broadus/Kenneth Edmonds/Antonio Reid] [BMI] (5/18/91 B-42)

***EXODUS** Ferrante & Teicher—United Artists 274 [Ernest Gold] [ASC] (11/7/60 BCtRt-1) [IM]*

***MAIN THEME FROM EXODUS (ARI'S THEME)** Mantovani And His Orchestra—London 1953 [Ernest Gold] [ASC] (11/7/60 BCtRt-1) [IM]*

***THE EXODUS SONG (THIS LAND IS MINE)** Pat Boone—Dot 16176 [Pat Boone/Ernest Gold] [ASC] (1/23/61 BCR-64)*

***EXODUS** The Medallion Strings—Medallion 602 [Ernest Gold] [ASC] (2/18/61 Ct-4) [IM]*

***EXODUS** Eddie Harris—Vee-Jay 378 [Ernest Gold] [ASC] (4/10/61 BCR-36) [IM]*

—EXORDIUM & TERMINUS see: IN THE YEAR 2525

EXPECTING TO FLY The Buffalo Springfield—Atco 6545 [Neil Young] [BMI] (12/23/67 BCR-91)

EXPERIENCE UNNECESSARY Sarah Vaughan—Mercury 70646 [Luigi Creatore/Hugo Peretti/Gladys Shelley/June Winters*] [ASC] (6/20/55 CR-31)

EXPERIMENTS WITH MICE Johnny Dankworth—Capitol 3499 [Johnny Dankworth/Traditional/Leslie Williams] [ASC] (8/25/56 B-61)

EXPLOSION IN YOUR SOUL Soul Survivors—Crimson 1012 [Kenneth Gamble/Leon Huff] [BMI] (12/23/67 BCR-28)

***EXPRESS** B.T. Express—Roadshow 7001 [Barbara Lomas/Louis Risbrook/William Risbrook/Dennis Rowe/Richard Thompson/Carlos Ward/Terrell Wood] [BMI] (1/25/75 BCR-4) [I]*

***EXPRESS** The Ritchie Family—Marlin 3306 [Barbara Lomas/Louis Risbrook/William Risbrook/Dennis Rowe/Richard Thompson/Carlos Ward/Terrell Wood] (Med) [BMI] (8/28/76 BCR-17)*

EXPRESS YOURSELF Charles Wright And The Watts 103rd Street Rhythm Band—Warner Bros. 7417 [Charles Wright] [BMI] (8/15/70 BCR-12)

EXPRESS YOURSELF Madonna—Sire 22948 [Stephen Bray/Madonna L. Ciccone] [ASC] (6/3/89 BC-1)

EXPRESSION Salt-N-Pepa—Next Plateau 329 [Cheryl James] [ASC] (3/10/90 BC-26)

EXPRESSWAY TO YOUR HEART Soul Survivors—Crimson 1010 [Kenneth Gamble/Leon Huff] [BMI] (9/2/67 BCR-4)

EYE IN THE SKY Alan Parsons Project—Arista 0696 [Alan Parsons/Eric Woolfson] [BMI] (7/3/82 BC-3)

EYE OF THE TIGER Survivor—Scotti Brothers 02912 [Jim Peterik/Frankie Sullivan] [ASC] (6/5/82 BC-1)

EYE OF THE ZOMBIE John Fogerty—Warner Bros. 28657 [John Fogerty] [ASC] (9/6/86 B-81)

EYE ON YOU Billy Squier—Capitol 5416 [Billy Squier] [ASC] (12/8/84 BC-69)

EYE TO EYE Go West—Chrysalis 42903 [Peter Cox/Richard Drummie] [ASC] (9/28/85 BC-73)

THE EYES OF A NEW YORK WOMAN B.J. Thomas—Scepter 12219 [Mark James] [BMI] (6/8/68 BCR-28)

EYES OF GOD The Four Lads—Columbia 40974 [Robert Allen/Al Stillman] [ASC] (8/26/57 CR-49)

EYES OF SILVER The Doobie Brothers—Warner Bros. 7832 [Tom Johnston] [BMI] (7/20/74 BCR-43)

EYES THAT SEE IN THE DARK Kenny Rogers—RCA 13774 [Barry Gibb/Maurice Gibb] [BMI] (4/28/84 B-79)

EYES WITHOUT A FACE Billy Idol—Chrysalis 42786 [Billy Idol/Steve Stevens] [ASC] (5/5/84 BC-4)

EYESIGHT TO THE BLIND Richie Havens—Ode 60032 [Sonny Boy Williamson II] [BMI] (3/24/73 R-97)

F

FA-FA-FA-FA-FA (SAD SONG) Otis Redding—Volt 138 [Steve Cropper/Otis Redding] [BMI] (9/24/66 BCR-29)

***FABULOUS** Charlie Gracie—Cameo 107 [Bernie Lowe/Kal Mann] [ASC] (5/6/57 BCRt-14)*

***FABULOUS** Steve Lawrence—Coral 61834 [Bernie Lowe/Kal Mann] [ASC] (5/11/57 BRt-16)*

FABULOUS CHARACTER Sarah Vaughan—Mercury 70885 [Bennie Benjamin/Sol Marcus] [ASC] (7/13/56 BR-27)

***FACE IN A CROWD** Jimmie Rodgers—Dot 16450 [Ramona Redd/Mitchell Torok] [BMI] (3/2/63 Rt-82)*

***FACE IN A CROWD** Dean Martin—Reprise 20,150 [Ramona Redd/Mitchell Torok] [BMI] (3/2/63 Rt-87)*

***A FACE IN THE CROWD** Andy Griffith—Capitol 3705 [Tom Glazer/Budd Schulberg] [ASC] (5/4/57 Rt-65)*

***A FACE IN THE CROWD** Art Mooney & His Orchestra—MGM 12461 [Tom Glazer/Budd Schulberg] [ASC] (5/4/57 Rt-65)*

***A FACE IN THE CROWD** Dick Lee—Vik 0269 [Tom Glazer/Budd Schulberg] [ASC] (5/4/57 Rt-65)*

***A FACE IN THE CROWD** Don Cornell—Coral 61819 [Tom Glazer/Budd Schulberg] [ASC] (5/4/57 Rt-65)*

A FACE IN THE CROWD Tom Petty—MCA 53781 [Jeff Lynne/Tom Petty] [ASC] (2/24/90 BC-42)

FACE IT GIRL, IT'S OVER Nancy Wilson—Capitol 2136 [Andy Badale/Frank Stanton] [ASC] (5/11/68 BCR-21)

FACE THE FACE Pete Townshend—Atco 99590 [Pete Townshend] [GL] (11/9/85 BC-26)

FACE THE MUSIC RTZ—Giant 19273 [Barry Goudreau/Brian Maes] [ASC] (8/17/91 BC-39)

FACTS OF LOVE Jeff Lorber—Warner Bros. 28588 [Evan Rogers/Carl Sturken] [BMI] (12/6/86 BC-27)

FADE AWAY Bruce Springsteen—Columbia 11431 [Bruce Springsteen] [ASC] (2/7/81 BCR-20)

FADE AWAY Loz Netto—21 Records 104 [Loz Netto] [BMI] (6/4/83 BC-82)

***FADED LOVE** Jackie de Shannon—Liberty 55526 [Bob Wills/Johnnie Lee Wills] [ASC] (1/26/63 BR-97)*

***FADED LOVE** Patsy Cline—Decca 31522 [Bob Wills/Johnnie Lee Wills] [ASC] (8/31/63 B-96)*

FADED ROSE The Hilltoppers—Dot 15459 [Billy Vaughn] [ASC] (6/1/56 R-84)

FADED SUMMER LOVE Georgie Shaw—Decca 30078 [Phil Baxter] [ASC] (12/1/56 BR-54)

FADING AWAY Will To Power—Epic 68543 [Bob Rosenberg] [BMI] (2/4/89 BC-65)

FADING LIKE A FLOWER (EVERY TIME YOU LEAVE) Roxette—EMI 50355 [Per Gessle] [BMI] (6/15/91 BC-2)

FAIR GAME Crosby, Stills & Nash—Atlantic 3432 [Stephen Stills] [BMI] (10/1/77 BCR-43)

FAIRWEATHER FRIEND Johnny Gill—Motown 2049 [Kenneth Edmonds/Antonio Reid/Daryl Simmons] [BMI] (10/20/90 BC-28)

FAIRY TALE Frank Sinatra—Capitol 3218 [Jerry Livingston/Dok Stanford] [ASC] (8/22/55 CR-14)

FAIRYTALE Pointer Sisters—ABC/Blue Thumb 254 [Anita Pointer/Bonnie Pointer] [BMI] (10/5/74 BCR-13)

FAITH Wallace Brothers—Sims 158 [Wallace Span] [BMI] (2/22/64 R-99)

FAITH George Michael—Columbia 07623 [George Michael] [ASC] (10/24/87 BC-1)

FAITHFUL AND TRUE Z.Z. Hill—Mankind 12003 [Jeanie Greene/Marlin Greene/Dan Penn] [BMI] (7/10/71 C-99)

***FAITHFUL HUSSAR** Ted Heath—London 1675 [Heinrich Frantzen] [ASC] (10/13/56 BR-52) [I]*

***DON'T CRY MY LOVE (THE FAITHFUL HUSSAR)** Vera Lynn—London 1729 [Heinrich Frantzen/Fred Jackson/W. Albert Poser] [ASC] (5/4/57 BCR-40) [FDE]*

FAITHFULLY Journey—Columbia 03840 [Jonathan Cain] [ASC] (4/16/83 BC-12)

FAKE Alexander O'Neal—Tabu 4-07100 [James Samuel Harris/Terry Lewis] [ASC] (7/18/87 BC-25)

FAKE FRIENDS Joan Jett & The Blackhearts—Blackheart/MCA 52256 [Joan Jett/Kenny Laguna] [BMI] (7/9/83 BC-35)

FAKE OUT Frankie Sardo—ABC-Paramount 9963 [Johnny Sardo] [BMI] (12/6/58 C-68)

FAKIN' IT Simon & Garfunkel—Columbia 44232 [Paul Simon] [BMI] (7/29/67 BCR-15)

FALL AT YOUR FEET Crowded House—Capitol 44747 [Neil Finn] [BMI] (10/19/91 B-75)

FALL AWAY Eddie Albert—Hickory 1278 [Boudleaux Bryant/Felice Bryant] [BMI] (1/9/65 R-92)

FALL IN LOVE WITH ME Bettye Swann—Money 129 [Bettye Swann] [BMI] (9/16/67 BCR-51)

FALL IN LOVE WITH ME Earth, Wind & Fire—Columbia 03375 [Wanda Hutchinson/Wayne Vaughn/Maurice White] [ASC] (1/22/83 BC-17)

THE FALL OF LOVE Johnny Mathis—Mercury 72263 [Dimitri Tiomkin/Ned Washington] [ASC] (4/11/64 R-96)

FALL ON ME R.E.M.—I.R.S. 52883 [Bill Berry/Peter Buck/Mike Mills/Michael Stipe] [BMI] (10/4/86 BC-88)

FALLEN ANGEL Webb Pierce—Decca 31165 [Wayne Walker/Marijohn Wilkin] [BMI] (11/21/60 B-99)

FALLEN ANGEL Frankie Valli—Private Stock 45,074 [Guy Fletcher/Doug Flett] [ASC] (4/3/76 BCR-36)

FALLEN ANGEL Poison—Enigma 44191 [Bobby Dall/C.C. DeVille/Bret Michaels/Rikki Rockett] [BMI] (7/30/88 BC-12)

***FALLEN STAR** Jimmy Newman—Dot 15574 [James Joiner] [BMI] (6/1/57 BCtRt-19)*

***FALLEN STAR** Nick Noble—Mercury 71124 [James Joiner] [BMI] (6/1/57 CtRt-19)*

***FALLEN STAR** Ferlin Husky—Capitol 3742 [James Joiner] [BMI] (6/22/57 BCtRt-19)*

***FALLEN STAR** The Hilltoppers—Dot 15594 [James Joiner] [BMI] (6/22/57 BCtRt-19)*

FALLIN' Connie Francis—MGM 12713 [Howard Greenfield/Neil Sedaka] [BMI] (9/29/58 BCR-30)

FALLIN' IN LOVE The Souther, Hillman, Furay Band—Asylum 45201 [Richie Furay] [ASC] (8/17/74 BCR-24)

FALLIN' IN LOVE Hamilton, Joe Frank & Reynolds—Playboy 6024 [Ann Marie Hamilton/Danny Hamilton] [BMI] (6/21/75 BCR-1)

FALLING Roy Orbison—Monument 815 [Roy Orbison] [BMI] (6/1/63 BCR-18)

FALLING Le Blanc & Carr—Big Tree 16100 [Lenny LeBlanc/Eddie Struzick] [BMI] (10/15/77 BCR-11)

FALLING APART AT THE SEAMS The Marmalade—Ariola America 7619 [Tony Macaulay] [ASC] (3/27/76 BCR-49)

FALLING IN LOVE Balance—Portrait 24-02608 [Peppy Castro] [BMI] (11/21/81 BCR-53)

FALLING IN LOVE Fat Boys—Tin Pan Apple 885 766 [Van Gibbs/Mark Anthony Morales/Darren Robinson/Eddison Sainsbury/Damon Wimbley] [ASC] (7/4/87 C-90)

FALLING IN LOVE AGAIN Michael Stanley Band—EMI America 8090 [Bob Pelander/Michael Stanley] [ASC] (8/8/81 BCR-55)

FALLING IN LOVE (UH-OH) Miami Sound Machine—Epic 06352 [Larry Dermer/Joe Galdo/Rafael Vigil] [BMI] (11/1/86 BC-23)

FALLING OUT OF LOVE Buster Brown—RCA 10023 [Buster (2) Brown] [BMI] (11/9/74 R-94)

FALLING OUT OF LOVE Ivan Neville—Polydor 871484 [Ivan Neville] [BMI] (2/25/89 BC-83)

FALLING TO PIECES Faith No More—Slash 19563 [Mike Bordin/Roddy Bottum/Billy Gould/Jim Martin/Michael Patton] [ASC] (11/10/90 BC-80)

FALLOUT Henry Mancini And His Orchestra—RCA Victor 47-7442 [Henry Mancini] [ASC] (1/19/59 R-38) [I]

FAME David Bowie—RCA Victor 10320 [Carlos Alomar/David Bowie/John Lennon] [ASC] (6/28/75 BCR-1)

FAME Irene Cara—RSO 1034 [Michael Gore/Dean Pitchford] [BMI] (6/14/80 BCR-3)

FAME AND FORTUNE Elvis Presley With The Jordanaires—RCA Victor 47-7740 [Ben Weisman/Fred Wise] [ASC] (4/4/60 BCR-17)

FAMILY AFFAIR Sly & The Family Stone—Epic 10805 [Sylvester Stewart] [BMI] (10/30/71 BCR-1)

FAMILY MAN Daryl Hall & John Oates—RCA Victor 13507 [Tim Cross/Richard Fenn/Mike Frye/Mike Oldfield/Morris Pert*/Maggie Reilly] [ASC] (4/30/83 BC-6)

FAMILY MAN Fleetwood Mac—Warner Bros. 28114 [Lindsey Buckingham/Richard Dashut] [ASC] (4/2/88 B-90)

THE FAMILY OF MAN Three Dog Night—Dunhill 4306 [Jack Conrad/Paul Williams] [ASC] (3/25/72 BCR-8)

THE FANATIC Felony—Rock 'n' Roll 03497 [Arthur Blea/Louis Ruiz/Dan Sands/Jeff Spry/Joe Spry] [ASC] (2/12/83 BC-42)

FANCY Bobbie Gentry—Capitol 2675 [Bobbie Gentry] [ASC] (11/15/69 BCR-31)

FANCY DANCER Commodores—Motown 1408 [Ronald LaPread/Lionel Richie] [ASC] (12/25/76 BCR-39)

FANCY DANCER Frankie Valli—Warner/Curb 8734 [L. Russell Brown/Bob Crewe] [BMI] (1/27/79 B-77)

FANCY FREE Oak Ridge Boys—MCA 51169 [Roy August/Jimbeau Hinson] [BMI] (9/26/81 C-95)

FANCY LADY Billy Preston—A&M 1735 [Billy Preston/Syreeta Wright] [BMI] (10/4/75 BC-71)

FANCY NANCY Skip & Flip—Brent 7005 [Clyde Battin/Gary S. Paxton] [BMI] (11/2/59 BC-71)

FANCY PANTS Al (He's The King) Hirt Trumpet with Chorus and Orchestra—RCA Victor 47-8487 [Floyd Cramer] [BMI] (1/16/65 BCR-37) [I]

***FANNIE MAE** Buster Brown—Fire 1008 [Buster Brown/Clarence L. Lewis‡/Morgan C. Robinson‡] [BMI] (2/1/60 BCR-34)*

***FANNIE MAE** Mighty Sam—Amy 963 [Buster Brown/Clarence L. Lewis‡/Morgan C. Robinson‡] [BMI] (9/17/66 CR-98)*

FANNY Eddie Fisher—RCA Victor 47-5871 [Harold Rome] [ASC] (10/4/54 CR-18)

***FANNY (BE TENDER WITH MY LOVE)** Bee Gees—RSO 519 [Barry Gibb/Maurice Gibb/Robin Gibb] [BMI] (12/20/75 BCR-9)*

***FANNY (BE TENDER WITH MY LOVE)** Gino Cunico—Arista 0162 [Barry Gibb/Maurice Gibb/Robin Gibb] [BMI] (12/20/75 C-91)*

FANTASTIC VOYAGE Lakeside—Solar 12129 [Fred Alexander/Norman Beavers/Marvin Craig/Bryan Dodds*/Tiemeyer McCain/Thomas Shelby/Stephen Shockley/Otis Stokes/Mark Wood] [BMI] (12/27/80 BCR-42)

FANTASTICALLY FOOLISH Tommy Sands—Capitol 3743 [R. Alan Edwards] [NA] (6/29/57 R-67)

FANTASY Earth, Wind & Fire—Columbia 10688 [Eddie Del Barrio/Maurice White/Verdine White] [ASC] (2/25/78 BCR-32)

FANTASY Aldo Nova—Portrait 24-02799 [Aldo Nova] [BMI] (3/20/82 BCR-23)

FANTASY GIRL .38 Special—A&M 2330 [Jeff Carlisi/Jim Peterik] [ASC] (6/6/81 BCR-52)

FANTASY LOVE AFFAIR Peter Brown—Drive 6274 [Peter H. Brown] [BMI] (1/13/79 R-91)

FAR FAR AWAY Don Gibson—RCA Victor 47-7762 [Don Gibson] [BMI] (7/18/60 BCR-55)

A FAR FAR BETTER THING Della Reese—RCA Victor 47-7884 [Luigi Creatore/Hugo Peretti/George David Weiss] [ASC] (7/24/61 R-74)

FAR FROM OVER Frank Stallone—RSO 815023 [Vince DiCola/Frank Stallone] [ASC] (7/30/83 BC-10)

FAR FROM THE LIGHTS OF TOWN Paul Anka—ABC-Paramount 10282 [Paul Anka] [BMI] (1/29/62 R-95)

FARAWAY BOY Della Reese—RCA Victor 47-7706 [Frank Loesser] [ASC] (3/7/60 R-74)

FARAWAY STAR The Chordettes—Cadence 1402 [Richard Carney/David (2) Martin] [ASC] (9/25/61 BR-80)

FAREWELL ANDROMEDA (WELCOME TO MY MORNING) John Denver—RCA Victor 0067 [John Denver] [ASC] (9/1/73 BCR-59)

FAREWELL LOVE SCENE Romeo & Juliet Soundtrack [Nino Rota]—Capitol 2502 [Nino Rota] [ASC] (8/9/69 B-86) [I]

FAREWELL MY SUMMER LOVE Michael Jackson—Motown 1739 [Keni St. Lewis] [BMI] (5/26/84 BC-34)

***A FAREWELL TO ARMS** Marty Gold & His Orchestra—Vik 0315 [Mario Nascimbene/Paul Francis Webster] [ASC] (2/10/58 Rt-81)*

***A FAREWELL TO ARMS** Gale Storm—Dot 15691 [Mario Nascimbene/Paul Francis Webster] [ASC] (2/10/58 Rt-81)*

***FARMER JOHN** The Premiers—Warner Bros. 5443 [Don Harris/Dewey Terry] [BMI] (6/20/64 BCR-19)*

***FARMER JOHN** Tidal Waves—HBR 482 [Don Harris/Dewey Terry] [BMI] (5/28/66 CR-76)*

FARTHER ON DOWN THE ROAD Joe Simon—Sound Stage 7 2656 [Jesse Edwin Davis III/Taj Mahal] [BMI] (4/18/70 BCR-56)

FARTHER UP THE ROAD Bobby "Blue" Bland, Bill Harvey Orchestra—Duke 170 [Deadric Malone/Joe Veasey] [BMI] (8/5/57 B-43)

FASCINATED Company B—Atlantic 89294 [Ish Ledesma] [BMI] (3/21/87 BC-21)

***FASCINATION** Dick Jacobs And His Chorus And Orchestra—Coral 61864 [Dick Manning/Dante Marchetti] [NA] (7/20/57 BCtRt-7) [FDE]*

FASCINATION *Dinah Shore—RCA Victor 47-6980*
[Dick Manning/Dante Marchetti] [NA] (8/3/57 BRt-14) [FDE]

FASCINATION *Jane Morgan with the Troubadors—Kapp 191*
[Dick Manning/Dante Marchetti] [NA] (8/3/57 BCtRt-5) [FDE]

FASCINATION *David Carroll Orch. And Chorus—Mercury 71152*
[Dante Marchetti] [NA] (8/3/57 BRt-16) [IM]

FASCINATION *Ray Ellis & His Gypsies—Columbia 40982*
[Dante Marchetti] [NA] (8/12/57 Rt-16) [IM]

FASCINATION *Ethel Smith—Decca 30421 [Dante Marchetti] [NA] (8/26/57 Rt-16) [IM]*

FASCINATION *Big Al Sears—Jubilee 5293 [Dante Marchetti] [NA] (9/2/57 Rt-16) [IM]*

FASCINATION *Nat "King" Cole—Capitol EAP 1-813*
[Dick Manning/Dante Marchetti] (EP) [NA] (9/9/57 R-55) [FDE]

FASCINATION STREET The Cure—Elektra 69300
[Simon Gallup/Roger O'Donnell/Robert James Smith/Porl Thompson/
Laurence Tolhurst/Boris Williams] [ASC] (5/13/89 BC-46)

FASHION David Bowie—RCA 12134 [David Bowie] [BMI] (12/6/80 BCR-70)

FAST CAR Tracy Chapman—Elektra 69412 [Tracy Chapman] [ASC] (6/4/88 BC-4)

—FASTER FASTER SONG see: NINE MORE MILES

FAT ALBERT (HEY, HEY, HEY)
The Fat Albert Orchestra and Chorus—Tetragrammaton 1500
[Bill Cosby/Samuel Denoff/William Allan Persky/Irwin Elliott Zucker] [BMI]
(4/27/68 R-82)

FAT BOTTOMED GIRLS Queen—Elektra 45541
[Brian May] (TSW) [BMI] (11/11/78 BCR-18)

—FAT see: BAD

FATHER COME ON HOME Pacific Gas & Electric—Columbia 45221
[Bill Soden] [BMI] (10/10/70 B-93)

FATHER FIGURE George Michael—Columbia 07682
[George Michael] [ASC] (1/16/88 BC-1)

FATHER KNOWS BEST The Radiants—Chess 1832
[Lee Jackson/Maurice McAlister] [BMI] (11/3/62 B-100)

THE FATHER OF GIRLS Perry Como—CA Victor 47-9448
[Ervin Drake] [ASC] (3/16/68 B-92)

FATHER SEBASTIAN The Ramblers (2)—Almont 311
[Keith Colley/Nancie Mantz] [BMI] (8/8/64 BCR-86)

FATHER TIME The Poni-Tails—ABC-Paramount 9995
[George Mysels/Morty Neff] [ASC] (2/9/59 R-92)

FAVORITE WASTE OF TIME Bette Midler—Atlantic 89761
[Marshall Crenshaw] [ASC] (10/22/83 BC-78)

FEE-FI-FO-FUM Hungry Tiger—White Whale 313 [Marie S. Moffit] [ASC] (7/26/69 R-95)

FEEL ALRIGHT Cargoe—Ardent 2901 [Tommy Richard] [ASC] (8/19/72 CR-91)

FEEL GOOD Ike & Tina Turner—United Artists 50913
[Jesse James*/Ike Turner/Tina Turner] [BMI] (5/27/72 R-95)

FEEL IT *Sam Cooke—RCA Victor 47-7927 [Sam Cooke] [BMI] (9/11/61 BCR-44)*

FEEL IT *Sam Cooke—RCA Victor 47-8751 [Sam Cooke] [BMI] (2/19/66 B-95)*

FEEL IT AGAIN Honeymoon Suite—Warner Bros. 28779
[Ray Coburn] [BMI] (3/8/86 BC-32)

FEEL LIKE A NUMBER Bob Seger & The Silver Bullet Band—Capitol 4581
[Bob Seger] [ASC] (12/19/81 BCR-48)

FEEL LIKE MAKIN' LOVE Bad Company—Swan Song 70106
[Mick Ralphs/Paul Rodgers] [ASC] (6/21/75 BCR-10)

FEEL LIKE MAKIN' LOVE *Roberta Flack—Atlantic 3025*
[Gene McDaniels] [BMI] (6/15/74 BCR-1)

FEEL LIKE MAKING LOVE *Bob James—CTI 24*
[Gene McDaniels] [BMI] (11/9/74 B-88) [IWM]

FEEL SO BAD Little Milton—Checker 1162 [Lightning Hopkins] [BMI] (2/4/67 B-91)

FEEL SO BAD Ray Charles—ABC/TRC 11308
[James E. Johnson/Leslie Temple] [BMI] (8/21/71 BCR-59)

FEEL SO FINE *Johnny Preston—Mercury 71651 [Leonard Lee] [BMI] (6/20/60 BCR-9)*

FEEL SO GOOD *Bunny Sigler—Parkway 153 [Leonard Lee] (Med) [BMI] (6/17/67 BCR-19)*

FEEL THAT YOU'RE FEELIN' Maze Featuring Frankie Beverly—Capitol 4686
[Frankie Beverly] [BMI] (5/5/79 BCR-67)

FEEL THE BEAT (EVERYBODY DISCO) Ohio Players—Mercury 73881
[William Beck/Leroy Bonner/Marshall Jones/Ralph Middlebrooks/
Andrew Noland/Marvin Pierce/James Rodger Williams] [BMI] (1/29/77 B-61)

FEEL THE FIRE Peabo Bryson—Capitol 4573 [Peabo Bryson] [BMI] (6/24/78 R-98)

FEEL THE GROOVE Cartouche—Scotti Brothers 5281
[Serge Ramaekers] [BMI] (4/13/91 BC-66)

FEEL THE HEAT Jean Beauvoir—Columbia 05904 [Jean Beauvoir] [ASC] (6/7/86 BC-66)

FEEL THE NEED IN ME *Detroit Emeralds—Westbound 209*
[Abrim Tilmon] [BMI] (12/2/72 CR-88)

FEEL THE NEED *Detroit Emeralds—Westbound 55401*
[Abrim Tilmon] [BMI] (5/14/77 B-90)

FEEL THE NEED *Leif Garrett—Scotti Brothers 407 [Abrim Tilmon] [BMI] (5/5/79 BCR-57)*

FEELIN' FRUGGY Al Hirt—RCA Victor 47-8684 [Teri Thornton] [BMI] (10/2/65 R-86)

—FEELIN' GROOVY see: FIFTY-NINTH STREET BRIDGE SONG

FEELIN' SATISFIED Boston—Epic 50677 [Tom Scholz] [ASC] (3/24/79 BCR-46)

FEELIN' SO GOOD (S.K.O.O.B.Y.-D.O.O.) The Archies—Calendar 1007
[Jeff Barry/Andy Kim] [BMI] (12/21/68 BCR-30)

FEELIN' STRONGER EVERY DAY Chicago—Columbia 45880
[Peter Cetera/James Pankow] [ASC] (6/23/73 BCR-8)

FEELIN' THAT GLOW Roberta Flack—Atlantic 3271
[Bobby Fusco/Charlotte Laws/Gene McDaniels/Maurice McKinley/Leon Pendarvis] [BMI]
(6/7/75 BC-65)

FEELING ALRIGHT *Joe Cocker—A&M 1063 [Dave Mason] [ASC] (6/21/69 BCR-69)*

FEELING ALRIGHT *Mongo Santamaria—Atlantic 2689*
[Dave Mason] [ASC] (11/29/69 B-96) [IWM]

FEELIN' ALRIGHT *Grand Funk Railroad—Capitol 3095*
[Dave Mason] [ASC] (5/1/71 BCR-45)

FEELING ALRIGHT *Joe Cocker—A&M 1063 [Dave Mason] [ASC] (1/1/72 BCR-28)*

THE FEELING IS GONE Bobby Bland—Duke 370 [Deadric Malone] [BMI] (12/28/63 B-91)

THE FEELING IS RIGHT Clarence Carter—Atlantic 2642
[Mickey Buckins/George Henry Jackson] [BMI] (6/14/69 BCR-39)

FEELINGS Barry Mann—Scepter 12281
[Barry Mann/Cynthia Weil] [BMI] (5/30/70 BCR-82)

FEELINGS *Morris Albert—RCA Victor 10279*
[Morris Albert/Louis Gasté] [ASC] (6/14/75 BCR-4)*

FEELINGS *Walter Jackson—Chi-Sound 908*
[Morris Albert/Louis Gasté] [ASC] (12/25/76 B-93)*

FEELINGS OF FOREVER Tiffany—MCA 53325
[John Duarte/Mark E. Paul] [BMI] (6/11/88 BC-50)

FEELS GOOD Tony! Toni! Toné!—Wing 877 436
[Clemon Timothy Riley/Raphael Saadiq/Carl Wheeler/Dwayne Wiggins] [ASC]
(9/1/90 BC-8)

FEELS LIKE ANOTHER ONE Patti LaBelle—MCA 54225
[Sharon Barnes/James R. Ellison/Patti LaBelle/Michael Lee Stokes] [BMI]
(11/9/91 C-86)

FEELS LIKE THE FIRST TIME Foreigner—Atlantic 3394
[Michael Leslie Jones] [ASC] (3/26/77 BCR-4)

FEELS SO GOOD Chuck Mangione—A&M 2001
[Chuck Mangione] [BMI] (1/28/78 BCR-4) [I]

FEELS SO GOOD Van Halen—Warner Bros. 27565
[Michael Anthony/Sammy Hagar/Alex Van Halen/Eddie Van Halen] [ASC]
(1/28/89 BC-35)

FEELS SO REAL (WON'T LET GO) Patrice Rushen—Elektra 69742
[Patrice Rushen/Freddie Washington] [ASC] (6/30/84 BC-78)

FEELS SO RIGHT Alabama—RCA 12236 [Randy Owen] [BMI] (6/6/81 BCR-20)

FEET DON'T FAIL ME NOW Utopia—Network 69859
[Doug Howard/Roger Powell/Todd Rundgren/John Griffitt Wilcox] [ASC] (1/8/83 B-82)

FEET START WALKING Doris Duke—Canyon 35
[Gary Anderson/Jerry Williams Jr.] [BMI] (5/9/70 CR-85)

FELICIDAD Sally Field—Colgems 1008
[Dominic Frontiere*/Diane Hilderbrand] [BMI] (11/11/67 BCR-91)

FELIZ NAVIDAD Jose Feliciano—RCA Victor 74-0404
[Jose Feliciano] [ASC] (12/26/70 C-71)

FELL FOR YOU The Dramatics—Volt 4099 [Tony Hester] [BMI] (10/27/73 BCR-45)

FELL IN LOVE ON MONDAY Fats Domino—Imperial 5734
[Fats Domino] [BMI] (3/20/61 BCR-32)

FEMALE INTUITION Mai Tai—Critique 722
[Jochem Fluitsma/Eric Van Tijn] [ASC] (5/24/86 BC-71)

FENCEWALK Mandrill—Polydor 14163
[Carlos Wilson/Louis Wilson/Ric Wilson] [ASC] (4/7/73 BCR-45)

FERNANDO Abba—Atlantic 3346
[Stig Anderson/Benny Andersson/Björn Ulvaeus] [ASC] (8/28/76 BCR-10)

THE FERRIS WHEEL The Everly Brothers—Warner Bros. 5441
[Dewayne Blackwell/Ronald Blackwell] [BMI] (6/20/64 BCR-54)

FERRY CROSS THE MERSEY Gerry And The Pacemakers—Laurie 3284
[Gerry Marsden] [BMI] (2/6/65 BCR-4)

FEVER *Little Willie John—King 4935*
[Otis Blackwell/Eddie Cooley] [BMI] (6/9/56 BCR-22)

FEVER *Earl Grant—Decca 30475 [Otis Blackwell/Eddie Cooley] [BMI] (12/21/57 CRt-3)*

FEVER *Ray Peterson—RCA Victor 47-7087*
[Otis Blackwell/Eddie Cooley] [BMI] (12/23/57 Rt-7)

FEVER *Peggy Lee—Capitol 3998 [Otis Blackwell/Eddie Cooley] [BMI] (7/7/58 BCRt-3)*

FEVER *Little Willie John—King 4935*
[Otis Blackwell/Eddie Cooley] [BMI] (9/1/58 Rt-7)

FEVER *Pete Bennett & The Embers—Sunset 1002*
[Otis Blackwell/Eddie Cooley] [BMI] (11/20/61 CR-93) [IWM]

FEVER *The McCoys—Bang 511 [Otis Blackwell/Eddie Cooley] [BMI] (11/6/65 BCR-6)*

FEVER *Rita Coolidge—A&M 1398*
[Otis Blackwell/Eddie Cooley] (TSW) [BMI] (1/6/73 BCR-62)

THE FEZ Steely Dan—ABC 12222
[Walter Becker/Donald Fagen/Paul Griffin] [ASC] (9/25/76 BCR-59)

FFUN Con Funk Shun—Mercury 73959 [Michael V. Cooper] [BMI] (11/19/77 BCR-18)

FIBBIN' Patti Page—Mercury 71355
[Michael Merlo/Patrick Welch] [ASC] (9/15/58 BCR-26)

FIDDLE AROUND Jan & Dean—Liberty 55905
[Clint Ballard Jr./Larry Kusik] [ASC] (8/27/66 BCR-73)

FIDDLER ON THE ROOF The Village Stompers—Epic 9740
[Jerry Bock] [BMI] (11/28/64 BCR-66) [IM]

FIELDS OF FIRE Big Country—Mercury 811450
[William Stuart Adamson/Mark Brzezicki/Anthony Earl Butler/Bruce William Watson] [ASC] (2/4/84 BC-52)

FIESTA Dave "Baby" Cortez—Emit 301
[David Clowney/Ken Wood] [BMI] (11/17/62 B-96) [I]

THE FIFE PIPER The Dynatones—HBR 494
[Eddie Evans/Ray Figlar/Gary Van Scyoc] [BMI] (8/20/66 BCR-53) [I]

FIFTEEN YEARS AGO Conway Twitty—Decca 32742
[Raymond Smith] [BMI] (10/24/70 BC-81)

A FIFTH OF BEETHOVEN Walter Murphy & The Big Apple Band—Private Stock 45,073
[Walter Murphy/Ludwig van Beethoven*] [BMI] (5/22/76 BCR-1) [I]

FIFTY FATHOMS Jack Fascinato—Fraternity 740
[Jack Fascinato/Larry Gordon/Al Trace] [ASC] (7/20/56 R-82)

THE 59TH STREET BRIDGE SONG (FEELIN' GROOVY) Harpers Bizarre—Warner Bros. 5890
[Paul Simon] [BMI] (2/18/67 BCR-13)

50 WAYS TO LEAVE YOUR LOVER Paul Simon—Columbia 10270
[Paul Simon] [BMI] (12/13/75 BCR-1)

FIGHT Barbra Streisand—Columbia 11008
[Bob Esty/Paul Jabara] (Med) [BMI] (6/16/79 BCR-3)

FIGHT FIRE WITH FIRE Kansas—CBS Associated 04057
[Dino Elefante/John Elefante] [BMI] (9/3/83 BC-58)

FIGHT THE POWER PART 1 The Isley Brothers—T-Neck 2256
[Ernie Isley/Marvin Isley/O'Kelly Isley/Ronald Isley/Rudolph Isley/Chris Jasper] [ASC] (6/14/75 BCR-4)

THE FIGHTIN' SIDE OF ME Merle Haggard And The Strangers—Capitol 2719
[Merle Haggard] [BMI] (2/14/70 BC-92)

FIGURE OF EIGHT Paul McCartney—Capitol 44489
[Paul McCartney] [ASC] (1/13/90 B-92)

FILL MY SOUL The Pop Explosion—We Make Rock 'n Roll Records 1603
[Fred Goodman/Richie Grasso] [BMI] (9/7/68 R-94)

THE FINAL COUNTDOWN Europe—Epic 06416 [Joey Tempest] [BMI] (1/24/87 BC-8)

FINALLY T.G. Sheppard—Warner/Curb 50041 [Gary Chapman] [ASC] (4/3/82 BCR-45)

FINALLY Ce Ce Peniston—A&M 1586
[Felipe Delgado/Elbert Linnear/Ce Ce Peniston] [BMI] (9/28/91 BC-5)

FINALLY GOT MYSELF TOGETHER (I'M A CHANGED MAN) The Impressions—Curtom 1997
[Ed Townsend] [BMI] (4/27/74 BCR-15)

FIND A WAY Amy Grant—A&M 2734
[Amy Grant/Michael W. Smith] [ASC] (5/18/85 BC-28)

FIND ANOTHER FOOL Quarterflash—Geffen 50006 [Marv Ross] [ASC] (2/13/82 BCR-16)

FIND ANOTHER GIRL Jerry Butler—Vee-Jay 375
[Jerry Butler/Curtis Mayfield] [BMI] (3/4/61 BCR-21)

—FIND ANOTHER LIKE YOU see: I'LL NEVER FIND ANOTHER

FIND 'EM, FOOL 'EM & FORGET 'EM Dobie Gray—Capricorn 0259
[Rick Hall/George Henry Jackson] [BMI] (10/23/76 B-94)

FIND MY WAY BACK HOME The Nashville Teens—London 9736
[Lou Courtney/Dennis Lambert] [BMI] (3/13/65 B-98)

FIND YOUR WAY BACK Jefferson Starship—Grunt 12211
[Thomas Borsdorf/Craig Chaquico] [BMI] (4/4/81 BCR-29)

FINDERS KEEPERS Salt Water Taffy—Buddah 37
[John Giametta/Rod McBrien] [BMI] (5/18/68 R-84)

FINDER'S KEEPERS Chairmen Of The Board—Invictus 1251
[Jeff Bowen/General Johnson] [BMI] (6/2/73 BCR-59)

FINDERS KEEPERS, LOSERS WEEPERS Nella Dodds—Wand 171
[Kenneth Gamble] [BMI] (1/9/65 B-96)

A FINE FINE BOY Darlene Love—Philles 117
[Jeff Barry/Ellie Greenwich/Phil Spector] [BMI] (10/19/63 BCR-53)

A FINE FINE DAY Tony Carey—MCA 52343 [Tony Carey] [ASC] (3/3/84 BC-22)

FINE ROMANCE Sammy Davis Jr. And Carmen McRae—Decca 29620
[Dorothy Fields/Jerome Kern] [ASC] (8/29/55 R-76)

THE FINER THINGS Steve Winwood—Island 28498
[Will Jennings/Steve Winwood] [BMI] (2/7/87 BC-7)

THE FINEST The S.O.S. Band—Tabu 4-05848
[James Samuel Harris/Terry Lewis] [ASC] (5/17/86 BC-44)

***THE FINGER OF SUSPICION** Dickie Valentine With The Stargazers—London 1498*
[Al Lewis/Paul Mann] [ASC] (1/10/55 CRt-13)

***THE FINGER OF SUSPICION** Dolores Gray—Decca 29353*
[Al Lewis/Paul Mann] [ASC] (1/10/55 Rt-13)

***THE FINGER OF SUSPICION POINTS AT YOU** Jane Froman—Capitol 2979*
[Al Lewis/Paul Mann] [ASC] (1/10/55 Rt-13)

***THE FINGER OF SUSPICION** Eddy Howard & His Orchestra—Mercury 70533*
[Al Lewis/Paul Mann] [ASC] (1/24/55 Rt-61)

—FINGER ON THE TRIGGER see: LOVE IS IN CONTROL

FINGER POPPIN' TIME Hank Ballard And The Midnighters—King 5341
[Hank Ballard] [BMI] (5/16/60 BCR-6)

***FINGERTIPS - PT 2** Little Stevie Wonder—Tamla 54080*
[Henry Cosby/Clarence Paul] [ASC] (6/22/63 BCR-1)

***FINGERTIPS** Stars On 45—Radio 4019*
[Henry Cosby/Clarence Paul] (Med) [ASC] (3/27/82 BCR-28)

FINISH WHAT YA STARTED Van Halen—Warner Bros. 27746
[Michael Anthony/Sammy Hagar/Alex Van Halen/Eddie Van Halen] [ASC] (10/1/88 BC-13)

FINS Jimmy Buffett—MCA 41109
[Jimmy Buffett/Barry Chance/Tom Corcoran/Deborah McColl] [BMI] (9/1/79 BCR-24)

FIRE (I'M KEEPING MY HEART AWAY FROM FIRE) Les Paul and Mary Ford—Capitol 3825
[Lee Silver] [BMI] (10/28/57 R-52)

FIRE The Crazy World Of Arthur Brown—Atlantic 2556
[Arthur Wilton Brown/Vincent Cheesman/Michael Finesilver/Peter Ker] [BMI] (9/7/68 BCR-2)

FIRE Five By Five—Paula 302 [Jimi Hendrix] [ASC] (9/28/68 BCR-31)

FIRE Ohio Players—Mercury 73643
[William Beck/Leroy Bonner/Marshall Jones/Ralph Middlebrooks/Andrew Noland/Marvin Pierce/James Rodger Williams] [BMI] (12/14/74 BCR-1)

FIRE Mother's Finest—Epic 50269
[Joyce Kennedy*/Glenn Murdock*/Jerry Seay] [ASC] (9/4/76 B-93)

***FIRE** Pointer Sisters—Planet 45901 [Bruce Springsteen] [ASC] (11/11/78 BCR-2)*

***FIRE** Bruce Springsteen & The E Street Band—Columbia 06657*
[Bruce Springsteen] [ASC] (1/31/87 BC-45)

FIRE AND ICE Pat Benatar—Chrysalis 2529
[Pat Benatar/Thomas F. Kelly/Scott Sheets] [ASC] (7/18/81 BCR-15)

***FIRE AND RAIN** R.B. Greaves—Atco 6745 [James Taylor] [ASC] (4/11/70 BCR-62)*

***FIRE AND RAIN** Johnny Rivers & Friends—Imperial 66453*
[James Taylor] [ASC] (8/22/70 BCR-68)

***FIRE AND RAIN** James Taylor—Warner Bros. 7423 [James Taylor] [ASC] (9/12/70 BCR-3)*

FIRE AND WATER Wilson Pickett—Atlantic 2852
[Andy Fraser/Paul Rodgers] [BMI] (12/18/71 BCR-17)

FIRE, BABY I'M ON FIRE Andy Kim—Capitol 3962 [Andy Kim] [BMI] (10/26/74 BCR-28)

***FIRE DOWN BELOW** Jeri Southern—Decca 30343*
[Lester Lee/Ned Washington] [ASC] (8/3/57 Rt-73)

***FIRE DOWN BELOW** Roger King Mozian—Decca 30349*
[Lester Lee/Ned Washington] [ASC] (8/3/57 Rt-73)

***FIRE DOWN BELOW** Gordon Jenkins & His Orchestra—Capitol 3751*
[Lester Lee] [ASC] (8/3/57 Rt-73) [IM]

FIRE IN THE MORNING Melissa Manchester—Arista 0485
[Steve Dorff/Gary Harju/Larry Herbstritt] [BMI] (2/9/80 BCR-32)

FIRE IN THE SKY The Dirt Band—Liberty 1429
[Robert Carpenter/Jeff Hanna] [ASC] (9/26/81 BCR-65)

FIRE LAKE Bob Seger—Capitol 4836 [Bob Seger] [ASC] (2/23/80 BCR-5)

FIRE OF LOVE Jody Reynolds—Demon 1509
[Jody Reynolds/Sonja Sturdivant] [BMI] (8/18/58 B-66)

FIRE ON THE MOUNTAIN The Marshall Tucker Band—Capricorn 0244
[George McCorkle] [BMI] (10/18/75 BCR-38)

FIRE SIGN Cory—Phantom 10856 [Cory Braverman/Rick Ulfik] [ASC] (1/22/77 BC-77)

FIRE WITH FIRE Wild Blue—Chrysalis 42985 [Chas Sandford] [ASC] (5/17/86 BC-71)

FIRE WOMAN The Cult—Sire 27543 [Ian Astbury/Billy Duffy] [ASC] (5/20/89 BC-46)

FIRECRACKER Mass Production—Cotillion 44254
[Ricardo Williams] [ASC] (7/28/79 BCR-33)

FIREFLIES Fleetwood Mac—Warner Bros. 49660 [Stevie Nicks] [BMI] (2/7/81 BCR-60)

FIREFLY Tony Bennett—Columbia 41237
[Cy Coleman/Carolyn Leigh] [ASC] (9/1/58 BCR-15)

FIRST ANNIVERSARY Cathy Carr—Roulette 4125
[Aaron Schroeder/Sid Wayne] [ASC] (1/12/59 BCR-24)

FIRST...BE A WOMAN Lenore O'Malley—Polydor 2055
[Michele Michaele/Lana Sebastian/Paul Sebastian] [BMI] (7/19/80 BCR-53)

FIRST BORN "Tennessee" Ernie Ford—Capitol 3553
[Johnny Lehmann] [BMI] (10/27/56 BCR-41)

***FIRST CUT IS THE DEEPEST** Keith Hampshire—A&M 1432*
[Cat Stevens] [BMI] (4/14/73 BCR-40)

***THE FIRST CUT IS THE DEEPEST** Rod Stewart—Warner Bros. 8321*
[Cat Stevens] [BMI] (2/12/77 BCR-17)

FIRST DATE FIRST KISS FIRST LOVE Sonny James—Capitol 3674
[Mary Stovall/Dan Welch] [BMI] (3/23/57 BCR-23)

FIRST DAY BACK AT SCHOOL Paul & Paula—Philips 40142
[Ray Hildebrand/Jill Jackson] [BMI] (10/5/63 BCR-60)

THE FIRST DAY OF SUMMER Tony Carey—MCA 52388 [Tony Carey] [ASC] (6/9/84 BC-33)

FIRST HYMN FROM GRAND TERRACE Mark Lindsay—Columbia 44875
[Jimmy Webb] [ASC] (7/12/69 BCR-81)

FIRST I LOOK AT THE PURSE The Contours—Gordy 7044
[Smokey Robinson/Robert Rogers] [ASC] (8/14/65 BCR-55)

THE FIRST KISS The Norman Petty Trio—Columbia 40929
[Norman Petty] [BMI] (8/12/57 B-81)

FIRST LOVE The Playmates—Roulette 4200
[Ray Allen/Wandra Merrell/Sam Saltzberg] [BMI] (10/26/59 R-82)

FIRST LOVE FIRST TEARS Duane Eddy His "Twangy" guitar and The Rebels—Jamie 1130
[Duane Eddy/Lee Hazlewood] [BMI] (9/21/59 BCR-43) [I]

FIRST NAME INITIAL Annette With The Afterbeats–Buena Vista 349
[Martin Kalmanoff/Aaron Schroeder] [ASC] (10/12/59 BCR-16)

FIRST NIGHT Survivor–Scotti Brothers 05579
[Jim Peterik/Frankie Sullivan] [ASC] (8/17/85 BC-52)

–FIRST NIGHT OF THE FULL MOON see: PEARLY SHELLS

FIRST OF MAY The Bee Gees–Atco 6657
[Barry Gibb/Maurice Gibb/Robin Gibb] [BMI] (3/22/69 BCR-16)

FIRST QUARREL Paul & Paula–Philips 40114
[Orville Couch/Eddie McDuff/Bill Smith] [BMI] (5/25/63 BCR-21)

FIRST TASTE OF LOVE Ben E. King–Atco 6185
[Doc Pomus/Phil Spector] [BMI] (12/24/60 BCR-53)

THE FIRST THING EV'RY MORNING (AND THE LAST THING EV'RY NIGHT)
Jimmy Dean–Columbia 43263
[Jimmy Dean/Ruth Roberts] [BMI] (6/26/65 B-79)

THE FIRST TIME Surface–Columbia 73502
[Bernard Leon Jackson/Brian Simpson] [ASC] (11/3/90 BC-1)

THE FIRST TIME EVER I SAW YOUR FACE Roberta Flack–Atlantic 2864
[Ewan MacColl] [BMI] (3/4/72 BCR-1)

FIRST TIME LOVE Livingston Taylor–Epic 50894
[Patrick Alger/Peter Kaminsky] [ASC] (7/26/80 BCR-38)

FIRST TRUE LOVE Tiana–MicMac 2537
[Mickey Garcia/Elvin Molina] [ASC] (7/14/90 B-81)

FISH Mindy Carson–Columbia 40438 [Philip Springer/Sid Wayne] [ASC] (3/5/55 CR-23)

THE FISH Bobby Rydell–Cameo 192
[Dave Appell/Bernie Lowe/Kal Mann] [BMI] (6/26/61 BCR-16)

FISH AIN'T BITIN' Lamont Dozier–ABC 11438
[McKinley Jackson/James Reddick] [BMI] (6/15/74 BCR-26)

FISHNET Morris Day–Warner Bros. 28201
[Morris Day/James Samuel Harris/Terry Lewis] [ASC] (2/20/88 BC-23)

FIVE Sammy Davis Jr.–Decca 29976
[Billy Martin/Larry (2) Martin] [ASC] (7/14/56 B-71)

FIVE BROTHERS Marty Robbins–Columbia 41771
[Tompall Glaser] [BMI] (8/29/60 BR-74)

FIVE CARD STUD Lorne Greene–RCA Victor 47-8757
[Wally Gold/David Hess] [ASC] (2/26/66 C-91)

5 D (FIFTH DIMENSION) The Byrds–Columbia 43702
[Roger McGuinn] [BMI] (7/9/66 BCR-32)

FIVE FEET HIGH AND RISING Johnny Cash–Columbia 41427
[Johnny Cash] [ASC] (8/15/59 BC-76)

5:15 The Who–Polydor 2022 [Pete Townshend] [BMI] (9/29/79 BCR-45)

FIVE FOOT TWO Don Johnson–Kandy 137
[Ray Henderson/Sam Lewis/Joe Young] [ASC] (2/29/60 R-45)

–FIVE FOR THE DJ see: MR. DJ

FIVE HUNDRED GUYS Frank Sinatra–Capitol 3423
[Don Canton/Ira Kosloff] [BMI] (5/18/56 BCR-38)

500 MILES AWAY FROM HOME *Bobby Bare–RCA Victor 47-8238*
[Bobby Bare/Hedy West/Charlie Williams] [BMI] (10/5/63 BCR-10)*

FIVE HUNDRED MILES *Heaven Bound With Tony Scotti–MGM 14314*
[Bobby Bare/Hedy West/Charlie Williams] [BMI] (11/27/71 BCR-79)*

500 MILES *Hooters–Columbia 73013*
[Bobby Bare/Hedy West/Charlie Williams*] [BMI] (12/9/89 B-97)*

–FIVE OAKS see: CINCO ROBLES

FIVE O'CLOCK WORLD The Vogues–Co & Ce 232
[Allen Reynolds] [BMI] (11/27/65 BCR-3)

THE FIVE PENNIES Dodie Stevens–Crystalette 728 [Sylvia Fine] [ASC] (5/23/59 BC-75)

5.7.0.5. City Boy–Mercury 73999 [Stephen Lunt/Lol Mason] [ASC] (7/15/78 BCR-27)

5-10-15-20 (25-30 YEARS OF LOVE) The Presidents–Sussex 207
[Tony Boyd/Archie Powell] [BMI] (10/3/70 BCR-6)

FLAME Steve Sperry–Mercury 73905 [Steve Sperry] [BMI] (7/2/77 BCR-91)

THE FLAME Cheap Trick–Epic 07745
[Alan Nicholas Graham/Bobby Mitchell] [ASC] (4/9/88 BC-1)

FLAMENCO LOVE *Tony Martin–RCA Victor 47-6493*
[Jimmy Eaton/Frank Shuman/Larry Wagner] [ASC] (3/30/56 Rt-48)

FLAMENCO LOVE *Don Costa His Orchestra And Chorus–ABC-Paramount 9693*
[Jimmy Eaton/Frank Shuman/Larry Wagner] [ASC] (3/30/56 CRt-44) [IMW]

FLAMENCO LOVE *Al Caiola and his Magic Guitar–Regent 7500*
[Jimmy Eaton/Frank Shuman/Larry Wagner] [ASC] (3/30/56 Rt-48) [IMW]

FLAMENCO LOVE *Richard Hayman–Mercury 70837*
[Jimmy Eaton/Frank Shuman/Larry Wagner] [ASC] (4/6/56 Rt-48) [IMW]

FLAMES OF PARADISE (DUET WITH ELTON JOHN) Jennifer Rush–Epic 07119
[Andy Goldmark/Bruce Roberts] [ASC] (5/16/87 BC-36)

FLAMETHROWER The J. Geils Band–EMI America 8108
[Seth Justman] (TSW) [ASC] (2/20/82 CR-4)

FLAMING STAR Elvis Presley With The Jordanaires–RCA Victor LPC-128
[Sherman Edwards/Sid Wayne] [ASC] (4/17/61 BCR-14)

FLAMING YOUTH Kiss–Casablanca 858
[Bob Ezrin/Ace Frehley/Gene Simmons/Paul Stanley] [BMI] (6/5/76 BC-74)

FLAMINGO L'AMORE *The Gaylords–Mercury 71369*
[Ed Anderson/Theodor Grouya] [ASC] (10/27/58 BCR-52) [F]

FLAMINGO *Herb Alpert & The Tijuana Brass–A&M 813*
[Theodor Grouya] [ASC] (9/3/66 BCR-20) [IM]

FLAMINGO EXPRESS The Royaltones–Goldisc 3011
[George Katsakis/Greg Popoff/Mike Popoff] [BMI] (12/24/60 BCR-44) [I]

FLASH LIGHT Parliament–Casablanca 909
[George Clinton/William Earl Collins/Bernie Worrell] [BMI] (2/4/78 BCR-14)

FLASHBACK *Paul Anka–Fame XW 345 [Alan O'Day/Artie Wayne] [ASC] (12/1/73 R-100)*

FLASHBACK *The 5th Dimension–Bell 45,425*
[Alan O'Day/Artie Wayne] [ASC] (12/15/73 BCR-82)

FLASHDANCE...WHAT A FEELING Irene Cara–Casablanca 811440
[Irene Cara/Keith Forsey/Giorgio Moroder] [ASC] (4/2/83 BC-1)

FLASHES Tiggi Clay–Morocco 1716
[Romeo McCall/Billy Peaches/Fizzy Qwick] [NA] (2/25/84 B-86)

FLASH'S THEME AKA FLASH Queen–Elektra 47092 [Brian May] [BMI] (1/17/81 BCR-39)

FLESH AND BLOOD Johnny Cash–Columbia 45269
[Johnny Cash] [NA] (12/12/70 BCR-49)

–FLESH FAILURES see: LET THE SUNSHINE IN

FLESH FOR FANTASY Billy Idol–Chrysalis 42809
[Billy Idol/Steve Stevens] [ASC] (8/25/84 BC-29)

–FLIGHT OF THE BUMBLE BEE see: BUMBLE BOOGIE

FLIGHT '76 The Walter Murphy Band–Private Stock 45,123
[Walter Murphy/Nikolai Rimsky-Korsakov] [BMI] (11/6/76 BCR-36) [I]

FLIM FLAM MAN Barbra Streisand–Columbia 45384
[Laura Nyro] [BMI] (5/15/71 BCR-69)

FLIP FLOP AND BOP Floyd Cramer–RCA Victor 47-7156
[Floyd Cramer] [BMI] (4/28/58 B-87) [I]

FLIP FLOP AND FLY *Joe Turner & His Blues Kings–Atlantic 1053*
[Jesse Stone/Lou Willie Turner] [BMI] (3/21/55 Rt-52)

FLIP FLOP AND FLY *Johnnie Ray–Columbia 40471*
[Jesse Stone/Lou Willie Turner] [BMI] (3/21/55 Rt-29)

FLIP FLOP AND FLY *The Goofers–Coral 61383*
[Jesse Stone/Lou Willie Turner] [BMI] (3/28/55 Rt-29)

FLIP TOP BOX Dicky Doo And The Don'ts–Swan 4006 [Marion Smith] [BMI] (6/9/58 B-61)

FLIRTIN' WITH DISASTER Molly Hatchet–Epic 50822
[Danny Joe Brown/Dave Hlubek/Banner Thomas] [BMI] (12/29/79 BCR-42)

THE FLOAT Hank Ballard And The Midnighters–King 5510
[Michael Cowan] [BMI] (6/19/61 BR-91)

FLOAT ON *The Floaters–ABC 12284*
[Arnold Ingram/James Mitchell Jr./Marvin Willis] [BMI] (6/25/77 BCR-2)

BLOAT ON FEATURING THE BLOATERS *(parody of Float On)*
Cheech & Chong–Ode 50471
[Tommy Chong/Arnold Ingram/Cheech Marin*/James Mitchell Jr./Marvin Willis] [BMI] (11/5/77 BCR-41) [P]*

THE FLOWER CHILDREN Marcia Strassman–Uni 55006
[Jerry Goldstein/Lord Tim Hudson/Russ Regan] [BMI] (5/27/67 CR-95)

FLOWER OF LOVE The Crests–Coed 511
[Alicia Evelyn/Billy Dawn Smith] [BMI] (6/8/59 BCR-72)

FLOWERS The Emotions–Columbia 10347
[Albert Philip McKay/Maurice White] (TSW) [ASC] (11/6/76 BR-62)

FLOWERS MEAN FORGIVENESS Frank Sinatra–Capitol 3350
[Al Frisch/Edward White/Mack Wolfson] [ASC] (2/24/56 BCR-16)

FLOWERS ON THE WALL The Statler Brothers–Columbia 43315
[Lewis DeWitt] [BMI] (11/13/65 BCR-4)

FLOY JOY The Supremes–Motown 1195 [Smokey Robinson] [ASC] (1/8/72 BCR-16)

THE FLY Chubby Checker–Parkway 830
[John Madara/David White] [BMI] (9/25/61 BCR-6)

THE FLY U2–Island 868 885
[Adam Clayton/Dave Evans/Paul Hewson/Larry Mullen] [ASC] (11/9/91 B-61)

FLY AT NIGHT Chilliwack–Mushroom 7024
[William A. Henderson/Ross Turney] [BMI] (4/16/77 BCR-57)

FLY AWAY John Denver–RCA Victor 10517 [John Denver] [ASC] (12/6/75 BCR-6)

FLY AWAY *Peter Allen–A&M 2288*
[Peter Allen/David Foster/Carole Bayer Sager] [BMI] (1/10/81 BCR-55)

FLY AWAY *Stevie Woods–Cotillion 47006*
[Peter Allen/David Foster/Carole Bayer Sager] [BMI] (5/15/82 BC-84)

FLY AWAY Blackfoot–Atco 7331 [Rick Medlocke/Jakson Spires] [BMI] (6/20/81 BCR-42)

FLY BY NIGHT Andy Williams–Columbia 42199
[Ritchie Adams/Neval Nader] [BMI] (10/16/61 BCR-73)

FLY BY NIGHT Rush–Mercury 73873 [Geddy Lee/Neil Peart] (Med) [ASC] (1/8/77 B-88)

FLY HIGH MICHELLE Enuff Z'Nuff–Atco 99135 [Donnie Vie] [ASC] (1/27/90 BC-47)

FLY LIKE AN EAGLE Steve Miller–Capitol 4372 [Steve Miller] [ASC] (12/11/76 BCR-2)

FLY LITTLE WHITE DOVE FLY The Bells–Polydor 15016
[Bob Bilyk/Martin Butler] [ASC] (12/26/70 BCR-65)

FLY ME TO THE MOON - BOSSA NOVA *Joe Harnell And His Orchestra–Kapp 497*
[Bart Howard] [ASC] (12/8/62 BCR-14) [IWM]

FLY ME TO THE MOON *LaVern Baker–Atlantic 2267 [Bart Howard] [ASC] (2/13/65 B-84)*

FLY ME TO THE MOON (IN OTHER WORDS) *Tony Bennett–Columbia 43331*
[Bart Howard] [ASC] (7/10/65 BCR-60)

FLY ME TO THE MOON *Sam & Bill–JoDa 104 [Bart Howard] [ASC] (1/29/66 BR-98)*

FLY ME TO THE MOON *Bobby Womack—Minit 32048*
[Bart Howard] [ASC] (8/17/68 BCR-49)

FLY, ROBIN, FLY *Silver Convention—Midland Int'l 10339*
[Sylvester Levay/Stephan Prager] [BMI] (10/4/75 BCR-1) [IWM]

FLY, ROBIN, FLY *The Ritchie Family—Marlin 3306*
[Sylvester Levay/Stephan Prager] (Med) [BMI] (8/28/76 BCR-17) [IWM]

FLY TO THE ANGELS Slaughter—Chrysalis 23527
[Mark Slaughter/Dana Strum] [BMI] (8/18/90 BC-18)

FLY WITH ME The Avant-Garde—Columbia 44701
[Chuck Woolery] [BMI] (12/21/68 CR-79)

THE FLYER Saga—Portrait 37-04178
[Jim Crichton/Michael Sadler] [ASC] (11/26/83 B-79)

FLYIN' Prism—Ariola America 7714
[John (2) Hall*/Allen Hawirko/Lindsay Mitchell*/Ronald Tabak*/Gary Wanstall*] [BMI] (7/22/78 BCR-53)

FLYING BLUE ANGELS George, Johnny And The Pilots—Coed 555
[Mark Barkan/Sandy Baron/George Eddy] [BMI] (1/15/62 R-93)

FLYING CIRCLE Frank Slay And His Orchestra—Swan 4085
[Frank Slay] [ASC] (11/13/61 BCR-43) [I]

FLYING HIGH The Blackbyrds—Fantasy 747 [Keith Killgo] [BMI] (7/26/75 BC-70)

FLYING HIGH Commodores—Motown 1452
[Thomas McClary/Lionel Richie] [ASC] (9/23/78 BCR-38)

THE FLYING SAUCER (PTS. 1 & 2) Buchanan And Goodman—Luniverse 101
[Bill Buchanan*/Dickie Goodman] [BMI] (8/4/56 BCR-3)

FLYING SAUCER THE SECOND Buchanan And Goodman—Luniverse 105
[Bill Buchanan*/Dickie Goodman] [BMI] (7/13/57 BCR-19)

FLYING WITH BROKEN WINGS (WITHOUT YOU) Angel—Casablanca 914
[Frank DiMino/Gregg Giuffria/Punky Meadows] [BMI] (4/1/78 R-89)

FM (NO STATIC AT ALL) Steely Dan—MCA 40894
[Walter Becker/Donald Fagen] [ASC] (6/3/78 BCR-22)

FOG CUTTER The Frantics—Dolton 6
[Don Fulton/Bob Hosko/Jim Manolides/Ron Peterson/Chuck Schoning] [BMI] (9/14/59 B-93) [I]

—FOGGY MOUNTAIN BREAKDOWN see: THEME FROM BONNIE AND CLYDE

THE FOLK SINGER Tommy Roe—ABC-Paramount 10423 [Merle Kilgore] [BMI] (5/4/63 BCR-84)

FOLLOW ME *The Four Esquires—Pilgrim 717 [Wally Gold] [ASC] (1/12/57 C-43)*

FOLLOW ME *Billy Williams Quartet—Coral 61751 [Wally Gold] [ASC] (1/19/57 R-75)*

FOLLOW ME The Drifters—Atlantic 2292 [Kenny Lynch/Mort Shuman] [BMI] (7/3/65 B-91)

FOLLOW ME Lyme & Cybelle—White Whale 228
[Violet Santangelo/Warren Zevon] [BMI] (3/19/66 BCR-65)

FOLLOW ME Mary Travers—Warner Bros. 7481 [John Denver] [ASC] (5/22/71 BCR-56)

FOLLOW MY HEARTBEAT A'me Lorain—RCA 2620 [Elliot Wolff] [ASC] (6/16/90 BC-56)

FOLLOW THAT DREAM Elvis Presley—RCA Victor EPA-4368
[Ben Weisman/Fred Wise] [ASC] (4/23/62 BCR-15)

FOLLOW THE BOYS Connie Francis—MGM 13127
[Benny Davis/Ted Murry] [ASC] (3/2/63 BCR-11)

FOLLOW YOU Glen Burtnick—A&M 2968
[Glen Burtnick/Jack Ponti] [ASC] (9/26/87 BC-65)

FOLLOW YOU FOLLOW ME Genesis—Atlantic 3474
[Tony Banks/Phil Collins/Mike Rutherford] [BMI] (4/22/78 BCR-22)

FOLLOW YOUR DAUGHTER HOME The Guess Who—RCA Victor 74-0880
[Burton Cummings/Don McDougall/Garry Peterson/Bill Wallace/Kurt Winter] [BMI] (2/3/73 BCR-61)

FOLLOW YOUR HEART The Four Coins—Epic 9253
[Bernie Lowe/Kal Mann] [ASC] (11/25/57 R-44)

FOLLOW YOUR HEART The Manhattans—Carnival 512
[Edward Bivins] [BMI] (12/18/65 BCR-70)

FOLLOW YOUR HEART Triumph—MCA 52540
[Rik Emmett/Mike Levine/Gil Moore] [ASC] (3/9/85 B-88)

FOLSOM PRISON BLUES Johnny Cash—Columbia 44513
[Johnny Cash] [BMI] (5/25/68 BCR-32)

THE FONZ SONG The Heyettes—London 232 [Michael Fein] [ASC] (4/10/76 BCR-66)

FOOL *Sanford Clark—Dot 15481 [Lee Hazlewood] [BMI] (7/20/56 BCtRt-7)*

FOOL *The Gallahads—Jubilee 5252 [Lee Hazlewood] [BMI] (7/27/56 BCtRt-7)*

FOOL Elvis Presley—RCA Victor 74-0910
[James Last/Carl Sigman] (TSW) [ASC] (4/14/73 BCR-16)

FOOL AND THE ANGEL Bobby Helms—Decca 30749
[Jimmy Duncan] [BMI] (12/8/58 B-75)

FOOL FOR A PRETTY FACE (HURT BY LOVE) Humble Pie—Atco 7216
[Steve Marriott/Jerry Shirley] [BMI] (4/26/80 BCR-52)

FOOL FOR THE CITY Foghat—Bearsville 0307 [Dave Peverett] [ASC] (5/22/76 BCR-44)

FOOL FOR YOU The Impressions—Curtom 1932 [Curtis Mayfield] [BMI] (9/7/68 BCR-17)

FOOL FOR YOUR LOVE Jimmy Hall—Epic 02857
[Michael Omartian/Leo Sayer] [ASC] (5/1/82 BC-74)

FOOL FOR YOUR LOVING *Whitesnake—Mirage 3672*
[David Coverdale/Bernie Marsden/Micky Moody] [ASC] (8/2/80 BCR-53)

FOOL FOR YOUR LOVING *Whitesnake—Geffen 22715*
[David Coverdale/Bernie Marsden/Micky Moody] [ASC] (11/4/89 BC-31)

FOOL (IF YOU THINK IT'S OVER) Chris Rea—United Artists/Magnet 1198
[Chris Rea] [ASC] (7/1/78 BCR-10)

FOOL IN LOVE Ike & Tina Turner—Sue 730 [Ike Turner] [BMI] (8/22/60 BCR-19)

FOOL IN LOVE WITH YOU Jim Photoglo—20th Century 2487
[Brian Neary/Jim Photoglo] [BMI] (4/11/81 BCR-23)

FOOL IN THE RAIN Led Zeppelin—Swan Song 71003
[John Paul Jones/Jimmy Page/Robert Plant] [ASC] (12/22/79 BCR-21)

FOOL LIKE YOU Tim Moore—Dunhill 4337 [Tim Moore] [NA] (4/7/73 BCR-81)

FOOL ME Joe South—Capitol 3204 [Joe South] [BMI] (11/6/71 BCR-78)

FOOL MOON FIRE Walter Egan—Backstreet 52200 [Walter Egan] [ASC] (4/9/83 BC-38)

A FOOL NEVER LEARNS Andy Williams—Columbia 42950
[Sonny Curtis] [BMI] (12/28/63 BCR-12)

FOOL #1 Brenda Lee—Decca 31309 [Kathryn Fulton] [BMI] (9/25/61 BCR-3)

A FOOL OF FOOLS Tony Bennett—Columbia 44443
[Mann Curtis/Joseph Meyer] [ASC] (3/9/68 CR-91)

FOOL OF THE YEAR Georgia Gibbs—Mercury 70850
[Martin Diamond/Arthur Korb] [ASC] (5/4/56 R-58)

THE FOOL ON THE HILL Sergio Mendes & Brasil '66—A&M 961
[John Lennon/Paul McCartney] [ASC] (8/10/68 BCR-6)

(NOW AND THEN THERE'S) A FOOL SUCH AS I *Elvis Presley—RCA Victor 47-7506*
[Bill Trader] [ASC] (3/23/59 BCR-1)

A FOOL SUCH AS I *Bob Dylan—Columbia 45982 [Bill Trader] [ASC] (12/15/73 BCR-47)*

FOOL THAT I AM Etta James—Argo 5390 [Floyd Hunt] [ASC] (6/3/61 BCR-50)

FOOL THAT I AM Rita Coolidge—A&M 2281
[Bruce Roberts/Carole Bayer Sager] [BMI] (12/13/80 BCR-46)

FOOL TO CRY The Rolling Stones—Rolling Stones 19304
[Mick Jagger/Keith Richards] (TSW) [ASC] (6/26/76 BCR-9)

FOOLED Perry Como—RCA Victor 47-6192
[Mann Curtis/Franz Lehár/Doris Tauber] (TSW) [ASC] (8/13/55 BCR-7)

FOOLED AROUND AND FELL IN LOVE Elvin Bishop—Capricorn 0252
[Elvin Bishop] [ASC] (3/6/76 BCR-3)

FOOLED BY A FEELING Barbara Mandrell—MCA 41077
[Kye Fleming/Dennis W. Morgan] [BMI] (10/6/79 B-89)

FOOLIN' Def Leppard—Mercury 814178
[Rick Allen/Steve Clark/Joe Elliott/Mutt Lange/Rick Savage/Pete Willis] [ASC] (9/3/83 BC-27)

FOOLIN' AROUND *Buck Owens—Capitol 4496*
[Harlan Howard/Buck Owens] [BMI] (3/27/61 Rt-90)

FOOLIN' AROUND *Kay Starr—Capitol 4542*
[Harlan Howard/Buck Owens] [BMI] (3/20/61 BCRt-29)

FOOLIN' YOURSELF Aldo Nova—Portrait 24-03001 [Aldo Nova] [BMI] (7/17/82 BC-65)

FOOLING YOURSELF (THE ANGRY YOUNG MAN) Styx—A&M 2007
[Tommy Shaw] [ASC] (2/11/78 BCR-20)

FOOLISH BEAT Debbie Gibson—Atlantic 89109 [Debbie Gibson] [ASC] (4/23/88 BC-1)

FOOLISH FOOL Dee Dee Warwick—Mercury 72880 [Ed Townsend] [BMI] (2/8/69 BCR-57)

FOOLISH HEART *Steve Perry—Columbia 04693*
[Randy Goodrum/Steve Perry] [ASC] (11/24/84 BC-18)

FOOLISH HEART *Sharon Bryant—Wing 889 878*
[Randy Goodrum/Steve Perry] [ASC] (12/16/89 BC-90)

FOOLISH LITTLE GIRL The Shirelles—Scepter 1248
[Howard Greenfield/Helen Miller] [BMI] (3/16/63 BCR-4)

FOOLISH PRIDE Daryl Hall—RCA 5038 [Daryl Hall] [BMI] (10/18/86 BC-29)

FOOLISHLY *The Three Chuckles— "X" 0095 [Cirino Colacrai] [BMI] (3/5/55 CRt-45)*

FOOLISHLY *Buddy Cole with The Wood Sisters—Columbia 40460*
[Cirino Colacrai] [BMI] (3/21/55 Rt-70)

FOOLISHLY Vic Damone—Mercury 70545
[Milton Berle/Bobby Kroll] [ASC] (3/7/55 Rt*-70)

FOOLISHLY YOURS *Doris Day—Columbia 40483*
[Leonard Joy/Alice D. Simms] [ASC] (4/4/55 CtRt-24)

FOOLISHLY YOURS *Kay Starr—RCA Victor 47-6079*
[Leonard Joy/Alice D. Simms] [ASC] (4/4/55 CtRt-24)

FOOLISHLY YOURS *The Four Knights—Capitol 3093*
[Leonard Joy/Alice D. Simms] [ASC] (4/4/55 Rt-47)

FOOLISHLY YOURS *Lee Raymond with The Costello Sisters—Decca 29492*
[Leonard Joy/Alice D. Simms] [ASC] (4/18/55 Rt-47)

FOOLS FALL IN LOVE *The Drifters—Atlantic 1123*
[Jerry Leiber/Mike Stoller] [BMI] (3/9/57 B-69)

FOOLS FALL IN LOVE *Elvis Presley—RCA Victor 47-9056*
[Jerry Leiber/Mike Stoller] [BMI] (2/11/67 R-100)

FOOL'S GAME Michael Bolton—Columbia 03800
[Michael Bolton/Mark Mangold/Craig Sprovach] [ASC] (5/14/83 B-82)

FOOLS HALL OF FAME Pat Boone—Dot 15982
[Wally Gold/Aaron Schroeder] [ASC] (9/7/59 BCR-25)

FOOLS HALL OF FAME Paul Anka—ABC-Paramount 10282
[Paul Anka] [BMI] (2/5/62 R-88)

FOOLS LIKE ME Lorenzo Lamas—Scotti Brothers 04686
[Phil Galdston/Andy Goldmark/Sylvester Levay] [ASC] (12/22/84 B-85)

FOOL'S PARADISE Buddy Holly / The Crickets—Brunswick 55072
[Sonny LeGlaire/Horace Linsley/Norman Petty] [BMI] (7/5/58 BC-58)

FOOL'S PARADISE The Sylvers—Pride 1001 [Leon Sylvers] [ASC] (9/2/72 BR-94)
FOOLS RUSH IN (WHERE ANGELS FEAR TO TREAD) *Brook Benton—Mercury 71722 [Rube Bloom/Johnny Mercer] [ASC] (10/31/60 BCR-15)*
FOOLS RUSH IN *Etta James—Argo 5424 [Rube Bloom/Johnny Mercer] [ASC] (10/13/62 B-87)*
FOOLS RUSH IN *Rick Nelson—Decca 31533 [Rube Bloom/Johnny Mercer] [ASC] (9/14/63 BCR-11)*
FOOT STOMPIN MUSIC Hamilton Bohannon—Dakar 4544 [Hamilton Bohannon] [ASC] (9/13/75 B-98)
FOOT STOMPING - PART 1 The Flares—Felsted 8624 [Aaron Collins] [BMI] (9/2/61 BCR-23)
THE FOOTBALL CARD Glenn Sutton—Mercury 55052 [Glenn Sutton] [BMI] (12/30/78 BCR-46)
FOOTLOOSE Kenny Loggins—Columbia 04310 [Kenny Loggins/Dean Pitchford] [BMI] (1/28/84 BC-1)
FOOTSTEPS Steve Lawrence—ABC-Paramount 10085 [Hank Hunter/Barry Mann] [BMI] (3/5/60 BCR-7)
FOOTSTOMPIN' MUSIC Grand Funk Railroad—Capitol 3255 [Mark Farner] [BMI] (12/25/71 BCR-28)
FOPP Ohio Players—Mercury 73775 [William Beck/Leroy Bonner/Marshall Jones/Ralph Middlebrooks/ Andrew Noland/Marvin Pierce/James Rodger Williams] [BMI] (2/21/76 BCR-30)
FOR A DANCER Prelude—Pye 71045 [Jackson Browne] [ASC] (11/29/75 BCR-63)
FOR A FRIEND The Bugaloos—Capitol 2946 [Joel Hirschhorn/Al Kasha] [ASC] (11/28/70 R-64)
FOR A PENNY Pat Boone—Dot 15914 [Charles Singleton] [BMI] (3/23/59 BCR-21)
FOR A ROCKER Jackson Browne—Asylum 69764 [Jackson Browne] [ASC] (1/14/84 BC-45)
FOR A WHILE Mary MacGregor—Ariola America 7667 [Kevin Hunter/Peter Yarrow] [ASC] (8/6/77 BC-90)
FOR ALL WE KNOW Dinah Washington—Roulette 4444 [J. Fred Coots/Sam Lewis] [ASC] (8/18/62 BR-84)
FOR ALL WE KNOW Carpenters—A&M 1243 [James Griffin/Fred Karlin/Robb Royer] [BMI] (2/6/71 BCR-3)
FOR AMERICA Jackson Browne—Asylum 69566 [Jackson Browne] [ASC] (3/1/86 BC-27)
FOR ELISE The Philarmonics—Capricorn 0268 [Ludwig van Beethoven] [NA] (3/12/77 B-100) [I]
FOR EMILY *The Arbors—Date 1645 [Paul Simon] (Med) [BMI] (5/24/69 BCR-67)*
FOR EMILY, WHENEVER I MAY FIND HER *Simon & Garfunkel—Columbia 45663 [Paul Simon] [BMI] (8/26/72 BCR-53)*
(FOR GOD'S SAKE) GIVE MORE POWER TO THE PEOPLE The Chi-Lites—Brunswick 55450 [Eugene Record] [BMI] (4/10/71 BCR-22)
FOR HE'S A JOLLY GOOD FELLOW Bobby Vinton—Epic 10136 [Ray Stevens] [BMI] (3/11/67 BCR-54)
—FOR JANIS JOPLIN see: IN THE QUIET MORNING
FOR LADIES ONLY Steppenwolf—Dunhill 4292 [Jerry Edmonton/Kent Henry/John Kay/Goldy McJohn] [BMI] (11/6/71 BCR-61)
FOR LOVE Lloyd Price And His Orchestra—ABC-Paramount 10102 [Harold Logan/Lloyd Price] [BMI] (4/18/60 BCR-43)
FOR LOVE Pousette-Dart Band—Capitol 4764 [David Finnerty] [ASC] (9/1/79 BCR-83)
FOR LOVIN' ME Peter, Paul & Mary—Warner Bros. 5496 [Gordon Lightfoot] [ASC] (1/23/65 BCR-24)
FOR MAMA *Jerry Vale—Columbia 43232 [Charles Aznavour/Don Black/Robert Gall] [ASC] (2/27/65 BCtRt-30) [FET]*
FOR MAMA *Matt Monro—Liberty 55763 [Charles Aznavour/Don Black/Robert Gall] [ASC] (2/27/65 CtRt-30) [FET]*
FOR MAMA (LA MAMMA) *Connie Francis—MGM 13325 [Charles Aznavour/Don Black/Robert Gall] [ASC] (2/27/65 BCtRt-30) [FET]*
FOR MAMA (LA MAMMA) *Vic Damone—Warner Bros. 5609 [Charles Aznavour/Don Black/Robert Gall] [ASC] (2/27/65 CtRt-30) [FET]*
FOR ME Sergio Mendes & Brasil '66—A&M 836 [Norman Gimbel/Edu Lobo] [BMI] (4/1/67 B-98) [FDE]
FOR ME AND MY GAL Freddy Cannon—Swan 4083 [Ray Goetz/Edgar Leslie/George Meyer] [ASC] (10/16/61 BCR-56)
FOR MY BABY Brook Benton—Mercury 71774 [Brook Benton*/Willie Dixon*/Clyde Otis] [BMI] (2/6/61 BCR-24)
FOR MY GOOD FORTUNE *Pat Boone—Dot 15825 [Otis Blackwell/Bobby Stevenson] [BMI] (9/15/58 BCRt-23)*
FOR MY GOOD FORTUNE *Mahalia Jackson—Columbia 41258 [Otis Blackwell/Bobby Stevenson] [BMI] (9/22/58 Rt-34)*
FOR OL' TIMES SAKE Elvis Presley—RCA Victor 74-0088 [Tony Joe White] (TSW) [ASC] (9/22/73 B-41)
FOR ONCE IN MY LIFE *Tony Bennett—Columbia 44258 [Ronald Norman Miller/Orlando Murden] [BMI] (10/14/67 BCR-91)*
FOR ONCE IN MY LIFE *Stevie Wonder—Tamla 54174 [Ronald Norman Miller/Orlando Murden] [BMI] (11/2/68 BCR-1)*
FOR ONCE IN MY LIFE *Jackie Wilson—Brunswick 55392 [Ronald Norman Miller/Orlando Murden] (TSW) [BMI] (11/2/68 BCR-57)*
FOR ONCE IN MY LIFE *Stars On 45—Radio 4019 [Ronald Norman Miller/Orlando Murden] (Med) [BMI] (3/27/82 BCR-28)*
(I LOVE YOU) FOR SENTIMENTAL REASONS *Sam Cooke—Keen 34002 [Pat Best/Deek Watson] [BMI] (12/16/57 BCR-25)*
FOR SENTIMENTAL REASONS *The Cleftones—Gee 1067 [Pat Best/Deek Watson] [BMI] (9/4/61 BCRt-60)*
FOR SENTIMENTAL REASONS *The Spaniels—Neptune 124 [Pat Best/Deek Watson] [BMI] (9/25/61 Rt-78)*
FOR THE GOOD TIMES Ray Price—Columbia 45178 [Kris Kristofferson] [BMI] (8/29/70 BCR-11)
FOR THE HEART Elvis Presley—RCA Victor 10601 [Dennis Linde] (TSW) [BMI] (4/3/76 B-28)
FOR THE LOVE OF HIM Bobbi Martin—United Artists 50602 [Henry Jerome/Bobbi Martin] [ASC] (3/14/70 BCR-8)
FOR THE LOVE OF IVY The Mamas & The Papas—Dunhill 4150 [Dennis Doherty/John Phillips] [ASC] (9/7/68 BCR-48)
FOR THE LOVE OF MONEY *The O'Jays—Philadelphia Int'l 3544 [Kenneth Gamble/Leon Huff/Anthony Jackson] [BMI] (4/13/74 BCR-7)*
FOR THE LOVE OF MONEY *Bulletboys—Warner Bros. 27554 [Kenneth Gamble/Leon Huff/Anthony Jackson] [BMI] (4/29/89 B-78)*
FOR THE LOVE OF YOU (PART 1 & 2) *The Isley Brothers—T-Neck 2259 [Ernie Isley/Marvin Isley/O'Kelly Isley/Ronald Isley/Rudolph Isley/Chris Jasper] [ASC] (11/8/75 BCR-22)*
FOR THE LOVE OF YOU *Houston Person—Westbound 5015 [Ernie Isley/Marvin Isley/O'Kelly Isley/Ronald Isley/Rudolph Isley/Chris Jasper] (TSW) [ASC] (1/17/76 B-91) [IWM]*
FOR TONIGHT Nancy Martinez—Atlantic 89371 [Phil George/Donna Pacifici] [BMI] (10/4/86 BC-32)
FOR WHAT IT'S WORTH (STOP, HEY WHAT'S THAT SOUND) *The Buffalo Springfield—Atco 6459 [Stephen Stills] [BMI] (1/14/67 BCR-7)*
FOR WHAT IT'S WORTH *The Staple Singers—Epic 10220 [Stephen Stills] [BMI] (9/9/67 BCR-56)*
FOR WHAT IT'S WORTH *King Curtis & The Kingpins—Atco 6534 [Stephen Stills] [BMI] (11/25/67 B-87) [IWM]*
FOR WHAT IT'S WORTH *Cher—Atco 6704 [Stephen Stills] [BMI] (8/23/69 R-89)*
FOR YASGUR'S FARM Mountain—Windfall 533 [Gail Collins/George Gardos/Corky Laing/Felix Pappalardi/Dave Rea/Gary Ship] [BMI] (9/5/70 CR-72)
FOR YOU Rick Nelson—Decca 31574 [Joe Burke/Al Dubin] [ASC] (12/28/63 BCR-6)
FOR YOU The Spellbinders—Columbia 43384 [Van McCoy] [BMI] (11/27/65 BCR-81)
FOR YOU Manfred Mann's Earth Band—Warner Bros.49678 [Bruce Springsteen] [ASC] (4/25/81 R-92)
FOR YOU The Outfield—Reunion 19103 [John Spinks] [ASC] (10/27/90 BC-21)
FOR YOU Michael W. Smith—MCA 53935 [Wayne Kirkpatrick/William Owsley/Michael W. Smith] [BMI] (8/31/91 BC-49)
FOR YOU AND I 10cc—Polydor 14528 [Graham Gouldman/Eric Stewart] [BMI] (1/20/79 BCR-73)
FOR YOU BLUE The Beatles—Apple 2832 [George Harrison] (TSW) [ASC] (5/16/70 BCR-1)
FOR YOUR EYES ONLY Sheena Easton—Liberty 1418 [Bill Conti/Mike Leeson] [ASC] (7/25/81 BCR-3)
FOR YOUR LOVE *Ed Townsend—Capitol 3926 [Ed Townsend] [BMI] (3/17/58 BCR-9)*
FOR YOUR LOVE *The Wanderers—Cub 9089 [Ed Townsend] [BMI] (4/17/61 BCR-56)*
FOR YOUR LOVE *Sam & Bill—JoDa 100 [Ed Townsend] [BMI] (8/7/65 BCR-40)*
FOR YOUR LOVE *Peaches & Herb—Date 1563 [Ed Townsend] [BMI] (6/24/67 BCR-20)*
FOR YOUR LOVE *Christopher Paul & Shawn—Casablanca 838 [Ed Townsend] [BMI] (8/2/75 B-91)*
FOR YOUR LOVE The Yardbirds—Epic 9790 [Graham Gouldman] [BMI] (5/8/65 BCR-4)
FOR YOUR MIND Robbie Nevil—EMI 50367 [Steven Dubin/Robbie Nevil] [ASC] (10/12/91 BC-63)
FOR YOUR PRECIOUS LOVE *Jerry Butler & The Impressions—Falcon 1013/Abner 1013 [Arthur Brooks/Richard Brooks/Jerry Butler] [ASC] (6/2/58 BCR-11)*
FOR YOUR PRECIOUS LOVE *Garnet Mimms & The Enchanters—United Artists 658 [Arthur Brooks/Richard Brooks/Jerry Butler] [ASC] (11/9/63 BCR-26)*
FOR YOUR PRECIOUS LOVE *Jerry Butler—Vee-Jay 715 [Arthur Brooks/Richard Brooks/Jerry Butler] [ASC] (3/26/66 B-99)*
FOR YOUR PRECIOUS LOVE *Oscar Toney, Jr.—Bell 672 [Arthur Brooks/Richard Brooks/Jerry Butler] [ASC] (5/27/67 BCR-19)*
FOR YOUR PRECIOUS LOVE *Jackie Wilson And Count Basie—Brunswick 55365 [Arthur Brooks/Richard Brooks/Jerry Butler] [ASC] (2/17/68 BCR-35)*
YOUR PRECIOUS LOVE *Linda Jones—Turbo 021 [Arthur Brooks/Richard Brooks/Jerry Butler] [ASC] (2/26/72 BCR-74)*
FOR YOUR SWEET LOVE The Cascades—RCA Victor 47-8268 [Jerry Fuller] [BMI] (12/28/63 BR-84)
FORBIDDEN FRUIT Anita Ellis—Epic 9204 [Joe Sherman/Noel Sherman] [ASC] (3/23/57 R-85)
—FORBIDDEN see: VERBOTEN!
FOREVER Sam Cooke—Specialty 619 [Alvin Tyler] [BMI] (12/23/57 B-60)

FOREVER *The Little Dippers—University 210 [Buddy Killen] [BMI] (1/25/60 BCRt-9)*

FOREVER *Billy Walker—Columbia 41548 [Buddy Killen] [BMI] (1/25/60 BRt-13)*

FOREVER *Pete Drake And His Talking Steel Guitar—Smash 1867 [Buddy Killen] [BMI] (3/7/64 BCR-16)*

FOREVER *Mercy—Warner Bros.-Seven Arts 7297 [Buddy Killen] [BMI] (6/28/69 BCR-75)*

FOREVER The Marvelettes—Tamla 54077 [Lamont Dozier/Freddie Gorman/Brian Holland] [BMI] (5/4/63 BCR-71)

FOREVER Little Steven and the Disciples Of Soul—EMI America 8144 [Steven Van Zandt] [ASC] (12/25/82 BC-63)

FOREVER Kenny Loggins—Columbia 04931 [David Foster/Kenny Loggins] [BMI] (5/25/85 BC-37)

FOREVER Kiss—Mercury 876 716 [Michael Bolton/Paul Stanley] [BMI] (2/3/90 BC-8)

FOREVER AMO'R D'Zyre—Atlantic 87685 [Troy Guy] [ASC] (6/8/91 B-77)

FOREVER AND A DAY Jackie Wilson—Brunswick 55233 [Hank Hunter/Al Kasha] [BMI] (9/15/62 BR-82)

FOREVER AND EVER Slik—Arista 0179 [Phil Coulter/William Wylie MacPherson Martin] [ASC] (5/1/76 C-98)

FOREVER AUTUMN Justin Hayward—Columbia 10799 [Gary Osborne/Paul Vigrass/Jeff Wayne] [BMI] (9/23/78 BCR-34)

FOREVER CAME TODAY *Diana Ross And The Supremes—Motown 1122 [Lamont Dozier/Brian Holland/Eddie Holland] [BMI] (3/16/68 BCR-13)*

FOREVER CAME TODAY *The Jackson 5—Motown 1356 [Lamont Dozier/Brian Holland/Eddie Holland] [BMI] (7/5/75 BCR-55)*

FOREVER DARLING *The Ames Brothers—RCA Victor 47-6400 [Sammy Cahn/Bronislaw Kaper] [ASC] (2/10/56 BCRt-27)*

FOREVER, DARLING *Desi Arnaz & His Orchestra—MGM 12144 [Sammy Cahn/Bronislaw Kaper] [ASC] (2/24/56 Rt-29)*

FOREVER IN BLUE JEANS Neil Diamond—Columbia 10897 [Richard Winchell Bennett/Neil Diamond] [ASC] (1/27/79 BCR-20)

(FOREVER) LIVE AND DIE Orchestral Manoeuvres In The Dark—A&M 2872 [Paul Humphreys/Graham Weir/Neil Weir] [ASC] (9/27/86 BC-19)

FOREVER LOVERS Mac Davis—Columbia 10304 [Sterling Whipple] [BMI] (4/10/76 B-76)

FOREVER MAN Eric Clapton—Duck/Warner 29081 [Eric Clapton*/Jerry Lynn Williams] [BMI] (3/9/85 BC-24)

FOREVER MINE The O'Jays—Philadelphia Int'l 3727 [Kenneth Gamble/Leon Huff] [BMI] (11/24/79 BCR-26)

FOREVER MINE The Motels—Capitol 5182 [Martha Davis] [BMI] (11/13/82 BC-60)

FOREVER MORE Stevie B—RCA 62112 [Warren Brooks] [BMI] (10/26/91 B-96)

FOREVER MY LADY Jodeci—Uptown/MCA 54197 [Albert Joseph Brown/Donald DeGrate] [ASC] (10/26/91 BC-25)

FOREVER YOUNG Rod Stewart—Warner Bros. 27796 [Jim Cregan/Bob Dylan/Kevin Savigar/Rod Stewart] [ASC] (8/6/88 BC-12)

FOREVER YOUNG *Alphaville—Atlantic 89578 [Marian Gold/Bernhard Lloyd/Frank Mertens] [BMI] (3/23/85 B-93)*

FOREVER YOUNG *Alphaville—Atlantic 89013 [Marian Gold/Bernhard Lloyd/Frank Mertens] [BMI] (10/29/88 BC-65)*

FOREVER YOUR GIRL Paula Abdul—Virgin 99230 [Oliver Leiber] [ASC] (3/11/89 BC-1)

FOREVER YOURS Tony Terry—Epic 07900 [Ted Currier/Gary Henry] [BMI] (6/25/88 BC-80)

FORGET DOMANI *Connie Francis—MGM 13363 [Norman Newell/Riz Ortolani/Katyna Ranieri] [ASC] (6/19/65 BCtRt-58) [FET]*

FORGET DOMANI *Frank Sinatra—Reprise 0380 [Norman Newell/Riz Ortolani/Katyna Ranieri] [ASC] (6/19/65 BCtRt-58) [FET]*

FORGET HER Tony Bennett with Percy Faith and His Orchestra—Columbia 40667 [Al Hoffman/Dick Manning] [ASC] (7/6/56 R-82)

FORGET HIM Bobby Rydell—Cameo 280 [Tony Hatch] [ASC] (11/2/63 BCR-4)

FORGET IT The Sandpebbles—Calla 134 [Teddy Vann/Calvin White] [BMI] (8/12/67 BCR-79)

FORGET ME NOT The Kalin Twins—Decca 30745 [Larry Kolber/Larry Martin] [BMI] (9/22/58 BCR-12)

FORGET ME NOT Martha Reeves & The Vandellas—Gordy 7070 [Richard Morris/Sylvia Moy] [BMI] (6/15/68 B-93)

FORGET ME NOT Bad English—Epic 68946 [Jonathan Cain/Mark Spiro/John Waite] [ASC] (7/22/89 BC-38)

FORGET ME NOTS Patrice Rushen—Elektra 47427 [Theresa McFaddin/Patrice Rushen/Freddie Washington] [ASC] (5/1/82 BC-22)

FORGET TO REMEMBER Frank Sinatra—Reprise 0865 [Victoria Pike/Teddy Randazzo] (TSW) [BMI] (11/29/69 B-79)

FORGIVE ME Kitty Kallen—Decca 29548 [Neal Arden/Christopher Neville] [ASC] (5/30/55 R-41)

FORGIVE ME Al Martino—Capitol 5506 [Milton Ager/Jack Yellen] [ASC] (10/9/65 BCR-61)

FORGIVE ME FOR DREAMING Elisa Fiorillo—Chrysalis 43237 [Scott Cutler/Gerry Goffin] [ASC] (5/7/88 BC-49)

FORGIVE ME (FOR GIVING YOU SUCH A BAD TIME) Babs Tino—Kapp 472 [Burt Bacharach/Hal David] [ASC] (8/18/62 C-97)

FORGIVE ME, GIRL The Spinners—Atlantic 3637 [Michael Zager] (Med) [BMI] (12/15/79 BCR-2)

FORGIVE MY HEART Nat "King" Cole—Capitol 3234 [Chester Conn/Sammy Gallop] (TSW) [ASC] (10/22/55 BCR-15)

FORGIVE THIS FOOL Roy Hamilton—Epic 9111 [William S. Cook] [NA] (7/11/55 CR-35)

FORGOTTEN DREAMS *Leroy Anderson And His "Pops" Concert Orchestra—Decca 30403 [Leroy Anderson] [ASC] (8/19/57 CtRt-43) [IM]*

FORGOTTEN DREAMS *Cyril Stapleton And His Orchestra—London 1754 [Leroy Anderson] [ASC] (8/19/57 CtRt-43) [IM]*

FORGOTTEN DREAMS *Frederick Fennell—Mercury 71170 [Leroy Anderson] [ASC] (9/9/57 Rt-55) [IM]*

FORTRESS AROUND YOUR HEART Sting—A&M 2767 [Sting] [BMI] (8/24/85 BC-8)

FORTUNATE SON Creedence Clearwater Revival—Fantasy 634 [John Fogerty] (TSW) [BMI] (10/25/69 BCR-3)

FORTUNE IN DREAMS Kay Starr—Capitol 2887 [Hal Stanley/Irving Taylor] [ASC] (9/11/54 CR-24)

FORTUNE TELLER The Hardtimes—World Pacific 77851 [Allen Toussaint] [BMI] (12/31/66 B-97)

FORTUNETELLER Bobby Curtola—Del-Fi 4177 [Basil Hurdon/Dyer Hurdon] [BMI] (5/5/62 BCR-41)

FORTY CUPS OF COFFEE Bill Haley And His Comets—Decca 30214 [Danny Overbea] [BMI] (3/23/57 BCR-45)

FORTY DAYS Ronnie Hawkins—Roulette 4154 [Chuck Berry] [BMI] (5/30/59 BCR-45)

48 CRASH Suzi Quatro—Bell 45,401 [Mike Chapman/Nicky Chinn] [ASC] (4/27/74 C-90)

FORTY MILES OF BAD ROAD Duane Eddy His "Twangy" guitar and The Rebels—Jamie 1126 [Al Casey/Duane Eddy] [BMI] (6/13/59 BCR-5) [I]

FORTY NINE SHADES OF GREEN The Ames Brothers—RCA Victor 47-6608 [Roy C. Bennett/Sid Tepper] [ASC] (9/8/56 BR-49)

FORTY TWO Rusty Draper—Mercury 70818 [Dorothy Jeffers/Ethel Phillips] [BMI] (4/13/56 R-82)

FOUND A CURE Ashford & Simpson—Warner Bros. 8870 [Nick Ashford/Valerie Simpson] [ASC] (8/4/79 BCR-26)

FOUND LOVE Jimmy Reed—Vee-Jay 347 [Jimmy Reed] [BMI] (5/23/60 BCR-73)

THE FOUNTAIN OF YOUTH The Four Lads—Columbia 41365 [Jerry Livingston/Paul Francis Webster] [ASC] (4/25/59 BC-76)

442 GLENWOOD AVENUE The Pixies Three—Mercury 72208 [John Madara/Artie Singer/David White] [BMI] (1/11/64 BCR-42)

FOUR IN THE MORNING (I CAN'T TAKE ANY MORE) Night Ranger—Camel/MCA 52661 [Jack Blades] [BMI] (8/24/85 BC-19)

FOUR LITTLE DIAMONDS ELO—Jet 04130 [Jeff Lynne] [ASC] (10/1/83 B-86)

FOUR LITTLE GIRLS IN BOSTON Jimmie Rodgers—Roulette 4260 [Jimmy Driftwood] [BMI] (7/4/60 R-79)

—FOUR LITTLE HEELS see: CLICKETY-CLACK SONG

409 *The Beach Boys—Capitol 4777 [Mike Love*/Gary Usher/Brian Wilson] [BMI] (10/13/62 B-76)*

409 *The Cantina Band—Millennium 11818 [Mike Love*/Gary Usher/Brian Wilson] (Med) [BMI] (7/25/81 B-81)*

FOUR STRONG WINDS *Bobby Bare—RCA Victor 47-8443 [Ian Tyson] [ASC] (10/31/64 BCR-54)*

FOUR STRONG WINDS *Neil Young—Reprise 1396 [Ian Tyson] [ASC] (2/3/79 BCR-61)*

FOUR WALLS *Jim Reeves—RCA Victor 47-6874 [George Campbell/Marvin Moore] [BMI] (4/20/57 BCtRt-7)*

FOUR WALLS *Jim Lowe—Dot 15569 [George Campbell/Marvin Moore] [BMI] (4/27/57 BCtRt-7)*

FOUR WALLS *Dorothy Collins—Coral 61828 [George Campbell/Marvin Moore] [BMI] (5/11/57 Rt-7)*

FOUR WALLS *Kay Starr—Capitol 4835 [George Campbell/Marvin Moore] [BMI] (10/6/62 BR-91)*

FOUR WALLS (THREE WINDOWS AND TWO DOORS) J.J. Jackson—Calla 133 [J.J. Jackson/Windsor King] [BMI] (7/1/67 CR-76)

FOURTEEN KARAT GOLD Don Cherry—Columbia 40958 [Sy Sandler/Eddie Zack] [BMI] (7/27/57 CR-60)

1492 Betty Johnson—Bally 1033 [Joe Csida/Charles Grean/Marvin Moore] [BMI] (5/6/57 B-70)

1432 FRANKLIN PIKE CIRCLE HERO Bobby Russell—Elf 90020 [Bobby Russell] [ASC] (10/5/68 BCR-36)

FOX HUNT Herb Alpert And The T.J.B.—A&M 1526 [Herb Alpert] [ASC] (5/18/74 BCR-70) [I]

FOX HUNTIN' (ON THE WEEKEND) Daddy Dewdrop—Sunflower 111 [Dick Monda] [BMI] (7/17/71 CR-87)

FOX ON THE RUN Manfred Mann—Mercury 72879 [Tony Hazzard] [BMI] (1/18/69 BR-94)

FOX ON THE RUN The Sweet—Capitol 4157 [Brian Connolly/Stephen Priest/Andrew Scott/Michael Tucker] [ASC] (11/8/75 BCR-4)

FOXEY LADY Jimi Hendrix—Reprise 0641 [Jimi Hendrix] [ASC] (12/23/67 BCR-67)

FOXY LADY Crown Heights Affair—De-Lite 1581 [Britt Britton/Freida Nerangis] [BMI] (5/22/76 BCR-49)

FRAMED Cheech & Chong—Ode 66124 [Jerry Leiber/Mike Stoller] [BMI] (6/5/76 BCR-41) [P]

FRANCENE ZZ Top—London 179 [Ken Cordray/Billy Gibbons/Steve Perron] [BMI] (5/20/72 BCR-69)

FRANKENSTEIN The Edgar Winter Group—Epic 10967 [Edgar Winter] [BMI] (3/10/73 BCR-1) [I]

FRANKENSTEIN OF '59 Buchanan And Goodman—Novelty 301
[Dickie Goodman/Susan Goodman] [BMI] (2/14/59 C-71)

FRANKIE Connie Francis—MGM 12793
[Howard Greenfield/Neil Sedaka] [BMI] (5/4/59 BCR-5)

FRANKIE Sister Sledge—Atlantic 89547 [Joy Denny] [ASC] (6/15/85 BC-75)

FRANKIE'S MAN JOHNNY *Johnny Cash—Columbia 41371*
[Hughie Cannon] [NA] (4/13/59 BCR-24)

FRANKIE AND JOHNNY *Sylvia Robbins—Jubilee 5386 [Hughie Cannon] [NA] (5/7/60 C-85)*

FRANKIE AND JOHNNY *Brook Benton—Mercury 71859*
[Hughie Cannon] [NA] (8/21/61 BCR-16)

FRANKIE AND JOHNNY *Sam Cooke—RCA Victor 47-8215*
[Hughie Cannon] [NA] (7/20/63 BCR-14)

THE NEW "FRANKIE AND JOHNNIE" SONG *The Greenwood County Singers—Kapp 591*
[Hughie Cannon/Bob Gibson/Shel Silverstein] [BMI] (8/1/64 BCR-62)*

FRANKIE AND JOHNNY *Elvis Presley—RCA Victor 47-8780*
[Hughie Cannon] [NA] (3/19/66 BCR-17)

FRAULEIN *Bobby Helms—Decca 30194 [Lawton Williams] [BMI] (7/15/57 BCtRt-29)*

FRAULEIN *Steve Lawrence—Coral 61876 [Lawton Williams] [BMI] (8/19/57 BCtRt-29)*

FRAULEIN *Don Estes—Decca 30386 [Lawton Williams] [BMI] (8/26/57 Rt-29)*

FRAULEIN *Vic Sabrino—Decca 30416 [Lawton Williams] [BMI] (8/26/57 Rt-67)*

FREAK-A-RISTIC Atlantic Starr—A&M 2718 [David E. Lewis] [ASC] (5/25/85 B-90)

FREAK-A-ZOID Midnight Star—Solar 69828
[Reggie Calloway/Vincent Calloway/Bill Simmons] [BMI] (8/13/83 BC-51)

—FREAK see: LE FREAK

FREAKSHOW ON THE DANCE FLOOR Bar-Kays—Mercury 818631
[James Edward Alexander/Michael Beard/Mark Bynum/Larry Dodson/
Harvey Henderson/Allen Alvoid Jones Jr./Lloyd Ed Smith/Winston Stewart/
Frank Thompson] [BMI] (5/26/84 BC-73)

FREAKY DANCIN' Cameo—Chocolate City 3225
[Larry Blackmon/Tomi Jenkins] [BMI] (6/13/81 R-75)

FREDDIE Charlene—Prodigal 0633
[Ken Hirsch/Ronald Norman Miller] [BMI] (5/14/77 B-96)

FREDDIE FEELGOOD (AND HIS FUNKY LITTLE FIVE PIECE BAND) Ray Stevens—
Monument 946 [Ray Stevens] [BMI] (7/9/66 BCR-80)

FREDDIE'S DEAD (THEME FROM "SUPERFLY") Curtis Mayfield—Curtom 1975
[Curtis Mayfield] [BMI] (8/19/72 BCR-4)

FREDDY *Annie Cordy—"X" 0154*
[Gisela Günther/Sheldon Harnick/Steve Kirk/Peter Pan] [BMI] (7/4/55 Rt-53)

FREDDY *Stan Kenton & His Orchestra—Capitol 3151*
[Gisela Günther/Sheldon Harnick/Steve Kirk/Peter Pan] [BMI] (7/4/55 Rt-63)

FREDDY *Guy Lombardo & His Royal Canadians—Decca 29587*
[Gisela Günther/Sheldon Harnick/Steve Kirk/Peter Pan] [BMI] (7/4/55 Rt-53)

FREDDY *Connie Francis—MGM 12015*
[Gisela Günther/Sheldon Harnick/Steve Kirk/Peter Pan] [BMI] (7/4/55 Rt-53)

FREDY *Eartha Kitt & Perez Prado—RCA Victor 47-6138*
[Gisela Günther/Sheldon Harnick/Steve Kirk/Peter Pan] [BMI] (7/4/55 Rt-63)

FREDERICK Patti Smith Group—Arista 0427 [Patti Smith] [ASC] (7/21/79 BR-87)

FREE *Tommy Leonetti—Capitol 3442 [Larry Conley/Johnny Marks] [ASC] (6/9/56 BRt-40)*

FREE *The Lancers—Coral 61665 [Larry Conley/Johnny Marks] [ASC] (7/13/56 Rt-72)*

FREE The Pearly Gate—Decca 732573 [Chris Frederick Andrews] [BMI] (11/1/69 R-88)

FREE Chicago—Columbia 45331 [Robert Lamm] [ASC] (2/20/71 BCR-19)

FREE Fresh Start—Dunhill/ABC 15002
[Fred Allen/Paul Frank/Bill Pratt] [ASC] (8/10/74 CR-89)

FREE Deniece Williams—Columbia 10429
[Susaye Greene/Henry Redd/Nathan Watts/Deniece Williams] [NA] (11/13/76 BCR-21)

FREE AGAIN Barbra Streisand—Columbia 43808
[Joss Baselli/Armand Canfora/Robert Colby] [ASC] (10/1/66 BCR-66) [FDE]

FREE AS THE WIND Brooklyn Bridge—Buddah 162
[Jerry Kasenetz/Jeff Katz/Sal Trimachi] [BMI] (3/7/70 CR-65)

FREE BIRD *Lynyrd Skynyrd—MCA 40328*
[Allen Collins/Ronnie Van Zant] [BMI] (11/16/74 BCR-19)

FREE BIRD (LIVE) *Lynyrd Skynyrd—MCA 40665*
[Allen Collins/Ronnie Van Zant] [BMI] (12/4/76 BCR-31)

FREE BIRD *Will To Power—Epic 08034*
[Allen Collins/Ronnie Van Zant] (Med) [BMI] (9/10/88 BC-1)

THE FREE ELECTRIC BAND Albert Hammond—Mums 6018
[Albert Hammond/Mike Hazlewood] [ASC] (4/28/73 BCR-31)

FREE FALLIN' Tom Petty—MCA 53748 [Jeff Lynne/Tom Petty] [ASC] (11/4/89 BC-6)

FREE MAN South Shore Commission—Wand 11287
[Bunny Sigler/Ronnie Tyson] [BMI] (6/28/75 BCR-61)

FREE MAN IN PARIS Joni Mitchell—Asylum 11041 [Joni Mitchell] [ASC] (7/20/74 BCR-22)

FREE ME Johnny Preston—Mercury 71908
[Jim Breedlove/Lynn Breedlove] [BMI] (12/25/61 BCR-74)

FREE ME Otis Redding—Atco 6700
[Gene Lawson/Otis Redding*/Bishop Robinson*/Tommy Star*] [BMI] (8/2/69 CR-60)

FREE ME Roger Daltrey—Polydor 2105 [Russ Ballard] [ASC] (7/5/80 BCR-44)

FREE ME FROM MY FREEDOM/TIE ME TO A TREE (HANDCUFF ME)
Bonnie Pointer—Motown 1451
[Angelo Bond/Truman Thomas] [BMI] (11/18/78 BCR-58)

FREE RIDE *The Edgar Winter Group—Epic 11024 [Dan Hartman] [BMI] (8/4/73 BCR-9)*

FREE RIDE *Tavares—Capitol 4184 [Dan Hartman] [BMI] (12/6/75 BCR-52)*

FREE SPIRIT Atlanta Rhythm Section—Polydor 14339
[Buddy Buie/Ronnie W. Hammond/Robert Nix] [BMI] (8/21/76 BC-76)

FREE THE PEOPLE Delaney & Bonnie & Friends—Atco 6756
[Barbara Keith] [ASC] (5/23/70 BR-75)

FREE TO CARRY ON The Sandpipers—A&M 1227
[Dale Bobbitt/Jim Brady] [ASC] (12/5/70 B-94)

FREE WHEELIN Bachman-Turner Overdrive—Mercury 73622
[Blair Thornton] (TSW) [BMI] (11/9/74 B-1) [I]

FREEDOM The Isley Brothers—T-Neck 927
[O'Kelly Isley/Ronald Isley/Rudolph Isley] [BMI] (1/2/71 BCR-53)

FREEDOM Jimi Hendrix—Reprise 1000
[Jimi Hendrix] [ASC] (3/27/71 BCR-59)

FREEDOM Grandmaster Flash And The Furious 5—Sugarhill 549
[Tyrone Armstrong/Melvin Glover/Nathaniel Glover/Eddie Morris/
Sylvia Robinson/Joseph Saddler/Ray Anthony Smith/Keith Wiggins/Guy T. Williams]
[BMI] (10/18/80 R-85)

FREEDOM *Wham!—Columbia 05409 [George Michael] [ASC] (7/27/85 BC-3)*

FREEDOM *George Michael—Columbia 73559 [George Michael] [ASC] (10/27/90 BC-7)*

FREEDOM Pointer Sisters—RCA 14224 [David McHugh] [ASC] (11/2/85 BC-52)

FREEDOM BLUES Little Richard—Reprise 0907 [Eskew Reeder] [BMI] (5/23/70 BCR-47)

FREEDOM COMES, FREEDOM GOES The Fortunes—Capitol 3179
[Roger Cook/Roger Greenaway/Albert Hammond/Mike Hazlewood] [BMI]
(10/2/71 BCR-72)

FREEDOM FOR THE STALLION The Hues Corporation—RCA Victor 74-0900
[Allen Toussaint] [BMI] (7/21/73 BCR-36)

FREEDOM OVERSPILL Steve Winwood—Island 28595
[George Fleming/James Hooker/Will Jennings*/Steve Winwood] [BMI] (9/27/86 BC-20)

FREEDOM TRAIN James Carr—Goldwax 338
[Steve Bogard/Larry Rogers/Carl Wells] [BMI] (1/18/69 C-96)

FREEWAY OF LOVE Aretha Franklin—Arista 1-9354
[Jeffrey E. Cohen/Narada Michael Walden] [ASC] (6/22/85 BC-3)

THE FREEZE Tony & Joe—Era 1075
[Joe Saraceno/Tony Savonne] [ASC] (7/12/58 BCRt*-33)

THE FREEZE Fention & The Castle Rockers—Duke 190
[David Dean] [NA] (7/21/58 Rt*-44) [IWM]

FREEZE-FRAME The J. Geils Band—EMI America 8108
[Seth Justman/Peter Wolf] (TSW) [ASC] (2/20/82 BCR-4)

FREIGHT TRAIN *The Chas. McDevitt Skiffle Group—Chic 1008*
[Elizabeth Cotten] [BMI] (5/11/57 BCtRt-17)

FREIGHT TRAIN *Rusty Draper—Mercury 71102*
[Elizabeth Cotten] [BMI] (5/18/57 BCtRt-11)

FREIGHT TRAIN *Steve Karmen—Bell 510 [Elizabeth Cotten] [BMI] (5/25/57 Rt-17)*

FREIGHT TRAIN *Margie Rayburn—Liberty 55072 [Elizabeth Cotten] [BMI] (5/25/57 Rt-17)*

FREIGHT TRAIN *Liz Winters with Bob Cort & His Skiffle Group—London 1742*
[Elizabeth Cotten] [BMI] (5/25/57 Rt-17)

FREIGHT TRAIN *Duane Eddy—Congress 6010*
[Elizabeth Cotten] [BMI] (1/17/70 C-95) [IWM]

FRENCH FOREIGN LEGION Frank Sinatra—Capitol 4155
[Aaron Schroeder/Guy Wood] [ASC] (3/2/59 BCR-32)

FRENCH KISS Lil Louis—Epic 73007 [Marvin Louis Burns] [ASC] (10/21/89 B-50)

FRENCH KISSIN Debbie Harry—Geffen 28546 [Chuck Lorre] [BMI] (11/22/86 BC-51)

THE FRENCH SONG (QUAND LE SOLEIL DIT BONJOUR AUX MONTAGNES)
Lucille Starr—Almo Int'l 204
[Harry Pease*/Lucille Starr*/Larry Vincent*] [ASC] (5/9/64 BCR-35) [FET]

FRESH Kool & The Gang—De-Lite 880623
[Robert Bell/Ronald Bell/James Bonneford/George M. Brown/Sandy Linzer/
Claydes Smith/J.T. Taylor/Curtis Fitzgerald Williams] [BMI] (3/23/85 BC-9)

FRESH AIR Quicksilver Messenger Service—Capitol 2920
[Chet Powers] [BMI] (10/3/70 BCR-49)

FRESH AS A DAISY Emitt Rhodes—Dunhill 4267 [Emitt Rhodes] [ASC] (12/26/70 BCR-38)

FRIDAY ON MY MIND The Easybeats—United Artists 50106
[Harry Vanda/George Young] [BMI] (3/18/67 BCR-16)

FRIDAY'S CHILD Nancy Sinatra—Reprise 0491 [Lee Hazlewood] [BMI] (7/9/66 BCR-36)

FRIED EGGS The Intruders—Fame 101
[Lee Gallo/George (2) Mitchell/Ben Smith] [BMI] (2/14/59 BCR-73) [I]

FRIED ONIONS Lord Rockingham's XI—London 1810
[McLeod Robertson] [BMI] (10/4/58 BC-96) [I]

FRIEND AND A LOVER The Partridge Family Starring Shirley Jones
& Featuring David Cassidy—Bell 45,336
[Wes Farrell/Bobby Hart/Danny Janssen] [BMI] (3/31/73 BCR-67)

A FRIEND IN THE CITY Andy Kim—Steed 723
[Jeff Barry/Andy Kim] [BMI] (1/24/70 BCR-58)

FRIEND, LOVER, WOMAN, WIFE O.C. Smith—Columbia 44859
[Mac Davis] [BMI] (5/10/69 BCR-47)

FRIEND OF MINE Bill Withers—Sussex 257 [Bill Withers] [BMI] (6/30/73 BR-80)

FRIEND OF MINE Little Milton—Glades 1734
[Milton Campbell/Joe Lewis/Jerry Puckett] [BMI] (5/22/76 R-91)

A FRIEND OF MINE IS GOING BLIND John Dawson Read—Chrysalis 2105 [John Dawson Read] [ASC] (8/30/75 BCR-58)

FRIENDLY PERSUASION (THEE I LOVE) *Pat Boone—Dot 15490 [Dimitri Tiomkin/Paul Francis Webster] [ASC] (9/15/56 BCtRt-8)*

FRIENDLY PERSUASION (THEE I LOVE) *Four Aces—Decca 30041 [Dimitri Tiomkin/Paul Francis Webster] [ASC] (9/15/56 BCtRt-9)*

FRIENDLY PERSUASION (THEE I LOVE) *Anthony Perkins—Epic 9181 [Dimitri Tiomkin/Paul Francis Webster] [ASC] (9/22/56 Rt-35)*

FRIENDLY PERSUASION (THEE I LOVE) *Lou Busch & His Orchestra—Capitol 3520 [Dimitri Tiomkin] [ASC] (9/22/56 Rt-35) [IM]*

FRIENDLY PERSUASION (THEE I LOVE) *Michel Legrand & His Orchestra—Columbia 40751 [Dimitri Tiomkin] [ASC] (9/22/56 Rt-35) [IM]*

FRIENDLY PERSUASION (THEE I LOVE) *George Cates & His Orchestra—Coral 61702 [Dimitri Tiomkin] [ASC] (9/29/56 Rt-35) [IM]*

FRIENDS The Beach Boys—Capitol 2160 [Alan Jardine/Brian Wilson/Carl Wilson/Dennis Wilson] [BMI] (4/20/68 BCR-34)

FRIENDS Feather—White Whale 353 [Peter Bregante/Barry Collings/Larry Sims/Roger White/Steve Woodard] [ASC] (5/16/70 BCR-76)

FRIENDS Elton John—Uni 55277 [Elton John/Bernie Taupin] [BMI] (3/20/71 BCR-17)

FRIENDS Bette Midler—Atlantic 2980 [Mark Klingman/Buzzy Linhart] (TSW) [BMI] (11/3/73 BCR-40)

FRIENDS Whodini—Jive 9276 [Jalil Hutchins/Lawrence Smith] [ASC] (1/5/85 B-87)

FRIENDS Jody Watley—MCA 53660 [Eric Barrier/André Cymone/William Griffin/Jody Watley] [BMI] (6/17/89 BC-8)

FRIENDS AND LOVERS Gloria Loring & Carl Anderson—USA Carrere 4-06122 [Paul Gordon/Jay Gruska] [ASC] (7/5/86 BC-2)

FRIENDS AND NEIGHBORS *Sammy Kaye & "Swing And Sway" Orchestra—Columbia 40269 [Sidney Colin/Malcolm Lockyer/Talbot Rothwell] [ASC] (7/10/54 Ct-PRE)*

FRIENDS AND NEIGHBORS *Plunkett Family—Essex 361 [Sidney Colin/Malcolm Lockyer/Talbot Rothwell] [ASC] (7/10/54 Ct-PRE)*

FRIENDS AND NEIGHBORS *Billy Cotton & Band—London 1473 [Sidney Colin/Malcolm Lockyer/Talbot Rothwell] [ASC] (7/10/54 Ct-PRE)*

FRIENDS AND NEIGHBORS *Tommy Prisco—Mercury 70396 [Sidney Colin/Malcolm Lockyer/Talbot Rothwell] [ASC] (7/10/54 Ct-PRE)*

FRIENDS IN LOVE Dionne Warwick And Johnny Mathis—Arista 0673 [Bill Champlin/David Foster/Jay Graydon] [ASC] (4/17/82 BC-38)

FRIENDS OR LOVERS Act I—Spring 132 [Raeford Gerald] [BMI] (3/31/73 C-99)

FRIENDS WITH YOU John Denver—RCA Victor 74-0567 [Bill Danoff/Taffy Danoff] [ASC] (11/6/71 BCR-27)

FRIENDSHIP TRAIN Gladys Knight & The Pips—Soul 35068 [Barrett Strong/Norman Whitfield] [BMI] (10/25/69 BCR-17)

FRIGHT NIGHT The J. Geils Band—Private I 4-05462 [Joe Lamont] [BMI] (8/10/85 B-91)

FRISCO BAY Navajo—Musicor 1449 [Lou Zerato] [ASC] (4/15/72 R-93)

FRISKY Sly & The Family Stone—Epic 11060 [Sylvester Stewart] [BMI] (11/24/73 BCR-65)

FRIVOLETTE The Hilltoppers—Dot 15318 [Edwin McMullen/Teddy Powell/Louis Shelly] [ASC] (1/24/55 R-82)

FROGG The Brothers Four—Columbia 41958 [Bob Flick/Dick Foley/Mike Kirkland/John Paine/Traditional] [BMI] (4/3/61 BCR-32)

FROM A DISTANCE Bette Midler—Atlantic 87820 [Julie Gold] [BMI] (10/6/90 BC-2)

FROM A JACK TO A KING Ned Miller—Fabor 114 [Ned Miller] [BMI] (12/15/62 BCR-6)

FROM A SCHOOL RING TO A WEDDING RING The Rover Boys—ABC-Paramount 9732 [Ted Kellem] [BMI] (8/17/56 BCR-24)

FROM A WINDOW *Billy J. Kramer With The Dakotas—Imperial 66051 [John Lennon/Paul McCartney] [ASC] (8/22/64 BCR-23)*

FROM A WINDOW *Chad & Jeremy—World Artists 1056 [John Lennon/Paul McCartney] [ASC] (6/26/65 BCR-79)*

—FROM BOTH SIDES NOW see: BOTH SIDES NOW

FROM GRACELAND TO THE PROMISED LAND Merle Haggard—MCA 40804 [Merle Haggard] [BMI] (10/1/77 BCR-58)

FROM HIS WOMAN TO YOU Barbara Mason—Buddah 441 [Bettye Crutcher/Lester Snell] [BMI] (11/30/74 BCR-28)

FROM ME TO YOU *Del Shannon—Big Top 3152 [John Lennon/Paul McCartney] [ASC] (6/29/63 BCR-67)*

FROM ME TO YOU *The Beatles—Vee-Jay 581 [John Lennon/Paul McCartney] [ASC] (2/8/64 BCR-41)*

FROM ME TO YOU *Stars On 45—Radio 3830 [John Lennon/Paul McCartney] (Med) [ASC] (7/11/81 BC-63)*

FROM ROCKING HORSE TO ROCKING CHAIR Paul Anka—RCA Victor 47-8311 [Burt Bacharach/Hal David] [ASC] (2/22/64 R-90)

FROM RUSSIA WITH LOVE *The Village Stompers—Epic 9674 [Lionel Bart] [BMI] (4/11/64 BCtR-67) [IWM]*

FROM RUSSIA WITH LOVE *Al Caiola—United Artists 711 [Lionel Bart] [BMI] (4/25/64 Ct-74) [IWM]*

FROM THE BEGINNING Emerson, Lake & Palmer—Cotillion 44158 [Greg Lake] [ASC] (8/26/72 BCR-34)

FROM THE BOTTOM OF MY HEART (DAMMI, DAMMI, DAMMI) Dean Martin—Reprise 20,116 [George Cardini/Danny DiMinno] [ASC] (12/1/62 BCR-84)

FROM THE BOTTOM OF MY HEART (I LOVE YOU) The Moody Blues—London 9764 [Denny Laine/Mike Pinder] [BMI] (6/5/65 BCR-70)

FROM THE CANDY STORE ON THE CORNER TO THE CHAPEL ON THE HILL Tony Bennett with Percy Faith and His Orchestra—Columbia 40726 [Bob Hilliard] [ASC] (8/18/56 BCR-33)

FROM THE FIRST HELLO TO THE LAST GOODBYE Jane Morgan and The 450 Collegians—Kapp 172 [Johnny Burke] [ASC] (1/19/57 R-72)

FROM THE TEACHER TO THE PREACHER Gene Chandler And Barbara Acklin—Brunswick 55387 [Barbara Acklin/Carl Davis/Eugene Record] [BMI] (10/19/68 BCR-40)

FROM THE VERY START The Children—Ode 66005 [Louis Cabaza/Steve Perron] [ASC] (1/30/71 R-93)

FROM US TO YOU The Stairsteps—Dark Horse 10005 [Clarence Burke Jr./Kenneth Burke] [BMI] (2/28/76 R-93)

FRONT PAGE STORY Neil Diamond—Columbia 03801 [Burt Bacharach/Neil Diamond/Carole Bayer Sager] [ASC] (4/23/83 BC-65)

FRUSTRATION The Zanies—Dore 632 [Robert Hemric/Jerry Styner] [ASC] (5/7/62 R-93)

FULL CIRCLE The Byrds—Asylum 11016 [Gene Clark] [BMI] (5/5/73 CR-77)

FULL MEASURE The Lovin' Spoonful—Kama Sutra 219 [Steve Boone/John Sebastian] [BMI] (1/7/67 BC-87)

FULL OF FIRE Al Green—Hi 2300 [Al Green/Mabon Hodges/Willie Mitchell] [BMI] (11/8/75 BCR-28)

FULL OF FIRE Shalamar—Solar 12152 [Joey Gallo/Richard Randolph/Jody Watley] [BMI] (12/20/80 BCR-55)

FULL TIME THING (BETWEEN DUSK AND DAWN) Whirlwind—Roulette 7195 [Melvin Steals/Mervin Steals] [BMI] (10/23/76 B-91)

FUN, FUN, FUN *The Beach Boys—Capitol 5118 [Mike Love/Brian Wilson] [BMI] (2/8/64 BCR-5)*

FUN, FUN, FUN *The Cantina Band—Millennium 11818 [Mike Love/Brian Wilson] (Med) [BMI] (7/25/81 B-81)*

FUN, FUN, FUN *The Beach Boys—Capitol 5030 [Mike Love/Brian Wilson] (Med) [BMI] (7/25/81 BCR-5)*

FUN TIME Joe Cocker—Asylum 45540 [Allen Toussaint] [BMI] (10/14/78 BCR-38)

FUNCTION AT THE JUNCTION Shorty Long—Soul 35021 [Lamont Dozier*/Brian Holland*/Eddie Holland/Frederick Long] [BMI] (9/24/66 B-97)

FUNK BOUTIQUE The Cover Girls—Epic 73698 [Tony Moran/Andy Tripoli] [BMI] (2/9/91 BC-55)

FUNK FACTORY Wilson Pickett—Atlantic 2878 [Luther Dixon/Wilson Pickett/Brad Shapiro] [BMI] (5/20/72 BCR-53)

FUNK #49 James Gang—ABC 11272 [Jim Fox/Dale Peters/Joe Walsh] [BMI] (8/29/70 BCR-54)

FUNK IT UP (DAVID'S SONG) The Sweet—Capitol 4454 [Brian Connolly/Stephen Priest/Andrew Scott/Michael Tucker] [ASC] (8/13/77 BC-88)

—FUNKTOWN see: CRANK IT UP

FUNKIN' FOR JAMAICA (N.Y.) Tom Browne—Arista/GRP 2506 [Tom Browne/Thomassina Smith] [BMI] (9/13/80 CR-74)

FUNK'N' ROLL (DANCIN' IN THE FUNKSHINE) Quazar—Arista 0349 [Jerome Brailey/Glenn Goins] [BMI] (11/25/78 R-96)

FUNKY The Chambers Brothers—Columbia 45277 [George Chambers*/Joe Chambers*/Lester Chambers/Willie Chambers*] [BMI] (2/27/71 C-96)

FUNKY BROADWAY PART 1 *Dyke And The Blazers—Original Sound 64 [Arlester Christian] [BMI] (4/15/67 BCR-65)*

FUNKY BROADWAY *Wilson Pickett—Atlantic 2430 [Arlester Christian] [BMI] (8/5/67 BCR-6)*

FUNKY CHICKEN Willie Henderson And The Soul Explosions—Brunswick 55429 [Carl Davis/Willie Henderson/Tom Washington] [BMI] (3/21/70 BR-86) [I]

FUNKY COLD MEDINA Tone Loc—Delicious Vinyl 104 [Matt Dike/Michael Ross/Marvin Young] [ASC] (3/4/89 BC-3)

FUNKY DONKEY Pretty Purdie—Date 1568 [Bernard Purdie] [BMI] (9/23/67 BR-87) [I]

FUNKY DRUMMER (PART 1) James Brown—King 6290 [James Brown] [BMI] (3/21/70 BCR-37)

FUNKY FEVER Clarence Carter—Atlantic 2508 [Clarence Carter/Marcus Daniel/Rick Hall/Joe Wilson] [BMI] (6/1/68 BCR-88)

THE FUNKY GIBBON The Goodies—20th Century 2189 [Evelyn Danzig*/Bill Oddie/Jack Segal*] [BMI] (5/3/75 BCR-79)

THE FUNKY JUDGE Bull & The Matadors—Toddlin' Town 108 [Leo Hutton/Andre Williams] [ASC] (8/24/68 BCR-39)

FUNKY L.A. Paul Humphrey & His Cool Aid Chemists—Lizard 21009 [Nolan Porter] [ASC] (7/24/71 C-97) [I]

FUNKY MAN Kool & The Gang—De-Lite 534 [Robert Bell/Ronald Bell/George M. Brown/Robert Mickens/Gene Redd Jr./Claydes Smith/Woodrow Sparrow/Dennis Thomas/Richard Westfield] [BMI] (9/5/70 BCR-84)

FUNKY MUSIC SHO NUFF TURNS ME ON *Edwin Starr—Gordy 7107 [Barrett Strong/Norman Whitfield] [BMI] (4/24/71 BCR-40)*

FUNKY MUSIC SHO NUFF TURNS ME ON *The Temptations—Gordy 7119 [Barrett Strong/Norman Whitfield] [BMI] (7/1/72 R-65)*

FUNKY NASSAU - PART 1 The Beginning Of The End—Alston 4595
[Tyrone Fitzgerald/Raphael Munnings] [BMI] (5/1/71 BCR-10)

FUNKY NORTH PHILLY Bill Cosby—Warner Bros. 7171/Warner Bros. Seven Arts 7171
[Bill Cosby*/Earl Nelson*] [BMI] (3/2/68 BR-80)

FUNKY PARTY Clarence Reid—Alston 4621 [Clarence Reid] [BMI] (7/27/74 BCR-91)

FUNKY PRESIDENT (PEOPLE IT'S BAD) James Brown—Polydor 14258
[James Brown] (TSW) [BMI] (12/7/74 BC-44)

FUNKY STREET Arthur Conley—Atco 6563
[Arthur Conley/Earl Simms] [BMI] (3/16/68 BCR-14)

FUNKY STUFF Kool & The Gang—De-Lite 557
[Robert Bell/Ronald Bell/George M. Brown/Robert Mickens/Claydes Smith/Dennis Thomas/Richard Westfield] [BMI] (9/8/73 BCR-29)

FUNKY WALK PART I (EAST) Dyke And The Blazers—Original Sound 79
[Arlester Christian] [BMI] (3/30/68 BCR-67)

FUNKY WAY Calvin Arnold—Venture 605 [Calvin Arnold] [BMI] (1/13/68 BCR-72)

FUNKY WEEKEND The Stylistics—Avco 4661
[Luigi Creatore/Hugo Peretti/George David Weiss] [ASC] (12/6/75 BC-76)

FUNKY WORM Ohio Players—Westbound 214
[Leroy Bonner/Marshall Jones/Ralph Middlebrooks/Walter Morrison/
Bruce Napier*/Andrew Noland/Marvin Pierce*/Greg Webster] [BMI] (2/17/73 BCR-13)

FUNKYTOWN *Lipps, Inc.—Casablanca 2233 [Steve Greenberg] [BMI] (3/29/80 BCR-1)*

FUNKY TOWN *Pseudo Echo—RCA 5217 [Steve Greenberg] [BMI] (5/16/87 BC-6)*

THE FUNNIEST THING Dennis Yost And The Classics IV—Imperial 66439
[Buddy Buie/J.R. Cobb] [BMI] (3/14/70 BCR-50)

FUNNY *Jesse Belvin—RCA Victor 47-7387*
[Lawrence Holofcener/Edward Scott] [ASC] (12/29/58 B-81)

FUNNY *Gene McDaniels—Liberty 55444*
[Lawrence Holofcener/Edward Scott] [ASC] (4/16/62 BR-92)

FUNNY Maxine Brown—Nomar 106
[Maxine M. Brown*/Sammy Taylor] [BMI] (3/13/61 BCR-15)

FUNNY FACE Donna Fargo—Dot 17429 [Donna Fargo] [BMI] (9/30/72 BCR-5)

FUNNY FAMILIAR FORGOTTEN FEELINGS Tom Jones—Parrot 40014
[Mickey Newbury] [BMI] (5/13/67 BCR-45)

FUNNY FEELING The Delfonics—Philly Groove 156
[Thom Bell/William Hart] [BMI] (5/31/69 BCR-87)

FUNNY GIRL Barbra Streisand—Columbia 43127
[Bob Merrill/Jule Styne] [ASC] (9/12/64 BCR-44)

FUNNY HOW LOVE CAN BE First Class—UK 49033
[John Carter/Ken Hawker/Gillian Shakespeare*] [ASC] (5/24/75 BC-74)

FUNNY HOW TIME SLIPS AWAY *Jimmy Elledge—RCA Victor 47-7946*
[Willie Nelson] [BMI] (11/13/61 BCR-22)

FUNNY HOW TIME SLIPS AWAY *Johnny Tillotson—Cadence 1441*
[Willie Nelson] [BMI] (10/19/63 BCR-50)

FUNNY *Joe Hinton—Back Beat 541 [Willie Nelson] [BMI] (8/8/64 BCR-10)*

FUNNY HOW TIME SLIPS AWAY *Dorothy Moore—Malaco 1033*
[Willie Nelson] [BMI] (7/24/76 BCR-58)

FUNNY HOW TIME SLIPS AWAY *The Spinners—Atlantic 89922*
[Willie Nelson] [BMI] (12/4/82 BC-60)

FUNNY LITTLE BUTTERFLIES Patty Duke—United Artists 915
[Lor Crane/Jack Gold/Bernice Ross] [BMI] (9/18/65 BCR-51)

FUNNY MAN Ray Stevens—Mercury 72098 [Ray Stevens] [BMI] (3/23/63 BCR-81)

FUNNY THING Tony Bennett with Percy Faith and His Orchestra—Columbia 40376
[Carl Sigman/Jimmy Van Heusen] [ASC] (12/4/54 CR-25)

FUNNY WAY OF LAUGHIN' Burl Ives—Decca 31371
[Hank Cochran] [BMI] (3/26/62 BCR-9)

FURRY MURRAY The Tradewinds—RCA Victor 47-7553
[Jack Hammer/Zelda Samuels] [ASC] (7/11/59 BCR-64)

FURTHER MORE Ray Stevens—Mercury 72039 [Ray Stevens] [BMI] (10/13/62 BCR-76)

FUTURE SHOCK Curtis Mayfield—Curtom 1987 [Curtis Mayfield] [BMI] (7/21/73 BCR-39)

FUTURE SHOCK Hello People—ABC/Dunhill 15023
[Greg Geddes/Robert Sedita/N.D. Smart II/Laurence Tasse] [ASC] (1/4/75 BCR-63)

THE FUTURE'S SO BRIGHT, I GOTTA WEAR SHADES Timbuk 3—I.R.S. 52940
[Pat MacDonald] [BMI] (10/25/86 BC-19)

G

THE GAL THAT GOT AWAY *Frank Sinatra—Capitol 2864*
[Harold Arlen/Ira Gershwin] [ASC] (7/24/54 CtR-PRE)

THE MAN THAT GOT AWAY *Jeri Southern—Decca 29184*
[Harold Arlen/Ira Gershwin] [ASC] (7/24/54 Ct-PRE)

GAL WITH THE YALLER SHOES Four Aces—Decca 29809
[Nicholas Brodszky/Sammy Cahn] [ASC] (2/10/56 BR-30)

GALAXY War—MCA 40820
[Thomas Allen/Harold Brown/Morris Dickerson/Jerry Goldstein/Lonnie Jordan/
Charles Miller/Lee Oskar/Howard Scott] [ASC] (12/17/77 BCR-39)

GALE WINDS Egyptian Combo—Norman 549
[Lloyd Rainey/Paul J. Scott] [BMI] (10/17/64 R-96) [IWM]

GALLANT MEN Senator Everett McKinley Dirksen—Capitol 5805
[John Cacavas/Charles Osgood] [ASC] (12/17/66 BCR-29)

GALVESTON *Glen Campbell—Capitol 2428 [Jimmy Webb] [ASC] (3/1/69 BCR-3)*

GALVESTON *Roger Williams—Kapp 2007 [Jimmy Webb] [ASC] (6/7/69 BCR-97) [IWM]*

THE GAMBLER Kenny Rogers—United Artists 1250 [Don Schlitz] [ASC] (11/4/78 BCR-13)

THE GAME IS OVER (WHAT'S THE MATTER WITH YOU) Brown Sugar—Capitol 4198
[Vincent Montana/Ron Walker] [BMI] (2/21/76 BC-76)

GAME OF LOVE Wayne Fontana & The Mindbenders—Fontana 1503/1509
[Clint Ballard Jr.] [ASC] (3/20/65 BCR-1)

GAMES Redeye—Pentagram 204 [David Hodgkins] [BMI] (10/24/70 BCR-22)

GAMES Phoebe Snow—Mirage 3800
[Andrea Farber/Vince Melamed] [ASC] (2/21/81 BCR-46)

GAMES PEOPLE PLAY Joe South—Capitol 2248 [Joe South] [BMI] (12/28/68 BCR-8)

GAMES PEOPLE PLAY Alan Parsons Project—Arista 0573
[Alan Parsons/Eric Woolfson] [BMI] (12/6/80 BCR-13)

—GAMES PEOPLE PLAY see: THEY JUST CAN'T STOP IT

GAMES THAT LOVERS PLAY *Wayne Newton—Capitol 5754*
[Larry Kusik/James Last/Eddie Snyder] [ASC] (10/15/66 BCRt-86) [FDE]

GAMES THAT LOVERS PLAY *Eddie Fisher—RCA Victor 47-8956*
[Larry Kusik/James Last/Eddie Snyder] [ASC] (10/15/66 BCRt-17) [FDE]

GAMES THAT LOVERS PLAY *Mantovani And His Orchestra—London 20015*
[James Last] [ASC] (11/5/66 CR-80) [IM]

GAMES WITHOUT FRONTIERS Peter Gabriel—Mercury 76063
[Peter Gabriel] [BMI] (8/2/80 BCR-48)

THE GANGS BACK AGAIN Kool & The Gang—De-Lite 523
[Robert Bell/Ronald Bell/George M. Brown/Robert Mickens/Gene Redd Jr./
Claydes Smith/Woodrow Sparrow/Dennis Thomas/Richard Westfield] [BMI]
(12/27/69 BR-85) [I]

THE GAP Thompson Twins—Arista 1-9290
[Tom Bailey/Alannah Currie/Joe Leeway] [ASC] (11/10/84 BC-69)

GARDEN IN THE RAIN Vic Dana—Dolton 99
[James Dyrenforth/Carroll Gibbons] [ASC] (10/10/64 BCR-90)

GARDEN OF EDEN *Joe Valino—Vik 0226*
[Dennise Norwood] [BMI] (9/15/56 BCRt-12)

GARDEN OF EDEN *Winifred Atwell—London 1724*
[Dennise Norwood] [BMI] (2/9/57 Rt-51)

GARDEN PARTY Rick Nelson & The Stone Canyon Band—Decca 32980
[Rick Nelson] [BMI] (7/29/72 BCR-3)

GARDEN PARTY Herb Alpert—A&M 2562 [Eythor Gunnarsson] [BMI] (8/20/83 B-81) [I]

GAS LAMPS AND CLAY Blues Image—Atco 6777
[Dennis Correll/Frank Konte] [ASC] (9/12/70 BCR-64)

GAS MONEY Jan & Arnie—Arwin 111
[Don Altfeld/Jan Berry/Arnie Ginsburg] [BMI] (7/21/58 BR-41)

GATOR TAILS AND MONKEY RIBS
The Spats Featuring Dick Johnson—ABC-Paramount 10585
[Alonzo Willis] [BMI] (9/12/64 BR-85)

GAZACHSTAHAGEN *Wild-Cats—United Artists 154 [Billy Mure] [BMI] (1/5/59 BCRt-52) [I]*

GAZACHSTAHAGEN *The Keymen—ABC-Paramount 9991*
[Billy Mure] [BMI] (1/19/59 Rt-52) [I]

GEE George Hamilton IV—ABC-Paramount 10028 [Dick Flood] [BMI] (8/1/59 BCR-73)

GEE *Jan & Dean—Dore 576*
[William Davis/Morris Levy‡/Daniel Norton/Viola Watkins*] [BMI] (11/14/60 BR-81)*

GEE *The Pixies Three—Mercury 72250*
[William Davis/Morris Levy‡/Daniel Norton/Viola Watkins*] [BMI] (4/18/64 BCR-78)*

GEE BABY *Joe & Ann—Ace 577 [Joe Joseph/Alvin Tyler] [BMI] (12/31/60 C-97)*

BABY YOU'RE SO FINE *Mickey And Sylvia—Willow 23000*
[Mickey Baker/Joe Joseph/Sylvia Robinson*/Alvin Tyler] [BMI] (8/21/61 BC-52)*

GEE BABY Peter Shelley—Bell 45,614 [Peter Shelley] [BMI] (11/30/74 BCR-81)

GEE BABY (I'M SORRY) The 3° Degrees—Swan 4197
[Richard Barrett] [BMI] (2/27/65 BCR-69)

GEE, BUT I'M LONESOME Ron Holden—Donna 1324
[Bruce Johnston] [BMI] (8/13/60 C-74)

GEE BUT IT'S LONELY Pat Boone—Dot 15825 [Phil Everly] [BMI] (9/15/58 BCR-25)

GEE, IT'S WONDERFUL Bobby Rydell—Cameo 217
[Dave Appell/Bernie Lowe/Kal Mann] [ASC] (6/9/62 R-96)

GEE WHITTAKERS *The Five Keys—Capitol 3267 [Winfield Scott] [BMI] (11/7/55 Rt-24)*

GEE WHITTAKERS *Pat Boone—Dot 15435 [Winfield Scott] [BMI] (12/1/55 BCRt-20)*

GEE WHIZ *The Innocents—Indigo 111*
[Leon René/Rafael René] [BMI] (11/14/60 BCtRt-28)

GEE WHIZ *Bobby Day (with Earl Nelson)—Rendezvous 136*
[Leon René/Rafael René] [BMI] (11/14/60 CtRt-33)

GEE WHIZ (LOOK AT HIS EYES) *Carla Thomas—Atlantic 2086*
[Carla Thomas] [BMI] (1/16/61 BCRt-5)

GEE WHIZ *Bernadette Peters—MCA 41210 [Carla Thomas] [BMI] (3/29/80 BCR-31)*

GEISHA GIRL Hank Locklin—RCA Victor 47-6984
[Lawton Williams] [BMI] (12/30/57 B-66)

GEMINI DREAM The Moody Blues—Threshold 601
[Justin Hayward/John Lodge] [ASC] (6/6/81 BCR-12)

GENERAL HOSPI-TALE The Afternoon Delights—MCA 51148
[Harry Francis King/Lisa Tedesco] [ASC] (7/25/81 BCR-27)

GENIUS OF LOVE Tom Tom Club—Sire 49882
[Adrian Belew*/Christopher Frantz/Steven J.C. Stanley/Tina Weymouth] [ASC] (1/23/82 BCR-31)

GENTLE Dino—Island 878 472 [Gerald Mims] [BMI] (11/10/90 BC-30)

***GENTLE ON MY MIND** Glen Campbell—Capitol 5939*
[John Hartford] [BMI] (7/8/67 BCR-62)

***GENTLE ON MY MIND** Patti Page—Columbia 44353 [John Hartford] [BMI] (2/10/68 B-66)*

***GENTLE ON MY MIND** Glen Campbell—Capitol 5939*
[John Hartford] [BMI] (9/14/68 BR-39)

***GENTLE ON MY MIND** Dean Martin—Reprise 0812 [John Hartford] [BMI] (3/1/69 CR-93)*

***GENTLE ON MY MIND** Aretha Franklin—Atlantic 2619*
[John Hartford] [BMI] (5/10/69 BCR-76)

GENUINE LOVE Les Paul and Mary Ford—Capitol 3108
[Rose Marie McCoy/Charles Singleton] [BMI] (4/25/55 R-17)

GEORGE JACKSON Bob Dylan—Columbia 45516 [Bob Dylan] [SE] (12/4/71 BCR-30)

***GEORGIA ON MY MIND** Ray Charles—ABC-Paramount 10135*
[Hoagy Carmichael/Stuart Gorrell] [BMI] (9/5/60 BCR-1)

***GEORGIA ON MY MIND** The Righteous Brothers—Moonglow 244*
[Hoagy Carmichael/Stuart Gorrell] [BMI] (2/5/66 BCR-62)

***GEORGIA ON MY MIND** Wes Montgomery—A&M 940*
[Hoagy Carmichael] [BMI] (7/6/68 BR-81) [IM]

***GEORGIA ON MY MIND** Willie Nelson—Columbia 10704*
[Hoagy Carmichael/Stuart Gorrell] [BMI] (5/27/78 BCR-84)

***GEORGIA ON MY MIND** Michael Bolton—Columbia 73490*
[Hoagy Carmichael/Stuart Gorrell] [BMI] (8/25/90 BC-33)

GEORGIA PINES The Candymen—ABC 10995
[John Adkins/Buddy Buie] [BMI] (11/4/67 BCR-44)

GEORGIA PORCUPINE George Fischoff—United Artists 410
[George Fischoff] [ASC] (5/25/74 BCR-65) [I]

GEORGIA RHYTHM Atlanta Rhythm Section—Polydor 14432
[Buddy Buie/J.R. Cobb/Robert Nix] [BMI] (10/1/77 BCR-68)

GEORGIA ROSE Tony Bennett—Columbia 43715
[Jimmy Flynn/Harry Rosenthal/Alex Sullivan] [ASC] (7/23/66 BCR-87)

GEORGIA TOOK HER BACK R.B. Greaves—Atco 6778
[Jonathan Rowlands] [BMI] (9/5/70 BCR-78)

GEORGIANNA The Princetons—Colpix 793 [Don Ciccone] [BMI] (2/5/66 R-90)

GEORGIE PORGIE Jewel Akens—Era 3142 [Herbert Newman] [ASC] (5/1/65 BCR-65)

***GEORGY GIRL** The Seekers—Capitol 5756*
[Jim Dale/Tom Springfield] [ASC] (12/3/66 BCR-1)

***GEORGY GIRL** Baja Marimba Band—A&M 843*
[Tom Springfield] [ASC] (4/29/67 B-98) [IM]

GEORGY PORGY Toto—Columbia 10944 [David Paich] [ASC] (4/28/79 BCR-44)

GERALDINE Jack Scott—Carlton 483 [Jack Scott] [BMI] (10/13/58 B-96)

GERONIMO'S CADILLAC Michael Murphey—A&M 1368
[Michael Murphey/Charles Quarto] [BMI] (8/5/72 BCR-37)

***GET A JOB** The Silhouettes—Ember 1029*
[Earl Beal/Ray Edwards/William Horton/Richard Lewis] [BMI] (1/6/58 BCRt-1)

***GET A JOB** The Mills Brothers—Dot 15695*
[Earl Beal/Ray Edwards/William Horton/Richard Lewis] [BMI] (2/3/58 Rt-2)

***GET A JOB** Nino & the Ebb Tides—Madison 166*
[Earl Beal/Ray Edwards/William Horton/Richard Lewis] (Med) [BMI] (8/26/61 BCR-57)

GET A LEG UP John Mellencamp—Mercury 867 890
[John Mellencamp] [ASC] (10/5/91 BC-13)

GET A LIFE Soul II Soul—Virgin 98981
[Hayden Browne/Beresford Romeo] [ASC] (4/14/90 BC-54)

GET A MOVE ON Eddie Money—Columbia 11064
[Lloyd Chiate/Paul Collins/Eddie Money] [BMI] (8/25/79 BCR-46)

GET AWAY Georgie Fame & The Blue Flames—Imperial 66189
[Georgie Fame] [BMI] (8/20/66 BCR-55)

GET BACK Roy Head—Scepter 12124 [Jimmy McCracklin] [BMI] (1/15/66 B-88)

***GET BACK** The Beatles With Billy Preston—Apple 2490*
[John Lennon/Paul McCartney] (TSW) [ASC] (5/3/69 BCR-1)

***GET BACK** Billy Preston—A&M 2071*
[John Lennon/Paul McCartney] [ASC] (10/28/78 B-86)

***GET BACK** The Beatles—Capitol 5107*
[John Lennon/Paul McCartney] (Med) [ASC] (3/27/82 BCR-12)

GET CLOSER Seals & Crofts (Featuring Carolyn Willis)—Warner Bros. 8190
[Dash Crofts/Jim Seals] [BMI] (4/10/76 BCR-4)

GET CLOSER Linda Ronstadt—Asylum 69948 [Jonathan Carroll] [ASC] (10/2/82 BC-20)

GET DANCIN'
Disco Tex & The Sex-O-Lettes Featuring Sir Monti Rock III—Chelsea 3004
[Bob Crewe/Kenny Nolan] [BMI] (11/23/74 BCR-10)

GET DOWN Harvey Scales & The 7 Sounds—Magic Touch 2007
[Harvey Scales/Monnie Smith/Albert Vance] [BMI] (10/14/67 BCR-79)

GET DOWN Curtis Mayfield—Curtom 1966 [Curtis Mayfield] [BMI] (11/13/71 BCR-52)

GET DOWN Gilbert O'Sullivan—MAM 3629 [Gilbert O'Sullivan] [BMI] (6/16/73 BCR-4)

GET DOWN Gene Chandler—20th Century Fox/Chi-Sound 2386
[James A. Thompson Jr.] [BMI] (12/2/78 BCR-48)

GET DOWN, GET DOWN (GET ON THE FLOOR) Joe Simon—Spring 156
[Raeford Gerald/Joe Simon] [BMI] (3/29/75 BCR-8)

GET DOWN ON IT Kool & The Gang—De-Lite 818
[Robert Bell/Ronald Bell/George M. Brown/Eumir Deodato/Robert Mickens/Claydes Smith/J.T. Taylor] [BMI] (2/27/82 BCR-10)

GET DOWN PEOPLE Fabulous Counts—Moira 108
[Demetrius Cates/Mose Davis/Leroy Emmanuel] [BMI] (4/25/70 BCR-87)

GET DOWN TONIGHT K.C. & The Sunshine Band—TK 1009
[Harry Wayne Casey/Rick Finch] [BMI] (6/21/75 BCR-1)

—GET FRESH AT THE WEEKEND see: SHOWING OUT

GET HERE Oleta Adams—Fontana 878 476 [Brenda Russell] [ASC] (12/15/90 BC-5)

GET HIM The Exciters—United Artists 604
[Bert Berns/Jerry Leiber/Ray Passman/Mike Stoller] [BMI] (6/22/63 B-76)

GET INTO SOMETHING The Isley Brothers—T-Neck 924
[O'Kelly Isley/Ronald Isley/Rudolph Isley] [BMI] (10/17/70 BC-89)

GET IT Stevie Wonder & Michael Jackson—Motown 1930
[Stevie Wonder] [ASC] (5/7/88 BC-80)

GET IT FROM THE BOTTOM The Steelers—Date 1642
[Albert B. Smith/Louis Smith/Wes Wells] [BMI] (11/8/69 BCR-49)

GET IT ON Chase—Epic 10738 [Bill Chase/Terry Richards] [ASC] (5/22/71 BCR-19)

GET IT ON Kingdom Come—Polydor 887436
[Lenny Wolf/Martin Wolff] [BMI] (4/2/88 B-69)

—GET IT ON see: BANG A GONG

GET IT RIGHT Aretha Franklin—Arista 1-9034
[Marcus Miller/Luther Vandross] [ASC] (7/30/83 BC-61)

GET IT RIGHT NEXT TIME Gerry Rafferty—United Artists 1316
[Gerry Rafferty] [BMI] (8/11/79 BCR-18)

GET IT TOGETHER (PART 1) James Brown And The Famous Flames—King 6122
[James Brown/Alfred James Ellis/Bud Hobgood] [BMI] (10/28/67 BCR-18)

GET IT TOGETHER The Jackson 5—Motown 1277
[Hal Davis/Donald Fletcher/Berry Gordy/Mel Larson/Jerry Marcellino] [ASC] (8/25/73 BCR-24)

GET IT UP Ben E. King and AWB—Atlantic 3402
[Ned Doheny] [ASC] (7/23/77 R-89)

GET IT UP Ronnie Milsap—RCA 11695
[Tom Brasfield/Robert Byrne] [ASC] (9/22/79 BCR-43)

GET IT UP The Time—Warner Bros. 49774 [Prince] [ASC] (10/10/81 R-72)

GET IT WHILE YOU CAN Janis Joplin—Columbia 45433
[Jerry Ragovoy/Mort Shuman] [BMI] (8/28/71 BCR-51)

GET ME TO THE CHURCH ON TIME Julius La Rosa—RCA Victor 47-6567
[Alan Jay Lerner/Frederick Loewe] [ASC] (7/14/56 B-89)

GET ME TO THE WORLD ON TIME The Electric Prunes—Reprise 0564
[Jill Jones/Annette Tucker] [BMI] (3/25/67 BCR-27)

GET OFF Foxy—Dash 5046 [Carl Driggs/Ish Ledesma] [BMI] (7/1/78 BCR-8)

GET OFF MY BACK WOMAN B.B. King—BluesWay 61026
[B.B. King/Ferdinand Washington] [BMI] (8/30/69 BCR-74)

GET OFF OF MY CLOUD The Rolling Stones—London 9792
[Mick Jagger/Keith Richards] [BMI] (10/2/65 BCR-1)

GET ON THE GOOD FOOT - PART 1 James Brown—Polydor 14139
[James Brown/Joe Mims/Fred Wesley] [BMI] (7/29/72 BCR-9)

GET ON UP The Esquires—Bunky 7750
[Gilbert Moorer/Bill Sheppard/Johnny (2) Taylor] [BMI] (8/19/67 BCR-11)

GET ON UP Tyrone Davis—Columbia 10648 [Leo Graham] [BMI] (4/22/78 R-91)

GET ON YOUR FEET Gloria Estefan—Epic 69064
[Jorge Casas/John DeFaria/Clay Ostwald] [BMI] (9/30/89 BC-9)

GET OUT NOW Tommy James And The Shondells—Roulette 7000
[Ritchie Cordell/Bo Gentry] [BMI] (1/27/68 BCR-26)

GET OUT OF BED Livingston Taylor—Capricorn 8025
[Livingston Taylor] [ASC] (2/5/72 BR-90)

GET OUT OF DENVER Bob Seger—Palladium 1205 [Bob Seger] [ASC] (7/27/74 BCR-80)

GET OUT OF MY LIFE, WOMAN Lee Dorsey—Amy 945
[Allen Toussaint] [BMI] (1/1/66 BCR-34)

GET OUT OF THE CAR The Treniers—Okeh 7050
[Claude Trenier/Cliff Trenier] [BMI] (3/7/55 R-76)

GET OUTTA MY DREAMS, GET INTO MY CAR Billy Ocean—Jive 9678
[Mutt Lange/Billy Ocean] [ASC] (2/13/88 BC-1)

***GET READY** The Temptations—Gordy 7049 [Smokey Robinson] [ASC] (2/26/66 BCR-23)*

***GET READY** Rare Earth—Rare Earth 5012 [Smokey Robinson] [ASC] (3/14/70 BCR-2)*

GET RHYTHM Johnny Cash—Sun 1103 [Johnny Cash] [BMI] (10/11/69 BCR-60)

GET SERIOUS Cut 'N' Move—Epic 73878
[Christine Christiansen/Per Holm-Petersen/Herman Wesley Kelley/Joern Volsgaard Kristensen/Jens Kjaer Larsen] [ASC] (8/3/91 B-76)

GET THAT GASOLINE BLUES NRBQ—Kama Sutra 586
[Terry Adams/Charlie Craig] [BMI] (1/26/74 BCR-55)

GET THAT LOVE Thompson Twins—Arista 1-9577
[Tom Bailey/Alannah Currie] [ASC] (3/28/87 BC-28)

GET THE CREAM OFF THE TOP Eddie Kendricks—Tamla 54260
[Brian Holland/Eddie Holland] [BMI] (7/5/75 BCR-50)

GET THE FUNK OUT MA FACE The Brothers Johnson—A&M 1851
[George Johnson/Louis E. Johnson/Quincy Jones] [BMI] (8/14/76 BCR-30)

GET THE MESSAGE Brian Hyland—Philips 40472
[Michael Gordon/James Griffin] [BMI] (8/12/67 B-91)

LET'S GET TOGETHER *We Five—A&M 784 [Chet Powers] [BMI] (11/13/65 BCR-31)*

GET TOGETHER *The Youngbloods—RCA Victor 47-9264*
[Chet Powers] [BMI] (9/2/67 BCR-62)

GET TOGETHER *The Youngbloods—RCA Victor 47-9752*
[Chet Powers] [BMI] (6/28/69 BCR-4)

GET TOUGH Kleeer—Atlantic 3788
[Woody Cunningham/Norman Durham] [ASC] (4/25/81 R-91)

GET UP AND BOOGIE (THAT'S RIGHT) Silver Convention—Midland Int'l 10571
[Sylvester Levay/Stephan Prager] [BMI] (3/13/76 BCR-1)

GET UP AND GET DOWN The Dramatics—Volt 4071
[Tony Hester] [BMI] (12/11/71 BCR-69)

GET UP AND GO Go-Go's—I.R.S. 9910
[Charlotte Caffey/Jane Wiedlin] [ASC] (9/25/82 BC-50)

GET UP! (BEFORE THE NIGHT IS OVER) Technotronic—SBK 07315
[Jo Bogaert/James Brown*/Bobby Byrd*/Manuela Kamosi/Ron Lenhoff*] [BMI] (1/27/90 BC-7)

GET UP, GET INTO IT, GET INVOLVED PT. 1 James Brown—King 6347
[James Brown/Bobby Byrd/Ron Lenhoff] [BMI] (12/26/70 BCR-32)

GET UP! GET UP! (YOU SLEEPYHEAD) *Jaye P. Morgan—RCA Victor 47-6441*
[Jim Breedlove/Joan White] [BMI] (3/31/56 BRt-80)

GET UP GET UP (YOU SLEEPY HEAD) *LaVern Baker with The Gliders—Atlantic 1087*
[Jim Breedlove/Joan White] [BMI] (4/6/56 Rt-80)

GET UP I FEEL LIKE BEING LIKE A SEX MACHINE (PART 1) *James Brown—King 6318*
[James Brown/Bobby Byrd/Ron Lenhoff] [BMI] (7/11/70 BCR-15)

GET UP I FEEL LIKE BEING A SEX MACHINE *James Brown—Polydor 14270*
[James Brown/Bobby Byrd/Ron Lenhoff] [BMI] (5/17/75 B-61)

GET UP OFFA THAT THING James Brown—Polydor 14326
[Deanna Brown/Deidra Brown/Yamma Brown] [BMI] (7/17/76 BCR-45)

GET USED TO IT Roger Voudouris—Warner Bros. 8762
[Michael Omartian/Roger Voudouris] [ASC] (3/17/79 BCR-21)

GET YOUR LIE STRAIGHT Bill Coday—Galaxy 777 [Denise LaSalle] [BMI] (3/13/71 R-93)

GETAWAY Earth, Wind & Fire—Columbia 10373
[Peter Cor/Bernard Taylor] [ASC] (7/10/76 BCR-10)

GETCHA BACK The Beach Boys—Caribou 04913
[Mike Love/Terry Melcher] [BMI] (5/25/85 BC-25)

GETT OFF Prince—Paisley Park 4-19225 [Prince] [ASC] (8/17/91 B-21)

GETTIN' READY FOR LOVE Diana Ross—Motown 1427
[Franne Golde/Tom Snow] [BMI] (10/29/77 BCR-27)

GETTIN' TOGETHER Tommy James And The Shondells—Roulette 4762
[Ritchie Cordell] [BMI] (8/26/67 BCR-14)

GETTING AWAY WITH IT Electronic—Warner Bros. 19880
[Johnny Marr/Bernard Sumner/Neil Tennant] [ASC] (3/31/90 BC-31)

GETTING CLOSER Wings—Columbia 11020 [Paul McCartney] [ASC] (6/16/79 BCR-20)

GETTING IT ON Dennis Coffey—Sussex 237
[Dennis Coffey/Mike Theodore] (TSW) [BMI] (6/3/72 B-93) [I]

GETTING MIGHTY CROWDED Betty Everett—Vee-Jay 628
[Van McCoy] [BMI] (11/28/64 BCR-65)

GETTING READY FOR THE HEARTBREAK Chuck Jackson—Wand 128
[Lockie Edwards/Larry Weiss] [BMI] (11/17/62 B-88)

GETTING THE CORNERS The T.S.U. Toronadoes—Atlantic 2579
[Leroy Lewis] [BMI] (1/18/69 BCR-73) [I]

GETTING TO KNOW YOU Sajid Khan—Colgems 1026
[Oscar Hammerstein/Richard Rodgers] [ASC] (10/26/68 R-93)

THE GHETTO - PART 1 Donny Hathaway—Atco 6719
[Donny Hathaway/Leroy Hutson] [BMI] (1/17/70 BC-87)

THE GHETTO Too Short—Jive/RCA 1414
[Al Eaton/Donny Hathaway/Leroy Hutson/Todd Shaw] [ASC] (11/17/90 BC-42)

GHETTO CHILD The Spinners—Atlantic 2973
[Thom Bell/Linda Creed] [BMI] (8/18/73 BCR-24)

GHETTO WOMAN B.B. King—ABC 11310
[Dave (2) Clark/B.B. King] [BMI] (8/28/71 BCR-56)

GHOST DANCER The Addrisi Brothers—Scotti Brothers 500
[Dick Addrisi/Don Addrisi] [BMI] (8/11/79 BCR-45)

THE GHOST IN YOU Psychedelic Furs—Columbia 04416
[Richard Butler/Tim Butler] [BMI] (5/12/84 BC-55)

GHOST OF BILLY MALLOO Dorsey Burnette—Era 3025
[Herbert Newman] [ASC] (9/19/60 R-98)

(GHOST) RIDERS IN THE SKY *The Ramrods—Amy 813*
[Stan Jones] [ASC] (12/26/60 BCR-23) [I]

RIDERS IN THE SKY *Lawrence Welk And His Orchestra and Chorus—Dot 16237*
[Stan Jones] [ASC] (9/4/61 BCR-45) [I]

GHOST RIDERS IN THE SKY *Baja Marimba Band—A&M 824*
[Stan Jones] [ASC] (11/26/66 BCR-50) [I]

(GHOST) RIDERS IN THE SKY *The Outlaws—Arista 0582*
[Stan Jones] [ASC] (12/27/80 BCR-31)

GHOST TOWN Don Cherry—Columbia 40705
[Nick Acquaviva/Ted Varnick] [ASC] (7/13/56 BCR-26)

GHOST TOWN Cheap Trick—Epic 08089
[Rick Nielsen/Diane Warren] [BMI] (11/5/88 BC-20)

GHOST TRAIN Marty Robbins—Columbia 42008 [Joe Babcock] [BMI] (6/3/61 C-100)

GHOSTBUSTERS Ray Parker Jr.—Arista 1-9212 [Ray Parker Jr.] [ASC] (6/16/84 BC-1)

GI GI Hoke Simpson—ABC-Paramount 9876 [Hoke Simpson] [NA] (12/30/57 R-82)

GIANT *Les Baxter with His Chorus and Orchestra—Capitol 3526*
[Dimitri Tiomkin/Paul Francis Webster] [ASC] (10/6/56 BRt-63)

GIANT *Jack Pleis and His Orchestra and Chorus—Decca 30055*
[Dimitri Tiomkin/Paul Francis Webster] [ASC] (10/6/56 BRt-73)

GIANT *Art Mooney and His Orchestra and Chorus—MGM 12320*
[Dimitri Tiomkin/Paul Francis Webster] [ASC] (10/6/56 BRt-73)

GIANT *Ray Heindorf & The Warner Bros. Orchestra—Columbia 40761*
[Dimitri Tiomkin/Paul Francis Webster] [ASC] (10/6/56 Rt-73)

GIANT *Jimmy Wakely—Coral 61706*
[Dimitri Tiomkin/Paul Francis Webster] [ASC] (10/6/56 Rt-73)

GIANT *Rusty Draper—Mercury 70938*
[Dimitri Tiomkin/Paul Francis Webster] [ASC] (10/6/56 Rt-73)

LOVE THEME FROM "GIANT" (THERE'S NEVER BEEN ANYONE ELSE BUT YOU)
David Carroll & His Orchestra—Mercury 70952
[Dimitri Tiomkin/Paul Francis Webster] [ASC] (10/6/56 Rt-73)

GIDDYUP GO Red Sovine—Starday 737 [Tommy Hill/Red Sovine] [BMI] (1/8/66 BC-82)

GIDGET *The Four Preps—Capitol 4078*
[Fred Karger/Patti Washington] [ASC] (11/3/58 R-86)

GIDGET *James Darren—Colpix 113*
[Fred Karger/Patti Washington] [ASC] (4/27/59 BCR-24)

GIFT OF LOVE The Van Dykes (1)—Donna 1333
[George Arlotta/Vincent Catalano/F. Kulaga] [ASC] (1/16/61 B-91)

GIGI *Vic Damone—Columbia 41122*
[Alan Jay Lerner/Frederick Loewe] [ASC] (2/24/58 BCtRt-47)

GIGI *Billy Eckstine—Mercury 71250*
[Alan Jay Lerner/Frederick Loewe] [ASC] (2/24/58 CtRt-47)

GIGI *Bing Crosby—Decca 30555*
[Alan Jay Lerner/Frederick Loewe] [ASC] (2/24/58 Rt-47)

GIGI *The Strollers Featuring Artie Malvin—MGM 12614*
[Alan Jay Lerner/Frederick Loewe] [ASC] (2/24/58 Rt-47)

GIGI *Tony Martin—RCA Victor 47-7170*
[Alan Jay Lerner/Frederick Loewe] [ASC] (2/24/58 Rt-47)

GIGI *Charles Margulis—Carlton 456 [Frederick Loewe] [ASC] (2/24/58 CtRt-47) [IM]*

THE GIGOLO O'Bryan—Capitol 5067
[O'Bryan Burnette/Don Cornelius] [ASC] (3/27/82 BCR-57)

GILEE Sonny Spencer—Memo 17984
[John Bobby Berry/Don Covay] [BMI] (10/19/59 BR-80)

GILLIAN FRANK Jerry Hudson—Big Tree 159 [Jerry Hudson] [BMI] (2/3/73 R-84)

GILLY GILLY OSSENFEFFER KATZENELLEN BOGEN BY THE SEA
The Four Lads—Columbia 40236
[Al Hoffman/Dick Manning] [ASC] (7/3/54 C-PRE)

GIMME ALL YOUR LOVIN' ZZ Top—Warner Bros. 29693
[Frank Beard/Billy Gibbons/Dusty Hill] [BMI] (4/2/83 BC-37)

GIMME DAT DING The Pipkins—Capitol 2819
[Albert Hammond/Mike Hazlewood] [BMI] (5/16/70 BCR-7)

GIMME GIMME GOOD LOVIN' Crazy Elephant—Bell 763
[Ritchie Cordell/Joey Levine] [BMI] (2/22/69 BCR-4)

GIMME LITTLE SIGN Brenton Wood—Double Shot 116
[Joseph Hooven/Alfred J. Smith/Hal Winn] [ASC] (8/12/67 BCR-6)

GIMME SHELTER *Merry Clayton—Ode '70 66003*
[Mick Jagger/Keith Richards] [BMI] (6/6/70 BCR-73)

GIMME SHELTER *Grand Funk Railroad—Capitol 3160*
[Mick Jagger/Keith Richards] [BMI] (8/28/71 BCR-57)

GIMME SOME LOVIN' *Spencer Davis Group—United Artists 50108*
[Spencer Davis/Muff Winwood/Steve Winwood] [BMI] (12/31/66 BCR-5)

GIMME SOME LOVIN' PART ONE *Traffic, Etc.—United Artists 50841*
[Spencer Davis/Muff Winwood/Steve Winwood] [BMI] (10/23/71 BCR-56)

GIMME SOME LOVIN' *Kongas—Polydor 14461*
[Spencer Davis/Muff Winwood/Steve Winwood] (Med) [BMI] (4/8/78 BC-84)

GIMME SOME LOVIN' *Blues Brothers—Atlantic 3666*
[Spencer Davis/Muff Winwood/Steve Winwood] [BMI] (5/31/80 BCR-16)

GIMME SOME MORE Crazy Elephant—Bell 817
[Jerry Kasenetz/Jeff Katz/Bob Levine/J.J. Woods] [BMI] (9/6/69 R-77)

GIMME SOME MORE The J.B.'s—People 602
[Charles Bobbit/James Brown] [BMI] (1/22/72 BCR-55) [I]

—GIMME THE GOOD LIFE see: BON BON VIE

GIMME YOUR GOOD LOVIN' Diving For Pearls—Epic 69036
[Dan Malone/Jack Moran] [NA] (12/9/89 B-84)

GIMME YOUR MONEY PLEASE Bachman-Turner Overdrive—Mercury 73843
[C.F. Turner] [BMI] (9/18/76 BC-70)

GINA Johnny Mathis—Columbia 42582 [Leon Carr/Paul Vance] [ASC] (9/22/62 BCR-6)
GINGER BREAD Frankie Avalon—Chancellor 1021
[Clint Ballard Jr./Hank Hunter] [ASC] (7/7/58 BCRt*-9)
GINGERBREAD The Gingersnaps—Kapp 226
[Al Frisch/Fred Tobias] [ASC] (7/7/58 Rt*-12)
GINNIE BELL Paul Dino—Promo 2180 [Paul Dino] [BMI] (1/23/61 BCR-38)
GINNY COME LATELY Brian Hyland—ABC-Paramount 10294
[Gary Geld/Peter Udell] [ASC] (3/5/62 BCR-18)
GINO IS A COWARD Gino Washington—Ric-Tic 100 [Ronald Davis] [BMI] (8/1/64 R-98)
A GIRL, A GIRL (ZOOM-BA DI ALLI NELLA) Eddie Fisher—RCA Victor 47-5675
[Al Bandini/Bennie Benjamin/Pat Rossi*/George David Weiss] [ASC] (5/29/54 BC-PRE)
GIRL CALLIN Chocolate Milk—RCA 11222 [Allen Toussaint] [BMI] (5/27/78 R-97)
GIRL CAN'T HELP IT Little Richard—Specialty 591 [Bobby Troup] [ASC] (1/26/57 BR-49)
GIRL CAN'T HELP IT Journey—Columbia 06302
[Jonathan Cain/Steve Perry/Neal Schon] [ASC] (8/30/86 BC-17)
GIRL COME RUNNING
The 4 Seasons Featuring The "Sound" Of Frankie Valli—Philips 40305
[Bob Crewe/Bob Gaudio] [BMI] (6/12/65 BCR-23)
GIRL DON'T CARE Gene Chandler—Brunswick 55312
[Gene Chandler/Keni St. Lewis] [BMI] (2/18/67 BCR-50)
GIRL DON'T COME Sandie Shaw—Reprise 0342
[Chris Frederick Andrews] [BMI] (3/6/65 BCR-29)
GIRL, DON'T LET IT GET YOU DOWN The O'Jays—TSOP 4790
[Kenneth Gamble/Leon Huff] [BMI] (8/23/80 BCR-43)
THE GIRL FROM IPANEMA Getz/Gilberto—Verve 10323
[Vinicius De Moraes/Norman Gimbel/Antonio Carlos Jobim] [BMI] (6/6/64 BCR-5) [FET]
THE GIRL FROM PEYTON PLACE Dickey Lee—TCF Hall 111
[Dickey Lee/Allen Reynolds] [BMI] (9/4/65 BCR-73)
GIRL FROM SPANISH TOWN Marty Robbins—Columbia 42968
[Marty Robbins] [BMI] (2/15/64 CR-76)
A GIRL HAS TO KNOW The G-Clefs—Terrace 7503
[Barry Mann/Cynthia Weil] [BMI] (2/12/62 BCR-60)
GIRL I AM SEARCHING FOR YOU Stevie B—LMR 74005 [Stevie B] [BMI] (10/7/89 BC-56)
THE GIRL I KNEW SOMEWHERE The Monkees—Colgems 1004
[Michael Nesmith] [BMI] (3/25/67 BR-39)
GIRL I NEED YOU The Artistics—Brunswick 55315
[Thomas Green/Barbara Griffin/Daniel Reed] [BMI] (3/18/67 BCR-66)
THE GIRL I USED TO KNOW Brother Beyond—EMI 50287
[Evan Rogers/Carl Sturken] [BMI] (6/23/90 BC-23)
THE GIRL I'LL NEVER KNOW (ANGELS NEVER FLY THIS LOW)
Frankie Valli—Philips 40622
[Raymond Bloodworth/L. Russell Brown] [BMI] (6/7/69 BCR-23)
GIRL I'M GONNA MISS YOU Milli Vanilli—Arista 1-9870
[Peter Bischof-Fallenstein/Frank Farian/Dietmar Kawohl] [ASC] (8/5/89 BC-1)
GIRL IN LOVE The Outsiders—Capitol 5646
[Chet Kelley/Thomas R. King] [BMI] (5/14/66 BCR-21)
THE GIRL IN MY DREAMS *The Four Lovers—RCA Victor 47-6518*
[Maxwell Davis/Joe Josea‡/Sam Ling‡/Jules Taub‡] [BMI] (5/4/56 Rt-74)
THE GIRL IN MY DREAMS *The Cliques—Modern 987*
[Maxwell Davis/Joe Josea‡/Sam Ling‡/Jules Taub‡] [BMI] (5/11/56 BRt-45)
GIRL IN MY DREAMS *The Capris—Old Town 1107*
[Maxwell Davis/Joe Josea‡/Sam Ling‡/Jules Taub‡] [BMI] (9/18/61 B-92)
A GIRL IN TROUBLE (IS A TEMPORARY THING) Romeo Void—Columbia 04534
[Debora Iyall/David Kahne/Peter Woods/Frank Zincavage] [BMI] (9/1/84 BC-30)
THE GIRL IS MINE Michael Jackson/Paul McCartney—Epic 03288
[Michael Jackson] [BMI] (11/6/82 BC-2)
GIRL LIKE YOU Gary Stites—Carlton 516 [Gary Stites] [BMI] (7/20/59 BCR-70)
A GIRL LIKE YOU The Young Rascals—Atlantic 2424
[Eddie Brigati/Felix Cavaliere] [ASC] (7/8/67 BCR-5)
A GIRL LIKE YOU The Smithereens—Enigma 44480 [Pat DiNizio] [BMI] (12/9/89 BC-38)
THE GIRL MOST LIKELY Jeannie C. Riley—Plantation 7
[Margaret Lewis/Mira Smith] [BMI] (11/30/68 BCR-41)
GIRL OF MY BEST FRIEND Ral Donner & The Starfires—Gone 5102
[Sam Bobrick/Beverly Ross] [BMI] (4/15/61 BCR-19)
GIRL OF MY DREAMS Bram Tchaikovsky—Polydor 14575
[Ron Thomas] [ASC] (7/7/79 BCR-37)
GIRL ON A SWING Gerry And The Pacemakers—Laurie 3354
[Ralph Miranda] [BMI] (9/10/66 BCR-28)
GIRL ON PAGE 44 The Four Lads—Columbia 41310
[Richard Adler/Robert Allen] [ASC] (1/3/59 BCR-31)
GIRL ON THE BILLBOARD Del Reeves—United Artists 824
[Walter Haynes/Hank Mills] [BMI] (5/29/65 BCR-92)
THE GIRL THAT STOOD BESIDE ME Bobby Darin—Atlantic 2367
[Geoffrey Stevens] [BMI] (12/10/66 BCR-45)
GIRL WATCHER The O'Kaysions—ABC 11094
[Wayne Pittman/Buck Trail] [BMI] (8/10/68 BCR-4)
THE GIRL WHO LOVED ME WHEN The Glass Bottle—Avco 4584
[Neil Brian Goldberg] [ASC] (11/13/71 BCR-78)
GIRL (WHY YOU WANNA MAKE ME BLUE) The Temptations—Gordy 7035
[Eddie Holland/Norman Whitfield] [BMI] (9/12/64 BCR-25)
GIRL WITH THE GOLDEN BRAIDS Perry Como—RCA Victor 47-6904
[Stanley Kahan/Eddie Snyder] [ASC] (5/18/57 BCR-11)
GIRL WITH THE HUNGRY EYES Jefferson Starship—Grunt 11921
[Paul Kantner] [BMI] (2/23/80 BCR-55)
GIRL WITH THE STORY IN HER EYES The Safaris With The Phantom's Band—Eldo 105
[Bob Roberts] [BMI] (9/19/60 BR-77)
GIRL (YOU CAPTIVATE ME) ? & The Mysterians—Cameo 479
[Joey Day/Alan Dischel] [ASC] (6/3/67 BCR-81)
GIRL YOU KNOW IT'S TRUE Milli Vanilli—Arista 1-9781
[Kayode Adeyemo/Rodney Hollaman/Kevin Lyles/William Pettaway/Sean Spencer] [BMI] (12/31/88 BC-1)
GIRL YOU NEED A CHANGE OF MIND (PART 1) Eddie Kendricks—Tamla 54230
[Leonard Caston/Anita Poree] [BMI] (2/24/73 BCR-87)
GIRL, YOU'LL BE A WOMAN SOON Neil Diamond—Bang 542
[Neil Diamond] [SE] (4/8/67 BCR-8)
GIRL YOU'RE TOO YOUNG Archie Bell & The Drells—Atlantic 2644
[Archie Bell/Thom Bell/Kenneth Gamble] [BMI] (6/14/69 BCR-57)
GIRLFRIEND Bobby Brown—MCA 52866
[Kirk Crumpler/Lee Peters/Larry White] [ASC] (12/20/86 BC-57)
GIRLFRIEND Pebbles—MCA 53185
[Kenneth Edmonds/Antonio Reid] [BMI] (1/30/88 BC-5)
GIRLS Johnny Burnette—Liberty 55345 [Barry De Vorzon] [BMI] (7/24/61 R-80)
GIRLS Major Lance—Okeh 7197 [Curtis Mayfield] [BMI] (6/20/64 BC-68)
GIRLS (PART I) Moments And Whatnauts—Stang 5057
[Venus Dodson/Al Goodman/Walter Lee Morris*/Harry Ray/Jonathan Williams*] [BMI] (1/11/75 CR-85)
GIRLS Dwight Twilley—EMI America 8196 [Dwight Twilley] [ASC] (2/18/84 BC-16)
THE GIRL'S A DEVIL Dukays—NAT 4001 [Bernice Williams] [BMI] (5/15/61 BC-64)
GIRLS AIN'T NOTHING BUT TROUBLE D.J. Jazzy Jeff & The Fresh Prince—Jive 1147
[Buddy Kaye/Hugo Montenegro/Will Smith/Jeff Townes] [ASC] (10/29/88 BC-54)
THE GIRL'S ALRIGHT WITH ME The Temptations—Gordy 7032
[Eddie Holland/Norman Whitfield] [BMI] (5/23/64 CR-82)
GIRLS ARE MORE FUN Ray Parker Jr.—Arista 1-9352
[Ray Parker Jr.] [ASC] (10/5/85 BC-30)
GIRLS ARE OUT TO GET YOU The Fascinations—Mayfield 7714
[Curtis Mayfield] [BMI] (1/28/67 BCR-80)
GIRLS CAN GET IT Dr. Hook—Casablanca 2314 [Leslie Pearl] [BMI] (11/1/80 BCR-34)
GIRLS CAN'T DO WHAT THE GUYS DO Betty Wright—Alston 4569
[Willie Clarke/Clarence Reid] [BMI] (8/3/68 BCR-33)
GIRLS, GIRLS, GIRLS Steve Lawrence—United Artists 233
[Howard Greenfield/Barry Mann] [BMI] (7/2/60 C-82)
GIRLS GIRLS GIRLS (PART II) The Coasters—Atco 6204
[Jerry Leiber/Mike Stoller] [BMI] (8/12/61 BCR-84)
GIRLS, GIRLS, GIRLS Mötley Crüe—Elektra 69465
[Tommy Lee/Mick Mars/Nikki Sixx] [ASC] (5/30/87 BC-12)
(GIRLS, GIRLS, GIRLS) MADE TO LOVE Eddie Hodges—Cadence 1421
[Phil Everly] [BMI] (6/9/62 BCR-14)
GIRLS GROW UP FASTER THAN BOYS The Cookies—Dimension 1020
[Gerry Goffin/Jack Keller] [BMI] (11/30/63 BCR-33)
GIRLS IN LOVE Gary Lewis And The Playboys—Liberty 55971
[Garry Bonner/Alan Gordon] [BMI] (5/13/67 BCR-35)
GIRLS IT AIN'T EASY The Honey Cone—Hot Wax 6903
[Lamont Dozier/Ronald Dunbar/Brian Holland/Eddie Holland] [BMI] (11/1/69 BCR-68)
GIRLS JUST WANT TO HAVE FUN Cyndi Lauper—Portrait 37-04120
[Robert Hazard] [ASC] (12/17/83 BC-1)
GIRLS NITE OUT Tyler Collins—RCA 2630
[Sheri Byers/Darryl Ross] [BMI] (4/28/90 BC-6)
GIRLS' SCHOOL Wings—Capitol 4504
[Denny Laine*/Paul McCartney] (TSW) [ASC] (11/19/77 BCR-31)
THE GIRLS' SONG The 5th Dimension—Soul City 781
[Jimmy Webb] [BMI] (3/28/70 BCR-43)
GIRLS TALK Dave Edmunds—Swan Song 71001 [Elvis Costello] [ASC] (8/25/79 BCR-65)
GIRLS WILL BE GIRLS, BOYS WILL BE BOYS The Isley Brothers—T-Neck 921
[O'Kelly Isley/Ronald Isley/Rudolph Isley] [BMI] (7/25/70 BCR-64)
GIRLS WITH GUNS Tommy Shaw—A&M 2676 [Tommy Shaw] [ASC] (9/29/84 BC-30)
GIRL'S WORK IS NEVER DONE The Chordettes—Cadence 1366
[Richard Barrett/Don Raysor] [BMI] (8/17/59 BR-89)
GITARZAN Ray Stevens—Monument 1131 [Bill Justis/Ray Stevens] [BMI] (4/5/69 BCR-7)
GIVE Missing Persons—Capitol 5326
[Dale Bozzio/Terry Bozzio/Warren Cuccurullo/Patrick O'Hearn] [BMI] (3/17/84 BC-67)
GIVE A DAMN Spanky And Our Gang—Mercury 72831
[Stuart Scharf] [BMI] (8/3/68 BCR-27)
GIVE A LITTLE Robert John—Ariola America 7693
[Robert John/Tom Pedrick/Mike Piccirillo] [BMI] (4/29/78 C-89)
GIVE A LITTLE BIT Supertramp—A&M 1938
[Rick Davies/Roger Hodgson] [ASC] (5/14/77 BCR-12)

GIVE A LITTLE BIT MORE Cliff Richard—EMI America 8076
[Andy Hill/John Philip Hodge] [ASC] (4/25/81 BCR-36)

GIVE A LITTLE TIME Ella Mae Morse—Capitol 2959
[Joyce Bennett/Leroy Kirkland] [BMI] (11/29/54 R-77)

GIVE A WOMAN LOVE Bobbi Martin—United Artists 50687
[Henry Jerome/Bobbi Martin] [ASC] (6/27/70 BCR-58)

GIVE ALL YOUR LOVE TO ME Gerry And The Pacemakers—Laurie 3313
[Gerry Marsden] [BMI] (8/14/65 BCR-68)

GIVE EVERYBODY SOME Bar-Kays—Volt 154
[James Edward Alexander/Ronnie Caldwell/Ben Cauley/Carl Cunningham/Phalon Jones/Jimmy King/David Porter] [BMI] (10/14/67 BCR-64)

GIVE HIM A GREAT BIG KISS The Shangri-Las—Red Bird 10-018
[Shadow Morton] [BMI] (12/26/64 BCR-14)

GIVE IRELAND BACK TO THE IRISH Wings—Apple 1847
[Linda McCartney/Paul McCartney] [ASC] (3/11/72 BCR-21)

GIVE IT ALL YOU GOT Chuck Mangione—A&M 2211
[Chuck Mangione] [BMI] (1/19/80 BCR-18) [I]

GIVE IT AWAY The Chi-Lites—Brunswick 55398 [Eugene Record] [BMI] (2/15/69 BCR-74)

GIVE IT AWAY Red Hot Chili Peppers—Warner Bros. 19147
[Michael Balzary/John Frusciante/Anthony Kiedis/Chad Smith] [BMI] (12/21/91 B-76)

GIVE IT TO ME The Mob—Colossus 134
[Gary Beisbier/James Holvay] [BMI] (2/27/71 BCR-71)

GIVE IT TO ME The J. Geils Band—Atlantic 2953
[Seth Justman/Peter Wolf] [ASC] (3/24/73 BCR-15)

GIVE IT TO ME BABY Rick James—Gordy 7179 [Rick James] [ASC] (5/16/81 BCR-30)

GIVE IT TO ME GOOD Trixter—Mechanic 53863
[Steven James Brown] [BMI] (12/1/90 BC-65)

GIVE IT TO THE PEOPLE The Righteous Brothers—Haven 7004
[Dennis Lambert/Brian Potter] [BMI] (9/7/74 BCR-20)

GIVE IT UP (TURN IT LOOSE) Tyrone Davis—Columbia 10388
[Leo Graham] [BMI] (8/28/76 BCR-36)

GIVE IT UP Steve Miller Band—Capitol 5194
[Steve Miller] [ASC] (12/11/82 BC-60)

GIVE IT UP KC—Meca 1001
[Deborah Carter/Harry Wayne Casey] [BMI] (12/24/83 BC-17)

GIVE IT UP ZZ Top—Warner Bros. 21840
[Frank Beard/Billy Gibbons/Dusty Hill] [BMI] (2/9/91 B-79)

GIVE IT UP OR TURNIT A LOOSE James Brown—King 6213
[Charles Bobbit] [BMI] (1/25/69 BCR-15)

GIVE IT WHAT YOU GOT B.T. Express—Roadshow 7003
[Solomon Roberts] (TSW) [BMI] (10/4/75 BCR-40)

GIVE ME Eileen Rodgers—Columbia 40791 [Bob Merrill] [ASC] (12/15/56 BR-61)

GIVE ME A REASON TO BE GONE Maureen McGovern—20th Century 2109
[Marie Cain] [ASC] (9/21/74 BCR-61)

GIVE ME ALL NIGHT Carly Simon—Arista 1-9587
[Gerard McMahon/Carly Simon] [BMI] (5/16/87 BC-61)

GIVE ME ALL YOUR LOVE Whitesnake—Geffen 28103
[David Coverdale/John Sykes] [ASC] (2/13/88 BC-48)

***GIVE ME AN INCH GIRL** Robert Palmer—Island 049 [Robert Palmer] [ASC] (1/17/76 C-88)*

***GIVE ME AN INCH** Ian Matthews—Mushroom 7040*
[Robert Palmer] [ASC] (2/14/79 BCR-65)

GIVE ME JUST A LITTLE MORE TIME Chairmen Of The Board—Invictus 9074
[Lamont Dozier/Ronald Dunbar/Brian Holland/Eddie Holland] [BMI] (1/17/70 BCR-3)

GIVE ME LOVE The McGuire Sisters—Coral 61494 [Cindy Walker] [BMI] (9/10/55 BCR-30)

GIVE ME LOVE (GIVE ME PEACE ON EARTH) George Harrison—Apple 1862
[George Harrison] [ASC] (5/12/73 BCR-1)

GIVE ME ONE MORE CHANCE Wilmer Alexander Jr. And The Dukes—Aphrodisiac 260
[Douglas L. Brown] [BMI] (6/22/68 BCR-65)

GIVE ME THE KEYS (AND I'LL DRIVE YOU CRAZY)
Huey Lewis and the News—Chrysalis 43335
[Bill Gibson/Huey Lewis/Steve Lewis] [ASC] (1/21/89 BC-38)

GIVE ME THE NIGHT George Benson—Warner Bros. 49505
[Rod Temperton] [ASC] (6/28/80 BCR-4)

GIVE ME THE REASON Luther Vandross—Epic 06129
[Nat Adderley Jr./Luther Vandross] [BMI] (8/23/86 BC-51)

GIVE ME TIME (L'AMORE SE NE VA) Dusty Springfield—Philips 40465
[Peter Callander/Pietro Melfa/Amedeo Tommasi] [BMI] (7/1/67 BCR-60) [FDE]

GIVE ME TONIGHT Shannon—Mirage 99775
[Chris Barbosa/Ed Chisolm] [ASC] (3/31/84 BC-40)

GIVE ME YOUR HEART Vanity Kills—Hollywood 64898
[Steve Baca/Eric Daniels] [BMI] (5/18/91 C-85)

GIVE ME YOUR HEART FOR CHRISTMAS The McGuire Sisters—Coral 61303
[Bob Goodman] [ASC] (11/22/54 R-25)

GIVE ME YOUR LOVE Don Cornell—Coral 61367
[Charles Albert/Fred Jay/Irving Reid] [BMI] (2/28/55 CR-28)

GIVE ME YOUR LOVE Nat "King" Cole—Capitol 4125
[Robert Mosely/Mayme Watts] [BMI] (1/31/59 BCR-75)

GIVE ME YOUR LOVE Barbara Mason—Buddah 331
[Curtis Mayfield] [BMI] (12/30/72 BCR-18)

GIVE MY LOVE A TRY Linda Jones—Loma 2085
[Charles Harper*/Ray Lewis/Richard Poindexter/Robert Poindexter] [BMI] (12/30/67 BR-93)

GIVE MYSELF A PARTY Don Gibson—RCA Victor 47-7330
[Don Gibson] [BMI] (9/29/58 BR-46)

***GIVE PEACE A CHANCE** Plastic Ono Band—Apple 1809*
[John Lennon/Paul McCartney] [NA] (7/26/69 BCR-10)

***GIVE PEACE A CHANCE** Peace Choir—Virgin 98839*
[John Lennon/Sean Ono Lennon/Paul McCartney/Yoko Ono*] [NA] (3/9/91 B-54)*

GIVE THE BABY ANYTHING THE BABY WANTS Joe Tex—Dial 1008
[Joe Tex] [BMI] (10/2/71 CR-97)

GIVE THE PEOPLE WHAT THEY WANT The O'Jays—Philadelphia Int'l 3565
[Kenneth Gamble/Leon Huff] [BMI] (4/26/75 BCR-33)

GIVE TO LIVE Sammy Hagar—Geffen 28314 [Sammy Hagar] [ASC] (6/13/87 BC-23)

—GIVE UP THE FUNK see: TEAR THE ROOF OFF THE SUCKER

GIVE UP YOUR GUNS The Buoys—Scepter 12318
[Gerard Florio/Rupert Holmes] [ASC] (6/12/71 BCR-81)

***GIVE US THIS DAY** Joni James—MGM 12288*
[Robert Day/Buddy Kaye] [ASC] (7/6/56 BCRt-30)

***GIVE US THIS DAY** The Dream Weavers—Decca 29990*
[Robert Day/Buddy Kaye] [ASC] (7/20/56 Rt-34)

***GIVE US YOUR BLESSING** Ray Peterson—Dunes 2025*
[Jeff Barry/Ellie Greenwich] [BMI] (6/1/63 BCR-70)

***GIVE US YOUR BLESSINGS** The Shangri-Las—Red Bird 10-030*
[Jeff Barry/Ellie Greenwich] [BMI] (5/29/65 BCR-29)

GIVE YOUR BABY A STANDING OVATION The Dells—Cadet 5696
[Marv Johnson/Henry Williams] [ASC] (4/14/73 BCR-20)

GIVIN' IT ALL UP The J. Geils Band—Atlantic 3251
[Seth Justman/Peter Wolf] [ASC] (2/15/75 C-86)

GIVING IT ALL AWAY Roger Daltrey—Track 40053
[David Courtney/Leo Sayer] [ASC] (5/26/73 BCR-60)

GIVING IT UP FOR YOUR LOVE Delbert McClinton—Capitol/MSS 4948
[Jerry Lynn Williams] [BMI] (12/6/80 BCR-8)

***GIVING UP** Gladys Knight & The Pips—Maxx 326 [Van McCoy] [BMI] (5/9/64 BCR-38)*

***GIVING UP** Donny Hathaway—Atco 6884 [Van McCoy] [BMI] (5/13/72 BCR-72)*

GIVING UP, GIVING IN The 3° Degrees—Ariola 7721
[Pete Bellotte/Giorgio Moroder] [ASC] (1/13/79 R-91)

GIVING UP ON LOVE Jerry Butler—Vee-Jay 588
[Bob Feldman/Jerry Goldstein/Richard Gottehrer] [BMI] (3/28/64 BCR-56)

GIVING UP ON LOVE Rick Astley—RCA 8872 [Rick Astley] [BMI] (4/15/89 BC-34)

GIVING YOU THE BENEFIT Pebbles—MCA 53891
[Kenneth Edmonds/Antonio Reid] [BMI] (8/18/90 BC-3)

GIVING YOU THE BEST THAT I GOT Anita Baker—Elektra 69371
[Anita Baker/Randy Holland/Skip Scarborough] [BMI] (9/24/88 BC-2)

GLAD ALL OVER The Dave Clark Five—Epic 9656
[Dave Clark/Mike Smith] [ASC] (2/15/64 BCR-5)

GLAD RAG DOLL Crazy Otto—Decca 29403
[Milton Ager/Dan Dougherty] (TSW) [ASC] (4/9/55 BCR-19) [IM]

GLAD RAGS Tennessee Ernie Ford—Capitol 4107 [Johnny Bond] [BMI] (1/5/59 BR-85)

GLAD SHE'S A WOMAN Bobby Goldsboro—United Artists 50497
[Bodie Chandler] [BMI] (2/8/69 BCR-43)

GLAD TO BE UNHAPPY The Mamas & The Papas—Dunhill 4107
[Lorenz Hart/Richard Rodgers] [ASC] (10/21/67 BCR-19)

THE GLAMOROUS LIFE Sheila E.—Warner Bros. 29285 [Prince] [ASC] (6/16/84 BC-7)

GLAMOUR BOY The Guess Who—RCA Victor 74-0977
[Burton Cummings] [BMI] (7/14/73 CR-83)

GLAMOUR BOYS Living Colour—Epic 68548
[Vernon Reid] [ASC] (8/26/89 BC-26)

GLASSHOUSE The Temptations—Gordy 7144
[James Carmichael/Berry Gordy/Ronald Norman Miller/Kathy Wakefield] [BMI] (7/5/75 BCR-37)

GLENDORA Perry Como—RCA Victor 47-6554 [Ray Stanley] [BMI] (6/8/56 BCR-12)

GLIDE Pleasure—Fantasy 874
[Nathaniel Phillips/Bruce A. Smith*] [ASC] (12/8/79 BR-55)

GLOBETROTTIN' The Tornadoes—London 9579 [Joe Meek] [ASC] (2/2/63 CR-87) [I]

***GLORIA** Them—Parrot 9727 [Van Morrison] [BMI] (5/1/65 BCR-81)*

***GLORIA** The Shadows Of Knight—Dunwich 116 [Van Morrison] [BMI] (3/12/66 BCR-6)*

***GLORIA** Them—Parrot 9727 [Van Morrison] [BMI] (4/23/66 B-71)*

***GLORIA** The Doors—Elektra 69770 [Van Morrison] [BMI] (12/3/83 B-71)*

GLORIA Enchantment—United Artists 912
[Emanuel Johnson/Michael Lee Stokes] [BMI] (1/22/77 BCR-25)

GLORIA Laura Branigan—Atlantic 4048
[Giancarlo Bigazzi/Umberto Tozzi/Trevor Veitch] [BMI] (7/3/82 BC-1) [FET]

GLORIA'S THEME Adam Wade—Coed 541
[Mack David/Bronislaw Kaper] [ASC] (11/21/60 BCR-74)

GLORY BOUND The Grass Roots—Dunhill 4302
[Steve Barri/Harvey Price/Dennis Provisor/Dan Walsh] [ASC] (2/12/72 BCR-22)

GLORY DAYS Bruce Springsteen—Columbia 04924
[Bruce Springsteen] [ASC] (6/1/85 BC-5)

GLORY GLORY The Rascals—Atlantic 2743 [Felix Cavaliere] [ASC] (7/18/70 BCR-38)

GLORY, GLORY The Byrds—Columbia 45440 [Art Reynolds] [ASC] (9/18/71 C-65)

GLORY OF LOVE *The Roommates—Valmor 008 [Billy Hill] [ASC] (4/10/61 BCR-44)*

GLORY OF LOVE *Don Gardner And Dee Dee Ford—KC 106 [Billy Hill] [ASC] (8/11/62 BCR-75)*

GLORY OF LOVE *Otis Redding—Volt 152 [Billy Hill] [ASC] (7/22/67 BCR-35)*

THE GLORY OF LOVE *The Dells—Cadet 5679 [Billy Hill] [ASC] (1/16/71 BCR-84)*

GLORY OF LOVE (THEME FROM THE KARATE KID PART II) Peter Cetera—Full Moon 28662 [Peter Cetera/David Foster] [ASC] (6/7/86 BC-1)

GLORY RIVER Lou Christie—Buddah 192 [Lou Christie/Twyla Herbert] (TSW) [BMI] (10/24/70 R-96)

GO Asia—Geffen 28872 [Geoffrey Downes/John Wetton] [BMI] (12/7/85 BC-45)

GO AHEAD AND CRY The Righteous Brothers—Verve 10430 [Bill Medley] [BMI] (8/6/66 BCR-23)

GO ALL THE WAY Raspberries—Capitol 3348 [Eric Carmen] [BMI] (7/1/72 BCR-3)

GO AWAY 1910 Fruitgum Co.—Super K 15 [Ritchie Cordell/Jerry Kasenetz/Jeff Katz/Sal Trimachi] [BMI] (6/13/70 R-88)

GO AWAY FROM MY WORLD Marianne Faithfull—London 9802 [Jon Mark] [BMI] (12/11/65 BCR-75)

GO AWAY LITTLE GIRL *Steve Lawrence—Columbia 42601 [Gerry Goffin/Carole King] [BMI] (11/10/62 BCR-1)*

GO AWAY LITTLE GIRL *The Happenings—B.T. Puppy 522 [Gerry Goffin/Carole King] [BMI] (10/1/66 BCR-9)*

GO AWAY LITTLE GIRL *Donny Osmond—MGM 14285 [Gerry Goffin/Carole King] [BMI] (8/7/71 BCR-1)*

GO AWAY LITTLE BOY *Marlena Shaw—Columbia 10542 [Gerry Goffin/Carole King] (Med) [BMI] (5/28/77 C-76)*

GO BACK Crabby Appleton—Elektra 45687 [Michael Fennelly] [BMI] (5/2/70 BCR-21)

GO CHASE A MOONBEAM Jerry Vale—Columbia 41238 [Lee Pockriss/Paul Vance] [ASC] (10/13/58 BCR-60)

GO DOWN EASY Dan Fogelberg—Full Moon 04835 [Jay Bolotin] [BMI] (3/23/85 B-85)

GO DOWN GAMBLIN' Blood, Sweat & Tears—Columbia 45427 [David Clayton-Thomas/Fred Lipsius] [BMI] (7/31/71 BCR-21)

GO FOR IT Kim Wilde—MCA 52513 [Marty Wilde/Ricky Wilde] [ASC] (1/19/85 BC-63)

GO FOR IT (HEART AND FIRE) Joey B. Ellis & Tynetta Hare—Bust It/Capitol 44667 [James Earley/Joey B. Ellis/Tynetta Hare/Michael Kelly] [BMI] (12/8/90 BC-63)

GO FOR SODA Kim Mitchell—Bronze/Island 7-99652 [Pye Dubois/Kim Mitchell] [ASC] (5/18/85 BC-80)

GO FOR YOURS Lisa Lisa & Cult Jam with Full Force—Columbia 07982 [Curtis Bedeau/Gerard Charles/Hugh Clarke/Brian George/Lucien George/Paul George] [BMI] (8/6/88 C-85)

GO-GO GIRL Lee Dorsey—Amy 998 [Allen Toussaint] [BMI] (10/14/67 BCR-57)

GO HOME Stevie Wonder—Tamla 1817 [Stevie Wonder] [ASC] (11/23/85 BC-10)

GO INSANE Lindsey Buckingham—Elektra 69714 [Lindsey Buckingham] [ASC] (7/28/84 BC-23)

GO JIMMY GO Jimmy Clanton—Ace 575 [Doc Pomus/Mort Shuman] [BMI] (11/30/59 BCR-5)

GO LIKE ELIJAH Chi Coltrane—Columbia 45749 [Chi Coltrane] [ASC] (1/27/73 R-94)

GO NOW! The Moody Blues—London 9726 [Larry Banks/Milton Bennett] [BMI] (2/13/65 BCR-6)

GO ON BY The Cowboy Church Sunday School—Decca 29530 [Stuart Hamblen] [ASC] (6/6/55 R-78)

GO ON FOOL Marion Black—Avco Embassy 4559 [Marion Black] [BMI] (2/20/71 C-93)

GO ON HOME Patti Page—Mercury 71906 [Hank Cochran] [BMI] (12/11/61 BCR-19)

GO ON WITH THE WEDDING *Kitty Kallen & Georgie Shaw—Decca 29776 [Milt Gabler*/Arthur Korb/Charlie Purvis/Milton Yakus] [ASC] (12/30/55 BCtRt-13)*

GO ON WITH THE WEDDING *Patti Page—Mercury 70766 [Milt Gabler*/Arthur Korb/Charlie Purvis/Milton Yakus] [ASC] (12/30/55 BCtRt-11)*

GO ON WITH THE WEDDING *The Modernaires—Coral 61555 [Milt Gabler*/Arthur Korb/Charlie Purvis/Milton Yakus] [ASC] (1/6/56 Rt-13)*

GO SEE THE DOCTOR Kool Moe Dee—Jive/Rooftop 1041 [Mohandas DeWese] [BMI] (4/18/87 B-89)

GO WEST Village People—Casablanca 984 [Henri Belolo/Jacques Morali/Victor Willis] [BMI] (5/26/79 BCR-45)

GO WHERE YOU WANNA GO The 5th Dimension—Soul City 753 [John Phillips] [ASC] (1/14/67 BCR-13)

GO WITH ME Gene & Debbe—TRX 5002 [Gene Thomas] [BMI] (9/30/67 BCR-63)

GO YOUR OWN WAY Fleetwood Mac—Warner Bros. 8304 [Lindsey Buckingham] [ASC] (1/1/77 BCR-10)

GOD BLESS Arthur Conley—Atco 6747 [Jerry Williams Jr.] [BMI] (4/25/70 CR-91)

GOD BLESS AMERICA Connie Francis—MGM 12841 [Irving Berlin] [ASC] (11/9/59 BCR-29)

GOD BLESS OUR LOVE Charles Brimmer—Chelsea 3017 [Al Green/Willie Mitchell/Earl Randle] [BMI] (7/12/75 CR-85)

—GOD BLESS OUR LOVE see: BLESS OUR LOVE

GOD BLESS WHOEVER SENT YOU The Originals—Soul 35079 [Clay McMurray/Pam Sawyer] [ASC] (12/12/70 BCR-52)

GOD COUNTRY AND MY BABY *Chico Holiday—Coral 62291 [John Dolan/Chico Holiday] [ASC] (10/9/61 CtRt-34)*

GOD, COUNTRY AND MY BABY *Johnny Burnette—Liberty 55379 [John Dolan/Chico Holiday] [ASC] (10/9/61 BCtRt-18)*

GOD KNOWS Debby Boone—Warner/Curb 8554 [Franne Golde/Peter Noone/Allee Willis] (TSW) [BMI] (5/27/78 B-74)

GOD KNOWS I LOVE YOU Nancy Sinatra—Reprise 0813 [Delaney Bramlett/Mac Davis] [BMI] (3/8/69 BCR-97)

GOD, LOVE AND ROCK & ROLL Teegarden & Van Winkle—Westbound 170 [Skip Knapé/David Teegarden] [BMI] (9/12/70 BCR-14)

GOD ONLY KNOWS *The Beach Boys—Capitol 5706 [Tony Asher/Brian Wilson] [BMI] (8/6/66 BCR-38)*

GOD ONLY KNOWS *The Vogues—Reprise 0887 [Tony Asher/Brian Wilson] [BMI] (1/24/70 R-85)*

GOD ONLY KNOWS *Marilyn Scott—Big Tree 16105 [Tony Asher/Brian Wilson] [BMI] (12/10/77 BC-61)*

GOIN' AWAY The Fireballs—Atco 6569 [Barbara Tomsco/George Tomsco] [BMI] (4/6/68 BCR-54)

GOIN' BACK The Byrds—Columbia 44362 [Gerry Goffin/Carole King] [BMI] (11/11/67 BCR-56)

GOIN' CRAZY! David Lee Roth—Warner Bros. 28584 [David Lee Roth/Steve Vai] [ASC] (9/27/86 BC-66)

GOIN' DOWN Greg Guidry—Columbia 02691 [Greg Guidry/David C. Martin] [ASC] (2/13/82 BCR-17)

GOIN' DOWN (ON THE ROAD TO L.A.) Terry Black And Laurel Ward—Kama Sutra 540 [Andy Arthurs*/Roger Cook/Roger Greenaway] [ASC] (2/5/72 BCR-57)

GOIN' DOWN SLOW Bobby Blue Bland—Dunhill 4379 [James B. Oden] [BMI] (3/2/74 BCR-69)

—GOIN DOWN THAT HIGHWAY see: SETTLE DOWN

GOIN' HOME The Osmonds—MGM 14562 [Alan Osmond/Merrill Osmond/Wayne Osmond] [BMI] (6/9/73 BCR-21)

GOIN' HOME (SING A SONG OF CHRISTMAS CHEER) Bobby Sherman—Metromedia 204 [Tom Bahler] [BMI] (12/26/70 C-70)

GOIN' ON The Beach Boys—Caribou 9032 [Mike Love/Brian Wilson] [BMI] (4/12/80 B-83)

GOIN' OUT OF MY HEAD *Little Anthony And The Imperials—DCP 1119 [Teddy Randazzo/Bobby Weinstein] [BMI] (11/7/64 BCR-4)*

GOIN' OUT OF MY HEAD *The Lettermen—Capitol 2054 [Teddy Randazzo/Bobby Weinstein] (Med) [BMI] (12/9/67 BCR-6)*

GOIN' OUT OF MY HEAD *Frank Sinatra—Reprise 0865 [Teddy Randazzo/Bobby Weinstein] (TSW) [BMI] (11/29/69 BCR-79)*

GOIN' PLACES The Jacksons—Epic 50454 [Kenneth Gamble/Leon Huff] [BMI] (10/8/77 BCR-52)

GOIN' STEADY Tommy Sands—Capitol 3723 [Faron Young] [BMI] (5/18/57 BCR-19)

GOIN' TO THE BANK Commodores—Polydor 885358 [Franne Golde/Andy Goldmark/Dennis Lambert] [BMI] (11/1/86 BC-65)

GOING BACK TO CALI LL Cool J—Def Jam 07679 [Rick Rubin/James Todd Smith] [ASC] (2/20/88 BC-31)

GOING BACK TO LOUISIANA Bruce Channel—Le Cam 122 [Robert Eugene Osborn] [BMI] (2/22/64 BC-89)

GOING DOWN SLOWLY Pointer Sisters—ABC/Blue Thumb 268 [Allen Toussaint] [BMI] (11/22/75 BC-51)

GOING GOING GONE Brook Benton—Mercury 72230 [Emil Anton/Alan Thomas] [BMI] (1/18/64 BCR-30)

GOING HOME Kenny G—Arista 1-9913 [Walter Afanasieff/Kenny G] [ASC] (12/23/89 BC-50) [I]

GOING IN CIRCLES The Friends Of Distinction—RCA Victor 74-0204 [Jerry Peters/Anita Poree] [BMI] (8/16/69 BCR-14)

GOING IN WITH MY EYES OPEN David Soul—Private Stock 45,150 [Tony Macaulay] [ASC] (4/30/77 BCR-54)

GOING NOWHERE Los Bravos—Press 60003 [Estelle Levitt/Ruth Sexter] [ASC] (12/3/66 BCR-69)

GOING OUT WITH THE TIDE Jivin' Gene—Mercury 71680 [Gene Bourgeois/Huey P. Meaux*] [BMI] (11/12/60 C-94)

GOING THROUGH THE MOTIONS Hot Chocolate—Infinity 50,016 [Errol Brown] [ASC] (7/14/79 BCR-53)

GOING THROUGH THE MOTIONS Aftershock—Virgin 98868 [Peter Lord/Jose Rivera/Guy Charles Routte] [ASC] (3/30/91 BC-52)

GOING TO A GO-GO *The Miracles—Tamla 54127 [Warren Moore/Smokey Robinson/Robert Rogers/Marvin Tarplin] [ASC] (12/25/65 BCR-9)*

GOING TO A GO-GO *Shalamar—Soul Train 10885 [Warren Moore/Smokey Robinson/Robert Rogers/Marvin Tarplin] (Med) [ASC] (3/12/77 BCR-25)*

GOING TO A GO-GO *The Rolling Stones—Rolling Stones 21301 [Warren Moore/Smokey Robinson/Robert Rogers/Marvin Tarplin] [ASC] (6/12/82 BC-20)*

GOING TO CHICAGO BLUES Count Basie—Roulette 4088 [Count Basie/Jimmy Rushing] [ASC] (8/18/58 B-100)

GOING TO THE COUNTRY The Steve Miller Band—Capitol 2878
[Steve Miller/Ben Sidran] [ASC] (8/15/70 BCR-69)

GOING UP THE COUNTRY Canned Heat—Liberty 56077
[Alan C. Wilson] [BMI] (11/30/68 BCR-9)

GOLD John Stewart—RSO 931 [John Stewart] [BMI] (5/19/79 BCR-5)

GOLD Spandau Ballet—Chrysalis 42743 [Gary Kemp] [BMI] (11/19/83 BC-29)

THE GOLDEN AGE OF ROCK 'N' ROLL Mott The Hoople—Columbia 46035
[Ian Hunter] [ASC] (4/27/74 BCR-72)

GOLDEN BATON Dick Jacobs And His Chorus And Orchestra—Coral 61653
[King Guion] [BMI] (6/15/56 R-49) [I]

GOLDEN EARRINGS The Five Satins—Cub 9090
[Ray Evans/Jay Livingston/Victor Young] [ASC] (5/1/61 R-96)

GOLDEN GATE PARK Rejoice!—Dunhill 4158
[Nancy Brown/Thomas Harold Brown] [ASC] (10/26/68 B-96)

GOLDEN RAINBOW Looking Glass—Epic 10900 [Elliot Lurie] [ASC] (11/18/72 CR-75)

THE GOLDEN RULE *'Cile Turner—Colonial 7004*
[Orville B. Campbell/Wilton Mason/Cile Turner] [BMI] (12/7/59 CRt-61)

THE GOLDEN RULE *Don Rondo—Roulette 4216*
[Orville B. Campbell/Wilton Mason/Cile Turner] [BMI] (12/14/59 Rt-61)

GOLDEN WILDWOOD FLOWER Tom & Jerry—Mercury 71753
[Jerry Kennedy/Mike Terry/Gerald Tomlinson] [BMI] (2/20/61 R-93)

GOLDEN YEARS David Bowie—RCA Victor 10441 [David Bowie] [BMI] (12/13/75 BCR-10)

GOLDFINGER *Billy Strange—GNP Crescendo 334*
[John Barry] [BMI] (1/23/65 BCtRt-6) [IM]

GOLDFINGER *Shirley Bassey—United Artists 790*
[John Barry/Leslie Bricusse/Anthony Newley] [BMI] (1/30/65 BCtRt-6)

GOLDFINGER *Jack La Forge, His Piano And Orchestra—Regina 1323*
[John Barry] [BMI] (1/30/65 BCtRt-6) [IM]

GOLDFINGER *John Barry And His Orchestra—United Artists 791*
[John Barry] [BMI] (2/6/65 BCtRt-6) [IM]

GOLDFINGER *Jimmy Smith—Verve 10346 [John Barry] [BMI] (2/20/65 CtRt-11) [IM]*

GOLDFINGER *Meco—Arista 0660 [John Barry] (Med) [BMI] (2/13/82 BCR-35) [IM]*

GOLDMINE Pointer Sisters—RCA 5062
[Andy Goldmark/Bruce Roberts] [ASC] (11/1/86 BC-31)

GOLLY The Four Lads—Columbia 40914
[Nicolas Arditi*/Fred Grant/Al Hoffman/Dick Manning] [ASC] (5/11/57 R-65)

GONE *Ferlin Husky—Capitol 3628 [Smokey Rogers] [BMI] (2/23/57 BCRt-4)*

GONE *Joan Weber—Columbia 40852 [Smokey Rogers] [BMI] (3/2/57 Rt-4)*

GONE *Bobby Wayne—Mercury 71070 [Smokey Rogers] [BMI] (3/23/57 Rt-4)*

GONE *Joey Heatherton—MGM 14387 [Smokey Rogers] [BMI] (5/20/72 BCR-23)*

GONE The Rip Chords—Columbia 42812
[Bruce Johnston/Terry Melcher] [BMI] (8/17/63 BC-83)

GONE AT LAST Paul Simon/Phoebe Snow—Columbia 10197
[Paul Simon] [BMI] (8/9/75 BCR-20)

GONE, GONE, GONE The Everly Brothers—Warner Bros. 5478
[Don Everly/Phil Everly] [BMI] (10/17/64 BCR-31)

GONE, GONE, GONE Bad Company—Swan Song 71000
[Raymond Burrell] [ASC] (7/28/79 BCR-56)

—GONE GONE GONE see: MY GIRL

GONE LONG GONE Chicago—Columbia 10935 [Peter Cetera] [ASC] (4/14/79 BCR-73)

GONE MOVIN' ON Raiders—Columbia 45150
[Mark Lindsay/Terry Melcher] [BMI] (5/2/70 C-92)

GONE TOO FAR England Dan & John Ford Coley—Big Tree 16102
[John Ford Coley] [BMI] (10/1/77 BCR-17)

GONE TOO FAR Eddie Rabbitt—Elektra 46613
[David Malloy/Eddie Rabbitt/Even Stevens] [BMI] (5/3/80 BC-82)

GONE WITH THE WIND The Duprees Featuring Joey Vann—Coed 576
[Herb Magidson/Allie Wrubel] [ASC] (3/23/63 BC-77)

—GONG GONG SONG see: I'M BLUE

GONNA BACK UP BABY Gene Vincent and His Blue Caps—Capitol 3530
[Danny Wolfe] [NA] (9/8/56 R-56)

GONNA BE ALRIGHT NOW Gayle McCormick—Dunhill 4281
[Dennis Lambert/Brian Potter] [BMI] (7/10/71 BCR-84)

—GONNA BOOGIE TONIGHT see: STEPPIN' OUT

GONNA CATCH YOU Lonnie Gordon—SBK 07365
[Daniele Davoli/Mirko Limoni/Valerio Semplici] [ASC] (8/31/91 B-79)

GONNA FIND ME A BLUEBIRD *Joyce Hahn—Cadence 1318*
[Marvin Rainwater] [BMI] (5/11/57 BRt-22)

GONNA FIND ME A BLUEBIRD *Eddy Arnold—RCA Victor 47-6905*
[Marvin Rainwater] [BMI] (5/11/57 BRt-22)

GONNA FIND ME A BLUEBIRD *Marvin Rainwater—MGM 12412*
[Marvin Rainwater] [BMI] (5/20/57 BCRt-22)

—GONNA FLY NOW see: THEME FROM ROCKY

GONNA GET ALONG WITHOUT YA NOW *Patience and Prudence—Liberty 55040*
[Milton Kellem] [ASC] (11/24/56 BCR-10)

GONNA GET ALONG WITHOUT YOU NOW *Skeeter Davis—RCA Victor 47-8347*
[Milton Kellem] [ASC] (4/18/64 BCtR-35)

GONNA' GET ALONG WITHOUT YOU NOW *Tracey Dey—Amy 901*
[Milton Kellem] [ASC] (4/18/64 BCtR-35)

GONNA GET ALONG WITHOUT YA' NOW *Trini Lopez—Reprise 0547*
[Milton Kellem] [ASC] (2/11/67 BCR-93)

GONNA GIVE HER ALL THE LOVE I'VE GOT *Jimmy Ruffin—Soul 35032*
[Barrett Strong/Norman Whitfield] [BMI] (3/18/67 BCR-29)

GONNA GIVE HER ALL THE LOVE I'VE GOT *Marvin Gaye—Tamla 54190*
[Barrett Strong/Norman Whitfield] (TSW) [BMI] (2/14/70 BR-41)

GONNA LOVE YOU MORE George Benson—Warner Bros. 8377
[Morris Albert] [ASC] (7/2/77 B-71)

GONNA MAKE IT Sa-Fire—Cutting 874 278-7 [David Harris] [ASC] (6/24/89 BC-71)

GONNA MAKE YOU SWEAT C & C Music Factory (Featuring Freedom Williams)—
Columbia 73604 [Robert Clivillés/Frederick B. Williams] [ASC] (11/17/90 BC-1)

GONNA RAISE A RUKUS TONIGHT Jimmy Dean—Columbia 42600
[Jimmy Dean] [BMI] (12/1/62 BR-73)

GONNA SEND YOU BACK TO GEORGIA (A CITY SLICK) *Timmy Shaw—Wand 146*
[Jake Hammonds/Johnnie Matthews] [BMI] (1/18/64 BCR-40)

GONNA SEND YOU BACK TO WALKER *The Animals—MGM 13242*
[Jake Hammonds/Johnnie Matthews] [BMI] (9/12/64 BCR-57)

GONNA TAKE A CHANCE Tommy Roe—ABC-Paramount 10389
[Tommy Roe] [BMI] (1/26/63 R-94)

GONZO James Booker—Peacock 1697 [Deadric Malone] [BMI] (10/22/60 BCR-27) [I]

GOO GOO BARABAJAGAL (LOVE IS HOT) Donovan (With The Jeff Beck Group)—Epic 10510
[Donovan Leitch] [BMI] (7/26/69 BCR-28)

GOOD AND LONESOME Kay Starr—RCA Victor 47-6146
[Larry Coleman/Fred Ebb/Paul Klein] [BMI] (6/13/55 CR-28)

THE GOOD BOOK Kay Starr—RCA Victor 47-6617
[Hal Stanley/Irving Taylor] [BMI] (9/8/56 B-89)

THE GOOD BOOK Melanie—Buddah 224 [Melanie Safka] [ASC] (4/10/71 CR-60)

GOOD-BYE Bob Manning—Capitol 2772 [Gordon Jenkins] [ASC] (6/4/55 C-50)

GOOD CLEAN FUN The Monkees—Colgems 5005
[Michael Nesmith] (TSW) [BMI] (9/20/69 BCR-73)

GOOD COMBINATION Sonny & Cher—Atco 6541 [Mark Barkan] [BMI] (12/16/67 BCR-56)

GOOD DAY SUNSHINE *Claudine Longet—A&M 864*
[John Lennon/Paul McCartney] [ASC] (8/5/67 B-100)

GOOD DAY SUNSHINE *Stars On 45—Radio 3830*
[John Lennon/Paul McCartney] (Med) [ASC] (7/11/81 BC-63)

GOOD ENOUGH TO BE YOUR WIFE Jeannie C. Riley—Plantation 75
[Ralph Murphy] [ASC] (7/24/71 BCR-46)

GOOD FEELIN' TIME The Yellow Balloon—Canterbury 513
[Don Grady/Gary Zekley] [BMI] (7/8/67 CR-87)

GOOD FRIEND Mary MacGregor—RSO 938
[Elmer Bernstein/Norman Gimbel] [ASC] (8/11/79 BCR-39)

GOOD FRIENDS? The Poppy Family Vocal: Susan Jacks—London 172
[Terry Jacks] [BMI] (2/12/72 C-74)

GOOD FRIENDS Joni Mitchell—Geffen 28840 [Joni Mitchell] [ASC] (12/28/85 B-85)

GOOD GIRLS DON'T The Knack—Capitol 4771 [Doug Fieger] [ASC] (9/1/79 BCR-10)

GOOD GOLLY MISS MOLLY *Little Richard—Specialty 624*
[Robert Blackwell/John Marascalco] [BMI] (2/15/58 BCRt-10)

GOOD GOLLY MISS MOLLY *The Valiants—Keen 34004*
[Robert Blackwell/John Marascalco] [NA] (2/24/58 Rt-23)

GOOD GOLLY MISS MOLLY *The Swinging Blue Jeans—Imperial 66030*
[Robert Blackwell/John Marascalco] [BMI] (5/2/64 BCR-43)

GOOD GOLLY MISS MOLLY *Mitch Ryder And The Detroit Wheels—New Voice 817*
[Robert Blackwell/John Marascalco] (Med) [BMI] (10/8/66 BCR-3)

GOOD GOLLY MISS MOLLY *Jive Bunny & The Mastermixers—Music Factory/Atco 99122*
[Robert Blackwell/John Marascalco] (Med) [BMI] (2/3/90 BC-67)

GOOD, GOOD FEELIN' War—MCA 40995
[Thomas Allen/Harold Brown/Jerry Goldstein/Lonnie Jordan/Charles Miller/
Lee Oskar/Luther Rabb/Howard Scott/Tweed Smith*] [ASC] (4/28/79 CR-94)

GOOD, GOOD LOVIN' Chubby Checker—Parkway 822
[James Brown/Andy Gibson] [BMI] (4/17/61 BR-43)

GOOD GOODBY Bob Knight Four—Laurel 1020
[Tony Sepe/Vincent Zeccola] [ASC] (4/29/61 C-90)

GOOD GUYS ONLY WIN IN THE MOVIES Mel And Tim—Bamboo 109
[Gene Chandler/James A. Thompson Jr.*] [BMI] (1/31/70 BCR-42)

A GOOD HEART Feargal Sharkey—A&M 2804 [Maria McKee] [BMI] (3/15/86 BC-74)

GOOD HEART Starship—RCA 2796 [Martin Page] [ASC] (4/20/91 BC-73)

GOOD HEARTED WOMAN Waylon & Willie—RCA Victor 10529
[Waylon Jennings/Willie Nelson] [BMI] (1/24/76 BCR-25)

THE GOOD LIFE *Kathy Keegan—Malibu 1219*
[Sacha Distel/Jack Reardon] [ASC] (2/16/63 R-96)

THE GOOD LIFE *Tony Bennett—Columbia 42779*
[Sacha Distel/Jack Reardon] [ASC] (5/11/63 BCR-18)

GOOD LIFE Inner City—Virgin 99236
[Paris Grey/Roy Holman/Kevin Saunderson] [BMI] (3/4/89 BC-64)

THE GOOD LORD LOVES YOU Neil Diamond—Columbia 11232
[Richard Fagan] [NA] (4/5/80 BCR-67)

GOOD LOVER Jimmy Reed—Vee-Jay 449 [Mary Lee Reed] [BMI] (6/9/62 BCR-77)

GOOD LOVIN' *The Olympics—Loma 2013*
[Rudy Clark/Artie Resnick] [BMI] (5/1/65 BCR-81)

GOOD LOVIN' *The Young Rascals—Atlantic 2321*
[Rudy Clark/Artie Resnick] [BMI] (3/12/66 BCR-1)

GOOD LOVIN' *Grateful Dead—Arista 0383*
[Rudy Clark/Artie Resnick] [BMI] (12/16/78 CR-87)

GOOD LOVIN' AIN'T EASY TO COME BY Marvin Gaye & Tammi Terrell—Tamla 54179
[Nick Ashford/Valerie Simpson] [ASC] (2/1/69 BCR-30)

GOOD LOVIN' GONE BAD Bad Company—Swan Song 70103
[Mick Ralphs] [ASC] (4/19/75 BCR-32)

GOOD LUCK CHARM Elvis Presley With The Jordanaires—RCA Victor 47-7992
[Wally Gold/Aaron Schroeder] [ASC] (3/12/62 BCR-1)

GOOD MAN IS HARD TO FIND Teresa Brewer—Coral 61548
[Edward Green] [ASC] (12/31/55 CR-39)

GOOD MORNING Michael Redway—Philips 40720
[Michael Redway] [ASC] (1/27/73 BCR-49)

GOOD MORNING FREEDOM Daybreak—Uni 55234
[Roger Cook/Roger Greenaway/Albert Hammond/Mike Hazlewood] [BMI] (6/13/70 BCR-83)

GOOD MORNING GIRL Journey—Columbia 11339
[Steve Perry/Neal Schon] (Med) [BMI] (8/16/80 BCR-55)

GOOD MORNING HEARTACHE Diana Ross—Motown 1211
[Ervin Drake/Dan Fisher/Irene Higginbotham] [ASC] (1/6/73 BCR-28)

GOOD MORNING JUDGE 10CC—Mercury 73943
[Graham Gouldman/Eric Stewart] [BMI] (8/6/77 BCR-69)

GOOD MORNING STARSHINE *Oliver—Jubilee 5659*
[Galt MacDermot/James Rado/Gerome Ragni] [ASC] (5/17/69 BCR-3)

GOOD MORNING STARSHINE *Strawberry Alarm Clock—Uni 55125*
[Galt MacDermot/James Rado/Gerome Ragni] [ASC] (5/17/69 BCR-83)

GOOD MUSIC Joan Jett And The Blackhearts—Blackheart 4-06336
[Joan Jett/Kenny Laguna] [BMI] (10/11/86 BC-69)

GOOD NEWS Eugene Church—Rendezvous 132 [Eugene Church] [BMI] (11/12/60 C-96)

GOOD NEWS Sam Cooke—RCA Victor 47-8299 [Sam Cooke] [BMI] (1/25/64 BCR-9)

GOODNIGHT AND GOODMORNING *Cecilio & Kapono—Columbia 10223*
[Daryl Hall/John Oates] [ASC] (1/10/76 C-95)

GOOD NIGHT & GOOD MORNING *Jim Capaldi—Island 067*
[Daryl Hall/John Oates] [ASC] (10/2/76 C-81)

GOOD NIGHT BABY The Butterflys—Red Bird 10-009
[Jeff Barry/Ellie Greenwich/Steve Venet] [BMI] (9/12/64 BCR-44)

—GOOD OL' BOYS see: THEME FROM THE DUKES OF HAZZARD

GOOD OLD ROCK 'N ROLL Cat Mother And The All Night News Boys—Polydor 14002
[Charlie Chin/Michael Equine/Roy Michaels/Larry Packer/Robert William Smith] (Med) [BMI] (6/21/69 BCR-12)

—GOOD ROCKIN' TONIGHT see: ROCKIN' AT MIDNIGHT

THE GOOD, THE BAD AND THE UGLY *Hugo Montenegro, His Orchestra And Chorus—RCA Victor 47-9423 [Ennio Morricone] [BMI] (2/17/68 BCR-2) [I]*

THE GOOD, THE BAD AND THE UGLY *Meco—Arista 0660*
[Ennio Morricone] (Med) [BMI] (2/13/82 BCR-35) [I]

GOOD THING Paul Revere And The Raiders Featuring Mark Lindsay—Columbia 43907
[Mark Lindsay/Terry Melcher] [BMI] (12/3/66 BCR-4)

GOOD THING Fine Young Cannibals—I.R.S./MCA 53639
[Roland Gift/David Steele] [ASC] (5/6/89 BC-1)

GOOD THING MAN Frank Lucas—ICA 001
[Virginia Bland*/Frank Lucas] [BMI] (5/14/77 BCR-60)

GOOD THINGS DON'T LAST FOREVER Ecstasy, Passion & Pain—Roulette 7156
[Allan Felder/Norman Harris/Bunny Sigler] [BMI] (7/6/74 BCR-68)

GOOD TIME Ziggy Marley—Virgin 98735
[Cedella Marley/Sharon Marley/Stephen Marley/Ziggy Marley] [ASC] (9/21/91 BC-85)

GOOD TIME BABY Bobby Rydell—Cameo 186
[Dave Appell/Bernie Lowe/Kal Mann] [ASC] (1/23/61 BCR-10)

GOOD TIME CHARLIE Bobby Bland—Duke 402
[Gilbert Caple/Deadric Malone/Joe Scott] [BMI] (5/21/66 BCR-51)

GOOD TIME CHARLIE'S GOT THE BLUES Danny O'Keefe—Signpost 70006
[Danny O'Keefe] [BMI] (8/26/72 BCR-8)

GOOD TIME GIRL Nancy Sinatra—Reprise 0789 [Mac Davis] [BMI] (11/30/68 BCR-65)

GOOD TIME MUSIC The Beau Brummels—Autumn 24
[John Sebastian] [BMI] (12/18/65 BCR-85)

GOOD TIME SALLY Rare Earth—Rare Earth 5048 [Tom Baird] [ASC] (11/4/72 BCR-67)

GOOD TIME TONIGHT Soul Sisters—Sue 10-005
[Smokey McAllister] [BMI] (6/13/64 B-98)

GOOD TIMES Sam Cooke—RCA Victor 47-8368 [Sam Cooke] [BMI] (6/6/64 BCR-11)

GOOD TIMES Jerry Butler—Vee-Jay 651 [Ted Daryll] [BMI] (2/20/65 BCR-63)

GOOD TIMES Gene Chandler—Constellation 160 [Curtis Mayfield] [BMI] (8/21/65 BR-88)

GOOD TIMES Chic—Atlantic 3584
[Bernard Edwards/Nile Rodgers] [BMI] (6/16/79 BCR-1)

GOOD TIMES INXS And Jimmy Barnes—Atlantic 89237
[Harry Vanda/George Young] [ASC] (6/20/87 BC-47)

GOOD TIMES BAD TIMES Led Zeppelin—Atlantic 2613
[John Bonham/John Paul Jones/Jimmy Page/Robert Plant*] [ASC] (3/29/69 BCR-65)

GOOD TIMES, ROCK & ROLL Flash Cadillac & The Continental Kids—Private Stock 45,006 [Richard Burns] [BMI] (1/18/75 BCR-41)

GOOD TIMES ROLL The Cars—Elektra 46014
[Ric Ocasek] [ASC] (3/17/79 BCR-41)

GOOD TIMIN' Jimmy Jones—Cub 9067
[Clint Ballard Jr./Fred Tobias] [ASC] (4/11/60 BCR-3)

GOOD TIMIN' The Beach Boys—Caribou 9029
[Brian Wilson/Carl Wilson] [BMI] (4/28/79 BCR-33)

GOOD TO HAVE LOVE BACK Felix Cavaliere—Epic 50880
[Felix Cavaliere] [ASC] (6/28/80 R-98)

GOOD VIBRATIONS *The Beach Boys—Capitol 5676*
[Mike Love/Brian Wilson] [BMI] (10/22/66 BCR-1)

GOOD VIBRATIONS *Hugo Montenegro, His Orchestra And Chorus—RCA Victor 47-9712*
[Mike Love/Brian Wilson] [BMI] (2/1/69 R-87) [IWM]

GOOD VIBRATIONS *Todd Rundgren—Bearsville 0309*
[Mike Love/Brian Wilson] [BMI] (6/5/76 BCR-34)

GOOD VIBRATIONS *The Cantina Band—Millennium 11818*
[Mike Love/Brian Wilson] (Med) [BMI] (7/25/81 B-81)

GOOD VIBRATIONS *The Beach Boys—Capitol 5030*
[Mike Love/Brian Wilson] (Med) [BMI] (7/25/81 BCR-5)

GOOD VIBRATIONS Marky Mark & The Funky Bunch—Interscope 98764
[Dan Hartman/Amir Shakir/Donnie Wahlberg/Mark Wahlberg] [ASC] (7/20/91 BC-1)

GOODBY LITTLE DARLIN' Johnny Cash—Sun 331
[Gene Autry/Johnny Marvin] [ASC] (10/26/59 R-81)

GOODBYE Mary Hopkin—Apple 1806
[John Lennon/Paul McCartney] [ASC] (4/12/69 BCR-11)

GOODBYE Night Ranger—Camel/MCA 52729
[Jack Blades/Jeff Watson] [BMI] (11/9/85 BC-17)

GOODBYE AGAIN Ferrante & Teicher—United Artists 319
[Georges Auric] [ASC] (6/12/61 BCR-84) [IM]

GOODBYE AGAIN John Denver—RCA Victor 74-0737
[John Denver] [ASC] (7/22/72 BCR-87)

GOODBYE BABE The Castaways—Soma 1442 [Roy Hensley] [BMI] (11/20/65 CR-54)

GOODBYE BABY Jack Scott—Carlton 493 [Jack Scott] [BMI] (12/1/58 BCR-8)

GOODBYE BABY (BABY GOODBYE) Solomon Burke—Atlantic 2226
[Bert Berns/Wes Farrell] [BMI] (4/18/64 BCR-32)

GOODBYE BABY (I DON'T WANT TO SEE YOU CRY) Tommy Boyce & Bobby Hart—A&M 919
[Tommy Boyce/Bobby Hart] [BMI] (3/30/68 BCR-46)

GOODBYE CHARLIE Patti Page—Mercury 71510
[Ralph Care/Sol Marcus] [BMI] (9/21/59 BCR-70)

GOODBYE COLUMBUS The Association—Warner Bros.-Seven Arts 7267
[Jim Yester] [BMI] (3/1/69 BCR-78)

GOODBYE CRUEL WORLD James Darren—Colpix 609
[Gloria Shayne] [BMI] (10/16/61 BCR-2)

GOODBYE DAD The Castle Sisters—Terrace 7506
[Winston Bogart/Ray Petty] [BMI] (6/16/62 BCR-66)

GOODBYE GIRL David Gates—Elektra 45450 [David Gates] [ASC] (12/10/77 BCR-9)

GOODBYE, I LOVE YOU Firefall—Atlantic 3544 [Rick Roberts] [BMI] (1/20/79 BCR-40)

GOODBYE IS FOREVER Arcadia—Capitol 5542
[Simon Le Bon/Nick Rhodes/Roger Taylor] [ASC] (2/1/86 BC-29)

GOODBYE JIMMY GOODBYE Kathy Linden—Felsted 8571
[Jack Vaughn] [ASC] (4/11/59 BCR-10)

GOODBYE MEDIA MAN (PART 1) Tom Fogerty—Fantasy 661
[Tom Fogerty] [BMI] (8/7/71 C-93)

GOODBYE MY FRIEND Engelbert Humperdinck—Epic/MAM 50365
[Ritchie Adams/Alan Bernstein] [ASC] (7/9/77 B-97)

GOODBYE MY LOVE James Brown—King 6198 [James Brown] [BMI] (11/9/68 BCR-31)

GOODBYE MY LOVER GOODBYE The Searchers—Kapp 658
[Frances Aycock*/Robert Mosely/Lamar Simington/Leroy Swearingen] [BMI] (4/3/65 BCR-42)

GOODBYE STRANGER Supertramp—A&M 2162
[Rick Davies/Roger Hodgson] [ASC] (7/7/79 BCR-13)

GOODBYE TO ALL YOU WOMEN Bobby Goldsboro—United Artists 50183
[Bobby Goldsboro] [BMI] (4/15/67 R-91)

GOODBYE TO LOVE Carpenters—A&M 1367
[John Bettis/Richard Carpenter] [ASC] (7/8/72 BCR-6)

—GOODBYE TO ROME see: ARRIVEDERCI ROMA

GOODBYE TO TOYLAND The Vonnair Sisters—Vista 390
[Salvador Camarata/Gene Garf/Victor Herbert] [ASC] (3/3/62 C-87)

GOODBYE TO YOU Scandal—Columbia 03234 [Zack Smith] [BMI] (11/13/82 BC-60)

GOODBYE YELLOW BRICK ROAD Elton John—MCA 40148
[Elton John/Bernie Taupin] [BMI] (10/20/73 BCR-1)

GOODNIGHT The Elegants—Apt 25017 [Arthur Venosa] [BMI] (11/8/58 C-77)

GOODNIGHT Roy Orbison—Monument 873
[William Dees/Roy Orbison] [BMI] (2/13/65 BCR-17)

GOODNIGHT IRENE *Billy Williams—Coral 62101*
[Huddie Ledbetter/John Lomax‡] [BMI] (4/20/59 BCR-75)

GOODNIGHT, IRENE *Jerry Reed And The Hully Girlies—Columbia 42417*
[Huddie Ledbetter/John Lomax‡] [BMI] (6/30/62 BCR-72)

GOODNIGHT MY LOVE *The Happenings—B.T. Puppy 523*
[Sandy Linzer/Denny Randell] [BMI] (12/3/66 BCR-39)

GOODNIGHT MY LOVE *The Duprees—Heritage 805*
[Sandy Linzer/Denny Randell] [BMI] (11/23/68 CR-74)

GOODNIGHT MY LOVE Mike Pinera—Spector 00003
[Mike Pinera] [BMI] (12/22/79 BCR-70)

GOODNIGHT MY LOVE (PLEASANT DREAMS) *Mindy Carson—Columbia 40789*
[John Marascalco/George Motola] [BMI] (11/24/56 Rt-28)

GOODNIGHT MY LOVE PLEASANT DREAMS *The McGuire Sisters—Coral 61748*
[John Marascalco/George Motola] [BMI] (12/8/56 BCtRt-23)

GOODNIGHT MY LOVE PLEASANT DREAMS *Jesse Belvin—Modern 1005*
[John Marascalco/George Motola] [BMI] (12/8/56 CtRt-23)

GOODNIGHT MY LOVE, PLEASANT DREAMS *Earl Grant—Decca 30150*
[John Marascalco/George Motola] [BMI] (12/22/56 Rt-28)

GOODNIGHT MY LOVE (PLEASANT DREAMS) *Ray Peterson—RCA Victor 47-7635*
[John Marascalco/George Motola] [BMI] (10/26/59 BCR-50)

GOODNIGHT MY LOVE *The Fleetwoods—Dolton 75*
[John Marascalco/George Motola] [BMI] (6/1/63 BCR-32)

GOODNIGHT MY LOVE *Ben E. King—Atco 6390*
[John Marascalco/George Motola] [BMI] (1/8/66 BCR-65)

GOODNIGHT MY LOVE *Paul Anka—RCA Victor 47-9648*
[John Marascalco/George Motola] [BMI] (12/28/68 BCR-18)

GOODNIGHT SAIGON Billy Joel—Columbia 03780 [Billy Joel] [ASC] (3/19/83 BC-56)

GOODNIGHT SWEET DREAMS Gordon Jenkins And His Orchestra—"X" 0159
[Carl Barefoot/Edith Lindeman/Carl Stutz] [ASC] (9/5/55 CR-36)

GOODNIGHT, SWEETHEART, GOODNIGHT *The McGuire Sisters—Coral 61187*
[Calvin Carter/James Hudson] [BMI] (6/26/54 BCR-8)

GOODNIGHT, SWEETHEART, GOODNIGHT *Sunny Gale—RCA Victor 47-5746*
[Calvin Carter/James Hudson] [BMI] (7/3/54 BC-PRE)

GOODNIGHT TONIGHT Wings—Columbia 10939 [Paul McCartney] [ASC] (3/31/79 BCR-4)

GOODY GOODY *Frankie Lymon—Gee 1039*
[Matt Malneck/Johnny Mercer] [ASC] (7/20/57 BCRt-19)

GOODY GOODY *Ella Fitzgerald—Decca 30405*
[Matt Malneck/Johnny Mercer] [ASC] (8/12/57 Rt-19)

GOODY, GOODY *Jane Grant—Dot 15610*
[Matt Malneck/Johnny Mercer] [ASC] (8/12/57 Rt-19)

GOODY GOODY GUMDROPS 1910 Fruitgum Co.—Buddah 71
[Billy Carl/Jerry Kasenetz/Jeff Katz/Reid Whitelaw] [BMI] (10/26/68 BCR-28)

GOODY TWO SHOES Adam Ant—Epic 03367
[Adam Ant/Marco Pirroni] [ASC] (11/13/82 BC-12)

GOOFUS Carpenters—A&M 1859
[William Harold/Gus Kahn/Wayne King] [ASC] (9/4/76 BC-56)

THE GOONIES 'R' GOOD ENOUGH Cyndi Lauper—Portrait 34-04918
[Cyndi Lauper/Stephen Lunt/Arthur Stead] [BMI] (5/18/85 BC-10)

GOT A DATE WITH AN ANGEL Billy Williams—Coral 61886
[Clifford Grey/Sonny Miller/Joseph Tunbridge/Jack Waller] [ASC] (10/12/57 BCR-51)

GOT A GIRL The Four Preps—Capitol 4362
[Bruce Belland/Glen Larson] [BMI] (4/18/60 BCR-24)

GOT A HOLD ON ME Christine McVie—Warner Bros. 29372
[Christine McVie/Todd Sharp] [BMI] (1/28/84 BC-10)

GOT A LOVE FOR YOU Jomanda—Big Beat 5031
[Derek Jenkins/Dwayne Richardson/Paul Scott/Cassio Ware/Joel Washington/
Cheri Williams] [ASC] (7/6/91 BC-40)

GOT A MATCH *The Daddy-O's—Cabot 122*
[Billy Mure/Dick Wolf] [BMI] (6/2/58 BCtRt-31) [IM]

GOT A MATCH *Frank Gallop—ABC-Paramount 9931*
[Billy Mure/Dick Wolf] [BMI] (6/9/58 BCtRt-31) [IM]

GOT A MATCH *Lou Stein—Mercury 71328*
[Billy Mure/Dick Wolf] [BMI] (6/9/58 CtRt-31) [IM]

GOT A NEW LOVE Good Question—Paisley Park 7-27861
[Marc Douglas/Sean Douglas/Rick Neigher] [BMI] (10/22/88 BC-83)

GOT A RIGHT TO LOVE MY BABY B.B. King—Kent 333
[Joe Josea‡/B.B. King*] [BMI] (6/11/60 C-100)

GOT IT MADE Crosby, Stills, Nash & Young—Atlantic 88966
[Stephen Stills/Neil Young] [BMI] (1/28/89 BC-58)

GOT MY MIND SET ON YOU George Harrison—Dark Horse 28178
[Rudy Clark] [BMI] (10/24/87 BC-1)

GOT MY MOJO WORKING (PART 1) Jimmy Smith—Verve 10393
[Preston Foster] [BMI] (3/19/66 BCR-45)

GOT PLEASURE Ohio Players—Westbound 204
[Leroy Bonner/Marshall Jones/Ralph Middlebrooks/Walter Morrison/
Bruce Napier*/Andrew Noland/Marvin Pierce*/Greg Webster] [BMI] (6/24/72 C-90)

GOT THE FEELING Fabian—Chancellor 1041
[Richard Sherman/Robert Sherman] [BMI] (9/19/59 BCR-46)

GOT TO BE ENOUGH Con Funk Shun—Mercury 76051
[Michael V. Cooper/Felton Pilate] [BMI] (4/19/80 R-91)

GOT TO BE REAL Cheryl Lynn—Columbia 10808
[David Foster/Cheryl Lynn/David Paich] [BMI] (11/11/78 BCR-9)

GOT TO BE THERE *Michael Jackson—Motown 1191*
[Elliot Willensky] [ASC] (10/30/71 BCR-1)

GOT TO BE THERE *Chaka Khan—Warner Bros. 29881*
[Elliot Willensky] [ASC] (1/8/83 BC-67)

GOT TO BELIEVE IN LOVE Robin McNamara—Steed 728
[Neil Brian Goldberg] [ASC] (9/26/70 BCR-60)

GOT TO GET Leila K with Rob 'N' Raz—Arista 1-9931
[Martin Carboo/Leila El Khalifi/Rasmus Lindwall/Robert Watz] [BMI] (2/17/90 BC-46)

GOT TO GET YOU INTO MY LIFE *Blood, Sweat & Tears—Columbia 10151*
[John Lennon/Paul McCartney] [ASC] (6/7/75 BCR-62)

GOT TO GET YOU INTO MY LIFE *The Beatles—Capitol 4274*
[John Lennon/Paul McCartney] [ASC] (6/5/76 BCR-3)

GOT TO GET YOU INTO MY LIFE *Earth, Wind & Fire—Columbia 10796*
[John Lennon/Paul McCartney] [ASC] (7/22/78 BCR-9)

GOT TO GET YOU OFF MY MIND Solomon Burke—Atlantic 2276
[Delores Burke/Solomon Burke/Josephine Burke Moore] [BMI] (3/6/65 BCR-21)

GOT TO GIVE IN TO LOVE Bonnie Boyer—Columbia 11028
[Bruce Dees/Kye Fleming/Rob Galbraith/Dennis W. Morgan] [BMI] (7/28/79 BCR-43)

GOT TO GIVE IT UP PT. I Marvin Gaye—Tamla 54280 [Marvin Gaye] [ASC] (4/9/77 BCR-1)

GOT TO HAVE LOVING Don Ray—Polydor 14489
[Marc Cerrone/Don Ray] [BMI] (9/2/78 BCR-44)

GOT TO HAVE YOU BACK The Isley Brothers—Tamla 54146
[Steve Bowden/Ivy Jo Hunter/Leon Ware] [BMI] (4/29/67 BC-93)

GOT TO HAVE YOUR LOVE Mantronix (featuring Wondress)—Capitol 44466
[Kurtis el Khaleel/Johnny D. Rodriguez/Bryce Wilson] [ASC] (2/24/90 BC-75)

GOT TO HAVE YOUR LOVIN' King Floyd—Chimneyville 439
[Michael Adams/Joe Broussard] [BMI] (7/24/71 CR-56)

GOT TO LOVE SOMEBODY Sister Sledge—Cotillion 45007
[Bernard Edwards/Nile Rodgers] [BMI] (1/19/80 BCR-64)

GOT TO ROCK ON Kansas—Kirshner 4292
[Steve Walsh] [BMI] (12/20/80 BC-75)

GOT TO SEE IF I CAN'T GET MOMMY (TO COME BACK HOME) Jerry Butler—Mercury 73015
[Rose Marie McCoy/Helen Miller] [BMI] (1/17/70 BCR-54)

GOT TO TELL ME SOMETHING Ana—Parc 73317 [Maurice Starr] [ASC] (5/19/90 BC-64)

GOT WHAT YOU NEED The Fantastic Johnny C—Phil-L.A. Of Soul 309
[Jesse James] [BMI] (2/10/68 BCR-45)

GOT YOU ON MY MIND Cookie & His Cupcakes—Chess 1848
[Howard Biggs/Joe Thomas] [BMI] (5/4/63 BCR-94)

GOTTA BE FUNKY Monk Higgins & The Specialties—United Artists 50897
[Alex Brown/Monk Higgins] [BMI] (6/3/72 CR-86)

GOTTA BE THE ONE Maxine Nightingale—United Artists 820
[Pierre Tubbs] [ASC] (7/10/76 BC-53)

GOTTA FIND A WAY The Moments—Stang 5050
[Ray Dahrouge/Billy Terrell] [BMI] (9/22/73 BCR-68)

GOTTA GET AWAY Randy Meisner—Epic 02059
[Eric Kaz/Randy Meisner/Wendy Waldman] [ASC] (5/30/81 C-83)

GOTTA GET BACK TO YOU Tommy James And The Shondells—Roulette 7071
[Tommy James/Robert L. King] [BMI] (2/14/70 BCR-25)

GOTTA GET MY HANDS ON SOME (MONEY) Fatback—Spring 3008
[Bill Curtis/Gerald Thomas] [BMI] (5/24/80 R-94)

GOTTA GET TO KNOW YOU Bobby Bland—Duke 447
[Deadric Malone/Andre Williams] [BMI] (6/14/69 BCR-91)

GOTTA GET TO YOUR HOUSE David Seville—Liberty 55079
[David Seville] [ASC] (9/9/57 B-77)

GOTTA GET YOU HOME TONIGHT Eugene Wilde—Philly World 7-99710
[Ronnie E. Broomfield/McKinley Horton] [BMI] (1/12/85 B-83)

GOTTA GIVE A LITTLE LOVE (TEN YEARS AFTER) Timmy Thomas—Gold Mountain 82004
[Timmy Thomas] [BMI] (6/2/84 B-80)

GOTTA GIVE HER LOVE The Volume's—American Arts AA6
[Barney Duke Browner] [BMI] (10/24/64 R-90)

GOTTA HAVE MORE LOVE Climax Blues Band—Warner Bros. 49605
[Greg Guidry/Randy Guidry/Jeff Silbar] [ASC] (11/8/80 BCR-47)

GOTTA HAVE RAIN *Eydie Gorme—ABC-Paramount 9944*
[Max Bygraves] [ASC] (8/4/58 BCtRt-43)

GOTTA HAVE RAIN *Max Bygraves—London 1813 [Max Bygraves] [ASC] (8/4/58 CtRt-43)*

GOTTA HAVE YOU Stevie Wonder—Motown 2081 [Stevie Wonder] [ASC] (7/13/91 BC-83)

GOTTA HAVE YOUR LOVE The Sapphires—ABC-Paramount 10639
[Jack Keller/Tony Powers] [BMI] (4/24/65 BCR-77)

GOTTA HOLD ON TO THIS FEELING Jr. Walker & The All Stars—Soul 35070
[Johnny Bristol/Joe Hinton/Pam Sawyer] [ASC] (2/21/70 BCR-14)

GOTTA LOTTA LOVE Steve Alaimo—Imperial 66003
[Al Hoffman/Dick Manning] [ASC] (11/16/63 BCR-74)

GOTTA NEW GIRL Bobby Day—Class 252 [Bobby Day] [BMI] (6/6/59 BC-79)

GOTTA SEE JANE R. Dean Taylor—Rare Earth 5026
[Eddie Holland*/Ronald Alonzo Miller/R. Dean Taylor] [BMI] (4/10/71 BCR-48)

GOTTA SERVE SOMEBODY Bob Dylan—Columbia 11072
[Bob Dylan] [SE] (9/8/79 BCR-24)

GOTTA TRAVEL ON *Billy Grammer—Monument 400*
*[Paul Clayton/Larry Ehrlich/Ronnie Gilbert/Lee Hays/Fred Hellerman/Dave Lazar/
Pete Seeger] [BMI] (11/8/58 BCRt-4)*

GOTTA TRAVEL ON *Harry Belafonte—RCA Victor 47-7445*
[Paul Clayton/Larry Ehrlich/Ronnie Gilbert/Lee Hays/Fred Hellerman/Dave Lazar/ Pete Seeger] [BMI] (1/19/59 Rt-4)

GOTTA TRAVEL ON *Timi Yuro—Liberty 55634*
[Paul Clayton/Larry Ehrlich/Ronnie Gilbert/Lee Hays/Fred Hellerman/Dave Lazar/ Pete Seeger] [BMI] (10/12/63 BCR-64)

—GOUALANTE DU PAUVRE JEAN see: POOR PEOPLE OF PARIS

GRACELAND Paul Simon—Warner Bros. 28522 [Paul Simon] [BMI] (11/29/86 BC-69)

GRADUATION DAY *The Rover Boys—ABC-Paramount 9700*
[Joe Sherman/Noel Sherman] [ASC] (5/4/56 BCtRt-9)

GRADUATION DAY *The Four Freshmen—Capitol 3410*
[Joe Sherman/Noel Sherman] [ASC] (5/11/56 BCtRt-11)

GRADUATION DAY *The Lennon Sisters & The Sparklers—Coral 61648*
[Joe Sherman/Noel Sherman] [ASC] (8/10/56 Rt-68)

GRADUATION DAY *Bobby Pickett—Garpax 44175*
[Joe Sherman/Noel Sherman] [ASC] (6/22/63 BR-88)

GRADUATION DAY *The Arbors—Date 1561*
[Joe Sherman/Noel Sherman] [ASC] (6/3/67 BCR-59)

THE GRADUATION SONG...POMP AND CIRCUMSTANCE Adrian Kimberly—Calliope 6501
[Edward Elgar] [BMI] (6/19/61 BCR-34) [I]

GRADUATION'S HERE The Fleetwoods—Dolton 3
[Gretchen Christopher/Barbara Ellis/Gary Troxel] [BMI] (5/18/59 BCR-34)

GRANADA Frank Sinatra—Reprise 20,010
[Dorothy Dodd/Agustin Lara] [ASC] (6/26/61 BCR-35) [FDE]

GRANDDADDY (PART 1) The New Birth—Buddah 464
[James Baker/Tony Churchill/Melvin Wilson] [BMI] (5/10/75 BCR-87)

GRANDMA'S HANDS Bill Withers—Sussex 227 [Bill Withers] [BMI] (10/30/71 BCR-31)

GRANDMOTHER'S SONG Steve Martin—Warner Bros. 8503
[Steve Martin] [ASC] (11/26/77 BCR-68)

GRANNY'S PAD The Viceroys—Dot 16456
[Alan Berry/Duane Potter/Mike Rogers/Jim Valley/Fred Zeufeld] [BMI] (5/11/63 R-95) [I]

THE GRASS IS GREENER Brenda Lee—Decca 31539
[Mike Anthony/Barry Mann] [BMI] (9/21/63 BCR-17)

GRASSHOPPER Spin—Ariola America 7632
[Hans Jansen/Jan Vennik] [BMI] (8/28/76 B-95) [I]

GRAVITY James Brown—Scotti Brothers 06275
[Dan Hartman/Charles E. Kaufman] [BMI] (10/18/86 B-93)

GRAVY (FOR MY MASHED POTATOES) Dee Dee Sharp—Cameo 219
[Dave Appell/Kal Mann] [ASC] (6/9/62 BCR-9)

GRAVY WALTZ Steve Allen—Dot 16457 [Ray Brown] [BMI] (4/20/63 BCR-64) [IM]

GRAZING IN THE GRASS *Hugh Masekela—Uni 55066*
[Hugh Masekela] [BMI] (6/8/68 BCR-1) [IM]

GRAZING IN THE GRASS *The Friends Of Distinction—RCA Victor 74-0107*
[Harry Elston/Hugh Masekela] [BMI] (4/5/69 BCR-3)

GREASE Frankie Valli—RSO 897 [Barry Gibb] [BMI] (5/27/78 BCR-1)

GREASED LIGHTNIN' John Travolta—RSO 909
[Warren Casey/Jim Jacobs] [ASC] (9/30/78 BCR-45)

GREASY HEART Jefferson Airplane—RCA Victor 47-9496
[Grace Slick] [BMI] (4/6/68 BCR-70)

THE GREASY SPOON Hank Marr—Federal 12508
[Hank Marr/Gene Redd Sr.] [BMI] (12/28/63 C-68) [I]

THE GREAT AIRPLANE STRIKE
Paul Revere And The Raiders Featuring Mark Lindsay—Columbia 43810
[Mark Lindsay/Terry Melcher/Paul Revere] [BMI] (10/1/66 BCR-17)

GREAT BALLS OF FIRE *Jerry Lee Lewis—Sun 281*
[Otis Blackwell/Jack Hammer] [BMI] (11/23/57 BCRt-2)

GREAT BALLS OF FIRE *Georgia Gibbs—RCA Victor 47-7098*
[Otis Blackwell/Jack Hammer] [BMI] (12/2/57 Rt-2)

GREAT BALLS OF FIRE *Tiny Tim—Reprise 0802*
[Otis Blackwell/Jack Hammer] [BMI] (2/1/69 BCR-73)

GREAT BALLS OF FIRE *Jive Bunny & The Mastermixers—Music Factory/Atco 99122*
[Otis Blackwell/Jack Hammer] (Med) [BMI] (2/3/90 BC-67)

THE GREAT COMMANDMENT Camouflage—Atlantic 89031
[Oliver Kreyssig/Heiko Maile/Marcus Meyn] [BMI] (12/24/88 BC-59)

GREAT DAY Sarah Vaughan—Roulette 4397
[Edward Eliscu/Billy Rose/Vincent Youmans] [ASC] (10/23/61 R-97)

THE GREAT ESCAPE Ray Stevens—Monument 1099 [Ray Stevens] [BMI] (11/9/68 CR-88)

GREAT GOSH A'MIGHTY Little Richard—MCA 52780
[Richard Penniman/John Schuller/Sylvia Smith] [BMI] (3/8/86 BC-42)

—GREAT IMPOSTER see: THEME FROM THE GREAT IMPOSTER

THE GREAT PRETENDER *The Platters—Mercury 70753*
[Buck Ram] [ASC] (12/9/55 BCRt-1)

THE GREAT PRETENDER *Jackie Riggs—Media 1020 [Buck Ram] [ASC] (12/16/55 Rt-13)*

THE GREAT PRETENDER *Stan Freberg—Capitol 3396 [Buck Ram] [ASC] (4/13/56 Rt-21)*

THE GREAT SNOW MAN Bob Luman—Warner Bros. 5204
[John D. Loudermilk] [BMI] (5/6/61 C-95)

THE GREATEST FEELING IN THE WORLD Four Tunes—Jubilee 5152
[Sid Bass/Roy Jordan] [ASC] (8/21/54 C-23)

THE GREATEST GIFT OF ALL Kenny Rogers & Dolly Parton—RCA 13945
[John Jarvis] [BMI] (12/22/84 B-81)

THE GREATEST HURT Jackie Wilson—Brunswick 55221
[Billy Myles] [BMI] (1/8/62 BCR-24)

THE GREATEST LOVE Dorsey Burnette—Liberty 56087 [Joe South] [BMI] (1/25/69 BCR-56)

GREATEST LOVE Judy Clay—Atlantic 2697 [Allen Toussaint] [BMI] (3/21/70 CR-86)

THE GREATEST LOVE OF ALL *George Benson—Arista 0251*
[Linda Creed/Michael Masser] [BMI] (7/23/77 BCR-24)

GREATEST LOVE OF ALL *Whitney Houston—Arista 1-9466*
[Linda Creed/Michael Masser] [BMI] (3/29/86 BC-1)

THE GREATEST THING Georgia Gibbs—Mercury 70811
[Bernie Lowe/Kal Mann] [ASC] (3/2/56 R-54)

GREEN CHRITMA Stan Freberg—Capitol 4097 [Stan Freberg] [ASC] (12/27/58 BC-34)

GREEN DOOR *Jim Lowe—Dot 15486 [Bob Davie/Marvin Moore] [BMI] (8/25/56 BCR-1)*

GREEN DOOR *The Jerms—Honor Brigade 1*
[Bob Davie/Marvin Moore] [BMI] (5/24/69 R-97)

GREEN-EYED LADY Sugarloaf—Liberty 56183
[Jerry Corbetta/John C. Phillips/David Riordan] [ASC] (8/8/70 BCR-3)

GREEN EYES The Ravens Featuring Jimmy Ricks—Jubilee 5203
[Unknown] [NA] (8/29/55 R-73)

GREEN GRASS Gary Lewis And The Playboys—Liberty 55880
[Roger Cook/Roger Greenaway] [ASC] (5/7/66 BCR-6)

GREEN GRASS OF TEXAS The Texans—Infinity 001
[Dorsey Burnette/Johnny Burnette] [BMI] (3/6/61 BCR-72) [I]

THE GREEN GRASS STARTS TO GROW Dionne Warwick—Scepter 12300
[Burt Bacharach/Hal David] [ASC] (12/5/70 BCR-32)

GREEN, GREEN The New Christy Minstrels—Columbia 42805
[Barry McGuire/Randy Sparks] [BMI] (6/29/63 BCR-12)

GREEN, GREEN GRASS OF HOME Tom Jones—Parrot 40009
[Curly Putman] [BMI] (12/17/66 BCR-10)

—GREEN HILLS OF TYROL see: SCOTTISH SOLDIER

THE GREEN LEAVES OF SUMMER *The Brothers Four—Columbia 41808*
[Dimitri Tiomkin/Paul Francis Webster] [ASC] (10/17/60 BCRt-55)

THE GREEN LEAVES OF SUMMER *Bud & Travis—Liberty 55284*
[Dimitri Tiomkin/Paul Francis Webster] [ASC] (10/17/60 Rt-55)

THE GREEN LEAVES OF SUMMER *Nelson Riddle & His Orchestra—Capitol 4448*
[Dimitri Tiomkin] [ASC] (10/17/60 Rt-90) [IM]

THE GREEN LEAVES OF SUMMER *Nick Perito—United Artists 262*
[Dimitri Tiomkin] [ASC] (10/24/60 Rt-55) [IM]

THE GREEN LEAVES OF SUMMER *Kenny Ball And His Jazzmen—Kapp 460*
[Dimitri Tiomkin] [ASC] (5/26/62 BCR-68) [IM]

GREEN LIGHT The American Breed—Acta 821
[Nancie Mantz/Annette Tucker] [BMI] (2/24/68 BCR-22)

GREEN MOSQUITO The Tune Rockers—United Artists 139
[Art Roberts/Art Wander] [BMI] (8/18/58 BCR-40) [I]

GREEN ONIONS *Booker T. & The M.G.'s—Stax 127*
[Steve Cropper/Al Jackson/Booker T. Jones Jr./Lewis Steinberg] [BMI] (8/11/62 BCR-3) [I]

GREEN ONIONS *Dick Hyman—Command 4129 [Steve Cropper/Al Jackson/ Booker T. Jones Jr./Lewis Steinberg] BMI] (9/13/69 CR-88) [I]*

GREEN RIVER Creedence Clearwater Revival—Fantasy 625
[John Fogerty] (TSW) [BMI] (7/26/69 BCR-2)

GREEN TAMBOURINE The Lemon Pipers—Buddah 23
[Paul Leka/Shelley Pinz] [BMI] (12/2/67 BCR-1)

THE GREEN YEARS Eddie Fisher—RCA Victor 47-5748
[Arthur Altman/Don Reid] [ASC] (6/12/54 BC-PRE)

GREENBACK DOLLAR *The Kingston Trio—Capitol 4898*
[Hoyt Axton/Ken Ramsey] [BMI] (1/19/63 BCRt-17)

GREENBACK DOLLAR *The Virginians—Colpix 666*
[Hoyt Axton/Ken Ramsey] [BMI] (2/9/63 Rt-26)

GREENBACK DOLLAR The Merry Melody Singers—Mercury 72083
[Neal Matthews] [BMI] (1/26/63 Rt*-57)

GREENBURG, GLICKSTEIN, CHARLES, DAVID SMITH & JONES
The Cryan' Shames—Columbia 44638
[Jim Fairs/Isaac Guillory] [BMI] (10/5/68 CR-73)

GREENFIELDS *The Brothers Four—Columbia 41571*
[Richard Dehr/Terry Gilkyson/Frank Miller] [BMI] (2/22/60 BCRt-1)

GREENFIELDS *Julius La Rosa—Kapp 323*
[Richard Dehr/Terry Gilkyson/Frank Miller] [BMI] (3/7/60 Rt-17)

GREEN FIELDS *The Vogues—Reprise 0844*
[Richard Dehr/Terry Gilkyson/Frank Miller] [BMI] (8/16/69 BCR-84)

GREENSLEEVES *The Beverley Sisters—London 1703 [Traditional] [NA] (12/15/56 BCR-22)*

GREENSLEEVES *Mason Williams—Warner Bros.-Seven Arts 7272*
[Traditional] [NA] (4/26/69 BC-90) [I]

GREENWOOD MISSISSIPPI Little Richard—Reprise 0942
[Albert Lowe/Travis Wammack] [BMI] (8/29/70 BCR-79)

GREETINGS (THIS IS UNCLE SAM) *Valadiers—Miracle 6*
[Stuart Avig/Robert Bateman/Martin Coleman/Ronald Dunbar/Art Glasser/ Brian Holland/Jerry Light] [BMI] (11/20/61 B-89)*

GREETINGS (THIS IS UNCLE SAM) *The Monitors—V.I.P. 25032 [Stuart Avig/Robert Bateman/Martin Coleman/Ronald Dunbar*/Art Glasser/ Brian Holland/Jerry Light] [BMI] (4/2/66 BCR-94)*

GRETCHEN The Diamonds—Mercury 71449 [William S. Kutner/Richard Loring] [ASC] (4/25/59 C-95)

GRIM REAPER OF LOVE The Turtles—White Whale 231 [Al Nichol/Charles Portz] [BMI] (6/18/66 BCR-81)

GRITS AIN'T GROCERIES (ALL AROUND THE WORLD) Little Milton—Checker 1212 [Titus Turner] [BMI] (2/1/69 BCR-73)

GRITS 'N CORN BREAD Soul Runners—MoSoul 101 [Nathaniel Nathan/Fred Smith] [BMI] (1/28/67 CR-98) [I]

GRIZZLY BEAR The Youngbloods—RCA Victor 47-9015 [Jerry Corbitt] [BMI] (12/17/66 BCR-42)

GROOVE IS IN THE HEART Deee-Lite—Elektra 64934 [Dmitry Brill/Kamaal Fareed/Herbie Hancock/Kier Kirby/Towa Tei] [BMI] (9/15/90 BC-3)

THE GROOVE LINE Heatwave—Epic 50524 [Rod Temperton] [ASC] (4/15/78 BCR-7)

GROOVE ME *King Floyd—Chimneyville 435 [King Floyd] [BMI] (10/24/70 BCR-4)*

GROOVE ME *Fern Kinney—Malaco 1058 [King Floyd] [BMI] (8/18/79 BR-54)*

THE GROOVIEST GIRL IN THE WORLD The Fun And Games—Uni 55098 [Mitch Bottler/Gary Zekley] [ASC] (1/18/69 BCR-50)

GROOVIN' *The Young Rascals—Atlantic 2401 [Eddie Brigati/Felix Cavaliere] [ASC] (4/22/67 BCR-1)*

GROOVIN' *Booker T. & The M.G.'s—Stax 224 [Eddie Brigati/Felix Cavaliere] [ASC] (8/5/67 BCR-21) [IWM]*

GROOVIN' UB40—Virgin 98654 [Byron Lee/Lester Sterling] [BMI] (11/23/91 B-90)

GROOVIN' (OUT ON LIFE) The Newbeats—Hickory 1552 [Robert Guidry] [BMI] (12/13/69 BCR-72)

GROOVIN' WITH MR. BLOE Cool Heat—Forward/MGM 152 [Bo Gentry/Kenny Laguna/Paul Naumann] [BMI] (8/15/70 BCR-89) [I]

GROOVY Joe Dodo And The Groovers—RCA Victor 47-7207 [Gordon Charles] [BMI] (4/19/58 CR-55)

GROOVY BABY Billy Abbott And The Jewels—Parkway 874 [William E. Jackson III/Roy Straigis] [BMI] (7/13/63 BCR-55)

GROOVY GRUBWORM Harlow Wilcox And The Oakies—Plantation 28 [Bobby Warren/Harlow Wilcox] [BMI] (9/27/69 BCR-23) [I]

A GROOVY KIND OF LOVE *The Mindbenders—Fontana 1541 [Carole Bayer Sager/Toni Wine] [BMI] (4/2/66 BCR-1)*

GROOVY KIND OF LOVE *Phil Collins—Atlantic 89017 [Carole Bayer Sager/Toni Wine] [BMI] (9/3/88 BC-1)*

GROOVY PEOPLE Lou Rawls—Philadelphia Int'l 3604 [Kenneth Gamble/Leon Huff] [BMI] (10/16/76 BC-64)

GROOVY SITUATION Gene Chandler—Mercury 73083 [Herman R. Davis/Russ Lewis] [BMI] (6/27/70 BCR-10)

GROOVY SUMMERTIME The Love Generation—Imperial 66243 [Tom Bahler/Keith Colley/Dick Ross] [BMI] (6/24/67 BCR-61)

GROOVY TONIGHT Bobby Rydell—Cameo 182 [Bernie Lowe/Kal Mann] [ASC] (12/5/60 B-70)

GROOVY TRAIN The Farm—Sire 19209 [Steve Grimes/Peter Hooton] [ASC] (9/14/91 BC-25)

GROUND HOG The Browns Featuring Jim Edward Brown—RCA Victor 47-7820 [Kenneth Burns/Henry Haynes/Traditional] [BMI] (4/10/61 B-97)

GROVER HENSON FEELS FORGOTTEN Bill Cosby—Uni 55223 [Christian Wilde] [ASC] (4/18/70 BCR-70)

GROW CLOSER TOGETHER The Impressions—ABC-Paramount 10289 [Curtis Mayfield] [BMI] (2/17/62 B-99)

GROW SOME FUNK OF YOUR OWN Elton John—MCA 40505 [Elton John/Davey Johnstone/Bernie Taupin] (TSW) [BMI] (1/24/76 BCR-9)

GROWIN' Loggins & Messina—Columbia 10118 [Kenny Loggins/Ronnie Wilkins] [BMI] (3/29/75 BCR-45)

GROWIN' PRETTIER Johnny October—Capitol 4267 [Jesse Stone] [BMI] (9/21/59 R-95)

GROWIN' UP Dan Hill—20th Century 2254 [Dan Hill] [ASC] (1/24/76 BC-67)

G.T.O. Ronny & The Daytonas—Mala 481 [John Buck Wilkin] [BMI] (8/1/64 BCR-4)

—GUACHA GUARO see: SOUL SAUCE

GUAGLIONE *Mitchell Ayers and his Orchestra and Chorus—RCA Victor 47-6729 [Giuseppe Fucilli] [ASC] (12/1/56 Rt-77) [IM]*

GUAGLIONE (LITTLE BOY) *Ralph Marterie And His Orchestra—Mercury 71007 [Giuseppe Fucilli] [ASC] (12/1/56 Rt-77) [IM]*

GUAGLIONE *Perez Prado And His Orchestra—RCA Victor 47-7337 [Giuseppe Fucilli] [ASC] (9/22/58 BCR-16) [IM]*

GUANTANAMERA The Sandpipers—A&M 806 [Héctor Angulo/José Fernandez Diaz*/Jose Marti/Julian Orson*/Pete Seeger/ Traditional] [BMI] (7/23/66 BCR-7) [F]

GUARANTEED FOR LIFE Millions Like Us—Virgin 99412 [Jonathan Hook/John O'Kane] [BMI] (11/7/87 BC-69)

GUAVA JELLY *Capers & Carson—Janus 216 [Bob Marley] [ASC] (6/16/73 R-82)*

GUAVA JELLY *Barbra Streisand—Columbia 10075 [Bob Marley] [ASC] (1/4/75 C-83)*

GUDBUY T' JANE Slade—Polydor 15060 [Noddy Holder/Jim Lea] [ASC] (3/3/73 BCR-62)

GUESS I'VE BEEN AROUND TOO LONG Carl Smith—Columbia 41170 [Mel Tillis/Wayne Walker] [BMI] (9/8/58 B-93)

GUESS THINGS HAPPEN THAT WAY *Johnny Cash And The Tennessee Two—Sun 295 [Jack H. Clement] [BMI] (5/26/58 BCR-11)*

GUESS THINGS HAPPEN THAT WAY *June Valli—Mercury 71750 [Jack H. Clement] [BMI] (1/16/61 R-92)*

GUESS WHO *Jesse Belvin—RCA Victor 47-7469 [Jesse Belvin/JoAnn Belvin] [BMI] (3/23/59 BCR-28)*

GUESS WHO *Ruby Winters—Diamond 269 [Jesse Belvin/JoAnn Belvin] [BMI] (12/27/69 BCR-69)*

GUESS WHO *B.B. King—ABC 11330 [Jesse Belvin/JoAnn Belvin] [BMI] (8/19/72 BCR-62)*

GUESS WHO? Dusty Springfield—Philips 40245 [Gary Klein/Artie Kornfeld] [BMI] (12/26/64 C-92)

GUILTY The Crests—Selma 311 [Harry Akst/Gus Kahn/Richard Whiting] [ASC] (12/22/62 R-88)

GUILTY Jim Reeves—RCA Victor 47-8193 [Alex Zanetis] [BMI] (6/29/63 BR-91)

GUILTY Al Green—Bell 45,258 [Robert Earl Williams] [BMI] (9/16/72 BCR-46)

GUILTY Barbra Streisand & Barry Gibb—Columbia 11390 [Barry Gibb/Maurice Gibb/Robin Gibb] [BMI] (11/1/80 BCR-3)

GUILTY OF LOVING YOU Jerry Fuller—Challenge 9114 [Jerry Fuller] [BMI] (9/23/61 BCR-94)

GUITAR BOOGIE SHUFFLE *The Virtues—Hunt 324 [Arthur Smith] [ASC] (3/2/59 BCR-5) [I]*

GUITAR BOOGIE SHUFFLE TWIST *The Virtues—Sure 1733 [Arthur Smith] [ASC] (3/24/62 B-96) [I]*

GUITAR MAN *Elvis Presley—RCA Victor 47-9425 [Jerry Reed] [BMI] (1/27/68 BCR-36)*

GUITAR MAN *Elvis Presley—RCA 12158 [Jerry Reed] [BMI] (1/24/81 BCR-28)*

THE GUITAR MAN Bread—Elektra 45803 [David Gates] [ASC] (7/22/72 BCR-9)

GUM DROP *The Crew-Cuts—Mercury 70668 [Rudy Toombs] [BMI] (7/25/55 BCRt-10)*

GUM DROP *Otis Williams & His New Group—DeLuxe 6090 [Rudy Toombs] [BMI] (7/25/55 Rt-21)*

GUM DROP *The Mills Brothers—Decca 29686 [Rudy Toombs] [BMI] (11/14/55 Rt-51)*

GUN SLINGER Bo Diddley—Checker 965 [Ellas McDaniel] [BMI] (12/5/60 R-71)

GUNS FOR HIRE AC/DC—Atlantic 89774 A [Brian Johnson/Angus Young/Malcolm Young] [ASC] (10/1/83 B-84)

GUNS, GUNS, GUNS The Guess Who—RCA Victor 74-0708 [Burton Cummings] [BMI] (5/20/72 BCR-66)

THE GUNS OF NAVARONE *Joe Reisman And His Orchestra—Landa 674 [Dimitri Tiomkin] [ASC] (7/3/61 BCt-74) [IM]*

THE GUNS OF NAVARONE *Mitch Miller and The Gang—GNP Crescendo 315 [Dimitri Tiomkin/Paul Francis Webster] [ASC] (8/5/61 Ct-89)*

GYPSY Van Morrison—Warner Bros. 7665 [Van Morrison] [BMI] (1/13/73 CR-89)

GYPSY Abraham's Children—Buddah 340 [Paul Gross] [ASC] (3/3/73 C-78)

GYPSY Fleetwood Mac—Warner Bros. 29918 [Stevie Nicks] [BMI] (9/4/82 BC-12)

THE GYPSY CRIED Lou Christie—Roulette 4457 [Lou Christie/Twyla Herbert] [BMI] (1/5/63 BCR-15)

GYPSY DAVY Arlo Guthrie—Reprise 1158 [Woody Guthrie] [BMI] (5/26/73 R-85)

GYPSY MAN War—United Artists 281 [Thomas Allen/Harold Brown/Morris Dickerson/Lonnie Jordan/Charles Miller/ Lee Oskar/Howard Scott] [ASC] (7/14/73 BCR-7)

GYPSY QUEEN (PART 1) Gypsy—Metromedia 202 [Enrico Rosenbaum] [BMI] (12/5/70 BCR-51)

GYPSY ROAD Cinderella—Mercury 874578 [Tom Keifer] [ASC] (8/5/89 B-51)

THE GYPSY ROVER The Highwaymen—United Artists 370 [Leo Maguire] [ASC] (10/30/61 BCR-38)

GYPSY SPIRIT Pendulum—Venture 131 [David Barrow*/James Kenny*/David Quintana] [BMI] (11/29/80 B-89)

GYPSY WOMAN *The Impressions—ABC-Paramount 10241 [Curtis Mayfield] [BMI] (10/16/61 BCR-13)*

GYPSY WOMAN *Brian Hyland—Uni 55240 [Curtis Mayfield] [BMI] (8/29/70 BCR-3)*

GYPSY WOMAN Rick Nelson—Decca 31495 [Dorsey Burnette/Joe Osborn] [BMI] (5/18/63 BCR-62)

GYPSY WOMAN (SHE'S HOMELESS) Crystal Waters—Mercury 868 208 [Neal Conway/Crystal Waters] [ASC] (5/4/91 BC-8)

GYPSY WOMAN TOLD ME Eddie Powers—Sims 187 [Henry R. Hines/Earl Stanley/Laverne Tardo] [BMI] (5/30/64 R-76)

GYPSYS, TRAMPS & THIEVES Cher—Kapp 2146 [Bob Stone] [BMI] (9/18/71 BCR-1)

H

HA CHA CHA (FUNKTION) Brass Construction—United Artists 921 [Randy Muller] [BMI] (12/25/76 BR-51) [I]

HAI HAI HAI ("CHE LLA LAI") *Lou Monte—RCA Victor 47-7061 [Al Hoffman/Dick Manning/Alessandro Taccani] [ASC] (10/21/57 Rt-54) [FDE]*

HAI HAI HAI (CHELLA LLA) *Kay Armen—Decca 30474 [Al Hoffman/Dick Manning/Alessandro Taccani] [ASC] (10/21/57 BRt-54) [FDE]*

HA HA HA (CHELLA LLA) *Sammy Kaye & His "Swing And Sway" Orchestra—Columbia 41028 [Al Hoffman/Dick Manning/Alessandro Taccani] [ASC] (10/28/57 Rt-54) [FDE]*

HA HA SAID THE CLOWN The Yardbirds—Epic 10204
[Tony Hazzard] [BMI] (8/5/67 BCR-45)

HAD A DREAM (SLEEPING WITH THE ENEMY) Roger Hodgson—A&M 2678
[Roger Hodgson] [ASC] (10/13/84 BC-44)

HAIL! HAIL! ROCK AND ROLL! Starland Vocal Band—Windsong 10855
[Bill Danoff/Taffy Danoff] [ASC] (1/1/77 BC-71)

HAIL TO THE CONQUERING HERO James Darren—Colpix 655
[Howard Greenfield/Gloria Shayne] [BMI] (9/15/62 BR-86)

HAIR The Cowsills—MGM 14026
[Galt MacDermot/James Rado/Gerome Ragni] [ASC] (3/15/69 BCR-1)

THE HAIR ON MY CHINNY CHIN CHIN Sam The Sham And The Pharaohs—MGM 13581
[Ronald Blackwell] [BMI] (10/1/66 BCR-14)

HAJJI BABA (PERSIAN LAMENT) Nat "King" Cole—Capitol 2949
[Dimitri Tiomkin/Ned Washington] [ASC] (10/11/54 BCR-11)

HALF A MILLION MILES FROM HOME Albert Hammond—Mums 6024
[Albert Hammond/Mike Hazlewood] [ASC] (11/24/73 BCR-72)

HALF AS LOVELY (TWICE AS TRUE) Frank Sinatra—Capitol 2864
[Sammy Gallop/Lew Spence] [ASC] (7/31/54 C-20)

HALF-BREED Marvin Rainwater—MGM 12803 [John D. Loudermilk] [BMI] (7/4/59 BC-66)

HALF-BREED Cher—MCA 40102 [Al Capps/Mary Dean] [BMI] (7/21/73 BCR-1)

HALF HEAVEN - HALF HEARTACHE Gene Pitney—Musicor 1026
[George Goehring/Wally Gold/Aaron Schroeder] [ASC] (12/15/62 BCR-12)

HALF MOON SILVER Hotel—MCA 41277
[Lee Bargeron/Tom Calton/Marc Phillips] [BMI] (7/12/80 BC-72)

HALF THE WAY Crystal Gayle—Columbia 11087
[Ralph Murphy/Bobby Wood] [ASC] (9/22/79 BCR-15)

HALFWAY TO PARADISE *Tony Orlando—Epic 9441*
[Gerry Goffin/Carole King] [BMI] (4/8/61 BCR-17)

HALFWAY TO PARADISE *Bobby Vinton—Epic 10350*
[Gerry Goffin/Carole King] [BMI] (7/13/68 BCR-16)

HALLELUIAH MAN Love and Money—Mercury 870596
[James (2) Grant] [BMI] (2/18/89 BC-74)

HALLELUJAH The Invitations—DynoVoice 206
[Sandy Linzer/Denny Randell] [BMI] (7/3/65 CR-98)

HALLELUJAH Sweathog—Columbia 45492
[Mitch Bottler/Roberta Twain/Gary Zekley] [ASC] (11/13/71 BCR-28)

HALLELUJAH CHORUS The Royal Philharmonic Orchestra—RCA 12304
[Georg Friederic Handel] (Med) [NA] (10/31/81 BCR-9) [I]

HALLELUJAH DAY The Jackson 5—Motown 1224
[Freddie Perren/Christine Yarian] [ASC] (3/17/73 BCR-21)

HALLELUJAH I LOVE HIM SO *Peggy Lee—Capitol 4189*
[Ray Charles] [BMI] (5/16/59 BCR-77)

HALLELUJAH I LOVE HER SO *Eddie Cochran—Liberty 55217*
[Ray Charles] [BMI] (11/30/59 CR-98)

HALLWAYS OF MY MIND The Dells—Cadet 5636
[Robert Eugene Miller] [BMI] (3/1/69 BCR-82)

HALO OF LOVE Nick Noble—Mercury 71233 [Don Shoemate] [BMI] (12/9/57 R-81)

HAND CLAPPIN' Red Prysock—Mercury 70698 [Red Prysock] [BMI] (9/26/55 R-73)

HAND CLAPPING SONG The Meters—Josie 1021
[Joseph Modeliste/Art Neville/Leo Nocentelli/George Porter] [BMI] (6/20/70 BCR-74)

HAND IT OVER Chuck Jackson—Wand 149
[Frances Aycock*/Robert Mosely] [BMI] (3/7/64 BC-72)

—HAND JIVE see: WILLIE AND THE HAND JIVE

HAND ME DOWN WORLD The Guess Who—RCA Victor 74-0367
[Kurt Winter] [BMI] (7/18/70 BCR-13)

HAND TO HOLD ON TO John Cougar—Riva 211 [John Mellencamp] [ASC] (11/6/82 BC-19)

HANDBAGS AND GLADRAGS *Chase—Epic 10775*
[Michael D'Abo] [ASC] (9/11/71 BCR-74)

HANDBAGS AND GLADRAGS *Rod Stewart—Mercury 73031*
[Michael D'Abo] [ASC] (2/5/72 BCR-38)

HANDFUL OF MEMORIES Baby Washington—Sue 767
[Ronald Alonzo Miller/Lee Porter] [ASC] (9/22/62 C-96)

HANDLE WITH CARE Traveling Wilburys—Wilbury 7-27732
[Bob Dylan/George Harrison/Jeff Lynne/Roy Orbison/Tom Petty] [SE] (10/22/88 BC-39)

HANDS ACROSS AMERICA Voices Of America—EMI America 8319
[Marc Blatte/John Carney/Larry Gottlieb] [ASC] (4/12/86 BC-65)

HANDS ACROSS THE SEA Modern English—Sire 29339
[Richard Ian Brown/Michael Conroy/Robbie Grey/Gary McDowell/Stephen Walker] [BMI] (4/7/84 B-91)

HANDS OFF *Johnny Maddox Orchestra—Dot 15432*
[Priscilla Bowman/Jay McShann] [ASC] (12/9/55 Rt-30)

HANDS OFF *Jay McShann's Orchestra—Vee-Jay 155*
[Priscilla Bowman/Jay McShann] [ASC] (12/9/55 Rt-30)

HANDS OFF *Frankie Castro—Wing 90037*
[Priscilla Bowman/Jay McShann] [ASC] (12/9/55 Rt-34)

HANDS OFF *Nan Wynn—RCA Victor 47-6336*
[Priscilla Bowman/Jay McShann] [ASC] (12/16/55 Rt-30)

KEEP YOUR HANDS OFF OF HIM *Damita Jo—Mercury 71760*
[Priscilla Bowman/Jay McShann] [BMI] (1/28/61 BCR-74)

HANDS ON THE RADIO Henry Lee Summer—CBS Associated 07986
[Henry Lee Summer] [BMI] (9/17/88 B-85)

HANDS TIED Scandal Featuring Patty Smyth—Columbia 04650
[Mike Chapman/Holly Knight] [ASC] (10/20/84 BC-39)

HANDS TO HEAVEN Breathe—A&M 2991
[Michael Delahunty/David Glasper/Marcus Lillington/Ian Spice] [ASC] (4/16/88 BC-2)

HANDY MAN *Jimmy Jones—Cub 9049*
[Andrew Barksdale/Otis Blackwell/Jimmy Jones/Charles Merenstein] [BMI] (12/14/59 BCR-2)

HANDY MAN *Del Shannon—Amy 905*
[Andrew Barksdale/Otis Blackwell/Jimmy Jones/Charles Merenstein] [BMI] (7/4/64 BCR-13)

HANDY MAN *James Taylor—Columbia 10557*
[Andrew Barksdale/Otis Blackwell/Jimmy Jones/Charles Merenstein] [BMI] (6/11/77 BCR-2)

HANG 'EM HIGH *Hugo Montenegro, His Orchestra And Chorus—RCA Victor 47-9554*
[Dominic Frontiere] [BMI] (6/15/68 BCR-70) [I]

HANG 'EM HIGH *Booker T. & The MG's—Stax 0013*
[Dominic Frontiere] [BMI] (11/9/68 BCR-9) [I]

HANG FIRE The Rolling Stones—Rolling Stones 21300
[Mick Jagger/Keith Richards] [ASC] (3/20/82 BCR-20)

HANG IN LONG ENOUGH Phil Collins—Atlantic 87800
[Phil Collins] [ASC] (11/10/90 BC-11)

HANG LOOSE Mandrill—Polydor 14187
[Claude Cave] [ASC] (8/11/73 BCR-83) [IWM]

HANG ON Floyd Cramer—RCA Victor 47-7907 [Floyd Cramer] [BMI] (9/30/61 BCR-73) [I]

HANG ON IN THERE BABY Johnny Bristol—MGM 14715
[Johnny Bristol] [ASC] (6/29/74 BCR-8)

HANG ON NOW Kajagoogoo—EMI America 8171
[Steven Askew/Nick Beggs/Christopher Hamill/Stuart Neale/Jeremy Strode] [ASC] (8/27/83 B-78)

MY GIRL SLOOPY *The Vibrations—Atlantic 2221*
[Bert Berns/Wes Farrell] [BMI] (3/28/64 BCR-26)

(MY GIRL) SLOOPY *Little Caesar And The Consuls—Mala 512*
[Bert Berns/Wes Farrell] [BMI] (8/14/65 BCRt-50)

HANG ON SLOOPY *The McCoys—Bang 506*
[Bert Berns/Wes Farrell] [BMI] (8/14/65 BCRt-1)

HANG ON SLOOPY *Ramsey Lewis Trio—Cadet 5522*
[Bert Berns/Wes Farrell] [BMI] (11/13/65 BCR-8) [IWM]

HANG ON SLOOPY *The Lettermen—Capitol 2774*
[Bert Berns/Wes Farrell] [BMI] (3/28/70 BR-77)

HANG ON SLOOPY *Rick Derringer—Blue Sky 2755*
[Bert Berns/Wes Farrell] [BMI] (3/29/75 BCR-67)

HANG ON TO YOUR LIFE The Guess Who—RCA Victor 74-0414
[Burton Cummings/Kurt Winter] [BMI] (1/30/71 BCR-22)

HANG UP MY ROCK AND ROLL SHOES Chuck Willis—Atlantic 1179
[Chuck Willis] [BMI] (4/28/58 BR-24)

HANGIN' AROUND The Edgar Winter Group—Epic 11069
[Dan Hartman/Edgar Winter] [BMI] (12/8/73 BCR-39)

HANGIN' ON A STRING (CONTEMPLATING) Loose Ends—MCA 52570
[Jane Eugene/Carl McIntosh/Steve Nichol] [BMI] (7/20/85 BC-43)

HANGIN' TOUGH New Kids On The Block—Columbia 68960
[Maurice Starr] [ASC] (7/15/89 BC-1)

HANGING ON A HEART ATTACK Device—Chrysalis 42996
[Mike Chapman/Holly Knight] [ASC] (6/14/86 BC-27)

HANGING TREE Marty Robbins—Columbia 41325
[Mack David/Jerry Livingston] [ASC] (2/2/59 BCR-31)

HANKY PANKY Tommy James And The Shondells—Roulette 4686
[Jeff Barry/Ellie Greenwich] [BMI] (5/28/66 BCR-1)

HANKY PANKY Madonna—Sire 19789
[Madonna L. Ciccone/Patrick Raymond Leonard] [ASC] (6/23/90 BC-8)

THE HAPPENING *The Supremes—Motown 1107*
[Frank DeVol/Lamont Dozier/Brian Holland/Eddie Holland] [BMI] (4/8/67 BCR-1)

THE HAPPENING *Herb Alpert & The Tijuana Brass—A&M 860*
[Frank DeVol] [ASC] (7/8/67 BCR-30) [IM]

HAPPENINGS TEN YEARS TIME AGO The Yardbirds—Epic 10094
[Jeff Beck/Jim McCarty/Jimmy Page/Keith Relf] [ASC] (11/26/66 BCR-29)

HAPPIER Paul Anka—United Artists 911 [Paul Anka] [BMI] (12/18/76 BCR-60)

HAPPIER THAN THE MORNING SUN B.J. Thomas—Scepter 12364
[Stevie Wonder] [ASC] (9/16/72 BCR-86)

HAPPIEST CHRISTMAS TREE Nat "King" Cole—Capitol 4301
[Lee Cathy] [BMI] (12/21/59 R-98)

THE HAPPIEST GIRL IN THE WHOLE U.S.A. Donna Fargo—Dot 17409
[Donna Fargo] [BMI] (5/27/72 BCR-7)

HAPPINESS Billy & Lillie—Swan 4005 [Bob Crewe/Frank Slay] [BMI] (5/5/58 B-56)

HAPPINESS Shades Of Blue—Impact 1015 [John Rhys] [BMI] (9/24/66 BCR-78)

HAPPINESS Pointer Sisters—Planet 45902 [Allen Toussaint] [BMI] (3/10/79 BCR-28)

HAPPINESS IS JUST AROUND THE BEND The Main Ingredient—RCA Victor 0305
[Brian Auger] [BMI] (6/15/74 BCR-26)

HAPPINESS IS ME AND YOU Gilbert O'Sullivan—MAM 3636
[Gilbert O'Sullivan] [ASC] (3/9/74 BCR-34)

HAPPINESS STREET *Tony Bennett with Percy Faith and His Orchestra—Columbia 40726*
[Edward White/Mack Wolfson] [ASC] (8/10/56 BCtRt-17)

HAPPINESS STREET *Georgia Gibbs—Mercury 70920*
[Edward White/Mack Wolfson] [ASC] (8/10/56 BCtRt-17)

HAPPINESS TRAIN The Sugar Bears—Big Tree 143
[Michael McGinnis] [BMI] (9/9/72 R-86)

HAPPY *The Sunshine Company—Imperial 66247*
[Vinny Gormann/Tony Michaels] [BMI] (7/15/67 BCR-31)

HAPPY *The Blades Of Grass—Jubilee 5582*
[Vinny Gormann/Tony Michaels] [BMI] (7/15/67 BCR-52)

HAPPY Nancy Sinatra—Reprise 0756 [Lee Hazlewood] [ASC] (7/20/68 BCR-44)

HAPPY Paul Anka—RCA Victor 47-9767 [Tony Romeo] [BMI] (11/15/69 BCR-71)

HAPPY Hog Heaven—Roulette 7101 [Peter Lucia/Mike Vale] [BMI] (4/24/71 BR-98)

HAPPY The Rolling Stones—Rolling Stones 19104
[Mick Jagger/Keith Richards] [ASC] (7/8/72 BCR-12)

HAPPY Bobby Darin—Motown 1217
[Michel Legrand/Smokey Robinson] [ASC] (12/23/72 BCR-59)

HAPPY Eddie Kendricks—Tamla 54263
[Leonard Caston/Kathy Wakefield] [BMI] (10/11/75 BCR-59)

HAPPY Surface—Columbia 06611
[Dave Conley/Bernard Leon Jackson/David Townsend] [ASC] (5/23/87 BC-20)

HAPPY AND ME Don And The Goodtimes—Epic 10199
[Buzz Overman] [BMI] (7/29/67 BR-95)

HAPPY ANNIVERSARY *The Four Lads—Columbia 41497*
[Robert Allen/Al Stillman] [ASC] (10/24/59 BCtRt-34)

HAPPY ANNIVERSARY *Jane Morgan—Kapp 305*
[Robert Allen/Al Stillman] [ASC] (10/24/59 BCtRt-34)

HAPPY ANNIVERSARY Little River Band—Harvest 4524
[Beeb Birtles/David John Briggs] [BMI] (12/17/77 BCR-16)

HAPPY BABY *Bill Haley And His Comets—Decca 29317*
[Frank Pingatore] [ASC] (11/1/54 Rt-39)

HAPPY BABY *Les Baxter & The Bombers—Capitol 3002*
[Frank Pingatore] [ASC] (12/13/54 Rt-PRE)

HAPPY BIRTHDAY BLUES Kathy Young With The Innocents—Indigo 115
[James Lee] [BMI] (2/6/61 BCR-30)

HAPPY BIRTHDAY, SWEET SIXTEEN Neil Sedaka—RCA Victor 47-7957
[Howard Greenfield/Neil Sedaka] [BMI] (11/6/61 BCR-6)

THE HAPPY COWBOY Billy Vaughn And His Orchestra—Dot 16477
[Werner Last/Wolfgang Roloff] [BMI] (6/1/63 R-96) [I]

HAPPY DAYS Marv Johnson—United Artists 273
[Berry Gordy/Alma McKnight] [ASC] (11/21/60 BCR-39)

HAPPY DAYS Pratt & McClain—Reprise 1351
[Charles Fox/Norman Gimbel] [BMI] (4/3/76 BCR-5)

HAPPY DAYS AND LONELY NIGHTS
The Fontane Sisters with Billy Vaughn's Orchestra—Dot 15171
[Fred Fisher/Billy Rose] [ASC] (8/7/54 CR-36)

HAPPY DAYS AND LONELY NIGHTS *Connie Francis—MGM 12713*
[Fred Fisher/Billy Rose] [ASC] (10/6/58 CR-70)

HAPPY ENDING Joe Jackson—A&M 2635 [Joe Jackson] [ASC] (7/14/84 BC-57)

HAPPY FEET TIME The Monclairs—Sunburst 106 [Don Jones] [ASC] (7/17/65 CR-90) [I]

THE HAPPY GIRLS Helen Reddy—Capitol 4487
[Kim Fowley/Rick Henn/Earle Mankey/Helen Reddy] [BMI] (10/8/77 BCR-57)

HAPPY GO LUCKY ME Paul Evans—Guaranteed 208
[Al Byron/Paul Evans] [ASC] (5/2/60 BCR-8)

A HAPPY GUY Rick Nelson—Decca 31703
[Larry Kusik/Kenny Rankin] [BMI] (11/28/64 BCR-82)

HAPPY HAPPY BIRTHDAY BABY *The Tune Weavers—Checker 872*
[Gilbert Lopez/Margo Sylvia] [BMI] (9/2/57 BCRt-5)

HAPPY, HAPPY BIRTHDAY BABY *Kay Cee Jones—Decca 30432*
[Gilbert Lopez/Margo Sylvia] [BMI] (9/2/57 Rt-7)

HAPPY, HAPPY BIRTHDAY BABY *Dottie Ferguson—Mercury 71182*
[Gilbert Lopez/Margo Sylvia] [BMI] (9/30/57 Rt-7)

HAPPY HAPPY BIRTHDAY *Wanda Jackson—Capitol 4469*
[Gilbert Lopez/Margo Sylvia] [BMI] (11/28/60 R-94)

HAPPY HEART *Andy Williams—Columbia 44818*
[James Last/Jackie Rae] [ASC] (4/5/69 BCRt-22)

HAPPY HEART *Petula Clark—Warner Bros.-Seven Arts 7275*
[James Last/Jackie Rae] [ASC] (4/5/69 BCRt-62)

HAPPY HOUR Deodato—Warner Bros. 29984
[Jerry Barnes/Katreese Barnes] [BMI] (6/19/82 B-70)

HAPPY JACK The Who—Decca 32114 [Pete Townshend] [ASC] (4/8/67 BCR-13)

HAPPY JOSE (CHING-CHING) *Jack Ross—Dot 16302*
[Jesus Escamilla/Norman Malkin] [ASC] (12/25/61 BCtRt-29) [IM]*

HAPPY JOSE (CHING-CHING) *Dave Appell and his Orchestra—Cameo 207*
[Jesus Escamilla/Norman Malkin] [ASC] (1/1/62 CtRt-29) [IM]*

HAPPY MAN (PART 1) Impact—Atco/WMOT 7049
[Bobby Eli/Charles Kelly] [BMI] (6/19/76 B-94)

HAPPY MAN Greg Kihn Band—Beserkley 47463
[Greg Kihn/Steve Wright] [ASC] (5/22/82 BC-62)

HAPPY MULETEER Ivo Robic—Laurie 3045
[Peter Mösser/Noel Sherman] [ASC] (1/9/60 BCR-50)

HAPPY MUSIC The Blackbyrds—Fantasy 762 [Donald Byrd] [BMI] (3/6/76 BCR-19)

HAPPY ORGAN Dave "Baby" Cortez—Clock 1009
[David Clowney/Jim Kriegsmann/Ken Wood] [BMI] (3/2/59 BCR-1) [I]

HAPPY PAIR The Ames Brothers—RCA Victor 47-7742
[Ollie Jones/Bert Keyes] [BMI] (6/6/60 R-94)

HAPPY PEOPLE The Temptations—Gordy 7138
[Donald Baldwin/Jeff Bowen/Lionel Richie] [ASC] (12/14/74 BCR-40)

THE HAPPY PUPPY Bent Fabric—Atco 6271
[Bent Fabricius-Bjerre/Ethelbert Nevin] [BMI] (8/10/63 CR-95) [I]

H.A.P.P.Y. RADIO Edwin Starr—20th Century 2408 [Edwin Starr] [BMI] (8/4/79 B-79)

HAPPY REINDEER Dancer, Prancer And Nervous—Capitol 4300
[Robert Plaisted/Harold Rustigian] [ASC] (11/23/59 BCR-26)

HAPPY SHADES OF BLUE Freddie Cannon—Swan 4057
[Bob Crewe/Frank Slay] [BMI] (7/25/60 BCR-54)

THE HAPPY SONG (DUM-DUM) Otis Redding—Volt 163
[Steve Cropper/Otis Redding] [BMI] (4/27/68 BCR-16)

HAPPY SUMMER DAYS Ronnie Dove—Diamond 205
[Ritchie Adams/Wes Farrell/Larry Kusik] [BMI] (6/18/66 BCR-24)

HAPPY TIMES (ARE HERE TO STAY) Tony Orlando—Epic 9476
[Gerry Goffin/Carole King/Cynthia Weil] [BMI] (11/13/61 BCR-55)

HAPPY TOGETHER *The Turtles—White Whale 244*
[Garry Bonner/Alan Gordon] [BMI] (2/11/67 BCR-1)

HAPPY TOGETHER *Dawn Featuring Tony Orlando—Bell 45,175*
[Garry Bonner/Alan Gordon] (Med) [BMI] (1/22/72 BCR-41)

HAPPY TOGETHER (A FANTASY) *Captain & Tennille—Casablanca 2264*
[Garry Bonner/Alan Gordon] [BMI] (5/10/80 BCR-53)

HAPPY TOGETHER *The Nylons—Open Air 0024*
[Garry Bonner/Alan Gordon] [BMI] (8/29/87 BC-75)

HAPPY VACATION Jackie Lee (1)—Swan 4034 [Earl Nelson] [BMI] (6/29/59 B-95) [I]

THE HAPPY WANDERER *Frank Weir & His Orchestra—London 1448*
[Friedrich W. Möller/Antonia Ridge/Florenz Siegesmund] [ASC] (5/29/54 BC-PRE)

THE HAPPY WANDERER *Henri René's Musette—RCA Victor 47-5715*
[Friedrich W. Möller/Antonia Ridge/Florenz Siegesmund] [ASC] (5/29/54 BC-PRE)

HAPPY WEEKEND Dave "Baby" Cortez—Chess 1834
[David Clowney] [BMI] (10/13/62 BCR-64) [I]

HAPPY WHISTLER Don Robertson—Capitol 3391
[Don Robertson] [ASC] (4/13/56 BCR-5) [I]

HAPPY XMAS (WAR IS OVER)
John & Yoko & Plastic Ono Band with Harlem Community Choir—Apple 1842
[John Lennon/Yoko Ono] [GL] (12/18/71 CR-28)

HAPPY YEARS The Diamonds—Mercury 71330
[Brook Benton/Oscar Liese/Clyde Otis] [BMI] (8/4/58 B-73)

HARBOR LIGHTS *The Mulcays—Essex 400*
[Jimmy Kennedy/Hugh Williams] [NA] (9/12/55 R-78) [IWM]

HARBOR LIGHTS *Seymour & His Heartbeat Trumpet—Argo 5334*
[Jimmy Kennedy/Hugh Williams] [NA] (10/12/59 R-97)

HARBOR LIGHTS *The Platters—Mercury 71563*
[Jimmy Kennedy/Hugh Williams] [NA] (1/25/60 BCR-7)

A HARD DAY'S NIGHT *The Beatles—Capitol 5222*
[John Lennon/Paul McCartney] [ASC] (7/11/64 BCR-1)

A HARD DAY'S NIGHT *Ramsey Lewis Trio—Cadet 5525*
[John Lennon/Paul McCartney] [ASC] (1/15/66 BCR-29) [IWM]

A HARD DAY'S NIGHT *Stars On 45—Radio 3830*
[John Lennon/Paul McCartney] (Med) [ASC] (7/11/81 BC-63)

A HARD DAY'S NIGHT *The Beatles—Capitol 5107*
[John Lennon/Paul McCartney] (Med) [ASC] (3/27/82 BCR-12)

HARD HABIT TO BREAK Chicago—Warner/Full Moon 29214
[Steve Kipner/John Lewis Parker] [ASC] (8/4/84 BC-2)

HARD HEAD Louis Jordan—Tangerine 930 [Eddie Curtis] [ASC] (4/6/63 R-87)

HARD HEADED WOMAN Elvis Presley—RCA Victor 47-7280
[Claude DeMetrius] [ASC] (6/23/58 BCR-2)

HARD LOVIN' LOSER Judy Collins—Elektra 45610 [Richard Farina] [ASC] (1/21/67 B-97)

HARD LUCK WOMAN Kiss—Casablanca 873 [Paul Stanley] [ASC] (12/18/76 BCR-15)

HARD ROCK CAFE Carole King—Capitol 4455 [Carole King] [ASC] (7/23/77 BCR-25)

HARD TIMES Peter Skellern—Private Stock 45,054
[Peter Skellern] [ASC] (1/31/76 C-90)

HARD TIMES Boz Scaggs—Columbia 10606 [Boz Scaggs] [ASC] (10/15/77 BCR-58)

HARD TIMES James Taylor—Columbia 02093 [James Taylor] [ASC] (6/6/81 BCR-72)

HARD TIMES FOR LOVERS Judy Collins—Elektra 46020
[Hugh Prestwood] [BMI] (3/10/79 BCR-63)

HARD TIMES FOR LOVERS Jennifer Holliday—Geffen 28958
[Lotti Golden/Richard C. Scher] [ASC] (9/21/85 BC-69)

HARD TIMES (THE SLOP) Noble "Thin Man" Watts & His Rhythm Sparks—Baton 249
[Noble Watts] [BMI] (12/23/57 B-48) [I]

HARD TO GET Gisele MacKenzie—"X" 0137 [Jack Segal] [ASC] (6/4/55 BCR-2)

HARD TO HANDLE Otis Redding—Atco 6592
[Alvertis Isbell/Allen Alvoid Jones Jr./Otis Redding] [BMI] (7/13/68 BC-51)

HARD TO HANDLE Patti Drew—Capitol 2339
[Alvertis Isbell/Allen Alvoid Jones Jr./Otis Redding] [BMI] (11/16/68 BR-93)

HARD TO HANDLE The Black Crowes—Def American 19668
[Alvertis Isbell/Allen Alvoid Jones Jr./Otis Redding] [BMI] (10/27/90 BC-45)

HARD TO HANDLE The Black Crowes—Def American 19245
[Alvertis Isbell/Allen Alvoid Jones Jr./Otis Redding] [BMI] (6/22/91 BC-21)

HARD TO SAY Dan Fogelberg—Full Moon 02488 [Dan Fogelberg] [ASC] (8/29/81 BCR-7)

HARD TO SAY I'M SORRY Chicago—Full Moon 29979
[Peter Cetera/David Foster] [ASC] (6/5/82 BC-1)

HARD WORK John Handy—ABC/Impulse 31005 [John Handy] [BMI] (6/19/76 BCR-46) [I]

HARDEN MY HEART Quarterflash—Geffen 49824 [Marv Ross] [ASC] (10/17/81 BCR-3)

THE HARDER I TRY (THE BLUER I GET) The Free Movement—Columbia 45512
[Frank F. Robinson] [BMI] (12/11/71 BCR-43)

THE HARDEST PART Blondie—Chrysalis 2408
[Clement A. Bozewski*/Deborah Harry/Christopher Stein] [ASC] (1/26/80 BCR-72)

HARDHEARTED HANNAH Ray Charles Orchestra & Chorus—ABC-Paramount 10164
[Milton Ager*/Charles Bates/Bob Bigelow*/Jack Yellen] [ASC] (11/21/60 BCR-50)

HAREM DANCE Armenian Jazz Sextet—Kapp 181
[Hank Beducci/Arthur Melkonian] [BMI] (4/27/57 BCRt-28) [I]

HAREM DANCE Roger King Mozian—Decca 30330
[Hank Beducci/Arthur Melkonian] [BMI] (6/1/57 Rt-82) [I]

HARLAN COUNTY Jim Ford—Sundown 115 [Jim Ford] [BMI] (9/13/69 CR-82)

HARLEM The 5th Dimension—Bell 45,612 [Bill Withers] [BMI] (11/23/74 C-92)

HARLEM NOCTURNE The Viscounts—Madison 123
[Earle Hagen] [ASC] (12/7/59 BCR-28) [IM]

HARLEM NOCTURNE The Viscounts—Amy 940
[Earle Hagen] [ASC] (10/30/65 BCR-39) [IM]

HARLEM SHUFFLE Bob & Earl—Marc 104
[Earl Nelson/Bob Relf] [BMI] (12/21/63 BCR-36)

HARLEM SHUFFLE The Traits—Scepter 12169
[Earl Nelson/Bob Relf] [BMI] (11/12/66 BCR-88)

HARLEM SHUFFLE The Rolling Stones—Rolling Stones 38-05802
[Earl Nelson/Bob Relf] [BMI] (3/15/86 BC-5)

HARMONY Billy Bland—Old Town 1088 [Gene Pitney] [BMI] (10/10/60 B-91)

HARPER VALLEY P.T.A. Jeannie C. Riley—Plantation 3
[Tom T. Hall] [BMI] (8/24/68 BCR-1)

HARPER VALLEY P.T.A. Bobbi Martin—United Artists 50443
[Tom T. Hall] [BMI] (8/24/68 R-94)

HARPER VALLEY P.T.A. King Curtis & The Kingpins—Atco 6613
[Tom T. Hall] [BMI] (10/12/68 BR-93) [IWM]

CONTINUING STORY OF HARPER VALLEY P.T.A. (response to Harper Valley P.T.A.)
Dee Mullins—SSS Int'l 749
[Clark Bentley/Jerri Clark/Tom T. Hall] [BMI] (11/16/68 R-96) [R]

HARPER VALLEY P.T.A. (LATER THAT SAME DAY) (parody of Harper Valley P.T.A)
Ben Colder—MGM 13997
[Jack H. Clement*/Tom T. Hall/Sheb Wooley*] [BMI] (10/19/68 BCR-67) [P]

HARPO'S BLUES Phoebe Snow—Shelter 40400 [Phoebe Snow] [ASC] (5/24/75 C-81)

HARRY HIPPIE Bobby Womack & Peace—United Artists 50946
[Jim Ford] [BMI] (12/9/72 BCR-25)

—HARRY LIME THEME see: THIRD MAN THEME

HARRY THE HAIRY APE Ray Stevens—Mercury 72125
[Ray Stevens] [BMI] (6/15/63 BCR-17)

HARRY TRUMAN Chicago—Columbia 10092 [Robert Lamm] [ASC] (2/15/75 BCR-13)

HARVEST FOR THE WORLD The Isley Brothers—T-Neck 2261
[Ernie Isley/Marvin Isley/O'Kelly Isley/Ronald Isley/Rudolph Isley/Chris Jasper] [ASC] (8/21/76 BCR-63)

HARVEY'S GOT A GIRLFRIEND Royal Teens—ABC-Paramount 9945
[Tom Austin/Bill Dalton/Bob Gaudio/Larry Qualiano] [BMI] (8/11/58 B-78)

HAS ANYONE EVER WRITTEN ANYTHING FOR YOU Stevie Nicks—Modern 99532
[Stevie Nicks/Keith Olsen] [BMI] (5/17/86 BC-60)

HATS OFF TO LARRY Del Shannon—Big Top 3075 [Del Shannon] [BMI] (6/5/61 BCR-2)

HAUNTED GUITAR The Three Suns—RCA Victor 47-6574
[Guy Wood] [ASC] (6/29/56 R-58) [IM]

HAUNTED HOUSE Gene Simmons—Hi 2076 [Bob Geddins] [BMI] (7/4/64 BCR-11)

HAVE A DRINK ON ME Buddy Thomas—Todd 1063
[Peter Buchanan/Lonnie Donegan/Huddie Ledbetter/Alan Lomax‡/John Lomax‡] [BMI] (6/26/61 CR-74)

HAVE A GOOD TIME Sue Thompson—Hickory 1174
[Boudleaux Bryant/Felice Bryant] [BMI] (6/9/62 BCR-27)

HAVE A HEART Bonnie Raitt—Capitol 44501 [Bonnie Hayes] [ASC] (3/10/90 BC-45)

HAVE A LITTLE FAITH David Houston—Epic 10291
[Billy Sherrill/Glenn Sutton] [BMI] (3/9/68 BR-96)

HAVE FAITH Gene Allison—Vee-Jay 273
[Henry Stone/Sonny Thompson] [BMI] (5/5/58 B-73)

HAVE I STAYED AWAY TOO LONG Bobby Bare—RCA Victor 47-8358
[Frank Loesser] [ASC] (5/16/64 B-94)

HAVE I STAYED TOO LONG Sonny & Cher—Atco 6420
[Sonny Bono] [BMI] (6/4/66 BCR-49)

HAVE I THE RIGHT? The Honeycombs—Interphon 7707
[Alan Blaikley/Ken Howard] [ASC] (9/12/64 BCR-4)

HAVE I TOLD YOU LATELY THAT I LOVE YOU? Crazy Otto—Decca 29753B
[Scott Wiseman] (Med) [BMI] (2/3/56 R-91) [I]

HAVE I TOLD YOU LATELY THAT I LOVE YOU Ricky Nelson—Imperial 5463
[Scott Wiseman] [BMI] (9/30/57 BCR-21)

HAVE MERCY BABY The Bobbettes—Triple-X 106 [Billy Ward] [BMI] (10/10/60 BCR-66)

HAVE MERCY BABY James Brown And The Famous Flames—King 5968
[Billy Ward] [BMI] (12/26/64 B-92)

HAVE YOU EVER BEEN LONELY Jerry Cooper & The Johnny Guarnieri Quintet—Anchor 14
[Peter DeRose/Billy Hill] [ASC] (5/9/55 Rt-34)

HAVE YOU EVER BEEN LONELY (HAVE YOU EVER BEEN BLUE) Karen Chandler—Coral 61386
[Peter DeRose/Billy Hill] [ASC] (5/9/55 CRt-47)

HAVE YOU EVER BEEN LONELY (HAVE YOU EVER BEEN BLUE)
Jaye P. Morgan—Decca 29501
[Peter DeRose/Billy Hill] [ASC] (5/9/55 Rt-34)

HAVE YOU EVER BEEN LONELY (HAVE YOU EVER BEEN BLUE) Teresa Brewer—Coral 62236
[Peter DeRose/Billy Hill] [ASC] (11/28/60 BR-77)

HAVE YOU EVER BEEN LONELY (HAVE YOU EVER BEEN BLUE) The Caravelles—Smash 1869
[Peter DeRose/Billy Hill] [ASC] (2/8/64 BCR-75)

HAVE YOU EVER LOVED SOMEBODY The Searchers—Kapp 783
[Allan Clarke/Tony Hicks/Graham Nash] [BMI] (11/12/66 BCR-53)

HAVE YOU EVER LOVED SOMEBODY Freddie Jackson—Capitol 5661
[Barry Eastmond/Jolyon Skinner] [ASC] (2/7/87 BC-69)

HAVE YOU EVER SEEN THE RAIN Creedence Clearwater Revival—Fantasy 655
[John Fogerty] (TSW) [BMI] (1/30/71 BCR-3)

HAVE YOU HEARD The Duprees Featuring Joey Vann—Coed 585
[Lew Douglas/Frank LaVere/LeRoy W. Rodde] [ASC] (11/2/63 BCR-18)

HAVE YOU LOOKED INTO YOUR HEART Jerry Vale—Columbia 43181
[Billy Barberis/Teddy Randazzo/Bobby Weinstein] [BMI] (12/12/64 BCR-23)

HAVE YOU NEVER BEEN MELLOW Olivia Newton-John—MCA 40349
[John Farrar] [BMI] (1/25/75 BCR-1)

HAVE YOU SEEN HER The Chi-Lites—Brunswick 55462
[Barbara Acklin/Eugene Record] [BMI] (10/23/71 BCR-1)

HAVE YOU SEEN HER Band Of Gold—RCA 13866
[Barbara Acklin/Eugene Record] (Med) [BMI] (10/13/84 BC-64)

HAVE YOU SEEN HER M.C. Hammer—Capitol 44573
[Barbara Acklin/Stanley Burrell*/Eugene Record] [BMI] (6/30/90 BC-4)

HAVE YOU SEEN HER FACE The Byrds—Columbia 44157
[Chris Hillman] [BMI] (6/3/67 BCR-58)

HAVE YOU SEEN YOUR MOTHER, BABY, STANDING IN THE SHADOW?
The Rolling Stones—London 903
[Mick Jagger/Keith Richards] [BMI] (10/1/66 BCR-3)

HAVEN'T GOT TIME FOR THE PAIN Carly Simon—Elektra 45887
[Jacob Brackman/Carly Simon] [ASC] (5/4/74 BCR-7)

HAVEN'T STOPPED DANCING YET Gonzalez—Capitol 4674
[Gloria Jones] [ASC] (1/6/79 BCR-26)

HAVEN'T YOU HEARD Patrice Rushen—Elektra 46551
[Sheree Brown/Charles Mims/Patrice Rushen/Freddie Washington] [BMI] (1/26/80 BCR-42)

HAVIN' FUN Dion—Laurie 3081 [Doc Pomus/Mort Shuman] [BMI] (1/30/61 BCR-42)

HAVING A PARTY Sam Cooke—RCA Victor 47-8036 [Sam Cooke] [BMI] (5/26/62 BCR-16)

HAVING A PARTY The Ovations—MGM 14623
[Sam Cooke] (Med) [BMI] (10/13/73 BCR-56)

HAVING A PARTY Luther Vandross—Epic 03205
[Sam Cooke] (Med) [BMI] (10/30/82 BC-55)

HAWAII FIVE-O The Ventures—Liberty 56068 [Mort Stevens] [ASC] (3/8/69 BCR-4) [I]

HAWAII 5-O Jive Bunny & The Mastermixers—Music Factory/Atco 99122
[Mort Stevens] (Med) [ASC] (2/3/90 BC-67) [I]

HAWAII 5-O Jive Bunny & The Mastermixers—Music Factory/Atco 99122
[Mort Stevens] (Med) [ASC] (2/3/90 BC-67) [I]

HAWAII HONEYMOON The Waikikis—Kapp 52
[Michel Cassez/Gérard Gustin] [BMI] (3/27/65 BC-91) [I]

HAWAII TATTOO The Waikikis—Kapp 30 [Michael Thomas] [BMI] (11/21/64 BCtR-23) [I]

HAWAII TATTOO The Exotic Sounds Of Martin Denny—Liberty 55754
[Michael Thomas] [BMI] (11/28/64 Ct-34) [I]

HAWAIIAN WAR CHANT Billy Vaughn And His Orchestra—Dot 15900
[Prince Leleiohoku/Johnny Noble] [BMI] (2/21/59 BCR-51) [IM]

HAWAIIAN WEDDING SONG Andy Williams—Cadence 1358
[Al Hoffman/Charles King/Dick Manning] [ASC] (12/22/58 BCR-5)

HAWK-EYE Frankie Laine—Columbia 40558 [Boudleaux Bryant] [BMI] (9/5/55 BCRt-19)

HAWK-EYE Chuck Miller—Mercury 70697 [Boudleaux Bryant] [BMI] (9/5/55 Rt-19)

HAWK-EYE Bobby Lord—Columbia 21437 [Boudleaux Bryant] [BMI] (9/19/55 Rt-27)

A HAZY SHADE OF WINTER Simon & Garfunkel—Columbia 43873
[Paul Simon] [BMI] (11/5/66 BCR-13)

HAZY SHADE OF WINTER Bangles—Def Jam 07630 [Paul Simon] [BMI] (11/14/87 BC-2)

***HE** Al Hibbler—Decca 29660 [Richard Mullan/Jack Richards] [ASC] (8/29/55 BCtRt-4)*

***HE** The McGuire Sisters—Coral 61501 [Richard Mullan/Jack Richards] [ASC] (10/3/55 BCtRt-4)*

***HE** The Righteous Brothers—Verve 10406 [Richard Mullan/Jack Richards] [ASC] (6/4/66 BCR-15)*

HE Today's People—20th Century 2032 [Michele Michaele/Lana Sebastian/Paul Sebastian] [BMI] (8/25/73 BR-83)

HE AIN'T GIVE YOU NONE Freddie Scott—Shout 220 [Van Morrison] [BMI] (11/11/67 BCR-93)

***HE AIN'T HEAVY, HE'S MY BROTHER** Hollies—Epic 10532 [Bob Russell/Bobby Scott] [ASC] (12/20/69 BCR-7)*

***HE AIN'T HEAVY...HE'S MY BROTHER** Neil Diamond—Uni 55264 [Bob Russell/Bobby Scott] [ASC] (11/7/70 BCR-13)*

***HE AIN'T HEAVY...HE'S MY BROTHER** Olivia Newton-John—MCA 40495 [Bob Russell/Bobby Scott] (TSW) [ASC] (12/6/75 BCR-30)*

HE AIN'T NO ANGEL The Ad Libs—Blue Cat 114 [Jeff Barry/Ellie Greenwich] [BMI] (5/1/65 B-100)

HE CAN'T LOVE YOU Michael Stanley Band—EMI America 8063 [Kevin Raleigh] [ASC] (11/15/80 BCR-27)

HE CHA CHA'D IN Kay Starr—RCA Victor 47-7414 [Johnny Burke/Al Frisch] [ASC] (12/22/58 R-96)

HE COULD BE THE ONE Josie Cotton—Elektra 47481 [Bobby Paine/Larson Paine] [ASC] (8/21/82 BC-67)

—HE CRIED see: SHE CRIED

HE DID ME WRONG, BUT HE DID IT RIGHT Patti Dahlstrom—20th Century 2113 [Patti Dahlstrom/Al Staehely] [ASC] (10/12/74 C-100)

HE DID WITH ME Vicki Lawrence—Bell 45,362 [Harry Lloyd/Gloria Sklerov] [ASC] (6/9/73 BCR-45)

—HE DON'T LOVE YOU LIKE I LOVE YOU see: HE WILL BREAK...

HE DON'T REALLY LOVE YOU The Delfonics—Moon Shot 6703 [Thom Bell/William Hart/Stan Watson] [BMI] (5/4/68 BR-89)

HE GIVES ME LOVE (LA LA LA) Lesley Gore—Mercury 72819 [Ramon Arcusa/Manuel De La Calva/Michael Julien] [BMI] (6/29/68 CR-91)

HE GOT YOU Ronnie Milsap—RCA 13296 [Ralph Murphy/Bobby Wood] [ASC] (8/21/82 BC-59)

HE KNOWS (BY THE WAY I LIVE EACH DAY) Gisele MacKenzie—Vik 0249 [Hal Spina] [ASC] (2/9/57 R-63)

HE KNOWS I LOVE HIM TOO MUCH The Paris Sisters—Gregmark 10 [Gerry Goffin/Carole King] [BMI] (1/22/62 BCR-34)

HE LOVES ME ALL THE WAY Tammy Wynette—Epic 10612 [Billy Sherrill/Carmol Taylor/Norro Wilson] [BMI] (6/13/70 B-97)

HE MADE A WOMAN OUT OF ME Bobbie Gentry—Capitol 2788 [Fred Burch/Don Hill] [BMI] (4/11/70 BCR-69)

HE NEEDS ME Gloria Lynne—Everest 19409 [Arthur Hamilton] [ASC] (4/24/61 CR-72)

HE SAYS THE SAME THINGS TO ME Skeeter Davis—RCA Victor 47-8288 [Gary Geld/Peter Udell] [ASC] (1/11/64 BCR-31)

***HE THINKS I STILL CARE** Connie Francis—MGM 13096 [Steve Duffy*/Dickey Lee] [BMI] (10/6/62 BCR-51)*

***SHE THINKS I STILL CARE** Elvis Presley—RCA 10857 [Steve Duffy*/Dickey Lee] (TSW) [BMI] (12/25/76 BR-31)*

HE TOUCHED ME Barbra Streisand—Columbia 43403 [Ira Levin/Milton Schafer] [NA] (10/2/65 BCR-51)

HE WALKS LIKE A MAN Jody Miller—Capitol 5090 [Diane Hilderbrand] [BMI] (2/8/64 BR-66)

HE WANTS MY BODY Starpoint—Elektra 69489 [Preston Glass] [BMI] (3/14/87 B-89)

HE WAS REALLY SAYIN' SOMETHIN' The Velvelettes—V.I.P. 25013 [Eddie Holland/William Stevenson/Norman Whitfield] [BMI] (1/30/65 BCR-61)

***HE WILL BREAK YOUR HEART** Jerry Butler—Vee-Jay 354 [Jerry Butler/Calvin Carter/Curtis Mayfield] [BMI] (10/15/60 BCR-3)*

***HE WILL BREAK YOUR HEART** The Righteous Brothers—Verve 10406 [Jerry Butler/Calvin Carter/Curtis Mayfield] [BMI] (6/4/66 B-91)*

***HE DON'T LOVE YOU (LIKE I LOVE YOU)** Tony Orlando & Dawn—Elektra 45240 [Jerry Butler/Calvin Carter/Curtis Mayfield] [BMI] (3/8/75 BCR-1)*

***HE DON'T LOVE YOU** Jim Croce—Lifesong 45001 [Jerry Butler/Calvin Carter/Curtis Mayfield] (Med) [BMI] (1/3/76 BCR-56)*

HE WON'T ASK ME Cilla Black—Capitol 5258 [Bobby Willis] [BMI] (9/19/64 C-91)

HE WORE THE GREEN BERET Nancy Ames—Epic 10003 [Peggy Barsella/Frank Catana] [BMI] (3/19/66 B-89)

***HE CALLED ME BABY** Ella Washington—Sound Stage 7 2621 [Harlan Howard] [BMI] (1/18/69 BC-77)*

***HE CALLED ME BABY** Candi Staton—Fame 1476 [Harlan Howard] [BMI] (12/26/70 BCR-44)*

***SHE CALLED ME BABY** Charlie Rich—RCA Victor 10062 [Harlan Howard] [BMI] (9/28/74 BC-47)*

HEAD FIRST The Babys—Chrysalis 2323 [Tony Brock/Wally Stocker/John Waite] [BMI] (5/26/79 BC-71)

HEAD GAMES Foreigner—Atlantic 3633 [Lou Gramm/Michael Leslie Jones] [ASC] (11/10/79 BCR-12)

HEAD OVER HEELS Go-Go's—I.R.S. 9926 [Charlotte Caffey/Kathy Valentine] [ASC] (3/17/84 BC-10)

HEAD OVER HEELS Tears For Fears—Mercury 880899 [Roland Orzabal/Curt Smith] [BMI] (9/14/85 BC-3)

HEAD TO TOE Lisa Lisa And Cult Jam—Columbia 07008 [Curtis Bedeau/Gerard Charles/Hugh Clarke/Brian George/Lucien George/Paul George] [BMI] (4/11/87 BC-1)

HEADED FOR A FALL Firefall—Atlantic 3657 [Rick Roberts] [BMI] (4/12/80 BCR-34)

HEADED FOR A HEARTBREAK Winger—Atlantic 88922 [Kip Winger] [BMI] (6/3/89 BC-18)

HEADED FOR THE FUTURE Neil Diamond—Columbia 05889 [Neil Diamond/Tom Hensley/Alan Lindgren] [SE] (5/24/86 BC-46)

HEADLINE NEWS Edwin Starr—Ric-Tic 114 [Al Hamilton/Richard Morris/Edwin Starr] [BMI] (4/30/66 BCR-84)

HEADLINES Midnight Star—Solar 69547 [Reggie Calloway/Vincent Calloway/Melvin Gentry/Belinda Lipscomb/Bobby Lovelace/Bill Simmons] [BMI] (6/14/86 BC-69)

HEALING HANDS Elton John—MCA 53692 [Elton John/Bernie Taupin] [BMI] (8/26/89 BC-11)

(HEAR MY SONG) VIOLETTA Ray Adams And Orchestra—Laurie 3118 [Othmar Klose/Rudolf Lukesch/Harry Pepper/Giuseppe Verdi] [ASC] (4/30/62 R-89)

HEAR THE BELLS The Tokens—RCA Victor 47-8210 [Bob Gibson*/Sammy Lowe/Mitch Margo/Phil Margo/Hank Medress/Jay Siegel/Traditional] [BMI] (8/3/63 BCR-51)

HEAR THE WORDS, FEEL THE FEELING Margie Joseph—Cotillion 44201 [Lamont Dozier/McKinley Jackson] [BMI] (7/3/76 R-96)

HEARD IT IN A LOVE SONG The Marshall Tucker Band—Capricorn 0270 [Toy Caldwell] [BMI] (3/12/77 BCR-10)

HEARSAY The Soul Children—Stax 0119 [John Colbert/Norman West] [BMI] (3/18/72 BCR-22)

***HEART** Four Aces—Decca 29476 [Richard Adler/Jerry Ross] [ASC] (4/25/55 BCtRt-7)*

***HEART** Eddie Fisher—RCA Victor 47-6097 [Richard Adler/Jerry Ross] [ASC] (4/25/55 BCtRt-7)*

***HEART** Norman Brooks—"X" 0125 [Richard Adler/Jerry Ross] [ASC] (5/2/55 Rt-7)*

***HEART** Peggy Lee—Capitol 4349 [Richard Adler/Jerry Ross] [ASC] (3/28/60 CR-80)*

***HEART** Kenny Chandler—Laurie 3158 [Barry Mann/Cynthia Weil] [BMI] (3/30/63 BCtRt-45)*

***HEART! (I HEAR YOU BEATING)** Wayne Newton—Capitol 4920 [Barry Mann/Cynthia Weil] [BMI] (4/6/63 BCtRt-45)*

HEART Neneh Cherry—Virgin 99153 [Neneh Cherry/Cameron McVey] [BMI] (12/9/89 BC-54)

***HEART AND SOUL** Johnny Maddox—Dot 15488 [Hoagy Carmichael] [ASC] (9/22/56 BRt-57) [IM]*

***HEART AND SOUL** Tom & Dan—Unique 340 [Hoagy Carmichael] [ASC] (9/22/56 Rt-80) [IM]*

***HEART AND SOUL** The Cleftones—Gee 1064 [Hoagy Carmichael/Frank Loesser] [ASC] (5/8/61 BCtRt-16)*

***HEART AND SOUL** Jan & Dean—Challenge 9111 [Hoagy Carmichael/Frank Loesser] [ASC] (6/26/61 BCtRt-16)*

HEART AND SOUL Huey Lewis and the News—Chrysalis 42726 [Mike Chapman/Nicky Chinn] [ASC] (9/10/83 BC-8)

HEART AND SOUL T'Pau—Virgin 99466 [Carol Decker/Ron Rogers] [ASC] (5/2/87 BC-4)

HEART AND SOUL The Monkees—Rhino 74408 [Simon Byrne/Andy Howell] [ASC] (9/26/87 B-87)

HEART ATTACK Olivia Newton-John—MCA 52100 [Paul Steven Bliss/Steve Kipner] [ASC] (9/4/82 BC-2)

HEART BE STILL Lorraine Ellison—Loma 2074 [Bert Berns/Jerry Ragovoy] [BMI] (10/7/67 B-89)

HEART BREAKER Dean Christie—Select 715 [Dean Christie] [BMI] (11/3/62 BC-77)

HEART DON'T FAIL ME NOW Holly Knight—Columbia 07932 [Holly Knight] [ASC] (9/3/88 BC-59)

HEART DON'T LIE La Toya Jackson—Private I 4-04439 [Amir Bayyan/LaToya Jackson/Donna Johnson] [BMI] (5/5/84 BC-56)

HEART FULL OF SOUL The Yardbirds—Epic 9823 [Graham Gouldman] [BMI] (7/31/65 BCR-9)

HEART HIDEAWAY Cathy Carr—Fraternity 743 [Joe Raye] [BMI] (7/13/56 BCR-45)

HEART HOTELS Dan Fogelberg—Full Moon/Epic 50862 [Dan Fogelberg] [ASC] (3/22/80 BCR-20)

HEART IN HAND Brenda Lee—Decca 31407 [Jackie DeShannon/Sharon Sheeley] [BMI] (7/7/62 BCR-14)

A HEART IN NEW YORK Art Garfunkel—Columbia 02307 [Benny Gallagher/Graham Lyle] [BMI] (8/8/81 BCR-58)

THE HEART IS NOT SO SMART El DeBarge with DeBarge—Gordy 1822 [Diane Warren] [ASC] (12/7/85 BC-73)

HEART LIKE A WHEEL Steve Miller Band—Capitol 5068 [Steve Miller] [ASC] (10/31/81 BCR-24)

HEART LIKE A WHEEL The Human League—A&M/Virgin 1520 [John William Callis/Eugene Reynolds] [ASC] (9/22/90 BC-30)

HEART OF GLASS Blondie—Chrysalis 2295
[Clement A. Bozewski*/Deborah Harry/Christopher Stein] [ASC] (2/10/79 BCR-1)

HEART OF GOLD The Twins—Lancer 106 [Doc Pomus/Mort Shuman] [BMI] (1/9/60 C-89)

HEART OF GOLD Neil Young—Reprise 1065 [Neil Young] [ASC] (1/29/72 BCR-1)

HEART OF MINE Boz Scaggs—Columbia 07780
[Bobby Caldwell/Dennis Matkosky/Jason Scheff] [BMI] (4/30/88 BC-35)

HEART OF MY HEART Frank Fontaine—ABC-Paramount 10384
[Ben Ryan] [NA] (1/12/63 R-80)

THE HEART OF ROCK & ROLL Huey Lewis and the News—Chrysalis 42782
[Johnny Colla/Huey Lewis] [ASC] (4/21/84 BC-6)

HEART OF STONE The Rolling Stones—London 9725
[Mick Jagger/Keith Richards] [BMI] (1/9/65 BCR-15)

HEART OF STONE Cher—Geffen 19953 [Andy Hill/Peter Sinfield] [ASC] (2/10/90 BC-19)

HEART OF STONE Taylor Dayne—Arista 2057
[Carolyn Bowden/Gregg Tripp/Elliot Wolff] [BMI] (8/4/90 BC-10)

THE HEART OF THE MATTER Don Henley—Geffen 19898
[Mike Campbell/Don Henley/J.D. Souther] [ASC] (2/17/90 BC-18)

HEART OF THE NIGHT Poco—MCA 41023 [Paul Cotton] [ASC] (5/12/79 BCR-13)

HEART OF THE NIGHT Juice Newton—Capitol 5192
[John Bettis/Michael Clark] [ASC] (11/27/82 BC-22)

HEART ON MY SLEEVE *Gallagher and Lyle—A&M 1850*
[Benny Gallagher/Graham Lyle] [BMI] (8/21/76 BCR-67)

HEART ON MY SLEEVE *Bryan Ferry—Atlantic 3364*
[Benny Gallagher/Graham Lyle] [BMI] (12/11/76 B-86)

HEART TO HEART Errol Sober—Number 1 Record 215
[Barry Mann/Cynthia Weil] [BMI] (3/17/79 BCR-65)

HEART TO HEART Kenny Loggins—Columbia 03377
[David Foster/Kenny Loggins/Michael McDonald] [BMI] (11/27/82 BC-15)

HEART TURNS TO STONE Foreigner—Atlantic 89046
[Lou Gramm/Michael Leslie Jones] [ASC] (7/16/88 BC-54)

HEART WITHOUT A SWEETHEART Gale Storm—Dot 15492
[Tommie Connor/Frank Stanton] [ASC] (9/29/56 BCR-46)

HEARTACHE Pepsi & Shirlie—Polydor 885470
[Wayne Brown/Iris Fernando/Tambi Fernando] [ASC] (8/15/87 BC-78)

HEARTACHE ALL OVER THE WORLD Elton John—Geffen 28578
[Elton John/Bernie Taupin] [BMI] (10/18/86 BC-48)

HEARTACHE AWAY Don Johnson—Epic 06426 [Steve Cochran] [ASC] (11/22/86 BC-43)

HEARTACHE TONIGHT Eagles—Asylum 46545
[Glenn Frey/Don Henley/Bob Seger/J.D. Souther] [BMI] (10/6/79 BCR-1)

HEARTACHES *Somethin' Smith & The Redheads—Epic 9179*
[Al Hoffman/John Klenner] [ASC] (9/8/56 BRt-71)

HEARTACHES *Ted Weems And His Orchestra—Decca 25017*
[Al Hoffman] [ASC] (9/22/56 Rt-75) [IM]

HEARTACHES *Sam Sideburn—Carlton 478*
[Al Hoffman/John Klenner] [ASC] (9/22/58 R-99)

HEARTACHES *The Marcels—Colpix 612*
[Al Hoffman/John Klenner] [ASC] (10/9/61 BCR-7)

HEARTACHES *(parody of Heartaches) The Four Preps—Capitol 4716*
[Al Hoffman/John Klenner] (Med) [ASC] (3/17/62 BCR-61) [P]

HEARTACHES *Patsy Cline—Decca 31429*
[Al Hoffman/John Klenner] [ASC] (10/6/62 BCR-44)

HEARTACHES BTO—Mercury 74046 [C.F. Turner] [BMI] (2/24/79 BCR-57)

HEARTACHES BY THE NUMBER *Guy Mitchell—Columbia 41476*
[Harlan Howard] [BMI] (10/5/59 BCR-1)

HEARTACHES BY THE NUMBER *Johnny Tillotson—MGM 13376*
[Harlan Howard] [BMI] (8/21/65 BCRt-29)

HEARTACHES BY THE NUMBER *Pat Zill—Boone 1903*
[Harlan Howard] [BMI] (8/21/65 Rt-29)

HEARTBEAT Buddy Holly / The Crickets—Coral 62051
[Bob Montgomery/Norman Petty] [BMI] (11/17/58 BR-78)

HEARTBEAT *Taana Gardner—West End 1232 [Kenton Nix] [ASC] (5/30/81 R-68)*

HEARTBEAT *Seduction—Vendetta 1473 [Kenton Nix] [ASC] (2/24/90 BC-12)*

HEARTBEAT Don Johnson—Epic 06285 [Eric Kaz/Wendy Waldman] [ASC] (8/23/86 BC-4)

HEARTBEAT - IT'S A LOVEBEAT
The Defranco Family Featuring Tony Defranco—20th Century 2030
[William Hudspeth/Michael Kennedy] [ASC] (8/25/73 BCR-1)

HEARTBREAK AHEAD The Murmaids—Chattahoochee 636
[David Gates] [BMI] (2/29/64 R-96)

HEARTBREAK AVENUE Don Gibson—RCA Victor 47-7566 [Mel Foree] [BMI] (8/3/59 R-86)

HEARTBREAK BEAT Psychedelic Furs—Columbia 06420
[John Ashton/Richard Butler/Tim Butler] [BMI] (3/14/87 BC-26)

HEARTBREAK HARRY Alis Leslie—Era 1034
[Dede Fairbanks/Herbert Newman] [NA] (4/27/57 R-80)

HEARTBREAK HILL Fats Domino—ABC-Paramount 10596
[Fats Domino/Al Downing] [BMI] (10/31/64 B-99)

HEARTBREAK HOTEL *Elvis Presley—RCA Victor 47-6420*
[Mae Boren Axton/Thomas Durden/Elvis Presley] [BMI] (3/3/56 BCRt-1)

HEARTBREAK HOTEL *(parody of Heartbreak Hotel) Stan Freberg—Capitol 3480*
[Mae Boren Axton/Thomas Durden/Elvis Presley] [BMI] (7/13/56 BRt-19) [P]

HEARTBREAK HOTEL *Roger Miller—Smash 2066*
[Mae Boren Axton/Thomas Durden/Elvis Presley] [BMI] (10/29/66 BCR-84)

HEARTBREAK HOTEL *Frijid Pink—Parrot 352*
[Mae Boren Axton/Thomas Durden/Elvis Presley] [BMI] (12/5/70 BCR-50)

HEARTBREAK HOTEL The Jacksons—Epic 50959
[Michael Jackson] [BMI] (12/6/80 BCR-19)

HEARTBREAK (IT'S HURTIN' ME) *Little Willie John—King 5356*
[Carlee Hoyles/Jon Thomas] [BMI] (5/30/60 BCtRt-27)

HEARTBREAK (IT'S HURTIN' ME) *Jon Thomas And Orchestra—ABC-Paramount 10122*
[Carlee Hoyles/Jon Thomas] [BMI] (6/6/60 BCtRt-27)

THE HEARTBREAK KID Bo Donaldson And The Heywoods—ABC 12039
[Harvey Price/Dan Walsh] [ASC] (11/16/74 BCR-39)

HEARTBREAK ROAD Bill Withers—Sussex 629 [Bill Withers] [ASC] (12/28/74 B-89)

HEARTBREAK STATION Cinderella—Mercury 878 796 [Tom Keifer] [ASC] (3/16/91 BC-44)

HEARTBREAKER Grand Funk Railroad—Capitol 2732
[Mark Farner] [BMI] (2/7/70 BCR-72)

HEARTBREAKER Dolly Parton—RCA 11296
[Carole Bayer Sager/David Wolfert] [BMI] (8/19/78 BCR-37)

HEARTBREAKER Pat Benatar—Chrysalis 2395
[Geoff Gill/Cliff Wade] [BMI] (12/15/79 BCR-19)

HEARTBREAKER Dionne Warwick—Arista 1015
[Barry Gibb/Maurice Gibb/Robin Gibb] [BMI] (10/9/82 BC-10)

HEARTBROKEN BOPPER The Guess Who—RCA Victor 74-0659
[Burton Cummings/Kurt Winter] [BMI] (2/26/72 BCR-26)

HEARTLESS Tommy Leonetti—Capitol 3274
[Marian Banks/Ernesto Lecuona] [BMI] (12/10/55 B-99) [FDE]

HEARTLESS Heart—Mushroom 7031 [Ann Wilson/Nancy Wilson] [ASC] (4/8/78 BCR-18)

HEARTLIGHT Neil Diamond—Columbia 03219
[Burt Bacharach/Neil Diamond/Carole Bayer Sager] [ASC] (9/11/82 BC-5)

HEARTLINE Robin George—Bronze/Island 7-99658 [Robin George] [BMI] (4/13/85 B-92)

HEARTS Jackie Wilson—Brunswick 55225
[Riccardo Drigo*/Larry Stock] [ASC] (4/16/62 BCR-58)

HEARTS Marty Balin—EMI America 8084 [Jesse Barish] [BMI] (5/23/81 BCR-8)

HEARTS AWAY Night Ranger—Camel/MCA 53131 [Jack Blades] [BMI] (7/4/87 B-90)

HEART'S DESIRE Billy Joe Royal—Columbia 43622 [Joe South] [BMI] (5/21/66 BCR-88)

HEARTS DON'T THINK (THEY FEEL) Natural Selection—EastWest 98652
[Elliot Erickson/Frederick Thomas] [ASC] (11/30/91 BC-15)

HEARTS IN TROUBLE Chicago—DGC 19679
[Bill Champlin/Kevin Dukes/Dennis Matkosky] [ASC] (7/28/90 BC-57)

HEARTS OF STONE *The Charms—DeLuxe 6062*
[Rudy Jackson/Eddy Ray] [BMI] (11/22/54 BCtRt-1)

HEARTS OF STONE *The Fontane Sisters with Billy Vaughn's Orchestra—Dot 15265*
[Rudy Jackson/Eddy Ray] [BMI] (11/22/54 BCtRt-1)

HEARTS OF STONE *Vicki Young—Capitol 3008*
[Rudy Jackson/Eddy Ray] [BMI] (12/13/54 Rt-PRE)

HEARTS OF STONE *The McGuire Sisters—Coral 61335*
[Rudy Jackson/Eddy Ray] [BMI] (1/3/55 Rt-5)

HEARTS OF STONE *Bill Black's Combo—Hi 2028 [Eddy Ray] [BMI] (2/13/61 BCR-15) [IM]*

HEARTS OF STONE *The Blue Ridge Rangers—Fantasy 700*
[Rudy Jackson/Eddy Ray] [BMI] (3/31/73 BCR-30)

HEARTS ON FIRE Randy Meisner—Epic 50964
[Eric Kaz/Randy Meisner] [ASC] (1/24/81 BCR-15)

HEART'S ON FIRE John Cafferty—Scotti Brothers 05774
[Vince DiCola/Joe Esposito/Ed Frugé] [ASC] (2/22/86 BC-69)

HEARTS ON FIRE Bryan Adams—A&M 2948
[Bryan Adams/Jim Vallance] [BMI] (6/13/87 BC-26)

HEARTS ON FIRE Steve Winwood—Virgin 99234
[Jim Capaldi/Steve Winwood] [ASC] (3/18/89 BC-53)

THE HEAT IS ON Glenn Frey—MCA 52512
[Harold Faltermeyer/Keith Forsey] [ASC] (12/8/84 BC-2)

THE HEAT OF HEAT Patti Austin—Qwest 28788
[James Samuel Harris/Terry Lewis] [ASC] (5/3/86 BC-55)

HEAT OF THE MOMENT Asia—Geffen 50040
[Geoffrey Downes/John Wetton] [ASC] (4/17/82 BC-4)

HEAT OF THE MOMENT *After 7—Virgin 99204*
[Kenneth Edmonds/Antonio Reid] [BMI] (10/21/89 B-74)

HEAT OF THE MOMENT *After 7—Virgin 99204*
[Kenneth Edmonds/Antonio Reid] [BMI] (11/24/90 BC-15)

HEAT OF THE NIGHT Bryan Adams—A&M 2921
[Bryan Adams/Jim Vallance] [BMI] (3/28/87 BC-6)

HEAT WAVE *Martha & The Vandellas—Gordy 7022*
[Lamont Dozier/Brian Holland/Eddie Holland] [BMI] (7/27/63 BCR-3)

HEAT WAVE *Linda Ronstadt—Asylum 45282*
[Lamont Dozier/Brian Holland/Eddie Holland] (TSW) [BMI] (9/20/75 BCR-4)

HEATHER HONEY Tommy Roe—ABC 11211 [Tommy Roe] [BMI] (4/26/69 BCR-12)

HEAVEN The Rascals—Atlantic 2599
[Felix Cavaliere] [ASC] (2/8/69 BCR-14)

HEAVEN Bryan Adams—A&M 2729
[Bryan Adams/Jim Vallance] [BMI] (4/20/85 BC-1)

HEAVEN Warrant—Columbia 68985
[Joseph Cagle*/Steven Chamberlin*/Jerry Dixon*/John Oswald/Eric Turner*] [BMI] (7/22/89 BC-2)
HEAVEN AND HELL The Easybeats—United Artists 50187
[Harry Vanda/George Young] [ASC] (7/15/67 CR-92)
HEAVEN CAN BE ANYWHERE (TWIN PINES THEME) Charlie Daniels Band—Epic 50456
[Charlie Daniels] [BMI] (10/22/77 R-86)
HEAVEN HELP ME Deon Estus—Mika 871 538-7
[Deon Estus/George Michael] [ASC] (2/25/89 BC-4)
HEAVEN HELP US ALL Stevie Wonder—Tamla 54200
[Ronald Norman Miller] [BMI] (10/17/70 BCR-8)
HEAVEN IN THE BACK SEAT Eddie Money—Columbia 73976
[Craig Joiner/Mutt Lange] [ASC] (9/14/91 BC-52)
HEAVEN IN YOUR ARMS Dan Hartman—Blue Sky 70053
[Dan Hartman] [BMI] (4/11/81 B-86)
HEAVEN IN YOUR EYES Loverboy—Columbia 06178
[Paul Dean/John Dexter/Debra Mae Moore/Mike Reno] [BMI] (8/2/86 BC-10)
HEAVEN IS A 4 LETTER WORD Bad English—Epic 73307
[Jonathan Cain/Neal Schon/Mark Spiro/John Waite] [ASC] (4/7/90 BC-60)
HEAVEN IS A PLACE ON EARTH Belinda Carlisle—MCA 53181
[Rick Nowels/Ellen Shipley] [ASC] (9/26/87 BC-1)
HEAVEN KNOWS The Grass Roots—Dunhill 4217
[Harvey Price/Dan Walsh] [ASC] (11/1/69 BCR-12)
HEAVEN KNOWS Donna Summer With Brooklyn Dreams—Casablanca 959
[Pete Bellotte/Greg Mathieson/Giorgio Moroder/Donna Summer] [ASC] (1/13/79 BCR-4)
HEAVEN KNOWS When In Rome—Virgin 99253
[Clive Farrington/Mike Floreale/Andrew Mann] [BMI] (1/28/89 BC-66)
HEAVEN MUST BE MISSING AN ANGEL (PART 1) Tavares—Capitol 4270
[Freddie Perren/Keni St. Lewis] [ASC] (6/5/76 BCR-10)
HEAVEN (MUST BE THERE) Eurogliders—Columbia 64626
[Bernie Lynch] [ASC] (11/10/84 BC-59)
HEAVEN MUST HAVE SENT YOU *The Elgins—V.I.P. 25037*
[Lamont Dozier/Brian Holland/Eddie Holland] [BMI] (10/22/66 BCR-47)
HEAVEN MUST HAVE SENT YOU *Bonnie Pointer—Motown 1459*
[Lamont Dozier/Brian Holland/Eddie Holland] [BMI] (6/16/79 BCR-10)
HEAVEN ON EARTH The Platters—Mercury 70893 [Buck Ram] [ASC] (7/6/56 BR-39)
HEAVEN ON EARTH (SO FINE) The Spinners—Atlantic 3425
[Casey James] [BMI] (10/8/77 B-89)
HEAVEN ON THE 7TH FLOOR *Paul Nicholas—RSO 878*
[Dominic Bugatti/Frank Musker] [BMI] (8/13/77 BCR-5)
HEAVEN ON THE SEVENTH FLOOR *The Mighty Pope—Private Stock 45,157*
[Dominic Bugatti/Frank Musker] [BMI] (8/13/77 C-83)
HEAVEN WAS NEVER LIKE THIS Eddie Fisher—RCA Victor 47-5830
[Mack David] [ASC] (8/28/54 CR-22)
HEAVENLY The Temptations—Gordy 7135 [Norman Whitfield] [BMI] (3/9/74 BCR-43)
HEAVENLY LOVER Teresa Brewer—Coral 62084
[Hal David/Carlo Alberto Rossi] [ASC] (2/23/59 BCR-34) [FDE]
HEAVEN'S JUST A SIN AWAY The Kendalls—Ovation 1103
[Jerry Gillespie] [BMI] (10/15/77 BCR-47)
HEAVEN'S ON FIRE KISS—Mercury 880205
[Desmond Child/Paul Stanley] [ASC] (10/13/84 BC-49)
HEAVY FALLIN' OUT The Stylistics—Avco 4647
[Luigi Creatore/Hugo Peretti/George David Weiss] [ASC] (10/19/74 BCR-31)
HEAVY LOVE David Ruffin—Motown 1388
[Joe Cobb/Van McCoy] [BMI] (3/20/76 BCR-47)
HEAVY MAKES YOU HAPPY (SHA-NA-BOOM BOOM) *The Staple Singers—Stax 0083*
[Jeff Barry/Bobby Bloom] [BMI] (2/6/71 BCR-24)
SHA LA BOOM BOOM *Bobby Bloom—MGM 14437*
[Jeff Barry/Bobby Bloom] [BMI] (2/3/73 C-100)
HEAVY METAL (TAKIN' A RIDE) Don Felder—Full Moon 47175
[Don Felder] [ASC] (7/25/81 BCR-42)
HEAVY MUSIC (PART 1) Bob Seger & The Last Heard—Cameo 494
[Bob Seger] [ASC] (9/9/67 CR-70)
HE'D RATHER HAVE THE RAIN Heaven Bound With Tony Scotti—MGM 14284
[Terry Cashman/Tommy West] [ASC] (8/21/71 BCR-80)
HEEBY JEEBIES Little Richard—Specialty 584
[Maybelle Jackson/John Marascalco] [BMI] (10/20/56 CR-50)
HEED THE CALL Kenny Rogers And The First Edition—Reprise 0953
[Kin Vassy] [ASC] (10/10/70 BCR-20)
HEIGH-HO The Fifth Estate—Jubilee 5595
[Frank Churchill/Larry Morey] [ASC] (10/21/67 C-91)
HEIGHDY-HO PRINCESS The Neon Philharmonic—Warner Bros. 7380
[Tupper Saussy] [BMI] (5/30/70 B-94)
HEIGHTY HI Lee Michaels—A&M 1095 [Lee Eugene Michaels] [ASC] (9/20/69 CR-90)
HELD FOR QUESTIONING Rusty Draper—Mercury 70818
[Bernie Baum/Florence Kaye] [BMI] (3/30/56 BCR-42)
HELEN WHEELS Paul McCartney & Wings—Apple 1869
[Linda McCartney/Paul McCartney] [ASC] (11/17/73 BCR-4)
HE'LL BE BACK The Players—Minit 32001
[Colis Gordon/John September Thomas] [BMI] (9/10/66 C-100)
HELL CAT Bellamy Brothers—Warner/Curb 8220 [David Bellamy] [ASC] (7/10/76 BC-70)
HE'LL HAVE TO GO *Jim Reeves—RCA Victor 47-7643*
[Audrey Allison/Joe Allison] [BMI] (12/21/59 BCR-1)
HE'LL HAVE TO STAY *(response to He'll Have To Go) Jeanne Black—Capitol 4368*
[Audrey Allison/Joe Allison/Charles Grean] [BMI] (4/18/60 BCRt-2) [R]
HE'LL HAVE TO STAY *(response to He'll Have To Go)*
Corina Minette—ABC-Paramount 10097
[Audrey Allison/Joe Allison/Charles Grean] [BMI] (4/18/60 Rt-4) [R]
HE'LL HAVE TO GO *(parody of He'll Have To Go) Homer & Jethro—*
RCA Victor 47-7744 [Audrey Allison/Joe Allison/Kenneth Burns/Henry Haynes*] [BMI] (6/20/60 R-88) [P]*
HE'LL HAVE TO GO *Solomon Burke—Atlantic 2218*
[Audrey Allison/Joe Allison] [BMI] (2/8/64 BCR-51)
—HE'LL HAVE TO STAY see: HE'LL HAVE TO GO
HE'LL NEVER LOVE YOU (LIKE I DO) Freddie Jackson—Capitol 5535
[Keith Diamond/Barry Eastmond] [BMI] (12/14/85 BC-25)
HELL ON WHEELS Cher—Casablanca 2208
[Michele Aller/Bob Esty] [BMI] (9/15/79 BCR-59)
HE'LL UNDERSTAND (AND SAY "WELL DONE") Pat Boone—Dot DEP-1056
[Lucie Campbell] (EP) [BMI] (5/11/57 R-60)
HELLO Lionel Richie—Motown 1722 [Lionel Richie] [ASC] (2/25/84 BC-1)
HELLO AGAIN Neil Diamond—Capitol 4960
[Neil Diamond/Alan Lindgren] [SE] (1/31/81 BCR-6)
HELLO AGAIN The Cars—Elektra 69681 [Ric Ocasek] [ASC] (10/27/84 BC-19)
HELLO DARLIN' Conway Twitty—Decca 32661 [Conway Twitty] [BMI] (6/27/70 BCR-60)
HELLO, DOLLY! *Louis Armstrong And The All-Stars—Kapp 573*
[Jerry Herman] [ASC] (2/15/64 BCtR-1)
HELLO, DOLLY! *Pete King Chorale and Orchestra—RCA Victor 47-8290*
[Jerry Herman] [ASC] (2/22/64 Ct-68)
HELLO, DOLLY! *Bobby Darin—Capitol 5359 [Jerry Herman] [ASC] (2/6/65 BR-79)*
HELLO ENEMY Johnny Tillotson—MGM 13445
[Salvatore D'Amico/Wilbur Meshel/Charlotte Parson] [BMI] (2/19/66 R-99)
HELLO FOOL Ralph Emery—Liberty 55352
[Jim Coleman/Willie Nelson] [BMI] (8/28/61 CR-84)
HELLO GOODBYE The Beatles—Capitol 2056
[John Lennon/Paul McCartney] [ASC] (12/2/67 BCR-1)
HELLO HEARTACHE, GOODBYE LOVE Little Peggy March—RCA Victor 47-8221
[Luigi Creatore/Hugo Peretti/George David Weiss] [ASC] (8/24/63 BCR-26)
HELLO HELLO *The Sopwith "Camel"—Kama Sutra 217*
[Peter Kraemer/Terry MacNeil] [BMI] (12/10/66 BCR-25)
HELLO, HELLO *Claudine Longet—A&M 846*
[Peter Kraemer/Terry MacNeil] [BMI] (5/27/67 B-91)
HELLO, HELLO, HELLO New England—Infinity 50,021
[John Fannon] [ASC] (9/1/79 BCR-69)
HELLO HURRAY Alice Cooper—Warner Bros. 7673 [Rolf Kempf] [ASC] (2/3/73 BCR-25)
HELLO, I LOVE YOU The Doors—Elektra 45635
[John Densmore/Robby Krieger/Ray Manzarek/Jim Morrison] [ASC] (6/29/68 BCR-1)
HELLO IT'S ME *Nazz—SGC 001 [Todd Rundgren] [BMI] (1/18/69 BCR-47)*
HELLO IT'S ME *Nazz—SGC 001 [Todd Rundgren] [BMI] (1/24/70 CR-69)*
HELLO IT'S ME *Todd Rundgren—Bearsville 0009 [Todd Rundgren] [BMI] (9/29/73 BCR-2)*
HELLO JIM Paul Anka—RCA Victor 47-8195 [Paul Anka] [BMI] (6/22/63 BCR-65)
HELLO MARY LOU Ricky Nelson—Imperial 5741
[Cayet Mangiaracina*/Gene Pitney] [BMI] (4/22/61 BCR-9)
HELLO MUDDUH, HELLO FADDUH! (A LETTER FROM CAMP) *Allan Sherman—*
Warner Bros. 5378 [Louis F. Bush/Allan Sherman] [ASC] (7/27/63 BCR-1)
HELLO MUDDUH, HELLO FADDUH! (A LETTER FROM CAMP) (NEW 1964 VERSION) *Allan Sherman—Warner Bros. 5449 [Louis F. Bush/Allan Sherman] [ASC] (7/25/64 BCR-55)*
HELLO OLD FRIEND Eric Clapton—RSO 861 [Eric Clapton] [BMI] (10/16/76 BCR-24)
HELLO OUT THERE *Carl Belew—RCA Victor 47-8058*
[Wayne Walker/Kent Westberry] [BMI] (10/6/62 CtRt-85)
HELLO OUT THERE *Nick Noble—Liberty 55488*
[Wayne Walker/Kent Westberry] [BMI] (10/6/62 CtRt-85)
HELLO PRETTY GIRL Ronnie Dove—Diamond 176
[Tommy Boyce/Wes Farrell] [BMI] (1/9/65 BCR-50)
HELLO STRANGER *Barbara Lewis—Atlantic 2184 [Barbara Lewis] [BMI] (4/20/63 BCR-3)*
HELLO STRANGER *Fire And Rain—Mercury 73373 [Barbara Lewis] [BMI] (6/9/73 BR-95)*
HELLO STRANGER *Yvonne Elliman—RSO 871 [Barbara Lewis] [BMI] (3/19/77 BCR-14)*
HELLO THERE Gisele MacKenzie—Vik 0249
[Eugene Cines/Buddy Kaye] [ASC] (2/9/57 R-64)
HELLO WALL NO. 2 *(parody of Hello Wall) Ben Colder—MGM 13122*
[Willie Nelson/Sheb Wooley] [BMI] (3/9/63 CR-85) [P]
HELLO WALLS *Faron Young—Capitol 4533 [Willie Nelson] [BMI] (3/27/61 BCR-7)*
HELLO YOUNG LOVERS Paul Anka—ABC-Paramount 10132
[Oscar Hammerstein/Richard Rodgers] [ASC] (7/25/60 BCR-12)
HELP! The Beatles—Capitol 5476 [John Lennon/Paul McCartney] [ASC] (7/31/65 BCR-1)
HELP FOR MY WAITING The Dorians—Big Tree 110
[Floyd Jones/Guido Marasco*/John Unger] [BMI] (2/13/71 R-90)

HELP IS ON ITS WAY Little River Band—Harvest 4428
[Glenn Shorrock] [BMI] (7/30/77 BCR-14)

HELP ME Andy Williams—Columbia 42265
[Carole King/Cynthia Weil] [BMI] (3/5/62 R-85)

HELP ME Joni Mitchell—Asylum 11034 [Joni Mitchell] [ASC] (3/2/74 BCR-7)

HELP ME Elvis Presley—RCA Victor 0280 [Larry Gatlin] (TSW) [BMI] (6/1/74 R-87)

HELP ME! Marcy Levy & Robin Gibb—RSO 1047
[Robin Gibb/Blue Weaver] [BMI] (11/8/80 BCR-50)

HELP ME FIND A WAY (TO SAY I LOVE YOU)
Little Anthony And The Imperials—United Artists 50720
[Thom Bell/Linda Creed] [BMI] (11/21/70 BCR-65)

HELP ME (GET MYSELF BACK TOGETHER AGAIN) The Spellbinders—Columbia 43830
[Ralph Newman*/Ken Williams] [BMI] (11/19/66 BR-100)

HELP ME GIRL *The Outsiders—Capitol 5759*
[Scott English/Larry Weiss] [BMI] (10/29/66 BCR-31)

HELP ME GIRL *Eric Burdon And The Animals—MGM 13636*
[Scott English/Larry Weiss] [BMI] (11/26/66 BCR-29)

HELP ME MAKE IT THROUGH THE NIGHT *Sammi Smith—Mega 0015*
[Kris Kristofferson] [BMI] (1/16/71 BCR-7)

HELP ME MAKE IT THROUGH THE NIGHT *Joe Simon—Spring 113*
[Kris Kristofferson] [BMI] (4/17/71 BCR-54)

HELP ME MAKE IT THROUGH THE NIGHT *O.C. Smith—Columbia 45435*
[Kris Kristofferson] [BMI] (11/13/71 BR-83)

HELP ME MAKE IT THROUGH THE NIGHT *Gladys Knight & The Pips—Soul 35094*
[Kris Kristofferson] [BMI] (3/25/72 BCR-31)

HELP ME MAKE IT (TO MY ROCKIN' CHAIR) B.J. Thomas—ABC 12121
[Bobby Emmons] [BMI] (9/20/75 BCR-62)

HELP ME, RHONDA *The Beach Boys—Capitol 5395*
[Mike Love/Brian Wilson] [BMI] (4/17/65 BCR-1)*

HELP ME RHONDA *Johnny Rivers—Soul City/Epic 50121*
[Mike Love/Brian Wilson] [BMI] (7/5/75 BCR-22)*

HELP ME RHONDA *The Cantina Band—Millennium 11818*
[Mike Love/Brian Wilson] (Med) [BMI] (7/25/81 B-81)*

HELP ME RHONDA *The Beach Boys—Capitol 5030*
[Mike Love/Brian Wilson] (Med) [BMI] (7/25/81 BCR-5)*

HELP THE POOR *B.B. King—ABC-Paramount 10552*
[Charles Singleton] [BMI] (6/27/64 B-98)

HELP THE POOR *B.B. King—ABC 11302 [Charles Singleton] [BMI] (6/5/71 BCR-65) [IWM]*

HELP WANTED Hudson Brothers—Arista 0208 [Chris Bond] [BMI] (10/30/76 BCR-70)

HELP YOURSELF Tom Jones—Parrot 40029
[Carlo Donida/Jack Fishman] [ASC] (8/17/68 BCR-31) [FDE]

HELP YOURSELF The Undisputed Truth—Gordy 7134
[Norman Whitfield] [BMI] (4/27/74 BCR-63)

HELP YOURSELF (TO ALL OF MY LOVIN') James & Bobby Purify—Bell 735
[Mark Barkan/Scott English/Jerry J. Ross] [BMI] (8/31/68 BR-84)

HELPLESS The Platters—Mercury 71246 [Buck Ram] [ASC] (1/6/58 BCR-38)

HELPLESS Kim Weston—Gordy 7050
[Lamont Dozier/Brian Holland/Eddie Holland] [BMI] (3/12/66 BCR-53)

HELPLESS Jackie Wilson—Brunswick 55418
[Carl Davis/Eugene Record] [BMI] (9/13/69 C-93)

HENRIETTA Jimmy Dee And The Offbeats—Dot 15664
[Jimmy Dee Fore/Larry Hitzfeld] [BMI] (1/6/58 BCR-49)

HEP DEE HOOTIE (CUTIE WOOTIE) Tommy Sands—Capitol 3639
[Larry Coleman/Charles Singleton] [BMI] (3/16/57 R-84)

HER ROYAL MAJESTY James Darren—Colpix 622
[Gerry Goffin/Carole King] [BMI] (2/3/62 BCR-6)

HER TOWN TOO James Taylor And J.D. Souther—Columbia 60514
[J.D. Souther/James Taylor/Waddy Wachtel] [ASC] (3/14/81 BCR-8)

HERE Tony Martin—RCA Victor 47-5665
[Dorcas Cochran/Harold Grant] [ASC] (5/29/54 BC-PRE)

HERE AND NOW Luther Vandross—Epic 73029
[David Leland Elliott/Terry Steele] [ASC] (12/23/89 BC-6)

HERE COME DA JUDGE The Buena Vistas—Marquee 443
[Nick Ameno/Carl Cisco] [BMI] (6/1/68 BCR-82) [I]

HERE COME THE JUDGE The Magistrates—MGM 13946
[Mike Freda/Jerry Gross] [BMI] (6/1/68 BCR-45)

HERE COME THE TEARS Gene Chandler—Constellation 164
[Gerald Sims] [BMI] (10/2/65 R-95)

HERE COME THOSE TEARS AGAIN Jackson Browne—Asylum 45379
[Jackson Browne/Nancy Farnsworth] [ASC] (1/29/77 BCR-18)

HERE COMES HEAVEN Eddy Arnold—RCA Victor 47-9368
[Joy Byers Johnston/Bob Tubert] [ASC] (11/18/67 BCR-68)

HERE COMES MY BABY The Tremeloes—Epic 10139 [Cat Stevens] [BMI] (4/8/67 BCR-11)

HERE COMES MY GIRL Tom Petty And The Heartbreakers—Backstreet 41227
[Mike Campbell/Tom Petty] [ASC] (4/26/80 BCR-59)

HERE COMES SANTA CLAUS (RIGHT DOWN SANTA CLAUS LANE)
Elvis Presley—RCA Victor LOC-1035
[Gene Autry/Oakley Haldeman] (EP) [ASC] (12/30/57 R-49)

HERE COMES SUMMER *Jerry Keller—Kapp 277 [Jerry Keller] [ASC] (6/22/59 BCR-14)*

HERE COMES SUMMER *Wildfire—Casablanca 885 [Jerry Keller] [ASC] (6/18/77 BCR-43)*

HERE COMES THAT FEELIN' Brenda Lee—Decca 31379
[Dorsey Burnette/Joe Osborn] [BMI] (4/14/62 BCR-57)

HERE COMES THAT RAINY DAY FEELING AGAIN The Fortunes—Capitol 3086
[Roger Cook/Roger Greenaway/Tony Macaulay] [ASC] (5/15/71 BCR-8)

HERE COMES THE BOY Tracey Dey—Amy 894
[Eddie Rambeau/Bud Rehak] [BMI] (12/28/63 BCR-84)

HERE COMES THE HAMMER M.C. Hammer—Capitol 44572
[Stanley Burrell] [BMI] (12/22/90 BC-54)

HERE COMES THE JUDGE Shorty Long—Soul 35044
[Billie Jean Brown/Suzanne DePasse/Frederick Long] [BMI] (6/1/68 BCR-8)

HERE COMES THE JUDGE Pigmeat Markham—Chess 2049
[Dick Alen/Robert Dade/Sarah Harvey/Pigmeat Markham] [BMI] (6/15/68 BCR-19)

HERE COMES THE NIGHT Ben E. King—Atco 6207
[Doc Pomus/Mort Shuman] [BMI] (10/9/61 B-81)

HERE COMES THE NIGHT Them—Parrot 9749 [Bert Berns] [BMI] (5/15/65 BCR-18)

HERE COMES THE NIGHT Nick Gilder—Chrysalis 2264
[Nick Gilder/James McCulloch] [BMI] (10/28/78 BCR-39)

HERE COMES THE NIGHT The Beach Boys—Caribou 9026
[Mike Love/Brian Wilson] [BMI] (3/3/79 BCR-44)

HERE COMES THE RAIN AGAIN Eurythmics—RCA 13725
[Annie Lennox/David A. Stewart] [ASC] (1/28/84 BC-4)

HERE COMES THE RAIN, BABY Eddy Arnold—RCA Victor 47-9437
[Mickey Newbury] [BMI] (2/3/68 BCR-53)

HERE COMES THE SUN *Richie Havens—Stormy Forest 656*
[George Harrison] [ASC] (3/20/71 BCR-14)

HERE COMES THE SUN *Stars On 45—Radio 3830*
[George Harrison] (Med) [ASC] (7/11/81 BC-63)

HERE I AM Dionne Warwick—Scepter 12104
[Burt Bacharach/Hal David] [ASC] (6/26/65 BCR-65)

HERE I AM BABY The Marvelettes—Tamla 54166
[Smokey Robinson] [ASC] (5/25/68 BCR-39)

HERE I AM (COME AND TAKE ME) *Al Green—Hi 2247*
[Al Green/Mabon Hodges] [BMI] (6/30/73 BCR-10)

HERE I AM (COME AND TAKE ME) *UB40—Virgin 99141*
[Al Green/Mabon Hodges] [BMI] (3/23/91 BC-7)

HERE I AM (JUST WHEN I THOUGHT I WAS OVER YOU) Air Supply—Arista 0626
[Norman Sallitt] [BMI] (9/19/81 BCR-4)

HERE I GO AGAIN Smokey Robinson & The Miracles—Tamla 54183
[Al Cleveland/Terry Johnson/Warren Moore/Smokey Robinson] [ASC] (8/23/69 BC-37)

HERE I GO AGAIN Whitesnake—Geffen 28339
[David Coverdale/Bernie Marsden] [ASC] (7/4/87 BC-1)

HERE I GO (FALLIN' IN LOVE AGAIN) Frannie Golde—Portrait 70031
[Franne Golde/Albert Hammond] [BMI] (7/7/79 B-76)

HERE I STAND *Wade Flemons and the Newcomers—Vee-Jay 295*
[Wade Flemons] [BMI] (12/22/58 BC-58)

HERE I STAND *The Rip Chords—Columbia 42687*
[Wade Flemons] [BMI] (3/30/63 BCR-51)

HERE IN MY HEART Al Martino—Capitol 4593
[Bill Borrelli/Pat Genaro/Lou Levinson] [ASC] (7/24/61 BR-86)

HERE IS WHERE YOUR LOVE BELONGS Sons Of Champlin—Ariola America 7653
[Bill Champlin] [ASC] (1/29/77 BCR-69)

HERE IT COMES AGAIN The Fortunes—Press 9798
[Barry Mason/Les Reed] [ASC] (11/6/65 BCR-27)

HERE SHE COMES The Tymes—Parkway 924
[William E. Jackson III/Roy Straigis/Jimmy Wisner] [BMI] (11/7/64 BCR-88)

HERE SHE COMES Bonnie Tyler—Columbia 04548
[Pete Bellotte/Giorgio Moroder] [ASC] (8/11/84 BC-76)

HERE, THERE AND EVERYWHERE *The Fourmost—Capitol 5738*
[John Lennon/Paul McCartney] [ASC] (9/17/66 CR-90)

HERE, THERE AND EVERYWHERE *Emmylou Harris—Reprise 1346*
[John Lennon/Paul McCartney] [ASC] (3/13/76 BC-65)

(HERE THEY COME) FROM ALL OVER THE WORLD Jan & Dean—Liberty 55766
[Steve Barri/P.F. Sloan] [ASC] (2/27/65 BCR-50)

HERE TO LOVE YOU The Doobie Brothers—Warner Bros. 50001
[Michael McDonald] [ASC] (2/6/82 BCR-65)

HERE WE ARE Gloria Estefan—Epic 73084
[Gloria Estefan] [BMI] (12/16/89 BC-6)

HERE WE GO
C & C Music Factory (Featuring Freedom Williams And Zelma Davis)—Columbia 73690
[Robert Clivillés/Frederick B. Williams] [ASC] (3/2/91 BC-1)

HERE WE GO AGAIN *Ray Charles—ABC 10938*
[Donnie Lanier/Russell Steagall] [BMI] (5/6/67 BCR-13)

HERE WE GO AGAIN *Nancy Sinatra—Reprise 0821*
[Donnie Lanier/Russell Steagall] [BMI] (5/24/69 B-98)

HERE WITH ME REO Speedwagon—Epic 07901
[Rick Braun/Kevin Cronin] [BMI] (6/25/88 BC-20)

HERE YOU COME AGAIN Dolly Parton—RCA 11123
[Barry Mann/Cynthia Weil] [BMI] (10/8/77 BCR-3)

HERE'S A HEART The Diplomats—Arock 1004
[William Collier/Samuel Orvitt Culley/Ervan Waters] [BMI] (2/1/64 BR-81)

HERE'S MY CONFESSION Wyatt (Earp) McPherson—Savoy 1599
[Wyatt McPherson/Paul Hucklebuck Williams] [BMI] (5/15/61 B-97)

HERE'S SOME LOVE Tanya Tucker—MCA 40598
[Richard Mainegra/Jack Roberts] [BMI] (8/28/76 BR-82)

HERE'S TO YOU Hamilton Camp—Warner Bros.-Seven Arts 7165
[Hamilton Camp] [ASC] (4/13/68 BCR-74)

HERNANDO'S HIDEAWAY *Archie Bleyer—Cadence 1241*
[Richard Adler/Jerry Ross] [ASC] (5/29/54 BCR-2)

HERNANDO'S HIDEAWAY *Johnnie Ray—Columbia 40224*
[Richard Adler/Jerry Ross] [ASC] (6/12/54 BC-PRE)

HERNANDO'S HIDEAWAY *Guy Lombardo & His Royal Canadians—Decca 29173*
[Richard Adler/Jerry Ross] [ASC] (7/10/54 B-PRE)

HEROES Commodores—Motown 1495
[Darrell Jones/Lionel Richie] [ASC] (9/20/80 BCR-50)

HEROES AND VILLAINS The Beach Boys—Brother 1001
[Van Dyke Parks/Brian Wilson] [BMI] (8/5/67 BCR-8)

HE'S A BAD BOY Carole King—Dimension 1009
[Gerry Goffin/Carole King] [BMI] (4/27/63 BCR-93)

HE'S A FOOL Jackie Wilson—Brunswick 55246
[Alan Lorber/Alonzo Tucker/Jackie Wilson] [BMI] (7/6/63 R-98)

HE'S A FRIEND Eddie Kendricks—Tamla 54266
[Talmadge Conway/Allan Felder/Bruce Gray] [BMI] (2/14/76 BCR-36)

HE'S A GOOD GUY (YES HE IS) The Marvelettes—Tamla 54091
[Smokey Robinson] [ASC] (2/22/64 BCR-55)

HE'S A LIAR Bee Gees—RSO 1066
[Barry Gibb/Maurice Gibb/Robin Gibb] [BMI] (9/26/81 BCR-29)

HE'S A LOVER Mary Wells—20th Century 590
[Ronald Alonzo Miller/Lee Porter] [ASC] (6/12/65 BCR-71)

—HE'S A MOOCHER see: BROTHER-IN-LAW

HE'S A PRETENDER High Inergy—Gordy 1662
[Gary Goetzman/Mike Piccirillo] [BMI] (5/21/83 B-82)

HE'S A REBEL *The Crystals—Philles 106 [Gene Pitney] [BMI] (9/8/62 BCRt-1)*

HE'S A REBEL *Vikki Carr—Liberty 55493 [Gene Pitney] [BMI] (9/8/62 Rt-1)*

HE'S AN INDIAN COWBOY IN THE RODEO Buffy Sainte-Marie—Vanguard 35156
[Buffy Sainte-Marie] [ASC] (8/5/72 BR-96)

HE'S GONE The Chantels—End 1001
[Richard Barrett/George Goldner*/Arlene Smith] [BMI] (9/30/57 B-71)

—HE'S GONNA STEP ON YOU AGAIN see: STEP ON

HE'S GOT NO LOVE The Searchers—Kapp 686
[Chris Curtis/Mike Pender] [BMI] (7/31/65 BCR-79)

HE'S GOT THE POWER The Exciters—United Artists 572
[Ellie Greenwich/Tony Powers] [BMI] (2/23/63 BCR-57)

HE'S GOT THE WHOLE WORLD (IN HIS HANDS) *Laurie London—Capitol 3891*
[Traditional] [NA] (3/10/58 BCRt-1)

HE'S GOT THE WHOLE WORLD IN HIS HANDS *Barbara McNair—Coral 61972*
[Traditional] [NA] (3/17/58 Rt-1)

HE'S GOT THE WHOLE WORLD IN HIS HANDS *Mahalia Jackson—Columbia 41150*
[Traditional] [NA] (3/31/58 BRt-1)

HE'S GOT THE WHOLE WORLD (IN HIS HANDS) *Jo March—Kapp 215*
[Traditional] [NA] (4/7/58 Rt-1)

HE'S IN TOWN The Tokens—B.T. Puppy 502
[Gerry Goffin/Carole King] [BMI] (8/1/64 BCR-43)

HE'S MINE The Platters—Mercury 71032
[Buck Ram/Paul Robi/Zola Taylor] [BMI] (3/16/57 BCR-23)

HE'S MINE (I LOVE HIM, I LOVE HIM, I LOVE HIM) Alice Wonder Land—Bardell 774
[Steve Schlaks/Charles Weiss] [BMI] (8/24/63 BCR-58)

(HE'S MY) DREAMBOAT Connie Francis—MGM 13039
[John D. Loudermilk] [BMI] (9/11/61 BCR-14)

HE'S MY GIRL David Hallyday—Scotti Brothers 07299
[Cecelia Bullard/Kim Bullard/Richie Wise] [BMI] (8/22/87 BC-72)

HE'S MY GUY Irma Thomas—Imperial 66080 [Van McCoy] [BMI] (12/19/64 BCR-63)

HE'S NOT JUST A SOLDIER Little Richard—Mercury 71884
[Richard Penniman/William P. Pitt] [BMI] (11/13/61 CR-91)

(HE'S) RAINING IN MY SUNSHINE Jay & The Americans—United Artists 50094
[Gene Allan/Ron Dante] [BMI] (11/19/66 BCR-61)

HE'S READY *The Poppies—Epic 10019*
[Billy Sherrill/Glenn Sutton] [BMI] (5/28/66 CR-94)

SHE'S READY *The Spiral Starecase—Columbia 45048*
[Billy Sherrill/Glenn Sutton] [BMI] (12/13/69 BCR-68)

HE'S SO FINE *The Chiffons—Laurie 3152 [Ronnie Mack] [BMI] (2/23/63 BCR-1)*

HE'S SO FINE *Jody Miller—Epic 10734 [Ronnie Mack] [BMI] (6/26/71 BCR-46)*

HE'S SO FINE *Jane Olivor—Columbia 10724 [Ronnie Mack] [BMI] (5/20/78 BCR-67)*

HE'S SO FINE *Kristy And Jimmy McNichol—RCA 11271*
[Ronnie Mack] [BMI] (7/22/78 BCR-70)

HE'S SO HEAVENLY Brenda Lee—Decca 31478
[Jackie DeShannon/Sharon Sheeley] [BMI] (4/13/63 BR-66)

HE'S SO SHY Pointer Sisters—Planet 47916
[Tom Snow/Cynthia Weil] [BMI] (7/19/80 BCR-3)

HE'S SURE THE BOY I LOVE The Crystals—Philles 109
[Barry Mann/Cynthia Weil] [BMI] (12/29/62 BCR-11)

(HE'S) THE GREAT IMPOSTER The Fleetwoods—Dolton 45
[Jackie DeShannon/Sharon Sheeley] [BMI] (8/28/61 BCR-30)

HE'S THE GREATEST DANCER Sister Sledge—Cotillion 44245
[Bernard Edwards/Nile Rodgers] [BMI] (2/3/79 BCR-8)

HE'S THE ONE YOU LOVE Inez Foxx—Symbol 922
[Charlie Foxx/Inez Foxx] [BMI] (11/2/63 R-93)

HEY AMERICA James Brown And The Famous Flames—King 6339
[Addie Williams Jones/Nat Jones] [BMI] (12/19/70 R-68)

HEY! BABY *Bruce Channel—Smash 1731*
[Bruce Channel/Margaret Cobb] [BMI] (1/20/62 BCR-1)

HEY! BABY *Jose Feliciano—RCA Victor 47-9714*
[Bruce Channel/Margaret Cobb] (TSW) [BMI] (1/25/69 BCR-30)

HEY BABY *Ringo Starr—Atlantic 3371*
[Bruce Channel/Margaret Cobb] [BMI] (12/18/76 BCR-62)

HEY BABY Ted Nugent—Epic 50197 [Derek St. Holmes] [ASC] (3/27/76 BCR-72)

HEY BABY J.J. Cale—Shelter 62002 [J.J. Cale] [BMI] (12/25/76 B-96)

HEY BABY Henry Lee Summer—CBS Associated 68891
[Henry Lee Summer] [BMI] (5/20/89 BC-18)

HEY BABY (THEY'RE PLAYING OUR SONG) The Buckinghams—Columbia 44254
[Gary Beisbier/James Holvay] [BMI] (9/9/67 BCR-5)

HEY BIG BROTHER Rare Earth—Rare Earth 5038
[Dino Fekaris/Nick Zesses] [ASC] (11/20/71 BCR-19)

HEY, BOBBA NEEDLE Chubby Checker—Parkway 907
[Dave Appell/Kal Mann] [ASC] (3/14/64 BCR-18)

HEY BOY TAKE A CHANCE ON LOVE Ruby Andrews—Zodiac 1006
[Fred Bridges/Bobby Eaton/Richard Knight] [BMI] (12/30/67 BR-92)

HEY-DA-DA-DOW The Dolphins—Fraternity 937
[Carl Edmondson] [BMI] (12/12/64 BCR-69)

HEY DEANIE Shaun Cassidy—Warner/Curb 8488 [Eric Carmen] [BMI] (11/12/77 BCR-7)

HEY DONNA Rythm Syndicate—Impact 54208
[Evan Rogers/Carl Sturken] [BMI] (9/7/91 BC-11)

HEY, E.T. Dickie Goodman—Extran 601
[Dickie Goodman*/Susan Goodman] [BMI] (9/11/82 C-92)

HEY, GIRL *Freddie Scott—Colpix 692 [Gerry Goffin/Carole King] [BMI] (7/20/63 BCR-9)*

HEY GIRL *Bobby Vee—Liberty 56033*
[Gerry Goffin/Carole King] (Med) [BMI] (4/13/68 BCR-17)

HEY GIRL *The Lettermen—Capitol 2938 [Gerry Goffin/Carole King] [BMI] (11/14/70 R-88)*

HEY GIRL *Donny Osmond—MGM 14322*
[Gerry Goffin/Carole King] (TSW) [BMI] (11/27/71 BCR-9)

HEY GIRL DON'T BOTHER ME The Tams—ABC-Paramount 10573
[Ray Whitley] [BMI] (7/18/64 BCR-41)

HEY GIRL-HEY BOY Oscar McLollie and Jeannette Baker—Class 228
[Oscar McLollie/Leon René] [BMI] (8/4/58 B-61)

HEY GIRL (I LIKE YOUR STYLE) The Temptations—Gordy 7131
[Norman Whitfield] [BMI] (8/18/73 BCR-27)

HEY GRANDMA Moby Grape—Columbia 44174
[Jerry Miller/Don Stevenson] [BMI] (7/8/67 C-94)

HEY HARMONICA MAN Stevie Wonder—Tamla 54096
[Marty Cooper/Lou Josie] [BMI] (6/13/64 BCR-29)

HEY HEY BUNNY John Fred & His Playboy Band—Paula 294
[Andrew Bernard/John Fred] [BMI] (2/24/68 BCR-39)

—HEY HEY JOHNNY see: EMPTY GARDEN

—HEY HEY MY MY [INTO THE BLACK] see: RUST NEVER SLEEPS

HEY HEY WOMAN Joe Jeffrey—Wand 11213
[Johnny Christopher/Red West] [BMI] (12/6/69 R-82)

HEY JEALOUS LOVER Frank Sinatra—Capitol 3552
[Sammy Cahn/Kay Twomey/Bee Walker] [ASC] (10/20/56 BCR-5)

HEY JEAN, HEY DEAN Dean And Jean—Rust 5075
[Ernie Maresca/Lou Zerato] [BMI] (2/22/64 BCR-32)

HEY JOE *The Leaves—Mira 222 [Billy Roberts] [BMI] (5/21/66 BCR-31)*

HEY JOE *Cher—Imperial 66252 [Billy Roberts] [BMI] (8/26/67 BCR-94)*

HEY JOE *Wilson Pickett—Atlantic 2648 [Billy Roberts] [BMI] (7/5/69 BCR-39)*

HEY JOYCE Lou Courtney—Popside 4954
[Robert Bateman/Lou Courtney] [BMI] (1/6/68 R-97)

HEY JUDE *The Beatles—Apple 2276*
[John Lennon/Paul McCartney] (TSW) [ASC] (9/7/68 BCR-1)

HEY JUDE *Wilson Pickett—Atlantic 2591*
[John Lennon/Paul McCartney] [ASC] (12/21/68 BCR-17)

HEY LA BAS Fats Domino—Imperial IMP-147
[Dave Bartholomew] (EP) [BMI] (5/11/57 R-53)

HEY LADIES Beastie Boys—Capitol 44454
[Barbarella Bishop/Mike Diamond/Matt Dike/Ronald Ford/Adam Horovitz/
John King/Garrett Clinton Shider/Garry Marshall Shider/Mike Simpson/
Larry Troutman/Roger Troutman/Adam Yauch] [BMI] (8/5/89 BC-36)

HEY LAWDY MAMA Steppenwolf—Dunhill 4234
[Larry Byrom/Jerry Edmonton/John Kay] [BMI] (4/4/70 BCR-21)
HEY, LEROY, YOUR MAMA'S CALLIN' YOU Jimmy Castor—Smash 2069
[Jimmy Castor/Johnny Pruitt] [BMI] (12/24/66 BCR-28)
HEY, LET'S TWIST Joey Dee & The Starliters—Roulette 4408
[Joey Dee/Henry Glover/Morris Levy‡] [BMI] (2/5/62 BCR-20)
HEY LITTLE COBRA The Rip Chords—Columbia 42921
[Carol Connors/Marshall Connors] [BMI] (12/14/63 BCR-2)
HEY LITTLE GIRL Techniques—Roulette 4030 [Buddy Funk] [BMI] (11/18/57 BCR-33)
HEY LITTLE GIRL Gary Stites—Carlton 516 [Gary Stites] [BMI] (8/8/59 C-86)
HEY LITTLE GIRL *Dee Clark—Abner 1029*
[Otis Blackwell/Bobby Stevenson] [BMI] (8/22/59 BCR-20)
HEY, LITTLE GIRL *Foster Sylvers—MGM 14630*
[Otis Blackwell/Dorian Burton/Eugene Randolph/Bobby Stevenson] [BMI] (10/6/73 BCR-92)
HEY! LITTLE GIRL Del Shannon—Big Top 3091
[Del Shannon] [BMI] (11/25/61 BCR-38)
HEY LITTLE GIRL Major Lance—Okeh 7181 [Curtis Mayfield] [BMI] (10/19/63 BCR-13)
HEY LITTLE LUCY! (DON'TCHA PUT NO LIPSTICK ON) Conway Twitty—MGM 12785
[Aaron Schroeder/Sharon Silbert/George David Weiss] [ASC] (4/20/59 BCR-43)
HEY LITTLE ONE *Dorsey Burnette—Era 3019*
[Dorsey Burnette/Barry De Vorzon] [BMI] (6/6/60 BCR-40)
HEY LITTLE ONE *J. Frank Wilson And The Cavaliers—Josie 926*
[Dorsey Burnette/Barry De Vorzon] [BMI] (11/28/64 BR-74)
HEY LITTLE ONE *Glen Campbell—Capitol 2076*
[Dorsey Burnette/Barry De Vorzon] [BMI] (1/20/68 BCR-54)
HEY LONELY ONE Baby Washington—Sue 794
[Betty Jackson/Henry Murray] [BMI] (10/12/63 B-100)
HEY, LOOK ME OVER Pete King Chorale and Orchestra—Kapp 367
[Cy Coleman/Carolyn Leigh] [ASC] (3/27/61 R-91)
HEY LOVE Stevie Wonder—Tamla 54147
[Morris Broadnax/Clarence Paul/Stevie Wonder] [BMI] (4/22/67 BCR-77)
HEY! LOVE The Delfonics—Philly Groove 166
[Wilbert Hart] (TSW) [BMI] (6/19/71 BR-52)
HEY LOVER Debbie Dovale—Roulette 4521
[John Bobby Berry/Don Covay] [BMI] (11/2/63 BCR-75)
HEY MAMBO Barry Manilow with Kid Creole And The Coconuts—Arista 1-9666
[Jack Feldman/Thomas F. Kelly/Barry Manilow/Bruce Sussman] [BMI] (3/19/88 B-90)
HEY, MISTER SUN Bobby Sherman—Metromedia 188
[Danny Janssen] [BMI] (5/9/70 BCR-22)
HEY MR. BANJO *The Sunnysiders—Kapp 113*
[Norman Malkin/Freddy Morgan] [ASC] (4/11/55 BCRt-4)
HEY, MR. BANJO *Lawrence Welk & His Champagne Music—Coral 61408*
[Norman Malkin/Freddy Morgan] [ASC] (5/16/55 Rt-7)
HEY, MR. BANJO *Guy Lombardo & His Royal Canadians—Decca 29516*
[Norman Malkin/Freddy Morgan] [ASC] (5/16/55 Rt-4)
HEY, MR. BANJO *The Banjo Boys—Capitol 3103*
[Norman Malkin/Freddy Morgan] [ASC] (6/6/55 Rt-4)
HEY, MR. SAX MAN Boots Randolph—Monument 835
[Harold Bradley/Boots Randolph/Nicollet Tady] [BMI] (4/4/64 BCR-67)
HEY NAUGHTY PAPA Sarah Vaughan—Mercury 70693
[Albert Beach] [ASC] (9/12/55 R-80)
HEY NINETEEN Steely Dan—MCA 51036
[Walter Becker/Donald Fagen] [ASC] (11/29/80 BCR-10)
HEY NOW Lesley Gore—Mercury 72352 [Sonny Gordon] [BMI] (10/17/64 BCR-40)
—HEY-O see: OUT IN THE SUN
HEY PAULA Paul & Paula—Philips 40084 [Ray Hildebrand] [BMI] (12/29/62 BCR-1)
HEY SCHOOLGIRL Tom & Jerry—Big 613
[Art Garfunkel/Paul Simon] [BMI] (12/2/57 BCR-41)
HEY SHIRLEY (THIS IS SQUIRRELY) Shirley & Squirrely—GRT 054
[Jimmie Green/Danny Wolfe] [BMI] (6/26/76 BC-48)
HEY, ST. PETER Flash & The Pan—Epic 50715
[Harry Vanda/George Young] [ASC] (7/14/79 BCR-65)
HEY, STELLA! (WHO ZAT DOWN YOUR CELLAR?) The Crew-Cuts—RCA Victor 47-7320
[Ray Allen/George Brown*/Wandra Merrell*/Sam Saltzberg] [BMI] (8/25/58 CR-82)
HEY STOOPID Alice Cooper—Epic 73845
[Alice Cooper/Vic Pepe/Bob Pfeifer/Jack Ponti] [BMI] (7/27/91 BC-78)
HEY THERE *Rosemary Clooney—Columbia 40266*
[Richard Adler/Jerry Ross] [ASC] (7/3/54 BCtR-1)
HEY THERE *Sammy Davis Jr.—Decca 29199*
[Richard Adler/Jerry Ross] [ASC] (8/21/54 BCtR-1)
HEY THERE LITTLE FIREFLY PART I Firefly—A&M 1736
[Kenny Nolan] [BMI] (10/18/75 BCR-67)
HEY THERE LONELY BOY *Ruby And The Romantics—Kapp 544*
[Leon Carr/Earl Shuman] [ASC] (8/3/63 BCR-27)
HEY THERE LONELY GIRL *Eddie Holman—ABC 11240*
[Leon Carr/Earl Shuman] [ASC] (12/20/69 BCR-2)
HEY THERE LONELY GIRL *Robert John—EMI America 8049*
[Leon Carr/Earl Shuman] [ASC] (7/19/80 BCR-31)
HEY TONIGHT Creedence Clearwater Revival—Fantasy 655
[John Fogerty] (TSW) [BMI] (1/30/71 BR-3)
HEY, WESTERN UNION MAN Jerry Butler—Mercury 72850
[Jerry Butler/Kenneth Gamble/Leon Huff] [BMI] (8/31/68 BCR-16)
(HEY WON'T YOU PLAY) ANOTHER SOMEBODY DONE SOMEBODY WRONG SONG
B.J. Thomas—ABC-Paramount 12054
[Larry Lee Butler/Chips Moman] [BMI] (2/1/75 BCR-1)
HEY YOU Bachman-Turner Overdrive—Mercury 73683
[Randy Bachman] [ASC] (5/17/75 BCR-16)
HEY YOU! GET OFF MY MOUNTAIN The Dramatics—Volt 4090
[Tony Hester] [BMI] (4/21/73 BCR-43)
HEY YOU! LITTLE BOO-GA-LOO Chubby Checker—Parkway 989
[Len Barry/Leon Huff/John Madara/David White] [BMI] (6/25/66 BCR-53)
HEY, YOU LOVE Mouth & MacNeal—Philips 40717
[Hans Van Hemert/Harry Van Hoof] [ASC] (10/7/72 BCR-68)
HI-DE-HO Blood, Sweat & Tears—Columbia 45204
[Gerry Goffin/Carole King] [BMI] (8/1/70 BCR-8)
HI DIDDLE DIDDLE Inez Foxx—Symbol 924 [Charlie Foxx] [BMI] (12/7/63 B-98)
HI HI HAZEL Gary And The Hornets—Smash 2061
[Phil Coulter/William Wylie MacPherson Martin] [BMI] (11/19/66 BCR-92)
HI, HI, HI Wings—Apple 1857
[Linda McCartney/Paul McCartney] [ASC] (12/16/72 BCR-6)
—HI LEE HI LO HI LUP UP UP see: LEFT RIGHT OUT OF YOUR HEART
HI LILI HI LO *Dick Hyman Trio—MGM 12207*
[Bronislaw Kaper] [ASC] (4/21/56 BCtRt-41) [IM]
HI LILI HI LO *Roger Williams—Kapp 144*
[Bronislaw Kaper] [ASC] (5/5/56 BCtRt-41) [IM]
HI-LILI, HI-LO *Richard Chamberlain—MGM 13121*
[Helen Deutsch/Bronislaw Kaper] [ASC] (2/9/63 BCR-55)
HICKORY Frankie Valli And The 4 Seasons—Motown 1288
[Bob Crewe/Kenny Nolan] [BMI] (5/11/74 CR-90)
HICKORY, DICK AND DOC Bobby Vee—Liberty 55700
[Dewayne Blackwell] [BMI] (5/30/64 BCR-63)
HICKORY DICKERY DOCK Baby Jane And The Rock-A-Byes—Spokane 4001
[Jeff Barry/Ellie Greenwich] [BMI] (9/21/63 R-94)
HIDE & GO SEEK, PART 1 *Bunker Hill—Mala 451 [Bunker Hill] [BMI] (8/25/62 BCR-33)*
HIDE & SEEK *The Sheep—Boom 60,000 [Bunker Hill] [BMI] (1/29/66 BCR-53)*
HIDE AND SEEK Pajama Party—Atlantic 87973
[Jim Klein/Peggy Sendars] [ASC] (3/10/90 BC-67)
HIDE AWAY Freddy King—Federal 12401
[Freddy King/Sonny Thompson] [BMI] (3/4/61 BCR-29) [I]
HIDE 'NOR HAIR Ray Charles And His Orchestra—ABC-Paramount 10314
[Morty Craft*/Percy Mayfield] [BMI] (3/26/62 BCR-20)
HIDE YOUR HEART KISS—Mercury 876146
[Desmond Child/Holly Knight/Paul Stanley] [ASC] (11/25/89 BC-66)
HIDEAWAY The Four Esquires—Paris 520 [Bob Goodman] [ASC] (9/20/58 BCR-14)
HIDEAWAY John Sebastian—Reprise 1355 [John Sebastian] [BMI] (7/31/76 B-95)
HIGH Skyy—Salsoul 2113 [Randy Muller] [ASC] (4/26/80 R-93)
—HIGH AND THE MIGHTY see: THEME FROM...
HIGH ENERGY Evelyn Thomas—TSR 106 [Ian Levine/Fiachra Trench] [BMI] (9/29/84 B-85)
HIGH ENOUGH Damn Yankees—Warner Bros. 19595
[Jack Blades/Ted Nugent/Tommy Shaw] [BMI] (9/22/90 BC-2)
HI-HEEL SNEAKERS *Tommy Tucker—Checker 1067*
[Robert Higginbotham] [BMI] (2/8/64 BCR-10)
SLIP-IN MULES (NO HIGH HEEL SNEAKERS) *(Response to Hi-Heel Sneakers)*
Sugar Pie Desanto—Checker 1073
[Billy Davis/Robert Higginbotham] [BMI] (4/11/64 BCR-48) [R]
HIGH HEEL SNEAKERS *Jerry Lee Lewis—Smash 1930*
[Robert Higginbotham] [BMI] (11/21/64 B-91)
HIGH HEEL SNEAKERS *Stevie Wonder—Tamla 54119*
[Robert Higginbotham] [BMI] (8/28/65 BCR-54)
HI HEEL SNEAKERS - PT. 1 *Ramsey Lewis Trio—Cadet 5531*
[Robert Higginbotham] [BMI] (3/26/66 BCR-60) [IWM]
HIGH HEEL SNEAKERS *Elvis Presley—RCA Victor 47-9425*
[Robert Higginbotham] [BMI] (2/3/68 CR-69)
HI-HEEL SNEAKERS *Jose Feliciano—RCA Victor 47-9641*
[Robert Higginbotham] [BMI] (10/12/68 BCR-9)
HIGH HOPES Frank Sinatra "and a bunch of kids"—Capitol 4214
[Sammy Cahn/Jimmy Van Heusen] [ASC] (6/8/59 BCR-22)
HIGH ON A HILL Scott English—Spokane 4003
[Frank Cari/Anna Vito] [BMI] (2/15/64 BCR-77)
HIGH ON EMOTION Chris DeBurgh—A&M 2643 [Chris de Burgh] [BMI] (6/30/84 BC-44)
HIGH ON LOVE The Knickerbockers—Challenge 59332
[Keith Colley/Linda Jo Colley/Annette Tucker] [BMI] (7/2/66 BR-94)
HIGH ON LOVE Elliott Randall—Kirshner 4269 [Mitch Margo] [ASC] (4/23/77 C-91)
HIGH ON THE HILL OF HOPE Patti Page—Mercury 72078
[Leon Carr/Earl Shuman] [ASC] (1/12/63 R-87)
HIGH ON YOU Survivor—Scotti Brothers 04685
[Jim Peterik/Frankie Sullivan] [ASC] (1/26/85 BC-8)

HIGH ON YOUR LOVE Debbie Jacobs—MCA 41167 [Paul Sabu] [BMI] (3/15/80 B-70)
HIGH ON YOUR LOVE SUITE Rick James—Gordy 7164 [Rick James] [ASC] (3/31/79 BR-72)
HIGH OUT OF TIME Carole King—Ode 66123
[Gerry Goffin/Carole King] [BMI] (5/22/76 B-76)
HIGH SCHOOL CONFIDENTIAL Jerry Lee Lewis And His Pumping Piano—Sun 296
[Ron Hargrave/Jerry Lee Lewis] [BMI] (5/26/58 BCR-20)
HIGH SCHOOL DANCE The Sylvers—Capitol 4405
[Edmund Sylvers/James Sylvers/Leon Sylvers/Ricky Sylvers] [ASC] (4/16/77 BCR-11)
HIGH SCHOOL NIGHTS Dave Edmunds—Columbia 04762
[John David/Dave Edmunds/Steve Gould] [BMI] (4/20/85 B-91)
HIGH SCHOOL ROMANCE George Hamilton IV—ABC-Paramount 9838
[George Hamilton IV] [BMI] (8/5/57 BR-77)
HIGH SCHOOL USA Tommy Facenda—Atlantic 51-78
[Frank Guida/Joseph Royster] [BMI] (10/12/59 BCR-28)
HIGH SIGN The Diamonds—Mercury 71291
[Carl Stevens/George Stone] [BMI] (3/31/58 BCR-21)
HIGH TIDE BOOGIE Richard Maltby And His Orchestra—"X" 0135
[Harry Eldridge/Virginia Jirik] [BMI] (6/27/55 R-78) [IM]
HIGH TIME Styx—A&M 2568 [Dennis DeYoung] [ASC] (8/13/83 BC-48)
HIGH TIME WE WENT Joe Cocker—A&M 1258
[Joe Cocker/Chris Stainton] (TSW) [ASC] (6/12/71 BCR-19)
(YOUR LOVE KEEPS LIFTING ME) HIGHER AND HIGHER *Jackie Wilson—Brunswick 55336*
[Gary Jackson/Raynard Miner/Carl William Smith] [BMI] (8/5/67 BCR-6)
HIGHER AND HIGHER *Canada Goose—Tonsil 0002*
[Gary Jackson/Raynard Miner/Carl William Smith] [BMI] (6/6/70 R-92)
(YOUR LOVE HAS LIFTED ME) HIGHER AND HIGHER *Rita Coolidge—A&M 1922*
[Gary Jackson/Raynard Miner/Carl William Smith] [BMI] (5/7/77 BCR-1)
HIGHER GROUND Stevie Wonder—Tamla 54235 [Stevie Wonder] [ASC] (8/18/73 BCR-1)
HIGHER LOVE Steve Winwood—Island 28710
[Will Jennings/Steve Winwood] [BMI] (6/14/86 BC-1)
HIGHER PLANE Kool & The Gang—De-Lite 1562
[Robert Bell/Ronald Bell/George M. Brown/Robert Mickens/Claydes Smith/
Dennis Thomas/Richard Westfield] [BMI] (8/31/74 BCR-37)
HIGHER THAN HOPE Daryl Braithwaite—Epic Associated 73788
[Daryl Braithwaite/Simon Hussey] [ASC] (5/25/91 BC-44)
HIGHFLY John Miles—London 20084 [Bob Marshall/John Miles] [ASC] (2/7/76 BCR-58)
HIGHWAY SONG Blackfoot—Atco 7104
[Rick Medlocke/Jakson Spires] [BMI] (6/23/79 BCR-26)
HIGHWAY TO HELL AC/DC—Atlantic 3617
[Bon Scott/Angus Young/Malcolm Young] [ASC] (10/13/79 BCR-47)
HIGHWIRE The Rolling Stones—Rolling Stones 73742
[Mick Jagger/Keith Richards] [ASC] (3/9/91 BC-49)
HIJACK Herbie Mann—Atlantic 3246 [Fernando Arbex] [ASC] (2/8/75 BCR-14) [F]
HIJACKIN' LOVE Johnnie Taylor—Stax 0096
[Tony Hester/Richard Wylie] [BMI] (8/28/71 BCR-52)
HIKKY BURR - PART ONE Bill Cosby With The Bunions Bradford Band—Uni 55184
[Bill Cosby/Quincy Jones] [BMI] (12/20/69 CR-92)
HILL WHERE THE LORD HIDES Chuck Mangione—Mercury 73208
[Chuck Mangione] [BMI] (7/3/71 BCR-61) [I]
HIM Rupert Holmes—MCA 41173 [Rupert Holmes] [ASC] (1/19/80 BCR-6)
HIM OR ME - WHAT'S IT GONNA BE?
Paul Revere And The Raiders Featuring Mark Lindsay—Columbia 44094
[Mark Lindsay/Terry Melcher] [BMI] (4/29/67 BCR-5)
—HIMNO A LA ALEGRIA see: SONG OF JOY
HIP CITY - PT. 2 Jr. Walker & The All Stars—Soul 35048
[Janie Bradford/Jr. Walker] [BMI] (8/10/68 BCR-27)
HIP HUG-HER Booker T. & The M.G.'s—Stax 211
[Steve Cropper/Donald "Duck" Dunn/Al Jackson/Booker T. Jones Jr.] [BMI]
(3/25/67 BCR-36) [I]
HIP TO BE SQUARE Huey Lewis and the News—Chrysalis 43065
[Bill Gibson/Sean Hopper/Huey Lewis] [ASC] (10/18/86 BC-3)
HIPPIE FROM OLEMA The Youngbloods—Warner Bros. 7445
[Lowell Levenger] [ASC] (12/12/70 R-98)
HIPPY HIPPY SHAKE *The Swinging Blue Jeans—Imperial 66021*
[Chan Romero] [BMI] (3/7/64 BCR-20)
HIPPY HIPPY SHAKE *The Georgia Satellites—Elektra 69366*
[Chan Romero] [BMI] (10/22/88 BC-45)
HIPPYCHICK Soho—Atco 98908 [Tim Brinkhurst/Johnny Marr*] [ASC] (9/8/90 BC-14)
HIS HANDS *"Tennessee" Ernie Ford—Capitol 3135*
[Stuart Hamblen] [ASC] (5/23/55 Rt-33)
HIS HANDS *Mahalia Jackson—Columbia 40529 [Stuart Hamblen] [ASC] (6/27/55 Rt-38)*
HIS KISS Betty Harris—Jubilee 5465 [Bert Berns/Mike Stoller] [BMI] (1/4/64 BCR-74)
HIS NAME WAS DEAN *Nathan Russell—Forest 5603*
[Eddie Cohen/Murray Walberg] [ASC] (8/25/56 Rt-73)*
HIS NAME WAS DEAN *Jimmy Wakely—Coral 61706*
[Eddie Cohen/Murray Walberg] [ASC] (9/29/56 Rt-74)*
HIS SONG SHALL BE SUNG Lou Rawls—MGM 14349
[Sandy Baron/Bobby Hebb] [BMI] (2/19/72 C-93)

HISTORY REPEATS ITSELF *Buddy Starcher—Boone 1038*
[Buddy Starcher] [BMI] (3/26/66 BCR-26)
HISTORY REPEATS ITSELF *Cab Calloway—Boom 60,006*
[Buddy Starcher] [BMI] (4/2/66 BCR-82)
HIT AND RUN Bar-Kays—Mercury 76123
[James Edward Alexander/Charles Leonard Allen/Michael Beard/Mark Bynum/
Larry Dodson/Sherman Guy/Harvey Henderson/Allen Alvoid Jones Jr./
Lloyd Ed Smith/Winston Stewart/Frank Thompson] [BMI] (12/5/81 R-82)
HIT AND RUN AFFAIR Perry Como—RCA Victor 47-5749
[Ray Cormier/Don Genson/Don Roseland] [BMI] (7/3/54 BC-PRE)
HIT ME WITH YOUR BEST SHOT Pat Benatar—Chrysalis 2464
[Eddie Schwartz] [ASC] (10/4/80 BCR-5)
HIT RECORD Brook Benton—Mercury 71962 [Malcolm Dodds] [ASC] (4/23/62 BCR-35)
—HIT RECORD see: OVERNIGHT SENSATION
HIT THE ROAD JACK
Ray Charles And His Orchestra With The Raeletts—ABC-Paramount 10244
[Percy Mayfield] [BMI] (9/4/61 BCR-1)
HIT THE ROAD JACK *Stampeders—Quality 501 [Percy Mayfield] [BMI] (2/14/76 BCR-32)*
HITCH HIKE Marvin Gaye—Tamla 54075
[Marvin Gaye/Clarence Paul/William Stevenson] [ASC] (1/12/63 BCR-30)
HITCH IT TO THE HORSE The Fantastic Johnny C—Phil-L.A. Of Soul 315
[Jesse James] [BMI] (6/22/68 BCR-30)
HITCHCOCK RAILWAY Jose Feliciano—RCA Victor 47-9641
[Don Dunn/Tony McCashen] [ASC] (10/12/68 BR-77)
HITCHIN' A RIDE Vanity Fare—Page One 21,029
[Peter Callander/Mitch Murray] [BMI] (3/21/70 BCR-3)
HITHER AND THITHER AND YON Brook Benton—Mercury 71566
[Wally Gold/Aaron Schroeder] [ASC] (4/9/60 BCR-36)
HOBO FLATS - PART I Jimmy Smith—Verve 10283
[Oliver Nelson] [BMI] (5/11/63 BCR-69) [I]
HOCUS POCUS Patti Page—Mercury 70511
[Norman Gimbel/David Saxon] [ASC] (12/13/54 R-81)
HOCUS POCUS Focus—Sire 704 [Jan Akkerman/Thijs Van Leer] [ASC] (3/3/73 BCR-4) [I]
HOLD BACK THE NIGHT *The Trammps—Buddah 507*
[Ron Baker/Allan Felder/Norman Harris/Earl Young*] [BMI] (1/10/76 BCR-35)*
HOLD BACK THE NIGHT *Graham Parker And The Rumour—Mercury 74000*
[Ron Baker/Allan Felder/Norman Harris/Earl Young*] [BMI] (4/9/77 BC-58)*
HOLD BACK THE TEARS The Delacardos—United Artists 310
[Christopher C. Harris Jr.] [BMI] (6/5/61 BCR-78)
HOLD 'EM JOE Harry Belafonte—RCA Victor 47-5617
[Harry Belafonte] [ASC] (2/9/57 BCR-31)
HOLD HER TIGHT The Osmonds—MGM 14405
[Alan Osmond/Merrill Osmond/Wayne Osmond] [BMI] (6/24/72 BCR-10)
HOLD IT Bill Doggett—King 5149
[Billy Butler/Clifford Scott] [BMI] (9/29/58 BCR-92) [I]
HOLD ME *P.J. Proby—London 9688*
[Jack Little/David Oppenheim/Ira Schuster] [ASC] (8/29/64 BCR-70)
HOLD ME *The Baskerville Hounds—Avco Embassy 4504*
[Jack Little/David Oppenheim/Ira Schuster] [ASC] (9/13/69 BCR-68)
HOLD ME Fleetwood Mac—Warner Bros. 29966
[Christine McVie/Robbie Patton] [BMI] (6/19/82 BC-3)
HOLD ME Teddy Pendergrass—Asylum 69720
[Linda Creed/Michael Masser] [BMI] (6/9/84 BC-46)
HOLD ME Menudo—RCA 14087 [Howard Lee Rice/Allan Rich] [BMI] (5/11/85 BC-61)
HOLD ME Laura Branigan—Atlantic 89496
[Beth Andersen/Bill Bodine] [ASC] (10/19/85 BC-79)
HOLD ME Sheila E.—Paisley Park 7-28580
[Connie Guzman/Eddie Mininfield/Sheila E.] [BMI] (2/7/87 BC-68)
HOLD ME Colin James Hay—Columbia 06580 [Colin James Hay] [ASC] (3/7/87 B-99)
HOLD ME IN YOUR ARMS Doris Day—Columbia 40371
[Ray Heindorf/Charles E. Henderson/Donald Pippin] [ASC] (12/18/54 C-39)
HOLD ME NOW Thompson Twins—Arista 1-9164
[Tom Bailey/Alannah Currie/Joe Leeway] [ASC] (2/11/84 BC-3)
HOLD ME TENDERLY Bobby Bland—Duke 318 [Deadric Malone] [BMI] (4/16/60 C-95)
HOLD ME, THRILL ME, KISS ME Mel Carter—Imperial 66113
[Harry Noble] [ASC] (6/19/65 BCR-8)
HOLD ME TIGHT Johnny Nash—JAD 207 [Johnny Nash] [ASC] (9/7/68 BCR-4)
HOLD ME 'TIL THE MORNING COMES Paul Anka—Columbia 03897
[Paul Anka/David Foster] [BMI] (6/18/83 BC-38)
HOLD ME, TOUCH ME Paul Stanley—Casablanca 940
[Paul Stanley] [ASC] (11/4/78 BCR-41)
HOLD MY HAND *Don Cornell—Coral 61206*
[Jack Lawrence/Richard Myers] [ASC] (8/7/54 BCR-3)
HOLD MY HAND *Guy Lombardo & His Royal Canadians—Decca 29301*
[Jack Lawrence/Richard Myers] [ASC] (11/1/54 Rt-PRE)
HOLD ON The Radiants—Chess 2037
[Leonard Caston/Lloyd Webber] [BMI] (5/25/68 BR-68)
HOLD ON The Rascals—Atlantic 2695 [Felix Cavaliere] [ASC] (12/27/69 BCR-27)

HOLD ON Sons Of Champlin–Ariola America 7627
[Laurie Allen/Bill Champlin] [ASC] (6/19/76 BCR-47)
HOLD ON Wild Cherry–Epic/Sweet City 50401 [Robert Parissi] [ASC] (7/30/77 BCR-51)
HOLD ON Triumph–RCA 11569 [Rik Emmett] [ASC] (6/2/79 BCR-36)
HOLD ON Ian Gomm–Stiff/Epic 50747 [Ian Gomm] [NA] (9/1/79 BCR-18)
HOLD ON Kansas–Kirshner 4291 [Kerry Livgren] [BMI] (9/20/80 BCR-38)
HOLD ON Badfinger–Radio 3793 [Tom Evans/Joseph Tansini*] [ASC] (2/28/81 BCR-56)
HOLD ON Santana–Columbia 03160 [Ian Thomas] [ASC] (8/14/82 BC-9)
HOLD ON Donny Osmond–Capitol 44423
[Donny Osmond/Evan Rogers/Carl Sturken] [BMI] (9/30/89 BC-72)
HOLD ON Wilson Phillips–SBK 07322
[Glen Ballard/Chynna Phillips/Carnie Wilson] [ASC] (3/17/90 BC-1)
HOLD ON En Vogue–Atlantic 87984
[Terry Lynn Ellis/Denzil Foster/Cindy Herron/Maxine Jones/Thomas McElroy/
Dawn Robinson] [BMI] (5/5/90 BC-2)
HOLD ON, HOLD OUT Jackson Browne–Asylum 11477
[Jackson Browne/Craig Doerge] [ASC] (12/27/80 C-87)
HOLD ON! I'M A COMIN' *Sam & Dave–Stax 189*
[Isaac Hayes/David Porter] [BMI] (4/16/66 BCR-15)
HOLD ON I'M COMING *Chuck Jackson & Maxine Brown–Wand 1148*
[Isaac Hayes/David Porter] [BMI] (2/18/67 BCR-77)
HOLD ON LOOSELY .38 Special–A&M 2316
[Don Barnes/Jeff Carlisi/Jim Peterik] [ASC] (2/28/81 BCR-27)
HOLD ON TIGHT ELO–Jet 02408 [Jeff Lynne] [ASC] (7/25/81 BCR-8)
HOLD ON TO MY LOVE Jimmy Ruffin–RSO 1021
[Robin Gibb/Blue Weaver] [BMI] (3/1/80 BCR-10)
HOLD ON TO THE NIGHT Starz–Capitol 4566
[Jeffrey Warren Grob*/Richie Ranno/Michael Lee Smith/Pieter Sweval] [ASC]
(5/20/78 B-78)
HOLD ON TO THE NIGHT Hotel–MCA 41113
[Barry Mann/Marc Phillips] [BMI] (9/22/79 BC-77)
HOLD ON TO THE NIGHTS Richard Marx–EMI-Manhattan 50106
[Richard Marx] [ASC] (5/21/88 BC-1)
HOLD THE LINE Toto–Columbia 10830 [David Paich] [ASC] (10/7/78 BCR-5)
HOLD TIGHT Vicki Sue Robinson–RCA Victor 11028 [David Gates] [ASC] (8/6/77 B-67)
HOLD TIGHT Change–RFC/Atlantic 3832
[Mauro Malavasi/Davide Romani/Paul Slade] [ASC] (8/8/81 B-89)
HOLD WHAT YOU'VE GOT Joe Tex–Dial 4001 [Joe Tex] [BMI] (12/19/64 BCR-5)
HOLD YOU TIGHT Tara Kemp–Giant 19458
[Will Hammond Jr./Tuhin Roy/Jake Smith] [BMI] (1/19/91 BC-3)
HOLD YOUR HEAD UP Argent–Epic 10852 [Rod Argent/Chris White] [BMI]
(6/3/72 BCR-4)
HOLDIN' ON Tané Cain–RCA 13287 [Pug Baker/Jonathan Cain] [ASC] (8/14/82 BC-36)
HOLDIN' ON FOR DEAR LOVE Lobo–MCA/Curb 41152
[Larry Henley/Steve Pippin/Johnny Slate] [BMI] (12/22/79 BCR-75)
HOLDIN' ON TO YESTERDAY Ambrosia–20th Century 2207
[David Pack/Joe Puerta] [BMI] (6/14/75 BCR-17)
HOLDING BACK THE YEARS Simply Red–Elektra 69564
[Mick Hucknall/Neil Moss] [ASC] (4/5/86 BC-1)
HOLDING MY HEART Bang (2)–Vendetta 1504
[Billy Adams/Paul Calliris/Paul Voudouris] [BMI] (8/11/90 BC-76)
HOLDING ON Steve Winwood–Virgin 99261
[Will Jennings/Steve Winwood] [BMI] (11/26/88 BC-9)
HOLDING ON (WHEN LOVE IS GONE) L.T.D.–A&M 2057
[John McGhee/Jeffrey Osborne] [ASC] (7/29/78 BCR-31)
HOLDING OUT FOR A HERO Bonnie Tyler–Columbia 04370
[Dean Pitchford/Jim Steinman] [BMI] (2/25/84 BC-34)
HOLE HEARTED Extreme–A&M 1564
[Nuno Bettencourt/Gary Cherone] [ASC] (8/3/91 BC-4)
HOLE IN MY HEART (ALL THE WAY TO CHINA) Cyndi Lauper–Epic 07940
[Richard Orange] [BMI] (7/9/88 BC-51)
HOLE IN MY POCKET Barry Goldberg Reunion–Buddah 59
[Danny Whitten] [BMI] (9/21/68 CR-77)
HOLE IN THE WALL The Packers–Pure Soul 1107
[Steve Cropper/Al Jackson/Booker T. Jones Jr./Nathaniel Nathan] [BMI]
(11/13/65 BCR-29) [I]
HOLIDAY The Bee Gees–Atco 6521 [Barry Gibb/Robin Gibb] [BMI] (9/30/67 BCR-12)
HOLIDAY Nazareth–A&M 2219
[Pete Agnew/Jeff Baxter*/Manny Charlton/Alistair Cleminson/Dan McCafferty/
Darrell Sweet] [BMI] (3/8/80 BCR-74)
HOLIDAY Madonna–London-Sire 7-29478
[Curtis Hudson/Lisa Stevens] [BMI] (10/29/83 BC-12)
HOLIDAY Kool & The Gang–Mercury 888712
[Robert Bell/Ronald Bell/George M. Brown/Claydes Smith/J.T. Taylor/
Curtis Fitzgerald Williams] [BMI] (6/27/87 BC-65)
HOLIDAY The Other Ones–Virgin 99428
[Stephan Gottwald/Uwe Hoffmann/Alf Klimek/Jayney Klimek/Johnny Klimek/
Andreas Schwarz-Ruszczynski] [BMI] (8/1/87 BC-29)
HOLIDAY FOR CLOWNS Brian Hyland–Philips 40444
[Sonny Curtis/Glen Hardin] [BMI] (5/20/67 BCR-84)
HOLIDAY FOR TROMBONES David Rose and His Orchestra–MGM 12376
[David Rose] [ASC] (2/2/57 B-84) [I]
HOLIDAY ROAD Lindsey Buckingham–Warner Bros. 29570
[Lindsey Buckingham] [ASC] (8/6/83 B-82)
HOLLY GO SOFTLY Cornerstone–Liberty 56148
[Irwin Levine/Toni Wine] [BMI] (3/28/70 C-92)
HOLLY HOLY *Neil Diamond–Uni 55175 [Neil Diamond] [SE] (10/25/69 BCR-4)*
HOLLY HOLY *Jr. Walker & The All Stars–Soul 35081*
[Neil Diamond] [SE] (12/26/70 BCR-67)
HOLLYWOOD Connie Francis–MGM 13039 [John D. Loudermilk] [BMI] (9/18/61 BCR-20)
HOLLYWOOD Rufus Featuring Chaka Khan–ABC 12269
[André Fischer/David Wolinski] [ASC] (4/30/77 BCR-31)
HOLLYWOOD Boz Scaggs–Columbia 10679
[Michael Omartian/Boz Scaggs] [ASC] (2/4/78 BCR-49)
HOLLYWOOD Shooting Star–Epic/Virgin 02755
[Van McLain/Gary West] [BMI] (3/27/82 BCR-70)
HOLLYWOOD HOT The Eleventh Hour–20th Century 2215
[Cindy Bullens/Bob Crewe] [BMI] (8/30/75 BC-55)
HOLLYWOOD NIGHTS Bob Seger & The Silver Bullet Band–Capitol 4618
[Bob Seger] [ASC] (8/12/78 BCR-12)
HOLLYWOOD SWINGING Kool & The Gang–De-Lite 561
[Robert Bell/Ronald Bell/George M. Brown/Robert Mickens/Claydes Smith/
Dennis Thomas/Richard Westfield] [BMI] (4/13/74 BCR-6)
HOLY COW *Lee Dorsey–Amy 965 [Allen Toussaint] [BMI] (10/22/66 BCR-21)*
HOLY COW *Stefan–Stax 0145 [Allen Toussaint] [BMI] (10/21/72 C-96)*
HOLY MAN Scott McKenzie–Ode 107 [John Phillips] [ASC] (4/13/68 CR-95)
HOLY MAN Diane Kolby–Columbia 45169 [Diane Kolby] [NA] (9/19/70 BCR-61)
–HOLY MOSES see: BORDER SONG
HOLY WATER Bad Company–Atco 98944
[Brian Howe/Terry Thomas] [ASC] (7/14/90 B-89)
HOLYANNA Toto–Columbia 04752 [David Paich/Jeff Porcaro] [ASC] (2/2/85 BC-64)
HOMBURG Procol Harum–A&M 885 [Gary Brooker/Keith Reid] [BMI] (10/21/67 BCR-34)
HOME AND DRY Gerry Rafferty–United Artists 1266
[Gerry Rafferty] [BMI] (11/25/78 BCR-23)
HOME BOUND Ted Nugent–Epic 50493 [Ted Nugent] [ASC] (2/4/78 B-70) [I]
HOME COOKIN Jr. Walker & The All Stars–Soul 35055
[Henry Cosby/Melvin Moy/Eddie Willis] [ASC] (1/18/69 BCR-42)
HOME FROM THE HILL The Kingston Trio–Capitol 4338
[Mack David/Bronislaw Kaper] [ASC] (2/27/60 C-73)
HOME IS WHERE THE HATRED IS Esther Phillips–Kudu 904
[Gil Scott-Heron] [ASC] (4/1/72 C-86)
HOME IS WHERE THE HEART IS Elvis Presley with the Jordanaires–
RCA Victor EPA-4371 [Hal David/Sherman Edwards] (EP) [ASC] (9/8/62 CR-26)
HOME OF THE BLUES Johnny Cash–Sun 279
[Johnny Cash/Glenn Douglas/Lillie McAlpin] [BMI] (9/9/57 BR-77)
HOME OF THE BRAVE *Jody Miller–Capitol 5483*
[Barry Mann/Cynthia Weil] [BMI] (8/28/65 BCRt-25)
HOME OF THE BRAVE *Bonnie And The Treasures–Phi-Dan 5005*
[Barry Mann/Cynthia Weil] [BMI] (8/28/65 BCRt-32)
HOME SWEET HOME *Mötley Crüe–Elektra 69591*
[Tommy Lee/Nikki Sixx] [ASC] (10/26/85 BC-80)
HOME SWEET HOME '91 *Mötley Crüe–Elektra 64818*
[Tommy Lee/Nikki Sixx] [ASC] (11/2/91 BC-19)
HOME SWEET HOME ON THE RANGE Kay Starr–RCA Victor 47-6247
[Traditional] [NA] (9/5/55 R-37)
HOME TO YOU Earth Opera–Elektra 45650 [Peter Rowan] [BMI] (4/26/69 B-97)
HOME TONIGHT Aerosmith–Columbia 10407 [Steven Tyler] [BMI] (9/25/76 BC-71)
THE HOMECOMING Hagood Hardy–Capitol 4156
[Hagood Hardy] [BMI] (12/6/75 BCR-41) [I]
HOMELY GIRL The Chi-Lites–Brunswick 55505
[Stan McKenney/Eugene Record] [BMI] (2/2/74 BCR-53)
HOMEWARD BOUND Simon & Garfunkel–Columbia 43511
[Paul Simon] [BMI] (2/12/66 BCR-5)
HONEST I DO Jimmy Reed–Vee-Jay 253
[Ewart Abner/Jimmy Reed] [BMI] (9/30/57 BR-32)
HONEST I DO The Innocents–Indigo 105
[Al Candelaria/Darron Stankey/James West] [BMI] (8/8/60 BCR-28)
HONESTLY Kitty Kallen–Decca 29417
[Harold Adamson/Carlo Rossi] [BMI] (2/7/55 CR-31) [FET]
HONESTLY Stryper–Enigma 75009 [Michael Sweet] [BMI] (11/7/87 BC-23)
HONESTLY AND TRULY Tommy Edwards–MGM 12837 [Tommy Edwards] [ASC]
(10/19/59 BCR-56)
HONESTY Billy Joel–Columbia 10959 [Billy Joel] [ASC] (4/21/79 BCR-17)
HONEY *Bobby Goldsboro–United Artists 50283 [Bobby Russell] [ASC] (3/23/68 BCR-1)*
HONEY (I MISS YOU) *O.C. Smith–Columbia 44751*
[Bobby Russell] [ASC] (2/8/69 BCR-44)

HONEY BABE *Art Mooney And His Orchestra—MGM 11900*
[Max Steiner/Traditional/Paul Francis Webster] [ASC] (1/10/55 BCtRt-5)

HONEY BABE *The Sauter-Finegan Orchestra—RCA Victor 47-6025*
[Max Steiner/Traditional/Paul Francis Webster] [ASC] (4/9/55 CtRt-6)

HONEY BUNCH The Four Knights—Capitol 3024
[Rose Marie McCoy/Charles Singleton] [BMI] (1/31/55 R-84)

HONEY CHILD Bad Company—Swan Song 70109
[Raymond Burrell/Simon Kirke/Mick Ralphs/Paul Rodgers] [ASC] (7/10/76 BCR-59)

HONEY CHILE Fats Domino—Imperial 5407
[Dave Bartholomew/Fats Domino] [BMI] (9/29/56 R-47)

HONEY CHILE Martha Reeves & The Vandellas—Gordy 7067
[Richard Morris/Sylvia Moy] [BMI] (11/18/67 BCR-11)

HONEY COME BACK Glen Campbell—Capitol 2718
[Jimmy Webb] [ASC] (1/17/70 BCR-10)

HONEY DO The Strangeloves—Sire 4102
[Jeff Barry/Marty Sanders] [BMI] (12/14/68 CR-83)

HONEY DON'T The Beatles—Capitol R-5365
[Carl Perkins] (EP) [BMI] (2/13/65 BCR-67)

HONEY DON'T LEAVE L.A. James Taylor—Columbia 10689
[Danny Kortchmar] [ASC] (2/25/78 BCR-61)

HONEY HAIR SUGAR LIPS EYES OF BLUE The Crew-Cuts—Mercury 70840
[Dick Richards] [BMI] (4/20/56 R-76)

HONEY HONEY *Sweet Dreams—ABC 12008*
[Stig Anderson/Benny Andersson/Björn Ulvaeus] [BMI] (8/31/74 BCR-68)

HONEY, HONEY *Abba—Atlantic 3209*
[Stig Anderson/Benny Andersson/Björn Ulvaeus] [BMI] (9/14/74 BCR-27)

HONEY, HONEY David Hudson—Alston 3750
[Earl Kenneth King Jr.] [BMI] (6/28/80 BCR-59)

HONEY HUSH Joe Turner—Atlantic 2044 [Joe Turner] [BMI] (12/28/59 BCR-53)

HONEY I George McCrae—TK 1016
[Harry Wayne Casey/Rick Finch] [BMI] (1/10/76 BCR-65)

HONEY I STILL LOVE YOU The Mark IV—Mercury 73319
[Roy C. Hammond] [BMI] (9/30/72 CR-96)

HONEY I'M RICH Raydio—Arista 0353
[Thurlene Johnson/Ray Parker Jr.] [ASC] (9/2/78 R-84)

HONEY LOVE *Bunny Paul with The Harptones—Essex 364*
[Clyde McPhatter/Jerry Wexler] [BMI] (8/7/54 CtR-PRE)

HONEY LOVE *The Drifters Featuring Clyde McPhatter—Atlantic 1029*
[Clyde McPhatter/Jerry Wexler] [BMI] (9/11/54 CtR-21)

HONEY LOVE *Vicki Young—Capitol 2865*
[Clyde McPhatter/Jerry Wexler] [BMI] (10/4/54 R-PRE)

HONEY LOVE *The Four Lovers—RCA Victor 47-6519*
[Clyde McPhatter/Jerry Wexler] [BMI] (5/4/56 R-82)

HONEY LOVE *Narvel Felts—Pink 702 [Clyde McPhatter/Jerry Wexler] [BMI] (2/8/60 B-90)*

HONEY PLEASE, CAN'T YA SEE Barry White—20th Century 2077
[Barry White] [BMI] (2/16/74 BCR-23)

HONEY TRIPPIN' The Mystic Moods—Sound Bird 5002
[Don McGinnis/Bob Todd/Hal Winn] [ASC] (7/12/75 BC-84) [I]

HONEYCOMB *Jimmie Rodgers—Roulette 4015 [Bob Merrill] [ASC] (8/3/57 BCRt-1)*

HONEYCOMB *Georgie Shaw—Decca 30418 [Bob Merrill] [ASC] (8/26/57 Rt-7)*

THE HONEYTHIEF Hipsway—Columbia 06579
[Johnny McElhone/Ali McLeod/Grahame Skinner/Harry Travers] [BMI] (1/24/87 BC-19)

HONKY CAT Elton John—Uni 55343 [Elton John/Bernie Taupin] [BMI] (8/12/72 BCR-7)

HONKY TONK (PTS. 1 & 2) *Bill Doggett—King 4950*
[Billy Butler/Bill Doggett/Clifford Scott/Shep Shepherd] [BMI] (8/18/56 BCRt-2) [IM]

HONKY TONK (PT. 2) *Rusty Bryant & The Carolyn Club Band—Dot 15494*
[Billy Butler/Bill Doggett/Clifford Scott/Shep Shepherd] [BMI] (9/8/56 Rt-12) [IM]

HONKY TONK (PART 2) *Bill Doggett—King 5444*
[Billy Butler/Bill Doggett/Clifford Scott/Shep Shepherd] [BMI] (1/30/61 B-57) [IM]

HONKY TONK '65 *Lonnie Mack—Fraternity 951*
[Billy Butler/Bill Doggett/Clifford Scott/Shep Shepherd] [BMI] (10/23/65 BCR-78) [IM]

HONKY TONK - PART 1 *The James Brown Soul Train—Polydor 14129*
[Billy Butler/Bill Doggett/Clifford Scott/Shep Shepherd] [BMI] (6/17/72 BCR-38) [IM]

HONKY TONK GIRL Johnny Cash—Columbia 41707
[Chuck Harding/Hank Thompson] [BMI] (6/27/60 BR-75)

HONKY-TONK MAN Johnny Horton—Columbia 42302
[Tillman Franks/Howard Hausey/Johnny Horton] [BMI] (3/31/62 B-96)

HONKY TONK WOMEN The Rolling Stones—London 910
[Mick Jagger/Keith Richards] [BMI] (7/19/69 BCR-1)

HONKY TRAIN Bill Black's Combo—Hi 2038 [Bill Black] [BMI] (9/25/61 B-92) [I]

HONOLULU LULU Jan & Dean—Liberty 55613
[Lou Adler/Jan Berry/Roger Christian] [BMI] (9/7/63 BCR-9)

HONOLULU NITES Arthur Lyman Group—HiFi 5040 [Arthur Lyman] [BMI] (9/25/61 R-92) [I]

HOOCHI COOCHI COO Hank Ballard And The Midnighters—King 5430
[Hank Ballard/Billy Myles] [BMI] (12/5/60 BCR-14)

HOOK Rita Robbins—RCA Victor 47-5856
[Larry Coleman/Fred Ebb/Paul Klein] [BMI] (10/4/54 R-PRE)

HOOK AND SLING-PART 1 Eddie Bo—Scram 117
[Edwin Bocage/Al Scramuzza] [BMI] (8/2/69 BCR-70)

HOOKA TOOKA Chubby Checker—Parkway 890
[Chubby Checker/Judy Henske] [BMI] (12/7/63 BCR-16)

HOOKED ON A FEELING *B.J. Thomas—Scepter 12230*
[Mark James] [BMI] (10/26/68 BCR-5)

HOOKED ON A FEELING *Blue Swede—EMI 3627 [Mark James] [BMI] (2/9/74 BCR-1)*

HOOKED ON YOU Bread—Elektra 45389 [David Gates] [ASC] (4/16/77 BCR-60)

HOOKED ON YOU *Sweet Sensation—Next Plateau 308*
[Joseph E. Malloy/David Sanchez] [BMI] (1/17/87 BC-64)

HOOKED ON YOU *Sweet Sensation—Atco 99210*
[Joseph E. Malloy/David Sanchez] [BMI] (6/3/89 BC-23)

HOOKED ON YOUR LOVE Aretha Franklin—Atlantic 3358
[Curtis Mayfield] (TSW) [BMI] (10/30/76 R-89)

HOOPA HOOLA Betty Johnson—Atlantic 2002
[Bob Davie/Charles Grean] [BMI] (10/6/58 BCR-56)

HOORAY FOR HAZEL Tommy Roe—ABC 10852 [Tommy Roe] [BMI] (9/17/66 BCR-4)

—HOORAY FOR THE SALVATION ARMY BAND see: PURPLE HAZE

HOOTENANNY The Glencoves—Select 724
[Eddie V. Deane/George Goehring/Peg Horther] [ASC] (6/15/63 BCR-34)

HOOTENANNY GRANNY Jim Lowe—20th Fox 426
[Charles Grean/Fred Hertz*] [BMI] (9/21/63 R-91)

HOOTENANNY SATURDAY NIGHT The Brothers Four—Columbia 42927
[Richard Lewine/Alfred Uhry] [ASC] (12/14/63 B-89)

HOP SCOTCH Santo & Johnny—Canadian-American 124
[Ann Farina/Johnny Farina/Santo Farina] [BMI] (3/27/61 BCR-75) [IWM]

HOP SCOTCH BOOGIE Johnny Maddox—Dot 15432
[Billy Vaughn] [ASC] (1/13/56 R-75) [I]

HOPE THAT WE CAN BE TOGETHER SOON
Sharon Paige And Harold Melvin And The Blue Notes—Philadelphia Int'l 3569
[Kenneth Gamble/Leon Huff] [BMI] (6/28/75 BCR-31)

HOPE YOU LOVE ME LIKE YOU SAY YOU DO Huey Lewis and the News—Chrysalis 2604
[Mike Duke] [BMI] (5/15/82 BC-33)

HOPELESS Andy Williams—Columbia 42784
[Alan Jeffreys/Doc Pomus] [BMI] (6/15/63 BCR-13)

HOPELESSLY The Ames Brothers—RCA Victor 47-5840
[Robert Mellin/Ed Penney/Jack Richards] [BMI] (9/18/54 CR-26)

HOPELESSLY DEVOTED TO YOU Olivia Newton-John—RSO 903
[John Farrar] [BMI] (7/8/78 BCR-3)

—HOPELESSLY IN LOVE see: PARTY'S OVER

HOPPY, GENE AND ME Roy Rogers—20th Century 2154
[Milton L. Brown/Steve Dorff/Snuff Garrett] [BMI] (12/21/74 BCR-59)

THE HORIZONTAL BOP Bob Seger—Capitol 4951 [Bob Seger] [ASC] (11/8/80 BCR-42)

THE HORSE Cliff Nobles & Co.—Phil-L.A. Of Soul 313
[Jesse James] [BMI] (5/25/68 BCR-2) [I]

HORSE FEVER Cliff Nobles & Co.—Phil-L.A. Of Soul 318
[Jesse James] [BMI] (9/14/68 BCR-68) [I]

A HORSE WITH NO NAME *America—Warner Bros. 7555*
[Dewey Bunnell] [ASC] (2/19/72 BCR-1)

A HORSE WITH NO NAME *Stars On 45—Radio 3863*
[Dewey Bunnell] (Med) [ASC] (9/19/81 BCR-55)

HOT AND COLD RUNNING TEARS Sarah Vaughan—Mercury 70846
[Teddy Powell/Bobby Sharp] [ASC] (6/9/56 B-92)

HOT BLOODED Foreigner—Atlantic 3488
[Lou Gramm/Michael Leslie Jones] [ASC] (7/1/78 BCR-3)

HOT CAKES! 1ST SERVING Dave "Baby" Cortez—Chess 1850
[David Clowney/Shirley Hall] [BMI] (4/13/63 B-91) [I]

HOT CHILD IN THE CITY Nick Gilder—Chrysalis 2226
[Nick Gilder/James McCulloch] [BMI] (6/10/78 BCR-1)

HOT DAWGIT Ramsey Lewis And Earth, Wind & Fire—Columbia 10056
[Charles Stepney/Maurice White] [ASC] (12/28/74 BCR-50) [I]

HOT DIGGITY (DOG ZIGGITY BOOM) Perry Como—RCA Victor 47-6427
[Al Hoffman/Dick Manning] [ASC] (3/2/56 BCR-2)

HOT DOG BUDDY BUDDY Bill Haley And His Comets—Decca 29948
[Bill Haley] [ASC] (6/15/56 BCR-35)

HOT FOR TEACHER Van Halen—Warner Bros. 29199
[Michael Anthony*/David Lee Roth/Alex Van Halen/Eddie Van Halen] [ASC] (10/27/84 BC-56)

HOT FUN IN THE SUMMERTIME *Sly & The Family Stone—Epic 10497*
[Sylvester Stewart] [BMI] (8/2/69 BCR-2)

HOT FUN IN THE SUMMERTIME *David T. Walker—Ode 66025*
[Sylvester Stewart] [BMI] (5/20/72 CR-66) [IWM]

HOT FUN IN THE SUMMERTIME *Dayton—Liberty 1468*
[Sylvester Stewart] [BMI] (7/24/82 BC-58)

HOT GIRLS IN LOVE Loverboy—Columbia 03941
[Paul Dean/Bruce Fairbairn] [BMI] (6/11/83 BC-11)

HOT HOT HOT (RADIO EDIT) Buster Poindexter And His Banshees Of Blue—RCA 5357
[Alphonsus Cassell] [ASC] (12/12/87 BC-45)

HOT HOT HOT!!! The Cure—Elektra 69424
[Simon Gallup/Robert James Smith/Porl Thompson/Laurence Tolhurst/Boris Williams] [ASC] (3/5/88 BC-65)

***HOT IN THE CITY** Billy Idol—Chrysalis 2605 [Billy Idol] [ASC] (7/3/82 BC-23)*

***HOT IN THE CITY** Billy Idol—Chrysalis 43203 [Billy Idol] [ASC] (12/12/87 BC-48)*

HOT LEGS Rod Stewart—Warner Bros. 8535 [Rod Stewart] [ASC] (2/11/78 BCR-25)

HOT LINE The Sylvers—Capitol 4336 [Freddie Perren/Keni St. Lewis] [ASC] (10/9/76 BCR-2)

HOT LIPS Grady Martin And The Slew Foot Five—Decca 29558 [Henry Busse/Lou Davis/Henry Lange] [NA] (8/22/55 R-72) [IWM]

HOT LOVE T. Rex—Reprise 1006 [Marc Bolan] [ASC] (5/1/71 BCR-52)

HOT LOVE, COLD WORLD Bob Welch—Capitol 4588 [John Henning/Bob Welch] [BMI] (6/3/78 BCR-31)

HOT 'N' NASTY Humble Pie—A&M 1349 [Clem Clempson/Steve Marriott/Greg Ridley/Jerry Shirley] [ASC] (4/29/72 BCR-44)

HOT NUMBER Foxy—Dash 5050 [Ish Ledesma] [BMI] (3/24/79 BCR-21)

HOT PANTS Salvage—Odax 420 [Lee Pockriss/Paul Vance] [ASC] (2/27/71 BCR-51)

HOT PANTS - I'M COMING, COMING, I'M COMING Bobby Byrd—BrownStone 4203 [James Brown] [BMI] (9/25/71 BCR-72)

HOT PANTS PT. 1 (SHE GOT TO USE WHAT SHE GOT TO GET WHAT SHE WANTS) James Brown—People 2501 [James Brown/Fred Wesley] [BMI] (7/3/71 BCR-10)

HOT PASTRAMI The Dartells—Dot 16453 [James Brown] [BMI] (3/23/63 BCR-11)

HOT PASTRAMI WITH MASHED POTATOES - PART 1 Joey Dee & The Starliters—Roulette 4488 [James Brown] [BMI] (4/20/63 BCR-35) [I]

HOT PEPPER Floyd Cramer—RCA Victor 47-8051 [Floyd Cramer] [BMI] (7/7/62 BCR-63) [I]

HOT POTATO (MAMBO) Jayne and Audrey Meadows—RCA Victor 47-6132 [Fred Patrick/George Snowhill] [ASC] (5/16/55 R-53)

HOT ROD HEARTS Robbie Dupree—Elektra 47005 [Stephen Geyer/Bill LaBounty] [BMI] (7/19/80 BCR-7)

***HOT ROD LINCOLN** Charlie Ryan And The Timberline Riders—4 Star 1733 [Charlie Ryan/W.S. Stevenson‡] [BMI] (5/9/60 BCtRt-21)*

***HOT ROD LINCOLN** Johnny Bond—Republic 2005 [Charlie Ryan/W.S. Stevenson‡] [BMI] (8/1/60 BCtRt-21)*

***HOT ROD LINCOLN** Commander Cody And His Lost Planet Airmen—Paramount 0146 [Charlie Ryan/W.S. Stevenson‡] [BMI] (3/25/72 BCR-6)*

HOT SHOT The Buena Vistas—Swan 4255 [Nick Ameno/Carl Cisco/Tom Shannon] [BMI] (6/25/66 BCR-82) [I]

HOT SHOT Karen Young—West End 1211 [Kurt Borusiewicz/Andy Kahn] [ASC] (8/26/78 BCR-51)

HOT SMOKE & SASAFRASS The Bubble Puppy—Int'l Artists 128 [Roy Cox/Rod Prince] [BMI] (1/25/69 BCR-13)

HOT STUFF The Rolling Stones—Rolling Stones 19304 [Mick Jagger/Keith Richards] (TSW) [ASC] (6/26/76 BC-10)

HOT STUFF Donna Summer—Casablanca 978 [Pete Bellotte/Harold Faltermeyer/Keith Forsey] [BMI] (4/21/79 BCR-1)

***HOT SUMMER NIGHTS** Walter Egan—Columbia 10824 [Walter Egan] [ASC] (10/14/78 BCR-55)*

***HOT SUMMER NIGHTS** Night—Planet 45903 [Walter Egan] [ASC] (6/23/79 BCR-18)*

HOT THING Prince—Paisley Park 7-28288 [Prince] [ASC] (2/6/88 BC-63)

HOT TO TROT Wild Cherry—Epic 50362 [Robert Parissi] [ASC] (5/14/77 B-95)

HOT WATER Level 42—Polydor 885155 [Wally Badarou/Phil Gould/Mark King/Mike Lindup] [BMI] (7/26/86 BC-78)

HOT WIRE Al Green—Bell 45,305 [Palmer James] [BMI] (1/20/73 BC-71)

HOTEL CALIFORNIA Eagles—Asylum 45386 [Don Felder/Glenn Frey/Don Henley] [ASC] (2/26/77 BCR-1)

HOTEL HAPPINESS Brook Benton—Mercury 72055 [Leon Carr/Earl Shuman] [ASC] (11/24/62 BCR-3)

HOUDINI Walter Brennan—Liberty 55477 [Cliff Crofford] [BMI] (8/4/62 B-100)

***HOUND DOG** Elvis Presley—RCA Victor 47-6604 [Jerry Leiber/Mike Stoller] [BMI] (7/27/56 BCR-1)*

***HOUND DOG** Elvis Presley—RCA 13351 [Jerry Leiber/Mike Stoller] (Med) [BMI] (11/20/82 BC-71)*

***HOUND DOG** Jive Bunny And The Mastermixers—Music Factory 99140 [Jerry Leiber/Mike Stoller] (Med) [BMI] (10/28/89 BC-11)*

HOUND DOG MAN Fabian—Chancellor 1044 [Doc Pomus/Mort Shuman] [BMI] (11/9/59 BCR-9)

HOUND DOG MAN (PLAY IT AGAIN) Lenny Le Blanc—Big Tree 16062 [Tommy Stuart] [ASC] (9/3/77 BCR-56)

HOURGLASS Squeeze—A&M 2967 [Chris Difford/Glenn Tilbrook] [ASC] (9/19/87 BC-15)

***A HOUSE A CAR AND A WEDDING RING** Dale Hawkins—Checker 906 [Jerry Lordan] [BMI] (11/8/58 BCtRt-50)*

***A HOUSE A CAR AND A WEDDING RING** Mike Preston—London 1834 [Jerry Lordan] [BMI] (11/8/58 BCtRt-57)*

HOUSE AT POOH CORNER Nitty Gritty Dirt Band—United Artists 50769 [Kenny Loggins] [ASC] (4/24/71 BCR-38)

HOUSE FULL OF REASONS Jude Cole—Reprise 19530 [Jude Cole] [BMI] (12/1/90 BC-59)

***A HOUSE IS NOT A HOME** Brook Benton—Mercury 72303 [Burt Bacharach/Hal David] [ASC] (7/18/64 BCtR-50)*

***A HOUSE IS NOT A HOME** Dionne Warwick—Scepter 1282 [Burt Bacharach/Hal David] [ASC] (7/25/64 BCtR-48)*

***HOUSE OF BAMBOO** Andy Williams—Cadence 1358 [Bill Crompton/Norman Murrells] [ASC] (12/15/58 CR-86)*

***HOUSE OF BAMBOO** Earl Grant—Decca 31044 [Bill Crompton/Norman Murrells] [ASC] (3/7/60 BCR-76)*

***THE HOUSE OF BLUE LIGHTS** Chuck Miller—Mercury 70627 [Don Raye/Freddie Slack] [ASC] (6/13/55 BCRt-9)*

***THE HOUSE OF BLUE LIGHTS** Pat Morrisey—Decca 29594 [Don Raye/Freddie Slack] [ASC] (8/1/55 Rt-17)*

HOUSE OF BROKEN LOVE Great White—Capitol 44491 [Michael Lardie/Alan Niven/Jack Russell] [ASC] (3/17/90 BC-78)

HOUSE OF FIRE Alice Cooper—Epic 73085 [Desmond Child/Joan Jett] [ASC] (1/20/90 BC-50)

HOUSE OF LOVE Scott Garrett—Laurie 3023 [Milton Kellem] [ASC] (2/28/59 BCR-87)

HOUSE OF PAIN Faster Pussycat—Elektra 64995 [Taime Downe/Greg Steele] [ASC] (2/24/90 BC-28)

HOUSE OF STRANGERS Jim Gilstrap—Roxbury 2013 [Dave Appell/Sandy Linzer] [ASC] (8/9/75 BCR-93)

***THE HOUSE OF THE RISING SUN** The Animals—MGM 13264 [Traditional] [BMI] (8/8/64 BCR-1)*

***HOUSE OF THE RISING SUN** Frijid Pink—Parrot 341 [Traditional] [ASC] (1/24/70 BCR-5)*

***THE HOUSE OF THE RISING SUN** Santa Esmeralda—Casablanca 913 [Traditional] [NA] (3/11/78 BR-78)*

***THE HOUSE OF THE RISING SUN** Dolly Parton—RCA 12282 [Traditional] [BMI] (9/19/81 B-77)*

THE HOUSE ON TELEGRAPH HILL Bo Donaldson And The Heywoods—ABC 12072 [Dennis Lambert/Brian Potter] [BMI] (4/12/75 C-89)

THE HOUSE THAT JACK BUILT Aretha Franklin—Atlantic 2546 [Bobby Lance/Fran Robins] [BMI] (8/10/68 BCR-6)

HOUSE WITH LOVE IN IT The Four Lads—Columbia 40736 [Sylvia Dee/Sid Lippman] [ASC] (9/1/56 BCR-14)

HOUSECALL Shabba Ranks—Epic 73928 [Michael Bennett/Clifton Dillon/Sly Dunbar/Rexton Gordon/Maxi Priest/Brian Thompson] [ASC] (10/26/91 BC-37)

HOUSTON Dean Martin—Reprise 0393 [Lee Hazlewood] [ASC] (8/7/65 BCR-15)

HOUSTON (I'M COMIN' TO SEE YOU) Glen Campbell—Capitol 3808 [David Paich] [ASC] (2/2/74 BCR-54)

HOW ABOUT ME Kitty Kallen—Decca 30049 [Irving Berlin] [ASC] (10/6/56 R-72)

HOW ABOUT THAT Dee Clark—Abner 1032 [Frank Augustus/Doris Payne] [BMI] (11/30/59 BCR-26)

***HOW AM I SUPPOSED TO LIVE WITHOUT YOU** Laura Branigan—Atlantic 89805 [Michael Bolton/Doug James] [BMI] (7/2/83 BC-12)*

***HOW AM I SUPPOSED TO LIVE WITHOUT YOU** Michael Bolton—Columbia 73017 [Michael Bolton/Doug James] [BMI] (10/28/89 BC-1)*

HOW ARE YA' FIXED FOR LOVE Frank Sinatra and Keely Smith—Capitol 3952 [Sammy Cahn/Jimmy Van Heusen] [ASC] (3/31/58 BR-59)

HOW BAD DO YOU WANT IT? Don Henley—Geffen 19699 [Don Henley/Danny Kortchmar/Stan Lynch] [ASC] (7/7/90 BC-39)

HOW BLUE The Mills Brothers—Decca 29185 [Moose Charlap/Johann Strauss/Chuck Sweeney] [NA] (7/24/54 CR-37)

HOW BLUE CAN YOU GET B.B. King—ABC-Paramount 10527 [Jack H. Clement] [BMI] (3/21/64 BC-92)

(HOW BOUT A LITTLE HAND FOR) THE BOYS IN THE BAND The Boys In The Band—Spring 103 [Jerry Leiber/Mike Stoller] [BMI] (5/16/70 BCR-38)

***HOW 'BOUT US** Champaign—Columbia 11433 [Dana Walden] [BMI] (2/7/81 BCR-10)*

***HOW 'BOUT US** Grayson Hugh and Betty Wright—RCA 9163 [Dana Walden] [BMI] (3/31/90 BC-59)*

***HOW CAN I BE SURE** The Young Rascals—Atlantic 2438 [Eddie Brigati/Felix Cavaliere] [ASC] (9/9/67 BCR-2)*

***HOW CAN I BE SURE** David Cassidy—Bell 45,220 [Eddie Brigati/Felix Cavaliere] [ASC] (5/13/72 BCR-15)*

HOW CAN I EASE THE PAIN Lisa Fischer—Elektra 64897 [Lisa Fischer/Narada Michael Walden] [ASC] (4/13/91 BC-11)

HOW CAN I FALL? Breathe—A&M 1224 [Michael Delahunty/David Glasper/Marcus Lillington/Ian Spice] [ASC] (9/10/88 BC-2)

***HOW CAN I FORGET** Ben E. King—Atco 6256 [Murray Cohen‡/Bernard Solomon‡/Ed Townsend] [BMI] (3/9/63 BCtRt-50)*

***HOW CAN I FORGET** Jimmy Holiday—Everest 2022 [Murray Cohen‡/Bernard Solomon‡/Ed Townsend] [BMI] (3/9/63 BCtRt-50)*

HOW CAN I FORGET Marvin Gaye—Tamla 54190 [Barrett Strong/Norman Whitfield] (TSW) [BMI] (2/14/70 BCR-27)

HOW CAN I FORGET YOU Elisa Fiorillo—Chrysalis 43189 [Gardner Cole] [BMI] (1/23/88 BC-60)

HOW CAN I LEAVE YOU AGAIN John Denver—RCA 11036 [John Denver] [ASC] (11/19/77 BCR-38)

HOW CAN I LIVE WITHOUT HER Christopher Atkins—Polydor 2210 [Terry Britten/Sue Shifrin] [BMI] (8/7/82 BC-69)

HOW CAN I MEET HER? The Everly Brothers—Warner Bros. 5273 [Gerry Goffin/Jack Keller] [BMI] (5/7/62 BCR-54)

HOW CAN I REFUSE Heart—Epic 04047
[Mark Andes/Denny Carmassi/Sue Ennis/Howard Leese/Ann Wilson/Nancy Wilson] [ASC] (8/13/83 BC-44)

HOW CAN I TELL HER Lobo—Big Tree 16,004
[Kent LaVoie] [ASC] (6/16/73 BCR-20)

HOW CAN I TELL MY MOM AND DAD The Lovelites—Uni 55181
[Patti Hamilton/Clarence Johnson Jr.] [BMI] (1/3/70 BCR-60)

HOW CAN I TELL YOU Travis Wammack—Fame 91008
[Cat Stevens] [ASC] (12/30/72 BCR-59)

HOW CAN I UNLOVE YOU Lynn Anderson—Columbia 45429
[Joe South] [BMI] (8/14/71 BCR-57)

(HOW CAN I WRITE ON PAPER) WHAT I FEEL IN MY HEART
Jim Reeves—RCA Victor 47-7950
[Don Carter/Danny Harrison/George Kent/Jim Reeves] [BMI] (10/23/61 BR-92)

HOW CAN WE BE LOVERS Michael Bolton—Columbia 73318
[Michael Bolton/Desmond Child/Diane Warren] [BMI] (3/3/90 BC-3)

HOW CAN WE TELL HIM Marv Johnson—United Artists 322
[Berry Gordy] [ASC] (7/3/61 R-95)

HOW CAN YOU EXPECT TO BE TAKEN SERIOUSLY Pet Shop Boys—EMI 50343
[Chris Lowe/Neil Tennant] [ASC] (2/16/91 B-93)

HOW CAN YOU LOVE ME Ambrosia—Warner Bros. 29996
[David Pack/Joe Puerta] [BMI] (6/5/82 B-86)

HOW CAN YOU MEND A BROKEN HEART Bee Gees—Atco 6824
[Barry Gibb/Robin Gibb] [BMI] (6/19/71 BCR-1)

HOW CAN YOU MISTREAT THE ONE YOU LOVE Jean & The Darlings—Volt 151
[Isaac Hayes/David Porter] [BMI] (8/26/67 B-96)

HOW COULD I LET YOU GET AWAY The Spinners—Atlantic 2904
[Yvette Davis] (TSW) [BMI] (9/16/72 BCR-74)

HOW COULD THIS GO WRONG Exile—Warner/Curb 8796
[Mike Chapman/Nicky Chinn/Lynda Lawley/James P. Pennington] [BMI] (4/28/79 B-88)

HOW DEEP IS THE OCEAN Miss Toni Fisher—Signet 276
[Irving Berlin] [ASC] (4/11/60 BC-90)

HOW DEEP IS YOUR LOVE Bee Gees—RSO 882
[Barry Gibb/Maurice Gibb/Robin Gibb] [BMI] (9/24/77 BCR-1)

HOW DID WE LOSE IT BABY Jerry Butler—Mercury 73210
[William Earl Butler/Charles Jones] [ASC] (7/10/71 BCR-85)

HOW DO I MAKE YOU Linda Ronstadt—Asylum 46602
[Billy Steinberg] [ASC] (2/2/80 BCR-6)

HOW DO I SURVIVE Amy Holland—Capitol 4884
[Paul Steven Bliss] [ASC] (8/9/80 BCR-22)

HOW DO YOU CATCH A GIRL Sam The Sham And The Pharaohs—MGM 13649
[Ronald Blackwell] [BMI] (12/24/66 BCR-22)

HOW DO YOU DO? Mouth & MacNeal—Philips 40715
[Hans Van Hemert/Harry Van Hoof] [ASC] (4/29/72 BCR-5)

HOW DO YOU DO IT? Gerry And The Pacemakers—Laurie 3261
[Mitch Murray] [BMI] (7/11/64 BCR-9)

HOW DO YOU FEEL THE MORNING AFTER Millie Jackson—Spring 147
[Raeford Gerald/Luther Lynch] [BMI] (6/8/74 BCR-56)

HOW DO YOU KEEP THE MUSIC PLAYING James Ingram And Patti Austin—Qwest 29618
[Alan Bergman/Marilyn Bergman/Michel Legrand] [ASC] (5/7/83 BC-45)

HOW DO YOU KNOW IT'S LOVE Teresa Brewer—Coral 62197
[Ben Raleigh/Don Wolf] [ASC] (5/16/60 R-96)

HOW DO YOU QUIT (SOMEONE YOU LOVE) Carla Thomas—Atlantic 2272
[Isaac Hayes/Raymond Moore/David Porter] [BMI] (2/13/65 R-85)

HOW DOES IT FEEL The Illusion—Steed 721
[Jeff Barry/Richie Cerniglia/Mike Maniscalco] [BMI] (10/11/69 R-81)

HOW DOES IT FEEL TO BE BACK Daryl Hall & John Oates—RCA 12048
[John Oates] [BMI] (7/19/80 BCR-30)

HOW DOES THAT GRAB YOU, DARLIN'? Nancy Sinatra—Reprise 0461
[Lee Hazlewood] [ASC] (4/16/66 BCR-6)

(YOU DON'T KNOW) HOW GLAD I AM *Nancy Wilson—Capitol 5198*
[Larry Harrison/Jimmy Williams] [BMI] (6/20/64 BCR-11)

HOW GLAD I AM *The Kiki Dee Band—Rocket/MCA 40401*
[Larry Harrison/Jimmy Williams] [BMI] (5/17/75 BC-74)

HOW HIGH THE MOON *David Rose and His Orchestra—MGM 12714*
[Morgan Lewis] [ASC] (1/26/59 R-81) [IM]

HOW HIGH THE MOON PART ONE *Ella Fitzgerald—Verve 10220*
[Nancy Hamilton/Morgan Lewis] [ASC] (8/15/60 BR-76)

HOW HIGH THE MOON *Floyd Cramer—RCA Victor 47-8217*
[Morgan Lewis] [ASC] (8/3/63 R-89) [IM]

HOW HIGH THE MOON *Gloria Gaynor—MGM 14838*
[Nancy Hamilton/Morgan Lewis] [ASC] (11/29/75 BC-75)

HOW I MISS YOU BABY Bobby Womack—Minit 32081
[Darryl Carter/Bobby Womack] [BMI] (12/13/69 BCR-73)

(HOW I SPENT MY SUMMER VACATION) OR A DAY AT THE BEACH WITH PEDRO AND MAN - PART I Cheech & Chong—Ode 66115
[Tommy Chong/Cheech Marin] [ASC] (10/18/75 BCR-53)

HOW IMPORTANT CAN IT BE *Sarah Vaughan—Mercury 70534*
[Bennie Benjamin/George David Weiss] [ASC] (1/24/55 BCtRt-4)

HOW IMPORTANT CAN IT BE *Joni James—MGM 11919*
[Bennie Benjamin/George David Weiss] [ASC] (1/24/55 BCtRt-4)

HOW IMPORTANT CAN IT BE *Lou Monte—RCA Victor 47-5993*
[Bennie Benjamin/George David Weiss] [ASC] (1/24/55 Rt-29)

HOW IMPORTANT CAN IT BE? *Teresa Brewer—Coral 61362*
[Bennie Benjamin/George David Weiss] [ASC] (2/7/55 Rt-4)

HOW IMPORTANT CAN IT BE? *Connee Boswell—Decca 29412*
[Bennie Benjamin/George David Weiss] [ASC] (2/7/55 Rt-17)

HOW IS JULIE? The Lettermen—Capitol 4746
[Eddie Carroll/Barry De Vorzon] [BMI] (4/30/62 BCR-42)

(HOW LITTLE IT MATTERS) HOW LITTLE WE KNOW Frank Sinatra—Capitol 3423
[Carolyn Leigh/Philip Springer] [ASC] (5/11/56 BCR-23)

HOW LONELY CAN I GET *Kitty Kallen—Decca 29708*
[Alex Kramer/Joan Whitney] [ASC] (10/24/55 Rt-33)

HOW LONELY CAN I GET? *The Lancers—Coral 61527*
[Alex Kramer/Joan Whitney] [ASC] (12/1/55 Rt-33)

HOW LONELY CAN ONE BE Teresa Brewer—Coral 61776
[Joe Shapiro/Lou Stallman] [NA] (3/2/57 C-49)

HOW LONG *Ace—Anchor 21000 [Paul Carrack] [ASC] (3/1/75 BCR-1)*

HOW LONG *Rod Stewart—Warner Bros. 50051 [Paul Carrack] [ASC] (4/24/82 BC-49)*

HOW LONG (BETCHA' GOT A CHICK ON THE SIDE) Pointer Sisters—ABC/Blue Thumb 265
[Anita Pointer/Bonnie Pointer/June Pointer/Ruth Pointer/David Rubinson] [BMI] (7/19/75 BCR-7)

HOW LOVELY IS CHRISTMAS Bing Crosby—Kapp 196
[Arnold Sundgaard/Alec Wilder] [BMI] (12/30/57 B-97)

HOW LUCKY YOU ARE Joni James—MGM 12288
[Ed Kassner/Desmond O'Connor] [ASC] (7/21/56 B-70)

HOW MANY Bill Haley & His Comets—Decca 30461
[Howard Ellington Riddiford Barnes/Hal Blair] [BMI] (11/11/57 R-79)

HOW MANY OTHERS Dick Roman—Double AA 116
[Richard George/Mel Leven/Don Reed] [BMI] (10/31/55 R-73)

HOW MANY TEARDROPS Lou Christie—Roulette 4504
[Rick Rodell] [BMI] (7/6/63 BCR-41)

HOW MANY TEARS Bobby Vee—Liberty 55325
[Gerry Goffin/Carole King] [BMI] (5/8/61 BCR-39)

HOW MANY TIMES CAN WE SAY GOODBYE
Dionne Warwick And Luther Vandross—Arista 1-9073
[Steve Goldman] [ASC] (10/8/83 BC-27)

HOW MUCH The Skyliners—Calico 114
[James Beaumont/Walter Lester/Joseph Rock/John L. Taylor/Joseph Verscharen/Janet Vogel] [ASC] (2/6/60 C-98)

HOW MUCH CAN A LONELY HEART STAND Skeeter Davis—RCA Victor 47-8288
[Sandra Rhodes] [BMI] (2/22/64 B-92)

HOW MUCH I FEEL Ambrosia—Warner Bros. 8640 [David Pack] [BMI] (9/2/78 BCR-2)

HOW MUCH IS ENOUGH The Fixx—Impact 54028
[Dan Brown*/Cy Cumin/Scott Cutler/Ashley Hall] [ASC] (3/23/91 BC-33)

HOW MUCH IS THAT DOGGIE IN THE WINDOW
Baby Jane & The Rockabyes—United Artists 560
[Bob Merrill] [ASC] (1/5/63 BCR-65)

HOW MUCH LOVE Leo Sayer—Warner Bros. 8319
[Barry Mann/Leo Sayer] [BMI] (7/9/77 BCR-9)

HOW MUCH LOVE Survivor—Scotti Brothers 06705
[Jim Peterik/Frankie Sullivan] [ASC] (2/14/87 BC-51)

HOW MUCH LOVE Vixen—EMI 50302
[Jack Conrad/Jan Kuehnemund/Steve Plunkett] [BMI] (8/11/90 BC-41)

HOW NICE IT IS Billy Stewart—Chess 1941 [Billy Stewart] [BMI] (9/18/65 BCR-60)

HOW SWEET IT IS TO BE LOVED BY YOU *Marvin Gaye—Tamla 54107*
[Lamont Dozier/Brian Holland/Eddie Holland] [BMI] (11/21/64 BCR-6)

HOW SWEET IT IS (TO BE LOVED BY YOU) *Jr. Walker & The All Stars—Soul 35024*
[Lamont Dozier/Brian Holland/Eddie Holland] [BMI] (7/30/66 BCR-18)

HOW SWEET IT IS (TO BE LOVED BY YOU) *James Taylor—Warner Bros. 8109*
[Lamont Dozier/Brian Holland/Eddie Holland] [BMI] (6/21/75 BCR-5)

HOW THE TIME FLIES Jerry Wallace—Challenge 59013
[Thomas J. Coe] [ASC] (7/19/58 BCR-11)

(HOW TO BE A) MILLIONAIRE ABC—Mercury 884382
[Martin Fry/Mark White] [BMI] (1/18/86 BC-20)

HOW TO DANCE Bingoboys—Atlantic 87756
[Klaus Biedermann/Jennece Moore/Martin Neumayer/Peter Pfab/Helmut Wolfgruber] [ASC] (2/16/91 BC-25)

HOW TO HANDLE A WOMAN Johnny Mathis—Columbia 41866
[Alan Jay Lerner/Frederick Loewe] [ASC] (11/28/60 BCR-64)

HOW WILL I KNOW Whitney Houston—Arista 1-9434
[George Merrill/Shannon Rubicam/Narada Michael Walden] [BMI] (12/7/85 BC-1)

HOW WILL I KNOW MY LOVE *Annette—Disneyland 102*
[Thomas Adair/Frances Jeffords/Bill Walsh] [ASC] (5/5/58 CRt-55)

HOW WILL I KNOW MY LOVE? *The Lennon Sisters—Brunswick 55063*
[Thomas Adair/Frances Jeffords/Bill Walsh] [ASC] (6/23/58 Rt-82)

HOW YOU GONNA SEE ME NOW Alice Cooper—Warner Bros. 8695
[Alice Cooper/Bernie Taupin/Dick Wagner] [BMI] (10/21/78 BCR-12)

HOW'D WE EVER GET THIS WAY Andy Kim—Steed 707 [Jeff Barry/Andy Kim] [BMI] (4/13/68 BCR-16)

HOWZAT Sherbet—MCA 40610 [Tony Mitchell/Garth Porter] [BMI] (8/21/76 BCR-61)

—HUCKLE BUCK (ITALIAN STYLE) see: HUCKLE BUCK

ITALIAN HUCKLE BUCK *Lou Monte—RCA Victor 47-5832 [Roy Alfred/Andy Gibson] [ASC] (8/14/54 C-15)*

THE HUCKLEBUCK *Chubby Checker—Parkway 813 [Roy Alfred/Andy Gibson] [ASC] (10/10/60 BCRt-10)*

THE HUCKLE-BUCK (ITALIAN STYLE) *Lou Monte—Roulette 4294 [Roy Alfred/Andy Gibson] [ASC] (10/17/60 Rt-20)*

HULA HOOP Steve Allen—Dot 15831 [Leon Carr/Buddy Kaye] [ASC] (10/6/58 Rt*-50)

HULA HOOP SONG *Teresa Brewer—Coral 62033 [Carl Maduri/James Testa] [ASC] (9/22/58 BCtRt-36)*

HULA HOOP SONG *Georgia Gibbs—Roulette 4106 [Carl Maduri/James Testa] [ASC] (9/22/58 BCtRt-32)*

HULA LOVE Buddy Knox with The Rhythm Orchids—Roulette 4018 [Dave Alldred/Jimmy Bowen/Buddy Knox/Donnie Lanier/Edward Madden/Percy Wenrich] [BMI] (8/24/57 BCR-9)

HULLY GULLY AGAIN Little Caesar And The Romans—Del-Fi 4164 [Cliff Goldsmith/Fred Smith] [BMI] (8/7/61 B-54)

HULLY GULLY BABY The Dovells—Parkway 845 [Dave Appell/Kal Mann] [ASC] (8/11/62 BCR-21)

HULLY GULLY GUITAR Jerry Reed And The Hully Girlies—Columbia 42533 [Jerry Reed] [BMI] (10/13/62 B-99) [I]

HUM A SONG (FROM YOUR HEART) Lulu With The Dixie Flyers—Atco 6749 [Richard H. Ross] [ASC] (4/18/70 BCR-40)

HUM ALONG AND DANCE The Temptations—Gordy 7102 [Barrett Strong/Norman Whitfield] [BMI] (10/31/70 CR-26)

HUMAN Tommy Hunt—Scepter 1219 [Luther Dixon] [BMI] (8/26/61 BCR-41)

HUMAN The Human League—A&M/Virgin 2861 [James Samuel Harris/Terry Lewis] [ASC] (9/13/86 BC-1)

HUMAN NATURE Michael Jackson—Epic 04026 [John Bettis/Steve Porcaro] [ASC] (7/23/83 BC-7)

HUMAN TOUCH Rick Springfield—RCA 13576 [Rick Springfield] [BMI] (7/9/83 BC-18)

HUMDINGER Freddy Cannon—Swan 4061 [Bob Crewe/Frank Slay] [BMI] (10/10/60 BCR-59)

HUMMIN' AND WALTZIN' Les Paul and Mary Ford—Capitol 3725 [Larry Coleman/Charles Singleton] [BMI] (6/15/57 R-76)

HUMMING BIRD *Les Paul and Mary Ford—Capitol 3165 [Don Robertson] [ASC] (6/13/55 BCtRt-6)*

HUMMING BIRD *Frankie Laine—Columbia 40526 [Don Robertson] [ASC] (6/13/55 CtRt-6)*

HUMMING BIRD *The Chordettes—Cadence 1267 [Don Robertson] [ASC] (6/20/55 CtRt-6)*

HUMMINGBIRD B.B. King—ABC 11268 [Leon Russell] [BMI] (7/18/70 BCR-31)

HUMMINGBIRD Seals & Crofts—Warner Bros. 7671 [Dash Crofts/Jim Seals] [BMI] (1/20/73 BCR-15)

HUMPHREY THE CAMEL Jack Blanchard & Misty Morgan—Wayside 013 [Jack Blanchard] [BMI] (6/27/70 BCR-78)

THE HUMPTY DANCE Digital Underground—Tommy Boy 7944 [George Clinton/William Earl Collins/Gregory Jacobs/Walter Morrison] [BMI] (3/17/90 BC-11)

HUMPTY DUMPTY HEART *LaVern Baker—Atlantic 1150 [Henry Boye] [BMI] (8/31/57 BCRt-53)*

HUMPTY DUMPTY HEART *Kay Cee Jones—Decca 30432 [Henry Boye] [BMI] (9/2/57 Rt-72)*

HUNCH *Paul Gayten—Anna 1106 [Larry Kerrin*/Joe Pyatt] [BMI] (10/19/59 BCtRt-33) [I]*

HUNCH *Bobby Peterson Quintet—V-Tone 205 [Larry Kerrin*/Joe Pyatt] [BMI] (10/19/59 BCtRt-33) [I]*

A HUNDRED POUNDS OF CLAY Gene McDaniels—Liberty 55308 [Luther Dixon/Stanley Kahan/Eddie Snyder] [BMI] (3/13/61 BCR-1)

HUNG ON YOU The Righteous Brothers—Philles 129 [Gerry Goffin/Carole King/Phil Spector] [BMI] (7/17/65 BCR-43)

HUNG UP IN YOUR EYES Brian Hyland—Philips 40424 [Sonny Curtis/Glen Hardin] [BMI] (2/11/67 BCR-58)

HUNGRY Paul Revere And The Raiders Featuring Mark Lindsay—Columbia 43678 [Barry Mann/Cynthia Weil] [BMI] (6/18/66 BCR-6)

HUNGRY Winger—Atlantic 88859 [Reb Beach/Kip Winger] [BMI] (9/23/89 BC-85)

HUNGRY Lita Ford—RCA 2607 [M. Dan Ehmig/Lita Ford] [BMI] (7/14/90 B-98)

HUNGRY EYES Eric Carmen—RCA 5315 [John DeNicola/Franke Previte] [ASC] (11/7/87 BC-3)

HUNGRY FOR LOVE San Remo Golden Strings—Ric-Tic 104 [Joanne Bratton/Al Hamilton/Bob Hamilton/Eugene Hamilton*] [BMI] (9/11/65 BCR-26) [I]

HUNGRY HEART Bruce Springsteen—Columbia 11391 [Bruce Springsteen] [ASC] (11/8/80 BCR-5)

HUNGRY LIKE THE WOLF Duran Duran—Harvest 5195 [Simon Le Bon/Nick Rhodes/Andy Taylor/Nigel John Taylor/Roger Taylor] [ASC] (12/25/82 BC-3)

THE HUNGRY YEARS Wayne Newton—Chelsea 3041 [Howard Greenfield/Neil Sedaka] [BMI] (5/29/76 BC-81)

HUNK OF FUNK Gene Dozier And The Brotherhood—Minit 32026 [Gene Dozier] [BMI] (11/4/67 R-97) [I]

THE HUNTER Ike & Tina Turner—Blue Thumb 102 [Steve Cropper/Donald "Duck" Dunn/Al Jackson/Booker T. Jones Jr./Carl Wells] [BMI] (6/28/69 BR-93)

THE HUNTER GTR—Arista 1-9512 [Geoffrey Downes] [BMI] (8/23/86 BC-80)

THE HUNTER GETS CAPTURED BY THE GAME The Marvelettes—Tamla 54143 [Smokey Robinson] [ASC] (1/21/67 BCR-13)

HUNTERS OF THE NIGHT Mr. Mister—RCA 13741 [Steve George/George Ghiz/John Lang/Richard Page] [ASC] (3/17/84 BC-57)

HURDY GURDY MAN Donovan—Epic 10345 [Donovan Leitch] [BMI] (6/15/68 BCR-3)

HURRICANE Dave "Baby" Cortez—Clock 1031 [David Clowney/Ken Wood] [BMI] (11/21/60 R-95) [I]

HURRICANE (PART I) Bob Dylan—Columbia 10245 [Bob Dylan/Jacques Levy] [SE] (11/22/75 BCR-27)

A HURRICANE IS COMING TONITE Carol Douglas—Midland Int'l 10229 [Alan Bernstein/Ed O'Loughlin] [ASC] (4/5/75 BC-81)

HURRY SUNDOWN The Outlaws—Arista 0258 [Hughie Thomasson] [BMI] (7/16/77 BCR-60)

HURRY UP AND TELL ME Paul Anka—RCA Victor 47-8237 [Eddie Snyder/Paul Vance] [ASC] (9/28/63 CR-97)

HURRY UP AND WAIT The Isley Brothers—T-Neck 02033 [Ernie Isley/Marvin Isley/O'Kelly Isley/Ronald Isley/Rudolph Isley/Chris Jasper] [ASC] (4/18/81 BCR-48)

HURT *Roy Hamilton—Epic 9086 [Jimmie Crane/Al Jacobs] [ASC] (12/27/54 R-71)*

HURT *Timi Yuro—Liberty 55343 [Jimmie Crane/Al Jacobs] [ASC] (7/17/61 BCR-3)*

HURT *Little Anthony And The Imperials—DCP 1154 [Jimmie Crane/Al Jacobs] [ASC] (1/1/66 BCR-51)*

HURT *The Manhattans—Columbia 10140 [Jimmie Crane/Al Jacobs] [ASC] (5/17/75 BC-70)*

HURT *Elvis Presley—RCA Victor 10601 [Jimmie Crane/Al Jacobs] (TSW) [ASC] (4/3/76 BCR-28)*

THE HURT Cat Stevens—A&M 1418 [Cat Stevens] [BMI] (6/30/73 BCR-20)

HURT Re-Flex—Capitol 5348 [Paul Fishman] [ASC] (5/5/84 BC-82)

HURT BY LOVE Inez Foxx—Symbol 20-001 [Charlie Foxx/Inez Foxx*] [BMI] (4/25/64 BCR-48)

HURT SO BAD *Little Anthony And The Imperials—DCP 1128 [Bobby Hart/Teddy Randazzo/Bobby Weinstein] [BMI] (2/6/65 BCR-10)*

HURT SO BAD *The Lettermen—Capitol 2482 [Bobby Hart/Teddy Randazzo/Bobby Weinstein] [BMI] (5/31/69 BCR-12)*

HURT SO BAD *Jackie DeShannon—Imperial 66452 [Bobby Hart/Teddy Randazzo/Bobby Weinstein] (Med) [BMI] (5/30/70 B-96)*

HURT SO BAD *Linda Ronstadt—Asylum 46624 [Bobby Hart/Teddy Randazzo/Bobby Weinstein] [BMI] (4/5/80 BCR-8)*

HURTIN' INSIDE Brook Benton—Mercury 71394 [Brook Benton/Cirino Colacrai/Clyde Otis/Teddy Randazzo] [BMI] (2/9/59 BR-78)

HURTING EACH OTHER Carpenters—A&M 1322 [Gary Geld/Peter Udell] [ASC] (1/15/72 BCR-1)

HURTING KIND (I'VE GOT MY EYES ON YOU) Robert Plant—Es Paranza 98985 [Christopher Blackwell/Doug Boyle/Phil Johnstone/Stephen Charles Jones/Robert Plant] [ASC] (3/24/90 BC-46)

HURTS SO GOOD Millie Jackson—Spring 139 [Phillip Mitchell] [BMI] (8/25/73 BCR-18)

HURTS SO GOOD John Cougar—Riva 209 [George Green/John Mellencamp] [ASC] (4/24/82 BC-1)

HURTS TO BE IN LOVE Gino Vannelli—CBS Associated 05586 [Gino Vannelli] [BMI] (9/21/85 BC-53)

HUSBANDS AND WIVES *Roger Miller—Smash 2024 [Roger Miller] [BMI] (2/12/66 BCR-20)*

HUSBANDS AND WIVES *Wayne Newton—MGM 14014 [Roger Miller] [BMI] (12/14/68 C-97)*

HUSH *Billy Joe Royal—Columbia 44277 [Joe South] [BMI] (9/30/67 BCR-48)*

HUSH *Deep Purple—Tetragrammaton 1503 [Joe South] [BMI] (8/3/68 BCR-4)*

HUSH *Blue Swede—EMI 4029 [Joe South] (Med) [BMI] (2/22/75 BCR-54)*

HUSH HUSH Jimmy Reed—Vee-Jay 357 [Jimmy Reed] [BMI] (9/26/60 BCR-75)

HUSH, HUSH, SWEET CHARLOTTE Patti Page—Columbia 43251 [Mack David/Frank DeVol] [ASC] (4/24/65 BCR-8)

HUSHABYE *The Mystics—Laurie 3028 [Doc Pomus/Mort Shuman] [BMI] (5/25/59 BCR-18)*

HUSHABYE *The Beach Boys—Capitol R-5267 [Doc Pomus/Mort Shuman] (EP) [BMI] (10/10/64 C-57)*

HUSHABYE *Jay & The Americans—United Artists 50535 [Doc Pomus/Mort Shuman] [BMI] (5/24/69 BCR-41)*

HUSHABYE *Robert John—Atlantic 2884 [Doc Pomus/Mort Shuman] [BMI] (6/10/72 BCR-59)*

HUSHABYE LITTLE GUITAR Paul Evans—Guaranteed 213 [Paul Evans/Matt Williams] [ASC] (11/7/60 R-96)

THE HUSTLE Van Mc Coy & The Soul City Symphony—Avco 4653 [Van McCoy] [BMI] (4/19/75 BCR-1) [I]

HUSTLE!!! (DEAD ON IT) James Brown—Polydor 14281
[James Brown] [BMI] (7/26/75 CR-95)

HYMN 43 Jethro Tull—Reprise 1024 [Ian Anderson] [ASC] (7/24/71 BCR-77)

HYMN NO. 5 Mighty Hannibal—Josie 964 [James T. Shaw] [BMI] (11/5/66 CR-79)

HYPERACTIVE Thomas Dolby—Capitol 5321 [Thomas Dolby] [ASC] (2/25/84 BC-59)

HYPERACTIVE Robert Palmer—Island 99545
[Tony Haynes/Dennis Nelson/Robert Palmer] [BMI] (6/7/86 BC-27)

HYPNOTIZE ME Wang Chung—Geffen 28359
[Nick Feldman/Jack Hues] [BMI] (6/6/87 BC-36)

HYPNOTIZED The Drifters—Atlantic 1141
[Terry Noland/Norman Petty] [BMI] (7/1/57 B-79)

HYPNOTIZED Linda Jones—Loma 2070
[Richard Poindexter/Gloria Spolan] [BMI] (6/17/67 BCR-21)

HYSTERIA Def Leppard—Mercury 870004
[Rick Allen*/Steve Clark/Phil Collen/Joe Elliott/Mutt Lange/Rick Savage] [ASC] (1/23/88 BC-10)

I

I ADORE HIM The Angels—Smash 1854
[Jan Berry/Artie Kornfeld] [BMI] (10/12/63 BCR-22)

I ADORE MI AMOR Color Me Badd—Giant 19204
[Bryan Abrams/Mark Calderon/Hamza Lee/Kevin Thornton/Sam Watters] [ASC] (7/27/91 BC-1)

I AIN'T GIVING UP NOTHING Ben Hewitt—Mercury 71413
[Brook Benton/Clyde Otis] [BMI] (3/21/59 C-84)

I AIN'T GONNA EAT OUT MY HEART ANYMORE *The Young Rascals—Atlantic 2312*
[Lori Burton/Pam Sawyer] [BMI] (12/11/65 BCR-52)

AIN'T GONNA EAT OUT MY HEART ANYMORE *Angel—Casablanca 914*
[Lori Burton/Pam Sawyer] [BMI] (4/1/78 BCR-44)

I AIN'T GONNA LEAD THIS LIFE NO MORE Dean Martin—Capitol 4287
[Ervin Drake] [ASC] (10/19/59 R-81)

I AIN'T GONNA STAND FOR IT Stevie Wonder—Tamla 54320
[Stevie Wonder] [ASC] (12/13/80 BCR-11)

I AIN'T GOT NOBODY David Lee Roth—Warner Bros. 29040
[Roger Graham/Spencer Williams] (Med) [NA] (3/23/85 BC-12)

I AIN'T GOT TIME ANYMORE The Glass Bottle Featuring Gary Criss—
Avco Embassy 4575 [Mike Leander/Ed Seago] [BMI] (7/10/71 BCR-26)

I AIN'T GOT TO LOVE NOBODY ELSE The Masqueraders—Bell 733
[Lee Jones/Charlie Lee Moore/Robert Wrightsil] [BMI] (9/21/68 BCR-57)

I AIN'T MUCH Atlanta Rhythm Section—Polydor/BGO 2125
[Buddy Buie/J.R. Cobb] [BMI] (9/20/80 CR-80)

I AIN'T NEVER *Webb Pierce—Decca 30923*
[Webb Pierce/Mel Tillis] [BMI] (8/10/59 BCR-22)

I AIN'T NEVER *The Four Preps—Capitol 4256*
[Webb Pierce/Mel Tillis] [BMI] (9/14/59 B-79)

I AIN'T SHARIN' SHARON Buddy Knox—Roulette 4179
[Doc Pomus/Mort Shuman] [BMI] (11/7/59 C-100)

I ALMOST CALLED YOUR NAME Margaret Whiting—London 115
[Margaret Lewis/Mira Smith] [BMI] (11/4/67 CR-95)

I ALMOST LOST MY MIND Pat Boone—Dot 15472 [Ivory Joe Hunter] [BMI] (6/1/56 BCR-1)

I AM Tony Bennett with Ray Ellis and His Orchestra—Columbia 40965
[Sherman Edwards/Earl Shuman] [ASC] (7/20/57 BCR-35)

I AM A ROCK Simon & Garfunkel—Columbia 43617 [Paul Simon] [BMI] (4/30/66 BCR-2)

I AM A WITNESS Tommy Hunt—Scepter 1261 [Ed Townsend] [BMI] (11/9/63 BCR-65)

I AM BY YOUR SIDE Corey Hart—EMI America 8348 [Corey Hart] [ASC] (9/20/86 BC-18)

I AM I AM Smokey Robinson—Tamla 54251
[Smokey Robinson] [ASC] (12/14/74 BCR-56)

I AM...I SAID Neil Diamond—Uni 55278 [Neil Diamond] [SE] (3/20/71 BCR-4)

I AM LOVE The Jackson 5—Motown 1310
[Don Fenceton/Mel Larson/Jerry Marcellino/Rod Rancifer] [ASC] (1/18/75 BCR-15)

I AM LOVE Jennifer Holliday—Geffen 29522
[David Foster/Maurice White/Allee Willis] [BMI] (10/15/83 BC-42)

I AM SOMEBODY PART II Johnnie Taylor—Stax 0078
[Arthur Snyder] [BMI] (10/3/70 BCR-30)

I AM SOMEBODY Jimmy James & The Vagabonds—Pye 71057
[Biddu Appaiah] [ASC] (2/21/76 B-94)

—I AM THE JAPANESE SANDMAN see: RANG TANG DING DONG

I AM THE MAN FOR YOU BABY Edwin Starr—Gordy 7071
[Steve Bowden/James Anthony Dean/William Weatherspoon] [ASC] (4/20/68 CR-86)

I AM THE WALRUS The Beatles—Capitol 2056
[John Lennon/Paul McCartney] [ASC] (12/2/67 BCR-44)

I AM WHAT I AM Lois Fletcher—Playboy 50049
[Scott English/Richard Kerr] [BMI] (3/23/74 BCR-53)

I AM WOMAN Barbra Streisand—Columbia 42965
[Bob Merrill/Jule Styne] [ASC] (2/22/64 R-89)

I AM WOMAN Helen Reddy—Capitol 3350
[Ray Burton/Helen Reddy] [BMI] (6/24/72 BCR-1)

I AM YOUR MAN Bobby Taylor & The Vancouvers—Gordy 7073
[Nick Ashford/Valerie Simpson] [ASC] (7/20/68 BCR-82)

I APOLOGIZE Timi Yuro—Liberty 55343
[Al Goodhart/Al Hoffman/Ed Nelson] [ASC] (10/9/61 B-72)

I BEEN MOVED Andy Kim—Steed 734 [Jeff Barry/Andy Kim] [BMI] (7/3/71 BCR-82)

I' BEEN WATCHIN' YOU The South Side Movement—Wand 11251
[Bobby Rush/James Vanleer] [BMI] (2/24/73 BCR-54)

I BEG OF YOU Elvis Presley—RCA Victor 47-7150
[Rose Marie McCoy/Kelly Owens] [BMI] (1/20/58 BCR-7)

I BEG YOUR PARDON Kon Kan—Atlantic 88969
[Barry Harris/Joe South] [BMI] (12/24/88 BC-15)

I BELIEVE *Roy Hamilton—Epic 9092*
[Ervin Drake/Irvin Graham/Jimmy Shirl/Al Stillman] [ASC] (2/21/55 R-82)

I BELIEVE *Elvis Presley—RCA Victor LOC-1035*
[Ervin Drake/Irvin Graham/Jimmy Shirl/Al Stillman] (EP) [ASC] (12/30/57 R-49)

I BELIEVE *The Bachelors—London 9672*
[Ervin Drake/Irvin Graham/Jimmy Shirl/Al Stillman] [ASC] (6/27/64 BCR-17)

I BELIEVE Chilliwack—Millennium 13102
[William A. Henderson] [BMI] (1/16/82 BCR-29)

I BELIEVE I'LL LOVE ON Jackie Wilson—Brunswick 55283
[Eddie Singleton] [BMI] (10/16/65 BCR-71)

I BELIEVE I'M GONNA LOVE YOU Frank Sinatra—Reprise 1335
[Harry Lloyd/Gloria Sklerov] [ASC] (7/26/75 BCR-42)

I BELIEVE I'M GONNA MAKE IT Joe Tex—Dial 4033 [Joe Tex] [BMI] (7/16/66 BCR-50)

I BELIEVE IN ALL I FEEL The G-Clefs—Regina 1314 [Arnold Scott] [BMI] (8/8/64 R-93)

I BELIEVE IN FATHER CHRISTMAS Greg Lake—Atlantic 3305
[Greg Lake/Sergei Prokofiev/Peter Sinfield] [ASC] (12/20/75 BCR-91)

I BELIEVE IN LOVE Kenny Loggins—Columbia 10569
[Alan Bergman/Marilyn Bergman/Kenny Loggins] [ASC] (7/16/77 BCR-53)

I BELIEVE IN MUSIC *Marian Love—A&R 7100/505 [Mac Davis] [BMI] (3/6/71 CR-94)*

I BELIEVE IN MUSIC *Gallery—Sussex 239 [Mac Davis] [BMI] (8/5/72 BCR-12)*

I BELIEVE IN YOU Robert & Johnny—Old Town 1052
[Robert Carr/Johnny Mitchell/Sam Weiss*] [BMI] (8/4/58 B-93)

I BELIEVE IN YOU Don Williams—MCA 41304
[Roger Cook/Sam Hogin] [ASC] (9/20/80 BCR-12)

I BELIEVE IN YOU Stryper—Enigma 75028 [Michael Sweet] [BMI] (11/5/88 B-88)

I BELIEVE IN YOU (YOU BELIEVE IN ME) Johnnie Taylor—Stax 0161
[Don Davis] [BMI] (6/23/73 BCR-5)

(I BELIEVE) THERE'S NOTHING STRONGER THAN OUR LOVE
Paul Anka With Odia Coates—United Artists 685
[Paul Anka] [BMI] (7/19/75 BCR-13)

I BELIEVE YOU *Dorothy Moore—Malaco 1042*
[Dick Addrisi/Don Addrisi] [BMI] (7/23/77 BCR-27)

I BELIEVE YOU *Carpenters—A&M 2097*
[Dick Addrisi/Don Addrisi] [BMI] (11/25/78 BCR-68)

I BELIEVED IT ALL Pozo Seco Singers—Columbia 44041
[Alan Bergman/Marilyn Bergman/Al Ham] [ASC] (5/6/67 B-96)

I BELONG TO YOU Ralph Flanagan and his Orchestra—RCA Victor 47-6023
[Jack Brooks/Alex North] [ASC] (6/11/55 CR-40)

I BELONG TO YOU Love Unlimited—20th Century 2141
[Barry White] [BMI] (11/16/74 BCR-27)

I BET HE DON'T LOVE YOU (LIKE I LOVE YOU) The Intruders—Gamble 4016
[Kenneth Gamble/Leon Huff] [BMI] (10/23/71 BCR-77)

I BET'CHA (COULDN'T LOVE ME) The Manhattans—Carnival 522
[Greg Gaskins/Winfred Lovett] [BMI] (11/5/66 CR-99)

I CALL IT LOVE The Manhattans—Carnival 533 [Edward Bivins] [BMI] (12/2/67 BC-93)

I CALL MY BABY CANDY The Jaggerz—Kama Sutra 509
[Donnie Iris] [BMI] (5/2/70 BCR-52)

I CALL YOUR NAME Switch—Gordy 7175
[Bobby DeBarge/Greg Williams] [ASC] (11/3/79 BCR-80)

—I CAME I SAW I CONQUERED see: VENI-VIDI-VICI

I CAN DREAM ABOUT YOU Dan Hartman—MCA 52378
[Dan Hartman] [BMI] (5/5/84 BC-6)

(I CAN FEEL THOSE VIBRATIONS) THIS LOVE IS REAL Jackie Wilson—Brunswick 55443
[Jack Daniels/John Edward Moore] [BMI] (12/19/70 BCR-42)

I CAN FEEL YOU The Addrisi Brothers—Columbia 45610
[Dick Addrisi/Don Addrisi] [BMI] (6/10/72 C-90)

(I CAN FEEL YOUR LOVE) SLIPPING AWAY Barbara Mason—Arctic 142
[Barbara Mason] [BMI] (9/14/68 B-97)

I CAN HEAR MUSIC *The Ronettes Featuring Veronica—Philles 133*
[Jeff Barry/Ellie Greenwich/Phil Spector] [BMI] (10/29/66 BR-90)

I CAN HEAR MUSIC *The Beach Boys—Capitol 2432*
[Jeff Barry/Ellie Greenwich/Phil Spector] [BMI] (3/8/69 BCR-18)

I CAN HELP Billy Swan—Monument 8621 [Billy Swan] [BMI] (9/28/74 BCR-1)

I CAN MAKE IT THRU THE DAYS (BUT OH THOSE LONELY NIGHTS)
Ray Charles—ABC/TRC 11351
[Ray Charles/Dee Ervin/Ruth Robinson] [BMI] (6/2/73 BCR-79)

I CAN MAKE IT WITH YOU *Pozo-Seco Singers—Columbia 43784*
[Chip Taylor] [BMI] (9/10/66 BCRt-32)

I CAN MAKE IT WITH YOU *Jackie de Shannon—Imperial 66202*
[Chip Taylor] [BMI] (9/10/66 BCRt-58)

I CAN NEVER GO HOME ANYMORE The Shangri-Las—Red Bird 10-043
[Shadow Morton] [BMI] (11/6/65 BCR-5)

I CAN REMEMBER *James & Bobby Purify—Bell 721*
[Richie Grasso/Gary Illingworth/Myrna March] [BMI] (4/20/68 BCR-44)

I CAN REMEMBER *Oliver—Crewe 346*
[Richie Grasso/Gary Illingworth/Myrna March] [BMI] (7/18/70 CR-94)

I CAN SEE CLEARLY NOW Johnny Nash—Epic 10902
[Johnny Nash] [ASC] (8/26/72 BCR-1)

I CAN SEE FOR MILES The Who—Decca 32206
[Pete Townshend] [ASC] (10/7/67 BCR-8)

I CAN SING A RAINBOW The Dells—Cadet 5641
[Arthur Hamilton] (Med) [ASC] (5/17/69 BCR-14)

I CAN STAND A LITTLE RAIN Joe Cocker—A&M 1626 [Jim Price] [ASC] (10/26/74 C-91)

I CAN SURVIVE Triumph—RCA 11945
[Rik Emmett/Mike Levine/Gil Moore] [ASC] (4/12/80 BCR-90)

I CAN TAKE CARE OF MYSELF Billy & The Beaters—Alfa 7002
[Billy Vera] [ASC] (4/25/81 BCR-39)

I CAN TAKE OR LEAVE YOUR LOVING Herman's Hermits—MGM 13885
[Rick Jones] [ASC] (1/13/68 BCR-20)

I CAN UNDERSTAND IT The New Birth—RCA Victor 74-0912
[Bobby Womack] [BMI] (3/17/73 BCR-28)

I CANNOT BELIEVE IT'S TRUE Phil Collins—Atlantic 89864
[Phil Collins] [ASC] (5/7/83 BC-79)

I CANNOT STOP YOU The Cherry Slush—U.S.A. 895 [Dick Wagner] [BMI] (2/24/68 R-93)

I CAN'T ASK FOR ANYMORE THAN YOU Cliff Richard—Rocket/MCA 40652
[Michael Denne/Ken Gold] [ASC] (12/18/76 B-80)

I CAN'T BE ALL BAD Johnny Adams—SSS Int'l 780
[Margaret Lewis/Mira Smith] [BMI] (10/11/69 BCR-83)

I CAN'T BE YOU (YOU CAN'T BE ME) The Glass House—Invictus 9076
[Ronald Dunbar/General Johnson/Greg Perry] [BMI] (7/18/70 BCR-88)

I CAN'T BEGIN TO TELL YOU Jane Morgan—Kapp 284
[Mack Gordon/James V. Monaco] [ASC] (6/29/59 R-86)

I CAN'T BELIEVE I'M LOSING YOU Frank Sinatra—Reprise 0677
[Don Costa/Phil Zeller] [ASC] (4/6/68 BCR-50)

I CAN'T BELIEVE THAT YOU'VE STOPPED LOVING ME Charley Pride—RCA Victor 47-9902
[Dallas Frazier/A.L. "Doodle" Owens] [BMI] (10/24/70 BCR-71)

I CAN'T BELIEVE WHAT YOU SAY (FOR SEEING WHAT YOU DO) Ike & Tina Turner—
Kent 402 [Ike Turner] [BMI] (10/3/64 B-95)

I CAN'T BELIEVE YOU LOVE ME Tammi Terrell—Motown 1086
[Johnny Bristol/Harvey Fuqua] [ASC] (1/8/66 BCR-72)

I CAN'T CONTROL MYSELF The Troggs—Atco 6444 / Fontana 1557
[Reg Presley] [BMI] (10/15/66 BCR-35)

I CAN'T DANCE TO THAT MUSIC YOU'RE PLAYIN'
Martha Reeves & The Vandellas—Gordy 7075
[Debbie Dean/Deke Richards] [ASC] (8/10/68 BCR-40)

I CAN'T DO ENOUGH The Dells—Cadet 5636
[Robert Eugene Miller] [BMI] (4/12/69 BC-93)

I CAN'T DO IT BY MYSELF Anita Bryant—Carlton 547
[Jo Davis/B.L. Porter] [BMI] (5/1/61 BR-87)

I CAN'T DRIVE 55 Sammy Hagar—Geffen 29173 [Sammy Hagar] [ASC] (9/29/84 BC-26)

I CAN'T EXPLAIN The Who—Decca 31725 [Pete Townshend] [BMI] (2/20/65 BCR-57)

I CAN'T FACE THE FACT Gina Go-Go—Capitol 44233
[Desmond Foster/Gina Gomez/Nick Mundy] [BMI] (2/25/89 BC-77)

I CAN'T GET NEXT TO YOU *The Temptations—Gordy 7093*
[Barrett Strong/Norman Whitfield] [BMI] (8/16/69 BCR-1)

I CAN'T GET NEXT TO YOU *Al Green—Hi 2182*
[Barrett Strong/Norman Whitfield] [BMI] (11/14/70 BCR-60)

(I CAN'T GET NO) SATISFACTION *The Rolling Stones—London 9766*
[Mick Jagger/Keith Richards] [BMI] (6/12/65 BCR-1)

SATISFACTION *Otis Redding—Volt 132*
[Mick Jagger/Keith Richards] [BMI] (3/5/66 BCR-29)

(I CAN'T GET NO) SATISFACTION *Tight Fit—Arista 0638*
[Mick Jagger/Keith Richards] (Med) [BMI] (10/10/81 B-89)

I CAN'T GET OVER YOU The Dramatics—ABC 12258
[John Brinson/Floyd Fleshman/Edward McGhee] [ASC] (6/11/77 C-84)

I CAN'T GET YOU OUT OF MY HEART *Al Martino—20th Fox 132*
[Jimmie Crane/Danny DiMinno] [ASC] (3/16/59 BCRt-25)

I CAN'T GET YOU OUT OF MY HEART *Bob Carroll—Unart 2012*
[Jimmie Crane/Danny DiMinno] [ASC] (3/30/59 Rt-25)

I CAN'T GET YOU OUT OF MY HEART *Al Martino—20th Fox 530*
[Jimmie Crane/Danny DiMinno] [ASC] (8/15/64 B-99)

I CAN'T GIVE YOU ANYTHING BUT LOVE *The Johnston Brothers—London 1526*
[Dorothy Fields/Jimmy McHugh] (Med) [ASC] (7/11/55 R-61)

I CAN'T GIVE YOU ANYTHING BUT LOVE *Bert Kaempfert And His Orchestra—Decca 32008*
[Jimmy McHugh] [ASC] (10/1/66 BC-97) [IM]

I CAN'T GO FOR THAT (NO CAN DO) Daryl Hall & John Oates—RCA 12357
[Sara Allen/Daryl Hall/John Oates] [BMI] (11/14/81 BCR-1)

I CAN'T GO ON LIVIN' WITHOUT YOU BABY
Nino Tempo & April Stevens—White Whale 252
[Jerry Riopelle/Nino Tempo] [BMI] (7/22/67 BR-86)

I CAN'T GROW PEACHES ON A CHERRY TREE Just Us—Minuteman 203/Colpix 803
[Estelle Levitt/Camille Monte] [ASC] (3/5/66 BCR-34)

I CAN'T HEAR YOU *Betty Everett—Vee-Jay 599*
[Gerry Goffin/Carole King] [BMI] (6/27/64 BCR-66)

I CAN'T HEAR YOU NO MORE *Helen Reddy—Capitol 4312*
[Gerry Goffin/Carole King] (TSW) [BMI] (8/14/76 BCR-29)

—I CAN'T HELP FALLING IN LOVE see: CAN'T HELP FALLING...

I CAN'T HELP IT The Moments—Stang 5020
[Joyce Bennett/Shena DeMell*/Sylvia Robinson] [BMI] (4/10/71 C-90)

I CAN'T HELP IT Andy Gibb & Olivia Newton-John—RSO 1026
[Barry Gibb] [BMI] (3/29/80 BCR-12)

I CAN'T HELP IT Bananarama—London 886212
[Matt Aitken/Sarah Dallin/Siobhan Fahey/Mike Stock/Pete Waterman/
Keren Woodward] [BMI] (11/21/87 BC-47)

I CAN'T HELP IT (IF I'M STILL IN LOVE WITH YOU) *Margaret Whiting—Dot 15680*
[Hank Williams] [BMI] (3/10/58 B-74)

I CAN'T HELP IT *Adam Wade—Coed 530 [Hank Williams] [BMI] (5/23/60 BCR-39)*

I CAN'T HELP IT (IF I'M STILL IN LOVE WITH YOU) *Johnny Tillotson—Cadence 1432*
[Hank Williams] [BMI] (10/27/62 BCR-12)

I CAN'T HELP IT (IF I'M STILL IN LOVE WITH YOU) *B.J. Thomas—Scepter 12194*
[Hank Williams] [BMI] (5/13/67 BCR-93)

I CAN'T HELP IT (IF I'M STILL IN LOVE WITH YOU) *Al Martino—Capitol 2355*
[Hank Williams] [BMI] (12/28/68 BCR-84)

I CAN'T HELP MYSELF *Four Tops—Motown 1076*
[Lamont Dozier/Brian Holland/Eddie Holland] [BMI] (5/15/65 BCR-1)

I CAN'T HELP MYSELF *The Magnificent Men—Capitol 5976*
[Lamont Dozier/Brian Holland/Eddie Holland] (Med) [BMI] (9/9/67 BCR-90)

I CAN'T HELP MYSELF (SUGAR PIE, HONEY BUNCH) *Donnie Elbert—Avco 4587*
[Lamont Dozier/Brian Holland/Eddie Holland] [BMI] (1/22/72 BCR-16)

I CAN'T HELP MYSELF (SUGAR PIE, HONEY BUNCH) *Shalamar—Soul Train 10885*
[Lamont Dozier/Brian Holland/Eddie Holland] (Med) [BMI] (3/12/77 BCR-25)

I CAN'T HELP MYSELF (SUGAR PIE, HONEY BUNCH) *Bonnie Pointer—Motown 1478*
[Lamont Dozier/Brian Holland/Eddie Holland] [BMI] (12/22/79 BCR-40)

I CAN'T HELP MYSELF Eddie Rabbitt—Elektra 45390
[Eddie Rabbitt/Even Stevens] [BMI] (6/25/77 B-77)

I CAN'T HOLD BACK Survivor—Scotti Brothers 04603
[Jim Peterik/Frankie Sullivan] [ASC] (9/15/84 BC-13)

I CAN'T HOLD ON Karla Bonoff—Columbia 10618 [Karla Bonoff] [BMI] (1/28/78 BCR-69)

I CAN'T LEAVE YOU ALONE George McCrae—TK 1007
[Harry Wayne Casey/Rick Finch] [BMI] (10/12/74 BCR-50)

I CAN'T LEAVE YOUR LOVE ALONE Clarence Carter—Atlantic 2726
[Clarence Carter/George Henry Jackson] [BMI] (4/11/70 BCR-42)

I CAN'T LET GO *The Hollies—Imperial 66158*
[Al Gorgoni/Chip Taylor] [BMI] (3/19/66 BCR-42)

I CAN'T LET GO *Linda Ronstadt—Asylum 46654*
[Al Gorgoni/Chip Taylor] [BMI] (6/28/80 BCR-27)

I CAN'T LIVE A DREAM The Osmonds—Polydor/Kolob 14348
[Arnold Capitanelli] [ASC] (9/25/76 BCR-46)

I CAN'T LIVE WITHOUT YOUR LOVE Teddy Pendergrass—Philadelphia Int'l 5 02462
[Leon Huff/Cecil Womack] [BMI] (10/17/81 R-91)

I CAN'T LOVE YOU ENOUGH LaVern Baker—Atlantic 1104
[LaVern Baker/Dorian Burton/Howard Plummer] [BMI] (9/15/56 BCR-37)

I CAN'T MAKE IT ALONE *Bill Medley—MGM 13931*
[Gerry Goffin/Carole King] [BMI] (5/4/68 BCR-63)

I CAN'T MAKE IT ALONE *Lou Rawls—Capitol 2668*
[Gerry Goffin/Carole King] [BMI] (11/1/69 BCR-63)

I CAN'T MAKE IT ANYMORE Spyder Turner—MGM 13692
[Gordon Lightfoot] [ASC] (3/25/67 BCR-95)

I CAN'T MAKE YOU LOVE ME Bonnie Raitt—Capitol 44729
[Mike Reid/Allen Shamblin] [ASC] (11/9/91 BC-7)

I CAN'T MOVE NO MOUNTAINS Blood, Sweat & Tears—Columbia 45755
[Michael Gately/Robert John] [BMI] (12/30/72 CR-78)

I CAN'T PLEASE YOU Jimmy Robins—Jerhart 207 [Jimmy Robins] [BMI] (1/14/67 CR-77)

I CAN'T QUIT HER The Arbors—Date 1645
[Al Kooper/Irwin Levine] (Med) [BMI] (5/24/69 BCR-67)

I CAN'T ROCK AND ROLL TO SAVE MY SOUL Pearl Bailey—Mercury 70926
[Fred Tobias] [ASC] (8/17/56 R-44)

I CAN'T SAY GOODBYE Fireflies Featuring Ritchie Adams—Ribbon 6904
[Jimmie Crane/Paul Giacalone/Phil Tucker] [ASC] (12/21/59 BCR-49)

I CAN'T SAY GOODBYE Bobby Vee—Liberty 55419
[Gerry Goffin/Carole King] [BMI] (2/24/62 BC-90)

I CAN'T SAY GOODBYE TO YOU Helen Reddy—MCA 51106
[Becky Hobbs] [BMI] (5/23/81 BC-88)

I CAN'T SAY NO TO YOU Betty Everett—Uni 55122 [Bob Stone] [BMI] (4/26/69 BCR-73)

I CAN'T SEE MYSELF LEAVING YOU Aretha Franklin—Atlantic 2619
[Ronnie Shannon] [BMI] (4/19/69 BCR-20)

I CAN'T SIT DOWN Marie & Rex—Carlton 502
[Jack Keller/Noel Sherman] [BMI] (2/16/59 BCR-84)

I CAN'T STAND IT Soul Sisters—Sue 799 [Smokey McAllister] [BMI] (2/22/64 BCR-42)

I CAN'T STAND IT Eric Clapton And His Band—RSO 1060
[Eric Clapton] [BMI] (2/28/81 BCR-10)

I CAN'T STAND IT NO MORE Peter Frampton—A&M 2148
[Peter Frampton] [ASC] (5/26/79 BCR-14)

I CAN'T STAND MYSELF (WHEN YOU TOUCH ME)
James Brown And The Famous Flames—King 6144
[James Brown] [BMI] (12/9/67 BCR-19)

I CAN'T STAND STILL Don Henley—Asylum 69931
[Don Henley/Danny Kortchmar] [ASC] (1/15/83 BC-38)

I CAN'T STAND THE RAIN *Ann Peebles—Hi 2248*
[Donald Bryant/Bernard Miller/Ann Peebles] [BMI] (9/1/73 BCR-33)

I CAN'T STAND THE RAIN *Eruption—Ariola America/Hansa 7686*
[Donald Bryant/Bernard Miller/Ann Peebles] [BMI] (3/11/78 BCR-18)

I CAN'T STAND TO SEE YOU CRY Smokey Robinson & The Miracles—Tamla 54225
[Johnny Bristol/Wade Brown/David H. Jones] [ASC] (12/9/72 BCR-45)

I CAN'T STAY AWAY FROM YOU The Impressions—ABC 10964
[Curtis Mayfield] [BMI] (8/19/67 BCR-80)

I CAN'T STAY MAD AT YOU Skeeter Davis—RCA Victor 47-8219
[Gerry Goffin/Carole King] [BMI] (8/24/63 BCR-5)

I CAN'T STOP The Honeycombs—Interphon 7713
[Alan Blaikley/Ken Howard] [ASC] (12/19/64 BCR-45)

I CAN'T STOP The Osmond Brothers—Uni 55276
[Wes Farrell/Jerry Goldstein] [BMI] (3/13/71 B-96)

I CAN'T STOP DANCING Archie Bell & The Drells—Atlantic 2534
[Kenneth Gamble/Leon Huff] [BMI] (7/20/68 BCR-5)

I CAN'T STOP LOVING YOU *Don Gibson—RCA Victor 47-7133*
[Don Gibson] [BMI] (2/24/58 B-81)

I CAN'T STOP LOVING YOU *Ray Charles—ABC-Paramount 10330*
[Don Gibson] [BMI] (4/30/62 BCRt-1)

I CAN'T STOP LOVING YOU *Gene Ammons—Argo 5417*
[Don Gibson] [BMI] (6/30/62 Rt-1) [IWM]

I CAN'T STOP LOVING YOU *Count Basie—Reprise 20,170*
[Don Gibson] [BMI] (6/1/63 BCR-77) [IWM]

—I CAN'T STOP LOVING YOU see also: CAN'T STOP LOVING YOU

I CAN'T STOP SINGING Bobby Bland—Duke 370
[Deadric Malone] [BMI] (1/4/64 C-98)

I CAN'T STOP TALKING ABOUT YOU Steve And Eydie—Columbia 42932
[Gerry Goffin/Carole King] [BMI] (11/30/63 BCR-31)

I CAN'T STOP THINKING OF YOU Bobbi Martin—Coral 62447
[Lee Bayer/Guy Louis] [BMI] (3/13/65 BCR-44)

I CAN'T STOP THIS FEELIN' Pure Prairie League—Casablanca 2319
[Daniel Fleishour/James Sandefur] [BMI] (12/6/80 BCR-77)

I CAN'T TAKE IT Mary Ann Fisher—Seg-Way 1001
[Tony Bruno/Gerry Granahan] [BMI] (8/28/61 BC-92)

I CAN'T TELL A WALTZ FROM A TANGO Patti Page—Mercury 70458
[Al Hoffman/Dick Manning] [ASC] (10/4/54 CR-24)

I CAN'T TELL THE BOTTOM FROM THE TOP The Hollies—Epic 10613
[Guy Fletcher/Doug Flett] [ASC] (5/23/70 BCR-64)

I CAN'T TELL YOU WHY Eagles—Asylum 46608
[Glenn Frey/Don Henley/Timothy B. Schmit] [ASC] (2/23/80 BCR-7)

I CAN'T TURN YOU LOOSE *The Chambers Brothers—Columbia 44679*
[Otis Redding] [BMI] (11/16/68 BCR-32)

I CAN'T TURN YOU LOOSE *Edgar Winter's White Trash—Epic 10855*
[Otis Redding] [BMI] (5/6/72 BCR-81)

I CAN'T WAIT Stevie Nicks—Modern 99565
[Stevie Nicks/Rick Nowels/Eric Pressly] [BMI] (2/22/86 BC-13)

I CAN'T WAIT Nu Shooz—Atlantic 89446 [John Robert Smith] [BMI] (3/8/86 BC-3)

I CAN'T WAIT Deniece Williams—Columbia 08014 [Skylark] [ASC] (9/24/88 BC-56)

I CAN'T WAIT ANOTHER MINUTE Hi-Five—Jive 1445
[Eric Foster White] [ASC] (6/22/91 BC-8)

I CAN'T WAIT ANY LONGER Bill Anderson—MCA 40893
[Bill Anderson/Buddy Killen] [BMI] (7/15/78 B-80)

I CAN'T WAIT UNTIL I SEE MY BABY Justine Washington—Sue 797
[Jerry Ragovoy/Chip Taylor] [BMI] (3/21/64 B-93)

I CAN'T WORK NO LONGER Billy Butler & The Chanters—Okeh 7221
[Curtis Mayfield] [NA] (7/3/65 BCR-58)

I CAUGHT YOUR ACT The Hues Corporation—Warner/Curb 8334
[Wally Holmes] [BMI] (4/30/77 B-92)

I CHEAT THE HANGMAN The Doobie Brothers—Warner Bros. 8161
[Patrick Simmons] [ASC] (11/29/75 BC-60)

I CHOSE TO SING THE BLUES Ray Charles & The Raeletts—ABC 10840
[Ray Charles/Jimmy Holiday] [BMI] (8/27/66 BCR-32)

I COME OFF Young M.C.—Delicious Vinyl 98993
[Matt Dike/Michael Ross*/Marvin Young] [ASC] (3/10/90 BC-55)

I CONFESS The New Colony Six—Centaur 1201
[Ray Graffia/Jerry Kollenburg] [BMI] (2/5/66 BCR-64)

I COULD BE GOOD FOR YOU 707—Casablanca 2280
[Jim McClarty/Duke McFadden] [ASC] (10/4/80 BCR-52)

I COULD BE SO GOOD TO YOU Don And The Goodtimes—Epic 10145
[Greg Dempsey/Jack Nitzsche] [BMI] (4/22/67 BCR-56)

I COULD BE SO HAPPY The Magnificent Men—Capitol 5905
[David Bupp/Adrian King] [BMI] (6/3/67 BC-93)

I COULD CONQUER THE WORLD The Shevelles—World Artists 1025
[Paul Evans/Paul Parnes] [ASC] (9/19/64 R-82)

I COULD HAVE DANCED ALL NIGHT *Dinah Shore—RCA Victor 47-6469*
[Alan Jay Lerner/Frederick Loewe] [ASC] (4/28/56 BRt-12)

I COULD HAVE DANCED ALL NIGHT *Rosemary Clooney—Columbia 40676*
[Alan Jay Lerner/Frederick Loewe] [ASC] (5/4/56 BCtRt-12)

I COULD HAVE DANCED ALL NIGHT *Sylvia Syms—Decca 29903*
[Alan Jay Lerner/Frederick Loewe] [ASC] (5/4/56 BCtRt-12)

I COULD HAVE DANCED ALL NIGHT *Lawrence Welk & His Champagne Music—Coral 61644*
[Alan Jay Lerner/Frederick Loewe] [ASC] (6/1/56 Rt-12)

I COULD HAVE DANCED ALL NIGHT
Sammy Kaye & His "Swing And Sway" Orchestra—Columbia 40707
[Frederick Loewe] [ASC] (6/22/56 Rt-12) [IM]

I COULD HAVE DANCED ALL NIGHT *Ben E. King—Atco 6275*
[Alan Jay Lerner/Frederick Loewe] [ASC] (11/2/63 B-72)

I COULD HAVE DANCED ALL NIGHT *Biddu Orchestra—Epic 50173*
[Frederick Loewe] (TSW) [ASC] (1/10/76 B-72) [IM]

I COULD HAVE LOVED YOU The Moments—Stang 5075
[Bette Midler/Bruce Roberts/Carole Bayer Sager] [BMI] (4/8/78 CR-94)

I COULD HAVE LOVED YOU SO WELL Ray Peterson—Dunes 2009
[Gerry Goffin/Barry Mann] [BMI] (12/16/61 BCR-57)

I COULD NEVER BE HAPPY The Emotions—Volt 4083
[Homer Banks/Carl Hampton/Raymond Earl Jackson] [BMI] (7/22/72 BC-92)

I COULD NEVER BE PRESIDENT Johnnie Taylor—Stax 0046
[Homer Banks/Bettye Crutcher/Raymond Earl Jackson] [BMI] (8/9/69 BCR-48)

I COULD NEVER LIE TO YOU The New Colony Six—Mercury 72920
[Pat McBride/Ronnie Rice] [BMI] (5/3/69 BCR-40)

I COULD NEVER LOVE ANOTHER (AFTER LOVING YOU) The Temptations—Gordy 7072
[Rodger Penzabene/Barrett Strong/Norman Whitfield] [BMI] (5/4/68 BCR-10)

I COULD NEVER MISS YOU (MORE THAN I DO) Lulu—Alfa 7006
[Neil Harrison] [BMI] (8/1/81 BCR-14)

I COULD NEVER TAKE THE PLACE OF YOUR MAN Prince—Paisley Park 7-28288
[Prince] [ASC] (11/14/87 BC-10)

I COULD WRITE A BOOK Jerry Butler—Mercury 73045
[Jerry Butler/Kenneth Gamble/Leon Huff] [BMI] (3/14/70 BCR-45)

I COULDN'T LIVE WITHOUT YOUR LOVE Petula Clark—Warner Bros. 5835
[Tony Hatch/Jackie Trent] [ASC] (7/16/66 BCR-8)

I COULDN'T SAY NO Robert Ellis Orrall With Carlene Carter—RCA 13431
[Robert Ellis Orrall] [ASC] (3/26/83 BC-32)

I COUNT THE TEARS The Drifters—Atlantic 2087
[Doc Pomus/Mort Shuman] [BMI] (12/19/60 BCR-11)

I CRIED *Patti Page—Mercury 70416*
[Michael Elias/William Tesone] [ASC] (8/7/54 BCR-14)

I CRIED *Joe Damiano—Chancellor 1039*
[Michael Elias/William Tesone] [ASC] (8/31/59 BC-90)

I CRIED *Tammy Montgomery—Try Me 28001*
[James Brown/Bobby Byrd] [BMI] (8/17/63 B-99)

I CRIED *James Brown—King 6363 [James Brown/Bobby Byrd] [BMI] (5/1/71 BCR-38)*

I CRIED A TEAR LaVern Baker—Atlantic 2007 [Fred Jay/Al Julia] [BMI] (12/8/58 BCR-6)

(I CRIED AT) LAURA'S WEDDING Barbara Lynn—Jamie 1260
[Dick Manning/Kay Twomey] [ASC] (8/10/63 BCR-68)

I CRIED MY LAST TEAR *Ernie K-Doe—Minit 634 [Allen Toussaint] [BMI] (11/6/61 B-69)*

I'VE CRIED MY LAST TEAR *The O'Jays—Imperial 66121*
[Allen Toussaint] [BMI] (8/7/65 BCR-93)

I CRY MYSELF TO SLEEP AT NIGHT Romeo's Daughter—Jive 1176
[Craig Joiner/Mutt Lange/Anthony Mitman] [ASC] (2/25/89 C-72)

I DID IT FOR LOVE Night Ranger—Camel/MCA 53364
[Russ Ballard] [ASC] (10/1/88 BC-75)

I DIDN'T FIGURE ON HIM (TO COME BACK) Ral Donner—Gone 5114
[Chesley Howard*/Douglas Lapham] [BMI] (10/7/61 C-97)

I DIDN'T KNOW I LOVED YOU (TILL I SAW YOU ROCK AND ROLL)
Gary Glitter—Bell 45,276
[Gary Glitter/Mike Leander] [BMI] (10/28/72 BCR-28)

I DIDN'T KNOW WHAT TIME IT WAS *The Crampton Sisters—DCP 1001*
[Lorenz Hart/Richard Rodgers] [ASC] (2/8/64 BCR-81)

I DIDN'T KNOW WHAT TIME IT WAS *Ray Charles—ABC/TRC 11193*
[Lorenz Hart/Richard Rodgers] [ASC] (3/1/69 CR-69)

I DIDN'T MEAN TO STAY ALL NIGHT Starship—RCA 9109
[Mutt Lange] [ASC] (11/25/89 B-75)

I DIDN'T MEAN TO TURN YOU ON *Cherrelle—Tabu 4-04406*
[James Samuel Harris/Terry Lewis] [ASC] (7/7/84 BC-71)

I DIDN'T MEAN TO TURN YOU ON *Robert Palmer—Island 99537*
[James Samuel Harris/Terry Lewis] [ASC] (8/16/86 BC-2)

—I DIDN'T WANT TO HAVE TO BE THE ONE see: SOMEDAY

I DIDN'T WANT TO NEED YOU Heart—Capitol 44553
[Diane Warren] [ASC] (6/23/90 BC-21)

I DIG EVERYTHING ABOUT YOU The Mob—Colossus 130
[Gary Beisbier/James Holvay] [BMI] (12/26/70 BCR-83)

I DIG GIRLS Bobby Rydell—Cameo 169
[Doc Pomus/Mort Shuman] [BMI] (10/5/59 BCR-44)

I DIG GIRLS J.J. Jackson—Calla 125 [Ed King] [BMI] (12/31/66 BCR-71)

I DIG ROCK AND ROLL MUSIC Peter, Paul & Mary—Warner Bros. 7067
[David George Dixon/James Howard Mason/Paul Stookey] [ASC] (8/19/67 BCR-9)

I DIG YOU BABY Marivn Rainwater—MGM 12665
[Marvin Rainwater/Bobby Stevenson] [BMI] (6/23/58 R-85)

***I DIG YOU BABY** Lorraine Ellison—Mercury 72472*
[Samuel Bell/Lorraine Ellison/Dennis Lambert] [BMI] (2/5/66 CR-80)

***I DIG YOU BABY** Jerry Butler—Mercury 72648*
[Samuel Bell/Lorraine Ellison/Dennis Lambert] [BMI] (1/21/67 BCR-60)

***I DO** The Marvelows—ABC-Paramount 10629*
[Melvin Mason/Frank Paden/Johnny Paden/Jesse Smith/Willie Stephenson] [BMI] (5/15/65 BCR-28)

***I DO (LIVE VERSION)** The J. Geils Band—EMI America 8148*
[Melvin Mason/Frank Paden/Johnny Paden/Jesse Smith/Willie Stephenson] [BMI] (11/20/82 BC-24)

I DO The Moments (2)—Stang 5005 [Kenneth Ruffin] [BMI] (8/16/69 BCR-50)

I DO BELIEVE IN YOU Pages—Epic 50769
[Steve George/John Lang/Jerry Manfredi/Richard Page] [ASC] (11/10/79 BCR-76)

I DO, I DO, I DO, I DO, I DO Abba—Atlantic 3310
[Stig Anderson/Benny Andersson/Björn Ulvaeus] [BMI] (2/14/76 BCR-15)

***I DO LOVE YOU** Billy Stewart—Chess 1922 [Billy Stewart] [BMI] (3/13/65 BCR-22)*

***I DO LOVE YOU** Billy Stewart—Chess 1922 [Billy Stewart] [BMI] (2/22/69 BR-94)*

***I DO LOVE YOU** GQ—Arista 0426 [Billy Stewart] [BMI] (6/30/79 BCR-18)*

I DO TAKE YOU The Three Degrees—Roulette 7088
[Myrna March] [ASC] (9/12/70 BCR-42)

I DO THE ROCK Tim Curry—A&M 2166
[Tim Curry/Michael Kamen] [BMI] (11/3/79 BCR-77)

—I DO THE SHIMMY SHIMMY see: SHIMMY SHIMMY

I DO' WANNA KNOW REO Speedwagon—Epic 04659
[Kevin Cronin] [ASC] (10/27/84 BC-28)

I DO WHAT I DO John Taylor—Capitol 5551
[Michael Des Barres/Jonathan Elias/Nigel John Taylor] [ASC] (3/8/86 BC-23)

I DO YOU The Jets—MCA 53193 [Rick Kelly/Linda Mallah] [ASC] (10/17/87 BC-20)

I DON'T BELIEVE The Guilloteens—HBR 446 [Louis E. Paul] [BMI] (7/10/65 R-65)

I DON'T BELIEVE I'LL FALL IN LOVE TODAY Bobby Bare—RCA Victor 47-8083
[Harlan Howard] [BMI] (10/27/62 CR-88)

I DON'T BELIEVE YOU WANT TO GET UP AND DANCE (OOPS, UP SIDE YOUR HEAD)
The Gap Band—Mercury 76037
[Lonnie Simmons/Rudy Taylor/Charles K. Wilson/Robert Wilson/Ronnie Wilson] [BMI] (3/22/80 R-92)

I DON'T BLAME YOU AT ALL Smokey Robinson & The Miracles—Tamla 54205
[Smokey Robinson] [ASC] (3/13/71 BCR-18)

—I DON'T CARE ABOUT YOU see: I DON'T LOVE YOU NO MORE

I DON'T CARE ANYMORE Phil Collins—Atlantic 89877
[Phil Collins] [ASC] (2/12/83 BC-39)

I DON'T CARE IF THE SUN DON'T SHINE Elvis Presley—RCA Victor 47-6381
[Mack David] [ASC] (10/6/56 BCR-46)

I DON'T CARE (JUST AS LONG AS YOU LOVE ME) Buck Owens—Capitol 5240
[Buck Owens] [BMI] (8/22/64 BCR-86)

***(I DON'T CARE) ONLY LOVE ME** Steve Lawrence—ABC-Paramount 10005*
[Mann Curtis/Virgilio Panzuti] [ASC] (3/21/59 BCRt-62) [FDE]

***(I DON'T CARE) ONLY LOVE ME** Kay Starr—RCA Victor 47-7521*
[Mann Curtis/Virgilio Panzuti] [ASC] (5/4/59 Rt-87) [FDE]

I DON'T HAVE THE HEART James Ingram—Warner Bros. 19911
[Jud Friedman/Allan Rich] [ASC] (8/4/90 BC-1)

***I DON'T HURT ANYMORE** Ray Anthony & His Orchestra—Capitol 2860*
[Don Robertson/Jack Rollins] [ASC] (11/8/54 Rt-PRE)

I DON'T HURT ANYMORE
Hank Snow The Singing Ranger And The Rainbow Ranch Boys—RCA Victor 47-5698
[Don Robertson/Jack Rollins] [ASC] (11/8/54 Rt-78)

***I DON'T HURT ANYMORE** Eddie Fisher—RCA Victor 47-7135*
[Don Robertson/Jack Rollins] [ASC] (1/13/58 R-80)

I DON'T KNOW Ruth Brown—Atlantic 2035
[Brook Benton/Bobby Stevenson] [BMI] (9/26/59 BCR-55)

I DON'T KNOW Michael Morales—Wing 873 282
[Michael Morales] [ASC] (12/9/89 B-81)

I DON'T KNOW ANYBODY ELSE Black Box—RCA 2735
[Daniele Davoli/Mirko Limoni/Valerio Semplici] [ASC] (12/8/90 BC-23)

I DON'T KNOW ENOUGH ABOUT YOU Peggy Lee—Decca 30059
[David M. Barbour/Peggy Lee] [ASC] (11/3/56 R-73)

***I DON'T KNOW HOW TO LOVE HIM** Helen Reddy—Capitol 3027*
[Tim Rice/Andrew Lloyd Webber] [ASC] (2/20/71 BCR-12)

***I DON'T KNOW HOW TO LOVE HIM** The Kimberlys—Happy Tiger 572*
[Tim Rice/Andrew Lloyd Webber] (Med) [ASC] (3/20/71 B-99)

***I DON'T KNOW HOW TO LOVE HIM** Yvonne Elliman—Decca 32785*
[Tim Rice/Andrew Lloyd Webber] [ASC] (4/17/71 BCR-23)

I DON'T KNOW IF IT'S RIGHT Evelyn "Champagne" King—RCA 11386
[John Fitch/Ted Life] [BMI] (12/9/78 BCR-17)

I DON'T KNOW WHAT IT IS The Bluenotes—Brooke 111
[Joe Tanner] [BMI] (12/14/59 BCR-61)

I DON'T KNOW WHAT IT IS, BUT IT SURE IS FUNKY Ripple—GRC 1004
[Simon Kenneth Carter/Walter Carter/Dave Ferguson/Bill Hull/Curtis Reynolds/Keith Samuels/Brian Sherrer] [BMI] (11/3/73 BCR-56)

I DON'T KNOW WHAT YOU'VE GOT BUT IT'S GOT ME - PART 1
Little Richard—Vee-Jay 698
[Don Covay/Horace Hall] [BMI] (11/13/65 BC-83)

I DON'T KNOW WHERE TO START Eddie Rabbitt—Elektra 47435
[Thom Schuyler] [BMI] (4/10/82 BC-35)

I DON'T KNOW WHY Linda Scott—Canadian-American 129
[Fred Ahlert/Roy Turk] [ASC] (10/23/61 BCR-11)

***I DON'T KNOW WHY** Stevie Wonder—Tamla 54180*
[Lula Mae Hardaway/Don Hunter/Paul Riser/Stevie Wonder] [BMI] (2/15/69 BCR-37)

***I DON'T KNOW WHY** The Rolling Stones—Abkco 4701*
[Lula Mae Hardaway/Don Hunter/Paul Riser/Stevie Wonder] [BMI] (6/7/75 BCR-37)

I DON'T LIKE MONDAYS The Boomtown Rats—Columbia 11117
[Bob Geldof] [ASC] (1/26/80 BCR-70)

I DON'T LIKE TO SLEEP ALONE Paul Anka—United Artists 615
[Paul Anka] [BMI] (3/15/75 BCR-5)

I DON'T LOVE YOU ANYMORE Teddy Pendergrass—Philadelphia Int'l 3622
[Kenneth Gamble/Leon Huff] [BMI] (4/30/77 BCR-41)

I DON'T LOVE YOU ANYMORE The London Quireboys—Capitol 44588
[Guy Bailey/Jonathan Gray] [ASC] (9/22/90 BC-69)

I DON'T LOVE YOU NO MORE (I DON'T CARE ABOUT YOU) Jimmy Norman—Little Star 113
[H.B. Barnum] [BMI] (5/26/62 BCR-43)

I DON'T MIND James Brown And The Famous Flames—King 5466
[James Brown] [BMI] (5/15/61 BCR-47)

I DON'T MIND AT ALL Bourgeois Tagg—Island 99409
[Brent Bourgeois/Lyle Workman] [ASC] (10/10/87 BC-38)

***I DON'T NEED NO DOCTOR** Ray Charles And His Orchestra—ABC 10865*
[Jo Armstead/Nick Ashford/Valerie Simpson] [BMI] (11/26/66 BR-72)

***I DON'T NEED NO DOCTOR** Humble Pie—A&M 1282*
[Jo Armstead/Nick Ashford/Valerie Simpson] [BMI] (9/25/71 BCR-70)

***I DON'T NEED NO DOCTOR** New Riders Of The Purple Sage—Columbia 45607*
[Jo Armstead/Nick Ashford/Valerie Simpson] [BMI] (6/10/72 BR-79)

I DON'T NEED YOU Rupert Holmes—MCA 51092 [Rupert Holmes] [ASC] (4/4/81 BCR-56)

I DON'T NEED YOU Kenny Rogers—Liberty 1415
[Ricky Lynn Christian] [BMI] (6/13/81 BCR-3)

I DON'T NEED YOU ANYMORE The Teddy Bears—Imperial 5562
[Phil Spector] [BMI] (1/31/59 BC-96)

I DON'T NEED YOU ANYMORE Together? With Jackie DeShannon—RCA 11902
[Paul Anka/Burt Bacharach] [BMI] (3/8/80 BR-86)

I DON'T SEE ME IN YOUR EYES ANYMORE Charlie Rich—RCA Victor 0260
[Bennie Benjamin/George David Weiss] [ASC] (5/4/74 BCR-47)

I DON'T THINK THAT MAN SHOULD SLEEP ALONE Ray Parker Jr.—Geffen 28417
[Ray Parker Jr.] [ASC] (8/29/87 BC-63)

I DON'T THINK YOU KNOW ME The American Breed—Acta 802
[Gerry Goffin/Carole King] [BMI] (4/8/67 R-89)

I DON'T WANNA BE A LOSER Lesley Gore—Mercury 72270
[Mark Barkan/Ben Raleigh] [BMI] (5/23/64 BCR-37)

I DON'T WANNA BE LEFT OUTSIDE Ellie Greenwich—Bell 855
[Ellie Greenwich/Mike Lendell] [BMI] (2/21/70 R-93)

I DON'T WANNA CRY Mariah Carey—Columbia 73743
[Mariah Carey/Narada Michael Walden] [ASC] (4/6/91 BC-1)

I DON'T WANNA DANCE Eddy Grant—Portrait 37-04039
[Eddy Grant] [ASC] (8/13/83 BC-53)

I DON'T WANNA GET DRAFTED Frank Zappa—Zappa 1001
[Frank Zappa] [ASC] (6/14/80 C-98)

I DON'T WANNA GO Joey Travolta—Millennium 615
[Bruce Roberts/Carole Bayer Sager] [BMI] (6/3/78 BCR-43)

I DON'T WANNA GO ON WITH YOU LIKE THAT Elton John—MCA 53345
[Elton John/Bernie Taupin] [BMI] (6/18/88 BC-2)

I DON'T WANNA LEAVE YOU Debbie Taylor—Arista 0144
[David Jordan/Andrew Smith] [ASC] (1/24/76 B-100)

I DON'T WANNA LIVE WITHOUT YOUR LOVE Chicago—Reprise/Full Moon 27855
[Albert Hammond/Diane Warren] [ASC] (6/4/88 BC-3)

I DON'T WANNA LOSE YOU Johnnie Taylor—Stax 0089
[Melvin Davis] [BMI] (5/22/71 BCR-64)

I DON'T WANNA LOSE YOU Daryl Hall & John Oates—RCA 11424
[Daryl Hall/John Oates] [BMI] (12/9/78 BCR-42)

I DON'T WANNA LOSE YOU BABY Chad & Jeremy—Columbia 43339
[Van McCoy] [BMI] (8/7/65 BCR-33)

I DON'T WANNA SEE YOU Michael Morales—Wing 867 396
[Michael Morales] [ASC] (7/13/91 BC-73)

I DON'T WANT A LOVER Texas—Mercury 872350
[Johnny McElhone/Sharleen Spiteri] [ASC] (9/9/89 BC-77)

I DON'T WANT NOBODY ELSE (TO DANCE WITH YOU) Narada Michael Walden—Atlantic 3541 [Narada Michael Walden] [ASC] (3/31/79 BCR-47)

I DON'T WANT NOBODY TO GIVE ME NOTHING (OPEN UP THE DOOR, I'LL GET IT MYSELF) (PART 1) James Brown—King 6224
[James Brown] [BMI] (3/29/69 BCR-16)

I DON'T WANT NOBODY (TO HAVE MY LOVE BUT YOU)
Woody Herman and His Orchestra—Capitol 3488
[Woodrow Buddy Johnson] [BMI] (8/18/56 B-75)

I DON'T WANT NOBODY (TO HAVE MY LOVE BUT YOU)
Ella Johnson With Buddy Johnson And His Orchestra—Mercury 71723
[Woodrow Buddy Johnson] [BMI] (12/31/60 B-78)

I DON'T WANT TO BE A HERO Johnny Hates Jazz—Virgin 99304
[Clark Datchler] [BMI] (7/9/88 BC-30)

I DON'T WANT TO BE A LONE RANGER Johnny "Guitar" Watson—Fantasy 739
[Johnny Watson] [BMI] (10/4/75 B-99)

I DON'T WANT TO BE HURT ANYMORE Nat King Cole—Capitol 5155
[Charlotte McCarthy] [ASC] (4/11/64 BCR-19)

I DON'T WANT TO BE LONELY Dana Valery—Scotti Brothers 509
[Mark Mueller] [BMI] (1/19/80 B-87)

I DON'T WANT TO CRY *Chuck Jackson—Wand 106*
[Luther Dixon/Chuck Jackson] [BMI] (2/11/61 BCR-24)

I DON'T WANT TO CRY *Ruby Winters—Diamond 255*
[Luther Dixon/Chuck Jackson] [BMI] (2/8/69 BCR-80)

I DON'T WANNA CRY *Ronnie Dyson—Columbia 45240*
[Luther Dixon/Chuck Jackson] [BMI] (10/17/70 BCR-35)

I DON'T WANT TO DO WRONG Gladys Knight & The Pips—Soul 35083
[Johnny Bristol/William Guest/Gladys Knight/Merald Knight/Katherine Schaffner] [ASC] (5/22/71 BCR-9)

I DON'T WANT TO HEAR ANYMORE *Jerry Butler—Vee-Jay 598*
[Randy Newman] [BMI] (6/27/64 B-95)

I DON'T WANT TO HEAR IT ANYMORE *Dusty Springfield—Atlantic 2623*
[Randy Newman] (TSW) [BMI] (4/26/69 CR-81)

I DON'T WANT TO KNOW YOUR NAME Glen Campbell—Capitol 4959
[Micheal Smotherman] [ASC] (1/24/81 BCR-65)

I DON'T WANT TO LIVE WITHOUT YOU Foreigner—Atlantic 89101
[Michael Leslie Jones] [ASC] (3/19/88 BC-5)

I DON'T WANT TO LOSE YOU Jackie Wilson—Brunswick 55309
[Carl Davis/Karl Tarleton] [BMI] (3/4/67 BCR-71)

I DON'T WANNA LOSE YOUR LOVE *The Emotions—Columbia 10347*
[Jeanette Hawes/Wanda Hutchinson] (TSW) [BMI] (11/6/76 BCR-51)

I DON'T WANT TO LOSE YOUR LOVE *B Angie B—Bust It 44658*
[Jeanette Hawes/Wanda Hutchinson] [BMI] (4/27/91 B-54)

(I DON'T WANT TO LOVE YOU BUT) YOU GOT ME ANYWAY
Sutherland Brothers And Quiver—Island 1217
[Iain Sutherland] [ASC] (8/4/73 BCR-20)

I DON'T WANT TO MAKE YOU WAIT The Delfonics—Philly Groove 176
[William Hart] [BMI] (4/28/73 BC-86)

I DON'T WANT TO SEE TOMORROW Nat King Cole—Capitol 5261
[Lee Morris/Bernie Wayne] [ASC] (9/19/64 BCR-34)

I DON'T WANT TO SEE YOU AGAIN Peter And Gordon—Capitol 5272
[John Lennon/Paul McCartney] [ASC] (10/3/64 BCR-16)

I DON'T WANT TO SET THE WORLD ON FIRE Somethin' Smith & The Redheads—Epic 9280
[Bennie Benjamin/Eddie Durham/Sol Marcus/Eddie Seiler] [ASC] (8/11/58 CR-34)

I DON'T WANT TO SPOIL THE PARTY The Beatles—Capitol 5371
[John Lennon/Paul McCartney] [ASC] (2/20/65 BCR-39)

I DON'T WANT TO TAKE A CHANCE Mary Wells—Motown 1011
[Berry Gordy/William Stevenson] [ASC] (7/8/61 BCR-33)

I DON'T WANT TO TALK ABOUT IT Rod Stewart—Warner Bros. 49138
[Danny Whitten] [BMI] (12/22/79 BCR-46)

I DON'T WANT TO WALK WITHOUT YOU *Phyllis McGuire—Reprise 0310*
[Frank Loesser/Jule Styne] [ASC] (12/5/64 BCR-79)

I DON'T WANT TO WALK WITHOUT YOU *Barry Manilow—Arista 0501*
[Frank Loesser/Jule Styne] [ASC] (4/12/80 BCR-36)

I DON'T WANT YOUR LOVE Duran Duran—Capitol 44237
[Simon Le Bon/Nick Rhodes/Nigel John Taylor] [ASC] (10/15/88 BC-3)

I DREAMED Betty Johnson—Bally 1020
[Charles Grean/Marvin Moore] [BMI] (11/24/56 BCR-12)

I DREAMED LAST NIGHT Justin Hayward And John Lodge—Threshold 67019
[Justin Hayward] [ASC] (5/10/75 BCR-45)

I DREAMED OF A HILL-BILLY HEAVEN Tex Ritter—Capitol 4567
[Eddie Dean/Hal Southern] [SE] (6/26/61 BCR-20)

I DROVE ALL NIGHT Cyndi Lauper—Epic 68759
[Thomas F. Kelly/Billy Steinberg] [ASC] (5/6/89 BC-5)

I EAT CANNIBALS Total Coelo—Chrysalis 42669
[Barry Blue/Paul Greedus/Roy Nicolson] [BMI] (3/26/83 BC-65)

I ENGINEER Animotion—Casablanca 884433
[Mike Chapman/Holly Knight/Bernie Taupin] [ASC] (3/8/86 B-76)

I ENJOY BEING A GIRL *Pat Suzuki—RCA Victor 47-7458*
[Oscar Hammerstein/Richard Rodgers] [ASC] (2/9/59 Rt-95)

I ENJOY BEING A GIRL *Doris Day—Columbia 41307*
[Oscar Hammerstein/Richard Rodgers] [ASC] (2/16/59 Rt-95)

I ENVY Nat "King" Cole—Capitol 2803
[Stan Brenders/Ralph Care/Sol Marcus] [BMI] (7/10/54 C-36)

I FALL TO PIECES Patsy Cline—Decca 31205
[Hank Cochran/Harlan Howard] [BMI] (4/10/61 BCR-12)

I FEEL A SIN COMING ON Solomon Burke—Atlantic 2327
[Orville Couch/Eddie McDuff] [BMI] (4/9/66 B-97)

I FEEL A SONG (IN MY HEART) Gladys Knight & The Pips—Buddah 433
[Tony Camillo/Mary Jane Sawyer] (TSW) [BMI] (1/25/75 BCR-11)

I FEEL FINE The Beatles—Capitol 5327
[John Lennon/Paul McCartney] [ASC] (12/5/64 BCR-1)

I FEEL FOR YOU Chaka Khan—Warner Bros. 29195 [Prince] [ASC] (9/8/84 BC-1)

I FEEL FREE Belinda Carlisle—MCA 53377
[Peter Ronald Brown/Jack Bruce] [BMI] (7/30/88 BC-81)

I FEEL GOOD Shirley & Lee—Aladdin 3338 [Leonard Lee] [BMI] (12/1/56 BCR-38)

I FEEL GOOD (I FEEL BAD) Lewis & Clarke Expedition—Colgems 1006
[Boomer Castleman/Michael Murphey] [BMI] (8/19/67 BCR-63)

I FEEL LIKE A BULLET (IN THE GUN OF ROBERT FORD) Elton John—MCA 40505
[Elton John/Bernie Taupin] (TSW) [BMI] (1/24/76 BCR-14)

I FEEL LOVE Donna Summer—Casablanca 884
[Pete Bellotte/Giorgio Moroder/Donna Summer] [ASC] (8/6/77 BCR-4)

I FEEL SANCTIFIED Commodores—Motown 1319
[Jeff Bowen*/Ronald LaPread/Thomas McClary/William Roderick Miller*/Walter Orange/Lionel Richie/Milan Williams] [ASC] (11/16/74 BC-75)

I FEEL SO BAD Elvis Presley—RCA Victor 47-7880 [Chuck Willis] [BMI] (5/15/61 BCR-5)

I FEEL THAT I'VE KNOWN YOU FOREVER
Elvis Presley With The Jordanaires—RCA Victor EPA-4383
[Alan Jeffreys/Doc Pomus] (EP) [BMI] (7/10/65 BCR-70)

I FEEL THE BEAT Jim Lowe—Dot 15525
[Bob Davie/Marvin Moore] [BMI] (12/15/56 BR-49)

I FEEL THE EARTH MOVE *Carole King—Ode '70 66015/Ode 66015*
[Carole King] (TSW) [ASC] (6/12/71 B-1)

I FEEL THE EARTH MOVE *Martika—Columbia 68996 [Carole King] [ASC] (9/2/89 BC-25)*

I FEEL THE MAGIC Belinda Carlisle—I.R.S. 52889
[Charlotte Caffey/Jonathan Segal] [ASC] (9/20/86 BC-77)

I FOOLED YOU THIS TIME Gene Chandler—Checker 1155
[Gene Chandler/Keni St. Lewis] [BMI] (11/26/66 BCR-45)

I FORGOT MORE THAN YOU'LL EVER KNOW Sonny James—Capitol 4307
[Cecil Null] [BMI] (1/18/60 B-80)

I FORGOT TO BE YOUR LOVER William Bell—Stax 0015
[William Bell/Booker T. Jones Jr.] [BMI] (1/4/69 BCR-31)

I FOUGHT THE LAW *Paul Stefen and the Royal Lancers—Citation 15003*
[Sonny Curtis] [BMI] (10/6/62 R-99)

I FOUGHT THE LAW *Bobby Fuller Four—Mustang 3014*
[Sonny Curtis] [BMI] (1/29/66 BCR-9)

I FOUGHT THE LAW *Sam Neely—A&M 1651 [Sonny Curtis] [BMI] (1/25/75 BCR-39)*

I FOUND A DAISY IN THE CITY Barry Darvell—World Artists 1058
[Artie Resnick/Kenny Young] [BMI] (6/26/65 R-92)

I FOUND A GIRL Jan & Dean—Liberty 55833
[Steve Barri/P.F. Sloan] [ASC] (10/9/65 BCR-30)

I FOUND A LOVE *The Falcons & Band (Ohio Untouchables)—Lu Pine 1003*
[Wilson Pickett/Willie Schofield/Robert West] [BMI] (3/31/62 BCR-51)

I FOUND A LOVE - PART 1 *Wilson Pickett—Atlantic 2394*
[Wilson Pickett/Willie Schofield/Robert West] [BMI] (4/1/67 BCR-22)

I FOUND A LOVE OH WHAT A LOVE Jo Ann & Troy—Atlantic 2256
[Jeanie Allen] [BMI] (12/12/64 BCR-67)

I FOUND A MILLION DOLLAR BABY IN A FIVE AND TEN CENT STORE
The Mills Brothers—Dot 15695
[Fred Fisher/Billy Rose] [ASC] (2/10/58 R-71)

I FOUND A NEW BABY Bobby Darin—Atco 6244
[Jack Palmer/Spencer Williams] [ASC] (12/15/62 B-90)

I FOUND A NEW LOVE The Blue Belles—Newtown 5006
[Marsha Levinson/Bobby Martin] [NA] (9/29/62 R-80)

I FOUND A RAINBOW Swingin' Medallions—Smash 2084
[Ray Whitley] [BMI] (4/15/67 C-95)

I FOUND A TRUE LOVE Wilson Pickett—Atlantic 2558
[Bobby Womack/Reggie Young] [BMI] (9/14/68 BCR-40)

I FOUND LOVE Jackie Wilson And Linda Hopkins—Brunswick 55224
[Alonzo Tucker/Jackie Wilson] [BMI] (4/21/62 B-96)

I FOUND LOVE The Party—Hollywood 4-64931 [Anne Preven] [BMI] (11/3/90 B-79)

I FOUND MY DAD Joe Simon—Spring 130
[Phil Hurtt/Bunny Sigler] (TSW) [BMI] (11/18/72 BCR-62)

I FOUND SOMEBODY Glenn Frey—Asylum 47466
[Glenn Frey/Jack Tempchin] [ASC] (6/5/82 BC-23)

I FOUND SOMEONE *Laura Branigan—Atlantic 89451*
[Michael Bolton/Mark Mangold] [BMI] (2/22/86 BC-81)

I FOUND SOMEONE *Cher—Geffen 28191*
[Michael Bolton/Mark Mangold] [BMI] (11/21/87 BC-10)

I FOUND SUNSHINE The Chi-Lites—Brunswick 55503
[Eugene Record] [BMI] (11/17/73 BCR-47)

I FOUND THAT GIRL The Jackson 5—Motown 1166
[Berry Gordy/Fonce Mizell/Freddie Perren/Deke Richards] (TSW) [ASC] (6/6/70 BR-6)

I FOUND YOU Frankie Laine—ABC 11057 [Craig Evans] [ASC] (3/23/68 CR-92)

I GET AROUND *The Beach Boys—Capitol 5174*
[Mike Love/Brian Wilson] [BMI] (5/23/64 BCR-1)*

I GET AROUND *The Cantina Band—Millennium 11818*
[Mike Love/Brian Wilson] (Med) [BMI] (7/25/81 B-81)*

I GET AROUND *The Beach Boys—Capitol 5030*
[Mike Love/Brian Wilson] (Med) [BMI] (7/25/81 BCR-5)*

I GET EXCITED Rick Springfield—RCA 13303 [Rick Springfield] [BMI] (9/11/82 BC-32)

I GET HIGH ON YOU Sly Stone—Epic 50135 [Sylvester Stewart] [BMI] (8/23/75 BCR-48)

I GET LIFTED George McCrae—TK 1007
[Harry Wayne Casey/Rick Finch] [BMI] (1/11/75 BCR-37)

I GET OFF ON IT Tony Joe White—Casablanca 2279
[Leann White/Tony Joe White] [ASC] (6/21/80 BCR-75)

I GET SO LONELY (WHEN I DREAM ABOUT YOU) The Four Knights—Capitol 2654
[Pat Ballard] [NA] (5/29/54 BC-PRE)

I GET THE SWEETEST FEELING Jackie Wilson—Brunswick 55381
[Alicia Evelyn/Van McCoy] [BMI] (7/13/68 BCR-34)

I GET WEAK Belinda Carlisle—MCA 53242 [Diane Warren] [ASC] (1/16/88 BC-2)

I GO APE Neil Sedaka—RCA Victor 47-7473
[Howard Greenfield/Neil Sedaka] [BMI] (3/2/59 BCR-40)

I GO CRAZY Paul Davis—Bang 733 [Paul Davis] [BMI] (8/27/77 BCR-7)

I GO TO EXTREMES Billy Joel—Columbia 73091 [Billy Joel] [ASC] (1/13/90 BC-6)

I GO TO PIECES *Peter And Gordon—Capitol 5335 [Del Shannon] [BMI] (1/9/65 BCR-4)*

I GO TO PIECES *Cotton, Lloyd and Christian—20th Century 2217*
[Del Shannon] [BMI] (9/27/75 BCR-66)

I GO TO RIO Pablo Cruise—A&M 2112
[Peter Allen/Adrienne Anderson] [BMI] (1/13/79 BCR-46)

I GOT A BAG OF MY OWN James Brown—Polydor 14153
[James Brown] [BMI] (11/11/72 BCR-32)

I GOT A FEELING Ricky Nelson—Imperial 5545 [Baker Knight] [BMI] (10/6/58 BCR-7)

I GOT A LINE ON YOU Spirit—Ode 115 [Randy California] [BMI] (1/18/69 BCR-25)

I GOT A NAME Jim Croce—ABC 11389
[Charles Fox/Norman Gimbel] [BMI] (9/29/73 BCR-3)

I GOT A PROBLEM Jesse Anderson—Thomas 805
[Jesse Anderson/Gene Barge] [BMI] (4/25/70 B-95)

I GOT A SURE THING Ollie & The Nightingales—Stax 245
[William Bell/Ollie Hoskins/Booker T. Jones Jr.] [BMI] (4/6/68 BR-73)

—I GOT A SWEETIE see: I GOT A WOMAN

I GOT A THING, YOU GOT A THING, EVERYBODY'S GOT A THING
Funkadelic—Westbound 158
[Clarence Haskins] [BMI] (3/14/70 BCR-80)

I GOT A WIFE The Mark IV—Mercury 71403
[Eddie Mascari/Erwin Wenzlaff] [BMI] (1/19/59 BCR-9)

I GOT A SWEETIE (NOTE I GOTTA WOMAN-CHARLES) *Jo Stafford—Columbia 40451*
[Ray Charles] [BMI] (2/28/55 CR-16)

I'VE GOT A WOMAN PART 1 *Jimmy McGriff—Sue 770*
[Ray Charles/Renald Richard] [BMI] (10/13/62 BCR-20) [IWM]*

I GOT A WOMAN *Rick Nelson—Decca 31475*
[Ray Charles/Renald Richard] [BMI] (3/9/63 BCR-40)*

I GOT A WOMAN *Freddie Scott—Colpix 709*
[Ray Charles/Renald Richard] [BMI] (11/2/63 BCR-48)*

I GOTTA WOMAN (PART ONE) *Ray Charles And His Orchestra—ABC-Paramount 10649*
[Ray Charles/Renald Richard] [BMI] (4/17/65 BCR-78)*

I GOT ANTS IN MY PANTS - PART 1 AND I WANT TO DANCE James Brown—Polydor 14162
[James Brown] [BMI] (1/20/73 BCR-27)

I GOT IT Gene Vincent and His Blue Caps—Capitol 3839
[Dick Glasser] [BMI] (11/18/57 R-78)

I GOT LIFE Nina Simone—RCA Victor 47-9686
[Galt MacDermot/James Rado/Gerome Ragni] (Med) [ASC] (1/4/69 BR-94)

I GOT LOVE Melba Moore—Mercury 73072
[Gary Geld/Peter Udell] [ASC] (6/13/70 CR-87)

I GOT LUCKY Elvis Presley with the Jordanaires—RCA Victor EPA-4371
[Dolores Fuller/Ben Weisman/Fred Wise] (EP) [ASC] (9/8/62 CR-26)

I GOT MY MIND MADE UP (YOU CAN GET IT GIRL) Instant Funk—Salsoul 2078
[Raymond Earl/Kim Miller/Scottie Miller] [BMI] (2/17/79 BCR-20)

I GOT OVER LOVE Major Harris—Atlantic 3303
[Joseph Jefferson/Charles Simmons] [BMI] (1/10/76 C-86)

I GOT RHYTHM The Happenings—B.T. Puppy 527
[George Gershwin/Ira Gershwin] [ASC] (4/8/67 BCR-1)

I GOT SOME HELP I DON'T NEED B.B. King—ABC 11321
[Dave (2) Clark/B.B. King] [BMI] (4/22/72 BCR-68)

I GOT STONED AND I MISSED IT Jim Stafford—MGM 14819
[Shel Silverstein] [BMI] (8/16/75 BCR-37)

I GOT STRIPES Johnny Cash—Columbia 41427
[Johnny Cash/Charlie Williams] [BMI] (7/27/59 BCR-43)

I GOT STUNG Elvis Presley—RCA Victor 47-7410
[David Hess/Aaron Schroeder] [ASC] (11/3/58 BCR-5)

I GOT THE FEELIN' James Brown And The Famous Flames—King 6155
[James Brown] [BMI] (3/16/68 BCR-5)

I GOT THE FEELIN' (IT'S OVER) Gregory Abbott—Columbia 06632
[Gregory Abbott] [BMI] (2/21/87 BC-55)

I GOT THE FEELIN' (OH NO NO) Neil Diamond—Bang 536
[Neil Diamond] [SE] (10/29/66 BCR-16)

I GOT TO GO BACK (AND WATCH THAT LITTLE GIRL DANCE) The McCoys—Bang 538
[Jeff Barry/Bert Berns] [BMI] (12/31/66 BCR-69)

I GOT TO HANDLE IT The Capitols—Karen 1525
[Barney Duke Browner] [BMI] (8/27/66 BR-74)

I GOT TO KNOW Starbuck—Private Stock 45,104
[Bruce Blackman] [ASC] (8/28/76 BCR-40)

I GOT TO TELL SOMEBODY Betty Everett—Fantasy 652
[Dee Ervin/Lynne Farr] [BMI] (12/19/70 BCR-83)

I GOT TO TRY IT ONE TIME Millie Jackson—Spring 144
[Millie Jackson/Brad Shapiro] [BMI] (3/2/74 R-76)

I GOT WHAT I WANTED Brook Benton—Mercury 72099
[Brook Benton/Margie Singleton] [BMI] (3/9/63 BCR-22)

I GOT WHAT YOU NEED Kim Weston—MGM 13720
[Douglas Fontaine Brown/William Stevenson] [BMI] (4/29/67 BCR-76)

I GOT YOU Split Enz—A&M 2252
[Neil Finn] [BMI] (8/23/80 BCR-50)

I GOT YOU BABE *Sonny & Cher—Atco 6359 [Sonny Bono] [BMI] (7/10/65 BCR-1)*

I GOT YOU BABE *Etta James—Cadet 5606 [Sonny Bono] [BMI] (5/18/68 BCR-51)*

I GOT YOU BABE *UB40 With Chrissie Hynde—A&M 2758*
[Sonny Bono] [BMI] (7/27/85 BC-28)

I GOT YOU (I FEEL GOOD) James Brown And The Famous Flames—King 6015
[James Brown] [BMI] (11/6/65 BCR-1)

I GOTCHA Joe Tex—Dial 1010 [Joe Tex] [BMI] (1/22/72 BCR-2)

I GOTTA DANCE TO KEEP FROM CRYING The Miracles—Tamla 54089
[Lamont Dozier/Brian Holland/Eddie Holland] [BMI] (11/23/63 BCR-35)

I GOTTA GO GET MY BABY Teresa Brewer—Coral 61339
[Kay Adelman/Marvin Rainwater] [BMI] (1/17/55 CR-21)

I GOTTA KEEP DANCIN' Carrie—Soul Train 10891
[Malcolm Anthony] [BMI] (4/30/77 BR-64)

I GOTTA KNOW Elvis Presley With The Jordanaires—RCA Victor 47-7810
[Paul Evans/Matt Williams] [ASC] (11/14/60 BCR-20)

I GOTTA LET YOU GO Martha Reeves & The Vandellas—Gordy 7103
[Norman Whitfield] [BMI] (11/7/70 BCR-83)

I GOTTA ROBE Laurie London—Capitol 3973 [Traditional] [NA] (5/19/58 R-80)

I GOTTA TRY Michael McDonald—Warner Bros. 29862
[Kenny Loggins/Michael McDonald] [ASC] (11/13/82 BC-31)

I GUESS I'LL ALWAYS LOVE YOU The Isley Brothers—Tamla 54135
[Lamont Dozier/Brian Holland/Eddie Holland] [BMI] (7/16/66 BCR-52)

I GUESS I'LL HAVE TO CRY, CRY, CRY James Brown And The Famous Flames—King 6141
[James Brown] [BMI] (7/20/68 BCR-31)

I GUESS I'LL MISS THE MAN The Supremes—Motown 1213
[Stephen Schwartz] [ASC] (10/21/72 BCR-85)

I GUESS I'M CRAZY Jim Reeves—RCA Victor 47-8383
[Werly Fairburn] [BMI] (8/22/64 BC-82)

I GUESS THAT'S WHY THEY CALL IT THE BLUES Elton John—Geffen 29460
[Elton John/Davey Johnstone/Bernie Taupin] [BMI] (10/29/83 BC-4)

I GUESS THE LORD MUST BE IN NEW YORK CITY Nilsson—RCA Victor 74-0261
[Harry Nilsson] [BMI] (10/25/69 BCR-33)

I HAD A DREAM Bruce Hayes with Mary Mayo—Dwain 812
[Unknown] (EP) [NA] (2/15/60 R-63)

I HAD A DREAM Paul Revere And The Raiders Featuring Mark Lindsay—Columbia 44227
[Mark Lindsay/Terry Melcher] [BMI] (8/19/67 BCR-13)

I HAD A DREAM Shorty Long—Soul 35054
[Frederick Long/Sylvia Moy] [BMI] (3/15/69 C-97)

I HAD A TALK WITH MY MAN Mitty Collier—Chess 1907
[Leonard Caston/Billy Davis] [BMI] (9/26/64 BCR-41)

I HAD IT ALL THE TIME Tyrone Davis—Dakar 4501
[Willie Henderson/Richard Parker] [BMI] (3/25/72 BCR-49)

I HAD TOO MUCH TO DREAM (LAST NIGHT) The Electric Prunes—Reprise 0532
[Nancie Mantz/Annette Tucker] [BMI] (12/10/66 BCR-11)

I HATE HATE Razzy—MGM 14728 [Razzy Bailey] [BMI] (5/25/74 BCR-49)

I HATE MYSELF FOR LOVING YOU Joan Jett and the Blackhearts—Blackheart 4-07919
[Desmond Child/Joan Jett] [ASC] (6/25/88 BC-8)

I HAVE A BOYFRIEND The Chiffons—Laurie 3212
[Jeff Barry/Ellie Greenwich/Hank Medress] [BMI] (11/16/63 BCR-34)

I HAVE A DREAM Rev. Martin Luther King—Gordy 7023
[Martin Luther King] [ASC] (5/4/68 B-88)

I HAVE A DREAM Donny Osmond—MGM 14781
[Selassie Burke/Solomon Burke Jr.] [BMI] (2/15/75 BCR-50)

I HAVE DREAMED Chad & Jeremy—Columbia 43414
[Oscar Hammerstein/Richard Rodgers] [ASC] (10/16/65 BC-91)

I HAVE LEARNED TO DO WITHOUT YOU Mavis Staples—Volt 4044
[J.J. Barnes/Don Davis/David Jordan] [BMI] (9/5/70 BCR-86)

I HAVE LEARNED TO RESPECT THE POWER OF LOVE Stephanie Mills—MCA 52799
[Angela Winbush] [BMI] (5/24/86 C-88)

(I HAVE LIVED, I HAVE LOVED) I HAVE YOU Sunny Gale—Decca 30157
[Aaron Schroeder] [ASC] (1/19/57 R-84)

I HAVE THE SKILL Sherbs—Atco 7325
[Daryl Braithwaite/Tony Mitchell/Garth Porter] [ASC] (3/7/81 BC-61)

I HEAR A RHAPSODY The Knightsbridge Strings—Top Rank 2082
[Jack Baker/George Fragos/Dick Gasparre*] [ASC] (11/14/60 R-94) [IWM]

I HEAR A SYMPHONY The Supremes—Motown 1083
[Lamont Dozier/Brian Holland/Eddie Holland] [BMI] (10/23/65 BCR-1)

I HEAR THOSE BELLS Dinah Washington—Mercury 70653
[Cy Crane/Ira Lee/Herb Wiener] [ASC] (7/11/55 R-72)

I HEAR THOSE CHURCH BELLS RINGING Dusk—Bell 990
[L. Russell Brown/Irwin Levine] [BMI] (5/29/71 BCR-41)

I HEAR TRUMPETS BLOW The Tokens—B.T. Puppy 518
[Mitch Margo/Phil Margo/Hank Medress/Jay Siegel] [ASC] (3/12/66 BCR-28)

I HEAR YOU KNOCKING *Gale Storm—Dot 15412*
[Dave Bartholomew/Fats Domino‡/Earl King Johnson] [BMI] (10/8/55 BCRt-2)

I HEAR YOU KNOCKING *Smiley Lewis—Imperial 5356*
[Dave Bartholomew/Fats Domino‡/Earl King Johnson] [BMI] (10/24/55 Rt-3)

I HEAR YOU KNOCKING *Fats Domino—Imperial 5796*
[Dave Bartholomew/Fats Domino‡/Earl King Johnson] [BMI] (12/4/61 BR-67)

I HEAR YOU KNOCKING *Dave Edmunds—MAM 3601*
[Dave Bartholomew/Fats Domino‡/Earl King Johnson] [BMI] (12/19/70 BCR-3)

I HEAR YOU NOW Jon And Vangelis—Polydor 2098
[Jon Anderson/Vangelis] [ASC] (7/26/80 BCR-58)

I HEARD A RUMOUR Bananarama—London 886165
[Matt Aitken/Sarah Dallin/Siobhan Fahey/Mike Stock/Pete Waterman/
Keren Woodward] [BMI] (7/11/87 BC-4)

I HEARD IT THROUGH THE GRAPEVINE *Gladys Knight & The Pips—Soul 35039*
[Barrett Strong/Norman Whitfield] [BMI] (10/21/67 BCR-1)

I HEARD IT THRU THE GRAPEVINE *King Curtis & The Kingpins—Atco 6598*
[Barrett Strong/Norman Whitfield] [BMI] (8/10/68 B-83) [IWM]

I HEARD IT THROUGH THE GRAPEVINE *Marvin Gaye—Tamla 54176*
[Barrett Strong/Norman Whitfield] [BMI] (11/16/68 BCR-1)

I HEARD IT THROUGH THE GRAPEVINE *Creedence Clearwater Revival—Fantasy 759*
[Barrett Strong/Norman Whitfield] [BMI] (1/24/76 BCR-43)

I HEARD IT THROUGH THE GRAPEVINE (PART 1) *Roger—Warner Bros. 49786*
[Barrett Strong/Norman Whitfield] [BMI] (10/3/81 BCR-56)

I HEARD IT THROUGH THE GRAPEVINE *The California Raisins—Priority 9719*
[Barrett Strong/Norman Whitfield] [BMI] (1/23/88 B-84)

I HEARD THE BELLS ON CHRISTMAS DAY Bing Crosby—Decca 30126
[Henry Wadsworth Longfellow/Johnny Marks] [ASC] (12/15/56 R-55)

I HEARD THE VOICE OF JESUS Turley Richards—Warner Bros. 7397
[Traditional] [NA] (6/20/70 B-99)

I HONESTLY LOVE YOU *Olivia Newton-John—MCA 40280*
[Peter Allen/Jeff Barry] [BMI] (8/17/74 BCR-1)

I HONESTLY LOVE YOU *Olivia Newton-John—MCA 40811*
[Peter Allen/Jeff Barry] [BMI] (11/5/77 BCR-48)

I HOPE WE GET TO LOVE IN TIME Marilyn McCoo & Billy Davis Jr.—ABC 12170
[James Anthony Dean/John Henry Glover] [BMI] (3/27/76 BCR-71)

I IDOLIZE YOU Ike & Tina Turner—Sue 735 [Ike Turner] [BMI] (12/10/60 BCR-49)

I JUST CALLED TO SAY I LOVE YOU Stevie Wonder—Motown 1745
[Stevie Wonder] [ASC] (8/18/84 BC-1)

I JUST CAN'T CONTROL MYSELF Nature's Divine—Infinity 50,027
[Robert William Carter/Lynn Marie Smith/Michael Lee Stokes] [NA] (10/20/79 BCR-65)

I JUST CAN'T GET YOU OUT OF MY MIND Four Tops—Dunhill 4377
[Dennis Lambert/Brian Potter] [BMI] (1/19/74 BCR-41)

I JUST CAN'T HELP BELIEVING B.J. Thomas—Scepter 12283
[Barry Mann/Cynthia Weil] [BMI] (6/13/70 BCR-9)

I JUST CAN'T HELP IT Jackie Wilson—Brunswick 55229
[Alonzo Tucker/Jackie Wilson] [BMI] (6/23/62 BC-70)

I JUST CAN'T HELP IT Major Lance—Okeh 7233 [Curtis Mayfield] [BMI] (12/4/65 R-100)

I JUST CAN'T SAY GOODBYE Bobby Rydell—Capitol 5305
[Gerry Goffin/Carole King] [BMI] (12/19/64 B-94)

I JUST CAN'T SAY GOODBYE Philly Devotions—Columbia 10076
[John E. Davis] [ASC] (2/8/75 BC-95)

I JUST CAN'T SAY NO TO YOU Parker McGee—Big Tree 16082
[Steve Gibson/Parker McGee] [BMI] (1/15/77 BCR-42)

I JUST CAN'T STOP LOVING YOU Cornelius Brothers & Sister Rose—
United Artists 313 [Eddie Cornelius] [BMI] (10/6/73 CR-88)

I JUST CAN'T STOP LOVING YOU Michael Jackson—Epic 07253
[Michael Jackson] [BMI] (8/8/87 BC-1)

I JUST CAN'T TURN MY HABIT INTO LOVE Buckwheat—London 189
[Micheal Smotherman] [ASC] (5/19/73 C-100)

I JUST CAN'T WALK AWAY Four Tops—Motown 1706
[Lamont Dozier/Brian Holland/Eddie Holland] [BMI] (10/22/83 BC-70)

I JUST CRY Fats Domino—Imperial 5753
[Dave Bartholomew/Fats Domino] [BMI] (5/15/61 R-92)

(I JUST) DIED IN YOUR ARMS Cutting Crew—Virgin 99481
[Nick Van Eede] [BMI] (3/7/87 BC-1)

I JUST DON'T KNOW The Four Lads—Columbia 40914
[Robert Allen/Joseph Stone] [ASC] (5/6/57 BCR-22)

I JUST DON'T KNOW WHAT TO DO WITH MYSELF *Tommy Hunt—Scepter 1236*
[Burt Bacharach/Hal David] [ASC] (9/8/62 CR-93)

I JUST DON'T KNOW WHAT TO DO WITH MYSELF *Dionne Warwick—Scepter 12167*
[Burt Bacharach/Hal David] [ASC] (10/1/66 BCR-17)

I JUST DON'T KNOW WHAT TO DO WITH MYSELF *Gary Puckett—Columbia 45249*
[Burt Bacharach/Hal David] [ASC] (10/17/70 BCR-44)

I JUST DON'T UNDERSTAND Ann-Margret—RCA Victor 47-7894
[Kent Westberry/Marijohn Wilkin] [BMI] (7/10/61 BCR-10)

I JUST FALL IN LOVE AGAIN Anne Murray—Capitol 4675
[Steve Dorff/Larry Herbstritt/Harry Lloyd/Gloria Sklerov] [BMI] (1/20/79 BCR-11)

I JUST GO FOR YOU Jimmy Jones—Cub 9072 [Don Covay] [BMI] (7/23/60 C-88)

I JUST LOVE THE MAN The Jones Girls—Philadelphia Int'l 3121
[Kenneth Gamble/Leon Huff] [BMI] (1/24/81 R-72)

I JUST THOUGHT YOU'D LIKE TO KNOW Johnny Cash—Sun 309
[Charlie Rich] [BMI] (12/15/58 B-85)

I JUST WANNA BE YOUR FRIEND Lighthouse—Evolution 1058
[Bob McBride/Skip Prokop] [BMI] (4/29/72 BR-91)

I JUST WANNA KEEP IT TOGETHER Paul Davis—Bang 579
[Paul Davis] [BMI] (9/5/70 BCR-42)

I JUST WANNA STOP Gino Vannelli—A&M 2072
[Ross Vannelli] [BMI] (9/9/78 BCR-2)

I JUST WANT TO BE Cameo—Chocolate City 019
[Larry Blackmon/Gregory Johnson] [ASC] (8/25/79 CR-86)

I JUST WANT TO BE YOUR EVERYTHING Andy Gibb—RSO 872
[Barry Gibb] [BMI] (4/23/77 BCR-1)

I JUST WANT TO CELEBRATE Rare Earth—Rare Earth 5031
[Dino Fekaris/Nick Zesses] [ASC] (7/17/71 BCR-7)

I JUST WANT TO LOVE YOU Clyde McPhatter—Mercury 71692
[Brook Benton/Clyde Otis] [BMI] (10/24/60 R-91)

I JUST WANT TO MAKE LOVE TO YOU *Foghat—Bearsville 0008*
[Willie Dixon] [BMI] (10/7/72 BR-83)

I JUST WANT TO MAKE LOVE TO YOU *Foghat—Bearsville 0319*
[Willie Dixon] [BMI] (8/27/77 BCR-31)

I KEEP CRYING The Hurricanes—Audiovox 109 [Norman Kaye] [ASC] (11/8/54 R-32)

I KEEP FORGETTIN' *Chuck Jackson—Wand 126*
[Jerry Leiber/Mike Stoller] [BMI] (8/11/62 BCR-48)

I KEEP FORGETTIN' *Michael McDonald—Warner Bros. 29933*
[Jerry Leiber/Michael McDonald/Ed Sanford/Mike Stoller] [ASC] (8/7/82 BC-4)

I KINDA MISS YOU The Manhattans—Columbia 10430
[Winfred Lovett] [BMI] (10/30/76 BCR-46)

I KNEEL AT YOUR THRONE Joe Medlin—Mercury 71415
[Addy Baron/Marvin Scott] [ASC] (3/9/59 BCR-49)

I KNEW HIM Joe Tex—Dial 1001 [Joe Tex] [BMI] (4/17/71 R-83)

I KNEW IT ALL THE TIME The Dave Clark Five—Congress 212
[Mitch Murray] [BMI] (4/25/64 BCR-53)

I KNEW JESUS (BEFORE HE WAS A STAR) Glen Campbell—Capitol 3548
[Neal Hefti/Stanley H. Styne] [ASC] (3/17/73 BCR-37)

I KNEW THE BRIDE (WHEN SHE USED TO ROCK 'N ROLL) Nick Lowe—Columbia 05570
[Nick Lowe] [BMI] (11/30/85 B-77)

I KNEW YOU WERE WAITING (FOR ME) Aretha Franklin & George Michael—Arista 1-9559
[Simon Climie/Dennis W. Morgan] [BMI] (2/21/87 BC-1)

I KNEW YOU WHEN *Billy Joe Royal—Columbia 43390 [Joe South] [BMI] (9/18/65 BCR-12)*

I KNEW YOU WHEN *Donny Osmond—MGM 14322*
[Joe South] (TSW) [BMI] (11/27/71 BCR-9)

I KNEW YOU WHEN *Linda Ronstadt—Asylum 69853 [Joe South] [BMI] (12/11/82 BC-30)*

I KNOW Perry Como—RCA Victor 47-7541
[Edith Lindeman/Carl Stutz] [ASC] (6/1/59 BCR-22)

I KNOW A HEARTACHE WHEN I SEE ONE Jennifer Warnes—Arista 0430
[Charlie Black/Rory Bourke/Kerry Chater] [ASC] (6/30/79 BCR-19)

I KNOW A MAN Rolf Harris—Epic 9615 [Max Frith/Galt MacDermot] [ASC] (9/14/63 R-99)

I KNOW A PLACE Petula Clark—Warner Bros. 5612 [Tony Hatch] [BMI] (3/20/65 BCR-2)

I KNOW I KNOW "Pookie" Hudson—Double-L 711
[Richard Barrett/Samuel Strain] [BMI] (5/25/63 B-96)

I KNOW I'M IN LOVE Chee-Chee And Peppy—Buddah 225
[Jesse James] [BMI] (5/22/71 BCR-35)

(I KNOW) I'M LOSING YOU *The Temptations—Gordy 7057*
[Cornelius Grant/Eddie Holland/Norman Whitfield] [BMI] (11/19/66 BCR-8)

(I KNOW) I'M LOSING YOU *Rare Earth—Rare Earth 5017*
[Cornelius Grant/Eddie Holland/Norman Whitfield] [BMI] (8/1/70 BCR-5)

(I KNOW) I'M LOSING YOU *Rod Stewart With Faces—Mercury 73244 [Cornelius Grant/Eddie Holland/Norman Whitfield] [BMI] (11/20/71 BCR-13)*

(I KNOW) I'M LOSING YOU *Uptown—Oak Lawn 3810 [Cornelius Grant/Eddie Holland/Norman Whitfield] [BMI] (12/27/86 B-80)*

I KNOW ONE Jim Reeves—RCA Victor 47-7756 [Jack H. Clement] [BMI] (7/9/60 BC-82)

I KNOW THERE'S SOMETHING GOING ON Frida—Atlantic 89984 [Russ Ballard] [ASC] (11/6/82 BC-13)

I KNOW WHAT BOYS LIKE The Waitresses—Polydor 2196 [Chris Butler] [BMI] (5/8/82 BC-62)

I KNOW WHAT GOD IS Perry Como—RCA Victor 47-7670 [John G. Bowen/Ned Freeman/Don Raye] [ASC] (1/25/60 BCR-81)

I KNOW WHAT I LIKE Huey Lewis and the News—Chrysalis 43108 [Chris Hayes/Huey Lewis] [ASC] (4/4/87 BC-9)

I KNOW WHERE I'M GOIN' George Hamilton IV—ABC-Paramount 9924 [Randy Starr/Dick Wolf] [ASC] (5/12/58 BCR-43)

I KNOW YOU BETTER THAN THAT Bobby Goldsboro—United Artists 50018 [Bobby Goldsboro] [BMI] (5/14/66 BCR-56)

I KNOW (YOU DON'T LOVE ME NO MORE) Barbara George—A.F.O. 302 [Barbara George] [BMI] (11/13/61 BCR-3)

I KNOW YOU'RE OUT THERE SOMEWHERE The Moody Blues—Polydor 887600 [Justin Hayward] [ASC] (6/4/88 BC-30)

I LEARNED A LESSON I'LL NEVER FORGET Joe Pica—Original 518 [Joseph M. Davis] [ASC] (5/9/55 R-54)

(I LEFT MY HEART) IN SAN FRANCISCO Tony Bennett—Columbia 42332 [George Cory/Douglass Cross] [ASC] (4/14/62 BCR-19)

I LEFT MY HEART IN THE BALCONY Linda Scott—Congress 106 [Jeff Barry/Artie Resnick] [BMI] (9/22/62 BCR-72)

I LIE AWAKE The New Colony Six—Sentaur 1202 [Ray Graffia/Jerry Kollenburg/Pat McBride] [BMI] (4/30/66 R-97)

I LIED TO MY HEART The Enchanters (1)—Musitron 1072 [Larry Fawcett] [BMI] (3/6/61 B-96)

I LIKE Men Without Hats—MCA 52293 [Ivan Doroschuk] [BMI] (11/12/83 BC-84)

I LIKE Guy—MCA 53490 [Timmy Gatling/Gene Griffin/Aaron Hall/Teddy Riley] [ASC] (5/6/89 B-70)

I LIKE DREAMIN' Kenny Nolan—20th Century 2287 [Kenny Nolan] [BMI] (11/6/76 BCR-3)

I LIKE GIRLS Johnny Restivo—RCA Victor 47-7601 [Eddie V. Deane/Ben Weisman] [ASC] (10/5/59 R-88)

I LIKE GIRLS The Fatback Band—Spring 181 [Bill Curtis] [BMI] (7/29/78 R-82)

I LIKE IT Gerry And The Pacemakers—Laurie 3271 [Mitch Murray] [BMI] (9/26/64 BCR-17)

I LIKE IT DeBarge—Gordy 1645 [Bunny DeBarge/El DeBarge/Randy DeBarge] [ASC] (2/5/83 BC-24)

I LIKE IT Dino—4th & Broadway 7483 [Dino Esposito] [BMI] (5/13/89 BC-4)

I LIKE IT LIKE THAT, PART 1 *Chris Kenner—Instant 3229 [Chris Kenner] [BMI] (5/22/61 BCR-2)*

I DON'T LIKE IT LIKE THAT *(response to I Like It Like That) The Bobbettes—Gone 5112 [Chris Kenner] [BMI] (9/4/61 BR-72) [R]*

I LIKE IT LIKE THAT *The Dave Clark Five—Epic 9811 [Chris Kenner/Allen Toussaint*] [BMI] (6/19/65 BCR-5)*

I LIKE IT LIKE THAT *Loggins & Messina—Columbia 10188 [Chris Kenner/Allen Toussaint*] [BMI] (8/30/75 BC-84)*

I LIKE IT LIKE THAT The Miracles—Tamla 54098 [Smokey Robinson/Marvin Tarplin] [ASC] (6/27/64 BCR-25)

I LIKE THE WAY Tommy James And The Shondells—Roulette 4756 [Ritchie Cordell/Bo Gentry*] [BMI] (7/1/67 BCR-20)

I LIKE THE WAY (THE KISSING GAME) Hi-Five—Jive 1424 [Bernard Belle/Teddy Riley/Dave Way] [ASC] (2/23/91 BC-1)

I LIKE THEM ALL Dean Martin—Capitol 3238 [Larry Coleman/Fred Ebb/Paul Klein] [BMI] (10/24/55 R-77)

I LIKE TO DO IT KC & The Sunshine Band—TK 1020 [Harry Wayne Casey/Rick Finch] [BMI] (12/4/76 BCR-37)

I LIKE TO LIVE THE LOVE B.B. King—ABC 11406 [Dave Crawford/Charles Mann] [ASC] (12/8/73 BCR-15)

I LIKE TO ROCK April Wine—Capitol 4828 [Myles Goodwyn] [BMI] (2/2/80 BCR-82)

I LIKE WHAT YOU GIVE Nolan—Lizard 21008 [Nolan Porter] [ASC] (9/18/71 BCR-67)

I LIKE WHAT YOU'RE DOING (TO ME) Carla Thomas—Stax 0024 [Homer Banks/Bettye Crutcher/Raymond Earl Jackson] [BMI] (2/15/69 BCR-49)

I LIKE YOU Donovan—Epic 10983 [Donovan Leitch] [BMI] (4/28/73 BCR-57)

I LIKE YOU Phyllis Nelson—Carrere 4-05719 [Phyllis Nelson] [ASC] (2/8/86 BC-61)

I LIKE YOUR KIND OF LOVE *Andy Williams—Cadence 1323 [Melvin Endsley] [BMI] (5/20/57 BCRt-7)*

I LIKE YOUR KIND OF LOVE *Melvin Endsley—RCA Victor 47-6891 [Melvin Endsley] [BMI] (6/8/57 Rt-7)*

I LIKE YOUR LOVIN' (DO YOU LIKE MINE) Chi-Lites—Brunswick 55438 [Eugene Record/Sandy Wilburn] [BMI] (7/18/70 BCR-51)

I LIKES TO DO IT People's Choice—Phil-L.A. Of Soul 349 [Frank Brunson] [BMI] (7/24/71 BCR-38)

I LIVE BY THE GROOVE Paul Carrack—Chrysalis 23427 [Paul Carrack/Eddie Schwartz] [ASC] (10/21/89 BC-27)

I LIVE FOR THE SUN The Sunrays—Tower 148 [Rick Henn] [BMI] (8/7/65 BCR-28)

I LIVE FOR YOUR LOVE Natalie Cole—Manhattan 50094 [Pam Reswick/Allan Rich/Steve Werfel] [ASC] (11/7/87 BC-13)

I LOOK AT YOU The Lassies—Decca 29868 [Charles Aznavour/Jean Louis Constantin/Rainey Robinson] [BMI] (6/23/56 B-66) [FET]

I LOOKED AT HEAVEN Tommy Edwards—MGM 12814 [Tommy Edwards] [ASC] (7/27/59 BR-84)

I LOST MY BABY Joey Dee—Roulette 4456 [Johnny Nash] [ASC] (11/3/62 BCR-58)

—I LOST ON JEOPARDY see: JEOPARDY

I LOVE Tom T. Hall—Mercury 73436 [Tom T. Hall] [BMI] (12/8/73 BCR-12)

I LOVE A RAINY NIGHT Eddie Rabbitt—Elektra 47066 [David Malloy/Eddie Rabbitt/Even Stevens] [BMI] (11/8/80 BCR-1)

I LOVE AN ANGEL Little Bill & The Bluenotes—Dolton 4 [Bill Engelhart] [BMI] (6/22/59 BR-66)

I LOVE HOW YOU LOVE ME *The Paris Sisters—Gregmark 6 [Larry Kolber/Barry Mann] [BMI] (9/2/61 BCR-5)*

I LOVE HOW YOU LOVE ME *Bobby Vinton—Epic 10397 [Larry Kolber/Barry Mann] [BMI] (10/26/68 BCR-4)*

—I LOVE LUCY THEME see: DISCO LUCY

I LOVE MAKIN' LOVE TO YOU Evie Sands—Haven 7013 [Richard Germinaro/Evie Sands/Ben Weisman] [BMI] (8/2/75 BCR-44)

I LOVE MICKEY Mickey Mantle And Teresa Brewer—Coral 61700 [Teresa Brewer/Bill Katz/Ruth Roberts] [ASC] (9/15/56 BC-50)

I LOVE MUSIC (PART 1) *The O'Jays—Philadelphia Int'l 3577 [Kenneth Gamble/Leon Huff] [BMI] (10/25/75 BCR-5)*

I LOVE MUSIC *The Ritchie Family—Marlin 3306 [Kenneth Gamble/Leon Huff] (Med) [BMI] (8/28/76 BCR-17)*

I LOVE MY BABY Archie Bell & The Drells—Atlantic 2612 [Kenneth Gamble/Leon Huff] [BMI] (3/29/69 BCR-80)

I LOVE MY BABY (MY BABY LOVES ME) *Jill Corey—Columbia 40794 [Bud Green/Harry Warren] [ASC] (12/8/56 BCRt-13)*

I LOVE MY BABY (MY BABY LOVES ME) *Benny Strong & His Orchestra—Decca 30234 [Bud Green/Harry Warren] [ASC] (3/16/57 Rt-38)*

I LOVE MY FRIEND Charlie Rich—Epic 20006 [Billy Sherrill/Norro Wilson] [BMI] (8/3/74 BCR-24)

I LOVE MY GIRL *Cozy Morley—ABC-Paramount 9811 [Peter DeAngelis/Bob Marcucci] [ASC] (4/6/57 BCtRt-31)*

I LOVE MY GIRL *The Hilltoppers—Dot 15560 [Peter DeAngelis/Bob Marcucci] [ASC] (4/20/57 BCtRt-31)*

I LOVE MY GIRL The Metronomes—Cadence 1310 [Stanley Wright] [BMI] (4/6/57 Rt*-31)

I LOVE MY MUSIC Wild Cherry—Epic/Sweet City 50500 [Robert Parissi] [ASC] (2/25/78 BCR-69)

I LOVE MY TRUCK Glen Campbell—Mirage 3845 [Joe Rainey] [BMI] (8/22/81 B-94)

I LOVE MY WIFE Frank Sinatra—Reprise 1383 [Cy Coleman/Michael Stewart] [ASC] (1/15/77 C-92)

I LOVE ONIONS Susan Christie—Columbia 43595 [Don Cochrane/John Michael Hill] [BMI] (6/4/66 BCR-63)

I LOVE ROCK 'N ROLL *Joan Jett & The Blackhearts—Boardwalk 7-11-135 [Jake Hooker/Alan Merrill] [ASC] (2/6/82 BCR-1)*

I LOVE ROCKY ROAD *(parody of I Love Rock 'N' Roll) "Weird Al" Yankovic—Rock 'n' Roll 03998 [Jake Hooker/Alan Merrill/Al Yankovic] [ASC] (7/30/83 C-78) [P]*

I LOVE THE BASS Bardeux—Enigma 75047 [Michael Eckart/Stacy Smith/Jon St. James] [BMI] (9/16/89 BC-64)

I LOVE THE NIGHTLIFE (DISCO 'ROUND) Alicia Bridges—Polydor 14483 [Alicia Bridges/Susan Hutcheson] [BMI] (7/1/78 BCR-5)

I LOVE THE WAY YOU LOVE Marv Johnson—United Artists 208 [Al Abrams*/Berry Gordy/John O'Den*/Stanley Ossman*] [BMI] (2/22/60 BCR-8)

I LOVE THE WAY YOU LOVE Betty Wright—Alston 4594 [Willie Clarke/William Hale] [BMI] (7/24/71 CR-84)

I LOVE TO DANCE WITH YOU Patti Page—Mercury 70607 [Joseph Francis Burke/Don Raye] [ASC] (4/25/55 CR-38)

I LOVE TO SING Jack Fascinato—Fraternity 740 [Jack Fascinato/Al Trace] [ASC] (7/20/56 R-83)

I LOVE WOMEN Jim Hurt—Scotti Brothers 605 [Michael D. Stewart/Dan Edward Williams] [BMI] (10/11/80 B-90)

I LOVE YOU Bob Stewart—Dot 15616 [Unknown] [NA] (8/19/57 R-80)

I LOVE YOU The Volume's—Chex 1002 [Willie Ewing/Ernest Newson] [BMI] (4/9/62 BCR-20)

I LOVE YOU People—Capitol 2078 [Chris White] [BMI] (3/23/68 BCR-13)

I LOVE YOU Otis Leavill—Dakar 614 [Barbara Acklin/Carl Davis/Eugene Record] [BMI] (11/29/69 BCR-63)

I LOVE YOU Donna Summer—Casablanca 907 [Pete Bellotte/Giorgio Moroder/Donna Summer] [ASC] (12/10/77 BCR-26)

I LOVE YOU Climax Blues Band—Warner Bros. 49669 [Derek Holt] [ASC] (2/14/81 BCR-9)

I LOVE YOU Vanilla Ice—SBK 07346 [Kim Sharp/Robert Van Winkle] [BMI] (2/23/91 BC-52)

I LOVE YOU BABY Paul Anka—ABC-Paramount 9855 [Paul Anka] [BMI] (9/30/57 BCR-48)

I LOVE YOU BABY Dottie And Ray—LeSage 701 [Cecil Bowen] [BMI] (1/23/65 C-86)

***I LOVE YOU BECAUSE** Johnny Cash—Sun 334 [Leon Payne] [BMI] (2/15/60 R-85)*
***I LOVE YOU BECAUSE** Al Martino—Capitol 4930 [Leon Payne] [BMI] (3/16/63 BCR-3)*
(I LOVE YOU) DON'T YOU FORGET IT Perry Como—RCA Victor 47-8186 [Henry Mancini/Al Stillman] [ASC] (6/1/63 BCR-35)
I LOVE YOU DROPS Vic Dana—Dolton 319 [Bill Anderson] [BMI] (4/30/66 BCR-30)
I LOVE YOU FOR ALL SEASONS The Fuzz—Calla 174 [Sheila Young] [BMI] (1/23/71 BCR-10)
—I LOVE YOU FOR SENTIMENTAL REASONS see: SENTIMENTAL REASONS
I LOVE YOU, I LOVE YOU, I LOVE YOU Ronnie McDowell—Scorpion 149 [Ronnie McDowell] [BMI] (3/18/78 B-81)
I LOVE YOU IN THE SAME OLD WAY Paul Anka—ABC-Paramount 10132 [Paul Anka] [BMI] (8/1/60 BCR-40)
I LOVE YOU LADY DAWN The Bells—Polydor 15027 [Marty Cooper] [BMI] (6/12/71 BCR-40)
I LOVE YOU MADLY The Four Coins—Epic 9082 [Charles R. Jones] [BMI] (12/13/54 BCR-27)
I LOVE YOU MADLY Fantastic Four—Ric-Tic 144/Soul 35052 [William Garrett/Mike Hanks] [BMI] (9/21/68 BCR-44)
—I LOVE YOU MADLY see: BONG BONG
I LOVE YOU MORE René & Angela—Capitol 5010 [René Moore/Angela Winbush] [ASC] (8/22/81 R-92)
I LOVE YOU MORE AND MORE EVERY DAY Al Martino—Capitol 5108 [Don Robertson] [ASC] (1/25/64 BCR-9)
I LOVE YOU MORE THAN WORDS CAN SAY Otis Redding—Volt 146 [Eddie Floyd/Booker T. Jones Jr.] [BMI] (4/8/67 BCR-59)
I LOVE YOU MORE THAN YOU'LL EVER KNOW Donny Hathaway—Atco 6903 [Al Kooper] [BMI] (10/21/72 BCR-50)
I LOVE YOU 1000 TIMES The Platters—Musicor 1166 [Luther Dixon/Inez Foxx] [BMI] (4/23/66 BCR-30)
I LOVE YOU SO The Chantels—End 1020 [George Goldner*/Morris Levy‡/Daniel Norton] [BMI] (6/16/58 BC-42)
I LOVE YOU SO Bobbi Martin—Coral 62452 [Henry Jerome] [ASC] (5/29/65 BCR-70)
I LOVE YOU SO MUCH IT HURTS Charlie Gracie—Cameo 111 [Floyd Tillman] [BMI] (8/12/57 BR-41)
I LOVE YOU THE WAY YOU ARE Bobby Vinton—Diamond 121 [Bobby Vinton] [BMI] (8/4/62 BCR-38)
I LOVE YOU YES I DO Bull Moose Jackson—7 Arts 705 [Henry Glover/Sally Nix] [BMI] (9/11/61 B-98)
I LOVE YOUR SMILE Shanice—Motown 2093 [Jarvis Baker/Sylvester Jackson/Narada Michael Walden/Shanice Wilson] [ASC] (11/23/91 BC-2)
I LOVED AND I LOST The Impressions—ABC 11103 [Curtis Mayfield] [BMI] (7/13/68 BCR-49)
I LOVED 'EM EVERY ONE T.G. Sheppard—Warner/Curb 49690 [Phil Sampson] [BMI] (3/14/81 BCR-35)
I LOVES YOU PORGY Nina Simone—Bethlehem 11021 [George Gershwin/Ira Gershwin*/DuBose Heyward] [ASC] (8/1/59 BCR-11)
I MADE IT THROUGH THE RAIN Barry Manilow—Arista 0566 [Jack Feldman/Gerard Kenny/Barry Manilow/Drey Shepperd/Bruce Sussman] [BMI] (11/22/80 BCR-10)
I MAKE A FOOL OF MYSELF Frankie Valli—Philips 40484 [Bob Crewe/Bob Gaudio] [BMI] (8/26/67 BCR-18)
I MAY NEVER PASS THIS WAY AGAIN Perry Como—RCA Victor 47-7628 [Irving Melsher/Murray Wizell] [BMI] (11/9/59 R-100)
I MAY NOT LIVE TO SEE TOMORROW Brian Hyland—ABC-Paramount 10374 [Gary Geld/Peter Udell] [ASC] (11/24/62 BCR-69)
***I MELT WITH YOU** Modern English—Sire 29775 [Richard Ian Brown/Michael Conroy/Robbie Grey/Gary McDowell/Stephen Walker] [BMI] (3/26/83 BC-68)*
***I MELT WITH YOU** Modern English—TVT 2812 [Richard Ian Brown/Michael Conroy/Robbie Grey/Gary McDowell/Stephen Walker] [BMI] (6/23/90 BC-75)*
I MET HER IN CHURCH The Box Tops—Mala 12,017 [Spooner Oldham/Dan Penn] [BMI] (9/14/68 BCR-29)
I MET HIM ON A SUNDAY (RONDE-RONDE) The Shirelles—Decca 30588 [Doris Coley/Addie Harris/Beverly Lee/Shirley Owens] [BMI] (3/22/58 BCR-24)
I MISS THE BOY Betty Madigan—MGM 12214 [Evelyn Danzig/Sylvia Dee] [ASC] (4/20/56 R-80)
I MISS YOU (PART I) Harold Melvin And The Blue Notes—Philadelphia Int'l 3516 [Kenneth Gamble/Leon Huff] [BMI] (6/24/72 BCR-40)
I MISS YOU The Dells—Cadet 5700 [Tony Hester] [BMI] (11/24/73 BCR-52)
I MISS YOU Klymaxx—Constellation 52606 [Lynn Malsby] [ASC] (9/14/85 BC-5)
I MISS YOU BABY Millie Jackson—Spring 131 [Raeford Gerald] [BMI] (12/2/72 BCR-69)
***I MISS YOU SO** Chris Connor—Atlantic 1105 [Jimmy Henderson/Sid Robin/Bertha Scott*] [ASC] (10/27/56 BCR-34)*
***I MISS YOU SO** Paul Anka—ABC-Paramount 10011 [Jimmy Henderson/Sid Robin/Bertha Scott*] [ASC] (3/16/59 BCR-24)*
***I MISS YOU SO** Little Anthony & The Imperials With The 101 Strings—DCP 1149 [Jimmy Henderson/Sid Robin/Bertha Scott*] [ASC] (10/2/65 BCR-32)*
I MISSED AGAIN Phil Collins—Atlantic 3790 [Phil Collins] [ASC] (3/14/81 BCR-19)
I MISSED ME Jim Reeves—RCA Victor 47-7800 [Bill Anderson] [BMI] (11/12/60 BCR-44)
I MUST BE DREAMING Nat "King" Cole—Capitol 4184 [Noel Sherman/Dick Wolf] [ASC] (5/9/59 BCR-54)
I MUST BE DREAMING Giuffria—MCA 52794 [Willy DeVille] [BMI] (5/3/86 BC-52)
—I MUST BE FALLING IN LOVE see: SPINNING AROUND
I MUST BE SEEING THINGS Gene Pitney—Musicor 1070 [Bob Brass/Al Kooper/Irwin Levine] [BMI] (2/20/65 BCR-26)
I NEED A CHANGE The Miracles—Chess 1768 [Berry Gordy/Smokey Robinson] [ASC] (11/21/60 R-96)
I NEED A LOVER John Cougar—Riva 202 [John Mellencamp] [ASC] (9/15/79 BCR-28)
I NEED A MAN Grace Jones—Beam Junction 104 [Pierre Papadiamandis/Paul Slade] [ASC] (5/7/77 B-83)
I NEED A MAN Eurythmics—RCA 5361 [Annie Lennox/David A. Stewart] [ASC] (12/19/87 BC-46)
I NEED HELP (I CAN'T DO IT ALONE) (PART 1) Bobby Byrd—King 6323 [Teddy Brown] [BMI] (10/10/70 BCR-61)
I NEED LOVE Barbara Mason—Arctic 120 [James A. Bishop/Barbara Mason] [BMI] (6/11/66 BC-98)
I NEED LOVE The Third Booth—Independence 86 [John C. Clore] [BMI] (6/22/68 CR-84)
I NEED LOVE LL Cool J—Def Jam 07350 [Bobby Ervin/Steve Ettinger/Darryl Pierce/Dwayne Simon/James Todd Smith] [ASC] (8/1/87 BC-14)
I NEED SOME ONE The Belmonts—Sabrina 502 [Peter Falciglia/Carlo Mastrangelo] [BMI] (11/27/61 BCR-57)
I NEED SOMEBODY ? & The Mysterians—Cameo 441 [Bobby Balderama/Frank Lugo/Rudy Martinez/Frank Rodriguez/Eddie Serrato] [BMI] (11/19/66 BCR-15)
I NEED SOMEBODY TO LEAN ON Elvis Presley—RCA Victor EPA-4382 [Doc Pomus/Mort Shuman] (EP) [BMI] (7/4/64 B-92)
I NEED SOMEONE (TO LOVE ME) Z.Z. Hill—Kent 4547 [Z.Z. Hill] [BMI] (6/19/71 BCR-86)
I NEED TO BE IN LOVE Carpenters—A&M 1828 [John Bettis/Richard Carpenter/Albert Hammond] [ASC] (6/5/76 BCR-25)
I NEED TO KNOW Tom Petty And The Heartbreakers—Shelter 62010 [Tom Petty] [ASC] (6/17/78 BCR-41)
I NEED YOU Rick Nelson—Imperial 5901 [Baker Knight] [BMI] (12/22/62 BC-83)
***I NEED YOU** Chuck Jackson—Wand 179 [Gerry Goffin/Carole King] [BMI] (4/3/65 BCR-75)*
***I NEED YOU** The Rationals—Capitol 2124 [Gerry Goffin/Carole King] [BMI] (3/2/68 C-91)*
I NEED YOU The Impressions—ABC-Paramount 10710 [Curtis Mayfield] [BMI] (8/14/65 BCR-47)
I NEED YOU The Friends Of Distinction—RCA Victor 74-0416 [Jerry Peters] [BMI] (1/16/71 BCR-47)
I NEED YOU America—Warner Bros. 7580 [Gerry Beckley] [ASC] (5/13/72 BCR-8)
I NEED YOU Euclid Beach Band—Epic/Cleveland Int'l 50676 [Eric Carmen] [BMI] (3/31/79 BC-81)
I NEED YOU Paul Carrack—Epic 03146 [Martin Belmont/Paul Carrack/Nick Lowe] [ASC] (9/4/82 BC-26)
I NEED YOU Pointer Sisters—Planet 13639 [John Alden Black/Richard Feldman/Nan O'Byrne] [BMI] (10/8/83 BC-48)
I NEED YOU Maurice White—Columbia 05726 [Priscilla Coolidge/William Daniel Smith/Mary Unobsky] [BMI] (2/8/86 B-95)
***I NEED YOU NOW** Eddie Fisher—RCA Victor 47-5830 [Jimmie Crane/Al Jacobs] [ASC] (8/21/54 BCR-1)*
***I NEED YOU NOW** 100 Strings And Joni—MGM 12885 [Jimmie Crane/Al Jacobs] [ASC] (3/28/60 B-98)*
***I NEED YOU NOW** Ronnie Dove—Diamond 260 [Jimmie Crane/Al Jacobs] [ASC] (5/24/69 BCR-90)*
***I NEED YOU SO** Ted Taylor—Top Rank 2048 [Ivory Joe Hunter] [BMI] (7/25/60 CR-81)*
***I NEED YOU SO** Chuck Jackson & Maxine Brown—Wand 198 [Ivory Joe Hunter] [BMI] (10/23/65 B-98)*
I NEED YOU SO BAD B.B. "Blues Boy" King and his orchestra—RPM 498 [B.B. King/Sam Ling‡] [BMI] (11/18/57 B-85)
I NEED YOU TONIGHT Peter Wolf—EMI America 8241 [Peter S. Bliss/Peter Wolf] [ASC] (10/13/84 BC-36)
I NEED YOU, YOU NEED ME Joe Simon—Spring 163 [Raeford Gerald/Billy Kennedy/Joe Simon] [BMI] (1/17/76 CR-63)
I NEED YOUR HELP BARRY MANILOW Ray Stevens—Warner Bros. 8785 [Dale Gonyea] [BMI] (3/24/79 BCR-34)
I NEED YOUR LOVE TONIGHT Elvis Presley—RCA Victor 47-7506 [Bickley Reichner/Sid Wayne] [ASC] (3/23/59 BCR-3)
I NEED YOUR LOVIN' Conway Twitty—Mercury 71086 [Jimmy Ray Paulman/Conway Twitty] [BMI] (5/4/57 BC-57)
***I NEED YOUR LOVIN'** Roy Hamilton—Epic 9307 [Kenny Martin*/Clarence Paul/Sonny Woods] [BMI] (4/6/59 BCRt-46)*
***I NEED YOUR LOVIN'** Clarence Paul—Hanover 4519 [Kenny Martin*/Clarence Paul/Sonny Woods] [BMI] (4/13/59 Rt-53)*
I NEED YOUR LOVIN' Teena Marie—Gordy 7189 [Teena Marie] [ASC] (10/25/80 BCR-37)

I NEED YOUR LOVING Don Gardner And Dee Dee Ford—Fire 508
[Don Gardner/Clarence L. Lewis*/James McDougal*/Morgan C. Robinson] [BMI] (6/2/62 BCR-16)

I NEED YOUR LOVING The Human League—A&M 2893
[Herman R. Davis/Dave Eiland/James Samuel Harris/Terry Lewis/Langston Richey/Danny Williams] [ASC] (12/6/86 BC-40)

I NEVER CRY Alice Cooper—Warner Bros. 8228
[Alice Cooper/Dick Wagner] [BMI] (7/3/76 BCR-8)

I NEVER FELT LIKE THIS Jack Scott—Carlton 504 [Jack Scott] [BMI] (3/28/59 BCR-69)

I NEVER FELT MORE LIKE FALLING IN LOVE
Tony Bennett with Ray Ellis and His Orchestra—Columbia 41032
[Robert Allen/Ralph Freed] [ASC] (10/21/57 CR-19)

I NEVER KNEW Clyde McPhatter—Mercury 71841
[Clyde McPhatter/Jimmy Oliver] [BMI] (7/24/61 BCR-37)

I NEVER LOVED A MAN (THE WAY I LOVE YOU) Aretha Franklin—Atlantic 2386
[Ronnie Shannon] [BMI] (3/4/67 BCR-8)

I NEVER SAID GOODBYE Engelbert Humperdinck—Parrot 40072
[Barry Mason/Les Reed] [ASC] (10/28/72 BCR-61)

I NEVER SAID I LOVE YOU Orsa Lia—Infinity 50,004
[Hal David/Archie Jordan] [ASC] (3/24/79 BC-84)

I.O.I.O. Bee Gees—Atco 6752
[Barry Gibb/Maurice Gibb] [BMI] (6/27/70 BR-94)

I.O.U. Jimmy Dean—Casino 052 [Jimmy Dean/Larry Markes] [BMI] (5/15/76 BCR-33)

I.O.U. Lee Greenwood—MCA 52199 [Kerry Chater/Austin Roberts] [BMI] (5/28/83 BC-53)

I ONLY HAVE EYES FOR YOU *The Flamingos—End 1046*
[Al Dubin/Harry Warren] [ASC] (5/4/59 BCR-10)

I ONLY HAVE EYES FOR YOU *Cliff Richard—Epic 9670*
[Al Dubin/Harry Warren] [ASC] (4/25/64 R-89)

I ONLY HAVE EYES FOR YOU *The Lettermen—Capitol 5649*
[Al Dubin/Harry Warren] [ASC] (6/18/66 BCR-72)

I ONLY HAVE EYES FOR YOU *Jerry Butler—Mercury 73290*
[Al Dubin/Harry Warren] [ASC] (5/13/72 BCR-67)

I ONLY HAVE EYES FOR YOU *Art Garfunkel—Columbia 10190*
[Al Dubin/Harry Warren] [ASC] (8/23/75 BCR-17)

I ONLY KNOW I LOVE YOU *Four Aces—Decca 29989*
[Ugo Calise/Carlo Alberto Rossi/Al Stillman] [ASC] (7/13/56 BCRt-35) [FDE]

I ONLY KNOW I LOVE YOU *Johnny Desmond—Coral 61663*
[Ugo Calise/Carlo Alberto Rossi/Al Stillman] [ASC] (8/17/56 Rt-46) [FDE]

I ONLY WANT TO BE WITH YOU *Dusty Springfield—Philips 40162*
[Mike Hawker/Ivor Raymonde] [ASC] (1/11/64 BCR-12)

I ONLY WANT TO BE WITH YOU *Bay City Rollers—Arista 0205*
[Mike Hawker/Ivor Raymonde] [ASC] (9/4/76 BCR-8)

I ONLY WANT TO BE WITH YOU *The Tourists—Epic 50850*
[Mike Hawker/Ivor Raymonde] [ASC] (5/10/80 BR-83)

I ONLY WANT TO BE WITH YOU *Nicolette Larson—Warner Bros. 29948*
[Mike Hawker/Ivor Raymonde] [ASC] (7/31/82 BC-48)

I ONLY WANNA BE WITH YOU *Samantha Fox—Jive 1192*
[Mike Hawker/Ivor Raymonde] [ASC] (3/18/89 BC-31)

I ONLY WANT YOU The Passions—Audicon 105 [Harry Evans] [BMI] (3/5/60 C-93)

I PITY THE FOOL *Bobby Bland—Duke 332 [Deadric Malone] [BMI] (2/11/61 BCR-45)*

I PITY THE FOOL *Ann Peebles—Hi 2186 [Deadric Malone] [BMI] (3/6/71 BCR-84)*

I PLAY AND SING Dawn—Bell 970
[L. Russell Brown/Irwin Levine] [BMI] (3/20/71 BCR-20)

I PLEDGE ALLEGIANCE TO YOUR HEART *Ginny Gibson—ABC-Paramount 9786*
[Bill Norvas] [ASC] (2/2/57 Rt-55)

I PLEDGE ALLEGIANCE TO YOUR HEART *Monique Cadou—Kapp 171*
[Bill Norvas] [ASC] (2/2/57 Rt-55)

I PLEDGE ALLEGIANCE TO YOUR HEART *Jaye P. Morgan—RCA Victor 47-6798*
[Bill Norvas] [ASC] (2/2/57 Rt-55)

I PLEDGE MY LOVE Peaches & Herb—Polydor/MVP 2053
[Dino Fekaris/Freddie Perren] [ASC] (1/19/80 BCR-19)

I PREDICT Sparks—Atlantic 4030 [Ron Mael/Russell Mael] [ASC] (5/15/82 BC-60)

I PRETEND Kim Carnes—EMI America 8202
[Brian Fairweather/Martin Page] [ASC] (5/19/84 B-74)

I PROMISE TO REMEMBER *Frankie Lymon and the Teenagers—Gee 1018*
[Jimmy Castor/James O. Smith] [BMI] (7/20/56 BCRt-33)

I PROMISE *Jimmy Castor & The Juniors—Wing 90078*
[Jimmy Castor/James O. Smith] [BMI] (8/10/56 Rt-42)

I PROMISE TO WAIT MY LOVE Martha Reeves & The Vandellas—Gordy 7070
[Billie Jean Brown/George Gordy/Margaret Johnson/Allen Story] [BMI] (4/20/68 BCR-37)

I PUT A SPELL ON YOU *Alan Price Set—Parrot 3001*
[Screamin' Jay Hawkins] [BMI] (7/30/66 B-80)

I PUT A SPELL ON YOU *Creedence Clearwater Revival—Fantasy 617*
[Screamin' Jay Hawkins] [BMI] (11/9/68 BCR-55)

I PUT A SPELL ON YOU *The Crazy World Of Arthur Brown—Track 2582*
[Screamin' Jay Hawkins] [BMI] (12/7/68 C-99)

I RAN (SO FAR AWAY) A Flock Of Seagulls—Jive 102
[Frank Maudsley/Paul Reynolds/Ali Score/Mike Score] [ASC] (7/10/82 BC-9)

I REALLY DON'T NEED NO LIGHT Jeffrey Osborne—A&M 2410
[Jeffrey Osborne/David Wolinski] [ASC] (6/5/82 BC-39)

I REALLY DON'T WANT TO KNOW *Les Paul and Mary Ford—Capitol 2735*
[Howard Lee Barnes/Don Robertson] [ASC] (5/29/54 B-PRE)

I REALLY DON'T WANT TO KNOW *Tommy Edwards—MGM 12890*
[Howard Lee Barnes/Don Robertson] [ASC] (5/2/60 BCR-18)

I REALLY DON'T WANT TO KNOW *Solomon Burke—Atlantic 2157*
[Howard Lee Barnes/Don Robertson] [ASC] (9/8/62 BR-93)

I REALLY DON'T WANT TO KNOW *"Little Esther" Phillips—Lenox 5560*
[Howard Lee Barnes/Don Robertson] [ASC] (2/9/63 BCR-61)

I REALLY DON'T WANT TO KNOW *Ronnie Dove—Diamond 208*
[Howard Lee Barnes/Don Robertson] [ASC] (9/3/66 BCR-22)

I REALLY DON'T WANT TO KNOW *Elvis Presley—RCA Victor 47-9960*
[Howard Lee Barnes/Don Robertson] (TSW) [ASC] (12/26/70 BCR-13)

I REALLY LOVE YOU The Danleers—Mercury 71356 [Danny Webb] [ASC] (10/4/58 C-58)

I REALLY LOVE YOU The Stereos—Cub 9095 [Leroy Swearingen] [BMI] (9/11/61 BCR-25)

I REALLY LOVE YOU Dee Dee Sharp—Cameo 375
[James A. Bishop/Kenneth Gamble] [BMI] (11/6/65 BCR-67)

I REALLY LOVE YOU Davy Jones—Bell 45,136 [Bob Gundry] [ASC] (10/23/71 C-96)

I RECEIVED A LETTER Delbert & Glen—Clean 60003
[Delbert McClinton] [BMI] (11/18/72 BCR-68)

I REFUSE TO SMILE Mandrill—Polydor 14127
[Carlos Wilson/Louis Wilson/Ric Wilson] [ASC] (7/1/72 C-100)

I REMEMBER Maurice Williams & The Zodiacs—Herald 556
[Maurice Williams] [BMI] (1/16/61 BCR-78)

I REMEMBER HOLDING YOU Boys Club—MCA 53430
[Joe Pasquale] [ASC] (10/22/88 BC-4)

(I REMEMBER) SUMMER MORNING Vanity Fare—Page One 21,033
[Jacky Arthur/Michael Kent] [NA] (8/8/70 BCR-61)

I REMEMBER YOU Frank Ifield—Vee-Jay 457
[Johnny Mercer/Victor Schertzinger] [ASC] (9/1/62 BCR-5)

I REMEMBER YOU Skid Row—Atlantic 88886
[Rachel Bolan/Dave Sabo] [ASC] (11/18/89 BC-6)

I RISE, I FALL Johnny Tillotson—MGM 13232 [Paul Hampton] [BMI] (5/2/64 BCR-35)

I SAW A MAN AND HE DANCED WITH HIS WIFE Cher—MCA 40273
[John Durrill] [ASC] (8/3/74 BCR-33)

I SAW ESAU The Ames Brothers—RCA Victor 47-6720
[Cy Coben] [ASC] (11/24/56 BCR-49)

I SAW HER AGAIN The Mamas & The Papas—Dunhill 4031
[Dennis Doherty/John Phillips] [ASC] (7/2/66 BCR-4)

I SAW HER STANDING THERE *The Beatles—Capitol 5112*
[John Lennon/Paul McCartney] [ASC] (2/8/64 BCR-14)

I SAW HIM STANDING THERE *Tiffany—MCA 53285*
[John Lennon/Paul McCartney] [ASC] (2/27/88 BC-7)

—I SAW HIM STANDING THERE see: I SAW HER STANDING THERE

I SAW LINDA YESTERDAY Dickey Lee—Smash 1791
[Dickey Lee/Allen Reynolds] [BMI] (12/8/62 BCR-8)

I SAW MOMMY DO THE MAMBO (WITH YOU KNOW WHO) Jimmy Boyd—Columbia 40365
[Robert Allen/Tommie Connor/Al Stillman] [ASC] (12/13/54 R-71)

I SAW MOMMY KISSING SANTA CLAUS Jimmy Boyd—Columbia 40070
[Tommie Connor] [ASC] (12/27/54 R-51)

I SAW RED Warrant—Columbia 73597
[Joseph Cagle*/Steven Chamberlin*/Jerry Dixon*/John Oswald/Eric Turner*] [BMI] (11/24/90 BC-10)

I SAW THE LIGHT Todd Rundgren—Bearsville 0003
[Todd Rundgren] [BMI] (4/1/72 BCR-11)

I SAY A LITTLE PRAYER *Dionne Warwick—Scepter 12203*
[Burt Bacharach/Hal David] [ASC] (10/21/67 BCR-4)

I SAY A LITTLE PRAYER *Aretha Franklin—Atlantic 2546*
[Burt Bacharach/Hal David] [ASC] (8/17/68 BCR-10)

I SAY A LITTLE PRAYER *Glen Campbell—Capitol 3200*
[Burt Bacharach/Hal David] (Med) [ASC] (10/23/71 BCR-72)

I SAY LOVE The Royal Guardsmen—Laurie 3428
[Billy (2) Taylor/Barry Winslow] [BMI] (2/17/68 BCR-72)

I SECOND THAT EMOTION Smokey Robinson & The Miracles—Tamla 54159
[Al Cleveland/Smokey Robinson] [ASC] (11/4/67 BCR-3)

I SEE THE LIGHT The Five Americans—HBR 454
[John Durrill/Norman Ezell/Michael Rabon] [BMI] (12/25/65 BCR-26)

I SEE YOU Cathy And Joe—Smash 1929 [Jimmy Duncan] [BMI] (10/3/64 BCR-75)

I SEND A MESSAGE INXS—Atco 99731
[Andy Farriss/Michael Hutchence] [BMI] (7/21/84 B-77)

I SHALL BE RELEASED The Box Tops—Mala 12,038 [Bob Dylan] [SE] (4/26/69 BCR-67)

I SHALL SING Garfunkel—Columbia 45983 [Van Morrison] [BMI] (12/22/73 BCR-18)

—I SHOT MR. LEE see: MR. LEE

I SHOT THE SHERIFF Eric Clapton—RSO 409 [Bob Marley] [ASC] (7/13/74 BCR-1)

I SHOULD BE SO LUCKY Kylie Minogue—Geffen 27922
[Matt Aitken/Mike Stock/Pete Waterman] [BMI] (5/7/88 BC-28)

I SHOULD CARE Gloria Lynne—Everest 2042
[Sammy Cahn/Axel Stordahl/Paul Weston] [ASC] (4/4/64 BCR-63)

I SHOULD HAVE KNOWN BETTER *The Beatles—Capitol 5222*
[John Lennon/Paul McCartney] [ASC] (7/18/64 BCR-43)

I SHOULD HAVE KNOWN BETTER *Stars On 45—Radio 3810*
[John Lennon/Paul McCartney] (Med) [ASC] (4/11/81 BCR-1)

I SHOULD HAVE KNOWN BETTER *The Beatles—Capitol 5107*
[John Lennon/Paul McCartney] (Med) [ASC] (3/27/82 BCR-12)

I SHOULDA LOVED YA Narada Michael Walden—Atlantic 3631
[Thomas M. Stevens/Narada Michael Walden/Allee Willis] [ASC] (2/2/80 BCR-66)

I SIT IN MY WINDOW *Russ Miller—VIP 1006 [Otis Blackwell] [BMI] (8/3/57 Rt-66)*

I SIT IN MY WINDOW *The Crew-Cuts—Mercury 71168*
[Otis Blackwell] [BMI] (8/26/57 Rt-66)

I SOLD MY HEART TO THE JUNKMAN Patti Labelle And The Blue Belles—Newtown 5000
[Leon René/Otis René] [ASC] (4/9/62 BCR-12)

I SPOKE TOO SOON The Crew-Cuts—Mercury 70404
[Ira Kosloff/Alice D. Simms] [ASC] (10/18/54 CR-49)

I SPY (FOR THE FBI) Jamo Thomas & His Party Brothers Orchestra—Thomas 303
[Herman Wesley Kelley/Richard Wylie] [BMI] (3/19/66 BC-94)

I STAND ACCUSED *Jerry Butler—Vee-Jay 598*
[Jerry Butler/William Earl Butler] [BMI] (8/1/64 BCR-44)

I STAND ACCUSED *Isaac Hayes—Enterprise 9017*
[Jerry Butler/William Earl Butler] [BMI] (8/29/70 BCR-29)

I STAND ACCUSED (OF LOVING YOU) The Glories—Date 1553
[Warren Levine] [BMI] (6/10/67 BCR-62)

I STARTED A JOKE The Bee Gees—Atco 6639
[Barry Gibb/Maurice Gibb/Robin Gibb] [BMI] (12/14/68 BCR-5)

—I STARTED LOVING YOU AGAIN see: TODAY I STARTED...

I STILL BELIEVE Brenda K. Starr—MCA 53288
[Antonina Armato/Giuseppe Cantarelli] [ASC] (4/2/88 BC-13)

I STILL BELIEVE IN TOMORROW John & Anne Ryder—Decca 732506
[Ronnie Scott/Marty Wilde] [BMI] (9/20/69 BCR-55)

I STILL CAN'T GET OVER LOVING YOU Ray Parker Jr.—Arista 1-9116
[Ray Parker Jr.] [ASC] (11/12/83 BC-12)

I STILL GET A THRILL (THINKING OF YOU) Joni James—MGM 12779
[J. Fred Coots/Benny Davis] [ASC] (3/30/59 BCR-33)

I STILL GET JEALOUS *Joni James—MGM 12807*
[Sammy Cahn/Jule Styne] [ASC] (6/22/59 BCR-50)

I STILL GET JEALOUS *Louis Armstrong And The All-Stars—Kapp 597*
[Sammy Cahn/Jule Styne] [ASC] (6/13/64 BCR-18)

I STILL HAVE DREAMS Richie Furay—Asylum 46534
[Billy Batstone] [ASC] (10/20/79 BCR-39)

I STILL HAVEN'T FOUND WHAT I'M LOOKING FOR U2—Island 99430
[Adam Clayton/Dave Evans/Paul Hewson/Larry Mullen] [ASC] (6/13/87 BC-1)

I STILL LOVE YOU Fats Domino—Imperial 5467
[Dave Bartholomew/Fats Domino/Earl Palmer/Wilbert Watson] [BMI]
(10/12/57 BCR-60)

I STILL LOVE YOU The Vejtables—Autumn 15 [Jan Ashton] [BMI] (10/23/65 B-84)

I STILL LOVE YOU Jackie Wilson—Brunswick 55402
[Carl Davis/Eugene Record] [BMI] (3/15/69 CR-67)

I STILL WANT YOU The Del Fuegos—Slash 28822
[Tom Lloyd/Dan Zanes] [ASC] (5/31/86 BC-81)

I STRUCK IT RICH Len Barry—Decca 32011
[Len Barry/Kenneth Gamble/Leon Huff] [BMI] (9/17/66 B-98)

I SURRENDER Fontella Bass—Checker 1137
[Billy Davis/Shena DeMell/Sugar Pie DeSanto] [ASC] (3/26/66 BCR-78)

I SURRENDER Arlan Day—Pasha 02480 [Arlan Day] [ASC] (10/10/81 BCR-61)

I SURRENDER, DEAR Aretha Franklin—Columbia 42266
[Harry Barris/Gordon Clifford] [ASC] (2/3/62 BCR-76)

I TAKE A LOT OF PRIDE IN WHAT I AM Dean Martin—Reprise 0841
[Merle Haggard] [BMI] (8/9/69 BCR-66)

I TAKE IT BACK Sandy Posey—MGM 13744
[Buddy Buie/J.R. Cobb] [BMI] (6/3/67 BCR-11)

I TAKE WHAT I WANT James & Bobby Purify—Bell 680
[Isaac Hayes/Mabon Hodges/David Porter] [BMI] (7/15/67 BCR-41)

I TALK TO THE TREES Edmundo Ros and His Orchestra—London 1831
[Frederick Loewe] [ASC] (12/13/58 BCR-46) [IM]

I THANK YOU *Sam & Dave—Stax 242 [Isaac Hayes/David Porter] [BMI] (1/27/68 BCR-8)*

I THANK YOU *ZZ Top—Warner Bros. 49163*
[Isaac Hayes/David Porter] [BMI] (1/19/80 BCR-34)

I THANK YOU Donny Hathaway And June Conquest—Curtom 1971
[Donny Hathaway/Curtis Mayfield] [BMI] (5/27/72 B-94)

I THINK ABOUT YOU ALL THE TIME Paul Evans—Decca 30680
[Paul Evans/Jack Reardon] [ASC] (7/21/58 R-76)

I THINK I CAN BEAT MIKE TYSON D.J. Jazzy Jeff & The Fresh Prince—Jive 1282
[Peter Brian Harris/Will Smith/Jeff Townes] [ASC] (11/4/89 B-58)

I THINK I LOVE YOU
The Partridge Family Starring Shirley Jones & Featuring David Cassidy—Bell 910
[Tony Romeo] [BMI] (9/26/70 BCR-1)

I THINK I LOVE YOU AGAIN Brenda Lee—Decca 32675
[Irwin Levine/Toni Wine] [BMI] (5/16/70 BCR-84)

I THINK I'M GONNA KILL MYSELF Buddy Knox—Roulette 4140
[Buddy Knox] [BMI] (3/30/59 BCR-55)

I THINK IT'S LOVE Jermaine Jackson—Arista 1-9444
[Jermaine Jackson/Michael Omartian/Stevie Wonder] [ASC] (2/22/86 BC-15)

I THINK OF YOU Perry Como—RCA Victor 74-0444
[Francis Lai/Rod McKuen] [ASC] (3/13/71 BCR-45)

I THINK SOMEBODY LOVES ME Noble Downs—Roulette 7115
[Tommy Ingram] [BMI] (1/22/72 R-99)

I THINK WE'RE ALONE NOW *Tommy James And The Shondells—Roulette 4720*
[Ritchie Cordell] [BMI] (2/4/67 BCR-3)

I THINK WE'RE ALONE NOW *The Rubinoos—Beserkley 5741*
[Ritchie Cordell] [BMI] (2/26/77 BCR-45)

I THINK WE'RE ALONE NOW *Tiffany—MCA 53167 [Ritchie Cordell] [BMI] (8/29/87 BC-1)*

I THINK YOU NEED LOVE Dionne Warwicke—Warner Bros. 7669
[Lamont Dozier/Brian Holland/Eddie Holland] [BMI] (2/3/73 R-87)

I THINK YOU'LL REMEMBER TONIGHT Axe—Atco 99823
[Bobby Barth/Michael Osborne] [BMI] (10/22/83 B-94)

I THOUGHT IT TOOK A LITTLE TIME (BUT TODAY I FELL IN LOVE)
Diana Ross—Motown 1387
[Michael Masser/Pam Sawyer] [ASC] (3/20/76 BC-47)

I THREW IT ALL AWAY Bob Dylan—Columbia 44826 [Bob Dylan] [SE] (5/17/69 BCR-60)

I TOLD MYSELF A LIE Clyde McPhatter—MGM 12780
[Otis Blackwell/Jimmy Williams] [BMI] (3/30/59 BCR-46)

I TOLD THE BROOK Marty Robbins—Columbia 42246
[Marty Robbins] [BMI] (12/25/61 BCR-81)

I TOLD THE STARS The Lettermen—Capitol 4810
[Johnny Colonna/Jerry Wallace] [BMI] (7/28/62 R-98)

I TOLD YOU SO Jimmy Jones—Cub 9085 [Gary Geld/Peter Udell] [ASC] (2/20/61 BCR-63)

I TOUCH MYSELF Divinyls—Virgin 98873
[Christina Amphlett/Tom Kelly/Mark McEntee/Billy Steinberg] [BMI] (3/9/91 BC-4)

I TRULY, TRULY BELIEVE The Temptations—Gordy 7068
[George Gordy/Margaret Johnson/Allen Story] [BMI] (3/30/68 C-93)

I TRUSTED YOU Jimmy Bowen With The Rhythm Orchids—Roulette 4010
[Dave Alldred*/Jimmy Bowen/Buddy Knox/Donnie Lanier*] [BMI] (5/11/57 CR-43)

I TURNED YOU ON The Isley Brothers—T-Neck 902
[O'Kelly Isley/Ronald Isley/Rudolph Isley] [ASC] (5/31/69 BCR-17)

I UNDERSTAND Fred Hughes—Brunswick 55438 [Fred Hughes] [BMI] (7/25/70 R-82)

I UNDERSTAND JUST HOW YOU FEEL *The Four Tunes—Jubilee 5132*
[Pat Best] [BMI] (5/29/54 BCR-PRE)

I UNDERSTAND JUST HOW YOU FEEL *June Valli—RCA Victor 47-5740*
[Pat Best] [BMI] (6/12/54 BC-7)

I UNDERSTAND (JUST HOW YOU FEEL) *The G-Clefs—Terrace 7500*
[Pat Best] [BMI] (9/11/61 BCR-9)

I UNDERSTAND (JUST HOW YOU FEEL) *Freddie And The Dreamers—Mercury 72377*
[Pat Best] [BMI] (3/13/65 BCR-36)

I WAITED TOO LONG LaVern Baker—Atlantic 2021
[Howard Greenfield/Neil Sedaka] [BMI] (4/20/59 BCR-33)

I WAKE UP CRYING Chuck Jackson—Wand 110
[Burt Bacharach/Hal David] [ASC] (8/5/61 BCR-41)

I WALK ALONE Marty Robbins—Columbia 44633
[Herbert Wilson] [BMI] (10/26/68 BC-65)

I WALK THE LINE *Johnny Cash and the Tennessee Two—Sun 241*
[Johnny Cash] [BMI] (9/15/56 BCRt-19)

I WALK THE LINE *Hoagy Carmichael—Coral 61717 [Johnny Cash] [BMI] (10/13/56 Rt-21)*

I WALK THE LINE *Carole Bennett—Capitol 3564 [Johnny Cash] [BMI] (10/20/56 Rt-21)*

I'LL WALK THE LINE *Don Costa And His Orchestra And Chorus—United Artists 190*
[Johnny Cash] [BMI] (10/12/59 BCR-27) [IWM]

I WALK THE LINE *Jaye P. Morgan—MGM 12924 [Johnny Cash] [BMI] (8/15/60 BCR-27)*

I WANNA The Platters—Mercury 71093 [Buck Ram/Zola Taylor] [NA] (6/1/57 R-35)

I WANNA BE A COWBOY Boys Don't Cry—Profile 5084
[Brian Chatton/Nico Ramsden/Nick Richards/Jeff Seopardie] [ASC] (4/5/86 BC-12)

I WANNA BE A FREE GIRL Dusty Springfield—Atlantic 2729
[Thom Bell/Linda Creed/Kenneth Gamble/Leon Huff] [BMI] (5/16/70 R-76)

I WANNA BE AROUND Tony Bennett—Columbia 42634
[Johnny Mercer/Sadie Vimmerstedt] [ASC] (1/12/63 BCR-14)

I WANNA BE FREE Loretta Lynn—Decca 32796 [Loretta Lynn] [BMI] (4/24/71 B-94)

I WANNA BE LOVED Ricky Nelson—Imperial 5614
[Baker Knight] [BMI] (11/21/59 BCR-20)

I WANNA BE LOVED House Of Lords—RCA 8805
[Steve Johnstad/Michael Meyer] [ASC] (12/17/88 BC-58)

I WANNA BE RICH Calloway—Solar 74005
[Reggie Calloway/Vincent Calloway/Melvin Gentry/Belinda Lipscomb] [BMI]
(2/10/90 BC-2)

I WANNA BE THE ONE Stevie B—LMR 74003
[Dadgel Atabay*/Stevie B] [BMI] (2/18/89 BC-32)

I WANNA BE WHERE YOU ARE Michael Jackson—Motown 1202
[Arthur Ross/Leon Ware] [ASC] (5/20/72 BCR-7)

I WANNA BE WITH YOU Raspberries—Capitol 3473
[Eric Carmen] [BMI] (11/11/72 BCR-7)

I WANNA BE WITH YOU (PART I) The Isley Brothers—T-Neck 2279
[Ernie Isley/Marvin Isley/O'Kelly Isley/Ronald Isley/Rudolph Isley/Chris Jasper] [ASC] (5/5/79 CR-76)

I WANNA BE YOUR BABY The Three Degrees—Roulette 7125
[Leon Huff] [BMI] (7/15/72 CR-94)

I WANNA BE (YOUR EVERYTHING) The Manhattans—Carnival 507
[Winfred Lovett] [BMI] (1/16/65 BCR-68)

I WANNA BE YOUR GIRL Icy Blu—Giant 19170 [Tyrone Fleming] [ASC] (11/2/91 BC-46)

I WANNA BE YOUR LOVER Prince—Warner Bros. 49050 [Prince] [ASC] (11/3/79 BCR-11)

—I WANNA CRY see: PLAY ME HEARTS AND FLOWERS

I WANNA DANCE WIT' CHOO (DOO DAT DANCE)
Disco Tex & The Sex-O-Lettes Featuring Sir Monti Rock III—Chelsea 3015
[Bob Crewe/Denny Randell] [BMI] (4/12/75 BCR-23)

I WANNA DANCE WITH SOMEBODY (WHO LOVES ME) Whitney Houston—Arista 1-9598
[George Merrill/Shannon Rubicam] [BMI] (5/16/87 BC-1)

(I WANNA) DANCE WITH THE TEACHER The Olympics—Demon 1512
[Cliff Goldsmith/Fred Smith] [BMI] (12/8/58 B-71)

I WANNA DO IT TO YOU Jerry Butler—Motown 1414
[Jerry Butler/Patricia Henley/Homer Talbert] [ASC] (3/5/77 BCR-51)

I WANNA GET BACK WITH YOU Louie Louie—WTG 73472
[Philip Bailey/Louie Cordero/Danny Sembello/Marti Sharron] [ASC] (8/18/90 BC-61)

I WANNA GET NEXT TO YOU Rose Royce—MCA 40662
[Norman Whitfield] [BMI] (2/26/77 BCR-8)

I WANNA GET WITH U Guy—MCA 53928
[Aqil Davidson/Aaron Hall/Damion Hall/Teddy Riley] [ASC] (11/10/90 BC-49)

I WANNA GO BACK *Billy Satellite—Capitol 5409*
[Monty Byrom/Danny Chauncey/Ira Walker] [BMI] (12/1/84 BC-72)

I WANNA GO BACK *Eddie Money—Columbia 06569*
[Monty Byrom/Danny Chauncey/Ira Walker] [BMI] (12/13/86 BC-14)

I WANNA GO WHERE YOU GO, DO WHAT YOU DO (THEN I'LL BE HAPPY)
Eddie Fisher—RCA Victor 47-6264
[Lew Brown/Sidney Clare/Cliff Friend] [ASC] (9/26/55 BCR-20)

I WANNA HAVE SOME FUN Samantha Fox—Jive 1154
[Curtis Bedeau/Gerard Charles/Hugh Clarke/Brian George/Lucien George/Paul George] [BMI] (11/5/88 BC-8)

I WANNA HEAR IT FROM YOUR LIPS Eric Carmen—Geffen 29118
[Eric Carmen/Dean Pitchford] [BMI] (1/19/85 BC-35)

I WANNA KNOW IF IT'S GOOD TO YOU? Funkadelic—Westbound 167
[George Clinton/Clarence Haskins/Eddie Hazel/Billy Nelson] [BMI] (8/22/70 BCR-81)

I WANNA KNOW YOUR NAME The Intruders—Gamble 2508
[Kenneth Gamble/Leon Huff] [BMI] (10/27/73 BCR-60)

I WANNA LEARN A LOVE SONG Harry Chapin—Elektra 45236
[Harry Chapin] [ASC] (2/15/75 BCR-40)

I WANNA LIVE Glen Campbell—Capitol 2146
[John D. Loudermilk] [BMI] (3/30/68 BCR-28)

I WANNA LOVE HIM SO BAD The Jelly Beans—Red Bird 10-003
[Jeff Barry/Ellie Greenwich] [BMI] (6/20/64 BCR-9)

—I WANNA LOVE MY LIFE AWAY see: LOVE MY LIFE AWAY

I WANNA MEET YOU Cryan' Shames—Columbia 43836
[Jim Fairs] [BMI] (10/29/66 BCR-62)

I WANNA ROCK Twisted Sister—Atlantic 89617 [Dee Snider] [ASC] (10/20/84 BC-68)

I WANNA SEX YOU UP Color Me Badd—Giant 19382
[Bryan Abrams*/Mark Calderon*/Willie Clarke*/Elliot Straite/Kevin Thornton*/Sam Watters*/Betty Wright*] [BMI] (4/6/91 BC-2)

I WANNA STAY WITH YOU Gallagher And Lyle—A&M 1778
[Benny Gallagher/Graham Lyle] [BMI] (4/10/76 BCR-49)

(I WANNA) TESTIFY *The Parliaments—Revilot 207*
[George Clinton/Daron Taylor] [BMI] (6/17/67 BCR-18)

TESTIFY (I WONNA) *Johnnie Taylor—Stax 0033*
[George Clinton/Daron Taylor] [BMI] (5/10/69 BCR-36)

I WANNA THANK YOU Bobby Rydell—Cameo 201
[Dave Appell/Bernie Lowe/Kal Mann] [ASC] (10/16/61 BCR-21)

I WANNA THANK YOU The Enchanters (2)—Warner Bros. 5460
[Samuel Bell/Jerry Ragovoy] [BMI] (9/5/64 B-91)

I WANT A GIRL (JUST LIKE THE GIRL THAT MARRIED DEAR OLD DAD)
Crazy Otto—Decca 29753A
[Harry Von Tilzer] (Med) [NA] (2/3/56 R-90) [IM]

I WANT A GIRL *Bruce Hayes with Mary Mayo—Dwain 812*
[Will Dillon/Harry Von Tilzer] (EP) [NA] (2/15/60 R-63)

I WANT A NEW DRUG Huey Lewis and the News—Chrysalis 42766
[Chris Hayes/Huey Lewis] [ASC] (1/14/84 BC-5)

I WANT ACTION Poison—Enigma 44004
[Bobby Dall/C.C. DeVille/Bret Michaels/Rikki Rockett] [BMI] (6/13/87 BC-50)

I WANT CANDY *The Strangeloves—Bang 501*
[Bert Berns/Bob Feldman/Jerry Goldstein/Richard Gottehrer] [BMI] (6/19/65 BCR-6)

I WANT CANDY *Bow Wow Wow—RCA 13204*
[Bert Berns/Bob Feldman/Jerry Goldstein/Richard Gottehrer] [BMI] (5/29/82 BC-61)

I WANT EDDIE FISHER FOR CHRISTMAS *Betty Johnson—New-Disc 10013*
[Joan Javits/Philip Springer] [ASC] (10/18/54 Rt-28)

I WANT EDDIE FISHER FOR CHRISTMAS
Spike Jones with Linda Strangis—RCA Victor 47-5920
[Joan Javits/Philip Springer] [ASC] (11/22/54 Rt-PRE)

I WANT HER Keith Sweat—Vintertainment 7-69431
[Teddy Riley/Keith Sweat] [ASC] (1/16/88 BC-5)

I WANT IT ALL Queen—Capitol 44372
[John Deacon/Brian May/Freddie Mercury/Roger Taylor] [BMI] (5/13/89 BC-48)

I WANT MY BABY BACK Jimmy Cross—Tollie 9039
[Perry Botkin Jr./Gil Garfield] [BMI] (1/23/65 BCR-80)

I WANT MY GIRL Jesse Johnson's Revue—A&M 2749
[Jesse Woods Johnson] [ASC] (7/20/85 BC-76)

I WANT SOME MORE Jon & Robin and The In Crowd—Abnak 124
[Wayne Carson Thompson] [BMI] (11/4/67 R-61)

I WANT SOMEONE The Mad Lads—Volt 131
[Estelle Stewart Axton/Willia Dean Parker] [BMI] (3/5/66 BCR-66)

I WANT TO BE FREE Ohio Players—Mercury 73675
[William Beck/Leroy Bonner/Marshall Jones/Ralph Middlebrooks/Andrew Noland/Marvin Pierce/James Rodger Williams] [BMI] (4/5/75 BCR-32)

I WANT TO BE HAPPY CHA CHA *Enoch Light & The Light Brigade—Grand Award 1020*
[Vincent Youmans] [ASC] (10/27/58 BCtRt-18) [IM]

I WANT TO BE HAPPY CHA CHA
Tommy Dorsey Orchestra starring Warren Covington—Decca 30790
[Irving Caesar/Vincent Youmans] [ASC] (11/3/58 BCtRt-18)

I WANT TO BE LOVED *Dinah Washington—Mercury 72015*
[Johnny Green/Edward Heyman/Billy Rose] [ASC] (8/18/62 BR-76)

I WANNA BE LOVED *Dean And Jean—Rust 5081*
[Johnny Green/Edward Heyman/Billy Rose] [ASC] (5/30/64 BC-89)

I WANT TO BE WANTED Brenda Lee—Decca 31149
[Kim Gannon/Giuseppe Spotti] [ASC] (9/12/60 BCR-1) [FDE]

I WANNA BE WITH YOU *Nancy Wilson—Capitol 5254*
[Lee Adams/Charles Strouse] [ASC] (9/26/64 BCR-50)

I WANT TO BE WITH YOU *Dee Dee Warwick—Mercury 72584*
[Lee Adams/Charles Strouse] [ASC] (8/6/66 BCR-41)

I WANT TO BE YOUR MAN Roger—Reprise 28229
[Larry Troutman/Roger Troutman] [BMI] (11/14/87 BC-3)

I WANT TO BE YOUR PROPERTY Blue Mercedes—MCA 53262
[Duncan Millar/David Titlow] [ASC] (3/5/88 BC-66)

I WANT TO BREAK FREE Queen—Capitol 5350
[John Deacon] [BMI] (4/28/84 BC-45)

I WANT TO DANCE WITH YOU (DANCE WITH ME) The Ritchie Family—20th Century 2252
[Henri Belolo/Jacques Morali/Peter Whitehead] [BMI] (12/6/75 BC-81)

I WANT TO (DO EVERYTHING FOR YOU) *Joe Tex—Dial 4016*
[Joe Tex] [BMI] (8/21/65 BCR-17)

I WANT TO (DO EVERYTHING FOR YOU) *The Raeletts—Tangerine 1006*
[Joe Tex] [BMI] (5/9/70 BCR-83)

I WANT TO GO BACK THERE AGAIN Chris Clark—V.I.P. 2504
[Chris Clark*/Berry Gordy] [ASC] (4/22/67 R-94)

I WANT TO GO WITH YOU Eddy Arnold—RCA Victor 47-8749
[Hank Cochran] [BMI] (2/5/66 BCR-36)

I WANT TO HOLD YOUR HAND *The Beatles—Capitol 5112*
[John Lennon/Paul McCartney] [ASC] (1/11/64 BCR-1)

I WANT TO HOLD YOUR HAND
Boston Pops Orchestra Arthur Fiedler Conductor—RCA Victor 47-8378
[John Lennon/Paul McCartney] [ASC] (7/4/64 BCR-55) [IWM]

I WANT TO HOLD YOUR HAND *Stars On 45—Radio 3830*
[John Lennon/Paul McCartney] (Med) [ASC] (7/11/81 BC-63)

I WANT TO KNOW Sugar Pie DeSanto—Check 103
[Ronald Badger/Sugar Pie DeSanto/Bob Geddins] [BMI] (8/22/60 CR-80)

I WANT TO KNOW WHAT LOVE IS Foreigner—Atlantic 89596
[Michael Leslie Jones] [ASC] (12/8/84 BC-1)

I WANT TO LIVE John Denver—RCA 11267 [John Denver] [ASC] (4/22/78 BCR-55)

I WANT TO LOVE YOU BABY Peggy Scott & Jo Jo Benson—SSS Int'l 769
[Don Hill] [ASC] (4/26/69 BCR-70)

I WANT TO LOVE YOU FOR WHAT YOU ARE Ronnie Dove—Diamond 227
[Andy Badale/Norm Simon] [ASC] (7/29/67 BCR-41)

I WANT TO MAKE THE WORLD TURN AROUND Steve Miller Band—Capitol 5646
[Steve Miller] [ASC] (11/8/86 BC-79)

I WANT TO MEET HIM The Royalettes—MGM 13405
[Teddy Randazzo/Lou Stallman/Bobby Weinstein] [BMI] (10/23/65 BCR-58)

I WANT TO PAY YOU BACK (FOR LOVING ME) The Chi-Lites—Brunswick 55458
[Eugene Record] [BMI] (9/25/71 BCR-64)

I WANT TO STAY HERE Steve And Eydie—Columbia 42815
[Gerry Goffin/Carole King] [BMI] (7/20/63 BCR-28)

I WANT TO TAKE YOU HIGHER *Sly & The Family Stone—Epic 10450*
[Sylvester Stewart] [BMI] (5/24/69 BCR-60)

I WANT TO TAKE YOU HIGHER *Sly & The Family Stone—Epic 10450*
[Sylvester Stewart] [BMI] (5/23/70 BCRt-38)

I WANT TO TAKE YOU HIGHER *Ike & Tina Turner & The Ikettes—Liberty 56177*
[Sylvester Stewart] [BMI] (5/23/70 BCRt-34)

I WANT TO TALK ABOUT YOU Ray Charles—ABC 10901
[Billy Eckstine] [ASC] (3/18/67 B-98)

I WANT TO WALK YOU HOME Fats Domino—Imperial 5606
[Fats Domino] [BMI] (8/1/59 BCR-7)

I WANT YOU Bob Dylan—Columbia 43683
[Bob Dylan] [SE] (7/2/66 BCR-20)

I WANT YOU *Marvin Gaye—Tamla 54264*
[Arthur Ross/Leon Ware] [ASC] (4/17/76 BCR-15)

I WANT YOU *Robert Palmer—EMI 50344*
[Arthur Ross/Leon Ware] (Med) [ASC] (2/16/91 BC-13)

I WANT YOU Animotion—Casablanca 884729
[Rick Neigher/Bill Wadhams] [BMI] (5/10/86 BC-74)

I WANT YOU Shana—Vision 4511 [Steven Gordon] [BMI] (10/7/89 B-40)

I WANT YOU Jody Watley—MCA 54137
[André Cymone/Jody Watley] [ASC] (11/30/91 BC-61)

I WANT YOU ALL TO MYSELF (JUST YOU) Kitty Kallen—Decca 29268
[Milt Gabler/John James Koch] [ASC] (10/4/54 BCR-22)

I WANT YOU BACK The Jackson 5—Motown 1157
[Berry Gordy/Fonce Mizell/Freddie Perren/Deke Richards] [ASC] (11/15/69 BCR-1)

I WANT YOU BACK AGAIN The Zombies—Parrot 9769 [Rod Argent] [BMI] (6/26/65 BC-92)

I WANT YOU FOREVER Brook Benton—Mercury 71512
[Brook Benton/Luchi DeJesus/Clyde Otis] [BMI] (10/5/59 R-45)

I WANT YOU, I NEED YOU Chris Christian—Boardwalk 7-11-126
[Chris Christian/J.C. Crowley/Shannon Smith] [ASC] (10/3/81 BCR-36)

I WANT YOU I NEED YOU I LOVE YOU Elvis Presley—RCA Victor 47-6540
[Ira Kosloff/Maurice Mysels] [ASC] (5/11/56 BCR-3)

I WANT YOU 'ROUND Marvin Gaye & Kim Weston—Tamla 54104
[Smokey Robinson/William Stevenson] [ASC] (10/24/64 C-98)

I WANT YOU SO BAD B.B. King—BluesWay 61026 [B.B. King] [BMI] (8/2/69 CR-76)

I WANT YOU SO BAD Heart—Capitol 44116
[Thomas F. Kelly/Billy Steinberg] [ASC] (2/20/88 BC-49)

I WANT YOU TO BE MINE Kayak—Janus 274 [Ton Scherpenzeel] [BMI] (4/8/78 BCR-50)

I WANT YOU TO BE MY BABY *Lillian Briggs—Epic 9115*
[Jon Hendricks] [ASC] (8/15/55 BCtRt-9)

I WANT YOU TO BE MY BABY *Georgia Gibbs—Mercury 70685*
[Jon Hendricks] [ASC] (8/15/55 BCtRt-9)

I WANT YOU TO BE MY BABY *Ellie Greenwich—United Artists 50151*
[Jon Hendricks] [ASC] (4/29/67 BCR-63)

I WANT YOU TO BE MY BOY The Exciters—Roulette 4591
[Richard Barrett/George Goldner*/Morris Levy‡] [BMI] (1/16/65 BR-86)

I WANT YOU TO BE MY GIRL Frankie Lymon and the Teenagers—Gee 1012
[Richard Barrett/George Goldner*/Morris Levy‡] [BMI] (4/20/56 BCR-10)

I WANT YOU TO HAVE EVERYTHING Lee Rogers—D-Town 1035
[Cara Bell/Mike Hanks] [BMI] (12/5/64 CR-87)

I WANT YOU TO KNOW Fats Domino—Imperial 5477
[Dave Bartholomew/Fats Domino] [BMI] (12/21/57 BCR-37)

I WANT YOU TO KNOW The New Colony Six—Mercury 72961
[Les Kummel] [BMI] (8/30/69 BCR-62)

I WANT YOU TO MEET MY BABY Eydie Gorme—Columbia 43082
[Barry Mann/Cynthia Weil] [BMI] (7/25/64 BCR-43)

I WANT YOU TO WANT ME Cheap Trick—Epic 50680 [Rick Nielsen] [BMI] (4/21/79 BCR-3)

I WANT YOU TONIGHT Pablo Cruise—A&M 2195
[David Jenkins/Cory Lerios/Allee Willis] [ASC] (10/13/79 BCR-19)

I WANT YOUR LOVE Chic—Atlantic 3557
[Bernard Edwards/Nile Rodgers] [BMI] (2/10/79 BCR-5)

I WANT YOUR SEX George Michael—Columbia 07164
[George Michael] [ASC] (6/6/87 BC-2)

I WANT'A DO SOMETHING FREAKY TO YOU Leon Haywood—20th Century 2228
[Leon Haywood] [BMI] (9/6/75 BCR-15)

I WAS A BOY (WHEN YOU NEEDED A MAN) Billy Shields—Harbour 304
[Michael Leonard/Bobby Weinstein] [BMI] (4/26/69 CR-89)

I WAS BORN A LOSER Bobby Lee—Sue 144 [Tom DeCillis] [BMI] (7/23/66 R-89)

(I WAS) BORN TO CRY Dion—Laurie 3123 [Dion DiMucci] [ASC] (4/16/62 BCR-35)

I WAS BORN TO LOVE YOU Freddie Mercury—Columbia 04869
[Freddie Mercury] [BMI] (4/27/85 BC-70)

I WAS CHECKIN' OUT SHE WAS CHECKIN' IN Don Covay—Mercury 73385
[Don Covay] [BMI] (6/23/73 BCR-28)

I WAS COUNTRY WHEN COUNTRY WASN'T COOL Barbara Mandrell—MCA 51107
[Kye Fleming/Dennis W. Morgan] [BMI] (7/18/81 C-95)

I WAS HOPING YOU'D ASK ME Janice Harper—Capitol 4087
[Al Hoffman/Dick Manning] [ASC] (11/17/58 R-57)

I WAS KAISER BILL'S BATMAN Whistling Jack Smith—Deram 85005
[Roger Cook/Roger Greenaway] [ASC] (4/22/67 BCR-14) [I]

I WAS LOOKING FOR SOMEONE TO LOVE Leif Garrett—Scotti Brothers 516
[Howard Greenfield/Michael Lloyd] [BMI] (4/12/80 B-78)

I WAS MADE FOR DANCIN' Leif Garrett—Scotti Brothers 403
[Michael Lloyd] [ASC] (11/4/78 BCR-10)

I WAS MADE FOR LOVIN' YOU Kiss—Casablanca 983
[Desmond Child/Vini Poncia/Paul Stanley] [ASC] (5/26/79 BCR-5)

I WAS MADE TO LOVE HER *Stevie Wonder—Tamla 54151*
[Henry Cosby/Lula Mae Hardaway/Sylvia Moy/Stevie Wonder] [ASC] (6/3/67 BCR-2)

I WAS MADE TO LOVE HER *King Curtis & The Kingpins—Atco 6547*
[Henry Cosby/Lula Mae Hardaway/Sylvia Moy/Stevie Wonder] [ASC] (12/30/67 BCR-76) [IWM]

I WAS MADE TO LOVE HER *Stars On 45—Radio 4019*
[Henry Cosby/Lula Mae Hardaway/Sylvia Moy/Stevie Wonder] (Med) [ASC] (3/27/82 BCR-28)

I WAS MEANT FOR YOU (THE WAH-WAH SONG) The Four Knights—Capitol 2782
[Sadie Hurwitz/Lou Stallman] [NA] (8/14/54 C-43)

I WAS ONLY JOKING Rod Stewart—Warner Bros. 8568
[Gary Grainger/Rod Stewart] [ASC] (4/29/78 BCR-19)

I WAS SUCH A FOOL (TO FALL IN LOVE WITH YOU) *The Flamingos—End 1062*
[Michael Canosa/Danny Stradella] [ASC] (1/4/60 BCR-67)

I WAS SUCH A FOOL (TO FALL IN LOVE WITH YOU) *Connie Francis—MGM 13096*
[Michael Canosa/Danny Stradella] [ASC] (10/6/62 BCR-18)

I WAS TELLING HER ABOUT YOU Al Hibbler—Decca 29982
[Moose Charlap/Don George] [ASC] (7/27/56 R-74)

I WAS THE ONE Elvis Presley—RCA Victor 47-6420
[Hal Blair/Claude DeMetrius/Bill Peppers/Aaron Schroeder] [ASC] (3/10/56 BCR-16)

I WAS WONDERING The Poppy Family Vocal: Susan Jacks—London 148
[Terry Jacks] [BMI] (4/3/71 BCR-87)

I WASH MY HANDS OF THE WHOLE DAMN DEAL (PART 1) The New Birth—RCA Victor 10017
[James Baker/Allen Frey] [BMI] (10/12/74 B-88)

(I WASHED MY HANDS IN) MUDDY WATER Johnny Rivers—Imperial 66175
[Joe Babcock] [BMI] (6/11/66 BCR-16)

I WASN'T THE ONE (WHO SAID GOODBYE) Agnetha Faltskog—Atlantic 89145
[Mark Mueller/Aaron Zigman] [ASC] (4/23/88 B-93)

I (WHO HAVE NOTHING) *Ben E. King—Atco 6267*
[Carlo Donida/Jerry Leiber/Giulio Rapetti/Mike Stoller] [ASC] (6/29/63 BCR-25) [FET]

I (WHO HAVE NOTHING) *Terry Knight And The Pack—Lucky Eleven 230*
[Carlo Donida/Jerry Leiber/Giulio Rapetti/Mike Stoller] [ASC] (10/15/66 BCR-42) [FET]

I WHO HAVE NOTHING *Liquid Smoke—Avco Embassy 4522*
[Carlo Donida/Jerry Leiber/Giulio Rapetti/Mike Stoller] [ASC] (4/11/70 BCR-78) [FET]

I (WHO HAVE NOTHING) *Tom Jones—Parrot 40051*
[Carlo Donida/Jerry Leiber/Giulio Rapetti/Mike Stoller] [ASC] (8/15/70 BCR-10) [FET]

I (WHO HAVE NOTHING) *Sylvester—Fantasy 855*
[Carlo Donida/Jerry Leiber/Giulio Rapetti/Mike Stoller] [ASC] (4/7/79 BCR-40) [FET]

I WILL *Vic Dana—Dolton 51 [Dick Glasser] [BMI] (3/19/62 BCR-31)*

I WILL *Dean Martin—Reprise 0415 [Dick Glasser] [BMI] (10/30/65 BCR-9)*

I WILL ALWAYS LOVE YOU Dolly Parton—RCA 13260 [Dolly Parton] [BMI] (7/31/82 BC-41)

I WILL ALWAYS THINK ABOUT YOU The New Colony Six—Mercury 72775
[Les Kummel/Ronnie Rice] [BMI] (3/16/68 BCR-19)

I WILL BE IN LOVE WITH YOU Livingston Taylor—Epic 50604
[Livingston Taylor] [ASC] (10/14/78 BCR-28)

I WILL BE THERE Glass Tiger—Manhattan 50066
[Al Connelly/Alan Frew/Michael Hanson/Wayne Parker/Sam Reid] [ASC] (2/28/87 BC-33)

(I WILL BE YOUR) SHADOW IN THE STREET Allan Clarke—Atlantic 3459
[Gary Benson/Allan Clarke] [BMI] (3/25/78 BCR-39)

I WILL FOLLOW U2—Island 99789
[Adam Clayton/Dave Evans/Paul Hewson/Larry Mullen] [ASC] (1/14/84 BC-80)

I WILL FOLLOW HIM Little Peggy March—RCA Victor 47-8139
[Arthur Altman/Norman Gimbel/Paul Mauriat/Franck Pourcel] [ASC] (3/16/63 BCR-1) [FDE]

I WILL LIVE MY LIFE FOR YOU Tony Bennett—Columbia 42634
[Henri Salvador/Marcel Stellman] [BMI] (1/5/63 BCR-58) [FDE]

I WILL LOVE YOU Richard Chamberlain—MGM 13148
[Barry De Vorzon/Shelby Flint] [BMI] (6/22/63 BCR-63)

I WILL NEVER PASS THIS WAY AGAIN Glen Campbell—Capitol 3411
[Ronnie Gaylord] [BMI] (8/26/72 BCR-61)

I WILL STILL LOVE YOU Stonebolt—Parachute 512 [Bob Strauss] [ASC] (7/29/78 BCR-29)

I WILL SURVIVE *Gloria Gaynor—Polydor 14508*
[Dino Fekaris/Freddie Perren] [ASC] (12/16/78 BCR-1)

I WILL SURVIVE *Sa-Fire—Mercury 876369*
[Dino Fekaris/Freddie Perren] [ASC] (12/16/89 BC-49)

I WISH *The Platters—Mercury 71353 [Tito Madi/Buck Ram] [ASC] (9/13/58 BCRt-34)*

I WISH *Della Reese—Jubilee 5332 [Tito Madi/Buck Ram] [ASC] (9/15/58 Rt-76)*

I WISH *Stevie Wonder—Tamla 54274 [Stevie Wonder] [ASC] (12/4/76 BCR-1)*

I WISH *Stars On 45—Radio 4019 [Stevie Wonder] (Med) [ASC] (3/27/82 BCR-28)*

I WISH I HAD A GIRL Henry Lee Summer—CBS Associated 07720
[Henry Lee Summer] [BMI] (2/13/88 BC-20)

I WISH I KNEW (HOW IT WOULD FEEL TO BE FREE) Solomon Burke—Atlantic 2507
[Dick Dallas/Billy Taylor] [ASC] (4/27/68 BCR-68)

I WISH I WAS EIGHTEEN AGAIN George Burns—Mercury 57011
[Sonny Throckmorton] [BMI] (12/29/79 BCR-49)

I WISH I WERE Andy Kim—Steed 731 [Jeff Barry/Andy Kim] [BMI] (3/20/71 BCR-53)

I WISH I WERE A PRINCESS Little Peggy March—RCA Victor 47-8189
[Luigi Creatore/Hugo Peretti/George David Weiss] [ASC] (6/1/63 BCR-24)

I WISH I'D NEVER BEEN BORN Patti Page—Mercury 71695
[Howard Greenfield/Jack Keller] [BMI] (10/1/60 BCR-52)

I WISH IT WAS ME Tyrone Davis—Dakar 4529
[Leo Graham/Raymond Haley] [BMI] (2/2/74 BCR-57)

I WISH IT WAS ME YOU LOVED The Dells—Cadet 5702
[Jackie Avery] [BMI] (6/1/74 BCR-78)

I WISH IT WOULD RAIN *The Temptations—Gordy 7068*
[Rodger Penzabene/Barrett Strong/Norman Whitfield] [BMI] (1/6/68 BCR-2)

I WISH IT WOULD RAIN *Gladys Knight & The Pips—Soul 35047*
[Rodger Penzabene/Barrett Strong/Norman Whitfield] [BMI] (8/24/68 BCR-37)

I WISH IT WOULD RAIN DOWN Phil Collins—Atlantic 88738
[Phil Collins] [ASC] (2/3/90 BC-3)

I WISH THAT WE WERE MARRIED Ronnie And The Hi-Lites—Joy 260
[Edna Lewis/Marion Weiss] [ASC] (3/26/62 BCR-16)

I WISH YOU COULD BE HERE The Cyrkle—Columbia 43965
[Paul Simon/Bruce Woodley] [BMI] (1/14/67 BCR-57)

I WISH YOU LOVE Gloria Lynne—Everest 2036
[Albert Beach/Charles Trenet] [ASC] (1/11/64 BCR-22) [FET]

I WOKE UP CRYING Joni James—MGM 12213 [Paul Insetta] [ASC] (4/27/56 BCR-37)

I WOKE UP IN LOVE THIS MORNING
The Partridge Family Starring Shirley Jones & Featuring David Cassidy—Bell 45,130
[L. Russell Brown/Irwin Levine] [BMI] (8/7/71 BCR-9)

I WONDER Brenda Lee—Decca 31510
[Cecil Gant/Raymond Leveen] [ASC] (6/29/63 BCR-19)

I WONDER The Butterflys—Red Bird 10-016
[Jeff Barry/Ellie Greenwich/Phil Spector] [BMI] (1/30/65 C-91)

I WONDER IF I TAKE YOU HOME
Lisa Lisa and Cult Jam with Full Force—Columbia 04886
[Curtis Bedeau/Gerard Charles/Hugh Clarke/Brian George/Lucien George/Paul George] [BMI] (6/8/85 BC-33)

I WONDER (IF YOUR LOVE WILL EVER BELONG TO ME) The Pentagons—Jamie 1201
[Ken Goodloe/Ted Goodloe/Joe C. Jones/Carl McGinnis/Otis Munson] [BMI] (10/30/61 B-84)

I WONDER WHAT SHE'S DOING TONIGHT Barry And The Tamerlanes—Valiant 6034
[Bodie Chandler/Barry De Vorzon] [BMI] (10/19/63 BCR-16)

I WONDER WHAT SHE'S DOING TONITE Tommy Boyce & Bobby Hart—A&M 893
[Tommy Boyce/Bobby Hart] [BMI] (12/23/67 BCR-6)

I WONDER WHO'S KISSING HER NOW Bobby Darin—Capitol 5126
[Frank Adams/Will Hough/Joe Howard] [NA] (2/22/64 BCR-64)

I WONDER WHY Dion and The Belmonts—Laurie 3013
[Melvin Anderson/Ricardo Weeks] [ASC] (5/10/58 BCR-20)

I WONDER WHY Curtis Stigers—Arista 12331
[Glen Ballard/Curtis Stigers] [ASC] (9/7/91 BC-9)

I WON'T BACK DOWN Tom Petty—MCA 53369
[Jeff Lynne/Tom Petty] [ASC] (4/29/89 BC-11)

I WON'T BE HOME TONIGHT Tony Carey—Rocshire 95030
[Tony Carey] [ASC] (3/19/83 BC-79)

I WON'T BE THERE Del Shannon—Big Top 3098 [Del Shannon] [BMI] (3/12/62 R-75)

I WON'T FORGET YOU Jim Reeves—RCA Victor 47-8461
[Harlan Howard] [BMI] (11/21/64 B-93)

I WON'T FORGET YOU Poison—Enigma 44038
[Bobby Dall/C.C. DeVille/Bret Michaels/Rikki Rockett] [BMI] (9/5/87 BC-13)

I WON'T GIVE UP ON YOU TKA—Tommy Boy 19730
[Steve Lironi/Dan Navarro] [BMI] (8/11/90 BC-65)

I WON'T HOLD YOU BACK Toto—Columbia 03597
[Steve Lukather] [ASC] (3/12/83 BC-10)

I WON'T LAST A DAY WITHOUT YOU *Maureen McGovern—20th Century 2051*
[Roger Nichols/Paul Williams] [ASC] (10/13/73 BCR-72)

I WON'T LAST A DAY WITHOUT YOU *Carpenters—A&M 1521*
[Roger Nichols/Paul Williams] [ASC] (4/6/74 BCR-9)

I WON'T LAST A DAY WITHOUT YOU *Al Wilson—Rocky Road 30202*
[Roger Nichols/Paul Williams] (Med) [ASC] (1/11/75 BCR-61)

I WON'T LOVE YOU ANYMORE (SORRY) Lesley Gore—Mercury 72513
[Lesley Gore/Michael Gore] [BMI] (11/27/65 BCR-61)

I WON'T MENTION IT AGAIN Ray Price—Columbia 45329
[Cameron L. Mullins/Carolyn Jean Yates*] [BMI] (3/13/71 BCR-42)

I WON'T STAND IN YOUR WAY Stray Cats—EMI America 8185
[Brian Setzer] [BMI] (10/29/83 BC-35)

I WORRY ABOUT YOU Joe Simon—Sound Stage 7 2617
[Norman Mapp] [BMI] (11/16/68 B-98)

I WOULD BE IN LOVE (ANYWAY) Frank Sinatra—Reprise 0895
[Bob Gaudio/Jake Holmes] [ASC] (3/21/70 B-88)

I WOULD DIE 4 U Prince and the Revolution—Warner Bros. 29121
[Prince] [ASC] (12/15/84 BC-8)

I WOULDN'T BEG FOR WATER Sheena Easton—EMI America 8142
[Mike Leeson/Peter Vale] [BMI] (10/30/82 BC-64)

I WOULDN'T GIVE YOU UP Ecstasy, Passion & Pain—Roulette 7151
[Barbara Jean Gaskins] [BMI] (4/20/74 R-100)

I WOULDN'T HAVE MISSED IT FOR THE WORLD Ronnie Milsap—RCA 12342
[Kye Fleming/Dennis W. Morgan/Charles Quillen] [BMI] (10/24/81 BCR-19)

I WOULDN'T KNOW (WHAT TO DO) Dinah Washington—Roulette 4444
[Rose Marie McCoy] [BMI] (8/18/62 BR-93)

I WOULDN'T KNOW WHERE TO BEGIN Eddy Arnold—RCA Victor 47-6699
[Johnny Marks] [ASC] (11/24/56 B-64)

I WOULDN'T LIE Yarbrough & Peoples—Total Experience 2437
[George Adams/Jimmy Hamilton/Maurice Hayes/Lonnie Simmons] [BMI] (6/28/86 BC-82)

I WOULDN'T TRADE YOU FOR THE WORLD The Bachelors—London 9693
[Curt Kirk/Bill Smith*/Bill Taylor] [BMI] (9/12/64 BCR-64)

I WOULDN'T TREAT A DOG (THE WAY YOU TREATED ME) Bobby Bland—Dunhill/ABC 15015
[Steve Barri/Michael Omartian/Harvey Price/Dan Walsh] [ASC] (11/23/74 BC-82)

I WOULDN'T WANT TO BE LIKE YOU Alan Parsons—Arista 0260
[Alan Parsons/Eric Woolfson] [BMI] (8/13/77 BCR-27)

I WRITE THE SONGS Barry Manilow—Arista 0157 [Bruce Johnston] [BMI] (11/8/75 BCR-1)

I WROTE A SIMPLE SONG Billy Preston—A&M 1320
[Joe Greene/Billy Preston] [BMI] (1/22/72 BCR-77)

ICE CREAM SONG The Dynamics—Cotillion 44021
[Ronnie Shannon] [BMI] (3/15/69 BCR-49)

ICE ICE BABY Vanilla Ice—SBK 07335
[David Bowie/Floyd Brown/John Deacon/Brian May/Freddie Mercury/Roger Taylor/Robert Van Winkle] [BMI] (9/8/90 BC-1)

ICE IN THE SUN The Status Quo—Cadet Concept 7006
[Ronnie Scott/Marty Wilde] [BMI] (9/14/68 BCR-54)

I'D BETTER BE CAREFUL Bob Manning—Capitol 3242
[Rose Marie McCoy/Charles Singleton] [ASC] (10/3/55 R-75)

I'D DO IT ALL AGAIN Vikki Carr—Columbia 45510
[Richard Ahlert/Leon Carr] [ASC] (1/22/72 R-91)

I'D DO IT ALL AGAIN Sam Harris—Motown 1829
[Sam Harris*/Mary Unobsky] [BMI] (2/1/86 BC-52)

I'D GIVE A MILLION TOMORROWS (FOR JUST ONE YESTERDAY)
Billy Vaughn and His Orchestra—Dot 15430
[Milton Berle/Jerry Livingston] [ASC] (12/1/55 Rt-40)

I'D GIVE A MILLION TOMORROWS (FOR JUST ONE YESTERDAY) *Frank Verna—Decca 29767*
[Milton Berle/Jerry Livingston] [ASC] (12/30/55 Rt-40)

I'D GIVE A MILLION TOMORROWS (FOR JUST ONE YESTERDAY)
Arthur Godfrey—Decca 29765
[Milton Berle/Jerry Livingston] [ASC] (1/13/56 Rt-40)

I'D HAVE TO BE CRAZY Willie Nelson—Columbia 10327
[Steven Fromholz] [ASC] (6/5/76 R-93)

(I'D KNOW YOU) ANYWHERE Ashford & Simpson—Warner Bros. 7745
[Nick Ashford/Valerie Simpson] [ASC] (1/19/74 B-88)

I'D LIKE TO TEACH THE WORLD TO SING (IN PERFECT HARMONY)
The Hillside Singers—Metromedia 231
[Bill Backer/Roger Cook/Billy Davis/Roger Greenaway] [ASC] (11/27/71 BCR-10)

I'D LIKE TO TEACH THE WORLD TO SING (IN PERFECT HARMONY)
The New Seekers—Elektra 45762
[Bill Backer/Roger Cook/Billy Davis/Roger Greenaway] [ASC] (11/27/71 BCR-7)

I'D LOVE TO CHANGE THE WORLD Ten Years After—Columbia 45457
[Alvin Lee] [ASC] (9/18/71 BCR-28)

I'D LOVE YOU TO WANT ME Lobo—Big Tree 147 [Kent LaVoie] [ASC] (9/16/72 BCR-1)

I'D NEVER FORGIVE MYSELF *Jerry Martin—Coral 61349*
[Roy Gould/Matty Martin/Bob McAvoy] [BMI] (10/4/54 R-PRE)

I'D NEVER FORGIVE MYSELF *Kitty Kallen—Decca 29417*
[Roy Gould/Matty Martin/Bob McAvoy] [BMI] (2/7/55 Rt-32)

I'D RATHER BE A COWBOY John Denver—RCA Victor 74-0955
[John Denver] [ASC] (5/19/73 BCR-27)

I'D RATHER BE AN OLD MAN'S SWEETHEART (THAN A YOUNG MAN'S FOOL)
Candi Staton—Fame 1456
[Clarence Carter/George Henry Jackson/Raymond Moore] [BMI] (6/21/69 BCR-38)

I'D RATHER BE HERE IN YOUR ARMS The Duprees—Coed 574
[Frank Reardon/Johnny Robba] [BMI] (1/19/63 BCR-70)

I'D RATHER BE SORRY Ray Price—Columbia 45425
[Kris Kristofferson] [BMI] (8/7/71 BCR-63)

I'D RATHER GO BLIND Sydney Youngblood—Arista 2055
[Billy Foster/Ellington Jordan] [BMI] (8/25/90 BC-42)

I'D RATHER LEAVE WHILE I'M IN LOVE Rita Coolidge—A&M 2199
[Peter Allen/Carole Bayer Sager] [BMI] (11/10/79 BCR-38)

I'D RATHER LOVE YOU Charley Pride—RCA Victor 47-9952
[Johnny Duncan] [BMI] (3/13/71 B-79)

I'D REALLY LOVE TO SEE YOU TONIGHT England Dan & John Ford Coley—Big Tree 16069
[Parker McGee] [BMI] (6/12/76 BCR-2)

I'D STILL SAY YES Klymaxx—Constellation 53028
[Kenneth Edmonds/Joyce Irby/Greg Scelsa] [BMI] (5/2/87 BC-18)

I'D WAIT A MILLION YEARS The Grass Roots—Dunhill 4198
[Mitch Bottler/Gary Zekley] [ASC] (6/21/69 BCR-11)

IDA JANE Fats Domino—Imperial 5816 [Fats Domino] [BMI] (3/3/62 B-90)

IDAHO The 4 Seasons Featuring Frankie Valli—Philips 40597
[Bob Gaudio/Jake Holmes] (TSW) [ASC] (3/29/69 BCR-64)

IDOL WITH THE GOLDEN HEAD The Coasters—Atco 6098
[Jerry Leiber/Mike Stoller] [BMI] (10/7/57 BR-64)

IESHA Another Bad Creation—Motown 2070
[Dallas Austin/Michael Bivins] [ASC] (1/12/91 BC-9)

IF *The Paragons—Tap 500*
[Stan Damerell/Tolchard Evans/Robert Hargreaves] [ASC] (7/17/61 B-82)

IF *Roy Hamilton—Epic 9466*
[Stan Damerell/Tolchard Evans/Robert Hargreaves] [ASC] (9/11/61 R-93)

IF *Timi Yuro—Mercury 72316*
[Stan Damerell/Tolchard Evans/Robert Hargreaves] [ASC] (8/15/64 CR-79)

IF *Al Hirt—RCA Victor 47-9717 [Tolchard Evans] [ASC] (1/25/69 CR-77) [IM]*

IF *Bread—Elektra 45720 [David Gates] [ASC] (3/20/71 BCR-4)*

IF *Telly Savalas—MCA 40301 [David Gates] [ASC] (11/23/74 C-89)*

IF A MAN ANSWERS Bobby Darin—Capitol 4837 [Bobby Darin] [BMI] (9/22/62 BCR-27)

IF A WOMAN ANSWERS (HANG UP THE PHONE) Leroy Van Dyke—Mercury 71926
[Barry Mann/Cynthia Weil] [BMI] (3/3/62 BCR-26)

IF ANYBODY HAD A HEART John Waite—EMI America 8315
[Danny Kortchmar/J.D. Souther] [ASC] (6/21/86 BC-64)

IF ANYONE FALLS Stevie Nicks—Modern 99832
[Stevie Nicks/Sandy Stewart] [BMI] (9/10/83 BC-14)

IF ANYONE FINDS THIS I LOVE YOU Kay Starr—RCA Victor 47-5999
[Sylvia Dee/Sid Lippman] [ASC] (2/26/55 CR-44)

IF DREAMS CAME TRUE Pat Boone—Dot 15785
[Robert Allen/Al Stillman] [ASC] (6/30/58 BCR-11)

IF EVER A LOVE THERE WAS Four Tops—Arista 1-9766
[Todd Cerney/Pamela Phillips Oland] [ASC] (12/24/88 C-88)

IF EVER I SEE YOU AGAIN Roberta Flack—Atlantic 3483
[Joe Brooks] [ASC] (5/20/78 BCR-24)

IF EVER YOU'RE IN MY ARMS AGAIN Peabo Bryson—Elektra 69728
[Michael Masser/Tom Snow/Cynthia Weil] [ASC] (5/12/84 BC-10)

IF EVERY DAY WAS LIKE CHRISTMAS Elvis Presley—RCA Victor 47-8950
[Red West] [BMI] (12/24/66 R-99)

IF I CAN DREAM Elvis Presley—RCA Victor 47-9670
[Walter Earl Brown] [ASC] (11/30/68 BCR-9)

IF I CAN HELP SOMEBODY Billy Eckstine—Mercury 71217
[Alma Bazel Androzzo] [ASC] (11/4/57 CR-50)

IF I CAN'T HAVE YOU Etta & Harvey—Chess 1760
[Harvey Fuqua/Etta James] [BMI] (8/1/60 BCR-32)

IF I CAN'T HAVE YOU Yvonne Elliman—RSO 884
[Barry Gibb/Maurice Gibb/Robin Gibb] [BMI] (1/28/78 BCR-1)

IF I COULD BUILD MY WHOLE WORLD AROUND YOU
Marvin Gaye & Tammi Terrell—Tamla 54161
[Johnny Bristol/Vernon Bullock/Harvey Fuqua] [ASC] (12/2/67 BCR-10)

IF I COULD GET YOU (INTO MY LIFE) Gene Cotton—Knoll 5002
[Gene Cotton] [ASC] (3/13/82 BC-76)

IF I COULD ONLY BE SURE Nolan Porter—ABC 11343
[Gabriel Mekler/Nolan Porter] [ASC] (3/31/73 B-89)

IF I COULD ONLY WIN YOUR LOVE Emmylou Harris—Reprise 1332
[Charlie Louvin/Ira Louvin] [BMI] (8/23/75 BCR-58)

IF I COULD REACH YOU The 5th Dimension—Bell 45,261
[Randall McNeill] [ASC] (9/2/72 BCR-9)

IF I COULD SEE THE LIGHT The 8th Day—Invictus 9107
[General Johnson/Greg Perry] [BMI] (12/25/71 BCR-77)

IF I COULD TURN BACK TIME Cher—Geffen 22886 [Diane Warren] [ASC] (7/8/89 BC-3)

IF I CRIED EVERY TIME YOU HURT ME Wanda Jackson—Capitol 4723
[Harlan Howard] [BMI] (4/2/62 BCR-58)

IF I DIDN'T CARE *The Hilltoppers—Dot 15220 [Jack Lawrence] [ASC] (7/31/54 C-18)*

IF I DIDN'T CARE *Connie Francis—MGM 12769 [Jack Lawrence] [ASC] (3/2/59 BCR-9)*

IF I DIDN'T CARE *The Platters—Mercury 71749 [Jack Lawrence] [ASC] (1/2/61 BCR-30)*

IF I DIDN'T CARE *The Moments—Stang 5016 [Jack Lawrence] [ASC] (8/15/70 BCR-37)*

IF I DIDN'T HAVE A DIME (TO PLAY THE JUKEBOX) Gene Pitney—Musicor 1022
[Bert Berns/Phil Medley] [BMI] (8/25/62 BCR-49)

IF I DIDN'T LOVE YOU Chuck Jackson—Wand 188
[Mark Barkan/Pam Sawyer] [BMI] (7/31/65 BCR-46)

IF I EVER LOSE THIS HEAVEN AWB—Atlantic 3285
[Pam Sawyer/Leon Ware] [ASC] (8/9/75 BCR-39)

IF I FELL The Beatles—Capitol 5235
[John Lennon/Paul McCartney] [ASC] (8/1/64 BCR-53)

IF I GIVE MY HEART TO YOU *Doris Day—Columbia 40300*
[Jimmie Crane/Milt Gabler/Al Jacobs] [ASC] (8/28/54 BCtR-1)

IF I GIVE MY HEART TO YOU *Denise Lor—Majar 27*
[Jimmie Crane/Milt Gabler/Al Jacobs] [ASC] (8/28/54 BCtR-1)

IF I GIVE MY HEART TO YOU *Connee Boswell—Decca 29148*
[Jimmie Crane/Milt Gabler/Al Jacobs] [ASC] (9/4/54 BCtR-1)

IF I GIVE MY HEART TO YOU *Dinah Shore—RCA Victor 47-5838*
[Jimmie Crane/Milt Gabler/Al Jacobs] [ASC] (9/4/54 CR-1)

IF I GIVE MY HEART TO YOU *Kitty Kallen—Columbia 41473*
[Jimmie Crane/Milt Gabler/Al Jacobs] [ASC] (9/28/59 BCR-25)

IF I HAD A GIRL Rod Lauren—RCA Victor 47-7645
[Roy C. Bennett/Sid Tepper] [ASC] (11/23/59 BCR-24)

IF I HAD A HAMMER (THE HAMMER SONG) *Peter, Paul & Mary—Warner Bros. 5296*
[Lee Hays/Pete Seeger] [BMI] (8/11/62 BCR-10)

IF I HAD A HAMMER *Trini Lopez—Reprise 20,198*
[Lee Hays/Pete Seeger] [BMI] (7/27/63 BCR-3)

IF I HAD A REASON The Bubble Puppy—International Artists 133
[Gene Corbin/Roy Cox] [BMI] (5/31/69 R-81)

IF I HAD A ROCKET LAUNCHER Bruce Cockburn—Gold Mountain 82013
[Bruce Cockburn] [BMI] (2/2/85 BC-71)

IF I HAD MY WISH TONIGHT David Lasley—EMI America 8111
[Randy Goodrum/Dave Loggins] [ASC] (3/13/82 BCR-36)

IF I HAVE TO GO AWAY Jigsaw—20th Century 2347
[Tetsuji Hayashi/Marci Sutin] [ASC] (8/27/77 BC-89)

IF I KNEW Nat King Cole—Capitol 4481 [Meredith Willson] [ASC] (12/31/60 B-86)

IF I LOVED YOU Chad & Jeremy—World Artists 1041
[Oscar Hammerstein/Richard Rodgers] [ASC] (2/20/65 BCR-17)

IF I MAY Nat "King" Cole And The Four Knights—Capitol 3095
[Rose Marie McCoy/Charles Singleton] (TSW) [BMI] (5/21/55 BCR-2)

IF I NEVER KNEW YOUR NAME Vic Dana—Liberty 56150
[Neil Diamond] [SE] (1/10/70 BCR-39)

IF I ONLY COULD The Rowans—Elektra 45237 [Chris Rowan] [BMI] (10/9/76 BC-69)

IF I ONLY HAD TIME Nick Decaro—A&M 1000
[Michel Fugain] [BMI] (12/21/68 BCR-71) [IM]

IF I ONLY KNEW Curt Jensen—Pet 806 [Bob Saffer] [ASC] (9/27/58 C-71)

IF I ONLY KNEW The Ozark Mountain Daredevils—A&M 1772
[Steve Cash/Larry Michael Lee] [BMI] (1/17/76 BCR-65)

IF I POSSESSED A PRINTING PRESS George Hamilton IV—ABC-Paramount 9782
[Willey Gale] [BMI] (2/2/57 R-57)

IF I RULED THE WORLD Tony Bennett—Columbia 43220
[Leslie Bricusse/Cyril Ornadel] [ASC] (2/13/65 BCR-34)

IF I SAID YOU HAD A BEAUTIFUL BODY WOULD YOU HOLD IT AGAINST ME
Bellamy Brothers—Warner/Curb 8790
[David Bellamy] [ASC] (5/26/79 BCR-39)

IF I SAY Kingofthehill—SBK 07358
[Jimmy Griffin/Frankie Muriel] [BMI] (8/10/91 B-63)

IF I SAY YES Five Star—RCA 5083 [Michael Jay/Marvin Morrow] [BMI] (12/27/86 BC-67)

IF I SHOULD LOSE YOU The Dreamlovers—End 1114
[Donald Hogan/Jerry J. Ross/Murray Wecht] [BMI] (6/23/62 BCR-62)

IF I WAS YOUR GIRLFRIEND Prince—Paisley Park 7-28334
[Prince] [ASC] (5/23/87 BC-67)

IF I WERE A BELL
The Big Three: Sarah Vaughan/Joe Williams/Count Basie—Roulette 4273
[Frank Loesser] [ASC] (9/12/60 R-88)

IF I WERE A CARPENTER *Bobby Darin—Atlantic 2350 [Tim Hardin] [BMI] (9/24/66 BCR-5)*

IF I WERE A CARPENTER *Four Tops—Motown 1124 [Tim Hardin] [BMI] (4/20/68 BCR-15)*

IF I WERE A CARPENTER *Johnny Cash & June Carter—Columbia 45064*
[Tim Hardin] [BMI] (1/17/70 BCR-26)

IF I WERE A CARPENTER *Bob Seger—Palladium 1079 [Tim Hardin] [BMI] (7/1/72 BCR-76)*

IF I WERE A CARPENTER *Leon Russell—Shelter 40210*
[Tim Hardin] [BMI] (4/20/74 BCR-73)

IF I WERE ONLY A CHILD AGAIN Curtis Mayfield—Curtom 1991
[Curtis Mayfield] [BMI] (10/20/73 BCR-71)

IF I WERE YOU *Toby Beau—RCA 11964 [Jerry Fuller/John Hobbs] [BMI] (7/5/80 BR-70)*

IF I WERE YOU *Lulu—Alfa 7011 [Jerry Fuller/John Hobbs] [BMI] (11/21/81 BCR-42)*

IF I WERE YOUR WOMAN Gladys Knight & The Pips—Soul 35078
[Gloria Jones/Clay McMurray/Pam Sawyer] [ASC] (11/21/70 BCR-5)

IF I'D BEEN THE ONE 38 Special—A&M 2584
[Don Barnes/Jeff Carlisi/Larry Steele/Donnie Van Zant] [ASC] (11/12/83 BC-19)

IF I'M A FOOL FOR LOVING YOU Bobby Wood—Joy 285
[Stanley A. Kesler] [BMI] (6/20/64 BCR-57)

IF I'M ELECTED Eddie Fisher—RCA Victor 47-6615
[Al Frisch/Sid Wayne] [ASC] (8/17/56 R-59)

IF IT AIN'T ONE THING...IT'S ANOTHER
Richard "Dimples" Fields—Boardwalk 7-11-139
[Richard "Dimples" Fields/Belinda Wilson] [ASC] (4/3/82 BCR-41)

IF IT DON'T FIT, DON'T FORCE IT Kellee Patterson—Shady Brook 1041
[Larry Farrow/Carolyn Johns] [BMI] (11/19/77 BCR-75)

IF IT FEELS GOOD, DO IT Ian Lloyd & Stories—Kama Sutra 588
[John Stevenson] [ASC] (3/2/74 BCR-69)

IF IT ISN'T LOVE New Edition—MCA 53264
[James Samuel Harris/Terry Lewis] [ASC] (7/2/88 BC-5)

IF IT WASN'T FOR BAD LUCK Ray Charles & Jimmy Lewis—ABC/TRC 11170
[Ray Charles/James E. Lewis] (TSW) [BMI] (1/25/69 BCR-71)

IF IT'S A DREAM *The McGuire Sisters—Coral 61454*
[Stella Unger/Victor Young] [ASC] (8/15/55 Rt-52)

IF IT'S A DREAM *Kitty Kallen—Decca 29548*
[Stella Unger/Victor Young] [ASC] (8/22/55 Rt-52)

IF IT'S ALRIGHT WITH YOU *Rose Colored Glass—Bang 588*
[Larry Henley/Kenny O'Dell] [BMI] (10/23/71 BCR-92)

IF IT'S ALL RIGHT WITH YOU *Dottie West—RCA Victor 74-0828*
[Larry Henley/Kenny O'Dell] [BMI] (1/13/73 BC-90)

IF IT'S GOOD TO YOU (IT'S GOOD FOR YOU) Flaming Ember—Hot Wax 7109
[Lamont Dozier/Brian Holland/Eddie Holland] [BMI] (11/6/71 C-91)

IF IT'S REAL WHAT I FEEL Jerry Butler Featuring Brenda Lee
[Eager]—Mercury 73169 [Charles Henry Jackson Jr.] [BMI] (2/27/71 BCR-69)

IF IT'S THE LAST THING I DO Thelma Houston—Tamla 54283
[Sammy Cahn/Saul Chaplin] [ASC] (6/4/77 BCR-47)

IF LOOKS COULD KILL Player—RCA 13006
[Peter Beckett/Dennis Lambert] [BMI] (1/23/82 BCR-48)

IF LOOKS COULD KILL Heart—Capitol 5605
[Jack Conrad/Bob Garrett] [BMI] (7/19/86 BC-54)

IF LOVE IS IN YOUR HEART Friend And Lover—Verve Forecast 5091
[Jim Post] [BMI] (8/24/68 BCR-47)

IF LOVE MUST GO Dobie Gray—Capricorn 0249 [Will Jennings] [BMI] (2/14/76 B-78)

IF LOVE RULED THE WORLD Bobby Bland—Duke 460
[Deadric Malone/Joe Veasey] [BMI] (5/23/70 CR-82)

IF LOVE SHOULD GO Streets—Atlantic 89760
[Mike Slamer/Steve Walsh] [BMI] (12/3/83 B-87)

(IF LOVING YOU IS WRONG) I DON'T WANT TO BE RIGHT *Luther Ingram—KoKo 2111*
[Homer Banks/Carl Hampton/Raymond Earl Jackson] [BMI] (5/20/72 BCR-3)

IF LOVING YOU IS WRONG I DON'T WANT TO BE RIGHT *Millie Jackson—Spring 155*
[Homer Banks/Carl Hampton/Raymond Earl Jackson] [BMI] (1/25/75 BCR-42)

(IF LOVING YOU IS WRONG) I DON'T WANT TO BE RIGHT
Barbara Mandrell—ABC/MCA 12451
[Homer Banks/Carl Hampton/Raymond Earl Jackson] [BMI] (3/17/79 BCR-25)

IF MARY'S THERE Brian Hyland—ABC-Paramount 10400
[Gary Geld/Peter Udell] [ASC] (2/16/63 BCR-63)

IF MY FRIENDS COULD SEE ME NOW Linda Clifford—Curtom 0140
[Cy Coleman/Dorothy Fields] [ASC] (8/26/78 BR-54)

IF MY HEART COULD SPEAK Manhattans—DeLuxe 122
[Eddie Jones/Kenneth Kelley] [BMI] (6/20/70 BCR-97)

IF MY PILLOW COULD TALK Connie Francis—MGM 13143
[Robert Mosely/Jimmie Steward] [BMI] (5/18/63 BCR-14)

IF MY WORLD FALLS THROUGH The Rose Garden—Atco 6564
[Kenny O'Dell] [BMI] (3/23/68 R-87)

IF NOT FOR YOU Olivia Newton-John—Uni 55281 [Bob Dylan] [SE] (5/29/71 BCR-23)

IF NOT YOU Dr. Hook—Capitol 4364 [Dennis Locorriere] [BMI] (11/27/76 BCR-55)

IF ONLY I COULD LIVE MY LIFE AGAIN Jane Morgan—Kapp 253
[Louis Amade/Gilbert Bécaud/Pierre Delanoë/Elly Leighton] [ASC] (1/12/59 R-84)

IF ONLY I HAD MY MIND ON SOMETHING ELSE Bee Gees—Atco 6741
[Barry Gibb/Maurice Gibb] [BMI] (3/14/70 BCR-76)

IF ONLY YOU KNEW Patti LaBelle—Philadelphia Int'l 4248
[Cynthia Biggs/Kenneth Gamble/Dexter Wansel] [BMI] (1/7/84 BC-39)

IF SHE KNEW WHAT SHE WANTS Bangles—Columbia 05886
[Jules Shear] [BMI] (5/10/86 BC-28)

—IF SHE SHOULD COME TO YOU see: LA MONTANA

IF SHE WOULD HAVE BEEN FAITHFUL... Chicago—Warner/Full Moon 28424
[Randy Goodrum/Steve Kipner] [ASC] (3/21/87 BC-16)

IF SOMEBODY TOLD YOU Anna King—Smash 1858
[James Brown] [BMI] (12/28/63 BCR-67)

IF THAT'S HOW NATURE MADE HIM Helen Grayco—Number 1 Record 001
[Hod David/Ben Raleigh] [ASC] (11/26/77 R-90)

IF THAT'S THE WAY YOU WANT IT Diamond Head—Dunhill 4342
[Dennis Lambert/Brian Potter] [BMI] (5/26/73 C-95)

IF THE LOVE FITS WEAR IT Leslie Pearl—RCA 13235
[Leslie Pearl/Phil Redrow] [BMI] (5/22/82 BC-25)

IF THE WORLD DON'T END TOMORROW (I'M COMIN' AFTER YOU)
Doug Warren—Image 1011
[Billy Sherrill] [BMI] (8/1/60 Rt-95)

IF THE WORLD DON'T END TOMORROW (I'M COMIN' AFTER YOU)
Carl Smith—Columbia 41729
[Billy Sherrill] [BMI] (8/1/60 Rt-87)

IF THE WORLD DON'T END TOMORROW (I'M COMIN' AFTER YOU)
The Fairlanes—Argo 5357
[Billy Sherrill] [BMI] (8/8/60 Rt-87)

(IF THERE WAS) ANY OTHER WAY Celine Dion—Epic 73665
[Paul Steven Bliss] [ASC] (4/6/91 BC-32)

IF THIS IS IT Huey Lewis and the News—Chrysalis 42803
[Johnny Colla/Huey Lewis] [ASC] (7/21/84 BC-6)

IF THIS IS LOVE (I'D RATHER BE LONELY) The Precisions—Drew 1003
[Charles Bassoline/Martin Coleman/Mike Valvano] [BMI] (9/30/67 BCR-60)

IF THIS WORLD WERE MINE Marvin Gaye & Tammi Terrell—Tamla 54161
[Marvin Gaye] [ASC] (3/2/68 BCR-68)

IF U WERE MINE U-Krew—Enigma 75051
[Larry Bell/James McClendon/Hakim Rashad Muhammad] [BMI] (1/27/90 BC-24)

IF WALLS COULD TALK Little Milton—Checker 1226
[Robert Miller] [BMI] (1/3/70 BCR-52)

IF WE MAKE IT THROUGH DECEMBER Merle Haggard—Capitol 3746
[Merle Haggard] [BMI] (11/10/73 BCR-27)

IF WE NEVER MEET AGAIN Tommy Conwell And The Young Rumblers—Columbia 08505
[Jules Shear] [BMI] (12/10/88 BC-48)

IF WE ONLY HAVE LOVE Dionne Warwicke—Warner Bros. 7560
[Eric Blau/Jacques Brel/Mort Shuman] [BMI] (3/4/72 BCR-68) [FET]

IF WE TRY Don McLean—United Artists 206 [Don McLean] [BMI] (3/24/73 BCR-49)

IF WISHES CAME TRUE Sweet Sensation—Atco 98953
[Deena Charles/Russ DeSalvo/Robert Steele] [ASC] (6/9/90 BC-1)

(IF YOU ADD) ALL THE LOVE IN THE WORLD Mac Davis—Columbia 10111
[Ian Page] [BMI] (3/22/75 BC-54)

IF YOU ASKED ME TO Patti LaBelle—MCA 53358 [Diane Warren] [ASC] (10/7/89 BC-79)

IF YOU BELIEVE Johnnie Ray—Columbia 40391 [Irving Berlin] [ASC] (12/20/54 R-73)

IF YOU CAN BEAT ME ROCKIN' (YOU CAN HAVE MY CHAIR) Laura Lee—Hot Wax 7207
[Lamont Dozier/Ronald Dunbar/Brian Holland] [BMI] (9/30/72 BCR-65)

IF YOU CAN DREAM *Four Aces—Decca 29809*
[Nicholas Brodszky/Sammy Cahn] [ASC] (2/17/56 BCRt-34)

IF YOU CAN DREAM *Lena Horne—RCA Victor 47-6431*
[Nicholas Brodszky/Sammy Cahn] [ASC] (2/24/56 Rt-35)

IF YOU CAN WANT Smokey Robinson & The Miracles—Tamla 54162
[Smokey Robinson] [ASC] (2/24/68 BCR-11)

IF YOU CAN'T GIVE ME LOVE Suzi Quatro—RSO 929
[Mike Chapman/Nicky Chinn] [ASC] (5/26/79 BCR-45)

IF YOU CAN'T ROCK ME Ricky Nelson—Imperial 5935
[Willie Jacobs] [BMI] (4/20/63 B-100)

IF YOU COULD READ MY MIND Gordon Lightfoot—Reprise 0974
[Gordon Lightfoot] [ASC] (12/26/70 BCR-3)

(IF YOU CRY) TRUE LOVE, TRUE LOVE The Drifters—Atlantic 2040
[Doc Pomus/Mort Shuman] [BMI] (10/24/59 BCR-23)

IF YOU DO BELIEVE IN LOVE The Tee Set—Colossus 114
[Peter Tetteroo/Hans Van Eijck] [ASC] (5/2/70 BCR-45)

IF YOU DON'T KNOW ME BY NOW
Harold Melvin And The Blue Notes—Philadelphia Int'l 3520
[Kenneth Gamble/Leon Huff] [BMI] (9/30/72 BCR-2)

IF YOU DON'T KNOW ME BY NOW *Simply Red—Elektra 69297*
[Kenneth Gamble/Leon Huff] [BMI] (5/6/89 BC-1)

IF YOU DON'T (LOVE ME, TELL ME SO) Barbara Mason—Arctic 112
[Barbara Mason] [BMI] (11/6/65 B-85)

IF YOU DON'T WANT MY LOVE Jaye P. Morgan—RCA Victor 47-6282
[George R. Brown/Albert Von Tilzer] [ASC] (10/17/55 BCR-21)

IF YOU DON'T WANT MY LOVE Robert John—Columbia 44435
[Michael Gately/Robert John/Lou Stallman] [BMI] (4/6/68 BCR-34)

IF YOU DON'T WANT MY LOVIN' Carl Dobkins, Jr.—Decca 30656
[Carl Dobkins Jr] [NA] (9/5/59 BCR-67)

IF YOU EVER LEAVE ME Jack Jones—RCA Victor 9441
[Tony Hatch/Jackie Trent] [ASC] (2/17/68 B-92)

IF YOU FEEL IT Denise Lopez—Vendetta 7213 [Eric Li] [BMI] (11/12/88 BC-81)

IF YOU GO AWAY *Damita Jo—Epic 10061*
[Jacques Brel/Rod McKuen] [BMI] (12/3/66 BCR-63)

IF YOU GO AWAY *Terry Jacks—Bell 45,467*
[Jacques Brel/Rod McKuen] [BMI] (6/1/74 BCR-45)

IF YOU GOTTA BREAK ANOTHER HEART Albert Hammond—Mums 6015
[Albert Hammond/Mike Hazlewood] [ASC] (2/24/73 BCR-53)

IF YOU GOTTA GO, GO NOW Manfred Mann—Ascot 2194
[Bob Dylan] [SE] (10/16/65 C-100)

IF YOU GOTTA MAKE A FOOL OF SOMEBODY *James Ray—Caprice 110*
[Rudy Clark] [BMI] (11/18/61 BCR-18)

IF YOU GOTTA MAKE A FOOL OF SOMEBODY *Maxine Brown—Wand 1104*
[Rudy Clark] [BMI] (12/4/65 BCR-63)

IF YOU KNEW SUSIE The Johnston Brothers—London 1526
[Buddy DeSylva/Joseph Meyer] (Med) [ASC] (7/11/55 R-61)

IF YOU KNOW WHAT I MEAN Neil Diamond—Columbia 10366
[Neil Diamond] [SE] (6/12/76 BCR-11)

IF YOU LEAVE Orchestral Manoeuvres In The Dark—A&M 2811
[Martin H. Cooper/Paul Humphreys/Andrew McCluskey] [ASC] (3/8/86 BC-4)

IF YOU LEAVE ME NOW Chicago—Columbia 10390 [Peter Cetera] [ASC] (8/7/76 BCR-1)

IF YOU LEAVE ME NOW Jaya—LMR 77000
[Dadgel Atabay/Glenn Gutierrez/Stevie B] [BMI] (10/14/89 BC-44)

IF YOU LEAVE ME TONIGHT I'LL CRY Jerry Wallace—Decca 32989
[Hal Mooney/Gerald Sanford] [ASC] (7/22/72 BCR-38)

IF YOU LET ME Eddie Kendricks—Tamla 54222
[Frank Edward Wilson] [BMI] (9/23/72 BCR-50)

(IF YOU LET ME MAKE LOVE TO YOU THEN) WHY CAN'T I TOUCH YOU? Ronnie Dyson—
Columbia 45110 [Charles Cane Courtney/Peter Link] [ASC] (6/13/70 BCR-7)

IF YOU LET ME STAY Terence Trent D'Arby—Columbia 07398 [Terence Trent D'Arby] [BMI] (10/24/87 BC-68)

IF YOU LOVE ME (REALLY LOVE ME) *Kay Starr—Capitol 2769 [Marguerite Monnot/Geoffrey Parsons/Edith Piaf] [ASC] (5/29/54 BC-PRE) [FET]*

IF YOU LOVE ME (REALLY LOVE ME) *Vera Lynn—London 1412 [Marguerite Monnot/Geoffrey Parsons/Edith Piaf] [ASC] (5/29/54 BC-PRE) [FET]*

IF YOU LOVE ME *LaVern Baker—Atlantic 2033 [Marguerite Monnot/Geoffrey Parsons/Edith Piaf] [ASC] (8/15/59 BC-79) [FET]*

IF YOU LOVE ME (LET ME KNOW) Olivia Newton-John—MCA 40209 [John Rostill] [BMI] (4/6/74 BCR-5)

IF YOU LOVE ME LIKE YOU SAY YOU LOVE ME Betty Wright—Alston 4609 [Willie Clarke/Clarence Reid] [BMI] (4/8/72 CR-69)

IF YOU LOVE SOMEBODY SET THEM FREE Sting—A&M 2738 [Sting] [BMI] (6/8/85 BC-2)

IF YOU NEED ME Fats Domino—Imperial 5645 [Dave Bartholomew/Fats Domino] [BMI] (2/15/60 B-98)

IF YOU NEED ME *Solomon Burke—Atlantic 2185 [Robert Bateman/Wilson Pickett/William Nelson Sanders] [BMI] (4/20/63 BCtRt-22)*

IF YOU NEED ME *Wilson Pickett—Double-L 713 [Robert Bateman/Wilson Pickett/William Nelson Sanders] [BMI] (4/20/63 BCtRt-22)*

IF YOU NEEDED SOMEBODY Bad Company—Atco 98914 [Brian Howe/Terry Thomas] [ASC] (11/10/90 BC-15)

IF YOU ONLY BELIEVE (JESUS FOR TONITE) Michel Polnareff—Atlantic 3314 [Jacob Brackman/George S. Clinton/Michel Polnareff] [ASC] (2/21/76 BCR-48)

IF YOU ONLY KNEW The Teddy Bears—Imperial 5581 [Phil Spector] [BMI] (4/25/59 C-96)

IF YOU REALLY LOVE ME Stevie Wonder—Tamla 54208 [Stevie Wonder/Syreeta Wright] [ASC] (8/7/71 BCR-4)

IF YOU REALLY WANT ME TO, I'LL GO The Ron-Dels—Smash 1986 [Delbert McClinton] [BMI] (7/3/65 BCR-91)

IF YOU REMEMBER ME Chris Thompson & Night—Planet 45909 [Marvin Hamlisch/Carole Bayer Sager] [ASC] (8/18/79 BCR-17)

IF YOU SEE MY LOVE Lenny Welch—Cadence 1446 [Dash Crofts/Jim Seals] [BMI] (7/4/64 B-92)

IF YOU SEE MY LOVE DANCING Bonnie Guitar—Dot 15587 [Bonnie Guitar] [BMI] (7/6/57 R-78)

IF YOU SHOULD SAIL Nielsen/Pearson—Capitol 4910 [Reed Nielsen/Mark Pearson] [BMI] (9/13/80 BCR-38)

IF YOU TALK IN YOUR SLEEP Elvis Presley—RCA Victor 0280 [Johnny Christopher/Red West] (TSW) [BMI] (6/1/74 BCR-17)

IF YOU THINK I DON'T NEED YOU Elvis Presley—RCA Victor EPA-4382 [Joey Cooper/Red West] (EP) [BMI] (7/4/64 B-92)

IF YOU THINK YOU KNOW HOW TO LOVE ME Smokey—MCA 40429 [Mike Chapman/Nicky Chinn] [BMI] (7/26/75 B-96)

IF YOU THINK YOU'RE LONELY NOW Bobby Womack—Beverly Glen 2000 [Richard Griffin*/Patrick L. Moten/Sandra E. Sully*/Bobby Womack] [BMI] (12/26/81 CR-73)

IF YOU TRY The Chantels—End 1030 [Richard Barrett/Nate Nelson] [BMI] (9/1/58 R-88)

IF YOU WAIT FOR LOVE Bobby Goldsboro—United Artists 908 [Bobby Goldsboro] [BMI] (8/21/65 BC-75)

IF YOU WANNA BE HAPPY Jimmy Soul—S.P.Q.R. 3305 [Carmela Guida/Frank Guida/Joseph Royster] [BMI] (3/23/63 BCR-1)

IF YOU WANNA DO A DANCE The Spinners—Atlantic 3493 [Leroy Bell/Thom Bell/Tony Bell/Casey James] [BMI] (7/22/78 BCR-49)

IF YOU WANNA GET BACK YOUR LADY Pointer Sisters—Planet 13430 [John Lewis Parker/Brian Potter] [BMI] (3/26/83 BC-60)

IF YOU WANNA GET TO HEAVEN Ozark Mountain Daredevils—A&M 1515 [Steve Cash/John Dillon] [BMI] (4/20/74 BCR-21)

IF YOU WANNA SEE MAMIE TONIGHT The Ames Brothers—RCA Victor 47-6481 [Sammy Fain/Paul Francis Webster] [ASC] (4/20/56 BR-56)

IF YOU WANT IT Niteflyte—Ariola America 7747 [Howard Williams Johnson/Sandy Torano] [BMI] (9/15/79 BCR-37)

(IF YOU WANT IT) DO IT YOURSELF Gloria Gaynor—MGM 14823 [James Bolden/Jack Robinson] [ASC] (10/25/75 B-98)

IF YOU WANT ME TO STAY Sly & The Family Stone—Epic 11017 [Sylvester Stewart] [BMI] (6/23/73 BCR-12)

IF YOU WANT MY LOVE Cheap Trick—Epic 02968 [Rick Nielsen] [BMI] (6/5/82 BC-42)

IF YOU WANT THIS LOVE Sonny Knight—Aura 403 [Baker Knight] [BMI] (9/26/64 BCR-71)

IF YOU WERE A ROCK AND ROLL RECORD Freddy Cannon—Swan 4122 [Jay Goodis] [ASC] (11/3/62 BCR-67)

IF YOU WERE A WOMAN (AND I WAS A MAN) Bonnie Tyler—Columbia 05839 [Desmond Child] [ASC] (4/12/86 B-77)

IF YOU WERE MINE Ray Charles—ABC/TRC 11271 [James E. Lewis] [BMI] (9/19/70 BCR-40)

IF YOUR HEART ISN'T IN IT Atlantic Starr—A&M 2822 [Hamish Stuart] [ASC] (4/19/86 BC-57)

IF YOU'RE NOT BACK IN LOVE BY MONDAY Millie Jackson—Spring 175 [Glenn Martin/Sonny Throckmorton] [BMI] (10/22/77 BCR-33)

IF YOU'RE READY (COME GO WITH ME) The Staple Singers—Stax 0179 [Homer Banks/Carl Hampton/Raymond Earl Jackson] [BMI] (10/27/73 BCR-8)

IF YOU'RE READY (HERE IT COMES) Enchantment—Roadshow 1212 [Verdell Lanier/Michael Lee Stokes] [BMI] (7/15/78 R-83)

IF YOU'RE SERIOUS Riff—SBK 07361 [Pam Reswick/Steve Werfel] [ASC] (9/14/91 B-88)

IF YOU'VE GOT A HEART Bobby Goldsboro—United Artists 908 [Bobby Goldsboro] [BMI] (9/11/65 BCR-54)

IF YOU'VE GOT A HEART Bobby Bland—Duke 458 [Deadric Malone] [BMI] (1/31/70 BCR-71)

IF YOU'VE GOT THE TIME The Babys—Chrysalis 2132 [Tony Brock/Mike Corby/Wally Stocker/John Waite] [BMI] (2/26/77 BCR-86)

IF'N *Richard Hayes—ABC-Paramount 9754 [Matt Dubey/Harold Karr] [ASC] (1/5/57 Rt-83)*

IF'N *Jeannie Carson—Decca 30113 [Matt Dubey/Harold Karr] [ASC] (1/5/57 Rt-83)*

IF'N *Jaye P. Morgan and Eddy Arnold—RCA Victor 47-6708 [Matt Dubey/Harold Karr] [ASC] (1/5/57 Rt-83)*

IGMOO (THE PRIDE OF SOUTH CENTRAL HIGH) Stonewall Jackson—Columbia 41488 [Wayne Walker/Marijohn Wilkin] [BMI] (10/17/59 BC-79)

I.G.Y. (WHAT A BEAUTIFUL WORLD) Donald Fagen—Warner Bros. 29900 [Donald Fagen] [ASC] (10/9/82 BC-19)

IKO IKO *The Dixie Cups—Red Bird 10-024 [James Crawford*/Barbara Anne Hawkins/Rosa Lee Hawkins/ Joan Marie Johnson/Traditional] [BMI] (4/3/65 BCR-19)*

IKO IKO *Dr. John—Atco 6882 [James Crawford*/Barbara Anne Hawkins/Rosa Lee Hawkins/ Joan Marie Johnson/Traditional] [BMI] (4/1/72 BCR-50)*

IKO IKO *The Belle Stars—Capitol 44343 [James Crawford*/Barbara Anne Hawkins/Rosa Lee Hawkins/ Joan Marie Johnson/Traditional] [BMI] (3/4/89 BC-14)*

—IL CIELO IN UNA STANZA see: THIS WORLD WE LOVE IN

—IL NOSTRO CONCERTO see: OUR CONCERTO

THE SILENCE (IL SILENZIO) *Al Hirt—RCA Victor 47-8653 [Guglielmo Brezza/Nini Rosso] [BMI] (9/11/65 B-96) [I]*

IL SILENZIO *Nini Rosso—Columbia 43363 [Guglielmo Brezza/Nini Rosso] [BMI] (10/30/65 CR-84) [I]*

I'LL ALWAYS BE IN LOVE WITH YOU *Jack Pleis and His Orchestra and Chorus—Decca 30086 [Bud Green/Herman Ruby/Sam H. Stept] [ASC] (10/27/56 BCRt-50) [IWM]*

I'LL ALWAYS BE IN LOVE WITH YOU *Rosemary June—Paris 516 [Bud Green/Herman Ruby/Sam H. Stept] [ASC] (5/12/58 Rt-55)*

I'LL ALWAYS BE IN LOVE WITH YOU *The Stroll Kings—Coral 61989 [Bud Green/Herman Ruby/Sam H. Stept] [ASC] (5/19/58 Rt-55)*

I'LL ALWAYS CALL YOUR NAME Little River Band—Harvest 4380 [Beeb Birtles] [BMI] (2/5/77 BC-62)

I'LL ALWAYS HAVE FAITH IN YOU Carla Thomas—Stax 222 [Eddie Floyd/Alvertis Isbell] [BMI] (6/17/67 BCR-70)

I'LL ALWAYS LOVE MY MAMA (PART I) The Intruders—Gamble 2506 [Kenneth Gamble/Leon Huff/Gene McFadden/John Whitehead] [BMI] (5/19/73 BCR-24)

I'LL ALWAYS LOVE YOU Brenda Holloway—Tamla 54099 [Ed Cobb] [BMI] (8/8/64 BR-60)

I'LL ALWAYS LOVE YOU The Spinners—Motown 1078 [Ivy Jo Hunter/William Stevenson] [ASC] (7/3/65 BCR-30)

I'LL ALWAYS LOVE YOU Taylor Dayne—Arista 1-9700 [Jimmy George] [ASC] (6/11/88 BC-3)

I'LL BE ALRIGHT WITHOUT YOU Journey—Columbia 06301 [Jonathan Cain/Steve Perry/Neal Schon] [ASC] (12/6/86 BC-12)

I'LL BE AROUND Don Cherry—Columbia 40705 [Alec Wilder] [BMI] (8/25/56 B-78)

I'LL BE AROUND *The Spinners—Atlantic 2904 [Thom Bell/Phil Hurtt] (TSW) [BMI] (9/16/72 BCR-1)*

I'LL BE AROUND *What Is This—MCA 52593 [Thom Bell/Phil Hurtt] [BMI] (8/17/85 BC-62)*

I'LL BE BACK Stars On 45—Radio 3810 [John Lennon/Paul McCartney] (Med) [ASC] (4/11/81 BCR-1)

I'LL BE BY YOUR SIDE Stevie B—LMR/RCA 2758 [Dadgel Atabay/Stevie B] [BMI] (2/2/91 BC-12)

I'LL BE DOGGONE Marvin Gaye—Tamla 54112 [Warren Moore/Smokey Robinson/Marvin Tarplin] [ASC] (3/20/65 BCR-8)

I'LL BE GONE Pozo-Seco Singers—Columbia 43646 [Michael Merchant] [BMI] (6/18/66 BR-92)

I'LL BE GOOD Joe Valino—Vik 0275 [Robert Griener/Ed Marshall/Joseph Scussa] [NA] (5/18/57 R-81)

I'LL BE GOOD René and Angela—Mercury 884009 [René Moore/Angela Winbush] [ASC] (9/28/85 BC-47)

I'LL BE GOOD TO YOU *The Brothers Johnson—A&M 1806 [George Johnson/Louis E. Johnson/Senora Sam] [BMI] (5/1/76 BCR-3)*

I'LL BE GOOD TO YOU *Quincy Jones—Qwest 22697 [George Johnson/Louis E. Johnson/Senora Sam] [BMI] (11/18/89 BC-18)*

I'LL BE HOLDING ON Al Downing—Chess 2158 [Al Downing/Andrew Smith] [BMI] (2/8/75 BCR-48)

I'LL BE HOME *Pat Boone—Dot 15443 [Stanley J. Lewis/Ferdinand Washington] [BMI] (1/20/56 BCtRt-5)*

I'LL BE HOME *The Flamingos—Checker 830 [Stanley J. Lewis/Ferdinand Washington] [BMI] (2/4/56 CtRt-5)*

I'LL BE HOME *The Platters—Musicor 1211 [Stanley J. Lewis/Ferdinand Washington] [BMI] (11/12/66 BC-92)*

I'LL BE HOME Vikki Carr—Columbia 45296 [Randy Newman] [BMI] (1/23/71 BR-96)

I'LL BE HOME FOR CHRISTMAS Elvis Presley—RCA Victor LOC-1035 [Kim Gannon/Walter Kent/Buck Ram] (EP) [NA] (12/30/57 R-49)

I'LL BE IN TROUBLE The Temptations—Gordy 7032 [Smokey Robinson] [ASC] (5/30/64 BCR-32)

I'LL BE LOVING YOU (FOREVER) New Kids On The Block—Columbia 68671 [Maurice Starr] [ASC] (4/1/89 BC-1)

I'LL BE OVER YOU Toto—Columbia 06280 [Randy Goodrum/Steve Lukather] [ASC] (8/30/86 BC-11)

I'LL BE RIGHT HERE Tyrone Davis—Dakar 618 [Jack Daniels/John Edward Moore] [BMI] (6/20/70 BCR-28)

I'LL BE SATISFIED Jackie Wilson—Brunswick 55136 [Billy Davis/Berry Gordy/Gwen Gordy*] [BMI] (6/15/59 BCR-20)

I'LL BE SEEING YOU *The Four Freshmen & Stan Kenton & Orchestra—Capitol 2832 [Sammy Fain/Irving Kahal] [ASC] (7/10/54 C-37)*

I'LL BE SEEING YOU *Tommy Sands—Capitol 4259 [Sammy Fain/Irving Kahal] [ASC] (9/26/59 BCtRt-48)*

I'LL BE SEEING YOU *Poni-Tails—ABC-Paramount 10047 [Sammy Fain/Irving Kahal] [ASC] (10/3/59 BCtRt-48)*

I'LL BE SEEING YOU *The Five Satins—Ember 1061 [Sammy Fain/Irving Kahal] [ASC] (5/9/60 B-79)*

I'LL BE SEEING YOU *Frank Sinatra—Reprise 20,023 [Sammy Fain/Irving Kahal] [ASC] (10/2/61 BCR-43)*

I'LL BE STANDING BY Foghat—Bearsville 0315 [Dave Peverett/Roderick Price] [ASC] (3/5/77 BCR-67)

I'LL BE SWEETER TOMORROW (THAN I WAS TODAY) The O'Jays—Bell 691 [Jackie Members/Robert Poindexter/Stan Poindexter/Emma Thomas] [BMI] (11/18/67 BCR-35)

I'LL BE THE OTHER WOMAN The Soul Children—Stax 0182 [Homer Banks/Carl Hampton] [BMI] (2/2/74 BCR-36)

I'LL BE THERE *Bobby Darin—Atco 6167 [Bobby Darin] [BMI] (7/11/60 B-79)*

I'LL BE THERE *Gerry And The Pacemakers—Laurie 3279 [Bobby Darin] [BMI] (12/12/64 BCR-14)*

I'LL BE THERE Damita Jo—Mercury 71840 [Ollie Jones/Ben E. King/Jerry Leiber/Mike Stoller] [BMI] (7/3/61 BCR-12)

I'LL BE THERE Eddie Holman—ABC 11265 [Peter DeAngelis/Earl Shuman] [ASC] (6/27/70 R-62)

I'LL BE THERE The Jackson 5—Motown 1171 [Hal Davis/Berry Gordy/Willie Hutch/Bob West] [ASC] (9/19/70 BCR-1)

I'LL BE THERE Kenny Loggins—Columbia 05625 [David Foster/E. Ein Loggins/Kenny Loggins] [BMI] (10/12/85 B-88)

I'LL BE THERE Joyce "Fenderella" Irby—Motown 2032 [Joyce Irby/Reginald Jones/Kenneth Wright] [ASC] (2/17/90 BC-70)

I'LL BE THERE The Escape Club—Atlantic 87683 [Johnnie Christo/John Holliday/Trevor Steel/Milan Zekavica] [BMI] (5/25/91 BC-8)

I'LL BE THERE FOR YOU Bon Jovi—Mercury 872564 [Jon Bon Jovi/Richie Sambora] [ASC] (3/4/89 BC-1)

—I'LL BE THERE see also: TRULY JULIE'S BLUES

I'LL BE THERE (TO BRING YOU LOVE) The Majors—Imperial 66009 [Jerry Ragovoy/Winifred Robinson] [BMI] (2/15/64 C-93)

I'LL BE TRUE The Orlons—Cameo 198 [Kal Mann] [ASC] (10/28/61 CR-79)

(I'LL BE WITH YOU) IN APPLE BLOSSOM TIME *Four Aces—Decca 29344 [Neville Fleeson/Albert Von Tilzer] [ASC] (11/22/54 R-75)*

(I'LL BE WITH YOU IN) APPLE BLOSSOM TIME *Tab Hunter—Warner Bros. 5032 [Neville Fleeson/Albert Von Tilzer] [ASC] (1/26/59 BCR-22)*

I'LL BE WITH YOU IN APPLE BLOSSOM TIME *Wayne Newton—Capitol 5419 [Neville Fleeson/Albert Von Tilzer] [ASC] (5/22/65 BCR-51)*

I'LL BE WORTHY OF YOU Cab Calloway—ABC Paramount 9757 [Edgar DeLange/Larry Stock] [ASC] (10/13/56 R-82)

I'LL BE YOU The Replacements—Sire 22992 [Paul Westerberg] [ASC] (4/8/89 BC-51)

I'LL BE YOUR EVERYTHING Percy Sledge—Capricorn 0209 [George Soule] [BMI] (11/2/74 BCR-59)

I'LL BE YOUR EVERYTHING Tommy Page—Sire 19959 [Jordan Knight/Tommy Page/Danny Wood] [BMI] (2/17/90 BC-1)

I'LL BE YOUR SHELTER Taylor Dayne—Arista 2005 [Diane Warren] [ASC] (5/5/90 BC-4)

I'LL BE YOUR SHELTER (IN TIME OF STORM) Luther Ingram—KoKo 2113 [Homer Banks/Carl Hampton/Raymond Earl Jackson] [BMI] (11/25/72 BCR-32)

I'LL BET YOU Funkadelic—Westbound 150 [Sid Barnes/George Clinton/Theresa Lindsey] [BMI] (9/20/69 BCR-63)

I'LL BRING IT HOME TO YOU Carla Thomas—Atlantic 2163 [Sam Cooke] [BMI] (10/13/62 BCR-41)

I'LL COME RUNNING Livingston Taylor—Epic 50667 [Livingston Taylor] [ASC] (3/31/79 BCR-72)

I'LL COME RUNNING BACK TO YOU Sam Cooke—Specialty 619 [William S. Cook] [BMI] (12/9/57 BCR-12)

I'LL CRY INSTEAD The Beatles—Capitol 5234 [John Lennon/Paul McCartney] [ASC] (7/25/64 BCR-22)

I'LL DO ANYTHING FOR YOU Denroy Morgan—Becket 45-5 [Ronald Dean Miller/Bert Reid] [BMI] (8/22/81 CR-63)

I'LL DO 4 U Father MC—Uptown/MCA 53914 [Timothy Brown*/David Foster/Cheryl Lynn/David Paich] [ASC] (1/12/91 BC-20)

I'LL DO FOR YOU ANYTHING YOU WANT ME TO Barry White—20th Century 2208 [Barry White] [BMI] (5/24/75 BCR-32)

I'LL DO IT FOR YOU Toussaint McCall—Ronn 9 [Toussaint McCall/Patrick Robinson*] [BMI] (7/1/67 BCR-77)

I'LL DRINK TO YOU Duke Jupiter—Coast To Coast 02801 [Marshall James Styler] [BMI] (3/20/82 BCR-53)

I'LL ERASE AWAY YOUR PAIN The Whatnauts—Stang 5023 [George Kerr/Sylvia Robinson] [BMI] (4/17/71 BCR-64)

I'LL FALL IN LOVE AGAIN Sammy Hagar—Geffen 49881 [Sammy Hagar] [ASC] (1/30/82 BCR-43)

I'LL FEEL A WHOLE LOT BETTER The Byrds—Columbia 43332 [Gene Clark] [BMI] (8/7/65 R-93)

I'LL FIND MY WAY HOME Jon & Vangelis—Polydor 2205 [Jon Anderson/Vangelis] [ASC] (5/22/82 BC-51)

I'LL FLY AWAY Lonnie Sattin & Orchestra—Warner Bros. 5158 [Albert E. Brumley Sr.] [BMI] (7/23/60 C-98)

I'LL GET BY Eddie Money—Columbia 74109 [Antonina Armato/Andy Hill/Eddie Money] [ASC] (12/7/91 BC-6)

I'LL GET BY (AS LONG AS I HAVE YOU) Billy Williams—Coral 61999 [Fred Ahlert/Roy Turk] [ASC] (6/16/58 BCR-34)

I'LL GET OVER YOU Crystal Gayle—United Artists 781 [Richard Leigh] [ASC] (6/12/76 BR-71)

I'LL GIVE ALL MY LOVE TO YOU Keith Sweat—Vintertainment 64915 [Keith Sweat/Bobby Wooten] [ASC] (12/1/90 BC-7)

I'LL GO CRAZY James Brown And The Famous Flames—King 6020 [James Brown] [BMI] (2/12/66 BC-73)

I'LL GO TO MY GRAVE LOVING YOU The Statler Brothers—Mercury 73687 [Don S. Reid] [BMI] (10/11/75 BC-93)

I'LL HAVE TO GO AWAY Skylark—Capitol 3661 [Renée Armand/Kerry Chater] [BMI] (9/8/73 CR-85)

I'LL HAVE TO SAY I LOVE YOU IN A SONG Jim Croce—ABC 11424 [Jim Croce] [ASC] (2/23/74 BCR-6)

I'LL HOLD OUT MY HAND *The Clique—White Whale 333 [Al Gorgoni/Chip Taylor] [BMI] (11/15/69 BCR-29)*

I'LL HOLD OUT MY HAND *Wind—Life 202 [Al Gorgoni/Chip Taylor] [BMI] (12/27/69 R-96)*

I'LL JUST HAVE A CUP OF COFFEE (THEN I'LL GO) Claude Gray—Mercury 71732 [Bill Brock] [BMI] (4/1/61 BCR-78)

I'LL KEEP HOLDING ON The Marvelettes—Tamla 54116 [Ivy Jo Hunter/William Stevenson] [ASC] (5/29/65 BCR-34)

I'LL KEEP YOU SATISFIED Billy J. Kramer With The Dakotas—Imperial 66048 [John Lennon/Paul McCartney] [ASC] (7/25/64 BCR-30)

I'LL KNOW Sammy Davis Jr.—Decca 29672 [Frank Loesser] [ASC] (11/26/55 B-87)

I'LL KNOW HER WHEN I SEE HER Cooper Brothers Band—Capricorn 0325 [Richard Cooper] [ASC] (6/23/79 BCR-72)

I'LL LOVE YOU FOREVER The Holidays—Golden World 36 [Don Davis/Tony Gray*/Robert Earl Johnson*] [BMI] (5/7/66 BCR-48)

I'LL LOVE YOU TILL THE COWS COME HOME Clyde McPhatter—Mercury 71783 [Joy Kennedy] [BMI] (3/13/61 R-92)

I'LL MAKE ALL YOUR DREAMS COME TRUE Ronnie Dove—Diamond 188 [Wes Farrell/Bernice Ross] [BMI] (8/28/65 BCR-19)

I'LL MAKE HIM LOVE ME Barbara Lewis—Atlantic 2400 [Howard Greenfield/Helen Miller] [BMI] (4/22/67 BR-72)

I'LL MAKE IT ALL UP TO YOU Jerry Lee Lewis And His Pumping Piano—Sun 303 [Charlie Rich] [BMI] (9/8/58 B-85)

I'LL MAKE IT ALRIGHT Valentinos (The Lovers)—SAR 137 [Curtis Womack] [BMI] (3/30/63 B-97)

I'LL MAKE YOU MINE Bobby Vee With The Eligibles—Liberty 55670 [Bobby Vee] [BMI] (2/22/64 BCR-52)

I'LL MAKE YOU MUSIC Beverly Bremers—Scepter 12363 [Bruce Roberts] [BMI] (9/16/72 BCR-54)

I'LL MEET YOU HALFWAY The Partridge Family Starring Shirley Jones & Featuring David Cassidy—Bell 996 [Wes Farrell/Gerry Goffin] [BMI] (5/8/71 BCR-2)

I'LL NEVER BE FREE Kay Starr—Capitol 4583 [Bennie Benjamin/George David Weiss] [ASC] (6/19/61 BCR-55)

I'LL NEVER DANCE AGAIN Bobby Rydell—Cameo 217 [Mike Anthony/Barry Mann] [BMI] (5/26/62 BCR-14)

I'LL NEVER DO YOU WRONG Joe Tex—Dial 4076 [Joe Tex] [BMI] (5/18/68 BCR-45)

I'LL NEVER FALL IN LOVE AGAIN Johnnie Ray—Columbia 41438 [Johnnie Ray] [ASC] (9/14/59 BCR-75)

I'LL NEVER FALL IN LOVE AGAIN *Tom Jones—Parrot 40018 [Jimmy Currie/Lonnie Donegan] [BMI] (9/9/67 BCR-42)*

I'LL NEVER FALL IN LOVE AGAIN *Tom Jones—Parrot 40018*
[Jimmy Currie/Lonnie Donegan] [BMI] (7/19/69 BCR-5)

I'LL NEVER FALL IN LOVE AGAIN *Burt Bacharach—A&M 1064*
[Burt Bacharach/Hal David] [ASC] (7/5/69 B-93)

I'LL NEVER FALL IN LOVE AGAIN *Dionne Warwick—Scepter 12273*
[Burt Bacharach/Hal David] [ASC] (12/27/69 BCR-6)

I'LL NEVER FIND ANOTHER (FIND ANOTHER LIKE YOU) The Manhattans—Columbia 11398
[Leo Graham/Paul Richmond] [BMI] (12/20/80 R-92)

I'LL NEVER FIND ANOTHER YOU *The Seekers—Capitol 5383*
[Tom Springfield] [ASC] (3/27/65 BCR-4)

I'LL NEVER FIND ANOTHER YOU *Sonny James The Southern Gentleman—Capitol 5914*
[Tom Springfield] [ASC] (7/22/67 B-97)

—I'LL NEVER GO BACK TO GEORGIA see: EL PITO

I'LL NEVER KNOW The Four Lads—Columbia 40629
[Roy Jordan/Ulpio Minucci] [BMI] (2/25/56 B-52)

I'LL NEVER LET YOU GO Steelheart—MCA 53801
[Michael Matijevic] [ASC] (3/16/91 BC-23)

I'LL NEVER LOVE THIS WAY AGAIN Dionne Warwick—Arista 0419
[Will Jennings/Richard Kerr] [BMI] (6/23/79 BCR-5)

I'LL NEVER SMILE AGAIN *The Modernaires—Coral 61779*
[Ruth Lowe] (Med) [ASC] (2/16/57 R-72)

I'LL NEVER SMILE AGAIN *The Platters—Mercury 71847*
[Ruth Lowe] [ASC] (7/24/61 BCtRt-25)

I'LL NEVER SMILE AGAIN *The Wanderers—Cub 9094*
[Ruth Lowe] [ASC] (7/24/61 CtRt-30)

I'LL NEVER SMILE AGAIN *(parody of I'll Never Smile Again) The Four Preps—Capitol 4716*
[Ruth Lowe] (Med) [ASC] (3/17/62 BCR-61) [P]

I'LL NEVER STAND IN YOUR WAY *The Four Tophatters—Cadence 1289*
[Hy Heath/Fred Rose] [ASC] (9/1/56 R-80)

I'LL NEVER STAND IN YOUR WAY *Jimmie Rodgers—Dot 16428*
[Hy Heath/Fred Rose] [ASC] (1/26/63 R-91)

I'LL NEVER STOP LOVING YOU *Doris Day—Columbia 40505*
[Nicholas Brodszky/Sammy Cahn] [ASC] (6/4/55 BCRt-11)

I'LL NEVER STOP LOVING YOU *Les Baxter & His Orchestra—Capitol 3120*
[Nicholas Brodszky/Sammy Cahn] [ASC] (6/20/55 Rt-11)

I'LL NEVER STOP LOVING YOU
David Whitfield with The Roland Shaw Orchestra—London 1572
[Nicholas Brodszky/Sammy Cahn] [ASC] (6/20/55 Rt-11)

I'LL NEVER STOP WANTING YOU Brian Hyland—ABC-Paramount 10262
[Gary Geld/Peter Udell] [ASC] (11/27/61 BR-83)

I'LL PLAY FOR YOU Seals & Crofts—Warner Bros. 8075
[Dash Crofts/Jim Seals] [BMI] (3/22/75 BCR-18)

I'LL PLAY THE BLUES FOR YOU Albert King—Stax 0135
[Jerry Beach] [BMI] (7/22/72 C-73)

I'LL PLAY THE FOOL Dr. Buzzard's Original "Savannah" Band—RCA 10762
[Stony Browder/August Darnell] [BMI] (9/25/76 BC-80)

—I'LL RELEASE YOU see: RELEASE ME

I'LL REMEMBER CAROL Tommy Boyce—RCA Victor 47-8074
[Tommy Boyce] [BMI] (10/13/62 BCR-78)

I'LL REMEMBER TODAY Patti Page—Mercury 71189
[William Engvick/Edith Piaf] [BMI] (9/23/57 BCR-15)

I'LL REMEMBER TONIGHT Pat Boone—Dot 15840
[Sammy Fain/Paul Francis Webster] [ASC] (10/20/58 BCR-22)

I'LL SAIL MY SHIP ALONE Jerry Lee Lewis And His Pumping Piano—Sun 312
[Henry Glover/Lois Mann/Moon Mullican/Henry Thurston] [BMI] (1/19/59 B-93)

I'LL SAVE THE LAST DANCE FOR YOU Damita Jo—Mercury 71690
[Doc Pomus/Mort Shuman] [BMI] (10/24/60 BCR-12)

I'LL SAY FOREVER MY LOVE Jimmy Ruffin—Soul 35043
[Steve Bowden/James Anthony Dean/William Weatherspoon] [ASC] (3/9/68 BCR-70)

I'LL SEARCH MY HEART Johnny Mathis—Columbia 42916
[Allyn Ferguson/Ernie Richman/Neil Westen] [ASC] (12/14/63 B-90)

I'LL SEE HIM THROUGH Tammy Wynette—Epic 10571
[Billy Sherrill/Norro Wilson] [BMI] (1/31/70 B-100)

I'LL SEE YOU IN MY DREAMS *Seymour & His Heartbeat Trumpet—Heartbeat 11*
[Isham Jones/Gus Kahn] [ASC] (12/8/58 R-77)

I'LL SEE YOU IN MY DREAMS *Pat Boone—Dot 16312*
[Isham Jones/Gus Kahn] [ASC] (1/15/62 BCR-30)

I'LL SEE YOU IN MY DREAMS Giant—A&M 1495
[Alan Pasqua/Mark Spiro] [BMI] (3/24/90 BC-18)

I'LL STEP ASIDE Georgie Shaw—Decca 29462
[Bennie Benjamin/George David Weiss] [ASC] (4/11/55 R-76)

I'LL STILL BE LOVING YOU Restless Heart—RCA 5065
[Pat Bunch/Todd Cerney/Mary Ann Kennedy/Pam Rose] [BMI] (4/11/87 BC-33)

I'LL STILL LOVE YOU Jim Weatherly—Buddah 444
[Jim Weatherly] [ASC] (1/25/75 BCR-68)

I'LL SUPPLY THE LOVE Toto—Columbia 10898
[David Paich] [ASC] (2/3/79 BCR-43)

I'LL TAKE CARE OF YOU Bobby Bland—Duke 314
[Brook Benton] [BMI] (12/28/59 BCR-82)

I'LL TAKE CARE OF YOUR CARES Frankie Laine—ABC 10891
[Mort Dixon/James V. Monaco] [ASC] (1/7/67 BCR-39)

I'LL TAKE GOOD CARE OF YOU Garnet Mimms—United Artists 995
[Bert Berns/Jerry Ragovoy] [BMI] (3/26/66 BCR-28)

I'LL TAKE ROMANCE Eydie Gorme—ABC-Paramount 9780
[Oscar Hammerstein/Ben Oakland] [ASC] (4/13/57 BR-65)

I'LL TAKE YOU HOME Corsairs Featuring Jay "Bird" Uzzell—Tuff 1818
[Luigi Creatore/Hugo Peretti/George David Weiss] [ASC] (4/14/62 BCR-55)

I'LL TAKE YOU HOME The Drifters—Atlantic 2201
[Barry Mann/Cynthia Weil] [BMI] (9/7/63 BCR-21)

I'LL TAKE YOU HOME AGAIN KATHLEEN Slim Whitman—Imperial 8310
[Thomas P. Westendorf] [BMI] (9/16/57 B-93)

I'LL TAKE YOU THERE The Staple Singers—Stax 0125
[Alvertis Isbell] [BMI] (4/1/72 BCR-1)

I'LL TAKE YOU WHERE THE MUSIC'S PLAYING The Drifters—Atlantic 2298
[Jeff Barry/Ellie Greenwich] [BMI] (8/14/65 BCR-51)

I'LL TEACH YOU HOW TO CRY Kitty Kallen—RCA Victor 47-8202
[Alan Brandt/Bob Haymes] [BMI] (7/6/63 R-99)

I'LL THINK OF YOU The McGuire Sisters—Coral 62047
[Clint Ballard Jr./Noel Sherman] [BMI] (10/27/58 R-85)

I'LL TOUCH A STAR Terry Stafford—Crusader 105
[Dolores Fuller/Ben Weisman/Fred Wise] [ASC] (5/23/64 BCR-22)

I'LL TRY ANYTHING Dusty Springfield—Philips 40439
[Mark Barkan/Vic Millrose] [BMI] (3/18/67 BCR-29)

I'LL TRY SOMETHING NEW *The Miracles—Tamla 54059*
[Smokey Robinson] [ASC] (5/7/62 BCR-33)

I'LL TRY SOMETHING NEW
Diana Ross And The Supremes & The Temptations—Motown 1142
[Smokey Robinson] [ASC] (3/15/69 BCR-18)

I'LL TRY SOMETHING NEW *A Taste Of Honey—Capitol 5099*
[Smokey Robinson] [ASC] (3/13/82 BCR-41)

I'LL TUMBLE 4 YA Culture Club—Virgin 03912
[Michael Craig/Roy Hay/Jon Moss/George O'Dowd] [ASC] (7/2/83 BC-8)

I'LL TURN TO STONE Four Tops—Motown 1110
[Lamont Dozier/Brian Holland/Eddie Holland/R. Dean Taylor] [BMI] (7/15/67 BC-76)

I'LL WAIT Betty Johnson—Bally 1000 [Fred Ebb/Paul Klein] [BMI] (3/3/56 BR-83)

I'LL WAIT Van Halen—Warner Bros. 29307
[Michael Anthony/David Lee Roth/Alex Van Halen/Eddie Van Halen] [ASC]
(4/14/84 BC-13)

I'LL WAIT FOR YOU Frankie Avalon—Chancellor 1026
[Peter DeAngelis/Bob Marcucci] [ASC] (10/13/58 BCR-15)

I'LL WALK ALONE Johnny Nash—ABC-Paramount 9844
[Sammy Cahn/Jule Styne] [ASC] (8/12/57 R-41)

ILLEGAL ALIEN Genesis—Atlantic 89698
[Tony Banks/Phil Collins/Mike Rutherford] [ASC] (3/10/84 BC-44)

I'M A BELIEVER *The Monkees—Colgems 1002 [Neil Diamond] [SE] (12/3/66 BCR-1)*

I'M A BELIEVER *Neil Diamond—Bang 586 [Neil Diamond] [SE] (6/19/71 BCR-45)*

I'M A BELIEVER Giant—A&M 1454
[Dann Huff/David Lyndon Huff/Philip Naish/Alan Pasqua/Mark Spiro] [BMI]
(9/30/89 BC-56)

I'M A BETTER MAN Engelbert Humperdinck—Parrot 40040
[Burt Bacharach/Hal David] [ASC] (8/16/69 BCR-35)

—I'M A CHANGED MAN see: FINALLY GOT MYSELF TOGETHER

I'M A DRIFTER Bobby Goldsboro—United Artists 50525
[Bobby Goldsboro] [BMI] (4/19/69 BCR-44)

I'M A FOOL Dino, Desi & Billy—Reprise 0367
[Joey Cooper/Red West] [BMI] (6/19/65 BCR-12)

I'M A FOOL FOR YOU James Carr—Goldwax 328
[Earl Cage/Quinton Claunch/Dan Greer/George Henry Jackson/Rudolph Russell] [BMI]
(9/23/67 BR-95)

I'M A FOOL TO CARE *Les Paul and Mary Ford—Capitol 2839*
[Ted Daffan] [BMI] (7/3/54 BCR-10)

I'M A FOOL TO CARE *Joe Barry—Smash 1702 [Ted Daffan] [BMI] (4/24/61 BCtRt-19)*

I'M A FOOL TO CARE *Oscar Black—Savoy 1600 [Ted Daffan] [BMI] (4/24/61 BCtRt-64)*

I'M A FOOL TO CARE *Ray Charles—ABC-Paramount 10700*
[Ted Daffan] [BMI] (7/17/65 BCR-77)

I'M A GREEDY MAN - PART 1 James Brown—Polydor 14100
[Charles Bobbit/James Brown] [BMI] (11/6/71 BCR-28)

I'M A HAPPY MAN The Jive Five—United Artists 853
[Casey Spencer] [BMI] (7/17/65 BCR-23)

I'M A HOG FOR YOU The Coasters—Atco 6146
[Jerry Leiber/Mike Stoller] [BMI] (8/29/59 BC-38)

I'M A LOSER The Beatles—Capitol R-5365
[John Lennon/Paul McCartney] (EP) [ASC] (2/13/65 BCR-67)

I'M A MAN Fabian—Chancellor 1029
[Doc Pomus/Mort Shuman] [BMI] (12/29/58 BCR-31)

I'M A MAN The Yardbirds—Epic 9857 [Ellas McDaniel] [BMI] (10/30/65 BCR-17)

I'M A MAN *Spencer Davis Group—United Artists 50144*
[Jimmy Miller/Steve Winwood] [BMI] (3/25/67 BCR-6)

I'M A MAN *Chicago—Columbia 45467*
[Jimmy Miller/Steve Winwood] (TSW) [BMI] (10/9/71 BCR-17)

I'M A MIDNIGHT MOVER Wilson Pickett—Atlantic 2528
[Wilson Pickett/Bobby Womack] [BMI] (6/22/68 BCR-19)

I'M A NUT Leroy Pullins—Kapp 758 [Leroy Pullins] [ASC] (6/25/66 BCR-57)

I'M A PRACTICAL GUY Lee Rogers—D-Town 1212
[Ronald Abner/Cody Black*/Mike Hanks*/Donald Parker*/Rudy Robinson/Lee Rogers] [BMI] (7/16/66 R-91)

I'M A RAMBLIN' MAN Waylon Jennings—RCA Victor 10020
[Ray Pennington] [BMI] (9/7/74 BCR-75)

(I'M A) ROAD RUNNER Jr. Walker & The All Stars—Soul 35015
[Lamont Dozier/Brian Holland/Eddie Holland] [BMI] (4/9/66 BCR-18)

I'M A ROCKER Raspberries—Capitol 3765 [Eric Carmen] [BMI] (11/24/73 BC-75)

I'M A STRANGER HERE Five Man Electrical Band—Lion 149
[Les Emmerson] [BMI] (3/31/73 BCR-57)

I'M A SUCKER FOR YOUR LOVE Teena Marie—Gordy 7169
[Rick James] [ASC] (7/7/79 R-96)

I'M A TELLING YOU Jerry Butler—Vee-Jay 390
[Jerry Butler/Curtis Mayfield] [BMI] (7/22/61 BCR-25)

I'M A TRAIN Albert Hammond—Mums 6026
[Albert Hammond/Mike Hazlewood] [ASC] (2/23/74 BCR-25)

I'M A WOMAN *Peggy Lee—Capitol 4888*
[Jerry Leiber/Mike Stoller] [BMI] (12/22/62 BCR-45)

I'M A WOMAN *Maria Muldaur—Reprise 1319*
[Jerry Leiber/Mike Stoller] [BMI] (12/21/74 BCR-12)

(I'M A) YOYO MAN Rick Cunha—GRC 2016
[Marty Cooper/Rick Cunha] [BMI] (4/20/74 BCR-45)

I'M AFRAID TO GO HOME Brian Hyland—ABC-Paramount 10452
[Gary Geld/Peter Udell] [ASC] (6/22/63 BCR-59)

I'M ALIVE *The Hollies—Imperial 66119 [Clint Ballard Jr.] [ASC] (7/17/65 CR-84)*

I'M ALIVE *Gamma—Elektra 46555 [Clint Ballard Jr.] [ASC] (12/22/79 BCR-58)*

I'M ALIVE Blue Swede—EMI 4029
[Tommy James/Peter Lucia] (Med) [BMI] (2/22/75 BCR-54)

I'M ALIVE Electric Light Orchestra—MCA 41246 [Jeff Lynne] [BMI] (5/24/80 BCR-14)

I'M ALIVE Neil Diamond—Columbia 03503
[Neil Diamond/David Foster] [SE] (1/15/83 BC-30)

I'M ALMOST READY Pure Prairie League—Casablanca 2294
[Vince Gill] [BMI] (8/16/80 BCR-34)

I'M ALRIGHT Kenny Loggins—Columbia 11317 [Kenny Loggins] [ASC] (7/12/80 BCR-4)

I'M ALWAYS CHASING RAINBOWS Joe Pica—Anchor 148
[Harry Carroll/Frederic Chopin/Joseph McCarthy] [NA] (12/15/58 R-96)

(I'M ALWAYS HEARING) WEDDING BELLS *Eddie Fisher—RCA Victor 47-6015*
[Herbert Jarczyk/Robert Mellin/Fred Rauch] [NA] (2/7/55 CRt-13)

(I'M ALWAYS HEARING) WEDDING BELLS *Frankie Lester—"X" 0077*
[Herbert Jarczyk/Robert Mellin/Fred Rauch] [NA] (2/14/55 Rt-16)

(I'M ALWAYS HEARING) WEDDING BELLS
Guy Lombardo & His Royal Canadians—Decca 29434
[Herbert Jarczyk/Robert Mellin/Fred Rauch] [NA] (2/28/55 Rt-19)

I'M AVAILABLE Margie Rayburn—Liberty 55102
[Dave Burgess/Don Earl*] [BMI] (9/23/57 BCR-13)

I'M BAD LL Cool J—Def Jam 07120
[Bobby Ervin/Dwayne Simon/James Todd Smith] [ASC] (7/11/87 B-84)

I'M BETTER OFF WITHOUT YOU The Main Ingredient—RCA Victor 74-0382
[Donald McPherson/Tony Silvester/Luther Simmons] [BMI] (10/10/70 BCR-83)

I'M BEWILDERED The DeCastro Sisters—Abbott 3002
[Danny Daniels/Herbert Dell] [BMI] (3/7/55 R-75)

I'M BLUE (THE GONG-GONG SONG) The Ikettes—Atco 6212
[Ike Turner] [BMI] (12/25/61 BCR-16)

I'M COMIN' HOME Sammy Davis Jr.—Decca 30536
[Bob Crewe/Frank Slay] [ASC] (12/30/57 R-85)

I'M COMIN' HOME Dave Edmunds—MAM 3608 [Traditional] [NA] (5/1/71 BCR-53)

I'M COMIN' HOME Tommy James—Roulette 7110
[Tommy James/Robert L. King] [BMI] (9/11/71 BCR-19)

I'M COMIN' HOME, CINDY Trini Lopez—Reprise 0455
[Trini Lopez/Phil Zeller] [BMI] (4/2/66 BCR-39)

I'M COMIN' ON BACK TO YOU Jackie Wilson—Brunswick 55216
[Al Kasha/Horace Ott] [BMI] (6/12/61 BCR-19)

I'M COMING HOME Marv Johnson—United Artists 175
[Berry Gordy] [NA] (6/22/59 BCR-81)

I'M COMING HOME Paul Anka—ABC-Paramount 10338
[Paul Anka] [BMI] (8/25/62 B-94)

I'M COMING HOME Tom Jones—Parrot 40024
[Barry Mason/Les Reed] [ASC] (12/23/67 BCR-52)

I'M COMING HOME Stories—Kama Sutra 545
[Ian Lloyd/Michael David Lookofsky] [ASC] (6/10/72 BCR-26)

I'M COMING HOME *Johnny Mathis—Columbia 45908*
[Thom Bell/Linda Creed] [BMI] (9/8/73 BCR-61)

I'M COMING HOME *The Spinners—Atlantic 3027*
[Thom Bell/Linda Creed] [BMI] (5/11/74 BCR-14)

I'M COMING OUT Diana Ross—Motown 1491
[Bernard Edwards/Nile Rodgers] [BMI] (9/6/80 BCR-5)

I'M CONFESSIN' (THAT I LOVE YOU) *Terri Dean—Laurel 1003*
[Doc Daugherty/Al Neiburg/Ellis Reynolds] [ASC] (5/30/59 CRt-89)

I'M CONFESSIN' THAT I LOVE YOU *Barbara Lantz—Palladium 603*
[Doc Daugherty/Al Neiburg/Ellis Reynolds] [ASC] (6/15/59 Rt-96)

I'M CONFESSIN' (THAT I LOVE YOU) *Frank Ifield—Capitol 5032*
[Doc Daugherty/Al Neiburg/Ellis Reynolds] [ASC] (9/7/63 BCR-37)

I'M CONFESSIN' (THAT I LOVE YOU) *Nino Tempo & April Stevens—Atco 6294*
[Doc Daugherty/Al Neiburg/Ellis Reynolds] [ASC] (4/25/64 BR-94)

I'M CRAZY 'BOUT MY BABY Marvin Gaye—Tamla 54087
[William Stevenson] [BMI] (10/19/63 B-77)

I'M CRYING The Animals—MGM 13274 [Eric Burdon/Alan Price] [BMI] (9/26/64 BCR-17)

I'M DOIN' FINE NOW New York City—Chelsea 0113
[Thom Bell/Sherman Marshall] [BMI] (2/24/73 BCR-12)

I'M DOWN TO MY LAST HEARTBREAK Wilson Pickett—Double-L 724
[Dee Ervin/James Willingham] [BMI] (11/9/63 B-95)

I'M DREAMIN' Christopher Williams—Giant 19441 [Stanley Brown] [BMI] (5/11/91 B-89)

I'M DREAMING Jennifer Warnes—Arista 0252
[Richard Kerr/Gary Osborne] [ASC] (7/23/77 BCR-50)

I'M DROWNING MY SORROWS Teresa Brewer—Coral 61776
[Eddie Brandt/Paul Frees] [ASC] (3/2/57 CR-40)

I'M EASY Keith Carradine—ABC 12117 [Keith Carradine] [ASC] (5/8/76 BCR-10)

I'M EVERY WOMAN Chaka Khan—Warner Bros. 8683
[Nick Ashford/Valerie Simpson] [ASC] (10/7/78 BCR-17)

I'M FALLING IN LOVE Hodges, James & Smith—London 256
[William Stevenson] (Med) [BMI] (7/9/77 BC-96)

I'M FALLING IN LOVE WITH YOU Little Anthony And The Imperials—Avco 4635
[Jean H. Davis] [BMI] (6/1/74 BCR-75)

—I'M FALLING TOO see: PLEASE HELP ME...

I'M FOR REAL Howard Hewett—Elektra 69527
[Stanley Clarke/Howard Hewett] [BMI] (11/8/86 B-90)

I'M FREE Al Hibbler—Decca 30100 [Richard Mullan] [NA] (11/10/56 CR-33)

I'M FREE The Who—Decca 732519 [Pete Townshend] [BMI] (7/12/69 BCR-29)

I'M FREE The Soup Dragons—Big Life 877 568
[Mick Jagger/Keith Richards] [BMI] (11/17/90 BC-75)

I'M FREE (HEAVEN HELPS THE MAN) Kenny Loggins—Columbia 04452
[Kenny Loggins/Dean Pitchford] [BMI] (6/16/84 BC-17)

I'M GETTIN' BETTER Jim Reeves—RCA Victor 47-7756
[Jim Reeves] [BMI] (6/20/60 BCR-18)

I'M GETTIN' SENTIMENTAL OVER YOU *The Modernaires—Coral 61779*
[George Bassman/Ned Washington] (Med) [ASC] (2/16/57 R-72)

I'M GETTIN' SENTIMENTAL OVER YOU *Nelson Riddle and His Orchestra—Capitol 3877*
[George Bassman/Ned Washington] [ASC] (3/3/58 R-80) [IWM]

I'M GIRL SCOUTIN' The Intruders—Gamble 4009
[Kenneth Gamble/Leon Huff] [BMI] (3/20/71 BCR-74)

—I'M GLAD THAT YOU'RE FALLING see: PLEASE HELP ME...

I'M GOIN' DOWN Bruce Springsteen—Columbia 05603
[Bruce Springsteen] [ASC] (9/7/85 BC-9)

I'M GOING BACK TO SCHOOL Dee Clark—Vee-Jay 462
[Dee Clark] [BMI] (10/6/62 BCR-52)

(I'M GOING BY) THE STARS IN YOUR EYES Ron Banks And The Dramatics—ABC 12125
[Tony Hester] [BMI] (11/1/75 BR-81)

I'M GOING DOWN Rose Royce—MCA 40721 [Norman Whitfield] [BMI] (5/7/77 BCR-61)

I'M GOING HOME Mickey & Sylvia—Groove 0175 [Billy Valentine] [BMI] (2/2/57 R-85)

I'M GONNA BE A COUNTRY GIRL AGAIN Buffy Sainte-Marie—Vanguard 35143
[Buffy Sainte-Marie] [ASC] (11/27/71 BCR-81)

I'M GONNA BE A WHEEL SOME DAY Fats Domino—Imperial 5606
[Dave Bartholomew/Fats Domino*/Roy Hayes] [BMI] (7/27/59 BCR-17)

I'M GONNA BE STRONG Gene Pitney—Musicor 1045
[Barry Mann/Cynthia Weil] [BMI] (10/24/64 BCR-9)

I'M GONNA' BE WARM THIS WINTER Connie Francis—MGM 13116
[Mark Barkan/Hank Hunter] [BMI] (12/15/62 BCR-17)

I'M GONNA CHANGE EVERYTHING Jim Reeves—RCA Victor 47-8080
[Alex Zanetis] [BMI] (9/8/62 BR-93)

I'M GONNA CHANGE HIM Cathy Carr—Roulette 4152
[Jack Segal/Paul Vance] [ASC] (5/11/59 BCR-62)

I'M GONNA DO ALL I CAN (TO DO RIGHT BY MY MAN) Ike & Tina Turner—Minit 32060
[Wayne Carson Thompson] [BMI] (5/10/69 B-98)

I'M GONNA DO WHAT THEY DO TO ME B.B. King—BluesWay 61018
[B.B. King] [BMI] (7/20/68 BCR-74)

I'M GONNA GET MARRIED Lloyd Price—ABC-Paramount 10032
[Harold Logan/Lloyd Price] [BMI] (8/3/59 BCR-2)

I'M GONNA HIRE A WINO TO DECORATE OUR HOME David Frizzell—Warner/Viva 50063
[Dewayne Blackwell] [BMI] (8/14/82 C-85)

I'M GONNA HOLD ON LONG AS I CAN The Marvelettes—Tamla 54177
[Lena M. Manns/Frank Edward Wilson] [BMI] (1/18/69 BCR-49)

I'M GONNA KNOCK ON YOUR DOOR Eddie Hodges—Cadence 1397
[Aaron Schroeder/Sid Wayne] [ASC] (5/27/61 BCR-9)

I'M GONNA LAUGH YOU RIGHT OUT OF MY LIFE Nat "King" Cole—Capitol 3305
[Cy Coleman/Joseph Allen McCarthy] [ASC] (12/31/55 BCR-42)

I'M GONNA LET MY HEART DO THE WALKING The Supremes—Motown 1391
[Harold Beatty/Brian Holland/Eddie Holland] [ASC] (5/29/76 BCR-40)

I'M GONNA LIVE TILL I DIE Frank Sinatra and Ray Anthony and his Orchestra—Capitol 3018
[Mann Curtis/Al Hoffman/Walter Kent] [ASC] (1/24/55 R-84)

I'M GONNA LOVE HER FOR BOTH OF US Meat Loaf—Cleveland International/Epic 02490
[Jim Steinman] [BMI] (9/19/81 B-84)

I'M GONNA LOVE YOU The Ames Brothers—RCA Victor 47-6400
[Ray Passman/Arthur Shaftel] [BMI] (3/3/56 B-84)

I'M GONNA LOVE YOU The Intrigues—Yew 1002
[Jerry Akines/Victor Drayton/Reginald Turner] [BMI] (11/29/69 BCR-68)

I'M GONNA LOVE YOU JUST A LITTLE MORE BABY Barry White—20th Century 2018
[Barry White] [BMI] (3/31/73 BCR-3)

I'M GONNA LOVE YOU TOO *Buddy Holly / The Crickets—Coral 61947*
[Joe Mauldin/Norman Petty/Niki Sullivan] [BMI] (3/15/58 C-56)

I'M GONNA LOVE YOU TOO *The Hullaballoos—Roulette 4587*
[Joe Mauldin/Norman Petty/Niki Sullivan] [BMI] (11/28/64 BCR-50)

I'M GONNA LOVE YOU TOO *Terry Jacks—London 188*
[Joe Mauldin/Norman Petty/Niki Sullivan] [BMI] (1/6/73 R-86)

I'M GONNA MAKE YOU LOVE ME *Dee Dee Warwick—Mercury 72638*
[Kenneth Gamble/Leon Huff/Jerry J. Ross] [BMI] (11/26/66 BCR-77)

I'M GONNA MAKE YOU LOVE ME *Madeline Bell—Philips 40517*
[Kenneth Gamble/Leon Huff/Jerry J. Ross] [BMI] (2/10/68 BCR-26)

I'M GONNA MAKE YOU LOVE ME
Diana Ross And The Supremes & The Temptations—Motown 1137
[Kenneth Gamble/Leon Huff/Jerry J. Ross] [BMI] (12/7/68 BCR-1)

I'M GONNA MAKE YOU LOVE ME Blend—MCA 40961
[James Drown] [BMI] (12/16/78 B-91)

I'M GONNA MAKE YOU MINE The Shadows Of Knight—Dunwich 141
[William Carr/Carl D'Errico/Carole Bayer Sager] [BMI] (12/24/66 BR-90)

I'M GONNA MAKE YOU MINE Lou Christie—Buddah 116
[Tony Romeo] [BMI] (8/16/69 BCR-5)

I'M GONNA MISS YOU The Artistics—Brunswick 55301
[Jesse Bolian/Larry Johnson/Marvin Smith] [BMI] (12/3/66 BCR-45)

I'M GONNA MISS YOU Kenny Loggins—Columbia 08091
[Jeff Pescetto/Pam Reswick/Steve Werfel] [ASC] (11/12/88 BC-76)

I'M GONNA MOVE TO THE OUTSKIRTS OF TOWN Ray Charles—Impulse 202
[Roy Jacobs/William Weldon] [ASC] (6/19/61 BR-57)

I'M GONNA SIT IN TILL YOU GIVE IN B.B. King—ABC-Paramount 10216
[Dave (2) Clark/B.B. King] [BMI] (4/9/62 R-100)

I'M GONNA SIT RIGHT DOWN AND WRITE MYSELF A LETTER *Billy Williams—Coral 61830*
[Fred Ahlert/Joe Young] [ASC] (6/3/57 BCRt-2)

I'M GONNA SIT RIGHT DOWN AND WRITE MYSELF A LETTER *Larry Storch—Roulette 4014*
[Fred Ahlert/Joe Young] [ASC] (8/3/57 Rt-2)

I'M GONNA SIT RIGHT DOWN AND WRITE MYSELF A LETTER *Harry The Hipster—Hip 501*
[Fred Ahlert/Joe Young] [ASC] (8/5/57 Rt-2)

I'M GONNA SIT RIGHT DOWN AND WRITE MYSELF A LETTER
Hop A Long Wong—Decca 30462
[Fred Ahlert/Joe Young] [ASC] (10/14/57 Rt-54)

I'M GONNA SIT RIGHT DOWN AND WRITE MYSELF A LETTER *Fabian—Chancellor 1051*
[Fred Ahlert/Joe Young] [ASC] (6/4/60 C-85)

I'M GONNA TAKE CARE OF EVERYTHING Rubicon—20th Century 2362
[Max Haskett] [BMI] (2/18/78 BCR-26)

I'M GONNA TEAR YOU A NEW HEART Clarence Reid—Alston 4578
[Clarence Reid/Brad Shapiro] [BMI] (11/1/69 C-97)

I'M GONNA TEAR YOUR PLAYHOUSE DOWN Paul Young—Columbia 05577
[Earl Randle] [BMI] (9/7/85 BC-10)

I'M HANGING UP MY HEART FOR YOU Solomon Burke—Atlantic 2147
[John Bobby Berry/Don Covay] [BMI] (7/7/62 B-85)

I'M HAPPY The Four Dates—Chancellor 1014
[Peter DeAngelis/Bob Marcucci] [ASC] (5/12/58 B-87)

I'M HAPPY JUST TO DANCE WITH YOU *The Beatles—Capitol 5234*
[John Lennon/Paul McCartney] [ASC] (8/1/64 BCR-91)

I'M HAPPY JUST TO DANCE WITH YOU *Anne Murray—Capitol 4878*
[John Lennon/Paul McCartney] [ASC] (6/14/80 BR-64)

I'M HAPPY THAT LOVE HAS FOUND YOU Jimmy Hall—Epic 50931
[Ellison Chase/William Haberman/Arthur Jacobson] [BMI] (9/27/80 BCR-23)

I'M HENRY VIII, I AM Herman's Hermits—MGM 13367
[Fred Murray/Robert Patrick Weston] [ASC] (7/3/65 BCR-1)

I'M HER FOOL Billy Swan—Monument 8641
[Dennis Linde/Billy Swan] [BMI] (3/15/75 BCR-53)

I'M HERE TO GET MY BABY OUT OF JAIL The Everly Brothers—Cadence 1429
[Karl Davis/Harty Taylor*] [BMI] (10/6/62 BCR-74)

I'M HURTIN' Roy Orbison—Monument 433
[Joe Melson/Roy Orbison] [BMI] (12/12/60 BCR-16)

I'M HYPNOTIZED Anthony And The Imperials—Veep 1278
[Victoria Pike/Teddy Randazzo/Kenny Seymour] [BMI] (2/17/68 B-98)

I'M IN A DIFFERENT WORLD Four Tops—Motown 1132
[Lamont Dozier/Brian Holland/Eddie Holland] [BMI] (10/5/68 BCR-32)

—I'M IN HEAVEN WHEN YOU SMILE see: JACKIE WILSON SAID

I'M IN LOVE *Wilson Pickett—Atlantic 2448 [Bobby Womack] [BMI] (12/2/67 BCR-23)*

I'M IN LOVE *Aretha Franklin—Atlantic 2999 [Bobby Womack] [BMI] (4/6/74 BCR-16)*

I'M IN LOVE Evelyn King—RCA 12243 [Michael Jones] [BMI] (7/25/81 BCR-33)

I'M IN LOVE AGAIN *Fats Domino—Imperial 5386*
[Dave Bartholomew/Fats Domino] [BMI] (4/28/56 BCRt-3)

I'M IN LOVE AGAIN *The Fontane Sisters—Dot 15462*
[Dave Bartholomew/Fats Domino] [BMI] (5/4/56 BRt-6)

I'M IN LOVE AGAIN *Rick Nelson—Imperial 5910*
[Dave Bartholomew/Fats Domino] [BMI] (2/23/63 BCR-51)

I'M IN LOVE AGAIN The Deb-Tones—RCA Victor 47-7539
[Cole Porter] [ASC] (6/29/59 R-95)

I'M IN LOVE AGAIN Pia Zadora—Elektra/Curb 47428
[Linda Laurie/Jacques Morali/Dan Schmidt] [BMI] (3/27/82 BCR-45)

I'M IN LOVE (AND I LOVE THE FEELING) Rose Royce—Whitfield 8629
[Norman Whitfield] [BMI] (9/9/78 R-68)

I'M IN LOVE WITH YOU Pat Boone—Dot 15472
[Nick Boldi/Dick Glasser] [BMI] (6/9/56 BR-50)

I'M IN LOVE WITH YOU Kasenetz-Katz Super Cirkus—Buddah 82
[Joey Levine/Kris Resnick] [BMI] (1/25/69 CR-77)

I'M IN THE MOOD FOR LOVE *Spike Jones & City Slickers—RCA Victor 47-5742*
[Dorothy Fields/Jimmy McHugh] [NA] (7/3/54 C-PRE)

I'M IN THE MOOD FOR LOVE *Fats Domino—Imperial 5428*
[Dorothy Fields/Jimmy McHugh] [NA] (3/2/57 R-64)

I'M IN THE MOOD FOR LOVE *The Chimes—Tag 445*
[Dorothy Fields/Jimmy McHugh] [NA] (3/27/61 BCR-37)*

I'M IN YOU Peter Frampton—A&M 1941
[Peter Frampton] [ASC] (5/28/77 BCR-1)

I'M INDESTRUCTIBLE Jack Jones—Kapp 818
[Mark Barkan/Vic Millrose] [BMI] (4/15/67 BCR-81)

I'M INTO LOOKIN' FOR SOMEONE TO LOVE ME Bobby Vee—Liberty 56080
[Carole Bayer Sager/Toni Wine] [BMI] (11/30/68 BCR-90)

I'M INTO SOMETHIN' GOOD *Earl-Jean—Colpix 729*
[Gerry Goffin/Carole King] [BMI] (6/27/64 BCR-35)

I'M INTO SOMETHING GOOD *Herman's Hermits—MGM 13280*
[Gerry Goffin/Carole King] [BMI] (10/10/64 BCR-7)

I'M JEALOUS Ike & Tina Turner—Sue 740
[Jane Bossung/Ike Turner] [BMI] (3/11/61 C-83)

I'M JUST A COUNTRY BOY *Harry Belafonte—RCA Victor 47-5617*
[Marshall Barer/Fred Hellerman] [ASC] (2/16/57 R-81)

I'M JUST A COUNTRY BOY *George McCurn—A&M 705*
[Marshall Barer/Fred Hellerman] [ASC] (3/2/63 BCR-55)

I'M JUST A DANCING PARTNER The Platters—Mercury 70753
[Cy Crane/Herb Weiner] [ASC] (1/13/56 BR-46)

(I'M JUST A) FOOL FOR YOU Gene Chandler—Constellation 167
[Carl Davis/Gerald Sims] [BMI] (3/12/66 BC-88)

I'M JUST A PRISONER (OF YOUR GOOD LOVIN') Candi Staton—Fame 1460
[Edward Harris Jr./George Henry Jackson] [BMI] (1/3/70 BCR-56)

I'M JUST A SINGER (IN A ROCK AND ROLL BAND) The Moody Blues—Threshold 67012
[John Lodge] [ASC] (1/20/73 BCR-8)

I'M JUST ME Charley Pride—RCA Victor 47-9996 [Glenn Martin] [BMI] (8/21/71 B-94)

I'M JUST TOO SHY Jermaine Jackson—Motown 1525
[Jermaine Jackson/Paul M. Jackson Jr.] [ASC] (10/31/81 BCR-60)

—I'M KEEPING MY HEART AWAY FROM FIRE see: FIRE

I'M LEARNIN' Mary Wells—20th Century 590
[Raynard Miner/Carl William Smith] [BMI] (6/26/65 R-96)

I'M LEARNING ABOUT LOVE Brenda Lee—Decca 31195
[Louis Innis/Grady Martin] [BMI] (1/30/61 B-33)

I'M LEAVIN' Elvis Presley—RCA Victor 47-9998
[Sonny Charles/Michael Jarrett] [BMI] (7/10/71 BCR-34)

I'M LEAVIN' YOU Engelbert Humperdinck—Parrot 40073
[Floyd Huddleston] [ASC] (5/12/73 BC-90)

I'M LEAVING IT UP TO YOU *Dale & Grace—Montel 921*
[Don Harris/Dewey Terry] [BMI] (10/5/63 BCR-1)

I'M LEAVING IT (ALL) UP TO YOU *Donny And Marie Osmond—MGM 14735*
[Don Harris/Dewey Terry] [BMI] (7/6/74 BCR-4)

I'M LIVIN' IN SHAME Diana Ross And The Supremes—Motown 1139
[Henry Cosby/Berry Gordy/Pam Sawyer/R. Dean Taylor/Frank Edward Wilson] [BMI]
(1/25/69 BCR-8)

I'M LIVING IN TWO WORLDS Bonnie Guitar—Dot 16811
[Jan Crutchfield] [BMI] (4/2/66 BCR-89)

—I'M LOSING YOU see: I KNOW I'M LOSING YOU

I'M MANDY FLY ME 10cc—Mercury 73779
[Kevin Godley/Graham Gouldman/Eric Stewart] [BMI] (3/27/76 BC-60)

I'M MOVIN' ON *Ray Charles And His Orchestra—Atlantic 2043*
[Hank Snow] [BMI] (10/26/59 BCtRt-40)

I'M MOVIN' ON *Don Gibson—RCA Victor 47-7629*
[Hank Snow] [BMI] (11/2/59 CtRt-41)

I'M MOVIN' ON *Matt Lucas—Smash 1813 [Hank Snow] [BMI] (4/27/63 BCR-43)*

I'M MOVIN' ON *John Kay—Dunhill 4309 [Hank Snow] [BMI] (4/15/72 BCR-45)*

I'M NEVER GONNA BE ALONE ANYMORE
Cornelius Brothers & Sister Rose—United Artists 50996
[Carter Cornelius*/Eddie Cornelius] [BMI] (12/16/72 BCR-31)

I'M NEVER GONNA GIVE YOU UP Brat Pack—Vendetta 8037
[David Cole] [ASC] (6/30/90 BCR-71)

I'M NEVER GONNA SAY GOODBYE Billy Preston—Motown 1625
[Artie Butler/Molly Ann Leikin] [BMI] (9/25/82 B-88)

I'M NEVER GONNA TELL Jimmie Rodgers—Roulette 4129
[Luigi Creatore/Al Hoffman/Dick Manning/Hugo Peretti] [ASC] (2/21/59 BCR-36)

I'M NEW AT THE GAME OF ROMANCE Jane Morgan with the Troubadors—Kapp 200
[Paul Brenner/David Pollock] [ASC] (11/25/57 R-53)

I'M NO ANGEL Gregg Allman Band—Epic 06998
[Tony Colton/Phil Palmer] [BMI] (4/4/87 BC-49)

I'M NO GONNA SAY Ronnie Gaylord—Mercury 70425
[Ronnie Gaylord] [ASC] (8/21/54 C-39)

I'M NOT A FOOL ANYMORE T.K. Hulin—Smash 1830
[Robert Thibodeaux] [BMI] (8/17/63 B-92)

I'M NOT AFRAID Ricky Nelson—Imperial 5685 [Felice Bryant] [BMI] (9/3/60 BCR-25)

I'M NOT GONNA CRY ANYMORE Nancy Brooks—Arista 0385
[Bobby David] [ASC] (2/17/79 BCR-62)

I'M NOT GONNA LET IT BOTHER ME TONIGHT Atlanta Rhythm Section—Polydor 14484
[Buddy Buie/Dean Daughtry/Robert Nix] [BMI] (6/10/78 BCR-14)

I'M NOT IN LOVE *10cc—Mercury 73678*
[Graham Gouldman/Eric Stewart] [BMI] (5/10/75 BCR-2)

I'M NOT IN LOVE *Will To Power—Epic 73636*
[Graham Gouldman/Eric Stewart] [BMI] (11/17/90 BC-7)

I'M NOT LISA Jessi Colter—Capitol 4009 [Jessi Colter] [BMI] (3/29/75 BCR-4)

I'M NOT MY BROTHER'S KEEPER The Flaming Ember—Hot Wax 7006
[Ronald Dunbar/Raynard Miner/William Weatherspoon] [BMI] (10/17/70 BCR-21)

I'M NOT PERFECT (BUT I'M PERFECT FOR YOU) Grace Jones—Manhattan 50052
[Grace Jones/Bruce Woolley] [ASC] (11/29/86 BC-62)

I'M NOT SATISFIED Fine Young Cannibals—I.R.S./MCA 53789
[Roland Gift/David Steele] [ASC] (2/17/90 BC-84)

I'M NOT THE MAN I USED TO BE Fine Young Cannibals—MCA 53686
[Roland Gift/David Steele] [ASC] (10/28/89 BC-47)

I'M NOT THE ONE The Cars—Elektra 69569 [Ric Ocasek] [ASC] (2/1/86 BC-32)

I'M NOT YOUR MAN Tommy Conwell And The Young Rumblers—Columbia 07980
[Tommy Conwell/Robert Dewald/Marci Rauer] [ASC] (9/24/88 BC-74)

I'M NOT YOUR PUPPET Hi-C—Hollywood 4-64849
[Tony Alvarez/Crawford Wilkerson/Steve Yano] [ASC] (8/17/91 B-63)

(I'M NOT YOUR) STEPPIN' STONE The Monkees—Colgems 1002
[Tommy Boyce/Bobby Hart] [BMI] (12/10/66 BCR-20)

I'M ON FIRE Jerry Lee Lewis—Smash 1886
[Bob Feldman/Jerry Goldstein/Richard Gottehrer] [BMI] (4/4/64 BCR-98)

I'M ON FIRE Dwight Twilley Band—Shelter 40380
[Dwight Twilley] [ASC] (4/26/75 BCR-16)

I'M ON FIRE *5000 Volts—Philips 40801 [Tony Eyers] [ASC] (10/18/75 BCR-24)*

I'M ON FIRE *Jim Gilstrap—Roxbury 2016 [Tony Eyers] [ASC] (10/25/75 BCR-78)*

I'M ON FIRE Bruce Springsteen—Columbia 04772
[Bruce Springsteen] [ASC] (2/16/85 BC-6)

I'M ON MY WAY The Highwaymen—United Artists 439
[Dave Fisher/Traditional] [BMI] (4/2/62 BCR-56)

I'M ON MY WAY Captain & Tennille—A&M 2027
[Mark Safan] [ASC] (4/22/78 BC-74)

—I'M ON MY WAY TO A STAR see: DREAM ALONG WITH ME

I'M ON THE OUTSIDE (LOOKING IN) Little Anthony And The Imperials—DCP 1104
[Teddy Randazzo/Bobby Weinstein] [BMI] (8/22/64 BCR-15)

I'M OVER YOU Jan Bradley—Chess 1919 [Jan Bradley/Don Talty] [BMI] (1/30/65 BCR-61)

I'M READY Fats Domino—Imperial 5585
[Sylvester Bradford/Fats Domino/Al Lewis] [ASC] (5/4/59 BCR-15)

I'M READY FOR LOVE Martha & The Vandellas—Gordy 7056
[Lamont Dozier/Brian Holland/Eddie Holland] [BMI] (10/22/66 BCR-8)

I'M SATISFIED San Remo Golden Strings—Ric-Tic 108
[Don Davis/Tony Hester*/Clarence McCloud/George McGregor] [BMI]
(11/20/65 BCR-89) [I]

I'M SATISFIED Otis Clay—One-derful! 4841 [Morris Dollison] [BMI] (4/16/66 C-95)

I'M SAVING MY LOVE Skeeter Davis—RCA Victor 47-8176
[Alex Zanetis] [BMI] (4/27/63 BCR-35)

I'M SCARED Burton Cummings—Portrait 70002
[Burton Cummings] [BMI] (2/19/77 BC-61)

I'M SERIOUS The Hilltoppers—Dot 15560
[William E. Cantrell/Quinton Claunch] [BMI] (4/29/57 B-74)

I'M SINCERE *Alan Dale—Coral 61373*
[Frank Bell/Herman Fairbanks/Jack Wolf Fine] [NA] (3/14/55 CRt-35)

I'M SINCERE *Joe Barrett—Decca 29450*
[Frank Bell/Herman Fairbanks/Jack Wolf Fine] [NA] (3/14/55 Rt-35)

I'M SINCERE *The Shannon Sisters—"X" 0106*
[Frank Bell/Herman Fairbanks/Jack Wolf Fine] [NA] (4/4/55 Rt-42)

(I'M SO) AFRAID OF LOSING YOU AGAIN Charley Pride—RCA Victor 74-0265
[Dallas Frazier/A.L. "Doodle" Owens] [BMI] (11/8/69 B-74)

I'M SO ANXIOUS Southside Johnny And The Asbury Jukes—Mercury 76007
[Billy Rush] [ASC] (9/22/79 BCR-71)

I'M SO EXCITED *Pointer Sisters—Planet 13327*
[Trevor Lawrence/Anita Pointer/June Pointer/Ruth Pointer] [BMI] (9/18/82 BC-30)

I'M SO EXCITED '84 *Pointer Sisters—Planet 13857*
[Trevor Lawrence/Anita Pointer/June Pointer/Ruth Pointer] [BMI] (8/4/84 BC-9)

I'M SO GLAD The Fuzz—Calla 179 [Joe Tate/Sheila Young] [BMI] (9/18/71 BCR-66)

I'M SO GLAD I FELL FOR YOU David Ruffin—Motown 1158
[Art Posey/Glenna Session] [BMI] (12/6/69 BCR-53)

I'M SO GLAD I'M STANDING HERE TODAY The Crusaders—MCA 51177
[Will Jennings/Joe Sample] [BMI] (9/26/81 B-97)

I'M SO INTO YOU Peabo Bryson—Capitol 4656 [Peabo Bryson] [ASC] (12/23/78 R-86)

I'M SO LONESOME I COULD CRY *Johnny Tillotson—Cadence 1432*
[Hank Williams] [BMI] (12/1/62 BC-89)

I'M SO LONESOME I COULD CRY *B.J. Thomas And The Triumphs—Scepter 12129*
[Hank Williams] [BMI] (2/19/66 BCR-5)

I'M SO LONESOME I COULD CRY *Hank Wilson—Shelter 7336*
[Hank Williams] (TSW) [BMI] (10/6/73 B-78)

I'M SO LONESOME I COULD CRY *Terry Bradshaw—Mercury 73760*
[Hank Williams] [BMI] (3/6/76 B-91)

I'M SO PROUD *The Impressions—ABC-Paramount 10544*
[Curtis Mayfield] [BMI] (3/28/64 BCR-14)

I'M SO PROUD *The Main Ingredient—RCA Victor 74-0401*
[Curtis Mayfield] [BMI] (12/12/70 BCR-31)

I'M SO THANKFUL The Ikettes—Modern 1011
[Marc Gordon/Frank Edward Wilson] [BMI] (9/25/65 BCR-57)

I'M SORRY The Platters—Mercury 71032
[Buck Ram/Peter Tinturin/William White] [BMI] (3/9/57 BCR-15)

I'M SORRY *Brenda Lee—Decca 31093*
[Dub Allbritten/Ronnie Self] [BMI] (5/30/60 BCR-1)*

I'M SORRY *Joey Heatherton—MGM 14434*
[Dub Allbritten/Ronnie Self] [BMI] (11/25/72 BCR-76)*

I'M SORRY The Delfonics—Philly Groove 151
[Thom Bell/William Hart] [BMI] (4/27/68 BCR-36)

I'M SORRY Bobby Bland—Duke 466 [Sonny Thompson] [BMI] (6/19/71 B-97)

I'M SORRY John Denver—RCA Victor 10353 [John Denver] (TSW) [ASC] (9/27/75 BCR-1)

—I'M SORRY see: SO. CENTRAL RAIN

I'M SORRY (I DID YOU WRONG) The Royal Holidays—Carlton 472
[Chester Scott/Vernon Williams] [BMI] (8/25/58 R-82)

I'M SORRY I MADE YOU CRY Connie Francis—MGM 12647
[N.J. Clesi] [ASC] (4/21/58 BCR-10)

I'M SPINNING Kripp Johnson—Dot 15636 [Don Bray/Pat Dicesare] [BMI] (9/23/57 R-84)

I'M STANDING BY Ben E. King—Atco 6237
[Johnny Taylor/Jerry Wexler/Ellen Woods] [BMI] (10/27/62 R-75)

I'M STEPPING OUT John Lennon—Polydor 821107 [John Lennon] [GL] (3/31/84 BC-55)

I'M STICKIN' WITH YOU *Jimmy Bowen With The Rhythm Orchids—Roulette 4001*
[Dave Alldred/Jimmy Bowen/Buddy Knox/Donnie Lanier*] [BMI] (2/9/57 BCRt-9)*

I'M STICKIN' WITH YOU *Roy Brown—Imperial 5427*
[Dave Alldred/Jimmy Bowen/Buddy Knox/Donnie Lanier*] [BMI] (2/23/57 Rt-9)*

I'M STICKIN' WITH YOU *The Fontane Sisters—Dot 15555*
[Dave Alldred/Jimmy Bowen/Buddy Knox/Donnie Lanier*] [BMI] (3/30/57 BRt-9)*

I'M STILL A KING TO YOU Don Cherry—Columbia 40665
[Bernie Lowe/Kal Mann] [ASC] (4/21/56 BR-72)

I'M STILL A STRUGGLING MAN Edwin Starr—Gordy 7087
[Johnny Bristol/Doris McNeil] [ASC] (6/14/69 BCR-50)

I'M STILL IN LOVE WITH YOU Al Green—Hi 2216
[Al Green/Al Jackson/Willie Mitchell] [BMI] (7/1/72 BCR-1)

I'M STILL SEARCHING Glass Tiger—EMI 50116
[Alan Frew/Michael Hanson/Sam Reid] [ASC] (4/9/88 BC-31)

I'M STILL STANDING Elton John—Geffen 29639
[Elton John/Bernie Taupin] [BMI] (5/7/83 BC-12)

I'M STILL WAITING Diana Ross—Motown 1192 [Deke Richards] [ASC] (10/30/71 BCR-62)

I'M STONE IN LOVE WITH YOU The Stylistics—Avco 4603
[Thom Bell/Tony Bell/Linda Creed] [BMI] (10/7/72 BCR-9)

I'M TELLING YOU NOW Freddie And The Dreamers—Tower 125
[Freddie Garrity/Mitch Murray] [ASC] (3/13/65 BCR-1)

I'M THAT TYPE OF GUY LL Cool J—Def Jam 68902
[Steve Ettinger/Dwayne Simon/James Todd Smith] [ASC] (6/10/89 BC-15)

I'M THE BOSS Burl Ives—Decca 31504 [Harlan Howard] [BMI] (6/8/63 R-83)

—I'M THE GIRL ON WOLVERTON MOUNTAIN see: WOLVERTON MOUNTAIN

I'M THE LEADER OF THE GANG Brownsville Station—Big Tree 15005
[Gary Glitter/Mike Leander] [BMI] (5/18/74 BCR-26)

I'M THE LONELY ONE Cliff Richard—Epic 9670
[Gordon Mills] [BMI] (4/18/64 BC-90)

I'M THE MIDNIGHT SPECIAL Clarence Carter—Fame 330
[Larry Chambers/George Henry Jackson/Argentry Mitchell/Raymond Moore] [BMI] (12/8/73 C-87)

I'M THE ONE Gerry And The Pacemakers—Laurie 3233
[Gerry Marsden] [BMI] (7/11/64 B-82)

I'M THE ONE Roberta Flack—Atlantic 4068
[William Eaton/Ralph MacDonald/William Salter] [ASC] (7/24/82 BC-36)

I'M THE ONE WHO LOVES YOU The Impressions—ABC-Paramount 10386
[Curtis Mayfield] [BMI] (2/9/63 BR-73)

I'M THE ONLY ONE Lobo—Big Tree 116 [Kent LaVoie] (TSW) [ASC] (6/12/71 BCR-39)

I'M THE SKY Eddie Rambeau—DynoVoice 217
[Norma Kutzer*/Norma Tanega] [BMI] (4/2/66 CR-97)

I'M THROUGH WITH LOVE Eric Carmen—Geffen 29032
[Eric Carmen] [BMI] (4/20/85 BC-79)

I'M TIRED Ray Peterson—RCA Victor 47-7845
[A.R. Peddy/Ray Price/Mel Tillis] [BMI] (1/30/61 R-74)

I'M TIRED Savoy Brown—Parrot 40042 [Chris Youlden] [ASC] (11/22/69 BCR-42)

I'M TOO FAR GONE (TO TURN AROUND) Bobby Bland—Duke 393
[Belford Hendricks/Clyde Otis] [BMI] (1/8/66 BCR-47)

I'M TOO SEXY Right Said Fred—Charisma 98671
[Fred Fairbrass/Richard Fairbrass/Rob Manzoli] [BMI] (12/21/91 BC-1)

I'M TOSSIN' AND TURNIN' AGAIN Bobby Lewis—Beltone 2023
[Bob Feldman/Jerry Goldstein/Richard Gottehrer] [BMI] (7/28/62 B-98)

I'M WAITING JUST FOR YOU *Pat Boone—Dot 15545*
[Henry Glover/Carolyn Leigh/Lucky Millinder] [BMI] (3/9/57 BCRt-16)*

I'M WAITING JUST FOR YOU *Hoagy Carmichael & Cass Daley—Decca 30260*
[Henry Glover/Carolyn Leigh/Lucky Millinder] [BMI] (5/11/57 Rt-49)*

I'M WALKIN' *Fats Domino—Imperial 5428*
[Dave Bartholomew/Fats Domino] [BMI] (3/2/57 BCtRt-5)

I'M WALKIN' *Ricky Nelson—Verve 10047*
[Dave Bartholomew/Fats Domino] [BMI] (5/6/57 BCtRt-12)

I'M WALKIN' *Larry Storch—Roulette 4014*
[Dave Bartholomew/Fats Domino] [BMI] (7/27/57 Rt-67)

I'M WALKING BEHIND YOU Crazy Otto—Decca 29753B
[Billy Reid] (Med) [ASC] (2/3/56 R-91) [I]

I'M WALKING OUT ON YOU Ruben Wright—Capitol 5588
[Ruben Wright] [BMI] (6/4/66 C-92)

(I'M WATCHING) EVERY LITTLE MOVE YOU MAKE Little Peggy March—RCA Victor 47-8302
[Paul Anka] [BMI] (2/1/64 BR-84)

I'M WITH YOU The "5" Royales—King 5329 [Lowman Pauling] [BMI] (6/11/60 C-97)

I'M WONDERING Stevie Wonder—Tamla 54157
[Henry Cosby/Sylvia Moy/Stevie Wonder] [ASC] (9/30/67 BCR-10)

I'M YOUR BABY TONIGHT Whitney Houston—Arista 2108
[Kenneth Edmonds/Antonio Reid] [BMI] (10/20/90 BC-1)

I'M YOUR BOOGIE MAN K C & The Sunshine Band—TK 1022
[Harry Wayne Casey/Rick Finch] [BMI] (2/26/77 BCR-1)

I'M YOUR BREAD MAKER, BABY Slim Harpo—Excello 2282
[Slim Harpo] [BMI] (12/17/66 C-100)

I'M YOUR HOOCHIE COOCHE MAN *Dion Di Muci—Columbia 42977*
[Willie Dixon] [BMI] (2/22/64 CR-68)

I'M YOUR HOOCHIE COOCHE MAN (PART 1) *Jimmy Smith—Verve 10426*
[Willie Dixon] [BMI] (8/6/66 BCR-93)

I'M YOUR MAN Wham!—Columbia 05721 [George Michael] [ASC] (11/30/85 BC-3)

I'M YOUR MAN Barry Manilow—RCA 14397
[Barry Manilow/Howard Lee Rice/Allan Rich] [BMI] (7/12/86 BC-69)

I'M YOUR MAN ROCK 'N' ROLL The Tarney/Spencer Band—Private Stock 45,108
[Trevor Spencer/Alan Tarney] [BMI] (7/24/76 C-71)

—I'M YOUR PART TIME LOVE see: PART TIME LOVE

I'M YOUR PUPPET James & Bobby Purify—Bell 648
[Spooner Oldham/Dan Penn] [BMI] (9/24/66 BCR-5)

I'M YOUR SUPERMAN All Sports Band—Radio 3871
[Michael Toste] [ASC] (11/28/81 B-93)

I'M YOURS Elvis Presley—RCA Victor 47-8657
[Hal Blair/Don Robertson] [ASC] (8/28/65 BCR-9)

I'M YOURS (USE ME ANYWAY YOU WANNA) Ike & Tina Turner—United Artists 50837
[Calvin Lane/Philip Reese] [BMI] (11/6/71 CR-80)

IMAGE - PART 1 Hank Levine And Orchestra—ABC-Paramount 10256
[Joe Glenn/Larry Greene*/Bob Sande] [BMI] (10/9/61 B-98) [I]

IMAGE OF A GIRL The Safaris With The Phantom's Band—Eldo 101
[Richard Clasky/Marvin Rosenberg] [BMI] (6/6/60 BCR-6)

IMAGINARY LOVER Atlanta Rhythm Section—Polydor 14459
[Buddy Buie/Dean Daughtry/Robert Nix] [BMI] (2/25/78 BCR-7)

IMAGINATION The Quotations—Verve 10245
[Johnny Burke/Jimmy Van Heusen] [ASC] (1/13/62 CR-72)

IMAGINATION Belouis Some—Capitol 5464 [Belouis Some] [ASC] (5/4/85 B-88)

IMAGINATION Xymox—Wing 873 000
[Ronny Moorings/Anka Wolbert] [BMI] (3/3/90 BC-81)

IMAGINE *John Lennon Plastic Ono Band—Apple 1840*
[John Lennon] [GL] (10/16/71 BCR-1)

IMAGINE *Tracie Spencer—Capitol 44268*
[John Lennon] [GL] (2/11/89 BC-82)

IMAGINE THAT Patsy Cline—Decca 31377 [Justin Tubb] [BMI] (5/5/62 BCR-78)

IMAGINE THE SWAN The Zombies—Date 1644
[Rod Argent/Chris White] [BMI] (5/17/69 CR-77)

THE IMMIGRANT Neil Sedaka—Rocket/MCA 40370
[Phil Cody/Neil Sedaka] [BMI] (3/22/75 BCR-22)

IMMIGRANT SONG Led Zeppelin—Atlantic 2777
[Jimmy Page/Robert Plant] [ASC] (11/14/70 BCR-8)

IMMIGRATION MAN Graham Nash & David Crosby—Atlantic 2873
[Graham Nash] [BMI] (5/6/72 BCR-25)

IMPOSSIBLE Gloria Lynne—Everest 19418 [B.F. Flip/Ollie Jones] [BMI] (9/11/61 B-95)

THE IMPOSSIBLE DREAM (THE QUEST) *Jack Jones—Kapp 755*
[Joseph Darion/Mitch Leigh] [ASC] (6/4/66 BCR-32)

THE IMPOSSIBLE DREAM *The Hesitations—Kapp 899*
[Joseph Darion/Mitch Leigh] [ASC] (3/16/68 BCR-38)

THE IMPOSSIBLE DREAM *Roger Williams—Kapp 907*
[Mitch Leigh] [ASC] (7/13/68 BCR-51) [IM]

THE IMPOSSIBLE HAPPENED Little Peggy March—RCA Victor 47-8267
[Luigi Creatore/Hugo Peretti/George David Weiss] [ASC] (11/16/63 BCR-52)

IMPOSSIBLE MISSION (MISSION IMPOSSIBLE) Soul Survivors—Crimson 1016
[Kenneth Gamble/Leon Huff] [BMI] (4/20/68 BCR-68)

IMPULSIVE Wilson Phillips—SBK 07337
[Steve Kipner/Clif Magness] [ASC] (10/13/90 BC-3)

IN A BIG COUNTRY Big Country—Mercury 814467
[William Stuart Adamson/Mark Brzezicki/Anthony Earl Butler/Bruce William Watson] [ASC] (10/22/83 BC-11)

IN A BROKEN DREAM Python Lee Jackson—GNP Crescendo 449
[David Keith Bentley] [ASC] (5/27/72 BCR-56)

IN-A-GADDA-DA-VIDA *Iron Butterfly—Atco 6606 [Doug Ingle] [BMI] (8/24/68 BCR-30)*

IN-A-GADDA-DA-VIDA *Iron Butterfly—Atco 6606 [Doug Ingle] [BMI] (5/10/69 BC-68)*

IN A GARDEN OF ROSES Joni James—MGM 11753
[Mary Jane Babbitt] [BMI] (7/3/54 C-PRE)

IN A LITTLE SPANISH TOWN *Russ Carlyle And His Orchestra—"X" 0055*
[Mabel Wayne] [NA] (10/2/54 CtR-PRE) [IM]

IN A LITTLE SPANISH TOWN *David Carroll & His Orchestra—Mercury 70444*
[Mabel Wayne] [NA] (10/4/54 CtR-PRE) [IM]

IN A LITTLE SPANISH TOWN *Al Lombardy—Dot 15227*
[Mabel Wayne] [NA] (10/4/54 R-PRE) [IM]

IN A LITTLE SPANISH TOWN *The Smith Brothers—"X" 0070*
[Sam Lewis/Mabel Wayne/Joe Young] [NA] (11/1/54 Rt-PRE)

IN A LITTLE SPANISH TOWN ('TWAS ON A NIGHT LIKE THIS)
Lawrence Welk & His Sparklers—Coral 61287
[Sam Lewis/Mabel Wayne/Joe Young] [NA] (11/15/54 Rt-PRE)

IN A LITTLE SPANISH TOWN ('TWAS ON A NIGHT LIKE THIS)
Bing Crosby And The Buddy Cole Trio—Decca 29850
[Sam Lewis/Mabel Wayne/Joe Young] [NA] (3/16/56 BCR-18)

IN A LITTLE SPANISH TOWN CHA CHA *Sy Oliver—Jubilee 5439*
[Mabel Wayne] [ASC] (12/20/58 C-95) [IM]

IN A LITTLE SPANISH TOWN *The Blue Diamonds—London 2002*
[Sam Lewis/Mabel Wayne/Joe Young] [NA] (9/11/61 R-74)

IN A MOMENT The Intrigues—Yew 1001
[Alfred Brown/Ronald Hamilton/James Harris/James Lee] [BMI] (7/26/69 BCR-28)

IN A PERSIAN MARKET LeRoy Holmes And His Orchestra—MGM 12733
[Albert W. Ketelbey] [BMI] (11/17/58 R-93) [IWM]

IN A SHANTY IN OLD SHANTY TOWN *Somethin' Smith & The Redheads—Epic 9168*
[Jack Little/Ira Schuster/Joe Young] [ASC] (5/25/56 BCRt-24)

IN A SHANTY IN OLD SHANTY TOWN *Johnny Long & His Orchestra—Decca 23622*
[Jack Little/Ira Schuster/Joe Young] [ASC] (7/6/56 Rt-24)

IN AMERICA Charlie Daniels Band—Epic 50888
[Tom Crain/Charlie Daniels/Joel DiGregorio/Fred Edwards/Charles Hayward/James W. Marshall] [BMI] (5/31/80 BCR-10)

IN AND OUT OF LOVE Diana Ross And The Supremes—Motown 1116
[Lamont Dozier/Brian Holland/Eddie Holland] [BMI] (11/11/67 BCR-8)

IN AND OUT OF LOVE Bon Jovi—Mercury 880951 [Jon Bon Jovi] [ASC] (8/3/85 BC-69)

IN AND OUT OF MY LIFE Martha Reeves & The Vandellas—Gordy 7113
[Lawrence Brown/George Gordy] [ASC] (2/5/72 C-70)

IN ANOTHER LAND Bill Wyman—London 907 [Bill Wyman] [BMI] (12/9/67 BCR-52)

IN BETWEEN DAYS The Cure—Elektra 69604 [Robert James Smith] [ASC] (2/15/86 B-99)

IN BETWEEN TEARS Lenny Miles—Scepter 1218
[Luther Dixon/Stanley Kahan/Eddie Snyder] [BMI] (5/8/61 B-84)

THE "IN" CROWD *Dobie Gray—Charger 105 [Billy Page] [BMI] (1/2/65 BCR-13)*

THE "IN" CROWD *Ramsey Lewis Trio—Argo 5506*
[Billy Page] [BMI] (7/31/65 BCR-4) [IWM]

—IN DER ALTEN HAFENBAR see: IVORY RAG

IN DER NACHT IST DER MENSCH NICHT GERN ALLEINE *Crazy Otto—Polydor 22009B*
[Franz Grothe] (Med) [NA] (1/17/55 R-1) [IM]

IN DER NACHT IST DER MENSCH NICHT GERN ALLEINE
Johnny Maddox And The Rhythmasters—Dot 15325
[Franz Grothe] (Med) [NA] (1/24/55 BCR-1) [IM]

—IN DER SCHWEIZ see: IN THE ALPS

IN DREAMS Roy Orbison—Monument 806 [Roy Orbison] [BMI] (2/9/63 BCR-5)

IN FOR THE NIGHT Dirt Band—United Artists 1228
[Ed Sanford/John Townsend] [BMI] (8/26/78 BC-76)

IN FRANCE THEY KISS ON MAIN STREET Joni Mitchell—Asylum 45296
[Joni Mitchell] [ASC] (2/7/76 BCR-55)

IN GOD'S COUNTRY U2—Island 99385
[Adam Clayton/Dave Evans/Paul Hewson/Larry Mullen] [ASC] (12/5/87 BC-44)

IN HEAVEN THERE IS NO BEER Clean Living—Vanguard 35162
[Ernst Neubach/Ralph Siegel] [BMI] (10/21/72 BCR-31)

IN IT FOR LOVE England Dan & John Ford Coley—Big Tree 17002
[Greg Guidry/Denny Henson] [ASC] (3/8/80 B-75)

IN LOVE The Ames Brothers—RCA Victor 47-7142
[Roy C. Bennett/Sid Tepper] [ASC] (1/20/58 R-59)

IN LOVE WITH LOVE Debbie Harry—Geffen 28476
[Deborah Harry/Christopher Stein] [ASC] (7/4/87 BC-70)

IN MY DREAMS Dokken—Elektra 69563
[Mick Brown/Don Dokken/George Lynch/Jeff Pilson] [ASC] (2/22/86 BC-77)

IN MY DREAMS REO Speedwagon—Epic 07255
[Kevin Cronin/Thomas F. Kelly] [ASC] (7/18/87 BC-18)

IN MY DREAMS The Party—Hollywood 64832
[Mick Brown/Don Dokken/George Lynch/Jeff Pilson] [ASC] (11/9/91 BC-24)

IN MY EYES Stevie B—LMR 74004
[Stevie B] [BMI] (5/27/89 B-37)

IN MY FATHER'S FOOTSTEPS Terry Jacks—Private Stock 45,094
[Mel Mandel/Norman Sachs] [BMI] (6/26/76 CR-74)

IN MY HEART The Timetones—Times Square 421
[Clarence Johnson/Claude Smith] [BMI] (4/24/61 BR-51)

IN MY HOUSE Mary Jane Girls—Gordy 1741 [Rick James] [ASC] (3/9/85 BC-5)

IN MY LITTLE CORNER OF THE WORLD Anita Bryant—Carlton 530
[Bob Hilliard/Lee Pockriss] [ASC] (7/4/60 BCR-10)

IN MY LONELY ROOM Martha & The Vandellas—Gordy 7031
[Lamont Dozier/Brian Holland/Eddie Holland] [BMI] (4/11/64 BCR-42)

IN MY ROOM *The Beach Boys—Capitol 5069*
[Gary Usher/Brian Wilson] [BMI] (11/2/63 BCR-23)

IN MY ROOM *Sagittarius—Together 105*
[Gary Usher/Brian Wilson] [BMI] (7/12/69 BCR-75)

IN MY ROOM (EL AMOR) Verdelle Smith—Capitol 5567
[Lee Pockriss/Joaquin Prieto/Paul Vance] [ASC] (2/5/66 BCR-62) [FDE]

IN NEED OF A FRIEND The Cowsills—MGM 13909
[Bill Cowsill/Bob Cowsill] [BMI] (3/16/68 BCR-45)

IN NEON Elton John—Geffen 29111
[Elton John/Bernie Taupin] [BMI] (12/1/84 BC-34)

—IN OLD LISBON see: LISBON ANTIGUA

IN OUR TIME Nancy Sinatra—Reprise 0514 [Lee Hazlewood] [ASC] (9/17/66 BCR-46)

IN PARADISE Laissez Faire—Metropolitan 4475 [Joey Gold] [ASC] (12/7/91 B-64)

IN SELF DEFENSE Cornel Gunter and The Flairs—ABC-Paramount 9698
[Joe (2) Thomas] [BMI] (5/4/56 R-25)

IN SOME TIME Ronnie Dove—Diamond 240 [Lee Hazlewood] [ASC] (3/16/68 BCR-94)

IN THE AIR TONIGHT Phil Collins—Atlantic 3824 [Phil Collins] [ASC] (5/30/81 BCR-17)

IN THE ALPS (IN DER SCHWEIZ)
Lawrence Welk And His Champagne Music And The McGuire Sisters—Coral 61670
[Hans Carste/Mann Curtis] [ASC] (7/13/56 BR-63) [FET]

IN THE ARMS OF LOVE Andy Williams—Columbia 43737
[Ray Evans/Jay Livingston/Henry Mancini] [ASC] (8/27/66 BCR-49)

IN THE ARMS OF MY LOVE Joe Valino—Vik 0257
[Fred Ebb/Paul Klein/Ludwig van Beethoven] [BMI] (2/16/57 R-73)

IN THE BAD, BAD OLD DAYS (BEFORE YOU LOVED ME) The Foundations—Uni 55117
[Tony Macaulay/John Macleod] [ASC] (3/29/69 BCR-24)

IN THE BASEMENT - PART 1 Etta James & Sugar Pie Desanto—Cadet 5539
[Billy Davis/Raynard Miner/Carl William Smith] [BMI] (7/23/66 BC-93)

IN THE BEGINNING Frankie Laine—Columbia 40378
[Dorcas Cochran/Kay Twomey/Ben Weisman/Fred Wise] [ASC] (12/4/54 C-39)

IN THE BOTTLE Brother To Brother—Turbo 039 [Gil Scott-Heron] [ASC] (9/14/74 BCR-46)

IN THE BUSH Musique—Prelude 71110
[Patrick Adams/Sandy Cooper] [ASC] (10/7/78 BCR-44)

IN THE CHAPEL IN THE MOONLIGHT *Kitty Kallen—Decca 29130*
[Billy Hill] [ASC] (7/3/54 BCR-5)

IN THE CHAPEL IN THE MOONLIGHT *The Orioles—Jubilee 5154*
[Billy Hill] [ASC] (10/4/54 R-PRE)

CHAPEL IN THE MOONLIGHT *The Bachelors—London 9793*
[Billy Hill] [ASC] (10/2/65 BCR-32)

IN THE CHAPEL IN THE MOONLIGHT *Dean Martin—Reprise 0601*
[Billy Hill] [ASC] (7/1/67 BCR-25)

(IN THE) COLD LIGHT OF DAY Gene Pitney—Musicor 1200
[Scott English/Larry Weiss] [BMI] (10/1/66 CR-83)

IN THE COURT OF THE CRIMSON KING King Crimson—Atlantic 2703
[Robert Fripp*/Michael Giles*/Greg Lake*/Ian McDonald/Peter Sinfield] [BMI] (1/31/70 B-80)

IN THE DARK Billy Squier—Capitol 5040 [Billy Squier] [ASC] (9/12/81 BCR-35)

IN THE DRIVERS SEAT John Schneider—Scotti Brothers 03062
[Jeff Harrington/Jeff Pennig] [ASC] (8/14/82 B-72)

IN THE GHETTO *Elvis Presley—RCA Victor 47-9741 [Mac Davis] [BMI] (5/3/69 BCR-1)*

IN THE GHETTO *Candi Staton—Fame 91000 [Mac Davis] [BMI] (6/10/72 BCR-36)*

IN THE HEART OF A FOOL Johnnie Ray—Cadence 1387
[Mel Tillis/Wayne Walker] [BMI] (10/17/60 R-92)

IN THE HEAT OF THE NIGHT Ray Charles—ABC 10970
[Alan Bergman/Marilyn Bergman/Quincy Jones] [ASC] (8/26/67 BCR-33)

IN THE JAILHOUSE NOW Webb Pierce—Decca 29391
[Jimmie Rodgers] [BMI] (3/21/55 R-66)

IN THE MEANTIME Georgie Fame And The Blue Flames—Imperial 66104
[John Burch] [ASC] (5/1/65 BR-97)

IN THE MIDDLE Tim Moore—Asylum 45394 [Tim Moore] [NA] (7/9/77 BCR-68)

IN THE MIDDLE OF A DARK DARK NIGHT Guy Mitchell—Columbia 40940
[Bob Merrill] [ASC] (7/6/57 R-79)

IN THE MIDDLE OF A HEARTACHE Wanda Jackson—Capitol 4635
[Laurie Christenson/Pat Franzese/Wanda Jackson] [BMI] (10/9/61 BCR-25)

IN THE MIDDLE OF AN ISLAND
Tony Bennett with Ray Ellis and His Orchestra—Columbia 40965
[Nick Acquaviva/Ted Varnick] [ASC] (7/20/57 BCRt-5)

IN THE MIDDLE OF AN ISLAND *"Tennessee" Ernie Ford—Capitol 3762*
[Nick Acquaviva/Ted Varnick] [ASC] (7/27/57 BRt-5)

IN THE MIDDLE OF AN ISLAND *Stan Wilson—Verve 10068*
[Nick Acquaviva/Ted Varnick] [ASC] (8/3/57 Rt-6)

IN THE MIDDLE OF AN ISLAND *The Anita Kerr Quartet—Decca 30417*
[Nick Acquaviva/Ted Varnick] [ASC] (8/26/57 Rt-6)

IN THE MIDDLE OF THE HOUSE *Rusty Draper—Mercury 70921*
[Bob Hilliard] [ASC] (8/25/56 BCtRt-20)

IN THE MIDDLE OF THE HOUSE
Vaughn Monroe with Joe Reisman's Orchestra—RCA Victor 47-6619
[Bob Hilliard] [ASC] (8/25/56 BCtRt-21)

IN THE MIDDLE OF THE HOUSE *Milton Berle—Coral 61691*
[Bob Hilliard] [ASC] (9/1/56 Rt-36)

IN THE MIDNIGHT HOUR *Wilson Pickett—Atlantic 2289*
[Steve Cropper/Wilson Pickett] [BMI] (6/26/65 BCR-19)

IN THE MIDNIGHT HOUR *The Wanted—A&M 844*
[Steve Cropper/Wilson Pickett] [BMI] (4/8/67 C-78)

IN THE MIDNIGHT HOUR *The Mirettes—Revue 11004*
[Steve Cropper/Wilson Pickett] [BMI] (2/10/68 BCR-45)

IN THE MIDNIGHT HOUR *Cross Country—Atco 6934*
[Steve Cropper/Wilson Pickett] [BMI] (8/4/73 BCR-18)

IN THE MIDNIGHT HOUR *Samantha Sang—United Artists 1313*
[Steve Cropper/Wilson Pickett] [BMI] (7/28/79 B-88)

IN THE MISTY MOONLIGHT *Jerry Wallace—Challenge 59246*
[Cindy Walker] [BMI] (7/18/64 BCR-19)

IN THE MISTY MOONLIGHT *Dean Martin—Reprise 0640*
[Cindy Walker] [BMI] (12/2/67 BCR-46)

IN THE MOOD *Crazy Otto—Decca 29449 [Joe Garland] [ASC] (3/21/55 R-44) [IM]*

IN THE MOOD *Matys Brothers—Decca 29838*
[Joe Garland/Andy Razaf] [ASC] (4/13/56 R-76)

IN THE MOOD *Ernie Fields Orch.—Rendezvous 110*
[Joe Garland] [ASC] (9/21/59 BCR-3) [IM]

IN THE MOOD *Bette Midler—Atlantic 3004*
[Joe Garland/Barry Manilow/Bette Midler/Andy Razaf] [ASC] (1/19/74 BCR-31)

IN THE MOOD *Henhouse Five Plus Too—Warner Bros. 8301*
[Joe Garland/Andy Razaf] [ASC] (12/25/76 BCR-37)

IN THE MOOD *Frank Barber Orchestra—Victory 1001*
[Joe Garland] (Med) [ASC] (5/8/82 B-61) [IM]

IN THE MOOD *Frank Barber Orchestra—Victory 1001*
[Joe Garland] (Med) [ASC] (5/8/82 B-61) [IM]

IN THE MOOD *Larry Elgart And His Manhattan Swing Orchestra—RCA 13219*
[Joe Garland] (Med) [ASC] (6/5/82 BC-31) [IM]

IN THE MOOD *Jive Bunny And The Mastermixers—Music Factory 99140*
[Joe Garland] (Med) [ASC] (10/28/89 BC-11) [IM]

IN THE MOOD *Jive Bunny And The Mastermixers—Music Factory 99140*
[Joe Garland] (Med) [ASC] (10/28/89 BC-11) [IM]

IN THE MOOD Rush—Mercury 73873 [Geddy Lee] (Med) [ASC] (1/8/77 B-88)

IN THE MOOD Tyrone Davis—Columbia 10904
[Darryl Ellis/Ruben Locke Jr./Paul Richmond] [BMI] (4/7/79 R-82)

IN THE MOOD Robert Plant—Atlantic 99820
[Robbie Blunt/Paul Martinez/Robert Plant] [ASC] (11/19/83 BC-36)

IN THE NAME OF LOVE Ralph MacDonald (with Bill Withers)—Polydor 881221
[Ralph MacDonald/William Salter/Bill Withers] [ASC] (9/1/84 BC-54)

IN THE NAVY Village People—Casablanca 973
[Henri Belolo/Jacques Morali/Victor Willis] [BMI] (3/17/79 BCR-2)

IN THE QUIET MORNING (FOR JANIS JOPLIN) Joan Baez–A&M 1362
[Mimi Farina] [ASC] (7/22/72 BCR-62)

IN THE RAIN *The Dramatics–Volt 4075 [Tony Hester] [BMI] (2/19/72 BCR-3)*

IN THE RAIN *Arthur Prysock–Old Town 100 [Tony Hester] [BMI] (9/29/73 CR-95)*

IN THE ROOM Pat Boone–Dot 16416
[Jan Crutchfield] [BMI] (1/5/63 R-95)

IN THE SHAPE OF A HEART Jackson Browne–Asylum 69543
[Jackson Browne] [ASC] (6/7/86 BC-70)

IN THE STILL OF THE NITE *The Five Satins–Ember 1005*
[Fred Parris] [BMI] (8/25/56 BCR-26)

IN THE STILL OF THE NITE *The Five Satins–Ember 1005*
[Fred Parris] [BMI] (1/4/60 B-81)

IN THE STILL OF THE NITE/"I'LL REMEMBER" *The Five Satins–Ember 1005*
[Fred Parris] [BMI] (1/23/61 B-99)

I'LL REMEMBER (IN THE STILL OF THE NIGHT) *Santo & Johnny–Canadian-American 164*
[Fred Parris] [BMI] (1/18/64 BCR-58) [IWM]

IN THE STILL OF THE NIGHT *Paul Anka–RCA Victor 74-0126*
[Fred Parris] [BMI] (3/15/69 BCR-59)

IN THE STILL OF THE NIGHT *Fred Parris & The Five Satins–Elektra 47411*
[Fred Parris] (Med) [BMI] (2/27/82 BC-71)

IN THE STILL OF THE NIGHT Dion And The Belmonts–Laurie 3059
[Cole Porter] [ASC] (7/4/60 BCR-35)

IN THE STONE Earth, Wind & Fire–ARC 11093
[David Foster/Maurice White/Allee Willis] [ASC] (10/13/79 BCR-58)

IN THE SUMMER OF HIS YEARS *Connie Francis–MGM 13203*
[Herbert Kretzmer/David Lee] [ASC] (12/21/63 BCtR-30)

IN THE SUMMER OF HIS YEARS *Millicent Martin–ABC-Paramount 10514*
[Herbert Kretzmer/David Lee] [ASC] (12/21/63 CtR-57)

IN THE SUMMER OF HIS YEARS *Toni Arden–Decca 31576*
[Herbert Kretzmer/David Lee] [ASC] (12/21/63 R-89)

IN THE SUMMERTIME Mungo Jerry–Janus 125 [Ray Dorset] [ASC] (7/11/70 BCR-1)

IN THE TIME OF OUR LIVES Iron Butterfly–Atco 6676
[Ron Bushy/Doug Ingle] [BMI] (7/12/69 BCR-96)

IN THE WINTER Janis Ian–Columbia 10228 [Janis Ian] [BMI] (11/29/75 C-97)

IN THE YEAR 2525 (EXORDIUM & TERMINUS) Zager & Evans–RCA Victor 74-0174
[Rick Evans] [BMI] (6/14/69 BCR-1)

IN THEE Blue Öyster Cult–Columbia 11055 [Allen Lanier] [ASC] (9/1/79 BC-74)

IN THESE CHANGING TIMES Four Tops–Motown 1185
[Pam Sawyer/Frank Edward Wilson] [BMI] (6/26/71 BR-67)

IN THIS WHOLE WIDE WORLD The Four Preps–Capitol 4599
[Jacques Cascales/Gene Roland] (Med) [BMI] (8/14/61 BCR-14)

IN TIME Steve Lawrence–United Artists 335
[Billy Barberis/Teddy Randazzo/Pyotr Ilyich Tchaikovsky/Bobby Weinstein] [BMI] (7/3/61 BCR-37)

IN TIME Engelbert Humperdinck–Parrot 40071
[Don Backy/Gil King/Detto Mariano/Norman Newell] [ASC] (8/5/72 BCR-69) [FET]

IN TOO DEEP Genesis–Atlantic 89316
[Tony Banks/Phil Collins/Mike Rutherford] [BMI] (4/25/87 BC-3)

IN YOUR ARMS Little Caesar–DGC 19003
[Gregg Sutton/Ron Young] [ASC] (3/2/91 BC-75)

IN YOUR EYES *Peter Gabriel–Geffen 28622 [Peter Gabriel] [BMI] (8/30/86 BC-24)*

IN YOUR EYES *Peter Gabriel–WTG 31-68936 [Peter Gabriel] [BMI] (5/20/89 BC-39)*

IN YOUR LETTER REO Speedwagon–Epic 02457 [Gary Richrath] [ASC] (8/8/81 BCR-20)

IN YOUR ROOM Bangles–Columbia 08090
[Susanna Hoffs/Thomas F. Kelly/Billy Steinberg] [ASC] (10/15/88 BC-5)

IN YOUR SOUL Corey Hart–EMI 50134 [Corey Hart] [ASC] (6/11/88 BC-38)

INCENSE AND PEPPERMINTS Strawberry Alarm Clock–Uni 55018
[John S. Carter/Tim Gilbert] [ASC] (9/23/67 BCR-1)

INDESCRIBABLY BLUE
Elvis Presley With The Jordanaires And The Imperials Quartet –RCA Victor 47-9056
[Darrell Glenn] [BMI] (1/21/67 BCR-26)

INDESTRUCTIBLE Four Tops–Arista 1-9706
[Harvey Price/Bobby Sandstrom] [ASC] (8/20/88 BC-35)

INDIAN GIVER 1910 Fruitgum Co.–Buddah 91
[Bobby Bloom/Ritchie Cordell/Bo Gentry] [BMI] (1/18/69 BCR-3)

INDIAN LADY Lou Christie–Buddah 192 [Stan Vincent] (TSW) [BMI] (10/24/70 CR-75)

INDIAN LAKE The Cowsills–MGM 13944 [Tony Romeo] [BMI] (5/25/68 BCR-6)

INDIAN LOVE CALL *Ernie Freeman–Imperial 5518*
[Rudolf Friml] [ASC] (5/19/58 BR-59) [IM]

INDIAN LOVE CALL *Ray Stevens–Barnaby 616*
[Rudolf Friml/Oscar Hammerstein/Otto Harbach] [ASC] (9/20/75 BCR-63)

(THE LAMENT OF THE CHEROKEE) INDIAN RESERVATION *Don Fardon–GNP Crescendo 405*
[John D. Loudermilk] [BMI] (8/24/68 BCR-18)

INDIAN RESERVATION (THE LAMENT OF THE CHEROKEE) *Raiders–Columbia 45332*
[John D. Loudermilk] [BMI] (4/10/71 BCR-1)

INDIAN SUMMER Audience–Elektra 45732
[Howard Werth/Trevor Williams] [ASC] (7/17/71 BCR-74)

INDIAN SUMMER Poco–ABC 12295 [Paul Cotton] [ASC] (7/23/77 BCR-50)

INDIANA WALTZ Jack Scott–Guaranteed 209 [Fred Rose] [ASC] (6/20/60 R-82)

INDIANA WANTS ME R. Dean Taylor–Rare Earth 5013
[R. Dean Taylor] [BMI] (8/29/70 BCR-1)

INDUSTRIAL DISEASE Dire Straits–Warner Bros. 29880
[Mark Knopfler] [ASC] (1/8/83 B-75)

INFATUATION (SCAPRICCIATIELLO) *Renato Carosone–Capitol 71001*
[Fernando Albano/Pacifico Vento] [NA] (2/3/56 CRt-47) [F]

INFATUATION (SCAPRICCIATIELLO)
Paul Weston & His Music From Hollywood–Columbia 40675
[Fernando Albano] [NA] (4/13/56 Rt-71) [IM]

INFATUATION *Dick Contino–Mercury 70830 [Fernando Albano] [NA] (4/27/56 Rt-71) [IM]*

INFATUATION Rod Stewart–Warner Bros. 29256
[Duane Hitchings/Roland Robinson/Rod Stewart] [ASC] (5/26/84 BC-6)

INFORMATION Eric Martin–Capitol 5502
[Tony Fanucchi/Randall Darnell Jackson/Michael Mani/Eric Martin] [ASC] (8/24/85 BC-82)

INJURED IN THE GAME OF LOVE Donnie Iris–HME 04734
[Mark Avsec/Donnie Iris] [ASC] (3/23/85 B-91)

INKY DINKY SPIDER (THE SPIDER SONG)
The Kids Next Door–4 Corners Of The World 129
[Murray Wecht] [BMI] (10/9/65 BCR-66)

INNAMORATA *Frank Verna–Decca 29767*
[Jack Brooks/Harry Warren] [ASC] (2/3/56 Rt-24)

INNAMORATA (SWEETHEART) *Jerry Vale–Columbia 40634*
[Jack Brooks/Harry Warren] [ASC] (2/3/56 BCtRt-17)

INNAMORATA (SWEETHEART) *Dean Martin–Capitol 3352*
[Jack Brooks/Harry Warren] [ASC] (2/24/56 BCtRt-17)

INNER CITY BLUES (MAKE ME WANNA HOLLER) Marvin Gaye–Tamla 54209
[Marvin Gaye/James Nyx] [ASC] (10/2/71 BCR-6)

THE INNER LIGHT The Beatles–Capitol 2138 [George Harrison] [ASC] (3/30/68 B-96)

INNOCENT The Whispers–Capitol 44593
[Robert Brookins/Gordon Jones/Marva King] [ASC] (8/4/90 BC-51)

INNOCENT EYES Graham Nash–Atlantic 89434
[Paul Steven Bliss] [ASC] (4/26/86 BC-84)

AN INNOCENT MAN Billy Joel–Columbia 04259 [Billy Joel] [ASC] (12/17/83 BC-10)

INSANITY COMES QUIETLY TO THE STRUCTURED MIND Janis Ian–Verve Forecast 5072
[Janis Ian] [BMI] (12/9/67 CR-82)

INSATIABLE Prince–Paisley Park 4-19090 [Prince] [ASC] (12/14/91 B-77)

INSEPARABLE Natalie Cole–Capitol 4193
[Charles Henry Jackson Jr./Marvin Yancy] [ASC] (12/13/75 BCR-32)

INSIDE A DREAM Jane Wiedlin–EMI 50145
[Gardner Cole/Jane Wiedlin] [BMI] (8/27/88 BC-56)

INSIDE-LOOKING OUT The Animals–MGM 13468
[Eric Burdon/Chas Chandler/Alan Lomax‡/Traditional] [BMI] (2/26/66 BCR-32)

INSIDE LOVE (SO PERSONAL) George Benson–Warner Bros. 29649
[Michael Jones] [BMI] (5/14/83 BC-40)

–INSIDE ME/INSIDE YOU see: SOMETHING REAL

INSIDE MY LOVE Minnie Riperton–Epic 50128
[Minnie Riperton/Richard Rudolph/Leon Ware] [BMI] (8/2/75 BC-72)

INSIDE OF YOU Ray, Goodman & Brown–Polydor 2077
[Al Goodman/Henrietta Goodman/Walter Lee Morris/Harry Ray] [BMI] (5/10/80 BCR-66)

INSIDE OUTSIDE The Cover Girls–Fever 1916
[Albert Cabrera/Tony Moran/Andy Tripoli] [BMI] (7/23/88 BC-55)

INSIDE YOU (PART 1) The Isley Brothers–T-Neck 5 02351
[Ernie Isley/Marvin Isley/O'Kelly Isley/Ronald Isley/Rudolph Isley/Chris Jasper] [ASC] (11/14/81 R-82)

INSPIRATION Paul Williams–A&M 1479
[Ken Ascher/Paul Williams] [ASC] (12/8/73 C-69)

INSTANT KARMA (WE ALL SHINE ON) John Ono Lennon–Apple 1818
[John Lennon] [GL] (2/21/70 BCR-3)

INSTANT REPLAY Dan Hartman–Blue Sky 2772 [Dan Hartman] [BMI] (10/14/78 BCR-22)

INSTIGATING (TROUBLE MAKING FOOL) The Whatnauts–GSF 6897
[Wesaline Hopson Kerr] [BMI] (5/5/73 C-96)

INSULT TO INJURY Timi Yuro–Liberty 55552
[Lockie Edwards/Eddie Snyder/June Tansey/Larry Weiss] [BMI] (3/23/63 BR-81)

INTERMISSION RIFF Bernie Lowe Orchestra–Cameo 153
[Ray Wetzel] [BMI] (11/24/58 B-61) [I]

INTERNATIONAL PLAYBOY Wilson Pickett–Atlantic 2961
[Bernard Broomer/Gene Dozier/Lee Phillips/Bunny Sigler] [BMI] (4/21/73 R-93)

INTO EACH LIFE SOME RAIN MUST FALL Crazy Otto–Decca 29753B
[Doris Fisher/Allan Roberts] (Med) [ASC] (2/3/56 R-91) [IWM]

INTO MY LOVE Greg Guidry–Columbia 02984
[Cindy Guidry/Greg Guidry] [ASC] (7/17/82 B-92)

INTO MY SECRET Alisha–RCA 5219 [Mike Leeson/Peter Vale] [BMI] (8/22/87 B-97)

INTO THE GREAT WIDE OPEN Tom Petty and the Heartbreakers–MCA 54131
[Jeff Lynne/Tom Petty] [ASC] (11/16/91 BC-68)

INTO THE MYSTIC Johnny Rivers–Imperial 66448 [Van Morrison] [BMI] (5/2/70 BCR-38)

INTO THE NIGHT The Dream Weavers–Decca 29818
[Wade Buff/Lee Turner] [ASC] (3/2/56 BR-82)

INTO THE NIGHT *Benny Mardones—Polydor 2091*
[Benny Mardones/Robert Tepper] [ASC] (6/7/80 BCR-9)

INTO THE NIGHT *Benny Mardones—Polydor 889368*
[Benny Mardones/Robert Tepper] [ASC] (5/6/89 BC-20)

INTO YOU Giant Steps—A&M 1256
[Colin Campsie/Gardner Cole/George McFarlane] [BMI] (1/28/89 BC-55)

INVINCIBLE Pat Benatar—Chrysalis 41507
[Simon Climie/Holly Knight] [ASC] (7/6/85 BC-9)

INVISIBLE Alison Moyet—Columbia 04781 [Lamont Dozier] [BMI] (3/9/85 BC-30)

INVISIBLE HANDS Kim Carnes—EMI America 8181
[Brian Fairweather/Martin Page] [ASC] (10/15/83 BC-34)

INVISIBLE TEARS The Ray Conniff Singers—Columbia 43061
[Ned Miller/Sue Miller] [BMI] (7/11/64 BCR-36)

INVISIBLE TOUCH Genesis—Atlantic 89407
[Tony Banks/Phil Collins/Mike Rutherford] [ASC] (5/31/86 BC-1)

INVITATION TO DANCE Kim Carnes—EMI America 8250
[Kim Carnes/Dave Ellingson/Brian Fairweather/Martin Page] [ASC] (1/19/85 BC-62)

INVITATION TO THE BLUES Ray Price—Columbia 41191
[Roger Miller] [BMI] (9/8/58 B-92)

IRMA LA DOUCE *Karen Chandler—Carlton 534*
[Alexandre Breffort/David William Heneker/Marguerite Monnot/
Julian Bensley More/Monty Norman] [ASC] (10/31/60 Rt-93)

IRMA LA DOUCE *Mantovani And His Orchestra—London 1947*
[Marguerite Monnot] [ASC] (10/31/60 Rt-93) [IM]

IRON MAN Black Sabbath—Warner Bros. 7530
[Terry Butler/Tony Iommi/Ozzy Osbourne/Bill Ward] [ASC] (1/29/72 BCR-52)

IRRESISTABLE YOU *Bobby Peterson—V-Tone 214*
[Luther Dixon/Al Kasha] [BMI] (9/10/60 BCR-67)

IRRESISTIBLE YOU *Bobby Darin—Atco 6214*
[Luther Dixon/Al Kasha] [BMI] (12/11/61 BCR-15)

IS A BLUE BIRD BLUE Conway Twitty—MGM 12911 [Dan Penn] [BMI] (6/13/60 BCR-27)

IS ANYBODY GOIN' TO SAN ANTONE Charley Pride—RCA Victor 47-9806
[Dave Kirby/Glenn Martin] [BMI] (3/14/70 BCR-70)

IS IT BECAUSE I'M BLACK Syl Johnson—Twilight 125
[Syl Johnson/James Leonard Jones/Glenn Watts] [BMI] (12/13/69 BR-63)

IS IT GOOD TO YOU Heavy D & The Boyz—MCA 54200
[Heavy D/Teddy Riley] [ASC] (11/23/91 B-32)

IS IT LOVE Mr. Mister—RCA 14313
[Steve George/John Lang/Pat Mastelotto/Richard Page] [ASC] (3/29/86 BC-8)

IS IT LOVE J.J. Fad—Ruthless 7-99257
[Juana Burns/Michelle Franklin] [ASC] (12/10/88 BC-71)

IS IT LOVE THAT WE'RE MISSIN' Quincy Jones—A&M 1743
[George Johnson/Debbie Smith] [BMI] (10/11/75 BC-66) [IWM]

IS IT ME? Barbara Mason—Arctic 116 [Barbara Mason] [BMI] (1/29/66 BR-95)

IS IT REALLY OVER? Jim Reeves—RCA Victor 47-8625
[Jim Reeves] [BMI] (8/7/65 BCR-62)

IS IT SOMETHING YOU'VE GOT Tyrone Davis—Dakar 605
[Barry Despenza/Carl Wolfolk] [BMI] (3/22/69 BCR-22)

IS IT TRUE Brenda Lee—Decca 31690
[John Carter/Ken Hawker] [ASC] (10/10/64 BCR-14)

IS IT WRONG (FOR LOVING YOU) *Warner Mack—Decca 30301*
[Warner McPherson] [BMI] (7/29/57 BR-61)

IS IT WRONG (FOR LOVING YOU) *Webb Pierce—Decca 31058*
[Warner McPherson] [BMI] (5/2/60 B-69)

IS IT YOU Lee Ritenour—Elektra 47124
[Bill Champlin/Lee Ritenour/Eric Tagg] [ASC] (4/18/81 BCR-15)

IS SHE REALLY GOING OUT WITH HIM? Joe Jackson—A&M 2132
[Joe Jackson] [ASC] (5/12/79 BCR-16)

IS THAT ALL THERE IS Peggy Lee—Capitol 2602
[Jerry Leiber/Mike Stoller] [BMI] (9/27/69 BCR-8)

IS THAT IT? Katrina And The Waves—Capitol 5566 [Kimberly Rew] [BMI] (4/5/86 BC-70)

IS THAT THE WAY Tin Tin—Atco 6821
[Steve Groves/Steve Kipner/Billy Lawrie] [BMI] (8/28/71 BCR-53)

IS THERE ANY CHANCE Marty Robbins—Columbia 41686
[Marty Robbins] [BMI] (6/20/60 BCR-31)

IS THERE ANYONE HOME? Jimmy Druiett—Wheel 0034
[L. Russell Brown/Irwin Levine] [BMI] (6/24/72 R-96)

IS THERE SOMEBODY ELSE The Dream Weavers—Decca 29905
[Nelson Cogane/Sammy Mysels/Dick Robertson] [ASC] (5/19/56 B-87)

IS THERE SOMETHING I SHOULD KNOW Duran Duran—Capitol 5233
[Simon Le Bon/Nick Rhodes/Andy Taylor/Nigel John Taylor/Roger Taylor] [ASC]
(6/4/83 BC-4)

IS THERE SOMETHING ON YOUR MIND Jack Scott—Top Rank 2093
[Jack Scott] [SE] (12/26/60 BCR-72)

IS THIS LOVE Pat Travers Band—Polydor 2080 [Bob Marley] [ASC] (5/10/80 BCR-49)

IS THIS LOVE Survivor—Scotti Brothers 06381
[Jim Peterik/Frankie Sullivan] [ASC] (10/25/86 BC-9)

IS THIS LOVE Whitesnake—Geffen 28233
[David Coverdale/John Sykes] [ASC] (10/24/87 BC-2)

IS THIS ME? Jim Reeves—RCA Victor 47-8127
[Bill West/Dottie West] [BMI] (3/30/63 R-89)

IS THIS THE END New Edition—Streetwise 1111
[Michael Jonzun/Maurice Starr] [ASC] (10/15/83 B-85)

IS THIS THE END OF THE LINE Joni James—MGM 11960
[Nick Acquaviva/Bobby Worth] [ASC] (4/18/55 CR-23)

IS THIS THE WAY TO TREAT A GIRL (YOU BET IT IS) The Hesitations—GWP 504
[Wesaline Hopson Kerr] [BMI] (4/26/69 R-50)

IS THIS WHAT I GET FOR LOVING YOU? The Ronettes Featuring Veronica—Philles 128
[Gerry Goffin/Carole King/Phil Spector] [BMI] (5/29/65 BCR-75)

IS YOU IS OR IS YOU AIN'T MY BABY Buster Brown—Fire 1023
[Billy Austin/Louis Jordan] [ASC] (9/17/60 BCR-81)

—ISLA BONITA see: LA ISLA BONITA

ISLAND GIRL Elton John—MCA 40461
[Elton John/Bernie Taupin] [BMI] (10/11/75 BCR-1)

ISLAND IN THE SKY Troy Shondell—Liberty 55398 [Gary Shelton] [BMI] (1/13/62 BCR-92)

ISLAND IN THE SUN Harry Belafonte—RCA Victor 47-6885
[Harry Belafonte/Lord Burgess] [ASC] (5/18/57 BCR-32)

ISLAND OF DREAMS The Springfields—Philips 40099
[Tom Springfield] [ASC] (4/27/63 CR-86)

ISLAND OF LOST SOULS Blondie—Chrysalis 2603
[Clement A. Bozewski*/Deborah Harry/Christopher Stein] [ASC] (5/29/82 BC-37)

ISLANDS IN THE STREAM Kenny Rogers Duet with Dolly Parton—RCA 13615
[Barry Gibb/Maurice Gibb/Robin Gibb] [BMI] (8/27/83 BC-1)

ISLE OF CAPRI *The Gaylords—Mercury 70350*
[Will Grosz/Jimmy Kennedy] [ASC] (5/29/54 BC-PRE)

ISLE OF CAPRI *Jackie Lee & His Orchestra—Coral 61149*
[Will Grosz] [ASC] (5/29/54 BC-PRE) [IM]

—ISLE OF LOVE see: MAJORCA

ISLE OF SIRENS Jerry Butler—Vee-Jay 426 [Curtis Mayfield] [BMI] (3/5/62 R-89)

ISN'T IT A PITY George Harrison—Apple 2995
[George Harrison] (TSW) [ASC] (11/28/70 BCR-1)

ISN'T IT ABOUT TIME Stephen Stills -- Manassas—Atlantic 2959
[Stephen Stills] [BMI] (4/28/73 BCR-56)

ISN'T IT ALWAYS LOVE Karla Bonoff—Columbia 10710 [Karla Bonoff] [BMI] (4/8/78 C-85)

ISN'T IT AMAZING The Crests Featuring Johnny Maestro—Coed 537
[Bert Keyes/Billy Dawn Smith] [BMI] (10/24/60 BC-89)

ISN'T IT LONELY TOGETHER *Robert Knight—Elf 90019*
[Ray Stevens] [BMI] (10/19/68 BR-95)

ISN'T IT LONELY TOGETHER *O.C. Smith—Columbia 44705*
[Ray Stevens] [BMI] (12/7/68 BCR-42)

ISN'T IT LONELY TOGETHER Stark & McBrien—RCA Victor 10109
[Estelle Levitt/Rod McBrien] [ASC] (1/25/75 BCR-69)

ISN'T IT TIME The Babys—Chrysalis 2173
[Jack Conrad/Ray Kennedy] [BMI] (10/1/77 BCR-8)

ISN'T LIFE STRANGE The Moody Blues—Threshold 67009
[John Lodge] [ASC] (4/15/72 BCR-20)

ISN'T SHE LOVELY Stars On 45—Radio 4019
[Stevie Wonder] (Med) [ASC] (3/27/82 BCR-28)

ISRAELITES Desmond Dekker & The Aces—Uni 55129
[Desmond Dekker/Leslie Kong] [BMI] (5/10/69 BCR-6)

IT AIN'T EASY COMIN' DOWN Charlene—Prodigal 0632
[Ken Hirsch/Ronald Norman Miller] [BMI] (3/5/77 BC-97)

IT AIN'T ENOUGH Corey Hart—EMI America 8236 [Corey Hart] [ASC] (9/29/84 BC-17)

IT AIN'T LOVE Tom Powers—Big Tree 16103 [Tom Powers] [ASC] (10/8/77 B-92)

IT AIN'T ME, BABE *Johnny Cash—Columbia 43145 [Bob Dylan] [SE] (10/31/64 BCR-49)*

IT AIN'T ME BABE *The Turtles—White Whale 222 [Bob Dylan] [SE] (7/31/65 BCR-7)*

IT AIN'T NO BIG THING The Radiants—Chess 1925 [Gerald Sims] [BMI] (5/1/65 BCR-91)

IT AIN'T NO FUN Shirley Brown—Truth 3223 [Frederick Knight] [BMI] (5/10/75 B-94)

IT AIN'T NO USE Major Lance—Okeh 7197 [Curtis Mayfield] [BMI] (6/6/64 BCR-52)

IT AIN'T OVER TIL IT'S OVER Lenny Kravitz—Virgin 98795
[Lenny Kravitz] [ASC] (6/1/91 BC-2)

IT ALL DEPENDS ON YOU Jerry Lewis—Decca 30263
[Lew Brown/Buddy DeSylva/Ray Henderson] [ASC] (4/27/57 BR-68)

IT ALL STARTED WITH YOUR KISS Micki Marlo—ABC-Paramount 9762
[Al Jacobs/Eddie Snyder] [ASC] (1/5/57 R-59)

IT AMAZES ME John Denver—RCA 11214 [John Denver] [ASC] (2/25/78 BCR-59)

IT CAN HAPPEN Yes—Atco 99745
[Jon Anderson/Trevor Rabin*/Chris Squire] [BMI] (6/23/84 BC-51)

IT COULD BE WE'RE IN LOVE The Cryan Shames—Columbia 44191
[Jim Fairs/Lenny Kerley*] [BMI] (7/29/67 BCR-52)

IT COULD HAPPEN TO YOU Dinah Washington—Mercury 71560
[Johnny Burke/Jimmy Van Heusen] [ASC] (3/14/60 BCR-42)

IT COULD HAVE BEEN ME Sami Jo—MGM South 7034
[Harry Lloyd/Gloria Sklerov] [ASC] (7/6/74 BCR-46)

IT COULD'VE BEEN WORSE Jesse Belvin—RCA Victor 47-7543
[Robert Allen/Bob Russell] [ASC] (6/20/59 CR-58)

IT DIDN'T EVEN BRING ME DOWN Sir Douglas Quintet—Smash 2222
[Martin Fierro/Frank Morin/Doug Sahm] [BMI] (5/17/69 R-97)

IT DIDN'T TAKE LONG Spider—Dreamland 111 [Holly Knight] [ASC] (5/30/81 BCR-43)
IT DO FEEL GOOD Donna Fargo—ABC/Dot 17541 [Donna Fargo] [BMI] (3/22/75 B-98)
IT DO ME SO GOOD Ann-Margret—RCA Victor 47-7952 [Willie Dixon/Billy Emerson] [BMI] (11/6/61 BCR-58)
IT DOESN'T HAVE TO BE THAT WAY Jim Croce—ABC 11413 [Jim Croce] [ASC] (12/22/73 BCR-47)
IT DOESN'T MATTER Stephen Stills—Atlantic 2876 [Chris Hillman/Stephen Stills] [BMI] (5/13/72 BCR-46)
IT DOESN'T MATTER ANYMORE *Buddy Holly / The Crickets—Coral 62074 [Paul Anka] [BMI] (2/21/59 BCR-13)*
IT DOESN'T MATTER ANYMORE *Linda Ronstadt—Capitol 4050 [Paul Anka] (TSW) [BMI] (7/26/75 BCR-46)*
IT DON'T COME EASY Ringo Starr—Apple 1831 [Ringo Starr] [BMI] (4/24/71 BCR-1)
IT DON'T HURT NO MORE Nappy Brown—Savoy 1551 [Mark Jackson/Yolanda Paterno] [BMI] (10/18/58 BC-80)
IT DON'T MATTER TO ME Bread—Elektra 45701 [David Gates] [ASC] (9/26/70 BCR-6)
IT FEELS SO GOOD TO BE LOVED SO BAD The Manhattans—Columbia 10495 [Roger Joyce/Victoria Pike/Teddy Randazzo] [ASC] (3/26/77 BCR-65)
IT FEELS SO RIGHT Elvis Presley With The Jordanaires—RCA Victor 47-8585 [Ben Weisman/Fred Wise] [ASC] (6/19/65 BCR-55)
IT HAPPENED AGAIN Sarah Vaughan—Mercury 70947 [Luigi Creatore/Hugo Peretti] [ASC] (9/15/56 BR-64)
IT HAPPENED IN MONTEREY The Lancers—Coral 61769 [Billy Rose/Mabel Wayne] (Med) [ASC] (3/2/57 R-79)
IT HAPPENED JUST THAT WAY Roger Miller—Smash 1994 [Roger Miller] [BMI] (7/10/65 CR-60)
IT HAPPENED TODAY The Skyliners—Calico 109 [James Beaumont/Walter Lester/Joseph Rock/John L. Taylor/Joseph Verscharen/Janet Vogel] [ASC] (9/26/59 BCR-43)
IT HIT ME LIKE A HAMMER Huey Lewis & The News—EMI 50364 [Mutt Lange/Huey Lewis] [ASC] (7/20/91 BC-15)
IT HURTS A LITTLE EVEN NOW John Reid—Arista 0114 [John Reid] [BMI] (5/17/75 CR-86)
IT HURTS ME Elvis Presley With The Jordanaires—RCA Victor 47-8307 [Charlie Daniels/Joy Byers Johnston] [ASC] (2/29/64 BCR-29)
IT HURTS ME Bobby Goldsboro—United Artists 50056 [Bobby Goldsboro] [BMI] (9/3/66 BCR-66)
IT HURTS ME TOO Elmore James—Enjoy 2015 [Elmore James/Hudson Whittaker*] [BMI] (5/8/65 R-96)
IT HURTS SO BAD Kim Carnes—EMI America 8011 [Kim Carnes] [ASC] (2/10/79 BCR-54)
IT HURTS TO BE IN LOVE Annie Laurie—DeLuxe 6107 [Julius Dixon/Rudy Toombs] [BMI] (7/8/57 B-61)
IT HURTS TO BE IN LOVE *Gene Pitney—Musicor 1040 [Howard Greenfield/Helen Miller] [BMI] (7/18/64 BCR-6)*
IT HURTS TO BE IN LOVE *Dan Hartman—Blue Sky 02115 [Howard Greenfield/Helen Miller] [BMI] (6/27/81 BCR-72)*
IT HURTS TO BE SIXTEEN *Andrea Carroll—Big Top 3156 [Ronnie Grossman] [BMI] (7/20/63 BCtRt-45)*
IT HURTS TO BE SIXTEEN *Barbara Chandler—Kapp 542 [Ronnie Grossman] [BMI] (7/27/63 CtRt-46)*
IT HURTS TOO MUCH Eric Carmen—Arista 0506 [Eric Carmen] [BMI] (6/28/80 BCR-71)
IT ISN'T, IT WASN'T, IT AIN'T NEVER GONNA BE Aretha Franklin—Arista 1-9850 [Albert Hammond/Diane Warren] [ASC] (7/1/89 BC-37)
IT ISN'T RIGHT The Platters—Mercury 70948 [Robert Mellin] [BMI] (9/22/56 BCR-13)
IT JUST HAPPENED THAT WAY Dean Martin—Reprise 0516 [Fred Carter] [BMI] (10/1/66 CR-71)
IT KEEPS RAININ' Fats Domino—Imperial 5753 [Dave Bartholomew/Fats Domino/Robert Guidry] [BMI] (5/15/61 BCR-23)
IT KEEPS RIGHT ON A-HURTIN' Johnny Tillotson—Cadence 1418 [Johnny Tillotson] [BMI] (4/30/62 BCR-2)
IT KEEPS YOU RUNNIN' *Carly Simon—Elektra 45323 [Michael McDonald] [ASC] (6/12/76 BCR-46)*
IT KEEPS YOU RUNNIN' *The Doobie Brothers—Warner Bros. 8282 [Michael McDonald] [ASC] (11/13/76 BCR-37)*
IT LOOKS LIKE RAIN IN CHERRY BLOSSOM LANE Debbie Reynolds—Dot 16156 [Joe Burke/Edgar Leslie] [ASC] (11/21/60 R-91)
IT MAKES ME GIGGLE John Denver—RCA Victor 10687 [John Denver] [ASC] (5/8/76 BCR-60)
IT MAY BE WINTER OUTSIDE (BUT IN MY HEART IT'S SPRING) *Felice Taylor—Mustang 3024 [Paul Politi/Barry White] [BMI] (1/14/67 BCR-39)*
IT MAY BE WINTER OUTSIDE (BUT IN MY HEART IT'S SPRING) *Love Unlimited—20th Century 2062 [Paul Politi/Barry White] [BMI] (12/15/73 BCR-83)*
IT MAY SOUND SILLY *The McGuire Sisters—Coral 61369 [Ivory Joe Hunter] [BMI] (2/21/55 BCRt-13)*
IT MAY SOUND SILLY *Ivory Joe Hunter and his Ivorytones—Atlantic 1049 [Ivory Joe Hunter] [BMI] (2/21/55 Rt-42)*
IT MAY SOUND SILLY *Joan Weber—Columbia 40440 [Ivory Joe Hunter] [BMI] (2/21/55 Rt-42)*
IT MAY SOUND SILLY *Dolores Gray—Decca 29430 [Ivory Joe Hunter] [BMI] (2/21/55 Rt-13)*
IT MAY SOUND SILLY *Bill Farrell—Mercury 70539 [Ivory Joe Hunter] [BMI] (2/21/55 Rt-42)*
IT MIGHT AS WELL RAIN UNTIL SEPTEMBER Carole King—Dimension 2000 [Gerry Goffin/Carole King] [BMI] (8/25/62 BCR-22)
IT MIGHT BE YOU Stephen Bishop—Warner Bros. 29791 [Alan Bergman/Marilyn Bergman/Dave Grusin] [ASC] (1/29/83 BC-19)
IT MIGHT HAVE BEEN Joe London—Liberty 55209 [Ronnie Green/Harriet Kane] [BMI] (10/24/59 CR-65)
IT MUST BE HIM Vikki Carr—Liberty 55986 [Gilbert Bécaud/Mack David] [ASC] (8/26/67 BCR-3) [FDE]
IT MUST BE LOVE Alton McClain & Destiny—Polydor 14532 [John Footman/Judy Wieder] [BMI] (3/24/79 BCR-32)
IT MUST BE LOVE Madness—Geffen 29562 [Labi Siffre] [ASC] (8/20/83 BC-33)
IT MUST HAVE BEEN LOVE Roxette—EMI 50283 [Per Gessle] [BMI] (4/7/90 BC-1)
(IT NEVER HAPPENS) IN REAL LIFE Chuck Jackson—Wand 108 [Luther Dixon/Ollie Jones] [BMI] (4/10/61 BCR-46)
IT NEVER RAINS IN SOUTHERN CALIFORNIA Albert Hammond—Mums 6011 [Albert Hammond/Mike Hazlewood] [ASC] (10/14/72 BCR-2)
IT NEVER RAINS (IN SOUTHERN CALIFORNIA) Tony! Toni! Toné!—Wing 879 068 [Clemon Timothy Riley/Raphael Saadiq] [ASC] (12/22/90 BC-34)
IT ONLY HAPPENED YESTERDAY Jack Scott—Top Rank 2055 [Jack Scott] [BMI] (7/18/60 BCR-25)
IT ONLY HURTS FOR A LITTLE WHILE The Ames Brothers—RCA Victor 47-6481 [Mack David/Fred Spielman] [ASC] (4/20/56 BCR-14)
IT ONLY HURTS WHEN I TRY TO SMILE Dawn Featuring Tony Orlando—Bell 45,450 [L. Russell Brown/Irwin Levine] [BMI] (3/30/74 BCR-56)
IT ONLY TAKES A MINUTE Tavares—Capitol 4111 [Dennis Lambert/Brian Potter] [BMI] (7/26/75 BCR-8)
IT SEEMS TO HANG ON Ashford & Simpson—Warner Bros. 8651 [Nick Ashford/Valerie Simpson] [ASC] (9/23/78 R-90)
IT SHALL COME TO PASS Four Aces—Decca 29217 [Deeda Patrick/Don Ralke] [ASC] (9/11/54 C-37)
IT SHOULD HAVE BEEN ME *Gladys Knight & The Pips—Soul 35045 [William Stevenson/Norman Whitfield] [BMI] (6/1/68 BCR-38)*
IT SHOULD HAVE BEEN ME *Yvonne Fair—Motown 1384 [William Stevenson/Norman Whitfield] [BMI] (4/24/76 BC-85)*
IT STARTED ALL OVER AGAIN Brenda Lee—Decca 31407 [Gerry Goffin/Jack Keller] [NA] (6/30/62 BCR-26)
IT SURE TOOK A LONG, LONG TIME Lobo—Big Tree 16,001 [Kent LaVoie] [ASC] (4/7/73 BCR-27)
IT TAKES ONE TO KNOW ONE Brenda Lee—Decca 31970 [Dub Allbritten*/Ronnie Self] [BMI] (6/18/66 C-91)
IT TAKES SO LONG (TO SAY GOODBYE) Dean Martin—Capitol 4124 [Haven Gillespie/Larry Shay] [ASC] (1/31/59 CR-80)
IT TAKES TIME The Marshall Tucker Band—Warner Bros. 49215 [Toy Caldwell] [BMI] (4/26/80 B-79)
IT TAKES TWO Marvin Gaye & Kim Weston—Tamla 54141 [Sylvia Moy/William Stevenson] [BMI] (1/7/67 BCR-14)
IT TAKES TWO Rob Base & D.J. E-Z Rock—Profile 5186 [James Brown/Robert Ginyard] [ASC] (8/20/88 BC-36)
IT TEARS ME UP Percy Sledge—Atlantic 2358 [Spooner Oldham/Dan Penn] [BMI] (10/22/66 BCR-12)
(IT TOOK) ONE KISS Jaye P. Morgan—MGM 12786 [Roy C. Bennett/Sid Tepper] [ASC] (4/27/59 CR-70)
IT WAS A VERY GOOD YEAR *Frank Sinatra—Reprise 0429 [Ervin Drake] [ASC] (12/18/65 BCR-28)*
IT WAS A VERY GOOD YEAR *Della Reese—ABC 10841 [Ervin Drake] [ASC] (9/10/66 B-99)*
IT WAS ALMOST LIKE A SONG Ronnie Milsap—RCA 10976 [Hal David/Archie Jordan] [ASC] (6/18/77 BCR-11)
IT WAS I Skip & Flip—Brent 7002 [Gary S. Paxton] [BMI] (6/8/59 BCR-11)
IT WILL STAND *The Showmen—Minit 632 [General Johnson] [BMI] (11/13/61 BCR-58)*
IT WILL STAND *The Showmen—Imperial 66033 [General Johnson] [BMI] (7/4/64 BR-80)*
IT WON'T BE THIS WAY (ALWAYS) The King Pins—Federal 12484 [Robert Kelly/Sonny Thompson] [BMI] (8/3/63 BCR-79)
IT WON'T BE WRONG The Byrds—Columbia 43501 [Harvey Gerst/Roger McGuinn] [BMI] (2/5/66 BCR-39)
IT WORRIES ME Frank Sinatra—Capitol 2922 [Fritz Schulz-Reichel/Carl Sigman] [ASC] (10/2/54 CR-29)
IT WOULD TAKE A STRONG STRONG MAN Rick Astley—RCA 8663 [Matt Aitken/Mike Stock/Pete Waterman] [BMI] (7/16/88 BC-10)
—ITALIAN HUCKLE BUCK see: HUCKLE BUCK
ITALIAN JINGLE BELLS Lou Monte—RCA Victor 47-6320 [George Brown/Lou Monte/James Lord Pierpont] [ASC] (12/30/55 R-72)
THE ITALIAN THEME *Cyril Stapleton And His Orchestra—London 1672 [Angelo Giacomazzi/Cyril Stapleton] [ASC] (8/11/56 BCRt-25) [IM]*
THE ITALIAN THEME *Dorothy Collins—Coral 61711 [Angelo Giacomazzi/Buddy Kaye/Cyril Stapleton] [ASC] (9/29/56 Rt-25)*

THE ITALIAN THEME *Joe Reisman and His Orchestra—RCA Victor 47-6647*
[Angelo Giacomazzi/Cyril Stapleton] [ASC] (9/29/56 Rt-25) [IM]

THE ITALIAN THEME *Owen Bradley & His Quintet—Decca 30083*
[Angelo Giacomazzi/Buddy Kaye/Cyril Stapleton] [ASC] (10/13/56 Rt-26)

—ITALIAN WALLFLOWER see: WALLFLOWER

ITCHIN' Jimmy Jones—Cub 9076
[Margaret Reddy/Dorothy Stipe/Joseph Wyant] [BMI] (9/26/60 R-92)

ITCHY TWITCHY FEELING *Bobby Hendricks—Sue 706*
[Jimmy Oliver] [BMI] (8/4/58 BCRt-25)

ITCHY TWITCHY FEELING *The Swallows—Federal 12333*
[Jimmy Oliver] [BMI] (8/18/58 BRt-76)

ITCHYCOO PARK Small Faces—Immediate 501
[Ronnie Lane/Steve Marriott] [BMI] (11/11/67 BCR-12)

IT'LL NEVER BE OVER FOR ME Baby Washington—Sue 114
[Norm Blagman/Sam Bobrick] [ASC] (11/21/64 BCR-78)

IT'S A BETTER THAN GOOD TIME Gladys Knight & The Pips—Buddah 598
[Tony Macaulay] [ASC] (8/12/78 R-59)

IT'S A COTTON CANDY WORLD Jerry Wallace—Mercury 72292
[By Dunham/Henry Vars] [ASC] (7/18/64 BCR-77)

IT'S A CRAZY WORLD Mac McAnally—Ariola America 7665
[Mac McAnally] [ASC] (6/25/77 BCR-37)

IT'S A CRYIN' SHAME Gayle McCormick—Dunhill 4288
[Dennis Lambert/Brian Potter] [BMI] (9/18/71 BCR-39)

IT'S A DISCO NIGHT (ROCK DON'T STOP) The Isley Brothers—T-Neck 2287
[Ernie Isley/Marvin Isley/O'Kelly Isley/Ronald Isley/Rudolph Isley/Chris Jasper] [ASC] (10/20/79 B-90)

IT'S A FUNKY THING-RIGHT ON (PART 1) Herbie Mann—Atlantic 2671
[Herbie Mann/Charlie Scruggs/Milton Smith] [ASC] (11/22/69 B-95)

IT'S A FUNNY SITUATION Dee Dee Sharp—Cameo 382
[Barrett Strong] [BMI] (2/26/66 C-96)

IT'S A GAS The Hombres—Verve Forecast 5076
[B.B. Cunningham/John W. Hunter/Jerry Masters/Gary McEwen] [BMI] (1/20/68 C-98)

IT'S A GROOVY WORLD! The Unifics—Kapp 985 [Guy Draper] [BMI] (3/29/69 BCR-86)

IT'S-A-HAPPENING The Magic Mushrooms—A&M 815
[Sonny Casella/Stu Freeman/Josh Rice] [BMI] (11/12/66 B-93)

IT'S A HAPPENING THING The Peanut Butter Conspiracy—Columbia 43985
[Alan Brackett] [BMI] (3/11/67 B-93)

IT'S A HAPPENING WORLD The Tokens—Warner Bros. 7056
[Barry Mann/Cynthia Weil] [BMI] (7/22/67 BCR-69)

IT'S A HARD LIFE Queen—Capitol 5372 [Freddie Mercury] [BMI] (7/28/84 BC-72)

IT'S A HEARTACHE *Bonnie Tyler—RCA 11249*
[Ronnie Scott/Steve Wolfe] [BMI] (3/25/78 BCR-3)

IT'S A HEARTACHE *Juice Newton—Capitol 4552*
[Ronnie Scott/Steve Wolfe] [BMI] (4/8/78 BC-86)

IT'S A LAUGH Daryl Hall & John Oates—RCA 11371 [Daryl Hall] [BMI] (8/26/78 BCR-20)

IT'S A LONELY TOWN (LONELY WITHOUT YOU) Gene McDaniels—Liberty 55597
[Doc Pomus/Mort Shuman] [BMI] (8/10/63 BCR-64)

(IT'S A) LONG LONELY HIGHWAY Elvis Presley—RCA Victor 47-8657
[Doc Pomus/Mort Shuman] [BMI] (8/28/65 C-96)

IT'S A LONG WAY THERE Little River Band—Harvest 4318
[Graham Goble] [BMI] (9/18/76 BCR-28)

IT'S A LOVE THING The Whispers—Solar 12154
[Dana Meyers/William Shelby] [ASC] (2/7/81 BCR-24)

IT'S A MAD, MAD, MAD, MAD WORLD The Shirelles—Scepter 1260
[Mack David/Ernest Gold] [ASC] (10/19/63 B-92)

IT'S A MAN DOWN THERE G.L. Crockett—4 Brothers 445
[G.L. Crockett/Jack Daniels] [BMI] (7/24/65 BCR-56)

IT'S A MAN'S MAN'S MAN'S WORLD James Brown And The Famous Flames—King 6035
[James Brown/Betty Jean Newsome*] [BMI] (4/30/66 BCR-3)

IT'S A MEAN OLD MAN'S WORLD Dinah Washington—Roulette 4455
[Leroy Kirkland/Dinah Washington/Pearl Woods] [BMI] (10/27/62 R-77)

IT'S A MIRACLE Barry Manilow—Arista 0108
[Barry Manilow/Marty Panzer] [BMI] (3/1/75 BCR-10)

IT'S A MIRACLE Culture Club—Virgin/Epic 04457
[Michael Craig/Roy Hay/Jon Moss/George O'Dowd/Phil Pickett] [ASC] (5/12/84 BC-13)

IT'S A MISTAKE Men At Work—Columbia 03959 [Colin James Hay] [ASC] (7/2/83 BC-6)

IT'S A NEW DAY (PART 1) & (PART 2) James Brown—King 6292
[James Brown] [BMI] (2/14/70 BCR-26)

IT'S A NIGHT FOR BEAUTIFUL GIRLS The Fools—EMI America 8036
[Doug Forman/Mike Girard] [ASC] (3/29/80 BCR-66)

IT'S A SHAME The Spinners—V.I.P. 25057
[Lee Garrett/Stevie Wonder/Syreeta Wright] [BMI] (7/18/70 BCR-14)

IT'S A SHAME (MY SISTER) Monie Love—Warner Bros. 19515
[Lee Garrett/Simone Antoinette Johnson/David Steele/Stevie Wonder/Syreeta Wright] [BMI] (3/16/91 BC-26)

IT'S A SIN Bill Haley And His Comets—Decca 30530
[Fred Rose/Zeb Turner] [NA] (1/6/58 R-71)

IT'S A SIN Pet Shop Boys—EMI America 43027
[Chris Lowe/Neil Tennant] [ASC] (9/5/87 BC-9)

IT'S A SIN TO TELL A LIE *Somethin' Smith & The Redheads—Epic 9093*
[Billy Mayhew] [ASC] (4/2/55 BCRt-6)

IT'S A SIN TO TELL A LIE *Johnny Desmond—Coral 61436*
[Billy Mayhew] [ASC] (6/13/55 Rt-6)

IT'S A SIN TO TELL A LIE *Dave "Baby" Cortez—Clock 1014*
[Billy Mayhew] [ASC] (9/28/59 R-92) [IWM]

IT'S A SIN TO TELL A LIE *Tony Bennett—Columbia 43073*
[Billy Mayhew] [ASC] (7/11/64 BCR-62)

IT'S A SIN WHEN YOU LOVE SOMEBODY Joe Cocker—A&M 1641
[Jimmy Webb] (TSW) [ASC] (1/18/75 B-43)

IT'S A SMALL SMALL WORLD The Mike Curb Congregation—MGM 14494
[Richard Sherman/Robert Sherman] [BMI] (9/1/73 CR-79)

—IT'S A WOMAN'S WORLD see: WOMAN'S WORLD

IT'S A WONDERFUL THING TO BE LOVED Gogi Grant—RCA Victor 47-6996
[Gerald Marks/Milton Pascal] [ASC] (8/12/57 R-55)

IT'S ABOUT TIME The Dillards—Anthem 101 [Chip Douglas] [BMI] (7/31/71 BCR-92)

IT'S ALL BECAUSE Linda Scott—Canadian-American 129
[Bob Davie] [BMI] (11/11/61 BCR-50)

IT'S ALL DOWN TO GOODNIGHT VIENNA Ringo Starr—Apple 1882
[John Lennon] (TSW) [GL] (6/14/75 BCR-29)

IT'S ALL I CAN DO The Cars—Elektra 46546 [Ric Ocasek] [ASC] (10/13/79 BCR-40)

IT'S ALL I CAN DO Anne Murray—Capitol 5023
[Archie Jordan/Richard Leigh] [ASC] (9/26/81 BCR-53)

IT'S ALL IN THE GAME *Tommy Edwards—MGM 12688*
[Charles Dawes/Carl Sigman] [ASC] (8/11/58 BCR-1)

IT'S ALL IN THE GAME *Cliff Richard—Epic 9633*
[Charles Dawes/Carl Sigman] [ASC] (12/7/63 BCR-21)

IT'S ALL IN THE GAME *Four Tops—Motown 1164*
[Charles Dawes/Carl Sigman] [ASC] (4/25/70 BCR-14)

IT'S ALL IN YOUR MIND Clarence Carter—Atlantic 2774
[George Henry Jackson/Raymond Moore] [BMI] (10/31/70 BCR-39)

IT'S ALL OVER Ben E. King—Atco 6315
[Bert Berns/Mike Leander] [BMI] (9/12/64 BCR-72)

IT'S ALL OVER Walter Jackson—Okeh 7204 [Curtis Mayfield] [BMI] (11/7/64 BCR-52)

IT'S ALL OVER Wilson Pickett—Atlantic 2306
[Steve Cropper/Wilson Pickett] [BMI] (11/6/65 CR-99)

IT'S ALL OVER Casinos—Fraternity 985 [Don Everly] [BMI] (4/29/67 BCR-55)

IT'S ALL OVER The Independents—Wand 11263
[Charles Henry Jackson Jr./Marvin Yancy] [ASC] (11/10/73 BCR-65)

IT'S ALL OVER NOW *The Valentinos—SAR 152*
[Bobby Womack/Shirley Womack] [BMI] (6/27/64 BCR-30)

IT'S ALL OVER NOW *The Rolling Stones—London 9687*
[Bobby Womack/Shirley Womack] [BMI] (7/25/64 BC-25)

IT'S ALL RIGHT Sam Cooke—RCA Victor 47-7927
[Sam Cooke] [BMI] (9/25/61 B-93)

IT'S ALL RIGHT The Impressions—ABC-Paramount 10487
[Curtis Mayfield] [BMI] (9/28/63 BCR-4)

IT'S ALL RIGHT Jim Capaldi—Island 003 [Jim Capaldi] [ASC] (12/28/74 BCR-47)

IT'S ALL RIGHT (YOU'RE JUST IN LOVE) The Tams—ABC-Paramount 10533
[Cliff Thomas/Edward S. Thomas Jr.] [BMI] (3/28/64 BC-79)

IT'S ALL THE WAY LIVE Lakeside—Solar 11380 [Fred Lewis] [ASC] (2/3/79 R-95)

IT'S ALL UP TO YOU The Dells—Cadet 5689
[Terry Callier/Larry Wade] [ASC] (2/26/72 BCR-69)

IT'S ALMOST TOMORROW *The Dream Weavers—Decca 29683*
[Gene Adkinson/Wade Buff] [ASC] (10/29/55 BCtRt-6)

IT'S ALMOST TOMORROW *Snooky Lanson—Dot 15424*
[Gene Adkinson/Wade Buff] [ASC] (11/12/55 BRt-20)

IT'S ALMOST TOMORROW *Jo Stafford—Columbia 40595*
[Gene Adkinson/Wade Buff] [ASC] (11/14/55 BCtRt-6)

IT'S ALMOST TOMORROW *David Carroll And His Orchestra—Mercury 70717*
[Gene Adkinson/Wade Buff] [ASC] (11/14/55 BRt-30)

IT'S ALMOST TOMORROW *Lawrence Welk & His Champagne Music—Coral 61524*
[Gene Adkinson/Wade Buff] [ASC] (11/14/55 Rt-7)

IT'S ALMOST TOMORROW
Ray Anthony & His Orchestra with Don Durant—Capitol EAP 1-9131 (EP)
[Gene Adkinson/Wade Buff] [ASC] (3/9/56 Rt-17)

IT'S ALMOST TOMORROW *Jimmy Velvet—Philips 40285*
[Gene Adkinson/Wade Buff] [ASC] (5/15/65 BCR-49)

IT'S ALRIGHT Adam Faith With The Roulettes—Amy 913
[Chris Frederick Andrews] [BMI] (1/16/65 BCR-30)

IT'S ALRIGHT Graham Central Station—Warner Bros. 8148
[Larry Graham] [BMI] (11/29/75 BC-92)

IT'S ALRIGHT (BABY'S COMING BACK) Eurythmics—RCA 14284
[Annie Lennox/David A. Stewart] [ASC] (2/15/86 BC-78)

IT'S AN UPHILL CLIMB TO THE BOTTOM Walter Jackson—Okeh 7247
[Fangette Enzel] [BMI] (5/21/66 BCR-73)

IT'S BEEN A LONG LONG TIME The Elgins—V.I.P. 25043
[Billy Fulgrum/Harvey Fuqua/Art Kirkpatrick/Billy Strawbridge/James Rodger Williams/Woody Woodall] [BMI] (7/29/67 B-92)

IT'S BEEN A LONG TIME The New Birth–RCA Victor 0185
[James Baker/Melvin Wilson] [BMI] (2/16/74 BCR-50)

(IT'S BEEN A LONG TIME) PRETTY BABY Gino & Gina–Mercury 71283
[Harry Giosasi/Artie Zwirn] [BMI] (5/5/58 BCRt*-28)

IT'S BETTER IN THE DARK Tony Martin–RCA Victor 47-6597
[Sammy Cahn/Jimmy Van Heusen] [ASC] (9/1/56 B-60)

IT'S BETTER TO HAVE (AND DON'T NEED) Don Covay–Mercury 73469
[Don Covay/Erskin Watts] [BMI] (7/13/74 BC-63)

IT'S BETTER TO HAVE IT Barbara Lynn–Jamie 1292 [Barbara Lynn] [BMI] (1/9/65 BR-88)

IT'S BIGGER THAN YOU AND ME Sammy Davis Jr.–Decca 29649
[Leo Robin/Jule Styne] [NA] (9/5/55 R-52)

IT'S COLD OUTSIDE The Choir–Roulette 4738 [Denny Klawson] [BMI] (5/20/67 BCR-49)

IT'S COOL The Tymes–RCA Victor 10561
[Charles Henry Jackson Jr./Marvin Yancy] [ASC] (4/3/76 BR-68)

IT'S CRAZY Eddie Harris–Atlantic 2561 [Eddie Harris] [BMI] (10/26/68 BC-88) [I]

IT'S ECSTASY WHEN YOU LAY DOWN NEXT TO ME Barry White–20th Century 2350
[Ekundayo Paris/Nelson Pigford] [BMI] (8/20/77 BCR-4)

IT'S FOR YOU *Cilla Black–Capitol 5258*
[John Lennon/Paul McCartney] [ASC] (9/19/64 BR-79)

IT'S FOR YOU *Springwell–Parrot 359*
[John Lennon/Paul McCartney] [ASC] (9/18/71 BCR-44)

IT'S FOR YOU Player–Casablanca 2265 [Peter Beckett] [BMI] (6/7/80 BCR-46)

IT'S FOREVER The Ebonys–Philadelphia Int'l 3529 [Leon Huff] [BMI] (6/16/73 BCR-68)

IT'S FOUR IN THE MORNING Faron Young–Mercury 73250
[Jerry Chesnut] [BMI] (2/12/72 B-92)

IT'S GETTIN' LATE The Beach Boys–Caribou 05433
[Robert White Johnson/Myrna Smith-Schilling/Carl Wilson] [ASC] (8/3/85 BC-78)

IT'S GETTING BETTER Mama Cass–Dunhill 4195
[Barry Mann/Cynthia Weil] [BMI] (5/31/69 BCR-22)

IT'S GOING TO TAKE SOME TIME Carpenters–A&M 1351
[Carole King/Toni Stern] [ASC] (4/29/72 BCR-12)

IT'S GONNA BE ALRIGHT Maxine Brown–Wand 173
[Gerry Goffin/Carole King] [BMI] (2/13/65 BCR-56)

IT'S GONNA BE ALRIGHT Gerry And The Pacemakers–Laurie 3293
[Gerry Marsden] [BMI] (4/10/65 BCR-20)

IT'S GONNA BE FINE Glenn Yarbrough–RCA Victor 47-8619
[Barry Mann/Cynthia Weil] [BMI] (7/10/65 BCR-54)

IT'S GONNA BE SPECIAL Patti Austin–Qwest 29373
[Glen Ballard/Clif Magness] [ASC] (2/11/84 B-82)

IT'S GONNA TAKE A MIRACLE *The Royalettes–MGM 13366*
[Teddy Randazzo/Lou Stallman/Bobby Weinstein] [BMI] (7/17/65 BCR-37)

IT'S GONNA TAKE A MIRACLE *Deniece Williams–ARC 02812*
[Teddy Randazzo/Lou Stallman/Bobby Weinstein] [BMI] (4/3/82 BCR-10)

IT'S GONNA WORK OUT FINE Ike & Tina Turner–Sue 749
[Ike Turner] [BMI] (7/29/61 BCR-14)

IT'S GOOD NEWS WEEK Hedgehoppers Anonymous–Parrot 9800
[Jonathan King] [BMI] (12/4/65 BCR-44)

IT'S GOOD TO HAVE YOU BACK WITH ME Adam Wade–Coed 565
[Arthur Kent/Ed Warren] [ASC] (1/27/62 C-91)

IT'S GOT THE WHOLE WORLD SHAKIN' Sam Cooke–RCA Victor 47-8539
[Sam Cooke] [BMI] (4/10/65 BCR-36)

IT'S GOT TO BE MELLOW Leon Haywood–Decca 32164
[Leon Haywood] [BMI] (8/12/67 BCR-63)

IT'S GOTTA LAST FOREVER Billy J. Kramer With The Dakotas–Imperial 66085
[Bill Giant/Kenny Lynch/Clive Westlake] [BMI] (2/6/65 BCR-67)

IT'S GROWING The Temptations–Gordy 7040
[Warren Moore/Smokey Robinson] [ASC] (4/3/65 BCR-14)

IT'S HARD TO BE HUMBLE Mac Davis–Casablanca 2244
[Mac Davis] [BMI] (3/22/80 BCR-34)

–IT'S HARD TO BELIEVE see: CHILD OF GOD

IT'S HARD TO GET ALONG Joe Simon–Sound Stage 7 2641
[Allen Orange/Joe Simon] [BMI] (10/18/69 BCR-87)

IT'S HARD TO STOP (DOING SOMETHING WHEN IT'S GOOD TO YOU) Betty Wright–Alston 4617 [Willie Clarke/Clarence Reid/Betty Wright] [BMI] (3/31/73 BCR-72)

IT'S HER TURN TO LIVE Smokey Robinson–Tamla 54246
[Smokey Robinson/Marvin Tarplin] [ASC] (5/18/74 BCR-69)

IT'S IMPOSSIBLE *Perry Como–RCA Victor 74-0387*
[Armando Manzanero/Sid Wayne] [ASC] (10/31/70 BCR-7) [FDE]

IT'S IMPOSSIBLE *The New Birth–RCA Victor 74-0520*
[Armando Manzanero/Sid Wayne] [ASC] (10/9/71 BCR-46) [FDE]

–IT'S IN HIS KISS see: SHOOP SHOOP SONG

IT'S IN YOUR POWER Joe Odom–1-2-3 1710
[Edward S. Thomas Jr.] [BMI] (5/24/69 CR-76)

IT'S INEVITABLE Charlie–Mirage 99862 [Terry Thomas] [NA] (6/25/83 BC-38)

IT'S JUST A HOUSE WITHOUT YOU Brook Benton–Mercury 71859
[Brook Benton/Cirino Colacrai/Clyde Otis/Teddy Randazzo] [BMI] (10/2/61 BCR-45)

IT'S JUST A LITTLE BIT TOO LATE Wayne Fontana & The Mind-Benders–Fontana 1514
[Clint Ballard Jr./Les Ledo] [ASC] (6/12/65 BCR-44)

IT'S JUST A MATTER OF TIME *Brook Benton–Mercury 71394*
[Brook Benton/Belford Hendricks/Clyde Otis] [BMI] (1/19/59 BCR-2)

IT'S JUST A MATTER OF TIME *Sonny James, The Southern Gentleman–Capitol 2700*
[Brook Benton/Belford Hendricks/Clyde Otis] [BMI] (1/24/70 BCR-87)

IT'S JUST ABOUT TIME Johnny Cash And The Tennessee Two–Sun 309
[Jack H. Clement] [BMI] (12/13/58 BCR-47)

IT'S JUST THE SUN Don McLean–Millennium 11809 [Don McLean] [BMI] (8/8/81 B-83)

(IT'S JUST) THE WAY THAT YOU LOVE ME *Paula Abdul–Virgin 99282*
[Oliver Leiber] [ASC] (10/22/88 BC-1)

(IT'S JUST) THE WAY THAT YOU LOVE ME *Paula Abdul–Virgin 99282*
[Oliver Leiber] [ASC] (9/23/89 B-3)

IT'S LATE Ricky Nelson–Imperial 5565 [Dorsey Burnette] [BMI] (3/2/59 BCR-6)

IT'S LATE Queen–Elektra 45478 [Brian May] [BMI] (5/6/78 BCR-66)

IT'S LIKE WE NEVER SAID GOODBYE Crystal Gayle–Columbia 11198
[Roger Greenaway/Geoff Stephens] [ASC] (2/23/80 BCR-63)

IT'S MAGIC *Teddy Randazzo–ABC-Paramount 9983*
[Sammy Cahn/Jule Styne] [ASC] (12/1/58 CR-79)

IT'S MAGIC *The Platters–Mercury 71921*
[Sammy Cahn/Jule Styne] [ASC] (2/17/62 BCR-88)

IT'S MONEY THAT MATTERS Randy Newman–Reprise 27709
[Randy Newman] [ASC] (11/5/88 BC-52)

IT'S MY JOB Jimmy Buffett–MCA 51061 [Mac McAnally] [ASC] (2/14/81 BCR-57)

IT'S MY LIFE The Animals–MGM 13414
[Roger Atkins/Carl D'Errico] [BMI] (11/6/65 BCR-20)

IT'S MY LIFE Talk Talk–EMI America 8195
[Tim Friese-Greene/Mark Hollis] [BMI] (3/24/84 BC-31)

IT'S MY PARTY *Lesley Gore–Mercury 72119*
[Cy Crane/John Gluck/Wally Gold/Herb Weiner] [ASC] (5/4/63 BCR-1)*

IT'S MY PARTY *Dave Stewart With Barbara Gaskin–Platinum 4*
[Cy Crane/John Gluck/Wally Gold/Herb Weiner] [ASC] (12/5/81 BC-72)*

–IT'S MY THING (YOU CAN'T TELL ME...) see: IT'S YOUR THING

IT'S MY TURN Diana Ross–Motown 1496
[Michael Masser/Carole Bayer Sager] [ASC] (10/25/80 BCR-9)

IT'S NEVER TOO LATE Brenda Lee–Decca 31231 [Jim Seals] [BMI] (4/8/61 C-100)

IT'S NEVER TOO LATE Steppenwolf–Dunhill 4192
[John Kay/Nick St. Nicholas] [BMI] (5/10/69 BCR-35)

IT'S NICE TO BE WITH YOU The Monkees–Colgems 1023
[Jerry Goldstein] [BMI] (6/15/68 BCR-26)

IT'S NO CRIME Babyface–Solar 68966
[Kenneth Edmonds/Antonio Reid/Daryl Simmons] [BMI] (8/12/89 BC-7)

IT'S NO SECRET Kylie Minogue–Geffen 27651
[Matt Aitken/Mike Stock/Pete Waterman] [BMI] (12/3/88 BC-32)

IT'S NO SECRET WHAT GOD CAN DO Elvis Presley–RCA Victor LOC-1035
[Stuart Hamblen] (EP) [ASC] (12/30/57 R-49)

(IT'S NO) SIN *Billy Vaughn And His Orchestra–Dot 15993*
[George Hoven] [BMI] (11/2/59 CR-90) [IM]

(IT'S NO) SIN *The Duprees Featuring Joey Vann–Coed 587*
[George Hoven/Chester Shull] [BMI] (1/18/64 BCR-47)

IT'S NOT A WONDER Little River Band–Capitol 4862 [Graham Goble] [BMI] (5/3/80 BCR-51)

IT'S NOT EASY The Will-O-Bees–Date 1583
[Barry Mann/Cynthia Weil] [BMI] (1/20/68 BCR-90)

IT'S NOT ENOUGH Starship–RCA 9032
[Tommy Funderburk/Martin Page] [BMI] (8/5/89 BC-11)

IT'S NOT FOR ME TO SAY *Johnny Mathis–Columbia 40851*
[Robert Allen/Al Stillman] [ASC] (4/27/57 BCRt-2)

IT'S NOT FOR ME TO SAY *Jane Morgan–Kapp 185*
[Robert Allen/Al Stillman] [ASC] (6/15/57 Rt-3)

IT'S NOT FOR ME TO SAY *Cyril Stapleton & His Orchestra–London 1754*
[Robert Allen/Al Stillman] [ASC] (8/5/57 Rt-6)

IT'S NOT OVER ('TIL IT'S OVER) Starship–RCA 5225
[Phil Galdston/Robbie Nevil/John Van Tongeren] [ASC] (6/27/87 BC-9)

IT'S NOT THE END OF EVERYTHING Tommy Edwards–MGM 12688
[Bill Anderson] [BMI] (10/10/60 B-78)

IT'S NOT THE SAME Anthony And The Imperials–Veep 1248
[Ritchie Adams/Larry Kusik/Victoria Pike/Teddy Randazzo] [BMI] (11/12/66 BR-78)

IT'S NOT UNUSUAL Tom Jones–Parrot 9737 [Gordon Mills/Les Reed] [BMI] (4/3/65 BCR-8)

IT'S NOT YOU, IT'S NOT ME KBC Band–Arista 1-9526
[Phil Brown/Van Stephenson] [BMI] (11/29/86 BC-79)

IT'S NOW OR NEVER *Elvis Presley With The Jordanaires–RCA Victor 47-7777*
[Eduardo di Capua/Wally Gold/Aaron Schroeder] [ASC] (7/18/60 BCR-1) [FDE]

IT'S NOW OR NEVER *John Schneider–Scotti Brothers 02105*
[Eduardo di Capua/Wally Gold/Aaron Schroeder] [ASC] (5/30/81 BCR-14) [FDE]

IT'S NOW WINTER'S DAY Tommy Roe–ABC 10888
[Tommy Roe] [BMI] (12/24/66 BCR-21)

IT'S O.K. The Beach Boys–Brother/Reprise 1368
[Mike Love/Brian Wilson] [BMI] (8/21/76 BCR-29)

IT'S ONE OF THOSE NIGHTS (YES LOVE) The Partridge Family Starring Shirley Jones & Featuring David Cassidy–Bell 45,160 [Tony Romeo] [BMI] (12/11/71 BCR-13)

IT'S ONLY LOVE Tommy James And The Shondells—Roulette 4710
[Ritchie Cordell/Morris Levy*/Sal Trimachi] [BMI] (11/5/66 BCR-26)

IT'S ONLY LOVE *B.J. Thomas—Scepter 12244*
[Mark James/Steve Tyrell] [BMI] (3/22/69 BCR-23)

IT'S ONLY LOVE *Elvis Presley—RCA Victor 48-1017*
[Mark James/Steve Tyrell] [BMI] (10/9/71 BCR-42)

IT'S ONLY LOVE ZZ Top—London 241
[Frank Beard/Billy Gibbons/Dusty Hill] [BMI] (9/4/76 BCR-44)

IT'S ONLY LOVE Bryan Adams/Tina Turner—A&M 2791
[Bryan Adams/Jim Vallance] [BMI] (11/23/85 BC-14)

IT'S ONLY LOVE Simply Red—Elektra 69317
[Jimmie Cameron/Vella Cameron] [ASC] (2/18/89 BC-49)

IT'S ONLY MAKE BELIEVE *Conway Twitty—MGM 12677*
[Jack Nance/Conway Twitty] [BMI] (9/8/58 BCR-1)

IT'S ONLY MAKE BELIEVE *Glen Campbell—Capitol 2905*
[Jack Nance/Conway Twitty] [BMI] (9/5/70 BCR-8)

IT'S ONLY ROCK 'N ROLL (BUT I LIKE IT) The Rolling Stones—Rolling Stones 19301
[Mick Jagger/Keith Richards] [ASC] (8/3/74 BCR-11)

IT'S ONLY THE BEGINNING The Kalin Twins—Decca 30807
[Aaron Schroeder/Sid Wayne] [ASC] (1/12/59 BCR-42)

IT'S ONLY THE GOOD TIMES Tommy Edwards—MGM 12794
[Lee Pockriss/Peter Udell] [ASC] (6/1/59 BCR-59)

IT'S ORDACIOUS Buddy Johnson and His Orchestra—Mercury 70695
[Woodrow Buddy Johnson] [BMI] (11/12/55 B-94)

IT'S OVER Roy Orbison—Monument 837
[William Dees/Roy Orbison] [BMI] (4/11/64 BCR-8)

IT'S OVER *Jimmie Rodgers—Dot 16861*
[James Frederick Rodgers] [ASC] (5/14/66 BCR-31)

IT'S OVER *Eddy Arnold—RCA Victor 47-9525*
[James Frederick Rodgers] [ASC] (5/18/68 BCR-63)

IT'S OVER Boz Scaggs—Columbia 10319
[David Paich/Boz Scaggs] [ASC] (4/3/76 BCR-38)

IT'S OVER Electric Light Orchestra—Jet 5052 [Jeff Lynne] [BMI] (10/28/78 BR-75)

IT'S OVER Teddy Baker—Casablanca 2340 [Teddy Baker] [BMI] (9/26/81 C-81)

IT'S RAINING AGAIN Supertramp—A&M 2502
[Rick Davies/Roger Hodgson] [ASC] (10/30/82 BC-7)

IT'S RAINING MEN The Weather Girls—Columbia 03354
[Paul Jabara/Paul Shaffer] [BMI] (1/22/83 BC-46)

IT'S RAINING OUTSIDE The Platters—Mercury 71353
[Tito Madi/Buck Ram] [ASC] (9/8/58 BCR-59)

IT'S REALLY YOU The Tarney/Spencer Band—A&M 2049
[Tom Snow/Trevor Spencer/Alan Tarney] [BMI] (7/15/78 BC-86)

IT'S SAD TO BELONG England Dan & John Ford Coley—Big Tree 16088
[Randy Goodrum] [ASC] (5/7/77 BCR-13)

IT'S SERIOUS Cameo—Chocolate City 013
[Larry Blackmon/Gregory Johnson] [BMI] (5/13/78 R-98)

IT'S SO EASY Linda Ronstadt—Asylum 45438
[Buddy Holly/Norman Petty] [ASC] (10/8/77 BCR-5)

IT'S SO EASY TO FORGET The Four Lads—Columbia 40811
[Gordon Charles/Jean David] [NA] (2/9/57 R-60)

IT'S SO EASY TO SAY Johnny Nash—ABC-Paramount 9894
[Jack Keller/Noel Sherman] [ASC] (3/10/58 R-48)

—IT'S SO GOOD see: C'EST SI BON

IT'S SO HARD BEING A LOSER The Contours—Gordy 7059
[James Anthony Dean/Stan McMullen/William Weatherspoon] [BMI] (4/8/67 BCR-66)

IT'S SO HARD FOR ME TO SAY GOOD-BYE Eddie Kendricks—Tamla 54203
[Pam Sawyer/Frank Edward Wilson] [BMI] (5/15/71 BCR-61)

IT'S SO HARD TO SAY GOODBYE TO YESTERDAY Boyz II Men—Motown 2136
[Freddie Perren/Christine Yarian] [ASC] (9/21/91 BC-1)

IT'S SO NICE Jackie Deshannon—Liberty 56187
[Irvin Hunt/Sam Russell] [BMI] (8/8/70 BCR-84)

IT'S STILL ROCK AND ROLL TO ME Billy Joel—Columbia 11276
[Billy Joel] [ASC] (5/24/80 BCR-1)

IT'S SUMMER The Temptations—Gordy 7109
[Barrett Strong/Norman Whitfield] [BMI] (7/17/71 BCR-28)

IT'S THAT TIME OF THE YEAR Len Barry—Decca 31969
[Len Barry/Leon Huff/John Madara/David White] [BMI] (6/11/66 BCR-80)

IT'S THE END OF THE WORLD AS WE KNOW IT (AND I FEEL FINE) R.E.M.—I.R.S. 53220
[Bill Berry/Peter Buck/Mike Mills/Michael Stipe] [BMI] (1/30/88 BC-69)

IT'S THE LITTLE THINGS Sonny & Cher—Atco 6507 [Sonny Bono] [BMI] (8/5/67 BCR-50)

IT'S THE LOVE THAT REALLY COUNTS (IN THE LONG RUN) The Shirelles—Scepter 1237
[Burt Bacharach/Hal David] [ASC] (9/22/62 R-97)

IT'S THE REAL THING - PT I The Electric Express—Linco 1001
[Vick Hudson] [BMI] (7/10/71 BCR-65) [IM]

IT'S THE SAME OLD LOVE The Courtship—Tamla 54217
[Gene Allan/Gary Knight] [BMI] (5/27/72 BC-93)

IT'S THE SAME OLD SONG *Four Tops—Motown 1081*
[Lamont Dozier/Brian Holland/Eddie Holland] [BMI] (7/24/65 BCR-5)

IT'S THE SAME OLD SONG *Shalamar—Soul Train 10885*
[Lamont Dozier/Brian Holland/Eddie Holland] (Med) [BMI] (3/12/77 BCR-25)

IT'S THE SAME OLD SONG *KC & The Sunshine Band—TK 1028*
[Lamont Dozier/Brian Holland/Eddie Holland] [BMI] (5/6/78 BCR-35)

(IT'S THE WAY) NATURE PLANNED IT Four Tops—Motown 1210
[Pam Sawyer/Frank Edward Wilson] [BMI] (8/26/72 BCR-53)

IT'S TIME FOR LOVE The Chi-Lites—Brunswick 55520
[Eugene Record] [BMI] (11/8/75 B-94)

IT'S TIME TO CRY Paul Anka—ABC-Paramount 10064 [Paul Anka] [BMI] (11/9/59 BCR-4)

IT'S TIME TO SAY GOODBYE The Third Rail—Epic 10285
[Joe (2) Brooks/Kathy Cooper] [NA] (3/9/68 CR-82)

IT'S TOO LATE Wilson Pickett—Double-L 717 [Wilson Pickett] [BMI] (7/20/63 BCR-31)

IT'S TOO LATE Bobby Goldsboro—United Artists 980
[Bobby Goldsboro] [BMI] (2/12/66 BCR-22)

IT'S TOO LATE *Carole King—Ode '70 66015/Ode 66015*
[Carole King/Toni Stern] (TSW) [ASC] (6/12/71 BCR-1)

IT'S TOO LATE *Bill Deal & The Rhondels—Buddah 318*
[Carole King/Toni Stern] [ASC] (8/12/72 CR-81)

IT'S TOO LATE, BABY TOO LATE Arthur Prysock—Old Town 1183
[Gayle Candis Brown*/Hazel Johnson] [BMI] (7/10/65 BCR-48)

IT'S TOO SOON TO KNOW *Tony Bennett—Columbia 40427*
[Deborah Chessler] [ASC] (2/21/55 R-60)

IT'S TOO SOON TO KNOW *Pat Boone—Dot 15690*
[Deborah Chessler] [ASC] (1/27/58 BCR-6)

IT'S TOO SOON TO KNOW *Etta James—Argo 5402*
[Deborah Chessler] [ASC] (11/4/61 BCR-54)

IT'S TRICKY Run-D.M.C.—Profile 5131
[Darryl McDaniels/Jason Mizell/Rick Rubin/Joseph Ward Simmons] [ASC] (2/28/87 BC-57)

IT'S TRUE I'M GONNA MISS YOU Carolyn Franklin—RCA Victor 74-0188
[Mattie Simpkins/Ken Williams] [BMI] (9/13/69 CR-97)

IT'S UNBELIEVABLE The Larks(1)—Sheryl 334
[Herb Gordon/Steve Schulman] [BMI] (3/6/61 BCR-69)

IT'S UNCANNY Daryl Hall & John Oates—Atlantic 3397
[Daryl Hall] [BMI] (7/30/77 BC-80)

IT'S UP TO YOU Rick Nelson—Imperial 5901 [Jerry Fuller] [BMI] (12/15/62 BCR-6)

IT'S UP TO YOU PETULA Edison Lighthouse—Bell 960
[Chris Arnold/David Martin/Geoff Morrow] [BMI] (1/2/71 BCR-59)

IT'S WONDERFUL The Young Rascals—Atlantic 2463
[Eddie Brigati/Felix Cavaliere] [ASC] (12/9/67 BCR-12)

IT'S WONDERFUL TO BE IN LOVE The Ovations (Featuring Louis Wiliams)—Goldwax 113
[Elvin Jones/Nathaniel Lewis/Louis Williams] [BMI] (5/15/65 BCR-54)

IT'S YOU Bob Seger & The Silver Bullet Band—Capitol 5623
[Bob Seger] [ASC] (8/16/86 BC-52)

IT'S YOU I LOVE Fats Domino—Imperial 5442
[Dave Bartholomew/Fats Domino] [BMI] (5/18/57 BCR-19)

IT'S YOU THAT I NEED Enchantment—Roadshow 1124
[Verdell Lanier/Michael Lee Stokes] [BMI] (1/21/78 BCR-33)

IT'S YOUR LIFE Bob Manning—Capitol 3041
[Nat Simon/Charles Tobias] [ASC] (2/7/55 R-71)

IT'S YOUR LIFE Andy Kim—Steed 727 [Jeff Barry/Andy Kim] [BMI] (7/25/70 BCR-74)

IT'S YOUR THING The Isley Brothers—T-Neck 901
[O'Kelly Isley/Ronald Isley/Rudolph Isley] [BMI] (3/15/69 BCR-2)

IT'S MY THING (YOU CAN'T TELL ME WHO TO SOCK IT TO)
(R: It's Your Thing, Isleys not credited, not listed as Cover) Marva Whitney—King 6229
[James Brown/Marva Whitney] [BMI] (5/31/69 BCR-72) [R]

IT'S YOUR WORLD Marty Robbins—Columbia 42065
[Marty Robbins] [BMI] (8/28/61 BCR-51)

IT'S YOURS The DeCastro Sisters—RCA Victor 47-6661
[Arthur Altman/Charles Tobias] [ASC] (10/20/56 B-74)

ITSY BITSY TEENIE WEENIE YELLOW POLKADOT BIKINI *Brian Hyland—Kapp 342*
[Lee Pockriss/Paul Vance] [ASC] (6/27/60 BCRt-1)

ITSY BITSY TEENIE WEENIE YELLOW POLKADOT BIKINI *Buddy Hackett—Laurel 1014*
[Lee Pockriss/Paul Vance] [ASC] (6/27/60 Rt-68)

ITTY BITTY PIECES James Ray—Caprice 114 [Rudy Clark] [BMI] (4/7/62 BCR-41)

I'VE ALWAYS HAD YOU Benny Troy—De-Lite 1566
[Billy Terrell] [BMI] (4/19/75 R-83)

I'VE BEEN A LONG TIME LEAVIN' (BUT I'LL BE A LONG TIME GONE)
Roger Miller—Smash 2024
[Roger Miller] [BMI] (2/12/66 CR-92)

I'VE BEEN AROUND Fats Domino—Imperial 5629
[Fats Domino] [BMI] (10/26/59 BCR-33)

I'VE BEEN BORN AGAIN Johnnie Taylor—Stax 0208
[Don Davis/James Anthony Dean] [BMI] (6/8/74 BCR-62)

I'VE BEEN EVERYWHERE Hank Snow—RCA Victor 47-8072
[Geoff Mack] [BMI] (9/29/62 BCR-68)

I'VE BEEN HURT Bill Deal & The Rhondels—Heritage 812
[Ray Whitley] [BMI] (4/19/69 BCR-27)

I'VE BEEN IN LOVE BEFORE Cutting Crew—Virgin 99425
[Nick Van Eede] [BMI] (9/5/87 BC-9)

I'VE BEEN LONELY FOR SO LONG Frederick Knight—Stax 0117
[Posie Knight/Jerry Weaver] [BMI] (4/22/72 BCR-20)

I'VE BEEN LONELY TOO LONG The Young Rascals—Atlantic 2377
[Eddie Brigati/Felix Cavaliere] [ASC] (1/28/67 BCR-15)

(I'VE BEEN LOOKIN' FOR) A NEW WAY TO SAY I LOVE YOU Driver—A&M 1966
[Dennis Coats/Peter Glindeman/Stephen Rexford] [BMI] (8/6/77 C-83)

I'VE BEEN LOVED BEFORE Shirley & Lee—Warwick 535
[Leonard Lee] [BMI] (6/27/60 BCR-88)

I'VE BEEN LOVIN' YOU Easy Street—Capricorn 0255
[Richard Burgess/Peter Marsh/Ken Nicol/Pete Zorn] [BMI] (7/3/76 BCR-79)

I'VE BEEN LOVING YOU TOO LONG (TO STOP NOW) *Otis Redding—Volt 126*
[Jerry Butler/Otis Redding] [BMI] (5/15/65 BCR-12)

I'VE BEEN LOVING YOU TOO LONG *Ike & Tina Turner—Blue Thumb 101*
[Jerry Butler/Otis Redding] [BMI] (4/26/69 BCR-68)

(I'VE BEEN) SEARCHIN' SO LONG Chicago—Columbia 46020
[James Pankow] [ASC] (3/16/74 BCR-5)

I'VE BEEN THERE Tommy Edwards—MGM 12814
[Robert Allen/Mack David] [ASC] (7/27/59 BCR-25)

I'VE BEEN THINKING *The Four Lads—Columbia 40436*
[Boudleaux Bryant] [BMI] (3/5/55 CRt-33)

I'VE BEEN THINKIN' *Rusty Draper—Mercury 70555*
[Boudleaux Bryant] [BMI] (3/14/55 Rt-74)

I'VE BEEN THINKING *Eddy Arnold—RCA Victor 47-6000*
[Boudleaux Bryant] [BMI] (3/14/55 Rt-74)

I'VE BEEN THINKING ABOUT YOU Londonbeat—Radioactive 54005
[Jimmy Chambers/George Chandler/Jimmy Helms/William Henshall] [BMI] (2/9/91 BC-1)

I'VE BEEN THIS WAY BEFORE Neil Diamond—Columbia 10084
[Neil Diamond] [SE] (2/1/75 BCR-34)

I'VE BEEN TRYING The Impressions—ABC-Paramount 10622
[Curtis Mayfield] [BMI] (2/20/65 CR-84)

I'VE BEEN WAITING FOR YOU Guys Next Door—SBK 07340
[Antonina Armato/Scott Cutler] [ASC] (12/29/90 BC-42)

I'VE BEEN WAITING FOR YOU ALL OF MY LIFE Paul Anka—RCA 12225
[Linda J. Kimball/Mark Sherrill] [BMI] (4/18/81 BCR-48)

I'VE CHANGED MY MIND A THOUSAND TIMES *Kay Starr—RCA Victor 47-6359*
[Bob Hilliard] [ASC] (2/3/56 BRt-73)

I'VE CHANGED MY MIND A THOUSAND TIMES *The Mills Brothers—Decca 29781*
[Bob Hilliard] [ASC] (2/3/56 Rt-84)

I'VE COME OF AGE Billy Storm—Columbia 41356
[Sid Jacobson/Lou Stallman] [BMI] (4/13/59 BCR-24)

I'VE DONE EVERYTHING FOR YOU Rick Springfield—RCA 12166
[Sammy Hagar] [BMI] (8/22/81 BCR-6)

I'VE FALLEN IN LOVE (WITH YOU) Carla Thomas—Stax 0011
[Carla Thomas] [BMI] (8/23/69 R-92)

I'VE FOUND SOMEONE OF MY OWN The Free Movement—Decca 32818
[Frank F. Robinson] [BMI] (5/22/71 BCR-5)

I'VE GOT A FEELING (WE'LL BE SEEING EACH OTHER AGAIN) Al Wilson—Playboy 6062
[Homer Banks/Carl Hampton] [BMI] (3/20/76 BCR-29)

I'VE GOT A GAL IN KALAMAZOO Frank Barber Orchestra—Victory 1001
[Harry Warren] (Med) [ASC] (5/8/82 B-61) [IM]

I'VE GOT A LOT TO LEARN ABOUT LOVE The Storm—Interscope 98726
[Kevin Chalfant/Bob Marlette/Gregg Rolie] [BMI] (10/26/91 BC-18)

I'VE GOT A NOTION Marv Johnson—United Artists 322
[Robert Bateman/George Fowler/Brian Holland] [BMI] (7/1/61 C-93)

I'VE GOT A RIGHT TO CRY *Eydie Gorme—ABC-Paramount 9758*
[Joseph Liggins] [BMI] (11/10/56 Rt-49)

I'VE GOT A RIGHT TO CRY *Bob Carroll—Bally 1021*
[Joseph Liggins] [BMI] (11/10/56 Rt-49)

I'VE GOT A ROCK N' ROLL HEART Eric Clapton—Duck/Warner 29780
[Steve Diamond/Troy Seals/Eddie Setser] [BMI] (1/29/83 BC-18)

I GOT A THING ABOUT YOU BABY *Billy Lee Riley—Entrance 7508*
[Tony Joe White] [ASC] (10/7/72 BC-93)

I'VE GOT A THING ABOUT YOU BABY *Elvis Presley—RCA Victor 0196*
[Tony Joe White] (TSW) [ASC] (3/16/74 BCR-30)

I'VE GOT A TIGER BY THE TAIL Buck Owens—Capitol 5336
[Harlan Howard/Buck Owens] [BMI] (1/23/65 BCR-25)

I'VE GOT BELLS ON MY HEART *Don Cornell—Coral 61956*
[Sunny Skylar] [ASC] (3/17/58 Rt-35)

I'VE GOT BELLS ON MY HEART *The Three Pennies—Golden Crest 1311*
[Sunny Skylar] [ASC] (3/17/58 Rt-35)

I'VE GOT BELLS ON MY HEART *Jane Morgan—Kapp 214*
[Sunny Skylar] [ASC] (3/17/58 Rt-35)

I'VE GOT BELLS ON MY HEART *Don Rondo—Jubilee 5320*
[Sunny Skylar] [ASC] (4/14/58 Rt-35)

I'VE GOT BONNIE Bobby Rydell—Cameo 209
[Gerry Goffin/Carole King] [BMI] (1/29/62 BCR-17)

I'VE GOT DREAMS TO REMEMBER Otis Redding—Atco 6612
[Otis Redding/Zelma Redding/Joseph Rock] [BMI] (9/21/68 BCR-37)

I'VE GOT FIVE DOLLARS AND IT'S SATURDAY NIGHT
George & Gene; George Jones & Gene Pitney—Musicor 1066
[Ted Daffan] [BMI] (3/27/65 BC-97)

I'VE GOT FOUR BIG BROTHERS (TO LOOK AFTER ME)
The Four Lads & Cathy Johnson—Columbia 40532
[Rose Maddox/Dusty Rose] [BMI] (7/4/55 R-74)

I'VE GOT LOVE Julius La Rosa—RCA Victor 47-6499 [Bob Haymes] [BMI] (6/30/56 B-93)

I'VE GOT LOVE FOR MY BABY Young Hearts—Minit 32049
[Earl Carter/Charles Ingersoll/James Leon Moore/Ronald Preyer] [BMI] (11/9/68 BCR-82)

I'VE GOT LOVE ON MY MIND Natalie Cole—Capitol 4360
[Charles Henry Jackson Jr./Marvin Yancy] [ASC] (1/29/77 BCR-3)

—I'VE GOT MY EYES ON YOU see: HURTING KIND

I'VE GOT NEWS FOR YOU Ray Charles—Impulse 202 [Roy Alfred] [ASC] (6/19/61 BCR-58)

I'VE GOT NO TIME TO LOSE Carla Thomas—Atlantic 2238
[Steve Cropper/Willia Dean Parker] [BMI] (8/1/64 BCR-53)

I'VE GOT SAND IN MY SHOES The Drifters—Atlantic 2253
[Artie Resnick/Kenny Young] [BMI] (9/26/64 BCR-29)

I'VE GOT SO MANY MILLION YEARS (THAT I CAN'T COUNT THEM)
Johnnie Ray—Columbia 40528
[Stuart Hamblen] [ASC] (7/4/55 R-56)

I'VE GOT SO MUCH TO GIVE Barry White—20th Century 2042
[Barry White] [BMI] (8/4/73 BCR-32)

(I'VE GOT) SPRING FEVER Little Willie John—King 5503
[Shorty Long/Paul Tannen] [BMI] (5/15/61 BR-71)

I'VE GOT THE MUSIC IN ME The Kiki Dee Band—Rocket/MCA 40293
[Bias Boshell] [ASC] (9/14/74 BCR-12)

I'VE GOT THE NEXT DANCE Deniece Williams—ARC 10971
[Cheyenne Fowler/Keg Johnson/Deniece Williams] [BMI] (8/18/79 B-73)

I'VE GOT THE SKILL Jackie Ross—Chess 1913
[Billy Davis/Wilfred McKinley/Carl William Smith] [BMI] (11/7/64 BCR-69)

I'VE GOT TO BE SOMEBODY Billy Joe Royal—Columbia 43465
[Joe South] [BMI] (12/4/65 BCR-33)

I'VE GOT TO DO A LITTLE BIT BETTER Joe Tex—Dial 4045
[Joe Tex] [BMI] (10/8/66 BCR-57)

I'VE GOT TO GO ON WITHOUT YOU The Van Dykes (2)—Mala 530
[Rondalis Tandy] [BMI] (7/9/66 CR-100)

I'VE GOT TO HAVE A REASON The Dave Clark Five—Epic 10114
[Dave Clark/Lenny Davidson] [BMI] (1/7/67 BCR-44)

I'VE GOT TO HAVE YOU Sammi Smith—Mega 0079
[Kris Kristofferson] [BMI] (8/26/72 BCR-75)

I'VE GOT TO HAVE YOUR LOVE Eddie Floyd—Stax 0025
[Steve Cropper/Eddie Floyd] [BMI] (2/15/69 CR-57)

I'VE GOT TO USE MY IMAGINATION Gladys Knight & The Pips—Buddah 393
[Gerry Goffin/Barry Goldberg] [BMI] (11/24/73 BCR-4)

I'VE GOT YOU UNDER MY SKIN *Louis Prima And Keely Smith—Capitol 4140*
[Cole Porter] [ASC] (2/16/59 BCR-62)

I'VE GOT YOU UNDER MY SKIN
The 4 Seasons Featuring The "Sound" Of Frankie Valli—Philips 40393
[Cole Porter] [ASC] (9/3/66 BCR-6)

I'VE GOT YOU UNDER MY SKIN *Gidea Park—Profile 5003*
[Cole Porter] (Med) [ASC] (12/26/81 BC-82)

—I'VE GOT YOUR NUMBER see: BACK OF MY HAND

I'VE GOTTA BE ME Sammy Davis Jr.—Reprise 0779
[Walter Marks] [ASC] (12/7/68 BCR-11)

I'VE GOTTA GET A MESSAGE TO YOU The Bee Gees—Atco 6603
[Barry Gibb/Maurice Gibb/Robin Gibb] [BMI] (8/10/68 BCR-3)

I'VE GOTTA MAKE YOU LOVE ME Steam—Mercury 73020
[Gary DeCarlo/Dale Frashuer/Paul Leka] [BMI] (1/24/70 BCR-31)

I'VE GROWN ACCUSTOMED TO YOUR FACE *Gordon MacRae—Capitol 3384*
[Alan Jay Lerner/Frederick Loewe] [ASC] (3/30/56 BRt-24)

I'VE GROWN ACCUSTOMED TO YOUR FACE *Rosemary Clooney—Columbia 40676*
[Alan Jay Lerner/Frederick Loewe] [ASC] (3/30/56 BRt-24)

I'VE GROWN ACCUSTOMED TO HER FACE
Sid Feller & His Orchestra—ABC-Paramount 9692
[Alan Jay Lerner/Frederick Loewe] [ASC] (4/20/56 Rt-24)

I'VE GROWN ACCUSTOMED TO YOUR FACE
Bob Eberly with Enoch Light & His Orchestra—Grand Award 1003
[Alan Jay Lerner/Frederick Loewe] [ASC] (5/11/56 Rt-24)

I'VE GROWN ACCUSTOMED TO HER FACE
Lawrence Welk & His Champagne Music—Coral 61645
[Alan Jay Lerner/Frederick Loewe] [ASC] (6/8/56 Rt-24)

I'VE GROWN ACCUSTOMED TO HER FACE
Sammy Kaye & His "Swing And Sway" Orchestra—Columbia 40707
[Alan Jay Lerner/Frederick Loewe] [ASC] (6/22/56 Rt-24)

I'VE HAD ENOUGH Wings—Capitol 4594
[Paul McCartney] [ASC] (6/17/78 BCR-25)

I'VE HAD IT *The Bell Notes—Time 1004*
[Carl Bonura/Raymond Ceroni] [BMI] (1/3/59 BCR-6)

I'VE HAD IT *Fanny—Casablanca 0009*
[Carl Bonura/Raymond Ceroni] [BMI] (6/1/74 BCR-63)

(I'VE HAD) THE TIME OF MY LIFE Bill Medley And Jennifer Warnes—RCA 5224
[John DeNicola/Donald Markowitz/Franke Previte] [ASC] (9/19/87 BC-1)

I'VE JUST BEGUN TO CARE
Michael Nesmith & The First National Band—RCA Victor 74-0540 [Michael Nesmith] [BMI] (10/23/71 CR-89)

I'VE JUST BEGUN TO LOVE YOU Dynasty—Solar 12021
[William Shelby/Ricky Darnell Smith] [ASC] (8/16/80 BCR-72)

I'VE LOST EVERYTHING I'VE EVER LOVED David Ruffin—Motown 1149
[Johnny Bristol/Thomas Kemp] [ASC] (7/12/69 BCR-53)

I'VE LOST YOU Jackie Wilson—Brunswick 55321 [Van McCoy] [BMI] (5/6/67 BCR-56)

I'VE LOST YOU Elvis Presley—RCA Victor 47-9873
[Alan Blaikley/Ken Howard] (TSW) [ASC] (8/1/70 BCR-14)

I'VE LOVED YOU FOR A LONG TIME The Spinners—Atlantic 3664
[Michael Zager] (Med) [BMI] (5/17/80 BCR-4)

I'VE NEVER BEEN IN LOVE Suzi Quatro—RSO 1001
[Melissa Connell] [ASC] (9/8/79 BCR-44)

I'VE NEVER BEEN TO ME *Charlene—Prodigal 0636*
[Ken Hirsch/Ronald Norman Miller] [BMI] (9/24/77 B-97)

I'VE NEVER BEEN TO ME *Charlene—Motown 1611*
[Ken Hirsch/Ronald Norman Miller] [BMI] (3/6/82 BCR-3)

I'VE NEVER FOUND A GIRL (TO LOVE ME LIKE YOU DO) *Eddie Floyd—Stax 0002*
[Eddie Floyd/Alvertis Isbell/Booker T. Jones Jr.] [BMI] (7/27/68 BCR-40)

I'VE NEVER FOUND A MAN (TO LOVE ME LIKE YOU DO) *Esther Phillips—Kudu 910*
[Eddie Floyd/Alvertis Isbell/Booker T. Jones Jr.] [BMI] (12/23/72 C-72)

I'VE PASSED THIS WAY BEFORE Jimmy Ruffin—Soul 35027
[James Anthony Dean/William Weatherspoon] [BMI] (12/3/66 BCR-14)

I'VE TOLD EVERY LITTLE STAR Linda Scott—Canadian-American 123
[Oscar Hammerstein/Jerome Kern] [ASC] (2/27/61 BCR-3)

IVORY Bob Seger System—Capitol 2480 [Bob Seger] [ASC] (5/10/69 BR-97)

IVORY RAG (IN DER ALTEN HAFENBAR) *Crazy Otto—Polydor 22009B*
[Louis F. Bush/John M. Elliott] (Med) [ASC] (1/17/55 R-1) [IWM]

IVORY RAG (IN DER ALTEN HAFENBAR) *Johnny Maddox And The Rhythmasters—Dot 15325*
[Louis F. Bush/John M. Elliott] (Med) [ASC] (1/24/55 BCR-1) [IWM]

IVORY TOWER *Cathy Carr—Fraternity 734*
[Jack Fulton/Lois Steele] [ASC] (3/24/56 BCtRt-2)

IVORY TOWER *Otis Williams And His Charms—DeLuxe 6093*
[Jack Fulton/Lois Steele] [ASC] (3/30/56 BCtRt-2)

IVORY TOWER *Gale Storm—Dot 15458 [Jack Fulton/Lois Steele] [ASC] (4/20/56 BCtRt-2)*

IVY, IVY The Left Banke—Smash 2089
[Tom Feher/Michael David Lookofsky*] [BMI] (5/6/67 R-99)

IVY ROSE Perry Como—RCA Victor 47-7050
[Al Hoffman/Dick Manning] [ASC] (9/30/57 BCR-26)

J

JA-DA Johnny And The Hurricanes—Big Top 3063
[Bob Carleton] [ASC] (2/4/61 BCR-86) [I]

JACK & DIANE John Cougar—Riva 210 [John Mellencamp] [ASC] (7/24/82 BC-1)

JACK AND JILL Tommy Roe—ABC 11229 [Tommy Roe/Freddy Weller] [BMI] (7/12/69 BCR-31)

JACK AND JILL Raydio—Arista 0283 [Ray Parker Jr.] [ASC] (12/17/77 BCR-6)

JACK O' DIAMONDS Ruth Brown—Atlantic 2026
[Jerry Leiber/Mike Stoller] [BMI] (5/23/59 BCR-77)

JACK THE LAD 3 Man Island—Chrysalis 43231
[Tim Cox/Nigel Swanston/Mike Whitford] [BMI] (4/2/88 BC-90)

JACK THE RIPPER Link Wray & His Ray Men—Swan 4137
[Milton Grant*/Link Wray] [BMI] (5/25/63 BCR-58) [I]

JACKIE Blue Zone U.K.—Arista 1-9725
[Thomas F. Kelly/Billy Steinberg] [ASC] (8/13/88 BC-54)

JACKIE BLUE The Ozark Mountain Daredevils—A&M 1654
[Steve Cash/Larry Michael Lee] [BMI] (2/8/75 BCR-1)

JACKIE BROWN John Cougar Mellencamp—Mercury 874 644
[John Mellencamp] [ASC] (7/15/89 BC-45)

JACKIE WILSON SAID (I'M IN HEAVEN WHEN YOU SMILE)
Van Morrison—Warner Bros. 7616
[Van Morrison] [BMI] (8/19/72 BCR-61)

JACKSON Nancy Sinatra & Lee Hazlewood—Reprise 0595
[Jerry Leiber/Billy Edd Wheeler] [BMI] (6/24/67 BCR-13)

JACOB'S LADDER Huey Lewis and the News—Chrysalis 43097
[Bruce Hornsby/John Hornsby] [ASC] (1/17/87 BC-1)

JACQUELINE Bobby Helms—Decca 30619
[Mort Garson/Bob Hilliard] [ASC] (4/21/58 BCR-45)

JACQUES D'IRAQUE Sammy Davis Jr.—Decca 29861
[Jerry Bock/Lawrence Holofcener/George David Weiss] [ASC] (3/16/56 R-50)

JAGUAR AND THUNDERBIRD Chuck Berry—Chess 1767
[Chuck Berry] [BMI] (11/14/60 CR-78)

JAILER, BRING ME WATER Trini Lopez—Reprise 0260
[Bobby Darin] [BMI] (2/29/64 BR-83)

JAILHOUSE ROCK *Elvis Presley—RCA Victor 47-7035*
[Jerry Leiber/Mike Stoller] [BMI] (9/30/57 BCR-1)

JAILHOUSE ROCK *Elvis Presley—RCA 13351*
[Jerry Leiber/Mike Stoller] (Med) [BMI] (11/20/82 BC-71)

JAILHOUSE ROCK *Jive Bunny And The Mastermixers—Music Factory 99140*
[Jerry Leiber/Mike Stoller] (Med) [BMI] (10/28/89 BC-11)

JALOUSIE Caterina Valente—Decca 29467
[Vera Bloom/Jacob Gade] [ASC] (4/11/55 R-31)

THE JAM PART 1 Bobby Gregg And His Friends—Cotton 1003
[Bobby Gregg] [BMI] (3/17/62 BCR-26) [I]

THE JAM Graham Central Station—Warner Bros. 8175
[Larry Graham] [BMI] (2/7/76 BCR-63) [I]

JAM BAND Disco Tex & The Sex-O-Lettes—Chelsea 3026
[Bob Crewe/Denny Randell] [BMI] (8/30/75 BC-80)

JAM ON IT Newcleus—Sunnyview SUN 3010 [Maurice Cenac] [ASC] (6/2/84 BC-56)

JAM TONIGHT Freddie Jackson—Capitol 44037
[Freddie Jackson/Paul Laurence] [ASC] (6/27/87 BC-32)

JAM UP JELLY TIGHT Tommy Roe—ABC 11247
[Tommy Roe/Freddy Weller] [BMI] (11/15/69 BCR-4)

THE JAM WAS MOVING Debbie Harry—Chrysalis 2554
[Bernard Edwards/Nile Rodgers] [BMI] (10/31/81 B-82)

JAMAICA FAREWELL Harry Belafonte—RCA Victor 47-6663
[Lord Burgess] [ASC] (10/20/56 BCR-15)

JAMAICA SKA The Ska Kings—Atlantic 2232 [Byron Lee] [BMI] (7/11/64 BR-97)

JAMBALAYA (ON THE BAYOU) *Little Brenda Lee (9 Years Old)—Decca 30050*
[Hank Williams] [BMI] (10/6/56 R-72)

JAMBALAYA *Bobby Comstock & The Counts—Atlantic 2051*
[Hank Williams] [BMI] (3/7/60 B-90)

JAMBALAYA (ON THE BAYOU) *Fats Domino—Imperial 5796*
[Hank Williams] [BMI] (12/4/61 BCR-28)

JAMBALAYA (ON THE BAYOU) *Nitty Gritty Dirt Band—United Artists 50890*
[Hank Williams] [BMI] (4/1/72 BCR-77)

JAMBALAYA (ON THE BAYOU) *The Blue Ridge Rangers—Fantasy 689*
[Hank Williams] [BMI] (12/2/72 BCR-10)

THE JAMES BOND THEME *Billy Strange—GNP Crescendo 320*
[Monty Norman] [BMI] (8/22/64 BCR-58) [I]

THE JAMES BOND THEME *Meco—Arista 0660*
[Monty Norman] (Med) [BMI] (2/13/82 BCR-35) [I]

JAMES DEAN Eagles—Asylum 45202
[Jackson Browne/Glenn Frey/Don Henley/J.D. Souther] [ASC] (9/7/74 BCR-49)

JAMES (HOLD THE LADDER STEADY) Sue Thompson—Hickory 1183
[John D. Loudermilk] [BMI] (9/29/62 BCR-17)

JAMIE Eddie Holland—Motown 1021
[William Stevenson/Barrett Strong] [BMI] (1/15/62 BCR-30)

JAMIE Ray Parker Jr.—Arista 1-9293 [Ray Parker Jr.] [ASC] (11/17/84 BC-14)

JAMIE BOY Kay Starr—RCA Victor 47-6864
[Joe Shapiro/Lou Stallman] [BMI] (4/13/57 BCR-36)

JAMMIN Teena Marie—Epic 04738 [Teena Marie] [ASC] (4/27/85 B-81)

JAMMIN' ME Tom Petty and The Heartbreakers—MCA 53065
[Mike Campbell/Bob Dylan/Tom Petty] [ASC] (4/25/87 BC-18)

JANE Jefferson Starship—Grunt 11750
[Craig Chaquico/David Freiberg/Paul Kantner/Jim McPherson] [BMI] (11/3/79 BCR-6)

JANE, JANE, JANE The Kingston Trio—Capitol 4740
[Stanley C. Wilson] [ASC] (5/19/62 B-93)

JANE'S GETTING SERIOUS Jon Astley—Atlantic 89258 [Jon Astley] [ASC] (6/27/87 BC-77)

JANET Commodores—Motown 1802
[Bobby Caldwell/Paul Fox/Franne Golde] [BMI] (9/21/85 B-87)

JANIE IS HER NAME Roger Williams—Kapp 545
[Joseph Turner Henderson] [ASC] (7/20/63 R-99) [IM]

JANIE'S GOT A GUN Aerosmith—Geffen 22727
[Tom Hamilton/Steven Tyler] [ASC] (11/25/89 BC-3)

JANUARY Pilot—EMI 4202 [David Paton] [BMI] (1/31/76 BC-87)

THE JAPANESE FAREWELL SONG *Kay Cee Jones—Marquee 1031*
[Freddy Morgan/Freddy Morgan] [ASC] (12/3/55 BCRt-44)

THE JAPANESE FAREWELL SONG *Lois Winters—Dot 15441*
[Freddy Morgan/Freddy Morgan] [ASC] (1/27/56 Rt-81)

JAPANESE RHUMBA *Jayne and Audrey Meadows—RCA Victor 47-6132*
[Jerry Miller] [BMI] (5/30/55 Rt-51)

JAPANESE RHUMBA *The Twin-Tunes—Sound 115*
[Jerry Miller] [BMI] (5/30/55 Rt-51)

JASPER Jim Stafford—Polydor 14309 [Dave Loggins/Jim Stafford] [ASC] (4/3/76 BCR-69)

JAVA *Floyd Cramer—RCA Victor 47-8116*
[Freddy Friday‡/Marilyn Schack‡/Allen Toussaint/Alvin Tyler] [BMI] (12/8/62 BCR-39) [I]

JAVA
Al (He's The King) Hirt Trumpet With Chorus And Orchestra—RCA Victor 47-8280
[Freddy Friday‡/Marilyn Schack‡/Allen Toussaint/Alvin Tyler] [BMI] (1/4/64 BCR-4) [I]
JAVA JONES *Donna Lynn—Capitol 5156*
[Bugs Bower/Freddy Friday‡/Allen Toussaint/Alvin Tyler/Jack Wolf] [BMI] (5/9/64 R-94)
JAY-DEE'S BOOGIE WOOGIE Jimmy Dorsey Orchestra and Chorus—Fraternity 777
[Howard Gibeling/Julie Hilton] [BMI] (8/26/57 B-77) [I]
THE JAZZ IN YOU Gloria Lynne—Everest 19390
[Luther Dixon/Chris Towns] [BMI] (1/2/61 R-80)
JAZZMAN Carole King—Ode 66101 [Carole King/David Palmer] [ASC] (8/31/74 BCR-1)
JE T'AIME...MOI NON PLUS *Jane Birkin & Serge Gainsbourg—Fontana 1665*
[Serge Gainsbourg] [BMI] (11/29/69 BCR-58) [F]
SOUL JE T'AIME *Sylvia & Ralfi Pagan—Vibration 525*
[Serge Gainsbourg/Sylvia Robinson] [BMI] (9/8/73 B-99) [FDE]
JEALOUS Gene Loves Jezebel—Geffen 19688
[Jay Aston/Christopher Bell/Peter Risingham/James Stevenson] [ASC] (8/18/90 BC-66)
JEALOUS AGAIN The Black Crowes—Def American 19697
[Chris Robinson/Rich Robinson] [BMI] (5/12/90 BC-73)
JEALOUS GUY John Lennon—Capitol/EMI 44230 [John Lennon] [GL] (10/15/88 BC-64)
JEALOUS HEART *Tab Hunter—Warner Bros. 5008*
[Jenny Lou Carson] [BMI] (10/20/58 BCtRt-33)
JEALOUS HEART *The Fontane Sisters—Dot 15853*
[Jenny Lou Carson] [BMI] (10/27/58 BCtRt-33)
JEALOUS HEART *Les Paul and Mary Ford—Columbia 41278*
[Jenny Lou Carson] [BMI] (11/3/58 CtRt-40)
JEALOUS HEART *Connie Francis—MGM 13420*
[Jenny Lou Carson] [BMI] (11/27/65 BCR-25)
JEALOUS KIND OF FELLA Garland Green—Uni 55143
[Jo Armstead/Rudolph Browner/Morris Dollison/Garland Green] [BMI]
(8/16/69 BCR-19)
JEALOUS LOVE Wilson Pickett—Atlantic 2484
[King Curtis/Bobby Womack] [BMI] (2/17/68 BCR-38)
JEALOUS OF YOU (TANGO DELLA GELOSIA) Connie Francis—MGM 12899
[Marjorie Harper/Vittorio Mascheroni/Peppino Mendes] [BMI] (5/9/60 BCR-19) [F]
JEALOUSY Kitty Wells—Decca 30662 [Jim Anglin] [BMI] (7/14/58 B-78)
JEALOUSY Major Harris—Atlantic 3321
[Joseph Jefferson/Charles Simmons] [BMI] (3/27/76 BCR-72)
JEALOUSY Adventures Of Stevie V—Mercury 878662
[Stevie Vincent/Mick Walsh] [BMI] (1/19/91 B-94)
JEAN Oliver—Crewe 334 [Rod McKuen] [ASC] (8/9/69 BCR-1)
THE JEAN GENIE David Bowie—RCA Victor 74-0838
[David Bowie] [BMI] (11/25/72 BCR-71)
JEANNIE, JEANNIE, JEANNIE Eddie Cochran—Liberty 55123
[George Motola/Rickie Page] [BMI] (3/10/58 B-94)
JEANS ON David Dundas—Chrysalis 2094
[David Dundas/Roger Greenaway] [BMI] (9/18/76 BCR-14)
JELLY, JELLY, JELLY Bobby Bland—Duke 338
[Billy Eckstine/Earl Hines] [ASC] (3/5/62 R-90)
JELLY JUNGLE (OF ORANGE MARMALADE) The Lemon Pipers—Buddah 41
[Paul Leka/Shelley Pinz] [BMI] (5/11/68 BCR-26)
JELLYBREAD Booker T. & The MGs—Stax 131
[Steve Cropper*/Al Jackson*/Booker T. Jones Jr./Lewis Steinberg*] [BMI]
(12/22/62 BCR-72) [I]
JENNIE LEE *Jan & Arnie—Arwin 108 [Jan Berry/Arnie Ginsburg] [BMI] (5/17/58 BCtRt-3)*
JENNIE LEE *Billy Ward And His Dominoes—Liberty 55136*
[Jan Berry/Arnie Ginsburg] [BMI] (5/17/58 BCtRt-11)
JENNIFER Bobby Sherman—Metromedia 227
[Peter Allen/Carole Bayer Sager] [BMI] (10/9/71 BCR-25)
JENNIFER ECCLES The Hollies—Epic 10298
[Allan Clarke/Graham Nash] [BMI] (3/9/68 BCR-37)
JENNIFER JUNIPER Donovan—Epic 10300 [Donovan Leitch] [BMI] (3/9/68 BCR-18)
JENNIFER TOMKINS Street People (2)—Musicor 1365
[Gerard Florio/Rupert Holmes/Paul Vance] [ASC] (12/13/69 BCR-36)
JENNY BROWN The Smothers Brothers—Mercury 72182
[George Wood] [ASC] (9/28/63 BR-82)
JENNY JENNY *Little Richard—Specialty 606*
[Enotris Johnson/Richard Penniman] [BMI] (6/15/57 BCR-14)
JENNY, JENNY *Mitch Ryder And The Detroit Wheels—New Voice 806*
[Enotris Johnson/Richard Penniman] (Med) [BMI] (12/11/65 BCR-10)
JENNY LOU Sonny James—NRC 50
[Mark McIntyre/William Olofson] [ASC] (4/11/60 BCR-67)
JEOPARDY *Greg Kihn Band—Beserkley 69847*
[Greg Kihn/Steve Wright] [ASC] (1/29/83 BC-2)
I LOST ON JEOPARDY *(parody of Jeopardy) "Weird Al" Yankovic—Rock 'n' Roll 04469*
[Greg Kihn/Steve Wright/Al Yankovic] [ASC] (6/30/84 B-81) [P]
JEREMIAH PEABODY'S POLY UNSATURATED QUICK DISSOLVING FAST ACTING PLEASANT TASTING GREEN AND PURPLE PILLS Ray Stevens—Mercury 71843
[Ray Stevens] [BMI] (8/19/61 BCR-35)
THE JERK The Larks (2)—Money 106 [Don Julian] [BMI] (11/7/64 BCR-6)
JERK AND TWINE Jackie Ross—Chess 1920
[Billy Davis/Ronald Ellison/Carl William Smith] [BMI] (1/30/65 BCR-73)
JERK-OUT The Time—Paisley Park 19750
[Morris Day/James Samuel Harris/Terry Lewis/Prince] [ASC] (6/30/90 BC-5)
JERUSALEM Herb Alpert & The Tijuana Brass—A&M 1225
[Herb Alpert] [ASC] (10/10/70 BCR-63) [I]
JESAHEL The English Congregation—Signpost 70004
[Ivano Fossati/Brian Keith/Oscar Prudente] [BMI] (7/1/72 CR-74) [FET]
JESSE Roberta Flack—Atlantic 2982 [Janis Ian] [BMI] (9/22/73 BCR-12)
JESSE Carly Simon—Warner Bros. 49518
[Mike Mainieri/Carly Simon] [ASC] (8/2/80 BCR-6)
JESSE Julian Lennon—Atlantic 89529 [China Burton] [BMI] (8/3/85 BC-54)
JESSE BRADY The McCoys—Mercury 72843 [Randy Zehringer] [BMI] (10/26/68 BCR-94)
JESSICA The Allman Brothers Band—Capricorn 0036
[Dickey Betts] [BMI] (12/29/73 BCR-33) [I]
JESSIE'S GIRL Rick Springfield—RCA 12201 [Rick Springfield] [BMI] (3/28/81 BCR-1)
JESUS IS A SOUL MAN Lawrence Reynolds—Warner Bros.-Seven Arts 7322
[Jack Cardwell/Lawrence Reynolds] [BMI] (9/20/69 BCR-28)
JESUS IS JUST ALRIGHT *The Byrds—Columbia 45071*
[Art Reynolds] [ASC] (1/17/70 BR-76)
JESUS IS JUST ALRIGHT *The Doobie Brothers—Warner Bros. 7661*
[Art Reynolds] [ASC] (12/16/72 BCR-29)
JESUS WAS A CAPRICORN Kris Kristofferson—Monument 8558
[Kris Kristofferson] [BMI] (12/30/72 BCR-86)
JESUS WAS A CROSSMAKER The Hollies—Epic 10989 [Judee Sill] [BMI] (6/2/73 R-97)
JET Paul McCartney & Wings—Apple 1871
[Linda McCartney/Paul McCartney] [ASC] (2/2/74 BCR-5)
JET AIRLINER Steve Miller Band—Capitol 4424 [Paul Pena] [ASC] (4/30/77 BCR-3)
JET SET (SIGH) Stephen Stills -- Manassas—Atlantic 2888
[Stephen Stills] (Med) [BMI] (7/15/72 BR-86)
JILL Gary Lewis And The Playboys—Liberty 55985
[Garry Bonner/Alan Gordon] [BMI] (8/5/67 BCR-30)
JILTED Teresa Brewer—Coral 61152 [Robert Colby/Dick Manning] [BMI] (5/29/54 B-PRE)
JIM DANDY *LaVern Baker and The Gliders—Atlantic 1116*
[Lincoln Chase] [BMI] (12/22/56 BCR-15)
JIM DANDY *Black Oak Arkansas—Atco 6948*
[Lincoln Chase] [BMI] (12/8/73 BCR-12)
JIM DANDY GOT MARRIED LaVern Baker—Atlantic 1136
[Lincoln Chase/Billy Davis/Albert Green/Alonzo Tucker] [BMI] (5/25/57 BR-72)
JIMMY KISS AND RUN Diane Maxwell—Challenge 59039
[Richard Sherman] [BMI] (3/23/59 B-95)
JIMMY LEE Aretha Franklin—Arista 1-9546
[Jeffrey E. Cohen/Preston Glass/Lisa Walden/Narada Michael Walden] [ASC]
(12/6/86 BC-28)
JIMMY LOVE Cathy Carroll—Triodex 110
[Bert Carroll/J.J. Reynolds] [BMI] (6/24/61 CR-79)
JIMMY LOVES MARY-ANNE *Looking Glass—Epic 11001*
[Elliot Lurie] [ASC] (7/7/73 BCR-22)
JIMMY LOVES MARYANN *Josie Cotton—Elektra 69748 [Elliot Lurie] [ASC] (4/7/84 B-82)*
JIMMY MACK *Martha & The Vandellas—Gordy 7058*
[Lamont Dozier/Brian Holland/Eddie Holland] [BMI] (2/25/67 BCR-6)
JIMMY MACK *Sheena Easton—EMI America 8309*
[Lamont Dozier/Brian Holland/Eddie Holland] [BMI] (2/8/86 BC-65)
JIMMY MARTINEZ Marty Robbins—Columbia 42008
[Marty Robbins] [BMI] (5/22/61 BCR-45)
JIMMY'S GIRL Johnny Tillotson—Cadence 1391
[Lee Pockriss/Paul Vance] [ASC] (1/9/61 BCR-19)
JINE THE CAVALRY Mitch Miller and The Gang—Columbia 41424
[Carl Haverlin/Traditional] [NA] (7/18/59 C-96)
JINGLE BELL ROCK *Bobby Helms—Decca 30513*
[Joe Beal/Jim Boothe] [ASC] (12/9/57 BCR-6)
JINGLE BELL ROCK *Bobby Helms—Decca 30513*
[Joe Beal/Jim Boothe] [ASC] (12/8/58 BRt-25)
JINGLE BELL ROCK *Teresa Brewer—Coral 62058*
[Joe Beal/Jim Boothe] [ASC] (12/15/58 Rt-32)
JINGLE BELL ROCK *Bobby Helms—Decca 30513*
[Joe Beal/Jim Boothe] [ASC] (1/4/60 R-82)
JINGLE BELL ROCK *Bobby Helms—Decca 30513*
[Joe Beal/Jim Boothe] [ASC] (12/12/60 BR-27)
JINGLE BELL ROCK *Bobby Rydell Chubby Checker—Cameo 205*
[Joe Beal/Jim Boothe] [ASC] (12/11/61 BCtRt-20)
JINGLE BELL ROCK *Bobby Helms—Decca 30513*
[Joe Beal/Jim Boothe] [ASC] (12/11/61 BCtRt-32)
JINGLE BELL ROCK *Bobby Helms—Decca 30513*
[Joe Beal/Jim Boothe] [ASC] (12/8/62 BCtRt-37)
JINGLE BELL ROCK *Bobby Rydell Chubby Checker—Cameo 205*
[Joe Beal/Jim Boothe] [ASC] (12/15/62 BCtRt-44)
JINGLE BELLS *The Singing Dogs—RCA Victor 47-6344*
[James Lord Pierpont] (Med) [NA] (12/10/55 CR-23)

JINGLE BELLS *Bing Crosby and The Andrews Sisters—Decca 23281*
[James Lord Pierpont] [NA] (12/16/55 Rt-49)

JINGLE BELLS *Four Aces Featuring Al Alberts—Decca 29702*
[James Lord Pierpont] [NA] (12/16/55 Rt-49)

JINGLE BELLS *Bing Crosby and The Andrews Sisters—Decca 23281*
[James Lord Pierpont] [NA] (12/23/57 Rt-40)

JINGLE BELLS *Gisele MacKenzie—Vik 0300 [James Lord Pierpont] [NA] (12/23/57 Rt-40)*

JINGLE BELLS *Perry Como—RCA Victor 47-EPA-920*
[James Lord Pierpont] [NA] (12/30/57 B-74)

JINGLE BELLS *Ella Fitzgerald—Verve 10224 [James Lord Pierpont] [BMI] (12/5/60 R-99)*

TWISTIN' BELLS *Santo & Johnny—Canadian-American 120*
[Ann Farina/Johnny Farina/Santo Farina/James Lord Pierpont] [BMI]
(12/5/60 BCR-35) [IWM]

JINGLE BELLS IMITATIONS *Bobby Rydell - Chubby Checker—Cameo 205*
[Dave Appell/Kal Mann/James Lord Pierpont] [ASC] (12/11/61 R-94)

JINGLE BELLS *Don Charles Presents The Singing Dogs Directed By Carl Weissman*
With Instrumental Accomp.—RCA Victor 48-1020
[James Lord Pierpont] [NA] (1/1/72 C-72)

JINGLE JANGLE The Archies—Kirshner 5002
[Jeff Barry/Andy Kim] [BMI] (11/29/69 BCR-4)

JINGO Santana—Columbia 45010 [Michael Olatunji] [BMI] (10/25/69 BCR-37) [I]

THE JITTERBUG The Dovells—Parkway 855
[Len Barry/Jerry Gross] [BMI] (11/17/62 BCR-70)

JIVE AFTER FIVE Carl Perkins—Columbia 41131 [Carl Perkins] [BMI] (3/31/58 R-59)

THE JIVE SAMBA Cannonball Adderley Sextet—Riverside 4541
[Nat Adderley] [BMI] (2/2/63 BCR-66) [I]

JIVE TALKIN' Bee Gees—RSO 510
[Barry Gibb/Maurice Gibb/Robin Gibb] [BMI] (5/24/75 BCR-1)

JIVE TURKEY (PART 1) Ohio Players—Mercury 73480
[Leroy Bonner/Marshall Jones/Ralph Middlebrooks/Andrew Noland/Marvin Pierce/
James Rodger Williams] [BMI] (6/1/74 BCR-47)

JIVIN' AROUND Al Casey Combo—Stacy 936
[John Grayton Dolphin/Ernie Freeman] [BMI] (7/28/62 BCR-71) [I]

JIVIN' AROUND (PT. 2) Ernie Freeman Combo—Cash 1017
[John Grayton Dolphin/Ernie Freeman] [BMI] (3/2/56 R-85) [I]

JO ANN *The Playmates—Roulette 4037*
[James Cunningham/John Cunningham] [BMI] (1/6/58 BCRt-17)

JO ANN *The Twin-Tones—RCA Victor EPA 4107*
[James Cunningham/John Cunningham] [BMI] (1/6/58 Rt-17)

JO-ANN *The Lancers—Coral 61930*
[James Cunningham/John Cunningham] [BMI] (1/6/58 Rt-17)

JO JO GUN Chuck Berry—Chess 1709 [Chuck Berry] [BMI] (11/15/58 BCR-74)

JO JO THE DOG FACED BOY Annette—Buena Vista 336
[Bob Roberts/Richard Sherman/Robert Sherman] [BMI] (3/30/59 BCR-45)

JOANIE The Bay Bops—Coral 61975
[Hal Gordon/Francis Philip Military/Dan Zipfel] [ASC] (5/17/58 C-58)

JOANIE Frankie Calen—Spark 902 [Geri Barton/Mark Harris] [BMI] (6/12/61 B-78)

JOANNA Kool & The Gang—De-Lite 829
[Clifford Adams/Robert Bell/Ronald Bell/James Bonneford/George M. Brown/
Claydes Smith/J.T. Taylor/Curtis Fitzgerald Williams] [BMI] (11/5/83 BC-2)

JOANNE Michael Nesmith & The First National Band—RCA Victor 74-0368
[Michael Nesmith] [BMI] (8/8/70 BCR-13)

JODY Jermaine Stewart—Arista 1-9476
[Jeffrey E. Cohen/Jermaine Stewart/Narada Michael Walden] [ASC] (9/20/86 BC-42)

JODY'S GOT YOUR GIRL AND GONE Johnnie Taylor—Stax 0085
[Kent Barker/Don Davis/James Wilson] [BMI] (1/16/71 BCR-20)

JOEY Betty Madigan—MGM 11716
[Jim Kriegsmann/Bert Salmers-Bernstein/Herb Wiener] [ASC] (5/29/54 BC-PRE)

JOEY Concrete Blonde—I.R.S. 73014 [Johnette Lin Napolitano] [BMI] (8/18/90 BC-19)

JOEY BABY Anita And Th' So-And-So's—RCA Victor 47-7974
[Jane Connell/Arthur Smith*] [BMI] (1/22/62 BCR-44)

JOEY, JOEY, JOEY Peggy Lee—Decca 29877 [Frank Loesser] [ASC] (5/5/56 B-76)

JOEY'S SONG *Bill Haley And His Comets—Decca 30956*
[Joe Reisman] [ASC] (9/12/59 BCR-35) [IM]

JOEY'S SONG *Bill Black's Combo—Hi 2059 [Joe Reisman] [ASC] (12/8/62 R-80) [IM]*

THE JOHN BIRCH SOCIETY The Chad Mitchell Trio—Kapp 457
[Michael Martin Brown] [ASC] (5/7/62 BCR-72)

JOHNNIE'S COMIN' HOME Johnnie Ray—Columbia 40578
[Wayne Shanklin/Al Sherman] [ASC] (11/12/55 B-100)

JOHNNY ANGEL Shelley Fabares—Colpix 621
[Lyn Duddy/Lee Pockriss] [ASC] (2/26/62 BCR-1)

JOHNNY B Hooters—Columbia 07241
[Eric Bazilian/Rick Chertoff/Rob Hyman] [ASC] (7/18/87 BC-61)

JOHNNY B GOODE *Chuck Berry—Chess 1691 [Chuck Berry] [BMI] (4/21/58 BCR-8)*

JOHNNY B. GOODE *Dion Di Muci—Columbia 43096*
[Chuck Berry] [BMI] (8/22/64 BCR-66)

JOHNNY B. GOODE *The Coronados—Parliament 750 [Chuck Berry] [BMI] (8/26/67 R-88)*

JOHNNY B. GOODE *Johnny Winter—Columbia 45058 [Chuck Berry] [BMI] (1/10/70 B-92)*

JOHNNY B. GOODE *Peter Tosh—EMI America 8159 [Chuck Berry] [BMI] (6/25/83 BC-84)*

JOHNNY B GOODE *Jive Bunny & The Mastermixers—Music Factory/Atco 99122*
[Chuck Berry] (Med) [BMI] (2/3/90 BC-67)

JOHNNY BE SMART Sarah Vaughan—Mercury 70693
[Victor Abrams/Fred Jay/Irving Reid] [BMI] (9/12/55 R-77)

JOHNNY CAN'T READ Don Henley—Asylum 69971
[Don Henley/Danny Kortchmar] [ASC] (8/14/82 BC-33)

JOHNNY CASANOVA Jaye P. Morgan—RCA Victor 47-6565
[Martin Burns/Mack Discant/Ray Passman] [BMI] (7/21/56 B-81)

JOHNNY COME HOME Fine Young Cannibals—I.R.S. 52760
[Roland Gift/David Steele] [ASC] (4/5/86 BC-76)

JOHNNY CONCHO THEME (WAIT FOR ME) Frank Sinatra—Capitol 3469
[Nelson Riddle/Dok Stanford] [BMI] (7/28/56 B-75)

JOHNNY COOL Steve Gibbons Band—MCA 40551 [Steve Gibbons] [BMI] (6/5/76 BCR-72)

JOHNNY FREEDOM Johnny Horton—Columbia 41685
[Jule Styne/George David Weiss] [ASC] (6/20/60 BCR-57)

JOHNNY GET ANGRY Joanie Sommers—Warner Bros. 5275
[Hal David/Sherman Edwards] [ASC] (5/26/62 BCR-7)

JOHNNY JINGO Hayley Mills—Vista 395
[Dick Manning/Kay Twomey] [ASC] (3/12/62 BCR-21)

JOHNNY LOVES ME Shelley Fabares—Colpix 636
[Barry Mann/Cynthia Weil] [BMI] (6/9/62 BCR-21)

JOHNNY LOVES ME Florraine Darlin—Ric 105 [John L. Finneran] [BMI] (7/25/64 R-80)

JOHNNY ONE TIME Brenda Lee—Decca 32428
[Dallas Frazier/A.L. "Doodle" Owens] [BMI] (2/1/69 BCR-29)

JOHNNY REB Johnny Horton—Columbia 41437 [Merle Kilgore] [BMI] (8/15/59 BCR-54)

JOHNNY TREMAIN Billy Vaughn and His Orchestra—Dot 15598
[Tom Blackburn/George Bruns] [BMI] (7/6/57 R-85)

JOHNNY WILL Pat Boone—Dot 16284 [Paul Evans/Fred Tobias] [ASC] (11/13/61 BCR-35)

JOHNNY WILLOW Fred Darian—JAF 2023
[Fred Darian/Al DeLory/Joseph Van Winkle] [ASC] (8/5/61 BCR-79)

JOHNNY'S HOUSE PARTY *Jimmy Beasley and The Rockers—Modern 1021*
[Johnny Heartsman] [BMI] (7/13/57 Rt-81) [IM]

JOHNNY'S HOUSE PARTY (PT. 1) *John Heartsman & The Gaylarks—Music City 807*
[Johnny Heartsman] [BMI] (7/13/57 Rt-81) [IM]

JOIN TOGETHER The Who—Decca 32983 [Pete Townshend] [BMI] (7/15/72 BCR-17)

JOJO Boz Scaggs—Columbia 11281
[David Foster/David Lasley/Boz Scaggs] [BMI] (6/14/80 BCR-17)

THE JOKER Steve Miller Band—Capitol 3732
[Eddie Curtis*/Ahmet Ertegun*/Steve Miller] [ASC] (10/20/73 BCR-1)

JOKER Snail—Cream 7827 [Randall Zacuto] [BMI] (9/23/78 B-93)

THE JOKER (THAT'S WHAT THEY CALL ME) *The Hilltoppers—Dot 15662*
[Billy Myles] [BMI] (10/28/57 BCtRt-13)

THE JOKER (THAT'S WHAT THEY CALL ME) *Billy Myles—Ember 1026*
[Billy Myles] [BMI] (10/28/57 BCtRt-13)

THE JOKER WENT WILD Brian Hyland—Philips 40377
[Bobby Russell] [ASC] (7/9/66 BCR-19)

THE JOKERS Peter And Gordon—Capitol 5919
[Mike Leander/Charles Mills] [ASC] (6/24/67 BR-97)

JOLE BLON Gary U.S. Bonds—EMI America 8089
[Moon Mullican] [BMI] (7/18/81 BCR-65)

JOLENE Dolly Parton—RCA Victor 0145 [Dolly Parton] [BMI] (12/22/73 BC-60)

THE JOLLY GREEN GIANT The Kingsmen—Wand 172
[Lynn Easton/Don Harris*/Dewey Terry*] [BMI] (1/9/65 BCR-4)

JONES VS. JONES Kool & The Gang—De-Lite 813
[Robert Bell/Ronald Bell/George M. Brown/Eumir Deodato/Robert Mickens/Claydes
Smith/J.T. Taylor/Dennis Thomas/Earl Toon] [BMI] (5/16/81 BCR-39)

JOSEPHINE Bill Black's Combo—Hi 2022
[Burke Bivens/Wayne King] [ASC] (6/13/60 BCR-8) [IM]

JOSIE Kris Kristofferson—Monument 8536 [Kris Kristofferson] [BMI] (3/11/72 BCR-63)

JOSIE Steely Dan—ABC 12404 [Walter Becker/Donald Fagen] [ASC] (8/26/78 BCR-21)

JOURNEY OF LOVE The Crests Featuring Johnny Maestro—Coed 535
[Allyson Khent/Miriam Lewis/Billy Dawn Smith] [BMI] (9/5/60 BR-81)

JOURNEY TO THE CENTER OF THE MIND The Amboy Dukes—Mainstream 684
[Steve Farmer/Ted Nugent] [BMI] (6/22/68 BCR-16)

JOY Mitch Ryder—New Voice 824
[Raymond Bloodworth/L. Russell Brown/Mitch Ryder] [BMI] (7/1/67 BCR-38)

JOY Apollo 100—Mega 0050 [Johann Sebastian Bach] [NA] (12/25/71 BCR-6) [I]

JOY PT. I Isaac Hayes—Enterprise 9085 [Isaac Hayes] [BMI] (12/22/73 BCR-29)

JOY Teddy Pendergrass—Elektra 69401
[Reggie Calloway/Vincent Calloway/Joel Davis] [BMI] (6/18/88 BC-77)

JOY AND PAIN Rob Base & D.J. E-Z Rock—Profile 5247
[Robert Ginyard] [ASC] (5/27/89 B-58)

THE JOY AND THE TEARS Gidea Park—Profile 5003
[Adrian Baker] (Med) [BMI] (12/26/81 BC-82)

JOY TO THE WORLD Three Dog Night—Dunhill 4272 [Hoyt Axton] [BMI] (3/6/71 BCR-1)

JOYFUL RESURRECTION Tom Fogerty—Fantasy 702 [Tom Fogerty] [BMI] (9/22/73 C-84)

JOYRIDE Roxette—EMI 50342 [Per Gessle] [BMI] (3/2/91 BC-1)

JOYSTICK Dazz Band—Motown 1701
[Eric Fearman/Robert Lamont Harris] [ASC] (2/11/84 BC-59)

JU JU HAND Sam The Sham And The Pharaohs—MGM 13364
[Domingo Samudio] [BMI] (7/31/65 BCR-26)

JUANITA BANANA The Peels—Karate 522
[Tash Howard/Murray Kenton] [BMI] (3/5/66 BCR-41)

JUBILATION Paul Anka—Buddah 294 [Paul Anka/Johnny Harris] [BMI] (3/25/72 BCR-58)

JUDY Frankie Vaughan—Epic 9273
[Noel Regney/Gloria Shayne] [BMI] (5/31/58 BCRt*-42)

JUDY The Prodigals—Falcon 1011 [Chuck Collins] [BMI] (6/9/58 Rt*-78)

JUDY David Seville—Liberty 55193 [David Seville] [ASC] (5/18/59 BCR-50) [I]

JUDY Elvis Presley—RCA Victor 47-9287 [Teddy DeLano Riedel] [BMI] (9/9/67 B-78)

JUDY IN DISGUISE (WITH GLASSES) John Fred & His Playboy Band—Paula 282
[Andrew Bernard/John Fred] [BMI] (11/18/67 BCR-1)

JUDY LOVES ME Johnny Crawford—Del-Fi 4231
[Don Altfeld/Jan Berry/Artie Kornfeld] [BMI] (1/11/64 B-95)

JUDY MAE Boomer Castleman—Mums 6038 [Boomer Castleman] [BMI] (5/3/75 BCR-25)

JUDY'S TURN TO CRY Lesley Gore—Mercury 72143
[Edna Lewis/Beverly Ross] [BMI] (7/6/63 BCR-4)

JUICY FRUIT Mtume—Epic 03578 [James Mtume] [BMI] (6/11/83 BC-35)

JUKE BOX BABY Perry Como—RCA Victor 47-6427
[Joe Sherman/Noel Sherman] [ASC] (3/2/56 BCR-8)

JUKE BOX HERO Foreigner—Atlantic 4017
[Lou Gramm/Michael Leslie Jones] [ASC] (2/13/82 BCR-26)

JUKE BOX MUSIC The Kinks—Arista 0247 [Ray Davies] [ASC] (6/4/77 R-91)

JUKE BOX SATURDAY NIGHT Nino & the Ebb Tides—Madison 166
[Paul McGrane/Al Stillman] (Med) [ASC] (8/26/61 BCR-57)

JUKIN Atlanta Rhythm Section—Polydor 14323
[Buddy Buie/Robert Nix] [BMI] (5/22/76 BC-75)

JULIA Ramsey Lewis—Cadet 5640
[John Lennon/Paul McCartney] [ASC] (9/27/69 BCR-69) [IWM]

JULIANNA Five Man Electrical Band—Lionel 3224 [Les Emmerson] [BMI] (3/4/72 CR-61)

JULIE Doris Day—Columbia 40758
[Thomas Adair/Leith Stevens] [ASC] (10/20/56 BCR-40)

JULIE ANN Ginger—Shock 3
[Phil Coulter/William Wylie MacPherson Martin] [ASC] (9/18/76 C-89)

JULIE, DO YA LOVE ME Bobby Sherman—Metromedia 194
[Tom Bahler] [BMI] (7/25/70 BCR-1)

JULIE IS HER NAME Perez Prado and His Orchestra—RCA Victor 47-7826
[Bobby Troup] [ASC] (1/9/61 R-91) [I]

JULIE KNOWS Randy Sparks—Columbia 43138
[Leon Carr/Paul Vance] [ASC] (11/21/64 R-100)

JULY 12, 1939 Charlie Rich—Epic 10585 [Norro Wilson] [BMI] (3/21/70 BCR-71)

JULY YOU'RE A WOMAN Pat Boone—Tetragrammaton 1516
[John Stewart] [BMI] (4/5/69 BCR-90)

JUMBO The Bee Gees—Atco 6570
[Barry Gibb/Maurice Gibb/Robin Gibb] [BMI] (4/6/68 BCR-39)

JUMP Aretha Franklin—Atlantic 3358 [Curtis Mayfield] (TSW) [BMI] (10/30/76 BCR-72)

JUMP Loverboy—Columbia 03346
[Bryan Adams/Paul Dean/Matt Frenette/Mike Reno/Jim Vallance] [BMI] (12/4/82 C-71)

JUMP Van Halen—Warner Bros. 29384
[Michael Anthony*/David Lee Roth/Alex Van Halen/Eddie Van Halen] [ASC] (1/14/84 BC-1)

JUMP BACK *Rufus Thomas—Stax 157 [Rufus Thomas] [ASC] (10/3/64 BCR-49)*

JUMP BACK *King Curtis—Atco 6476 [Rufus Thomas] [ASC] (5/13/67 B-63) [IWM]*

JUMP FOR JOY Biddu Orchestra—Epic 50173
[Biddu Appaiah/Lee Vanderbilt] (TSW) [BMI] (1/10/76 B-72) [I]

JUMP (FOR MY LOVE) Pointer Sisters—Planet 13780
[Stephen Mitchell/Marti Sharron/Gary Skardina] [ASC] (4/28/84 BC-3)

JUMP INTO THE FIRE Nilsson—RCA Victor 74-0673
[Harry Nilsson] [BMI] (3/18/72 BCR-22)

JUMP OVER Freddy Cannon—Swan 4053 [Bob Crewe/Frank Slay] [BMI] (5/7/60 BCR-24)

JUMP START Natalie Cole—Manhattan 50073
[Reggie Calloway/Vincent Calloway] [BMI] (7/25/87 BC-13)

JUMP TO IT Aretha Franklin—Arista 0699
[Marcus Miller/Luther Vandross] [ASC] (8/21/82 BC-24)

JUMPIN' JACK FLASH *The Rolling Stones—London 908*
[Mick Jagger/Keith Richards] [BMI] (6/8/68 BCR-1)

JUMPIN' JACK FLASH *Johnny Winter—Columbia 45368*
[Mick Jagger/Keith Richards] [BMI] (5/1/71 BR-89)

JUMPIN' JACK FLASH *Aretha Franklin—Arista 1-9528*
[Mick Jagger/Keith Richards] [BMI] (9/27/86 BC-21)

JUMPIN' JACK The Kalin Twins—Decca 30552
[Clint Ballard Jr./Hank Hunter] [BMI] (2/3/58 R-54)

JUNE JULY AND AUGUST Rusty Draper—Mercury 71336
[Buddy Kaye/Murray Semos/Frank Stanton] [ASC] (7/19/58 CR-65)

JUNE NIGHT Jimmy Dorsey Orchestra and Chorus—Fraternity 777
[Abel Baer/Cliff Friend] [ASC] (8/3/57 BCR-19)

THE JUNGLE B.B. King—Kent 462 [Joe Josea‡/B.B. King] [BMI] (4/1/67 BCR-94)

JUNGLE BOOGIE Kool & The Gang—De-Lite 559
[Robert Bell/Ronald Bell/Donald Boyce/George M. Brown/Robert Mickens/Claydes Smith/Dennis Thomas/Richard Westfield] [BMI] (12/8/73 BCR-4)

JUNGLE BOY John Eddie—Columbia 05858 [John Eddie] [ASC] (6/7/86 BC-52)

JUNGLE DRUMS Clyde Otis—Mercury 71776 [Ernesto Lecuona] [BMI] (3/25/61 C-79) [IM]

JUNGLE FEVER Chakachas—Polydor 15030 [Bill Ador] [ASC] (12/25/71 BCR-5) [I]

JUNGLE LOVE Steve Miller Band—Capitol 4466
[Greg Douglass/Lonnie Turner] [BMI] (8/6/77 BCR-17)

JUNGLE LOVE The Time—Warner Bros. 29181
[Morris Day/Jesse Woods Johnson/Prince] [ASC] (10/27/84 BC-20)

JUNIOR JUNIOR JUNIOR Russ Regan-Laura Lane—ABC-Paramount 9949
[Russ Regan] [BMI] (8/25/58 R-89)

JUNIOR'S FARM Paul McCartney & Wings—Apple 1875
[Linda McCartney/Paul McCartney] (TSW) [ASC] (12/14/74 BCR-3)

JUNK FOOD JUNKIE Larry Groce—Warner/Curb 8165 [Larry Groce] [ASC] (1/3/76 BCR-9)

JUPITER-C Pat and the Satellites—Atco 6131
[Otis Antonelli/Dick Biondi‡/Clyde Dickerson] [NA] (2/9/59 B-81) [I]

JURA (I SWEAR I LOVE YOU) Les Paul and Mary Ford—Columbia 41994
[Jose Barbosa da Silva/Les Paul] [BMI] (4/24/61 BCR-37) [FET]

JUST A CLOSER WALK WITH THEE *Pat Boone—Dot DEP-1056*
[Traditional] (EP) [NA] (5/11/57 R-60)

JUST A CLOSER WALK WITH THEE *Andy Griffith—Capitol 3706*
[Traditional] [NA] (6/1/57 Rt-61)

CLOSER WALK *Pete Fountain—Coral 62154 [Traditional] [NA] (2/8/60 BRt-48) [IWM]*

JUST A CLOSER WALK WITH THEE *Jimmie Rodgers—Roulette 4234*
[Traditional] [NA] (3/28/60 BCRt-44)

JUST A DREAM *Jimmy Clanton—Ace 546 [Jimmy Clanton] [BMI] (7/5/58 BCRt-4)*

JUST A DREAM *Margaret Whiting—Dot 15804 [Jimmy Clanton] [BMI] (8/11/58 Rt-4)*

JUST A FRIEND Biz Markie—Cold Chillin' 22784 [Biz Markie] [ASC] (1/20/90 BC-9)

JUST A GIGOLO David Lee Roth—Warner Bros. 29040
[Irving Caesar/Leonello Casucci] (Med) [ASC] (3/23/85 BC-12) [FDE]

JUST A LITTLE Brenda Lee—Decca 31149 [Betty Chotas] [BMI] (9/26/60 BR-40)

JUST A LITTLE The Beau Brummels—Autumn 10
[Robert Durand/Ron Elliott] [BMI] (4/17/65 BCR-6)

JUST A LITTLE BIT *Rosco Gordon—Vee-Jay 332 [Rosco Gordon] [BMI] (2/15/60 BCR-64)*

JUST A LITTLE BIT *Roy Head—Scepter 12116 [Rosco Gordon] [BMI] (10/30/65 BCR-37)*

JUST A LITTLE BIT *Little Milton—Checker 1217*
[Ralph Bass‡/Piney Brown‡/Rosco Gordon/Jimmy McCracklin/Sylvester Thompson‡/John Thornton‡/Earl Washington‡] [BMI] (5/10/69 B-97)

JUST A LITTLE BIT Blue Cheer—Philips 40541 [Dickie Peterson] [ASC] (6/22/68 BCR-71)

JUST A LITTLE BIT BETTER Herman's Hermits—MGM 13398
[Kenny Young] [BMI] (9/18/65 BCR-6)

JUST A LITTLE BIT LONGER Maxi Priest—Charisma 98883
[Handel Tucker] [ASC] (12/8/90 BC-53)

JUST A LITTLE BIT MORE The Intrigues—Yew 1007
[Jerry Akines/Johnnie Bellmon/Victor Drayton/Reginald Turner] [BMI] (6/13/70 R-87)

JUST A LITTLE BIT OF YOU Michael Jackson—Motown 1349
[Brian Holland/Eddie Holland] [BMI] (5/17/75 BCR-23)

JUST A LITTLE LONESOME Bobby Helms—Decca 30557
[Cindy Walker] [BMI] (2/10/58 CR-57)

JUST A LITTLE LOVE B.B. King—BluesWay 61029 [B.B. King] [BMI] (10/18/69 BCR-74)

JUST A LITTLE MISUNDERSTANDING The Contours—Gordy 7052
[Morris Broadnax/Clarence Paul/Stevie Wonder] [BMI] (5/14/66 BCR-85)

JUST A LITTLE TOO MUCH Ricky Nelson—Imperial 5595
[Johnny Burnette] [BMI] (6/29/59 BCR-9)

JUST A MAN Tony Martin—RCA Victor 47-6039 [Stuart Hamblen] [ASC] (3/19/55 C-48)

JUST A MOMENT AGO Soul Sisters—Sue 111
[Smokey McAllister] [BMI] (10/10/64 B-100)

JUST A SMILE Pilot—EMI 4135 [Billy Lyall/David Paton] [BMI] (10/11/75 BC-75)

JUST A SONG BEFORE I GO Crosby, Stills & Nash—Atlantic 3401
[Graham Nash] [BMI] (5/28/77 BCR-7)

JUST A TOUCH OF LOVE Slave—Cotillion 45005
[Mark Adams/Steve Arrington/Mark Hicks/Tom Lockett*/Raye Turner/Danny Webster/Starleana Young] [BMI] (1/26/80 R-91)

JUST A TOUCH OF LOVE C & C Music Factory—Columbia 74033
[Robert Clivillés] [ASC] (11/9/91 BC-50)

JUST ABOUT THE SAME The Association—Warner Bros. 7372
[Ron Edgar/Michael Fennelly/Lee Mallory/Doug Rhodes/Joseph Stec] [BMI] (3/7/70 C-91)

JUST AIN'T ENOUGH LOVE Eddie Holland—Motown 1058
[Lamont Dozier/Brian Holland/Eddie Holland] [BMI] (5/23/64 BCR-54)

JUST AIN'T NO LOVE Barbara Acklin—Brunswick 55388
[Carl Davis/Eugene Record] [BMI] (11/16/68 BCR-55)

JUST ANOTHER DAY Oingo Boingo—MCA 52726 [Danny Elfman] [BMI] (12/21/85 BC-79)

JUST ANOTHER DAY IN PARADISE Bertie Higgins—Kat Family 02839
[Bertie Higgins/Columbia Jones/Sonny Limbo] [BMI] (5/1/82 BC-42)

JUST ANOTHER DREAM Cathy Dennis—Polydor 877 962
[Cathy Dennis/Danny Poku] [BMI] (10/27/90 BC-9)

JUST ANOTHER FACE The Blades Of Grass–Jubilee 5590 [Joey Day/Alan Dischel] [ASC] (9/23/67 R-94)

JUST ANOTHER GIRLFRIEND Hi-Five–Jive 42009 [Eric Foster White] [ASC] (11/23/91 B-88)

JUST ANOTHER NIGHT Ian Hunter–Chrysalis 2352 [Ian Hunter/Mick Ronson] [ASC] (8/4/79 BCR-68)

JUST ANOTHER NIGHT Mick Jagger–Columbia 04743 [Mick Jagger] [ASC] (2/9/85 BC-10)

JUST AS I AM Air Supply–Arista 1-9353 [Rob Hegel/Dick Wagner] [BMI] (5/25/85 BC-16)

JUST AS LONG AS I'M WITH YOU Pat Boone–Dot 15457 [Billy Vaughn] [ASC] (4/20/56 BR-21)

JUST AS LONG AS YOU NEED ME, PART I Independents–Wand 11245 [William Earl Butler/Charles Henry Jackson Jr./Marvin Yancy] [ASC] (5/6/72 BCR-77)

JUST AS MUCH AS EVER *Bob Beckham–Decca 30861 [Larry Coleman/Charles Singleton] [BMI] (8/10/59 BCR-32)*

JUST AS MUCH AS EVER *Bobby Vinton–Epic 10266 [Larry Coleman/Charles Singleton] [BMI] (12/30/67 BCR-13)*

JUST ASK ME TO Tevin Campbell–Qwest 19275 [Albert Joseph Brown/Kyle West] [ASC] (8/10/91 BC-87)

JUST ASK YOUR HEART Frankie Avalon–Chancellor 1040 [Pete Damato/Diane DeNota/Joe Ricci] [BMI] (8/24/59 BCR-7)

JUST BE GOOD TO ME *The S.O.S. Band–Tabu 4-03955 [James Samuel Harris/Terry Lewis] [ASC] (8/27/83 BC-42)*

DUB BE GOOD TO ME *Beats International–Elektra 64970 [James Samuel Harris/Terry Lewis] [ASC] (4/14/90 BC-69)*

JUST BE MY LADY Larry Graham–Warner Bros. 49744 [Larry Graham] [BMI] (8/1/81 BCR-67)

JUST BE SINCERE Jackie Wilson–Brunswick 55309 [Bernard Reed/Daniel Reed/Othie Wright] [BMI] (2/11/67 B-91)

JUST BE TRUE Gene Chandler–Constellation 130 [Curtis Mayfield] [BMI] (7/4/64 BCR-19)

JUST BECAUSE Elvis Presley–RCA Victor 47-6640 [Sid Robin/Bob Shelton/Joe Shelton] [BMI] (9/29/56 R-53)

JUST BECAUSE *Lloyd Price–ABC-Paramount 9792 [Lloyd Price] [BMI] (2/16/57 BCRt-15)*

JUST BECAUSE *Larry Williams–Specialty 597 [Lloyd Price] [BMI] (3/23/57 Rt-15)*

JUST BECAUSE The McGuire Sisters–Coral 62288 [Dick Jacobs/Murray Kane/Edna Lewis] [ASC] (10/9/61 BCR-89)

JUST BECAUSE Anita Baker–Elektra 69327 [Alex Brown/Sami McKinney/Michael O'Hara] [BMI] (1/21/89 BC-14)

JUST BETWEEN FRIENDS Kitty Kallen–Decca 29593 [Robert Mellin/Gerald Rogers] [BMI] (7/25/55 R-75)

JUST BETWEEN US Bill Woody–Hickory 54043 [Mickey Newbury] [NA] (5/19/79 R-77)

JUST BETWEEN YOU AND ME The Chordettes–Cadence 1330 [Lee Cathy/Jack Keller] [BMI] (8/3/57 BCR-12)

JUST BETWEEN YOU AND ME April Wine–Capitol 4975 [Myles Goodwyn] [ASC] (2/7/81 BCR-16)

JUST BETWEEN YOU AND ME Lou Gramm–Atlantic 88781 [Lou Gramm/Holly Knight] [ASC] (10/28/89 BC-6)

JUST BORN (TO BE YOUR BABY) Perry Como–RCA Victor 47-7050 [Luther Dixon/Billy Dawn Smith] [BMI] (9/30/57 BCR-8)

JUST CALL ME (AND I'LL UNDERSTAND) Lloyd Price And His Orchestra–ABC-Paramount 10139 [Harold Logan/Lloyd Price] [BMI] (9/5/60 BCR-62)

JUST CAN'T WAIT The J. Geils Band–EMI America 8047 [Seth Justman/Peter Wolf] [ASC] (7/12/80 BCR-78)

JUST CAN'T WIN 'EM ALL Stevie Woods–Cotillion 46030 [Bill Bowersock/Greg Mathieson/Trevor Veitch/Matt Vernon] [BMI] (1/23/82 BCR-38)

JUST COME HOME Hugo & Luigi–RCA Victor 47-7639 [Marguerite Monnot/Carl Sigman] [ASC] (12/7/59 BCR-35) [FDE]

JUST DON'T WANT TO BE LONELY *Ronnie Dyson–Columbia 45867 [Vinnie Barrett/Bobby Eli/John Freeman] [BMI] (8/11/73 BCR-58)*

JUST DON'T WANT TO BE LONELY *The Main Ingredient–RCA Victor 0205 [Vinnie Barrett/Bobby Eli/John Freeman] [BMI] (2/2/74 BCR-7)*

JUST DROPPED IN (TO SEE WHAT CONDITION MY CONDITION WAS IN) The First Edition–Reprise 0655 [Mickey Newbury] [BMI] (2/3/68 BCR-3)

JUST FOR ME AND YOU Poco–Epic 10804 [Richie Furay] [NA] (11/6/71 CR-86)

JUST FOR OLD TIME'S SAKE The McGuire Sisters–Coral 62249 [Hank Hunter/Jack Keller] [BMI] (3/11/61 BCR-14)

JUST FOR THE MOMENT Ray Kennedy–ARC 11242 [Jack Conrad/Ray Kennedy] [BMI] (5/3/80 B-82)

JUST GIVE ME A RING Clyde McPhatter–Atlantic 2049 [Clyde McPhatter] [BMI] (2/29/60 B-96)

JUST GOT LUCKY JoBoxers–RCA 13601 [Chris Bostock/Dig Wayne] [ASC] (9/10/83 BC-36)

JUST GOT PAID Johnny Kemp–Columbia 07744 [Gene Griffin/Johnny Kemp] [BMI] (5/14/88 BC-10)

JUST GOT TO KNOW Jimmy McCracklin–Art-Tone 825 [Jimmy McCracklin] [BMI] (11/18/61 BCR-64)

JUST IN TIME *Tony Bennett with Percy Faith and His Orchestra–Columbia 40770 [Betty Comden/Adolph Green/Jule Styne] [ASC] (11/10/56 BCRt-37)*

JUST IN TIME *Jeri Southern–Decca 30114 [Betty Comden/Adolph Green/Jule Styne] [ASC] (11/24/56 Rt-37)*

JUST IN TIME *Dean Martin–Capitol 4391 [Betty Comden/Adolph Green/Jule Styne] [ASC] (6/27/60 R-56)*

JUST KEEP IT UP Dee Clark–Abner 1026 [Otis Blackwell] [BMI] (5/4/59 BCR-14)

JUST KEEP WALKIN' AMBROSE Jimmy Valentine & His Orchestra–Cub 9024 [Linda Laurie/Wes McWain/Lou Sprung] [BMI] (2/2/59 R-76)

JUST LET IT COME Alive And Kicking–Roulette 7087 [Allen Martancik] [BMI] (9/12/70 BCR-48)

JUST LET ME CRY Lesley Gore–Mercury 72143 [Mark Barkan/Ben Raleigh] [BMI] (7/6/63 R-94)

JUST LET ME HOLD YOU FOR A NIGHT David Ruffin–Motown 1420 [Charles Kipps] [BMI] (9/24/77 R-94)

JUST LIKE A WOMAN *Manfred Mann–Mercury 72607 [Bob Dylan] [SE] (8/27/66 CRt-67)*

JUST LIKE A WOMAN *Bob Dylan–Columbia 43792 [Bob Dylan] [SE] (9/10/66 BCRt-26)*

JUST LIKE HEAVEN The Cure–Elektra 69443 [Simon Gallup/Robert James Smith/Porl Thompson/Laurence Tolhurst/Boris Williams] [ASC] (10/10/87 BC-40)

JUST LIKE IN THE MOVIES The Upbeats–Swan 4010 [Bernie Lowe/Kal Mann] [ASC] (7/19/58 BCR-58)

JUST LIKE JESSE JAMES Cher–Geffen 22844 [Desmond Child/Diane Warren] [ASC] (10/21/89 BC-4)

JUST LIKE ME Paul Revere And The Raiders Featuring Mark Lindsay–Columbia 43461 [Richard Dey/Roger Hart] [BMI] (12/4/65 BCR-11)

JUST LIKE PARADISE Larry John McNally–ARC 02200 [Larry John McNally] [ASC] (8/8/81 B-86)

JUST LIKE PARADISE David Lee Roth–Warner Bros. 28119 [David Lee Roth/Brett Tuggle] [ASC] (1/16/88 BC-6)

(JUST LIKE) ROMEO & JULIET *The Reflections–Golden World 9 [Freddie Gorman/Bob Hamilton] [BMI] (3/28/64 BCR-6)*

(JUST LIKE) ROMEO AND JULIET *Sha Na Na–Kama Sutra 602 [Freddie Gorman/Bob Hamilton] [BMI] (4/12/75 BCR-46)*

(JUST LIKE) STARTING OVER John Lennon–Geffen 49604 [John Lennon] [GL] (11/1/80 BCR-1)

–JUST LIKE THE WHITE WINGED DOVE see: EDGE OF SEVENTEEN

JUST LIKE YOU Robbie Nevil–EMI 50356 [Robbie Nevil] [ASC] (6/29/91 BC-25)

JUST LOOK WHAT YOU'VE DONE Brenda Holloway–Tamla 54148 [R. Dean Taylor/Frank Edward Wilson] [BMI] (4/22/67 BC-69)

JUST LOVE ME Jaye P. Morgan–RCA Victor 47-6653 [Bob Davie/Marvin Moore] [BMI] (10/27/56 B-97)

JUST MARRIED Marty Robbins–Columbia 41143 [Al Allen/Barry De Vorzon] [BMI] (4/14/58 BR-27)

JUST MY IMAGINATION (RUNNING AWAY WITH ME) The Temptations–Gordy 7105 [Barrett Strong/Norman Whitfield] [BMI] (1/30/71 BCR-1)

JUST ONCE Quincy Jones Featuring James Ingram–A&M 2357 [Barry Mann/Cynthia Weil] [BMI] (8/15/81 BCR-13)

JUST ONCE IN A LIFETIME Brenda & The Tabulations–Dionn 503 [Maurice Coates/Bob Finiz/Brenda J. Payton] [BMI] (8/12/67 BR-90)

JUST ONCE IN MY LIFE The Righteous Brothers–Philles 127 [Gerry Goffin/Carole King/Phil Spector] [BMI] (4/10/65 BCR-9)

JUST ONE KISS FROM YOU The Impressions–ABC-Paramount 10725 [Curtis Mayfield] [BMI] (10/2/65 BCR-70)

JUST ONE LOOK *Doris Troy–Atlantic 2188 [Greg Carroll/Doris Payne] [BMI] (6/8/63 BCR-9)*

JUST ONE LOOK *The Hollies–Imperial 66026 [Greg Carroll/Doris Payne] [BMI] (4/18/64 BCR-83)*

JUST ONE LOOK *The Hollies–Imperial 66258 [Greg Carroll/Doris Payne] [BMI] (9/30/67 BCR-44)*

JUST ONE LOOK *Anne Murray–Capitol 3955 [Greg Carroll/Doris Payne] [BMI] (10/5/74 BC-86)*

JUST ONE LOOK *Linda Ronstadt–Asylum 46011 [Greg Carroll/Doris Payne] [BMI] (2/10/79 BCR-44)*

JUST ONE MINUTE MORE Mike Finnigan–Columbia 10741 [Al Kooper/Richie Supa] [BMI] (7/1/78 C-84)

JUST ONE MORE DAY Otis Redding–Volt 130 [Steve Cropper/Otis Redding/McEvoy Robinson] [BMI] (12/4/65 BCR-65)

JUST ONE MORE TIME Eddie Fisher–RCA Victor 47-6071 [Al Jacobs] [ASC] (3/21/55 CR-27)

JUST ONE MORE TIME Headpins–SGR 90001 [Brian MacLeod/Darby Mills] [BMI] (12/24/83 BC-68)

JUST ONE SMILE Gene Pitney–Musicor 1219 [Randy Newman] [BMI] (12/3/66 BCR-64)

JUST ONE TIME Don Gibson–RCA Victor 47-7690 [Don Gibson] [BMI] (2/8/60 BCR-26)

JUST OUT OF REACH (OF MY TWO OPEN ARMS) *Solomon Burke–Atlantic 2114 [Virgil Stewart] [BMI] (9/18/61 BCR-17)*

JUST OUT OF REACH (OF MY TWO EMPTY ARMS) *Percy Sledge–Atlantic 2434 [Virgil Stewart] [BMI] (8/26/67 BCR-54)*

JUST REMEMBER I LOVE YOU Firefall—Atlantic 3420
[Rick Roberts] [BMI] (8/13/77 BCR-9)
JUST SEVEN NUMBERS (CAN STRAIGHTEN OUT MY LIFE) Four Tops—Motown 1175
[Gloria Jones/Pam Sawyer] [ASC] (1/16/71 BCR-26)
JUST SEVENTEEN Raiders—Columbia 45082 [Mark Lindsay] [BMI] (2/14/70 BCR-73)
JUST SO LONELY Get Wet—Boardwalk 8-02018
[Jose Augusto Esquibel] [ASC] (4/25/81 BCR-39)
JUST TELL HER JIM SAID HELLO Elvis Presley With The Jordanaires—
RCA Victor 47-8041 [Jerry Leiber/Mike Stoller] [BMI] (8/4/62 BCR-49)
JUST THE SAME WAY Journey—Columbia 10928
[Gregg Rolie/Neal Schon/Ross Valory] [BMI] (3/10/79 BCR-58)
JUST THE TWO OF US Grover Washington, Jr.—Elektra 47103
[Ralph MacDonald/William Salter/Bill Withers] [ASC] (2/7/81 BCR-2)
JUST THE WAY IT IS, BABY The Rembrandts—Atco 98874
[Phil Solem/Danny Wilde] [BMI] (2/9/91 BC-14)
JUST THE WAY YOU ARE Billy Joel—Columbia 10646 [Billy Joel] [ASC] (11/12/77 BCR-2)
JUST THE WAY YOU LIKE IT The S.O.S. Band—Tabu 4-04523
[James Samuel Harris/Terry Lewis] [ASC] (8/11/84 BC-64)
JUST TO BE CLOSE TO YOU Commodores—Motown 1402
[Lionel Richie] [ASC] (9/4/76 BCR-7)
JUST TO BE WITH YOU The Passions—Audicon 102 [Marvin Kalfin] [BMI] (9/5/59 BCR-48)
JUST TO HOLD MY HAND Clyde McPhatter—Atlantic 1133
[Deadric Malone/Paul Perryman*] [BMI] (5/4/57 BCR-30)
JUST TO SATISFY YOU Waylon & Willie—RCA 13073
[Don Bowman/Waylon Jennings] [BMI] (4/3/82 BC-52)
JUST TO SEE HER Smokey Robinson—Motown 1877
[Jimmy George/Louis Pardini] [ASC] (3/28/87 BC-7)
JUST TOO MANY PEOPLE Melissa Manchester—Arista 0146
[Melissa Manchester/Vini Poncia] [BMI] (9/20/75 BCR-30)
JUST WALKING IN THE RAIN Johnnie Ray—Columbia 40729
[Johnny Bragg/Buddy Killen*/Robert S. Riley] [BMI] (9/1/56 BCR-1)
JUST WANT TO HOLD YOU Jasmine Guy—Warner Bros. 19330
[Melanie Andrews/Tony Andrews/Cal Harris] [BMI] (8/3/91 BC-34)
JUST WHAT I NEEDED The Cars—Elektra 45491 [Ric Ocasek] [ASC] (6/17/78 BCR-24)
JUST WHEN I NEEDED YOU MOST Randy Vanwarmer—Bearsville 0334
[Randy Vanwarmer] [ASC] (3/17/79 BCR-4)
JUST YESTERDAY Jack Jones—Kapp 699
[Klaus Ogerman/Carl Sigman] [ASC] (10/2/65 BCR-73)
JUST YESTERDAY Al Martino—Capitol 5702
[Peter DeAngelis/Russell Faith] [ASC] (7/23/66 BCR-67)
JUST YOU Sonny & Cher—Atco 6345 [Sonny Bono] [BMI] (8/28/65 BCR-20)
JUST YOU AND I Melissa Manchester—Arista 0168
[Melissa Manchester/Carole Bayer Sager] [BMI] (2/7/76 BCR-27)
JUST YOU 'N' ME Chicago—Columbia 45933 [James Pankow] [ASC] (9/22/73 BCR-1)
JUST YOUNG *Andy Rose—Aamco 100 [Lya Roberts] [BMI] (9/15/58 BCtRt-28)*
JUST YOUNG *Paul Anka—ABC-Paramount 9956 [Lya Roberts] [BMI] (9/15/58 BCtRt-28)*
JUSTIFY MY LOVE Madonna—Sire 19485
[Ingrid Chavez*/Madonna L. Ciccone/Lenny Kravitz] [ASC] (11/17/90 BC-1)
JUSTINE The Righteous Brothers—Moonglow 242
[Don Harris/Dewey Terry] [BMI] (7/3/65 BCR-85)

K

K-JEE The Nite-Liters—RCA Victor 74-0461
[Harvey Fuqua/Charles Hearndon] [BMI] (7/3/71 BCR-34) [I]
KA DING DONG *The G-Clefs—Pilgrim 715*
[Joe Jordan/Jack McDermott] [BMI] (7/28/56 BCtRt-17)
KA DING DONG *The Hilltoppers—Dot 15489*
[Joe Jordan/Jack McDermott] [BMI] (8/25/56 BCtRt-17)
KA DING DONG *The Diamonds—Mercury 70934*
[Joe Jordan/Jack McDermott] [BMI] (8/25/56 BCtRt-17)
KALIMBA STORY Earth, Wind & Fire—Columbia 46070
[Maurice White/Verdine White] [ASC] (7/6/74 BCR-51)
KANSAS CITY *Wilbert Harrison—Fury 1023*
[Jerry Leiber/Mike Stoller] [BMI] (4/13/59 BCRt-1)
KANSAS CITY *Hank Ballard And The Midnighters—King 5195*
[Jerry Leiber/Mike Stoller] [BMI] (4/20/59 BRt-18)
KANSAS CITY *Rocky Olson—Chess 1723 [Jerry Leiber/Mike Stoller] [BMI] (5/4/59 B-60)*
KANSAS CITY *Little Richard—Specialty 664*
[Jerry Leiber/Mike Stoller] [BMI] (5/11/59 B-95)
KANSAS CITY *Trini Lopez—Reprise 20,236*
[Jerry Leiber/Mike Stoller] [BMI] (11/16/63 BCR-23)
KANSAS CITY *The Beatles—Capitol 6066*
[Jerry Leiber/Mike Stoller] [BMI] (10/23/65 C-75)
KANSAS CITY *James Brown And The Famous Flames—King 6086*
[Jerry Leiber/Mike Stoller] [BMI] (3/4/67 BCR-49)
KANSAS CITY STAR Roger Miller—Smash 1998
[Roger Miller] [BMI] (9/11/65 BCR-26)

KARATE The Emperor's—Mala 543
[Milton S. Brown Jr./Tyrone Moss] [BMI] (11/26/66 BCR-49)
KARATE-BOO-GA-LOO Jerryo—Shout 217
[Sammy Kaplan/Jerry Murray] [BMI] (9/16/67 BCR-34)
KARELIA SUITE The Royal Philharmonic Orchestra—RCA 12304
[Jean Sibelius] (Med) [NA] (10/31/81 BCR-9) [I]
KAREN B. E. Taylor Group—Epic 05851
[Joe Macre/B.E. Taylor/Rick Witkowski] [NA] (5/31/86 B-94)
KARMA CHAMELEON Culture Club—Virgin/Epic 04221
[Michael Craig/Roy Hay/Jon Moss/George O'Dowd/Phil Pickett] [ASC] (12/3/83 BC-1)
KATE Johnny Cash And The Tennessee Three—Columbia 45590
[Marty Robbins] [BMI] (5/13/72 BCR-75)
KATHLEEN Wally Lewis—Dot 15705 [Wally Lewis/Beverly Stewart] [BMI] (4/19/58 C-55)
KATHY O *The Diamonds—Mercury 71330*
[Larry Shayne/Jack Sherr/Charles Tobias] [ASC] (7/5/58 BCRt-37)
KATHY O *Earl Grant—Decca 30640*
[Larry Shayne/Jack Sherr/Charles Tobias] [ASC] (7/7/58 Rt-37)
KATMANDU Bob Seger—Capitol 4116 [Bob Seger] [ASC] (8/9/75 BCR-43)
KATY TOO Johnny Cash And The Tennessee Two—Sun 321
[Johnny Cash/Jack H. Clement] [BMI] (7/11/59 BCR-66)
KAW LIGA The Four Preps—Capitol 4435
[Fred Rose/Hank Williams] [ASC] (10/17/60 R-100)
KAY John Wesley Ryles I—Columbia 44682 [Hank Mills] [BMI] (12/14/68 BCR-83)
KAYLEIGH Marillion—Capitol 5493
[Derek Dick/Mark Kelly/Ian Mosley/Steve Rothery/Pete Trewavas] [BMI]
(10/5/85 BC-74)
KEEM-O-SABE The Electric Indian—United Artists 50563
[Bernard Binnick/Bernice Borisoff] [ASC] (8/2/69 BCR-14) [I]
KEEP A KNOCKIN' Little Richard—Specialty 611
[Richard Penniman] [BMI] (9/16/57 BCR-8)
KEEP A LIGHT IN THE WINDOW TILL I COME HOME Solomon Burke—Atlantic 2378
[James W. Alexander] [BMI] (1/28/67 BCR-64)
KEEP COMING BACK Richard Marx—Capitol 44753 [Richard Marx] [ASC] (11/2/91 BC-5)
(KEEP FEELING) FASCINATION The Human League—A&M/Virgin 2547
[John William Callis/Philip Oakey] [ASC] (5/21/83 BC-7)
KEEP HOLDING ON The Temptations—Gordy 7146
[Brian Holland/Eddie Holland] [BMI] (2/7/76 BCR-53)
KEEP IT COMIN' Keith Sweat—Elektra 64812
[Joe Carter/Lionel Job/Joe Sayles/Kevin Scott/Keith Sweat/Dwight Wyatt] [BMI]
(11/30/91 BC-16)
KEEP IT COMIN' LOVE KC & The Sunshine Band—TK 1023
[Harry Wayne Casey/Rick Finch] [BMI] (7/23/77 BCR-2)
KEEP IT CONFIDENTIAL Nona Hendryx—RCA 13438
[Ellen Foley/Ellie Greenwich/Jeff Kent] [BMI] (6/4/83 B-91)
KEEP IT HOT Cameo—Chocolate City 3219
[Larry Blackmon/Anthony Lockett] [BMI] (1/17/81 R-92)
KEEP IT IN THE FAMILY Leon Haywood—20th Century 2065
[Leon Haywood] [BMI] (3/9/74 BCR-44)
KEEP IT TIGHT Single Bullet Theory—Nemperor 03300
[Michael Garrett/Gary Holmes] [BMI] (3/5/83 B-78)
KEEP IT TOGETHER Madonna—Sire 19986
[Stephen Bray/Madonna L. Ciccone] [ASC] (2/3/90 BC-8)
KEEP LOOKING Solomon Burke—Atlantic 2349
[Delores Burke/Mark Burke/Solomon Burke] [BMI] (8/20/66 CR-93)
KEEP ME CRYIN' Al Green—Hi 2319 [Al Green/Willie Mitchell] [BMI] (10/23/76 BCR-37)
KEEP ME IN MIND Patti Page—Mercury 70579
[Burt Bacharach/Jack Wolf] [ASC] (3/28/55 CR-26)
KEEP ME IN MIND Lynn Anderson—Columbia 45768
[George Richey/Glenn Sutton] [BMI] (2/24/73 C-91)
KEEP ON DANCIN' Gary's Gang—Columbia 10884
[Eric Matthew/Gary Turnier] [ASC] (2/3/79 BCR-33)
KEEP ON DANCING Hank Ballard And The Midnighters—King 5535
[Hank Ballard/Nathaniel Nathan] [BMI] (8/21/61 BCR-66)
KEEP ON DANCING The Gentrys—MGM 13379
[Allen Alvoid Jones Jr./Andrew Love/Richard Shann/Willie David Young] [BMI]
(9/4/65 BCR-3)
KEEP ON DANCING Alvin Cash—Toddlin' Town 111
[Alvin Cash/Ira Gates/Howard Scott/Walter Lee Scott] [BMI] (11/23/68 BCR-66)
KEEP ON DOIN' The Isley Brothers—T-Neck 914
[O'Kelly Isley/Ronald Isley/Rudolph Isley] [BMI] (2/7/70 BCR-49)
KEEP ON DOIN' WHAT YOU'RE DOIN' Bobby Byrd—BrownStone 4205
[James Brown/Bobby Byrd/Hearlon Martin/Fred Wesley] [BMI] (2/26/72 BCR-81)
—KEEP ON FALLING see: CRAZY
KEEP ON KEEPING ON N.F. Porter—Lizard 1010
[Richard Flowers] [BMI] (12/18/71 BCR-77)
KEEP ON LOVIN' ME HONEY Marvin Gaye & Tammi Terrell—Tamla 54173
[Nick Ashford/Valerie Simpson] [ASC] (10/5/68 BCR-22)
KEEP ON LOVING ME (YOU'LL SEE THE CHANGE) Bobby Bland—Duke 464
[Clyde Wilson] [BMI] (12/5/70 BCR-71)

KEEP ON LOVING YOU REO Speedwagon—Epic 50953 [Kevin Cronin] [ASC] (11/29/80 BCR-1)

KEEP ON MOVIN' Soul II Soul—Virgin 99205 [Beresford Romeo] [ASC] (6/24/89 BC-8)

KEEP ON PUSHING The Impressions—ABC-Paramount 10554 [Curtis Mayfield] [BMI] (6/6/64 BCR-10)

KEEP ON RUNNING Spencer Davis Group—Atco 6400 [Jackie Edwards] [BMI] (2/26/66 BCR-76)

KEEP ON RUNNING Stevie Wonder—Tamla 54223 [Stevie Wonder] [ASC] (9/2/72 BCR-76)

KEEP ON RUNNING AWAY Lazy Racer—A&M 2152 [Tim Renwick/Chris White] [ASC] (7/7/79 BCR-81)

KEEP ON SINGING *Austin Roberts—Chelsea 0110 [Bobby Hart/Danny Janssen] [BMI] (1/27/73 BCR-35)*

KEEP ON SINGING *Helen Reddy—Capitol 3845 [Bobby Hart/Danny Janssen] [BMI] (3/9/74 BCR-9)*

KEEP ON SMILIN' Wet Willie—Capricorn 0043 [John David Anthony/Jack Hall/Jimmy Hall/Rick Hirsch/Lewis Ross] [BMI] (5/25/74 BCR-10)

KEEP ON TRUCKIN' (PART 1) Eddie Kendricks—Tamla 54238 [Leonard Caston/Anita Poree/Frank Edward Wilson] [BMI] (8/18/73 BCR-1)

KEEP ON TRYIN' Poco—ABC 12126 [Timothy B. Schmit] [ASC] (9/20/75 BCR-45)

KEEP ON TRYING Bobby Vee—Liberty 55790 [Van McCoy] [BMI] (5/8/65 BCR-84)

KEEP OUR LOVE ALIVE Paul Davis—Bang 718 [Paul Davis] [BMI] (6/28/75 BCR-78)

KEEP PLAYIN' THAT ROCK 'N' ROLL Edgar Winter's White Trash—Epic 10788 [Edgar Winter] [BMI] (12/18/71 BCR-58)

KEEP SEARCHIN' (WE'LL FOLLOW THE SUN) Del Shannon—Amy 915 [Del Shannon] [BMI] (11/21/64 BCR-7)

KEEP THAT SAME OLD FEELING Side Effect—Fantasy 792 [Wayne Henderson] [BMI] (6/4/77 C-98)

KEEP THE BALL ROLLING *Jay And The Techniques—Smash 2124 [Sandy Linzer/Denny Randell] [BMI] (10/21/67 BCR-6)*

KEEP THE BALL ROLLIN' *Al Hirt—RCA Victor 47-9417 [Sandy Linzer/Denny Randell] [BMI] (1/27/68 B-100)*

KEEP THE CUSTOMER SATISFIED Gary Puckett—Columbia 45303 [Paul Simon] [BMI] (1/30/71 BCR-49)

KEEP THE FIRE Kenny Loggins—Columbia 11215 [E. Ein Loggins/Kenny Loggins] [ASC] (2/23/80 BCR-36)

KEEP THE FIRE BURNIN' REO Speedwagon—Epic 02967 [Kevin Cronin] [ASC] (6/12/82 BC-7)

KEEP THE HOME FIRE BURNIN' Latimore—Glades 1726 [Steve Alaimo/Benny Latimore] [BMI] (5/17/75 R-98)

KEEP THE ONE YOU GOT Joe Tex—Dial 4083 [Joe Tex] [BMI] (8/10/68 BCR-49)

KEEP THIS TRAIN A-ROLLIN' The Doobie Brothers—Warner Bros. 49670 [Michael McDonald] [ASC] (2/14/81 BCR-62)

KEEP WARM Jinny—Next Plateau 50168 [Walt Cremonini/Alessandro Gilardi/Andrew Hinton] [BMI] (9/14/91 B-97)

KEEP YOUR COTTON PICKIN' PADDIES OFFA MY HEART Teresa Brewer—Coral 61700 [Jerry Bresler/Lyn Duddy/Joan Edwards] [ASC] (9/8/56 R-77)

KEEP YOUR EYE ON ME Herb Alpert—A&M 2915 [James Samuel Harris/Terry Lewis] [ASC] (2/28/87 BC-46)

—KEEP YOUR EYE ON THE SPARROW see: BARETTA'S THEME

KEEP YOUR HANDS IN YOUR POCKETS The Playmates—Roulette 4432 [Jack Segal/Paul Vance] [ASC] (7/14/62 BR-86)

KEEP YOUR HANDS OFF MY BABY Little Eva—Dimension 1003 [Gerry Goffin/Carole King] [BMI] (10/27/62 BCR-12)

—KEEP YOUR HANDS OFF OF HIM see: HANDS OFF

KEEP YOUR HANDS TO YOURSELF Georgia Satellites—Elektra 69502 [Dan Baird] [BMI] (11/22/86 BC-2)

KEEP YOUR HEAD TO THE SKY Earth, Wind & Fire—Columbia 45953 [Maurice White] [ASC] (11/17/73 BCR-34)

KEEP YOUR LOVE LOCKED (DEEP IN YOUR HEART) Paul Petersen—Colpix 632 [Gerry Goffin/Carole King] [BMI] (6/9/62 BCR-58)

KEEP YOURSELF ALIVE Queen—Elektra 45268 [Brian May] [ASC] (8/16/75 C-89)

KEEPER OF THE CASTLE Four Tops—Dunhill 4330 [Dennis Lambert/Brian Potter] [BMI] (11/4/72 BCR-9)

KEEPING OUR LOVE ALIVE Henry Paul Band—Atlantic 3883 [Steve Grisham/Henry Paul/Jim Peterik] [BMI] (12/12/81 BCR-50)

KEEPING THE FAITH Billy Joel—Columbia 04681 [Billy Joel] [ASC] (1/26/85 BC-18)

THE KENTUCKIAN SONG *The Hilltoppers—Dot 15375 [Irving Gordon] [ASC] (6/13/55 BCtRt-19)*

THE KENTUCKIAN SONG *Eddy Arnold with Hugo Winterhalter's Orch. And Chorus—RCA Victor 47-6139 [Irving Gordon] [ASC] (6/13/55 CtRt-19)*

THE KENTUCKIAN SONG *Bobby Sherwood—Coral 61439 [Irving Gordon] [ASC] (6/13/55 Rt-37)*

THE KENTUCKIAN SONG *Guy Cherney—Mercury 70637 [Irving Gordon] [ASC] (6/13/55 Rt-72)*

THE KENTUCKIAN SONG *Paul Weston & His Orchestra—Columbia 40527 [Irving Gordon] [ASC] (6/27/55 Rt-37)*

KENTUCKY Bob Moore and His Orch.—Monument 814 [Karl Davis] [ASC] (5/18/63 CR-67) [I]

KENTUCKY Sammi Smith—Mega 0056 [Sammi Smith] [BMI] (2/5/72 CR-92)

KENTUCKY MOONRUNNER Cledus Maggard And The Citizen's Band—Mercury 73789 [Jay Huguely/Jerry Kennedy] [BMI] (4/24/76 B-85)

KENTUCKY MORNIN' Al Martino—Capitol 4444 [Ritchie Adams/Alan Bernstein] [ASC] (8/20/77 R-96)

KENTUCKY RAIN Elvis Presley—RCA Victor 47-9791 [Dick Heard/Eddie Rabbitt] [BMI] (2/14/70 BCR-10)

KENTUCKY WOMAN *Neil Diamond—Bang 551 [Neil Diamond] [SE] (10/14/67 BCR-12)*

KENTUCKY WOMAN *Deep Purple—Tetragrammaton 1508 [Neil Diamond] [SE] (11/2/68 BCR-29)*

KEWPIE DOLL Perry Como—RCA Victor 47-7202 [Roy C. Bennett/Sid Tepper] [ASC] (4/7/58 BCRt*-7)

KEWPIE DOLL Jim Lowe—Dot 15693 [Pat Smith] [BMI] (4/7/58 Rt*-21)

KEY LARGO Bertie Higgins—Kat Family 02524 [Bertie Higgins/Sonny Limbo] [BMI] (11/7/81 BCR-7)

THE KEY TO MY HEART Rosemary Clooney—Columbia 40619 [Bob Merrill] [ASC] (1/21/56 B-82)

KICK IT OUT Heart—Portrait 70010 [Ann Wilson] [ASC] (11/12/77 BC-69)

KICK OUT THE JAMS MC5—Elektra 45648 [Michael Davis/Robert Derminer/Wayne Kambes/Frederick Dewey Smith/Dennis Tomich] [BMI] (2/22/69 BCR-61)

KICK THAT LITTLE FOOT SALLY ANN Round Robin—Domain 1404 [Steve Barri/P.F. Sloan] [BMI] (5/23/64 BCR-61)

KICK THE WALL Jimmy Davis & Junction—QMI 53107 [James O. Davis] [ASC] (11/7/87 BC-67)

KICKS Paul Revere And The Raiders Featuring Mark Lindsay—Columbia 43556 [Barry Mann/Cynthia Weil] [BMI] (3/19/66 BCR-3)

KICKSTART MY HEART Mötley Crüe—Elektra 69248 [Nikki Sixx] [ASC] (11/25/89 BC-27)

KID CHARLEMAGNE Steely Dan—ABC 12195 [Walter Becker/Donald Fagen] [ASC] (7/10/76 B-82)

THE KID IS HOT TONITE Loverboy—Columbia 02068 [Bernard Aubin/Paul Dean] [BMI] (6/20/81 BCR-55)

"KID" SANTA CLAUS *Patsy—Roperry 2255 [Patsy Maharam] [BMI] (12/24/83 C-98)*

"KID" SANTA CLAUS *Patsy—Roperry 2255 [Patsy Maharam] [BMI] (12/22/84 C-92)*

"KID" SANTA CLAUS *Patsy—Roperry 2255 [Patsy Maharam] [BMI] (12/21/85 C-94)*

KID STUFF *The McGuire Sisters—Coral 61771 [Sal Izzo/Bob Perper] [BMI] (2/16/57 CRt-36)*

KID STUFF *Bernadine Read—ABC-Paramount 9764 [Sal Izzo/Bob Perper] [BMI] (3/16/57 Rt-56)*

KID STUFF Barbara Fairchild—Columbia 45903 [Jerry Crutchfield/Don Earl] [BMI] (8/25/73 B-95)

KID STUFF Lenny White—Elektra 47043 [John Vernon Anderson/Eddie Martinez/Denzil Miller/Lenny White] [BMI] (11/22/80 R-88)

KIDDIO Brook Benton—Mercury 71652 [Brook Benton/Clyde Otis] [BMI] (8/1/60 BCR-3)

KIDS The Kirby Stone Four—Columbia 41668 [Lee Adams/Charles Strouse] [ASC] (6/18/60 C-91)

THE KID'S AMERICAN Matthew Wilder—Private I 4-04363 [Matthew Wilder] [ASC] (2/18/84 BC-33)

THE KIDS ARE ALRIGHT The Who—Decca 31988 [Pete Townshend] [BMI] (8/13/66 CR-85)

KIDS IN AMERICA Kim Wilde—EMI America 8110 [Marty Wilde/Ricky Wilde] [ASC] (5/22/82 BC-20)

KIDS SAY THE DARNDEST THINGS Tammy Wynette—Epic 10969 [Billy Sherrill/Glenn Sutton] [BMI] (6/16/73 BR-72)

KIKO Jimmy McGriff—Sue 10-001 [Jimmy McGriff] [BMI] (5/16/64 BCR-79) [I]

KILLER CUT Charlie—Arista 0449 [Terry Thomas] [NA] (9/1/79 BCR-57)

KILLER JOE *The Rocky Fellers—Scepter 1246 [Bert Berns/Stanley Kahan/Phil Medley] [BMI] (3/9/63 BCR-16)*

KILLER JOE *The Kingsmen—Wand 1115 [Bert Berns/Stanley Kahan/Phil Medley] [BMI] (4/2/66 BCR-66)*

KILLER JOE Quincy Jones—A&M 1163 [Benny Golson] [ASC] (4/25/70 BCR-55)

KILLER QUEEN Queen—Elektra 45226 [Freddie Mercury] [ASC] (2/8/75 BCR-11)

KILLIN' TIME Fred Knoblock & Susan Anton—Scotti Brothers 609 [Jeff Harrington/Jeff Pennig] [ASC] (11/22/80 BCR-28)

KILLING ME SOFTLY WITH HIS SONG *Roberta Flack—Atlantic 2940 [Charles Fox/Norman Gimbel] [BMI] (1/20/73 BCR-1)*

KILLING ME SOFTLY *Al B. Sure!—Warner Bros. 27772 [Charles Fox/Norman Gimbel] [BMI] (11/19/88 BC-80)*

THE KILLING OF GEORGIE (PART I AND II) Rod Stewart—Warner Bros. 8396 [Rod Stewart] [ASC] (6/4/77 BCR-30)

KIND OF A DRAG The Buckinghams—U.S.A. 860 [James Holvay] [BMI] (12/24/66 BCR-1)

THE KIND OF BOY YOU CAN'T FORGET The Raindrops—Jubilee 5455 [Jeff Barry/Ellie Greenwich] [BMI] (8/10/63 BCR-15)

A KIND OF MAGIC Queen—Capitol 5590 [Roger Taylor] [BMI] (6/21/86 BC-42)

KING CREOLE Elvis Presley with the Jordanaires—RCA Victor EPA-4319 [Jerry Leiber/Mike Stoller] (EP) [BMI] (7/26/58 CR-14)

KING CROESUS World Of Oz—Deram 85034
[Tony Clarkson/Chris Evans/David Kubinec/David Reay] [BMI] (11/9/68 C-94)
KING FOR A DAY Thompson Twins—Arista 1-9450
[Tom Bailey/Alannah Currie/Joe Leeway] [ASC] (1/18/86 BC-8)
KING HEROIN James Brown—Polydor 14116
[Charles Bobbit/James Brown/David Matthews/Manny Rosen] [BMI] (2/26/72 BCR-32)
THE KING IS GONE Ronnie McDowell—Scorpion 135
[Ronnie McDowell/Lee Morgan] [BMI] (9/10/77 BCR-12)
KING KONG - PT. 1 The Jimmy Castor Bunch—Atlantic 3295
[Jimmy Castor/Johnny Pruitt] [BMI] (10/4/75 BCR-69)
KING MIDAS IN REVERSE The Hollies—Epic 10234
[Allan Clarke/Tony Hicks/Graham Nash] [BMI] (9/30/67 BCR-46)
KING OF CLOWNS Neil Sedaka—RCA Victor 47-8007
[Howard Greenfield/Neil Sedaka] [BMI] (3/26/62 BCR-34)
KING OF LOVE Fabian—Chancellor 1055 [Russell Faith] [ASC] (8/8/60 CR-88)
KING OF NOTHING Seals & Crofts—Warner Bros. 7810
[Jim Seals] [BMI] (5/18/74 BCR-50)
KING OF PAIN *The Police—A&M 2569 [Sting] [BMI] (8/27/83 BC-3)*
KING OF SUEDE *(parody of King Of Pain) "Weird Al" Yankovic—Rock 'n' Roll 04451*
[Sting/Al Yankovic] [BMI] (5/5/84 BC-62) [P]
THE KING OF ROCK 'N' ROLL Cashman & West—Dunhill 4349
[Terry Cashman/Tommy West] [ASC] (8/4/73 CR-77)
—KING OF SUEDE see: KING OF PAIN
KING OF THE HILL Rick Pinette And Oak—Mercury 76049
[Rick Pinette] [BMI] (5/10/80 BCR-36)
KING OF THE ROAD *Roger Miller—Smash 1965 [Roger Miller] [BMI] (1/30/65 BCR-3)*
QUEEN OF THE HOUSE *(response to King Of The Road) Jody Miller—Capitol 5402*
[Roger Miller/Mary Taylor] [BMI] (4/24/65 BCR-12) [R]
KING OF THE WHOLE WIDE WORLD
Elvis Presley with the Jordanaires—RCA Victor EPA-4371
[Ruth Batchelor/Bob Roberts] (EP) [BMI] (9/8/62 BCR-30;26)
KING OF WISHFUL THINKING Go West—EMI 50307
[Peter Cox/Richard Drummie/Martin Page] [ASC] (5/19/90 BC-8)
KING TUT Steve Martin And The Toot Uncommons—Warner Bros. 8577
[Steve Martin] [ASC] (5/20/78 BCR-16)
KINGS AND QUEENS Aerosmith—Columbia 10699
[Jack Douglas/Tom Hamilton/Joey Kramer/Steven Tyler/Brad Whitford] [BMI]
(3/11/78 BCR-70)
KINGS OF THE PARTY Brownsville Station—Big Tree 16001
[Cub Koda/Michael Lutz/Henry Weck] [ASC] (8/17/74 BCR-31)
KISS *Prince And The Revolution—Paisley Park 7-28751 [Prince] [ASC] (2/22/86 BC-1)*
KISS *The Art Of Noise featuring Tom Jones—China 871038*
[Prince] [ASC] (11/26/88 BC-31)
KISS AN ANGEL GOOD MORNIN' Charley Pride—RCA Victor 74-0550
[Ben Peters] [BMI] (11/20/71 BCR-19)
KISS AND RUN Peggy King—Columbia 40638
[René Denoncin/William Engvick/Jack Ledru] [BMI] (3/3/56 B-88) [FDE]
KISS AND SAY GOODBYE *The Manhattans—Columbia 10310*
[Winfred Lovett] [BMI] (4/17/76 BCR-1)
KISS AND SAY GOODBYE *Band Of Gold—RCA 13866*
[Winfred Lovett] (Med) [BMI] (10/13/84 BC-64)
KISS AND TELL Isley, Jasper, Isley—CBS Associated 04741
[Ernie Isley/Marvin Isley/Chris Jasper] [ASC] (2/16/85 BC-60)
KISS AND TELL Breakfast Club—MCA 53128 [Dan Gilroy] [ASC] (7/11/87 BC-48)
KISS AND TELL Bryan Ferry—Reprise 28117 [Bryan Ferry] [BMI] (2/27/88 BC-31)
KISS AWAY Ronnie Dove—Diamond 191
[Billy Sherrill/Glenn Sutton] [BMI] (10/30/65 BCR-21)
A KISS FOR CHRISTMAS (O TANNENBAUM) Joe Dowell—Smash 1728
[Ben Weisman/Fred Wise] [ASC] (12/4/61 R-72)
KISS HER NOW Ed Ames—RCA Victor 47-9647 [Jerry Herman] [ASC] (10/19/68 CR-77)
—KISS HIM GOODBYE see: NA NA HEY HEY KISS HIM...
KISS IN THE DARK Pink Lady—Elektra/Curb 46040
[Michael Lloyd] [ASC] (6/2/79 BCR-37)
KISS ME AND KILL ME WITH LOVE *The Mills Brothers—Decca 29511*
[Sammy Fain/Dan Shapiro] [ASC] (5/23/55 Rt-50)
KISS ME AND KILL ME WITH LOVE *The McGuire Sisters—Coral 61454*
[Sammy Fain/Dan Shapiro] [ASC] (8/15/55 Rt-50)
KISS ME AND KISS ME AND KISS ME (TRE VOLTE BACIAMI)
Perry Como—RCA Victor 47-7464
[Luciano Beretta/Arturo Casadei/Al Hoffman/Dick Manning] [NA] (2/16/59 R-45)
KISS ME ANOTHER Georgia Gibbs—Mercury 70850
[Fred Ebb/Charles Friedman/Arnold Shaw*] [BMI] (5/4/56 BCR-18)
KISS ME DEADLY Lita Ford—RCA 6866 [Mick Smiley] [ASC] (4/2/88 BC-12)
KISS ME GOODBYE Petula Clark—Warner Bros. 7170/Warner Bros.-Seven Arts 7170
[Barry Mason/Les Reed] [ASC] (2/17/68 BCR-10)
(KISS ME) HONEY, HONEY (KISS ME) Gogi Grant—RCA Victor 47-7438
[Michael Julien/Al Timothy] [BMI] (2/2/59 R-98)
KISS ME IN THE RAIN Barbra Streisand—Columbia 11179
[Sandy Farina/Lisa Ratner] [ASC] (1/12/80 BCR-37)
KISS ME QUICK Elvis Presley With The Jordanaires—RCA Victor 447-0639
[Doc Pomus/Mort Shuman] [BMI] (4/18/64 BCR-29)
KISS ME SAILOR Diane Renay—20th Century 477
[Eddie Rambeau/Bud Rehak] [BMI] (4/4/64 BCR-28)
KISS ON MY LIST Daryl Hall & John Oates—RCA 12142
[Janna Allen/Daryl Hall] [BMI] (1/24/81 BCR-1)
KISS THE BRIDE Elton John—Geffen 29568
[Elton John/Bernie Taupin] [BMI] (8/6/83 BC-25)
KISS THE DIRT (FALLING DOWN THE MOUNTAIN) INXS—Atlantic 89418
[Andy Farriss/Michael Hutchence] [ASC] (8/2/86 C-87)
KISS THEM FOR ME Siouxsie And The Banshees—Geffen 19031
[Susan Ballion/Peter Clarke/Martin McCarrick/Steven Severin] [ASC] (8/17/91 BC-23)
KISS THIS THING GOODBYE Del Amitri—A&M 1485
[Justin Currie/Iain Harvie/Michael Slaven] [ASC] (5/19/90 BC-35)
KISS TOMORROW GOODBYE Lainie Kazan—MGM 13657
[Paul Anka/René Villard] [BMI] (2/18/67 CR-84)
KISS YOU ALL OVER Exile—Warner/Curb 8589
[Mike Chapman/Nicky Chinn] [ASC] (7/8/78 BCR-1)
KISS YOU BACK Digital Underground—Tommy Boy 993
[Ron Brooks/George Clinton/Gregory Jacobs/Philippe Wynn] [BMI] (11/16/91 B-40)
KISS YOU (WHEN IT'S DANGEROUS) Eight Seconds—Polydor 885352
[Marcello Cesare/Andres Del Castillo/Frank Lavigne/Scott Milks] [BMI]
(1/31/87 BC-62)
KISSES IN THE NIGHT Brandon—Alpha International 70718
[John Roselada] [ASC] (5/11/91 B-64)
KISSES ON THE WIND Neneh Cherry—Virgin 99183
[Neneh Cherry/Cameron McVey] [BMI] (7/22/89 BC-8)
KISSES SWEETER THAN WINE Jimmie Rodgers—Roulette 4031
[Ronnie Gilbert/Lee Hays/Fred Hellerman/Sam Kennedy/Huddie Ledbetter/
Pete Seeger/Traditional] [BMI] (11/4/57 BCR-5)
KISSIN' AND TWISTIN' Fabian—Chancellor 1061
[Howard Greenfield/Barry Mann] [BMI] (10/31/60 BCR-82)
KISSIN' COUSINS Elvis Presley—RCA Victor 47-8307
[Randy Starr/Fred Wise] [ASC] (2/8/64 BCR-9)
KISSIN' GAME Dion—Laurie 3090 [Terry Philips/Jerry Vance] [BMI] (4/29/61 BCR-71)
KISSIN' ON THE PHONE Paul Anka—ABC-Paramount 10239
[Leonard Whitcup/Earl Wilson] [ASC] (8/26/61 BCR-21)
KISSIN' TIME Bobby Rydell—Cameo 167
[Bernie Lowe/Kal Mann] [ASC] (6/29/59 BCR-11)
KISSIN' TIME Kiss—Casablanca 0011 [Bernie Lowe/Kal Mann] [ASC] (5/25/74 BCR-79)
K.I.S.S.I.N.G. Siedah Garrett—Qwest 27928
[Guy Babylon/Dana Merino] [ASC] (7/16/88 B-97)
KISSING A FOOL George Michael—Columbia 08050
[George Michael] [ASC] (10/8/88 BC-4)
—KISSING KISSING see: BACIARE BACIARE
KISSING MY LOVE Bill Withers—Sussex 250 [Bill Withers] [BMI] (2/3/73 BCR-26)
KISSING TREE Billy Grammer—Monument 403
[Edith Lindeman/Carl Stutz] [ASC] (3/23/59 BCR-42)
KISSING YOU Keith Washington—Qwest 19414
[Marsha Jenkins/Rodney Shelton/Keith Washington] [ASC] (5/25/91 BC-40)
KITTY DOYLE Dino, Desi & Billy—Reprise 0619
[Garry Bonner/Alan Gordon] [BMI] (9/23/67 C-98)
KITTY WHO Kitty Kallen—Decca 29473 [Joan Javits/Joe Sherman] [ASC] (5/2/55 R-83)
KNEE DEEP IN THE BLUES Guy Mitchell—Columbia 40820
[Melvin Endsley] [BMI] (1/19/57 BCR-10)
KNIGHT IN RUSTY ARMOUR Peter And Gordon—Capitol 5808
[Mike Leander/Charles Mills] [ASC] (12/24/66 BCR-12)
KNOCK! KNOCK! (WHO'S THERE?) The Orlons—Cameo 332
[Bob Crewe/Larry Santos] [BMI] (8/29/64 BCR-64)
KNOCK KNOCK WHO'S THERE Mary Hopkin—Apple 1855
[John Carter/Geoff Stephens] [BMI] (12/2/72 BCR-78)
KNOCK ON WOOD *Eddie Floyd—Stax 194*
[Steve Cropper/Eddie Floyd] [BMI] (8/27/66 BCR-10)
KNOCK ON WOOD *Otis & Carla—Stax 228*
[Steve Cropper/Eddie Floyd] [BMI] (8/12/67 BCR-30)
KNOCK ON WOOD *Amii Stewart—Ariola America/Hansa 7736*
[Steve Cropper/Eddie Floyd] [BMI] (1/27/79 BCR-1)
KNOCK THREE TIMES Dawn—Bell 938
[L. Russell Brown/Irwin Levine] [BMI] (11/14/70 BCR-1)
KNOCKED OUT Paula Abdul—Virgin 99329
[Kenneth Edmonds/Antonio Reid/Daryl Simmons] [BMI] (6/18/88 BC-41)
KNOCKIN' BOOTS Candyman—Epic 73450
[Willie Clarke/Al Hamilton*/Eugene Hamilton*/Norman Whitfield/Betty Wright/
Richard Wylie] [BMI] (9/1/90 BC-9)
KNOCKIN' ON HEAVEN'S DOOR Bob Dylan—Columbia 45913
[Bob Dylan] [SE] (9/1/73 BCR-10)
KNOCKING AT YOUR BACK DOOR Deep Purple—Mercury 880477
[Ritchie Blackmore/Ian Gillan/Roger Glover] [ASC] (12/29/84 BC-61)
—KNOW WHAT I MEAN JELLY BEAN see: OH PAIN! OH AGONY!

KNOWING ME, KNOWING YOU Abba—Atlantic 3387 [Stig Anderson/Benny Andersson/Björn Ulvaeus] [BMI] (5/14/77 BCR-11)

KNUCKLEHEAD Bar-Kays—Volt 148 [Steve Cropper/Booker T. Jones Jr.] [BMI] (8/19/67 BC-76) [I]

KO-KO JOE Jerry Reed—RCA Victor 48-1011 [Jerry Reed] [BMI] (8/28/71 BCR-46)

KO KO MO *The Dooley Sisters—Tampa 100 [Eunice Levy/Jake Porter/Forrest Wilson] [BMI] (1/10/55 Rt-28)*

KO KO MO (I LOVE YOU SO) *Perry Como—RCA Victor 47-5994 [Eunice Levy/Jake Porter/Forrest Wilson] [BMI] (1/17/55 BCtRt-3)*

KO KO MO (I LOVE YOU SO) *Bill Darnel & Betty Clooney—"X" 0087 [Eunice Levy/Jake Porter/Forrest Wilson] [BMI] (1/17/55 Rt-28)*

KO KO MO (I LOVE YOU SO) *The Hutton Sisters—Capitol 3031 [Eunice Levy/Jake Porter/Forrest Wilson] [BMI] (1/24/55 Rt-28)*

KO KO MO (I LOVE YOU SO) *The Crew-Cuts—Mercury 70529 [Eunice Levy/Jake Porter/Forrest Wilson] (TSW) [BMI] (4/9/55 BCtRt-3)*

KODACHROME Paul Simon—Columbia 45859 [Paul Simon] [BMI] (5/19/73 BCR-1)

KOKOMO The Flamingos—End 1085 [Sammy Taylor] [BMI] (3/13/61 B-92)

KOKOMO The Beach Boys—Elektra 69385 [Mike Love/Scott McKenzie/Terry Melcher/John Phillips] [BMI] (9/3/88 BC-1)

KOMMOTION Duane Eddy—Jamie 1163 [Duane Eddy/Lee Hazlewood] [BMI] (8/22/60 BCR-28) [I]

KONG Dickie Goodman—Shock 6 [Dickie Goodman/Bill Ramal*] [BMI] (1/29/77 BCR-48)

KOOKIE, KOOKIE (LEND ME YOUR COMB) Edward Byrnes and Connie Stevens—Warner Bros. 5047 [Irving Taylor] [ASC] (4/20/59 BCR-3)

KOOKIE LITTLE PARADISE *Jo Ann Campbell—ABC-Paramount 10134 [Bob Hilliard/Lee Pockriss] [ASC] (8/8/60 BCtRt-49)*

KOOKIE LITTLE PARADISE *The Tree Swingers—Guyden 2036 [Bob Hilliard/Lee Pockriss] [ASC] (8/8/60 BCtRt-49)*

KOOKIE'S MAD PAD Edd Byrnes—Warner Bros. 5087 [Deeda Patrick/Don Ralke] [ASC] (8/8/59 C-80)

KOOL AND THE GANG Kool & The Gang—De-Lite 519 [Robert Bell/Ronald Bell/George M. Brown/Robert Mickens/Claydes Smith/Woodrow Sparrow/Dennis Thomas/Richard Westfield] [BMI] (9/6/69 BCR-56) [I]

KOOL'S BACK AGAIN Kool & The Gang—De-Lite 523 [Jimmy Crosby/Gene Redd Jr.] [BMI] (1/10/70 C-80) [I]

KOZMIC BLUES Janis Joplin—Columbia 45023 [Janis Joplin/Gabriel Mekler] [ASC] (11/8/69 BCR-39)

KUFANYA MAPENZI (MAKING LOVE) Ramsey Lewis—Columbia 45766 [Edward Prince Green] [BMI] (3/17/73 B-93) [I]

KUM BA YAH Tommy Leonetti—Decca 32421 [Traditional] [NA] (1/4/69 BCR-54)

KUNG FU Curtis Mayfield—Curtom 1999 [Curtis Mayfield] [BMI] (6/22/74 BCR-32)

KUNG FU FIGHTING Carl Douglas—20th Century 2140 [Carl Douglas] [ASC] (10/12/74 BCR-1)

(KWA-NA-VA-KA) CUERNAVACA CHOO CHOO Freddy Cannon—Swan 4057 [Bob Crewe/Frank Slay] [BMI] (7/18/60 R-84)

KWELA KWELA Bill Hayes—Cadence 1274 [Nico Carstens/Anton De Waal/Charles Segal/Viv Styger] [BMI] (10/24/55 R-71)

KYRIE Mr. Mister—RCA 14258 [Steve George/John Lang/Richard Page] [ASC] (12/21/85 BC-1)

L

L.A. BREAKDOWN Larry Marks—A&M 969 [Larry Marks] [ASC] (9/14/68 R-83)

L.A. FREEWAY Jerry Jeff Walker—MCA 40054 [Guy Clark] [ASC] (7/14/73 BCR-72)

L.A. GOODBYE The Ides Of March—Warner Bros. 7466 [Jim Peterik] [ASC] (3/13/71 BCR-72)

L.A. INTERNATIONAL AIRPORT Susan Raye—Capitol 3035 [Leanne Scott] [BMI] (4/17/71 BCR-54)

L.A. SUNSHINE War—Blue Note 1009 [Thomas Allen/Harold Brown/Morris Dickerson/Jerry Goldstein/Lonnie Jordan/Charles Miller/Lee Oskar/Howard Scott] [ASC] (7/9/77 BCR-45)

L.A. WOMAN Billy Idol—Chrysalis 23571 [John Densmore/Robby Krieger/Ray Manzarek/Jim Morrison] [ASC] (9/8/90 BC-46)

L. DAVID SLOANE Michele Lee—Columbia 44413 [Angela Martin/Wilbur Meshel] [ASC] (2/24/68 BCR-52)

L-O-N-E-L-Y Bobby Vinton—Epic 9791 [Bobby Vinton] [BMI] (5/8/65 BCR-16)

L-O-V-E Nat King Cole—Capitol 5261 [Milt Gabler/Bert Kaempfert] [BMI] (9/26/64 B-81)

L-O-V-E (LOVE) Al Green—Hi 2282 [Al Green/Mabon Hodges/Willie Mitchell] [BMI] (2/22/75 BCR-10)

LA BAMBA *Ritchie Valens—Del-Fi 4110 [Traditional] [NA] (12/20/58 BCR-22) [F]*

LA BAMBA *Carlos Brothers—Del-Fi 4145 [Traditional] [NA] (9/10/60 C-81) [F]*

LA BOMBA *The Tokens—RCA Victor 47-8052 [Traditional] [NA] (6/30/62 BCR-73) [F]*

LA BAMBA - PART 1 *Trini Lopez—Reprise 0480 [Traditional] [NA] (6/25/66 BCR-86) [F]*

LA BAMBA *Los Lobos—Slash 28336 [Traditional] [NA] (6/27/87 BC-1) [F]*

—LA CACAHUATA see: PEANUTS

LA DEE DAH Billy & Lillie—Swan 4002 [Bob Crewe/Frank Slay] [BMI] (12/28/57 BCR-4)

LA-DI-DA Sad Café—Swan Song 72002 [John Stimpson/Paul Young] [BMI] (8/15/81 B-78)

LA DO DADA Dale Hawkins—Checker 900 [Dale Hawkins/Stanley J. Lewis] [BMI] (9/1/58 BCR-32)

LA DOLCE VITA (THE SWEET LIFE) *Ray Ellis And His Orchestra—RCA Victor 47-7888 [Nino Rota] [ASC] (5/15/61 BRt-79) [IM]*

LA DOLCE VITA (THE SWEET LIFE) *Harry Simeone Chorale—20th Fox 245 [Nino Rota/Les Vandyke*/Dino Verde] [ASC] (6/12/61 Rt-82) [FDE]*

LA GRANGE ZZ Top—London 203 [Frank Beard/Billy Gibbons/Dusty Hill] [BMI] (3/30/74 BCR-24)

LA ISLA BONITA Madonna—Sire 28425 [Madonna L. Ciccone/Bruce Gaitsch/Patrick Raymond Leonard] [BMI] (3/21/87 BC-4)

LA LA LA Gerry And The Pacemakers—Laurie 3337 [Gerry Marsden] [BMI] (4/2/66 BCR-87)

LA LA LA (IF I HAD YOU) Bobby Sherman—Metromedia 150 [Danny Janssen] [BMI] (11/15/69 BCR-8)

LA LA LA LA LA The Blendells—Reprise 0291 [Clarence Paul] [BMI] (9/5/64 BCR-61)

LA - LA - MEANS I LOVE YOU *The Delfonics—Philly Groove 150 [Thom Bell/William Hart] [BMI] (2/3/68 BCR-3)*

LA LA MEANS I LOVE YOU *Tierra—Boardwalk 129 [Thom Bell/William Hart] [BMI] (10/24/81 BCR-60)*

LA LA PEACE SONG *O.C. Smith—Columbia 10031 [Johnny Bristol/Liz Martin] [ASC] (9/28/74 BCR-62)*

LA LA PEACE SONG *Al Wilson—Rocky Road 30200 [Johnny Bristol/Liz Martin] [ASC] (10/5/74 BCR-29)*

—LA MER see: BEYOND THE SEA

LA MONTANA (IF SHE SHOULD COME TO YOU) *Frank Devol And His Rainbow Strings—Columbia 41620 [Augusto Alguero] [BMI] (5/2/60 BCtRt-62) [IM]*

LA MONTANA (IF SHE SHOULD COME TO YOU) *Roger Williams—Kapp 331 [Augusto Alguero] [BMI] (5/2/60 BCtRt-62) [IM]*

IF SHE SHOULD COME TO YOU (LA MONTANA) *Anthony Newley—London 1929 [Augusto Alguero/Georges Moreau/Alec Wilder] [BMI] (9/3/60 BCR-67) [FET]*

LA PACHANGA *Hugo & Luigi with their Children's Cho.—RCA Victor 47-7868 [Eduardo Davidson/Jeanne Pollock] [BMI] (4/10/61 Rt-90) [FDE?]*

LA PACHANGA *Audrey Arno And The Hazy Osterwald Sextet—Decca 31238 [Eduardo Davidson/Kurt Feltz] [BMI] (4/10/61 BRt-87) [F]*

LA PALOMA Billy Vaughn And His Orchestra—Dot 15795 [Sebastian Yradier] [NA] (8/4/58 BCR-13) [I]

LA PALOMA TWIST Chubby Checker—Parkway 835 [Kal Mann/Sebastian Yradier] [NA] (3/17/62 B-72)

LA PLUME DE MA TANTE Hugo & Luigi—RCA Victor 47-7518 [Al Hoffman/Dick Manning] [ASC] (5/18/59 BCR-31)

LA RAZA Kid Frost—Virgin 98947 [Antonio Gonzalez/Arturo Molina Jr./Gerald Wilson] [BMI] (7/7/90 BC-42)

—LA SHABLA see: SHOVEL

LA STRADA DEL' AMORE Caterina Valente—RCA Victor 47-7525 [Jack Reardon] [ASC] (5/30/59 CR-83)

THE LADDER OF LOVE *The Flamingos—Decca 30335 [Clint Ballard Jr.] [ASC] (7/13/57 Rt-35)*

THE LADDER OF LOVE *Johnny Nash—ABC-Paramount 9844 [Clint Ballard Jr.] [ASC] (8/5/57 Rt-35)*

LADIES NIGHT Kool & The Gang—De-Lite 801 [Robert Bell/Ronald Bell/George M. Brown/Meekaaeel Muhammed/Claydes Smith/J.T. Taylor/Dennis Thomas/Earl Toon] [BMI] (10/6/79 BCR-4)

LADY Jack Jones—Kapp 800 [Bert Kaempfert/Larry Kusik/Herbert Rehbein/Charles Singleton] [BMI] (1/21/67 BCR-34)

LADY Styx—Wooden Nickel 10102 [Dennis DeYoung] [ASC] (12/7/74 BCR-6)

LADY Little River Band—Harvest 4667 [Graham Goble] [BMI] (1/6/79 BCR-7)

LADY The Whispers—Solar 11928 [Nicholas Caldwell] [BMI] (4/12/80 BCR-28)

LADY Kenny Rogers—Liberty 1380 [Lionel Richie] [ASC] (10/4/80 BCR-1)

LADY BIRD Nancy Sinatra & Lee Hazlewood—Reprise 0629 [Lee Hazlewood] [ASC] (10/21/67 BCR-20)

LADY BLUE *Leon Russell—Shelter 40378 [Leon Russell] [BMI] (7/26/75 BCR-8)*

LADY BLUE *George Benson—Warner Bros. 8604 [Leon Russell] [BMI] (7/15/78 C-94)*

LADY BUMP *Penny McLean—Atco 7038 [Sylvester Levay/Stephan Prager] [BMI] (1/3/76 BC-48)*

LADY BUMP *The Ritchie Family—Marlin 3306 [Sylvester Levay/Stephan Prager] (Med) [BMI] (8/28/76 BCR-17)*

THE LADY CAME FROM BALTIMORE Bobby Darin—Atlantic 2395 [Tim Hardin] [BMI] (4/8/67 BCR-62)

LADY DOWN ON LOVE Alabama—RCA 13590 [Randy Owen] [BMI] (10/29/83 B-76)

LADY ELEANOR Lindisfarne—Elektra 45799 [Alan Hull] [ASC] (9/2/72 BCR-78)

LADY FRIEND The Byrds—Columbia 44230 [David Crosby] [BMI] (8/12/67 BCR-71)

LADY GODIVA Peter And Gordon—Capitol 5740 [Mike Leander/Charles Mills] [BMI] (10/8/66 BCR-5)

THE LADY IN RED Chris DeBurgh—A&M 2848 [Chris de Burgh] [ASC] (2/14/87 BC-2)

LADY JANE The Rolling Stones—London 902
[Mick Jagger/Keith Richards] [BMI] (7/9/66 BCR-24)
LADY, LADY, LADY Joe "Bean" Esposito—Casablanca 814430
[Keith Forsey/Giorgio Moroder] [ASC] (10/22/83 BC-82)
LADY LAY Wayne Newton—Chelsea 3003
[Pierre Groscolas/Michel Jourdan/Donny Marchand/M. McGinnis*] [BMI] (11/16/74 C-83) [FDE]
LADY LOVE The Klowns—RCA Victor 74-0393
[Mike Soles/Steve Soles] [BMI] (12/5/70 BCR-81)
LADY LOVE Lou Rawls—Philadelphia Int'l 3634
[Von Gray/Sherman Marshall] [BMI] (12/24/77 BCR-19)
LADY LOVE ME (ONE MORE TIME) George Benson—Warner Bros. 29563
[James Newton Howard/David Paich] [BMI] (7/23/83 BC-30)
LADY LUCK Lloyd Price And His Orchestra—ABC-Paramount 10075
[Harold Logan/Lloyd Price] [BMI] (1/25/60 BCR-11)
LADY MADONNA *The Beatles—Capitol 2138*
[John Lennon/Paul McCartney] [ASC] (3/16/68 BCR-2)
LADY MADONNA *Fats Domino—Reprise 0763*
[John Lennon/Paul McCartney] [ASC] (8/17/68 BC-87)
LADY MARMALADE *Labelle—Epic 50048 [Bob Crewe/Kenny Nolan] [BMI] (1/4/75 BCR-1)*
LADY MARMALADE *The Ritchie Family—Marlin 3306*
[Bob Crewe/Kenny Nolan] (Med) [BMI] (8/28/76 BCR-17)
LADY-O The Turtles—White Whale 334 [Judee Sill] [BMI] (11/22/69 BCR-67)
LADY OF MAGIC Maze Featuring Frankie Beverly—Capitol 4456
[Frankie Beverly] [BMI] (10/15/77 R-95)
LADY OF MY HEART Jack Wagner—Qwest 29085
[Glen Ballard/David Foster/Jay Graydon] [ASC] (5/25/85 BC-76)
LADY (PUT THE LIGHT ON ME) Brownsville Station—Private Stock 45,149
[John Goodison/Phil Wainman] [BMI] (5/28/77 BCR-44)
LADY SOUL The Temptations—Gordy 1856 [Mark Holden] [ASC] (10/11/86 BC-47)
LADY WILLPOWER Gary Puckett And The Union Gap—Columbia 44547
[Jerry Fuller] [BMI] (6/8/68 BCR-1)
LADY WRITER Dire Straits—Warner Bros. 49006 [Mark Knopfler] [ASC] (7/28/79 BCR-45)
LADY (YOU BRING ME UP) Commodores—Motown 1514
[Harold Hudson/Shirley King/William King] [ASC] (6/20/81 BCR-7)
LAID BACK LOVE Major Harris—WMOT 4002 [Len Barry/Bobby Eli] [BMI] (11/27/76 B-91)
—LAISSE MOI LE TEMPS see: LET ME TRY AGAIN
LALENA Donovan—Epic 10393 [Donovan Leitch] [BMI] (9/28/68 BCR-28)
LAMBADA Kaoma—Epic 73090 [Chico De Oliveira] [BMI] (3/3/90 BC-46) [F]
—LAMENT OF THE CHEROKEE see: INDIAN RESERVATION
—L'AMORE SE NE VA see: GIVE ME TIME
—L'AMOUR EST BLEU see: LOVE IS BLUE
LAMPLIGHT David Essex—Columbia 46041 [David Essex] [ASC] (5/25/74 BCR-61)
LANA Gene McCannon—Parkway 883 [Joe Melson/Roy Orbison] [BMI] (8/31/63 R-100)
LAND OF 1000 DANCES *Chris Kenner—Instant 3252*
[Chris Kenner] [BMI] (6/29/63 BCR-77)
LAND OF 1000 DANCES *Cannibal And The Headhunters—Rampart 642*
[Chris Kenner] [BMI] (2/27/65 BCtRt-25)
LAND OF A THOUSAND DANCES PART I *Thee Midniters—Chattahoochee 666*
[Chris Kenner] [BMI] (2/27/65 BCtRt-25)
LAND OF 1000 DANCES *Round Robin—Domain 1420 [Chris Kenner] [BMI] (5/8/65 Rt-25)*
LAND OF 1000 DANCES *Wilson Pickett—Atlantic 2348*
[Chris Kenner] [BMI] (7/30/66 BCR-6)
LAND OF 1000 DANCES *The Electric Indian—United Artists 50613*
[Chris Kenner] [BMI] (11/22/69 BCR-63) [IWM]
LAND OF A THOUSAND DANCES *The J. Geils Band—EMI America 8156*
[Chris Kenner] [BMI] (2/26/83 BC-60)
LAND OF CONFUSION Genesis—Atlantic 89336
[Tony Banks/Phil Collins/Mike Rutherford] [ASC] (11/1/86 BC-4)
LAND OF DREAMS Hugo Winterhalter's Orchestra And Chorus—RCA Victor 47-5888
[Norman Gimbel/Eddie Heywood] [BMI] (11/22/54 BR-16)
LAND OF LA LA Stevie Wonder—Tamla 1846 [Stevie Wonder] [ASC] (6/14/86 BC-83)
LAND OF MAKE BELIEVE Chuck Mangione—Mercury 73920
[Chuck Mangione] [BMI] (6/11/77 B-86)
THE LAND OF MILK AND HONEY The Vogues—Co & Ce 238
[John Hurley/Ronnie Wilkins] [BMI] (6/4/66 BCR-29)
LAND OF YOU AND ME The Four Esquires—Paris 526 [Wally Gold] [BMI] (1/3/59 C-81)
LANDLORD Gladys Knight & The Pips—Columbia 11239
[Nick Ashford/Valerie Simpson] [ASC] (5/24/80 BCR-46)
LANDSLIDE Olivia Newton-John—MCA 52069 [John Farrar] [BMI] (6/12/82 BC-52)
LANGUAGE OF LOVE Cindy And Lindy—ABC-Paramount 9847
[Al Frisch/Sid Wayne] [ASC] (9/23/57 R-78)
LANGUAGE OF LOVE John D. Loudermilk—RCA Victor 47-7938
[John D. Loudermilk] [BMI] (10/23/61 BCR-23)
THE LANGUAGE OF LOVE The Intrigues—Yew 1012
[Joe Cobb/Van McCoy] [BMI] (6/19/71 BCR-82)
THE LANGUAGE OF LOVE Dan Fogelberg—Full Moon 04314
[Dan Fogelberg] [ASC] (2/4/84 BC-13)
LAPLAND The Baltimore And Ohio Marching Band—Jubilee 5592
[Carl Hjelm/Mats Olsson] [BMI] (10/28/67 B-94) [IM]
—LARA'S THEME FROM DR. ZHIVAGO see: SOMEWHERE MY LOVE
THE LARGE LARGE HOUSE Mike Pedicin Quintet—RCA Victor 47-6369
[Bickley Reichner] [ASC] (3/17/56 B-79)
LAST CHANCE Collay And The Satellites—Sho-Biz 1002
[Allen Callais] [BMI] (4/25/60 B-82)
LAST CHANCE TO TURN AROUND Gene Pitney—Musicor 1093
[Tony Bruno/Stanley Kahan/Vic Millrose] [BMI] (5/8/65 BCR-12)
LAST CHILD Aerosmith—Columbia 10359
[Steven Tyler/Brad Whitford] [BMI] (6/5/76 BCR-21)
THE LAST DANCE The McGuire Sisters—Coral 62216
[Sammy Cahn/Jimmy Van Heusen] [ASC] (8/15/60 B-99)
LAST DANCE Donna Summer—Casablanca 926 [Paul Jabara] [BMI] (5/13/78 BCR-3)
LAST DATE *Floyd Cramer—RCA Victor 47-7775 [Floyd Cramer] [BMI] (10/3/60 BCRt-1) [I]*
LAST DATE *Lawrence Welk And His Orchestra—Dot 16145*
[Floyd Cramer] [BMI] (10/17/60 BRt-1) [I]
MY LAST DATE (WITH YOU) *Skeeter Davis—RCA Victor 47-7825*
[Boudleaux Bryant/Floyd Cramer/Skeeter Davis] [BMI] (12/12/60 BCtRt-26)
MY LAST DATE (WITH YOU) *Joni James—MGM 12933*
[Boudleaux Bryant/Floyd Cramer/Skeeter Davis] [BMI] (12/19/60 BCtRt-31)
THE LAST FAREWELL Roger Whittaker—RCA Victor 50030
[Ron Webster/Roger Whittaker] [ASC] (3/29/75 BCR-16)
THE LAST GAME OF THE SEASON (A BLIND MAN IN THE BLEACHERS)
David Geddes—Big Tree 16052
[Sterling Whipple] [BMI] (11/8/75 BCR-18)
THE BLIND MAN IN THE BLEACHERS *Kenny Starr—MCA 40474*
[Sterling Whipple] [BMI] (12/6/75 BC-58)
LAST KISS *J. Frank Wilson And The Cavaliers—Josie 923*
[Wayne Cochran] [BMI] (8/8/64 BCR-1)
LAST KISS *Wednesday—Sussex 507 [Wayne Cochran] [BMI] (11/10/73 BCR-33)*
LAST KISS *J. Frank Wilson And The Cavaliers—Virgo 506*
[Wayne Cochran] [BMI] (12/1/73 BCR-65)
THE LAST LEAF The Cascades—Valiant 6028
[Bodie Chandler/Edward McKendry] [BMI] (5/4/63 BCR-42)
THE LAST MILE Cinderella—Mercury 872148 [Tom Keifer] [ASC] (1/21/89 BC-36)
THE LAST MINUTE PT. I Jimmy McGriff—Sue 786
[Jimmy McGriff] [BMI] (5/25/63 BR-93) [I]
LAST MINUTE MIRACLE The Shirelles—Scepter 12198
[Gerald Harris/George Kerr] [BMI] (8/19/67 B-99)
LAST NIGHT Mar-Keys—Satellite 107
[Charles Axton/Gilbert Caple/Chips Moman/Floyd Newman/Jerald Leroy Smith] [BMI] (6/12/61 BCR-3) [I]
LAST NIGHT A D.J. SAVED MY LIFE Indeep—Sound Of New York 5102
[Mike Cleveland] [BMI] (3/5/83 C-91)
(LAST NIGHT) I DIDN'T GET TO SLEEP AT ALL The 5th Dimension—Bell 45,195
[Tony Macaulay] [BMI] (3/25/72 BCR-6)
LAST OF THE SINGING COWBOYS The Marshall Tucker Band—Warner Bros. 8841
[George McCorkle] [BMI] (6/23/79 BCR-42)
LAST OF THE WINE The Robbs—Dunhill 4233 [Dee Robb] [BMI] (4/25/70 R-95)
THE LAST ONE TO KNOW The Fleetwoods—Dolton 27
[Dewayne Blackwell] [BMI] (10/1/60 BC-79)
THE LAST SAFE PLACE ON EARTH Le Roux—RCA 13224
[Jeff Pollard] [BMI] (5/22/82 BC-71)
LAST SONG Edward Bear—Capitol 3452 [Larry Evoy] [ASC] (12/16/72 BCR-2)
LAST SONG AND DANCE Kay Starr—RCA Victor 47-7114
[Edgar Leslie] [ASC] (1/6/58 R-58)
LAST TANGO IN PARIS Herb Alpert & The TJB—A&M 1420
[Gato Barbieri] [BMI] (3/10/73 BCR-70) [IM]
THE LAST THING ON MY MIND Neil Diamond—MCA 40092
[Tom Paxton] [ASC] (8/18/73 BCR-42)
LAST TIME Sil Austin—Mercury 71027 [Sil Austin] [BMI] (1/26/57 R-74) [I]
THE LAST TIME *The Rolling Stones—London 9741*
[Mick Jagger/Keith Richards] [BMI] (3/27/65 BCR-9)
THE LAST TIME *The Buchanan Brothers—Event 3307*
[Mick Jagger/Keith Richards] [BMI] (12/6/69 CR-84)
THE LAST TIME I MADE LOVE Joyce Kennedy & Jeffrey Osborne—A&M 2656
[Jeff Barry/Barry Mann/Cynthia Weil] [BMI] (8/18/84 BC-40)
THE LAST TIME I SAW HER Glen Campbell—Capitol 3123
[Gordon Lightfoot] [ASC] (6/26/71 BCR-57)
LAST TIME I SAW HIM Diana Ross—Motown 1278
[Michael Masser/Pam Sawyer] [ASC] (12/22/73 BCR-9)
LAST TRAIN (BIDDI-BIDDI BUM-BUM) Ray Lang—Decca 30210
[Joe Sciacca/Bev Terry] [NA] (2/23/57 R-82)
LAST TRAIN TO CLARKSVILLE The Monkees—Colgems 1001
[Tommy Boyce/Bobby Hart] [BMI] (9/3/66 BCR-1)
LAST TRAIN TO LONDON Electric Light Orchestra—Jet 5067
[Jeff Lynne] [BMI] (12/1/79 BCR-36)

THE LAST WALTZ Engelbert Humperdinck—Parrot 40019
[Barry Mason/Les Reed] [ASC] (9/16/67 BCR-21)

THE LAST WORD IN LONESOME IS ME Eddy Arnold—RCA Victor 47-8818
[Roger Miller] [BMI] (5/7/66 BCR-34)

THE LAST WORTHLESS EVENING Don Henley—Geffen 22771
[John Corey/Don Henley/Stan Lynch] [ASC] (10/7/89 BC-20)

LASTING LOVE *Sal Mineo—Epic 9227*
[Jack Ackerman/Hunt Stevens] [BMI] (8/3/57 BCRt-35)

LASTING LOVE *Kitty Kallen—Decca 30404*
[Jack Ackerman/Hunt Stevens] [BMI] (8/3/57 Rt-39)

LATE AT NIGHT England Dan Seals—Atlantic 3674
[Dan Seals/Rafe Van Hoy] [BMI] (8/9/80 BCR-57)

LATE DATE The Parkays—ABC-Paramount 10242
[Walter Maynard] [NA] (10/9/61 B-89) [I]

LATE IN THE EVENING Paul Simon—Warner Bros. 49511
[Paul Simon] [BMI] (8/9/80 BCR-6)

LATELY Stevie Wonder—Tamla 54323 [Stevie Wonder] [ASC] (4/11/81 BCR-64)

LATIN ACTIVE A Lighter Shade Of Brown—Pump 15168
[Fabian Alfaro/James Carter/Darryl Cash/Robert Gutierrez/Luis Ortiz/
Bobby Ramirez/Humberto Vergara*] [BMI] (7/20/91 BC-59)

LAUGH The Velvets—Monument 448 [Joe Melson/Roy Orbison] [BMI] (9/25/61 BCR-78)

LAUGH AT ME Sonny—Atco 6369 [Sonny Bono] [BMI] (8/21/65 BCR-6)

LAUGH, LAUGH The Beau Brummels—Autumn 8 [Ron Elliott] [BMI] (12/26/64 BCR-15)

LAUGHIN AND CLOWNIN Ray Charles—ABC/TRC 11259
[Sam Cooke] [BMI] (3/14/70 BC-90)

LAUGHING The Guess Who—RCA Victor 74-0195
[Randy Bachman/Burton Cummings] [BMI] (7/5/69 BCR-5)

LAUGHING BOY Mary Wells—Motown 1039 [Smokey Robinson] [ASC] (2/23/63 BCR-15)

LAUGHTER IN THE RAIN Neil Sedaka—Rocket/MCA 40313
[Phil Cody/Neil Sedaka] [BMI] (10/19/74 BCR-1)

LAURA, WHAT'S HE GOT THAT I AIN'T GOT *Frankie Laine—ABC 10967*
[Leon Ashley/Margie Singleton] [BMI] (8/12/67 BCR-53)

LAURA (TELL ME WHAT HE'S GOT THAT I AIN'T GOT) *Brook Benton—Reprise 0611*
[Leon Ashley/Margie Singleton] [BMI] (8/19/67 BCR-78)

LAURIE, MY LOVE Johnny Mathis—Columbia 42048
[Jerry Livingston/Paul Francis Webster] [ASC] (7/10/61 R-78)

LAURIE (STRANGE THINGS HAPPEN) Dickey Lee—TCF Hall 102
[Milton Addington] [BMI] (5/15/65 BCR-11)

LAVENDER BLUE Sammy Turner—Big Top 3016
[Eliot Daniel/Larry Morey] [ASC] (6/22/59 BCR-3)

LAWDY MISS CLAWDY *Gary Stites—Carlton 525 [Lloyd Price] [BMI] (2/22/60 BCR-47)*

LAUDY MISS CLAUDY *The Buckinghams—U.S.A. 869*
[Lloyd Price] [BMI] (3/11/67 BCR-36)

LAWYERS IN LOVE Jackson Browne—Asylum 69826
[Jackson Browne] [ASC] (7/9/83 BC-13)

LAY A LITTLE LOVIN' ON ME Robin McNamara—Steed 724
[Jeff Barry/Jim Cretecos/Robin McNamara] [BMI] (5/16/70 BCR-6)

LAY ALL YOUR LOVE ON ME Information Society—Tommy Boy 27534
[Benny Andersson/Björn Ulvaeus] [BMI] (8/12/89 BC-61)

LAY-AWAY The Isley Brothers—T-Neck 934
[O'Kelly Isley/Ronald Isley/Rudolph Isley] [BMI] (3/18/72 BCR-36)

LAY DOWN (CANDLES IN THE RAIN)
Melanie With The Edwin Hawkins Singers—Buddah 167
[Melanie Safka] [ASC] (4/18/70 BCR-3)

LAY DOWN SALLY Eric Clapton—RSO 886
[Eric Clapton/Marcy Levy/George Terry] [BMI] (12/31/77 BCR-3)

LAY DOWN YOUR ARMS *Russ Morgan & His Orchestra—Decca 30070*
[Leon Landgren/Åke Gerhard Larsson/Paddy Roberts] [BMI] (9/29/56 Rt-21) [FDE]

LAY DOWN YOUR ARMS *The Chordettes—Cadence 1299*
[Leon Landgren/Åke Gerhard Larsson/Paddy Roberts] [BMI] (9/29/56 BCtRt-16) [FDE]

LAY DOWN YOUR ARMS *Anne Shelton—Columbia 40759*
[Leon Landgren/Åke Gerhard Larsson/Paddy Roberts] [BMI] (9/29/56 BCtRt-21) [FDE]

LAY DOWN YOUR ARMS The Graces—A&M 1440
[Charlotte Caffey/Ralph Schuckett/Ellen Shipley] [ASC] (8/12/89 BC-56)

LAY IT DOWN Ratt—Atlantic 89546
[Robbin Crosby/Juan Croucier/Warren DeMartini/Stephen Pearcy] [BMI]
(7/6/85 BC-40)

LAY IT ON THE LINE Triumph—RCA 11690 [Rik Emmett] [ASC] (11/3/79 BCR-66)

LAY LADY LAY *Bob Dylan—Columbia 44926 [Bob Dylan] [SE] (7/12/69 BCR-7)*

LAY LADY LAY *Ferrante & Teicher—United Artists 50646*
[Bob Dylan] [SE] (2/28/70 BCR-71) [IWM]

LAY LADY LAY *The Isley Brothers—T-Neck 933 [Bob Dylan] [SE] (11/27/71 BCR-57)*

LAY SOME HAPPINESS ON ME Dean Martin—Reprise 0571
[Jean Chapel/Bob Jennings] [BMI] (4/22/67 BCR-42)

LAY YOUR HANDS ON ME Thompson Twins—Arista 1-9396
[Tom Bailey/Alannah Currie/Joe Leeway] [ASC] (9/21/85 BC-6)

LAY YOUR HANDS ON ME Bon Jovi—Mercury 874452
[Jon Bon Jovi/Richie Sambora] [ASC] (6/3/89 BC-5)

LAYIN' IT ON THE LINE Jefferson Starship—Grunt 13872
[Craig Chaquico/Mickey Thomas] [BMI] (9/8/84 BC-66)

LAYLA *Derek And The Dominos—Atco 6809*
[Eric Clapton/Jim Gordon] [BMI] (3/20/71 BCR-50)

LAYLA *Derek And The Dominos—Atco 6809*
[Eric Clapton/Jim Gordon] [BMI] (5/13/72 BCR-10)

LAZY DAY Spanky And Our Gang—Mercury 72732
[George Fischoff/Tony Powers] [BMI] (10/14/67 BCR-14)

LAZY ELSIE MOLLY Chubby Checker—Parkway 920
[Tommy Boyce/Roberta Harris/Bobby Hart] [BMI] (6/6/64 BCR-39)

LAZY EYES T.M.G.—Atco 7096 [Ted Mulry] [ASC] (3/3/79 BC-91)

LAZY GONDOLIER *Mantovani And His Orchestra—London 1510*
[Georgio Forli/Mantovani/Angelo Piccioni] [ASC] (3/5/55 CRt-17) [IM]*

LAZY GONDOLIER *Lawrence Welk & His Champagne Music—Coral 61372*
[Georgio Forli/Mantovani/Angelo Piccioni] [ASC] (3/28/55 Rt-67) [IM]*

LAZY LADY Fats Domino—ABC-Paramount 10531
[Fats Domino/Reginald Hall*] [BMI] (2/29/64 BR-83)

LAZY MARY (LUNA MEZZO MARE) Lou Monte—RCA Victor 47-7160
[Paolo Citorello/Lou Monte] [ASC] (2/24/58 BCR-7) [F]

LAZY RIVER *Roberta Sherwood—Decca 29911*
[Sidney Arodin/Hoagy Carmichael] [ASC] (5/25/56 BRt-57)*

LAZY RIVER *Cathy Ryan—King 4916*
[Sidney Arodin/Hoagy Carmichael] [ASC] (5/25/56 Rt-78)*

LAZY RIVER *Bobby Darin—Atco 6188*
[Sidney Arodin/Hoagy Carmichael] [ASC] (2/6/61 BCR-11)*

UP A LAZY RIVER *Si Zentner And His Orchestra—Liberty 55374*
[Sidney Arodin/Hoagy Carmichael] [ASC] (11/6/61 BCR-27) [IWM]*

LAZY SUMMER NIGHT The Four Preps—Capitol 4023 [Hal Spina] [ASC] (7/28/58 BCR-21)

LE BEL AGE (THE BEST YEARS) Pat Benatar—Chrysalis 42968
[Guy Marshall/Robert Tepper] [ASC] (2/15/86 BC-54)

LE FREAK Chic—Atlantic 3519 [Bernard Edwards/Nile Rodgers] [BMI] (10/28/78 BCR-1)

—LE GRISBI see: TOUCH

LE PETIT REVEIL (THE LITTLE CLOCK) Domenico Modugno—Jubilee 5339
[Domenico Modugno] [ASC] (9/15/58 R-77)

LE SPANK Le Pamplemousse—AVI 153
[Gilbert Karson/W. Michael Lewis/Laurin Rinder/David Larry Williams] [BMI]
(11/26/77 BC-58) [IWM]

LEAD A DOUBLE LIFE Loverboy—Columbia 05867
[Paul Dean/Doug Johnson/Ted Johnson/Mike Reno/Davitt Sigerson/Bill Wray] [BMI]
(4/26/86 BC-65)

LEAD ME ON Bobby Bland—Duke 318 [Deadric Malone] [BMI] (5/2/60 R-99)

LEAD ME ON Maxine Nightingale—Windsong 11530
[David Lasley/Allee Willis] [ASC] (5/5/79 BCR-4)

LEAD ME ON Amy Grant—A&M 1218
[Amy Grant/Wayne Kirkpatrick/Michael W. Smith] [ASC] (8/6/88 B-96)

LEADER OF THE BAND Dan Fogelberg—Full Moon 02647
[Dan Fogelberg] [ASC] (11/28/81 BCR-9)

LEADER OF THE LAUNDROMAT The Detergents—Roulette 4590
[Lee Pockriss/Paul Vance] [ASC] (12/5/64 BCR-10)

LEADER OF THE PACK *The Shangri-Las—Red Bird 10-014*
[Jeff Barry/Ellie Greenwich/Shadow Morton] [BMI] (10/10/64 BCR-1)

LEADER OF THE PACK *Twisted Sister—Atlantic 89478*
[Jeff Barry/Ellie Greenwich/Shadow Morton] [BMI] (11/30/85 BC-51)

LEAH Roy Orbison—Monument 467 [Roy Orbison] [BMI] (9/29/62 BCR-25)

LEAN JEAN Bill Haley And His Comets—Decca 30681
[Johnny Grande/Ralph Jones/Stella Lee/Rudy Pompilli] [BMI] (8/2/58 BCR-54)

LEAN ON ME Bill Withers—Sussex 235 [Bill Withers] [BMI] (4/15/72 BCR-1)

LEAN ON ME Club Nouveau—King Jay/Warner 28430 [Bill Withers] [BMI] (2/14/87 BC-1)

LEANIN' ON YOU Joe South—Capitol 2491 [Joe South] [BMI] (5/10/69 R-64)

LEANING ON THE LAMP POST Herman's Hermits—MGM 13500
[Noel Gay] [ASC] (4/2/66 BCR-7)

LEAP FROG Chuck Alaimo Quartet—MGM 12449
[Joe Garland] [ASC] (4/13/57 BCR-56) [IM]

LEARNIN' THE BLUES Frank Sinatra—Capitol 3102
[Dolores Vicki Silvers] [ASC] (4/18/55 BCR-2)

LEARNING TO FLY Pink Floyd—Columbia 07363
[Jon Carin/Bob Ezrin/David Gilmour/Anthony Moore] [BMI] (10/10/87 BC-70)

LEARNING TO FLY Tom Petty and the Heartbreakers—MCA 54124
[Jeff Lynne/Tom Petty] [ASC] (6/22/91 BC-28)

LEARNING TO LOVE *LaFawn Paul with The Whippoorwills—Abbott 3009*
[John Harper] [BMI] (9/12/55 Rt-22)

LEARNING TO LOVE *Jean Dinning—Essex 401 [John Harper] [BMI] (9/12/55 Rt-63)*

LEARNING TO LOVE *Dori Anne Gray—Mercury 70689 [John Harper] [BMI] (9/12/55 Rt-22)*

LEARNING TO LOVE *Peggy King—Columbia 40562 [John Harper] [BMI] (9/19/55 BCRt-22)*

LEARNING TO LOVE *The Billy Williams Quartet—Coral 61498*
[John Harper] [BMI] (10/3/55 Rt-41)

LEATHER AND LACE Stevie Nicks (with Don Henley)—Modern 7341
[Stevie Nicks] [BMI] (10/24/81 BCR-6)

LEAVE A LIGHT ON Belinda Carlisle—MCA 53706
[Rick Nowels/Ellen Shipley] [ASC] (9/30/89 BC-11)

LEAVE A TENDER MOMENT ALONE Billy Joel—Columbia 04514
[Billy Joel] [ASC] (7/7/84 BC-27)

LEAVE IT Yes—Atco 99787
[Trevor Horn/Trevor Rabin/Chris Squire] [BMI] (3/3/84 BC-24)

LEAVE IT TO LOVE Sarah Vaughan—Mercury 71030
[Mack Discant/Dick Miles] [ASC] (3/2/57 B-91)

LEAVE IT TO YOUR HEART The Ames Brothers—RCA Victor 47-5764
[Kermit Goell/Fred Spielman] [ASC] (7/3/54 C-27)

LEAVE ME ALONE Baby Washington—Sue 790
[Lockie Edwards/Mat Maurer/Larry Weiss] [BMI] (7/6/63 BCR-62)

LEAVE ME ALONE (LET ME CRY) Dicky Doo And The Don'ts—Swan 4014
[Gerry Granahan/Marion Smith/Traditional] [BMI] (9/29/58 BCR-44)

LEAVE ME ALONE (RUBY RED DRESS) Helen Reddy—Capitol 3768
[Linda Laurie] [ASC] (10/27/73 BCR-1)

LEAVE MY KITTEN ALONE *Little Willie John—King 5219*
[Little Willie John/James McDougal/Titus Turner] [BMI] (8/3/59 B-60)

LEAVE MY KITTEN ALONE *Little Willie John—King 5452*
[Little Willie John/James McDougal/Titus Turner] [BMI] (1/23/61 BRt-60)

LEAVE MY KITTEN ALONE *Johnny Preston—Mercury 71761*
[Little Willie John/James McDougal/Titus Turner] [BMI] (1/28/61 BCRt-69)

LEAVE MY MAN (WOMAN) ALONE The Raeletts Featuring Vernita Moss—Tangerine 1017
[Ray Charles] [BMI] (9/4/71 C-99)

LEAVIN' ON YOUR MIND Patsy Cline—Decca 31455
[Webb Pierce/Wayne Walker] [BMI] (1/12/63 BCR-59)

LEAVING HERE Eddie Holland—Motown 1052
[Lamont Dozier/Brian Holland/Eddie Holland] [BMI] (2/8/64 BCR-71)

LEAVING L.A. Deliverance—Columbia 11320
[Ken Janz/Paul Janz] [BMI] (8/23/80 BCR-71)

LEAVING ME The Independents—Wand 11252
[Maurice Barge/Jimmie Jiles] [BMI] (3/24/73 BCR-18)

LEAVING ON A JET PLANE *Gloria Loring—Evolution 1012*
[John Denver] [ASC] (10/11/69 R-98)

LEAVING ON A JET PLANE *Peter, Paul & Mary—Warner Bros.-Seven Arts 7340*
[John Denver] [ASC] (10/25/69 BCR-1)

THE LEBANON The Human League—A&M/Virgin 2641
[John William Callis/Philip Oakey] [ASC] (6/9/84 BC-64)

THE LEFT ARM OF BUDDHA Les Baxter's Orchestra—Capitol 3573
[Les Baxter] [ASC] (12/22/56 B-82) [I]

LEFT IN THE DARK Barbra Streisand—Columbia 04605
[Jim Steinman] [BMI] (9/22/84 BC-37)

LEFT RIGHT OUT OF YOUR HEART (HI-LEE HI-LO HI-LUP-UP-UP)
Patti Page—Mercury 71331
[Mort Garson/Earl Shuman] [ASC] (6/16/58 BCRt-5)

LEFT RIGHT OUT OF YOUR HEART (HI-LEE HI-LO HI-LUP-UP-UP)
Vaughn Monroe—RCA Victor 47-7284
[Mort Garson/Earl Shuman] [ASC] (7/7/58 Rt-5)

LEFT TO MY OWN DEVICES Pet Shop Boys—EMI-Manhattan 50171
[Chris Lowe/Neil Tennant] [ASC] (1/28/89 BC-74)

LEFTOVERS Millie Jackson—Spring 161 [Phillip Mitchell] [BMI] (9/27/75 BC-74)

LEGAL TENDER The B-52's—Warner Bros. 29579
[Kate Pierson/Fred Schneider/Keith Strickland/Robert Waldrop/Cindy Wilson/
Ricky Wilson] [ASC] (7/16/83 BC-81)

LEGEND IN YOUR OWN TIME Carly Simon—Elektra 45774
[Carly Simon] [ASC] (3/18/72 BCR-50)

—LEGEND OF BILLY JACK see: ONE TIN SOLDIER

THE LEGEND OF WOOLEY SWAMP Charlie Daniels Band—Epic 50921
[Tom Crain/Charlie Daniels/Joel DiGregorio/Fred Edwards/Charles Hayward/
James W. Marshall] [BMI] (8/16/80 BCR-23)

LEGS ZZ Top—Warner Bros. 29272
[Frank Beard/Billy Gibbons/Dusty Hill] [BMI] (5/19/84 BC-8)

LEILA ZZ Top—Warner Bros. 49782
[Frank Beard/Billy Gibbons/Dusty Hill] [BMI] (9/26/81 BCR-76)

LEMON TREE *Peter, Paul & Mary—Warner Bros. 5274*
[Will Holt/Traditional] [ASC] (4/16/62 BCR-35)

LEMON TREE *Trini Lopez—Reprise 0336 [Will Holt/Traditional] [ASC] (1/16/65 BCR-20)*

LEND ME YOUR COMB *Bernie Nee—Columbia 41090*
[Kay Twomey/Ben Weisman/Fred Wise] [ASC] (1/13/58 Rt-81)

LEND ME YOUR COMB *Carol Hughes—Roulette 4041*
[Kay Twomey/Ben Weisman/Fred Wise] [ASC] (1/13/58 Rt-81)

LEND ME YOUR COMB *Carl Perkins—Sun 287*
[Kay Twomey/Ben Weisman/Fred Wise] [ASC] (1/25/58 CRt-60)

LEONA Wet Willie—Capricorn 0224 [Jack Hall/Jimmy Hall] [BMI] (2/22/75 BCR-65)

LEOPARD-SKIN PILL-BOX HAT Bob Dylan—Columbia 44069
[Bob Dylan] [SE] (5/20/67 BCR-81)

LEROY Jack Scott—Carlton 462 [Jack Scott] [BMI] (5/24/58 BCR-25)

LEROY Norma Tracey And The Cinderella Kids—Day Dell 1005
[William E. Jackson III/Jimmy Wisner] [BMI] (2/20/65 R-94)

LES BICYCLETTES DE BELSIZE Engelbert Humperdinck—Parrot 40032
[Barry Mason/Les Reed] [ASC] (10/12/68 BCR-22)

—LES LAVANDIERES DU PORTUGAL see: PORTUGUESE WASHERWOMEN

THE LESSON Vikki Carr—Liberty 56012 [Mack David] [ASC] (12/23/67 BCR-34)

A LESSON IN LEAVIN' Dottie West—United Artists 1339
[Randy Goodrum/Brent Maher] [ASC] (3/8/80 BC-73)

LESSONS IN LOVE Level 42—Polydor 883956
[Wally Badarou/Boon Gould/Mark King] [BMI] (4/4/87 BC-12)

LET A MAN COME IN AND DO THE POPCORN PART ONE James Brown—King 6255
[James Brown] [BMI] (10/11/69 BCR-21)

PART TWO (LET A MAN COME IN AND DO THE POPCORN) James Brown—King 6275
[James Brown] [BMI] (12/20/69 BCR-40)

LET A WOMAN BE A WOMAN - LET A MAN BE A MAN
Dyke And The Blazers—Original Sound 89
[Arlester Christian] [BMI] (9/13/69 BCR-36)

LET 'EM IN Wings—Capitol 4293
[Linda McCartney/Paul McCartney] [ASC] (6/26/76 BCR-1)

LET GO Sharon Bryant—Wing 871 722 [Darryl Duncan] [ASC] (8/19/89 BC-34)

LET HER IN John Travolta—Midland Int'l 10623 [Gary Benson] [ASC] (5/1/76 BCR-5)

LET HER LOVE ME Otis Leavill—Blue Rock 4002
[William Earl Butler] [BMI] (1/30/65 CR-71)

LET HIM GO Animotion—Mercury 880737 [Bill Wadhams] [ASC] (6/1/85 BC-35)

LET IT ALL BLOW Dazz Band—Motown 1760
[Robert Lamont Harris/Keith Harrison] [BMI] (12/1/84 B-84)

LET IT BE *The Beatles—Apple 2764*
[John Lennon/Paul McCartney] [ASC] (3/14/70 BCR-1)

LET IT BE *Joan Baez—Vanguard 35145*
[John Lennon/Paul McCartney] [ASC] (11/13/71 BCR-37)

LET IT BE ME *Jill Corey—Columbia 40878*
[Gilbert Bécaud/Mann Curtis/Pierre Delanoë] [ASC] (4/20/57 BCR-54) [FET/FDE]

LET IT BE ME *The Everly Brothers—Cadence 1376*
[Gilbert Bécaud/Mann Curtis/Pierre Delanoë] [ASC] (1/11/60 BCR-7) [FET/FDE]

LET IT BE ME *Betty Everett & Jerry Butler—Vee-Jay 613*
[Gilbert Bécaud/Mann Curtis/Pierre Delanoë] [ASC] (9/5/64 BCR-3) [FET/FDE]

LET IT BE ME *The Sweet Inspirations—Atlantic 2418*
[Gilbert Bécaud/Mann Curtis/Pierre Delanoë] [ASC] (7/22/67 B-94) [FET/FDE]

LET IT BE ME *Glen Campbell And Bobbie Gentry—Capitol 2387*
[Gilbert Bécaud/Mann Curtis/Pierre Delanoë] [ASC] (1/25/69 BCR-36) [FET/FDE]

LET IT BE ME *Willie Nelson—Columbia 03073*
[Gilbert Bécaud/Mann Curtis/Pierre Delanoë] [ASC] (8/7/82 BC-40) [FET/FDE]

LET IT GO, LET IT FLOW Dave Mason—Columbia 10662
[Dave Mason] [BMI] (1/14/78 BCR-45)

LET IT OUT (LET IT ALL HANG OUT) The Hombres—Verve Forecast 5058
[B.B. Cunningham/John W. Hunter/Jerry Masters/Gary McEwen] [BMI] (9/9/67 BCR-6)

LET IT RAIN Eric Clapton—Polydor 15049
[Bonnie Bramlett/Delaney Bramlett*/Eric Clapton] [BMI] (9/16/72 BCR-48)

LET IT RIDE Bachman-Turner Overdrive—Mercury 73457
[Randy Bachman/C.F. Turner] [BMI] (2/23/74 BCR-14)

LET IT RING Doris Day—Columbia 40618
[Lyn Duddy/Joan Edwards] [ASC] (12/30/55 BR-51)

LET IT ROCK Chuck Berry—Chess 1747 [Chuck Berry] [BMI] (2/1/60 BCR-60)

LET IT ROLL (LET THE GOOD TIMES ROLL)
Earl Knight & George Kelley—ABC-Paramount 10023
[Paul Winley] [BMI] (6/20/59 C-87)

LET IT SHINE Olivia Newton-John—MCA 40495
[Linda Ann Hargrove] (TSW) [BMI] (12/6/75 BC-28)

LET IT SHINE Santana—Columbia 10336
[David Brown/Ray Gardner] [BMI] (5/22/76 B-77)

LET IT WHIP Dazz Band—Motown 1609
[Reggie Andrews/Leon Chancler] [BMI] (4/24/82 BC-5)

LET LOVE COME BETWEEN US James & Bobby Purify—Bell 685
[Joe Sobotka/John Wyker] [BMI] (9/9/67 BCR-21)

LET LOVE GO BY Jeanette (Baby) Washington—ABC-Paramount 10223
[Jeanette Washington] [BMI] (6/19/61 R-92)

LET LOVE RULE Lenny Kravitz—Virgin 99166 [Lenny Kravitz] [ASC] (1/27/90 BC-85)

LET ME Paul Revere And The Raiders Featuring Mark Lindsay—Columbia 44854
[Mark Lindsay] [BMI] (5/10/69 BCR-14)

LET ME BACK IN Tyrone Davis—Dakar 621
[Morris Dollison] [BMI] (9/26/70 BCR-53)

LET ME BE The Turtles—White Whale 224 [P.F. Sloan] [ASC] (10/30/65 BCR-25)

LET ME BE Korona—United Artists 1341 [Bruce Blackman] [ASC] (3/22/80 BCR-43)

LET ME BE GOOD TO YOU Carla Thomas—Stax 188
[Isaac Hayes/David Porter/Carl Wells] [BMI] (4/30/66 BCR-62)

LET ME BE GOOD TO YOU Lou Rawls—Philadelphia Int'l 3684
[Kenneth Gamble/Leon Huff] [BMI] (6/16/79 CR-80)

LET ME BE LONELY Dionne Warwick—Scepter 12216
[Burt Bacharach/Hal David] [ASC] (6/8/68 BCR-71)

LET ME BE LOVED *Mantovani And His Orchestra—London 1761*
[Ray Evans/Jay Livingston] [ASC] (10/7/57 Rt-58) [IWM]

LET ME BE LOVED *Eydie Gorme—ABC-Paramount 9863*
[Ray Evans/Jay Livingston] [ASC] (10/28/57 Rt-58)

LET ME BE THE CLOCK Smokey Robinson—Tamla 54311
[Smokey Robinson] [ASC] (3/15/80 BCR-31)

LET ME BE THE MAN MY DADDY WAS The Chi-Lites—Brunswick 55414
[Barbara Acklin/Eugene Record] [BMI] (8/2/69 B-94)

LET ME BE THE ONE *The Paris Sisters—Gregmark 12*
[Larry Kolber/Barry Mann] [BMI] (5/12/62 BC-87)

LET ME BE THE ONE *Peaches & Herb—Date 1649*
[Larry Kolber/Barry Mann] [BMI] (8/9/69 BCR-74)

LET ME BE THE ONE Al Wilson—Rocky Road 30202
[Roger Nichols/Paul Williams] (Med) [ASC] (1/11/75 BCR-61)

LET ME BE THE ONE Five Star—RCA 14229 [Ian Foster] [ASC] (2/8/86 BC-59)

LET ME BE THE ONE Exposé—Arista 1-9617 [Lewis Martinée] [ASC] (8/15/87 BC-7)

LET ME BE THERE Olivia Newton-John—MCA 40101
[John Rostill] [BMI] (10/27/73 BCR-4)

LET ME BE YOUR ANGEL Stacy Lattisaw—Cotillion 46001
[Bunny Hull/Narada Michael Walden] [BMI] (8/9/80 BCR-21)

LET ME BE YOUR LOVEMAKER Betty Wright—Alston 4619
[Willie Clarke/Clarence Reid/Betty Wright] [BMI] (10/6/73 BCR-55)

LET ME BE YOUR LOVER U-Krew—Enigma 75069 [Larry Bell] [BMI] (6/9/90 BC-64)

(LET ME BE YOUR) TEDDY BEAR *Elvis Presley—RCA Victor 47-7000*
[Bernie Lowe/Kal Mann] [ASC] (6/24/57 BCR-1)

(LET ME BE YOUR) TEDDY BEAR *Elvis Presley—RCA 13351*
[Bernie Lowe/Kal Mann] (Med) [ASC] (11/20/82 BC-71)

LET ME BELONG TO YOU Brian Hyland—ABC-Paramount 10236
[Gary Geld/Peter Udell] [ASC] (8/7/61 BCR-20)

LET ME CALL YOU SWEETHEART *Bruce Hayes with Mary Mayo—Dwain 812*
[Leo Friedman/Beth Slater Whitson] (EP) [ASC] (2/15/60 R-63)

LET ME CALL YOU SWEETHEART *Timi Yuro—Liberty 55410*
[Leo Friedman/Beth Slater Whitson] [ASC] (2/3/62 BCR-66)

LET ME CRY ON YOUR SHOULDER Georgia Gibbs—Bell 615
[Joe Sherman/George David Weiss] [ASC] (5/22/65 CR-80)

LET ME DOWN EASY Betty LaVette—Calla 102
[Wrecia Holloway/James McDougal] [BMI] (5/8/65 CR-90)

LET ME DOWN EASY Cornelius Brothers & Sister Rose—United Artists 208
[Eddie Cornelius] [BMI] (4/7/73 BCR-72)

LET ME DOWN EASY American Flyer—United Artists 874
[Craig Fuller/Eric Kaz] [BMI] (10/30/76 B-80)

LET ME DOWN EASY Roger Daltrey—Atlantic 89471
[Bryan Adams/Jim Vallance] [BMI] (12/28/85 B-86)

LET ME ENTERTAIN YOU Ray Anthony—Capitol 4876
[Jule Styne] [ASC] (11/24/62 BR-84) [IM]

LET ME GET TO KNOW YOU Paul Anka—Fame 345 [Paul Anka] [BMI] (12/15/73 BCR-54)

LET ME GO The Rings—MCA 51069 [Mike Baker] [ASC] (2/21/81 BC-75)

LET ME GO Ray Parker Jr.—Arista 0695 [Ray Parker Jr.] [ASC] (7/17/82 BC-38)

LET ME GO Heaven 17—Arista/Virgin 1050
[Glenn Gregory/Ian Craig Marsh/Martyn Ware] [ASC] (3/12/83 B-74)

LET ME GO, LOVE Nicolette Larson—Warner Bros. 49130
[B.J. Cook Foster/Michael McDonald] [ASC] (12/29/79 BCR-35)

LET ME GO LOVER *Joan Weber—Columbia 40366*
[Jenny Lou Carson/Kay Twomey/Ben Weisman/Fred Wise] [BMI] (11/22/54 BCtRt-1)

LET ME GO LOVER *Patti Page—Mercury 70511*
[Jenny Lou Carson/Kay Twomey/Ben Weisman/Fred Wise] [BMI] (11/29/54 BRt-1)

LET ME GO LOVER *Teresa Brewer with The Lancers—Coral 61315*
[Jenny Lou Carson/Kay Twomey/Ben Weisman/Fred Wise] [BMI] (12/6/54 BCtRt-1)

LET ME GO, LOVER! *Sunny Gale—RCA Victor 47-5952*
[Jenny Lou Carson/Kay Twomey/Ben Weisman/Fred Wise] [BMI] (12/6/54 Rt-PRE)

LET ME GO, LOVER! *Peggy Lee—Decca 29373*
[Jenny Lou Carson/Kay Twomey/Ben Weisman/Fred Wise] [BMI] (1/3/55 Rt-1)

LET ME GO THE RIGHT WAY The Supremes—Motown 1034
[Berry Gordy] [ASC] (12/1/62 BCR-82)

LET ME GO TO HIM Dionne Warwick—Scepter 12276
[Burt Bacharach/Hal David] [ASC] (4/18/70 BCR-25)

LET ME IN The Sensations—Argo 5405
[Yvonne Baker/Alphonso Howell/George Minor] [BMI] (1/6/62 BCR-3)

LET ME IN The Osmonds—MGM 14617
[Alan Osmond/Merrill Osmond/Wayne Osmond] [BMI] (9/8/73 BCR-19)

LET ME IN Derringer—Blue Sky 2765
[Rick Derringer/Cynthia Weil] [BMI] (8/28/76 B-86)

LET ME IN Eddie Money—Columbia 68739
[Paul Gordon/Dennis Matkosky] [ASC] (4/15/89 BC-60)

LET ME KNOW (I HAVE A RIGHT) Gloria Gaynor—Polydor 2021
[Dino Fekaris/Freddie Perren] [ASC] (9/22/79 BCR-42)

LET ME LOVE YOU B.B. King—Kent 396 [B.B. King/Sam Ling‡] [BMI] (8/15/64 CR-91)

LET ME LOVE YOU Ray Charles—ABC/TRC 11213
[Jimmy Holiday] [ASC] (5/17/69 BCR-87)

LET ME LOVE YOU GOODBYE Bobby Vinton—Tapestry 006
[Stephen Allen Davis/Billy Sherrill] [BMI] (4/4/81 C-96)

LET ME LOVE YOU ONCE Greg Lake—Chrysalis 2571
[Steve Dorff/Molly Ann Leikin] [BMI] (11/21/81 BCR-38)

LET ME LOVE YOU TONIGHT Pure Prairie League—Casablanca 2266
[George Daniel Greer/Jeff Wilson/Steve Woodard] [BMI] (5/10/80 BCR-8)

LET ME MAKE LOVE TO YOU The O'Jays—Philadelphia Int'l 3573
[Allan Felder/Bunny Sigler] [BMI] (7/26/75 BCR-56)

LET ME PARTY WITH YOU (PART 1) (PARTY, PARTY, PARTY)
Bunny Sigler—Gold Mind 4008
[Raymond Earl/Kim Miller/Scottie Miller/Bunny Sigler] [BMI] (2/25/78 BCR-43)

LET ME SERENADE YOU Three Dog Night—Dunhill 4370
[John Finley] [BMI] (10/27/73 BCR-12)

LET ME SING AND I'M HAPPY Jerry Lewis—Decca 30263
[Irving Berlin] [ASC] (3/30/57 R-77)

LET ME SLEEP ALONE Cugini—Scotti Brothers 503
[Don Cugini/Andrew DiTaranto/Anthony Papa] [BMI] (12/22/79 B-88)

LET ME START TONITE Lamont Dozier—ABC 12044
[Lamont Dozier] [BMI] (1/4/75 BC-72)

LET ME STAY WITH YOU TONIGHT Point Blank—MCA 51083
[Rusty Burns/Kim Davis/Peter Gruen/Mike Hamilton/Bubba Keith/Bill Randolph] [BMI] (4/18/81 C-94)

LET ME TALK Earth, Wind & Fire—ARC 11366
[Philip Bailey/Lorenzo Dunn/Ralph Johnson/Albert Philip McKay/Maurice White/Verdine White] [ASC] (9/20/80 BCR-42)

LET ME TELL YOU, BABE Nat King Cole—Capitol 5683
[Joe Sherman/George David Weiss] [ASC] (8/6/66 BCR-90)

LET ME TICKLE YOUR FANCY Jermaine Jackson—Motown 1628
[Jermaine Jackson/Paul M. Jackson Jr./Marilyn McLeod/Pam Sawyer] [BMI] (7/24/82 BC-18)

LET ME TRY AGAIN (LAISSE MOI LE TEMPS) Frank Sinatra—Reprise 1181
[Paul Anka/Sammy Cahn/Romuald Figuier/Michel Jourdan/Claude Vasori] [BMI] (11/10/73 BCR-61) [FET]

LET MY LOVE OPEN THE DOOR Pete Townshend—Atco 7217
[Pete Townshend] [GL] (6/14/80 BCR-9)

LET THE BEAT HIT 'EM Lisa Lisa & Cult Jam—Columbia 73847
[Robert Clivillés/David Cole/Alan Friedman/Duran Ramos] [ASC] (6/22/91 BC-37)

LET THE BELLS KEEP RINGING Paul Anka—ABC-Paramount 9907
[Paul Anka] [BMI] (4/7/58 BCR-15)

LET THE DAY BEGIN The Call—MCA 53658 [Michael Been] [ASC] (7/22/89 BC-51)

LET THE FEELING FLOW Peabo Bryson—Capitol 5065
[Peabo Bryson] [ASC] (12/5/81 BCR-39)

LET THE FOUR WINDS BLOW *Roy Brown—Imperial 5439*
[Dave Bartholomew/Fats Domino] [BMI] (7/1/57 BCR-38)

LET THE FOUR WINDS BLOW *Fats Domino—Imperial 5764*
[Dave Bartholomew/Fats Domino] [BMI] (7/10/61 BCR-15)

LET THE GOOD TIMES ROLL *Shirley And Lee—Aladdin 3325*
[Shirley Goodman/Leonard Lee] [BMI] (8/11/56 BCR-16)*

LET THE GOOD TIMES ROLL *Shirley & Lee—Warwick 581*
[Shirley Goodman/Leonard Lee] [BMI] (9/5/60 BCR-48)*

LET THE GOOD TIMES ROLL *Roy Orbison—Monument 906*
[Shirley Goodman/Leonard Lee] [BMI] (11/13/65 BCR-81)*

LET THE GOOD TIMES ROLL *Bunny Sigler—Parkway 153*
[Shirley Goodman/Leonard Lee] (Med) [BMI] (6/17/67 BCR-19)*

LET THE GOOD TIMES ROLL Ray Charles—Atlantic 2047
[Fleecie Moore/Sam Theard] [ASC] (1/11/60 BC-78)

LET THE HEARTACHES BEGIN Long John Baldry—Warner Bros. 7098
[Tony Macaulay/John Macleod] [ASC] (1/13/68 BCR-84)

LET THE LITTLE GIRL DANCE Billy Bland—Old Town 1076
[Henry Glover/Carl Spencer] [BMI] (2/15/60 BCR-7)

LET THE MUSIC PLAY Barry White—20th Century 2265
[Barry White] [BMI] (12/20/75 BCR-31)

LET THE MUSIC PLAY Shannon—Mirage/Emergency 99810
[Chris Barbosa/Ed Chisolm] [ASC] (11/12/83 BC-8)

LET THE MUSIC TAKE YOUR MIND Kool & The Gang—De-Lite 529
[Robert Bell/Ronald Bell/George M. Brown/Robert Mickens/Gene Redd Jr./Claydes Smith/Woodrow Sparrow/Dennis Thomas/Richard Westfield] [BMI] (6/13/70 BCR-78)

LET THE RIVER RUN Carly Simon—Arista 1-9793 [Carly Simon] [ASC] (3/4/89 BC-49)

LET THE SONG LAST FOREVER Dan Hill—20th Century 2392
[Dan Hill/Barry Mann] [ASC] (11/25/78 B-91)

LET THE SUNSHINE IN (THE FLESH FAILURES) The 5th Dimension—Soul City 772
[Galt MacDermot/James Rado/Gerome Ragni] (Med) [ASC] (3/8/69 BCR-1)

—LET THE WIND PAY THE WAY see: EASY RIDER

LET THEM LOVE (AND BE LOVED) The Dreamlovers—Heritage 104
[Donald Hogan] [BMI] (10/23/61 R-83)

LET THEM TALK Little Willie John—King 5274 [Sonny Thompson] [BMI] (12/19/59 BC-96)

LET THERE BE DRUMS *Sandy Nelson—Imperial 5775*
[Sandy Nelson/Richard Podolor] [BMI] (10/30/61 BCR-7) [I]

LET THERE BE DRUMS *The Incredible Bongo Band—MGM 14635*
[Sandy Nelson/Richard Podolor] [BMI] (11/10/73 C-93) [I]

LET THERE BE MUSIC Orleans—Asylum 45243
[Johanna Hall/Larry Hoppen] [BMI] (4/19/75 BCR-49)

LET THERE BE YOU The Five Keys—Capitol 3660
[Dave Cavanaugh/Vicki Young] [BMI] (3/30/57 BR-69)

LET THIS BE A LESSON TO YOU The Independents—Wand 11279
[Charles Henry Jackson Jr./Marvin Yancy] [ASC] (10/5/74 BCR-63)

LET THIS BE A LETTER (TO MY BABY) Jackie Wilson—Brunswick 55435
[Eugene Record] [BMI] (5/2/70 BCR-78)

LET TRUE LOVE BEGIN Nat King Cole—Capitol 4623
[Mark Barkan/Sandy Baron/George Eddy] [BMI] (9/18/61 BR-69)

LET US LOVE Bill Withers—Sussex 247 [Bill Withers] [BMI] (12/2/72 BCR-39)

LET YOUR HAIR DOWN The Temptations—Gordy 7133
[Norman Whitfield] [BMI] (12/15/73 BCR-25)

LET YOUR LOVE FLOW Bellamy Brothers—Warner/Curb 8169
[Larry Williams] [BMI] (1/31/76 BCR-1)

LET YOUR LOVE GO Bread—Elektra 45711 [David Gates] [ASC] (12/26/70 BCR-18)

LET YOUR YEAH BE YEAH Brownsville Station—Big Tree 161
[Jimmy Cliff] [BMI] (2/24/73 BCR-57)

LET YOURSELF GO James Brown And The Famous Flames—King 6100
[James Brown/Bud Hobgood*] [BMI] (5/6/67 BCR-39)

LET YOURSELF GO Elvis Presley With The Jordanaires—RCA Victor 47-9547
[Joy Byers Johnston] [ASC] (6/15/68 BCR-51)

LET YOURSELF GO The Friends Of Distinction—RCA Victor 74-0204
[Willie Hutch] [BMI] (7/26/69 BCR-58)

LET'S ALL CHANT Michael Zager Band—Private Stock 45,184
[Alvin Fields/Michael Zager] [BMI] (2/25/78 BCR-25) [I]

LET'S ALL ROCK TOGETHER The Jodimars—Capitol 3285
[Marshall Lytle/Frank Pingatore] [BMI] (1/6/56 R-72)

LET'S BE LOVERS The Playmates—Roulette 4056
[Ben Raleigh/Don Wolf] [BMI] (3/24/58 BCR-45)

LET'S BE LOVERS AGAIN Eddie Money with Valerie Carter—Columbia 11377
[Jimmy Lyon/Eddie Money] [BMI] (10/18/80 BCR-65)

LET'S BE YOUNG TONIGHT Jermaine Jackson—Motown 1401
[Don Daniels/Michael Larry Smith] [BMI] (9/18/76 BCR-55)

LET'S CALL IT A DAY GIRL *The Razor's Edge—Pow! 101*
[Irwin Levine/Neil Sheppard] [BMI] (7/16/66 BCR-58)

LET'S CALL IT A DAY GIRL *Bobby Vee—Liberty 56124*
[Irwin Levine/Neil Sheppard] [BMI] (7/26/69 BC-92)

LET'S CHILL Guy—MCA 54051
[Bernard Belle/Teddy Riley/Keith Sweat] [ASC] (2/23/91 B-41)

LET'S CLEAN UP THE GHETTO Philadelphia International All Stars—Philadelphia Int'l 3627
[Kenneth Gamble/Cary Gilbert/Leon Huff] [BMI] (8/6/77 BCR-82)

LET'S DANCE *Chris Montez—Monogram 505 [James Lee] [BMI] (8/4/62 BCR-4)*

LET'S DANCE *Ola & The Janglers—GNP Crescendo 423*
[James Lee] [BMI] (5/24/69 BCR-91)

LET'S DANCE *Jive Bunny & The Mastermixers—Music Factory/Atco 99122*
[James Lee] (Med) [BMI] (2/3/90 BC-67)

LET'S DANCE David Bowie—EMI America 8158 [David Bowie] [ASC] (3/26/83 BC-1)

LET'S DANCE Chris Rea—Motown 1900 [Chris Rea] [ASC] (8/29/87 BC-81)

LET'S DANCE (MAKE YOUR BODY MOVE) West Street Mob—Sugar Hill 559
[Dan Brewster/Bruce Carter/Sherman Davis/Wayne Henderson/Donald Hepburn/
Augie Johnson/Marlon McClain/Jerry Peters/Nathaniel Phillips/Bruce A. Smith/
Dennis Springer] [BMI] (9/12/81 BCR-84)

LET'S DO IT AGAIN The Staple Singers—Curtom 0109
[Curtis Mayfield] [BMI] (10/18/75 BCR-1)

LET'S DO SOMETHING CHEAP AND SUPERFICIAL Burt Reynolds—MCA 51004
[Richard Levinson] [BMI] (10/18/80 BC-87)

LET'S DO THE FREDDIE Chubby Checker—Parkway 949
[Dave Appell/Doc Pomus] [ASC] (4/3/65 BCR-40)

(LET'S DO) THE HULLY GULLY TWIST Bill Doggett—Warner Bros. 5181
[Billy Butler/Bill Doggett] [BMI] (12/26/60 BC-66) [I]

LET'S FALL IN LOVE *Linda Scott—Congress 200*
[Harold Arlen/Ted Koehler] [ASC] (10/5/63 R-97)

LET'S FALL IN LOVE *Peaches & Herb—Date 1523*
[Harold Arlen/Ted Koehler] [ASC] (12/31/66 BCR-21)

LET'S FOOL AROUND General Johnson—Arista 0264
[General Johnson] [BMI] (12/24/77 R-73)

LET'S GET CRAZY TONIGHT Rupert Holmes—Private Stock 45,199
[Rupert Holmes] [ASC] (8/26/78 BCR-64)

LET'S GET IT ON Marvin Gaye—Tamla 54234
[Marvin Gaye*/Ed Townsend] [ASC] (7/7/73 BCR-1)

LETS GET IT TOGETHER El Coco—AVI 115 [Merria Ross] [BMI] (10/23/76 B-61) [I]

LET'S GET IT UP AC/DC—Atlantic 3894
[Brian Johnson/Angus Young/Malcolm Young] [ASC] (1/16/82 BCR-44)

LET'S GET MARRIED Al Green—Hi 2262 [Al Green] [BMI] (3/16/74 BCR-21)

LET'S GET SERIOUS Jermaine Jackson—Motown 1469
[Lee Garrett/Stevie Wonder] [BMI] (3/22/80 BCR-9)

LET'S GET TOGETHER Hayley Mills And Hayley Mills—Buena Vista 385
[Richard Sherman/Robert Sherman] [BMI] (9/4/61 BCR-5)

LET'S GIVE ADAM AND EVE ANOTHER CHANCE
Gary Puckett And The Union Gap—Columbia 45097
[Richard Mainegra/Red West] [BMI] (2/28/70 BCR-33)

LET'S GO Floyd Cramer—RCA Victor 47-7978 [Grady Martin] [BMI] (2/3/62 B-90) [I]

LET'S GO The Cars—Elektra 46063 [Ric Ocasek] [ASC] (6/30/79 BCR-12)

LET'S GO Wang Chung—Geffen 28531 [Nick Feldman/Jack Hues] [BMI] (1/24/87 BC-9)

LET'S GO AGAIN (WHERE WE WENT LAST NIGHT)
Hank Ballard And The Midnighters—King 5459
[Hank Ballard/Billy Myles] [BMI] (2/20/61 BCR-39)

(LET'S GO) ALL THE WAY The Whispers—Solar 11246
[Reggie Burke/Brian Holland/Eddie Holland/Art Posey/Josef Powell/Melvin Ragin] [ASC]
(5/27/78 R-81)

LET'S GO ALL THE WAY Sly Fox—Capitol 5552 [Gary Lee Cooper] [BMI] (12/28/85 BC-7)

LET'S GO CALYPSO Rusty Draper—Mercury 71039
[John Gluck/Diane Lampert] [BMI] (2/23/57 BR-53)

LET'S GO CRAZY Prince and the Revolution—Warner Bros. 29216
[Prince] [ASC] (8/4/84 BC-1)

LET'S GO DANCIN' (OOH LA, LA, LA) Kool & The Gang—De-Lite 824
[Clifford Adams/Amir Bayyan/Robert Bell/Ronald Bell/George M. Brown/
Eumir Deodato/Robert Mickens/Michael Ray/Claydes Smith/J.T. Taylor/
Curtis Fitzgerald Williams] [BMI] (10/30/82 BC-29)

LET'S GO DOWN TO THE DISCO The Undisputed Truth—Whitfield 8306
[Norman Whitfield] (TSW) [BMI] (2/19/77 B-48)

LET'S GO GET STONED Ray Charles Band With The Raelets—ABC-Paramount 10808
[Jo Armstead/Nick Ashford/Valerie Simpson] [BMI] (5/28/66 BCR-23)

LET'S GO LET'S GO LET'S GO Hank Ballard And The Midnighters—King 5400
[Hank Ballard] [BMI] (9/19/60 BCR-6)

LET'S GO OUT TONIGHT Nile Rodgers—Warner Bros. 29049
[Nile Rodgers] [ASC] (6/1/85 B-88)

LET'S GO (PONY) The Routers—Warner Bros. 5283
[Lanny Duncan/Robert Duncan] [BMI] (10/20/62 BCR-19) [I]

LET'S GO ROCK AND ROLL K.C. & The Sunshine Band—TK 1036
[Harry Wayne Casey/Rick Finch] [BMI] (2/16/80 R-89)

LET'S GO 'ROUND AGAIN Average White Band—Atlantic 3354
[Alan Gorrie] [ASC] (6/14/80 BCR-53)

LET'S GO STEADY AGAIN Neil Sedaka—RCA Victor 47-8169
[Howard Greenfield/Neil Sedaka] [BMI] (4/27/63 BCR-25)

LET'S GO STEADY AGAIN Sam Cooke—RCA Victor 47-8803
[James W. Alexander] [BMI] (4/30/66 B-97)

LET'S GO STEADY FOR THE SUMMER Three G's—Columbia 41175
[Dick Glasser] [BMI] (8/4/58 B-55)

LET'S GO TO SAN FRANCISCO Stars On 45—Radio 3863
[John Carter/Ken Hawker] (Med) [BMI] (9/19/81 BCR-55)

LET'S GO TRIPPIN' Dick Dale And The Del-Tones—Deltone 5017
[Dick Dale] [ASC] (11/27/61 BCR-60) [I]

LET'S GO UP Diana Ross—RCA 13671 [Franne Golde/Peter Ivers] [BMI] (12/17/83 B-77)

LET'S GROOVE Archie Bell & The Drells—TSOP 4775
[Victor Carstarphen/Leon Huff/Gene McFadden/John Whitehead] [BMI] (3/6/76 CR-77)

LET'S GROOVE Earth, Wind & Fire—ARC Columbia 18-02536
[Wayne Vaughn/Maurice White] [ASC] (10/3/81 BCR-3)

LET'S HANG ON!
The 4 Seasons Featuring The "Sound" Of Frankie Valli—Philips 40317
[Bob Crewe/Sandy Linzer/Denny Randell] [BMI] (10/2/65 BCR-1)

LET'S HANG ON *Gidea Park—Profile 5003*
[Bob Crewe/Sandy Linzer/Denny Randell] (Med) [BMI] (12/26/81 BC-82)

LET'S HANG ON *Barry Manilow—Arista 0675*
[Bob Crewe/Sandy Linzer/Denny Randell] [BMI] (3/20/82 BCR-32)

LET'S HAVE A PARTY *Wanda Jackson—Capitol 4397*
[Jessie Mae Robinson] [ASC] (8/8/60 BCR-30)

LET'S HAVE A PARTY *The Rivieras (2)—Riviera 1402*
[Jessie Mae Robinson] [ASC] (5/30/64 BR-99)

LET'S HAVE SOME FUN Bar-Kays—Mercury 73971
[James Edward Alexander/Charles Leonard Allen/Michael Beard/Larry Dodson/
Harvey Henderson/Allen Alvoid Jones Jr./Lloyd Ed Smith/Winston Stewart/
Frank Thompson] [BMI] (2/18/78 C-91)

LET'S HEAR IT FOR THE BOY Deniece Williams—Columbia 04417
[Dean Pitchford/Tom Snow] [BMI] (4/7/84 BC-1)

LET'S KISS AND MAKE UP Bobby Vinton—Epic 9561
[Van McCoy/Jerry Ragovoy] [BMI] (11/24/62 BCR-32)

LET'S LIGHT THE CHRISTMAS TREE *Ruby Wright—Fraternity 787*
[Ruth Lyons] [BMI] (12/2/57 BRt-54)

LET'S LIGHT THE CHRISTMAS TREE *The Lennon Sisters—Brunswick 55044*
[Ruth Lyons] [BMI] (12/9/57 Rt-77)

LET'S LIMBO SOME MORE Chubby Checker—Parkway 862
[Dave Appell/Kal Mann] [ASC] (2/16/63 BCR-15)

LET'S LIVE FOR TODAY The Grass Roots—Dunhill 4084
[Michael Julien/Giulio Rapetti/David Shapiro] [BMI] (5/13/67 BCR-5) [FDE]

LET'S LIVE TOGETHER *The Road Apples—Polydor 14285*
[David Finnerty] [ASC] (9/27/75 BCR-35)

LET'S LIVE TOGETHER *Cazz—Number 1 Record 210*
[David Finnerty] [ASC] (2/18/78 BC-70)

LET'S LOCK THE DOOR (AND THROW AWAY THE KEY)
Jay & The Americans—United Artists 805
[Roy Alfred/Wes Farrell] [ASC] (12/26/64 BCR-10)

LET'S LOVE Johnny Mathis—Columbia 41304
[Richard Ferraris/Norman Kaye] [ASC] (12/27/58 BCR-40)

LET'S LOVEDANCE TONIGHT Gary's Gang—Columbia 10970
[Eric Matthew/Gary Turnier] [ASC] (5/5/79 R-93)

LET'S MAKE A BABY Billy Paul—Philadelphia Int'l 3584
[Kenneth Gamble/Leon Huff] [BMI] (3/20/76 BCR-79)

LET'S MAKE A PROMISE Peaches & Herb—Date 1623
[Thom Bell/Mikki Farrow/Kenneth Gamble] [BMI] (10/26/68 BCR-53)

LET'S MAKE EACH OTHER HAPPY The Illusion—Steed 726
[Chuck Alder/Richie Cerniglia] [BMI] (6/27/70 BR-97)

—LET'S MAKE LOTS OF MONEY see: OPPORTUNITIES

LET'S MAKE LOVE TONIGHT Bobby Rydell—Cameo 272
[William E. Jackson III/Roy Straigis/George R. Williams] [BMI] (9/28/63 BC-92)

LET'S MOVE & GROOVE (TOGETHER) Johnny Nash—JoDa 102
[Margaret Nash] [BMI] (9/11/65 BCR-59)

LET'S PRETEND Raspberries—Capitol 3546 [Eric Carmen] [BMI] (3/17/73 BCR-14)

LET'S PRETEND WE'RE MARRIED Prince—Warner Bros. 29548
[Prince] [ASC] (12/17/83 BC-46)

LET'S PUT IT ALL TOGETHER *The Stylistics—Avco 4640*
[Luigi Creatore/Hugo Peretti/George David Weiss] [ASC] (7/20/74 BCR-14)

LET'S PUT IT ALL TOGETHER *Band Of Gold—RCA 13866*
[Luigi Creatore/Hugo Peretti/George David Weiss] (Med) [ASC] (10/13/84 BC-64)

LET'S PUT THE FUN BACK IN ROCK N ROLL
Freddy Cannon & The Belmonts—MiaSound 1002
[Bob Feldman/Joseph Nicoletti] [BMI] (9/26/81 BCR-77)

LET'S PUT THE X IN SEX KISS—Mercury 872246
[Desmond Child/Paul Stanley] [ASC] (1/14/89 BC-93)

LET'S ROCK Ellison Chase—Big Tree 16072
[Gary Askenas/Ellison Chase] [BMI] (8/28/76 BC-82)

LET'S SPEND THE NIGHT TOGETHER *The Rolling Stones—London 904*
[Mick Jagger/Keith Richards] [BMI] (1/21/67 BCR-28)

LET'S SPEND THE NIGHT TOGETHER *David Bowie—RCA Victor 0028*
[Mick Jagger/Keith Richards] [BMI] (8/4/73 CR-90)

LET'S START ALL OVER AGAIN Ronnie Dove—Diamond 198
[Joel Hirschhorn/Al Kasha] [ASC] (4/9/66 BCR-10)

LET'S START THE DANCE Hamilton Bohannon—Mercury 74105
[Hamilton Bohannon] [ASC] (9/2/78 R-72)

LET'S STAY TOGETHER *Al Green—Hi 2202*
[Al Green/Al Jackson/Willie Mitchell] [BMI] (11/27/71 BCR-1)

LET'S STAY TOGETHER *Isaac Hayes—Enterprise 9045*
[Al Green/Al Jackson/Willie Mitchell] [BMI] (3/18/72 BCR-45) [IWM]

LET'S STAY TOGETHER *Tina Turner—Capitol 5322*
[Al Green/Al Jackson/Willie Mitchell] [BMI] (1/21/84 BC-24)

LET'S STOMP Bobby Comstock—Lawn 202
[Bob Feldman/Jerry Goldstein/Richard Gottehrer] [BMI] (2/2/63 BCR-57)

LET'S STRAIGHTEN IT OUT Latimore—Glades 1722
[Benny Latimore] [BMI] (9/21/74 BCR-31)

LET'S TALK ABOUT ME Alan Parsons Project—Arista 1-9282
[Alan Parsons/Eric Woolfson] [BMI] (2/16/85 BC-47)

LET'S TALK ABOUT SEX Salt-N-Pepa—Next Plateau 333
[Hurby Azor] [ASC] (8/24/91 BC-13)

LET'S TALK ABOUT US Jerry Lee Lewis—Sun 324 [Otis Blackwell] [BMI] (8/1/59 C-83)

LET'S THINK ABOUT LIVING Bob Luman—Warner Bros. 5172
[Boudleaux Bryant] [BMI] (8/29/60 BCR-4)

LET'S TRY AGAIN Al Hibbler—Decca 29789 [Ruth Bishop] [NA] (3/9/56 R-61)

LET'S TRY AGAIN Clyde McPhatter—MGM 12843
[Billy Dawn Smith] [BMI] (11/9/59 BCR-48)

LET'S TRY IT AGAIN New Kids On The Block—Columbia 73443
[Maurice Starr] [ASC] (10/6/90 BC-53)

LET'S TURKEY TROT Little Eva—Dimension 1006
[Herbert Cox*/Gerry Goffin/Jack Keller/Morris Levy‡] [BMI] (1/26/63 BCR-20)

LET'S TWIST AGAIN *Chubby Checker—Parkway 824*
[Dave Appell/Kal Mann] [ASC] (6/19/61 BCR-3)

LET'S TWIST AGAIN *Jive Bunny And The Mastermixers—Music Factory 99140*
[Dave Appell/Kal Mann] (Med) [ASC] (10/28/89 BC-11)

LETS TWIST AGAIN *Jive Bunny & The Mastermixers—Music Factory/Atco 99122*
[Dave Appell/Kal Mann] (Med) [ASC] (2/3/90 BC-67)

LET'S WAIT AWHILE Janet Jackson—A&M 2906
[Melanie Andrews/James Samuel Harris/Janet Jackson/Terry Lewis] [BMI] (1/17/87 BC-2)

LET'S WALK AND TALK The Ames Brothers—RCA Victor 47-5764
[Joe Thomas] [BMI] (7/10/54 C-48)

LET'S WORK Mick Jagger—Columbia 07306
[Mick Jagger/David A. Stewart] [ASC] (9/12/87 BC-37)

LET'S WORK TOGETHER (PART 1) *Wilbert Harrison—Sue 11*
[Wilbert Harrison] [BMI] (12/6/69 BCR-29)

LET'S WORK TOGETHER *Canned Heat—Liberty 56151*
[Wilbert Harrison] [BMI] (9/26/70 BCR-17)

THE LETTER Sonny & Cher—Vault 916 [Don Harris/Dewey Terry] [BMI] (10/23/65 BR-75)

THE LETTER *The Box Tops—Mala 565 [Wayne Carson Thompson] [BMI] (8/12/67 BCR-1)*

THE LETTER *The Arbors—Date 1638 [Wayne Carson Thompson] [BMI] (2/15/69 BCR-20)*

THE LETTER *Joe Cocker With Leon Russell And The Shelter People—A&M 1174*
[Wayne Carson Thompson] [BMI] (4/18/70 BCR-5)

A LETTER FROM BETTY Bobby Vee—Liberty 55581
[Bob Feldman/Jerry Goldstein/Richard Gottehrer] [BMI] (6/29/63 BC-85)

LETTER FROM SHERRY Dale Ward—Dot 16520
[Noel Ball/Ken Moffitt] [BMI] (12/7/63 BCR-25)

LETTER FULL OF TEARS Gladys Knight & The Pips—Fury 1054
[Don Covay] [BMI] (12/11/61 BCR-17)

LETTER TO AN ANGEL Jimmy Clanton—Ace 551
[Jimmy Clanton/Cosimo Matassa] [BMI] (10/18/58 BCR-25)

A LETTER TO DAD Every Father's Teenage Son—Buddah 25
[Bill Dean/Ron Marshall] [BMI] (11/25/67 B-93)

LETTER TO LUCILLE Tom Jones—Parrot 40074 [Tony Macaulay] [ASC] (5/5/73 BCR-34)

A LETTER TO MYSELF The Chi-Lites—Brunswick 55491
[Sandra Drayton/Eugene Record] [BMI] (2/3/73 BCR-33)

A LETTER TO THE BEATLES The Four Preps—Capitol 5143
[Bruce Belland/Glen Larson/Ivan Ulz] [BMI] (3/21/64 BCR-76)

LETTING GO Wings—Capitol 4145
[Linda McCartney/Paul McCartney] [ASC] (10/4/75 BCR-39)

LEVON Elton John—Uni 55314 [Elton John/Bernie Taupin] [BMI] (12/11/71 BCR-17)

—L'HOMME ET L'ENFANT see: LITTLE CHILD

LIAR The Regents—Gee 1073 [Sal Cuomo] [BMI] (10/30/61 R-92)

LIAR Three Dog Night—Dunhill 4282 [Russ Ballard] [BMI] (7/3/71 BCR-6)

LIAR, LIAR The Castaways—Soma 1433
[Dennis Craswell*/James Donna] [BMI] (7/10/65 BCR-8)

LICENCE TO CHILL Billy Ocean—Jive 1283
[Mutt Lange/Billy Ocean] [ASC] (10/7/89 BC-32)

LICK IT UP KISS—Mercury 814671 [Paul Stanley/Vinnie Vincent] [ASC] (11/12/83 B-66)

LICKING STICK-LICKING STICK (PART 1)
James Brown And The Famous Flames—King 6166
[James Brown/Bobby Byrd/Alfred James Ellis] [BMI] (5/18/68 BCR-12)

LICORICE STICK Pete Fountain—Coral 62413
[Owen Bradley/Charles "Bud" Dant/Pete Fountain] [BMI] (6/20/64 C-94) [I]

LIDO SHUFFLE Boz Scaggs—Columbia 10491
[David Paich/Boz Scaggs] [ASC] (3/12/77 BCR-6)

LIE TO ME Brook Benton—Mercury 72024
[Brook Benton/Margie Singleton] [BMI] (8/18/62 BCR-10)

LIECHTENSTEINER POLKA *Will Glahe And His Orchestra And Chorus—London 1755*
[Edmund Koetscher/Rudi Lindt] [ASC] (10/14/57 BCRt-10) [F]

LIECHTENSTEINER POLKA *Lawrence Welk And His Champagne Music—Coral 61900*
[Edmund Koetscher/Rudi Lindt] [ASC] (10/28/57 BRt-10) [F]

LIECHTENSTEINER POLKA *Horst Wende & His Polka Boys—Decca 30506*
[Rudi Lindt] [ASC] (11/18/57 Rt-10) [IWM]

LIES Teddy Randazzo—ABC-Paramount 10043
[Billy Barberis/Teddy Randazzo] [ASC] (10/3/59 C-94)

LIES The Knickerbockers—Challenge 59321
[Beau Charles/Bill Crandall] [BMI] (12/4/65 BCR-17)

LIES J.J. Cale—Shelter 7326 [J.J. Cale] [BMI] (11/4/72 BCR-42)

LIES Thompson Twins—Arista 1024
[Tom Bailey/Alannah Currie/Joe Leeway] [ASC] (1/22/83 BC-30)

LIES Jonathan Butler—Jive 1038
[Jonathan Butler/Jolyon Skinner] [BMI] (6/27/87 BC-27)

LIES En Vogue—EMI 50363
[Terry Lynn Ellis/Denzil Foster/Cindy Herron/Maxine Jones/Thomas McElroy/Dawn Robinson] [BMI] (8/25/90 BC-36)

LIES EMF—Atlantic 87893
[James Atkin/Derry Brownson/Mark Decloedt/Ian Dench/Zac Foley] [BMI] (9/21/91 BC-18)

LIFE Sly & The Family Stone—Epic 10353 [Sylvester Stewart] [BMI] (7/6/68 BCR-59)

LIFE Elvis Presley—RCA Victor 47-9985 [Shirl Milete] (TSW) [BMI] (5/15/71 BCR-40)

LIFE AIN'T EASY Dr. Hook And The Medicine Show—Columbia 45925
[Ray Sawyer/Shel Silverstein] [BMI] (9/22/73 BCR-68)

LIFE AND BREATH Climax Featuring Sonny Geraci—Rocky Road 30061
[George S. Clinton] [BMI] (4/22/72 BCR-41)

LIFE AND DEATH IN G & A *Abaco Dream—A&M 1081*
[Sylvester Stewart] [BMI] (8/30/69 BCR-58)

LIFE AND DEATH IN G&A *Love Childs Afro Cuban Blues Band—Roulette 7172*
[Sylvester Stewart] [BMI] (7/19/75 B-90) [I]

LIFE DURING WARTIME (THIS AIN'T NO PARTY.. THIS AINT NO DISCO.. THIS AIN'T NO FOOLIN' AROUND) Talking Heads—Sire 49075
[David Byrne/Chris Frantz/Jerry Harrison/Tina Weymouth] [ASC] (11/3/79 B-80)

LIFE GETS BETTER Graham Parker—Arista 1-9065 [Graham Parker] [ASC] (9/24/83 B-94)

LIFE GOES ON Poison—Capitol 44705
[Bobby Dall/C.C. DeVille/Bret Michaels/Rikki Rockett] [BMI] (5/4/91 BC-35)

LIFE IN A NORTHERN TOWN The Dream Academy—Warner Bros. 28841
[Gilbert Gabriel/Nick Laird-Clowes] [BMI] (11/30/85 BC-6)

LIFE IN ONE DAY Howard Jones—Elektra 69631 [Howard Jones] [BMI] (7/6/85 BC-19)

LIFE IN THE FAST LANE Eagles—Asylum 45403
[Glenn Frey/Don Henley/Joe Walsh] [ASC] (5/14/77 BCR-11)

LIFE IS A CARNIVAL The Band—Capitol 3199
[Rick Danko/Levon Helm/Robbie Robertson] [ASC] (10/2/71 BCR-52)

LIFE IS A ROCK (BUT THE RADIO ROLLED ME) Reunion—RCA Victor 10056
[Paul DiFranco/Norman Dolph] [BMI] (9/7/74 BCR-7)

LIFE IS A SONG WORTH SINGING Johnny Mathis—Columbia 45975
[Thom Bell/Linda Creed] [BMI] (12/29/73 BCR-54)

LIFE IS BUT A DREAM The Earls—Rome 101
[Raoul Cita/Hy Weiss‡] [BMI] (5/29/61 CR-65)

LIFE IS JUST A BOWL OF CHERRIES Jaye P. Morgan—Decca 29611
[Lew Brown/Ray Henderson] [ASC] (9/5/55 R-33)

A LIFE OF ILLUSION Joe Walsh—Asylum 47144
[Kenny Passarelli/Joe Walsh] [BMI] (5/23/81 BCR-34)

LIFE'S A HOLIDAY Jerry Wallace—Challenge 9107
[George Callender*/Thomas J. Coe/Wayne Shanklin*/Jerry Wallace] [ASC] (4/22/61 BCR-53)

LIFE'S BEEN GOOD Joe Walsh—Asylum 45493 [Joe Walsh] [ASC] (6/3/78 BCR-6)

LIFE'S TOO SHORT The Lafayettes—RCA Victor 47-8044
[Lee Bonner/Phil Huth] [BMI] (7/14/62 BCR-78)

LIFE'S WHAT YOU MAKE IT Talk Talk—EMI America 8303
[Tim Friese-Greene/Mark Hollis] [BMI] (2/1/86 BC-88)

A LIFETIME OF LONELINESS Jackie De Shannon—Imperial 66132
[Burt Bacharach/Hal David] [ASC] (10/2/65 BCR-66)

LIFT ME UP Yes—Arista 2218 [Trevor Rabin*/Chris Squire] [BMI] (5/18/91 BC-64)

LIGHT MY FIRE *The Doors—Elektra 45615*
[John Densmore/Robby Krieger/Ray Manzarek/Jim Morrison] [ASC] (5/27/67 BCR-1)

LIGHT MY FIRE *Jose Feliciano—RCA Victor 47-9550*
[John Densmore/Robby Krieger/Ray Manzarek/Jim Morrison] [ASC] (7/20/68 BCR-3)

LIGHT MY FIRE *The Doors—Elektra 45615*
[John Densmore/Robby Krieger/Ray Manzarek/Jim Morrison] [ASC] (8/31/68 B-87)

LIGHT MY FIRE *Rhetta Hughes—Tetragrammaton 1513*
[John Densmore/Robby Krieger/Ray Manzarek/Jim Morrison] [ASC] (1/25/69 CR-78)

LIGHT MY FIRE *Amii Stewart—Ariola America/Hansa 7753*
[John Densmore/Robby Krieger/Ray Manzarek/Jim Morrison] (Med) [ASC] (6/23/79 BCR-69)

LIGHT OF A CLEAR BLUE MORNING Dolly Parton—RCA 10935
[Dolly Parton] [BMI] (6/18/77 B-87)

LIGHT OF DAY The Barbusters (Joan Jett & The Blackhearts)—Blackheart 4-06692
[Bruce Springsteen] [ASC] (2/21/87 BC-33)

LIGHT OF LOVE Peggy Lee—Capitol 4071 [Charles Singleton] [BMI] (10/20/58 BR-63)

LIGHT SINGS The 5th Dimension—Bell 999
[Gary Friedman/Will Holt] [BMI] (5/15/71 BCR-22)

LIGHT THE SKY ON FIRE Jefferson Starship—Grunt 11426
[Craig Chaquico] [BMI] (12/2/78 BCR-65)

LIGHT UP THE WORLD WITH SUNSHINE Hamilton, Joe Frank & Dennison—Playboy 6077
[Ben Findon/Geoff Wilkins] [BMI] (7/17/76 B-67)

LIGHTNIN' STRIKES Lou Christie—MGM 13412
[Lou Christie/Twyla Herbert] [BMI] (12/25/65 BCR-1)

LIGHTNING'S GIRL Nancy Sinatra—Reprise 0620 [Lee Hazlewood] [ASC] (9/23/67 BCR-18)

LIGHTS Journey—Columbia 10800 [Steve Perry/Neal Schon] [BMI] (8/19/78 BCR-63)

THE LIGHTS OF TUCSON Jim Campbell—Laurie 3546
[Linda Kay Zerato] [ASC] (7/18/70 BR-93)

LIGHTS OUT Billy Vaughn And His Orchestra—Dot 15936
[Billy Hill] [ASC] (5/2/59 C-100) [I]

LIGHTS OUT Peter Wolf—EMI America 8208
[Don Covay/Peter Wolf] [BMI] (7/14/84 BC-12)

(THE LIGHTS WENT OUT IN) MASSACHUSETTS The Bee Gees—Atco 6532
[Barry Gibb/Maurice Gibb/Robin Gibb] [BMI] (11/11/67 BCR-11)

LIKE A BABY Len Barry—Decca 31889
[Len Barry/John Madara/David White] [BMI] (12/25/65 BCR-13)

LIKE A CHILD Julie Rogers—Mercury 72380
[Jim Breedlove/Lynn Breedlove] [BMI] (2/6/65 BCR-58)

LIKE A CHILD Noel—4th & Broadway 7458
[Mary E. Kessler/Noel Pagan/Roman Ricardo] [ASC] (4/9/88 BC-67)

LIKE A PRAYER Madonna—Sire 27539
[Madonna L. Ciccone/Patrick Raymond Leonard] [BMI] (3/18/89 BC-1)

LIKE A ROCK Bob Seger & The Silver Bullet Band—Capitol 5592
[Bob Seger] [ASC] (5/24/86 BC-12)

LIKE A ROLLING STONE *Bob Dylan—Columbia 43346 [Bob Dylan] [SE] (7/24/65 BCR-1)*

LIKE A ROLLING STONE *Phil Flowers & The Flower Shop—A&M 1122*
[Bob Dylan] [SE] (10/11/69 CR-90)

LIKE A SAD SONG John Denver—RCA 10774 [John Denver] [ASC] (9/11/76 BCR-36)

LIKE A SUNDAY IN SALEM (THE AMOS & ANDY SONG) Gene Cotton—Ariola America 7723
[Gene Cotton] [ASC] (9/30/78 BCR-37)

LIKE A SUNDAY MORNING Lana Cantrell—Polydor 14261
[Alan Bernstein/Joel Diamond] [ASC] (2/15/75 BCR-63)

—LIKE A SURGEON see: LIKE A VIRGIN

LIKE A VIRGIN *Madonna—Sire 29210*
[Thomas F. Kelly/Billy Steinberg] [ASC] (11/17/84 BC-1)

LIKE A SURGEON *(parody of Like A Virgin "Weird Al" Yankovic—Rock 'n' Roll 04937 [Thomas F. Kelly/Billy Steinberg/Al Yankovic] [ASC] (6/22/85 BC-41) [P]*

LIKE AN OLD TIME MOVIE Scott McKenzie—Ode 105
[John Phillips] [ASC] (10/21/67 BCR-18)

LIKE AN OPEN DOOR The Fuzz—Calla 177 [Sheila Young] [BMI] (6/19/71 BCR-57)

LIKE COLUMBUS DID The Reflections—Golden World 12
[Joanne Bratton/Freddie Gorman/Bob Hamilton/Barbara Terry] [BMI] (7/11/64 BCR-72)

LIKE FLAMES Berlin—Geffen 28563 [Rob Brill] [ASC] (10/25/86 BC-82)

LIKE I LOVE YOU Edd Byrnes And Friend—Warner Bros. 5087
[Larry Markes/Don Ralke] [ASC] (8/10/59 BCR-41)

LIKE, LONG HAIR Paul Revere And The Raiders—Gardena 116
[Paul Revere] [BMI] (3/18/61 BCR-30) [I]

LIKE NO OTHER NIGHT 38 Special—A&M 2831
[Don Barnes/John Bettis/Jeff Carlisi/Jim Vallance] [ASC] (5/3/86 BC-14)

LIKE STRANGERS The Everly Brothers—Cadence 1388
[Boudleaux Bryant] [BMI] (10/24/60 BCR-21)

LIKE THE BIG GUYS DO The Rocky Fellers—Scepter 1254
[Stanley Kahan/Horace Ott] [BMI] (6/22/63 BCR-55)

LIKE THE WEATHER 10,000 Maniacs—Elektra 69418
[Natalie Merchant] [ASC] (5/7/88 BC-68)

LIKE THEY SAY IN L.A. East L.A. Car Pool—GRC 2064 [Jerry Rush] [ASC] (8/2/75 BC-72)

LIKE TO GET TO KNOW YOU Spanky And Our Gang—Mercury 72795
[Stuart Scharf] [ASC] (4/13/68 BCR-13)

LIKE TO GET TO KNOW YOU WELL Howard Jones—Elektra 69598
[Howard Jones] [BMI] (9/28/85 BC-46)

LIKE YOUNG Andre Previn & David Rose—MGM 12792
[André Previn] [ASC] (6/1/59 BCR-31) [IM]

LIL' RED RIDING HOOD Sam The Sham And The Pharaohs—MGM 13506
[Ronald Blackwell] [BMI] (6/11/66 BCR-1)

LILI MARLENE Al Martino—Capitol 2158
[Tommie Connor/Hans Leip/Norbert Schultze] [BMI] (4/27/68 BCR-74) [FET]

LILY WAS HERE David A. Stewart—Arista 2187
[David A. Stewart] [BMI] (5/18/91 BC-9) [I]

LIMBO The Capris—Mr. Peeke 118
[John Cassese/Mike Mincieli/Vinny Naccarato/Frank Reina] [BMI] (8/18/62 B-99)

LIMBO DANCE The Champs—Challenge 9162 [Dave Burgess] [BMI] (10/20/62 B-97)

LIMBO ROCK *The Champs—Challenge 9131 [Billy Strange] [BMI] (5/14/62 BCR-32) [IM]*

LIMBO ROCK *Chubby Checker—Parkway 849*
[Kal Mann/Billy Strange] [BMI] (9/8/62 BCR-1)

LIMELIGHT Rush—Mercury 76095
[Geddy Lee/Alex Lifeson/Neil Peart] [ASC] (3/14/81 BCR-55)

—LIMELIGHT see: ETERNALLY

LINDA *Adam Wade—Coed 556 [Jack Lawrence] [ASC] (9/18/61 BR-60)*

LINDA *Jan & Dean—Liberty 55531 [Jack Lawrence] [ASC] (2/23/63 BCR-26)*

LINDA LU Ray Sharpe—Jamie 1128 [Ray Sharpe] [BMI] (7/6/59 BCR-40)

LINDA ON MY MIND Conway Twitty—MCA 40339 [Conway Twitty] [BMI] (2/15/75 BC-48)

LING TING TONG *The Five Keys—Capitol 2945 [Mable Godwin] [BMI] (12/4/54 BCtR-21)*

LING, TING, TONG *The Charms—DeLuxe 6076 [Mable Godwin] [BMI] (1/15/55 BCt-26)*

LING-TING-TONG *Buddy Knox—Liberty 55305 [Mable Godwin] [BMI] (3/6/61 BCR-65)*

THE LION SLEEPS TONIGHT *The Tokens—RCA Victor 47-7954*
[Luigi Creatore/Solomon Linda/Hugo Peretti/Albert Stanton/George David Weiss] [ASC] (11/13/61 BCR-1)

THE LION SLEEPS TONIGHT *Robert John—Atlantic 2846*
[Luigi Creatore/Solomon Linda/Hugo Peretti/Albert Stanton/George David Weiss] [ASC] (12/25/71 BCR-2)

LIP SYNC (TO THE TONGUE TWISTERS) Len Barry—Decca 31788
[Len Barry/John Madara/David White] [BMI] (5/29/65 BCR-84)

LIPS OF WINE Andy Williams—Cadence 1336
[Sy Soloway/Shirley Wolfe] [BMI] (9/9/57 BCR-15)

LIPSTICK Michel Polnareff—Atlantic 3330 [Michel Polnareff] [ASC] (5/29/76 B-61) [I]

LIPSTICK Suzi Quatro—Dreamland 107
[Mike Chapman/Nicky Chinn] [BMI] (1/24/81 BCR-51)

LIPSTICK AND CANDY AND RUBBERSOLE SHOES Julius La Rosa—RCA Victor 47-6416
[Bob Haymes] [BMI] (2/11/56 BCR-21)

LIPSTICK ON YOUR COLLAR Connie Francis—MGM 12793
[George Goehring/Edna Lewis] [ASC] (5/16/59 BCR-3)

LIPSTICK TRACES (ON A CIGARETTE) *Benny Spellman—Minit 644*
[Allen Toussaint] [BMI] (5/5/62 BCR-80)

LIPSTICK TRACES (ON A CIGARETTE) *The O'Jays—Imperial 66102*
[Allen Toussaint] [BMI] (5/8/65 BCR-48)

LISA Jeanne Black—Capitol 4396 [Cindy Walker] [BMI] (7/18/60 BCR-34)
LISA Ferrante & Teicher—United Artists 470
[Malcolm Arnold] [ASC] (6/2/62 BCR-65) [I]
LISA, LISTEN TO ME Blood, Sweat & Tears—Columbia 45477
[David Clayton-Thomas/Dick Halligan] [BMI] (10/23/71 BCR-66)
LISBON ANTIGUA *Nelson Riddle And His Orchestra—Capitol 3287*
[Amadeu do Vale/Jose Galhardo/Raul Portela] [BMI] (12/10/55 BCRt-1) [IM]
LISBON ANTIGUA (IN OLD LISBON) *Alan Dale—Coral 61553*
[Amadeu do Vale/Harry Dupree/Jose Galhardo/Raul Portela] [BMI] (12/16/55 Rt-6)
LISBON ANTIGUA (IN OLD LISBON) *Mitch Miller & His Orchestra—Columbia 40635*
[Amadeu do Vale/Jose Galhardo/Raul Portela] [BMI] (2/3/56 BRt-3) [IM]
LISBON ANTIGUA *Lawrence Welk & His Champagne Music—Coral 61595*
[Amadeu do Vale/Jose Galhardo/Raul Portela] [BMI] (3/2/56 Rt-4) [IM]
LISTEN HERE *Eddie Harris—Atlantic 2487 [Eddie Harris] [BMI] (6/15/68 BCR-45) [IM]*
LISTEN HERE *Brian Auger & The Trinity—RCA Victor 0381*
[Eddie Harris] [BMI] (10/10/70 B-100) [IM]
LISTEN LIKE THIEVES INXS—Atlantic 89429
[Garry Beers/Andy Farriss/Michael Hutchence] [ASC] (5/10/86 BC-54)
LISTEN LONELY GIRL Johnny Mathis—Mercury 72339
[Richard Ahlert/James Lyons/Bobby Scott] [ASC] (10/10/64 BCR-59)
LISTEN PEOPLE Herman's Hermits—MGM 13462
[Graham Gouldman] [ASC] (2/12/66 BCR-3)
LISTEN, THEY'RE PLAYING MY SONG Ray Charles—ABC/TRC 11133
[Glen Garrison/Charlie Williams] [BMI] (10/19/68 B-92)
LISTEN TO HER HEART Tom Petty And The Heartbreakers—Shelter 62011
[Tom Petty] [ASC] (9/23/78 BCR-59)
LISTEN TO ME Buddy Holly / The Crickets—Coral 61947
[Buddy Holly/Norman Petty] [BMI] (2/17/58 R-76)
LISTEN TO THE BAND The Monkees—Colgems 5004
[Michael Nesmith] [BMI] (5/24/69 BCR-57)
LISTEN TO THE BUDDHA Ozo—DJM 1012 [Kenny George] [ASC] (7/17/76 BC-72)
LISTEN TO THE MUSIC The Doobie Brothers—Warner Bros. 7619
[Tom Johnston] [BMI] (9/2/72 BCR-9)
LISTEN TO THE PEOPLE Zager & Evans—RCA Victor 74-0299
[Rick Evans] [BMI] (12/27/69 C-100)
LISTEN TO WHAT THE MAN SAID Wings—Apple 4091
[Linda McCartney/Paul McCartney] [ASC] (5/31/75 BCR-1)
LISTEN TO YOUR HEART Roxette—EMI 50223
[Per Gessle/Mats Persson] [BMI] (8/26/89 BC-1)
LITTLE ALTAR BOY Vic Dana—Dolton 48 [Howlett Smith] [ASC] (11/27/61 BCR-42)
LITTLE ARROWS Leapy Lee—Decca 32380
[Albert Hammond/Mike Hazlewood] [BMI] (10/5/68 BCR-12)
LITTLE BAND OF GOLD James Gilreath—Joy 274
[James William Gilreath] [BMI] (3/23/63 BCR-21)
LITTLE BECKY'S CHRISTMAS WISH Becky Lamb—Warner Bros. 7154
[Clifford Casabon/Tom DeAngelo] [BMI] (12/23/67 CR-59)
LITTLE BELL The Dixie Cups—Red Bird 10-017
[Jeff Barry/Ellie Greenwich] [BMI] (12/19/64 BCR-51)
LITTLE BIRD Pete Jolly Trio and Friends—Ava 116
[Dick Grove/Pete Jolly] [ASC] (4/27/63 R-89) [IM]
A LITTLE BIT LIKE MAGIC King Harvest—Perception 527
[Ron Altbach/Sherman Kelly/David P. Robinson] [ASC] (5/5/73 BCR-73)
A LITTLE BIT ME, A LITTLE BIT YOU The Monkees—Colgems 1004
[Neil Diamond] [SE] (3/25/67 BCR-1)
A LITTLE BIT MORE Dr. Hook—Capitol 4280 [Bobby Gosh] [ASC] (6/19/76 BCR-9)
A LITTLE BIT NOW (A LITTLE BIT LATER) *The Majors—Imperial 5879*
[Celia Marshall/Jerry Ragovoy] [BMI] (11/10/62 BCR-61)
A LITTLE BIT NOW *The Dave Clark Five—Epic 10209*
[Celia Marshall/Jerry Ragovoy] [BMI] (8/5/67 BCR-52)
LITTLE BIT O' SOUL *The Music Explosion—Laurie 3380*
[John Carter/Ken Hawker] [ASC] (5/6/67 BCR-1)
LITTLE BIT O' SOUL *Bullet—Big Tree 140*
[John Carter/Ken Hawker] [ASC] (6/10/72 CR-71)
A LITTLE BIT OF HEAVEN Ronnie Dove—Diamond 184
[Artie Resnick/Kenny Young] [BMI] (6/5/65 BCR-9)
A LITTLE BIT OF HEAVEN Natalie Cole—Modern 99630
[Richard Kerr/Graham Lyle] [BMI] (9/7/85 B-81)
LITTLE BIT OF LOVE Dwight Twilley—EMI America 8206
[Dwight Twilley] [ASC] (5/19/84 BC-77)
A LITTLE BIT OF LOVE (IS ALL IT TAKES) New Edition—MCA 52768
[Richard Wyatt/Christine Yarian] [ASC] (2/22/86 BC-38)
A LITTLE BIT OF SOAP *The Jarmels—Laurie 3098 [Bert Berns] [BMI] (7/22/61 BCR-12)*
A LITTLE BIT OF SOAP *Garnet Mimms—United Artists 796*
[Bert Berns] [BMI] (1/2/65 BR-95)
A LITTLE BIT OF SOAP *The Exciters—Bang 515 [Bert Berns] [BMI] (1/22/66 BCR-56)*
A LITTLE BIT OF SOAP *Paul Davis—Bang 576 [Bert Berns] [BMI] (4/18/70 BCR-42)*
LITTLE BIT OF SOAP *Nigel Olsson—Bang 4800 [Bert Berns] [BMI] (4/7/79 BCR-33)*
LITTLE BITTY GIRL Bobby Rydell—Cameo 171
[Clint Ballard Jr./Fred Tobias] [ASC] (1/30/60 BCR-19)
LITTLE BITTY JOHNNY Travis & Bob—Sandy 1019 [Travis Pritchett] [BMI] (7/4/59 C-95)
LITTLE BITTY PRETTY ONE *Thurston Harris—Aladdin 3398*
[Bobby Day] [BMI] (10/12/57 BCtRt-6)
LITTLE BITTY PRETTY ONE *Bobby Day And The Satellites—Class 211*
[Bobby Day] [BMI] (10/12/57 BCtRt-9)
LITTLE BITTY PRETTY ONE *Frankie Lymon—Roulette 4257*
[Bobby Day] [BMI] (7/11/60 BCR-39)
LITTLE BITTY PRETTY ONE *Clyde McPhatter—Mercury 71987*
[Bobby Day] [BMI] (6/16/62 BCR-25)
LITTLE BITTY PRETTY ONE *The Jackson 5—Motown 1199*
[Bobby Day] [BMI] (4/22/72 BCR-5)
A LITTLE BITTY TEAR *Burl Ives—Decca 31330 [Hank Cochran] [BMI] (12/16/61 BCtRt-7)*
A LITTLE BITTY TEAR *Wanda Jackson—Capitol 4681*
[Hank Cochran] [BMI] (1/20/62 BCtRt-7)
LITTLE BLACK BOOK Jimmy Dean—Columbia 42529 [Jimmy Dean] [BMI] (9/8/62 BCR-29)
THE LITTLE BLACK EGG The Nightcrawlers—Kapp 709
[Chuck Conlon] [ASC] (12/24/66 BCR-78)
LITTLE BLONDE GIRL Don French—Lancer 105 [Don French] [BMI] (10/24/59 C-95)
LITTLE BLUE MAN Betty Johnson—Atlantic 1169
[Fred Ebb/Paul Klein] [BMI] (2/15/58 BCR-19)
LITTLE BOXES *Pete Seeger—Columbia 42940*
[Malvina Reynolds] [ASC] (1/11/64 BCR-70)
LITTLE BOXES *The Womenfolk—RCA Victor 47-8301*
[Malvina Reynolds] [ASC] (4/18/64 BC-83)
THE LITTLE BOY Tony Bennett—Columbia 42931
[Al Stillman/Guy Wood] [ASC] (12/21/63 BCR-33)
LITTLE BOY The Crystals—Philles 119
[Jeff Barry/Ellie Greenwich/Phil Spector] [BMI] (1/25/64 BCR-92)
LITTLE BOY BLUE Billy Vaughn and His Orchestra—Dot 15444
[Ed Bonner/Eugene Field*/Billy Vaughn] [ASC] (2/11/56 B-76)
LITTLE BOY BLUE Huelyn Duvall—Challenge 59014
[Jerry Arnold/Doyle Turner] [BMI] (6/15/59 B-88)
LITTLE BOY (IN GROWN UP CLOTHES) The 4 Seasons—Vee-Jay 713
[Bob Crewe/Bob Gaudio] [BMI] (12/25/65 BCR-60)
LITTLE BOY SAD Johnny Burnette—Liberty 55298 [Wayne Walker] [BMI] (2/4/61 BCR-16)
—LITTLE BOY see: GUAGLIONE
LITTLE BRASS BAND David Seville—Liberty 55153 [David Seville] [ASC] (8/25/58 BC-78)
LITTLE BROWN JUG *Frank Barber Orchestra—Victory 1001*
[Joseph Winner] (Med) [NA] (5/8/82 B-61) [IWM]
LITTLE BROWN JUG *Frank Barber Orchestra—RCA 13219*
[Joseph Winner] (Med) [NA] (6/5/82 BC-31) [IWM]
LITTLE BY LITTLE *Nappy Brown—Savoy 1506*
[Rose Marie McCoy/Kelly Owens] [BMI] (1/19/57 BCRt-14)
LITTLE BY LITTLE *Micki Marlo—ABC-Paramount 9762*
[Rose Marie McCoy/Kelly Owens] [BMI] (1/19/57 BRt-14)
LITTLE BY LITTLE *Toni Arden—Decca 30180*
[Rose Marie McCoy/Kelly Owens] [BMI] (1/19/57 Rt-14)
LITTLE BY LITTLE *The Crew-Cuts—Mercury 71022*
[Rose Marie McCoy/Kelly Owens] [BMI] (1/19/57 Rt-14)
LITTLE BY LITTLE Robert Plant—Es Paranza 7-99644
[Robert Plant/Jezz Woodroffe] [ASC] (5/18/85 BC-34)
L'HOMME ET L'ENFANT *Eddie Constantine & Tania—Kapp 133*
[René Rouzaud/Wayne Shanklin] [ASC] (2/3/56 Rt-73)
LITTLE CHILD *Lael & Cab Calloway—ABC-Paramount 9671*
[Wayne Shanklin] [ASC] (2/3/56 BCtRt-25)
LITTLE CHILD *Eddie Albert and Sondra Lee—Kapp 134*
[Wayne Shanklin] [ASC] (2/3/56 BCtRt-25)
LITTLE CHILD *Danny Kaye And Dena Kaye—Decca 29806*
[Wayne Shanklin] [ASC] (2/3/56 CtRt-25)
LITTLE CHILD *Gisele MacKenzie And Billy Quinn—Vik 0189*
[Wayne Shanklin] [ASC] (2/3/56 CtRt-25)
LITTLE CHILD *Frankie Laine & Jimmy Boyd—Columbia 40650*
[Wayne Shanklin] [ASC] (2/17/56 Rt-76)
LITTLE CHILDREN Billy J. Kramer With The Dakotas—Imperial 66027
[J. Leslie McFarland/Mort Shuman] [ASC] (4/18/64 BCR-7)
—LITTLE CLOCK see: LE PETIT REVEIL
LITTLE COCO PALM Jerry Wallace—Challenge 59060
[Wayne Shanklin] [ASC] (12/14/59 BCR-29)
LITTLE DARLIN' *The Diamonds—Mercury 71060*
[Maurice Williams] [BMI] (3/2/57 BCRt-1)
LITTLE DARLIN' *The Gladiolas—Excello 2101 [Maurice Williams] [BMI] (3/30/57 BRt-1)*
LITTLE DARLIN' Sheila—Carrere 02564
[Amanda Blue/Holly Knight] [ASC] (12/5/81 BCR-49)
LITTLE DARLING, I NEED YOU *Marvin Gaye—Tamla 54138*
[Lamont Dozier/Brian Holland/Eddie Holland] [BMI] (8/20/66 BCR-47)
LITTLE DARLING (I NEED YOU) *The Doobie Brothers—Warner Bros. 8408*
[Lamont Dozier/Brian Holland/Eddie Holland] [BMI] (7/23/77 BCR-39)
LITTLE DEUCE COUPE The Beach Boys—Capitol 5009
[Roger Christian/Brian Wilson] [BMI] (8/3/63 BCR-15)

LITTLE DEVIL Neil Sedaka—RCA Victor 47-7874
[Howard Greenfield/Neil Sedaka] [BMI] (4/17/61 BCR-9)

LITTLE DIANE Dion—Laurie 3134
[Dion DiMucci] [ASC] (7/7/62 BCR-8)

LITTLE DIPPER Mickey Mozart Quintet—Roulette 4148
[Robert Maxwell] [ASC] (5/4/59 BCR-25) [I]

A LITTLE DOG CRIED Jimmie Rodgers—Roulette 4384
[Eddie V. Deane/Al Dredick] [ASC] (8/21/61 BR-71)

LITTLE DONNA The Rivieras (2)—Riviera 1402 [Bill Dobslaw] [BMI] (4/25/64 BCR-84)

THE LITTLE DRUMMER BOY *Harry Simeone Chorale—20th Fox 121*
[Katherine Davis/Henry Onorati/Harry Simeone] [ASC] (12/22/58 BCR-10)

THE LITTLE DRUMMER BOY *Harry Simeone Chorale—20th Fox 121*
[Katherine Davis/Henry Onorati/Harry Simeone] [ASC] (11/9/59 BCtRt-15)

THE LITTLE DRUMMER BOY *Johnny Cash—Columbia 41481*
[Katherine Davis/Henry Onorati/Harry Simeone] [ASC] (11/9/59 BCtRt-24)

THE LITTLE DRUMMER BOY *Harry Simeone Chorale—20th Fox 121*
[Katherine Davis/Henry Onorati/Harry Simeone] [ASC] (12/12/60 BCR-24)

THE LITTLE DRUMMER BOY *Harry Simeone Chorale—20th Fox 121*
[Katherine Davis/Henry Onorati/Harry Simeone] [ASC] (12/11/61 BCR-22)

THE LITTLE DRUMMER BOY *Jack Halloran Singers—Dot 16275*
[Katherine Davis/Henry Onorati/Harry Simeone] [ASC] (1/6/62 B-96)

THE LITTLE DRUMMER BOY *Harry Simeone Chorale—20th Fox 121*
[Katherine Davis/Henry Onorati/Harry Simeone] [ASC] (12/8/62 BCR-14)

THE LITTLE DRUMMER BOY *Harry Simeone Chorale—20th Fox 429*
[Katherine Davis/Henry Onorati/Harry Simeone] [ASC] (12/28/63 C-96)

LITTLE DRUMMER BOY *Lou Rawls—Capitol 2026*
[Katherine Davis/Henry Onorati/Harry Simeone] [ASC] (12/23/67 C-78)

THE LITTLE DRUMMER BOY *Moonlion—P.I.P. 6513*
[Katherine Davis/Henry Onorati/Harry Simeone] [ASC] (12/27/75 BR-94) [IWM]

LITTLE EEEFIN ANNIE Joe Perkins—Sound Stage 7 2511
[Fred Aylor MacRae/Bob L. Moore] [BMI] (9/28/63 BCR-55)

LITTLE EGYPT (YING-YANG) The Coasters—Atco 6192
[Jerry Leiber/Mike Stoller] [BMI] (4/24/61 BCR-23)

A LITTLE FEELING (CALLED LOVE) Jack Scott—Capitol 4554
[Jack Scott] [SE] (5/1/61 BCR-51)

LITTLE FIGHTER White Lion—Atlantic 88874
[Vito Bratta/Mike Tramp] [ASC] (6/24/89 BC-52)

—LITTLE FLOWER see: PETITE FLEUR

LITTLE GAMES The Yardbirds—Epic 10156
[Harold Spiro/Phil Wainman] [ASC] (4/15/67 BCR-44)

LITTLE GHETTO BOY Donny Hathaway—Atco 6880
[Earl DeRouen/Edward Howard] [BMI] (4/1/72 R-100)

LITTLE GIRL Frankie Lymon—Roulette 4035
[Francis Henry/Madeline Hyde] [ASC] (12/9/57 R-73)

LITTLE GIRL Ritchie Valens—Del-Fi 4117
[Robert Kuhn/Ritchie Valens] [BMI] (7/13/59 BC-92)

LITTLE GIRL Syndicate Of Sound—Bell 640
[Don Baskin/Bob Gonzalez] [BMI] (5/28/66 BCR-8)

LITTLE GIRL The Critters—Kapp 853 [Chris Darway] [BMI] (11/4/67 R-95)

LITTLE GIRL GONE Donna Fargo—Dot 17476 [Donna Fargo] [BMI] (10/6/73 BCR-57)

THE LITTLE GIRL I ONCE KNEW The Beach Boys—Capitol 5540
[Brian Wilson] [BMI] (11/27/65 BCR-15)

LITTLE GIRL, LITTLE BOY Al Martino—20th Fox 237
[Aldo Provenzano] [BMI] (3/18/61 CR-89)

LITTLE GIRL OF MINE *The Cleftones—Gee 1011*
[Herbert Cox/George Goldner/Morris Levy‡] [BMI] (4/21/56 BCRt-24)*

LITTLE GIRL OF MINE *The Diamonds—Mercury 70835*
[Herbert Cox/George Goldner/Morris Levy‡] [BMI] (6/1/56 Rt-35)*

A LITTLE GOOD NEWS Anne Murray—Capitol 5264
[Charlie Black/Rory Bourke/Tommy Rocco] [ASC] (9/17/83 BC-74)

LITTLE GREEN APPLES *Roger Miller—Smash 2148*
[Bobby Russell] [ASC] (2/24/68 BCR-39)

LITTLE GREEN APPLES *Patti Page—Columbia 44556 [Bobby Russell] [ASC] (7/6/68 B-96)*

LITTLE GREEN APPLES *O.C. Smith—Columbia 44616*
[Bobby Russell] [ASC] (8/17/68 BCR-2)

LITTLE GREEN BAG George Baker Selection—Colossus 112
[George Baker/Jan Visser] [BMI] (3/14/70 BCR-16)

LITTLE GYPSY The Ames Brothers—RCA Victor 47-7142
[Luther Dixon/Bert Keyes/Billy Dawn Smith] [BMI] (1/20/58 BR-65)

A LITTLE HEARTACHE Eddy Arnold—RCA Victor 47-8048
[Wayne Walker] [BMI] (6/16/62 R-88)

LITTLE HONDA *The Hondells—Mercury 72324*
[Mike Love/Brian Wilson] [BMI] (9/12/64 BCR-7)

LITTLE HONDA *The Beach Boys—Capitol R-5267*
[Mike Love/Brian Wilson] (EP) [BMI] (10/10/64 BC-65;57)

A LITTLE IN LOVE Cliff Richard—EMI America 8068
[Alan Tarney] [BMI] (12/13/80 BCR-11)

A LITTLE IS ENOUGH Pete Townshend—Atco 7312
[Pete Townshend] [GL] (10/11/80 BC-72)

LITTLE JACKIE WANTS TO BE A STAR Lisa Lisa And Cult Jam—Columbia 68674
[Curtis Bedeau/Gerard Charles/Hugh Clarke/Brian George/Lucien George/Paul George] [BMI] (4/15/89 BC-29)

LITTLE JEANNIE Elton John—MCA 41236 [Elton John/Gary Osborne] [BMI] (5/3/80 BCR-3)

LITTLE LADY Duke Jupiter—Morocco 1736 [Marshall James Styler] [BMI] (5/12/84 BC-66)

LITTLE LATIN LUPE LU *The Righteous Brothers—Moonglow 215*
[Bill Medley] [BMI] (5/11/63 BCR-47)

LITTLE LATIN LUPE LU *The Kingsmen—Wand 157 [Bill Medley] [BMI] (7/11/64 BCR-46)*

LITTLE LATIN LUPE LU *Mitch Ryder And The Detroit Wheels—New Voice 808*
[Bill Medley] [BMI] (3/5/66 BCR-13)

A LITTLE LESS CONVERSATION
Elvis Presley With The Jordanaires—RCA Victor 47-9610
[Mac Davis/Billy Strange] [BMI] (9/28/68 BCR-53)

LITTLE LIAR Joan Jett and the Blackhearts—Blackheart 4-08095
[Desmond Child/Joan Jett] [ASC] (10/29/88 BC-19)

LITTLE LIES Fleetwood Mac—Warner Bros. 28291
[Christine McVie/Eddy Quintela] [BMI] (8/29/87 BC-4)

LITTLE LONELINESS Kay Starr—RCA Victor 47-6864
[Damita Jo Gibson] [BMI] (4/13/57 BCR-52)

LITTLE LONELY Chad Allen—Smash 1720
[Glen Campbell/Jerry Jackson] [BMI] (11/6/61 R-92)

LITTLE LONELY ONE Tom Jones—Tower 126
[Bob Brass/Irwin Levine] [BMI] (5/29/65 BCR-42)

A LITTLE LOVE Juice Newton—RCA 13823
[Danny Douma/Richard Feldman/Todd Sharp] [BMI] (6/2/84 BC-44)

A LITTLE LOVE Corey Hart—EMI 50239 [Corey Hart] [ASC] (3/17/90 BC-37)

A LITTLE LOVE CAN GO A LONG LONG WAY
The Dream Weavers Featuring Wade Buff—Decca 29905
[Sammy Fain/Paul Francis Webster] [ASC] (5/5/56 BCRt-33)

A LITTLE LOVE CAN GO A LONG, LONG WAY *Johnny Desmond—Coral 61632*
[Sammy Fain/Paul Francis Webster] [ASC] (5/25/56 Rt-74)

A LITTLE LOVIN' (KEEPS THE DOCTOR AWAY) The Raes—A&M 2091
[Dino Fekaris/Freddie Perren] [ASC] (11/25/78 BCR-60)

LITTLE MAN Sonny & Cher—Atco 6440 [Sonny Bono] [BMI] (10/1/66 BCR-16)

LITTLE MARIE Chuck Berry—Chess 1912 [Chuck Berry] [BMI] (10/24/64 BCR-51)

LITTLE MARY Fats Domino—Imperial 5526
[Dave Bartholomew/Fats Domino] [BMI] (7/7/58 B-49)

LITTLE MISS BELONG TO NO ONE Teresa Brewer—Coral 62278
[Mel Tillis*/Wayne Walker] [BMI] (7/17/61 R-97)

LITTLE MISS BLUE Dion—Laurie 3070
[Jimmy Isle*/Ronnie Isle/Kenny Marlowe*] [BMI] (12/5/60 B-96)

LITTLE MISS SAD The Five Emprees—Freeport 1001
[Dick Addrisi/Don Addrisi] [BMI] (8/21/65 BCR-56)

LITTLE MISS STUCK-UP The Playmates—Roulette 4322
[Lee Pockriss/Paul Vance] [ASC] (2/20/61 BCR-35)

LITTLE MISS SUNSHINE Tommy Roe—ABC 10945 [Tommy Roe] [BMI] (6/10/67 BCR-90)

LITTLE MISS U.S.A. Barry Mann—ABC-Paramount 10263
[Barry Mann/Cynthia Weil] [BMI] (11/6/61 CR-65)

A LITTLE MORE LOVE Olivia Newton-John—MCA 40975
[John Farrar] [BMI] (11/25/78 BCR-3)

THE LITTLE MUSICIANS
Hugo Winterhalter's Orchestra And Chorus—RCA Victor 47-6459
[Francesco Frontini] [ASC] (4/7/56 B-41) [I]

THE LITTLE OLD LADY (FROM PASADENA) Jan & Dean—Liberty 55704
[Don Altfeld/Jan Berry*/Roger Christian] [BMI] (6/27/64 BCR-3)

LITTLE OLD WINE DRINKER ME *Robert Mitchum—Monument 1006*
[Dick Jennings/Hank Mills] [BMI] (8/12/67 B-96)

LITTLE OLE WINE DRINKER, ME *Dean Martin—Reprise 0608*
[Dick Jennings/Hank Mills] [BMI] (8/19/67 BCR-38)

—LITTLE OLE MAN see: UPTIGHT

LITTLE ONE Chicago—Columbia 10683
[Danny Seraphine/David Wolinski] [ASC] (2/11/78 BCR-44)

LITTLE PEDRO The Olympics—Arvee 5023
[Cliff Goldsmith/Fred Smith/Bill Spitalsky] [BMI] (3/11/61 BCR-71)

LITTLE PIGEON *Sal Mineo—Epic 9260 [Ray Whitt] [BMI] (1/13/58 BCRt-47)*

LITTLE PIGEON *Chuck Sims—Trend 30-000 [Ray Whitt] [BMI] (1/20/58 Rt-77)*

LITTLE PIXIE *Moe Koffman Quartette—Jubilee 5324*
[Sal Baionno] [BMI] (5/24/58 BCRt-44) [IM]

LITTLE PIXIE *Johnnie Pate—Federal 12327 [Sal Baionno] [BMI] (5/26/58 Rt-78) [IM]*

LITTLE PIXIE *Frank D'Rone—Mercury 71329*
[Sal Baionno/Mel Mitchell] [BMI] (6/9/58 Rt-78)

LITTLE QUEEN Heart—Portrait 70008
[Michael Derosier/Roger Fisher/Steve Fossen/Howard Leese/Ann Wilson/Nancy Wilson] [ASC] (9/10/77 BCR-48)

LITTLE QUEENIE *Chuck Berry—Chess 1722 [Chuck Berry] [BMI] (4/4/59 BC-80)*

LITTLE QUEENIE *Bill Black's Combo—Hi 2079 [Chuck Berry] [BMI] (10/3/64 BR-73) [IWM]*

A LITTLE RAIN MUST FALL The Epic Splendor—Hot Biscuit 1450
[Richard Fishbaugh] [BMI] (12/9/67 BCR-59)

LITTLE RED CORVETTE Prince—Warner Bros. 29746 [Prince] [ASC] (2/26/83 BC-6)

LITTLE RED RENTED ROWBOAT Joe Dowell—Smash 1759
[Marvin Moore/Bernie Wayne] [BMI] (6/23/62 BCR-18)

LITTLE RED RIDING HOOD Big Bopper—Mercury 71375
[J.P. Richardson] [BMI] (11/24/58 BCR-63)

LITTLE RED ROOSTER Sam Cooke—RCA Victor 47-8247
[Willie Dixon] [BMI] (10/19/63 BCR-11)

A LITTLE RESPECT Erasure—Sire 27738 [Andy Bell/Vince Clarke] [ASC] (12/3/88 BC-14)

LITTLE SAINT NICK The Beach Boys—Capitol 5096
[Mike Love*/Brian Wilson] [BMI] (12/21/63 C-69)

LITTLE SANDY SLEIGHFOOT
Jimmy Dean with Ray Ellis and his Orchestra—Columbia 41025
[Philip M. Crane/Joe Savarino] [ASC] (12/9/57 BR-32)

LITTLE SERENADE *The Ames Brothers—RCA Victor 47-7268*
[Giovanni Ferrio/Geoffrey Parsons/John Turner] [ASC] (6/28/58 BCtRt-45) [FDE]

LITTLE SERENADE *Teddy Randazzo—Vik 0330*
[Antonio Amurri/Giovanni Ferrio/Geoffrey Parsons/John Turner] [ASC] (7/5/58 BCtRt-45) [FDE]

LITTLE SERENADE *The Johnston Brothers—London 1807*
[Giovanni Ferrio/Geoffrey Parsons/John Turner] [ASC] (7/14/58 Rt-50) [FDE]

LITTLE SERENADE *Ted Heath & His Music—London 1800*
[Giovanni Ferrio] [ASC] (7/14/58 Rt-50) [IM]

LITTLE SERENADE (PICCOLISSIMA SERENATA) *Eddie Calvert—ABC-Paramount 9939*
[Giovanni Ferrio] [ASC] (7/14/58 Rt-50) [IM]

LITTLE SHEILA Slade—CBS Associated 04865
[Noddy Holder/Jim Lea] [ASC] (5/4/85 B-86)

LITTLE SHOEMAKER *Hugo Winterhalter And His Orchestra—RCA Victor 47-5769*
[Francis Lemarque/Geoffrey Parsons/Rudi Revil/John Turner] [ASC] (7/3/54 BCR-2) [FET]

LITTLE SHOEMAKER *The Gaylords—Mercury 70403*
[Francis Lemarque/Geoffrey Parsons/Rudi Revil/John Turner] [ASC] (7/3/54 BCR-2) [FET]

LITTLE SISTER *Connie Stevens—Warner Bros. 5137*
[Robert I. Allen] [ASC] (1/11/60 Rt-84)

LITTLE SISTER *Cathy Carr—Roulette 4219 [Robert I. Allen] [ASC] (1/11/60 Rt-84)*

LITTLE SISTER Elvis Presley—RCA Victor 47-7908
[Doc Pomus/Mort Shuman] [BMI] (8/14/61 BCR-3)

LITTLE SPACE GIRL Jesse Lee Turner—Carlton 496
[Jesse Lee Turner] [BMI] (1/3/59 BCR-18)

LITTLE STAR The Elegants—Apt 25005
[Vito Picone/Arthur Venosa] [BMI] (6/30/58 BCR-1)

LITTLE STAR Bobby Callender—Roulette 4471
[Bobby Callender/Morris Levy‡/John Peabody] [BMI] (2/9/63 BR-58)

LITTLE SUSIE Ray Bryant Trio—Columbia 41553 / Signature 12026
[Ray Bryant] [BMI] (2/27/60 C-81) [I]

LITTLE SUZI Tesla—Geffen 28353 [James Diamond/Tony Hymas] [ASC] (5/9/87 BC-80)

LITTLE THING CALLED LOVE Neil Young—Geffen 29887
[Neil Young] [ASC] (1/29/83 BC-71)

LITTLE THINGS Bobby Goldsboro—United Artists 810
[Bobby Goldsboro] [BMI] (1/23/65 BCR-9)

LITTLE THINGS MEAN A LOT *Kitty Kallen—Decca 29037*
[Edith Lindeman/Carl Stutz] [ASC] (5/29/54 BCR-PRE)

LITTLE THINGS MEAN A LOT *Joni James—MGM 12849*
[Edith Lindeman/Carl Stutz] [ASC] (12/7/59 BCRt-35)

LITTLE THINGS MEAN A LOT *John Gary—Fraternity 858*
[Edith Lindeman/Carl Stutz] [ASC] (12/28/59 Rt-60)

LITTLE THINGS YOU DO Sam Cooke—Keen 3-2018
[James W. Alexander] [BMI] (2/16/59 R-92)

LITTLE TIN SOLDIER The Toy Dolls—Era 3093
[Fred Darian/Joseph Van Winkle] [ASC] (12/29/62 BCR-80)

LITTLE TOO LATE Pat Benatar—Chrysalis 03536 [Alex Call] [BMI] (2/5/83 BC-20)

A LITTLE TOO MUCH Clarence Henry—Argo 5408
[Robert Guidry/Clarence "Frogman" Henry*] [BMI] (1/13/62 BCR-74)

LITTLE TOWN FLIRT Del Shannon—Big Top 3131
[Maron McKenzie/Del Shannon] [BMI] (12/22/62 BCR-11)

A LITTLE TOY BALLOON Danny Williams—United Artists 729
[Lor Crane/Bernice Ross] [BMI] (6/20/64 BCR-82)

THE LITTLE TRAIN (DIE KLEINE BIMMELBAHN)
Marianne Vasel & Erich Storz—Mercury 71286
[Erich Storz] [ASC] (4/12/58 BCR-40) [F]

LITTLE TURTLE DOVE Otis Williams And His Charms—King 5455
[Lonnie Carter/Andy Gibson/Otis Williams] [BMI] (3/13/61 B-95)

LITTLE WALTER Tony! Toni! Toné!—Wing 887 385
[Denzil Foster/Thomas McElroy/Clemon Timothy Riley/Raphael Saadiq/Dwayne Wiggins] [BMI] (5/28/88 BC-47)

THE LITTLE WHITE CLOUD THAT CRIED Wayne Newton—Challenge 59238
[Johnnie Ray] [ASC] (5/2/64 B-99)

LITTLE WHITE LIES *Betty Johnson—Bally 1033*
[Walter Donaldson] [ASC] (4/29/57 BCR-40)

LITTLE WHITE LIES *The Kenjolairs—A&M 704 [Walter Donaldson] [ASC] (1/12/63 C-99)*

LITTLE WILLY The Sweet—Bell 45,251
[Mike Chapman/Nicky Chinn] [ASC] (1/20/73 BCR-3)

LITTLE WOMAN Bobby Sherman—Metromedia 121
[Danny Janssen] [BMI] (8/16/69 BCR-1)

LITTLE WOMAN LOVE Wings—Apple 1851
[Linda McCartney/Paul McCartney] (TSW) [ASC] (6/24/72 BC-28)

A LITTLE YOU Freddie And The Dreamers—Mercury 72462
[Gordon Mills] [BMI] (7/31/65 BCR-37)

LITTLE YOUNG LOVER The Impressions—ABC-Paramount 10328
[Curtis Mayfield] [BMI] (7/28/62 B-96)

LIVE The Merry-Go-Round—A&M 834 [Emitt Rhodes] [ASC] (4/1/67 BCR-57)

LIVE AND LET DIE *Wings—Apple 1863*
[Linda McCartney/Paul McCartney] [ASC] (6/30/73 BCR-1)

LIVE AND LET DIE *Guns N' Roses—Geffen 19114*
[Linda McCartney/Paul McCartney] [ASC] (12/21/91 BC-26)

LIVE EVERY MINUTE Ali Thomson—A&M 2260 [Ali Thomson] [ASC] (9/6/80 BCR-39)

LIVE EVERY MOMENT REO Speedwagon—Epic 05412
[Kevin Cronin] [ASC] (7/13/85 BC-34)

LIVE FOR LIFE Jack Jones—RCA Victor 9365
[Pierre Barouh/Norman Gimbel/Francis Lai] [BMI] (12/2/67 B-99) [FET]

LIVE FOR LOVING YOU Gloria Estefan—Epic 73962
[Emilio Estefan/Gloria Estefan/Diane Warren] [BMI] (10/12/91 BC-11)

LIVE IS LIFE Opus—Polydor 883730
[Guenter Grasmuck/Niki Gruber/Ewald Pfleger/Kurt Plisnier/Herwig Rudisser] [ASC] (1/25/86 BC-32)

LIVE IT UP Dusty Springfield—Philips 40245 [Leon Huff] [BMI] (12/19/64 CR-90)

LIVE IT UP PART 1 The Isley Brothers—T-Neck 2254
[Ernie Isley/Marvin Isley/O'Kelly Isley/Ronald Isley/Rudolph Isley/Chris Jasper] [ASC] (7/27/74 BCR-52)

LIVE IT UP Gardner Cole—Warner Bros. 27793
[Gardner Cole/Danny Sembello] [BMI] (10/15/88 BC-84)

LIVE MY LIFE Boy George—Virgin 99390
[Danny Sembello/Allee Willis] [ASC] (12/26/87 BC-40)

LIVE TO TELL Madonna—Sire 28717
[Madonna L. Ciccone/Patrick Raymond Leonard] [BMI] (4/12/86 BC-1)

LIVE WIRE Martha & The Vandellas—Gordy 7027
[Lamont Dozier/Brian Holland/Eddie Holland] [BMI] (2/8/64 BCR-34)

LIVE YOUR LIFE BEFORE YOU DIE Pointer Sisters—ABC/Blue Thumb 262
[Anita Pointer/Bonnie Pointer/Vincent Wayne] [BMI] (3/1/75 BCR-72)

LIVIN' ABOVE YOUR HEAD Jay & The Americans—United Artists 50046
[Jay Black/Marty Sanders/Kenny Vance] [BMI] (7/30/66 BCR-76)

LIVIN' AIN'T LIVIN' Firefall—Atlantic 3333 [Rick Roberts] [BMI] (6/5/76 BCR-41)

LIVIN' DANGEROUSLY The McGuire Sisters—Coral 62162
[Mack Discant/Doris Tauber] [ASC] (1/25/60 B-97)

LIVIN' FOR THE WEEKEND The O'Jays—Philadelphia Int'l 3587
[Kenneth Gamble/Cary Gilbert/Leon Huff] [BMI] (3/6/76 BCR-20)

LIVIN' FOR YOU Al Green—Hi 2257 [Al Green/Willie Mitchell] [BMI] (11/24/73 BCR-14)

LIVIN' IN DESPERATE TIMES Olivia Newton-John—MCA 52341
[Barry Alfonso/Tom Snow] [ASC] (2/11/84 BC-29)

LIVIN' IN THE LIFE The Isley Brothers—T-Neck 2264
[Ernie Isley/Marvin Isley/O'Kelly Isley/Ronald Isley/Rudolph Isley/Chris Jasper] [ASC] (6/18/77 BCR-40)

LIVIN' IN THE LIGHT Caron Wheeler—EMI 50286
[Nathaniel Hall/Caron Wheeler] [BMI] (9/29/90 BC-45)

LIVIN' IT UP (FRIDAY NIGHT) Bell & James—A&M 2069
[Leroy Bell/Casey James] [BMI] (1/27/79 BCR-15)

LIVIN' LOVIN' MAID Led Zeppelin—Atlantic 2690
[Jimmy Page/Robert Plant] [ASC] (3/14/70 B-65)

LIVIN' ON A PRAYER Bon Jovi—Mercury 888184
[Jon Bon Jovi/Desmond Child/Richie Sambora] [ASC] (12/13/86 BC-1)

LIVIN' RIGHT Glenn Frey—MCA 53497 [Glenn Frey/Jack Tempchin] [ASC] (3/18/89 B-90)

LIVIN' THING Electric Light Orchestra—United Artists 888
[Jeff Lynne] [BMI] (10/23/76 BCR-10)

LIVING A LIE Al Martino—Capitol 5060
[Peter DeAngelis/Norma Mendoza*/Jean Sawyer] [ASC] (10/12/63 BCR-13)

LIVING A LITTLE, LAUGHING A LITTLE The Spinners—Atlantic 3252
[Thom Bell/Linda Creed] [BMI] (3/1/75 BCR-33)

LIVING AFTER MIDNIGHT Judas Priest—Columbia 11308
[Kenneth Downing/Rob Halford/Glenn Tipton] [ASC] (7/12/80 R-95)

LIVING DOLL *Cliff Richard and The Drifters—ABC-Paramount 10042*
[Lionel Bart] [BMI] (8/24/59 BCtRt-30)

LIVING DOLL *David Hill—Kapp 293 [Lionel Bart] [BMI] (8/24/59 BCtRt-53)*

LIVING EYES Bee Gees—RSO 1067
[Barry Gibb/Maurice Gibb/Robin Gibb] [BMI] (11/7/81 BCR-40)

LIVING FOR THE CITY *Stevie Wonder—Tamla 54242*
[Stevie Wonder] [ASC] (11/10/73 BCR-5)

LIVING FOR THE CITY *Ray Charles—Crossover 981*
[Stevie Wonder] [ASC] (8/30/75 BCR-71)

LIVING FOR YOU Sonny & Cher—Atco 6449 [Sonny Bono] [BMI] (11/19/66 BCR-87)

LIVING IN A BOX Living In A Box–Chrysalis 43104
[Steve Pigott/Marcus Vere] [ASC] (6/20/87 BC-17)
LIVING IN A DREAM Pseudo Echo–RCA 5125 [Brian Canham] [BMI] (3/28/87 BC-55)
LIVING IN A FANTASY Leo Sayer–Warner Bros. 49657
[Leo Sayer/Alan Tarney] [ASC] (1/24/81 BCR-21)
LIVING IN A HOUSE DIVIDED Cher–Kapp 2171 [Tom Bahler] [BMI] (5/13/72 BCR-21)
LIVING IN AMERICA James Brown–Scotti Brothers 05682
[Dan Hartman/Charles E. Kaufman] [BMI] (12/7/85 BC-4)
LIVING IN OBLIVION Anything Box–Epic 73231 [Claudio Strilio] [BMI] (2/17/90 BC-65)
LIVING IN SIN Bon Jovi–Mercury 876070 [Jon Bon Jovi] [ASC] (10/7/89 BC-9)
LIVING IN THE BACKGROUND Baltimora–Manhattan 50029
[Maurizio Bassi/Naimy Hackett] [BMI] (4/12/86 B-87)
LIVING IN THE PAST Jethro Tull–Chrysalis 2006 [Ian Anderson] [ASC] (11/4/72 BCR-11)
LIVING IN THE U.S.A. *Steve Miller Band–Capitol 2287*
[Steve Miller] [ASC] (11/9/68 BCR-72)
LIVING IN THE U.S.A. *Steve Miller Band–Capitol 3884*
[Steve Miller] [ASC] (5/18/74 BCR-38)
LIVING INSIDE MYSELF Gino Vannelli–Arista 0588
[Gino Vannelli] [BMI] (3/21/81 BCR-6)
LIVING IT DOWN Freddy Fender–ABC/Dot 17652 [Ben Peters] [BMI] (10/30/76 BCR-72)
LIVING NEXT DOOR TO ALICE Smokie–RSO 860
[Mike Chapman/Nicky Chinn] [ASC] (12/4/76 BCR-18)
LIVING ON THE EDGE Jim Capaldi–Atlantic 89799 [Jim Capaldi] [ASC] (8/27/83 BC-68)
LIVING ON VIDEO Trans-X–Atco 99534 [Pascal Languirand] [ASC] (5/10/86 BC-61) [I]
LIVING TOGETHER, GROWING TOGETHER The 5th Dimension–Bell 45,310
[Burt Bacharach/Hal David] [ASC] (1/6/73 BCR-20)
LIVING WITHOUT YOU Manfred Mann's Earth Band–Polydor 14113
[Randy Newman] [BMI] (2/26/72 BCR-69)
THE LIVING YEARS Mike + The Mechanics–Atlantic 88964
[Brian A. Robertson/Mike Rutherford] [BMI] (12/31/88 BC-1)
LIVINGSTON SATURDAY NIGHT Jimmy Buffett–ABC 12391
[Jimmy Buffett] [BMI] (8/12/78 BCR-52)
LIZZIE AND THE RAINMAN Tanya Tucker–MCA 40402
[Larry Henley/Kenny O'Dell] [BMI] (5/3/75 BCR-35)
LIZZIE BORDEN The Chad Mitchell Trio–Kapp 439
[Michael Martin Brown] [ASC] (1/27/62 BCR-35)
LO MUCHO QUE TE QUIERO (THE MORE I LOVE YOU) René & René–White Whale 287
[René Herrera/Samuel Ibarra/René Ornelas] [BMI] (11/9/68 BCR-13) [F & E]
THE LOAD-OUT Jackson Browne–Asylum 45485
[Jackson Browne/Bryan Garofalo] (TSW) [ASC] (7/1/78 BCR-20)
LOADING COAL Johnny Cash–Columbia 41804 [Merle Travis] [BMI] (10/24/60 R-94)
LOCKING UP MY HEART The Marvelettes–Tamla 54077
[Lamont Dozier/Brian Holland/Eddie Holland] [BMI] (3/9/63 BCR-44)
LOCO MOTION *Irving Ashby–Imperial 5426*
[Irving Ashby/Edward Hall] [BMI] (4/20/57 Rt-44)
LOCO-MOTION *Joe "Fingers" Carr–Capitol 3681*
[Irving Ashby/Edward Hall] [BMI] (4/20/57 Rt-44)
THE LOCO-MOTION *Little Eva–Dimension 1000*
[Gerry Goffin/Carole King] [BMI] (6/30/62 BCR-1)
THE LOCO-MOTION *Grand Funk–Capitol 3840*
[Gerry Goffin/Carole King] [BMI] (3/9/74 BCR-1)
THE LOCO-MOTION *Kylie Minogue–Geffen 27752*
[Gerry Goffin/Carole King] [BMI] (8/27/88 BC-3)
LOCOMOTIVE BREATH Jethro Tull–Chrysalis 2110
[Ian Anderson] [ASC] (2/14/76 BCR-62)
LODDY LO Chubby Checker–Parkway 890
[Dave Appell/Kal Mann] [ASC] (11/2/63 BCR-12)
LODI *Creedence Clearwater Revival–Fantasy 622*
[John Fogerty] (TSW) [BMI] (5/3/69 BCR-46)
LODI *Al Wilson–Soul City 775 [John Fogerty] [BMI] (8/23/69 BCR-58)*
THE LOGICAL SONG *Supertramp–A&M 2128*
[Rick Davies/Roger Hodgson] [ASC] (3/24/79 BCR-4)
THE TOPICAL SONG *(parody of The Logical Song) The Barron Knights–Epic 50755*
[Rick Davies/Roger Hodgson/Robert White] [ASC] (8/25/79 BCR-70) [P]*
LOLA *The Kinks–Reprise 0930 [Ray Davies] [BMI] (8/15/70 BCR-7)*
LOLA (LIVE VERSION) *The Kinks–Arista 0541 [Ray Davies] [BMI] (8/30/80 BR-81)*
LOLA'S THEME *Muir Mathieson–Columbia 40725*
[Malcolm Arnold] [ASC] (8/3/56 BRt-67) [I]
LOLA'S THEME *Ralph Marterie & His Orchestra–Mercury 70917*
[Malcolm Arnold] [ASC] (8/10/56 Rt-85) [I]
LOLA'S THEME *Steve Allen–Coral 61681 [Malcolm Arnold] [ASC] (8/18/56 B-75) [I]*
LOLITA YA-YA The Ventures–Dolton 60
[Bob Harris/Nelson Riddle] [ASC] (8/4/62 BC-61) [I]
LOLLIPOP *The Chordettes–Cadence 1345*
[Julius Dixon/Beverly Ross] [BMI] (3/3/58 BCtRt-2)
LOLLIPOP *Ronald And Ruby–RCA Victor 47-7174*
[Julius Dixon/Beverly Ross] [BMI] (3/3/58 BCtRt-2)
LOLLIPOP Vince Edwards–Capitol 3826
[David Holt/Dok Stanford] [ASC] (3/24/58 Rt*-3)
LOLLIPOP (I LIKE YOU) The Intruders–Gamble 231
[Perry Green/Bob Morgan/Leon Swanson/Arthur West] [BMI] (6/7/69 CR-96)
LOLLIPOPS AND ROSES *Jack Jones–Kapp 435 [Tony Velona] [ASC] (2/5/62 BCR-30)*
LOLLIPOPS AND ROSES *Paul Petersen–Colpix 649*
[Tony Velona] [ASC] (8/25/62 BCR-54)
LONDON TOWN Wings–Capitol 4625
[Denny Laine/Paul McCartney] [BMI] (9/9/78 BCR-39)
THE LONE RANGER Oscar Brown Jr.–Atlantic 3001
[Oscar Brown Jr.] [BMI] (5/4/74 BCR-65)
THE LONE TEEN RANGER Jerry Landis–Amy 875 [Paul Simon] [BMI] (1/19/63 BR-92)
THE LONELIEST MAN ON THE MOON David Castle–Parachute 505
[David Castle/Graham Dee] [BMI] (12/31/77 BCR-65)
THE LONELIEST NIGHT Dale & Grace–Montel 928
[Louis Mathis/Marc Mathis] [BMI] (5/2/64 BCR-64)
(LONELINESS MADE ME REALIZE) IT'S YOU THAT I NEED The Temptations–Gordy 7065
[Eddie Holland/Norman Whitfield] [BMI] (10/7/67 BCR-8)
LONELY AGAIN Eddy Arnold–RCA Victor 47-9080 [Jean Chapel] [BMI] (3/18/67 BCR-87)
LONELY BLUE BOY Conway Twitty–MGM 12857
[Ben Weisman/Fred Wise] [ASC] (12/28/59 BCR-6)
LONELY BLUE NIGHTS Rosie Formerly With The Originals–Brunswick 55205
[Rosie Hamlin] [BMI] (2/20/61 BCR-48)
LONELY BOY *Paul Anka–ABC-Paramount 10022*
[Paul Anka/Alberto Curci] [BMI] (5/23/59 BCR-1)*
LONELY BOY *Donny Osmond–MGM 14424*
[Paul Anka/Alberto Curci] (TSW) [BMI] (9/16/72 B-13)*
LONELY BOY Andrew Gold–Asylum 45384 [Andrew Gold] [BMI] (3/19/77 BCR-3)
LONELY BOY, LONELY GUITAR Duane Eddy–RCA Victor 47-8180
[Duane Eddy/Lee Hazlewood] [BMI] (5/18/63 BCR-62)
THE LONELY BULL (EL SOLO TORRO) Herb Alpert & The Tijuana Brass–A&M 703
[Sol Lake] [ASC] (10/20/62 BCR-6) [IM]
LONELY CHAIR Lloyd Price–KRC 301 [William Boskent/Lloyd Price] [BMI] (9/30/57 B-88)
THE LONELY CROWD Teddy Vann–Columbia 41996 [Teddy Vann] [BMI] (6/5/61 BC-76)
LONELY DAYS Bee Gees–Atco 6795
[Barry Gibb/Maurice Gibb/Robin Gibb] [BMI] (11/28/70 BCR-1)
LONELY DRIFTER *The O'Jays–Imperial 5976*
[Eddie Levert/Walter Williams] [BMI] (9/14/63 BCR-93)
LONELY DRIFTER *Pieces Of Eight–A&M 854*
[Eddie Levert/Walter Williams] [BMI] (6/17/67 BCR-58)
LONELY EYES Robert John–EMI America 8030 [Mike Piccirillo] [BMI] (12/1/79 BCR-37)
LONELY FEELIN' War–United Artists 50746
[Thomas Allen/Harold Brown/Morris Dickerson/Lonnie Jordan/Charles Miller/
Lee Oskar/Howard Scott] [ASC] (4/17/71 CR-71)
LONELY FOR YOU Gary Stites–Carlton 508 [Gary Stites] [BMI] (4/11/59 BCR-24)
LONELY GUITAR Annette–Buena Vista 339 [Jimmie Dodd] [ASC] (6/15/59 BCR-40)
LONELY IN LOVE Giuffria–MCA 52558
[David Glen Eisley/Gregg Giuffria] [ASC] (3/23/85 BC-57)
LONELY IS THE NAME Sammy Davis Jr.–Reprise 0673
[Bert Kaempfert/Herbert Rehbein/Carl Sigman] [BMI] (5/25/68 B-93)
LONELY IS THE NIGHT Air Supply–Arista 1-9521
[Albert Hammond/Diane Warren] [ASC] (8/9/86 BC-67)
LONELY ISLAND Sam Cooke–Keen 34009 [Eden Ahbez] [ASC] (3/3/58 BCR-30)
LONELY LIFE Jackie Wilson–Brunswick 55216
[Al Kasha/Alan Thomas] [BMI] (6/12/61 BR-80)
LONELY LIPS The Chordettes–Cadence 1259
[Teddy Powell/Louis Shelly/Sol Winkler] [ASC] (4/9/55 CR-46)
LONELY LITTLE ROBIN The Browns Featuring Jim Edward Brown–RCA Victor 47-7755
[Cy Coben] [ASC] (6/27/60 CR-42)
LONELY LONELY GIRL AM I The Velvelettes–V.I.P. 25017
[Eddie Holland/Eddie Kendricks/Norman Whitfield] [BMI] (6/12/65 C-95)
LONELY MAN Elvis Presley With The Jordanaires–RCA Victor 47-7850
[Bennie Benjamin/Sol Marcus] [ASC] (2/13/61 BCR-32)
A LONELY MAN The Chi-Lites–Brunswick 55483
[Edward Haycraft/Eugene Record] (TSW) [BMI] (9/30/72 BCR-46)
LONELY NIGHT (ANGEL FACE) Captain & Tennille–A&M 1782
[Neil Sedaka] [BMI] (1/24/76 BCR-1)
LONELY NIGHTS Bryan Adams–A&M 2359
[Bryan Adams/Jim Vallance] [BMI] (3/13/82 BC-79)
LONELY OL' NIGHT John Cougar Mellencamp–Riva 880 984
[John Mellencamp] [ASC] (8/17/85 BC-6)
LONELY ONE Duane Eddy His "Twangy" guitar and The Rebels–Jamie 1117
[Duane Eddy/Lee Hazlewood] [BMI] (1/19/59 BCR-19) [I]
LONELY ONE Kai Winding–Verve 10301
[Peter Pavey/David Whitaker] [BMI] (10/12/63 R-94)
THE LONELY ONE Special Delivery Featuring Terry Huff–Mainstream 5581
[Adrian Clements/Terry Huff] [BMI] (5/22/76 BCR-67)
LONELY PEOPLE America–Warner Bros. 8048
[Catherine Peek/Dan Peek] [ASC] (12/21/74 BCR-5)
LONELY SATURDAY NIGHT Don French–Lancer 104
[Chick Barr/Ron Bloomberg] [BMI] (4/18/59 BCR-50)

LONELY SCHOOL Tommy Shaw—A&M 2696 [Tommy Shaw] [ASC] (12/15/84 BC-57)

LONELY SCHOOL YEAR Hudson Brothers—Rocket/MCA 40464 [Bill Hudson*/Brett Hudson*/Mark Hudson/Michael Parker*/Bernie Taupin] [ASC] (10/25/75 BCR-57)

A LONELY SOLDIER Jerry Butler—Abner 1035 [Calvin Carter] [BMI] (5/21/60 C-100)

LONELY SOLDIER Mike Williams—Atlantic 2339 [Rose Mary Gaines/Hattie Leeper] [BMI] (7/2/66 BCR-59)

LONELY STREET Andy Williams—Cadence 1370 [Carl Belew/Kenny Sowder/W.S. Stevenson‡] [BMI] (9/7/59 BCR-5)

LONELY STREET Clarence Henry—Argo 5395 [Joe Bisko] [BMI] (8/7/61 BCR-51)

LONELY SUMMER Shades Of Blue—Impact 1014 [Edwin Starr] [BMI] (7/30/66 BCR-65)

THE LONELY SURFER Jack Nitzsche—Reprise 20,202 [Marty Cooper/Jack Nitzsche] [BMI] (8/3/63 BCR-31) [I]

LONELY TEARDROPS *Jackie Wilson—Brunswick 55105 [Billy Davis/Berry Gordy/Gwen Gordy*] [ASC] (11/17/58 BCR-6)*

LONELY TEARDROPS *Brian Hyland—Uni 55272 [Billy Davis/Berry Gordy/Gwen Gordy*] [BMI] (2/6/71 BCR-35)*

LONELY TEARDROPS *Narvel Felts—ABC/Dot 17620 [Billy Davis/Berry Gordy/Gwen Gordy*] [ASC] (5/8/76 BCR-62)*

LONELY TEENAGER Dion—Laurie 3070 [Alfred DiPaola/Silvio Faraci/Salvatore Pippa] [BMI] (10/10/60 BCR-12)

LONELY TOGETHER Barry Manilow—Arista 0596 [Kenny Nolan] [ASC] (3/14/81 BCR-45)

LONELY WEEKENDS Charlie Rich—Phillips Int'l 3552 [Charlie Rich] [BMI] (3/14/60 BCR-19)

LONELY WIND Kansas—Kirshner 4280 [Steve Walsh] [BMI] (1/20/79 BCR-60)

LONELY WINDS The Drifters—Atlantic 2062 [Doc Pomus/Mort Shuman] [BMI] (5/23/60 BCR-40)

—LONELY WITHOUT YOU see: IT'S A LONELY TOWN

LONELY WON'T LEAVE ME ALONE Glenn Medeiros—Amherst 317 [David Foster/Jermaine Jackson/Tom Keane/Kathy Wakefield] [BMI] (12/19/87 B-67)

LONESOME Four Tunes—Jubilee 5152 [Pat Best] [NA] (8/21/54 C-45)

LONESOME LOSER Little River Band—Capitol 4748 [David John Briggs] [BMI] (7/14/79 BCR-4)

LONESOME LOVER BLUES The Fontane Sisters—Dot 15480 [Beasley Smith/Billy Vaughn] [ASC] (7/27/56 BR-74)

LONESOME MARY Chilliwack—A&M 1310 [William A. Henderson] [BMI] (1/22/72 BCR-75)

LONESOME NUMBER ONE Don Gibson—RCA Victor 47-7959 [Don Gibson] [BMI] (11/27/61 BCR-59)

LONESOME OLD HOUSE Don Gibson—RCA Victor 47-7505 [Don Gibson] [BMI] (4/20/59 BR-58)

LONESOME POLECAT *The McGuire Sisters—Coral 61278 [Gene DePaul/Johnny Mercer] [ASC] (10/4/54 BCR-28)*

LONESOME POLECAT *Jack Pleis and His Orchestra and Chorus—Decca 29227 [Gene DePaul/Johnny Mercer] [ASC] (10/4/54 R-PRE)*

LONESOME POLECAT *Freddy Martin & His Orchestra—RCA Victor 47-5833 [Gene DePaul/Johnny Mercer] [ASC] (10/4/54 R-PRE)*

LONESOME ROAD The Wonder Who ?—Philips 40471 [Gene Austin/Nat Shilkret] [ASC] (7/22/67 BCR-62)

LONESOME TOWN Ricky Nelson—Imperial 5545 [Baker Knight] [BMI] (10/6/58 BCR-7)

LONESOME WHISTLE BLUES Freddy King—Federal 12415 [Alan Moore/Elson Teat/Rudy Toombs] [BMI] (5/22/61 B-88)

LONG AGO AND FAR AWAY James Taylor—Warner Bros. 7521 [James Taylor] [ASC] (10/2/71 BCR-15)

LONG AGO TOMORROW B.J. Thomas—Scepter 12335 [Burt Bacharach/Hal David] [ASC] (10/30/71 BCR-57)

LONG AND LASTING LOVE (ONCE IN A LIFETIME) Glenn Medeiros—Amherst 324 [Gerry Goffin/Michael Masser] [BMI] (8/13/88 BC-68)

LONG AND LONESOME ROAD The Shocking Blue—Colossus 116 [Robbie Van Leeuwen] [ASC] (6/6/70 BCR-62)

THE LONG AND WINDING ROAD The Beatles—Apple 2832 [John Lennon/Paul McCartney] (TSW) [ASC] (5/16/70 BCR-1)

LONG AS I CAN SEE THE LIGHT Creedence Clearwater Revival—Fantasy 645 [John Fogerty] (TSW) [BMI] (8/8/70 BCR-1)

LONG AS THE ROSE IS RED Florraine Darlin—Epic 9529 [Al Byron/Paul Evans] [ASC] (8/25/62 BCR-45)

LONG COOL WOMAN (IN A BLACK DRESS) The Hollies—Epic 10871 [Allan Clarke/Roger Cook/Roger Greenaway] [ASC] (6/17/72 BCR-1)

LONG DARK ROAD The Hollies—Epic 10920 [Tony Hicks/Kenny Lynch] [ASC] (11/4/72 BCR-24)

—LONG DISTANCE LOVE AFFAIR see: TELEFONE

LONG GONE LONESOME BLUES Hank Williams, Jr.—MGM 13208 [Hank Williams] [BMI] (1/25/64 BCR-67)

LONG GREEN The Fireballs—Atco 6651 [Lynn Easton] [BMI] (2/22/69 BCR-43)

LONG HAIRED COUNTRY BOY Charlie Daniels Band—Kama Sutra 601 [Charlie Daniels] [BMI] (5/10/75 BCR-50)

LONG HAIRED LOVER FROM LIVERPOOL Little Jimmy Osmond—MGM 14376 [Christopher Kingsley] [BMI] (4/22/72 BCR-38)

LONG HOT SUMMER Jimmie Rodgers—Roulette 4045 [Sammy Cahn/Alex North] [ASC] (1/27/58 BCR-49)

LONG HOT SUMMER NIGHTS Wendy Waldman—Warner Bros. 8617 [Wendy Waldman] [BMI] (8/12/78 BCR-76)

LONG LEGGED GIRL (WITH THE SHORT DRESS ON) Elvis Presley With The Jordanaires—RCA Victor 47-9115 [J. Leslie McFarland/Winfield Scott] [BMI] (5/13/67 BCR-35)

LONG LINE RIDER Bobby Darin—Direction 350 [Bobby Darin] [BMI] (12/28/68 BCR-52)

LONG LIVE LOVE Sandie Shaw—Reprise 0375 [Chris Frederick Andrews] [BMI] (6/12/65 BC-88)

LONG LIVE OUR LOVE The Shangri-Las—Red Bird 10-048 [Sid Barnes/J.J. Jackson] [BMI] (1/29/66 BCR-33)

LONG LIVE ROCK The Who—MCA 41053 [Pete Townshend] [BMI] (6/30/79 BCR-54)

LONG LONELY NIGHTS *Clyde McPhatter—Atlantic 1149 [Lee Andrews/Bernice Davis/Douglas Henderson/Miriam Uniman] [BMI] (7/20/57 BCtRt-24)*

LONG LONELY NIGHTS *Lee Andrews And The Hearts—Chess 1665 [Lee Andrews/Bernice Davis/Douglas Henderson/Miriam Uniman] [BMI] (7/20/57 BCtRt-24)*

LONG, LONELY NIGHTS *The Kings (2)—Baton 245 [Lee Andrews/Bernice Davis/Douglas Henderson/Miriam Uniman] [BMI] (7/20/57 Rt-32)*

LONG LONELY NIGHTS *Kitty Kallen—Decca 30404 [Lee Andrews/Bernice Davis/Douglas Henderson/Miriam Uniman] [BMI] (8/3/57 Rt-24)*

LONG LONELY NIGHTS *The 4 Seasons—Vee-Jay 597 [Lee Andrews/Bernice Davis/Douglas Henderson/Miriam Uniman] [BMI] (6/6/64 C-74)*

LONG LONELY NIGHTS *Bobby Vinton—Epic 9768 [Lee Andrews/Bernice Davis/Douglas Henderson/Miriam Uniman] [BMI] (3/6/65 BCR-12)*

LONG LONELY NIGHTS *The Dells—Cadet 5672 [Lee Andrews/Bernice Davis/Douglas Henderson/Miriam Uniman] [BMI] (7/11/70 BCR-60)*

LONG LONESOME HIGHWAY Michael Parks—MGM 14104 [James Richard Hendricks] [BMI] (2/28/70 BCR-13)

LONG LONG TIME Linda Ronstadt—Capitol 2846 [Gary B. White] [ASC] (8/15/70 BCR-21)

LONG, LONG WAY FROM HOME Foreigner—Atlantic 3439 [Lou Gramm/Michael Leslie Jones/Ian McDonald] [ASC] (12/10/77 BCR-20)

—LONG NIGHTS see: BLUE COLLAR MAN

LONG PROMISED ROAD The Beach Boys—Brother/Reprise 1047 [Jack Rieley/Carl Wilson] [BMI] (10/30/71 BCR-79)

THE LONG RUN Eagles—Asylum 46569 [Glenn Frey/Don Henley] [ASC] (12/1/79 BCR-4)

LONG STROKE ADC Band—Cotillion 44243 [Curtis Hobson/Michael Judkins/James Maddox/Artwell Matthews/ Kaiya Matthews/Mark Patterson] [BMI] (11/25/78 R-84)

LONG TALL GLASSES (I CAN DANCE) Leo Sayer—Warner Bros. 8043 [David Courtney/Leo Sayer] [ASC] (2/22/75 BCR-6)

LONG TALL SALLY *Little Richard—Specialty 572 [Robert Blackwell/Enotris Johnson/Richard Penniman] [BMI] (3/30/56 BCtRt-5)*

LONG TALL SALLY *Pat Boone—Dot 15457 [Robert Blackwell/Enotris Johnson/Richard Penniman] [BMI] (3/31/56 BCtRt-5)*

LONG TALL SALLY *Cat Mother And The All Night News Boys—Polydor 14002 [Robert Blackwell/Enotris Johnson/Richard Penniman] (Med) [BMI] (6/21/69 BCR-12)*

LONG TALL SHORTY Tommy Tucker—Checker 1075 [Herb Abramson/Don Covay] [BMI] (5/16/64 BR-82)

LONG TALL TEXAN Murry Kellum—M.O.C. 653 [Henry Strzelecki] [ASC] (11/9/63 BCR-51)

LONG TIME Boston—Epic 50329 [Tom Scholz] [ASC] (1/22/77 BCR-12)

A LONG TIME, A LONG WAY TO GO Runt--Todd Rundgren—Ampex 31004 [Todd Rundgren] [BMI] (9/4/71 BR-86)

LONG TIME LOVIN' YOU McGuffey Lane—Atco 7319 [John Schwab] [BMI] (1/17/81 BC-85)

LONG TIME TO BE ALONE The New Colony Six—Sunlight 1004 [Jerry Kollenburg/Pat McBride/Ronnie Rice] [BMI] (12/11/71 BR-93)

LONG TRAIN RUNNIN' The Doobie Brothers—Warner Bros. 7698 [Tom Johnston] [BMI] (4/21/73 BCR-8)

THE LONG WAY AROUND Linda Ronstadt—Capitol 3021 [Kenny Edwards] (TSW) [BMI] (1/23/71 BCR-70)

THE LONG WAY HOME Neil Diamond—Bang 703 [Neil Diamond] [SE] (7/7/73 BCR-67)

LONG WAY TO LOVE Britny Fox—Columbia 07926 [Dean Davidson] [BMI] (10/1/88 B-100)

LONGER Dan Fogelberg—Full Moon/Epic 50824 [Dan Fogelberg] [ASC] (12/15/79 BCR-1)

THE LONGER YOU WAIT Gino Vannelli—Arista 0664 [Gino Vannelli] [BMI] (3/6/82 B-89)

THE LONGEST DAY Mitch Miller With His Orchestra and Chorus—Columbia 42585 [Paul Anka] [BMI] (11/10/62 C-86)

THE LONGEST TIME Billy Joel—Columbia 04400 [Billy Joel] [ASC] (3/24/84 BC-10)

LONGEST WALK Jaye P. Morgan—RCA Victor 47-6182 [Edward Pola/Fred Spielman] [ASC] (7/4/55 BCR-5)

LONGFELLOW SERENADE Neil Diamond—Columbia 10043
[Neil Diamond] [SE] (10/5/74 BCR-4)
THE LOOK Roxette—EMI 50190 [Per Gessle] [BMI] (2/11/89 BC-1)
LOOK AGAIN Roger Williams—Kapp 545 [André Previn] [ASC] (8/17/63 R-86) [IM]
LOOK AT 'ER *Ralph Young—Epic 9206 [Bob Merrill] [ASC] (5/4/57 Rt-79)*
LOOK AT 'ER *Tony Martin—RCA Victor 47-6888 [Bob Merrill] [ASC] (5/4/57 Rt-79)*
LOOK AT 'ER *Tommy Leonetti with The Ray Ellis Orchestra—Vik 0270*
[Bob Merrill] [ASC] (5/4/57 Rt-79)
LOOK AT GRANNY RUN, RUN Howard Tate—Verve 10464
[Jerry Ragovoy/Mort Shuman] [BMI] (12/17/66 BCR-61)
LOOK AT ME Dobie Gray—Cordak 1602 [Johnny Cole] [ASC] (1/12/63 B-91)
LOOK AT ME GIRL Bobby Vee And The Strangers—Liberty 55877
[James L. Williams] [BMI] (7/2/66 BCR-52)
LOOK AT ME (I'M IN LOVE) The Moments—Stang 5060
[Al Goodman/Walter Lee Morris/Harry Ray] [BMI] (5/31/75 BCR-39)
LOOK AT MINE Petula Clark—Warner Bros.-Seven Arts 7310
[Tony Hatch/Jackie Trent] [ASC] (7/26/69 BCR-62)
LOOK AT THAT CADILLAC Stray Cats—EMI America 8194
[Brian Setzer] [BMI] (1/28/84 BC-68)
LOOK AT YOU George McCrae—TK 1011
[Harry Wayne Casey/Rick Finch] [BMI] (5/17/75 BC-79)
LOOK AWAY Garnet Mimms—United Artists 773
[Bert Berns/Jerry Ragovoy] [BMI] (10/10/64 BCR-73)
LOOK AWAY The Ozark Mountain Daredevils—A&M 1623
[Randle Chowning] [BMI] (10/26/74 CR-88)
LOOK AWAY Big Country—Mercury 884645
[William Stuart Adamson] [BMI] (7/26/86 C-82)
LOOK AWAY Chicago—Reprise/Full Moon 27766 [Diane Warren] [ASC] (9/24/88 BC-1)
LOOK FOR A STAR *Deane Hawley—Dore 554 [Tony Hatch] [ASC] (6/20/60 BCtRt-13)*
LOOK FOR A STAR *Garry Miles—Liberty 55261 [Tony Hatch] [ASC] (6/20/60 BCtRt-13)*
LOOK FOR A STAR *Nicky Como—Laurie 3061 [Tony Hatch] [ASC] (7/16/60 Ct-13)*
LOOK FOR A STAR *Billy Vaughn And His Orchestra—Dot 16106*
[Tony Hatch] [ASC] (6/20/60 BCtRt-13) [IWM]
LOOK FOR A STAR PART ONE *Garry Mills—Imperial 5674*
[Tony Hatch] [ASC] (6/20/60 BCtRt-13)
LOOK FOR MY TRUE LOVE Bobby Darin—Atco 6196
[Bobby Darin] [BMI] (5/29/61 R-100)
LOOK, HERE COMES THE SUN The Sunshine Company—Imperial 66280
[John Boylan/Terence Boylan] [BMI] (2/3/68 BCR-56)
LOOK HOMEWARD ANGEL *The Four Esquires—London 1652*
[Wally Gold] [ASC] (4/28/56 BCR-46)
LOOK HOMEWARD ANGEL *Johnnie Ray—Columbia 40803*
[Wally Gold] [ASC] (1/12/57 BCR-34)
LOOK HOMEWARD ANGEL *The Monarchs—Sound Stage 7 2516*
[Wally Gold] [ASC] (2/15/64 BCR-47)
LOOK IN MY EYES *The Chantels—Carlton 555 [Richard Barrett] [BMI] (8/28/61 BCR-14)*
LOOK IN MY EYES *The 3° Degrees—Swan 4235 [Richard Barrett] [BMI] (1/1/66 BCR-97)*
LOOK IN MY EYES PRETTY WOMAN Tony Orlando And Dawn—Bell 45,620
[Dennis Lambert/Brian Potter] [BMI] (12/14/74 BCR-11)
LOOK INTO MY EYES George LaMond—Columbia 73486
[Phillip Andreula/Dominic Marabeti] [ASC] (8/18/90 BC-60)
LOOK INTO YOUR HEART Aretha Franklin—Atlantic 3373
[Curtis Mayfield] [BMI] (2/5/77 BCR-75)
LOOK-KA PY PY The Meters—Josie 1015
[Joseph Modeliste/Art Neville/Leo Nocentelli/George Porter] [BMI]
(12/6/69 BCR-53) [I]
LOOK MY WAY The Vels—Mercury 880547
[Alice DeSoto/Charles Hanson/Chris Larkin] [ASC] (2/23/85 BC-71)
LOOK OF LOVE Lesley Gore—Mercury 72372
[Jeff Barry/Ellie Greenwich] [BMI] (12/26/64 BCR-20)
THE LOOK OF LOVE *Dusty Springfield—Philips 40465*
[Burt Bacharach/Hal David] [ASC] (7/22/67 BCR-22)
THE LOOK OF LOVE *Sergio Mendes & Brasil '66—A&M 924*
[Burt Bacharach/Hal David] [ASC] (5/11/68 BCR-4)
THE LOOK OF LOVE *Isaac Hayes—Enterprise 9028*
[Burt Bacharach/Hal David] [ASC] (2/13/71 BCR-68)
THE LOOK OF LOVE - PART ONE ABC—Mercury 76168
[Martin Fry/David Gerald Palmer/Stephen Singleton/Mark White] [BMI] (9/11/82 BC-9)
LOOK OUT Ted Taylor—Top Rank 2076 [Ted Taylor] [BMI] (12/3/60 C-95)
LOOK OUT ANY WINDOW Bruce Hornsby & The Range—RCA 8678
[Bruce Hornsby/John Hornsby] [ASC] (7/23/88 BC-35)
LOOK OVER YOUR SHOULDER The O'Jays—Bell 704
[George Kerr/Larry Roberts] [BMI] (6/15/68 BCR-72)
LOOK SHARP—BE SHARP Boston Pops Orchestra—RCA Victor 49-4219
[Mahlon Merrick] [BMI] (8/7/54 C-27)
LOOK THROUGH ANY WINDOW The Hollies—Imperial 66134
[Graham Gouldman/Charles Silverman] [ASC] (11/20/65 BCR-32)
LOOK THROUGH MY WINDOW The Mamas & The Papas—Dunhill 4050
[John Phillips] [ASC] (10/22/66 BCR-14)
LOOK TO YOUR HEART Georgie Shaw—Decca 29679
[Sammy Cahn/Jimmy Van Heusen] [ASC] (9/19/55 R-72)
LOOK TO YOUR SOUL Johnny Rivers—Imperial 66286
[James Richard Hendricks] [BMI] (3/30/68 BCR-22)
LOOK UP Patrice Rushen—Elektra 47067
[Sheree Brown/Charles Mims/Patrice Rushen] [ASC] (12/13/80 CR-88)
LOOK WHAT THEY'VE DONE TO MY SONG MA
The New Seekers Featuring Eve Graham—Elektra 45699
[Melanie Safka] [ASC] (8/29/70 BCR-8)
LOOK WHAT THEY'VE DONE TO MY SONG, MA *Ray Charles—ABC/TRC 11329*
[Melanie Safka] [ASC] (7/1/72 BCR-49)
LOOK WHAT WE HAVE JOINED TOGETHER Sugar Blues—Bell 766
[Edward S. Thomas Jr.] [BMI] (3/22/69 R-94)
LOOK WHAT YOU DONE FOR ME Al Green—Hi 2211
[Al Green/Al Jackson/Willie Mitchell] [BMI] (3/25/72 BCR-3)
LOOK WHAT YOU'VE DONE Pozo-Seco Singers—Columbia 43927
[Wes Farrell/Bob Johnston] [BMI] (12/17/66 BCR-32)
LOOK WHAT YOU'VE DONE TO ME Boz Scaggs—Columbia 11349
[David Foster/Boz Scaggs] [ASC] (8/23/80 BCR-13)
LOOK WHAT YOU'VE DONE TO MY HEART Marilyn McCoo & Billy Davis Jr.—ABC 12298
[John Footman/Theresa McFaddin/Frank Edward Wilson] [BMI] (8/13/77 BCR-51)
LOOK WHO'S BLUE Don Gibson—RCA Victor 47-7330
[Don Gibson] [BMI] (9/27/58 BCR-57)
LOOKIN' BACK Bob Seger—Capitol 3187 [Bob Seger] [ASC] (10/30/71 BCR-95)
LOOKIN' FOR LOVE Ray Conniff And The Singers—Columbia 43814
[Johnny Rotella] [ASC] (10/8/66 B-94)
LOOKIN' FOR LOVE Johnny Lee—Full Moon/Asylum 47004
[Wanda Mallette/Bob Morrison/Patti Ryan] [ASC] (7/12/80 BCR-4)
LOOKIN' OUT FOR #1 Bachman-Turner Overdrive—Mercury 73784
[Randy Bachman] [BMI] (4/24/76 BC-65)
LOOKIN' OUT MY BACK DOOR Creedence Clearwater Revival—Fantasy 645
[John Fogerty] (TSW) [BMI] (8/8/70 BCR-1)
LOOKIN' THROUGH THE WINDOWS The Jackson 5—Motown 1205
[Clifton Davis] [ASC] (7/8/72 BCR-15)
LOOKING BACK *Nat "King" Cole—Capitol 3939*
[Brook Benton/Belford Hendricks/Clyde Otis] [BMI] (4/5/58 BCR-6)
LOOKING BACK *Dinah Washington—Mercury 71744*
[Brook Benton/Belford Hendricks/Clyde Otis] [BMI] (12/31/60 C-92)
LOOKING BACK *Joe Simon—Sound Stage 7 2622*
[Brook Benton/Belford Hendricks/Clyde Otis] [BMI] (12/7/68 BCR-70)
LOOKING FOR A FOX Clarence Carter—Atlantic 2461
[Clarence Carter/Marcus Daniel/Rick Hall/Wilbur Terrell] [BMI] (1/20/68 BCR-62)
LOOKIN' FOR A LOVE *The Valentinos—SAR 132*
[James W. Alexander/Zelda Samuels] [BMI] (8/18/62 BCR-63)
LOOKING FOR A LOVE *The J. Geils Band—Atlantic 2844*
[James W. Alexander/Zelda Samuels] [BMI] (11/27/71 BCR-30)
LOOKIN' FOR A LOVE *Bobby Womack—United Artists 375*
[James W. Alexander/Zelda Samuels] [BMI] (2/2/74 BCR-8)
LOOKING FOR A NEW LOVE Jody Watley—MCA 52956
[André Cymone/Jody Watley] [ASC] (3/7/87 BC-2)
LOOKING FOR A STRANGER Pat Benatar—Chrysalis 42688
[Franne Golde/Peter Mclan] [BMI] (4/23/83 BC-39)
LOOKING FOR LOVE Connie Francis—MGM 13256
[Hank Hunter/Stan Vincent] [BMI] (7/18/64 BCR-34)
LOOKING FOR SPACE John Denver—RCA Victor 10586
[John Denver] [ASC] (2/28/76 BCR-18)
LOOKING OVER MY SHOULDER til tuesday—Epic 04936
[Michael Hausman/Robert Holmes/Aimee Mann/Joey Pesce] [ASC] (8/24/85 BC-61)
LOOKING THROUGH THE EYES OF LOVE *Gene Pitney—Musicor 1103*
[Barry Mann/Cynthia Weil] [BMI] (7/24/65 BCR-23)
LOOKING THROUGH THE EYES OF LOVE
The Partridge Family Starring Shirley Jones & Featuring David Cassidy—Bell 45,301
[Barry Mann/Cynthia Weil] [BMI] (12/2/72 BCR-25)
LOOKING WITH MY EYES Dionne Warwick—Scepter 12111
[Burt Bacharach/Hal David] [ASC] (10/2/65 BCR-64)
LOOKS LIKE LOVE AGAIN Dann Rogers—IA 500 [Dana Merino] [ASC] (12/15/79 BCR-41)
LOOKS LIKE WE MADE IT Barry Manilow—Arista 0244
[Will Jennings/Richard Kerr] [BMI] (5/7/77 BCR-1)
LOOKS THAT KILL Mötley Crüe—Elektra 69756 [Nikki Sixx] [ASC] (1/28/84 BC-49)
LOOKY LOOKY (LOOK AT ME GIRL) The O'Jays—Neptune 31
[Kenneth Gamble/Leon Huff] [BMI] (8/22/70 BC-97)
THE LOOP Johnny Lytle—Tuba 2004 [Johnny Lytle] [BMI] (1/15/66 BCR-77) [I]
LOOP DE LOOP *Johnny Thunder—Diamond 129*
[Joe Dong/Teddy Vann] [BMI] (12/22/62 BCR-4)*
LOOP DE LOOP *Soul Sisters—Sue 107 [Joe Dong*/Teddy Vann] [BMI] (8/22/64 R-99)*
LOOSE BOOTY Sly & The Family Stone—Epic 50033
[Sylvester Stewart] [BMI] (10/19/74 BC-84)
THE LORD IS A BUSY MAN *The Merry Macs—Era 1007*
[Ray (2) Allen/Jerry Joyce] [BMI] (11/21/55 Rt-14)

THE LORD IS A BUSY MAN *Steve Lawrence—Coral 61537 [Ray (2) Allen/Jerry Joyce] [BMI] (11/21/55 Rt-14)*

THE LORD IS A BUSY MAN *Nan Wynn—RCA Victor 47-6336 [Ray (2) Allen/Jerry Joyce] [BMI] (12/1/55 Rt-14)*

THE LORD IS A BUSY MAN *Mahalia Jackson—Columbia 40610 [Ray (2) Allen/Jerry Joyce] [BMI] (12/9/55 Rt-38)*

THE LORD IS A BUSY MAN *Ralph Young—Decca 29741 [Ray (2) Allen/Jerry Joyce] [BMI] (12/9/55 Rt-38)*

THE LORD KNOWS I'M DRINKING Cal Smith—Decca 33040 [Bill Anderson] [BMI] (3/10/73 BCR-64)

LORD, MR. FORD Jerry Reed—RCA Victor 74-0960 [Dick Feller] [BMI] (6/30/73 BCR-52)

THE LORD'S PRAYER Sister Janet Mead—A&M 1491 [Arnold Strals/Traditional] [ASC] (2/9/74 BCR-4)

LORELEI Styx—A&M 1786 [Dennis DeYoung/James Young] [ASC] (2/14/76 BCR-27)

LOSE AGAIN Linda Ronstadt—Asylum 45402 [Karla Bonoff] [BMI] (6/4/77 B-76)

LOSE HER Bobby Rydell—Cameo 209 [Dave Appell/Bernie Lowe/Kal Mann] [ASC] (2/10/62 BCR-49)

THE LOSER The Skyliners—Jubilee 5506 [Debora Losak/Sharon Vanselow] [BMI] (6/26/65 BCR-42)

THE LOSER (WITH A BROKEN HEART) Gary Lewis And The Playboys—Liberty 55949 [Don Nix/Leon Russell] [BMI] (3/4/67 BCR-31)

LOSERS WEEPERS - PART I Etta James—Cadet 5676 [Leon Bonds] [BMI] (10/3/70 BCR-74)

LOSING MY RELIGION R.E.M.—Warner Bros. 19392 [Bill Berry/Peter Buck/Mike Mills/Michael Stipe] [BMI] (3/30/91 BC-4)

LOSING YOU Brenda Lee—Decca 31478 [Jean Renard/Carl Sigman] [ASC] (4/6/63 BCR-5) [FDE]

LOSING YOU Dusty Springfield—Philips 40270 [Tom Springfield/Clive Westlake] [ASC] (2/27/65 BCR-75)

LOSING YOUR LOVE Jim Reeves—RCA Victor 47-7950 [Bill Anderson/Buddy Killen] [BMI] (10/30/61 BR-65)

LOST Jerry Butler with Riley Hampton's Orchestra—Abner 1045 [Cortez Bateza/Alonzo Tucker/Theodore J. Twiggs] [BMI] (2/14/59 C-83)

LOST Jerry Butler—Mercury 72764 [Jerry Butler/Kenneth Gamble/Leon Huff] [BMI] (12/23/67 BCR-52)

LOST HER IN THE SUN John Stewart—RSO 1016 [John Stewart] [BMI] (12/8/79 BCR-34)

LOST HORIZON Shawn Phillips—A&M 1405 [Burt Bacharach/Hal David] [ASC] (2/10/73 BCR-63)

LOST IN EMOTION Lisa Lisa And Cult Jam—Columbia 07267 [Curtis Bedeau/Gerard Charles/Hugh Clarke/Brian George/Lucien George/Paul George] [BMI] (8/1/87 BC-1)

LOST IN LOVE Air Supply—Arista 0479 [Graham Russell] [BMI] (2/9/80 BCR-2)

LOST IN LOVE New Edition—MCA 52553 [Russ Kramer] [ASC] (3/30/85 BC-35)

LOST IN THE SHUFFLE Jaye P. Morgan—RCA Victor 47-6505 [Pat Mellin/Robert Mellin] [BMI] (5/26/56 B-69)

LOST IN YOU Rod Stewart—Warner Bros. 27927 [Rod Stewart/Andy Taylor] [ASC] (5/7/88 BC-12)

LOST IN YOUR EYES Debbie Gibson—Atlantic 88970 [Debbie Gibson] [ASC] (1/21/89 BC-1)

LOST IN YOUR LOVE John Paul Young—Scotti Brothers 405 [Harry Vanda/George Young] [ASC] (12/9/78 BCR-55)

LOST JOHN Lonnie Donegan and the Skiffle Group—Mercury 70872 [Traditional] [NA] (6/9/56 BCR-45)

LOST LOVE H.B. Barnum—Eldo 111 [H.B. Barnum] [BMI] (1/9/61 BCR-35) [I]

THE LOST PENNY Brook Benton—Mercury 71912 [J.T. Adams] [BMI] (1/8/62 BCR-72)

LOST SOMEONE *James Brown And The Famous Flames—King 5573 [James Brown/Bobby Byrd/Lloyd Stallworth] [BMI] (12/18/61 BCR-40)*

LOST SOMEONE *James Brown And The Famous Flames—King 6020 [James Brown/Bobby Byrd/Lloyd Stallworth] [BMI] (2/5/66 B-94)*

LOST SOUL Bruce Hornsby & The Range—RCA 2704 [Bruce Hornsby] [ASC] (10/27/90 B-84)

LOST WITHOUT YOUR LOVE Bread—Elektra 45365 [David Gates] [ASC] (11/20/76 BCR-9)

LOTTA LOVE Nicolette Larson—Warner Bros. 8664 [Frank Sampedro*/Neil Young] [ASC] (11/25/78 BCR-8)

LOTTA LOVIN' Gene Vincent and His Blue Caps—Capitol 3763 [Bernice Bedwell] [BMI] (8/17/57 BCR-10)

LOUDER THAN LOVE TKA—Tommy Boy 7998 [Joey Gardner/Mac Quayle/Louis Sharpe] [BMI] (8/10/91 B-62)

LOUELLA Pat Boone—Dot DEP-1057 [Harold Adamson/Jimmy McHugh] (EP) [ASC] (9/9/57 R-61)

LOUIE LOUIE *Paul Revere And The Raiders—Columbia 42814 [Richard Berry] [BMI] (11/9/63 Ct-1)*

LOUIE LOUIE *The Kingsmen—Wand 143 [Richard Berry] [BMI] (11/9/63 BCtR-1)*

LOUIE LOUIE *Travis Wammack—Atlantic 2322 [Richard Berry] [BMI] (3/26/66 C-88) [IWM]*

LOUIE LOUIE *The Kingsmen—Wand 143 [Richard Berry] [BMI] (4/23/66 BCR-65)*

LOUIE, LOUIE *The Sandpipers—A&M 819 [Richard Berry/Nick DeCaro/Carlos Ortega] [BMI] (10/15/66 BCR-30) [F]*

LOUIE, LOUIE *John Belushi—MCA 40950 [Richard Berry] [BMI] (9/30/78 BCR-89)*

LOUIE, LOUIE *Fat Boys—Tin Pan Apple 871 010 [Richard Berry] [BMI] (10/15/88 B-89)*

LOUISIANA LADY New Riders Of The Purple Sage—Columbia 45469 [John C. Dawson] [ASC] (10/30/71 C-100)

LOUISIANA LOU AND THREE CARD MONTY JOHN The Allman Brothers Band—Capricorn 0246 [Dickey Betts] (TSW) [BMI] (11/15/75 BR-67)

LOUISIANA MAMA Gene Pitney—Musicor 1006 [Gene Pitney] [BMI] (5/13/61 C-88)

LOUISIANA MAN *Rusty & Doug—Hickory 1137 [Billy Deaton‡/Doug Kershaw] [BMI] (7/3/61 R-97)*

LOUISIANA MAN *Pozo Seco Singers—Columbia 44263 [Billy Deaton‡/Doug Kershaw] [BMI] (9/16/67 B-97)*

LOUISIANA MAN *Bobbie Gentry—Capitol 2147 [Billy Deaton‡/Doug Kershaw] [BMI] (4/13/68 BCR-88)*

LOUISIANNA Mike Kennedy—ABC 11309 [Fernando Arbex] [ASC] (3/4/72 BCR-60)

LOVE The Lettermen—Capitol 3192 [John Lennon] [GL] (10/2/71 BCR-34)

LOVE ACTION (I BELIEVE IN LOVE) The Human League—A&M/Virgin 2425 [Ian Burden/Philip Oakey] [ASC] (8/14/82 C-77)

LOVE AGAIN John Denver—RCA 13931 [John Denver] [ASC] (11/10/84 B-85)

LOVE AIN'T RIGHT Kay Starr—RCA Victor 47-6541 [Hal Stanley/Irving Taylor] [BMI] (8/11/56 B-89)

LOVE ALL THE HURT AWAY Aretha Franklin—Arista 0624 [Sam Dees] [BMI] (8/29/81 BCR-43)

LOVE ALWAYS El DeBarge—Gordy 1857 [Burt Bacharach/Bruce Roberts/Carole Bayer Sager] [ASC] (8/9/86 BC-43)

LOVE AND DESIRE (PART I) Arpeggio—Polydor 14535 [Sid Barnes/Joe Cash/Simon Soussan] [BMI] (3/10/79 BCR-70)

LOVE AND EMOTION Stevie B—LMR/RCA 2645 [Warren Brooks] [BMI] (6/30/90 BC-15)

LOVE AND HAPPINESS Earnest Jackson—Stone 200 [Al Green/Mabon Hodges] [BMI] (6/2/73 BCR-58)

LOVE AND LIBERTY Laura Lee—Hot Wax 7111 [Angelo Bond/William Weatherspoon] [BMI] (1/22/72 B-94)

LOVE AND LONELINESS The Motors—Virgin 67007 [Nick Garvey/Gordon Hann] [BMI] (5/10/80 BCR-78)

LOVE AND MARRIAGE *Frank Sinatra—Capitol 3260 [Sammy Cahn/Jimmy Van Heusen] [ASC] (10/10/55 BCRt-5)*

LOVE AND MARRIAGE *Dinah Shore—RCA Victor 47-6266 [Sammy Cahn/Jimmy Van Heusen] [ASC] (10/10/55 BRt-5)*

LOVE AND MARRIAGE *Helen Grayco—"X" 0168 [Sammy Cahn/Jimmy Van Heusen] [ASC] (10/10/55 Rt-25)*

LOVE AND PRIDE King—Epic 04917 [Paul King/Mick Roberts] [BMI] (7/13/85 BC-49)

LOVE AND ROCK AND ROLL Greg Kihn—EMI America 8306 [Greg Kihn] [ASC] (3/29/86 B-92)

LOVE AND UNDERSTANDING (COME TOGETHER) Kool & The Gang—De-Lite 1579 [Robert Bell/Ronald Bell/George M. Brown/Claydes Smith/Dennis Thomas] [BMI] (3/20/76 BR-77)

LOVE AND UNDERSTANDING Cher—Geffen 19023 [Diane Warren] [ASC] (6/15/91 BC-12)

LOVE AT FIRST SIGHT Styx—A&M 1548 [Glen Burtnick/Dennis DeYoung/James Young] [ASC] (4/6/91 BC-19)

LOVE ATTACK James Carr—Goldwax 309 [Quinton Claunch/George Henry Jackson*] [BMI] (7/30/66 BC-99)

LOVE BALLAD *L.T.D.—A&M 1847 [Skip Scarborough] [BMI] (9/25/76 BCR-20)*

LOVE BALLAD *George Benson—Warner Bros. 8759 [Skip Scarborough] [BMI] (2/24/79 BCR-14)*

—LOVE BEING YOUR FOOL see: SHU-DOO-PA-POO-POOP

LOVE BITES Def Leppard—Mercury 870402 [Rick Allen*/Steve Clark/Phil Collen/Joe Elliott/Mutt Lange/Rick Savage] [ASC] (8/13/88 BC-1)

A LOVE BIZARRE Sheila E.—Paisley Park 7-28890 [Prince/Sheila E.] [ASC] (11/16/85 BC-11)

LOVE BONES Johnnie Taylor—Stax 0055 [Don Davis/Alvertis Isbell] [BMI] (12/20/69 BCR-32)

LOVE BROUGHT ME BACK D. J. Rogers—Columbia 10754 [D.J. Rogers] [ASC] (9/2/78 R-97)

LOVE BUG Jack Jones—Kapp 722 [Wayne Kemp/Curtis Wayne] [BMI] (11/27/65 BCR-56)

LOVE BUG Bumblebee Unlimited—Mercury 73864 [Patrick Adams] [ASC] (12/11/76 B-92)

LOVE BUG CRAWL Jimmy Edwards—Mercury 71209 [James Bullington/Jack Foshee] [ASC] (11/16/57 BCR-35)

LOVE BUG LEAVE MY HEART ALONE Martha & The Vandellas—Gordy 7062 [Richard Morris/Sylvia Moy] [BMI] (8/19/67 BCR-25)

LOVE CAME TO ME Dion—Laurie 3145 [Dion DiMucci/John Falbo] [ASC] (11/10/62 BCR-10)

LOVE (CAN MAKE YOU HAPPY) Mercy—Sundi 6811 [Jack Sigler] [BMI] (4/5/69 BCR-2)

LOVE CAN'T WAIT Marty Robbins—Columbia 42375 [Marty Robbins] [BMI] (4/2/62 BCR-69)

LOVE CHANGES EVERYTHING Honeymoon Suite—Warner Bros. 27935 [Johnnie Dee/Dermot Grehan/Rob Preuss] [BMI] (4/30/88 BC-89)

LOVE CHANGES (EVERYTHING) Climie Fisher—Capitol 44137 [Simon Climie/Rob Fisher/Dennis W. Morgan] [BMI] (5/14/88 BC-23)

LOVE CHILD *Diana Ross And The Supremes—Motown 1135 [Deke Richards/Pam Sawyer/R. Dean Taylor/Frank Edward Wilson] [ASC] (10/19/68 BCR-1)*

LOVE CHILD *Sweet Sensation—Atco 98983 [Deke Richards/Pam Sawyer/R. Dean Taylor/Frank Edward Wilson] [ASC] (3/17/90 BC-12)*

LOVE COME DOWN Evelyn King—RCA 13273 [Michael Jones] [BMI] (8/28/82 BC-17)

LOVE COMES QUICKLY Pet Shop Boys—EMI America 8338 [Stephen Hague/Chris Lowe/Neil Tennant] [BMI] (8/30/86 BC-56)

LOVE CORPORATION The Hues Corporation—RCA Victor 10200 [Wally Holmes] [BMI] (2/8/75 BCR-49)

LOVE CRAZY Atlantic Starr—Reprise 19150 [David E. Lewis/Wayne I. Lewis] [ASC] (11/23/91 B-75)

LOVE CRIES Stage Dolls—Chrysalis 23366 [Torstein Flakne/Bobby Icon] [BMI] (7/29/89 BC-46)

LOVE DESIRE Sandee—Fever/RAL 38-73755 [Elis Pacheco] [BMI] (6/1/91 B-49)

LOVE DON'T COME NO STRONGER (YOURS AND MINE) Jeff Perry—Arista 0133 [Leonard O. Perry/Kenny Stover] [ASC] (10/25/75 R-98)

LOVE DON'T LIVE HERE ANYMORE Rose Royce—Whitfield 8712 [Miles Gregory] [BMI] (11/11/78 BCR-18)

LOVE DON'T LOVE NOBODY - PT. I The Spinners—Atlantic 3206 [Joseph Jefferson/Charles Simmons] [BMI] (9/21/74 BCR-15)

LOVE DON'T MAKE IT RIGHT Ashford & Simpson—Warner Bros. 49269 [Nick Ashford/Valerie Simpson] [ASC] (8/23/80 R-81)

LOVE DON'T YOU GO THROUGH NO CHANGES ON ME Sister Sledge—Atco 7008 [Patrick Grant/Gwen Guthrie] [BMI] (1/4/75 B-92)

LOVE EXPLOSION Troy Keyes—ABC 11027 [Gerald Harris/George Kerr] [BMI] (1/27/68 BCR-76)

LOVE EYES Nancy Sinatra—Reprise 0559 [Lee Hazlewood] [ASC] (3/25/67 BCR-12)

LOVE FINDS ITS OWN WAY Gladys Knight & The Pips—Buddah 453 [Jim Weatherly] [ASC] (2/15/75 BCR-33)

LOVE FIRE Jigsaw—Chelsea 3037 [Des Dyer/Clive Scott] [ASC] (2/7/76 BCR-30)

LOVE FOR SALE Arthur Lyman Group—HiFi 5066 [Cole Porter] [ASC] (2/2/63 BCR-43) [IWM]

LOVE FOR YOU Sonoma—Dunhill 4365 [Charles D. Merriam] [ASC] (11/3/73 CR-79)

LOVE GETS ROUGH Troy Newman—EastWest 4-98801 [David Malloy/Troy Newman] [BMI] (6/15/91 B-92)

LOVE GONE BY Dan Fogelberg—Full Moon/Epic 50412 [Dan Fogelberg] [ASC] (7/16/77 C-75)

LOVE GONNA PACK UP (AND WALK OUT) The Persuaders—Win Or Lose 220 [Ray Lewis/Jackie Members/Richard Poindexter/Robert Poindexter] [BMI] (12/11/71 BCR-49)

LOVE GRAMMAR John Parr—Atlantic 89484 [John Parr] [BMI] (11/16/85 BC-82)

LOVE GROWS (WHERE MY ROSEMARY GOES) Edison Lighthouse—Bell 858 [Tony Macaulay/Barry Mason] [ASC] (2/14/70 BCR-4)

LOVE GUN Kiss—Casablanca 895 [Paul Stanley] [ASC] (9/24/77 BCR-55)

LOVE GUN Rick James—Gordy 7176 [Rick James] [ASC] (12/1/79 R-80)

LOVE HANGOVER *Diana Ross—Motown 1392 [Marilyn McLeod/Pam Sawyer] [ASC] (4/3/76 BCR-1)*

LOVE HANGOVER *The 5th Dimension—ABC 12181 [Marilyn McLeod/Pam Sawyer] [ASC] (4/3/76 BCR-80)*

LOVE HAS A MIND OF ITS OWN Donna Summer—Mercury 814922 [Michael Omartian/Donna Summer] [ASC] (1/14/84 BC-70)

—LOVE HAS DIED see: STAR IS BORN

LOVE HAS FINALLY COME AT LAST Bobby Womack and Patti LaBelle—Beverly Glen 2012 [Patrick L. Moten/Bobby Womack] [BMI] (3/24/84 BC-80)

LOVE HAS NO PRIDE Linda Ronstadt—Asylum 11026 [Eric Kaz/Libby Titus] [ASC] (11/24/73 BCR-45)

LOVE HAS TAKEN ITS TOLL Saraya—Polydor 889292 [Anthony Michael Bruno/Sandy Linzer*/Sandi Saraya] [BMI] (7/8/89 BC-57)

LOVE HEALS Colours—Dot 17132 [Jack Dalton/Gary Montgomery] [BMI] (8/24/68 CR-70)

LOVE HER MADLY The Doors—Elektra 45726 [John Densmore/Robby Krieger/Ray Manzarek/Jim Morrison] [ASC] (4/3/71 BCR-7)

LOVE HURTS *Nazareth—A&M 1671 [Boudleaux Bryant] [BMI] (11/15/75 BCR-8)*

LOVE HURTS *Jim Capaldi—Island 045 [Boudleaux Bryant] [BMI] (12/13/75 BC-95)*

THE LOVE I LOST (PART 1) Harold Melvin And The Blue Notes—Philadelphia Int'l 3533 [Kenneth Gamble/Leon Huff] [BMI] (9/22/73 BCR-6)

THE LOVE I SAW IN YOU WAS JUST A MIRAGE Smokey Robinson & The Miracles—Tamla 54145 [Smokey Robinson/Marvin Tarplin] [ASC] (2/18/67 BCR-20)

LOVE I YOU The Gaylords—Mercury 70350 [Sam Carlisi] [BMI] (6/5/54 B-PRE)

LOVE (I'M SO GLAD) I FOUND YOU The Spinners—Tri-Phi 1004 [Harvey Fuqua/Gwen Gordy] [BMI] (11/20/61 B-91)

LOVE IN A HOME *Doris Day—Columbia 40758 [Gene DePaul/Johnny Mercer] [ASC] (10/20/56 BRt-59)*

LOVE IN A HOME *Bing Crosby—Decca 30120 [Gene DePaul/Johnny Mercer] [ASC] (11/10/56 Rt-59)*

LOVE IN A HOME *The Crew-Cuts—Mercury 70977 [Gene DePaul/Johnny Mercer] [ASC] (11/10/56 Rt-59)*

LOVE IN A VACUUM 'til tuesday—Epic 05673 [Michael Hausman/Robert Holmes/Aimee Mann/Joey Pesce] [ASC] (11/30/85 C-88)

LOVE IN AN ELEVATOR Aerosmith—Geffen 22845 [Joe Perry/Steven Tyler] [ASC] (9/2/89 BC-5)

LOVE IN C MINOR *Heart and Soul Orchestra—Casablanca 876 [Marc Cerrone*/Alec R. Costandinos*] [BMI] (2/26/77 B-46) [IWM]*

LOVE IN 'C' MINOR - PT. 1 *Cerrone—Cotillion 44215 [Marc Cerrone*/Alec R. Costandinos] [BMI] (2/26/77 BC-36) [I]*

LOVE IN EVERY ROOM (MEME SI TU REVENAIS) Paul Mauriat And His Orchestra—Philips 40530 [Bernard Kesslair] [ASC] (5/4/68 BCR-47) [IM]

LOVE IN SIBERIA Laban—Critique 725 [Ivan Pedersen] [ASC] (11/8/86 BC-77)

LOVE IN STORE Fleetwood Mac—Warner Bros. 29848 [Christine McVie/Jim Recor] [BMI] (11/27/82 BC-22)

LOVE IN THE CITY The Turtles—White Whale 326 [Howard Kaylan/Al Nichol/Jim Pons/John Seiter/Mark Volman] [BMI] (9/20/69 BCR-48)

LOVE IN THE FIRST DEGREE Alabama—RCA 12288 [Tim DuBois/Jim Hurt] [BMI] (11/14/81 BCR-15)

LOVE IN THE FIRST DEGREE Bananarama—London 886255 [Matt Aitken/Sarah Dallin/Siobhan Fahey/Mike Stock/Pete Waterman/Keren Woodward] [BMI] (3/12/88 BC-48)

LOVE IN THE SHADOWS Neil Sedaka—Rocket/MCA 40543 [Phil Cody/Neil Sedaka] [BMI] (4/10/76 BCR-16)

LOVE IN THEM THERE HILLS The Vibrations—Okeh 7311 [Roland Chambers/Kenneth Gamble/Leon Huff] [BMI] (4/13/68 BCR-82)

THE LOVE IN YOUR EYES Eddie Money—Columbia 68532 [David Paul Bryant/Steven Dubin/Adrian Gurvitz] [ASC] (1/14/89 BC-15)

LOVE IS Maxine Starr—New Hits 3009 [Joe (2) Burke/Ralph Romano] [BMI] (9/29/62 R-92)

LOVE IS Alannah Myles—Atlantic 87945 [David Tyson/Christopher Ward] [BMI] (5/5/90 BC-32)

LOVE IS A BATTLEFIELD Pat Benatar—Chrysalis 42732 [Mike Chapman/Holly Knight] [ASC] (9/24/83 BC-4)

LOVE IS A DOGGONE GOOD THING Eddie Floyd—Stax 223 [Steve Cropper/Eddie Floyd] [BMI] (8/26/67 B-97)

LOVE IS A 5-LETTER WORD James Phelps—Argo 5499 [Gene Barge] [BMI] (5/1/65 BCR-48)

LOVE IS A GOLDEN RING Frankie Laine with The Easy Riders—Columbia 40856 [Richard Dehr/Terry Gilkyson/Frank Miller] [BMI] (3/16/57 BCR-11)

LOVE IS A HOUSE Force M.D.'s—Tommy Boy 28300 [Gina Foster/Geoff Gurd/Martin Lascelles] [BMI] (8/29/87 B-78)

LOVE IS A HURTIN' THING Lou Rawls—Capitol 5709 [Dave Linden/Ben Raleigh] [BMI] (9/3/66 BCR-13)

LOVE IS A KILLER Vixen—EMI 50332 [Harry Paress/Roxy Petrucci] [BMI] (11/3/90 BC-71)

LOVE IS A MANY SPLENDORED THING *Four Aces—Decca 29625 [Sammy Fain/Paul Francis Webster] [ASC] (8/1/55 BCtRt-1)*

LOVE IS A MANY SPLENDORED THING *Woody Herman and His Orchestra—Capitol 3202 [Sammy Fain] [ASC] (8/15/55 BRt-21) [IM]*

LOVE IS A MANY-SPLENDORED THING *Don Cornell—Coral 61467 [Sammy Fain/Paul Francis Webster] (TSW) [ASC] (9/24/55 BCtRt-1)*

LOVE IS A MANY-SPLENDORED THING *David Rose and His Orchestra—MGM 30883 [Sammy Fain] [ASC] (11/12/55 B-54) [IM]*

LOVE IS A MANY SPLENDORED THING *Don, Dick N' Jimmy—Crown 158 [Sammy Fain/Paul Francis Webster] [ASC] (12/3/55 B-96)*

LOVE IS A MANY-SPLENDORED THING *(parody of Love Is A Many Splendored Thing) The Four Preps—Capitol 4716 [Sammy Fain/Paul Francis Webster] (Med) [ASC] (3/17/62 BCR-61) [P]*

LOVE IS A ROCK REO Speedwagon—Epic 73540 [Kevin Cronin] [ASC] (10/6/90 BC-62)

LOVE IS A ROSE Linda Ronstadt—Asylum 45282 [Neil Young] (TSW) [ASC] (9/20/75 BCR-5)

LOVE IS A SACRED THING Kitty Kallen—Columbia 41236 [Ben Raleigh/Don Wolf] [ASC] (9/22/58 R-82)

LOVE IS A STRANGER Eurythmics—RCA 13618 [Annie Lennox/David A. Stewart] [BMI] (9/17/83 BC-23)

LOVE IS A TREASURE Mickey And Sylvia—Vik 0290 [Sylvia Robinson*/Carmen Taylor] [BMI] (9/16/57 R-75)

LOVE IS A WONDERFUL THING Michael Bolton—Columbia 73719 [Michael Bolton/Andy Goldmark] [BMI] (4/20/91 BC-3)

LOVE IS ALIVE Gary Wright—Warner Bros. 8143 [Gary Wright] [ASC] (4/17/76 BCR-2)

LOVE IS ALL Engelbert Humperdinck—Parrot 40076 [Barry Mason/Les Reed] [BMI] (9/22/73 BC-91)

LOVE IS ALL AROUND The Troggs—Fontana 1607 [Reg Presley] [BMI] (2/17/68 BCR-7)

LOVE IS ALL I HAVE TO GIVE The Checkmates, Ltd.—A&M 1039 [Phil Spector/Bobby Stevens] [BMI] (4/5/69 BCR-45)

LOVE IS ALL WE NEED *Tommy Edwards—MGM 12722 [Ben Raleigh/Don Wolf] [ASC] (10/20/58 BCR-8)*

LOVE IS ALL WE NEED *Vic Dana—Dolton 95 [Ben Raleigh/Don Wolf] [ASC] (6/27/64 BCR-53)*

LOVE IS ALL WE NEED *Mel Carter—Imperial 66148 [Ben Raleigh/Don Wolf] [ASC] (1/22/66 BCR-50)*

LOVE IS ALL YOU NEED High Inergy—Gordy 7157 [Clarence Drayton] [ASC] (3/4/78 B-89)

LOVE IS ALRIGHT TONITE Rick Springfield—RCA 13008 [Rick Springfield] [BMI] (12/5/81 BCR-13)

LOVE IS BETTER IN THE A.M. (PART 1) Johnnie Taylor—Columbia 10478 [Don Davis/Mel Griffin/Harvey Scales] [BMI] (2/26/77 BCR-65)

LOVE IS BLUE (L'AMOUR EST BLEU) *Paul Mauriat And His Orchestra—Philips 40495 [André Popp] [ASC] (12/30/67 BCR-1) [IM]*

LOVE IS BLUE (L'AMOUR EST BLEU) *Al Martino—Capitol 2102 [Bryan Blackburn/Pierre Lemaire/André Popp] [ASC] (2/10/68 BCR-54) [FET]*

LOVE IS BLUE (L'AMOUR EST BLEU) *Claudine Longet—A&M 909 [Pierre Lemaire/André Popp] [ASC] (2/24/68 B-71) [F]*

LOVE IS BLUE (L'AMOUR EST BLEU) *Manny Kellem, His Orchestra And Voices—Epic 10282 [Pierre Lemaire/André Popp] [ASC] (2/24/68 B-96) [F]*

LOVE IS BLUE *The Dells—Cadet 5641 [Bryan Blackburn/Pierre Lemaire/André Popp] (Med) [ASC] (5/17/69 BCR-14) [FET]*

LOVE IS CONTAGIOUS Taja Sevelle—Reprise 28257 [Taja Sevelle] [ASC] (9/12/87 BC-52)

LOVE IS FOR THE BEST IN US James Walsh Gypsy Band—RCA 11480 [Scott Fronsoe] [NA] (5/19/79 C-91)

LOVE IS FOREVER Billy Ocean—Jive 9540 [Wayne Brathwaite/Barry Eastmond/Billy Ocean] [ASC] (10/25/86 BC-16)

LOVE IS FUNNY THAT WAY Jackie Wilson—Brunswick 55461 [Lenny Crohet*/Floyd Smith/Richard Anthony Tufo] [BMI] (11/20/71 BCR-63)

LOVE IS GONNA COME AT LAST Badfinger—Elektra 46025 [Joey Molland] [ASC] (4/7/79 BCR-69)

LOVE IS HERE Ronnie Laws—United Artists 1264 [Ronnie Laws] [ASC] (12/9/78 R-63)

LOVE IS HERE AND NOW YOU'RE GONE The Supremes—Motown 1103 [Lamont Dozier/Brian Holland/Eddie Holland] [BMI] (1/28/67 BCR-1)

—LOVE IS HOT see: GOO GOO BARABAJAGAL

LOVE IS IN CONTROL (FINGER ON THE TRIGGER) Donna Summer—Geffen 29982 [Quincy Jones/Merria Ross/Rod Temperton] [BMI] (6/26/82 BC-10)

LOVE IS IN THE AIR John Paul Young—Scotti Brothers 402 [Harry Vanda/George Young] [ASC] (7/15/78 BCR-7)

LOVE IS JUST A FOUR-LETTER WORD Joan Baez—Vanguard 35088 [Bob Dylan] [SE] (4/12/69 BCR-75)

LOVE IS LIFE Earth, Wind & Fire—Warner Bros. 7492 [Wade Flemons/Maurice White/Don Whitehead] [BMI] (6/19/71 BCR-77)

(LOVE IS LIKE A) BASEBALL GAME The Intruders—Gamble 217 [Kenneth Gamble/Leon Huff] [BMI] (7/6/68 BCR-26)

LOVE IS LIKE A ROCK Donnie Iris—MCA/Carousel 51223 [Mark Avsec/Martin Lee Hoenes/Donnie Iris/Albritton McClain/Kevin Valentine] [ASC] (12/19/81 BCR-36)

LOVE IS LIKE AN ITCHING IN MY HEART The Supremes—Motown 1094 [Lamont Dozier/Brian Holland/Eddie Holland] [BMI] (4/23/66 BCR-9)

LOVE IS LIKE OXYGEN The Sweet—Capitol 4549 [Trevor Griffin/Andrew Scott] [ASC] (2/18/78 BCR-8)

LOVE IS ME, LOVE IS YOU Connie Francis—MGM 13470 [Tony Hatch] [BMI] (3/12/66 BCR-66)

LOVE IS STRANGE *Mickey & Sylvia—Groove 0175 [Mickey Baker/Ellas McDaniel/Sylvia Robinson*] [BMI] (12/22/56 BCR-7)*

LOVE IS STRANGE *The Everly Brothers—Warner Bros. 5649 [Mickey Baker/Ellas McDaniel/Sylvia Robinson*] [BMI] (8/28/65 C-96)*

LOVE IS STRANGE *Peaches & Herb—Date 1574 [Mickey Baker/Ellas McDaniel/Sylvia Robinson*] [BMI] (9/30/67 BCR-10)*

LOVE IS STRANGE *Buddy Holly / The Crickets—Coral 62558 [Mickey Baker/Ellas McDaniel/Sylvia Robinson*] [BMI] (5/3/69 CR-94)*

LOVE IS THE ANSWER Van Mc Coy & The Soul City Symphony—Avco 4639 [Luigi Creatore/Hugo Peretti/George David Weiss] [ASC] (8/3/74 CR-89) [IWM]

LOVE IS THE ANSWER England Dan & John Ford Coley—Big Tree 16131 [Todd Rundgren] [BMI] (3/10/79 BCR-10)

LOVE IS THE DRUG Roxy Music—Atco 7042 [Bryan Ferry/Andy Mackay] [BMI] (12/20/75 BCR-24)

LOVE IS THE HERO Billy Squier—Capitol 5619 [Billy Squier] [ASC] (9/27/86 BC-65)

LOVE IS THE KEY Maze—Capitol 5221 [Frankie Beverly] [BMI] (6/4/83 B-80)

LOVE IS THE MESSAGE MFSB Featuring The Three Degrees—Philadelphia Int'l 3547 [Kenneth Gamble/Leon Huff] [BMI] (6/29/74 BCR-48)

LOVE IS THE ONLY THING Mickey And Sylvia—RCA Victor 47-7877 [J. Leslie McFarland] [ASC] (5/1/61 R-95)

LOVE IS THE RITUAL Styx—A&M 1525 [Glen Burtnick/Sal Giglio Jr.] [ASC] (10/20/90 BC-74)

LOVE IS THE SEVENTH WAVE Sting—A&M 2787 [Sting] [BMI] (11/9/85 BC-17)

LOVE IS THE SWEETEST THING Saverio Saridis—Warner Bros. 5243 [Ray Noble] [ASC] (1/1/62 BCR-77)

(LOVE IS) THE TENDER TRAP *Frank Sinatra—Capitol 3290 [Sammy Cahn/Jimmy Van Heusen] [ASC] (12/1/55 BCRt-13)*

(LOVE IS) THE TENDER TRAP *Ella Fitzgerald—Decca 29746 [Sammy Cahn/Jimmy Van Heusen] [ASC] (12/1/55 Rt-38)*

(LOVE IS) THICKER THAN WATER Andy Gibb—RSO 883 [Andy Gibb/Barry Gibb] [BMI] (11/5/77 BCR-1)

LOVE IS WHAT YOU MAKE IT The Grass Roots—Dunhill 4335 [Harvey Price/Dan Walsh] [ASC] (1/27/73 BCR-27)

LOVE JONES *Brighter Side Of Darkness—20th Century 2002 [Ralph Eskridge/Clarence Johnson Jr./Randolph Murph] [BMI] (11/25/72 BCR-8)*

BASKETBALL JONES FEATURING TYRONE SHOELACES *(parody of Love Jones) Cheech & Chong—Ode 66038 [Tommy Chong/Cheech Marin] [ASC] (9/1/73 BCR-13) [P]*

LOVE KILLS Freddie Mercury—Columbia 04606 [Freddie Mercury/Giorgio Moroder] [BMI] (9/29/84 BC-61)

LOVE LAND Charles Wright And The Watts 103rd Street Rhythm Band—Warner Bros. 7365 [Luther Dixon*/James Lee*/Don Trotter/Charles Wright] [BMI] (3/28/70 BCR-16)

LOVE LETTERS *Joni James—MGM 12353 [Edward Heyman/Victor Young] [ASC] (11/17/56 R-83)*

LOVE LETTERS *Ketty Lester—Era 3068 [Edward Heyman/Victor Young] [ASC] (2/17/62 BCR-5)*

LOVE LETTERS *Elvis Presley—RCA Victor 47-8870 [Edward Heyman/Victor Young] [ASC] (6/25/66 BCR-18)*

LOVE LETTERS IN THE SAND Pat Boone—Dot 15570 [J. Fred Coots/Charles Kenny/Nick Kenny] [ASC] (5/4/57 BCR-1)

LOVE LIFTED ME Kenny Rogers—United Artists 746 [James Rowe/Howard E. Smith] [ASC] (3/13/76 B-97)

LOVE LIGHT Yutaka—Alfa 7004 [Marti McCall/Yutaka Yokokura] [ASC] (7/18/81 BC-81)

LOVE LIGHT IN FLIGHT Stevie Wonder—Tamla 1769 [Stevie Wonder] [ASC] (12/1/84 BC-16)

LOVE LIKE A FOOL *The Fontane Sisters—Dot 15682 [John Marascalco/George Motola/Hal Winn] [BMI] (1/27/58 Rt-82)*

LOVE LIKE A FOOL *The Georgettes—Ebb 125 [John Marascalco/George Motola/Hal Winn] [BMI] (1/27/58 Rt-82)*

LOVE LIKE A MAN Ten Years After—Deram 7529 [Alvin Lee] [ASC] (5/2/70 BCR-73)

LOVE LOOK AWAY Tony Bennett—Columbia 41298 [Oscar Hammerstein/Richard Rodgers] [ASC] (12/13/58 CR-83)

LOVE LOST Santo & Johnny—Canadian-American 118 [Ann Farina/Johnny Farina/Santo Farina] [BMI] (9/5/60 CR-76) [I]

LOVE LOVE LOVE *The Clovers—Atlantic 1094 [Sunny David*/Ted McRae/Sid Wyche] [BMI] (6/23/56 BCRt-20)*

LOVE LOVE LOVE *The Diamonds—Mercury 70889 [Sunny David*/Ted McRae/Sid Wyche] [BMI] (6/23/56 BRt-30)*

LOVE, LOVE, LOVE Donny Hathaway—Atco 6928 [Ralph Bailey/Ken Williams] [BMI] (6/30/73 BCR-44)

LOVE LOVE LOVE LOVE LOVE Terry Knight And The Pack—Lucky Eleven 235 [Terry Knight] [BMI] (5/20/67 R-92)

LOVE MACHINE The Roosters—Philips 40504 [Michael Gordon/James Griffin] [BMI] (4/20/68 CR-72) [IWM]

LOVE MACHINE The O'Kaysions—ABC 11153 [Thomas L. Dorsey] [BMI] (11/16/68 BCR-39)

LOVE MACHINE (PART 1) The Miracles—Tamla 54262 [Billy Griffin/Warren Moore] [ASC] (10/25/75 BCR-1)

LOVE MAKES A WOMAN Barbara Acklin—Brunswick 55379 [Carl Davis/Eugene Record/William Nelson Sanders/Gerald Sims*] [BMI] (6/29/68 BCR-9)

LOVE (MAKES ME DO FOOLISH THINGS) Martha & The Vandellas—Gordy 7045 [Lamont Dozier/Brian Holland/Eddie Holland] [BMI] (12/11/65 BCR-70)

LOVE MAKES THE WORLD GO 'ROUND Perry Como—RCA Victor 47-7353 [Ollie Jones] [BMI] (10/6/58 BCR-24)

LOVE (MAKES THE WORLD GO 'ROUND) Paul Anka—RCA Victor 47-8115 [Paul Anka] [BMI] (1/12/63 BCR-26)

LOVE MAKES THE WORLD GO ROUND *Deon Jackson—Carla 2526 [Deon Jackson] [BMI] (1/22/66 BCR-11)*

LOVE MAKES THE WORLD GO ROUND *Odds & Ends—Today 1003 [Deon Jackson] [BMI] (3/13/71 BCR-83)*

LOVE MAKES THE WORLD GO ROUND *Kiki Dee—Rare Earth 5025 [Deon Jackson] [BMI] (3/27/71 BC-87)*

—LOVE MAKES THE WORLD GO ROUND see: THEME FROM CARNIVAL

LOVE MAKES THINGS HAPPEN Pebbles—MCA 53973 [Kenneth Edmonds/Antonio Reid] [BMI] (12/1/90 BC-13)

LOVE MAN Otis Redding—Atco 6677 [Otis Redding] [BMI] (5/17/69 BCR-53)

LOVE ME *Connie Russell—Capitol 2933 [Jerry Leiber/Mike Stoller] [BMI] (10/25/54 Rt-PRE)*

LOVE ME *The Billy Williams Quartet—Coral 61264 [Jerry Leiber/Mike Stoller] [BMI] (10/25/54 Rt-PRE)*

LOVE ME *5 DeMarco Sisters—Decca 29299 [Jerry Leiber/Mike Stoller] [BMI] (10/25/54 Rt-73)*

LOVE ME *Georgia Gibbs—Mercury 70473 [Jerry Leiber/Mike Stoller] [BMI] (11/1/54 Rt-PRE)*

LOVE ME *Elvis Presley—RCA Victor EPA-992 [Jerry Leiber/Mike Stoller] [BMI] (11/17/56 BCR-6)*

LOVE ME Billy Eckstine—MGM 10982
[Ned Washington/Victor Young] [ASC] (10/25/54 Rt*-PRE)

LOVE ME Buddy Holly / The Crickets—Decca 30543
[Buddy Holly/Sue Parrish] [BMI] (1/6/58 R-80)

LOVE ME Bobby Hebb—Philips 40421
[Kenneth Gamble/Leon Huff*/Jerry J. Ross] [BMI] (12/31/66 BCR-76)

LOVE ME The Rascals—Columbia 45400
[Felix Cavaliere] [ASC] (6/26/71 BCR-74)

LOVE ME The Impressions—Curtom 1959 [Curtis Mayfield] [BMI] (7/31/71 BR-91)

LOVE ME Yvonne Elliman—RSO 858 [Barry Gibb/Robin Gibb] [BMI] (10/2/76 BCR-10)

LOVE ME AGAIN Rita Coolidge—A&M 2090
[David Lasley/Allee Willis] [ASC] (11/4/78 BC-68)

LOVE ME AGAIN John Hall Band—EMI America 8151 [John Hall] [BMI] (1/22/83 BC-64)

LOVE ME ALL THE WAY Kim Weston—Tamla 54076
[Barney Ales*/William Stevenson] [BMI] (7/6/63 BCR-65)

LOVE ME ALL UP Stacy Earl—RCA 62116
[Stacy Earl/Richard Rudolph/Danny Sembello] [ASC] (11/16/91 BC-26)

LOVE ME AS I LOVE YOU George Maharis—Epic 9522
[Gwynn Elias/Ira Kosloff/Irving Reid] [BMI] (7/21/62 BCR-54)

LOVE ME AS THOUGH THERE WERE NO TOMORROW Sonny Knight—Aura 4505
[Harold Adamson/Jimmy McHugh] [ASC] (2/6/65 B-100)

LOVE ME DO The Beatles—Tollie 9008
[John Lennon/Paul McCartney] [GL] (4/4/64 BCR-1)

LOVE ME FOR A REASON The Osmonds—MGM 14746
[Johnny Bristol/Wade Brown/David H. Jones] [ASC] (8/31/74 BCR-8)

LOVE ME FOR LIFE Stevie B—LMR 84006
[Dadgel Atabay/Stevie B*] [BMI] (2/3/90 BC-29)

LOVE ME FOR WHAT I AM Lobo—Big Tree 16,012
[Kent LaVoie] (TSW) [ASC] (12/8/73 B-86)

***LOVE ME FOREVER** Eydie Gorme—ABC-Paramount 9863*
[Beverly Guthrie/Gary Lynes] [BMI] (10/28/57 BCtRt-21)

***LOVE ME FOREVER** The Four Esquires—Paris 509*
[Beverly Guthrie/Gary Lynes] [BMI] (10/28/57 BCtRt-21)

***LOVE ME FOREVER** Roger Williams—Kapp 821*
[Beverly Guthrie/Gary Lynes] [BMI] (5/6/67 BCR-60)

LOVE ME FOREVER OR LOVE ME NOT Trilogy—Atco 98876
[Robert Clivillés/David Cole] [ASC] (3/30/91 B-82)

LOVE ME GOOD Jo Stafford—Columbia 40745
[Robert Allen/Al Stillman] [ASC] (11/17/56 B-62)

LOVE ME IN A SPECIAL WAY DeBarge—Gordy 1723 [El DeBarge] [ASC] (3/17/84 BC-45)

LOVE ME IN THE DAYTIME Doris Day—Columbia 41354
[Robert Allen/Bob Hilliard] [ASC] (4/11/59 BCR-51)

LOVE ME JUST FOR ME Special Generation—Capitol 44604
[Stanley Burrell/Chip Carter/Maurice Dowdell/Felton Pilate/Maquet Robinson/ Charles Salter/Kendrick Washington] [BMI] (12/8/90 B-91)

LOVE ME, LOVE ME LOVE Frank Mills—Sunflower 118
[Frank Mills] [ASC] (1/22/72 BCR-35)

(LOVE ME) LOVE THE LIFE I LEAD The Fantastics—Bell 45,157
[Roger Greenaway/Tony Macaulay] [ASC] (2/19/72 BCR-86)

LOVE ME MY LOVE Dean Martin—Capitol 4328
[Victor Abrams/Phil Medley] [BMI] (1/11/60 R-92)

LOVE ME NOW Brook Benton—Mercury 72446 [Brook Benton] [BMI] (7/3/65 BCR-96)

LOVE ME NOW Ruby Winters—Polydor 14249 [Paul Kelly] [BMI] (11/23/74 CR-91)

LOVE ME ONE MORE TIME (JUST FOR OLD TIMES SAKE)
Karen Nelson And Billy T—Amherst 724
[Karen Nelson/Billy Tragesser] [BMI] (8/13/77 BCR-79)

***LOVE ME OR LEAVE ME** Lena Horne—RCA Victor 47-6073*
[Walter Donaldson/Gus Kahn] [ASC] (5/2/55 CtRt-13)

***LOVE ME OR LEAVE ME** Billy Eckstine—MGM 11984*
[Walter Donaldson/Gus Kahn] [ASC] (5/2/55 Rt-32)

***LOVE ME OR LEAVE ME** Lawrence Welk & His Champagne Music—Coral 61408*
[Walter Donaldson] [ASC] (5/9/55 Rt-22) [IM]

***LOVE ME OR LEAVE ME** Sammy Davis Jr.—Decca 29484*
[Walter Donaldson/Gus Kahn] (TSW) [ASC] (6/4/55 BCtRt-9)

LOVE ME RIGHT Denise LaSalle—ABC 12312 [Denise LaSalle] [BMI] (1/14/78 BCR-80)

***LOVE ME SO I'LL KNOW** Jimmy Dean with Ray Ellis and his Orchestra—Columbia 40995*
[Paul Hampton] [ASC] (9/16/57 Rt-78)

***LOVE ME, SO I'LL KNOW** Bob Denton—Dot 15622 [Paul Hampton] [ASC] (9/16/57 Rt-78)*

***LOVE ME TENDER** Elvis Presley—RCA Victor 47-6643*
[Ken Darby/George R. Poulton/Elvis Presley] [BMI] (10/13/56 BCRt-1)

***LOVE ME TENDER** Henri René—RCA Victor 47-6728*
[Ken Darby/George R. Poulton/Elvis Presley] [BMI] (12/8/56 BRt-5) [IWM]

***LOVE ME TENDER** Richard Chamberlain—MGM 13097*
[Ken Darby/George R. Poulton/Elvis Presley] [BMI] (10/6/62 BCR-21)

***LOVE ME TENDER** Percy Sledge—Atlantic 2414*
[Ken Darby/George R. Poulton/Elvis Presley] [BMI] (6/17/67 BCR-40)

LOVE ME TO PIECES Jill Corey—Columbia 40955 [Melvin Endsley] [BMI] (8/3/57 BCR-13)

LOVE ME TOMORROW Chicago—Full Moon 29911
[Peter Cetera/David Foster] [ASC] (9/25/82 BC-22)

LOVE ME TONIGHT Tom Jones—Parrot 40038
[Barry Mason/Mario Panzeri/Lorenzo Pilat] [BMI] (5/24/69 BCR-7) [FDE]

LOVE ME TONIGHT Head East—A&M 1784 [Michael Somerville] [ASC] (2/7/76 BC-54)

LOVE ME TONIGHT Blackjack—Polydor 14572
[Michael Bolton/Bruce Kulick/Robert Kulick] [ASC] (7/14/79 BCR-62)

LOVE ME TWO TIMES The Doors—Elektra 45624
[John Densmore/Robby Krieger/Ray Manzarek/Jim Morrison] [ASC] (12/2/67 BCR-21)

LOVE ME WARM AND TENDER Paul Anka—RCA Victor 47-7977
[Paul Anka] [BMI] (2/19/62 BCR-8)

CUANDO CALIENTA EL SOL (WHEN THE SUN IS HOT)
Steve Allen And His Orchestra With The Copacabana Trio—Dot 16507
[Carlos Martinoli/Carlos Rigual/Mario Rigual] [BMI] (10/12/63 BR-80) [F]*

LOVE ME WITH ALL YOUR HEART (CUANDO CALIENTE EL SOL)
Ray Charles Singers—Command 4046
[Carlos Rigual/Sunny Skylar] [BMI] (4/11/64 BCR-3) [FDE]

***LOVE ME WITH ALL OF YOUR HEART** The Bachelors—London 9828*
[Carlos Rigual/Sunny Skylar] [BMI] (4/9/66 BCR-37) [FDE]

LOVE MEANS (YOU NEVER HAVE TO SAY YOU'RE SORRY)
Sounds Of Sunshine—Ranwood 896
[Warner Wilder] [ASC] (5/29/71 BCR-32)

LOVE MINUS ZERO - NO LIMIT Turley Richards—Warner Bros. 7376
[Bob Dylan] [SE] (3/14/70 BCR-69)

***LOVE MUSIC** Raiders—Columbia 45759*
[Dennis Lambert/Brian Potter] [BMI] (1/13/73 BCR-56)

***LOVE MUSIC** Sergio Mendes & Brasil '77—Bell 45,335*
[Dennis Lambert/Brian Potter] [BMI] (5/19/73 C-99)

LOVE MY LADY Bobby Helms—Decca 30557
[Lee Emerson/Bobby Helms] [BMI] (2/3/58 R-79)

***(I WANNA) LOVE MY LIFE AWAY** Gene Pitney—Musicor 1002*
[Gene Pitney] [BMI] (1/14/61 BCR-31)

***LOVE MY LIFE AWAY** The Hagers—Elektra 45209 [Gene Pitney] [BMI] (10/26/74 CR-79)*

LOVE MY WAY Psychedelic Furs—Columbia 03340
[John Ashton/Richard Butler/Tim Butler/Vince Ely] [BMI] (3/5/83 BC-41)

LOVE NEVER CHANGES The Chordettes—Cadence 1291
[Mary Jo Rush] [ASC] (6/8/56 R-66)

LOVE NEVER FAILS Greg Kihn Band—Beserkley 69820
[Greg Douglass/Greg Kihn/Larry Lynch/Gary Philippet/Steve Wright] [ASC] (6/4/83 BC-59)

THE LOVE OF A BOY Timi Yuro—Liberty 55519
[Burt Bacharach/Hal David] [ASC] (11/24/62 BCR-44)

LOVE OF A LIFETIME Chaka Khan—Warner Bros. 28671
[David Gamson/Green Gartside] [ASC] (7/12/86 BC-45)

LOVE OF A LIFETIME Firehouse—Epic 73771
[Bill Leverty/Carl J. Snare] [ASC] (6/29/91 BC-5)

LOVE OF MY LIFE The Everly Brothers—Cadence 1355
[Boudleaux Bryant/Felice Bryant] [BMI] (11/22/58 BCR-40)

LOVE OF MY LIFE Gino Vannelli—A&M 1861 [Gino Vannelli] [ASC] (9/4/76 BCR-57)

THE LOVE OF MY MAN Theola Kilgore—Serock 2004
[Ed Townsend] [BMI] (4/13/63 BCR-21)

A LOVE OF MY OWN Carla Thomas—Atlantic 2101 [Carla Thomas] [BMI] (5/1/61 BCR-56)

***LOVE OF THE COMMON PEOPLE** The Winstons—Metromedia 142*
[John Hurley/Ronnie Wilkins] [BMI] (9/13/69 BCR-37)

***LOVE OF THE COMMON PEOPLE** Paul Young—Columbia 04453*
[John Hurley/Ronnie Wilkins] [BMI] (5/19/84 BC-45)

LOVE ON A ROOFTOP Desmond Child—Elektra 64883
[Desmond Child/Paul Stanley*/Diane Warren] [ASC] (6/22/91 BC-34)

LOVE ON A SHOESTRING Captain & Tennille—Casablanca 2243
[Kerry Chater/Douglas Foxworthy] [BMI] (3/8/80 BCR-55)

***LOVE ON A TWO-WAY STREET** Moments—Stang 5012*
[Bert Keyes/Sylvia Robinson] [BMI] (4/4/70 BCR-3)

***LOVE ON A TWO WAY STREET** Stacy Lattisaw—Cotillion 46015*
[Bert Keyes/Sylvia Robinson] [BMI] (6/20/81 BCR-20)

LOVE ON MY MIND TONIGHT The Temptations—Gordy 1666
[Peter Beckett/Dennis Lambert] [BMI] (4/16/83 B-88)

LOVE ON THE AIRWAVES Night—Planet 47921
[Chris Thompson/Robert Watson] [ASC] (2/21/81 B-87)

LOVE ON THE PHONE Suzanne Fellini—Casablanca 2242
[Johanna Deneroff*/Suzanne Fellini/David Sonenberg/Jeff Waxman] [ASC] (3/1/80 BR-85)

LOVE ON THE ROCKS Neil Diamond—Capitol 4939
[Gilbert Bécaud/Neil Diamond] [SE] (11/1/80 BCR-2)

LOVE ON YOUR SIDE Thompson Twins—Arista 1056
[Tom Bailey/Alannah Currie/Joe Leeway] [ASC] (4/30/83 BC-45)

LOVE OR LEAVE The Spinners—Atlantic 3309
[Bruce Hawes/Joseph Jefferson/Charles Simmons] [BMI] (12/20/75 BCR-35)

***LOVE OR LET ME BE LONELY** The Friends Of Distinction—RCA Victor 74-0319*
[Jerry Peters/Anita Poree/Skip Scarborough] [BMI] (3/7/70 BCR-5)

***LOVE OR LET ME BE LONELY** Paul Davis—Arista 0697*
[Jerry Peters/Anita Poree/Skip Scarborough] [BMI] (7/17/82 BC-40)

LOVE OR MONEY The Blackwells—Jamie 1179
[Dewayne Blackwell] [BMI] (4/15/61 CR-87)

LOVE OR SOMETHING LIKE IT Kenny Rogers—United Artists 1210
[Steve Glassmeyer/Kenny Rogers] [ASC] (6/3/78 BCR-32)

LOVE OVER AND OVER AGAIN Switch—Gordy 7193
[Bobby DeBarge/Bunny DeBarge] [ASC] (12/13/80 R-80)

LOVE OVERBOARD Gladys Knight And The Pips—MCA 53210
[Reggie Calloway] [BMI] (12/26/87 BC-13)

LOVE PAINS Yvonne Elliman—RSO 1007
[Steve Barri/Harvey Price/Dan Walsh] [ASC] (10/13/79 BCR-34)

THE LOVE PARADE The Dream Academy—Reprise 28750
[Gilbert Gabriel/Nick Laird-Clowes] [BMI] (4/19/86 BC-32)

LOVE, PEACE AND HAPPINESS The Chambers Brothers—Columbia 45088
[George Chambers/Joe Chambers/Lester Chambers/Willie Chambers] [BMI] (2/28/70 B-96)

LOVE PLUS ONE Haircut One Hundred—Arista 0672
[Nicholas Heyward] [ASC] (5/15/82 BC-37)

LOVE POTION NUMBER NINE *The Clovers—United Artists 180*
[Jerry Leiber/Mike Stoller] [BMI] (8/24/59 BCR-21)

LOVE POTION NUMBER NINE *The Searchers—Kapp 27*
[Jerry Leiber/Mike Stoller] [BMI] (11/28/64 BCR-1)

LOVE POTION NUMBER NINE *The Coasters—King 6385*
[Jerry Leiber/Mike Stoller] [BMI] (12/11/71 BCR-71)

LOVE POWER *The Sandpebbles—Calla 141 [Teddy Vann] [BMI] (11/11/67 BCR-22)*

LOVE POWER *Luther Vandross—Epic 73778 [Teddy Vann] (Med) [BMI] (4/27/91 BC-4)*

LOVE POWER Willie Hutch—Motown 1360 [Frankie L. Hutchison] [BMI] (10/4/75 BCR-41)

LOVE POWER Dionne Warwick & Jeffrey Osborne—Arista 1-9567
[Burt Bacharach/Carole Bayer Sager] [ASC] (7/11/87 BC-11)

LOVE REALLY HURTS WITHOUT YOU Billy Ocean—Ariola America 7621
[Ben Findon/Billy Ocean] [BMI] (4/3/76 BCR-16)

LOVE, REIGN O'ER ME The Who—Track 40152
[Pete Townshend] [BMI] (11/17/73 BCR-54)

LOVE RESURRECTION Alison Moyet—Columbia 05411
[Steve Jolley/Alison Moyet/Tony Swain] [BMI] (7/20/85 BC-81)

LOVE ROLLERCOASTER Ohio Players—Mercury 73734
[William Beck/Leroy Bonner/Marshall Jones/Ralph Middlebrooks/Andrew Noland/Marvin Pierce/James Rodger Williams] [BMI] (11/8/75 BCR-1)

LOVE SHACK The B-52's—Reprise 22817
[Kate Pierson/Fred Schneider/Keith Strickland/Cindy Wilson] [ASC] (8/26/89 BC-3)

A LOVE SHE CAN COUNT ON The Miracles—Tamla 54078
[Smokey Robinson] [ASC] (3/30/63 BCR-31)

A LOVE SO FINE The Chiffons—Laurie 3195
[Sid Barnes/George Kerr/Mitch Margo/Phil Margo/Hank Medress/Jay Siegel] [BMI] (9/7/63 BCR-38)

LOVE SO RIGHT Bee Gees—RSO 859
[Barry Gibb/Maurice Gibb/Robin Gibb] [BMI] (9/18/76 BCR-3)

LOVE SOMEBODY Rick Springfield—RCA 13738 [Rick Springfield] [BMI] (3/10/84 BC-3)

LOVE SONG The Artistics—Brunswick 55326
[Carl Davis/Larry Johnson] [BMI] (5/27/67 CR-68)

LOVE SONG Tommy James—Roulette 7130
[Tommy James/Robert L. King] [BMI] (7/29/72 BCR-50)

LOVE SONG Anne Murray—Capitol 3776
[Dona Lyn George/Kenny Loggins] [ASC] (12/15/73 BCR-10)

A LOVE SONG Kenny Rogers—Liberty 1485 [Lee Greenwood] [BMI] (10/9/82 BC-44)

LOVE SONG The Cure—Elektra 69280
[Simon Gallup/Roger O'Donnell/Robert James Smith/Porl Thompson/Laurence Tolhurst/Boris Williams] [ASC] (8/5/89 BC-2)

LOVE SONG Tesla—Geffen 22856 [Frank Hannon/Jeff Keith] [ASC] (9/30/89 BC-9)

LOVE SONG FROM "HOUSEBOAT" (ALMOST IN YOUR ARMS) *Sam Cooke—Keen 3-2006*
[Ray Evans/Jay Livingston] [ASC] (7/21/58 Rt-76)

LOVE SONG FROM "HOUSEBOAT" (ALMOST IN YOUR ARMS)
Don Costa & His Orchestra—ABC-Paramount 9943
[Ray Evans/Jay Livingston] [ASC] (7/28/58 Rt-76) [IWM]

LOVE SONG FROM "HOUSEBOAT" (ALMOST IN YOUR ARMS)
Les Baxter & His Orchestra—Capitol 4011
[Ray Evans/Jay Livingston] [ASC] (8/11/58 Rt-80) [IWM]

LOVE SONGS ARE BACK AGAIN *Band Of Gold—RCA 13866*
[Sander Cult/Thomas Hempel/Paco Saval] (Med) [BMI] (10/13/84 BC-64)

LOVE SONGS ARE BACK AGAIN *Band Of Gold—RCA 13866*
[Sander Cult/Thomas Hempel/Paco Saval] (Med) [BMI] (10/13/84 BC-64)

LOVE STINKS The J. Geils Band—EMI America 8039
[Seth Justman/Peter Wolf] [ASC] (4/12/80 BCR-37)

LOVE STREET The Doors—Elektra 45635
[John Densmore/Robby Krieger/Ray Manzarek/Jim Morrison] [ASC] (6/29/68 C-81)

LOVE STRUCK Stonebolt—Parachute 522
[Ray Roper/Dave Wills] [BMI] (2/10/79 BCR-70)

LOVE STRUCK Jesse Johnson—A&M 3020 [Jesse Woods Johnson] [ASC] (4/23/88 BC-75)

LOVE TAKES A LONG TIME GROWING Deon Jackson—Carla 2527
[Roger Atkins/Helen Miller] [BMI] (4/30/66 BCR-72)

LOVE TAKES TIME Orleans—Infinity 50,006
[Larry Hoppen/Marilyn Mason] [BMI] (3/24/79 BCR-11)

LOVE TAKES TIME Mariah Carey—Columbia 73455
[Mariah Carey/Ben Margulies] [BMI] (9/15/90 BC-1)

LOVE THAT GOT AWAY Firefall—Atlantic 3670 [Rick Roberts] [BMI] (6/28/80 BCR-50)

LOVE THAT REALLY COUNTS Natural Four—Curtom 1995
[Michael J. Hawkins/Janice Hutson/Leroy Hutson/Joe Reaves] [ASC] (4/6/74 BR-58)

A LOVE THAT'S REAL The Intruders—Gamble 209
[Kenneth Gamble/Leon Huff] [BMI] (12/2/67 BC-82)

LOVE THE ONE YOU'RE WITH *Stephen Stills—Atlantic 2778*
[Stephen Stills] [BMI] (12/5/70 BCR-10)

LOVE THE ONE YOU'RE WITH *The Isley Brothers—T-Neck 930*
[Stephen Stills] [BMI] (6/19/71 BCR-10)

LOVE THE WORLD AWAY Kenny Rogers—United Artists 1359
[Bob Morrison/Johnny Wilson] [ASC] (6/14/80 BCR-8)

—LOVE THEME FROM "CHANCES ARE" see: AFTER ALL

—LOVE THEME FROM "FOOTLOOSE" see: ALMOST PARADISE

—LOVE THEME FROM "TOP GUN" see: TAKE MY BREATH AWAY

LOVE THEME FROM "A STAR IS BORN" (EVERGREEN) Barbra Streisand—Columbia 10450
[Barbra Streisand/Paul Williams] [ASC] (12/11/76 BCR-1)

PRISONER (CAPTURED BY YOUR EYES) *L.A. Jets—RCA 10826*
[John Desautels/Karen Lawrence] [BMI] (12/18/76 BCR-80)

LOVE THEME FROM "EYES OF LAURA MARS" (PRISONER)
Barbra Streisand—Columbia 10777
[John Desautels/Karen Lawrence] [BMI] (7/29/78 BCR-21)

—LOVE THEME FROM GOYA see: TILL I LOVED YOU

LOVE THEME FROM "LA STRADA" (THE ROAD)
Michel Legrand And His Orchestra—Columbia 40732
[Nino Rota] [ASC] (8/10/56 Rt-78) [IM]

LOVE THEME FROM "LA STRADA" *Jo Moutet & His Orchestra—London 1687*
[Nino Rota] [ASC] (10/6/56 Rt-78) [IM]

LOVE THEME FROM "LA STRADA" (THE ROAD)
Paul Weston And His Music From Hollywood—Columbia 40737
[Nino Rota] [ASC] (10/6/56 Rt-78) [IM]

LOVE THEME FROM ONE EYED JACKS Ferrante & Teicher—United Artists 300
[Hugo Friedhofer] [ASC] (3/6/61 BCR-18) [I]

LOVE THEME FROM ROMEO & JULIET
Henry Mancini, His Orchestra And Chorus—RCA Victor 74-0131
[Nino Rota] [ASC] (4/26/69 BCR-1) [IM]

LOVE THEME FROM "ROMEO AND JULIET" (A TIME FOR US)
Johnny Mathis—Columbia 44915
[Larry Kusik/Nino Rota/Eddie Snyder] [ASC] (7/5/69 BCR-88)

LOVE THEME FROM SHOGUN (MARIKO'S THEME) Meco—RSO 1052
[Maurice Jarre] [ASC] (10/11/80 B-70) [I]

LOVE THEME FROM ST. ELMO'S FIRE David Foster—Atlantic 89528
[David Foster] [BMI] (8/24/85 BC-15) [I]

LOVE THEME FROM "THE GODFATHER" (SPEAK SOFTLY LOVE)
Andy Williams—Columbia 45579
[Larry Kusik/Nino Rota] [ASC] (4/8/72 BCR-24)

LOVE THEME FROM "THE GODFATHER"
The Music Of Nino Rota Conducted By Carlo Savina—Paramount 0152
[Nino Rota] [ASC] (4/22/72 BCR-63) [IM]

SPEAK SOFTLY LOVE *Al Martino—Capitol 3313*
[Larry Kusik/Nino Rota] [ASC] (4/22/72 BCR-77)

—LOVE THEME FROM THE SANDPIPER see: SHADOW OF YOUR SMILE

—LOVE THEME see: SEDUCTION

LOVE THING Tina Turner—Capitol 44778
[Albert Hammond/Holly Knight] [ASC] (10/26/91 C-77)

LOVE... THY WILL BE DONE Martika—Columbia 73853
[Martika/Prince] [ASC] (8/10/91 BC-10)

LOVE T.K.O. Teddy Pendergrass—Philadelphia Int'l 3116
[Gip Noble/Cecil Womack/Linda Womack] [BMI] (10/25/80 BCR-39)

LOVE TO LOVE YOU BABY *Donna Summer—Oasis 401*
[Pete Bellotte/Giorgio Moroder/Donna Summer] [ASC] (11/8/75 BCR-1)

LOVE TO LOVE YOU BABY *The Ritchie Family—Marlin 3306*
[Pete Bellotte/Giorgio Moroder/Donna Summer] (Med) [ASC] (8/28/76 BCR-17)

LOVE TO THE WORLD L.T.D.—A&M 1897
[Fonce Mizell/Larry Mizell/Rodney Mizell] [ASC] (1/29/77 B-91)

LOVE TOUCH Rod Stewart—Warner Bros. 28668
[Gene Black/Mike Chapman/Holly Knight] [ASC] (5/31/86 BC-6)

LOVE TRAIN The O'Jays—Philadelphia Int'l 3524
[Kenneth Gamble/Leon Huff] [BMI] (1/13/73 BCR-1)

LOVE TRAIN Holly Johnson—Uni 50023 [Holly Johnson] [ASC] (6/17/89 BC-65)

LOVE, TRUTH AND HONESTY Bananarama—London 886362
[Matt Aitken/Sarah Dallin/Jacquie O'Sullivan/Mike Stock/Pete Waterman/Keren Woodward] [BMI] (11/12/88 BC-72)

LOVE UPRISING Otis Leaville—Dakar 620 [Eugene Record] [BMI] (9/19/70 BCR-69)

LOVE VIBRATION Joe Simon—Spring 190
[Teddy Randazzo/Joe Simon] [BMI] (1/20/79 R-94)

LOVE WALKED IN *The Flamingos—End 1055*
[George Gershwin/Ira Gershwin] [ASC] (9/14/59 BCR-54)

LOVE WALKED IN *Dinah Washington—Mercury 71696*
[George Gershwin/Ira Gershwin] [ASC] (10/3/60 BCR-18)

LOVE WALKS IN Van Halen—Warner Bros. 28626
[Michael Anthony/Sammy Hagar/Alex Van Halen/Eddie Van Halen] [ASC] (8/9/86 BC-18)

THE LOVE WE HAD (STAYS ON MY MIND) The Dells—Cadet 5683
[Terry Callier/Larry Wade] [ASC] (8/14/71 BCR-30)

LOVE WILL CONQUER ALL Lionel Richie—Motown 1866
[Greg Phillinganes/Lionel Richie/Cynthia Weil] [ASC] (10/4/86 BC-9)

LOVE WILL FIND A WAY Jackie De Shannon—Imperial 66419
[Jackie DeShannon/Jimmy Holiday/Randy Myers] [BMI] (10/25/69 BCR-30)

LOVE WILL FIND A WAY Pablo Cruise—A&M 2048
[David Jenkins/Cory Lerios] [ASC] (5/27/78 BCR-5)

LOVE WILL FIND A WAY Yes—Atco 99449 [Trevor Rabin] [BMI] (10/3/87 BC-30)

LOVE WILL KEEP US TOGETHER *The Captain & Tennille—A&M 1672*
[Howard Greenfield/Neil Sedaka] [BMI] (4/19/75 BCR-1)

POR AMOR VIVIREMOS *The Captain & Tennille—A&M 1715*
[Howard Greenfield/Armando Martinez/Neil Sedaka] [BMI] (8/9/75 BCR-49) [F]

LOVE WILL LEAD YOU BACK Taylor Dayne—Arista 1-9938
[Diane Warren] [ASC] (1/27/90 BC-1)

LOVE WILL MAKE YOU FAIL IN SCHOOL Mickey And Sylvia—Vik 0280
[Cornell Muldrow/Sylvia Robinson] [BMI] (7/6/57 R-77)

LOVE WILL NEVER DO (WITHOUT YOU) Janet Jackson—A&M 1538
[James Samuel Harris/Terry Lewis] [ASC] (11/17/90 BC-1)

LOVE WILL SAVE THE DAY Whitney Houston—Arista 1-9720
[Toni Colandreo] [BMI] (7/2/88 BC-9)

LOVE WILL SHOW US HOW Christine McVie—Warner Bros. 29313
[Christine McVie/Todd Sharp] [BMI] (4/28/84 BC-30)

LOVE WILL SURVIVE Donny Osmond—Capitol 44707
[Donny Osmond/Evan Rogers/Carl Sturken] [BMI] (4/20/91 C-79)

LOVE WILL TURN YOU AROUND Kenny Rogers—Liberty 1471
[David Malloy/Kenny Rogers/Thom Schuyler/Even Stevens] [BMI] (7/3/82 BC-12)

LOVE WITH THE PROPER STRANGER Jack Jones—Kapp 571
[Elmer Bernstein/Johnny Mercer] [ASC] (2/8/64 BCR-56)

LOVE WON'T LET ME WAIT Major Harris—Atlantic 3248
[Vinnie Barrett/Bobby Eli] [BMI] (3/29/75 BCR-3)

LOVE X LOVE George Benson—Warner Bros./Qwest 49570
[Rod Temperton] [ASC] (10/18/80 BCR-57)

LOVE YOU DIDN'T DO RIGHT BY ME *Rosemary Clooney—Columbia 40305*
[Irving Berlin] [ASC] (10/2/54 CRt-41)

LOVE, YOU DIDN'T DO RIGHT BY ME *Peggy Lee—Decca 29250*
[Irving Berlin] [ASC] (11/8/54 Rt-82)

LOVE YOU DOWN Ready For The World—MCA 52947
[Melvin Riley] [ASC] (11/29/86 BC-9)

LOVE YOU FUNNY THING Tony Martin—RCA Victor 47-6368
[Fred Ahlert/Roy Turk] [ASC] (2/17/56 R-89)

LOVE YOU INSIDE OUT Bee Gees—RSO 925
[Barry Gibb/Maurice Gibb/Robin Gibb] [BMI] (4/21/79 BCR-1)

LOVE YOU LIKE I NEVER LOVED BEFORE John O'Banion—Elektra 47125
[Joey Carbone/Kathi Pinto/Richie Zito] [BMI] (3/21/81 BCR-24)

LOVE YOU MOST OF ALL Sam Cooke—Keen 3-2008
[Sam Cooke] [BMI] (11/17/58 BCR-26)

THE LOVE YOU SAVE The Jackson 5—Motown 1166
[Berry Gordy/Fonce Mizell/Freddie Perren/Deke Richards] (TSW) [ASC] (6/6/70 BCR-1)

THE LOVE YOU SAVE (MAY BE YOUR OWN) Joe Tex—Dial 4026
[Joe Tex] [BMI] (3/5/66 BCR-41)

LOVE YOU SO Ron Holden With The Thunderbirds—Donna 1315
[Ron Holden] [BMI] (3/28/60 BCR-5)

LOVE YOU SO MUCH The New Colony Six—Sentar 1205
[Ray Graffia/Jerry Kollenburg/Pat McBride] [BMI] (1/28/67 BCR-55)

THE LOVE YOU TAKE Dan Hartman And Denise Lopez—A&M 1264
[Dan Hartman] [ASC] (12/17/88 C-75)

LOVE ZONE Billy Ocean—Jive 9510
[Wayne Brathwaite/Barry Eastmond/Billy Ocean] [ASC] (7/26/86 BC-10)

LOVEDROPS Mickey And Sylvia—Willow 23000
[Mickey Baker/Sylvia Robinson] [BMI] (8/7/61 B-97)

LOVELAND Paul Anka—ABC-Paramount 10279 [Paul Anka] [BMI] (11/27/61 R-78)

LOVELINE Dr. Hook—Casablanca 2351
[David Malloy/Eddie Rabbitt/Even Stevens] [BMI] (6/12/82 BC-60)

LOVELY DAY Bill Withers—Columbia 10627
[Skip Scarborough/Bill Withers] [BMI] (11/19/77 BCR-23)

LOVELY LADIES OF MILANO Dick Jacobs And His Chorus And Orchestra—Coral 61907
[Hans Bradtke/Erwin Halletz/Mel Mitchell] [BMI] (11/4/57 R-50)

LOVELY LIES *Manhattan Brothers And Miriam Makeba—London 1610*
[Sherwood Mackay Davashe/Tom Glazer] [ASC] (2/10/56 BCRt-44)

LOVELY LIES *Nick Noble—Wing 90042*
[Sherwood Mackay Davashe/Tom Glazer] [ASC] (2/10/56 Rt-72)

LOVELY, LOVELY (LOVERLY, LOVERLY) Chubby Checker—Parkway 936
[Sherman Rothman/Robyn Supraner] [BMI] (12/19/64 BCR-70)

LOVELY ONE The Four Voices—Columbia 40643
[Fred Weismantel] [BMI] (2/24/56 BCR-19)

LOVELY ONE Jacksons—Epic 50938
[Michael Jackson/Steven Randall Jackson] [BMI] (9/27/80 BCR-9)

LOVELY WAY SHE LOVES The Moments—Stang 5009
[William A. Brown/Al Goodman/Sylvia Robinson] [BMI] (1/31/70 R-90)

LOVER Michael Stanley Band—EMI America 8064
[Michael Stanley] [ASC] (3/28/81 BCR-68)

LOVER COME BACK Doris Day—Columbia 42295
[Frank DeVol/Alan Spilton] [ASC] (4/7/62 B-98)

LOVER COME BACK TO ME The Cleftones—Gee 1079
[Oscar Hammerstein/Sigmund Romberg] [ASC] (11/24/62 BCR-88)

LOVER COME BACK TO ME Dead Or Alive—Epic 05607
[Pete Burns/Steve Coy/Wayne Hussey/Tim Lever/Mike Percy] [ASC] (9/21/85 BC-72)

LOVER DOLL Elvis Presley with the Jordanaires—RCA Victor EPA-4319
[Abner Silver/Sid Wayne] (EP) [ASC] (7/26/58 CR-14)

THE LOVER IN ME Sheena Easton—MCA 53416
[Kenneth Edmonds/Antonio Reid/Daryl Simmons] [BMI] (10/29/88 BC-2)

LOVER PLEASE Clyde McPhatter—Mercury 71941 [Billy Swan] [BMI] (2/24/62 BCR-4)

LOVERBOY Karen Kamon—Columbia 04474
[Billy Alessi/Bobby Alessi] [BMI] (7/28/84 B-88)

LOVERBOY Billy Ocean—Jive 9284
[Keith Diamond/Mutt Lange/Billy Ocean] [BMI] (12/1/84 BC-2)

LOVERGIRL Teena Marie—Epic 04619 [Teena Marie] [ASC] (12/15/84 BC-4)

LOVERS AFTER ALL Melissa Manchester And Peabo Bryson—Arista 0587
[Melissa Manchester/Leon Ware] [BMI] (2/28/81 BCR-54)

LOVERS ALWAYS FORGIVE Gladys Knight & The Pips—Maxx 329
[Van McCoy] [BMI] (8/22/64 BR-89)

LOVERS BY NIGHT, STRANGERS BY DAY The Fleetwoods—Dolton 62
[John Gluck/Neval Nader] [BMI] (9/15/62 BCR-34)

A LOVER'S CONCERTO *The Toys—DynoVoice 209*
[Johann Sebastian Bach/Sandy Linzer/Denny Randell] [BMI] (9/11/65 BCR-1)

A LOVER'S CONCERTO *Sarah Vaughan—Mercury 72543*
[Johann Sebastian Bach/Sandy Linzer/Denny Randell] [BMI] (4/2/66 BCR-63)

A LOVER'S CONCERTO *Mrs. Miller—Capitol 5640*
[Johann Sebastian Bach/Sandy Linzer/Denny Randell] [BMI] (5/7/66 BCR-94)

A LOVER'S CONCERTO *Stars On 45—Radio 3863*
[Johann Sebastian Bach/Sandy Linzer/Denny Randell] (Med) [BMI] (9/19/81 BCR-55)

LOVER'S CROSS Melanie—Neighborhood 4215 [Jim Croce] [ASC] (7/27/74 CR-70)

LOVER'S HOLIDAY Peggy Scott & Jo Jo Benson—SSS Int'l 736
[Bob McRee/Cliff Thomas/Edward S. Thomas Jr.] [BMI] (5/4/68 BCR-15)

A LOVER'S HOLIDAY Change—Warner Bros./RFC 49208
[Davide Romani/Tanyayette Willoughby] [ASC] (5/17/80 BCR-40)

LOVER'S HYMN The Fontane Sisters—Dot 15943
[Charles Singleton] [BMI] (7/18/59 CR-91)

LOVER'S ISLAND The Blue Jays—Milestone 2008
[Alex Manigo/Leon Peels] [BMI] (7/29/61 BCR-26)

LOVER'S LANE Georgio—Motown 1906 [Georgio Allentini] [BMI] (12/5/87 BC-59)

LOVERS NEVER SAY GOODBYE The Flamingos—End 1035
[Terry Johnson/Paul Wilson] [BMI] (12/6/58 BC-52)

LOVER'S PRAYER Dion and The Belmonts—Laurie 3035
[Ernie Maresca] [BMI] (9/7/59 BCR-41)

LOVER'S PRAYER Wallace Brothers—Sims 189
[Cooky Wallace*/Ernest Wallace Jr.] [BMI] (8/22/64 BCR-64)

A LOVER'S QUESTION *Clyde McPhatter—Atlantic 1199*
[Brook Benton/Jimmy Williams] [BMI] (10/6/58 BCR-6)

A LOVER'S QUESTION *Ernestine Anderson—Mercury 71772*
[Brook Benton/Jimmy Williams] [BMI] (2/6/61 BR-84)

A LOVER'S QUESTION *Otis Redding—Atco 6654*
[Brook Benton/Jimmy Williams] [BMI] (2/15/69 BCR-35)

A LOVER'S QUESTION *Loggins & Messina—Columbia 10222*
[Brook Benton/Jimmy Williams] [BMI] (10/18/75 BC-89)

A LOVER'S QUESTION *Jacky Ward—Mercury 55018*
[Brook Benton/Jimmy Williams] [BMI] (3/4/78 CR-77)

LOVERS WHO WANDER Dion—Laurie 3123
[Dion DiMucci/Ernie Maresca] [ASC] (4/21/62 BCR-3)

LOVE'S A HURTING GAME Ivory Joe Hunter—Atlantic 1128
[Julius Dixon*/Ivory Joe Hunter/Ollie Jones] [BMI] (4/13/57 R-77)

LOVE'S ABOUT TO CHANGE MY HEART Donna Summer—Atlantic 88840
[Matt Aitken/Mike Stock/Pete Waterman] [BMI] (9/16/89 B-85)

LOVE'S BEEN A LITTLE BIT HARD ON ME Juice Newton—Capitol 5120
[Gary Burr] [ASC] (5/8/82 BC-5)

LOVE'S BEEN GOOD TO ME Frank Sinatra—Reprise 0852
[Rod McKuen] [ASC] (9/6/69 BCR-53)

LOVE'S BURNING FIRE Beverly Ann Gibson—Deb 506 [Julius Dixon] [BMI] (3/23/59 R-79)

LOVE'S GOT A LINE ON YOU Scandal—Columbia 03615
[Kathe Green/Zack Smith] [BMI] (4/2/83 BC-38)

LOVE'S GROWN DEEP Kenny Nolan—20th Century 2331 [Kenny Nolan] [BMI] (4/2/77 BCR-20)

LOVE'S LINES, ANGLES AND RHYMES The 5th Dimension—Bell 965 [Dorothea Joyce] [ASC] (2/20/71 BCR-11)

LOVE'S MADE A FOOL OF YOU *Bobby Fuller Four—Mustang 3016 [Buddy Holly/Bob Montgomery] [ASC] (4/16/66 BCR-20)*

LOVE'S MADE A FOOL OF YOU *Cochise—United Artists 50756 [Buddy Holly/Bob Montgomery] [ASC] (5/1/71 BCR-89)*

LOVES ME LIKE A ROCK Paul Simon (with The Dixie Hummingbirds)—Columbia 45907 [Paul Simon] [BMI] (7/28/73 BCR-1)

LOVE'S ONLY LOVE Engelbert—Epic 50844 [Paul Ryan] [NA] (3/15/80 B-83)

LOVE'S STREET AND FOOL'S ROAD Solomon Burke—MGM 14353 [Solomon Burke] [BMI] (4/15/72 BCR-75)

—LOVE'S TAKING OVER see: VIOLENCE OF LOVE

LOVE'S THEME Love Unlimited Orchestra—20th Century 2069 [Barry White] [BMI] (12/1/73 BCR-1) [I]

LOVESICK BLUES *Sonny James—Capitol 3734 [Cliff Friend/Irving Mills] [ASC] (6/29/57 CRt-52)*

LOVESICK BLUES *Sonny Knight—Dot 15597 [Cliff Friend/Irving Mills] [ASC] (8/3/57 Rt-58)*

LOVESICK BLUES *Floyd Cramer—RCA Victor 47-8013 [Cliff Friend/Irving Mills] [ASC] (4/2/62 BR-85) [IWM]*

LOVESICK BLUES *Frank Ifield—Vee-Jay 477 [Cliff Friend/Irving Mills] [ASC] (12/22/62 BCR-32)*

LOVEY The Clovers—United Artists 209 [Jerry Leiber/Mike Stoller] [BMI] (4/11/60 R-98)

LOVEY DOVEY *Clyde McPhatter—Atlantic 2018 [Eddie Curtis/Ahmet Ertegun] [ASC] (3/28/59 BCR-49)*

LOVEY DOVEY *Buddy Knox—Liberty 55290 [Eddie Curtis/Ahmet Ertegun] [ASC] (12/10/60 BCR-25)*

LOVEY DOVEY *Bunny Sigler—Parkway 6000 [Eddie Curtis/Ahmet Ertegun] (Med) [ASC] (10/7/67 BCR-72)*

LOVEY DOVEY *Otis & Carla—Stax 244 [Eddie Curtis/Ahmet Ertegun] [ASC] (2/10/68 BCR-46)*

LOVEY DOVEY KINDA LOVIN' Brenton Wood—Double Shot 126 [Joseph Hooven/Alfred J. Smith/Hal Winn] [ASC] (3/9/68 B-99)

LOVIN' EVERY MINUTE OF IT Loverboy—Columbia 05569 [Mutt Lange] [ASC] (8/24/85 BC-9)

LOVIN' IS REALLY MY GAME Brainstorm—Tabu 10961 [Tranita Womack/Belita Woods] [BMI] (6/11/77 R-83)

LOVIN' NATURALLY Sandalwood—Bell 45,348 [Brian Tabach/Byron Walls] [ASC] (6/9/73 R-87)

LOVIN' PLACE Gale Garnett—RCA Victor 47-8472 [Gale Garnett] [BMI] (12/5/64 BCR-36)

LOVIN' SEASON Gene & Debbe—TRX 5010 [Gene Thomas] [BMI] (6/15/68 BCR-51)

LOVIN' SOUND Ian & Sylvia—MGM 13686 [Ian Tyson] [ASC] (8/19/67 C-96)

LOVIN' THE NIGHT AWAY The Dillman Band—RCA 12206 [Patrick Frederick/Steve Seamans] [BMI] (5/9/81 BCR-45)

LOVIN' THINGS The Grassroots—Dunhill 4180 [Jet Loring/Artie Schroeck] [BMI] (2/8/69 BCR-30)

LOVIN' TOUCH Mark Dinning—MGM 12929 [Gerry Goffin/Jack Keller] [BMI] (8/22/60 BCR-64)

LOVIN', TOUCHIN', SQUEEZIN' Journey—Columbia 11036 [Steve Perry] [BMI] (7/14/79 BCR-12)

LOVIN' UP A STORM Jerry Lee Lewis—Sun 317 [Luther Dixon/Allyson Khent] [BMI] (3/21/59 C-81)

LOVIN' YOU Bobby Darin—Atlantic 2376 [John Sebastian] [BMI] (1/14/67 BCR-31)

LOVIN' YOU Minnie Riperton—Epic 50057 [Minnie Riperton/Richard Rudolph] [BMI] (1/18/75 BCR-1)

LOVIN' YOU BABY White Plains—Deram 85066 [Roger Cook/Roger Greenaway] [ASC] (9/12/70 BCR-63)

LOVIN' YOU, LOVIN' ME Candi Staton—Fame 91005 [Barbara Wyrick] [ASC] (11/4/72 BCR-70)

LOVING ARMS *Dobie Gray—MCA 40100 [Tom Jans] [ASC] (7/28/73 BCR-36)*

LOVING ARMS *Kris Kristofferson & Rita Coolidge—A&M 1498 [Tom Jans] [ASC] (3/23/74 BCR-86)*

LOVING HER WAS EASIER (THAN ANYTHING I'LL EVER DO AGAIN) Kris Kristofferson—Monument 8525 [Kris Kristofferson] [BMI] (8/21/71 BCR-26)

LOVING POWER The Impressions—Curtom 0110 [Charles Henry Jackson Jr./Marvin Yancy] [ASC] (1/17/76 CR-79)

LOVING YOU Elvis Presley—RCA Victor 47-7000 [Jerry Leiber/Mike Stoller] [BMI] (6/24/57 BCR-21)

LOVING YOU Johnny Nash—Epic 11070 [William Stevenson] [BMI] (2/23/74 BCR-64)

LOVING YOU Chris Rea—Columbia 02727 [Chris Rea] [ASC] (4/3/82 BC-75)

LOVING YOU HAS MADE ME BANANAS Guy Marks—ABC 11055 [Guy Marks] [ASC] (4/6/68 BCR-38)

LOVING YOU IS A NATURAL THING Ronnie Milsap—Chips 2889 [Mark James/George Klein/Glenn Spreen] [BMI] (9/12/70 BR-87)

LOVING YOU IS JUST AN OLD HABIT Jim Weatherly—RCA Victor 74-0822 [Jim Weatherly] [ASC] (12/23/72 CR-90)

LOVING YOU IS SWEETER THAN EVER Four Tops—Motown 1096 [Ivy Jo Hunter/Stevie Wonder] [ASC] (5/28/66 BCR-44)

LOVING YOU JUST CROSSED MY MIND Sam Neely—Capitol 3381 [Sam Neely] [BMI] (8/12/72 BCR-29)

LOVING YOU MORE EVERY DAY Etta James—Argo 5465 [Ronny Mitchell] [BMI] (4/11/64 BCR-65)

LOVING YOU WITH MY EYES Starland Vocal Band—Windsong 11899 [Taffy Danoff/Margot Kunkel] [ASC] (2/23/80 BCR-71)

LOVING YOU'S A DIRTY JOB BUT SOMEBODY'S GOTTA DO IT Bonnie Tyler (Duet with Todd Rundgren)—Columbia 06151 [Jim Steinman] [BMI] (7/12/86 C-82)

LOW RIDER War—United Artists 706 [Thomas Allen/Harold Brown/Morris Dickerson/Jerry Goldstein/Lonnie Jordan/Charles Miller/Lee Oskar/Howard Scott] [ASC] (9/13/75 BCR-5)

LOW RIDER (ON THE BOULEVARD) Latin Alliance—Virgin 98751 [Albin*/Thomas Allen/Harold Brown/Morris Dickerson/Jerry Goldstein/Lonnie Jordan/Charles Miller/Arturo Molina Jr./Lee Oskar/Sergio Reyes/Howard Scott/Al Trivette] [ASC] (8/10/91 B-54)

LOWDOWN Chicago—Columbia 45370 [Peter Cetera/Danny Seraphine] [ASC] (5/8/71 BCR-25)

LOWDOWN Boz Scaggs—Columbia 10367 [David Paich/Boz Scaggs] [ASC] (7/3/76 BCR-1)

LOWDOWN POPCORN James Brown—King 6250 [James Brown] [BMI] (8/23/69 BCR-41) [I]

LU Peggy Lipton—Ode 124 [Laura Nyro] [BMI] (12/27/69 CR-70)

LUANNE Foreigner—Atlantic 4072 [Lou Gramm/Michael Leslie Jones] [ASC] (7/31/82 B-75)

LUCIFER Bob Seger System—Capitol 2748 [Bob Seger] [ASC] (4/4/70 BCR-72)

LUCILLE *Little Richard—Specialty 598 [Albert Collins/Richard Penniman] [BMI] (3/16/57 BCR-22)*

LUCILLE *The Everly Brothers—Warner Bros. 5163 [Albert Collins/Richard Penniman] [BMI] (9/3/60 BCR-21)*

LUCILLE Kenny Rogers—United Artists 929 [Roger Bowling/Hal Bynum] [BMI] (3/19/77 BCR-5)

LUCKENBACH, TEXAS (BACK TO THE BASICS OF LOVE) Waylon Jennings—RCA 10924 [Bobby Emmons/Chips Moman] [BMI] (4/23/77 BCR-23)

LUCKY Eye To Eye—Warner Bros. 29455 [Deborah Berg/Julian Marshall] [ASC] (10/29/83 B-88)

LUCKY Greg Kihn—EMI America 8255 [Greg Kihn/Steve Wright] [ASC] (2/16/85 BC-30)

LUCKY DEVIL Carl Dobkins, Jr.—Decca 31020 [Wally Gold/Aaron Schroeder] [ASC] (11/30/59 BCR-20)

A LUCKY GUY Rickie Lee Jones—Warner Bros. 49816 [Rickie Lee Jones] [ASC] (9/26/81 BCR-53)

LUCKY IN LOVE Mick Jagger—Columbia 04893 [Carlos Alomar*/Mick Jagger] [ASC] (4/27/85 BC-36)

LUCKY LADYBUG Billy & Lillie—Swan 4020 [Bob Crewe/Frank Slay] [BMI] (12/20/58 BCR-14)

LUCKY LIPS *Ruth Brown—Atlantic 1125 [Jerry Leiber/Mike Stoller] [BMI] (2/9/57 BCRt-13)*

LUCKY LIPS *Gale Storm—Dot 15539 [Jerry Leiber/Mike Stoller] [BMI] (2/23/57 BRt-13)*

LUCKY LIPS *Cliff Richard—Epic 9597 [Jerry Leiber/Mike Stoller] [BMI] (8/3/63 BCR-62)*

LUCKY MAN *Emerson, Lake & Palmer—Cotillion 44106 [Greg Lake] [ASC] (3/13/71 BCR-48)*

LUCKY MAN *Emerson, Lake & Palmer—Cotillion 44106 [Greg Lake] [ASC] (12/30/72 BCR-51)*

LUCKY MAN Starbuck—Private Stock 45,125 [Bruce Blackman] [ASC] (11/27/76 BCR-48)

LUCKY ME The Moments—Stang 5031 [George Kerr/Sylvia Robinson] [BMI] (8/21/71 BCR-93)

LUCKY ME Anne Murray—Capitol 4848 [Charlie Black/Rory Bourke] [ASC] (3/29/80 BCR-42)

THE LUCKY ONE Laura Branigan—Atlantic 89636 [Bruce Roberts] [BMI] (8/4/84 BC-20)

LUCKY STAR Madonna—Sire 29177 [Madonna L. Ciccone] [ASC] (8/18/84 BC-4)

LUCRETIA MAC EVIL Blood, Sweat & Tears—Columbia 45235 [David Clayton-Thomas] [BMI] (9/26/70 BCR-17)

LUCY IN THE SKY WITH DIAMONDS Elton John—MCA 40344 [John Lennon/Paul McCartney] [ASC] (11/30/74 BCR-1)

LUCY, LUCY George Hamilton IV—ABC-Paramount 9966 [Wally Gold] [ASC] (11/10/58 R-90)

LUKA Suzanne Vega—A&M 2937 [Suzanne Vega] [ASC] (6/6/87 BC-3)

LULLABY The Cure—Elektra 69249 [Simon Gallup/Roger O'Donnell/Robert James Smith/Porl Thompson/Laurence Tolhurst/Boris Williams] [ASC] (11/25/89 BC-57)

LULLABY OF BIRDLAND (54) *Ella Fitzgerald—Decca 29198 [George Shearing/George David Weiss] [ASC] (9/4/54 C-31)*

LULLABY OF BIRDLAND *Blue Stars—Mercury 70742*
[George Shearing/George David Weiss] [ASC] (12/17/55 BCRt-20) [F]

LULLABY OF BIRDLAND *Pee Wee Hunt & His Orchestra—Capitol 3309*
[George Shearing] [ASC] (1/13/56 Rt-21) [IM]

LULLABY OF BIRDLAND *Ella Fitzgerald—Decca 29198*
[George Shearing/George David Weiss] [ASC] (2/17/56 Rt-21)

LULLABY OF BIRDLAND *Ray Anthony & His Orchestra with Don Durant—Capitol EAP 1-9131 (EP) [George Shearing/George David Weiss] [ASC] (3/9/56 Rt-27)*

LULLABY OF BIRDLAND *The George Shearing Quintet—MGM 11354*
[George Shearing] [ASC] (3/30/56 Rt-34) [IM]

LULLABY OF LOVE Frank Gari—Crusade 1021
[Sy Mann/Don Michals/Sy Muskin] [ASC] (4/10/61 BCR-23)

LULLABY OF LOVE The Poppies—Epic 9893
[Larry Lee Butler/Billy Sherrill] [BMI] (2/26/66 BCR-48)

LULLABY OF THE LEAVES The Ventures—Dolton 41
[Bernice Petkere] [ASC] (4/24/61 BCR-69) [IM]

LULLABYE The Chevrons—Brent 7007
[Mickey Baker/Lee Greenlee/Booker Lee*] [BMI] (1/18/60 CR-87)

LULU HAD A BABY Chico Holiday—RCA Victor 47-7549
[Luigi Creatore/Al Hoffman/Dick Manning/Hugo Peretti] [ASC] (6/22/59 R-96)

LUMBERJACK Brook Benton—Mercury 72333
[Charles Allen*/Charles Arrington] [BMI] (11/7/64 BCR-42)

LUMBERJACK Hal Willis—Sims 207 [Ginger Willis/Hal Willis] [BMI] (11/7/64 R-83)

LUNA TRIP Dickie Goodman—Cotique 173 [Dickie Goodman] [BMI] (9/6/69 BR-95)

LYIN' EYES Eagles—Asylum 45279 [Glenn Frey/Don Henley] [ASC] (9/13/75 BCR-2)

LYIN' TO MYSELF David Cassidy—Enigma 75084
[David Cassidy/Sue Shifrin] [ASC] (9/22/90 BC-27)

LYING Peter Frampton—Atlantic 89463 [Peter Frampton] [ASC] (2/1/86 BC-74)

M

MA BAKER Boney M—Atlantic 3422
[Frank Farian/Fred Jay/Hans-Jörg Mayer] [ASC] (8/27/77 B-96)

MA BELLE AMIE The Tee Set—Colossus 107
[Peter Tetteroo/Hans Van Eijck] [BMI] (1/3/70 BCR-4)

MA! (HE'S MAKING EYES AT ME) Lena Zavaroni—Stax 0206
[Sidney Clare/Con Conrad] [ASC] (7/13/74 BCR-81)

MACARTHUR PARK *Richard Harris—Dunhill 4134 [Jimmy Webb] [ASC] (5/4/68 BCR-2)*

MACARTHUR PARK *Waylon Jennings And The Kimberlys—RCA Victor 74-0210*
[Jimmy Webb] [ASC] (8/30/69 BC-93)

MACARTHUR PARK *Al Capps Band—Columbia 45219*
[Jimmy Webb] (Med) [ASC] (10/10/70 C-97) [IWM]

MAC ARTHUR PARK (PART II) *Four Tops—Motown 1189*
[Jimmy Webb] [ASC] (8/28/71 BCR-36)

MAC ARTHUR PARK *Donna Summer—Casablanca 939*
[Jimmy Webb] [ASC] (9/9/78 BCR-1)

MACHINE GUN Commodores—Motown 1307
[Milan Williams] [ASC] (6/15/74 BCR-13) [I]

MACHINERY Sheena Easton—EMI America 8131 [Julia Downes] [BMI] (9/4/82 BC-57)

MACHINES John Livigni—Raintree 2204
[John LiVigni/Danny Meehan] [ASC] (10/18/75 BC-83)

MACHO MAN Village People—Casablanca 922
[Henri Belolo/Jacques Morali/Peter Whitehead/Victor Willis] [BMI] (6/24/78 BCR-25)

MORITAT (A THEME FROM "THE THREE PENNY OPERA") *Dick Hyman Trio—MGM 12149*
[Kurt Weill] [ASC] (1/6/56 BCtRt-5) [IM]

A THEME FROM THREEPENNY OPERA (MACK THE KNIFE)
Louis Armstrong And His All-Stars—Columbia 40587
[Marc Blitzstein/Berthold Brecht/Kurt Weill] [ASC] (1/13/56 BRt-6)

A THEME FROM "THE THREE PENNY OPERA" (MORITAT)
Richard Hayman And Jan August—Mercury 70781
[Kurt Weill] [ASC] (1/20/56 BCtRt-6) [IM]

A THEME FROM (THE THREE PENNY OPERA) 'MORITAT'
Billy Vaughn and His Orchestra—Dot 15444
[Kurt Weill] [ASC] (1/20/56 BRt-8) [IM]

MORITAT (THEME FROM "THREE PENNY OPERA") *Les Paul—Capitol 3329*
[Kurt Weill] [ASC] (1/20/56 BRt-5) [IM]

MORITAT (A THEME FROM "THE THREE PENNY OPERA") *Lawrence Welk And His Sparkling Strings—Coral 61574 [Kurt Weill] [ASC] (1/27/56 BRt-5) [IM]*

MORITAT (A THEME FROM "THREE PENNY OPERA")
Owen Bradley & His Orchestra—Decca 29816
[Kurt Weill] [ASC] (3/9/56 Rt-6) [IM]

MACK THE KNIFE *Bobby Darin—Atco 6147*
[Marc Blitzstein/Berthold Brecht/Kurt Weill] [ASC] (8/24/59 BCR-1)

MACK THE KNIFE *Ella Fitzgerald—Verve 10209*
[Marc Blitzstein/Berthold Brecht/Kurt Weill] [ASC] (4/18/60 BCR-27)

MAD ABOUT YOU Belinda Carlisle—I.R.S. 52815
[Paula Brown/Mitchel Evans/James Whelan] [ASC] (5/17/86 BC-3)

MADALAINE Winger—Atlantic 89041 [Reb Beach/Kip Winger] [BMI] (12/24/88 C-85)

MADE TO LOVE YOU Gary Wright—Warner Bros. 8250
[Gary Wright] [ASC] (9/18/76 BC-79)

MADE UP MY MIND Sa-Fire—Mercury 878 784 [Ernie Gold] [ASC] (3/2/91 BC-82)

MADEIRA *Ray Anthony—Capitol 3335 [Maximiano de Sousa] [NA] (1/27/56 Rt-72) [IWM]*

MADEIRA *Mitch Miller And His Orchestra—Columbia 40655*
[Maximiano De Sousa] [NA] (3/10/56 BCRt-39) [IWM]

MADEIRA *LeRoy Holmes & His Orchestra—MGM 12157*
[Maximiano de Sousa] [NA] (3/30/56 Rt-83) [IWM]

MADELAINE Stu Nunnery—Evolution 1088 [Stu Nunnery] [ASC] (3/16/74 CR-86)

MADEMOISELLE Styx—A&M 1877
[Dennis DeYoung/Tommy Shaw] [ASC] (11/6/76 BCR-36)

MADISON Al Brown's Tunetoppers Featuring Cookie Brown—Amy 804
[Al Brown] [BMI] (3/21/60 BCR-13)

MADISON TIME PART ONE Ray Bryant Combo—Columbia 41628
[Ray Bryant/Eddie Morrison] [BMI] (3/28/60 BCR-25)

MADONNA, MADONNA Tony Bennett with Percy Faith and His Orchestra—Columbia 40311
[Bob Merrill] [ASC] (9/18/54 CR-23)

MADRID Nat "King" Cole—Capitol 4125
[Georges Bizet/Nat "King" Cole/Léon Halévy/Johnny Lange/Henri Meilhac] [ASC] (1/26/59 BCR-45)

MAGGIE Redbone—Epic 10670 [Lolly Vegas] [BMI] (12/5/70 BCR-45)

MAGGIE MAY Rod Stewart—Mercury 73224
[Martin Quittenton/Rod Stewart] (TSW) [ASC] (8/14/71 BCR-1)

MAGIC Pilot—EMI 3992 [Billy Lyall/David Paton] [BMI] (4/5/75 BCR-5)

MAGIC Olivia Newton-John—MCA 41247 [John Farrar] [BMI] (5/24/80 BCR-1)

MAGIC The Cars—Elektra 69724 [Ric Ocasek] [ASC] (5/19/84 BC-12)

MAGIC BUS The Who—Decca 32362 [Pete Townshend] [ASC] (8/3/68 BCR-10)

MAGIC CARPET RIDE Steppenwolf—Dunhill 4161
[John Kay/Rushton Moreve] [BMI] (10/5/68 BCR-2)

MAGIC CARPET RIDE Bardeux—Enigma 75016
[Stacy Smith/Jon St. James] [BMI] (2/20/88 BC-78)

MAGIC FINGERS Eddie Fisher—RCA Victor 47-6264
[Don Robertson] [ASC] (9/26/55 BCR-26)

MAGIC IS THE NIGHT Kathy Young With The Innocents—Indigo 125
[James Lee] [BMI] (9/18/61 B-80)

MAGIC MAN Heart—Mushroom 7011 [Ann Wilson/Nancy Wilson] [ASC] (7/10/76 BCR-5)

MAGIC MAN Robert Winters & Fall—Buddah 624
[Lloyd Chiate/Ray Dewey/Jimmy George/Robert L. Winters] [BMI] (4/4/81 R-71)

MAGIC MAN Herb Alpert—A&M 2356
[Herb Alpert/Melvin Ragin/Michael Lee Stokes] [ASC] (9/5/81 B-79) [I]

MAGIC MELODY Les Paul and Mary Ford—Capitol 3248
[Les Paul] [NA] (9/19/55 BCR-39) [IM]

MAGIC MOMENT Nat King Cole—Capitol 4672
[Howard Dietz/Arthur Schwartz] [ASC] (12/18/61 R-87)

MAGIC MOMENTS Perry Como—RCA Victor 47-7128
[Burt Bacharach/Hal David] [ASC] (12/30/57 BCR-21)

—MAGIC MOON see: CLAIR DE LUNE

THE MAGIC OF OUR SUMMER LOVE The Tymes—Parkway 919
[William E. Jackson III/Jimmy Wisner] [BMI] (6/13/64 B-99)

MAGIC POWER Triumph—MCA 12298
[Rik Emmett/Mike Levine/Gil Moore] [ASC] (10/3/81 BCR-46)

THE MAGIC TANGO Hugo Winterhalter & Orchestra—RCA Victor 47-5769
[Philippe Gerard Bloch/Jimmy Kennedy] [ASC] (7/3/54 BC-25)

THE MAGIC TOUCH Bobby Fuller Four—Mustang 3018 [Ted Daryll] [BMI] (7/16/66 R-83)

MAGIC TOWN The Vogues—Co & Ce 234
[Barry Mann/Cynthia Weil] [BMI] (2/19/66 BCR-16)

MAGIC WAND Don & Juan—Big Top 3121 [Claude Johnson] [BMI] (10/27/62 B-91)

MAGIC WOMAN TOUCH The Hollies—Epic 10951
[Colin Horton-Jennings/Garth Watt-Roy] [BMI] (2/10/73 BCR-43)

MAGICAL John Parr—Atlantic 89568 [Marvin Lee Aday/John Parr] [BMI] (4/6/85 BC-69)

MAGICAL MYSTERY TOUR *Ambrosia—20th Century 2327*
[John Lennon/Paul McCartney] [ASC] (2/26/77 BCR-39)

MAGICAL MYSTERY TOUR *The Beatles—Capitol 5107*
[John Lennon/Paul McCartney] (Med) [ASC] (3/27/82 BCR-12)

MAGNET AND STEEL Walter Egan—Columbia 10719
[Walter Egan] [ASC] (5/20/78 BCR-8)

MAGNETIC Earth, Wind & Fire—Columbia 04210 [Martin Page] [ASC] (11/12/83 BC-57)

THE MAGNIFICENT SEVEN *Al Caiola And His Orchestra—United Artists 261*
[Elmer Bernstein] [ASC] (11/21/60 BCR-21) [I]

THE MAGNIFICENT SEVEN *Meco—Arista 0660*
[Elmer Bernstein] (Med) [ASC] (2/13/82 BCR-35) [I]

MAH-NA-MAH-NA Piero Umiliani—Ariel 500 [Piero Umiliani] [BMI] (8/30/69 BCR-38) [I]

—MAID OF NOVGOROD see: THEME FROM WAR AND PEACE

MAIN EVENT Barbra Streisand—Columbia 11008
[Paul Jabara/Bruce Roberts] (Med) [BMI] (6/16/79 BCR-3)

MAIN STREET Gary Lewis And The Playboys—Liberty 56075
[Michael Gordon/James Griffin] [BMI] (11/2/68 CR-67)

MAIN TITLE (THEME FROM "JAWS") John Williams—MCA 40439
[John Williams] [BMI] (8/9/75 BCR-25) [I]

(MAIN TITLE THEME FROM) "THE RAT RACE"
Richard Maltby And His Orchestra—Roulette 4270
[Elmer Bernstein] [ASC] (11/19/60 CR-83) [I]

MAINSTREET Bob Seger—Capitol 4422 [Bob Seger] [ASC] (4/23/77 BCR-19)

MAIRZY DOATS *Dodie Stevens—Dot 16002*
[Milton Drake/Al Hoffman/Jerry Livingston] [ASC] (11/23/59 R-98)

MAIRZY DOATS *The Innocence—Kama Sutra 222*
[Milton Drake/Al Hoffman/Jerry Livingston] [ASC] (2/25/67 BCR-75)

THE MAJESTIC Dion—Laurie 3115
[Brenda Lee Jones/Welton Young] [BMI] (11/27/61 BCR-30)

MAJESTY OF LOVE Marvin Rainwater and Connie Francis—MGM 12555
[Ben Raleigh/Don Wolf] [ASC] (9/30/57 BR-76)

MAJOR TOM (COMING HOME) Peter Schilling—Elektra 69811
[David Lodge/Peter Schilling] [ASC] (9/24/83 BC-10)

MAJORCA *Monty Kelly & His Orchestra—Essex 375*
[Louis Gasté] [BMI] (2/21/55 Rt-76) [IM]

MAJORCA (ISLE OF LOVE) *Bob Manning—Capitol 3041*
[Georges Bonnet/Louis Gasté/Johnny Lehmann] [BMI] (2/21/55 Rt-76) [FET]

MAKE A CIRCLE Kay Starr—Capitol 5046
[Ruth Freed/David Saxon] [ASC] (9/28/63 R-94)

MAKE A LITTLE LOVE Lowell Fulsom—Kent 463
[Mike Akopoff/Jimmy Holiday] [BMI] (4/1/67 B-97)

MAKE A LITTLE MAGIC The Dirt Band—United Artists 1356
[Robert Carpenter/Jeff Hanna/Richard Hathaway] [ASC] (6/14/80 BCR-25)

MAKE A MOVE ON ME Olivia Newton-John—MCA 52000
[John Farrar/Tom Snow] [BMI] (2/13/82 BCR-5)

MAKE BELIEVE Wind—Life 200 [Bo Gentry/Joey Levine] [BMI] (8/30/69 BCR-17)

MAKE BELIEVE Toto—Columbia 03143 [David Paich] [ASC] (8/7/82 BC-19)

MAKE BELIEVE IT'S YOUR FIRST TIME Bobby Vinton—Tapestry 002
[Bob Morrison/Johnny Wilson] [ASC] (12/22/79 BCR-78)

MAKE BELIEVE WEDDING The Castells—Era 3057
[William Landau/Irving Roth] [BMI] (10/9/61 B-98)

MAKE HER MINE Nat "King" Cole—Capitol 2803
[Chester Conn/Sammy Gallop] [ASC] (7/3/54 CR-PRE)

MAKE IT BETTER (FORGET ABOUT ME) Tom Petty and The Heartbreakers—MCA 52605
[Tom Petty/David A. Stewart] [ASC] (6/8/85 BC-53)

MAKE IT EASY ON YOURSELF *Jerry Butler—Vee-Jay 451*
[Burt Bacharach/Hal David] [ASC] (7/7/62 BCR-20)

MAKE IT EASY ON YOURSELF *The Walker Bros.—Smash 2000*
[Burt Bacharach/Hal David] [ASC] (10/9/65 BCR-16)

MAKE IT EASY ON YOURSELF *Dionne Warwick—Scepter 12294*
[Burt Bacharach/Hal David] [ASC] (10/3/70 BCR-25)

MAKE IT FUNKY (PART 1) James Brown—Polydor 14088
[Charles Bobbit/James Brown] [BMI] (8/21/71 BCR-18)

MAKE IT FUNKY (PART 3) James Brown—Polydor 14098
[Charles Bobbit/James Brown] (Med) [BMI] (10/23/71 BCR-68) [IWM]

MAKE IT LAST Brooklyn Dreams—Casablanca 962
[Joe Esposito/Bruce Sudano] [BMI] (2/24/79 BCR-69)

MAKE IT LAST FOREVER Keith Sweat—Vintertainment 7-69386
[Teddy Riley/Keith Sweat] [ASC] (7/23/88 BC-55)

MAKE IT LIKE IT WAS Regina Belle—Columbia 73022
[Carvin Winans] [ASC] (2/24/90 BC-43)

MAKE IT MEAN SOMETHING Rob Jungklas—Manhattan 50054
[Chad Cromwell/Jack Holder/Rob Jungklas] [ASC] (2/7/87 BC-81)

MAKE IT REAL The Jets—MCA 53311
[Rick Kelly/Linda Mallah/Don Powell] [ASC] (4/16/88 BC-4)

MAKE IT WITH YOU *Bread—Elektra 45686 [David Gates] [ASC] (6/13/70 BCR-1)*

MAKE IT WITH YOU *Ralfi Pagan—Wand 11326 [David Gates] [ASC] (7/24/71 R-93)*

MAKE IT WITH YOU *The Whispers—Soul Train 10996 [David Gates] [ASC] (8/13/77 BC-90)*

MAKE LIKE A BUNNY, HONEY Jill Corey—Columbia 40878
[Joe Sherman/Noel Sherman] [ASC] (4/29/57 B-95)

MAKE LOVE STAY Dan Fogelberg—Full Moon 03525
[Dan Fogelberg] [ASC] (2/5/83 BC-26)

MAKE LOVE TO ME! *Jo Stafford—Columbia 40143*
[George Brunies/Allan Copeland/Paul Mares/Walter Melrose/Bill Norvas/ Ben Pollack/Leon Rappolo/Mel Stitzel] [ASC] (5/29/54 BC-PRE)

MAKE LOVE TO ME *Johnny Thunder & Ruby Winters—Diamond 218*
[George Brunies/Allan Copeland/Paul Mares/Walter Melrose/Bill Norvas/ Ben Pollack/Leon Rappolo/Mel Stitzel] [ASC] (3/18/67 BCR-94)

MAKE LOVE TO ME Helen Reddy—Capitol 4712
[Mike Tinsley/Steve Voice/Peter Yellowstone] [BMI] (5/19/79 BCR-59)

MAKE LOVE TO YOUR MIND Bill Withers—Columbia 10255
[Bill Withers] [ASC] (12/13/75 BCR-67)

MAKE ME A CHILD AGAIN Frankie Laine—Columbia 40720
[Ned Washington/Paul Weston] [ASC] (7/13/56 R-79)

MAKE ME A MIRACLE Jimmie Rodgers—Roulette 4070
[Luigi Creatore/Al Hoffman/Dick Manning/Hugo Peretti] [ASC] (5/3/58 BCR-27)

MAKE ME BELONG TO YOU Barbara Lewis—Atlantic 2346
[Chip Taylor/Billy Vera] [BMI] (7/23/66 BCR-28)

MAKE ME FEEL LIKE A WOMAN Jackie Moore—Kayvette 5122
[Clarence Reid] [BMI] (8/16/75 CR-81)

MAKE ME FORGET Bobby Rydell—Cameo 309
[Jan Douglas/Ray Merrell/Hal Shaper] [ASC] (3/21/64 BCR-43)

MAKE ME HAPPY Bobby Bloom—MGM 14212
[Jeff Barry/Bobby Bloom] [BMI] (1/9/71 BCR-68)

MAKE ME LOSE CONTROL Eric Carmen—Arista 1-9686
[Eric Carmen/Dean Pitchford] [BMI] (5/21/88 BC-3)

MAKE ME SMILE Chicago—Columbia 45127 [James Pankow] [ASC] (3/28/70 BCR-9)

MAKE ME SMILE AGAIN Cathy Jean—Valmor 009 [Ray Stevens] [BMI] (6/12/61 R-98)

MAKE ME SMILE (COME UP AND SEE ME) Steve Harley And Cockney Rebel—EMI 4201
[Steve Harley] [ASC] (2/28/76 B-96)

MAKE ME THE WOMAN THAT YOU GO HOME TO Gladys Knight & The Pips—Soul 35091
[Clay McMurray] [ASC] (12/11/71 BCR-22)

MAKE ME TWICE THE MAN New York City—Chelsea 0025
[Tim McQueen] [BMI] (8/4/73 BCR-78)

MAKE ME YOUR BABY Barbara Lewis—Atlantic 2300
[Roger Atkins/Helen Miller] [BMI] (9/11/65 BCR-11)

MAKE ME YOURS Bettye Swann—Money 126 [Bettye Swann] [BMI] (5/13/67 BCR-19)

MAKE MY DAY T.G. Sheppard with Clint Eastwood—Warner/Curb 29343 A
[Dewayne Blackwell] [BMI] (2/18/84 BC-62)

MAKE MY LIFE A LITTLE BIT BRIGHTER Chester—Bell 45,379
[Michael Argue/Glen Morrow*] [ASC] (9/1/73 C-100)

MAKE NO MISTAKE, HE'S MINE
Barbra Streisand (Duet With Kim Carnes)—Columbia 04695
[Kim Carnes] [ASC] (12/15/84 BC-42)

MAKE OUT ALRIGHT Divinyls—Virgin 98780
[Christina Amphlett/Mark McEntee/Martyn Watson] [BMI] (7/6/91 C-87)

MAKE SOMEONE HAPPY Perry Como—RCA Victor 47-7812
[Betty Comden/Adolph Green/Jule Styne] [ASC] (11/21/60 BCR-80)

MAKE THAT MOVE Shalamar—Solar 12192
[William Shelby/Ricky Darnell Smith/Kevin Spencer] [ASC] (4/11/81 BCR-53)

MAKE THE MUSIC PLAY Dionne Warwick—Scepter 1253
[Burt Bacharach/Hal David] [NA] (8/3/63 B-81)

MAKE THE WORLD GO AWAY *Timi Yuro—Liberty 55587*
[Hank Cochran] [BMI] (7/13/63 BCR-19)

MAKE THE WORLD GO AWAY *Ray Price—Columbia 42827*
[Hank Cochran] [BMI] (8/31/63 B-100)

MAKE THE WORLD GO AWAY *Eddy Arnold—RCA Victor 47-8679*
[Hank Cochran] [BMI] (10/16/65 BCR-6)

MAKE THE WORLD GO AWAY *Donny And Marie Osmond—MGM/Kolob 14807*
[Hank Cochran] [BMI] (6/7/75 BCR-44)

MAKE UP YOUR MIND The J. Geils Band—Atlantic 2974
[Seth Justman/Peter Wolf] [ASC] (8/4/73 BCR-76)

MAKE UP YOUR MIND Aurra—Salsoul 7017
[George Curtis Jones/Stephen C. Washington/Starleana Young] [BMI] (3/20/82 BCR-71)

(MAKE WITH) THE SHAKE The Mark IV—Cosmic 704
[Eddie Mascari/Erwin Wenzlaff] [BMI] (2/22/58 BCR-51)

MAKE YOU FEEL LOVE AGAIN Wet Willie—Epic 50528
[George Henry Jackson/Thomas Earl Jones III] [BMI] (4/1/78 BCR-41)

MAKE YOU SWEAT Keith Sweat—Vintertainment 64961
[Timmy Gatling/Keith Sweat/Bobby Wooten] [ASC] (6/2/90 BC-12)

MAKE YOUR OWN KIND OF MUSIC *Mama Cass Elliot—Dunhill 4214*
[Barry Mann/Cynthia Weil] [BMI] (10/18/69 BCR-22)

MAKE YOUR OWN KIND OF MUSIC *Barbra Streisand—Columbia 45686*
[Barry Mann/Cynthia Weil] (Med) [BMI] (9/30/72 BR-94)

MAKE YOURSELF COMFORTABLE *Sarah Vaughan—Mercury 70469*
[Bob Merrill] [ASC] (11/8/54 BCtRt-4)

MAKE YOURSELF COMFORTABLE *Peggy King—Columbia 40363*
[Bob Merrill] [ASC] (12/6/54 BRt-8)

MAKE YOURSELF COMFORTABLE *Eydie Gorme & Steve Lawrence—Coral 61313*
[Bob Merrill] [ASC] (12/13/54 Rt-PRE)

MAKE YOURSELF COMFORTABLE *Andy Griffith—Capitol 3057*
[Bob Merrill] [ASC] (3/19/55 BCt-25)

MAKES YOU BLIND Glitter Band—Arista 0207
[Mike Leander/Peter Phipps/Gerry Shephard] [ASC] (11/6/76 B-91) [I]

MAKIN' IT David Naughton—RSO 916
[Dino Fekaris/Freddie Perren] [ASC] (3/17/79 BCR-5)

MAKIN' LOVE Floyd Robinson—RCA Victor 47-7529
[Floyd Robinson] [BMI] (7/13/59 BCR-17)

MAKIN' LOVE Climax Blues Band—Sire 1026
[Colin Cooper/John Cuffley/Peter Haycock/Derek Holt] [ASC] (7/8/78 B-91)

MAKIN' THE BEST OF A BAD SITUATION Dick Feller—Asylum 11037
[Dick Feller] [BMI] (6/15/74 BCR-80)

MAKIN' WHOOPEE Ray Charles—ABC-Paramount 10609
[Walter Donaldson/Gus Kahn] [ASC] (12/12/64 BCR-39)

MAKING A GOOD THING BETTER Olivia Newton-John—MCA 40737
[Pete Wingfield] [ASC] (6/18/77 B-87)

MAKING BELIEVE Ray Charles—ABC-Paramount 10481
[Jimmy Work] [BMI] (9/7/63 CR-70)
MAKING EVERY MINUTE COUNT Spanky And Our Gang—Mercury 72714
[John Morier] [BMI] (8/19/67 BCR-17)
MAKING LOVE Roberta Flack—Atlantic 4005
[Burt Bacharach/Bruce Roberts/Carole Bayer Sager] [ASC] (3/6/82 BCR-13)
MAKING LOVE IN THE RAIN Herb Alpert—A&M 2949
[James Samuel Harris/Terry Lewis] [ASC] (7/18/87 BC-35)
MAKING LOVE OUT OF NOTHING AT ALL Air Supply—Arista 1-9056
[Jim Steinman] [BMI] (7/30/83 BC-2)
—MAKING LOVE see: KUFANYA MAPENZI
MAKING MEMORIES Frankie Laine—ABC 10924
[Larry Kusik/Eddie Snyder] [ASC] (4/8/67 BCR-28)
MAKING OUR DREAMS COME TRUE Cyndi Grecco—Private Stock 45,086
[Charles Fox/Norman Gimbel] [BMI] (4/24/76 BCR-21)
ALWAYS YOU *Betty Madigan—MGM 11812*
[Walter Gary/Jim Kriegsmann/Johnny Mario/Totò] [BMI] (10/9/54 CR-36) [FET]*
MALA FEMMENA *Jimmy Roselli—Lenox 5571 [Totò] [BMI] (8/24/63 Rt-85) [F]*
MALA FEMMENA *Connie Francis—MGM 13160*
[Ray Allen/George Brown*/Totò] [BMI] (8/24/63 Rt-85) [F,FET]*
MALAGUENA *Caterina Valente—Decca 29394*
[Ernesto Lecuona/Ralph Siegel] [BMI] (1/17/55 CRt-22) [F]
MALAGUENA *Stan Kenton & His Orchestra—Capitol 3047*
[Ernesto Lecuona] [BMI] (2/28/55 Rt-23) [IM]
MALAGUEÑA *Connie Francis—MGM 12923*
[Ernesto Lecuona] [BMI] (8/15/60 BCR-42) [F]
—MALATIA see: ONE KISS AWAY FROM HEAVEN
MALAYISHA Miriam Makeba—Reprise 0654
[Miriam Makeba/Jerry Ragovoy*] [ASC] (1/20/68 BCR-60)
MALINDA Bobby Taylor & The Vancouvers—Gordy 7079
[Al Cleveland/Terry Johnson/Smokey Robinson] [ASC] (12/7/68 BCR-48)
MAMA Connie Francis—MGM 12878
[Harold Barlow/Cesare Bixio/Phil Brito/Bixio Cherubini] [ASC] (2/22/60 BCR-7) [F,FDE]
MAMA B.J. Thomas—Scepter 12139 [Mark Charron] [BMI] (5/14/66 BCR-15)
MAMA Genesis—Atlantic 89770
[Tony Banks/Phil Collins/Mike Rutherford] [ASC] (10/1/83 BC-60)
A MAMA AND A PAPA Ray Stevens—Barnaby 2029 [Tom Autry] [BMI] (5/1/71 BCR-58)
MAMA CAN'T BUY YOU LOVE Elton John—MCA 41042
[Leroy Bell/Casey James] [BMI] (6/9/79 BCR-7)
(MAMA COME QUICK, AND BRING YOUR) LICKIN' STICK
George Torrence & The Naturals—Shout 224
[Charles Manley/George Torrence] [BMI] (2/17/68 BCR-91)
MAMA DIDN'T LIE *Jan Bradley—Chess 1845*
[Curtis Mayfield] [BMI] (1/5/63 BCtRt-13)
MAMA DIDN'T LIE *The Fasinations—ABC-Paramount 10387*
[Curtis Mayfield] [BMI] (1/12/63 CtRt-13)
THE MAMA DOLL SONG *Patti Page—Mercury 70458*
[Nat Simon/Charles Tobias] [ASC] (10/4/54 BCR-14)
THE MAMA DOLL SONG *Guy Lombardo & His Royal Canadians—Decca 29301*
[Nat Simon/Charles Tobias] [ASC] (11/1/54 Rt-PRE)
MAMA DON'T ALLOW The Rooftop Singers—Vanguard 35020
[Erik Darling/Willard Svanoe/Lynne Taylor] [BMI] (7/13/63 BCR-48)
MAMA DON'T ALLOW NO PARKIN' Brownsville Station—Big Tree 16029
[Cub Koda/Michael Lutz] [ASC] (12/7/74 CR-74)
MAMA DON'T CRY AT MY WEDDING Joni James—MGM 11802
[Helene Hudgins] [BMI] (9/11/54 CR-19)
MAMA FROM THE TRAIN Patti Page—Mercury 70971
[Irving Gordon] [ASC] (10/13/56 BCR-11)
MAMA GUITAR *Don Cornell—Coral 61819*
[Tom Glazer/Budd Schulberg] [ASC] (4/20/57 BCtRt-44)
MAMA GUITAR *Julius La Rosa—RCA Victor 47-6878*
[Tom Glazer/Budd Schulberg] [ASC] (4/20/57 BCtRt-44)
MAMA GUITAR *Andy Griffith—Capitol 3705*
[Tom Glazer/Budd Schulberg] [ASC] (4/27/57 Rt-44)
MAMA (HE TREATS YOUR DAUGHTER MEAN) *The Dinning Sisters Featuring Jean Dinning—*
Essex 388 [Herb Lance/Charles Singleton/Johnny Wallace] [BMI] (3/12/55 CRt-36)*
(MAMA) HE TREATS YOUR DAUGHTER MEAN *Ruth Brown—Atlantic 986*
[Herb Lance/Charles Singleton/Johnny Wallace] [BMI] (3/14/55 Rt-71)*
MAMA (HE TREATS YOUR DAUGHTER MEAN) *Bette Anne Steele—Capitol 3073*
[Herb Lance/Charles Singleton/Johnny Wallace] [BMI] (3/28/55 Rt-71)*
MAMA (HE TREATS YOUR DAUGHTER MEAN) *Ruth Brown—Philips 40056*
[Herb Lance/Charles Singleton/Johnny Wallace] [BMI] (9/8/62 B-99)*
MAMA LET HIM PLAY Doucette—Mushroom 7030 [Jerry Doucette] [ASC] (4/1/78 BCR-66)
MAMA LIKED THE ROSES Elvis Presley—RCA Victor 47-9835
[Johnny Christopher] (TSW) [BMI] (5/16/70 BC-9)
MAMA LOOK AT BUBU *Harry Belafonte—RCA Victor 47-6830*
[Lord Melody] [ASC] (3/16/57 BCRt-6)
MAMA LOOKA BOO BOO *Robert Mitchum—Capitol 3672*
[Lord Melody] [ASC] (3/16/57 Rt-6)
MAMA, LOOKA BOO BOO (BOO BOO MAN)
Calypso Carnival Featuring King Flash—Columbia 40866
[Lord Melody] [ASC] (3/16/57 Rt-6)
MAMA LOOK A BOOBOO *Marty Franklin—Cadence 1321*
[Lord Melody] [ASC] (5/4/57 Rt-10)
(MAMA, MAMA) WISH ME GOOD LUCK Carla Thomas—Atlantic 2113
[Carla Thomas] [BMI] (8/28/61 R-97)
MAMA ROSA Julius La Rosa—Cadence 1265 [Nicola Paone] [ASC] (6/25/55 CR-37)
MAMA SAID The Shirelles—Scepter 1217
[Willie Denson/Luther Dixon] [BMI] (4/10/61 BCR-4)
MAMA SAID KNOCK YOU OUT LL Cool J—Def Jam 73706
[George Clinton*/William Earl Collins*/Gregory Jacobs*/James McCants*/
Leroy McCants*/Walter Morrison*/James Todd Smith/Sylvester Stewart*/
Marlon Williams] [ASC] (4/13/91 BC-17)
MAMA SANG A SONG *Stan Kenton—Capitol 4847*
[Bill Anderson] [BMI] (10/13/62 BCtRt-22)
MAMA SANG A SONG *Bill Anderson—Decca 31404*
[Bill Anderson] [BMI] (10/20/62 BCtRt-22)
MAMA SANG A SONG *Walter Brennan—Liberty 55508*
[Bill Anderson] [BMI] (10/20/62 BCtRt-22)
MAMA TEACH ME TO DANCE *Eydie Gorme—ABC-Paramount 9722*
[Al Hoffman/Dick Manning] [ASC] (7/6/56 BCRt-16)
MAMA, TEACH ME TO DANCE *Bobby Madera & His Orchestra—ABC-Paramount 9731*
[Al Hoffman/Dick Manning] [ASC] (9/22/56 Rt-21)
MAMA TOLD ME (NOT TO COME) *Three Dog Night—Dunhill 4239*
[Randy Newman] [BMI] (5/23/70 BCR-1)
MAMA TOLD ME NOT TO COME *Wilson Pickett—Atlantic 2909*
[Randy Newman] [BMI] (11/11/72 BCR-81)
MAMA USED TO SAY Junior—Mercury 76132
[Robert Ashley Carter/Junior Giscombe] [ASC] (2/13/82 BCR-30)
MAMA WAS A COTTON PICKER Jimmie Rodgers—Dot 16561
[Marty Cooper] [ASC] (1/4/64 R-91)
MAMA WAS A ROCK AND ROLL SINGER, PAPA USED TO WRITE ALL HER SONGS
Sonny & Cher—MCA 40026
[Sonny Bono] [BMI] (3/17/73 BCR-60)
MAMA WEER ALL CRAZEE NOW *Slade—Polydor 15053*
[Noddy Holder/Jim Lea] [ASC] (11/18/72 BCR-60)
MAMA WEER ALL CRAZEE NOW *Quiet Riot—Pasha 04505*
[Noddy Holder/Jim Lea] [ASC] (7/7/84 BC-49)
MAMA (WHEN MY DOLLIES HAVE BABIES) Cher—Imperial 66223
[Sonny Bono] [BMI] (12/17/66 CR-70)
MAMACITA The Grass Roots—Haven 7015
[Barry Mann/Cynthia Weil] [BMI] (8/2/75 BCR-71)
—MAMA'S GOT THE RHYTHM—PAPA'S GOT THE BLUES see: RHYTHM 'N' BLUES
MAMA'S PEARL The Jackson 5—Motown 1177
[Berry Gordy/Fonce Mizell/Freddie Perren/Deke Richards] [ASC] (1/23/71 BCR-1)
MAMA'S PLACE Bing Day—Mercury 71446
[Murray Allen/Dan Belloc/Bing Day] [ASC] (5/18/59 CR-98)
MAMBO BABY *Ruth Brown And Her Rhythmakers with Orchestra—Atlantic 1044*
[Rose Marie McCoy/Charles Singleton] [BMI] (11/13/54 C-41)
MAMBO BABY *Georgia Gibbs—Mercury 70473*
[Rose Marie McCoy/Charles Singleton] [BMI] (11/13/54 C-41)
MAMBO IN THE MOONLIGHT Gary Crosby And The Cheer Leaders—Decca 29272
[Buddy Kaye/Jules Loman/René Touzet] [ASC] (10/4/54 CR-47)
MAMBO ITALIANO Rosemary Clooney—Columbia 40361
[Bob Merrill] [ASC] (10/18/54 BCR-8)
—MAMBO NUMBER FIVE see: SEVEN ELEVEN
MAMBO ROCK *The Mike Pedicin Quintette—RCA Victor 47-6051*
[Jimmy Ayre/Mildred Phillips/Bickley Reichner] [ASC] (3/7/55 Rt-14)
MAMBO ROCK *Bill Haley And His Comets—Decca 29418*
[Jimmy Ayre/Mildred Phillips/Bickley Reichner] (TSW) [ASC] (4/16/55 BCRt-14)
MAME *Bobby Darin—Atlantic 2329 [Jerry Herman] [ASC] (4/30/66 BCRt-53)*
MAME *Louis Armstrong—Mercury 72574 [Jerry Herman] [ASC] (5/7/66 BCRt-57)*
MAME *Herb Alpert & The Tijuana Brass—A&M 823*
[Jerry Herman] [ASC] (11/12/66 BCR-17)
MAMMA MIA Abba—Atlantic 3315
[Stig Anderson/Benny Andersson/Björn Ulvaeus] [BMI] (5/22/76 BCR-32)
MAMMAS DON'T LET YOUR BABIES GROW UP TO BE COWBOYS
Waylon & Willie—RCA 11198
[Ed Bruce*/Patsy Bruce] [BMI] (2/11/78 BCR-42)
MAMMY BLUE *Pop-Tops—ABC 11311*
[Hubert Giraud/Phil Trim] [ASC] (10/2/71 BCR-44) [FET]
MAMMY BLUE *James Darren—Kirshner 5015*
[Hubert Giraud/Phil Trim] [ASC] (10/9/71 CR-60) [FET]
MAMMY BLUE *Stories—Kama Sutra 584*
[Hubert Giraud/Phil Trim] [ASC] (10/20/73 BCR-21) [FET]
THE MAN Lorne Greene—RCA Victor 47-8490 [Merle Kilgore] [BMI] (1/30/65 BCR-72)
MAN AGAINST THE WORLD Survivor—Scotti Brothers 07070
[Jimi Jamison/Jim Peterik/Frankie Sullivan] [ASC] (5/9/87 BC-81)

A MAN AND A HALF Wilson Pickett—Atlantic 2575
[Larry Chambers/George Henry Jackson/Melvin Leakes/Raymond Moore] [BMI] (11/16/68 BCR-42)

A MAN AND A WOMAN Tamiko Jones With Herbie Mann—Atlantic 2362
[Pierre Barouh/Jerry Keller/Francis Lai] [ASC] (11/12/66 B-88)

THE MAN & THE WOMAN The Chi-Lites—Brunswick 55483
[Eugene Record] (TSW) [BMI] (9/30/72 B-57)

A MAN CHASES A GIRL (UNTIL SHE CATCHES HIM) Eddie Fisher—RCA Victor 47-6015
[Irving Berlin] [ASC] (2/7/55 BCR-16)

MAN FROM LARAMIE *The Voices Of Walter Schumann—RCA Victor 47-6157*
[Lester Lee/Ned Washington] [ASC] (8/29/55 CRt-50)

THE MAN FROM LARAMIE *Al Martino—Capitol 3171*
[Lester Lee/Ned Washington] [ASC] (8/29/55 Rt-74)

THE MAN FROM LARAMIE *Ralph Young—Decca 29615*
[Lester Lee/Ned Washington] [ASC] (8/29/55 Rt-74)

THE MAN FROM LARAMIE *Eddy Howard & His Orchestra—Mercury 70639*
[Lester Lee/Ned Washington] [ASC] (9/5/55 Rt-74)

A MAN I'LL NEVER BE Boston—Epic 50638 [Tom Scholz] [ASC] (11/11/78 BCR-31)

MAN IN BLACK Johnny Cash—Columbia 45339 [Johnny Cash] [ASC] (3/13/71 BCR-44)

—MAN IN MOTION see: ST. ELMO'S FIRE

MAN IN THE MIRROR Michael Jackson—Epic 07668
[Glen Ballard/Siedah Garrett] [ASC] (2/6/88 BC-1)

MAN IN THE PHONE BOOTH The Wanderer—Flair-X 5003
[Lee Pines*/Herb Zane] [BMI] (2/23/57 R-84)

MAN IN THE RAINCOAT *Priscilla Wright—Unique 303*
[Warwick Webster] [BMI] (6/6/55 BCtRt-12)

THE MAN IN THE RAINCOAT *Karen Chandler—Coral 61433*
[Warwick Webster] [BMI] (6/6/55 Rt-19)

MAN IN THE RAINCOAT *Marion Marlowe—Cadence 1266*
[Warwick Webster] [BMI] (6/20/55 CtRt-12)

THE MAN IN THE RAINCOAT *Lita Roza with Bob Sharples & His Music—London 1589*
[Warwick Webster] [BMI] (7/4/55 Rt-12)

A MAN NEEDS A WOMAN James Carr—Goldwax 332
[Quinton Claunch/O.B. McClinton] [BMI] (12/30/67 BCR-57)

MAN OF CONSTANT SORROW Ginger Baker's Air Force—Atco 6750
[Traditional] [NA] (5/16/70 BCR-79)

THE MAN ON PAGE 602 Zoot Fenster—Antique 106
[Helen Ann Fischer/Eugene Strasser/George Dodson Winters] [BMI] (11/29/75 C-91)

MAN ON THE CORNER Genesis—Atlantic 4025 [Phil Collins] [ASC] (3/20/82 BCR-40)

MAN ON YOUR MIND Little River Band—Capitol 5061
[Glenn Shorrock/Kerryn Tolhurst] [BMI] (4/3/82 BCR-13)

MAN SIZE LOVE Klymaxx—MCA 52841 [Rod Temperton] [ASC] (7/5/86 BC-15)

MAN SIZED JOB Denise LaSalle—Westbound 206
[Denise LaSalle] [BMI] (9/30/72 BCR-40)

MAN SMART, WOMAN SMARTER Robert Palmer—Island 075
[Norman Span] [BMI] (11/27/76 BCR-63)

—MAN THAT GOT AWAY see: GAL THAT GOT AWAY

THE MAN THAT TURNED MY MAMA ON Tanya Tucker—Columbia 46047
[Ed Bruce*/Patsy Bruce] [BMI] (7/27/74 BCR-62)

MAN THAT'S CHOICE Sam (The Man) Taylor And His Orchestra—MGM 12696
[Stan Lebowsky/Johnny Lehmann] [BMI] (8/18/58 R-100)

THE MAN UPSTAIRS Kay Starr—Capitol 2769
[Bill Anson/Dorinda Morgan/Hal Stanley] [ASC] (5/29/54 BC-PRE)

(THE MAN WHO SHOT) LIBERTY VALANCE Gene Pitney—Musicor 1020
[Burt Bacharach/Hal David] [ASC] (4/9/62 BCR-4)

A MAN WHO SINGS Richard Landis—Dunhill 4300
[Richard Landis/Joan Meltzer] [ASC] (3/4/72 R-83)

THE MAN WITH THE BANJO The Ames Brothers—RCA Victor 47-5644
[Hans Bradtke/Robert Mellin/Fritz Schulz-Reichel] [BMI] (5/29/54 BC-PRE)

THE MAN WITH THE CHILD IN HIS EYES Kate Bush—EMI America 8006
[Kate Bush] [BMI] (2/17/79 B-85)

A MAN WITHOUT LOVE (QUANDO M'INNAMORO) Engelbert Humperdinck—Parrot 40027
[Roberto Livraghi/Barry Mason/Daniele Pace/Mario Panzeri] [ASC] (5/11/68 BCR-13) [FDE]

MANANA Jimmy Buffett—ABC 12428 [Jimmy Buffett] [BMI] (12/2/78 BR-84)

MANDOLIN RAIN Bruce Hornsby And The Range—RCA 5087
[Bruce Hornsby/John Hornsby] [ASC] (1/17/87 BC-4)

MANDOLINO Les Paul and Mary Ford—Capitol 2928
[Les Paul] [BMI] (10/4/54 CR-22) [IM]

MANDOLINS IN THE MOONLIGHT Perry Como—RCA Victor 47-7353
[Aaron Schroeder/George David Weiss] [ASC] (10/6/58 BCR-32)

MANDRILL Mandrill—Polydor 14070
[Claude Cave/Fudgie Kae/Omar Mesa/Charlie Pardo/Carlos Wilson/Louis Wilson/Ric Wilson] [ASC] (5/22/71 BCR-82) [I]

BRANDY *Scott English—Janus 171 [Scott English/Richard Kerr] [BMI] (3/4/72 BCR-70)*

MANDY *Barry Manilow—Bell 45,613*
[Scott English/Richard Kerr] [BMI] (11/16/74 BCR-1)

MANEATER Daryl Hall & John Oates—RCA Victor 13354
[Sara Allen/Daryl Hall/John Oates] [BMI] (10/16/82 BC-1)

MANGOS *Rosemary Clooney—Columbia 40835*
[Dee Libbey/Sid Wayne] [ASC] (3/16/57 BCRt-23)

MANGOS *Buddy Morrow & His Orchestra—Mercury 71091*
[Dee Libbey/Sid Wayne] [ASC] (4/20/57 Rt-28)

MANGOS *Roger King Mozian—Decca 30330 [Dee Libbey] [ASC] (6/1/57 Rt-28) [IM]*

MANHATTAN SPIRITUAL *Reg Owen And His Orchestra—Palette 5005*
[Billy Maxted] [BMI] (12/8/58 BCR-10) [I]

MANHATTAN SPIRITUAL *Mike Post—MGM 14829 [Billy Maxted] [BMI] (9/27/75 BC-56) [I]*

MANIAC Michael Sembello—Casablanca 812516
[Dennis Matkosky/Michael Sembello] [ASC] (6/4/83 BC-1)

MANIC MONDAY Bangles—Columbia 05757 [Prince] [ASC] (1/25/86 BC-2)

MAN'S TEMPTATION Gene Chandler—Vee-Jay 536
[Curtis Mayfield] [BMI] (8/3/63 BCR-49)

MANY A TIME Steve Lawrence—Coral 62025
[Paul Koy/Frank Mader] [BMI] (9/8/58 BCR-66)

MANY A WONDERFUL MOMENT Rosemary Clooney—RCA Victor 47-7754
[Hal David/Sid Lippman] [ASC] (8/29/60 B-84)

MANY RIVERS TO CROSS Nilsson—RCA Victor 10001 [Jimmy Cliff] [BMI] (7/27/74 CR-78)

MANY TEARS AGO Connie Francis—MGM 12964 [Winfield Scott] [BMI] (10/31/60 BCR-6)

MARBLE BREAKS AND IRON BENDS Drafi—London 10825
[Christian Bruhn/Drafi Deutscher/Rudolf Loose/Marcel Stellman] [ASC] (4/30/66 BCR-60) [FET]

MARCH OF THE SIAMESE CHILDREN Kenny Ball And His Jazzmen—Kapp 451
[Richard Rodgers] [ASC] (4/2/62 BCR-74) [I]

MARCH OF THE TOREADORS The Royal Philharmonic Orchestra—RCA 12304
[Georges Bizet] (Med) [NA] (10/31/81 BCR-9) [I]

MARCHING ALONG TO THE BLUES Perry Como—RCA Victor 47-6991
[Allan Roberts] [ASC] (8/17/57 CR-42)

—MARCHING SAINTS see: WHEN THE SAINTS...

MARCHING THRU MADRID Herb Alpert's Tijuana Brass—A&M 706
[Sol Lake] [ASC] (3/23/63 BC-90) [I]

MARE, TAKE ME HOME Matthews' Southern Comfort—Decca 32845
[Al Anderson] [BMI] (7/24/71 B-96)

MARGARITA Chuck Rio And The Originals—Jackpot 48016
[Kay Thompson] [BMI] (3/30/59 R-88)

MARGARITAVILLE Jimmy Buffett—ABC 12254 [Jimmy Buffett] [BMI] (3/26/77 BCR-7)

MARGIE Fats Domino—Imperial 5585
[Con Conrad/Benny Davis/J. Russel Robinson] [ASC] (5/11/59 BCR-32)

MARGO (THE NINTH OF MAY)
The Browns Featuring Jim Edward Brown—RCA Victor 47-7755
[Boudleaux Bryant] [BMI] (7/23/60 C-89)

MARIA *Johnny Mathis—Columbia 41684*
[Leonard Bernstein/Stephen Sondheim] [ASC] (5/30/60 BCR-50)

MARIA *Roger Williams—Kapp 437 [Leonard Bernstein] [ASC] (11/27/61 BCtRt-40) [IM]*

MARIA *The Clebanoff Strings—Mercury 71905*
[Leonard Bernstein] [ASC] (11/27/61 CtRt-40) [IM]

MARIA *Johnny Mathis—Columbia 41684*
[Leonard Bernstein/Stephen Sondheim] [ASC] (12/11/61 BCt-40)

MARIA ELENA *Los Indios Tabajaras—RCA Victor 47-8216*
[Lorenzo Barcelata] [ASC] (8/10/63 BCRt-6) [IM]

MARIA ELENA *Billy Mure—MGM 13161 [Lorenzo Barcelata] [ASC] (8/31/63 Rt-60) [IM]*

MARIA (YOU WERE THE ONLY ONE) Jimmy Ruffin—Soul 35077
[Lawrence Brown/Linda Glover/George Gordy/Allen Story] [BMI] (2/13/71 BCR-90)

MARIANNA Lou Monte—RCA Victor 47-7346 [Wandra Merrell] [NA] (9/22/58 R-87)

MARIANNA Johnny Mathis—Columbia 42420
[Alfred Newman/Paul Francis Webster] [ASC] (5/26/62 BR-85)

MARIANNE *Terry Gilkyson And The Easy Riders—Columbia 40817*
[Rafael de Leon/Richard Dehr/Terry Gilkyson/Frank Miller/Traditional] [BMI] (1/19/57 BCtRt-1)*

MARIANNE *The Hilltoppers—Dot 15537*
[Rafael de Leon/Richard Dehr/Terry Gilkyson/Frank Miller/Traditional] [BMI] (1/26/57 BCtRt-1)*

MARIANNE *The Lane Brothers—RCA Victor 47-6810*
[Rafael de Leon/Richard Dehr/Terry Gilkyson/Frank Miller/Traditional] [BMI] (2/2/57 BRt-1)*

MARY ANN *The Talbot Brothers—Audio Fidelity 071*
[Rafael de Leon/Richard Dehr/Terry Gilkyson/Frank Miller/Traditional] [BMI] (2/9/57 Rt-12)*

MARY ANN *Edmundo Ros & His Orchestra—London 1730*
[Rafael de Leon/Richard Dehr/Terry Gilkyson/Frank Miller/Traditional] [BMI] (2/9/57 Rt-12)*

MARIANNE *Burl Ives—Decca 30217*
[Rafael de Leon/Richard Dehr/Terry Gilkyson/Frank Miller/Traditional] [BMI] (2/23/57 BRt-1)*

MARIANNE Stephen Stills—Atlantic 2820
[Stephen Stills] [BMI] (8/14/71 BCR-31)

MARIE *The Modernaires—Coral 61779 [Irving Berlin] (Med) [ASC] (2/16/57 R-72)*

MARIE *The Four Tunes—Jubilee 6000 [Irving Berlin] [ASC] (10/24/59 C-90)*

MARIE *The Bachelors—London 9762 [Irving Berlin] [ASC] (6/5/65 BCR-14)*

MARIE'S THE NAME HIS LATEST FLAME Elvis Presley—RCA Victor 47-7908
[Doc Pomus/Mort Shuman] [BMI] (8/21/61 BCR-4)

—MARIKO'S THEME see: LOVE THEME FROM SHOGUN

MARILYN MONROE MAMBO Perez Prado And His Orchestra—RCA Victor 47-5892
[Perez Prado] [BMI] (10/18/54 R-53) [I]

MARIMBA CHARLESTON Marimba Chiapas—Capitol 3447
[Hermisendo Paniagua] [BMI] (7/14/56 B-82) [I]

MARINA *Rocco Granata and the International Quintet—Laurie 3041*
[Rocco Granata] [ASC] (10/26/59 BCtRt-12) [F]

MARINA *Willy Alberti—London 1888 [Rocco Granata] [ASC] (10/26/59 BCtRt-12) [F]*

MARINA *Joe Vina—Allied 7778 [Rocco Granata] [ASC] (10/26/59 Rt-66) [F]*

MARINA *Jacky Noguez and His Orchestra—Jamie 1137*
[Rocco Granata] [ASC] (10/26/59 BRt-12) [I]

MARINA *Tony Martin—RCA Victor 47-7633 [Rocco Granata] [ASC] (11/2/59 Rt-42) [F]*

MARJOLAINA Gogi Grant—RCA Victor 47-7294
[Francis Lemarque/Rudi Revil/Sunny Skylar] [ASC] (7/28/58 R-77)

MARLENA The 4 Seasons—Vee-Jay 539 [Bob Gaudio] [ASC] (7/6/63 BCR-35)

MARLEY PURT DRIVE Jose Feliciano—RCA Victor 47-9739
[Barry Gibb/Maurice Gibb/Robin Gibb] [BMI] (4/26/69 BCR-60)

MARNIE Nat King Cole—Capitol 5219
[Bernard Herrmann/Peter Jason/Gloria Shayne] [BMI] (7/11/64 R-96)

MARRAKESH EXPRESS Crosby, Stills & Nash—Atlantic 2652
[Graham Nash] [BMI] (7/12/69 BCR-17)

MARRIED BUT NOT TO EACH OTHER Denise LaSalle—Westbound 5019
[Denise LaSalle/Frances H. Miller] [BMI] (5/15/76 R-84)

MARRIED I CAN ALWAYS GET *Teddi King—RCA Victor 47-6660*
[Gordon Jenkins] [ASC] (11/3/56 BRt-75)

MARRIED I CAN ALWAYS GET *Gordon Jenkins & His Orchestra—Capitol 3556*
[Gordon Jenkins] [ASC] (11/3/56 Rt-75)

MARRIED I CAN ALWAYS GET *Jeri Southern—Decca 30106*
[Gordon Jenkins] [ASC] (11/3/56 Rt-75)

MARRIED MAN Richard Burton—MGM 13307
[Marian Grudeff/Ray Jessel] [BMI] (1/23/65 BCR-56)

MARRIED MEN Bette Midler—Atlantic 3582
[Dominic Bugatti/Frank Musker] [BMI] (6/2/79 BCR-40)

MARRIED TO A MEMORY *Judy Lynn—Amaret 131 [Alex Harvey] [ASC] (4/10/71 R-76)*

MARRIED TO A MEMORY *Arlene Harden—Columbia 45635*
[Alex Harvey] [ASC] (4/24/71 R-87)

MARTA The Bachelors—London 20027
[L. Wolfe Gilbert/Moises Simons] [BMI] (7/15/67 CR-97)

MARTHA (YOUR LOVERS COME AND GO) Gabriel—Epic 50594
[Terry Lauber] [ASC] (9/30/78 BCR-73)

THE MARTIAN BOOGIE Brownsville Station—Private Stock 45,167
[Cub Koda/Michael Lutz/Bruce Nazarian/Henry Weck] [ASC] (8/20/77 BCR-45)

MARTIAN HOP The Ran-Dells—Chairman 4403
[Robert Rappaport/Steve Rappaport/John Spirt] [BMI] (8/3/63 BCR-13)

MARTIKA'S KITCHEN Martika—Columbia 74094 [Prince] [ASC] (11/30/91 C-74)

MARTINIQUE The Exotic Sounds Of Martin Denny—Liberty 55199
[Norman Warren] [ASC] (7/11/59 BCR-78) [I]

THE MARVELOUS TOY The Chad Mitchell Trio—Mercury 72197
[Tom Paxton] [ASC] (11/30/63 BCR-41)

MARY AND MAN-O Lloyd Price And His Great Orchestra—ABC-Paramount 10221
[Harold Logan/Lloyd Price] [BMI] (6/5/61 R-98)

MARY ANN REGRETS Burl Ives—Decca 31433 [Harlan Howard] [BMI] (10/27/62 BCR-20)

MARY ANN THOMAS *Bobby Freeman—Josie 863*
[Ben Raleigh/Don Wolf] [BMI] (6/1/59 BCRt-82)

MARY ANN THOMAS *Buddy Heart—Decca 30892*
[Ben Raleigh/Don Wolf] [BMI] (6/15/59 Rt-89)

MARY ANNE The Fallenrock—Capricorn 0227
[Larry Keith/Steve Pippin] [BMI] (5/31/75 R-90)

MARY DON'T YOU WEEP Stonewall Jackson—Columbia 41533
[Mel Tillis/Marijohn Wilkin] [BMI] (12/28/59 BCR-41)

MARY HAD A LITTLE LAMB Wings—Apple 1851
[Linda McCartney/Paul McCartney] (TSW) [ASC] (6/24/72 BCR-28)

MARY HARTMAN, MARY HARTMAN The Deadly Nightshade—Phantom 10709
[Robert Kingston] [ASC] (7/3/76 BCR-65)

MARY IN THE MORNING Al Martino—Capitol 5904
[Johnny Cymbal/Mike Lendell] [ASC] (5/27/67 BCR-27)

MARY JANE Ernie Maresca—Seville 119 [Ernie Maresca] [ASC] (6/30/62 R-81)

MARY JANE Rick James—Gordy 7162 [Rick James] [ASC] (10/28/78 BCR-41)

MARY LOU Ronnie Hawkins and The Hawks—Roulette 4177
[Ronnie Hawkins/Jacqueline Magill] [BMI] (8/10/59 BCR-24)

MARY, MARY Run-D.M.C.—Profile 5211 [Michael Nesmith] [BMI] (7/30/88 BC-75)

MARY, MARY LOU Bill Haley & His Comets—Decca 30530
[Cayet Mangiaracina] [BMI] (12/23/57 R-54)

MARY'S BOY CHILD *Harry Belafonte—RCA Victor 47-6735*
[Jester Hairston] [BMI] (12/15/56 BCRt-14)

MARY'S LITTLE BOY CHILE *Mahalia Jackson—Columbia 40777*
[Jester Hairston] [BMI] (12/15/56 Rt-14)

MARY'S LITTLE BOY CHILE *The Four Lads—Columbia 40788*
[Jester Hairston] [BMI] (12/15/56 Rt-14)

MARY'S BOY CHILD *Boney M—Sire 1036 [Jester Hairston] (Med) [BMI] (12/23/78 B-85)*

MARY'S LITTLE LAMB James Darren—Colpix 644
[Barry Mann/Cynthia Weil] [BMI] (6/30/62 BCR-39)

MARY'S PRAYER Danny Wilson—Virgin 99465 [Gary Clark] [BMI] (6/6/87 BC-23)

MAS QUE NADA Sergio Mendes & Brasil '66—A&M 807
[Jorge Ben] [BMI] (9/24/66 BCR-47) [F]

MASHED POTATO TIME Dee Dee Sharp—Cameo 212
[Robert Bateman/Georgia Dobbins/William Garrett/Freddie Gorman/Brian Holland/
Bernie Lowe/Kal Mann] [BMI] (2/19/62 BCR-1)

(DO THE) MASHED POTATOES (PART 1) *Nat Kendrick And The Swans—Dade 1804*
[James Brown] [BMI] (1/23/60 BCR-52)

MASHED POTATOES (PART 1) *Steve Alaimo—Checker 1006*
[James Brown] [BMI] (3/12/62 BR-81)

MASHED POTATOES U.S.A. James Brown And The Famous Flames—King 5672
[James Brown] [BMI] (9/29/62 B-82)

MASHUGA Louis Prima & Keely Smith—Dot 16042
[Sid Danoff/Edward White/Mack Wolfson] [ASC] (1/25/60 R-79)

MASQUERADE Berlin—Geffen 29504 [Chris Ruiz-Velasco] [ASC] (9/24/83 BC-79)

MASTER AND SERVANT Depeche Mode—Sire 28918 [Martin L. Gore] [BMI] (9/7/85 B-87)

MASTER BLASTER (JAMMIN') *Stevie Wonder—Tamla 54317*
[Stevie Wonder] [ASC] (9/20/80 BCR-1)

MASTER BLASTER *Stars On 45—Radio 4019*
[Stevie Wonder] (Med) [ASC] (3/27/82 BCR-28)

MASTER JACK Four Jacks And A Jill—RCA Victor 47-9473
[Spiro Marks] [ASC] (3/16/68 BCR-9)

MASTER OF EYES (THE DEEPNESS OF YOUR EYES) Aretha Franklin—Atlantic 2941
[Aretha Franklin/Bernice Hart] [BMI] (2/10/73 BCR-31)

MASTERPIECE The Temptations—Gordy 7126 [Norman Whitfield] [BMI] (2/17/73 BCR-7)

THE MATADOR Johnny Cash—Columbia 42880
[June Carter/Johnny Cash] [NA] (10/19/63 BCR-39)

THE MATADOR Major Lance—Okeh 7191
[William Earl Butler/Carl Davis/Major Lance] [BMI] (3/28/64 BCR-20)

MATCHBOX The Beatles—Capitol 5255 [Carl Perkins] [BMI] (9/5/64 BCR-17)

MATERIAL GIRL Madonna—Sire 29083
[Peter H. Brown/Robert Rans] [BMI] (2/9/85 BC-1)

MATHEMATICS Melissa Manchester—MCA 52575
[Melissa Manchester/Robbie Nevil/Brock Walsh] [BMI] (4/27/85 BC-72)

MATILDA HAS FINALLY COME BACK Cookie & His Cupcakes—Mercury 71748
[George Khoury/Huey Thierry] [BMI] (1/19/59 B-47)

A MATTER OF TRUST Billy Joel—Columbia 06108 [Billy Joel] [ASC] (8/9/86 BC-10)

MATTHEW AND SON Cat Stevens—Deram 7505 [Cat Stevens] [ASC] (3/25/67 CR-92)

MAU-MAU The Wailers—Golden Crest 526
[Rich Dangel/John Greek/Kent Morrill*] [BMI] (8/17/59 B-68) [I]

MAY I Bill Deal & The Rhondels—Heritage 803
[Maurice Williams] [BMI] (12/28/68 BCR-33)

MAY I NEVER LOVE AGAIN
Tony Bennett with Percy Faith and His Orchestra—Columbia 40523
[Jack Erickson/Sano Marco] [BMI] (6/13/55 CR-33)

MAY I TAKE A GIANT STEP (INTO YOUR HEART) 1910 Fruitgum Co.—Buddah 39
[Elliot Chiprut] [BMI] (4/20/68 BCR-45)

MAY MY HEART BE CAST INTO STONE The Toys—DynoVoice 218
[Sandy Linzer/Denny Randell] [BMI] (4/2/66 B-85)

MAY THE BIRD OF PARADISE FLY UP YOUR NOSE
"Little" Jimmy Dickens—Columbia 43388
[Neal Merritt] [BMI] (10/16/65 BCR-15)

MAY YOU ALWAYS The McGuire Sisters—Coral 62059
[Dick Charles/Larry Markes] [ASC] (12/22/58 BCR-11)

MAYBE *The Chantels—End 1005*
[Richard Barrett/George Goldner‡/Arlene Smith] [BMI] (1/6/58 BCR-15)

MAYBE *The Shangri-Las—Red Bird 10-019*
[Richard Barrett/George Goldner‡/Arlene Smith] [BMI] (12/26/64 B-91)

MAYBE *The Three Degrees—Roulette 7079*
[Richard Barrett/George Goldner‡/Arlene Smith] [BMI] (6/6/70 BCR-15)

MAYBE Betty Everett—Uni 55141 [Lee Simmons/Floyd Smith] [BMI] (8/30/69 R-91)

MAYBE BABY Buddy Holly / The Crickets—Brunswick 55053
[Buddy Holly/Norman Petty] [ASC] (2/17/58 BCR-9)

MAYBE I KNOW Lesley Gore—Mercury 72309
[Jeff Barry/Ellie Greenwich] [BMI] (7/25/64 BCR-10)

MAYBE I'M A FOOL Eddie Money—Columbia 10900
[Lloyd Chiate/Lee Garrett/Eddie Money/Robert Percy Taylor] [BMI] (1/27/79 BCR-22)

MAYBE I'M AMAZED Wings—Capitol 4385 [Paul McCartney] [ASC] (2/12/77 BCR-10)

MAYBE IT'S BECAUSE (I LOVE YOU TOO MUCH) Sarah Vaughan—Mercury 71519
[Irving Berlin] [ASC] (10/19/59 R-72)

MAYBE JUST TODAY Bobby Vee And The Strangers—Liberty 56014
[Martha Sharp] [BMI] (2/10/68 BCR-29)

MAYBE THE RAIN WILL FALL The Cascades—Uni 55152
[Carl Storie] [BMI] (8/9/69 BCR-49)

MAYBE THIS DAY Kissing The Pink—Atlantic 89796
[Peter Barnett/Stephen Cusack/Sylvia Griffin/Jon Kingsley Hall/Peter Stewart/Josephine Wells/Nick Whitecross] [BMI] (8/6/83 B-87)

MAYBE TOMORROW The Everly Brothers—Cadence 1337
[Don Everly/Phil Everly*] [BMI] (9/23/57 R-83)

MAYBE TOMORROW The Iveys—Apple 1803 [Tom Evans] [ASC] (2/8/69 BCR-32)

MAYBE TOMORROW The Jackson 5—Motown 1186
[Berry Gordy/Fonce Mizell/Freddie Perren/Deke Richards] [ASC] (7/10/71 BCR-16)

MAYBE TONIGHT The Shirelles—Scepter 1284 [Van McCoy] [BMI] (10/31/64 B-88)

MAYBE YOU'LL BE THERE Billy And The Essentials—Jamie 1239
[Rube Bloom/Sammy Gallop] [ASC] (12/15/62 C-90)

MAYBELLENE *Chuck Berry—Chess 1604*
[Chuck Berry/Russ Fratto‡/Alan Freed‡] [BMI] (8/8/55 BCRt-4)

MAYBELLENE *Johnny Long & His Orchestra—Coral 61478*
[Chuck Berry/Russ Fratto‡/Alan Freed‡] [BMI] (8/8/55 Rt-4)

MAYBELLENE *Jim Lowe—Dot 15407*
[Chuck Berry/Russ Fratto‡/Alan Freed‡] [BMI] (8/8/55 Rt-4)

MAYBELLENE *Ralph Marterie & His Orchestra—Mercury 70682*
[Chuck Berry/Russ Fratto‡/Alan Freed‡] [BMI] (8/29/55 Rt-14)

MAYBELLINE *Johnny Rivers—Imperial 66056*
[Chuck Berry/Russ Fratto‡/Alan Freed‡] [BMI] (8/15/64 BCR-11)

THE MAYOR OF SIMPLETON XTC—Geffen 27552 [Andy Partridge] [BMI] (4/29/89 BC-67)

ME - U = BLUE Glenn Medeiros—MCA 53945
[Franne Golde/Andy Goldmark/Bruce Roberts] [BMI] (11/3/90 BC-69)

ME ABOUT YOU *The Mojo Men—Reprise 0580*
[Garry Bonner/Alan Gordon] [BMI] (5/27/67 BCR-83)

ME ABOUT YOU *The Lovin' Spoonful—Kama Sutra 255*
[Garry Bonner/Alan Gordon] [BMI] (1/25/69 BCR-82)

ME ABOUT YOU *The Turtles—White Whale 364*
[Garry Bonner/Alan Gordon] [BMI] (11/14/70 R-96)

ME AND BABY BROTHER War—United Artists 350
[Thomas Allen/Harold Brown/Morris Dickerson/Lonnie Jordan/Charles Miller/Lee Oskar/Howard Scott] [ASC] (11/10/73 BCR-12)

ME AND BOBBY MCGEE *Janis Joplin—Columbia 45314*
[Fred Foster/Kris Kristofferson] [BMI] (1/30/71 BCR-1)

ME AND BOBBY MCGEE *Jerry Lee Lewis—Mercury 73248*
[Fred Foster/Kris Kristofferson] [BMI] (11/27/71 BCR-40)

ME AND JESUS Tom T. Hall—Mercury 73278 [Tom T. Hall] [BMI] (5/13/72 B-98)

ME AND JULIO DOWN BY THE SCHOOLYARD Paul Simon—Columbia 45585
[Paul Simon] [BMI] (4/1/72 BCR-7)

ME AND MRS. JONES *Billy Paul—Philadelphia Int'l 3521*
[Kenneth Gamble/Cary Gilbert/Leon Huff] [BMI] (10/21/72 BCR-1)

ME AND MRS. JONES *Ron Banks And The Dramatics—ABC 12090*
[Kenneth Gamble/Cary Gilbert/Leon Huff] [BMI] (4/26/75 BCR-46)

ME AND MY ARROW Nilsson—RCA Victor 74-0443
[Harry Nilsson] [BMI] (3/20/71 BCR-22)

ME AND MY BABY GOT A GOOD THING GOING Lyn Collins—People 615
[Charles Bobbit/James Brown/Lyn Collins/Fred Wesley] [BMI] (12/2/72 B-86)

ME AND MY SHADOW Frank Sinatra And Sammy Davis Jr.—Reprise 20,128
[Dave Dreyer/Al Jolson/Billy Rose] [ASC] (12/1/62 BCR-57)

ME AND YOU O.C. Smith—Columbia 45038 [Jerry Fuller] [BMI] (11/22/69 C-93)

ME AND YOU AND A DOG NAMED BOO Lobo—Big Tree 112
[Kent LaVoie] [ASC] (3/27/71 BCR-5)

ME JAPANESE BOY I LOVE YOU Bobby Goldsboro—United Artists 742
[Burt Bacharach/Hal David] [ASC] (8/8/64 BCR-74)

—ME LO DIJO ADELA see: SWEET AND GENTLE

ME MYSELF AND I De La Soul—Tommy Boy 7926
[Edwin Birdsong*/George Clinton/Paul Huston/David Jolicoeur/Vincent Mason/Kelvin Mercer/Abrim Tilmon*/Philippe Wynn] [BMI] (6/3/89 BC-34)

ME SO HORNY 2 Live Crew—Skywalker 130
[Luther Campbell/David Hobbs/Mark Ross/Ricardo Williams/Chris Wong Won] [BMI] (9/9/89 BC-26)

ME, THE PEACEFUL HEART Lulu—Epic 10302 [Tony Hazzard] [BMI] (3/23/68 BCR-40)

ME WITHOUT YOU Mary Wells—20th Century 606
[Sid Barnes/J.J. Jackson] [BMI] (9/11/65 BCR-91)

ME (WITHOUT YOU) Andy Gibb—RSO 1056 [Andy Gibb] [BMI] (3/14/81 BCR-40)

MEADOWS Joe Walsh—Dunhill 4373 [Joe Walsh] [BMI] (12/15/73 BCR-71)

MEAN LITTLE WOMAN, ROSALIE Tommy Roe—MGM South 7001
[R.W. Laws] [BMI] (9/23/72 BR-91)

MEAN MEAN MAN Wanda Jackson—Capitol 4469 [Wanda Jackson] [BMI] (12/5/60 R-87)

MEAN MISTREATER Grand Funk Railroad—Capitol 2996
[Mark Farner] [BMI] (12/12/70 BCR-44)

MEAN OLD WORLD Rick Nelson—Decca 31756 [Billy Vera] [BMI] (3/20/65 BCR-92)

MEAN WOMAN BLUES Roy Orbison—Monument 824
[Claude DeMetrius] [ASC] (9/7/63 BCR-5)

—MEANING OF LOVE see: TO EV'RY GIRL—TO EV'RY BOY

MECCA Gene Pitney—Musicor 1028 [John Gluck/Neval Nader] [BMI] (3/16/63 BCR-12)

MECHANICAL WORLD Spirit—Ode 108 [Mark Andes/Jay Ferguson] [BMI] (6/1/68 C-92)

MEDICINE MAN (PART 1) Buchanan Brothers—Event 3302
[Terry Cashman/Eugene Pistilli/Tommy West] [ASC] (4/19/69 BCR-18)

THE MEDICINE SONG Stephanie Mills—Casablanca 880180
[David Wolinski] [ASC] (10/13/84 BC-61)

—MEDITAÇAO see: MEDITATION

MEDITATION (MEDITAÇAO) *Charlie Byrd—Riverside 4544*
[Antonio Carlos Jobim] [BMI] (1/26/63 BCtRt-66) [IM]

MEDITATION (MEDITAÇAO) *Pat Boone—Dot 16439*
[Norman Gimbel/Antonio Carlos Jobim] [BMI] (2/9/63 BCtRt-70) [FDE]

MEDITATION (MEDITAÇAO) *Billy Vaughn And His Orchestra—Dot 16436*
[Antonio Carlos Jobim] [BMI] (2/16/63 Rt-71) [IM]

MEDITATION (MEDITACAO) *Claudine Longet—A&M 817*
[Norman Gimbel/Antonio Carlos Jobim] [BMI] (11/5/66 BR-98) [FDE]

THE MEDITATION TNT Band—Cotique 136 [Tito Ramos/Tony Rojas] [BMI] (1/4/69 R-85)

MEDITERRANEAN MOON The Rays—XYZ 605
[Bob Crewe/Frank Slay] [BMI] (1/25/60 B-95)

MEET EL PRESIDENTE Duran Duran—Capitol 44001
[Simon Le Bon/Nick Rhodes/Nigel John Taylor] [ASC] (5/2/87 BC-70)

MEET ME AT THE TWISTIN' PLACE Johnnie Morisette—SAR 126
[Sam Cooke] [BMI] (4/14/62 BCR-63)

MEET ME HALF WAY Kenny Loggins—Columbia 06690
[Giorgio Moroder/Tom Whitlock] [ASC] (3/7/87 BC-10)

MEETING IN THE LADIES ROOM Klymaxx—Constellation 52545
[Reggie Calloway/Vincent Calloway/Bo Watson] [BMI] (5/11/85 BC-59)

MEETING OVER YONDER The Impressions—ABC-Paramount 10670
[Curtis Mayfield] [BMI] (5/29/65 BCR-46)

MEGA FORCE 707—Boardwalk 7-11-146
[Jonathan Cain*/Tod Howarth/Jim McClarty/Kevin Russell] [BMI] (7/3/82 BC-59)

MELANCHOLY MUSIC MAN The Righteous Brothers—Verve 10507
[Garry Bonner/Alan Gordon] [BMI] (4/22/67 BCR-43)

MELANIE MAKES ME SMILE *Tony Burrows—Bell 884*
[Tony Macaulay/Barry Mason] [ASC] (6/6/70 BCR-87)

MELANIE MAKES ME SMILE *Terry Williams—MGM/Verve 10686*
[Tony Macaulay/Barry Mason] [ASC] (12/9/72 CR-94)

MELISSA The Allman Brothers Band—Capricorn 0007
[Gregg Allman] [BMI] (8/12/72 B-86)

MELLOW LOVIN' Judy Cheeks—Salsoul 2063
[Judy Cheeks/Anthony Monn/Ronnie Lee Williams] [ASC] (9/30/78 BR-65)

MELLOW MOONLIGHT Leon Haywood—Decca 32230
[Leon Haywood] [BMI] (12/30/67 B-92)

MELLOW YELLOW *Donovan—Epic 10098 [Donovan Leitch] [BMI] (11/12/66 BCR-1)*

MELLOW YELLOW *Senator Bobby & Senator McKinley—Parkway 137*
[Donovan Leitch] [BMI] (3/11/67 B-99)

MELODIE D'AMOUR (MELODY OF LOVE) *The Ames Brothers—RCA Victor 47-7046*
[Marcel Stellman/Traditional] [BMI] (9/9/57 BCRt-3) [FDE]

MELODIE D'AMOUR *Edmundo Ros & His Orchestra—London 1751*
[Marcel Stellman/Traditional] [BMI] (9/23/57 Rt-3) [FDE]

MELODIE D'AMOUR *Marty Gold & His Orchestra—Vik 0303*
[Marcel Stellman/Traditional] [BMI] (10/14/57 Rt-3) [FET]

—MELODIE PERDUE see: WILLINGLY

MELODY David Johansen—Blue Sky 9 2781
[Ronnie Guy/David Johansen] [BMI] (11/10/79 R-91)

MELODY FOR AN UNKNOWN GIRL The Unknowns—Parrot 307
[Mark Lindsay/Paul Revere*] [BMI] (9/24/66 BCR-74)

A MELODY FOR YOU The Grass Roots—Dunhill 4122 [P.F. Sloan] [ASC] (3/2/68 R-75)

MELODY OF LOVE *Billy Vaughn and His Orchestra—Dot 15247*
[Hans Engelmann] [ASC] (12/11/54 BCtRt-1) [IM]

MELODY OF LOVE *David Carroll And His Orchestra—Mercury 70516*
[Hans Engelmann] [ASC] (12/20/54 BCtRt-1) [IM]

MELODY OF LOVE *Four Aces—Decca 29395*
[Hans Engelmann/Tom Glazer] [ASC] (12/27/54 BCtRt-1)

MELODY OF LOVE *Frank Sinatra & Ray Anthony—Capitol 3018*
[Hans Engelmann] [ASC] (1/3/55 Rt-3)

MELODY OF LOVE *Tony Martin & Dinah Shore—RCA Victor 47-5975*
[Hans Engelmann/Tom Glazer] [ASC] (1/3/55 Rt-3)

MELODY OF LOVE *Sammy Kaye & His "Swing & Sway" Orchestra—Columbia 40417*
[Hans Engelmann] [ASC] (1/3/55 Rt-13) [IM]

MELODY OF LOVE *Leo Diamond—RCA Victor 47-5973*
[Hans Engelmann] [ASC] (2/19/55 B-30) [IM]

—MELODY OF LOVE see: MELODIE D'AMOUR

MELT IN YOUR MOUTH Candyman—Epic 73652
[John B. Shaffer III/Melvin Steals/Mervin Steals] [BMI] (12/15/90 BC-69)

MELTING POT Blue Mink Featuring Madeleine Bell—Philips 40658
[Roger Cook/Roger Greenaway] [ASC] (2/14/70 CR-71)

MELTING POT Booker T. & The M.G.'s—Stax 0082
[Steve Cropper/Donald "Duck" Dunn/Al Jackson/Booker T. Jones Jr.] [BMI] (3/13/71 BC-45) [I]

—MEME SI TU REVENAIS see: LOVE IN EVERY ROOM

MEMORIES *Elvis Presley—RCA Victor 47-9731*
[Mac Davis/Billy Strange] [BMI] (3/15/69 BCR-21)

MEMORIES *The Lettermen—Capitol 2697*
[Mac Davis/Billy Strange] (Med) [BMI] (12/13/69 BCR-47)

MEMORIES Tierra—Boardwalk 70073 [Rudy Salas] [BMI] (3/14/81 BCR-62)

MEMORIES ARE MADE OF THIS *Dean Martin—Capitol 3295*
[Richard Dehr/Terry Gilkyson/Frank Miller] [BMI] (11/21/55 BCtRt-1)

MEMORIES ARE MADE OF THIS *Mindy Carson—Columbia 40573*
[Richard Dehr/Terry Gilkyson/Frank Miller] [BMI] (11/21/55 BRt-19)

MEMORIES ARE MADE OF THIS *Gale Storm—Dot 15436*
[Richard Dehr/Terry Gilkyson/Frank Miller] [BMI] (12/9/55 BCtRt-1)

MEMORIES ARE MADE OF THIS *Roger Williams—Kapp 265*
[Richard Dehr/Terry Gilkyson/Frank Miller] [BMI] (4/6/59 R-81) [IWM]

MEMORIES ARE MADE OF THIS *The Drifters—Atlantic 2325*
[Richard Dehr/Terry Gilkyson/Frank Miller] [BMI] (3/19/66 BCR-45)

MEMORIES OF A BROKEN PROMISE Motherlode—Buddah 144
[Dianne Brooks] [BMI] (11/15/69 CR-92)

MEMORIES OF DAYS GONE BY *Fred Parris & The Five Satins—Elektra 47411*
[Marty Markiewicz] (Med) [ASC] (2/27/82 BC-71)

MEMORIES OF DAYS GONE BY *Fred Parris & The Five Satins—Elektra 47411*
[Marty Markiewicz] (Med) [ASC] (2/27/82 BC-71)

MEMORIES OF MARIA The Music Of Jerry Byrd—Monument 449
[Joe Melson/Roy Orbison] [BMI] (3/17/62 BCR-63) [I]

MEMORIES OF YOU *The Four Coins—Epic 9129*
[Eubie Blake/Andy Razaf] [ASC] (11/19/55 BCRt-9)

MEMORIES OF YOU *The Benny Goodman Trio with Rosemary Clooney—Columbia 40616*
[Eubie Blake/Andy Razaf] [ASC] (12/16/55 BRt-12)

MEMORIES OF YOU *Joe Carr—Capitol 3304 [Eubie Blake] [ASC] (12/16/55 Rt-25) [IM]*

MEMORIES OF YOU *Paul Weston & His Orchestra—Columbia 40605*
[Eubie Blake] [ASC] (12/16/55 Rt-25) [IM]

MEMORIES OF YOU *The Ink Spots—Decca 29750*
[Eubie Blake/Andy Razaf] [ASC] (12/23/55 Rt-25)

MEMORIES OF YOU *Glen Gray & His Orchestra—Decca 29763*
[Eubie Blake] [ASC] (1/6/56 Rt-12) [IM]

MEMORIES OF YOU *Hugo Winterhalter's Orchestra And Chorus—RCA Victor 47-6339*
[Eubie Blake] [ASC] (1/28/56 B-62) [IM]

MEMORIZE YOUR NUMBER Leif Garrett—Scotti Brothers 510
[Billy Kirkland] [ASC] (12/15/79 BR-60)

MEMORY - THE THEME FROM ANDREW LLOYD WEBBER'S MUSICAL "CATS"
Barbra Streisand—Columbia 02717
[T.S. Eliot/Trevor Nunn/Andrew Lloyd Webber] [BMI] (2/20/82 BCR-48)

MEMORY *Barry Manilow—Arista 1025*
[T.S. Eliot/Trevor Nunn/Andrew Lloyd Webber] [BMI] (11/20/82 BC-37)

MEMORY LANE The Hippies (Formerly The Tams)—Parkway 863
[Howard Boggess/John Felker] [ASC] (3/30/63 BCR-57)

MEMORY LANE Minnie Riperton—Capitol 4706
[Gene Dozier/Minnie Riperton/Richard Rudolph/Keni St. Lewis] [BMI] (7/7/79 R-96)

MEMPHIS, TENNESSEE *Chuck Berry—Chess 1729 [Chuck Berry] [BMI] (7/25/59 C-87)*

MEMPHIS *Lonnie Mack—Fraternity 906 [Chuck Berry] [BMI] (6/1/63 BCR-5) [IWM]*

MEMPHIS *Johnny Rivers—Imperial 66032 [Chuck Berry] [BMI] (5/30/64 BCR-2)*

MEMPHIS Donnie Brooks—Era 3042 [Jesse D. Hodges] [BMI] (3/13/61 BCR-81)

MEMPHIS Joe Jackson—A&M 2601 [Joe Jackson] [ASC] (11/26/83 B-85)

MEMPHIS AT SUNRISE Bar-Kays—Volt 4081
[Allen Alvoid Jones Jr./Jerome McLaughlin] [BMI] (10/21/72 C-90)

MEMPHIS SOUL STEW King Curtis—Atco 6511
[King Curtis] [BMI] (8/26/67 BCR-33) [I]

MEMPHIS TRAIN Buddy Miles Express—Mercury 72945
[Bonny Rice/Willie Sparks/Rufus Thomas] [BMI] (8/23/69 B-100)

MEMPHIS UNDERGROUND Herbie Mann—Atlantic 2621
[Herbie Mann] [ASC] (5/24/69 BCR-44) [I]

THE MEN ALL PAUSE Klymaxx—Constellation 52486
[Bernadette Cooper/Joyce Irby] [ASC] (2/15/86 BC-70)

MEN ARE GETTIN' SCARCE Joe Tex—Dial 4069 [Joe Tex] [BMI] (2/10/68 BCR-26)

MEN ARE GETTING SCARCE Chairmen Of The Board—Invictus 9103
[General Johnson/Greg Perry] [BMI] (11/27/71 CR-68)

THE MEN IN MY LITTLE GIRL'S LIFE Mike Douglas—Epic 9876
[Mary Candy/Eddie V. Deane/Gloria Shayne] [ASC] (12/18/65 BCR-4)

MEN OF LEARNING Vigrass & Osborne—Uni 55330
[Gary Osborne/Paul Vigrass/Jeff Wayne] [BMI] (6/10/72 BCR-45)

MEN OF WAR The Rouzan Sisters—Frisco 113 [Al Reed] [BMI] (4/2/66 R-100)

MENDELSSOHN'S 4TH (SECOND MOVEMENT) Apollo 100—Mega 0069
[Felix Mendelssohn] [ASC] (4/15/72 BCR-92) [I]

MENDOCINO Sir Douglas Quintet—Smash 2191 [Doug Sahm] [BMI] (1/18/69 BCR-14)

MENTIROSA Mellow Man Ace—Capitol 44533
[Tony Gonzalez/Sergio Reyes] [BMI] (5/12/90 BC-14)

MERCEDES BOY Pebbles—MCA 53279 [Perri Arlette Reid] [ASC] (5/7/88 BC-2)

MERCY Ohio Express—Buddah 102 [Steve Feldman/Joey Levine] [BMI] (3/22/69 BCR-26)

MERCY, MERCY *Don Covay & The Goodtimers—Rosemart 801*
[Don Covay/Ronald Alonzo Miller] [BMI] (9/5/64 BCR-26)

MERCY, MERCY, MERCY *Phoebe Snow—Mirage 3818*
[Don Covay/Ronald Alonzo Miller] [BMI] (5/2/81 BCR-52)

MERCY MERCY ME (THE ECOLOGY) *Marvin Gaye—Tamla 54207*
[Marvin Gaye] [ASC] (6/26/71 BCR-2)

MERCY MERCY ME (THE ECOLOGY) *Robert Palmer—EMI 50344*
[Marvin Gaye] (Med) [ASC] (2/16/91 BC-13)

MERCY, MERCY, MERCY *"Cannonball" Adderley—Capitol 5798*
[Joe Zawinul] [BMI] (12/31/66 BCR-11) [IM]

MERCY, MERCY, MERCY *Larry Williams & Johnny Watson—Okeh 7274*
[Gail Levy/Vincent Levy/Joe Zawinul] [BMI] (2/25/67 BC-81)

MERCY, MERCY, MERCY *Marlena Shaw—Cadet 5557*
[Gail Levy/Vincent Levy/Joe Zawinul] [BMI] (3/11/67 BCR-58)

MERCY, MERCY, MERCY *The Buckinghams—Columbia 44182*
[Gail Levy/Vincent Levy/Joe Zawinul] [BMI] (6/17/67 BCR-5)

MERRY CHRISTMAS BABY Chuck Berry—Chess 1714
[Lou Baxter/Johnny Moore] [ASC] (12/15/58 BC-71)

MERRY CHRISTMAS DARLING Carpenters—A&M 1236
[Richard Carpenter/Frank Pooler] [BMI] (12/12/70 C-41)

MERRY CHRISTMAS IN THE NFL Willis "The Guard" and Vigorish—Handshake 5308
[Jerry Buckner/Gary Garcia] [ASC] (12/27/80 B-82)

—MERRY CHRISTMAS see: SANTO NATALE

MERRY-GO-ROUND Marv Johnson—United Artists 294
[Berry Gordy] [ASC] (3/11/61 BCR-44)

THE MESS AROUND Bobby Freeman—Josie 887 [Jack Cortes] [BMI] (4/17/61 B-89)

MESS OF BLUES Elvis Presley With The Jordanaires—RCA Victor 47-7777
[Doc Pomus/Mort Shuman] [BMI] (7/25/60 BCR-32)

THE MESSAGE Cymande—Janus 203
[Patrick Patterson/Steve Scipio] [BMI] (1/6/73 BCR-39)

THE MESSAGE Grandmaster Flash & The Furious Five—Sugar Hill 584
[Clifton Chase/Edward Fletcher/Melvin Glover/Sylvia Robinson] [BMI]
(10/16/82 BC-62)

MESSAGE FROM A BLACK MAN The Whatnauts—A & I 001
[Barrett Strong/Norman Whitfield] [BMI] (2/28/70 B-99)

MESSAGE FROM MARIA Joe Simon—Sound Stage 7 2617
[Al Reed] [BMI] (9/28/68 BCR-75)

MESSAGE IN A BOTTLE The Police—A&M 2190 [Sting] [BMI] (11/17/79 BCR-62)

MESSAGE IN OUR MUSIC The O'Jays—Philadelphia Int'l 3601
[Kenneth Gamble/Leon Huff] [BMI] (9/11/76 BCR-49)

MESSAGE TO MICHAEL Dionne Warwick—Scepter 12133
[Burt Bacharach/Hal David] [ASC] (4/2/66 BCR-7)

METHOD OF MODERN LOVE Daryl Hall & John Oates—RCA 13970
[Janna Allen/Daryl Hall] [BMI] (12/15/84 BC-5)

THE METRO Berlin—Geffen 29638 [John Crawford] [BMI] (5/28/83 BC-50)

MEXICALI ROSE Dick Contino—Mercury 70911 [Jack Tenney] [ASC] (9/22/56 R-83) [IWM]

MEXICAN DIVORCE The Drifters—Atlantic 2134
[Burt Bacharach/Bob Hilliard] [ASC] (2/12/62 R-100)

MEXICAN DRUMMER MAN Herb Alpert's Tijuana Brass—A&M 732
[Scott Turner] [BMI] (3/28/64 BR-77)

MEXICAN HAT ROCK The Applejacks (S)—Cameo 149
[Kal Mann/Jesús Gonzáles Rubio] [BMI] (9/15/58 BCR-16) [I]

MEXICAN HAT TWIST The Applejacks (S)—Cameo 203
[Dave Appell/Kal Mann/Jesús Gonzáles Rubio] [ASC] (11/13/61 R-98)

MEXICAN JOE *Mitchell Torok—Guyden 2028 [Mitchell Torok] [BMI] (10/24/59 C-77)*

MEXICAN JOE *Pat Boone—Dot 16416 [Mitchell Torok] [BMI] (12/22/62 R-95)*

MEXICAN PEARLS *Billy Vaughn And His Orchestra—Dot 16706*
[Joe Mikolas/Don Randi] [BMI] (3/27/65 BCtRt-79) [I]*

MEXICAN PEARLS *Don Randi—Palomar 2203*
[Joe Mikolas/Don Randi] [BMI] (4/3/65 CtRt-79) [I]*

MEXICAN RADIO Wall Of Voodoo—I.R.S. 9912
[Charles Gray/Marc Moreland/Joe Nanini/Stan Ridgway] [BMI] (3/19/83 BC-55)

THE MEXICAN SHUFFLE Herb Alpert's Tijuana Brass—A&M 742
[Sol Lake] [ASC] (6/27/64 BC-85) [IM]

MEXICO Bob Moore And His Orch.—Monument 446
[Boudleaux Bryant] [BMI] (8/14/61 BCR-5) [I]

MEXICO James Taylor—Warner Bros. 8137 [James Taylor] [ASC] (10/4/75 BCR-38)

M.G. BLUES Jimmy McGriff—Sue 777 [Jimmy McGriff] [BMI] (12/29/62 BR-79) [I]

MI CASA, SU CASA (MY HOUSE IS YOUR HOUSE) Perry Como—RCA Victor 47-6815
[Al Hoffman/Dick Manning] [ASC] (3/9/57 BCR-50)

MIAMI Eugene Church—Class 254 [Eugene Church/Paul Clifton] [BMI] (8/3/59 BC-67)

MIAMI Bob Seger & The Silver Bullet Band—Capitol 5658
[Bob Seger] [ASC] (11/15/86 BC-60)

MIAMI VICE THEME Jan Hammer—MCA 52666 [Jan Hammer] [ASC] (9/7/85 BC-1) [I]

MICHAEL *The Highwaymen—United Artists 258 [Traditional] [NA] (6/24/61 BCR-1)*

MICHAEL *(parody of Michael) The Four Preps—Capitol 4716*
[Traditional] (Med) [NA] (3/17/62 BCR-61) [P]

MICHAEL - PT. 1 *Steve Alaimo—Checker 1054 [Traditional] [NA] (10/5/63 B-100)*

MICHAEL *Trini Lopez—Reprise 0300 [Traditional] [NA] (8/15/64 BCR-36)*

MICHAEL The C.O.D.'s—Kellmac 1003
[Larry Brownlee/Charles (Pete) Matthews] [BMI] (11/27/65 BCR-41)

MICHELLE *David & Jonathan—Capitol 5563*
[John Lennon/Paul McCartney] [ASC] (1/8/66 BCR-12)

MICHELLE *Billy Vaughn His Orchestra & Chorus—Dot 16809*
[John Lennon/Paul McCartney] [ASC] (1/8/66 BCR-52)

MICHELLE *Bud Shank—World Pacific 77814*
[John Lennon/Paul McCartney] [ASC] (1/22/66 BCR-65) [IWM]

MICHIGAN HARRY SLAUGHTER Wadsworth Mansion—Sussex 215
[Steve Jablecki] [BMI] (4/24/71 C-99)

MICKEY *Toni Basil—Chrysalis 2638 [Mike Chapman/Nicky Chinn] [ASC] (9/4/82 BC-1)*

RICKY *(parody of Mickey) "Weird Al" Yankovic—Rock 'n' Roll 03849*
[Mike Chapman/Nicky Chinn/Eliot Daniel/Al Yankovic] [BMI] (4/30/83 BC-58) [P]

MICKEY'S MONKEY The Miracles—Tamla 54083
[Lamont Dozier/Brian Holland/Eddie Holland] [BMI] (8/17/63 BCR-7)

MIDAS TOUCH Midnight Star—Solar 69525
[Bo Watson/June Watson Williams] [BMI] (9/20/86 BC-42)

MIDDLE OF THE ROAD The Pretenders—Sire 29444
[Chrissie Hynde] [ASC] (12/17/83 BC-13)

MIDNIGHT Hugo Winterhalter's Orch. & Chorus—RCA Victor 47-7182
[Luther Dixon/Ollie Jones] [BMI] (4/5/58 C-60) [IWM]

MIDNIGHT Paul Anka—ABC-Paramount 9937 [Paul Anka] [BMI] (7/7/58 BR-47) [I]

MIDNIGHT Johnny Gibson—Big Top 3088
[Johnny Gibson/Tom King/Ira Mack‡/John Pocisk] [BMI] (1/27/62 BCR-76) [I]

MIDNIGHT Dennis Yost And The Classics IV—Imperial 66424
[Buddy Buie/J.R. Cobb/Emory Gordy] [BMI] (11/8/69 BCR-36)

MIDNIGHT AT THE OASIS Maria Muldaur—Reprise 1183
[David Nichtern] [ASC] (2/9/74 BCR-4)

MIDNIGHT BLUE Melissa Manchester—Arista 0116
[Melissa Manchester/Carole Bayer Sager] [BMI] (5/10/75 BCR-5)

MIDNIGHT BLUE Louise Tucker—Arista 1-9022
[Charlie Skarbek/Tim Smit/Ludwig van Beethoven] [BMI] (6/18/83 BC-46)

MIDNIGHT BLUE Lou Gramm—Atlantic 89304
[Lou Gramm/Bruce Turgon] [ASC] (1/31/87 BC-5)

MIDNIGHT BUS Billy Graves—Monument 404 [John D. Loudermilk] [BMI] (3/30/59 R-60)

MIDNIGHT CONFESSIONS The Grass Roots—Dunhill 4144
[Lou Josie] [BMI] (8/17/68 BCR-3)

MIDNIGHT COWBOY Ferrante & Teicher—United Artists 50554
[John Barry] [ASC] (11/1/69 BCR-10) [I]

MIDNIGHT FLOWER Four Tops—Dunhill/ABC 15005
[Reggie Dozier/McKinley Jackson] [BMI] (8/3/74 BCR-55)

MIDNIGHT FLYER Nat "King" Cole—Capitol 4248
[Robert Mosely/Mayme Watts] [BMI] (8/3/59 BCR-24)

MIDNIGHT IN MOSCOW *Kenny Ball And His Jazzmen—Kapp 442*
[Mikhail Matusovskij/Vasilj Solovev-Sedoj] [ASC] (1/20/62 BCtR-2) [IWM]

MIDNIGHT IN MOSCOW *Jan Burgens & His New Orleans Syncopators—London 10503*
[Mikhail Matusovskij/Vasilj Solovev-Sedoj] [ASC] (1/20/62 Ct-85) [IWM]

MIDNIGHT LACE *David Carroll And His Orchestra—Mercury 71703*
[Jerome Howard/Joe Lubin] [BMI] (10/10/60 BCtRt-56) [IWM]

MIDNIGHT LACE *Ray Ellis And His Orchestra—MGM 12942*
[Jerome Howard/Joe Lubin] [BMI] (10/10/60 BCtRt-56) [IWM]

MIDNIGHT LACE *Sid Feller & His Orchestra—ABC-Paramount 10145*
[Jerome Howard/Joe Lubin] [BMI] (10/10/60 Rt-68) [IWM]

MIDNIGHT LACE PART ONE *Ray Conniff & His Orch. & Chorus—Columbia 41800*
[Jerome Howard/Joe Lubin] [BMI] (10/10/60 BCtRt-56) [IWM]

MIDNIGHT LIGHT Le Blanc & Carr—Big Tree 16114
[Lenny LeBlanc/Eddie Struzick] [BMI] (6/3/78 BC-91)

MIDNIGHT LOVE AFFAIR *Tony Orlando And Dawn—Elektra 45319*
[Pierre Groscolas/Michel Jourdan/Estelle Levitt] [BMI] (5/15/76 C-93)

MIDNIGHT LOVE AFFAIR *Carol Douglas—Midland Int'l 10753*
[Pierre Groscolas/Michel Jourdan/Estelle Levitt] [BMI] (12/25/76 C-96)

—MIDNIGHT LOVE see: CLAIR DE LUNE

MIDNIGHT MAN The James Gang—ABC 11312
[Joe Walsh] [BMI] (9/25/71 BCR-50)

MIDNIGHT MARY Joey Powers—Amy 892
[Ben Raleigh/Artie Wayne] [ASC] (11/2/63 BCR-10)

MIDNIGHT OIL Charlie Blackwell—Warner Bros. 5031
[Richard Sherman/Robert Sherman] [BMI] (2/2/59 BCR-53) [IWM]

MIDNIGHT RAIN Poco—MCA 41326 [Paul Cotton] [ASC] (10/11/80 BC-74)

MIDNIGHT RENDEZVOUS The Babys—Chrysalis 2425
[Jonathan Cain/John Waite] [ASC] (4/26/80 BCR-68)

MIDNIGHT RIDER *Joe Cocker And The Chris Stainton Band—A&M 1370*
[Gregg Allman] [BMI] (9/9/72 BCR-26)

MIDNIGHT RIDER *Gregg Allman—Capricorn 0035*
Gregg Allman] [BMI] (12/22/73 BCR-16)

MIDNIGHT ROCKS Al Stewart—Arista 0552
[Al Stewart/Peter White] [BMI] (8/23/80 BCR-24)

MIDNIGHT SHOW *Ron Dante—Arista 0111 [Gene Allan/Ron Dante] [BMI] (3/1/75 C-94)*

MIDNIGHT SHOW *Bobby Vinton—ABC 12131*
[Gene Allan/Ron Dante] [BMI] (9/27/75 C-78)

MIDNIGHT SKY (PART 1) The Isley Brothers—T-Neck 2255
[Ernie Isley/Marvin Isley/O'Kelly Isley/Ronald Isley/Rudolph Isley/Chris Jasper] [ASC] (1/4/75 BC-65)

MIDNITE SPECIAL *Paul Evans—Guaranteed 205 [Traditional] [NA] (1/18/60 BCR-14)*

MIDNIGHT SPECIAL *Johnny Rivers—Imperial 66087 [Traditional] [NA] (2/6/65 BCR-20)*

MIDNIGHT SPECIAL PART 1 Jimmy Smith—Blue Note 1819
[James O. Smith] [BMI] (3/3/62 BR-69) [I]

MIDNIGHT STROLL The Revels—Norgolde 103
[Thomas Coman*/Michael Guerra*/William E. Jackson III] [BMI] (10/12/59 BCR-35)

MIDNIGHT SUN The Five Whispers—Dolton 61
[Joseph Francis Burke/Lionel Hampton] [BMI] (10/20/62 C-99) [IM]

MIDNIGHT TRAIN TO GEORGIA Gladys Knight & The Pips—Buddah 383
[Jim Weatherly] [ASC] (8/25/73 BCR-1)

MIDNIGHT WIND John Stewart—RSO 1000 [John Stewart] [BMI] (8/25/79 BCR-28)

MIDNIGHTER The Champs—Challenge 59007 [Dave Burgess] [BMI] (8/11/58 B-94) [I]

MIDNITE MANIAC Krokus—Arista 1-9248
[Marc Storace/Fernando Von Arb] [ASC] (9/15/84 BC-70)

MIGHT JUST TAKE YOUR LIFE Deep Purple—Warner Bros. 7784
[Ritchie Blackmore/David Coverdale/Jon Lord/Ian Paice] [BMI] (3/9/74 BCR-87)

MIGHTY CLOUDS OF JOY B.J. Thomas—Scepter 12320
[Buddy Buie/Robert Nix] [BMI] (6/26/71 BCR-33)

MIGHTY GOOD Ricky Nelson—Imperial 5614 [Baker Knight] [BMI] (11/16/59 BCR-38)

MIGHTY GOOD LOVIN' The Miracles—Tamla 54044
[Smokey Robinson] [ASC] (7/10/61 BR-51)

MIGHTY HIGH Mighty Clouds Of Joy—ABC 12164
[Dave Crawford/Rich Downing] [ASC] (2/21/76 BCR-69)

MIGHTY JOE The Shocking Blue—Colossus 111
[Robbie Van Leeuwen] [ASC] (3/7/70 BCR-27)

MIGHTY LOVE - PT. I The Spinners—Atlantic 3006
[Bruce Hawes/Joseph Jefferson/Charles Simmons] [BMI] (1/19/74 BCR-15)

MIGHTY MIGHTY Earth, Wind & Fire—Columbia 46007
[Maurice White/Verdine White] [ASC] (3/9/74 BCR-29)

MIGHTY QUINN (QUINN THE ESKIMO) Manfred Mann—Mercury 72770
[Bob Dylan] [SE] (3/2/68 BCR-4)

MILES AWAY Fotomaker—Atlantic 3531 [Frankie Vinci] [BMI] (11/18/78 BCR-63)

MILES AWAY Winger—Atlantic 87824 [Paul Taylor] [BMI] (10/13/90 BC-12)

MILITARY MADNESS Graham Nash—Atlantic 2827 [Graham Nash] [BMI] (9/4/71 BCR-66)

MILK AND HONEY The Limeliters—RCA Victor 47-7942
[Jerry Herman] [ASC] (10/9/61 R-90)

MILK COW BLUES Ricky Nelson—Imperial 5707 [Kokomo Arnold] [ASC] (12/31/60 B-79)

MILL VALLEY
Miss Abrams And The Strawberry Point School Third Grade Class—Reprise 0928
[Rita Abrams] [ASC] (8/1/70 BR-90)

MILLER'S CAVE Bobby Bare—RCA Victor 47-8294
[Jack H. Clement] [BMI] (2/1/64 BCR-31)

A MILLION AND ONE *Dean Martin—Reprise 0500*
[Yvonne Devaney] [BMI] (7/23/66 BCRt-38)

A MILLION AND ONE *Vic Dana—Dolton 322 [Yvonne Devaney] [BMI] (7/23/66 BCRt-38)*

A MILLION MILES AWAY The Plimsouls—Geffen 29600
[Joey Alkes/Peter Case/Chris Fradkin] [BMI] (7/30/83 B-82)

A MILLION MILES FROM NOWHERE Brook Benton—Vik 0311
[Daryl Petty] [BMI] (3/10/58 B-82)

A MILLION TEARDROPS Conway Twitty—MGM 13011 [Fred Carter] [BMI] (6/12/61 R-89)

A MILLION TO ONE *Jimmy Charles And The Revellettes—Promo 1002*
[Phil Medley] [BMI] (7/11/60 BCR-5)

A MILLION TO ONE *The Five Stairsteps & Cubie—Buddah 26*
[Phil Medley] [BMI] (1/27/68 BCR-58)

A MILLION TO ONE *Brian Hyland—Dot 17222 [Phil Medley] [BMI] (3/29/69 BCR-76)*

A MILLION TO ONE *Donny Osmond—MGM 14583*
[Phil Medley] (TSW) [BMI] (7/28/73 BCR-21)

MILLIONAIRE Perez Prado And His Orchestra—RCA Victor 47-7456
[Perez Prado] [BMI] (2/9/59 CR-82) [I]

THE MILLIONAIRE Dr. Hook—Capitol 4104 [Dennis Tracy] [ASC] (8/23/75 BC-95)

MILORD *Edith Piaf—Capitol 4493*
[Marguerite Monnot/Giuseppe Mustacchi] [ASC] (1/9/61 BR-87) [F]

MILORD *Teresa Brewer—Coral 62265*
[Bunny Lewis/Marguerite Monnot/Giuseppe Mustacchi] [ASC] (5/8/61 BR-65) [FET]

MILORD *Bobby Darin—Atco 6297*
[Marguerite Monnot/Giuseppe Mustacchi] [ASC] (5/16/64 BCR-29) [F]

MIND BENDER Stillwater—Capricorn 0280
[Buddy Buie/Rob Roy Walker] [BMI] (11/5/77 BCR-43)

MIND, BODY AND SOUL The Flaming Ember—Hot Wax 6902
[Lamont Dozier/Ronald Dunbar/Brian Holland/Eddie Holland] [BMI] (9/27/69 BCR-19)

MIND EXCURSION The Trade Winds—Kama Sutra 212
[Pete Andreoli/Vini Poncia] [BMI] (9/3/66 BCR-50)

MIND GAMES John Lennon—Apple 1868 [John Lennon] [GL] (11/10/73 BCR-10)

MIND OVER MATTER (I'M GONNA MAKE YOU MINE) Nolan Strong—Fortune 546
[Devora Brown] [BMI] (11/3/62 C-82)

MIND PLAYING TRICKS ON ME Geto Boys—Rap-A-Lot 7241
[Willie Dennis/Isaac Hayes/Brad Jordan/Doug King] [ASC] (10/5/91 B-23)

MINE EXCLUSIVELY The Olympics—Mirwood 5513
[Sherlie Mae Matthews] [BMI] (4/23/66 BCR-65)

MINE FOR ME Rod Stewart—Mercury 73636
[Linda McCartney/Paul McCartney] [ASC] (12/14/74 B-91)

MINI-SKIRT MINNIE Wilson Pickett—Atlantic 2611
[Earl Cage/Steve Cropper*/Lindell Hill/George Henry Jackson] [BMI] (3/22/69 BCR-38)

MINIMUM LOVE Mac McAnally—Geffen 29736
[Mac McAnally/Jerry Wexler] [ASC] (3/5/83 BC-38)

MINK SCHMINK Eartha Kitt—RCA Victor 47-5756
[Sid Cutner/Leo Shuken] [ASC] (7/17/54 C-23)

MINNESOTA Northern Light—Columbia 10136
[Spencer Peterson/Dave Stuart] [NA] (5/3/75 BCR-72)

THE MINOTAUR Dick Hyman & His Electric Eclectics—Command 4126
[Dick Hyman] [ASC] (5/10/69 BCR-29) [I]

MINSTREL AND QUEEN The Impressions—ABC-Paramount 10357
[Curtis Mayfield] [BMI] (10/20/62 R-92)

MINSTREL IN THE GALLERY Jethro Tull—Chrysalis 2106
[Ian Anderson/Martin Barre] [ASC] (10/11/75 B-79)

MINUTE BY MINUTE The Doobie Brothers—Warner Bros. 8828
[Lester Abrams/Michael McDonald] [ASC] (5/5/79 BCR-12)

A MINUTE OF YOUR TIME Tom Jones—Parrot 40035
[Clive Westlake] [BMI] (12/14/68 BCR-37)

THE MINUTE YOU'RE GONE *Sonny James—Capitol 4969*
[Jimmy Gateley] [BMI] (7/13/63 BCR-70)

THE MINUTE YOU'RE GONE *Cliff Richard—Epic 9757*
[Jimmy Gateley] [BMI] (4/10/65 C-98)

MIO AMORE The Flamingos—End 1073
[Jake Carey/Zeke Carey/Tommy Hunt/Terry Johnson/Nate Nelson/Paul Wilson] [BMI] (7/11/60 BCR-45)

A MIRACLE Frankie Avalon—Chancellor 1115
[Billy Barberis/Teddy Randazzo/Bobby Weinstein] [BMI] (7/14/62 BCR-75)

MIRACLE Jon Bon Jovi—Mercury 878 392 [Jon Bon Jovi] [ASC] (10/13/90 BC-12)

MIRACLE Whitney Houston—Arista 2222
[Kenneth Edmonds/Antonio Reid] [BMI] (4/13/91 BC-9)

MIRACLE OF LOVE *Eileen Rodgers—Columbia 40708*
[Bob Merrill] [ASC] (8/18/56 BCtRt-17)

MIRACLE OF LOVE *Ginny Gibson—ABC-Paramount 9739*
[Bob Merrill] [ASC] (9/22/56 BCtRt-17)

MIRACLE OF LOVE *Bonnie Lake & Her Beaus—Decca 30081*
[Bob Merrill] [ASC] (10/6/56 Rt-17)

MIRACLES Jefferson Starship—Grunt 10367 [Marty Balin] [BMI] (8/23/75 BCR-2)

MIRACLES Stacy Lattisaw—Cotillion 7-99855
[Gary Benson/Frank Wildhorn] [ASC] (8/13/83 BC-35)

MIRAGE Tommy James And The Shondells—Roulette 4736
[Ritchie Cordell/Bo Gentry] [BMI] (4/29/67 BCR-7)

MIRAGE Eric Troyer—Chrysalis 2445 [Eric Troyer] [BMI] (7/19/80 BCR-91)

MIRROR MAN The Human League—A&M 2587
[Ian Burden/John William Callis/Philip Oakey] [ASC] (10/1/83 BC-28)

MIRROR, MIRROR Diana Ross—RCA 13021
[Dennis Matkosky/Michael Sembello] [ASC] (1/9/82 BCR-7)

MIRROR STAR Fabulous Poodles—Epic 50666
[Tony DeMeur/John Parsons] [BMI] (4/28/79 B-81)

MISDEMEANOR Foster Sylvers—Pride 1031/MGM 14580
[Leon Sylvers] [ASC] (5/26/73 BCR-14)

MISERY The Dynamics—Big Top 3161
[George E. Stratton/Anthony Wilson] [BMI] (10/19/63 BCR-40)

MISFIT Curiosity Killed The Cat—Mercury 888674
[Tobias Andersen/Julian Brookhouse/Michael Drummond/Nick Thorp/Ben Volpeliere-Pierrot] [BMI] (8/1/87 BC-42)

THE MISFITS Don Costa And His Orchestra And Chorus—United Artists 286
[Alex North] [ASC] (1/9/61 CR-68) [I]

MISLED Kool & The Gang—De-Lite 880431
[Robert Bell/Ronald Bell/James Bonneford/George M. Brown/Claydes Smith/J.T. Taylor/Curtis Fitzgerald Williams] [BMI] (11/24/84 BC-10)

MISS AMERICA Mark Lindsay—Columbia 45125 [James Kelly] [BMI] (4/4/70 BCR-31)

MISS ANN Little Richard—Specialty 606
[Enotris Johnson/Richard Penniman] [BMI] (7/1/57 B-56)

MISS BROADWAY Belle Epoque—Big Tree 16109
[Evelyne Lenton/Albert Weyman] [ASC] (3/11/78 B-92)

MISS FINE The New Yorkers—Wall 547 [Andre Scott] [BMI] (5/15/61 BC-69)

MISS KATY CRUEL The New Christy Minstrels—Columbia 43000
[Art Podell/Traditional/Nick Woods] [ASC] (4/4/64 R-94)

MISS ME BLIND Culture Club—Virgin/Epic 04388
[Michael Craig/Roy Hay/Jon Moss/George O'Dowd] [ASC] (3/3/84 BC-5)

MISS SUN Boz Scaggs—Columbia 11406 [David Paich] [ASC] (11/29/80 BCR-14)

MISS YOU *The Mulcays—Essex 407*
[Henry H. Tobias] [ASC] (1/13/56 R-49) [IM]

MISS YOU *The Keymen—ABC-Paramount 9991*
[Henry H. Tobias] [ASC] (1/24/59 CtRt-42) [IM]

MISS YOU *Jaye P. Morgan—MGM 12752*
[Charles Tobias/Harry Tobias/Henry H. Tobias] [ASC] (1/26/59 BCtRt-42)

MISS YOU The Rolling Stones—Rolling Stones 19307
[Mick Jagger/Keith Richards] [ASC] (5/27/78 BCR-1)

MISS YOU LIKE CRAZY Natalie Cole—EMI 50185
[Preston Glass/Gerry Goffin/Michael Masser] [BMI] (4/15/89 BC-7)

MISS YOU MUCH Janet Jackson—A&M 1445
[James Samuel Harris/Terry Lewis] [ASC] (9/2/89 BC-1)

MISS YOU SO Lillian Offitt—Excello 2104 [Morgan Babb] [BMI] (7/29/57 B-66)

MISSED OPPORTUNITY Daryl Hall & John Oates—Arista 1-9727
[Sara Allen/Daryl Hall/John Oates] [BMI] (7/9/88 BC-29)

MISSING The McGuire Sisters—Coral 61587 [Robert Mellin] [BMI] (2/24/56 BCR-36)

MISSING YOU Ray Peterson—Dunes 2006
[Dale Noe/Red Sovine] [BMI] (6/24/61 BCR-27)

MISSING YOU Luther Ingram—KoKo 2110
[Luther Ingram/J. Leslie McFarland] [BMI] (2/5/72 CR-72)

MISSING YOU Dan Fogelberg—Full Moon 03289 [Dan Fogelberg] [ASC] (10/9/82 BC-23)

MISSING YOU John Waite—EMI America 8212
[Mark Leonard/Chas Sandford/John Waite] [ASC] (6/23/84 BC-1)

MISSING YOU Diana Ross—RCA 13966 [Lionel Richie] [ASC] (12/1/84 BC-10)

MISSION BELL Donnie Brooks—Era 3018
[Jesse D. Hodges*/William Michael] [BMI] (6/13/60 BCR-7)

MISSION: IMPOSSIBLE Lalo Schifrin—Dot 17059
[Lalo Schifrin] [BMI] (1/6/68 BCR-36) [I]

—MISSION IMPOSSIBLE see: IMPOSSIBLE MISSION

MISSIONARY MAN Eurythmics—RCA 14414
[Annie Lennox/David A. Stewart] [BMI] (7/19/86 BC-14)

MISSISSIPPI John Phillips—Dunhill 4236 [John Phillips] [ASC] (5/9/70 BCR-32)

MISSISSIPPI COTTON PICKING DELTA TOWN Charley Pride—RCA Victor 10030
[Harold Dorman/Wiley Gann] [BMI] (11/16/74 B-70)

MISSISSIPPI MAMA Owen B.—Janus 107 [Tom Zinser] [BMI] (2/21/70 BCR-76)

MISSISSIPPI QUEEN Mountain—Windfall 532
[Corky Laing/Felix Pappalardi/Dave Rea/Leslie West] [ASC] (4/4/70 BCR-21)

MISSUNDERSTANDING Al B. Sure!—Warner Bros. 19590
[Albert Joseph Brown/Edward Ferrell/Nevelle Hodge] [ASC] (10/13/90 BC-41)

MISTAKE NO. 3 Culture Club—Virgin/Epic 04727
[Michael Craig/Roy Hay/Jon Moss/George O'Dowd] [ASC] (12/15/84 BC-33)

MISTAKEN IDENTITY Kim Carnes—EMI America 8098
[Kim Carnes] [ASC] (10/24/81 BCR-60)

MISTER CAN'T YOU SEE Buffy Sainte-Marie—Vanguard 35151
[Mickey Newbury/Townes Van Zandt] [BMI] (3/25/72 BCR-29)

MISTER FIRE EYES Bonnie Guitar—Dot 15612
[Bonnie Guitar/Ned Miller] [BMI] (9/28/57 BCR-43)

MISTER LIVINGSTON Larry Verne—Era 3034
[Thomas J. Coe/Fred Darian/Al DeLory/Joseph Van Winkle] [ASC] (12/5/60 BCR-71)

MISTER LONELY The Videls—JDS 5004
[Pete Andreoli/Vini Poncia] [BMI] (4/16/60 BCR-66)

MISTER MAGIC Grover Washington, Jr.—Kudu 924
[Ralph MacDonald/William Salter] [ASC] (5/3/75 BCR-54) [I]

MISTER NICO Four Jacks And A Jill—RCA Victor 47-9572
[Spiro Marks] [ASC] (8/10/68 B-96)

MR. SANDMAN *The Chordettes—Cadence 1247 [Pat Ballard] [ASC] (10/11/54 BCtRt-1)*

MISTER SANDMAN *The Lancers—Coral 61288 [Pat Ballard] [ASC] (11/1/54 Rt-PRE)*

MISTER SANDMAN *Vaughn Monroe & His Orchestra—RCA Victor 47-5767*
[Pat Ballard] [ASC] (11/1/54 Rt-PRE)

MR. SANDMAN *Buddy Morrow & His Orchestra—Mercury 70477*
[Pat Ballard] [ASC] (11/1/54 Rt-PRE)

MISTER SANDMAN *Four Aces—Decca 29344 [Pat Ballard] [ASC] (11/15/54 BCtRt-1)*

MR. SANTA *(parody of Mister Sandman) Dorothy Collins—Coral 61539*
[Pat Ballard] [NA] (12/23/55 R-51) [P]

MISTER SANDMAN *Emmylou Harris—Warner Bros. 49684*
[Pat Ballard] [ASC] (2/28/81 BCR-37)

—MISTER see also: MR.

MISTRUSTED LOVE Mistress—RSO 1009
[Barry Kenneth Hopkins] [BMI] (11/10/79 BCR-49)

MISTY *Sarah Vaughan—Mercury 71477*
[Johnny Burke/Erroll Garner] [ASC] (7/18/59 C-77)

MISTY *Johnny Mathis—Columbia 41483*
[Johnny Burke/Erroll Garner] [ASC] (9/28/59 BCR-12)

MISTY *Lloyd Price—Double-L 722 [Johnny Burke/Erroll Garner] [ASC] (9/28/63 BCR-20)*

MISTY *The Vibrations—Okeh 7230*
[Johnny Burke/Erroll Garner] [ASC] (10/23/65 BCR-63)

MISTY *"Groove" Holmes—Prestige 401 [Erroll Garner] [ASC] (6/25/66 BCR-32) [IM]*

MISTY *Ray Stevens—Barnaby 614 [Johnny Burke/Erroll Garner] [ASC] (4/5/75 BCR-14)*

MISTY BLUE *Eddy Arnold—RCA Victor 47-9182 [Bob Montgomery] [BMI] (5/6/67 BCR-48)*

MISTY BLUE *Joe Simon—Sound Stage 7 1508*
[Bob Montgomery] [BMI] (10/7/72 BCR-62)

MISTY BLUE *Dorothy Moore—Malaco 1029 [Bob Montgomery] [BMI] (3/6/76 BCR-3)*
MISUNDERSTANDING Genesis—Atlantic 3662 [Phil Collins] [ASC] (5/17/80 BCR-9)
MIXED EMOTIONS The Rolling Stones—Columbia 69008 [Mick Jagger/Keith Richards] [ASC] (9/2/89 BC-3)
MIXED UP GUY Joey Scarbury—Lionel 3208 [Jimmy Webb] [ASC] (1/16/71 BCR-73)
MIXED-UP, SHOOK-UP, GIRL Patty & The Emblems—Herald 590 [Leon Huff/Ralston McGriff] [BMI] (6/20/64 BCR-28)
M'LADY Sly & The Family Stone—Epic 10353 [Sylvester Stewart] [BMI] (8/10/68 BCR-90)
MO-ONIONS Booker T. & The MG's—Stax 142 [Steve Cropper/Al Jackson/Booker T. Jones Jr./Lewis Steinberg] [BMI] (2/22/64 B-97) [I]
MOBILE Julius La Rosa—Cadence 1251 [David Holt/Robert Wells] [ASC] (11/20/54 CR-21)
THE MOCKING BIRD *The Four Lads—Epic 9150 [Anton Dvorak/Dazz Jordan] [ASC] (5/19/56 B-67)*
THE MOCKING BIRD *The Four Lads—Columbia 41266 [Anton Dvorak/Dazz Jordan] [ASC] (10/20/58 BCR-32)*
MOCKINGBIRD *Inez Foxx—Symbol 919 [Charlie Foxx/Inez Foxx] [BMI] (6/22/63 BCR-7)*
MOCKINGBIRD *Aretha Franklin—Columbia 44381 [Charlie Foxx/Inez Foxx] [BMI] (12/23/67 BCR-90)*
MOCKINGBIRD *Carly Simon & James Taylor—Elektra 45880 [Charlie Foxx/Inez Foxx] [BMI] (2/2/74 BCR-3)*
MODEL GIRL Johnny Maestro The Voice Of The Crests—Coed 545 [Lockie Edwards/Ollie Jones] [BMI] (2/6/61 BCR-20)
MODERN DAY DELILAH Van Stephenson—MCA 52376 [Jan Buckingham/Van Stephenson] [BMI] (4/21/84 BC-22)
MODERN GIRL Sheena Easton—EMI America 8080 [Dominic Bugatti/Frank Musker] [BMI] (5/9/81 BCR-12)
MODERN LOVE David Bowie—EMI America 8177 [David Bowie] [ASC] (9/17/83 BC-14)
MODERN WOMAN Billy Joel—Epic 06118 [Billy Joel] [ASC] (6/7/86 BC-10)
MOHAIR SAM Charlie Rich—Smash 1993 [Dallas Frazier] [BMI] (8/21/65 BCR-17)
MOJO WORKOUT (DANCE) Larry Bright—Tide 006 [Larry Bright/Paula DePores/Orena D. Fulmer/Ruth Stratchborneo] [BMI] (5/16/60 BC-90)
MOLLY Bobby Goldsboro—Laurie 3148 [Steve Karliski] [BMI] (12/22/62 BCR-60)
—MOLLY-O see: THEMES FROM MAN WITH THE GOLDEN ARM
MOM AND DAD'S WALTZ Patti Page—Mercury 71823 [Lefty Frizzell] [BMI] (6/12/61 B-58)
MOMENT BY MOMENT Yvonne Elliman—RSO 915 [Lee Holdridge/Molly Ann Leikin] [ASC] (12/23/78 B-59)
MOMENT I SAW YOU Joni James—MGM 12020 [Robert Mellin/Richard Savage] [NA] (7/11/55 CR-36)
THE MOMENT OF TRUTH Survivor—Casablanca 880053 [Peter Beckett/Bill Conti/Dennis Lambert] [BMI] (6/16/84 BC-63)
MOMENTS TO REMEMBER *The Four Lads—Columbia 40539 [Robert Allen/Al Stillman] [ASC] (8/27/55 BCR-2)*
MOMENTS TO REMEMBER *The Vogues—Reprise 0831 [Robert Allen/Al Stillman] [ASC] (6/21/69 BCR-40)*
MOMENTS *Jennell Hawkins—Amazon 1003 [Richard Berry] [BMI] (2/10/62 BCtR-50)*
MOMENTS TO REMEMBER *Joyce Davis—United Artists 425 [Richard Berry] [BMI] (3/3/62 Ct-78)*
MOMMY AND DADDY The Monkees—Colgems 5005 [Micky Dolenz] (TSW) [BMI] (9/20/69 R-76)
MOMMY AND DADDY WERE TWISTIN' Susan Summers—Diamond 106 [Paul Vance/Artie Wayne] [BMI] (1/15/62 R-95)
MONA LISA *Carl Mann—Phillips Int'l 3539 [Ray Evans/Jay Livingston] [ASC] (6/1/59 BCtRt-25)*
MONA LISA *Conway Twitty—MGM 12804 [Ray Evans/Jay Livingston] [ASC] (6/22/59 BCtRt-29)*
MONDAY IN MAY Third Condition—Sundi 6815 [Charles Robinette] [BMI] (9/12/70 R-95)
MONDAY, MONDAY *The Mama's & The Papa's—Dunhill 4026 [John Phillips] [ASC] (4/9/66 BCR-1)*
MONDAY, MONDAY *Stars On 45—Radio 3863 [John Phillips] (Med) [ASC] (9/19/81 BCR-55)*
MONEY (THAT'S WHAT I WANT) *Barrett Strong—Anna 1111 [Janie Bradford/Berry Gordy] [BMI] (1/30/60 BCR-14)*
MONEY *The Kingsmen—Wand 150 [Janie Bradford/Berry Gordy] [BMI] (3/7/64 BCR-16)*
MONEY (THAT'S WHAT I WANT) PART 1 *Jr. Walker & The All Stars—Soul 35026 [Janie Bradford/Berry Gordy] [BMI] (11/19/66 BCR-32)*
MONEY *The Flying Lizards—Virgin 67003 [Janie Bradford/Berry Gordy] [BMI] (12/1/79 BCR-34)*
MONEY The Lovin' Spoonful—Kama Sutra 241 [John Sebastian] [BMI] (1/6/68 BCR-34)
MONEY Pink Floyd—Harvest 3609 [Roger Waters] [ASC] (5/12/73 BCR-10)
MONEY Gladys Knight & The Pips—Buddah 487 [Gene McDaniels] [BMI] (8/23/75 BCR-40)
MONEY BACK GUARANTEE Five Man Electrical Band—Lion 127 [Les Emmerson] [BMI] (9/2/72 BCR-54)
MONEY BURNS A HOLE IN MY POCKET Dean Martin—Capitol 2818 [Bob Hilliard/Jule Styne] [ASC] (10/4/54 R-PRE)
MONEY CHANGES EVERYTHING Cyndi Lauper—Portrait 37-04737 [Thomas Gray] [BMI] (12/22/84 BC-27)
MONEY FOR NOTHING Dire Straits—Warner Bros. 28950 [Mark Knopfler/Sting] [ASC] (7/13/85 BC-1)
MONEY HONEY Elvis Presley—RCA Victor EPA-821 [Jesse Stone] [NA] (5/12/56 B-76)
MONEY HONEY Bay City Rollers—Arista 0170 [Eric Faulkner/Stuart John Wood] [ASC] (2/7/76 BCR-7)
MONEY, MONEY, MONEY ABBA—Atlantic 3434 [Benny Andersson/Björn Ulvaeus] [ASC] (10/15/77 BCR-54)
MONEY MUSIC The Boys In The Band—Spring 106 [Bob Feldman/Richard Gottehrer] [BMI] (10/3/70 R-81)
MONEY RUNNER Quincy Jones—Reprise 1072 [Quincy Jones] [BMI] (3/11/72 BCR-57) [I]
—MONEY TALKS see: DIRTY CASH
THE MONEY TREE *Margaret Whiting—Capitol 3586 [Cliff Ferré/Mark McIntyre] [ASC] (12/8/56 BRt-48)*
THE MONEY TREE *Patience and Prudence—Liberty 55040 [Cliff Ferré/Mark McIntyre] [ASC] (12/8/56 BRt-48)*
THE MONEY TREE *Frankie Lester—Vik 0242 [Cliff Ferré/Mark McIntyre] [ASC] (12/8/56 Rt-48)*
THE MONEY TREE *Annisteen Allen—Decca 30146 [Cliff Ferré/Mark McIntyre] [ASC] (12/29/56 Rt-48)*
MONEY WON'T CHANGE YOU PART 1 James Brown And The Famous Flames—King 6048 [James Brown/Nat Jones] [BMI] (7/30/66 BCR-35)
MONEY$ TOO TIGHT (TO MENTION) Simply Red—Elektra 69528 [John Valentine/William Valentine/Caroline Wiggins] [BMI] (7/19/86 BC-27)
MONEYTALKS AC/DC—Atco 98881 [Angus Young/Malcolm Young] [ASC] (12/8/90 BC-23)
MONGOOSE Elephant's Memory—Metromedia 182 [Stan Bronstein/David Cohen*/Rick Frank] [BMI] (7/25/70 BCR-40)
—MONIQUE see: SONG FROM "KINGS GO FORTH"
MONKEY George Michael—Columbia 07941 [George Michael] [ASC] (7/9/88 BC-1)
MONKEY-SHINE Bill Black And His Combo—Hi 2069 [Carl McVoy] [BMI] (9/14/63 BCR-47) [I]
THE MONKEY TIME *Major Lance—Okeh 7175 [Curtis Mayfield] [BMI] (7/13/63 BCR-7)*
THE MONKEY TIME *The Tubes—Capitol 5254 [Curtis Mayfield] [BMI] (10/1/83 BC-68)*
MONSTER Steppenwolf—Dunhill 4221 [Jerry Edmonton/John Kay] [BMI] (12/27/69 BCR-21)
MONSTER Fred Schneider—Reprise 19262 [John Cote/Fred Schneider] [BMI] (6/29/91 BC-81)
MONSTER MASH *Bobby (Boris) Pickett And The Crypt-Kickers—Garpax 44167 [Leonard L. Capizzi/Bobby Pickett] [BMI] (9/1/62 BCR-1)*
MONSTER MASH *Bobby (Boris) Pickett And The Crypt-Kickers—Parrot 348 [Leonard L. Capizzi/Bobby Pickett] [BMI] (7/11/70 BC-72)*
MONSTER MASH *Bobby (Boris) Pickett And The Crypt-Kickers—Parrot 348 [Leonard L. Capizzi/Bobby Pickett] [BMI] (5/5/73 BCR-10)*
MONSTERS AND ANGELS Voice Of The Beehive—London 869 428 [Tracey Bryn/Mike Jones/Brad Nack] [BMI] (10/19/91 BC-73)
MONSTERS' HOLIDAY Bobby (Boris) Pickett And The Crypt-Kickers—Garpax 44171 [Charles Underwood] [BMI] (12/1/62 BCR-24)
MONTAGE FROM HOW SWEET IT IS (I KNOW THAT YOU KNOW) *The Love Generation—Imperial 66310 [Jimmy Webb] [ASC] (8/3/68 BCR-81)*
MONTAGE *Picardy—Dunhill 4146 [Jimmy Webb] [ASC] (8/10/68 R-84)*
MONTE CARLO MELODY Werner Müller And His Orchestra—Decca 29992 [Al Frisch] [ASC] (7/27/56 R-82)
MONTEGO BAY *Bobby Bloom—L&R/MGM 157 [Jeff Barry/Bobby Bloom] [BMI] (9/5/70 BCR-6)*
MONTEGO BAY *Amazulu—Mango 121 [Jeff Barry/Bobby Bloom] [BMI] (7/25/87 BC-88)*
MONTEREY Eric Burdon & The Animals—MGM 13868 [Vic Briggs/Eric Burdon/Barry Jenkins/Danny McCulloch/John Weider] [BMI] (12/16/67 BCR-10)
MONY MONY *Tommy James And The Shondells—Roulette 7008 [Bobby Bloom/Ritchie Cordell/Bo Gentry/Tommy James] [BMI] (3/30/68 BCR-3)*
MONY MONY *Billy Idol—Chrysalis 2543 [Bobby Bloom/Ritchie Cordell/Bo Gentry/Tommy James] [BMI] (9/19/81 CR-81)*
MONY MONY *Tight Fit—Arista 0638 [Bobby Bloom/Ritchie Cordell/Bo Gentry/Tommy James] (Med) [BMI] (10/10/81 B-89)*
MONY MONY "LIVE" *Billy Idol—Chrysalis 43161 [Bobby Bloom/Ritchie Cordell/Bo Gentry/Tommy James] [BMI] (9/5/87 BC-1)*
MOOD INDIGO *The Norman Petty Trio—"X" 0040 [Barney Bigard/Duke Ellington/Irving Mills] [ASC] (9/18/54 BCR-19) [I]*
MOOD INDIGO *The Modernaires & George Auld—Coral 61265 [Barney Bigard/Duke Ellington/Irving Mills] [ASC] (10/25/54 Rt-PRE)*
MOOD INDIGO MAMBO *Perez Prado And His Orchestra—RCA Victor 47-6085 [Barney Bigard/Duke Ellington/Irving Mills] [ASC] (5/2/55 R-81) [I]*
MOODY BLUE Elvis Presley—RCA 10857 [Mark James] (TSW) [BMI] (12/25/76 BCR-31)
MOODY RIVER Pat Boone—Dot 16209 [Gary Bruce] [BMI] (5/1/61 BCR-1)
MOODY WOMAN Jerry Butler—Mercury 72929 [Jerry Butler/Kenneth Gamble/Leon Huff] [BMI] (5/24/69 BCR-19)

MOON IS ON FIRE Teresa Brewer—Coral 61315 [Bob Merrill] [ASC] (12/27/54 R-63)
—MOON OVER NAPLES see: SPANISH EYES
MOON RIVER *Jerry Butler—Vee-Jay 405 [Henry Mancini/Johnny Mercer] [ASC] (9/25/61 BCtRt-5)*
MOON RIVER *The Fuller Brothers—Challenge 9119 [Henry Mancini/Johnny Mercer] [ASC] (9/25/61 Rt-79)*
MOON RIVER *Henry Mancini, His Orchestra And Chorus—RCA Victor 47-7916 [Henry Mancini/Johnny Mercer] [ASC] (9/30/61 BCtRt-5)*
MOON RIVER *Jean Thomas—Cadence 1419 [Henry Mancini/Johnny Mercer] [ASC] (5/7/62 Rt-58)*
MOON SHADOW Cat Stevens—A&M 1265 [Cat Stevens] [ASC] (6/19/71 BCR-22)
MOON TALK Perry Como—RCA Victor 47-7274 [Al Hoffman/Dick Manning] [ASC] (7/14/58 BCR-24)
MOON WALK PART I Joe Simon—Sound Stage 7 2651 [Alfred James Ellis*/Joe Simon] [BMI] (12/27/69 BCR-40)
THE MOON WAS YELLOW Frank Sinatra—Capitol 4677 [Fred Ahlert/Edgar Leslie] [ASC] (1/15/62 BR-76)
MOONBEAM Men Without Hats—Mercury 870153 [Ivan Doroschuk] [BMI] (4/9/88 C-89)
MOONDANCE Van Morrison—Warner Bros. 8450 [Van Morrison] [BMI] (11/5/77 BCR-91)
MOONFLIGHT Vik Venus Alias: Your Main Moon Man—Buddah 118 [Barry Siegal] [BMI] (6/14/69 BCR-23)
MOONGLOW *George Cates & His Orchestra—Coral 61618 [Will Hudson/Irving Mills] (Med) [ASC] (3/30/56 BCR-1) [IM]*
MOONGLOW *Morris Stoloff Conducting The Columbia Pictures Orchestra—Decca 29888 [Will Hudson/Irving Mills] (Med) [ASC] (4/13/56 BCR-1) [IM]*
MOONLIGHT AND ROSES (BRING MEM'RIES OF YOU) *The Three Suns—RCA Victor 47-5768 [Ben Black/Charles N. Daniels/Edwin Lemare] [ASC] (7/10/54 BCR-17) [I]*
MOONLIGHT AND ROSES (BRING MEM'RIES OF YOU) *Vic Dana—Dolton 309 [Ben Black/Charles N. Daniels/Edwin Lemare] [ASC] (8/7/65 BCR-51)*
MOONLIGHT BAY *The Drifters—Atlantic 1187 [Edward Madden/Percy Wenrich] [NA] (6/2/58 BCRt-53)*
MOONLIGHT BAY *Joe Leahy & His Orchestra—Felsted 8518 [Edward Madden/Percy Wenrich] [NA] (6/2/58 Rt-53)*
MOONLIGHT BAY *Jimmie Haskell & His Orchestra—Imperial 5519 [Edward Madden/Percy Wenrich] [NA] (6/30/58 Rt-55)*
MOONLIGHT FEELS RIGHT Starbuck—Private Stock 45,039 [Bruce Blackman] [ASC] (4/17/76 BCR-3)
MOONLIGHT GAMBLER *Frankie Laine—Columbia 40780 [Bob Hilliard/Philip Springer] [ASC] (12/1/56 BCRt-3)*
MOONLIGHT GAMBLER *Winifred Atwell And Her Piano—London 1724 [Philip Springer] [ASC] (2/9/57 Rt-3) [IM]*
MOONLIGHT LOVE Perry Como—RCA Victor 47-6670 [Claude Debussy*/Mitchell Parish/Domenico Savino] [ASC] (10/20/56 BCR-33)
MOONLIGHT MOUNTAIN Faron Young—Capitol 3753 [Bud Freeman/Leon Pober] [ASC] (8/5/57 R-81)
MOONLIGHT MOUNTAIN Faron Young—Capitol 3753 [Bud Freeman/Leon Pober] [ASC] (8/14/61 R-63)
MOONLIGHT ON WATER *Kevin Raleigh—Atlantic 88962 [Andy Goldmark/Steve Kipner] [ASC] (5/20/89 B-60)*
MOONLIGHT ON WATER *Laura Branigan—Atlantic 87969 [Andy Goldmark/Steve Kipner] [ASC] (3/31/90 BC-58)*
MOONLIGHT SERENADE *The Rivieras (1)—Coed 508 [Glenn Miller/Mitchell Parish] [ASC] (2/9/59 BCRt-47)*
MOONLIGHT SERENADE *Tommy Leonetti—RCA Victor 47-7455 [Glenn Miller/Mitchell Parish] [ASC] (2/9/59 Rt-76)*
MOONLIGHT SERENADE *Bobby Vinton—ABC 12178 [Glenn Miller/Mitchell Parish] [ASC] (5/1/76 B-97)*
MOONLIGHT SERENADE *Frank Barber Orchestra—Victory 1001 [Glenn Miller] (Med) [ASC] (5/8/82 B-61) [IM]*
MOONLIGHT SONATA Henry Mancini And His Orchestra—RCA Victor 74-0212 [Henry Mancini/Ludwig van Beethoven] [ASC] (8/9/69 BCR-87) [I]
MOONLIGHT SPECIAL Ray Stevens—Barnaby 604 [Ray Stevens] [BMI] (7/27/74 BCR-49)
MOON LIGHT SWIM *Tony Perkins—RCA Victor 47-7020 [Sylvia Dee/Ben Weisman] [ASC] (9/2/57 BCtRt-41)*
MOONLIGHT SWIM *Nick Noble—Mercury 71169 [Sylvia Dee/Ben Weisman] [ASC] (9/2/57 BCtRt-37)*
MOONLIGHT SWIM *Joel Grey—Capitol 3777 [Sylvia Dee/Ben Weisman] [ASC] (9/23/57 Rt-42)*
MOONLIGHTING (THEME) Al Jarreau—MCA 53124 [Lee Holdridge/Al Jarreau] [BMI] (5/30/87 BC-23)
MOONSHINE (FRIEND OF MINE) John Kay—Dunhill 4351 [Les Emmerson] [BMI] (5/26/73 CR-67)
MOOVIN' N' GROOVIN' Duane Eddy—Jamie 1101 [Duane Eddy/Lee Hazlewood] [BMI] (3/1/58 BC-54) [I]
MORE Perry Como—RCA Victor 47-6554 [Alex Alstone/Tom Glazer] [ASC] (6/8/56 BCR-7)
MORE (THEME FROM "MONDO CANE") *Della Reese—RCA Victor 47-8187 [Norman Newell/Nino Oliviero/Riz Ortolani] [BMI] (6/1/63 Rt-90) [FDE]*
MORE (THEME FROM THE FILM "MONDO CANE") *Steve Lawrence—Columbia 42795 [Norman Newell/Nino Oliviero/Riz Ortolani] [BMI] (6/1/63 CtRt-10) [FDE]*
MORE THEME FROM MONDO CANE *Martin Denny—Liberty 55571 [Nino Oliviero/Riz Ortolani] [BMI] (6/8/63 Rt-90) [IM]*
MORE *Kai Winding & Orchestra—Verve 10295 [Nino Oliviero/Riz Ortolani] [BMI] (7/6/63 BCtRt-7) [IM]*
MORE (FROM THE FILM "MONDO CANE") *Danny Williams—United Artists 601 [Norman Newell/Nino Oliviero/Riz Ortolani] [BMI] (7/6/63 Ct-10) [FDE]*
MORE *Vic Dana—Dolton 81 [Norman Newell/Nino Oliviero/Riz Ortolani] [BMI] (7/27/63 BCtRt-7) [FDE]*
MORE AND MORE Andy Williams—Columbia 44202 [Tommy Karen/Allan Reuss/Rainey Robinson] [BMI] (7/8/67 BCR-88)
MORE AND MORE Carly Simon—Elektra 45278 [Mac Rebennack/Alvin Robinson] [BMI] (10/18/75 BC-90)
MORE AND MORE OF YOUR AMOR Nat King Cole—Capitol 5219 [Joe Sherman/George David Weiss] [ASC] (8/1/64 C-97)
MORE BOUNCE TO THE OUNCE (PART 1) Zapp—Warner Bros. 49534 [Roger Troutman] [BMI] (9/20/80 BCR-56)
—MORE I LOVE YOU see: LO MUCHO QUE TE QUIERO
THE MORE I SEE YOU Chris Montez—A&M 796 [Mack Gordon/Harry Warren] [ASC] (4/16/66 BCR-14)
MORE LOVE *Smokey Robinson & The Miracles—Tamla 54152 [Smokey Robinson] [ASC] (6/17/67 BCR-19)*
MORE LOVE *Kim Carnes—EMI America 8045 [Smokey Robinson] [ASC] (5/31/80 BCR-9)*
MORE MONEY FOR YOU AND ME The Four Preps—Capitol 4599 [Bruce Belland/Glen Larson] (Med) [BMI] (8/14/61 BCR-14)
MORE, MORE, MORE (PT. 1) Andrea True Connection—Buddah 515 [Gregg Diamond] [ASC] (3/13/76 BCR-1)
MORE MORE MORE OF YOUR LOVE Bob Brady—Chariot 101 [Smokey Robinson] [ASC] (5/20/67 R-77)
MORE POWER TO YOU Tommy Tate—KoKo 2114 [Johnny Baylor/Tommy Tate] [BMI] (12/9/72 CR-90)
MORE THAN A FEELING Boston—Epic 50266 [Tom Scholz] [ASC] (9/11/76 BCR-4)
MORE THAN A MIRACLE Roger Williams—Kapp 843 [Larry Kusik/Gian Piccioni/Eddie Snyder] [ASC] (11/25/67 C-100)
MORE THAN A WOMAN Tavares—Capitol 4500 [Barry Gibb/Maurice Gibb/Robin Gibb] [BMI] (11/19/77 BCR-32)
MORE THAN EVER Georgia Gibbs—Mercury 70430 [Don George/Joe Marsala] [ASC] (10/4/54 R-PRE)
MORE THAN EVER Nelson—DGC 19002 [Gunnar Nelson/Matthew Nelson/Marc Tanner] [ASC] (3/9/91 BC-11)
MORE THAN I CAN SAY *Bobby Vee—Liberty 55296 [Jerry Allison/Sonny Curtis] [BMI] (2/27/61 BCR-48)*
MORE THAN I CAN SAY *Leo Sayer—Warner Bros. 49565 [Jerry Allison/Sonny Curtis] [BMI] (9/27/80 BCR-2)*
MORE THAN I CAN STAND Bobby Womack—Minit 32093 [Darryl Carter/Bobby Womack] [BMI] (4/11/70 BCR-84)
MORE THAN JUST THE TWO OF US Sneaker—Handshake 02557 [Mitch Crane/Michael Schneider] [BMI] (10/31/81 BCR-34)
MORE THAN PHYSICAL Bananarama—London 886080 [Matt Aitken/Sarah Dallin/Siobhan Fahey/Mike Stock/Pete Waterman/Keren Woodward] [BMI] (10/18/86 BC-72)
MORE THAN THE EYE CAN SEE Al Martino—Capitol 5989 [Bob Crewe/Larry Weiss] [BMI] (9/16/67 BCR-41)
MORE THAN WORDS Extreme—A&M 1552 [Nuno Bettencourt/Gary Cherone] [ASC] (3/23/91 BC-1)
MORE THAN WORDS CAN SAY Alias—EMI 50324 [Freddy Curci/Steve DeMarchi] [BMI] (9/8/90 BC-2)
MORE THAN YOU KNOW The Platters—Mercury 71986 [Edward Eliscu/Billy Rose/Vincent Youmans] [ASC] (6/2/62 R-97)
MORE THAN YOU KNOW Martika—Columbia 08103 [Michael Jay/Martika/Marvin Morrow] [BMI] (12/24/88 BC-17)
MORE TODAY THAN YESTERDAY Spiral Starecase—Columbia 44741 [Pat Upton] [BMI] (3/29/69 BCR-7)
THE MORE YOU DO IT (THE MORE I LIKE IT DONE TO ME) Ronnie Dyson—Columbia 10356 [Charles Henry Jackson Jr./Marvin Yancy] [ASC] (7/10/76 BCR-59)
THE MORE YOU LIVE, THE MORE YOU LOVE A Flock Of Seagulls—Jive 9220 [Frank Maudsley/Paul Reynolds/Ali Score/Mike Score] [ASC] (8/11/84 BC-56)
MORGEN *Ivo Robic and The Song-Masters—Laurie 3033 [Peter Mösser] [ASC] (8/10/59 BCRt-9) [F]*
MORGEN (ONE MORE SUNRISE) *Rex Allen—Buena Vista 347 [Peter Mösser/Noel Sherman] [ASC] (8/17/59 Rt-9)*
MORGEN (ONE MORE SUNRISE) *Leslie Uggams—Columbia 41451 [Peter Mösser/Noel Sherman] [ASC] (9/14/59 B-98)*
—MORITAT see: MACK THE KNIFE
MORNIN' Jarreau—Warner Bros. 29720 [David Foster/Jay Graydon/Al Jarreau] [BMI] (3/19/83 BC-21)
MORNIN' BEAUTIFUL Tony Orlando & Dawn—Elektra 45260 [Dave Appell/Sandy Linzer] [ASC] (6/21/75 BCR-14)
MORNIN' GLORY Bobbie Gentry & Glen Campbell—Capitol 2314 [Bobbie Gentry] [ASC] (10/26/68 BCR-56)

MORNIN' MORNIN' Bobby Goldsboro—United Artists 50614
[Dennis Linde] [BMI] (12/20/69 BCR-61)

MORNING Jim Ed Brown—RCA Victor 47-9909
[Willis S. Graham] [BMI] (11/14/70 BCR-42)

MORNING AFTER The Mar-Keys—Stax 112
[Earl Forest/Robert Talley] [BMI] (10/2/61 BCR-58) [I]

THE MORNING AFTER Maureen McGovern—20th Century 2010
[Joel Hirschhorn/Al Kasha] [ASC] (6/16/73 BCR-1)

MORNING DANCE Spyro Gyra—Infinity 50,011
[Jay Beckenstein] [BMI] (6/2/79 BCR-24) [I]

MORNING DESIRE Kenny Rogers—RCA 14194 [Dave Loggins] [ASC] (11/23/85 B-72)

MORNING DEW Lulu—Epic 10367 [Bonnie Dobson/Tim Rose] [BMI] (8/3/68 BCR-52)

MORNING GIRL The Neon Philharmonic—Warner Bros.-Seven Arts 7261
[Tupper Saussy] [BMI] (4/5/69 BCR-15)

MORNING HAS BROKEN Cat Stevens—A&M 1335
[Eleanor Farjeon/Traditional] [BMI] (3/25/72 BCR-6)

MORNING MAN Rupert Holmes—MCA 51019 [Rupert Holmes] [ASC] (11/8/80 BC-68)

MORNING MUCH BETTER Ten Wheel Drive With Genya Ravan—Polydor 14037
[Aram Schefrin/Michael Zager] [BMI] (7/4/70 BCR-53)

THE MORNING OF OUR LIVES Arkade—Dunhill 4268
[Steve Barri/Barry Gross/Harvey Price*/Dan Walsh] [BMI] (2/6/71 BCR-60)

MORNING SIDE OF THE MOUNTAIN *Tommy Edwards—MGM 12757*
[Dick Manning/Larry Stock] [ASC] (2/28/59 BCR-27)

MORNING SIDE OF THE MOUNTAIN *Donny And Marie Osmond—MGM 14765*
[Dick Manning/Larry Stock] [ASC] (11/16/74 BCR-6)

MORNING TRAIN (NINE TO FIVE) Sheena Easton—EMI America 8071
[Florrie Palmer] [ASC] (2/14/81 BCR-1)

MORNINGTOWN RIDE The Seekers—Capitol 5787
[Malvina Reynolds] [ASC] (2/18/67 BCR-41)

THE MOSQUITO The Doors—Elektra 45807
[John Densmore/Robby Krieger/Ray Manzarek] [ASC] (9/30/72 BCR-82)

THE MOST BEAUTIFUL GIRL Charlie Rich—Epic 11040
[Rory Bourke/Billy Sherrill/Norro Wilson] [BMI] (9/29/73 BCR-1)

THE MOST BEAUTIFUL WORDS Della Reese—RCA Victor 47-7833
[Stan Lebowsky/Johnny Lehmann] [BMI] (1/16/61 BCR-56)

MOST LIKELY YOU GO YOUR WAY (AND I'LL GO MINE)
Bob Dylan / The Band—Asylum 11043
[Bob Dylan] [SE] (7/27/74 BCR-47)

MOST OF ALL *The Fontane Sisters with Billy Vaughn's Orchestra—Dot 15352*
[Alan Freed‡/Harvey Fuqua] [BMI] (4/4/55 CtRt-7)

MOST OF ALL *The Moonglows—Chess 126*
[Alan Freed‡/Harvey Fuqua] [BMI] (4/4/55 Rt-20)

MOST OF ALL *Don Cornell—Coral 61393*
[Alan Freed‡/Harvey Fuqua] (TSW) [BMI] (5/21/55 BCtRt-7)

MOST OF ALL B.J. Thomas—Scepter 12299
[Buddy Buie/J.R. Cobb] [BMI] (11/28/70 BCR-22)

MOST OF ALL Jody Watley—MCA 53258
[Gardner Cole/Patrick Raymond Leonard] [BMI] (4/30/88 BC-60)

MOST PEOPLE GET MARRIED Patti Page—Mercury 71950
[Leon Carr/Earl Shuman] [ASC] (4/2/62 BCR-20)

MOSTLY MARTHA The Crew-Cuts—Mercury 70741
[David Carroll/Dorcas Cochran] [BMI] (11/14/55 BCR-28)

MOTHER *John Lennon/Plastic Ono Band—Apple 1827*
[John Lennon] [GL] (1/2/71 BCR-16)

MOTHER *Barbra Streisand—Columbia 45471 [John Lennon] [GL] (10/9/71 BCR-59)*

MOTHER AND CHILD REUNION Paul Simon—Columbia 45547
[Paul Simon] [BMI] (2/5/72 BCR-4)

A MOTHER FOR MY CHILDREN The Whispers—Janus 231
[Ron Baker/Allan Felder/Norman Harris/Bunny Sigler] [BMI] (2/2/74 BC-92)

MOTHER FREEDOM Bread—Elektra 45740 [David Gates] [ASC] (7/10/71 BCR-31)

MOTHER-IN-LAW *Ernie K-Doe—Minit 623 [Allen Toussaint] [BMI] (3/13/61 BCR-1)*

MOTHER-IN-LAW *Clarence Carter—Fame 250*
[Allen Toussaint] (TSW) [BMI] (7/7/73 BCR-65)

MOTHER NATURE The Temptations—Gordy 7119
[Dino Fekaris/Nick Zesses] [ASC] (7/1/72 BCR-65)

MOTHER NATURE, FATHER TIME Brook Benton—RCA Victor 47-8693
[Brook Benton/Clyde Otis] [BMI] (11/13/65 BCR-40)

MOTHER NATURE'S WINE Sugarloaf—United Artists 50784
[Jerry Corbetta/John C. Phillips/David Riordan] [ASC] (6/26/71 BC-88)

MOTHER, PLEASE! Jo Ann Campbell—Cameo 249
[Dave Appell/Kal Mann] [ASC] (4/20/63 BC-88)

MOTHER POPCORN (YOU GOT TO HAVE A MOTHER FOR ME) PART 1
James Brown—King 6245
[James Brown/Alfred James Ellis] [BMI] (6/14/69 BCR-7)

MOTHERLAND Quincy Jones—A&M 1909 [Quincy Jones] (Med) [ASC] (2/19/77 BCR-57)

MOTHER'S EYES Enuff Z'Nuff—Atco 98845
[Derek Frigo/Donnie Vie] [ASC] (5/25/91 C-84)

MOTHER'S LITTLE HELPER The Rolling Stones—London 902
[Mick Jagger/Keith Richards] [BMI] (7/9/66 BCR-4)

MOTHER'S LOVE The Diamonds—Mercury 71449 [Clyde Otis] [NA] (4/13/59 R-83)

MOTHER'S PRIDE George Michael—Columbia 73663 TSW
[George Michael] [ASC] (2/2/91 B-46)

MOTHERS TALK Tears For Fears—Mercury 884638
[Roland Orzabal/Ian Stanley] [BMI] (4/12/86 BC-25)

THE MOTION OF LOVE Gene Loves Jezebel—Geffen 28183
[Jay Aston/Michael Aston/Peter Risingham/James Stevenson] [ASC] (2/6/88 B-87)

MOTORCYCLE Tico And The Triumphs—Amy 835 [Paul Simon] [BMI] (1/6/62 BR-97)

MOTORCYCLE MAMA Sailcat—Elektra 45782 [John Wyker] [BMI] (6/10/72 BCR-12)

MOTORTOWN The Kane Gang—Capitol 44062
[Martin Brammer/David Brewis/Paul Woods] [BMI] (10/17/87 BC-36)

MOTOWN REVIEW Philly Cream—Fantasy/WMOT 862
[Len Barry/Butch Ingram] [BMI] (6/30/79 B-67)

THE MOTOWN SONG Rod Stewart—Warner Bros. 19322
[Larry John McNally] [ASC] (7/6/91 BC-9)

MOTOWNPHILLY Boyz II Men—Motown 2090
[Dallas Austin/Michael Bivins/Nathan Morris/Shawn Stockman] [BMI] (6/15/91 BC-3)

MOULTY The Barbarians—Laurie 3326
[Barbara Baer/Eliot Greenberg/Douglas Morris/Robert Schwartz] [BMI]
(2/26/66 BCR-82)

MOUNTAIN OF LOVE *Harold Dorman—Rita 1003*
[Harold Dorman] [BMI] (2/29/60 BCR-17)

MOUNTAIN OF LOVE *Johnny Rivers—Imperial 66075*
[Harold Dorman] [BMI] (10/31/64 BCR-7)

MOUNTAIN OF LOVE *Ronnie Dove—Diamond 244*
[Harold Dorman] [BMI] (6/1/68 BCR-49)

MOUNTAIN OF LOVE Billy Stewart—Chess 1948
[Shena DeMell/Sugar Pie DeSanto] [BMI] (12/18/65 BC-81)

MOUNTAINS Prince And The Revolution—Paisley Park 7-28711
[Lisa Coleman/Wendy Melvoin/Prince] [ASC] (5/24/86 BC-19)

THE MOUNTAIN'S HIGH *Dick And Deedee—Liberty 55350*
[Dick Gosting] [BMI] (7/31/61 BCR-2)

THE MOUNTAIN'S HIGH *(parody of The Mountain's High)*
The Four Preps—Capitol 4716
[Dick Gosting] (Med) [BMI] (3/17/62 BCR-61) [P]

THE MOUSE Soupy Sales—ABC-Paramount 10646
[Sandy Linzer/Denny Randell] [BMI] (4/3/65 BCR-37)

MOVE ANY MOUNTAIN The Shamen—Epic 74044
[Colin Angus/Will Sinott/Richard West] [NA] (12/14/91 BC-34)

MOVE AWAY Culture Club—Virgin/Epic 05847
[Michael Craig/Roy Hay/Jon Moss/George O'Dowd/Phil Pickett] [ASC] (4/5/86 BC-12)

MOVE 'EM OUT Delaney & Bonnie—Atco 6866
[Steve Cropper/Bettye Crutcher] [BMI] (1/8/72 BCR-55)

MOVE IN A LITTLE CLOSER, BABY Mama Cass—Dunhill 4184
[Arnold Capitanelli/Robert O'Connor] [ASC] (3/8/69 BCR-49)

MOVE ME, O WONDROUS MUSIC The Ray Charles Singers—Command 4135
[Buddy Kaye/Charles Raymond Offenberg] [ASC] (5/30/70 BCR-87)

MOVE OVER Steppenwolf—Dunhill 4205
[John Kay/Gabriel Mekler] [BMI] (8/9/69 BCR-16)

MOVE OVER ROVER The Mark IV—Mercury 71445
[Eddie Mascari/Erwin Wenzlaff] [BMI] (4/25/59 CR-93)

MOVE RIGHT OUT Rick Astley—RCA 2839 [Rick Astley/Rob Fisher] [BMI] (6/15/91 BC-75)

MOVE YOUR BOOGIE BODY Bar-Kays—Mercury 76015
[James Edward Alexander/Charles Leonard Allen/Michael Beard/Mark Bynum/
Larry Dodson/Sherman Guy/Harvey Henderson/Allen Alvoid Jones Jr./
Lloyd Ed Smith/Winston Stewart/Frank Thompson] [BMI] (11/10/79 BCR-57)

MOVIN' Bill Black's Combo—Hi 2038
[Bill Black] [BMI] (9/11/61 BCR-34) [I]

MOVIN' Brass Construction—United Artists 775
[Randy Muller/Wade Williamston] [BMI] (3/20/76 BCR-14) [I]

MOVIN' ON Bad Company—Swan Song 70101 [Mick Ralphs] [ASC] (1/18/75 BCR-19)

MOVIN' OUT (ANTHONY'S SONG) Billy Joel—Columbia 10708
[Billy Joel] [ASC] (3/18/78 BCR-14)

MOZAMBIQUE Bob Dylan—Columbia 10298
[Bob Dylan/Jacques Levy] [SE] (3/6/76 BCR-43)

MR. AND MRS. UNTRUE Candi Staton—Fame 1478
[Irwin Levine/Toni Wine] [BMI] (4/10/71 CR-56)

MR. BASS MAN Johnny Cymbal—Kapp 503 [Johnny Cymbal] [ASC] (2/16/63 BCR-16)

MR. BIG STUFF Jean Knight—Stax 0088
[Joe Broussard/Carrol Washington/Ralph Williams] [BMI] (5/29/71 BCR-1)

MR. BLUE *The Fleetwoods—Dolton 5 [Dewayne Blackwell] [BMI] (9/7/59 BCR-1)*

MR. BLUE *(parody of Mr. Blue) The Four Preps—Capitol 4599*
[Dewayne Blackwell] (Med) [BMI] (8/14/61 BCR-14) [P]

MR. BLUE SKY Electric Light Orchestra—Jet 5050 [Jeff Lynne] [BMI] (6/24/78 BCR-27)

MR. BOJANGLES *Jerry Jeff Walker—Atco 6594 [Jerry Jeff Walker] [BMI] (7/6/68 BCR-50)*

MISTER BOJANGLES *Bobby Cole—Date 1613 [Jerry Jeff Walker] [BMI] (7/13/68 BCR-65)*

MR. BOJANGLES (PROLOGUE: UNCLE CHARLIE AND HIS DOG TEDDY)
Nitty Gritty Dirt Band—Liberty 56197
[Jerry Jeff Walker] [BMI] (10/31/70 BCR-6)

MR. BUS DRIVER *Bruce Channel—Mala 579*
[Wayne Carson Thompson] [BMI] (12/9/67 BCR-74)

MR. BUS DRIVER *Neal Dover—Diamond 270*
[Wayne Carson Thompson] [BMI] (1/31/70 R-91)

MR. BUSINESSMAN Ray Stevens—Monument 1083
[Ray Stevens] [BMI] (8/3/68 BCR-15)

MR. CUSTER Larry Verne—Era 3024
[Fred Darian/Al DeLory/Joseph Van Winkle] [ASC] (8/22/60 BCR-1)

MR. DIEINGLY SAD The Critters—Kapp 769 [Don Ciccone] [BMI] (8/6/66 BCR-12)

MR. D.J. (5 FOR THE D.J.) Aretha Franklin—Atlantic 3289
[Aretha Franklin] [BMI] (9/20/75 BCR-50)

—MR. DREAM MERCHANT see: DREAM MERCHANT

MR. FARMER The Seeds—GNP Crescendo 383 [Sky Saxon] [BMI] (3/11/67 BR-86)

MR. GRILLON The Archibald Players—Arch 1606
[George Atkins/George Garabedian*] [BMI] (12/20/58 C-100)

MR. HAPPINESS Johnny Maestro With The Coeds—Coed 552
[Mark Barkan/Sandy Baron/George Eddy] [BMI] (7/24/61 BCR-57)

MR. JAWS Dickie Goodman—Cash 451
[Dickie Goodman/Bill Ramal*] [BMI] (8/23/75 BCR-1)

MR. JONES The Grass Roots—Dunhill 4013 [Bob Dylan] [SE] (10/16/65 R-95)

MR. LEE *The Bobbettes—Atlantic 1144*
[Reather Dixon/Helen Gathers/Emma Pought/Jannie Pought/Laura Webb] [BMI] (8/3/57 BCR-6)

I SHOT MR. LEE *The Bobbettes—Triple-X 104*
[Reather Dixon/Helen Gathers/Emma Pought/Jannie Pought/Laura Webb] [BMI] (7/4/60 BCR-52)

MR. LIMOUSINE DRIVER Grand Funk Railroad—Capitol 2691
[Mark Farner] [BMI] (12/20/69 BC-97)

MR. LONELY *Buddy Greco—Epic 9536*
[Gene Allan/Bobby Vinton] [BMI] (9/22/62 BCR-59)

MR. LONELY *Bobby Vinton—Epic 9730*
[Gene Allan/Bobby Vinton] [BMI] (10/31/64 BCR-1)

MR. LUCKY *Henry Mancini And His Orchestra—RCA Victor 47-7705*
[Henry Mancini] [ASC] (3/14/60 BCRt-20) [I]

MR. LUCKY *Georgie Auld—Top Rank 2037 [Henry Mancini] [ASC] (3/14/60 Rt-21) [I]*

MR. MAGIC MAN Wilson Pickett—RCA Victor 74-0898
[Bobby Eli/Carl Fisher] [BMI] (3/17/73 BCR-83)

MR. MELODY Natalie Cole—Capitol 4328
[Charles Henry Jackson Jr./Marvin Yancy] [ASC] (9/11/76 BCR-49)

MR. MOONLIGHT The Beatles—Capitol R-5365
[Roy Lee Johnson] (EP) [BMI] (2/13/65 BCR-67)

MR. NATURAL Bee Gees—RSO 408 [Barry Gibb/Robin Gibb] [BMI] (3/2/74 BCR-87)

MR. PAGANINI (YOU'LL HAVE TO SWING IT) Ella Fitzgerald—Verve 10237
[Sam Coslow] [ASC] (7/31/61 R-57)

MR. PENGUIN - PT. 1 Lunar Funk—Bell 45,172
[Janice Davis/William Flemister/Linda Williams] [ASC] (1/29/72 BCR-56)

MR. PITIFUL Otis Redding—Volt 124
[Steve Cropper/Otis Redding] [BMI] (2/6/65 BCR-41)

MR. PLEASANT The Kinks—Reprise 0587 [Ray Davies] [BMI] (7/1/67 BCR-64)

MR. PRESIDENT Dickie Goodman—Rainy Wednesday 207
[M. Alexander*/Dickie Goodman] [BMI] (6/8/74 BCR-73)

MR. PRIDE Chuck (2) Jackson—Beltone 1005
[Ed Davis/Robert Head] [BMI] (4/10/61 B-91)

MR. ROBOTO Styx—A&M 2525 [Dennis DeYoung] [ASC] (2/12/83 BC-1)

—MR. see: MISTER

MR. SKIN Spirit—Epic 10701 [Jay Ferguson] [BMI] (7/21/73 BCR-84)

MR. SONGWRITER Connie Stevens—Warner Bros. 5289
[Russell Murray/Eddie Snyder] [BMI] (7/21/62 BCR-43)

MR. SPACEMAN The Byrds—Columbia 43766 [Roger McGuinn] [BMI] (9/17/66 BCR-29)

MR. SUCCESS Frank Sinatra—Capitol 4070
[Edwin Greines/Henry Sanicola/Frank Sinatra] [ASC] (10/13/58 BCR-25)

MR. SUN, MR. MOON
Paul Revere And The Raiders Featuring Mark Lindsay—Columbia 44744
[Mark Lindsay] [BMI] (2/8/69 BCR-15)

MR. TAMBOURINE MAN The Byrds—Columbia 43271 [Bob Dylan] [SE] (5/8/65 BCR-1)

MR. TELEPHONE MAN New Edition—MCA 52484 [Ray Parker Jr.] [ASC] (12/22/84 BC-9)

MR. TURNKEY Zager & Evans—RCA Victor 74-0246 [Rick Evans] [BMI] (10/4/69 CR-67)

MR. UNRELIABLE The Cryan' Shames—Columbia 44037
[Jim Fairs*/Lenny Kerley] [BMI] (5/6/67 R-100)

MR. WALKER, IT'S ALL OVER Billie Jo Spears—Capitol 2436
[Gene Crysler] [BMI] (4/26/69 BCR-80)

MR. WISHING WELL Nat King Cole—Capitol 5027
[Lockie Edwards/Larry Weiss] [BMI] (8/24/63 BCR-64)

MR. WONDERFUL *Sarah Vaughan—Mercury 70777*
[Jerry Bock/Lawrence Holofcener/George David Weiss] [BMI] (2/11/56 BCtRt-22)

MR. WONDERFUL *Peggy Lee—Decca 29834*
[Jerry Bock/Lawrence Holofcener/George David Weiss] [BMI] (2/17/56 BCtRt-22)

MR. WONDERFUL *Teddi King—RCA Victor 47-6392*
[Jerry Bock/Lawrence Holofcener/George David Weiss] [BMI] (2/17/56 BCtRt-22)

MR. WONDERFUL *Bette Anne Steele—ABC-Paramount 9669*
[Jerry Bock/Lawrence Holofcener/George David Weiss] [BMI] (2/17/56 Rt-41)

MR. WONDERFUL *The Mello-Larks—Epic 9146*
[Jerry Bock/Lawrence Holofcener/George David Weiss] [BMI] (2/17/56 Rt-41)

MRS. BLUEBIRD Eternity's Children—Tower 416
[Bruce Blackman*/Johnny Walker*] [ASC] (6/29/68 BCR-54)

MRS. BROWN YOU'VE GOT A LOVELY DAUGHTER Herman's Hermits—MGM 13341
[Trevor Peacock] [BMI] (4/17/65 BCR-1)

MRS. LENNON Yoko Ono—Apple 1839 [Yoko Ono] [BMI] (10/23/71 R-86)

MRS. ROBINSON *Simon & Garfunkel—Columbia 44511*
[Paul Simon] [BMI] (4/27/68 BCR-1)

MRS. ROBINSON *Booker T. & The M.G.'s—Stax 0037*
[Paul Simon] [BMI] (6/7/69 BCR-23) [IWM]

MS. David Oliver—Mercury 73973 [David Oliver/Ruth Robinson] [BMI] (5/13/78 R-92)

MS. GRACE The Tymes—RCA Victor 10128
[Johanna Hall/John Hall] [BMI] (12/21/74 BC-91)

M. T. A. *The Kingston Trio—Capitol 4221*
[Bess Hawes/Jacqueline Steiner] [BMI] (6/1/59 BCRt-15)

THE M.T.A. *The Gateway Singers—Warner Bros. 5073*
[Bess Hawes/Jacqueline Steiner] [BMI] (6/15/59 Rt-16)

MUDDY MISSISSIPPI LINE Bobby Goldsboro—United Artists 50565
[Bobby Goldsboro] [BMI] (8/9/69 BCR-41)

MUDDY RIVER Johnny Rivers—Imperial 66386
[James Richard Hendricks] [BMI] (6/28/69 BCR-30)

THE MULE The James Boys—Phil-L.A. Of Soul 316
[Jesse James] [BMI] (8/31/68 BCR-82) [I]

MULE SKINNER BLUES *The Fendermen—Soma 1137*
[Vaughn Horton/Jimmie Rodgers] [BMI] (5/23/60 BCtRt-5)*

MULE SKINNER BLUES *Rusty Draper—Mercury 71634*
[Vaughn Horton/Jimmie Rodgers] [BMI] (5/23/60 CtRt-5)*

MULL OF KINTYRE Wings—Capitol 4504
[Denny Laine/Paul McCartney] (TSW) [ASC] (11/19/77 CR-31)

MULTIPLICATION Bobby Darin—Atco 6214 [Bobby Darin] [BMI] (12/18/61 BCR-20)

MUMBLIN' MOSIE Johnny Otis Show—Capitol 4326 [Johnny Otis] [BMI] (2/15/60 B-80)

MUMMY Bob McFadden & Dor—Brunswick 55140
[Rod McKuen] [ASC] (8/17/59 BCR-39)

MURPHY'S LAW Cheri—Venture 149
[Geraldine Hunt/Daniel Joseph] [BMI] (4/10/82 BCR-37)

MUSCLES Diana Ross—RCA 13348 [Michael Jackson] [BMI] (10/2/82 BC-7)

MUSEUM Herman's Hermits—MGM 13787 [Donovan Leitch] [BMI] (8/26/67 BCR-21)

MUSIC John Miles—London 20086 [John Miles] [BMI] (5/15/76 BC-88)

MUSIC BOX Evelyn "Champagne" King—RCA 11586
[John Fitch/Ted Life/Sam Peake] [BMI] (5/26/79 B-75)

MUSIC BOX DANCER Frank Mills—Polydor 14517 [Frank Mills] [ASC] (1/27/79 BCR-1) [I]

MUSIC EVERYWHERE Tufano & Giammarese—Ode 66033
[Carl Giammarese] [ASC] (4/21/73 BCR-68)

MUSIC EYES Heartsfield—Mercury 73449 [Perry Jordan] [ASC] (3/2/74 BCR-85)

MUSIC FROM ACROSS THE WAY James Last—Polydor 15028
[James Last/Carl Sigman] [ASC] (1/8/72 BR-82) [FDE]

MUSIC GOES 'ROUND AND AROUND Joe Pica—Original 512
[Edward J. Farley/William Hodgson/Mike Riley] [ASC] (11/8/54 R-77)

MUSIC, HARMONY AND RHYTHM Brooklyn Dreams—Millennium 610
[Joe Esposito/Bruce Sudano] [BMI] (3/25/78 BCR-57)

MUSIC IN MY BONES Joe Simon—Spring 159
[Raeford Gerald/Joe Simon] [BMI] (8/23/75 BCR-60)

MUSIC IS LOVE David Crosby—Atlantic 2792
[David Crosby/Graham Nash/Neil Young] [BMI] (4/24/71 BCR-76)

MUSIC IS MY LIFE Helen Reddy—Capitol 4312
[Alan Gordon] (TSW) [BMI] (8/14/76 BCR-29)

MUSIC, MUSIC, MUSIC *Crazy Otto—Polydor 22009A*
[Bernie Baum/Stephan Weiss] (Med) [ASC] (1/10/55 R-30) [IWM]

MUSIC, MUSIC, MUSIC *The Sensations Featuring Yvonne Baker—Argo 5391*
[Bernie Baum/Stephan Weiss] [ASC] (8/14/61 BCR-54)

MUSIC MUSIC MUSIC *The Happenings—B.T. Puppy 538*
[Bernie Baum/Stephan Weiss] [ASC] (2/10/68 BCR-84)

MUSIC, MUSIC, MUSIC *Teresa Brewer—Amsterdam 64405*
[Bernie Baum/Stephan Weiss] [ASC] (7/21/73 R-90)

THE MUSIC NEVER STOPPED Grateful Dead—Grateful Dead 718
[John Perry Barlow/Bob Weir] [ASC] (10/18/75 BC-78)

MUSIC OF HOME Bing Crosby—RCA Victor 47-7695 [Frank Loesser] [ASC] (2/22/60 R-96)

MUSIC TIME Styx—A&M 2625 [Dennis DeYoung] [ASC] (5/5/84 BC-40)

MUSIC TO MY HEART The Obsession—Happy Tiger 531
[Gary Knight/Francine Neiman] [BMI] (2/28/70 R-95)

MUSIC TO WATCH GIRLS BY *The Bob Crewe Generation—DynoVoice 229*
[Sid Ramin] [ASC] (12/31/66 BCR-9) [IM]

MUSIC TO WATCH GIRLS BY *Andy Williams—Columbia 44065*
[Sid Ramin/Tony Velona] [ASC] (3/25/67 BCR-34)

MUSKRAT The Everly Brothers—Warner Bros. 5501
[Tex Ann/Harold G. Hensley/Traditional/Merle Travis] [BMI] (9/18/61 BCR-69)

MUSKRAT LOVE *America—Warner Bros. 7725*
[Willis Alan Ramsey] [ASC] (8/11/73 BCR-33)

MUSKRAT LOVE *Captain & Tennille—A&M 1870*
[Willis Alan Ramsey] [ASC] (9/25/76 BCR-2)

MUSKRAT RAMBLE *The McGuire Sisters—Coral 61258*
[Ray Gilbert/Edward Ory] [ASC] (9/25/54 BCR-9)

MUSKRAT RAMBLE *The Matys Brothers—Essex 369*
[Ray Gilbert/Edward Ory] [ASC] (9/25/54 CR-12)

MUSKRAT RAMBLE *Rusty Draper—Mercury 70446*
[Ray Gilbert/Edward Ory] [ASC] (10/4/54 R-PRE)

MUSKRAT RAMBLE *Louis Armstrong & His All-Stars—Decca 29280*
[Ray Gilbert/Edward Ory] [ASC] (10/25/54 Rt-PRE)

MUSKRAT RAMBLE *Freddy Cannon—Swan 4066*
[Ray Gilbert/Edward Ory] [ASC] (1/9/61 BCR-48)

MUST BE LOVE The James Gang—Atco 6953
[Tommy Bolin/Jeffrey Cook] [BMI] (1/19/74 BCR-45)

MUST HAVE BEEN CRAZY Chicago—Columbia 11061
[Donnie Dacus] [BMI] (8/25/79 BCR-83)

MUST OF GOT LOST The J. Geils Band—Atlantic 3214
[Seth Justman/Peter Wolf] [ASC] (11/2/74 BCR-12)

A MUST TO AVOID Herman's Hermits—MGM 13437
[Steve Barri*/P.F. Sloan] [ASC] (12/18/65 BCR-6)

MUSTANG SALLY Wilson Pickett—Atlantic 2365 [Bonny Rice] [BMI] (11/19/66 BCR-16)

MUTUAL ADMIRATION SOCIETY *Teresa Brewer—Coral 61737*
[Matt Dubey/Harold Karr] [ASC] (11/3/56 BCtRt-20)

MUTUAL ADMIRATION SOCIETY *Eddy Arnold And Jaye P. Morgan—RCA Victor 47-6708*
[Matt Dubey/Harold Karr] [ASC] (11/17/56 BCtRt-20)

MUTUAL SURRENDER (WHAT A WONDERFUL WORLD) Bourgeois Tagg—Island 99558
[Larry Tagg] [ASC] (4/12/86 BC-62)

MY ADORABLE ONE *Joe Simon—Vee-Jay 609*
[Irral Berger/Clara Thompson] [BMI] (10/17/64 C-76)*

WARM AND TENDER LOVE *Percy Sledge—Atlantic 2342*
[Irral Berger/Morgan C. Robinson*/Clara Thompson*] [BMI] (7/16/66 BCR-12)*

—MY AIRPLANE see: AIRPLANE SONG

MY ANGEL BABY Toby Beau—RCA 11250
[Danny McKenna/Balde Silva] [BMI] (5/13/78 BCR-10)

MY ANSWER Jimmy McCracklin—Imperial 66147
[Deadric Malone/Jimmy McCracklin] [BMI] (1/22/66 BCR-89)

MY ANXIOUS HEART The Four Coins—Epic 9091
[Ollie Jones/William Sanford*] [BMI] (3/5/55 C-45)

MY ARMS ARE A HOUSE Hank Snow—RCA Victor 47-6955
[Alex Alstone/Jimmy Kennedy] [ASC] (7/20/57 R-78)

MY BABE The Righteous Brothers—Moonglow 223
[Bobby Hatfield/Bill Medley] [BMI] (9/7/63 BCR-66)

MY BABE Roy Head And The Traits—Back Beat 560 [Willie Dixon] [BMI] (3/12/66 B-99)

MY BABE Ronnie Dove—Diamond 221 [Neil Diamond] [SE] (4/15/67 BCR-40)

MY BABY The Temptations—Gordy 7047
[Warren Moore/Smokey Robinson/Robert Rogers] [ASC] (10/23/65 BCR-13)

MY BABY The Pretenders—Sire 28496 [Chrissie Hynde] [ASC] (2/7/87 BC-64)

MY BABY DON'T DIG ME
Ray Charles And His Orchestra With The Raelettes—ABC-Paramount 10557
[Percy Mayfield] [BMI] (5/30/64 BCR-50)

MY BABY LEFT ME Elvis Presley—RCA Victor 47-6540
[Arthur Crudup] [BMI] (5/11/56 BCR-14)

MY BABY LOVES LOVIN' White Plains—Deram 85058
[Roger Cook/Roger Greenaway] [ASC] (4/11/70 BCR-10)

MY BABY LOVES ME *Martha & The Vandellas—Gordy 7048*
[Ivy Jo Hunter/Sylvia Moy/William Stevenson] [ASC] (1/22/66 BCR-17)

MY BABY LOVES ME *David T. Walker—Revue 11060*
[Ivy Jo Hunter/Sylvia Moy/William Stevenson] [ASC] (11/22/69 R-52) [IWM]

MY BABY MUST BE A MAGICIAN The Marvelettes—Tamla 54158
[Smokey Robinson] [ASC] (12/16/67 BCR-10)

MY BABY'S BABY Liquid Gold—Parachute 524
[Adrian Baker/Ed Seago] [BMI] (4/28/79 BCR-45)

MY BABY'S GOT SUCH LOVIN' WAYS The McGuire Sisters—Coral 61532
[Leon Carr/Hal David] [ASC] (1/7/56 CR-40)

MY BACK PAGES The Byrds—Columbia 44054 [Bob Dylan] [SE] (4/1/67 BCR-26)

MY BACK SCRATCHER Frank Frost—Jewel 765
[Frank Frost/Chip Young] [BMI] (7/16/66 CR-97)

MY BALLOON'S GOING UP Archie Bell & The Drells—Atlantic 2663
[Kenneth Gamble/Leon Huff] [BMI] (8/30/69 BCR-63)

MY BAMBINO Tony Martin—RCA Victor 47-5907
[Marjorie Goetschius/Al Hoffman] [ASC] (11/1/54 CR-36)

MY BELIEVING HEART Joni James—MGM 12126
[Jimmie Crane/Al Jacobs] [ASC] (12/1/55 BCR-31)

MY BEST FRIEND Jefferson Airplane—RCA Victor 47-9063
[Skip Spence] [BMI] (2/4/67 CR-76)

MY BEST FRIEND'S GIRL The Cars—Elektra 45537
[Ric Ocasek] [ASC] (10/21/78 BCR-35)

MY BEST FRIEND'S WIFE Paul Anka—United Artists 972
[Paul Anka] [BMI] (4/23/77 BC-74)

MY BEWILDERED HEART Jaye P. Morgan—RCA Victor 47-6329
[Joan Javits/Philip Springer/Hans Zeeman] [BMI] (1/14/56 C-47)

MY BIG BROTHER'S FRIEND *Cecelia Batten—Colonial 431*
[John D. Loudermilk] [BMI] (5/4/57 Rt-59)

MY BIG BROTHER'S FRIEND *Carol Hughes—Mercury 71095*
[John D. Loudermilk] [BMI] (5/11/57 Rt-59)

MY BLOCK The Four Pennies—Rust 5071
[Bert Berns*/Jimmy Radcliffe/Carl Spencer] [BMI] (6/22/63 BCR-67)

MY BLUE ANGEL Michael Learns To Rock—Impact 54160
[Harvey Price/Jascha Richter/Richard C. Scher] [BMI] (8/31/91 C-70)

MY BLUE HEAVEN *Fats Domino—Imperial 5386*
[Walter Donaldson/George Whiting] [ASC] (4/28/56 BCR-14)

MY BLUE HEAVEN *Bobby Day—Class 263*
[Walter Donaldson/George Whiting] [ASC] (1/18/60 CR-86)

MY BLUE HEAVEN *Duane Eddy—Jamie 1200*
[Walter Donaldson] [ASC] (8/28/61 BCR-50) [IM]

MY BLUE HEAVEN *The String-A-Longs—Dot 16379*
[Walter Donaldson] [ASC] (9/15/62 R-95) [IM]

MY BODY SAYS YES Titiyo Featuring Papa D—Arista 2224
[Magnus Frykberg/Dan Wahlgren] [ASC] (6/8/91 BC-42)

MY BONNIE (MY BONNIE LIES OVER THE OCEAN)
The Beatles With Tony Sheridan—MGM 13213
[Traditional] [NA] (2/1/64 BCR-26)

MY BONNIE LASSIE The Ames Brothers—RCA Victor 47-6208
[Roy C. Bennett/Marion McClurg/Sid Tepper] [ASC] (9/3/55 BCR-11)

MY BOOMERANG WON'T COME BACK Charlie Drake—United Artists 398
[Max Diamond/Charlie Drake] [BMI] (12/18/61 BCR-21)

MY BOY *Richard Harris—Dunhill 4293*
[Jean-Pierre Bourtayre/Phil Coulter/Claude François/Yves-Jacques Lavot/William Wylie MacPherson Martin] [ASC] (11/13/71 BCR-41) [FET]

MY BOY *Elvis Presley—RCA Victor 10191*
[Jean-Pierre Bourtayre/Phil Coulter/Claude François/Yves-Jacques Lavot/William Wylie MacPherson Martin] [ASC] (1/25/75 BCR-17) [FET]

MY BOY FLAT TOP *Boyd Bennett And His Rockets—King 1494*
[Boyd Bennett/John Young] [BMI] (9/24/55 BCtRt-18)

MY BOY FLAT TOP *Dorothy Collins—Coral 61510*
[Boyd Bennett/John Young] [BMI] (10/3/55 BCtRt-18)

MY BOY LOLLIPOP Millie Small—Smash 1893
[Barbie Gaye/Morris Levy‡/Johnnie B. Roberts*/Robert Spencer] [BMI]
(5/16/64 BCR-2)

MY BOYFRIEND GOT A BEATLE HAIRCUT Donna Lynn—Capitol 5127
[Bugs Bower/Rose Mehlman/Jack Wolf] [ASC] (2/22/64 BR-79)

MY BOYFRIEND'S BACK The Angels—Smash 1834
[Bob Feldman/Jerry Goldstein/Richard Gottehrer] [BMI] (7/27/63 BCR-1)

YOUR BOYFRIEND'S BACK Bobby Comstock & The Counts—Lawn 219
[Bob Feldman/Jerry Goldstein/Richard Gottehrer] [BMI] (9/14/63 B-100) [R]

MY BRAVE FACE Paul McCartney—Capitol 44367
[Elvis Costello/Paul McCartney] [ASC] (5/27/89 BC-22)

MY BUCKET'S GOT A HOLE IN IT Ricky Nelson—Imperial 5503
[Clarence Williams] [ASC] (3/29/58 BCR-18)

MY BUDDY Eddie Harris—Vee-Jay 407 [Walter Donaldson] [ASC] (10/2/61 R-88) [IM]

MY BUDDY SEAT The Hondells—Mercury 72366
[Gary Usher/Brian Wilson] [BMI] (12/12/64 BCR-61)

MY CHERIE Al Martino—Capitol 5434
[Peter DeAngelis/Jean Sawyer] [ASC] (6/12/65 BCR-76)

MY CHERIE AMOUR *Stevie Wonder—Tamla 54180*
[Henry Cosby/Sylvia Moy/Stevie Wonder] [ASC] (5/31/69 BCR-3)

MY CHERIE AMOUR *Soul Train Gang—Soul Train 10995*
[Henry Cosby/Sylvia Moy/Stevie Wonder] [ASC] (8/13/77 B-92)

MY CHERIE AMOUR *Stars On 45—Radio 4019*
[Henry Cosby/Sylvia Moy/Stevie Wonder] (Med) [ASC] (3/27/82 BCR-28)

—MY CLAIR DE LUNE see: CLAIR DE LUNE

MY COLORING BOOK *Sandy Stewart—Colpix 669*
[Fred Ebb/John Kander] [BMI] (12/22/62 BCtRt-8)

MY COLORING BOOK *Kitty Kallen—RCA Victor 47-8124*
[Fred Ebb/John Kander] [BMI] (12/22/62 BCtRt-8)

MY COLORING BOOK *George Chakiris—Capitol 4892*
[Fred Ebb/John Kander] [BMI] (12/22/62 Ct-41)

MY COLORING BOOK *Barbra Streisand—Columbia 42648*
[Fred Ebb/John Kander] [BMI] (12/22/62 CtRt-8)

MY COUNTRY Jud Strunk—Capitol 3960
[Dennis McCarthy/Jud Strunk] [ASC] (9/28/74 BCR-59)

MY CREW Rita Coolidge—A&M 1398
[Priscilla Coolidge/Booker T. Jones Jr.] (TSW) [BMI] (1/6/73 BCR-60)

MY CUP RUNNETH OVER Ed Ames—RCA Victor 47-9002
[Tom Jones/Harvey Schmidt] [ASC] (1/14/67 BCR-8)

MY DAD Paul Petersen—Colpix 663 [Barry Mann/Cynthia Weil] [BMI] (11/10/62 BCR-6)

MY DADDY IS PRESIDENT Little Jo Ann—Kapp 467
[David DeNoon/Emanuel Vardi] [ASC] (6/30/62 BCR-67)
MY DADDY KNOWS BEST The Marvelettes—Tamla 54082
[Berry Gordy] [ASC] (7/27/63 BCR-67)
MY DEAREST DARLING Etta James—Argo 5368
[Edwin Bocage/Paul Gayten] [BMI] (9/12/60 BCR-25)
MY DECEIVING HEART The Impressions—Curtom 1937
[Curtis Mayfield] [BMI] (2/22/69 CR-79)
MY DING-A-LING Chuck Berry—Chess 2131 [Chuck Berry] [BMI] (7/29/72 BCR-1)
MY DREAM The Platters—Mercury 71093 [Buck Ram] [ASC] (5/25/57 BCR-19)
MY DREAM COME TRUE Jack Scott—Capitol 4597 [Jack Scott] [SE] (8/28/61 B-83)
MY DREAM SONATA *Nat "King" Cole—Capitol 3456*
[Mack David/Jimmy Van Heusen] [ASC] (6/22/56 BCRt-37)
MY DREAM SONATA *Roger Williams—Kapp 144*
[Jimmy Van Heusen] [ASC] (7/27/56 Rt-56) [IM]
MY DREAMS Brenda Lee—Decca 31628
[David Paul Briggs/Dan Penn] [BMI] (6/6/64 BR-55)
MY ELUSIVE DREAMS *David Houston And Tammy Wynette—Epic 10194*
[Curly Putman/Billy Sherrill] [BMI] (7/8/67 BCR-89)
MY ELUSIVE DREAMS *Bobby Vinton—Epic 10576*
[Curly Putman/Billy Sherrill] [BMI] (1/31/70 BCR-34)
MY ELUSIVE DREAMS *Charlie Rich—Epic 50064*
[Curly Putman/Billy Sherrill] [BMI] (2/1/75 BCR-49)
MY EMPTY ARMS Jackie Wilson—Brunswick 55201
[Hank Hunter/Al Kasha] [BMI] (1/2/61 BCR-9)
MY EMPTY ROOM Little Anthony And The Imperials—End 1067
[Michael Merlo/Patrick Welch] [BMI] (4/16/60 BCR-81)
MY EVER CHANGING MOODS The Style Council—Geffen 29359
[Paul Weller] [BMI] (4/7/84 BC-29)
MY EYES ADORED YOU Frankie Valli—Private Stock 45,003
[Bob Crewe/Kenny Nolan] [BMI] (11/9/74 BCR-1)
MY EYES GET BLURRY Kenny Nolan—20th Century 2352
[Kenny Nolan] [ASC] (10/15/77 B-97)
MY FAIR SHARE Seals & Crofts—Warner Bros. 8405
[Charles Fox/Paul Williams] [BMI] (9/3/77 BCR-25)
MY FAITH, MY HOPE, MY LOVE Don Cornell—Coral 61811
[Douglas Burford/Colin Ronald] [NA] (4/13/57 C-57)
MY FALLEN ANGEL Coro—Cutting/Charisma 98772
[Deborah Tariq/Zahid Tariq] [ASC] (7/13/91 B-54)
MY FANTASY Teddy Riley featuring Guy—Motown 1968
[William Aquart/Gene Griffin/Teddy Riley] [BMI] (9/23/89 B-62)
MY FAVORITE THINGS Herb Alpert & The Tijuana Brass—A&M 1001
[Richard Rodgers] [ASC] (12/14/68 BCR-30) [IM]
MY FIRST DAY WITHOUT HER Dennis Yost And The Classics IV—MGM 14785
[Jim Weatherly] [ASC] (3/29/75 BC-88)
MY FIRST FORMAL GOWN Patti Page—Mercury 70820
[Roy Alfred/Abner Silver] [ASC] (3/16/56 BR-48)
MY FIRST NIGHT WITHOUT YOU Cyndi Lauper—Epic 68945
[Thomas F. Kelly/Cyndi Lauper/Billy Steinberg] [ASC] (8/5/89 BC-55)
MY FOOLISH HEART The Demensions—Coral 62344
[Ned Washington/Victor Young] [ASC] (2/23/63 BCR-87)
MY FORBIDDEN LOVER Chic—Atlantic 3620
[Bernard Edwards/Nile Rodgers] [BMI] (10/6/79 B-43)
MY FRIEND Eddie Fisher—RCA Victor 47-5748
[Ervin Drake/Jimmy Shirl] [ASC] (6/12/54 BC-PRE)
MY GENERATION The Who—Decca 31877 [Pete Townshend] [BMI] (12/18/65 BCR-74)
MY GIRL Frankie Lymon—Roulette 4026
[Bill Harrington/Bob Saffer] [ASC] (10/19/57 C-60)
MY GIRL Robin Luke—Dot 15839 [Bob Bertram] [ASC] (11/8/58 C-97)
MY GIRL *The Temptations—Gordy 7038*
[Smokey Robinson/Ronnie White] [ASC] (1/9/65 BCR-1)
MY GIRL *Bobby Vee—Liberty 56033*
[Smokey Robinson/Ronnie White] (Med) [ASC] (4/13/68 BCR-17)
MY GIRL *Eddie Floyd—Stax 0072*
[Smokey Robinson/Ronnie White] [ASC] (7/18/70 CR-62)
MY GIRL *Amii Stewart & Johnny Bristol—Handshake 5300*
[Smokey Robinson/Ronnie White] (Med) [ASC] (8/30/80 BCR-58)
MY GIRL *Daryl Hall & John Oates Featuring David Ruffin & Eddie Kendricks—RCA 14178 [Smokey Robinson/Ronnie White] (Med) [ASC] (8/31/85 BC-20)*
MY GIRL *Suavé—Capitol 44124*
[Smokey Robinson/Ronnie White] [ASC] (3/12/88 BC-20)
MY GIRL Donnie Iris—MCA/Carousel 52031
[Mark Avsec/Donnie Iris] [ASC] (3/27/82 BCR-25)
MY GIRL (GONE, GONE, GONE) Chilliwack—Millennium 11813
[William A. Henderson/Brian MacLeod] [BMI] (9/26/81 BCR-19)
MY GIRL BILL Jim Stafford—MGM 14718 [Jim Stafford] [ASC] (4/13/74 BCR-10)
MY GIRL HAS GONE The Miracles—Tamla 54123
[Warren Moore/Smokey Robinson/Robert Rogers*/Marvin Tarplin/Ronnie.38 White] [ASC] (10/9/65 BCR-14)
MY GIRL JOSEPHINE *Fats Domino—Imperial 5704*
[Dave Bartholomew/Fats Domino] [BMI] (10/24/60 BCR-14)
MY GIRL JOSEPHINE *Jerry Jaye—Hi 2120*
[Dave Bartholomew/Fats Domino] [BMI] (4/8/67 BCR-22)
—MY GIRL SLOOPY see: HANG ON SLOOPY
MY GUY *Mary Wells—Motown 1056 [Smokey Robinson] [ASC] (3/28/64 BCR-1)*
MY GUY *Petula Clark—MGM 14392 [Smokey Robinson] [ASC] (6/10/72 BCR-70)*
MY GUY *Amii Stewart & Johnny Bristol—Handshake 5300*
[Smokey Robinson] (Med) [ASC] (8/30/80 BCR-58)
MY GUY *Sister Sledge—Cotillion 47000 [Smokey Robinson] [ASC] (1/30/82 BCR-23)*
MY HAPPINESS *Fats Domino—Imperial IMP-147*
[Borney Bergantine/Betty Peterson] (EP) [ASC] (5/11/57 R-53)*
MY HAPPINESS *Connie Francis—MGM 12738*
[Borney Bergantine/Betty Peterson] [ASC] (12/1/58 BCR-2)*
MY HEART BECAME OF AGE Annette With The Afterbeats—Buena Vista 349
[Richard Sherman/Robert Sherman] [BMI] (10/26/59 B-74)
MY HEART BELONGS TO ME Barbra Streisand—Columbia 10555
[Alan Gordon] [BMI] (5/21/77 BCR-4)
MY HEART BELONGS TO ONLY YOU *Mary Swan—Swan 4016*
[Dorothy Daniels/Frank Daniels] [BMI] (10/20/58 R-90)
MY HEART BELONGS TO ONLY YOU *Jackie Wilson—Brunswick 55220*
[Dorothy Daniels/Frank Daniels] [BMI] (10/16/61 BCR-46)
MY HEART BELONGS TO ONLY YOU *Bobby Vinton—Epic 9662*
[Dorothy Daniels/Frank Daniels] [BMI] (2/29/64 BCR-8)
MY HEART BELONGS TO YOU Russ Irwin—SBK 07363 [Russ Irwin] [BMI] (9/14/91 BC-28)
MY HEART CAN'T TELL YOU NO Rod Stewart—Warner Bros. 27729
[Simon Climie/Dennis W. Morgan] [BMI] (12/3/88 BC-4)
MY HEART CRIES FOR YOU *Ray Stevens—NRC 042*
[Percy Faith/Carl Sigman] [ASC] (11/23/59 R-80)
MY HEART CRIES FOR YOU *Ray Charles—ABC-Paramount 10530*
[Percy Faith/Carl Sigman] [ASC] (2/22/64 BCR-38)
MY HEART CRIES FOR YOU *Connie Francis—MGM 13773*
[Percy Faith/Carl Sigman] [ASC] (7/29/67 C-96)
MY HEART HAS A MIND OF ITS OWN Connie Francis—MGM 12923
[Howard Greenfield/Jack Keller] [BMI] (8/15/60 BCR-1)
MY HEART IS AN OPEN BOOK Carl Dobkins, Jr.—Decca 30803
[Hal David/Lee Pockriss] [ASC] (4/13/59 BCR-1)
MY HEART IS BLEEDING Fats Domino—Imperial 5833
[Dave Bartholomew/Earl King Johnson] [BMI] (5/14/62 CR-99)
MY HEART IS FAILING ME Riff—SBK 07342
[Albert Hammond/Holly Knight] [ASC] (3/23/91 BC-25)
MY HEART IS YOURS Wilbert Harrison—SSS Int'l 830
[Wilbert Harrison] [BMI] (3/13/71 B-98)
MY HEART JUST KEEPS ON BREAKIN' The Chi-Lites—Brunswick 55496
[Stan McKenney/Eugene Record] [BMI] (5/26/73 BR-83)
—MY HEART REMINDS ME see: AND THAT REMINDS ME
—MY HEART SINGS see: ALL OF A SUDDEN MY HEART SINGS
MY HEART SKIPS A BEAT Buck Owens—Capitol 5136 [Buck Owens] [BMI] (7/4/64 B-94)
MY HEART SKIPS A BEAT The Cover Girls—Capitol 44436
[David Cole] [ASC] (9/9/89 BC-38)
MY HEART WOULD KNOW Al Martino—Capitol 5341
[Hank Williams] [BMI] (1/16/65 BCR-49)
MY HEART'S ON FIRE Billy Bland—Old Town 1105 [Billy Bland] [BMI] (8/7/61 B-90)
MY HEART'S SYMPHONY Gary Lewis And The Playboys—Liberty 55898
[Glen Hardin] [BMI] (7/30/66 BCR-10)
MY HERO The Blue Notes—Val-ue 213
[Stanislaus Stange*/Oskar Strauss] [ASC] (10/3/60 B-78)
MY HERO (THAT'S WHAT YOU ARE) Sue Thompson—Hickory 3008
[Boudleaux Bryant/Felice Bryant] [BMI] (9/22/62 R-90)
MY HEROES HAVE ALWAYS BEEN COWBOYS Willie Nelson—Columbia 11186
[Sharon Vaughn] [ASC] (2/9/80 BCR-44)
MY HOME TOWN Paul Anka—ABC-Paramount 10106 [Paul Anka] [BMI] (5/9/60 BCR-8)
MY HOME TOWN Steve Lawrence—Columbia 42952 [Ervin Drake] [ASC] (12/28/63 R-72)
MY HOMETOWN Bruce Springsteen—Columbia 05728
[Bruce Springsteen] [ASC] (12/7/85 BC-6)
MY HONEY AND ME *Luther Ingram—KoKo 2104*
[Luther Ingram/J. Leslie McFarland] [BMI] (1/3/70 BCR-42)
MY HONEY AND ME *The Emotions—Volt 4077*
[Luther Ingram/J. Leslie McFarland] [BMI] (3/11/72 CR-85)
—MY HOUSE IS YOUR HOUSE see: MI CASA SU CASA
MY HOW THE TIME GOES BY Patti Page—Mercury 71189
[Cy Coleman/Carolyn Leigh] [ASC] (10/7/57 R-81)
MY JIMMIE Jeanie Johnson—RCA Victor 47-7163 [Dave Rich] [BMI] (3/17/58 R-62)
MY KIND OF GIRL Matt Monro—Warwick 636 [Leslie Bricusse] [BMI] (5/8/61 BCR-18)
MY KIND OF LADY Supertramp—A&M 2517
[Rick Davies/Roger Hodgson] [ASC] (1/29/83 BC-23)
MY KINDA GIRL Babyface—Solar 74515
[Kenneth Edmonds/Antonio Reid/Daryl Simmons] [BMI] (6/16/90 BC-30)
MY KINDA LOVER Billy Squier—Capitol 5037 [Billy Squier] [ASC] (11/21/81 BCR-43)

—MY LAST DATE WITH YOU see: LAST DATE

MY LAST NIGHT IN ROME *Eddie Dano—Vik 0237 [Ralph Freed/Jerry Livingston] [ASC] (12/8/56 Rt-79)*

MY LAST NIGHT IN ROME *The Motifs—Motif 003 [Jerry Livingston] [ASC] (12/8/56 Rt-79) [IM]*

MY LIFE Chuck Willis—Atlantic 1192 [Chuck Willis] [BMI] (8/18/58 BC-56)

MY LIFE Billy Joel—Columbia 10853 [Billy Joel] [ASC] (11/4/78 BCR-3)

MY LITTLE ANGEL The Four Lads—Columbia 40674 [Gordon Charles/Dazz Jordan] [ASC] (4/28/56 BCR-16)

MY LITTLE BABY Perry Como—RCA Victor 47-6904 [Joe Shapiro/Lou Stallman] [BMI] (5/18/57 BCR-23)

MY LITTLE CHICKADEE The Foundations—Uni 55137 [Tony Macaulay/John Macleod] [ASC] (6/21/69 BCR-64)

—MY LITTLE DOLL see: PUPALINA

MY LITTLE LADY Bloodstone—London 1061 [Charles E. McCormick] [BMI] (2/22/75 BCR-41)

MY LITTLE MARINE Jamie Horton—Joy 234 [Jamie Horton/Ed Warren] [ASC] (1/23/60 BCR-58)

MY LITTLE RED BOOK Love—Elektra 45603 [Burt Bacharach/Hal David] [ASC] (4/30/66 BCR-35)

MY LITTLE TOWN Simon & Garfunkel—Columbia 10230 [Paul Simon] [BMI] (10/18/75 BCR-7)

MY LOVE Nat King Cole-Stan Kenton—Capitol 4393 [Ollie Jones] [BMI] (7/4/60 BCR-42)

MY LOVE Petula Clark—Warner Bros. 5684 [Tony Hatch] [BMI] (12/25/65 BCR-1)

MY LOVE *Paul McCartney & Wings—Apple 1861 [Linda McCartney/Paul McCartney] [ASC] (4/14/73 BCR-1)*

MY LOVE *Margie Joseph—Atlantic 3032 [Linda McCartney/Paul McCartney] [ASC] (7/6/74 BCR-69)*

MY LOVE Lionel Richie—Motown 1677 [Lionel Richie] [ASC] (4/9/83 BC-5)

MY LOVE Julio Iglesias Featuring Stevie Wonder—Columbia 07781 [Stevie Wonder] [ASC] (5/14/88 BC-80)

MY LOVE FOR YOU Johnny Mathis—Columbia 41764 [Abner Silver/Sid Wayne] [ASC] (8/15/60 BCR-35)

MY LOVE, FORGIVE ME (AMORE, SCUSAMI) Robert Goulet—Columbia 43131 [Sydney Lee/Gino Mescoli/Vito Pallavicini] [BMI] (10/24/64 BCR-15)

MY LOVE IS A FIRE Donny Osmond—Capitol 44634 [Evan Rogers/Carl Sturken] [BMI] (10/13/90 BC-21)

MY LOVE IS MUSIC Space—Casablanca 974 [Paul Greedus/Didier Marouani] [BMI] (4/28/79 BCR-60) [FET]

MY LOVE IS REAL Marvin Rainwater—MGM 12511 [Marvin Rainwater] [BMI] (8/5/57 R-55)

MY LOVE SONG Tommy Sands—Capitol 3690 [Guy Singer] [ASC] (4/13/57 BCR-25)

MY LOVE SONG TO YOU Bob Manning—Capitol 3014 [Roy Alfred/Al Frisch] [ASC] (12/20/54 CR-18)

—MY LOVE WILL LIFT YOU UP see: AT MIDNIGHT

MY LOVER'S PRAYER Otis Redding—Volt 136 [Otis Redding] [BMI] (6/4/66 BCR-48)

MY LOVE'S A GENTLE MAN Dorothy Collins—Audiovox 113 [Roy Jordan/Ulpio Minucci] [ASC] (2/28/55 R-75)

MY LUCKY LOVE Doug Franklin with The Bluenotes—Colonial 7777 [Joe Tanner] [BMI] (8/30/58 BCR-72)

MY MAIN MAN The Staple Singers—Stax 0227 [Bettye Crutcher/Bobby Manuel/Larry Nix/Bonny Rice] [BMI] (12/7/74 BCR-70)

MY MAMMY The Happenings—B.T. Puppy 530 [Walter Donaldson/Sam Lewis/Joe Young] [ASC] (7/8/67 BCR-12)

MY MAN *Peggy Lee—Capitol 4115 [Jacques Charles/Channing Pollock/Albert Willemetz/Maurice Yvain] [ASC] (1/12/59 BCR-35) [FET]*

MY MAN *Barbra Streisand—Columbia 43323 [Jacques Charles/Channing Pollock/Albert Willemetz/Maurice Yvain] [ASC] (6/26/65 BCR-48) [FET]*

MY MAN, A SWEET MAN Millie Jackson—Spring 127 [Raeford Gerald] [BMI] (7/29/72 BCR-28)

MY MAN—HE'S A LOVIN' MAN Betty LaVett—Atlantic 2160 [James Bennett/Johnnie Matthews] [BMI] (1/5/63 C-97)

MY MARIA B.W. Stevenson—RCA Victor 0030 [Daniel Moore/B.W. Stevenson] [BMI] (7/28/73 BCR-7)

MY MARIE Engelbert Humperdinck—Parrot 40049 [Tony Macaulay/Barry Mason] [BMI] (6/27/70 BCR-24)

MY MELANCHOLY BABY *Willie Gibson & The Boys—Benida 5016 [Ernie Burnette/George Norton/Maybelle Watson] [NA] (3/21/55 Rt-49)*

MY MELANCHOLY BABY *Crazy Otto—Decca 29449 [Ernie Burnette] [NA] (3/21/55 Rt-46) [IM]*

MY MELANCHOLY BABY *Tommy Edwards—MGM 12794 [Ernie Burnette/George Norton/Maybelle Watson] [NA] (5/4/59 BCR-15)*

MY MELANCHOLY BABY *The Marcels—Colpix 624 [Ernie Burnette/George Norton/Maybelle Watson] [NA] (1/29/62 BCR-58)*

MY MELODY OF LOVE Bobby Vinton—ABC 12022 [Henry Mayer/Bobby Vinton] [BMI] (9/21/74 BCR-1) [FDE]

MY MEMORIES OF YOU Donnie And The Dreamers—Whale 505 [Raoul Cita] [BMI] (7/17/61 B-79)

MY MERRY-GO-ROUND Johnny Nash—Epic 11003 [Diane Brodsky/Johnny Nash/Dann Rogers] [ASC] (6/16/73 BCR-60)

MY MIND KEEPS TELLING ME (THAT I REALLY LOVE YOU, GIRL) Eddie Holman—GSF 6873 [Ron Baker] [BMI] (7/29/72 CR-98)

MY MISTAKE The Kingbees—RSO 1032 [Jamie James] [BMI] (6/14/80 BCR-69)

MY MISTAKE (WAS TO LOVE YOU) Diana Ross & Marvin Gaye—Motown 1269 [Gloria Jones/Pam Sawyer] [ASC] (2/16/74 BCR-19)

MY MOTHER'S EYES Russ Hamilton—Kapp 204 [Abel Baer/L. Wolfe Gilbert] [NA] (1/27/58 R-83)

MY MOTHER'S EYES Bette Midler—Atlantic 3771 [Tom Jans] [ASC] (11/22/80 BCR-39)

MY MUSIC Loggins & Messina—Columbia 45952 [Kenny Loggins/Jim Messina] [ASC] (10/27/73 BCR-13)

MY, MY, MY Johnny Gill—Motown 2033 [Kenneth Edmonds/Daryl Simmons] [BMI] (8/4/90 BC-9)

MY NAME IS JACK Manfred Mann—Mercury 72822 [John S. Simon] [ASC] (7/13/68 CR-57)

MY NAME IS NOT SUSAN Whitney Houston—Arista 12259 [Eric Foster White] [ASC] (7/27/91 BC-20)

MY OBSESSION Icehouse—Chrysalis 43240 [Iva Davies/Robert Kretschmer] [ASC] (7/9/88 BC-86)

MY OH MY Slade—CBS Associated 04528 [Noddy Holder/Jim Lea] [ASC] (7/7/84 BC-37)

MY OLD CAR Lee Dorsey—Amy 987 [Allen Toussaint] [BMI] (5/6/67 BCR-95)

MY OLD SCHOOL Steely Dan—ABC 11396 [Walter Becker/Donald Fagen] [ASC] (10/27/73 BCR-56)

MY ONE AND ONLY, JIMMY BOY The Girlfriends—Colpix 712 [David Gates] [ASC] (12/14/63 BCR-39)

MY ONE AND ONLY LOVE Roy Hamilton—Epic 9294 [Robert Mellin/Guy Wood] [BMI] (11/22/58 C-98)

MY ONE SIN *Nat "King" Cole—Capitol 3136 [Vittorio Mascheroni/Robert Mellin/Giancarlo Testoni] [BMI] (5/30/55 BCR-21) [FET]*

MY ONE SIN *The Four Coins—Epic 9229 [Vittorio Mascheroni/Robert Mellin/Giancarlo Testoni] [BMI] (9/14/57 BCR-20) [FET]*

MY ONE TEMPTATION Mica Paris—Island 99252 [Mike Leeson/Peter Vale/Miles Waters] [BMI] (6/24/89 B-97)

MY OWN TRUE LOVE (TARA'S THEME) *LeRoy Holmes And His Orchestra—MGM 11854 [Max Steiner] [ASC] (11/15/54 CtRt-PRE) [IM]*

TARA'S THEME *Paul Weston & His Orchestra—Columbia 40385 [Max Steiner] [ASC] (11/15/54 Rt-PRE) [IM]*

MY OWN TRUE LOVE (TARA'S THEME) *Johnny Desmond—Coral 61301 [Mack David/Max Steiner] [ASC] (12/4/54 CtRt-PRE)*

TARA'S THEME *Bill Doggett—King 4759 [Max Steiner] [ASC] (12/27/54 Rt-PRE) [IM]*

MY OWN TRUE LOVE *Jimmy Clanton—Ace 567 [Mack David/Max Steiner] [ASC] (7/13/59 BCRt-25)*

MY OWN TRUE LOVE *The Four Coachmen—MGM 12810 [Mack David/Max Steiner] [ASC] (7/13/59 Rt-82)*

MY OWN TRUE LOVE *The Duprees—Coed 571 [Mack David/Max Steiner] [ASC] (10/20/62 BCR-13)*

TARA'S THEME *Meco—Arista 0660 [Max Steiner] (Med) [ASC] (2/13/82 BCR-35) [IM]*

MY OWN WAY TO ROCK Burton Cummings—Portrait 70007 [Burton Cummings] [BMI] (9/10/77 B-74)

MY PARADISE The Outfield—Columbia 68943 [John Spinks] [ASC] (7/22/89 B-72)

MY PART James Brown—Polydor 14098 [Charles Bobbit/James Brown] (Med) [BMI] (10/23/71 BCR-68) [IWM]

MY PEARL Automatic Man—Island 063 [Todd Cochran/Doni Harvey/Michael Shrieve/Pat Thrall] [BMI] (12/25/76 BC-88)

MY PERSONAL POSSESSION *Nat "King" Cole And The Four Knights—Capitol 3737 [Rose Marie McCoy/Charles Singleton] [BMI] (6/15/57 BCRt-21)*

MY PERSONAL POSSESSION *Andy Bey—Decca 30361 [Rose Marie McCoy/Charles Singleton] [BMI] (7/13/57 Rt-21)*

MY PLEDGE OF LOVE Joe Jeffrey Group—Wand 11200 [Joe Stafford Jr.] [BMI] (5/31/69 BCR-9)

MY PRAYER *The Platters—Mercury 70893 [Georges Boulanger/Jimmy Kennedy] [ASC] (6/29/56 BCRt-1)*

MY PRAYER *The Ink Spots—Decca 29991 [Georges Boulanger/Jimmy Kennedy] [ASC] (7/20/56 Rt-1)*

MY PRAYER *Johnny Thunder—Diamond 196 [Georges Boulanger/Jimmy Kennedy] [ASC] (3/12/66 CR-80)*

MY PRAYER *Ray, Goodman & Brown—Polydor 2116 [Georges Boulanger/Jimmy Kennedy] [ASC] (8/23/80 BCR-47)*

MY PREROGATIVE Bobby Brown—MCA 53383 [Bobby Brown/Gene Griffin] [BMI] (10/22/88 BC-1)

MY PRETENDING DAYS ARE OVER The Dells—Cadet 5698 [Don Davis/James Anthony Dean/Herbie Ross] [BMI] (9/29/73 BCR-51)

MY REAL NAME Fats Domino—Imperial 5833 [Fats Domino] [BMI] (5/12/62 BCR-59)

MY SECRET The Platters—Mercury 71538 [Buck Ram] [ASC] (12/12/59 C-98)

MY SHARONA The Knack—Capitol 4731 [Berton Averre/Doug Fieger] [ASC] (6/23/79 BCR-1)

MY SHIP Tavares—Capitol 4010 [Dennis Lambert/Brian Potter] (TSW) [BMI] (4/12/75 B-40)

MY SHIP IS COMIN' IN The Walker Bros.—Smash 2016 [Joey Brooks] [BMI] (1/29/66 BCR-62)

***MY SHOES KEEP WALKING BACK TO YOU** Ray Price—Columbia 40951 [Lee Ross/Bob Wills] [ASC] (10/14/57 B-63)*

***MY SHOES KEEP WALKING BACK TO YOU** Guy Mitchell—Columbia 41725 [Lee Ross/Bob Wills] [ASC] (7/11/60 BR-41)*

MY SHY VIOLET The Mills Brothers—Dot 17096 [Leon Carr/Earl Shuman] [ASC] (5/11/68 BCR-62)

MY SIDE OF THE BED Susanna Hoffs—Columbia 73529 [Susanna Hoffs/Thomas F. Kelly/Billy Steinberg] [ASC] (2/2/91 BC-26)

MY SON, MY SON Vera Lynn—London 1501 [Albert Calvert/Robert Howard/Gordon Rees] [ASC] (10/18/54 CR-22)

MY SONG Aretha Franklin—Atlantic 2574 [John Alexander/David Mattis] [BMI] (11/30/68 B-31)

MY SONG Glass Tiger—EMI-Manhattan 50172 [Alan Frew/Sam Reid/Jim Vallance] [ASC] (11/26/88 C-71)

MY SOUL'S GOT A HOLE IN IT Howard Tate—Turntable 1018 [Titus Turner] [BMI] (4/4/70 B-100)

***MY SPECIAL ANGEL** Bobby Helms—Decca 30423 [Jimmy Duncan] [BMI] (9/9/57 BCRt-7)*

***MY SPECIAL ANGEL** The Sonny Land Trio—Prep 115 [Jimmy Duncan] [BMI] (9/9/57 Rt-7)*

***MY SPECIAL ANGEL** The Vogues—Reprise 0766 [Jimmy Duncan] [BMI] (9/7/68 BCR-6)*

***MY SPECIAL PRAYER** Joe Simon—Sound Stage 7 2577 [Wini Scott] [BMI] (1/21/67 BCR-87)*

***MY SPECIAL PRAYER** Percy Sledge—Atlantic 2594 [Wini Scott] [BMI] (2/1/69 B-93)*

MY SUMMER LOVE Ruby And The Romantics—Kapp 525 [Mort Garson/Bob Hilliard] [ASC] (5/11/63 BCR-16)

***MY SWEET LADY** Cliff DeYoung—MCA 40156 [John Denver] [ASC] (12/22/73 BCR-17)*

***MY SWEET LADY** John Denver—RCA 10911 [John Denver] [ASC] (3/12/77 BCR-32)*

***MY SWEET LORD** George Harrison—Apple 2995 [George Harrison] (TSW) [ASC] (11/28/70 BCR-1)*

***MY SWEET LORD** Billy Preston—Apple 1826 [George Harrison] [ASC] (2/13/71 BC-82)*

***MY SWEET LORD** Stars On 45—Radio 3830 [George Harrison] (Med) [ASC] (7/11/81 BC-63)*

MY SWEET POTATO Booker T. & The M.G.'s—Stax 196 [Steve Cropper/Al Jackson/Booker T. Jones Jr.] [BMI] (8/27/66 BCR-72) [I]

MY SWEET SUMMER SUITE Love Unlimited Orchestra—20th Century 2301 [Barry White] [BMI] (9/11/76 BC-48) [I]

MY TANI The Brothers Four—Columbia 41692 [August Goupil/Dick Gump/Johnny Noble] [ASC] (6/13/60 BCR-50)

MY THANG James Brown—Polydor 14244 [James Brown] [BMI] (6/8/74 BCR-29)

MY TIME FOR CRYIN' Maxine Brown—ABC-Paramount 10327 [Sid Bass/Bob Crewe] [ASC] (6/30/62 B-98)

MY TOOT TOOT Jean Knight—Mirage 99643 [Sidney Simien] [BMI] (5/4/85 BC-50)

MY TOWN Michael Stanley Band—EMI America 8178 [Michael Stanley] [ASC] (10/1/83 BC-39)

MY TOWN, MY GUY AND ME Lesley Gore—Mercury 72475 [Lesley Gore/Stanley Kahan/Paul Kaufman] [BMI] (9/4/65 BCR-32)

***MY TREASURE** The Hilltoppers—Dot 15437 [Cy Coben/Bill Templeton] [ASC] (12/31/55 BCtRt-31)*

***MY TREASURE** Connie Francis—MGM 12122 [Cy Coben/Bill Templeton] [ASC] (12/31/55 CtRt-37)*

MY TRUE CARRIE, LOVE Nat King Cole—Capitol 5125 [Paula Frances/Gary Romero] [ASC] (2/15/64 BCR-36)

MY TRUE CONFESSION Brook Benton—Mercury 72135 [Margie Singleton/Ray Stevens] [BMI] (6/15/63 BCR-22)

MY TRUE LOVE Jack Scott—Carlton 462 [Jack Scott] [BMI] (6/14/58 BCR-3)

MY TRUE STORY The Jive Five—Beltone 1006 [Phil Belmonte*/Eugene Pitt/Oscar Waltzer] [BMI] (7/3/61 BCR-3)

MY UNCLE USED TO LOVE ME BUT SHE DIED Roger Miller—Smash 2055 [Roger Miller] [BMI] (9/10/66 BCR-45)

***MY WAY** Frank Sinatra—Reprise 0817 [Paul Anka/Claude François/Jacques Revaux] [BMI] (3/22/69 BCR-27) [FDE]*

***MY WAY** Brook Benton—Cotillion 44072 [Paul Anka/Claude François/Jacques Revaux] [BMI] (4/18/70 BCR-42) [FDE]*

***MY WAY** Elvis Presley—RCA 11165 [Paul Anka/Claude François/Jacques Revaux] [BMI] (11/12/77 BCR-22) [FDE]*

MY WAY OF LIFE Frank Sinatra—Reprise 0764 [Bert Kaempfert/Herbert Rehbein/Carl Sigman] [BMI] (8/24/68 BCR-60)

MY WHEELS WON'T TURN Bachman-Turner Overdrive—Mercury 73903 [Randy Bachman] [BMI] (4/30/77 CR-84)

MY WHOLE WORLD ENDED (THE MOMENT YOU LEFT ME) David Ruffin—Motown 1140 [Johnny Bristol/Harvey Fuqua/Jimmy Roach/Pam Sawyer] [ASC] (2/8/69 BCR-9)

MY WHOLE WORLD IS FALLING DOWN Brenda Lee—Decca 31510 [Bill Anderson/Jerry Crutchfield] [BMI] (7/6/63 BCR-22)

MY WIFE CAN'T COOK Lonnie Russ—4J 501 [Lonnie Russ] [BMI] (12/8/62 BCR-57)

MY WIFE, MY DOG, MY CAT The Maskman & The Agents—Dynamo 131 [Harmon Bethea] [BMI] (5/17/69 BR-90)

MY WIFE, THE DANCER Eddie & Dutch—Ivanhoe 502 [Eddie Mascari/Erwin Wenzlaff] [BMI] (4/4/70 BCR-52)

MY WISH CAME TRUE Elvis Presley—RCA Victor 47-7600 [Ivory Joe Hunter] [BMI] (6/29/59 BCR-12)

***MY WOMAN, MY WOMAN, MY WIFE** Marty Robbins—Columbia 45091 [Marty Robbins] [BMI] (3/7/70 BCR-38)*

***MY WOMAN, MY WOMAN, MY WIFE** Dean Martin—Reprise 0934 [Marty Robbins] [BMI] (8/15/70 C-97)*

MY WORLD Bee Gees—Atco 6871 [Barry Gibb/Robin Gibb] [BMI] (1/22/72 BCR-15)

MY WORLD FELL DOWN Sagittarius—Columbia 44163 [John Carter/Geoff Stephens] [ASC] (6/24/67 BCR-59)

***MY WORLD IS EMPTY WITHOUT YOU** The Supremes—Motown 1089 [Lamont Dozier/Brian Holland/Eddie Holland] [BMI] (1/15/66 BCR-4)*

***MY WORLD IS EMPTY WITHOUT YOU** Jose Feliciano—RCA Victor 47-9714 [Lamont Dozier/Brian Holland/Eddie Holland] (TSW) [BMI] (1/25/69 BCR-47)*

MYSTERIOUS WAYS U2—Island 866 188 [Adam Clayton/Dave Evans/Paul Hewson/Larry Mullen] [ASC] (11/23/91 BC-3)

MYSTERY GIRL The Dukes—Atlantic 89999 [Dominic Bugatti/Frank Musker] [BMI] (8/28/82 C-96)

MYSTERY LADY Billy Ocean—Jive 9374 [Keith Diamond/Billy Ocean/James Woodley] [BMI] (7/6/85 BC-24)

MYSTERY OF YOU The Platters—Mercury 71184 [George Goehring/Gerald Frederick Grant] [BMI] (9/23/57 CR-45)

MYSTIC EYES Them—Parrot 9796 [Van Morrison] [BMI] (10/30/65 BCR-25)

N

N-E-R-V-O-U-S! Ian Whitcomb—Tower 155 [Willie Dixon*/Ian Whitcomb] [BMI] (8/28/65 BCR-40)

***NA NA HEY HEY KISS HIM GOODBYE** Steam—Fontana 1667 [Gary DeCarlo/Dale Frashuer/Paul Leka] [BMI] (9/27/69 BCR-1)*

***KISS HIM GOODBYE** The Nylons—Open Air 0022 [Gary DeCarlo/Dale Frashuer/Paul Leka] [BMI] (5/9/87 BC-12)*

NADIA'S THEME (THE YOUNG AND THE RESTLESS) Barry De Vorzon and Perry Botkin, Jr.—A&M 1856 [Perry Botkin Jr./Barry De Vorzon] [BMI] (8/28/76 BCR-5) [I]

NADINE The Dells—Cadet 5667 [Alan Freed] (TSW) [BMI] (5/2/70 BR-49)

NADINE (IS IT YOU?) Chuck Berry—Chess 1883 [Chuck Berry] [BMI] (2/29/64 BCR-23)

NAG The Halos—7 Arts 709 [Arthur Crier] [BMI] (7/17/61 BCR-25)

NAIL IT TO THE WALL Stacy Lattisaw—Motown 1859 [Stephen Lunt/Arnie Roman] [ASC] (10/18/86 BC-48)

—NAIVE MELODY see: THIS MUST BE THE PLACE

NAME AND NUMBER Big Noise—Atco 99168 [Anthony Fennell/Paul Morais Johnson/Huw Lucas] [ASC] (11/4/89 B-97)

THE NAME GAME Shirley Ellis—Congress 230 [Lincoln Chase/Shirley Ellis] [BMI] (12/12/64 BCR-3)

THE NAME OF THE GAME Abba—Atlantic 3449 [Stig Anderson/Benny Andersson/Björn Ulvaeus] [BMI] (12/24/77 BCR-12)

***NAMELY YOU** Julius La Rosa—RCA Victor 47-6648 [Gene DePaul/Johnny Mercer] [ASC] (9/8/56 Rt-51)*

***NAMELY YOU** Don Cherry—Columbia 40746 [Gene DePaul/Johnny Mercer] [ASC] (10/6/56 BRt-51)*

***NAMELY YOU** Carmen McRae—Decca 30075 [Gene DePaul/Johnny Mercer] [ASC] (10/13/56 Rt-51)*

NAMES, TAGS, NUMBERS & LABELS The Association—Mums 6016 [Albert Hammond/Mike Hazlewood] [ASC] (2/17/73 BCR-85)

NANCY'S MINUET The Everly Brothers—Warner Bros. 5346 [Don Everly] [BMI] (3/23/63 R-82)

NANU, NANU, (I WANNA GET FUNKY WICH YOU) Daddy Dewdrop—Inphasion 7201 [Dick Monda] [BMI] (2/10/79 CR-93)

NASHVILLE CATS The Lovin' Spoonful—Kama Sutra 219 [John Sebastian] [BMI] (12/17/66 BCR-8)

NASTY Janet Jackson—A&M 2830 [James Samuel Harris/Terry Lewis] [ASC] (5/17/86 BC-3)

NATHAN JONES The Supremes—Motown 1182 [Leonard Caston/Kathy Wakefield] [BMI] (5/1/71 BCR-8)

NATIONAL CITY Joiner, Arkansas Junior High School Band—Liberty 55244 [Traditional] [BMI] (5/9/60 BCR-53) [I]

(NATIVE GIRL) ELEPHANT WALK Donald Jenkins & The Delighters—Cortland 109 [Bob Catron/Donald Jenkins] [BMI] (9/14/63 BCR-54)

NATIVE NEW YORKER Odyssey—RCA 11129 [Sandy Linzer/Denny Randell] [BMI] (10/29/77 BCR-15)

NATURAL BORN LOVER Fats Domino—Imperial 5704 [Dave Bartholomew/Fats Domino] [BMI] (10/31/60 BCR-38)

NATURAL HIGH Bloodstone—London 1046 [Charles E. McCormick] [BMI] (4/7/73 BCR-5)

NATURAL LOVE Petula Clark—Scotti Brothers 02676 [Kim Espy/Phil Gernhard/Jeff Harrington/Jeff Pennig] [BMI] (2/6/82 BR-66)

A NATURAL MAN Lou Rawls—MGM 14262
[Sandy Baron/Bobby Hebb] [BMI] (8/28/71 BCR-17)
A NATURAL WOMAN (YOU MAKE ME FEEL LIKE) Aretha Franklin—Atlantic 2441
[Gerry Goffin/Carole King/Jerry Wexler] [BMI] (9/30/67 BCR-8)
NATURALLY STONED The Avant-Garde—Columbia 44590
[Chuck Woolery] [BMI] (8/24/68 BCR-35)
NATURE BOY *The Shields—Dot 15856 [Eden Ahbez] [ASC] (11/17/58 R-93)*
NATURE BOY *Bobby Darin—Atco 6196 [Eden Ahbez] [ASC] (5/29/61 BCR-31)*
NATURE OF LOVE Waterfront—Polydor 871414
[Phil Cilia/Chris Duffy] [BMI] (7/29/89 BC-58)
NAUGHTY GIRLS (NEED LOVE TOO) Samantha Fox—Jive 1089
[Curtis Bedeau/Gerard Charles/Hugh Clarke/Brian George/Lucien George/Paul George] [BMI] (2/27/88 BC-3)
NAUGHTY LADY OF SHADY LANE *The Ames Brothers—RCA Victor 47-5897*
[Roy C. Bennett/Sid Tepper] [ASC] (7/10/54 BCtRt-3)
NAUGHTY LADY OF SHADY LANE *Archie Bleyer—Cadence 1254*
[Roy C. Bennett/Sid Tepper] [ASC] (11/8/54 BCtRt-3)
NAUGHTY LITTLE FLEA Lord Flea and His Calypsonians—Capitol 3659
[Norman Thomas] [NA] (3/16/57 R-81)
NAUGHTY NAUGHTY John Parr—Atlantic 89612 [John Parr] [BMI] (12/15/84 BC-23)
NAVY BLUE Diane Renay—20th Century 456
[Bob Crewe/Eddie Rambeau/Bud Rehak] [BMI] (1/18/64 BCR-5)
NEANDERTHAL MAN Hotlegs—Capitol 2886
[Lol Crème/Kevin Godley/Eric Stewart] [BMI] (8/15/70 BCR-11)
NEAR TO YOU *Patti Page—Mercury 70607*
[Richard Adler/Jerry Ross] [ASC] (4/25/55 CRt-46)
NEAR TO YOU *Eddie Fisher—RCA Victor 47-6097*
[Richard Adler/Jerry Ross] [ASC] (4/25/55 Rt-56)
NEAR YOU *Roger Williams—Kapp 233 [Francis Craig] [ASC] (8/18/58 BCRt-9) [IM]*
NEAR YOU *Cliffie Stone & His Orchestra—Capitol 4044*
[Francis Craig/Kermit Goell] [ASC] (9/15/58 Rt-9)
NEAR YOU *The Mulcays—GNP 136 [Francis Craig] [ASC] (9/29/58 Rt-9) [IM]*
NEAR YOU Boz Scaggs—Columbia 45408 [Boz Scaggs] [ASC] (7/3/71 B-96)
NEARER TO YOU Betty Harris—Sansu 466 [Allen Toussaint] [BMI] (7/22/67 BCR-73)
NEE NEE NA NA NA NA NU NU Dicky Doo And The Don'ts—Swan 4006
[Eddie V. Deane/Al Dredick] [ASC] (5/3/58 BC-40) [I]
NEED A LITTLE TASTE OF LOVE The Doobie Brothers—Capitol 44441
[Ernie Isley/Marvin Isley/O'Kelly Isley/Ronald Isley/Rudolph Isley/Chris Jasper] [ASC] (8/12/89 BC-38)
—NEED FOR LOVE see: THEME FROM THE UNFORGIVEN
NEED LOVE Vanilla Fudge—Atco 6703
[Carmine Appice/Tim Bogert/Vince Martell/Mark Stein] [ASC] (8/9/69 R-84)
NEED ME Kitty Kallen—Columbia 41546 [Jim Reeves] [BMI] (1/18/60 R-91)
THE NEED TO BE Jim Weatherly—Buddah 420 [Jim Weatherly] [ASC] (8/24/74 BCR-11)
NEED TO BELONG Jerry Butler—Vee-Jay 567 [Curtis Mayfield] [BMI] (11/16/63 BCR-28)
NEED YOU Donnie Owens—Guyden 2001 [Buddy Wheeler] [BMI] (9/27/58 BCR-20)
NEED YOU BAD Ted Nugent—Epic 50648 [Ted Nugent] [ASC] (1/6/79 BR-84)
NEED YOU TONIGHT INXS—Atlantic 89188
[Andy Farriss/Michael Hutchence] [ASC] (10/24/87 BC-1)
NEED YOUR LOVE Bobby Freeman—Josie 844 [Bobby Freeman] [BMI] (11/24/58 BC-54)
NEED YOUR LOVING TONIGHT Queen—Elektra 47086
[John Deacon] [BMI] (11/29/80 BCR-44)
NEEDLE IN A HAYSTACK The Velvelettes—V.I.P. 25007
[William Stevenson/Norman Whitfield] [BMI] (10/17/64 BCR-32)
NEEDLES AND PINS *Jackie de Shannon—Liberty 55563*
[Sonny Bono/Jack Nitzsche] [BMI] (5/11/63 BCR-58)
NEEDLES AND PINS *The Searchers—Kapp 577*
[Sonny Bono/Jack Nitzsche] [BMI] (2/29/64 BCR-12)
NEEDLES AND PINS *Smokie—RSO 881*
[Sonny Bono/Jack Nitzsche] [BMI] (9/17/77 BCR-68)
NEEDLES AND PINS *Tom Petty and The Heartbreakers—MCA 52772*
[Sonny Bono/Jack Nitzsche] [BMI] (2/1/86 BC-37)
NEIGHBOR, NEIGHBOR Jimmy Hughes—Fame 1003
[Huey P. Meaux] [BMI] (5/21/66 BCR-54)
NEITHER ONE OF US (WANTS TO BE THE FIRST TO SAY GOODBYE)
Gladys Knight & The Pips—Soul 35098
[Jim Weatherly] [ASC] (1/20/73 BCR-1)
—NEL BLU DIPINTO DI BLU see: VOLARE
NEON NITES Atlanta Rhythm Section—Polydor 14397
[Buddy Buie/Robert Nix] [BMI] (6/4/77 BCR-42)
NEON RAINBOW The Box Tops—Mala 580
[Wayne Carson Thompson] [BMI] (11/11/67 BCR-16)
NERVOUS BOOGIE Paul Gayten—Argo 5277 [Paul Gayten] [BMI] (12/2/57 B-68) [I]
NESSUNO MI PUO' GIUDCARE Gene Pitney—Musicor 1155
[Luciano Beretta/Michele Del Prete/Daniele Pace/Mario Panzeri] [ASC] (3/5/66 C-87) [F]
NEUTRON DANCE Pointer Sisters—Planet 13951
[Danny Sembello/Allee Willis] [ASC] (11/24/84 BC-6)
NEVADA FIGHTER Michael Nesmith & The First National Band—RCA Victor 74-0453
[Michael Nesmith] [BMI] (4/17/71 BCR-63)
NEVER The Earls—Old Town 1133
[Robert Del Din/Larry Figueiredo/Stan Vincent] [BMI] (3/16/63 C-82)
NEVER Heart—Capitol 5512
[Gene Black/Holly Knight/Ann Wilson/Nancy Wilson] [ASC] (9/14/85 BC-4)
NEVER AGAIN Dinah Washington—Mercury 71317
[Edward Grossman/Neil Sedaka] [BMI] (8/16/58 C-74)
NEVER AS GOOD AS THE FIRST TIME Sade—Portrait 37-05761
[Helen Adu/Stuart Matthewman] [BMI] (3/29/86 BC-20)
NEVER BE AFRAID Bing Crosby with The Arthur Norman Choir—Kapp 195
[Alan Bergman/Marilyn Bergman/Lew Spence] [ASC] (11/9/57 CR-50)
NEVER BE ANYONE ELSE BUT YOU Ricky Nelson—Imperial 5565
[Baker Knight] [BMI] (2/23/59 BCR-5)
NEVER BE THE SAME Christopher Cross—Warner Bros. 49580
[Christopher Cross] [ASC] (10/11/80 BCR-10)
NEVER BEEN ANY REASON Head East—A&M 1718
[Michael Somerville] [ASC] (10/18/75 BCR-68)
NEVER BEEN IN LOVE Randy Meisner—Epic 03032
[Craig Bickhardt] [ASC] (7/31/82 BC-23)
NEVER BEEN TO SPAIN Three Dog Night—Dunhill 4299
[Hoyt Axton] [BMI] (12/25/71 BCR-3)
NEVER BEFORE Connie Francis—MGM 12738
[Moose Charlap/Norman Gimbel] [ASC] (12/13/58 C-99)
NEVER CAN SAY GOODBYE *The Jackson 5—Motown 1179*
[Clifton Davis] [ASC] (4/3/71 BCR-1)
NEVER CAN SAY GOODBYE *Isaac Hayes—Enterprise 9031*
[Clifton Davis] [ASC] (5/8/71 BCR-22)
NEVER CAN SAY GOODBYE *Gloria Gaynor—MGM 14748*
[Clifton Davis] [ASC] (11/2/74 BCR-8)
NEVER CAN SAY GOODBYE *Communards—MCA/London 53224*
[Clifton Davis] [ASC] (1/30/88 BC-51)
NEVER COMES THE DAY The Moody Blues—Deram 85044
[Justin Hayward] [ASC] (5/10/69 BCR-89)
NEVER DIE YOUNG James Taylor—Columbia 07616 [James Taylor] [ASC] (4/2/88 B-80)
NEVER DREAMED YOU'D LEAVE IN SUMMER Stevie Wonder—Tamla 54202
[Stevie Wonder/Syreeta Wright] [ASC] (6/19/71 BR-78)
NEVER ENDING SONG OF LOVE Delaney & Bonnie & Friends—Atco 6804
[Bonnie Bramlett*/Delaney Bramlett] [BMI] (5/22/71 BCR-9)
NEVER ENDING STORY Limahl—EMI America 8230
[Keith Forsey/Giorgio Moroder] [ASC] (3/23/85 BC-17)
NEVER ENOUGH Patty Smyth—Columbia 06643
[Eric Bazilian/Rick Chertoff/Rob Hyman/David Kagan/Patty Smyth] [BMI] (2/28/87 BC-57)
NEVER ENOUGH The Cure—Fiction/Elektra 64928
[Simon Gallup/Robert James Smith/Porl Thompson/Boris Williams] [ASC] (11/3/90 BC-72)
NEVER EVER Peter And Gordon—Capitol 2071 [Gordon Waller] [BMI] (1/20/68 CR-95)
NEVER GET ENOUGH OF YOUR LOVE Oscar Toney, Jr.—Bell 714
[Eddie Floyd] [BMI] (4/20/68 BR-95)
NEVER GET ENOUGH OF YOUR LOVE L.T.D.—A&M 2005
[Ray Dahrouge] [ASC] (3/11/78 BCR-56)
NEVER GIVE UP Sammy Hagar—Geffen 29718
[Keith Olsen/Alan Pasqua] [BMI] (3/26/83 BC-46)
NEVER GIVE UP ON A GOOD THING George Benson—Warner Bros. 50005
[Michael Garvin/Tom Shapiro] [BMI] (2/20/82 BCR-52)
NEVER GIVE YOU UP Jerry Butler—Mercury 72798
[Jerry Butler/Kenneth Gamble/Leon Huff] [BMI] (5/4/68 BCR-17)
NEVER GOING BACK The Lovin' Spoonful—Kama Sutra 250
[John Stewart] [BMI] (7/13/68 BCR-56)
NEVER GONNA FALL IN LOVE AGAIN Eric Carmen—Arista 0184
[Eric Carmen/Sergei Rachmaninoff*] [BMI] (5/1/76 BCR-9)
NEVER GONNA GIVE YOU UP Rick Astley—RCA 5347
[Matt Aitken/Mike Stock/Pete Waterman] [BMI] (12/19/87 BC-1)
NEVER GONNA LET HIM KNOW Debbie Taylor—GWP 501
[Ray Dahrouge/Billy Terrell] [BMI] (3/29/69 BCR-56)
NEVER GONNA LET YOU DOWN Surface—Columbia 73643
[Bernard Leon Jackson] [ASC] (4/27/91 BC-17)
NEVER GONNA LET YOU GO Sergio Mendes—A&M 2540
[Barry Mann/Cynthia Weil] [BMI] (4/16/83 BC-3)
NEVER HAD A DREAM COME TRUE Stevie Wonder—Tamla 54191
[Henry Cosby/Sylvia Moy/Stevie Wonder] [ASC] (1/31/70 BCR-18)
NEVER HAD A LOT TO LOSE Cheap Trick—Epic 68563
[Thomas John Peterson/Robin Zander] [BMI] (2/18/89 BC-54)
NEVER HAD A LOVE Pablo Cruise—A&M 1999
[David Jenkins/Cory Lerios] [ASC] (1/28/78 BCR-85)
NEVER HAD A LOVE LIKE THIS BEFORE Tavares—Capitol 4658
[Zane Grey/Len Hanks/Arnold McCuller*] [BMI] (1/20/79 R-93)

NEVER HAD IT SO GOOD Ronnie Milsap—Scepter 12109
[Jo Armstead/Nick Ashford/Valerie Simpson] [BMI] (10/23/65 C-94)

—NEVER HAVE TO SAY GOODBYE AGAIN see: WE'LL NEVER HAVE TO SAY GOODBYE AGAIN

NEVER IN A MILLION YEARS Linda Scott—Congress 103
[Mack Gordon/Harry Revel] [ASC] (6/16/62 BCR-47)

NEVER KNEW LOVE LIKE THIS Alexander O'Neal—Tabu 4-07646
[James Samuel Harris/Terry Lewis] [ASC] (1/23/88 BC-28)

NEVER KNEW LOVE LIKE THIS BEFORE Stephanie Mills—20th Century Fox 2460
[Reggie Lucas/James Mtume] [BMI] (8/9/80 BCR-6)

***NEVER LEAVE ME** Gale Storm—Dot 15412
[Nick Acquaviva/Ted Varnick] [ASC] (2/3/56 Rt-88)*

***NEVER LEAVE ME** Bob Presto—Fraternity 726
[Nick Acquaviva/Ted Varnick] [ASC] (2/3/56 Rt-88)*

***NEVER LEAVE ME** Dick Roman—ABC-Paramount 9748
[Gordon Jenkins] [ASC] (10/20/56 Rt-31)*

***NEVER LEAVE ME** Dick Haymes—Capitol 3547 [Gordon Jenkins] [ASC] (10/20/56 Rt-31)*

***NEVER LEAVE ME** The Lancers—Coral 61712 [Gordon Jenkins] [ASC] (10/20/56 Rt-31)*

NEVER LET HER GO David Gates—Elektra 45223 [David Gates] [ASC] (12/28/74 BCR-26)

NEVER LET HER SLIP AWAY Andrew Gold—Asylum 45489
[Andrew Gold] [BMI] (6/17/78 BCR-61)

NEVER LET ME DOWN David Bowie—EMI America 43031
[Carlos Alomar/David Bowie] [ASC] (8/8/87 BC-27)

NEVER LET ME DOWN AGAIN Depeche Mode—Sire 28189
[Martin L. Gore] [BMI] (12/26/87 BC-63)

NEVER LET ME GO Nat "King" Cole—Capitol 3390
[Ray Evans/Jay Livingston] [ASC] (4/21/56 B-79)

NEVER LET ME GO Lloyd Price And His Orchestra—ABC-Paramount 10075
[Luther Dixon] [BMI] (3/7/60 B-82)

NEVER LET YOU GO Bloodstone—London 1051 [Harry Williams Jr.] [BMI] (9/1/73 BCR-35)

NEVER LET YOU GO Sweet Sensation—Atco 99284
[Joseph E. Malloy] [BMI] (9/17/88 B-58)

NEVER LOVE A ROBIN Bobby Vee—Liberty 55636
[Mickey Gentile/Artie Resnick] [BMI] (12/28/63 B-99)

NEVER MARRY A RAILROAD MAN The Shocking Blue—Colossus 123
[Robbie Van Leeuwen] [ASC] (1/30/71 C-93)

***NEVER MY LOVE** The Association—Warner Bros. 7074
[Dick Addrisi/Don Addrisi] [BMI] (8/26/67 BCR-1)*

***NEVER MY LOVE** The Sandpebbles—Calla 155
[Dick Addrisi/Don Addrisi] [BMI] (10/19/68 BR-98)*

***NEVER MY LOVE** The 5th Dimension—Bell 45,134
[Dick Addrisi/Don Addrisi] [BMI] (9/11/71 BCR-12)*

***NEVER MY LOVE** Blue Swede—EMI 3938
[Dick Addrisi/Don Addrisi] [BMI] (8/24/74 BCR-6)*

***NEVER MY LOVE** The Addrisi Brothers—Buddah 587
[Dick Addrisi/Don Addrisi] [BMI] (11/26/77 BC-69)*

NEVER, NEVER The Jive Five—Beltone 1014
[Eugene Pitt/Malou René] [BMI] (11/13/61 BC-74)

NEVER, NEVER GONNA GIVE YA UP Barry White—20th Century 2058
[Barry White] [BMI] (10/27/73 BCR-7)

NEVER, NEVER LEAVE ME Mary Wells—20th Century 570
[Mickey Gentile/Jennie Lee Lambert] [BMI] (3/13/65 BCR-53)

NEVER, NEVER, NEVER (GRANDE, GRANDE, GRANDE) Shirley Bassey—United Artists 211
[Norman Newell/Tony Renis/Al Testa] [BMI] (5/5/73 BCR-42) [FET]

***NEVER ON SUNDAY** Don Costa And His Orchestra And Chorus—United Artists 234
[Manos Hadjidakis] [ASC] (7/30/60 BCRt-12) [IM]*

***NEVER ON SUNDAY** Marty Gold & His Orchestra—RCA Victor 47-7769
[Manos Hadjidakis] [ASC] (8/1/60 Rt-22) [IM]*

***NEVER ON SUNDAY** Ray Martin & His Orchestra—RCA Victor 47-7769
[Manos Hadjidakis] [ASC] (8/1/60 Rt-22) [IM]*

***NEVER ON SUNDAY** Raymond Lefevre—Jamie 1161
[Manos Hadjidakis] [ASC] (8/8/60 Rt-22) [IM]*

***(A SHIP WILL COME) EIN SCHIFF WIRD KOMMEN** Lale Anderson—King 5478
[Fini Busch/Manos Hadjidakis] [BMI] (4/24/61 BR-88) [F]*

***NEVER ON SUNDAY** The Chordettes—Cadence 1402
[Manos Hadjidakis/Billy Towne] [ASC] (6/12/61 BCRt-10) [FDE]*

NEVER SAY DIE (GIVE A LITTLE BIT MORE) Cliff Richard—EMI America 8180
[Terry Britten/Sue Shifrin] [ASC] (10/8/83 BC-73)

NEVER STOP Brand New Heavies—Delicious Vinyl 868 552-4 [Simon Bartholomew*/
N'Dea Davenport*/Jan Kincaid/Andrew Levy*] [ASC] (9/7/91 B-54)

NEVER SURRENDER Corey Hart—EMI America 8268
[Corey Hart] [ASC] (6/8/85 BC-3)

NEVER TEAR US APART INXS—Atlantic 89038
[Andy Farriss/Michael Hutchence] [ASC] (8/13/88 BC-7)

NEVER TELL AN ANGEL (WHEN YOUR HEART'S ON FIRE) The Stompers—Boardwalk 177
[Sal Baglio] [ASC] (6/18/83 B-88)

NEVER THOUGHT I'D FALL IN LOVE The Spinners—Atlantic 4007
[Dean Gant] [BMI] (3/6/82 B-95)

NEVER THOUGHT (THAT I COULD LOVE) Dan Hill—Columbia 07618
[Dan Hill] [ASC] (12/12/87 BC-43)

NEVER TOO MUCH Luther Vandross—Epic 02409
[Luther Vandross] [ASC] (9/19/81 BCR-22)

NEVER TOO MUCH LOVE The Bards—Capitol 2041
[Curtis Mayfield] [BMI] (11/25/67 R-87)

NEVER 2 MUCH OF U Dino—4th & Broadway 7495
[Dino Esposito] [BMI] (12/16/89 BC-58)

NEVER TRUST A WOMAN B.B. King—ABC-Paramount 10599
[Bill Doggett/Louis Jordan] [BMI] (11/7/64 BR-90)

NEVER TURN BACK Al Hibbler—Decca 29950
[Irving Berger/Herbert L. Miller] [BMI] (6/8/56 BCR-31)

NEVERTHELESS The Allman Brothers Band—Capricorn 0246
[Gregg Allman] (TSW) [BMI] (11/15/75 B-67)

NEW ATTITUDE Patti LaBelle—MCA 52517
[Jonathan Gilutin/Bunny Hull/Sharon Robinson] [BMI] (2/16/85 BC-17)

NEW BREED (PART 1) (THE BOO-GA-LOO) James Brown—Smash 2028
[James Brown/Nat Jones] [BMI] (4/16/66 C-100) [I]

NEW DAY FOR YOU Basia—Epic 08112
[Peter Ross/Basia Trzetrzelewska/Danny White] [ASC] (11/19/88 BC-53)

NEW FRONTIER Donald Fagen—Warner Bros. 29792
[Donald Fagen] [ASC] (1/29/83 BC-68)

THE NEW GIRL IN SCHOOL Jan & Dean—Liberty 55672
[Jan Berry/Roger Christian/Bob Norman/Brian Wilson] [BMI] (3/7/64 BCR-26)

NEW GIRL NOW Honeymoon Suite—Warner Bros. 29208
[Dermot Grehan] [BMI] (9/8/84 BC-57)

(NEW IN) THE WAYS OF LOVE Tommy Edwards—MGM 12837
[Hal David/Lee Pockriss] [ASC] (10/26/59 BCR-42)

NEW JACK HUSTLER (NINO'S THEME) Ice-T—Giant/Sire 19442
[Alphonso Henderson/Tracy Marrow] [ASC] (4/27/91 B-67)

NEW KID IN TOWN Eagles—Asylum 45373
[Glenn Frey/Don Henley/J.D. Souther] [BMI] (12/11/76 BCR-1)

NEW MEXICAN ROSE The 4 Seasons—Vee-Jay 562
[Charlie Calello/Bob Crewe] [ASC] (9/28/63 BCR-30)

NEW MOON ON MONDAY Duran Duran—Capitol 5309
[Simon Le Bon/Nick Rhodes/Andy Taylor/Nigel John Taylor/Roger Taylor] [ASC]
(1/14/84 BC-10)

NEW ORLEANS Elvis Presley with the Jordanaires—RCA Victor EPA-4319
[Roy C. Bennett/Sid Tepper] (EP) [ASC] (7/26/58 CR-14)

***NEW ORLEANS** U.S. Bonds—Legrand 1003
[Frank Guida/Joseph Royster] [BMI] (10/17/60 BCR-3)*

***NEW ORLEANS** Eddie Hodges—Aurora 153
[Frank Guida/Joseph Royster] [BMI] (6/19/65 BCRt-36)*

***NEW ORLEANS** The Chartbusters—Crusader 118
[Frank Guida/Joseph Royster] [BMI] (6/19/65 Rt-37)*

***NEW ORLEANS** Neil Diamond—Bang 554
[Frank Guida/Joseph Royster] [BMI] (1/6/68 BCR-36)*

NEW ORLEANS The Staple Singers—Curtom 0113
[Curtis Mayfield] [BMI] (2/21/76 BCR-57)

NEW ORLEANS LADIES Louisiana's Le Roux—Capitol 4586
[Hoyt Garrick/Leon Medica] [BMI] (6/17/78 BCR-49)

NEW PHILOSOPHER Eddie Lawrence—Coral 61713
[Eddie Lawrence] [BMI] (11/3/56 R-81)

NEW POWER GENERATION Prince—Paisley Park 19525 [Prince] [ASC] (10/20/90 BC-54)

NEW RIVER TRAIN Bobby Helms—Decca 30831 [Maggie Andrews] [ASC] (2/9/59 R-82)

A NEW ROCK AND ROLL Mahogany Rush—20th Century 2111
[Frank Marino] [BMI] (8/3/74 CR-88)

NEW ROMANCE (IT'S A MYSTERY) Spider—Dreamland 100
[Anton Fig/Holly Knight] [ASC] (4/19/80 BCR-35)

NEW SENSATION INXS—Atlantic 89080
[Andy Farriss/Michael Hutchence] [ASC] (5/14/88 BC-3)

NEW SONG Howard Jones—Elektra 69766 [Howard Jones] [BMI] (1/21/84 BC-27)

—NEW SWINGOVA RHYTHM see: BABY DON'T YOU CRY

NEW THING Enuff Z'Nuff—Atco 99207
[Ron Fajerstein/Donnie Vie/Chip Z'Nuff] [ASC] (10/21/89 BC-67)

NEW WORLD COMING Mama Cass Elliot—Dunhill 4225
[Barry Mann/Cynthia Weil] [BMI] (1/24/70 BCR-24)

NEW WORLD MAN Rush—Mercury 76179
[Geddy Lee/Alex Lifeson/Neil Peart] [ASC] (9/18/82 BC-21)

NEW YEAR'S DAY U2—Island 99915
[Adam Clayton/Dave Evans/Paul Hewson/Larry Mullen] [ASC] (4/2/83 BC-50)

NEW YORK CITY Zwol—EMI America 8005 [Walter Zwol] [ASC] (9/16/78 BCR-75)

NEW YORK GROOVE Ace Frehley—Casablanca 941
[Russ Ballard] [ASC] (10/14/78 BCR-13)

NEW YORK MINING DISASTER 1941 HAVE YOU SEEN MY WIFE, MR. JONES
The Bee Gees—Atco 6487
[Barry Gibb/Robin Gibb] [BMI] (5/27/67 BCR-14)

NEW YORK MINUTE Don Henley—Geffen 19660
[Don Henley/Danny Kortchmar/Jai Winding] [ASC] (11/10/90 BC-43)

NEW YORK'S A LONELY TOWN The Trade Winds—Red Bird 10-020
[Pete Andreoli/Vini Poncia] [BMI] (2/6/65 BCR-32)

NEW YORK'S MY HOME Sammy Davis Jr.—Decca 30111 [Gordon Jenkins] [ASC] (11/3/56 BR-59)

NEWSY NEIGHBORS First Choice—Philly Groove 183 [Allan Felder/Norman Harris] [BMI] (3/2/74 BCR-93)

NEXT DOOR TO AN ANGEL Neil Sedaka—RCA Victor 47-8086 [Howard Greenfield/Neil Sedaka] [BMI] (10/6/62 BCR-5)

NEXT DOOR TO THE BLUES Etta James—Argo 5424 [Leroy Kirkland/Pearl Woods] [BMI] (10/13/62 BCR-63)

THE NEXT HUNDRED YEARS Al Martino—Capitol 4508 [Ritchie Adams/Alan Bernstein] [ASC] (12/3/77 BCR-49)

NEXT IN LINE Johnny Cash—Sun 266 [Johnny Cash] [BMI] (7/1/57 B-99)

THE NEXT KISS (IS THE LAST GOODBYE) Conway Twitty—MGM 12998 [Bill Giant/David Hess/Buddy Kaye] [ASC] (4/3/61 BCR-53)

NEXT LOVE Deniece Williams—Columbia 04537 [George Duke/Deniece Williams] [ASC] (8/11/84 BC-79)

NEXT PLANE TO LONDON The Rose Garden—Atco 6510 [Kenny O'Dell] [BMI] (10/21/67 BCR-15)

THE NEXT STEP IS LOVE Elvis Presley—RCA Victor 47-9873 [Paul Evans/Paul Parnes] (TSW) [ASC] (8/1/70 BCR-14)

NEXT STOP PARADISE Teddy Randazzo—Vik 0277 [Oramay Diamond/Dave Dreyer/Clyde Otis] [ASC] (6/22/57 CR-47)

THE NEXT TIME I FALL Peter Cetera—Full Moon 28597 [Bobby Caldwell/Paul Gordon] [BMI] (9/20/86 BC-1)

THE NEXT TIME IT HAPPENS Carmen McRae—Decca 29749 [Oscar Hammerstein/Richard Rodgers] [ASC] (2/4/56 B-75)

NEXT TIME YOU SEE ME Little Junior Parker—Duke 164 [Earl Forest/Bill Harvey] [BMI] (7/8/57 B-74)

NEXT TIME YOU'LL KNOW Sister Sledge—Cotillion 46012 [Narada Michael Walden/Allee Willis] [ASC] (5/9/81 B-82)

NIAGARA FALLS Chicago—Warner/Full Moon 28283 [Bobby Caldwell/Steve Kipner] [BMI] (7/11/87 B-91)

NICE GIRLS Eye To Eye—Warner Bros. 50050 [Deborah Berg/Julian Marshall] [ASC] (5/22/82 BC-33)

NICE GIRLS Melissa Manchester—Arista 1045 [Jan Buckingham/Steve Buckingham/Mark Eugene Gray] [BMI] (2/5/83 BC-40)

NICE 'N' EASY Frank Sinatra—Capitol 4408 [Alan Bergman/Marilyn Bergman/Lew Spence] [ASC] (7/25/60 BCR-35)

NICE 'N' NAASTY The Salsoul Orchestra—Salsoul 2011 [Vincent Montana] [BMI] (9/18/76 BCR-30)

NICE 'N' SLOW Freddie Jackson—Capitol 44171 [Barry Eastmond/Jolyon Skinner] [ASC] (7/23/88 BC-61)

NICE, NICE, VERY NICE Ambrosia—20th Century 2244 [Burleigh Drummond/Christopher North/David Pack/Joe Puerta/Kurt Vonnegut] [BMI] (10/25/75 BC-63)

NICE TO BE AROUND Maureen McGovern—20th Century 2072 [John Williams/Paul Williams] [ASC] (2/16/74 C-96)

NICE TO BE WITH YOU Gallery—Sussex 232 [Jim Gold] [BMI] (2/26/72 BCR-1)

NICETY Michel'le—Ruthless 98980 [Michel'le Toussant/Andre Romell Young] [ASC] (4/14/90 BC-26)

NICK OF TIME Bonnie Raitt—Capitol 44364 [Bonnie Raitt] [ASC] (5/19/90 BC-70)

NICK TEEN AND AL K. HALL Rolf Harris—Epic 9615 [Rolf Harris] [BMI] (9/28/63 B-95)

NICKEL SONG *The New Seekers Featuring Eve Graham—Elektra 45719 [Melanie Safka] [ASC] (3/20/71 BCR-78)*

THE NICKEL SONG *Melanie—Buddah 268 [Melanie Safka] [ASC] (1/22/72 BCR-25)*

NICOLE Point Blank—MCA 51132 [Rusty Burns/Kim Davis/Peter Gruen/Mike Hamilton/Bubba Keith/Bill Randolph] [BMI] (6/27/81 BCR-39)

NIGHT Jackie Wilson—Brunswick 55166 [Johnny Lehmann/Herbert L. Miller] [BMI] (3/7/60 BCR-2)

THE NIGHT The Animals—I.R.S. 9920 [Eric Burdon/Don Evans/John Sterling] [BMI] (8/13/83 BC-48)

NIGHT (FEEL LIKE GETTING DOWN) Billy Ocean—Epic 02053 [Nigel Martinez/Billy Ocean] [BMI] (6/13/81 R-71)

NIGHT AND DAY *Louis Prima And Keely Smith—Dot 15978 [Cole Porter] [ASC] (8/31/59 R-91)*

NIGHT AND DAY *Sergio Mendes & Brasil '66—A&M 853 [Cole Porter] [ASC] (5/27/67 BCR-82)*

NIGHT AND DAY Bette Midler—Atlantic 87825 [Bill Hughes/Roxanne Seeman] [ASC] (1/19/91 BC-54)

THE NIGHT CHICAGO DIED Paper Lace—Mercury 73492 [Peter Callander/Mitch Murray] [BMI] (6/15/74 BCR-1)

NIGHT DANCIN' Taka Boom—Ariola America 7748 [Lenny Macaluso/Pat Summerson*] [BMI] (4/28/79 BC-74)

NIGHT FEVER Bee Gees—RSO 889 [Barry Gibb/Maurice Gibb/Robin Gibb] [BMI] (2/4/78 BCR-1)

NIGHT FO' LAST Shorty Long—Soul 35040 [Frederick Long/Clarence Paul] [BMI] (2/3/68 BCR-71)

THE NIGHT HAS A THOUSAND EYES Bobby Vee—Liberty 55521 [Marilyn Garrett/Dottie Wayne/Ben Weisman] [ASC] (12/1/62 BCR-3)

THE NIGHT I CRIED Brian Hyland—ABC-Paramount 10262 [Gary Geld/Peter Udell] [ASC] (11/6/61 R-86)

THE NIGHT IS STILL YOUNG Billy Joel—Columbia 05657 [Billy Joel] [ASC] (10/5/85 BC-34)

NIGHT LIFE Rusty Draper—Monument 823 [Walter Breeland*/Paul Buskirk*/Willie Nelson] [BMI] (9/14/63 BCR-57)

NIGHT LIGHTS Nat "King" Cole—Capitol 3551 [Chester Conn/Sammy Gallop] [ASC] (10/20/56 BCR-16)

NIGHT MOVES Bob Seger—Capitol 4369 [Bob Seger] [ASC] (12/4/76 BCR-4)

NIGHT MOVES Marilyn Martin—Atlantic 89465 [Marilyn Martin/John Parr] [ASC] (1/18/86 BC-27)

—NIGHT OF THE MOSSACIN see: ROOSEVELT AND IRA LEE

THE NIGHT OWLS Little River Band—Capitol 5033 [Graham Goble] [BMI] (8/22/81 BCR-6)

NIGHT PULSE Double Image—CBS Associated 03942 [Patrick Bolen/William Eugene Butler/Gabriel Katona] [ASC] (7/2/83 B-92)

NIGHT RIDER Elvis Presley With The Jordanaires—RCA Victor EPA-4383 [Doc Pomus/Mort Shuman] (EP) [BMI] (7/10/65 BCR-70)

NIGHT SHIFT Quarterflash—Warner Bros. 29932 [Burt Bacharach/Marv Ross/Carole Bayer Sager] [ASC] (8/14/82 BC-57)

THE NIGHT THE LIGHTS WENT OUT IN GEORGIA Vicki Lawrence—Bell 45,303 [Bobby Russell] [ASC] (2/3/73 BCR-1)

NIGHT THEME The Mark II—Wye 1001 [Wayne Cogswell/Ray Peterson] [BMI] (10/10/60 BCR-42) [I]

THE NIGHT THEY DROVE OLD DIXIE DOWN Joan Baez—Vanguard 35138 [Robbie Robertson] [ASC] (8/7/71 BCR-1)

NIGHT TIME Pete Antell—Cameo 234 [Pete Antel/John Linde] [BMI] (11/17/62 BCR-68)

NIGHT TIME The Strangeloves—Bang 514 [Bob Feldman/Jerry Goldstein/Richard Gottehrer] [BMI] (1/15/66 BCR-18)

NIGHT TIME IS THE RIGHT TIME *Ray Charles—Atlantic 2010 [Nappy Brown/James B. Oden/Roosevelt Sykes] [BMI] (2/9/59 B-95)*

NIGHT TIME IS THE RIGHT TIME *Rufus & Carla—Stax 151 [Nappy Brown/James B. Oden/Roosevelt Sykes] [BMI] (6/20/64 B-94)*

A NIGHT TO REMEMBER Shalamar—Solar 48005 [Nidra Beard/Dana Meyers/Charmaine Sylvers] [ASC] (4/10/82 BC-31)

NIGHT TRAIN *Ernie Englund—Cadence 1269 [Jimmy Forrest] [BMI] (11/14/55 Rt-72) [IM]*

NIGHT TRAIN MAMBO *Jimmy Forrest—Dot 15340 [Jimmy Forrest] [BMI] (11/14/55 Rt-72) [IM]*

ALL NITE LONG *Billy Vaughn And His Orchestra—Dot 15960 [Jimmy Forrest] [BMI] (7/6/59 CR-60) [IM]*

NIGHT TRAIN *The Viscounts—Madison 133 [Jimmy Forrest] [BMI] (7/18/60 BCR-46) [IM]*

NIGHT TRAIN *Richard Hayman And His Orchestra—Mercury 71869 [Jimmy Forrest] [BMI] (9/18/61 BR-80) [IM]*

NIGHT TRAIN *James Brown And The Famous Flames—King 5614 [Jimmy Forrest] [BMI] (4/2/62 BCR-35)*

NIGHT WALK Van McCoy—H&L 4667 [Van McCoy] [BMI] (5/29/76 B-96) [I]

NIGHTBIRD Stevie Nicks—Modern 99799 [Stevie Nicks/Sandy Stewart] [BMI] (12/17/83 BC-33)

NIGHTFALL Al Hibbler—Decca 30100 [Charles H. Cuppett/Peter DeRose/Sam Lewis] [ASC] (11/10/56 R-80)

NIGHTGOWN Candyman—Epic 73721 [Seth Justman/Prince/John B. Shaffer III] [ASC] (4/13/91 B-91)

NIGHTIME Pretty Poison—Virgin 99350 [Vincent Corea/Jeanne Roberts] [ASC] (4/2/88 BC-34)

NIGHTINGALE Carole King—Ode 66106 [Carole King/David Palmer] [ASC] (12/28/74 BCR-9)

NIGHTINGALE MELODY Little Johnny Taylor—Galaxy 731 [Little Johnny Taylor] [BMI] (7/18/64 R-93)

NIGHTMARE The Crazy World Of Arthur Brown—Track 2582 [Arthur Wilton Brown] [BMI] (11/30/68 CR-74)

A NIGHTMARE ON MY STREET D.J. Jazzy Jeff & The Fresh Prince—Jive 1124 [Peter Brian Harris/Will Smith/Jeff Townes] [ASC] (7/30/88 BC-15)

NIGHTRAIN Guns N' Roses—Geffen 22869 [Steven Adler/Saul Hudson/Duff McKagan/Axl Rose/Izzy Stradlin] [ASC] (7/29/89 B-93)

NIGHTS ARE FOREVER WITHOUT YOU England Dan & John Ford Coley—Big Tree 16079 [Parker McGee] [BMI] (10/9/76 BCR-9)

NIGHTS IN WHITE SATIN *The Moody Blues—Deram 85023 [Justin Hayward] [ASC] (3/9/68 C-93)*

NIGHTS IN WHITE SATIN *The Moody Blues—Deram 85023 [Justin Hayward] [ASC] (8/5/72 BCR-1)*

NIGHTS LIKE THIS After 7—Virgin 98798 [Jesse Woods Johnson/Keith Lewis] [ASC] (5/25/91 BC-24)

NIGHTS ON BROADWAY *Bee Gees—RSO 515 [Barry Gibb/Maurice Gibb/Robin Gibb] [BMI] (10/4/75 BCR-4)*

NIGHTS ON BROADWAY *Candi Staton—Warner Bros. 8387 [Barry Gibb/Maurice Gibb/Robin Gibb] [BMI] (8/6/77 R-91)*

NIGHTSHIFT Commodores—Motown 1773 [Franne Golde/Dennis Lambert/Walter Orange] [BMI] (1/26/85 BC-3)

NIGHTWALKER Gino Vannelli—Arista 0613 [Gino Vannelli] [BMI] (6/27/81 BCR-41)

NIKI HOEKY P.J. Proby—Liberty 55936
[Jim Ford/Lolly Vegas/Pat Vegas] [BMI] (1/28/67 BCR-23)
NIKITA Elton John—Geffen 28800 [Elton John/Bernie Taupin] [BMI] (1/18/86 BC-7)
992 ARGUMENTS The O'Jays—Philadelphia Int'l 3522
[Kenneth Gamble/Leon Huff] [BMI] (11/11/72 BCR-43)
9,999,999 TEARS Dickey Lee—RCA 10764 [Razzy Bailey] [BMI] (11/13/76 BCR-52)
NINE MORE MILES (THE "FASTER-FASTER" SONG)
Georgie Young And The Rockin' Bocs—Cameo 150
[Kal Mann] [ASC] (9/22/58 BCR-53)
NINE O'CLOCK The McGuire Sisters—Coral 62216
[Michael Merlo/Patrick Welch] [NA] (7/11/60 R-96)
9 LB. HAMMER Sanford Clark—Dot 15534 [Merle Travis] [BMI] (3/2/57 C-48)
NINE POUND STEEL Joe Simon—Sound Stage 7 2589
[Dan Penn/Wayne Carson Thompson] [BMI] (9/23/67 BCR-70)
9 TO 5 Dolly Parton—RCA 12133 [Dolly Parton] [BMI] (11/29/80 BCR-1)
19 Paul Hardcastle—Chrysalis 42860
[William Couturie/Paul Hardcastle/Jonas McCord/Mike Oldfield*] [ASC]
(6/1/85 BC-15)
NINETEEN DAYS The Dave Clark Five—Epic 10076
[Dave Clark/Denny Payton] [BMI] (10/15/66 BCR-45)
1984 Spirit—Ode 128 [Randy California] [BMI] (1/17/70 BCR-69)
1984 David Bowie—RCA Victor 10026 [David Bowie] [ASC] (8/31/74 C-96)
1941 Tom Northcott—Warner Bros. 7160/Warner Bros.-Seven Arts 7160
[Harry Nilsson] [BMI] (3/16/68 B-88)
1900 YESTERDAY Liz Damon's Orient Express—White Whale 368
[John Cameron/Lee Simmons*] [BMI] (12/19/70 BCR-29)
1999 Prince—Warner Bros. 29896 [Prince] [ASC] (10/30/82 BC-12)
1927 KANSAS CITY Mike Reilly—Paramount 0053 [Mike Reilly] [ASC] (3/13/71 BCR-88)
19TH NERVOUS BREAKDOWN The Rolling Stones—London 9823
[Mick Jagger/Keith Richards] [BMI] (2/26/66 BCR-1)
90 DAY FREEZE (ON HER LOVE) 100 Proof Aged In Soul—Hot Wax 7108
[Angelo Bond/Ronald Dunbar] [BMI] (11/6/71 C-83)
98.6 Keith—Mercury 72639 [George Fischoff/Tony Powers] [BMI] (12/3/66 BCR-4)
99 Toto—Columbia 11173 [David Paich] [ASC] (12/22/79 BCR-15)
99 1/2 Carol Lynn Townes—Polydor 881008
[Maxi Anderson/John Footman] [BMI] (7/7/84 BC-77)
NINETY-NINE AND A HALF (WON'T DO) Wilson Pickett—Atlantic 2334
[Steve Cropper/Eddie Floyd/Wilson Pickett] [BMI] (5/28/66 BCR-45)
99 LUFTBALLONS Nena—Epic 04108
[Jörn Fahrenkrog-Petersen/Carlo Karges] [ASC] (12/10/83 BC-1) [F]
99 MILES FROM L.A. Albert Hammond—Mums 6037
[Hal David/Albert Hammond] [ASC] (4/26/75 BCR-78)
99 + 1 J. Gardner—Blue Rock 4026
[Wardell Quezergue] [BMI] (7/24/65 R-92) [I]
NINETY NINE WAYS *Tab Hunter—Dot 15548*
[Bernie Lowe/Kal Mann] [ASC] (3/23/57 BCRt-11)
NINETY-NINE WAYS *Charlie Gracie—Cameo 105*
[Bernie Lowe/Kal Mann] [ASC] (4/13/57 Rt-12)
99 WORLDS Peter Wolf—MCA 53726
[Robert White Johnson/Taylor Rhodes/Peter Wolf] [ASC] (3/3/90 BC-59)
NINETY NINE YEARS (DEAD OR ALIVE) Guy Mitchell—Columbia 40631
[John Benson Brooks/Sid Wayne] [ASC] (1/20/56 BCR-12)
96 TEARS *? (Question Mark) & The Mysterians—Cameo 428*
[Rudy Martinez] [BMI] (8/27/66 BCR-1)
96 TEARS *Big Maybelle—Rojac 112 [Rudy Martinez] [BMI] (1/14/67 BCR-93)*
96 TEARS *Garland Jeffreys—Epic 51008 [Rudy Martinez] [BMI] (3/14/81 BC-66)*
—NINTEEN EIGHTY-FOUR see: SEXCRIME
NITE AND DAY Al B. Sure!—Warner Bros. 28192
[Albert Joseph Brown/Kyle West] [ASC] (4/9/88 BC-7)
NITE OWL *Dukays—NAT 4002 [Bernice Williams] [BMI] (1/20/62 BCR-73)*
NITE OWL *Dukays—Vee-Jay 430 [Bernice Williams] [BMI] (3/31/62 B-88)*
NITE ROCK (LONELY TRAIN) Nite Rockers—RCA Victor 47-7323
[Robert Abdinoor/Patrick Kaloustian/Robert Maderios] [BMI] (8/25/58 R-94)
THE NITTY GRITTY *Shirley Ellis—Congress 202 [Lincoln Chase] [BMI] (11/9/63 BCR-7)*
NITTY GRITTY *Ricardo Ray—Alegre 4024 [Lincoln Chase] [BMI] (9/28/68 BCR-80)*
THE NITTY GRITTY *Gladys Knight & The Pips—Soul 35063*
[Lincoln Chase] [BMI] (7/19/69 BCR-19)
NO Dodie Stevens—Dot 16103 [Lee Pockriss/Paul Vance] [ASC] (8/8/60 BCR-60)
NO Bulldog—Decca 32996 [Billy Hocher/John Turi] [ASC] (10/14/72 BCR-44)
NO ARMS CAN EVER HOLD YOU (LIKE THESE ARMS OF MINE) *Georgie Shaw—Decca 29679*
[Art Crafer/Jimmy Nebb] [BMI] (9/26/55 BCtRt-11)
NO OTHER ARMS *Pat Boone—Dot 15422*
[Art Crafer/Jimmy Nebb] [BMI] (9/26/55 BCtRt-11)
NO ARMS CAN EVER HOLD YOU (LIKE THESE ARMS OF MINE)
The Gaylords—Mercury 70706
[Art Crafer/Jimmy Nebb] [BMI] (10/3/55 BCtRt-11)
NO ARMS CAN EVER HOLD YOU
Jimmy Young with Bob Sharples & His Music—London 1609
[Art Crafer/Jimmy Nebb] [BMI] (10/17/55 Rt-17)
NO ARMS CAN EVER HOLD YOU *The Bachelors—London 9724*
[Art Crafer/Jimmy Nebb] [BMI] (12/26/64 BCR-26)
NO ARMS CAN EVER HOLD YOU *Bobby Vinton—Epic 10629*
[Art Crafer/Jimmy Nebb] [BMI] (7/4/70 BCR-58)
NO BIG DEAL Love and Rockets—Big Time 9045
[Daniel Ash/David Haskins/Kevin Haskins] [BMI] (9/23/89 BC-82)
NO CHANCE Moon Martin—Capitol 4794 [Moon Martin] [BMI] (11/3/79 BCR-50)
NO CHARGE *Melba Montgomery—Elektra 45883*
[Harlan Howard] [BMI] (3/30/74 BCR-39)
NO CHARGE *Shirley Caesar—Hob/Scepter 12402*
[Harlan Howard] [BMI] (5/17/75 BC-91)
NO CHEMISE PLEASE Gerry Granahan—Sunbeam 102
[Jodi D'Amour/Arnie Goland/Gerry Granahan] [BMI] (6/2/58 BCR-14)
NO EASY WAY OUT Robert Tepper—Scotti Brothers 05750
[Robert Tepper] [ASC] (1/25/86 BC-22)
NO FAIR AT ALL The Association—Valiant 758 [Jim Yester] [BMI] (2/4/67 BCR-51)
NO FAITH, NO LOVE Mitty Collier—Chess 1918
[Leonard Caston/Billy Davis] [BMI] (1/9/65 BCR-72)
NO FRILLS LOVE Jennifer Holliday—Geffen 28845
[Arthur Baker/Tina Baker/Gary Henry] [BMI] (2/8/86 B-87)
NO GOOD TO CRY *The Wildweeds—Cadet 5561 [Al Anderson] [BMI] (5/13/67 BCR-85)*
NO GOOD TO CRY *The Poppy Family—London 164*
[Al Anderson] [BMI] (12/11/71 BCR-80)
NO IF'S NO AND'S Lloyd Price And His Orchestra—ABC-Paramount 10102
[Harold Logan/Lloyd Price] [BMI] (4/23/60 BCR-36)
NO LETTER TODAY Les Paul and Mary Ford—Capitol 3108
[Ted Daffan] [BMI] (5/9/55 CR-27)
NO LOOKIN' BACK Michael McDonald—Warner Bros. 28960
[Kenny Loggins/Michael McDonald/Ed Sanford] [ASC] (7/27/85 BC-31)
NO LOVE AT ALL B.J. Thomas—Scepter 12307
[Johnny Christopher/Wayne Carson Thompson] [BMI] (2/20/71 BCR-14)
NO LOVE (BUT YOUR LOVE) Johnny Mathis—Columbia 41060
[Billy Myles] [BMI] (12/2/57 BCR-26)
NO LOVE HAVE I Webb Pierce—Decca 31021 [Mel Tillis] [BMI] (12/14/59 BCR-40)
NO LOVE IN THE ROOM The 5th Dimension—Arista 0101
[Patrick J. McManus/Lefty Pedroski] [ASC] (2/22/75 C-99)
NO MAN IS AN ISLAND Don Cornell—Coral 61253
[Ted Lehrman/Phil Sheer] [ASC] (11/22/54 CR-21)
NO MAN IS AN ISLAND The Van Dykes (2)—Mala 520
[Rondalis Tandy] [BMI] (3/19/66 BC-94)
NO MATTER WHAT Badfinger—Apple 1822 [Pete Ham] [ASC] (10/17/70 BCR-4)
NO MATTER WHAT George LaMond—Columbia 73603
[Ann Godwin/Larry Lange] [ASC] (12/1/90 BC-42)
NO MATTER WHAT SHAPE (YOUR STOMACH'S IN) The T-Bones—Liberty 55836
[Sascha Burland] [BMI] (12/4/65 BCR-3) [I]
NO MATTER WHAT SIGN YOU ARE Diana Ross And The Supremes—Motown 1148
[Henry Cosby/Berry Gordy] [ASC] (5/24/69 BCR-25)
NO MILK TODAY Herman's Hermits—MGM 13681
[Graham Gouldman] [BMI] (2/18/67 BCR-29)
NO MORE *The DeJohn Sisters—Epic 9085*
[Dux DeJohn/Julie DeJohn/Leo DeJohn] [BMI] (12/13/54 BCtRt-7)
NO MORE *The McGuire Sisters—Coral 61323*
[Dux DeJohn/Julie DeJohn/Leo DeJohn] [BMI] (12/20/54 BCtRt-7)
NO MORE *Guy Lombardo & His Royal Canadians—Decca 29381*
[Leo DeJohn] [BMI] (12/27/54 Rt-PRE) [IM]
NO MORE "I LOVE YOU'S" The Lover Speaks—A&M 2846
[David Freeman/Joseph Hughes] [BMI] (9/6/86 C-88)
NO MORE LIES Michel'le—Ruthless 7-99149
[Larry Goodman/Michel'le Toussant/Andre Romell Young] [ASC] (11/18/89 BC-7)
NO MORE LONELY NIGHTS Paul McCartney—Columbia 04581
[Paul McCartney] [ASC] (10/13/84 BC-6)
—NO MORE LOVE ON THE RUN see: CARIBBEAN QUEEN
NO MORE MR. NICE GUY Alice Cooper—Warner Bros. 7691
[Michael Bruce/Alice Cooper] [BMI] (4/7/73 BCR-19)
NO MORE RHYME Debbie Gibson—Atlantic 88885
[Debbie Gibson] [ASC] (6/17/89 BC-17)
NO MORE TEARS Ozzy Osbourne—Epic 73973
[Ozzy Osbourne/John Purdell/Zakk Wylde] [ASC] (11/30/91 B-71)
NO MORE TEARS (ENOUGH IS ENOUGH)
Barbra Streisand/Donna Summer—Columbia 11125
[Paul Jabara/Bruce Roberts] [BMI] (10/20/79 BCR-1)
NO MORE WORDS Berlin—Geffen 29360 [John Crawford] [BMI] (3/10/84 BC-16)
NO MYTH Michael Penn—RCA 9111 [Michael Penn] [BMI] (1/6/90 BC-13)
NO NIGHT SO LONG Dionne Warwick—Arista 0527
[Will Jennings/Richard Kerr] [BMI] (7/26/80 BCR-23)
NO, NO Fats Domino—Imperial 5515
[Dave Bartholomew/Fats Domino] [BMI] (5/5/58 B-55)
(NO, NO) I'M LOSING YOU Aretha Franklin—Columbia 43333
[Joy Byers Johnston] [ASC] (7/17/65 C-100)

NO, NO, JOE Silver Convention–Midland Int'l 10723
[Sylvester Levay/Stephan Prager] [BMI] (8/7/76 BCR-60)

NO, NO, NO The Chanters–DeLuxe 6191 [Bud Johnson Jr.] [BMI] (6/19/61 BCR-41)

NO NO SONG Ringo Starr–Apple 1880
[Hoyt Axton/David P. Jackson] (TSW) [BMI] (2/8/75 BCR-1)

***NO NOT MUCH** The Four Lads–Columbia 40629*
[Robert Allen/Al Stillman] [ASC] (1/20/56 BCR-3)

***NO NOT MUCH** The Smoke Ring–Buddah 77*
[Robert Allen/Al Stillman] [ASC] (1/25/69 BCR-58)

***NO, NOT MUCH** The Vogues–Reprise 0803*
[Robert Allen/Al Stillman] [ASC] (3/1/69 BCR-29)

***NO ONE** Connie Francis–MGM 12971*
[Doc Pomus/Mort Shuman] [BMI] (1/16/61 BCR-34)

***NO ONE** Ray Charles With The Raeletts–ABC-Paramount 10453*
[Doc Pomus/Mort Shuman] [BMI] (6/22/63 BCR-21)

***NO ONE** Brenda Lee–Decca 31792 [Doc Pomus/Mort Shuman] [BMI] (5/22/65 BC-95)*

NO ONE BETTER THAN YOU Petula Clark–Warner Bros.-Seven Arts 7343
[Clive Westlake] [BMI] (11/15/69 BCR-83)

NO ONE BUT YOU Charlie Applewhite–Decca 29125
[Nicholas Brodszky/Jack Lawrence] [ASC] (8/7/54 C-46)

NO ONE BUT YOU (IN MY HEART) The Ames Brothers–RCA Victor 47-7315
[Robert Mellin/Otto Riedlmayer] [BMI] (9/8/58 BCR-34) [FDE]

NO ONE (CAN EVER TAKE YOUR PLACE) Sam Cooke–Keen 82111
[Sam Cooke] [BMI] (1/18/60 R-95)

NO ONE CAN LOVE YOU MORE THAN ME Melissa Manchester–Arista 1-9087
[Terry Britten/Billy Livsey] [ASC] (10/29/83 B-78)

NO ONE CAN MAKE MY SUNSHINE SMILE The Everly Brothers–Warner Bros. 5297
[Gerry Goffin/Jack Keller] [BMI] (11/3/62 R-68)

NO ONE FOR ME TO TURN TO Spiral Starecase–Columbia 44924
[Pat Upton] [BMI] (8/16/69 BCR-37)

NO ONE HAS TO CRY The Fixx–Impact 54106
[Dan Brown/Cy Curnin/Scott Cutler] [ASC] (8/24/91 C-85)

NO ONE IN THE WORLD Anita Baker–Elektra 69456
[Ken Hirsch/Marti Sharron] [BMI] (8/22/87 BC-44)

NO ONE IS TO BLAME Howard Jones–Elektra 69549 [Howard Jones] [BMI] (4/5/86 BC-3)

NO ONE KNOWS Dion and The Belmonts–Laurie 3015
[Ken Hecht/Ernie Maresca] [ASC] (8/11/58 BCR-15)

NO ONE KNOWS Every Mother's Son–MGM 13887
[Ritchie Adams/Wes Farrell/Larry Kusik] [BMI] (1/27/68 BR-95)

NO ONE LIKE YOU Scorpions–Mercury 76153
[Klaus Meine/Rudolf Schenker] [ASC] (6/12/82 BC-65)

NO ONE TO CRY TO Ray Charles–ABC-Paramount 10571
[Sid Robin/Foy Willing] [ASC] (7/18/64 BCR-53)

NO ONE TO DEPEND ON Santana–Columbia 45552
[Michael Carabello/Coke Escovedo/Gregg Rolie] [BMI] (2/5/72 BCR-17)

NO ONE WILL EVER KNOW Jimmie Rodgers–Dot 16378
[Mel Foree/Fred Rose] [ASC] (8/25/62 BCR-43)

***NO OTHER ARMS NO OTHER LIPS** The Chordettes–Cadence 1361*
[Alex Kramer/Joan Whitney/Hy Zaret] [ASC] (2/23/59 BCtRt-22)

***NO OTHER ARMS NO OTHER LIPS** Four Aces–Decca 30822*
[Alex Kramer/Joan Whitney/Hy Zaret] [ASC] (2/28/59 BCtRt-26)

—NO OTHER ARMS see: NO ARMS CAN EVER...

NO OTHER ONE Eddie Fisher–RCA Victor 47-6470
[Ivory Joe Hunter/Clyde Otis] [BMI] (3/23/56 BCR-29)

NO PARKING (ON THE DANCE FLOOR) Midnight Star–Solar 69753
[Vincent Calloway/Bobby Lovelace/Bill Simmons] [BMI] (3/3/84 B-81)

NO PARTICULAR PLACE TO GO Chuck Berry–Chess 1898
[Chuck Berry] [BMI] (5/23/64 BCR-6)

NO PITY (IN THE NAKED CITY) Jackie Wilson–Brunswick 55280
[Johnnie B. Roberts/Alonzo Tucker/Jackie Wilson] [BMI] (6/19/65 BCR-54)

NO PROMISES Icehouse–Chrysalis 42978
[Iva Davies/Robert Kretschmer] [ASC] (7/5/86 BC-79)

NO REBATE ON LOVE The Dramatics–Mainstream 5571
[Jimmie Abston/Stella Petty] [BMI] (11/15/75 R-96)

NO REGRETS Jimmy Barnes–Gibraltar 101 [Otis Blackwell] [BMI] (3/9/59 B-90)

NO REPLY Stars On 45–Radio 3810
[John Lennon/Paul McCartney] (Med) [ASC] (4/11/81 BCR-1)

NO REPLY AT ALL Genesis–Atlantic 3858
[Tony Banks/Phil Collins/Mike Rutherford] [ASC] (9/26/81 BCR-28)

NO RETURN Megan McDonough–Wooden Nickel 73-0112
[Barry Fasman/Megan McDonough] [NA] (4/28/73 R-91)

NO ROCK 'N ROLL TONIGHT Dorothy Collins–Coral 61669
[Jerry Graziano] [BMI] (7/20/56 R-85)

NO SAD SONG Helen Reddy–Capitol 3231
[Carole King/Toni Stern] [ASC] (11/27/71 BCR-50)

NO SAD SONGS Joe Simon–Sound Stage 7 2602
[Darryl Carter] [BMI] (12/30/67 BCR-48)

NO SIGNS OF LONELINESS HERE Marty Robbins–Columbia 42781
[Lee Emerson] [BMI] (5/18/63 R-87)

NO SON OF MINE Genesis–Atlantic 87571
[Tony Banks/Phil Collins/Mike Rutherford] [BMI] (11/2/91 BC-6)

NO SOUVENIRS Melissa Etheridge–Island 99176
[Melissa Etheridge] [ASC] (11/4/89 B-95)

—NO STATIC AT ALL see: FM

NO SUBSTITUTE FOR LOVE Roy Hamilton–Epic 9449
[William S. Cook] [BMI] (7/15/61 C-81)

NO SUGAR TONIGHT The Guess Who–RCA Victor 74-0325
[Randy Bachman] (TSW) [BMI] (3/21/70 BCR-1)

NO TELL LOVER Chicago–Columbia 10879
[Peter Cetera/Lee Loughnane/Danny Seraphine] [ASC] (12/23/78 BCR-14)

NO TIME The Guess Who–RCA Victor 74-0300
[Randy Bachman/Burton Cummings] [BMI] (12/13/69 BCR-3)

NO TIME FOR TALK Christopher Cross–Warner Bros. 29662
[Christopher Cross] [ASC] (4/30/83 BC-33)

NO TIME LIKE THE RIGHT TIME The Blues Project–Verve Folkways 5040
[Al Kooper] [BMI] (4/1/67 BCR-66)

***NO TIME TO LOSE** The Tarney/Spencer Band–A&M 2124*
[Trevor Spencer/Alan Tarney] [BMI] (5/19/79 BCR-66)

***NO TIME TO LOSE** The Tarney/Spencer Band–A&M 2366*
[Trevor Spencer/Alan Tarney] [BMI] (9/12/81 BCR-68)

NO WAY OUT Jefferson Starship–Grunt 13811
[Ina Wolf/Peter F. Wolf] [BMI] (5/12/84 BC-23)

NO WHEELS The Chordettes–Cadence 1366
[Nancy Lee/Bobby Stevenson] [BMI] (8/29/59 C-92)

***NOBODY** Perry Como–RCA Victor 47-6059*
[Alex Rogers/Bert A. Williams] [NA] (3/14/55 CRt-15)

***NOBODY** Bing Crosby–Decca 29493 [Alex Rogers/Bert A. Williams] [NA] (4/18/55 Rt-17)*

NOBODY Three Dog Night–Dunhill 4168
[Dick Cooper/Ernie Shelby] [BMI] (11/23/68 CR-72)

NOBODY The Doobie Brothers–Warner Bros. 8041
[Tom Johnston] [BMI] (10/26/74 BCR-51)

NOBODY Doucette–Mushroom 7042 [Jerry Doucette/Duris Maxwell] [SO] (7/14/79 C-91)

NOBODY Sylvia (2)–RCA 13223 [Kye Fleming/Dennis W. Morgan] [BMI] (8/21/82 BC-9)

NOBODY BUT ME The Human Beinz–Capitol 5990
[O'Kelly Isley/Ronald Isley/Rudolph Isley] [ASC] (11/4/67 BCR-5)

NOBODY BUT YOU Dee Clark–Abner 1019 [Dee Clark] [ASC] (11/10/58 BCR-21)

NOBODY BUT YOU The Lafayettes–RCA Victor 47-8044
[Frank Bonarrigo/Lee Bonner] [BMI] (6/9/62 R-93)

NOBODY BUT YOU Kenny Loggins With Jim Messina–Columbia 45617
[Jim Messina] [ASC] (6/10/72 BCR-70)

NOBODY BUT YOU BABE Clarence Reid–Alston 4574
[Willie Clarke/Clarence Reid] [BMI] (7/26/69 BCR-32)

NOBODY CARES (ABOUT ME) Jeanette (Baby) Washington–Neptune 122
[Jeanette Washington] [BMI] (4/24/61 BCR-60)

NOBODY DOES IT BETTER Carly Simon–Elektra 45413
[Marvin Hamlisch/Carole Bayer Sager] [ASC] (7/23/77 BCR-2)

NOBODY I KNOW Peter And Gordon–Capitol 5211
[John Lennon/Paul McCartney] [ASC] (6/27/64 BCR-12)

NOBODY KNOWS WHAT'S GOIN' ON (IN MY MIND BUT ME) The Chiffons–Laurie 3301
[Stephen Friedland] [BMI] (6/19/65 BCR-46)

***NOBODY KNOWS YOU WHEN YOU'RE DOWN AND OUT** Nina Simone–Colpix 158*
[Jimmie Cox] [ASC] (9/5/60 B-93)

***NOBODY WANTS YOU WHEN YOU'RE DOWN AND OUT** Bobby Womack–United Artists 255*
[Jimmie Cox] [ASC] (6/9/73 BCR-29)

NOBODY LOVES ME LIKE YOU The Flamingos–End 1068
[Sam Cooke] [BMI] (4/9/60 BCR-30)

NOBODY SAID IT WAS EASY (LOOKIN' FOR THE LIGHTS) Le Roux–RCA 13059
[Tony Haselden] [BMI] (2/13/82 BCR-18)

NOBODY (TELLIN' ME 'BOUT MY BABY)
Charles Wright And The Watts 103rd Street Rhythm Band–Warner Bros. 7504
[Grady Esked/Charles Wright] [ASC] (7/24/71 C-81)

NOBODY TOLD ME John Lennon–Polydor 817254 [John Lennon] [GL] (1/21/84 BC-5)

—NOBODY WANTS YOU WHEN YOU'RE DOWN AND OUT see: NOBODY KNOWS YOU...

NOBODY WINS Brenda Lee–MCA 40003
[Kris Kristofferson] [BMI] (3/24/73 BCR-70)

NOBODY WINS Elton John–Geffen 49722
[Jean-Paul Dreau/Gary Osborne] [ASC] (5/9/81 BCR-21)

NOBODY'S BABY AGAIN Dean Martin–Reprise 0516
[Baker Knight] [BMI] (10/1/66 BCR-52)

NOBODY'S FOOL Cinderella–Mercury 884851 [Tom Keifer] [ASC] (11/8/86 BC-13)

NOBODY'S FOOL Kenny Loggins–Columbia 07971
[Kenny Loggins/Mike Towers] [BMI] (7/9/88 BC-8)

NOBODY'S PERFECT Mike + The Mechanics–Atlantic 88990
[Brian A. Robertson/Mike Rutherford] [BMI] (11/5/88 BC-58)

***NOBODY'S SWEETHEART** Jerry Cooper with The Johnny Guarnieri Swingtet–Anchor 26*
[Ernie Erdman/Gus Kahn/Billy Meyers/Elmer Schoebel] [ASC] (1/10/55 Rt-77)

***NOBODY'S SWEETHEART** Johnnie Ray–Columbia 40392*
[Ernie Erdman/Gus Kahn/Billy Meyers/Elmer Schoebel] [ASC] (1/10/55 Rt-77)

NOLA *Billy Williams—Coral 62069*
[Felix Arndt/Nola Arndt/Sunny Skylar] [ASC] (1/12/59 BCtRt-27)

NOLA *The Morgan Brothers—MGM 12747*
[Felix Arndt/Nola Arndt/Sunny Skylar] [ASC] (1/12/59 BCtRt-27)

NON DIMENTICAR (DON'T FORGET) Nat "King" Cole—Capitol 4056
[Shelley Dobbins/Michele Galdieri/Gino Redi] [BMI] (9/29/58 BCR-10) [F,FET]

—NON PENSARE A ME see: TIME ALONE WILL TELL

NORMA JEAN WANTS TO BE A MOVIE STAR Sundown Company—Polydor 14312
[John Collins Cunningham] [ASC] (5/8/76 BC-84)

NORMAN Sue Thompson—Hickory 1159 [John D. Loudermilk] [BMI] (12/4/61 BCR-3)

NORTH TO ALASKA Johnny Horton—Columbia 41782
[Mike Phillips] [ASC] (9/12/60 BCR-4)

—NOT ANOTHER LONELY NIGHT see: WITHOUT YOU

NOT AS A STRANGER Tony Bennett with Percy Faith and His Orchestra—
Columbia 40311 [John Schroeder/Abner Silver] [ASC] (10/4/54 R-PRE)

NOT AS A STRANGER The McGuire Sisters—Coral 61258
[Lawrence Elow/Linda Roberts/Phyllis Taff*] [ASC] (10/4/54 R-PRE)

NOT AS A STRANGER *Frank Sinatra—Capitol 3130*
[Buddy Kaye/Jimmy Van Heusen] [ASC] (6/6/55 CRt-27)

NOT AS A STRANGER *Henri René & His Orchestra—RCA Victor 47-6159*
[Buddy Kaye/Jimmy Van Heusen] [ASC] (8/8/55 Rt-47)

NOT ENOUGH INDIANS Dean Martin—Reprise 0780
[Baker Knight] [BMI] (10/26/68 BCR-42)

NOT ENOUGH LOVE IN THE WORLD Don Henley—Geffen 29012
[Don Henley/Danny Kortchmar/Benmont Tench] [ASC] (5/25/85 BC-29)

NOT FADE AWAY *The Rolling Stones—London 9657*
[Buddy Holly/Norman Petty] [ASC] (5/2/64 BCR-44)

NOT FADE AWAY *Tanya Tucker—MCA 40976*
[Buddy Holly/Norman Petty] [ASC] (12/30/78 BCR-70)

NOT FADE AWAY *Eric Hine—Montage 1200*
[Buddy Holly/Norman Petty] [ASC] (8/22/81 BC-73)

NOT FOR ALL THE MONEY IN THE WORLD The Shirelles—Scepter 1248
[Ronald Alonzo Miller/Lee Porter] [ASC] (4/13/63 B-100)

NOT JUST ANOTHER GIRL Ivan Neville—Polydor 887814
[Ivan Neville] [BMI] (10/1/88 BC-26)

(NOT JUST) KNEE DEEP - PART 1 Funkadelic—Warner Bros. 49040
[George Clinton/Philippe Wynn] [BMI] (9/8/79 BCR-45)

NOT ME The Orlons—Cameo 257 [Gary Anderson/Frank Guida] [BMI] (6/8/63 BCR-12)

NOT ON THE OUTSIDE The Moments (2)—Stang 5000
[Larry Roberts/Sylvia Robinson] [BMI] (12/21/68 BCR-42)

NOT ONE GOODBYE Jaye P. Morgan—RCA Victor 47-6329
[Redd Evans/Philip Springer] [ASC] (12/24/55 BR-48)

NOT ONE MINUTE MORE Della Reese—RCA Victor 47-7644
[Hal Blair/Lou Dinning/Don Robertson] [ASC] (11/30/59 BCR-15)

NOT RESPONSIBLE Tom Jones—Parrot 40006 [Gordon Mills] [BMI] (6/18/66 BCR-58)

NOT SO SWEET MARTHA LORRAINE Country Joe And The Fish—Vanguard 35052
[Joe McDonald] [BMI] (8/5/67 B-95)

NOT THE LOVIN' KIND Dino, Desi & Billy—Reprise 0401
[Lee Hazlewood] [ASC] (9/18/65 BCR-23)

NOT TOO LONG AGO The Uniques Featuring Joe Stampley—Paula 219
[Merle Kilgore/Joe Stampley] [BMI] (2/27/65 BCR-62)

NOT TOO YOUNG TO GET MARRIED Bob B. Soxx And The Blue Jeans—Philles 113
[Jeff Barry/Ellie Greenwich/Phil Spector] [BMI] (6/1/63 BCR-61)

NOT WRONG LONG Nazz—SGC 006 [Todd Rundgren] [BMI] (4/12/69 CR-97)

NOT YET Susan Hunter—Decca 29512
[Milton Berle/Elaine Mazlish/Robert Mellin] [BMI] (5/14/55 CR-22)

NOTHIN' AT ALL Heart—Capitol 5572
[Mark Mueller] [ASC] (4/19/86 BC-10)

NOTHIN' BUT A GOOD TIME Poison—Enigma 44145
[Bobby Dall/C.C. DeVille/Bret Michaels/Rikki Rockett] [BMI] (4/23/88 BC-6)

NOTHIN' HEAVY David Bellamy—Warner/Curb 8123
[David Bellamy] [ASC] (9/20/75 BC-77)

NOTHIN' SHAKIN Eddie Fontaine—Argo 5309
[Cirino Colacrai/Eddie Fontaine/John Gluck/Diane Lampert] [BMI] (9/22/58 B-64)

NOTHIN (THAT COMPARES 2 U) Jacksons—Epic 68688
[Kenneth Edmonds/Antonio Reid] [BMI] (6/3/89 BC-72)

NOTHIN' TO HIDE Poco—RCA 9131 [Bruce Gaitsch/Richard Marx] [ASC] (12/2/89 B-39)

NOTHING BUT A BREEZE Jesse Winchester—Bearsville 0318
[Jesse Winchester] [ASC] (8/6/77 BCR-72)

NOTHING BUT A HEARTACHE The Flirtations—Deram 85038
[Wayne Bickerton/Tony Waddington] [ASC] (3/8/69 BCR-25)

NOTHING BUT GOOD Hank Ballard And The Midnighters—King 5535
[Hank Ballard] [BMI] (8/21/61 B-49)

NOTHING BUT HEARTACHES The Supremes—Motown 1080
[Lamont Dozier/Brian Holland/Eddie Holland] [BMI] (7/31/65 BCR-8)

NOTHING CAN CHANGE THIS LOVE Sam Cooke—RCA Victor 47-8088
[Sam Cooke] [BMI] (9/29/62 BCR-12)

NOTHING CAN STOP ME Gene Chandler—Constellation 149
[Curtis Mayfield] [BMI] (4/10/65 BCR-18)

NOTHING TAKES THE PLACE OF YOU *Toussaint McCall—Ronn 3*
[Toussaint McCall/Patrick Robinson] [BMI] (3/25/67 BCR-33)*

NOTHING CAN TAKE THE PLACE OF YOU *Brook Benton—Cotillion 44034*
[Toussaint McCall/Patrick Robinson] [BMI] (6/28/69 BCR-61)*

NOTHING COMPARES 2 U Sinead O'Connor—Ensign/Chrysalis 23488
[Prince] [ASC] (3/17/90 BC-1)

NOTHING EVER CHANGES MY LOVE FOR YOU Nat "King" Cole—Capitol 3328
[Marvin Fisher/Jack Segal] [ASC] (1/27/56 BCR-21)

NOTHING EVER GOES AS PLANNED Styx—A&M 2348
[Dennis DeYoung] [ASC] (7/11/81 BCR-54)

NOTHING FROM NOTHING Billy Preston—A&M 1544
[Bruce Fisher/Billy Preston] [ASC] (7/13/74 BCR-1)

NOTHING GOES UP (WITHOUT COMING DOWN) Nat King Cole—Capitol 4919
[Larry Harrison/Clyde Otis/Jimmy Williams] [BMI] (3/2/63 BC-81)

NOTHING IN COMMON Thompson Twins—Arista 1-9511
[Tom Bailey/Alannah Currie] [ASC] (7/26/86 BC-47)

NOTHING IN THE WORLD Nat "King" Cole—Capitol 4004
[Brook Benton/Belford Hendricks/Clyde Otis] [BMI] (7/26/58 BC-51)

NOTHING IS TOO GOOD FOR YOU The Harvey Boys—Cadence 1306
[Johnny Brandon] [BMI] (3/9/57 B-84)

NOTHING NEW (SAME OLD THING) Fats Domino—Imperial 5863
[Dave Bartholomew/Fats Domino/Jack Jessup/Pee Wee Maddux] [BMI]
(6/30/62 BR-77)

NOTHING REMAINS THE SAME The Spinners—Atlantic 3798
[Michael Zager] (Med) [BMI] (2/14/81 BCR-52)

NOTHING SUCCEEDS LIKE SUCCESS Bill Deal & The Rhondels—Heritage 821
[Raymond Bloodworth/L. Russell Brown] [BMI] (3/14/70 BCR-60)

NOTHING TO HIDE Tommy James—Roulette 7114
[Tommy James/Robert L. King] [BMI] (11/20/71 BCR-24)

NOTHING WILL EVER CHANGE Joni James—MGM 12627
[Otis Blackwell/Jacqueline Burks] [BMI] (4/14/58 R-79)

NOTHING'S GONNA CHANGE MY LOVE FOR YOU Glenn Medeiros—Amherst 311
[Gerry Goffin/Michael Masser] [BMI] (2/14/87 BC-12)

NOTHING'S GONNA STOP ME NOW Samantha Fox—Jive 1072
[Matt Aitken/Mike Stock/Pete Waterman] [BMI] (10/10/87 BC-80)

NOTHING'S GONNA STOP US NOW Starship—Grunt 5109-7
[Albert Hammond/Diane Warren] [ASC] (1/31/87 BC-1)

NOTHING'S TOO GOOD FOR MY BABY Stevie Wonder—Tamla 54130
[Henry Cosby/Sylvia Moy/William Stevenson] [ASC] (4/16/66 BCR-20)

NOTICE ME Nikki—Geffen 19946 [Nikki Lee/Paul David Wilson] [ASC] (4/28/90 BC-18)

NOTORIOUS Duran Duran—Capitol 5648
[Simon Le Bon/Nick Rhodes/Nigel John Taylor] [ASC] (11/1/86 BC-2)

NOTORIOUS Loverboy—Columbia 07324
[Jon Bon Jovi/Todd Cerney/Paul Dean/Mike Reno/Richie Sambora] [ASC]
(8/22/87 BC-38)

NOVEMBER SNOW Rejoice!—Dunhill 4176 [Thomas Harold Brown] [ASC] (3/1/69 R-95)

NOW! Lena Horne—20th Century 449
[Betty Comden/Adolph Green/Jule Styne] [ASC] (11/16/63 BCR-58)

NOW AND FOR ALWAYS George Hamilton IV—ABC-Paramount 9898
[Roy Alfred] [ASC] (3/10/58 BCR-22)

NOW AND FOREVER Bert Kaempfert And His Orchestra—Decca 31279
[Milt Gabler/Bert Kaempfert] [BMI] (7/31/61 BCR-37) [IWM]

NOW AND FOREVER (YOU AND ME) Anne Murray—Capitol 5547
[David Foster/Randy Goodrum/Jim Vallance] [BMI] (3/1/86 B-92)

—NOW AND THEN THERE'S A FOOL SUCH AS I see: FOOL SUCH AS I

NOW I KNOW Jack Jones—Kapp 833
[Scott English/Stan Gelber/James Last/Harald Werner*] [BMI] (6/3/67 BCR-71)

NOW I'M A WOMAN Nancy Wilson—Capitol 2934
[Kenneth Gamble/Leon Huff] [BMI] (1/2/71 B-93)

NOW IS THE HOUR Gale Storm—Dot 15492
[Maewa Kaihan/Clement Scott/Dorothy Stewart] [ASC] (9/15/56 BC-50)

NOW IS THE TIME *The Paulette Sisters—Capitol 3211*
[Floyd Huddleston/Al Rinker] [ASC] (8/22/55 Rt-73)

NOW IS THE TIME *Eileen Rodgers—Columbia 40549*
[Floyd Huddleston/Al Rinker] [ASC] (8/22/55 Rt-73)

NOW IT'S MY TURN Berlin—Geffen 29283 [John Crawford] [BMI] (6/30/84 B-74)

NOW OR NEVER Axe—Atco 7408 [Bobby Barth] [BMI] (7/17/82 BC-56)

NOW RUN AND TELL THAT Denise LaSalle—Westbound 201
[Denise LaSalle] [BMI] (1/22/72 BCR-32)

NOW THAT SUMMER IS HERE The Videls—JDS 5005
[Pete Andreoli/Vini Poncia] [BMI] (8/8/60 R-86)

NOW THAT WE FOUND LOVE *Third World—Island 8663*
[Kenneth Gamble/Leon Huff] [BMI] (12/23/78 BCR-37)

NOW THAT WE FOUND LOVE *Heavy D & The Boyz—Uptown/MCA 54090*
[Kenneth Gamble/Leon Huff] [BMI] (6/29/91 BC-11)

NOW THAT YOU'VE GONE Connie Stevens—Warner Bros. 5610
[Hubert Ballay/Petula Clark/Norman Newell] [ASC] (4/24/65 BCR-53) [FET]

NOW YOU HAS JAZZ Bing Crosby and Louis Armstrong—Capitol 3506
[Cole Porter] [ASC] (8/25/56 BR-73)

NOW YOU KNOW Little Willie John—King 5516
[Sy Soloway/Shirley Wolfe] [BMI] (7/17/61 B-93)

NOW YOU'RE GONE Whitesnake—Geffen 19976
[David Coverdale/Adrian Vandenberg] [ASC] (6/2/90 BC-81)

NOW YOU'RE IN HEAVEN Julian Lennon—Atlantic 88925
[Julian Lennon/John McCurry] [ASC] (4/29/89 BC-72)

NOWHERE MAN *The Beatles—Capitol 5587*
[John Lennon/Paul McCartney] [ASC] (3/5/66 BCR-1)

NOWHERE MAN *Stars On 45—Radio 3810*
[John Lennon/Paul McCartney] (Med) [ASC] (4/11/81 BCR-1)

NOWHERE TO RUN Martha & The Vandellas—Gordy 7039
[Lamont Dozier/Brian Holland/Eddie Holland] [BMI] (2/27/65 BCR-6)

NOWHERE TO RUN Santana—Columbia 03376 [Russ Ballard] [ASC] (11/27/82 BC-66)

NUEVO LAREDO Les Paul and Mary Ford—Capitol 3329
[Bill Carey/Johnny Hicks/Jim Lowe/Marvin Moore] [BMI] (1/27/56 BR-88)

#9 DREAM John Lennon—Apple 1878 [John Lennon] [GL] (12/21/74 BCR-9)

NUMBER ONE Billy Swan—Monument 8697
[Billy Swan/Marlu Swan] [BMI] (5/22/76 CR-74)

NUMBER ONE Eloise Laws—ABC 12341 [Lolly Vegas/Pat Vegas] [BMI] (3/18/78 B-97)

#1 DEE JAY Goody Goody—Atlantic 3504
[Vincent Montana/Len Rocco/Bud Ross] [BMI] (10/28/78 BR-82)

NUMBER ONE MAN Bruce Channel—Smash 1752
[Bruce Channel/Margaret Cobb/Marvin Montgomery] [BMI] (4/9/62 BCR-34)

NUMBER ONE STREET (SIDES 1 & 2) Bob Corley—Stars 4773
[Bob Corley] [BMI] (11/19/55 B-95)

NUMBER WONDERFUL Rock Flowers—Wheel 0032
[L. Russell Brown/Irwin Levine] [BMI] (12/11/71 BCR-56)

NURSERY RHYMES (PART I) People's Choice—TSOP 4773
[Cary Gilbert/Leon Huff] [BMI] (1/31/76 BCR-78)

NUTBUSH CITY LIMITS *Ike & Tina Turner—United Artists 298*
[Tina Turner] [BMI] (8/25/73 BCR-22)

NUTBUSH CITY LIMITS *Bob Seger—Capitol 4269 [Tina Turner] [BMI] (6/5/76 BCR-69)*

NUT ROCKER *B. Bumble & The Stingers—Rendezvous 166*
[Kim Fowley/Pyotr Ilyich Tchaikovsky] [BMI] (2/12/62 BCtRt-20) [I]

NUT ROCKER *Jack B. Nimble & Quicks—Dot 16319*
[Kim Fowley/Pyotr Ilyich Tchaikovsky] [BMI] (2/12/62 CtRt-20) [I]

NUTROCKER *Emerson, Lake & Palmer—Cotillion 44151*
[Kim Fowley/Pyotr Ilyich Tchaikovsky] [BMI] (3/11/72 BCR-70) [I]

NOTHIN' FOR CHRISTMAS *Eartha Kitt—RCA Victor 47-6319*
[Roy C. Bennett/Sid Tepper] [ASC] (12/1/55 Rt-20)

NUTTIN' FOR CHRISTMAS *Joe Ward—King 4854*
[Roy C. Bennett/Sid Tepper] [ASC] (12/1/55 BCtRt-5)

NUTTIN' FOR CHRISTMAS
Art Mooney And His Orchestra, Vocal By Barry Gordon—MGM 12092
[Roy C. Bennett/Sid Tepper] [ASC] (12/1/55 BCtRt-5)

NUTTIN' FOR CHRISTMAS *Stan Freberg—Capitol 3280*
[Roy C. Bennett/Sid Tepper] [ASC] (12/1/55 BRt-20)

NUTTIN' FOR CHRISTMAS *The Fontane Sisters—Dot 15434*
[Roy C. Bennett/Sid Tepper] [ASC] (12/9/55 BRt-20)

NUTTIN' FOR CHRISTMAS *Ricky Zahnd And The Blue Jeaners—Columbia 40576*
[Roy C. Bennett/Sid Tepper] [ASC] (12/10/55 BCtRt-5)

NUTTIN' FOR CHRISTMAS *Kenny & Corky—Big Top 3031*
[Roy C. Bennett/Sid Tepper] [ASC] (12/21/59 CR-100)

N.Y., YOU GOT ME DANCING Andrea True Connection—Buddah 564
[Gregg Diamond] [ASC] (2/19/77 BCR-27)

O

—O' CANGACIERO see: BANDIT

O DIO MIO Annette—Buena Vista 354 [Al Hoffman/Dick Manning] [ASC] (2/8/60 BCR-10)

O FALLING STAR The Four Knights—Coral 62045
[Jody Cameron Malis] [BMI] (12/29/58 BCR-56)

O-H-I-O Ohio Players—Mercury 73932
[William Beck/Leroy Bonner/Marshall Jones/Ralph Middlebrooks/Andrew Noland/Marvin Pierce/James Rodger Williams] [BMI] (7/23/77 BCR-45) [I]

O-O-H CHILD The Five Stairsteps—Buddah 165
[Stan Vincent] (TSW) [BMI] (5/2/70 BCR-4)

O-O, I LOVE YOU The Dells—Cadet 5574 [Robert Eugene Miller] [BMI] (11/4/67 BCR-50)

O.P.P. Naughty By Nature—Tommy Boy 988
[Vincent Brown/Anthony Criss/Keir Gist/Berry Gordy/Fonce Mizell/Freddie Perren/Deke Richards] [ASC] (9/7/91 BC-6)

THE OAK TREE Morris Day—Warner Bros. 28899 [Morris Day] [ASC] (9/28/85 BC-65)

OB-LA-DI, OB-LA-DA *Arthur Conley—Atco 6640*
[John Lennon/Paul McCartney] [ASC] (12/28/68 BCR-46)

OB-LA-DI, OB-LA-DA *The Beatles—Capitol 4347*
[John Lennon/Paul McCartney] [ASC] (11/13/76 BCR-47)

THE OBJECT OF MY AFFECTION Pee Wee Hunt & His Orchestra—Capitol 3426
[Jimmie Grier/Coy Poe/Pinky Tomlin] [NA] (6/1/56 R-75)

OBJECT OF MY DESIRE Starpoint—Elektra 69621
[Kayode Adeyemo/Keith Diamond/Ernesto Phillips] [BMI] (9/28/85 BC-25)

OBSCENE PHONE CALLER Rockwell—Motown 1731
[Kennedy Gordy] [ASC] (5/5/84 BC-30)

OBSESSION Animotion—Mercury 880266
[Michael Des Barres/Holly Knight] [ASC] (1/26/85 BC-6)

THE OBVIOUS CHILD Paul Simon—Warner Bros. 19549
[Paul Simon] [BMI] (12/15/90 BC-78)

AN OCCASIONAL MAN *Jeri Southern—Decca 29647*
[Ralph Blane/Hugh Martin] [ASC] (9/24/55 BCRt-47)

AN OCCASIONAL MAN *Billy May & His Orchestra with Ella Mae Morse—Capitol 3210*
[Ralph Blane/Hugh Martin] [ASC] (10/17/55 Rt-77)

OCEAN OF THOUGHTS AND DREAMS The Dramatics—ABC 12331
[Don Davis/Eddie Robinson] [BMI] (4/15/78 C-89)

ODDS AND ENDS Dionne Warwick—Scepter 12256
[Burt Bacharach/Hal David] [ASC] (7/19/69 BCR-37)

ODE TO BILLIE JOE *Bobbie Gentry—Capitol 5950 [Bobbie Gentry] [ASC] (8/5/67 BCR-1)*

ODE TO BILLIE JOE *The Kingpins—Atco 6516*
[Bobbie Gentry] [ASC] (9/23/67 BCR-27) [IWM]

ODE TO BILLY JOE *Ray Bryant—Cadet 5575 [Bobbie Gentry] [ASC] (9/30/67 B-89) [IWM]*

ODE TO BILLIE JOE *Bobbie Gentry—Capitol 4294*
[Bobbie Gentry] [ASC] (7/17/76 BCR-54)

ODE TO BILLY JOE - MAIN TITLE *Bobbie Gentry—Warner Bros. 8210*
[Bobbie Gentry] [ASC] (7/31/76 BR-65)

ODE TO THE LITTLE BROWN SHACK OUT BACK Billy Edd Wheeler—Kapp 617
[Billy Edd Wheeler] [ASC] (12/26/64 BCR-50)

OF THIS I'M SURE Four Aces—Decca 29725
[Bennie Benjamin/Sol Marcus] [ASC] (11/19/55 BC-47)

OFF AND RUNNING Lesley Gore—Mercury 72580
[Carole Bayer Sager/Toni Wine] [BMI] (6/4/66 CR-94)

OFF ON YOUR OWN (GIRL) Al B. Sure!—Warner Bros. 27870
[Albert Joseph Brown/Kyle West] [ASC] (8/6/88 BC-45)

OFF THE WALL Michael Jackson—Epic 50838 [Rod Temperton] [ASC] (2/16/80 BCR-10)

OFF TO DUBLIN IN THE GREEN The Abbey Tavern Singers—HBR 498
[Dominic Behan/Traditional] [BMI] (9/10/66 BCR-68)

OH ATLANTA Little Feat—Warner Bros. 8566 [Bill Payne] [ASC] (5/6/78 C-92)

OH, BABE, WHAT WOULD YOU SAY? Hurricane Smith—Capitol 3383
[Hurricane Smith] [ASC] (11/18/72 BCR-1)

OH BABY Cathy Carr—Fraternity 750
[Bobby Lewis/Joseph L. Syracuse/Nat Tarnopol] [BMI] (10/13/56 R-60)

OH BABY Nite Rockers—RCA Victor 47-7323 [Robert Abdinoor] [BMI] (8/25/58 R-98)

OH BABY DOLL Chuck Berry—Chess 1664 [Chuck Berry] [BMI] (7/20/57 BCR-45)

OH BABY DON'T YOU WEEP (PART 1) James Brown And The Famous Flames—King 5842
[James Brown] [BMI] (1/25/64 BCR-23)

OH! BABY (WE GOT A GOOD THING GOIN') Barbara Lynn—Jamie 1277
[Barbara Lynn] [BMI] (6/20/64 BC-69)

OH BOY Buddy Holly / The Crickets—Brunswick 55035
[Norman Petty/Bill Tilghman/Sonny West] [BMI] (11/16/57 BCR-7)

OH CAROL Neil Sedaka—RCA Victor 47-7595
[Howard Greenfield/Neil Sedaka] [BMI] (9/28/59 BCR-5)

—OH COME ALL YE FAITHFUL see: ADESTE FIDELES

OH DADDY Adrian Belew—Atlantic 88904 [Adrian Belew] [ASC] (8/5/89 BC-58)

OH! DARLING Robin Gibb—RSO 907
[John Lennon/Paul McCartney] [ASC] (8/12/78 BCR-15)

OH FATHER Madonna—Sire 22723
[Madonna L. Ciccone/Patrick Raymond Leonard] [BMI] (11/4/89 BC-15)

OH GIRL *The Chi-Lites—Brunswick 55471 [Eugene Record] [BMI] (4/1/72 BCR-1)*

OH GIRL *Paul Young—Columbia 73377 [Eugene Record] [BMI] (7/14/90 BC-6)*

OH GIRL Boy Meets Girl—A&M 2713
[George Merrill/Shannon Rubicam] [BMI] (4/6/85 BC-32)

OH HAPPY DAY
Edwin Hawkins Singers Featuring: Dorothy Combs Morrison—Pavilion 20001
[Edwin Hawkins] [ASC] (4/26/69 BCR-2)

OH HAPPY DAY *Glen Campbell—Capitol 2787 [Edwin Hawkins] [ASC] (4/11/70 BCR-34)*

OH HONEY Delegation—Shady Brook 1048
[Michael Denne/Ken Gold] [BMI] (1/27/79 BCR-45)

OH HOW HAPPY *Shades Of Blue—Impact 1007 [Edwin Starr] [BMI] (4/30/66 BCR-8)*

OH HOW HAPPY *Blinky & Edwin Starr—Gordy 7090 [Edwin Starr] [BMI] (8/16/69 BCR-83)*

OH HOW HAPPY *The Skyliners—Tortoise Int'l 11243 [Edwin Starr] [BMI] (4/15/78 CR-89)*

OH HOW I MISS YOU TONIGHT Jeanne Black—Capitol 4492
[Joe Burke/Benny Davis/Mark Fisher] [ASC] (12/19/60 BCR-63)

OH, HOW IT HURTS Barbara Mason—Arctic 137
[Bernard Broomer/Barbara Mason] [BMI] (12/23/67 BCR-48)

OH JOHNNY OH *Kathy Linden—Felsted 8533 [Abe Olman/Ed Rose] [ASC] (7/14/58 Rt-84)*

OH JOHNNY! *Sparkley Betty Barkley—Keen 3-4020*
[Abe Olman/Ed Rose] [ASC] (7/14/58 Rt-84)

OH JOHNNY *Janie Grant—Caprice 113 [Abe Olman/Ed Rose] [ASC] (3/5/62 R-89)*

OH JULIE *The Crescendos—Nasco 6005 [Noel Ball/Ken Moffitt] [BMI] (12/16/57 BCRt-5)*

OH JULIE *Sammy Salvo—RCA Victor 47-7097*
[Noel Ball/Ken Moffitt] [BMI] (12/23/57 BRt-9)

OH JULIE *Otis Williams & His Charms—DeLuxe 6158*
[Noel Ball/Ken Moffitt] [BMI] (1/27/58 Rt-12)

OH JULIE Barry Manilow—Arista 0698 [Shakin' Stevens] [ASC] (7/31/82 BC-38)

OH LA DE DA The Staple Singers—Stax 0156 [Phillip Mitchell] [BMI] (3/3/73 BCR-33)

OH LITTLE ONE Jack Scott—Top Rank 2041 [Jack Scott] [BMI] (4/23/60 BCR-34)

OH LITTLE TOWN OF BETHLEHEM Elvis Presley—RCA Victor LOC-1035
[Phillips Brooks/Lewis Redner] (EP) [NA] (12/30/57 R-49)

OH LONESOME ME *Don Gibson—RCA Victor 47-7133*
[Don Gibson] [BMI] (2/22/58 BCRt-3)

OH LONESOME ME *Jackie Walker—Imperial 5490 [Don Gibson] [BMI] (2/24/58 Rt-32)*

OH! LONESOME ME *The Swallows—Federal 12319 [Don Gibson] [BMI] (4/7/58 Rt-4)*

OH LONESOME ME *Bob Luman—Warner Bros. 5184 [Don Gibson] [BMI] (12/12/60 R-85)*

OH LONESOME ME *Johnny Cash—Sun 355 [Don Gibson] [BMI] (12/31/60 BRt-74)*

OH! LOOK AT ME NOW The Modernaires—Coral 61779
[Joseph Bushkin/John DeVries] (Med) [ASC] (2/16/57 R-72)

OH LORD, WHY LORD Los Pop Tops—Calla 154
[Luis Angulo/Johann Pachelbel/Phil Trim] [BMI] (9/7/68 BCR-65)

(OH LORD WON'T YOU BUY ME A) MERCEDES BENZ Goose Creek Symphony—Capitol 3246
[Janis Joplin/Michael McClure/Bob Neuwirth] [ASC] (1/29/72 BCR-64)

OH LORI Alessi—A&M 1955 [Billy Alessi/Bobby Alessi] [BMI] (9/10/77 CR-84)

MA MA MA MARIE *The Gaylords—Mercury 71337*
[Harold Barlow/Eduardo di Capua/Emmanuele Mazzucchi/Ferdinando Russo] [ASC] (7/12/58 BCR-43)

OH MARIE *The Village Stompers—Epic 9718*
[Eduardo di Capua] [ASC] (10/17/64 R-82) [IM]

OH ME Fields-Madera Orchestra—Catalina 1000
[Sabu Evertez/Bobby Madera/Marcelina Valdes] [BMI] (4/13/59 R-88) [IWM]

OH ME, OH MY (DREAMS IN MY ARMS) Al Green—Hi 2288
[Al Green/Mabon Hodges/Willie Mitchell] [BMI] (6/28/75 BCR-40)

OH ME OH MY (I'M A FOOL FOR YOU BABY) *Lulu—Atco 6722*
[Jim Doris] [ASC] (12/13/69 BCR-17)

OH ME OH MY (I'M A FOOL FOR YOU BABY) *Aretha Franklin—Atlantic 2838*
[Jim Doris] [ASC] (1/8/72 BCR-60)

OH MEIN PAPA Dick Lee—Blue Bell 503
[Paul Burkhard/Geoffrey Parsons/John Turner] [ASC] (3/13/61 B-94) [FDE]

OH MY ANGEL Bertha Tillman—Brent 7029 [June Jackson] [BMI] (5/5/62 BCR-61)

OH MY GOODNESS The Kalin Twins—Decca 30807
[Harold Kalin/Herbie Kalin] [BMI] (1/5/59 R-78)

OH MY LORD Boney M—Sire 1036 [Frank Farian/Fred Jay] (Med) [ASC] (12/23/78 B-85)

OH! MY LOVE (KEEP YOUR DREAMS JUST FOR ME) June Valli—RCA Victor 47-6215
[Michael Carr/Frankie Russell] [NA] (8/1/55 R-80)

OH MY MARIA Eddie Fisher—RCA Victor 47-6615
[Sammy Cahn/Peter Herz/Hans Lang] [ASC] (9/8/56 B-80) [FET]

OH MY MY The Monkees—Colgems 5011 [Jeff Barry/Andy Kim] [BMI] (5/2/70 BC-94)

OH MY MY Ringo Starr—Apple 1872 [Vini Poncia/Ringo Starr] [BMI] (3/2/74 BCR-5)

OH NO Commodores—Motown 1527 [Lionel Richie] [ASC] (9/19/81 BCR-4)

OH NO NOT MY BABY *Maxine Brown—Wand 162*
[Gerry Goffin/Carole King] [BMI] (10/24/64 BCR-22)

OH NO, NOT MY BABY *Merry Clayton—Ode 66030*
[Gerry Goffin/Carole King] [BMI] (12/23/72 BCR-60)

OH! NO NOT MY BABY *Rod Stewart—Mercury 73426*
[Gerry Goffin/Carole King] [BMI] (10/6/73 BCR-56)

OH OH I'M FALLING IN LOVE AGAIN Jimmie Rodgers—Roulette 4045
[Luigi Creatore/Al Hoffman/Dick Manning/Hugo Peretti] [ASC] (1/27/58 BCR-8)

OH PAIN! OH AGONY! (KNOW WHAT I MEAN JELLY BEAN) Gisele MacKenzie—Vik 0274
[Jimmy Kennedy/Nat Simon] [ASC] (6/8/57 R-76)

OH, PEOPLE Patti LaBelle—MCA 52877
[Andy Goldmark/Bruce Roberts] [ASC] (7/19/86 BC-29)

OH, PRETTY WOMAN *Roy Orbison And The Candy Men—Monument 851*
[William Dees/Roy Orbison] [BMI] (8/29/64 BCR-1)

(OH) PRETTY WOMAN *Van Halen—Warner Bros. 50003*
[William Dees/Roy Orbison] [BMI] (2/6/82 BCR-10)

OH, ROCK MY SOUL (PART I) Peter, Paul & Mary—Warner Bros. 5442
[Traditional] [NA] (6/27/64 BR-93)

OH SHEILA Ready For The World—MCA 52636
[Melvin Riley/Gordon Strozier/Gerald Valentine] [BMI] (8/3/85 BC-1)

OH SHERRIE Steve Perry—Columbia 04391
[Bill Cuomo/Randy Goodrum/Craig Krampf/Steve Perry] [BMI] (4/7/84 BC-3)

OH, SINGER Jeannie C. Riley—Plantation 72
[Margaret Lewis/Mira Smith] [BMI] (3/27/71 BCR-54)

OH! SUSANNA
Don Charles presents the Singing Dogs, directed by Carl Weisman—RCA Victor 47-6344
[Stephen Foster] [NA] (12/10/55 B-37)

OH THAT'S GOOD, NO THAT'S BAD Sam The Sham And The Pharaohs—MGM 13713
[Dewayne Blackwell] [BMI] (3/18/67 BCR-50)

OH VERY YOUNG Cat Stevens—A&M 1503 [Cat Stevens] [ASC] (3/16/74 BCR-10)

OH WELL - PART I *Fleetwood Mac—Reprise 0883*
[Peter Green] [BMI] (1/31/70 BCR-55) [IWM]

OH WELL *The Rockets—RSO 935 [Peter Green] [BMI] (7/7/79 BCR-30)*

OH WHAT A DAY The Dells—Cadet 5663 [Michael McGill] [BMI] (1/17/70 BCR-36)

OH WHAT A FEELING The Everly Brothers—Cadence 1369
[Don Everly] [BMI] (8/17/59 CR-82)

OH WHAT A FOOL The Impalas—Cub 9033
[Harry Giosasi/Artie Zwirn] [BMI] (6/22/59 BCR-86)

OH, WHAT A NIGHT The Dells—Cadet 5649
[Johnny Funches/Marvin Junior] [BMI] (8/9/69 BCR-10)

OH WHAT A NIGHT FOR DANCING Barry White—20th Century 2365
[Barry White/Vance Wilson] [BMI] (4/22/78 BCR-23)

—OH WHAT A NIGHT see: DECEMBER, 1963

OH! WHAT IT SEEMED TO BE The Castells—Era 3083
[Bennie Benjamin/Frankie Carle/George David Weiss] [ASC] (8/25/62 B-91)

OH WHY The Teddy Bears—Imperial 5562 [Phil Spector] [BMI] (1/19/59 BCR-50)

OH WOMAN OH WHY Paul McCartney—Apple 1829
[Paul McCartney] (TSW) [ASC] (2/27/71 BCR-5)

OH YEAH Tommy Danton & The Echoes—Dot 15650
[Fred Coupland] [BMI] (11/18/57 Rt*-45)

OH YEAH The Shadows Of Knight—Dunwich 122 [Ellas McDaniel] [BMI] (6/4/66 BCR-39)

OH YEAH! The Joe Cuba Sextet—Tico 490 [Jaime Sabater] [BMI] (12/24/66 BCR-60)

OH YEAH Yello—Mercury 884930 [Boris Blank] [ASC] (8/8/87 BC-49) [IM]

—OH YOU CAN'T GET TO HEAVEN see: YOU CAN'T GET...

OHIO Crosby, Stills, Nash & Young—Atlantic 2740 [Neil Young] [BMI] (6/20/70 BCR-13)

OKEFENOKEE Freddy Cannon—Swan 4038
[Bob Crewe/Frank Slay] [BMI] (8/24/59 BCR-41)

OKIE FROM MUSKOGEE Merle Haggard—Capitol 2626
[Eddie Burris/Merle Haggard] [BMI] (11/1/69 BR-41)

OKLAHOMA SUNDAY MORNING Glen Campbell—Capitol 3254
[Albert Hammond/Mike Hazlewood/Tony Macaulay] [BMI] (1/15/72 R-95)

OKOLONA RIVER BOTTOM BAND Bobbie Gentry—Capitol 2044
[Bobbie Gentry] [ASC] (11/25/67 BCR-39)

OL' MAN RIVER *Bing Crosby And The Buddy Cole Trio—Decca 29850*
[Oscar Hammerstein/Jerome Kern] [ASC] (3/16/56 R-17)

OL' MAN RIVER *Earl Grant—Decca 30640*
[Oscar Hammerstein/Jerome Kern] [ASC] (6/23/58 R-56)

OL' MAN RIVER *Jimmy Smith—Verve 10262 [Jerome Kern] [ASC] (9/1/62 BCtRt-82) [IM]*

OL' MAN RIVER *Johnny Nash—Warner Bros. 5301*
[Oscar Hammerstein/Jerome Kern] [ASC] (9/22/62 CtRt-78)

THE OL' RACE TRACK The Mills Brothers—Dot 17162
[Don Christopher/Stan Gelber] [ASC] (11/2/68 BCR-77)

OLD BETSY (DAVY CROCKETT'S GUN)
The Voices Of Walter Schumann—RCA Victor 47-6125
[George Bruns/Gil George] [ASC] (5/23/55 Rt-42)

OLD BETSY (DAVY CROCKETT'S GUN) *The Sons Of The Pioneers—RCA Victor WBY 27*
[George Bruns/Gil George] [ASC] (5/23/55 Rt-65)

OLD BETSY (DAVY CROCKETT'S RIFLE) *Fess Parker & Buddy Ebsen—Columbia 40510*
[George Bruns/Gil George] [ASC] (5/23/55 Rt-42)

OLD BETSY *Burl Ives—Decca 29549 [George Bruns/Gil George] [ASC] (6/13/55 Rt-49)*

—OLD BLACK MAGIC see: THAT OLD BLACK MAGIC

OLD CAPE COD Patti Page—Mercury 71101
[Irwin Pincus/Claire Rothrock/Milton Yakus] [ASC] (5/20/57 BCR-7)

OLD DAYS Chicago—Columbia 10131 [James Pankow] [ASC] (4/26/75 BCR-5)

OLD ENOUGH TO LOVE Rick Nelson—Imperial 5935
[Al Jones/Bill Jones/Merle Kilgore] [BMI] (4/27/63 BC-86)

OLD-FASHION LOVE Commodores—Motown 1489
[Milan Williams] [ASC] (6/21/80 BCR-17)

OLD FASHIONED BOY (YOU'RE THE ONE) Stallion—Casablanca 877
[Wally Damrick] [BMI] (3/12/77 BCR-37)

OLD FASHIONED LOVE Smokey Robinson—Tamla 1615
[Gary Goetzman/Mike Piccirillo] [BMI] (4/17/82 BC-60)

AN OLD FASHIONED LOVE SONG Three Dog Night—Dunhill 4294
[Paul Williams] [ASC] (11/6/71 BCR-4)

OLD HOME FILLER-UP AN' KEEP ON-A-TRUCKIN' CAFE C.W. McCall—MGM 14738
[Chip Davis/Bill Fries] [SE] (6/29/74 BCR-52)

OLD LAMPLIGHTER The Browns Featuring Jim Edward Brown—RCA Victor 47-7700
[Nat Simon/Charles Tobias] [ASC] (3/12/60 BCR-5)

OLD MACDONALD *The Chargers—RCA Victor 47-7301*
[Jesse Belvin/JoAnn Belvin/Traditional] [NA] (9/1/58 BC-95)

OL' MAC DONALD *Frank Sinatra—Capitol 4466*
[Alan Bergman/Marilyn Bergman/Lew Spence/Traditional] [NA] (11/7/60 BCR-22)

OLD MAN Neil Young—Reprise 1084 [Neil Young] [ASC] (4/29/72 BCR-26)

THE OLD MAN DOWN THE ROAD John Fogerty—Warner Bros. 29100
[John Fogerty] [ASC] (12/22/84 BC-10)

OLD OAKEN BUCKET Tommy Sands—Capitol 4405 [Ervin Drake] [ASC] (8/8/60 BCR-57)

THE OLD PAYOLA ROLL BLUES (LIKE THE BEGINNING) Stan Freberg Featuring Jesse White—Capitol 4329 [Stan Freberg] [ASC] (2/29/60 B-99)

OLD PHILOSOPHER Eddie Lawrence—Coral 61671
[Eddie Lawrence] [BMI] (7/28/56 BCR-33)

OLD PIANO ROLL BLUES Johnny Maddox And The Rhythmasters—Dot 15365
[Cy Coben] (Med) [ASC] (5/28/55 C-43) [IWM]

OLD RIVERS Walter Brennan—Liberty 55436
[Cliff Crofford] [BMI] (4/2/62 BCR-5)

OLD SHEP *Elvis Presley—RCA Victor EPA-993 [Red Foley] [BMI] (12/29/56 B-47)*

OLD SHEP *Ralph DeMarco—Guaranteed 202 [Red Foley] [BMI] (11/2/59 BCR-56)*

OLD SHOES Frankie Laine—Columbia 40378
[Richard Adler/Jerry Ross] [ASC] (12/25/54 C-28)

OLD SLEW FOOT Johnny Horton—Columbia 42063
[Howard Hausey/Traditional/Jay Webb] [BMI] (8/7/61 R-77)

OLD SMOKIE *Johnny And The Hurricanes—Big Top 3076*
[Traditional] [BMI] (6/26/61 R-91) [I]

OLD SMOKEY LOCOMOTION *Little Eva—Dimension 1011*
[Gerry Goffin/Carole King/Traditional] [BMI] (5/18/63 BCR-42)

ON TOP OF SPAGHETTI *(parody of On Top Of Old Smokey)*
Tom Glazer And The Do-Re-Mi Children's Chorus—Kapp 526
[Tom Glazer/Traditional] [ASC] (6/1/63 BCR-11) [P]

THE OLD SONGS Barry Manilow—Arista 0633
[Buddy Kaye/David Pomeranz] [ASC] (10/10/81 BCR-15)

OLD SPANISH TOWN The Bell Notes—Time 1010
[Fred Johnson/Leroy Kirkland] [BMI] (4/27/59 BCR-48)

OLD TIME ROCK & ROLL *Bob Seger & The Silver Bullet Band—Capitol 4702*
[George Henry Jackson/Thomas Earl Jones III] [BMI] (4/7/79 BCR-28)

OLD TIME ROCK & ROLL *Bob Seger & The Silver Bullet Band—Capitol 5276*
[George Henry Jackson/Thomas Earl Jones III] [BMI] (9/17/83 BC-38)

OLE BUTTERMILK SKY Bill Black's Combo—Hi 2036
[Jack Brooks/Hoagy Carmichael] [ASC] (6/5/61 BCR-17) [IWM]

OLE MUMMER'S STRUT The Nu Tornados—Carlton 497
[Bill Borrelli/Danny DiMinno] [ASC] (1/26/59 CR-82)

OLE PAPPY TIME *Stuart Hamblen—RCA Victor 47-5918*
[Stuart Hamblen] [ASC] (12/25/54 Ct-29)

OLE PAPPY TIME *June Valli—RCA Victor 47-5924*
[Stuart Hamblen] [ASC] (12/25/54 Ct-23)

OLENA Don Nix—Elektra 45746 [Don Nix] [BMI] (10/9/71 BCR-91)

OLIVER COOL Oliver Cool—Roulette 4292
[Lee Pockriss/Paul Vance] [ASC] (10/24/60 R-88)

OLIVER TWIST Rod McKuen—Spiral 1407
[Rod McKuen/Gladys Shelley] [ASC] (1/20/62 BCR-59)

OLIVIA (LOST AND TURNED OUT) The Whispers—Solar 11353
[Malcolm Anthony] [ASC] (10/14/78 R-95)

OLYMPIA Sergio Mendes—A&M 2623 [Barry Mann/Cynthia Weil] [BMI] (4/7/84 BC-58)

OMAHA Moby Grape—Columbia 44173 [Skip Spence] [BMI] (7/8/67 BCR-70)

ON A CAROUSEL *The Hollies—Imperial 66231*
[Allan Clarke/Tony Hicks/Graham Nash] [BMI] (3/11/67 BCR-7)

ON A CAROUSEL *Glass Moon—Radio 4022*
[Allan Clarke/Tony Hicks/Graham Nash] [BMI] (3/13/82 BCR-50)

ON A CLEAR DAY YOU CAN SEE FOREVER Johnny Mathis—Mercury 72493
[Burton Lane/Alan Jay Lerner] [ASC] (12/18/65 B-98)

ON A NIGHT LIKE THIS Bob Dylan—Asylum 11033 [Bob Dylan] [SE] (2/16/74 BCR-30)

ON A SATURDAY NIGHT Eddie Floyd—Stax 233
[Steve Cropper/Eddie Floyd] [BMI] (10/21/67 BC-92)

ON A SUNDAY AFTERNOON A Lighter Shade Of Brown—Pump 15186
[Eddie Brigati/Felix Cavaliere/Ed Gray/Tommy James/Barrett Strong/Mike Vale/
Norman Whitfield] [BMI] (11/30/91 B-39)

ON AN EVENING IN ROMA Dean Martin—Capitol 4222
[Umberto Bertini/Nan Fredrics/Alessandro Taccani] [BMI] (6/1/59 BCR-27) [FET]

ON AND OFF (PART 1) Anacostia—Columbia 45685 [Van McCoy] [BMI] (12/9/72 BC-76)

ON AND ON Gladys Knight & The Pips—Buddah 423
[Curtis Mayfield] [BMI] (5/11/74 BCR-5)

ON AND ON Stephen Bishop—ABC 12260 [Stephen Bishop] [ASC] (5/7/77 BCR-5)

ON AND ON AND ON ABBA—Atlantic 3826
[Benny Andersson/Björn Ulvaeus] [BMI] (6/27/81 B-90)

ON BENDED KNEES Clarence Henry—Argo 5401
[Robert Guidry] [BMI] (10/23/61 BCR-64)

ON BROADWAY *The Drifters—Atlantic 2182*
[Jerry Leiber/Barry Mann/Mike Stoller/Cynthia Weil] [BMI] (3/16/63 BCR-9)

ON BROADWAY *George Benson—Warner Bros. 8542*
[Jerry Leiber/Barry Mann/Mike Stoller/Cynthia Weil] [BMI] (3/11/78 BCR-5)

ON CAMPUS Dickie Goodman—Cotique 158
[George Goldner*/Dickie Goodman/Bill Ramal] [BMI] (6/28/69 BCR-45)

ON LONDON BRIDGE Jo Stafford—Columbia 40782
[Roy C. Bennett/Sid Tepper] [ASC] (11/24/56 BCR-33)

ON MY OWN Patti LaBelle And Michael McDonald—MCA 52770
[Burt Bacharach/Carole Bayer Sager] [ASC] (3/22/86 BC-1)

—ON MY WAY TO SUNNY CALIFORN-I-A see: CALIFORNIA SAGA

ON MY WORD OF HONOR The Platters—Mercury 71011
[Claude Baum/Buck Ram] [BMI] (12/15/56 BCR-13)

ON OUR OWN Bobby Brown—MCA 53662
[Kenneth Edmonds/Antonio Reid/Daryl Simmons] [BMI] (6/10/89 BC-2)

ON THE ALAMO The Norman Petty Trio—"X" 0071
[Isham Jones/Gus Kahn] [ASC] (12/25/54 C-31)

ON THE BEACH *The Playmates—Roulette 4211*
[Steve Allen/Ernest Gold] [ASC] (12/28/59 Rt-90)

ON THE BEACH *Frank Chacksfield And His Orch.—London 1901*
[Ernest Gold] [ASC] (12/28/59 BCRt-47) [IM]

ON THE BEACH Southside Johnny & Asbury Jukes—Mercury 76074
[Billy Rush] [ASC] (8/2/80 C-92)

ON THE BEACH (IN THE SUMMERTIME) The 5th Dimension—Bell 913
[Landy McNeil] [BMI] (8/15/70 BCR-41)

ON THE BEAT B. B. & Q Band—Capitol 4993
[Mauro Malavasi/Paul Slade] [ASC] (9/19/81 R-86)

ON THE BORDER Al Stewart—Janus 267 [Al Stewart] [BMI] (4/23/77 BCR-39)

ON THE DARK SIDE *Eddie And The Cruisers—Scotti Brothers 04107*
[John Cafferty] [BMI] (10/8/83 BC-64)

ON THE DARK SIDE *John Cafferty And The Beaver Brown Band—Scotti Brothers 04594*
[John Cafferty] [BMI] (8/18/84 BC-7)

ON THE GOOD SHIP LOLLIPOP The Wonder Who ?—Philips 40380
[Sidney Clare/Richard Whiting] [ASC] (7/2/66 B-87)

ON THE LINE Tangier—Atco 99208 [Doug Gordon] [BMI] (8/12/89 BC-67)

ON THE LOOSE Saga—Portrait 37-03359
[Ian Stevenson Crichton/Jim Crichton/Jim Gilmour/Steve Negus/Michael Sadler] [ASC]
(12/4/82 BC-26)

ON THE OTHER SIDE The Seekers—Capitol 5974
[Gary Osborne/Bob Sage*/Tom Springfield] [ASC] (9/9/67 CR-69)

ON THE RADIO Donna Summer—Casablanca 2236
[Giorgio Moroder/Donna Summer] [ASC] (1/12/80 BCR-1)

ON THE REBOUND Floyd Cramer—RCA Victor 47-7840
[Floyd Cramer] [BMI] (3/4/61 BCR-4) [I]

ON THE REBOUND Russ Ballard—Epic 50883 [Russ Ballard] [ASC] (6/14/80 BCR-58)

ON THE ROAD AGAIN Canned Heat—Liberty 56038
[Tommy Johnson/Floyd Jones/Alan C. Wilson] [BMI] (8/3/68 BCR-9)

ON THE ROAD AGAIN Willie Nelson—Columbia 11351
[Willie Nelson] [BMI] (9/6/80 BCR-16)

ON THE SHELF Donny & Marie—Polydor/Kolob 14510
[Steve Voice/Peter Yellowstone] [ASC] (10/7/78 BCR-38)

ON THE STREET WHERE YOU LIVE *Vic Damone—Columbia 40654*
[Alan Jay Lerner/Frederick Loewe] [ASC] (4/21/56 BCRt-4)

ON THE STREET WHERE YOU LIVE *Eddie Fisher—RCA Victor 47-6529*
[Alan Jay Lerner/Frederick Loewe] [ASC] (5/25/56 BRt-4)

ON THE STREET WHERE YOU LIVE *Lawrence Welk And His Champagne Music—Coral 61644*
[Alan Jay Lerner/Frederick Loewe] [ASC] (6/1/56 BRt-4)

ON THE STREET WHERE YOU LIVE *Andy Williams—Columbia 43128*
[Alan Jay Lerner/Frederick Loewe] [ASC] (9/12/64 BCR-28)

ON THE STRIP Paul Nicholas—RSO 887
[Dominic Bugatti/Frank Musker] [BMI] (7/22/78 BC-67)

ON THE SUNNY SIDE OF THE STREET The Modernaires—Coral 61779
[Dorothy Fields/Jimmy McHugh] (Med) [ASC] (2/16/57 R-72)

ON THE WAY HOME The Buffalo Springfield—Atco 6615
[Neil Young] [BMI] (10/12/68 BC-82)

ON THE WAY OUT Walter Scott—Eagle 1003
[Robert I. Allen/Joseph Meyer] [ASC] (10/13/58 R-97)

ON THE WAY TO THE SKY Neil Diamond—Columbia 02712
[Neil Diamond/Carole Bayer Sager] [SE] (2/13/82 BCR-27)

ON THE WAY UP Elisa Fiorillo—Chrysalis 23497
[Elisa Fiorillo/Prince/David Rivkin/Levi Seacer] [BMI] (9/29/90 BC-27)

ON THE WINGS OF A NIGHTINGALE The Everly Brothers—Mercury 880213
[Paul McCartney] [ASC] (9/1/84 BC-47)

ON THE WINGS OF LOVE Jeffrey Osborne—A&M 2434
[Jeffrey Osborne/Peter Schless] [ASC] (9/25/82 BC-23)

ON THE WRONG TRACK Kevin Lamb—Arista 0316 [Kevin Lamb] [ASC] (6/17/78 BCR-71)

ON THIS SIDE OF GOODBYE The Righteous Brothers—Verve 10449
[Gerry Goffin/Carole King] [BMI] (10/22/66 BCR-45)

—ON TOP OF SPAGHETTI see: OLD SMOKEY

ON TREASURE ISLAND Gale Storm—Dot 15539
[Joe Burke/Edgar Leslie] [ASC] (3/16/57 B-74)

ONCE A DAY Connie Smith—RCA Victor 47-8416 [Bill Anderson] [BMI] (10/10/64 C-96)

ONCE A FOOL Kiki Dee—Rocket/MCA 40506
[Dennis Lambert/Brian Potter] [BMI] (3/6/76 BC-82)

ONCE A NIGHT Jackie English—Venture 135
[Beverly Bremers/Jackie English] [ASC] (12/20/80 B-94)

ONCE BITTEN TWICE SHY Great White—Capitol 44366 [Ian Hunter] [ASC] (5/13/89 BC-5)

ONCE IN A LIFETIME Talking Heads—Sire 29163
[David Byrne/Brian Eno/Chris Frantz/Jerry Harrison/Tina Weymouth] [ASC]
(4/12/86 BC-82)

ONCE IN A WHILE *The Modernaires—Coral 61779*
[Michael Edwards/Bud Green] (Med) [ASC] (2/16/57 R-72)

ONCE IN A WHILE *Clyde Stacy—Bullseye 1014 [Michael Edwards/Bud Green] [ASC] (9/22/58 R-100)*

ONCE IN A WHILE *The Chimes—Tag 444 [Michael Edwards/Bud Green] [ASC] (10/31/60 BCR-11)*

ONCE UPON A TIME Dean Martin—Capitol 4065 [Benny Carter/John V. Moen] [ASC] (10/6/58 CR-80)

ONCE UPON A TIME Rochell And The Candles With Johnny Wyatt—Swingin' 623 [Rochell Henderson/Johnny Wyatt] [BMI] (2/6/61 BCR-24)

ONCE UPON A TIME Marvin Gaye & Mary Wells—Motown 1057 [Barney Ales*/Dave Hamilton/Clarence Paul/William Stevenson] [BMI] (5/2/64 BCR-19)

ONCE YOU GET STARTED Rufus Featuring Chaka Khan—ABC 12066 [Gavin Christopher] [ASC] (2/8/75 BCR-6)

ONCE YOU HIT THE ROAD Dionne Warwick—Warner Bros. 8154 [Joseph Jefferson/Charles Simmons] [BMI] (12/27/75 BCR-75)

ONCE YOU UNDERSTAND *Think—Laurie 3583 [Lou Stallman/Bob Susser] [BMI] (12/4/71 BCR-21)*

ONCE YOU UNDERSTAND *Think (Featuring Lou Stallman)—Big Tree 15000 [Lou Stallman/Bob Susser] [BMI] (3/2/74 BCR-42)*

ONE Three Dog Night—Dunhill 4191 [Harry Nilsson] [BMI] (4/26/69 BCR-1)

ONE Metallica—Elektra 69329 [James Hetfield/Lars Ulrich] [ASC] (2/18/89 BC-35)

ONE Bee Gees—Warner Bros. 22899 [Barry Gibb/Maurice Gibb/Robin Gibb] [BMI] (7/29/89 BC-7)

A-ONE A-TWO A-CHA CHA CHA Lawrence Welk And His Orchestra and Chorus—Dot 16285 [George Cates] [ASC] (11/20/61 CR-91) [I]

ONE AMONG THE MANY Ned Miller—Fabor 116 [Ned Miller] [BMI] (3/30/63 R-83)

THE ONE AND ONLY Chesney Hawkes—Chrysalis 23730 [Nik Kershaw] [BMI] (8/3/91 BC-10)

ONE AND ONLY MAN Steve Winwood—Virgin 98892 [Jim Capaldi/Steve Winwood] [ASC] (11/3/90 BC-16)

ONE BAD APPLE The Osmonds—MGM 14193 [George Henry Jackson] [BMI] (12/26/70 BCR-1)

ONE BEAUTIFUL DAY Ecstasy, Passion & Pain—Roulette 7163 [Melvin Steals/Mervin Steals] [BMI] (3/22/75 BCR-41)

ONE BOY Joanie Sommers—Warner Bros. 5157 [Lee Adams/Charles Strouse] [ASC] (7/4/60 BCR-54)

ONE BOY TOO LATE Mike Clifford—United Artists 588 [Ellie Greenwich/Tony Powers] [BMI] (5/11/63 BCR-96)

ONE BROKEN HEART FOR SALE Elvis Presley With The Mello Men—RCA Victor 47-8134 [Otis Blackwell/Winfield Scott] [BMI] (2/9/63 BCR-8)

ONE BY ONE Blues Magoos—Mercury 72692 [Ronald Gilbert/Emil Thielhelm] [BMI] (6/10/67 BCR-63)

ONE CHAIN DON'T MAKE NO PRISON *Four Tops—Dunhill 4386 [Dennis Lambert/Brian Potter] [BMI] (4/27/74 BCR-36)*

ONE CHAIN (DON'T MAKE NO PRISON) *Santana—Columbia 10938 [Dennis Lambert/Brian Potter] [BMI] (4/14/79 BCR-59)*

ONE CUP OF HAPPINESS (AND ONE PEACE OF MIND) Dean Martin—Reprise 0857 [Baker Knight] [BMI] (10/18/69 CR-82)

ONE DAY AT A TIME Marilyn Sellars—Mega 1205 [Kris Kristofferson/Marijohn Wilkin] [BMI] (8/24/74 BCR-37)

ONE DAY IN YOUR LIFE Michael Jackson—Motown 1512 [Renée Armand/Samuel F. Brown III] [BMI] (4/18/81 BCR-55)

ONE DAY OF YOUR LIFE Andy Williams—Columbia 45175 [Howard Greenfield/Neil Sedaka] [BMI] (6/13/70 BCR-77)

ONE DYIN' AND A BURYIN' Roger Miller—Smash 1994 [Roger Miller] [BMI] (7/10/65 BCR-30)

ONE EYE OPEN The Maskman & The Agents—Dynamo 125 [Harmon Bethea/James Burston] [BMI] (2/8/69 BCR-89)

ONE FINE DAY *The Chiffons—Laurie 3179 [Gerry Goffin/Carole King] [BMI] (6/1/63 BCR-5)*

ONE FINE DAY *Julie—Tom Cat 10454 [Gerry Goffin/Carole King] [BMI] (1/17/76 BC-91)*

ONE FINE DAY *Rita Coolidge—A&M 2169 [Gerry Goffin/Carole King] [BMI] (9/1/79 BCR-66)*

ONE FINE DAY *Carole King—Capitol 4864 [Gerry Goffin/Carole King] [BMI] (5/17/80 BCR-12)*

ONE FINE MORNING Lighthouse—Evolution 1048 [Skip Prokop] [BMI] (9/11/71 BCR-13)

ONE FOOT BACK IN YOUR DOOR Roman Holliday—Jive 9287 [Mutt Lange] [ASC] (2/9/85 B-76)

ONE FOR MY BABY (AND ONE MORE FOR THE ROAD) Tony Bennett with Ray Conniff—Columbia 40907 [Harold Arlen/Johnny Mercer] [ASC] (5/11/57 BCR-32)

ONE FOR THE MOCKINGBIRD Cutting Crew—Virgin 99464 [Nick Van Eede] [BMI] (6/6/87 BC-32)

ONE FOR THE MONEY (PART 1) The Whispers—Soul Train 10700 [Jerry Akines/Johnnie Bellmon/Victor Drayton/Reginald Turner] [BMI] (7/31/76 BR-87)

ONE GIRL Garnet Mimms—United Artists 715 [Bert Berns/Jerry Ragovoy] [BMI] (5/16/64 BCR-60)

ONE GOOD REASON Paul Carrack—Chrysalis 43204 [Paul Carrack/Chris Difford] [ASC] (3/19/88 BC-28)

ONE GOOD WOMAN Hamilton, Joe Frank & Reynolds—Dunhill 4305 [Dennis Lambert/Brian Potter] [BMI] (4/8/72 R-99)

ONE GOOD WOMAN Peter Cetera—Full Moon 27824 [Peter Cetera/Patrick Raymond Leonard] [ASC] (7/23/88 BC-4)

ONE HAS MY NAME (THE OTHER HAS MY HEART) Barry Young—Dot 16756 [Hal Blair/Eddie Dean/Lorene Dean] [ASC] (10/16/65 BCR-10)

ONE HEART George Hamilton IV—ABC-Paramount 9898 [Frank Cari/Sonny Wells] [NA] (3/24/58 R-68)

ONE HEARTBEAT Smokey Robinson—Motown 1897 [Steve LeGassick/Brian Ray] [BMI] (7/18/87 BC-10)

ONE HELL OF A WOMAN Mac Davis—Columbia 46004 [Mac Davis/Mark James] [BMI] (3/30/74 BCR-11)

ONE HIT (TO THE BODY) The Rolling Stones—Rolling Stones 38-05906 [Mick Jagger/Keith Richards/Ron Wood] [ASC] (5/17/86 BC-28)

ONE HUNDRED WAYS Quincy Jones—A&M 2387 [Tony Coleman/Kathy Wakefield/Ben Wright] [BMI] (12/19/81 BCR-14)

100 YEARS Nancy Sinatra—Reprise 0670 [Lee Hazlewood] [ASC] (3/23/68 BCR-51)

ONE HURT DESERVES ANOTHER The Raeletts—Tangerine 972 [Ralph Bailey/Johnny Northern/Sammy Turner] [BMI] (4/8/67 BCR-55)

THE ONE I LOVE R.E.M.—I.R.S. 53171 [Bill Berry/Peter Buck/Mike Mills/Michael Stipe] [BMI] (9/19/87 BC-9)

ONE IN A MILLION The Platters—Mercury 71011 [Buck Ram/Tony Williams] [BMI] (12/15/56 BCR-31)

ONE IN A MILLION The Romantics—Nemperor 04373 [Coz Canler/Jimmy Marinos/Wally Palmar/Mike Skill] [ASC] (2/25/84 BC-37)

ONE IN A MILLION Eddie And The Tide—Atco 99617 [Eddie Rice] [BMI] (9/21/85 B-85)

ONE IN A MILLION Trixter—Mechanic 54044 [Steven James Brown/Bill Wray/Jim Wray] [ASC] (3/16/91 BC-74)

ONE IN A MILLION YOU Larry Graham—Warner Bros. 49221 [Sam Dees] [BMI] (6/21/80 BCR-9)

ONE KISS AWAY FROM HEAVEN (MALATIA) Tony Bennett with Percy Faith—Columbia 40849 [Sam Coslow/Armando Romeo] [ASC] (3/9/57 R-85) [FDE]

ONE KISS FOR OLD TIMES' SAKE Ronnie Dove—Diamond 179 [Artie Resnick/Kenny Young] [BMI] (3/13/65 BCR-6)

ONE KISS LED TO ANOTHER *The Coasters—Atco 6073 [Jerry Leiber/Mike Stoller] [BMI] (9/15/56 BRt-73)*

ONE KISS LED TO ANOTHER *Sunny Gale—Decca 30063 [Jerry Leiber/Mike Stoller] [BMI] (9/15/56 Rt-76)*

ONE LAST KISS Bobby Vee—Liberty 55251 [Lee Adams/Charles Strouse] [ASC] (5/9/60 CR-91)

ONE LAST KISS The J. Geils Band—EMI America 8007 [Seth Justman/Peter Wolf] [ASC] (11/18/78 BCR-35)

ONE LAST TIME Glen Campbell—Capitol 3483 [Dick Addrisi/Don Addrisi] [BMI] (12/9/72 BCR-78)

ONE LESS BELL TO ANSWER The 5th Dimension—Bell 940 [Burt Bacharach/Hal David] [ASC] (10/17/70 BCR-2)

ONE LESS SET OF FOOTSTEPS Jim Croce—ABC 11346 [Jim Croce] [ASC] (2/3/73 BCR-29)

ONE LIFE TO LIVE The Manhattans—DeLuxe 139 [Winfred Lovett] [BMI] (10/28/72 CR-67)

ONE LIFE TO LIVE Wayne Massey—Polydor 2112 [Ritchie Adams/Gloria Nissenson] [ASC] (10/4/80 BC-92)

ONE LIGHT TWO LIGHTS The Satisfactions—Lionel 3205 [Landy McNeil] [BMI] (10/31/70 B-94)

ONE LITTLE KISS The Playmates—Roulette 4393 [Bob Goodman/Earl Shuman] [ASC] (10/9/61 R-99)

ONE LONELY NIGHT REO Speedwagon—Epic 04848 [Neal Doughty] [ASC] (3/30/85 BC-19)

ONE LOVE IN MY LIFETIME Diana Ross—Motown 1398 [Lawrence Brown/Theresa McFaddin/Leonard O. Perry] [ASC] (7/31/76 BCR-25)

ONE LOVE, ONE HEART The Four Coins—Epic 9314 [Guy D'Hardelot/Albert Locke/Teddy Powell] [ASC] (5/30/59 BC-69)

ONE LOVER AT A TIME Atlantic Starr—Warner Bros. 28327 [Richard Feldman/James Scott] [BMI] (8/15/87 BC-58)

ONE MAN BAND Three Dog Night—Dunhill 4262 [Billy Fox/Tommy Kaye/January Tyme] [BMI] (11/14/70 BCR-11)

ONE MAN BAND Leo Sayer—Warner Bros. 8097 [David Courtney/Leo Sayer] [ASC] (6/28/75 B-96)

ONE MAN BAND (PLAYS ALL ALONE) Ronnie Dyson—Columbia 45776 [Thom Bell/Linda Creed] [BMI] (2/10/73 BCR-20)

ONE MAN PARADE James Taylor—Warner Bros. 7682 [James Taylor] [BMI] (2/24/73 BCR-53)

ONE MAN WOMAN/ONE WOMAN MAN Paul Anka with Odia Coates—United Artists 569 [Paul Anka] [BMI] (11/2/74 BCR-7)

ONE MAN'S LEFTOVERS (IS ANOTHER MAN'S FEAST) 100 Proof Aged In Soul—Hot Wax 7009 [Angelo Bond/General Johnson/Greg Perry] [BMI] (2/27/71 BCR-79)

ONE MINT JULEP *Chet Atkins—RCA Victor 47-7684 [Rudy Toombs] [BMI] (1/4/60 BR-82) [IWM]*

ONE MINT JULEP *Ray Charles—Impulse 200 [Rudy Toombs] [BMI] (3/6/61 BCR-8) [IWM]*

ONE MINT JULEP *Sarah Vaughan—Roulette 4413 [Rudy Toombs] [BMI] (3/26/62 R-89)*

ONE MOMENT IN TIME Whitney Houston—Arista 1-9743
[John Bettis/Albert Hammond] [ASC] (9/10/88 BC-5)

ONE MONKEY DON'T STOP NO SHOW Joe Tex—Dial 4011
[Joe Tex] [BMI] (6/26/65 BCR-65)

ONE MONKEY DON'T STOP NO SHOW PART 1 The Honey Cone—Hot Wax 7110
[General Johnson/Greg Perry] [BMI] (11/13/71 BCR-14)

ONE MORE CHANCE Rod Bernard—Mercury 71507
[J.P. Richardson] [BMI] (11/9/59 B-74)

ONE MORE CHANCE Ocean—Kama Sutra 556
[Roger Cook/Roger Greenaway/Albert Hammond*/Mike Hazlewood*] [ASC] (9/16/72 BCR-70)

ONE MORE CHANCE Diana Ross—Motown 1508
[Gerry Goffin/Michael Masser] [ASC] (4/11/81 B-79)

ONE MORE HEARTACHE Marvin Gaye—Tamla 54129
[Warren Moore/Smokey Robinson/Robert Rogers/Marvin Tarplin/Ronnie White] [ASC] (2/19/66 BCR-23)

ONE MORE MINUTE Saint Tropez—Butterfly 41080
[Barry Blue/Dave Jordan] [ASC] (4/14/79 BCR-49)

ONE MORE MOUNTAIN TO CLIMB Ronnie Dove—Diamond 217
[Joel Hirschhorn/Al Kasha] [ASC] (2/11/67 BCR-44)

ONE MORE NIGHT Streek—Columbia 02529 [Bill DeMartines] [BMI] (10/10/81 BCR-47)

ONE MORE NIGHT Phil Collins—Atlantic 89588 [Phil Collins] [ASC] (2/9/85 BC-1)

—ONE MORE SUNRISE see: MORGEN

ONE MORE TEAR The Raindrops—Jubilee 5487
[Jeff Barry/Ellie Greenwich] [BMI] (9/12/64 B-97)

ONE MORE TIME *Dean Martin—Capitol 2910*
[Horst Heinz Henning/Kay Twomey/Ben Weisman/Fred Wise] [BMI] (9/18/54 CtR-PRE)

ONE MORE TIME *The Ames Brothers—RCA Victor 47-5840*
[Horst Heinz Henning/Kay Twomey/Ben Weisman/Fred Wise] [BMI] (9/18/54 CtR-PRE)

ONE MORE TIME Ray Charles Singers—Command 4057
[Bill Angelos/Alan Kohan] [BMI] (10/24/64 BCR-29)

ONE MORE TIME FOR LOVE Billy Preston & Syreeta—Tamla 54312
[Jerry Peters] [BMI] (6/14/80 BCR-50)

ONE MORE TOMORROW Henry Gross—A&M 1682
[Henry Gross] [ASC] (4/26/75 BCR-92)

ONE MORE TOWN The Kingston Trio—Capitol 4842
[John Stewart] [BMI] (9/29/62 BCR-81)

ONE MORE TRY George Michael—Columbia 07773
[George Michael] [ASC] (4/16/88 BC-1)

ONE MORE TRY Timmy T—Quality 15114
[Russell Hildreth/Timmy Torres] [BMI] (12/22/90 BC-1)

(ONE MORE YEAR OF) DADDY'S LITTLE GIRL Ray Sawyer—Capitol 4344
[Hazel Smith] [BMI] (10/30/76 BCR-68)

ONE NATION UNDER A GROOVE - PART I Funkadelic—Warner Bros. 8618
[George Clinton/Walter Morrison/Garry Marshall Shider] [BMI] (9/2/78 BCR-7)

ONE NIGHT Elvis Presley—RCA Victor 47-7410
[Dave Bartholomew/Earl King Johnson/Anita Steinman*] [BMI] (11/3/58 BCR-3)

ONE NIGHT AFFAIR *The O'Jays—Neptune 12*
[Kenneth Gamble/Leon Huff] [BMI] (8/9/69 BCR-68)

ONE NIGHT AFFAIR *Jerry Butler—Mercury 73335*
[Kenneth Gamble/Leon Huff] [BMI] (11/4/72 BCR-52)

ONE NIGHT IN BANGKOK *Murray Head—RCA 13988*
[Benny Andersson/Tim Rice/Björn Ulvaeus] [ASC] (2/23/85 BC-3)

ONE NIGHT IN BANGKOK *Robey—Silver Blue 4-04774*
[Benny Andersson/Tim Rice/Björn Ulvaeus] [ASC] (3/2/85 BC-75)

ONE NIGHT LOVE AFFAIR Bryan Adams—A&M 2770
[Bryan Adams/Jim Vallance] [BMI] (9/14/85 BC-13)

ONE NIGHT ONLY Otis Williams And His Charms—DeLuxe 6095
[Rose Marie McCoy/Charles Singleton] [BMI] (7/13/56 R-76)

ONE NIGHT STAND The Magic Lanterns—Big Tree 109 / Atlantic 2715
[Albert Hammond/Mike Hazlewood] [BMI] (12/26/70 BCR-62)

ONE OF A KIND (LOVE AFFAIR) The Spinners—Atlantic 2962
[Joseph Jefferson] [BMI] (4/21/73 BCR-8)

ONE OF THE BOYS Mott The Hoople—Columbia 45754
[Ian Hunter/Mick Ralphs] [ASC] (1/27/73 B-96)

ONE OF THE LIVING Tina Turner—Capitol 5518 [Holly Knight] [ASC] (10/5/85 BC-15)

ONE OF THE LUCKY ONES Anita Bryant—Carlton 535
[George Goehring/Ed Warren] [ASC] (10/10/60 BCR-40)

(ONE OF THESE DAYS) SUNDAY'S GONNA' COME ON TUESDAY
The New Establishment—Colgems 5006
[Jack Keller/Ernie Sheldon] [ASC] (11/29/69 B-92)

ONE OF THESE NIGHTS Eagles—Asylum 45257
[Glenn Frey/Don Henley] [ASC] (5/31/75 BCR-1)

ONE OF US (WILL WEEP TONIGHT) Patti Page—Mercury 71639
[Clint Ballard Jr./Fred Tobias] [ASC] (6/6/60 BCR-22)

ONE ON ONE Daryl Hall & John Oates—RCA Victor 13421
[Daryl Hall] [BMI] (1/29/83 BC-5)

THE ONE ON THE RIGHT IS ON THE LEFT Johnny Cash—Columbia 43496
[Jack H. Clement] [BMI] (2/19/66 BCR-46)

ONE PIECE AT A TIME Johnny Cash And The Tennessee Three—Columbia 10321
[Wayne Kemp] [BMI] (4/10/76 BCR-29)

ONE PIECE TOPLESS BATHING SUIT The Rip Chords—Columbia 43093
[Don Altfeld/Steve Barri/P.F. Sloan] [BMI] (8/8/64 B-96)

THE ONE ROSE (THAT'S LEFT IN MY HEART) Teresa Brewer—Coral 62057
[Del Lyon/Lani McIntyre] [ASC] (12/15/58 BCR-54)

ONE SIMPLE THING Stabilizers—Columbia 06700
[Dave Christenson/Rich Nevens] [BMI] (4/4/87 B-93)

ONE STEP AT A TIME Brenda Lee—Decca 30198 [Hugh Ashley] [BMI] (2/2/57 BR-42)

ONE STEP AT A TIME Maxine Brown—Wand 185
[Jo Armstead/Nick Ashford/Valerie Simpson] [BMI] (7/3/65 BCR-49)

ONE STEP CLOSER The Doobie Brothers—Warner Bros. 49622
[Carlene Carter/Keith Knudsen/John McFee] [ASC] (11/22/80 BCR-24)

ONE STEP CLOSER TO YOU Gavin Christopher—Manhattan 50028
[David Grant/Jeff Pescetto/Evan Rogers/Carl Sturken] [ASC] (5/24/86 BC-22)

ONE STEP UP Bruce Springsteen—Columbia 07726
[Bruce Springsteen] [ASC] (2/27/88 BC-13)

ONE SUIT "Tennessee" Ernie Ford—Capitol 3649
[Larry Coleman/Charles Singleton] [BMI] (2/23/57 BR-63)

ONE SUMMER NIGHT *The Danleers—Mercury 71322*
[Danny Webb] [ASC] (5/31/58 BCR-9)

ONE SUMMER NIGHT *The Diamonds—Mercury 71831*
[Danny Webb] [ASC] (7/1/61 BCR-22)

ONE SUNNY DAY/DUELING BIKES FROM QUICKSILVER Ray Parker Jr.—Atlantic 89456
[Dean Pitchford/Bill Wolfer] [BMI] (2/15/86 B-96)

ONE TEAR Eddie Kendricks—Tamla 54255 [Leonard Caston] [BMI] (12/7/74 BC-55)

THE ONE THAT REALLY MATTERS Survivor—Scotti Brothers 03485
[Jim Peterik] [ASC] (1/22/83 B-74)

THE ONE THAT YOU LOVE Air Supply—Arista 0604
[Graham Russell] [BMI] (5/16/81 BCR-1)

THE ONE THING INXS—Atco 99905
[Andy Farriss/Michael Hutchence] [BMI] (3/26/83 BC-30)

ONE THING LEADS TO ANOTHER The Fixx—MCA 52264
[Alfie Agius/Cy Curnin/Peter John Greenall/Jamie West-Oram/Adam Woods] [ASC] (8/27/83 BC-4)

137 DISCO HEAVEN Amii Stewart—Ariola America/Hansa 7753
[Barry Leng/Simon May] (Med) [BMI] (6/23/79 BCR-69)

ONE THOUSAND CONCRETE BLOCKS Johnny Dee—Colonial 435
[John D. Loudermilk] [BMI] (8/3/57 R-71)

1,000 LAUGHS Eloise Laws—ABC 12313 [Linda Creed] [BMI] (1/14/78 B-91)

ONE TIN SOLDIER *The Original Caste—T-A 186*
[Dennis Lambert/Brian Potter] [BMI] (10/18/69 BCR-34)

ONE TIN SOLDIER THE LEGEND OF BILLY JACK *Coven—Warner Bros. 7509*
[Dennis Lambert/Brian Potter] [BMI] (9/11/71 BCR-18)

ONE TIN SOLDIER (THE LEGEND OF BILLY JACK) *Coven—MGM 14308*
[Dennis Lambert/Brian Potter] [BMI] (7/7/73 BCR-63)

ONE TIN SOLDIER THE LEGEND OF BILLY JACK *Coven—Warner Bros. 0101*
[Dennis Lambert/Brian Potter] [BMI] (12/29/73 BCR-73)

ONE TO ONE Carole King—Atlantic 4026
[Carole King/Cynthia Weil] [ASC] (3/27/82 BCR-45)

ONE TOKE OVER THE LINE Brewer & Shipley—Kama Sutra 516
[Michael Brewer/Tom Shipley] [BMI] (2/6/71 BCR-8)

ONE TOO MANY MORNINGS The Beau Brummels—Warner Bros. 5813
[Bob Dylan] [SE] (6/4/66 BCR-88)

ONE TRACK MIND Bobby Lewis—Beltone 1012
[Bobby Lewis/Malou René] [BMI] (8/28/61 BCR-9)

ONE TRACK MIND The Knickerbockers—Challenge 59326
[Keith Colley/Linda Jo Colley] [BMI] (3/19/66 BCR-46)

ONE-TRICK PONY Paul Simon—Warner Bros. 49601
[Paul Simon] [BMI] (10/25/80 BCR-40)

1-2-3 *Len Barry—Decca 31827*
[Len Barry/Lamont Dozier/Brian Holland*/Eddie Holland*/John Madara/David White] [BMI] (9/18/65 BCR-1)*

ONE, TWO, THREE *Ramsey Lewis—Cadet 5556*
[Len Barry/Lamont Dozier/Brian Holland*/Eddie Holland*/John Madara/David White] [BMI] (2/11/67 BCR-67) [IWM]*

1-2-3 Gloria Estefan and Miami Sound Machine—Epic 07921
[Gloria Estefan/Enrique Garcia] [BMI] (6/4/88 BC-3)

1-2-3 The Chimes (2)—Columbia 73087
[Pauline Henry/James Locke/Mike Peden] [BMI] (2/3/90 BC-82)

(1-2-3-4-5-6-7) COUNT THE DAYS Inez & Charlie Foxx—Dynamo 112
[Charlie Foxx/Brooks O'Dell/Yvonne Williams] [BMI] (12/16/67 BCR-73)

1, 2, 3, RED LIGHT 1910 Fruitgum Co.—Buddah 54
[Bobbi Trimachi/Sal Trimachi] [BMI] (7/13/68 BCR-3)

ONE VISION Queen—Capitol 5530
[John Deacon/Brian May/Freddie Mercury/Roger Taylor] [BMI] (12/7/85 BC-52)

ONE WAY LOVE The Drifters—Atlantic 2225
[Bert Berns/Jerry Ragovoy] [BMI] (5/2/64 BCR-56)

ONE WAY LOVE Bandit—Ariola America 7731 [Tony Lester] [ASC] (3/10/79 B-77)

ONE WAY LOVE TKA–Tommy Boy 866 [Jeff Mann/Marco Olivo] [ASC] (6/7/86 BC-75)

ONE WAY OR ANOTHER Blondie–Chrysalis 2336
[Clement A. Bozewski*/Nigel Harrison/Deborah Harry] [ASC] (6/2/79 BCR-22)

ONE WAY OUT The Allman Brothers Band–Capricorn 0014
[Elmore James/Marshall Sehorn/Sonny Boy Williamson II] [BMI] (12/2/72 B-86)

ONE WAY SUNDAY Mark-Almond–Blue Thumb 206 [Jon Mark] [ASC] (2/19/72 BCR-94)

ONE-WAY TICKET Tyrone Davis–Dakar 624
[Jack Daniels/John Edward Moore] [BMI] (6/26/71 BCR-68)

THE ONE WHO REALLY LOVES YOU Mary Wells–Motown 1024
[Smokey Robinson] [ASC] (3/5/62 BCR-4)

ONE WOMAN Johnny Rivers–Imperial 66418
[Charlie Chalmers/Sandra Rhodes] [BMI] (10/25/69 BCR-69)

ONE WOMAN BAND Carol Chase–Janus 256 [John Lombardo] [BMI] (12/27/75 C-92)

ONE WONDERFUL LOVE Ray Smith–Judd 1019
[Charles Adams/Earl Cage/Bill Justis/Willie Murphy/Earl Shelton/William Yancey*] [BMI] (8/20/60 C-99)

THE ONE YOU LOVE Glenn Frey–Asylum 69974
[Glenn Frey/Jack Tempchin] [ASC] (8/21/82 BC-12)

ONION SONG Marvin Gaye & Tammi Terrell–Tamla 54192
[Nick Ashford/Valerie Simpson] (TSW) [ASC] (4/25/70 BR-50)

ONLY A FOOL BREAKS HIS OWN HEART Arthur Prysock–Old Town 1185
[Norman Bergen/Shelly Coburn] [BMI] (10/23/65 R-100)

ONLY A GIRL LIKE YOU Brook Benton–RCA Victor 47-8768
[Frank Augustus/Clyde Otis] [BMI] (3/19/66 R-96)

ONLY A HEARTBEAT T'Pau–Charisma 98787
[Carol Decker/Ron Rogers] [NA] (6/15/91 C-82)

ONLY A LONELY HEART SEES Felix Cavaliere–Epic 50829
[Felix Cavaliere/Jay Tran] [ASC] (3/1/80 BCR-34)

ONLY A MEMORY The Smithereens–Enigma 44150 [Pat DiNizio] [BMI] (5/21/88 B-92)

ONLY BECAUSE The Platters–Mercury 71184
[Buck Ram/Jonathan Small/Ralph Yates] [BMI] (9/23/57 BCR-36)

ONLY BELIEVE Elvis Presley–RCA Victor 47-9985
[Elvis Presley*/Paul Rader] (TSW) [ASC] (5/15/71 B-53)

THE ONLY FLAME IN TOWN Elvis Costello & The Atractions–Columbia 04502
[Elvis Costello] [ASC] (7/28/84 BC-56)

ONLY FOR LOVE Limahl–EMI America 8277 [Christopher Hamill] [ASC] (7/20/85 BC-47)

ONLY IN AMERICA Jay & The Americans–United Artists 626
[Jerry Leiber/Barry Mann/Mike Stoller/Cynthia Weil] [BMI] (8/17/63 BCR-21)

ONLY IN MY DREAMS Debbie Gibson–Atlantic 89322
[Debbie Gibson] [ASC] (5/9/87 BC-4)

ONLY IN YOUR HEART America–Warner Bros. 7694
[Gerry Beckley] [ASC] (4/21/73 BCR-58)

ONLY LONELY Bon Jovi–Mercury 880736
[Jon Bon Jovi/Dave Bryan] [ASC] (4/20/85 BC-54)

ONLY LOVE Bill Quateman–Columbia 45792
[Bill Quateman] [BMI] (3/31/73 BCR-73)

ONLY LOVE CAN BREAK A HEART *Gene Pitney–Musicor 1022*
[Burt Bacharach/Hal David] [ASC] (9/1/62 BCR-2)

ONLY LOVE CAN BREAK A HEART *Margaret Whiting–London 108*
[Burt Bacharach/Hal David] [ASC] (5/20/67 BCR-94)

ONLY LOVE CAN BREAK A HEART *Bobby Vinton–ABC 12265*
[Burt Bacharach/Hal David] [ASC] (6/4/77 B-99)

ONLY LOVE CAN BREAK YOUR HEART *Neil Young–Reprise 0958*
[Neil Young] [BMI] (10/24/70 BCR-14)

ONLY LOVE CAN BREAK A HEART *Jackie Deshannon–Atlantic 2871*
[Neil Young] [BMI] (8/26/72 CR-96)

ONLY LOVE (CAN SAVE ME NOW) Solomon Burke–Atlantic 2308
[Larry Harrison/Jimmy Williams] [BMI] (11/13/65 BCR-73)

ONLY LOVE IS REAL Carole King–Ode 66119 [Carole King] [ASC] (2/14/76 BCR-27)

ONLY ME The First Edition–Reprise 0683
[Roger Nichols/Paul Williams] [BMI] (5/11/68 R-81)

ONLY MY HEART TALKIN' Alice Cooper–Epic 73268
[Alice Cooper/Andy Goldmark/Bruce Roberts] [ASC] (4/28/90 BC-85)

ONLY ONE Don "Red" Roberts–Rama 230 [Don W. Roberts] [NA] (7/6/57 R-83)

THE ONLY ONE I KNOW Charlatans UK–Beggars Banquet 2451
[Martin Blunt/Jon Brookes/Tim Burgess/Mark Collins/Jon Day] [ASC] (12/22/90 C-80)

ONLY ONE LOVE George Hamilton IV–ABC-Paramount 9782
[Joe Tanner] [BMI] (2/2/57 BCR-17)

ONLY ONE LOVE IN MY LIFE Ronnie Milsap–RCA 11270
[Royal C. Bannon/John Bettis] [BMI] (7/1/78 BCR-63)

ONLY ONE SONG Sha Na Na–Kama Sutra 522 [Scott Simon] [BMI] (5/8/71 CR-94)

ONLY ONE WOMAN Nigel Olsson–Rocket/MCA 40337
[Barry Gibb/Maurice Gibb/Robin Gibb] [BMI] (3/1/75 BCR-91)

ONLY ONE YOU T.G. Sheppard–Warner/Curb 49858
[Michael Garvin/Bucky Jones] [ASC] (1/30/82 BCR-67)

ONLY SIXTEEN *Sam Cooke–Keen 82022 [Sam Cooke] [BMI] (6/1/59 BCR-27)*

ONLY SIXTEEN *Dr. Hook–Capitol 4171 [Sam Cooke] [BMI] (1/3/76 BCR-5)*

ONLY THE BROKEN HEARTED Bob Beckham–Decca 31090
[J. George Johnson/Anne Spear] [ASC] (5/23/60 R-85)

ONLY THE GOOD DIE YOUNG Billy Joel–Columbia 10750
[Billy Joel] [ASC] (5/13/78 BCR-24)

ONLY THE LONELY (KNOW HOW I FEEL) *Roy Orbison–Monument 421*
[Joe Melson/Roy Orbison] [BMI] (5/23/60 BCR-2)

ONLY THE LONELY *Sonny James (The Southern Gentleman)–Capitol 2370*
[Joe Melson/Roy Orbison] [BMI] (1/25/69 BCR-92)

ONLY THE LONELY The Motels–Capitol 5114 [Martha Davis] [BMI] (4/24/82 BC-8)

ONLY THE LONELY (HAVE A REASON TO BE SAD) La Flavour–Sweet City 7377
[Mark Avsec] [ASC] (6/14/80 B-91)

ONLY THE LUCKY Walter Egan–Columbia 10531 [Walter Egan] [ASC] (6/11/77 BCR-74)

ONLY THE STRONG SURVIVE Jerry Butler–Mercury 72898
[Jerry Butler/Kenneth Gamble/Leon Huff] [BMI] (3/1/69 BCR-4)

ONLY THE STRONG SURVIVE REO Speedwagon–Epic 50790
[Gary Richrath] [ASC] (11/24/79 CR-66)

ONLY THE YOUNG Journey–Geffen 29090
[Jonathan Cain/Steve Perry/Neal Schon] [ASC] (1/26/85 BC-9)

ONLY THOSE IN LOVE Baby Washington–Sue 129
[Bert Kaempfert/Charles Singleton] [BMI] (7/3/65 BCR-43)

ONLY TIME WILL TELL Asia–Geffen 29970
[Geoffrey Downes/John Wetton] [ASC] (7/24/82 BC-16)

ONLY TIME WILL TELL Nelson–DGC 19014
[Gunnar Nelson/Matthew Nelson/Gregg Sutton/Marc Tanner] [ASC] (6/22/91 BC-28)

ONLY TRUST YOUR HEART *Dick Roman–ABC-Paramount 9793*
[Nicholas Brodszky/Sammy Cahn] [ASC] (3/23/57 Rt-43)

ONLY TRUST YOUR HEART *Joni James–MGM 12450*
[Nicholas Brodszky/Sammy Cahn] [ASC] (3/23/57 Rt-43)

ONLY TRUST YOUR HEART *Dean Martin–Capitol 3680*
[Nicholas Brodszky/Sammy Cahn] [ASC] (3/30/57 Rt-43)

ONLY TRUST YOUR HEART *Bob Winn–Imperial 7004*
[Nicholas Brodszky/Sammy Cahn] [ASC] (3/30/57 Rt-43)

THE ONLY WAY IS UP Yazz And The Plastic Population–Elektra 69365
[Johnny Henderson/George Henry Jackson] [BMI] (11/26/88 B-96)

THE ONLY WAY OUT Cliff Richard–EMI America 8135
[Ray Martinez] [ASC] (10/2/82 BC-64)

ONLY WHEN YOU LEAVE Spandau Ballet–Chrysalis 42792
[Gary Kemp] [BMI] (7/28/84 BC-32)

ONLY WHEN YOU'RE LONELY The Grass Roots–Dunhill 4043
[Steve Barri/P.F. Sloan] [ASC] (9/10/66 BCR-77)

ONLY WOMEN *Alice Cooper–Atlantic 3254*
[Alice Cooper/Dick Wagner] [BMI] (4/5/75 BCR-9)

ONLY WOMEN BLEED *Favorite Angel–Columbia 73476*
[Alice Cooper/Dick Wagner] [BMI] (8/11/90 BC-64)

ONLY YESTERDAY Carpenters–A&M 1677
[John Bettis/Richard Carpenter] [ASC] (3/29/75 BCR-4)

ONLY YOU (AND YOU ALONE) *The Platters–Mercury 70633*
[Buck Ram] [BMI] (8/1/55 BCtRt-3)

ONLY YOU (AND YOU ALONE) *Lola Dee–Wing 90015 [Buck Ram] [BMI] (9/19/55 Rt-9)*

ONLY YOU (AND YOU ALONE) *The Hilltoppers–Dot 15423*
[Buck Ram] [BMI] (10/29/55 BCtRt-3)

ONLY YOU *Franck Pourcel–Capitol 4165 [Buck Ram] [BMI] (3/23/59 BCR-8) [IWM]*

ONLY YOU (AND YOU ALONE) *Mr. Acker Bilk–Atco 6247*
[Buck Ram] [BMI] (1/26/63 BR-77) [IWM]

ONLY YOU *Wayne Newton–Capitol 5203 [Buck Ram] [BMI] (7/11/64 R-91)*

ONLY YOU (AND YOU ALONE) *Bobby Hatfield–Verve 10634*
[Buck Ram] [BMI] (3/1/69 BC-91)

ONLY YOU *Ringo Starr–Apple 1876 [Buck Ram] [BMI] (11/16/74 BCR-6)*

ONLY YOU *Fred Parris & The Five Satins–Elektra 47411*
[Buck Ram] (Med) [BMI] (2/27/82 BC-71)

ONLY YOU Loleatta Holloway and Bunny Sigler–Gold Mind 4012
[Bunny Sigler] [BMI] (11/4/78 B-87)

ONLY YOU Yaz–Sire 29844 [Vince Clarke] [BMI] (2/26/83 BC-67)

ONLY YOU Commodores–Motown 1694 [Milan Williams] [ASC] (9/17/83 BC-54)

ONLY YOU CAN Fox–Ariola America/GTO 7601 [Kenny Young] [BMI] (8/23/75 BCR-53)

ONLY YOU KNOW AND I KNOW *Dave Mason–Blue Thumb 114*
[Dave Mason] [ASC] (8/1/70 BCR-33)

ONLY YOU KNOW AND I KNOW *Delaney & Bonnie–Atco 6838*
[Dave Mason] [ASC] (9/25/71 BCR-15)

OO-EE-DIDDLEY-BOP! Peter Wolf–EMI America 8254
[Michael Jonzun/Peter Wolf/Gordon Worthy] [ASC] (4/27/85 BC-61)

OO-LA-LA-LIMBO Danny & The Juniors–Guyden 2076
[John Madara/David White] [BMI] (1/19/63 BCR-83)

OO-WEE Ringo Starr–Apple 1882 [Vini Poncia/Ringo Starr] (TSW) [BMI] (6/14/75 B-31)

OO WEE BABY, I LOVE YOU Fred Hughes–Vee-Jay 684
[Richard Parker] [BMI] (5/22/65 BCR-23)

OOBY DOOBY Roy Orbison And Teen Kings–Sun 242
[Wade Moore/Dick Penner] [BMI] (6/9/56 BCR-48)

THE OOGUM BOOGUM SONG Brenton Wood–Double Shot 111
[Alfred J. Smith] [ASC] (4/15/67 BCR-34)

OOH BABY Bo Diddley–Checker 1158 [Ellas McDaniel] [BMI] (1/21/67 BR-88)

OOH BABY Deon Jackson—Carla 2537
[Richard Barbary/Harold Thomas] [BMI] (11/18/67 BR-65)

OOH BABY Gilbert O'Sullivan—MAM 3633 [Gilbert O'Sullivan] [BMI] (10/13/73 BCR-11)

OOO BABY BABY *The Miracles—Tamla 54113*
[Warren Moore/Smokey Robinson] [ASC] (3/27/65 BCR-16)

OOOH, BABY BABY *The Five Stairsteps—Windy C 607*
[Warren Moore/Smokey Robinson] [ASC] (5/20/67 BCR-52)

OOH BABY BABY *The Magnificent Men—Capitol 5976*
[Warren Moore/Smokey Robinson] (Med) [ASC] (9/9/67 BCR-90)

OOH BABY BABY *Linda Ronstadt—Asylum 45546*
[Warren Moore/Smokey Robinson] [ASC] (11/11/78 BCR-7)

OOH BANG JIGGILLY JANG Doris Day—Columbia 40581
[Bob Merrill] [ASC] (11/26/55 B-83)

OOH BOY Rose Royce—Whitfield 8491 [Norman Whitfield] [BMI] (11/12/77 BCR-47)

OOH LA LA David Hallyday—Scotti Brothers 5282
[Lisa Cohen/David Hallyday] [ASC] (5/4/91 BC-51)

OOH LA LA (I CAN'T GET OVER YOU) Perfect Gentlemen—Columbia 73211
[Maurice Starr] [ASC] (4/14/90 BC-9)

OOH MY SOUL Little Richard—Specialty 633 [Richard Penniman] [BMI] (6/9/58 BCR-35)

OOH OOH OOH Sam & Dave—Atlantic 2668
[Donnie Fritts/John Reid] [BMI] (11/8/69 C-98)

OOH OOH SONG Pat Benatar—Chrysalis 42843
[Pat Benatar/Neil Geraldo] [ASC] (1/19/85 BC-35)

OOH POO PAH DOO PART TWO *Jessie Hill—Minit 607*
[Jessie Hill] [BMI] (3/26/60 BCR-28) [IWM]

OOH POO PAH DOO *Ike & Tina Turner—United Artists 50782*
[Jessie Hill] [BMI] (5/15/71 BCR-37)

OOH WHAT A DAY Sarah Vaughan—Roulette 4256
[Robert Mosely/Mayme Watts] [BMI] (6/6/60 R-83)

—OOM DOOBY DOOM see: SHE SAY

OOO-EEE Nicolette Larson—Warner Bros. 49666 [Annie McLoone] [ASC] (2/14/81 C-85)

OOOLA LA Betty Wright—Alston 3715
[Willie Clarke/Clarence Reid] [BMI] (9/13/75 R-91)

OOO LA LA LA Teena Marie—Epic 07708
[Teena Marie/Allen McGrier] [ASC] (3/12/88 B-85)

OOOH THIS I NEED Elisa Fiorillo—Chrysalis 23670 [Prince] [ASC] (3/9/91 B-90)

OOOPS UP Snap!—Arista 2060
[Benito Benites/Durron Butler/Penny Ford/John Virgo Garrett III/Lonnie Simmons/Rudy Taylor/Charles K. Wilson/Robert Wilson/Ronnie Wilson] [BMI] (9/8/90 BC-35)

OOP-SHOOP The Crew-Cuts—Mercury 70443
[Shirley Gunter/Joe Josea‡/Blondene Taylor] [BMI] (9/18/54 BCR-13)

OOWEE, OOWEE Perry Como—RCA Victor 47-8636
[Ronald Andre/Bonita Donato/Mona Donato/Sid Robin*] [ASC] (7/31/65 BCR-68)

OP The Honeycones—Ember 1036
[Margie Fisher] [ASC] (7/12/58 BC-65)

OPEN Smokey Robinson—Tamla 54267
[Pamela Moffett/Smokey Robinson/Marvin Tarplin] [ASC] (5/8/76 BR-81)

OPEN ARMS Journey—Columbia 02687
[Jonathan Cain/Steve Perry] [BMI] (1/16/82 BCR-1)

OPEN LETTER (TO A LANDLORD) Living Colour—Epic 68934
[Tracie Morris/Vernon Reid] [ASC] (7/1/89 BC-69)

AN OPEN LETTER TO MY TEENAGE SON Victor Lundberg—Liberty 55996
[Robert R. Thompson] [ASC] (11/11/67 BCR-6)

OPEN MY EYES Nazz—SGC 001 [Todd Rundgren] [BMI] (8/17/68 R-85)

OPEN SESAME - PART I Kool & The Gang—De-Lite 1586
[Robert Bell/Ronald Bell/George M. Brown/Claydes Smith/Dennis Thomas] [BMI] (11/6/76 BCR-47)

OPEN THE DOOR (SONG FOR JUDITH) Judy Collins—Elektra 45755
[Judy Collins] [ASC] (12/18/71 BCR-79)

OPEN THE DOOR TO YOUR HEART Darrell Banks—Revilot 201
[Donnie Elbert/Darrell Eubanks] [BMI] (7/16/66 BCR-24)

OPEN UP MY HEART The Dells—Cadet 5667
[Robert Eugene Miller] (TSW) [BMI] (5/2/70 BCR-49)

OPEN UP THE DOGHOUSE (TWO CATS ARE COMIN' IN)
Dean Martin And Nat "King" Cole—Capitol 2985
[Roy Alfred/Marvin Fisher] [ASC] (11/22/54 CR-22)

(OPEN UP THE DOOR) LET THE GOOD TIMES IN Dean Martin—Reprise 0538
[Ramona Redd/Mitchell Torok] [BMI] (12/10/66 BCR-50)

OPEN UP YOUR DOOR Richard and The Young Lions—Philips 40381
[Raymond Bloodworth/L. Russell Brown/Neval Nader] [BMI] (9/17/66 BCR-70)

OPEN UP YOUR HEART Rainbow—Evolution 1056
[David Victor Meyers/Les Vandyke] [ASC] (4/29/72 R-98)

OPEN UP YOUR HEART (AND LET THE SUNSHINE IN)
The Cowboy Church Sunday School—Decca 29367
[Stuart Hamblen] [ASC] (12/27/54 BCRt-7)

OPEN UP YOUR HEART (AND LET THE SUNSHINE IN) *The Lancers—Coral 61332*
[Stuart Hamblen] [ASC] (1/3/55 Rt-25)

OPEN UP YOUR HEART (AND LET THE SUNSHINE IN) *The McGuire Sisters—Coral 61334*
[Stuart Hamblen] [ASC] (1/10/55 Rt-25)

OPEN UP YOUR HEART (AND LET THE SUNSHINE IN)
Little Sister Gale & Big Sister Rosemary Clooney—Columbia 40422
[Stuart Hamblen] [ASC] (1/17/55 Rt-18)

OPEN YOUR HEART Madonna—Sire 28508
[Madonna L. Ciccone/Gardner Cole/Peter Rafelson] [BMI] (12/6/86 BC-1)

OPERATOR Gladys Knight & The Pips—Fury 1064
[Ray Jones/Stanley Kahan/Eddie Snyder] [BMI] (4/2/62 BCR-79)

OPERATOR Brenda Holloway—Tamla 54115 [Smokey Robinson] [ASC] (6/5/65 BCR-78)

OPERATOR The Manhattan Transfer—Atlantic 3292
[William Spivery] [BMI] (9/20/75 BCR-22)

OPERATOR Midnight Star—Solar 69684
[Reggie Calloway/Vincent Calloway/Belinda Lipscomb/Bo Watson] [BMI] (12/1/84 BC-18)

OPERATOR (THAT'S NOT THE WAY IT FEELS) Jim Croce—ABC 11335
[Jim Croce] [ASC] (10/14/72 BCR-10)

OPHELIA The Band—Capitol 4230 [Robbie Robertson] [ASC] (3/20/76 BCR-62)

OPPORTUNITIES (LET'S MAKE LOTS OF MONEY) Pet Shop Boys—EMI America 8330
[Chris Lowe/Neil Tennant] [ASC] (5/31/86 BC-9)

OPPORTUNITY The Jewels—Dimension 1034
[Raymond Augustus Evans/Randall Stewart] [BMI] (10/10/64 BCR-59)

OPPOSITES ATTRACT Paula Abdul—Virgin 99158 [Oliver Leiber] [ASC] (12/16/89 BC-1)

OPPOSITES DO ATTRACT All Sports Band—Radio 3892
[Cy Sulack/Michael Toste] [ASC] (2/6/82 B-78)

OPUS ONE *The Mills Brothers—Decca 29496*
[Sid Garris/Sy Oliver] [BMI] (4/25/55 CR-21)

OPUS ONE *The Modernaires—Coral 61779*
[Sid Garris/Sy Oliver] (Med) [BMI] (2/16/57 R-72)

OPUS #1 *Larry Elgart And His Manhattan Swing Orchestra—RCA 13219*
[Sy Oliver] (Med) [BMI] (6/5/82 BC-31) [IM]

OPUS 17 (DON'T YOU WORRY 'BOUT ME)
The 4 Seasons Featuring The "Sound" Of Frankie Valli—Philips 40370
[Sandy Linzer/Denny Randell] [BMI] (5/14/66 BCR-9)

OPUS 17 *Gidea Park—Profile 5003*
[Sandy Linzer/Denny Randell] (Med) [BMI] (12/26/81 BC-82)

ORANGE BLOSSOM SPECIAL *Billy Vaughn And His Orchestra—Dot 16174*
[Ervin Rouse] [ASC] (2/13/61 BCR-63) [I]

ORANGE BLOSSOM SPECIAL *Johnny Cash—Columbia 43206*
[Ervin Rouse] [ASC] (2/6/65 BCR-80)

—ORBITAL BE-BOP see: DANCING IN HEAVEN

ORGAN GRINDER'S SWING *Sam (The Man) Taylor And His Orchestra—MGM 12729*
[Will Hudson] [ASC] (12/8/58 R-94) [IM]

THE ORGAN GRINDER'S SWING
Jimmy Smith With Kenny Burrell And Grady Tate—Verve 10363
[Will Hudson] [ASC] (10/2/65 BCR-86) [IM]

ORGAN SHOUT Dave "Baby" Cortez—Chess 1861
[David Clowney/Julia Clowney] [BMI] (8/24/63 BCR-68) [I]

ORIGINAL SIN INXS—Atco 99766
[Andy Farriss/Michael Hutchence] [BMI] (4/28/84 BC-58)

ORINOCO FLOW Enya—Geffen 27633 [Enya/Roma Ryan] [BMI] (1/21/89 BC-24)

THE OTHER GUY Little River Band—Capitol 5185 [Graham Goble] [BMI] (11/20/82 BC-8)

THE OTHER MAN'S GRASS IS ALWAYS GREENER Petula Clark—Warner Bros. 7097
[Tony Hatch/Jackie Trent] [ASC] (12/2/67 BCR-28)

THE OTHER RINGO Larry Finnegan—Ric S-146 [John L. Finneran] [BMI] (12/26/64 R-91)

THE OTHER SIDE Aerosmith—Geffen 19927
[Lamont Dozier*/Brian Holland*/Eddie Holland*/Steven Tyler/Jim Vallance] [BMI] (6/23/90 BC-19)

THE OTHER SIDE OF LIFE The Moody Blues—Polydor 885201
[Justin Hayward] [ASC] (8/16/86 BC-58)

THE OTHER SIDE OF THIS LIFE Peter, Paul & Mary—Warner Bros. 5849
[Fred Neil] [BMI] (9/24/66 B-100)

THE OTHER WOMAN Sarah Vaughan—Mercury 70885
[Jessie Mae Robinson] [ASC] (8/4/56 B-86)

THE OTHER WOMAN Vicki Lawrence—Private Stock 45,036
[Tom Bahler/Harry Shannon] [BMI] (9/27/75 BCR-70)

THE OTHER WOMAN Ray Parker Jr.—Arista 0669 [Ray Parker Jr.] [ASC] (3/20/82 BCR-2)

OUR ANNIVERSARY Shep And The Limelites—Hull 748
[James Sheppard] [BMI] (2/10/62 BCR-59)

OUR CONCERTO *Umberto Bindi—Jamie 1159*
[Umberto Bindi/Giorgio Calabrese/Hal David] [ASC] (7/18/60 Rt-88) [FET]

OUR CONCERTO (IL NOSTRO CONCERTO) *Al Martino—20th Fox 213*
[Umberto Bindi/Giorgio Calabrese/Hal David] [ASC] (7/25/60 Rt-88)

OUR CONCERTO *Steve Lawrence—United Artists 403*
[Umberto Bindi/Giorgio Calabrese/Hal David] [ASC] (1/22/62 R-74) [FET]

OUR CORNER OF THE NIGHT Barbra Streisand—Columbia 44474
[George Goehring/Stan Rhodes] [ASC] (3/16/68 CR-74)

OUR DAY WILL COME *Ruby And The Romantics—Kapp 501*
[Mort Garson/Bob Hilliard] [ASC] (1/19/63 BCR-1)

OUR DAY WILL COME *Frankie Valli—Private Stock 45,043*
[Mort Garson/Bob Hilliard] [ASC] (10/18/75 BCR-11)

OUR EVERLASTING LOVE Ruby And The Romantics—Kapp 578
[Leon Carr/Earl Shuman] [ASC] (3/7/64 BCR-49)

OUR FADED LOVE The Royaltones—Mala 473
[Dennis Coffey/George Katsakis] [BMI] (4/18/64 CR-92) [IM]

OUR FIRST DANCE (PREMIER BAL) Gerard Calvi—Jamie 1165
[Sidney Bechet] [BMI] (9/12/60 R-99) [IM]

OUR HOUSE Crosby, Stills, Nash & Young—Atlantic 2760
[Graham Nash] [BMI] (9/19/70 BCR-20)

OUR HOUSE Madness—Geffen 29668
[Michael Barson*/Mark Bedford*/Christopher Foreman/Graham McPherson*/Charles Smyth/Lee Jay Thompson*/Daniel Woodgate*] [BMI] (4/30/83 BC-5)

OUR LAST SONG TOGETHER Bo Donaldson And The Heywoods—ABC 12108
[Howard Greenfield/Neil Sedaka] [BMI] (7/5/75 BC-95)

OUR LIPS ARE SEALED Go-Go's—I.R.S. 9901
[Terry Hall/Jane Wiedlin] [ASC] (8/29/81 BCR-20)

OUR LOVE Natalie Cole—Capitol 4509
[Charles Henry Jackson Jr./Marvin Yancy] [ASC] (12/24/77 BCR-6)

OUR LOVE AFFAIR Tommy Charles—Decca 29717
[Harry Edelstein/Cliff Parman] [ASC] (2/11/56 BCR-43)

—OUR LOVE AFFAIR see: AFFAIR TO REMEMBER

(OUR LOVE) DON'T THROW IT ALL AWAY Andy Gibb—RSO 911
[Barry Gibb/Blue Weaver] [BMI] (10/14/78 BCR-7)

OUR LOVE IS HERE TO STAY *Dinah Washington—Mercury 71812*
[George Gershwin/Ira Gershwin] [ASC] (5/8/61 BCR-48)

LOVE IS HERE TO STAY *Chris Montez—A&M 958*
[George Gershwin/Ira Gershwin] [ASC] (8/10/68 C-97)

OUR LOVE IS INSANE Desmond Child And Rouge—Capitol 4669
[Desmond Child] [ASC] (1/20/79 BCR-51)

—OUR MELODY see: PHONOGRAPH SONG

OUR NIGHT Shaun Cassidy—Warner/Curb 8634
[Bruce Roberts/Carole Bayer Sager] [BMI] (9/9/78 B-80)

OUR SONG Jack Jones—Kapp 847
[Umberto Bindi/Anthony Ralph Clarke] [BMI] (8/26/67 BCR-76) [FDE]

OUR WALTZ Sarah Vaughan—Mercury 71610
[Nat Burton/David Rose] [ASC] (5/7/60 C-83)

OUR WINTER LOVE *Bill Pursell—Columbia 42619*
[Johnny Cowell] [BMI] (1/26/63 BCR-7) [IM]

OUR WINTER LOVE *The Lettermen—Capitol 5813*
[Johnny Cowell/Bob Tubert] [BMI] (1/28/67 B-72)

OUR WORLD Johnny Tillotson—MGM 13408
[Paul Evans/Paul Parnes] [ASC] (11/20/65 BCR-54)

OUR WORLD Blue Mink—Philips 40686
[Herbie Flowers/Ken Pickett] [BMI] (9/12/70 BCR-56)

OUT AND ABOUT Tommy Boyce & Bobby Hart—A&M 858
[Tommy Boyce/Bobby Hart] [BMI] (7/1/67 BCR-30)

OUT HERE ON MY OWN Irene Cara—RSO 1048
[Lesley Gore/Michael Gore] [BMI] (8/16/80 BCR-19)

OUT IN THE COUNTRY Three Dog Night—Dunhill 4250
[Roger Nichols/Paul Williams] [BMI] (8/29/70 BCR-9)

OUT IN THE STREETS The Shangri-Las—Red Bird 10-025
[Jeff Barry/Ellie Greenwich] [BMI] (4/3/65 BCR-53)

OUT IN THE SUN (HEY-O) The Beach Nuts—Bang 504
[Bob Feldman/Jerry Goldstein/Richard Gottehrer] [BMI] (7/24/65 CR-77)

OUT OF A CLEAR BLUE SKY Lawrence Welk And His Orchestra—Dot 16198
[Harry Von Tilzer] [ASC] (3/20/61 R-83) [IM]

OUT OF LEFT FIELD Percy Sledge—Atlantic 2396
[Spooner Oldham/Dan Penn] [BMI] (4/8/67 BCR-41)

OUT OF LIMITS The Marketts—Warner Bros. 5391
[Michael Gordon] [BMI] (12/7/63 BCR-3) [I]

OUT OF MIND OUT OF SIGHT Models—Geffen 28762
[James Freud] [ASC] (4/26/86 BC-33)

OUT OF MY MIND Johnny Tillotson—Cadence 1434
[Johnny Tillotson] [BMI] (3/2/63 BCR-16)

OUT OF SIGHT James Brown And His Orchestra—Smash 1919
[Ted Wright] [BMI] (8/8/64 BCR-21)

OUT OF SIGHT OUT OF MIND *The Five Keys—Capitol 3502*
[Ivory Joe Hunter/Clyde Otis] [BMI] (9/15/56 BCR-16)

OUT OF SIGHT, OUT OF MIND *The Essex—Roulette 4530*
[Ivory Joe Hunter/Clyde Otis] [BMI] (11/16/63 C-97)

OUT OF SIGHT - OUT OF MIND *Sunny & The Sunliners—Tear Drop 3027*
[Ivory Joe Hunter/Clyde Otis] [BMI] (2/22/64 B-71)

OUT OF SIGHT, OUT OF MIND *Little Anthony And The Imperials—United Artists 50552*
[Ivory Joe Hunter/Clyde Otis] [BMI] (7/5/69 BCR-50)

OUT OF THE BLUE Tommy James And The Shondells—Roulette 4775
[Ritchie Cordell/Bo Gentry] [BMI] (10/28/67 BCR-31)

OUT OF THE BLUE Debbie Gibson—Atlantic 89129
[Debbie Gibson] [ASC] (1/30/88 BC-3)

OUT OF THE DARKNESS David Crosby / Graham Nash—ABC 12199
[David Crosby/Craig Doerge/Graham Nash] [BMI] (7/24/76 BC-77)

OUT OF THE PICTURE The Crew-Cuts—Mercury 70840
[Joe Lubin/Irving Roth] [ASC] (4/21/56 C-49)

OUT OF THE QUESTION Gilbert O'Sullivan—MAM 3628
[Gilbert O'Sullivan] [ASC] (3/3/73 BCR-17)

OUT OF THIS WORLD The Chiffons—Laurie 3350
[Barbara Baer/Eliot Greenberg/Douglas Morris/Robert Schwartz] [BMI] (8/6/66 BCR-67)

OUT OF TIME The Rolling Stones—Abkco 4702
[Mick Jagger/Keith Richards] [BMI] (8/16/75 BCR-65)

OUT OF TOUCH Daryl Hall & John Oates—RCA Victor 13916
[Daryl Hall/John Oates] [BMI] (9/29/84 BC-1)

OUT OF WORK Gary U.S. Bonds—EMI America 8117
[Bruce Springsteen] [ASC] (6/12/82 BC-21)

OUTA-SPACE Billy Preston—A&M 1320
[Joe Greene/Billy Preston] [BMI] (4/22/72 BCR-1) [I]

OUTLAW War—RCA 13238
[Thomas Allen/Harold Brown/Jerry Goldstein/Ronnie Hammon/Lonnie Jordan/Lee Oskar/Luther Rabb/Howard Scott] [ASC] (7/10/82 BC-94)

OUTLAW MAN *David Blue—Asylum 11015 [David Blue] [ASC] (4/21/73 BCR-73)*

OUTLAW MAN *Eagles—Asylum 11025 [David Blue] [ASC] (9/1/73 BCR-49)*

OUTSIDE MY WINDOW The Fleetwoods—Dolton 15
[Hal David/Sherman Edwards] [ASC] (2/1/60 BCR-28)

OUTSIDE MY WINDOW Stevie Wonder—Tamla 54308
[Stevie Wonder] [ASC] (3/1/80 BCR-52)

OUTSIDE THE GATES OF HEAVEN Lou Christie—Co & Ce 235
[Lou Christie/Twyla Herbert] [BMI] (3/5/66 BCR-45)

OUTSIDE WOMAN Bloodstone—London 1052 [Harry Williams Jr.] [BMI] (2/2/74 BCR-31)

OUTSTANDING The Gap Band—Total Experience 8205
[Ray Calhoun] [BMI] (3/5/83 BC-51)

OVER AND OVER *Thurston Harris—Aladdin 3430 [Bobby Day] [BMI] (8/4/58 BCtRt-51)*

OVER AND OVER *Bobby Day—Class 229 [Bobby Day] [BMI] (8/4/58 BCtRt-41)*

OVER AND OVER *The Dave Clark Five—Epic 9863 [Bobby Day] [BMI] (11/6/65 BCR-1)*

OVER AND OVER The Delfonics—Philly Groove 166
[Thom Bell/William Hart] (TSW) [BMI] (6/19/71 BCR-52)

OVER AND OVER Pajama Party—Atlantic 88799
[Jim Klein/Peggy Sendars] [ASC] (11/11/89 BC-59)

OVER AND OVER Timmy -T-—Quality 15111 [Carl King] [BMI] (5/11/91 BC-63)

OVER MY HEAD Fleetwood Mac—Warner Bros. 1339
[Christine McVie] [BMI] (10/25/75 BCR-18)

OVER MY HEAD Toni Basil—Chrysalis 42753
[Franne Golde/Sue Shifrin] [BMI] (1/21/84 BC-77)

OVER THE HILLS AND FAR AWAY Led Zeppelin—Atlantic 2970
[Jimmy Page/Robert Plant] [ASC] (6/9/73 BCR-28)

OVER THE LINE Eddie Schwartz—Atco 7402
[Eddie Schwartz/David Tyson] [BMI] (3/20/82 B-91)

OVER THE MOUNTAIN ACROSS THE SEA *Johnnie & Joe—Chess 1654*
[Rex Garvin] [BMI] (5/11/57 BCR-8)

OVER THE MOUNTAIN; ACROSS THE SEA *Johnnie & Joe—Chess 1654*
[Rex Garvin] [BMI] (9/26/60 B-89)

OVER THE MOUNTAIN (ACROSS THE SEA) *Bobby Vinton—Epic 9577*
[Rex Garvin] [BMI] (3/9/63 BCR-20)

OVER THE RAINBOW *The Demensions—Mohawk 116*
[Harold Arlen/E.Y. Harburg] [ASC] (6/20/60 BCRt-16)

OVER THE RAINBOW *The Baysiders—Everest 19366*
[Harold Arlen/E.Y. Harburg] [ASC] (7/4/60 Rt-17)

OVER THE RAINBOW *Gary Tanner—20th Century 2373*
[Harold Arlen/E.Y. Harburg] [ASC] (5/27/78 BCR-63)

OVER THE WEEKEND The Playboys—Cameo 142
[Don Canton/Teddy Powell/Tony Starr] [ASC] (7/12/58 BCR-29)

OVER UNDER SIDEWAYS DOWN The Yardbirds—Epic 10035
[Jeff Beck/Chris Dreja/Jim McCarty/Keith Relf/Paul Samwell-Smith] [ASC] (6/25/66 BCR-11)

OVER YOU Gary Puckett And The Union Gap—Columbia 44644
[Jerry Fuller] [BMI] (9/14/68 BCR-5)

OVER YOU Roxy Music—Atco 7301 [Bryan Ferry/Phil Manzanera] [BMI] (8/9/80 BCR-80)

OVERJOYED Stevie Wonder—Tamla 1832 [Stevie Wonder] [ASC] (2/22/86 BC-24)

OVERKILL Men At Work—Columbia 03795 [Colin James Hay] [ASC] (4/9/83 BC-3)

OVERNIGHT SENSATION (HIT RECORD) Raspberries—Capitol 3946
[Eric Carmen] [BMI] (9/14/74 BCR-18)

OVERTURE FROM TOMMY (A ROCK OPERA) The Assembled Multitude—Atlantic 2737
[Pete Townshend] [BMI] (6/13/70 BCR-16) [I]

OWN THE NIGHT Chaka Khan—MCA 52730
[Mary Dean/Franne Golde/Marti Sharron] [BMI] (12/21/85 BC-57)

OWNER OF A LONELY HEART Yes—Atco 99817
[Jon Anderson/Trevor Horn/Trevor Rabin/Chris Squire] [BMI] (11/5/83 BC-1)

OWWWW! Chunky A—MCA 53736 [Zane Giles/Arsenio Hall] [ASC] (12/2/89 B-77)

OYE COMO VA Santana—Columbia 45330 [Tito Puente] [ASC] (2/20/71 BCR-10) [F]

OYE MI CANTO (HEAR MY VOICE) Gloria Estefan—Epic 73269
[Jorge Casas/Gloria Estefan/Clay Ostwald] [BMI] (4/7/90 BC-45)

—OYE NEGRA see: BONGO GUITAR

P

P. S. I LOVE YOU The Classics (2)—Music Note 1118
[Gordon Jenkins/Johnny Mercer] [ASC] (9/21/63 R-95)

P.Y.T. (PRETTY YOUNG THING) Michael Jackson—Epic 04165
[James Ingram/Quincy Jones] [BMI] (10/8/83 BC-10)

PA PA PA Joni James—M-G-M 11802
[Lew Douglas/Jim Krum/Cliff Parman] [ASC] (9/11/54 C-42)

PAC-MAN FEVER Buckner & Garcia—Columbia 02673
[Jerry Buckner/Gary Garcia] [ASC] (12/26/81 BCR-7)

PACO PECO The Limeliters—RCA Victor 47-7913 [Neely Plumb] [ASC] (7/17/61 R-60)

PADRE *Valerie Carr—Roulette 4066*
[Marcel Ageron/Regis Gabriel Desplanques/Alain Romans/Paul Francis Webster] [ASC] (4/21/58 Rt-7) [FET]*

PADRE *Toni Arden—Decca 30628*
[Marcel Ageron/Regis Gabriel Desplanques/Alain Romans/Paul Francis Webster] [ASC] (4/21/58 BCRt-7) [FET]*

PADRE *Sarah Vaughan—Mercury 71303*
[Marcel Ageron/Regis Gabriel Desplanques/Alain Romans/Paul Francis Webster] [ASC] (4/28/58 Rt-8) [FET]*

PAIN (PART 1) Ohio Players—Westbound 188
[Leroy Bonner/Marshall Jones/Ralph Middlebrooks/Walter Morrison/
Bruce Napier*/Andrew Noland/Marvin Pierce*/Greg Webster] [BMI] (12/4/71 BCR-64)

THE PAIN GETS A LITTLE DEEPER Darrow Fletcher—Groovy 3001
[Ted Daniels/Darrow Fletcher] [BMI] (1/15/66 BCR-89)

PAIN IN MY HEART Otis Redding—Volt 112 [Allen Toussaint] [BMI] (11/23/63 BCR-47)

PAINT IT, BLACK The Rolling Stones—London 901
[Mick Jagger/Keith Richards] [BMI] (5/14/66 BCR-1)

PAINTED LADIES Ian Thomas—Janus 224 [Ian Thomas] [ASC] (10/13/73 BCR-27)

PAINTED MOON The Silencers—RCA 5220
[Charles Burns/James O'Neill] [ASC] (8/8/87 BC-82)

PAINTED PICTURE Commodores—Motown 1651
[Harold Hudson/Walter Orange] [ASC] (12/4/82 BC-70)

PAINTED, TAINTED ROSE Al Martino—Capitol 5000
[Peter DeAngelis/Jean Sawyer] [ASC] (7/20/63 BCR-14)

PAINTER Lou Christie—MGM 13533 [Lou Christie/Twyla Herbert] [BMI] (6/18/66 BCR-73)

PALACE GUARD Rick Nelson And The Stone Canyon Band—MCA 40001
[Rick Nelson] [BMI] (2/3/73 BCR-65)

PALISADES PARK Freddy Cannon—Swan 4106 [Chuck Barris] [ASC] (4/30/62 BCR-3)

PALOMA BLANCA George Baker Selection—Warner Bros. 8115
[George Baker] [ASC] (11/22/75 BCR-22)

—PALOMA see: LA PALOMA

—PALOMA TWIST see: LA PALOMA TWIST

PAMELA Toto—Columbia 07715
[David Paich/Joseph Stanley Williams] [ASC] (2/20/88 BC-22)

PAMELA THROWS A PARTY
Joe Reisman and His Orchestra And Chorus—RCA Victor 47-6826
[Robert Allen] [ASC] (3/16/57 BR-55)

PANAMA Van Halen—Warner Bros. 29250
[Michael Anthony*/David Lee Roth/Alex Van Halen/Eddie Van Halen] [ASC] (6/23/84 BC-13)

PANDORA'S GOLDEN HEEBIE JEEBIES The Association—Valiant 755
[Jules Alexander] [BMI] (11/26/66 BCR-19)

PANIC Otis Williams And His Charms—King 5527
[Marnie Ewald/Billy Oliver] [BMI] (9/18/61 B-99)

PAPA DON'T PREACH Madonna—Sire 28660
[Madonna L. Ciccone*/Brian Elliot] [ASC] (6/28/86 BC-1)

PAPA DON'T TAKE NO MESS - PART I James Brown—Polydor 14255
[Charles Bobbit*/James Brown/John Starks/Fred Wesley] [BMI] (8/24/74 BCR-27)

PAPA LOVES MAMBO Perry Como—RCA Victor 47-5857
[Al Hoffman/Dick Manning/Bickley Reichner] [ASC] (9/25/54 BCR-1)

PAPA-OOM-MOW-MOW *The Rivingtons—Liberty 55427*
[Al Frazier/John Earl (Sonny) Harris/Carl White/Turner Wilson] [BMI] (8/4/62 BCR-35)

PAPA OOM MOW MOW *(as part of Surfin' Bird) The Trashmen—Garrett 4002*
[Al Frazier/John Earl (Sonny) Harris/Carl White/Turner Wilson] (Med) [BMI] (12/7/63 BCR-2)

PAPA WAS A ROLLIN' STONE *The Undisputed Truth—Gordy 7117*
[Barrett Strong/Norman Whitfield] [BMI] (6/10/72 BCR-63)

PAPA WAS A ROLLIN' STONE *The Temptations—Gordy 7121*
[Barrett Strong/Norman Whitfield] [BMI] (10/14/72 BCR-1)

PAPA WAS A ROLLING STONE *Stars On 45—Radio 3863*
[Barrett Strong/Norman Whitfield] (Med) [BMI] (9/19/81 BCR-55)

PAPA WAS A ROLLIN' STONE *Wolf—Constellation 69849*
[Barrett Strong/Norman Whitfield] [BMI] (12/11/82 BC-55)

PAPA WAS TOO Joe Tex—Dial 4051
[Joe Tex] [BMI] (12/10/66 BCR-29)

PAPA'S GOT A BRAND NEW BAG PART I *James Brown And The Famous Flames—King 5999*
[James Brown] [BMI] (7/17/65 BCR-6)

PAPA'S GOT A BRAND NEW BAG *Otis Redding—Atco 6636*
[James Brown] [BMI] (11/30/68 BCR-20)

PAPER CUP The 5th Dimension—Soul City 760 [Jimmy Webb] [BMI] (11/4/67 BCR-32)

PAPER IN FIRE John Cougar Mellencamp—Mercury 888763
[John Mellencamp] [ASC] (8/15/87 BC-9)

PAPER LOVE Jack Gandy Trio—King 1388 [Howard Marks] [NA] (1/31/55 R-57)

PAPER MACHE Dionne Warwick—Scepter 12285
[Burt Bacharach/Hal David] [ASC] (7/11/70 BCR-31)

—PAPER OF PINS see: BUS STOP SONG

PAPER ROSES Lola Dee—Wing 90015
[Emery Altimus/Ronald Badger*/Fred Dexter] [BMI] (11/12/55 B-72)

PAPER ROSES *Anita Bryant—Carlton 528*
[Fred Spielman/Janice Torre] [ASC] (4/4/60 BCR-3)

PAPER ROSES *Marie Osmond—MGM 14609*
[Fred Spielman/Janice Torre] [ASC] (9/8/73 BCR-4)

PAPER SUN Traffic Featuring Stevie Winwood—United Artists 50195
[Jim Capaldi/Dave Mason*/Steve Winwood/Chris Wood*] [ASC] (8/12/67 BCR-67)

PAPER TIGER Sue Thompson—Hickory 1284
[John D. Loudermilk] [BMI] (12/26/64 BCR-18)

PAPER VALENTINE *The Mills Brothers—Decca 29382*
[David E. Coleman] [BMI] (1/10/55 Rt-53)

PAPER VALENTINE *The Crackerjacks—Kapp 106*
[David E. Coleman] [BMI] (1/31/55 Rt-53)

PAPERBACK WRITER The Beatles—Capitol 5651
[John Lennon/Paul McCartney] [ASC] (6/11/66 BCR-1)

PAPERLATE Genesis—Atlantic 4053
[Tony Banks/Phil Collins/Mike Rutherford] [ASC] (6/5/82 BC-31)

PARADISE Sammy Turner—Big Top 3032
[Nacio Herb Brown/Gordon Clifford] [ASC] (2/15/60 BCR-33)

PARADISE Change—RFC/Atlantic 3809
[Mauro Malavasi/Davide Romani/Tanyayette Willoughby] [ASC] (5/9/81 BCR-62)

PARADISE Sade—Epic 07904
[Helen Adu/Paul Denman/Andrew Hale/Stuart Matthewman] [BMI] (5/14/88 BC-16)

PARADISE BY THE DASHBOARD LIGHT Meat Loaf—Cleveland Int'l/Epic 50588
[Jim Steinman] [BMI] (8/12/78 BCR-37)

PARADISE CITY Guns N' Roses—Geffen 27570
[Steven Adler/Saul Hudson/Duff McKagan/Axl Rose/Izzy Stradlin] [ASC] (1/14/89 BC-4)

PARALYZED Elvis Presley—RCA Victor EPA-992
[Otis Blackwell/Elvis Presley] [BMI] (12/29/56 B-59)

PARANOID Black Sabbath—Warner Bros. 7437
[Terry Butler/Tony Iommi/Ozzy Osbourne/Bill Ward] [ASC] (11/28/70 BCR-58)

PARANOIMIA The Art Of Noise with Max Headroom—China 43002
[Anne Dudley/Jonathan Jeczalik/Gary Langan] [ASC] (8/16/86 BC-32)

PARDON ME Billy Bland—Old Town 1082 [Otis Blackwell] [BMI] (7/16/60 C-81)

PARDON ME SIR Joe Cocker—A&M 1407
[Joe Cocker/Chris Stainton] [ASC] (2/17/73 BCR-48)

PARENTS JUST DON'T UNDERSTAND D.J. Jazzy Jeff & The Fresh Prince—Jive 1099
[Peter Brian Harris/Will Smith/Jeff Townes] [ASC] (5/7/88 BC-12)

PARIS Perez Prado And His Orchestra—RCA Victor 47-7337
[Perez Prado] [BMI] (10/20/58 B-95) [I]

PARRTY (PART 1) Maceo And The Macks—People 624
[James Brown] [BMI] (9/1/73 BR-71)

PART OF ME Jimmy Clanton—Ace 551
[Jimmy Clanton/Cosimo Matassa] [BMI] (10/20/58 BCR-38)

PART OF ME, PART OF YOU Glenn Frey—MCA 54060
[Glenn Frey/Jack Tempchin] [ASC] (5/11/91 BC-49)

PART OF ME THAT NEEDS YOU MOST Jay Black—Midsong Int'l 72012
[Mike Chapman/Nicky Chinn] [ASC] (9/20/80 B-98)

PART OF THE PLAN Dan Fogelberg—Epic 50055
[Dan Fogelberg] [ASC] (12/28/74 BCR-24)

A PART OF YOU Brenda & The Tabulations—Top & Bottom 408
[Joe Cobb/Van McCoy] [BMI] (8/28/71 BCR-84)

PART TIME LOVE *Little Johnny Taylor—Galaxy 722*
[Clay Hammond] [BMI] (8/17/63 BCR-19)

I'M YOUR PART TIME LOVE *(response to Part Time Love) Mitty Collier—Chess 1871*
[Clay Hammond/Albert B. Smith] [BMI] (10/19/63 R-94) [R]

PART TIME LOVE *Ann Peebles—Hi 2178 [Clay Hammond] [BMI] (9/19/70 BCR-27)*

PART TIME LOVE Gladys Knight & The Pips—Buddah 513
[David Gates] [ASC] (11/1/75 BCR-22)

PART TIME LOVE Kerry Chater—Warner Bros. 8310
[Michael Omartian/Stormie Omartian] [ASC] (2/26/77 BC-80)

PART-TIME LOVE Elton John—MCA 40973
[Elton John/Gary Osborne] [BMI] (11/4/78 BCR-13)

PART-TIME LOVER Stevie Wonder—Tamla 1808 [Stevie Wonder] [ASC] (9/7/85 BC-1)

PARTIN' TIME B.B. King—Kent 346 [Joe Josea‡/B.B. King] [BMI] (7/30/60 C-89)

PARTNERS Jim Reeves—RCA Victor 47-7557 [Danny Dill] [BMI] (7/27/59 R-79)

PARTY Van McCoy—H&L 4670 [Van McCoy] [BMI] (7/17/76 BCR-62)

PARTY ALL THE TIME Eddie Murphy—Columbia 05609 [Rick James] [ASC] (10/5/85 BC-2)

PARTY BLUES
Count Basie Small Band with Ella Fitzgerald and Joe Williams—Clef 89172
[Count Basie/Ella Fitzgerald/Joe Williams] [BMI] (1/5/57 R-60)

***PARTY DOLL** Buddy Knox with The Rhythm Orchids—Roulette 4002*
[Dave Alldred/Jimmy Bowen/Buddy Knox/Donnie Lanier*] [BMI] (2/9/57 BCtRt-1)*

***PARTY DOLL** Wingy Manone And His Orchestra—Decca 30211*
[Dave Alldred/Jimmy Bowen/Buddy Knox/Donnie Lanier*] [BMI] (2/9/57 BRt-1)*

***PARTY DOLL** Steve Lawrence—Coral 61792*
[Dave Alldred/Jimmy Bowen/Buddy Knox/Donnie Lanier*] [BMI] (2/16/57 BCtRt-1)*

***PARTY DOLL** Roy Brown—Imperial 5427*
[Dave Alldred/Jimmy Bowen/Buddy Knox/Donnie Lanier*] [BMI] (4/29/57 B-89)*

***PARTY DOLL** Cat Mother And The All Night News Boys—Polydor 14002*
[Dave Alldred/Jimmy Bowen/Buddy Knox/Donnie Lanier*] (Med) [BMI]*
(6/21/69 BCR-12)

PARTY GIRL Bernadette Carroll—Laurie 3238
[Ernie Maresca/Lou Zerato*] [BMI] (5/16/64 BCR-45)

PARTY GIRL Tommy Roe—ABC-Paramount 10604
[Buddy Buie/William Gilmore] [BMI] (12/5/64 BR-85)

PARTY HEARTY Oliver Sain—Abet 9463 [Oliver Sain] (TSW) [BMI] (2/21/76 R-76) [I]

PARTY LIGHTS Claudine Clark—Chancellor 1113 [Claudine Clark] [BMI] (6/30/62 BCR-5)

PARTY LIGHTS Natalie Cole—Capitol 4439 [Tennyson Stephens] [BMI] (7/23/77 B-79)

PARTY LINE Andrea True Connection—Buddah 538
[Gregg Diamond] [ASC] (8/7/76 BC-80)

PARTY MUSIC Pat Lundi—Vigor 1723
[Melissa Manchester/David Wolfert] [BMI] (9/6/75 BC-78)

PARTY TIME Sal Mineo—Epic 9246 [Bernie Lowe/Kal Mann] [BMI] (11/2/57 BC-45)

PARTYMAN Prince—Warner Bros. 22814 [Prince] [ASC] (8/26/89 BC-15)

***THE PARTY'S OVER** Doris Day—Columbia 40798*
[Betty Comden/Adolph Green/Jule Styne] [ASC] (12/22/56 BCRt-47)

***THE PARTY'S OVER** Carmen McRae—Decca 30112*
[Betty Comden/Adolph Green/Jule Styne] [ASC] (2/9/57 Rt-74)

***THE PARTY'S OVER** Lurlean Hunter—Vik 0241*
[Betty Comden/Adolph Green/Jule Styne] [ASC] (2/9/57 Rt-74)

THE PARTY'S OVER (HOPELESSLY IN LOVE) Journey—Columbia 60505
[Steve Perry] [BMI] (2/28/81 BCR-34)

***PASS ME BY** Peggy Lee—Capitol 5346*
[Cy Coleman/Carolyn Leigh] [ASC] (2/20/65 BCtR-86)

***PASS ME BY** Mike Douglas—Epic 9760 [Cy Coleman/Carolyn Leigh] [ASC] (3/6/65 Ct-86)*

PASS THE APPLE EVE B.J. Thomas—Scepter 12255
[Johnny Christopher/Mark James] [BMI] (6/28/69 BCR-82)

PASS THE DUTCHIE Musical Youth—MCA 52149
[Headley Bennett*/Huford Benjamin Brown*/Lloyd Ferguson/Robert Lyn*/
Jackie Mittoo/Leroy Sibblis*/Fitzroy Simpson] [ASC] (12/11/82 BC-10)

PASS THE PEAS The J.B.'s—People 607
[Charles Bobbit/James Brown/John Starks] [BMI] (5/13/72 BCR-76) [I]

PASSING STRANGERS Sarah Vaughan & Billy Eckstine—Mercury 71122
[Stanley Applebaum/Mel Mitchell] [ASC] (7/6/57 BCR-36)

PASSION Rod Stewart—Warner Bros. 49617
[Phil Chen/Jim Cregan/Gary Grainger/Kevin Savigar/Rod Stewart] [ASC]
(11/22/80 BCR-4)

P.A.S.S.I.O.N. Rythm Syndicate—Impact 54046
[Evan Rogers/Carl Sturken] [BMI] (6/1/91 BC-2)

PASSION FLOWER Caterina Valente—Telefunken 4502
[Perry Botkin Jr./Gil Garfield/Patrick Murtagh/Ludwig van Beethoven] [ASC]
(8/10/59 R-98)

A PASSION PLAY (EDIT #8) Jethro Tull—Chrysalis 2012
[Ian Anderson] [ASC] (5/12/73 BCR-60)

PASSPORT TO THE FUTURE Jean Jacques Perrey—Vanguard 35105
[Andy Badale/Robert Colby/Paul Mauriat/Jean-Jacques Perrey] [ASC]
(5/30/70 CR-93) [I]

PAST, PRESENT AND FUTURE The Shangri-Las—Red Bird 10-068
[Artie Butler/Jerry Leiber/Shadow Morton] [BMI] (6/25/66 BCR-57)

PAT-A-CAKE The Singing Dogs—RCA Victor 47-6344
[Traditional] (Med) [NA] (12/10/55 CR-23)

PATA PATA Miriam Makeba—Reprise 0606
[Miriam Makeba/Jerry Ragovoy] [ASC] (10/7/67 BCR-12) [F]

PATCH IT UP Elvis Presley—RCA Victor 47-9916
[Rory Bourke/Eddie Rabbitt] (TSW) [BMI] (10/24/70 BR-7)

PATCH OF BLUE Frankie Valli & The 4 Seasons—Philips 40662
[Angelo M. Cifelli/Mike Petrillo] [BMI] (4/25/70 BCR-53)

PATCHES Dickey Lee—Smash 1758 [Larry Kolber/Barry Mann] [BMI] (8/18/62 BCR-4)

PATCHES Clarence Carter—Atlantic 2748
[Ronald Dunbar/General Johnson] [BMI] (7/18/70 BCR-1)

PATHS OF PARADISE Johnnie Ray—Columbia 40435
[Johnnie Ray] [ASC] (2/19/55 CR-42)

PATIENCE Guns N' Roses—Geffen 22996
[Steven Adler/Saul Hudson/Duff McKagan/Axl Rose/Izzy Stradlin] [ASC] (4/8/89 BC-4)

***PATRICIA** Perez Prado And His Orchestra—RCA Victor 47-7245*
[Perez Prado] [BMI] (6/9/58 BCRt-1) [I]

***PATRICIA** Morty Craft & His Orchestra—MGM 12672*
[Perez Prado] [BMI] (6/9/58 Rt-1) [I]

***PATRICIA** Jerry Martin—Chock 106 [Bob Marcus/Perez Prado] [BMI] (9/1/58 Rt-3)*

***PATRICIA** Ray Peterson—RCA Victor 47-7303*
[Bob Marcus/Perez Prado] [BMI] (9/1/58 Rt-3)

***PATRICIA - TWIST** Perez Prado And His Orchestra—RCA Victor 47-8006*
[Perez Prado] [BMI] (3/12/62 BR-65) [I]

PATSY Jack Scott—Top Rank 2075 [Clyde Otis] [BMI] (10/10/60 BCR-35)

PATTI ANN Johnny Crawford—Del-Fi 4172
[Cliff Goldsmith/Fred Smith] [BMI] (2/24/62 BCR-40)

***PATTY BABY** Terry Noland—Brunswick 55036*
[Walter Baker/Rick Tucker] [ASC] (1/20/58 Rt-81)

***PATTY BABY** Rick Tucker & The Picks—Columbia 41041*
[Walter Baker/Rick Tucker] [ASC] (1/20/58 Rt-81)

PATTY BABY Freddy Cannon—Swan 4139
[Freddy Cannon/Bob Feldman/Jerry Goldstein/Richard Gottehrer] [ASC]
(5/4/63 BCR-62)

PAY BACK Etta James—Argo 5445 [Billy Davis] [BMI] (8/10/63 BCR-75)

PAY THE DEVIL (OOO, BABY, OOO) The Knack—Capitol 5054
[Berton Averre] [ASC] (10/31/81 BCR-67)

PAY TO THE PIPER Chairmen Of The Board—Invictus 9081
[Angelo Bond/Ronald Dunbar/General Johnson/Greg Perry] [BMI] (11/7/70 BCR-7)

***PAY YOU BACK WITH INTEREST** The Hollies—Imperial 66240*
[Allan Clarke/Tony Hicks/Graham Nash] [BMI] (6/3/67 BCR-28)

***PAY YOU BACK WITH INTEREST** Gary O'—Capitol 5018*
[Allan Clarke/Tony Hicks/Graham Nash] [BMI] (7/18/81 BC-70)

THE PAYBACK - PART I James Brown—Polydor 14223
[James Brown/John Starks/Fred Wesley] [BMI] (3/9/74 BCR-23)

PAYING THE COST TO BE THE BOSS B.B. King—BluesWay 61015
[B.B. King] [BMI] (4/6/68 BCR-39)

PEACE The McGuire Sisters—Coral 62106
[Jack Fulton/Lois Steele] [ASC] (4/27/59 BCR-75)

PEACE BROTHER PEACE Bill Medley—MGM 14000
[Barry Mann/Cynthia Weil] [BMI] (10/26/68 BCR-48)

PEACE IN OUR TIME Eddie Money—Columbia 73047
[Andy Hill/Peter Sinfield] [ASC] (12/2/89 BC-8)

—PEACE IN THE VALLEY see: THERE'LL BE PEACE IN THE VALLEY FOR ME

PEACE IN THE VALLEY OF LOVE The Persuaders—Win Or Lose 225
[Jackie Members/Richard Poindexter/Robert Poindexter] [BMI] (11/18/72 CR-92)

PEACE OF MIND Teresa Brewer—Coral 62167 [Lou Fields] [ASC] (2/1/60 BCR-66)

PEACE OF MIND Paul Revere And The Raiders Featuring Mark Lindsay—Columbia 44335
[Mark Lindsay/Terry Melcher] [BMI] (11/18/67 BCR-35)

PEACE OF MIND Nancy Wilson—Capitol 2283 [Nick Woods] [ASC] (9/28/68 BCR-54)

PEACE OF MIND Boston—Epic 50381 [Tom Scholz] [ASC] (5/7/77 BCR-33)

PEACE PIPE B.T. Express—Roadshow 7003
[Mark Barkan/Sammy Taylor] (TSW) [BMI] (10/4/75 BCR-31)

PEACE TRAIN Cat Stevens—A&M 1291 [Cat Stevens] [ASC] (9/25/71 BCR-4)

PEACE WILL COME (ACCORDING TO PLAN) Melanie—Buddah 186
[Melanie Safka] [ASC] (8/15/70 BCR-20)

PEACEFUL Helen Reddy—Capitol 3527 [Kenny Rankin] [BMI] (2/3/73 BCR-11)

PEACEFUL EASY FEELING Eagles—Asylum 11013
[Jack Tempchin] [ASC] (12/23/72 BCR-18)

THE PEACEMAKER Albert Hammond—Mums 6021
[Albert Hammond/Mike Hazlewood] [ASC] (8/4/73 BCR-80)

PEACHES 'N' CREAM The Ikettes—Modern 1005
[Tommy Boyce/Steve Venet] [BMI] (3/13/65 BCR-34)

PEAK OF LOVE Bobby McClure—Checker 1152
[Billy Davis/Sugar Pie DeSanto] [BMI] (12/10/66 BC-97)

PEANUT BUTTER The Marathons—Arvee 5027
[H.B. Barnum/Marty Cooper/Cliff Goldsmith/Fred Smith] [BMI] (4/24/61 BCR-20)

PEANUT BUTTER Twennynine Featuring Lenny White—Elektra 46552
[Donald Blackman/Lenny White*] [BMI] (12/29/79 BCR-66)

***PEANUTS** Little Joe And The Thrillers—Okeh 7088 [Joe Cook] [BMI] (9/16/57 BCR-23)*

***PEANUTS** Rick And The Keens—Smash 1705 [Joe Cook] [BMI] (7/3/61 BCR-60)*

***PEANUTS** The Four Seasons—Vee-Jay EP 901 [Joe Cook] [BMI] (1/4/64 R-72)*

PEANUTS (LA CACAHUATA) The Sunglows—Sunglow 107
[Luis Guerrero] [BMI] (4/24/65 BCR-54) [I]

PEARL Tommy Roe—ABC 11266 [Tommy Roe/Freddy Weller] [BMI] (6/20/70 BCR-30)

PEARL TIME Andre Williams—Sport 105 [Andre Williams] [BMI] (7/29/67 BCR-90)

***THE FIRST NIGHT OF THE FULL MOON** Jack Jones—Kapp 589*
[Hal David/Alfred Kealoha Perry/Traditional] [ASC] (5/30/64 BCR-54) [FDE]

***PEARLY SHELLS (POPO O EWA)** Burl Ives—Decca 31659*
[Webley Edwards/Leon Pober/Traditional] [ASC] (8/29/64 BCtR-60) [FDE]

***PEARLY SHELLS** Arthur Lyman—GNP Crescendo 315*
[Webley Edwards/Leon Pober/Traditional] [ASC] (10/24/64 Ct-62) [IWM]

PEAS 'N' RICE Freddie McCoy—Prestige 450
[Freddie McCoy] [BMI] (10/7/67 B-92) [IM]

THE PEDDLER MAN (TEN I LOVED) Dean Martin—Capitol 2870 [Nicholas Brodszky/Jack Lawrence] [ASC] (8/21/54 C-33)

PEEK A BOO The Cadillacs—Josie 846 [Jack Hammer] [ASC] (11/17/58 BCR-28)

PEEK-A-BOO The New Vaudeville Band—Fontana 1573 [John Carter/Geoff Stephens] [ASC] (2/18/67 BCR-72)

PEEK-A-BOO Siouxsie & The Banshees—Geffen 27760 [Susan Ballion/Peter Clarke/Steven Severin] [ASC] (10/15/88 BC-53)

PEEP PEEP POP POP Dearly Beloveds—Columbia 43797 [Edward Harry Deo/Kinder Nolen/Arthur Shorter] [BMI] (10/29/66 CR-93)

PEEPIN' 'N HIDIN' Count Victors Featuring Danny Harrison—Coral 62324 [Jimmy Reed] [BMI] (9/15/62 C-91)

PEG Steely Dan—ABC 12320 [Walter Becker/Donald Fagen] [ASC] (11/19/77 BCR-8)

PEG O' MY HEART *Seymour & His Heartbeat Trumpet—Heartbeat 7 [Fred Fisher] [NA] (8/4/58 R-35) [IM]*

PEG O' MY HEART *Robert Maxwell, His Harp And Orchestra—Decca 25637 [Fred Fisher] [NA] (6/20/64 BCR-51) [IM]*

PEGGY SUE *Buddy Holly / The Crickets—Coral 61885 [Jerry Allison/Buddy Holly*/Norman Petty] [ASC] (10/21/57 BCRt-2)*

PEGGY SUE *Jackie Walker—Imperial 5473 [Jerry Allison/Buddy Holly*/Norman Petty] [ASC] (12/9/57 Rt-3)*

PEGGY SUE *The Beach Boys—Brother/Reprise 1394 [Jerry Allison/Buddy Holly*/Norman Petty] [ASC] (9/2/78 BCR-59)*

PENETRATION The Pyramids—Best 13002 [Steve Leonard] [ASC] (1/11/64 BCR-17) [I]

PENNIES FROM HEAVEN The Skyliners—Calico 117 [Johnny Burke/Arthur Johnston] [ASC] (5/7/60 BCR-24)

PENNSYLVANIA 6-5000 Frank Barber Orchestra—Victory 1001 [Jerry Gray/Carl Sigman*] (Med) [ASC] (5/8/82 B-61) [IWM]

PENNSYLVANIA WALTZ *Wayne King—Decca 30171 [Sunny Skylar] [ASC] (1/19/57 Rt-83) [IWM]*

PENNSYLVANIA WALTZ *Billy Vaughn and His Orchestra—Dot 15530 [Sunny Skylar] [ASC] (1/19/57 Rt-83) [IWM]*

PENNY ARCADE The Cyrkle—Columbia 44224 [Sandy Linzer/Denny Randell] [BMI] (8/5/67 BCR-60)

A PENNY FOR YOUR THOUGHTS Tavares—RCA 13292 [Kenny Nolan] [ASC] (9/18/82 BC-28)

PENNY LANE The Beatles—Capitol 5810 [John Lennon/Paul McCartney] [ASC] (2/25/67 BCR-1)

PENNY LOAFERS AND BOBBY SOCKS Joe Bennett And The Sparkletones—ABC-Paramount 9867 [Joe Bennett] [BMI] (12/2/57 BCR-41)

PENNY LOVER Lionel Richie—Motown 1762 [Brenda Richie/Lionel Richie] [ASC] (10/6/84 BC-8)

PEOPLE *Nat King Cole—Capitol 5155 [Bob Merrill/Jule Styne] [ASC] (4/4/64 BCtR-49)*

PEOPLE *Barbra Streisand—Columbia 42965 [Bob Merrill/Jule Styne] [ASC] (4/4/64 BCtR-5)*

PEOPLE *The Tymes—Columbia 44630 [Bob Merrill/Jule Styne] [ASC] (11/16/68 BCR-34)*

PEOPLE ARE CHANGIN' Timmy Thomas—Glades 1709 [Timmy Thomas] [BMI] (4/7/73 BCR-75)

PEOPLE ARE PEOPLE Depeche Mode—Sire 29221 [Martin L. Gore] [BMI] (5/18/85 BC-13)

PEOPLE ARE STILL HAVING SEX LaTour—Smash 879 666 [William LaTour] [BMI] (4/6/91 BC-35)

PEOPLE ARE STRANGE The Doors—Elektra 45621 [John Densmore/Robby Krieger/Ray Manzarek/Jim Morrison] [ASC] (9/16/67 BCR-10)

PEOPLE GET READY *The Impressions—ABC-Paramount 10622 [Curtis Mayfield] [BMI] (2/13/65 BCR-14)*

PEOPLE GET READY *Jeff Beck And Rod Stewart—Epic 05416 [Curtis Mayfield] [BMI] (6/15/85 BC-44)*

PEOPLE GOT TO BE FREE *The Rascals—Atlantic 2537 [Eddie Brigati/Felix Cavaliere] [ASC] (7/13/68 BCR-1)*

PEOPLE GOTTA BE FREE *The 5th Dimension—Bell 860 [Eddie Brigati/Felix Cavaliere] (Med/TSW) [ASC] (2/28/70 BR-54)*

PEOPLE GOTTA MOVE Gino Vannelli—A&M 1614 [Gino Vannelli] [ASC] (9/7/74 BCR-22)

PEOPLE IN LOVE 10cc—Mercury 73917 [Graham Gouldman/Eric Stewart] [BMI] (5/21/77 BCR-40)

THE PEOPLE IN ME The Music Machine—Original Sound 67 [Sean Bonniwell] [BMI] (1/28/67 BCR-65)

PEOPLE LIKE YOU Eddie Fisher—RCA Victor 47-9070 [Larry Kusik/Eddie Snyder] [ASC] (2/11/67 BCR-61)

PEOPLE MAKE THE WORLD GO ROUND The Stylistics—Avco 4595 [Thom Bell/Linda Creed] [BMI] (5/27/72 BCR-16)

PEOPLE OF THE SOUTH WIND Kansas—Kirshner 4284 [Kerry Livgren] [BMI] (6/2/79 BCR-23)

PEOPLE SAY The Dixie Cups—Red Bird 10-006 [Jeff Barry/Ellie Greenwich] [BMI] (7/11/64 BCR-7)

PEOPLE SURE ACT FUNNY Arthur Conley—Atco 6588 [James McDougal/Titus Turner] [BMI] (6/15/68 BCR-37)

THE PEOPLE TREE Sammy Davis, Jr. With The Mike Curb Congregation—MGM 14426 [Leslie Bricusse/Anthony Newley] [BMI] (10/21/72 BCR-87)

PEOPLE WORLD Jim & Jean—Verve Forecast 5073 [Jean Glover] [BMI] (2/3/68 BCR-85)

PEPE Duane Eddy His "Twangy" Guitar And The Rebels—Jamie 1175 [Hans Wittstatt] [ASC] (12/12/60 BCR-15) [IM]

PEPINO THE ITALIAN MOUSE Lou Monte—Reprise 20,106 [Ray Allen/Wandra Merrell] [BMI] (11/24/62 BCR-4)

PEPINO'S FRIEND PASQUAL (THE ITALIAN PUSSY-CAT) Lou Monte—Reprise 20,146 [Ray Allen/Wandra Merrell] [BMI] (2/23/63 BCR-45)

PEPPER BOX The Peppers—Event 213 [Mat Camison/Pierre-Alain Dahan] [BMI] (2/16/74 BCR-61) [I]

PEPPER HOT BABY *Jaye P. Morgan—RCA Victor 47-6282 [Alicia Evelyn] [BMI] (10/17/55 BCRt-14)*

PEPPER HOT BABY *Gisele MacKenzie—"X" 0172 [Alicia Evelyn] [BMI] (10/17/55 BRt-14)*

PEPPER-HOT BABY *Bonnie Davis—Decca 29718 [Alicia Evelyn] [BMI] (10/24/55 Rt-14)*

PEPPERMINT MAN Dick Dale And His Del-Tones—Deltone 5020 [Alonzo Willis] [BMI] (1/12/63 C-91)

PEPPERMINT TWIST - PART 1 Joey Dee & The Starliters—Roulette 4401 [Joey Dee/Henry Glover] [BMI] (11/13/61 BCR-1)

THE PEPPERMINT TWIST Danny Peppermint And The Jumping Jacks—Carlton 565 [Danny Peppermint] [ASC] (12/4/61 B-54)

PER-SO-NAL-LY Bobby Paris—Tetragrammaton 1504 [Bobby Paris] [BMI] (9/14/68 CR-82)

PERCOLATIN' Willie Mitchell—Hi 2083 [Jerry Arnold] [BMI] (12/19/64 BR-85) [I]

PERCOLATOR (TWIST) *Billy Joe & The Checkmates—Dore 620 [Lou Bideu/Ernie Freeman] [ASC] (1/13/62 BCR-10) [I]*

PERCOLATOR *Hot Butter—Musicor 1473 [Lou Bideu/Ernie Freeman] [ASC] (4/21/73 CR-82) [I]*

PERFECT Fairground Attraction—RCA 8789 [Mark Nevin] [ASC] (12/17/88 BC-80)

PERFECT COMBINATION Stacy Lattisaw & Johnny Gill—Cotillion [Preston Glass/Narada Michael Walden] [ASC] (3/10/84 BC-75)

PERFECT LOVE Frankie Avalon—Chancellor 1065 [Peter DeAngelis/Bob Marcucci/Jimmy Wisner] [ASC] (11/21/60 BCR-47)

PERFECT WAY Scritti Politti—Warner Bros. 28949 [David Gamson/Green Gartside] [ASC] (9/7/85 BC-10)

PERFECT WORLD Huey Lewis and the News—Chrysalis 43265 [Alex Call] [BMI] (7/16/88 BC-3)

PERFECT WORLD Alias—Giant 19249 [Glen Burtnick/Steve Krikorian] [ASC] (6/29/91 BC-79)

PERFIDIA The Ventures—Dolton 28 [Alberto Dominguez] [BMI] (10/31/60 BCR-12) [I]

PERHAPS LOVE Placido Domingo And John Denver—Columbia 02679 [John Denver] [ASC] (1/16/82 BCR-59)

PERIOD The Four Knights—Capitol 2847 [Jenny Lou Carson] [BMI] (7/24/54 C-29)

PERMANENTLY LONELY Timi Yuro—Liberty 55665 [Willie Nelson] [BMI] (2/29/64 R-97)

PERSONAL JESUS Depeche Mode—Sire 4-19941 [Martin L. Gore] [BMI] (12/9/89 BC-28)

PERSONALITY *Lloyd Price—ABC-Paramount 10018 [Harold Logan/Lloyd Price] [BMI] (4/27/59 BCR-2)*

(YOU'VE GOT) PERSONALITY *Mitch Ryder—DynoVoice 905 [Harold Logan/Lloyd Price] (Med) [BMI] (1/27/68 BCR-58)*

PERSONALLY Karla Bonoff—Columbia 02805 [Paul Kelly] [BMI] (5/1/82 BC-12)

PET ME, PAPPA Rosemary Clooney—Columbia 40579 [Frank Loesser] [ASC] (11/12/55 B-62)

PETE KELLY'S BLUES *Ray Anthony—Capitol 3176 [Ray Heindorf] [ASC] (8/8/55 CRt-45) [IM]*

PETE KELLY'S BLUES *June Christy—Capitol 3213 [Sammy Cahn/Ray Heindorf] [ASC] (8/29/55 Rt-71)*

PETE KELLY'S BLUES *Ella Fitzgerald—Decca 29609 [Sammy Cahn/Ray Heindorf] [ASC] (8/29/55 Rt-71)*

PETE KELLY'S BLUES *Ray Heindorf & The Warner Bros. Orchestra—Columbia 40533 [Ray Heindorf] [ASC] (8/29/55 Rt-71) [IM]*

PETER AND THE WOLF Charles Randolph Grean Sounde—Ranwood 864 [Sergei Prokofiev] [NA] (3/7/70 R-91) [I]

PETER GUNN *Ray Anthony—Capitol 4041 [Henry Mancini] [ASC] (12/29/58 BCRt-7) [I]*

PETER GUNN THEME *Henry Mancini And His Orchestra—RCA Victor 47-7460 [Henry Mancini] [ASC] (3/2/59 Rt-10) [I]*

PETER GUNN *Duane Eddy His "Twangy" Guitar And The Rebels—Jamie 1168 [Henry Mancini] [ASC] (10/3/60 BCR-23) [I]*

PETER GUNN *Deodato—MCA 40631 [Henry Mancini] [ASC] (10/23/76 BC-84) [I]*

PETER GUNN *The Art Of Noise featuring Duane Eddy—China 42986 [Henry Mancini] [ASC] (5/17/86 BC-49) [I]*

PETER PIPER Frank Mills—Polydor 2002 [Frank Mills] [BMI] (10/27/79 BCR-48) [I]

PETER RABBIT Dee Jay And The Runaways—Smash 2034 [Myron Wachendorf] [BMI] (5/7/66 BCR-39)

—PETIT REVEIL see: LE PETIT REVEIL

PETITE FLEUR (LITTLE FLOWER) *Chris Barber's Jazz Band—Laurie 3022 [Sidney Bechet] [ASC] (1/10/59 BCRt-3) [IM]*

PETITE FLEUR *Bob Crosby & The Bob Cats—Dot 15890 [Sidney Bechet] [ASC] (1/26/59 Rt-4) [IM]*

PETITE FLEUR (LITTLE FLOWER) *Bob Wilber's Jazz Quartet—Cub 9021 [Sidney Bechet] [ASC] (1/26/59 Rt-36) [IM]*

***A TIME TO LOVE-A TIME TO CRY (PETITE FLEUR)** Lou Johnson—Big Top 101 [Bernie Baum/Sidney Bechet/Bill Giant/Florence Kaye] [ASC] (10/30/65 BCR-56)*

PETTICOAT WHITE (SUMMER SKY BLUE) Bobby Vinton—Epic 10048 [Doc Pomus/Mort Shuman] [BMI] (7/23/66 BCR-73)

***PETTICOATS OF PORTUGAL** Dick Jacobs And His Chorus And Orchestra—Coral 61724 [Michael Durso/Marvin Kahn/Mel Mitchell] [ASC] (10/13/56 BCtRt-10)*

***PETTICOATS OF PORTUGAL** Caesar Giovannini & Sextette—Bally 1018 [Michael Durso/Marvin Kahn/Mel Mitchell] [ASC] (10/13/56 CtRt-10) [IWM]*

***PETTICOATS OF PORTUGAL** Billy Vaughn and His Orchestra—Dot 15506 [Michael Durso/Marvin Kahn/Mel Mitchell] [ASC] (10/20/56 BRt-11) [IWM]*

***PETTICOATS OF PORTUGAL** Florian Zabach—Mercury 70975 [Michael Durso/Marvin Kahn/Mel Mitchell] [ASC] (10/20/56 Rt-32) [IWM]*

PHANTOM WRITER Gary Wright—Warner Bros. 8331 [Gary Wright] [ASC] (2/26/77 BCR-43)

PHILADELPHIA B.B. King—ABC 12029 [Dave Crawford] [ASC] (11/30/74 BC-64) [I]

PHILADELPHIA FREEDOM The Elton John Band—MCA 40364 [Elton John/Bernie Taupin] [BMI] (3/8/75 BCR-1)

***PHILADELPHIA USA** The Nu Tornados—Carlton 492 [Anthony Antonucci/Bill Borrelli] [ASC] (11/17/58 BCRt-16)*

***PHILADELPHIA USA** Art Lund—Coral 62054 [Anthony Antonucci/Bill Borrelli] [ASC] (11/17/58 BRt-16)*

***PHILADELPHIA U.S.A.** Milton DeLugg & His Orchestra—Dot 15865 [Anthony Antonucci/Bill Borrelli] [ASC] (11/24/58 Rt-41) [IWM]*

***PHILLY DOG** The Mar-Keys—Stax 185 [Rufus Thomas] [ASC] (3/5/66 BCR-89) [I]*

***PHILLY DOG** Herbie Mann—Atlantic 5074 [Rufus Thomas] [ASC] (10/1/66 B-93) [I]*

THE PHILLY FREEZE Alvin Cash & The Registers—Mar-V-Lus 6012 [Otha Hayes/James Leonard Jones] [BMI] (7/23/66 BCR-44)

THE PHOENIX LOVE THEME (SENZA FINE) Brass Ring Featuring Phil Bodner—Dunhill 4023 [Gino Paoli] [BMI] (3/12/66 BCR-32) [IM]

***THE PHONOGRAPH SONG** Guy Lombardo And His Royal Canadians—Capitol 3371 [Joe Dixie/H. Evans/L. Hughes/Rudi Lindt] [NA] (3/2/56 Rt-75)*

***THE PHONOGRAPH SONG (OUR MELODY)** Billy May & His Orchestra—Capitol 3372 [Joe Dixie/H. Evans/L. Hughes/Rudi Lindt] [NA] (3/2/56 Rt-75)*

***THE PHONOGRAPH SONG (OUR MELODY)** Lou Stein—Epic 9156 [Joe Dixie/Rudi Lindt] [NA] (3/2/56 Rt-75) [IM]*

***WHISTLIN' WILLIE (OUR MELODY)** The Chordettes—Cadence 1284 [Archie Bleyer/Joe Dixie/Rudi Lindt] [NA] (3/2/56 Rt-75)*

***THE PHONOGRAPH SONG (OUR MELODY)** Art Mooney & His Orchestra—MGM 12190 [Joe Dixie/H. Evans/L. Hughes/Rudi Lindt] [NA] (3/23/56 Rt-75)*

PHOTOGRAPH Ringo Starr—Apple 1865 [George Harrison/Ringo Starr] [ASC] (10/6/73 BCR-1)

PHOTOGRAPH Def Leppard—Mercury 811215 [Rick Allen/Steve Clark/Joe Elliott/Mutt Lange/Rick Savage/Pete Willis] [ASC] (3/12/83 BC-12)

PHYSICAL Olivia Newton-John—MCA 51182 [Steve Kipner/Terry Shaddick] [ASC] (10/3/81 BCR-1)

PIANO CONCERTO IN A MINOR The Royal Philharmonic Orchestra—RCA 12304 [Edvard Grieg] (Med) [NA] (10/31/81 BCR-9) [I]

PIANO CONCERTO NO. 1 The Royal Philharmonic Orchestra—RCA 12304 [Pyotr Ilyich Tchaikovsky] (Med) [NA] (10/31/81 BCR-9) [I]

PIANO IN THE DARK Brenda Russell—A&M 3003 [Scott Cutler/Jeff Hull/Brenda Russell] [ASC] (2/13/88 BC-6)

PIANO MAN Billy Joel—Columbia 45963 [Billy Joel] [ASC] (2/9/74 BCR-16)

PIANO SHUFFLE Dave "Baby" Cortez—Clock 1014 [David Clowney/Ken Wood] [BMI] (10/31/59 C-99) [I]

—PICCOLISSIMA SERENATA see: LITTLE SERENADE

PICK ME UP ON YOUR WAY DOWN Pat Zill—Indigo 119 [Harlan Howard] [BMI] (4/29/61 BCR-85)

PICK UP THE PACE 1990 Young M.C.—Delicious Vinyl 440 113 [Matt Dike/Marvin Young] [ASC] (12/29/90 C-83)

PICK UP THE PIECES Carla Thomas—Stax 239 [Kent Barker/Fred Briggs/Don Davis] [BMI] (12/23/67 BCR-68)

PICK UP THE PIECES AWB—Atlantic 3229 [Roger Ball/Malcolm Duncan/Alan Gorrie/Robbie McIntosh/Onnie McIntyre/Hamish Stuart] [ASC] (11/23/74 BCR-1) [I]

PICKIN' WILD MOUNTAIN BERRIES Peggy Scott & Jo Jo Benson—SSS Int'l 748 [Bob McRee/Cliff Thomas/Edward S. Thomas Jr.] [BMI] (10/12/68 BCR-24)

PICKLE UP A DOODLE Teresa Brewer—Coral 62013 [Jeannie Joy] [BMI] (8/11/58 BR-87)

—PICNIC see: THEME FROM PICNIC

PICTURES IN THE FIRE Pat Boone—Dot 16312 [Martin Kalmanoff/Lenore Rosenblatt] [ASC] (1/20/62 BCR-63)

PICTURES OF LILY The Who—Decca 32156 [Pete Townshend] [ASC] (7/1/67 BCR-49)

PICTURES OF MATCHSTICK MEN The Status Quo—Cadet Concept 7001 [Francis Rossi] [ASC] (5/11/68 BCR-11)

PICTURES OF YOU The Cure—Elektra 64974 [Simon Gallup/Roger O'Donnell/Robert James Smith/Porl Thompson/Laurence Tolhurst/Boris Williams] [ASC] (4/21/90 BC-67)

***PIDDILY PATTER** Nappy Brown—Savoy 1162 [Rose Marie McCoy/Charles Singleton] [BMI] (7/11/55 Rt-23)*

***PIDDILY PATTER PATTER** Patti Page—Mercury 70657 [Rose Marie McCoy/Charles Singleton] [BMI] (7/11/55 CRt-23)*

***PIDDILY PATTER PATTER** The Burton Sisters—RCA Victor 47-6186 [Rose Marie McCoy/Charles Singleton] [BMI] (7/11/55 Rt-31)*

***PIDDILY PATTER PATTER** Helene Dixon—Epic 9113 [Rose Marie McCoy/Charles Singleton] [BMI] (8/15/55 Rt-29)*

PIDDLE DE PAT Tommy Roe—ABC-Paramount 10362 [Felton Jarvis*/Tommy Roe] [BMI] (10/6/62 R-79)

PIECE BY PIECE The Tubes—Capitol 5443 [Rick Anderson/Michael Cotten/Charles Prince/Todd Rundgren/Tom Snow/William Spooner/Roger Steen/Fee Waybill/Vince Welnick] [BMI] (3/9/85 B-87)

***PIECE OF MY HEART** Erma Franklin—Shout 221 [Bert Berns/Jerry Ragovoy] [BMI] (11/4/67 BCR-61)*

***PIECE OF MY HEART** Big Brother And The Holding Company—Columbia 44626 [Bert Berns/Jerry Ragovoy] [BMI] (8/31/68 BCR-12)*

***PIECE OF MY HEART** Sammy Hagar—Geffen 50059 [Bert Berns/Jerry Ragovoy] [BMI] (5/15/82 B-73)*

PIECE OF MY HEART Tara Kemp—Giant 19364 [Tara Kemp/Tuhin Roy/Jake Smith] [BMI] (5/11/91 BC-7)

A PIECE OF PAPER Gladstone—ABC 11327 [Tom Russell/Richard Sellers] [BMI] (8/12/72 BCR-38)

PIECES OF APRIL Three Dog Night—Dunhill 4331 [Dave Loggins] [ASC] (11/11/72 BCR-18)

PIECES OF ICE Diana Ross—RCA 13549 [John Capek/Marc Jordan] [ASC] (6/25/83 BC-30)

THE PIED PIPER Billy Williams—Coral 61795 [Lee Denson] [BMI] (3/23/57 B-50)

***PIED PIPER** The Changin' Times—Philips 40320 [Steve Duboff/Artie Kornfeld] [BMI] (10/9/65 BCR-66)*

***THE PIED PIPER** Crispian St. Peters—Jamie 1320 [Steve Duboff/Artie Kornfeld] [BMI] (6/11/66 BCR-2)*

THE PILL Loretta Lynn—MCA 40358 [Lorene Allen/T.D. Bayless/Don McHan] [BMI] (3/1/75 BCR-49)

PILLOW TALK Sylvia—Vibration 521 [Michael Burton/Sylvia Robinson] [BMI] (3/24/73 BCR-2)

PILOT OF THE AIRWAVES Charlie Dore—Island 49166 [Charlie Dore] [ASC] (2/16/80 BCR-12)

PILTDOWN RIDES AGAIN The Piltdown Men—Capitol 4460 [Howard Adelman/Ed Cobb/Lincoln Mayorga] [BMI] (11/7/60 R-97) [I]

PIN A MEDAL ON JOEY James Darren—Colpix 672 [Ralph Montello/Billy Dawn Smith] [BMI] (2/9/63 BCR-51)

PIN THE TAIL ON THE DONKEY Paul Peek—Columbia 43527 [Dave Morrison/Henry Strzelecki] [BMI] (4/16/66 BR-90)

PIN THE TAIL ON THE DONKEY The Newcomers—Stax 0099 [Bettye Crutcher/Marvell Thomas] [BMI] (9/11/71 BCR-74)

PINBALL Brian Protheroe—Chrysalis 2104 [Brian Protheroe] [ASC] (3/29/75 BCR-60)

PINBALL, THAT'S ALL Bill Wray—ABC 12449 [Bill Wray] [ASC] (5/19/79 B-96)

***PINBALL WIZARD** The Who—Decca 732465 [Pete Townshend] [BMI] (3/29/69 BCR-15)*

***PINBALL WIZARD** The New Seekers—MGM/Verve 10709 [Pete Townshend] (Med) [BMI] (2/17/73 BCR-21)*

PINCH ME (BABY, CONVINCE ME) Ohio Express—Buddah 117 [Jerry Kasenetz/Jeff Katz/J.J. Woods] [BMI] (6/7/69 BCR-58)

—PINE TOP'S BOOGIE see: BOOGIE WOOGIE

PINEAPPLE PRINCESS Annette With The Afterbeats—Buena Vista 362 [Richard Sherman/Robert Sherman] [BMI] (8/8/60 BCR-11)

PINK CADILLAC Natalie Cole—EMI-Manhattan 50117 [Bruce Springsteen] [ASC] (3/5/88 BC-5)

PINK CHIFFON Mitchell Torok—Guyden 2034 [Ramona Redd/Mitchell Torok] [BMI] (4/18/60 BCR-56)

PINK DOMINOS The Crescents—Era 3116 [Bill Eucker] [BMI] (12/28/63 BCR-69) [I]

PINK HOUSES John Cougar Mellencamp—Riva 215 [John Mellencamp] [ASC] (12/10/83 BC-8)

THE PINK PANTHER THEME Henry Mancini And His Orchestra—RCA Victor 47-8286 [Henry Mancini] [ASC] (4/4/64 BCR-31) [I]

PINK PEDAL PUSHERS Carl Perkins—Columbia 41131 [Carl Perkins] [BMI] (3/31/58 BR-81)

PINK SHOE LACES Dodie Stevens—Crystalette 724 [Mickie Grant] [BMI] (2/16/59 BCR-3)

PINK SWEATER ANGEL Johnnie Ray with Ray Conniff & His Orch.—Columbia 41002 [Aaron Schroeder/Guy Wood] [ASC] (10/21/57 R-77)

PIPE DREAM Blues Magoos—Mercury 72660 [Ronald Gilbert/Ralph Scala] [BMI] (3/18/67 BCR-47)

PIPE DREAMS Jimmy Beck & His Orchestra—Champion 1002 [Alan Bubis/Harriet Bubis*] [BMI] (4/20/59 B-82) [I]

PIPELINE Chantay's—Dot 16440 [Brian Carman] [BMI] (3/2/63 BCR-4) [I]

PIRATE Cher—Warner Bros. 8311 [Steve Dorff/Gary Harju/Larry Herbstritt] [BMI] (1/15/77 B-93)

A PIRATE LOOKS AT FORTY Jimmy Buffett—ABC/Dunhill 15029 [Jimmy Buffett] [BMI] (4/12/75 C-97)

—PITIE SENORITA see: DON'T TELL ME WHY

PITTER-PATTER The Four Sportsmen—Sunnybrook 4
[Norman Brown/John Mobley] [BMI] (8/14/61 B-76)
PITTY PAT BAND Dori Anne Gray—Mercury 70801 [Dave Williams] [NA] (3/23/56 R-90)
PLACE IN THE SUN Johnny Nash—ABC-Paramount 10076
[Jack Delgado/Ira Kosloff/Vance Packard/Tom Pray] [BMI] (2/1/60 R-93)
A PLACE IN THE SUN Stevie Wonder—Tamla 54139
[Ronald Norman Miller/Bryan Wells] [BMI] (11/12/66 BCR-7)
A PLACE IN THE SUN Pablo Cruise—A&M 1976
[Bud Cockrell/Cory Lerios] [BMI] (9/17/77 BCR-42)
PLACE IN THIS WORLD Michael W. Smith—Reunion 19019
[Amy Grant/Wayne Kirkpatrick/Michael W. Smith] [ASC] (5/4/91 BC-3)
PLAIN AND SIMPLE GIRL Garland Green—Cotillion 44098
[Joe Cato] [BMI] (4/10/71 C-90)
PLAIN JANE Bobby Darin—Atco 6133
[Doc Pomus/Mort Shuman] [BMI] (1/26/59 BCR-30)
PLAIN JANE Sammy Hagar—Capitol 4757 [Sammy Hagar] [BMI] (9/15/79 BR-77)
PLANET ROCK Afrika Bambaataa And The Soul Sonic Force—Tommy Boy 823
[Arthur Baker/Afrika Bambaataa/John Robie] [BMI] (7/17/82 BC-48)
PLANTATION BOOGIE *Lenny Dee—Decca 29360 [Lenny Dee] [BMI] (2/5/55 BCRt-19) [IM]*
PLANTATION BOOGIE *Shay Torrent—Mercury 70542 [Lenny Dee] [BMI] (2/7/55 Rt-42)*
PLANTATION BOOGIE *Georgie Auld & His Rockin' Rhythm—Coral 61381*
[Lenny Dee] [BMI] (3/21/55 Rt-23) [IM]
PLANTATION BOOGIE *Buddy Cole with The Wood Sisters—Columbia 40460*
[Lenny Dee] [BMI] (3/28/55 Rt-23)
PLASTIC MAN Sonny & Cher—Atco 6486 [Sonny Bono] [BMI] (6/10/67 BCR-61)
THE PLASTIC MAN The Temptations—Gordy 7129
[Norman Whitfield] [BMI] (6/2/73 BCR-28)
PLATINUM HEROES Bruce Foster—Millennium 602
[Bruce Foster] [BMI] (6/25/77 BCR-63)
PLAY A SIMPLE MELODY (SPIEL MIR EINE ALTE MELODIE ES SPIELT)
Crazy Otto—Polydor 22009B
[Irving Berlin] (Med) [ASC] (1/17/55 R-1) [IWM]
PLAY A SIMPLE MELODY (SPIEL MIR EINE ALTE MELODIE ES SPIELT)
Johnny Maddox And The Rhythmasters—Dot 15325
[Irving Berlin] (Med) [ASC] (1/24/55 BCR-1) [IWM]
PLAY FOR KEEPS Jaye P. Morgan—RCA Victor 47-6505
[Robert Allen] [ASC] (5/26/56 B-79)
PLAY ME Neil Diamond—Uni 55346 [Neil Diamond] [SE] (8/5/72 BCR-11)
PLAY ME HEARTS AND FLOWERS (I WANNA CRY) *Johnny Desmond—Coral 61379*
[Mann Curtis/Sanford Green] [ASC] (3/14/55 BCRt-7)
PLAY ME HEARTS AND FLOWERS (I WANNA CRY) *Dick Jacobs & His Orchestra—*
Coral 61380 [Mann Curtis/Sanford Green] [ASC] (3/21/55 Rt-12)
PLAY ON LOVE Jefferson Starship—Grunt 10456
[Pete Sears/Grace Slick] [BMI] (12/6/75 BC-47)
PLAY SOME MUSIC FOR BROKEN HEARTS Don Cornell—Dot 15829
[Marino Marini/Al Neiburg] [ASC] (11/1/58 CR-95) [FDE]
PLAY SOMETHING SWEET (BRICKYARD BLUES) Three Dog Night—Dunhill/ABC 15013
[Allen Toussaint] [BMI] (9/21/74 BCR-24)
PLAY THAT FUNKY MUSIC *Wild Cherry—Epic 50225*
[Robert Parissi] [ASC] (6/12/76 BCR-1)
PLAY THAT FUNKY MUSIC *Roxanne—Scotti Brothers 07724*
[Robert Parissi] [ASC] (3/12/88 BC-63)
PLAY THAT FUNKY MUSIC *Vanilla Ice—SBK 07339 [Robert Parissi] [ASC] (12/8/90 BC-4)*
PLAY THE GAME Queen—Elektra 46652 [Freddie Mercury] [BMI] (6/28/80 BCR-38)
PLAY THE GAME TONIGHT Kansas—Kirshner 2903
[Phil Ehart/Daniel Fleishour/Robert Frazier/Kerry Livgren/Richard John Williams] [BMI] (5/8/82 BC-17)
PLAY THE THING Marlowe Morris Quintet—Columbia 42218
[Marlowe Morris] [BMI] (3/17/62 BC-81) [I]
—PLAY TO ME MY DARLING see: DUSELDACK SONG
PLAY WITH FIRE The Rolling Stones—London 9741
[Mick Jagger/Brian Jones*/Keith Richards/Charlie Watts*/Bill Wyman*] [BMI] (5/22/65 B-96)
PLAYBOY The Marvelettes—Tamla 54060
[Robert Bateman/Brian Holland/William Stevenson*] [BMI] (4/23/62 BCR-7)
PLAYBOY Gene & Debbe—TRX 5006 [Gene Thomas] [BMI] (2/17/68 BCR-11)
THE PLAYER - PART 1 First Choice—Philly Groove 200
[Allan Felder/Norman Harris] [BMI] (9/14/74 BCR-70)
PLAYGIRL Thee Prophets—Kapp 962
[Keith Colley/Linda Jo Colley] [BMI] (3/1/69 BCR-39)
PLAYGROUND Another Bad Creation—Motown 2088
[Dallas Austin/Michael Bivins/Kevin Wales] [ASC] (4/27/91 B-10)
PLAYGROUND IN MY MIND Clint Holmes—Epic 10891
[Lee Pockriss/Paul Vance] [ASC] (2/17/73 BCR-2)
PLAYING FOR KEEPS Elvis Presley—RCA Victor 47-6800
[Stanley A. Kesler] [BMI] (1/19/57 BCR-25)
PLAYING TO WIN LRB—Capitol 5411
[John Farnham/Graham Goble/David Hirschfelder/Stephen Housden/
Wayne Nelson/Stephen Prestvich/Spencer Proffer] [BMI] (1/26/85 BC-49)
PLAYING WITH LIGHTNING Shot In The Dark—RSO 1061
[Robin Lamble/Adam Yurman] [BMI] (4/4/81 BC-71)
PLAYING WITH THE BOYS Kenny Loggins—Columbia 05902
[Kenny Loggins/Ina Wolf/Peter F. Wolf] [BMI] (8/16/86 BC-56)
PLAYING YOUR GAME, BABY Barry White—20th Century 2361
[Smead Hudman/Austin Johnson] [BMI] (2/4/78 CR-95)
PLAYMATES *The Fontane Sisters with Billy Vaughn's Orchestra—Dot 15370*
[Saxie Dowell] [ASC] (5/2/55 CRt-17)
PLAYMATES *Hack Swain—Cardinal 1036 [Saxie Dowell] [ASC] (5/23/55 Rt-17)*
PLAYTHING *Ted Newman—Rev 3505*
[Henry Underwood/Samuel Underwood] [BMI] (9/2/57 BCtRt-22)
PLAYTHING *Chuck Miller—Mercury 71173*
[Henry Underwood/Samuel Underwood] [BMI] (9/2/57 Rt-34)
PLAYTHING *Nick Todd—Dot 15643*
[Henry Underwood/Samuel Underwood] [BMI] (9/14/57 BCtRt-22)
PLAYTHING *Judy Faye—RCA Victor 47-7029*
[Henry Underwood/Samuel Underwood] [BMI] (9/30/57 Rt-22)
THE PLEA The Jesters—Winley 225
[Richard Barrett/George Goldner*/Arlene Smith] [BMI] (3/3/58 B-74)
PLEASANT VALLEY SUNDAY The Monkees—Colgems 1007
[Gerry Goffin/Carole King] [BMI] (7/22/67 BCR-2)
PLEASE Frank Ifield—Capitol 5089
[Ralph Rainger/Leo Robin] [ASC] (11/30/63 BCR-55)
PLEASE BE THE ONE Karla Bonoff—Columbia 03172
[Karla Bonoff] [BMI] (9/25/82 BC-63)
PLEASE BELIEVE ME The Elegants—Apt 25017
[Vito Picone] [BMI] (10/13/58 CR-83)
PLEASE COME HOME FOR CHRISTMAS *Charles Brown—King 5405*
[Charles Mose Brown/Gene Redd Sr.] [BMI] (12/31/60 C-90)
PLEASE COME HOME FOR CHRISTMAS *Charles Brown—King 5405*
[Charles Mose Brown/Gene Redd Sr.] [BMI] (12/25/61 BC-76)
PLEASE COME HOME FOR CHRISTMAS *Eagles—Asylum 45555*
[Charles Mose Brown/Gene Redd Sr.] [BMI] (12/9/78 BCR-18)
PLEASE COME TO BOSTON Dave Loggins—Epic 11115
[Dave Loggins] [ASC] (5/11/74 BCR-5)
PLEASE, DADDY John Denver—RCA Victor 0182
[Bill Danoff/Taffy Danoff] [ASC] (11/24/73 BCR-51)
PLEASE DON'T ASK ABOUT BARBARA Bobby Vee—Liberty 55419
[Bill Buchanan/Jack Keller] [BMI] (2/19/62 BCR-15)
PLEASE DON'T BLAME ME Marty Robbins—Columbia 40969
[Marty Robbins] [BMI] (8/5/57 CR-60)
PLEASE DON'T DESERT ME BABY Gloria Walker & The Chevelles—Flaming Arrow 36
[Eugene Davis] [BMI] (1/25/69 BR-96)
PLEASE DON'T DO IT Dale Wright—Fraternity 818 [Dale Wright] [ASC] (9/1/58 BR-77)
PLEASE DON'T EVER LEAVE ME The Cyrkle—Columbia 43871
[Susan Haber] [ASC] (11/26/66 BCR-50)
PLEASE DON'T FIGHT IT Dino, Desi & Billy—Reprise 0426
[Jerry Fuller] [BMI] (12/11/65 BCR-52)
PLEASE DON'T GO Ral Donner—Gone 5114
[Chesley Howard*/Douglas Lapham] [BMI] (9/25/61 BCR-30)
PLEASE DON'T GO K.C. & The Sunshine Band—TK 1035
[Harry Wayne Casey/Rick Finch] [BMI] (8/25/79 BCR-1)
PLEASE DON'T GO GIRL New Kids On The Block—Columbia 07700
[Maurice Starr] [ASC] (6/25/88 BC-10)
PLEASE DON'T GO SO SOON (WENN DIE LIEBE WILL) Jo Stafford—Columbia 40451
[Heinz Gietz/Carl Sigman] [ASC] (2/28/55 R-59) [FDE]
PLEASE DON'T KISS ME AGAIN The Charmettes—Kapp 547
[Kenny Young] [BMI] (9/21/63 BCR-62)
PLEASE DON'T LEAVE Lauren Wood—Warner Bros. 49043
[Lauren Wood] [BMI] (9/22/79 BCR-24)
PLEASE DON'T LEAVE ME The Fontane Sisters—Dot 15501
[Fats Domino] [BMI] (10/13/56 BCR-31)
PLEASE DON'T SELL MY DADDY NO MORE WINE The Greenwoods—Kapp 742
[Tom Lane] [BMI] (4/30/66 BCR-64)
PLEASE DON'T STOP LOVING ME Elvis Presley—RCA Victor 47-8780
[Joy Byers Johnston] [ASC] (3/19/66 BCR-45)
PLEASE DON'T TALK TO THE LIFEGUARD Diane Ray—Mercury 72117
[Sylvia Dee/George Goehring] [ASC] (8/3/63 BCR-31)
PLEASE DON'T TELL ME HOW THE STORY ENDS Ronnie Milsap—RCA Victor 0313
[Kris Kristofferson] [BMI] (9/14/74 BC-95)
PLEASE DRIVER (ONCE AROUND THE PARK AGAIN) Tony Bennett—Columbia 40213
[Chilton Price] [BMI] (7/3/54 C-PRE)
PLEASE HELP ME I'M FALLING *Hank Locklin—RCA Victor 47-7692*
[Hal Blair/Don Robertson] [ASC] (5/23/60 BCRt-5)
PLEASE HELP ME I'M FALLING *Rusty Draper—Mercury 71634*
[Hal Blair/Don Robertson] [ASC] (5/30/60 BRt-5)
(I CAN'T HELP YOU) I'M FALLING TOO *(response to Please Help Me I'm Falling)*
Skeeter Davis—RCA Victor 47-7767
[Hal Blair/Don Robertson] [ASC] (8/15/60 BCR-24) [R]

I'M GLAD THAT YOUR FALLING *(response to Please Help Me I'm Falling)*
Betty Madigan—United Artists 246
[Hal Blair/Don Robertson] [ASC] (9/12/60 R-97) [R]

PLEASE LET ME WONDER The Beach Boys—Capitol 5372
[Mike Love/Brian Wilson] [BMI] (2/27/65 BCR-46)

PLEASE LOVE ME FOREVER *Tommy Edwards—MGM 12688*
[Ollie Blanchard/Johnnie Malone] [BMI] (10/20/58 B-61)

PLEASE LOVE ME FOREVER *Cathy Jean And The Roommates—Valmor 007*
[Ollie Blanchard/Johnnie Malone] [BMI] (2/6/61 BCR-9)

PLEASE LOVE ME FOREVER *Bobby Vinton—Epic 10228*
[Ollie Blanchard/Johnnie Malone] [BMI] (9/23/67 BCR-5)

PLEASE MR. BROWN Sarah Vaughan—Mercury 71157
[Gene DePaul/Don Raye] [ASC] (9/21/57 CR-47)

PLEASE MR. PLEASE Olivia Newton-John—MCA 40418
[John Rostill/Bruce Welch] [ASC] (5/31/75 BCR-1)

PLEASE MR. POSTMAN *The Marvelettes—Tamla 54046*
[Robert Bateman/Georgia Dobbins/William Garrett/Freddie Gorman/Brian Holland] [BMI] (9/4/61 BCR-1)

PLEASE MR. POSTMAN *The Beatles—Capitol EAP-2121*
[Robert Bateman/Georgia Dobbins/William Garrett/Freddie Gorman/Brian Holland] (EP) [BMI] (5/30/64 BCR-86)

PLEASE MR. POSTMAN *Carpenters—A&M 1646*
[Robert Bateman/Georgia Dobbins/William Garrett/Freddie Gorman/Brian Holland] [BMI] (11/23/74 BCR-1)

PLEASE MR. POSTMAN *Gentle Persuasion—Capitol 5207*
[Robert Bateman/Georgia Dobbins/William Garrett/Freddie Gorman/Brian Holland] [BMI] (2/26/83 BC-79)

PLEASE, MR. PRESIDENT Paula Webb—20th Century/Westbound 5001
[Randall Carlisle] [BMI] (2/1/75 BCR-54)

PLEASE MR. SUN *Tommy Edwards—MGM 12757*
[Sid Frank/Ray Getzov] [BMI] (2/9/59 BCR-11)

PLEASE MR. SUN *The Vogues—Co & Ce 240*
[Sid Frank/Ray Getzov] [BMI] (9/24/66 BCR-48)

PLEASE PARDON ME (YOU REMIND ME OF A FRIEND)
Rufus Featuring Chaka Khan—ABC 12099
[Brenda Russell/Brian Russell] [ASC] (5/24/75 BCR-44)

PLEASE PLEASE BELIEVE ME Cathy Carr—Fraternity 734
[Marge Stafford/Al Trace/Ben Trace] [ASC] (3/23/56 R-80)

PLEASE PLEASE ME *The Beatles—Vee-Jay 581*
[John Lennon/Paul McCartney] [GL] (2/1/64 BCR-3)

PLEASE PLEASE ME *Stars On 45—Radio 3830*
[John Lennon/Paul McCartney] (Med) [GL] (7/11/81 BC-63)

PLEASE, PLEASE, PLEASE James Brown And The Famous Flames—King 5853
[James Brown/Johnny Terry] [BMI] (2/15/64 B-95)

PLEASE RETURN YOUR LOVE TO ME The Temptations—Gordy 7074
[Barrett Strong/Norman Whitfield] [BMI] (7/27/68 BCR-21)

PLEASE SAY YOU'RE FOOLING Ray Charles And His Orchestra—ABC 10865
[Bobby Stevenson] [BMI] (11/5/66 BCR-64)

PLEASE SEND ME SOMEONE TO LOVE The Moonglows—Chess 1661
[Percy Mayfield] [BMI] (7/8/57 B-73)

PLEASE STAY *The Drifters—Atlantic 2105*
[Burt Bacharach/Bob Hilliard] [ASC] (6/5/61 BCR-13)

PLEASE STAY *The Dave Clark Five—Epic 10325*
[Burt Bacharach/Bob Hilliard] [ASC] (5/25/68 CR-88)

PLEASE TELL HIM THAT I SAID HELLO Debbie Campbell—Playboy 6037
[Peter Dibbens/Michael Shepstone] [ASC] (7/5/75 B-84)

PLEASE TELL ME WHY Betty Johnson—Bally 1000 [Jim Leisy] [BMI] (4/6/56 R-86)

PLEASE TELL ME WHY Jackie Wilson—Brunswick 55208
[Joyce Lee] [NA] (3/13/61 BCR-20)

PLEASE TELL ME WHY The Dave Clark Five—Epic 10031
[Dave Clark/Mike Smith] [BMI] (6/4/66 BCR-18)

PLEASURE AND PAIN Divinyls—Chrysalis 42916
[Mike Chapman/Holly Knight] [ASC] (1/25/86 BC-76)

—PLEASURE IS A FREEDOM SONG/ON LOVE see: THEME FROM THE PROPHET

THE PLEASURE PRINCIPLE Janet Jackson—A&M 2927
[Monte Moir] [ASC] (5/23/87 BC-13)

THE PLEDGE OF ALLEGIANCE Red Skelton—Columbia 44798
[Traditional] [NA] (3/15/69 BCR-44)

PLEDGE OF LOVE *Mitchell Torok—Decca 30230*
[Ramona Redd] [BMI] (3/30/57 BCtRt-11)

PLEDGE OF LOVE *Ken Copeland—Imperial 5432*
[Ramona Redd] [BMI] (3/30/57 BCtRt-11)

PLEDGE OF LOVE *Dick Contino—Mercury 71079*
[Ramona Redd] [BMI] (3/30/57 BCtRt-11)

PLEDGE OF LOVE *Johnny Janis—ABC-Paramount 9800*
[Ramona Redd] [BMI] (3/30/57 BRt-11)

PLEDGE OF LOVE *The Penguins—Atlantic 1132 [Ramona Redd] [BMI] (5/18/57 Rt-14)*

PLEDGE OF LOVE Bobby Goldsboro—United Artists 50224
[Bobby Goldsboro] [BMI] (1/13/68 R-98)

PLEDGE PIN Robert Plant—Swan Song 99952
[Robbie Blunt/Robert Plant] [ASC] (11/13/82 BC-74)

PLEDGING MY LOVE *Teresa Brewer—Coral 61362*
[Deadric Malone/Ferdinand Washington] [BMI] (2/7/55 BCtRt-8)

PLEDGING MY LOVE *The Four Lads—Columbia 40436*
[Deadric Malone/Ferdinand Washington] [BMI] (2/7/55 Rt-8)

PLEDGING MY LOVE *Tommy Mara—MGM 11931*
[Deadric Malone/Ferdinand Washington] [BMI] (2/7/55 Rt-8)

PLEDGING MY LOVE *Johnny Ace—Duke 136*
[Deadric Malone/Ferdinand Washington] [BMI] (2/14/55 BCtRt-8)

PLEDGING MY LOVE *Ronnie Gaylord—Mercury 70551*
[Deadric Malone/Ferdinand Washington] [BMI] (2/14/55 Rt-20)

PLEDGING MY LOVE *Roy Hamilton—Epic 9294*
[Deadric Malone/Ferdinand Washington] [BMI] (11/3/58 BCRt-45)

PLEDGING MY LOVE *Jesse Belvin—RCA Victor 47-7387*
[Deadric Malone/Ferdinand Washington] [BMI] (11/10/58 Rt-59)

PLEDGING MY LOVE *Johnny Tillotson—Cadence 1377*
[Deadric Malone/Ferdinand Washington] [BMI] (3/21/60 BCRt-44)

PLEDGING MY LOVE *Sanford Clark—Jamie 1153*
[Deadric Malone/Ferdinand Washington] [BMI] (3/21/60 Rt-44)

PLENTY GOOD LOVIN' Connie Francis—MGM 12824
[Connie Francis] [ASC] (8/24/59 BCR-39)

—PLUME DE MA TANTE see: LA PLUME DE MA TANTE

POCKETFUL OF MIRACLES Frank Sinatra—Reprise 20,040
[Sammy Cahn/Jimmy Van Heusen] [ASC] (12/18/61 BCR-26)

POCKETFUL OF RAINBOWS Deane Hawley—Liberty 55359
[Ben Weisman/Fred Wise] [ASC] (10/2/61 BC-93)

POCO LOCO Gene & Eunice—Case 1001
[Eunice Levy/Forrest Wilson] [BMI] (8/24/59 BCR-48)

POETRY IN MOTION Johnny Tillotson—Cadence 1384
[Mike Anthony/Paul Kaufman] [BMI] (10/3/60 BCR-2)

POETRY MAN Phoebe Snow—Shelter 40353 [Phoebe Snow] [ASC] (1/4/75 BCR-5)

POINCIANA Ahmad Jamal Trio—Argo 5306 [Nat Simon] [BMI] (10/13/58 R-88) [IM]

POINT IT OUT Smokey Robinson & The Miracles—Tamla 54189
[Al Cleveland/Smokey Robinson/Marvin Tarplin] [ASC] (12/6/69 BCR-32)

POINT OF KNOW RETURN Kansas—Kirshner 4273
[Phil Ehart/Robby Steinhardt/Steve Walsh] [BMI] (11/5/77 BCR-17)

POINT OF NO RETURN Adam Wade—Coed 550
[Robert Mosely/Mayme Watts] [BMI] (6/19/61 B-85)

POINT OF NO RETURN Gene McDaniels—Liberty 55480
[Gerry Goffin/Carole King] [BMI] (8/4/62 BCR-21)

POINT OF NO RETURN Nu Shooz—Atlantic 89392
[Valerie Day/John Robert Smith] [BMI] (7/5/86 BC-28)

POINT OF NO RETURN Exposé—Arista 1-9579 [Lewis Martinée] [ASC] (5/9/87 BC-5)

POINT OF ORDER Stan Freberg & Daws Butler—Capitol 2838
[Daws Butler/Stan Freberg] [BMI] (6/26/54 BC-PRE)

POINT PANIC The Surfaris—Decca 31538
[Bob Berryhill/Pat Connolly/Jim Fuller/Jim Pash/Ron Wilson] [BMI] (9/14/63 BCR-49) [I]

POINTED TOE SHOES Carl Perkins—Columbia 41379
[Carl Perkins] [BMI] (5/23/59 BCR-86)

POISON Alice Cooper—Epic 68958
[Desmond Child/Alice Cooper/John McCurry] [ASC] (9/9/89 BC-7)

POISON Bell Biv DeVoe—MCA 53772 [Elliot Straite] [BMI] (4/7/90 BC-2)

POISON ARROW ABC—Mercury 810340
[Martin Fry/Mark Lickley/Stephen Singleton/Mark White] [ASC] (1/29/83 BC-24)

POISON IVY The Coasters—Atco 6146 [Jerry Leiber/Mike Stoller] [BMI] (8/22/59 BCR-6)

POLICY OF TRUTH Depeche Mode—Sire 19842 [Martin L. Gore] [BMI] (8/11/90 BC-15)

THE POLITICS OF DANCING Re-Flex—Capitol 5301
[Paul Fishman] [ASC] (11/26/83 BC-23)

POLK SALAD ANNIE Tony Joe White—Monument 1104
[Tony Joe White] [BMI] (7/5/69 BCR-8)

POLLYANNA The Classics (1)—Capitol 5710 [Joe South] [BMI] (9/24/66 CR-83)

—POMP AND CIRCUMSTANCE see: GRADUATION SONG

PONY EXPRESS Danny & The Juniors—Swan 4068
[Bob Crewe/Frank Slay] [ASC] (2/20/61 BCR-40)

PONY TIME *Chubby Checker—Parkway 818*
[John Bobby Berry/Don Covay] [BMI] (1/23/61 BCtRt-1)

PONY TIME *Don Covay and The Goodtimers—Arnold 1002*
[John Bobby Berry/Don Covay] [BMI] (1/23/61 BCtRt-20)

PONY TRAIN Titus Turner—Jamie 1177
[Mort Garson/Priscilla Turner] [ASC] (4/17/61 R-82)

PONY WITH THE GOLDEN MANE Every Mothers' Son—MGM 13844
[Dennis Larden/Lary Larden] [BMI] (11/4/67 BCR-59)

POOL OF BAD LUCK Joe Simon—Spring 124
[Kenneth Gamble/Leon Huff] [BMI] (3/25/72 BCR-32)

POOR BABY The Cowsills—MGM 13981 [Tony Romeo] [BMI] (9/7/68 BCR-33)

POOR BOY Elvis Presley—RCA Victor EPA-4006
[Ken Darby/Elvis Presley] [BMI] (12/29/56 BR-35)

POOR BOY *The Royaltones—Jubilee 5338*
[David Sanderson] [BMI] (9/15/58 BCRt-17) [IM]

POOR BOY *The Cardigans—Mercury 71367*
[Mel Mitchell/David Sanderson] [BMI] (10/27/58 Rt-73)

POOR BOY The Royalettes—MGM 13327
[Teddy Randazzo/Bobby Weinstein] [BMI] (5/1/65 C-90)

POOR BOY Casey Kelly—Elektra 45804 [Casey Kelly] [ASC] (9/23/72 BCR-52)

POOR BUTTERFLY *The Hilltoppers—Dot 15156*
[John L. Golden/Raymond Hubbell] [NA] (5/29/54 BC-PRE)

POOR BUTTERFLY *Sarah Vaughan—Mercury 71085*
[John L. Golden/Raymond Hubbell] [NA] (4/20/57 R-52)

POOR FOOL Ike & Tina Turner—Sue 753 [Ike Turner] [BMI] (11/25/61 BCR-23)

POOR JENNY The Everly Brothers—Cadence 1364
[Boudleaux Bryant/Felice Bryant] [BMI] (3/30/59 BCR-21)

POOR LITTLE CUPID Joe Dowell—Smash 1786 [Ronnie Wilkins] [BMI] (10/6/62 R-87)

POOR LITTLE FOOL Ricky Nelson—Imperial 5528 [Sharon Sheeley] [BMI] (6/21/58 BCR-1)

—POOR LITTLE FOOL LIKE ME see: DON'T EVER BE LONELY

POOR LITTLE PUPPET Cathy Carroll—Warner Bros. 5284
[Howard Greenfield/Jack Keller] [BMI] (7/28/62 BR-91)

POOR LITTLE RICH GIRL Steve Lawrence—Columbia 42795
[Gerry Goffin/Carole King] [BMI] (5/18/63 BCR-27)

A POOR MAN'S ROSES (OR A RICH MAN'S GOLD) *Patti Page—Mercury 71059*
[Milton DeLugg/Bob Hilliard] [BMI] (2/23/57 BCRt-25)

A POOR MAN'S ROSES (OR A RICH MAN'S GOLD) *Patsy Cline—Decca 30221*
[Milton DeLugg/Bob Hilliard] [ASC] (2/23/57 Rt-28)

POOR MAN'S SON The Reflections—Golden World 20
[Joanne Bratton/Bob Hamilton/Eugene Hamilton/Steve Venet] [BMI] (3/6/65 BCR-53)

POOR MAN'S SON Survivor—Scotti Brothers 02560
[Jim Peterik/Frankie Sullivan] [ASC] (10/17/81 BCR-33)

POOR ME *Fats Domino—Imperial 5369*
[Dave Bartholomew/Fats Domino] [BMI] (12/3/55 CRt-44)

POOR ME *Bill Carey—Coral 61540*
[Dave Bartholomew/Fats Domino] [BMI] (12/16/55 Rt-44)

POOR MOON Canned Heat—Liberty 56127 [Alan C. Wilson] [BMI] (8/9/69 C-95)

THE POOR PEOPLE OF PARIS (LA GOUALANTE DU PAUVRE JEAN)
Les Baxter His Chorus And Orchestra—Capitol 3336
[Marguerite Monnot] [ASC] (1/27/56 BCRt-1) [IM]

THE POOR PEOPLE OF PARIS *Russ Morgan And His Orchestra—Decca 29835*
[Marguerite Monnot] [ASC] (2/24/56 BRt-1) [IM]

THE POOR PEOPLE OF PARIS *Chet Atkins—RCA Victor 47-6366*
[Marguerite Monnot] [ASC] (2/25/56 B-52) [IM]

THE POOR PEOPLE OF PARIS *Lawrence Welk And His Champagne Music—Coral 61592*
[Marguerite Monnot] [ASC] (3/2/56 BRt-1) [IM]

THE POOR PEOPLE OF PARIS *Winifred Atwell—London 1628*
[Marguerite Monnot] [ASC] (3/23/56 Rt-1) [IM]

POOR POOR PITIFUL ME Linda Ronstadt—Asylum 45462
[Warren Zevon] [BMI] (1/28/78 BCR-26)

POOR SIDE OF TOWN *Johnny Rivers—Imperial 66205*
[Lou Adler/Johnny Rivers] [BMI] (9/17/66 BCR-1)

POOR SIDE OF TOWN *Al Wilson—Soul City 771*
[Lou Adler/Johnny Rivers] [BMI] (12/28/68 BCR-65)

POP-EYE Huey Smith—Ace 649
[Huey P. Smith/Cliff Thomas/Edward S. Thomas Jr.] [BMI] (2/12/62 BCR-46)

POP-EYE STROLL The Mar-Keys—Stax 121
[Steve Cropper/Booker T. Jones Jr.] [BMI] (3/31/62 B-94) [I]

POP GOES THE WEASEL Anthony Newley—London 9501
[Traditional] [NA] (11/6/61 BCR-55)

POP GOES THE WEASEL 3rd Bass—Def Jam 73728
[Michael Berrin/John Dajani/Peter Gabriel/John Gamble/Pete Nash/Dante Ross/Stevie Wonder] [ASC] (7/13/91 BC-29)

POP GOES THE WORLD Men Without Hats—Mercury 888859
[Ivan Doroschuk] [BMI] (10/24/87 BC-20)

POP LIFE Prince & the Revolution—Paisley Park 7-28998 [Prince] [ASC] (7/27/85 BC-7)

POP MUZIK M—Sire 49033 [Robin Scott] [ASC] (8/11/79 BCR-1)

POP POP POP-PIE The Sherrys—Guyden 2068
[John Madara/David White] [BMI] (9/29/62 BCR-35)

POP SINGER John Cougar Mellencamp—Mercury 874 012
[John Mellencamp] [ASC] (4/29/89 BC-11)

POP SONG 89 R.E.M.—Warner Bros. 27640
[Bill Berry/Peter Buck/Mike Mills/Michael Stipe] [BMI] (6/10/89 BC-80)

POP THAT COOCHIE 2 Live Crew—Luke 98712
[Luther Campbell/David Hobbs/Mark Ross/Chris Wong Won] [BMI] (11/2/91 B-58)

POP THAT THANG The Isley Brothers—T-Neck 935
[O'Kelly Isley*/Ronald Isley*/Rudolph Isley*/Herman Wesley Kelley/Clyde Otis] [BMI] (7/1/72 BCR-23)

THE POPCORN James Brown—King 6240 [James Brown] [BMI] (5/31/69 BCR-30) [I]

POPCORN Hot Butter—Musicor 1458 [Gershon Kingsley] [ASC] (6/17/72 BCR-7) [I]

POPCORN SONG *Cliffie Stone And His Orchestra—Capitol 3131*
[Bob Roubian] [BMI] (6/6/55 BCRt-18)

THE POPCORN SONG *Russ Morgan & His Scranton Seven—Decca 29606*
[Bob Roubian] [BMI] (8/8/55 Rt-18)

POPEYE JOE Ernie K-Doe—Minit 641 [Ernie K-Doe] [BMI] (2/24/62 B-99)

POPEYE THE HITCHHIKER Chubby Checker—Parkway 849
[Dave Appell/Kal Mann] [ASC] (9/8/62 BCR-8)

THE POPEYE WADDLE Don Covay—Cameo 239
[Dave Appell/Kal Mann] [ASC] (12/29/62 BCR-65)

POPS, WE LOVE YOU (A TRIBUTE TO FATHER)
Diana Ross, Marvin Gaye, Smokey Robinson & Stevie Wonder—Motown M 1455F
[Marilyn McLeod/Pam Sawyer] [ASC] (1/20/79 BCR-59)

POPSICLE Jan & Dean—Liberty 55886
[Buzz Cason/Bobby Russell] [BMI] (5/28/66 BCR-21)

POPSICLE TOES Michael Franks—Reprise 1360 [Michael Franks] [BMI] (7/31/76 BCR-43)

POPSICLES AND ICICLES The Murmaids—Chattahoochee 628
[David Gates] [ASC] (11/16/63 BCR-1)

—POR AMOR VIVIREMOS see: LOVE WILL KEEP US TOGETHER

POR FAVOR Vic Damone—Mercury 70699
[Joe Sherman/Noel Sherman] [ASC] (10/15/55 BCR-44)

PORPOISE SONG The Monkees—Colgems 1031
[Gerry Goffin/Carole King] (TSW) [BMI] (10/5/68 BCR-30)

PORT AU PRINCE *Nelson Riddle And His Orchestra—Capitol 3374*
[Bernie Wayne] [BMI] (3/16/56 BCRt-26) [I]

PORT-AU-PRINCE
Winifred Atwell with Frank Chacksfield & His Orchestra—London 1667
[Bernie Wayne] [BMI] (5/11/56 Rt-42)

PORTRAIT (HE KNEW) Kansas—Kirshner 4276
[Kerry Livgren/Steve Walsh] [BMI] (6/3/78 BCR-53)

PORTRAIT OF A FOOL Conway Twitty—MGM 13050
[Louis Innis/Buddy Killen] [BMI] (1/15/62 BR-91)

PORTRAIT OF MY LOVE *Steve Lawrence—United Artists 291*
[Norman Newell/Cyril Ornadel] [BMI] (3/6/61 BCR-9)

PORTRAIT OF MY LOVE *The Tokens—Warner Bros. 5900*
[Norman Newell/Cyril Ornadel] [BMI] (4/15/67 BCR-25)

THE PORTUGUESE WASHERWOMEN *Joe "Fingers" Carr—Capitol 3418*
[André Popp] [ASC] (5/4/56 BCRt-23) [IM]

PORTUGUESE WASHERWOMEN *Joe Sherman, his Orchestra and Chorus—Kapp 149*
[André Popp] [ASC] (5/25/56 Rt-23) [IM]

THE PORTUGUESE WASHERWOMEN (LES LAVANDIERES DU PORTUGAL)
Jacqueline François with Michel Legrand & His Orchestra—Columbia 40713
[Roger Lucchesi/André Popp] [ASC] (7/6/56 Rt-24)

THE PORTUGUESE WASHERWOMEN *Baja Marimba Band—A&M 816*
[André Popp] [ASC] (10/8/66 C-98) [IM]

POSITIVELY 4TH STREET Bob Dylan—Columbia 43389 [Bob Dylan] [SE] (9/25/65 BCR-7)

POSSE' ON BROADWAY Sir Mix-A-Lot—Nastymix 75555
[Anthony Ray] [BMI] (12/17/88 BC-70)

POSSESSION Bad English—Epic 73398
[Jonathan Cain/Ricky Phillips/John Waite] [ASC] (6/9/90 BC-20)

POSSESSION OBSESSION Daryl Hall & John Oates—RCA 14098
[Sara Allen/Daryl Hall/John Oates] [BMI] (6/1/85 BC-29)

POSTCARD The Who—Track/MCA 40330
[John Entwhistle] [NA] (11/23/74 C-64)

POSTCARD FROM JAMAICA The Sopwith "Camel"—Kama Sutra 224
[Peter Kraemer/Terry MacNeil] [BMI] (3/18/67 BCR-86)

—POSTILLION see: ANGEL PIE

—POSTMAN SONG see: BECAUSE I LOVE YOU

POTATO PEELER Bobby Gregg And His Friends—Cotton 1006
[Bobby Gregg] [BMI] (6/30/62 B-89) [I]

POUR SOME SUGAR ON ME Def Leppard—Mercury 870298
[Rick Allen*/Steve Clark/Phil Collen/Joe Elliott/Mutt Lange/Rick Savage] [ASC] (4/23/88 BC-1)

POURING WATER ON A DROWNING MAN James Carr—Goldwax 311
[Drew Baker/Danny McCormick] [BMI] (10/22/66 B-85)

POVERTY Bobby Bland—Duke 407 [Dave (2) Clark/Pearl Woods] [BMI] (9/17/66 BCR-65)

POW WOW Cory Daye—New York Int'l. 11748
[L. Russell Brown/Sandy Linzer] [BMI] (10/27/79 B-76)

POWDER BLUE MERCEDES QUEEN Raiders—Columbia 45601
[Richard Burns*/Mark Lindsay/Bob Siller*] [BMI] (5/13/72 BCR-43)

POWER The Temptations—Gordy 7183
[Angelo Bond/Berry Gordy/Jean Mayer] [BMI] (5/3/80 BCR-43)

POWER Kansas—MCA 53027
[Randy Goodrum/Steve Morse/Steve Walsh] [ASC] (2/14/87 BC-84)

THE POWER Snap!—Arista 2013
[Benito Benites/Toni Colandreo*/John Virgo Garrett III] [BMI] (5/12/90 BC-2)

THE POWER OF GOLD Dan Fogelberg / Tim Weisberg—Full Moon/Epic 50606
[Dan Fogelberg] [ASC] (10/7/78 BCR-23)

POWER OF LOVE *Joe Simon—Spring 128*
[Kenneth Gamble/Leon Huff/Joe Simon] [BMI] (7/1/72 BCR-6)

POWER OF LOVE *Martha Reeves—MCA 40194*
[Kenneth Gamble/Leon Huff/Joe Simon] [BMI] (3/9/74 BCR-71)

THE POWER OF LOVE Huey Lewis and the News—Chrysalis 42876
[Johnny Colla/Chris Hayes/Huey Lewis] [ASC] (6/29/85 BC-1)

THE POWER OF LOVE (YOU ARE MY LADY) *Air Supply—Arista 1-9391 [Mary Applegate/Candy DeRouge/Gunther Mende/Jennifer Rush] [ASC] (8/10/85 BC-68)*

THE POWER OF LOVE *Jennifer Rush—Epic 05754 [Mary Applegate/Candy DeRouge/Gunther Mende/Jennifer Rush] [ASC] (2/8/86 BC-57)*

POWER OF LOVE *Laura Branigan—Atlantic 89191 [Mary Applegate/Candy DeRouge/Gunther Mende/Jennifer Rush] [ASC] (10/24/87 BC-26)*

POWER OF LOVE Deee-Lite—Elektra 64912
[Dmitry Brill/Kier Kirby/Towa Tei] [ASC] (12/22/90 BC-47)

POWER OF LOVE Luther Vandross—Epic 73778
[Marcus Miller/Luther Vandross] (Med) [ASC] (4/27/91 BC-4)

POWER PLAY Molly Hatchet—Epic 02680
[Steve Holland] [BMI] (2/6/82 BC-89)

POWER TO THE PEOPLE John Lennon Plastic Ono Band—Apple 1830
[John Lennon] [GL] (3/27/71 BCR-8)

POWER WINDOWS Billy Falcon—Jambco 868 672
[Billy Falcon] [BMI] (8/3/91 BC-31)

POWERFUL STUFF The Fabulous Thunderbirds—Elektra 69384
[Robert Field/Michael James Henderson/Kim Wilson] [ASC] (8/27/88 BC-65)

PRAY M.C. Hammer—Capitol 44609 [Stanley Burrell/Prince] [BMI] (9/15/90 BC-2)

PRAY FOR ME The Intruders—Gamble 4014
[Kenneth Gamble/Leon Huff] [BMI] (7/10/71 C-88)

PRAYER AND A JUKE BOX Little Anthony And The Imperials—End 1047
[Gary Shelton] [BMI] (6/1/59 BCR-71)

PRAYER MEETIN' Willie Mitchell—Hi 2147 [James O. Smith] [BMI] (7/13/68 BCR-45) [I]

PRAYING FOR TIME George Michael—Columbia 73512
[George Michael] [ASC] (9/1/90 BC-1)

PRAYING TO A NEW GOD Wang Chung—Geffen 22969
[David Chandler/Nick Feldman/Jack Hues] [BMI] (5/27/89 BC-57)

PREACHER MAN The Impressions—Curtom 1982
[Richard Anthony Tufo] [BMI] (3/30/63 CR-74)

PREACHERMAN Charlie Russo—Diamond 131
[June Astor/Charley Russo] [BMI] (3/23/63 BC-82) [I]

PRECIOUS AND FEW Climax—Carousel 30,055/Rocky Road 30055
[Walter Nims] [ASC] (12/25/71 BCR-1)

PRECIOUS LOVE Bob Welch—Capitol 4685 [Bob Welch] [ASC] (2/10/79 BCR-17)

PRECIOUS LOVE Jody Watley—MCA 53790
[André Cymone/Jody Watley] [ASC] (3/24/90 BC-54)

PRECIOUS MEMORIES The Romeos—Mark II 101
[Martin Montague] [ASC] (4/1/67 BCR-65) [I]

PRECIOUS, PRECIOUS Jackie Moore—Atlantic 2681
[Dave Crawford/Jackie Moore] [ASC] (11/21/70 BCR-11)

PRECIOUS TO ME Phil Seymour—Boardwalk 8-5703
[Phil Seymour] [BMI] (1/17/81 BCR-22)

PRECIOUS WORDS Wallace Brothers—Sims 174
[Claudia Robinson] [BMI] (5/16/64 CR-55)

—PREMIER BAL see: OUR FIRST DANCE

PREPARE YE THE WAY OF THE LORD Holly Sherwood—Carousel 30,057
[Stephen Schwartz/John Tebelak] (Med) [ASC] (10/2/71 CR-91)

PRESENCE OF LOVE The Alarm—I.R.S. 53259
[Eddie MacDonald/Mike Peters] [BMI] (3/26/88 BC-77)

PRESENT FOR BOB The DeJohn Sisters—Epic 9097
[Bob Crystal/Dux DeJohn/Julie DeJohn] [BMI] (4/9/55 CR-46)

THE PRESIDENT ON THE DOLLAR Mitch Miller & His Orchestra—Columbia 40715
[Bob Hilliard/Philip Springer] [ASC] (7/21/56 B-88)

PRESIDENTIAL PRESS CONFERENCE The Sickniks—Amy 824
[Sandy Baron/George Eugene/Sid Jacobson/Lou Stallman] [BMI] (6/12/61 R-83)

PRESS Paul McCartney—Capitol 5597 [Paul McCartney] [ASC] (8/2/86 BC-21)

PRESSURE Billy Joel—Columbia 03244 [Billy Joel] [ASC] (9/25/82 BC-20)

PRETEND *Tab Smith His Fabulous Alto and His Band—United 205 [Lew Douglas/Frank LaVere/Cliff Parman] [ASC] (3/30/57 B-89) [I]*

PRETEND *Carl Mann—Phillips Int'l 3546 [Dan Belloc*/Lew Douglas/Frank LaVere/Cliff Parman] [ASC] (10/17/59 BCR-56)*

PRETEND YOU DON'T SEE HER *Jerry Vale—Columbia 41010 [Steve Allen] [ASC] (10/21/57 BCRt-25)*

PRETEND YOU DON'T SEE HER *Steve Allen—Coral 61909 [Steve Allen] [ASC] (12/30/57 Rt-25)*

PRETEND YOU DON'T SEE HER *Bobby Vee—Liberty 55751 [Steve Allen] [ASC] (12/5/64 BCR-80)*

THE PRETENDER Jackson Browne—Asylum 45399
[Jackson Browne] [ASC] (5/14/77 BCR-58)

PRETENDING Eric Clapton—Duck/Reprise 22732
[Jerry Lynn Williams] [BMI] (11/11/89 BC-50)

THE PRETTIEST GIRL IN SCHOOL Randy Starr—Dale 103
[Lee Pockriss/Paul Vance] [ASC] (6/7/58 C-60)

PRETTY AS YOU FEEL Jefferson Airplane—Grunt 0500
[Jack Casady/Joey Covington/Jorma Kaukonen/Carlos Santana*/Michael Shrieve*] [BMI] (11/13/71 BCR-35)

PRETTY BABY - OH Austin Smiley—Brunswick 55061
[Joan Robbins/Berl Rotfeld] [BMI] (5/5/58 Rt*-28)

PRETTY BALLERINA The Left Banke—Smash 2074
[Michael David Lookofsky] [BMI] (12/31/66 BCR-12)

PRETTY BLUE EYES Steve Lawrence—ABC-Paramount 10058
[Teddy Randazzo/Bobby Weinstein] [BMI] (11/9/59 BCR-5)

PRETTY BOY LONELY Patti Page—Columbia 42671
[Neval Nader/Jimmy Radcliffe] [BMI] (2/16/63 BR-98)

PRETTY BOYS AND PRETTY GIRLS Book Of Love—Sire 27858
[Ted Ottaviano] [BMI] (9/3/88 B-90)

PRETTY FLAMINGO Manfred Mann—United Artists 50040
[Mark Barkan] [BMI] (7/2/66 BCR-27)

—PRETTY GIRL see: B'WA NINA

PRETTY GIRLS Melissa Manchester—Arista 0456
[Lisa Dal Bello] [ASC] (10/13/79 BCR-39)

PRETTY GIRLS EVERYWHERE Eugene Church and The Fellows—Class 235
[Eugene Church/Thomas Williams] [BMI] (12/15/58 BCR-36)

PRETTY IN PINK Psychedelic Furs—A&M 2826
[John Ashton/Richard Butler/Tim Butler/Vince Ely/Duncan Kilburn/Roger Morris] [BMI] (4/12/86 BC-41)

PRETTY LADY Lighthouse—Polydor 14198 [Skip Prokop] [BMI] (10/13/73 BCR-31)

PRETTY LITTLE ANGEL EYES Curtis Lee—Dunes 2007
[Tommy Boyce/Curtis Lee] [BMI] (7/1/61 BCR-6)

PRETTY LITTLE BABY Marvin Gaye—Tamla 54117
[Marvin Gaye/Dave Hamilton/Clarence Paul] [ASC] (7/3/65 BCR-13)

PRETTY LITTLE PEARLY The Click-Clacks—Apt 25010
[Bob Johnston/Diane Johnston] [BMI] (10/4/58 C-96)

PRETTY MESS Vanity—Motown 1752 [Denise Matthews/Bill Wolfer] [ASC] (9/8/84 BC-70)

PRETTY PAPER Roy Orbison—Monument 830 [Willie Nelson] [BMI] (11/30/63 BCR-11)

PRETTY WORLD Sergio Mendes & Brasil '66—A&M 1049
[Antonio Adolfo/Alan Bergman/Marilyn Bergman/Tiberio Gaspar] [ASC] (4/26/69 BCR-59)

PRETZEL LOGIC Steely Dan—ABC 12033
[Walter Becker/Donald Fagen] [ASC] (9/28/74 BCR-57)

PREVIEW OF PARADISE Adam Wade—Coed 560
[Clint Ballard Jr./Fred Tobias] [ASC] (11/25/61 C-73)

THE PRICE Solomon Burke—Atlantic 2259
[Solomon Burke/Solomon Burke Jr./Josephine Burke Moore] [BMI] (11/21/64 BCR-48)

PRICE OF LOVE Bad English—Epic 73094
[Jonathan Cain/John Waite] [ASC] (12/23/89 BC-4)

THE PRIDE (PART 1) The Isley Brothers—T-Neck 2262
[Ernie Isley/Marvin Isley/O'Kelly Isley/Ronald Isley/Rudolph Isley/Chris Jasper] [ASC] (4/2/77 BCR-63)

PRIDE & PASSION John Cafferty and the Beaver Brown Band—Scotti Brothers 68999
[John Cafferty] [BMI] (7/29/89 BC-66)

PRIDE AND JOY Marvin Gaye—Tamla 54079
[Marvin Gaye/William Stevenson/Norman Whitfield] [ASC] (5/18/63 BCR-9)

PRIDE (IN THE NAME OF LOVE) U2—Island 99704
[Adam Clayton/Dave Evans/Paul Hewson/Larry Mullen] [ASC] (10/27/84 BC-33)

PRIMAL SCREAM Mötley Crüe—Elektra 4-64848
[Tommy Lee/Mick Mars/Vince Neil/Nikki Sixx] [ASC] (9/21/91 B-63)

PRIME TIME Alan Parsons Project—Arista 1-9208
[Alan Parsons/Eric Woolfson] [BMI] (5/19/84 BC-33)

PRIMITIVE LOVE RITES Mondo Rock—Columbia 06981
[J.J. Hackett/Ross Wilson] [NA] (5/16/87 BC-71)

PRIMROSE LANE *Jerry Wallace with The Jewels—Challenge 59047 [George Callender/Wayne Shanklin] [ASC] (8/15/59 BCR-4)*

PRIMROSE LANE *O.C. Smith—Columbia 45160 [George Callender/Wayne Shanklin] [ASC] (5/23/70 BCR-72)*

PRINCE OF PLAYERS Tommy Frederick and the Hi-Notes—Carlton 450
[Arthur Korb/Ralph Spurlin Jr.] [BMI] (2/3/58 R-76)

PRINCESS Frank Gari—Crusade 1022
[Eddie V. Deane/Vince Familio/Patrick Leonard] [ASC] (7/3/61 BCR-30)

THE PRINCESS AND THE PUNK Barry Mann—Arista 0194
[Barry Mann/Cynthia Weil] [BMI] (8/14/76 BC-78)

PRINCESS IN RAGS Gene Pitney—Musicor 1130
[Roger Atkins/Helen Miller] [BMI] (11/13/65 BCR-32)

PRINCIPAL'S OFFICE Young M.C.—Delicious Vinyl 99137
[Matt Dike/Michael Ross*/Marvin Young] [ASC] (11/25/89 BC-33)

PRISCILLA *Julius La Rosa—RCA Victor 47-6700 [Eddie Cooley] [BMI] (10/20/56 CtRt-22)*

PRISCILLA *Eddie Cooley And The Dimples—Royal Roost 621 [Eddie Cooley] [BMI] (10/27/56 BCtRt-22)*

PRISCILLA *Les Brown & His Band Of Renown—Capitol 3587 [Eddie Cooley] [BMI] (11/10/56 Rt-22) [IWM]*

THE PRISONER Howard Jones—Elektra 69288
[Howard Jones] [ASC] (7/1/89 BC-22)

—PRISONER CAPTURED BY YOUR EYES see: LOVE THEME FROM "EYES OF LAURA MARS"

PRISONER OF LOVE James Brown And The Famous Flames—King 5739
[Russ Columbo/Clarence Gaskill/Leo Robin] [ASC] (4/20/63 BCR-16)

PRISONER OF YOUR LOVE Player—RSO 908
[Peter Beckett/J.C. Crowley] [BMI] (9/9/78 BCR-27)

PRISONER'S SONG Warren Storm—Nasco 6015
[Guy Massey/Robert Massey] [ASC] (8/25/58 BC-81)

PRIVATE DANCER Tina Turner—Capitol 5433 [Mark Knopfler] [ASC] (1/19/85 BC-7)

PRIVATE EYE The Olympics—Arvee 562
[Cliff Goldsmith/Fred Smith] [BMI] (9/14/59 B-95)

PRIVATE EYES Daryl Hall & John Oates—RCA 12296
[Janna Allen/Sara Allen/Daryl Hall/Warren Pash] [BMI] (8/29/81 BCR-1)

PRIVATE IDAHO The B-52's—Warner Bros. 49537
[Kate Pierson/Fred Schneider/Keith Strickland/Cindy Wilson] [BMI] (10/18/80 BCR-74)

PRIVATE NUMBER Judy Clay & William Bell—Stax 0005
[William Bell/Booker T. Jones Jr.] [BMI] (8/31/68 BCR-75)

PRIVATE NUMBER The Jets—MCA 52846
[Jerry Knight/Aaron Zigman] [BMI] (8/2/86 BC-45)

PROBLEM CHILD Mark Lindsay—Columbia 45286
[Mac Davis] [BMI] (12/26/70 BCR-59)

PROBLEMS The Everly Brothers—Cadence 1355
[Boudleaux Bryant/Felice Bryant] [BMI] (11/10/58 BCR-2)

THE PROMISE When In Rome—Virgin 99323
[Clive Farrington/Mike Floreale/Andrew Mann] [BMI] (9/3/88 BC-11)

PROMISE HER ANYTHING Dean Martin—Capitol 3787 [Roy Alfred] [ASC] (9/23/57 R-64)

PROMISE HER ANYTHING Tom Jones—Parrot 9809
[Burt Bacharach/Hal David] [ASC] (2/19/66 BCR-72)

PROMISE ME The Cover Girls—Fever 1917
[Albert Cabrera/Tony Moran/Andy Tripoli] [BMI] (3/26/88 BC-40)

PROMISE ME A ROSE (A SLIGHT DETAIL) Anita Bryant—Carlton 518
[Bob Merrill] [ASC] (12/28/59 B-78)

PROMISE ME LOVE Andy Williams—Cadence 1351
[Kay Thompson] [ASC] (9/1/58 BCR-17)

THE PROMISE OF A NEW DAY Paula Abdul—Captive/Virgin 98752
[Paula Abdul/Peter Lord/V. Jeffrey Smith/Sandra St. Victor] [BMI] (7/20/91 BC-1)

PROMISED LAND *Chuck Berry—Chess 1916 [Chuck Berry] [BMI] (12/12/64 BCR-35)*

PROMISED LAND *Elvis Presley—RCA Victor 10074*
[Chuck Berry] [BMI] (10/19/74 BCR-14)

PROMISES Carla Thomas—Atlantic 2101 [Chips Moman] [BMI] (5/1/61 R-80)

PROMISES Eric Clapton And His Band—RSO 910
[Richard Feldman/Roger Linn] [BMI] (10/14/78 BCR-9)

PROMISES Barbra Streisand—Columbia 02065
[Barry Gibb/Robin Gibb] [BMI] (5/23/81 BCR-48)

PROMISES Basia—Epic 68608
[Peter Ross/Basia Trzetrzelewska/Danny White] [BMI] (4/22/89 C-86)

PROMISES IN THE DARK Pat Benatar—Chrysalis 2555
[Pat Benatar/Neil Geraldo] [ASC] (10/3/81 BCR-35)

PROMISES, PROMISES Dionne Warwick—Scepter 12231
[Burt Bacharach/Hal David] [ASC] (11/2/68 BCR-15)

PROMISES, PROMISES Naked Eyes—EMI-America 8170
[Pete Byrne/Rob Fisher] [ASC] (7/16/83 BC-11)

THE PROPHECY OF DANIEL AND JOHN THE DIVINE (SIX-SIX-SIX) The Cowsills—MGM 14063
[Remo Capra] [ASC] (6/14/69 BCR-55)

PROUD Johnny Crawford—Del-Fi 4193
[Barry Mann/Cynthia Weil] [BMI] (12/29/62 BCR-28)

PROUD Joe Chemay Band—Unicorn 95001
[Bunny Hull/Andrew Woolfolk] [BMI] (2/7/81 BC-68)

PROUD MARY *Creedence Clearwater Revival—Fantasy 619*
[John Fogerty] [BMI] (1/18/69 BCR-1)

PROUD MARY *Solomon Burke—Bell 783 [John Fogerty] [BMI] (4/26/69 BCR-41)*

PROUD MARY *The Checkmates, Ltd. Featuring Sonny Charles—A&M 1127*
[John Fogerty] [BMI] (10/18/69 BCR-69)

PROUD MARY *Ike & Tina Turner—Liberty 56216 [John Fogerty] [BMI] (1/30/71 BCR-4)*

THE PROUD ONE *Frankie Valli—Philips 40407*
[Bob Crewe/Bob Gaudio] [BMI] (11/5/66 BCR-54)

THE PROUD ONE *The Osmonds—MGM 14791*
[Bob Crewe/Bob Gaudio] [BMI] (7/26/75 BCR-22)

PROVE IT ALL NIGHT Bruce Springsteen—Columbia 10763
[Bruce Springsteen] [ASC] (6/10/78 BCR-33)

PROVE ME WRONG David Pack—Warner Bros. 28802
[James Newton Howard/David Pack] [BMI] (1/25/86 B-95)

PROVE YOUR LOVE Taylor Dayne—Arista 1-9676
[Arnie Roman/Seth Swirsky] [ASC] (2/20/88 BC-7)

P.S. I LOVE YOU The Beatles—Tollie 9008
[John Lennon/Paul McCartney] [GL] (5/2/64 BCR-10)

PSYCHEDELIC SHACK The Temptations—Gordy 7096
[Barrett Strong/Norman Whitfield] [BMI] (1/17/70 BCR-4)

PSYCHO Bobby Hendricks—Sue 732
[Clyde McPhatter/Jimmy Oliver] [BMI] (10/24/60 BCR-73)

PSYCHO KILLER Talking Heads—Sire 1013
[David Byrne/Chris Frantz/Tina Weymouth] [ASC] (2/18/78 B-92)

PSYCHOBABBLE Alan Parsons Project—Arista 1029
[Alan Parsons/Eric Woolfson] [BMI] (11/27/82 BC-57)

PSYCHOTIC REACTION Count Five—Double Shot 104
[Craig Atkinson/John Byrne/Roy Chaney/Kenn Ellner/John Michalski] [BMI] (9/10/66 BCR-4)

P.T. 109 Jimmy Dean—Columbia 42338
[Fred Burch/Marijohn Wilkin] [BMI] (3/31/62 BCR-7)

PUCKER UP BUTTERCUP Jr. Walker & The All Stars—Soul 35030
[Johnny Bristol/Danny Coggins/Harvey Fuqua] [ASC] (2/4/67 BCR-31)

PUDDIN N' TAIN (ASK ME AGAIN I'LL TELL YOU THE SAME) The Alley Cats—Philles 108
[Brice Coefield/Gary Pipkin/Alonzo Willis] [BMI] (1/12/63 BCR-39)

PUFF OF SMOKE Roy Head—TMI 9000 [Steve Cropper/Bonny Rice] [BMI] (6/26/71 B-96)

PUFF (THE MAGIC DRAGON) Peter, Paul & Mary—Warner Bros. 5348
[Leonard Lipton/Peter Yarrow] [ASC] (3/16/63 BCR-2)

PUFFIN' ON DOWN THE TRACK Hugh Masekela—Uni 55085
[Lemmy Mabaso] [BMI] (9/28/68 BCR-50) [I]

PULL UP TO THE BUMPER Grace Jones—Island 49697
[Sly Dunbar/Grace Jones*/Dana Manno/Robbie Shakespeare*] [BMI] (6/6/81 CR-66)

PUMP IT (NICE AN' HARD) Icy Blu—Giant 19377
[Hurby Azor/Tyrone Fleming] [ASC] (7/6/91 B-78)

PUMP UP THE JAM Technotronic—SBK 07311
[Jo Bogaert/Manuela Kamosi] [ASC] (10/14/89 BC-1)

PUMP UP THE VOLUME M/A/R/R/S—4th & Broadway 7452
[Andrew Martyn Biggs/Steven Anthony Biggs] [ASC] (11/28/87 BC-13)

PUNCH AND JUDY LOVE Tony Bennett with Percy Faith and His Orchestra—
Columbia 40491 [Bob Merrill] [ASC] (4/18/55 R-71)

PUNISH HER Bobby Vee—Liberty 55479
[John Gluck/Neval Nader] [BMI] (8/25/62 BCR-20)

PUPALINA *The Gaylords—Mercury 70479*
[Luigi Creatore/C. DeMarinis/Alex Kramer/Hugo Peretti*/Joan Whitney] [ASC] (11/13/54 CRt-22) [FET]*

PUPALINA (MY LITTLE DOLL) *Jimmy Durante—Decca 29354*
[Luigi Creatore/C. DeMarinis/Alex Kramer/Hugo Peretti*/Joan Whitney] [ASC] (12/20/54 Rt-PRE) [FET]*

PUPALINA (MY LITTLE DOLL) *Guy Lombardo & His Royal Canadians—Decca 29381*
[Luigi Creatore/C. DeMarinis/Alex Kramer/Hugo Peretti*/Joan Whitney] [ASC] (12/27/54 Rt-PRE) [FET]*

PUPPET MAN *The 5th Dimension—Bell 880*
[Howard Greenfield/Neil Sedaka] [BMI] (4/11/70 BCR-19)

PUPPET MAN *Tom Jones—Parrot 40062 / 40064*
[Howard Greenfield/Neil Sedaka] (TSW) [BMI] (7/3/71 BCR-14)

PUPPET ON A STRING Elvis Presley With The Jordanaires—RCA Victor 447-0650
[Roy C. Bennett/Sid Tepper] [ASC] (11/13/65 BCR-13)

THE PUPPET SONG Frankie Avalon—Chancellor 1065
[Peter DeAngelis/Bob Marcucci] [ASC] (12/12/60 BCR-56)

(THE PUPPET SONG) WHISKEY ON A SUNDAY The Irish Rovers—Decca 32333
[Glyn Hughes] [NA] (6/15/68 BCR-48)

PUPPY LOVE *Paul Anka—ABC-Paramount 10082 [Paul Anka] [BMI] (2/20/60 BCR-2)*

PUPPY LOVE *Donny Osmond—MGM 14367 [Paul Anka] [BMI] (2/19/72 BCR-2)*

PUPPY LOVE Barbara Lewis—Atlantic 2214 [Barbara Lewis] [BMI] (1/11/64 BCR-38)

PURE Lightning Seeds—MCA 53816 [Ian Broudie] [ASC] (5/19/90 BC-29)

—PURE ENERGY see: WHAT'S ON YOUR MIND

PURPLE HAZE *The Jimi Hendrix Experience—Reprise 0597*
[Jimi Hendrix] [ASC] (8/26/67 BCR-64)

HOORAY FOR THE SALVATION ARMY BAND *(parody of Purple Haze)*
Bill Cosby—Warner Bros. 7096
[Bill Cosby/Jimi Hendrix/Fred Smith*] [BMI] (12/2/67 BCR-60) [P]*

PURPLE HAZE *Dion—Laurie 3478 [Jimi Hendrix] [ASC] (1/25/69 BCR-63)*

PURPLE PEOPLE EATER Sheb Wooley—MGM 12651
[Sheb Wooley] [ASC] (5/19/58 BCR-1)

PURPLE PEOPLE EATER MEETS THE WITCH DOCTOR Joe South—NRC 5000
[J.P. Richardson/Gordon Ritter] [BMI] (7/28/58 B-71)

PURPLE RAIN Prince and the Revolution—Warner Bros. 29174
[Prince] [ASC] (10/6/84 BC-1)

PUSH One Way—MCA 51110 [Kevin McCord] [BMI] (6/20/81 R-90)

THE PUSH AND KICK Mark Valentino—Swan 4121
[Eddie Rambeau/Bud Rehak/Frank Slay] [ASC] (11/3/62 BCR-27)

PUSH IT Salt-N-Pepa—Next Plateau 315
[Hurby Azor/Ray Davies*] [ASC] (11/21/87 BC-19)

PUSH PUSH Austin Taylor—Laurie 3067
[Bert Berns/Phil Medley] [BMI] (11/14/60 BC-90)

PUSHBIKE SONG The Mixtures—Sire 350
[Evan Jones/Idris Jones] [ASC] (2/27/71 BCR-29)

PUSHIN' TOO HARD The Seeds—GNP Crescendo 372
[Sky Saxon] [BMI] (11/26/66 BCR-36)

PUSHIN' YOUR LUCK Sleepy King—Joy 257
[David E. Parker/Maurice Vann] [BMI] (11/4/61 BC-84)

PUSHOVER Etta James—Argo 5437 [Tony Clarke/Billy Davis] [BMI] (4/6/63 BCR-24)

PUSS N BOOTS Kon Kan—Atlantic 88828
[Barry Harris/Jimmy Page/Robert Plant/Kevin Wynne] (Med) [ASC] (9/2/89 BC-58)

PUSSY CAT The Ames Brothers—RCA Victor 47-7315
[Tom Glazer/Sunny Skylar] [ASC] (9/20/58 BCR-17)

PUT A LIGHT IN THE WINDOW The Four Lads—Columbia 41058
[Kenny Jacobson/Rhoda Roberts] [ASC] (11/18/57 BCR-14)

PUT A LITTLE LOVE AWAY The Emotions—Volt 4106
[Dennis Lambert/Brian Potter] [BMI] (3/16/74 BCR-72)

PUT A LITTLE LOVE IN YOUR HEART *Jackie DeShannon—Imperial 66385*
[Jackie DeShannon/Jimmy Holiday/Randy Myers] [BMI] (6/14/69 BCR-3)

PUT A LITTLE LOVE IN YOUR HEART *Annie Lennox & Al Green—A&M 1255*
[Jackie DeShannon/Jimmy Holiday/Randy Myers] [BMI] (11/5/88 BC-5)

PUT A RING ON MY FINGER Les Paul and Mary Ford—Columbia 41222
[Joe Meek] [BMI] (8/11/58 BCR-21)

PUT AWAY YOUR LOVE Alessi—Qwest 50055
[Billy Alessi/Bobby Alessi] [BMI] (5/1/82 BC-71)

PUT IT IN A MAGAZINE Sonny Charles—Highrise 2001
[Sonny Charles/Bobby Paris] [BMI] (11/13/82 BC-40)

PUT IT WHERE YOU WANT IT *The Crusaders—Blue Thumb 208*
[Joe Sample] [BMI] (5/13/72 BCR-37) [I]

PUT IT WHERE YOU WANT IT *Nino & April—A&M 1443*
[Joe Sample/Nino Tempo] [BMI] (6/9/73 CR-72)*

PUT ME IN THE MOOD The Fontane Sisters with Billy Vaughn's Orchestra—Dot 15352
[Bernie Lowe/Al Lubar] [BMI] (4/4/55 R-23)

PUT ON YOUR SHOES AND WALK Clarence Carter—Fame 179
[Ralph Bailey/Rudy Clark/Ken Williams] [BMI] (2/17/73 CR-77)

PUT OUT THE LIGHT Joe Cocker—A&M 1539 [Daniel Moore] [BMI] (6/15/74 BCR-38)

PUT THE BLAME ON ME Elvis Presley—RCA Victor EPA-4383
[Norm Blagman/Kay Twomey/Fred Wise] (EP) [ASC] (7/10/65 BCR-70)

PUT THIS LOVE TO THE TEST Jon Astley—Atlantic 89027
[Jon Astley/Richard King] [BMI] (10/15/88 BC-70)

PUT YOUR ARMS AROUND ME HONEY *Ray Smith—Judd 1017*
[Junie McCree/Albert Von Tilzer] [NA] (4/25/60 BCR-91)

PUT YOUR ARMS AROUND ME HONEY *Fats Domino—Imperial 5687*
[Junie McCree/Albert Von Tilzer] [NA] (9/5/60 BCR-28)

PUT YOUR HAND IN THE HAND Ocean—Kama Sutra 519
[Gene MacLellan] [BMI] (3/13/71 BCR-2)

PUT YOUR HANDS TOGETHER The O'Jays—Philadelphia Int'l 3535
[Kenneth Gamble/Leon Huff] [BMI] (12/22/73 BCR-10)

PUT YOUR HEAD ON MY SHOULDER *Paul Anka—ABC-Paramount 10040*
[Paul Anka] [BMI] (8/24/59 BCR-2)

PUT YOUR HEAD ON MY SHOULDER *The Lettermen—Capitol 2324*
[Paul Anka] [BMI] (11/9/68 BCR-35)

PUT YOUR HEAD ON MY SHOULDER *Leif Garrett—Atlantic 3466*
[Paul Anka] [BMI] (2/25/78 BCR-58)

PUT YOUR MIND AT EASE Every Mothers' Son—MGM 13788
[Dennis Larden/Lary Larden] [BMI] (8/26/67 BCR-36)

PUT YOUR MOUTH ON ME Eddie Murphy—Columbia 68897
[Jeffrey E. Cohen/Eddie Murphy/Narada Michael Walden] [ASC] (7/29/89 BC-27)

PUT YOURSELF IN MY PLACE The Elgins—V.I.P. 25029
[Lamont Dozier/Brian Holland/Eddie Holland/John Thornton*] [BMI] (2/12/66 BCR-88)

PUTTIN' ON THE RITZ Taco—RCA 13574 [Irving Berlin] [ASC] (6/25/83 BC-1)

THE PUZZLE Gene McDaniels—Liberty 55541
[Cliff Crofford/Nick Savorese/Warren Schatz] [BMI] (2/23/63 R-100)

THE PUZZLE SONG (A PUZZLE IN SONG) Shirley Ellis—Congress 238
[Lincoln Chase] [BMI] (5/29/65 BCR-53)

Q

—QUAND LE SOLEIL DIT BONJOUR AUX MONTAGNES see: FRENCH SONG

—QUANDO M'INNAMORO see: MAN WITHOUT LOVE

QUANDO, QUANDO, QUANDO (TELL ME WHEN) Pat Boone—Dot 16349
[Pat Boone/Tony Renis/Al Testa] [ASC] (5/19/62 B-95) [FET]

QUARTER TO FOUR STOMP The Stompers—Landa 684
[Gary S. Paxton/Bob Todd] [BMI] (2/26/62 BCR-65)

QUARTER TO THREE U.S. Bonds—Legrand 1008
[Gary Anderson/Gene Barge/Frank Guida/Joseph Royster] [BMI] (5/22/61 BCR-1)

—QUE C'EST TRISTE VENISE see: VENICE BLUE

WHATEVER WILL BE WILL BE (QUE SERÁ SERÁ) *Eddy Howard—Mercury 70881*
[Ray Evans/Jay Livingston] [ASC] (6/22/56 Rt-2)

WHATEVER WILL BE, WILL BE (QUE SERA, SERA) *Doris Day—Columbia 40704*
[Ray Evans/Jay Livingston] [ASC] (6/22/56 BCRt-2)

QUE SERA, SERA (WHATEVER WILL BE, WILL BE) *The High Keys—Atco 6268*
[Ray Evans/Jay Livingston] [ASC] (7/27/63 BCR-47)

QUE SERA, SERA (WHATEVER WILL BE, WILL BE) *Mary Hopkin—Apple 1823*
[Ray Evans/Jay Livingston] [ASC] (6/27/70 BCR-45)

QUE TE QUIERO Katrina And The Waves—Capitol 5528
[Kimberly Rew] [BMI] (10/12/85 BC-71)

QUEEN OF CLUBS K.C. & The Sunshine Band—TK 1005
[Harry Wayne Casey/Willie Clarke/Rick Finch] [BMI] (3/13/76 BCR-63)

QUEEN OF HEARTS Juice Newton—Capitol 4997 [Hank DeVito] [ASC] (5/30/81 BCR-2)

QUEEN OF MY HEART René And Ray—Donna 1360
[Paul Buff/Ray Quinones/Pablo Venezuela] [BMI] (5/19/62 BCR-75)

QUEEN OF MY SOUL Average White Band—Atlantic 3354
[Hamish Stuart] [ASC] (9/4/76 BCR-40)

—QUEEN OF THE BLUES see: BRIDGET THE MIDGET

QUEEN OF THE BROKEN HEARTS Loverboy—Columbia 04096
[Paul Dean/Mike Reno] [BMI] (9/17/83 BC-33)

QUEEN OF THE HOP Bobby Darin—Atco 6127 [Woody Harris] [ASC] (10/4/58 BCR-9)

—QUEEN OF THE HOUSE see: KING OF THE ROAD

QUEEN OF THE ROLLER DERBY Leon Russell—Shelter 7337
[Leon Russell] [BMI] (9/1/73 BCR-87)

QUEEN OF THE SENIOR PROM *The Mills Brothers—Decca 30299*
[Stella Lee/Ed Penney/Jack Richards] [BMI] (5/27/57 BCR-39)

QUEEN OF THE SENIOR PROM *The Mills Brothers—Dot 16360*
[Stella Lee/Ed Penney/Jack Richards] [BMI] (6/30/62 R-98)

QUENTIN'S THEME Charles Randolph Grean Sounde—Ranwood 840
[Robert W. Cobert] [BMI] (6/7/69 BCR-6) [I]

QUESTION Lloyd Price And His Orchestra—ABC-Paramount 10123
[Harold Logan/Lloyd Price] [BMI] (6/25/60 BCR-19)

QUESTION The Moody Blues—Threshold 67004 [Justin Hayward] [ASC] (5/2/70 BCR-19)

A QUESTION OF TEMPERATURE The Balloon Farm—Laurie 3405
[Mike Appel/Don Henny/Ed Schnug] [BMI] (2/3/68 BCR-37)

QUESTIONS Bang—Capitol 3304
[Anthony D'Iorio/Frank Ferrara/Frank Gilcken] [BMI] (4/22/72 BC-90)

QUESTIONS AND ANSWERS The In Crowd—Viva 604
[Wally Gold/Philip Springer/Pyotr Ilyich Tchaikovsky*] [ASC] (11/26/66 BCR-87)

QUESTIONS 67 AND 68 *Chicago—Columbia 44909*
[Robert Lamm] [ASC] (8/9/69 BCR-71)

QUESTIONS 67 AND 68 *Chicago—Columbia 45467*
[Robert Lamm] (TSW) [ASC] (10/9/71 BCR-13)

QUICK, FAST, IN A HURRY New York City—Chelsea 0150
[Thom Bell/Linda Creed] [BMI] (1/26/74 BCR-78)

QUICK JOEY SMALL (RUN JOEY RUN) Kasenetz-Katz Singing Orchestral Circus—
Buddah 64 [Joey Levine/Artie Resnick] [BMI] (9/21/68 BCR-18)

QUICKSAND Martha & The Vandellas—Gordy 7025
[Lamont Dozier/Brian Holland/Eddie Holland] [BMI] (11/23/63 BCR-8)

—QUIEN SERA see: SWAY

QUIET NIGHTS OF QUIET STARS Andy Williams—Columbia 43456
[Antonio Carlos Jobim/Gene Lees] [BMI] (11/27/65 BCR-92)

A QUIET PLACE Garnet Mimms & The Enchanters—United Artists 715
[Samuel Bell/Jerry Ragovoy] [NA] (5/30/64 BCR-73)

QUIET STORM Smokey Robinson—Tamla 54265
[Rose Ella Jones/Smokey Robinson] [ASC] (1/17/76 BCR-61)

QUIET THREE Duane Eddy His "Twangy" guitar and The Rebels—Jamie 1126
[Duane Eddy/Lee Hazlewood] [BMI] (6/20/59 BCR-46) [I]

QUIET VILLAGE The Exotic Sounds Of Martin Denny—Liberty 55162
[Les Baxter] [ASC] (4/11/59 BCR-3) [I]

—QUINN THE ESKIMO see: MIGHTY QUINN

QUITE A PARTY The Fireballs—Warwick 644 [George Tomsco] [BMI] (6/24/61 BC-27) [I]

—QU'L FAIT BON VIVRE see: DOWN BY THE RIVERSIDE

R

R O C K Bill Haley And His Comets—Decca 29870
[Bill Haley/Arrett Keefer/Ruth Keefer] [ASC] (3/30/56 BCR-16)

R.O.C.K. IN THE U.S.A. (A SALUTE TO 60'S ROCK)
John Cougar Mellencamp—Riva 884 455
[John Mellencamp] [ASC] (2/1/86 BC-2)

RACE AMONG THE RUINS Gordon Lightfoot—Reprise 1380
[Gordon Lightfoot] [ASC] (2/19/77 BC-65)

THE RACE IS ON *George Jones—United Artists 751 [Don Rollins] [BMI] (1/23/65 B-96)*

THE RACE IS ON *Jack Jones—Kapp 651 [Don Rollins] [BMI] (2/27/65 BCR-12)*

RACE WITH THE DEVIL Gene Vincent and His Blue Caps—Capitol 3530
[William Douchette/Gene Vincent] [BMI] (9/8/56 BCR-40)

RACE WITH THE WIND The Robbs—Mercury 72579 [Dee Robb] [BMI] (6/18/66 R-93)

RADAR LOVE *Golden Earring—Track/MCA 40202*
[Barry Hay/George Kooymans] [ASC] (5/11/74 BCR-9)

RADAR LOVE *White Lion—Atlantic 88836*
[Barry Hay/George Kooymans] [ASC] (9/23/89 BC-59)

RADIO FREE EUROPE R.E.M.—I.R.S. 9916
[Bill Berry/Peter Buck/Mike Mills/Michael Stipe] [BMI] (7/23/83 B-78)

RADIO GA-GA Queen—Capitol 5317 [Roger Taylor] [BMI] (2/18/84 BC-14)

RADIO ROMANCE Tiffany—MCA 53623
[John Duarte/Mark E. Paul] [BMI] (2/25/89 BC-35)

RADIO SONG R.E.M.—Warner Bros. 19246
[Bill Berry/Peter Buck/Mike Mills/Michael Stipe] [BMI] (11/2/91 C-75)

RADIOACTIVE Gene Simmons—Casablanca 951
[Gene Simmons] [ASC] (12/2/78 BCR-47)

RADIOACTIVE The Firm—Atlantic 89586 [Paul Rodgers] [ASC] (2/9/85 BC-28)

RAG DOLL The 4 Seasons Featuring The "Sound" Of Frankie Valli—Philips 40211
[Bob Crewe/Bob Gaudio] [BMI] (6/20/64 BCR-1)

RAG DOLL Sammy Johns—GRC 2062 [Steve Eaton] [ASC] (5/31/75 BCR-49)

RAG DOLL Aerosmith—Geffen 27915
[Holly Knight/Joe Perry/Steven Tyler/Jim Vallance] [ASC] (6/4/88 BC-17)

RAG MAMA RAG The Band—Capitol 2705 [Robbie Robertson] [ASC] (2/14/70 BCR-44)

RAGS TO RICHES *The Rays Featuring Hal Miller—Cameo 133*
[Richard Adler/Jerry Ross] [ASC] (5/5/58 R-82)

RAGS TO RICHES *Sunny & The Sunliners—Tear Drop 3022*
[Richard Adler/Jerry Ross] [ASC] (11/16/63 BCR-45)

RAGS TO RICHES *Lenny Welch—Kapp 740*
[Richard Adler/Jerry Ross] [ASC] (2/26/66 CR-85)

RAGS TO RICHES *Elvis Presley—RCA Victor 47-9980*
[Richard Adler/Jerry Ross] (TSW) [ASC] (3/13/71 BCR-25)

RAGTIME COWBOY JOE David Seville And The Chipmunks—Liberty 55200
[Maurice Abrahams/Grant Clarke/Lewis Muir] [BMI] (7/4/59 BCR-14)

RAIN The Beatles—Capitol 5651 [John Lennon/Paul McCartney] [ASC] (6/11/66 BCR-23)

RAIN Jose Feliciano—RCA Victor 47-9757
[Hilda Feliciano/Jose Feliciano] [BMI] (8/23/69 BCR-68)

RAIN Dragon—Polydor 817292
[Marc Hunter/Todd Hunter/Johanna Pigott] [BMI] (8/18/84 B-88)

THE RAIN Oran "Juice" Jones—Def Jam 06209 [Vincent Bell] [ASC] (9/13/86 BC-9)

RAIN DANCE The Guess Who—RCA Victor 74-0522
[Burton Cummings/Kurt Winter] [BMI] (8/7/71 BCR-11)

RAIN FOREST Paul Hardcastle—Profile 7059
[Paul Hardcastle] [BMI] (1/12/85 BC-43) [I]

RAIN IN MAY Max Werner—Radio 3821
[Chris Meldon*/Chris Pilgram] [ASC] (5/16/81 BCR-74)

RAIN IN MY HEART Frank Sinatra—Reprise 0798
[Victoria Pike/Teddy Randazzo] [BMI] (12/28/68 BCR-51)

RAIN IN THE SUMMERTIME The Alarm—I.R.S. 53219
[Eddie MacDonald/Mike Peters/Dave Sharp/Nigel Twist] [BMI] (12/19/87 BC-71)

RAIN, OH RAIN Fools Gold—Morning Sky 700 [Denny Henson] [ASC] (5/15/76 BCR-67)

RAIN ON THE ROOF The Lovin' Spoonful—Kama Sutra 216
[John Sebastian] [BMI] (10/15/66 BCR-6)

RAIN ON THE SCARECROW John Cougar Mellencamp—Riva 884 635
[George Green/John Mellencamp] [ASC] (4/26/86 BC-21)

RAIN RAIN GO AWAY Bobby Vinton—Epic 9532
[Noel Regney/Gloria Shayne] [BMI] (8/25/62 BCR-12)

RAIN, RAIN, RAIN
Frankie Laine & The Four Lads with The Buddy Cole Quartet—Columbia 40295
[Jay McConlogue] [NA] (9/11/54 BCR-18)

THE RAIN, THE PARK & OTHER THINGS The Cowsills—MGM 13810
[Steve Duboff/Artie Kornfeld] [BMI] (9/30/67 BCR-1)

RAINBOW *Russ Hamilton—Kapp 184 [Russ Hamilton] [ASC] (6/17/57 BCRt-3)*

RAINBOW *Bill Darnel—Jubilee 5290 [Russ Hamilton] [ASC] (7/13/57 Rt-3)*

RAINBOW *Bobby Breen—Chic 1013 [Russ Hamilton] [ASC] (8/3/57 Rt-3)*

RAINBOW *Gene Chandler—Vee-Jay 468 [Curtis Mayfield] [BMI] (2/23/63 BCR-47)*

RAINBOW '65 PART I *Gene Chandler—Constellation 158*
[Curtis Mayfield] [BMI] (11/13/65 BCR-69)

RAINBOW The Marmalade—London 20059
[Junior Campbell/Thomas McAleese] [BMI] (7/25/70 BCR-48)

RAINBOW AT MIDNIGHT Jimmie Rodgers—Dot 16407
[John A. Miller] [ASC] (11/17/62 BCR-51)

RAINBOW CONNECTION Kermit (Jim Henson)—Atlantic 3610
[Ken Ascher/Paul Williams] [ASC] (9/15/79 BCR-25)

RAINBOW IN YOUR EYES Leon & Mary Russell—Paradise 8208
[Leon Russell] [BMI] (6/19/76 BCR-52)

RAINBOW MAN Looking Glass—Epic 10953 [Pieter Sweval] [ASC] (2/24/73 CR-91)

RAINBOW RIDE Andy Kim—Steed 711
[Jeff Barry/Andy Kim] [BMI] (11/30/68 BCR-45)

RAINBOW'S END Sergio Mendes—A&M 2563
[David Batteau/Don Freeman] [ASC] (8/13/83 BC-51)

RAINDROPS Dee Clark—Vee-Jay 383 [Dee Clark] [BMI] (5/1/61 BCR-2)

RAINDROPS KEEP FALLIN' ON MY HEAD B.J. Thomas—Scepter 12265
[Burt Bacharach/Hal David] [ASC] (10/25/69 BCR-1)

RAININ' IN MY HEART Slim Harpo—Excello 2194
[Slim Harpo/Jerry West] [BMI] (5/27/61 BCR-24)

RAINING IN MY HEART *Buddy Holly / The Crickets—Coral 62074*
[Boudleaux Bryant/Felice Bryant] [BMI] (2/21/59 BC-88)

RAINING IN MY HEART *Leo Sayer—Warner Bros. 8682*
[Boudleaux Bryant/Felice Bryant] [BMI] (9/23/78 BCR-43)

THE RAINS CAME *Big Sambo And The House Wreckers—Eric 7003*
[Huey P. Meaux] [BMI] (2/26/62 BCR-72)

THE RAINS CAME *Sir Douglas Quintet—Tribe 8314*
[Huey P. Meaux] [BMI] (1/22/66 BCR-31)

RAINY DAY PEOPLE Gordon Lightfoot—Reprise 1328
[Gordon Lightfoot] [ASC] (3/29/75 BCR-26)

RAINY DAY WOMEN #12 & 35 Bob Dylan—Columbia 43592
[Bob Dylan] [SE] (4/16/66 BCR-2)

RAINY DAYS AND MONDAYS Carpenters—A&M 1260
[Roger Nichols/Paul Williams] [ASC] (5/8/71 BCR-2)

RAINY JANE Davy Jones—Bell 45,111
[Howard Greenfield/Neil Sedaka] [BMI] (6/19/71 BCR-31)

RAINY NIGHT IN GEORGIA Brook Benton—Cotillion 44057
[Tony Joe White] [BMI] (1/3/70 BCR-2)

RAISE A LITTLE HELL Trooper—MCA 40924
[Ra McGuire/Brian Smith] [BMI] (8/5/78 BCR-51)

RAISE YOUR HAND Eddie Floyd—Stax 208
[Steve Cropper/Eddie Floyd/Alvertis Isbell] [BMI] (2/4/67 BCR-63)

RAISED ON ROBBERY Joni Mitchell—Asylum 11029
[Joni Mitchell] [ASC] (12/22/73 BCR-50)

RAISED ON ROCK Elvis Presley—RCA Victor 74-0088
[Mark James] (TSW) [BMI] (9/22/73 BCR-27)

RAISIN' SUGAR CANE The Untouchables—Madison M147
[Leon Carr/Ed Warren] [ASC] (2/6/61 R-94)

RAM BUNK SHUSH *Bill Doggett—King 5020*
[Henry Glover/Lucky Millinder/Jim Mundy] [BMI] (2/16/57 BR-26) [I]

RAM-BUNK-SHUSH *The Ventures—Dolton 32*
[Henry Glover/Lucky Millinder/Jim Mundy] [BMI] (1/23/61 BCR-29) [I]

RAMA LAMA DING DONG The Edsels—Twin 700
[George Wydell Jones Jr.] [BMI] (5/1/61 BCR-21)

THE RAMBLER Molly Hatchet—Epic 50965
[Jimmy Farrar/Dave Hlubek] [BMI] (3/7/81 B-91)

RAMBLIN' GAMBLIN' MAN Bob Seger System—Capitol 2297
[Bob Seger] [ASC] (11/16/68 BCR-16)

RAMBLIN' MAN The Allman Brothers Band—Capricorn 0027
[Dickey Betts] [BMI] (8/18/73 BCR-1)

RAMBLIN' ROSE Nat King Cole—Capitol 4804
[Joe Sherman/Noel Sherman] [ASC] (7/28/62 BCR-1)

RAMBLING The Ramblers (1)—Addit 1257
[Mike Borchetta/Kip Martin] [BMI] (8/22/60 BCR-62) [I]

RAMONA *The Lancers—Coral 61769*
[L. Wolfe Gilbert/Mabel Wayne] (Med) [NA] (3/2/57 R-79)

RAMONA *The Blue Diamonds—London 1954*
[L. Wolfe Gilbert/Mabel Wayne] [ASC] (11/28/60 BCR-52)

RAMROD Duane Eddy his "twangy" guitar and The Rebels—Jamie 1109
[Al Casey] [BMI] (8/18/58 BCR-28) [I]

RANDY The Happenings—B.T. Puppy 540
[David Libert/Ralph Miranda] [BMI] (5/18/68 CR-90)

RANG TANG DING DONG (I AM THE JAPANESE SANDMAN) *The Cellos—Apollo 510*
[Alvin Williams] [BMI] (5/18/57 BCRt-46)

RANG TANG DING DONG *Chuck Miller—Mercury 71118*
[Alvin Williams] [BMI] (6/29/57 Rt-74)

RANG TANG DING DONG (I'M THE JAPANESE SANDMAN) *Ray Stevens—Prep 108*
[Alvin Williams] [BMI] (6/29/57 Rt-74)

THE RAPPER The Jaggerz—Kama Sutra 502 [Donnie Iris] [BMI] (1/24/70 BCR-1)

RAPPER'S DELIGHT Sugarhill Gang—Sugar Hill 542
[Bernard Edwards/Nile Rodgers] [BMI] (10/27/79 BCR-36)

RAPPIN' RODNEY Rodney Dangerfield—RCA 13656
[Dennis Blair/Rodney Dangerfield/Robert Arthur Ford Jr./Scott Henry/Doug Hoyt/
James B. Moore/Lawrence Smith*] [BMI] (12/3/83 BC-59)

RAPTURE Blondie—Chrysalis 2485
[Clement A. Bozewski*/Deborah Harry/Christopher Stein] [ASC] (1/31/81 BCR-1)

RASPBERRIES STRAWBERRIES The Kingston Trio—Capitol 4114
[Will Holt] [ASC] (1/12/59 BCR-43)

RASPBERRY BERET Prince and the Revolution—Paisley Park 7-28972
[Prince] [ASC] (5/18/85 BC-1)

RAT RACE The Drifters—Atlantic 2191
[Jerry Leiber/Van McCoy/Mike Stoller] [BMI] (6/8/63 BCR-71)

RATTLESNAKE Ohio Players—Westbound 5018
[Leroy Bonner/Marshall Jones/Ralph Middlebrooks/Walter Morrison/
Bruce Napier/Andrew Noland/Marvin Pierce] [BMI] (2/21/76 B-90) [I]

RAUNCHY *Bill Justis—Phillips Int'l 3519*
[Bill Justis/Sid Manker] [BMI] (10/28/57 BCtRt-1) [I]

RAUNCHY *Ernie Freeman—Imperial 5474*
[Bill Justis/Sid Manker] [BMI] (11/4/57 BCtRt-1) [I]

RAUNCHY *Billy Vaughn and His Orchestra—Dot 15661*
[Bill Justis/Sid Manker] [BMI] (11/11/57 BCtRt-1) [I]

RAUNCHY *Muvva "Guitar" Hubbard—ABC-Paramount 9869*
[Bill Justis/Sid Manker] [BMI] (11/11/57 Rt-48) [I]

RAVE ON Buddy Holly / The Crickets—Coral 61985
[Norman Petty/Bill Tilghman/Sonny West] [BMI] (5/17/58 BCR-37)

RAVEL'S BOLERO Henry Mancini And His Orchestra—Warner Bros. 49139
[Maurice Ravel] [NA] (1/12/80 CR-59) [I]

RAVEN Alan Parsons—20th Century 2308
[Alan Parsons/Eric Woolfson] [BMI] (10/16/76 B-80)

RAW HIDE Link Wray & His Ray Men—Epic 9300
[Milton Grant/Link Wray] [BMI] (1/26/59 BCRt*-23) [I]

RAWHIDE Bill & Doree Post—Crest 1054 [Bill Post/Doree Post] [BMI] (3/2/59 Rt*-35)

A RAY OF HOPE The Rascals—Atlantic 2584
[Eddie Brigati/Felix Cavaliere] [ASC] (11/30/68 BCR-14)

—RAZA see: LA RAZA

RAZZLE-DAZZLE *Bill Haley And His Comets—Decca 29552*
[Jesse Stone] (TSW) [BMI] (7/23/55 BCRt-15)

RAZZLE-DAZZLE *Ella Mae Morse—Capitol 3199 [Jesse Stone] [BMI] (8/29/55 Rt-23)*

RAZZLE DAZZLE Jive Bunny & The Mastermixers—Music Factory/Atco 99122
[Jesse Stone] (Med) [ASC] (2/3/90 BC-67)

REACH Orleans—Asylum 45375 [Johanna Hall/John Hall] [BMI] (1/22/77 BCR-45)

REACH FOR IT George Duke—Epic 50463
[Leon Chancler/George Duke/Charles Icarus Johnson/Byron Lee Miller] [ASC] (11/19/77 BCR-54)

REACH OUT Giorgio Moroder—Columbia 04511
[Paul Engemann/Giorgio Moroder/Richie Zito] [BMI] (7/21/84 BC-76)

REACH OUT AND TOUCH (SOMEBODY'S HAND) Diana Ross—Motown 1165
[Nick Ashford/Valerie Simpson] [ASC] (4/18/70 BCR-9)

REACH OUT FOR ME *Lou Johnson—Big Top 3153*
[Burt Bacharach/Hal David] [ASC] (9/28/63 BCR-52)

REACH OUT FOR ME *Dionne Warwick—Scepter 1285*
[Burt Bacharach/Hal David] [ASC] (10/24/64 BCR-20)

REACH OUT I'LL BE THERE *Four Tops—Motown 1098*
[Lamont Dozier/Brian Holland/Eddie Holland] [BMI] (9/3/66 BCR-1)

REACH OUT *Merrilee Rush—AGP 107*
[Lamont Dozier/Brian Holland/Eddie Holland] [BMI] (11/23/68 BCR-79)

REACH OUT I'LL BE THERE *Diana Ross—Motown 1184*
[Lamont Dozier/Brian Holland/Eddie Holland] [BMI] (5/1/71 BCR-19)

REACH OUT I'LL BE THERE *The New Seekers—MGM 14683*
[Lamont Dozier/Brian Holland/Eddie Holland] [BMI] (1/19/74 C-99)

REACH OUT, I'LL BE THERE *Gloria Gaynor—MGM 14790*
[Lamont Dozier/Brian Holland/Eddie Holland] [BMI] (3/15/75 BCR-60)

REACH OUT, I'LL BE THERE *The Ritchie Family—Marlin 3306*
[Lamont Dozier/Brian Holland/Eddie Holland] (Med) [BMI] (8/28/76 BCR-17)

REACH OUT I'LL BE THERE *Stars On 45—Radio 3863*
[Lamont Dozier/Brian Holland/Eddie Holland] (Med) [BMI] (9/19/81 BCR-55)

REACH OUT OF THE DARKNESS Friend And Lover—Verve Forecast 5069
[Jim Post] [BMI] (5/4/68 BCR-7)

REACH OUT YOUR HAND The Brotherhood Of Man—Deram 85073
[Tony Hiller] [ASC] (4/24/71 BC-73)

REACHING FOR THE SKY Peabo Bryson—Capitol 4522
[Peabo Bryson] [BMI] (2/25/78 CR-60)

REACHING FOR THE WORLD Harold Melvin And The Blue Notes—ABC 12240
[Derek Floyd] [BMI] (2/12/77 BCR-73)

REACTION TO ACTION Foreigner—Atlantic 89542
[Lou Gramm/Michael Leslie Jones] [ASC] (6/1/85 BC-49)

READ 'EM AND WEEP Barry Manilow—Arista 1-9101
[Jim Steinman] [BMI] (11/19/83 BC-18)

READY Cat Stevens—A&M 1645 [Cat Stevens] [ASC] (11/30/74 BCR-26)

READY FOR LOVE Silverado—Pavillion 02077
[Buzz Goodwin/Carl Shillo] [BMI] (7/4/81 B-92)

READY FOR THE '80S Village People—Casablanca 2220
[Henri Belolo/Phil Hurtt/Jacques Morali/Peter Whitehead] [BMI] (11/3/79 BCR-52)

READY FOR THE TIMES TO GET BETTER Crystal Gayle—United Artists 1136
[Allen Reynolds] [BMI] (2/18/78 BCR-52)

READY FOR YOUR LOVE Shep And The Limelites—Hull 742
[James Sheppard] [BMI] (7/10/61 BCR-42)

READY OR NOT Helen Reddy—Capitol 4582
[Amber DiLena/Jack Keller] [ASC] (7/15/78 BCR-73)

READY OR NOT Lou Gramm—Atlantic 89269
[Lou Gramm/Bruce Turgon] [ASC] (5/9/87 BC-54)

READY OR NOT After 7—Virgin 98995 [Kenneth Edmonds] [BMI] (3/31/90 BC-4)

READY OR NOT HERE I COME (CAN'T HIDE FROM LOVE) The Delfonics—Philly Groove 154
[Thom Bell/William Hart] [BMI] (12/7/68 BCR-24)

READY TEDDY Little Richard—Specialty 579
[Robert Blackwell/John Marascalco] [BMI] (6/29/56 BCR-28)

READY TO RIDE Southwind—Blue Thumb 108
[Douglas Fontaine Brown] [BMI] (11/22/69 R-92)

READY TO TAKE A CHANCE AGAIN Barry Manilow—Arista 0357
[Charles Fox/Norman Gimbel] [BMI] (9/9/78 BCR-5)

READY WILLING AND ABLE *Doris Day—Columbia 40371*
[Dick Gleason/Floyd Huddleston/Al Rinker] [BMI] (11/22/54 CRt-31)

READY, WILLING AND ABLE *Gary Crosby—Decca 29291*
[Dick Gleason/Floyd Huddleston/Al Rinker] [BMI] (11/22/54 Rt-75)

READY, WILLING AND ABLE The American Breed—Acta 824
[Bob Stone] [BMI] (5/11/68 BCR-73)

THE REAL END Rickie Lee Jones—Warner Bros. 29191
[Rickie Lee Jones] [ASC] (9/29/84 B-83)

REAL HUMDINGER J.J. Barnes—Ric-Tic 110
[Al Hamilton/Bob Hamilton/Richard Morris] [BMI] (3/26/66 BCR-80)

REAL LIVE GIRL Steve Alaimo—ABC-Paramount 10620
[Cy Coleman/Carolyn Leigh] [ASC] (1/30/65 BCR-77)

REAL LOVE The Cretones—Planet 45911 [Mark Goldenberg] [BMI] (4/12/80 BCR-72)

REAL LOVE The Doobie Brothers—Warner Bros. 49503
[Patrick Henderson/Michael McDonald] [ASC] (9/6/80 BCR-5)

REAL LOVE Dolly Parton (Duet With Kenny Rogers)—RCA 14058
[Richard Brannan/David Malloy/Randy McCormick] [ASC] (6/8/85 B-91)

REAL LOVE Jody Watley—MCA 53484 [André Cymone/Jody Watley] [ASC] (3/18/89 BC-1)

REAL LOVE Skyy—Atlantic 88816 [Solomon Roberts] [ASC] (1/20/90 BC-47)

THE REAL LOVE Bob Seger And The Silver Bullet Band—Capitol 44743
[Bob Seger] [ASC] (8/24/91 BC-24)

REAL MAN Ernie K-Doe—Minit 627 [Allen Toussaint] [BMI] (6/5/61 R-76)

REAL MAN Todd Rundgren—Bearsville 0304 [Todd Rundgren] [BMI] (4/12/75 BCR-83)

THE REAL ME The Who—Track/MCA 40182 [Pete Townshend] [BMI] (1/26/74 BC-82)

A REAL MOTHER FOR YA Johnny "Guitar" Watson—DJM 1024
[Johnny Watson] [BMI] (7/2/77 BCR-41)

REAL PEOPLE Chic—Atlantic 3768
[Bernard Edwards/Nile Rodgers] (TSW) [BMI] (11/22/80 B-79)

REAL, REAL, REAL Jesus Jones—SBK/Food 07364
[Michael James Edwards] [BMI] (8/24/91 BC-4)

THE REAL THING Tina Britt—Eastern 604
[Jo Armstead/Nick Ashford/Valerie Simpson] [BMI] (5/22/65 R-85)

THE REAL THING The Brothers Johnson—A&M 2343
[George Johnson/Louis E. Johnson] [ASC] (6/20/81 BCR-60)

THE REAL THING Jellybean—Chrysalis 43167
[Toni Colandreo/Arnie Roman] [BMI] (11/7/87 B-82)

REAL WILD CHILD Ivan—Coral 62017
[John Greenan/John O'Keefe/David Owens] [BMI] (9/22/58 B-68)

REALISTIC Shirley Lewis—Vendetta 1448
[Richard Darbyshire/Charles Mole] [ASC] (10/28/89 B-84)

REALITY James Brown—Polydor 14268
[James Brown/Fred Wesley/Gertie Wesley] [BMI] (2/22/75 BC-73)

REALLY WANNA KNOW YOU Gary Wright—Warner Bros. 49769
[Ali Thomson/Gary Wright] [ASC] (7/4/81 BCR-16)

REAP THE WILD WIND Ultravox—Chrysalis 42682
[Warren Cann/Chris Cross/Billy Currie/Midge Ure] [ASC] (3/26/83 BC-58)

REAP WHAT YOU SOW Billy Stewart—Chess 1820 [Billy Stewart] [BMI] (7/14/62 BCR-50)

REASON 5 Chanels—Deb 500 [Julius Dixon] [BMI] (11/10/58 BR-80)

REASON TO BE Kansas—Kirshner 4285 [Kerry Livgren] [BMI] (9/1/79 BCR-45)

REASON TO BELIEVE Rod Stewart—Mercury 73224
[Tim Hardin] (TSW) [BMI] (8/14/71 BCR-1)

REASON TO LIVE KISS—Mercury 870022
[Desmond Child/Paul Stanley] [ASC] (12/5/87 BC-64)

REASON TO TRY Eric Carmen—Arista 1-9746
[Phil Galdston/Jon Lind] [ASC] (10/8/88 B-87)

REBEL *Carol Jarvis—Dot 15586*
[Al Chorney/Hal Shrager/Sid Shrager] [BMI] (9/2/57 BCRt-44)

REBEL *Jill Whitney—ABC-Paramount 9851*
[Al Chorney/Hal Shrager/Sid Shrager] [BMI] (9/16/57 Rt-69)

REBEL IN TOWN The Crew-Cuts—Mercury 70890
[Lenny Adelson/Les Baxter] [ASC] (7/13/56 R-80)

THE REBEL - JOHNNY YUMA Johnny Cash—Columbia 41995
[Andrew Fenady/Richard Markowitz] [ASC] (5/8/61 R-92)

REBEL REBEL David Bowie—RCA Victor 0287 [David Bowie] [ASC] (6/1/74 BCR-53)

REBEL 'ROUSER Duane Eddy—Jamie 1104
[Duane Eddy/Lee Hazlewood] [BMI] (6/16/58 BCR-6) [I]

REBEL YELL Billy Idol—Chrysalis 42762
[Billy Idol/Steve Stevens] [ASC] (1/28/84 BC-29)

REBELS Tom Petty and The Heartbreakers—MCA 52658
[Tom Petty] [ASC] (8/17/85 BC-74)

REBELS ARE WE Chic—Atlantic 3665
[Bernard Edwards/Nile Rodgers] [BMI] (8/16/80 BCR-61)

RECONSIDER ME *Johnny Adams—SSS Int'l 770*
[Margaret Lewis/Mira Smith] [BMI] (6/28/69 BCR-18)

RECONSIDER ME *Narvel Felts—ABC/Dot 17549*
[Margaret Lewis/Mira Smith] [BMI] (5/24/75 BC-67)

THE RECORD (BABY, I LOVE YOU) Ben E. King—Atco 6343
[Artie Resnick/Kenny Young] [BMI] (4/3/65 BR-84)

RECORD HOP BLUES Quarter Notes—Wizz 715 [Anthony Sperry] [BMI] (3/23/59 BR-82) [I]

RECOVERY Fontella Bass—Checker 1131
[Billy Davis/Raynard Miner/Carl William Smith] [BMI] (12/25/65 BCR-32)

RED AND BLUE The Dave Clark Five—Epic 10244
[Dave Clark/Lenny Davidson] [BMI] (11/4/67 BCR-69)

THE RED BACK SPIDER Brownsville Station—Big Tree 156
[Slim Newton] [BMI] (12/9/72 BCR-85)

RED EYE BLUES Redeye—Pentagram 206 [David Hodgkins] [BMI] (4/10/71 BCR-77)

RED GRAPES Sammy Davis Jr.—Decca 29310
[Frank Cady/David Seville] [ASC] (11/29/54 R-73)

RED HEAD *Cliff Steward And His Boro Lounge Boys—Coral 61399*
[Merrill Gridley/Thomas J. Jordan] [NA] (8/1/55 Rt-73)

RED HEAD *The Cloverleafs—MGM 12026*
[Merrill Gridley/Thomas J. Jordan] [NA] (8/1/55 Rt-73)

RED HEAD *Somethin' Smith & The Redheads—Epic 9140*
[Merrill Gridley/Thomas J. Jordan] [NA] (2/17/56 R-85)

RED HOT *Sam The Sham And The Pharaohs—MGM 13452*
[Billy Emerson] [BMI] (2/5/66 BCR-60)

RED HOT *Robert Gordon With Link Wray—Private Stock 45,156*
[Billy Emerson] [BMI] (9/10/77 BCR-69)

RED HOT Herb Alpert—A&M 2593 [Howard Massey] [ASC] (12/10/83 B-77) [I]

RED LIGHT Linda Clifford—RSO 1041
[Michael Gore/Dean Pitchford] [BMI] (8/9/80 BCR-41)

RED PEPPER I Roosevelt Fountain And Pens Of Rhythm—Prince-Adams 447
[Rudy Robinson] [BMI] (1/5/63 BR-78) [I]

RED RED WINE *Neil Diamond—Bang 556 [Neil Diamond] [SE] (3/23/68 BCR-55)*

RED RED WINE *Vic Dana—Liberty 56163 [Neil Diamond] [SE] (4/25/70 BCR-72)*

RED RED WINE *UB40—A&M 2600 [Neil Diamond] [SE] (1/28/84 BC-34)*

RED RED WINE *UB40—A&M 1244 [Neil Diamond] [SE] (8/13/88 BC-1)*

RED RIVER ROCK Johnny And The Hurricanes—Warwick 509
[Tom King/Ira Mack‡/Fred Mendelsohn/John Pocisk/Traditional] [BMI]
(7/27/59 BCR-5) [IM]

RED RIVER ROSE The Ames Brothers—RCA Victor 47-7413
[Tommie Connor/Johnny Reine] [BMI] (12/15/58 BCR-13)

RED ROSES John Laurenz—Jubilee 5190
[Jim Kriegsmann/Douglas Walters] [BMI] (4/18/55 R-77)

RED ROSES FOR A BLUE LADY *Bert Kaempfert And His Orchestra—Decca 31722*
[Roy C. Bennett/Sid Tepper] [ASC] (1/23/65 BCRt-8) [IWM]

RED ROSES FOR A BLUE LADY *Vic Dana—Dolton 304*
[Roy C. Bennett/Sid Tepper] [ASC] (2/6/65 BCtRt-8)

RED ROSES FOR A BLUE LADY *Wayne Newton—Capitol 5366*
[Roy C. Bennett/Sid Tepper] [ASC] (2/13/65 BCtRt-8)

RED ROSES FOR MOM Bobby Vinton—Epic 10168
[Gene Allan/Bobby Vinton] [BMI] (5/20/67 BCR-85)

RED RUBBER BALL The Cyrkle—Columbia 43589
[Paul Simon/Bruce Woodley] [BMI] (5/21/66 BCR-2)

RED SAILS IN THE SUNSET *Tab Hunter—Dot 15533*
[Jimmy Kennedy/Hugh Williams] [ASC] (2/2/57 BR-57)

RED SAILS IN THE SUNSET *The Platters Featuring Tony Williams—Mercury 71656*
[Jimmy Kennedy/Hugh Williams] [ASC] (7/11/60 BCR-27)

RED SAILS IN THE SUNSET *Fats Domino—ABC-Paramount 10484*
[Jimmy Kennedy/Hugh Williams] [ASC] (9/14/63 BCR-35)

RED TOP The Teen Queens—RPM 470
[Lionel Hampton/Ben Kynard] [BMI] (10/20/56 R-85)

REDNECK FRIEND Jackson Browne—Asylum 11023
[Jackson Browne] [ASC] (9/29/73 BCR-72)

RED'S DREAM Louisiana Red—Roulette 4469
[Henry Glover/Morris Levy‡/Teddy Reig] [BMI] (1/12/63 R-93)

REDWOOD TREE Van Morrison—Warner Bros. 7638
[Van Morrison] [BMI] (10/28/72 BR-96)

REELIN' AND ROCKIN' *The Dave Clark Five—Epic 9786*
[Chuck Berry] [BMI] (4/17/65 BCR-13)

REELIN' & ROCKIN' *Chuck Berry—Chess 2136*
[Chuck Berry] [BMI] (11/25/72 BCR-27)

REELING IN THE YEARS Steely Dan—ABC 11352
[Walter Becker/Donald Fagen] [ASC] (3/10/73 BCR-6)

REET PETITE (THE FINEST GIRL YOU EVER WANT TO MEET)
Jackie Wilson—Brunswick 55024
[Billy Davis/Berry Gordy] [BMI] (9/23/57 BCR-23)

REFLECTIONS Diana Ross And The Supremes—Motown 1111
[Lamont Dozier/Brian Holland/Eddie Holland] [BMI] (8/5/67 BCR-2)

REFLECTIONS OF MY LIFE The Marmalade—London 20058
[Junior Campbell/Thomas McAleese] [BMI] (2/28/70 BCR-7)

THE REFLEX Duran Duran—Capitol 5345
[Simon Le Bon/Nick Rhodes/Andy Taylor/Nigel John Taylor/Roger Taylor] [ASC]
(4/21/84 BC-1)

REFUGEE Tom Petty And The Heartbreakers—Backstreet 41169
[Mike Campbell/Tom Petty] [ASC] (1/26/80 BCR-11)

REGGAE ROCK 'N ROLL B. E. Taylor Group—Epic 04862
[Joe Macre/B.E. Taylor/Rick Witkowski] [ASC] (5/11/85 C-80)

RELAX *Frankie Goes To Hollywood—Island 99805*
[Peter Gill/Holly Johnson/Mark O'Toole] [BMI] (4/7/84 BC-13)

RELAX (MIX) *Frankie Goes To Hollywood—ZTT/Island 7-99805*
[Peter Gill/Holly Johnson/Mark O'Toole] [BMI] (1/19/85 B-10)

THE RELAY The Who—Track 33041 [Pete Townshend] [BMI] (12/9/72 BCR-33)

RELEASE ME *Jivin' Gene—Mercury 71680*
[Eddie Miller/Dub Williams/Robert Gene Yount] [BMI] (10/15/60 C-90)

RELEASE ME *Esther Phillips "Little Esther"—Lenox 5555*
[Eddie Miller/Dub Williams/Robert Gene Yount] [BMI] (10/27/62 BCR-5)

RELEASE ME (AND LET ME LOVE AGAIN) *Engelbert Humperdinck—Parrot 40011*
[Eddie Miller/Dub Williams/Robert Gene Yount] [BMI] (4/8/67 BCR-3)

RELEASE ME *Esther Phillips—Atlantic 2411*
[Eddie Miller/Dub Williams/Robert Gene Yount] [BMI] (6/3/67 B-93)

I'LL RELEASE YOU *(response to Release Me) Joann Bon And The Coquettes—MTA 129*
[Joann Bongiorno/Ruth Calkins/Eddie Miller/Dub Williams/Robert Gene Yount] [BMI]
(9/16/67 CR-84) [R]

RELEASE ME *Johnny Adams—SSS Int'l 750*
[Eddie Miller/Dub Williams/Robert Gene Yount] [BMI] (12/14/68 BR-82)

RELEASE ME Wilson Phillips—SBK 07327
[Chynna Phillips/Carnie Wilson/Wendy Wilson] [BMI] (6/30/90 BC-1)

REMEMBER The Velours—Onyx 520
[Arthur Crier/Gary Morrison/Jerry Winston] [BMI] (3/17/58 B-83)

REMEMBER BABY Shep And The Limelites—Hull 756
[Charles Baskerville/Clarence Bassett/James Sheppard] [BMI] (2/9/63 B-91)

REMEMBER (CHRISTMAS) Nilsson—RCA Victor 74-0855
[Harry Nilsson] [BMI] (12/9/72 BCR-40)

REMEMBER DIANA Paul Anka—RCA Victor 47-8170 [Paul Anka] [BMI] (4/13/63 BCR-35)

REMEMBER ME Rita Pavone—RCA Victor 47-8365
[Shelly Coburn] [BMI] (5/30/64 BCR-19)

REMEMBER ME Diana Ross—Motown 1176
[Nick Ashford/Valerie Simpson] [ASC] (12/26/70 BCR-8)

REMEMBER ME Willie Nelson—Columbia 10275 [Scott Wiseman] [BMI] (1/10/76 BC-67)

(REMEMBER ME) I'M THE ONE WHO LOVES YOU *The Fontane Sisters—Dot 15547*
[Stuart Hamblen] [ASC] (3/23/57 R-80)

(REMEMBER ME) I'M THE ONE WHO LOVES YOU *Dean Martin—Reprise 0369*
[Stuart Hamblen] [ASC] (5/22/65 BCR-26)

REMEMBER MY NAME House Of Lords—RCA/Simmons 2736
[Alan Nicholas Graham/Bobby Mitchell] [ASC] (12/15/90 BC-65)

(REMEMBER THE DAYS OF THE) OLD SCHOOLYARD Cat Stevens—A&M 1948
[Cat Stevens] [ASC] (6/18/77 BCR-33)

REMEMBER THE NIGHTS The Motels—Capitol 5246
[Martha Davis/Scott Thurston] [BMI] (12/3/83 BC-36)

REMEMBER THE RAIN Bob Lind—World Pacific 77822
[Bob Lind] [BMI] (4/23/66 BCR-55) [FDE]

REMEMBER THE RAIN? 21st Century—RCA Victor 10201
[Marvin Smith] [ASC] (5/31/75 B-100)

REMEMBER THEN The Earls—Old Town 1130
[Tony Powers/Beverly Ross/Stan Vincent*] [BMI] (12/8/62 BCR-24)

REMEMBER (WALKIN' IN THE SAND) *The Shangri-Las—Red Bird 10-008*
[Shadow Morton] [BMI] (8/22/64 BCR-4)

REMEMBER (WALKING IN THE SAND) *Louise Goffin—Asylum 46521*
[Shadow Morton] [BMI] (8/18/79 BCR-43)

REMEMBER (WALKING IN THE SAND) *Aerosmith—Columbia 11181*
[Shadow Morton] [BMI] (12/22/79 BCR-67)

REMEMBER WHAT I TOLD YOU TO FORGET Tavares—Capitol 4010
[Dennis Lambert/Brian Potter] (TSW) [BMI] (4/12/75 BCR-21)

REMEMBER WHAT YOU LIKE Jenny Burton—Atlantic 89748
[John Robie] [BMI] (1/28/84 B-81)

REMEMBER WHEN The Platters—Mercury 71467
[Mickey Addy/Buck Ram] [BMI] (6/15/59 BCR-26)

REMEMBER WHEN Wayne Newton—Capitol 5514
[Bert Kaempfert/Herbert Rehbein/Charles Singleton/Eddie Snyder] [BMI]
(10/16/65 BCR-69)

REMEMBER YOU'RE MINE Pat Boone—Dot 15602
[Bernie Lowe/Kal Mann] [ASC] (8/3/57 BCR-10)

REMEMB'RING Peter Lind Hayes & Mary Healy—Columbia 40547
[Rosetta Duncan/Vivian Duncan] [ASC] (11/12/55 BC-47)

REMINISCING Little River Band—Harvest 4605 [Graham Goble] [BMI] (7/22/78 BCR-3)

REMO'S THEME (WHAT IF) Tommy Shaw—A&M 2773
[Richie Cannata/Tommy Shaw] [ASC] (10/5/85 BC-81)

REMOTE CONTROL The Reddings—Believe In A Dream 5600
[William Ray Beard/Chet Fortune/Nick Mann] [BMI] (11/8/80 BCR-65)

RENDEZVOUS Hudson Brothers—Rocket/MCA 40417
[Bill Hudson/Brett Hudson/Mark Hudson/Bruce Johnston] [BMI] (6/21/75 BCR-26)

RENEGADE Michael Murphey—Epic 50184 [Michael Murphey] [BMI] (1/17/76 BCR-39)

RENEGADE Styx—A&M 2110 [Tommy Shaw] (TSW) [ASC] (3/17/79 BCR-16)

REPEAT AFTER ME *Patti Page—Mercury 71015*
[Gordon Jenkins] [ASC] (11/10/56 BRt-45)

REPEAT AFTER ME *Gordon Jenkins & His Orchestra—Capitol 3556*
[Gordon Jenkins] [ASC] (11/10/56 Rt-82)

REPETITION Information Society—Tommy Boy 27659 [Paul Robb] [ASC] (4/1/89 BC-66)

REPORT TO THE NATION Winkly & Nutly—MK 101 [Bob Krasnow] [BMI] (10/31/60 CR-80)

REQUIEM FOR THE MASSES The Association—Warner Bros. 7074 [Terry Kirkman] [BMI] (9/2/67 B-100)

RESCUE ME *Fontella Bass—Checker 1120 [Raynard Miner/Carl William Smith] [BMI] (9/18/65 BCR-2)*

RESCUE ME *Cher—MCA 40375 [Raynard Miner/Carl William Smith] [BMI] (3/29/75 CR-84)*

RESCUE ME *Melissa Manchester—Arista 0196 [Raynard Miner/Carl William Smith] [BMI] (8/7/76 B-78)*

RESCUE ME Madonna—Sire 19490 [Madonna L. Ciccone/Shep Pettibone] [ASC] (1/19/91 BC-9)

RESERVATIONS FOR TWO Dionne Warwick—Arista 1-9638 [Tena Clark/Nathan East/Gary Prim] [ASC] (10/31/87 BC-62)

RESPECT *Otis Redding—Volt 128 [Otis Redding] [BMI] (9/4/65 BCR-35)*

RESPECT *The Rationals—Cameo 437 [Otis Redding] [BMI] (10/15/66 BCR-75)*

RESPECT *Aretha Franklin—Atlantic 2403 [Otis Redding] [BMI] (4/29/67 BCR-1)*

RESPECT YOURSELF *The Staple Singers—Stax 0104 [Luther Ingram/Bonny Rice] [BMI] (10/2/71 BCR-9)*

RESPECT YOURSELF *Bruce Willis—Motown 1876 [Luther Ingram/Bonny Rice] [BMI] (1/17/87 BC-5)*

RESPECTABLE *The Isley Brothers—RCA Victor 47-7657 [O'Kelly Isley/Ronald Isley/Rudolph Isley] [ASC] (1/11/60 R-87)*

RESPECTABLE *The Chants—MGM 13008 [O'Kelly Isley/Ronald Isley/Rudolph Isley] [ASC] (5/22/61 R-79)*

RESPECTABLE *The Outsiders—Capitol 5701 [O'Kelly Isley/Ronald Isley/Rudolph Isley] [ASC] (8/6/66 BCR-13)*

RESPECTFULLY MISS BROOKS Marty Robbins—Columbia 40706 [Marty Robbins] [BMI] (6/29/56 R-72)

—RESTA CU 'MME see: STAY HERE WITH ME

RESTLESS Starpoint—Elektra 69561 [Keith Diamond/Ernesto Phillips] [BMI] (3/22/86 BC-46)

RESTLESS HEART John Waite—EMI America 8252 [John Waite] [ASC] (1/26/85 BC-58)

RESURRECTION SHUFFLE *Ashton, Gardner & Dyke—Capitol 3060 [Tony Ashton] [ASC] (6/19/71 BCR-24)*

RESURRECTION SHUFFLE *Tom Jones—Parrot 40064 [Tony Ashton] (TSW) [ASC] (7/3/71 BCR-26)*

—RETURN OF THE NATIVE see: SAN FRANCISCO GIRLS

THE RETURN OF THE RED BARON The Royal Guardsmen—Laurie 3379 [Phil Gernhard/James McCullough/John McCullough] [BMI] (2/25/67 BCR-14)

RETURN TO ME Dean Martin—Capitol 3894 [Danny DiMinno/Carmen Lombardo] [ASC] (3/17/58 BCR-2)

RETURN TO SENDER Elvis Presley With The Jordanaires—RCA Victor 47-8100 [Otis Blackwell/Winfield Scott] [BMI] (10/13/62 BCR-1)

REUBEN JAMES Kenny Rogers And The First Edition—Reprise 0854 [Barry Etris/Alex Harvey] [BMI] (9/20/69 BCR-14)

REUNITED *Peaches & Herb—Polydor/MVP 14547 [Dino Fekaris/Freddie Perren] [ASC] (3/17/79 BCR-1)*

REUNITED *Band Of Gold—RCA 13866 [Dino Fekaris/Freddie Perren] (Med) [ASC] (10/13/84 BC-64)*

REV IT UP Newcity Rockers—Critique 7-99437 [Robert Emlund/Anders Wikström/Gregg Winter] [ASC] (9/12/87 B-86)

REVEILLE ROCK Johnny And The Hurricanes—Warwick 513 [Carl Conaster/Tom King/John Pocisk/Traditional] [BMI] (10/31/59 BCR-22) [I]

REVENGE Brook Benton—Mercury 71903 [Brook Benton/Marnie Ewald/Oliver Hall] [BMI] (11/20/61 BCR-15)

REVEREND MR. BLACK The Kingston Trio—Capitol 4951 [Jerry Leiber*/Mike Stoller*/Billy Edd Wheeler] [BMI] (4/6/63 BCR-4)

REVIVAL (LOVE IS EVERYWHERE) The Allman Brothers Band—Capricorn 8011 [Dickey Betts] [BMI] (1/9/71 BR-92)

—REVIVAL see: WHEN THE SAINTS GO MARCHING IN

REVOLUTION The Beatles—Apple 2276 [John Lennon/Paul McCartney] (TSW) [ASC] (9/7/68 BCR-2)

THE REVOLUTION KIND Sonny—Atco 6386 [Sonny Bono] [BMI] (11/27/65 BCR-55)

RHAPSODY IN BLUE Deodato—CTI 16 [George Gershwin] [ASC] (8/11/73 BCR-41) [I]

RHAPSODY IN BLUE The Royal Philharmonic Orchestra—RCA 12304 [George Gershwin] (Med) [ASC] (10/31/81 BCR-9) [I]

RHAPSODY IN THE RAIN Lou Christie—MGM 13473 [Lou Christie/Twyla Herbert] [BMI] (3/26/66 BCR-16)

RHAPSODY IN WHITE Love Unlimited Orchestra—20th Century 2090 [Barry White] [BMI] (4/27/74 BCR-63) [I]

RHIANNON (WILL YOU EVER WIN) Fleetwood Mac—Reprise 1345 [Stevie Nicks] [BMI] (3/6/76 BCR-9)

RHINESTONE COWBOY Glen Campbell—Capitol 4095 [Larry Weiss] [ASC] (5/31/75 BCR-1)

RHUMBA GIRL Nicolette Larson—Warner Bros. 8795 [Jesse Winchester] [ASC] (3/31/79 BCR-41)

RHYME TYME PEOPLE Kool & The Gang—De-Lite 1563 [Robert Bell/Ronald Bell/George M. Brown/Robert Mickens/Penni Saunders/Claydes Smith/Dennis Thomas/Richard Westfield] [BMI] (1/4/75 BCR-52)

RHYTHM Major Lance—Okeh 7203 [Curtis Mayfield] [BMI] (8/22/64 BCR-23)

RHYTHM IS GONNA GET YOU Gloria Estefan and Miami Sound Machine—Epic 07059 [Gloria Estefan/Enrique Garcia] [BMI] (5/30/87 BC-5)

RHYTHM 'N' BLUES (MAMA'S GOT THE RHYTHM—PAPA'S GOT THE BLUES) The McGuire Sisters—Coral 61423 [Buddy Kaye/Jules Loman] (TSW) [ASC] (6/25/55 BCR-6)

RHYTHM NATION Janet Jackson—A&M 1455 [James Samuel Harris/Janet Jackson/Terry Lewis] [BMI] (11/11/89 BC-2)

RHYTHM OF LOVE Yes—Atco 99419 [Jon Anderson/Tony Kaye/Trevor Rabin/Chris Squire/Alan (2) White*] [BMI] (12/19/87 BC-40)

RHYTHM OF LOVE Scorpions—Mercury 870323 [Klaus Meine/Rudolf Schenker] [ASC] (6/4/88 BC-75)

RHYTHM OF MY HEART Rod Stewart—Warner Bros. 19366 [John Capek/Marc Jordan] [ASC] (3/16/91 BC-1)

RHYTHM OF THE NIGHT DeBarge—Gordy 1770 [Diane Warren] [ASC] (2/16/85 BC-3)

RHYTHM OF THE RAIN *The Cascades—Valiant 6026 [John Gummoe] [BMI] (1/12/63 BCR-2)*

RHYTHM OF THE RAIN *Gary Lewis And The Playboys—Liberty 56093 [John Gummoe] [BMI] (3/29/69 BCR-49)*

RIB TIP'S (PART 1) Andre Williams & His Orch.—Avin 103 [Andre Williams] [BMI] (1/29/66 BCR-82) [I]

RIBBON IN THE SKY Stevie Wonder—Tamla 1639 [Stevie Wonder] [ASC] (9/18/82 BC-54)

RICE IS NICE The Lemon Pipers—Buddah 31 [Paul Leka/Shelley Pinz] [BMI] (3/9/68 BCR-26)

RICH GIRL Daryl Hall & John Oates—RCA 10860 [Daryl Hall] [BMI] (1/22/77 BCR-1)

RICH MAN Terri Gibbs—MCA 51119 [Ed Mattson] [BMI] (6/20/81 BC-89)

RICHARD AND ME Gene & Tommy—ABC 10981 [Eugene Pistilli/Tommy West] [ASC] (10/14/67 CR-98)

THE RICHEST MAN (IN THE WORLD) Eddy Arnold—RCA Victor 47-6290 [Boudleaux Bryant] [BMI] (10/31/55 BR-74)

—RICKY see: MICKEY

RICO SUAVE Gerardo—Interscope 98871 [Fabian Cooke*/Gerardo Mejia/Alberto Slezynger/Rosa Soy*/Christian Warren*] [ASC] (2/2/91 BC-7)

RIDE! Dee Dee Sharp—Cameo 230 [Dave Appell/Kal Mann] [ASC] (10/20/62 BCR-5)

RIDE A WHITE SWAN Tyrannosaurus Rex—Blue Thumb 7121 [Marc Bolan] [ASC] (1/9/71 BCR-58)

RIDE AWAY Roy Orbison—MGM 13386 [William Dees/Roy Orbison] [BMI] (8/21/65 BCR-17)

RIDE CAPTAIN RIDE Blues Image—Atco 6746 [Frank Konte/Mike Pinera] [ASC] (4/25/70 BCR-4)

RIDE 'EM COWBOY Paul Davis—Bang 712 [Paul Davis] [BMI] (10/5/74 BCR-23)

RIDE LIKE THE WIND Christopher Cross—Warner Bros. 49184 [Christopher Cross] [ASC] (2/9/80 BCR-2)

RIDE MY SEE-SAW The Moody Blues—Deram 85033 [John Lodge] [BMI] (10/5/68 BCR-46)

RIDE, RIDE, RIDE Brenda Lee—Decca 32079 [Liz Anderson] [BMI] (1/7/67 BCR-37)

RIDE, SALLY, RIDE Dennis Coffey—Sussex 237 [Dennis Coffey] (TSW) [BMI] (6/3/72 BCR-55) [I]

RIDE THE TIGER Jefferson Starship—Grunt 10080 [Paul Kantner/Grace Slick/Byong Yu] [BMI] (11/16/74 BC-84)

RIDE THE WILD SURF Jan & Dean—Liberty 55724 [Jan Berry/Roger Christian/Brian Wilson] [BMI] (9/19/64 BCR-16)

RIDE THE WIND Poison—Enigma 44616 [Bobby Dall/C.C. DeVille/Bret Michaels/Rikki Rockett] [BMI] (2/2/91 BC-36)

RIDE WITH ME Steppenwolf—Dunhill 4283 [Mars Bonfire] [BMI] (7/17/71 BCR-31)

RIDE YOUR PONY Lee Dorsey—Amy 927 [Allen Toussaint] [BMI] (6/19/65 BCR-28)

—RIDERS IN THE SKY see: GHOST RIDERS...

RIDERS ON THE STORM The Doors—Elektra 45738 [John Densmore/Robby Krieger/Ray Manzarek/Jim Morrison] [ASC] (7/3/71 BCR-12)

RIDIN' MY THUMB TO MEXICO Johnny Rodriguez—Mercury 73416 [Johnny Rodriguez] [BMI] (9/29/73 BCR-70)

RIDIN' THE STORM OUT REO Speedwagon—Epic 50367 [Gary Richrath] [BMI] (5/7/77 BCR-79)

RIDIN' THE WIND The Tornadoes—London 9581 [George Bellamy] [ASC] (2/2/63 BCR-59) [I]

RIDING HIGH Faze-O—SHE 8700 [Ralph Aikens/Tyrone Crum/Keith Harrison/Robert Neal Jr./Andrew Noland/Roger Parker] [BMI] (4/29/78 R-95)

RIDING THE RAINBOW Elvis Presley with the Jordanaires—RCA Victor EPA-4371 [Ben Weisman/Fred Wise] (EP) [ASC] (9/8/62 CR-26)

RIGHT AND HYPE Abstrac'—Reprise 22872 [Gene Griffin/Teddy Riley] [BMI] (12/23/89 B-89)

RIGHT AWAY Hawks—Columbia 60500 [Dave Steen] [ASC] (3/14/81 BCR-63)

RIGHT AWAY Kansas—Kirshner 3084 [Dino Elefante/John Elefante] [BMI] (8/21/82 BC-73)

RIGHT BACK WHERE WE STARTED FROM *Maxine Nightingale—United Artists 752 [J. Vincent Edwards/Pierre Tubbs] [BMI] (2/14/76 BCR-1)*

RIGHT BACK WHERE WE STARTED FROM *Sinitta—Atlantic 88807 [J. Vincent Edwards/Pierre Tubbs] [BMI] (9/23/89 B-84)*

RIGHT BEFORE YOUR EYES America—Capitol 5177 [Ian Thomas] [ASC] (11/27/82 BC-45)

RIGHT BETWEEN THE EYES Wax—RCA 14306 [Andrew Gold/Graham Gouldman] [BMI] (3/15/86 BC-42)

RIGHT BY MY SIDE Ricky Nelson—Imperial 5663 [Baker Knight] [BMI] (4/23/60 BCR-59)

RIGHT BY YOUR SIDE Eurythmics—RCA 13695 [Annie Lennox/David A. Stewart] [ASC] (7/21/84 BC-29)

THE RIGHT COMBINATION Seiko & Donnie Wahlberg—Columbia 73417 [Michael Cruz/Michael Jay] [BMI] (6/16/90 BC-54)

RIGHT DOWN THE LINE Gerry Rafferty—United Artists 1233 [Gerry Rafferty] [BMI] (8/12/78 BCR-8)

RIGHT DOWN TO IT Damian Dame—LaFace 2-4002 [Kenneth Edmonds/Antonio Reid/Daryl Simmons] [BMI] (12/14/91 B-90)

RIGHT FEELING AT THE WRONG TIME Hot—Big Tree 16099 [Kevin Lamb/Barbara Wyrick] [BMI] (8/27/77 B-65)

RIGHT HERE AND NOW Bill Medley—Planet 13317 [Barry Mann/Cynthia Weil] [BMI] (10/2/82 BC-58)

RIGHT HERE, RIGHT NOW Jesus Jones—SBK/Food 07345 [Michael James Edwards] [BMI] (4/13/91 BC-1)

RIGHT HERE WAITING Richard Marx—EMI 50219 [Richard Marx] [ASC] (7/8/89 BC-1)

RIGHT KIND OF LOVE Quarterflash—Geffen 29994 [Marv Ross] [ASC] (5/29/82 BC-47)

RIGHT NEXT DOOR (BECAUSE OF ME) The Robert Cray Band—Mercury 888327 [Dennis Walker] [BMI] (5/16/87 BC-80)

RIGHT NEXT TO ME Whistle—Select 2005 [Shiller Shaun Fequiere] [BMI] (6/3/89 BC-60)

RIGHT NOW AND NOT LATER The Shangri-Las—Red Bird 10-036 [Robert Bateman/Ken Hollon/Ronald Moseley] [BMI] (10/9/65 B-99)

RIGHT NOW, RIGHT NOW Alan Freed—Coral 61626 [Al Sears/Jesse Stone*] [BMI] (5/25/56 R-85)

RIGHT ON The Rascals—Atlantic 2773 [Felix Cavaliere] [ASC] (12/19/70 R-94)

RIGHT ON THE TIP OF MY TONGUE Brenda & The Tabulations—Top & Bottom 407 [Joe Cobb/Van McCoy] [BMI] (4/3/71 BCR-14)

RIGHT ON TRACK Breakfast Club—MCA 52954 [Stephen Bray/Dan Gilroy] [ASC] (3/14/87 BC-7)

RIGHT OR LEFT AT OAK STREET Roy Clark—Dot 17324 [Joe Nixon/Charlie Williams] [BMI] (12/13/69 C-96)

RIGHT OR WRONG *Wanda Jackson—Capitol 4553 [Wanda Jackson] [BMI] (6/5/61 BCRt-29)*

RIGHT OR WRONG *Debbie Reynolds—Dot 16225 [Wanda Jackson] [BMI] (7/3/61 Rt-68)*

RIGHT OR WRONG *Ronnie Dove—Diamond 173 [Wanda Jackson] [BMI] (10/24/64 BCR-12)*

RIGHT PLACE WRONG TIME Dr. John—Atco 6914 [Mac Rebennack] [ASC] (4/14/73 BCR-9)

RIGHT RELATIONS Johnny Rivers—Imperial 66335 [Bob Ray] [BMI] (11/9/68 BCR-42)

RIGHT STRING BUT THE WRONG YO-YO Dr. Feelgood And The Interns—Okeh 7156 [Willie Perryman] [NA] (8/4/62 B-84)

THE RIGHT STUFF Vanessa Williams—Wing 887 386 [Kevin Jones/Rex Salas] [ASC] (7/23/88 BC-44)

—RIGHT STUFF see: YOU GOT IT

RIGHT THE FIRST TIME Gamma—Elektra 47423 [Mitchell Froom/Ronnie Montrose/Jerry Stahl] [BMI] (4/3/82 BC-77)

THE RIGHT THING Simply Red—Elektra 69487 [Mick Hucknall] [ASC] (2/28/87 BC-27)

THE RIGHT THING TO DO Carly Simon—Elektra 45843 [Carly Simon] [ASC] (3/24/73 BCR-10)

RIGHT TIME OF THE NIGHT Jennifer Warnes—Arista 0223 [Peter McCann] [ASC] (1/29/77 BCR-5)

RIKI TIKI TAVI Donovan—Epic 10649 [Donovan Leitch] [BMI] (8/15/70 BCR-35)

RIKKI DON'T LOSE THAT NUMBER Steely Dan—ABC 11439 [Walter Becker/Donald Fagen] [ASC] (5/4/74 BCR-3)

RING A DING A DING Tommy Sands—Capitol 3690 [Gordon Charles/Billy Towne] [BMI] (4/6/57 BCR-30)

RING A LING A LARIO Jimmie Rodgers—Roulette 4158 [Gerald Frederick Grant/Arthur Kent/Joe Reisman] [ASC] (5/25/59 BCR-32)

RING DANG DOO Sam The Sham And The Pharaohs—MGM 13397 [Joy Byers Johnston/Bob Tubert] [ASC] (10/2/65 BCR-24)

RING MY BELL *Anita Ward—Juana 3422 [Frederick Knight] [BMI] (5/12/79 BCR-1)*

RING MY BELL *DJ Jazzy Jeff & The Fresh Prince—Jive 42024 [Frederick Knight] [BMI] (10/12/91 BC-20)*

RING OF FIRE Duane Eddy—Jamie 1187 [Duane Eddy] [BMI] (5/15/61 BCR-49) [I]

RING OF FIRE Johnny Cash—Columbia 42788 [June Carter/Merle Kilgore] [BMI] (6/1/63 BCR-13)

—RING RING GOES THE BELL see: SCHOOL DAY

RING THE LIVING BELL Melanie—Neighborhood 4202 [Melanie Safka] [ASC] (1/22/72 BCR-21)

RINGO Lorne Greene—RCA Victor 47-8444 [Hal Blair/Don Robertson] [ASC] (10/31/64 BCR-1)

THIS BOY *The Beatles—Capitol EAP-2121 [John Lennon/Paul McCartney] (EP) [ASC] (5/30/64 BCR-86)*

RINGO'S THEME (THIS BOY) *George Martin And His Orch.—United Artists 745 [John Lennon/Paul McCartney] [ASC] (7/25/64 BCR-53) [IWM]*

RINGS *Cymarron—Entrance 7500 [Alex Harvey/Eddie Reeves] [BMI] (6/5/71 BCR-17)*

RINGS *Reuben Howell—Motown 1305 [Alex Harvey/Eddie Reeves] [BMI] (7/20/74 BC-86)*

RINGS *Lobo—Big Tree 15008 [Alex Harvey/Eddie Reeves] [BMI] (7/20/74 BCR-37)*

RINKY DINK Baby Cortez—Julia/Chess 1829 [David Clowney/Paul Winley] [BMI] (7/7/62 BCR-9) [I]

RIO Duran Duran—Capitol 5215 [Simon Le Bon/Nick Rhodes/Andy Taylor/Nigel John Taylor/Roger Taylor] [ASC] (3/26/83 BC-14)

RIO BRAVO Dean Martin—Capitol 4174 [Dimitri Tiomkin/Paul Francis Webster] [ASC] (4/13/59 R-85)

RIOT Hugh Masekela—Uni 55102 [Hugh Masekela] [BMI] (1/11/69 BCR-47) [I]

RIP IT UP *Little Richard—Specialty 579 [Robert Blackwell/John Marascalco] [BMI] (6/29/56 BCtRt-15)*

RIP IT UP *Bill Haley And His Comets—Decca 30028 [Robert Blackwell/John Marascalco] [BMI] (8/10/56 BCtRt-15)*

RIP OFF Laura Lee—Hot Wax 7204 [Angelo Bond/William Weatherspoon] [BMI] (5/27/72 BCR-51)

RIP VAN WINKLE The Devotions—Roulette 4541 [Ray Sanchez] [BMI] (2/8/64 BCR-27)

RISE Herb Alpert—A&M 2151 [Andy Armer/Randy Badazz] [ASC] (7/28/79 BCR-1) [IWM]

RISE TO IT Kiss—Mercury 875 098 [Bob Halligan/Paul Stanley] [BMI] (6/9/90 BC-79)

RITUAL Dan Reed Network—Mercury 870183 [Dan Edward Reed] [ASC] (3/12/88 BC-38)

RITZY MAMBO The Salsoul Orchestra—Salsoul 2018 [Vincent Montana] [BMI] (2/26/77 B-99)

RIVER Joe Simon—Spring 141 [Gene McDaniels] [BMI] (11/3/73 BCR-42)

RIVER DEEP-MOUNTAIN HIGH *Ike & Tina Turner—Philles 131 [Jeff Barry/Ellie Greenwich/Phil Spector] [BMI] (5/28/66 BR-88)*

RIVER DEEP-MOUNTAIN HIGH *Deep Purple—Tetragrammaton 1514 [Jeff Barry/Ellie Greenwich/Phil Spector] [BMI] (1/25/69 BCR-38)*

RIVER DEEP-MOUNTAIN HIGH *Ike & Tina Turner—A&M 1118 [Jeff Barry/Ellie Greenwich/Phil Spector] [BMI] (10/11/69 R-95)*

RIVER DEEP-MOUNTAIN HIGH *The Supremes & Four Tops—Motown 1173 [Jeff Barry/Ellie Greenwich/Phil Spector] [BMI] (11/21/70 BCR-12)*

THE RIVER IS WIDE *The Forum—Mira 232 [Billy Joe Admire/Gary Knight] [BMI] (6/24/67 BCR-44)*

THE RIVER IS WIDE *The Grassroots—Dunhill 4187 [Billy Joe Admire/Gary Knight] [BMI] (4/5/69 BCR-16)*

MARCH FROM THE RIVER KWAI *Mitch Miller And His Orchestra—Columbia 41066 [Malcolm Arnold] (Med) [ASC] (12/30/57 BCR-15) [I]*

RIVER KWAI MARCH *Carlson's Raiders—Capitol 3857 [Malcolm Arnold] (Med) [ASC] (12/30/57 R-16) [I]*

THE RIVER KWAI MARCH *Art Mooney And His Orchestra—MGM 12590 [Malcolm Arnold] (Med) [ASC] (12/30/57 BCR-16) [I]*

MARCH FROM THE RIVER KWAI *David Terry & His Orchestra—RCA Victor 47-7153 [Malcolm Arnold] (Med) [ASC] (2/24/58 R-20) [I]*

THE RIVER OF LOVE B.W. Stevenson—RCA Victor 0171 [Daniel Moore] [BMI] (11/17/73 BCR-36)

THE RIVER OF NO RETURN Marilyn Monroe—RCA Victor 47-5745 [Ken Darby/Lionel Newman] [BMI] (7/24/54 C-PRE)

RIVER ROAD Uncle Dog—MCA 40005 [David Skinner] [ASC] (3/3/73 BCR-82)

RIVER STAY 'WAY FROM MY DOOR Frank Sinatra—Capitol 4376 [Mort Dixon/Harry Woods] [ASC] (5/23/60 BCR-45)

RIVERBOAT Faron Young—Capitol 4291 [Bill Anderson] [BMI] (1/4/60 B-83)

RIVER'S INVITATION Percy Mayfield—Tangerine 931 [Percy Mayfield] [BMI] (6/1/63 B-99)

RIVERS OF BABYLON Boney M—Sire 1027 [Brent Dowe/Frank Farian/Hans-Jörg Mayer/James McNaughton] [BMI] 6/3/78 BCR-30)

RIVER'S RISIN' Edgar Winter—Epic 11143 [Dan Hartman] [BMI] (7/20/74 BCR-33)

RIVIERA CONCERTO Roger Williams—Kapp 345 [Charles Wildman] [ASC] (8/15/60 R-97) [I]

RO RO ROSEY Van Morrison—Bang 552 [Van Morrison] [BMI] (11/4/67 R-97)

ROAD HOG John D. Loudermilk—RCA Victor 47-8101 [Gwen Loudermilk/John D. Loudermilk] [BMI] (11/10/62 BCR-65)

ROAD RUNNER *Bo Diddley—Checker 942 [Ellas McDaniel] [BMI] (2/29/60 BC-75)*

ROAD RUNNER *The Gants—Liberty 55829 [Ellas McDaniel] [BMI] (9/25/65 BCR-40)*

—ROAD see: LOVE THEME FROM LA STRADA

THE ROAD WE DIDN'T TAKE Freda Payne—Invictus 9109 [Lamont Dozier/Daphne Dumas/Brian Holland] [BMI] (1/1/72 BR-60)

ROADHOUSE BLUES The Doors—Elektra 45685 [John Densmore/Robby Krieger/Ray Manzarek/Jim Morrison] (TSW) [ASC] (4/11/70 BC-50)

ROAM The B-52's—Reprise 22667 [Kate Pierson/Fred Schneider/Keith Strickland/Robert Waldrop/Cindy Wilson] [ASC] (12/23/89 BC-3)

ROBBIN' THE CRADLE Tony Bellus—NRC 023 [Tony Bellus] [BMI] (4/27/59 BCR-25)

ROBERT DENIRO'S WAITING Bananarama—London 820033 [Sarah Dallin*/Siobhan Fahey/Steve Jolley/Tony Swain/Keren Woodward] [BMI] (5/19/84 B-95)

ROBERTA Barry And The Tamerlanes—Valiant 6040 [Bodie Chandler/Barry De Vorzon] [BMI] (2/1/64 CR-72)

ROBERTA Bones—Signpost 70008 [Huey P. Smith/John Vincent] [BMI] (10/21/72 BCR-85)

ROBOT MAN Jamie Horton—Joy 241 [Sylvia Dee/George Goehring] [ASC] (8/8/60 R-87)

***ROC A CHICKA** Warner Mack—Decca 30471 [Warner McPherson] [BMI] (11/4/57 BCRt-25)*

***ROCK-A-CHICKA** Jim Lowe—Dot 15665 [Warner McPherson] [BMI] (11/11/57 Rt-25)*

ROCK & ROLL RUNAWAY Ace—Anchor 21002 [Paul Carrack/Terry Comer/Phil Harris/Alan King] [ASC] (7/26/75 BC-63)

ROCK & ROLL STEW (PART 1) Traffic—Island 1201 [Jim Gordon/Rick Grech] [BMI] (1/15/72 B-93)

ROCK & ROLL STRATEGY Thirty Eight Special—A&M 1246 [Max Carl/Donnie Van Zant] [BMI] (10/29/88 BC-57)

***ROCK-A-BEATIN' BOOGIE** Esquire Boys—Guyden 705 [Bill Haley] [ASC] (10/30/54 C-42)*

***ROCK A BEATIN' BOOGIE** Bill Haley And His Comets—Decca 29713 [Bill Haley] [ASC] (11/5/55 BCR-24)*

***ROCK A BEATIN' BOOGIE** Jive Bunny And The Mastermixers—Music Factory 99140 [Bill Haley] (Med) [ASC] (10/28/89 BC-11)*

ROCK A BILLY Guy Mitchell—Columbia 40877 [Eddie V. Deane/Woody Harris] [ASC] (3/30/57 BCR-7)

***ROCK A BYE YOUR BABY WITH A DIXIE MELODY** Jerry Lewis—Decca 30124 [Sam Lewis/Jean Schwartz/Joe Young] [NA] (11/10/56 BCR-4)*

***ROCK A BYE YOUR BABY WITH A DIXIE MELODY** Judy Garland—Columbia 40010 [Sam Lewis/Jean Schwartz/Joe Young] [NA] (9/25/61 CtRt-60)*

***ROCK-A-BYE YOUR BABY WITH A DIXIE MELODY** Aretha Franklin—Columbia 42157 [Sam Lewis/Jean Schwartz/Joe Young] [NA] (9/25/61 BCtRt-21)*

ROCK-A-HULA BABY ("TWIST" SPECIAL) Elvis Presley With The Jordanaires—RCA Victor 47-7968 [Dolores Fuller/Ben Weisman/Fred Wise] [ASC] (11/27/61 BCR-14)

ROCK-A-LOTT Aretha Franklin—Arista 1-9574 [Preston Glass/Joe Johnson/Narada Michael Walden] [ASC] (6/20/87 BC-82)

ROCK AND A HARD PLACE The Rolling Stones—Columbia 73057 [Mick Jagger/Keith Richards] [NA] (11/4/89 BC-18)

ROCK AND CRY Clyde McPhatter—Atlantic 1158 [Joyce Heath] [ASC] (12/2/57 B-93)

ROCK AND ROLL Led Zeppelin—Atlantic 2865 [John Bonham/John Paul Jones/Jimmy Page/Robert Plant] [ASC] (3/11/72 BCR-38)

ROCK AND ROLL PART 2 Gary Glitter—Bell 45,237 [Gary Glitter/Mike Leander] [BMI] (7/15/72 BCR-3) [I]

***ROCK AND ROLL ALL NITE (STUDIO)** Kiss—Casablanca 829 [Gene Simmons/Paul Stanley] [ASC] (5/17/75 BCR-57)*

***ROCK AND ROLL ALL NITE (LIVE)** Kiss—Casablanca 850 [Gene Simmons/Paul Stanley] [ASC] (11/8/75 BCR-12)*

ROCK AND ROLL DANCIN' Beckmeier Brothers—Casablanca 1000 [Fred Beckmeier/Steve Beckmeier] [ASC] (7/21/79 BCR-53)

ROCK AND ROLL DREAMS COME THROUGH Jim Steinman—Cleveland International 19-02111 [Jim Steinman] [BMI] (5/30/81 BCR-28)

ROCK AND ROLL GIRLS John Fogerty—Warner Bros. 29053 [John Fogerty] [ASC] (3/16/85 BC-20)

ROCK AND ROLL HEAVEN The Flares—Press 2800 [Aaron Collins/Buck Ram] [BMI] (1/29/62 R-98)

ROCK AND ROLL HEAVEN The Righteous Brothers—Haven 7002 [Alan O'Day/John Stevenson] [ASC] (5/18/74 BCR-3)

ROCK AND ROLL, HOOCHIE KOO Rick Derringer—Blue Sky 2751 [Rick Derringer] [BMI] (1/19/74 BCR-15)

ROCK AND ROLL IS HERE TO STAY Danny And The Juniors—ABC-Paramount 9888 [David White] [BMI] (2/10/58 BCR-19)

ROCK AND ROLL LOVE LETTER Bay City Rollers—Arista 0185 [Tim Moore] [NA] (4/24/76 BCR-28)

ROCK AND ROLL LULLABY B.J. Thomas—Scepter 12344 [Barry Mann/Cynthia Weil] [BMI] (2/5/72 BCR-11)

***ROCK AND ROLL MUSIC** Chuck Berry—Chess 1671 [Chuck Berry] [BMI] (11/4/57 BCR-8)*

***ROCK AND ROLL MUSIC** The Beach Boys—Brother/Reprise 1354 [Chuck Berry] [BMI] (6/5/76 BCR-5)*

ROCK AND ROLL NEVER FORGETS Bob Seger—Capitol 4449 [Bob Seger] [ASC] (7/9/77 BCR-41)

ROCK AND ROLL RHAPSODY Four Aces—Decca 30575 [Bob Davie/Marvin Moore] [BMI] (3/24/58 B-66)

ROCK AND ROLL STAR Champagne—Ariola America 7658 [Martin Duiser/Wally Tax] [ASC] (3/12/77 BCR-68)

ROCK AND ROLL WALTZ Kay Starr—RCA Victor 47-6359 [Roy Alfred/Shorty Allen] [ASC] (12/23/55 BCR-1)

***ROCK AND ROLL WEDDING** Sunny Gale—RCA Victor 47-6479 [Eddie Brandt/George Motola] [ASC] (4/13/56 BRt-66)*

***ROCK AND ROLL WEDDING** Ella Mae Morse—Capitol 3387 [Eddie Brandt/George Motola] [ASC] (4/13/56 Rt-73)*

***ROCK AND ROLL WEDDING** Helen Grayco—Vik 0199 [Eddie Brandt/George Motola] [ASC] (4/13/56 Rt-73)*

ROCK AND STROLL ROOM Mickey & Sylvia—Vik 0324 [Norman Mapp] [BMI] (5/5/58 R-63)

ROCK AROUND MOTHER GOOSE Barry Gordon—MGM 12166 [Roy C. Bennett/Sid Tepper] [ASC] (2/11/56 BCR-30)

—ROCK AROUND THE CLOCK see: WE'RE GONNA ROCK...

ROCK BOTTOM The McGuire Sisters—Coral 61842 [Bill Katz/Ruth Roberts] [ASC] (6/29/57 R-84)

ROCK BRIGADE Def Leppard—Mercury 76064 [Rick Allen*/Steve Clark/Joe Elliott/Rick Savage/Pete Willis*] [ASC] (6/28/80 CR-91)

ROCK CREEK PARK The Blackbyrds—Fantasy 771 [Joe Hall/Steve Johnson/Keith Killgo/Orville Saunders/Kevin Toney] [BMI] 7/17/76 B-93)

—ROCK DON'T STOP see: IT'S A DISCO NIGHT

—ROCK-FREAK see: DISCO NIGHTS

***ROCK ISLAND LINE** The Lonnie Donegan Skiffle Group—London 1650 [Traditional] [NA] (3/23/56 BCRt-5)*

***ROCK ISLAND LINE** Don Cornell—Coral 61613 [Traditional] [NA] (3/30/56 BRt-5)*

***ROCK ISLAND LINE** Len Dresslar—Mercury 70831 [Traditional] [NA] (3/30/56 Rt-5)*

***ROCK ISLAND LINE** Bobby Darin & The Jaybirds—Decca 29883 [Traditional] [NA] (4/6/56 Rt-5)*

***ROCK ISLAND LINE** Merrill Moore—Capitol 3397 [Traditional] [NA] (4/13/56 Rt-16)*

***ROCK ISLAND LINE** Jimmy Gavin—Epic 9161 [Traditional] [NA] (4/13/56 Rt-16)*

***ROCK ISLAND LINE** The Lonnie Donegan Skiffle Group—London 1650 [Traditional] [NA] (10/23/61 R-97)*

***ROCK ISLAND LINE** Johnny Cash—Sun 1111 [Traditional] [NA] (2/28/70 B-93)*

ROCK IT Lipps, Inc.—Casablanca 2281 [Steve Greenberg] [BMI] (8/2/80 BCR-64)

ROCK LOBSTER The B-52's—Warner Bros. 49173 [Kate Pierson*/Fred Schneider/Keith Strickland*/Cindy Wilson*/Ricky Wilson] [BMI] (4/12/80 BCR-56)

***ROCK LOVE** The Fontane Sisters with Billy Vaughn's Orchestra—Dot 15333 [Henry Glover] [BMI] (1/31/55 BCRt-9)*

***ROCK LOVE** Elaine Gay—DeLuxe 2029 [Henry Glover] [BMI] (1/31/55 Rt-15)*

***ROCK LOVE** Bill Farrell—Mercury 70539 [Henry Glover] [BMI] (1/31/55 Rt-17)*

***ROCK LOVE** Eddie Fontaine—"X" 0096 [Henry Glover] [BMI] (2/14/55 Rt-9)*

***ROCK LOVE** Teresa Brewer—Coral 61366 [Henry Glover] [BMI] (2/28/55 Rt-9)*

***ROCK LOVE** Dolores Gray—Decca 29430 [Henry Glover] [BMI] (2/28/55 Rt-17)*

ROCK ME Steppenwolf—Dunhill 4182 [John Kay] [BMI] (3/1/69 BCR-7)

ROCK ME Nick Gilder—Chrysalis 2332 [Nick Gilder/James McCulloch] [BMI] (5/26/79 BCR-53)

ROCK ME Great White—Capitol 44042 [Mark Kendall/Michael Lardie/Alan Niven/Jack Russell] [ASC] (8/22/87 BC-60)

ROCK ME AMADEUS Falco—A&M 2821 [Ferdi Bolland/Rob Bolland/Falco] [ASC] (2/8/86 BC-1)

ROCK ME BABY B.B. King—Kent 393 [Joe Josea‡/B.B. King] [BMI] (5/2/64 BCR-28)

ROCK ME BABY David Cassidy—Bell 45,260 [Peggy Clinger/Johnny Cymbal] [BMI] (8/26/72 BCR-26)

—ROCK ME BABY AND ROLL ME AWAY see: SO HIGH

ROCK ME GENTLY Andy Kim—Capitol 3895 [Andy Kim] [BMI] (6/15/74 BCR-1)

ROCK ME IN THE CRADLE OF LOVE Dee Dee Sharp—Cameo 260 [Dave Appell/Kal Mann] [ASC] (6/29/63 BCR-38)

***ROCK ME ON THE WATER** Linda Ronstadt—Capitol 3273 [Jackson Browne] [ASC] (3/4/72 B-85)*

***ROCK ME ON THE WATER** Jackson Browne—Asylum 11006 [Jackson Browne] [ASC] (8/5/72 BCR-43)*

ROCK ME TONIGHT (FOR OLD TIMES SAKE) Freddie Jackson—Capitol 5459 [Paul Laurence] [ASC] (5/25/85 BC-18)

ROCK ME TONITE Billy Squier—Capitol 5370 [Billy Squier] [ASC] (7/7/84 BC-10)

ROCK 'N ROLL Detroit featuring Mitch Ryder—Paramount 0133 [Lou Reed] [BMI] (1/22/72 CR-84)

A ROCK 'N' ROLL FANTASY The Kinks—Arista 0342 [Ray Davies] [ASC] (7/15/78 BCR-30)

ROCK 'N' ROLL FANTASY Bad Company—Swan Song 70119 [Paul Rodgers] [ASC] (3/17/79 BCR-11)

***ROCK 'N ROLL (I GAVE YOU THE BEST YEARS OF MY LIFE)** Kevin Johnson—Mainstream 5548 [Kevin Johnson] [BMI] (10/13/73 BCR-63)*

***ROCK 'N ROLL (I GAVE YOU THE BEST YEARS OF MY LIFE)** Terry Jacks—Bell 45,606 [Kevin Johnson] [BMI] (11/23/74 BC-92)*

***ROCK N' ROLL (I GAVE YOU THE BEST YEARS OF MY LIFE)** Mac Davis—Columbia 10070 [Kevin Johnson] [BMI] (11/30/74 BCR-15)*

ROCK 'N' ROLL IS KING ELO—Jet 03964 [Jeff Lynne] [ASC] (6/25/83 BC-19)

ROCK 'N ROLL SOUL Grand Funk Railroad—Capitol 3363 [Mark Farner] [BMI] (9/16/72 BCR-24)

ROCK 'N' ROLL TO THE RESCUE The Beach Boys—Capitol 5595 [Mike Love/Terry Melcher] [BMI] (6/28/86 BC-68)

ROCK OF AGES Def Leppard—Mercury 812604
[Rick Allen/Steve Clark/Joe Elliott/Mutt Lange/Rick Savage/Pete Willis] [ASC] (6/11/83 BC-16)

ROCK OF LIFE Rick Springfield—RCA 6853 [Rick Springfield] [ASC] (2/6/88 BC-22)

***ROCK ON** David Essex—Columbia 45940 [David Essex] [ASC] (11/10/73 BCR-1)*

***ROCK ON** Michael Damian—Cypress 1420 [David Essex] [ASC] (3/18/89 BC-1)*

ROCK 'N' ROLL WOMAN The Buffalo Springfield—Atco 6519
[Stephen Stills] [BMI] (9/23/67 BCR-39)

ROCK RIGHT Georgia Gibbs—Mercury 70811
[Sherman Edwards/Ben Raleigh] [ASC] (3/2/56 BCR-29)

ROCK ROLL BOOGIE "Tennessee" Ernie Ford—Capitol 3474
[Roy Alfred/Abner Silver] [ASC] (8/3/56 R-81)

ROCK STEADY Aretha Franklin—Atlantic 2838 [Aretha Franklin] [BMI] (10/23/71 BCR-6)

ROCK STEADY The Whispers—Solar 70006
[Kenneth Edmonds/Antonio Reid/Bo Watson] [BMI] (6/6/87 BC-7)

ROCK THE BOAT The Hues Corporation—RCA Victor 0232
[Wally Holmes] [BMI] (5/18/74 BCR-1)

ROCK THE CASBAH The Clash—Epic 03245
[Nicky Headon/Michael Geoffrey Jones/Paul Simonon*/Joe Strummer] [ASC] (10/2/82 BC-8)

***ROCK THE JOINT** Bill Haley With Haley's Comets—Essex 399
[Harry Bagby/Harry Crafton/Don Keene] [NA] (7/4/55 R-53)*

***ROCK THE JOINT** Bill Haley & His Comets—Decca 30461
[Harry Bagby/Harry Crafton/Don Keene] [NA] (11/11/57 R-78)*

ROCK THE NIGHT Europe—Epic 07091 [Joey Tempest] [BMI] (5/2/87 BC-30)

ROCK THIS TOWN Stray Cats—EMI America 8132 [Brian Setzer] [BMI] (9/18/82 BC-9)

ROCK WIT' CHA Bobby Brown—MCA 53652
[Kenneth Edmonds/Daryl Simmons] [BMI] (8/26/89 BC-7)

ROCK WITH YOU Michael Jackson—Epic 50797 [Rod Temperton] [ASC] (11/3/79 BCR-1)

ROCK YOU LIKE A HURRICANE Scorpions—Mercury 818440
[Klaus Meine/Herman Rarebell/Rudolf Schenker] [ASC] (3/24/84 BC-20)

ROCK YOUR BABY George McCrae—TK 1004
[Harry Wayne Casey/Rick Finch] [BMI] (5/25/74 BCR-1)

ROCK YOUR LITTLE BABY TO SLEEP Buddy Knox with The Rhythm Orchids—Roulette 4009
[Dave Alldred*/Jimmy Bowen*/Buddy Knox/Donnie Lanier*] [BMI] (5/4/57 BCR-23)

ROCKA CONGA The Applejacks (S)—Cameo 155
[Dave Appell/Kal Mann] [ASC] (12/20/58 BCR-31)

ROCKAWAY BEACH The Ramones—Sire 1008
[Doug Colvin/John Cummings/Tom Erdelyi/Jeff Hyman] [ASC] (12/3/77 B-66)

ROCKET Joe Bennett And The Sparkletones—ABC-Paramount 9867
[Joe Bennett] [BMI] (12/2/57 R-75)

ROCKET Def Leppard—Mercury 872614
[Rick Allen*/Steve Clark/Phil Collen/Joe Elliott/Mutt Lange/Rick Savage] [ASC] (3/4/89 BC-11)

ROCKET MAN Elton John—Uni 55328
[Elton John/Bernie Taupin] [BMI] (4/29/72 BCR-6)

ROCKET RIDE Kiss—Casablanca 915
[Prentice DeLaney/Ace Frehley] [ASC] (2/25/78 BCR-39)

ROCKET 2 U The Jets—MCA 53254 [Bobby Nunn] [BMI] (1/23/88 BC-5)

THE ROCKFORD FILES Mike Post—MGM 14772
[Pete Carpenter/Mike Post] [BMI] (5/17/75 BCR-10) [I]

ROCKHOUSE (PART 2) Ray Charles—Atlantic 2006
[Ray Charles] [BMI] (12/8/58 BR-79) [I]

ROCKIN' ALL OVER THE WORLD John Fogerty—Asylum 45274
[John Fogerty] [ASC] (8/30/75 BCR-25)

ROCKIN' AND ROLLIN' ON THE STREETS OF HOLLYWOOD Buddy Miles—Casablanca 839
[Buddy Miles] [ASC] (9/13/75 BCR-80)

***ROCKIN' AROUND THE CHRISTMAS TREE** Brenda Lee—Decca 30776
[Johnny Marks] [ASC] (11/28/60 BCR-14)*

***ROCKIN' AROUND THE CHRISTMAS TREE** Brenda Lee—Decca 30776
[Johnny Marks] [ASC] (12/11/61 BCR-50)*

***ROCKIN' AROUND THE CHRISTMAS TREE** Brenda Lee—Decca 30776
[Johnny Marks] [ASC] (12/15/62 BCR-44)*

***GOOD ROCKIN' TONIGHT** Pat Boone—Dot 15888 [Roy Brown] [BMI] (1/12/59 BCR-49)*

***ROCKIN' AT MIDNIGHT** The Honeydrippers—Es Paranza 7-99686
[Roy Brown] [BMI] (1/5/85 BC-25)*

ROCKIN' BICYCLE Fats Domino—Imperial 5779
[Fats Domino/Jack Jessup/Pee Wee Maddux] [BMI] (10/9/61 BCR-83)

ROCKIN' CHAIR Gwen McCrae—Cat 1996
[Willie Clarke/Clarence Reid] [BMI] (4/26/75 BCR-9)

***ROCKIN' CRICKETS** The Hot-Toddys Featuring Bill Pennell—Shan-Todd 0056
[Tom Shannon/Phil Todaro] [BMI] (3/30/59 BCR-57) [I]*

***ROCKIN' CRICKETS** Rockin' Rebels—Swan 4140
[Tom Shannon/Phil Todaro] [BMI] (4/27/63 BCR-74) [I]*

THE ROCKIN' GHOST Archie Bleyer—Cadence 1293
[Steve Allen/Ira Lee] [ASC] (6/30/56 B-61)

A ROCKIN' GOOD WAY (TO MESS AROUND AND FALL IN LOVE)
Dinah Washington & Brook Benton—Mercury 71629
[Brook Benton/Luchi DeJesus/Clyde Otis] [BMI] (5/21/60 BCR-5)

ROCKIN' IN THE CONGO Hank Thompson And His Brazos Valley Boys—Capitol 3623
[Hank Thompson] [BMI] (3/2/57 R-83)

ROCKIN' IN THE JUNGLE The Eternals—Hollywood 68
[Carlos Girona/William Rever Martin] [BMI] (5/25/59 BCR-78)

ROCKIN' IN THE SAME OLD BOAT Bobby Bland—Duke 440
[Deadric Malone/Vernon Morrison] [BMI] (11/2/68 BCR-57)

ROCKIN' INTO THE NIGHT 38 Special—A&M 2205
[Jim Peterik/Gary Smith/Frankie Sullivan] [ASC] (12/29/79 BCR-43)

THE ROCKIN' LADY (FROM NEW ORLEANS) Penny Candy—Flippin' 201
[Rose Felicio/Sid Prosen] [BMI] (8/29/59 C-96)

ROCKIN' LITTLE ANGEL Ray Smith—Judd 1016 [Jimmie O. Rogers] [BMI] (1/2/60 BCR-19)

ROCKIN' OVER THE BEAT Technotronic—SBK 07338
[Jo Bogaert/Manuela Kamosi] [ASC] (11/17/90 B-95)

***ROCKIN' PNEUMONIA AND THE BOOGIE WOOGIE FLU**
Huey Smith and The Clowns—Ace 530
[Huey P. Smith/John Vincent*] [BMI] (8/12/57 B-52)*

***ROCKIN' PNEUMONIA - BOOGIE WOOGIE FLU** Johnny Rivers—United Artists 50960
[Huey P. Smith/John Vincent*] [BMI] (10/7/72 BCR-4)*

ROCKIN' RED WING Sammy Masters—Lode 108 [Chapel Haynes] [ASC] (4/4/60 BR-56)

***ROCKIN ROBIN** Bobby Day—Class 229 [Leon René] [BMI] (7/26/58 BCR-2)*

***ROCKIN' ROBIN** The Rivieras (2)—Riviera 1403 [Leon René] [BMI] (9/5/64 BR-83)*

***ROCKIN' ROBIN** Michael Jackson—Motown 1197 [Leon René] [BMI] (3/4/72 BCR-1)*

ROCKIN' ROLL BABY The Stylistics—Avco 4625
[Thom Bell/Linda Creed] [BMI] (10/13/73 BCR-14)

ROCKIN', ROLLIN' OCEAN Hank Snow—RCA Victor 47-7702
[Ted Daffan/Theda Roush*] [BMI] (12/5/60 B-87)

ROCKIN' SHOES The Ames Brothers—RCA Victor 47-6930
[David Hess/Bobby Stevenson] [ASC] (6/8/57 BCR-41)

ROCKIN' SOUL The Hues Corporation—RCA Victor 10066
[Wally Holmes] [BMI] (10/12/74 BCR-18)

ROCKIN' THE CHA CHA Alan Dale—Coral 61495
[Larry Coleman/Fred Ebb/Paul Klein] [BMI] (9/5/55 CR-39)

ROCKIN' THROUGH THE RYE Bill Haley And His Comets—Decca 29948
[Bill Haley/Arrett Keefer] [ASC] (6/15/56 BCR-39)

ROCKIN' WITH THE KING Canned Heat—United Artists 50892
[Richard Penniman/Skip Taylor] [BMI] (3/18/72 BR-88)

ROCKING GOOSE Johnny And The Hurricanes—Big Top 3051
[T.J. Fowler/Tom King/Ira Mack‡/John Pocisk] [BMI] (8/29/60 BCR-60) [I]

ROCKIT Herbie Hancock—Columbia 04054
[Michael Beinhorn/Herbie Hancock/Bill Laswell] [BMI] (9/10/83 BC-64) [IWM]

ROCK'N ME Steve Miller—Capitol 4323 [Steve Miller] [ASC] (8/14/76 BCR-1)

ROCKY Austin Roberts—Private Stock 45,020 [Jay Stevens] [ASC] (7/12/75 BCR-6)

ROCKY II DISCO Maynard Ferguson—Columbia 11037
[Carol Connors/Bill Conti/Ayn Robbins] [BMI] (8/4/79 B-82)

ROCKY MOUNTAIN HIGH John Denver—RCA Victor 74-0829
[John Denver/Michael C. Taylor] [ASC] (11/25/72 BCR-7)

ROCKY MOUNTAIN MUSIC Eddie Rabbitt—Elektra 45315
[Eddie Rabbitt] [BMI] (6/26/76 BCR-76)

ROCKY MOUNTAIN WAY Joe Walsh—Dunhill 4361
[Rocke Grace/Kenny Passarelli/Joe Vitale/Joe Walsh] [BMI] (8/4/73 BCR-13)

ROCKY RACCOON Richie Havens—Stormy Forest 650
[John Lennon/Paul McCartney] [ASC] (10/11/69 C-92)

ROLAND THE ROADIE AND GERTRUDE THE GROUPIE Dr. Hook And The Medicine Show—Columbia 45878 [Shel Silverstein] [BMI] (6/23/73 BCR-52)

ROLENE Moon Martin—Capitol 4765 [Moon Martin] [BMI] (8/18/79 BCR-28)

ROLL AWAY THE STONE Leon Russell—Shelter 301
[Greg Dempsey/Leon Russell] [BMI] (6/20/70 CR-89)

ROLL CALL COMPANY J The Balladeers—Del-Fi 4138
[Fred Darian/Al DeLory/Joseph Van Winkle] [BMI] (5/2/60 R-94)

ROLL IN MY SWEET BABY'S ARMS Hank Wilson—Shelter 7336
[Buster Carter/Lester Flatt/Traditional] (TSW) [BMI] (10/6/73 BCR-66)

ROLL ME AWAY Bob Seger and The Silver Bullet Band—Capitol 5235
[Bob Seger] [ASC] (5/28/83 BC-27)

ROLL ON The New Colony Six—Sunlight 1001
[Billy Herman/Jerry Kollenburg] [BMI] (8/21/71 BCR-56)

ROLL ON DOWN THE HIGHWAY Bachman-Turner Overdrive—Mercury 73656
[Robbie Bachman/C.F. Turner] [BMI] (1/18/75 BCR-8)

***ROLL OVER BEETHOVEN** Chuck Berry—Chess 1626 [Chuck Berry] [BMI] (6/1/56 BCRt-29)*

***ROLL OVER BEETHOVEN** Helene Dixon—Vik 0212 [Chuck Berry] [BMI] (6/1/56 Rt-71)*

***ROLL OVER BEETHOVEN** The Velaires—Jamie 1198 [Chuck Berry] [BMI] (8/14/61 BCR-51)*

***ROLL OVER BEETHOVEN** The Beatles—Capitol of Canada 72133
[Chuck Berry] [BMI] (3/14/64 BCR-30)*

***ROLL OVER BEETHOVEN** The Beatles—Capitol EAP-2121
[Chuck Berry] (EP) [BMI] (5/30/64 BCR-86)*

***ROLL OVER BEETHOVEN** Electric Light Orchestra—United Artists 173
[Chuck Berry] [BMI] (4/28/73 BCR-31)*

ROLL WITH IT Steve Winwood—Virgin 99326
[Lamont Dozier*/Brian Holland*/Eddie Holland*/Will Jennings/Steve Winwood] [BMI] (6/11/88 BC-1)

ROLL WITH THE CHANGES REO Speedwagon—Epic 50545
[Kevin Cronin] [ASC] (5/13/78 BCR-42)

ROLLER April Wine—Capitol 4660 [Myles Goodwyn] [BMI] (3/3/79 BCR-34)

ROLLER COASTER The Ides Of March—Parrot 310 [Jim Peterik] [BMI] (9/10/66 B-92)

ROLLER COASTER Blood, Sweat & Tears—Columbia 45937
[Mark James] [BMI] (10/27/73 C-90)

ROLLER-SKATIN' MATE (PART 1) Peaches & Herb—Polydor/MVP 2031
[Dino Fekaris/Freddie Perren] [ASC] (11/24/79 B-66)

ROLLIN' STONE *The Fontane Sisters with Billy Vaughn's Orchestra—Dot 15370*
[Robert S. Riley] [BMI] (5/16/55 CRt-18)

ROLLIN' STONE *Eddie Fontaine with The Excels—"X" 0128*
[Robert S. Riley] [BMI] (5/16/55 Rt-18)

ROLLIN' WITH THE FLOW Charlie Rich—Epic 50392 [Jerry Hayes] [BMI] (9/17/77 C-94)

ROLLING DOWN A MOUNTAINSIDE The Main Ingredient—RCA Victor 10224
[Jacqueline Hilliard/Leon Ware] [ASC] (5/10/75 BCR-80)

ROLY POLY Joey Dee & The Starliters—Roulette 4408
[Joey Dee/Henry Glover/Morris Levy‡] [BMI] (2/19/62 BCR-74)

ROMAN GUITAR (CHITARRA ROMANA) Lou Monte—RCA Victor 47-6769
[Bruno Cherubini/Eldo Di Lazzaro/Marjorie Harper] [ASC] (1/19/57 CR-38) [FET]

ROMANCE IN THE DARK Dinah Washington—Roulette 4476
[Lillian Green] [BMI] (2/16/63 R-96)

—ROMANCE IS NOT OVER see: WE'VE ONLY JUST BEGUN

ROMANCING THE STONE Eddy Grant—Portrait 37-04433
[Eddy Grant] [ASC] (5/19/84 BC-22)

ROMANTIC Karyn White—Warner Bros. 19319
[James Samuel Harris/Terry Lewis/Karyn White] [ASC] (8/17/91 BC-1)

ROMANTICA *Gordon Jenkins And His Orchestra and Chorus—Kapp 326*
[Dino Verde] [ASC] (5/2/60 Rt-81) [IM]

ROMANTICA *Jane Morgan—Kapp 332*
[Al Stillman/Dino Verde] [ASC] (5/16/60 Rt-81) [FDE]

ROME WILL NEVER LEAVE YOU Richard Chamberlain—MGM 13285
[Burt Bacharach/Hal David] [ASC] (12/5/64 B-99)

ROMEO Janie Grant—Caprice 109 [Janie Grant] [BMI] (8/28/61 B-75)

ROMEO Mr. Big—Arista 0229 [Edward Carter/Jeffrey Robert Pain] [BMI] (3/5/77 BCR-64)

ROMEO Dino—Island 878 012
[Dino Esposito/Frederick Douglass Reeves] [BMI] (8/11/90 BC-6)

ROMEO AND JULIET The Royal Philharmonic Orchestra—RCA 12304
[Pyotr Ilyich Tchaikovsky] (Med) [NA] (10/31/81 BCR-9) [I]

ROMEO'S TUNE Steve Forbert—Nemperor 7525 [Steve Forbert] [ASC] (12/1/79 BCR-10)

—RONDE-RONDE see: I MET HIM ON A SUNDAY

RONI Bobby Brown—MCA 53463
[Darnell Bristol/Kenneth Edmonds] [BMI] (12/10/88 BC-3)

RONNIE Marcy Joe—Robbee 110 [Marcy Sockel] [BMI] (5/1/61 BCR-64)

RONNIE The 4 Seasons Featuring The "Sound" Of Frankie Valli—Philips 40185
[Bob Crewe/Bob Gaudio] [BMI] (4/11/64 BCR-6)

RONNIE, CALL ME WHEN YOU GET A CHANCE Shelley Fabares—Colpix 682
[Mike Anthony/Ted Cooper] [BMI] (4/27/63 BCR-71)

RONNIE'S RAPP Ron And The D.C. Crew—Profile 5130
[Inez J. Kitts/Paul (2) Klein/Mark Mosseley/Joseph Louis Stone] [BMI] (1/24/87 B-93)

ROOM AT THE TOP Adam Ant—MCA 53679
[Adam Ant/André Cymone/Marco Pirroni] [ASC] (3/10/90 BC-17)

ROOM FULL OF ROSES Mickey Gilley—Playboy 50056
[Tim Spencer] [BMI] (6/8/74 BCR-50)

ROOM FULL OF TEARS The Drifters—Atlantic 2127
[Doc Pomus/Mort Shuman] [BMI] (11/27/61 BR-58)

ROOM TO MOVE John Mayall—Polydor 14010 [John Mayall] [BMI] (12/20/69 CR-91)

ROOM TO MOVE Animotion—Polydor 871418
[Simon Climie/Rob Fisher/Dennis W. Morgan] [BMI] (2/18/89 BC-9)

ROOMS ON FIRE Stevie Nicks—Modern 99216
[Stevie Nicks/Rick Nowels] [BMI] (5/6/89 BC-16)

ROOSEVELT AND IRA LEE (NIGHT OF THE MOSSACIN) Tony Joe White—Monument 1169
[Tony Joe White] [BMI] (10/18/69 BCR-32)

THE ROOSTER SONG Fats Domino—Imperial IMP-147
[Dave Bartholomew/Fats Domino] (EP) [BMI] (5/11/57 R-53)

ROOTS, ROCK, REGGAE Bob Marley & The Wailers—Island 060
[Vincent Ford] [ASC] (7/3/76 BC-51)

ROOTY TOOT TOOT John Cougar Mellencamp—Mercury 870 327
[John Mellencamp] [ASC] (5/14/88 BC-61)

ROSALIE Sam Neely—Capitol 3510 [Sam Neely] [BMI] (1/27/73 BCR-43)

ROSANNA The Capreez—Sound 126 [Harold Bowen/Charlie Rich] [BMI] (10/15/66 CR-92)

ROSANNA Dennis Yost And The Classics IV—MGM South 7012
[Buddy Buie/J.R. Cobb] [BMI] (3/3/73 BCR-83)

ROSANNA Toto—Columbia 02811 [David Paich] [ASC] (4/17/82 BC-2)

ROSANNA'S GOING WILD Johnny Cash—Columbia 44373
[Anita Carter/Helen Carter/June Carter] [ASC] (1/27/68 B-91)

THE ROSE Bette Midler—Atlantic 3656 [Amanda McBroom] [BMI] (3/22/80 BCR-1)

A ROSE AND A BABY RUTH *Eddie Fontaine—Decca 30108*
[John D. Loudermilk] [BMI] (10/27/56 Rt-6)

A ROSE AND A BABY RUTH *George Hamilton IV—ABC-Paramount 9765*
[John D. Loudermilk] [BMI] (10/27/56 BCRt-6)

ROSE GARDEN *Dobie Gray—White Whale 300 [Joe South] [BMI] (5/17/69 CR-98)*

ROSE GARDEN *Lynn Anderson—Columbia 45252 [Joe South] [BMI] (11/28/70 BCR-1)*

ROSE OF CIMARRON Poco—ABC 12204 [Rusty Young] [ASC] (8/14/76 B-94)

THE ROSE TATTOO *Perry Como—RCA Victor 47-6294*
[Jack Brooks/Harry Warren] [ASC] (10/24/55 BCRt-33)

THE ROSE TATTOO *Percy Faith & His Orchestra—Columbia 40588*
[Jack Brooks/Harry Warren] [ASC] (11/21/55 Rt-34)

ROSEMARIE Pat Boone—Dot 16598 [Henry Mayer/Claus Ritter] [ASC] (5/23/64 R-83) [F]

ROSES AND RAINBOWS Danny Hutton—HBR 447
[Danny Hutton] [BMI] (9/18/65 BCR-57)

ROSES ARE RED (MY LOVE) Bobby Vinton—Epic 9509
[Al Byron/Paul Evans] [ASC] (6/2/62 BCR-1)

ROSES ARE RED MY LOVE The "You Know Who" Group!—4 Corners Of The World 113
[Robert Esposito] [BMI] (11/28/64 BCR-39)

ROSES OF PICARDY Buddy Greco—Epic 9472
[Fred Weatherly/Haydn Wood] [NA] (10/30/61 R-95)

ROSES OF RIO Four Aces—Decca 30721
[Heino Gaze/Carl Sigman] [ASC] (9/13/58 C-89) [FDE]

ROSIE Chubby Checker—Parkway 920
[William E. Jackson III/Jimmy Wisner] [BMI] (6/20/64 C-89)

ROSIE LEE *The Mello-Tones—Gee 1037 [Jerry Carr] [BMI] (5/4/57 BCRt-21)*

ROSIE LEE *The Tunedrops—Gone 5003 [Jerry Carr] [BMI] (5/18/57 Rt-21)*

THE ROSY DANCE Johnny Thunder—Diamond 132 [Teddy Vann] [BMI] (3/9/63 R-78)

ROTATION Herb Alpert—A&M 2202
[Andy Armer/Randy Badazz] [ASC] (11/17/79 BCR-30) [I]

ROUGH BOY ZZ Top—Warner Bros. 28733
[Frank Beard/Billy Gibbons/Dusty Hill] [BMI] (3/29/86 BC-22)

ROUGH BOYS Pete Townshend—Atco 7318 [Pete Townshend] [GL] (11/15/80 BC-89)

ROUGH LOVER Aretha Franklin—Columbia 42266
[J. Leslie McFarland] [ASC] (2/10/62 B-94)

ROUND & ROUND New Order—Qwest 27524
[Gillian Gilbert/Peter Hook/Stephen Morris/Bernard Sumner] [ASC] (4/8/89 BC-54)

ROUND AND ROUND Perry Como—RCA Victor 47-6815
[Joe Shapiro/Lou Stallman] [BMI] (2/23/57 BCR-1)

ROUND AND ROUND Ratt—Atlantic 89693
[Robbin Crosby/Warren DeMartini/Stephen Pearcy] [BMI] (6/16/84 BC-12)

ROUND AND ROUND
Tevin Campbell—Paisley Park 21740 [Prince] [ASC] (12/8/90 BC-10)

ROUND EVERY CORNER Petula Clark—Warner Bros. 5661
[Tony Hatch] [BMI] (10/9/65 BCR-18)

ROUND THE BAY OF MEXICO Harry Belafonte—RCA Victor 47-7550
[Lord Burgess] [ASC] (6/15/59 R-65)

ROUNDABOUT Connie Francis—MGM 13389 [Tony Hatch] [BMI] (8/28/65 BCR-80)

ROUNDABOUT Yes—Atlantic 2854 [Jon Anderson/Steve Howe] [ASC] (2/5/72 BCR-10)

ROUTE 101 Herb Alpert—A&M 2422 [Juan Carlos Calderón] [BMI] (6/26/82 BC-30) [I]

ROUTE 66 *The Manhattan Transfer—Atlantic 4034 [Bobby Troup] [ASC] (5/29/82 BC-78)*

ROUTE 66 *Depeche Mode—Sire 27991 [Bobby Troup] (Med) [ASC] (5/7/88 BC-61)*

ROUTE 66 THEME Nelson Riddle And His Orchestra—Capitol 4741
[Nelson Riddle] [BMI] (6/2/62 BCR-30) [I]

ROVIN' GAMBLER "Tennessee" Ernie Ford—Capitol 3421
[Traditional] [NA] (5/18/56 BR-60)

ROXANNE The Police—A&M 2096 [Sting] [BMI] (2/10/79 BCR-31)

ROXANNE, ROXANNE UTFO—Select 1182
[Curtis Bedeau/Jeff Campbell/Gerard Charles/Hugh Clarke/Shiller Shaun Fequiere/
Brian George/Lucien George/Paul George/Frederick Douglass Reeves] [BMI]
(3/9/85 B-77)

ROXY ROLLER *Sweeney Todd—London 240*
[Nick Gilder/James McCulloch] [BMI] (8/21/76 BCR-90)

ROXY ROLLER (BRYAN ADAMS) *Sweeney Todd—London 240*
[Nick Gilder/James McCulloch] [BMI] (9/18/76 B-99)

THE ROYAL MILE (SWEET DARLIN') Gerry Rafferty—United Artists 1366
[Gerry Rafferty] [BMI] (7/19/80 BCR-54)

RUB IT IN *Layng Martine—Barnaby 2041 [Layng Martine Jr.] [BMI] (9/18/71 BCR-49)*

RUB IT IN *Billy "Crash" Craddock—ABC 12013*
[Layng Martine Jr.] [BMI] (6/29/74 BCR-16)

RUB YOU THE RIGHT WAY Johnny Gill—Motown 1982
[James Samuel Harris/Terry Lewis] [ASC] (5/12/90 BC-3)

RUBBER BALL Bobby Vee—Liberty 55287
[Gene Pitney/Aaron Schroeder] [BMI] (11/28/60 BCR-5)

RUBBER BISCUIT Blues Brothers—Atlantic 3564
[Nathaniel Epps/Paul Fulton/Kinrod Charles Johnson/Shedrick Lincoln/Samuel Strain]
[BMI] (3/3/79 BCR-37)

RUBBER BULLETS 10 C. C.—UK 49015
[Lol Crème/Kevin Godley/Graham Gouldman] [BMI] (9/8/73 BCR-43)

RUBBER DUCKIE Ernie (Jim Henson)—Columbia 45207
[Jeffrey Moss] [ASC] (8/8/70 BCR-11)

THE RUBBERBAND MAN The Spinners—Atlantic 3355
[Thom Bell/Linda Creed] [BMI] (9/11/76 BCR-2)

RUBBERNECKIN' Elvis Presley—RCA Victor 47-9768
[Dory Jones/Bunny Warren] (TSW) [BMI] (11/29/69 BCR-5)

RUBY *Adam Wade—Coed 526 [Mitchell Parish/Heinz Roemheld] [ASC] (3/7/60 BCRt-43)*

RUBY *Bobby Milano—Time 1019*
[Mitchell Parish/Heinz Roemheld] [ASC] (3/21/60 Rt-63)

RUBY *Ray Charles Orchestra & Chorus—ABC-Paramount 10164*
[Mitchell Parish/Heinz Roemheld] [ASC] (11/14/60 BCR-17)

RUBY ANN Marty Robbins—Columbia 42614
[Roberta Bellamy] [BMI] (11/17/62 BCR-18)

RUBY BABY *Dion—Columbia 42662 [Jerry Leiber/Mike Stoller] [BMI] (1/12/63 BCR-2)*

RUBY, BABY *Billy "Crash" Craddock—ABC 12036*
[Jerry Leiber/Mike Stoller] [BMI] (11/23/74 BCR-33)

RUBY, DON'T TAKE YOUR LOVE TO TOWN *Kenny Rogers And The First Edition—Reprise 0829 [Mel Tillis] [BMI] (6/7/69 BCR-6)*

BILLY, I'VE GOT TO GO TO TOWN *(Response to Ruby, Don't Take...)*
Geraldine Stevens—World Pacific 77927
[Vic Dana/Mel Tillis] [BMI] (9/6/69 C-89) [R]

RUBY DUBY DU *Tobin Matthews & Co.—Chief 7022*
[Charles Wolcott] [ASC] (10/24/60 BCtRt-27) [IM]

RUBY DUBY DU *The Pepper Pots—Panlin 7320*
[Charles Wolcott] [ASC] (10/24/60 Rt-30) [IM]

RUBY DUBY DU FROM KEY WITNESS *Charles Wolcott—MGM 12944*
[Charles Wolcott] [ASC] (10/24/60 BCtRt-27) [IM]

RUBY TUESDAY *The Rolling Stones—London 904*
[Mick Jagger/Keith Richards] [BMI] (1/21/67 BCR-1)

RUBY TUESDAY *Melanie—Buddah 202*
[Mick Jagger/Keith Richards] [BMI] (11/28/70 BCR-34)

RUDOLPH THE RED NOSED REINDEER *Gene Autry—Columbia 38610*
[Johnny Marks] [ASC] (12/13/54 Rt-PRE)

RUDOLPH THE RED NOSED REINDEER *The Mulcays—Cardinal 1025*
[Johnny Marks] [ASC] (12/13/54 Rt-PRE) [IWM]

RUDOLPH THE RED NOSED REINDEER *The Mulcays—Cardinal 1025*
[Johnny Marks] [ASC] (12/30/55 Rt-73) [IWM]

RUDOLPH THE RED-NOSED REINDEER *Les Paul & Mary Ford—Capitol 3302*
[Johnny Marks] [ASC] (12/30/55 Rt-73)

RUDOLPH, THE RED-NOSED REINDEER *Gene Autry & The Pinafores—Columbia 39463*
[Johnny Marks] [ASC] (12/30/55 Rt-73)

RUDOLPH THE RED-NOSED REINDEER *Gene Autry—Challenge 1010*
[Johnny Marks] [ASC] (12/30/57 B-70)

RUDOLPH THE RED NOSED REINDEER CHA CHA *Hugo Winterhalter and his Orchestra—RCA Victor 47-7397 [Johnny Marks] [ASC] (11/24/58 Rt-50) [IWM]*

RUDOLPH THE RED-NOSED REINDEER CHA CHA
Hernando Hopkins—ABC-Paramount 9973
[Johnny Marks] [ASC] (12/15/58 Rt-50) [IWM]

RUDOLPH THE RED NOSED REINDEER *David Seville And The Chipmunks—Liberty 55289*
[Johnny Marks] [ASC] (12/12/60 BCtRt-21)

RUDOLPH THE RED NOSED REINDEER *The Melodeers—Studio 9908*
[Johnny Marks] [ASC] (12/12/60 BCtRt-25)

RUDOLPH THE RED NOSED REINDEER *Paul Anka—ABC-Paramount 10169*
[Johnny Marks] [ASC] (12/12/60 CtRt-51)

RUDOLPH THE RED NOSED REINDEER *David Seville And The Chipmunks—Liberty 55289*
[Johnny Marks] [ASC] (12/18/61 BCR-47)

RUDOLPH THE RED NOSED REINDEER *David Seville And The Chipmunks—Liberty 55289*
[Johnny Marks] [ASC] (12/15/62 BR-69)

RUDY'S ROCK Bill Haley And His Comets—Decca 30085
[Bill Haley/Rudy Pompilli] [ASC] (10/20/56 BCR-34) [IWM]

RULES OF LOVE The Orlons—Cameo 319
[Dave Appell/Kal Mann] [ASC] (5/16/64 BCR-66)

RUMBLE *Link Wray & His Ray Men—Cadence 1347*
[Milton Grant/Link Wray] [BMI] (4/7/58 BCR-16) [I]

RUMBLE *Jack Nitzsche—Reprise 20,225*
[Milton Grant/Link Wray] [BMI] (11/23/63 B-91) [I]

RUMBLE BOOGIE Don Cherry—Columbia 40597 [Eddie Curtis] [BMI] (2/24/56 R-82)

RUMBLESEAT John Cougar Mellencamp—Riva 884 856
[John Mellencamp] [ASC] (6/28/86 BC-28)

RUMMY POLKA Matys Bros.—Sunnyside 3102
[John Matys/Walt Matys] [BMI] (1/24/59 CR-63)

RUMOR AT THE HONKY TONK Spellbound—EMI America 8002
[Barry Flast] [BMI] (7/29/78 BCR-89)

RUMORS Johnny Crawford—Del-Fi 4188
[Howard Greenfield/Helen Miller] [BMI] (11/3/62 BCR-12)

RUMORS Syndicate Of Sound—Bell 646 [John Sharkey] [BMI] (8/20/66 BCR-55)

RUMORS Timex Social Club—Jay 7001
[Alex Hill/Michael Marshall/Marcus Thompson] [BMI] (6/14/86 BC-8)

THE RUMOUR Olivia Newton-John—MCA 53294
[Elton John/Bernie Taupin] [BMI] (8/20/88 BC-62)

RUMOUR HAS IT Donna Summer—Casablanca 916
[Pete Bellotte/Giorgio Moroder/Donna Summer] [ASC] (3/4/78 BC-53)

RUN AND HIDE The Uniques—Paula 245
[Kenneth Freeman/Joe Stampley/David Wade] [BMI] (10/29/66 C-100)

RUN AWAY CHILD, RUNNING WILD The Temptations—Gordy 7084
[Barrett Strong/Norman Whitfield] [BMI] (2/15/69 BCR-6)

RUN, BABY RUN (BACK INTO MY ARMS) The Newbeats—Hickory 1332
[Don Gant/Joe Melson] [BMI] (9/25/65 BCR-10)

RUN FOR HOME Lindisfarne—Atco 7093 [Alan Hull] [ASC] (9/30/78 BCR-33)

RUN FOR THE ROSES Dan Fogelberg—Full Moon 02821
[Dan Fogelberg] [ASC] (4/3/82 BCR-14)

RUN HOME GIRL Sad Café—A&M 2111 [Ian Wilson/Paul Young] [ASC] (1/13/79 BCR-71)

RUN JOEY RUN David Geddes—Big Tree 16044
[Jack Perricone/Paul Vance] [ASC] (7/26/75 BCR-1)

—RUN JOEY RUN see: QUICK JOEY SMALL

RUN LIKE HELL Pink Floyd—Columbia 11265
[David Gilmour/Roger Waters] [BMI] (5/10/80 BCR-53)

RUN RED RUN The Coasters—Atco 6153
[Jerry Leiber/Mike Stoller] [BMI] (11/30/59 BCR-36)

RUN, RUDOLPH, RUN Chuck Berry—Chess 1714
[Marvin Lee Brodie/Johnny Marks] [ASC] (12/15/58 B-69)

RUN, RUN, LOOK AND SEE Brian Hyland—Philips 40405
[Marty Cooper/Ray Whitley] [BMI] (10/22/66 BCR-25)

RUN, RUN, RUN Ronny Douglas—Everest 19413
[Wes Farrell*/Larry Kusik] [BMI] (6/19/61 BR-75)

RUN, RUN, RUN The Supremes—Motown 1054
[Lamont Dozier/Brian Holland/Eddie Holland] [BMI] (2/29/64 BCR-86)

RUN, RUN, RUN The Gestures—Soma 1417 [Dale Menten] [BMI] (11/14/64 BCR-38)

RUN, RUN, RUN The Third Rail—Epic 10191
[Joey Levine/Artie Resnick/Kris Resnick] [BMI] (7/29/67 BCR-53)

RUN RUN RUN Jo Jo Gunne—Asylum 11003
[Matt Andes/Jay Ferguson] [BMI] (3/18/72 BCR-27)

RUN RUNAWAY Slade—CBS Associated 04398
[Noddy Holder/Jim Lea] [ASC] (4/7/84 BC-20)

RUN SALLY RUN The Cuff Links—Decca 32639
[Lee Pockriss/Paul Vance] [ASC] (2/28/70 BCR-40)

RUN SAMSON RUN Neil Sedaka—RCA Victor 47-7781
[Howard Greenfield/Neil Sedaka] [BMI] (8/8/60 BCR-24)

RUN TELL THE PEOPLE Daniel Boone—Pye 12105
[Daniel Boone/Rod McQueen] [ASC] (5/24/75 B-93)

RUN THROUGH THE JUNGLE Creedence Clearwater Revival—Fantasy 641
[John Fogerty] (TSW) [BMI] (4/25/70 BCR-2)

RUN TO HIM Bobby Vee—Liberty 55388
[Gerry Goffin/Jack Keller] [BMI] (11/13/61 BCR-2)

RUN TO ME The Montanas—Independence 89
[Tony Hatch/Jackie Trent] [BMI] (11/16/68 C-96)

RUN TO ME Bee Gees—Atco 6896
[Barry Gibb/Maurice Gibb/Robin Gibb] [BMI] (7/22/72 BCR-9)

RUN TO ME Savoy Brown—Town House 1055
[Chris Norman/Pete Spencer] [NA] (10/10/81 BCR-68)

RUN TO MY LOVIN' ARMS Lenny Welch—Kapp 712
[George Fischoff/Tony Powers] [BMI] (11/6/65 BCR-85)

RUN TO PARADISE Choirboys—WTG 31-68564
[Brad Carr/Mark Gable] [ASC] (3/11/89 BC-80)

RUN TO YOU Bryan Adams—A&M 2686
[Bryan Adams/Jim Vallance] [BMI] (11/3/84 BC-4)

RUN, WOMAN, RUN Tammy Wynette—Epic 10653
[Ann Booth/Duke Goff/Dan Hoffman] [BMI] (10/24/70 B-92)

RUNAROUND *The Three Chuckles—"X" 0066 [Cirino Colacrai] [BMI] (10/30/54 BCRt-20)*

RUNAROUND *Karen Chandler—Coral 61289 [Cirino Colacrai] [BMI] (11/1/54 Rt-PRE)*

RUNAROUND *The Fleetwoods—Dolton 22 [Cirino Colacrai] [BMI] (5/14/60 BCR-19)*

RUNAROUND The Regents—Gee 1071 [Ernie Maresca] [BMI] (7/10/61 BCR-26)

RUNAROUND SUE *Dion—Laurie 3110*
[Dion DiMucci/Ernie Maresca] [ASC] (9/18/61 BCR-1)

RUNAROUND SUE *(parody of Runaround Sue) The Four Preps—Capitol 4716*
[Dion DiMucci/Ernie Maresca] (Med) [ASC] (3/17/62 BCR-61) [P]

RUNAROUND SUE *Leif Garrett—Atlantic 3440*
[Dion DiMucci/Ernie Maresca] [ASC] (11/5/77 BCR-13)

RUNAROUND SUE *Jive Bunny & The Mastermixers—Music Factory/Atco 99122*
[Dion DiMucci/Ernie Maresca] (Med) [ASC] (2/3/90 BC-67)

RUNAWAY *Del Shannon—Big Top 3067 [Max Crook/Del Shannon] [BMI] (3/6/61 BCR-1)*

RUNAWAY *Lawrence Welk And His Orchestra—Dot 16336*
[Max Crook/Del Shannon] [BMI] (4/2/62 BCR-56) [IWM]

RUNAWAY *Dawn Featuring Tony Orlando—Bell 45,175*
[Max Crook/Del Shannon] (Med) [BMI] (1/22/72 BCR-41)

RUNAWAY *Charlie Kulis—Playboy 6023 [Max Crook/Del Shannon] [BMI] (3/1/75 BCR-42)*

RUNAWAY *Bonnie Raitt—Warner Bros. 8382*
[Max Crook/Del Shannon] [BMI] (5/21/77 BCR-50)

RUNAWAY *Luis Cardenas—Allied Artists 72500 [Max Crook/Del Shannon] [BMI] (9/13/86 BC-68)*

RUNAWAY Jefferson Starship—Grunt 11274 [Nicholas Dewey] [BMI] (5/27/78 BCR-12)

RUNAWAY Bon Jovi—Mercury 818309 [Jon Bon Jovi/George Karak] [ASC] (2/25/84 BC-37)

RUNAWAY LOVE Linda Clifford—Curtom 0138 [Gilbert Askey] [BMI] (6/3/78 BCR-68)

RUNAWAY PEOPLE Dyke And The Blazers—Original Sound 96 [Arlester Christian] [BMI] (7/18/70 R-86)

RUNAWAY RITA Leif Garrett—Scotti Brothers 02579 [Jeff Harrington/Jeff Pennig/Shunichi Tokura] [ASC] (12/5/81 B-84)

RUNNER Manfred Mann's Earth Band—Arista 1-9143 [Ian Thomas] [NA] (1/21/84 BC-22)

RUNNIN' AWAY Sly & The Family Stone—Epic 10829 [Sylvester Stewart] [BMI] (2/5/72 BCR-11)

RUNNIN' BACK TO SASKATOON The Guess Who—RCA Victor 74-0803 [Burton Cummings/Kurt Winter] [BMI] (10/7/72 BCR-74)

RUNNIN' BLUE The Doors—Elektra 45675 [Robby Krieger] [ASC] (8/30/69 BCR-36)

RUNNIN' DOWN A DREAM Tom Petty—MCA 53682 [Mike Campbell/Jeff Lynne/Tom Petty] [ASC] (7/29/89 BC-22)

RUNNIN' OUT OF FOOLS Aretha Franklin—Columbia 43113 [Richard Ahlert/Eddie Snyder] [ASC] (9/19/64 BCR-57)

RUNNIN' WILD Les Paul and Mary Ford—Capitol 3570 [A. Harrington Gibbs/Joe Grey/Leo Wood] [NA] (11/3/56 R-79)

RUNNIN' WITH THE DEVIL Van Halen—Warner Bros. 8556 [Michael Anthony/David Lee Roth/Alex Van Halen/Eddie Van Halen] [ASC] (5/6/78 B-84)

RUNNING Chubby Checker—MCA 51233 [Joe Russo] [BMI] (2/13/82 BCR-79)

RUNNING AWAY Maze Featuring Frankie Beverly—Capitol 5000 [Frankie Beverly] [BMI] (6/27/81 R-87)

RUNNING BACK Eddie Money—Columbia 11325 [Radcliffe Bryan] [NA] (9/6/80 BCR-78)

RUNNING BACK Urgent—Manhattan 50005 [Don Kehr/Michael Kehr/Steve Kehr] [BMI] (8/10/85 BC-79)

RUNNING BACK TO YOU Vanessa Williams—Wing 867 518 [Trevor Gale/Kenni Hairston] [ASC] (8/10/91 BC-18)

RUNNING BEAR *Johnny Preston—Mercury 71474 [J.P. Richardson] [BMI] (10/12/59 BCR-1)*

RUNNING BEAR *Sonny James The Southern Gentleman—Capitol 2486 [J.P. Richardson] [BMI] (5/17/69 BCR-79)*

RUNNING IN THE FAMILY Level 42—Polydor 885957 [Wally Badarou/Phil Gould/Mark King] [BMI] (8/8/87 BC-79)

RUNNING ON EMPTY Jackson Browne—Asylum 45460 [Jackson Browne] [ASC] (2/11/78 BCR-6)

RUNNING SCARED *Roy Orbison—Monument 438 [Joe Melson/Roy Orbison] [BMI] (4/10/61 BCR-1)*

RUNNING SCARED *The Fools—EMI America 8072 [Joe Melson/Roy Orbison] [BMI] (3/7/81 BCR-50)*

RUNNING UP THAT HILL Kate Bush—EMI America 8285 [Kate Bush] [BMI] (9/7/85 BC-28)

RUNNING WITH THE NIGHT Lionel Richie—Motown 1710 [Lionel Richie/Cynthia Weil] [ASC] (11/26/83 BC-7)

RUNWAY David Rose—MGM 13118 [David Rose] [ASC] (1/12/63 R-95) [I]

THE RUNWAY The Grass Roots—Dunhill 4316 [Dennis Lambert/Brian Potter] [BMI] (6/10/72 BCR-29)

RUSH Big Audio Dynamite II—Columbia 73987 [Michael Leslie Jones] [BMI] (9/21/91 BC-32)

THE RUSH Luther Vandross—Epic 74049 [Marcus Miller/Luther Vandross] [ASC] (12/28/91 C-64)

RUSH HOUR Jane Wiedlin—EMI 50118 [Peter Rafelson/Jane Wiedlin] [ASC] (5/7/88 BC-9)

RUSH RUSH Paula Abdul—Virgin 98828 [Peter Lord] [ASC] (5/11/91 BC-1)

RUSSIAN BANDSTAND Spencer & Spencer—Argo 5331 [Dickie Goodman] [BMI] (5/18/59 B-91)

RUSSIAN RADIO Red Flag—Enigma 75035 [Chris Reynolds/Mark Reynolds] [BMI] (3/18/89 C-83)

RUSSIANS Sting—A&M 2799 [Sergei Prokofiev*/Sting] [BMI] (1/18/86 BC-16)

RUST NEVER SLEEPS (HEY HEY, MY MY [INTO THE BLACK]) Neil Young & Crazy Horse—Reprise 49031 [Neil Young] [BMI] (10/6/79 BCR-72)

RUSTY BELLS Brenda Lee—Decca 31849 [Richard Ahlert/Eddie Snyder] [ASC] (10/2/65 BCR-25)

A RUSTY OLD HALO *Mahalia Jackson & The Falls-Jones Ensemble—Columbia 40411 [Bob Merrill] [ASC] (2/5/55 CRt-26)*

A RUSTY OLD HALO *Pat O'Day—MGM 11930 [Bob Merrill] [ASC] (2/7/55 Rt-66)*

RUTHLESS PEOPLE Mick Jagger—Epic 06211 [Daryl Hall/Mick Jagger/David A. Stewart] [BMI] (8/2/86 BC-51)

S

S'-ALL RIGHT? S'-ALL RIGHT! Senor Wences—Joy 228 [Al Hoffman/Dick Manning/Señor Wences] [ASC] (3/21/59 C-86)

S-W-I-M Bobby Freeman—Autumn 5 [Thomas Coman/Sylvester Stewart] [BMI] (10/24/64 BCR-56)

'S WONDERFUL Ray Conniff & His Orchestra and Chorus—Columbia 40827 [George Gershwin] [ASC] (3/16/57 B-73) [IM]

S.Y.S.L.J.F.M. (THE LETTER SONG) Joe Tex—Dial 4028 [Joe Tex] [BMI] (5/14/66 BCR-39)

SACK DRESS The Beavers—Capitol 3956 [Warner Wilder] [ASC] (4/21/58 R-68)

SACRED The Castells—Era 3048 [William Landau/Irving Roth] [BMI] (5/29/61 BCR-20)

SACRED EMOTION Donny Osmond—Capitol 44379 [Evan Rogers/Carl Sturken] [BMI] (6/17/89 BC-10)

SACRIFICE Elton John—MCA 53750 [Elton John/Bernie Taupin] [BMI] (1/13/90 BC-18)

SAD EYES Brooklyn Dreams—Millennium 606 [Joe Esposito/Eddie Hokenson/Bruce Sudano] [BMI] (11/12/77 BCR-63)

SAD EYES Robert John—EMI America 8015 [Robert John] [BMI] (5/19/79 BCR-1)

SAD EYES (DON'T YOU CRY) The Echoes—Seg-Way 106 [Addy Baron/Bernice Ross] [BMI] (6/12/61 B-88)

SAD GIRL *Jay Wiggins—IPG 1008 [Lloyd Smith/Jay Wiggins] [BMI] (10/5/63 R-99)*

SAD GIRL *The Intruders—Gamble 235 [Lloyd Smith/Jay Wiggins] [BMI] (8/23/69 BCR-47)*

SAD GIRL *GQ—Arista 0659 [Lloyd Smith/Jay Wiggins] [BMI] (3/6/82 BR-75)*

SAD GIRL Carl Graves—Ariola America 7660 [Alan Gordon] [BMI] (4/9/77 BCR-68)

SAD HEARTS Four Tops—Casablanca 2353 [Marc Blatte/Larry Gottlieb] [ASC] (8/28/82 BC-84)

SAD MOOD Sam Cooke—RCA Victor 47-7816 [Sam Cooke] [BMI] (11/21/60 BCR-22)

SAD MOVIES (MAKE ME CRY) *The Lennon Sisters—Dot 16255 [John D. Loudermilk] [BMI] (8/28/61 BCtRt-5)*

SAD MOVIES (MAKE ME CRY) *Sue Thompson—Hickory 1153 [John D. Loudermilk] [BMI] (8/28/61 BCtRt-5)*

SAD, SAD GIRL Barbara Mason—Arctic 108 [Barbara Mason] [BMI] (8/7/65 BCR-24)

SAD, SAD GIRL AND BOY The Impressions—ABC-Paramount 10431 [Curtis Mayfield] [BMI] (5/25/63 B-84)

—SAD SONG see: FA-FA-FA-FA-FA

SAD SONGS (SAY SO MUCH) Elton John—Geffen 29292 [Elton John/Bernie Taupin] [BMI] (6/9/84 BC-5)

SAD SWEET DREAMER Sweet Sensation—Pye 71002 [David Parton] [BMI] (1/11/75 BCR-14)

SAD TOMORROWS Trini Lopez—Reprise 0328 [John Greenbach/Jerry Marcellino] [BMI] (4/17/65 BCR-81)

SADENESS PART 1 Enigma—Charisma 98864 [Michael Cretu/Fabrice Cuitad/Frank Peterson] [ASC] (2/9/91 BC-5) [FET]

SADIE The Spinners—Atlantic 3268 [Bruce Hawes/Joseph Jefferson/Charles Simmons] [BMI] (5/3/75 BCR-44)

SADIE TAKE A LOVER Sam Neely—A&M 1523 [Sam Neely] [BMI] (5/25/74 R-84)

SADIE'S SHAWL *Bob Sharples And His Music—London 1661 [Nico Carstens/Harold Fields/Joseph Roncoroni] [ASC] (9/8/56 BCRt-42) [I]*

SADIE'S SHAWL *Richard Hayman And Jan August—Mercury 70937 [Nico Carstens/Harold Fields/Joseph Roncoroni] [ASC] (9/8/56 Rt-51) [I]*

SADIE'S SHAWL *Philip Green & His Gob Music—Capitol 3529 [Nico Carstens/Harold Fields/Joseph Roncoroni] [ASC] (9/22/56 Rt-51) [I]*

SAFE AND SOUND Fontella Bass—Checker 1147 [Billy Davis/Raynard Miner/Carl William Smith] [BMI] (8/27/66 B-100)

SAFE AT HOME The Souther, Hillman, Furay Band—Asylum 45217 [Chris Hillman] [BMI] (12/7/74 CR-80)

SAFE IN MY GARDEN The Mamas & The Papas—Dunhill 4125 [John Phillips] [ASC] (6/1/68 BCR-33)

THE SAFETY DANCE Men Without Hats—Backstreet 52232 [Ivan Doroschuk] [BMI] (6/25/83 BC-1)

SAGINAW, MICHIGAN Lefty Frizzell—Columbia 42924 [Bill Anderson/Don Wayne] [BMI] (1/18/64 BCR-79)

SAID I WASN'T GONNA TELL NOBODY Sam & Dave—Stax 198 [Isaac Hayes/David Porter] [BMI] (9/10/66 BCR-64)

SAIL ALONG SILVERY MOON *Billy Vaughn and His Orchestra—Dot 15661 [Harry Tobias/Percy Wenrich] [ASC] (12/7/57 BCRt-4) [IWM]*

SAIL ALONG SILV'RY MOON *Karen Chandler & Her Jacks—Decca 30537 [Harry Tobias/Percy Wenrich] [ASC] (12/30/57 Rt-12)*

SAIL AROUND THE WORLD David Gates—Elektra 45868 [David Gates] [ASC] (10/13/73 BCR-49)

SAIL AWAY Sam Neely—Elektra 45419 [Rafe Van Hoy] [BMI] (8/27/77 BR-84)

SAIL AWAY The Temptations—Gordy 1720 [Angelo Bond/Norman Whitfield] [BMI] (4/7/84 BC-54)

SAIL ON Commodores—Motown 1466 [Lionel Richie] [ASC] (8/11/79 BCR-1)

SAIL ON SAILOR *The Beach Boys—Brother/Reprise 1138 [Tandyn Almer/Ray Kennedy/Van Dyke Parks/Jack Rieley/Brian Wilson] [BMI] (2/24/73 BC-79)*

SAIL ON SAILOR *The Beach Boys—Brother/Reprise 1325 [Tandyn Almer/Ray Kennedy/Van Dyke Parks/Jack Rieley/Brian Wilson] [BMI] (4/12/75 BCR-49)*

SAILING Rod Stewart—Warner Bros. 8146 [Gavin Sutherland] [ASC] (10/11/75 BCR-49)

SAILING Christopher Cross—Warner Bros. 49507 [Christopher Cross] [ASC] (6/7/80 BCR-1)

SAILING SHIPS Mesa—Ariola America 7654
[Jeff Des Enfants/Carmine Notaro/Evan Pace/Roger Paglia/Ed Rekers] [BMI] (2/12/77 BCR-55)

SAILOR BOY The Chiffons—Laurie 3262
[Gerry Goffin/Russ Titelman] [BMI] (7/11/64 BCR-75)

SAILOR BOYS HAVE TALK TO ME IN ENGLISH *Rosemary Clooney—Columbia 40534*
[Milton DeLugg/Bob Hilliard] [BMI] (7/25/55 CRt-42)

SAILOR BOYS HAVE TALK TO ME IN ENGLISH *The 5 DeMarco Sisters—Decca 29607*
[Milton DeLugg/Bob Hilliard] [BMI] (7/25/55 Rt-42)

SAILOR BOYS HAVE TALK TO ME IN ENGLISH *Helen O'Connell—Kapp 119*
[Milton DeLugg/Bob Hilliard] [BMI] (7/25/55 Rt-52)

SAILOR (YOUR HOME IS THE SEA) Lolita—Kapp 349
[Fini Busch/Mickey Leader/Werner Scharfenberger] [ASC] (10/8/60 BCR-5) [F, FET]

—SAINTS ROCK AND ROLL see: WHEN THE SAINTS...

SALLY The Kingston Trio—Capitol 4114
[Woody Guthrie/Malvina Reynolds] [BMI] (1/17/59 C-80)

SALLY Grand Funk Railroad—Capitol 4235 [Mark Farner] [BMI] (3/20/76 BC-69)

SALLY FROM SYRACUSE Stu Nunnery—Evolution 1084
[Stu Nunnery] [ASC] (11/3/73 CR-67)

SALLY G Paul McCartney & Wings—Apple 1875
[Linda McCartney/Paul McCartney] (TSW) [ASC] (12/14/74 BCR-3)

SALLY, GO 'ROUND THE ROSES The Jaynetts—Tuff 369
[Zell Sanders/Lona Stevens] [ASC] (8/24/63 BCR-1)

SALLY HAD A PARTY Flavor—Columbia 44521
[Timothy O'Brien/Gary St. Clair] [ASC] (7/6/68 BCR-66)

SALLY WAS A GOOD OLD GIRL *Fats Domino—ABC-Paramount 10584*
[Harlan Howard] [BMI] (9/19/64 B-99)

SALLY WAS A GOOD OLD GIRL *Trini Lopez—Reprise 0659*
[Harlan Howard] [BMI] (3/2/68 B-99)

SAL'S GOT A SUGAR LIP Johnny Horton—Columbia 41437
[Jimmy Driftwood] [BMI] (8/10/59 BCR-54)

SALSOUL HUSTLE The Salsoul Orchestra—Salsoul 2002
[Vincent Montana] [BMI] (9/13/75 BC-76) [I]

THE SALT IN MY TEARS Martin Briley—Mercury 812165
[Martin Briley] [ASC] (5/21/83 BC-36)

SALT WATER TAFFY Morty Jay And The Surferin' Cats—Legend 124
[Arline J. Quier/Mack Wolfson] [ASC] (11/9/63 B-93) [I]

SALTY TEARS Mara Lynn Brown—Laurie 3604
[Victoria Pike/Teddy Randazzo] [BMI] (2/3/73 R-86)

SALVATION ROCK Marv Meredith And His Orchestra—Strand 25021
[Mort Garson/Grace Lane] [ASC] (12/19/60 R-94)

SAM Olivia Newton-John—MCA 40670
[Don Black/John Farrar/Hank Marvin] [BMI] (1/29/77 BCR-20)

SAM, YOU MADE THE PANTS TOO LONG (parody of Lawd, You Made The Night Too Long)
Barbra Streisand—Columbia 43612
[Milton Berle/Sam Lewis/Fred Whitehouse/Victor Young] [ASC] (5/7/66 BC-79) [P]

SAMANTHA (WHAT YOU GONNA DO?) Cellarful Of Noise—CBS Associated 07731
[Mark Avsec] [ASC] (3/5/88 BC-69)

THE SAME LOVE The Jets—MCA 53734 [Diane Warren] [ASC] (10/21/89 B-87)

THE SAME LOVE THAT MADE ME LAUGH Bill Withers—Sussex 513
[Bill Withers] [BMI] (4/13/74 BCR-43)

SAME OL' SITUATION (S.O.S.) Mötley Crüe—Elektra 64942
[Tommy Lee/Mick Mars/Vince Neil/Nikki Sixx] [ASC] (9/1/90 BC-50)

THE SAME OLD HURT Burl Ives—Decca 31453 [Hank Cochran] [BMI] (1/26/63 B-91)

SAME OLD LANG SYNE Dan Fogelberg—Full Moon/Epic 50961
[Dan Fogelberg] [ASC] (12/13/80 BCR-7)

SAME OLD LOOK Jimmy Ryser—Arista 2039
[Diane Ryser/Jimmy Ryser] [ASC] (7/14/90 BC-66)

SAME OLD ME Guy Mitchell—Columbia 41576 [Fuzzy Owen] [BMI] (2/22/60 BR-51)

SAME OLD SATURDAY NIGHT Frank Sinatra—Capitol 3218
[Sammy Cahn/Frank Reardon] [ASC] (8/22/55 BCR-11)

THE SAME OLD SONG AND DANCE Frank Sinatra—Capitol 4003
[Sammy Cahn/Jimmy Van Heusen/Bobby Worth] [ASC] (7/26/58 C-74)

SAME OLE LOVE (365 DAYS A YEAR) Anita Baker—Elektra 69484
[Marilyn McLeod/Darryl Keith Roberts] [ASC] (3/21/87 BC-43)

SAME ONE Brook Benton—Mercury 71652
[Brook Benton/Clyde Otis] [BMI] (8/8/60 BCR-16)

SAME THING IT TOOK The Impressions—Curtom 0106
[Charles Henry Jackson Jr./Ed Townsend/Marvin Yancy] [ASC] (10/4/75 BCR-62)

SAM'S PLACE Buck Owens And The Buckaroos—Capitol 5865
[Buck Owens/Red Simpson] [BMI] (4/15/67 BC-92)

SAM'S SONG Dean Martin And Sammy Davis Jr.—Reprise 20,128
[John M. Elliott/Lew Quadling] [ASC] (12/22/62 B-94)

SAN ANTONIO ROSE *Johnny Maddox And The Rhythmasters—Dot 15365*
[Bob Wills] (Med) [ASC] (5/28/55 C-43) [IWM]

SAN ANTONIO ROSE *Floyd Cramer—RCA Victor 47-7893*
[Bob Wills] [ASC] (6/5/61 BCR-8) [IWM]

SAN BERNADINO Christie—Epic 10695 [Jeff Christie] [BMI] (1/30/71 BCR-86)

SAN FRANCISCAN NIGHTS Eric Burdon And The Animals—MGM 13769
[Vic Briggs/Eric Burdon/Barry Jenkins/Danny McCulloch/John Weider] [BMI] (8/5/67 BCR-8)

SAN FRANCISCO (BE SURE TO WEAR FLOWERS IN YOUR HAIR) *Scott McKenzie—Ode 103*
[John Phillips] [ASC] (5/27/67 BCR-3)

SAN FRANCISCO (WEAR SOME FLOWERS IN YOUR HAIR)
Paul Mauriat and His Orchestra—Philips 40550
[John Phillips] [ASC] (8/17/68 CR-88) [IWM]

SAN FRANCISCO GIRLS (RETURN OF THE NATIVE) Fever Tree—Uni 55060
[Scott Holtzman/Vivian Holtzman/Michael Knust] [BMI] (4/20/68 BCR-65)

SAN FRANCISCO IS A LONELY TOWN Joe Simon—Sound Stage 7 2641
[Ben Peters] [BMI] (9/6/69 BR-76)

SAN-HO-ZAY Freddy King—Federal 12428
[Freddy King/Sonny Thompson] [BMI] (8/7/61 B-47) [I]

SANCTIFY YOURSELF Simple Minds—A&M 2810
[Charles Burchill/Jim Kerr/Michael MacNeil] [ASC] (1/25/86 BC-10)

THE SAND AND THE SEA *Nat "King" Cole—Capitol 3027*
[Hal Hester/Barry Parker] (TSW) [BMI] (4/9/55 BCRt-10)

THE SAND AND THE SEA *Bob Santa Maria—MGM 11925*
[Hal Hester/Barry Parker] [BMI] (4/11/55 Rt-25)

SANDY Larry Hall—Strand 25007 [Terry Fell] [BMI] (11/9/59 BCR-14)

SANDY Dion—Laurie 3153 [Steve Brandt/Dion DiMucci] [BMI] (3/2/63 BCR-21)

SANDY Ronny & The Daytonas—Mala 513
[Buzz Cason/John Buck Wilkin] [BMI] (12/4/65 BCR-27)

SANDY The Hollies—Epic 50086 [Bruce Springsteen] [ASC] (4/12/75 BC-85)

SANTA AND THE PURPLE PEOPLE EATER Sheb Wooley—MGM 12733
[Sheb Wooley] [ASC] (12/27/58 C-93)

SANTA AND THE SATELLITE Buchanan And Goodman—Luniverse 107
[Bill Buchanan*/Dickie Goodman] [BMI] (12/14/57 BC-32)

SANTA & THE TOUCHABLES Dickie Goodman—Rori 701
[Robert Arkin*/Dickie Goodman] [BMI] (12/25/61 B-99)

SANTA BRING MY BABY BACK TO ME Elvis Presley—RCA Victor LOC-1035
[Claude DeMetrius/Aaron Schroeder] (EP) [ASC] (12/30/57 R-49)

—SANTA CATALINA see: 26 MILES

SANTA CLAUS IS BACK IN TOWN Elvis Presley—RCA Victor LOC-1035
[Jerry Leiber/Mike Stoller] (EP) [ASC] (12/30/57 R-49)

SANTA CLAUS IS COMIN' TO TOWN *Bing Crosby and the Andrews Sisters—Decca 23281*
[J. Fred Coots/Haven Gillespie] [ASC] (12/20/54 Rt-80)

SANTA CLAUS IS COMIN' TO TOWN *Fred Waring presents The Teen Trio—Decca 29351*
[J. Fred Coots/Haven Gillespie] [ASC] (12/20/54 Rt-80)

SANTA CLAUS IS COMING TO TOWN *The 4 Seasons—Vee-Jay 478*
[J. Fred Coots/Haven Gillespie] [ASC] (12/15/62 BCR-12)

SANTA CLAUS IS COMIN' TO TOWN *The Jackson 5—Motown 1174*
[J. Fred Coots/Haven Gillespie] [ASC] (12/19/70 C-51)

SANTA CLAUS IS WATCHING YOU Ray Stevens—Mercury 72058
[Ray Stevens] [BMI] (12/15/62 BCR-26)

SANTA JAWS (PART I) Homemade Theatre—A&M 1776
[Fred Mollin/Larry Mollin/Phil Savath] [ASC] (1/3/76 R-95)

SANTA LOOKED A LOT LIKE DADDY Buck Owens—Capitol
[Buck Owens/Don Rich] [BMI] (12/18/65 R-97)

SANTO DOMINGO The Sandpipers—A&M 1208
[Rudi Lindt/Michael Piano/Peter Poll] [BMI] (9/5/70 C-94) [F]

SANTO NATALE (MERRY CHRISTMAS)
David Whitfield with Stanley Black And His Orchestra—London 1508
[Al Hoffman/Dick Manning/Belle Nardone] [ASC] (11/22/54 BRt-26)

SANTO NATALE *Ronnie Gaylord—Mercury 70504*
[Al Hoffman/Dick Manning/Belle Nardone] [ASC] (12/13/54 Rt-PRE)

SARA Fleetwood Mac—Warner Bros. 49150 [Stevie Nicks] [BMI] (12/15/79 BCR-6)

SARA Bill Champlin—Elektra 47456 [Bill Champlin/Alan Thicke] [ASC] (7/31/82 BC-61)

SARA Starship—Grunt 14253 [Ina Wolf/Peter F. Wolf] [BMI] (12/28/85 BC-1)

SARA SMILE Daryl Hall & John Oates—RCA Victor 10530
[Daryl Hall/John Oates] [BMI] (1/31/76 BCR-4)

(SARTORIAL ELOQUENCE) DON'T YA WANNA PLAY THIS GAME NO MORE?
Elton John—MCA 41293
[Elton John/Tom Robinson] [BMI] (8/9/80 BCR-39)

SATELLITE Hooters—Columbia 07607
[Eric Bazilian/Rick Chertoff/Rob Hyman] [ASC] (10/3/87 BC-61)

SATIN PILLOWS Bobby Vinton—Epic 9869
[Sonny James/Bob Tubert] [BMI] (11/27/65 BCR-20)

SATIN RED AND BLACK VELVET WOMAN Dave Mason—Blue Thumb 7117
[Dave Mason] [BMI] (11/14/70 BCR-65)

SATIN SHEETS Jeanne Pruett—MCA 40015 [John Volinkaty] [BMI] (5/12/73 BCR-24)

SATIN SHEETS Bellamy Brothers—Warner/Curb 8248
[Willis Alan Ramsey] [ASC] (9/4/76 BCR-73)

SATIN SOUL Love Unlimited Orchestra—20th Century 2162
[Barry White] [BMI] (2/1/75 BCR-22) [I]

SATISFACTION Smokey Robinson & The Miracles—Tamla 54211
[Smokey Robinson] [ASC] (11/13/71 BCR-43)

SATISFACTION GUARANTEED The Firm—Atlantic 89561 [Jimmy Page/Paul Rodgers] [ASC] (5/4/85 BC-73)

SATISFACTION GUARANTEED (OR TAKE YOUR LOVE BACK) Harold Melvin And The Blue Notes—Philadelphia Int'l 3543 [Kenneth Gamble/Leon Huff] [BMI] (4/6/74 BCR-58)

—SATISFACTION see: I CAN'T GET NO...

SATISFIED Richard Marx—EMI 50189 [Richard Marx] [ASC] (5/6/89 BC-1)

SATISFIED (PART 2) *Cashmeres—Lake 705 [Ernest Kelley/Windsor King] [BMI] (10/10/60 CtRt-64)*

SATISFIED (PART 2) *Debbie Reynolds—Dot 16156 [Ernest Kelley/Windsor King] [BMI] (11/21/60 CtRt-70)*

SATISFIED MAN Molly Hatchet—Epic 04648 [Thomas DeLuca/Tom Jans] [BMI] (10/20/84 B-81)

SATISFIED MIND *Jack And Betty—Teen 107 [Joe Hayes/Jack Rhodes] [BMI] (8/15/55 Rt-25)*

A SATISFIED MIND *Jeffrey Clay—Coral 61482 [Joe Hayes/Jack Rhodes] [BMI] (8/22/55 Rt-25)*

A SATISFIED MIND *Porter Wagoner—RCA Victor 47-6105 [Joe Hayes/Jack Rhodes] [BMI] (8/22/55 Rt-25)*

SATISFIED MIND *Ella Fitzgerald—Decca 29648 [Joe Hayes/Jack Rhodes] [BMI] (8/22/55 Rt-25)*

SATISFIED MIND *Mahalia Jackson—Columbia 40554 [Joe Hayes/Jack Rhodes] [BMI] (8/29/55 Rt-61)*

A SATISFIED MIND *Bobby Hebb—Philips 40400 [Joe Hayes/Jack Rhodes] [BMI] (10/8/66 BCR-33)*

SATISFIED WITH YOU The Dave Clark Five—Epic 10053 [Dave Clark/Denny Payton] [BMI] (8/13/66 BCR-44)

SATISFY ME Billy Satellite—Capitol [Monty Byrom/Danny Chauncey/Ira Walker] [BMI] (8/18/84 BC-64)

SATURDAY Norma Jean Wright—Bearsville 0326 [Bobby Cotter/Bernard Edwards/Nile Rodgers] [BMI] (7/29/78 R-66)

SATURDAY IN THE PARK Chicago—Columbia 45657 [Robert Lamm] [ASC] (7/29/72 BCR-3)

SATURDAY LOVE Cherrelle—Tabu 4-05767 [James Samuel Harris/Terry Lewis] [ASC] (2/15/86 BC-26)

SATURDAY MORNING CONFUSION Bobby Russell—United Artists 50788 [Bobby Russell] [ASC] (7/10/71 BCR-24)

SATURDAY NIGHT The New Christy Minstrels—Columbia 42887 [Randy Sparks] [ASC] (10/26/63 BCR-29)

SATURDAY NIGHT Bay City Rollers—Arista 0149 [Phil Coulter/William Wylie MacPherson Martin] [ASC] (10/4/75 BCR-1)

SATURDAY NIGHT AT THE MOVIES The Drifters—Atlantic 2260 [Barry Mann/Cynthia Weil] [BMI] (11/14/64 BCR-14)

SATURDAY NIGHT AT THE WORLD Mason Williams—Warner Bros.-Seven Arts 7248 [Mason Williams] [BMI] (2/1/69 B-99)

SATURDAY NIGHT SPECIAL Lynyrd Skynyrd—MCA 40416 [Ed King/Ronnie Van Zant] [BMI] (6/7/75 BCR-27)

SATURDAY NIGHT, SUNDAY MORNING Thelma Houston—Tamla 54297 [Mitch Bottler/Norma Helms] [ASC] (3/10/79 BCR-34)

SATURDAY NIGHT'S ALRIGHT FOR FIGHTING Elton John—MCA 40105 [Elton John/Bernie Taupin] [BMI] (7/28/73 BCR-8)

SATURDAY NITE Earth, Wind & Fire—Columbia 10439 [Philip Bailey/Albert Philip McKay/Maurice White] [ASC] (11/20/76 BCR-21)

SATURDAY SUNSHINE Burt Bacharach—Kapp 532 [Burt Bacharach/Hal David] [ASC] (7/27/63 BCR-93)

SATURDAYNIGHT Herman Brood—Ariola America 7754 [Herman Brood/Dan Lademacher] [ASC] (7/14/79 BCR-35)

SATURDAY'S FATHER The 4 Seasons—Philips 40542 [Bob Gaudio/Jake Holmes] [ASC] (6/22/68 CR-50)

SAUSALITO Al Martino—Capitol 2468 [Terry Cashman/Eugene Pistilli/Tommy West] [ASC] (4/19/69 BCR-59)

SAUSALITO (IS THE PLACE TO GO) Ohio Express—Buddah 129 [Graham Gouldman] [BMI] (8/23/69 BCR-59)

SAUSALITO SUMMERNIGHT Diesel—Regency 7339 [Mark Boon/Rob Vunderink] [ASC] (9/12/81 BCR-25)

—SAVAGE SEVEN THEME see: ANYONE FOR TENNIS

SAVANNAH NIGHTS Tom Johnston—Warner Bros. 49096 [Tom Johnston] [BMI] (11/10/79 BCR-34)

SAVE A PRAYER Duran Duran—Capitol 5438 [Simon Le Bon/Nick Rhodes/Andy Taylor/Nigel John Taylor/Roger Taylor] [ASC] (2/2/85 BC-16)

SAVE ALL YOUR LOVIN' FOR ME Brenda Lee—Decca 31424 [Gerald Nelson/Chuck Taylor] [BMI] (9/22/62 BCR-38)

SAVE IT FOR A RAINY DAY Stephen Bishop—ABC 12232 [Stephen Bishop] [ASC] (12/4/76 BCR-21)

SAVE IT FOR ME The 4 Seasons Featuring The "Sound" Of Frankie Valli—Philips 40225 [Bob Crewe/Bob Gaudio] [BMI] (8/29/64 BCR-8)

SAVE ME Silver Convention—Midland Int'l 10212 [Sylvester Levay/Stephan Prager] [BMI] (4/19/75 CR-88)

SAVE ME *Merrilee Rush—United Artists 993 [Guy Fletcher/Doug Flett] [ASC] (6/4/77 BCR-54)*

SAVE ME *Donna McDaniel—Midsong Int'l 11005 [Guy Fletcher/Doug Flett] [ASC] (6/18/77 BCR-80)*

SAVE ME Dave Mason—Columbia 11289 [Jim Krueger] [BMI] (7/5/80 BCR-71)

SAVE ME Fleetwood Mac—Warner Bros. 19866 [Christine McVie/Eddy Quintela] [BMI] (4/7/90 BC-29)

SAVE ME Lisa Fischer—Atco 98799 [Lisa Fischer/Narada Michael Walden] [ASC] (9/7/91 BC-72)

SAVE ME Rembrandts—Elektra 64854 [Phil Solem/Danny Wilde] [BMI] (9/28/91 C-84)

—SAVE ME FROM TOMORROW see: SHIP OF FOOLS

SAVE MY SOUL Jack Scott—Carlton 493 [Jack Scott] [BMI] (12/13/58 BC-73)

SAVE SOME LOVE Keedy—Arista 2153 [Greg Gerard] [BMI] (3/16/91 BC-14)

SAVE THE COUNTRY *Thelma Houston—Dunhill 4222 [Laura Nyro] [BMI] (1/17/70 BCR-59)*

SAVE THE COUNTRY *The 5th Dimension—Bell 895 [Laura Nyro] [BMI] (6/6/70 BCR-18)*

SAVE THE LAST DANCE FOR ME *The Drifters—Atlantic 2071 [Doc Pomus/Mort Shuman] [BMI] (9/5/60 BCR-1)*

SAVE THE LAST DANCE FOR ME *The Defranco Family Featuring Tony Defranco—20th Century 2088 [Doc Pomus/Mort Shuman] [BMI] (4/27/74 BCR-16)*

SAVE THE LAST DANCE FOR ME *Dolly Parton—RCA 13703 [Doc Pomus/Mort Shuman] [BMI] (12/10/83 BC-45)*

SAVE THE NIGHT FOR ME Maureen Steele—Motown 1787 [Harvey Price/Bobby Sandstrom] [ASC] (5/4/85 BC-76)

SAVE THE OVERTIME (FOR ME) Gladys Knight & The Pips—Columbia 03761 [Sam Dees/Joey Gallo/Gladys Knight/Merald Knight/Ricky Darnell Smith] [BMI] (5/21/83 BC-61)

SAVE UP ALL YOUR TEARS Cher—Geffen 19105 [Desmond Child/Diane Warren] [ASC] (10/19/91 BC-27)

SAVE YOUR HEART FOR ME Gary Lewis And The Playboys—Liberty 55809 [Gary Geld/Peter Udell] [ASC] (7/3/65 BCR-2)

SAVE YOUR KISSES FOR ME *The Brotherhood Of Man—Pye 71066 [Tony Hiller/Martin Lee/Lee Sheriden] [ASC] (5/8/76 BCR-27)*

SAVE YOUR KISSES FOR ME *Bobby Vinton—ABC 12186 [Tony Hiller/Martin Lee/Lee Sheriden] [ASC] (5/29/76 B-75)*

SAVE YOUR LOVE Great White—Capitol 44104 [Jack Russell/Stephan Williams] [ASC] (1/23/88 BC-57)

SAVE YOUR SUGAR FOR ME Tony Joe White—Monument 1206 [Tony Joe White] [BMI] (7/18/70 BC-94)

SAVED LaVern Baker—Atlantic 2099 [Jerry Leiber/Mike Stoller] [BMI] (4/10/61 BCR-37)

SAVED BY THE BELL Robin Gibb—Atco 6698 [Robin Gibb] [BMI] (7/26/69 R-87)

SAVED BY THE GRACE OF YOUR LOVE Sons Of Champlin—Ariola America 7664 [David Palmer/William Daniel Smith] [BMI] (6/18/77 C-89)

SAVED BY ZERO The Fixx—MCA 52213 [Alfie Agius/Cy Curnin/Peter John Greenall/Jamie West-Oram/Adam Woods] [ASC] (5/28/83 BC-19)

SAVIN' MYSELF Eria Fachin—Critique 7-99356 [David Lodge] [ASC] (2/27/88 BC-50)

SAVING ALL MY LOVE FOR YOU Whitney Houston—Arista 1-9381 [Gerry Goffin/Michael Masser] [BMI] (8/17/85 BC-1)

SAW A NEW MORNING Bee Gees—RSO 401 [Barry Gibb/Maurice Gibb/Robin Gibb] [BMI] (3/10/73 BCR-69)

SAX FIFTH AVENUE *Johnny Beecher And His Buckingham Road Quintet—Warner Bros. 5341 [Victor Harris] [BMI] (3/2/63 BCtR-62) [I]*

SAX FIFTH AVENUE *Jack Cole Quintet—Wall 553 [Victor Harris] [BMI] (3/16/63 Ct-82) [I]*

SAY A PRAYER Breathe—A&M 1519 [David Glasper/Marcus Lillington] [ASC] (8/25/90 BC-16)

SAY GOODBYE TO HOLLYWOOD Billy Joel—Columbia 02518 [Billy Joel] [ASC] (9/12/81 BCR-17)

SAY GOODBYE TO LITTLE JO Steve Forbert—Nemperor 7529 [Steve Forbert] [ASC] (4/12/80 BCR-82)

SAY, HAS ANYBODY SEEN MY SWEET GYPSY ROSE Dawn Featuring Tony Orlando—Bell 45,374 [L. Russell Brown/Irwin Levine] [BMI] (7/14/73 BCR-3)

SAY HELLO April Wine—Capitol 4802 [Myles Goodwyn] [BMI] (1/19/80 R-93)

SAY HELLO TO RONNIE Janey Street—Arista 1-9265 [Dennis Pereca/Janey Street] [ASC] (10/6/84 BC-68)

SAY I AM (WHAT I AM) Tommy James And The Shondells—Roulette 4695 [Barbara Tomsco/George Tomsco] [BMI] (7/30/66 BCR-15)

SAY IT AGAIN Santana—Columbia 04758 [Val Garay/Steve Goldstein/Anthony La Peau] [BMI] (2/23/85 BC-40)

SAY IT AGAIN Jermaine Stewart—Arista 1-9636 [Carol Davis/Bunny Sigler] [BMI] (3/19/88 BC-27)

SAY IT ISN'T SO Teddi King—RCA Victor 47-6866 [Irving Berlin] [ASC] (5/6/57 B-98)

SAY IT ISN'T SO Daryl Hall & John Oates—RCA Victor 13654 [Daryl Hall] [BMI] (10/29/83 BC-2)

SAY IT LOUD - I'M BLACK AND I'M PROUD (PART 1) James Brown—King 6187 [James Brown/Alfred James Ellis*] [BMI] (9/7/68 BCR-9)

SAY IT, SAY IT E.G. Daily—A&M 2825 [Stephen Bray/Toni Colandreo/E.G. Daily] [ASC] (4/26/86 BC-70)

SAY IT'S GONNA RAIN Will To Power—Epic 07908 [Bob Rosenberg] [BMI] (6/18/88 BC-49)

SAY MAN Bo Diddley—Checker 931 [Ellas McDaniel] [BMI] (9/12/59 BCR-20)

SAY MAN BACK AGAIN Bo Diddley—Checker 936 [Ellas McDaniel] [BMI] (11/30/59 CR-83)

SAY MAYBE Neil Diamond—Columbia 10945 [Neil Diamond] [SE] (5/19/79 BCR-55)

SAY SAY SAY Paul McCartney and Michael Jackson—Columbia 04168 [Michael Jackson/Paul McCartney] [BMI] (10/15/83 BC-1)

SAY SOMETHING FUNNY Patty Duke—United Artists 915 [Lor Crane/Bernice Ross] [BMI] (10/2/65 BCR-22)

SAY THE WORDS I LOVE TO HEAR Les Paul and Mary Ford—Capitol 3389 [Jesse Stone] [BMI] (3/30/56 R-73)

SAY WHAT Jesse Winchester—Bearsville 49711 [Jesse Winchester] [ASC] (4/18/81 BCR-32)

SAY WONDERFUL THINGS *Ronnie Carroll—Phillips 40110 [Phil Green/Norman Newell] [BMI] (5/25/63 BCtRt-64)*

SAY WONDERFUL THINGS *Patti Page—Columbia 42791 [Phil Green/Norman Newell] [BMI] (6/1/63 BCtRt-64)*

SAY YEAH *Ollie Shepard—Gee 1044 [Wayne Handy] [BMI] (11/4/57 Rt-68)*

SAY YEAH *Wayne Handy—Renown 102 [Wayne Handy] [BMI] (11/4/57 Rt-45)*

SAY YEAH *The Southerners—Columbia 41052 [Wayne Handy] [BMI] (11/18/57 Rt-45)*

SAY YEAH *Sammy Salvo—RCA Victor 47-7097 [Wayne Handy] [BMI] (12/2/57 Rt-45)*

SAY YOU Ronnie Dove—Diamond 167 [Johnnie B. Hicks] [BMI] (7/18/64 BCR-29)

SAY YOU LOVE ME The Impressions—Curtom 1946 [Curtis Mayfield] [BMI] (10/18/69 BCR-58)

SAY YOU LOVE ME D. J. Rogers—RCA Victor 10568 [D.J. Rogers] [ASC] (7/3/76 B-98)

SAY YOU LOVE ME Fleetwood Mac—Reprise 1356 [Christine McVie] [BMI] (7/3/76 BCR-11)

SAY YOU REALLY WANT ME Kim Wilde—MCA 53130 [Richard Rudolph/Danny Sembello/Donnell Spencer] [BMI] (7/18/87 BC-44)

SAY YOU, SAY ME Lionel Richie—Motown 1819 [Lionel Richie] [ASC] (11/9/85 BC-1)

SAY YOU WILL Foreigner—Atlantic 89169 [Lou Gramm/Michael Leslie Jones] [ASC] (12/5/87 BC-6)

SAY YOU'LL BE MINE Christopher Cross—Warner Bros. 49705 [Christopher Cross] [ASC] (3/28/81 BCR-20)

SAY YOU'LL STAY UNTIL TOMORROW Tom Jones—Epic 50308 [Roger Greenaway/Barry Mason] [BMI] (12/25/76 BCR-13)

(SAY) YOU'RE MY GIRL Roy Orbison—Monument 891 [William Dees/Roy Orbison] [BMI] (7/10/65 BCR-39)

SAY YOU'RE WRONG Julian Lennon—Atlantic 89567 [Julian Lennon] [ASC] (4/20/85 BC-21)

SAYIN' SORRY (DON'T MAKE IT RIGHT) Denise Lopez—Vendetta 7200 [David Bowler/Eric Li] [BMI] (6/11/88 BC-31)

SAYONARA *Eddie Fisher—RCA Victor 47-7051 [Irving Berlin] [ASC] (10/26/57 CRt-56)*

SAYONARA *Gordon MacRae—Capitol 3816 [Irving Berlin] [ASC] (11/11/57 Rt-79)*

SAYONARA *Pat Kirby—Decca 30464 [Irving Berlin] [ASC] (11/11/57 Rt-79)*

SCANDAL RCR—Radio 711 [Donna Rhodes/Perry Rhodes/Sandra Rhodes] [BMI] (4/5/80 B-94)

SCANDINAVIAN SHUFFLE The Swe-Danes—Warner Bros. 5144 [Svend Asmussen] [ASC] (3/14/60 R-80) [I]

—SCAPRICCIATIELLO see: DO YOU LOVE ME LIKE YOU KISS ME

—SCAPRICCIATIELLO see: INFATUATION

SCARBOROUGH FAIR (/CANTICLE) *Simon & Garfunkel—Columbia 44465 [Art Garfunkel/Paul Simon] [BMI] (3/2/68 BCR-11)*

SCARBOROUGH FAIR *Sergio Mendes & Brasil '66—A&M 986 [Art Garfunkel/Paul Simon] [BMI] (11/16/68 BCR-14)*

SCARLET FEVER Kenny Rogers—Liberty 1503 [Mike Dekle] [ASC] (8/20/83 B-94)

SCARLET RIBBONS (FOR HER HAIR) *The Browns—RCA Victor 47-7614 [Evelyn Danzig/Jack Segal] [ASC] (10/26/59 BCRt-10)*

SCARLET RIBBONS (FOR HER HAIR) *Enoch Light & The Light Brigade—Grand Award 1035 [Evelyn Danzig/Jack Segal] [ASC] (10/26/59 Rt-33)*

SCARLETT O'HARA *Lawrence Welk And His Orchestra—Dot 16488 [Jerry Lordan] [BMI] (6/29/63 BCtR-79) [IM]*

SCARLET O'HARA *Bobby Gregg—Epic 9601 [Jerry Lordan] [BMI] (7/6/63 Ct-100) [IM]*

THE SCAVENGER Dick Dale And The Del-Tones—Capitol 5048 [Paul Nuckles/Gary S. Paxton] [BMI] (10/19/63 BCR-87)

SCENE OF THE CRIME Dinah Shore—RCA Victor 47-7349 [Robert Allen/Al Stillman] [ASC] (10/11/58 CR-41)

SCHEMER-DREAMER Steve Walsh—Kirschner 4287 [Steve Walsh] (Med) [BMI] (4/26/80 R-100)

SCHOOL BOY CRUSH AWB—Atlantic 3304 [Roger Ball/Malcolm Duncan/Steve Ferrone/Alan Gorrie/Onnie McIntyre/Hamish Stuart] [ASC] (11/15/75 BCR-31)

SCHOOL DAY *Chuck Berry—Chess 1653 [Chuck Berry] [BMI] (4/6/57 BCRt-3)*

SCHOOL DAY (RING! RING! GOES THE BELL) *"Big" Tiny Little—Brunswick 55007 [Chuck Berry] [BMI] (5/4/57 Rt-3)*

SCHOOL IS IN Gary (U.S.) Bonds—Legrand 1012 [Gary Anderson/Gene Barge] [BMI] (10/16/61 BCR-28)

SCHOOL IS OUT Gary (U.S.) Bonds—Legrand 1009 [Gary Anderson/Gene Barge] [BMI] (7/17/61 BCR-2)

SCHOOL OF LIFE Tommy Tate—KoKo 2112 [Mickey Gregory/Tommy Tate] [BMI] (6/3/72 CR-68)

SCHOOL TEACHER Kenny Rogers And The First Edition—Reprise 1069 [Larry Cansler/Michael Murphey] [BMI] (4/1/72 B-91)

SCHOOL'S BACK Philadelphia—Warner Bros. 8470 [Don Cugini/Andrew DiTaranto] [BMI] (10/15/77 C-99)

SCHOOL'S OUT *Alice Cooper—Warner Bros. 7596 [Michael Bruce/Glen Buxton*/Alice Cooper/Dennis Dunaway*/Neal Smith*] [BMI] (5/27/72 BCR-6)*

SCHOOL'S OUT *Krokus—Arista 1-9468 [Michael Bruce/Glen Buxton*/Alice Cooper/Dennis Dunaway*/Neal Smith*] [BMI] (6/7/86 BC-66)*

SCHUBERT'S SERENADE Ray Conniff & His Orch. & Chorus—Columbia 41242 [Franz Schubert] [NA] (10/20/58 R-94) [I]

SCHWEIZER KANTON POLKA Will Glahe And His Orchestra—London 1755 [Fred Oldörp/Eddi Rothé] [BMI] (10/21/57 R-71) [F]

SCIENTIFIC LOVE Midnight Star—Solar 69659 [Vincent Calloway/Kenneth Gant/Melvin Gentry/Belinda Lipscomb/Bo Watson] [BMI] (3/2/85 BC-80)

SCORPIO Dennis Coffey And The Detroit Guitar Band—Sussex 226 [Dennis Coffey] [BMI] (10/30/71 BCR-4) [IWM]

SCOTCH AND SODA *The Kingston Trio—Capitol 4740 [Dave Guard] [BMI] (4/9/62 BCR-81)*

SCOTCH AND SODA *The Kingston Trio—Tetragrammaton 1526 [Dave Guard] [BMI] (4/26/69 R-87)*

SCOTCH ON THE ROCKS The Band Of The Black Watch—Private Stock 45,055 [Bill Bates] [BMI] (1/31/76 BCR-75) [I]

A SCOTTISH SOLDIER (GREEN HILLS OF TYROL) Andy Stewart—Warwick 627 [Andy Stewart] [BMI] (4/3/61 BCR-69)

SCRATCH The Crusaders—Blue Thumb 249 [Wayne Henderson] [BMI] (4/27/74 BCR-72) [I]

SCRATCH MY BACK (AND MUMBLE IN MY EAR) Clarence Carter—Atlantic 2842 [Earl Cage/Raymond Moore/Marcell Strong] [BMI] (12/18/71 CR-95)

SCRATCHY Travis Wammack—ARA 204 [Gene Chrisman/Prentiss McPhail/Travis Wammack] [BMI] (10/17/64 BCR-69) [I]

SCREAMING NIGHT HOG Steppenwolf—Dunhill 4248 [John Kay] [BMI] (8/15/70 BCR-38)

THE SCREAMS OF PASSION The Family—Paisley Park 7-28953 [Prince] [ASC] (9/28/85 BC-63)

SE LA Lionel Richie—Motown 1883 [Greg Phillinganes/Lionel Richie] [ASC] (3/28/87 BC-20)

SEA CRUISE *Frankie Ford—Ace 554 [Huey P. Smith] [BMI] (2/7/59 BCR-12)*

SEA CRUISE *Johnny Rivers—United Artists 50778 [Huey P. Smith] [BMI] (5/1/71 BCR-74)*

SEA CRUISE *John Fogerty—Asylum 45291 [Huey P. Smith] (TSW) [BMI] (12/6/75 R-84)*

SEA OF HEARTBREAK *Don Gibson—RCA Victor 47-7890 [Hal David/Paul Hampton] [ASC] (6/5/61 BCR-16)*

SEA OF HEARTBREAK *Poco—MCA 52001 [Hal David/Paul Hampton] [ASC] (3/20/82 C-95)*

SEA OF LOVE *Phil Phillips with The Twilights—Mercury 71465 [Phil Baptiste/George Khoury] [BMI] (6/27/59 BCR-2)*

SEA OF LOVE *Del Shannon—Network 47951 [Phil Baptiste/George Khoury] [BMI] (12/5/81 BCR-33)*

SEA OF LOVE *The Honeydrippers—Es Paranza 7-99701 [Phil Baptiste/George Khoury] [BMI] (10/13/84 BC-3)*

SEA SHELL Strawberry Alarm Clock—Uni 55093 [John S. Carter/Tim Gilbert] [ASC] (11/30/68 CR-97)

SEAL OUR FATE Gloria Estefan—Epic 73769 [Gloria Estefan] [BMI] (4/20/91 BC-40)

SEALED WITH A KISS *Brian Hyland—ABC-Paramount 10336 [Gary Geld/Peter Udell] [ASC] (6/9/62 BCR-3)*

SEALED WITH A KISS *Gary Lewis And The Playboys—Liberty 56037 [Gary Geld/Peter Udell] [ASC] (6/15/68 BCR-8)*

SEALED WITH A KISS *The Toys—Musicor 1319 [Gary Geld/Peter Udell] [ASC] (7/6/68 C-93)*

SEALED WITH A KISS *Bobby Vinton—Epic 10861 [Gary Geld/Peter Udell] [ASC] (6/3/72 BCR-14)*

SEARCH Dean Reed—Capitol 4121 [Dean Reed] [BMI] (3/2/59 B-96)

THE SEARCH IS OVER Survivor—Scotti Brothers 04871 [Jim Peterik/Frankie Sullivan] [ASC] (4/20/85 BC-4)

SEARCHIN' *The Coasters—Atco 6087 [Jerry Leiber/Mike Stoller] [BMI] (5/13/57 BCR-5)*

SEARCHING *Jack Eubanks And The Sound Of The South—Monument 451 [Jerry Leiber/Mike Stoller] [BMI] (11/27/61 BCR-69) [IWM]*

SEARCHIN' *Ace Cannon—Hi 2074 [Jerry Leiber/Mike Stoller] [BMI] (3/7/64 BCR-79) [IWM]*

SEARCHIN' *Johnny Rivers—United Artists XW226-W [Jerry Leiber/Mike Stoller] (Med) [BMI] (7/14/73 R-75)*

SEARCHIN' *Jim Croce—Lifesong 45001 [Jerry Leiber/Mike Stoller] (Med) [BMI] (1/3/76 BCR-56)*

SEARCHIN' Santana—Columbia 18 02519 [Alex Ligertwood/Alan Pasqua/Carlos Santana/Chris Solberg] [BMI] (9/19/81 R-83)

SEARCHING The Hilltoppers—Dot 15415 [Billy Vaughn/Randy Wood] [ASC] (10/1/55 BCR-43)

SEARCHING Change—Warner/RFC 49512 [Mauro Malavasi/Paul Slade] [ASC] (8/23/80 R-98)

SEARCHING FOR A THRILL Starbuck—United Artists 1245 [Bruce Blackman/James E. Cobb] [ASC] (9/23/78 BCR-45)

SEARCHING FOR MY LOVE Bobby Moore & The Rhythm Aces—Checker 1129 [Bobby Moore] [BMI] (4/9/66 BCR-20)

THE SEARCHING IS OVER Joe Henderson—Todd 1079 [Joe Lee Henderson/Don Schroeder] [BMI] (11/24/62 B-94)

SEASIDE WOMAN Suzy And The Red Stripes—Epic 50403 [Linda McCartney] [ASC] (6/11/77 BCR-58)

SEASON OF THE WITCH, PT. 1 Vanilla Fudge—Atco 6632 [Donovan Leitch] [BMI] (12/7/68 BCR-65)

SEASONS Grace Slick—RCA Victor 11939 [Grace Slick] [BMI] (4/19/80 B-95)

SEASONS Charles Fox—Handshake 5307 [Charles Fox/Ed Newmark] [BMI] (12/27/80 BCR-75) [I]

SEASONS CHANGE Exposé—Arista 1-9640 [Lewis Martinée] [ASC] (11/28/87 BC-1)

SEASONS IN THE SUN Terry Jacks—Bell 45,432 [Jacques Brel/Rod McKuen] [BMI] (1/5/74 BCR-1)

SEASONS OF THE HEART John Denver—RCA 13270 [John Denver] [ASC] (7/31/82 B-78)

SEATTLE Perry Como—RCA Victor 47-9722 [Jack Keller/Hugo Montenegro/Ernie Sheldon] [ASC] (4/12/69 BCR-36)

SECOND AVENUE *Tim Moore—A Small Record Co. 0601/Asylum 45208 [Tim Moore] [NA] (7/20/74 BCR-58)*

SECOND AVENUE *Garfunkel—Columbia 10020 [Tim Moore] [NA] (9/7/74 BCR-34)*

SECOND AVENUE *Tim Moore—Asylum 45427 [Tim Moore] [NA] (12/10/77 CR-83)*

SECOND CHANCE Thirty Eight Special—A&M 1273 [Max Carl/Jeff Carlisi/Cal Curtis] [BMI] (2/4/89 BC-6)

SECOND CHANCE Tyler Collins—RCA 2639 [Wardell Potts/Melissa Ritter] [ASC] (9/1/90 BC-47)

SECOND FIDDLE Kay Starr—RCA Victor 47-6541 [James Cavanaugh/John Redmond/Irving Taylor/Frank Weldon] [ASC] (6/1/56 BCR-30)

SECOND FIDDLE GIRL Barbara Lynn—Jamie 1233 [Barbara Lynn] [BMI] (9/15/62 BCR-63)

SECOND HAND LOVE Connie Francis—MGM 13074 [Hank Hunter/Phil Spector] [BMI] (4/30/62 BCR-6)

SECOND HAND ROSE Barbra Streisand—Columbia 43469 [Grant Clarke/James Hanley] [ASC] (12/18/65 BCR-29)

SECOND HONEYMOON Johnny Cash—Columbia 41707 [Autry Inman] [BMI] (7/4/60 BC-79)

SECOND NATURE Dan Hartman—MCA 52519 [Dan Hartman/Charles E. Kaufman] [BMI] (2/9/85 BC-38)

THE SECOND TIME AROUND Frank Sinatra—Reprise 20,001 [Sammy Cahn/Jimmy Van Heusen] [ASC] (2/20/61 BCR-34)

THE SECOND TIME AROUND Shalamar—Solar 11709 [William Shelby/Leon Sylvers] [ASC] (12/8/79 BCR-8)

SECRET *Gordon MacRae—Capitol 4033 [Joe Lubin/Irving Roth] [BMI] (9/8/58 BCtRt-17)*

SECRET *The Gainors—Cameo 151 [Joe Lubin/Irving Roth] [BMI] (10/11/58 CtRt-17)*

THE SECRET Clint Ballard Jr.—Guyden 2047 [B.L. Porter] [BMI] (1/23/61 R-85)

SECRET Orchestral Manoeuvres In The Dark—A&M 2794 [Paul Humphreys] [ASC] (12/14/85 BC-63)

SECRET Heart—Capitol 44614 [Franne Golde/Bruce Roberts] [BMI] (1/26/91 BC-41)

SECRET AGENT MAN *The Ventures—Dolton 316 [Steve Barri/P.F. Sloan] [ASC] (2/26/66 BCR-54) [IWM]*

SECRET AGENT MAN *Johnny Rivers—Imperial 66159 [Steve Barri/P.F. Sloan] [ASC] (3/12/66 BCR-3)*

THE SECRET GARDEN (SWEET SEDUCTION SUITE) Quincy Jones featuring Al B. Sure!, James Ingram, El DeBarge & Barry White—Qwest 19992 [El DeBarge/Siedah Garrett/Quincy Jones/Rod Temperton] [ASC] (3/10/90 BC-30)

SECRET JOURNEY The Police—A&M 2408 [Sting] [BMI] (4/10/82 BCR-46)

SECRET LOVE *Doris Day—Columbia 40108 [Sammy Fain/Paul Francis Webster] [ASC] (5/29/54 B-PRE)*

SECRET LOVE *Jimmy Ricks—Felsted 8560 [Sammy Fain/Paul Francis Webster] [ASC] (3/21/59 C-82)*

SECRET LOVE *Richard "Groove" Holmes—Pacific Jazz 88130 [Sammy Fain] [ASC] (10/1/66 B-99) [IM]*

SECRET LOVE *Billy Stewart—Chess 1978 [Sammy Fain/Paul Francis Webster] [ASC] (10/15/66 BCR-29)*

SECRET LOVE *Freddy Fender—ABC/Dot 17585 [Sammy Fain/Paul Francis Webster] [ASC] (10/18/75 BCR-20)*

SECRET LOVERS Atlantic Starr—A&M 2788 [David E. Lewis/Wayne I. Lewis] [ASC] (12/28/85 BC-3)

SECRET OF LOVE Elton Anderson With Sid Lawrence Combo—Mercury 71542 [Eddie Shuler/William Willdridge] [BMI] (1/25/60 B-88)

THE SECRET OF MY SUCCESS Night Ranger—Camel/MCA 53013 [Jack Blades/David Foster/Tom Keane/Mike Landau] [BMI] (3/21/87 BC-60)

SECRET RENDEZVOUS Karyn White—Warner Bros. 27863 [Kenneth Edmonds/Antonio Reid/Daryl Simmons] [BMI] (5/27/89 BC-6)

SECRET SEPARATION The Fixx—MCA 52832 [Dan Brown/Cy Curnin/Peter John Greenall/Jeannette Obstoj/Jamie West-Oram/Adam Woods] [ASC] (5/24/86 BC-19)

SECRETARY Betty Wright—Alston 4622 [Willie Clarke/Clarence Reid] [BMI] (6/29/74 BCR-48)

SECRETLY *Jimmie Rodgers—Roulette 4070 [Luigi Creatore/Al Hoffman/Dick Manning/Hugo Peretti] [ASC] (4/28/58 BCR-2)*

SECRETLY *The Lettermen—Capitol 5499 [Luigi Creatore/Al Hoffman/Dick Manning/Hugo Peretti] [ASC] (9/25/65 BCR-56)*

SECRETS Sutherland Brothers & Quiver—Columbia 10460 [Iain Sutherland] [BMI] (1/8/77 C-97)

SECRETS Mac Davis—Casablanca 2336 [Sam Lorber/Mike Noble/Jeff Silbar] [ASC] (7/11/81 BC-76)

SECURITY *Otis Redding—Volt 117 [Otis Redding] [BMI] (5/23/64 B-97)*

SECURITY *Etta James—Cadet 5594 [Otis Redding] [BMI] (3/2/68 BCR-32)*

SEDUCED Leon Redbone—Emerald City 7326 [Gary Tigerman] [BMI] (4/11/81 BC-72)

THE SEDUCTION (LOVE THEME) The James Last Band—Polydor 2071 [Giorgio Moroder] [BMI] (3/22/80 BCR-26) [I]

SEE The Rascals—Atlantic 2634 [Felix Cavaliere] [ASC] (5/17/69 BCR-11)

SEE ME, FEEL ME *The Who—Decca 32729 [Pete Townshend] [BMI] (9/19/70 BCR-8)*

SEE ME, FEEL ME *The New Seekers—MGM/Verve 10709 [Pete Townshend] (Med) [BMI] (2/17/73 BCR-21)*

SEE RUBY FALL Johnny Cash—Columbia 45020 [Johnny Cash/Roy Orbison] (TSW) [ASC] (11/29/69 BCR-37)

SEE SAW *The Moonglows—Chess 1629 [Billy Davis/Harvey Fuqua/Charles Sutton] [BMI] (9/1/56 BCRt-25)*

SEE SAW *Don Cornell—Coral 61721 [Billy Davis/Harvey Fuqua/Charles Sutton] [BMI] (10/13/56 BRt-57)*

SEESAW *Don Covay & The Goodtimers—Atlantic 2301 [Don Covay/Steve Cropper] [BMI] (10/23/65 BCR-40)*

SEE SAW *Aretha Franklin—Atlantic 2574 [Don Covay/Steve Cropper] [BMI] (11/16/68 BCR-11)*

C C RIDER *Chuck Willis—Atlantic 1130 [Ma Rainey/Traditional/Chuck Willis] [BMI] (4/20/57 BCR-12)*

SEE SEE RIDER *LaVern Baker—Atlantic 2167 [Ma Rainey/Traditional] [BMI] (12/1/62 BCR-34)*

C.C. RIDER *Bobby Powell—Whit 714 [Ma Rainey/Traditional] [BMI] (11/13/65 BCR-38)*

C. C. RIDER *Mitch Ryder And The Detroit Wheels—New Voice 806 [Ma Rainey/Traditional] (Med) [BMI] (12/11/65 BCR-10)*

SEE SEE RIDER *Eric Burdon And The Animals—MGM 13582 [Ma Rainey/Traditional] [BMI] (9/10/66 BCR-10)*

SEE THE FUNNY LITTLE CLOWN Bobby Goldsboro—United Artists 672 [Bobby Goldsboro] [BMI] (1/11/64 BCR-9)

SEE THE LIGHT The Flame—Brother 3500 [Blondie Chaplin/Edries Fataar/Rikki Fataar/Steve Fataar] [BMI] (11/7/70 BC-95)

SEE THE LIGHTS Simple Minds—A&M 1553 [Charles Burchill/Jim Kerr] [ASC] (5/11/91 BC-40)

SEE WHAT LOVE CAN DO Eric Clapton—Duck/Warner 28986 [Jerry Lynn Williams] [BMI] (6/29/85 B-89)

SEE YOU AT THE "GO-GO" Dobie Gray—Charger 107 [Billy Page] [BMI] (4/3/65 BCR-56)

SEE YOU IN SEPTEMBER *The Tempos—Climax 102 [Sherman Edwards/Sid Wayne] [ASC] (6/29/59 BCR-22)*

SEE YOU IN SEPTEMBER *The Happenings—B.T. Puppy 520 [Sherman Edwards/Sid Wayne] [ASC] (7/9/66 BCR-1)*

SEE YOU LATER ALLIGATOR Bill Haley And His Comets—Decca 29791 [Robert Guidry] [BMI] (1/13/56 BCR-6)

SEE YOU WHEN I GIT THERE Lou Rawls—Philadelphia Int'l 3623 [Kenneth Gamble/Leon Huff] [BMI] (6/11/77 BCR-55)

SEEIN' IS BELIEVIN' Eddie Hodges—Columbia 42649 [Bodie Chandler/Edward McKendry] [BMI] (12/22/62 R-97)

SEEIN' THE RIGHT LOVE GO WRONG Jack Jones—Kapp 672 [Joey Brooks/Aaron Schroeder] [BMI] (6/5/65 BCR-41)

SEEING IS BELIEVING Mike + The Mechanics—Atlantic 88921 [Brian A. Robertson/Mike Rutherford] [BMI] (4/22/89 BC-53)

THE SEEKER The Who—Decca 32670 [Pete Townshend] [BMI] (4/11/70 BCR-30)

THE SEEKER Dolly Parton—RCA Victor 10310 [Dolly Parton] [BMI] (7/26/75 CR-89)

SEEMS LIKE I CAN'T LIVE WITH YOU, BUT I CAN'T LIVE WITHOUT YOU The Guess Who—RCA Victor 10075 [Burton Cummings/Domenic Troiano] [BMI] (5/10/75 C-88)

SEEMS LIKE I GOTTA DO WRONG The Whispers—Soul Clock 1004 [Dee Ervin/Lynne Farr/Jerry Williams Jr.*] [BMI] (9/12/70 BCR-38)

SELF CONTROL Laura Branigan—Atlantic 89676
[Giancarlo Bigazzi/Steve Piccolo/Raffaele Riefoli] [BMI] (4/14/84 BC-4)

SELFISH ONE Jackie Ross—Chess 1903
[Wilfred McKinley/Carl William Smith] [BMI] (7/25/64 BCR-9)

SEMPRE AMORE Don Cornell—Signature 12002 [Buddy Greco] [ASC] (8/3/59 R-80)

SEND A LITTLE LOVE MY WAY Anne Murray—Capitol 3648
[Hal David/Henry Mancini] [ASC] (8/4/73 BCR-72)

SEND FOR ME Nat "King" Cole And The Four Knights—Capitol 3737
[Ollie Jones] [BMI] (6/17/57 BCR-6)

SEND FOR ME Atlantic Starr—A&M 2340 [Sam Dees/Ron Kersey] [BMI] (7/25/81 R-92)

SEND FOR ME (IF YOU NEED SOME LOVIN) Barbara George—Sue 766
[Barbara George] [BMI] (9/8/62 B-96)

SEND HER MY LOVE Journey—Columbia 04151
[Jonathan Cain/Steve Perry] [ASC] (9/24/83 BC-23)

SEND IN THE CLOWNS *Judy Collins—Elektra 45253*
[Stephen Sondheim] [ASC] (6/21/75 BCR-36)

SEND IN THE CLOWNS *Judy Collins—Elektra 45253*
[Stephen Sondheim] [ASC] (9/24/77 BCR-17)

SEND IT Ashford & Simpson—Warner Bros. 8453
[Nick Ashford/Valerie Simpson] [ASC] (11/26/77 R-81)

SEND ME AN ANGEL *Real Life—Curb/MCA 52287*
[David Sterry/Richard Zatorski] [BMI] (11/12/83 BC-22)

SEND ME AN ANGEL '89 *Real Life—Curb 10531*
[David Sterry/Richard Zatorski] [BMI] (5/13/89 BC-20)

SEND ME AN ANGEL Scorpions—Mercury 868 956
[Klaus Meine/Rudolf Schenker] [ASC] (11/9/91 BC-30)

SEND ME SOME LOVIN' (PEEPIN' AND HIDIN') *Little Richard—Specialty 598*
[John Marascalco/Leo Price] [BMI] (4/6/57 B-54)

SEND ME SOME LOVIN' *Sam Cooke—RCA Victor 47-8129*
[John Marascalco/Leo Price] [BMI] (1/19/63 BCR-13)

SEND ME SOME MONEY Les Paul and Mary Ford—Capitol 3389
[Zeke Clements] [BMI] (3/30/56 R-54)

SEND ME THE PILLOW YOU DREAM ON *Hank Locklin—RCA Victor 47-7127*
[Hank Locklin] [BMI] (6/2/58 B-77)

SEND ME THE PILLOW YOU DREAM ON
The Browns Featuring Jim Edward Brown—RCA Victor 47-7804
[Hank Locklin] [BMI] (11/7/60 BCR-50)

SEND ME THE PILLOW YOU DREAM ON *Johnny Tillotson—Cadence 1424*
[Hank Locklin] [BMI] (8/11/62 BCR-10)

SEND ME THE PILLOW YOU DREAM ON *Dean Martin—Reprise 0344*
[Hank Locklin] [BMI] (2/20/65 BCR-20)

SEND MY BABY BACK Freddie Hughes—Wand 1182
[Lonnie Hewitt/Ernest Marbray] [BMI] (7/6/68 BCR-85)

SEND ONE YOUR LOVE Stevie Wonder—Tamla 54303
[Stevie Wonder] [ASC] (11/3/79 BCR-4)

SENDIN' ALL MY LOVE The Jets—MCA 53380
[Stephen Bray/Linda Mallah] [ASC] (8/6/88 BC-80)

SENDING ALL MY LOVE Linear—Atlantic 87961
[Tolga Katas/Charlie Pennachio] [BMI] (2/17/90 BC-5)

THE SENSITIVE KIND Santana—Columbia 02178 [J.J. Cale] [BMI] (8/1/81 BCR-56)

SENSITIVITY Ralph Tresvant—MCA 53932
[James Samuel Harris/Terry Lewis] [ASC] (11/3/90 BC-3)

SENTIMENTAL BABY Frank Sinatra—Capitol 4546
[Alan Bergman/Marilyn Bergman/Lew Spence] [ASC] (4/3/61 R-48)

SENTIMENTAL LADY Bob Welch—Capitol 4479 [Bob Welch] [ASC] (10/8/77 BCR-4)

SENTIMENTAL STREET Night Ranger—Camel/MCA 52591
[Jack Blades/Alan Fitzgerald] [BMI] (5/25/85 BC-8)

SENZA MAMMA (WITH NO ONE) Connie Francis—MGM 12964
[Luigi Donadio/Connie Francis] [ASC] (11/7/60 BR-87) [FDE]

SEPARATE LIVES Phil Collins and Marilyn Martin—Atlantic 89498
[Stephen Bishop] [ASC] (10/5/85 BC-1)

SEPARATE TABLES *Eydie Gorme—ABC-Paramount 9971*
[Harold Adamson/Harry Warren] [ASC] (11/17/58 Rt-83)

SEPARATE TABLES *Vic Damone—Columbia 41287*
[Harold Adamson/Harry Warren] [ASC] (1/5/59 Rt-83)

SEPARATE WAYS Sarah Vaughan—Mercury 71433
[Vince Corso/Clyde Otis] [BMI] (5/4/59 BC-96)

SEPARATE WAYS Elvis Presley—RCA Victor 74-0815
[Richard Mainegra/Red West] [BMI] (11/25/72 BCR-15)

SEPARATE WAYS (WORLDS APART) Journey—Columbia 03513
[Jonathan Cain/Steve Perry] [ASC] (2/5/83 BC-8)

SEPTEMBER Earth, Wind & Fire—ARC 10854
[Albert Philip McKay/Maurice White/Allee Willis] [ASC] (11/18/78 BCR-4)

SEPTEMBER IN THE RAIN Dinah Washington—Mercury 71876
[Al Dubin/Harry Warren] [ASC] (10/9/61 BCR-16)

SEPTEMBER MORN' Neil Diamond—Columbia 11175
[Gilbert Bécaud/Neil Diamond] [SE] (12/22/79 BCR-7)

SEPTEMBER SONG *Jimmy Durante—Warner Bros. 5382*
[Maxwell Anderson/Kurt Weill] [ASC] (9/7/63 BCR-47)

SEPTEMBER SONG *Roy Clark—Dot 17299*
[Maxwell Anderson/Kurt Weill] [ASC] (9/20/69 CR-54)

SEQUEL Harry Chapin—Boardwalk 5700 [Harry Chapin] [ASC] (11/1/80 BCR-23)

SERENADE *Mario Lanza—RCA Victor 49-4218*
[Dorothy Donnelly/Sigmund Romberg] [ASC] (4/13/56 Rt-75)

SERENADE
Eddie Calvert, his Trumpet and the Norris Paramor Orchestra—Capitol 3407
[Sigmund Romberg] [ASC] (4/20/56 Rt-75) [IM]

SERENADE *Slim Whitman—Imperial 8305*
[Nicholas Brodszky/Sammy Cahn] [ASC] (4/20/56 Rt-75)

SERENADE *Dick Lee—Vik 0200 [Nicholas Brodszky/Sammy Cahn] [ASC] (4/27/56 Rt-77)*

SERENADE *Ray Heindorf & His Orchestra with The Mellomen—Columbia 40681*
[Nicholas Brodszky/Sammy Cahn] [ASC] (5/11/56 Rt-82)

SERENADE OF THE BELLS The Four Coins—Epic 9348
[Al Goodhart/Kay Twomey/Al Urbano] [ASC] (1/11/60 R-86)

SERENATA Sarah Vaughan—Roulette 4285
[Leroy Anderson/Mitchell Parish] [ASC] (10/10/60 BCR-72)

SERIOUS Donna Allen—21 Records 99497
[Donna Allen/Emridge Jones/Gary King/Harry J. King/Louis Pace/Reggie White] [BMI] (2/14/87 BC-20)

SERIOUS KINDA GIRL Christopher Max—EMI 50229
[Christopher Max/Nile Rodgers] [BMI] (12/2/89 BC-67)

SERMONETTE Della Reese—Jubilee 5345
[Julian Adderley/Jon Hendricks] [ASC] (1/5/59 B-99)

SERPENTINE FIRE Earth, Wind & Fire—Columbia 10625
[Reggie Burke/Maurice White/Verdine White] [ASC] (10/15/77 BCR-10)

SET ADRIFT ON MEMORY BLISS PM Dawn—Gee Street 866 094
[Attrell Cordes/Gary Kemp] [ASC] (10/19/91 BC-1)

SET ME FREE The Kinks—Reprise 0379 [Ray Davies] [BMI] (6/12/65 BCR-21)

SET ME FREE Utopia—Bearsville 49180
[Roger Powell/Todd Rundgren/Kasim Sulton/John Griffitt Wilcox] [BMI] (2/16/80 BCR-22)

SET THE NIGHT ON FIRE Oak—Mercury 76087
[Jeff Silbar/Van Stephenson] [BMI] (12/13/80 B-71)

SET THE NIGHT TO MUSIC Roberta Flack—Atlantic 87607
[Diane Warren] [ASC] (9/21/91 BC-5)

SET THE WORLD ON FIRE Liar—Bearsville 0328 [David John Taylor] [ASC] (8/19/78 R-89)

SET YOU FREE THIS TIME The Byrds—Columbia 43501
[Gene Clark] [BMI] (2/5/66 BCR-79)

SETTLE DOWN (GOIN' DOWN THAT HIGHWAY) Peter, Paul & Mary—Warner Bros. 5334
[Mike Settle] [BMI] (1/19/63 BCR-56)

7 AND 7 IS Love—Elektra 45605 [Arthur Taylor Lee] [BMI] (7/30/66 BCR-33)

SEVEN BRIDGES ROAD Eagles—Asylum 47100 [Steve Young] [BMI] (12/20/80 BCR-21)

SEVEN DAY FOOL Etta James—Argo 5402
[Billy Davis/Berry Gordy*/Sonny Woods*] [BMI] (10/23/61 BCR-61)

SEVEN DAY WEEKEND Gary (U.S.) Bonds—Legrand 1019
[Doc Pomus/Mort Shuman] [BMI] (6/16/62 BCR-27)

SEVEN DAYS *Dorothy Collins—Coral 61562*
[Willis Carroll/Carmen Taylor] [BMI] (1/13/56 BCtRt-15)

SEVEN DAYS *Clyde McPhatter—Atlantic 1081*
[Willis Carroll/Carmen Taylor] [BMI] (1/20/56 BCtRt-15)

SEVEN DAYS *The Crew-Cuts—Mercury 70782*
[Willis Carroll/Carmen Taylor] [BMI] (1/28/56 BCtRt-15)

SEVEN DAYS *Snooky Lanson—Dot 15445*
[Willis Carroll/Carmen Taylor] [BMI] (2/3/56 Rt-20)

SEVEN ELEVEN *The Gone All Stars—Gone 5016 [Perez Prado] [BMI] (2/8/58 BCRt-31) [I]*

7-11 (MAMBO #5) *Dick Jacobs & His Orchestra—Coral 61951*
[Perez Prado] [BMI] (3/24/58 Rt-84) [I]

SEVEN LETTERS Ben E. King—Atco 6328 [Ben E. King] [BMI] (12/12/64 BCR-45)

(SEVEN LITTLE GIRLS) SITTING IN THE BACK SEAT
Paul Evans and The Curls—Guaranteed 200
[Bob Hilliard/Lee Pockriss] [ASC] (9/7/59 BCR-5)

SEVEN LONELY NIGHTS Four Tops—ABC 12096
[Ralph Bailey/Rudy Clark/Ken Williams] [BMI] (5/24/75 BC-71)

SEVEN MINUTES IN HEAVEN Poni-Tails—ABC-Paramount 9969
[Jack Keller/Noel Sherman] [ASC] (11/29/58 BC-77)

7-ROOMS OF GLOOM Four Tops—Motown 1110
[Lamont Dozier/Brian Holland/Eddie Holland] [BMI] (5/20/67 BCR-9)

777-9311 The Time—Warner Bros. 29952 [Prince] [ASC] (10/9/82 B-88)

7-6-5-4-3-2-1 (BLOW YOUR WHISTLE) Gary Toms Empire—Pickwick Int'l 6504
[Roger Cook] [BMI] (6/7/75 BCR-35)

7:30 GUIDED TOUR The Five Americans—Abnak 126
[Robin Brians] [BMI] (1/13/68 BR-87)

SEVEN WONDERS Fleetwood Mac—Warner Bros. 28317
[Stevie Nicks/Sandy Stewart] [BMI] (6/13/87 BC-19)

SEVEN YEAR ACHE Rosanne Cash—Columbia 11426
[Rosanne Cash] [BMI] (4/11/81 BCR-21)

SEVEN YEARS The Impressions—Curtom 1940
[Curtis Mayfield] [BMI] (4/26/69 BCR-83)

***SEVENTEEN** Boyd Bennett And His Rockets—King 1470*
[Boyd Bennett/Chuck Gorman/John Young] [BMI] (7/4/55 BCtRt-2)*
***SEVENTEEN** Rusty Draper—Mercury 70651*
[Boyd Bennett/Chuck Gorman/John Young] [BMI] (7/4/55 BCtRt-2)*
***SEVENTEEN** The Fontane Sisters with Billy Vaughn's Orchestra—Dot 15386*
[Boyd Bennett/Chuck Gorman/John Young] [BMI] (7/25/55 BCtRt-2)*
***SEVENTEEN** Ella Mae Morse—Capitol 3199*
[Boyd Bennett/Chuck Gorman/John Young] [BMI] (8/15/55 Rt-4)*
***SEVENTEEN** Frankie Ford—Imperial 5735*
[Boyd Bennett/Chuck Gorman/John Young] [BMI] (3/20/61 B-72)*
17 Rick James—Gordy 1730 [Rick James] [ASC] (7/14/84 BC-36)
SEVENTEEN Winger—Atlantic 88958
[Reb Beach/Beau Hill/Kip Winger] [BMI] (2/25/89 BC-26)
SEVENTH SON Johnny Rivers—Imperial 66112 [Willie Dixon] [BMI] (5/29/65 BCR-7)
***SEVENTY SEVEN SUNSET STRIP** The Big Sound of Don Ralke—Warner Bros. 5025*
[Mack David/Jerry Livingston] [ASC] (3/7/59 BCtRt-38) [IWM]
***SEVENTY SEVEN SUNSET STRIP** Frank Ortega Trio—Jubilee 5365*
[Mack David/Jerry Livingston] [ASC] (3/23/59 CtRt-38) [IWM]
***SEVENTY SIX TROMBONES** Billy May and His Orchestra—Capitol 3846*
[Meredith Willson] [ASC] (2/17/58 Rt-36)
SEVENTY SIX TROMBONES
Arthur Godfrey with Norman Leyden & His Orchestra—Columbia 41113
[Meredith Willson] [ASC] (2/17/58 Rt-49)
***SEVENTY SIX TROMBONES** Jimmy McPartland's All-Stars—Epic 9261*
[Meredith Willson] [ASC] (2/17/58 Rt-36)
***SEVENTY SIX TROMBONES** Hugo & Luigi—Roulette 4050*
[Meredith Willson] [ASC] (2/17/58 Rt-36)
***SEVENTY SIX TROMBONES** The Jonah Jones Quartet—Capitol 3893*
[Meredith Willson] [ASC] (2/24/58 Rt-36) [IWM]
***SEVENTY-SIX TROMBONES** Vera Lynn—London 1793*
[Meredith Willson] [ASC] (3/17/58 Rt-36)
***SEVENTY SIX TROMBONES** The King Sisters—Capitol 3933*
[Meredith Willson] [ASC] (3/31/58 Rt-36)
SEX AS A WEAPON Pat Benatar—Chrysalis 42927
[Thomas F. Kelly/Billy Steinberg] [ASC] (11/23/85 BC-27)
SEX (I'M A...) Berlin—Geffen 29747
[John Crawford/David Samuel Diamond/Terri Nunn] [BMI] (3/5/83 BC-57)
SEX SHOOTER Apollonia 6—Warner Bros. 29182 [Prince] [ASC] (10/20/84 B-85)
SEXAPPEAL Georgio—Motown 1882 [Georgio Allentini] [BMI] (2/28/87 BC-58)
SEXCRIME (NINETEEN EIGHTY-FOUR) Eurythmics—RCA 13956
[Annie Lennox/David A. Stewart] [BMI] (11/24/84 B-81)
SEXUAL HEALING Marvin Gaye—Columbia 03302
[Odell Brown/Marvin Gaye/David Ritz*] [ASC] (10/30/82 BC-3)
SEXY MFSB—Philadelphia Int'l 3567
[Kenneth Gamble/Leon Huff] [BMI] (6/7/75 BCR-42) [I]
SEXY EYES Dr. Hook—Capitol 4831
[Robert Mather/Keith Stegall/Chris Waters] [BMI] (2/16/80 BCR-3)
SEXY GIRL Glenn Frey—MCA 52413
[Glenn Frey/Jack Tempchin] [ASC] (6/30/84 BC-20)
SEXY IDA (PART 2) Ike & Tina Turner—United Artists 528
[Tina Turner] [BMI] (11/2/74 BCR-62)
SEXY MAMA The Moments—Stang 5052
[Al Goodman/Harry Ray/Sylvia Robinson] [BMI] (1/5/74 BCR-17)
SEXY, SEXY, SEXY James Brown—Polydor 14194 [James Brown] [BMI] (8/18/73 BCR-46)
SGT. PEPPER'S LONELY HEARTS CLUB BAND The Beatles—Capitol 4612
[John Lennon/Paul McCartney] (Med) [ASC] (9/9/78 BC-71)
***SH-BOOM** The Chords—Cat 104*
[James Edwards/Carl Feaster/Claude Feaster/James C. Keyes/Floyd F. McRae] [BMI] (7/3/54 BCtR-1)
***SH-BOOM** The Crew-Cuts—Mercury 70404*
[James Edwards/Carl Feaster/Claude Feaster/James C. Keyes/Floyd F. McRae] [BMI] (7/3/54 BCtR-1)
***SHA-LA-LA** The Shirelles—Scepter 1267*
[Frances Aycock/Robert Mosely/Robert Napoleon Taylor] [BMI] (3/14/64 BCR-59)*
***SHA LA LA** Manfred Mann—Ascot 2165*
[Frances Aycock/Robert Mosely/Robert Napoleon Taylor] [BMI] (11/7/64 BCR-12)*
SHA-LA-LA (MAKE ME HAPPY) Al Green—Hi 2274 [Al Green] [BMI] (9/28/74 BCR-7)
—SHA NA BOOM BOOM see: HEAVY MAKES YOU HAPPY
SHABBY LITTLE HUT The Reflections—Golden World 19 [Van McCoy] [BMI] (1/2/65 CR-78)
SHACKIN' UP Barbara Mason—Buddah 459 [Jackie Avery] [BMI] (4/19/75 BCR-76)
SHADDAP YOU FACE Joe Dolce—MCA 51053 [Joe Dolce] [ASC] (4/25/81 BCR-24)
SHADES OF GREEN The Flaming Ember—Hot Wax 6907
[Lamont Dozier/Ronald Dunbar/Brian Holland/Eddie Holland] [BMI] (1/17/70 BCR-53)
SHADOW DANCING Andy Gibb—RSO 893
[Andy Gibb/Barry Gibb/Maurice Gibb/Robin Gibb] [BMI] (4/15/78 BCR-1)
SHADOW KNOWS The Coasters—Atco 6126
[Jerry Leiber/Mike Stoller] [BMI] (9/8/58 R-89)
THE SHADOW OF YOUR LOVE The Five Stairsteps & Cubie—Buddah 35
[Ted Daryll] [BMI] (4/20/68 BCR-92)
LOVE THEME FROM "THE SANDPIPER" (THE SHADOW OF YOUR SMILE)
Tony Bennett—Columbia 43431
[Johnny Mandel/Paul Francis Webster] [ASC] (11/13/65 B-95)
***THE SHADOW OF YOUR SMILE** Boots Randolph—Monument 976*
[Johnny Mandel/Paul Francis Webster] [ASC] (12/17/66 BCR-90)
SHADOWS The Five Satins—Ember 1056 [Fred Parris] [BMI] (11/7/59 BC-87)
SHADOWS IN THE MOONLIGHT Anne Murray—Capitol 4716
[Charlie Black/Rory Bourke] [ASC] (5/19/79 BCR-19)
SHADOWS OF LOVE LaVern Baker—Atlantic 2059 [Otis Blackwell] [BMI] (5/23/60 B-83)
SHADOWS OF THE NIGHT Pat Benatar—Chrysalis 2647
[David Leigh Byron] [ASC] (10/16/82 BC-13)
SHADRACK Brook Benton—Mercury 71912 [Robert MacGimsey] [ASC] (1/8/62 BCR-19)
SHADY LADY Shepstone & Dibbens—Buddah 379
[Peter Dibbens/Michael Shepstone] [ASC] (9/15/73 CR-68)
THE SHAG (IS TOTALLY COOL) Billy Graves—Monument 401
[Dick Flood/Fred Foster] [BMI] (1/5/59 BCR-45)
SHAGGY DOG Mickey Lee Lane—Swan 4183
[Bernie Lane/Mickey Lee Lane] [BMI] (10/10/64 BCR-38)
***SHAKE** Sam Cooke—RCA Victor 47-8486 [Sam Cooke] [BMI] (1/9/65 BCR-5)*
***SHAKE** The British Walkers—Cameo 466 [Sam Cooke] [BMI] (4/15/67 CR-83)*
***SHAKE** Otis Redding—Volt 149 [Sam Cooke] [BMI] (5/20/67 BCR-37)*
SHAKE The Shadows Of Knight—Team 520
[Joey Levine/Kris Resnick] [BMI] (10/19/68 BCR-39)
SHAKE The Gap Band—Mercury 74053 [Charles K. Wilson] [BMI] (6/16/79 R-96)
SHAKE Andrew Ridgeley—Columbia 73337
[David Austin/Andrew Ridgeley] [ASC] (5/5/90 BC-68)
***SHAKE A HAND** Mike Pedicin Quintet—Cameo 125 [Joe Morris] [BMI] (1/20/58 BR-71)*
***SHAKE A HAND** LaVern Baker—Atlantic 2048 [Joe Morris] [BMI] (1/30/60 CR-83)*
***SHAKE A HAND** Ruth Brown—Philips 40028 [Joe Morris] [BMI] (6/9/62 BCR-83)*
***SHAKE A HAND** Jackie Wilson And Linda Hopkins—Brunswick 55243*
[Joe Morris] [BMI] (5/25/63 BCR-34)
SHAKE A LEG Sea Level—Capricorn 0272 [Edward R. Hoerner] [BMI] (6/18/77 C-100)
SHAKE A POO POO Chet "Poison" Ivey And His Fabulous Avengers—Tangerine 989
[Chet Ivey] [BMI] (1/18/69 C-100)
***SHAKE A TAIL FEATHER** The Five Du-Tones—One-derful! 4815*
[Otha Hayes/Verlie Rice/Andre Williams] [BMI] (5/18/63 BCR-46)
***SHAKE A TAIL FEATHER** James & Bobby Purify—Bell 669*
[Otha Hayes/Verlie Rice/Andre Williams] [BMI] (4/15/67 BCR-23)
SHAKE AND DANCE WITH ME Con Funk Shun—Mercury 74008
[Michael V. Cooper] [BMI] (7/29/78 BCR-57)
SHAKE AND FINGERPOP Jr. Walker & The All Stars—Soul 35013
[Lawrence Horn/Jr. Walker/Willie Woods] [BMI] (7/31/65 BCR-29)
SHAKE FOR THE SHEIK The Escape Club—Atlantic 88983
[Johnnie Christo/John Holliday/Trevor Steel/Milan Zekavica] [BMI] (12/3/88 BC-26)
SHAKE HANDS (AND COME OUT CRYING) The Newbeats—Hickory 1366
[Doug Kershaw] [BMI] (2/26/66 BCR-62)
SHAKE HANDS AND WALK AWAY CRYIN' Lou Christie—Columbia 44062
[Lou Christie/Twyla Herbert] [BMI] (4/29/67 B-95)
SHAKE HANDS WITH A FOOL June Valli—RCA Victor 47-7149
[Lee Pockriss/Paul Vance] [ASC] (2/10/58 R-84)
SHAKE IT Ian Matthews—Mushroom 7039 [Terence Boylan] [BMI] (11/18/78 BCR-10)
SHAKE IT (LIKE A WHITE GIRL) Jesse Jaymes—Delicious Vinyl 868 214-4
[Harry Wayne Casey/Matt Dike/Rick Finch*/Jesse Eric Itzler] [ASC] (7/6/91 B-74)
SHAKE IT UP The Cars—Elektra 47250 [Ric Ocasek] [ASC] (7/11/81 BCR-3)
SHAKE IT UP Bad Company—Atlantic 88939
[Brian Howe/Terry Thomas] [ASC] (4/22/89 B-82)
SHAKE IT UP TONIGHT Cheryl Lynn—Columbia 02102
[Brenda Sutton/Mike Sutton] [ASC] (8/8/81 BC-68)
SHAKE IT WELL The Dramatics—ABC 12299
[Don Davis/Eddie Robinson] [BMI] (10/1/77 BCR-63)
***SHAKE ME I RATTLE (SQUEEZE ME I CRY)** The Lennon Sisters—Brunswick 55028*
[Hal Hackady/Charles Naylor] [BMI] (9/9/57 R-71)
***SHAKE ME I RATTLE (SQUEEZE ME I CRY)** Marion Worth—Columbia 42640*
[Hal Hackady/Charles Naylor] [BMI] (12/22/62 BCR-32)
SHAKE ME, WAKE ME (WHEN IT'S OVER) Four Tops—Motown 1090
[Lamont Dozier/Brian Holland/Eddie Holland] [BMI] (2/19/66 BCR-15)
SHAKE OFF THE DEMON Brewer And Shipley—Kama Sutra 539
[Michael Brewer/Tom Shipley] [BMI] (2/5/72 B-98)
***SHAKE RATTLE AND ROLL** Bill Haley And His Comets—Decca 29204*
[Jesse Stone] [BMI] (8/7/54 BCR-6)
***SHAKE, RATTLE & ROLL** Arthur Conley—Atco 6494 [Jesse Stone] [BMI] (6/10/67 BCR-27)*
***SHAKE, RATTLE & ROLL** Jive Bunny And The Mastermixers—Music Factory 99140*
[Jesse Stone] (Med) [BMI] (10/28/89 BC-11)
SHAKE! SHAKE! SHAKE! Jackie Wilson—Brunswick 55246
[Bobby Adams/Bobby Stevenson] [BMI] (7/13/63 BCR-33)
(SHAKE, SHAKE, SHAKE) SHAKE YOUR BOOTY K C & The Sunshine Band—TK 1019
[Harry Wayne Casey/Rick Finch] [BMI] (7/3/76 BCR-1)
SHAKE SHAKE SONORA Lord Flea and His Calypsonians—Capitol 3659
[Sam Manning] [NA] (3/2/57 R-44)

SHAKE SHERRY The Contours—Gordy 7012 [Berry Gordy] [ASC] (12/22/62 BCR-37)

SHAKE YOU DOWN Gregory Abbott—Columbia 06191
[Gregory Abbott] [BMI] (10/18/86 BC-1)

SHAKE YOUR BODY (DOWN TO THE GROUND) Jacksons—Epic 50656
[Michael Jackson/Steven Randall Jackson] [BMI] (1/20/79 BCR-3)

SHAKE YOUR GROOVE THING Peaches & Herb—Polydor/MVP 14514
[Dino Fekaris/Freddie Perren] [ASC] (12/9/78 BCR-5)

SHAKE YOUR HIPS Slim Harpo—Excello 2278 [Slim Harpo] [BMI] (7/2/66 CR-91)

SHAKE YOUR LOVE Debbie Gibson—Atlantic 89187
[Debbie Gibson] [ASC] (10/3/87 BC-4)

SHAKE YOUR PANTS Cameo—Chocolate City 3210
[Larry Blackmon] [ASC] (8/30/80 R-90)

SHAKE YOUR RUMP TO THE FUNK Bar-Kays—Mercury 73833
[James Edward Alexander/Charles Leonard Allen/Michael Beard/Larry Dodson/Harvey Henderson/Lloyd Ed Smith/Winston Stewart/Frank Thompson] [BMI] (10/16/76 BCR-23)

SHAKEDOWN Bob Seger—MCA 53094
[Harold Faltermeyer/Keith Forsey/Bob Seger] [ASC] (5/23/87 BC-1)

SHAKEDOWN CRUISE Jay Ferguson—Asylum 46041
[Jay Ferguson] [BMI] (5/5/79 BCR-27)

SHAKER SONG Spyro Gyra—Amherst 730 [Jay Beckenstein] [BMI] (6/17/78 BC-90) [I]

SHAKEY GROUND *The Temptations—Gordy 7142*
[Jeff Bowen/Alphonso Boyd/Eddie Hazel] [BMI] (3/22/75 BCR-26)

SHAKEY GROUND *Phoebe Snow—Columbia 10463*
[Jeff Bowen/Alphonso Boyd/Eddie Hazel] [BMI] (1/22/77 B-70)

SHAKIN' Eddie Money—Columbia 03252
[Ralph Carter/Eddie Money/Elizabeth Myers] [BMI] (10/9/82 BC-62)

SHAKIN' ALL OVER Guess Who?—Scepter 1295 [Johnny Kidd] [ASC] (4/17/65 BCR-13)

SHALOM Eddie Fisher—ABC-Paramount 10264 [Jerry Herman] [ASC] (10/30/61 R-96)

SHAMBALA *Three Dog Night—Dunhill 4352 [Daniel Moore] [BMI] (5/12/73 BCR-1)*

SHAMBALA *B.W. Stevenson—RCA Victor 74-0952*
[Daniel Moore] [BMI] (5/12/73 BCR-66)

SHAME Evelyn "Champagne" King—RCA 11122
[Reuben Cross/John Fitch] [BMI] (5/27/78 BCR-8)

SHAME The Motels—Capitol 5497 [Martha Davis] [BMI] (7/20/85 BC-21)

SHAME ON ME *Bobby Bare—RCA Victor 47-8032*
[Bill Enis/Lawton Williams] [BMI] (7/14/62 BCR-13)

SHAME ON ME *Chuck Jackson—Wand 1166*
[Bill Enis/Lawton Williams] [BMI] (10/14/67 BCR-76)

SHAME ON THE MOON Bob Seger & The Silver Bullet Band—Capitol 5187
[Rodney Crowell] [ASC] (12/18/82 BC-2)

SHAME, SHAME Magic Lanterns—Atlantic 2560
[Keith Colley/Linda Jo Colley/Knox Henderson] [BMI] (10/19/68 BCR-17)

SHAME, SHAME, SHAME Jimmy Reed—Vee-Jay 509
[Jimmy Reed] [BMI] (4/13/63 BCR-52)

SHAME, SHAME, SHAME Shirley (And Company)—Vibration 532
[Sylvia Robinson] [BMI] (1/11/75 BCR-8)

SHANDI Kiss—Casablanca 2282 [Vini Poncia/Paul Stanley] [BMI] (6/21/80 BCR-47)

SHANGHAI BREEZES John Denver—RCA 13071
[John Denver] [ASC] (3/6/82 BCR-25)

SHANGRI LA *The Four Coins—Epic 9213*
[Matt Malneck/Robert Maxwell/Carl Sigman] [ASC] (5/27/57 BCR-12)

SHANGRI-LA *Vic Dana—Dolton 92*
[Matt Malneck/Robert Maxwell/Carl Sigman] [ASC] (3/21/64 BCtR-9)

SHANGRI-LA *Robert Maxwell, His Harp And Orchestra—Decca 25622*
[Matt Malneck/Robert Maxwell] [ASC] (3/21/64 BCtR-9) [IM]

SHANGRI-LA *The Lettermen—Capitol 2643*
[Matt Malneck/Robert Maxwell/Carl Sigman] [ASC] (10/11/69 BCR-51)

SHANGRI-LA Steve Miller Band—Capitol 5407
[Kenny Lee Lewis/Steve Miller] [ASC] (10/6/84 BC-53)

SHANNON Henry Gross—Lifesong 45002 [Henry Gross] [ASC] (2/21/76 BCR-4)

SHAPE I'M IN Johnny Restivo—RCA Victor 47-7559
[Otis Blackwell/Lee Cathy] [BMI] (8/3/59 BCR-49)

SHAPE OF THINGS TO COME Max Frost And The Troopers—Tower 419
[Barry Mann/Cynthia Weil] [BMI] (8/31/68 BCR-16)

SHAPE OF THINGS TO COME Headboys—RSO 1005
[George Boyter/Brian Lewis/Calum Malcolm/Davy Ross] [ASC] (11/10/79 B-67)

SHAPES OF THINGS The Yardbirds—Epic 10006
[Jim McCarty/Keith Relf/Paul Samwell-Smith] [BMI] (3/12/66 BCR-10)

SHARE THE LAND The Guess Who—RCA Victor 74-0388
[Burton Cummings] [BMI] (10/17/70 BCR-5)

SHARE YOUR LOVE WITH ME *Bobby Bland—Duke 377*
[Al Braggs/Deadric Malone] [BMI] (6/13/64 BCR-37)

TO SHARE YOUR LOVE *Fantastic Four—Ric-Tic 130*
[Al Braggs/Deadric Malone] [BMI] (9/23/67 BR-68)

SHARE YOUR LOVE WITH ME *Aretha Franklin—Atlantic 2650*
[Al Braggs/Deadric Malone] [BMI] (7/26/69 BCR-11)

SHARE YOUR LOVE WITH ME *Kenny Rogers—Liberty 1430*
[Al Braggs/Deadric Malone] [BMI] (9/5/81 BCR-14)

SHARING THE LOVE Rufus With Chaka Khan—MCA 51203
[Kevin Murphy] [ASC] (12/5/81 B-91)

SHARING THE NIGHT TOGETHER *Arthur Alexander—Buddah 522*
[Ava Aldridge/Eddie Struzick] [BMI] (5/29/76 C-94)

SHARING THE NIGHT TOGETHER *Lenny LeBlanc—Big Tree 16062*
[Ava Aldridge/Eddie Struzick] [BMI] (6/5/76 C-99)

SHARING THE NIGHT TOGETHER *Dr. Hook—Capitol 4621*
[Ava Aldridge/Eddie Struzick] [BMI] (9/16/78 BCR-4)

SHARING YOU Bobby Vee—Liberty 55451
[Gerry Goffin/Carole King] [BMI] (5/19/62 BCR-12)

SHARING YOU Mitty Collier—Chess 1953 [Ronald Saunders] [BMI] (3/19/66 BCR-80)

SHARP DRESSED MAN ZZ Top—Warner Bros. 29576
[Frank Beard/Billy Gibbons/Dusty Hill] [BMI] (7/23/83 BC-56)

SHATTERED The Rolling Stones—Rolling Stones 19310
[Mick Jagger/Keith Richards] [ASC] (12/16/78 BCR-27)

SHATTERED DREAMS Johnny Hates Jazz—Virgin 99383
[Clark Datchler] [BMI] (3/19/88 BC-2)

SHATTERED GLASS Laura Branigan—Atlantic 89245
[Steve Coe/Bobby Mitchell] [ASC] (7/4/87 BC-48)

SHAVING CREAM Benny Bell—Vanguard 35183 [Benny Bell] [BMI] (3/1/75 BCR-30)

SHAZAM Duane Eddy His "Twangy" Guitar And The Rebels—Jamie 1151
[Duane Eddy/Lee Hazlewood] [BMI] (3/14/60 BCR-41) [I]

SHE Tommy James And The Shondells—Roulette 7066
[Ritchie Cordell/Tommy James/Jerry Kasenetz/Jeff Katz/Mike Vale] [BMI] (12/6/69 BCR-18)

SHE Southcote—Buddah 399 [Beau David] [ASC] (3/9/74 BCR-80)

SHE AIN'T LOVIN' YOU The Distant Cousins—Date 1514
[Raymond Bloodworth/L. Russell Brown/Bob Crewe] [BMI] (9/10/66 C-90)

SHE AIN'T PRETTY Northern Pikes—Scotti Brothers 75287
[Bryan Potvin] [ASC] (12/21/91 C-69)

SHE AIN'T WORTH IT Glenn Medeiros featuring Bobby Brown—MCA 53831
[Antonina Armato/Bobby Brown/Ian Prince] [ASC] (5/19/90 BC-1)

SHE BELIEVES IN ME Kenny Rogers—United Artists 1273
[Steve Gibb] [ASC] (4/21/79 BCR-4)

SHE BELONGS TO ME Rick Nelson And The Stone Canyon Band—Decca 32550
[Bob Dylan] [SE] (10/11/69 BCR-23)

SHE BLEW A GOOD THING The Poets—Symbol 214
[Ronnie Lewis/Henry Murray] [BMI] (3/19/66 BCR-30)

SHE BLINDED ME WITH SCIENCE Thomas Dolby—Capitol 5204
[Thomas Dolby/Jo Kerr] [ASC] (2/19/83 BC-4)

SHE BOP Cyndi Lauper—Portrait 37-04516
[Rick Chertoff/Gary Corbett/Cyndi Lauper/Stephen Lunt] [BMI] (7/21/84 BC-3)

—SHE CALLED ME BABY see: HE CALLED ME BABY

SHE CAME IN THROUGH THE BATHROOM WINDOW Joe Cocker—A&M 1147
[John Lennon/Paul McCartney] [ASC] (11/29/69 BCR-30)

SHE CAN'T FIND HER KEYS Paul Petersen—Colpix 620
[Roy Alfred/Wally Gold] [ASC] (2/19/62 BCR-19)

SHE CRIED *Jay & The Americans—United Artists 415*
[Ted Daryll/Greg Richards] [BMI] (3/5/62 BCR-4)

HE CRIED *The Shangri-Las—Red Bird 10-053*
[Ted Daryll/Greg Richards] [BMI] (4/9/66 BCR-54)

SHE CRIED *The Lettermen—Capitol 2820*
[Ted Daryll/Greg Richards] [BMI] (6/6/70 BCR-54)

SHE DID IT Eric Carmen—Arista 0266 [Eric Carmen] [BMI] (8/27/77 BCR-15)

SHE DID IT Michael Damian—LEG 007 [Eric Carmen] [BMI] (5/30/81 BC-69)

SHE DIDN'T DO MAGIC Lobo—Big Tree 116 [Kent LaVoie] (TSW) [ASC] (6/12/71 BCR-39)

SHE DIDN'T KNOW (SHE KEPT ON TALKING) Dee Dee Warwick—Atco 6754
[Gary Anderson/Charlie Whitehead/Jerry Williams Jr.] [BMI] (5/9/70 BCR-48)

SHE DON'T KNOW ME Bon Jovi—Mercury 818958 [Mark Avsec] [ASC] (5/26/84 BC-46)

SHE DON'T LET NOBODY (BUT ME) Curtis Mayfield—Boardwalk 122
[Dino Fekaris/Curtis Mayfield] [BMI] (9/26/81 CR-66)

SHE DON'T LOOK BACK Dan Fogelberg—Full Moon 07044
[Dan Fogelberg] [ASC] (5/30/87 BC-76)

SHE DRIVES ME CRAZY Fine Young Cannibals—I.R.S./MCA 53483
[Roland Gift/David Steele] [ASC] (1/28/89 BC-1)

SHE DRIVES ME OUT OF MY MIND Swingin' Medallions—Smash 2050
[Freddy Weller] [BMI] (8/20/66 BCR-68)

SHE GOT THE GOLDMINE (I GOT THE SHAFT) Jerry Reed—RCA 13268
[Tim DuBois] [BMI] (7/24/82 BC-57)

SHE IS STILL A MYSTERY The Lovin' Spoonful—Kama Sutra 239
[John Sebastian] [BMI] (10/28/67 BCR-16)

SHE KNOWS ME TOO WELL The Beach Boys—Capitol 5245
[Mike Love*/Brian Wilson] [BMI] (9/26/64 R-93)

SHE LETS HER HAIR DOWN (EARLY IN THE MORNING) *The Tokens—Buddah 151*
[Leon Carr/Paul Vance] [ASC] (12/6/69 BCRt-59)

SHE LETS HER HAIR DOWN (EARLY IN THE MORNING) *Gene Pitney—Musicor 1384*
[Leon Carr/Paul Vance] [ASC] (12/6/69 BCRt-76)

SHE LETS HER HAIR DOWN (EARLY IN THE MORNING) *Don Young—Bang 574*
[Leon Carr/Paul Vance] [ASC] (12/13/69 Rt-76)

SHE LOOKS A LOT LIKE YOU Clocks—Boulevard 03075
[Steve Swaim] [NA] (8/28/82 BC-67)

SHE LOVES MY CAR Ronnie Milsap—RCA 13847
[Roy Freeland/Bill LaBounty] [BMI] (8/4/84 BC-80)

SHE LOVES TO BE IN LOVE Charlie—Janus 276 [Terry Thomas] [BMI] (7/29/78 BCR-54)

SHE LOVES TO ROCK Cornel Gunter and The Flairs—ABC-Paramount 9698
[Buck Ram] [BMI] (5/4/56 R-50)

SHE LOVES YOU *The Beatles—Swan 4152*
[John Lennon/Paul McCartney] [ASC] (1/25/64 BCR-1)

SIE LIEBT DICH (SHE LOVES YOU) *Die Beatles—Swan 4182*
[Otto Demmlar/J. Nicolas Felgen*/John Lennon/Paul McCartney] [BMI] (6/27/64 B-97) [F]*

SHE REALLY LOVES YOU Timi Yuro—Liberty 55375
[Clyde Otis/Timi Yuro] [BMI] (12/4/61 B-93)

SHE SAID YES Wilson Pickett—Atlantic 2753
[Don Covay/Johnny Nash/Wilson Pickett/William Stevenson] [BMI] (8/22/70 BCR-52)

SHE SAY (OOM DOOBY DOOM) The Diamonds—Mercury 71404
[Mike Anthony/Barry Mann] [BMI] (1/19/59 BCR-12)

SHE SHOT A HOLE IN MY SOUL Clifford Curry—Elf 90002
[Mac Gayden/Chuck Neese] [BMI] (5/6/67 BCR-95)

SHE TALKS TO ANGELS The Black Crowes—Def American 19403
[Chris Robinson/Rich Robinson] [BMI] (3/16/91 BC-30)

—SHE THINKS I STILL CARE see: HE THINKS...

SHE TOOK YOU FOR A RIDE Aaron Neville—Par-Lo 103
[George Richard Davis Jr./Lee Diamond] [BMI] (3/25/67 BCR-92)

SHE UNDERSTANDS ME *Johnny Tillotson—MGM 13284*
[Merle Kilgore/Margie Singleton] [BMI] (10/31/64 BCR-28)

DUM-DE-DA *(She Understands Me) Bobby Vinton—Epic 10014*
[Merle Kilgore/Margie Singleton] [BMI] (4/23/66 BCR-32)

SHE WANTS T' SWIM Chubby Checker—Parkway 922
[Dave Appell/Kal Mann] [ASC] (8/29/64 BCR-50)

SHE WANTS TO DANCE WITH ME Rick Astley—RCA 8838
[Rick Astley] [BMI] (12/17/88 BC-6)

SHE WAS HOT The Rolling Stones—Rolling Stones 99788
[Mick Jagger/Keith Richards] [ASC] (2/4/84 BC-44)

SHE WAS ONLY SEVENTEEN (HE WAS ONE YEAR MORE) Marty Robbins—Columbia 41208
[Marty Robbins] [BMI] (8/4/58 BCR-27)

SHE WEARS MY RING Solomon King—Capitol 2114
[Boudleaux Bryant/Felice Bryant] [BMI] (4/6/68 C-92)

SHE WILL SURVIVE (POLAND) Bobby Vinton—Tapestry 008
[Edilio Capotosti/Antoniette Desimone/Bobby Vinton] [NA] (3/13/82 C-93)

SHE WON'T TALK TO ME Luther Vandross—Epic 08513
[Hubert Eaves III/Luther Vandross] [BMI] (1/28/89 BC-30)

SHE WORKS HARD FOR THE MONEY Donna Summer—Mercury 812370
[Michael Omartian/Donna Summer] [ASC] (5/28/83 BC-3)

SHE'D RATHER BE WITH ME The Turtles—White Whale 249
[Garry Bonner/Alan Gordon] [BMI] (5/13/67 BCR-1)

SHEENA IS A PUNK ROCKER The Ramones—Sire 746
[Doug Colvin/John Cummings/Tom Erdelyi/Jeff Hyman] [ASC] (7/2/77 BC-81)

THE SHEIK OF ARABY (ITALIAN STYLE) Lou Monte—RCA Victor 47-7265
[Harry B. Smith/Ted Snyder/Francis Wheeler] [NA] (6/16/58 BCR-33) [F]

SHEILA Tommy Roe—ABC-Paramount 10329
[Tommy Roe] [BMI] (7/14/62 BCR-1)

SHEILA ANN Bobby Skel—Uni 55071 [Robert Doyle Skelton] [BMI] (7/6/68 R-86)

SHE'LL BE THERE Vikki Carr—Liberty 56026 [Mack David] [ASC] (3/23/68 BCR-83)

SHE'LL NEVER KNOW Brenda Lee—Decca 31454 [Rick Hall] [BMI] (1/26/63 BCR-36)

SHELTER Lone Justice—Geffen 28520
[Maria McKee/Steven Van Zandt] [BMI] (1/10/87 BC-47)

SHELTER ME Joe Cocker—Capitol 5557 [Nicholas DiStefano] [BMI] (3/1/86 BC-80)

SHELTER ME Cinderella—Mercury 878 700 [Tom Keifer] [ASC] (12/8/90 BC-31)

THE SHELTER OF YOUR ARMS Sammy Davis Jr.—Reprise 20,216
[Jerry Samuels] [ASC] (11/30/63 BCR-17)

SHENANDOAH ROSE *Hugo & Luigi—Roulette 4012*
[Jerry Livingston/Paul Francis Webster] [ASC] (6/22/57 CRt-40)

SHENANDOAH ROSE *Johnny Desmond—Coral 61846*
[Jerry Livingston/Paul Francis Webster] [ASC] (6/29/57 Rt-40)

SHENANDOAH ROSE *Peter Hanley—Verve 10058*
[Jerry Livingston/Paul Francis Webster] [ASC] (6/29/57 Rt-40)

SHENANDOAH ROSE *The Jack Halloran Singers—Dot 15599*
[Jerry Livingston/Paul Francis Webster] [ASC] (7/6/57 Rt-40)

SHERRY *The 4 Seasons—Vee-Jay 456 [Bob Gaudio] [ASC] (8/18/62 BCR-1)*

SHERRY *Robert John—EMI America 8061 [Bob Gaudio] [ASC] (10/25/80 BCR-70)*

SHERRY *Gidea Park—Profile 5003 [Bob Gaudio] (Med) [ASC] (12/26/81 BC-82)*

SHERRY The Keane Brothers—20th Century 2302 [Dwayne Ford] [BMI] (11/13/76 B-84)

SHERRY DON'T GO The Lettermen—Capitol 2132
[Danny Janssen/Myrna Janssen/Walt Keske] [BMI] (3/23/68 BCR-35)

SHE'S A BAD MAMA JAMA (SHE'S BUILT, SHE'S STACKED)
Carl Carlton—20th Century 2488
[Leon Haywood] [BMI] (8/1/81 BCR-20)

SHE'S A BEAUTY The Tubes—Capitol 5217
[David Foster/Steve Lukather/Fee Waybill] [BMI] (4/9/83 BC-8)

SHE'S A DISCO QUEEN Oliver Sain—Abet 9463 [Oliver Sain] (TSW) [BMI] (2/21/76 CR-76)

SHE'S A FOOL Lesley Gore—Mercury 72180
[Mark Barkan/Ben Raleigh] [BMI] (9/21/63 BCR-3)

SHE'S A HEARTBREAKER Gene Pitney—Musicor 1306
[Charlie Foxx/Jerry Williams Jr.] [BMI] (5/4/68 BCR-16)

SHE'S A LADY John Sebastian—Kama Sutra 254
[John Sebastian] [BMI] (12/14/68 BCR-54)

SHE'S A LADY Tom Jones—Parrot 40058 [Paul Anka] [BMI] (1/30/71 BCR-1)

SHE'S A RAINBOW The Rolling Stones—London 906
[Mick Jagger/Keith Richards] [BMI] (12/30/67 BCR-9)

SHE'S A RUNNER Billy Squier—Capitol 5202 [Billy Squier] [ASC] (2/5/83 BC-75)

SHE'S A TROUBLEMAKER The Majors—Imperial 5879
[Van McCoy/Jerry Ragovoy] [BMI] (11/24/62 BCR-72)

—SHE'S A VERY LOVELY WOMAN see: YOU'RE A VERY...

SHE'S A WOMAN The Beatles—Capitol 5327
[John Lennon/Paul McCartney] [ASC] (12/5/64 BCR-4)

SHE'S A WOMAN José Feliciano—RCA Victor 47-9757
[John Lennon/Paul McCartney] [ASC] (8/2/69 R-89)

SHE'S ABOUT A MOVER *Sir Douglas Quintet—Tribe 8308*
[Doug Sahm] [BMI] (4/3/65 BCR-13)

SHE'S ABOUT A MOVER *Otis Clay—Cotillion 44001 [Doug Sahm] [BMI] (8/17/68 BC-96)*

SHE'S ALL I GOT *Freddie North—Mankind 12004*
[Gary Anderson/Jerry Williams Jr.] [BMI] (9/25/71 BCR-30)

SHE'S ALL I GOT *Johnny Paycheck—Epic 10783*
[Gary Anderson/Jerry Williams Jr.] [BMI] (12/18/71 B-91)

SHE'S ALL RIGHT Jackie Wilson—Brunswick 55273
[Eddie Singleton] [BMI] (12/19/64 R-91)

SHE'S ALMOST YOU Billy Harner—Open 1253 [Joe South] [BMI] (2/22/69 R-84)

SHE'S ALWAYS A WOMAN Billy Joel—Columbia 10788 [Billy Joel] [ASC] (8/5/78 BCR-17)

—SHE'S BUILT SHE'S STACKED see: SHE'S A BAD MAMA JAMA

SHE'S COMING HOME The Zombies—Parrot 9747 [Rod Argent] [BMI] (4/10/65 BCR-48)

SHE'S EVERYTHING (I WANTED YOU TO BE) Ral Donner—Gone 5121
[Chesley Howard/Douglas Lapham] [BMI] (12/16/61 BCR-10)

SHE'S FLY Tony Terry—Epic 07417
[George Dick/Gary Henry/David Sanchez/Tony Terry] [BMI] (11/28/87 B-80)

SHE'S GONE *Daryl Hall & John Oates—Atlantic 2993*
[Daryl Hall/John Oates] [BMI] (1/26/74 BCR-48)

SHE'S GONE *Tavares—Capitol 3957 [Daryl Hall/John Oates] [BMI] (10/5/74 BCR-50)*

SHE'S GONE *Daryl Hall & John Oates—Atlantic 3332*
[Daryl Hall/John Oates] [BMI] (7/17/76 BCR-6)

SHE'S GONE (LADY) Steelheart—MCA 54167 [Michael Matijevic] [ASC] (8/31/91 BC-59)

SHE'S GOT A WAY Billy Joel—Columbia 02628 [Billy Joel] [ASC] (11/21/81 BCR-23)

SHE'S GOT A WHOLE NUMBER Keith Herman—Radio 418
[Keith Herman/Robert Eugene Walker] [ASC] (10/20/79 BCR-87)

SHE'S GOT EVERYTHING The Essex Featuring Anita Humes—Roulette 4530
[Oramay Diamond/Jimmy Radcliffe] [BMI] (11/9/63 BCR-50)

SHE'S GOT IT Little Richard—Specialty 584
[John Marascalco/Richard Penniman] [BMI] (1/5/57 R-84)

SHE'S GOT LOVE Thomas & Richard Frost—Imperial 66405
[Richard Frost/Thomas Frost] [ASC] (10/11/69 BCR-79)

SHE'S GOT TO BE A SAINT Ray Price—Columbia 45724
[Mario DiNapoli/Joseph Paulini] [ASC] (1/6/73 BCR-75)

SHE'S GOT YOU Patsy Cline—Decca 31354 [Hank Cochran] [BMI] (1/27/62 BCR-6)

SHE'S IN LOVE WITH YOU Suzi Quatro—RSO 1014
[Mike Chapman/Nicky Chinn] [ASC] (11/24/79 BCR-41)

(SHE'S JUST A) FALLEN ANGEL Starz—Capitol 4343
[Prentice DeLaney/Larry Gonsky*/Jeffrey Warren Grob/Brendan Harkin/
Richie Ranno/Michael Lee Smith/Pieter Sweval] [ASC] (11/27/76 BC-95)

SHE'S JUST A WHOLE LOT LIKE YOU Hank Thompson—Capitol 4386
[Hank Thompson] [BMI] (7/18/60 BR-98)

SHE'S JUST MY STYLE Gary Lewis And The Playboys—Liberty 55846
[Al Capps/Snuff Garrett/Gary Lewis/Leon Russell] [BMI] (12/4/65 BCR-2)

SHE'S LIKE THE WIND Patrick Swayze—RCA 5363
[Patrick Swayze/Stacey Widelitz] [BMI] (12/19/87 BC-2)

SHE'S LOOKING GOOD *Rodger Collins—Galaxy 750*
[Rodger Collins] [ASC] (3/11/67 CR-56)

SHE'S LOOKIN' GOOD *Wilson Pickett—Atlantic 2504*
[Rodger Collins] [ASC] (4/13/68 BCR-15)

SHE'S LOST YOU The Zephyrs—Rotate 5006 [Peter Gage] [BMI] (4/10/65 R-88)

SHE'S MINE Conway Twitty—MGM 12911
[Jack Nance/Conway Twitty] [BMI] (8/8/60 B-98)

SHE'S MINE Steve Perry—Columbia 04496
[Randy Goodrum/Steve Perry] [ASC] (6/30/84 BC-21)

SHE'S MY GIRL Bobby Shafto—Rust 5082
[Len Beadle/Peter Callander] [BMI] (6/20/64 BCR-86)

SHE'S MY GIRL The Turtles—White Whale 260
[Garry Bonner/Alan Gordon] [BMI] (11/4/67 BCR-14)

SHE'S NEAT Dale Wright With The Rock-Its—Fraternity 792 [Dale Wright] [ASC] (1/13/58 BCR-39)

SHE'S NOT JUST ANOTHER WOMAN The 8th Day—Invictus 9087 [Ronald Dunbar/Clyde Wilson] [BMI] (5/8/71 BCR-8)

SHE'S NOT THERE *The Zombies—Parrot 9695 [Rod Argent] [BMI] (10/3/64 BCR-1)*

SHE'S NOT THERE *The Road—Kama Sutra 256 [Rod Argent] [BMI] (2/1/69 CR-81)*

SHE'S NOT THERE *Santana—Columbia 10616 [Rod Argent] [BMI] (10/1/77 BCR-20)*

SHE'S NOT YOU Elvis Presley With The Jordanaires—RCA Victor 47-8041 [Jerry Leiber/Doc Pomus/Mike Stoller] [BMI] (7/28/62 BCR-4)

SHE'S ON THE LEFT Jeffrey Osborne—A&M 1227 [Clinton Blanson/Robert Brookins/Tony Haynes/Jeffrey Osborne] [ASC] (8/20/88 BC-48)

SHE'S ONLY 20 Tami Show—Chrysalis 43146 [Tommy Gawenda/Cathy Massey/Claire Massey] [ASC] (3/12/88 B-88)

SHE'S OUT OF MY LIFE Michael Jackson—Epic 50871 [Tom Bahler] [BMI] (4/12/80 BCR-7)

—SHE'S READY see: HE'S READY

(SHE'S) SEXY + 17 Stray Cats—EMI America 8168 [Brian Setzer] [BMI] (8/6/83 BC-4)

SHE'S SO COLD The Rolling Stones—Rolling Stones 21001 [Mick Jagger/Keith Richards] [ASC] (9/27/80 BCR-21)

SHE'S STRANGE Cameo—Atlanta Artists 818384 [Larry Blackmon/Tomi Jenkins/Nathan Leftenant/Charles L. Singleton] [BMI] (4/7/84 BC-43)

SHE'S THE ONE The Chartbusters—Mutual 502 [John Joseph Dubas] [BMI] (7/4/64 BCR-33)

SHE'S TIGHT Cheap Trick—Epic 03233 [Rick Nielsen] [BMI] (10/9/82 B-65)

SHE'S TROUBLE Musical Youth—MCA 52312 [Terry Britten/Billy Livsey/Sue Shifrin] [BMI] (12/31/83 BC-56)

SHE'S WITH HER OTHER LOVE Leon Hayward—Imperial 66123 [Leon Haywood/Nathaniel Nathan] [BMI] (10/23/65 BC-92)

SHIFTING WHISPERING SANDS *Billy Vaughn and His Orchestra—Dot 15409 [Mary Hadler Gilbert/V.C. Gilbert] [BMI] (8/29/55 BCtRt-4)*

SHIFTING WHISPERING SANDS *Rusty Draper—Mercury 70696 [Mary Hadler Gilbert/V.C. Gilbert] [BMI] (9/3/55 BCtRt-4)*

SHILO Neil Diamond—Bang 575 [Neil Diamond] [SE] (1/31/70 BCR-23)

SHIMMY LIKE KATE The Olympics—Arvee 5006 [Armond J. Piron] [ASC] (9/5/60 BCR-33)

(I DO THE) SHIMMY SHIMMY *Bobby Freeman—King 5373 [Andy Gibson/Bill Massey] [BMI] (8/15/60 BCR-37)*

SHIMMY SHIMMY *The Orlons—Cameo 295 [Andy Gibson/Bill Massey] [BMI] (2/1/64 BCR-62)*

SHIMMY SHIMMY KO KO BOP Little Anthony And The Imperials—End 1060 [Robert T. Smith] [BMI] (11/2/59 BCR-19)

SHIMMY, SHIMMY WALK, PART 1 The Megatons—Dodge 808 [Billy Lee Riley] [BMI] (1/27/62 B-88) [I]

SHINE Bar-Kays—Mercury 74048 [James Edward Alexander/Charles Leonard Allen/Michael Beard/Larry Dodson/ Harvey Henderson/Allen Alvoid Jones Jr./Lloyd Ed Smith/Winston Stewart/ Frank Thompson] [BMI] (4/7/79 R-94)

SHINE A LITTLE LOVE Electric Light Orchestra—Jet 5057 [Jeff Lynne] [BMI] (5/19/79 BCR-7)

SHINE ON L.T.D.—A&M 2283 [Richard Kerr/Billy Osborne/Jeffrey Osborne] [BMI] (11/15/80 BCR-38)

SHINE ON George Duke—Epic 02701 [George Duke] [ASC] (2/20/82 BCR-41)

SHINE ON HARVEST MOON *Four Aces—Decca 29625 [Nora Bayes/Jack Norworth] [ASC] (8/1/55 CR-21)*

SHINE ON HARVEST MOON *Googie René And His Band—Class 227 [Nora Bayes/Jack Norworth] [ASC] (5/26/58 R-82) [IWM]*

SHINE SHINE Barry Gibb—MCA 52443 [George Bitzer/Barry Gibb/Maurice Gibb] [BMI] (9/1/84 BC-37)

SHININ' ON Grand Funk—Capitol 3917 [Don Brewer/Mark Farner] [BMI] (7/6/74 BCR-11)

SHINING STAR Earth, Wind & Fire—Columbia 10090 [Philip Bailey/Lorenzo Dunn/Maurice White] [ASC] (2/8/75 BCR-1)

SHINING STAR The Manhattans—Columbia 11222 [Leo Graham/Paul Richmond] [BMI] (4/26/80 BCR-4)

SHINING STAR INXS—Atlantic 87576 [Andy Farriss] [NA] (11/23/91 C-84)

SHINY HAPPY PEOPLE R.E.M.—Warner Bros. 19242 [Bill Berry/Peter Buck/Mike Mills/Michael Stipe] [BMI] (7/27/91 BC-8)

SHINY SHINY Haysi Fantayzee—RCA 13534 [Paul Caplin/Kate Garner/Jeremy Healy] [BMI] (7/23/83 B-74)

SHIP OF FOOLS (SAVE ME FROM TOMORROW) World Party—Chrysalis 43052 [Karl Wallinger] [ASC] (2/14/87 BC-27)

SHIP OF FOOLS Robert Plant—Es Paranza 7-99333 [Phil Johnstone/Robert Plant] [ASC] (8/27/88 B-84)

THE SHIP THAT NEVER SAILED *Billy Vaughn and His Orchestra—Dot 15546 [Art Kassel] [ASC] (3/16/57 BCtRt-41)*

THE SHIP THAT NEVER SAILED *Johnny Ridge—Epic 9205 [Art Kassel] [ASC] (3/16/57 Rt-43)*

THE SHIP THAT NEVER SAILED *David Carroll And His Orchestra—Mercury 71069 [Art Kassel] [ASC] (3/16/57 BCtRt-41) [IWM]*

THE SHIP THAT NEVER SAILED *Sammy Kaye & His "Swing And Sway" Orchestra—Columbia 40869 [Art Kassel] [ASC] (3/16/57 Rt-43) [IWM]*

SHIP TO SHORE Chris DeBurgh—A&M 2565 [Chris de Burgh] [BMI] (8/20/83 BC-71)

—SHIP WILL COME (EIN SCHIFF WIRD KOMMEN) see: NEVER ON SUNDAY

SHIPS Barry Manilow—Arista 0464 [Ian Hunter] [ASC] (10/13/79 BCR-9)

SHIRL GIRL Wayne Newton & The Newton Brothers —Capitol 5058 [Rudy Clark/Bobby Darin] [BMI] (10/26/63 BCR-58)

SHIRLEY The Schoolboys—Okeh 7076 [Arnold Maxin/Gene Redd Sr.] [BMI] (2/16/57 BCR-50)

SHIRLEY John Fred and the Playboys—Montel 1002 [Thomas Bryan/John Fred] [BMI] (2/23/59 BC-78)

SHISH KEBAB Ralph Marterie And His Orchestra—Mercury 71092 [David Carroll/George Stone] [BMI] (4/27/57 BCR-29) [I]

SHIVER AND SHAKE The Silencers—Precision 9800 [Cathi Capiola/Warren King] [NA] (7/19/80 BCR-81)

SHO NUFF BOOGIE (PART 1) Sylvia & The Moments—All Platinum 2350 [Al Goodman/Harry Ray/Sylvia Robinson] [BMI] (5/25/74 BCR-59)

SHOCK The Motels—Capitol 5529 [Martha Davis/Scott Thurston] [BMI] (10/26/85 BC-83)

SHOCK THE MONKEY Peter Gabriel—Geffen 29883 [Peter Gabriel] [BMI] (10/23/82 BC-29)

SHOE SHOE SHINE Dynamic Superiors—Motown 1324 [Nick Ashford/Valerie Simpson] [ASC] (11/2/74 BCR-68)

SHOES Brook Benton With The Dixie Flyers—Cotillion 44093 [Don Covay/George Soule] [BMI] (12/19/70 BCR-52)

SHOES Reparata—Polydor 14271 [Eric Beam] [BMI] (7/5/75 BC-92)

SHOESHINE BOY Eddie Kendricks—Tamla 54257 [Linda Allen/Harry Booker] [BMI] (2/8/75 BCR-18)

SHOO-BE-DOO-BE-DOO-DA-DAY Stevie Wonder—Tamla 54165 [Henry Cosby/Sylvia Moy/Stevie Wonder] [ASC] (4/6/68 BCR-7)

THE SHOOP SHOOP SONG (IT'S IN HIS KISS) *Betty Everett—Vee-Jay 585 [Rudy Clark] [BMI] (2/29/64 BCR-5)*

IT'S IN HIS KISS (THE SHOOP SHOOP SONG) *Kate Taylor—Columbia 10596 [Rudy Clark] [BMI] (9/3/77 BCR-49)*

THE SHOOP SHOOP SONG (IT'S IN HIS KISS) *Cher—Geffen 19659 [Rudy Clark] [BMI] (11/17/90 BC-33)*

SHOOT FOR THE MOON Poco—Atlantic 89919 [Rusty Young] [ASC] (12/18/82 BC-44)

SHOOT IT AGAIN Teresa Brewer—Coral 61528 [Marshall Brown/Earl Shuman] [ASC] (11/19/55 BCR-39)

SHOOT ME (WITH YOUR LOVE) Tasha Thomas—Atlantic 3542 [James R. Glaser] [BMI] (1/27/79 B-91)

SHOOT YOUR SHOT Jr. Walker & The All Stars—Soul 35036 [James Graves/Lawrence Horn/Jr. Walker] [BMI] (7/15/67 BCR-37)

SHOOT 'EM UP, BABY Andy Kim—Steed 710 [Jeff Barry/Andy Kim] [BMI] (8/24/68 BCR-31)

SHOOTING SHARK Blue Öyster Cult—Columbia 04298 [Donald Roeser/Patti Smith] [ASC] (2/11/84 B-83)

SHOOTING STAR Dollar—Atco 7208/Carrere 7208 [David Courtney] [ASC] (12/15/79 BCR-74)

SHOP AROUND *The Miracles (Featuring Bill "Smokey" Robinson) —Tamla 54034 [Berry Gordy/Smokey Robinson] [ASC] (11/28/60 BCR-2)*

DON'T LET HIM SHOP AROUND *Debbie Dean—Motown 1007 [Berry Gordy/Smokey Robinson/Loucye Gordy Wakefield] [ASC] (2/6/61 BR-91) [R]*

SHOP AROUND *Captain & Tennille—A&M 1817 [Berry Gordy/Smokey Robinson] [ASC] (4/24/76 BCR-4)*

SHOPPIN' FOR CLOTHES The Coasters—Atco 6178 [Kent Harris*/Jerry Leiber/Mike Stoller] [BMI] (10/3/60 BCR-57)

SHOPPIN' FROM A TO Z Toni Basil—Chrysalis 03537 [Toni Basil/Bruce Roberts/Allee Willis] [ASC] (2/26/83 BC-77)

SHORT FAT FANNIE Larry Williams—Specialty 608 [Larry Williams] [BMI] (6/24/57 BCR-6)

SHORT PEOPLE Randy Newman—Warner Bros. 8492 [Randy Newman] [ASC] (11/12/77 BCR-1)

SHORT SHORTS *Royal Teens—ABC-Paramount 9882 [Tom Austin/Bill Crandall/Bill Dalton/Bob Gaudio] [BMI] (1/13/58 BCRt-3)*

SHORT SHORTS *The Four Winds—Decor 175 [Tom Austin/Bill Crandall/Bill Dalton/Bob Gaudio] [BMI] (1/20/58 Rt-15)*

SHORT SHORTS *Tiny Bradshaw & His Orchestra—King 5114 [Tom Austin/Bill Crandall/Bill Dalton/Bob Gaudio] [BMI] (3/24/58 Rt-14)*

SHORTNIN' BREAD *Paul Chaplain & His Emeralds—Harper 100 [Traditional] [NA] (8/22/60 BCtRt-50)*

SHORTNIN' BREAD *The Bell Notes—Madison 136 [Traditional] [NA] (8/22/60 BCtRt-50)*

A SHOT IN THE DARK Henry Mancini And His Orchestra—RCA Victor 47-8381 [Henry Mancini] [ASC] (7/18/64 B-97) [I]

SHOT IN THE DARK Ozzy Osbourne—CBS Associated 05810 [Ozzy Osbourne/Phil Soussan] [ASC] (3/22/86 BC-68)

SHOT OF POISON Lita Ford—RCA 62074
[Lita Ford/Myron Grombacher/Jim Vallance] [ASC] (10/26/91 BC-26)

SHOTGUN *Jr. Walker & The All Stars—Soul 35008 [Jr. Walker] [BMI] (2/13/65 BCR-3)*

SHOTGUN *Vanilla Fudge—Atco 6655 [Jr. Walker] [BMI] (2/22/69 BCR-59)*

SHOTGUN RIDER *Joe Sun—Ovation 1141*
[Larry Henley/Jim Hurt/Johnny Slate] [BMI] (5/31/80 BR-71)

SHOTGUN RIDER *Delbert McClinton—Capitol/MSS 4984*
[Larry Henley/Jim Hurt/Johnny Slate] [BMI] (3/28/81 BC-70)

SHOTGUN SHUFFLE The Sunshine Band—TK 1010
[Harry Wayne Casey/Rick Finch] [BMI] (9/6/75 BC-84) [I]

SHOULD ANYBODY ASK Garry Bonner—Atlantic 3234
[Ritchie Adams/Bob Levine] [BMI] (12/28/74 C-85)

SHOULD I The String-A-Longs—Warwick 654
[Nacio Herb Brown] [ASC] (6/12/61 BCR-42) [IM]

SHOULD I Chad & Jeremy—Columbia 43414
[Jeremy Clyde/Chad Stuart] [BMI] (10/30/65 C-100)

SHOULD I DO IT The Pointer Sisters—Planet 47960
[Layng Martine Jr.] [BMI] (1/16/82 BCR-13)

SHOULD I LOVE YOU Cee Farrow—Rocshire 95032
[Cee Farrow/Lothar Krell] [ASC] (9/24/83 B-82)

SHOULD I SAY YES? Nu Shooz—Atlantic 89108
[Valerie Day/John Robert Smith] [BMI] (4/16/88 BC-41)

SHOULD I SEE Frozen Ghost—Atlantic 89279 [Arnold Lanni] [BMI] (4/11/87 BC-64)

SHOULD I STAY OR SHOULD I GO? *The Clash—Epic 03006*
[Nicky Headon/Michael Geoffrey Jones/Paul Simonon*/Joe Strummer] [ASC]*
(7/17/82 BC-45)

SHOULD I STAY OR SHOULD I GO? *The Clash—Epic 03547*
[Nicky Headon/Michael Geoffrey Jones/Paul Simonon*/Joe Strummer] [ASC]*
(2/19/83 BC-50)

—SHOULD I TIE A YELLOW RIBBON...see: TIE A YELLOW RIBBON...

SHOULD WE TELL HIM The Everly Brothers—Cadence 1342
[Don Everly/Phil Everly*] [BMI] (1/20/58 R-55)

A SHOULDER TO CRY ON Tommy Page—Sire 27645 [Tommy Page] [BMI] (2/11/89 BC-29)

SHOULD'VE KNOWN BETTER Richard Marx—Manhattan 50083
[Richard Marx] [ASC] (9/26/87 BC-3)

SHOULD'VE NEVER LET YOU GO Neil Sedaka & Dara Sedaka—Elektra 46615
[Phil Cody/Neil Sedaka] [BMI] (3/29/80 BCR-19)

SHOUT PART ONE *The Isley Brothers—RCA Victor 47-7588*
[O'Kelly Isley/Ronald Isley/Rudolph Isley] [BMI] (9/7/59 BCR-28)

SHOUT - PART 1 *Joey Dee & The Starliters—Roulette 4416*
[O'Kelly Isley/Ronald Isley/Rudolph Isley] [BMI] (3/19/62 BCR-6)

SHOUT - PART 1 *The Isley Brothers—RCA Victor 47-0589*
[O'Kelly Isley/Ronald Isley/Rudolph Isley] [BMI] (3/24/62 B-94)

SHOUT *Lulu And The Luvers—Parrot 9678*
[O'Kelly Isley/Ronald Isley/Rudolph Isley] [BMI] (7/25/64 BCR-83)

SHOUT *Lulu—Parrot 40021*
[O'Kelly Isley/Ronald Isley/Rudolph Isley] [BMI] (12/9/67 B-96)

SHOUT! - PART 1 *The Chambers Brothers—Vault 945*
[O'Kelly Isley/Ronald Isley/Rudolph Isley] [BMI] (12/21/68 B-83)

SHOUT Tears For Fears—Mercury 880294
[Roland Orzabal/Ian Stanley] [BMI] (6/15/85 BC-1)

SHOUT AND SHIMMY James Brown And The Famous Flames—King 5657
[James Brown] [BMI] (7/7/62 BCR-61)

SHOUT BAMALAMA Mickey Murray—SSS Int'l 715
[Otis Redding] [BMI] (9/30/67 BCR-41)

SHOUT IT OUT B.T. Express—Columbia 10649
[Billy Nichols/Maxwell Romer/Allen Williams] [BMI] (2/11/78 C-89)

SHOUT IT OUT LOUD *Kiss—Casablanca 854*
[Bob Ezrin/Gene Simmons/Paul Stanley] [BMI] (3/13/76 BCR-24)

SHOUT IT OUT LOUD (LIVE) *Kiss—Casablanca 906*
[Bob Ezrin/Gene Simmons/Paul Stanley] [BMI] (12/31/77 BR-54)

SHOUT! SHOUT! (KNOCK YOURSELF OUT) Ernie Maresca—Seville 117
[Thomas Bogdany/Ernie Maresca] [BMI] (3/17/62 BCR-6)

LA SHABLA *Danny Roma—Hanover 4532 [Danny Guglielmi] [NA] (9/7/59 Rt-76)*

THE SHOVEL (LA SHABLA) *The Gaylords —Mercury 71503*
[Steve Allen/Danny Guglielmi] [ASC] (9/7/59 Rt-76)

SHOW AND TELL Al Wilson—Rocky Road 30073 [Jerry Fuller] [BMI] (10/6/73 BCR-1)

SHOW BIZ KIDS Steely Dan—ABC 11382
[Walter Becker/Donald Fagen] [ASC] (7/28/73 BCR-30)

SHOW BUSINESS Lou Rawls—Capitol 5941 [June Jackson] [BMI] (7/1/67 BCR-42)

SHOW FOLK Paul Evans—Carlton 539 [Robert Allen/Bob Hilliard] [ASC] (1/16/61 CR-79)

SHOW ME Joe Tex—Dial 4055 [Joe Tex] [BMI] (2/25/67 BCR-35)

SHOW ME The Pretenders—Sire 29317 [Chrissie Hynde] [ASC] (3/17/84 BC-28)

SHOW ME The Cover Girls—Fever 1911
[Albert Cabrera/Bob Khozouri/Tony Moran/Andy Tripoli] [BMI] (2/28/87 BC-44)

SHOW ME Howard Hewett—Elektra 64978
[Terry Coffey/Howard Hewett/Jon Nettlesbey] [BMI] (5/26/90 BC-59)

SHOW ME HOW The Emotions—Volt 4066
[Isaac Hayes/David Porter] [BMI] (11/6/71 BCR-33)

SHOW ME THE WAY Peter Frampton—A&M 1693/1795
[Peter Frampton] [ASC] (7/12/75 BCR-4)

SHOW ME THE WAY Regina Belle—Columbia 07080
[Joey Gallo/Sue Pomerantz/Wardell Potts] [BMI] (7/18/87 BC-62)

SHOW ME THE WAY Styx—A&M 1536 [Dennis DeYoung] [ASC] (12/8/90 BC-3)

THE SHOW MUST GO ON Three Dog Night—Dunhill 4382
[David Courtney/Leo Sayer] [ASC] (3/16/74 BCR-1)

SHOW SOME RESPECT Tina Turner—Capitol 5461
[Terry Britten/Sue Shifrin] [ASC] (4/20/85 BC-37)

SHOW TIME Detroit Emeralds—Ric-Tic 135
[William Garrett/Al Hamilton/Hermon Weems] [BMI] (2/24/68 BCR-80)

SHOW YOU THE WAY TO GO The Jacksons—Epic 50350
[Kenneth Gamble/Leon Huff] [BMI] (4/2/77 BCR-28)

SHOWDOWN *Electric Light Orchestra—United Artists 337*
[Jeff Lynne] [ASC] (11/24/73 BCR-51)

SHOWDOWN *Odia Coates—United Artists 601 [Jeff Lynne] [ASC] (2/22/75 BCR-61)*

SHOWDOWN *Electric Light Orchestra—United Artists 842*
[Jeff Lynne] [ASC] (8/7/76 BCR-59)

SHOWER ME WITH YOUR LOVE Surface—Columbia 68746
[Bernard Leon Jackson] [ASC] (7/1/89 BC-5)

SHOWER THE PEOPLE James Taylor—Warner Bros. 8222
[James Taylor] [ASC] (7/3/76 BCR-22)

SHOWING OUT (GET FRESH AT THE WEEKEND) Mel & Kim—Atlantic 89329
[Matt Aitken/Mike Stock/Pete Waterman] [BMI] (2/21/87 BC-78)

SHRINE OF ST. CECILIA Faron Young—Capitol 3696
[Carroll Loveday/Nils Perne] [SE] (4/20/57 BR-52)

SHRINER'S CONVENTION Ray Stevens—RCA 11911 [Ray Stevens] [BMI] (3/15/80 C-95)

(SHU-DOO-PA-POO-POOP) LOVE BEING YOUR FOOL Travis Wammack—Capricorn 0239
[Charlie Whitehead/Jerry Williams Jr.] [BMI] (6/21/75 BCR-38)

SHU RAH Fats Domino—Imperial 5734
[Dave Bartholomew/Fats Domino] [BMI] (3/20/61 BCR-32)

—SHUDD UP! see: SISTER MARY ELEPHANT

SHUT DOWN *The Beach Boys—Capitol 4932*
[Roger Christian/Brian Wilson] [BMI] (4/6/63 BCR-23)

SHUT DOWN *The Beach Boys—Capitol 5030*
[Roger Christian/Brian Wilson] (Med) [BMI] (7/25/81 BCR-5)

SHUTTERS AND BOARDS Jerry Wallace—Challenge 9171
[Audie Murphy/Scott Turner] [BMI] (11/10/62 BCR-20)

SHY AWAY Jerry Fuller—Challenge 9104 [Dave Burgess] [BMI] (4/24/61 B-71)

SHY BOY (DON'T IT MAKE YOU FEEL GOOD) Bananarama—London 810112
[Steve Jolley/Tony Swain] [ASC] (6/25/83 BC-74)

SHY BOYS Ana—Parc 07056 [Sue Shifrin/Frank Wildhorn] [ASC] (7/11/87 B-94)

SHY GIRL The Cascades—Valiant 6028
[Bodie Chandler/Barry De Vorzon] [BMI] (4/13/63 BCR-76)

SHY GIRL Stacey Q—On The Spot 110
[Skip Hahn/Jon St. James/Stacey Swain] [BMI] (4/11/87 B-89)

SIBONEY Caterina Valente—Decca 29760
[Ernesto Lecuona/Dolly Morse] [ASC] (2/10/56 R-89)

SICK AND TIRED Fats Domino—Imperial 5515
[Dave Bartholomew/Chris Kenner] [BMI] (4/26/58 BC-30)

SIDE BY SIDE Earth, Wind & Fire—Columbia 03814
[Wanda Hutchinson/Wayne Vaughn/Maurice White] [ASC] (4/30/83 BC-75)

SIDE CAR CYCLE Charlie Ryan And The Timberline Riders—4 Star 1745
[Charlie Ryan/W.S. Stevenson‡] [BMI] (10/17/60 B-84)

SIDE SADDLE *Freddy Morgan—Challenge 59044 [Trevor Stanford] [ASC] (4/20/59 Rt-91)*

SIDE SADDLE *Russ Conway—Capitol 4188 [Trevor Stanford] [ASC] (4/20/59 Rt-91) [I]*

SIDESHOW *Blue Magic—Atco 6961 [Vinnie Barrett/Bobby Eli] [BMI] (5/4/74 BCR-5)*

SIDESHOW *Band Of Gold—RCA 13866*
[Vinnie Barrett/Bobby Eli] (Med) [BMI] (10/13/84 BC-64)

SIDEWALK SURFIN' Jan & Dean—Liberty 55727
[Roger Christian/Brian Wilson] [BMI] (10/31/64 BCR-25)

SIDEWALK TALK Jellybean—EMI America 8297
[Madonna L. Ciccone] [ASC] (11/16/85 BC-18)

THE SIDEWINDER, PART 1 Lee Morgan—Blue Note 1911
[Edward Lee Morgan] [BMI] (12/19/64 B-81) [I]

—SIE LIEBT DICH see: SHE LOVES YOU

SIGN O' THE TIMES Prince—Paisley Park 7-28399 [Prince] [ASC] (3/7/87 BC-3)

THE SIGN OF FIRE The Fixx—MCA 52316
[Alfie Agius/Cy Curnin/Peter John Greenall/Jamie West-Oram/Adam Woods] [ASC]
(11/26/83 BC-32)

SIGN OF THE GYPSY QUEEN April Wine—Capitol 5001
[Lorence Hud] [BMI] (5/23/81 BCR-56)

A SIGN OF THE TIMES Petula Clark—Warner Bros. 5802
[Tony Hatch] [BMI] (3/19/66 BCR-9)

SIGN OF THE TIMES The Belle Stars—Warner Bros. 29672
[Stella Barker/Clare Hirst/Miranda Joyce/Theresa Matthias/Sarah Jane Owen/
Judy Parsons/Lesley Shone] [ASC] (5/7/83 BC-75)

SIGN YOUR NAME Terence Trent D'Arby—Columbia 07911
[Terence Trent D'Arby] [BMI] (5/28/88 BC-3)

__SIGNED, SEALED AND DELIVERED__ Rusty Draper—Mercury 71854 [Cowboy Copas/Lois Mann] [BMI] (9/11/61 B-91)

__SIGNED, SEALED, AND DELIVERED__ James Brown And The Famous Flames—King 5803 [Cowboy Copas/Lois Mann] [BMI] (10/12/63 BC-77)

__SIGNED, SEALED, DELIVERED I'M YOURS__ Stevie Wonder—Tamla 54196 [Lee Garrett/Lula Mae Hardaway/Stevie Wonder/Syreeta Wright] [BMI] (6/20/70 BCR-1)

__SIGNED, SEALED, DELIVERED (I'M YOURS)__ Peter Frampton—A&M 1972 [Lee Garrett/Lula Mae Hardaway/Stevie Wonder/Syreeta Wright] [BMI] (8/27/77 BCR-13)

SIGNS Five Man Electrical Band—Lionel 3213 [Les Emmerson] [BMI] (5/15/71 BCR-3)

SIGNS Tesla—Geffen 19653 [Les Emmerson] [BMI] (12/22/90 BC-8)

SILENCE IS GOLDEN The Tremeloes—Epic 10184 [Bob Crewe/Bob Gaudio] [BMI] (6/17/67 BCR-9)

—SILENCE see: IL SILENZIO

SILENT LIPS Georgia Gibbs—Mercury 71058 [Vince Corso/Clyde Otis] [BMI] (3/16/57 BCR-50)

SILENT LUCIDITY Queensryche—EMI 50345 [Chris DeGarmo] [BMI] (3/23/91 BC-9)

SILENT MORNING Noel—4th & Broadway 7439 [Noel Pagan] [ASC] (8/22/87 BC-47)

__SILENT NIGHT (CHRISTMAS HYMN)__ Bing Crosby—Decca 23777 [Franz Gruber/Josef Mohr] [NA] (11/29/54 Rt-PRE)

__SILENT NIGHT, HOLY NIGHT__ The Mulcays—Cardinal 1024 [Franz Gruber] [NA] (12/13/54 Rt-PRE) [IM]

__SILENT NIGHT (CHRISTMAS HYMN)__ Bing Crosby—Decca 23777 [Franz Gruber/Josef Mohr] [NA] (12/23/55 Rt-45)

__SILENT NIGHT__ Al Hibbler—Decca 30127 [Franz Gruber/Josef Mohr] [NA] (12/22/56 Rt-38)

__SILENT NIGHT (CHRISTMAS HYMN)__ Bing Crosby—Decca 23777 [Franz Gruber/Josef Mohr] [NA] (12/22/56 Rt-38)

__SILENT NIGHT, HOLY NIGHT__ Mahalia Jackson—Columbia 40777 [Franz Gruber/Josef Mohr] [NA] (12/22/56 Rt-38)

__SILENT NIGHT (CHRISTMAS HYMN)__ Bing Crosby—Decca 23777 [Franz Gruber/Josef Mohr] [NA] (12/23/57 BRt-30)

__SILENT NIGHT__ Elvis Presley—RCA Victor LOC-1035 [Franz Gruber/Josef Mohr] (EP) [NA] (12/30/57 R-49)

__SILENT NIGHT (CHRISTMAS HYMN)__ Bing Crosby—Decca 23777 [Franz Gruber/Josef Mohr] [NA] (12/8/58 Rt-48)

__SILENT NIGHT__ Pat Holliday—LaVista 101 [Franz Gruber/Josef Mohr] [NA] (12/22/58 Rt-67)

__SILENT NIGHT (CHRISTMAS HYMN)__ Bing Crosby—Decca 23777 [Franz Gruber/Josef Mohr] [NA] (12/12/60 BR-36)

__SILENT NIGHT, HOLY NIGHT__ Mahalia Jackson—Apollo 750 [Franz Gruber/Josef Mohr] [NA] (12/29/62 B-99)

__SLEEP IN HEAVENLY PEACE (SILENT NIGHT)__ Barbra Streisand—Columbia 43896 [Franz Gruber/Josef Mohr] [NA] (12/24/66 R-98)

SILENT RUNNING (ON DANGEROUS GROUND) Mike + The Mechanics—Atlantic 89488 [Brian A. Robertson/Mike Rutherford] [BMI] (11/23/85 BC-5)

SILHOUETTE Kenny G—Arista 1-9751 [Kenny G] [BMI] (10/22/88 BC-13) [I]

__SILHOUETTES__ The Rays—Cameo 117 [Bob Crewe/Frank Slay] [BMI] (10/7/57 BCRt-2)

__SILHOUETTES__ Steve Gibson & the Red Caps—ABC-Paramount 9856 [Bob Crewe/Frank Slay] [BMI] (10/7/57 BRt-2)

__SILHOUETTES__ The Diamonds—Mercury 71197 [Bob Crewe/Frank Slay] [BMI] (10/7/57 BRt-2)

__SILHOUETTES__ Herman's Hermits—MGM 13332 [Bob Crewe/Frank Slay] [BMI] (4/3/65 BCR-4)

__SILK STOCKINGS__ Perry Como—RCA Victor 47-5950 [Cole Porter] [ASC] (11/29/54 CRt-20)

__SILK STOCKINGS__ Vic Damone—Mercury 70480 [Cole Porter] [ASC] (11/29/54 Rt-PRE)

__SILK STOCKINGS__ Fred Waring's Pennsylvanians—Decca 29331 [Cole Porter] [ASC] (12/6/54 Rt-PRE)

SILLY Deniece Williams—ARC 02406 [Fritz Baskett/Clarence McDonald/Deniece Williams] [BMI] (8/15/81 BCR-46)

SILLY BOY (SHE DOESN'T LOVE YOU) The Lettermen—Capitol 4810 [Dave Burgess/Mamie Thomas] [BMI] (8/18/62 BCR-74)

SILLY LITTLE GIRL The Tams—ABC-Paramount 10601 [Joe South] [BMI] (11/28/64 B-87)

SILLY LOVE SONGS Wings—Capitol 4256 [Linda McCartney/Paul McCartney] [ASC] (4/10/76 BCR-1)

SILLY MILLY Blue Swede—EMI 3893 [Harald Braschoss/Christian Bruhn/Hartmut Priess] [ASC] (6/1/74 BCR-56)

SILLY OL' SUMMERTIME The New Christy Minstrels—Columbia 43092 [Randy Sparks/Scott Turner] [BMI] (8/8/64 B-92)

SILLY PEOPLE Litter—Probe 461 [Mark Gallagher/Jim Kane/Ray Melina/Tom Murray] [BMI] (8/2/69 R-88)

SILLY, SILLY, FOOL Dusty Springfield—Atlantic 2705 [Kenneth Gamble/Leon Huff] [BMI] (2/21/70 BCR-52)

SILLY WASN'T I Valerie Simpson—Tamla 54224 [Jo Armstead/Nick Ashford/Valerie Simpson] [BMI] (12/9/72 BCR-58)

__SILVER BELLS__ Bing Crosby and Carol Richards—Decca 27229 [Ray Evans/Jay Livingston] [ASC] (12/20/54 R-43)

__SILVER BELLS__ Bing Crosby and Carol Richards—Decca 27229 [Ray Evans/Jay Livingston] [ASC] (12/30/57 B-78)

SILVER BIRD Mark Lindsay—Columbia 45180 [Kenny Young] [ASC] (6/13/70 BCR-20)

__SILVER DOLLAR__ Teresa Brewer—Coral 61394 [Jack Palmer/Clarke Van Ness] [ASC] (5/7/55 CRt-27)

__SILVER DOLLAR__ Johnny Long—King 1472 [Jack Palmer/Clarke Van Ness] [ASC] (5/9/55 Rt-65)

__SILVER DOLLAR__ Barry Darvell—Atlantic 2128 [Jack Palmer/Clarke Van Ness] [ASC] (1/1/62 R-80)

SILVER DREAMS The Babys—Chrysalis 2201 [Tony Brock/John Waite] [BMI] (1/28/78 BCR-48)

SILVER HEELS Blaze—Epic 50292 [Bob Welch] [ASC] (11/6/76 BCR-88)

SILVER LADY David Soul—Private Stock 45,163 [Tony Macaulay/Geoff Stephens] [ASC] (9/10/77 BCR-52)

SILVER LINING Player—RSO 914 [Peter Beckett] [BMI] (12/16/78 BCR-62)

__SILVER MOON__ Billy Vaughn and His Orchestra—Dot 15347 [Sigmund Romberg] [ASC] (3/21/55 CRt-18) [IM]

__SILVER MOON__ Russ Morgan & His Orchestra—Decca 27415 [Sigmund Romberg] [ASC] (3/28/55 Rt-21) [IM]

__SILVER MOON__ Bing Crosby—Decca 29493 [Dorothy Donnelly/Sigmund Romberg] [ASC] (4/11/55 Rt-18)

__SILVER MOON__ Ralph Marterie & His Orchestra—Mercury 70588 [Sigmund Romberg] [ASC] (4/11/55 Rt-18) [IM]

SILVER MOON Michael Nesmith & The First National Band—RCA Victor 74-0399 [Michael Nesmith] [BMI] (11/21/70 BCR-28)

SILVER STAR The Four Seasons—Warner/Curb 8203 [Bob Gaudio/Judy Parker] [ASC] (5/29/76 BCR-38)

__SILVER THREADS AND GOLDEN NEEDLES__ The Springfields—Philips 40038 [Dick Reynolds/Jack Rhodes] [BMI] (7/28/62 BCR-20)

__SILVER THREADS AND GOLDEN NEEDLES__ Jody Miller—Capitol 5429 [Dick Reynolds/Jack Rhodes] [BMI] (6/26/65 BCR-54)

__SILVER THREADS AND GOLDEN NEEDLES__ The Cowsills—MGM 14084 [Dick Reynolds/Jack Rhodes] [BMI] (9/27/69 BCR-57)

__SILVER THREADS AND GOLDEN NEEDLES__ Linda Ronstadt—Asylum 11032 [Dick Reynolds/Jack Rhodes] [BMI] (4/6/74 BC-67)

SILVER THUNDERBIRD Marc Cohn—Atlantic 87678 [Marc Cohn] [ASC] (8/3/91 BC-44)

SIMILAR FEATURES Melissa Etheridge—Island 99251 [Melissa Etheridge] [ASC] (4/8/89 B-94)

SIMON SAYS 1910 Fruitgum Co.—Buddah 24 [Elliot Chiprut] [BMI] (1/13/68 BCR-1)

SIMON ZEALOTES The Assembled Multitude—Atlantic 2780 [Tim Rice/Andrew Lloyd Webber] (Med) [ASC] (2/6/71 BR-87) [IWM]

SIMONE Henry Gross—A&M 1494 [Henry Gross] [ASC] (3/30/74 CR-94)

SIMPEL GIMPEL Horst Jankowski—Mercury 72465 [Horst Jankowski/Bernd Rabe] [BMI] (8/7/65 BCR-66) [I]

SIMPLE Johnny Mathis—Columbia 04468 [Marvin Morrow/Keith Stegall] [ASC] (6/23/84 B-81)

A SIMPLE GAME Four Tops—Motown 1196 [Mike Pinder] [BMI] (2/5/72 BCR-80)

A SIMPLE MAN Lobo—Big Tree 141 [Kent LaVoie] [ASC] (6/24/72 BCR-48)

__SIMPLE SONG OF FREEDOM__ Tim Hardin—Columbia 44920 [Bobby Darin] [BMI] (7/12/69 BCR-47)

__SIMPLE SONG OF FREEDOM__ Buckwheat—London 176 [Bobby Darin] [BMI] (3/25/72 BCR-69)

SIMPLY CALL IT LOVE Gene Chandler—Mercury 73121 [Gene Chandler/James A. Thompson Jr.] [BMI] (10/24/70 BCR-62)

SIMPLY IRRESISTIBLE Robert Palmer—EMI-Manhattan 50133 [Robert Palmer] [ASC] (7/2/88 BC-2)

__SINCE I DON'T HAVE YOU__ The Skyliners—Calico 103 [James Beaumont/Walter Lester/Lennie Martin/Joseph Rock/John L. Taylor/Joseph Verscharen/Janet Vogel] [ASC] (2/14/59 BCR-7)*

__SINCE I DON'T HAVE YOU__ Chuck Jackson—Wand 169 [James Beaumont/Walter Lester/Lennie Martin/Joseph Rock/John L. Taylor/Joseph Verscharen/Janet Vogel] [ASC] (11/14/64 BCR-42)*

__SINCE I DON'T HAVE YOU__ Eddie Holman—ABC 11261 [James Beaumont/Walter Lester/Lennie Martin/Joseph Rock/John L. Taylor/Joseph Verscharen/Janet Vogel] (TSW) [ASC] (5/2/70 BR-32)*

__SINCE I DON'T HAVE YOU__ Art Garfunkel—Columbia 10999 [James Beaumont/Walter Lester/Lennie Martin/Joseph Rock/John L. Taylor/Joseph Verscharen/Janet Vogel] [ASC] (6/2/79 BCR-52)*

__SINCE I DON'T HAVE YOU__ Don McLean—Millennium 11804 [James Beaumont/Walter Lester/Lennie Martin/Joseph Rock/John L. Taylor/Joseph Verscharen/Janet Vogel] [ASC] (4/11/81 BCR-23)*

__SINCE I DON'T HAVE YOU__ Fred Parris & The Five Satins—Elektra 47411 [James Beaumont/Walter Lester/Lennie Martin/Joseph Rock/John L. Taylor/Joseph Verscharen/Janet Vogel] (Med) [ASC] (2/27/82 BC-71)*

__SINCE I FELL FOR YOU__ Lenny Welch—Cadence 1439 [Woodrow Buddy Johnson] [ASC] (10/26/63 BCR-4)

__SINCE I FELL FOR YOU__ Laura Lee—Hot Wax 7201 [Woodrow Buddy Johnson] [ASC] (2/26/72 BCR-43)

SINCE I FELL FOR YOU *Charlie Rich—Epic 50182*
[Woodrow Buddy Johnson] [ASC] (1/17/76 BCR-71)
SINCE I FELL FOR YOU *Hodges, James & Smith—London 256*
[Woodrow Buddy Johnson] (Med) [ASC] (7/9/77 BC-96)
SINCE I FOUND A NEW LOVE Little Johnny Taylor—Galaxy 725
[Little Johnny Taylor] [BMI] (1/4/64 BC-78)
SINCE I LOST MY BABY The Temptations—Gordy 7043
[Warren Moore/Smokey Robinson] [ASC] (7/24/65 BCR-17)
SINCE I LOST THE ONE I LOVE The Impressions—ABC-Paramount 10761
[Curtis Mayfield] [BMI] (2/5/66 BCR-62)
SINCE I MADE YOU CRY The Rivieras (1)—Coed 522
[Robert Mosely/Mayme Watts] [BMI] (1/18/60 B-93)
SINCE I MET YOU BABY *Ivory Joe Hunter—Atlantic 1111*
[Ivory Joe Hunter] [BMI] (11/17/56 BCRt-7)
SINCE I MET YOU BABY *Molly Bee—Dot 15517 [Ivory Joe Hunter] [BMI] (11/17/56 Rt-7)*
SINCE I MET YOU BABY *Mindy Carson—Columbia 40789*
[Ivory Joe Hunter] [BMI] (11/24/56 BRt-7)
SINCE I MET YOU BABY *Bobby Vee—Liberty 55270*
[Ivory Joe Hunter] [BMI] (9/12/60 B-81)
SINCE I MET YOU, BABY *Sonny James, The Southern Gentleman—Capitol 2595*
[Ivory Joe Hunter] [BMI] (9/20/69 BCR-64)
SINCE I MET YOU BABY *Freddy Fender—GRT 031*
[Ivory Joe Hunter] [BMI] (10/18/75 BCR-44)
SINCE YOU BEEN GONE *Head East—A&M 2026 [Russ Ballard] [ASC] (4/8/78 BCR-46)*
SINCE YOU'VE BEEN GONE *(Since You Been Gone)*
Cherie & Marie Currie—Capitol 4754
[Russ Ballard] [ASC] (10/13/79 BCR-91)
SINCE YOU BEEN GONE *Rainbow (2)—Polydor 2014*
[Russ Ballard] [ASC] (10/27/79 BCR-42)
SINCE YOU BROKE MY HEART The Everly Brothers—Cadence 1376
[Don Everly] [BMI] (1/11/60 CR-85)
SINCE YOU SHOWED ME HOW TO BE HAPPY Jackie Wilson—Brunswick 55354
[Gary Jackson/Gerald Sims/Floyd Smith] [BMI] (11/25/67 BCR-29)
SINCE YOU'RE GONE The Cars—Elektra 47433 [Ric Ocasek] [ASC] (3/27/82 BCR-41)
SINCE YOU'VE BEEN GONE Clyde McPhatter—Atlantic 2028
[Howard Greenfield/Neil Sedaka] [BMI] (6/6/59 BCR-31)
(SWEET SWEET BABY) SINCE YOU'VE BEEN GONE *Aretha Franklin—Atlantic 2486*
[Aretha Franklin/Ted White] [BMI] (3/2/68 BCR-4)
SINCE YOU'VE BEEN GONE *Ramsey Lewis—Cadet 5609*
[Aretha Franklin/Ted White] [BMI] (8/31/68 BC-92) [IWM]
SINCE YOU'VE BEEN GONE The Outfield—Columbia 07170
[John Spinks] [ASC] (6/13/87 BC-31)
SINCERELY *The McGuire Sisters—Coral 61323*
[Alan Freed/Harvey Fuqua] [BMI] (12/20/54 BCRt-1)
SINCERELY *The Moonglows—Chess 1581 [Alan Freed/Harvey Fuqua] [BMI] (2/7/55 Rt-1)*
SINCERELY *The Tokens—RCA Victor 47-7925*
[Alan Freed/Harvey Fuqua] [BMI] (9/4/61 R-87)
SINCERELY *The 4 Seasons—Vee-Jay 608*
[Alan Freed/Harvey Fuqua] [BMI] (8/22/64 BCR-60)
SINCERELY *Paul Anka—RCA Victor 74-0164*
[Alan Freed/Harvey Fuqua] [BMI] (5/24/69 BCR-78)
SINCERELY YOURS Sweet Sensation—Atco 99246
[Joseph E. Malloy/Ricardo Pagan] [BMI] (2/4/89 BC-14)
SING A SONG *Barbra Streisand—Columbia 45686*
[Joe Raposo] (Med) [BMI] (9/30/72 BR-94)
SING *Carpenters—A&M 1413 [Joe Raposo] [BMI] (2/17/73 BCR-3)*
SING Tony Orlando & Dawn—Elektra 45387 [Leo Gianangelo] [ASC] (3/12/77 BCR-58)
SING Mickey Thomas—Columbia 68558
[Jonathan Cain/Martin Page/Dean Pitchford] [ASC] (2/4/89 C-73)
SING A HAPPY SONG The O'Jays—Philadelphia Int'l 3707
[Kenneth Gamble/Leon Huff] [BMI] (9/29/79 R-95)
SING A SIMPLE SONG *Sly & The Family Stone—Epic 10407*
[Sylvester Stewart] [BMI] (3/8/69 B-89)
SING A SIMPLE SONG *West Street Mob—Sugar Hill 576*
[Sylvester Stewart] [BMI] (4/17/82 B-89)
SING A SONG David Clayton-Thomas—Columbia 45569
[Gary Wright] [BMI] (4/1/72 CR-83)
SING A SONG Earth, Wind & Fire—Columbia 10251
[Albert Philip McKay/Maurice White] [ASC] (11/22/75 BCR-5)
SING A SONG FOR FREEDOM Frijid Pink—Parrot 349
[Tom Beaudry/Rich Stevers/Gary Thompson] [BMI] (7/18/70 BCR-39)
SING ALONG Jimmy Dean—Columbia 41395 [Robert Allen] [ASC] (5/25/59 CR-43)
SING ALONG WITH ME Tommy Roe—ABC 10908 [Tommy Roe] [BMI] (3/11/67 BCR-91)
SING BOY SING Tommy Sands—Capitol 3867
[Rod McKuen/Tommy Sands] [ASC] (2/8/58 BCR-46)
SING FOR THE DAY Styx—A&M 2110 [Tommy Shaw] (TSW) [ASC] (3/17/79 BCR-22)
SING HIGH—SING LOW Anne Murray—Capitol 2988
[Brent Titcomb] [BMI] (12/5/70 BCR-83)
SING IT, SHOUT IT Starz—Capitol 4434
[Prentice DeLaney/Jeffrey Warren Grob/Brendan Harkin/Richie Ranno/
Michael Lee Smith/Pieter Sweval] [ASC] (6/18/77 BCR-53)
SING ME AWAY Night Ranger—Boardwalk
[Jack Blades/Kelly Keagy] [BMI] (4/9/83 BC-54)
SING OUT THE LOVE (IN MY HEART) Arkade—Dunhill 4247
[Harvey Price/Dan Walsh] [BMI] (8/22/70 B-99)
SING SING SING *Bernie Lowe Orchestra—Cameo 153*
[Louis Prima] [ASC] (11/24/58 BCR-46) [IWM]
SING, SING, SING *Larry Elgart And His Manhattan Swing Orchestra—RCA 13219*
[Louis Prima] (Med) [ASC] (6/5/82 BC-31) [IWM]
SING YOU SINNERS Tony Bennett with Percy Faith and His Orchestra—Columbia 40632
[Sam Coslow/W. Franke Harling] [ASC] (1/20/56 R-78)
SINGING HILLS *Billy Vaughn and His Orchestra—Dot 15771*
[Mack David/Sammy Mysels/Dick Sanford] [ASC] (6/16/58 BCRt-48) [IWM]
THE SINGING HILLS *Don Cogan & LeRoy Holmes & His Orchestra—MGM 12676*
[Mack David/Sammy Mysels/Dick Sanford] [ASC] (6/30/58 Rt-48)
SINGING MY SONG Tammy Wynette—Epic 10462
[Billy Sherrill/Glenn Sutton/Tammy Wynette] [BMI] (4/12/69 BCR-75)
SINGING THE BLUES *Guy Mitchell—Columbia 40769*
[Melvin Endsley] [BMI] (10/20/56 BCtRt-1)
SINGING THE BLUES *Marty Robbins—Columbia 21545*
[Melvin Endsley] [BMI] (10/27/56 BCtRt-1)
SINGLE GIRL Sandy Posey—MGM 13612 [Martha Sharp] [BMI] (11/19/66 BCR-10)
SINGLES GAME Jay And The Techniques—Smash 2171
[Raymond Bloodworth/L. Russell Brown] [BMI] (8/10/68 CR-95)
SINK THE BISMARCK Johnny Horton—Columbia 41568
[Tillman Franks/Johnny Horton] [BMI] (2/15/60 BCR-3)
SINNER MAN Les Baxter, His Chorus and Orchestra—Capitol 3404
[Les Baxter/Will Holt] [ASC] (4/20/56 BR-78) [IWM]
SINNER MAN Trini Lopez—Reprise 0405
[Billy Barberis/Bobby Hart/Trini Lopez/Teddy Randazzo/Bobby Weinstein] [BMI]
(10/16/65 BCR-54)
SINNER MAN Sarah Dash—Kirshner 4278
[Carol George/Rob Hegel] [BMI] (2/10/79 BCR-71)
THE SINS OF A FAMILY P.F. Sloan—Dunhill 4007 [P.F. Sloan] [ASC] (9/11/65 BCR-74)
SIPPIN' 'N CHIPPIN' The T-Bones—Liberty 55867
[Sascha Burland] [BMI] (3/19/66 BCR-62) [I]
SIR DUKE *Stevie Wonder—Tamla 54281 [Stevie Wonder] [ASC] (4/2/77 BCR-1)*
SIR DUKE *Stars On 45—Radio 4019 [Stevie Wonder] (Med) [ASC] (3/27/82 BCR-28)*
SISTER CHRISTIAN Night Ranger—Camel/MCA 52350
[Kelly Keagy] [BMI] (3/10/84 BC-5)
SISTER GOLDEN HAIR America—Warner Bros. 8086 [Gerry Beckley] [ASC] (4/5/75 BCR-1)
SISTER JAMES Nino Tempo And 5th Ave. Sax—A&M 1461
[Jeff Barry/Nino Tempo] [BMI] (9/8/73 BCR-40) [IWM]
SISTER MARY ELEPHANT (SHUDD-UP!) Cheech & Chong—Ode 66041
[Tommy Chong/Cheech Marin] [ASC] (11/17/73 BCR-22)
SISTERS
Rosemary Clooney & Betty Clooney with Paul Weston & His Orch.—Columbia 40305
[Irving Berlin] [ASC] (10/16/54 CRt-24)
SISTERS *Peggy Lee—Decca 29250 [Irving Berlin] [ASC] (10/18/54 Rt-PRE)*
SISTERS ARE DOIN' IT FOR THEMSELVES Eurythmics And Aretha Franklin—RCA 14214
[Annie Lennox/David A. Stewart] [ASC] (10/19/85 BC-18)
SISTERS OF THE MOON Fleetwood Mac—Warner Bros. 49500
[Stevie Nicks] [BMI] (6/7/80 B-86)
SIT DOWN, I THINK I LOVE YOU The Mojo Men—Reprise 0539
[Stephen Stills] [BMI] (1/28/67 BCR-32)
SIT WITH THE GURU Strawberry Alarm Clock—Uni 55055
[Roy Freeman/Ed King/Mark Weitz] [ASC] (3/16/68 BCR-36)
SIT YOURSELF DOWN Stephen Stills—Atlantic 2790
[Stephen Stills] [BMI] (3/6/71 BCR-31)
SITTIN' BY SITTIN' BULL Eddy Arnold—RCA Victor 47-7619
[Jimmy Driftwood] [BMI] (11/16/59 R-99)
SITTIN' IN THE BALCONY *Johnny Dee—Colonial 430*
[John D. Loudermilk] [BMI] (2/23/57 BCtRt-13)
SITTIN' IN THE BALCONY *Eddie Cochran—Liberty 55056*
[John D. Loudermilk] [BMI] (3/2/57 BCtRt-13)
SITTIN' IN THE BALCONY *Don Cornell—Coral 61811*
[John D. Loudermilk] [BMI] (4/13/57 Rt-13)
SITTIN' IN THE LAP OF LUXURY Louie Louie—WTG 73266
[Louie Cordero/Les Pierce] [ASC] (4/28/90 BC-18)
SITTIN' ON A FENCE Twice As Much—MGM 13530
[Mick Jagger/Keith Richards] [BMI] (6/25/66 CR-87)
SITTIN' ON A TIME BOMB (WAITIN' FOR THE HURT TO COME)
The Honey Cone—Hot Wax 7205
[General Johnson/Greg Perry] [BMI] (7/29/72 BC-75)
(SITTIN' ON) THE DOCK OF THE BAY *Otis Redding—Volt 157*
[Steve Cropper/Otis Redding] [BMI] (1/27/68 BCR-1)

***(SITTIN' ON) THE DOCK OF THE BAY** King Curtis & The Kingpins—Atco 6562*
[Steve Cropper/Otis Redding] [BMI] (3/9/68 BR-84) [IWM]
***(SITTIN' ON) THE DOCK OF THE BAY** Sergio Mendes & Brasil '66—A&M 1073*
[Steve Cropper/Otis Redding] [BMI] (6/21/69 BCR-66)
***ON THE DOCK OF THE BAY** The Dells—Cadet 5658*
[Steve Cropper/Otis Redding] [BMI] (10/25/69 BCR-42)
***(SITTIN' ON) THE DOCK OF THE BAY** Sammy Hagar—Capitol 4699*
[Steve Cropper/Otis Redding] [BMI] (4/7/79 BCR-65)
***(SITTIN' ON) THE DOCK OF THE BAY** The Reddings—Believe In a Dream 5-02836*
[Steve Cropper/Otis Redding] [BMI] (6/12/82 BC-55)
***(SITTIN' ON) THE DOCK OF THE BAY** Michael Bolton—Columbia 07680*
[Steve Cropper/Otis Redding] [BMI] (1/23/88 BC-11)
SITTIN' ON TOP OF THE WORLD Jerry Mar—Amp 3 131
[Ray Henderson/Sam Lewis/Joe Young] [ASC] (8/19/57 R-79)
SITTING Cat Stevens—A&M 1396 [Cat Stevens] [ASC] (11/11/72 BCR-15)
SITTING AT THE WHEEL The Moody Blues—Threshold 604
[John Lodge] [ASC] (9/3/83 BC-27)
SITTING IN LIMBO Don Brown—1st American 102
[Plummer Guillermo Bright/Jimmy Cliff] [BMI] (3/11/78 BCR-64)
***SITTING IN THE PARK** Billy Stewart—Chess 1932*
[Billy Stewart] [BMI] (6/19/65 BCR-19)
***SITTING IN THE PARK** GQ—Arista 0510*
[Billy Stewart] [BMI] (6/7/80 CR-85)
SITUATION Yazoo—Sire 29953 [Vince Clarke/Alison Moyet] [BMI] (9/18/82 B-73)
SIX BOYS J. Frank Wilson—Josie 929
[Marvin Montgomery/Mary Tarver] [BMI] (1/30/65 CR-95)
SIX BOYS AND SEVEN GIRLS Anita Bryant—Carlton 518
[Carl Sigman] [ASC] (9/21/59 BCR-62)
SIX DAYS ON THE ROAD Dave Dudley—Golden Wing 3020
[Earl Greene/Carl Montgomery] [BMI] (5/25/63 BCR-26)
SIX MAN BAND The Association—Warner Bros.-Seven Arts 7229
[Terry Kirkman] [BMI] (8/24/68 BCR-26)
6 MINUTES OF PLEASURE LL Cool J—Def Jam 73821
[James Todd Smith/Marlon Williams] [ASC] (9/14/91 B-95)
SIX MONTHS IN A LEAKY BOAT Split Enz—A&M 2411 [Tim Finn] [BMI] (6/12/82 C-81)
SIX NIGHTS A WEEK The Crests—Coed 509
[Alicia Evelyn/Billy Dawn Smith] [BMI] (3/16/59 BCR-28)
SIX O'CLOCK The Lovin' Spoonful—Kama Sutra 225
[John Sebastian] [BMI] (4/29/67 BCR-11)
SIX PACK TO GO Hank Thompson—Capitol 4334
[Dick Hart/Johnny Lowe/Hank Thompson] [BMI] (3/21/60 R-67)
SIX PACKS A DAY Billy Lemmons—Ariola America 7661
[Billy Lemmons] [BMI] (3/26/77 BC-93)
634-5789 (SOULSVILLE, U.S.A) Wilson Pickett—Atlantic 2320
[Steve Cropper/Eddie Floyd] [BMI] (2/12/66 BCR-6)
SIX WHITE HORSES Tommy Cash—Epic 10540 [Larry Murray] [BMI] (12/13/69 BCR-70)
***SIXTEEN CANDLES** Crests—Coed 506*
[Luther Dixon/Allyson Khent] [BMI] (11/24/58 BCR-2)
***16 CANDLES** Fred Parris & The Five Satins—Elektra 47411*
[Luther Dixon/Allyson Khent] (Med) [BMI] (2/27/82 BC-71)
***SIXTEEN REASONS** Connie Stevens—Warner Bros. 5137*
[Bill Post/Doree Post] [BMI] (2/1/60 BCR-3)
***SIXTEEN REASONS** Laverne & Shirley—Atlantic 3367*
[Bill Post/Doree Post] [BMI] (11/20/76 BCR-65)
***SIXTEEN TONS** "Tennessee" Ernie Ford—Capitol 3262*
[Merle Travis] [BMI] (10/24/55 BCRt-1)
***SIXTEEN TONS** Johnny Desmond—Coral 61529 [Merle Travis] [BMI] (11/7/55 BRt-1)*
***SIXTEEN TONS** Lou Monte—Reprise 20,015 [Merle Travis] [BMI] (9/11/61 R-99)*
***SIXTEEN TONS** Tom Jones—Parrot 40016 [Merle Travis] [BMI] (8/12/67 BCR-68)*
***SIXTEEN TONS** The Don Harrison Band—Atlantic 3323*
[Merle Travis] [BMI] (4/17/76 BCR-47)
'65 LOVE AFFAIR Paul Davis—Arista 0661 [Paul Davis] [BMI] (2/27/82 BCR-6)
***SIXTY MINUTE MAN** Bill Darnel—Paris 541 [Rose Marks*/Billy Ward] [BMI] (1/4/60 R-97)*
***SIXTY MINUTE MAN** Rufus Thomas—Stax 0071*
[Rose Marks/Billy Ward] [BMI] (7/4/70 CR-72)*
***SIXTY MINUTE MAN** Clarence Carter—Fame 250*
[Rose Marks/Billy Ward] (TSW) [BMI] (7/7/73 BCR-43)*
SKAT STRUT M.C. Skat Kat And The Stray Mob—Virgin 98770
[Romany Malco/Wayne Vaughn/Maurice White] [ASC] (10/12/91 B-80)
SKATE NOW Lou Courtney—Riverside 4588
[Robert Bateman/Lou Courtney] [BMI] (1/21/67 BCR-54)
SKATEAWAY Dire Straits—Warner Bros. 49632 [Mark Knopfler] [ASC] (12/20/80 B-58)
SKATERS' WALTZ Billy Vaughn And His Orchestra—Dot 16064
[Émile Waldteufel] [ASC] (4/18/60 R-87) [I]
SKATING AWAY ON THE THIN ICE OF THE NEW DAY Jethro Tull—Chrysalis 2103
[Ian Anderson] [ASC] (3/8/75 C-75)
SKELETONS Stevie Wonder—Motown 1907 [Stevie Wonder] [ASC] (10/17/87 BC-19)
SKI KING E. C. Beatty—Colonial 7003 [E.C. Beatty] [BMI] (9/14/59 BCR-40)
SKIN DEEP Cher—Geffen 27894 [Mark Goldenberg/Jon Lind] [BMI] (7/30/88 BC-78)
SKIN TIGHT Ohio Players—Mercury 73609
[Leroy Bonner/Marshall Jones/Ralph Middlebrooks/Andrew Noland/Marvin Pierce/ James Rodger Williams] [BMI] (8/3/74 BCR-11)
SKIN TIGHT, PIN STRIPED, PURPLE PEDAL PUSHERS Sheb Wooley—MGM 13013
[Sheb Wooley] [ASC] (6/12/61 R-84)
SKIN TRADE Duran Duran—Capitol 5670
[Simon Le Bon/Nick Rhodes/Nigel John Taylor] [ASC] (1/31/87 BC-39)
SKINNIE MINNIE (FISH TAIL) Teresa Brewer—Coral 61197
[Vince Fiorino/Dennise Norwood] [BMI] (7/3/54 C-PRE)
SKINNY LEGS AND ALL Joe Tex—Dial 4063 [Joe Tex] [BMI] (10/28/67 BCR-7)
SKINNY MINNIE Bill Haley And His Comets—Decca 30592
[Catherine Cafra/Milt Gabler/Bill Haley/Arrett Keefer] [ASC] (4/5/58 BCRt*-22)
SKINNY MINNIE The Sprouts—RCA Victor 47-7172
[Walter P. Maynard Jr.] [BMI] (4/21/58 Rt*-41)
SKIP A ROPE Henson Cargill—Monument 1041
[Jack (2) Moran/Glenn Tubb] [BMI] (12/16/67 BCR-15)
SKIP TO M'LIMBO The Ventures—Dolton 68 [Don Wilson] [BMI] (4/20/63 R-89) [I]
***SKOKIAAN** Bulawayo Sweet Rhythms Band—London 1491*
[August Msarurgwa] [ASC] (8/21/54 BCtR-2) [IM]
***SKOKIAAN** Ralph Marterie And His Orchestra—Mercury 70432*
[August Msarurgwa] [ASC] (8/21/54 BCtR-2) [IM]
***SKOKIAAN** The Four Lads—Columbia 40306*
[Tom Glazer/August Msarurgwa] [ASC] (9/4/54 BCtR-2)
***SKOKIAAN** Ray Anthony & His Orchestra—Capitol 2896*
[August Msarurgwa] [ASC] (9/25/54 B-PRE) [IM]
***SKOKIAAN (SOUTH AFRICAN SONG)** Bill Haley And His Comets—Decca 31030*
[August Msarurgwa] [ASC] (1/4/60 BCR-70) [IM]
SKY HIGH Jigsaw—Chelsea 3022 [Des Dyer/Clive Scott] [BMI] (8/30/75 BCR-3)
SKY PILOT (PART ONE) Eric Burdon & The Animals—MGM 13939
[Vic Briggs/Eric Burdon/Barry Jenkins/Danny McCulloch/John Weider] [BMI] (5/18/68 BCR-14)
SKYBIRD Neil Diamond—Columbia 45998 [Neil Diamond] [SE] (3/2/74 BCR-48)
SKYBIRD Tony Orlando And Dawn—Arista 0156
[Bruce Roberts/Carole Bayer Sager] [BMI] (10/18/75 BC-49)
SKYLINER Carmen McRae—Decca 30004 [Dale Bennett] [BMI] (3/2/57 B-92)
SKYSCRAPER COMMANDO Elephant's Memory—Metromedia 210
[Stan Bronstein/David Cohen*/Rick Frank] [BMI] (4/3/71 R-88)
SLAM! BAM! The Crew-Cuts—Mercury 70710
[Rose Marie McCoy/Charles Singleton] [BMI] (10/22/55 C-48)
SLAUGHTER Billy Preston—A&M 1380 [Billy Preston] [BMI] (9/2/72 BCR-40)
SLAUGHTER ON TENTH AVENUE The Ventures—Dolton 300
[Richard Rodgers] [ASC] (10/17/64 BCR-35) [I]
SLEDGEHAMMER Peter Gabriel—Geffen 28718 [Peter Gabriel] [BMI] (5/10/86 BC-1)
SLEEP Little Willie John—King 5394
[Earl Burtnett/Adam Geibel] [ASC] (9/5/60 BCR-13)
***SLEEP WALK** Santo & Johnny—Canadian-American 103*
[Ann Farina/Johnny Farina/Santo Farina] [BMI] (7/18/59 BCR-1) [I]
***SLEEPWALK** Larry Carlton—Warner Bros. 50019*
[Ann Farina/Johnny Farina/Santo Farina] [BMI] (2/27/82 BCR-74) [I]
SLEEPIN' Diana Ross—Motown 1295
[Terry Etlinger/Ronald Norman Miller] [BMI] (4/27/74 BCR-53)
SLEEPING BAG ZZ Top—Warner Bros. 28884
[Frank Beard/Billy Gibbons/Dusty Hill] [BMI] (10/19/85 BC-8)
—SLEEPING WITH THE ENEMY see: HAD A DREAM
SLEEPLESS NIGHTS Tony Williams—Reprise 20,019 [Buck Ram] [ASC] (8/28/61 R-87)
SLEEPWALKER The Kinks—Arista 0240 [Ray Davies] [BMI] (4/2/77 BCR-48)
SLEEPY-EYED JOHN Johnny Horton—Columbia 41963
[Tex Atchison] [BMI] (3/27/61 BCR-49)
SLEEPY JOE Herman's Hermits—MGM 13934
[Russell Alquist/John Carter] [BMI] (5/4/68 BCR-51)
SLEEPY LAGOON The Platters—Mercury 71563
[Eric Coates/Jack Lawrence] [ASC] (2/22/60 B-65)
SLICK Willie Hutch—Motown 1252 [Willie Hutch] [BMI] (8/11/73 BCR-65)
SLIDE Slave—Cotillion 44218
[Mark Adams/Carter Bradley/Tim Dozier/Mark Hicks/Tom Lockett/Floyd Miller/ Stephen C. Washington/Danny Webster/Orion Wilhoite] [BMI] (6/11/77 BCR-27) [IWM]
—SLIGHT DETAIL see: PROMISE ME A ROSE
—SLIGHTLY OUT OF TUNE see: DESAFINADO
SLIM JENKIN'S PLACE Booker T. & The M.G.'s—Stax 224
[Steve Cropper/Donald "Duck" Dunn/Al Jackson/Booker T. Jones Jr.] [BMI] (7/29/67 B-70) [I]
SLIP AWAY Clarence Carter—Atlantic 2508
[William Armstrong/Marcus Daniel/Wilbur Terrell] [BMI] (7/13/68 BCR-6)
SLIP AWAY Ian Lloyd—Scotti Brothers 505 [Ric Ocasek] [ASC] (10/13/79 BCR-50)
SLIP AWAY Pablo Cruise—A&M 2373
[David Jenkins/Chuck Lutz/John Pierce] [ASC] (10/17/81 BC-75)
—SLIP-IN MULES see: HIGH HEEL SNEAKERS
SLIP 'N SLIDE Rufus—ABC 11356 [Ron Stockert] [ASC] (4/21/73 CR-82)
SLIP SLIDIN' AWAY Paul Simon—Columbia 10630 [Paul Simon] [BMI] (10/15/77 BCR-5)

SLIPPIN' AND SLIDIN' (PEEPIN' AND HIDIN') *Little Richard—Specialty 572*
[Edwin Bocage/Albert Collins/Richard Penniman/James Smith] [BMI] (4/21/56 B-33)

SLIPIN' AND SLIDIN' *Sing Along With Jim And Monica—Betty 1207*
[Edwin Bocage/Albert Collins/Richard Penniman/James Smith] [BMI] (1/18/64 B-96)

SLIPPIN' & SLIDIN' *Willie Mitchell—Hi 2125*
[Edwin Bocage/Albert Collins/Richard Penniman/James Smith] [BMI] (7/22/67 B-96) [IWM]

SLIPPED, TRIPPED AND FELL IN LOVE Clarence Carter—Atlantic 2818
[George Henry Jackson] [BMI] (7/31/71 BCR-50)

SLIPPERY WHEN WET Commodores—Motown 1338
[Thomas McClary/Walter Orange] [ASC] (5/10/75 BCR-19)

SLIPPIN' AWAY Jean Shepard—United Artists 248 [Bill Anderson] [BMI] (9/15/73 B-81)

SLIPPIN' INTO DARKNESS *War—United Artists 50867*
[Thomas Allen/Harold Brown/Morris Dickerson/Lonnie Jordan/Charles Miller/ Lee Oskar/Howard Scott] [ASC] (12/25/71 BCR-12)

SLIPPING INTO DARKNESS *Ramsey Lewis—Columbia 45634*
[Thomas Allen/Harold Brown/Morris Dickerson/Lonnie Jordan/Charles Miller/ Lee Oskar/Howard Scott] [ASC] (7/29/72 CR-79) [IWM]

SLIPPING AWAY Dave Edmunds—Columbia 03877 [Jeff Lynne] [ASC] (5/14/83 BC-32)

SLIPPING INTO CHRISTMAS Leon Russell—Shelter 7328
[Leon Russell] [BMI] (12/9/72 C-94)

SLIPSTREAM Allan Clarke—Elektra/Curb 46617
[Gary Benson/Allan Clarke] [ASC] (4/26/80 BCR-70)

WRECK OF THE JOHN B *Jimmie Rodgers—Roulette 4260*
[Traditional] [BMI] (7/23/60 BCR-41)

SLOOP JOHN B *The Beach Boys—Capitol 5602 [Traditional] [BMI] (4/2/66 BCR-2)*

THE SLOP Chet Atkins—RCA Victor 47-7847 [Wayne Cogswell] [BMI] (2/27/61 R-79) [I]

SLOP TIME The Sherrys—Guyden 2077 [John Madara/David White] [BMI] (1/12/63 B-97)

SLOW DANCIN' Peabo Bryson—Elektra 69699 [Peabo Bryson] [ASC] (9/29/84 B-82)

SLOW DANCIN' DON'T TURN ME ON The Addrisi Brothers—Buddah 566
[Dick Addrisi/Don Addrisi] [BMI] (3/26/77 BCR-18)

SLOW DANCING *Funky Kings—Arista 0209 [Jack Tempchin] [ASC] (11/6/76 BCR-61)*

SWAYIN' TO THE MUSIC (SLOW DANCIN') *Johnny Rivers—Big Tree 16094*
[Jack Tempchin] [ASC] (6/25/77 BCR-6)

SLOW DOWN *The Beatles—Capitol 5255 [Larry Williams] [BMI] (9/5/64 BCR-23)*

SLOW DOWN *Crow—Amaret 119 [Larry Williams] [BMI] (3/14/70 CR-84)*

SLOW DRAG The Intruders—Gamble 221
[Kenneth Gamble/Leon Huff] [BMI] (11/2/68 BCR-54)

SLOW HAND Pointer Sisters—Planet 47929
[John Bettis/Michael Clark] [ASC] (5/30/81 BCR-2)

SLOW LOVE Doc Box & B. Fresh—Motown 2028
[Marcus Dare/Jon Gordon/Brenard Stallworth] [ASC] (7/21/90 B-51)

SLOW MOTION Wade Flemons—Vee-Jay 321 [Otis Blackwell] [BMI] (8/22/59 C-91)

SLOW MOTION (PART 1) Johnny Williams—Philadelphia Int'l 3518
[Kenneth Gamble/Leon Huff] [BMI] (1/6/73 BCR-78)

SLOW RIDE Foghat—Bearsville 0306 [Dave Peverett] [ASC] (12/6/75 BCR-15)

SLOW TWISTIN' Chubby Checker—Parkway 835 [Kal Mann] [ASC] (2/26/62 BCR-1)

SLOW WALK *Sil Austin—Mercury 70963*
[Sil Austin/Irving Siders‡] [BMI] (10/27/56 BCtRt-11) [I]

SLOW WALK *Bill Doggett—King 5000*
[Sil Austin/Irving Siders‡] [BMI] (11/24/56 BCtRt-11) [I]

SLOW WALK *Ocie Smith—Cadence 1304 [Sil Austin/Irving Siders‡] [BMI] (1/5/57 Rt-17)*

SLOWDOWN John Miles—London 20092
[Bob Marshall/John Miles] [BMI] (3/26/77 BCR-34)

SLOWLY BUT SURELY Gordon Jenkins And His Orchestra and Chorus—Decca 29244
[Al Lewis/Vincent Rose/Larry Stock] [ASC] (10/18/54 R-85)

SLOWLY BUT SURELY Elvis Presley With The Jordanaires—RCA Victor EPA-4383
[Sid Wayne/Ben Weisman] (EP) [ASC] (7/10/65 BCR-70)

SLUEFOOT *Ray Anthony—Capitol 3096 [Johnny Mercer] [ASC] (4/25/55 Rt-57)*

SLUEFOOT *Four Aces—Decca 29476 [Johnny Mercer] [ASC] (4/25/55 Rt-57)*

SLUE FOOT *The Modernaires—Coral 61412 [Johnny Mercer] [ASC] (5/23/55 Rt-57)*

SLUM BABY Booker T. & The M.G.'s—Stax 0049
[Homer Banks/Bettye Crutcher/Raymond Earl Jackson] [BMI] (9/6/69 BCR-75) [IWM]

THE SLY, SLICK, AND THE WICKED The Lost Generation—Brunswick 55436
[Larry Brownlee/Gus Redmond*/Lowrell Simon] [BMI] (6/6/70 BCR-10)

SMACK DAB IN THE MIDDLE *The Mills Brothers—Decca 29511*
[Jesse Stone] [BMI] (5/9/55 CRt-20)

SMACK DAB IN THE MIDDLE *Ella Mae Morse—Capitol 3105*
[Jesse Stone] [BMI] (5/9/55 Rt-20)

SMACK DAB IN THE MIDDLE *Charlie Calhoun—MGM 11989*
[Jesse Stone] [BMI] (5/23/55 Rt-36)

SMACK DAB IN THE MIDDLE
Ray Charles And His Orchestra With The Raelettes—ABC-Paramount 10588
[Jesse Stone] [BMI] (9/26/64 BCR-52)

SMACKWATER JACK Carole King—Ode 66019
[Gerry Goffin/Carole King] (TSW) [BMI] (9/4/71 B-14)

SMALL BEGINNINGS Flash—Capitol 3345
[Peter W. Banks/Colin Carter] [ASC] (6/10/72 BCR-26)

SMALL PARADISE John Cougar—Riva 203 [John Mellencamp] [ASC] (1/26/80 BCR-76)

SMALL SAD SAM Phil McLean—Versatile 107
[Eddie V. Deane/Sunny Skylar] [ASC] (12/4/61 BCR-16)

SMALL TOWN John Cougar Mellencamp—Riva 884 202
[John Mellencamp] [ASC] (11/2/85 BC-6)

SMALL TOWN GIRL John Cafferty And The Beaver Brown Band—Scotti Brothers 05668
[John Cafferty] [BMI] (11/9/85 BC-56)

SMALL WORLD Johnny Mathis—Columbia 41410
[Stephen Sondheim/Jule Styne] [ASC] (6/13/59 BCR-19)

SMALL WORLD Huey Lewis and the News—Chrysalis 43306
[Chris Hayes/Huey Lewis] [ASC] (10/8/88 BC-21)

SMALLTOWN BOY Bronski Beat—MCA 52494
[Steve Bronski/Jimmy Somerville/Larry Steinbachek] [ASC] (12/22/84 BC-32)

SMARTY PANTS First Choice—Philly Groove 179
[Allan Felder/Norman Harris] [BMI] (10/13/73 BCR-38)

SMASHED! BLOCKED! John's Children—White Whale 239
[John Hewlett/Simon Napier-Bell] [BMI] (1/22/67 R-99)

SMELL OF INCENSE Southwest F.O.B.—Hip 8002
[Bob Markley/Ron Morgan] [BMI] (9/21/68 BCR-55)

SMELLS LIKE TEEN SPIRIT Nirvana—DGC 19050
[Kurt Cobain/Dave Grohl/Chris Novoselic] [BMI] (11/30/91 BC-5)

SMILE *Nat "King" Cole—Capitol 2897*
[Charles Chaplin/Geoffrey Parsons/John Turner] [ASC] (9/4/54 BCtR-10)

SMILE *Sunny Gale—RCA Victor 47-5836*
[Charles Chaplin/Geoffrey Parsons/John Turner] [ASC] (9/4/54 CtR-PRE)

SMILE *Tony Bennett—Columbia 41434*
[Charles Chaplin/Geoffrey Parsons/John Turner] [ASC] (7/27/59 BCR-43)

SMILE *Timi Yuro—Liberty 55375*
[Charles Chaplin/Geoffrey Parsons/John Turner] [ASC] (11/6/61 BCR-33)

SMILE *Ferrante & Teicher—United Artists 431*
[Charles Chaplin] [ASC] (3/12/62 BCR-68) [IM]

SMILE *Betty Everett & Jerry Butler—Vee-Jay 633*
[Charles Chaplin/Geoffrey Parsons/John Turner] [ASC] (12/5/64 BCR-42)

SMILE The Emotions—Columbia 10791
[Albert Philip McKay/Maurice White] [ASC] (8/26/78 R-75)

SMILE A LITTLE SMILE FOR ME The Flying Machine—Congress 6000
[Tony Macaulay/Geoff Stephens] [ASC] (9/20/69 BCR-4)

THE SMILE HAS LEFT YOUR EYES Asia—Geffen 29475
[John Wetton] [ASC] (10/15/83 BC-34)

SMILES Crazy Otto—Decca 29403 [Lee S. Roberts] (TSW) [NA] (4/9/55 BCR-21) [I]

SMILIN' Sly & The Family Stone—Epic 10850
[Sylvester Stewart] [BMI] (4/15/72 BCR-25)

SMILING FACES SOMETIMES Undisputed Truth—Gordy 7108
[Barrett Strong/Norman Whitfield] [BMI] (6/26/71 BCR-1)

SMILING ISLANDS Robbie Patton—Atlantic 89955
[David Adelstein/Robbie Patton] [ASC] (3/5/83 BC-46)

SMOKE FROM A DISTANT FIRE The Sanford/Townsend Band—Warner Bros. 8370
[Ed Sanford/Steven Stewart/John Townsend] [BMI] (6/18/77 BCR-9)

(WHEN YOUR HEART'S ON FIRE) SMOKE GETS IN YOUR EYES
Richard Barrett—MGM 12616
[Otto Harbach/Jerome Kern] [ASC] (4/14/58 BR-77)

SMOKE GETS IN YOUR EYES *The Platters—Mercury 71383*
[Otto Harbach/Jerome Kern] [ASC] (11/17/58 BCR-1)

SMOKE GETS IN YOUR EYES *The Four Preps—Capitol 4599*
[Otto Harbach/Jerome Kern] (Med) [ASC] (8/14/61 BCR-14)

SMOKE GETS IN YOUR EYES *Blue Haze—A&M 1357*
[Otto Harbach/Jerome Kern] [ASC] (11/4/72 BCR-14)

SMOKE ON THE WATER Deep Purple—Warner Bros. 7710
[Ritchie Blackmore/Ian Gillan/Roger Glover/Jon Lord/Ian Paice] [ASC] (5/26/73 BCR-2)

SMOKE! SMOKE! SMOKE! (THAT CIGARETTE)
Commander Cody And His Lost Planet Airmen—Paramount 0216
[Merle Travis/Tex Williams] [BMI] (6/23/73 BCR-71)

SMOKEY JOE'S CAFE The Robins—Atco 6059
[Jerry Leiber/Mike Stoller] [BMI] (12/10/55 B-79)

SMOKEY JOE'S LA LA Googie René Combo—Class 1517
[Rafael René] [ASC] (2/26/66 BCR-77) [I]

SMOKIE PART TWO *Bill Black's Combo—Hi 2018 [Bill Black] [BMI] (11/2/59 BCR-13) [I]*

SMOKIE-PART 2 *Bill Doggett—King 5310 [Bill Black] [BMI] (1/4/60 B-95) [I]*

SMOKIN' IN THE BOY'S ROOM *Brownsville Station—Big Tree 16,011*
[Cub Koda/Michael Lutz] [ASC] (10/13/73 BCR-2)

SMOKIN' IN THE BOYS ROOM *Mötley Crüe—Elektra 69625*
[Cub Koda/Michael Lutz] [ASC] (7/13/85 BC-16)

SMOKIN' ROOM Carl Carlton—ABC 12059 [Dennis Belfield] [ASC] (2/15/75 B-91)

SMOKING GUN The Robert Cray Band—Mercury 888343
[Bruce Bromberg/Richard Cousins/Robert Cray] [BMI] (2/7/87 BC-22)

SMOKY MOUNTAIN RAIN Ronnie Milsap—RCA 12084
[Kye Fleming/Dennis W. Morgan] [BMI] (11/29/80 BCR-16)

SMOKY PLACES Corsairs Featuring The Voice Of Jay "Bird" Uzzell—Tuff 1808
[Abner Spector] [ASC] (12/25/61 BCR-11)

SMOOTH CRIMINAL Michael Jackson—Epic 08044
[Michael Jackson] [BMI] (11/12/88 BC-7)
SMOOTH OPERATOR Sarah Vaughan—Mercury 71519
[Clyde Otis/Murray Stein] [BMI] (10/26/59 BCR-32)
SMOOTH OPERATOR Sade—Portrait 37-04807
[Helen Adu/Ray St. John] [BMI] (3/2/85 BC-5)
SMOOTH UP Bulletboys—Warner Bros. 22876
[Jimmy D'Anda/Mick Sweda/Marq Torien/Lonnie Vencent] [ASC] (7/22/89 B-71)
SMUGGLER'S BLUES Glenn Frey—MCA 52546
[Glenn Frey/Jack Tempchin] [ASC] (4/6/85 BC-12)
THE SNAKE Al Wilson—Soul City 767 [Oscar Brown Jr.] [BMI] (7/27/68 BCR-26)
SNAKE EYES Alan Parsons Project—Arista 0635
[Alan Parsons/Eric Woolfson] [BMI] (10/17/81 BR-67)
SNAP-OUT The Interpertations—Bell 757
[Carl Simpson/Lewis Smith/Joe Stevenson] [BMI] (2/8/69 CR-92) [I]
SNAP SHOT Slave—Cotillion 46022
[Mark Adams/Steve Arrington/Charles Carter/Jimmy Douglass/Floyd Miller] [BMI] (10/24/81 BR-67)
SNAP YOUR FINGERS *Joe Henderson—Todd 1072*
[Grady Martin/Alex Zanetis] [BMI] (5/7/62 BCR-6)
SNAP YOUR FINGERS *Barbara Lewis—Atlantic 2214*
[Grady Martin/Alex Zanetis] [BMI] (12/28/63 BCR-65)
SNATCHING IT BACK Clarence Carter—Atlantic 2605
[Clarence Carter/George Henry Jackson] [BMI] (2/22/69 BCR-16)
SNEAKIN' SALLY THROUGH THE ALLEY Robert Palmer—Island 006
[Allen Toussaint] [BMI] (7/19/75 C-96)
SNEAKIN' UP BEHIND YOU The Brecker Brothers—Arista 0122
[Michael Brecker/Randy Brecker/Don Grolnick/Will Lee/David Sanborn] [BMI] (6/7/75 BCR-47) [I]
SNEAKY SNAKE Tom T. Hall—Mercury 73641 [Tom T. Hall] [BMI] (3/1/75 BCR-55)
SNOOKEROO Ringo Starr—Apple 1880
[Elton John/Bernie Taupin] (TSW) [BMI] (2/8/75 BR-3)
SNOOPY FOR PRESIDENT The Royal Guardsmen—Laurie 3451
[Phil Gernhard/Dick Holler/Arnold Shapiro] [BMI] (7/13/68 BR-85)
SNOOPY VS. THE RED BARON The Royal Guardsmen—Laurie 3366
[Phil Gernhard/Dick Holler] [BMI] (12/10/66 BCR-1)
SNOOPY'S CHRISTMAS The Royal Guardsmen—Laurie 3416
[Luigi Creatore/Hugo Peretti/George David Weiss] [ASC] (12/9/67 CR-10)
SNOW BLIND FRIEND Steppenwolf—Dunhill 4269 [Hoyt Axton] [BMI] (2/27/71 BCR-44)
SNOW FLAKE Jim Reeves—RCA Victor 47-8719 [Ned Miller] [BMI] (1/1/66 BCR-56)
SNOWBIRD Anne Murray—Capitol 2738 [Gene MacLellan] [BMI] (7/18/70 BCR-4)
SNOWBOUND FOR CHRISTMAS The DeCastro Sisters—Abbott 3012
[Al Chorney/Hal Shrager/Sid Shrager] [BMI] (12/31/55 B-84)
SO ALIVE Love and Rockets—RCA 8956
[Daniel Ash/David Haskins/Kevin Haskins] [BMI] (5/20/89 BC-3)
SO ALL ALONE The Teen Queens—RPM 460
[Aaron Collins/Maxwell Davis/Sam Ling‡] [BMI] (5/11/56 R-50)
SO BAD Paul McCartney—Columbia 04296 [Paul McCartney] [ASC] (12/24/83 BC-21)
SO BLUE The Vibrations—Checker 954
[Lew Brown/Helen Crawford/Buddy DeSylva/Ray Henderson] [ASC] (6/27/60 R-83)
SO CLOSE Brook Benton—Mercury 71443
[Brook Benton/Luther Dixon/Clyde Otis] [BMI] (5/2/59 BCR-38)
SO CLOSE Jake Holmes—Polydor 14041 [Jake Holmes] [ASC] (9/26/70 BCR-27)
SO CLOSE Diana Ross—RCA 13424
[Rob Mounsey/Diana Ross/Bill Wray] [ASC] (2/5/83 BC-35)
SO CLOSE Daryl Hall & John Oates—Arista 2085
[Jon Bon Jovi/Rick Giles*/George Green/Daryl Hall/Danny Kortchmar] [ASC] (9/29/90 BC-11)
SO CLOSE TO MY HEART Kathy Linden—Felsted 8587
[Jimmie Crane/Al Jacobs/Phil Tucker] [ASC] (8/8/59 C-84)
SO DEEP Brenda Lee—Decca 31348
[Jackie DeShannon/Sharon Sheeley] [BMI] (1/8/62 BCR-40)
SO EMOTIONAL Whitney Houston—Arista 1-9642
[Thomas F. Kelly/Billy Steinberg] [ASC] (10/31/87 BC-1)
SO EXCITED B.B. King—BluesWay 61035
[Gerald Jemmott/B.B. King] [BMI] (4/11/70 BCR-50)
SO FAR AWAY Hank Jacobs—Sue 795
[Kent Harris*/Henry Jacobs] [BMI] (1/18/64 BCR-63) [I]
SO FAR AWAY Carole King—Ode 66019 [Carole King] (TSW) [ASC] (9/4/71 BCR-5)
SO FAR AWAY Dire Straits—Warner Bros. 28789 [Mark Knopfler] [ASC] (3/1/86 BC-15)
SO FAR SO GOOD Sheena Easton—EMI America 8332
[Tom Snow/Cynthia Weil] [BMI] (7/26/86 BC-42)
SO FINE *The Fiestas—Old Town 1062 [Johnny Otis] [BMI] (4/4/59 BCR-11)*
SO FINE *Johnny Rivers—United Artists XW226-W*
[Johnny Otis] (Med) [BMI] (7/14/73 R-75)
SO FINE *Oak Ridge Boys—MCA 52065*
[Johnny Otis] [BMI] (6/12/82 BC-76)
SO GOOD The Eleventh Hour—20th Century 2076
[Bob Crewe/Kenny Nolan] [BMI] (4/6/74 B-94)
SO GOOD, SO RIGHT Brenda Russell—Horizon 123
[Brenda Russell] [ASC] (8/11/79 BCR-26)
SO GOOD TOGETHER Andy Kim—Steed 720
[Jeff Barry/Andy Kim] [BMI] (9/20/69 BCR-18)
SO HARD Pet Shop Boys—EMI 50329 [Chris Lowe/Neil Tennant] [ASC] (10/20/90 BC-62)
SO HARD LIVIN' WITHOUT YOU Airwaves—A&M 2032
[John Bettis/Kerry Chater] [ASC] (5/13/78 BCR-62)
SO HIGH (ROCK ME BABY AND ROLL ME AWAY) Dave Mason—Columbia 10509
[Jack Conrad/Mentor Williams] [BMI] (5/14/77 BCR-69)
SO HIGH SO LOW LaVern Baker—Atlantic 2033
[LaVern Baker/Traditional] [BMI] (7/27/59 BCR-52)
SO I CAN LOVE YOU The Emotions—Volt 4010
[Sheila Hutchinson] [BMI] (5/24/69 BCR-39)
SO IN LOVE Curtis Mayfield—Curtom 0105 [Curtis Mayfield] [BMI] (9/27/75 BCR-58)
SO IN LOVE Orchestral Manoeuvres In The Dark—A&M 2746
[Stephen Hague/Paul Humphreys/Andrew McCluskey] [BMI] (8/31/85 BC-26)
SO IN TO YOU Atlanta Rhythm Section—Polydor 14373
[Buddy Buie/Dean Daughtry/Robert Nix] [BMI] (1/22/77 BCR-5)
SO LONG Fats Domino—Imperial 5396
[Dave Bartholomew/Fats Domino] [BMI] (7/28/56 BCR-44)
SO LONG Firefall—Atlantic 3452 [Rick Roberts] [BMI] (1/14/78 BCR-48)
SO LONG BABE Nancy Sinatra—Reprise 0407 [Lee Hazlewood] [ASC] (10/16/65 BCR-81)
SO LONG BABY Del Shannon—Big Top 3083 [Del Shannon] [BMI] (9/11/61 BCR-28)
SO LONG DEARIE Louis Armstrong—Mercury 72338
[Jerry Herman] [ASC] (9/26/64 BCR-31)
SO LONG DIXIE Blood, Sweat & Tears—Columbia 45661
[Barry Mann/Cynthia Weil] [BMI] (9/30/72 BCR-44)
SO LONG I'M GONE Warren Smith—Sun 268
[Roy Orbison/Sam Phillips*] [BMI] (6/10/57 B-72)
SO LONG, MARIANNE Brian Hyland—Uni 55287 [Leonard Cohen] [BMI] (7/3/71 CR-93)
SO LONG MY LOVE Frank Sinatra—Capitol 3703
[Sammy Cahn/Lew Spence] [ASC] (4/27/57 BCR-51)
SO MANY MEN, SO LITTLE TIME Miquel Brown—TSR 102
[Ian Levine/Fiachra Trench] [BMI] (9/24/83 C-94)
SO MANY PEOPLE Chase—Epic 10806
[Roger Nichols/Paul Williams] [BMI] (12/11/71 BCR-62)
SO MANY WAYS Brook Benton—Mercury 71512
[Bobby Stevenson] [BMI] (10/5/59 BCR-3)
SO MUCH Little Anthony And The Imperials—End 1036
[Richard Barrett] [BMI] (11/22/58 BC-73)
SO MUCH FOR LOVE The Venetians—Chrysalis 43056 [Rik Swinn] [ASC] (2/28/87 B-88)
SO MUCH IN LOVE *The Tymes—Parkway 871*
[William E. Jackson III/Roy Straigis/George R. Williams] [BMI] (6/1/63 BCR-1)
SO MUCH IN LOVE *Timothy B. Schmit—Full Moon 69939*
[William E. Jackson III/Roy Straigis/George R. Williams] [BMI] (10/2/82 BC-59)
SO MUCH LOVE *Steve Alaimo—ABC-Paramount 10805*
[Gerry Goffin/Carole King] [BMI] (5/7/66 BCRt-72)
SO MUCH LOVE *Ben E. King—Atco 6413*
[Gerry Goffin/Carole King] [BMI] (5/7/66 BCRt-54)
SO MUCH LOVE Faith, Hope & Charity—Maxwell 805
[Joe Cobb/Van McCoy] [BMI] (5/16/70 BCR-35)
—SO NICE see: SUMMER SAMBA
SO RARE *Jimmy Dorsey with Orchestra and Chorus—Fraternity 755*
[Jerry Herst/Jack Sharpe] [ASC] (2/23/57 BCR-2)
SO RARE *Mavis Rivers—Capitol 4333 [Jerry Herst/Jack Sharpe] [ASC] (2/29/60 R-92)*
SO RARE *Andy Williams—Cadence 1433*
[Jerry Herst/Jack Sharpe] [ASC] (11/24/62 R-93)
SO SAD THE SONG Gladys Knight & The Pips—Buddah 544
[Gerry Goffin/Michael Masser] [BMI] (10/9/76 BCR-47)
SO SAD (TO WATCH GOOD LOVE GO BAD) The Everly Brothers—Warner Bros. 5163
[Don Everly] [BMI] (8/29/60 BCR-5)
SO STRANGE The Jesters—Winley 218
[Ethel Byrd*/David Clowney*/Adam Jackson/Paul Winley] [BMI] (7/15/57 B-100)
SO THE STORY GOES Living In A Box—Chrysalis 43162
[Richard Darbyshire/Marcus Vere] [ASC] (10/17/87 B-81)
SO THIS IS LOVE The Castells—Era 3073 [Herbert Newman] [ASC] (4/14/62 BCR-21)
SO TOUGH *The Original Casuals—Back Beat 503 [Gary Mears] [BMI] (2/1/58 BCRt-28)*
SO TOUGH *Kuf-Linx—Challenge 1013 [Gary Mears] [BMI] (2/24/58 BRt-37)*
SO TRUE Peaches & Herb—Date 1633 [Diana Allen/Robert (2) Allen] [ASC] (1/18/69 R-96)
SO VERY HARD TO GO Tower Of Power—Warner Bros. 7687
[Emilio Castillo/Steve Kupka] [ASC] (5/5/73 BCR-15)
SO WHAT *Bill Black's Combo—Hi 2055 [Bill Black] [BMI] (7/28/62 BCR-65) [I]*
SO WHAT *Bill Black's Combo—Hi 2055 [Bill Black] [BMI] (1/2/65 BR-89) [I]*
SO WILL I The Ames Brothers—RCA Victor 47-6208
[George Kelly/Mayme Watts] [BMI] (8/29/55 R-75)
SO WRONG Patsy Cline—Decca 31406
[Danny Dill*/Carl Perkins/Mel Tillis*] [BMI] (7/14/62 BCR-44)
SO WRONG Patrick Simmons—Elektra 69839
[Patrick Simmons/Chris Thompson] [ASC] (3/19/83 BC-30)

SO YOU ARE A STAR Hudson Brothers—Casablanca 0108
[Bill Hudson/Brett Hudson/Mark Hudson] [BMI] (9/7/74 BCR-20)
SO YOU RAN Orion The Hunter—Portrait 04483
[Fran Cosmo/Barry Goudreau] [ASC] (6/2/84 BC-58)
SO YOU WANT TO BE A ROCK 'N' ROLL STAR The Byrds—Columbia 43987
[Chris Hillman/Roger McGuinn] [BMI] (1/28/67 BCR-28)
SO YOU WIN AGAIN Hot Chocolate—Big Tree 16096
[Russ Ballard] [ASC] (7/9/77 BCR-31)
SO YOUNG *Clyde Stacy—Candlelight 1015 [Dwight Sherman] [BMI] (6/17/57 B-68)*
SO YOUNG *Clyde Stacy—Argyle 1001 [Dwight Sherman] [BMI] (11/16/59 B-99)*
SO YOUNG, SO BAD Starz—Capitol 4637 [Michael Lee Smith] [ASC] (10/21/78 BCR-73)
SOCIETY GIRL (vague parody of Rag Doll) The Rag Dolls—Parkway 921
[Bob Crewe/Sandy Linzer/Denny Randell] [BMI] (9/5/64 BCR-91) [P]
SOCIETY'S CHILD (BABY I'VE BEEN THINKING) Janis Ian—Verve Forecast 5027
[Janis Ian] [BMI] (5/20/67 BCR-12)
SOCK IT TO ME-BABY! Mitch Ryder And The Detroit Wheels—New Voice 820
[L. Russell Brown/Bob Crewe] [BMI] (2/4/67 BCR-4)
SOCKIN' 1-2-3-4 John Roberts—Duke 425
[Robert Garner/John Roberts] [BMI] (11/18/67 BCR-71)
SOFT Bill Doggett—King 5080 [Tiny Bradshaw] [BMI] (11/4/57 BR-51) [I]
SOFT AND WET Prince—Warner Bros. 8619
[Christopher Moon/Prince] [ASC] (9/30/78 BCR-74)
SOFT SANDS *The Chordettes—Cadence 1330*
[Carroll Coates/Lou Stein] [BMI] (8/3/57 BCRt-56)
SOFT SANDS *Dorothy Collins—Coral 61865*
[Carroll Coates/Lou Stein] [BMI] (8/3/57 Rt-73)
SOFT SANDS *The Rover Boys—Vik 0283 [Carroll Coates/Lou Stein] [BMI] (8/3/57 Rt-73)*
SOFT SANDS *Oscar Peterson—Verve 10056 [Lou Stein] [BMI] (8/3/57 Rt-73) [I]*
SOFT SANDS *Ray Ellis & His Orchestra—Columbia 40982*
[Carroll Coates/Lou Stein] [BMI] (8/12/57 Rt-73)
SOFT SANDS *The Voices Of Walter Schumann—RCA Victor 47-6986*
[Carroll Coates/Lou Stein] [BMI] (8/12/57 Rt-73)
SOFT SUMMER BREEZE *Eddie Heywood—Mercury 70863*
[Eddie Heywood] [BMI] (6/30/56 BCRt-7) [IM]
SOFT SUMMER BREEZE *The Diamonds—Mercury 70934*
[Eddie Heywood/Judy Spencer] [BMI] (8/25/56 BRt-7)
SOFT SUMMER BREEZE *Romaine Brown & His Romaines—Decca 30054*
[Eddie Heywood/Judy Spencer] [BMI] (9/22/56 Rt-10)
SOFT SUMMER BREEZE *Eddie Heywood—Mercury 71462*
[Eddie Heywood] [BMI] (7/11/59 C-100) [IM]
SOFTLY AS I LEAVE YOU *Matt Monro—Liberty 55449*
[Giorgio Calabrese/Antonio De Vita/Hal Shaper] [ASC] (8/25/62 C-84) [FET]
SOFTLY, AS I LEAVE YOU *Frank Sinatra—Reprise 0301*
[Giorgio Calabrese/Antonio De Vita/Hal Shaper] [ASC] (9/5/64 BCR-27) [FET]
SOFTLY, SOFTLY *Guy Lombardo & His Royal Canadians—Decca 29434*
[Pierre Dudan/Mark Paul/Paddy Roberts] [ASC] (2/28/55 Rt-54)
SOFTLY, SOFTLY *Jaye P. Morgan—RCA Victor 47-6016*
[Pierre Dudan/Mark Paul/Paddy Roberts] (TSW) [ASC] (4/9/55 BCRt-18)
SOFTLY SOFTLY The Equals—President 109 [Eddy Grant] [BMI] (12/7/68 R-94)
SOFTLY WHISPERING I LOVE YOU The English Congregation—Atco 6865
[Roger Cook/Roger Greenaway] [ASC] (1/8/72 BCR-25)
SOLD ME DOWN THE RIVER The Alarm—I.R.S. 73002
[Eddie MacDonald/Mike Peters] [ASC] (10/7/89 BC-50)
SOLD TO THE MAN WITH THE BROKEN HEART Tony Bennett with Percy Faith—
Columbia 40849 [Sammy Cahn/Jimmy Van Heusen] [ASC] (3/16/57 R-76)
SOLDIER BOY *The Four Fellows—Glory 234*
[David P. Jones/Theodore Williams Jr.] [BMI] (8/15/55 Rt-21)
SOLDIER BOY *Eydie Gorme—Coral 61481*
[David P. Jones/Theodore Williams Jr.] [BMI] (8/22/55 Rt-71)
SOLDIER BOY *Ella Fitzgerald—Decca 29648*
[David P. Jones/Theodore Williams Jr.] [BMI] (8/22/55 Rt-21)
SOLDIER BOY *Pat O'Day—MGM 12025*
[David P. Jones/Theodore Williams Jr.] [BMI] (8/22/55 Rt-71)
SOLDIER BOY *Sunny Gale—RCA Victor 47-6227*
[David P. Jones/Theodore Williams Jr.] [BMI] (8/22/55 Rt-21)
SOLDIER BOY The Shirelles—Scepter 1228
[Luther Dixon/Florence Green] [BMI] (3/17/62 BCR-1)
SOLDIER OF LOVE Donny Osmond—Capitol 44369
[Evan Rogers/Carl Sturken] [BMI] (3/25/89 BC-2)
SOLDIER'S JOY Hawkshaw Hawkins—Columbia 41419 [Traditional] [BMI] (8/3/59 B-87)
SOLDIER'S LAST LETTER Merle Haggard & The Strangers—Capitol 3024
[Redd Stewart/Ernest Tubb] [BMI] (3/20/71 B-90)
SOLE SOLE SOLE Siw Malmkvist - Umberto Marcato—Jubilee 5479
[Arturo Casadei/Laura Zanin] [ASC] (7/18/64 BCR-58) [F]
SOLEDAD Eric Burdon & Jimmy Witherspoon—MGM 14296
[Eric Burdon/John Sterling] [BMI] (10/30/71 CR-88)
SOLID Ashford & Simpson—Capitol 5397
[Nick Ashford/Valerie Simpson] [ASC] (11/10/84 BC-12)
SOLID ROCK Goanna—Atco 99895 [Shane Howard] [NA] (6/11/83 B-71)
SOLITAIRE The Embers—Empress 101
[Renée Borek/King Guion/Carl Nutter] [BMI] (7/29/61 CR-36)
SOLITAIRE Carpenters—A&M 1721 [Phil Cody/Neil Sedaka] [BMI] (8/2/75 BCR-15)
SOLITAIRE Peter Mclan—ARC 11214 [Anne Mclan/Peter Mclan] [ASC] (3/29/80 BCR-52)
SOLITAIRE Laura Branigan—Atlantic 89868
[Martine Clémenceau/Diane Warren] [ASC] (3/19/83 BC-7)
SOLITARY MAN *Neil Diamond—Bang 519 [Neil Diamond] [SE] (5/14/66 BCR-55)*
SOLITARY MAN *Neil Diamond—Bang 578 [Neil Diamond] [SE] (7/11/70 BCR-16)*
SOLITARY MAN *T.G. Sheppard—Hitsville 6032 [Neil Diamond] [SE] (7/3/76 BR-91)*
SOLITUDE STANDING Suzanne Vega—A&M 2960
[Stephen Ferrera/Anton Sanko/Marc Shulman/Suzanne Vega/Michael Visceglia] [BMI]
(9/12/87 B-94)
SOLO Billy Sans—Invictus 9102
[Paschal Cusimano/Sam DiMaggio] [BMI] (9/11/71 BR-91)
—SOLO TORRO see: LONELY BULL
SOLSBURY HILL *Peter Gabriel—Atco 7079 [Peter Gabriel] [BMI] (4/30/77 BCR-68)*
SOLSBURY HILL *Peter Gabriel—Geffen 29542 [Peter Gabriel] [BMI] (8/27/83 B-84)*
SOLUTION FOR POLLUTION
Charles Wright And The Watts 103rd Street Rhythm Band—Warner Bros. 7451
[Charles Wright] [BMI] (1/2/71 BCR-61)
SOME BEAUTIFUL Jack Wild—Capitol 2742 [Billy Page] [BMI] (5/30/70 BCR-92)
SOME BROKEN HEARTS NEVER MEND Don Williams—ABC/Dot 17683
[Wayland Holyfield] [ASC] (5/21/77 C-99)
SOME CHANGES ARE FOR GOOD Dionne Warwick—Arista 0602
[Michael Masser/Carole Bayer Sager] [ASC] (6/20/81 BCR-61)
SOME COME RUNNING Jim Capaldi—Island 99220
[Jim Capaldi/Peter Vale/Miles Waters] [ASC] (11/19/88 C-88)
SOME DAY Frankie Laine—Columbia 40235
[Rudolf Friml/Brian Hooker] [ASC] (7/3/54 BC-PRE)
SOME DAY I'LL BE A FARMER Melanie—Neighborhood 4204
[Melanie Safka] [ASC] (5/20/72 CR-73)
SOME DAY SOON Eddie Fisher—RCA Victor 47-6746
[Mack Gordon/Josef Myrow] [ASC] (1/5/57 BR-78)
SOME DAY WE'RE GONNA LOVE AGAIN The Searchers—Kapp 609
[Sharon McMahan] [BMI] (8/15/64 BCR-34)
SOME DAYS ARE DIAMONDS (SOME DAYS ARE STONES) John Denver—RCA 12246
[Dick Feller] [BMI] (6/13/81 BCR-36)
SOME ENCHANTED EVENING *Jay & The Americans—United Artists 919*
[Oscar Hammerstein/Richard Rodgers] [ASC] (9/4/65 BCR-13)
SOME ENCHANTED EVENING *Jane Olivor—Columbia 10527*
[Oscar Hammerstein/Richard Rodgers] [ASC] (9/3/77 BC-89)
SOME GUYS HAVE ALL THE LUCK *The Persuaders—Atco 6943*
[Jeff Fortgang] [ASC] (10/20/73 BCR-35)
SOME GUYS HAVE ALL THE LUCK *Rod Stewart—Warner Bros. 29215*
[Jeff Fortgang] [ASC] (8/25/84 BC-10)
SOME KIND A EARTHQUAKE
Duane Eddy His "Twangy" guitar and The Rebels—Jamie 1130
[Duane Eddy/Lee Hazlewood] [BMI] (10/3/59 BCR-28) [I]
SOME KIND OF FRIEND Barry Manilow—Arista 1046
[Adrienne Anderson/Barry Manilow] [BMI] (2/26/83 BC-26)
SOME KIND OF LOVER Jody Watley—MCA 53235
[André Cymone/Jody Watley] [ASC] (1/30/88 BC-9)
SOME KIND OF WONDERFUL The Drifters—Atlantic 2096
[Gerry Goffin/Carole King] [BMI] (3/20/61 BCR-11)
SOME KIND OF WONDERFUL *Soul Brothers Six—Atlantic 2406*
[John Ellison] [BMI] (6/24/67 BCR-91)
(SHE'S) SOME KIND OF WONDERFUL *The Fantastic Johnny C—Phil-L.A. Of Soul 320*
[John Ellison] [BMI] (11/16/68 B-87)
SOME KIND OF WONDERFUL *Grand Funk—Capitol 4002*
[John Ellison] [BMI] (12/14/74 BCR-3)
SOME KINDA FUN Chris Montez—Monogram 507
[James Lee/Chris Montez] [BMI] (12/1/62 BCR-43)
SOME LIKE IT HOT The Power Station—Capitol 5444
[Robert Palmer/Andy Taylor/Nigel John Taylor] [ASC] (3/16/85 BC-6)
SOME OF SHELLY'S BLUES *Nitty Gritty Dirt Band—Liberty 56134*
[Michael Nesmith] [BMI] (11/22/69 R-95)
SOME OF SHELLY'S BLUES *Nitty Gritty Dirt Band—United Artists 50817*
[Michael Nesmith] [BMI] (9/11/71 BCR-64)
SOME OF YOUR LOVIN' Johnny Nash—ABC-Paramount 10181
[Terry Philips/Phil Spector] [BMI] (2/27/61 CR-93)
SOME PEOPLE Belouis Some—Capitol 5492 [Belouis Some] [ASC] (8/3/85 BC-67)
SOME PEOPLE Paul Young—Columbia 06423
[Ian Kewley/Paul Young] [NA] (11/15/86 BC-59)
SOME SUNDAY MORNING Wayne Newton—Capitol 5553
[Ray Heindorf/M.K. Jerome/Ted Koehler] [ASC] (12/25/65 CR-96)
SOME THINGS A MAN'S GOTTA DO Shango—Dunhill 4242
[Richie Hernandez/Lynn Lundgren] [BMI] (7/25/70 C-90)
SOME THINGS ARE BETTER LEFT UNSAID Daryl Hall & John Oates—RCA 14035
[Daryl Hall] [BMI] (3/16/85 BC-15)

SOME THINGS YOU NEVER GET USED TO Diana Ross And The Supremes—Motown 1126 [Nick Ashford/Valerie Simpson] [ASC] (6/8/68 BCR-21)

SOME VELVET MORNING *Nancy Sinatra & Lee Hazlewood—Reprise 0651 [Lee Hazlewood] [ASC] (1/6/68 BCR-26)*

SOME VELVET MORNING *Vanilla Fudge—Atco 6679 [Lee Hazlewood] [ASC] (5/24/69 C-81)*

SOMEBODY Bryan Adams—A&M 2701 [Bryan Adams/Jim Vallance] [BMI] (2/2/85 BC-9)

SOMEBODY CARES Tommy James And The Shondells—Roulette 7016 [Ritchie Cordell/Bo Gentry/Harvey Weisenfeld] [BMI] (7/13/68 BCR-35)

SOMEBODY ELSE IS TAKING MY PLACE *Jaye P. Morgan—MGM 12815 [Bob Ellsworth/Richard Howard/Russ Morgan] [ASC] (8/17/59 R-81)*

SOMEBODY ELSE IS TAKING MY PLACE *Joni James—MGM 13037 [Bob Ellsworth/Richard Howard/Russ Morgan] [ASC] (9/25/61 R-62)*

SOMEBODY ELSE IS TAKING MY PLACE *Al Martino—Capitol 5384 [Bob Ellsworth/Richard Howard/Russ Morgan] [ASC] (3/27/65 BCR-53)*

SOMEBODY ELSE'S GUY Jocelyn Brown—Vinyl Dreams 71 [Annette E. Brown/Jocelyn Brown] [BMI] (6/16/84 B-75)

SOMEBODY ELSE'S LOVE SONG Georgie Shaw—Decca 29160 [Norman Kaye/Ethel Marsh] [ASC] (7/10/54 C-49)

SOMEBODY ELSE'S SWEETHEART The Wanderers—Cub 9099 [Burt Bacharach/Hal David] [ASC] (11/6/61 R-97)

SOMEBODY HAVE MERCY Sam Cooke—RCA Victor 47-8088 [Sam Cooke] [BMI] (10/20/62 BCR-59)

SOMEBODY HELP ME Spencer Davis Group—United Artists 50162 [Jackie Edwards] [BMI] (6/17/67 BCR-45)

SOMEBODY LIKE ME Eddy Arnold—RCA Victor 47-8965 [Wayne Carson Thompson] [BMI] (10/8/66 BCR-36)

SOMEBODY LIKE YOU 38 Special—A&M 2854 [Don Barnes/Jeff Carlisi/Larry Steele/Jim Vallance/Donnie Van Zant] [ASC] (7/19/86 BC-47)

SOMEBODY LIKE YOU Robbie Nevil—EMI 50176 [Richard Feldman/Robbie Nevil/Jeff Pescetto] [ASC] (3/18/89 BC-54)

SOMEBODY LOVES YOU The Delfonics—Philly Groove 154 [Thom Bell/William Hart] [BMI] (2/8/69 BCR-72)

SOMEBODY LOVES YOU The Whispers—Janus 200 [Theresa McFaddin/Warren Sams] [ASC] (1/27/73 B-94)

SOMEBODY NEW Chuck Jackson—Wand 161 [Luther Dixon/Robert Mosely*] [BMI] (10/3/64 B-93)

SOMEBODY NOBODY WANTS Dion—Laurie 3101 [Sylvia Dee/George Goehring] [ASC] (7/3/61 CR-73)

SOMEBODY SAVE ME Cinderella—Mercury 888483 [Tom Keifer] [ASC] (4/25/87 BC-66)

SOMEBODY SEND MY BABY HOME Lenny LeBlanc—Capitol/MSS 4979 [Ava Aldridge/Lenny LeBlanc] [BMI] (3/28/81 BCR-55)

SOMEBODY SOMEWHERE *Doris Day—Columbia 40673 [Frank Loesser] [ASC] (5/25/56 Rt-75)*

SOMEBODY SOMEWHERE *Pat Kirby—Decca 29884 [Frank Loesser] [ASC] (5/25/56 Rt-75)*

SOMEBODY SOMEWHERE *Roy Hamilton—Epic 9160 [Frank Loesser] [ASC] (5/25/56 Rt-75)*

SOMEBODY SOMEWHERE Platinum Blonde—Epic 05804 [Mark Holmes] [ASC] (4/12/86 B-82)

SOMEBODY (SOMEWHERE) NEEDS YOU Darrell Banks—Revilot 203 [Marc Gordon/Frank Edward Wilson] [BMI] (10/15/66 BCR-55)

SOMEBODY SPECIAL Rod Stewart—Warner Bros. 49686 [Phil Chen/Jim Cregan/Gary Grainger/Steve Harley/Kevin Savigar/Rod Stewart] [ASC] (3/21/81 BC-71)

SOMEBODY STOLE MY DOG Rufus Thomas—Stax 149 [Steve Cropper/Rufus Thomas] [BMI] (4/11/64 BR-86)

SOMEBODY STOLE MY GAL The Johnston Brothers—London 1526 [Leo Wood] (Med) [ASC] (7/11/55 R-61)

SOMEBODY TO LOVE Bobby Darin—Atco 6179 [Bobby Darin] [BMI] (9/26/60 BCR-45)

SOMEBODY TO LOVE Jefferson Airplane—RCA Victor 47-9140 [Darby Slick] [BMI] (4/1/67 BCR-5)

SOMEBODY TO LOVE Queen—Elektra 45362 [Freddie Mercury] [BMI] (11/20/76 BCR-9)

SOMEBODY TOUCHED ME Buddy Knox with The Rhythm Orchids—Roulette 4082 [Ahmet Ertegun] [BMI] (6/30/58 BCR-22)

SOMEBODY UP THERE LIKES ME Perry Como—RCA Victor 47-6590 [Sammy Cahn/Bronislaw Kaper] [ASC] (7/20/56 BCR-18)

SOMEBODY'S BABY Jackson Browne—Asylum 69982 [Jackson Browne/Danny Kortchmar] [ASC] (7/31/82 BC-5)

SOMEBODY'S BEEN SLEEPING 100 Proof Aged In Soul—Hot Wax 7004 [Angelo Bond/General Johnson/Greg Perry] [BMI] (8/29/70 BCR-6)

SOMEBODY'S GETTIN' IT Johnnie Taylor—Columbia 10334 [Clarence Coulter/Don Davis/Chico Jones] [BMI] (6/5/76 BCR-33)

SOMEBODY'S GONNA LOVE YOU Lee Greenwood—MCA 52257 [Don Cook/Rafe Van Hoy] [BMI] (10/1/83 B-96)

SOMEBODY'S GOTTA WIN, SOMEBODY'S GOTTA LOSE The Controllers—Juana 3414 [David Camon] [BMI] (11/26/77 CR-84)

SOMEBODY'S KNOCKIN' Terri Gibbs—MCA 41309 [Jerry Gillespie/Ed Penney*] [SE] (1/17/81 BCR-10)

SOMEBODY'S OUT THERE Triumph—MCA 52898 [Rik Emmett/Mike Levine/Gil Moore] [ASC] (8/30/86 BC-27)

SOMEBODY'S SLEEPING IN MY BED Johnnie Taylor—Stax 235 [Bettye Crutcher/Allen Alvoid Jones Jr.] [BMI] (12/2/67 BCR-95)

SOMEBODY'S WATCHING ME Rockwell—Motown 1702 [Kennedy Gordy] [ASC] (1/28/84 BC-2)

SOMEBODY'S WATCHING YOU Little Sister—Stone Flower 9001 [Sylvester Stewart] [BMI] (12/5/70 BCR-22)

SOMEDAY Dave Loggins—Epic 50035 [Dave Loggins] [ASC] (10/26/74 BCR-57)

SOMEDAY (I DIDN'T WANT TO HAVE TO BE THE ONE) Henry Gross—Lifesong 45014 [Henry Gross] [ASC] (10/30/76 B-85)

SOMEDAY Glass Tiger—Manhattan 50048 [Al Connelly/Alan Frew/Jim Vallance] [ASC] (11/1/86 BC-7)

SOMEDAY Mariah Carey—Columbia 73561 [Mariah Carey/Ben Margulies] [BMI] (1/19/91 BC-1)

SOMEDAY MAN The Monkees—Colgems 5004 [Roger Nichols/Paul Williams] [BMI] (5/10/69 BCR-74)

SOMEDAY NEVER COMES Creedence Clearwater Revival—Fantasy 676 [John Fogerty] [ASC] (4/29/72 BCR-25)

SOMEDAY, SOMEWAY *Robert Gordon—RCA 12239 [Marshall Crenshaw] [ASC] (6/27/81 BCR-72)*

SOMEDAY, SOMEWAY *Marshall Crenshaw—Warner Bros. 29974 [Marshall Crenshaw] [ASC] (7/10/82 BC-31)*

SOMEDAY SOON Judy Collins—Elektra 45649 [Ian Tyson] [ASC] (1/25/69 BCR-39)

SOMEDAY SWEETHEART Les Paul—Capitol 3015 [Benjamin Spikes*/John C. Spikes] [ASC] (1/10/55 CR-39) [IWM]

SOMEDAY WE'LL BE TOGETHER Diana Ross And The Supremes—Motown 1156 [Jackey Beavers/Johnny Bristol/Harvey Fuqua] [BMI] (11/1/69 BCR-1)

SOMEDAY (WHEN I'M GONE FROM YOU) Bobby Vee And The Crickets—Liberty 55479 [Snuff Garrett/Dick Glasser] [BMI] (9/22/62 B-99)

SOMEDAY (YOU'LL WANT ME TO WANT YOU) *Jodie Sands—Chancellor 1023 [Jimmie Hodges] [BMI] (9/8/58 BCR-52)*

SOMEDAY (YOU'LL WANT ME TO WANT YOU) *Della Reese—RCA Victor 47-7706 [Jimmie Hodges] [BMI] (3/14/60 BCR-31)*

SOMEDAY YOU'LL WANT ME TO WANT YOU *Brook Benton—Mercury 71722 [Jimmie Hodges] [BMI] (12/26/60 B-93)*

SOMEONE Johnny Mathis—Columbia 41355 [William Tennyson] [ASC] (3/23/59 BCR-33)

SOMEONE Billy Vaughn And His Orchestra—Dot 16397 [Milt Gabler/Bert Kaempfert] [BMI] (10/27/62 R-89) [I]

SOMEONE El DeBarge—Gordy 1867 [Jay Graydon/Mark Mueller/Robbie Nevil] [ASC] (12/27/86 B-70)

SOMEONE The Rembrandts—Atco 98786 [Phil Solem/Danny Wilde] [BMI] (5/25/91 BC-54)

SOMEONE BELONGING TO SOMEONE Bee Gees—RSO 815235 [Barry Gibb/Maurice Gibb/Robin Gibb] [BMI] (8/20/83 BC-49)

SOMEONE COULD LOSE A HEART TONIGHT Eddie Rabbitt—Elektra 47239 [David Malloy/Eddie Rabbitt/Even Stevens] [BMI] (11/14/81 BCR-15)

SOMEONE ELSE'S BOY Connie Francis—MGM 12995 [Hal Gordon/Athena Hosey] [ASC] (5/1/61 R-93)

SOMEONE ELSE'S ROSES Doris Day—Columbia 40234 [Howard Ellington Riddiford Barnes/Harold Fields/Joseph Roncoroni] [ASC] (7/3/54 C-PRE)

SOMEONE IS WATCHING Solomon Burke—Atlantic 2299 [Solomon Burke/Eddie Floyd/Alvertis Isbell] [BMI] (8/21/65 BCR-89)

SOMEONE LIKE YOU Michael Stanley Band—EMI America 8189 [Kevin Raleigh] [ASC] (12/24/83 B-75)

SOMEONE LIKE YOU Daryl Hall—RCA 5105 [Daryl Hall] [BMI] (1/24/87 BC-57)

SOMEONE LOVES YOU JOE The Singing Belles—Madison 126 [Larry Kolber/Norman Strassberg] [BMI] (3/19/60 BCR-53)

SOMEONE ON YOUR MIND Champ Butler—Coral 61496 [Doris Houck/Arthur Valando*] [BMI] (11/19/55 B-77)

SOMEONE SAVED MY LIFE TONIGHT Elton John—MCA 40421 [Elton John/Bernie Taupin] [BMI] (7/5/75 BCR-1)

SOMEONE, SOMEONE Brian Poole & The Tremeloes—Monument 846 [Edwin Greines/Violet Petty] [ASC] (8/15/64 BCR-59)

SOMEONE SOMEWHERE Junior Parker—Duke 357 [Junior Parker] [BMI] (1/12/63 B-95)

SOMEONE THAT I USED TO LOVE Natalie Cole—Capitol 4869 [Gerry Goffin/Michael Masser] [BMI] (6/21/80 BCR-21)

SOMEONE TO COME HOME TO The Ames Brothers—RCA Victor 47-7526 [Jimmie Steward/Jimmy Williams] [BMI] (5/18/59 BCR-78)

SOMEONE TO LAY DOWN BESIDE ME *Linda Ronstadt—Asylum 45361 [Karla Bonoff] [BMI] (12/4/76 BCR-42)*

SOMEONE TO LAY DOWN BESIDE ME *Karla Bonoff—Columbia 10751 [Karla Bonoff] [BMI] (6/3/78 R-88)*

SOMEONE TO LOVE Four Aces—Decca 30123 [Francis Lemarque/Norman Newell] [ASC] (11/10/56 BR-45) [FDE]

SOMEONE TO LOVE ME FOR ME Lisa Lisa & Cult Jam—Columbia 07619
[Curtis Bedeau/Gerard Charles/Hugh Clarke/Brian George/Lucien George/Paul George/Lisa Velez] [BMI] (11/14/87 B-78)

SOMEONE TO WATCH OVER ME Frank Sinatra—Capitol 2993
[George Gershwin/Ira Gershwin] [ASC] (11/22/54 R-63)

SOMEONE WHO CARES Kenny Rogers And The First Edition—Reprise 0999
[Alex Harvey] [BMI] (3/20/71 BCR-39)

SOMEONE YOU LOVE Nat "King" Cole—Capitol 3234
[Stephen Michaels] (TSW) [BMI] (10/22/55 BCR-14)

SOMETHIN' 'BOUT 'CHA Latimore—Glades 1739
[Benny Latimore] [BMI] (1/29/77 BCR-37)

***SOMETHIN' 'BOUT YOU BABY I LIKE** Trini Lopez—Private Stock 45,024*
[Richie Supa] [ASC] (6/21/75 CR-76)

***SOMETHIN' 'BOUT YOU BABY I LIKE** Glen Campbell and Rita Coolidge—Capitol 4865*
[Richie Supa] [ASC] (5/17/80 BCR-42)

SOMETHIN' ELSE Eddie Cochran—Liberty 55203
[Bob Cochran/Sharon Sheeley] [BMI] (8/29/59 BCR-56)

SOMETHIN' STUPID Nancy Sinatra & Frank Sinatra—Reprise 0561
[C. Carson Parks] [BMI] (3/18/67 BCR-1)

***SOMETHING** The Beatles—Apple 2654 [George Harrison] (TSW) [ASC] (10/25/69 BCR-1)*

***SOMETHING** Booker T. & The M.G.'s—Stax 0073*
[George Harrison] [ASC] (7/25/70 BCR-76) [IWM]

***SOMETHING** Shirley Bassey—United Artists 50698*
[George Harrison] [ASC] (9/19/70 BCR-55)

***SOMETHING** Johnny Rodriguez—Mercury 73471 [George Harrison] [ASC] (5/4/74 B-85)*

***SOMETHING ABOUT YOU** Four Tops—Motown 1084*
[Lamont Dozier/Brian Holland/Eddie Holland] [BMI] (11/6/65 BCR-11)

***SOMETHING ABOUT YOU** Le Blanc & Carr—Big Tree 16092*
[Lamont Dozier/Brian Holland/Eddie Holland] [BMI] (6/25/77 BCR-48)

SOMETHING ABOUT YOU Level 42—Polydor 883362
[Wally Badarou/Boon Gould/Phil Gould/Mark King/Mike Lindup] [BMI] (2/15/86 BC-7)

—SOMETHING ABOUT YOUR LOVE see: ATLANTA LADY

SOMETHING BETTER Chilliwack—Mushroom 7025
[William A. Henderson/Ross Turney] [BMI] (9/3/77 C-92)

SOMETHING BETTER TO DO Olivia Newton-John—MCA 40459
[John Farrar] [BMI] (9/20/75 BCR-13)

SOMETHING GOOD (IS GOING TO HAPPEN TO YOU) Carla Thomas—Stax 207
[Isaac Hayes/David Porter] [BMI] (1/14/67 BCR-62)

SOMETHING GOT ME STARTED Simply Red—EastWest 98711
[Mick Hucknall/Fritz McIntyre] [ASC] (9/21/91 BC-20)

SOMETHING HAPPENED Paul Anka—ABC-Paramount 10106
[Gloria Van Cleve/Bob Wilson] [BMI] (5/16/60 BCR-41)

SOMETHING HAPPENED ON THE WAY TO HEAVEN Phil Collins—Atlantic 87885
[Phil Collins/Daryl Stuermer] [ASC] (8/4/90 BC-3)

SOMETHING HE CAN FEEL Aretha Franklin—Atlantic 3326
[Curtis Mayfield] [BMI] (5/29/76 BCR-27)

SOMETHING I WANT TO TELL YOU Johnny and The Expressions—Josie 946
[Ralph Weeks] [BMI] (1/15/66 BCR-60)

SOMETHING I'LL REMEMBER Sandy Posey—MGM 13892
[Buddy Buie/J.R. Cobb] [BMI] (2/24/68 CR-74)

SOMETHING IN MY HEART Michel'le—Ruthless 4-98885
[Andre Bolton/Michel'le Toussant/Andre Romell Young] [ASC] (1/12/91 B-31)

SOMETHING IN MY HOUSE Dead Or Alive—Epic 07022
[Pete Burns/Steve Coy/Wayne Hussey/Tim Lever/Mike Percy] [ASC] (4/25/87 BC-85)

SOMETHING IN THE AIR Thunderclap Newman—Track 2656
[Speedy Keen] [BMI] (7/26/69 BCR-35)

SOMETHING IN YOU Manitoba—RCA Victor 47-9908 [Joe Dowen] [BMI] (11/21/70 C-98)

SOMETHING JUST AIN'T RIGHT Keith Sweat—Vintertainment 7-69411
[Teddy Riley/Keith Sweat] [ASC] (5/7/88 BC-78)

SOMETHING OLD, SOMETHING NEW Paul & Paula—Philips 40130
[Marvin Montgomery/Mary Tarver] [BMI] (8/17/63 BCR-59)

SOMETHING REAL (INSIDE ME/INSIDE YOU) Mr. Mister—RCA 5273
[Steve George/John Lang/Richard Page] [ASC] (8/22/87 BC-29)

SOMETHING SO STRONG Crowded House—Capitol 5695
[Neil Finn/Mitchell Froom] [BMI] (5/2/87 BC-7)

SOMETHING THERE IS ABOUT YOU Bob Dylan—Asylum 11035
[Bob Dylan] [SE] (5/4/74 C-76)

SOMETHING TO BELIEVE IN Poison—Enigma 44617
[Bobby Dall/C.C. DeVille/Bret Michaels/Rikki Rockett] [BMI] (10/6/90 BC-4)

SOMETHING TO GRAB FOR Ric Ocasek—Geffen 29784
[Ric Ocasek] [ASC] (2/12/83 BC-47)

SOMETHING TO TALK ABOUT Bonnie Raitt—Capitol 44724
[Shirley Eikhard] [BMI] (7/13/91 BC-5)

SOMETHING WONDERFUL HAPPENS IN SUMMER Frank Sinatra—Capitol 3744
[Joseph Bushkin/John DeVries] [ASC] (6/29/57 R-67)

***SOMETHING YOU GOT** Alvin Robinson—Tiger 104 [Chris Kenner] [BMI] (5/23/64 BCR-46)*

***SOMETHING YOU GOT** Ramsey Lewis Trio—Argo 5481*
[Chris Kenner] [BMI] (10/10/64 BCR-63) [I]

***SOMETHING YOU GOT** Chuck Jackson & Maxine Brown—Wand 181*
[Chris Kenner] [BMI] (4/24/65 BCR-45)

SOMETHING'S BURNING Kenny Rogers And The First Edition—Reprise 0888
[Mac Davis] [BMI] (2/7/70 BCR-5)

SOMETHING'S GOT A HOLD ON ME Etta James—Argo 5409
[Etta James/Leroy Kirkland/Pearl Woods] [BMI] (2/5/62 BCR-20)

***SOMETHING'S GOTTA GIVE** Ray Anthony—Capitol 3096*
[Johnny Mercer] [ASC] (5/16/55 Rt-48)

***SOMETHING'S GOTTA GIVE** Sammy Davis Jr.—Decca 29484*
[Johnny Mercer] (TSW) [ASC] (6/4/55 BCtRt-4)

***SOMETHING'S GOTTA GIVE** The McGuire Sisters—Coral 61423*
[Johnny Mercer] (TSW) [ASC] (6/25/55 BCtRt-4)

SOMETHING'S MISSING The Five Stairsteps & Cubie—Buddah 20
[Clarence Burke Jr./Clarence Burke Sr.] [BMI] (12/2/67 BCR-70)

SOMETHING'S ON HER MIND The 4 Seasons Featuring Frankie Valli—Philips 40597
[Bob Gaudio/Jake Holmes] (TSW) [ASC] (3/29/69 BR-92)

SOMETHING'S ON YOUR MIND D Train—Prelude 8080
[Hubert Eaves III/James N. Williams] [BMI] (1/7/84 B-79)

SOMETHING'S WRONG WITH ME Austin Roberts—Chelsea 0101
[Bobby Hart/Danny Janssen] [BMI] (9/9/72 BCR-9)

SOMETIMES Gene Thomas—United Artists 338 [Gene Thomas] [BMI] (9/9/61 BCR-53)

SOMETIMES Facts Of Life—Kayvette 5128 [Bill Anderson] [BMI] (2/19/77 BCR-31)

SOMETIMES A FANTASY Billy Joel—Columbia 11379 [Billy Joel] [ASC] (10/11/80 BCR-36)

SOMETIMES GOOD GUYS DON'T WEAR WHITE The Standells—Tower 257
[Ed Cobb] [BMI] (8/13/66 BCR-43)

SOMETIMES I WISH I WERE A BOY Lesley Gore—Mercury 72352
[Cy Crane/Herb Weiner] [ASC] (10/31/64 B-86)

SOMETIMES I WONDER Major Lance—Okeh 7209
[Curtis Mayfield] [BMI] (12/5/64 BCR-36)

SOMETIMES (IT'S A BITCH) Stevie Nicks—Modern 98758
[Jon Bon Jovi/Billy Falcon] [ASC] (9/7/91 BC-43)

SOMETIMES IT'S GOT TO RAIN Jackie Moore With The Dixie Flyers—Atlantic 2798
[Dave Crawford/Willie Martin/Jackie Moore] [ASC] (5/8/71 CR-72)

SOMETIMES SHE CRIES Warrant—Columbia 73095
[Joseph Cagle*/Steven Chamberlin*/Jerry Dixon*/John Oswald/Eric Turner*] [BMI] (12/16/89 BC-16)

SOMETIMES SHE'S A LITTLE GIRL Tommy Boyce & Bobby Hart—A&M 874
[Tommy Boyce/Bobby Hart] [BMI] (9/23/67 CR-72)

SOMETIMES WHEN WE TOUCH Dan Hill—20th Century 2355
[Dan Hill/Barry Mann] [ASC] (11/26/77 BCR-3)

SOMETIMES YOU GOTTA CRY A LITTLE Bobby Bland—Duke 366
[Deadric Malone] [BMI] (7/13/63 BCR-56)

SOMEWHERE The Tymes—Parkway 891
[Norma Mendoza/Wolfgang Amadeus Mozart*/Jimmy Wisner] [ASC] (12/7/63 BCR-14)

***SOMEWHERE** P.J. Proby—Liberty 55757*
[Leonard Bernstein/Stephen Sondheim] [ASC] (1/30/65 BCR-69)

***SOMEWHERE** Len Barry—Decca 31923*
[Leonard Bernstein/Stephen Sondheim] [ASC] (3/19/66 BCR-17)

***SOMEWHERE (FROM WEST SIDE STORY)** Barbra Streisand—Columbia 05680*
[Leonard Bernstein/Stephen Sondheim] [ASC] (12/7/85 BC-43)

***SOMEWHERE ALONG THE WAY** Roy Hamilton—Epic 9301*
[Sammy Gallop/Jimmy Van Heusen] [ASC] (1/26/59 R-89)

***SOMEWHERE ALONG THE WAY** Steve Lawrence—United Artists 364*
[Sammy Gallop/Jimmy Van Heusen] [ASC] (10/9/61 BR-64)

SOMEWHERE BETWEEN LOVE AND TOMORROW Roy Clark—Dot 17480
[Tom Lazaros/Bud Reneau] [ASC] (12/15/73 BCR-81)

SOMEWHERE DOWN THE ROAD Barry Manilow—Arista 0658
[Tom Snow/Cynthia Weil] [BMI] (12/19/81 BCR-21)

SOMEWHERE IN AMERICA Survivor—Scotti Brothers 511
[Jim Peterik] [ASC] (2/23/80 B-70)

***SOMEWHERE IN THE NIGHT** Helen Reddy—Capitol 4192*
[Will Jennings/Richard Kerr] [BMI] (11/29/75 BCR-19)

***SOMEWHERE IN THE NIGHT** Batdorf & Rodney—Arista 0159*
[Will Jennings/Richard Kerr] [BMI] (11/29/75 BCR-69)

***SOMEWHERE IN THE NIGHT** Barry Manilow—Arista 0382*
[Will Jennings/Richard Kerr] [BMI] (12/16/78 BCR-9)

SOMEWHERE IN YOUR HEART Frank Sinatra—Reprise 0332
[Russell Faith/Clarence Kehner] [ASC] (12/19/64 BCR-31)

***LARA'S THEME FROM "DR. ZHIVAGO"** Roger Williams—Kapp 738*
[Maurice Jarre] [ASC] (6/11/66 BC-65) [I]

***SOMEWHERE, MY LOVE** Ray Conniff And The Singers—Columbia 43626*
[Maurice Jarre/Paul Francis Webster] [ASC] (6/11/66 BCR-9)

SOMEWHERE OUT THERE Linda Ronstadt And James Ingram—MCA 52973
[James Horner/Barry Mann/Cynthia Weil] [ASC] (12/20/86 BC-2)

SOMEWHERE, SOMEBODY Aaron Neville—A&M 1577
[Max Carl/Andrew Kastner/Larry John McNally] [BMI] (12/7/91 C-66)

SOMEWHERE THERE'S A SOMEONE Dean Martin—Reprise 0443
[Baker Knight] [BMI] (2/12/66 BCR-30)

SON-IN-LAW (response to Mother-In-Law) The Blossoms—Challenge 9109
[Dave Burgess/Jerry Fuller] [BMI] (5/8/61 BCt*R-78) [R]

SON-IN-LAW (response to Mother-In-Law) Louise Brown—Witch 101
[Bill Erman] [BMI] (5/8/61 BCt*R-76) [R]

SON OF A LOVIN' MAN Buchanan Brothers—Event 3305
[Terry Cashman/Eugene Pistilli/Tommy West] [ASC] (8/23/69 BCR-51)

SON-OF-A PREACHER MAN *Dusty Springfield—Atlantic 2580*
[John Hurley/Ronnie Wilkins] [BMI] (11/23/68 BCR-8)

SON OF A PREACHER MAN *Aretha Franklin—Atlantic 2706*
[John Hurley/Ronnie Wilkins] (TSW) [BMI] (2/14/70 B-41)

SON OF A TRAVELIN' MAN Ed Ames—RCA Victor 74-0156
[Robert I. Allen/Mauro Lusini] [ASC] (5/31/69 BCR-92) [FDE]

THE SON OF HICKORY HOLLER'S TRAMP O.C. Smith—Columbia 44425
[Dallas Frazier] [BMI] (2/24/68 BCR-38)

SON OF ICE BAG Hugh Masekela—Uni 55037 [Hugh Masekela] [BMI] (12/9/67 R-81) [I]

SON OF MY FATHER *Giorgio—Dunhill 4304*
[Pete Bellotte/Giorgio Moroder] [ASC] (2/19/72 BCR-34) [FDE]

SON OF MY FATHER *Chicory—Epic 10837*
[Pete Bellotte/Giorgio Moroder] [ASC] (2/26/72 BC-82) [FDE]

THE SON OF REBEL ROUSER Duane Eddy—RCA Victor 47-8276
[Duane Eddy] [BMI] (11/30/63 BCR-90) [I]

SON OF SAGITTARIUS Eddie Kendricks—Tamla 54247
[Leonard Caston/Anita Poree/Frank Edward Wilson] [BMI] (5/4/74 BCR-20)

SON OF SHAFT Bar-Kays—Volt 4073
[Homer Banks/William C. Brown III/Allen Alvoid Jones Jr.] [BMI]
(12/25/71 BCR-53) [IWM]

SONG FOR ANNA (CHANSON D'ANNA) Herb Ohta—A&M 1505
[André Popp] [ASC] (7/6/74 CR-88) [IM]

SONG FOR THE LONELY The Platters—Mercury 71904
[Joseph S. Lewis/William Wheeler] [ASC] (11/20/61 R-71)

—SONG FOR THE NINTH DAY see: VERY SPECIAL LOVE

A SONG FOR YOU *Andy Williams—Columbia 45434*
[Leon Russell] [BMI] (8/21/71 BCR-78)

A SONG FOR YOU *Jaye P. Morgan—Beverly Hills 9367*
[Leon Russell] [BMI] (9/11/71 R-92)

THE SONG FROM DESIREE (WE MEET AGAIN) *Johnny Desmond—Coral 61301*
[Ken Darby/Alfred Newman] [ASC] (12/25/54 CtRt-17)

THE SONG FROM DESIREE (WE MEET AGAIN) *Paul Weston And His Orchestra—*
Columbia 40359 [Alfred Newman] [ASC] (12/25/54 CtRt-17) [IM]

THE SONG FROM DESIREE (WE MEET AGAIN)
Bing Crosby And Alfred Newman—Decca 29357
[Ken Darby/Alfred Newman] [ASC] (12/27/54 Rt-PRE)

THE SONG FROM DESIREE (WE MEET AGAIN) *Jane Froman—Capitol 2979*
[Ken Darby/Alfred Newman] [ASC] (12/27/54 Rt-PRE)

THE SONG FROM "KINGS GO FORTH" (MONIQUE) Frank Sinatra—Capitol 4003
[Elmer Bernstein/Sammy Cahn] [ASC] (6/30/58 R-39)

SONG FROM M*A*S*H Al DeLory—Capitol 2811
[Johnny Mandel] [ASC] (6/13/70 BCR-63) [IM]

A SONG I'D LIKE TO SING Kris Kristofferson & Rita Coolidge—A&M 1475
[Kris Kristofferson] [BMI] (11/10/73 BCR-33)

SONG IN BLUE Les Paul and Mary Ford—Capitol 3015
[Mary Ford*/Les Paul/Celia Ryland*] [ASC] (1/15/55 CR-17)

A SONG OF JOY (HIMNO A LA ALEGRIA) Miguel Rios—A&M 1193
[Waldo De Los Rios/Ross Parker/Ludwig van Beethoven] [ASC] (6/6/70 BCR-9) [FET]

—SONG OF LOVE see: CHANSON D'AMOUR

(THE SONG OF) RAINTREE COUNTY Nat "King" Cole—Capitol 3782
[Johnny Green/Paul Francis Webster] [ASC] (9/9/57 CR-46)

SONG OF THE BAREFOOT CONTESSA Hugo Winterhalter's Orchestra And Chorus—
RCA Victor 47-5888 [Mario Nascimbene] [ASC] (11/22/54 BCR-14) [I]

SONG OF THE BAREFOOT MAILMAN Billy Leach—Bally 1039
[Jonny Graff/Billy Leach] [BMI] (9/16/57 B-86)

SONG OF THE DREAMER *Johnnie Ray—Columbia 40528*
[Eddie Curtis] [ASC] (7/25/55 CtRt-10)

SONG OF THE DREAMER *Bunny Paul—Capitol 3178 [Eddie Curtis] [ASC] (7/25/55 Rt-16)*

SONG OF THE DREAMER *Billy Brooks—Duke 142 [Eddie Curtis] [ASC] (8/8/55 Rt-16)*

SONG OF THE DREAMER *Eddie Fisher—RCA Victor 47-6196*
[Eddie Curtis] (TSW) [ASC] (9/3/55 BCtRt-10)

SONG OF THE NAIROBI TRIO The Fortune Tellers—Music Makers 105
[Robert Maxwell] [ASC] (8/12/61 CR-69) [I]

SONG ON THE RADIO Al Stewart—Arista 0389 [Al Stewart] [BMI] (1/27/79 BCR-27)

SONG SELLER Raiders—Columbia 45688 [Jimmy Webb] [ASC] (10/14/72 BCR-89)

SONG SUNG BLUE Neil Diamond—Uni 55326 [Neil Diamond] [SE] (4/29/72 BCR-1)

A SONG THAT NEVER COMES Mama Cass Elliot—Dunhill 4264
[Terry Cashman/Eugene Pistilli/Tommy West] [ASC] (8/1/70 BR-99)

SONGBIRD Barbra Streisand—Columbia 10756
[Stephen Nelson/David Wolfert] [BMI] (6/10/78 BCR-25)

SONGBIRD Kenny G—Arista 1-9588 [Kenny G] [BMI] (4/4/87 BC-4) [I]

SONGMAN Cashman & West—Dunhill 4333
[Terry Cashman/Tommy West] [ASC] (12/16/72 BCR-54)

SONS AND LOVERS Percy Faith—Columbia 41731
[Mario Nascimbene] [ASC] (7/25/60 R-90) [I]

SOOLAIMON (AFRICAN TRILOGY II) Neil Diamond—Uni 55224
[Neil Diamond] [SE] (4/25/70 BCR-24)

SOON (I'LL BE HOME AGAIN) The 4 Seasons Featuring Frankie Valli—Vee-Jay 512
[Bob Crewe/Bob Gaudio] [BMI] (4/27/63 BCR-59)

SOON I'LL WED MY LOVE John Gary—RCA Victor 47-8413
[Buddy Bregman*/Phillipa Fallon] [NA] (9/12/64 B-89)

SOONER OR LATER Johnny Mathis—Columbia 42836
[Thomas Garlock/Alan Jeffreys] [ASC] (8/24/63 BR-78)

SOONER OR LATER The Grass Roots—Dunhill 4279
[Mitch Bottler/Ted McNamara/Adeneyi Paris/Ekundayo Paris/Gary Zekley] [BMI]
(5/29/71 BCR-9)

SOONER OR LATER The Impressions—Curtom 0103
[Ed Townsend] [BMI] (5/31/75 BCR-63)

SOOTHE ME *Sims Twins—Sar 117 [Sam Cooke] [BMI] (10/23/61 BCR-42)*

SOOTHE ME *Sam & Dave—Stax 218 [Sam Cooke] [BMI] (6/17/67 BCR-47)*

SOOTHE ME *The Ovations—MGM 14623 [Sam Cooke] (Med) [BMI] (10/13/73 BCR-56)*

SOPHISTICATED CISSY The Meters—Josie 1001
[Joseph Modeliste/Art Neville/Leo Nocentelli/George Porter] [BMI] (2/1/69 BCR-34) [I]

SOPHISTICATED LADY (SHE'S A DIFFERENT LADY) Natalie Cole—Capitol 4259
[Natalie Cole/Charles Henry Jackson Jr./Marvin Yancy] [BMI] (5/29/76 BCR-25)

SORROW David Bowie—RCA Victor 0160
[Bob Feldman/Jerry Goldstein/Richard Gottehrer] [BMI] (11/17/73 C-69)

SORRY Grace Jones—Beam Junction 102
[Grace Jones/Pierre Papadiamandis] (TSW) [BMI] (1/22/77 B-71)

SORRY DOESN'T ALWAYS MAKE IT RIGHT Diana Ross—Motown 1335
[Michael Masser/Pam Sawyer] [BMI] (3/8/75 C-84)

SORRY (I RAN ALL THE WAY HOME) The Impalas—Cub 9022
[Harry Giosasi/Artie Zwirn] [BMI] (3/7/59 BCR-2)

SORRY SEEMS TO BE THE HARDEST WORD Elton John—MCA/Rocket 40645
[Elton John/Bernie Taupin] [BMI] (11/6/76 BCR-6)

SORRY SUZANNE The Hollies—Epic 10454
[Tony Macaulay/Geoff Stephens] [BMI] (4/12/69 BCR-53)

SOS Abba—Atlantic 3265
[Stig Anderson/Benny Andersson/Björn Ulvaeus] [BMI] (8/9/75 BCR-10)

S.O.S. (HEART IN DISTRESS) Christine Cooper—Parkway 971
[Ritchie Cordell/Sal Trimachi] [BMI] (2/5/66 CR-98)

SOUL CITY Partland Brothers—Manhattan 50065
[Chris Partland/George Partland] [ASC] (4/25/87 BC-27)

SOUL COAXING (AME CALINE)
Raymond Lefevre And His Orchestra—4 Corners Of The World 147
[Michel Polnareff] [ASC] (2/17/68 BCR-28) [I]

SOUL DANCE Tommy Leonetti—RCA Victor 47-8251 [Gene Lynd] [ASC] (1/4/64 C-99)

SOUL DANCE NUMBER THREE Wilson Pickett—Atlantic 2412
[Wilson Pickett/Jerry Wexler] [BMI] (6/17/67 BCR-55)

SOUL DEEP The Box Tops—Mala 12,040
[Wayne Carson Thompson] [BMI] (6/28/69 BCR-11)

SOUL DRESSING Booker T. & The MG's—Stax 153
[Steve Cropper/Al Jackson/Booker T. Jones Jr./Lewis Steinberg] [BMI]
(8/15/64 B-95) [I]

SOUL DRIPPIN' The Mauds—Mercury 72832 [Dick Monda] [BMI] (9/28/68 BCR-55)

SOUL EXPERIENCE Iron Butterfly—Atco 6647
[Erik Brann/Ron Bushy/Lee Dorman/Doug Ingle] [BMI] (2/22/69 BCR-65)

SOUL FINGER Bar-Kays—Volt 148
[James Edward Alexander/Ronnie Caldwell/Ben Cauley/Carl Cunningham/Phalon
Jones/Jimmy King] [BMI] (5/20/67 BCR-16) [I]

SOUL HEAVEN Dixie Drifter—Roulette 4641 [Teddy Vann] [BMI] (8/21/65 BCR-76)

—SOUL HOOTENANNY (PART ONE) see: BIG BOSS MAN

SOUL INSPIRATION Anita Baker—Elektra 64935
[Terry Britten/Graham Lyle] [ASC] (9/15/90 BC-64)

—SOUL JE T'AIME see JE T'AIME

SOUL KISS Olivia Newton-John—MCA 52686 [Mark Goldenberg] [BMI] (10/5/85 BC-20)

SOUL-LIMBO Booker T. & The M.G.'s—Stax 0001
[Steve Cropper/Donald "Duck" Dunn/Al Jackson/Booker T. Jones Jr.] [BMI]
(7/6/68 BCR-9) [I]

SOUL MAKOSSA *Afrique—Mainstream 5542 [Manu Dibango] [ASC] (6/9/73 BCR-41) [I]*

SOUL MAKOSSA *Manu Dibango—Atlantic 2971*
[Manu Dibango] [ASC] (6/16/73 BCR-22) [I]

SOUL MAN *Sam & Dave—Stax 231 [Isaac Hayes/David Porter] [ASC] (9/9/67 BCR-1)*

SOUL MAN *Ramsey Lewis—Cadet 5583*
[Isaac Hayes/David Porter] [ASC] (11/11/67 BCR-49) [IWM]

SOUL MAN *Blues Brothers—Atlantic 3545*
[Isaac Hayes/David Porter] [ASC] (12/9/78 BCR-9)

SOUL MEETING The Soul Clan—Atlantic 2530 [Don Covay] [BMI] (7/20/68 BR-91)

THE SOUL OF J. B. James Brown And The Famous Flames—King 6133
[James Brown/Bud Hobgood/Gladys Knochelman] [BMI] (12/16/67 R-97)

SOUL POWER PT. 1 James Brown—King 6368
[James Brown] [BMI] (2/20/71 BCR-21)

SOUL PRIDE (PART 1) James Brown—King 6222
[James Brown/Alfred James Ellis] [BMI] (3/22/69 CR-89) [I]

SOUL PROVIDER Michael Bolton—Columbia 68909
[Michael Bolton/Andy Goldmark] [BMI] (7/1/89 BC-17)

SOUL SAUCE (GUACHA GUARO) Cal Tjader—Verve 10345
[Dizzy Gillespie/Chano Pozo] [ASC] (5/15/65 BCR-69) [IM]

SOUL SERENADE *King Curtis—Capitol 5109*
[King Curtis/Luther Dixon] [BMI] (3/7/64 BCR-51) [I]

SOUL SERENADE *Willie Mitchell—Hi 2140*
[King Curtis/Luther Dixon] [BMI] (2/17/68 BCR-20) [I]

SOULSHAKE *Peggy Scott & Jo Jo Benson—SSS Int'l 761*
[Margaret Lewis/Mira Smith] [BMI] (1/18/69 BCR-26)

SOUL SHAKE *Delaney & Bonnie & Friends—Atco 6756*
[Margaret Lewis/Mira Smith] [BMI] (8/15/70 BCR-31)

SOUL SISTER, BROWN SUGAR Sam & Dave—Atlantic 2590
[Isaac Hayes/David Porter] [ASC] (12/21/68 BCR-41)

SOUL SONG Joe Stampley—Dot 17442
[George Richey/Billy Sherrill/Norro Wilson] [BMI] (1/6/73 BCR-29)

SOUL STRUTTIN' Jamie Lyons—Laurie 3422
[Tony Orlando/Marty Thau] [BMI] (12/16/67 R-80)

SOUL TIME Shirley Ellis—Columbia 44021 [Shirley Ellis] [BMI] (2/25/67 BCR-59)

SOUL TRAIN Classics IV—Imperial 66293 [Buddy Buie/J.R. Cobb] [BMI] (4/6/68 BCR-59)

SOUL TRAIN "75" Soul Train Gang—Soul Train 10400
[Don Cornelius/Dick Griffey] [NA] (11/22/75 BCR-74)

SOUL TWIST King Curtis And The Noble Knights—Enjoy 1000
[King Curtis] [BMI] (2/17/62 BCR-14) [I]

SOULFUL STRUT *Young-Holt Unlimited—Brunswick 55391*
[Eugene Record/William Nelson Sanders] [BMI] (11/16/68 BCR-1) [IWM]

AM I THE SAME GIRL *(Soulful Strut) Barbara Acklin—Brunswick 55399*
[Eugene Record/William Nelson Sanders] [BMI] (2/15/69 BCR-52)

SOULS Rick Springfield—RCA 13650 [Rick Springfield] [BMI] (10/15/83 BC-23)

SOULSVILLE Isaac Hayes—Enterprise 9045 [Isaac Hayes] [BMI] (4/29/72 C-94)

SOULVILLE *Dinah Washington—Roulette 4490*
[Henry Glover/Morris Levy‡/Titus Turner/Dinah Washington] [BMI] (5/25/63 BR-92)

SOULVILLE *Aretha Franklin—Columbia 44441*
[Henry Glover/Morris Levy‡/Titus Turner/Dinah Washington] [BMI] (2/24/68 B-83)

SOUND AND VISION David Bowie—RCA 10905
[David Bowie] [BMI] (4/9/77 BC-69)

SOUND ASLEEP The Turtles—White Whale 264
[John Barbata/Howard Kaylan/Al Nichol/Jim Pons/Mark Volman] [BMI] (3/2/68 BCR-30)

THE SOUND OF GOODBYE Crystal Gayle—Warner Bros. 29452
[Hugh Prestwood] [BMI] (12/10/83 B-84)

SOUND OF LOVE The Five Americans—Abnak 120
[John Durrill/Norman Ezell/Michael Rabon] [BMI] (5/13/67 BCR-24)

SOUND OF MUSIC *Patti Page—Mercury 71555*
[Oscar Hammerstein/Richard Rodgers] [ASC] (12/21/59 BCRt-74)

SOUND OF MUSIC *Doris Day—Columbia 41542*
[Oscar Hammerstein/Richard Rodgers] [ASC] (12/21/59 Rt-81)

SOUND OF MUSIC *David Whitfield—London 1905*
[Oscar Hammerstein/Richard Rodgers] [ASC] (1/25/60 Rt-88)

—SOUND OF PHILADELPHIA see: TSOP

THE SOUND OF SILENCE *Simon & Garfunkel—Columbia 43396*
[Paul Simon] [BMI] (11/20/65 BCR-1)

THE SOUND OF SILENCE *Peaches & Herb—Columbia 45386*
[Paul Simon] [BMI] (6/26/71 BC-94)

THE SOUND OF SILENCE *Paul Simon—Columbia 46038 [Paul Simon] [BMI] (5/4/74 C-97)*

SOUNDS OF SILENCE *Stars On 45—Radio 3863*
[Paul Simon] (Med) [BMI] (9/19/81 BCR-55)

THE SOUND OF SURF Percy Faith And His Orchestra—Columbia 42844
[Charles Albertine] [BMI] (9/28/63 R-94) [I]

THE SOUND OF YOUR VOICE .38 Special—Charisma 98773
[Max Carl/Jeff Carlisi/Danny Chauncey/Jim Peterik] [BMI] (7/13/91 BC-33)

SOUND-OFF Titus Turner—Jamie 1174
[Willie Lee Duckworth/Bernard Lentz] [ASC] (1/9/61 BCR-51)

SOUNDS OF YOUR VOICE Jon Butcher—Capitol 5534
[Jon Butcher/Thom Gimbel] [BMI] (11/30/85 B-94)

SOUP FOR ONE Chic—Mirage 4032 [Bernard Edwards/Nile Rodgers] [BMI] (6/5/82 B-80)

SOUR SUITE The Guess Who—RCA Victor 74-0578
[Burton Cummings] [BMI] (11/27/71 BCR-41)

SOUTH Johnny Maddox And The Rhythmasters—Dot 15365
[Thamon Hayes/Bennie Moten] (Med) [BMI] (5/28/55 C-43) [IM]

SO. CENTRAL RAIN (I'M SORRY) R.E.M.—I.R.S. 9927
[Bill Berry/Peter Buck/Mike Mills/Michael Stipe] [BMI] (6/23/84 BC-82)

SOUTH STREET The Orlons—Cameo 243 [Dave Appell/Kal Mann] [ASC] (2/9/63 BCR-3)

SOUTHBOUND TRAIN David Crosby & Graham Nash—Atlantic 2892
[Graham Nash] [BMI] (8/5/72 BR-75)

SOUTHERN COUNTRY BOY The Carter Brothers—Jewel 745
[Duke Coleman] [BMI] (7/3/65 R-66)

SOUTHERN CROSS The Ames Brothers—RCA Victor 47-6117
[Bob Hilliard/Dave Mann] [BMI] (5/30/55 R-72)

SOUTHERN CROSS Crosby, Stills & Nash—Atlantic 89969
[Michael Curtis/Richard Curtis/Stephen Stills] [BMI] (9/18/82 BC-18)

SOUTHERN GIRL Maze—Capitol 4891 [Frankie Beverly] [BMI] (9/20/80 R-90)

SOUTHERN LOVE Ronnie Hawkins and The Hawks—Roulette 4209
[Ronnie Hawkins/Levon Helm/Jacqueline Magill] [BMI] (12/21/59 CR-89)

SOUTHERN NIGHTS Glen Campbell—Capitol 4376
[Allen Toussaint] [BMI] (2/12/77 BCR-1)

SOUTHERN PACIFIC Neil Young & Crazy Horse—Reprise 49870
[Neil Young] [ASC] (12/19/81 BC-70)

THE SOUTH'S GONNA DO IT Charlie Daniels Band—Kama Sutra 598
[Charlie Daniels] [BMI] (1/18/75 BCR-26)

SOUTHTOWN, U.S.A. The Dixiebelles—Sound Stage 7 2517
[Billy Sherrill] [BMI] (1/11/64 BCR-15)

SOUVENIRS Barbara Evans—RCA Victor 47-7519 [Cy Coben] [ASC] (6/1/59 R-79)

SOUVENIRS Voyage—Marlin 3330
[Marc Chantereau/Pierre-Alain Dahan/Slim Pezin] [ASC] (2/17/79 BCR-41)

SOWING THE SEEDS OF LOVE Tears For Fears—Fontana 874 710
[Roland Orzabal/Curt Smith] [BMI] (9/2/89 BC-1)

SPACE AGE LOVE SONG A Flock Of Seagulls—Jive 2003
[Frank Maudsley/Paul Reynolds/Ali Score/Mike Score] [ASC] (11/13/82 BC-30)

SPACE AGE WHIZ KIDS Joe Walsh—Full Moon 29611
[Joe Vitale/Joe Walsh] [BMI] (6/11/83 BC-52)

SPACE CAPTAIN Barbra Streisand—Columbia 45511
[Matthew Moore] [BMI] (12/18/71 R-80)

SPACE INVADERS Uncle Vic—Prelude 8015 [Victor Blecman] [BMI] (8/2/80 R-91)

SPACE ODDITY David Bowie—RCA Victor 74-0876 [David Bowie] [ASC] (1/27/73 BCR-10)

SPACE RACE Billy Preston—A&M 1463 [Billy Preston] [BMI] (9/15/73 BCR-4) [I]

SPACEMAN Nilsson—RCA Victor 74-0788 [Harry Nilsson] [BMI] (9/16/72 BCR-22)

SPACESHIP SUPERSTAR Prism—Ariola America 7672
[Jim Vallance] [BMI] (10/22/77 BCR-82)

SPAGHETTI RAG Johnny Maddox And The Rhythmasters—Dot 15365
[George Lyons/Bob Yosco] (Med) [ASC] (5/28/55 C-43) [IM]

SPANISH EDDIE Laura Branigan—Atlantic 89531
[Charles E. Cochran/David Palmer] [ASC] (7/27/85 BC-37)

MOON OVER NAPLES *Bert Kaempfert And His Orchestra—Decca 31812*
[Bert Kaempfert] [BMI] (6/26/65 BCR-51) [IM]

SPANISH EYES *Al Martino—Capitol 5542*
[Bert Kaempfert/Charles Singleton/Eddie Snyder] [BMI] (11/27/65 BCR-11)

SPANISH FLEA Herb Alpert & The Tijuana Brass—A&M 792
[Julius Wechter] [ASC] (3/12/66 BCR-19) [I]

SPANISH HARLEM *Ben E. King—Atco 6185*
[Jerry Leiber/Phil Spector] [BMI] (12/31/60 BCR-9)

SPANISH HARLEM *Santo & Johnny—Canadian-American 137*
[Jerry Leiber/Phil Spector] [BMI] (4/2/62 R-80) [IWM]

SPANISH HARLEM *King Curtis—Atco 6387*
[Jerry Leiber/Phil Spector] [BMI] (12/25/65 B-89) [IWM]

SPANISH HARLEM *Aretha Franklin—Atlantic 2817*
[Jerry Leiber/Phil Spector] [BMI] (7/31/71 BCR-1)

SPANISH HUSTLE The Fatback Band—Event 229
[Gerald Thomas] [BMI] (3/27/76 CR-60) [I]

SPANISH LACE Gene McDaniels—Liberty 55510
[Doc Pomus/Mort Shuman] [BMI] (11/10/62 BCR-31)

SPANISH MARCHING SONG *Joe Reisman and His Orchestra—Roulette 4137*
[Isabel Hansen/Morris Levy‡/Traditional] [BMI] (3/16/59 Rt-94) [IM]

THE SPANISH MARCHING SONG *Ethel Smith—Decca 30851*
[Isabel Hansen/Morris Levy‡/Traditional] [BMI] (3/16/59 Rt-94) [IM]

SPANISH NIGHTS AND YOU Connie Francis—MGM 13610
[Ray Allen/Wandra Merrell] [BMI] (11/5/66 BC-81)

SPANISH WINE Lou Christie—Midsong Int'l 10959 [Chris White] [BMI] (6/11/77 C-95)

—SPANK see: LE SPANK

SPARKELIN' EYES Dean Martin—Capitol 4518
[Sy Soloway/Shirley Wolfe] [BMI] (2/25/61 C-98)

SPARKLE Cameo—Chocolate City 3202
[Larry Blackmon/Anthony Lockett] [BMI] (12/29/79 R-90)

SPARKLE AND SHINE The Four Coquettes—Capitol 4534
[Bruce Belland] [BMI] (4/24/61 R-79)

SPARKLE AND SHINE The Clique—White Whale 338
[Ritchie Cordell/Tommy James/Robert L. King*] [BMI] (2/21/70 BCR-68)

SPEAK HER NAME Walter Jackson—Okeh 7272 [Clint Ballard Jr.] [ASC] (4/8/67 BCR-83)

SPEAK, MY LOVE Vic Damone—Columbia 40733
[Roberta Heller/Perotti*/Eraldo Raviolo] [BMI] (8/17/56 R-77) [FDE]

—SPEAK SOFTLY LOVE see: LOVE THEME FROM THE GODFATHER

SPEAK TO THE SKY Rick Springfield—Capitol 3340
[Rick Springfield] [ASC] (7/29/72 BCR-14)

SPEAKING OF HER Adam Wade—Coed 536 [Jerry Samuels] [BMI] (8/29/60 R-81)

SPECIAL DELIVERY 1910 Fruitgum Co.—Buddah 114
[Bobby Bloom/Bo Gentry] [BMI] (5/10/69 BCR-28)

SPECIAL LADY Ray, Goodman & Brown—Polydor 2033
[Al Goodman/Walter Lee Morris/Harry Ray] [BMI] (1/26/80 BCR-5)

SPECIAL MEMORY Jerry Butler—Mercury 73131
[Jerry Butler/William Earl Butler/Larry Wade] [BMI] (10/24/70 C-96)

SPECIAL OCCASION Smokey Robinson & The Miracles—Tamla 54172
[Al Cleveland/Smokey Robinson] [ASC] (8/10/68 BCR-22)

SPECIAL SOMEONE The Heywoods—Family 0911 [Harold Jones] [BMI] (10/7/72 BCR-51)

SPECIAL WAY Kool & The Gang—Mercury 888867
[Ronald Bell/George M. Brown/Dwania Kyles/Kendal Stubbs/J.T. Taylor] [BMI] (10/10/87 BC-72)

SPEED BALL Ray Stevens—Mercury 72189 [Ray Stevens] [BMI] (10/5/63 BCR-46)

SPEEDOO *The Cadillacs—Josie 785 [Esther Navarro] [BMI] (12/10/55 BCRt-15)*

SPEEDO *The Commodores (2)—Dot 15439 [Esther Navarro] [BMI] (1/13/56 Rt-21)*

SPEEDOO *Steve Lawrence—Coral 61563 [Esther Navarro] [BMI] (1/13/56 Rt-21)*

SPEEDY GONZALES *David Dante—RCA Victor 47-7860*
[Bill Giant/David Hess/Buddy Kaye] [ASC] (4/3/61 R-84)

SPEEDY GONZALES *Pat Boone—Dot 16368*
[Bill Giant/David Hess/Buddy Kaye] [ASC] (6/16/62 BCR-6)

SPEND A LITTLE TIME Barbara Lewis—Atlantic 2227
[Eddie Singleton] [BMI] (5/16/64 C-94)

SPEND MY LIFE Slaughter—Chrysalis 23605
[Mark Slaughter/Dana Strum] [BMI] (12/15/90 BC-39)

SPEND SOME TIME Elvin Bishop Featuring Mickey Thomas—Capricorn 0266
[Elvin Bishop] [ASC] (12/25/76 B-93)

SPEND THE NIGHT IN LOVE The Four Seasons—Warner/Curb 49597
[Bob Gaudio/Lenny Lee Goldsmith/Judy Parker] [ASC] (12/13/80 B-91)

SPENDING MY TIME Roxette—EMI 50366
[Per Gessle/Mats Persson] [BMI] (10/26/91 BC-14)

SPICE OF LIFE The Manhattan Transfer—Atlantic 89786
[Derek Bramble/Rod Temperton] [ASC] (9/10/83 BC-40)

SPIDER JIVING Andy Fairweather Low—A&M 1649
[Andy Fairweather-Low] [ASC] (3/29/75 BC-83)

—SPIDER MAN see: WHAT'S THE NAME OF THIS FUNK

SPIDERS AND SNAKES Jim Stafford—MGM 14648
[David Bellamy/Jim Stafford] [ASC] (11/3/73 BCR-3)

—SPIEL MIR EINE ALTE MELODIE ES SPIELT see: PLAY A SIMPLE MELODY

SPIES LIKE US Paul McCartney—Capitol 5537 [Paul McCartney] [ASC] (11/23/85 BC-7)

SPILL THE WINE *Eric Burdon And War—MGM 14118*
[Thomas Allen/Harold Brown/Morris Dickerson/Lonnie Jordan/Charles Miller/Lee Oskar/Howard Scott] [ASC] (5/23/70 BCR-1)

SPILL THE WINE *The Isley Brothers—T-Neck 932*
[Thomas Allen/Harold Brown/Morris Dickerson/Lonnie Jordan/Charles Miller/Lee Oskar/Howard Scott] [ASC] (9/18/71 BCR-39)

SPIN THAT WHEEL Hi Tek 3 featuring Ya Kid K—SBK 07320
[Manuela Kamosi/Stijn Lauwers/Koenraad Van-Lishout] [ASC] (4/14/90 BC-62)

SPINNING AROUND (I MUST BE FALLING IN LOVE)
The Main Ingredient—RCA Victor 74-0456
[Donald McPherson/Tony Silvester/Luther Simmons] [BMI] (5/1/71 BCR-35)

SPINNING WHEEL *Blood, Sweat & Tears—Columbia 44871*
[David Clayton-Thomas] [BMI] (5/31/69 BCR-2)

SPINNING WHEEL PT. 1 *James Brown—King 6366*
[David Clayton-Thomas] [BMI] (2/13/71 BCR-78) [I]

SPINOUT Elvis Presley With The Jordanaires—RCA Victor 47-8941
[Dolores Fuller/Sid Wayne/Ben Weisman] [ASC] (10/1/66 BCR-25)

SPIRIT IN THE DARK Aretha Franklin With The Dixie Flyers—Atlantic 2731
[Aretha Franklin] [BMI] (5/23/70 BCR-20)

SPIRIT IN THE NIGHT *Manfred Mann's Earth Band—Warner Bros. 8176*
[Bruce Springsteen] [ASC] (4/3/76 B-97)

SPIRIT IN THE NIGHT *Manfred Mann's Earth Band—Warner Bros. 8355*
[Bruce Springsteen] [ASC] (4/23/77 BCR-40)

SPIRIT IN THE SKY *Norman Greenbaum—Reprise 0885*
[Norman Greenbaum] [BMI] (2/21/70 BCR-1)

SPIRIT IN THE SKY *Dorothy Morrison—Buddah 196*
[Norman Greenbaum] [BMI] (10/31/70 BR-99)

SPIRIT IN THE SKY *Doctor And The Medics—I.R.S. 52880*
[Norman Greenbaum] [BMI] (8/2/86 BC-62)

THE SPIRIT OF RADIO Rush—Mercury 76044
[Geddy Lee/Alex Lifeson/Neil Peart] [ASC] (2/9/80 BCR-51)

SPIRIT OF THE BOOGIE Kool & The Gang—De-Lite 1567
[Robert Bell/Ronald Bell/Donald Boyce/George M. Brown/Robert Mickens/Otha Nash/Claydes Smith/Dennis Thomas/Richard Westfield] (TSW) [BMI] (4/19/75 BCR-27)

SPIRITS IN THE MATERIAL WORLD The Police—A&M 2390
[Sting] [BMI] (1/16/82 BCR-11)

SPLISH SPLASH Bobby Darin—Atco 6117
[Bobby Darin/Murray Kaufman/Jean Murray] [BMI] (6/16/58 BCR-2)

SPOOKY *Mike Sharpe—Liberty 55922*
[Harry Middlebrooks/Mike Shapiro] [BMI] (1/28/67 BCR-57) [IM]

SPOOKY *Classics IV—Imperial 66259*
[Buddy Buie/J.R. Cobb/Harry Middlebrooks/Mike Shapiro] [BMI] (12/9/67 BCR-2)

SPOOKY *Atlanta Rhythm Section—Polydor/BGO 2001*
[Buddy Buie/J.R. Cobb/Harry Middlebrooks/Mike Shapiro] [BMI] (8/11/79 BCR-15)

SPOONFUL Etta & Harvey—Chess 1771 [Willie Dixon] [BMI] (12/12/60 BCR-76)

SPREAD IT ON THICK The Gentrys—MGM 13432
[William Cates/John Hurley/Ronnie Wilkins] [BMI] (12/25/65 BCR-36)

SPREADIN' HONEY The Watts 103rd Street Rhythm Band—Keymen 108
[Nathaniel Nathan/Fred Smith] [BMI] (9/9/67 BCR-57) [I]

SPRING Birdlegs & Pauline And Their Versatility Birds—Vee-Jay 510
[Sidney Banks] [BMI] (5/18/63 BCR-94)

SPRING AFFAIR *Donna Summer—Casablanca 872*
[Pete Bellotte/Giorgio Moroder/Donna Summer] [ASC] (12/18/76 BC-58)

SPRING AFFAIR *Donna Summer—Casablanca 874*
[Pete Bellotte/Giorgio Moroder/Donna Summer] (TSW) [ASC] (2/5/77 R-49)

SPRING IN MANHATTAN Tony Bennett—Columbia 42779
[Alice Reach/Anthony Scibetta] [ASC] (5/11/63 BCR-68)

SPRING LOVE The Cover Girls—Fever 1913 [Rainy Davis/Pete Warner] [SE] (8/1/87 B-98)

SPRING LOVE (COME BACK TO ME) Stevie B—LMR 74002
[Stevie B] [BMI] (7/9/88 BC-43)

SPRING RAIN Pat Boone—Dot 16073 [Fay Tishman] [ASC] (5/28/60 BCR-47)

SPRING RAIN Silvetti—Salsoul 2014 [Bebu Silvetti] [ASC] (1/22/77 BC-39) [I]

SPRINGFIELD PLANE Kenny O'Dell—Vegas 722
[Harold Gay/Kenny O'Dell] [BMI] (2/24/68 BCR-84)

SPRINGTIME MAMA Henry Gross—Lifesong 45008 [Henry Gross] [ASC] (7/10/76 BCR-37)

SPY IN THE HOUSE OF LOVE Was (Not Was)—Chrysalis 43266
[David Was/Don Was] [ASC] (10/1/88 BC-16)

SQUARE BIZ Teena Marie—Gordy 7202
[Teena Marie/Allen McGrier] [ASC] (7/18/81 BCR-49)

SQUARE ROOMS Al Corley—Mercury 822241
[Al Corley/Harold Faltermeyer/Peter John Wood] [BMI] (5/11/85 BC-80)

SQUEEZE BOX The Who—MCA 40475 [Pete Townshend] [GL] (11/15/75 BCR-11)

SQUEEZE HER-TEASE HER (BUT LOVE HER) Jackie Wilson—Brunswick 55269
[Alonzo Tucker/Jackie Wilson] [BMI] (8/22/64 B-89)

ST. CHARLES Jefferson Starship—Grunt 10791
[Marty Balin*/Jesse Barish/Craig Chaquico/Paul Kantner/Thunderhawk] [BMI] (12/4/76 B-64)

ST. ELMO'S FIRE (MAN IN MOTION) John Parr—Atlantic 89541
[David Foster/John Parr] [BMI] (6/22/85 BC-1)

ST. LOUIS The Easybeats—Rare Earth 5009
[Harry Vanda/George Young] [ASC] (11/8/69 BCR-71)

ST. LOUIS BLUES MAMBO *Richard Maltby And Orchestra—"X" 0042*
[W.C. Handy] [NA] (9/25/54 BCR-17) [IWM]

ST. LOUIS BLUES MAMBO *Perez Prado & His Orchestra—RCA Victor 47-5820*
[W.C. Handy] [NA] (10/4/54 R-PRE) [IWM]

ST. LOUIS BLUES MAMBO *Alberto Iznaga & His Orchestra—Decca 29294*
[W.C. Handy] [NA] (11/1/54 Rt-PRE) [IWM]

ST. LOUIS BLUES MAMBO *Les Brown & His Band Of Renown—Coral 61277*
[W.C. Handy] [NA] (11/15/54 Rt-PRE) [IWM]

ST. LOUIS BLUES *LaVern Baker—Atlantic 1163 [W.C. Handy] [NA] (12/7/57 CR-58)*

ST. LOUIS BLUES *The Cousins—Parkway 823 [W.C. Handy] [NA] (7/31/61 CR-95) [IWM]*

ST THERESE OF THE ROSES Billy Ward And His Dominoes—Decca 29933
[Remus Harris/Arthur Strauss] [ASC] (8/4/56 BCR-24)

STACY Fortune—MCA 52727 [Roger Craig/Larry Alan Greene] [BMI] (12/21/85 B-80)

STAGES ZZ Top—Warner Bros. 28810
[Frank Beard/Billy Gibbons/Dusty Hill] [BMI] (1/18/86 BC-21)

STAGGER LEE *Lloyd Price—ABC-Paramount 9972*
[Harold Logan/Lloyd Price/Traditional] [BMI] (11/24/58 BCR-1)

STAG-O-LEE *Wilson Pickett—Atlantic 2448*
[Harold Logan/Lloyd Price/Traditional] [BMI] (10/28/67 BCR-17)

STAGGER LEE *Tommy Roe—ABC 11307*
[Harold Logan/Lloyd Price/Traditional] [BMI] (8/14/71 BCR-19)

STAIRWAY OF LOVE Marty Robbins—Columbia 41143
[Roy C. Bennett/Sid Tepper] [ASC] (4/14/58 BCR-41)

STAIRWAY TO HEAVEN Neil Sedaka—RCA Victor 47-7709
[Howard Greenfield/Neil Sedaka] [BMI] (3/21/60 BCR-6)

STAIRWAY TO HEAVEN Far Corporation—Atco 99509
[Jimmy Page/Robert Plant] [ASC] (10/4/86 BC-82)

STAND! Sly & The Family Stone—Epic 10450 [Sylvester Stewart] [BMI] (4/12/69 BCR-20)

STAND R.E.M.—Warner Bros. 27688
[Bill Berry/Peter Buck/Mike Mills/Michael Stipe] [BMI] (1/21/89 BC-6)

STAND BACK Stevie Nicks—Modern 99863 [Stevie Nicks/Prince] [BMI] (6/4/83 BC-5)

STAND BACK The Fabulous Thunderbirds—CBS Associated 07230
[Kim Wilson] [BMI] (7/4/87 BC-73)

STAND BY Roman Holliday—Jive 9036
[Robert Lambert/Steve Lambert] [ASC] (6/18/83 BC-54)

STAND BY ME Little Junior Parker—Duke 330 [Junior Parker] [BMI] (12/31/60 C-87)

STAND BY ME *Ben E. King—Atco 6194*
[Ben E. King/Jerry Leiber/Mike Stoller] [BMI] (5/8/61 BCR-3)

STAND BY ME *Cassius Clay—Columbia 43007*
[Ben E. King/Jerry Leiber/Mike Stoller] [BMI] (3/28/64 CR-86)

STAND BY ME *Earl Grant—Decca 25674*
[Ben E. King/Jerry Leiber/Mike Stoller] [BMI] (10/9/65 BCR-66) [IWM]

STAND BY ME *Spyder Turner—MGM 13617*
[Ben E. King/Jerry Leiber/Mike Stoller] [BMI] (12/10/66 BCR-8)

STAND BY ME *David & Jimmy Ruffin—Soul 35076*
[Ben E. King/Jerry Leiber/Mike Stoller] [BMI] (10/24/70 BCR-57)

STAND BY ME *John Lennon—Apple 1881*
[Ben E. King/Jerry Leiber/Mike Stoller] [BMI] (3/15/75 BCR-20)

STAND BY ME *Mickey Gilley—Full Moon/Asylum 46640*
[Ben E. King/Jerry Leiber/Mike Stoller] [BMI] (5/17/80 BCR-12)

STAND BY ME *Maurice White—Columbia 05571*
[Ben E. King/Jerry Leiber/Mike Stoller] [BMI] (8/31/85 BC-48)

STAND BY ME *Ben E. King—Atlantic 89361*
[Ben E. King/Jerry Leiber/Mike Stoller] [BMI] (10/4/86 BC-9)

STAND BY MY WOMAN Lenny Kravitz—Virgin 98736
[Henry Hirsch/Lenny Kravitz/Anthony Krizan/Steve Pasch] [ASC] (10/12/91 BC-64)

STAND BY YOUR MAN *Tammy Wynette—Epic 10398*
[Billy Sherrill/Tammy Wynette] [BMI] (11/9/68 BCR-19)

STAND BY YOUR MAN *Candi Staton—Fame 1472*
[Billy Sherrill/Tammy Wynette] [BMI] (8/29/70 BCR-13)

STAND IN FOR LOVE The O'Jays—Imperial 66197 [Eddie Levert] [BMI] (10/22/66 BR-95)

STAND OR FALL The Fixx—MCA 52106
[Charles Barrett/Cy Curnin/Peter John Greenall/John Leroy Kinyon*/Jamie West-Oram/Adam Woods] [ASC] (10/16/82 BC-76)

STAND TALL Burton Cummings—Portrait 70001
[Burton Cummings] [BMI] (10/2/76 BCR-5)

STAND UP Atlantic Starr—A&M 2065 [Wayne I. Lewis] [ASC] (9/30/78 R-97)

STAND UP David Lee Roth—Warner Bros. 28108
[David Lee Roth/Brett Tuggle] [ASC] (4/16/88 BC-64)

STAND UP Underworld—Sire 22852
[Karl Hyde/Richard David Smith/Alfie Thomas] [ASC] (8/26/89 BC-66)

STANDING AT THE END OF THE LINE Lobo—Big Tree 15001
[Kent LaVoie] [ASC] (3/30/74 BCR-30)

STANDING HERE WONDERING WHICH WAY TO GO Marion Williams—Atlantic 2788
[Thomas A. Dorsey] [BMI] (2/27/71 C-93)

STANDING IN FOR JODY Johnnie Taylor—Stax 0114
[Kent Barker/Bobby Newsome] [BMI] (1/22/72 BCR-70)

STANDING IN THE RAIN The James Gang—Atco 6966
[Tommy Bolin] [ASC] (5/11/74 CR-82)

STANDING IN THE SHADOWS OF LOVE Four Tops—Motown 1102
[Lamont Dozier/Brian Holland/Eddie Holland] [BMI] (12/17/66 BCR-6)

STANDING ON GUARD The Falcons—Big Wheel 1967
[James Gibson/Frank Kocian/Carlis Munro] [BMI] (11/19/66 R-70)

STANDING ON THE CORNER *The Four Lads—Columbia 40674*
[Frank Loesser] [ASC] (4/20/56 BCRt-3)

STANDING ON THE CORNER *The Neal Hefti Singers—Epic 9158*
[Frank Loesser] [ASC] (4/20/56 Rt-8)

STANDING ON THE CORNER *The Mills Brothers—Decca 29897*
[Frank Loesser] [ASC] (4/27/56 BRt-3)

STANDING ON THE CORNER *Dean Martin—Capitol 3414*
[Frank Loesser] [ASC] (5/4/56 BRt-3)

STANDING ON THE CORNER *Andy Griffith—Capitol 3498*
[Frank Loesser] [ASC] (8/25/56 Rt-37)

STANDING ON THE TOP PART 1 The Temptations Featuring Rick James—Gordy 1616
[Rick James] [ASC] (5/8/82 BC-66)

STANDING OVATION GQ—Arista 0483
[Keith Crier/Herb Lane/Emanuel Rahiem LeBlanc/Paul Service] [BMI] (4/5/80 R-87)

STAR Stealers Wheel—A&M 1483
[Joe Egan] [ASC] (12/22/73 BCR-20)

STAR Earth, Wind & Fire—ARC 11165
[Eddie Del Barrio/Maurice White/Allee Willis] [ASC] (12/15/79 BCR-64)

STAR BABY The Guess Who—RCA Victor 0217
[Burton Cummings] [BMI] (2/16/74 BCR-30)

STAR DUST MAMBO *Richard Maltby And His Orchestra—"X" 0075*
[Hoagy Carmichael] [ASC] (12/20/54 CR-27) [IM]

VERSE OF STARDUST *Eddie Dexter and His Band—Capitol 3212*
[Hoagy Carmichael] [ASC] (8/29/55 R-55) [IM]

STAR DUST *Philip Green And His Orchestra—Coral 61497*
[Hoagy Carmichael] [ASC] (10/24/55 R-78) [IM]

STAR DUST *Connee Boswell—Decca 29944*
[Hoagy Carmichael/Mitchell Parish] [ASC] (9/15/56 R-75)

STARDUST *Nat "King" Cole—Capitol EAP 2-824*
[Hoagy Carmichael/Mitchell Parish] [ASC] (5/6/57 BRt-45)

STAR DUST *Billy Ward And His Dominoes—Liberty 55071*
[Hoagy Carmichael/Mitchell Parish] [ASC] (6/17/57 BCRt-10)

STAR DUST *Jaye P. Morgan And The Morgan Brothers—RCA Victor 47-7326*
[Hoagy Carmichael/Mitchell Parish] [ASC] (9/8/58 R-79)

STARDUST *Frank Sinatra—Reprise 20,059*
[Hoagy Carmichael/Mitchell Parish] [ASC] (3/12/62 BR-73)

STARDUST *Nino Tempo & April Stevens—Atco 6286*
[Hoagy Carmichael/Mitchell Parish] [ASC] (2/22/64 BCR-22)

A STAR IS BORN (A LOVE HAS DIED) Mark Dinning—MGM 12888
[Jean Dinning/Red Surrey] [BMI] (4/11/60 BCR-54)

STAR LOVE The Playmates—Roulette 4136
[Edward White/Mack Wolfson] [ASC] (3/30/59 B-75)

STAR LOVE Cheryl Lynn—Columbia 10907
[John Footman/Judy Wieder] [BMI] (4/7/79 BCR-62)

STAR O Harry Belafonte—RCA Victor 47-6771 [Traditional] [NA] (2/9/57 R-66)

STAR ON A TV SHOW The Stylistics—Avco 4649
[Luigi Creatore/Hugo Peretti/George David Weiss] [ASC] (1/18/75 BCR-47)

THE STAR-SPANGLED BANNER Jose Feliciano—RCA Victor 47-9665
[Francis Scott Key] [BMI] (11/2/68 BCR-46)

THE STAR SPANGLED BANNER Whitney Houston—Arista 2207
[Francis Scott Key] [ASC] (3/9/91 B-20)

THE STAR WARS STARS The Force—Lifesong 45031
[Gary Lee Coury/Wynn Jackson] [ASC] (7/23/77 CR-81)

STAR WARS (MAIN TITLE)
John Williams/London Symphony Orchestra—20th Century 2345
[John Williams] [BMI] (7/9/77 BCR-10) [I]

STAR WARS THEME *Meco—Millennium 604*
[John Williams] (Med) [BMI] (7/30/77 BCR-1) [I]

THE STAR YOU WISHED UPON LAST NIGHT *Gisele MacKenzie—Vik 0233*
[Buddy Kaye/Jimmy McHugh] [ASC] (11/10/56 BCRt-40)

THE STAR YOU WISHED UPON LAST NIGHT *Jeannie Carson—Decca 30113*
[Buddy Kaye/Jimmy McHugh] [ASC] (11/17/56 Rt-40)

THE STAR YOU WISHED UPON LAST NIGHT *Nick Noble—Mercury 70981*
[Buddy Kaye/Jimmy McHugh] [ASC] (11/17/56 Rt-40)

STARBRIGHT Johnny Mathis—Columbia 41583
[Lee Pockriss/Paul Vance] [ASC] (2/29/60 BCR-24)

STARGAZER Peter Brown—Drive 6281 [Peter H. Brown] [BMI] (12/15/79 B-59)

STARLIGHT Lee Greenlee—Brent 7003
[Mickey Baker/Lee Greenlee] [BMI] (8/31/59 CR-92)

STARLIGHT The Preludes Five—Pik 231 [Leroy R. Bates] [BMI] (8/14/61 B-80)

STARLIGHT, STARBRIGHT Linda Scott—Canadian-American 127
[Bob Davie/George David Weiss] [BMI] (7/8/61 BCR-44)

STARMAN David Bowie—RCA Victor 74-0719 [David Bowie] [BMI] (6/17/72 BCR-61)

STARRY EYED Gary Stites—Carlton 521
[Mort Garson/Earl Shuman] [ASC] (11/2/59 BC-77)

STARRY EYES The Records—Virgin 67000
[Will Birch/John Wicks] [ASC] (9/15/79 BCR-56)

STARS Simply Red—EastWest 98636 [Mick Hucknall] [ASC] (12/21/91 C-32)

STARS IN MY EYES Sugarloaf/Jerry Corbetta—Claridge 405
[Jerry Corbetta] [ASC] (6/7/75 B-87)

STARS ON 45 *Stars On 45—Radio 3810*
[Martin Duiser/Jaap Eggermont] (Med) [ASC] (4/11/81 BCR-1)

STARS ON 45 *Stars On 45—Radio 3810*
[Martin Duiser/Jaap Eggermont] (Med) [ASC] (4/11/81 BCR-1)

STARS ON 45 *Stars On 45—Radio 3830*
[Martin Duiser/Jaap Eggermont] (Med) [ASC] (7/11/81 BC-63)

STARS ON 45 *Stars On 45—Radio 3863*
[Martin Duiser/Jaap Eggermont] (Med) [ASC] (9/19/81 BCR-55)

STARS ON 45 *Stars On 45—Radio 3863*
[Martin Duiser/Jaap Eggermont] (Med) [ASC] (9/19/81 BCR-55)

STARS ON 45 *Stars On 45—Radio 4019*
[Martin Duiser/Jaap Eggermont] (Med) [ASC] (3/27/82 BCR-28)

START IT ALL OVER McGuffey Lane—Atco 7345 [Robert McNelley] [BMI] (2/6/82 B-97)

START ME UP The Rolling Stones—Rolling Stones 21003
[Mick Jagger/Keith Richards] [ASC] (8/22/81 BCR-2)

START MOVIN' (IN MY DIRECTION) Sal Mineo—Epic 9216
[David Hess/Bobby Stevenson] [BMI] (5/11/57 BCR-6)

STARTED OUT DANCING, ENDED UP MAKING LOVE Alan O'Day—Pacific 002
[Alan O'Day] [ASC] (10/1/77 BC-73)

STARTING ALL OVER AGAIN Mel And Tim—Stax 0127
[Phillip Mitchell] [BMI] (6/24/72 BCR-16)

STARTING OVER AGAIN Dolly Parton—RCA 11926
[Bruce Sudano/Donna Summer] [BMI] (3/29/80 BCR-36)

STASHU PANDOWSKI (SHE'S NOT VERY MUCH GOOD FOR PRETTY)
Russ Carlyle And The Coachmen—ABC-Paramount 9772
[Russ Carlyle/Irwin Pincus] [ASC] (1/26/57 CtRt-36)

STASHU PANDOWSKI (SHE'S NOT VERY MUCH GOOD FOR PRETTY)
Julius La Rosa—RCA Victor 47-6802
[Russ Carlyle/Irwin Pincus] [ASC] (2/2/57 CtRt-36)

STASHU PANDOWSKI (SHE'S NOT VERY MUCH GOOD FOR PRETTY)
The Toppers—Decca 30209
[Russ Carlyle/Irwin Pincus] [ASC] (2/23/57 Rt-41)

STASHU PANDOWSKI (SHE'S NOT VERY MUCH GOOD FOR PRETTY)
Ray Henry & His Orchestra—Dana 2119
[Russ Carlyle/Irwin Pincus] [ASC] (3/9/57 Rt-46)

STATE OF INDEPENDENCE Donna Summer—Geffen 29895
[Jon Anderson/Vangelis] [ASC] (10/2/82 BC-41)
STATE OF SHOCK Jacksons—Epic 04503
[Randy Hansen/Michael Jackson] [BMI] (6/30/84 BC-3)
STATE OF THE HEART Rick Springfield—RCA 14120
[Eric McCusker/Tim Pierce*/Rick Springfield*] [ASC] (6/8/85 BC-22)
STATE OF THE NATION Industry—Capitol 5268
[Jon Carin/Mercury Caronia] [BMI] (11/19/83 BC-79)
STATE OF THE WORLD Janet Jackson—A&M 8694
[James Samuel Harris/Janet Jackson/Terry Lewis] [BMI] (2/16/91 C-8)
STAY The Ames Brothers—RCA Victor 47-7268
[Roy C. Bennett/Sid Tepper] [ASC] (8/4/58 B-90)
STAY *Maurice Williams & The Zodiacs—Herald 552*
[Maurice Williams] [BMI] (9/17/60 BCR-1)
STAY *The 4 Seasons—Vee-Jay 582 [Maurice Williams] [BMI] (2/8/64 BCR-15)*
STAY *Jackson Browne—Asylum 45485 [Maurice Williams] (TSW) [BMI] (7/1/78 BCR-20)*
STAY Rufus/Chaka Khan—ABC 12349
[Richard Calhoun/Chaka Khan] [BMI] (4/8/78 BCR-38)
STAY AND LOVE ME ALL SUMMER Brian Hyland—Dot 17258
[Joel Hirschhorn/Al Kasha] [ASC] (5/31/69 BCR-69)
STAY AWAKE Ronnie Laws—Liberty 1424 [Ronnie Laws] [ASC] (9/5/81 BCR-47)
STAY AWAY Elvis Presley With The Jordanaires—RCA Victor 47-9465
[Roy C. Bennett/Sid Tepper] [ASC] (3/16/68 BCR-50)
STAY AWAY FROM ME The Sylvers—MGM 14579 [Leon Sylvers] [ASC] (8/18/73 BC-89)
STAY AWAY FROM ME (I LOVE YOU TOO MUCH) Major Lance—Curtom 1953
[Curtis Mayfield] [BMI] (7/25/70 BCR-67)
STAY AWAY FROM MY BABY Ted Taylor—Okeh 7231
[Ray Pennington] [BMI] (12/4/65 BCR-93)
STAY AWHILE *Dusty Springfield—Philips 40180*
[Mike Hawker/Ivor Raymonde] [BMI] (3/28/64 BCR-35)
STAY AWHILE *The Continental Miniatures—London 266*
[Mike Hawker/Ivor Raymonde] [BMI] (5/13/78 BCR-74)
STAY AWHILE The Bells—Polydor 15023 [Ken Tobias] [BMI] (3/6/71 BCR-4)
STAY AWHILE Journey—Columbia 11339
[Steve Perry/Neal Schon*] (Med) [BMI] (8/16/80 BCR-55)
STAY CLOSE TO ME The Five Stairsteps & Cubie—Curtom 1933
[Curtis Mayfield] [BMI] (12/21/68 B-91)
STAY HERE WITH ME (RESTA CU 'MME) Domenico Modugno—Decca 30747
[Milt Gabler/Domenico Modugno/Dino Verde] [ASC] (9/29/58 R-97)
STAY IN MY CORNER The Dells—Cadet 5612
[Wade Flemons/Robert Eugene Miller/Barrett Strong] [BMI] (6/29/68 BCR-10)
STAY IN TIME Off Broadway USA—Atlantic 3647 [Cliff Johnson] [BMI] (3/15/80 BCR-51)
STAY THE NIGHT The Faragher Brothers—Polydor 14533
[Jimmy Faragher/Tommy Faragher] [BMI] (2/24/79 BCR-48)
STAY THE NIGHT Chicago—Warner/Full Moon 29306
[Peter Cetera/David Foster] [ASC] (5/5/84 BC-15)
STAY THE NIGHT Benjamin Orr—Elektra 69506
[Benjamin Orr/Diane Page] [ASC] (11/8/86 BC-20)
STAY TOGETHER YOUNG LOVERS Brenda & The Tabulations—Dionn 501
[Samuel Bell/Lorraine Ellison] [BMI] (5/20/67 BR-66)
STAY TRUE Sly Fox—Capitol 5581 [Michael Camacho] [BMI] (6/7/86 B-94)
STAY WITH ME Frank Sinatra—Reprise 0249
[Carolyn Leigh/Jerome Moross] [ASC] (1/4/64 BR-79)
STAY WITH ME Lorraine Ellison—Warner Bros. 5850
[Jerry Ragovoy/George David Weiss] [ASC] (10/1/66 BCR-63)
STAY WITH ME Faces—Warner Bros. 7545
[Rod Stewart/Ron Wood] [ASC] (12/25/71 BCR-10)
STAY WITH ME TONIGHT Jeffrey Osborne—A&M 2591
[Raymond C. Jones] [ASC] (10/15/83 BC-27)
STAYIN' ALIVE Bee Gees—RSO 885
[Barry Gibb/Maurice Gibb/Robin Gibb] [BMI] (12/10/77 BCR-1)
STAYIN' IN Bobby Vee—Liberty 55296 [John D. Loudermilk] [BMI] (1/30/61 BCR-20)
STAYING TOGETHER Debbie Gibson—Atlantic 89034
[Debbie Gibson] [ASC] (8/6/88 BC-22)
STAYING WITH IT Firefall—Atlantic 3791
[John Lewis Parker/Tom Snow] [BMI] (1/24/81 BCR-37)
STEADY Jules Shear—EMI America 8259
[Cyndi Lauper/Jules Shear] [BMI] (4/6/85 BC-57)
STEAL AWAY Pat Boone—Dot DEP-1056
[Traditional/Wallace Willis] (EP) [BMI] (5/11/57 R-60)
STEAL AWAY *Jimmy Hughes—Fame 6401 [Jimmy Hughes] [BMI] (6/20/64 BCR-11)*
STEAL AWAY *Johnnie Taylor—Stax 0068 [Jimmy Hughes] [BMI] (5/23/70 BCR-23)*
STEAL AWAY Robbie Dupree—Elektra 46621
[Rick Chudacoff/Robbie Dupree] [BMI] (4/12/80 BCR-5)
STEAL THE NIGHT Stevie Woods—Cotillion 46016
[Bill Bowersock/Trevor Veitch/Matt Vernon] [BMI] (9/12/81 BCR-25)
STEALER Free—A&M 1230
[Andy Fraser/Paul Kossoff/Paul Rodgers] [BMI] (11/28/70 BCR-40)
STEALIN' Uriah Heep—Warner Bros. 7738 [Ken Hensley] [ASC] (10/6/73 BCR-62)
STEALING IN THE NAME OF THE LORD Paul Kelly—Happy Tiger 541
[Paul Kelly] [BMI] (6/13/70 BCR-44)
STEALING LOVE The Emotions—Volt 4031
[Isaac Hayes/David Porter] [ASC] (4/11/70 C-100)
STEALING MOMENTS FROM ANOTHER WOMAN'S LIFE The Glass House—Invictus 9082
[Lamont Dozier/Brian Holland] [BMI] (12/12/70 C-92)
STEAM HEAT *Patti Page—Mercury 70380*
[Richard Adler/Jerry Ross] [ASC] (6/5/54 BC-PRE)
STEAM HEAT *Pointer Sisters—ABC/Blue Thumb 248*
[Richard Adler/Jerry Ross] [ASC] (3/23/74 C-84)
STEAMROLLER BLUES Elvis Presley—RCA Victor 74-0910
[James Taylor] (TSW) [ASC] (4/14/73 BCR-10)
STEAMY WINDOWS Tina Turner—Capitol 44473 [Tony Joe White] [BMI] (11/25/89 BC-39)
A STEEL GUITAR AND A GLASS OF WINE Paul Anka—RCA Victor 47-8030
[Paul Anka] [BMI] (5/26/62 BCR-13)
STEEL GUITAR RAG The Dynatones (2)—Bomarc 303
[Leon McAuliffe] [ASC] (6/20/59 C-95) [IM]
STEEL MEN Jimmy Dean—Columbia 42483
[David Anthony Martins] [BMI] (6/16/62 BCR-41)
STEP BY STEP The Crests—Coed 525
[Ollie Jones/Billy Dawn Smith] [BMI] (2/29/60 BCR-13)
STEP BY STEP Joe Simon—Spring 133 [Raeford Gerald] [BMI] (2/17/73 BCR-23)
STEP BY STEP The Kiki Dee Band—Rocket/MCA 40355
[Bias Boshell] [ASC] (3/1/75 C-85)
STEP BY STEP Eddie Rabbitt—Elektra 47174
[David Malloy/Eddie Rabbitt/Even Stevens] [BMI] (7/25/81 BCR-5)
STEP BY STEP New Kids On The Block—Columbia 73343
[Maurice Starr] [ASC] (5/26/90 BC-1)
STEP BY STEP, LITTLE BY LITTLE Anita Bryant—Columbia 42257
[Lou Dinning] [ASC] (2/12/62 R-71)
STEP INSIDE LOVE Cilla Black—Bell 726
[John Lennon/Paul McCartney] [ASC] (6/29/68 CR-89)
STEP INTO CHRISTMAS Elton John—MCA 65018
[Elton John/Bernie Taupin] [BMI] (12/15/73 CR-56)
HE'S GONNA STEP ON YOU AGAIN *(Step On) John Kongos—Elektra 45729*
[Christos Demetriou/John Kongos] [ASC] (7/10/71 BCR-64)
STEP ON *Happy Mondays—Elektra 64899*
[Christos Demetriou/John Kongos] [ASC] (3/16/91 BC-55)
STEP OUT The Mamas & The Papas—Dunhill 4301 [John Phillips] [ASC] (2/12/72 BR-81)
STEP OUT OF YOUR MIND The American Breed—Acta 804
[Al Gorgoni/Chip Taylor] [BMI] (6/3/67 BCR-20)
SUCU SUCU *Ping-Ping and the Al Verlane Orchestra—Kapp 377*
[Tarateno Rojas] [BMI] (5/13/61 C-90) [F]
STEP RIGHT UP (AND SAY YOU LOVE ME) *(derived from Sucu Sucu)*
Teresa Brewer—Coral 62299
[Phil Belmonte/Ray Maxwell/Tarateno Rojas] [BMI] (1/8/62 Rt-72) [FDE]*
STEP RIGHT UP (AND SAY YOU LOVE ME) *(derived from Sucu Sucu)*
Nat King Cole—Capitol 4672
[Phil Belmonte/Ray Maxwell/Tarateno Rojas] [BMI] (1/8/62 Rt-71) [FDE]*
STEPPIN' IN A SLIDE ZONE The Moody Blues—London 270
[John Lodge] [ASC] (7/29/78 BCR-39)
STEPPIN' OUT Paul Revere And The Raiders—Columbia 43375
[Mark Lindsay/Paul Revere] [BMI] (9/4/65 BCR-41)
STEPPIN' OUT (GONNA BOOGIE TONIGHT) Tony Orlando And Dawn—Bell 45,601
[L. Russell Brown/Irwin Levine] [BMI] (8/17/74 BCR-7)
STEPPIN' OUT Neil Sedaka—Rocket/MCA 40582
[Phil Cody/Neil Sedaka] [BMI] (6/19/76 BCR-36)
STEPPIN' OUT Kool & The Gang—De-Lite 816
[Robert Bell/Ronald Bell/George M. Brown/Eumir Deodato/Amos Guider/
Robert Mickens/Claydes Smith/J.T. Taylor] [BMI] (2/13/82 B-89)
STEPPIN' OUT Joe Jackson—A&M 2428 [Joe Jackson] [ASC] (8/21/82 BC-5)
STEPS 1 AND 2 Jack Scott—Capitol 4637 [Jack Scott] [SE] (10/30/61 BCR-67)
STEREOTOMY Alan Parsons Project—Arista 1-9443
[Alan Parsons/Eric Woolfson] [BMI] (2/15/86 BC-71)
STEWBALL Peter, Paul & Mary—Warner Bros. 5399
[Elena Mezzetti/Milton Okun/Paul Stookey/Traditional/Mary Travers] [ASC]
(11/23/63 BCR-34)
STICK AROUND Julian Lennon—Atlantic 89437 [Julian Lennon] [ASC] (3/22/86 BC-32)
STICK SHIFT Duals—Sue 745 [Henry Bellinger] [BMI] (8/28/61 BCR-24) [I]
STICK-UP The Honey Cone—Hot Wax 7106
[Angelo Bond/General Johnson/Greg Perry] [BMI] (7/31/71 BCR-7)
STICK WITH ME BABY The Everly Brothers—Warner Bros. 5220
[Mel Tillis] [BMI] (6/5/61 BCR-41)
STICKS AND STONES Ray Charles And His Orchestra—ABC-Paramount 10118
[Titus Turner] [BMI] (6/25/60 BCR-27)
STICKY, STICKY Bobby Harris—Shout 203
[Bert Berns] [BMI] (9/24/66 C-99)
STILL *LaVern Baker—Atlantic 1104*
[Dorian Burton/Howard Plummer] [BMI] (9/29/56 BRt-30)

STILL *The Fontane Sisters—Dot 15501*
[Dorian Burton/Howard Plummer] [BMI] (9/29/56 BRt-30)

STILL *Bill Anderson—Decca 31458 [Bill Anderson] [BMI] (4/6/63 BCR-7)*

STILL NO. 2 *(parody of Still) Ben Colder—MGM 13147*
[Bill Anderson/Sheb Wooley] [BMI] (7/20/63 BCR-80) [P]

STILL *The Sunrays—Tower 224 [Bill Anderson] [BMI] (4/16/66 BCR-83)*

STILL *Commodores—Motown 1474 [Lionel Richie] [ASC] (9/29/79 BCR-1)*

STILL *John Schneider—Scotti Brothers 02489 [Lionel Richie] [ASC] (9/26/81 BCR-69)*

STILL A THRILL Jody Watley—MCA 53081
[André Cymone/Jody Watley] [ASC] (6/20/87 BC-56)

STILL AS THE NIGHT Sanford Clark—Jamie 1107 [Lee Hazlewood] [BMI] (9/13/58 C-80)

STILL CRAZY AFTER ALL THESE YEARS Paul Simon—Columbia 10332
[Paul Simon] [BMI] (5/1/76 BCR-40)

STILL CRUISIN' The Beach Boys—Capitol 44445
[Mike Love/Terry Melcher] [BMI] (8/26/89 B-93)

STILL GOT THE BLUES Gary Moore—Charisma 98854 [Gary Moore] [BMI] (2/16/91 B-97)

—STILL GOT THE LIGHT IN YOUR EYES see: DAYS GONE DOWN

STILL IN LOVE Boston—MCA 53029 [Brad Delp/Tom Scholz] (Med) [ASC] (3/7/87 BC-20)

STILL IN SAIGON Charlie Daniels Band—Epic 02828 [Dan Daley] [BMI] (3/27/82 BCR-22)

STILL IN THE GAME Steve Winwood—Island 29940
[Will Jennings/Steve Winwood] [BMI] (7/31/82 BC-44)

STILL LOVING YOU Scorpions—Mercury 880082
[Klaus Meine/Rudolf Schenker] [ASC] (7/7/84 BC-64)

STILL OF THE NIGHT Whitesnake—Geffen 28331
[David Coverdale/John Sykes] [ASC] (6/13/87 B-79)

STILL RIGHT HERE IN MY HEART Pure Prairie League—Casablanca 2332
[George Daniel Greer/Jeff Wilson] [BMI] (4/18/81 BCR-28)

STILL SMALL VOICE Perry Como—RCA Victor 47-7628
[Al Stillman/Ben Weisman] [ASC] (11/30/59 R-97)

STILL TAKING CHANCES Michael Martin Murphey—Liberty 1486
[Michael Murphey] [BMI] (1/8/83 B-76)

STILL THE LOVIN' IS FUN B.J. Thomas—MCA 40812
[Chris Christian] [ASC] (11/12/77 BC-77)

STILL THE ONE Orleans—Asylum 45336 [Johanna Hall/John Hall] [BMI] (7/24/76 BCR-5)

STILL THE SAME Bob Seger & The Silver Bullet Band—Capitol 4581
[Bob Seger] [ASC] (5/13/78 BCR-4)

STILL THEY RIDE Journey—Columbia 02883
[Jonathan Cain/Steve Perry/Neal Schon] [BMI] (5/22/82 BC-19)

STILL THINKING OF YOU The Three Chuckles—"X" 0162
[Teddy Randazzo] [BMI] (11/21/55 R-57)

STILL WATER (LOVE) Four Tops—Motown 1170
[Smokey Robinson/Frank Edward Wilson] [ASC] (8/29/70 BCR-8)

STILL WATERS RUN DEEP Brook Benton—Mercury 72055
[Paul Gasper/Bob Perper] [BMI] (11/17/62 BCR-65)

STILLSANE Carolyne Mas—Mercury 76004 [Carolyne Mas] [ASC] (9/8/79 BCR-71)

STIMULATION Wa Wa Nee—Epic 07671 [Paul Gray] [ASC] (1/30/88 B-86)

STING RAY The Routers—Warner Bros. 5349
[Dayton Howe/Jean Sharp Murphy] [BMI] (4/27/63 BCR-45) [I]

STIR IT UP Johnny Nash—Epic 10949 [Bob Marley] [ASC] (2/3/73 BCR-11)

STIR IT UP Patti LaBelle—MCA 52610
[Danny Sembello/Allee Willis] [ASC] (6/15/85 BC-41)

STIR IT UP AND SERVE IT Tommy Roe—ABC 11258
[Tommy Roe/Freddy Weller] [BMI] (2/21/70 BCR-27)

STOCKHOLM Lawrence Welk And His Orchestra—Dot 16582
[George Cates] [ASC] (3/7/64 BR-85) [I]

STOLEN ANGEL Scott Brothers—Ribbon 6905 [Warren Scott] [BMI] (2/27/60 C-88)

STOLEN LOVE Dinah Shore—RCA Victor 47-6360
[Bob Roberts/Robert Sherman] [BMI] (2/11/56 B-73)

STOMP! The Brothers Johnson—A&M 2216
[George Johnson/Louis E. Johnson/Valerie Johnson/Rod Temperton] [BMI] (3/8/80 BCR-7)

STONE BLUE Foghat—Bearsville 0325 [Dave Peverett] [ASC] (5/20/78 BCR-34)

STONE COLD Rainbow—Mercury 76146
[Ritchie Blackmore/Roger Glover/Joe Lynn Turner] [ASC] (4/24/82 BC-39)

STONE COLD GENTLEMAN Ralph Tresvant—MCA 54043
[Antonio Reid/Kevin Roberson/Daryl Simmons/Ralph Tresvant] [BMI] (2/23/91 BC-34)

STONE COLD SOBER Crawler—Epic 50442 [John Bundrick] [BMI] (10/1/77 BCR-62)

STONE LOVE Kool & The Gang—Mercury 888292
[Robert Bell/Ronald Bell/George M. Brown/Claydes Smith/J.T. Taylor/Dennis Thomas/Curtis Fitzgerald Williams] [BMI] (2/7/87 BC-10)

STONE OF YEARS Emerson, Lake & Palmer—Cotillion 44131
[Keith Emerson/Greg Lake] [ASC] (9/11/71 CR-84)

STONE TO THE BONE - PART 1 James Brown—Polydor 14210
[James Brown] [BMI] (11/17/73 BCR-46)

STONED COWBOY Fantasy—Liberty 56190
[Vincent DeMeo/Greg Kimple/David Robert Robbins/Mario Russo] [BMI] (9/19/70 BCR-72) [IM]

STONED LOVE The Supremes—Motown 1172
[Kenny Thomas/Frank Edward Wilson] [BMI] (10/31/70 BCR-5)

STONED OUT OF MY MIND The Chi-Lites—Brunswick 55500
[Barbara Acklin/Eugene Record] [BMI] (8/4/73 BCR-30)

STONED SOUL PICNIC The 5th Dimension—Soul City 766
[Laura Nyro] [BMI] (5/25/68 BCR-3)

STONES Neil Diamond—Uni 55310 [Neil Diamond] (TSW) [SE] (1/8/72 BCR-10)

STONEY END Barbra Streisand—Columbia 45236 [Laura Nyro] [BMI] (10/17/70 BCR-6)

STOOD UP Ricky Nelson—Imperial 5483
[Dub Dickerson/Erma Herrold] [BMI] (12/23/57 BCR-3)

STOP! The Moody Blues—London 9810
[Denny Laine/Mike Pinder] [BMI] (2/12/66 BCR-89)

STOP Howard Tate—Verve 10573 [Jerry Ragovoy/Mort Shuman] [BMI] (1/27/68 BCR-67)

STOP Sam Brown—A&M 1234
[Bruce Brody/Samantha Brown/Gregg Sutton] [ASC] (4/15/89 BC-65)

STOP! Erasure—Sire 22879 [Andy Bell/Vince Clarke] [ASC] (7/22/89 B-97)

STOP AND SMELL THE ROSES Mac Davis—Columbia 10018
[Mac Davis/Doc Severinsen] [BMI] (8/17/74 BCR-5)

STOP AND THINK IT OVER Dale & Grace—Montel 922
[Jake Graffagnino/Joseph Noel] [BMI] (1/25/64 BCR-8)

STOP! AND THINK IT OVER Perry Como—RCA Victor 47-9165
[Roy C. Bennett/Sid Tepper] [ASC] (5/13/67 BCR-82)

STOP DOGGIN' ME Johnnie Taylor—Stax 0142
[Bettye Crutcher/Don Davis/Arthur Snyder] [BMI] (9/9/72 CR-67)

—STOP DOGGIN' ME AROUND see: DOGGIN' AROUND

STOP DRAGGIN' MY HEART AROUND
Stevie Nicks (with Tom Petty And The Heartbreakers)—Modern 7336
[Mike Campbell/Tom Petty] [ASC] (7/25/81 BCR-3)

STOP FOOLIN' Brook Benton & Damita Jo—Mercury 72207
[Brook Benton] [BMI] (11/16/63 CR-72)

STOP! GET A TICKET Clefs Of Lavender Hill—Date 1510
[Coventry Fairchild/Travis Fairchild] [BMI] (6/25/66 BCR-72)

STOP HER ON SIGHT (S.O.S.) Edwin Starr—Ric-Tic 109
[Al Hamilton/Richard Morris/Edwin Starr] [BMI] (2/12/66 BCR-39)

STOP! IN THE NAME OF LOVE *The Supremes—Motown 1074*
[Lamont Dozier/Brian Holland/Eddie Holland] [BMI] (2/20/65 BCR-1)

STOP! IN THE NAME OF LOVE *Margie Joseph—Volt 4056*
[Lamont Dozier/Brian Holland/Eddie Holland] [BMI] (3/27/71 BC-66)

STOP! IN THE NAME OF LOVE *Shalamar—Soul Train 10885*
[Lamont Dozier/Brian Holland/Eddie Holland] (Med) [BMI] (3/12/77 BCR-25)

STOP IN THE NAME OF LOVE *Stars On 45—Radio 3863*
[Lamont Dozier/Brian Holland/Eddie Holland] (Med) [BMI] (9/19/81 BCR-55)

STOP IN THE NAME OF LOVE *The Hollies—Atlantic 89819*
[Lamont Dozier/Brian Holland/Eddie Holland] [BMI] (6/4/83 BC-29)

STOP, LOOK AND LISTEN The Chiffons—Laurie 3357
[Barbara Baer/Eliot Greenberg/Douglas Morris/Robert Schwartz] [BMI] (10/1/66 B-85)

STOP, LOOK, LISTEN (TO YOUR HEART) The Stylistics—Avco Embassy 4572
[Thom Bell/Linda Creed] [BMI] (5/29/71 BCR-32)

STOP! LOOK WHAT YOU'RE DOING Carla Thomas—Stax 172
[Eddie Floyd/Alvertis Isbell] [BMI] (7/3/65 BCR-87)

STOP MONKEYIN' AROUN' The Dovells—Parkway 889
[Dave Appell/Kal Mann] [ASC] (11/9/63 BR-94)

S.T.O.P. (STOP) The Lorelei—Columbia 45629
[Mark Barkan/Don Oriolo] [BMI] (11/4/72 CR-82)

STOP STOP STOP The Hollies—Imperial 66214
[Allan Clarke/Tony Hicks/Graham Nash] [BMI] (10/22/66 BCR-5)

STOP TAKIN' ME FOR GRANTED Mary Wells—20th Century 544
[Mickey Gentile/Jennie Lee Lambert] [BMI] (11/7/64 B-88)

STOP THE MUSIC The Shirelles—Scepter 1237
[Willie Denson/Van McCoy] [BMI] (9/8/62 BCR-36)

STOP THE WAR NOW Edwin Starr—Gordy 7104
[Barrett Strong/Norman Whitfield] [BMI] (12/5/70 BCR-22)

STOP THE WEDDING Etta James—Argo 5418
[Fred Johnson/Leroy Kirkland/Pearl Woods] [BMI] (7/21/62 BCR-22)

STOP THE WORLD AND LET ME OFF The Flaming Ember—Hot Wax 7010
[Angelo Bond/Lamont Dozier/Ronald Dunbar/Brian Holland/Eddie Holland] [BMI] (2/27/71 C-98)

STOP THIS GAME Cheap Trick—Epic 50942
[Rick Nielsen/Robin Zander] [BMI] (11/8/80 BCR-44)

STOP TO LOVE Luther Vandross—Epic 06523
[Nat Adderley Jr./Luther Vandross] [BMI] (11/15/86 BC-15)

STOP TO START Blue Magic—Atco 6949
[Allan Felder/James Grant] [BMI] (1/19/74 BCR-56)

STOP, WAIT AND LISTEN Circus—Metromedia 265 [Dan Hrdlicka] [BMI] (1/27/73 BCR-74)

STOP YOUR SOBBING The Pretenders—Sire 49506 [Ray Davies] [BMI] (6/14/80 BCR-64)

STORIES?? Chakachas—Avco 4596
[Bill Ador/Jean Joseph Kluger] [ASC] (7/29/72 CR-95) [I]

STORM WARNING The Volcanos—Arctic 106 [Carl Fisher] [BMI] (7/24/65 R-94)

STORMY *Classics IV Featuring Dennis Yost—Imperial 66328*
[Buddy Buie/J.R. Cobb] [BMI] (10/12/68 BCR-2)

STORMY *Santana—Columbia 10873 [Buddy Buie/J.R. Cobb] [BMI] (12/23/78 BCR-32)*

STORMY MONDAY Latimore—Glades 1716
[Bob Crowder/Billy Eckstine/Earl Hines] [ASC] (12/22/73 C-92)

STORMY MONDAY BLUES Bobby Bland—Duke 355
[Aaron Walker] [BMI] (9/8/62 BCR-36)

THE STORY IN YOUR EYES The Moody Blues—Threshold 67006
[Justin Hayward] [BMI] (8/7/71 BCR-14)

STORY OF MY LIFE Marty Robbins—Columbia 41013
[Burt Bacharach/Hal David] [ASC] (11/11/57 BCR-26)

STORY OF MY LOVE Conway Twitty—MGM 12748
[Jack Nance/Conway Twitty] [BMI] (1/26/59 BCR-28)

THE STORY OF MY LOVE Paul Anka—ABC-Paramount 10168
[Paul Anka] [BMI] (1/2/61 BCR-16)

THE STORY OF OUR LOVE Johnny Mathis—Columbia 41483
[Michael Colicchio/Anthony Piano] [ASC] (10/12/59 B-93)

THE STORY OF ROCK AND ROLL The Turtles—White Whale 273
[Harry Nilsson] [BMI] (6/15/68 BCR-36)

(THE STORY OF) WOMAN, LOVE AND A MAN (PART 1) Tony Clarke—Chess 1880
[Tony Clarke/Wilfred McKinley/Carl William Smith*] [BMI] (2/15/64 BC-83)

A STORY UNTOLD *The Crew-Cuts—Mercury 70634 [Leroy Griffin] [BMI] (6/6/55 BCtRt-14)*

STORY UNTOLD *The Nutmegs—Herald 452 [Leroy Griffin] [BMI] (6/11/55 CtRt-14)*

STORY UNTOLD *The Four Coins—Epic 9107 [Leroy Griffin] [BMI] (6/11/55 CtRt-14)*

A STORY UNTOLD *The Emotions—20th Century 430 [Leroy Griffin] [BMI] (10/5/63 CR-61)*

STORYBOOK CHILDREN Billy Vera & Judy Clay—Atlantic 2445
[Chip Taylor/Billy Vera] [BMI] (11/18/67 BCR-54)

STORYBOOK CHILDREN (DAYBREAK) Bette Midler—Atlantic 3431
[David Pomeranz/Spencer Proffer] [BMI] (1/14/78 BCR-57)

STOUT-HEARTED MEN Barbra Streisand—Columbia 44225
[Oscar Hammerstein/Sigmund Romberg] [ASC] (8/26/67 B-92)

—STRADA DEL' AMORE see: LA STRADA DEL' AMORE

STRAIGHT AHEAD Young-Holt Unlimited—Brunswick 55417
[Carl Davis/Raymond Haley/Willie Henderson] [BMI] (7/26/69 CR-94) [I]

STRAIGHT A'S IN LOVE Johnny Cash—Sun 334 [Johnny Cash] [ASC] (3/14/60 B-84)

STRAIGHT FLUSH The Frantics—Dolton 2
[Don Fulton/Eddie Goodman*/Bob Hosko/Jim Manolides*/Ron Peterson/
Chuck Schoning] [BMI] (5/25/59 B-91) [I]

STRAIGHT FROM THE HEART The Allman Brothers Band—Arista 0618
[Dickey Betts/Johnny Cobb] [BMI] (8/1/81 BCR-39)

STRAIGHT FROM THE HEART Bryan Adams—A&M 2536
[Bryan Adams/Eric Kagna] [BMI] (3/12/83 BC-10)

STRAIGHT FROM THE HEART (INTO YOUR LIFE) The Coyote Sisters—Morocco 1742
[Tony Berg/Leah Kunkel] [BMI] (7/28/84 BC-66)

THE STRAIGHT LIFE Bobby Goldsboro—United Artists 50461
[Sonny Curtis] [BMI] (10/19/68 BCR-22)

STRAIGHT ON Heart—Portrait 70020
[Sue Ennis/Ann Wilson/Nancy Wilson] [ASC] (9/16/78 BCR-15)

STRAIGHT SHOOTIN' WOMAN Steppenwolf—Mums 6031
[Jerry Edmonton] [BMI] (8/31/74 BCR-20)

STRAIGHT TO YOUR HEART Bad English—Epic 73982
[Jonathan Cain/Neal Schon/Mark Spiro/John Waite] [ASC] (8/31/91 BC-34)

STRAIGHT UP Paula Abdul—Virgin 99256 [Elliot Wolff] [ASC] (12/3/88 BC-1)

STRAIGHTEN UP AND FLY RIGHT The DeJohn Sisters—Sunbeam 106
[Nat "King" Cole/Irving Mills] [ASC] (8/18/58 BR-73)

STRAIGHTEN UP YOUR HEART Barbara Lewis—Atlantic 2200
[Sharon McMahan] [BMI] (8/10/63 BCR-43)

STRAIN ON MY HEART Roscoe Shelton—Sims 217 [Allen Orange] [BMI] (1/16/65 R-85)

STRANDED Heart—Capitol 44621 [Jeff Harrington/Jaime Kyle] [ASC] (9/22/90 BC-11)

STRANDED IN THE JUNGLE *The Jayhawks—Flash 109*
[James E. Johnson/Ernestine Smith] [BMI] (6/30/56 BCtRt-10)

STRANDED IN THE JUNGLE *The Gadabouts—Mercury 70898*
[James E. Johnson/Ernestine Smith] [BMI] (7/6/56 BRt-18)

STRANDED IN THE JUNGLE *The Cadets—Modern 994*
[James E. Johnson/Ernestine Smith] [BMI] (7/7/56 BCtRt-10)

STRANDED IN THE MIDDLE OF NOPLACE The Righteous Brothers—Verve 10551
[William Stevenson] [BMI] (9/30/67 BCR-55)

STRANGE Patsy Cline—Decca 31354 [Fred Burch/Mel Tillis] [BMI] (1/22/62 BR-90)

STRANGE Jellyroll—Kapp 2107 [David Wolinski] [BMI] (9/12/70 CR-97)

STRANGE ARE THE WAYS OF LOVE *Gogi Grant—RCA Victor 47-7294*
[Dimitri Tiomkin/Ned Washington] [ASC] (7/21/58 BCRt-53)

STRANGE ARE THE WAYS OF LOVE *Randy Sparks—Verve 10147*
[Dimitri Tiomkin/Ned Washington] [ASC] (9/8/58 Rt-65)

STRANGE BUT TRUE Times Two—Reprise 27998
[Gardner Cole/Shanti Jones] [BMI] (3/12/88 BC-21)

STRANGE FEELING Billy Stewart—Chess 1868 [Billy Stewart] [BMI] (9/28/63 BCR-70)

STRANGE I KNOW The Marvelettes—Tamla 54072
[Lamont Dozier/Freddie Gorman/Brian Holland] [BMI] (11/24/62 BCR-49)

STRANGE LADY IN TOWN *Frankie Laine—Columbia 40457*
[Dimitri Tiomkin/Ned Washington] [ASC] (4/16/55 CRt-49)

STRANGE LADY IN TOWN *Dimitri Tiomkin & His Orchestra—Coral 61388*
[Dimitri Tiomkin] [ASC] (4/25/55 Rt-71) [IM]

STRANGE MAGIC Electric Light Orchestra—United Artists 770
[Jeff Lynne] [BMI] (3/6/76 BCR-14)

STRANGE THINGS HAPPENING Little Junior Parker—Duke 371
[Percy Mayfield] [BMI] (1/18/64 BR-95)

STRANGE WAY Firefall—Atlantic 3518 [Rick Roberts] [BMI] (9/30/78 BCR-11)

STRANGELOVE *Depeche Mode—Sire 28366 [Martin L. Gore] [BMI] (7/25/87 B-76)*

STRANGELOVE *Depeche Mode—Sire 27777 [Martin L. Gore] [BMI] (9/10/88 BC-41)*

STRANGER Johnny Duncan—Columbia 10302 [Kris Kristofferson] [BMI] (7/10/76 R-78)

STRANGER L.T.D.—A&M 2192 [Jeffrey Osborne/Jake Riley] [ASC] (12/8/79 R-92)

STRANGER Jefferson Starship—Grunt 12275
[Jeannette Sears/Pete Sears] [BMI] (7/11/81 BCR-48)

STRANGER Stephen Stills—Atlantic 89633
[Christopher Stills/Stephen Stills] [BMI] (8/11/84 BC-61)

STRANGER FROM DURANGO Richie Allen—Imperial 5683
[Richard Podolor] [BMI] (11/21/60 B-90) [I]

STRANGER IN MY HOME TOWN Foghat—Bearsville 49510
[Dave Peverett] [ASC] (7/19/80 BCR-71)

STRANGER IN MY HOUSE Ronnie Milsap—RCA 13470 [Mike Reid] [ASC] (3/26/83 BC-23)

STRANGER IN TOWN Del Shannon—Amy 919 [Del Shannon] [BMI] (2/27/65 BCR-30)

STRANGER IN TOWN Toto—Columbia 04672
[David Paich/Jeff Porcaro] [ASC] (10/27/84 BC-26)

STRANGER IN YOUR ARMS Bobby Vee—Liberty 55654
[Hank Hunter/Vic Thomas] [BMI] (1/18/64 BCR-83)

A STRANGER IN YOUR TOWN The Shacklefords—Mercury 72112
[Marty Cooper/Lee Hazlewood] [BMI] (5/4/63 BCR-65)

STRANGER ON THE SHORE *Mr. Acker Bilk—Atco 6217*
[Acker Bilk] [BMI] (3/12/62 BCtR-1) [IM]

STRANGER ON THE SHORE *The Drifters—Atlantic 2143*
[Acker Bilk/Robert Mellin] [BMI] (5/12/62 BRt-71)

STRANGER ON THE SHORE *Andy Williams—Columbia 42451*
[Acker Bilk/Robert Mellin] [BMI] (6/2/62 BCtRt-2)

STRANGER TO LOVE St. Paul—Atlantic 87899
[Paul Peterson/Evan Rogers/Carl Sturken] [BMI] (7/7/90 BC-50)

STRANGERS IN A STRANGE WORLD Jenny Burton & Patrick Jude—Atlantic 89660
[Jake Holmes] [ASC] (6/9/84 BC-54)

STRANGERS IN THE NIGHT Frank Sinatra—Reprise 0470
[Bert Kaempfert/Charles Singleton/Eddie Snyder] [BMI] (5/7/66 BCR-1)

THE STRANGEST ROMANCE Patti Page—Mercury 70878
[Fay Tishman] [ASC] (7/7/56 B-93)

STRANGLEHOLD Paul McCartney—Capitol 5636
[Paul McCartney/Eric Stewart] [ASC] (11/15/86 BC-75)

STRAP ME IN The Cars—Elektra 69427 [Ric Ocasek] [ASC] (11/14/87 BC-84)

STRAWBERRY FIELDS FOREVER The Beatles—Capitol 5810
[John Lennon/Paul McCartney] [ASC] (2/25/67 BCR-8)

STRAWBERRY LETTER 23 The Brothers Johnson—A&M 1949
[Shuggie Otis] [BMI] (7/2/77 BCR-5)

STRAWBERRY SHORTCAKE Jay And The Techniques—Smash 2142
[Maurice Irby] [BMI] (1/20/68 BCR-29)

STRAY CAT STRUT Stray Cats—EMI America 8122 [Brian Setzer] [BMI] (12/25/82 BC-3)

THE STREAK Ray Stevens—Barnaby 600 [Ray Stevens] [BMI] (4/13/74 BCR-1)

STREET CORNER Ashford & Simpson—Capitol 5109
[Nick Ashford/Valerie Simpson] [ASC] (6/5/82 BC-56)

STREET CORNER SERENADE Wet Willie—Epic 50478
[Mike Duke/Jimmy Hall/Marshall Smith] [BMI] (11/19/77 BCR-21)

STREET FIGHTING MAN The Rolling Stones—London 909
[Mick Jagger/Keith Richards] [BMI] (9/7/68 BCR-28)

STREET LIFE The Crusaders—MCA 41054 [Joe Sample] [BMI] (8/18/79 BCR-29) [IM]

STREET OF DREAMS Rainbow—Mercury 815660
[Ritchie Blackmore/Joe Lynn Turner] [ASC] (11/5/83 BC-60)

STREET OF DREAMS Nia Peeples—Charisma 98690
[Evan Rogers/Carl Sturken] [BMI] (10/12/91 BC-8)

STREET SINGIN' Lady Flash—RSO 852
[Adrienne Anderson/Barry Manilow] [BMI] (7/17/76 BCR-27)

STREET TALK (VAR. III) B. C. G. (B.C. Generation)—20th Century 2271
[Cindy Bullens/Bob Crewe] [BMI] (3/6/76 BC-56) [IWM]

STRENGTH The Alarm—I.R.S. 52736
[Eddie MacDonald/Mike Peters/Dave Sharp/Nigel Twist] [BMI] (12/28/85 BC-61)

STRETCHIN' OUT Duane Eddy and The Rebelettes—RCA Victor 47-8087
[Duane Eddy/Lee Hazlewood] [BMI] (9/22/62 R-100) [I]

STRICTLY SENTIMENTAL June Valli—RCA Victor 47-6852
[Claude DeMetrius] [ASC] (4/13/57 CR-57)

STRIKE IT UP Black Box—RCA 2794
[Daniele Davoli/Mirko Limoni/Valerio Semplici] [ASC] (4/6/91 BC-8)

STRING ALONG *Fabian—Chancellor 1047*
[Bobby Doyle/Jimmy Duncan] [BMI] (2/22/60 BCR-35)

STRING ALONG *Rick Nelson—Decca 31495*
[Bobby Doyle/Jimmy Duncan] [BMI] (5/18/63 BCR-17)

STRING OF PEARLS Larry Elgart And His Manhattan Swing Orchestra—RCA 13219
[Jerry Gray] (Med) [ASC] (6/5/82 BC-31) [IM]

STRING OF TRUMPETS The Trumpeteers—Splash 800
[Billy Mure] [BMI] (4/25/59 BCR-59) [I]
STRIP Adam Ant—Epic 04337 [Adam Ant/Marco Pirroni] [ASC] (2/4/84 BC-41)
THE STRIPPER David Rose And His Orchestra—MGM 13064
[David Rose] [ASC] (4/30/62 BCR-1) [I]
THE STROKE Billy Squier—Capitol 5005 [Billy Squier] [ASC] (5/16/81 BCR-6)
STROKIN' Leon Haywood—20th Century 2285 [Leon Haywood] [BMI] (6/26/76 R-98)
***THE STROLL** The Diamonds—Mercury 71242*
[Nancy Lee/Clyde Otis] [BMI] (12/23/57 BCRt-1)
***THE STROLL** The Lancers—Coral 61930 [Nancy Lee/Clyde Otis] [BMI] (12/23/57 Rt-1)*
STROLL ME Kay Starr—RCA Victor 47-7218
[Kurt Feltz*/Heinz Gietz/Donald Simms] [BMI] (5/5/58 CR-46) [FDE]
STROLLIN' IN THE SPRINGTIME Fabian—Chancellor 1051
[Doc Pomus/Mort Shuman] [BMI] (5/23/60 CR-83)
STRONG ENOUGH TO BE GENTLE Black Oak Arkansas—MCA 40496
[Pat Daugherty/James David Henderson/Stan Knight/James Mangrum*/
Rickie Reynolds/Ronnie Smith/Norman Stone] [ASC] (1/10/76 B-89)
STRONGER THAN BEFORE Carole Bayer Sager—Boardwalk
[Burt Bacharach/Bruce Roberts/Carole Bayer Sager] [ASC] (5/16/81 BCR-30)
STRUNG OUT Steve Perry—Columbia 04598
[Craig Krampf/Steve Perry/Billy Steele] [BMI] (9/8/84 BC-38)
STRUT Sheena Easton—EMI America 8227
[Charlie Dore/Julian Littman] [BMI] (8/25/84 BC-4)
STRUTTIN' Billy Preston—A&M 1644
[George Johnson/Louis E. Johnson/Billy Preston] (TSW) [BMI] (12/14/74 BCR-22) [I]
STRUTTIN' MY STUFF Elvin Bishop—Capricorn 0256
[Phil Aaberg/Elvin Bishop] [ASC] (7/24/76 BR-68)
STRUTTIN' WITH SOME BARBECUE Louis Armstrong and Gary Crosby—Decca 29420
[Lillian Hardin Armstrong/Don Raye] [ASC] (2/21/55 R-77)
STUBBORN KIND OF FELLOW Marvin Gaye—Tamla 54068
[Marvin Gaye/George Gordy/William Stevenson] [ASC] (9/15/62 BCR-36)
STUCK IN THE MIDDLE WITH YOU Stealers Wheel—A&M 1416
[Joe Egan/Gerry Rafferty] [BMI] (3/3/73 BCR-3)
STUCK ON YOU Elvis Presley With The Jordanaires—RCA Victor 47-7740
[J. Leslie McFarland/Aaron Schroeder] [ASC] (4/4/60 BCR-1)
STUCK ON YOU Lionel Richie—Motown 1746 [Lionel Richie] [ASC] (6/23/84 BC-3)
STUCK WITH YOU Huey Lewis and the News—Chrysalis 43019
[Chris Hayes/Huey Lewis] [ASC] (8/2/86 BC-1)
STUFF LIKE THAT Quincy Jones—A&M 2043
[Nick Ashford/Steve Gadd/Eric Gale/Quincy Jones/Ralph MacDonald/Valerie Simpson/
Richard Tee] [BMI] (5/20/78 BCR-19)
STUMBLIN' IN Suzi Quatro And Chris Norman—RSO 917
[Mike Chapman/Nicky Chinn] [ASC] (1/27/79 BCR-4)
STUPID CUPID Connie Francis—MGM 12683
[Howard Greenfield/Neil Sedaka] [BMI] (7/28/58 BCR-16)
SUAVECITO Malo—Warner Bros. 7559
[Richard Bean/Pablo Tellez/Abel Zarate] [BMI] (2/26/72 BCR-12)
SUB-ROSA SUBWAY Klaatu—Capitol 4412
[Dino Tome/John Woloschuk] (TSW) [ASC] (4/2/77 BCR-57)
SUBSTITUTE Clout—Epic 50591 [Willie Wilson] [BMI] (9/2/78 BCR-52)
SUBTERRANEAN HOMESICK BLUES Bob Dylan—Columbia 43242
[Bob Dylan] [SE] (4/3/65 BCR-39)
SUBURBIA Pet Shop Boys—EMI America 8355
[Chris Lowe/Neil Tennant] [ASC] (11/22/86 BC-70)
***SUCH A DAY** Rita Raines—Deed 1010*
[Dorcas Cochran/Lotar Olias/Walter Rothenburg] [BMI] (1/28/56 BCtRt-45) [FET]*
***SUCH A DAY** Vera Lynn—London 1642*
[Dorcas Cochran/Lotar Olias/Walter Rothenburg] [BMI] (1/28/56 BCtRt-45) [FET]*
***SUCH A NIGHT** Dinah Washington—Mercury 71958 [Lincoln Chase] [BMI] (4/16/62 R-72)*
***SUCH A NIGHT** Elvis Presley With The Jordanaires—RCA Victor 47-8400*
[Lincoln Chase] [BMI] (7/25/64 BCR-13)
SUCH A NIGHT Dr. John—Atco 6937 [Mac Rebennack] [ASC] (9/8/73 BCR-42)
SUCH A SHAME Talk Talk—EMI America 8215 [Mark Hollis] [BMI] (6/30/84 B-89)
SUCH A SWEET THING Mary Wells—Atco 6423 [Barrett Strong] [BMI] (7/2/66 BCR-93)
SUCH A WOMAN Tycoon—Arista 0398
[Mark Kreider/Norman Mershon] [BMI] (3/10/79 BCR-21)
(SUCH AN) EASY QUESTION Elvis Presley With The Jordanaires—RCA Victor 47-8585
[Otis Blackwell/Winfield Scott] [BMI] (6/12/65 BCR-10)
SUDDEN STOP Percy Sledge—Atlantic 2539 [Bobby Russell] [ASC] (8/3/68 BCR-63)
SUDDENLY Jo Stafford—Columbia 40351
[Dorcas Cochran/Richard Heuberger*] [BMI] (11/6/54 CR-37) [FDE]
SUDDENLY Nicky DeMatteo—Guyden 2024 [Michael Pratt] [BMI] (2/8/60 BCR-74)
SUDDENLY Olivia Newton-John & Cliff Richard—MCA 51007
[John Farrar] [BMI] (10/18/80 BCR-19)
SUDDENLY Billy Ocean—Jive 9323 [Keith Diamond/Billy Ocean] [BMI] (3/23/85 BC-4)
SUDDENLY I'M ALL ALONE Walter Jackson—Okeh 7215
[Van McCoy] [BMI] (1/30/65 BCR-92)
SUDDENLY LAST SUMMER The Motels—Capitol 5271 [Martha Davis] [BMI] (9/3/83 BC-9)
***SUDDENLY THERE'S A VALLEY** Gogi Grant—Era 1003*
[Biff Jones/Chuck Meyer] [ASC] (9/3/55 BCtRt-7)
***SUDDENLY THERE'S A VALLEY** Julius La Rosa—Cadence 1270*
[Biff Jones/Chuck Meyer] [ASC] (9/5/55 BCtRt-7)
***SUDDENLY THERE'S A VALLEY** Jo Stafford—Columbia 40559*
[Biff Jones/Chuck Meyer] [ASC] (9/5/55 BCtRt-7)
***SUDDENLY THERE'S A VALLEY** Patty Andrews—Capitol 3228*
[Biff Jones/Chuck Meyer] [ASC] (9/5/55 BRt-12)
***SUDDENLY THERE'S A VALLEY** The Mills Brothers—Decca 29686*
[Biff Jones/Chuck Meyer] [ASC] (10/24/55 BRt-12)
SUDDENLY YOU LOVE ME The Tremeloes—Epic 10293
[Peter Callander/Daniele Pace/Mario Panzeri/Lorenzo Pilat] [BMI]
(2/17/68 BCR-40) [FDE]
SUE'S GOTTA BE MINE Del Shannon—Berlee 501
[Del Shannon] [BMI] (10/26/63 BCR-67)
SUGAH WOOGA The Three Playmates—Savoy 1528
[Dianne Brooks/Oscar Cadena] [BMI] (3/10/58 B-89)
***SUGAR AND SPICE** The Searchers—Liberty 55689 [Tony Hatch] [BMI] (4/25/64 BCR-44)*
***SUGAR AND SPICE** Cryan' Shames—Destination 624*
[Tony Hatch] [BMI] (7/23/66 BCR-39)
SUGAR BABE Buster Brown—Fire 507 [Morgan C. Robinson] [BMI] (2/3/62 B-99)
***SUGAR BABY LOVE** The Rubettes—Polydor 15089*
[Wayne Bickerton/Tony Waddington] [ASC] (7/6/74 BCR-24)
***SUGAR BABY LOVE** Stars On 45—Radio 3863*
[Wayne Bickerton/Tony Waddington] (Med) [ASC] (9/19/81 BCR-55)
SUGAR BEE Cleveland Crochet And Band—Goldband 1106
[Eddie Shuler] [BMI] (12/31/60 BR-80)
SUGAR BEE Mitch Ryder—Dot 17290
[Homer Banks/Bettye Crutcher/Raymond Earl Jackson] [BMI] (9/6/69 CR-85)
***SUGAR BLUES** Don Costa—Columbia 42307 [Clarence Williams] [NA] (3/5/62 R-88) [IM]*
***SUGAR BLUES** Ace Cannon—Santo 503 [Clarence Williams] [NA] (4/14/62 BC-92) [IM]*
SUGAR CANDY Georgia Gibbs—RCA Victor 47-6922
[Irving Fields/Kay Twomey] [ASC] (6/8/57 R-44)
***SUGAR CORSAGE** Bonnie Scott—RCA Victor 47-7025*
[Fred Ebb/Paul Klein] [BMI] (10/14/57 Rt-84)
***SUGAR CORSAGE** Chuck Reed—Roulette 4020*
[Fred Ebb/Paul Klein] [BMI] (10/14/57 Rt-84)
SUGAR DADDY The Jackson 5—Motown 1194
[Berry Gordy/Fonce Mizell/Freddie Perren/Deke Richards] [ASC] (12/11/71 BCR-6)
SUGAR DADDY Thompson Twins—Warner Bros. 22819
[Tom Bailey/Alannah Currie] [ASC] (9/23/89 BC-24)
SUGAR DON'T BITE Sam Harris—Motown 1743
[Bruce Roberts/Donna Weiss] [BMI] (9/15/84 BC-35)
SUGAR DUMPLING Sam Cooke—RCA Victor 47-8631
[Sam Cooke] [BMI] (7/24/65 BCR-30)
SUGAR FREE Wa Wa Nee—Epic 07283 [Paul Gray] [ASC] (9/12/87 BC-35)
SUGAR LIPS
Al (He's The King) Hirt Trumpet with Chorus and Orchestra—RCA Victor 47-8391
[Buddy Killen/Billy Sherrill] [BMI] (7/11/64 BCR-20) [I]
SUGAR LUMP Leon Haywood—20th Century 2103 [Billy Page] [BMI] (7/27/74 CR-68)
SUGAR MAGNOLIA Grateful Dead—Warner Bros. 7667
[Robert Hunter/Bob Weir] [ASC] (2/3/73 B-91)
SUGAR MOON Pat Boone—Dot 15750 [Danny Wolfe] [BMI] (4/28/58 BCR-7)
SUGAR ON SUNDAY The Clique—White Whale 323
[Tommy James/Mike Vale] [BMI] (8/9/69 BCR-15)
SUGAR PIE GUY PT. 1 The Joneses—Mercury 73614
[Glenn Dorsey] [BMI] (10/5/74 BCR-47)
—SUGAR PIE, HONEY BUNCH see: I CAN'T HELP MYSELF
SUGAR PLUM Ike Clanton—Mercury 71975 [Roger Schenzel] [BMI] (6/30/62 BCR-88)
SUGAR SHACK Jimmy Gilmer And The Fireballs—Dot 16487
[Keith McCormack/Faye Voss] [BMI] (9/21/63 BCR-1)
***SUGAR, SUGAR** The Archies—Calendar 1008*
[Jeff Barry/Andy Kim] [BMI] (7/19/69 BCR-1)
***SUGAR SUGAR** Wilson Pickett—Atlantic 2722*
[Jeff Barry/Andy Kim] (TSW) [BMI] (5/2/70 BCR-15)
***SUGAR SUGAR** Stars On 45—Radio 3810*
[Jeff Barry/Andy Kim] (Med) [BMI] (4/11/81 BCR-1)
SUGAR TOWN Nancy Sinatra—Reprise 0527 [Lee Hazlewood] [ASC] (11/12/66 BCR-4)
SUGAR WALLS Sheena Easton—EMI America 8253 [Prince] [ASC] (12/22/84 BC-5)
***SUGAREE** Rusty York—Chess 1730 [Marty Robbins] [BMI] (7/20/59 BCtRt-64)*
***SUGAREE** Hank Ballard And The Midnighters—King 5215*
[Marty Robbins] [BMI] (7/25/59 CtRt-64)
SUGAREE Jerry Garcia—Warner Bros. 7569
[Jerry Garcia/Robert Hunter] [ASC] (4/15/72 B-94)
***SUGARTIME** The McGuire Sisters—Coral 61924*
[Odis Echols/Charlie Phillips] [BMI] (12/23/57 BCRt-1)
***SUGARTIME** Charlie Phillips—Coral 61908*
[Odis Echols/Charlie Phillips] [BMI] (12/30/57 Rt-1)

SUICIDE BLONDE INXS—Atlantic 87860
[Andy Farriss/Michael Hutchence] [ASC] (9/8/90 BC-5)

SUITE: JUDY BLUE EYES Crosby, Stills & Nash—Atlantic 2676
[Stephen Stills] [BMI] (10/4/69 BCR-15)

SUITE: MAN AND WOMAN Tony Cole—20th Century 2001
[Tony Cole] [ASC] (10/28/72 BCR-95)

SUKIYAKI *Kyu Sakamoto—Capitol 4945*
[Rohusuke Ei/Hachidai Nakamura] [BMI] (5/4/63 BCR-1) [F]

SUKIYAKI *A Taste Of Honey—Capitol 4953*
[Buzz Cason/Snuff Garrett/Hachidai Nakamura] [BMI] (3/7/81 BCR-3) [FDE]

SULTANS OF SWING Dire Straits—Warner Bros. 8736
[Mark Knopfler] [ASC] (2/3/79 BCR-4)

SUMMER War—United Artists 834
[Thomas Allen/Harold Brown/Morris Dickerson/Jerry Goldstein/Lonnie Jordan/ Charles Miller/Lee Oskar/Howard Scott] [ASC] (7/10/76 BCR-7)

SUMMER AND SANDY Lesley Gore—Mercury 72683
[Raymond Bloodworth/L. Russell Brown/Bob Crewe] [BMI] (6/3/67 BCR-49)

SUMMER BREEZE *Seals & Crofts—Warner Bros. 7606*
[Dash Crofts/Jim Seals] [BMI] (9/9/72 BCR-6)

SUMMER BREEZE (PART 1) *The Isley Brothers—T-Neck 2253*
[Dash Crofts/Jim Seals] [BMI] (3/23/74 BCR-60)

SUMMER DAYS Lou Christie—Slipped Disc 45270
[Tony Romeo] [BMI] (8/30/75 R-89)

SUMMER DREAMS The McGuire Sisters—Coral 62106
[Dorcas Cochran/Rae Seymour] [BMI] (4/27/59 BCR-55)

SUMMER IN THE CITY *The Lovin' Spoonful—Kama Sutra 211*
[Steve Boone/John Sebastian/Mark Sebastian] [BMI] (7/9/66 BCR-1)

SUMMER IN THE CITY *Quincy Jones—A&M 1455*
[Steve Boone/John Sebastian/Mark Sebastian] [BMI] (9/1/73 C-87) [IWM]

SUMMER KISSES Floyd & Jerry With The Counterpoints—Presta 1006
[Floyd Westfall/Jerry Westfall] [BMI] (7/23/66 R-69)

—SUMMER KNOWS see: THEME FROM SUMMER OF '42

SUMMER LOVE Joni James—MGM 12480 [George David Weiss] [ASC] (6/8/57 BR-82)

SUMMER MADNESS Kool & The Gang—De-Lite 1567
[Robert Bell/Ronald Bell/George M. Brown/Robert Mickens/Claydes Smith/ Alton Taylor/Dennis Thomas/Richard Westfield] (TSW) [BMI] (4/19/75 BR-34) [I]

SUMMER MEANS FUN Bruce And Terry—Columbia 43055
[Steve Barri/P.F. Sloan] [ASC] (7/25/64 BR-72)

SUMMER NIGHTS Marianne Faithfull—London 9780
[Brian Henderson/Liza Strike] [BMI] (8/14/65 BCR-24)

SUMMER NIGHTS John Travolta, Olivia Newton-John & Cast—RSO 906
[Warren Casey/Jim Jacobs] [ASC] (8/5/78 BCR-3)

SUMMER NIGHTS Survivor—Scotti Brothers 02700
[Jim Peterik/Frankie Sullivan] [ASC] (2/20/82 BCR-62)

SUMMER OF '69 Bryan Adams—A&M 2739
[Bryan Adams/Jim Vallance] [BMI] (6/29/85 BC-5)

—SUMMER PLACE see: THEME FROM A SUMMER PLACE

SUMMER RAIN Johnny Rivers—Imperial 66267
[James Richard Hendricks] [BMI] (11/18/67 BCR-10)

SUMMER RAIN Belinda Carlisle—MCA 53783
[Robbie Seidman/Maria Vidal] [BMI] (1/20/90 BC-30)

SUMMER SAMBA (SO NICE) Walter Wanderley—Verve 10421
[Marcos Valle/Paulo Sergio Valle] [BMI] (8/27/66 BCR-26) [IM]

SUMMER SAND Dawn—Bell 45,107
[L. Russell Brown/Irwin Levine] [BMI] (6/12/71 BCR-19)

SUMMER SET *Mr. Acker Bilk—Atco 6160*
[Acker Bilk/David Collett] [ASC] (2/22/60 CtRt-36) [I]

SUMMER SET *Monty Kelly & His Orchestra—Carlton 527*
[Acker Bilk/David Collett] [ASC] (2/29/60 BCtRt-26) [I]

SUMMER SET *Ronnie Chamberlain—London 1911*
[Acker Bilk/David Collett] [ASC] (2/29/60 Rt-52) [I]

SUMMER SIDE OF LIFE Gordon Lightfoot—Reprise 1035
[Gordon Lightfoot] [ASC] (9/11/71 B-98)

A SUMMER SONG Chad Stuart & Jeremy Clyde—World Artists 1027
[Clive Metcalfe/Keith Noble/Chad Stuart] [BMI] (8/15/64 BCR-6)

SUMMER SOUNDS Robert Goulet—Columbia 43301
[Roy C. Bennett/Sid Tepper] [ASC] (5/29/65 BCR-43)

SUMMER SOUVENIRS Karl Hammel, Jr.—Arliss 1007
[Paul Evans/Jimmy Krondes] [ASC] (7/31/61 BCR-60)

SUMMER SUN Jamestown Massacre—Warner Bros. 7603
[Tom Powers] [ASC] (7/29/72 BCR-78)

SUMMER SWEETHEART The Ames Brothers—RCA Victor 47-6608
[Fred Ebb/Paul Klein] [BMI] (9/8/56 BR-67)

SUMMER (THE FIRST TIME) Bobby Goldsboro—United Artists 251
[Bobby Goldsboro] [BMI] (8/18/73 BCR-17)

SUMMER VACATION *The Party—Hollywood 64945*
[Matt Dike/Albert Fields/Chasen Cord Hampton/Damon Philip Pampolina/ Peter T. Paterno/Julian Raymond/Michael Ross] [ASC] (7/21/90 BC-68)

SUMMER VACATION *The Party—Hollywood 64945*
[Matt Dike/Albert Fields/Chasen Cord Hampton/Damon Philip Pampolina/ Peter T. Paterno/Julian Raymond/Michael Ross] [ASC] (6/15/91 B-86)

SUMMER WIND *Wayne Newton—Capitol 5470*
[Hans Bradtke/Henry Mayer/Johnny Mercer] [ASC] (8/7/65 BCRt-74) [FET]

SUMMER WIND *Roger Williams & The Harry Simeone Chorale—Kapp 55*
[Hans Bradtke/Henry Mayer/Johnny Mercer] [ASC] (8/7/65 CRt-74) [FET]

SUMMER WIND *Frank Sinatra—Reprise 0509*
[Hans Bradtke/Henry Mayer/Johnny Mercer] [ASC] (9/3/66 BCR-23) [FET]

SUMMER WINE Nancy Sinatra With Lee Hazlewood—Reprise 0527
[Lee Hazlewood] [ASC] (3/4/67 BR-49)

SUMMERGIRLS Dino—4th & Broadway 7468 [Dino Esposito] [BMI] (7/16/88 BC-50)

SUMMER'S COMIN' Kirby St. Romain—Inette 103
[Scotty McKay/Kirby St. Romain] [BMI] (6/15/63 BCR-42)

SUMMER'S GONE Paul Anka—ABC-Paramount 10147
[Paul Anka] [BMI] (9/26/60 BCR-11)

SUMMER'S LOVE Richard Barrett with the Chantels—Gone 5060
[Richard Barrett] [BMI] (7/20/59 B-93)

SUMMERTIME *Sam Cooke—Keen 34013*
[George Gershwin/Ira Gershwin/DuBose Heyward] [ASC] (11/4/57 B-81)*

SUMMERTIME (PART 2) *Sam Cooke—Keen 8-2101*
[George Gershwin/Ira Gershwin/DuBose Heyward] [ASC] (8/31/59 R-90)*

SUMMERTIME *The Marcels—Colpix 196*
[George Gershwin/Ira Gershwin/DuBose Heyward] [ASC] (5/15/61 BCRt-74)*

SUMMERTIME *Will Sanders—Regatta 2000*
[George Gershwin/Ira Gershwin/DuBose Heyward] [ASC] (5/15/61 Rt-74)*

SUMMERTIME *Rick Nelson—Imperial 5805*
[George Gershwin/Ira Gershwin/DuBose Heyward] [ASC] (3/10/62 B-89)*

SUMMERTIME *Chris Columbo Quintet—Strand 25056*
[George Gershwin] [ASC] (6/29/63 BCR-73) [IM]

SUMMERTIME *Billy Stewart—Chess 1966*
[George Gershwin/Ira Gershwin/DuBose Heyward] [ASC] (7/16/66 BCR-7)*

SUMMERTIME *Billy Hemmans & Clays Composite—Blue Fox 102*
[George Gershwin] [ASC] (11/14/70 C-97) [IM]

SUMMERTIME DJ Jazzy Jeff & The Fresh Prince—Jive 1465
[Robert Bell/Ronald Bell/George M. Brown/Lamar Mahone/Robert Mickens/ Craig Simpkins/Claydes Smith/Will Smith/Alton Taylor/Dennis Thomas/Jeff Townes*/ Richard Westfield] [BMI] (6/15/91 BC-4)

SUMMERTIME BLUES *Eddie Cochran—Liberty 55144*
[Jerry Capehart/Eddie Cochran] [BMI] (8/4/58 BCR-8)

SUMMERTIME BLUES *Blue Cheer—Philips 40516*
[Jerry Capehart/Eddie Cochran] [BMI] (2/10/68 BCR-8)

SUMMERTIME BLUES *The Who—Decca 32708*
[Jerry Capehart/Eddie Cochran] [BMI] (7/4/70 BCR-14)

SUMMERTIME BLUES *Jive Bunny & The Mastermixers—Music Factory/Atco 99122*
[Jerry Capehart/Eddie Cochran] (Med) [BMI] (2/3/90 BC-67)

SUMMERTIME GIRLS Y&T—A&M 2748
[Joey Alves/Leonard Haze/Philip Kennemore/Dave Meniketti] [BMI] (7/13/85 BC-51)

SUMMERTIME LIES The Four Preps—Capitol 4023
[Alan Hood/Richard Loring] [ASC] (8/23/58 CR-71)

SUMMERTIME SUMMERTIME *The Jamies—Epic 9281*
[Sherm Feller/Tom Jameson] [ASC] (8/11/58 BCR-26)

SUMMERTIME, SUMMERTIME *The Jamies—Epic 9281*
[Sherm Feller/Tom Jameson] [ASC] (6/23/62 BCR-38)

SUMMERTIME, SUMMERTIME Nocera—Sleeping Bag 7LX-22
[Floyd Fisher/Maria Nocera] [BMI] (1/17/87 BC-84)

THE SUN AIN'T GONNA SHINE (ANYMORE) *The Walker Bros.—Smash 2032*
[Bob Crewe/Bob Gaudio] [BMI] (4/9/66 BCR-13)

THE SUN AIN'T GONNA SHINE ANYMORE *Fuzzy Bunnies—Decca 32364*
[Bob Crewe/Bob Gaudio] [BMI] (9/7/68 CR-96)

THE SUN AIN'T GONNA SHINE ANYMORE *Nielsen/Pearson—Capitol 5032*
[Bob Crewe/Bob Gaudio] [BMI] (8/8/81 BCR-54)

THE SUN ALWAYS SHINES ON T.V. A-Ha—Warner Bros. 28846
[Pal Waaktaar] [BMI] (11/30/85 BC-20)

THE SUN AND THE RAIN Madness—Geffen 29350 [Michael Barson] [ASC] (3/3/84 B-72)

SUN ARISE Rolf Harris—Epic 9567
[Harry Butler/Rolf Harris] [BMI] (3/9/63 BCR-44)

SUN CITY Artists United Against Apartheid—Manhattan 50017
[Steven Van Zandt] [ASC] (11/2/85 BC-38)

SUN GODDESS Ramsey Lewis And Earth, Wind & Fire—Columbia 10103
[Jon Lind/Maurice White] [ASC] (3/15/75 BCR-44) [I]

THE SUN IS SHINING Jimmy Reed—Vee-Jay 248
[Ewart Abner*/Calvin Carter*/Jimmy Reed] [BMI] (7/8/57 B-65)

SUN, SUN, SUN (PART 1) Ja-Kki—Pyramid 8004 [Johnny Melfi] [ASC] (9/11/76 B-96)

SUNDAY The Moments (2)—Stang 5003
[Bert Keyes/Sylvia Robinson] [BMI] (5/10/69 BCR-84)

SUNDAY AND ME Jay & The Americans—United Artists 948
[Neil Diamond] [SE] (11/13/65 BCR-18)

SUNDAY BARBECUE Tennessee Ernie Ford—Capitol 3997
[Ira Cook/Mort Greene] [ASC] (8/11/58 B-97)

SUNDAY FOR TEA Peter And Gordon—Capitol 5864
[John Carter/Ken Hawker] [ASC] (3/18/67 BCR-22)

SUNDAY KIND OF LOVE *Fran Warren—MGM 12718*
[Barbara Belle/Anita Leonard/Louis Prima/Stan Rhodes] [ASC] (12/1/58 R-99)

SUNDAY KIND OF LOVE *Etta James—Argo 5393*
[Barbara Belle/Anita Leonard/Louis Prima/Stan Rhodes] [ASC] (8/7/61 R-89)

A SUNDAY KIND OF LOVE *Jan & Dean—Liberty 55397*
[Barbara Belle/Anita Leonard/Louis Prima/Stan Rhodes] [ASC] (1/8/62 BR-91)

A SUNDAY KIND OF LOVE *Lenny Welch—Atco 6894*
[Barbara Belle/Anita Leonard/Louis Prima/Stan Rhodes] [ASC] (8/12/72 BCR-90)

SUNDAY MORNIN' *Spanky And Our Gang—Mercury 72765*
[Margo Guryan] [ASC] (1/6/68 BCR-18)

SUNDAY MORNIN' *Oliver—Crewe 337 [Margo Guryan] [ASC] (11/15/69 BCR-17)*

SUNDAY MORNIN' COMIN' DOWN *Ray Stevens—Monument 1163*
[Kris Kristofferson] [BMI] (10/4/69 BC-76)

SUNDAY MORNING COMING DOWN *Johnny Cash—Columbia 45211*
[Kris Kristofferson] [BMI] (8/29/70 BCR-41)

SUNDAY MORNING SUNSHINE Harry Chapin—Elektra 45811
[Harry Chapin] [ASC] (10/21/72 BCR-75)

SUNDAY SUN Neil Diamond—Uni 55084 [Neil Diamond] [SE] (9/28/68 BCR-41)

SUNDAY SUNRISE Anne Murray—Capitol 4142 [Mark James] [BMI] (11/22/75 BC-94)

SUNDAY WILL NEVER BE THE SAME Spanky And Our Gang—Mercury 72679
[Terry Cashman/Eugene Pistilli] [ASC] (5/13/67 BCR-7)

SUNDOWN Gordon Lightfoot—Reprise 1194 [Gordon Lightfoot] [ASC] (4/6/74 BCR-1)

—SUNDOWNERS see: THEME FROM THE SUNDOWNERS

SUNFLOWER Glen Campbell—Capitol 4445 [Neil Diamond] [SE] (7/2/77 BCR-39)

SUNGLASSES AT NIGHT Corey Hart—EMI America 8203
[Corey Hart] [ASC] (5/26/84 BC-7)

SUNLIGHT The Youngbloods—RCA Victor 74-0270
[Jesse Colin Young] [ASC] (11/1/69 CR-85)

SUNNY Neil Sedaka—RCA Victor 47-8382
[Howard Greenfield/Neil Sedaka] [BMI] (7/11/64 BCR-63)

SUNNY Bobby Hebb—Philips 40365 [Bobby Hebb] [BMI] (6/11/66 BCR-1)

SUNNY AFTERNOON The Kinks—Reprise 0497 [Ray Davies] [BMI] (8/6/66 BCR-11)

SUNNY DAYS Lighthouse—Evolution 1069 [Skip Prokop] [BMI] (10/7/72 BCR-29)

SUNRISE Eric Carmen—Arista 0200 [Eric Carmen] [BMI] (8/14/76 BCR-34)

SUNRISE The Triplets—Mercury 868 414
[Martin Page/Diana Villegas/Sylvia Villegas/Vicky Villegas] [ASC] (6/29/91 C-76)

SUNRISE SERENADE Willie Mitchell—Hi 2058 [Frankie Carle] [ASC] (11/17/62 R-83) [IM]

SUNRISE, SUNSET Roger Williams—Kapp 801
[Jerry Bock/Sheldon Harnick] [BMI] (1/28/67 BCR-65)

SUNSET GRILL Don Henley—Geffen 28906
[Don Henley/Danny Kortchmar/Benmont Tench] [ASC] (8/31/85 BC-20)

SUNSET STRIP Ray Stevens—Barnaby 2021 [Ray Stevens] [BMI] (10/31/70 BCR-64)

SUNSHINE The Archies—Kirshner 1009
[Jeff Barry/Bobby Bloom] [BMI] (6/27/70 BCR-17)

SUNSHINE Jonathan Edwards—Capricorn 8021
[Jonathan Edwards] [ASC] (11/13/71 BCR-3)

SUNSHINE Mickey Newbury—Elektra 45853 [Mickey Newbury] [BMI] (6/23/73 BCR-60)

SUNSHINE (PART 2) The O'Jays—Philadelphia Int'l 3558
[Phil Hurtt/Bunny Sigler] [BMI] (12/14/74 B-48)

SUNSHINE Enchantment—Roadshow 991
[Emanuel Johnson/Michael Lee Stokes] [BMI] (7/2/77 BCR-45)

SUNSHINE Dino—4th & Broadway 7489 [Dino Esposito] [BMI] (9/9/89 BC-23)

SUNSHINE AND RAIN *Bob Whalen—Jubilee 5289*
[Joe Leahy/Rolande Young] [ASC] (7/20/57 Rt-56)

SUNSHINE AND RAIN *Teddy Bart—National 102*
[Joe Leahy/Rolande Young] [ASC] (7/20/57 Rt-56)

SUNSHINE GAMES The Music Explosion—Laurie 3400
[Eric Woolfson] [ASC] (9/9/67 BCR-62)

SUNSHINE GIRL Eddie Fisher—RCA Victor 47-6913 [Bob Merrill] [ASC] (6/10/57 B-94)

SUNSHINE GIRL The Parade—A&M 841
[Murray MacLeod/Jerry Riopelle/Smokey Roberds] [BMI] (4/15/67 BCR-20)

SUNSHINE GIRL Herman's Hermits—MGM 13973
[John Carter/Geoff Stephens] [BMI] (8/10/68 CR-66)

SUNSHINE IN THE SHADE The Fixx—MCA 52498
[Dan Brown/Cy Curnin/Peter John Greenall/Jamie West-Oram/Adam Woods] [ASC] (11/17/84 BC-68)

SUNSHINE, LOLLIPOPS AND RAINBOWS Lesley Gore—Mercury 72433
[Marvin Hamlisch/Howard Liebling] [ASC] (6/19/65 BCR-13)

SUNSHINE OF YOUR LOVE Cream—Atco 6544
[Peter Ronald Brown/Jack Bruce/Eric Clapton] [BMI] (1/6/68 BCR-4)

SUNSHINE ON MY SHOULDERS John Denver—RCA Victor 0213
[John Denver/Dick Kniss/Michael C. Taylor] [ASC] (1/19/74 BCR-1)

SUNSHINE, RED WINE Crazy Elephant—Bell 804
[Jerry Kasenetz/Jeff Katz/Bob Levine/J.J. Woods] [BMI] (6/21/69 CR-70)

SUNSHINE ROSES Gene Cotton—Myrrh 137 [Gene Cotton] [ASC] (11/16/74 BCR-63)

SUNSHINE SHIP Arthur, Hurley & Gottlieb—Columbia 45881
[Jeff Arthur] [NA] (7/21/73 CR-93)

SUNSHINE SUPERMAN *Donovan—Epic 10045 [Donovan Leitch] [BMI] (7/23/66 BCR-1)*

SUNSHINE SUPERMAN *Willie Bobo—Verve 10448*
[Donovan Leitch] [BMI] (11/26/66 C-98) [IWM]

SUPER BAD (PART 1 & PART 2) James Brown—King 6329
[James Brown] [BMI] (10/3/70 BCR-9)

SUPER BOWL SHUFFLE The Chicago Bears Shufflin' Crew—Red Label 71012
[Lloyd Barry/Bobby Daniels/Richard E. Meyer/Melvin Owens] [BMI] (1/11/86 BC-41)

SUPER-CALI-FRAGIL-ISTIC-EXPI-ALI-DOCIOUS
Julie Andrews - Dick Van Dyke And The Pearlies—Buena Vista 434
[Richard Sherman/Robert Sherman] [BMI] (4/24/65 BCR-66)

SUPER DUPER LOVE (ARE YOU DIGGIN' ON ME) PART 1 Sugar Billy—Fast Track 2501
[Willie Garner] [BMI] (1/18/75 R-92)

SUPER FLY MEETS SHAFT John & Ernest—Rainy Wednesday 201
[Dickie Goodman/Sal Passantino] [BMI] (4/7/73 BCR-31)

SUPER FREAK (PART I) Rick James—Gordy 7205
[Rick James/Alonzo H. Miller] [ASC] (8/8/81 BCR-14)

SUPER HIGHWAY Ballin' Jack—Columbia 45312
[Luther Rabb/Jim Walters] [ASC] (2/13/71 B-93)

SUPER TROUPER ABBA—Atlantic 3806
[Benny Andersson/Björn Ulvaeus] [BMI] (4/4/81 BCR-45)

SUPERFLY Curtis Mayfield—Curtom 1978 [Curtis Mayfield] [BMI] (11/11/72 BCR-6)

SUPERMAN Dino, Desi & Billy—Reprise 0444
[Lee Adams/Charles Strouse] [ASC] (2/26/66 BCR-94)

SUPERMAN The Ides Of March—Warner Bros. 7403 [Jim Peterik] [ASC] (6/27/70 BCR-48)

SUPERMAN Donna Fargo—Dot 17444 [Donna Fargo] [BMI] (2/17/73 BCR-31)

SUPERMAN *Celi Bee & The Buzzy Bunch—APA 17001*
[Pepe Luis Soto] [BMI] (6/11/77 BC-41)

SUPERMAN *Herbie Mann—Atlantic 3547 [Pepe Luis Soto] [BMI] (1/13/79 BCR-26)*

SUPERMAN'S SONG Crash Test Dummies—Arista 12339
[Brad Roberts] [ASC] (10/5/91 B-56)

SUPERNATURAL LOVE Donna Summer—Geffen 29142
[Michael Omartian/Bruce Sudano/Donna Summer] [ASC] (11/10/84 BC-75)

SUPERNATURAL THING - PART I Ben E. King—Atlantic 3241
[Patrick Grant/Gwen Guthrie] [BMI] (1/25/75 BCR-5)

SUPERNATURE Cerrone—Cotillion 44230
[Marc Cerrone/Lili Premilovich*/Alain Wisniak] [BMI] (1/21/78 B-70)

SUPERSONIC J.J. Fad—Ruthless 7-99328
[Dania Birks/Juana Burns/Juanita Lee/Kim Nazel/Fatimah Shaheed] [ASC] (4/23/88 BC-30)

SUPERSTAR *Murray Head With The Trinidad Singers—Decca 32603*
[Tim Rice/Andrew Lloyd Webber] [ASC] (12/20/69 BCR-8)

SUPERSTAR - JESUS CHRIST SUPERSTAR *Murray Head—Decca 32603*
[Tim Rice/Andrew Lloyd Webber] [ASC] (1/2/71 B-14)

SUPERSTAR *The Assembled Multitude—Atlantic 2780*
[Tim Rice/Andrew Lloyd Webber] (Med) [ASC] (2/6/71 BR-87) [IWM]

SUPERSTAR (REMEMBER HOW YOU GOT WHERE YOU ARE) The Temptations—Gordy 7111
[Barrett Strong/Norman Whitfield] [BMI] (11/6/71 BCR-12)

SUPERSTAR *Carpenters—A&M 1289*
[Bonnie Bramlett/Delaney Bramlett/Leon Russell] (TSW) [BMI] (11/20/71 BCR-1)*

SUPERSTAR *Luther Vandross—Epic 04969*
[Bonnie Bramlett/Delaney Bramlett/Leon Russell] (Med) [BMI] (4/28/84 B-87)*

SUPERSTAR Paul Davis—Bang 726 [Paul Davis] [BMI] (8/7/76 BCR-35)

SUPERSTITION *Stevie Wonder—Tamla 54226 [Stevie Wonder] [ASC] (11/11/72 BCR-1)*

SUPERSTITION *Stars On 45—Radio 4019 [Stevie Wonder] (Med) [ASC] (3/27/82 BCR-28)*

SUPERSTITIOUS Europe—Epic 07979 [Joey Tempest] [BMI] (8/13/88 BC-31)

SUPERWOMAN (WHERE WERE YOU WHEN I NEEDED YOU) Stevie Wonder—Tamla 54216
[Stevie Wonder] [ASC] (5/20/72 BCR-32)

SUPERWOMAN Karyn White—Warner Bros. 27783
[Kenneth Edmonds/Antonio Reid/Daryl Simmons] [BMI] (1/28/89 BC-8)

SURE AS I'M SITTIN' HERE Three Dog Night—Dunhill/ABC 15001
[John Hiatt] [BMI] (6/29/74 BCR-16)

SURE FEELS GOOD Elvin Bishop—Capricorn 0237 [Elvin Bishop] [ASC] (6/28/75 BCR-76)

SURE GONNA MISS HER Gary Lewis And The Playboys—Liberty 55865
[Bobby Russell] [ASC] (3/5/66 BCR-8)

SURE KNOW SOMETHING Kiss—Casablanca 2205
[Vini Poncia/Paul Stanley] [BMI] (9/1/79 BCR-39)

SURE LOOKIN' Donny Osmond—Capitol 44670
[David Gamson/Tony LeMans/Donny Osmond] [ASC] (1/19/91 BC-45)

SURF CITY Jan & Dean—Liberty 55580 [Jan Berry/Brian Wilson] [BMI] (6/8/63 BCR-1)

SURF PARTY Chubby Checker—Parkway 879
[Dave Appell/Kal Mann] [ASC] (7/13/63 BCR-48)

—SURFER BIRD see: BIRD'S THE WORD and PAPA OOM MOW MOW

SURFER GIRL *The Beach Boys—Capitol 5009 [Brian Wilson] [BMI] (7/20/63 BCR-5)*

SURFER GIRL *The Cantina Band—Millennium 11818*
[Brian Wilson] (Med) [BMI] (7/25/81 B-81)

SURFER JOE The Surfaris—Dot 16479
[Bob Berryhill*/Pat Connolly*/Jim Fuller*/Ron Wilson] [BMI] (8/31/63 BCR-56)

SURFER STREET The Allisons—Tip 1011 [Don Harris/Dewey Terry] [BMI] (12/14/63 B-93)
SURFER'S STOMP Kay Bell and The Tuffs—Dot 16304
[Sonny Anderson/John Schmidt] [BMI] (1/8/62 Rt*-57)
SURFER'S STOMP The Mar-Kets—Liberty 55401
[Michael Gordon/Joe Saraceno] [BMI] (1/8/62 BCRt*-31) [I]
SURFIN' The Beach Boys—Candix 331 [Mike Love/Brian Wilson] [BMI] (2/10/62 BC-75)
SURFIN' HOOTENANNY Al Casey with The K-C-Ettes—Stacy 962
[Lee Hazlewood] [BMI] (7/13/63 BCR-38)
***SURFIN' SAFARI** The Beach Boys—Capitol 4777*
[Mike Love/Brian Wilson] [BMI] (7/14/62 BCR-10)
***SURFIN' SAFARI** The Beach Boys—Capitol 5030*
[Mike Love/Brian Wilson] (Med) [BMI] (7/25/81 BCR-5)
***SURFIN' U.S.A.** The Beach Boys—Capitol 4932*
[Chuck Berry/Brian Wilson] [BMI] (3/23/63 BCR-2)*
***SURFIN' U.S.A.** The Beach Boys—Capitol 3924*
[Chuck Berry/Brian Wilson] [BMI] (8/10/74 BCR-36)*
***SURFIN' USA** Leif Garrett—Atlantic 3423*
[Chuck Berry/Brian Wilson] [BMI] (8/27/77 BCR-20)*
***SURFIN' USA** The Beach Boys—Capitol 5030*
[Chuck Berry/Brian Wilson] (Med) [BMI] (7/25/81 BCR-5)*
SURRENDER Elvis Presley With The Jordanaires—RCA Victor 47-7850
[Doc Pomus/Mort Shuman] [BMI] (2/13/61 BCR-1)
SURRENDER Diana Ross—Motown 1188
[Nick Ashford/Valerie Simpson] [ASC] (8/14/71 BCR-38)
SURRENDER Cheap Trick—Epic 50570 [Rick Nielsen] [BMI] (7/22/78 BCR-62)
SURRENDER Trixter—Mechanic 54105
[Steven James Brown/Bill Wray/Jim Wray] [ASC] (6/8/91 BC-72)
SURRENDER TO ME Ann Wilson and Robin Zander—Capitol 44288
[Richard Marx/Ross Vannelli] [ASC] (12/24/88 BC-6)
SURVIVE Jimmy Buffett—MCA 41199 [Jimmy Buffett/Mike Utley] [BMI] (3/8/80 BCR-71)
SURVIVOR Cindy Bullens—United Artists 1261 [Cindy Bullens] [BMI] (2/3/79 BCR-56)
SUSAN The Buckinghams—Columbia 44378
[Gary Beisbier/James William Guercio/James Holvay] [BMI] (12/9/67 BCR-6)
***SUSIE DARLIN'** Robin Luke—Dot 15781 [Robin Luke] [ASC] (8/2/58 BCR-3)*
***SUSIE DARLIN'** Tommy Roe—ABC-Paramount 10362*
[Robin Luke] [ASC] (10/6/62 BCR-34)
***SUSIE Q** Dale Hawkins—Checker 863*
[Eleanor Broadwater‡/Robert Chaisson/Dale Hawkins/Stanley J. Lewis‡] [BMI]*
(6/10/57 BCRt-29)
***SUSIE-Q** The Crew-Cuts—Mercury 71125*
[Eleanor Broadwater‡/Robert Chaisson/Dale Hawkins/Stanley J. Lewis‡] [BMI]*
(6/15/57 Rt-36)
***SUZIE Q (PART ONE)** Creedence Clearwater Revival—Fantasy 616*
[Eleanor Broadwater‡/Robert Chaisson/Dale Hawkins/Stanley J. Lewis‡] [BMI]*
(9/7/68 BCR-9)
***SUSIE-Q** José Feliciano—RCA Victor 74-0358*
[Eleanor Broadwater‡/Robert Chaisson/Dale Hawkins/Stanley J. Lewis‡] (TSW) [BMI]*
(7/4/70 BR-73)
SUSPICION Terry Stafford—Crusader 101
[Doc Pomus/Mort Shuman] [BMI] (2/22/64 BCR-2)
SUSPICIONS The Sidekicks—RCA Victor 47-8864
[Mike Burke/John Spirt] [BMI] (7/30/66 BCR-44)
SUSPICIONS Eddie Rabbitt—Elektra 46053
[David Malloy/Randy McCormick/Eddie Rabbitt/Even Stevens] [BMI] (6/9/79 BCR-13)
***SUSPICIOUS MINDS** Elvis Presley—RCA Victor 47-9764*
[Mark James] [BMI] (9/13/69 BCR-1)
***SUSPICIOUS MINDS** Dee Dee Warwick—Atco 6810*
[Mark James] [BMI] (6/19/71 BCR-76)
***SUSPICIOUS MINDS** Elvis Presley—RCA 13351*
[Mark James] (Med) [BMI] (11/20/82 BC-71)
SUSSUDIO Phil Collins—Atlantic 89560 [Phil Collins] [ASC] (5/11/85 BC-1)
SUZANNE Noel Harrison—Reprise 0615 [Leonard Cohen] [BMI] (10/21/67 BCR-56)
SUZANNE Journey—Columbia 06134 [Jonathan Cain/Steve Perry] [ASC] (6/21/86 BC-17)
SUZI Randy Vanwarmer—Bearsville 49752 [Randy Vanwarmer] [ASC] (6/20/81 BCR-54)
SUZIE BABY Bobby Vee and The Shadows—Liberty 55208
[Bobby Vee] [BMI] (8/31/59 B-77)
SUZIE GIRL Redbone—Epic 50015 [Lolly Vegas] [BMI] (8/31/74 CR-67)
THE SWALK Notorious—Geffen 19698
[Robin George/Sean Harris] [BMI] (12/8/90 BC-73)
SWAMP WITCH Jim Stafford—MGM 14496 [Jim Stafford] [ASC] (5/12/73 BCR-21)
SWANEE Jaye P. Morgan—RCA Victor 47-6182
[Irving Caesar/George Gershwin] [ASC] (7/4/55 CR-28)
SWANEE RIVER Ace Cannon—Hi 2070 [Stephen Foster] [BMI] (11/2/63 R-82) [I]
***SWANEE RIVER ROCK (TALKIN' 'BOUT THAT RIVER)** Ray Charles—Atlantic 1154*
[Ray Charles/Stephen Foster] [BMI] (10/19/57 BCRt-42)
***SWANEE RIVER ROCK** Sanford Clark—Dot 15646*
[Stephen Foster/Floyd Huddleston] [NA] (12/2/57 Rt-78)
***SWANEE RIVER ROCK** Plas Johnson & His Orchestra—Capitol 3835*
[Stephen Foster] [NA] (12/2/57 Rt-78) [IWM]
***SWAY (QUIEN SERA)** Dean Martin—Capitol 2818*
[Norman Gimbel/Pablo Beltran Ruiz] [NA] (7/3/54 BCR-13) [FDE]
***SWAY** Bobby Rydell—Cameo 182*
[Norman Gimbel/Pablo Beltran Ruiz] [BMI] (10/31/60 BCR-12) [FDE]
—SWAYIN' TO THE MUSIC see: SLOW DANCING
SWEAR Sheena Easton—EMI America 8263 [Tim Scott] [ASC] (3/23/85 BC-65)
SWEARIN' TO GOD Frankie Valli—Private Stock 45,021
[Bob Crewe/Denny Randell] [BMI] (5/10/75 BCR-6)
SWEAT (TIL YOU GET WET) Brick—Bang 02246
[Ambric Bridgeforth/James B. Brown/Regi Hargis/Eddie Irons/Ray Ransom] [ASC]
(8/29/81 R-85)
***SWEET AND GENTLE** Alan Dale—Coral 61435*
[Otilio Portal/George Thorn] [BMI] (6/6/55 BCtRt-5) [FDE]
***SWEET AND GENTLE** Georgia Gibbs—Mercury 70647*
[Otilio Portal/George Thorn] [BMI] (6/6/55 CtRt-5) [FDE]
SWEET AND GENTLE (ME LO DIJO ADELA)
Eartha Kitt & Perez Prado—RCA Victor 47-6138
[Otilio Portal/George Thorn] [BMI] (6/6/55 Rt-36) [FDE]
***SWEET AND GENTLE (ME LO DIJO ADELA)** Merv Griffin & Xavier Cugat—Columbia 40530*
[Otilio Portal/George Thorn] [BMI] (6/27/55 Rt-12) [FDE]
SWEET AND INNOCENT Donny Osmond—MGM 14227
[Rick Hall/Billy Sherrill] [BMI] (3/20/71 BCR-5)
SWEET AND LOVELY April Stevens & Nino Tempo—Atco 6224
[Gus Arnheim/Charles N. Daniels/Harry Tobias] [ASC] (7/7/62 BC-77)
SWEET ANNIE LAURIE Sammy Turner and The Twisters—Big Top 3007
[Rita Murphy/Traditional] [BMI] (3/23/59 B-100)
SWEET BABY Donnie Elbert—All Platinum 2333 [Donnie Elbert] [BMI] (1/15/72 BCR-69)
SWEET BABY Stanley Clarke/George Duke—Epic 01052
[George Duke] [ASC] (5/2/81 BCR-19)
SWEET BIRD OF YOUTH Nat "King" Cole—Capitol 4248
[Wally Gold/Aaron Schroeder] [ASC] (8/3/59 BCR-46)
SWEET BLINDNESS The 5th Dimension—Soul City 768
[Laura Nyro] [BMI] (9/21/68 BCR-11)
SWEET BROWN EYED BABY The Ames Brothers—RCA Victor 47-6044
[Al Frisch/Allan Roberts] [ASC] (3/14/55 CR-28)
***SWEET CAROLINE (GOOD TIMES NEVER SEEMED SO GOOD)** Neil Diamond—Uni 55136*
[Neil Diamond] [SE] (6/14/69 BCR-3)
SWEET CAROLINE (GOOD TIMES NEVER SEEMED SO GOOD)
Bobby Womack & Peace—United Artists 50946
[Neil Diamond] [SE] (8/26/72 BCR-39)
SWEET CHARLIE BABE Jackie Moore—Atlantic 2956
[Phil Hurtt/Bunny Sigler] [BMI] (6/30/73 BCR-24)
SWEET CHERRY WINE Tommy James And The Shondells—Roulette 7039
[Richie Grasso/Tommy James] [BMI] (3/22/69 BCR-5)
SWEET CHILD O' MINE Guns N' Roses—Geffen 27963
[Steven Adler/Saul Hudson/Duff McKagan/Axl Rose/Izzy Stradlin] [ASC]
(6/25/88 BC-1)
SWEET CHILE Sheb Wooley—MGM 12781
[Sheb Wooley] [ASC] (4/27/59 BCR-54)
SWEET CITY WOMAN Stampeders—Bell 45,120 [Rich Dodson] [ASC] (7/31/71 BCR-7)
SWEET CREAM LADIES, FORWARD MARCH The Box Tops—Mala 12,035
[Jon Stroll/Bobby Weinstein] [BMI] (12/28/68 BCR-22)
SWEET DARLIN' Martha Reeves & The Vandellas—Gordy 7080
[Richard Morris] [BMI] (11/2/68 BCR-73)
***SWEET DREAMS** Don Gibson—RCA Victor 47-7805 [Don Gibson] [BMI] (11/7/60 BCR-76)*
***SWEET DREAMS (OF YOU)** Patsy Cline—Decca 31483*
[Don Gibson] [BMI] (4/20/63 BCR-44)
***SWEET DREAMS** Tommy McLain—MSL 197 [Don Gibson] [BMI] (6/25/66 BCR-15)*
SWEET DREAMS Air Supply—Arista 0655 [Graham Russell] [BMI] (12/12/81 BCR-5)
SWEET DREAMS (ARE MADE OF THIS) Eurythmics—RCA 13533
[Annie Lennox/David A. Stewart] [ASC] (5/14/83 BC-1)
SWEET ELIZABETH Will Glahe And His Orchestra—London 1788
[Karl Theodor Uhlisch] [ASC] (2/24/58 BCR-43) [F]
SWEET EMOTION Aerosmith—Columbia 10155
[Tom Hamilton/Steven Tyler] [BMI] (5/31/75 BCR-36)
SWEET FEELING Candi Staton—Fame 1466
[Clarence Carter/Marcus Daniel/Rick Hall/Candi Staton] [BMI] (4/25/70 BCR-44)
SWEET FREEDOM Michael McDonald—MCA 52857
[Rod Temperton] [ASC] (6/14/86 BC-6)
***SWEET GEORGIE BROWN SWEET GEORGIA BROWN** Mindy Carson—Columbia 41021*
[Ben Bernie/Kenneth Casey/Maceo Pinkard] [ASC] (10/28/57 R-77)
***SWEET GEORGIA BROWN** Carroll Bros.—Cameo 221*
[Ben Bernie/Kenneth Casey/Maceo Pinkard] [ASC] (8/11/62 BCR-80) [IWM]
SWEET HARMONY Smokey Robinson—Tamla 54233
[Smokey Robinson] [ASC] (7/7/73 BCR-48)
SWEET HEARTACHES Eddie Fisher—RCA Victor 47-6529
[Jimmy Kennedy/Nat Simon] [ASC] (5/25/56 BCR-35)
SWEET HITCH-HIKER Creedence Clearwater Revival—Fantasy 665
[John Fogerty] [ASC] (7/17/71 BCR-3)

SWEET HOME ALABAMA Lynyrd Skynyrd—MCA 40258
[Ed King/Gary Rossington/Ronnie Van Zant] [BMI] (7/27/74 BCR-7)

SWEET IMPOSSIBLE YOU Brenda Lee—Decca 31539
[Dub Allbritten*/Ronnie Self] [BMI] (9/28/63 BCR-60)

SWEET INSPIRATION *The Sweet Inspirations—Atlantic 2476*
[Spooner Oldham/Dan Penn] [BMI] (3/2/68 BCR-14)

SWEET INSPIRATION *Barbra Streisand—Columbia 45626*
[Spooner Oldham/Dan Penn] (Med) [BMI] (6/24/72 BCR-30)

SWEET JANE Cowboy Junkies—RCA 8879 [Lou Reed] [BMI] (4/22/89 C-87)

SWEET KENTUCKY ROSE *Kitty Kallen—Decca 29708*
[Pat Noto] [ASC] (10/22/55 BCRt-23)

SWEET KENTUCKY ROSE *Jeffrey Clay—Coral 61511 [Pat Noto] [ASC] (10/24/55 Rt-23)*

SWEET KENTUCKY ROSE *Red Foley—Decca 29704 [Pat Noto] [ASC] (11/7/55 Rt-29)*

SWEET LIES Robert Palmer—Island 99377
[Frank Blair/Robert Palmer/Dony Wynn] [BMI] (3/26/88 B-94)

SWEET LIFE Paul Davis—Bang 738 [Susan Collins/Paul Davis] [BMI] (8/12/78 BCR-15)

SWEET LIPS Jaye P. Morgan—RCA Victor 47-6441
[Lillian Hardin Armstrong/Sid Robin] [ASC] (3/24/56 B-85)

SWEET LITTLE BABY BOY James Brown And The Famous Flames—King 6065
[James Brown/Nat Jones] [BMI] (12/10/66 R-96)

SWEET LITTLE KATHY Ray Peterson—Dunes 2004
[Tommy Boyce/Ray A. Peterson] [BMI] (3/25/61 BCR-83)

SWEET LITTLE ROCK AND ROLLER Chuck Berry—Chess 1709
[Chuck Berry] [BMI] (11/10/58 BCR-47)

SWEET LITTLE SIXTEEN *Chuck Berry—Chess 1683 [Chuck Berry] [BMI] (2/15/58 BCR-2)*

SWEET LITTLE SIXTEEN *Jerry Lee Lewis—Sun 379 [Chuck Berry] [BMI] (9/15/62 B-95)*

SWEET LITTLE SIXTEEN *Cat Mother And The All Night News Boys—Polydor 14002*
[Chuck Berry] (Med) [BMI] (6/21/69 BCR-12)

SWEET LITTLE YOU Neil Sedaka—RCA Victor 47-7922
[Larry Kolber/Barry Mann] [BMI] (8/14/61 BCR-40)

SWEET LORRAINE Uriah Heep—Mercury 73349
[Mick Box/David John Byron/Gary Thain] (TSW) [ASC] (1/20/73 BCR-87)

SWEET LOVE Commodores—Motown 1381 [Lionel Richie] [ASC] (12/20/75 BCR-5)

SWEET LOVE Anita Baker—Elektra 69557
[Anita Baker/Gary Bias/Louis A. Johnson] [BMI] (8/16/86 BC-8)

SWEET LOVING MAN Morris Albert—RCA Victor 10437
[Morris Albert] [ASC] (12/20/75 BC-85)

SWEET LUI-LOUISE Ironhorse—Scotti Brothers 406
[Randy Bachman] [BMI] (3/17/79 BCR-36)

SWEET MARIA The Billy Vaughn Singers—Dot 16985
[Milt Gabler/Bert Kaempfert/Herbert Rehbein] [BMI] (2/18/67 CR-82)

SWEET MARY Wadsworth Mansion—Sussex 209 [Steve Jablecki] [BMI] (12/5/70 BCR-5)

SWEET MAXINE The Doobie Brothers—Warner Bros. 8126
[Tom Johnston/Patrick Simmons] [BMI] (8/2/75 BCR-40)

SWEET MEMORIES Andy Williams—Columbia 44527
[Mickey Newbury] [BMI] (6/8/68 BCR-75)

SWEET MERILEE Donnie Iris—MCA/Carousel 51198
[Mark Avsec/Donnie Iris] [ASC] (10/31/81 BCR-65)

SWEET MUSIC MAN Kenny Rogers—United Artists 1095
[Kenny Rogers] [ASC] (12/17/77 BCR-44)

SWEET 'N' SASSY Jerry Smith—ABC 11230 [Jerry Dean Smith] [ASC] (8/9/69 CR-94)

SWEET NOTHIN'S Brenda Lee—Decca 30967 [Ronnie Self] [BMI] (12/21/59 BCR-3)

SWEET OLD FASHIONED GIRL Teresa Brewer—Coral 61636
[Bob Merrill] [ASC] (6/1/56 BCR-9)

SWEET PEA Tommy Roe—ABC-Paramount 10762 [Tommy Roe] [BMI] (5/28/66 BCR-5)

SWEET RACHEL Beau Coup—Amherst 318 [Dennis Lewin] [ASC] (10/31/87 B-80)

SWEET SEASONS Carole King—Ode 66022
[Carole King/Toni Stern] [ASC] (1/22/72 BCR-8)

—SWEET SEDUCTION SUITE see: SECRET GARDEN

SWEET SENSATION Stephanie Mills—20th Century Fox 2449
[Reggie Lucas/James Mtume] [BMI] (5/10/80 BCR-52)

SWEET SEPTEMBER The Lettermen—Capitol 5544
[Phyllis Kasha/Bill McGuffie/Stan Mills] [ASC] (12/18/65 CR-97)

SWEET SIXTEEN B.B. King—ABC 11319 [Joe Josea‡/B.B. King] [BMI] (3/4/72 BCR-63)

SWEET SIXTEEN Billy Idol—Chrysalis 43114 [Billy Idol] [ASC] (4/25/87 BC-20)

SWEET SIXTEEN BARS Earl Grant—Decca 25574 [Ray Charles] [BMI] (9/8/62 BCR-54) [I]

SWEET SOMEONE Eddie And Betty—Warner Bros. 5054
[Baron Keyes/George Waggner] [ASC] (6/29/59 BCR-83)

SWEET SONG OF INDIA The McGuire Sisters—Coral 61494
[Buddy Kaye/Nikolai Rimsky-Korsakov/Bob Thiele] [ASC] (9/12/55 CR-34)

SWEET SOUL MUSIC *Arthur Conley—Atco 6463*
[Arthur Conley/Sam Cooke/Otis Redding] [BMI] (3/11/67 BCR-2)

SWEET SOUL MUSIC *The Magnificent Men—Capitol 5976*
[Arthur Conley/Sam Cooke/Otis Redding] (Med) [BMI] (9/9/67 BCR-90)

SWEET STICKY THING Ohio Players—Mercury 73713
[William Beck/Leroy Bonner/Marshall Jones/Ralph Middlebrooks/Andrew Noland/Marvin Pierce/James Rodger Williams] [BMI] (9/6/75 BCR-31)

SWEET STUFF Guy Mitchell—Columbia 40940
[Aaron Schroeder/Ben Weisman] [ASC] (6/17/57 BCR-51)

SWEET SUGAR LIPS The Kalin Twins—Decca 30911
[Boudleaux Bryant/Felice Bryant] [BMI] (7/6/59 B-97)

SWEET SUMMER LOVIN' Dolly Parton—RCA 11705
[Bud Reneau/Blaise Tosti] [ASC] (9/29/79 B-77)

SWEET SUMMER MUSIC Attitudes—Dark Horse 10011
[Gilbert Bottiglier/Charles Higgins/Paul Stallworth] [BMI] (9/4/76 B-94)

SWEET SURRENDER Bread—Elektra 45818 [David Gates] [ASC] (11/4/72 BCR-11)

SWEET SURRENDER John Denver—RCA Victor 10148
[John Denver] [ASC] (12/28/74 BCR-13)

SWEET, SWEET BABY (I'M FALLING) Lone Justice—Geffen 28965
[Maria McKee/Benmont Tench/Steven Van Zandt] [BMI] (7/27/85 BC-73)

SWEET, SWEET LOVIN' The Platters—Musicor 1275
[Ralph Bailey/Vernon Harrell] [BMI] (10/21/67 BCR-66)

SWEET, SWEET SMILE Carpenters—A&M 2008
[Juice Newton/Otha Young] [ASC] (2/4/78 BCR-42)

SWEET SWEETHEART Bobby Vee—Liberty 56208
[Gerry Goffin/Carole King] [BMI] (11/7/70 BCR-88)

SWEET TALKIN' GUY The Chiffons—Laurie 3340
[Barbara Baer/Eliot Greenberg/Douglas Morris/Robert Schwartz] [BMI] (5/7/66 BCR-9)

SWEET TALKIN' WOMAN Electric Light Orchestra—Jet 1145
[Jeff Lynne] [BMI] (2/18/78 BCR-17)

SWEET THING Rufus Featuring Chaka Khan—ABC 12149
[Chaka Khan/Tony Maiden] [ASC] (12/27/75 BCR-5)

SWEET THURSDAY Johnny Mathis—Columbia 42261
[Jerry Livingston/Paul Francis Webster] [ASC] (2/19/62 BCR-75)

SWEET TIME REO Speedwagon—Epic 03264 [Kevin Cronin] [ASC] (8/28/82 BC-26)

SWEET UNDERSTANDING LOVE Four Tops—Dunhill 4366
[Renaldo Benson/Val Benson/Ivy Jo Hunter] [BMI] (10/13/73 BCR-28)

SWEET WATER Stereos—Cub 9103 [Otis Blackwell] [BMI] (12/4/61 R-82)

SWEET WILLIAM Millie Small—Smash 1920
[Buddy Kaye/Philip Springer] [ASC] (8/1/64 BCR-33)

A SWEET WOMAN LIKE YOU Joe Tex—Dial 4022 [Joe Tex] [BMI] (12/4/65 BCR-20)

SWEET YOUNG THING LIKE YOU Ray Charles—ABC/TRC 11133
[Dee Ervin] [BMI] (9/21/68 BCR-55)

THE SWEETER HE IS PART I The Soul Children—Stax 0050
[Isaac Hayes/David Porter] [ASC] (10/11/69 BCR-52)

SWEETER THAN SUGAR Ohio Express—Buddah 92
[Steve Feldman/Joey Levine] [BMI] (2/1/69 BCR-60)

SWEETER THAN YOU Ricky Nelson—Imperial 5595 [Baker Knight] [BMI] (6/29/59 BCR-9)

SWEETEST ONE The Crests—Joyce 103
[Al Browne/John Mastrangelo] [BMI] (7/15/57 B-86)

SWEETEST ONE The Metros—RCA Victor 47-8994
[Jesse Anderson] [BMI] (1/14/67 BCR-76)

THE SWEETEST TABOO Sade—Portrait 37-05713
[Helen Adu/Martin Ditcham] [BMI] (11/23/85 BC-5)

THE SWEETEST THING (I'VE EVER KNOWN) Juice Newton—Capitol 5046
[Otha Young] [ASC] (10/17/81 BCR-7)

THE SWEETEST THING THIS SIDE OF HEAVEN Chris Bartley—Vando 101
[Van McCoy] [BMI] (7/15/67 BCR-24)

SWEETHEART Peggy Lee—Capitol 4071 [Winfield Scott] [BMI] (11/8/58 BC-92)

SWEETHEART Engelbert Humperdinck—Parrot 40054
[Barry Gibb/Maurice Gibb] [BMI] (9/26/70 BCR-35)

SWEETHEART Franke & The Knockouts—Millennium 11801
[Billy Elworthy/Franke Previte] [ASC] (3/7/81 BCR-10)

SWEETHEART LIKE YOU Bob Dylan—Columbia 04301 [Bob Dylan] [SE] (12/17/83 BC-55)

—SWEETHEART see: ALSO INNAMORATA

SWEETHEART TREE *Henry Mancini And His Orchestra—RCA Victor 47-8624*
[Henry Mancini/Johnny Mercer] [ASC] (7/24/65 CRt-79)

SWEETHEART TREE *Johnny Mathis—Mercury 72464*
[Henry Mancini/Johnny Mercer] [ASC] (7/24/65 CRt-75)

SWEETHEART (WILL YOU REMEMBER) The Hilltoppers—Dot 15201
[Sigmund Romberg/Rida Johnson Young] [NA] (7/3/54 C-PRE)

SWEETHEARTS ON PARADE *Dick Jacobs And His Chorus And Orchestra—Coral 61479*
[Carmen Lombardo/Charles Newman] [ASC] (9/12/55 Rt-72)

SWEETHEARTS ON PARADE *Billy Ward & The Dominoes—Jubilee 5213*
[Carmen Lombardo/Charles Newman] [ASC] (9/12/55 Rt-72)

SWEETS FOR MY SWEET *The Drifters—Atlantic 2117*
[Doc Pomus/Mort Shuman] [BMI] (9/4/61 BCR-16)

SWEETS FOR MY SWEET *Central Park West—Event 3301*
[Doc Pomus/Mort Shuman] [BMI] (1/4/69 R-97)

SWEETS FOR MY SWEET *Tony Orlando—Casablanca 991*
[Doc Pomus/Mort Shuman] [BMI] (7/7/79 BCR-54)

SWEPT AWAY Diana Ross—RCA 13864 [Sara Allen/Daryl Hall] [BMI] (9/1/84 BC-19)

SWING The Tokens—B.T. Puppy 500 [Henry Jamiph] [BMI] (5/9/64 CR-47)

SWING LOW Floyd Cramer—RCA Victor 47-8084 [Traditional] [BMI] (9/22/62 R-87) [I]

SWING YOUR DADDY Jim Gilstrap—Roxbury 2006
[Kenny Nolan] [ASC] (3/1/75 BCR-55)

SWINGIN' John Anderson—Warner Bros. 29788
[John David Anderson/Lionel Delmore] [BMI] (3/5/83 BC-30)

SWINGIN' DADDY Buddy Knox with The Rhythm Orchids—Roulette 4042
[Jimmy Bowen/Buddy Knox/Donnie Lanier] [BMI] (1/11/58 BCR-47)

SWINGIN' DOWN THE LANE Jerry Wallace—Challenge 59082
[Isham Jones/Gus Kahn] [ASC] (7/11/60 BCR-79)

SWINGIN' GENTLY Earl Grant—Decca 25560 [Earl Grant] [BMI] (5/14/62 BCR-37) [I]

SWINGIN' ON A RAINBOW Frankie Avalon—Chancellor 1045
[Peter DeAngelis/Bob Marcucci] [ASC] (12/14/59 BCR-39)

A SWINGIN' SAFARI Billy Vaughn And His Orchestra—Dot 16374
[Bert Kaempfert] [BMI] (7/7/62 BCR-11) [IM]

SWINGIN' SCHOOL Bobby Rydell—Cameo 175
[Dave Appell/Bernie Lowe/Kal Mann] [ASC] (4/25/60 BCR-5)

THE SWINGIN' SHEPHERD BLUES *Moe Koffman Quartette—Jubilee 5311*
[Moe Koffman] [BMI] (1/13/58 BCtRt-17) [I]

SWINGING SHEPHERD BLUES *David Rose And His Orchestra—MGM 12608*
[Moe Koffman] [BMI] (1/13/58 BCtRt-17) [I]

SWINGING SHEPHERD BLUES *Johnny Pate Quintet—Federal 12312*
[Moe Koffman] [BMI] (1/18/58 BCtRt-17) [I]

SWINGIN' SHEPHERD BLUES *David Terry & His Orchestra—RCA Victor 47-7153*
[Moe Koffman] [BMI] (2/10/58 Rt-17) [I]

THE SWINGIN' SHEPHERD BLUES *Ella Fitzgerald & Her Shepherds—Verve 10130*
[Kenny Jacobson/Moe Koffman/Rhoda Roberts] [BMI] (4/14/58 Rt-63)

SWINGIN' SHEPHERD BLUES TWIST *Moe Koffman—Ascot 2100*
[Moe Koffman] [BMI] (4/16/62 R-99) [I]

SWINGIN' TIGHT Bill Deal & The Rhondels—Heritage 818
[Bob Barash/Mark Barkan] [BMI] (11/8/69 BCR-51)

SWINGING ON A STAR Big Dee Irwin—Dimension 1010
[Johnny Burke/Jimmy Van Heusen] [ASC] (5/18/63 BCR-21)

SWINGIN' SWEETHEARTS *David Carroll & His Orchestra—Mercury 71152*
[Ron Goodwin] [ASC] (8/3/57 Rt-31) [IM]

SWINGIN' SWEETHEARTS *Hugo Winterhalter And His Orchestra—RCA Victor 47-6982*
[Ron Goodwin] [ASC] (8/3/57 Rt-31) [IM]

SWINGING SWEETHEARTS *Ron Goodwin And His Orchestra—Capitol 3748*
[Ron Goodwin] [ASC] (8/3/57 BCRt-30) [IM]

SWINGING SWEETHEARTS *Richard Hayes—Decca 30436*
[Ron Goodwin/Carolyn Leigh] [ASC] (9/9/57 Rt-31)

SWINGTOWN Steve Miller Band—Capitol 4496
[Chris McCarty/Steve Miller] [ASC] (10/15/77 BCR-13)

THE SWISS MAID Del Shannon—Big Top 3117 [Roger Miller] [BMI] (8/25/62 BCR-64)

THE SWITCH-A-ROO Hank Ballard And The Midnighters—King 5510
[Hank Ballard] [BMI] (6/24/61 BCR-26)

SWITCH IT ON Cliff Nobles & Co.—Phil-L.A. Of Soul 324
[Jesse James] [BMI] (2/8/69 BCR-93) [I]

SWITCHIN' TO GLIDE The Kings—Elektra 47006/47052
[David Diamond/Aryan Zero] (TSW) [ASC] (8/23/80 BCR-43)

SYLVIA Focus—Sire 708 [Thijs Van Leer] [ASC] (7/14/73 BCR-58) [I]

SYLVIA'S MOTHER Dr. Hook And The Medicine Show—Columbia 45562
[Shel Silverstein] [BMI] (3/18/72 BCR-1)

SYMPATHETIC EYES The Ames Brothers—RCA Victor 47-6044
[Ervin Drake/Jimmy Shirl] [ASC] (3/7/55 R-61)

SYMPATHY Rare Bird—Probe 477
[David Franklin Ewer/Steve Gould/Mark McVey/Graham Stansfield] [BMI]
(4/4/70 CR-82)

SYMPHONY Sammy Turner—Big Top 3029
[Alex Alstone/Roger Bernstein/Jack Lawrence/André Tabet] [ASC]
(11/30/59 B-82) [FET]

A SYMPHONY FOR SUSAN The Arbors—Date 1529
[Bill Stegmeyer] [ASC] (10/15/66 BCR-44)

MOZART SYMPHONY NO. 40 IN G MINOR K.550, 1ST MOVEMENT
Waldo De Los Rios—United Artists 50772
[Wolfgang Amadeus Mozart] [NA] (5/22/71 BCR-57) [I]

SYMPHONY NO. 40 IN G MINOR *The Royal Philharmonic Orchestra—RCA 12304*
[Wolfgang Amadeus Mozart] (Med) [NA] (10/31/81 BCR-9) [I]

SYMPHONY NO. 9 The Royal Philharmonic Orchestra—RCA 12304
[Ludwig van Beethoven] (Med) [NA] (10/31/81 BCR-9) [I]

SYMPTOMS OF TRUE LOVE Tracie Spencer—Capitol 44198
[Irmgard Klarmann/Felix Weber] [ASC] (10/1/88 BC-38)

SYNCHRONICITY II The Police—A&M 2571 [Sting] [BMI] (11/5/83 BC-15)

(THE SYSTEM OF) DOCTOR TARR AND PROFESSOR FETHER
Alan Parsons Project—20th Century 2297
[Alan Parsons/Eric Woolfson] [BMI] (7/24/76 BCR-37)

SYSTEM OF SURVIVAL Earth, Wind & Fire—Columbia 07608
[Skylark] [ASC] (10/31/87 BC-60)

T

T'AIN'T NOTHIN' TO ME The Coasters—Atco 6287 [Leon Payne] [BMI] (3/7/64 BCR-64)

T-R-O-U-B-L-E Elvis Presley—RCA Victor 10278 [Jerry Chesnut] [BMI] (5/10/75 BCR-35)

TA TA Clyde McPhatter—Mercury 71660
[Clyde McPhatter/Jimmy Oliver] [BMI] (7/11/60 BCR-22)

TABOO Arthur Lyman—HiFi 550 [Margarita Lecuona] [BMI] (6/13/59 BCR-36) [IM]

TAINTED LOVE Soft Cell—Sire 49855 [Ed Cobb] [BMI] (1/16/82 BCR-7)

TAKE A BOW Alan Dean—MGM 12189 [Edwin Kimmel/Al Vann] [ASC] (4/20/56 R-82)

TAKE A CHANCE Jaye P. Morgan—RCA Victor 47-7064
[Mort Garson/Bob Hilliard] [ASC] (11/11/57 R-68)

TAKE A CHANCE ON ME ABBA—Atlantic 3457
[Benny Andersson/Björn Ulvaeus] [ASC] (4/22/78 BCR-3)

TAKE A CLOSER LOOK AT THE WOMAN YOU'RE WITH Wilson Pickett—RCA Victor 0049
[Wilson Pickett] [BMI] (9/15/73 BCR-58)

TAKE A FOOL'S ADVICE Nat King Cole—Capitol 4582
[Charles Singleton] [BMI] (6/26/61 BCR-67)

TAKE A HAND Rick Springfield—Chelsea 3051 [Rick Springfield] [BMI] (8/21/76 BCR-41)

TAKE A HEART Don Fardon—GNP Crescendo 418 [Miki Dallon] [ASC] (12/14/68 C-95)

TAKE A LETTER MARIA R.B. Greaves—Atco 6714 [R.B. Greaves] [BMI] (10/4/69 BCR-2)

TAKE A LITTLE RHYTHM Ali Thomson—A&M 2243 [Ali Thomson] [ASC] (6/7/80 BCR-15)

TAKE A LOOK Aretha Franklin—Columbia 44270 [Clyde Otis] [BMI] (9/2/67 BCR-54)

TAKE A LOOK AROUND Smith—Dunhill 4228
[Jerry Carter/James Cliburn] [BMI] (2/14/70 BCR-26)

TAKE A LOOK AROUND The Temptations—Gordy 7115
[Barrett Strong/Norman Whitfield] [BMI] (2/19/72 BCR-25)

—TAKE A LOOK AT ME NOW see: AGAINST ALL ODDS

TAKE A MESSAGE TO MARY The Everly Brothers—Cadence 1364
[Boudleaux Bryant/Felice Bryant] [BMI] (3/30/59 BCR-15)

TAKE A MINUTE The String-A-Longs—Warwick 654 [Jimmy Torres] [BMI] (6/5/61 R-99) [I]

TAKE ALL OF MY LIFE Carrie Grant And The Grandeurs—New-Art 1002
[Morris Bailey/Bobby Martin] [BMI] (12/22/62 R-96)

TAKE ANOTHER PICTURE Quarterflash—Geffen 29523 [Marv Ross] [ASC] (10/1/83 BC-58)

TAKE AWAY Big Ric—Scotti Brothers 04084
[Kevin DiSimone/Bud Harner/John Pondel] [BMI] (9/3/83 BC-77)

TAKE CARE OF YOUR HOMEWORK Johnnie Taylor—Stax 0023
[Homer Banks/Don Davis/Raymond Earl Jackson/Thomas Kelly] [BMI]
(1/11/69 BCR-12)

TAKE EVERYTHING BUT YOU Kitty Kallen—Decca 29130
[Maurice Abrahams/Lew Brown*/Elmer Colby*] [ASC] (7/24/54 CR-24)

TAKE FIVE Dave Brubeck Quartet—Columbia 41479
[Paul Desmond] [BMI] (7/29/61 BCR-23) [I]

TAKE GOOD CARE OF HER *Adam Wade—Coed 546*
[Arthur Kent/Ed Warren] [ASC] (3/4/61 BCR-7)

TAKE GOOD CARE OF HER *Mel Carter—Imperial 66208*
[Arthur Kent/Ed Warren] [ASC] (9/24/66 BC-78)

TAKE GOOD CARE OF HER *Elvis Presley—RCA Victor 0196*
[Arthur Kent/Ed Warren] (TSW) [ASC] (3/16/74 BC-39)

TAKE GOOD CARE OF MY BABY *Bobby Vee—Liberty 55354*
[Gerry Goffin/Carole King] [BMI] (8/7/61 BCR-1)

TAKE GOOD CARE OF MY BABY *Bobby Vinton—Epic 10305*
[Gerry Goffin/Carole King] [BMI] (3/30/68 BCR-19)

TAKE IT ANY WAY YOU WANT IT The Outlaws—Arista 0378
[William Harlin Jones/Hughie Thomasson] [BMI] (12/23/78 C-94)

TAKE IT AWAY Paul McCartney—Columbia 03018 [Paul McCartney] [ASC] (7/10/82 BC-6)

TAKE IT BACK The J. Geils Band—EMI America 8012
[Seth Justman/Peter Wolf] [ASC] (3/10/79 BCR-67)

TAKE IT EASY Eagles—Asylum 11005
[Jackson Browne/Glenn Frey] [ASC] (5/20/72 BCR-6)

TAKE IT EASY Andy Taylor—Atlantic 89414
[Stephen Jones/Andy Taylor] [ASC] (5/31/86 BC-16)

TAKE IT EASY ON ME Little River Band—Capitol 5057
[Graham Goble] [BMI] (12/5/81 BCR-10)

TAKE IT FROM ME Dionne Warwicke—Warner Bros. 8088
[Jerry Ragovoy] [ASC] (5/17/75 R-87)

TAKE IT LIKE A MAN Bachman-Turner Overdrive—Mercury 73766
[Blair Thornton/C.F. Turner] [BMI] (1/31/76 BCR-33)

TAKE IT OFF HIM AND PUT IT ON ME Clarence Carter—Atlantic 2702
[Mickey Buckins/George Henry Jackson/Herman Jones/Robert Owens/Larry Pierce]
[BMI] (1/24/70 BC-94)

TAKE IT OFF THE TOP The Dixie Dregs—Capricorn 0291
[Steve Morse] [BMI] (5/20/78 C-92) [I]

TAKE IT ON THE RUN REO Speedwagon—Epic 01054
[Gary Richrath] [ASC] (3/21/81 BCR-3)

TAKE IT SLOW (OUT IN THE COUNTRY) Lighthouse—Evolution 1052
[Ralph Cole/Keith Jollimore/Larry Edward Smith] [BMI] (12/11/71 BCR-41)

TAKE IT TO HEART Michael McDonald—Reprise 19828
[Michael McDonald/Diane Warren] [ASC] (6/9/90 BC-88)

TAKE IT TO THE LIMIT Eagles—Asylum 45293
[Glenn Frey/Don Henley/Randy Meisner] [ASC] (12/20/75 BCR-4)

TAKE IT WHILE IT'S HOT Sweet Sensation—Atco 99352
[Joseph E. Malloy] [BMI] (4/9/88 BC-57)

TAKE LIFE A LITTLE EASIER Rodney Allen Rippy—Bell 45,403
[John Annarino/Sid Woloshin] [ASC] (10/13/73 C-75)

TAKE ME Brenda Lee—Decca 32119 [George Jones/Leon Payne] [BMI] (4/1/67 C-91)

TAKE ME Grand Funk Railroad—Capitol 4199
[Don Brewer/Craig Frost] [BMI] (1/24/76 BC-50)

TAKE ME ALONG *The Ames Brothers—RCA Victor 47-7604*
[Bob Merrill] [ASC] (10/12/59 Rt-56)

TAKE ME ALONG *Lonnie Sattin—Warner Bros. 5112 [Bob Merrill] [ASC] (10/12/59 Rt-56)*

TAKE ME BACK Little Anthony And The Imperials—DCP 1136
[Teddy Randazzo] [BMI] (6/26/65 BCR-16)

TAKE ME BACK Frankie Laine—ABC-Paramount 11097 [Lou Garisto] [ASC] (7/6/68 R-98)

TAKE ME BACK Bonnie Tyler—Columbia 04246 [Billy Cross] [ASC] (12/3/83 BC-46)

TAKE ME BACK AGAIN Tony Bennett—Columbia 40272
[Arthur Berman/Redd Evans/Marvin Kahn] [ASC] (7/31/54 C-33)

TAKE ME BACK BABY Guy Mitchell—Columbia 40820
[Claude DeMetrius] [ASC] (1/26/57 BCR-36)

TAKE ME BACK TO CHICAGO Chicago—Columbia 10737
[Danny Seraphine/David Wolinski] [ASC] (5/13/78 BCR-55)

TAKE ME BACK TO TOYLAND Nat "King" Cole—Capitol 3305
[Bob Horn*/Bernie Lowe/Kal Mann] [BMI] (12/23/55 BCR-32)

TAKE ME BAK 'OME Slade—Polydor 15046
[Noddy Holder/Jim Lea] [ASC] (9/23/72 BCR-80)

TAKE ME DOWN Alabama—RCA 13210
[Mark Eugene Gray/James P. Pennington] [BMI] (5/22/82 BC-17)

TAKE ME FOR A LITTLE WHILE *Patti LaBelle And The Blue Belles—Atlantic 2373*
[Trade Martin] [BMI] (12/24/66 BCR-82)

TAKE ME FOR A LITTLE WHILE *Vanilla Fudge—Atco 6616*
[Trade Martin] [BMI] (10/5/68 BCR-38)

TAKE ME FOR WHAT I'M WORTH The Searchers—Kapp 729
[Steve Barri/P.F. Sloan] [ASC] (1/22/66 BCR-57)

TAKE ME GIRL, I'M READY Jr. Walker & The All Stars—Soul 35084
[Johnny Bristol/Gloria Jones/Pam Sawyer] [ASC] (8/7/71 BCR-44)

TAKE ME HOME Balcones Fault—Cream 7714 [Jack Jacobs] [BMI] (7/30/77 C-93)

TAKE ME HOME Cher—Casablanca 965 [Michele Aller/Bob Esty] [BMI] (2/10/79 BCR-8)

TAKE ME HOME Phil Collins—Atlantic 89472 [Phil Collins] [ASC] (3/15/86 BC-7)

TAKE ME HOME, COUNTRY ROADS John Denver—RCA Victor 74-0445
[Bill Danoff/Taffy Danoff/John Denver] [ASC] (4/10/71 BCR-1)

TAKE ME HOME TONIGHT Eddie Money—Columbia 06231
[Jeff Barry/Ellie Greenwich/Mike Leeson/Phil Spector/Peter Vale] [BMI] (8/16/86 BC-4)

TAKE ME I'M YOURS Michael Henderson—Buddah 597
[Michael E. Henderson] [ASC] (8/5/78 BR-54)

TAKE ME IN YOUR ARMS AND LOVE ME Gladys Knight & The Pips—Soul 35033
[Cornelius Grant/Rodger Penzabene/Barrett Strong] [BMI] (5/6/67 B-98)

TAKE ME IN YOUR ARMS (ROCK ME A LITTLE WHILE) *Kim Weston—Gordy 7046*
[Lamont Dozier/Brian Holland/Eddie Holland] [BMI] (9/25/65 BCR-42)

TAKE ME IN YOUR ARMS (ROCK ME A LITTLE WHILE) *The Isley Brothers—Tamla 54164*
[Lamont Dozier/Brian Holland/Eddie Holland] [BMI] (4/20/68 C-97)

TAKE ME IN YOUR ARMS (ROCK ME) *The Doobie Brothers—Warner Bros. 8092*
[Lamont Dozier/Brian Holland/Eddie Holland] [BMI] (5/3/75 BCR-5)

TAKE ME (JUST AS I AM) Solomon Burke—Atlantic 2416
[Spooner Oldham/Dan Penn] [BMI] (7/1/67 BCR-49)

TAKE ME NOW David Gates—Arista 0615 [David Gates] [ASC] (9/26/81 BCR-62)

TAKE ME TO HEART Quarterflash—Geffen 29603 [Marv Ross] [ASC] (6/18/83 BC-14)

TAKE ME TO THE KAPTIN Prism—Ariola America 7678
[Jim Vallance] [BMI] (12/24/77 BCR-56)

TAKE ME TO THE NEXT PHASE The Isley Brothers—T-Neck 2272
[Ernie Isley/Marvin Isley/O'Kelly Isley/Ronald Isley/Rudolph Isley/Chris Jasper] [ASC] (4/29/78 CR-66)

TAKE ME TO THE RIVER *Syl Johnson—Hi 2285*
[Al Green/Mabon Hodges] [BMI] (5/31/75 BCR-48)

TAKE ME TO THE RIVER *Talking Heads—Sire 1032*
[Al Green/Mabon Hodges] [BMI] (11/4/78 BCR-26)

TAKE ME TO YOUR HEART Monkey Meeks—Roxbury 0133
[Billy Wade McKnight] [BMI] (12/8/73 CR-91)

TAKE ME WITH U Prince and the Revolution—Warner Bros. 29079
[Prince] [ASC] (2/9/85 BC-25)

TAKE ME WITH YOU The Honey Cone—Hot Wax 7001
[Lamont Dozier/Ronald Dunbar/Brian Holland/Eddie Holland] [BMI] (5/2/70 CR-73)

TAKE MY BREATH AWAY (LOVE THEME FROM TOP GUN) Berlin—Columbia 05903
[Giorgio Moroder/Tom Whitlock] [ASC] (6/21/86 BC-1)

TAKE MY HAND Kenny Rogers And The First Edition—Reprise 1018
[Kenny Rogers] [ASC] (6/26/71 BR-91)

TAKE MY HAND, PRECIOUS LORD Elvis Presley—RCA Victor LOC-1035
[Thomas A. Dorsey] (EP) [BMI] (12/30/57 R-49)

TAKE MY HEART (YOU CAN HAVE IT IF YOU WANT IT) Kool & The Gang—De-Lite 815
[Robert Bell/Ronald Bell/George M. Brown/Eumir Deodato/Claydes Smith/J.T. Taylor] [BMI] (10/10/81 BCR-17)

TAKE MY LOVE Eddie Fisher—RCA Victor 47-6071
[Helen Deutsch/Bronislaw Kaper] [ASC] (3/21/55 CR-36)

TAKE MY LOVE (I WANT TO GIVE IT ALL TO YOU) Little Willie John—King 5516
[Mertis John] [BMI] (9/18/61 B-87)

TAKE NO PRISONERS (IN THE GAME OF LOVE) Peabo Bryson—Elektra 69632
[Billy Livsey/Sue Shifrin] [BMI] (6/29/85 BC-78)

TAKE OFF Bob & Doug McKenzie—Mercury 76134
[Kerry Crawford/Marc Giacomelli/Jonathan Goldsmith/Rick Moranis/Dave Thomas] [BMI] (1/30/82 BCR-14)

TAKE ON ME A-Ha—Warner Bros. 29011
[Magne Furuholmen/Morten Harket/Pal Waaktaar] [BMI] (7/13/85 BC-1)

TAKE SOME TIME OUT FOR LOVE The Isley Brothers—Tamla 54133
[Robert Gordy/Thomas Kemp] [ASC] (5/21/66 BCR-66)

TAKE THAT TO THE BANK Shalamar—Solar 11379
[Kevin Spencer/Leon Sylvers] [ASC] (12/9/78 BCR-54)

TAKE THE L The Motels—Capitol 5149
[John S. Carter/Martha Davis/Marty Jourard] [ASC] (9/4/82 BC-48)

TAKE THE LONG WAY HOME Supertramp—A&M 2193
[Rick Davies/Roger Hodgson] [ASC] (10/13/79 BCR-10)

TAKE THE MONEY AND RUN Steve Miller—Capitol 4260
[Steve Miller] [ASC] (5/8/76 BCR-9)

TAKE THE SHORT WAY HOME Dionne Warwick—Arista 1040
[Albhy Galuten/Barry Gibb] [BMI] (2/26/83 BC-32)

TAKE THE TIME Johnny Mathis—Mercury 72432 [Robert Allen] [ASC] (5/29/65 CR-82)

TAKE THE TIME Michael Stanley Band—EMI America 8146
[Michael Stanley] [ASC] (12/25/82 B-81)

TAKE THESE CHAINS FROM MY HEART
Ray Charles With The Jack Halloran Singers And The Ray Charles Orchestra—ABC-Paramount 10435
[Hy Heath/Fred Rose] [ASC] (4/13/63 BCR-8)

TAKE THIS HEART OF MINE Marvin Gaye—Tamla 54132
[Warren Moore/Smokey Robinson/Marvin Tarplin] [ASC] (5/21/66 BCR-32)

TAKE THIS HURT OFF ME Don Covay—Rosemart 802
[Don Covay/Ronald Norman Miller] [BMI] (12/26/64 B-97)

TAKE TIME TO KNOW HER Percy Sledge—Atlantic 2490
[Stephen Allen Davis] [BMI] (3/9/68 BCR-11)

TAKE YOU TONIGHT Ozark Mountain Daredevils—Columbia 11247
[Steve Cash/John Dillon/Larry Michael Lee] [BMI] (5/10/80 BCR-67)

TAKE YOUR LOVE (AND SHOVE IT) Kane's Cousins—Shove Love 500
[Terrence Kane/Richard Vrabcak] [BMI] (7/5/69 C-97)

TAKE YOUR TIME (DO IT RIGHT) (PART 1) The S.O.S. Band—Tabu 5522
[Sigidi Abdullah/Harold Clayton] [BMI] (5/24/80 BCR-1)

TAKEN IN Mike + The Mechanics—Atlantic 89404
[Christopher Neil/Mike Rutherford] [ASC] (6/28/86 BC-30)

THE TAKER Waylon Jennings—RCA Victor 47-9885
[Kris Kristofferson/Shel Silverstein] [BMI] (10/17/70 BC-84)

—TAKIN' A RIDE see: HEAVY METAL

TAKIN' ALL I CAN GET Mitch Ryder And The Detroit Wheels—New Voice 814
[Bob Crewe/Gary Knight] [BMI] (7/30/66 B-100)

TAKIN' CARE OF BUSINESS Bachman-Turner Overdrive—Mercury 73487
[Randy Bachman] [ASC] (5/18/74 BCR-6)

TAKIN' IT BACK Breathless—EMI America 8020 [Jonah Koslen] [ASC] (12/15/79 BCR-86)

TAKIN' IT EASY Seals & Crofts—Warner Bros. 8639
[Sean MacLeod/Bob Phillips] [ASC] (8/26/78 BR-79)

TAKIN' IT TO THE STREETS The Doobie Brothers—Warner Bros. 8196
[Michael McDonald] [ASC] (4/17/76 BCR-13)

TAKING A CHANCE ON LOVE Ahmad Jamal Trio—Argo 5317
[Vernon Duke] [ASC] (11/10/58 R-88) [IM]

TAKING IT ALL TOO HARD Genesis—Atlantic 89656
[Tony Banks/Phil Collins/Mike Rutherford] [ASC] (6/16/84 BC-49)

TAKING MY LOVE (AND LEAVING ME) Martha Reeves & The Vandellas—Gordy 7094
[George Gordy/Allen Story] [BMI] (9/20/69 C-86)

TALK ABOUT IT Boom Crash Opera—Giant 19476
[Peter Farnan*/Peter Maslen*/Greg O'Connor*/Richard Pleasance/Dale Ryder*] [BMI] (2/23/91 C-85)

TALK ABOUT LOVE Adam Faith—Amy 922
[Chris Frederick Andrews] [BMI] (4/17/65 BCR-96)

TALK BACK TREMBLING LIPS *Ernest Ashworth—Hickory 1214*
[John D. Loudermilk] [BMI] (10/19/63 CtRt-20)

TALK BACK TREMBLING LIPS *Johnny Tillotson—MGM 13181*
[John D. Loudermilk] [BMI] (10/26/63 BCtRt-7)

TALK DIRTY TO ME Poison—Enigma 5686
[Bobby Dall/C.C. DeVille/Bret Michaels/Rikki Rockett] [BMI] (3/14/87 BC-9)

TALK IT OVER Grayson Hugh—RCA 8802
[Irwin Levine/Sandy Linzer] [BMI] (6/24/89 BC-19)

TALK IT OVER IN THE MORNING Anne Murray—Capitol 3159
[Roger Nichols/Paul Williams] [ASC] (9/11/71 BCR-57)

TALK OF THE SCHOOL Sonny James—Capitol 4178
[Bobbie Carrol/Sonny James] [BMI] (5/4/59 B-85)

TALK TALK The Music Machine—Original Sound 61
[Sean Bonniwell] [BMI] (10/29/66 BCR-15)

TALK TALK Talk Talk–EMI America 8136 [Ed Hollis/Mark Hollis] [BMI] (10/16/82 BC-75)
TALK THAT TALK Jackie Wilson–Brunswick 55165 [Sid Wyche] [BMI] (11/14/59 BCR-33)
TALK TO ME, TALK TO ME *Little Willie John–King 5108 [Joe Seneca] [BMI] (4/7/58 BC-20)*
TALK TO ME *Sunny & The Sunglows–Tear Drop 3014 [Joe Seneca] [BMI] (9/7/63 BCR-9)*
TALK TO ME Frank Sinatra–Capitol 4284 [Stanley Kahan/Eddie Snyder/Rudy Vallee*] [ASC] (9/28/59 BCR-27)
TALK TO ME Fiona–Atlantic 89572 [Beau Hill/Michael Pfeifer] [BMI] (4/13/85 BC-64)
TALK TO ME Quarterflash–Geffen 28908 [Marv Ross/Rindy Ross] [ASC] (10/19/85 B-83)
TALK TO ME Stevie Nicks–Modern 99582 [Chas Sandford] [ASC] (11/16/85 BC-4)
TALK TO ME Chico DeBarge–Motown 1858 [Paul Fox/Franne Golde/Nick Mundy] [BMI] (11/8/86 BC-21)
TALK TO ME Anita Baker–Elektra 64964 [Anita Baker/Vernon Fails/Michael Powell] [BMI] (6/23/90 BC-39)
TALK TO ME BABY Annette With The Afterbeats–Buena Vista 369 [Paul Anka] [BMI] (10/31/60 BCR-73)
TALK TO ME BABY Barry Mann–Red Bird 10-015 [Barry Mann/Cynthia Weil] [BMI] (12/5/64 B-94)
TALK TO MYSELF Christopher Williams–Geffen 22936 [Timmy Gatling/Alton Stewart] [ASC] (9/9/89 BC-49)
TALKIN' BOUT A REVOLUTION Tracy Chapman–Elektra 39383 [Tracy Chapman] [ASC] (9/24/88 BC-67)
–TALKIN' 'BOUT THAT RIVER see: SWANEE RIVER ROCK
TALKIN' TO THE BLUES Jim Lowe–Dot 15569 [Jim Lowe/Marvin Moore] [BMI] (5/6/57 BCR-21)
TALKING ABOUT MY BABY The Impressions–ABC-Paramount 10511 [Curtis Mayfield] [BMI] (1/11/64 BCR-12)
TALKING ABOUT MY BABY Gloria Walker–Flaming Arrow 35 [Eugene Davis/Billy Foster*/Ellington Jordan*] [BMI] (10/26/68 BCR-55)
TALKING BACK TO THE NIGHT Steve Winwood–Island 28122 [Will Jennings/Steve Winwood] [BMI] (2/13/88 BC-57)
TALKING IN YOUR SLEEP Gordon Lightfoot–Reprise 1020 [Gordon Lightfoot] [ASC] (6/19/71 BCR-64)
TALKING IN YOUR SLEEP Crystal Gayle–United Artists 1214 [Roger Cook/Bobby Wood] [ASC] (7/8/78 BCR-16)
TALKING IN YOUR SLEEP The Romantics–Nemperor 04135 [Coz Canler/Jimmy Marinos/Wally Palmar/Mike Skill/Pete Solley] [ASC] (10/8/83 BC-3)
TALKING LOUD AND SAYING NOTHING - PT. I James Brown–Polydor 14109 [James Brown/Bobby Byrd] [BMI] (1/29/72 BCR-27)
TALKING OUT OF TURN The Moody Blues–Threshold 603 [John Lodge] [ASC] (11/7/81 BCR-60)
TALL COOL ONE *The Wailers–Golden Crest 518 [Rich Dangel/John Greek/Kent Morrill] [BMI] (5/4/59 BCR-36) [I]*
TALL COOL ONE *The Wailers–Golden Crest 518 [Rich Dangel/John Greek/Kent Morrill] [BMI] (3/28/64 BCR-36) [I]*
TALL COOL ONE Robert Plant–Es Paranza 7-99348 [Phil Johnstone/Robert Plant] [ASC] (4/16/88 BC-25)
TALL PAUL Annette With The Afterbeats–Disneyland 118 [Bob Roberts/Richard Sherman/Robert Sherman] [BMI] (12/29/58 BCR-7)
TALLAHASSEE LASSIE Freddy Cannon–Swan 4031 [Freddy Cannon/Bob Crewe/Frank Slay] [BMI] (5/9/59 BCR-5)
TAMIAMI Bill Haley And His Comets–Warner Bros. 5145 [Mort Garson/Earl Shuman] [ASC] (2/8/60 CR-79) [I]
TAMMY *The Ames Brothers–RCA Victor 47-6930 [Ray Evans/Jay Livingston] [ASC] (7/1/57 BCtRt-1)*
TAMMY *Debbie Reynolds–Coral 61851 [Ray Evans/Jay Livingston] [ASC] (7/6/57 BCtRt-1)*
MAIN TITLE/TAMMY *Joseph Gershenson & The Universal-International Orchestra–Coral 61845 [Ray Evans/Jay Livingston] [ASC] (7/20/57 Rt-12) [IWM]*
TAMMY *Pat Kirby–Decca 30317 [Ray Evans/Jay Livingston] [ASC] (7/20/57 Rt-12)*
TAMMY *Richard Hayman, His Orchestra And Chorus–Mercury 71123 [Ray Evans/Jay Livingston] [ASC] (7/20/57 CtRt-1) [IWM]*
TAMMY *Bill Snyder & His Orchestra–Decca 30433 [Ray Evans/Jay Livingston] [ASC] (9/9/57 Rt-1) [IWM]*
TAMOURÉ Bill Justis–Smash 1812 [Birgit Helmer/Bill Justis/Wolf Petersen/Margie Singleton] [NA] (5/18/63 R-78) [FET]
TANGERINE *Ahmad Jamal–Argo 5337 [Victor Schertzinger] [ASC] (6/29/59 R-78) [IM]*
TANGERINE *The Salsoul Orchestra–Salsoul 2004 [Victor Schertzinger] [ASC] (1/24/76 BCR-18) [IM]*
TANGLED UP IN BLUE Bob Dylan–Columbia 10106 [Bob Dylan] [SE] (3/8/75 BCR-31)
TANGO OF THE DRUMS Les Baxter His Chorus And Orchestra–Capitol 3404 [Peter Mösser*/Lotar Olias] [ASC] (5/11/56 BCR-36) [I]
TAOS NEW MEXICO R. Dean Taylor–Rare Earth 5041 [R. Dean Taylor] [BMI] (4/8/72 BCR-82)
TAPIOCA TUNDRA The Monkees–Colgems 1019 [Michael Nesmith] [BMI] (3/9/68 BCR-34)
TAR AND CEMENT Verdelle Smith–Capitol 5632 [Luciano Beretta/Adriano Celentano/Michele Del Prete/Lee Pockriss/Paul Vance] [ASC] (6/25/66 BCR-38) [FET]
–TARA'S THEME see: MY OWN TRUE LOVE
TARKIO ROAD Brewer And Shipley–Kama Sutra 524 [Michael Brewer/Tom Shipley] [BMI] (5/15/71 BCR-39)
TARZAN BOY Baltimora–Manhattan 50018 [Maurizio Bassi/Naimy Hackett] [BMI] (10/19/85 BC-13)
A TASTE OF HONEY *Martin Denny And His Orchestra–Liberty 55470 [Bobby Scott] [ASC] (6/30/62 BCtRt-45) [IM]*
A TASTE OF HONEY *Eddie Cano–Reprise 20,075 [Bobby Scott] [ASC] (6/30/62 CtRt-55) [IM]*
A TASTE OF HONEY *The Victor Feldman Quartet–Infinity 020 [Bobby Scott] [ASC] (7/14/62 BCtRt-45) [IM]*
A TASTE OF HONEY *Quincy Jones–Mercury 72012 [Bobby Scott] [ASC] (7/14/62 CtRt-55) [IM]*
A TASTE OF HONEY *Tony Bennett–Columbia 43073 [Ric Marlow/Bobby Scott] [ASC] (7/18/64 BCtR-65)*
TASTE OF HONEY *Herb Alpert & The Tijuana Brass–A&M 775 [Bobby Scott] [ASC] (8/28/65 BCR-1) [IM]*
TASTE OF TEARS Johnny Mathis–Mercury 72287 [Teddy Bart/Paul Wyatt] [ASC] (6/20/64 B-87)
TASTY LOVE Freddie Jackson–Capitol 5616 [Freddie Jackson/Paul Laurence] [ASC] (11/8/86 BC-41)
TAURUS Dennis Coffey And The Detroit Guitar Band–Sussex 233 [Dennis Coffey] [BMI] (2/12/72 BCR-13) [I]
TAXI Harry Chapin–Elektra 45770 [Harry Chapin] [ASC] (3/4/72 BCR-20)
TAXI J. Blackfoot–Sound Town 0004 [Homer Banks/Chuck Brooks] [BMI] (3/3/84 B-90)
TAXI DANCING Rick Springfield & Randy Crawford–RCA 13861 [Rick Springfield] [BMI] (11/17/84 BC-59)
TAXMAN Stars On 45–Radio 3830 [George Harrison] (Med) [ASC] (7/11/81 BC-63)
TE AMO *Dick Jacobs And His Chorus And Orchestra–Coral 61653 [Jimmy Mulcay/Mildred Mulcay] [ASC] (7/7/56 BRt-70) [IWM]*
TE AMO *The Mulcays–Trans-World 711 [Jimmy Mulcay/Mildred Mulcay] [ASC] (7/20/56 Rt-75) [IWM]*
TE-TA-TE-TA-TA Ernie K-Doe–Minit 627 [Ernie K-Doe] [BMI] (6/12/61 BCR-43)
TEA FOR TWO CHA CHA *Tommy Dorsey Orchestra Starring Warren Covington–Decca 30704 [Vincent Youmans] [ASC] (8/18/58 BCRt-2) [IM]*
TEA FOR TWO CHA CHA *Bill Ador & His Orchestra–Verve 10155 [Vincent Youmans] [ASC] (12/22/58 Rt-33) [IM]*
TEA FOR TWO *Nino Tempo & April Stevens–Atco 6294 [Irving Caesar/Vincent Youmans] [ASC] (4/25/64 BCR-56)*
TEACH ME TIGER April Stevens–Imperial 5626 [April Stevens*/Nino Tempo] [ASC] (11/30/59 B-86)
TEACH ME TO TWIST Bobby Rydell - Chubby Checker–Cameo 214 [Dave Appell/Kal Mann] [ASC] (4/23/62 CR-60)
TEACH ME TONIGHT *The DeCastro Sisters–Abbott 3001 [Sammy Cahn/Gene DePaul] [ASC] (10/4/54 BCR-2)*
TEACH ME TONIGHT *Jo Stafford–Columbia 40351 [Sammy Cahn/Gene DePaul] [ASC] (10/18/54 BRt-PRE)*
TEACH ME TONIGHT *The Modernaires Featuring Paula Kelly & George Auld–Coral 61265 [Sammy Cahn/Gene DePaul] [ASC] (11/1/54 Rt-PRE)*
TEACH ME TONIGHT *Janet Brace–Decca 28990 [Sammy Cahn/Gene DePaul] [ASC] (12/6/54 Rt-PRE)*
TEACH ME TONIGHT CHA CHA *The DeCastro Sisters–ABC-Paramount 9988 [Sammy Cahn/Gene DePaul] [ASC] (12/8/58 BCR-62)*
TEACH ME TONIGHT *The Big Three: Sarah Vaughan/Joe Williams/Count Basie–Roulette 4273 [Sammy Cahn/Gene DePaul] [ASC] (9/5/60 R-98)*
TEACH ME TONIGHT *George Maharis–Epic 9504 [Sammy Cahn/Gene DePaul] [ASC] (4/16/62 BCR-25)*
TEACH ME TONIGHT *Al Jarreau–Warner Bros. 50032 [Sammy Cahn/Gene DePaul] [ASC] (4/3/82 BC-70)*
TEACH YOUR CHILDREN Crosby, Stills, Nash & Young–Atlantic 2735 [Graham Nash] [BMI] (6/6/70 BCR-16)
TEACHER The Falcons–United Artists 229 [Dave Braithwaite/Eddie Powell] [BMI] (7/9/60 CR-84)
TEACHER TEACHER Johnny Mathis–Columbia 41152 [Robert Allen/Al Stillman] [ASC] (4/7/58 BCR-20)
TEACHER TEACHER Rockpile–Columbia 11388 [Eddie Phillips/Ken Pickett] [ASC] (11/22/80 BCR-51)
TEACHER, TEACHER 38 Special–Capitol 5405 [Bryan Adams/Jim Vallance] [BMI] (9/29/84 BC-25)
TEACHER'S PET Doris Day–Columbia 41123 [Joe Lubin] [BMI] (3/3/58 BCR-36)
A TEAR Gene McDaniels–Liberty 55344 [Willie Denson/Luther Dixon] [BMI] (7/3/61 BCR-19)

TEAR AFTER TEAR Patty LaBelle & Her Blue Belles—Newtown 5007
[Morris Bailey/Bobby Martin] [BMI] (7/14/62 CR-72)

TEAR DROP Santo & Johnny—Canadian-American 107
[Ann Farina/Johnny Farina/Santo Farina] [BMI] (11/9/59 BCR-22) [I]

TEAR DROP CITY The Monkees—Colgems 5000
[Tommy Boyce/Bobby Hart] [BMI] (2/15/69 BCR-33)

TEAR DROPS Lee Andrews And The Hearts—Chess 1675
[Larry Brown/Roy Calhoun/Barry Golder/Helen Stanley] [BMI] (11/25/57 BCR-20)

A TEAR FELL *Teresa Brewer—Coral 61590*
[Dorian Burton/Eugene Randolph] [BMI] (2/17/56 BCRt-7)

A TEAR FELL *Ivory Joe Hunter—Atlantic 1086*
[Dorian Burton/Eugene Randolph] [BMI] (2/24/56 Rt-7)

A TEAR FELL *Ray Charles—ABC-Paramount 10571*
[Dorian Burton/Eugene Randolph] [BMI] (7/18/64 BCR-35)

THE TEAR OF THE YEAR Jackie Wilson—Brunswick 55201
[Gary Geld/Peter Udell] [ASC] (1/14/61 BCR-40)

TEAR THE ROOF OFF THE SUCKER (GIVE UP THE FUNK) *Parliament—Casablanca 856*
[Jerome Brailey/George Clinton/William Earl Collins] [BMI] (5/8/76 BCR-8)

WE WANT THE FUNK *Gerardo—Interscope 98815*
[Jerome Brailey/George Clinton/William Earl Collins/Fabian Cooke/Gerardo Mejia] [BMI] (5/4/91 BC-15)*

TEARDROPS The Hurricanes—Audiovox 109 [Unknown] [NA] (11/8/54 R-31)

TEARDROPS George Harrison—Dark Horse 49785 [George Harrison] [ASC] (8/8/81 C-88)

TEARDROPS IN MY HEART *Teresa Brewer—Coral 61850*
[Vaughn Horton] [ASC] (6/17/57 BCRt-40)

TEARDROPS IN MY HEART *Tommy Prisco—Epic 9219*
[Vaughn Horton] [ASC] (6/29/57 Rt-72)

TEARDROPS IN MY HEART *Joe Barry—Smash 1710*
[Vaughn Horton] [ASC] (7/24/61 BCR-47)

TEARDROPS ON YOUR LETTER Hank Ballard And The Midnighters—King 5171
[Henry Glover] [BMI] (3/9/59 B-87)

TEARDROPS WILL FALL Dicky Doo And The Don'ts—Swan 4025
[Gerry Granahan/Marion Smith] [BMI] (2/2/59 BC-61)

TEARS (FOR SOUVENIRS) *Ken Dodd—Liberty 55835*
[Frank Capano/Billy Uhr] [ASC] (1/15/66 R-95)

TEARS *Bobby Vinton—Epic 9894 [Frank Capano/Billy Uhr] [ASC] (2/12/66 BCR-43)*

TEARS John Waite—EMI America 8238
[Vince Cusano/Adam Mitchell] [BMI] (10/20/84 BC-37)

TEARS AND LAUGHTER Dinah Washington—Mercury 71922
[Yvette Ball/John Howard/Miriam Lewis] [BMI] (1/29/62 BCR-56)

TEARS AND ROSES Al Martino—Capitol 5183
[Dick Heard/Hank Hunter] [BMI] (5/16/64 BCR-9)

TEARS ARE FALLING KISS—Mercury 884141 [Paul Stanley] [ASC] (10/19/85 BC-51)

TEARS BROKE OUT ON ME Eddy Arnold—RCA Victor 47-7984
[Hank Cochran] [BMI] (2/5/62 R-89)

TEARS FROM AN ANGEL Troy Shondell—Liberty 55398
[Jackie DeShannon/Sharon Sheeley] [BMI] (12/25/61 BCR-68)

TEARS FROM MY HEART Thurston Harris—Aladdin 3435
[Bob Berry/Pearl White] [BMI] (10/4/58 C-82)

TEARS KEEP ON FALLING Jerry Vale—Columbia 43252
[Lee Madison] [ASC] (5/15/65 BCR-63)

THE TEARS OF A CLOWN *Smokey Robinson & The Miracles—Tamla 54199*
[Henry Cosby/Smokey Robinson/Stevie Wonder] [ASC] (10/10/70 BCR-1)

TEARS OF A CLOWN *Stars On 45—Radio 3863*
[Henry Cosby/Smokey Robinson/Stevie Wonder] (Med) [ASC] (9/19/81 BCR-55)

TEARS OF JOY Chuck Jackson—Wand 138
[Chuck Jackson*/Ed Townsend] [BMI] (7/6/63 B-85)

TEARS ON MY PILLOW *Little Anthony And The Imperials—End 1027*
[Sylvester Bradford/Al Lewis] [ASC] (8/11/58 BCR-4)

TEARS ON MY PILLOW *Johnny Tillotson—Amos 117*
[Sylvester Bradford/Al Lewis] [ASC] (6/21/69 CR-96)

TEARS ON MY PILLOW *Fred Parris & The Five Satins—Elektra 47411*
[Sylvester Bradford/Al Lewis] (Med) [ASC] (2/27/82 BC-71)

TEARS ON MY PILLOW The McGuire Sisters—Coral 62276
[Gene Autry/Fred Rose] [ASC] (7/10/61 BCR-40)

TEARS RUN RINGS Marc Almond—Capitol 44240 [Marc Almond] [ASC] (12/31/88 BC-67)

TEARS, TEARS, TEARS Ben E. King—Atco 6472 [Fred Parris] [BMI] (4/15/67 BR-93)

TEASABLE, PLEASABLE YOU Buddy Knox—Roulette 4120
[Jack Dixon] [BMI] (1/19/59 B-85)

THE TEASER Bob Kuban And The In-Men—Musicland U.S.A. 20,006
[Greg Hoeltzel/John Krenski] [BMI] (4/23/66 BCR-70)

TEASIN' Quaker City Boys—Swan 4023
[Irving Fields/Al Hoffman] [ASC] (12/22/58 BCR-24)

TEASIN' YOU Willie Tee—Atlantic 2273 [Earl King Johnson] [BMI] (3/6/65 BCR-88)

TECHNIQUE Pat Boone—Dot DEP-1057 [Johnny Mercer] (EP) [ASC] (9/9/57 R-61)

TEDDY Connie Francis—MGM 12878 [Paul Anka] [BMI] (2/27/60 BCR-17)

TEDDY BEAR Red Sovine—Starday 142
[Billy Joe Burnette/Tommy Hill/Dale Royal/Red Sovine] [BMI] (7/3/76 BCR-35)

—TEDDY BEAR see: (LET ME BE YOUR) TEDDY BEAR

TEDDY BEAR SONG Barbara Fairchild—Columbia 45743
[Don Earl/Nick Nixon] [BMI] (2/24/73 BCR-27)

TEDDY BEAR'S LAST RIDE Diana Williams—Capitol 4317
[Billy Joe Burnette/Dale Royal] [BMI] (9/4/76 BCR-66)

TEEN AGE CRUSH Tommy Sands—Capitol 3639
[Audrey Allison/Joe Allison] [BMI] (2/16/57 BCR-1)

TEEN AGE DOLL Tommy Sands—Capitol 3953 [Bobbie Carrol] [BMI] (5/12/58 BR-81)

TEEN AGE GOODNIGHT The Chordettes—Cadence 1299
[Dale Fitzsimmons/Ray Stanley] [BMI] (10/20/56 B-45)

TEEN AGE IDOL Rick Nelson—Imperial 5864 [Jack Lewis] [ASC] (8/11/62 BCR-5)

TEEN AGE PRAYER *Gloria Mann—Sound 126*
[Bernie Lowe/Bickley Reichner] [ASC] (12/1/55 BCtRt-8)

TEEN AGE PRAYER *Gale Storm—Dot 15436*
[Bernie Lowe/Bickley Reichner] [ASC] (12/9/55 BCtRt-8)

TEEN AGE PRAYER *Kitty White—Mercury 70750*
[Bernie Lowe/Bickley Reichner] [ASC] (12/16/55 BRt-32)

TEEN AGER'S WALTZ Eddy Howard And His Orchestra—Mercury 70700
[Teddy Powell/Tony Starr] [ASC] (11/21/55 BR-73)

TEEN ANGEL *Mark Dinning—MGM 12845*
[Jean Dinning/Red Surrey] [BMI] (12/21/59 BCR-1)*

TEEN ANGEL *Wednesday—Sussex 515*
[Jean Dinning/Red Surrey] [BMI] (5/4/74 BCR-67)*

TEEN BEAT *Sandy Nelson—Original Sound 5*
[Arthur Egnoian/Sandy Nelson] [BMI] (9/5/59 BCR-3) [I]

TEEN BEAT '65 *Sandy Nelson—Imperial 66060*
[Arthur Egnoian/Sandy Nelson] [BMI] (9/19/64 BCR-37) [I]

TEEN COMMANDMENTS
Paul Anka-George Hamilton IV-Johnny Nash—ABC-Paramount 9974
[Nancy Becker] [BMI] (11/22/58 BCR-29)

TEEN EX The Browns Featuring Jim Edward Brown—RCA Victor 47-7700
[Boudleaux Bryant/Felice Bryant] [BMI] (3/7/60 BR-47)

TEEN PRAYER The Velveteens—Stark 102 [Charles Liddell] [BMI] (6/26/61 R-86)

TEEN QUEEN OF THE WEEK Freddy Cannon—Swan 4096
[Bob Crewe/Frank Slay] [ASC] (1/22/62 BCR-64)

TEENAGE CLEOPATRA Tracey Dey—Liberty 55604 [Beverly Ross] [BMI] (9/14/63 BCR-66)

TEENAGE HAYRIDE Tender Slim—Grey Cliff 723 [Teddy Vann] [BMI] (1/2/60 BC-93) [I]

TEENAGE HEARTACHE Ray Peterson—RCA Victor 47-7779
[Doc Pomus/Mort Shuman] [BMI] (9/19/60 R-75)

TEENAGE HEAVEN Eddie Cochran—Liberty 55177
[Jerry Capehart/Eddie Cochran] [BMI] (3/16/59 B-99)

TEENAGE HEAVEN Johnny Cymbal—Kapp 524
[Johnny Cymbal/Jack Gale] [BMI] (5/4/63 BCR-50)

TEENAGE LAMENT '74 Alice Cooper—Warner Bros. 7762
[Alice Cooper/Neal Smith] [BMI] (12/22/73 BCR-24)

TEENAGE LOVE AFFAIR Rick Derringer—Blue Sky 2752
[Rick Derringer] [BMI] (4/27/74 BCR-60)

TEENAGE MEETING (GONNA ROCK IT UP RIGHT) *Don Cornell—Coral 61584*
[Julius Dixon/Alan Freed/Ollie Jones] [BMI] (2/18/56 BRt-80)

TEENAGE MEETING (GONNA ROCK IT UP RIGHT)
Dave Appell & His Applejacks—President 1006
[Julius Dixon/Alan Freed/Ollie Jones] [BMI] (3/9/56 Rt-80)

TEENAGE QUEEN Johnny Dee with the Bluenotes—Colonial 433
[Orville B. Campbell/John D. Loudermilk] [BMI] (6/29/57 R-85)

TEENAGE SONATA Sam Cooke—RCA Victor 47-7701 [Jeff Barry] [BMI] (2/29/60 BCR-40)

TEENAGE VOWS OF LOVE The Dreamers—Goldisc 3015
[Artie Ripp/Nick Smith/Neil Stevens] [BMI] (2/6/61 CR-87)

A TEENAGER FEELS IT TOO Denny Reed—3 Trey 3007
[Connie Conway/Norma Conway] [BMI] (8/29/60 B-94)

TEENAGER IN LOVE *Dion and The Belmonts—Laurie 3027*
[Doc Pomus/Mort Shuman] [BMI] (4/18/59 BCR-5)

A TEENAGER IN LOVE *(parody of A Teenager In Love) The Four Preps—Capitol 4599*
[Doc Pomus/Mort Shuman] (Med) [BMI] (8/14/61 BCR-14) [P]

TEENAGER'S MOTHER (ARE YOU RIGHT?) Bill Haley And His Comets—Decca 30028
[Curtis Reginald Lewis/J. Leslie McFarland] [BMI] (8/3/56 BCR-24)

TEENAGER'S PRAYER Joe Simon—Sound Stage 7 2564
[Leonard Allen] [BMI] (6/18/66 BCR-66)

TEENAGER'S ROMANCE Ricky Nelson—Verve 10047
[David Gillam] [ASC] (5/20/57 BCR-8)

TEENSVILLE Chet Atkins—RCA Victor 47-7684
[Wayne Cogswell] [BMI] (1/11/60 BCR-62) [I]

TELEFONE (LONG DISTANCE LOVE AFFAIR) Sheena Easton—EMI America 8172
[Greg Mathieson/Trevor Veitch] [BMI] (8/20/83 BC-8)

TELEGRAM SAM T. Rex—Reprise 1078 [Marc Bolan] [ASC] (4/15/72 BCR-58)

TELEPHONE LINE Electric Light Orchestra—United Artists 1000
[Jeff Lynne] [BMI] (6/11/77 BCR-4)

TELEPHONE MAN Meri Wilson—GRT 127 [Meri Wilson] [ASC] (6/4/77 BCR-18)

TELL ALL THE PEOPLE The Doors—Elektra 45663 [Robby Krieger] [ASC] (6/14/69 BCR-32)

TELL 'EM I'M SURFIN Fantastic Baggys—Imperial 66047
[Steve Barri/P.F. Sloan] [ASC] (8/15/64 R-99)

TELL 'EM WILLIE BOY 'S A'COMIN' Tommy James—Roulette 7119
[Tommy James/Robert L. King] [BMI] (2/12/72 BCR-52)

TELL HER ABOUT IT Billy Joel—Columbia 04012 [Billy Joel] [ASC] (7/30/83 BC-1)

TELL HER FOR ME Adam Wade—Coed 520
[Morty Craft/Selma Craft] [BMI] (12/14/59 BCR-45)

TELL HER LOVE HAS FELT THE NEED Eddie Kendricks—Tamla 54249
[Leonard Caston/Kathy Wakefield] [BMI] (7/27/74 BCR-38)

TELL HER NO *The Zombies—Parrot 9723 [Rod Argent] [BMI] (1/9/65 BCR-6)*

TELL HER NO *Juice Newton—Capitol 5265 [Rod Argent] [BMI] (8/13/83 BC-27)*

TELL HER SHE'S LOVELY El Chicano—MCA 40104
[David Batteau] [ASC] (11/17/73 BCR-28)

TELL HER YOU LOVE HER Frank Sinatra—Capitol 3859
[Homer Denison/Hugh Halliday/Barry Parker] [BMI] (12/30/57 CR-48)

TELL HER (YOU LOVE HER EVERY DAY) Frank Sinatra—Reprise 0373
[Gil Ward] [BMI] (5/22/65 BCR-53)

TELL HIM *The Exciters—United Artists 544 [Bert Berns] [BMI] (11/24/62 BCR-4)*

TELL HER *Dean Parrish—Boom 60012 [Bert Berns] [BMI] (7/16/66 BC-94)*

TELL HER *Kenny Loggins—Columbia 68531 [Bert Berns] [BMI] (1/28/89 BC-64)*

TELL HIM *The Drew-Vels—Capitol 5055 [Carlton Black] [BMI] (2/8/64 BCR-76)*

TELL HIM *Patti Drew—Capitol 5861 [Carlton Black] [BMI] (8/26/67 BCR-81)*

TELL HIM I'M NOT HOME Chuck Jackson—Wand 132
[Sanford Bellini/Brenda Bruno/Tony Bruno] [BMI] (1/26/63 BCR-42)

TELL HIM NO *Travis & Bob—Sandy 1017 [Travis Pritchett] [BMI] (3/21/59 BCRt-8)*

TELL HIM NO *Dean & Marc—Bullseye 1025 [Travis Pritchett] [BMI] (3/23/59 BRt-15)*

TELL HIM NO *The Jackson Brothers—Atco 6139 [Travis Pritchett] [BMI] (4/20/59 Rt-11)*

TELL IT ALL BROTHER Kenny Rogers And The First Edition—Reprise 0923
[Alex Harvey] [BMI] (7/4/70 BCR-12)

TELL IT LIKE IT IS *Aaron Neville—Par-Lo 101*
[George Richard Davis Jr./Lee Diamond] [BMI] (11/26/66 BCR-2)

TELL IT LIKE IT IS *Andy Williams—Columbia 10263*
[George Richard Davis Jr./Lee Diamond] [BMI] (1/17/76 BCR-72)

TELL IT LIKE IT IS *Heart—Epic 50950*
[George Richard Davis Jr./Lee Diamond] [BMI] (11/22/80 BCR-8)

TELL IT ON THE MOUNTAIN Peter, Paul & Mary—Warner Bros. 5418
[Milton Okun/Paul Stookey/Traditional/Mary Travers/Peter Yarrow] [ASC]
(3/7/64 BCR-31)

TELL IT TO MY HEART Taylor Dayne—Arista 1-9612
[Ernie Gold/Seth Swirsky] [ASC] (10/10/87 BC-7)

TELL IT TO THE RAIN
The 4 Seasons Featuring The "Sound" Of Frankie Valli—Philips 40412
[Angelo M. Cifelli/Mike Petrillo] [BMI] (12/10/66 BCR-10)

TELL LAURA I LOVE HER *Ray Peterson—RCA Victor 47-7745*
[Jeff Barry/Ben Raleigh] [BMI] (6/13/60 BCR-5)

TELL LAURA I LOVE HER *Johnny T. Angel—Bell 45,472*
[Jeff Barry/Ben Raleigh] [BMI] (6/1/74 BC-80)

TELL MAMA Etta James—Cadet 5578
[Clarence Carter/Marcus Daniel*/Wilbur Terrell*] [BMI] (11/11/67 BCR-23)

TELL MAMA Savoy Brown—Parrot 40066
[Paul Raymond/Kim Simmonds] [BMI] (11/6/71 BCR-83)

TELL ME Dick And Deedee—Liberty 55412 [Dick Gosting] [BMI] (3/12/62 BCR-22)

TELL ME White Lion—Atlantic 89051 [Vito Bratta/Mike Tramp] [ASC] (7/2/88 BC-58)

TELL ME A LIE Sami Jo—MGM South 7029
[Mickey Buckins/Barbara Wyrick] [BMI] (2/2/74 BCR-21)

TELL ME BABY Garnet Mimms—United Artists 694
[Bob Halley/Carl Spencer] [BMI] (2/15/64 BCR-69)

TELL ME IF YOU STILL CARE The S.O.S. Band—Tabu 4-04160
[James Samuel Harris/Terry Lewis] [ASC] (11/19/83 BC-65)

TELL ME I'M NOT DREAMING Robert Palmer—EMI 50206
[Jay Gruska/Michael Omartian/Bruce Sudano] [ASC] (7/1/89 BC-50)

TELL ME MAMMA Christine Quaite—World Artists 1022
[Charles Gambel/Gerry Granahan/Ellen May] [BMI] (5/9/64 BCR-62)

TELL ME NOW The McGuire Sisters—Coral 61587
[Hal Gordon/Ruth Kardon/Horace Linsley] [BMI] (3/16/56 R-84)

TELL ME SOMETHING Indecent Obsession—MCA 53830
[David Lincoln Dixon/Michael Szumowski] [ASC] (7/28/90 BC-27)

TELL ME SOMETHING GOOD Rufus—ABC 11427 [Stevie Wonder] [ASC] (6/8/74 BCR-1)

TELL ME TELL ME June Valli—RCA Victor 47-5837 [Bob Merrill] [ASC] (9/4/54 CR-23)

TELL ME THAT I'M WRONG Blood, Sweat & Tears—Columbia 46059
[Patricia Cosby] [BMI] (6/29/74 B-83)

TELL ME THAT YOU LOVE ME Paul Anka—ABC-Paramount 9855
[Paul Anka] [BMI] (10/7/57 R-47)

TELL ME THAT YOU LOVE ME Fats Domino—Imperial 5660
[Dave Bartholomew/Fats Domino] [BMI] (4/23/60 BCR-51)

TELL ME THE TRUTH Nancy Wilson—Capitol 4991
[Dimple M. Jackson/George Harold Jackson] [BMI] (8/3/63 BCR-72)

TELL ME THIS IS A DREAM The Delfonics—Philly Groove 172
[William Hart] [BMI] (5/27/72 BCR-73)

TELL ME TO MY FACE Keith—Mercury 72652
[Allan Clarke/Tony Hicks/Graham Nash] [BMI] (3/11/67 BCR-26)

TELL ME TOMORROW - PART 1 Smokey Robinson—Tamla 1601
[Gary Goetzman/Mike Piccirillo] [BMI] (1/16/82 BCR-29)

TELL ME WHAT SHE SAID The Playmates—Roulette 4370
[Jeff Barry] [BMI] (6/19/61 R-100)

TELL ME WHAT YOU WANT ME TO DO Tevin Campbell—Qwest 19131
[Tevin Campbell/Sally Jo Dakota/Narada Michael Walden] [ASC] (11/9/91 BC-6)

—TELL ME WHEN see: QUANDO QUANDO QUANDO

TELL ME WHY *Gale Storm—Dot 15474 [Titus Turner] [BMI] (6/15/56 BCtRt-32)*

TELL ME WHY *The Crew-Cuts—Mercury 70890 [Titus Turner] [BMI] (6/15/56 BCtRt-32)*

TELL ME WHY *Marie Knight—Wing 90069 [Titus Turner] [BMI] (6/15/56 Rt-32)*

TELL ME WHY *Elvis Presley With The Jordanaires—RCA Victor 47-8740*
[Titus Turner] [BMI] (1/1/66 BCR-20)

TELL ME WHY The Belmonts—Sabrina 500
[Don Carter/Marshall Helfand] [BMI] (5/22/61 BCR-18)

TELL ME WHY Bobby Vinton—Epic 9687 [Al Alberts/Marty Gold] [ASC] (5/23/64 BCR-8)

TELL ME WHY Matthews' Southern Comfort—Decca 32874
[Neil Young] [BMI] (10/16/71 BR-95)

TELL ME WHY Exposé—Arista 1-9916 [Lewis Martinée] [BMI] (12/9/89 BC-6)

TELL ME (YOU'RE COMING BACK) The Rolling Stones—London 9682
[Mick Jagger/Keith Richards] [ASC] (7/4/64 BCR-24)

TELL SOMEONE YOU LOVE THEM Dino, Desi & Billy—Reprise 0698
[Billy Hinsche/Dean Martin Jr.*] [BMI] (8/3/68 BCR-69)

TELL THAT GIRL TO SHUT UP Transvision Vamp—Uni 50001
[Holly Beth Vincent] [ASC] (10/1/88 BC-82)

TELL THE TRUTH Ray Charles—Atlantic 2068 [Ray Charles] [BMI] (7/30/60 C-72)

TELL THE WORLD HOW I FEEL ABOUT 'CHA BABY
Harold Melvin And The Blue Notes—Philadelphia Int'l 3588
[Victor Carstarphen/Gene McFadden/John Whitehead] [BMI] (4/3/76 BCR-67)

TELLING LIES Fats Domino—Imperial 5569
[Fats Domino/Earl Palmer] [BMI] (2/16/59 BCR-35)

TELSTAR The Tornadoes—London 9561 [Joe Meek] [ASC] (10/27/62 BCR-1) [I]

TEMMA HARBOUR Mary Hopkin—Apple 1816
[Philamore Lincoln] [ASC] (2/21/70 BCR-39)

THE TEMPLE The Assembled Multitude—Atlantic 2780
[Tim Rice/Andrew Lloyd Webber] (Med) [ASC] (2/6/71 BCR-87) [IWM]

TEMPLE OF LOVE Harriet—EastWest 98863
[Simon Franglen/Harriet Roberts] [BMI] (2/16/91 BC-39)

TEMPTATION *Roger Williams—Kapp 347*
[Nacio Herb Brown] [ASC] (8/29/60 BCR-53) [IM]

TEMPTATION *The Everly Brothers—Warner Bros. 5220*
[Nacio Herb Brown/Arthur Freed] [ASC] (5/22/61 BCR-14)

TEMPTATION *Boots Randolph—Monument 1009*
[Nacio Herb Brown] [ASC] (6/10/67 BCR-91) [IM]

TEMPTATION Corina—Cutting/Atco 98775
[Corina Ayala/Carlos Berrios*/Inez Diaz/Luis Duprey*/Franc Reyes*] [ASC]
(5/18/91 BC-5)

TEMPTATION 'BOUT TO GET ME The Knight Bros.—Checker 1107
[James Leon Diggs] [BMI] (5/29/65 BCR-56)

TEMPTATION EYES The Grass Roots—Dunhill 4263
[Harvey Price/Dan Walsh] [ASC] (12/19/70 BCR-11)

TEMPTED Squeeze—A&M 2345 [Chris Difford/Glenn Tilbrook] [ASC] (7/25/81 BCR-49)

TEN COMMANDMENTS Prince Buster—Philips 40427
[Buster Campbell] [BMI] (1/21/67 BCR-48)

TEN COMMANDMENTS OF LOVE *Harvey and The Moonglows—Chess 1705*
[Marshall Paul] [BMI] (9/13/58 BCR-22)

THE TEN COMMANDMENTS OF LOVE *James Macarthur—Scepter 1250*
[Marshall Paul] [BMI] (6/22/63 BCR-87)

THE TEN COMMANDMENTS OF LOVE *Peaches & Herb—Date 1592*
[Marshall Paul] [BMI] (2/24/68 BCR-45)

THE TEN COMMANDMENTS OF LOVE *Little Anthony And The Imperials—*
United Artists 50598 [Marshall Paul] [BMI] (11/8/69 BCR-78)

—TEN I LOVED see: PEDDLER MAN

10 LITTLE BOTTLES Johnny Bond—Starday 704 [Johnny Bond] [BMI] (2/27/65 BCR-34)

TEN LITTLE INDIANS The Beach Boys—Capitol 4880
[Gary Usher/Brian Wilson] [BMI] (11/24/62 BCR-42)

TEN LITTLE INDIANS The Yardbirds—Epic 10248 [Harry Nilsson] [BMI] (11/4/67 BCR-62)

TEN LONELY GUYS *Pat Boone—Dot 16391*
[Cliff Adams/Neil Diamond/Lockie Edwards/Wes Farrell/Bob Feldman/Jerry Goldstein/
Richard Gottehrer/Stanley Kahan/Eddie Snyder/Larry Weiss] [BMI] (9/15/62 BCR-43)

TEN LONELY GUYS *Ten Broken Hearts—Diamond 123*
[Cliff Adams/Neil Diamond/Lockie Edwards/Wes Farrell/Bob Feldman/Jerry Goldstein/
Richard Gottehrer/Stanley Kahan/Eddie Snyder/Larry Weiss] [BMI] (9/22/62 R-43)

10-9-8 Face To Face—Epic 04430 [Angelo Petraglia] [ASC] (6/2/84 BC-38)

TEN PERCENT Double Exposure—Salsoul 2008
[Talmadge Conway/Allan Felder] [BMI] (6/19/76 B-54)

TEN POUND NOTE Steel River—Evolution 1030 [Jay Telfer] [BMI] (10/31/70 R-86)

TEN THOUSAND DRUMS Carl Smith—Columbia 41417
[Carl M. Smith/Mel Tillis] [BMI] (6/22/59 BCR-43)

TEN TO EIGHT David Castle—Parachute 501 [David Castle] [BMI] (9/24/77 BC-68)

—TEN YEARS AFTER see: GOTTA GIVE A LITTLE LOVE

TENDER IS THE NIGHT Jackson Browne—Asylum 69791 [Jackson Browne/Danny Kortchmar/Russ Kunkel] [ASC] (9/24/83 BC-25)

TENDER KISSES Tracie Spencer—Capitol 44680 [Matt Sherrod/Paul Sherrod/Marty Spencer/Tracie Spencer] [ASC] (10/19/91 B-42)

TENDER LOVE Force M.D.'s—Warner Bros. 28818 [James Samuel Harris/Terry Lewis] [ASC] (2/1/86 BC-10)

TENDER LOVER Babyface—Solar 74003 [Kenneth Edmonds/Antonio Reid/Perri Arlette Reid] [BMI] (11/18/89 BC-14)

***TENDER YEARS** George Jones—Mercury 71804 [Darrell Edwards] [BMI] (7/3/61 BR-76)*

***TENDER YEARS** Brook Benton—Mercury 72135 [Darrell Edwards] [BMI] (6/22/63 C-87)*

***TENDER YEARS** John Cafferty And The Beaver Brown Band—Scotti Brothers 04327 [John Cafferty] [BMI] (1/28/84 BC-75)*

***TENDER YEARS** John Cafferty And The Beaver Brown Band—Scotti Brothers 04682 [John Cafferty] [BMI] (11/17/84 BC-29)*

TENDERLY Bert Kaempfert And His Orchestra—Decca 31236 [Walter Gross] [ASC] (3/27/61 BCR-28) [IM]

TENDERNESS General Public—I.R.S. 9934 [Micky Billingham/Roger Charlery/Dave Wakeling] [ASC] (11/17/84 BC-24)

TENNESSEE Jan & Dean—Liberty 55454 [Buzz Cason/Bobby Russell] [BMI] (5/26/62 BCR-69)

TENNESSEE BIRD WALK Jack Blanchard & Misty Morgan—Wayside 010 [Jack Blanchard] [BMI] (2/28/70 BCR-14)

TENNESSEE FLAT-TOP BOX Johnny Cash—Columbia 42147 [Johnny Cash] [ASC] (11/13/61 BC-84)

TENNESSEE STUD Eddy Arnold—RCA Victor 47-7542 [Jimmy Driftwood] [BMI] (6/22/59 BCR-47)

***TENNESSEE WALTZ** Bobby Comstock & The Counts—Blaze 349 [Pee Wee King/Redd Stewart] [BMI] (10/12/59 BCtRt-34)*

***TENNESSEE WALTZ** Jerry Fuller—Challenge 59057 [Pee Wee King/Redd Stewart] [BMI] (10/19/59 BCtRt-34)*

***TENNESSEE WALTZ** The Jupiter Serenaders—Hickory 1104 [Pee Wee King] [BMI] (10/19/59 Rt-63) [IM]*

***TENNESSEE WALTZ** Don Robertson—RCA Victor 47-7909 [Pee Wee King] [BMI] (7/17/61 R-96) [IM]*

***TENNESSEE WALTZ** Sam Cooke—RCA Victor 47-8368 [Pee Wee King/Redd Stewart] [BMI] (6/6/64 BCR-35)*

TENTH AVENUE FREEZE-OUT Bruce Springsteen—Columbia 10274 [Bruce Springsteen] [ASC] (1/10/76 BC-63)

***TEQUILA** The Champs—Challenge 1016 [Chuck Rio] [BMI] (2/17/58 BCRt-1) [I]*

***TEQUILA** Eddie Platt And His Orchestra—ABC-Paramount 9899 [Chuck Rio] [BMI] (2/17/58 BRt-1) [I]*

***TEQUILA** Stan Kenton & His Orchestra—Capitol 3928 [Chuck Rio] [BMI] (2/24/58 Rt-1) [I]*

***TEQUILA TWIST** The Champs—Challenge 9131 [Chuck Rio] [BMI] (2/3/62 B-99) [I]*

***TEQUILA** Bill Black's Combo—Hi 2077 [Chuck Rio] [BMI] (5/16/64 B-91) [I]*

***TEQUILA** Hot Butter—Musicor 1468 [Chuck Rio] [BMI] (12/16/72 R-79) [I]*

TEQUILA SUNRISE Eagles—Asylum 11017 [Glenn Frey/Don Henley] [ASC] (6/9/73 BCR-40)

TEST OF TIME The Romantics—Nemperor 05587 [Coz Canler/Wally Palmar/Mike Skill] [ASC] (8/31/85 BC-64)

—TESTIFY see: I WANNA TESTIFY

A TEXAN AND A GIRL FROM MEXICO Anita Bryant—Carlton 538 [Doc Pomus/Mort Shuman] [BMI] (1/23/61 BCR-48)

TEXAS Charlie Daniels Band—Kama Sutra 607 [Charlie Daniels] [BMI] (2/7/76 BC-91)

TEXAS IN MY REAR VIEW MIRROR Mac Davis—Casablanca 2305 [Mac Davis] [BMI] (10/18/80 BCR-51)

TEXAS LADY Les Paul and Mary Ford—Capitol 3301 [Johnny Mann/Paul Sawtell] [ASC] (12/24/55 BCR-47)

THANK GOD AND GREYHOUND Roy Clark—Dot 17355 [Larry Kingston/Ed Nix] [BMI] (10/31/70 BC-90)

THANK GOD FOR YOU BABY PG&E—Columbia 45519 [Charles Edward Allen/John Michael Hill] [BMI] (2/26/72 BCR-82)

THANK GOD I'M A COUNTRY BOY John Denver—RCA Victor 10239 [John Martin Sommers] [ASC] (3/22/75 BCR-1)

THANK GOD IT'S FRIDAY Love And Kisses—Casablanca 925 [Alec R. Costandinos] [ASC] (5/6/78 BCR-22)

THANK THE LORD FOR THE NIGHT TIME Neil Diamond—Bang 547 [Neil Diamond] [SE] (7/15/67 BCR-10)

THANK U VERY MUCH Scaffold—Bell 701 [Mike McGear] [BMI] (2/3/68 BCR-43)

THANK YOU AND GOODNIGHT The Angels—Smash 1854 [Bob Feldman/Jerry Goldstein/Richard Gottehrer/Marty Sanders] [BMI] (12/7/63 BC-84)

THANK YOU BABY The Shirelles—Scepter 1278 [Luther Dixon*/Beverly Lee] [BMI] (7/18/64 BCR-63)

THANK YOU BABY The Stylistics—Avco 4652 [Luigi Creatore/Hugo Peretti/George David Weiss] [ASC] (4/19/75 BCR-67)

THANK YOU (FALETTINME BE MICE ELF AGIN) Sly & The Family Stone—Epic 10555 [Sylvester Stewart] (TSW) [BMI] (1/3/70 BCR-1)

THANK YOU FOR BEING A FRIEND Andrew Gold—Asylum 45456 [Andrew Gold] [BMI] (2/11/78 BCR-11)

THANK YOU FOR CALLING Jo Stafford—Columbia 40250 [Cindy Walker] [BMI] (6/19/54 BC-PRE)

THANK YOU FOR LOVING ME Al Martino—Capitol 5239 [Don Robertson] [ASC] (8/22/64 C-96)

THANK YOU GIRL The Beatles—Vee-Jay 587 [John Lennon/Paul McCartney] [ASC] (3/28/64 BCR-35)

THANK YOU GIRL Street People—Musicor 1401 [Gerard Florio/Rupert Holmes/Paul Vance] [ASC] (4/25/70 B-96)

THANK YOU PRETTY BABY Brook Benton—Mercury 71478 [Brook Benton/Clyde Otis] [BMI] (7/13/59 BCR-9)

THANKS A LOT Brenda Lee—Decca 31728 [Eddie Miller/Don Sessions] [BMI] (1/16/65 BCR-33)

THANKS FOR MY CHILD Cheryl "Pepsii" Riley—Columbia 07996 [Curtis Bedeau/Gerard Charles/Hugh Clarke/Brian George/Lucien George/Paul George] [BMI] (10/29/88 BC-32)

THANKS FOR SAVING MY LIFE Billy Paul—Philadelphia Int'l 3538 [Kenneth Gamble/Leon Huff] [BMI] (1/26/74 BCR-26)

THANKS FOR THE SMILES Charlie Ross—Big Tree 16025 [Kenny O'Dell] [BMI] (1/4/75 BCR-61)

THANKS TO THE FOOL Brook Benton—Mercury 71962 [Bennie Benjamin/Sol Marcus] [ASC] (5/19/62 C-86)

THAT ACAPULCO GOLD The Rainy Daze—Uni 55002 [John S. Carter/Tim Gilbert] [ASC] (2/25/67 BCR-59)

THAT AIN'T LOVE REO Speedwagon—Epic 06656 [Kevin Cronin] [ASC] (1/31/87 BC-16)

THAT BOY JOHN The Raindrops—Jubilee 5466 [Jeff Barry/Ellie Greenwich] [BMI] (11/16/63 BCR-64)

THAT CRAZY FEELING Kenneth Rogers—Carlton 454 [Ray Doggett] [BMI] (4/26/58 CR-51)

THAT DID IT Bobby Bland—Duke 421 [Pearl Woods] [BMI] (8/5/67 CR-95)

THAT DIDN'T HURT TOO BAD Dr. Hook—Casablanca 2325 [Tom Brasfield/Robert Byrne] [ASC] (4/4/81 BC-69)

THAT DO MAKE IT NICE Eddy Arnold—RCA Victor 47-6198 [Eddy Arnold/Fred Ebb/Paul Klein] [BMI] (10/3/55 R-79)

THAT EVIL CHILD B.B. King—Kent 4542 [Joe Josea‡/B.B. King] [BMI] (4/24/71 B-97)

THAT GIRL Stevie Wonder—Tamla 1602 [Stevie Wonder] [ASC] (1/16/82 BCR-1)

THAT GIRL BELONGS TO YESTERDAY Gene Pitney—Musicor 1036 [Mick Jagger/Keith Richards] [BMI] (1/18/64 BCR-49)

THAT GIRL COULD SING Jackson Browne—Asylum 47036 [Jackson Browne] [ASC] (9/20/80 BCR-22)

THAT GREASY KID STUFF Janie Grant—Caprice 115 [Cy Coben] [ASC] (6/2/62 BCR-70)

THAT HAPPY FEELING Bert Kaempfert And His Orchestra—Decca 31388 [Guy Warren] [ASC] (4/30/62 BCR-67) [I]

THAT KIND OF WOMAN Merrilee Rush & The Turnabouts—Bell 738 [Mary Unobsky/Donna Weiss] [BMI] (8/24/68 BCR-39)

—THAT KISS see: ESO BESO

THAT LADY (PART 1) The Isley Brothers—T-Neck 2251 [O'Kelly Isley/Ronald Isley/Rudolph Isley] [BMI] (7/14/73 BCR-6)

THAT LOVIN' YOU FEELIN' AGAIN Roy Orbison & Emmylou Harris—Warner Bros. 49262 [Roy Orbison/Chris Price] [BMI] (6/21/80 BCR-55)

***THAT LUCKY OLD SUN** The Velvets—Monument 435 [Haven Gillespie/Beasley Smith] [ASC] (3/6/61 CR-92)*

***THAT LUCKY OLD SUN** The Floridians—ABC-Paramount 10185 [Haven Gillespie/Beasley Smith] [ASC] (3/6/61 R-97)*

***THAT LUCKY OLD SUN** Ray Charles—ABC-Paramount 10509 [Haven Gillespie/Beasley Smith] [ASC] (11/30/63 BCR-18)*

THAT MAGIC TOUCH Angel—Casablanca 878 [Frank DiMino/Gregg Giuffria/Punky Meadows] [BMI] (4/2/77 BC-74)

***THAT OLD BLACK MAGIC** Sammy Davis Jr.—Decca 29541 [Harold Arlen/Johnny Mercer] [ASC] (6/18/55 BCR-16)*

***THAT OLD BLACK MAGIC** Louis Prima And Keely Smith—Capitol 4063 [Harold Arlen/Johnny Mercer] [ASC] (10/13/58 BCR-9)*

***OLD BLACK MAGIC** The Clovers—United Artists 174 [Harold Arlen/Johnny Mercer] [ASC] (7/13/59 R-91)*

***THAT OLD BLACK MAGIC** Bobby Rydell—Cameo 190 [Harold Arlen/Johnny Mercer] [ASC] (4/24/61 BCR-17)*

THAT OLD FEELING Kitty Kallen—Columbia 41546 [Lew Brown/Sammy Fain] [ASC] (2/1/60 BCR-55)

THAT OLD SONG Ray Parker Jr. And Raydio—Arista 0616 [Ray Parker Jr.] [ASC] (7/11/81 BCR-21)

THAT ONCE IN A LIFETIME Demis Roussos—Mercury 73992 [Dino Fekaris/Freddie Perren] [ASC] (5/27/78 BCR-47)

***THAT SAME OLD FEELING** Pickettywitch—Janus 118 [Tony Macaulay/John Macleod] [ASC] (5/16/70 BCRt-40)*

***THAT SAME OLD FEELING** The Fortunes—World Pacific 77937 [Tony Macaulay/John Macleod] [ASC] (5/16/70 BCRt-56)*

THAT SONG IS DRIVING ME CRAZY Tom T. Hall—Mercury 73488 [Tom T. Hall] [BMI] (6/15/74 BCR-60)

THAT STRANGER USED TO BE MY GIRL Trade Martin—Coed 570
[Sandy Baron/Fred Weismantel] [BMI] (10/6/62 BCR-28)

THAT SUNDAY, THAT SUMMER Nat King Cole—Capitol 5027
[Joe Sherman/George David Weiss] [ASC] (8/31/63 BCR-12)

THAT WAS THEN BUT THIS IS NOW ABC—Mercury 814631
[Martin Fry/Stephen Singleton/Mark White] [BMI] (2/4/84 B-89)

THAT WAS THEN, THIS IS NOW
Micky Dolenz And Peter Tork (Of The Monkees)—Arista 1-9505
[Vance Brescia] [ASC] (7/5/86 BC-20)

THAT WAS YESTERDAY Foreigner—Atlantic 89571
[Lou Gramm/Michael Leslie Jones] [ASC] (3/16/85 BC-10)

—THAT'S MY BOY see: THAT'S MY HEART STRINGS

THAT'LL BE THE DAY *Buddy Holly / The Crickets—Brunswick 55009*
[Jerry Allison/Buddy Holly/Norman Petty] [ASC] (7/27/57 BCRt-3)*

THAT'LL BE THE DAY *Jeff Allen—Verve 10064*
[Jerry Allison/Buddy Holly/Norman Petty] [ASC] (7/27/57 Rt-3)*

THAT'LL BE THE DAY *Buddy Holly & The Three Tunes—Decca 30434*
[Jerry Allison/Buddy Holly/Norman Petty] [ASC] (9/2/57 Rt-3)*

THAT'LL BE THE DAY *The Everly Brothers—Warner Bros. 5611*
[Jerry Allison/Buddy Holly/Norman Petty] [ASC] (3/27/65 C-90)*

THAT'LL BE THE DAY *Linda Ronstadt—Asylum 45340*
[Jerry Allison/Buddy Holly/Norman Petty] [ASC] (8/21/76 BCR-11)*

THAT'S A LIE Ray Charles—ABC 11045
[Ray Charles/Jimmy Holiday] [BMI] (2/24/68 BCR-46)

THAT'S ALL "Tennessee" Ernie Ford—Capitol 3343
[Merle Travis] [BMI] (2/10/56 BCR-30)

THAT'S ALL Rick Nelson—Imperial 5910
[Alan Brandt/Bob Haymes] [BMI] (2/23/63 BC-48)

THAT'S ALL Genesis—Atlantic 89724
[Tony Banks/Phil Collins/Mike Rutherford] [ASC] (11/26/83 BC-6)

THAT'S ALL I NEED *Dorothy Collins—Audiovox 117*
[LaVern Baker/Howard Biggs/Lincoln Chase] [BMI] (5/9/55 Rt-38)

THAT'S ALL I NEED *LaVern Baker & The Gliders—Atlantic 1057*
[LaVern Baker/Howard Biggs/Lincoln Chase] [BMI] (5/16/55 Rt-48)

THAT'S ALL I NEED *Rusty Draper—Mercury 70619*
[LaVern Baker/Howard Biggs/Lincoln Chase] [BMI] (5/16/55 Rt-68)

THAT'S ALL I NEED *Jill Corey—Columbia 40502*
[LaVern Baker/Howard Biggs/Lincoln Chase] [BMI] (5/23/55 Rt-38)

THAT'S ALL I WANT Bobby Day—Class 245 [Bobby Day] [BMI] (4/20/59 B-98)

THAT'S ALL I WANT FROM YOU *Jaye P. Morgan—RCA Victor 47-5896*
[Fritz Rotter/Fritz Rotter] [BMI] (11/15/54 BCR-4)

THAT'S ALL I WANT FROM YOU *The Silva-Tones—Argo 5281*
[Fritz Rotter/Fritz Rotter] [BMI] (12/16/57 B-86)

THAT'S ALL RIGHT Steve Walsh—Kirschner 4287
[Arthur Crudup] (Med) [BMI] (4/26/80 R-100)

THAT'S ALL THERE IS TO THAT Nat "King" Cole And The Four Knights—Capitol 3456
[Clyde Otis/Kelly Owens] [BMI] (6/22/56 BCR-7)

THAT'S ALL YOU GOTTA DO Brenda Lee—Decca 31093
[Jerry Reed] [BMI] (5/23/60 BCR-6)

THAT'S ALRIGHT Little Junior Parker—Duke 168 [Jimmy Rogers] [BMI] (1/27/58 B-78)

THAT'S ENOUGH Rosco Robinson—Wand 1125 [Gene Barge] [BMI] (7/9/66 BCR-52)

THAT'S FREEDOM Tom Kimmel—Mercury 888571
[Jean Chapman/Tom Kimmel] [BMI] (6/20/87 BC-61)

THAT'S HOW HEARTACHES ARE MADE *Baby Washington—Sue 783*
[Bob Halley/Ben Raleigh] [BMI] (3/23/63 BCR-40)

THAT'S HOW HEARTACHES ARE MADE *The Marvelettes—Tamla 54186*
[Bob Halley/Ben Raleigh] [BMI] (11/8/69 BC-81)

THAT'S HOW IT GOES George Maharis—Epic 9613
[Ray Allen/Wandra Merrell] [BMI] (9/14/63 BCR-84)

THAT'S HOW LONG The Chi-Lites—Brunswick 55515
[Tony Boyd/Archie Powell] (TSW) [BMI] (3/1/75 B-78)

THAT'S HOW LOVE GOES Jermaine Jackson—Motown 1201
[Johnny Bristol/Wade Brown/David H. Jones] [ASC] (9/9/72 BCR-39)

THAT'S HOW MUCH Brian Hyland—Kapp 352
[Brooks Arthur/Art Kaplan/Jack Keller] [BMI] (10/3/60 BCR-71)

THAT'S HOW MUCH I LOVE YOU Pat Boone—Dot 15785
[Eddy Arnold/Wally Fowler/J. Graydon Hall*] [BMI] (7/5/58 BCR-31)

THAT'S HOW STRONG MY LOVE IS Otis Redding—Volt 124
[Roosevelt Jamison] [BMI] (1/30/65 BCR-74)

THAT'S IT-I QUIT-I'M MOVIN' ON Sam Cooke—RCA Victor 47-7853
[Roy Alfred/Del Serino] [ASC] (3/6/61 BCR-20)

THAT'S LIFE *Frank Sinatra—Reprise 0531*
[Kelly Gordon/Dean Kay] [ASC] (11/12/66 BCR-1)

THAT'S LIFE *David Lee Roth—Warner Bros. 28511*
[Kelly Gordon/Dean Kay] [ASC] (11/22/86 BC-85)

THAT'S LIFE (THAT'S TOUGH) Gabriel And The Angels—Swan 4118
[Richard Kellis] [BMI] (10/27/62 BCR-44)

THAT'S LOVE Jim Capaldi—Atlantic 89849 [Jim Capaldi] [ASC] (4/23/83 BC-27)

THAT'S MY DESIRE *Pat Boone—Dot 16244*
[Helmy Kresa/Carroll Loveday] [ASC] (8/7/61 R-99)

THAT'S MY DESIRE *Yvonne Baker And The Sensations—Argo 5412*
[Helmy Kresa/Carroll Loveday] [ASC] (4/28/62 BCR-69)

THAT'S MY HEART STRINGS (THAT'S MY BOY) Burl Ives—Decca 30046
[Wiley Patterson/Maurice J. Reis] [BMI] (10/27/56 R-33)

THAT'S MY LITTLE SUZIE Ritchie Valens—Del-Fi 4114
[Robert Kuhn/Ritchie Valens] [BMI] (4/4/59 BCR-43)

THAT'S MY PA Sheb Wooley—MGM 13046 [Sheb Wooley] [ASC] (12/11/61 BCR-38)

THAT'S NOT HER STYLE Billy Joel—Columbia 73442 [Billy Joel] [ASC] (7/28/90 BC-52)

THAT'S NOT HOW IT GOES Bloodstone—London 1055
[Willis Draffen] [BMI] (7/27/74 BCR-50)

THAT'S OK WITH ME Susan Hunter—Decca 29643
[Larry Coleman/Fred Ebb/Paul Klein] [BMI] (9/5/55 R-61)

THAT'S OLD FASHIONED (THAT'S THE WAY LOVE SHOULD BE)
The Everly Brothers—Warner Bros. 5273
[Bernie Baum/Bill Giant/Florence Kaye] [BMI] (5/12/62 BCR-9)

THAT'S REALLY SOME GOOD Rufus & Carla—Stax 151
[Rufus Thomas] [ASC] (6/6/64 BC-90)

THAT'S ROCK 'N' ROLL Shaun Cassidy—Warner/Curb 8423
[Eric Carmen] [BMI] (7/23/77 BCR-3)

THAT'S SOMEONE YOU NEVER FORGET
Elvis Presley With The Jordanaires—RCA Victor 47-9115
[Elvis Presley/Red West] [BMI] (5/27/67 B-92)

THAT'S THE ONLY WAY The 4 Seasons—Vee-Jay 562
[Robert Boulanger/Bob Crewe] [BMI] (10/5/63 BC-65)

THAT'S THE SOUND THAT LONELY MAKES Tavares—Capitol 3794
[Johnny Bristol/James Anthony Dean/John Henry Glover] [ASC] (2/2/74 BCR-70)

THAT'S THE TROUBLE Grace Jones—Beam Junction 102
[Grace Jones/Pierre Papadiamandis] (TSW) [BMI] (1/22/77 B-71)

THAT'S THE TUNE The Vogues—Co & Ce 242
[Joey Levine/Artie Resnick] [BMI] (12/24/66 BR-97)

THAT'S THE WAY Joe Tex—Dial 4093 [Joe Tex] [BMI] (7/5/69 BCR-56)

THAT'S THE WAY Katrina And The Waves—SBK 07303
[Katrina Leskanich/Kimberly Rew] [BMI] (7/22/89 BC-16)

THAT'S THE WAY A WOMAN IS The Messengers—Rare Earth 5032
[John Hoier/Michael Morgan] [BMI] (9/11/71 BCR-42)

THAT'S THE WAY BOYS ARE Lesley Gore—Mercury 72259
[Mark Barkan/Ben Raleigh] [BMI] (3/21/64 BCR-12)

THAT'S THE WAY GOD PLANNED IT *Billy Preston—Apple 1808*
[Billy Preston] [BMI] (7/26/69 BCR-62)

THAT'S THE WAY GOD PLANNED IT *Billy Preston—Apple 1808*
[Billy Preston] [BMI] (7/8/72 BCR-65)

THAT'S THE WAY I FEEL ABOUT CHA
(The Preacher) Bobby Womack (& Peace)—United Artists 50847
[John Grisby/Joe Hicks/Bobby Womack] [BMI] (11/20/71 BCR-18)

THAT'S THE WAY (I LIKE IT) *K.C. & The Sunshine Band—TK 1015*
[Harry Wayne Casey/Rick Finch] [BMI] (10/18/75 BCR-1)

THAT'S THE WAY I LIKE IT *The Ritchie Family—Marlin 3306*
[Harry Wayne Casey/Rick Finch] (Med) [BMI] (8/28/76 BCR-17)

THAT'S THE WAY I WANT OUR LOVE Joe Simon—Sound Stage 7 2667
[Jackey Beavers/Jack Hill] [BMI] (10/24/70 BCR-92)

THAT'S THE WAY IT GOES Eddie Fisher—RCA Victor 47-7051
[Heino Gaze/Al Stillman] [ASC] (10/7/57 CR-55) [FDE]

THAT'S THE WAY I'VE ALWAYS HEARD IT SHOULD BE Carly Simon—Elektra 45724
[Jacob Brackman/Carly Simon] [ASC] (4/17/71 BCR-7)

THAT'S THE WAY LOVE GOES Young M.C.—Capitol 44740
[Marvin Young] [ASC] (8/3/91 BC-54)

THAT'S THE WAY LOVE IS Bobby Bland—Duke 360
[Deadric Malone] [BMI] (1/5/63 BCR-30)

THAT'S THE WAY LOVE IS Marvin Gaye—Tamla 54185
[Barrett Strong/Norman Whitfield] [BMI] (8/23/69 BCR-7)

—THAT'S THE WAY LOVE SHOULD BE see: THAT'S OLD FASHIONED

THAT'S THE WAY OF THE WORLD Earth, Wind & Fire—Columbia 10172
[Charles Stepney/Maurice White/Verdine White] [ASC] (7/5/75 BCR-6)

THAT'S THE WAY OF THE WORLD D Mob With Cathy Dennis—ffrr 886 980
[Cathy Dennis/Danny Poku] [BMI] (4/28/90 BC-55)

THAT'S THE WAY WITH LOVE *Piero Soffici—Kip 224*
[Gualtiero Malgoni/Carl Sigman/Pietro Soffici] [ASC] (4/24/61 BR-59) [IWM]*

THAT'S THE WAY WITH LOVE
Don Costa And His Orchestra And Chorus—United Artists 313
[Gualtiero Malgoni/Carl Sigman/Pietro Soffici] [ASC] (5/8/61 R-80) [IWM]*

THAT'S WHAT FRIENDS ARE FOR B.J. Thomas—Scepter 12354
[Paul Williams] [ASC] (7/8/72 BCR-74)

THAT'S WHAT FRIENDS ARE FOR Dionne & Friends—Arista 1-9422
[Burt Bacharach/Carole Bayer Sager] [ASC] (11/9/85 BC-1)

THAT'S WHAT GIRLS ARE MADE FOR The Spinners—Tri-Phi 1001
[Harvey Fuqua/Gwen Gordy] [BMI] (6/26/61 BCR-25)

THAT'S WHAT I LIKE *Dean Martin—Capitol 2870*
[Bob Hilliard/Jule Styne] [ASC] (8/7/54 CRt-23)
THAT'S WHAT I LIKE *Don, Dick N' Jimmy—Crown 125*
[Bob Hilliard/Jule Styne] [ASC] (10/9/54 BCRt-20)
THAT'S WHAT LOVE IS ALL ABOUT Michael Bolton—Columbia 7322
[Michael Bolton/Eric Kaz] [BMI] (8/29/87 BC-19)
THAT'S WHAT LOVE IS FOR Amy Grant—A&M 1566
[Amy Grant/Mark Mueller/Michael Omartian] [ASC] (9/28/91 BC-2)
THAT'S WHAT LOVE IS MADE OF The Miracles—Tamla 54102
[Warren Moore/Smokey Robinson/Robert Rogers] [ASC] (9/19/64 BCR-35)
THAT'S WHAT LOVE WILL MAKE YOU DO Little Milton—Stax 0111
[Milton Campbell] [BMI] (2/12/72 BCR-59)
(THAT'S) WHAT THE NITTY GRITTY IS Shirley Ellis—Congress 208
[Lincoln Chase] [BMI] (2/22/64 BCR-70)
—THAT'S WHAT THE WORLD IS TODAY see: BALL OF CONFUSION
THAT'S WHEN I CRIED Jimmy Jones—Cub 9072
[Lockie Edwards/Waldense Hall] [BMI] (7/4/60 BCR-44)
THAT'S WHEN I THINK OF YOU 1927—Atlantic 88878
[Garry Frost/Eric Weideman] [BMI] (8/26/89 B-100)
THAT'S WHEN IT HURTS Ben E. King—Atco 6288
[Bert Berns/Jerry Wexler] [BMI] (3/21/64 BCR-57)
THAT'S WHEN THE MUSIC TAKES ME Neil Sedaka—Rocket/MCA 40426
[Neil Sedaka] [BMI] (6/28/75 BCR-27)
THAT'S WHEN YOUR HEARTACHES BEGIN Elvis Presley—RCA Victor 47-6870
[Fred Fisher/Billy Hill/William Raskin] [ASC] (4/6/57 BR-43)
THAT'S WHERE I WENT WRONG The Poppy Family (Featuring Susan Jacks)—London 139
[Terry Jacks] [BMI] (8/1/70 BCR-20)
THAT'S WHERE IT'S AT Sam Cooke—RCA Victor 47-8426
[James W. Alexander/Sam Cooke] [BMI] (9/26/64 BCR-55)
THAT'S WHERE THE HAPPY PEOPLE GO The Trammps—Atlantic 3306
[Ron Baker] [BMI] (3/27/76 BCR-27)
THAT'S WHY The Party—Hollywood 64903
[Stephen Bray/Linda Mallah] [ASC] (2/23/91 BC-52)
THAT'S WHY I CRY Buddy Knox—Roulette 4120 [Jack Dixon] [BMI] (12/29/58 BR-88)
THAT'S WHY I LOVE YOU Andrew Gold—Asylum 45286
[Gene Garfin/Andrew Gold] [BMI] (1/3/76 BC-68)
THAT'S WHY (I LOVE YOU SO) Jackie Wilson—Brunswick 55121
[Billy Davis/Berry Gordy/Gwen Gordy*] [BMI] (3/21/59 BCR-13)
THAT'S WHY I WAS BORN *Janice Harper—Prep 123*
[Oliver Merritt/Vincent Rodomista] [ASC] (11/18/57 BCRt-27)
THAT'S WHY I WAS BORN *Billy Scott—Cameo 121*
[Oliver Merritt/Vincent Rodomista] [ASC] (12/9/57 Rt-27)
THAT'S WHY I WAS BORN *Margaret Whiting—Dot 15680*
[Oliver Merritt/Vincent Rodomista] [ASC] (12/16/57 Rt-27)
THAT'S WHY YOU REMEMBER Kenny Karen—Big Tree 16,007
[Ed Labunski] [BMI] (8/25/73 BCR-60)
THAT'S YOU Nat King Cole—Capitol 4369
[Chester Conn/Sammy Gallop/Nelson Riddle] [ASC] (4/25/60 R-63)
THAT'S YOUR BABY Joe Tex—Dial 4089 [Joe Tex] [BMI] (1/11/69 BCR-79)
THAT'S YOUR MISTAKE *Otis Williams And His Charms—DeLuxe 6091*
[Rudy Toombs] [BMI] (1/28/56 BCRt-39)
THAT'S YOUR MISTAKE *The Crew-Cuts—Mercury 70782*
[Rudy Toombs] [BMI] (2/10/56 Rt-43)
THAT'S YOUR SECRET Sea Level—Capricorn 0287
[Randall Bramblett/Davis Causey] [BMI] (2/25/78 BCR-50)
(THE CLICKITY CLACK SONG) FOUR LITTLE HEELS Brian Hyland—Kapp 352
[Lee Pockriss/Paul Vance] [ASC] (10/10/60 BCR-73)
THEM CHANGES *Buddy Miles & The Freedom Express—Mercury 73008*
[Buddy Miles] [BMI] (5/2/70 BC-81)
THEM CHANGES *Buddy Miles—Mercury 73228 [Buddy Miles] [BMI] (7/17/71 BCR-62)*
THEM CHANGES *Carlos Santana & Buddy Miles—Columbia 45666*
[Buddy Miles] (TSW) [ASC] (9/16/72 B-95)
THEM THAT GOT Ray Charles And His Orchestra—ABC-Paramount 10141
[Ray Charles/Ricci Harper] [BMI] (1/2/61 BCR-38)
THEME FOR YOUNG LOVERS Percy Faith And His Orchestra—Columbia 41655
[Percy Faith] [ASC] (5/9/60 BCR-35) [I]
—THEME FROM "CATS" see: MEMORY
THEME FROM THE MEDIC *Victor Young And His Singing Strings—Decca 29433*
[Victor Young] [ASC] (3/21/55 CtRt-26) [IM]
THEME FROM "MEDIC" *Les Baxter His Chorus And Orchestra—Capitol 3055*
[Victor Young] (TSW) [ASC] (4/30/55 BCtRt-5) [IM]
BLUE STAR (THE "MEDIC" THEME) *Felicia Sanders—Columbia 40508*
[Edward Heyman/Victor Young] [ASC] (5/28/55 BCRt-17)
BLUE STAR (THE "MEDIC" THEME)
Charlie Applewhite with Victor Young & His Orchestra—Decca 29553
[Edward Heyman/Victor Young] [ASC] (6/20/55 Rt-17)
BLUE STAR *The Ventures—Dolton 320*
[Victor Young] [ASC] (6/4/66 CR-81) [IM]
—THEME FROM "THE CIRCUS" see: COMPUTER GAME
—THEME FROM 2001 see: ALSO SPRACH ZARATHUSTRA
THEME FROM A SUMMER PLACE *Percy Faith And His Orchestra—Columbia 41490*
[Max Steiner] [ASC] (1/11/60 BCRt-1) [IM]
THEME FROM "A SUMMER PLACE" *Hugo Winterhalter And His Orchestra—*
RCA Victor 47-7599 [Max Steiner] [ASC] (1/18/60 Rt-3) [IM]
THEME FROM "A SUMMER PLACE" *Don Ralke—Warner Bros. 5108*
[Max Steiner] [ASC] (1/18/60 Rt-30) [IM]
(THEME FROM) "A SUMMER PLACE" *LeRoy Holmes & His Orchestra—MGM 12833*
[Max Steiner] [ASC] (2/15/60 Rt-7) [IM]
THEME FROM "A SUMMER PLACE" *Lolita—Kapp 370*
[Hans Bradtke/Mack Discant/Max Steiner] [ASC] (1/30/61 R-91) [F]
THEME FROM A SUMMER PLACE *Dick Roman—Harmon 1004*
[Mack Discant/Max Steiner] [ASC] (7/21/62 BCR-53)
THEME FROM "A SUMMER PLACE" *The Lettermen—Capitol 5437*
[Mack Discant/Max Steiner] [ASC] (6/19/65 BCR-11)
THEME FROM "A SUMMER PLACE" *The Ventures—Liberty 56115*
[Max Steiner] [ASC] (6/21/69 BCR-54) [IM]
THEME FROM ADVENTURES IN PARADISE Jerry Byrd And His Steel Guitar—Monument 419
[Lionel Newman] [BMI] (7/16/60 BCR-79) [I]
THEME FROM ANY NUMBER CAN WIN Jimmy Smith—Verve 10299
[Michel Magne] [ASC] (11/2/63 B-96) [I]
(THEME FROM) AROUND THE WORLD *Victor Young & Orchestra—Decca 30262*
[Stella Unger/Victor Young] (TSW) [ASC] (5/20/57 BCtRt-6) [IWM]*
AROUND THE WORLD *Bing Crosby—Decca 30262*
[Harold Adamson/Stella Unger/Victor Young] (TSW) [ASC] (5/20/57 BRt-7)*
(THEME FROM) AROUND THE WORLD *Mantovani And His Orchestra—London 1746*
[Stella Unger/Victor Young] [ASC] (6/8/57 BCtRt-6) [IWM]*
AROUND THE WORLD *Don Costa & His Orchestra—ABC-Paramount 9770*
[Harold Adamson/Stella Unger/Victor Young] [ASC] (6/8/57 Rt-22)*
AROUND THE WORLD *Jane Morgan—Kapp 185*
[Harold Adamson/Stella Unger/Victor Young] [ASC] (6/8/57 Rt-7)*
AROUND THE WORLD *Manny Lopez & His Orchestra—RCA Victor 47-6853*
[Stella Unger/Victor Young] [ASC] (6/8/57 Rt-29) [IWM]
AROUND THE WORLD *Lawrence Welk & His Champagne Music—Coral 61741*
[Stella Unger/Victor Young] [ASC] (6/8/57 Rt-18) [IWM]*
AROUND THE WORLD *Eddie Fisher—RCA Victor 47-6677*
[Harold Adamson/Stella Unger/Victor Young] [ASC] (7/6/57 Rt-7)*
AROUND THE WORLD IN EIGHTY DAYS *The McGuire Sisters—Coral 61856*
[Harold Adamson/Stella Unger/Victor Young] [ASC] (7/20/57 BRt-7)*
AROUND THE WORLD *Nat "King" Cole—Capitol EAP 1-813*
[Harold Adamson/Stella Unger/Victor Young] (EP) [ASC] (9/9/57 R-55)*
THEME FROM "BAA BAA BLACK SHEEP" Mike Post—Epic 50325
[Pete Carpenter/Mike Post] [BMI] (4/2/77 C-96) [I]
THEME FROM BEN CASEY Valjean—Carlton 573
[David Raksin] [ASC] (4/30/62 BCR-28) [I]
THEME FROM BONNIE AND CLYDE (FOGGY MOUNTAIN BREAKDOWN)
Flatt & Scruggs—Columbia 44380/Mercury 72739
[Earl Scruggs] [BMI] (3/2/68 BCR-55) [I]
(THEME FROM "CARNIVAL") LOVE MAKES THE WORLD GO ROUND
Jane Morgan—Kapp 390
[Bob Merrill] [ASC] (5/29/61 R-93)
THEME FROM CHARLIE'S ANGELS Henry Mancini And His Orchestra—RCA 10888
[Allyn Ferguson/Irwin Elliott Zucker] [BMI] (3/19/77 BCR-45) [I]
THEME FROM CLEOPATRA JONES Joe Simon—Spring 138
[Joe Simon] [BMI] (7/21/73 BCR-14)
THEME FROM CLOSE ENCOUNTERS Meco—Millennium 608
[John Williams] [BMI] (12/24/77 BCR-24) [I]
THEME FROM "CLOSE ENCOUNTERS OF THE THIRD KIND" John Williams—Arista 0300
[John Williams] [BMI] (12/24/77 BCR-10) [I]
THEME FROM "COME SEPTEMBER" *Dick Jacobs And His Orchestra—Coral 72436*
[Bobby Darin] [BMI] (7/3/61 Rt-84) [I]
THEME FROM COME SEPTEMBER *Bobby Darin & His Orchestra—Atco 6200*
[Bobby Darin] [BMI] (7/3/61 CtRt-55) [I]
COME SEPTEMBER *Billy Vaughn And His Orchestra—Dot 16262*
[Bobby Darin] [BMI] (9/30/61 BCtR-55) [I]
THEME FROM DOCTOR DETROIT Devo—Backstreet 52215
[Jerry Casale/Mark Mothersbaugh] [BMI] (5/21/83 BC-59)
THEME FROM DR. KILDARE (THREE STARS WILL SHINE TONIGHT)
Richard Chamberlain—MGM 13075
[Jerry Goldsmith/Pete Rugolo/Hal Winn] [BMI] (5/26/62 BCR-10)
THEME FROM DYNASTY Bill Conti—Arista 1021 [Bill Conti] [ASC] (11/6/82 BC-52) [I]
THEME FROM "EAST OF EDEN" Dick Jacobs And His Chorus And Orchestra—Coral 61692
[Leonard Rosenman] [ASC] (10/6/56 B-73) [I]
THEME FROM ELECTRIC SURFBOARD Brother Jack McDuff—Blue Note 1953
[Jack McDuff] [BMI] (12/27/69 B-95) [I]
THEME FROM "HARLOW" (LONELY GIRL) Bobby Vinton—Epic 9814
[Ray Evans/Neal Hefti/Jay Livingston] [ASC] (7/3/65 BCR-61)
THEME FROM "HATARI!" *Henry Mancini And His Orchestra—RCA Victor 47-8037*
[Henry Mancini] [ASC] (6/23/62 BCRt-76) [I]

THEME FROM HATARI *Roger Williams—Kapp 470*
[Henry Mancini] [ASC] (6/30/62 Rt-76) [I]

THE THEME FROM HILL STREET BLUES Mike Post—Elektra 47186
[Mike Post] [BMI] (8/22/81 BCR-10) [I]

THEME FROM ICE CASTLES (THROUGH THE EYES OF LOVE)
Melissa Manchester—Arista 0405
[Marvin Hamlisch/Carole Bayer Sager] [ASC] (4/28/79 BC-76)

—THEME FROM JAWS see: MAIN TITLE

THEME FROM KING KONG (PT. 1) Love Unlimited Orchestra—20th Century 2325
[John Barry] [BMI] (1/22/77 BC-68) [I]

THEME FROM LAWRENCE OF ARABIA *Ferrante & Teicher—United Artists 563*
[Maurice Jarre] [ASC] (2/2/63 BRt-84) [I]

THEME FROM LAWRENCE OF ARABIA *Bernie Leighton—Colpix 673*
[Maurice Jarre] [ASC] (3/2/63 Rt-89) [I]

THEME FROM LAWRENCE OF ARABIA *Percy Faith and his Orchestra—Columbia 42677*
[Maurice Jarre] [ASC] (3/9/63 Rt-89) [I]

THEME FROM "LOLITA" Orchestra Del Oro—Sonodor 207
[Bob Harris] [ASC] (4/23/62 R-93) [I]

(THEME FROM) LOVE STORY
Henry Mancini, His Orchestra & Chorus Henry Mancini, Piano Soloist—
RCA Victor 47-9927
[Francis Lai] [ASC] (1/9/71 BCR-9) [IM]

THEME FROM LOVE STORY *Francis Lai And His Orchestra—Paramount 0064*
[Francis Lai] [ASC] (1/23/71 BCR-26) [IM]

(WHERE DO I BEGIN) LOVE STORY *Andy Williams—Columbia 45317*
[Francis Lai/Carl Sigman] [ASC] (2/6/71 BCR-5)

THEME FROM MAGNUM P.I. Mike Post—Elektra 47400
[Pete Carpenter/Mike Post] [BMI] (2/6/82 BCR-25) [I]

THEME FROM MAHOGANY (DO YOU KNOW WHERE YOU'RE GOING TO)
Diana Ross—Motown 1377
[Gerry Goffin/Michael Masser] [BMI] (11/1/75 BCR-1)

—THEME FROM MONDO CANE see: MORE

THEME FROM MY THREE SONS *Lawrence Welk And His Orchestra—Dot 16198*
[Frank DeVol] [ASC] (3/20/61 BCtRt-20) [I]

(THEME FROM) MY THREE SONS *Bob Moore and His Orch.—Monument 437*
[Frank DeVol] [ASC] (3/27/61 CtRt-20) [I]

THEME FROM NEW YORK, NEW YORK Frank Sinatra—Reprise 49233
[Fred Ebb/John Kander] [BMI] (5/3/80 BCR-32)

THEME FROM ORDINARY PEOPLE Marvin Hamlisch—Planet 47922
[Johann Pachelbel] [ASC] (12/27/80 C-95) [I]

THEME FROM "PICNIC" *George Cates & His Orchestra—Coral 61618*
[George Duning] (Med) [ASC] (3/30/56 BCR-1) [IM]

PICNIC *Buddy Bregman & His Orchestra—RCA Victor 47-6471*
[George Duning] [ASC] (4/6/56 Rt-2) [IM]

THEME FROM "PICNIC" (MEDLEY)
Morris Stoloff Conducting The Columbia Pictures Orchestra—Decca 29888
[George Duning] (Med) [ASC] (4/13/56 BCR-1) [IM]

PICNIC *The McGuire Sisters—Coral 61627*
[Steve Allen/George Duning] [ASC] (5/4/56 BCRt-2)

THEME FROM PICNIC *Ralph Marterie And His Orchestra—Mercury 70836*
[George Duning] [ASC] (5/19/56 B-64) [IM]

THEME FROM RAGING BULL (CAVALLERIA RUSTICANA) Joel Diamond—Motown 1504
[Pietro Mascagni] [ASC] (2/14/81 BC-82) [I]

THEME FROM ROCKY (GONNA FLY NOW) *Rhythm Heritage—ABC 12243*
[Carol Connors/Bill Conti/Ayn Robbins] [BMI] (2/26/77 BC-94)

GONNA FLY NOW (THEME FROM "ROCKY") *Bill Conti—United Artists 940*
[Carol Connors/Bill Conti/Ayn Robbins] [BMI] (4/16/77 BCR-1)

GONNA FLY NOW (THEME FROM "ROCKY") *Maynard Ferguson—Columbia 10468*
[Carol Connors/Bill Conti/Ayn Robbins] [BMI] (4/16/77 BCR-28)

THEME FROM "ROCKY" (GONNA FLY NOW) *Current—Playboy 6098*
[Bill Conti] [BMI] (4/30/77 B-94) [IM]

THEME FROM ROOTS Quincy Jones—A&M 1909
[Gerald Fried] (Med) [ASC] (2/19/77 BCR-57)

THEME FROM S-EXPRESS S-Express—Capitol 44181
[Pascal Gabriel/Miles Gregory*/Mark Moore/Matt Noble*/Thomassina Smith*] [BMI]
(6/18/88 B-91)

THEME FROM SHAFT Isaac Hayes—Enterprise 9038
[Isaac Hayes] [BMI] (10/16/71 BCR-1)

(THEME FROM) SILVER CITY The Ventures—Dolton 44
[Hank Levine] [BMI] (8/7/61 BCR-76) [I]

(THEME FROM) SONG OF THE SPARROW (INSTRUMENTAL)
Mitch Miller And His Orchestra—Columbia 40772
[Margaret Miller/Mike Miller] [BMI] (10/20/56 BCR-46) [IM]

(THEME FROM) SONG OF THE SPARROW (VOCAL) Mitch Miller And His Orchestra—
Columbia 40772 [Margaret Miller/Mike Miller] [BMI] (10/20/56 R-79)

THEME FROM "SUMMER OF '42" *Peter Nero—Columbia 45399*
[Michel Legrand] [ASC] (10/16/71 BCR-21) [IM]

SUMMER OF '42 *Biddu Orchestra—Epic 50139*
[Michel Legrand] [ASC] (9/13/75 BCR-54) [IM]

THEME FROM SUPERMAN (MAIN TITLE)
John Williams/London Symphony Orchestra—Warner Bros. 8729
[John Williams] [BMI] (1/20/79 BCR-65) [I]

THEME FROM S.W.A.T. Rhythm Heritage—ABC 12135
[Barry De Vorzon] [BMI] (11/15/75 BCR-1) [I]

THEME FROM TARAS BULBA (THE WISHING STAR) *Jerry Butler—Vee-Jay 475*
[Mack David/Franz Waxman] [ASC] (11/24/62 BRt-87)

THEME FROM TARAS BULBA (THE WISHING STAR) *Maxine Starr—New Hits 3010*
[Mack David/Franz Waxman] [ASC] (11/24/62 Rt-87)

THEME FROM TARAS BULBA (THE WISHING STAR)
Ferrante & Teicher—United Artists 537
[Franz Waxman] [ASC] (11/24/62 Rt-87) [IM]

THEME FROM "TAXI" (ANGELA) Bob James—Tappan Zee 3 10896
[Bob James] [NA] (2/24/79 R-83) [I]

THEME FROM "TERMS OF ENDEARMENT" Michael Gore—Capitol 5334
[Michael Gore] [BMI] (4/14/84 BC-80) [I]

THEME FROM THE APARTMENT
Ferrante & Teicher With Their Orch. & Chrous—United Artists 231
[Charles Williams] [ASC] (7/9/60 BCR-6) [I]

THEME FROM THE APARTMENT *Meco—Arista 0660*
[Charles Williams] (Med) [ASC] (2/13/82 BCR-35) [I]

THEME FROM THE BLACK HOLE Parliament—Casablanca 2235
[George Clinton/William Earl Collins/Walter Morrison/James Vitti] [BMI] (3/15/80 R-99)

(THEME FROM) "THE DARK AT THE TOP OF THE STAIRS"
Percy Faith and his Orchestra—Columbia 41796
[Max Steiner] [ASC] (10/10/60 CtRt-72) [I]

(THEME FROM) "THE DARK AT THE TOP OF THE STAIRS"
Frank Chacksfield & His Orchestra—London 1945
[Max Steiner] [ASC] (10/10/60 Rt-73) [I]

(THEME FROM) THE DARK AT THE TOP OF THE STAIRS
Bob Crosby & The Bobcats—Dot 16141
[Max Steiner] [ASC] (10/10/60 Rt-91) [I]

THEME FROM THE DARK AT THE TOP OF THE STAIRS *Chet Atkins—RCA Victor 47-7796*
[Max Steiner] [ASC] (10/10/60 Rt-72) [I]

THEME FROM THE DARK AT THE TOP OF THE STAIRS *Ernie Freeman—Imperial 5693*
[Max Steiner] [ASC] (10/22/60 BCtRt-70) [I]

THEME FROM THE DUKES OF HAZZARD (GOOD OL' BOYS) Waylon—RCA 12067
[Waylon Jennings] [BMI] (9/13/80 BCR-7)

GREAT IMPOSTER *The Piltdown Men—Capitol 4488*
[Henry Mancini] [ASC] (2/13/61 Rt-83) [I]

THEME FROM THE GREAT IMPOSTER
Henry Mancini And His Orchestra—RCA Victor 47-7830
[Henry Mancini] [ASC] (2/13/61 BCRt-83) [I]

THE THEME FROM "THE GREATEST AMERICAN HERO" (BELIEVE IT OR NOT)
Joey Scarbury—Elektra 47147
[Stephen Geyer/Mike Post] [BMI] (5/9/81 BCR-1)

THE HIGH AND THE MIGHTY *Les Baxter & His Orchestra—Capitol 2845*
[Dimitri Tiomkin] [ASC] (7/10/54 BCtR-4) [IM]

THE HIGH AND THE MIGHTY *Johnny Desmond—Coral 61232*
[Dimitri Tiomkin/Ned Washington] [ASC] (7/24/54 BCt-PRE)

THE HIGH AND THE MIGHTY *Victor Young And His Singing Strings—Decca 29203*
[Dimitri Tiomkin] [ASC] (7/24/54 BCtR-PRE) [IM]

THE HIGH AND THE MIGHTY *LeRoy Holmes & His Orchestra—MGM 11761*
[Dimitri Tiomkin] [ASC] (7/24/54 CtR-PRE) [IM]

THEME FROM THE HIGH AND THE MIGHTY *Meco—Arista 0660*
[Dimitri Tiomkin] (Med) [ASC] (2/13/82 BCR-35) [IM]

—THEME FROM THE KARATE KID PART II see: GLORY OF LOVE

THEME FROM THE MEN Isaac Hayes—Enterprise 9058
[Isaac Hayes] [BMI] (10/7/72 BCR-34) [I]

THEME FROM "THE PROPHET" (PLEASURE IS A FREEDOM SONG/ON LOVE)
Richard Harris—Atlantic 3238
[Kahlil Gibran] [BMI] (3/1/75 CR-86)

THEME FROM THE PROUD ONES *Nelson Riddle And His Orchestra—Capitol 3472*
[Lionel Newman] [BMI] (7/7/56 BCRt-27) [IM]

THEME FROM "THE PROUD ONES" *Johnny Desmond—Coral 61663*
[Johnny Desmond/Ruth Keddington/Lionel Newman] [BMI] (7/13/56 Rt-57)

THEME FROM "THE PROUD ONES" *The Three Suns—RCA Victor 47-6574*
[Lionel Newman] [BMI] (7/13/56 Rt-33) [IM]

THEME FROM "THE PROUD ONES" *Buddy Morrow & His Orchestra—Wing 90079*
[Lionel Newman] [BMI] (7/13/56 Rt-57) [IM]

THEME FROM THE PROUD ONES *LeRoy Holmes And His Orchestra—MGM 12275*
[Lionel Newman] [BMI] (7/13/56 BRt-39) [IM]

THEME FROM "THE PROUD ONES" *Lionel Newman & His Orchesra—Columbia 40717*
[Lionel Newman] [BMI] (8/4/56 B-72) [IM]

(THEME FROM) THE PROUD ONES *Fred Lowery—Decca 30001*
[Lionel Newman] [BMI] (8/25/56 Rt-41) [IM]

—THEME FROM THE RAT RACE see: MAIN TITLE

SUNDOWNERS *Billy Vaughn And His Orchestra—Dot 16133*
[Dimitri Tiomkin] [ASC] (9/26/60 BCtRt-34) [I]

***THEME FROM THE SUNDOWNERS** Felix Slatkin Orchestra And Chorus—Liberty 55282 [Dimitri Tiomkin] [ASC] (9/26/60 BCtRt-34) [I]*

***THEME FROM THE SUNDOWNERS** Eddie Calvert—ABC-Paramount 10157 [Dimitri Tiomkin] [ASC] (10/10/60 Rt-52) [I]*

***THEME FROM THE SUNDOWNERS** Mantovani And His Orchestra—London 1946 [Dimitri Tiomkin] [ASC] (11/7/60 BRt-34) [I]*

—THEME FROM THE THREE PENNY OPERA see: MACK THE KNIFE

THEME FROM THE TV SHOW CHEERS (WHERE EVERYBODY KNOWS YOUR NAME) Gary Portnoy—Applause 106 [Judy Hart Angelo/Gary Portnoy] [BMI] (4/30/83 BC-83)

***THEME FROM "THE UNFORGIVEN" (THE NEED FOR LOVE)** Don Costa And His Orchestra And Chorus—United Artists 221 [Dimitri Tiomkin] [ASC] (5/2/60 BCRt-18) [IM]*

***THE UNFORGIVEN (THE NEED FOR LOVE)** The McGuire Sisters—Coral 62196 [Dimitri Tiomkin/Ned Washington] [ASC] (5/9/60 Rt-43)*

THEME FROM THE WILD ANGELS Davie Allan And The Arrows—Tower 267 [Mike Curb] [BMI] (11/12/66 B-99) [I]

THEME FROM "THE WONDERFUL WORLD OF THE BROTHERS GRIMM" David Rose And His Orchestra—MGM 13086 [Bob Merrill] [ASC] (8/4/62 R-100) [I]

***THEME FROM TUNES OF GLORY** Cambridge Strings & Singers—London 1960 [Traditional] [BMI] (1/30/61 BCtRt-40) [I]*

***TUNES OF GLORY** Mitch Miller & His Orch. And Chorus—Columbia 41941 [Traditional] [BMI] (1/30/61 BCtRt-40) [I]*

***(THEME FROM) VALLEY OF THE DOLLS** Dionne Warwick—Scepter 12203 [André Previn/Dory Previn] [ASC] (1/20/68 BCR-1)*

***VALLEY OF THE DOLLS** King Curtis & The Kingpins—Atco 6582 [André Previn] [ASC] (6/15/68 B-83) [IM]*

THEME FROM "WAR AND PEACE" (THE MAID OF NOVGOROD) Richard Maltby And His Orchestra—Vik 0229 [Nino Rota] [ASC] (11/17/56 Rt*-83) [IM]

THEME OF STAR TREK II (MAIN TITLE) Soundtrack—Atlantic 4057 [Alexander Courage*/James Horner] [ASC] (7/31/82 C-95)

THEME SONG FROM SONG FOR A SUMMER NIGHT (PTS. 1 & 2) Mitch Miller with His Orch. & Chorus—Columbia 40730 [Robert Allen] [ASC] (7/28/56 BCR-9) [I]

THEME SONG FROM "WHICH WAY IS UP" Stargard—MCA 40825 [Norman Whitfield] [BMI] (1/14/78 BCR-21)

THEMES FROM E.T. (THE EXTRA-TERRESTRIAL) Walter Murphy—MCA 52099 [John Williams] [BMI] (7/31/82 BC-32) [I]

***MAIN TITLE AND MOLLY O FROM THE MAN WITH THE GOLDEN ARM** Dick Jacobs And His Chorus And Orchestra—Coral 61606 [Elmer Bernstein/Sylvia Fine] [ASC] (3/9/56 BCtRt-9)*

***MOLLY-O** Ralph Young—Decca 29833 [Elmer Bernstein/Sylvia Fine] [ASC] (3/9/56 Rt-14)*

***MAIN TITLE GOLDEN ARM** Les Elgart and His Orchestra—Columbia 40664 [Elmer Bernstein/Sylvia Fine] [ASC] (3/16/56 BRt-14) [I]*

***THEMES FROM THE MAN WITH THE GOLDEN ARM** Billy May And His Orchestra—Capitol 3372 [Elmer Bernstein/Sylvia Fine] [ASC] (3/16/56 BCtRt-12) [I]*

***THEMES FROM THE MAN WITH THE GOLDEN ARM** Richard Maltby And His Orchestra—Vik 0196 [Elmer Bernstein/Sylvia Fine] [ASC] (3/17/56 BCtRt-9) [I]*

***MAIN TITLE FROM THE MAN WITH THE GOLDEN ARM** Elmer Bernstein And Orchestra—Decca 29869 [Elmer Bernstein/Sylvia Fine] [ASC] (3/23/56 BCtRt-9) [I]*

***MAIN TITLE FROM "THE MAN WITH THE GOLDEN ARM"** Buddy Morrow And His Orchestra—Wing 90063 [Elmer Bernstein/Sylvia Fine] [ASC] (4/21/56 B-82) [I]*

THEMES FROM THE WIZARD OF OZ Meco—Millennium 620 [Harold Arlen/E.Y. Harburg] [NA] (9/2/78 BCR-34)

THEN CAME YOU Dionne Warwicke And Spinners—Atlantic 3029 [Sherman Marshall/Phil Pugh] [BMI] (7/20/74 BCR-1)

THEN CAME YOU T.P.E.—MicMac 2564 [Amy Friedman] [ASC] (11/30/91 B-91)

THEN HE KISSED ME The Crystals—Philles 115 [Jeff Barry/Ellie Greenwich/Phil Spector] [BMI] (8/17/63 BCR-4)

THEN I'LL COUNT AGAIN Johnny Tillotson—MGM 13344 [Chip Taylor] [BMI] (5/15/65 BCR-57)

THEN SHE'S A LOVER Roy Clark—Dot 17335 [Bobby Russell] [ASC] (1/17/70 BCR-71)

***THEN YOU CAN TELL ME GOODBYE** The Casinos—Fraternity 977 [John D. Loudermilk] [BMI] (1/7/67 BCR-2)*

***THEN YOU CAN TELL ME GOODBYE** Eddy Arnold—RCA Victor 47-9606 [John D. Loudermilk] [BMI] (8/24/68 BCR-69)*

***THEN YOU CAN TELL ME GOODBYE** Glen Campbell—Capitol 4245 [John D. Loudermilk] (Med) [BMI] (3/27/76 BCR-27)*

***THEN YOU CAN TELL ME GOODBYE** Toby Beau—RCA 11670 [John D. Loudermilk] [BMI] (8/4/79 BCR-57)*

THERE AIN'T NO WAY Lobo—Big Tree 16,012 [Kent LaVoie] (TSW) [ASC] (12/8/73 BCR-50)

THERE ARE SUCH THINGS The Modernaires—Coral 61779 [Stanley Adams/Abel Baer/George Meyer] (Med) [ASC] (2/16/57 R-72)

THERE BUT FOR FORTUNE Joan Baez—Vanguard 35031 [Phil Ochs] [ASC] (9/4/65 BCR-31)

THERE BUT FOR THE GRACE OF GOD GO I Machine—RCA/Hologram 11456 [August Darnell/Kevin Nance] [BMI] (3/17/79 BCR-77)

THERE COMES A TIME Jack Scott—Carlton 519 [Jack Scott] [BMI] (10/10/59 BCR-54)

THERE GOES ANOTHER LOVE SONG The Outlaws—Arista 0150 [Hughie Thomasson/Monte Yoho] [BMI] (9/6/75 BCR-26)

***THERE GOES MY BABY** The Drifters—Atlantic 2025 [Ben E. King/Jerry Leiber*/Lover Patterson/Mike Stoller*/George Treadwell] [BMI] (6/1/59 BCR-1)*

***THERE GOES MY BABY** Donna Summer—Geffen 29291 [Ben E. King/Jerry Leiber*/Lover Patterson/Mike Stoller*/George Treadwell] [BMI] (8/11/84 BC-21)*

***THERE GOES MY EVERYTHING** Jack Greene—Decca 32023 [Dallas Frazier] [BMI] (1/7/67 B-65)*

***THERE GOES MY EVERYTHING** Engelbert Humperdinck—Parrot 40015 [Dallas Frazier] [BMI] (6/24/67 BCR-20)*

***THERE GOES MY EVERYTHING** Elvis Presley—RCA Victor 47-9960 [Dallas Frazier] (TSW) [BMI] (12/26/70 BCR-15)*

***THERE GOES MY HEART** Four Aces—Decca 29435 [Benny Davis/Abner Silver] [ASC] (2/21/55 CR-15)*

***THERE GOES MY HEART** Joni James—MGM 12706 [Benny Davis/Abner Silver] [ASC] (9/8/58 BCR-8)*

THERE GOES (MY HEART AGAIN) Fats Domino—ABC-Paramount 10444 [Fats Domino] [BMI] (5/18/63 BCR-59)

THERE GOES MY LOVE The Fantastics—RCA Victor 47-7572 [William Forrest] [NA] (12/28/59 R-100)

THERE GOES THE LOVER Gene Chandler—Brunswick 55339 [Carl Davis/Otis Leavill] [BMI] (9/2/67 BR-96)

THERE IS The Dells—Cadet 5590 [Robert Eugene Miller/Raynard Miner] [BMI] (1/20/68 BCR-17)

THERE IS A MOUNTAIN Donovan—Epic 10212 [Donovan Leitch] [BMI] (8/12/67 BCR-9)

THERE IS A TAVERN IN THE TOWN Four Aces—Decca 29395 [Traditional] [NA] (1/17/55 R-47)

THERE IS NO GREATER LOVE The Wanderers—MGM 13082 [Isham Jones/Marty Symes] [ASC] (7/28/62 BCR-65)

***THERE IS SOMETHING ON YOUR MIND** Big Jay McNeely and Band—Swingin' 614 [Cecil (Big Jay) McNeely] [BMI] (5/25/59 BCR-41)*

***THERE IS SOMETHING ON YOUR MIND PART TWO** Bobby Marchan—Fire 1022 [Cecil (Big Jay) McNeely] [BMI] (6/13/60 BCR-17)*

***THERE'S SOMETHING ON YOUR MIND** Baby Ray—Imperial 66216 [Cecil (Big Jay) McNeely] [BMI] (12/3/66 BCR-69)*

THERE IT GOES AGAIN Barbara And The Uniques—Arden 3001 [Eugene Record] [BMI] (11/28/70 BCR-73)

THERE IT IS - PART 1 James Brown—Polydor 14125 [James Brown] [BMI] (4/29/72 BCR-38)

THERE IT IS Tyrone Davis—Dakar 4523 [Leo Graham/Raymond Haley] [BMI] (7/28/73 BCR-32)

***THERE I'VE SAID IT AGAIN** Sam Cooke—Keen 82105 [Redd Evans/Dave Mann] [ASC] (10/12/59 BCR-64)*

***THERE! I'VE SAID IT AGAIN** Bobby Vinton—Epic 9638 [Redd Evans/Dave Mann] [ASC] (11/23/63 BCR-1)*

***THERE MUST BE A WAY** Joni James—MGM 12746 [Sammy Gallop/David Saxon] [ASC] (1/12/59 BCR-15)*

***THERE MUST BE A WAY** Jimmy Roselli—United Artists 50179 [Sammy Gallop/David Saxon] [ASC] (7/1/67 BCR-87)*

THERE MUST BE AN ANGEL (PLAYING WITH MY HEART) Eurythmics—RCA 14160 [Annie Lennox/David A. Stewart] [ASC] (8/3/85 BC-22)

THERE NEVER WAS A NIGHT SO BEAUTIFUL Perry Como—RCA Victor 47-5749 [John Rox] [BMI] (7/3/54 C-PRE)

THERE NEVER WAS A TIME Jeannie C. Riley—Plantation 16 [Margaret Lewis/Mira Smith] [BMI] (3/22/69 BCR-75)

THERE OUGHTA BE A LAW Mickey & Sylvia—Vik 0267 [Mickey Baker/Joyce Bennett] [BMI] (3/30/57 BCR-13)

THERE SHE GOES Jerry Wallace—Challenge 59098 [Durwood Haddock/Eddie Miller/W.S. Stevenson‡] [BMI] (12/5/60 BCR-13)

THERE SHE GOES The La's—London 869 370 [Lee Mavers] [BMI] (7/20/91 BC-47)

THERE SHOULD BE RULES (PROTECTING FOOLS WHO FALL IN LOVE) Betty Madigan—MGM 12094 [Robert I. Allen/John Benson Brooks/Joseph Darion] [ASC] (11/19/55 BR-54)

THERE STANDS THE DOOR We Five—A&M 800 [Herb Jackson] [BMI] (6/4/66 CR-95)

THERE WAS A FUNGUS AMONG US Hugh Barrett and The Victors—Madison 164 [Terry Noland] [BMI] (7/15/61 C-98)

(THERE WAS A) TALL OAK TREE Dorsey Burnette—Era 3012 [Dorsey Burnette] [BMI] (2/1/60 BCR-18)

***THERE WAS A TIME** James Brown And The Famous Flames—King 6144 [James Brown/Bud Hobgood] [BMI] (1/20/68 BCR-23)*

THERE WAS A TIME *The Dapps Featuring Alfred Ellis—King 6169 [James Brown/Bud Hobgood] [BMI] (7/27/68 R-82) [IWM]*

THERE WAS A TIME *Gene Chandler—Brunswick 55383 [James Brown/Bud Hobgood] [BMI] (9/21/68 BCR-63)*

THERE WILL COME A DAY (I'M GONNA HAPPEN TO YOU) Smokey Robinson—Tamla 54279 [Brenda Sutton/Mike Sutton/Kathy Wakefield] [ASC] (2/19/77 BCR-42)

THERE WILL NEVER BE ANOTHER TONIGHT Bryan Adams—A&M 1588 [Bryan Adams/Mutt Lange/Jim Vallance] [ASC] (12/21/91 BC-8)

THERE WILL NEVER BE ANOTHER YOU Chris Montez—A&M 810 [Mack Gordon/Harry Warren] [ASC] (8/13/66 BCR-31)

THERE WILL NEVER BE ANY PEACE (UNTIL GOD IS SEATED AT THE CONFERENCE TABLE) The Chi-Lites—Brunswick 55512 [Barbara Acklin/Eugene Record] [BMI] (6/1/74 BR-63)

THERE WON'T BE ANY SNOW (CHRISTMAS IN THE JUNGLE) Derrik Roberts—Roulette 4656 [Lee Pockriss/Paul Vance] [ASC] (12/11/65 CR-58)

THERE WON'T BE ANYMORE Charlie Rich—RCA Victor 0195 [Charlie Rich] [BMI] (1/26/74 BCR-15)

THERE WON'T BE NO COUNTRY MUSIC (THERE WON'T BE NO ROCK 'N' ROLL) C.W. McCall—Polydor 14310 [Chip Davis/Bill Fries] [SE] (3/20/76 BC-52)

THERE YOU ARE Johnny Mathis—Columbia 42156 [Clyde Otis/Chris Towns] [BMI] (9/25/61 R-94)

THERE YOU GO Johnny Cash and the Tennessee Two—Sun 258 [Johnny Cash] [BMI] (12/29/56 CR-45)

THERE YOU GO Edwin Starr—Soul 35103 [Chuck Middleton*/Edwin Starr] [BMI] (6/30/73 BCR-74)

THERE'LL BE NO BACKIN' OUT Mickey And Sylvia—Vik 0297 [Mickey Baker/Joseph Robinson] [BMI] (11/11/57 R-76)

THERE'LL BE NO NEXT TIME Jackie Wilson—Brunswick 55221 [Bobby Adams/Alonzo Tucker] [BMI] (1/8/62 BCR-75)

THERE'LL BE NO TEARDROPS TONIGHT *Tony Bennett—Columbia 40169 [Hank Williams] [BMI] (5/29/54 B-PRE)*

THERE'LL BE NO TEARDROPS TONIGHT *Adam Wade—Epic 9557 [Hank Williams] [BMI] (12/29/62 C-95)*

(THERE'LL BE) PEACE IN THE VALLEY (FOR ME) *Elvis Presley—RCA Victor EPA-4054 [Thomas A. Dorsey] [BMI] (4/6/57 BCR-25)*

(THERE'LL BE) PEACE IN THE VALLEY (FOR ME) *Pat Boone—Dot DEP-1056 [Thomas A. Dorsey] (EP) [BMI] (5/11/57 R-60)*

(THERE'LL BE) PEACE IN THE VALLEY (FOR ME) *Elvis Presley—RCA Victor LOC-1035 [Thomas A. Dorsey] (EP) [BMI] (12/30/57 R-49)*

(THERE'LL BE) PEACE IN THE VALLEY (FOR ME) *Red Foley—Decca 30080 [Thomas A. Dorsey] [BMI] (11/3/56 R-78)*

THERE'LL BE SAD SONGS (TO MAKE YOU CRY) Billy Ocean—Jive 9465 [Wayne Brathwaite/Barry Eastmond/Billy Ocean] [ASC] (4/19/86 BC-1)

(THERE'LL COME A DAY WHEN) EV'RY LITTLE BIT HURTS Bobby Vee—Liberty 55751 [Marilyn Garrett/Dottie Wayne/Ben Weisman] [ASC] (12/5/64 BCR-84)

THERE'LL COME A TIME Betty Everett—Uni 55100 [Eugene Record/Floyd Smith] [BMI] (1/18/69 BCR-26)

THERE'LL NEVER BE Switch—Gordy 7159 [Bobby DeBarge] [ASC] (9/16/78 BCR-36)

THERE'S A BETTER DAY COMIN' Crazy Elephant—Bell 846 [Ritchie Cordell/Jerry Kasenetz/Jeff Katz/Robert L. King] [BMI] (11/29/69 R-82)

THERE'S A CHANCE WE CAN MAKE IT Blues Magoos—Mercury 72660 [Ronald Gilbert/Ralph Scala] [BMI] (3/11/67 BCR-76)

THERE'S A GIRL Jan & Dean—Dore 531 [Lou Adler/Herb Alpert] [BMI] (10/24/59 BC-80)

THERE'S A GOLD MINE IN THE SKY *Pat Boone—Dot 15602 [Charles Kenny/Nick Kenny] [ASC] (8/3/57 BCRt-8)*

THERE'S A GOLD MINE IN THE SKY *Bing Crosby—Decca 25001 [Charles Kenny/Nick Kenny] [ASC] (8/26/57 Rt-10)*

THERE'S A GOLD MINE IN THE SKY *Nat "King" Cole—Capitol EAP 1-813 [Charles Kenny/Nick Kenny] (EP) [ASC] (9/9/57 R-55)*

THERE'S A KIND OF HUSH *Herman's Hermits—MGM 13681 [Les Reed/Geoff Stephens] [BMI] (2/11/67 BCR-3)*

THERE'S A KIND OF HUSH (ALL OVER THE WORLD) *Carpenters—A&M 1800 [Les Reed/Geoff Stephens] [BMI] (2/28/76 BCR-12)*

THERE'S A MOON OUT TONIGHT The Capris—Old Town 1094 [Alfonso Gentile/Joseph Luccisano/Alfred Striano] [BMI] (12/26/60 BCR-3)

THERE'S A NEW MOON OVER MY SHOULDER Bonnie Guitar—Dot 15612 [Lee Blastic/Jimmie H. Davis/Ekko Whelan] [BMI] (8/19/57 R-38)

THERE'S A PARTY GOING ON Yvonne—Cutting 228 [Elis Pacheco] [BMI] (1/27/90 BC-88)

THERE'S A PLACE The Beatles—Tollie 9001 [John Lennon/Paul McCartney] [ASC] (4/11/64 B-74)

THERE'S A STAR SPANGLED BANNER WAVING #2 (THE BALLAD OF FRANCIS POWERS) *Red River Dave—Savoy 3020 [Shelby Darnell/Dave McEnery/Paul Roberts] [ASC] (6/27/60 BCRt-64)*

THERE'S A STAR SPANGLED BANNER WAVING SOMEWHERE *Tommy Dee—Challenge 59083 [Shelby Darnell/Dave McEnery/Paul Roberts] [ASC] (7/4/60 Rt-87)*

THERE'S A STAR SPANGLED BANNER WAVING SOMEWHERE *Betty Johnson—Coed 532 [Shelby Darnell/Dave McEnery/Paul Roberts] [ASC] (7/11/60 Rt-87)*

THERE'S ALWAYS ME Elvis Presley With The Jordanaires—RCA Victor 47-9287 [Don Robertson] [ASC] (8/26/67 BCR-45)

(THERE'S) ALWAYS SOMETHING THERE TO REMIND ME *Lou Johnson—Big Hill 552 [Burt Bacharach/Hal David] [ASC] (8/8/64 BCR-49)*

(THERE'S) ALWAYS SOMETHING THERE TO REMIND ME *Sandie Shaw—Reprise 0320 [Burt Bacharach/Hal David] [ASC] (11/28/64 BCR-49)*

(THERE'S) ALWAYS SOMETHING THERE TO REMIND ME *Dionne Warwick—Scepter 12226 [Burt Bacharach/Hal David] [ASC] (8/24/68 BCR-60)*

ALWAYS SOMETHING THERE TO REMIND ME *R.B. Greaves—Atco 6726 [Burt Bacharach/Hal David] [ASC] (1/24/70 BCR-20)*

ALWAYS SOMETHING THERE TO REMIND ME *Naked Eyes—EMI-America 8155 [Burt Bacharach/Hal David] [ASC] (3/12/83 BC-7)*

"THERE'S GONNA BE A" SHOWDOWN Archie Bell & The Drells—Atlantic 2583 [Kenneth Gamble/Leon Huff] [BMI] (12/14/68 BCR-18)

THERE'S GOT TO BE A WORD! The Innocence—Kama Sutra 214 [Don Ciccone] [BMI] (11/19/66 BCR-33)

THERE'S GOT TO BE RAIN IN YOUR LIFE (TO APPRECIATE THE SUNSHINE) Dorothy Norwood—GRC 1011 [Dorothy Norwood] [BMI] (1/19/74 BCR-74)

—THERE'S NEVER BEEN ANYONE ELSE BUT YOU see: GIANT

THERE'S NO EASY WAY James Ingram—Qwest 29318 [Barry Mann] [BMI] (4/7/84 BC-58)

THERE'S NO FOOL LIKE A YOUNG FOOL Tab Hunter—Warner Bros. 5051 [Craig Shane/Rod Sherwood] [ASC] (4/20/59 BCR-52)

(THERE'S) NO GETTIN' OVER ME Ronnie Milsap—RCA 12264 [Walt Aldridge/Tom Brasfield] [ASC] (6/27/81 BCR-5)

THERE'S NO LIVING WITHOUT YOUR LOVING Peter And Gordon—Capitol 5650 [Jerome Harris/Paul Kaufman] [BMI] (5/7/66 BCR-50)

THERE'S NO ME WITHOUT YOU The Manhattans—Columbia 45838 [Edward Bivins] [BMI] (5/5/73 BCR-29)

THERE'S NO OTHER (LIKE MY BABY) The Crystals—Philles 100 [Leroy R. Bates/Phil Spector] [BMI] (11/4/61 BCR-18)

THERE'S NO OTHER WAY Blur—SBK/Food 07374 [Damon Albarn/Graham Coxon/Alex James/Dave Rowntree] [ASC] (12/28/91 C-61)

(THERE'S NO PLACE LIKE) HOME FOR THE HOLIDAYS Perry Como—RCA Victor 47-5950 [Robert Allen/Al Stillman] [ASC] (11/22/54 BCR-12)

THERE'S NO SUCH THING AS LOVE Anthony Newley—London 5201 [Ian Fraser/Anthony Newley] [BMI] (3/30/63 R-99)

THERE'S NO SURF IN CLEVELAND The Euclid Beach Band—Epic/Cleveland Int'l 50584 [Jim Girard/Richard Reising] [BMI] (8/12/78 R-80)

THERE'S NOTHING BETTER THAN LOVE Luther Vandross (Duet With Gregory Hines)—Epic 06978 [John Vernon Anderson/Luther Vandross] [ASC] (3/14/87 BC-46)

THERE'S NOTHING I CAN SAY Rick Nelson—Decca 31656 [Christian Sarrel/Al Stillman] [ASC] (8/22/64 BCR-47) [FDE]

THERE'S NOTHING LIKE LOVE Jackie Wilson And Linda Hopkins—Brunswick 55224 [Leroy Kirkland/Pearl Woods] [BMI] (3/31/62 C-95)

THERE'S ONLY ONE OF YOU The Four Lads—Columbia 41136 [Robert Allen/Al Stillman] [ASC] (3/10/58 BCR-13)

THERE'S ONLY YOU *Don Rondo—Jubilee 5297 [Billy Mure] [BMI] (9/9/57 BCRt-41)*

THERE'S ONLY YOU *Don Cornell—Coral 61879 [Billy Mure] [BMI] (9/16/57 Rt-41)*

THERE'S SO MUCH LOVE ALL AROUND ME The Three Degrees—Roulette 7102 [Gary Illingworth/Paul Vance] [ASC] (5/8/71 BCR-90)

THERE'S THE GIRL Heart—Capitol 44089 [Holly Knight/Nancy Wilson] [ASC] (11/7/87 BC-12)

THESE ARE NOT MY PEOPLE Johnny Rivers—Imperial 66360 [Joe South] [BMI] (2/22/69 BCR-42)

(THESE ARE) THE CLOSING CREDITS Robert Goulet—Columbia 42740 [Bugs Bower/Jack Wolf] [ASC] (4/20/63 R-95)

(THESE ARE) THE YOUNG YEARS Floyd Cramer—RCA Victor 47-8171 [Johnny Cowell] [BMI] (5/4/63 CR-97) [I]

THESE ARMS OF MINE Otis Redding—Volt 103 [Otis Redding] [BMI] (5/4/63 BCR-80)

THESE BOOTS ARE MADE FOR WALKIN' *Nancy Sinatra—Reprise 0432 [Lee Hazlewood] [ASC] (1/22/66 BCR-1)*

THESE BOOTS (ARE MADE FOR WALKIN') *Kon Kan—Atlantic 88828 [Lee Hazlewood] (Med) [ASC] (9/2/89 BC-58)*

THESE DREAMS Heart—Capitol 5541 [Martin Page/Bernie Taupin] [ASC] (1/18/86 BC-1)

THESE EYES *The Guess Who—RCA Victor 74-0102 [Randy Bachman/Burton Cummings] [BMI] (4/5/69 BCR-3)*

THESE EYES *Jr. Walker & The All Stars—Soul 35067 [Randy Bachman/Burton Cummings] [BMI] (10/25/69 BCR-16)*

THESE FOOLISH THINGS James Brown And The Famous Flames—King 5767 [Harry Link/Holt Marvell/Jack Strachey] [ASC] (7/27/63 BCR-55)

THESE HANDS *Len Dresslar—Mercury 70774 [Eddie Noack] [BMI] (1/28/56 BCRt-40)*

THESE HANDS *Jeffrey Clay—Coral 61567 [Eddie Noack] [BMI] (2/3/56 Rt-40)*

THESE HANDS *Johnny Oliver—MGM 12164 [Eddie Noack] [BMI] (2/3/56 Rt-40)*

THESE HANDS *Hank Snow The Singing Ranger And The Rainbow Ranch Boys—RCA Victor 47-6379 [Eddie Noack] [BMI] (2/3/56 Rt-40)*

THESE HANDS *Tex Ritter—Capitol 3324 [Eddie Noack] [BMI] (3/9/56 Rt-45)*

THESE HANDS (SMALL BUT MIGHTY) Bobby Bland—Duke 385
[Deadric Malone] [BMI] (8/28/65 BCR-53)

THESE THINGS I OFFER YOU (FOR A LIFETIME) The Playmates—Roulette 4227
[Bennie Benjamin/Morty Nevins/George David Weiss] [ASC] (3/7/60 R-88)

THESE THINGS WILL KEEP ME LOVING YOU The Velvelettes—Soul 35025
[Johnny Bristol/Harvey Fuqua] [ASC] (10/22/66 CR-88)

THESE TIMES ARE HARD FOR LOVERS John Waite—EMI America 43018
[Desmond Child/John Waite] [ASC] (6/20/87 BC-52)

THESE WORLDLY WONDERS Patti Page—Mercury 71294
[Phil Medley] [BMI] (3/31/58 R-36)

THEY CAN'T TAKE AWAY OUR MUSIC
Eric Burdon And War Featuring Sharon Scott And The Beautiful New Born Children Of Southern California—MGM 14196
[Thomas Allen/Harold Brown/Morris Dickerson/Jerry Goldstein*/Lonnie Jordan/Charles Miller/Lee Oskar/Howard Scott] [ASC] (12/19/70 BCR-37)

THEY DON'T KNOW Tracey Ullman—MCA/Stiff 52347
[Kirsty MacColl] [BMI] (2/25/84 BC-8)

THEY DON'T MAKE 'EM LIKE THAT ANY MORE Reunion—RCA Victor 10252
[Marc Bellack/Tony Jaffe/Joey Levine] [BMI] (5/10/75 R-94)

THEY DON'T MAKE LOVE LIKE THEY USED TO Eddy Arnold—RCA Victor 47-9667
[Red Lane] [BMI] (11/30/68 BCR-73)

—THEY DON'T WRITE 'EM see: BREAKUP SONG

THEY JUST CAN'T STOP IT THE (GAMES PEOPLE PLAY) The Spinners—Atlantic 3284
[Bruce Hawes/Joseph Jefferson/Charles Simmons] [BMI] (8/2/75 BCR-1)

—THEY LONG TO BE CLOSE TO YOU see: CLOSE TO YOU

THEY REMIND ME TOO MUCH OF YOU
Elvis Presley With The Mello Men—RCA Victor 47-8134
[Don Robertson] [ASC] (2/23/63 BC-53)

THEY SAY YOU'RE LAUGHING AT ME (WHILE I'M CRYING FOR YOU)
Al Hibbler—Decca 29543
[Jerry Livingston/Dok Stanford] [ASC] (6/20/55 R-29)

THEY WERE DOIN' THE MAMBO Vaughn Monroe with Orchestra—RCA Victor 47-5767
[Joseph Francis Burke/Don Raye] [ASC] (7/10/54 BCR-8)

THEY'RE COMING TO TAKE ME AWAY, HA-HAAA! *Napoleon XIV—Warner Bros. 5831*
[Jerry Samuels] [ASC] (7/23/66 BCR-1)

THEY'RE COMING TO TAKE ME AWAY, HA-HAAA! *Napoleon XIV—Warner Bros. 7726*
[Jerry Samuels] [ASC] (8/18/73 BR-73)

THEY'RE HERE Boots Walker—Rust 5115 [Lou Zerato] [ASC] (6/10/67 BR-77)

THIEF OF HEARTS Melissa Manchester—Casablanca 880308
[Keith Forsey/Melissa Manchester/Giorgio Moroder] [ASC] (11/24/84 B-86)

THIEVES IN THE TEMPLE Prince—Paisley Park 19751 [Prince] [ASC] (8/4/90 BC-1)

THIGHS HIGH (GRIP YOUR HIPS AND MOVE) Tom Browne—Arista/GRP 2510
[Tom Browne/Sekou Bunch/Dave Grusin*/Thomassina Smith] [BMI] (2/28/81 R-70)

THIN LINE BETWEEN LOVE AND HATE *The Persuaders—Atco 6822*
[Jackie Members/Richard Poindexter/Robert Poindexter] [BMI] (8/14/71 BCR-9)

THIN LINE BETWEEN LOVE AND HATE *The Pretenders—Sire 29249*
[Jackie Members/Richard Poindexter/Robert Poindexter] [BMI] (6/30/84 B-83)

A THING OF THE PAST The Shirelles—Scepter 1220
[Bob Brass/Irwin Levine] [BMI] (7/1/61 BCR-22)

THINGS *Bobby Darin—Atco 6229 [Bobby Darin] [BMI] (7/7/62 BCR-3)*

THINGS *Anne Murray—Capitol 4329 [Bobby Darin] [BMI] (10/30/76 B-89)*

THINGS CAN ONLY GET BETTER Howard Jones—Elektra 69651
[Howard Jones] [BMI] (3/23/85 BC-5)

THINGS I DIDN'T DO Perry Como—RCA Victor 47-5857
[Fred Jay/Ira Kosloff/Irving Reid] [BMI] (10/4/54 BCR-20)

THINGS I DIDN'T SAY The Jordan Brothers—Jamie 1169
[Mort Garson/Earl Shuman] [ASC] (11/19/60 C-83)

THINGS I LOVE The Fidelity's—Baton 252
[Harold Barlow/Lew Harris] [ASC] (5/5/58 BR-60)

THE THINGS I NEVER HAD Kay Starr—RCA Victor 47-6617
[Hal Stanley/Irving Taylor] [BMI] (9/8/56 B-89)

THINGS I SHOULD HAVE SAID The Grass Roots—Dunhill 4094
[Steve Barri/P.F. Sloan] [ASC] (8/12/67 BCR-23)

THINGS I'D LIKE TO SAY The New Colony Six—Mercury 72858
[Les Kummel/Ronnie Rice] [BMI] (12/14/68 BCR-13)

THE THINGS IN THIS HOUSE Bobby Darin—Capitol 5257
[Bobby Darin] [BMI] (9/19/64 BC-86)

THE THINGS THAT I USED TO DO James Brown—Smash 1908
[Eddie Jones] [BMI] (6/20/64 BC-92)

THINGS THAT MAKE YOU GO HMMMM
C & C Music Factory (Featuring Freedom Williams)—Columbia 73687
[Robert Clivillés/Frederick B. Williams] [ASC] (7/20/91 BC-4)

THINGS THEY DON'T TEACH YOU IN SCHOOL Connie Freed—Challenge 59031
[Ralph Freed/Craig Shane/Rod Sherwood/Sharon Silbert] [ASC] (12/8/58 R-88)

THE THINGS WE DID LAST SUMMER Shelley Fabares—Colpix 654
[Sammy Cahn/Jule Styne] [ASC] (9/15/62 BCR-46)

THE THINGS WE DO FOR LOVE 10CC—Mercury 73875
[Graham Gouldman/Eric Stewart] [BMI] (1/1/77 BCR-3)

THINK *The 5 Royales—King 5053 [Lowman Pauling] [BMI] (8/5/57 B-66)*

THINK *James Brown And The Famous Flames—Federal 12370*
[Lowman Pauling] [BMI] (5/2/60 BC-33)

THINK *Vicki Anderson And James Brown—King 6091*
[Lowman Pauling] [BMI] (4/8/67 BR-98)

THINK *James Brown—Polydor 14177 [Lowman Pauling] [BMI] (5/19/73 B-77)*

THINK *James Brown—Polydor 14185 [Lowman Pauling] [BMI] (8/11/73 B-80)*

THINK Brenda Lee—Decca 31599 [Peggy Whittington] [BMI] (3/7/64 BCR-17)

THINK Jimmy McCracklin—Imperial 66129
[Deadric Malone/Jimmy McCracklin] [BMI] (10/2/65 BCR-72)

THINK Aretha Franklin—Atlantic 2518
[Aretha Franklin/Ted White] [BMI] (5/18/68 BCR-7)

THINK Information Society—Tommy Boy 19591 [Paul Robb] [ASC] (9/29/90 BC-24)

THINK (ABOUT IT) Lyn Collins—People 608 [James Brown] [BMI] (8/12/72 BCR-55)

THINK ABOUT ME Fleetwood Mac—Warner Bros. 49196
[Christine McVie] [BMI] (3/8/80 BCR-17)

THINK ABOUT YOUR CHILDREN Mary Hopkin—Apple 1825
[Errol Brown/Margaret Wilson/Tony Wilson] [ASC] (11/21/70 BR-87)

THINK HIS NAME Johnny Rivers—United Artists 50822
[Thomas J. Coe/Dwain Mincy/Wayne Mincy/Timothy Michael Shanklin/Wayne Shanklin] [ASC] (8/28/71 BCR-61)

THINK I'LL GO SOMEWHERE AND CRY MYSELF TO SLEEP Al Martino—Capitol 5598
[Bill Anderson] [BMI] (3/5/66 BCR-25)

THINK I'M IN LOVE Eddie Money—Columbia 02964
[Eddie Money/Randy Oda] [BMI] (6/26/82 BC-16)

THINK IT OVER Buddy Holly / The Crickets—Brunswick 55072
[Jerry Allison*/Buddy Holly/Norman Petty] [BMI] (7/5/58 BC-27)

THINK IT OVER The Delfonics—Philly Groove 174 [William Hart] [BMI] (1/13/73 C-75)

THINK IT OVER Cheryl Ladd—Capitol 4599
[Brenda Russell/Brian Russell] [ASC] (7/22/78 BCR-34)

THINK ME A KISS Clyde McPhatter—MGM 12877 [Ray Stanley] [BMI] (3/7/60 BCR-66)

THINK OF LAURA Christopher Cross—Warner Bros. 29658
[Christopher Cross] [ASC] (12/10/83 BC-6)

THINK OF ME Maxine Brown—ABC-Paramount 10235
[Sammy Taylor] [BMI] (7/8/61 C-82)

THINK OF ME Buck Owens And The Buckaroos—Capitol 5647
[Estella Olson/Don Rich] [BMI] (5/21/66 BCR-72)

THINK OF THE GOOD TIMES Jay & The Americans—United Artists 845
[Roy Alfred/Wes Farrell] [ASC] (3/27/65 BCR-54)

THINK TWICE Brook Benton—Mercury 71774
[Clyde Otis/Joe Shapiro/Jimmy Williams] [BMI] (2/6/61 BCR-7)

THINK TWICE Jackie Wilson And Lavern Baker—Brunswick 55287
[Eddie Singleton] [BMI] (1/15/66 BC-93)

THINKING ABOUT YOUR LOVE Skipworth & Turner—4th & Broadway 7414
[Rodney Skipworth/Phil Turner] [ASC] (7/20/85 C-80)

THINKING OF YOU Loggins & Messina—Columbia 45815
[Jim Messina] [ASC] (3/24/73 BCR-11)

THINKING OF YOU Paul Davis—Bang 724 [Paul Davis] [BMI] (4/17/76 BCR-45)

THINKING OF YOU Earth, Wind & Fire—Columbia 07695
[Wanda Hutchinson/Wayne Vaughn/Maurice White] [ASC] (2/6/88 BC-67)

THINKING OF YOU Sa-Fire—Cutting 872 502-7
[Wilma Cosmé/Russ DeSalvo/Robert Steele] [ASC] (2/4/89 BC-11)

THINKING OF YOU Grandmaster Slice—Jive 42034
[David Ellis Martin/Stacey Rogers] [ASC] (10/26/91 B-85)

THIRD FINGER - LEFT HAND Eileen Rodgers—Columbia 40956
[Eddie V. Deane/Ben Weisman] [ASC] (9/16/57 B-82)

HARRY LIME THEME *(Third Man Theme) Crazy Otto—Polydor 22009A*
[Anton Karas] (Med) [ASC] (1/10/55 R-30) [I]

3RD MAN THEME *Herb Alpert & The Tijuana Brass—A&M 775*
[Anton Karas] [ASC] (8/28/65 BCR-47) [I]

THIRD RATE ROMANCE The Amazing Rhythm Aces—ABC 12078
[Howard Russell Smith] [ASC] (6/21/75 BCR-14)

THIRD TIME LUCKY (FIRST TIME I WAS A FOOL) Foghat—Bearsville 49125
[Dave Peverett] [ASC] (11/10/79 BCR-19)

THIRTEEN GOING ON FOURTEEN The Crew-Cuts—Mercury 70922
[Al Hoffman/Dick Manning] [ASC] (8/10/56 R-77)

13 QUESTIONS Seatrain—Capitol 3067
[Andrew Kulberg/Jim Roberts] [BMI] (4/3/71 BCR-44)

THIRTY DAYS (TO COME BACK HOME) *Chuck Berry—Chess 1610*
[Chuck Berry] [BMI] (10/29/55 CRt-42)

THIRTY DAYS (TO COME BACK HOME) *Ernest Tubb—Decca 29731*
[Chuck Berry] [BMI] (2/3/56 Rt-89)

39-21-46 The Showmen—Minit 32007 [General Johnson] [BMI] (7/15/67 R-92)

31 FLAVORS The Shirelles—Scepter 1260
[Mack David/Ernest Gold] [ASC] (11/2/63 BCR-90)

30-60-90 Willie Mitchell—Hi 2154
[Howard Grimes/Leroy Hodges/Mabon Hodges/James Mitchell/Willie Mitchell] [BMI] (1/18/69 BC-69) [I]

THIS & THAT Michael Penn—RCA 2512 [Michael Penn] [BMI] (4/28/90 BC-49)

—THIS AIN'T NO PARTY...THIS AINT NO DISCO... see: LIFE DURING WARTIME

THIS BEAT GOES ON The Kings—Elektra 47006/47052
[David Diamond/Aryan Zero] (TSW) [ASC] (8/23/80 BC-43)

THIS BEAT IS HOT B.G. Prince Of Rap—Epic 73950
[Rolf Ellmer/Bernard Greene] [ASC] (8/17/91 B-72)

THIS BITTER EARTH *Dinah Washington—Mercury 71635*
[Clyde Otis] [BMI] (6/18/60 BCR-23)

THIS BITTER EARTH *The Satisfactions—Lionel 3201 [Clyde Otis] [BMI] (6/20/70 BCR-87)*

—THIS BOY see: RINGO'S THEME

THIS CAN'T BE TRUE Eddie Holman—Parkway 960
[Eddie Holman/James Solomon] [BMI] (1/15/66 BCR-47)

THIS COULD BE THE NIGHT Loverboy—Columbia 05765
[Jonathan Cain/Paul Dean/Mike Reno/Bill Wray] [ASC] (1/18/86 BC-10)

THIS COULD BE THE RIGHT ONE April Wine—Capitol 5319
[Myles Goodwyn/David Henman*/Jim Henman*/Richie Henman*] [BMI]
(2/11/84 BC-58)

THIS DIAMOND RING Gary Lewis And The Playboys—Liberty 55756
[Bob Brass/Al Kooper/Irwin Levine] [BMI] (1/9/65 BCR-1)

THIS DOOR SWINGS BOTH WAYS Herman's Hermits—MGM 13548
[Estelle Levitt/Don Thomas] [BMI] (7/9/66 BCR-8)

THIS EMPTY PLACE Dionne Warwick—Scepter 1247
[Burt Bacharach/Hal David] [ASC] (3/23/63 BCR-84)

THIS FRIENDLY WORLD Fabian—Chancellor 1044 [Ken Darby] [ASC] (11/14/59 BCR-12)

THIS GIRL (HAS TURNED INTO A WOMAN) Mary MacGregor—Ariola America 7662
[Mary MacGregor/Peter Yarrow] [ASC] (4/23/77 BCR-46)

THIS GIRL IS A WOMAN NOW Gary Puckett And The Union Gap—Columbia 44967
[Alan Bernstein/Vic Millrose] [ASC] (8/16/69 BCR-3)

THIS GOLDEN RING The Fortunes—Press 9811
[Roger Cook/Roger Greenaway] [ASC] (2/5/66 BCR-82)

THIS GUY'S IN LOVE WITH YOU *Herb Alpert—A&M 929*
[Burt Bacharach/Hal David] [ASC] (5/11/68 BCR-1)

THIS GIRL'S IN LOVE WITH YOU *Dionne Warwick—Scepter 12241*
[Burt Bacharach/Hal David] [ASC] (2/1/69 BCR-7)

THIS HEART Gene Redding—Haven 7000
[Dennis Lambert/Brian Potter] [BMI] (3/16/74 BCR-22)

THIS HOUSE Tracie Spencer—Capitol 44652
[Matt Sherrod/Paul Sherrod/Marty Spencer] [ASC] (12/22/90 BC-3)

THIS I SWEAR The Skyliners—Calico 106
[James Beaumont/Walter Lester/Lennie Martin*/Joseph Rock/John L. Taylor/
Joseph Verscharen/Janet Vogel] [ASC] (5/25/59 BCR-26)

THIS I SWEAR Tyrone Davis—Columbia 10528 [Leo Graham] [BMI] (6/18/77 CR-86)

THIS IS ALL I ASK *Tony Bennett—Columbia 42820*
[Gordon Jenkins] [ASC] (7/13/63 BCtRt-36)

THIS IS ALL I ASK *Burl Ives—Decca 31518 [Gordon Jenkins] [ASC] (7/13/63 BCtRt-36)*

THIS IS IT Jay & The Americans—United Artists 479
[Ellie Greenwich/Tony Powers] [BMI] (7/21/62 CR-83)

THIS IS IT Jim Reeves—RCA Victor 47-8508 [Cindy Walker] [BMI] (3/13/65 BC-88)

THIS IS IT Melba Moore—Buddah 519 [Van McCoy] [BMI] (4/24/76 BR-90)

THIS IS IT Dan Hartman—Blue Sky 2775 [Dan Hartman] [BMI] (2/24/79 BR-91)

THIS IS IT Kenny Loggins—Columbia 11109
[Kenny Loggins/Michael McDonald] [ASC] (10/13/79 BCR-8)

THIS IS LIVING Elvis Presley with the Jordanaires—RCA Victor EPA-4371
[Ben Weisman/Fred Wise] (EP) [ASC] (9/8/62 CR-26)

THIS IS LOVE Paul Anka—RCA 11395
[Madeline Sunshine/Robert Tepper] [ASC] (10/7/78 BCR-35)

THIS IS LOVE Oak—Mercury 74076 [Rick Pinette] [BMI] (7/14/79 BCR-55)

—THIS IS LOVE see also: ESO ES EL AMOR

—THIS IS LOVE see also: THIS IS REAL

THIS IS MY CONFESSION Joni James—MGM 11919
[Marjorie Goetschius/Edward Pola] [ASC] (2/7/55 R-52)

THIS IS MY COUNTRY The Impressions—Curtom 1934
[Curtis Mayfield] [BMI] (11/30/68 BCR-23)

THIS IS MY COUNTRY, THANK YOU CANADA Shelley Looney—Mercury 76050
[T. DeAngelo/Shelley Looney] [BMI] (3/1/80 C-98)

THIS IS MY LOVE The Passions—Audicon 105 [Billy Dawn Smith] [BMI] (3/21/60 R-92)

THIS IS MY LOVE SONG The Intruders—Gamble 4007
[Kenneth Gamble/Leon Huff] [BMI] (10/24/70 BCR-80)

THIS IS MY NIGHT Chaka Khan—Warner Bros. 29097
[David Frank/Mic Murphy] [ASC] (1/19/85 BC-58)

THIS IS MY PRAYER Theola Kilgore—Serock 2006 [Ed Townsend] [BMI] (8/10/63 BCR-60)

THIS IS MY PRAYER Ray Charles Singers—Command 4059
[Buddy Kaye/Nicola Salerno/Philip Springer] [ASC] (2/27/65 BCR-69) [FDE]

THIS IS MY SONG Petula Clark—Warner Bros. 7002
[Charles Chaplin] [ASC] (3/4/67 BCR-3)

THIS IS MY STORY Mickey And Sylvia—RCA Victor 47-7811
[Eunice Levy/Forrest Wilson] [BMI] (12/31/60 B-100)

THIS IS NOT AMERICA David Bowie/Pat Metheny Group—EMI America 8251
[David Bowie/Lyle Mays/Pat Metheny] [BMI] (2/2/85 BC-24)

THIS IS PONDEROUS 2NU—Atlantic 87771
[Jock Blaney/Phil DeVault*/Tom Martin*/Michael Nealy*] [ASC] (12/15/90 BC-46)

THIS IS REAL (THIS IS LOVE) *Malcolm Dodds—Decca 30766*
[Louise Bell] [ASC] (11/3/58 Rt-38)

THIS IS REAL (THIS IS LOVE) *Billy Dawn—Coed 504*
[Louise Bell] [ASC] (11/17/58 Rt-82)

THIS IS THE NITE The Valiants—Keen 34004
[Brice Coefield*/Chester Pipkin*/Sheridan Spencer/Billy Storm] [BMI]
(12/30/57 B-69)

THIS IS THE RIGHT TIME Lisa Stansfield—Arista 2049
[Ian Devaney/Andy Morris/Lisa Stansfield] [BMI] (8/18/90 BC-18)

THIS IS THE THANKS I GET Barbara Lynn—Atlantic 2450
[Barbara Lynn] [BMI] (2/17/68 BR-65)

THIS IS THE TIME Dennis DeYoung—A&M 2839 [Dennis DeYoung] [ASC] (6/28/86 BC-84)

THIS IS THE TIME Billy Joel—Columbia 06526 [Billy Joel] [ASC] (11/15/86 BC-18)

THIS IS THE WAY THAT I FEEL Marie Osmond—Polydor/Kolob 14385
[George Henry Jackson] [BMI] (4/16/77 BCR-39)

THIS IS THE WORLD CALLING Bob Geldof—Atlantic 89341
[Bob Geldof] [ASC] (12/13/86 BC-79)

THIS IS WHAT YOU MEAN TO ME Engelbert Humperdinck—Parrot 40085
[Terry Collins/Bobby Eli] [BMI] (11/15/75 C-87)

THIS IS YOUR LIFE Commodores—Motown 1361 [Lionel Richie] [ASC] (10/25/75 CR-77)

THIS IS YOUR SONG Don Goodwin—Silver Blue 806 [Paul Anka] [BMI] (12/8/73 BCR-75)

THIS LAND IS YOUR LAND *Paul Clayton—Monument 416*
[Woody Guthrie] [BMI] (4/11/60 R-79)

THIS LAND IS YOUR LAND *The New Christy Minstrels—Columbia 42592*
[Woody Guthrie] [BMI] (12/1/62 B-93)

THIS LAND IS YOUR LAND *Ketty Lester—Era 3094 [Woody Guthrie] [BMI] (12/1/62 B-97)*

THIS LITTLE BIRD Marianne Faithfull—London 9759
[John D. Loudermilk] [BMI] (6/5/65 BCR-32)

THIS LITTLE GIRL Dion—Columbia 42776
[Gerry Goffin/Carole King] [BMI] (4/20/63 BCR-19)

THIS LITTLE GIRL Gary U.S. Bonds—EMI America 8079
[Bruce Springsteen] [ASC] (4/25/81 BCR-7)

THIS LITTLE GIRL OF MINE The Everly Brothers—Cadence 1342
[Ray Charles] [BMI] (1/20/58 BCR-25)

THIS LITTLE GIRL'S GONE ROCKIN' Ruth Brown—Atlantic 1197
[Mann Curtis/Bobby Darin] [BMI] (9/8/58 BCR-24)

THIS LOVE Bad Company—Atlantic 89355
[Chris Fretwell/Brian Howe] [ASC] (10/18/86 BC-82)

THIS LOVE OF MINE *5 DeMarco Sisters—Decca 29388*
[Barry Parker/Henry Sanicola/Frank Sinatra] [ASC] (11/21/55 R-75)

THIS LOVE OF MINE *The Modernaires—Coral 61779*
[Barry Parker/Henry Sanicola/Frank Sinatra] (Med) [ASC] (2/16/57 R-72)

THIS MAGIC MOMENT *The Drifters—Atlantic 2050*
[Doc Pomus/Mort Shuman] [BMI] (2/13/60 BCR-9)

THIS MAGIC MOMENT *Jay & The Americans—United Artists 50475*
[Doc Pomus/Mort Shuman] [BMI] (12/14/68 BCR-4)

THIS MAGIC MOMENT *Richie Furay—Asylum 45487*
[Doc Pomus/Mort Shuman] [BMI] (6/10/78 C-92)

THIS MAN IS MINE Heart—Epic 02925
[Sue Ennis/Ann Wilson/Nancy Wilson] [ASC] (5/15/82 BC-29)

THIS MASQUERADE George Benson—Warner Bros. 8209
[Leon Russell] [BMI] (6/5/76 BCR-8)

THIS MOMENT IN TIME Engelbert Humperdinck—Epic 50632
[Ritchie Adams/Alan Bernstein] [ASC] (12/16/78 BCR-58)

THIS MUCH I KNOW Tony Martin—RCA Victor 47-6731
[Matt Dubey/Harold Karr] [ASC] (12/1/56 R-81)

THIS MUST BE THE PLACE (NAÏVE MELODY) Talking Heads—London-Sire 7-29451
[David Byrne/Chris Frantz/Jerry Harrison/Tina Weymouth] [ASC] (11/26/83 BC-62)

THIS MUST BE WRONG (OHO-AHA) Caterina Valente—Decca 29570
[Kurt Feltz*/Heinz Gietz/Kermit Goell] [ASC] (8/1/55 R-37)

THIS NIGHT WON'T LAST FOREVER *Bill LaBounty—Warner/Curb 8529*
[Roy Freeland/Bill LaBounty] [BMI] (5/20/78 BC-65)

THIS NIGHT WON'T LAST FOREVER *Michael Johnson—EMI America 8019*
[Roy Freeland/Bill LaBounty] [BMI] (8/4/79 BCR-18)

THIS OL' COWBOY The Marshall Tucker Band—Capricorn 0228
[Toy Caldwell] [BMI] (4/26/75 B-78)

THIS OLD HEART James Brown And The Famous Flames—Federal 12378
[James Brown] [BMI] (8/29/60 BCR-79)

THIS OLD HEART OF MINE (IS WEAK FOR YOU) *The Isley Brothers—Tamla 54128*
[Lamont Dozier/Brian Holland/Eddie Holland/Sylvia Moy] [BMI] (2/19/66 BCR-12)*

THIS OLD HEART OF MINE (IS WEAK FOR YOU) *Tammi Terrell—Motown 1138*
[Lamont Dozier/Brian Holland/Eddie Holland/Sylvia Moy] [BMI] (1/11/69 BCR-67)*

THIS OLD HEART OF MINE *Rod Stewart—Warner Bros. 8170*
[Lamont Dozier/Brian Holland/Eddie Holland/Sylvia Moy] [BMI] (1/10/76 BC-72)*

THIS OLD HEART OF MINE *Rod Stewart (with Ronald Isley)—Warner Bros. 19983*
[Lamont Dozier/Brian Holland/Eddie Holland/Sylvia Moy] [BMI] (3/24/90 BC-10)*

—THIS OLD MAN see: CHILDREN'S MARCHING SONG

THIS OLE HOUSE *Rosemary Clooney—Columbia 40266*
[Stuart Hamblen] [ASC] (7/10/54 BCR-1)

THIS OLE HOUSE *Stuart Hamblen—RCA Victor 47-5739 [Stuart Hamblen] [ASC] (11/13/54 B-26)*

THIS ONE Paul McCartney—Capitol 44438 [Paul McCartney] [ASC] (9/9/89 BC-90)

THIS ONE'S FOR THE CHILDREN New Kids On The Block—Columbia 73064 [Maurice Starr] [ASC] (11/11/89 BC-7)

THIS ONE'S FOR YOU Barry Manilow—Arista 0206 [Barry Manilow/Marty Panzer] [BMI] (9/18/76 BCR-21)

THIS PRECIOUS TIME Terry Knight And The Pack—Lucky Eleven 235 [Steve Barri/P.F. Sloan] [ASC] (2/11/67 CR-82)

THIS SHOULD GO ON FOREVER Rod Bernard—Argo 5327 [Bernard Jolivette/Jerry West] [BMI] (3/7/59 BCR-8)

THIS SONG George Harrison—Dark Horse 8294 [George Harrison] [ASC] (11/20/76 BCR-25)

THIS SPORTING LIFE Ian Whitcomb & Bluesville—Tower 120 [Ian Whitcomb] [BMI] (2/20/65 BCR-61)

THIS THING CALLED LOVE The Webs—Pop-Side 4593 [Marshall Boxley/Willie Cooper] [BMI] (12/9/67 CR-83)

THIS TIME *Thomas Wayne—Mercury 71454 [Chips Moman] [BMI] (7/13/59 R-70)*

THIS TIME *Troy Shondell—Liberty 55353 / Goldcrest 161 [Chips Moman] [BMI] (8/28/61 BCR-5)*

THIS TIME John Cougar—Riva 205 [John Mellencamp] [ASC] (9/20/80 BCR-27)

THIS TIME Bryan Adams—A&M 2574 [Bryan Adams/Jim Vallance] [BMI] (9/3/83 BC-24)

THIS TIME INXS—Atlantic 89497 [Andy Farriss] [NA] (11/16/85 BC-80)

THIS TIME Kiara—Arista 1-9772 [Charles L. Singleton] [ASC] (2/25/89 BC-78)

THIS TIME BABY Jackie Moore—Columbia 10993 [Leroy Bell/Casey James] [BMI] (8/25/79 R-94)

THIS TIME I KNOW IT'S FOR REAL Donna Summer—Atlantic 88899 [Matt Aitken/Mike Stock/Donna Summer/Pete Waterman] [BMI] (4/22/89 BC-6)

THIS TIME I'M GONE FOR GOOD Bobby Blue Bland—Dunhill 4369 [Deadric Malone/Oscar Perry] [BMI] (11/17/73 BCR-39)

THIS TIME I'M IN IT FOR LOVE Player—RSO 890 [Larry Keith/Steve Pippin] [BMI] (3/11/78 BCR-10)

THIS TIME IT'S REAL Tower Of Power—Warner Bros. 7733 [David Bartlett/Emilio Castillo/Steve Kupka] [ASC] (9/15/73 BCR-62)

THIS TIME MAKE IT FUNKY Tracie Spencer—Capitol 44699 [Lyndell Blake*/Crystal Carlisle/Matt Sherrod/Paul Sherrod/Marty Spencer] [ASC] (5/18/91 BC-54)

THIS TIME OF THE YEAR *Brook Benton—Mercury 71558 [Brook Benton/Clyde Otis] [BMI] (12/14/59 BCR-44)*

THIS TIME OF THE YEAR *Brook Benton—Mercury 71558 [Brook Benton/Clyde Otis] [BMI] (12/12/60 R-69)*

THIS TOWN Frank Sinatra—Reprise 0631 [Lee Hazlewood] [ASC] (10/28/67 BCR-40)

THIS TRAIN The Brothers Four—Columbia 42450 [Traditional] [NA] (6/16/62 R-87)

THIS WILL BE Natalie Cole—Capitol 4109 [Charles Henry Jackson Jr./Marvin Yancy] [ASC] (8/9/75 BCR-6)

THIS WILL BE A NIGHT TO REMEMBER Eddie Holman—Salsoul 2026 [Ron Baker/Ronnie Tyson] [BMI] (6/25/77 B-90)

THIS WOMAN Kenny Rogers—RCA 13710 [Albhy Galuten/Barry Gibb] [BMI] (1/14/84 BC-23)

THIS WORLD *The Sweet Inspirations—Atlantic 2750 [Gary Friedman/Herb Schapiro] [BMI] (10/10/70 R-96)*

THIS WORLD *The Staple Singers—Stax 0137 [Gary Friedman/Herb Schapiro] [BMI] (7/22/72 BCR-28)*

THIS WORLD WE LOVE IN *June Valli—Mercury 71800 [Gino Paoli/Don Raye] [ASC] (4/3/61 Rt-85) [FET]*

THIS WORLD WE LOVE IN (IL CIELO IN UNA STANZA) *Mina—Time 1030 [Gino Paoli] [ASC] (4/10/61 BCRt-82) [F]*

THIS YEAR'S SANTA BABY (response to Santa Baby) Eartha Kitt—RCA Victor 47-5914 [Joan Javits/Philip Springer/Tony Springer] [ASC] (11/1/54 R-68) [R]

THORN IN MY SIDE Eurythmics—RCA 5058 [Annie Lennox/David A. Stewart] [BMI] (11/15/86 BC-56)

THOSE GOOD OLD DREAMS Carpenters—A&M 2386 [John Bettis/Richard Carpenter] [ASC] (12/19/81 BCR-63)

THOSE LAZY-HAZY-CRAZY DAYS OF SUMMER Nat King Cole—Capitol 4965 [Hans Carste/Charles Tobias] [ASC] (5/4/63 BCR-6) [FDE]

THOSE OLDIES BUT GOODIES (REMIND ME OF YOU) *Little Caesar And The Romans—Del-Fi 4158 [Nick Curinga/Paul Politi] [BMI] (5/1/61 BCtR-9)*

THOSE OLDIES BUT GOODIES (REMIND ME OF YOU) *Nino and the Ebb Tides—Madison 162 [Nick Curinga/Paul Politi] [BMI] (5/27/61 Ct-9)*

THOSE WERE THE DAYS Mary Hopkin—Apple 1801 [Boris Fomin/Gene Raskin] [ASC] (9/21/68 BCR-1) [FET]

THOSE WERE THE DAYS Carroll O'Connor And Jean Stapleton (As The Bunkers)—Atlantic 2847 [Lee Adams/Charles Strouse] [ASC] (12/11/71 BCR-43)

THOU SHALT NOT STEAL *John D. Loudermilk—RCA Victor 47-7993 [John D. Loudermilk] [BMI] (4/7/62 BC-73)*

THOU SHALT NOT STEAL *Dick And Deedee—Warner Bros. 5482 [John D. Loudermilk] [BMI] (11/21/64 BCR-13)*

THE THOUGHT OF LOVING YOU Crystal Mansion—Capitol 2275 [David White] [BMI] (12/7/68 BCR-79)

A THOUSAND CUPS OF HAPPINESS Joe Hinton—Back Beat 532 [Deadric Malone] [BMI] (11/7/64 CR-85)

A THOUSAND MILES AWAY *The Heartbeats—Rama 216 [William Henry Miller/James Sheppard] [BMI] (12/8/56 BCRt-36)*

A THOUSAND MILES AWAY *The Diamonds—Mercury 71021 [William Henry Miller/James Sheppard] [BMI] (12/22/56 Rt-56)*

A THOUSAND MILES AWAY *The Heartbeats—Rama 216 [William Henry Miller/James Sheppard] [BMI] (11/7/60 B-96)*

A THOUSAND MILES AWAY *Fred Parris & The Five Satins—Elektra 47411 [William Henry Miller/James Sheppard] (Med) [BMI] (2/27/82 BC-71)*

A THOUSAND SHADOWS The Seeds—GNP Crescendo 394 [Daryl Hooper/Jan Savage/Sky Saxon] [BMI] (7/15/67 BCR-56)

A THOUSAND STARS Kathy Young With The Innocents—Indigo 108 [Eugene Pearson] [BMI] (10/24/60 BCR-3)

THREAD THE NEEDLE Clarence Carter—Fame 1013 [Clarence Carter] [BMI] (6/24/67 B-98)

3 A.M. ETERNAL The KLF—Arista 2230 [James Cauty/William Ernest Drummond] [ASC] (6/22/91 BC-5)

THE THREE BELLS *The Browns—RCA Victor 47-7555 [Bert Reisfeld/Jean Villard] [ASC] (7/20/59 BCRt-1) [FET]*

THE THREE BELLS *Dick Flood—Monument 408 [Bert Reisfeld/Jean Villard] [ASC] (8/3/59 BRt-1) [FET]*

THE THREE BELLS *The Tokens—B.T. Puppy 516 [Bert Reisfeld/Jean Villard] [ASC] (11/20/65 R-77) [FET]*

THREE BLIND MICE The Singing Dogs—RCA Victor 47-6344 [Traditional] (Med) [NA] (12/10/55 CR-23)

THREE CIGARETTES IN AN ASHTRAY Patsy Cline—Decca 30406 [Eddie Miller/W.S. Stevenson‡] [BMI] (8/19/57 R-57)

THREE COINS IN THE FOUNTAIN *Four Aces—Decca 29123 [Sammy Cahn/Jule Styne] [ASC] (5/29/54 BCR-PRE)*

THREE COINS IN THE FOUNTAIN *Frank Sinatra—Capitol 2816 [Sammy Cahn/Jule Styne] [ASC] (6/5/54 BC-PRE)*

THREE FOOLS Patti Page—Mercury 72013 [Horace Ott/Charles Singleton] [BMI] (7/21/62 R-57)

THREE HEARTS IN A TANGLE *Roy Drusky—Decca 31193 [Ray Pennington/Sonny Thompson] [BMI] (4/10/61 BC-35)*

THREE HEARTS IN A TANGLE *James Brown And The Famous Flames—King 5701 [Ray Pennington/Sonny Thompson] [BMI] (12/8/62 B-93)*

THREE LITTLE FISHES *Buzz Clifford—Columbia 41979 [Saxie Dowell] [ASC] (4/22/61 C-98)*

THREE LITTLE FISHES *Mitch Ryder And The Detroit Wheels—New Voice 822 [Saxie Dowell] (Med) [ASC] (4/29/67 BCR-20)*

THREE LITTLE PIGS Lloyd Price—ABC-Paramount 10032 [Harold Logan/Lloyd Price] [BMI] (8/8/59 CR-76)

THREE NIGHTS A WEEK Fats Domino—Imperial 5687 [Fats Domino] [BMI] (9/3/60 BCR-14)

THREE O'CLOCK IN THE MORNING *Bert Kaempfert And His Orchestra—Decca 31778 [Julian Robledo] [ASC] (5/1/65 BCR-28) [IM]*

THREE O'CLOCK IN THE MORNING *Lou Rawls—Capitol 5424 [Julian Robledo/Dorothy Terriss] [ASC] (6/5/65 B-83)*

THREE RING CIRCUS Blue Magic—Atco 7004 [Vinnie Barrett/Bobby Eli] [BMI] (10/12/74 BCR-36)

THREE STARS *Tommy Dee—Crest 1057 [Tommy Dee] [BMI] (3/30/59 BCR-11)*

THREE STARS *Ruby Wright—King 5192 [Tommy Dee] [BMI] (5/4/59 B-99)*

—THREE STARS WILL SHINE TONIGHT see: THEME FROM DR. KILDARE

THREE STEPS FROM THE ALTAR Shep And The Limelites—Hull 747 [James Sheppard] [BMI] (10/2/61 BCR-51)

THREE STEPS FROM TRUE LOVE The Reflections—Capitol 4078 [Ralph Bailey/Ken Williams] [BMI] (7/12/75 BC-90)

THREE STEPS TO HEAVEN Eddie Cochran—Liberty 55242 [Bob Cochran/Eddie Cochran] [BMI] (5/28/60 C-99)

3000 MILES Brian Hyland—Philips 40354 [Artie Wayne] [BMI] (3/26/66 BCR-75)

THREE TIMES A LADY Commodores—Motown 1443 [Lionel Richie] [ASC] (6/17/78 BCR-1)

THREE TIMES IN LOVE Tommy James—Millennium 11785 [Tommy James/Ronald Serota] [BMI] (1/19/80 BCR-17)

THREE WINDOW COUPE The Rip Chords—Columbia 43035 [Jan Berry/Roger Christian] [BMI] (4/25/64 BCR-28)

THE THRILL IS GONE B.B. King—BluesWay 61032 [Rick Darnell/Roy Hawkins] [BMI] (12/20/69 BCR-13)

THRILLER Michael Jackson—Epic 04363 [Rod Temperton] [ASC] (2/4/84 BC-4)

—THROUGH THE EYES OF LOVE see: THEME FROM ICE CASTLES

THROUGH THE FIRE Chaka Khan—Warner Bros. 29025 [David Foster/Tom Keane/Cynthia Weil] [BMI] (4/27/85 BC-60)

THROUGH THE STORM Aretha Franklin And Elton John—Arista 1-9809 [Albert Hammond/Diane Warren] [ASC] (4/15/89 BC-15)

THROUGH THE YEARS Kenny Rogers—Liberty 1444 [Steve Dorff/Marty Panzer] [BMI] (12/26/81 BCR-12)

THROWAWAY Mick Jagger—Columbia 07653 [Mick Jagger] [ASC] (11/28/87 BC-67)
THROWING IT ALL AWAY Genesis—Atlantic 89372
[Tony Banks/Phil Collins/Mike Rutherford] [ASC] (8/16/86 BC-3)
THUNDER AND LIGHTNING Chi Coltrane—Columbia 45640
[Chi Coltrane] [ASC] (9/2/72 BCR-14)
THUNDER AND LIGHTNING Chicago—Columbia 11345
[Peter Cetera/Robert Lamm/Danny Seraphine] [ASC] (8/23/80 BCR-56)
THUNDER IN MY HEART Leo Sayer—Warner Bros. 8465
[Leo Sayer/Tom Snow] [ASC] (10/1/77 BCR-35)
THUNDER ISLAND Jay Ferguson—Asylum 45444 [Jay Ferguson] [BMI] (12/17/77 BCR-6)
THUNDERBALL Tom Jones—Parrot 9801 [John Barry/Don Black] [BMI] (12/4/65 BCR-19)
—THUNDERDOME see: WE DON'T NEED ANOTHER HERO
TI AMO Laura Branigan—Atlantic 89608
[Giancarlo Bigazzi/Umberto Tozzi/Diane Warren] [ASC] (11/3/84 BC-54) [FET]
TIC-A-TEE, TIK-A-TAY Dean Martin—Reprise 25508
[Mike Andre/Francesco Feola/Gaetano Lama] [BMI] (3/12/62 R-100) [FET]
TIC-TAC-TOE Kyper—Atlantic 87910 [Randall Kiper] [NA] (6/30/90 BC-14)
TIC TOC Lee Allen And His Band—Ember 1039 [Lee Allen] [BMI] (9/29/58 BCR-87) [I]
TIC TOC POLLY WOC Perez Prado And His Orchestra—RCA Victor 47-7540
[Evangelina Reyes] [BMI] (7/6/59 R-84) [I]
TICK TOCK The Vaughan Brothers—Epic Associated 73576
[Nile Rodgers/Jimmie Vaughan/Jerry Lynn Williams] [BMI] (10/20/90 BC-50)
TICKET TO RIDE *The Beatles—Capitol 5407*
[John Lennon/Paul McCartney] [ASC] (4/17/65 BCR-1)
TICKET TO RIDE *Carpenters—A&M 1142*
[John Lennon/Paul McCartney] [ASC] (2/14/70 BCR-54)
TICKET TO RIDE *The Beatles—Capitol 5107*
[John Lennon/Paul McCartney] (Med) [ASC] (3/27/82 BCR-12)
THE TIDE IS HIGH Blondie—Chrysalis 2465
[John Holt/Duke Reid] [ASC] (11/15/80 BCR-1)
TIE A STRING AROUND YOUR FINGER The Marvelettes—Tamla 54082
[Janie Bradford*/Lamont Dozier/Brian Holland/Eddie Holland] [BMI] (7/27/63 R-100)
TIE A YELLOW RIBBON ROUND THE OLE OAK TREE
Dawn Featuring Tony Orlando—Bell 45,318
[L. Russell Brown/Irwin Levine] [BMI] (2/3/73 BCR-1)
SHOULD I TIE A YELLOW RIBBON ROUND THE OLE OAK TREE? THE ANSWER
(response to Tie A Yellow Ribbon...) Connie Francis—GSF 6901
[L. Russell Brown/Irwin Levine] [BMI] (7/14/73 C-99) [R]
TIE ME KANGAROO DOWN, SPORT Rolf Harris—Epic 9596
[Rolf Harris] [BMI] (6/8/63 BCR-3)
TIE YOUR MOTHER DOWN Queen—Elektra 45385 [Brian May] [BMI] (3/19/77 BCR-49)
TIED UP Olivia Newton-John—MCA 52155
[John Farrar/Lee Ritenour] [BMI] (1/15/83 BC-38)
TIES THAT BIND Brook Benton—Mercury 71566
[Vince Corso/Clyde Otis] [BMI] (4/4/60 BCR-23)
TIGER *Fabian—Chancellor 1037 [Ollie Jones] [BMI] (6/8/59 BCRt-3)*
TIGER *Nick Todd—Dot 15951 [Ollie Jones] [BMI] (6/8/59 Rt-11)*
TIGER IN THE TANK The Chariots—RSVP 1105
[Peter Greco/Rod Salazar/Jerry Simon] [BMI] (1/9/65 R-87)
TIGER LILY Rusty Draper—Mercury 70989
[Aaron Schroeder/Ben Weisman] [ASC] (2/16/57 B-88)
TIGHT ROPE Leon Russell—Shelter 7325 [Leon Russell] [BMI] (8/19/72 BCR-9)
TIGHTEN UP Archie Bell & The Drells—Atlantic 2478
[Archie Bell/Billy Buttier] [BMI] (3/30/68 BCR-1)
TIGHTER, TIGHTER Alive And Kicking—Roulette 7078
[Tommy James/Robert L. King] [BMI] (5/30/70 BCR-3)
TIGHTROPE RIDE The Doors—Elektra 45757
[Robby Krieger/Ray Manzarek] [ASC] (11/27/71 BCR-64)
TIJUANA JAIL The Kingston Trio—Capitol 4167
[Denny Thompson] [BMI] (3/16/59 BCR-11)
TIJUANA TAXI Herb Alpert & The Tijuana Brass—A&M 787
[Bud Coleman] [BMI] (12/25/65 BCR-34) [I]
'TIL I CAN MAKE IT ON MY OWN Tammy Wynette—Epic 50196
[George Richey/Billy Sherrill/Tammy Wynette] [BMI] (4/10/76 BCR-67)
('TIL) I KISSED YOU The Everly Brothers—Cadence 1369
[Don Everly] [BMI] (8/15/59 BCR-4)
TIL IT'S TIME TO SAY GOODBYE Jonathan Cain—October 1001
[Jonathan Cain] [BMI] (1/10/76 BCR-44)
TIL MY BABY COMES HOME Luther Vandross—Epic 04760
[Marcus Miller/Luther Vandross] [ASC] (3/16/85 BC-29)
TIL THE WORLD ENDS Three Dog Night—ABC 12114
[Dave Loggins] [ASC] (7/5/75 BCR-22)
TIL TOMORROW Janice Harper—Capitol 4356
[Jerry Bock/Sheldon Harnick] [BMI] (4/4/60 R-79)
TIL YOU AND YOUR LOVER ARE LOVERS AGAIN Engelbert Humperdinck—Epic 03817
[Jan Buckingham/Mark Eugene Gray] [BMI] (7/16/83 B-77)
TILL *Percy Faith And His Orchestra and Chorus—Columbia 40826*
[Charles Danvers/Carl Sigman] [ASC] (4/13/57 BCRt-42) [FDE]
TILL *Dinah Shore—RCA Victor 47-6980*
[Charles Danvers/Carl Sigman] [ASC] (8/19/57 Rt-53) [FDE]
TILL *Leo Diamond His Harmonica & Orch—Roulette 4025*
[Charles Danvers/Carl Sigman] [ASC] (10/7/57 Rt-53) [IWM]*
TILL *Roger Williams—Kapp 197*
[Charles Danvers/Carl Sigman] [ASC] (10/14/57 BCRt-24) [FDE]
TILL *Kay Armen—Decca 30474*
[Charles Danvers/Carl Sigman] [ASC] (10/21/57 Rt-53) [FDE]
'TIL *The Angels—Caprice 107*
[Charles Danvers/Carl Sigman] [ASC] (9/18/61 BCR-14) [FDE]
TILL *The Tokens—Warner Bros. 7169*
[Charles Danvers/Carl Sigman] [ASC] (3/9/68 C-97) [FDE]
TILL *The Vogues—Reprise 0788*
[Charles Danvers/Carl Sigman] [ASC] (11/16/68 BCR-14) [FDE]
TILL *Tom Jones—Parrot 40067*
[Charles Danvers/Carl Sigman] [ASC] (10/23/71 BCR-38) [FDE]
TILL DEATH DO US PART Bob Braun—Decca 31355 [Eric Leiser] [ASC] (6/30/62 BCR-24)
TILL I LOVED YOU (THE LOVE THEME FROM GOYA)
Barbra Streisand And Don Johnson—Columbia 08062
[Maury Yeston] [BMI] (10/22/88 BC-25)
TILL SOMEBODY LOVES YOU Henry Lee Summer—Epic Associated 73893
[Michael Bolton/Henry Lee Summer/Diane Warren] [BMI] (8/10/91 BC-42)
TILL THE END OF THE DAY The Kinks—Reprise 0454 [Ray Davies] [BMI] (3/26/66 BCR-37)
TILL THE END OF TIME The Nobles—ABC-Paramount 9984
[Buddy Kaye/Ted Mossman] [ASC] (12/8/58 R-91)
TILL THE END OF TIME Ray Charles Singers—Command 4049
[Frederic Chopin/Buddy Kaye/Ted Mossman] [ASC] (9/19/64 B-83)
TILL THEN The Classics (2)—Musicnote 1116
[Sol Marcus/Eddie Seiler/Guy Wood] [ASC] (6/1/63 BCR-20)
TILL THERE WAS YOU *Anita Bryant—Carlton 512*
[Meredith Willson] [ASC] (6/15/59 BCR-14)
TILL THERE WAS YOU *Valjean (At The Piano)—Carlton 576*
[Meredith Willson] [ASC] (8/25/62 BCR-92) [IWM]
TILL YOU GET ENOUGH
The Watts 103rd Street Rhythm Band—Warner Bros.-Seven Arts 7298
[Melvin Dunlap/James Gadson/Albert Philip McKay/John Rayford/Charles Wright] [BMI] (6/28/69 BCR-62)
TILL YOU'RE BACK IN MY ARMS Vince Carson—Essex 410
[Bill Borrelli/Tony Starr] [ASC] (2/17/56 R-81)
TIME Teresa Brewer—Coral 61286 [Cliff Friend/Jack Reynolds] [ASC] (11/20/54 C-43)
TIME Pozo-Seco Singers—Columbia 43437 [Michael Merchant] [BMI] (1/8/66 BCR-44)
TIME Alan Parsons Project—Arista 0598
[Alan Parsons/Eric Woolfson] [BMI] (4/18/81 BCR-13)
TIME (CLOCK OF THE HEART) Culture Club—Virgin 03796
[Michael Craig/Roy Hay/Jon Moss/George O'Dowd] [ASC] (4/16/83 BC-2)
TIME AFTER TIME *Frankie Ford—Ace 580*
[Sammy Cahn/Jule Styne] [ASC] (1/16/60 BCR-48)
TIME AFTER TIME *Chris Montez—A&M 822*
[Sammy Cahn/Jule Styne] [ASC] (10/29/66 BCR-28)
TIME AFTER TIME Cyndi Lauper—Portrait 37-04432
[Rob Hyman/Cyndi Lauper] [BMI] (4/14/84 BC-1)
TIME AFTER TIME Timmy -T-—Jam City 5003 [Timmy Torres] [BMI] (3/10/90 B-40)
TIME ALONE WILL TELL *Connie Francis—MGM 13718*
[Norman Newell/Eros Sciorilli/Al Testa] [ASC] (4/15/67 B-94) [F,FDE]
TIME ALONE WILL TELL (NON PENSARE A ME) *Jerry Vale—Columbia 44087*
[Norman Newell/Eros Sciorilli/Al Testa] [ASC] (4/15/67 C-95) [F,FDE]
TIME AND LOVE Barbra Streisand—Columbia 45341
[Laura Nyro] [BMI] (3/13/71 BCR-47)
TIME AND THE RIVER Nat King Cole—Capitol 4325
[Wally Gold/Aaron Schroeder] [ASC] (1/4/60 BCR-30)
TIME AND TIDE Basia—Epic 07730
[Basia Trzetrzelewska/Danny White] [BMI] (7/23/88 BC-26)
TIME BOMB Lake—Columbia 10614
[James Hopkins-Harrison/Geoffrey Peacey] [BMI] (10/1/77 BCR-70)
TIME FOR LETTING GO Jude Cole—Reprise 19743 [Jude Cole] [BMI] (7/28/90 BC-32)
TIME FOR LIVIN' The Association—Warner Bros.-Seven Arts 7195
[Dick Addrisi/Don Addrisi] [BMI] (5/11/68 BCR-23)
TIME FOR LIVIN' Sly & The Family Stone—Epic 11140
[Sylvester Stewart] [BMI] (6/29/74 BCR-32)
TIME FOR ME TO FLY *REO Speedwagon—Epic 50582*
[Kevin Cronin] [ASC] (7/15/78 BCR-56)
TIME FOR ME TO FLY *REO Speedwagon—Epic 50858*
[Kevin Cronin] [ASC] (5/17/80 BCR-59)
—TIME FOR US see: LOVE THEME FROM ROMEO AND JULIET
TIME HAS COME TODAY The Chambers Brothers—Columbia 44414
[Joe Chambers/Willie Chambers] [BMI] (8/10/68 BCR-11)
TIME IN A BOTTLE Jim Croce—ABC 11405 [Jim Croce] [ASC] (11/17/73 BCR-1)
TIME IS MOVIN' The Blackbyrds—Fantasy 787 [Keith Killgo] [BMI] (3/12/77 B-95)

TIME IS ON MY SIDE The Rolling Stones—London 9708
[Jimmy Norman/Jerry Ragovoy] [BMI] (10/10/64 BCR-6)

TIME IS TIGHT Booker T. & The M.G.'s—Stax 0028
[Steve Cropper*/Donald "Duck" Dunn*/Al Jackson*/Booker T. Jones Jr.] [BMI] (3/15/69 BCR-6) [I]

TIME IS TIME Andy Gibb—RSO 1059 [Andy Gibb/Barry Gibb] [BMI] (11/22/80 BCR-15)

TIME, LOVE AND TENDERNESS Michael Bolton—Columbia 73889
[Diane Warren] [ASC] (7/13/91 BC-3)

TIME MACHINE Danté And The Evergreens—Madison 135
[Howard Greenfield/Barry Mann] [BMI] (9/12/60 BC-73)

TIME MACHINE Grand Funk Railroad—Capitol 2567
[Mark Farner] [BMI] (9/27/69 BCR-42)

TIME MARCHES ON Roy Hamilton—Epic 9323
[Howard Greenfield/Neil Sedaka] [BMI] (7/25/59 BCR-55)

TIME OF THE SEASON The Zombies—Date 1628 [Rod Argent] [BMI] (2/8/69 BCR-1)

TIME OUT FOR TEARS *The Four Tunes—Jubilee 5200*
[Irving Berman/Abe Schiff] [BMI] (6/6/55 R-74)

TIME OUT FOR TEARS *Chris Connor—Atlantic 1121*
[Irving Berman/Abe Schiff] [BMI] (3/9/57 R-84)

TIME OUT OF MIND Steely Dan—MCA 51082
[Walter Becker/Donald Fagen] [ASC] (3/14/81 BCR-22)

TIME PASSAGES Al Stewart—Arista 0362 [Al Stewart/Peter White] [BMI] (9/30/78 BCR-7)

TIME SELLER Spencer Davis Group—United Artists 50202
[Spencer Davis/Ed Hardin/Phil Sawyer*] [BMI] (9/16/67 BCR-90)

TIME STOPPED Marvin Smith—Brunswick 55299
[Carl Davis/Marvin Smith] [BMI] (10/1/66 C-79)

TIME, TIME Ed Ames—RCA Victor 47-9178
[Joss Baselli/Armand Canfora/Earl Shuman] [ASC] (5/6/67 BCR-61) [FDE]

TIME TO GET DOWN The O'Jays—Philadelphia Int'l 3531
[Kenneth Gamble/Leon Huff] [BMI] (5/19/73 BCR-26)

TIME TO GET IT TOGETHER Country Coalition—BluesWay 61034
[Smokey Roberds] [ASC] (3/7/70 BCR-58)

TIME TO KILL The Band—Capitol 2870 [Robbie Robertson] [ASC] (10/3/70 BCR-69)

—TIME TO LOVE, A TIME TO CRY see: PETITE FLEUR

TIME WAITS FOR NO ONE The Hilltoppers—Dot 15249
[Cliff Friend/Charles Tobias] [ASC] (10/4/54 CR-26)

TIME WAITS FOR NO ONE The Friends Of Distinction—RCA Victor 74-0385
[Howard Greenfield/Neil Sedaka] [BMI] (10/3/70 BCR-41)

TIME WAS The Flamingos—End 1092
[Gabriel Luna/Miguel Prado/Bob Russell] [BMI] (7/3/61 BC-45) [FDE]

TIME WAS Canned Heat—Liberty 56097
[Fito De La Parra/Bob Hite/Larry Taylor/Henry Vestine/Alan C. Wilson] [BMI] (3/8/69 BCR-45)

TIME WILL REVEAL DeBarge—Gordy 1705
[Bunny DeBarge/El DeBarge] [ASC] (10/15/83 BC-18)

TIME WILL TELL Tower Of Power—Warner Bros. 7796
[Emilio Castillo/Steve Kupka] [ASC] (4/27/74 BCR-69)

TIME WON'T LET ME The Outsiders—Capitol 5573
[Chet Kelley/Thomas R. King] [BMI] (2/19/66 BCR-5)

TIMELESS LOVE Saraya—SBK 07316 [Desmond Child] [ASC] (12/30/89 BC-82)

TIMES HAVE CHANGED Irma Thomas—Imperial 66069
[Van McCoy] [BMI] (10/24/64 BCR-94)

TIMES OF YOUR LIFE Paul Anka—United Artists 737
[Bill Lane/Roger Nichols] [ASC] (11/15/75 BCR-7)

TIMES TWO I LOVE YOU The Three Chuckles—"X" 0162
[Jack Fulton/Lois Steele] [ASC] (11/12/55 BR-61)

TIMOTHY The Buoys—Scepter 12275 [Rupert Holmes] [ASC] (11/28/70 BCR-13)

TIN MAN America—Warner Bros. 7839 [Dewey Bunnell] [ASC] (8/10/74 BCR-4)

TIN SOLDIER Small Faces—Immediate 5003
[Ronnie Lane/Steve Marriott] [BMI] (3/16/68 BCR-52)

TINA The Easy Riders—Columbia 40910
[Boudleaux Bryant/Felice Bryant] [BMI] (5/27/57 B-96)

TINA CHERRY Georgio—Motown 1892 [Georgio Allentini] [BMI] (8/29/87 B-96)

TINA MARIE Perry Como—RCA Victor 47-6192 [Bob Merrill] (TSW) [ASC] (8/13/55 BCR-4)

TINA'S DILEMMA Ike & Tina Turner—Sue 768 [Ike Turner] [BMI] (9/15/62 R-87)

TINY BUBBLES Don Ho And The Aliis—Reprise 0507
[Leon Pober] [ASC] (11/26/66 BCR-55)

TINY DANCER Elton John—Uni 55318 [Elton John/Bernie Taupin] [BMI] (3/4/72 BCR-29)

TINY TIM LaVern Baker—Atlantic 2041
[LaVern Baker/Alex Bradford] [BMI] (11/2/59 BCR-63)

TIP OF MY FINGERS *Nick Noble—Coral 62213 [Bill Anderson] [BMI] (7/25/60 CR-72)*

THE TIPS OF MY FINGERS *Roy Clark—Capitol 4956*
[Bill Anderson] [BMI] (5/18/63 BCR-36)

THE TIP OF MY FINGERS *Eddy Arnold—RCA Victor 47-8869*
[Bill Anderson] [BMI] (7/16/66 BCR-35)

TIP OF MY TONGUE The Tubes—Capitol 5258
[Michael Snyder/William Spooner/Maurice White] [ASC] (7/23/83 BC-52)

TIP ON IN (PART 1) Slim Harpo—Excello 2285
[Slim Harpo/Robert Lee Holmes] [BMI] (7/22/67 C-97)

TIP TOE Robert Parker—Nola 729 [Robert Parker] [BMI] (1/21/67 B-83)

TIP-TOE THRU' THE TULIPS WITH ME Tiny Tim—Reprise 0679
[Joe Burke/Al Dubin] [ASC] (5/18/68 BCR-17)

TIPPY TOEING The Harden Trio—Columbia 43463
[Bobby Harden] [BMI] (3/12/66 BCR-33)

THE TIPSY PIANO Helmut Zacharias—Decca 30795 [Lotar Olias] [BMI] (1/24/59 C-98) [I]

TIRED OF BEING ALONE Al Green—Hi 2194 [Al Green] [BMI] (7/24/71 BCR-6)

TIRED OF BEING BLONDE Carly Simon—Epic 05419
[Larry Raspberry] [BMI] (6/29/85 BC-63)

TIRED OF BEING LONELY Sharpees—One-derful! 4839
[James Leonard Jones/Larry Nestor] [BMI] (1/15/66 BCR-79)

TIRED OF TOEIN' THE LINE Rocky Burnette—EMI America 8043
[Rocky Burnette/Ron Coleman] [BMI] (5/10/80 BCR-6)

TIRED OF WAITING FOR YOU The Kinks—Reprise 0347
[Ray Davies] [BMI] (3/13/65 BCR-5)

TIT FOR TAT (AIN'T NO TAKING BACK) James Brown—King 6204
[James Brown/Nat Jones] [BMI] (12/21/68 BCR-47)

—TITLE NUMBER ONE AGAIN see: BIRDMAN PART ONE

TLC TENDER LOVE AND CARE Jimmie Rodgers—Roulette 4218
[Herb Clarke/Stan Lebowsky/Johnny Lehmann] [BMI] (1/4/60 BCR-23)

TO A SLEEPING BEAUTY Jimmy Dean—Columbia 42282
[Gus Kahn/Larry Markes/Egbert Van Alstyne] [ASC] (1/20/62 BCR-26)

TO A SOLDIER BOY The Tassels—Madison 117
[Mary Glen Gaudet] [BMI] (5/30/59 BCR-47)

TO ALL THE GIRLS I'VE LOVED BEFORE
Julio Iglesias & Willie Nelson—Columbia 04217
[Hal David/Albert Hammond] [ASC] (3/3/84 BC-3)

TO BE A LOVER Gene Chandler—Checker 1165 [Karl Tarleton] [BMI] (5/27/67 BCR-88)

TO BE A LOVER Billy Idol—Chrysalis 43024
[William Bell/Booker T. Jones Jr.] [BMI] (10/4/86 BC-6)

TO BE LOVED Jackie Wilson—Brunswick 55052
[Billy Davis/Berry Gordy/Gwen Gordy] [BMI] (4/5/58 BCR-22)

TO BE LOVED (FOREVER) The Pentagons—Donna 1337
[Ken Goodloe/Ted Goodloe*/Joe C. Jones*/Carl McGinnis*/Otis Munson*] [BMI] (2/20/61 BCR-48)

TO BE WITH YOU The Highlights—Bally 1027 [Frank McNulty] [ASC] (4/20/57 B-84)

TO BE WITH YOU Mr. Big—Atlantic 87580
[David Grahame/Eric Martin] [ASC] (12/14/91 BC-1)

TO BE YOUNG, GIFTED AND BLACK Nina Simone—RCA Victor 74-0269
[Weldon Irvine/Nina Simone] [BMI] (12/13/69 BCR-76)

TO DREAM THE DREAM Frankie Miller—Capitol/MSS 5131
[Francis John Miller] [ASC] (6/19/82 BC-60)

TO EACH HIS OWN *The Platters—Mercury 71697*
[Ray Evans/Jay Livingston] [ASC] (10/3/60 BCR-11)

TO EACH HIS OWN *The Tymes—Parkway 908*
[Ray Evans/Jay Livingston] [ASC] (3/7/64 BCR-69)

TO EACH HIS OWN *Frankie Laine—ABC 11032*
[Ray Evans/Jay Livingston] [ASC] (1/6/68 BCR-54)

TO EACH HIS OWN Faith, Hope & Charity—RCA Victor 10343
[Van McCoy] [BMI] (8/9/75 BCR-42)

TO EV'RY GIRL—TO EV'RY BOY (THE MEANING OF LOVE) Johnnie Ray—Columbia 40252
[Barry Parker/Jerry Samuels] [BMI] (8/14/54 C-40)

TO GET TO YOU Jerry Wallace—Decca 32914 [Jean Chapel] [BMI] (3/18/72 BCR-48)

TO GIVE (THE REASON I LIVE) Frankie Valli—Philips 40510
[Bob Crewe/Bob Gaudio] [BMI] (12/23/67 BCR-17)

TO KNOW HIM IS TO LOVE HIM *The Teddy Bears—Dore 503*
[Phil Spector] [BMI] (9/22/58 BCRt-1)

TO KNOW HIM, IS TO LOVE HIM *Cathy Carr—Roulette 4107*
[Phil Spector] [BMI] (10/20/58 Rt-29)

TO KNOW YOU IS TO LOVE YOU *Peter And Gordon—Capitol 5461*
[Phil Spector] [BMI] (7/10/65 BCR-24)

TO KNOW YOU IS TO LOVE YOU *Bobby Vinton—Epic 10461*
[Phil Spector] [BMI] (3/29/69 BCR-19)

TO KNOW SOMEONE DEEPLY IS TO KNOW SOMEONE SOFTLY Terence Trent D'Arby—Columbia 73217 [Terence Trent D'Arby] [BMI] (1/27/90 C-80)

TO KNOW YOU IS TO LOVE YOU B.B. King—ABC 11373
[Stevie Wonder/Syreeta Wright] [ASC] (8/4/73 BCR-38)

TO LIVE AND DIE IN L.A. Wang Chung—Geffen 28891
[Nick Feldman/Jack Hues] [ASC] (10/12/85 BC-38)

TO LOVE AGAIN *Four Aces—Decca 29889*
[Frederic Chopin/George Sidney/Morris Stoloff/Ned Washington] [ASC] (4/21/56 BCRt-26)

TO LOVE AGAIN *Bob Manning—RCA Victor 47-6462*
[Frederic Chopin/George Sidney/Morris Stoloff/Ned Washington] [ASC] (4/27/56 Rt-45)

TO LOVE AGAIN *Carmen Cavallaro—Decca 29907*
[Frederic Chopin/George Sidney/Morris Stoloff/Ned Washington] [ASC] (5/4/56 Rt-45)

TO LOVE AGAIN *Vic Damone—Columbia 40682*
[Frederic Chopin/George Sidney/Morris Stoloff/Ned Washington] [ASC] (6/8/56 Rt-45)

TO LOVE AGAIN *Marc Fredericks—Dot 15465 [Frederic Chopin/George Sidney/Morris Stoloff/Ned Washington] [ASC] (6/8/56 Rt-45)*

TO LOVE AND BE LOVED *Jane Morgan—Kapp 253 [Sammy Cahn/Jimmy Van Heusen] [ASC] (12/29/58 R-84)*

TO LOVE AND BE LOVED *Frank Sinatra—Capitol 4103 [Sammy Cahn/Jimmy Van Heusen] [ASC] (1/3/59 C-100)*

TO LOVE SOMEBODY *The Bee Gees—Atco 6503 [Barry Gibb/Robin Gibb] [BMI] (7/8/67 BCR-17)*

TO LOVE SOMEBODY *The Sweet Inspirations—Atlantic 2529 [Barry Gibb/Robin Gibb] [BMI] (7/6/68 BCR-74)*

TO LOVE YOU Country Store—T-A 189 [Dennis Lambert/Brian Potter] [BMI] (1/31/70 R-85)

TO MAKE A BIG MAN CRY Roy Head—Back Beat 571 [Peter Callander/Les Reed] [BMI] (9/17/66 B-95)

TO SAY YOU'RE MINE The DeCastro Sisters—Abbott 3002 [Arthur Grover/Lanny Shore/Max Solis] [BMI] (1/24/55 CR-49)

—TO SHARE YOUR LOVE see: SHARE YOUR LOVE WITH ME

TO SHOW I LOVE YOU Peter And Gordon—Capitol 5684 [Tony Hatch] [ASC] (7/30/66 BCR-92)

TO SIR WITH LOVE *Lulu—Epic 10187 [Don Black/Mark London] [BMI] (9/2/67 BCR-1)*

TO SIR, WITH LOVE *Herbie Mann—Atlantic 2444 [Mark London] [BMI] (10/21/67 B-93) [IM]*

TO SUSAN ON THE WEST COAST WAITING Donovan—Epic 10434 [Donovan Leitch] [BMI] (2/1/69 BCR-27)

TO THE AISLE *The Five Satins—Ember 1019 [Billy Dawn Smith/Stuart Wiener] [BMI] (6/29/57 BCtRt-25)*

AISLE *Roy Hamilton—Epic 9224 [Billy Dawn Smith/Stuart Wiener] [BMI] (7/13/57 CtRt-29)*

TO THE DOOR OF THE SUN (ALLE PORTE DEL SOLE) Al Martino—Capitol 3987 [Corrado Conti/Norman Newell/Daniele Pace/Mario Panzeri/Lorenzo Pilat] [BMI] (12/14/74 BCR-17) [F,FET]

TO THE ENDS OF THE EARTH Nat "King" Cole—Capitol 3551 [Joe Sherman/Noel Sherman] [ASC] (10/20/56 BCR-23)

TO THE OTHER MAN Luther Ingram—KoKo 2106 [Johnny Baylor/Luther Ingram/Johnny Northern/Randall Stewart] [BMI] (10/17/70 C-97)

TO THE OTHER WOMAN (I'M THE OTHER WOMAN) Doris Duke—Canyon 28 [Gary Anderson/Jerry Williams Jr.] [BMI] (2/21/70 BCR-50)

TO WAIT FOR LOVE Herb Alpert—A&M 964 [Burt Bacharach/Hal David] [ASC] (8/31/68 BCR-36)

TO YOU MY LOVE *Nick Noble—Wing 90045 / Mercury 70821 [Louis Gasté/Jack Lawrence] [ASC] (2/25/56 BCtRt-20) [FDE]*

TO YOU MY LOVE *Georgie Shaw—Decca 29839 [Louis Gasté/Jack Lawrence] [ASC] (3/2/56 BCtRt-20) [FDE]*

TO YOU, MY LOVE *Betty Madigan—MGM 12156 [Louis Gasté/Jack Lawrence] [ASC] (4/13/56 Rt-20) [FDE]*

TOAST AND MARMALADE FOR TEA Tin Tin—Atco 6794 [Steve Groves] [BMI] (3/27/71 BCR-15)

TOAST TO THE FOOL The Dramatics—Volt 4082 [Don Davis/Arthur Snyder] [BMI] (8/5/72 BCR-52)

TOBACCO ROAD *The Nashville Teens—London 9689 [John D. Loudermilk] [BMI] (9/5/64 BCR-11)*

TOBACCO ROAD *Jamul—Lizard 21001 [John D. Loudermilk] [BMI] (5/9/70 B-93)*

TOBY The Chi-Lites—Brunswick 55515 [Barbara Acklin/Eugene Record] (TSW) [BMI] (3/1/75 BR-78)

TOCCATA Sky—Arista 0568 [Johann Sebastian Bach] [BMI] (1/10/81 B-83) [I]

TODAY *The New Christy Minstrels—Columbia 43000 [Randy Sparks] [ASC] (4/18/64 BCR-17)*

TODAY *Jimmie Rodgers—A&M 976 [Randy Sparks] [ASC] (10/26/68 CR-89)*

TODAY HAS BEEN CANCELLED Billy Meshel—Probe 462 [Jay Fishman/Wilbur Meshel] [BMI] (6/21/69 R-98)

(TODAY I MET) THE BOY I'M GONNA MARRY Darlene Love—Philles 111 [Ellie Greenwich/Tony Powers/Phil Spector] [BMI] (3/30/63 BCR-35)

TODAY I SING THE BLUES Aretha Franklin—Columbia 41793 [Curtis Reginald Lewis] [BMI] (12/3/60 C-72)

I STARTED LOVING YOU AGAIN *Al Martino—Capitol 2674 [Merle Haggard/Bonnie Owens] [BMI] (11/15/69 BCR-73)*

TODAY I STARTED LOVING YOU AGAIN *Bettye Swann—Atlantic 2921 [Merle Haggard/Bonnie Owens] [BMI] (1/13/73 BCR-44)*

TODAY I STARTED LOVING YOU AGAIN *Bobby Bland—ABC 12156 [Merle Haggard/Bonnie Owens] [BMI] (3/27/76 R-97)*

TODAY IS THE DAY Bar-Kays—Mercury 76036 [James Edward Alexander/Charles Leonard Allen/Michael Beard/Mark Bynum/ Larry Dodson/Sherman Guy/Harvey Henderson/Allen Alvoid Jones Jr./ Lloyd Ed Smith/Winston Stewart/Frank Thompson] [BMI] (3/15/80 BCR-60)

TODAY, TOMORROW AND FOREVER Elvis Presley—RCA Victor EPA-4382 [Bernie Baum/Bill Giant/Florence Kaye] (EP) [BMI] (7/4/64 B-92)

TODAY'S TEARDROPS Rick Nelson—Imperial 66004 [Gene Pitney/Aaron Schroeder] [BMI] (11/30/63 BCR-54)

TODAY'S THE DAY America—Warner Bros. 8212 [Dan Peek] [ASC] (5/15/76 BCR-23)

TOGETHER Connie Francis—MGM 13019 [Lew Brown/Buddy DeSylva/Ray Henderson] [ASC] (6/26/61 BCR-4)

TOGETHER *The Intruders—Gamble 205 [Kenneth Gamble/Leon Huff] [BMI] (4/29/67 BCR-48)*

TOGETHER *Tierra—Boardwalk 5702 [Kenneth Gamble/Leon Huff] [BMI] (11/8/80 BCR-18)*

TOGETHER The Illusion—Steed 722 [Chuck Alder/Richie Cerniglia/Mike Maniscalco] [BMI] (12/13/69 BCR-47)

TOGETHER AGAIN Ray Charles—ABC-Paramount 10785 [Buck Owens] [BMI] (3/26/66 BCR-16)

TOGETHER AGAIN Bobby Sherman—Metromedia 240 [Larry Weiss] [ASC] (2/12/72 BCR-53)

TOGETHER ALONE Melanie—Neighborhood 4207 [Melanie Safka] [ASC] (10/7/72 BCR-47)

TOGETHER FOREVER Lisette Melendez—Fever 38-73630 [Carlos Berrios/Frankie Malave/Franc Reyes] [ASC] (2/2/91 B-35)

TOGETHER FOREVER (REMIX) Rick Astley—RCA 8319 [Matt Aitken/Mike Stock/Pete Waterman] [BMI] (4/16/88 BC-1)

TOGETHER LET'S FIND LOVE The 5th Dimension—Bell 45,170 [James W. Alexander/Willie Hutch] [BMI] (12/25/71 BCR-24)

TOGETHER WE CAN MAKE SUCH SWEET MUSIC The Spinners—Motown 1235 [Martin Coleman/Richard Drapkin] [BMI] (4/28/73 BCR-76)

TOGETHERNESS Frankie Avalon—Chancellor 1056 [Russell Faith] [ASC] (9/19/60 BCR-15)

TOM CAT The Rooftop Singers—Vanguard 35019 [Erik Darling/Tom Geraci/Willard Svanoe/Lynne Taylor] [BMI] (3/23/63 BCR-20)

TOM DOOLEY *The Kingston Trio—Capitol 4049 [Traditional] [BMI] (9/27/58 BCR-1)*

TOM DOOLEY *(parody of Tom Dooley) The Four Preps—Capitol 4599 [Traditional] (Med) [BMI] (8/14/61 BCR-14) [P]*

TOM HARK *Elias & His Zig Zag Jive Flutes—Capitol 3989 [Rupert Bopape] [BMI] (6/30/58 Rt-76) [I]*

TOM HARK *Ted Heath and His Orchestra—London 1809 [Rupert Bopape] [BMI] (6/30/58 Rt-76) [I]*

TOM SAWYER Rush—Mercury 76109 [Pye Dubois/Geddy Lee/Alex Lifeson/Neil Peart] [ASC] (6/6/81 BCR-44)

TOM THUMB'S TUNE *Russ Tamblyn—Metro 20012 [Peggy Lee] [ASC] (1/5/59 CRt-86)*

TOM THUMB'S TUNE *Patience & Prudence—Liberty 55169 [Peggy Lee] [ASC] (1/12/59 Rt-91)*

TOMBOY Perry Como—RCA Victor 47-7464 [Jim Conway/Joseph T. Farrell] [ASC] (2/16/59 BCR-26)

TOMBOY Ronnie Dove—Diamond 249 [Charles Segal/Frank Stanton] [ASC] (9/14/68 BCR-76)

TOMMY Reparata And The Delrons—World Artists 1051 [Ted Daryll/Chip Taylor] [BMI] (4/3/65 BCR-50)

TOMMY JONES Johnny Tillotson—MGM 13684 [Fred Haber] [BMI] (2/25/67 C-91)

TOMORROW Donnie Owens—Guyden 2006 [Buddy Wheeler] [BMI] (12/15/58 CR-86)

TOMORROW Strawberry Alarm Clock—Uni 55046 [Ed King/Mark Weitz] [ASC] (12/23/67 BCR-14)

TOMORROW (A BETTER YOU, BETTER ME) Quincy Jones featuring Tevin Campbell—Qwest 19881 [Siedah Garrett/George Johnson/Louis E. Johnson] [ASC] (5/26/90 BC-70)

TOMORROW DOESN'T MATTER TONIGHT Starship—Grunt 14332 [Steven Cristol/Robin Randall] [ASC] (4/5/86 BC-24)

TOMORROW NEVER COMES B.J. Thomas—Scepter 12165 [Johnny Bond/Ernest Tubb] [BMI] (9/10/66 BCR-80)

TOMORROW NIGHT Damita Jo—Epic 9766 [Sam Coslow/Hugh Williams] [ASC] (3/20/65 CR-88)

TOMORROW PEOPLE Ziggy Marley And The Melody Makers—Virgin 99347 [Ziggy Marley] [ASC] (5/14/88 BC-39)

—TOMORROW see: DOMANI

TOMORROW TOMORROW The Bee Gees—Atco 6682 [Barry Gibb/Maurice Gibb] [BMI] (5/24/69 BCR-32)

TOM'S DINER DNA—A&M 1529 [Suzanne Vega] [ASC] (10/6/90 BC-4)

TONGUE IN CHEEK Sugarloaf—Liberty 56218 [Robert Yeazel] [BMI] (2/27/71 BCR-40)

TONI The Tradewinds—RCA Victor 47-7511 [Del Morris/Mel Phillips] [ASC] (5/11/59 R-97)

TONIGHT *Ferrante & Teicher—United Artists 373 [Leonard Bernstein/Stephen Sondheim] [ASC] (10/16/61 BCtRt-6)*

TONIGHT *Eddie Fisher—7 Arts 719 [Leonard Bernstein/Stephen Sondheim] [ASC] (10/30/61 BCtRt-6)*

TONIGHT *Jay & The Americans—United Artists 353 [Leonard Bernstein/Stephen Sondheim] [ASC] (11/11/61 CtRt-6)*

TONIGHT Raspberries—Capitol 3610 [Eric Carmen] [BMI] (8/18/73 BCR-37)

TONIGHT The Whispers—Solar 69842 [Jerry Knight] [ASC] (4/30/83 B-84)

TONIGHT Kool & The Gang—De-Lite 830 [Clifford Adams*/Robert Bell*/Ronald Bell*/James Bonneford*/George M. Brown*/ Michael Ray*/Claydes Smith*/J.T. Taylor/Curtis Fitzgerald Williams] [BMI] (2/25/84 BC-13)

TONIGHT David Bowie—EMI America 8246
[David Bowie/Iggy Pop] [BMI] (12/1/84 BC-51)

TONIGHT New Kids On The Block—Columbia 73461
[Al Lancellotti/Maurice Starr] [ASC] (7/21/90 BC-7)

TONIGHT (COULD BE THE NIGHT) The Velvets—Monument 441
[Virgil Johnson] [BMI] (5/29/61 BCR-18)

TONIGHT, I CELEBRATE MY LOVE Peabo Bryson/Roberta Flack—Capitol 5242
[Gerry Goffin/Michael Masser] [BMI] (7/9/83 BC-14)

TONIGHT I FELL IN LOVE The Tokens—Warwick 615
[Mitch Margo/Phil Margo/Hank Medress] [ASC] (3/6/61 BCR-12)

TONIGHT I WON'T BE THERE Adam Wade—Coed 556
[Arthur Kent/Ed Warren] [ASC] (9/18/61 BCR-57)

TONIGHT I'LL BE STAYING HERE WITH YOU Bob Dylan—Columbia 45004
[Bob Dylan] [SE] (11/1/69 BCR-39)

TONIGHT I'LL SAY A PRAYER Eydie Gorme—RCA Victor 74-0250
[Robert I. Allen/Tony Renis] [ASC] (11/29/69 BCR-45) [FDE]

TONIGHT I'M YOURS (DON'T HURT ME) Rod Stewart—Warner Bros. 49886
[Jim Cregan/Kevin Savigar/Rod Stewart] [ASC] (1/23/82 BCR-15)

TONIGHT IS THE NIGHT PT. 2 Betty Wright—Alston 3740
[Willie Clarke/Betty Wright] [BMI] (10/7/78 R-87)

TONIGHT IS WHAT IT MEANS TO BE YOUNG Fire Inc.—MCA 52377
[Jim Steinman] [BMI] (6/2/84 B-80)

TONIGHT IT'S YOU Cheap Trick—Epic 05431
[Jon Brant/Rick Nielsen/Mark Radice/Robin Zander] [ASC] (7/27/85 BC-44)

TONIGHT MY HEART WILL BE CRYING *Eddie Fisher—RCA Victor 47-6849*
[Victor Abrams/Morris Levy‡/Irving Reid] [BMI] (3/16/57 BRt-50)

TONIGHT MY HEART SHE IS CRYING *Shirley Bassey—Columbia 40848*
[Victor Abrams/Morris Levy‡/Irving Reid] [BMI] (4/6/57 Rt-50)

TONIGHT MY HEART SHE IS CRYING
El Boy with The Ralph Sayho Calypso Singers—Rama 220
[Victor Abrams/Morris Levy‡/Irving Reid] [BMI] (4/6/57 Rt-50)

TONIGHT MY LOVE, TONIGHT Paul Anka—ABC-Paramount 10194
[Paul Anka] [BMI] (3/6/61 BCR-10)

TONIGHT SHE COMES The Cars—Elektra 69589 [Ric Ocasek] [ASC] (11/2/85 BC-7)

TONIGHT TONIGHT Bill Champlin—Elektra 47240
[Bill Champlin/David Foster/Ray Kennedy] [BMI] (12/26/81 BCR-55)

TONIGHT, TONIGHT, TONIGHT Genesis—Atlantic 89290
[Tony Banks/Phil Collins/Mike Rutherford] [ASC] (2/14/87 BC-3)

TONIGHT YOU BELONG TO ME *Patience and Prudence—Liberty 55022*
[Lee David/Billy Rose] [ASC] (8/4/56 BCtRt-3)

TONIGHT YOU BELONG TO ME *The Tracey Twins—Reserve 110*
[Lee David/Billy Rose] [ASC] (9/1/56 Rt-17)

TONIGHT YOU BELONG TO ME *Lawrence Welk And His Sparkling Strings—Coral 61701*
[Lee David/Billy Rose] [ASC] (9/15/56 BCtRt-3)

TONIGHT YOU BELONG TO ME *Karen Chandler & Jimmy Wakely—Decca 30040*
[Lee David/Billy Rose] [ASC] (9/22/56 BRt-4)

TONIGHT YOU'RE GONNA FALL IN LOVE WITH ME The Shirelles—Scepter 1264
[Artie Kornfeld/Toni Wine] [BMI] (1/4/64 BCR-35)

TONIGHT'S THE NIGHT *The Shirelles—Scepter 1208*
[Luther Dixon/Shirley Owens] [BMI] (9/10/60 BCRt-20)

TONIGHT'S THE NIGHT *The Chiffons—Big Deal 6003*
[Luther Dixon/Shirley Owens] [BMI] (9/12/60 BRt-59)

TONIGHT'S THE NIGHT Solomon Burke—Atlantic 2288
[Solomon Burke/Don Covay] [BMI] (5/29/65 BCR-22)

TONIGHT'S THE NIGHT S.S.O.—Shady Brook 019
[Doug Lucas/François Weyer] [BMI] (1/10/76 B-99)

TONIGHT'S THE NIGHT (GONNA BE ALRIGHT) Rod Stewart—Warner Bros. 8262
[Rod Stewart] [ASC] (10/2/76 BCR-1)

TONITE DJ Quik—Profile 5338 [David Marvin Blake] [ASC] (8/24/91 B-49)

TONITE, TONITE *The Mello-Kings—Herald 502 [Billy Myles] [BMI] (8/19/57 B-77)*

TONITE, TONITE *Mello-Kings—Herald 502 [Billy Myles] [BMI] (1/23/61 B-95)*

TONY ROME Nancy Sinatra—Reprise 0636 [Lee Hazlewood] [ASC] (12/2/67 BR-83)

TOO BAD Ben E. King—Atco 6231 [Betty Woods] [BMI] (7/28/62 BCR-67)

TOO BEAUTIFUL TO LAST Engelbert Humperdinck—Parrot 40069
[Richard Rodney Bennett/Paul Francis Webster] [ASC] (4/1/72 BCR-75)

TOO BLIND TO SEE IT Kym Sims—Atco 98667 [Steve Hurley] [ASC] (11/16/91 BC-38)

TOO BUSY THINKING ABOUT MY BABY Marvin Gaye—Tamla 54181
[Janie Bradford/Barrett Strong/Norman Whitfield] [BMI] (4/19/69 BCR-4)

TOO CLOSE FOR COMFORT *Sammy Davis Jr.—Decca 29861*
[Jerry Bock/Lawrence Holofcener/George David Weiss] [BMI] (3/16/56 Rt-40)

TOO CLOSE FOR COMFORT *Eydie Gorme—ABC-Paramount 9684*
[Jerry Bock/Lawrence Holofcener/George David Weiss] [BMI] (4/20/56 BCRt-39)

TOO CLOSE FOR COMFORT *Lillian Briggs—Epic 9166*
[Jerry Bock/Lawrence Holofcener/George David Weiss] [BMI] (6/1/56 Rt-58)

TOO EXPERIENCED Eddie Lovette—Steady 124
[Keith Anderson/Luther Dixon] [NA] (5/10/69 BCR-79)

TOO GOOD TO TURN BACK NOW Rick Bowles—Polydor 2209
[Rick Bowles/Richard Putnam] [BMI] (7/3/82 BC-75)

TOO HOT Kool & The Gang—De-Lite 802 [George M. Brown] [BMI] (1/19/80 BCR-5)

TOO HOT Loverboy—Columbia 73066 [Paul Dean/Mike Reno] [ASC] (12/2/89 BC-78)

TOO HOT TA TROT Commodores—Motown 1432
[William King/Ronald LaPread/Thomas McClary/Walter Orange/Lionel Richie/Milan Williams] [ASC] (12/17/77 BCR-24)

TOO HOT TO HANDLE UFO—Chrysalis 2157 [Phil Mogg/Pete Way] [ASC] (8/27/77 C-94)

TOO HOT TO HOLD Major Lance—Okeh 7226 [Gerald Sims] [BMI] (8/28/65 BCR-80)

TOO HOT TO STOP Bar-Kays—Mercury 73888
[James Edward Alexander/Charles Leonard Allen/Michael Beard/Larry Dodson/Frederick Freeman/Harvey Henderson/Harry Nehls/Lloyd Ed Smith/Winston Stewart/Frank Thompson] [BMI] (2/12/77 BR-74)

TOO LATE Gene Austin—RCA Victor 47-6880 [Gene Austin] [ASC] (5/27/57 B-75)

TOO LATE Tavares—Capitol 3882 [Dennis Lambert/Brian Potter] [BMI] (6/1/74 BCR-54)

TOO LATE Shoes—Elektra 46557 [Gary Klebe] [BMI] (11/3/79 BCR-74)

TOO LATE Journey—Columbia 11143 [Steve Perry/Neal Schon] [BMI] (12/22/79 BCR-70)

TOO LATE FOR GOODBYES Julian Lennon—Atlantic 89589
[Julian Lennon] [ASC] (1/19/85 BC-5)

TOO LATE NOW The DeCastro Sisters—Abbott 3011
[Burton Lane/Alan Jay Lerner] [ASC] (12/17/55 B-66)

TOO LATE TO SAY GOODBYE Richard Marx—EMI 50234
[Richard Marx/Fee Waybill] [ASC] (1/20/90 BC-12)

TOO LATE TO TURN BACK NOW Brook Benton—Mercury 72266
[Clyde Otis] [BMI] (5/9/64 BCR-38)

TOO LATE TO TURN BACK NOW Cornelius Brothers & Sister Rose—United Artists 50910
[Eddie Cornelius] [BMI] (5/20/72 BCR-1)

TOO LATE TO WORRY - TOO BLUE TO CRY *Glen Campbell—Capitol 4783*
[Al Dexter] [BMI] (7/28/62 BCR-73)

TOO LATE TO WORRY, TOO BLUE TO CRY *Ronnie Milsap—RCA Victor 10228*
[Al Dexter] [BMI] (4/19/75 C-87)

2 LEGIT 2 QUIT M.C. Hammer—Capitol 44785
[Louis Burrell/Stanley Burrell/James Earley/Michael Kelly/Felton Pilate] [BMI] (11/2/91 BC-5)

TOO LITTLE TIME Brenda Lee—Decca 31917
[Marvin Hamlisch/Howard Liebling] [ASC] (3/19/66 R-96)

TOO MANY COOKS (SPOIL THE SOUP) 100 Proof Aged In Soul—Hot Wax 6904
[Angelo Bond/Lamont Dozier/Ronald Dunbar/Brian Holland/Eddie Holland] [BMI] (12/20/69 B-94)

TOO MANY FISH IN THE SEA *The Marvelettes—Tamla 54105*
[Eddie Holland/Norman Whitfield] [BMI] (11/7/64 BCR-21)

TOO MANY FISH IN THE SEA *Mitch Ryder And The Detroit Wheels—New Voice 822*
[Eddie Holland/Norman Whitfield] (Med) [BMI] (4/29/67 BCR-20)

TOO MANY LOVERS Shack—Volt 4051
[Homer Banks/Raymond Earl Jackson] [BMI] (3/6/71 CR-81)

TOO MANY RIVERS Brenda Lee—Decca 31792 [Harlan Howard] [BMI] (5/22/65 BCR-13)

TOO MANY RULES Connie Francis—MGM 13019
[Gary Knight/Don Stirling] [BMI] (7/1/61 BCR-64)

TOO MANY WALLS Cathy Dennis—Polydor 867 134
[Cathy Dennis/Anne Dudley] [ASC] (6/29/91 BC-8)

TOO MUCH Elvis Presley—RCA Victor 47-6800
[Bill Beasley/Joan Norris/Lee Rosenberg‡/Bernard Weinman‡] [BMI] (1/19/57 BCR-1)

TOO MUCH Tara Kemp—Giant 19168
[Tara Kemp/Tuhin Roy] [BMI] (10/26/91 B-95)

TOO MUCH AIN'T ENOUGH LOVE Jimmy Barnes—Geffen 27920
[Jimmy Barnes/Tony Brock/Jonathan Cain/Randall Darnell Jackson/Neal Schon] [BMI] (7/9/88 B-91)

TOO MUCH HEAVEN Bee Gees—RSO 913
[Barry Gibb/Maurice Gibb/Robin Gibb] [BMI] (11/18/78 BCR-1)

TOO MUCH LOVE TO HIDE Crosby, Stills & Nash—Atlantic 89888
[Stephen Stills/Gerry Tolman] [BMI] (1/29/83 BC-69)

TOO MUCH OF NOTHING Peter, Paul & Mary—Warner Bros. 7092
[Bob Dylan] [SE] (11/25/67 BCR-35)

TOO MUCH TALK Paul Revere And The Raiders Featuring Mark Lindsay—Columbia 44444
[Mark Lindsay] [BMI] (2/10/68 BCR-11)

TOO MUCH TEQUILA The Champs—Challenge 59063
[Dave Burgess] [BMI] (1/11/60 BCR-21) [I]

TOO MUCH TIME ON MY HANDS Styx—A&M 2323 [Tommy Shaw] [ASC] (3/21/81 BCR-7)

TOO MUCH, TOO LITTLE, TOO LATE Johnny Mathis/Deniece Williams—Columbia 10693
[Nat Kipner/John Vallins] [BMI] (3/18/78 BCR-1)

TOO POOPED TO POP "CASEY" Chuck Berry—Chess 1747
[Billy Davis/Alonso Mitchell*] [BMI] (2/6/60 BCR-42)

TOO SHY Kajagoogoo—EMI America 8161
[Steven Askew/Nick Beggs/Christopher Hamill/Stuart Neale/Jeremy Strode] [ASC] (4/23/83 BC-5)

TOO SLOW The Impressions—ABC-Paramount 10789
[Curtis Mayfield] [BMI] (4/2/66 BCR-91)

TOO SOON TO KNOW Roy Orbison—MGM 13549 [Don Gibson] [BMI] (7/23/66 BCR-62)

TOO TIGHT Con Funk Shun—Mercury 76089
[Michael V. Cooper] [BMI] (12/27/80 BCR-34)

TOO WEAK TO FIGHT Clarence Carter—Atlantic 2569
[Clarence Carter/Rick Hall/George Henry Jackson/John Keyes] [BMI] (11/2/68 BCR-7)

TOO YOUNG Donny Osmond—MGM 14407
[Sylvia Dee/Sid Lippman] [ASC] (6/10/72 BCR-8)

TOO YOUNG Jack Wagner—Qwest 28931
[David Foster/Jay Graydon/Steve Kipner/Donny Osmond] [BMI] (10/26/85 BC-52)

TOO YOUNG TO FALL IN LOVE Mötley Crüe—Elektra 69732
[Nikki Sixx] [ASC] (6/16/84 B-90)

TOO YOUNG TO GO STEADY *Nat "King" Cole—Capitol 3390*
[Harold Adamson/Jimmy McHugh] [ASC] (3/24/56 BCRt-20)

TOO YOUNG TO GO STEADY *Patti Page—Mercury 70820*
[Harold Adamson/Jimmy McHugh] [ASC] (3/30/56 BRt-20)

TOO YOUNG TO GO STEADY *Connie Stevens—Warner Bros. 5159*
[Harold Adamson/Jimmy McHugh] [ASC] (7/4/60 BC-71)

TOO YOUNG TO LOVE YOU Timmy -T-—Quality 15116 [Timmy Torres] [BMI] (9/14/91 C-85)

TOOK THE LAST TRAIN David Gates—Elektra 45500
[David Gates/Larry Knechtel] [ASC] (8/12/78 BCR-30)

TOOT, TOOT, TOOTSIE The Johnston Brothers—London 1526
[Ernie Erdman/Gus Kahn/Dan Russo] (Med) [NA] (7/11/55 R-61)

TOP FORTY, NEWS, WEATHER AND SPORTS Mark Dinning—MGM 12980
[John D. Loudermilk] [BMI] (2/20/61 BCR-59)

TOP FORTY (OF THE LORD) Sha Na Na—Kama Sutra 528
[Scott Simon] [BMI] (8/7/71 BCR-84)

TOP OF THE WORLD *Lynn Anderson—Columbia 45857*
[John Bettis/Richard Carpenter] [ASC] (6/23/73 BC-74)

TOP OF THE WORLD *Carpenters—A&M 1468*
[John Bettis/Richard Carpenter] [ASC] (9/29/73 BCR-1)

TOP OF THE WORLD Van Halen—Warner Bros. 19151
[Michael Anthony/Sammy Hagar/Alex Van Halen/Eddie Van Halen] [ASC]
(10/5/91 BC-15)

TOP OF THE WORLD (MAKE MY RESERVATION) Canyon—Magna-Glide 323
[Ellison Chase/William Haberman] [BMI] (6/14/75 BC-98)

—TOPICAL SONG see: LOGICAL SONG

TOPSY I Cozy Cole—Love 5004 [Edgar Battle/Eddie Durham] [ASC] (9/15/58 B-27) [IM]

TOPSY II Cozy Cole—Love 5004 [Edgar Battle/Eddie Durham] [ASC] (8/25/58 BCR-1) [IM]

TORERO *Renato Carosone—Capitol 71080*
[Renato Carosone/Nicola Salerno] [ASC] (4/26/58 BCRt-19) [F]

TORERO *Julius La Rosa—RCA Victor 47-7227*
[Renato Carosone/Al Hoffman/Dick Manning/Nicola Salerno] [ASC]
(4/28/58 Rt-21) [FDE]

TORERO *The Andrews Sisters—Capitol 3965*
[Renato Carosone/Al Hoffman/Dick Manning/Nicola Salerno] [ASC]
(6/2/58 Rt-21) [FDE]

TORN BETWEEN TWO LOVERS Mary MacGregor—Ariola America 7638
[Phil Jarrell/Peter Yarrow] [ASC] (11/13/76 BCR-1)

TORQUAY Fireballs—Top Rank 2008
[George Tomsco] [BMI] (9/7/59 BCR-34) [I]

TORTURE Kris Jensen—Hickory 1173 [John D. Loudermilk] [BMI] (8/18/62 BCR-17)

TORTURE Jacksons—Epic 04575
[Jackie Jackson/Kathy Wakefield] [ASC] (8/18/84 BC-16)

TOSSIN' AND TURNIN' *Bobby Lewis—Beltone 1002*
[Ritchie Adams/Malou René] [BMI] (4/24/61 BCR-1)

TOSSIN' AND TURNIN' *Bunny Sigler—Philadelphia Int'l 3523*
[Ritchie Adams/Malou René] [BMI] (2/10/73 B-97)

TOSSING & TURNING The Ivy League—Cameo 377
[John Carter/Perry Ford*/Ken Hawker] [ASC] (9/11/65 BCR-48)

TOTAL ECLIPSE OF THE HEART Bonnie Tyler—Columbia 03906
[Jim Steinman] [BMI] (7/16/83 BC-1)

TOTAL STRANGERS Hank Thompson And His Brazos Valley Boys—Capitol 4182
[Hank Thompson] [BMI] (5/4/59 R-84)

TOTALLY HOT Olivia Newton-John—MCA 41074 [John Farrar] [BMI] (7/28/79 BCR-52)

THE TOUCH (LE GRISBI) *The Three Suns—RCA Victor 47-5874*
[Jean Wiener] [BMI] (10/16/54 CRt-21) [IM]

THE TOUCH *Betty Johnson—New-Disc 10012*
[Norman Gimbel/Jean Wiener] [BMI] (10/18/54 Rt-79)

TOUCH The Supremes—Motown 1190
[Pam Sawyer/Frank Edward Wilson] [BMI] (10/2/71 BCR-53)

TOUCH A FOUR LEAF CLOVER Atlantic Starr—A&M 2580
[David E. Lewis/Wayne I. Lewis] [ASC] (12/10/83 B-87)

TOUCH A HAND, MAKE A FRIEND The Staple Singers—Stax 0196
[Homer Banks/Carl Hampton/Raymond Earl Jackson] [BMI] (2/23/74 BCR-18)

TOUCH AND GO Al Wilson—Rocky Road 30076 [Jerry Fuller] [BMI] (3/2/74 BCR-48)

TOUCH AND GO Ecstasy, Passion & Pain Featuring Barbara Roy—Roulette 7182
[Allan Felder/Norman Harris/Bunny Sigler] [BMI] (6/5/76 B-98)

TOUCH AND GO The Cars—Elektra 47039 [Ric Ocasek] [ASC] (9/6/80 BCR-37)

TOUCH AND GO Emerson, Lake & Powell—Polydor 885101
[Keith Emerson/Greg Lake] [ASC] (6/21/86 BC-60)

TOUCH AND GONE Gary Wright—Warner Bros. 8494
[Richard Reicheg/Gary Wright] [ASC] (1/21/78 B-73)

TOUCH ME The Doors—Elektra 45646
[John Densmore/Robby Krieger/Ray Manzarek/Jim Morrison] [ASC] (12/28/68 BCR-1)

TOUCH ME Fancy—Big Tree 16026
[Raymond Fenwick/Mike Hurst] [BMI] (10/12/74 BCR-19)

TOUCH ME (ALL NIGHT LONG) Cathy Dennis—Polydor 879 466
[Patrick Adams/Cathy Dennis*/C. Delyle Gregory] [ASC] (3/2/91 BC-2)

TOUCH ME BABY Ultimate—Casablanca 966 [Giuliano Salerni] [ASC] (4/14/79 BR-82)

TOUCH ME BABY (REACHING OUT FOR YOUR LOVE) Tamiko Jones—Arista 0110
[Johnny Bristol] [ASC] (3/8/75 BCR-60)

TOUCH ME (I WANT YOUR BODY) Samantha Fox—Jive 1006
[Jon Astrop/Peter Brian Harris/Mark Shreeve] [ASC] (11/1/86 BC-4)

TOUCH ME IN THE MORNING Diana Ross—Motown 1239
[Michael Masser/Ronald Norman Miller] [BMI] (5/26/73 BCR-1)

TOUCH ME TONIGHT Shooting Star—Enigma 75054 [Van McLain] [BMI] (11/4/89 B-67)

TOUCH ME WHEN WE'RE DANCING *Bama—Free Flight 11629*
[Kenneth Edward Bell/Terry Skinner/J.L. Wallace] [BMI] (10/6/79 BC-86)

TOUCH ME WHEN WE'RE DANCING *Carpenters—A&M 2344*
[Kenneth Edward Bell/Terry Skinner/J.L. Wallace] [BMI] (6/20/81 BCR-16)

TOUCH OF GREY Grateful Dead—Arista 1-9606
[Jerry Garcia/Robert Hunter] [ASC] (7/25/87 BC-9)

TOUCH OF MAGIC James Leroy—Janus 219 [James Leroy] [ASC] (7/28/73 CR-80)

A TOUCH OF PINK *Dick Jacobs & His Orchestra—Coral 62086*
[Diane Lampert/Richard Loring] [ASC] (3/23/59 Rt-93)

A TOUCH OF PINK *Jerry Wallace—Challenge 59040*
[Diane Lampert/Richard Loring] [ASC] (3/23/59 BRt-92)

THE TOUCH OF YOU Brenda & The Tabulations—Top & Bottom 401
[Eddie L. Jackson/Jerry Jones] [BMI] (1/17/70 BCR-50)

TOUCH THE FIRE Icehouse—Chrysalis 23414 [Iva Davies] [ASC] (10/7/89 B-84)

TOUCH THE HAND Conway Twitty—MCA 40407
[Ronald Robert Peterson*/Conway Twitty] [BMI] (6/28/75 C-75)

—TOUCH THE WIND see: ERES TU

THE TOUCHABLES Dickie Goodman—Mark-X 8009
[Robert Arkin*/Melvin Glazer*/Dickie Goodman] [BMI] (2/6/61 BCR-23)

THE TOUCHABLES IN BROOKLYN Dickie Goodman—Mark-X 8010
[Robert Arkin*/Melvin Glazer*/Dickie Goodman] [BMI] (4/24/61 BCR-42)

TOUGH ALL OVER John Cafferty And The Beaver Brown Band—Scotti Brothers 04891
[John Cafferty] [BMI] (5/11/85 BC-20)

TOUGH WORLD Donnie Iris—MCA 52127
[Mark Avsec/Martin Lee Hoenes/Donnie Iris] [ASC] (10/23/82 BC-57)

TOUS LES CHEMINS (ALL THE ROADS) The Singing Nun (Soeur Sourire)—Philips 40165
[Jeanine Deckers] [ASC] (1/25/64 CR-87) [F]

TOWER OF STRENGTH Gene McDaniels—Liberty 55371
[Burt Bacharach/Bob Hilliard] [ASC] (9/25/61 BCR-5)

TOWER TROT (AND THEN YOU DO THAT STEP)
Dick Jacobs And His Chorus And Orchestra—Coral 61794
[Gary Belkin/Mel Brooks/Sid Caesar/Larry Gelbart/Bernard Green/Sheldon Keller/
Neil Simon/Michael Stewart/Mel Tolkin] [ASC] (3/9/57 B-73)

TOWN CRIER Al Hibbler—Decca 30176
[Moose Charlap/Milton Drake] [ASC] (1/26/57 R-73)

TOWN WITHOUT PITY Gene Pitney—Musicor 1009
[Dimitri Tiomkin/Ned Washington] [ASC] (10/23/61 BCR-11)

TOY SOLDIER The 4 Seasons Featuring The "Sound" Of Frankie Valli—Philips 40278
[Bob Crewe/Bob Gaudio] [BMI] (4/3/65 BCR-54)

TOY SOLDIERS Martika—Columbia 68747 [Michael Jay/Martika] [BMI] (5/20/89 BC-1)

TOY TIGER *Les Baxter & His Orchestra—Capitol 3195*
[Henry Mancini/Herman Stein] [ASC] (9/12/55 Rt-76) [IM]

TOY TIGER *Johnny Long & His Orchestra—Coral 61478*
[Henry Mancini/Herman Stein] [ASC] (9/12/55 Rt-76) [IM]

TOY TIGER *Victor Young And His Singing Strings—Decca 29653*
[Henry Mancini/Herman Stein] [ASC] (9/12/55 Rt-76) [IM]

TOY TIGER *Ralph Marterie & His Orchestra—Mercury 70692*
[Henry Mancini/Herman Stein] [ASC] (9/12/55 Rt-76) [IM]

TOYLAND Alan Bown—Music Factory 402
[Tony Catchpole/Jess Roden] [BMI] (1/20/68 CR-84)

TOYS ARE MADE FOR CHILDREN The Uniques—Paula 324
[Spooner Oldham/Dan Penn] [BMI] (8/16/69 R-84)

TOYS IN THE ATTIC *Jack Jones—Kapp 551*
[George Duning/Joe Sherman/George David Weiss] [ASC] (10/5/63 BCtRt-76)

TOYS IN THE ATTIC *Joe Sherman, His Orchestra And Chorus—World Artists 1008*
[George Duning/Joe Sherman/George David Weiss] [ASC] (10/5/63 BCtRt-76)

TOYS IN THE ATTIC *Dennis Regor—Contempo 904*
[George Duning/Joe Sherman/George David Weiss] [ASC] (10/12/63 CtRt-88) [IWM]

TRA LA LA *Georgia Gibbs—Mercury 70998 [Johnny Parker] [BMI] (11/24/56 BCRt-25)*

TRA LA LA *LaVern Baker—Atlantic 1116 [Johnny Parker] [BMI] (11/24/56 BRt-25)*

TRA LA LA LA LA Ike & Tina Turner—Sue 757 [Ike Turner] [BMI] (3/24/62 BCR-50)

TRA LA LA SUZY Dean And Jean—Rust 5067
[Brenda Lee Jones/Welton Young] [BMI] (11/2/63 BCR-34)

THE TRA LA LA SONG (ONE BANANA, TWO BANANA) The Banana Splits—Decca 32429
[Ritchie Adams/Mark Barkan] [BMI] (2/8/69 B-96)

TRACES *Classics IV Featuring Dennis Yost—Imperial 66352*
[Buddy Buie/J.R. Cobb/Emory Gordy] [BMI] (2/1/69 BCR-2)

TRACES *The Lettermen—Capitol 2697 [Buddy Buie/J.R. Cobb/Emory Gordy] (Med) [BMI] (12/13/69 BCR-47)*

THE TRACKS OF MY TEARS *The Miracles—Tamla 54118 [Warren Moore/Smokey Robinson/Marvin Tarplin] [ASC] (7/10/65 BCR-16)*

THE TRACKS OF MY TEARS *Johnny Rivers—Imperial 66244 [Warren Moore/Smokey Robinson/Marvin Tarplin] [ASC] (6/3/67 BCR-10)*

TRACKS OF MY TEARS *Aretha Franklin—Atlantic 2603 [Warren Moore/Smokey Robinson/Marvin Tarplin] [ASC] (3/15/69 BR-69)*

TRACKS OF MY TEARS *Linda Ronstadt—Asylum 45295 [Warren Moore/Smokey Robinson/Marvin Tarplin] [ASC] (12/20/75 BCR-25)*

TRACY The Cuff Links—Decca 32533 [Lee Pockriss/Paul Vance] [ASC] (8/30/69 BCR-4)

TRACY'S THEME Spencer Ross—Columbia 41532 [Robert Ascher] [BMI] (12/28/59 BCR-13) [I]

TRADE WINDS Billy Vaughn And His Orchestra—Dot 15900 [Cliff Friend/Charles Tobias] [ASC] (2/16/59 CR-43) [IWM]

TRADE WINDS, TRADE WINDS Aki Aleong—Reprise 20,021 [Aki Aleong/Craig Jenkins/Tony Wynn] [BMI] (11/25/61 C-93)

TRAGEDY *Thomas Wayne with The DeLons—Fernwood 109 [Fred Burch/Gerald Nelson] [BMI] (1/19/59 BCR-5)*

TRAGEDY *The Fleetwoods—Dolton 40 [Fred Burch/Gerald Nelson] [BMI] (4/17/61 BCR-10)*

TRAGEDY *Brian Hyland—Dot 17176 [Fred Burch/Gerald Nelson] [BMI] (12/14/68 BCR-34)*

TRAGEDY Argent—Epic 10919 [Russ Ballard] [BMI] (11/11/72 C-81)

TRAGEDY Bee Gees—RSO 918 [Barry Gibb/Maurice Gibb/Robin Gibb] [BMI] (2/10/79 BCR-1)

TRAGEDY John Hunter—Private I 4-04643 [John Martin Hunter Jr.] [BMI] (12/8/84 BC-31)

THE TRAIN 1910 Fruitgum Co.—Buddah 130 [Ritchie Cordell/Jerry Kasenetz/Jeff Katz] [BMI] (8/9/69 BCR-52)

TRAIN CALLED FREEDOM South Shore Commission—Wand 11294 [Bunny Sigler/Ronnie Tyson] [BMI] (2/28/76 BCR-86)

TRAIN IN VAIN (STAND BY ME) The Clash—Epic 50851 [Nicky Headon*/Michael Geoffrey Jones/Paul Simonon*/Joe Strummer] [ASC] (3/22/80 BCR-23)

TRAIN OF GLORY Jonathan Edwards—Atco 6881 [Jonathan Edwards] [ASC] (3/18/72 CR-69)

TRAIN OF LOVE Annette With The Afterbeats—Buena Vista 359 [Paul Anka] [BMI] (5/23/60 BCR-36)

TRAIN OF THOUGHT Cher—MCA 40245 [Alan O'Day] [ASC] (5/18/74 BCR-18)

TRAIN, TRAIN Blackfoot—Atco 7207 [Shorty Medlocke] [BMI] (10/20/79 BCR-36)

TRAINS AND BOATS AND PLANES *Billy J. Kramer & The Dakotas—Imperial 66115 [Burt Bacharach/Hal David] [ASC] (6/19/65 BCR-47)*

TRAINS AND BOATS AND PLANES *Dionne Warwick—Scepter 12153 [Burt Bacharach/Hal David] [ASC] (7/2/66 BCR-22)*

TRAMP *Lowell Fulsom—Kent 456 [Lowell Fulsom/Jimmy McCracklin] [BMI] (1/14/67 BCR-51)*

TRAMP *Otis & Carla—Stax 216 [Lowell Fulsom/Jimmy McCracklin] [BMI] (5/6/67 BCR-18)*

TRAMPLED UNDER FOOT Led Zeppelin—Swan Song 70102 [John Paul Jones/Jimmy Page/Robert Plant] [ASC] (4/12/75 BCR-28)

TRANQUILLO Carly Simon—Elektra 45544 [Arif Mardin/Carly Simon/James Taylor] [BMI] (12/9/78 C-86)

TRANS-EUROPE EXPRESS Kraftwerk—Capitol 4460 [Ralf Hutter] [ASC] (6/3/78 BCR-67) [IM]

TRANSFUSION *Nervous Norvus—Dot 15470 [Jimmy Drake] [BMI] (6/1/56 BCRt-10)*

TRANSFUSION *The Four Jokers—Diamond 3004 [Jimmy Drake] [BMI] (6/15/56 Rt-24)*

TRANSISTOR SISTER Freddy Cannon—Swan 4078 [Chuck Dougherty/Frank Slay] [ASC] (7/24/61 BCR-31)

TRAPPED BY A THING CALLED LOVE Denise LaSalle—Westbound 182 [Denise LaSalle] [BMI] (8/21/71 BCR-9)

TRAVELIN' BAND Creedence Clearwater Revival—Fantasy 637 [John Fogerty] (TSW) [BMI] (1/31/70 BCR-2)

TRAVELIN' MAN Ricky Nelson—Imperial 5741 [Jerry Fuller] [BMI] (4/22/61 BCR-1)

TRAVELIN' PRAYER Billy Joel—Columbia 10015 [Billy Joel] [ASC] (8/17/74 BCR-59)

TRAVELIN' SHOES Elvin Bishop—Capricorn 0202 [Elvin Bishop] [ASC] (9/14/74 BCR-44)

TRAVELING BOY Garfunkel—Columbia 46030 [Roger Nichols/Paul Williams] [ASC] (4/6/74 C-70)

TRAVELING DOWN A LONELY ROAD Teddi King—RCA Victor 47-6660 [Michele Galdieri/Don Raye/Nino Rota] [ASC] (10/6/56 R-79)

—TRAVELLER see: DAYS ARE NUMBERS

TRAVLIN' MAN Stevie Wonder—Tamla 54147 [Ronald Norman Miller/Bryan Wells] [BMI] (3/4/67 BCR-32)

—TRE VOLTE BACIAMI see: KISS ME AND KISS ME AND KISS ME

TREASURE The Brothers Johnson—A&M 2254 [Rod Temperton] [ASC] (8/16/80 B-73)

TREASURE OF LOVE *Clyde McPhatter—Atlantic 1092 [Joe Shapiro/Lou Stallman] [BMI] (5/11/56 BCRt-13)*

TREASURE OF LOVE *Dorothy Collins—Coral 61647 [Joe Shapiro/Lou Stallman] [BMI] (5/18/56 Rt-15)*

TREASURE OF YOUR LOVE Eileen Rodgers—Columbia 41214 [Barry De Vorzon] [BMI] (8/25/58 BCR-26)

TREAT 'EM RIGHT Chubb Rock—Select 5009 [McKinley Jackson*/Richard Simpson/Melvin Steals*/Mervin Steals*/Howard Thompson] [BMI] (5/18/91 B-95)

TREAT 'EM TOUGH Jimmy Soul—S.P.Q.R. 3310 [Frank Guida/Joseph Royster] [BMI] (7/13/63 CR-79)

TREAT HER LIKE A LADY Cornelius Brothers & Sister Rose—United Artists 50721 [Eddie Cornelius] [BMI] (3/13/71 BCR-2)

TREAT HER LIKE A LADY The Temptations—Gordy 1765 [Otis Clayburne Williams/Ollie Woodson] [ASC] (12/15/84 BC-48)

TREAT HER RIGHT Roy Head And The Traits—Back Beat 546 [Roy Head/Gene Kurtz*] [BMI] (9/4/65 BCR-2)

TREAT ME LIKE A GOOD PIECE OF CANDY Dusk—Bell 45,148 [L. Russell Brown/Irwin Levine] [BMI] (11/27/71 CR-71)

TREAT ME NICE Elvis Presley—RCA Victor 47-7035 [Jerry Leiber/Mike Stoller] [BMI] (9/30/57 BCR-27)

TREAT ME RIGHT Pat Benatar—Chrysalis 2487 [Pat Benatar*/Doug Lubahn] [BMI] (1/17/81 BCR-10)

TREAT MY BABY GOOD Bobby Darin—Capitol 5019 [Bobby Darin] [BMI] (8/17/63 BCR-29)

TREES *Al Hibbler—Decca 30176 [Joyce Kilmer/Oscar Rasbach] [NA] (2/2/57 BR-76)*

TREES *The Platters—Mercury 71791 [Joyce Kilmer/Oscar Rasbach] [NA] (3/27/61 BCR-51)*

TRES CHIC Geoff Gilmore & The Sheiks—Jamie 1132 [Jack Hoffman/Buddy Motola/Charles Rosoff] [ASC] (8/29/59 CR-84)

TRIANGLE Janie Grant—Caprice 104 [Janie Grant] [BMI] (3/27/61 BCR-23)

TRIANGLE OF LOVE (HEY DIDDLE DIDDLE) The Presidents—Sussex 212 [Joe Cobb/Van McCoy] [BMI] (1/23/71 BCR-52)

TRIBUTE Anthony Newley—Acappella 778 [Anthony Newley] [BMI] (1/4/64 CR-89)

TRIBUTE (RIGHT ON) The Pasadenas—Columbia 68575 [Jon Banfield/Jeffrey Aaron Brown/David Milliner/Michael Milliner/Hammish Seelochan/Pete Wingfield] [BMI] (2/25/89 BC-42)

A TRIBUTE TO A KING William Bell—Stax 248 [William Bell/Booker T. Jones Jr.] [BMI] (4/27/68 BCR-79)

TRICIA TELL YOUR DADDY Andy Kim—Steed 715 [Jeff Barry/Marty Sanders] [BMI] (3/15/69 CR-83)

A TRICK OF THE NIGHT Bananarama—London 886119 [Steve Jolley/Tony Swain] [BMI] (12/13/86 BC-71)

TRICKLE, TRICKLE *The Videos—Casino 102 [Clarence Bassett] [BMI] (9/13/58 C-90)*

TRICKLE TRICKLE *The Manhattan Transfer—Atlantic 3772 [Clarence Bassett] [BMI] (11/29/80 BCR-73)*

TRICKY *Gus Jenkins—Flash 115 [Gus Jenkins] [BMI] (12/1/56 B-79) [I]*

TRICKY *Ralph Marterie And His Orchestra—Mercury 71050 [Gus Jenkins] [BMI] (3/9/57 BCRt-37) [I]*

TRICKY *The Rhythm Rockers Featuring Chet Atkins—RCA Victor 47-6808 [Gus Jenkins] [BMI] (4/13/57 Rt-59) [I]*

TRIED TO LOVE Peter Frampton—A&M 1988 [Peter Frampton] [ASC] (12/3/77 BCR-41)

TROGLODYTE (CAVE MAN) The Jimmy Castor Bunch—RCA Victor 48-1029 [Jimmy Castor/Langdon Fridie/Douglas Gibson/Harry Jensen/Robert Manigault/Gerald Thomas] [BMI] (5/6/72 BCR-2)

TROPICAL MERENGUE Percy Faith And His Orchestra—Columbia 40543 [Rafael Munoz Sr.] [BMI] (9/12/55 R-79) [I]

TROUBLE Elvis Presley with the Jordanaires—RCA Victor EPA-4321 [Jerry Leiber/Mike Stoller] (EP) [BMI] (8/18/58 R-56)

TROUBLE Frederick Knight—Stax 0139 [Frederick Knight/Aaron Varnell] [BMI] (9/16/72 CR-80)

TROUBLE Lindsey Buckingham—Asylum 47223 [Lindsey Buckingham] [ASC] (10/24/81 BCR-8)

TROUBLE Nia Peeples—Mercury 870154 [Stephen Laurence Harvey] [ASC] (5/7/88 BC-35)

TROUBLE DOWN HERE BELOW Lou Rawls—Capitol 5824 [John W. Anderson] [BMI] (1/28/67 BC-91)

TROUBLE IN MIND *Nina Simone—Colpix 175 [Richard M. Jones] [ASC] (1/14/61 BC-92)*

TROUBLE IN MIND *Aretha Franklin—Columbia 42625 [Richard M. Jones] [ASC] (12/15/62 B-86)*

TROUBLE IN MY HOME Joe Simon—Spring 130 [Raeford Gerald/Joe Simon] (TSW) [BMI] (11/18/72 BCR-47)

TROUBLE IN PARADISE The Crests—Coed 531 [Allyson Khent/Billy Dawn Smith] [BMI] (6/13/60 BCR-20)

TROUBLE IN PARADISE Al Jarreau—Warner Bros. 29501 [Jay Graydon/Greg Mathieson/Trevor Veitch] [ASC] (9/10/83 BC-63)

TROUBLE IS MY MIDDLE NAME Bobby Vinton—Epic 9561 [John Gluck/Neval Nader] [BMI] (11/24/62 BCR-33)

TROUBLE I'VE HAD Clarence Ashe—J&S 1466 [Clarence Ashe] [BMI] (5/30/64 BR-87)

TROUBLE MAKER Lee Hazlewood—LHI 20 [Bruce Belland/Dave Somerville] [ASC] (11/29/69 C-91)

—TROUBLE MAKING FOOL see: INSTIGATING

TROUBLE MAN Marvin Gaye—Tamla 54228 [Marvin Gaye] [ASC] (12/16/72 BCR-6)

TROUBLE ME 10,000 Maniacs—Elektra 69298 [Dennis Drew/Natalie Merchant] [ASC] (6/17/89 BC-42)

THE TROUBLE WITH HARRY *Jack Pleis and His Orchestra and Chorus—Decca 29766 [Herb Eiseman/Floyd Huddleston/Mark McIntyre] [ASC] (1/13/56 Rt-72)*

TROUBLE WITH HARRY *Les Baxter, His Chorus and Orchestra—Capitol 3291 [Herb Eiseman/Floyd Huddleston/Mark McIntyre] [ASC] (1/13/56 BRt-72)*

TROUBLE WITH HARRY *Alfi & Harry—Liberty 55008 [Herb Eiseman/Floyd Huddleston/Mark McIntyre] [ASC] (1/13/56 BRt-44)*

TRUCK STOP Jerry Smith and his Pianos—ABC 11162 [Jerry Dean Smith] [ASC] (4/26/69 BCR-71) [IM]

TRUCKIN' Grateful Dead—Warner Bros. 7464 [Jerry Garcia/Robert Hunter/Phil Lesh/Bob Weir] [ASC] (11/27/71 BCR-64)

TRUDIE *Owen Bradley And His Orchestra—Decca 30702 [Joseph Turner Henderson] [BMI] (8/18/58 Rt-91) [I]*

TRUDIE *Joe Henderson—Cub 9013 [Joseph Turner Henderson] [BMI] (8/25/58 Rt-88) [I]*

TRUDY *Joe Bushkin—Capitol 4027 [Joseph Turner Henderson] [BMI] (8/25/58 Rt-91) [I]*

TRUDIE *Jorgen Ingmann with Camarata & His Orchestra—Buena Vista 331 [Joseph Turner Henderson] [BMI] (9/29/58 Rt-93) [I]*

TRUDIE *Eric Rogers & His Music—London 1829 [Joseph Turner Henderson] [BMI] (10/13/58 Rt-93) [I]*

TRUDY The Cleftones—Roulette 4094 [Herbert Cox/Charles McGhee] [BMI] (8/18/58 Rt*-91) [IM]

TRUE Spandau Ballet—Chrysalis 42720 [Gary Kemp] [BMI] (7/30/83 BC-4)

TRUE BLUE Madonna—Sire 28591 [Stephen Bray/Madonna L. Ciccone] [ASC] (10/4/86 BC-3)

TRUE BLUE LOU Tony Bennett—Columbia 42820 [Sam Coslow/Leo Robin/Richard Whiting] [ASC] (7/27/63 B-99)

TRUE BLUE LOVE Lou Gramm—Atlantic 88768 [Lou Gramm/Peter F. Wolf] [ASC] (2/17/90 BC-39)

TRUE COLORS Cyndi Lauper—Portrait 37-06247 [Thomas F. Kelly/Billy Steinberg] [ASC] (8/30/86 BC-1)

TRUE COMPANION Marc Cohn—Atlantic 87583 [Marc Cohn] [ASC] (10/19/91 BC-60)

TRUE FAITH New Order—Qwest 28271 [Gillian Gilbert/Stephen Hague/Peter Hook/Stephen Morris/Bernard Sumner] [ASC] (10/24/87 BC-30)

TRUE, FINE MAMA Little Richard—Specialty 633 [Richard Penniman] [BMI] (6/30/58 B-68)

TRUE GRIT Glen Campbell—Capitol 2573 [Elmer Bernstein/Don Black] [ASC] (7/19/69 BCR-28)

TRUE LOVE *Jane Powell—Verve 2018 [Cole Porter] [ASC] (8/25/56 BCtRt-3)*

TRUE LOVE *Bing Crosby and Grace Kelly—Capitol 3507 [Cole Porter] [ASC] (9/8/56 BCtRt-3)*

TRUE LOVE *Margaret Whiting—Capitol 3473 [Cole Porter] [ASC] (9/29/56 Rt-8)*

TRUE LOVE *Richard Chamberlain—MGM 13148 [Cole Porter] [ASC] (7/27/63 B-98)*

TRUE LOVE Glenn Frey—MCA 53363 [Glenn Frey/Jack Tempchin] [ASC] (8/20/88 BC-13)

TRUE LOVE GOES ON AND ON Burl Ives—Decca 31571 [Richard Adler/Jerry Ross] [ASC] (12/14/63 BCR-66)

TRUE LOVE GONE (COME ON HOME) Betty Madigan—Coral 61812 [Alton Hollowell/Gerald Hollowell/Ulysses Hollowell/Jack Edward Thomas/George Wade] [ASC] (4/20/57 B-78)

TRUE LOVE NEVER RUNS SMOOTH Gene Pitney—Musicor 1032 [Burt Bacharach/Hal David] [ASC] (7/6/63 BCR-21)

TRUE LOVE WAYS *Peter And Gordon—Capitol 5406 [Buddy Holly/Norman Petty] [ASC] (4/17/65 BCR-12)*

TRUE LOVE WAYS *Mickey Gilley—Epic 50876 [Buddy Holly/Norman Petty] [ASC] (8/16/80 BCR-66)*

TRUE TO YOU Ric Ocasek—Geffen 28504 [Ric Ocasek] [ASC] (12/13/86 BC-69)

TRUE TRUE HAPPINESS Johnny Tillotson—Cadence 1365 [Hal Greene/Dick Wolf] [BMI] (8/24/59 BCR-49)

TRUE, TRUE LOVE Frankie Avalon—Chancellor 1087 [Frankie Avalon/Harvey Lembeck/Sonny Troy] [BMI] (9/25/61 B-90)

TRULY The Dinning Sisters Featuring Jean Dinning—Essex 392 [Richard Berry/Joe Josea‡/Jules Taub‡] [BMI] (3/28/55 R-69)

TRULY Lionel Richie—Motown 1644 [Lionel Richie] [ASC] (10/9/82 BC-1)

TRULY JULIE'S BLUES (I'LL BE THERE) Bob Lind—World Pacific 77822 [Bob Lind] [BMI] (4/23/66 BCR-65)

TRULY LOVE Johnny Nash—ABC-Paramount 9942 [Robert Mosely/Mayme Watts] [BMI] (7/28/58 R-79)

TRULY, TRULY, TRUE Brenda Lee—Decca 31762 [Arthur Altman/Dalibor Basler/Al Stillman] [ASC] (4/3/65 BCR-41) [FDE]

TRULY YOURS The Spinners—Motown 1093 [Ivy Jo Hunter/William Stevenson] [ASC] (5/28/66 CR-67)

TRUMPET CHA-CHA-CHA Danny Davis—Cabot 126 [Billy Mure] [BMI] (11/15/58 C-90) [I]

TRUMPET VOLUNTARY The Royal Philharmonic Orchestra—RCA 12304 [Jeremiah Clarke] (Med) [NA] (10/31/81 BCR-9) [I]

TRUST IN ME *Chris Connor—Atlantic 1138 [Milton Ager/Jean Schwartz/Ned Wever] [ASC] (6/10/57 B-95)*

TRUST IN ME *Patti Page—Mercury 71400 [Milton Ager/Jean Schwartz/Ned Wever] [ASC] (1/3/59 BCR-32)*

TRUST IN ME *Etta James—Argo 5385 [Milton Ager/Jean Schwartz/Ned Wever] [ASC] (3/13/61 BCR-24)*

TRUST ME Cindy Bullens—Casablanca 2217 [Cindy Bullens] [BMI] (12/29/79 BCR-82)

THE TRUTH Tami Show—RCA 2694 [Mike Chapman/Tommy Gawenda/Mark Jiaras/Cathy Massey/Claire Massey] [ASC] (8/3/91 BC-28)

TRY A LITTLE KINDNESS Glen Campbell—Capitol 2659 [Bobby Austin/Curt Sapaugh] [BMI] (10/11/69 BCR-15)

TRY A LITTLE TENDERNESS *Aretha Franklin—Columbia 42520 [Jimmy Campbell/Reg Connelly/Harry Woods] [ASC] (9/29/62 B-100)*

TRY A LITTLE TENDERNESS *Otis Redding—Volt 141 [Jimmy Campbell/Reg Connelly/Harry Woods] [ASC] (12/3/66 BCR-20)*

TRY A LITTLE TENDERNESS *Three Dog Night—Dunhill 4177 [Jimmy Campbell/Reg Connelly/Harry Woods] [ASC] (2/8/69 BCR-22)*

TRY A LITTLE TENDERNESS *The Commitments—Beacon/MCA 54128 [Jimmy Campbell/Reg Connelly/Harry Woods] [ASC] (10/5/91 BC-56)*

TRY AGAIN Dean Martin—Capitol 2911 [Edith Bergdahl*/Otto Kollman/Johnny May] [NA] (10/2/54 C-36)

TRY AGAIN Patsy Cline—Decca 30339 [Jerry LeFors/Bob Summers] [BMI] (6/15/57 R-72)

TRY AGAIN Champaign—Columbia 03563 [Michael Day/Rocky Maffit/Dana Walden] [BMI] (4/2/83 BC-18)

TRY IT Ohio Express—Cameo 2001 [Marc Bellack*/Joey Levine] [BMI] (1/27/68 BCR-51)

TRY IT BABY Marvin Gaye—Tamla 54095 [Berry Gordy] [ASC] (6/6/64 BCR-15)

TRY IT ON Exile—Atco 7072 [Mike Chapman/Nicky Chinn] [ASC] (3/5/77 B-97)

TRY (JUST A LITTLE BIT HARDER) Janis Joplin—Columbia 45080 [Jerry Ragovoy/Chip Taylor] [BMI] (2/7/70 R-66)

TRY ME *James Brown And The Famous Flames—Federal 12337 [James Brown] [BMI] (12/15/58 BC-48)*

TRY ME *Jimmy Hughes—Fame 6403 [James Brown] [BMI] (9/26/64 BCR-63)*

TRY ME *James Brown At The Organ—Smash 2008 [James Brown] [BMI] (11/13/65 BCR-53) [IWM]*

TRY ME, I KNOW WE CAN MAKE IT Donna Summer—Oasis 406 [Pete Bellotte/Giorgio Moroder/Donna Summer] [ASC] (7/10/76 BR-80)

TRY MY LOVE AGAIN Bobby Moore's Rhythm Aces Featuring Chico—Checker 1156 [Bobby Moore] [BMI] (12/17/66 BR-81)

TRY MY LOVE ON FOR SIZE Chairmen Of The Board—Invictus 9099 [Lamont Dozier/Brian Holland] [BMI] (10/16/71 R-97)

TRY SOME, BUY SOME Ronnie Spector—Apple 1832 [George Harrison] [ASC] (5/8/71 BCR-50)

TRY THE IMPOSSIBLE Lee Andrews And The Hearts—United Artists 123 [Thomas Curry/Barry Golder] [BMI] (5/5/58 BCR-32)

TRY TO FIND ME Gorky Park—Mercury 876 488 [Alexei Belov/Andrei Grigoriev/Nikolai Noskov] [BMI] (4/28/90 B-81)

TRY TO REMEMBER *Ed Ames—RCA Victor 47-8483 [Tom Jones/Harvey Schmidt] [ASC] (1/16/65 BCR-73)*

TRY TO REMEMBER *Roger Williams—Kapp 48 [Tom Jones/Harvey Schmidt] [ASC] (4/10/65 BCR-97)*

TRY TO REMEMBER *The Brothers Four—Columbia 43404 [Tom Jones/Harvey Schmidt] [ASC] (11/6/65 B-91)*

TRY TO REMEMBER *Gladys Knight & The Pips—Buddah 463 [Tom Jones/Harvey Schmidt] (Med) [ASC] (4/26/75 BCR-9)*

TRY TOO HARD The Dave Clark Five—Epic 10004 [Dave Clark/Mike Smith] [BMI] (4/2/66 BCR-9)

TRY (TRY TO FALL IN LOVE) Cooker—Scepter 12388 [Norman Desrosiers] [BMI] (2/2/74 BCR-67)

TRY, TRY, TRY Jim Valley—Dunhill 4096 [Jim Valley] [BMI] (8/12/67 CR-85)

TRYIN' TO BEAT THE MORNING HOME T.G. Sheppard—Melodyland 6006 [Elroy Kahanek/T.G. Sheppard/Red Williams] [BMI] (5/10/75 BC-94)

TRYIN' TO GET THE FEELING AGAIN Barry Manilow—Arista 0172 [David Pomeranz] [ASC] (3/13/76 BCR-10)

TRYING TO LIVE MY LIFE WITHOUT YOU *Otis Clay—Hi 2226 [Eugene Williams] [BMI] (12/16/72 CR-70)*

TRYIN' TO LIVE MY LIFE WITHOUT YOU *Bob Seger—Capitol 5042 [Eugene Williams] [BMI] (9/12/81 BCR-5)*

TRYIN' TO LOVE TWO William Bell—Mercury 73839 [William Bell/Paul Mitchell] [BMI] (2/12/77 BCR-7)

TRYIN' TO STAY 'LIVE The Asylum Choir—Shelter 7313 [Marc Benno/Leon Russell] [BMI] (2/5/72 C-98)

TRYING Billy Vaughn and His Orchestra—Dot 15710 [Billy Vaughn] [ASC] (4/14/58 B-77) [I]

TRYING TO HOLD ON TO MY WOMAN Lamont Dozier—ABC 11407 [McKinley Jackson/James Reddick] [BMI] (12/15/73 BCR-14)

TRYING TO MAKE A FOOL OF ME The Delfonics—Philly Groove 162 [Thom Bell/William Hart] [BMI] (5/30/70 BCR-40)

TRYING TO SLIP (AWAY) Lloyd Price—GSF 6904 [Frederick Knight/Lloyd Price] [BMI] (8/25/73 C-95)

TSOP (THE SOUND OF PHILADELPHIA) *MFSB Featuring The Three Degrees—Philadelphia Int'l 3540 [Kenneth Gamble/Leon Huff] [BMI] (2/23/74 BCR-1) [IWM]*

T.S.O.P. *The Ritchie Family—Marlin 3306 [Kenneth Gamble/Leon Huff] (Med) [BMI] (8/28/76 BCR-17)*

TUBULAR BELLS *Mike Oldfield—Virgin 55100 [Mike Oldfield] [ASC] (2/23/74 BCR-5) [I]*

TUBULAR BELLS *Champs' Boys Orchestra—Janus 259 [Mike Oldfield] [ASC] (5/29/76 B-98) [I]*

TUCUMCARI Jimmie Rodgers—Roulette 4191 [Mark McIntyre/William Olofson] [ASC] (9/19/59 BCR-32)

TUESDAY AFTERNOON (FOREVER AFTERNOON) The Moody Blues—Deram 85028 [Justin Hayward] [ASC] (6/29/68 BCR-24)

TUFF Ace Cannon—Hi 2040 [Ace Cannon] [BMI] (12/9/61 BCR-13) [I]

TUFF ENUFF The Fabulous Thunderbirds—CBS Associated 05838 [Kim Wilson] [BMI] (4/19/86 BC-10)

TUG OF WAR Paul McCartney—Columbia 03235 [Paul McCartney] [ASC] (10/2/82 BC-53)

TULSA Billy Joe Royal—Columbia 45289 [Wayne Carson Thompson] [BMI] (2/20/71 BCR-83)

TULSA TIME *Don Williams—ABC 12425 [Danny Flowers] [ASC] (11/25/78 C-96)*

TULSA TIME *Eric Clapton And His Band—RSO 1039 [Danny Flowers] (TSW) [ASC] (6/14/80 BCR-30)*

TUMBLING DICE *The Rolling Stones—Rolling Stones 19103 [Mick Jagger/Keith Richards] [ASC] (4/22/72 BCR-4)*

TUMBLING DICE *Linda Ronstadt—Asylum 45479 [Mick Jagger/Keith Richards] [ASC] (4/22/78 BCR-32)*

TUMBLING TUMBLEWEEDS *Roger Williams—Kapp 156 [Bob Nolan] [BMI] (8/17/56 BCR-34) [IWM]*

TUMBLING TUMBLEWEEDS *Billy Vaughn and His Orchestra—Dot 15710 [Bob Nolan] [BMI] (3/17/58 BCR-13) [IWM]*

—TUNES OF GLORY see: THEME FROM TUNES OF GLORY

TUNNEL OF LOVE Doris Day—Columbia 41252 [Ruth Freed/Bob Roberts] [BMI] (10/20/58 BCR-43)

TUNNEL OF LOVE Bruce Springsteen—Columbia 07663 [Bruce Springsteen] [ASC] (12/5/87 BC-9)

TUPELO HONEY Van Morrison—Warner Bros. 7543 [Van Morrison] [BMI] (12/25/71 BCR-40)

TURN AND WALK AWAY The Babys—Chrysalis 2467 [Jonathan Cain/John Waite] [ASC] (11/15/80 BCR-42)

TURN AROUND Dick And Deedee—Warner Bros. 5396 [Harry Belafonte/Alan Greene/Malvina Reynolds] [ASC] (11/23/63 BCR-22)

TURN AROUND Neil Diamond—Columbia 04541 [Burt Bacharach/Neil Diamond/Carole Bayer Sager] [ASC] (8/18/84 BC-62)

TURN AROUND AND LOVE YOU Rita Coolidge—Pepper 443 [Donna Weiss] [BMI] (5/10/69 B-96)

TURN AROUND, LOOK AT ME *Glen Campbell—Crest 1087 [Jerry Capehart] [BMI] (10/30/61 BCR-48)*

TURN AROUND, LOOK AT ME *The Lettermen—Capitol 4746 [Jerry Capehart] [BMI] (5/12/62 C-85)*

TURN AROUND, LOOK AT ME *The Vogues—Reprise 0686 [Jerry Capehart] [BMI] (6/8/68 BCR-4)*

TURN BACK THE HANDS OF TIME Tyrone Davis—Dakar 616 [Jack Daniels/John Edward Moore] [BMI] (3/7/70 BCR-1)

TURN BACK THE PAGES Stephen Stills—Columbia 10179 [Donnie Dacus/Stephen Stills] [BMI] (8/2/75 BC-76)

TURN-DOWN DAY The Cyrkle—Columbia 43729 [David Blume/Jerry Keller] [ASC] (8/13/66 BCR-16)

—TURN IT LOOSE see: GIVE IT UP

TURN IT ON AGAIN Genesis—Atlantic 3751 [Tony Banks/Phil Collins/Mike Rutherford] [ASC] (8/30/80 BCR-55)

TURN IT UP Oaktown's 3.5.7—Bust It/Capitol 44717 [James Earley/Djuana Johnican/Michael Kelly] [BMI] (8/3/91 B-66)

TURN LOOSE OF MY LEG Jim Stafford—Warner/Curb 8299 [Willie Hammond/Jim Stafford] [ASC] (1/29/77 B-98)

TURN ME LOOSE Fabian—Chancellor 1033 [Doc Pomus/Mort Shuman] [BMI] (3/23/59 BCR-8)

TURN ME LOOSE Loverboy—Columbia 11421 [Paul Dean/Mike Reno] [BMI] (1/31/81 BCR-33)

TURN OFF THE LIGHTS Teddy Pendergrass—Philadelphia Int'l 3696 [Kenneth Gamble/Leon Huff] [BMI] (6/23/79 BCR-48)

TURN OFF THE LIGHTS The World Class Wreckin' Cru—Kru-Cut 006 [Alonzo Williams] [BMI] (3/26/88 B-84)

TURN ON A DREAM The Box Tops—Mala 12,042 [Mark James] [BMI] (10/11/69 BCR-31)

TURN ON YOUR LOVE LIGHT *Bobby Bland—Duke 344 [Deadric Malone/Joe Scott] [BMI] (11/27/61 BCR-24)*

TURN ON YOUR LOVE LIGHT *Oscar Toney, Jr.—Bell 681 [Deadric Malone/Joe Scott] [BMI] (8/12/67 BCR-65)*

TURN ON YOUR LOVE LIGHT *The Human Beinz—Capitol 2119 [Deadric Malone/Joe Scott] [BMI] (3/9/68 BCR-55)*

TURN ON YOUR LOVE LIGHT *Bill Black's Combo—Hi 2145 [Deadric Malone/Joe Scott] [BMI] (6/22/68 BCR-78) [IWM]*

TURN ON YOUR LOVE LIGHT *Jerry Lee Lewis—Mercury 73296 [Deadric Malone/Joe Scott] [BMI] (7/22/72 B-95)*

TURN ON YOUR RADAR Prism—Capitol 5106 [Morgan Walker] [ASC] (4/17/82 BC-64)

TURN RIGHT Kay Starr—RCA Victor 47-5999 [Marty Dorn Roberts/Hal Stanley] [NA] (1/31/55 CR-23)

TURN THE BEAT AROUND Vicki Sue Robinson—RCA Victor 10562 [Gerald Jackson/Pete Jackson] [BMI] (4/10/76 BCR-10)

TURN THE WORLD AROUND Eddy Arnold—RCA Victor 47-9265 [Ben Peters] [BMI] (8/12/67 BCR-61)

TURN TO STONE Joe Walsh—ABC/Dunhill 15026 [Terry Trabandt/Joe Walsh] [BMI] (2/15/75 BCR-64)

TURN TO STONE Electric Light Orchestra—Jet 1099 [Jeff Lynne] [BMI] (11/19/77 BCR-9)

TURN TO YOU Go-Go's—I.R.S. 9928 [Charlotte Caffey/Jane Wiedlin] [ASC] (6/16/84 BC-28)

TURN! TURN! TURN! (TO EVERYTHING THERE IS A SEASON) *The Byrds—Columbia 43424 [Pete Seeger] [BMI] (10/23/65 BCR-1)*

TURN! TURN! TURN!/TO EVERYTHING THERE IS A SEASON *Judy Collins—Elektra 45680 [Pete Seeger] [BMI] (11/22/69 BCR-50)*

TURN UP THE RADIO Autograph—RCA 13953 [Steve Isham/Steve Lynch/Steve Plunkett/Randy Rand/Keni Richards] [BMI] (12/22/84 BC-25)

TURN YOUR LOVE AROUND George Benson—Warner Bros. 49846 [Bill Champlin/Jay Graydon/Steve Lukather] [ASC] (10/24/81 BCR-5)

TURN YOUR RADIO ON Ray Stevens—Barnaby 2048 [Albert E. Brumley Sr.] [BMI] (11/20/71 BR-63)

TURNED AWAY Chuckii Booker—Atlantic 88917 [Chuckii Booker/Donnell Spencer] [BMI] (7/8/89 BC-42)

TURNING JAPANESE The Vapors—United Artists 1364 [David Fenton] [ASC] (9/13/80 BCR-31)

TURNING POINT Tyrone Davis—Dakar 4550 [Leo Graham] [BMI] (12/27/75 CR-64)

TURNING TO YOU Charlie—Janus 270 [Terry Thomas] [BMI] (7/30/77 BC-88)

TURTLE POWER! Partners In Kryme—SBK 07325 [James Alpern/Richard Usher] [BMI] (4/21/90 BC-12)

TURVY II Cozy Cole—Love 5014 [Dick Hyman] [ASC] (11/24/58 BCR-25) [I]

TUSH ZZ Top—London 220 [Frank Beard/Billy Gibbons/Dusty Hill] [BMI] (7/19/75 BCR-12)

TUSK Fleetwood Mac—Warner Bros. 49077 [Lindsey Buckingham] [ASC] (10/6/79 BCR-8)

TUTTI FRUTTI *Little Richard—Specialty 561 [Dorothy LaBostrie/Joe Lubin*/Richard Penniman] [BMI] (1/14/56 BCtRt-10)*

TUTTI FRUTTI *Pat Boone—Dot 15443 [Dorothy LaBostrie/Joe Lubin*/Richard Penniman] [BMI] (1/20/56 BCtRt-10)*

TUTTI-FRUTTI *Art Mooney & His Orchestra—MGM 12165 [Dorothy LaBostrie/Joe Lubin*/Richard Penniman] [BMI] (2/17/56 Rt-10)*

TUTTI FRUTTI *Jive Bunny And The Mastermixers—Music Factory 99140 [Dorothy LaBostrie/Joe Lubin*/Richard Penniman] (Med) [BMI] (10/28/89 BC-11)*

TUTTI-FRUTTI *Jive Bunny And The Mastermixers—Music Factory 99140 [Dorothy LaBostrie/Joe Lubin*/Richard Penniman] (Med) [BMI] (10/28/89 BC-11)*

TUXEDO JUNCTION Frankie Avalon—Chancellor 1052 [Julian Dash/Buddy Feyne/Erskine Hawkins/William Luther Johnson] [ASC] (6/13/60 BCR-69)

TVC 15 David Bowie—RCA Victor 10664 [David Bowie] [BMI] (5/22/76 B-64)

TWEEDLE DEE *Georgia Gibbs—Mercury 70517 [Winfield Scott] [BMI] (1/3/55 BCtRt-3)*

TWEEDLEE DEE *LaVern Baker and The Gliders—Atlantic 1047 [Winfield Scott] [BMI] (1/3/55 BCtRt-3)*

TWEEDLEE DEE *Vicki Young—Capitol 3046 [Winfield Scott] [BMI] (1/3/55 Rt-12)*

TWEEDLEE DEE *The Lancers—Coral 61332 [Winfield Scott] [BMI] (1/3/55 Rt-10)*

TWEEDLEE DEE *Dave "Baby" Cortez—Chess 1842 [Winfield Scott] [BMI] (12/15/62 R-87) [IWM]*

TWEEDLEE DEE *Little Jimmy Osmond—MGM 14468 [Winfield Scott] [BMI] (12/30/72 BCR-49)*

THE TWELFTH OF NEVER *Johnny Mathis—Columbia 40993 [Jerry Livingston/Paul Francis Webster] [ASC] (9/7/57 BCR-38)*

THE TWELFTH OF NEVER *Donny Osmond—MGM 14503 [Jerry Livingston/Paul Francis Webster] [ASC] (3/3/73 BCR-5)*

TWELFTH STREET RAG *Crazy Otto—Polydor 22009A [Euday L. Bowman] (Med) [ASC] (1/10/55 R-30) [I]*

TWELFTH STREET RAG *Crazy Otto—Decca 29503 [Euday L. Bowman] [ASC] (5/2/55 R-79) [I]*

TWELFTH STREET RAG *The Mulcays—Essex 407 [Euday L. Bowman] [ASC] (2/17/56 R-81) [I]*

THE TWELVE GIFTS OF CHRISTMAS Allan Sherman—Warner Bros. 5406 [Allan Sherman] [ASC] (12/28/63 C-93)

TWELVE O'CLOCK TONIGHT Doris Day—Columbia 40870 [Pat Ballard] [ASC] (4/20/57 BR-68)

TWELVE THIRTY (YOUNG GIRLS ARE COMING TO THE CANYON) The Mamas & The Papas—Dunhill 4099 [John Phillips] [ASC] (8/26/67 BCR-12)

20TH CENTURY FOX TRADEMARK Meco—Arista 0660 [Alfred Newman] (Med) [ASC] (2/13/82 BCR-35) [I]

25TH OF LAST DECEMBER Roberta Flack—Atlantic 3441
[Gene McDaniels] [BMI] (12/17/77 C-92)

TWENTY-FIVE MILES *Edwin Starr—Gordy 7083*
[Bert Berns/Johnny Bristol/Harvey Fuqua/Edwin Starr/Jerry Wexler] [ASC] (2/15/69 BCR-5)

TWENTY-FIVE MILES *Mongo Santamaria—Columbia 44886*
[Bert Berns/Johnny Bristol/Harvey Fuqua/Edwin Starr/Jerry Wexler] [ASC] (6/28/69 C-99) [IWM]

25 MINUTES TO GO The Brothers Four—Columbia 42586
[Shel Silverstein] [BMI] (11/10/62 R-100)

25 OR 6 TO 4 *Chicago—Columbia 45194 [Robert Lamm] [ASC] (7/18/70 BCR-4)*

25 OR 6 TO 4 *Chicago—Warner/Full Moon 27-28628*
[Robert Lamm] [ASC] (9/6/86 BC-46)

24 HOURS A DAY (365 A YEAR) Georgia Gibbs—Mercury 70743
[Henry Glover/Rudy Toombs] [BMI] (11/7/55 BCR-33)

TWENTY FOUR HOURS FROM TULSA Gene Pitney—Musicor 1034
[Burt Bacharach/Hal David] [ASC] (10/19/63 BCR-17)

24/7 Dino—4th & Broadway 7471
[Dino Esposito] [BMI] (2/4/89 BC-42)

TWENTY MILES Chubby Checker—Parkway 862
[Bernie Lowe/Kal Mann] [ASC] (2/23/63 BCR-15)

20-75 Willie Mitchell—Hi 2075 [Willie Mitchell] [BMI] (8/22/64 BCR-31) [I]

26 MILES (SANTA CATALINA) The Four Preps—Capitol 3845
[Bruce Belland/Glen Larson] [BMI] (1/18/58 BCR-3)

20/20 George Benson—Warner Bros. 29120
[Randy Goodrum/Steve Kipner] [ASC] (12/15/84 BC-46)

TWICE AS NICE Clyde McPhatter—MGM 12816
[Charles Singleton] [BMI] (7/27/59 BCR-79)

TWILIGHT ELO—Jet 02559 [Jeff Lynne] [ASC] (10/24/81 BCR-38)

TWILIGHT TIME *Dick Contino—Mercury 70911*
[Artie Dunn/Al Nevins/Morty Nevins/Buck Ram] [ASC] (8/17/56 R-36) [IWM]

TWILIGHT TIME *The Platters—Mercury 71289*
[Artie Dunn/Al Nevins/Morty Nevins/Buck Ram] [ASC] (3/24/58 BCR-1)

TWILIGHT TIME *Andy Williams—Cadence 1433*
[Artie Dunn/Al Nevins/Morty Nevins/Buck Ram] [ASC] (12/1/62 BCR-86)

TWILIGHT WORLD Swing Out Sister—Mercury 888484
[Andy Connell/Corinne Drewery/Martin Jackson] [BMI] (12/19/87 BC-31)

TWILIGHT ZONE The Manhattan Transfer—Atlantic 3649
[Jay Graydon/Alan Paul] (Med) [ASC] (4/5/80 BCR-30)

TWILIGHT ZONE Golden Earring—21 Records 103
[George Kooymans] [ASC] (11/27/82 BC-10)

TWILIGHT ZONE (THEME) The Manhattan Transfer—Atlantic 3649
[Bernard Herrmann] (Med) [BMI] (4/5/80 BCR-30)

TWILLEY DON'T MIND Dwight Twilley Band—Arista 0278
[Dwight Twilley] [ASC] (10/29/77 R-94)

TWINE TIME Alvin Cash & The Crawlers—Mar-V-Lus 6002
[Verlie Rice/Andre Williams] [BMI] (1/2/65 BCR-9) [I]

TWINKLE TOES Roy Orbison—MGM 13498
[William Dees/Roy Orbison] [BMI] (4/23/66 BCR-35)

THE TWIST *Hank Ballard And The Midnighters—King 5171*
[Hank Ballard] [BMI] (7/18/60 BCtRt-1)

THE TWIST *Chubby Checker—Parkway 811 [Hank Ballard] [BMI] (7/18/60 BCtRt-1)*

THE TWIST *Chubby Checker—Parkway 811 [Hank Ballard] [BMI] (11/13/61 BCR-1)*

THE TWIST *Ernie Freeman—Imperial 5793 [Hank Ballard] [BMI] (1/6/62 B-93) [IWM]*

THE TWIST (YO, TWIST) *Fat Boys—Tin Pan Apple 887 571*
[Hank Ballard] [BMI] (6/18/88 BC-16)

THE TWIST *Jive Bunny & The Mastermixers—Music Factory/Atco 99122*
[Hank Ballard] (Med) [BMI] (2/3/90 BC-67)

TWIST AND SHOUT *The Isley Brothers—Wand 124*
[Bert Berns/Phil Medley] [BMI] (6/2/62 BCR-7)

TWIST AND SHOUT *The Beatles—Tollie 9001*
[Bert Berns/Phil Medley] [BMI] (3/7/64 BCR-1)

TWIST AND SHOUT *The Beatles—Capitol 5624*
[Bert Berns/Phil Medley] [BMI] (8/9/86 BC-23)

TWIST-HER Bill Black's Combo—Hi 2042 [Bill Black] [BMI] (12/11/61 BCR-26) [I]

TWIST IT UP Chubby Checker—Parkway 879
[Dave Appell/Kal Mann] [ASC] (7/20/63 BCR-23)

TWIST MY ARM Pointer Sisters—RCA 14197
[Andy Goldmark/Bruce Roberts] [ASC] (3/1/86 BC-82)

TWIST OF FATE Olivia Newton-John—MCA 52284
[Peter Beckett/Steve Kipner] [BMI] (11/5/83 BC-5)

TWIST, TWIST SENORA Gary (U.S.) Bonds—Legrand 1018
[Gene Barge/Frank Guida/Joseph Royster/Steve Samuel] [BMI] (3/19/62 BCR-9)

TWISTIN' ALL NIGHT LONG
Danny & The Juniors With Guest Artist Freddy Cannon—Swan 4092
[Bob Crewe/Frank Slay] [ASC] (1/6/62 BR-68)

—TWISTIN' BELLS see: JINGLE BELLS

TWISTIN' MATILDA (AND THE CHANNEL) Jimmy Soul—S.P.Q.R. 3300
[Frank Guida/Norman Span] [BMI] (3/19/62 BCR-17)

TWISTIN' POSTMAN The Marvelettes—Tamla 54054
[Robert Bateman/Brian Holland/William Stevenson] [BMI] (1/22/62 BCR-32)

TWISTIN' THE NIGHT AWAY *Sam Cooke—RCA Victor 47-7983*
[Sam Cooke] [BMI] (1/22/62 BCR-5)

TWISTING THE NIGHT AWAY *Rod Stewart—Mercury 73412*
[Sam Cooke] [BMI] (8/4/73 BCR-35)

TWISTIN' THE NIGHT AWAY *Rod Stewart—Geffen 28303*
[Sam Cooke] [BMI] (7/11/87 BC-72)

TWISTIN' USA *Danny & The Juniors—Swan 4060 [Kal Mann] [ASC] (9/5/60 BCR-27)*

TWISTIN' U.S.A. *Chubby Checker—Parkway 811 [Kal Mann] [ASC] (12/4/61 BR-68)*

TWISTIN' WITH LINDA The Isley Brothers—Wand 127
[O'Kelly Isley/Ronald Isley/Rudolph Isley] [ASC] (9/22/62 BCR-54)

TWITCHY Rene Hall's Orchestra Featuring Willie Joe—Specialty 618
[Willie Joe Duncan] [BMI] (1/6/58 R-82)

TWIXT TWELVE AND TWENTY Pat Boone—Dot 15955
[Fredda Gold/Aaron Schroeder] [ASC] (6/15/59 BCR-16)

TWO-BIT MANCHILD Neil Diamond—Uni 55075 [Neil Diamond] [SE] (7/6/68 BCR-51)

TWO BROTHERS David Hill—Kapp 266 [Irving Gordon] [ASC] (4/11/59 BCR-89)

TWO DIFFERENT WORLDS *Don Rondo—Jubilee 5256*
[Al Frisch/Sid Wayne] [ASC] (9/29/56 BCtRt-10)

TWO DIFFERENT WORLDS *Roger Williams And Jane Morgan—Kapp 161*
[Al Frisch/Sid Wayne] [ASC] (10/6/56 BCtRt-10)

TWO DIFFERENT WORLDS *Dick Kallman—Decca 30036*
[Al Frisch/Sid Wayne] [ASC] (10/6/56 Rt-63)

TWO DIFFERENT WORLDS *Dick Haymes—Capitol 3565*
[Al Frisch/Sid Wayne] [ASC] (12/29/56 B-80)

TWO DIFFERENT WORLDS *Lenny Welch—Kapp 689*
[Al Frisch/Sid Wayne] [ASC] (8/21/65 BCR-47)

TWO DIVIDED BY LOVE The Grass Roots—Dunhill 4289
[Marty Kupps/Dennis Lambert/Brian Potter] [BMI] (10/9/71 BCR-8)

TWO DOORS DOWN Dolly Parton—RCA 11240 [Dolly Parton] [BMI] (3/18/78 BCR-19)

TWO FACES HAVE I Lou Christie—Roulette 4481
[Lou Christie/Twyla Herbert] [BMI] (3/23/63 BCR-3)

TWO FINE PEOPLE Cat Stevens—A&M 1700 [Cat Stevens] [ASC] (7/12/75 BCR-33)

TWO FOOLS Frankie Avalon—Chancellor 1040
[Doc Pomus/Mort Shuman] [BMI] (9/5/59 BC-51)

TWO HEARTS Stephanie Mills featuring Teddy Pendergrass—20th Century 2492
[Tawatha Agee/Reggie Lucas/James Mtume] [BMI] (5/9/81 BCR-39)

TWO HEARTS Phil Collins—Atlantic 88980
[Phil Collins/Lamont Dozier] [ASC] (11/19/88 BC-1)

TWO HEARTS *Pat Boone—Dot 15338 [Henry Stone/Otis Williams] [BMI] (3/7/55 BCRt-5)*

TWO HEARTS *The Charms—DeLuxe 6065*
[Henry Stone/Otis Williams] [BMI] (3/7/55 Rt-21)

TWO HEARTS, TWO KISSES (MAKE ONE LOVE) *The 5 DeMarco Sisters—Decca 29470*
[Henry Stone/Otis Williams] [BMI] (3/21/55 Rt-5)

TWO HEARTS, TWO KISSES (MAKE ONE LOVE) *Doris Day—Columbia 40483*
[Henry Stone/Otis Williams] [BMI] (4/4/55 Rt-5)

TWO HEARTS, TWO KISSES (MAKE ONE LOVE)
Frank Sinatra with The Nuggets—Capitol 3084
[Henry Stone/Otis Williams] [BMI] (4/11/55 Rt-5)

TWO HOUND DOGS Bill Haley And His Comets—Decca 29552
[Bill Haley/Frank Pingatore] (TSW) [ASC] (7/23/55 BCR-15)

TWO IN THE AFTERNOON Dino, Desi & Billy—Reprise 0579
[Garry Bonner/Alan Gordon] [BMI] (6/3/67 BC-99)

TWO INNOCENT HEARTS Ginny Gibson—ABC-Paramount 9739
[Dorian Burton/Lee Pincus] [BMI] (10/13/56 C-50)

TWO KINDS OF TEARDROPS Del Shannon—Big Top 3143
[Maron McKenzie/Del Shannon] [BMI] (4/13/63 BCR-50)

TWO LANE HIGHWAY Pure Prairie League—RCA Victor 10302
[Larry Goshorn] [ASC] (6/14/75 BC-87)

TWO LESS LONELY PEOPLE IN THE WORLD Air Supply—Arista 1004
[Howard Greenfield/Ken Hirsch] [BMI] (11/13/82 BC-33)

TWO LITTLE KIDS Peaches & Herb—Date 1586
[Barbara Acklin/Carl Davis/Eugene Record] [BMI] (12/16/67 BCR-31)

TWO LONG YEARS Dick Caruso—MGM 12900
[Clint Ballard Jr./Fred Tobias] [ASC] (6/11/60 C-95)

TWO LOST SOULS Perry Como & Jaye P. Morgan—RCA Victor 47-6137
[Richard Adler/Jerry Ross] (TSW) [ASC] (6/25/55 BCR-24)

TWO LOVERS Mary Wells—Motown 1035 [Smokey Robinson] [ASC] (11/24/62 BCR-7)

TWO OCCASIONS The Deele—Solar 70015
[Darnell Bristol/Kenneth Edmonds/Sid Johnson] [BMI] (2/27/88 BC-10)

TWO OF A KIND Sue Thompson—Hickory 1166
[Bob Montgomery/Earl Sinks] [BMI] (3/12/62 BCR-25)

TWO OF HEARTS Stacey Q—Atlantic 89381
[Sue Gatlin/Tim Greene/John Mitchell] [NA] (7/12/86 BC-3)

TWO OUT OF THREE AIN'T BAD Meat Loaf—Cleveland Int'l/Epic 50513
[Jim Steinman] [BMI] (3/18/78 BCR-7)

TWO PEOPLE Tina Turner—Capitol 5644
[Terry Britten/Graham Lyle] [BMI] (11/22/86 BC-29)

TWO PLACES AT THE SAME TIME Ray Parker Jr. and Raydio—Arista 0494
[Ray Parker Jr.] [ASC] (3/22/80 BCR-27)

2 + 2 = ? Bob Seger System—Capitol 2143 [Bob Seger] [ASC] (6/8/68 C-90)

TWO SHADOWS ON YOUR WINDOW *Jim Reeves—RCA Victor 47-6973*
[Mickey Baker/Joseph Robinson] [BMI] (8/12/57 Rt-79)

TWO SHADOWS ON YOUR WINDOW *Mickey & Sylvia—Vik 0280*
[Mickey Baker/Joseph Robinson] [BMI] (8/12/57 Rt-79)

TWO SIDES OF LOVE Sammy Hagar—Geffen 29446
[Sammy Hagar] [ASC] (7/14/84 BC-38)

TWO SIDES (TO EVERY STORY) Etta James—Argo 5452
[Tony Clarke/Billy Davis] [BMI] (10/5/63 BCR-63)

TWO-TEN, SIX-EIGHTEEN (DOESN'T ANYBODY KNOW MY NAME)
Jimmie Rodgers—Dot 16527
[Rod McKuen] [ASC] (10/12/63 BCR-62)

THE 2,000 POUND BEE (PART 2) The Ventures—Dolton 67
[Don Wilson] [BMI] (12/29/62 BC-91) [I]

TWO THOUSAND TWO HUNDRED TWENTY THREE MILES Patti Page—Mercury 71597
[Leon Carr/Paul Vance] [ASC] (3/7/60 BR-67)

TWO TICKETS TO PARADISE Brook Benton—Mercury 72177
[Brook Benton/Malcolm Dodds] [BMI] (9/7/63 BCR-29)

TWO TICKETS TO PARADISE Eddie Money—Columbia 10765
[Eddie Money] [BMI] (6/24/78 BCR-20)

TWO TO MAKE IT RIGHT Seduction—Vendetta 1464 [David Cole] [ASC] (11/11/89 BC-1)

TWO TRIBES Frankie Goes To Hollywood—ZTT/Island 7-99695
[Peter Gill/Holly Johnson/Mark O'Toole] [BMI] (10/20/84 BC-37)

TWO WRONGS DON'T MAKE A RIGHT Mary Wells—Motown 1039
[Berry Gordy/Smokey Robinson] [ASC] (3/23/63 B-100)

TYPICAL MALE Tina Turner—Capitol 5615
[Terry Britten/Graham Lyle] [BMI] (8/30/86 BC-1)

U

U CAN'T TOUCH THIS M.C. Hammer—Capitol 15571
[Stanley Burrell/Rick James/Alonzo H. Miller] [BMI] (4/7/90 BC-4)

U GOT THE LOOK Prince—Paisley Park 7-28289 [Prince] [ASC] (7/25/87 BC-2)

THE "U-T" Harry M. And The Marvels—ABC-Paramount 10243
[Harry Middlebrooks] [BMI] (10/7/61 C-95)

UH HUH MM Sonny James—Capitol 3840
[Sylvester Bradford/Al Lewis] [ASC] (12/9/57 BCR-42)

UH-HUH OH YEAH *Steve Lawrence—Coral 61950*
[Jerry Bock/Sheldon Harnick] [BMI] (2/10/58 BCRt-52)

UH-HUH, OH YEAH *Jill Corey—Columbia 41108*
[Jerry Bock/Sheldon Harnick] [BMI] (2/10/58 Rt-81)

UH YUH OH YEAH *Bill Hayes—ABC-Paramount 9895*
[Jerry Bock/Sheldon Harnick] [BMI] (2/17/58 Rt-81)

UH! OH! (PART 2) *The Nutty Squirrels—Hanover 4540*
[Sascha Burland/Don Elliot] [BMI] (11/2/59 BCR-3)

UH! OH! (PART 1) *The Nutty Squirrels—Hanover 4540*
[Sascha Burland/Don Elliot] [BMI] (12/7/59 B-45)

UHH Dyke And The Blazers—Original Sound 89
[Arlester Christian] [BMI] (4/18/70 CR-81)

UHH AHH Boyz II Men—Motown 2141
[Michael Bivins/Nathan Morris/Wanya Morris] [ASC] (12/14/91 B-16)

UM, UM, UM, UM, UM, UM *Major Lance—Okeh 7187*
[Curtis Mayfield] [BMI] (12/28/63 BCR-4)

CURIOUS MIND (UM, UM, UM, UM, UM, UM) *Johnny Rivers—Big Tree 16106*
[Curtis Mayfield] [BMI] (12/17/77 BCR-34)

UNBELIEVABLE Nat "King" Cole—Capitol 2949
[Irving Gordon/Jerry Livingston] [ASC] (10/11/54 CR-25)

UNBELIEVABLE EMF—EMI 50350
[James Atkin/Derry Brownson/Mark Decloedt/Ian Dench/Zac Foley] [BMI]
(4/13/91 BC-1)

UNBORN CHILD Seals & Crofts—Warner Bros. 7771
[Lana Bogan/Jim Seals] [BMI] (2/23/74 BCR-65)

UNCHAIN MY HEART *Ray Charles And His Orchestra—ABC-Paramount 10266*
[Teddy Powell/Bobby Sharp] [ASC] (11/20/61 BCR-9)

UNCHAIN MY HEART *Herbie Mann—A&M 896*
[Teddy Powell/Bobby Sharp] [ASC] (2/17/68 BCR-71) [IWM]

UNCHAINED MELODY *Al Hibbler—Decca 29441*
[Alex North/Hy Zaret] [NA] (3/21/55 BCtRt-1)

UNCHAINED MELODY *Roy Hamilton—Epic 9102*
[Alex North/Hy Zaret] [NA] (3/28/55 BCtRt-1)

UNCHAINED MELODY *LeRoy Holmes & His Orchestra—MGM 11962*
[Alex North] [NA] (3/28/55 Rt-19) [IM]

UNCHAINED MELODY *June Valli—RCA Victor 47-6078*
[Alex North/Hy Zaret] [NA] (4/18/55 BRt-2)

UNCHAINED MELODY *Les Baxter His Chorus And Orchestra—Capitol 3055*
[Alex North/Hy Zaret] (TSW) [NA] (4/30/55 BCtRt-1)

UNCHAINED MELODY *The Blackwells—Jamie 1157*
[Alex North/Hy Zaret] [NA] (5/30/60 CR-83)

UNCHAINED MELODY *Vito & The Salutations—Herald 583*
[Alex North/Hy Zaret] [NA] (10/12/63 BCR-50)

UNCHAINED MELODY *The Righteous Brothers—Philles 129*
[Alex North/Hy Zaret] [NA] (7/10/65 BCR-4)

UNCHAINED MELODY *The Sweet Inspirations—Atlantic 2551*
[Alex North/Hy Zaret] [NA] (8/31/68 BR-73)

UNCHAINED MELODY (LIVE) *Heart—Epic 51010*
[Alex North/Hy Zaret] [NA] (3/28/81 B-83)

UNCHAINED MELODY *The Righteous Brothers—Verve Forecast 871 882*
[Alex North/Hy Zaret] [NA] (8/25/90 BC-9)

UNCHAINED MELODY (1990) *The Righteous Brothers—Curb 76842*
[Alex North/Hy Zaret] [NA] (10/6/90 B-19)

UNCLE ALBERT/ADMIRAL HALSEY Paul & Linda McCartney—Apple 1837
[Linda McCartney/Paul McCartney] [ASC] (8/14/71 BCR-1)

UNCLE JOHN'S BAND Grateful Dead—Warner Bros. 7410
[Jerry Garcia/Robert Hunter] [ASC] (8/8/70 BCR-66)

UNCLE TOM'S CABIN Warrant—Columbia 73644
[Joseph Cagle*/Steven Chamberlin*/Jerry Dixon*/John Oswald/Eric Turner*] [BMI]
(4/20/91 BC-76)

UNCONDITIONAL LOVE Donna Summer—Mercury 814088
[Michael Omartian/Donna Summer] [ASC] (9/3/83 BC-40)

UNDENIABLE Ms. Adventures—Atco 98938
[Arthur Baker/Tommy Faragher/Lotti Golden] [BMI] (9/1/90 BC-67)

UNDER MY THUMB *Del Shannon—Liberty 55904*
[Mick Jagger/Keith Richards] [BMI] (9/17/66 C-99)

UNDER MY THUMB *Hounds—Columbia 11159*
[Mick Jagger/Keith Richards] [BMI] (1/9/80 R-99)

UNDER MY WHEELS Alice Cooper—Warner Bros. 7529
[Michael Bruce/Dennis Dunaway/Bob Ezrin*] [BMI] (12/25/71 BCR-59)

UNDER PRESSURE Queen & David Bowie—Elektra 47235
[David Bowie/John Deacon/Brian May/Freddie Mercury/Roger Taylor] [BMI]
(11/7/81 BCR-22)

UNDER THE BOARDWALK *The Drifters—Atlantic 2237*
[Artie Resnick/Kenny Young] [BMI] (6/27/64 BCR-4)

UNDER THE BOARDWALK *Billy Joe Royal—Private Stock 45,192*
[Artie Resnick/Kenny Young] [BMI] (5/27/78 BCR-60)

UNDER THE BOARDWALK *Bruce Willis—Motown 1896*
[Artie Resnick/Kenny Young] [BMI] (6/13/87 BC-59)

UNDER THE BRIDGES OF PARIS Dean Martin—Capitol 3036
[Dorcas Cochran/Jean Coulon*/Jean Rodor*/Vincent Scotto] [BMI] (1/31/55 R-75)

UNDER THE COVERS Janis Ian—Columbia 02176
[Janis Ian] [BMI] (7/11/81 BCR-71)

UNDER THE GUN Poco—MCA 41269 [Paul Cotton] [ASC] (7/12/80 BCR-42)

UNDER THE INFLUENCE Vanity—Motown 1833
[Tommy Faragher/Tony Haynes/Robbie Nevil] [BMI] (4/19/86 BC-56)

UNDER THE INFLUENCE OF LOVE Love Unlimited—20th Century 2082
[Paul Politi/Barry White] [BMI] (3/30/74 BC-76)

UNDER THE MILKY WAY The Church—Arista 1-9673
[Karin Jansson/Steve Kilbey] [ASC] (4/9/88 BC-24)

UNDER THE MOON OF LOVE Curtis Lee—Dunes 2008
[Tommy Boyce/Curtis Lee] [BMI] (10/7/61 BCR-42)

UNDER THE SUN VALLEY MOON Patti Page—Mercury 71400
[Jimmy Kennedy/Nat Simon] [ASC] (1/10/59 CR-70)

UNDER YOUR SPELL AGAIN Johnny Rivers—Imperial 66144
[Buck Owens/Dusty Rhodes] [BMI] (12/11/65 BCR-35)

UNDERCOVER ANGEL Alan O'Day—Pacific 001 [Alan O'Day] [ASC] (4/2/77 BCR-1)

UNDERCOVER OF THE NIGHT The Rolling Stones—Rolling Stones 99813
[Mick Jagger/Keith Richards] [ASC] (11/12/83 BC-9)

UNDERNEATH THE RADAR Underworld—Sire 27968
[Karl Hyde/Richard David Smith/Alfie Thomas] [ASC] (4/16/88 BC-74)

UNDERSTAND YOUR MAN Johnny Cash—Columbia 42964
[Johnny Cash] [ASC] (2/15/64 BCR-35)

UNDERSTANDING Ray Charles—ABC/TRC 11090
[Ray Charles/Jimmy Holiday] [BMI] (6/15/68 BR-46)

UNDERSTANDING Bob Seger & The Silver Bullet Band—Capitol 5413
[Bob Seger] [ASC] (11/10/84 BC-17)

UNDERWATER The Frogmen—Candix 314 [Jack Andrews] [BMI] (4/3/61 BCR-34) [I]

UNDUN The Guess Who—RCA Victor 74-0195
[Randy Bachman] [BMI] (10/11/69 BCR-22)

UNEASY RIDER Charlie Daniels—Kama Sutra 576 [Charlie Daniels] [BMI] (6/2/73 BCR-9)

UNFAITHFULLY YOURS (ONE LOVE) Stephen Bishop—Warner Bros. 29345
[Stephen Bishop] [ASC] (3/31/84 B-87)

UNFORGETTABLE *Dinah Washington—Mercury 71508*
[Irving Gordon] [ASC] (9/28/59 BCR-6)

UNFORGETTABLE *Natalie Cole—Elektra 64875 [Irving Gordon] [ASC] (7/13/91 BC-14)*

THE UNFORGIVEN Metallica—Elektra 64814
[Kirk Hammett/James Hetfield/Lars Ulrich] [ASC] (12/7/91 BC-35)

UNGENA ZA ULIMWENGU (UNITE THE WORLD) The Temptations—Gordy 7102 [Barrett Strong/Norman Whitfield] [BMI] (10/3/70 BCR-28)

THE UNICORN The Irish Rovers—Decca 32254 [Shel Silverstein] [BMI] (3/16/68 BCR-4)

UNION MAN Cate Brothers—Asylum 45294 [Earl Cate/Ernie Cate] [BMI] (2/7/76 BCR-24)

UNION OF THE SNAKE Duran Duran—Capitol 5290 [Simon Le Bon/Nick Rhodes/Andy Taylor/Nigel John Taylor/Roger Taylor] [ASC] (11/5/83 BC-1)

—UNITE THE WORLD see: UNGENA ZA ULIMWENGU

(WE'LL BE) UNITED *The Intruders—Gamble 201 [Kenneth Gamble/Leon Huff] [BMI] (7/16/66 BCR-78)*

UNITED (PART 1) *The Music Makers—Gamble 210 [Kenneth Gamble/Leon Huff] [BMI] (12/23/67 BCR-78) [IWM]*

UNITED *Peaches & Herb—Date 1603 [Kenneth Gamble/Leon Huff] [BMI] (5/18/68 BCR-25)*

UNITED TOGETHER Aretha Franklin—Arista 0569 [Charles Henry Jackson Jr./Phil Perry] [ASC] (12/20/80 BCR-52)

UNITED WE STAND The Brotherhood Of Man—Deram 85059 [Tony Hiller/Peter Simons] [ASC] (4/18/70 BCR-13)

THE UNIVERSAL SOLDIER *Glen Campbell—Capitol 5504 [Buffy Sainte-Marie] [ASC] (9/18/65 BCRt-30)*

UNIVERSAL SOLDIER *Donovan—Hickory 1338 [Buffy Sainte-Marie] [ASC] (9/18/65 BCRt-30)*

UNIVERSAL SOLDIER *The Roemans—ABC-Paramount 10723 [Buffy Sainte-Marie] [ASC] (9/25/65 Rt-30)*

THE UNKNOWN SOLDIER The Doors—Elektra 45628 [John Densmore/Robby Krieger/Ray Manzarek/Jim Morrison] [ASC] (3/23/68 BCR-22)

UNLESS YOU CARE Terry Black—Tollie 9026 [Steve Barri/P.F. Sloan] [ASC] (11/14/64 BCR-85)

UNLOVED Walter Egan—Columbia 10916 [Walter Egan] [ASC] (3/10/79 C-93)

UNO Tony Martin—RCA Victor 47-5841 [Enrique Santos Discepolo/Marianito Mores/Geoffrey North] [BMI] (9/25/54 CR-37)

UNSKINNY BOP Poison—Enigma 44584 [Bobby Dall/C.C. DeVille/Bret Michaels/Rikki Rockett] [BMI] (7/7/90 BC-3)

UNSQUARE DANCE Dave Brubeck Quartet—Columbia 42228 [Dave Brubeck] [BMI] (12/4/61 BCR-74) [I]

UNSUSPECTING HEART *Sunny Gale—RCA Victor 47-5952 [Joe Beal/Teddy Powell/Joe Shank/Bob Singer] [ASC] (12/13/54 CtRt-PRE)*

UNSUSPECTING HEART *Georgie Shaw—Decca 29368 [Joe Beal/Teddy Powell/Joe Shank/Bob Singer] [ASC] (12/13/54 Rt-PRE)*

UNSUSPECTING HEART *Terri Stevens—Double AA 101 [Joe Beal/Teddy Powell/Joe Shank/Bob Singer] [ASC] (12/27/54 CtRt-14)*

UNTIE ME The Tams—Arlen 11 [Joe South] [BMI] (10/13/62 BCR-60)

UNTIL IT'S TIME FOR YOU TO GO *Neil Diamond—Uni 55204 [Buffy Sainte-Marie] [ASC] (2/21/70 BCR-40)*

UNTIL IT'S TIME FOR YOU TO GO *Buffy Sainte-Marie—Vanguard 35116 [Buffy Sainte-Marie] [ASC] (11/14/70 R-78)*

UNTIL IT'S TIME FOR YOU TO GO *Elvis Presley—RCA Victor 74-0619 [Buffy Sainte-Marie] (TSW) [ASC] (1/29/72 BCR-31)*

UNTIL IT'S TIME FOR YOU TO GO *The New Birth—RCA Victor 0003 [Buffy Sainte-Marie] [ASC] (8/25/73 B-97)*

UNTIL NOW Bobby Arvon—First Artists 41000 [Bobby Arvon] [ASC] (12/3/77 BC-59)

(UNTIL THEN) I'LL SUFFER Barbara Lynn—Atlantic 2812 [Barbara Lynn] [BMI] (8/21/71 C-98)

UNTIL YOU COME BACK TO ME (THAT'S WHAT I'M GONNA DO) *Aretha Franklin—Atlantic 2995 [Morris Broadnax/Clarence Paul/Stevie Wonder] [BMI] (11/17/73 BCR-3)*

UNTIL YOU COME BACK TO ME (THAT'S WHAT I'M GONNA DO) (MEDLEY) *Luther Vandross—Epic 04969 [Morris Broadnax/Clarence Paul/Stevie Wonder] (Med) [BMI] (4/28/84 B-87)*

UNWIND Ray Stevens—Monument 1048 [Ray Stevens] [BMI] (3/16/68 BCR-44)

—UP A LAZY RIVER see: LAZY RIVER

UP ABOVE MY HEAD (I HEAR MUSIC IN THE AIR) Al (He's The King) Hirt Trumpet with Chorus and Orchestra—RCA Victor 47-8439 [Rosetta Tharpe] [ASC] (10/10/64 BCR-84)

UP ALL NIGHT Slaughter—Chrysalis 23486 [Mark Slaughter/Dana Strum] [BMI] (4/28/90 BC-24)

UP AND DOWN The McCoys—Bang 516 [Lou Courtney/Dennis Lambert] [BMI] (2/12/66 BCR-39)

UP AROUND THE BEND Creedence Clearwater Revival—Fantasy 641 [John Fogerty] (TSW) [BMI] (4/25/70 BCR-2)

UP FOR THE DOWN STROKE Parliament—Casablanca 0013 [George Clinton/William Earl Collins/Clarence Haskins/Bernie Worrell] [BMI] (8/31/74 B-63)

UP FROM THE SKIES The Jimi Hendrix Experience—Reprise 0665 [Jimi Hendrix] [ASC] (3/16/68 BR-82)

UP-HARD Willie Mitchell—Hi 2151 [Art Miller] [BMI] (9/28/68 BCR-63) [I]

UP IN A PUFF OF SMOKE Polly Brown—GTO 1002 [Ron Roker*/Gerry Shury/Phillip Swern] [ASC] (12/28/74 BCR-16)

UP IN HEAH Ike & Tina Turner—United Artists 50881 [Tina Turner/Leon Ware] [BMI] (2/19/72 BCR-70)

UP JUMPED A RABBIT Frankie Lymon—Roulette 4128 [John Gluck] [ASC] (2/28/59 C-81)

UP ON CRIPPLE CREEK The Band—Capitol 2635 [Robbie Robertson] [ASC] (10/18/69 BCR-25)

UP ON THE MOUNTAIN The Magnificents—Vee Jay 183 [Ewart Abner/Nathaniel Nathan] [BMI] (9/1/56 R-79)

UP ON THE ROOF *The Drifters—Atlantic 2162 [Gerry Goffin/Carole King] [BMI] (11/3/62 BCR-5)*

UP ON THE ROOF *The Cryan' Shames—Columbia 44457 [Gerry Goffin/Carole King] [BMI] (3/16/68 BCR-60)*

UP ON THE ROOF *Laura Nyro—Columbia 45230 [Gerry Goffin/Carole King] [BMI] (10/10/70 B-92)*

UP ON THE ROOF *James Taylor—Columbia 11005 [Gerry Goffin/Carole King] [BMI] (6/2/79 BCR-28)*

UP THE CREEK (WITHOUT A PADDLE) Matys Brothers—Decca 29838 [Bill Haley/Bickley Reichner] [BMI] (4/13/56 R-77)

UP THE CREEK (WITHOUT A PADDLE) The Temptations—Gordy 7150 [Jeff Bowen/Jim Ford/Truman Thomas] [BMI] (7/3/76 BR-81)

UP THE LADDER TO THE ROOF The Supremes—Motown 1162 [Vince DiMirco/Frank Edward Wilson*] [BMI] (3/7/70 BCR-7)

UP TIGHT, GOOD MAN Laura Lee—Chess 2030 [Jimmy Ray Johnson/Spooner Oldham/Dan Penn] [BMI] (12/23/67 BC-90)

UP TO MY NECK IN HIGH MUDDY WATER Linda Ronstadt And The Stone Poneys—Capitol 2110 [John Herald/Frank Wakefield/Robert Yellin] [BMI] (3/30/68 B-93)

UP TOWN Roy Orbison—Monument 412 [Joe Melson/Roy Orbison] [BMI] (12/28/59 BCR-70)

UP UNTIL NOW Johnnie Ray—Columbia 41213 [Otis Blackwell] [BMI] (9/1/58 BCR-81)

UP-UP AND AWAY *The 5th Dimension—Soul City 756 [Jimmy Webb] [BMI] (6/3/67 BCR-4)*

UP-UP AND AWAY *Johnny Mann Singers—Liberty 55972 [Jimmy Webb] [BMI] (6/24/67 B-91)*

UP-UP AND AWAY *Hugh Masekela—Uni 55037 [Jimmy Webb] [BMI] (12/9/67 BCR-66) [IWM]*

UP WHERE WE BELONG Joe Cocker and Jennifer Warnes—Island 99996 [Will Jennings/Jack Nitzsche/Buffy Sainte-Marie] [BMI] (8/21/82 BC-1)

UP YOUR NOSE Gabriel Kaplan—Elektra 45369 [Gabe Kaplan/Greg Prestopino/Justus G. Roe] [BMI] (1/8/77 BCR-82)

UPS AND DOWNS Paul Revere And The Raiders—Columbia 44018 [Mark Lindsay/Terry Melcher] [BMI] (2/18/67 BCR-19)

UPSETTER Grand Funk Railroad—Capitol 3316 [Mark Farner] [BMI] (4/15/72 BCR-73)

UPSIDE DOWN Diana Ross—Motown 1494 [Bernard Edwards/Nile Rodgers] [BMI] (7/12/80 BCR-1)

UPTIGHT (EVERYTHING'S ALRIGHT) *Stevie Wonder—Tamla 54124 [Henry Cosby/Sylvia Moy/Stevie Wonder] [ASC] (12/11/65 BCR-3)*

UPTIGHT (EVERYTHING'S ALRIGHT) *The Jazz Crusaders—Pacific Jazz 88125 [Henry Cosby/Sylvia Moy/Stevie Wonder] [ASC] (4/2/66 B-95) [IWM]*

UPTIGHT (EVERYTHING'S ALRIGHT) *Nancy Wilson—Capitol 5673 [Henry Cosby/Sylvia Moy/Stevie Wonder] [ASC] (7/16/66 B-84)*

UP TIGHT *Ramsey Lewis—Cadet 5547 [Henry Cosby/Sylvia Moy/Stevie Wonder] [ASC] (10/8/66 BCR-49) [IWM]*

LITTLE OLE MAN (UPTIGHT - EVERYTHING'S ALRIGHT) *(parody of Uptight) Bill Cosby—Warner Bros. 7072 [Bill Cosby/Henry Cosby/Sylvia Moy/Stevie Wonder] [BMI] (9/2/67 BCR-4) [P]*

UPTIGHT *Shalamar—Soul Train 10885 [Henry Cosby/Sylvia Moy/Stevie Wonder] (Med) [ASC] (3/12/77 BCR-25)*

UPTIGHT EVERYTHING'S ALL RIGHT *Stars On 45—Radio 4019 [Henry Cosby/Sylvia Moy/Stevie Wonder] (Med) [ASC] (3/27/82 BCR-28)*

UPTOWN The Crystals—Philles 102 [Barry Mann/Cynthia Weil] [BMI] (3/19/62 BCR-10)

UPTOWN Prince—Warner Bros. 49559 [Prince] [ASC] (11/1/80 R-78)

UPTOWN & COUNTRY Tom Scott—Ode 66118 [Tom Scott] [BMI] (3/6/76 B-80) [I]

UPTOWN GIRL Billy Joel—Columbia 04149 [Billy Joel] [ASC] (9/24/83 BC-3)

URGE Freddy Cannon—Swan 4053 [Bob Crewe/Frank Slay] [BMI] (4/25/60 BCR-60)

URGENT Foreigner—Atlantic 3831 [Michael Leslie Jones] [ASC] (7/4/81 BCR-3)

US AND LOVE (WE GO TOGETHER) Kenny Nolan—Casablanca 2234 [Kenny Nolan] [BMI] (2/2/80 BCR-44)

US AND THEM Pink Floyd—Harvest 3832 [Roger Waters/Rick Wright] [ASC] (2/23/74 C-72)

U.S. MALE Elvis Presley With The Jordanaires—RCA Victor 47-9465 [Jerry Reed] [BMI] (3/16/68 BCR-26)

U.S. OF A. Donna Fargo—Dot 17523 [Donna Fargo] [BMI] (11/9/74 B-86)

USE IT UP AND WEAR IT OUT Pat & Mick—Charisma 98870 [L. Russell Brown/Sandy Linzer] [BMI] (12/15/90 BC-69)

USE ME Bill Withers—Sussex 241 [Bill Withers] [BMI] (8/19/72 BCR-2)

—USE ME ANYWAY YOU WANNA see: I'M YOURS

USE TA BE MY GIRL The O'Jays—Philadelphia Int'l 3642 [Kenneth Gamble/Leon Huff] [BMI] (4/22/78 BCR-3)

USE YOUR HEAD Mary Wells—20th Century 555 [Chuck Barksdale/Wade Flemons/Barrett Strong] [BMI] (1/2/65 BCR-33)

USED TO BE Charlene & Stevie Wonder—Motown 1650 [Ken Hirsch/Ronald Norman Miller] [BMI] (10/30/82 BC-46)

UTOPIA Frank Gari—Crusade 1020
[Wally Gold/Martin Kalmanoff/Aaron Schroeder] [ASC] (12/19/60 BCR-27)

V

VACATION Connie Francis—MGM 13087
[Connie Francis/Hunk Hunter/Gary Knight] [BMI] (7/21/62 BCR-9)

VACATION Go-Go's—I.R.S. 9907
[Charlotte Caffey/Kathy Valentine/Jane Wiedlin] [ASC] (7/3/82 BC-6)

—VADO VIA see: WORDS ARE IMPOSSIBLE

VAHEVALA (PRONOUNCED VA-HÊÊ-VA-LA)
Kenny Loggins With Jim Messina—Columbia 45550
[Dan Loggins/Dann Lottermoser] [ASC] (4/15/72 BCR-83)

VALENTINE LOVE
Norman Connors (Featuring Michael Henderson And Jean Cain)—Buddah 499
[Michael E. Henderson] [ASC] (11/29/75 BC-81)

VALERIE Cymarron—Entrance 7502 [Richard Mainegra] [BMI] (10/2/71 BCR-93)

VALERIE Steve Winwood—Island 29879
[Will Jennings/Steve Winwood] [BMI] (11/6/82 BC-70)

VALERIE Steve Winwood—Island 28231
[Will Jennings/Steve Winwood] [BMI] (10/10/87 BC-9)

VALLERI The Monkees—Colgems 1019 [Tommy Boyce/Bobby Hart] [BMI] (3/9/68 BCR-1)

VALLEY GIRL Frank Zappa—Barking Pumpkin 9-02972
[Frank Zappa/Moon Unit Zappa] [ASC] (7/17/82 BC-32)

VALLEY OF TEARS Fats Domino—Imperial 5442
[Dave Bartholomew/Fats Domino] [BMI] (5/13/57 BCR-13)

—VALLEY OF THE DOLLS see: THEME FROM VALLEY OF THE DOLLS

THE VALLEY ROAD Bruce Hornsby & The Range—RCA 7645
[Bruce Hornsby/John Hornsby] [ASC] (4/30/88 BC-5)

VALLEY TO PRAY Arlo Guthrie—Reprise 0951
[Arlo Guthrie/John Pilla/Traditional/Doc Watson] [BMI] (10/31/70 CR-79)

VALLEY VALPARAISO Percy Faith And His Orchestra and Chorus—Columbia 40633
[Lee Berke/René Denoncin/Louis Ferrari] [BMI] (1/27/56 BCR-29) [FDE]

VALOTTE Julian Lennon—Atlantic 89609
[Justin Clayton/Julian Lennon/Carlton Morales] [ASC] (10/20/84 BC-9)

VANCE Roger Miller—Smash 2197 [Bobby Russell] [ASC] (11/30/68 BCR-52)

VANILLA OLAY Jackie Deshannon—Atlantic 2871
[Jackie DeShannon] [ASC] (6/3/72 BCR-76)

VANISHING POINT The Marketts—Warner Bros. 5423
[Michael Gordon] [BMI] (3/28/64 B-90) [I]

VANITY KILLS ABC—Mercury 884714 [Martin Fry/Mark White] [BMI] (5/17/86 BC-85)

VAQUERO (COWBOY) The Fireballs—Top Rank 2054
[Norman Petty/George Tomsco] [BMI] (8/15/60 BCR-86) [I]

VARIETY TONIGHT REO Speedwagon—Epic 07055 [Neal Doughty] [ASC] (5/9/87 BC-60)

VAYA CON DIOS *The Drifters—Atlantic 2216*
[Inez James/Buddy Pepper/Larry Russell] [ASC] (1/25/64 BCR-42)

VAYA CON DIOS *Dawn Featuring Tony Orlando—Bell 45,225*
[Inez James/Buddy Pepper/Larry Russell] [ASC] (6/17/72 BCR-60)

VAYA CON DIOS *Freddy Fender—ABC/Dot 17627*
[Inez James/Buddy Pepper/Larry Russell] [ASC] (5/29/76 BC-59)

VEHICLE The Ides Of March—Warner Bros. 7378 [Jim Peterik] [ASC] (3/21/70 BCR-2)

VELCRO FLY ZZ Top—Warner Bros. 28650
[Frank Beard/Billy Gibbons/Dusty Hill] [BMI] (7/26/86 BC-34)

VELVET WATERS The Megatrons—Acousticon 101
[William Plunkett] [BMI] (5/23/59 BCR-51) [I]

VENGEANCE Carly Simon—Elektra 46051 [Carly Simon] [ASC] (6/9/79 BCR-48)

VENI-VIDI-VICI (I CAME, I SAW, I CONQUERED) The Gaylords—Mercury 70427
[Jerry Livingston/Paul Francis Webster] [ASC] (9/4/54 CR-25)

VENICE BLUE (QUE C'EST TRISTE VENISE) Bobby Darin—Capitol 5399
[Charles Aznavour/Françoise Dorin/Gene Lees] [ASC] (4/10/65 C-94) [FET]

VENTURA HIGHWAY America—Warner Bros. 7641
[Dewey Bunnell] [ASC] (10/14/72 BCR-7)

VENUS *Frankie Avalon—Chancellor 1031 [Ed Marshall] [ASC] (2/9/59 BCR-1)*

VENUS *Johnny Mathis—Columbia 44517 [Ed Marshall] [ASC] (6/1/68 C-97)*

VENUS *Frankie Avalon—De-Lite 1578 [Ed Marshall] [ASC] (1/24/76 BCR-32)*

VENUS *Shocking Blue—Colossus 108 [Robbie Van Leeuwen] [ASC] (12/6/69 BCR-1)*

VENUS *Stars On 45—Radio 3810 [Robbie Van Leeuwen] (Med) [ASC] (4/11/81 BCR-1)*

VENUS *Bananarama—London 886056 [Robbie Van Leeuwen] [ASC] (6/28/86 BC-1)*

VENUS AND MARS ROCK SHOW Wings—Capitol 4175
[Linda McCartney/Paul McCartney] [ASC] (11/1/75 BCR-12)

VENUS IN BLUE JEANS Jimmy Clanton—Ace 8001
[Howard Greenfield/Jack Keller] [BMI] (8/18/62 BCR-7)

VERBOTEN! (FORBIDDEN) Paul Anka—ABC-Paramount 9937
[Mack David/Harry Sukman] [ASC] (8/11/58 R-85)

VERDIE MAE Phil Phillips—Mercury 71531
[Phil Baptiste/George Khoury] [BMI] (11/2/59 R-84)

VERONICA Elvis Costello—Warner Bros. 22981
[Elvis Costello/Paul McCartney] [ASC] (4/15/89 BC-19)

THE VERY BEST IN YOU Change—RFC/Atlantic 4027
[Mauro Malavasi/Herb Smith] [ASC] (5/29/82 B-84)

THE VERY LAST TIME Utopia—Bearsville 49247
[Roger Powell/Todd Rundgren/Kasim Sulton/John Griffitt Wilcox] [BMI] (5/31/80 BCR-76)

VERY MUCH IN LOVE Johnny Mathis—Columbia 41355
[Ray Ellis/Al Stillman] [ASC] (4/11/59 C-88)

A VERY PRECIOUS LOVE *The Ames Brothers—RCA Victor 47-7167*
[Sammy Fain/Paul Francis Webster] [ASC] (3/10/58 BCRt-50)

A VERY PRECIOUS LOVE *Doris Day—Columbia 41123*
[Sammy Fain/Paul Francis Webster] [ASC] (3/10/58 Rt-50)

A VERY PRECIOUS LOVE *Bonnie Guitar—Dot 15708*
[Sammy Fain/Paul Francis Webster] [ASC] (3/10/58 Rt-50)

A VERY PRECIOUS LOVE *The Johnston Brothers—London 1796*
[Sammy Fain/Paul Francis Webster] [ASC] (3/17/58 Rt-50)

A VERY PRECIOUS LOVE *Jack Jones—Capitol 3929*
[Sammy Fain/Paul Francis Webster] [ASC] (3/31/58 Rt-50)

VERY SPECIAL Debra Laws—Elektra 47142
[William Jeffery/Lisa Peters] [ASC] (7/4/81 BR-81)

A VERY SPECIAL LOVE (SONG FOR THE NINTH DAY)
Mitch Miller & His Orchestra—Columbia 40831
[Robert Allen] [ASC] (3/2/57 B-94) [I]

A VERY SPECIAL LOVE (SONG FOR THE NINTH DAY) *The Hi-Lo's—Columbia 41050*
[Robert Allen] [ASC] (12/9/57 Rt-15)

A VERY SPECIAL LOVE *Johnny Nash—ABC-Paramount 9874*
[Robert Allen] [ASC] (12/9/57 BCtRt-15)

A VERY SPECIAL LOVE *Debbie Reynolds—Coral 61897*
[Robert Allen] [ASC] (12/9/57 BCtRt-15)

A VERY SPECIAL LOVE SONG Charlie Rich—Epic 11091
[Billy Sherrill/Norro Wilson] [BMI] (2/16/74 BCR-8)

THE VERY THOUGHT OF YOU *Little Willie John—King 5458*
[Ray Noble] [ASC] (3/13/61 B-61)

THE VERY THOUGHT OF YOU *Rick Nelson—Decca 31612*
[Ray Noble] [ASC] (4/25/64 BCR-17)

A VERY TRUE STORY Chris Kenner—Instant 3234 [Chris Kenner] [BMI] (9/4/61 R-89)

VICTIM Candi Staton—Warner Bros. 8582
[Dave Crawford] [ASC] (7/29/78 R-88)

VICTIM OF A FOOLISH HEART Bettye Swann—Atlantic 2869
[Mickey Buckins/George Henry Jackson] [BMI] (5/27/72 BCR-63)

VICTIM OF LOVE Elton John—MCA 41126
[Pete Bellotte/Sylvester Levay/Jerry Rix] [ASC] (9/29/79 BCR-31)

VICTIM OF LOVE Bryan Adams—A&M 2964
[Bryan Adams/Jim Vallance] [BMI] (8/22/87 BC-32)

VICTORIA The Kinks—Reprise 0863 [Ray Davies] [BMI] (1/31/70 BCR-54)

VICTORY Kool & The Gang—Mercury 888074
[Robert Bell/Ronald Bell/George M. Brown/Claydes Smith/J.T. Taylor/Curtis Fitzgerald Williams] [BMI] (11/1/86 BC-10)

VICTORY LINE Limited Warranty—Atco 99541
[Gerald Brunskill/Dale Goulett/Paul Hartwig/Jon Erik Newman/Greg Sotebeer] [BMI] (6/28/86 BC-79)

VIDEO Jeff Lynne—Virgin/Epic 04570 [Jeff Lynne] [ASC] (8/18/84 B-85)

VIDEO KILLED THE RADIO STAR The Buggles—Island 49114
[Geoffrey Downes/Trevor Horn/Bruce Woolley] [BMI] (11/10/79 BCR-40)

VIENI VIENI *Werner Müller And His Orchestra—Decca 29670*
[Vincent Scotto] [ASC] (9/19/55 R-35) [IM]

VIENI VIENI *Terri Stevens—Felsted 8586*
[Géo Koger/Vincent Scotto/Rudy Vallee/Henri Varna] [ASC] (7/27/59 R-94)

VIENNA CALLING Falco—A&M 2832
[Ferdi Bolland/Rob Bolland/Falco] [ASC] (4/26/86 BC-17)

A VIEW TO A KILL Duran Duran—Capitol 5475
[John Barry/Simon Le Bon/Nick Rhodes/Andy Taylor/Nigel John Taylor/Roger Taylor] [BMI] (5/18/85 BC-1)

VILLAGE OF LOVE Nathaniel Mayer And The Fabulous Twilights—Fortune 449
[Devora Brown/Nathaniel Mayer] [BMI] (4/7/62 BCR-22)

THE VILLAGE OF ST. BERNADETTE *Rosemary June—United Artists 197*
[Eula Parker] [BMI] (12/7/59 Rt-7)

THE VILLAGE OF ST. BERNADETTE *Andy Williams—Cadence 1374*
[Eula Parker] [BMI] (12/7/59 BCRt-7)

THE VILLAGE OF ST. BERNADETTE *Toni Arden—Decca 31025*
[Eula Parker] [BMI] (12/21/59 Rt-7)

VINCENT Don McLean—United Artists 50887
[Don McLean] (TSW) [BMI] (4/22/72 BCR-11)

VIOLENCE OF SUMMER (LOVE'S TAKING OVER) Duran Duran—Capitol 44608
[Sterling Campbell/Warren Cuccurullo/Simon Le Bon/Nick Rhodes/Nigel John Taylor] [ASC] (8/25/90 BC-56)

VIRGIN MAN Smokey Robinson—Tamla 54250
[Rose Ella Jones/Smokey Robinson] [ASC] (9/7/74 BCR-56)

VIRGINIA (TOUCH ME LIKE YOU DO) Bill Amesbury—Casablanca 0001
[Bill Amesbury] [BMI] (2/2/74 BCR-38)

VISION OF LOVE Mariah Carey—Columbia 73348
[Mariah Carey/Ben Margulies] [BMI] (6/2/90 BC-1)

THE VISITORS ABBA—Atlantic 4031
[Benny Andersson/Björn Ulvaeus] [BMI] (4/17/82 BC-63)

VITAMIN L B. E. Taylor Group—MCA 52311
[Debbie Witkowski/Rick Witkowski] [ASC] (1/28/84 BC-66)

VIVA LAS VEGAS Elvis Presley With The Jordanaires—RCA Victor 47-8360
[Doc Pomus/Mort Shuman] [BMI] (5/2/64 BCR-16)

VIVA TIRADO - PART 1 El Chicano—Kapp 2085 [Gerald Wilson] [BMI] (4/4/70 BCR-27) [I]

VOGUE Madonna—Sire 19863
[Madonna L. Ciccone/Shep Pettibone] [ASC] (4/14/90 BC-1)

THE VOICE The Moody Blues—Threshold 602 [Justin Hayward] [ASC] (8/8/81 BCR-15)

THE VOICE IN MY HEART Eydie Gorme—ABC-Paramount 9971
[Dave Franklin] [ASC] (11/22/58 BC-68)

A VOICE IN THE CHOIR Al Martino—Capitol 2053
[Danny DiMinno/Johnny Tucker] [ASC] (12/9/67 BCR-78)

VOICE OF AMERICA'S SONS
John Cafferty And The Beaver Brown Band—Scotti Brothers 06048
[John Cafferty] [BMI] (6/14/86 BC-52)

VOICE OF FREEDOM Jim Kirk And The TM Singers—Capitol 4834
[Jim Kirk] [ASC] (2/16/80 BCR-71)

VOICE ON THE RADIO Conductor—Montage 1210
[Franne Golde/Peter Mclan] [ASC] (1/30/82 BCR-63)

VOICE YOUR CHOICE The Radiants—Chess 1904
[Maurice McAlister/Gerald Sims] [BMI] (12/26/64 BCR-38)

VOICES The Fontane Sisters—Dot 15480 [Larry Coleman] [BMI] (7/6/56 BCR-34)

VOICES Cheap Trick—Epic 50814 [Rick Nielsen] [BMI] (12/1/79 BCR-28)

VOICES CARRY 'til tuesday—Epic 04795
[Michael Hausman/Robert Holmes/Aimee Mann/Joey Pesce] [ASC] (4/13/85 BC-8)

VOICES OF BABYLON The Outfield—Columbia 68601
[John Spinks] [ASC] (3/25/89 BC-25)

VOICES THAT CARE Voices That Care—Giant 19350
[Peter Cetera/David Foster/Linda Thompson] [ASC] (3/16/91 BC-11)

NEL BLU DIPINTO DI BLU (VOLARE) *Domenico Modugno—Decca 30677*
[Franco Migliacci/Domenico Modugno] [ASC] (7/7/58 BCtRt-1) [F]

NEL BLU DIPINTO DI BLU *Rosa Linda—Challenge 59016*
[Franco Migliacci/Domenico Modugno] [ASC] (7/28/58 Rt-22) [F]

VOLARE (NEL BLU DIPINTO DI BLU) *Dean Martin—Capitol 4028*
[Franco Migliacci/Domenico Modugno/Mitchell Parish] [ASC] (8/4/58 BCtRt-1) [FDE]

VOLARE (NEL BLU, DIPINTO DI BLU) *Alan Dale—MGM 12699*
[Franco Migliacci/Domenico Modugno/Mitchell Parish] [ASC] (8/4/58 Rt-7) [FDE]

VOLARE (NEL BLU DI PINTO DI BLU) *The McGuire Sisters—Coral 62021*
[Franco Migliacci/Domenico Modugno/Mitchell Parish] [ASC] (8/11/58 BRt-1) [FDE]

VOLARE (NEL BLU DIPINTO DI BLU) *Jesse Belvin—RCA Victor 47-7310*
[Franco Migliacci/Domenico Modugno/Mitchell Parish] [ASC] (8/11/58 Rt-1) [FDE]

(NEL BLU DIPINTO DI BLU) VOLARE *Umberto Marcato—Kapp 228*
[Franco Migliacci/Domenico Modugno] [ASC] (8/25/58 Rt-1) [F]

VOLARE *Bobby Rydell—Cameo 179*
[Franco Migliacci/Domenico Modugno/Mitchell Parish] [ASC] (7/11/60 BCR-4) [FDE]

VOLARE *Ace Cannon—Hi 2057 [Domenico Modugno] [ASC] (11/3/62 CR-77) [IM]*

VOLARE *Al Martino—Capitol 4134*
[Franco Migliacci/Domenico Modugno/Mitchell Parish] [ASC] (11/1/75 BCR-33) [FDE]

VOLCANO Jimmy Buffett—MCA 41161
[Jimmy Buffett/Harry Dailey/Keith Sykes] [BMI] (12/15/79 BCR-61)

VOLUNTEERS Jefferson Airplane—RCA Victor 74-0245
[Marty Balin/Paul Kantner] [BMI] (11/8/69 BCR-58)

VOO DOO Rachel Sweet—Columbia 03411
[Marc Blatte/Larry Gottlieb/Rachel Sweet] [ASC] (2/5/83 B-72)

VOODOO WOMAN Bobby Goldsboro—United Artists 862
[Bobby Goldsboro] [BMI] (5/1/65 BCR-21)

VOODOO WOMAN Simon Stokes & The Nighthawks—Elektra 45670
[Randall Keith/Simon Stokes] [ASC] (12/13/69 BCR-85)

VOULEZ-VOUS ABBA—Atlantic 3609
[Benny Andersson/Björn Ulvaeus] (TSW) [ASC] (9/8/79 BCR-77)

VOX HUMANA Kenny Loggins—Columbia 04849
[E. Ein Loggins/Kenny Loggins] [ASC] (3/23/85 BC-22)

VOYEUR Kim Carnes—EMI America 8127
[Kim Carnes/Dave Ellingson/Duane Hitchings] [ASC] (8/21/82 BC-25)

W

WABASH BLUES *Billy Vaughn and his Orchestra—Dot 15976*
[Fred Meinken] [ASC] (8/24/59 R-80) [IM]

WABASH BLUES *The Viscounts—Madison 140*
[Fred Meinken] [ASC] (12/5/60 BCR-77) [IM]

WABASH CANNONBALL Rusty Draper—Mercury 70757
[William Kindt] [ASC] (1/27/56 R-86)

WACK WACK Young Holt Trio—Brunswick 55305
[Isaac Holt/Donald Storball*/Hysear Don Walker/Eldee Young] [BMI]
(12/17/66 BCR-35) [I]

WADE IN THE WATER *Ramsey Lewis—Cadet 5541 [Traditional] [BMI] (7/9/66 BCR-18) [I]*

WADE IN THE WATER *Herb Alpert & The Tijuana Brass—A&M 840*
[Traditional] [BMI] (3/11/67 BCR-37) [I]

—WAH-WAH SONG see: I WAS MEANT FOR YOU

THE WAH-WATUSI The Orlons—Cameo 218 [Dave Appell/Kal Mann] [ASC] (6/9/62 BCR-2)

WAIT Jimmy Clanton—Ace 600 [Doc Pomus/Mort Shuman] [BMI] (9/26/60 B-91)

WAIT White Lion—Atlantic 89126 [Vito Bratta/Mike Tramp] [ASC] (2/27/88 BC-8)

WAIT A MINUTE The Coasters—Atco 6186
[Bobby Darin/Don Kirshner] [BMI] (1/23/61 BCR-37)

WAIT A MINUTE Tim Tam And The Turn-Ons—Palmer 5002
[Tom DeAngelo/Rick Wiesend] [BMI] (3/5/66 BR-76)

WAIT AND SEE Fats Domino—Imperial 5467
[Dave Bartholomew/Fats Domino] [BMI] (10/12/57 BCR-27)

WAIT FOR ME The Playmates—Roulette 4276
[Lee Pockriss/Paul Vance] [ASC] (10/8/60 BCR-28)

WAIT FOR ME Rita Pavone—RCA Victor 47-8420
[Sylvia Dee/Arthur Kent] [ASC] (10/17/64 C-97)

WAIT FOR ME Daryl Hall & John Oates—RCA 11747 [Daryl Hall] [BMI] (10/27/79 BCR-18)

WAIT FOR TOMORROW Jill Corey—Columbia 40627
[Larry Coleman/Fred Ebb/Paul Klein] [NA] (1/20/56 R-80)

WAIT FOR YOU Bonham—WTG 73034
[Jason Bonham/Bob Ezrin/Ian Hatton/Dan MacMaster/John Smithson] [ASC]
(11/25/89 BC-55)

WAIT ON LOVE Michael Bolton—Columbia 07794
[Michael Bolton/Jonathan Cain] [BMI] (5/28/88 BC-79)

WAIT 'TIL MY BOBBY GETS HOME Darlene Love—Philles 114
[Jeff Barry/Ellie Greenwich/Phil Spector] [BMI] (7/20/63 BCR-26)

WAIT TIL THE SUN SHINES NELLIE Crazy Otto—Decca 29753A
[Harry Von Tilzer] (Med) [ASC] (2/3/56 R-90) [IM]

WAITIN' IN SCHOOL Ricky Nelson—Imperial 5483
[Dorsey Burnette/Johnny Burnette] [BMI] (12/23/57 BCR-6)

WAITIN' IN YOUR WELFARE LINE Buck Owens—Capitol 5566
[Buck Owens/Don Rich/Nat Stuckey] [BMI] (1/29/66 BCR-57)

THE WAITING Tom Petty and the Heartbreakers—Backstreet 51100
[Tom Petty] [ASC] (5/2/81 BCR-14)

WAITING AT THE BUS STOP Bobby Sherman—Metromedia 222
[Ronald Boutwell/Bobby Sherman] [ASC] (8/14/71 BCR-44)

WAITING FOR A GIRL LIKE YOU Foreigner—Atlantic 3868
[Lou Gramm/Michael Leslie Jones] [ASC] (10/10/81 BCR-2)

WAITING FOR A STAR TO FALL Boy Meets Girl—RCA 8691
[George Merrill/Shannon Rubicam] [BMI] (9/3/88 BC-4)

WAITING FOR CHARLIE *Etta James—Argo 5409*
[Burt Bacharach/Bob Hilliard] [ASC] (1/29/62 R-80)

WAITING FOR CHARLIE TO COME HOME *Marlena Shaw—Cadet 5571*
[Burt Bacharach/Bob Hilliard] [ASC] (9/9/67 C-97)

WAITING FOR LOVE Alias—EMI 50337
[Jeff Paris/Brett Walker] [BMI] (1/19/91 BC-10)

WAITING FOR THAT DAY George Michael—Columbia 73663
[Mick Jagger/George Michael/Keith Richards] (Med) [ASC] (1/19/91 BC-21)

WAITING FOR YOUR LOVE Toto—Columbia 03981
[Bobby Kimball/David Paich] [BMI] (7/2/83 BC-73)

THE WAITING GAME Harry Belafonte—RCA Victor 47-7289
[Robert Allen/Bob Hilliard] [ASC] (7/19/58 C-57)

THE WAITING GAME Brenda Lee—Decca 31599 [Buzz Cason] [BMI] (3/14/64 CR-81)

WAITING GAME Swing Out Sister—Fontana 874 190
[Andy Connell/Corinne Drewery] [BMI] (6/3/89 B-86)

WAITING ON A FRIEND The Rolling Stones—Rolling Stones 21004
[Mick Jagger/Keith Richards] [ASC] (12/5/81 BCR-13)

WAKE ME SHAKE ME The Coasters—Atco 6168 [Billy Guy] [BMI] (6/20/60 BCR-34)

WAKE ME UP BEFORE YOU GO-GO Wham!—Columbia 04552
[George Michael] [ASC] (9/8/84 BC-1)

WAKE ME WHEN IT'S OVER Andy Williams—Cadence 1378
[Sammy Cahn/Jimmy Van Heusen] [ASC] (3/14/60 BCR-50)

WAKE THE TOWN AND TELL THE PEOPLE
Les Baxter His Chorus And Orchestra—Capitol 3120 [Sammy Gallop/Jerry Livingston]
[ASC] (7/9/55 BCtRt-4)

WAKE THE TOWN AND TELL THE PEOPLE *Mindy Carson—Columbia 40537*
[Sammy Gallop/Jerry Livingston] [ASC] (7/25/55 BCtRt-4)

WAKE UP The Chambers Brothers—Columbia 44890
[Marvin Hamlisch/Joel Hirschhorn/Al Kasha*] [ASC] (7/12/69 B-92)

WAKE UP Law—GRC 2072 [Ronnie Cunningham] [BMI] (10/11/75 CR-91)

WAKE UP AND BE SOMEBODY Brainstorm—Tabu 10811
[Gerald Kent] [BMI] (3/12/77 B-86)

WAKE UP AND LOVE ME April—A&M 1528
[Jeff Barry/April Stevens/Nino Tempo] [BMI] (6/15/74 BCR-81)

WAKE UP EVERYBODY (PART 1) Harold Melvin And The Blue Notes—Philadelphia Int'l 3579 [Victor Carstarphen/Gene McFadden/John Whitehead] [BMI] (11/15/75 BCR-12)

WAKE UP LITTLE SUSIE *The Everly Brothers—Cadence 1337 [Boudleaux Bryant/Felice Bryant] [BMI] (9/16/57 BCR-1)*

WAKE UP LITTLE SUSIE *Simon and Garfunkel—Warner Bros. 50053 [Boudleaux Bryant/Felice Bryant] [BMI] (4/3/82 BCR-27)*

WAKE UP LITTLE SUZIE *Jive Bunny And The Mastermixers—Music Factory 99140 [Boudleaux Bryant/Felice Bryant] (Med) [BMI] (10/28/89 BC-11)*

WAKE UP MY LOVE George Harrison—Dark Horse 29864 [George Harrison] [ASC] (11/13/82 BC-53)

WAKE UP (NEXT TO YOU) Graham Parker And The Shot—Elektra 69654 [Graham Parker] [ASC] (5/4/85 BC-38)

WAKE UP SUSAN The Spinners—Atlantic 3341 [Thom Bell/Sherman Marshall] [BMI] (7/10/76 BCR-56)

WAKE UP, WAKE UP The Grass Roots—Dunhill 4105 [Steve Barri/P.F. Sloan] [ASC] (10/21/67 BCR-43)

WAKING UP ALONE Paul Williams—A&M 1325 [Paul Williams] [ASC] (2/12/72 BCR-51)

THE WALK *Jimmy McCracklin—Checker 885 [V. Garlic*/Jimmy McCracklin] [BMI] (2/17/58 BCR-7)*

THE WALK *The Inmates—Polydor 2058 [V. Garlic*/Jimmy McCracklin] [BMI] (2/2/80 CR-84)*

WALK A MILE IN MY SHOES Joe South And The Believers—Capitol 2704 [Joe South] [BMI] (12/20/69 BCR-11)

WALK ALONG WITH KINGS *Johnnie Ray—Columbia 40649 [Bob Merrill] [ASC] (2/24/56 Rt-52)*

WALK ALONG WITH KINGS *Roy Hamilton—Epic 9147 [Bob Merrill] [ASC] (2/24/56 Rt-52)*

WALK AWAY Matt Monro—Liberty 55745 [Don Black/Udo Jürgens] [BMI] (11/21/64 BCR-23) [FDE]

WALK AWAY The James Gang—ABC 11301 [Joe Walsh] [BMI] (5/22/71 BCR-29)

WALK AWAY Donna Summer—Casablanca 2300 [Pete Bellotte/Harold Faltermeyer] [BMI] (9/13/80 BCR-36)

WALK AWAY FROM LOVE David Ruffin—Motown 1376 [Charles Kipps] [BMI] (11/8/75 BCR-8)

WALK AWAY RENEE *The Left Banke—Smash 2041 [Bob Calilli/Michael David Lookofsky/Tony Sansone] [BMI] (9/10/66 BCR-2)*

WALK AWAY RENEE *Four Tops—Motown 1119 [Bob Calilli/Michael David Lookofsky/Tony Sansone] [BMI] (2/3/68 BCR-8)*

WALK AWAY RENEE *Southside Johnny & The Jukes—Atlantic 89394 [Bob Calilli/Michael David Lookofsky/Tony Sansone] [BMI] (8/9/86 BC-82)*

WALK DON'T RUN *The Ventures—Dolton 25 [Johnny Smith] [BMI] (7/18/60 BCR-2) [I]*

WALK—DON'T RUN '64 *The Ventures—Dolton 96 [Johnny Smith] [BMI] (7/11/64 BCR-8) [I]*

WALK EASY MY SON Jerry Butler—Mercury 73241 [Charles Henry Jackson Jr./Eutrice Shell] [BMI] (10/9/71 BCR-92)

WALK HAND IN HAND *Andy Williams—Cadence 1288 [Johnny Cowell] [BMI] (4/13/56 BCtRt-16)*

WALK HAND IN HAND *Tony Martin—RCA Victor 47-6493 [Johnny Cowell] [BMI] (4/13/56 BCtRt-10)*

WALK HAND IN HAND *Denny Vaughn—Kapp 143 [Johnny Cowell] [BMI] (4/13/56 BRt-27)*

A WALK IN THE BLACK FOREST Horst Jankowski—Mercury 72425 [Horst Jankowski] [BMI] (5/1/65 BCR-9) [I]

WALK IN THE NIGHT Jr. Walker & The All Stars—Soul 35095 [Johnny Bristol/Marilyn McLeod] [ASC] (4/1/72 BCR-46) [I]

WALK IN THE PARK Claudine Longet—A&M 967 [William Sievers] [BMI] (8/31/68 C-94)

WALK LIKE A MAN *The 4 Seasons—Vee-Jay 485 [Bob Crewe/Bob Gaudio] [BMI] (1/19/63 BCR-1)*

WALK LIKE A MAN *Gidea Park—Profile 5003 [Bob Crewe/Bob Gaudio] (Med) [BMI] (12/26/81 BC-82)*

WALK LIKE A MAN *Mary Jane Girls—Motown 1851 [Bob Crewe/Bob Gaudio] [BMI] (7/12/86 BC-41)*

WALK LIKE A MAN Grand Funk—Capitol 3760 [Don Brewer/Mark Farner] [BMI] (11/17/73 BCR-17)

WALK LIKE AN EGYPTIAN Bangles—Columbia 06257 [Liam Sternberg] [BMI] (9/27/86 BC-1)

WALK OF LIFE Dire Straits—Warner Bros. 28878 [Mark Knopfler] [ASC] (11/2/85 BC-7)

WALK ON Roy Orbison—MGM 13950 [William Dees/Roy Orbison] [BMI] (7/6/68 CR-93)

WALK ON Neil Young—Reprise 1209 [Neil Young] [ASC] (7/13/74 BCR-54)

WALK ON BY Leroy Van Dyke—Mercury 71834 [Kendall L. Hayes] [BMI] (10/28/61 BCR-2)

WALK ON BY *Dionne Warwick—Scepter 1274 [Burt Bacharach/Hal David] [ASC] (4/18/64 BCR-6)*

WALK ON BY *Isaac Hayes—Enterprise 9003 [Burt Bacharach/Hal David] [ASC] (8/23/69 BCR-30)*

WALK ON BY *Gloria Gaynor—MGM 14808 [Burt Bacharach/Hal David] [ASC] (6/28/75 B-98)*

WALK ON BY *AWB—Atlantic 3563 [Burt Bacharach/Hal David] [ASC] (4/14/79 B-92)*

WALK ON BY *Sybil—Next Plateau 327 [Burt Bacharach/Hal David] [ASC] (1/27/90 BC-68)*

WALK ON THE WILD SIDE *Brook Benton—Mercury 71925 [Elmer Bernstein/Mack David] [ASC] (2/12/62 BCtR-32)*

WALK ON THE WILD SIDE (PART 1) *Elmer Bernstein and Orchestra—Choreo 101 [Elmer Bernstein] [ASC] (5/19/62 Ct-71) [IM]*

WALK ON THE WILD SIDE - PART 1 *Jimmy Smith And The Big Band—Verve 10255 [Elmer Bernstein] [ASC] (5/7/62 BCR-15) [IM]*

WALK ON THE WILD SIDE *Lou Reed—RCA Victor 74-0887 [Lou Reed] [BMI] (2/17/73 BCR-16)*

WILDSIDE *Marky Mark & The Funky Bunch—Interscope 98673 [Lou Reed/Amir Shakir] [BMI] (11/2/91 BC-10)*

WALK ON WATER Neil Diamond—Uni 55352 [Neil Diamond] [SE] (11/4/72 BCR-14)

WALK ON WATER Eddie Money—Columbia 08060 [Jesse Harms] [ASC] (10/1/88 BC-7)

WALK ON WITH THE DUKE The Duke Of Earl—Vee-Jay 440 [Calvin Carter/Gene Chandler/Earl Edwards/Bob Finiz/Irving Nahan/Joe Pirollo/Ernie Spano/James Testa/Bernice Williams] [BMI] (4/16/62 BCR-70)

WALK RIGHT BACK *The Everly Brothers—Warner Bros. 5199 [Sonny Curtis] [BMI] (1/30/61 BCR-7)*

WALK RIGHT BACK *Anne Murray—Capitol 4527 [Sonny Curtis] [BMI] (3/25/78 C-92)*

WALK RIGHT IN *The Rooftop Singers—Vanguard 35017 [Gus Cannon/Erik Darling/Willard Svanoe/Hosea Woods] [BMI] (12/29/62 BCR-1)*

WALK RIGHT IN *The Moments (1)—Era 3099 [Gus Cannon/Erik Darling/Willard Svanoe/Hosea Woods] [BMI] (1/12/63 B-82)*

WALK RIGHT IN *Dr. Hook—Capitol 4423 [Gus Cannon/Erik Darling/Willard Svanoe/Hosea Woods] [BMI] (6/18/77 BCR-46)*

WALK RIGHT NOW Jacksons—Epic 02132 [Jackie Jackson/Michael Jackson/Steven Randall Jackson] [BMI] (6/27/81 BCR-73)

WALK RIGHT UP TO THE SUN The Delfonics—Philly Groove 169 [Allan Felder/Norman Harris] [BMI] (10/9/71 BCR-62)

WALK SLOW Little Willie John—King 5428 [Darlynn John/Little Willie John] [BMI] (11/28/60 BCR-48)

WALK TALL 2 Of Clubs—Fraternity 975 [Lee Pockriss/Paul Vance] [ASC] (12/24/66 BCR-62)

WALK THE DINOSAUR Was (Not Was)—Chrysalis 43331 [Randy Jacobs/David Was/Don Was] [ASC] (1/28/89 BC-7)

WALK THIS WAY *Aerosmith—Columbia 10449 [Joe Perry/Steven Tyler] [BMI] (11/20/76 BCR-5)*

WALK THIS WAY *Run-D.M.C.—Profile 5112 [Joe Perry/Steven Tyler] [BMI] (7/26/86 BC-4)*

WALK THROUGH FIRE Bad Company—Atco 98748 [Brian Howe/Terry Thomas] [ASC] (8/24/91 BC-18)

WALK WITH FAITH IN YOUR HEART *Johnny Nash—ABC-Paramount 9989 [Teddy Powell/Tony Starr] [ASC] (1/10/59 CR-48)*

WALK WITH FAITH IN YOUR HEART *The Bachelors—London 20018 [Teddy Powell/Tony Starr] [ASC] (12/31/66 BCR-83)*

WALKIN' AFTER MIDNIGHT *Patsy Cline—Decca 30221 [Alan Block/Don Hecht] [BMI] (2/9/57 BCRt-7)*

WALKIN' AFTER MIDNIGHT *Otis Williams & His Charms—DeLuxe 6115 [Alan Block/Don Hecht] [BMI] (3/2/57 Rt-12)*

WALKIN' BACK TO HAPPINESS Helen Shapiro—Capitol 4662 [Mike Hawker/John Schroeder] [ASC] (12/4/61 B-100)

WALKIN' HOME FROM SCHOOL Gene Vincent and His Blue Caps—Capitol 3874 [Sylvester Bradford/Al Lewis] [ASC] (2/10/58 R-52)

WALKING IN THE RAIN *The Ronettes—Philles 123 [Barry Mann/Phil Spector/Cynthia Weil] [BMI] (10/24/64 BCR-20)*

WALKIN' IN THE RAIN *Jay And The Americans—United Artists 50605 [Barry Mann/Phil Spector/Cynthia Weil] [BMI] (11/15/69 BCR-10)*

WALKIN' IN THE RAIN WITH THE ONE I LOVE Love Unlimited—Uni 55319 [Barry White] [BMI] (3/18/72 BCR-7)

WALKIN' IN THE SUNSHINE Roger Miller—Smash 2081 [Roger Miller] [BMI] (3/18/67 BCR-37)

A WALKIN' MIRACLE The Essex Featuring Anita Humes—Roulette 4515 [Luigi Creatore/Adam Levy/Hugo Peretti/George David Weiss] [ASC] (8/24/63 BCR-8)

WALKIN' MY CAT NAMED DOG Norma Tanega—New Voice 807 [Norma Tanega] [ASC] (2/26/66 BCR-18)

WALKIN' PROUD Pete Klint Quintet—Mercury 72709 [Gordon Evans/Joe Simmons] [BMI] (10/7/67 BR-98)

WALKIN' SHOES Tora Tora—A&M 1425 [Anthony Corder/Keith Douglas/Patrick Francis/John Patterson] [BMI] (8/12/89 B-86)

WALKIN' THE FENCE Couchois—Warner Bros. 8749 [Chris Couchois/Mike Couchois/Pat Couchois/Howard Messer] [ASC] (3/24/79 CR-83)

WALKIN' THE LOW ROAD Randy Sparks—Verve 10116 [Randy Sparks] [ASC] (3/29/58 C-57)

WALKIN' TO MOTHER'S Ray Anthony and his Orchestra—Capitol 4176 [Henry Mancini] [ASC] (4/20/59 B-96) [I]

WALKIN' TO SCHOOL The Kalin Twins—Decca 30552 [Harold Kalin/Herbie Kalin] [BMI] (2/3/58 R-63)

WALKIN' WITH MR. LEE Lee Allen And His Band—Ember 1027 [Lee Allen] [BMI] (12/23/57 BCR-32) [I]

WALKIN' WITH MY ANGEL Bobby Vee—Liberty 55388 [Gerry Goffin/Carole King] [BMI] (11/25/61 BCR-53)

WALKING ALONG *The Diamonds—Mercury 71366*
[Bobby Baylor/Pat Gaston/Milton Love/Monte Owens/Hy Weiss‡/Sam Weiss‡/Winston Willis] [BMI] (10/11/58 BCRt-19)

WALKING ALONG *The Solitaires—Argo 5316*
[Bobby Baylor/Pat Gaston/Milton Love/Monte Owens/Hy Weiss‡/Sam Weiss‡/Winston Willis] [BMI] (11/3/58 Rt-45)

WALKING AWAY Information Society—Tommy Boy 27736
[Paul Robb] [ASC] (11/26/88 BC-9)

WALKING DOWN YOUR STREET Bangles—Columbia 06674
[Louis Gutierrez/Susanna Hoffs/David Kahne] [BMI] (2/14/87 BC-9)

WALKING IN L.A. Missing Persons—Capitol 5212 [Terry Bozzio] [ASC] (3/12/83 BC-62)

WALKING IN MEMPHIS Marc Cohn—Atlantic 87747 [Marc Cohn] [ASC] (3/30/91 BC-11)

WALKING IN MY SLEEP Roger Daltrey—Atlantic 89704
[Leslie Adey/Jack Green] [BMI] (2/18/84 BC-62)

WALKING IN RHYTHM The Blackbyrds—Fantasy 736 [Barney Perry] [BMI] (2/8/75 BCR-6)

WALKING INTO SUNSHINE Central Line—Mercury 76126
[Linton Beckles/Roy Carter/Lipson Francis] [ASC] (11/14/81 BR-79)

WALKING ON A THIN LINE Huey Lewis and the News—Chrysalis 42825
[André Pessis/Kevin Wells] [ASC] (10/20/84 BC-18)

WALKING ON BACK Edward Bear—Capitol 3683 [Robert Kendall] [BMI] (8/25/73 C-77)

WALKING ON SUNSHINE Katrina And The Waves—Capitol 5466
[Kimberly Rew] [BMI] (3/23/85 BC-9)

WALKING ON THE CHINESE WALL Philip Bailey—Columbia 04826
[Bill Hughes/Marcy Levy*/Roxanne Seeman] [ASC] (4/6/85 BC-46)

WALKING ON THIN ICE Yoko Ono—Geffen 49683 [Yoko Ono] [BMI] (2/28/81 BCR-41)

WALKING PROUD Steve Lawrence—Columbia 42865
[Gerry Goffin/Carole King] [BMI] (10/5/63 BCR-17)

WALKING THE BLUES Jack DuPree and Mr. Bear—King 4812
[Jack Dupree/Ted McRae] [ASC] (10/17/55 R-76)

WALKING THE DOG Rufus Thomas—Stax 140 [Rufus Thomas] [ASC] (10/5/63 BCR-10)

I'M WALKING THE FLOOR OVER YOU *Georgia Gibbs—RCA Victor 47-6922*
[Ernest Tubb] [BMI] (6/3/57 BR-46)

WALKING THE FLOOR OVER YOU *Pat Boone—Dot 16073*
[Ernest Tubb] [BMI] (5/9/60 BCR-21)

WALKING THROUGH THE COUNTRY The Grass Roots—Dunhill 4227
[Dennis Provisor] [ASC] (2/7/70 BCR-27)

WALKING THROUGH WALLS The Escape Club—Atlantic 88951
[Johnnie Christo/John Holliday/Trevor Steel/Milan Zekavica] [ASC] (3/25/89 BC-71)

WALKING TO NEW ORLEANS Fats Domino—Imperial 5675
[Dave Bartholomew/Fats Domino/Robert Guidry] [BMI] (6/20/60 BCR-6)

WALKS LIKE A LADY Journey—Columbia 11275 [Steve Perry] [BMI] (5/24/80 BCR-32)

THE WALL *Eileen Rodgers—Columbia 40850*
[Oramay Diamond/Dave Dreyer/Clyde Otis] [ASC] (2/23/57 BCtRt-42)

THE WALL *Patti Page—Mercury 71059*
[Oramay Diamond/Dave Dreyer/Clyde Otis] [ASC] (2/23/57 BCtRt-42)

THE WALL *Brook Benton—Epic 9199*
[Oramay Diamond/Dave Dreyer/Clyde Otis] [ASC] (2/23/57 Rt-45)

THE WALL STREET SHUFFLE 10 C. C.—UK 49023
[Graham Gouldman/Eric Stewart] [BMI] (7/13/74 C-84)

DANCE WITH ME HENRY (WALLFLOWER) *Georgia Gibbs—Mercury 70572*
[Hank Ballard/Etta James/Johnny Otis] [BMI] (3/7/55 BCRt-1)

THE WALLFLOWER *The Three Rays—Coral 61370*
[Hank Ballard/Etta James/Johnny Otis] [BMI] (3/14/55 Rt-9)

THE WALLFLOWER *Etta James & The Peaches—Modern 947*
[Hank Ballard/Etta James/Johnny Otis] [BMI] (3/14/55 Rt-9)

THE WALLFLOWER (DANCE WITH ME HENRY) *Lee Winters—Crown 142*
[Hank Ballard/Etta James/Johnny Otis] [BMI] (3/14/55 Rt-44)

THE ITALIAN WALLFLOWER (I'LL DANCE WITH HER HENRY) *(response to Wallflower)*
Lou Monte—RCA Victor 47-6072
[Hank Ballard/Etta James/Johnny Otis] [BMI] (4/11/55 Rt-3) [R]

DANCE WITH ME GEORGIE *(Wallflower) The Bobbettes—Triple-X 106*
[Hank Ballard/Etta James/Johnny Otis] [BMI] (10/24/60 B-95)

THE WALLS CAME DOWN The Call—Mercury 811487
[Michael Been] [ASC] (5/7/83 BC-74)

WALLS HAVE EARS Patti Page—Mercury 71428 [Irving Gordon] [ASC] (3/30/59 BCR-52)

THE WALTZ YOU SAVED FOR ME *Billy Vaughn and His Orchestra—Dot 15374*
[Emil Flindt/Wayne King] [ASC] (6/18/55 C-50) [IM]*

THE WALTZ YOU SAVED FOR ME *Ferlin Husky—Capitol 4650*
[Emil Flindt/Gus Kahn/Wayne King] [ASC] (11/27/61 BR-82)*

WALTZING MATILDA *David Carroll And His Orchestra—Mercury 71535*
[Marie Cowan/A.B. Patterson/Traditional] [NA] (11/23/59 Rt-67)

WALTZING MATILDA *Jimmie Rodgers—Roulette 4218*
[Marie Cowan/A.B. Patterson/Traditional] [NA] (1/18/60 BRt-41)

WALTZING MATILDA *The Merrill Staton Choir—Epic 9344*
[Marie Cowan/A.B. Patterson/Traditional] [NA] (2/1/60 Rt-89)

THE WANDERER *Dion—Laurie 3115 [Ernie Maresca] [ASC] (12/4/61 BCR-2)*

THE WANDERER *Leif Garrett—Atlantic 3476 [Ernie Maresca] [ASC] (4/22/78 BCR-49)*

THE WANDERER Donna Summer—Geffen 49563
[Giorgio Moroder/Donna Summer] [ASC] (9/20/80 BCR-2)

WANDERIN' EYES Charlie Gracie—Cameo 111
[Bernie Lowe/Kal Mann] [ASC] (8/12/57 R-80)

WANG DANG DOODLE *Ko Ko Taylor—Checker 1135 [Willie Dixon] [BMI] (4/9/66 BCR-36)*

WANG DANG DOODLE *Pointer Sisters—Blue Thumb 243*
[Willie Dixon] [BMI] (12/22/73 BCR-61)

THE WANG DANG TAFFY-APPLE TANGO (MAMBO CHA CHA CHA) Pat Boone—Dot 15914
[J. Leslie McFarland/Aaron Schroeder] [ASC] (3/28/59 BCR-61)

WANGO TANGO Ted Nugent—Epic 50907 [Ted Nugent] [ASC] (7/26/80 B-86)

WANNA BE STARTIN' SOMETHIN' Michael Jackson—Epic 03914
[Michael Jackson] [BMI] (5/28/83 BC-5)

WANNA BE WITH YOU Earth, Wind & Fire—ARC 02688
[Wayne Vaughn/Maurice White] [ASC] (1/23/82 BCR-51)

WANNA DANCE Yasmin—Geffen 19022
[Mich Hansen/Peter Meldgaard/Carsten Schack/Lucas Secon/Yasmin Elvira Steenholdt] [ASC] (7/20/91 B-76)

WANNA MAKE LOVE (COME FLIC MY BIC) Sun—Capitol 4254
[Byron Byrd] [ASC] (9/25/76 B-76)

WANT ADS The Honey Cone—Hot Wax 7011
[General Johnson/Barney Perkins/Greg Perry] [BMI] (4/10/71 BCR-1)

(WANT YOU) BACK IN MY LIFE AGAIN Carpenters—A&M 2370
[Kerry Chater/Chris Christian] [BMI] (9/12/81 BC-72)

WANT YOU FOR MY GIRLFRIEND 4 By Four—Capitol 5690
[Chris Dixon/Charles Henry Jackson Jr.] [BMI] (6/13/87 BC-79)

WANT YOU TO KNOW Rotary Connection—Cadet Concept 7018
[Jon Stocklin] [BMI] (12/13/69 BCR-73)

WANTED Perry Como—RCA Victor 47-5647
[Jack Fulton/Lois Steele] [ASC] (5/29/54 BC-PRE)

WANTED DEAD OR ALIVE Bon Jovi—Mercury 888467
[Jon Bon Jovi/Richie Sambora] [ASC] (4/11/87 BC-7)

WANTED MAN Ratt—Atlantic 89618
[Joe Cristofanilli/Robbin Crosby/Stephen Pearcy] [BMI] (10/6/84 B-87)

WANTED: LOVER, NO EXPERIENCE NECESSARY Laura Lee—Chess 2030
[Leonard Caston/Lloyd Webber] [BMI] (11/25/67 BCR-84)

WANTING YOU Roger Williams—Kapp 127
[Sigmund Romberg] [ASC] (12/3/55 BCR-30) [IM]

WAR *Edwin Starr—Gordy 7101 [Barrett Strong/Norman Whitfield] [BMI] (7/11/70 BCR-1)*

WAR *Bruce Springsteen & The E Street Band—Columbia 06432*
[Barrett Strong/Norman Whitfield] [BMI] (11/22/86 BC-8)

WAR AND PEACE Vic Damone—Columbia 40733
[Nino Rota/Wilson Stone] [ASC] (9/22/56 BRt*-59)

WAR GAMES Crosby, Stills & Nash—Atlantic 89912
[Stephen Stills] [BMI] (6/25/83 BC-45)

WAR SONG Neil Young And Graham Nash With The Stray Gators—Reprise 1099
[Neil Young] [ASC] (6/24/72 BCR-51)

THE WAR SONG Culture Club—Virgin/Epic 04638
[Michael Craig/Roy Hay/Jon Moss/George O'Dowd] [ASC] (10/6/84 BC-14)

—WARM AND TENDER LOVE see: MY ADORABLE ONE

WARM RIDE Rare Earth—Prodigal 0640
[Barry Gibb/Maurice Gibb/Robin Gibb] [BMI] (4/29/78 BCR-39)

WARM UP TO ME BABY Jimmy Bowen With The Rhythm Orchids—Roulette 4010
[Don Kirshner/Lou Stallman] [BMI] (5/18/57 BCR-33)

WARMED OVER KISSES (LEFT OVER LOVE) Brian Hyland—ABC-Paramount 10359
[Gary Geld/Peter Udell] [ASC] (9/15/62 BCR-24)

WARMIN' UP THE BAND Don Everly—Ode 66046
[Tony Colton/Pete Gavin/Charles Nicholas Hodges/Albert Lee/Raymond Barry Smith] [ASC] (7/6/74 C-92)

WARPATH The Isley Brothers—T-Neck 929
[Ernie Isley*/O'Kelly Isley*/Ronald Isley/Rudolph Isley/Harrison Pennington] [BMI] (3/27/71 CR-76)

THE WARRIOR Scandal Featuring Patty Smyth—Columbia 04424
[Nick Gilder/Holly Knight] [BMI] (6/30/84 BC-5)

WAS DOG A DOUGHNUT Cat Stevens—A&M 1971
[Bruce Lynch/Jean Roussel/Cat Stevens] [BMI] (11/12/77 BCR-68) [I]

WAS IT GOOD TO YOU The Isley Brothers—T-Neck 908
[O'Kelly Isley/Ronald Isley/Rudolph Isley] [ASC] (9/27/69 BCR-52)

WAS IT NOTHING AT ALL Michael Damian—Cypress 1451
[Michael Damian] [BMI] (10/28/89 BC-23)

WAS MACHT DER ALTE SEEMANN *Crazy Otto—Polydor 22009B*
[Heino Gaze] (Med) [NA] (1/17/55 R-1) [IM]

WAS MACHT DER ALTE SEEMANN *Johnny Maddox And The Rhythmasters—Dot 15325*
[Heino Gaze] (Med) [NA] (1/24/55 BCR-1) [IM]

WASHED ASHORE (ON A LONELY ISLAND IN THE SEA) The Platters—Musicor 1251
[Tony Hester/Richard Wylie] [BMI] (7/1/67 BCR-54)

WASHINGTON SQUARE The Village Stompers—Epic 9617
[Bob Goldstein/David Shire*] [ASC] (9/21/63 BCR-2) [IWM]

WASN'T BORN TO FOLLOW The Byrds—Columbia 44990
[Gerry Goffin/Carole King] [BMI] (11/29/69 R-66)

WASN'T IT GOOD Cher—Casablanca 987
[Michele Aller/Bob Esty] [BMI] (6/2/79 BCR-49)

WASN'T IT NICE IN NEW YORK CITY Tommy Leonetti—Columbia 45807
[Ken Gold] [ASC] (6/2/73 R-100)

WASN'T THAT A PARTY The Rovers—Epic 51007 [Tom Paxton] [ASC] (2/21/81 BCR-37)

WASN'T THE SUMMER SHORT? Johnny Mathis—Columbia 42156
[Ruth Lyons] [ASC] (10/23/61 B-89)

***WASTED DAYS AND WASTED NIGHTS** Freddy Fender—Imperial 5670*
[Wayne Duncan/Freddy Fender] [BMI] (7/9/60 C-82)*

***WASTED DAYS AND WASTED NIGHTS** Freddy Fender—ABC/Dot 17558*
[Wayne Duncan/Freddy Fender] [BMI] (6/14/75 BCR-3)*

WASTED ON THE WAY Crosby, Stills & Nash—Atlantic 4058
[Graham Nash] [BMI] (6/26/82 BC-8)

WATCH CLOSELY NOW Kris Kristofferson—Columbia 10525
[Ken Ascher/Paul Williams] [ASC] (5/21/77 BCR-52)

WATCH HER RIDE Jefferson Airplane—RCA Victor 47-9389
[Paul Kantner] [BMI] (12/9/67 BCR-37)

WATCH OUT FOR LUCY Eric Clapton And His Band—RSO 910
[Eric Clapton] [BMI] (2/17/79 BCR-40)

WATCH OUT, SALLY! Diane Renay—MGM 13296
[Bob Crewe/Sandy Linzer/Denny Randell] [BMI] (11/28/64 CR-95)

WATCH THE FLOWERS GROW
The 4 Seasons Featuring The "Sound" Of Frankie Valli—Philips 40490
[Raymond Bloodworth/L. Russell Brown] [BMI] (10/28/67 BCR-14)

WATCH YOUR STEP Bobby Parker—V-Tone 223
[Phil Belmonte*/Robert Lee Parker] [BMI] (6/12/61 B-51)

WATCH YOUR STEP Brooks O'Dell—Gold 214 [Kenneth Gamble] [BMI] (12/7/63 BCR-58)

WATCHING OVER YOU Glenn Medeiros—Amherst 314 [Paul Gordon] [ASC] (8/1/87 B-80)

WATCHING SCOTTY GROW Bobby Goldsboro—United Artists 50727
[Mac Davis] [BMI] (12/19/70 BCR-6)

WATCHING THE DETECTIVES Elvis Costello—Columbia 10705
[Elvis Costello] (TSW) [ASC] (3/11/78 CR-61)

WATCHING THE RIVER FLOW Bob Dylan—Columbia 45409
[Bob Dylan] [SE] (6/26/71 BCR-31)

WATCHING THE RIVER RUN Loggins & Messina—Columbia 46010
[Kenny Loggins/Jim Messina] [ASC] (2/23/74 BCR-41)

WATCHING THE WHEELS John Lennon—Geffen 49695
[John Lennon] [GL] (3/28/81 BCR-7)

WATCHING THE WORLD GO BY Dean Martin—Capitol 3414
[Jean Senn/Sunny Skylar] [ASC] (6/2/56 BR-71) [FDE]

WATCHING YOU Slave—Cotillion 46006
[Mark Adams/Steve Arrington/Raye Turner/Stephen C. Washington/Danny Webster] [BMI] (12/27/80 BCR-66)

WATER BOY Don Shirley Trio—Cadence 1392 [Traditional] [ASC] (7/3/61 BCR-40) [I]

THE WATER TUMBLER TUNE
Henri René And His Orchestra And Chorus—RCA Victor 47-6027
[Rudi Revil*/Fred Tobias] [ASC] (4/2/55 C-41)

WATERFALL Carly Simon—Elektra 45263 [Carly Simon] [ASC] (7/26/75 BC-76)

WATERFALL Wendy & Lisa—Columbia 07243
[Lisa Coleman/Wendy Melvoin/Robert Rivkin] [ASC] (9/19/87 BC-54)

WATERFALLS Paul McCartney—Columbia 11335 [Paul McCartney] [ASC] (8/16/80 R-83)

WATERGRATE Dickie Goodman—Rainy Wednesday 202
[Dickie Goodman] [BMI] (6/16/73 BCR-42)

WATERLOO Stonewall Jackson—Columbia 41393
[John D. Loudermilk/Marijohn Wilkin] [BMI] (5/23/59 BCR-3)

WATERLOO Abba (Björn, Benny, Anna & Frida)—Atlantic 3035
[Stig Anderson/Benny Andersson/Björn Ulvaeus] [BMI] (5/25/74 BCR-6)

***WATERMELON MAN** Mongo Santamaria Band—Battle 45909*
[Herbie Hancock] [BMI] (3/9/63 BCRt-9) [IM]

***WATERMELON MAN** Xavier Cugat—Mercury 72108*
[Herbie Hancock] [BMI] (3/23/63 Rt-9) [IM]

***WATERMELON MAN** Herbie Hancock—Blue Note 1862*
[Herbie Hancock] [BMI] (3/23/63 Rt-16) [IM]

***WATERMELON MAN** Gloria Lynne—Fontana 1511*
[Herbie Hancock/Gloria Lynne] [BMI] (6/12/65 BCR-62)

WATERMELON SONG "Tennessee" Ernie Ford—Capitol 3649
[Bill Norvas] [BMI] (2/23/57 BR-45)

THE WATUSI The Vibrations—Checker 969
[Shirley Hall/James E. Johnson/Leslie Temple] [BMI] (1/23/61 BCR-25)

WAVELENGTH Van Morrison—Warner Bros. 8661 [Van Morrison] [BMI] (9/16/78 BCR-42)

***WAY BACK HOME** The Jazz Crusaders—Chisa 8010*
[Wilton Felder] [BMI] (12/5/70 BCR-73) [I]

***WAY BACK HOME** Jr. Walker & The All Stars—Soul 35090*
[Johnny Bristol/Wilton Felder/Gladys Knight] [BMI] (12/4/71 BCR-52)

WAY COOL JR. Ratt—Atlantic 88985
[Warren DeMartini/Beau Hill/Stephen Pearcy] [BMI] (12/17/88 BC-67)

WAY DOWN Elvis Presley—RCA 10998 [Layng Martine Jr.] [BMI] (6/18/77 BCR-10)

WAY DOWN YONDER IN NEW ORLEANS Freddie Cannon—Swan 4043
[Henry Creamer/J. Turner Layton] [ASC] (11/23/59 BCR-3)

THE WAY HE MAKES ME FEEL Barbra Streisand—Columbia 04177
[Alan Bergman/Marilyn Bergman/Michel Legrand] [ASC] (10/22/83 BC-26)

THE WAY I AM Jackie Wilson—Brunswick 55220
[Gary Geld/Peter Udell] [ASC] (10/23/61 BCR-52)

THE WAY I FEEL ABOUT YOU Karyn White—Warner Bros. 19088
[William Harmon/Bruce Sterling/Christopher Troy/Karyn White] [BMI] (11/30/91 BC-3)

THE WAY I FEEL TONIGHT Bay City Rollers—Arista 0272
[Harvey Shield] [ASC] (10/8/77 BCR-19)

WAY I WALK Jack Scott—Carlton 514 [Jack Scott] [BMI] (6/27/59 BCR-25)

THE WAY I WANT TO TOUCH YOU Captain & Tennille—A&M 1725
[Toni Tennille] [BMI] (9/20/75 BCR-3)

THE WAY IT IS Bruce Hornsby And The Range—RCA Victor 5023
[Bruce Hornsby] [ASC] (9/20/86 BC-1)

THE WAY IT IS Tesla—Geffen 19948
[Frank Hannon/Jeff Keith/Troy Luccketta/Tommy Skeoch] [ASC] (3/10/90 BC-55)

THE WAY IT USED TO BE Engelbert Humperdinck—Parrot 40036
[Gianni Argenio/Francesco Cassano/Corrado Conti/Roger Cook/Roger Greenaway] [BMI] (3/1/69 BCR-24) [FET]

WAY OF A CLOWN Teddy Randazzo—ABC-Paramount 10088
[Howard Greenfield/Barry Mann] [BMI] (3/12/60 BCR-30)

***THE WAY OF LOVE** Kathy Kirby—Parrot 9775*
[Jack Diéval/Al Stillman] [ASC] (9/4/65 BCR-84) [FDE]

***THE WAY OF LOVE** Cher—Kapp 2158*
[Jack Diéval/Al Stillman] [ASC] (1/22/72 BCR-7) [FDE]

WAY OUT J.J. Fad—Ruthless 7-99285 [Juana Burns] [ASC] (9/17/88 BC-61)

WAY OVER THERE The Miracles—Tamla 54069
[Smokey Robinson] [ASC] (9/15/62 BR-85)

THE WAY TO YOUR HEART Soulsister—EMI 50217
[Jan Leyers/Paul Michiels] [BMI] (9/23/89 BC-41)

***THE WAY WE WERE** Barbra Streisand—Columbia 45944*
[Alan Bergman/Marilyn Bergman/Marvin Hamlisch] [ASC] (11/24/73 BCR-1)

***THE WAY WE WERE** Gladys Knight & The Pips—Buddah 463*
[Alan Bergman/Marilyn Bergman/Marvin Hamlisch] (Med) [ASC] (4/26/75 BCR-9)

***THE WAY YOU DO THE THINGS YOU DO** The Temptations—Gordy 7028*
[Smokey Robinson/Robert Rogers] [ASC] (2/22/64 BCR-10)

***THE WAY YOU DO THE THINGS YOU DO** Rita Coolidge—A&M 2004*
[Smokey Robinson/Robert Rogers] [ASC] (1/14/78 BCR-18)

THE WAY YOU DO THE THINGS YOU DO
Daryl Hall & John Oates Featuring David Ruffin & Eddie Kendricks—RCA 14178
[Smokey Robinson/Robert Rogers] (Med) [ASC] (8/31/85 BC-20)

***THE WAY YOU DO THE THINGS YOU DO** UB40—Virgin 98978*
[Smokey Robinson/Robert Rogers] [ASC] (9/15/90 BC-4)

THE WAY YOU LOOK TONIGHT The Lettermen—Capitol 4586
[Dorothy Fields/Jerome Kern] [ASC] (8/14/61 BCR-8)

THE WAY YOU LOVE ME Karyn White—Warner Bros. 27773
[Kenneth Edmonds/Antonio Reid/Daryl Simmons] [BMI] (10/15/88 BC-5)

THE WAY YOU MAKE ME FEEL Michael Jackson—Epic 07645
[Michael Jackson] [BMI] (11/21/87 BC-1)

WAYS OF A WOMAN IN LOVE Johnny Cash And The Tennessee Two—Sun 302
[Bill Justis/Charlie Rich] [BMI] (8/11/58 BCR-24)

WAYS TO BE WICKED Lone Justice—Geffen 29023
[Mike Campbell/Tom Petty] [ASC] (5/11/85 BC-59)

THE WAYS TO LOVE A MAN Tammy Wynette—Epic 10512
[Billy Sherrill/Glenn Sutton/Tammy Wynette] [BMI] (8/30/69 BCR-81)

***THE WAYWARD WIND** Gogi Grant—Era 1013*
[Stan Lebowsky/Herbert Newman] [ASC] (4/28/56 BCRt-1)

***THE WAYWARD WIND** Tex Ritter—Capitol 3430*
[Stan Lebowsky/Herbert Newman] [ASC] (6/29/56 BRt-1)

***THE WAYWARD WIND** Gogi Grant—Era 3046*
[Stan Lebowsky/Herbert Newman] [ASC] (4/24/61 BCR-50)

WE Shawn Phillips—A&M 1402 [Shawn Phillips] [BMI] (1/13/73 B-89)

(WE AIN'T GOT) NOTHIN' YET Blues Magoos—Mercury 72622
[Michael Esposito/Ronald Gilbert/Ralph Scala/Emil Thielhelm] [BMI] (11/26/66 BCR-5)

WE ALL GOTTA STICK TOGETHER Four Tops—ABC 12123
[Richard Beasley/Fred Bridges/Richard Knight/Lawrence Payton] [BMI] (10/25/75 BCR-64)

WE ALL NEED LOVE Percy Faith And His Orchestra and Chorus—Columbia 40644
[Henri Contet/Paul Durand/Carl Sigman] [ASC] (4/14/56 B-67) [FDE]

WE ALL NEED LOVE Troiano—Capitol 4709 [Domenic Troiano] [BMI] (6/23/79 C-93)

—WE ALL SHINE ON see: INSTANT KARMA

WE ALL SLEEP ALONE Cher—Geffen 27986
[Jon Bon Jovi/Desmond Child/Richie Sambora] [ASC] (4/9/88 BC-12)

WE ARE FAMILY Sister Sledge—Cotillion 44251
[Bernard Edwards/Nile Rodgers] [BMI] (4/28/79 BCR-2)

WE ARE NEIGHBORS The Chi-Lites—Brunswick 55455
[Quinton Joseph*/Eugene Record] [BMI] (7/24/71 BCR-70)

WE ARE THE CHAMPIONS Queen—Elektra 45441
[Freddie Mercury] [BMI] (10/22/77 BCR-1)

WE ARE THE WORLD USA for Africa—Columbia 7-04839
[Michael Jackson/Lionel Richie] [BMI] (3/23/85 BC-1)

WE ARE THE YOUNG Dan Hartman—MCA 52471
[Dan Hartman/Charles E. Kaufman] [BMI] (10/6/84 BC-25)

WE ARE WHAT WE ARE The Other Ones—Virgin 99473
[Stephan Gottwald/Uwe Hoffmann/Alf Klimek/Jayney Klimek/Johnny Klimek/Andreas Schwarz-Ruszczynski] [BMI] (4/18/87 BC-49)

WE BEEN SINGIN' SONGS Baron Stewart—United Artists 686
[Baron Stewart] [BMI] (8/16/75 BCR-91)

WE BELONG Pat Benatar—Chrysalis 42826
[Eric Lowen/Dan Navarro] [BMI] (10/27/84 BC-5)

WE BELONG TOGETHER *Robert & Johnny—Old Town 1047*
[Robert Carr/Johnny Mitchell/Hy Weiss‡] [BMI] (2/24/58 BCR-33)

WE BELONG TOGETHER *Robert & Johnny—Old Town 1047*
[Robert Carr/Johnny Mitchell/Hy Weiss‡] [BMI] (1/30/61 Rt-89)

WE BELONG TOGETHER *The Belmonts—Laurie 3080*
[Robert Carr/Johnny Mitchell/Hy Weiss‡] [BMI] (1/30/61 Rt-89)

WE BELONG TOGETHER *Jimmy Velvet—ABC-Paramount 10488*
[Robert Carr/Johnny Mitchell/Hy Weiss‡] [BMI] (12/7/63 BCR-74)

WE BOTH DESERVE EACH OTHER'S LOVE L.T.D.—A&M 2095
[James Edward Davis/Jeffrey Osborne] [ASC] (12/16/78 R-95)

WE BOTH NEED EACH OTHER Norman Connors—Buddah 534
[Michael E. Henderson] [ASC] (8/21/76 C-98)

WE BUILT THIS CITY Starship—Grunt 14170
[Dennis Lambert/Martin Page/Bernie Taupin/Peter F. Wolf] [BMI] (9/7/85 BC-1)

WE CAN FLY The Cowsills—MGM 13886
[Bill Cowsill/Bob Cowsill/Steve Duboff/Artie Kornfeld] [BMI] (1/13/68 BCR-17)

WE CAN GET TOGETHER Icehouse—Chrysalis 2530 [Iva Davies] [ASC] (8/1/81 BCR-62)

WE CAN LAST FOREVER Chicago—Reprise/Full Moon 22985
[John Dexter/Jason Scheff] [BMI] (5/6/89 BC-53)

WE CAN MAKE IT Ray Charles—ABC/TRC 11239 [James E. Lewis] [BMI] (9/6/69 CR-90)

WE CAN MAKE IT BABY The Originals—Soul 35074
[Marvin Gaye/James Nyx] [ASC] (8/22/70 B-74)

WE CAN MAKE IT TOGETHER Steve & Eydie Featuring The Osmonds—MGM 14383
[Alan Osmond/Merrill Osmond/Wayne Osmond] [BMI] (9/16/72 BCR-64)

WE CAN MAKE MUSIC Tommy Roe—ABC 11273 [Lou Josie] [BMI] (9/5/70 BCR-35)

WE CAN MAKE THE MORNING Elvis Presley—RCA Victor 74-0619
[Jay Ramsey] (TSW) [BMI] (1/29/72 R-59)

WE CAN MAKE THE WORLD Gravy—GRT 34
[Michael Gately/Robert John] [BMI] (2/20/71 R-94)

WE CAN WORK IT OUT *The Beatles—Capitol 5555*
[John Lennon/Paul McCartney] [ASC] (12/11/65 BCR-1)

WE CAN WORK IT OUT *Stevie Wonder—Tamla 54202*
[John Lennon/Paul McCartney] [ASC] (3/13/71 BCR-9)

WE CAN WORK IT OUT *Stars On 45—Radio 3810*
[John Lennon/Paul McCartney] (Med) [ASC] (4/11/81 BCR-1)

WE CAN'T BELIEVE YOU'RE GONE Bobby Harris—Atlantic 2270
[Brook Benton/Benny Hall Jr.] [BMI] (2/13/65 R-97)

WE CAN'T DANCE TO YOUR MUSIC The Grass Roots—Dunhill 4371
[Jeff Barry/Mentor Williams] [BMI] (12/15/73 C-97)

WE CAN'T GO ON THIS WAY *Teddy And The Pandas—Musicor 1190*
[Bob Stone] [BMI] (9/10/66 C-99)

WE CAN'T GO ON THIS WAY *Unchained Mynds—Buddah 111*
[Bob Stone] [BMI] (4/26/69 CR-96)

WE CAN'T GO WRONG The Cover Girls—Capitol 44498
[David Cole/Tony Moran/Andy Tripoli] [ASC] (12/9/89 BC-5)

WE CAN'T HIDE IT ANYMORE Larry Santos—Casablanca 844
[Barry Murphy] [BMI] (1/31/76 BCR-36)

WE CLOSE OUR EYES Go West—Chrysalis 42850
[Peter Cox/Richard Drummie] [ASC] (2/23/85 BC-33)

WE CONNECT Stacey Q—Atlantic 89331 [John Griffitt Wilcox] [ASC] (12/13/86 BC-35)

WE COULD Al Martino—Capitol 5293 [Felice Bryant] [BMI] (10/24/64 BCR-40)

WE COULD BE TOGETHER Debbie Gibson—Atlantic 88896
[Debbie Gibson] [ASC] (9/23/89 BC-71)

WE DID IT Syl Johnson—Hi 2229 [John E. Moore] [BMI] (2/3/73 BCR-72)

WE DIDN'T START THE FIRE Billy Joel—Columbia 73021
[Billy Joel] [ASC] (10/14/89 BC-1)

WE DON'T HAVE TO TAKE OUR CLOTHES OFF Jermaine Stewart—Arista 1-9424
[Preston Glass/Narada Michael Walden] [ASC] (5/17/86 BC-5)

WE DON'T NEED ANOTHER HERO (THUNDERDOME) Tina Turner—Capitol 5491
[Terry Britten/Graham Lyle] [BMI] (7/6/85 BC-2)

WE DON'T TALK ANYMORE Cliff Richard—EMI America 8025
[Alan Tarney] [BMI] (10/20/79 BCR-6)

WE FELL IN LOVE WHILE DANCING Bill Brandon—Prelude 71102
[Jesse Boyce/Moses Dillard] [BMI] (2/25/78 B-80)

WE GO TOGETHER Jan & Dean—Dore 555
[Shelley Haims/Perry Stevens] [ASC] (7/30/60 BCR-39)

WE GOT A DREAM Ocean—Kama Sutra 529
[Roger Cook/Roger Greenaway] [ASC] (7/31/71 BCR-82)

WE GOT A THING THAT'S IN THE GROOVE The Capitols—Karen 1526
[Donald Storball] [BMI] (11/12/66 BCR-65)

WE GOT LOVE Bobby Rydell—Cameo 169
[Bernie Lowe/Kal Mann] [ASC] (10/12/59 BCR-2)

WE GOT MORE SOUL Dyke And The Blazers—Original Sound 86
[Arlester Christian] [BMI] (5/17/69 BCR-35)

WE GOT THE BEAT Go-Go's—I.R.S. 9903 [Charlotte Caffey] [ASC] (1/23/82 BCR-2)

WE GOT THE WINNING HAND Little Milton—Checker 1132
[Billy Davis/Shena DeMell] [BMI] (2/5/66 BCR-84)

WE GOT TO HAVE PEACE Curtis Mayfield—Curtom 1968
[Curtis Mayfield] [BMI] (3/4/72 C-81)

WE GOT TO LIVE TOGETHER - PART I Buddy Miles—Mercury 73159
[Buddy Miles] [ASC] (12/12/70 BC-81)

WE GOTTA ALL GET TOGETHER
Paul Revere And The Raiders Featuring Mark Lindsay—Columbia 44970
[Freddy Weller] [BMI] (8/30/69 BCR-25)

WE GOTTA GET OUT OF THIS PLACE The Animals—MGM 13382
[Barry Mann/Cynthia Weil] [BMI] (8/14/65 BCR-12)

WE GOTTA GET YOU A WOMAN Runt—Ampex 31001
[Todd Rundgren] [BMI] (10/17/70 BCR-17)

WE GOTTA GO HOME The Music Explosion—Laurie 3414
[Ritchie Cordell/Bo Gentry] [BMI] (10/21/67 R-70)

WE HAD A GOOD THING GOIN' The Cyrkle—Columbia 44108
[Howard Greenfield/Neil Sedaka] [BMI] (5/13/67 BCR-65)

WE HAVE LOVE Jackie Wilson—Brunswick 55086
[Billy Davis/Berry Gordy/Gwen Gordy] [ASC] (9/13/58 BC-76)

WE HAVE LOVE Dinah Washington—Mercury 71744
[Alfonso Higgins/Dinah Washington] [BMI] (12/12/60 BCR-36)

WE HAVE SOMETHING MORE Connie Francis—MGM 13287
[Mickey Gentile/Jennie Lee Lambert] [BMI] (10/24/64 R-81)

WE JUST DISAGREE Dave Mason—Columbia 10575 [Jim Krueger] [BMI] (9/3/77 BCR-12)

WE KNOW Joni James—MGM 12895
[Nick Acquaviva/Peter Udell] [ASC] (7/25/60 R-98)

WE KNOW WE'RE IN LOVE Lesley Gore—Mercury 72530
[Lesley Gore/Michael Gore] [BMI] (1/22/66 BCR-58)

WE LIVE FOR LOVE Pat Benatar—Chrysalis 2419 [Neil Geraldo] [ASC] (4/5/80 BCR-26)

WE LOVE YOU The Rolling Stones—London 905
[Mick Jagger/Keith Richards] [BMI] (9/9/67 BCR-50)

WE LOVE YOU BEATLES (parody of We Love You Conrad)
The Carefrees—London Int'l 10614
[Lee Adams/Charles Strouse] [ASC] (3/14/64 BCR-36) [P]

WE LOVE YOU, CALL COLLECT Art Linkletter—Capitol 2678
[Ralph Carmichael/Martin Wark] [ASC] (11/1/69 BCR-38)

WE MAY NEVER LOVE LIKE THIS AGAIN Maureen McGovern—20th Century 2158
[Joel Hirschhorn/Al Kasha] [BMI] (1/25/75 BCR-72)

WE MAY NEVER PASS THIS WAY (AGAIN) Seals & Crofts—Warner Bros. 7740
[Dash Crofts/Jim Seals] [BMI] (9/22/73 BCR-18)

—WE MEET AGAIN see: SONG FROM DESIREE

WE MUST BE IN LOVE The Five Stairsteps & Cubie—Curtom 1945
[Curtis Mayfield] [BMI] (10/18/69 BCR-81)

WE NEED ORDER The Chi-Lites—Brunswick 55489
[Quinton Joseph/Eugene Record] [BMI] (12/2/72 BCR-55)

WE NEVER DANCED TO A LOVE SONG The Manhattans—Columbia 10586
[Gerald Alston/Edward Bivins] [BMI] (8/27/77 BR-77)

WE SHALL OVERCOME Joan Baez—Vanguard 35023
[Guy Carawan/Frank Hamilton/Zilphia Horton/Pete Seeger/Traditional] [BMI] (11/9/63 B-90)

WE SHOULD BE SLEEPING Eddie Money—Columbia 07359
[Kevin Burns/Greg Lowry/Eddie Money/Glenn Thompson] [BMI] (9/19/87 B-90)

WE TOLD YOU NOT TO MARRY Titus Turner—Glover 201
[Henry Glover] [BMI] (11/9/59 BCR-77)

WE TWO Little River Band—Capitol 5231 [Graham Goble] [BMI] (5/7/83 BC-22)

—WE WANT THE FUNK see: TEAR THE ROOF OFF THE SUCKER

WE WERE ALWAYS SWEETHEARTS Boz Scaggs—Columbia 45353
[Boz Scaggs] [ASC] (4/17/71 BCR-44)

WE WERE MEANT TO BE LOVERS Photoglo—20th Century Fox 2446
[Brian Neary/Jim Photoglo] [BMI] (3/29/80 BCR-31)

WEAPONS OF LOVE The Truth—I.R.S. 53084
[Dennis Greaves/Mick Lister] [BMI] (5/9/87 BC-59)

WEAR IT ON OUR FACE The Dells—Cadet 5599
[Robert Eugene Miller] [BMI] (4/13/68 BCR-41)

WEAR MY RING AROUND YOUR NECK Elvis Presley—RCA Victor 47-7240
[Bert Carroll/Russell Moody/Marilyn Schack‡] [BMI] (4/14/58 BCR-3)

WEAR THIS RING (WITH LOVE) Detroit Emeralds—Westbound 181
[James Mitchell Jr./Abrim Tilmon] [BMI] (8/14/71 BCR-70)

WEAR YOUR LOVE LIKE HEAVEN Donovan—Epic 10253
[Donovan Leitch] [BMI] (11/25/67 BCR-23)

WEARY BLUES The McGuire Sisters And Lawrence Welk—Coral 61670
[George Cates/Mort Greene/Artie Matthews] [NA] (7/20/56 BCR-31)

WEATHERMAN *Nick Jameson—Motown 1853*
[Nick Jameson/Kim O'Leary] [ASC] (8/16/86 BC-81)

WEATHERMAN SAYS *Jack Wagner—Qwest 28387*
[Nick Jameson/Kim O'Leary] [ASC] (4/25/87 BC-65)

THE WEDDING *The Solitaires—Old Town 1014*
[Pat Gaston/Jacqueline McCoy/Bobby Williams] [BMI] (10/22/55 CRt-43)

THE WEDDING *The Chordettes—Cadence 1273*
[Pat Gaston/Jacqueline McCoy/Bobby Williams] [BMI] (11/14/55 BRt-75)

THE WEDDING June Valli—Mercury 71382
[Albert Beach/Guy Wood] [ASC] (11/24/58 BCR-18)

THE WEDDING Julie Rogers—Mercury 72332
[Fred Jay/Joaquin Prieto] [BMI] (11/14/64 BCR-7)

WEDDING BELL BLUES *Laura Nyro—Verve Folkways 5024*
[Laura Nyro] [BMI] (12/3/66 C-96)

WEDDING BELL BLUES *The 5th Dimension—Soul City 779*
[Laura Nyro] [BMI] (9/20/69 BCR-1)

WEDDING BELLS (ARE BREAKING UP THAT OLD GANG OF MINE) Four Aces—Decca 29123
[Sammy Fain/Irving Kahal/William Raskin] [ASC] (5/29/54 BC-PRE)

—WEDDING BELLS see: I'M ALWAYS HEARING...

THE WEDDING CAKE Connie Francis—MGM 14034
[Margaret Lewis/Mira Smith] [BMI] (2/22/69 BCR-91)

WEDDING RING Russ Hamilton—Kapp 194 [Russ Hamilton] [BMI] (10/14/57 R-81)

—WEDDING SONG see: DOWN THE AISLE

WEDDING SONG (THERE IS LOVE) *Paul Stookey—Warner Bros. 7511*
[Paul Stookey] [ASC] (7/31/71 BCR-19)

WEDDING SONG (THERE IS LOVE) *Petula Clark—MGM 14431*
[Paul Stookey] [ASC] (10/7/72 BCR-61)

THE WEDDING SONG (THERE IS LOVE) *Mary MacGregor—Ariola America 7726*
[Paul Stookey] [ASC] (11/25/78 B-81)

WEDNESDAY The Royal Guardsmen—Laurie 3397 [Charles Souza] [BMI] (8/26/67 BR-80)

WEEK END The Kingsmen—East West 115
[Franny Beecher/Rudy Pompilli/Billy Williamson] [BMI] (9/1/58 BCR-56) [I]

THE WEEKEND Jack Jones—Kapp 736
[Teddy Randazzo/Lou Stallman/Bobby Weinstein] [BMI] (2/19/66 C-100)

WEEKEND Wet Willie—Epic 50714
[Mick Jackson/Tommy Mayer] [ASC] (5/26/79 BCR-29)

WEEKEND IN NEW ENGLAND Barry Manilow—Arista 0212
[Randy Edelman] [BMI] (11/27/76 BCR-6)

WEEKEND LOVER Odyssey—RCA 11245
[Sandy Linzer/Denny Randell] [BMI] (4/29/78 BCR-57)

THE WEIGHT *Jackie DeShannon—Imperial 66313*
[Robbie Robertson] [ASC] (8/17/68 BCR-35)

THE WEIGHT *The Band—Capitol 2269 [Robbie Robertson] [ASC] (8/31/68 BCR-46)*

THE WEIGHT *Aretha Franklin—Atlantic 2603 [Robbie Robertson] [ASC] (2/22/69 BCR-8)*

THE WEIGHT *Diana Ross And The Supremes & The Temptations—Motown 1153*
[Robbie Robertson] [ASC] (9/13/69 BCR-34)

WEIRD SCIENCE Oingo Boingo—MCA 52633 [Danny Elfman] [BMI] (8/31/85 BC-42)

WELCOME BACK John Sebastian—Reprise 1349 [John Sebastian] [BMI] (3/27/76 BCR-1)

WELCOME HOME Sammy Kaye & His Orchestra—Decca 31204
[Jean Evans/Marcel Stellman/Lieve Van Steyvoort] [NA] (2/27/61 BR-68) [FET]

WELCOME HOME Shelley Fabares—Colpix 705
[Buddy Kaye/Philip Springer] [ASC] (10/5/63 C-100)

WELCOME HOME Walter Jackson—Okeh 7219 [Chip Taylor] [BMI] (6/5/65 BCR-78)

WELCOME HOME BABY The Shirelles—Scepter 1234
[Luther Dixon] [BMI] (6/16/62 BCR-22)

WELCOME ME LOVE The Brooklyn Bridge Featuring Johnny Maestro—Buddah 95
[Tony Romeo] [BMI] (5/10/69 BCR-42)

(WELCOME) NEW LOVERS Pat Boone—Dot 16048
[Charles Singleton] [BMI] (2/1/60 BCR-18)

WELCOME TO HEARTLIGHT Kenny Loggins—Columbia 03555
[Kenny Loggins] [ASC] (3/5/83 BC-24)

—WELCOME TO MY MORNING see: FAREWELL ANDROMEDA

WELCOME TO MY NIGHTMARE Alice Cooper—Atlantic 3298
[Alice Cooper/Dick Wagner] [BMI] (10/25/75 BCR-37)

WELCOME TO MY WORLD Jim Reeves—RCA Victor 47-8289
[Johnny Hathcock/Ray Winkler] [BMI] (3/28/64 R-94)

WELCOME TO OUR WORLD (OF MERRY MUSIC) Mass Production—Cotillion 44213
[Tyrone Williams] [ASC] (2/19/77 B-68)

WELCOME TO PARADISE John Waite—EMI America 8278
[John Waite] [BMI] (10/19/85 BC-81)

WELCOME TO THE BOOMTOWN David & David—A&M 2857
[David Baerwald/David Ricketts] [ASC] (9/27/86 BC-37)

WELCOME TO THE JUNGLE Guns N' Roses—Geffen 27759
[Steven Adler/Saul Hudson/Duff McKagan/Axl Rose/Izzy Stradlin] [ASC]
(10/22/88 BC-7)

WELCOME TO THE PLEASUREDOME (TREVOR HORN REMIX)
Frankie Goes To Hollywood—ZTT/Island 7-99653
[Peter Gill/Holly Johnson/Brian Nash/Mark O'Toole] [BMI]
(4/6/85 BC-48)

WELCOME TO THE REAL WORLD Jane Child—Warner Bros. 19834
[Jane Child] [BMI] (6/2/90 BC-46)

WELFARE CADILAC Guy Drake—Royal American 1 [Guy Drake] [BMI] (1/31/70 BCR-63)

WELL-A, WELL-A Shirley & Lee—Warwick 664 [Arthur Crier] [BMI] (8/7/61 B-77)

WELL ALL RIGHT Santana—Columbia 10839
[Jerry Allison/Buddy Holly/Joe Mauldin/Norman Petty] [ASC] (11/11/78 B-69)

WE'LL BE TOGETHER Sting—A&M 2983 [Sting] [BMI] (10/10/87 BC-7)

WE'LL BE TOGETHER AGAIN *Rosemary Clooney—Columbia 40361*
[Carl T. Fischer/Frankie Laine] [ASC] (10/16/54 CR-43)

WE'LL BE TOGETHER AGAIN *Ray Charles And Betty Carter—ABC-Paramount 10298*
[Carl T. Fischer/Frankie Laine] [ASC] (2/12/62 R-89)

—WE'LL BE UNITED see: UNITED

WE'LL CRY TOGETHER Maxine Brown—Commonwealth United 3001
[Rose Marie McCoy/Helen Miller] [BMI] (9/27/69 BCR-73)

WELL DID YOU EVAH Bing Crosby—Capitol 3507 [Cole Porter] [ASC] (9/22/56 B-92)

WE'LL HAVE IT MADE The Spinners—V.I.P. 25060
[Stevie Wonder/Syreeta Wright] [ASC] (1/16/71 BCR-75)

WELL I ASK YOU *Eden Kane—London 1993 [Les Vandyke] [BMI] (9/11/61 Rt-95)*

WELL, I ASK YA *Kay Starr—Capitol 4620 [Les Vandyke] [BMI] (9/11/61 Rt-72)*

WELL, I TOLD YOU The Chantels—Carlton 564 [Richard Barrett] [BMI] (11/13/61 BCR-28)

WELL I'M YOUR MAN Johnny Tillotson—Cadence 1353
[Johnny Tillotson] [BMI] (10/6/58 BR-87)

(WE'LL MEET IN THE) "YELLOW FOREST" Jay & The Americans—United Artists 50196
[Billy Carl/Reid Whitelaw] [BMI] (8/12/67 CR-81)

NEVER HAVE TO SAY GOODBYE AGAIN *Deardorff & Joseph—Arista 0230*
[Jeffrey Comanor] [BMI] (4/16/77 CR-94)

WE'LL NEVER HAVE TO SAY GOODBYE AGAIN
England Dan & John Ford Coley—Big Tree 16110
[Jeffrey Comanor] [BMI] (2/25/78 BCR-9)

A WELL RESPECTED MAN The Kinks—Reprise 0420 [Ray Davies] [BMI] (11/27/65 BCR-9)

WE'LL SING IN THE SUNSHINE Gale Garnett—RCA Victor 47-8388
[Gale Garnett] [ASC] (8/1/64 BCR-1)

WENDEGAHL THE WARLOCK The Rugbys—Amazon 4
[Ed Vernon] [BMI] (11/29/69 R-84)

WENDY The Beach Boys—Capitol R-5267
[Mike Love*/Brian Wilson] (EP) [BMI] (10/10/64 BCR-44;57)

WENDY WENDY The Four Coins—Epic 9286
[Burt Bacharach/Hal David] [ASC] (9/22/58 B-72)

—WENN DIE LIEBE WILL see: PLEASE DON'T GO SOON

WE'RE A WINNER The Impressions—ABC 11022
[Curtis Mayfield] [BMI] (12/23/67 BCR-7)

WE'RE ALL ALONE *Frankie Valli—Private Stock 45,098*
[Boz Scaggs] [ASC] (8/7/76 BC-74)

WE'RE ALL ALONE *Rita Coolidge—A&M 1965 [Boz Scaggs] [ASC] (9/10/77 BCR-4)*

WE'RE ALL GOIN' HOME Bobby Bloom—MGM 14246
[Jeff Barry/Bobby Bloom/Neil Brian Goldberg] [BMI] (6/26/71 B-93)

WE'RE ALL IN THE SAME GANG West Coast Rap All-Stars—Warner Bros. 19819
[West Coast Rap All-Stars] [NA] (6/23/90 BC-35)

WE'RE ALL PLAYING IN THE SAME BAND Bert Sommer—Eleuthera 470
[Bert Sommer] [BMI] (7/25/70 BCR-44)

WE'RE ALMOST THERE Michael Jackson—Motown 1341
[Brian Holland/Eddie Holland] [BMI] (2/22/75 BCR-50)

WE'RE AN AMERICAN BAND Grand Funk—Capitol 3660
[Don Brewer] [BMI] (7/21/73 BCR-1)

WE'RE DOING FINE Dee Dee Warwick—Blue Rock 4027
[Horace Ott] [BMI] (7/3/65 BCR-65)

WE'RE FREE Beverly Bremers—Scepter 12348
[L. Russell Brown/Irwin Levine] [BMI] (4/22/72 BCR-40)

WE'RE FRIENDS BY DAY (AND LOVERS BY NIGHT) The Whatnauts—Stang 5030
[George Kerr/Larry Saunders] [BMI] (9/4/71 B-100)

WE'RE GETTING CARELESS WITH OUR LOVE Johnnie Taylor—Stax 0193
[Don Davis/Frank L. Johnson] [BMI] (1/26/74 BCR-34)

WE'RE GOIN' OUT TONIGHT Cameo—Chocolate City 3206
[Larry Blackmon/Tomi Jenkins/Nathan Leftenant] [BMI] (6/21/80 R-90)

WE'RE GOING ALL THE WAY Jeffrey Osborne—A&M 2618
[Barry Mann/Cynthia Weil] [BMI] (2/25/84 BC-47)

WE'RE GONNA HAVE A GOOD TIME Rare Earth—Rare Earth 5052
[Tom Baird/Gil Bridges/Ed Guzman/Ray Monette/Mark Olson/Pete Rivera] [ASC]
(1/27/73 B-93)

WE'RE GONNA MAKE IT Little Milton—Checker 1105
[Gene Barge/Billy Davis/Raynard Miner/Carl William Smith] [BMI] (3/27/65 BCR-18)

(WE'RE GONNA) ROCK AROUND THE CLOCK *Bill Haley and His Comets—Decca 29124*
[Jimmy DeKnight/Max C. Freedman] [ASC] (7/3/54 C-36)

(WE'RE GONNA) ROCK AROUND THE CLOCK *Bill Haley And His Comets—Decca 29124*
[Jimmy DeKnight/Max C. Freedman] [ASC] (5/14/55 BCR-1)

(WE'RE GONNA) ROCK AROUND THE CLOCK *Bill Haley And His Comets—MCA 60025*
[Jimmy DeKnight/Max C. Freedman] [ASC] (3/16/74 BCR-36)

ROCK AROUND THE CLOCK *Jive Bunny And The Mastermixers—Music Factory 99140*
[Jimmy DeKnight/Max C. Freedman] (Med) [ASC] (10/28/89 BC-11)

WE'RE IN THIS LOVE TOGETHER Al Jarreau—Warner Bros. 49746
[Roger Murrah/Keith Stegall] [BMI] (8/1/81 BCR-13)

WE'RE NOT GONNA TAKE IT Twisted Sister—Atlantic 89641
[Dee Snider] [ASC] (7/28/84 BC-18)

WE'RE ON OUR WAY Chris Hodge—Apple 1850 [Chris Hodge] [BMI] (5/27/72 BCR-35)

WE'RE ON THE RIGHT TRACK South Shore Commission—Wand 11291
[Allan Felder/Norman Harris] [BMI] (1/10/76 B-94)

WE'RE READY Boston—MCA 52985 [Tom Scholz] [ASC] (12/6/86 BC-9)

WE'RE ROLLING ON (PART 1) The Impressions—ABC 11071
[Curtis Mayfield] [BMI] (4/13/68 BCR-40)

WE'RE TOGETHER The Hillside Singers—Metromedia 241
[Kevin Gavin/Al Ham/Nat Kipner/Sid Woloshin] [ASC] (2/12/72 BCR-73)

WEREWOLF The Frantics—Dolton 16
[Gary Hodge/Terry Wadsworth] [BMI] (2/29/60 B-83) [I]

WEREWOLF Five Man Electrical Band—Polydor 14221
[Les Emmerson] [BMI] (3/30/74 BCR-44)

WEREWOLVES OF LONDON Warren Zevon—Asylum 45472
[LeRoy Marinell/Waddy Wachtel/Warren Zevon] [BMI] (3/25/78 BCR-15)

WEST COAST SUMMER NIGHTS Tony Carey—Rocshire 95037
[Tony Carey] [ASC] (7/2/83 BC-64)

WEST COAST WOMAN Painter—Elektra 45862
[Doran Beattie/Danny Lowe] [BMI] (9/15/73 BCR-60)

WEST END GIRLS Pet Shop Boys—EMI America 8307
[Chris Lowe/Neil Tennant] [ASC] (3/1/86 BC-1)

WEST OF THE WALL Toni Fisher—Big Top 3097 [Wayne Shanklin] [ASC] (5/7/62 BCR-23)

WESTBOUND #9 The Flaming Ember—Hot Wax 7003
[Lamont Dozier/Daphne Dumas/Ronald Dunbar/Brian Holland/Eddie Holland] [BMI] (5/16/70 BCR-23)

WESTERN MOVIES The Olympics—Demon 1508
[Cliff Goldsmith/Fred Smith] [BMI] (7/19/58 BCR-8)

WESTERN UNION The Five Americans—Abnak 118
[John Durrill/Norman Ezell/Michael Rabon] [BMI] (2/25/67 BCR-5)

WET MY WHISTLE Midnight Star—Solar 69790 [Reggie Calloway] [BMI] (11/26/83 BC-53)

WE'VE COME TOO FAR TO END IT NOW Smokey Robinson & The Miracles—Tamla 54220
[Johnny Bristol/Wade Brown/David H. Jones] [ASC] (6/3/72 BCR-46)

(WE'VE GOT) HONEY LOVE Martha Reeves & The Vandellas—Gordy 7085
[Richard Morris/Sylvia Moy] [BMI] (4/12/69 BCR-50)

WE'VE GOT LOVE Peaches & Herb—Polydor/MVP 14577
[Dino Fekaris/Freddie Perren] [ASC] (6/30/79 BCR-44)

WE'VE GOT TO GET IT ON AGAIN The Addrisi Brothers—Columbia 45521
[Dick Addrisi/Don Addrisi] [BMI] (1/15/72 BCR-15)

WE'VE GOT TONITE *Bob Seger & The Silver Bullet Band—Capitol 4653*
[Bob Seger] [ASC] (10/28/78 BCR-11)

WE'VE GOT TONIGHT *Kenny Rogers And Sheena Easton—Liberty 1492*
[Bob Seger] [ASC] (1/29/83 BC-6)

WE'VE ONLY JUST BEGUN Carpenters—A&M 1217
[Roger Nichols/Paul Williams] [BMI] (9/12/70 BCR-1)

WE'VE ONLY JUST BEGUN (THE ROMANCE IS NOT OVER) Glenn Jones—Jive 1049
[Timmy Allen/Glenn Jones] [BMI] (10/31/87 BC-66)

WE'VE SAVED THE BEST FOR LAST Kenny G—Arista 1-9785
[Paul Gordon/Dennis Matkosky/Louis Pardini] [ASC] (2/4/89 BC-40)

WHAM! Lonnie Mack—Fraternity 912 [Lonnie Mack] [BMI] (8/24/63 BCR-24) [I]

WHAM BAM SHANG-A-LANG Silver—Arista 0189 [Rick Giles] [ASC] (6/19/76 BCR-16)

—WHAT A BEAUTIFUL WORLD see: IGY

WHAT A BUMMER The Jaggerz—Kama Sutra 513 [Donnie Iris] [BMI] (8/22/70 B-88)

WHAT A DIFFERENCE YOU'VE MADE IN MY LIFE Ronnie Milsap—RCA 11146
[Archie Jordan] [ASC] (12/24/77 BC-80)

WHAT A DIFF'RENCE A DAY MADE *Jerry Martin—Coral 61349*
[Stanley Adams/Maria Grever] [ASC] (3/7/55 Rt-42) [FDE]

WHAT A DIFF'RENCE A DAY MADE *Vaughn Monroe & His Orchestra—RCA Victor 47-6002*
[Stanley Adams/Maria Grever] [ASC] (3/7/55 Rt-60) [FDE]

WHAT A DIFF'RENCE A DAY MAKES *Dinah Washington—Mercury 71435*
[Stanley Adams/Maria Grever] [ASC] (5/9/59 BCR-4) [FDE]

WHAT A DIFF'RENCE A DAY MAKES *Esther Phillips—Kudu 925*
[Stanley Adams/Maria Grever] [ASC] (8/16/75 BCR-20) [FDE]

WHAT A DREAM *Patti Page—Mercury 70416 [Chuck Willis] [BMI] (8/7/54 BCtR-14)*

(OH) WHAT A DREAM *Ruth Brown & Rhythmakers—Atlantic 1036*
[Chuck Willis] [BMI] (8/28/54 Ct-PRE)

WHAT A DREAM *Conway Twitty—MGM 12918 [Chuck Willis] [BMI] (9/19/60 CR-82)*

WHAT A FOOL BELIEVES The Doobie Brothers—Warner Bros. 8725
[Kenny Loggins/Michael McDonald] [ASC] (1/20/79 BCR-1)

WHAT A FOOL I'VE BEEN Carla Thomas—Atlantic 2189
[William Bell/Steve Cropper] [BMI] (7/20/63 B-93)

WHAT A FOOL WAS I Georgie Shaw—Decca 29906 [Jerry Holmes] [BMI] (5/11/56 R-51)

WHAT A GUY The Raindrops—Jubilee 5444
[Jeff Barry/Ellie Greenwich] [BMI] (4/13/63 BCR-34)

WHAT A HEAVENLY NIGHT FOR LOVE
Lawrence Welk And His Champagne Music—Coral 61621
[Sammy Gallop/Frankie Masters] [ASC] (6/22/56 Rt-80)

WHAT A HEAVENLY NIGHT FOR LOVE *Dinah Shore—RCA Victor 47-6469*
[Sammy Gallop/Frankie Masters] [ASC] (6/22/56 Rt-80)

WHAT A HEAVENLY NIGHT FOR LOVE *Frankie Masters & His Orchestra—Utopia 1954*
[Sammy Gallop/Frankie Masters] [ASC] (6/22/56 Rt-80)

WHAT A MAN, MY MAN IS Lynn Anderson—Columbia 10041
[Glenn Sutton] [BMI] (1/4/75 BC-93)

WHAT A PARTY Fats Domino—Imperial 5779
[Dave Bartholomew/Earl King Johnson] [BMI] (10/2/61 BCR-22)

WHAT A PRICE Fats Domino—Imperial 5723
[Fats Domino/Jack Jessup/Pee Wee Maddux] [BMI] (1/23/61 BCR-21)

WHAT A PRICE TO PAY Michael Damian—A&M 1559
[Michael Damian] [BMI] (6/8/91 BC-57)

(WHAT A SAD WAY) TO LOVE SOMEBODY Ral Donner—Gone 5125
[Norm Blagman/Sam Bobrick] [ASC] (3/24/62 BCR-74)

WHAT A SHAME Foghat—Bearsville 0014 [Roderick Price] [ASC] (4/28/73 BCR-81)

WHAT A SURPRISE Johnny Maestro The Voice Of The Crests—Coed 549
[Steve (2) Lewis/Dave Pasternack/Peter Scerra] [BMI] (4/24/61 BCR-33)

WHAT A SWEET THING THAT WAS The Shirelles—Scepter 1220
[Gerry Goffin/Carole King] [BMI] (6/26/61 BCR-30)

WHAT A WALK Bobby Lewis—Beltone 1015
[Ritchie Adams/Malou René] [BMI] (11/20/61 BCR-77)

WHAT A WOMAN IN LOVE WON'T DO Sandy Posey—MGM 13702
[John D. Loudermilk] [BMI] (3/11/67 BCR-31)

WHAT A WONDERFUL THING WE HAVE The Fabulous Rhinestones—Just Sunshine 500
[Harvey Brooks/Martin Grebb] [ASC] (7/1/72 BCR-67)

WHAT A WONDERFUL WORLD Louis Armstrong—A&M 3010
[Bob Thiele/George David Weiss] [ASC] (2/20/88 BC-32)

—WHAT A WONDERFUL WORLD see: WONDERFUL WORLD

WHAT ABOUT LOVE? Heart—Capitol 5481
[Brian Allen/Sheron Alton/Jim Vallance] [ASC] (6/1/85 BC-10)

WHAT ABOUT LOVE 'til tuesday—Epic 06289 [Aimee Mann] [ASC] (9/20/86 BC-26)

WHAT ABOUT ME Don Gibson—RCA Victor 47-7841 [Don Gibson] [BMI] (2/13/61 B-100)

WHAT ABOUT ME Quicksilver Messenger Service—Capitol 3046
[Chet Powers] [BMI] (3/6/71 B-100)

WHAT ABOUT ME Anne Murray—Capitol 3600 [Scott McKenzie] [BMI] (5/19/73 BCR-37)

WHAT ABOUT ME *Moving Pictures—Network 69952*
[Frances Frost/Garry Frost] [BMI] (9/18/82 BC-21)

WHAT ABOUT ME *Moving Pictures—Geffen 22859*
[Frances Frost/Garry Frost] [BMI] (8/12/89 BC-46)

WHAT ABOUT ME? Kenny Rogers—RCA 13899
[David Foster/Richard Marx/Kenny Rogers] [BMI] (9/15/84 BC-15)

WHAT ABOUT US The Coasters—Atco 6153
[Jerry Leiber/Mike Stoller] [BMI] (12/7/59 BCR-31)

WHAT AM I CRYING FOR? Dennis Yost And The Classics IV—MGM South 7002
[Buddy Buie/J.R. Cobb] [BMI] (10/14/72 BCR-30)

WHAT AM I GOING TO DO WITHOUT YOUR LOVE Martha & The Vandellas—Gordy 7053
[Sylvia Moy/William Stevenson] [BMI] (6/11/66 BCR-64)

WHAT AM I GONNA DO Jimmy Clanton—Ace 607
[Howard Greenfield/Neil Sedaka] [BMI] (1/2/61 BCR-50)

WHAT AM I GONNA DO Smith—Dunhill 4238
[Carole King/Toni Stern] [ASC] (5/16/70 BCR-49)

WHAT AM I GONNA DO (I'M SO IN LOVE WITH YOU) Rod Stewart—Warner Bros. 29564
[Tony Brock/Jay Davis/Rod Stewart] [BMI] (8/27/83 BC-35)

WHAT AM I GONNA DO WITH YOU Barry White—20th Century 2177
[Barry White] [BMI] (3/8/75 BCR-8)

WHAT AM I LIVING FOR *Chuck Willis—Atlantic 1179*
[Art Harris/Fred Jay] [BMI] (5/12/58 BCR-15)

WHAT AM I LIVING FOR *Conway Twitty—MGM 12886*
[Art Harris/Fred Jay] [BMI] (3/28/60 BCR-16)

WHAT AM I LIVING FOR *Percy Sledge—Atlantic 2414*
[Art Harris/Fred Jay] [BMI] (7/8/67 B-91)

WHAT AM I LIVING FOR *Ray Charles—ABC/TRC 11317*
[Art Harris/Fred Jay] [BMI] (12/25/71 BCR-49)

WHAT AM I SUPPOSED TO DO Ann-Margret—RCA Victor 47-7986
[Helen Carter] [BMI] (3/5/62 BCR-82)

WHAT ARE BOYS MADE OF The Percells—ABC-Paramount 10401
[Pete Antel/John Linde] [BMI] (3/2/63 BCR-52)

WHAT ARE WE DOIN' IN LOVE Dottie West—Liberty 1404
[Randy Goodrum] [ASC] (3/28/81 BCR-14)

WHAT ARE WE GOING TO DO? David Jones—Colpix 784
[Hank Levine/Murray MacLeod/Smokey Roberds] [BMI] (8/7/65 BCR-66)

WHAT ARE YOU DOING SUNDAY Dawn Featuring Tony Orlando—Bell 45,141
[Irwin Levine/Toni Wine] [BMI] (9/25/71 BCR-26)

WHAT ARE YOU DOING WITH A FOOL LIKE ME Joe Cocker—Capitol 44543
[Diane Warren] [ASC] (6/16/90 BC-69)

WHAT BECOMES OF THE BROKENHEARTED Jimmy Ruffin—Soul 35022
[James Anthony Dean/Paul Riser/William Weatherspoon] [BMI] (8/20/66 BCR-7)

WHAT CAN A MAN DO Ben E. King—Atco 6303 [Rudy Clark] [BMI] (7/25/64 R-76)

WHAT CAN I DO Donnie Elbert—DeLuxe 6125 [Donnie Elbert] [BMI] (7/8/57 B-61)

WHAT CAN I DO FOR YOU? Labelle—Epic 50097
[Edward Batts/James R. Ellison] [BMI] (5/10/75 BCR-48)

WHAT CAN I DO WITH THIS BROKEN HEART
England Dan & John Ford Coley—Big Tree 17000
[John Ford Coley/Bob Gundry/Dan Seals] [BMI] (10/27/79 BCR-50)

WHAT CAN I SAY Boz Scaggs—Columbia 10440
[David Paich/Boz Scaggs] [ASC] (11/20/76 BCR-42)

WHAT CAN YOU GET A WOOKIEE FOR CHRISTMAS (WHEN HE ALREADY OWNS A COMB?)
Star Wars Intergalactic Droid Choir & Chorale—RSO 1058
[Maury Yeston] [BMI] (12/13/80 BCR-69)

WHAT CHA' GONNA DO FOR ME Chaka Khan—Warner Bros. 49692
[Ned Doheny/Hamish Stuart] [ASC] (5/9/81 BCR-41)

WHAT COLOR (IS A MAN) Bobby Vinton—Epic 9846
[Marge Barton] [BMI] (9/11/65 BCR-33)

WHAT COMES NATURALLY Sheena Easton—MCA 53742
[Antonina Armato/Nick Mundy] [ASC] (3/30/91 BC-18)

WHAT DID DADDY DO Shep And The Limelites—Hull 751
[James Sheppard] [BMI] (6/30/62 B-94)

WHAT DO ALL THE PEOPLE KNOW The Monroes—Alfa 7119
[Bob Monroe] [ASC] (5/29/82 BC-50)

WHAT DO I CARE Johnny Cash—Columbia 41251 [Johnny Cash] [ASC] (9/29/58 BCR-52)

WHAT DO YOU KNOW ABOUT LOVE Apple & Appleberry—ABC 11415
[Harris Apple/Bobby Ray Appleberry] [BMI] (4/6/74 C-97)

WHAT DO YOU WANT? Bobby Vee—Liberty 55234 [Les Vandyke] [ASC] (4/4/60 B-93)

WHAT DO YOU WANT TO MAKE THOSE EYES AT ME FOR *Kenny Rankin—Decca 31054*
[Howard Johnson/Joseph McCarthy/James V. Monaco] [NA] (2/29/60 Rt-80)

WHAT DO YOU WANT TO MAKE THOSE EYES AT ME FOR *Ray Peterson—RCA Victor 47-7703*
[Howard Johnson/Joseph McCarthy/James V. Monaco] [NA] (2/29/60 Rt-77)

WHAT DO YOU WANT TO MAKE THOSE EYES AT ME FOR? *Sunny Gale—Warwick 526*
[Howard Johnson/Joseph McCarthy/James V. Monaco] [NA] (3/7/60 Rt-77)

WHAT DO YOU WANT WITH ME Chad & Jeremy—World Artists 1052
[Jeremy Clyde/Chad Stuart] [BMI] (4/10/65 BCR-48)

WHAT DOES A GIRL DO? Marcie Blane—Seville 123
[Henry Hoffman/Gary Klein] [BMI] (2/9/63 BCR-68)

WHAT DOES A GIRL DO? The Shirelles—Scepter 1259
[Ed Townsend] [BMI] (9/7/63 BCR-52)

WHAT DOES IT MATTER The Platters—Mercury 71538
[Cy Crane/Terry Symms*/Herb Weiner] [ASC] (12/19/59 CR-83)

WHAT DOES IT TAKE Honeymoon Suite—Warner Bros. 28670
[Dermot Grehan] [BMI] (7/12/86 BC-51)

WHAT DOES IT TAKE (TO WIN YOUR LOVE) Jr. Walker & The All Stars—Soul 35062
[Johnny Bristol/Vernon Bullock/Harvey Fuqua] [ASC] (5/17/69 BCR-4)

WHAT GOES ON The Beatles—Capitol 5587
[John Lennon/Paul McCartney/Ringo Starr] [ASC] (3/12/66 BR-81)

WHAT GOES UP Alan Parsons Project—Arista 0352
[Alan Parsons/Eric Woolfson] [BMI] (9/23/78 B-87)

WHAT GOES UP (MUST COME DOWN) Tyrone Davis—Dakar 4532
[Leo Graham/John Sibley] [BMI] (7/6/74 B-89)

WHAT GOOD AM I WITHOUT YOU Marvin Gaye & Kim Weston—Tamla 54104
[Alphonso Higdon/William Stevenson] [BMI] (10/24/64 BCR-61)

WHAT HAPPENS NOW Mona Carol—Kent 5001
[Peter DeAngelis/Bob Marcucci] [ASC] (7/27/56 R-41)

—WHAT HAPPENS WHEN YOUR LOVE HAS GONE see: DIDDLE-DEE-DUM

WHAT HAVE I DONE TO DESERVE THIS?
Pet Shop Boys And Dusty Springfield—EMI-Manhattan 50107
[Chris Lowe/Neil Tennant/Allee Willis] [ASC] (12/12/87 BC-1)

WHAT HAVE I GOT OF MY OWN Trini Lopez—Reprise 0276
[John Herring/Paul Sawtell] [ASC] (5/9/64 BCR-43)

WHAT HAVE THEY DONE TO THE RAIN The Searchers—Kapp 644
[Malvina Reynolds] [ASC] (1/30/65 BCR-25)

WHAT HAVE YOU DONE FOR ME LATELY Janet Jackson—A&M 2812
[James Samuel Harris/Terry Lewis] [ASC] (2/22/86 BC-4)

WHAT I AM Edie Brickell & The New Bohemians—Geffen 27696
[Alan Aly*/Edie Brickell/John Bush*/John Houser*/Ken Withrow] [ASC]
(11/26/88 BC-6)

WHAT I GOTTA DO (TO MAKE YOU JEALOUS) Little Eva—Dimension 1013
[Gerry Goffin/Carole King] [BMI] (8/10/63 C-91)

WHAT I LIKE ABOUT YOU *The Romantics—Nemperor 7527*
[Jimmy Marinos/Wally Palmar/Mike Skill] [ASC] (2/16/80 BCR-49)

WHAT I LIKE ABOUT YOU *Michael Morales—Wing 889 678*
[Jimmy Marinos/Wally Palmar/Mike Skill] [ASC] (8/12/89 BC-25)

WHAT I WOULDN'T DO (FOR THE LOVE OF YOU) Angela Bofill—Arista/GRP 2503
[Jack Perricone/Denise Utt] [ASC] (3/1/80 R-93)

WHAT IF (I SAID I LOVE YOU) Unipop—Kat Family 03533
[Sonny Limbo/Manny Loiacono/Phyllis Loiacono] [BMI] (12/25/82 B-71)

—WHAT IF see: REMO'S THEME

(WHAT) IN THE NAME OF LOVE Naked Eyes—EMI-America 8219
[Pete Byrne/Rob Fisher] [ASC] (8/11/84 BC-39)

—WHAT IN THE WORLD'S COME OVER US see: ANGEL

WHAT IN THE WORLD'S COME OVER YOU Jack Scott—Top Rank 2028
[Jack Scott] [BMI] (12/28/59 BCR-3)

WHAT IS A HUSBAND? Jane Meadows—Coral 61554
[Bill Katz/Gene Piller/Ruth Roberts] [ASC] (1/27/56 Rt*-77)

WHAT IS A MAN Four Tops—Motown 1147
[Johnny Bristol/Doris McNeil] [ASC] (5/3/69 BCR-48)

WHAT IS A TEENAGE BOY? Tom Edwards—Coral 61773
[Tom Edwards/Buddy Kaye] [ASC] (2/9/57 B-96)

WHAT IS A TEENAGE GIRL? Tom Edwards—Coral 61773
[Tom Edwards/Buddy Kaye] [NA] (2/2/57 B-57)

WHAT IS A WIFE Steve Allen—Coral 61542
[Bill Katz/Gene Piller/Ruth Roberts] [ASC] (12/17/55 BCRt*-32)

WHAT IS HIP? Tower Of Power—Warner Bros. 7748
[Emilio Castillo/David Garibaldi/Steve Kupka] [ASC] (2/23/74 B-91)

WHAT IS LIFE George Harrison—Apple 1828
[George Harrison] (TSW) [ASC] (2/27/71 BCR-7)

WHAT IS LOVE The Playmates—Roulette 4160
[Lee Pockriss/Paul Vance] [ASC] (6/22/59 BCR-15)

WHAT IS LOVE? Howard Jones—Elektra
[William Bryant/Howard Jones] [BMI] (4/21/84 BC-33)

WHAT IS TRUTH Johnny Cash—Columbia 45134
[Johnny Cash] [ASC] (4/4/70 BCR-11)

WHAT IT COMES DOWN TO The Isley Brothers—T-Neck 2252
[Ernie Isley/Marvin Isley/O'Kelly Isley/Ronald Isley/Rudolph Isley/Chris Jasper] [ASC]
(12/15/73 BCR-55)

WHAT IT IS The Undisputed Truth—Gordy 7114
[Barrett Strong/Norman Whitfield] [BMI] (2/26/72 BCR-66)

WHAT IT TAKES Aerosmith—Geffen 19944
[Desmond Child/Joe Perry/Steven Tyler] [ASC] (3/17/90 BC-8)

WHAT IT TAKES TO GET A GOOD WOMAN (THAT'S WHAT IT'S GONNA TAKE TO KEEP HER)
Denise LaSalle—Westbound 215
[Dorothy Hoskins/Albert Lowe/O.B. McClinton] [BMI] (5/12/73 C-97)

WHAT KIND OF FOOL Barbra Streisand & Barry Gibb—Columbia 11430
[Albhy Galuten/Barry Gibb] [BMI] (1/31/81 BCR-10)

WHAT KIND OF FOOL AM I *Robert Goulet—Columbia 42519*
[Leslie Bricusse/Anthony Newley] [BMI] (8/18/62 BCtRt-73)

WHAT KIND OF FOOL AM I *Anthony Newley—London 9546*
[Leslie Bricusse/Anthony Newley] [BMI] (8/18/62 BCtRt-14)

WHAT KIND OF FOOL AM I *Sammy Davis Jr.—Reprise 20,048*
[Leslie Bricusse/Anthony Newley] [BMI] (8/18/62 BCtRt-14)

WHAT KIND OF FOOL AM I *Billy Eckstine—Mercury 72022*
[Leslie Bricusse/Anthony Newley] [BMI] (8/18/62 CtRt-16)

WHAT KIND OF FOOL AM I *Mantovani And His Orchestra—London 9552*
[Leslie Bricusse/Anthony Newley] [BMI] (8/18/62 Rt-86) [IWM]

WHAT KIND OF FOOL AM I *Burt Farber—Felsted 8652*
[Leslie Bricusse/Anthony Newley] [BMI] (8/25/62 Rt-86)

WHAT KIND OF FOOL AM I *Vic Damone—Capitol 4827*
[Leslie Bricusse/Anthony Newley] [BMI] (8/25/62 Rt-86)

WHAT KIND OF FOOL AM I *The Cordials—Felsted 8653*
[Leslie Bricusse/Anthony Newley] [BMI] (9/1/62 Rt-86)

WHAT KIND OF FOOL AM I *Billy Daniels—Jubilee 5437*
[Leslie Bricusse/Anthony Newley] [BMI] (9/1/62 Rt-86)

WHAT KIND OF FOOL AM I *Ronnie Aldrich—London 9553*
[Leslie Bricusse/Anthony Newley] [BMI] (9/1/62 Rt-86)

WHAT KIND OF FOOL AM I Rick Springfield—RCA 13245
[Rick Springfield] [BMI] (6/5/82 BC-19)

WHAT KIND OF FOOL (DO YOU THINK I AM) *The Tams—ABC-Paramount 10502*
[Ray Whitley] [BMI] (12/14/63 BCR-9)

WHAT KIND OF FOOL DO YOU THINK I AM *Bill Deal & The Rhondels—Heritage 817*
[Ray Whitley] [BMI] (8/9/69 BCR-20)

WHAT KIND OF LOVE IS THIS Joey Dee & The Starliters—Roulette 4438
[Johnny Nash] [ASC] (8/18/62 BCR-17)

WHAT KIND OF MAN WOULD I BE? Chicago—Reprise/Full Moon 22741
[Bobby Caldwell/Chas Sandford/Jason Scheff] [BMI] (12/2/89 BC-5)

WHAT LITTLE GIRL Frankie Avalon—Chancellor 1026
[Frankie Avalon/Sal Ponti] [BMI] (10/13/58 BR-58)

WHAT LOVE IS Marty Balin—EMI America 8153
[Greg Prestopino/Brock Walsh] [ASC] (2/19/83 BC-63)

WHAT MADE AMERICA FAMOUS Harry Chapin—Elektra 45893
[Harry Chapin] [ASC] (7/6/74 C-87)

WHAT MAKES LITTLE GIRLS CRY The Victorians—Liberty 55574
[Lou Josie] [BMI] (7/13/63 C-84)

WHAT MY BABY NEEDS NOW IS A LITTLE MORE LOVIN'
James Brown & Lyn Collins—Polydor 14157
[James Brown/Lyn Collins/David Matthews] [BMI] (12/16/72 BCR-51)

WHAT NOW Gene Chandler—Constellation 141
[Curtis Mayfield] [BMI] (11/28/64 BCR-40)

WHAT NOW MY LOVE *Sonny & Cher—Atco 6395*
[Gilbert Bécaud/Pierre Delanoë/Carl Sigman] [ASC] (1/29/66 BCR-14) [FET]

WHAT NOW MY LOVE *Herb Alpert & The Tijuana Brass—A&M 792*
[Gilbert Bécaud/Pierre Delanoë/Carl Sigman*] [ASC] (3/12/66 BCR-24) [IWM]*

WHAT NOW MY LOVE *"Groove" Holmes—Prestige 427*
[Gilbert Bécaud/Pierre Delanoë/Carl Sigman*] [ASC] (10/1/66 B-96) [IWM]*

WHAT NOW MY LOVE *Mitch Ryder—DynoVoice 901*
[Gilbert Bécaud/Pierre Delanoë/Carl Sigman] [ASC] (9/9/67 BCR-22) [FET]

WHAT SHE DOES TO ME (THE DIANA SONG) The Producers—Portrait 12-02092
[Wayne Famous/Kyle Henderson/Bryan Holmes/Van Temple] [BMI] (6/13/81 BCR-61)

WHAT THE BIG GIRLS DO Van Stephenson—MCA 52437
[Jan Buckingham/Steve Buckingham/Van Stephenson] [BMI] (8/4/84 BC-44)

WHAT THE WORLD NEEDS NOW IS LOVE *Jackie deShannon—Imperial 66110*
[Burt Bacharach/Hal David] [ASC] (5/22/65 BCR-7)

WHAT THE WORLD NEEDS NOW IS LOVE *Tom Clay—Mowest 5002*
[Burt Bacharach/Hal David] (Med) [ASC] (7/10/71 BCR-7)

WHAT TIME IS IT? The Jive Five—Beltone 2024
[Bob Feldman/Jerry Goldstein/Richard Gottehrer] [BMI] (9/15/62 BCR-67)

WHAT TIME IS LOVE? The KLF—Arista 2365
[Isaac Bello/James Cauty/William Ernest Drummond] [BMI] (10/26/91 B-57)

WHAT TIME OF DAY Billy Thunderkloud & The Chieftones—20th Century 2181
[Ronel McCown] [BMI] (6/28/75 BC-92)

WHAT TO DO WITH LAURIE Mike Clifford—United Artists 557
[Jerry Leiber/Mike Stoller/Billy Edd Wheeler] [BMI] (12/29/62 BCR-67)

WHAT WILL I DO Timmy -T-—Quality 4-15102 [Timmy Torres] [BMI] (7/21/90 B-96)

WHAT WILL I TELL MY HEART *Fats Domino—Imperial 5454*
[Irving Gordon/Jack Lawrence/Peter Tinturin] [ASC] (8/3/57 BCR-37)*

WHAT WILL I TELL MY HEART *The Harptones—Companion 103*
[Irving Gordon/Jack Lawrence/Peter Tinturin] [ASC] (5/8/61 B-96)*

WHAT WILL MARY SAY Johnny Mathis—Columbia 42666
[Eddie Snyder/Paul Vance] [ASC] (1/26/63 BCR-8)

WHAT WOULD I DO Mickey And Sylvia—RCA Victor 47-7811
[Mickey Baker/Leonard Lee/Sylvia Robinson] [BMI] (12/19/60 BCR-34)

WHAT WOULD THE CHILDREN THINK Rick Springfield—Capitol 3466
[Rick Springfield] [ASC] (11/4/72 BCR-70)

WHAT WOULD YOU DO? Jim Reeves—RCA Victor 47-7905
[Jim Reeves] [BMI] (7/3/61 BCR-50)

WHAT YOU DO TO ME Carl Wilson—Caribou 03590
[Johanna Hall/John Hall] [BMI] (5/14/83 BC-72)

WHAT YOU DON'T KNOW Exposé—Arista 1-9836 [Lewis Martinée] [ASC] (5/20/89 BC-8)

WHAT YOU GAVE ME Marvin Gaye & Tammi Terrell—Tamla 54187
[Nick Ashford/Valerie Simpson] [ASC] (11/22/69 BCR-43)

WHAT YOU GET IS WHAT YOU SEE Tina Turner—Capitol 5668
[Terry Britten/Graham Lyle] [ASC] (2/7/87 BC-13)

WHAT YOU GOT Duke & The Drivers—ABC 12110
[Charles Armstrong] [BMI] (8/16/75 BCR-76)

WHAT YOU NEED INXS—Atlantic 89460
[Andy Farriss/Michael Hutchence] [ASC] (1/18/86 BC-4)

WHAT YOU SEE IS WHAT YOU GET Stoney And Meatloaf—Rare Earth 5027
[Patti Jerome/Mike Valvano] [ASC] (5/22/71 BCR-59)

WHAT YOU SEE IS WHAT YOU GET Brenda K. Starr—MCA 53367
[Stephen Lunt/Arthur Stead] [ASC] (8/6/88 BC-24)

WHAT YOU WAITIN' FOR Stargard—MCA 40932 [Norman Whitfield] [BMI] (8/26/78 R-94)

WHAT YOU WON'T DO FOR LOVE Bobby Caldwell—Clouds 11
[Bobby Caldwell/Alfons Kettner] [BMI] (12/2/78 BCR-9)

WHAT YOU'RE MISSING Chicago—Full Moon 29798
[Jay Gruska/Joseph Amos Williams] [ASC] (1/29/83 B-81)

WHATCHA' GONNA DO Nat King Cole—Capitol 4325
[Nat "King" Cole] [ASC] (2/13/60 BC-92) [I]

WHATCHA GONNA DO? Pablo Cruise—A&M 1920
[David Jenkins/Cory Lerios] [ASC] (4/9/77 BCR-3)

WHATCHA GONNA DO Chilliwack—Millennium 13110
[William A. Henderson/Brian MacLeod] [BMI] (10/16/82 BC-32)

WHAT'CHA GONNA DO ABOUT IT Doris Troy—Atlantic 2206
[Greg Carroll/Rex Garvin/Doris Payne] [BMI] (11/9/63 R-100)

WHAT CHA GONNA DO WITH MY LOVIN' *Stephanie Mills—20th Century Fox 2403*
[Reggie Lucas/James Mtume] [BMI] (7/7/79 BCR-22)

WHATCHA GONNA DO WITH MY LOVIN' *Inner City—Virgin 98999*
[Reggie Lucas/James Mtume] [BMI] (3/3/90 BC-76)

WHATCHA SEE IS WHATCHA GET The Dramatics—Volt 4058
[Tony Hester] [BMI] (7/3/71 BCR-9)

WHAT'D I SAY (PART 1) *Ray Charles And His Orchestra—Atlantic 2031*
[Ray Charles] [BMI] (7/4/59 BCR-6)

WHAT'D I SAY *Jerry Lee Lewis And His Pumping Piano —Sun 356*
[Ray Charles] [BMI] (4/3/61 BCtR-30)

WHAT'D I SAY *Jack Eubanks, His Orchestra and Singers—Monument 434*
[Ray Charles] [BMI] (4/8/61 Ct-41) [IWM]

WHAT'D I SAY (PART 1) *Bobby Darin—Atco 6221 [Ray Charles] [BMI] (3/19/62 BCR-24)*

WHAT I SAY *Etta James—Argo 5459*
[Ray Charles] [BMI] (1/11/64 R-96)

WHAT'D I SAY
Elvis Presley With The Jubilee Four And Carole Lombard Quartet —RCA Victor 47-8360
[Ray Charles] [BMI] (5/16/64 BCR-13)

WHAT'D I SAY *Rare Earth—Rare Earth 5043*
[Ray Charles] [BMI] (4/8/72 BCR-61)

WHATEVER GETS YOU THRU THE NIGHT
John Lennon With The Plastic Ono Nuclear Band—Apple 1874
[John Lennon] [GL] (9/28/74 BCR-1)

WHATEVER HAPPENED TO BENNY SANTINI? Chris Rea—United Artists/Magnet 1252
[Chris Rea] [ASC] (11/11/78 BCR-71)

WHATEVER HAPPENED TO OLD FASHIONED LOVE
B.J. ThomasCleveland International 03492
[Lewis J. Anderson] [BMI] (5/21/83 B-93)

WHATEVER LOLA WANTS (LOLA GETS) *Sarah Vaughan—Mercury 70595*
[Richard Adler/Jerry Ross] [ASC] (4/4/55 BCtRt-3)

WHATEVER LOLA WANTS (LOLA GETS) *Dinah Shore—RCA Victor 47-6077*
[Richard Adler/Jerry Ross] [ASC] (4/4/55 BCtRt-3)

WHATEVER LOLA WANTS (LOLA GETS) *Ginny Gibson—MGM 11961*
[Richard Adler/Jerry Ross] [ASC] (4/4/55 Rt-4)

WHATEVER LOLA WANTS *Carmen McRae—Decca 29472*
[Richard Adler/Jerry Ross] [ASC] (4/11/55 Rt-4)

WHATEVER TURNS YOU ON Travis Wammack—Fame 91001
[George Henry Jackson/Raymond Moore] [BMI] (7/29/72 BCR-65)

—WHATEVER WILL BE, WILL BE see: QUE SERA SERA

WHATEVER YOU DECIDE Randy Vanwarmer—Bearsville 49258
[Randy Vanwarmer] [ASC] (7/19/80 BCR-69)

WHATEVER YOU GOT, I WANT The Jackson 5—Motown 1308
[Mel Larson/Gene Marcellino/Jerry Marcellino] [ASC] (10/19/74 BCR-27)

WHATEVER YOU WANT Jerry Butler—Vee-Jay 486
[Bob Crewe/Bob Gaudio] [BMI] (3/30/63 B-68)

WHATEVER YOU WANT Tony! Toni! Toné!—Wing 879 590
[Carl Wheeler/Dwayne Wiggins] [ASC] (4/13/91 B-48)

WHAT'S A MATTER BABY (IS IT HURTING YOU) *Timi Yuro—Liberty 55469*
[Joy Byers Johnston/Clyde Otis] [BMI] (7/7/62 BCR-12)

WHAT'S A MATTER BABY *Ellen Foley—Cleveland Int'l/Epic 50770*
[Joy Byers Johnston/Clyde Otis] [BMI] (11/3/79 BCR-85)

WHAT'S COME OVER ME Margie Joseph & Blue Magic—Atco/WMOT 7030
[Ted "Wizard" Mills] [BMI] (12/6/75 C-89)

WHAT'S COME OVER THIS WORLD? Billy Carr—Colpix 791
[Howard Greenfield/Jack Keller] [BMI] (12/4/65 C-100)

WHAT'S EASY FOR TWO IS SO HARD FOR ONE Mary Wells—Motown 1048
[Smokey Robinson] [ASC] (10/19/63 BCR-29)

WHAT'S FOREVER FOR Michael Murphey—Liberty 1466
[Rafe Van Hoy] [BMI] (7/24/82 BC-19)

WHAT'S GOING ON *Marvin Gaye—Tamla 54201*
[Renaldo Benson/Al Cleveland/Marvin Gaye] [BMI] (2/20/71 BCR-1)

WHAT'S GOING ON *Quincy Jones—A&M 1316*
[Renaldo Benson/Al Cleveland/Marvin Gaye] [BMI] (12/18/71 CR-96)

WHAT'S GOING ON *Cyndi Lauper—Portrait 37-06970*
[Renaldo Benson/Al Cleveland/Marvin Gaye] [BMI] (3/14/87 BC-12)

WHAT'S GONNA HAPPEN WHEN SUMMER'S DONE Freddy Cannon—Swan 4117
[Bob Feldman/Jerry Goldstein/Richard Gottehrer] [BMI] (8/25/62 BCR-45)

WHAT'S HAPPENED TO BLUE EYES Jessi Colter—Capitol 4087
[Jessi Colter] (TSW) [BMI] (10/11/75 BC-57)

WHAT'S HAPPENING Wade Flemons—Vee-Jay 335
[Whelock Bisson] [BMI] (2/15/60 B-94)

WHAT'S HAPPENING TO ME Dale & Grace—Montel 930
[June Sparks] [BMI] (7/18/64 C-91)

WHAT'S HE DOING IN MY WORLD Eddy Arnold—RCA Victor 47-8516
[Carl Belew/Eddie Bush/Billy Joe Moore] [BMI] (5/15/65 BCR-60)

WHAT'S IT GONNA BE Dusty Springfield—Philips 40498
[Jerry Ragovoy/Mort Shuman] [ASC] (11/18/67 BCR-48)

WHAT'S IT GONNA BE Jellybean—Atlantic 87782
[Wardell Potts/Anne Preven] [ASC] (2/9/91 B-90)

WHAT'S LOVE GOT TO DO WITH IT Tina Turner—Capitol 5354
[Terry Britten/Graham Lyle] [BMI] (5/19/84 BC-1)

WHAT'S MADE MILWAUKEE FAMOUS (HAS MADE A LOSER OUT OF ME)
Jerry Lee Lewis—Smash 2164
[Glenn Sutton] [BMI] (6/22/68 BC-94)

WHAT'S NEW Linda Ronstadt & The Nelson Riddle Orchestra—Asylum 69780
[Johnny Burke/Bob Haggart] [ASC] (10/29/83 BC-38)

WHAT'S NEW PUSSYCAT? Tom Jones—Parrot 9765
[Burt Bacharach/Hal David] [ASC] (6/12/65 BCR-2)

WHAT'S ON MY MIND Kansas—Kirshner 4270 [Kerry Livgren] [BMI] (6/25/77 CR-85)

WHAT'S ON YOUR MIND (PURE ENERGY) Information Society—Tommy Boy 27826
[Paul Robb/Kurt Valaquen] [ASC] (7/16/88 BC-3)

WHAT'S SHE GOT Liquid Gold—Critique 701
[George Stanley Alexander/Rob Davis] [ASC] (9/3/83 BC-86)

WHAT'S SO GOOD ABOUT GOOD-BY The Miracles—Tamla 54053
[Smokey Robinson] [ASC] (1/1/62 BCR-22)

WHAT'S THE MATTER HERE? 10,000 Maniacs—Elektra 69388
[Robert Buck/Natalie Merchant] [ASC] (9/3/88 B-80)

WHAT'S THE MATTER WITH YOU BABY Marvin Gaye & Mary Wells—Motown 1057
[Barney Ales*/Clarence Paul/William Stevenson/Andre Williams*] [BMI] (5/9/64 BCR-17)

—WHAT'S THE MATTER WITH YOU see: GAME IS OVER

WHAT'S THE NAME OF THIS FUNK (SPIDER MAN) Ramsey Lewis—Columbia 10235
[Derf Reklaw Raheem/Charles Stepney/Morris Stewart] [BMI] (1/24/76 BC-69) [I]

WHAT'S THE REASON I'M NOT PLEASING YOU *Fats Domino—Imperial 5417*
[Jimmie Grier/Earl Hatch/Coy Poe/Pinky Tomlin] [ASC] (12/22/56 BCR-22)

WHAT'S THE REASON *Bobby Edwards—Capitol 4674*
[Jimmie Grier/Earl Hatch/Coy Poe/Pinky Tomlin] [ASC] (1/8/62 BCR-43)

WHAT'S THE USE OF BREAKING UP Jerry Butler—Mercury 72960
[Jerry Butler/Kenneth Gamble/Leon Huff] [BMI] (8/23/69 BCR-20)

WHAT'S THE USE OF CRYIN' Eddie Fisher—RCA Victor 47-7135
[Noel Regney/Gloria Shayne] [BMI] (1/13/58 CR-43)

WHAT'S TOO MUCH Smokey Robinson—Motown 1911
[Lonnie Kirtz/Smokey Robinson/Ivory Stone/Homer Talbert] [ASC] (11/14/87 BC-79)

WHAT'S YOUR HURRY DARLIN' Ironhorse—Scotti Brothers 512
[Randy Bachman/Carl Wilson] [NA] (4/26/80 B-89)

WHAT'S YOUR MAMA'S NAME Tanya Tucker—Columbia 45799
[Dallas Frazier/Earl Montgomery] [BMI] (5/26/73 BCR-86)

WHAT'S YOUR NAME *Don & Juan—Big Top 3079*
[Claude Johnson] [BMI] (1/29/62 BCR-5)

WHAT'S YOUR NAME *Andy & David Williams—Barnaby 601*
[Claude Johnson] [BMI] (6/22/74 BCR-73)

WHAT'S YOUR NAME Lynyrd Skynyrd—MCA 40819
[Gary Rossington/Ronnie Van Zant] [BMI] (11/26/77 BCR-7)

WHAT'S YOUR NAME, WHAT'S YOUR NUMBER Andrea True Connection—Buddah 582
[Roger Cook/Bobby Wood] [BMI] (1/14/78 BC-56)

WHAT'VE I DONE (TO MAKE YOU MAD) Linda Jones—Loma 2077
[Ken Hollon/George Kerr] [BMI] (9/30/67 BCR-61)

WHEEL IN THE SKY Journey—Columbia 10700
[Robert Fleischman/Neal Schon/Diane Valory] [BMI] (4/1/78 BCR-52)

WHEEL OF FORTUNE *The Knightsbridge Strings—Top Rank 2014*
[Bennie Benjamin/George David Weiss] [ASC] (11/2/59 BC-88) [IWM]

WHEEL OF FORTUNE *LaVern Baker—Atlantic 2059*
[Bennie Benjamin/George David Weiss] [ASC] (5/2/60 B-83)

THE WHEEL OF HURT *Margaret Whiting—London 101*
[Charles Singleton/Eddie Snyder] [BMI] (10/1/66 BCR-26)

THE WHEEL OF HURT *Al Martino—Capitol 5741*
[Charles Singleton/Eddie Snyder] [BMI] (10/15/66 BCR-42)

WHEELS *The String-A-Longs—Warwick 603*
[Richard Stephens/Jimmy Torres] [BMI] (12/26/60 BCtRt-3) [I]

WHEELS *Billy Vaughn And His Orchestra—Dot 16174*
[Richard Stephens/Jimmy Torres] [BMI] (1/23/61 BCtRt-4) [I]

WHEELS OF FORTUNE The Doobie Brothers—Warner Bros. 8233
[Jeff Baxter/John Hartman/Patrick Simmons] [ASC] (8/28/76 B-87)

WHEELS OF LIFE Gino Vannelli—A&M 2114 [Gino Vannelli] [ASC] (2/17/79 BCR-78)

WHEN The Kalin Twins—Decca 30642 [Paul Evans/Jack Reardon] [ASC] (5/19/58 BCR-4)

WHEN A BOY FALLS IN LOVE *Mel Carter—Derby 1003*
[Sam Cooke/Clint Lavert] [BMI] (6/29/63 BCR-38)

WHEN A BOY FALLS IN LOVE *Sam Cooke—RCA Victor 47-8586*
[Sam Cooke/Clint Lavert] [BMI] (6/5/65 BCR-52)

WHEN A CHILD IS BORN Michael Holm—Mercury 73642
[Fred Jay/Zacar] [BMI] (12/14/74 BCR-24)

WHEN A MAN LOVES A WOMAN *Percy Sledge—Atlantic 2326*
[Calvin Lewis/Andrew Wright] [BMI] (4/9/66 BCR-1)

WHEN A WOMAN LOVES A MAN *Esther Phillips—Atlantic 2335*
[Calvin Lewis/Andrew Wright] [BMI] (5/28/66 BCR-59)

WHEN A MAN LOVES A WOMAN *Bette Midler—Atlantic 3643*
[Calvin Lewis/Andrew Wright] [BMI] (1/19/80 BCR-35)

WHEN A MAN LOVES A WOMAN *Michael Bolton—Columbia 74020*
[Calvin Lewis/Andrew Wright] [BMI] (10/12/91 BC-1)

WHEN ALL IS SAID AND DONE ABBA—Atlantic 3889
[Benny Andersson/Björn Ulvaeus] [BMI] (1/9/82 BCR-27)

WHEN ALL THE STREETS ARE DARK Somethin' Smith & The Redheads—Epic 9119
[Bob Merrill] [ASC] (11/12/55 B-90)

WHEN DOVES CRY Prince—Warner Bros. 29286 [Prince] [ASC] (6/2/84 BC-1)

WHEN HE SHINES Sheena Easton—EMI America 8113
[Dominic Bugatti/Florrie Palmer] [BMI] (4/3/82 BCR-24)

WHEN HE TOUCHES ME (NOTHING ELSE MATTERS) Peaches & Herb—Date 1637
[Carolyn Varga] [BMI] (2/15/69 BCR-40)

WHEN HE'S GONE Bee Gees—Warner Bros. 19369
[Barry Gibb/Maurice Gibb/Robin Gibb] [BMI] (5/25/91 C-86)

WHEN I DIE Motherlode—Buddah 131
[Steve Kennedy/William Daniel Smith] [BMI] (8/2/69 BCR-12)

WHEN I DREAM Crystal Gayle—United Artists 1288
[Sandy Theoret] [ASC] (7/7/79 B-84)

WHEN I DREAM OF YOU Tommy Page—Sire 19839
[Tommy Page] [BMI] (5/12/90 BC-31)

WHEN I FALL IN LOVE *Etta Jones—King 5424*
[Edward Heyman/Victor Young] [ASC] (1/16/61 BR-65)

WHEN I FALL IN LOVE *The Lettermen—Capitol 4658*
[Edward Heyman/Victor Young] [ASC] (11/20/61 BCR-7)

WHEN I FALL IN LOVE *Donny Osmond—MGM 14677*
[Edward Heyman/Victor Young] (TSW) [ASC] (11/24/73 BCR-14)

WHEN I FALL IN LOVE *Natalie Cole—EMI-Manhattan 50138*
[Edward Heyman/Victor Young] [ASC] (8/27/88 B-95)

WHEN I GET THRU WITH YOU (YOU'LL LOVE ME TOO) Patsy Cline—Decca 31377
[Harlan Howard] [BMI] (4/30/62 BCR-36)

WHEN I GET YOU BABY Ruth Brown—Atlantic 1140
[Ruth Brown/Jimmy Lewis] [BMI] (5/25/57 R-66)

WHEN I GO TO SLEEP AT NIGHT The Tokens—RCA Victor 47-7896
[Mitch Margo/Phil Margo*/Hank Medress] [BMI] (6/19/61 R-68)

WHEN I GROW TOO OLD TO DREAM *Ed Townsend—Capitol 4048*
[Oscar Hammerstein/Sigmund Romberg] [ASC] (9/8/58 BCRt-47)

WHEN I GROW TOO OLD TO DREAM *Duke Mitchell—Liberty 55158*
[Oscar Hammerstein/Sigmund Romberg] [ASC] (9/22/58 Rt-47)

WHEN I GROW UP (TO BE A MAN) The Beach Boys—Capitol 5245
[Mike Love*/Brian Wilson] [BMI] (9/5/64 BCR-7)

WHEN I HOLD YOU IN MY ARMS
Lou Monte with Hugo Winterhalter And His Orchestra—RCA Victor 47-5883
[George Brown/Rodolfo Falvo] [BMI] (10/4/54 R-PRE)

WHEN I LET YOU GO Jerry Vale—Columbia 40463 [Paul Insetta] [ASC] (4/2/55 C-44)

WHEN I LOOKED AT HIM Exposé—Arista 1-9868 [Lewis Martinée] [BMI] (8/19/89 BC-10)

WHEN I NEED YOU Leo Sayer—Warner Bros. 8332
[Albert Hammond/Carole Bayer Sager] [BMI] (2/26/77 BCR-1)

WHEN I SEE YOU Fats Domino—Imperial 5454
[Dave Bartholomew/Fats Domino] [BMI] (8/3/57 BCR-29)

WHEN I SEE YOU SMILE Bad English—Epic 69082 [Diane Warren] [ASC] (9/16/89 BC-1)

WHEN I STOP DREAMING Ray Charles & Jimmy Lewis—ABC/TRC 11170
[Charlie Louvin/Ira Louvin] (TSW) [BMI] (1/25/69 R-71)

WHEN I THINK OF YOU *James & Michael—London 5N 257*
[James L. Williams] [BMI] (9/3/77 R-84)

WHEN I THINK OF YOU *Leif Garrett—Scotti Brothers 502*
[James L. Williams] [BMI] (11/3/79 B-78)

WHEN I THINK OF YOU Janet Jackson—A&M 2855
[James Samuel Harris/Terry Lewis] [ASC] (8/9/86 BC-1)

WHEN I WANTED YOU Barry Manilow—Arista 0481
[Gino Cunico] [BMI] (12/15/79 BCR-20)

WHEN I WAS YOUNG Eric Burdon & The Animals—MGM 13721
[Vic Briggs/Eric Burdon/Barry Jenkins/Danny McCulloch/John Weider] [BMI] (4/8/67 BCR-15)

WHEN I'M BACK ON MY FEET AGAIN Michael Bolton—Columbia 73342
[Diane Warren] [ASC] (5/26/90 BC-7)

WHEN I'M DEAD AND GONE McGuinness Flint—Capitol 3014
[Benny Gallagher/Graham Lyle] [BMI] (12/26/70 BCR-35)

WHEN I'M GONE Brenda Holloway—Tamla 54111
[Smokey Robinson] [ASC] (3/6/65 BCR-24)

WHEN I'M HOLDING YOU TIGHT Michael Stanley Band—EMI America 8130
[Kevin Raleigh] [ASC] (9/11/82 B-78)

WHEN I'M NOT WITH YOU Conway Twitty—MGM 12785
[Jack Nance/Conway Twitty] [BMI] (5/2/59 C-98)

WHEN I'M WITH YOU *Sheriff—Capitol 5199 [Arnold Lanni] [BMI] (4/23/83 BC-61)*

WHEN I'M WITH YOU *Sheriff—Capitol 44302 [Arnold Lanni] [BMI] (11/19/88 BC-1)*

WHEN IRISH EYES ARE SMILING Bruce Hayes with Mary Mayo—Dwain 812
[Ernest R. Ball/George Graff Jr./Chauncey Olcott] (EP) [ASC] (2/15/60 R-63)

WHEN IT'S LOVE Van Halen—Warner Bros. 27827
[Michael Anthony/Sammy Hagar/Alex Van Halen/Eddie Van Halen] [ASC] (7/2/88 BC-5)

WHEN IT'S OVER Loverboy—Columbia 02814
[Paul Dean/Mike Reno] [BMI] (4/10/82 BCR-25)

WHEN IT'S SPRINGTIME IN ALASKA (IT'S FORTY BELOW) Johnny Horton—Columbia 41308
[Tillman Franks/Johnny Horton*] [BMI] (4/6/59 R-85)

WHEN JOANNA LOVED ME Tony Bennett—Columbia 42996
[Jack Segal/Robert Wells] [ASC] (3/14/64 BCR-54)

(WHEN JOHNNY COMES MARCHING HOME AGAIN) I CAN'T SEE YOU NO MORE
Joe Tex—Dial 4095
[Joe Tex] [BMI] (11/29/69 C-95)

WHEN JULIE COMES AROUND The Cuff Links—Decca 732592
[Lee Pockriss/Paul Vance] [ASC] (11/29/69 BCR-24)

WHEN LIKING TURNS TO LOVING Ronnie Dove—Diamond 195
[Jay Fishman*/Kenny Young] [BMI] (1/22/66 BCR-15)

WHEN LOVE CALLS Atlantic Starr—A&M 2312
[David E. Lewis/Wayne I. Lewis] [ASC] (4/4/81 R-61)

WHEN LOVE COMES TO TOWN U2 With B. B. King—Island 99225
[Adam Clayton/Dave Evans/Paul Hewson/Larry Mullen] [ASC] (4/1/89 BC-68)

WHEN LOVE CRIES Donna Summer—Atlantic 87624
[Keith Diamond/Larry Henley/Eve Nelson/Anthony L. Smith/Donna Summer] [BMI] (8/17/91 B-77)

WHEN LOVE HAS GONE AWAY Richard Cocciante—20th Century 2275
[Amerigo Cassella/Riccardo Cocciante/Marco Luberti/Danielle Rouby] [ASC] (4/3/76 BCR-41) [FET]

WHEN LOVE IS NEW Arthur Prysock—Old Town 1000
[Kenneth Gamble/Leon Huff] [BMI] (12/25/76 BCR-64)

WHEN LOVE SLIPS AWAY Dee Dee Warwick—Mercury 72667
[Scott English/Vic Millrose/Jerry J. Ross] [BMI] (4/29/67 BC-92)

WHEN MABEL COMES IN THE ROOM Michael Allen—Warner Bros. 7833
[Jerry Herman] [ASC] (11/9/74 R-73)

WHEN MY BABY SMILES AT ME Crazy Otto—Decca 29753A
[Bill Munro] (Med) [NA] (2/3/56 R-90) [IM]

WHEN MY BLUE MOON TURNS TO GOLD AGAIN Elvis Presley—RCA Victor EPA-992
[Gene Sullivan/Wiley Walker] [BMI] (12/1/56 BR-27)

***WHEN MY DREAMBOAT COMES HOME** Fats Domino—Imperial 5396*
[Dave Franklin/Cliff Friend] [ASC] (7/20/56 BCRt-12)

***WHEN MY DREAM BOAT COMES HOME** Grady Martin & His Slew Foot Five—Decca 30022*
[Dave Franklin/Cliff Friend] [ASC] (8/10/56 Rt-12) [IWM]

***WHEN MY LITTLE GIRL IS SMILING** The Drifters—Atlantic 2134*
[Gerry Goffin/Carole King] [BMI] (2/19/62 BCR-18)

***WHEN MY LITTLE GIRL IS SMILING** Steve Alaimo—Entrance 7501*
[Gerry Goffin/Carole King] [BMI] (6/26/71 BR-72)

WHEN ROCK AND ROLL COME TO TRINIDAD Nat "King" Cole—Capitol 3702
[Roy Alfred/Marvin Fisher] [ASC] (4/13/57 BCR-31)

WHEN SCHOOL STARTS AGAIN Tony Perkins—RCA Victor 47-7078
[Joe Benedetti/Dick Scher] [BMI] (11/30/57 C-60)

WHEN SHE DANCES Joey Scarbury—Elektra 47201
[Brian Blugerman] [ASC] (10/10/81 BCR-49)

***(WHEN SHE WANTS GOOD LOVIN') MY BABY COMES TO ME** The Coasters—Atco 6098*
[Jerry Leiber/Mike Stoller] [BMI] (9/9/57 R-76)

***(WHEN SHE NEEDS GOOD LOVIN') SHE COMES TO ME** The Chicago Loop—DynoVoice 226*
[Jerry Leiber/Mike Stoller] [BMI] (11/5/66 BCR-33)

WHEN SHE WAS MY GIRL Four Tops—Casablanca 2338
[Marc Blatte/Larry Gottlieb] [ASC] (8/15/81 BCR-10)

WHEN SMOKEY SINGS ABC—Mercury 888604
[Martin Fry/Mark White] [BMI] (7/4/87 BC-5)

WHEN SOMEBODY LOVES YOU Frank Sinatra—Reprise 0398
[Howard Greenfield/Jack Keller/Keely Smith] [BMI] (10/2/65 R-97)

***WHEN SOMETHING IS WRONG WITH MY BABY** Sam & Dave—Stax 210*
[Isaac Hayes/David Porter] [BMI] (2/11/67 BCR-42)

***WHEN SOMETHING IS WRONG WITH MY BABY** Otis & Carla—Atco 6665*
[Isaac Hayes/David Porter] [BMI] (4/26/69 R-81)

WHEN SOMETHING IS WRONG WITH MY BABY
Linda Ronstadt (featuring Aaron Neville)—Elektra 64968
[Isaac Hayes/David Porter] [BMI] (5/12/90 BC-78)

WHEN THE BOY IN YOUR ARMS (IS THE BOY IN YOUR HEART) Connie Francis—MGM 13051
[Roy C. Bennett/Sid Tepper] [ASC] (11/20/61 BCR-7)

WHEN THE BOYS GET TOGETHER Joanie Sommers—Warner Bros. 5308
[Hal David/Sherman Edwards] [ASC] (10/6/62 B-94)

WHEN THE BOY'S HAPPY (THE GIRL'S HAPPY TOO) The Four Pennies—Rust 5070
[Jeff Barry/Ellie Greenwich] [BMI] (11/9/63 B-95)

WHEN THE BOYS TALK ABOUT THE GIRLS Valerie Carr—Roulette 4066
[Bob Merrill] [ASC] (4/21/58 BCR-23)

WHEN THE CHILDREN CRY White Lion—Atlantic 89015
[Vito Bratta/Mike Tramp] [ASC] (11/5/88 BC-3)

WHEN THE FEELING COMES AROUND Jennifer Warnes—Arista 0497
[Rick Cunha] [BMI] (3/29/80 BCR-45)

WHEN THE GOING GETS TOUGH, THE TOUGH GET GOING Billy Ocean—Jive 9432
[Wayne Brathwaite/Barry Eastmond/Mutt Lange/Billy Ocean] [ASC] (11/30/85 BC-1)

WHEN THE GOOD SUN SHINES Elmo & Almo—Daddy Best Presents 2501
[Garry Bonner/Alan Gordon] [BMI] (6/3/67 B-98)

WHEN THE HEART RULES THE MIND GTR—Arista 1-9470
[Steve Hackett/Steve Howe] [BMI] (5/10/86 BC-14)

WHEN THE LADY SMILES Golden Earring—21 Records 112
[Barry Hay/George Kooymans] [ASC] (3/24/84 B-76)

WHEN THE LIGHTS GO OUT Naked Eyes—EMI-America 8183
[Pete Byrne/Rob Fisher] [ASC] (10/22/83 BC-37)

WHEN THE LIGHTS GO OUT Gerardo—Interscope 4-98734
[Fabian Cooke*/Gerardo Mejia/Danny Sembello/Michael Sembello] [ASC] (8/24/91 B-98)

WHEN THE LOVELIGHT STARTS SHINING THROUGH HIS EYES
The Supremes—Motown 1051
[Lamont Dozier/Brian Holland/Eddie Holland] [BMI] (11/30/63 BCR-19)

WHEN THE MORNING COMES Hoyt Axton—A&M 1497
[Hoyt Axton] [BMI] (6/1/74 BCR-54)

WHEN THE NIGHT COMES Joe Cocker—Capitol 44437
[Bryan Adams/Jim Vallance/Diane Warren] [BMI] (10/28/89 BC-11)

WHEN THE PARTY IS OVER Robert John—A&M 1210
[Michael Gately/Robert John] [BMI] (11/14/70 BCR-69)

WHEN THE RADIO IS ON Paul Shaffer—Capitol 44413
[Kevin Calhoun/Matt Noble] [BMI] (8/12/89 BC-77)

WHEN THE RAIN BEGINS TO FALL Jermaine Jackson And Pia Zadora—Curb/MCA 52521
[Michael Bradley/Peggy March/Steve Wittmack] [BMI] (2/2/85 BC-48)

WHEN THE RAIN COMES DOWN Andy Taylor—MCA 52946
[Stephen Jones/Andy Taylor] [ASC] (10/18/86 BC-58)

***SAINTS ROCK 'N ROLL** Bill Haley And His Comets—Decca 29870*
[Traditional] [NA] (3/30/56 BCR-20)

***MARCHING SAINTS** Harry Belafonte—RCA Victor 47-7176*
[Traditional] [NA] (3/22/58 CR-57)

***WHEN THE SAINTS GO MARCHING IN** Fats Domino—Imperial 5569*
[Traditional] [NA] (2/14/59 BCR-40)

***REVIVAL** (Based on When The Saints...) Johnny And The Hurricanes—Big Top 3051*
[Traditional] [BMI] (8/29/60 B-97) [I]

WHEN THE SHIP COMES IN Peter, Paul & Mary—Warner Bros. 5625
[Bob Dylan] [SE] (5/8/65 BCR-74)

WHEN THE SHIP HIT THE SAND "Little" Jimmy Dickens—Columbia 43514
[Larry Kingston] [BMI] (2/12/66 C-83)

WHEN THE SNOW IS ON THE ROSES Ed Ames—RCA Victor 47-9319
[Larry Kusik/James Last/Eddie Snyder] [ASC] (9/30/67 BCR-69) [FDE]

WHEN THE SWALLOWS COME BACK TO CAPISTRANO Pat Boone—Dot 15660
[Leon René] [ASC] (10/14/57 BCR-33)

WHEN THE TIDE IS HIGH Gogi Grant—Era 1019
[Buddy Bregman/Herbert Newman] [ASC] (9/1/56 BR-32)

***WHEN THE WHITE LILACS BLOOM AGAIN** Helmut Zacharias And His Magic Violins—*
Decca 30039 [Franz Doelle] [ASC] (8/25/56 BCtRt-8) [IM]

***WHEN THE WHITE LILACS BLOOM AGAIN** Billy Vaughn and His Orchestra—Dot 15491*
[Franz Doelle] [ASC] (8/25/56 BCtRt-8) [IM]

***WHEN THE WHITE LILACS BLOOM AGAIN** Florian Zabach—Mercury 70936*
[Franz Doelle] [ASC] (8/25/56 BCtRt-8) [IM]

***WHEN THE WHITE LILACS BLOOM AGAIN** LeRoy Holmes And His Orchestra—MGM 12317*
[Franz Doelle] [ASC] (8/25/56 BCtRt-8) [IM]

WHEN THE WHITE LILACS BLOOM AGAIN
Lawrence Welk And His Sparkling Strings—Coral 61701
[Franz Doelle] [ASC] (8/25/56 BCtRt-14) [IM]

WHEN THERE'S NO LOVE LEFT The New Seekers featuring Eve Graham—Elektra 45710
[Robert John Lovett/Brian Peacock] (TSW) [ASC] (12/12/70 R-58)

WHEN THERE'S NO YOU Engelbert Humperdinck—Parrot 40059
[Jackie Rae/Les Reed] [ASC] (3/6/71 BCR-36)

WHEN THINGS GO WRONG Robin Lane & The Chartbusters—Warner Bros. 49246
[Joanne Cipolla/Robin Lane] [ASC] (6/28/80 BCR-83)

WHEN TOMORROW COMES Carla Thomas—Stax 214
[Isaac Hayes/David Porter] [BMI] (5/6/67 B-99)

WHEN WE COME OF AGE Joni James—MGM 11865
[Nick Acquaviva/Norman Gimbel] [ASC] (8/21/54 CR-19)

***WHEN WE GET MARRIED** The Dreamlovers—Heritage 102*
[Donald Hogan] [BMI] (7/31/61 BCR-10)

***WHEN WE GET MARRIED** The Intruders—Gamble 4004*
[Donald Hogan] [BMI] (6/20/70 BCR-39)

***WHEN WE GET MARRIED** Larry Graham—Warner Bros. 49581*
[Donald Hogan] [BMI] (10/25/80 BR-76)

WHEN WE GET MARRIED 1910 Fruitgum Co.—Buddah 146
[Ritchie Cordell/J.J. Woods] [BMI] (11/29/69 CR-74)

WHEN WE KISS Bardeux—Enigma 75018
[Stacy Smith/Jon St. James] [BMI] (4/9/88 BC-36)

WHEN WE MAKE LOVE Alabama—RCA 13763
[Troy Seals/Mentor Williams] [ASC] (5/19/84 B-72)

WHEN WE WAS FAB George Harrison—Dark Horse 28131
[George Harrison/Jeff Lynne] [ASC] (2/6/88 BC-23)

WHEN WILL I BE FAMOUS Bros—Epic 07905
[Nicky Graham/Tom Watkins] [ASC] (6/25/88 B-83)

***WHEN WILL I BE LOVED** The Everly Brothers—Cadence 1380*
[Phil Everly] [BMI] (5/30/60 BCR-8)

***WHEN WILL I BE LOVED** Linda Ronstadt—Capitol 4050*
[Phil Everly] (TSW) [BMI] (7/26/75 BCR-1)

WHEN WILL I KNOW George Hamilton IV—ABC-Paramount 9946
[Billy Mure/Dick Wolf] [BMI] (8/11/58 BR-52)

WHEN WILL I SEE YOU AGAIN The Three Degrees—Philadelphia Int'l 3550
[Kenneth Gamble/Leon Huff] [BMI] (9/21/74 BCR-1)

WHEN WILL I SEE YOU SMILE AGAIN? Bell Biv DeVoe—MCA 53976
[Timmy Gatling/Alton Stewart] [ASC] (1/19/91 B-63)

WHEN YOU CLOSE YOUR EYES Night Ranger—Camel/MCA 52420
[Jack Blades/Alan Fitzgerald/Brad Gillis] [BMI] (7/14/84 BC-14)

WHEN YOU COME TO THE END OF THE DAY Red Foley—Decca 29667
[Gus Kahn/Frank C. Westphal] [ASC] (9/19/55 R-77)

***WHEN YOU DANCE** The Turbans—Herald 458 [Andrew Jones] [BMI] (11/7/55 BCRt-31)*

***WHEN YOU DANCE** The Laurie Sisters—Mercury 70751*
[Andrew Jones] [BMI] (12/9/55 Rt-36)

WHEN YOU DANCE *Jay & The Americans—United Artists 50510*
[Andrew Jones] [BMI] (3/29/69 BCR-36)

WHEN YOU DANCE I CAN REALLY LOVE Neil Young—Reprise 0992
[Neil Young] [BMI] (3/13/71 BCR-59)

WHEN YOU FEEL LOVE Bob McGilpin—Butterfly 1211
[John Hoke/Bob McGilpin] [BMI] (9/23/78 BC-91)

WHEN YOU GET RIGHT DOWN TO IT *The Delfonics—Philly Groove 163*
[Barry Mann] [BMI] (9/5/70 BCR-38)

WHEN YOU GET RIGHT DOWN TO IT *Ronnie Dyson—Columbia 45387*
[Barry Mann] [BMI] (7/3/71 BCR-81)

WHEN YOU GET RIGHT DOWN TO IT *Barry Mann—New Design 1005*
[Barry Mann] [BMI] (1/15/72 R-90)

WHEN YOU LOSE THE ONE YOU LOVE
David Whitfield with Mantovani And His Orchestra—London 1617
[James S. Hancock/Don Pelosi/Dave Silver] [ASC] (1/28/56 BCR-41)

WHEN YOU LOVED ME Brenda Lee—Decca 31654
[Joy Byers Johnston/Bob Tubert] [ASC] (8/8/64 BCR-36)

WHEN YOU SAY LOVE Sonny & Cher—Kapp 2176
[Jerry Foster/Steve Karmen*/Bill Rice] [ASC] (7/8/72 BCR-30)

WHEN YOU TOOK YOUR LOVE (FROM ME) Jimmy Dorsey Orchestra—Fraternity 797
[Harry Carlson/Lew Douglas/Erwin King] [ASC] (2/3/58 R-55)

WHEN YOU WAKE UP Cash McCall—Thomas 307
[Morris Dollison/Monk Higgins] [BMI] (7/16/66 C-86)

WHEN YOU WAKE UP TOMORROW Candi Staton—Warner Bros. 8821
[Patrick Adams/Wayne Garfield/Ken Morris/Candi Staton] [ASC] (7/28/79 R-83)

WHEN YOU WALK IN THE ROOM *Jackie deShannon—Liberty 55645*
[Jackie DeShannon] [BMI] (1/4/64 BCR-81)

WHEN YOU WALK IN THE ROOM *The Searchers—Kapp 618*
[Jackie DeShannon] [BMI] (10/10/64 BCR-29)

WHEN YOU WALK IN THE ROOM *Tight Fit—Arista 0638*
[Jackie DeShannon] (Med) [BMI] (10/10/81 B-89)

WHEN YOU WALK IN THE ROOM *Paul Carrack—Chrysalis 43252*
[Jackie DeShannon] [BMI] (6/11/88 BC-90)

WHEN YOU WERE MINE Mitch Ryder—Riva 213 [Prince] [ASC] (7/16/83 B-87)

WHEN YOU WISH UPON A STAR *Joni James—MGM 11960*
[Leigh Harline/Ned Washington] [ASC] (4/30/55 CRt-48)

WHEN YOU WISH UPON A STAR *Rosemary Clooney & Harry James—Columbia 40496*
[Leigh Harline/Ned Washington] [ASC] (5/23/55 Rt-76)

WHEN YOU WISH UPON A STAR *Jack Pleis and His Orchestra and Chorus—Decca 29457*
[Leigh Harline/Ned Washington] [ASC] (5/23/55 Rt-77)

WHEN YOU WISH UPON A STAR *Cliff Edwards—Decca 29487*
[Leigh Harline/Ned Washington] [ASC] (5/23/55 Rt-77)

WHEN YOU WISH UPON A STAR *Dion And The Belmonts—Laurie 3052*
[Leigh Harline/Ned Washington] [ASC] (4/23/60 BCR-25)

WHEN YOUR HEART IS WEAK Cock Robin—Columbia 04875
[Peter Kingsbery] [BMI] (6/15/85 BC-33)

—WHEN YOUR HEART'S ON FIRE see: SMOKE GETS IN YOUR EYES

WHEN YOUR OLD WEDDING RING WAS NEW Bruce Hayes with Mary Mayo—Dwain 812
[Bert Douglas/Charles McCarthy/Joe Solieri] (EP) [ASC] (2/15/60 R-63)

WHEN YOU'RE GONE Brenda & The Tabulations—Dionn 504
[Bob Finiz/Leonard Pakula*/Palmer C. Rakes*] [BMI] (11/4/67 BCR-58)

WHEN YOU'RE HOT, YOU'RE HOT Jerry Reed—RCA Victor 47-9976
[Jerry Reed] [BMI] (4/24/71 BCR-8)

WHEN YOU'RE IN LOVE WITH A BEAUTIFUL WOMAN Dr. Hook—Capitol 4705
[Even Stevens] [BMI] (4/14/79 BCR-4)

WHEN YOU'RE #1 Gene Chandler—20th Century 2411
[Gene Chandler/James A. Thompson Jr.] [BMI] (10/6/79 B-99)

WHEN YOU'RE SMILING *Dick Hyman Trio—MGM 12258*
[Larry Shay] [ASC] (7/13/56 R-75) [I]

WHEN YOU'RE SMILING *Bobby Freeman—Josie 855*
[Mark Fisher/Joe Goodwin/Larry Shay] [ASC] (2/7/59 C-87)

WHEN YOU'RE YOUNG AND IN LOVE *Ruby And The Romantics—Kapp 615*
[Van McCoy] [BMI] (10/3/64 BCR-48)

WHEN YOU'RE YOUNG AND IN LOVE *The Marvelettes—Tamla 54150*
[Van McCoy] [BMI] (4/22/67 BCR-23)

WHEN YOU'RE YOUNG AND IN LOVE *The Choice Four—RCA Victor 10342*
[Van McCoy] [BMI] (8/30/75 B-91)

WHEN YOU'RE YOUNG AND IN LOVE *Ralph Carter—Mercury 73695*
[Van McCoy] [BMI] (9/6/75 B-94)

WHENEVER A TEENAGER CRIES Reparata And The Delrons—World Artists 1036
[Ernie Maresca] [BMI] (12/26/64 BCR-35)

WHENEVER HE HOLDS YOU *Bobby Goldsboro—United Artists 710*
[Bobby Goldsboro] [BMI] (4/11/64 BCR-39)

WHENEVER SHE HOLDS YOU *Patty Duke—United Artists 978*
[Bobby Goldsboro] [BMI] (2/19/66 BCR-63)

WHENEVER I CALL YOU "FRIEND" Kenny Loggins—Columbia 10794
[Kenny Loggins/Melissa Manchester] [ASC] (7/29/78 BCR-5)

WHENEVER I'M AWAY FROM YOU John Travolta—Midland Int'l 10780
[Gary Benson/Dave Mindel] [ASC] (10/9/76 BCR-38)

WHENEVER YOU CLOSE YOUR EYES Tommy Page—Sire 19323
[Michael Bolton/Diane Warren] [BMI] (6/1/91 C-89)

WHERE The Platters—Mercury 71502
[Buck Ram/Pyotr Ilyich Tchaikovsky] [BMI] (8/31/59 BCR-38)

WHERE AM I GOING? Barbra Streisand—Columbia 43518
[Cy Coleman/Dorothy Fields] [ASC] (2/12/66 BCR-94)

WHERE ARE ALL MY FRIENDS
Harold Melvin And The Blue Notes—Philadelphia Int'l 3552
[Victor Carstarphen/Gene McFadden/John Whitehead] [BMI] (11/9/74 BCR-67)

WHERE ARE WE GOING Bobby Bloom—Roulette 7095
[Mickey Lee Lane/John Linde] [BMI] (12/26/70 BCR-70)

WHERE ARE YOU Frankie Avalon—Chancellor 1052
[Peter DeAngelis/Bob Marcucci] [ASC] (6/13/60 BCR-22)

WHERE ARE YOU *Dinah Washington—Roulette 4424*
[Harold Adamson/Jimmy McHugh] [ASC] (4/23/62 BCR-27)

WHERE ARE YOU *The Duprees featuring Joey Vann—Coed 591*
[Harold Adamson/Jimmy McHugh] [ASC] (4/11/64 CR-94)

WHERE ARE YOU Cat Stevens—Deram 85079 [Cat Stevens] [ASC] (1/29/72 C-98)

WHERE ARE YOU GOING Jerry Butler—Mercury 73101
[Danny Meehan/Bobby Scott] [ASC] (8/15/70 BCR-74)

WHERE ARE YOU GOING TO MY LOVE The Brotherhood Of Man—Deram 85065
[Bill Davidson/Mike Davies/John Goodison/Tony Hiller] [BMI] (8/8/70 BCR-54)

WHERE ARE YOU NOW? *Synch—Columbia 05788*
[Richard Congdon/Jimmy Harnen] [ASC] (3/1/86 B-77)

WHERE ARE YOU NOW? *Jimmy Harnen w/Synch—WTG 31-68625*
[Richard Congdon/Jimmy Harnen] [ASC] (2/25/89 BC-10)

WHERE CAN YOU BE *Jerry Martin—Coral 61274*
[John M. Anthony/Milt Gabler/Pinky Herman] [ASC] (10/4/54 R-PRE)

WHERE CAN YOU BE *Don Cherry—Decca 29322*
[John M. Anthony/Milt Gabler/Pinky Herman] [ASC] (11/15/54 Rt-65)

WHERE CAN YOU GO (FOR A BROKEN HEART) George Maharis—Epic 9600
[Ricky Layne] [BMI] (6/22/63 CR-89)

WHERE DID ALL THE GOOD TIMES GO Dennis Yost And The Classics IV—Liberty 56200
[Buddy Buie/J.R. Cobb] [BMI] (10/24/70 BCR-67)

WHERE DID I GO WRONG Dee Dee Sharp—Cameo 296
[Dave Appell/Kal Mann] [ASC] (2/1/64 BCR-82)

WHERE DID I MAKE MY MISTAKE Clyde McPhatter—MGM 12816
[Clint Ballard Jr./Fred Tobias] [ASC] (7/27/59 R-89)

WHERE DID OUR LOVE GO *The Supremes—Motown 1060*
[Lamont Dozier/Brian Holland/Eddie Holland] [BMI] (7/11/64 BCR-1)

WHERE DID OUR LOVE GO *Donnie Elbert—All Platinum 2330*
[Lamont Dozier/Brian Holland/Eddie Holland] [BMI] (10/9/71 BCR-15)

WHERE DID OUR LOVE GO *The J. Geils Band—Atlantic 3320*
[Lamont Dozier/Brian Holland/Eddie Holland] [BMI] (3/27/76 BCR-62)

WHERE DID THE GOOD TIMES GO Dick And Deedee—Warner Bros. 5383
[Dick Gosting*/Deedee Sperling] [BMI] (10/5/63 B-93)

WHERE DID THEY GO, LORD Elvis Presley—RCA Victor 47-9980
[Dallas Frazier/A.L. "Doodle" Owens] (TSW) [BMI] (3/13/71 BCR-25)

WHERE DID WE GO WRONG Frankie Valli Introducing Chris Forde—MCA/Curb 41253
[Richard Kerr/Marty Panzer] [BMI] (7/19/80 B-90)

WHERE DID WE GO WRONG L.T.D.—A&M 2250
[Sam Dees/Jeffrey Osborne] [BMI] (9/27/80 R-76)

WHERE DID YOUR HEART GO? Wham!—Columbia 06294
[David Was/Don Was] [ASC] (10/11/86 BC-49)

WHERE DO BROKEN HEARTS GO Whitney Houston—Arista 1-9674
[Charles Henry Jackson Jr./Frank Wildhorn] [ASC] (2/27/88 BC-1)

—WHERE DO I BEGIN see: THEME FROM LOVE STORY

WHERE DO I GO *Carla Thomas—Stax 0011*
[Galt MacDermot/James Rado/Gerome Ragni] [ASC] (10/19/68 BR-75)

WHERE DO I GO *The Happenings—Jubilee 5666*
[Galt MacDermot/James Rado/Gerome Ragni] (Med) [ASC] (6/28/69 BCR-29)

WHERE DO THE CHILDREN GO Hooters—Columbia 05854
[Eric Bazilian/Rob Hyman] [ASC] (4/5/86 BC-37)

WHERE DO YOU COME FROM Elvis Presley With The Jordanaires—RCA Victor 47-8100
[Ruth Batchelor/Bob Roberts] [ASC] (10/27/62 B-99)

WHERE DO YOU GO Cher—Imperial 66136 [Sonny Bono] [BMI] (10/16/65 BCR-25)

WHERE DO YOU GO TO (MY LOVELY) Peter Sarstedt—World Pacific 77911
[Peter Sarstedt] [BMI] (3/22/69 BCR-61)

WHERE DOES LOVE GO Freddie Scott—Colpix 724
[Gerry Goffin/Carole King] [BMI] (3/14/64 BCR-82)

WHERE DOES MY HEART BEAT NOW Celine Dion—Epic 73536
[Robert White Johnson/Taylor Rhodes] [ASC] (12/8/90 BC-4)

WHERE DOES THE LOVIN' GO David Gates—Elektra 46588
[David Gates] [ASC] (2/9/80 BCR-46)

—WHERE EVERYBODY KNOWS YOUR NAME see: THEME FROM THE TV SHOW CHEERS

WHERE EVIL GROWS The Poppy Family Vocal: Susan And Terry Jacks—London 148
[Terry Jacks] [BMI] (7/31/71 BCR-45)

WHERE HAVE ALL OUR HEROES GONE Bill Anderson—Decca 32744
[Bill Anderson/Bob Talbert] [BMI] (11/21/70 B-93)

WHERE HAVE ALL THE FLOWERS GONE *The Kingston Trio—Capitol 4671 [Pete Seeger] [BMI] (1/8/62 BCR-19)*

WHERE HAVE ALL THE FLOWERS GONE *Johnny Rivers—Imperial 66133 [Pete Seeger] [BMI] (10/2/65 BCR-26)*

WHERE HAVE THEY GONE Jimmie Beaumont And The Skyliners—Capitol 3979 [Ken Hirsch/Doc Pomus] [BMI] (3/1/75 BR-96)

WHERE HAVE YOU BEEN (ALL MY LIFE) Arthur Alexander—Dot 16357 [Barry Mann/Cynthia Weil] [BMI] (5/26/62 BCR-58)

WHERE HAVE YOU BEEN ALL MY LIFE Fotomaker—Atlantic 3471 [James Cawley] [BMI] (4/22/78 BCR-81)

WHERE I FELL IN LOVE The Capris—Old Town 1099 [John Cassese/Mike Mincieli/Vinny Naccarato/Frank Reina/Nick Santamaria] [BMI] (3/27/61 BCR-74)

WHERE IS JOHNNY NOW The Sapphires—Swan 4143 [Roland Smith] [BMI] (7/13/63 C-100)

WHERE IS MY MIND Vanilla Fudge—Atco 6554 [Carmine Appice*/Tim Bogert*/Vince Martell*/Mark Stein*] [BMI] (2/3/68 BCR-73)

—WHERE IS SANTA CLAUS see: DONDE ESTA SANTA CLAUS

WHERE IS THAT SOMEONE FOR ME Joni James—MGM 12020 [Stella Unger/Victor Young] [ASC] (8/8/55 R-64)

WHERE IS THE LOVE Roberta Flack & Donny Hathaway—Atlantic 2879 [Ralph MacDonald/William Salter] [ASC] (6/3/72 BCR-5)

WHERE IS THE LOVE Betty Wright—Alston 3713 [Harry Wayne Casey/Willie Clarke/Rick Finch/Betty Wright] [BMI] (4/5/75 BC-73)

WHERE IS THE PARTY Helena Ferguson—Compass 7009 [Billy Frazier] [BMI] (11/4/67 BCR-79)

WHERE LOVE HAS GONE Jack Jones—Kapp 608 [Sammy Cahn/Jimmy Van Heusen] [ASC] (8/15/64 BCR-58)

WHERE OR WHEN *Dion And The Belmonts—Laurie 3044 [Lorenz Hart/Richard Rodgers] [ASC] (12/26/59 BCR-3)*

WHERE OR WHEN *The Lettermen—Capitol 5091 [Lorenz Hart/Richard Rodgers] [ASC] (12/28/63 B-98)*

WHERE PEACEFUL WATERS FLOW Gladys Knight & The Pips—Buddah 363 [Jim Weatherly] [ASC] (6/9/73 BCR-23)

WHERE THE BLUE OF THE NIGHT Tommy Mara—Felsted 8532 [Fred Ahlert/Bing Crosby/Roy Turk] [ASC] (8/18/58 BCR-51)

WHERE THE BOYS ARE Connie Francis—MGM 12971 [Howard Greenfield/Neil Sedaka] [BMI] (1/16/61 BCR-2)

WHERE THE STREETS HAVE NO NAME *U2—Island 99408 [Adam Clayton/Dave Evans/Paul Hewson/Larry Mullen] [ASC] (9/12/87 BC-13)*

WHERE THE STREETS HAVE NO NAME *Pet Shop Boys—EMI 50351 [Adam Clayton/Dave Evans/Paul Hewson/Larry Mullen] (Med) [ASC] (5/25/91 BC-72)*

WHERE THE SUN HAS NEVER SHONE Jonathan King—Parrot 9804 [Jonathan King] [BMI] (12/25/65 BCR-71)

WHERE THERE'S A WILL THERE'S A WAY Delaney & Bonnie—Atco 6883 [Bonnie Bramlett/Delaney Bramlett*/Bobby Whitlock] [BMI] (4/29/72 B-99)

WHERE THERE'S LIFE George Cates And His Orchestra And Chorus—Coral 61683 [George Cates/Russ David] [ASC] (9/15/56 B-75) [I]

WHERE THERE'S SMOKE THERE'S FIRE The Grass Roots—Dunhill 4345 [Harvey Price/Dan Walsh] [ASC] (6/30/73 CR-88)

WHERE WERE YOU (ON OUR WEDDING DAY)? Lloyd Price—ABC-Paramount 9997 [Harold Logan/John Patton/Lloyd Price] [BMI] (2/16/59 BCR-15)

WHERE WERE YOU WHEN I NEEDED YOU Jerry Vale—Columbia 43337 [Marvin Moore/Bernie Wayne] [BMI] (8/7/65 BCR-92)

WHERE WERE YOU WHEN I NEEDED YOU The Grass Roots—Dunhill 4029 [Steve Barri/P.F. Sloan] [ASC] (6/18/66 BCR-26)

—WHERE WERE YOU WHEN I NEEDED YOU see: SUPERWOMAN

WHERE WERE YOU WHEN I WAS FALLING IN LOVE Lobo—MCA/Curb 41065 [Steve Jobe/Sam Lorber/Jeff Silbar] [BMI] (7/28/79 BCR-16)

WHERE WILL THE DIMPLE BE Rosemary Clooney—Columbia 40434 [Al Hoffman/Bob Merrill] [ASC] (3/7/55 CR-21)

WHERE WILL THE WORDS COME FROM Gary Lewis And The Playboys—Liberty 55933 [Sonny Curtis/Glen Hardin] [BMI] (12/10/66 BCR-20)

WHERE WILL YOUR HEART TAKE YOU Buckeye—Polydor 14578 [Ronn Price] [BMI] (8/18/79 BCR-63)

WHERE YOU LEAD *Barbra Streisand—Columbia 45414 [Carole King/Toni Stern] [ASC] (7/24/71 BCR-33)*

WHERE YOU LEAD *Barbra Streisand—Columbia 45626 [Carole King/Toni Stern] (Med) [ASC] (6/24/72 BCR-30)*

WHERE'S THE PLAYGROUND SUSIE Glen Campbell—Capitol 2494 [Jimmy Webb] [ASC] (5/3/69 BCR-13)

WHERE'S YOUR ANGEL? Lani Hall—A&M 2305 [Greg Phillinganes/Allee Willis] [ASC] (3/14/81 BC-88)

WHEREVER I LAY MY HAT (THAT'S MY HOME) Paul Young—Columbia 04071 [Marvin Gaye/Barrett Strong/Norman Whitfield] [ASC] (10/1/83 BC-70)

WHEREVER WOULD I BE Cheap Trick—Epic 73580 [Diane Warren] [ASC] (10/27/90 BC-44)

WHICH WAY YOU GOIN' BILLY? The Poppy Family (Featuring Susan Jacks)—London 129 [Terry Jacks] [BMI] (3/14/70 BCR-2)

WHIFFENPOOF SONG Bob Crewe—Warwick 519 [Tod Galloway/Meade Minnigerode/George Pomeroy] [ASC] (12/21/59 BR-47)

WHILE I'M ALONE Maze Featuring Frankie Beverly—Capitol 4392 [Frankie Beverly] [BMI] (5/14/77 BCR-71)

WHILE MY GUITAR GENTLY WEEPS Stars On 45—Radio 3830 [George Harrison] (Med) [ASC] (7/11/81 BC-63)

WHILE YOU SEE A CHANCE Steve Winwood—Island 49656 [Will Jennings/Steve Winwood] [BMI] (2/7/81 BCR-7)

WHILE YOU'RE OUT LOOKING FOR SUGAR? The Honey Cone—Hot Wax 6901 [Lamont Dozier/Ronald Dunbar/Brian Holland/Eddie Holland] [BMI] (6/21/69 BCR-62)

WHIP APPEAL Babyface—Solar 74007 [Kenneth Edmonds/Perri Arlette Reid] [BMI] (2/24/90 BC-5)

WHIP IT Devo—Warner Bros. 49550 [Jerry Casale/Mark Mothersbaugh] [BMI] (8/30/80 BCR-13)

WHIP IT ON ME Jessie Hill—Minit 611 [Jessie Hill] [BMI] (7/25/60 BC-91)

WHIPPED CREAM *Herb Alpert's Tijuana Brass—A&M 760 [Allen Toussaint] [BMI] (2/20/65 BCRt-68) [I]*

WHIPPED CREAM *The Stokes—Alon 1197 [Allen Toussaint] [BMI] (3/6/65 Rt-87) [I]*

WHIPPOORWILL Keely Smith—Capitol 3975 [Robert Mitchum/Don Raye] [ASC] (6/30/58 R-77)

WHIRLY GIRL Oxo—Geffen 29765 [Ish Ledesma] [BMI] (2/19/83 BC-28)

WHISPER IN THE DARK Dionne Warwick—Arista 1-9460 [Edgar Bronfman/Bruce Roberts] [ASC] (3/15/86 BC-72)

WHISPER TO A SCREAM (BIRDS FLY) Icicle Works—Arista 1-9155 [Robert Ian McNabb] [BMI] (4/21/84 BC-34)

WHISPERING *Paul Whiteman & The New Ambassador Hotel Orchestra—Coral 61228 [Richard Coburn/Vincent Rose/John Schonberger] [ASC] (8/28/54 CR-24) [IM]*

WHISPERING *Nino Tempo & April Stevens—Atco 6281 [Richard Coburn/Vincent Rose/John Schonberger] [ASC] (12/21/63 BCRt-9)*

WHISPERING *The Bachelors—London 9623 [Richard Coburn/Vincent Rose/John Schonberger] [ASC] (12/21/63 Rt-40)*

WHISPERING *Dr. Buzzard's Original "Savannah" Band—RCA 10827 [Richard Coburn/Vincent Rose/John Schonberger] (Med) [ASC] (11/6/76 BCR-23) [IM]*

WHISPERING BELLS The Dell-Vikings—Dot 15592 [Clarence Quick] [BMI] (6/29/57 BCR-9)

WHISPERING HEART Sherry Parsons—Jubilee 5265 [Al Lewis/Larry Stock] [ASC] (12/29/56 R-75)

WHISPERS Corina—Cutting/Atco 98709 [Peter Zizzo] [BMI] (9/28/91 BC-51)

WHISPERS (GETTIN' LOUDER) Jackie Wilson—Brunswick 55300 [Barbara Acklin/David Scott] [BMI] (10/8/66 BCR-10)

THE WHISTLER Jethro Tull—Chrysalis 2135 [Ian Anderson] [ASC] (4/9/77 BCR-52)

—WHISTLIN WILLIE see: PHONOGRAPH SONG

WHISTLING ORGAN Dave "Baby" Cortez—Clock 1012 [David Clowney/Jim Kriegsmann/Ken Wood] [BMI] (6/8/59 BCR-29) [I]

A WHISTLING TUNE Elvis Presley with the Jordanaires—RCA Victor EPA-4371 [Hal David/Sherman Edwards] (EP) [ASC] (9/8/62 CR-26)

WHITE BIRD David Laflamme—Amherst 717 [David Laflamme/Linda Laflamme] [ASC] (12/11/76 BC-85)

WHITE BUCKS AND SADDLE SHOES Bobby Pedrick, Jr.—Big Top 3004 [Doc Pomus/Mort Shuman] [BMI] (11/1/58 BC-74)

WHITE CHRISTMAS *Bing Crosby—Decca 23778 [Irving Berlin] [ASC] (11/22/54 BRt-11)*

WHITE CHRISTMAS *The Mulcays—Cardinal 1024 [Irving Berlin] [ASC] (11/22/54 Rt-PRE) [IWM]*

WHITE CHRISTMAS (FINALE) *Bing Crosby, Danny Kaye, Peggy Lee & Trudy Stevens—Decca 29342 [Irving Berlin] [ASC] (11/22/54 Rt-PRE)*

WHITE CHRISTMAS *Rosemary Clooney—Columbia 40370 [Irving Berlin] [ASC] (12/13/54 Rt-PRE)*

WHITE CHRISTMAS *Bing Crosby—Decca 23778 [Irving Berlin] [ASC] (12/16/55 BRt-18)*

WHITE CHRISTMAS *Les Paul & Mary Ford—Capitol 2617 [Irving Berlin] [ASC] (12/16/55 Rt-42)*

WHITE CHRISTMAS *The Drifters—Atlantic E701048 [Irving Berlin] [ASC] (12/31/55 B-80)*

WHITE CHRISTMAS *Bing Crosby—Decca 23778 [Irving Berlin] [ASC] (12/15/56 BRt-26)*

WHITE CHRISTMAS *Al Hibbler—Decca 30127 [Irving Berlin] [ASC] (12/15/56 Rt-33)*

WHITE CHRISTMAS *Joni James—MGM 12368 [Irving Berlin] [ASC] (12/15/56 Rt-33)*

WHITE CHRISTMAS *Bing Crosby—Decca 23778 [Irving Berlin] [ASC] (12/16/57 BR-23)*

WHITE CHRISTMAS *Elvis Presley—RCA Victor LOC-1035 [Irving Berlin] (EP) [ASC] (12/30/57 R-49)*

WHITE CHRISTMAS *Bing Crosby—Decca 23778 [Irving Berlin] [ASC] (12/1/58 BR-27)*

WHITE CHRISTMAS *Bing Crosby—Decca 23778 [Irving Berlin] [ASC] (12/28/59 B-59)*

WHITE CHRISTMAS *Bing Crosby—Decca 23778 [Irving Berlin] [ASC] (12/12/60 BR-20)*

WHITE CHRISTMAS *The Drifters Featuring Clyde McPhatter And Bill Pinckney—Atlantic 1048 [Irving Berlin] [ASC] (12/19/60 B-96)*

WHITE CHRISTMAS *Bing Crosby—Decca 23778 [Irving Berlin] [ASC] (12/11/61 BCR-12)*

WHITE CHRISTMAS *Bing Crosby—Decca 23778 [Irving Berlin] [ASC] (12/15/62 BCR-34)*

WHITE CHRISTMAS *The Drifters Featuring Clyde McPhatter And Bill Pinckney—Atlantic 1048 [Irving Berlin] [ASC] (12/22/62 B-88)*

WHITE CHRISTMAS *Andy Williams—Columbia 42894*
[Irving Berlin] [ASC] (12/21/63 C-81)

THE WHITE CLIFFS OF DOVER The Righteous Brothers—Philles 132
[Nat Burton/Walter Kent] [NA] (10/1/66 CR-87)

WHITE HORSE Laid Back—Sire 29346 [John Guldberg/Tim Stahl] [ASC] (2/25/84 BC-22)

WHITE HOT Red Rider—Capitol 4845 [Tom Cochrane/Ken Greer] [ASC] (4/5/80 BCR-48)

WHITE HOUSES Eric Burdon and The Animals—MGM 14013
[Eric Burdon] [BMI] (11/23/68 BCR-53)

THE WHITE KNIGHT Cledus Maggard and The Citizen's Band—Mercury 73751
[Jay Huguely] [BMI] (12/27/75 BCR-19)

WHITE LIES Grin—Spindizzy 4005 [Nils Lofgren] [ASC] (2/5/72 BCR-69)

WHITE LIES, BLUE EYES Bullet—Big Tree 123
[Bobby Flax/Lanny Lambert] [BMI] (10/23/71 BCR-22)

WHITE LIGHTNING George Jones—Mercury 71406
[J.P. Richardson] [BMI] (5/4/59 BCR-73)

WHITE ON WHITE Danny Williams—United Artists 685
[Lor Crane/Bernice Ross] [BMI] (3/7/64 BCR-9)

WHITE RABBIT Jefferson Airplane—RCA Victor 47-9248
[Grace Slick] [BMI] (6/24/67 BCR-6)

WHITE RHYTHM AND BLUES J.D. Souther—Columbia 11196
[J.D. Souther] [BMI] (3/8/80 R-93)

WHITE ROOM Cream—Atco 6617
[Peter Ronald Brown/Jack Bruce] [BMI] (9/28/68 BCR-5)

THE WHITE ROSE OF ATHENS *David Carroll And His Orchestra—Mercury 71917*
[Manos Hadjidakis] [BMI] (2/24/62 BCtRt-40) [IM]

THE WHITE ROSE OF ATHENS *Nana Mouskouri—Riverside 4513*
[Archie Bleyer/Hans Bradtke/Manos Hadjidakis/Norman Newell] [BMI]
(2/26/62 CtRt-40) [FET]

THE WHITE ROSE OF ATHENS *The Chordettes—Cadence 1417*
[Archie Bleyer/Hans Bradtke/Manos Hadjidakis/Norman Newell] [BMI]
(3/12/62 Rt-40) [FET]

WHITE SILVER SANDS *Don Rondo—Jubilee 5288*
[Charles G. Matthews/Gladys Reinhardt] [BMI] (6/29/57 BCtRt-2)*

WHITE SILVER SANDS *Dave Gardner—OJ 1002*
[Charles G. Matthews/Gladys Reinhardt] [BMI] (6/29/57 BCtRt-2)*

WHITE SILVER SANDS *Owen Bradley Quintet—Decca 30363*
[Charles G. Matthews/Gladys Reinhardt] [BMI] (6/29/57 BRt-2)*

WHITE SILVER SANDS *The Lennon Sisters—Brunswick 55013*
[Charles G. Matthews/Gladys Reinhardt] [BMI] (7/6/57 Rt-2)*

WHITE SILVER SANDS *Bill Black's Combo—Hi 2021*
[Charles G. Matthews/Gladys Reinhardt] [BMI] (2/22/60 BCR-4) [IWM]*

-TWISTIN'-WHITE SILVER SANDS *Bill Black's Combo—Hi 2052*
[Charles G. Matthews/Gladys Reinhardt] [BMI] (4/23/62 BCR-54) [IWM]*

A WHITE SPORT COAT (AND A PINK CARNATION) *Marty Robbins—Columbia 40864*
[Marty Robbins] [BMI] (3/30/57 BCRt-3)

A WHITE SPORT COAT (AND A PINK CARNATION) *Johnny Desmond—Coral 61835*
[Marty Robbins] [BMI] (5/11/57 BRt-4)

WHITE WEDDING Billy Idol—Chrysalis 2648 [Billy Idol] [ASC] (5/21/83 BC-36)

A WHITER SHADE OF PALE *Procol Harum—Deram 7507*
[Gary Brooker/Matthew Fisher/Keith Reid] [ASC] (6/17/67 BCR-3)*

A WHITER SHADE OF PALE *The Hesitations—Kapp 948*
[Gary Brooker/Matthew Fisher/Keith Reid] [ASC] (11/9/68 BCR-85)*

A WHITER SHADE OF PALE *Shorty Long—Soul 35064*
[Gary Brooker/Matthew Fisher/Keith Reid] [ASC] (9/20/69 C-100)*

A WHITER SHADE OF PALE *R.B. Greaves—Atco 6789*
[Gary Brooker/Matthew Fisher/Keith Reid] [ASC] (12/5/70 BCR-73)*

A WHITER SHADE OF PALE *Procol Harum—A&M 1389*
[Gary Brooker/Matthew Fisher/Keith Reid] [ASC] (11/18/72 CR-86)*

WHITER SHADE OF PALE *Hagar, Schon, Aaronson, Shrieve—Geffen 29280*
[Gary Brooker/Matthew Fisher/Keith Reid] [ASC] (5/19/84 B-94)*

WHITHER THOU GOEST Les Paul and Mary Ford—Capitol 2928
[Guy Singer] [ASC] (10/2/54 BCR-10)

WHO AM I Petula Clark—Warner Bros. 5863
[Tony Hatch/Jackie Trent] [BMI] (10/22/66 BCR-18)

WHO ARE THEY TO SAY The DeCastro Sisters—ABC-Paramount 9932
[Sammy Cahn/Gene DePaul] [ASC] (8/18/58 B-99)

WHO ARE WE Gogi Grant—Era 1008
[Jerry Livingston/Paul Francis Webster] [ASC] (2/4/56 BR-62)

WHO ARE YOU Stacey Cane—Jubilee 5500 [Ted Daryll/Chip Taylor] [BMI] (3/27/65 R-83)

WHO ARE YOU B.B. King—ABC 11433
[Dave Crawford/Horace Johnson] [ASC] (6/8/74 BCR-78)

WHO ARE YOU The Who—MCA 40948 [Pete Townshend] [GL] (8/26/78 BCR-9)

WHO CAN EXPLAIN Frankie Lymon and the Teenagers—Gee 1018
[Roy Alfred/Abner Silver] [ASC] (7/27/56 R-81)

WHO CAN I COUNT ON Patsy Cline—Decca 31317
[Sammy Masters] [BMI] (10/23/61 B-99)

WHO CAN I TURN TO (WHEN NOBODY NEEDS ME) *Tony Bennett—Columbia 43141*
[Leslie Bricusse/Anthony Newley] [BMI] (10/3/64 BCR-33)

WHO CAN I TURN TO *Dionne Warwick—Scepter 1298*
[Leslie Bricusse/Anthony Newley] [BMI] (2/27/65 BR-62)

WHO CAN IT BE NOW? Men At Work—Columbia 02888
[Colin James Hay] [BMI] (7/10/82 BC-1)

WHO CARES *Don Gibson—RCA Victor 47-7437 [Don Gibson] [BMI] (1/19/59 BCR-33)*

WHO CARES *Fats Domino—ABC-Paramount 10512*
[Don Gibson] [BMI] (12/28/63 BCR-55)

WHO COULD BE LOVIN' YOU Al Wilson—Soul City 759 [Willie Hutch] [BMI] (9/9/67 CR-91)

WHO COULDA' TOLD YOU (THEY LIED) Lloyd Price—ABC-Paramount 10139
[Harold Logan/Lloyd Price] [BMI] (9/24/60 CR-95)

WHO DO YA LOVE KC & The Sunshine Band—TK 1031
[Harry Wayne Casey/Rick Finch] [BMI] (12/16/78 BCR-64)

WHO DO YOU GIVE YOUR LOVE TO? Michael Morales—Wing 887 743
[Michael Morales] [ASC] (4/29/89 BC-14)

WHO DO YOU LOVE The Sapphires—Swan 4162
[Kenneth Gamble/Jerry J. Ross] [BMI] (1/11/64 BCR-22)

WHO DO YOU LOVE *The Woolies—Dunhill 4052 [Ellas McDaniel] [BMI] (2/25/67 BCR-82)*

WHO DO YOU LOVE *Quicksilver Messenger Service—Capitol 2557*
[Ellas McDaniel] [BMI] (8/9/69 BR-91)

WHO DO YOU LOVE *George Thorogood And The Destroyers—Rounder 4519*
[Ellas McDaniel] [BMI] (3/24/79 CR-71)

WHO DO YOU THINK YOU ARE The Shindogs—Viva 601
[Delaney Bramlett/Joey Cooper] [ASC] (7/30/66 BR-91)

WHO DO YOU THINK YOU ARE Bo Donaldson And The Heywoods—ABC 12006
[Des Dyer/Clive Scott] [ASC] (7/27/74 BCR-13)

WHO DO YOU THINK YOU'RE FOOLIN' Donna Summer—Geffen 49664
[Pete Bellotte/Sylvester Levay/Jerry Rix] [ASC] (2/21/81 BCR-38)

WHO-DUN-IT? Monk Higgins—St. Lawrence 1013 [Monk Higgins] [BMI] (7/30/66 C-69) [I]

WHO ELSE BUT YOU Frankie Avalon—Chancellor 1077
[Russell Faith/Clarence Kehner] [ASC] (5/15/61 BCR-76)

WHO FOUND WHO Jellybean—Chrysalis 43120 [Paul Gurvitz] [BMI] (7/11/87 BC-16)

WHO GETS THE GUY Dionne Warwick—Scepter 12309
[Burt Bacharach/Hal David] [ASC] (3/20/71 BCR-57)

WHO GETS YOUR LOVE Dusty Springfield—Dunhill 4341
[Dennis Lambert/Brian Potter] [BMI] (3/17/73 C-93)

WHO IS GONNA LOVE ME? Dionne Warwick—Scepter 12226
[Burt Bacharach/Hal David] [ASC] (8/24/68 BCR-22)

WHO IS HE AND WHAT IS HE TO YOU Creative Source—Sussex 509
[Stan McKenney/Bill Withers] [BMI] (3/16/74 BCR-60)

WHO LISTENS TO THE RADIO The Sports—Arista 0468
[Stephen Cummings/Andrew Pendlebury] [BMI] (10/6/79 BCR-45)

WHO LOVES YOU *Four Seasons—Warner/Curb 8122*
[Bob Gaudio/Judy Parker] [ASC] (8/23/75 BCR-3)

WHO LOVES YOU *Gidea Park—Profile 5003*
[Bob Gaudio/Judy Parker] (Med) [ASC] (12/26/81 BC-82)

WHO LOVES YOU BETTER - PART 1 The Isley Brothers—T-Neck 2260
[Ernie Isley/Marvin Isley/O'Kelly Isley/Ronald Isley/Rudolph Isley/Chris Jasper] [ASC]
(5/29/76 BCR-47)

WHO NEEDS IT Gene Pitney—Musicor 1036
[Len Beadle/Peter Callander] [BMI] (1/18/64 R-95)

WHO NEEDS YA Steppenwolf—Dunhill 4261
[Larry Byrom/John Kay] [BMI] (11/7/70 BCR-42)

WHO NEEDS YOU The Four Lads—Columbia 40811
[Robert Allen/Al Stillman] [ASC] (1/12/57 BCR-9)

WHO PUT THE BOMP (IN THE BOMP, BOMP, BOMP) Barry Mann—ABC-Paramount 10237
[Gerry Goffin/Barry Mann] [BMI] (7/31/61 BCR-5)

WHO SAID I WOULD Phil Collins—Atlantic 84881 [Phil Collins] [ASC] (1/26/91 BC-67)

WHO SAYS Device—Chrysalis 43063
[Mike Chapman/Holly Knight] [ASC] (9/27/86 BC-73)

WHO SHOT J.R.? Gary Burbank with Band McNally—Ovation 1150
[Gary Burbank/Ron Reed/Ed Vanover] [BMI] (6/14/80 BCR-67)

WHO SHOT SAM George Jones—Mercury 71464
[Darrell Edwards/Ray Jackson/George Jones] [BMI] (7/27/59 BC-83)

WHO STOLE THE KEESHKA? The Matys Bros.—Select 719
[Walter Dana/Walter Solek] [BMI] (1/12/63 BCR-47)

WHO WAS IT? Hurricane Smith—Capitol 3455
[Gilbert O'Sullivan] [ASC] (3/17/73 BCR-41)

WHO WEARS THESE SHOES? Elton John—Geffen 29189
[Elton John/Bernie Taupin] [BMI] (9/8/84 BC-16)

WHO WERE YOU THINKIN' OF The Doolittle Band—Columbia 11355
[Paul Gauvin/James W. Glaser/Cathie Pelletier] [BMI] (10/11/80 BCR-49)

WHO WILL ANSWER? Ed Ames—RCA Victor 47-9400
[Luis Eduardo Aute Gutiérrez/Sheila Davis] [ASC] (12/16/67 BCR-14)

WHO WILL THE NEXT FOOL BE Bobby Bland—Duke 347
[Charlie Rich] [BMI] (2/26/62 BR-76)

WHO WILL YOU RUN TO Heart—Capitol 44040 [Diane Warren] [ASC] (8/15/87 BC-6)

WHO YOU GONNA' LOVE Ray Charles And His Orchestra—ABC-Paramount 10081
[Ray Charles] [BMI] (2/20/60 C-92)

WHOA MABEL Bill Haley And His Comets—Decca 30741
[Catherine Cafra/Milt Gabler/Bill Haley/Arrett Keefer] [ASC] (9/15/58 R-94)

WHO'D SHE COO? Ohio Players—Mercury 73814
[William Beck/Leroy Bonner/Marshall Jones/Ralph Middlebrooks/Andrew Noland/Marvin Pierce/James Rodger Williams] [BMI] (6/26/76 BCR-18)

WHODUNIT Tavares—Capitol 4398
[Freddie Perren/Keni St. Lewis] [ASC] (3/19/77 BCR-16)

WHOEVER FINDS THIS, I LOVE YOU Mac Davis—Columbia 45117
[Mac Davis] [BMI] (5/2/70 BCR-53)

***WHOLE LOT OF SHAKIN' GOING ON** Jerry Lee Lewis—Sun 267*
[Dave Williams] [BMI] (6/24/57 BCR-3)

***WHOLE LOTTA SHAKIN' GOIN' ON** Chubby Checker—Parkway 813*
[Dave Williams] [BMI] (10/10/60 BCtRt-33)

***WHOLE LOT OF SHAKIN' GOING ON** Conway Twitty—MGM 12962*
[Dave Williams] [BMI] (10/17/60 BCtRt-33)

WHOLE LOTTA SHAKIN' GOIN' ON
Cat Mother And The All Night News Boys—Polydor 14002
[Dave Williams] (Med) [BMI] (6/21/69 BCR-12)

WHOLE LOT OF SHAKIN' IN MY HEART (SINCE I MET YOU) The Miracles—Tamla 54134
[Frank Edward Wilson] [BMI] (6/18/66 BCR-46)

***WHOLE LOTTA LOVE** Led Zeppelin—Atlantic 2690*
[John Bonham/John Paul Jones/Jimmy Page/Robert Plant] [ASC] (11/15/69 BCR-2)

***WHOLE LOTTA LOVE** King Curtis & The Kingpins—Atco 6779*
[John Bonham/John Paul Jones/Jimmy Page/Robert Plant] [ASC] (1/23/71 BCR-51) [IWM]

***WHOLE LOTTA LOVE** C.C.S.—Rak 4501*
[John Bonham/John Paul Jones/Jimmy Page/Robert Plant] [ASC] (1/30/71 BCR-45) [IWM]

***WHOLE LOTTA LOVE** The Wonder Band—Atco DK 4719*
[John Bonham/John Paul Jones/Jimmy Page/Robert Plant] [ASC] (3/3/79 B-87)

WHOLE LOTTA LOVING Fats Domino—Imperial 5553
[Dave Bartholomew/Fats Domino] [BMI] (11/3/58 BCR-6)

WHOLE LOTTA WOMAN Marvin Rainwater—MGM 12609
[Marvin Rainwater] [BMI] (2/3/58 BR-42)

WHOLE LOTTA WOMAN Arthur Conley—Atco 6529
[Arthur Conley] [BMI] (11/4/67 BCR-73)

THE WHOLE TOWN'S LAUGHING AT ME Teddy Pendergrass—Philadelphia Int'l 3633
[Sherman Marshall/Ted Wortham] [BMI] (9/10/77 R-93)

WHOLE WIDE WORLD A'me Lorain—RCA 9098
[Arnie Roman/Elliot Wolff] [ASC] (1/20/90 BC-9)

THE WHOLE WORLD IS A STAGE Fantastic Four—Ric-Tic 122
[Al Hamilton/Eugene Hamilton/Ed Wingate] [BMI] (3/25/67 BCR-45)

WHOLESALE LOVE Buddy Miles—Mercury 73205 [Otis Redding] [BMI] (5/15/71 BCR-62)

WHO'LL BE THE FOOL TONIGHT Larsen-Feiten Band—Warner Bros. 49282
[Buzz Feiten] [BMI] (7/26/80 BCR-22)

WHO'LL BE THE NEXT IN LINE The Kinks—Reprise 0366
[Ray Davies] [BMI] (8/7/65 BCR-34)

WHO'LL STOP THE RAIN Creedence Clearwater Revival—Fantasy 637
[John Fogerty] (TSW) [BMI] (1/31/70 BCR-2)

WHOLY HOLY Aretha Franklin—Atlantic 2901
[Renaldo Benson/Al Cleveland/Marvin Gaye] [BMI] (8/12/72 BCR-51)

WHO'S AFRAID OF VIRGINIA WOOLF? (PART 1) Jimmy Smith—Verve 10314
[Don Kirkpatrick/Kevin Knox] [ASC] (4/25/64 BR-72) [I]

WHO'S BEEN SLEEPING IN MY BED? Linda Scott—Congress 204
[Burt Bacharach/Hal David] [ASC] (1/25/64 BR-99)

WHO'S BEHIND THE DOOR? Zebra—Atlantic 89821
[Randolph Lynch Jackson] [ASC] (7/9/83 BC-61)

WHO'S CHEATING WHO? Little Milton—Checker 1113
[Billy Davis/Raynard Miner/Carl William Smith] [BMI] (6/12/65 BCR-38)

WHO'S CRYING NOW Journey—Columbia 02241
[Jonathan Cain/Steve Perry] [BMI] (7/18/81 BCR-3)

WHO'S GOING TO TAKE CARE OF ME Justine Washington—Sue 797
[Jeanette Washington] [BMI] (3/7/64 C-86)

WHO'S GONNA TAKE THE BLAME Smokey Robinson & The Miracles—Tamla 54194
[Nick Ashford/Valerie Simpson] [ASC] (5/16/70 BCR-46)

WHO'S GONNA TAKE THE WEIGHT (PART ONE) Kool & The Gang—De-Lite 538
[Robert Bell*/Ronald Bell*/George M. Brown/Robert Mickens*/Gene Redd Jr.*/Claydes Smith*/Woodrow Sparrow*/Dennis Thomas*/Richard Westfield] [BMI] (1/16/71 C-94) [IWM]

WHO'S GONNA TAKE YOU TO THE PROM The Gaylords—Mercury 70834
[Roy Alfred/Abner Silver] [ASC] (4/13/56 R-79)

WHO'S HOLDING DONNA NOW DeBarge—Gordy 1793
[David Foster/Randy Goodrum/Jay Graydon] [ASC] (6/1/85 BC-6)

WHO'S IN THE STRAWBERRY PATCH WITH SALLY Tony Orlando And Dawn—Bell 45,424
[L. Russell Brown/Irwin Levine] [BMI] (11/10/73 BCR-13)

WHO'S JOHNNY (SHORT CIRCUIT THEME) El DeBarge—Gordy 1842
[Ina Wolf/Peter F. Wolf] [BMI] (4/26/86 BC-3)

WHO'S LOVIN' YOU Brenda And The Tabulations—Dionn 501
[Smokey Robinson] [ASC] (5/20/67 BCR-64)

***WHO'S MAKING LOVE** Johnnie Taylor—Stax 0009*
[Homer Banks/Bettye Crutcher/Don Davis/Raymond Earl Jackson] [BMI] (10/19/68 BCR-4)

***WHO'S MAKING LOVE** Young-Holt Unlimited—Brunswick 55400*
[Homer Banks/Bettye Crutcher/Don Davis/Raymond Earl Jackson] [BMI] (2/15/69 BCR-46) [IWM]

***WHO'S MAKING LOVE** Blues Brothers—Atlantic 3785*
[Homer Banks/Bettye Crutcher/Don Davis/Raymond Earl Jackson] [BMI] (12/20/80 BCR-39)

***WHO'S SORRY NOW** Connie Francis—MGM 12588*
[Bert Kalmar/Harry Ruby/Ted Snyder] [ASC] (2/3/58 BCR-2)

***WHO'S SORRY NOW** Marie Osmond—MGM 14786*
[Bert Kalmar/Harry Ruby/Ted Snyder] [ASC] (3/1/75 BCR-39)

WHO'S THAT GIRL? Eurythmics—RCA 13800
[Annie Lennox/David A. Stewart] [ASC] (5/5/84 BC-21)

WHO'S THAT GIRL Madonna—Sire 28341
[Madonna L. Ciccone/Patrick Raymond Leonard] [BMI] (7/11/87 BC-1)

WHO'S THAT KNOCKING Genies—Shad 5002
[Claude Johnson/Fred O. Jones] [BMI] (3/7/59 BCR-33)

WHO'S YOUR BABY? The Archies—Kirshner 5003
[Jeff Barry/Andy Kim] [BMI] (2/28/70 BCR-25)

WHO'S ZOOMIN' WHO Aretha Franklin—Arista 1-9410
[Aretha Franklin/Preston Glass/Narada Michael Walden] [BMI] (9/28/85 BC-7)

WHOSE HEART ARE YOU BREAKING NOW Johnny Love—Tee Pee 395
[Teddy Powell] [ASC] (8/25/58 CR-55)

WHOSE HEART ARE YOU BREAKING TONIGHT Connie Francis—MGM 13303
[Benny Davis/Ted Murry] [ASC] (1/16/65 BCR-42)

WHY The Cues—Capitol 3582 [Jesse Stone] [BMI] (1/19/57 B-77)

WHY Gary Lee—Time 1009 [Connie Conway/Norma Conway] [BMI] (5/16/59 CR-57)

***WHY** Frankie Avalon—Chancellor 1045*
[Peter DeAngelis/Bob Marcucci] [ASC] (11/16/59 BCR-1)

***WHY** Donny Osmond—MGM 14424*
[Peter DeAngelis/Bob Marcucci] (TSW) [ASC] (9/16/72 BCR-13)

WHY The Beatles With Tony Sheridan—MGM 13227
[Bill Crompton/Tony Sheridan] [BMI] (4/18/64 B-88)

WHY Carly Simon—Mirage 4051 [Bernard Edwards/Nile Rodgers] [BMI] (7/10/82 BC-73)

***WHY? (AM I TREATED SO BAD)** "Cannonball" Adderley—Capitol 5877*
[Roebuck Staples] [BMI] (4/8/67 BCR-73) [IWM]

***WHY (AM I TREATED SO BAD)** The Sweet Inspirations—Atlantic 2410*
[Roebuck Staples] [BMI] (6/3/67 BR-57)

***WHY? (AM I TREATED SO BAD)** The Staple Singers—Epic 9880*
[Roebuck Staples] [BMI] (6/3/67 B-95)

***WHY (AM I TREATED SO BAD)** Bobby Powell—Whit 730*
[Roebuck Staples] [BMI] (6/17/67 B-91)

WHY (ARE THERE THINGS WE CAN'T EXPLAIN) Jane Morgan—Kapp 107
[Tony Burello/Tom (2) Murray] [BMI] (11/15/54 R-47)

WHY BABY WHY Pat Boone—Dot 15545
[Luther Dixon/Larry Harrison] [BMI] (3/9/57 BCRt*-6)

WHY BABY WHY Red Sovine & Webb Pierce—Decca 29739
[Darrell Edwards/George Jones] [BMI] (5/11/57 Rt*-11)

WHY CAN'T I BE YOU? The Cure—Elektra 69474
[Simon Gallup/Robert James Smith/Porl Thompson/Laurence Tolhurst/Boris Williams] [ASC] (6/20/87 BC-47)

WHY CAN'T I HAVE YOU The Cars—Elektra 69657 [Ric Ocasek] [ASC] (1/26/85 BC-33)

WHY CAN'T THIS BE LOVE Van Halen—Warner Bros. 28740
[Michael Anthony/Sammy Hagar/Alex Van Halen/Eddie Van Halen] [ASC] (3/15/86 BC-1)

WHY CAN'T THIS NIGHT GO ON FOREVER Journey—Columbia 07043
[Jonathan Cain/Steve Perry] [ASC] (4/25/87 BC-60)

WHY CAN'T WE BE FRIENDS? War—United Artists 629
[Thomas Allen/Harold Brown/Morris Dickerson/Jerry Goldstein/Lonnie Jordan/Charles Miller/Lee Oskar/Howard Scott] [ASC] (4/26/75 BCR-5)

WHY CAN'T WE BE LOVERS Holland-Dozier—Invictus 9125
[Lamont Dozier/Brian Holland/Eddie Holland] [BMI] (9/23/72 BCR-48)

WHY CAN'T WE LIVE TOGETHER Timmy Thomas—Glades 1703
[Timmy Thomas] [BMI] (11/25/72 BCR-2)

WHY CAN'T YOU BRING ME HOME Jay & The Americans—United Artists 992
[Wes Farrell/Joel Hirschhorn/Al Kasha] [BMI] (2/19/66 BCR-55)

WHY CAN'T YOU COME HOME Ex-Girlfriend—Reprise 40065
[Curtis Bedeau/Gerard Charles/Hugh Clarke/Brian George/Lucien George/Paul George] [BMI] (9/7/91 B-78)

WHY DID I CHOOSE YOU Barbra Streisand—Columbia 43248
[Michael Leonard/Herb Martin] [ASC] (3/27/65 BCR-72)

—WHY DID YOU DO IT see: DISCIPLINE OF LOVE

WHY DID YOU LEAVE ME? Vince Edwards—Russ-Fi 7001
[Frank Russell] [BMI] (6/30/62 BCR-68)

***WHY DO FOOLS FALL IN LOVE** The Teenagers Featuring Frankie Lymon—Gee 1002*
[George Goldner‡/Morris Levy‡/Frankie Lymon/Jimmy Merchant/Herman Santiago] [ASC] (2/4/56 BCtRt-2)

WHY DO FOOLS FALL IN LOVE *Gale Storm—Dot 15448*
[George Goldner‡/Morris Levy‡/Frankie Lymon/Jimmy Merchant/Herman Santiago] [ASC] (2/17/56 BCtRt-2)

WHY DO FOOLS FALL IN LOVE *The Diamonds—Mercury 70790*
[George Goldner‡/Morris Levy‡/Frankie Lymon/Jimmy Merchant/Herman Santiago] [ASC] (2/17/56 BCtRt-2)

WHY DO FOOLS FALL IN LOVE *Gloria Mann—Decca 29832*
[George Goldner‡/Morris Levy‡/Frankie Lymon/Jimmy Merchant/Herman Santiago] [ASC] (2/17/56 BRt-2)

WHY DO FOOLS FALL IN LOVE *The Beach Boys—Capitol 5118*
[George Goldner‡/Morris Levy‡/Frankie Lymon/Jimmy Merchant/Herman Santiago] [ASC] (2/22/64 CR-94)

WHY DO FOOLS FALL IN LOVE *The Happenings—B.T. Puppy 532*
[George Goldner‡/Morris Levy‡/Frankie Lymon/Jimmy Merchant/Herman Santiago] [ASC] (9/23/67 BCR-39)

WHY DO FOOLS FALL IN LOVE *Summer Wine—Sire 701*
[George Goldner‡/Morris Levy‡/Frankie Lymon/Jimmy Merchant/Herman Santiago] [ASC] (2/24/73 C-100)

WHY DO FOOLS FALL IN LOVE *Diana Ross—RCA 12349*
[George Goldner‡/Morris Levy‡/Frankie Lymon/Jimmy Merchant/Herman Santiago] [ASC] (10/17/81 BCR-6)

WHY DO I Lee Andrews And The Hearts—United Artists 136
[Barry Golder/Ted Weems] [BMI] (8/11/58 CR-72)

WHY DO I LOVE YOU SO Johnny Tillotson—Cadence 1372
[Clifford Rhodes] [BMI] (1/16/60 BCR-31)

WHY DO KIDS GROW UP Randy And The Rainbows—Rust 5073
[Neil Levenson] [BMI] (12/14/63 BR-95)

WHY DO LOVERS BREAK EACH OTHER'S HEART?
Bob B. Soxx And The Blue Jeans—Philles 110
[Ellie Greenwich/Tony Powers/Phil Spector] [BMI] (2/9/63 BCR-30)

WHY DO LOVERS (BREAK EACH OTHER'S HEART?) Daryl Hall & John Oates—RCA 11132
[Sara Allen/Daryl Hall] [BMI] (10/22/77 BCR-73)

WHY (DONCHA BE MY GIRL) The Chartbusters—Mutual 508
[Vernon Sandusky] [BMI] (11/7/64 BCR-72)

WHY DON'T THEY UNDERSTAND *George Hamilton IV—ABC-Paramount 9862*
[Jack Fishman/Joseph Turner Henderson] [BMI] (11/4/57 BCR-6)

WHY DON'T THEY UNDERSTAND *Bobby Vinton—Epic 10651*
[Jack Fishman/Joseph Turner Henderson] [BMI] (9/26/70 CR-90)

WHY DON'T YOU BELIEVE ME *The Duprees Featuring Joey Vann—Coed 584*
[Lew Douglas/Luther King Laney/LeRoy W. Rodde] [ASC] (8/17/63 BCR-23)

WHY DON'T YOU BELIEVE ME *Vic Damone—Warner Bros. 5644*
[Lew Douglas/Luther King Laney/LeRoy W. Rodde] [ASC] (7/10/65 C-90)

WHY DON'T YOU WRITE ME *Snooky Lanson—Dot 15385*
[Laura Hollins] [BMI] (8/22/55 CtRt-39)

WHY DON'T YOU WRITE ME *The Jacks—RPM 428 [Laura Hollins] [BMI] (9/3/55 BCtRt-33)*

WHY DON'T YOU WRITE ME? *Buddy Greco—Coral 61483*
[Laura Hollins] [BMI] (9/26/55 Rt-71)

WHY I SING THE BLUES B.B. King—BluesWay 61024
[Dave (2) Clark/B.B. King] [BMI] (5/10/69 BCR-57)

WHY I'M WALKIN' Stonewall Jackson—Columbia 41591
[Melvin Endsley*/Stonewall Jackson] [BMI] (3/28/60 B-83)

WHY IS THE WINE SWEETER (ON THE OTHER SIDE) Eddie Floyd—Stax 0051
[Eddie Floyd/Booker T. Jones Jr.] [BMI] (10/25/69 BCR-80)

WHY LEAVE US ALONE Five Special—Elektra 46032
[Ron Banks/Tony Green/Raymond Johnson] [ASC] (7/14/79 BCR-55)

WHY ME Kris Kristofferson—Monument 8571 [Kris Kristofferson] [BMI] (4/7/73 BCR-16)

WHY ME Styx—A&M 2206 [Dennis DeYoung] [ASC] (12/15/79 BCR-18)

WHY ME? Planet P—Geffen 29705 [Tony Carey] [ASC] (4/2/83 BC-51)

WHY ME? Irene Cara—Geffen 29464
[Irene Cara/Keith Forsey/Giorgio Moroder] [ASC] (10/22/83 BC-13)

WHY NOT ME Fred Knoblock—Scotti Brothers 600
[Fred Knoblock/Carson Whitsett] [ASC] (6/28/80 BCR-18)

WHY NOT NOW Matt Monro—Warwick 669
[Harold Fields/Peter G.D. Ling/Joseph Roncoroni] [BMI] (10/2/61 BCR-65)

WHY NOT START ALL OVER AGAIN The Counts—Westbound 191
[Leroy Emmanuel] [BMI] (3/11/72 C-89)

WHY NOT TONIGHT Jimmy Hughes—Fame 1011
[James William Gilreath] [BMI] (2/18/67 BCR-82)

WHY PICK ON ME The Standells—Tower 282 [Ed Cobb] [BMI] (10/22/66 BCR-52)

WHY SHOULD I CRY The Gentrys—Sun 1108 [Jimmy Hart] [BMI] (1/24/70 BCR-46)

WHY SHOULD I CRY? Nona Hendryx—EMI America 8382
[Nona Hendryx/Garry Johnson/Lisa Keith] [BMI] (5/23/87 BC-58)

WHY SHOULD I CRY FOR YOU? Sting—A&M 1560 [Sting] [BMI] (5/4/91 C-87)

WHY SHOULD I CRY OVER YOU Frank Sinatra—Capitol 3050
[Chester Conn/Nathan Miller] [ASC] (3/7/55 R-70)

WHY SHOULD I LOVE YOU *The Harptones with The Shytans—Bruce 109*
[Harold Barlow] [ASC] (10/4/54 R-PRE)

WHY SHOULD I LOVE YOU? *The Four Lads—Columbia 40306*
[Harold Barlow] [ASC] (10/4/54 R-PRE)

WHY WHY WHY Steve Lawrence—ABC-Paramount 10113
[Salvatore D'Amico/Teddy Randazzo] [BMI] (6/6/60 R-85)

WHY YOU TREAT ME SO BAD Club Nouveau—King Jay/Warner 28360
[Denzil Foster/Jay King/Thomas McElroy] [BMI] (5/30/87 BC-39)

—WHY YOU WANNA HURT ME see: BURN RUBBER

WHY YOU WANNA TRY ME Commodores—Motown 1604
[David Cochrane/Lionel Richie] [ASC] (2/6/82 BCR-61)

WHY'D YOU WANNA MAKE ME CRY Connie Stevens—Warner Bros. 5265
[Gerry Goffin/Carole King] [BMI] (5/5/62 BCR-52)

WICHITA LINEMAN *Glen Campbell—Capitol 2302 [Jimmy Webb] [ASC] (11/2/68 BCR-2)*

WICHITA LINEMAN *Sergio Mendes & Brasil '66—A&M 1132*
[Jimmy Webb] [ASC] (11/29/69 B-95)

WICKED GAME Chris Isaak—Reprise 19704 [Chris Isaak] [ASC] (12/1/90 BC-6)

WICKED RUBY Danny Zella & his Zell Rocks—Fox 10057
[Danny Zella] [BMI] (11/15/58 BC-71)

WIDE RECEIVER (PART I) Michael Henderson—Buddah 622
[Michael E. Henderson/Randy Jacobs] [ASC] (8/30/80 R-82)

WIEDERSEH'N Al Martino—Capitol 5652
[Milt Gabler/Bert Kaempfert/Herbert Rehbein] [BMI] (5/14/66 BCR-53)

WIGGLE IT 2 In A Room—Cutting 98887
[George Morel/Rafael Vargas] [BMI] (10/6/90 BC-15)

WIGGLE-TAIL (PTS. 1 & 2) Googie René—Class 221 [Leon René] [BMI] (3/15/58 C-60)

WIGGLE WIGGLE The Accents—Brunswick 55100
[Robert Draper] [ASC] (12/22/58 BCR-51)

WIGGLE WOBBLE Les Cooper And The Soulrockers—Everlast 5019
[Les Cooper] [BMI] (10/6/62 BCR-18) [I]

WIGWAM Bob Dylan—Columbia 45199 [Bob Dylan] [SE] (7/18/70 BCR-28) [I]

WILD! Dee Dee Sharp—Cameo 274 [Dave Appell/Kal Mann] [ASC] (9/28/63 BCR-29)

WILD AGAIN Starship—Elektra 69349
[John Bettis/Michael Clark] [ASC] (12/17/88 BC-73)

WILD AND CRAZY LOVE Mary Jane Girls—Gordy 1798
[Kenny Hawkins*/Rick James] [ASC] (7/20/85 BC-42)

THE WILD BOYS Duran Duran—Capitol 5417
[Simon Le Bon/Nick Rhodes/Andy Taylor/Nigel John Taylor/Roger Taylor] [ASC] (11/3/84 BC-1)

WILD CHERRY Don Cherry—Columbia 40665 [Eddie Curtis] [ASC] (3/30/56 BCR-24)

WILD HONEY The Beach Boys—Capitol 2028
[Mike Love/Brian Wilson] [BMI] (11/4/67 BCR-22)

WILD HORSES The Rolling Stones—Rolling Stones 19101
[Mick Jagger/Keith Richards] [BMI] (6/19/71 BCR-18)

WILD HORSES Gino Vannelli—CBS Associated 06699
[Roy Freeland/Gino Vannelli] [BMI] (4/18/87 BC-55)

WILD IN THE COUNTRY Elvis Presley With The Jordanaires—RCA Victor 47-7880
[Luigi Creatore/Hugo Peretti/George David Weiss] [ASC] (5/20/61 BCR-26)

WILD IN THE STREETS British Lions—RSO 898
[Peter Casperson*/Garland Jeffreys] [ASC] (7/22/78 B-87)

WILD IS THE WIND *Johnny Mathis—Columbia 41060*
[Dimitri Tiomkin/Ned Washington] [ASC] (11/25/57 BCRt-14)

WILD IS THE WIND *Henri René & His Orchestra—RCA Victor 47-7101*
[Dimitri Tiomkin] [ASC] (12/2/57 Rt-14) [IM]

WILD IS THE WIND *LeRoy Holmes & His Orchestra—MGM 12587*
[Dimitri Tiomkin] [ASC] (12/9/57 Rt-14) [IM]

THE WILD LIFE Bananarama—London 882019
[Sarah Dallin/Siobhan Fahey*/Steve Jolley/Tony Swain/Keren Woodward*] [BMI] (11/10/84 BC-70)

WILD NIGHT Van Morrison—Warner Bros. 7518 [Van Morrison] [BMI] (10/9/71 BCR-22)

WILD ONE Bobby Rydell—Cameo 171
[Dave Appell/Bernie Lowe/Kal Mann] [ASC] (1/30/60 BCR-2)

WILD ONE Martha & The Vandellas—Gordy 7036
[Ivy Jo Hunter/William Stevenson] [ASC] (12/5/64 BC-31)

WILD ROSIE The Four Tophatters—Cadence 1268
[Hal Hackady/Billy Mure] [BMI] (10/17/55 R-79)

WILD THING *The Troggs—Atco 6415 / Fontana 1548 [Chip Taylor] [BMI] (6/18/66 BCR-1)*

WILD THING *Senator Bobby—Parkway 127 [Chip Taylor] [BMI] (1/7/67 BCR-13)*

WILD THING *Fancy—Big Tree 15004 [Chip Taylor] [BMI] (6/1/74 BCR-12)*

WILD THING Tone Loc—Delicious Vinyl 102
[Matt Dike/Michael Ross*/Anthony Terrell Smith/Marvin Young] [ASC] (12/3/88 BC-2)

WILD WEEKEND The Rebels—Swan 4125
[Tom Shannon/Phil Todaro] [BMI] (12/29/62 BCR-8) [I]

WILD WILD LIFE Talking Heads—Sire 28629
[David Byrne/Chris Frantz*/Jerry Harrison*/Tina Weymouth*] [ASC] (8/30/86 BC-25)

WILD, WILD WEST Kool Moe Dee—Jive 1086 [Mohandas DeWese] [BMI] (4/30/88 BC-62)

WILD, WILD WEST The Escape Club—Atlantic 89048
[Johnnie Christo/John Holliday/Amos Pizzey*/Trevor Steel/Milan Zekavica] [ASC] (8/20/88 BC-1)

WILD WOMEN DO Natalie Cole—EMI 50275
[Sam Lorber/Greg Prestopino/Matthew Wilder] [ASC] (2/17/90 BC-34)

WILD WORLD *Cat Stevens—A&M 1231 [Cat Stevens] [ASC] (2/13/71 BCR-11)*

WILD WORLD *The Gentrys—Sun 1122 [Cat Stevens] [ASC] (2/13/71 BCR-78)*

WILD WORLD Maxi Priest—Virgin 99269 [Cat Stevens] [ASC] (10/29/88 BC-25)

WILDFIRE Michael Murphey—Epic 50084 [Larry Cansler/Michael Murphey] [BMI] (3/22/75 BCR-2)

WILDFLOWER Skylark—Capitol 3511 [Doug Edwards/David Richardson] [BMI] (2/17/73 BCR-8)

WILDFLOWER The New Birth—RCA Victor 0265 [Doug Edwards/David Richardson] [BMI] (4/27/74 BCR-45)

—WILDSIDE see: WALK ON THE WILD SIDE

WILDWOOD DAYS Bobby Rydell—Cameo 252 [Dave Appell/Kal Mann] [ASC] (5/11/63 BCR-17)

WILDWOOD WEED Jim Stafford—MGM 14737 [Don Bowman/Jim Stafford] [BMI] (7/6/74 BCR-4)

WILL I ALWAYS BE YOUR SWEETHEART Mona Carol—Casino 170 [Peter DeAngelis/Bob Marcucci] [ASC] (5/11/56 Rt-71)

WILL I ALWAYS BE YOUR SWEETHEART Kitty Kallen—Decca 29959 [Peter DeAngelis/Bob Marcucci] [ASC] (7/13/56 Rt-74)

WILL IT GO ROUND IN CIRCLES Billy Preston—A&M 1411 [Bruce Fisher/Billy Preston] [ASC] (2/24/73 BCR-1)

WILL POWER The Cookies—Dimension 1012 [Gerry Goffin/Carole King] [BMI] (7/6/63 BCR-61)

WILL THE WOLF SURVIVE? Los Lobos—Slash 29093 [David Hidalgo/Louie Perez] [BMI] (3/23/85 BC-78)

WILL YOU BE STAYING AFTER SUNDAY The Peppermint Rainbow—Decca 32410 [Joel Hirschhorn/Al Kasha] [BMI] (12/28/68 BCR-20)

WILL YOU LOVE ME TOMORROW The Shirelles—Scepter 1211 [Gerry Goffin/Carole King] [BMI] (11/21/60 BCR-1)

WILL YOU LOVE ME TOMORROW The 4 Seasons Featuring The "Sound" Of Frankie Valli—Philips 40523 [Gerry Goffin/Carole King] [BMI] (2/24/68 BCR-13)

WILL YOU LOVE ME TOMORROW? Linda Ronstadt—Capitol 2767 [Gerry Goffin/Carole King] [BMI] (3/28/70 C-98)

WILL YOU STILL LOVE ME TOMORROW Roberta Flack—Atlantic 2851 [Gerry Goffin/Carole King] [BMI] (1/8/72 BCR-49)

WILL YOU LOVE ME TOMORROW? Melanie—Neighborhood 4213 [Gerry Goffin/Carole King] [BMI] (11/24/73 BCR-54)

WILL YOU LOVE ME TOMORROW Dana Valery—Phantom 10566 [Gerry Goffin/Carole King] [BMI] (6/19/76 BC-95)

WILL YOU STILL LOVE ME TOMORROW Dave Mason—Columbia 10749 [Gerry Goffin/Carole King] [BMI] (5/27/78 BCR-39)

WILL YOU STILL LOVE ME? Chicago—Warner/Full Moon 28512 [Richard Baskin/David Foster/Tom Keane] [ASC] (11/15/86 BC-3)

WILL YOU WILLYUM Janis Martin—RCA Victor 47-6491 [Carl Barefoot/Carl Stutz] [ASC] (5/4/56 Rt-46)

WILL YOU, WILLYUM? Joan Hager—Decca 29928 [Carl Barefoot/Carl Stutz] [ASC] (6/15/56 Rt-54)

WILLIE Bill Black's Combo—Hi 2027 [Bill Black] [BMI] (12/31/60 C-82) [I]

WILLIE & LAURA MAE JONES Dusty Springfield—Atlantic 2647 [Tony Joe White] [BMI] (6/28/69 BCR-64)

WILLIE AND THE HAND JIVE Johnny Otis Show—Capitol 3966 [Johnny Otis] [BMI] (5/19/58 BCR-9)

HAND JIVE The Strangeloves—Bang 524 [Johnny Otis] [BMI] (6/18/66 BR-96)

WILLIE AND THE HAND JIVE Eric Clapton—RSO 503 [Johnny Otis] [BMI] (10/26/74 BCR-26)

WILLIE AND THE HAND JIVE George Thorogood & The Destroyers—EMI America 8270 [Johnny Otis] [BMI] (6/15/85 BC-61)

WILLIE CAN Sue Thompson—Hickory 1196 [Boudleaux Bryant/Felice Bryant] [BMI] (1/5/63 BCR-74)

WILLIE DID THE CHA CHA Johnny Otis Show—Capitol 4060 [Johnny Otis] [BMI] (10/27/58 R-79)

WILLIE JEAN The Sunshine Company—Imperial 66324 [Hoyt Axton] [BMI] (2/15/69 R-95)

WILLIE PASS THE WATER Ripple—GRC 1013 [Dee Ervin/Ruth Robinson] [BMI] (2/9/74 C-94)

WILLING AND EAGER Pat Boone—Dot 16349 [Richard Rodgers] [ASC] (4/23/62 CR-76)

WILLINGLY (MELODIE PER DUE) Johnny Desmond—Columbia 41302 [Hubert Giraud/Carl Sigman] [ASC] (12/15/58 Rt-66)

WILLINGLY (MELODIE PERDUE) Monty Kelly And His Orchestra—Carlton 495 [Hubert Giraud/Carl Sigman*] [ASC] (12/15/58 Rt-63) [IWM]

WILLOW WEEP FOR ME The Fontane Sisters with Billy Vaughn's Orchestra—Dot 15248 [Ann Ronell] [ASC] (10/4/54 R-PRE)

WILLOW WEEP FOR ME Chad & Jeremy—World Artists 1034 [Ann Ronell] [ASC] (11/14/64 BCR-15)

WILLPOWER WEAK, TEMPTATION STRONG Bullet—Big Tree 131 [Bobby Flax/Lanny Lambert] [BMI] (2/19/72 BCR-68)

THE WILLY The Willies—Co & Ce 239 [Irving Roth] [BMI] (10/22/66 CR-94)

WILLYAM, WILLYAM Dee Dee Sharp—Cameo 296 [Tracy Lee Alexander/William E. Jackson III] [BMI] (2/29/64 B-97)

WIN YOUR LOVE FOR ME Sam Cooke—Keen 2006 [Sam Cooke] [BMI] (8/4/58 BCR-33)

WINCHESTER CATHEDRAL The New Vaudeville Band—Fontana 1562 [Geoff Stephens] [ASC] (10/29/66 BCR-1)

WINCHESTER CATHEDRAL Dana Rollin—Tower 283 [Geoff Stephens] [ASC] (11/5/66 BCR-60)

WIND BENEATH MY WINGS Lou Rawls—Epic 03758 [Larry Henley/Jeff Silbar] [ASC] (3/26/83 BC-54)

WIND BENEATH MY WINGS Bette Midler—Atlantic 88972 [Larry Henley/Jeff Silbar] [ASC] (3/4/89 BC-1)

WIND HIM UP Saga—Portrait 37-03791 [Ian Stevenson Crichton/Jim Crichton/Jim Gilmour/Steve Negus/Michael Sadler] [ASC] (4/2/83 BC-51)

WIND IN THE WILLOW Jo Stafford—Columbia 40832 [Edwin Brown‡/Artie Singer/Harold Singer/Murray Wecht] [BMI] (3/23/57 BCtRt-33)

WIND IN THE WILLOW Ann Reynolds—Kapp 179 [Edwin Brown‡/Artie Singer/Harold Singer/Murray Wecht] [BMI] (4/20/57 CtRt-38)

WIND OF CHANGE Scorpions—Mercury 868 180 [Klaus Meine] [BMI] (6/1/91 BC-4)

THE WINDMILLS OF YOUR MIND Dusty Springfield—Atlantic 2623 [Alan Bergman/Marilyn Bergman/Michel Legrand] (TSW) [ASC] (4/26/69 BCR-22)

WINDOWS Missing Persons—Capitol 5200 [Dale Bozzio/Terry Bozzio] [BMI] (1/15/83 BC-62)

WINDOWS OF THE WORLD Dionne Warwick—Scepter 12196 [Burt Bacharach/Hal David] [ASC] (7/29/67 BCR-32)

WINDS OF CHANGE Jefferson Starship—Grunt 13439 [Jeannette Sears/Pete Sears] [BMI] (1/29/83 BC-37)

WINDY Paul Gayten—Argo 5300 [Rupert Bopape] [NA] (7/21/58 B-78) [I]

WINDY The Association—Warner Bros. 7041 [Ruthann Friedman] [BMI] (5/27/67 BCR-1)

WINDY Wes Montgomery—A&M 883 [Ruthann Friedman] [BMI] (11/25/67 BCR-44) [IWM]

WINDY AND WARM Boots Randolph And His Combo—Monument 821 [John D. Loudermilk] [BMI] (9/7/63 R-97) [I]

WINGS OF A DOVE Ferlin Husky—Capitol 4406 [Bob Ferguson] [BMI] (11/28/60 BCRt-9)

WINGS OF A DOVE Paul Clayton—Monument 432 [Bob Ferguson] [BMI] (12/12/60 Rt-12)

WINNER TAKE ALL The Platters—Mercury 70819 [Al Frisch/Sid Wayne] [ASC] (3/16/56 BCRt-13)

WINNER TAKE ALL Sunny Gale—RCA Victor 47-6479 [Al Frisch/Sid Wayne] [ASC] (3/30/56 Rt-13)

THE WINNER TAKES IT ALL ABBA—Atlantic 3776 [Benny Andersson/Björn Ulvaeus] [ASC] (11/22/80 BCR-8)

WINNER TAKES IT ALL Sammy Hagar—Columbia 06647 [Giorgio Moroder/Tom Whitlock] [ASC] (2/14/87 BC-54)

WINNERS AND LOSERS Hamilton, Joe Frank And Reynolds—Playboy 6054 [Ann Marie Hamilton/Danny Hamilton] [BMI] (11/8/75 BCR-18)

WINNING Santana—Columbia 01050 [Russ Ballard] [ASC] (4/11/81 BCR-14)

WINTER GAMES David Foster—Atlantic 89140 [David Foster] [BMI] (2/20/88 BC-78) [I]

WINTER MELODY Donna Summer—Casablanca 874 [Pete Bellotte/Giorgio Moroder/Donna Summer] (TSW) [ASC] (2/5/77 BCR-43)

WINTER WONDERLAND The Andrews Sisters—Decca 23722 [Felix Bernard/Richard B. Smith] [ASC] (12/20/54 Rt-38)

WINTER WONDERLAND Richard Hayman & His Orchestra—Mercury 70514 [Felix Bernard] [ASC] (12/20/54 Rt-38) [IM]

WINTER WONDERLAND The Ames Brothers—Coral 60113 [Felix Bernard/Richard B. Smith] [ASC] (1/3/55 Rt-39)

WINTER WORLD OF LOVE Engelbert Humperdinck—Parrot 40044 [Barry Mason/Les Reed] [ASC] (11/29/69 BCR-13)

WIPE OUT The Surfaris—Dot 16479 [Bob Berryhill/Pat Connolly/Jim Fuller/Ron Wilson] [BMI] (6/8/63 BCR-2) [I]

WIPE OUT The Surfaris—Dot 144 [Bob Berryhill/Pat Connolly/Jim Fuller/Ron Wilson] [BMI] (7/30/66 BCR-9) [I]

WIPE OUT The Surfaris—Dot 144 [Bob Berryhill/Pat Connolly/Jim Fuller/Ron Wilson] [BMI] (8/15/70 R-97) [I]

WIPEOUT Fat Boys—Tin Pan Apple 885 960 [Bob Berryhill/Pat Connolly/Jim Fuller/Ron Wilson] [BMI] (7/11/87 BC-12)

WIPE OUT Jive Bunny & The Mastermixers—Music Factory/Atco 99122 [Bob Berryhill/Pat Connolly/Jim Fuller/Ron Wilson] (Med) [BMI] (2/3/90 BC-67) [I]

WIRED FOR SOUND Cliff Richard—EMI America 8095 [Brian A. Robertson/Alan Tarney] [BMI] (10/10/81 BCR-70)

WISDOM OF A FOOL The Five Keys—Capitol 3597 [Roy Alfred/Abner Silver] [ASC] (12/1/56 BCR-24)

WISE UP Amy Grant—A&M 2762 [Wayne Kirkpatrick/Billy Simon] [BMI] (8/17/85 BC-66)

(WISH I COULD FLY LIKE) SUPERMAN The Kinks—Arista 0409 [Ray Davies] [ASC] (4/21/79 BCR-41)

WISH IT WERE ME The Platters—Mercury 71502 [Buck Ram] [ASC] (9/14/59 BC-61)

WISH ME A RAINBOW Gunter Kallmann Chorus—4 Corners Of The World 138 [Ray Evans/Jay Livingston] [ASC] (12/10/66 BCR-56)

WISH SOMEONE WOULD CARE Irma Thomas—Imperial 66013 [Irma Thomas] [BMI] (3/28/64 BCR-17)

WISH THAT I COULD TALK TO YOU The Sylvers—Pride 1019 [Leon Sylvers] [ASC] (12/23/72 BCR-46)

WISH YOU DIDN'T HAVE TO GO James & Bobby Purify—Bell 660
[Spooner Oldham/Dan Penn] [BMI] (1/28/67 BCR-35)

WISH YOU WERE HERE, BUDDY Pat Boone—Dot 16933
[Pat Boone] [ASC] (10/8/66 BCR-49)

WISHFUL SINFUL The Doors—Elektra 45656
[John Densmore*/Robby Krieger/Ray Manzarek*/Jim Morrison*] [ASC]
(3/29/69 BCR-28)

WISHFUL THINKING Little Anthony And The Imperials—End 1039
[Sylvester Bradford/Al Lewis] [ASC] (2/21/59 BCR-50)

WISHIN' AND HOPIN' Dusty Springfield—Philips 40207
[Burt Bacharach/Hal David] [ASC] (6/20/64 BCR-4)

WISHIN' ON A RAINBOW Phill Wilson—Huron 22000 [Phill Wilson] [BMI] (7/10/61 B-91)

WISHING FOR YOUR LOVE *The Voxpoppers—Mercury 71282*
[Sampson Horton] [BMI] (2/3/58 BCRt-17)

WISHING FOR YOUR LOVE *The Clovers—Atlantic 1175*
[Sampson Horton] [BMI] (4/7/58 Rt-17)

WISHING I WAS LUCKY Wet Wet Wet—Uni 50000
[Graeme Clark/Tommy Cunningham/Neil Mitchell/Marti Pellow] [ASC] (5/28/88 BC-58)

WISHING (IF I HAD A PHOTOGRAPH OF YOU) A Flock Of Seagulls—Jive 2006
[Frank Maudsley/Paul Reynolds/Ali Score/Mike Score] [ASC] (5/14/83 BC-26)

WISHING IT WAS YOU Connie Francis—MGM 13331
[Joy Byers Johnston/Clyde Otis] [BMI] (5/1/65 BCR-49)

WISHING ON THE SAME STAR Keedy—Arista 2255 [Diane Warren] [ASC] (8/17/91 B-86)

—WISHING STAR see: THEME FROM TARAS BULBA

WISHING WELL Terence Trent D'Arby—Columbia 07675
[Terence Trent D'Arby/Sean Oliver] [BMI] (1/16/88 BC-1)

WISHING YOU WERE HERE Chicago—Columbia 10049
[Peter Cetera] [ASC] (10/12/74 BCR-9)

THE WITCH The Rattles—Probe 480
[Herbert Hildebrand-Winhauer] [ASC] (6/20/70 BCR-69)

WITCH DOCTOR David Seville—Liberty 55132 [David Seville] [ASC] (4/7/58 BCR-1)

THE WITCH QUEEN OF NEW ORLEANS Redbone—Epic 10749
[Lolly Vegas/Pat Vegas] [BMI] (11/20/71 BCR-17)

WITCHCRAFT Frank Sinatra—Capitol 3859
[Cy Coleman/Carolyn Leigh] [ASC] (12/30/57 BCR-8)

WITCHCRAFT Elvis Presley With The Jordanaires—RCA Victor 47-8243
[Dave Bartholomew/Earl King Johnson] [BMI] (10/19/63 BCR-31)

WITCHI TAI TO Everything Is Everything—Vanguard Apostolic 35082
[Jim Pepper] [BMI] (1/25/69 BCR-50) [F]

WITCHY WOMAN Eagles—Asylum 11008
[Don Henley/Bernie Leadon] [ASC] (8/26/72 BCR-8)

WITH A CHILD'S HEART *Stevie Wonder—Tamla 54130*
[Vicki Basemore/Henry Cosby/Sylvia Moy] [BMI] (7/2/66 CR-94)

WITH A CHILD'S HEART *Michael Jackson—Motown 1218*
[Vicki Basemore/Henry Cosby/Sylvia Moy] [BMI] (5/5/73 BCR-37)

WITH A GIRL LIKE YOU The Troggs—Atco 6415 / Fontana 1552
[Reg Presley] [BMI] (8/6/66 BCR-29)

WITH A LITTLE BIT OF LUCK *Percy Faith And His Orchestra—Columbia 40696*
[Frederick Loewe] [ASC] (7/21/56 BRt-73) [IM]

WITH A LITTLE BIT OF LUCK *Jo Stafford—Columbia 40718*
[Alan Jay Lerner/Frederick Loewe] [ASC] (8/3/56 BRt-73)

WITH A LITTLE HELP FROM MY FRIENDS *Joe Cocker—A&M 991*
[John Lennon/Paul McCartney] [ASC] (11/9/68 BCR-49)

WITH A LITTLE HELP FROM MY FRIENDS *The Beatles—Capitol 4612*
[John Lennon/Paul McCartney] (Med) [ASC] (9/9/78 BC-71)

WITH A LITTLE LUCK Wings—Capitol 4559 [Paul McCartney] [ASC] (3/25/78 BCR-1)

WITH ALL MY HEART *Jodie Sands—Chancellor 1003*
[Peter DeAngelis/Bob Marcucci] [ASC] (5/11/57 BCRt-11)

WITH ALL MY HEART *Judy Scott—Decca 30324*
[Peter DeAngelis/Bob Marcucci] [ASC] (5/20/57 BRt-11)

WITH ALL MY HEART *Buddy Greco—Kapp 183*
[Peter DeAngelis/Bob Marcucci] [ASC] (5/25/57 Rt-11)

WITH ALL MY HEART *Al Martino—Capitol 5384*
[Peter DeAngelis/Bob Marcucci] [ASC] (3/20/65 CR-97)

WITH ALL MY LOVE The Five Keys—Capitol 3948 [Fanny Dosher] [ASC] (4/14/58 R-84)

WITH ALL OF MY HEART Brook Benton—Mercury 71478
[Brook Benton/Chris Towns] [BMI] (7/18/59 BCR-51)

WITH EVERY BEAT OF MY HEART Taylor Dayne—Arista 1-9895
[Arthur Baker/Tommy Faragher/Lotti Golden] [BMI] (10/21/89 BC-5)

WITH MY EYES WIDE OPEN I'M DREAMING
Enoch Light & The Light Brigade—Grand Award 1032
[Mack Gordon/Harry Revel] [ASC] (5/25/59 BCtRt-39) [IWM]

WITH MY EYES WIDE OPEN I'M DREAMING *Patti Page—Mercury 71469*
[Mack Gordon/Harry Revel] [ASC] (6/6/59 BCtRt-39)

—WITH NO ONE see: SENZA MAMMA

WITH OPEN ARMS Jane Morgan—Kapp 284
[Burt Bacharach/Hal David] [ASC] (7/27/59 BCR-39)

WITH OR WITHOUT YOU U2—Island 99469
[Adam Clayton/Dave Evans/Paul Hewson/Larry Mullen] [ASC] (3/21/87 BC-1)

WITH PEN IN HAND *Billy Vera—Atlantic 2526 [Bobby Goldsboro] [BMI] (6/15/68 BCR-25)*

WITH PEN IN HAND *Vikki Carr—Liberty 56092 [Bobby Goldsboro] [BMI] (3/29/69 BCR-34)*

WITH PEN IN HAND *Bobby Goldsboro—United Artists 50938*
[Bobby Goldsboro] [BMI] (9/9/72 BCR-87)

WITH PEN IN HAND *Dorothy Moore—Malaco 1047*
[Bobby Goldsboro] [BMI] (1/21/78 R-92)

WITH THE WIND AND THE RAIN IN YOUR HAIR Pat Boone—Dot 15888
[Clara Edwards/Jack Lawrence] [ASC] (1/5/59 BCR-16)

WITH THESE HANDS Tom Jones—Parrot 9787
[Benny Davis/Abner Silver] [ASC] (8/28/65 BCR-21)

WITH THIS RING The Platters—Musicor 1229
[Luther Dixon/Tony Hester/Richard Wylie] [BMI] (2/25/67 BCR-14)

WITH YOU Sam Cooke—Keen 82117 [Sam Cooke] [BMI] (8/1/60 R-99)

WITH YOU The Moments (2)—Stang 5068
[Ken Ascher/Carole Bayer Sager] [ASC] (12/4/76 R-93)

WITH YOU Tony Terry—Epic 73713 [Raymond Reeder] [ASC] (6/29/91 BC-14)

WITH YOU ALL THE WAY New Edition—MCA 52829 [Carl Wurtz] [BMI] (6/14/86 BC-51)

WITH YOU I'M BORN AGAIN Billy Preston & Syreeta—Motown 1477
[Carol Connors/David Shire] [BMI] (12/8/79 BCR-4)

WITH YOU ON MY MIND Nat "King" Cole—Capitol 3782
[Nat "King" Cole/Charlotte Hawkins] [ASC] (9/9/57 BCR-19)

WITH YOUR LOVE Jack Scott—Carlton 483 [Jack Scott] [BMI] (9/22/58 BCR-26)

WITH YOUR LOVE Jefferson Starship—Grunt 10746
[Marty Balin/Joey Covington/Victor Gabriel Smith] [BMI] (7/24/76 BCR-11)

WITHIN MY HEART Voyce—Atco 98759
[Carlos Berrios/Carlos Colon/Miguel Cordero/Angel LeBron] [ASC] (11/30/91 B-77)

WITHOUT A SONG *Kay Starr—RCA Victor 47-6247*
[Edward Eliscu/Billy Rose/Vincent Youmans] [ASC] (9/5/55 Rt-30)

WITHOUT A SONG *Roy Hamilton—Epic 9125*
[Edward Eliscu/Billy Rose/Vincent Youmans] [ASC] (10/1/55 BCRt-42)

WITHOUT A SONG (PART 1) *James Cleveland and the Cleveland Singers—Savoy 4269*
[Edward Eliscu/Billy Rose/Vincent Youmans] [ASC] (7/23/66 C-81)

WITHOUT HER Herb Alpert—A&M 1065
[Harry Nilsson] [BMI] (5/24/69 BCR-38)

WITHOUT LOVE Aretha Franklin—Atlantic 3224
[Carolyn Franklin/Ivy Jo Hunter] [ASC] (11/16/74 BCR-45)

WITHOUT LOVE (THERE IS NOTHING) *Clyde McPhatter—Atlantic 1117*
[Danny Small] [BMI] (1/12/57 BCRt-38)

WITHOUT LOVE (THERE IS NOTHING) *Toni Arden—Decca 30180*
[Danny Small] [BMI] (1/19/57 Rt-71)

WITHOUT LOVE (THERE IS NOTHING) *Ray Charles—ABC-Paramount 10453*
[Danny Small] [BMI] (6/15/63 BCR-29)

WITHOUT LOVE (THERE IS NOTHING) *Oscar Toney, Jr.—Bell 699*
[Danny Small] [BMI] (1/13/68 BCR-71)

WITHOUT LOVE (THERE IS NOTHING) *Tom Jones—Parrot 40045*
[Danny Small] [BMI] (12/27/69 BCR-3)

WITHOUT MY LOVE Pat Boone—Dot DEP-1057
[Billy Vaughn/Johnny Wood] (EP) [ASC] (9/9/57 R-61)

WITHOUT THE ONE YOU LOVE (LIFE'S NOT WORTH WHILE) Four Tops—Motown 1069
[Lamont Dozier/Brian Holland/Eddie Holland] [BMI] (11/28/64 BCR-43)

WITHOUT YOU *Eddie Fisher—RCA Victor 47-6470*
[Ornella Ferrari Colombi/Hal Hackady/Vittorio Mascheroni] [BMI]
(3/23/56 BCRt-27) [FET]

WITHOUT YOU *Johnny Desmond—Coral 61608*
[Ornella Ferrari Colombi/Hal Hackady/Vittorio Mascheroni] [BMI] (4/6/56 Rt-27) [FET]

WITHOUT YOU *Alan Dean—MGM 12189*
[Ornella Ferrari Colombi/Hal Hackady/Vittorio Mascheroni] [BMI] (4/27/56 Rt-27) [FET]

WITHOUT YOU Johnny Tillotson—Cadence 1404 [Johnny Tillotson] [BMI] (8/7/61 BCR-7)

WITHOUT YOU *Nilsson—RCA Victor 74-0604*
[Tom Evans/Pete Ham] [ASC] (12/11/71 BCR-1)

WITHOUT YOU *Heart—Mushroom 7035 [Tom Evans/Pete Ham] [ASC] (8/12/78 R-91)*

WITHOUT YOU David Bowie—EMI America 8190 [David Bowie] [ASC] (3/10/84 B-73)

WITHOUT YOU Peabo Bryson—Elektra 69426 [Lamont Dozier] [BMI] (2/6/88 B-89)

WITHOUT YOU Mötley Crüe—Elektra 64985 [Mick Mars/Nikki Sixx] [ASC] (2/24/90 BC-7)

WITHOUT YOU (NOT ANOTHER LONELY NIGHT) Franke & the Knockouts—Millennium 13105
[Billy Elworthy/Blake Levinsohn/Franke Previte] [ASC] (4/3/82 BCR-22)

WITHOUT YOU IN MY LIFE Tyrone Davis—Dakar 4519
[Leo Graham/Raymond Haley] [BMI] (4/14/73 BCR-48)

WITHOUT YOUR LOVE Roger Daltrey—Polydor 2121
[William Morris Nicholls] [ASC] (9/13/80 BCR-20)

WITHOUT YOUR LOVE Toto—Columbia 06570 [David Paich] [ASC] (12/27/86 BC-38)

WITHOUT YOUR LOVE (MR. JORDAN) Charlie Ross—Big Tree 16056
[Jack Perricone/Paul Vance] [ASC] (2/21/76 BCR-34)

WIVES AND LOVERS Jack Jones—Kapp 551
[Burt Bacharach/Hal David] [ASC] (11/2/63 BCR-12)

WIZARD OF LOVE The Ly-Dells—Master 251
[Chuck Hatfield/Paul O'Lone/Gary Young] [BMI] (7/24/61 BCR-54)

THE WIZARD Jimmie Rodgers—Roulette 4090
[Luigi Creatore/Mack David/Hugo Peretti] [ASC] (8/11/58 B-45)

WKRP IN CINCINNATI Steve Carlisle—MCA 51205
[Tom Wells/Hugh Wilson] [ASC] (11/21/81 BCR-65)

WOLD Harry Chapin—Elektra 45874 [Harry Chapin] [ASC] (12/29/73 BCR-26)

WOLF CREEK PASS C.W. McCall—MGM 14764
[Chip Davis/Bill Fries] [SE] (2/1/75 BCR-40)

WOLFMAN JACK Todd Rundgren—Bearsville 0301 [Todd Rundgren] [BMI] (1/18/75 C-94)

WOLVERTON MOUNTAIN *Claude King—Columbia 42352*
[Merle Kilgore/Claude King] [BMI] (5/14/62 BCR-4)

(I'M THE GIRL FROM) WOLVERTON MOUNTAIN *(response to Wolverton Mountain)*
Jo Ann Campbell—Cameo 223
[Merle Kilgore/Claude King] [BMI] (8/18/62 BCR-29) [R]

WOMAN Peter And Gordon—Capitol 5579 [Paul McCartney] [ASC] (2/12/66 BCR-12)

WOMAN John Lennon—Geffen 49644 [John Lennon] [GL] (1/17/81 BCR-1)

WOMAN A LOVER A FRIEND Jackie Wilson—Brunswick 55167
[Sid Wyche] [BMI] (7/9/60 BCR-12)

A WOMAN CAN CHANGE A MAN Joe Tex—Dial 4006 [Joe Tex] [BMI] (4/10/65 BCR-56)

WOMAN DON'T GO ASTRAY King Floyd—Chimneyville 443
[King Floyd] [BMI] (9/2/72 BCR-35)

WOMAN FROM LIBERIA Jimmie Rodgers—Roulette 4293
[James Frederick Rodgers/Art Whiting] [ASC] (10/24/60 R-87)

WOMAN FROM TOKYO Deep Purple—Warner Bros. 7672/Warner Bros. 7737
[Ritchie Blackmore/Ian Gillan/Roger Glover/Jon Lord/Ian Paice] [ASC]
(2/17/73 BCR-54)

WOMAN HELPING MAN The Vogues—Reprise 0803
[Mark Charron] [BMI] (1/25/69 BCR-27)

THE WOMAN I LOVE B.B. King—Kent 492 [Joe Josea‡/B.B. King] [BMI] (8/24/68 BR-88)

WOMAN IN CHAINS Tears For Fears—Fontana 876 248
[Roland Orzabal] [BMI] (12/2/89 BC-32)

A WOMAN IN LOVE *Gordon MacRae—Capitol 3284 [Frank Loesser] [ASC] (11/7/55 Rt-28)*

A WOMAN IN LOVE *Four Aces—Decca 29725 [Frank Loesser] [ASC] (11/7/55 BCtRt-7)*

A WOMAN IN LOVE *Frankie Laine—Columbia 40583*
[Frank Loesser] [ASC] (11/19/55 BCtRt-7)

WOMAN IN LOVE Barbra Streisand—Columbia 11364
[Barry Gibb/Robin Gibb] [BMI] (9/6/80 BCR-1)

A WOMAN IN LOVE (IT'S NOT ME) Tom Petty and the Heartbreakers—Backstreet 51136
[Mike Campbell/Tom Petty] [ASC] (7/25/81 BCR-62)

THE WOMAN IN ME Crystal Gayle—Columbia 02523 [Susan Thomas] [NA] (12/5/81 B-76)

THE WOMAN IN ME Donna Summer—Geffen 29805
[John Bettis/Michael Clark] [ASC] (12/18/82 BC-28)

THE WOMAN IN YOU Bee Gees—RSO 813173
[Barry Gibb/Maurice Gibb/Robin Gibb] [BMI] (5/21/83 BC-21)

WOMAN IS A MAN'S BEST FRIEND Teddy And The Twilights—Swan 4102
[Fred Cohen] [ASC] (5/12/62 BCR-59)

WOMAN IS THE NIGGER OF THE WORLD
John Lennon/Plastic Ono Band With Elephant's Memory And The Invisible Strings—
Apple 1848
[John Lennon/Yoko Ono] [GL] (5/20/72 BCR-57)

WOMAN LIKE THAT, YEAH Joe Tex—Dial 4059 [Joe Tex] [BMI] (6/3/67 BCR-51)

WOMAN LOVE Gene Vincent and His Blue Caps—Capitol 3450
[Jack Rhodes] [BMI] (6/15/56 R-47)

A WOMAN NEEDS LOVE (JUST LIKE YOU DO) Ray Parker Jr. & Raydio—Arista 0592
[Ray Parker Jr.] [ASC] (3/7/81 BCR-4)

A WOMAN OF THE WORLD The Gentrys—MGM 13561
[John Hurley/Ronnie Wilkins] [BMI] (9/10/66 R-95)

WOMAN TO WOMAN Joe Cocker And The Chris Stainton Band—A&M 1370
[Joe Cocker/Chris Stainton] [ASC] (12/2/72 BCR-52)

WOMAN TO WOMAN *Shirley Brown—Truth 3206*
[James Banks/Eddie Marion/Henderson Thigpen] [BMI] (10/12/74 BCR-22)

WOMAN TO WOMAN *Barbara Mandrell—ABC/Dot 17736*
[James Banks/Eddie Marion/Henderson Thigpen] [BMI] (3/4/78 BC-92)

WOMAN TONIGHT America—Warner Bros. 8157 [Dan Peek] [ASC] (11/22/75 BCR-42)

WOMAN, WOMAN The Union Gap Featuring Gary Puckett—Columbia 44297
[James W. Glaser/Jimmy Payne] [BMI] (11/11/67 BCR-2)

WOMAN'S GOT SOUL The Impressions—ABC-Paramount 10647
[Curtis Mayfield] [BMI] (4/3/65 BCR-29)

WOMAN'S GOTTA HAVE IT (The Preacher) Bobby Womack—United Artists 50902
[Darryl Carter/Bobby Womack/Linda Womack] [BMI] (4/22/72 BCR-32)

A WOMAN'S HANDS Joe Tex—Dial 4061 [Joe Tex] [BMI] (8/5/67 BCR-59)

A WOMAN'S LOVE Carla Thomas—Atlantic 2258
[Steve Cropper/Carla Thomas] [BMI] (11/28/64 BCR-62)

A WOMAN'S STORY Cher—Warner-Spector 0400
[Phil Spector/April Stevens/Nino Tempo] [BMI] (12/14/74 CR-66)

A WOMAN'S WAY Andy Williams—Columbia 45003
[Smokey Roberds] [ASC] (11/8/69 C-91)

A WOMAN'S WAY Rozetta Johnson—Clintone 001 [Lillian Dees] [BMI] (12/12/70 B-94)

IT'S A WOMAN'S WORLD *Four Aces—Decca 29269*
[Sammy Cahn/Cyril Mockridge] [ASC] (10/4/54 BCR-15)

WOMAN'S WORLD *Ray Anthony & His Orchestra—Capitol 2936*
[Sammy Cahn/Cyril Mockridge] [NA] (10/4/54 R-PRE)

WOMBLING SUMMER PARTY The Wombles—Columbia 10013
[Michael Philip Batt] [ASC] (8/3/74 BCR-55)

WOMEN Foreigner—Atlantic 3651 [Michael Leslie Jones] [ASC] (2/16/80 BCR-41)

WOMEN Def Leppard—Mercury 888757
[Steve Clark/Phil Collen/Joe Elliott/Mutt Lange/Rick Savage] [ASC] (8/22/87 B-80)

WOMEN'S LOVE RIGHTS Laura Lee—Hot Wax 7105
[Angelo Bond/William Weatherspoon] [BMI] (9/4/71 BCR-20)

WONDER COULD I LIVE THERE ANYMORE Charley Pride—RCA Victor 47-9855
[Bill Rice] [ASC] (7/4/70 B-87)

WONDER GIRL Sparks—Bearsville 0006 [Ron Mael] [ASC] (11/4/72 CR-89)

A WONDER LIKE YOU Rick Nelson—Imperial 5770 [Jerry Fuller] [BMI] (10/2/61 BCR-11)

THE WONDER OF YOU *Ray Peterson—RCA Victor 47-7513*
[Baker Knight] [BMI] (5/18/59 BCR-14)

THE WONDER OF YOU *Ray Peterson—RCA Victor 47-8333*
[Baker Knight] [BMI] (4/11/64 BCR-70)

THE WONDER OF YOU *Elvis Presley—RCA Victor 47-9835*
[Baker Knight] (TSW) [BMI] (5/16/70 BCR-4)

WONDERFUL Blackwell—Astro 1000
[John Bundrick/Glenn Gibson] [BMI] (10/25/69 BCR-69)

WONDERFUL Isaac Hayes—Enterprise 9095 [Isaac Hayes] [BMI] (5/4/74 B-71)

WONDERFUL BABY Don McLean—United Artists 614
[Don McLean] [BMI] (6/14/75 BC-93)

WONDERFUL CHRISTMASTIME Paul McCartney—Columbia 11162
[Paul McCartney] [ASC] (12/29/79 CR-83)

A WONDERFUL DREAM The Majors—Imperial 5855
[Celia Marshall/Jerry Ragovoy] [BMI] (8/4/62 BCR-20)

WONDERFUL SUMMER Robin Ward—Dot 16530
[Perry Botkin Jr./Gil Garfield] [BMI] (10/26/63 BCR-14)

WONDERFUL TIME UP THERE Pat Boone—Dot 15690
[Lee Roy Abernathy] [BMI] (1/27/58 BCR-6)

WONDERFUL TONIGHT Eric Clapton—RSO 895 [Eric Clapton] [BMI] (5/13/78 BCR-16)

WONDERFUL WONDERFUL *Johnny Mathis—Columbia 40784*
[Sherman Edwards/Ben Raleigh] [ASC] (2/9/57 BCRt-12)

WONDERFUL! WONDERFUL!
Jan Peerce with Joe Reisman & His Orchestra—RCA Victor 47-6916
[Sherman Edwards/Ben Raleigh] [ASC] (6/8/57 Rt-22)

WONDERFUL! WONDERFUL! *The Tymes—Parkway 884*
[Sherman Edwards/Ben Raleigh] [ASC] (8/17/63 BCR-7)

WONDERFUL WORLD *Sam Cooke—Keen 82112*
[Lou Adler/Herb Alpert/Sam Cooke] [BMI] (5/7/60 BCR-10)

WONDERFUL WORLD *Herman's Hermits—MGM 13354*
[Lou Adler/Herb Alpert/Sam Cooke] [BMI] (5/22/65 BCR-4)

WONDERFUL WORLD *The Ovations—MGM 14623*
[Lou Adler/Herb Alpert/Sam Cooke] (Med) [BMI] (10/13/73 BCR-56)

(WHAT A) WONDERFUL WORLD *Johnny Nash—Epic 50219*
[Lou Adler/Herb Alpert/Sam Cooke] [BMI] (4/24/76 C-82)

(WHAT A) WONDERFUL WORLD
Art Garfunkel With James Taylor & Paul Simon—Columbia 10676
[Lou Adler/Herb Alpert/Sam Cooke] [BMI] (1/21/78 BCR-15)

WONDERFUL WORLD, BEAUTIFUL PEOPLE Jimmy Cliff—A&M 1146
[Jimmy Cliff] [BMI] (11/29/69 BCR-18)

THE WONDERFUL WORLD OF THE YOUNG Andy Williams—Columbia 42265
[Roy C. Bennett/Sid Tepper] [ASC] (3/24/62 B-99)

WONDERFUL YOU Jimmie Rodgers—Roulette 4158
[Sid Jacobson/Lou Stallman] [BMI] (6/8/59 BCR-40)

WONDERING Patti Page—Mercury 71101 [Jack Schafer] [ASC] (5/20/57 BR-35)

WONDERING WHERE THE LIONS ARE Bruce Cockburn—Millennium 11786
[Bruce Cockburn] [BMI] (3/1/80 BCR-20)

WONDERLAND Commodores—Motown 1479 [Milan Williams] [ASC] (12/15/79 BCR-25)

WONDERLAND Big Country—Mercury 818834
[William Stuart Adamson/Mark Brzezicki/Anthony Earl Butler/Bruce William Watson]
[ASC] (6/2/84 B-86)

WONDERLAND BY NIGHT *Bert Kaempfert And His Orchestra—Decca 31141*
[Klaus-Günter Neumann] [BMI] (10/31/60 BCtRt-1) [IM]

WONDERLAND BY NIGHT *Louis Prima—Dot 16151*
[Klaus-Günter Neumann] [BMI] (11/7/60 BCtRt-1) [IM]

WONDERLAND BY NIGHT *Anita Bryant—Carlton 537*
[Lincoln Chase/Klaus-Günter Neumann] [BMI] (11/21/60 BCtRt-1)

WON'T BE LONG Aretha Franklin—Columbia 41923
[J. Leslie McFarland] [ASC] (1/28/61 BC-87)

WON'T FIND BETTER (THAN ME) The New Hope—Jamie 1381
[Carl Hausman/Kit Stewart] [BMI] (1/3/70 BCR-57)

WON'T GET FOOLED AGAIN The Who—Decca 32846
[Pete Townshend] [BMI] (7/10/71 BCR-8)

WON'T TALK ABOUT IT Beats International—Elektra 64948
[Billy Bragg/Norman Cook] [ASC] (8/25/90 BC-75)

—WON'T YOU COME HOME, BILL BAILEY see: BILL BAILEY WON'T YOU PLEASE...

WON'T YOU COME ON BACK Fats Domino—Imperial 5895
[Marion Carpenter/Fats Domino/Tim Gillis] [BMI] (12/15/62 C-94)

WONT'CHA COME HOME Lloyd Price—ABC-Paramount 10062 [Harold Logan/Lloyd Price] [BMI] (10/19/59 BCR-15)

WOO HOO The Rock-A-Teens—Roulette 4192 [George McGraw] [ASC] (9/21/59 BCR-16) [I]

WOOD BEEZ (PRAY LIKE ARETHA FRANKLIN) Scritti Politti—Warner Bros. 28811 [Green Gartside] [ASC] (2/8/86 BC-89)

WOODCHOPPER'S BALL *Hutch Davie And His Honky Tonkers—Atco 6110 [Joe Bishop/Woody Herman] [ASC] (4/28/58 BCRt-42) [I]*

WOODCHOPPER'S BALL *Winifred Atwell—London 1817 [Joe Bishop/Woody Herman] [ASC] (7/7/58 Rt-74) [I]*

WOODEN HEART *Joe Dowell—Smash 1708 [Bert Kaempfert/Kay Twomey/Ben Weisman/Fred Wise] [ASC] (6/26/61 BCR-1)*

WOODEN HEART *Bobby Vinton—ABC 12100 [Bert Kaempfert/Kay Twomey/Ben Weisman/Fred Wise] [ASC] (5/31/75 BCR-58)*

THE WOODPECKER SONG Bobby Rydell—Cameo 265 [Harold Adamson/Bruno Cherubini/Eldo Di Lazzaro] [BMI] (8/17/63 CR-81) [FET]

WOODSTOCK *Crosby, Stills, Nash & Young—Atlantic 2723 [Joni Mitchell] [ASC] (3/21/70 BCR-10)*

WOODSTOCK *The Assembled Multitude—Atlantic 2764 [Joni Mitchell] [ASC] (9/26/70 BCR-71) [IWM]*

WOODSTOCK *Matthews' Southern Comfort—Decca 32774 [Joni Mitchell] [ASC] (3/6/71 BCR-17)*

WOOLY BULLY Sam The Sham And The Pharaohs—MGM 13322 [Domingo Samudio] [BMI] (4/3/65 BCR-1)

A WORD IN SPANISH Elton John—MCA 53408 [Elton John/Bernie Taupin] [BMI] (9/17/88 BC-18)

THE WORD IS OUT Jermaine Stewart—Arista 1-9256 [Gregory Craig/Jermaine Stewart] [ASC] (2/2/85 BC-37)

WORD OF MOUTH Mike + The Mechanics—Atlantic 87714 [Christopher Neil/Mike Rutherford] [BMI] (3/30/91 BC-62)

WORD TO THE BADD!! Jermaine Jackson—LaFace 2-4011 [Kenneth Edmonds/Jermaine Jackson/Lisa Lopes/Antonio Reid/Daryl Simmons] [BMI] (11/30/91 B-78)

WORD UP Cameo—Atlanta Artists 884933 [Larry Blackmon/Tomi Jenkins] [BMI] (9/13/86 BC-6)

WORDS Pat Boone—Dot 16048 [Jessie Cavanaugh/Charles Singleton] [BMI] (2/13/60 BC-94)

WORDS The Monkees—Colgems 1007 [Tommy Boyce/Bobby Hart] [BMI] (7/22/67 BCR-5)

WORDS The Bee Gees—Atco 6548 [Barry Gibb/Maurice Gibb/Robin Gibb] [BMI] (1/20/68 BCR-15)

WORDS Missing Persons—Capitol 5127 [Terry Bozzio/Warren Cuccurullo] [ASC] (7/3/82 BC-37)

WORDS F.R. David—Carrere 101 [Robert Fitoussi/Marty Sanders/Louis Yaguda] [BMI] (7/23/83 BC-59)

VADO VIA *Drupi—A&M 1460 [Luigi Albertelli/Enrico Riccardi] [BMI] (10/20/73 BC-88) [F]*

WORDS (ARE IMPOSSIBLE) *Margie Joseph—Atlantic 3220 [Bobby Hart/Danny Janssen/Enrico Riccardi] [BMI] (12/21/74 B-91) [FDE]*

WORDS (ARE IMPOSSIBLE) *Donny Gerrard—Greedy 101 [Bobby Hart/Danny Janssen/Enrico Riccardi] [BMI] (3/27/76 BC-87) [FDE]*

WORDS GET IN THE WAY Miami Sound Machine—Epic 06120 [Gloria Estefan] [BMI] (6/14/86 BC-5)

WORDS OF LOVE The Diamonds—Mercury 71128 [Buddy Holly] [ASC] (6/15/57 BCR-47)

WORDS OF LOVE The Mamas & The Papas—Dunhill 4057 [John Phillips] [ASC] (12/3/66 BCR-5)

WORK ON ME The O'Jays—Philadelphia Int'l 3631 [Kenneth Gamble/Leon Huff] [BMI] (8/13/77 R-76)

WORK OUT, PART I & II Ricky Dee & the Embers—Newtown 5001 [Marsha Levinson*/Bobby Martin] [BMI] (6/9/62 R-87) [I]

THE WORK SONG Herb Alpert & The Tijuana Brass—A&M 805 [Nat Adderley] [BMI] (7/2/66 BCR-13) [IM]

WORK THAT BODY Diana Ross—RCA 13201 [Ray Chew/Paul Jabara/Diana Ross] [BMI] (4/10/82 BCR-41)

WORK TO DO The Isley Brothers—T-Neck 936 [O'Kelly Isley/Ronald Isley/Rudolph Isley] [ASC] (10/28/72 BCR-43)

WORK, WORK, WORK Lee Dorsey—Amy 939 [Allen Toussaint] [BMI] (10/2/65 C-100)

WORKIN' AT THE CAR WASH BLUES Jim Croce—ABC 11447 [Jim Croce] [ASC] (6/8/74 BCR-20)

WORKIN' FOR A LIVIN' Huey Lewis and the News—Chrysalis 2630 [Mario Cipollina/Johnny Colla/Bill Gibson/Chris Hayes/Sean Hopper/Huey Lewis] [ASC] (8/14/82 BC-41)

WORKIN' FOR THE MAN Roy Orbison—Monument 467 [Roy Orbison] [BMI] (9/15/62 BCR-30)

WORKIN' ON A GROOVY THING *Patti Drew—Capitol 2197 [Roger Atkins/Neil Sedaka] [BMI] (8/3/68 BCR-41)*

WORKIN' ON A GROOVY THING *The 5th Dimension—Soul City 776 [Roger Atkins/Neil Sedaka] [BMI] (7/19/69 BCR-19)*

WORKIN' TOGETHER Ike & Tina Turner—Liberty 56207 [Ike Turner] [BMI] (11/28/70 CR-80)

WORKING CLASS HERO Tommy Roe—MGM South 7013 [Tommy Roe] [BMI] (4/7/73 BCR-67)

WORKING CLASS MAN Jimmy Barnes—Geffen 28749 [Jonathan Cain] [ASC] (3/22/86 B-74)

WORKING FOR THE WEEKEND Loverboy—Columbia 02589 [Paul Dean/Matt Frenette/Mike Reno] [BMI] (11/14/81 BCR-25)

WORKING IN THE COAL MINE *Lee Dorsey—Amy 958 [Allen Toussaint] [BMI] (7/23/66 BCR-8)*

WORKING IN THE COAL MINE *Devo—Full Moon 47204 [Allen Toussaint] [BMI] (9/5/81 BCR-27)*

A WORKING MAN'S PRAYER Arthur Prysock—Verve 10574 [Ed Bruce] [BMI] (1/6/68 BCR-61)

WORKING MY WAY BACK TO YOU *The 4 Seasons Featuring The "Sound" Of Frankie Valli—Philips 40350 [Sandy Linzer/Denny Randell] [BMI] (1/29/66 BCR-9)*

WORKING MY WAY BACK TO YOU *The Spinners—Atlantic 3637 [Sandy Linzer/Denny Randell] (Med) [BMI] (12/15/79 BCR-2)*

WORKING MY WAY BACK TO YOU *Gidea Park—Profile 5003 [Sandy Linzer/Denny Randell] (Med) [BMI] (12/26/81 BC-82)*

WORKING ON IT Chris Rea—Geffen 27535 [Chris Rea] [ASC] (3/25/89 BC-65)

WORKOUT STEVIE, WORKOUT Little Stevie Wonder—Tamla 54086 [Henry Cosby/Clarence Paul] [ASC] (9/28/63 BCR-33)

WORLD (PART 1) James Brown—King 6258 [James Brown] [BMI] (9/6/69 BCR-26)

THE WORLD I USED TO KNOW Jimmie Rodgers—Dot 16595 [Rod McKuen] [ASC] (5/23/64 BCR-51)

WORLD IN MY EYES Depeche Mode—Sire 19580 [Martin L. Gore] [BMI] (11/24/90 BC-48)

THE WORLD IS A GHETTO War—United Artists 50975 [Thomas Allen/Harold Brown/Morris Dickerson/Lonnie Jordan/Charles Miller/Lee Oskar/Howard Scott] [ASC] (11/18/72 BCR-7)

THE WORLD IS WAITING FOR THE SUNRISE Don Gibson—RCA Victor 47-7841 [Eugene Lockhart/Ernest Seitz] [ASC] (1/30/61 R-43)

WORLD OF FANTASY The Five Stairsteps—Windy C 602 [Clarence Burke Sr./Gregory Keith Fowler] [BMI] (7/23/66 BCR-42)

THE WORLD OF LONELY PEOPLE Anita Bryant—Columbia 43037 [Mort Garson/Buddy Kaye] [ASC] (5/16/64 BCR-59)

A WORLD OF OUR OWN The Seekers—Capitol 5430 [Tom Springfield] [ASC] (5/29/65 BCR-19)

WORLD OUTSIDE *Four Aces—Decca 30764 [Richard Addinsell/Carl Sigman] [ASC] (10/27/58 BCtRt-17)*

WORLD OUTSIDE *The Four Coins—Epic 9295 [Richard Addinsell/Carl Sigman] [ASC] (11/3/58 BCRt-17)*

WORLD OUTSIDE *Roger Williams—Kapp 246 [Richard Addinsell/Carl Sigman] [ASC] (11/10/58 BCtRt-17)*

WORLD SHUT YOUR MOUTH Julian Cope—Island 99479 [Julian Cope] [BMI] (3/14/87 BC-83)

THE WORLD THROUGH A TEAR Neil Sedaka—RCA Victor 47-8637 [Chris Allen/Peter Allen*/Dick Everitt] [ASC] (8/28/65 BCR-69)

THE WORLD WE KNEW (OVER AND OVER) Frank Sinatra—Reprise 0610 [Bert Kaempfert/Herbert Rehbein/Carl Sigman] [BMI] (8/5/67 BCR-22)

WORLD WHERE YOU LIVE Crowded House—Capitol 44033 [Neil Finn] [BMI] (8/8/87 BC-65)

A WORLD WITHOUT HEROES KISS—Casablanca 2343 [Bob Ezrin/Lou Reed/Gene Simmons/Paul Stanley] [BMI] (12/12/81 BCR-56)

A WORLD WITHOUT LOVE *Peter And Gordon—Capitol 5175 [John Lennon/Paul McCartney] [ASC] (5/9/64 BCtR-1)*

A WORLD WITHOUT LOVE *Bobby Rydell—Cameo 320 [John Lennon/Paul McCartney] [ASC] (5/9/64 BCtR-2)*

A WORLD WITHOUT MUSIC Archie Bell & The Drells—Atlantic 2693 [Kenneth Gamble/Leon Huff] [BMI] (4/18/70 B-100)

—WORLDS APART see: SEPARATE WAYS

THE WORM Jimmy McGriff—Solid State 2524 [Fats Theus] [BMI] (12/14/68 BR-97) [IWM]

WORRIED GUY Johnny Tillotson—MGM 13193 [Paul Evans/Jack Reardon] [ASC] (2/8/64 BCR-29)

WORRIED LIFE BLUES Ray Charles And His Orchestra—ABC-Paramount 10118 [Maceo Merriweather] [BMI] (7/9/60 C-88)

A WORRIED MAN *The Kingston Trio—Capitol 4271 [Tom Glazer/Dave Guard] [ASC] (9/7/59 BCR-15)*

A WORRIED MAN *(parody of A Worried Man) The Four Preps—Capitol 4599 [Tom Glazer/Dave Guard] (Med) [ASC] (8/14/61 BCR-14) [P]*

WORRIED MIND Ray Anthony—Capitol 4742 [Ted Daffan/Jimmie H. Davis] [BMI] (6/23/62 BCR-66) [IWM]

WORRY Johnny Tillotson—MGM 13255 [Chip Taylor] [BMI] (7/18/64 BCR-45)

THE WORRYIN' KIND Tommy Sands—Capitol 4082 [Diane Lampert/Scott Turner] [BMI] (12/29/58 BC-69)

WORSE COMES TO WORST Billy Joel—Columbia 46055 [Billy Joel] [ASC] (6/22/74 BC-70)

WORST THAT COULD HAPPEN Brooklyn Bridge—Buddah 75 [Jimmy Webb] [BMI] (12/7/68 BCR-3)

WOT'S IT TO YA Robbie Nevil—EMI 50075
[Robbie Nevil/Brock Walsh] [ASC] (5/30/87 BC-10)

WOULD I LIE TO YOU? Eurythmics—RCA 14078
[Annie Lennox/David A. Stewart] [ASC] (4/27/85 BC-5)

WOULD IT MAKE ANY DIFFERENCE TO YOU Etta James—Argo 5430
[Bob Forshee] [BMI] (12/22/62 BCR-64)

WOULD YOU LAY WITH ME (IN A FIELD OF STONE) Tanya Tucker—Columbia 45991
[David Allan Coe] [BMI] (2/16/74 BCR-45)

WOULDN'T CHANGE A THING Kylie Minogue—Geffen 22794
[Matt Aitken/Mike Stock/Pete Waterman] [BMI] (2/3/90 C-83)

WOULDN'T I BE SOMEONE Bee Gees—RSO 404
[Barry Gibb/Maurice Gibb/Robin Gibb] [BMI] (7/21/73 R-100)

WOULDN'T IT BE GOOD Nik Kershaw—MCA 52371 [Nik Kershaw] [BMI] (3/31/84 BC-46)

WOULDN'T IT BE NICE *The Beach Boys—Capitol 5706*
[Tony Asher/Mike Love/Brian Wilson] [BMI] (7/30/66 BCR-5)*

WOULDN'T IT BE NICE *The Cantina Band—Millennium 11818*
[Tony Asher/Mike Love/Brian Wilson] (Med) [BMI] (7/25/81 B-81)*

WOW Andre Gagnon—London 230 [André Gagnon] [ASC] (3/6/76 B-95) [I]

WOW WOW WEE (HE'S THE BOY FOR ME) The Angels—Smash 1870
[Peggy Farina/Bob Feldman/Jerry Goldstein/Richard Gottehrer/Robert Spencer] [BMI] (1/18/64 BCR-28)

WRACK MY BRAIN Ringo Starr—Boardwalk 7-11-130
[George Harrison] [ASC] (11/7/81 BCR-37)

WRAP HER UP Elton John—Geffen 28873
[Elton John/Davey Johnstone/Fred Mandel/Charlie Morgan/Bernie Taupin/Paul Westwood] [BMI] (10/26/85 BC-14)

WRAP IT UP *Archie Bell & The Drells—Atlantic 2768*
[Isaac Hayes/David Porter] [BMI] (12/12/70 BR-87)

WRAP IT UP *The Fabulous Thunderbirds—CBS Associated 06270*
[Isaac Hayes/David Porter] [BMI] (8/9/86 BC-41)

WRAP MY BODY TIGHT Johnny Gill—Motown 2077
[James Samuel Harris/Terry Lewis] [ASC] (3/23/91 BC-84)

WRAP YOUR ARMS AROUND ME K C & The Sunshine Band—TK 1022
[Harry Wayne Casey/Rick Finch] [BMI] (11/26/77 BCR-48)

WRAPPED AROUND YOUR FINGER The Police—A&M 2614 [Sting] [BMI] (1/7/84 BC-8)

WRAPPED UP IN YOUR WARM AND TENDER LOVE Tyrone Davis—Dakar 4526
[Carl Davis/Richard Parker] [BMI] (10/20/73 CR-83)

THE WRECK OF THE EDMUND FITZGERALD Gordon Lightfoot—Reprise 1369
[Gordon Lightfoot] [ASC] (8/28/76 BCR-1)

—WRECK OF THE JOHN B. see: SLOOP JOHN B.

WRINGLE WRANGLE *Bill Hayes—ABC-Paramount 9785*
[Stan Jones] [ASC] (1/19/57 BCtRt-12)

WRINGLE WRANGLE *Fess Parker—Disneyland 43 [Stan Jones] [ASC] (1/19/57 BCtRt-12)*

WRINGLE WRANGLE *Merv Griffin—Decca 30131 [Stan Jones] [ASC] (1/19/57 Rt-15)*

WRINGLE WRANGLE *Rex Allen—Decca 30205 [Stan Jones] [ASC] (2/9/57 Rt-15)*

WRINGLE WRANGLE *Vaughn Monroe—RCA Victor 47-6822*
[Stan Jones] [ASC] (3/2/57 Rt-15)

WRITE TO ME FROM NAPLES Dean Martin—Capitol 3752
[Alex Alstone/Jimmy Kennedy] [ASC] (7/27/57 R-77)

THE WRITING ON THE WALL Adam Wade—Coed 550
[Mark Barkan/Sandy Baron/George Eddy] [BMI] (5/15/61 BCR-5)

WRITTEN ALL OVER YOUR FACE Rude Boys—Atlantic 87805
[Larry Marcus] [BMI] (3/9/91 BC-16)

WRITTEN ON THE WIND Four Aces—Decca 30123
[Sammy Cahn/Victor Young] [ASC] (12/1/56 BCR-39)

WRONG AGAIN The Ames Brothers—RCA Victor 47-6156
[Stanley Applebaum/Elsie Simmons] [ASC] (7/4/55 R-74)

WRONG FOR EACH OTHER Andy Williams—Columbia 43015
[Doc Pomus/Mort Shuman] [BMI] (4/4/64 BCR-27)

WUN'ERFUL, WUN'ERFUL! (SIDES UH-ONE & UH-TWO) (parody of Lawrence Welk)
Stan Freberg—Capitol 3815
[Bob Calame/Stan Freberg/Fred Hollander/Frank Loesser/Ralph Rainger/Leo Robin/Lawrence Welk/Richard Whiting] [ASC] (10/26/57 BCR-22) [P]

WINKIN', BLINKIN' AND NOD *The Simon Sisters—Kapp 586*
[Eugene Field/Lucy Simon] [BMI] (4/25/64 B-73)

WYNKEN, BLYNKEN AND NOD *The Doobie Brothers—Sesame Street 49642*
[Eugene Field/Lucy Simon] [BMI] (1/17/81 BCR-76)

X

XANADU Olivia Newton-John/Electric Light Orchestra—MCA 41285
[Jeff Lynne] [BMI] (8/9/80 BCR-4)

Y

YA MAMA Wuf Ticket—Prelude 644
[Mustafa Ahmed/James Mason/Earl McField/Karin Wolf] [BMI] (2/19/83 C-94)

YA YA Lee Dorsey—Fury 1053
[Lee Dorsey/Morris Levy‡/Clarence L. Lewis*/Morgan C. Robinson*] [BMI] (9/2/61 BCR-7)

YAH MO B THERE James Ingram—Qwest 29394
[James Ingram/Quincy Jones/Michael McDonald/Rod Temperton] [BMI] (12/10/83 BC-19)

YAKETY SAX *Boots Randolph—Monument 804*
[Boots Randolph/James Rich] [BMI] (2/23/63 BCR-23) [I]

YAKETY AXE *Chet Atkins—RCA Victor 47-8590*
[Boots Randolph/James Rich] [BMI] (7/10/65 BC-85) [I]

YAKETY YAK The Coasters—Atco 6116
[Jerry Leiber/Mike Stoller] [BMI] (5/31/58 BCRt*-1)

YAKKITY YAK The Markeys Featuring Georgie Morton—RCA Victor 47-7256
[Jack Hammer] [ASC] (6/2/58 Rt*-7)

YANCY DERRINGER Tommy Mara—Felsted 8561
[Don Quinn/Henry Russell] [ASC] (3/9/59 R-80)

YANK ME, CRANK ME Ted Nugent—Epic 50533 [Ted Nugent] [ASC] (4/1/78 BCR-56)

YANKEE LADY Brewer And Shipley—Kama Sutra 547
[Jesse Winchester] [ASC] (7/22/72 C-90)

YANKEE ROSE David Lee Roth—Warner Bros. 28656
[David Lee Roth/Steve Vai] [ASC] (7/5/86 BC-16)

THE YARD WENT ON FOREVER Richard Harris—Dunhill 4170
[Jimmy Webb] [ASC] (11/2/68 BCR-43)

YEA, YEA The Kendall Sisters—Argo 5291
[Hillman Baker/Vlad Maleckar] [BMI] (3/24/58 B-73)

YEAH, YEAH, YEAH Judson Spence—Atlantic 88999
[Monroe Jones/Judson Spence] [BMI] (10/15/88 BC-30)

YEAR AGO TONIGHT The Crests—Coed 521
[Allyson Khent/Billy Dawn Smith] [BMI] (12/7/59 BCR-40)

YEAR OF THE CAT Al Stewart—Janus 266
[Al Stewart/Peter John Wood] [BMI] (12/11/76 BCR-4)

THE YEAR THAT CLAYTON DELANEY DIED Tom T. Hall—Mercury 73221
[Tom T. Hall] [BMI] (8/21/71 BCR-42)

YEARNING FOR YOUR LOVE The Gap Band—Mercury 76101
[Oliver Scott/Ronnie Wilson] [ASC] (5/16/81 BCR-60)

YEARNING (JUST FOR YOU) Georgie Shaw—Decca 29245
[Joe Burke/Benny Davis] [ASC] (9/25/54 C-42)

YEARS Wayne Newton—Aries II 108
[Kye Fleming/Dennis W. Morgan] [BMI] (1/26/80 BCR-32)

YEARS FROM NOW Jackie Wilson—Brunswick 55219
[Bobby Adams/Horace Ott/Alonzo Tucker] [BMI] (8/19/61 BCR-37)

YEARS FROM NOW Dr. Hook—Capitol 4885
[Charles Lincoln Cochran/Roger Cook] [BMI] (7/5/80 BCR-51)

YEH-YEH! *Mongo Santamaria Orch.—Battle 45917*
[Rodgers Grant/Pat Patrick] [BMI] (6/22/63 B-92) [IM]

YEH, YEH *Georgie Fame And The Blue Flames—Imperial 66086*
[Rodgers Grant/Jon Hendricks/Pat Patrick] [BMI] (2/13/65 BCR-13)

YELLOW BALLOON The Yellow Balloon—Canterbury 508
[Dick Gosting/Jay Lee/Gary Zekley] [BMI] (3/11/67 BCR-25)

THE YELLOW BANDANA Faron Young—Mercury 72085
[Al Gorgoni/Steve Karliski/Larry Kolber] [BMI] (2/16/63 CR-65)

YELLOW BIRD *The Mills Brothers—Dot 15858*
[Alan Bergman/Marilyn Bergman/Norman Luboff] [ASC] (12/6/58 BCR-70)

YELLOW BIRD *Arthur Lyman Group—HiFi 5024*
[Norman Luboff] [ASC] (5/27/61 BCtRt-4) [IM]

YELLOW BIRD *Lawrence Welk And His Orchestra—Dot 16222*
[Norman Luboff] [ASC] (5/29/61 BCtRt-5) [IM]

YELLOW DOG BLUES *Joe Darensbourg And His Dixie Flyers—Lark 452*
[W.C. Handy] [NA] (12/23/57 BCRt-24) [I]

YELLOW DOG BLUES *Pete Fountain—Brunswick 55045*
[W.C. Handy] [NA] (12/23/57 Rt-24) [I]

YELLOW DOG BLUES *Bob Crosby & His Orchestra—Coral 61929*
[W.C. Handy] [NA] (12/23/57 Rt-24) [I]

YELLOW DOG BLUES *Johnny Maddox—Dot 15683*
[W.C. Handy] [NA] (12/30/57 BRt-24) [I]

YELLOW RIVER Christie—Epic 10626 [Jeff Christie] [BMI] (7/4/70 BCR-16)

THE YELLOW ROSE OF TEXAS *Mitch Miller with His Orch. & Chorus—Columbia 40540*
[Don George/Traditional] [ASC] (7/25/55 BCtRt-1)

THE YELLOW ROSE OF TEXAS *Johnny Desmond—Coral 61476*
[Don George/Traditional] [ASC] (7/25/55 BCtRt-1)

THE YELLOW ROSE OF TEXAS *Stan Freberg—Capitol 3249*
[Don George/Traditional] [ASC] (10/22/55 BCt-2)

YELLOW SUBMARINE The Beatles—Capitol 5715
[John Lennon/Paul McCartney] [ASC] (8/20/66 BCR-1)

YEN YET SONG Gary Cane And His Friends—Shell 719
[Sid Jacobson/Lou Stallman] [BMI] (6/6/60 BCR-93)

YEP Duane Eddy His "Twangy" guitar and The Rebels—Jamie 1122
[Duane Eddy/Lee Hazlewood] [BMI] (3/23/59 BCR-27) [I]

YES Merry Clayton—RCA 6989
[Neal Cavanaugh/Terry Fryer/Thomas Graf] [ASC] (3/5/88 BC-42)
YES I DO Solomon Burke—Atlantic 2254 [Bert Berns] [BMI] (10/10/64 BR-90)
YES, I WANT YOU Ivory Joe Hunter—Atlantic 1191
[Ivory Joe Hunter] [BMI] (9/8/58 B-94)
—YES I'M LONESOME TONIGHT see: ARE YOU LONESOME TONIGHT
YES, I'M READY *Barbara Mason—Arctic 105 [Barbara Mason] [BMI] (5/8/65 BCR-3)*
YES, I'M READY *Teri DeSario with K.C.—Casablanca 2227*
[Barbara Mason] [BMI] (11/17/79 BCR-1)
YES INDEED *The Modernaires—Coral 61779 [Sy Oliver] (Med) [BMI] (2/16/57 R-72)*
YES INDEED *Pete Fountain—Coral 65549 [Sy Oliver] [BMI] (2/5/62 BCR-69) [IWM]*
YES IT IS The Beatles—Capitol 5407
[John Lennon/Paul McCartney] [ASC] (5/1/65 BR-46)
YES MY DARLING Fats Domino—Imperial 5492
[Dave Bartholomew/Fats Domino] [BMI] (3/1/58 BCR-53)
YES OR NO Go-Go's—I.R.S. 9933
[Ron Mael/Russell Mael/Jane Wiedlin] [ASC] (9/22/84 B-84)
YES SIR The Music Explosion—Laurie 3454
[Joey Levine/Kris Resnick] [BMI] (6/22/68 R-97)
YES SIR EE Dodie Stevens—Crystalette 728
[Dorothy Brandes/Sanger Shafer/Albert Stella] [BMI] (5/25/59 BCR-79)
YES SIR THAT'S MY BABY *Ralph Marterie And His Orchestra—Mercury 70917*
[Walter Donaldson] [ASC] (8/17/56 R-81) [IM]
YES SIR THAT'S MY BABY *Four Aces—Decca 30348*
[Walter Donaldson/Gus Kahn] [ASC] (6/15/57 R-78)
YES SIR THAT'S MY BABY *Ricky Nelson—Imperial 5685*
[Walter Donaldson/Gus Kahn] [ASC] (8/29/60 BCR-34)
YES SIR, THAT'S MY BABY *Julius Wechter & The Baja Marimba Band—A&M 937*
[Walter Donaldson/Gus Kahn] [ASC] (6/15/68 CR-87)
YES SIREE!! Earl Grant—Decca 31468
[Charles "Bud" Dant/Bill Grant/Earl Grant] [BMI] (3/9/63 R-84)
YES TONIGHT JOSEPHINE Johnnie Ray—Columbia 40893
[Dorothy Goodman/Winfield Scott] [BMI] (4/13/57 BCR-18)
YES WE CAN CAN The Pointer Sisters—Blue Thumb 229
[Allen Toussaint] [BMI] (8/18/73 BCR-10)
YES, YES, YES Bill Cosby—Capitol 4258
[Bill Cosby/Stu Gardner] [BMI] (5/1/76 BCR-46)
YES YOU ARE The Mills Brothers—Decca 29496 [Bob Merrill] [ASC] (5/2/55 R-50)
YESSIREE Linda Scott—Congress 101 [Linda Scott] [BMI] (2/5/62 BCR-48)
YESTER LOVE Smokey Robinson & The Miracles—Tamla 54167
[Al Cleveland/Smokey Robinson] [ASC] (6/1/68 BCR-22)
YESTER-ME, YESTER-YOU, YESTERDAY *Stevie Wonder—Tamla 54188*
[Ronald Norman Miller/Bryan Wells] [ASC] (10/18/69 BCR-7)
YESTER-ME, YESTER-YOU, YESTERDAY *Stars On 45—Radio 4019*
[Ronald Norman Miller/Bryan Wells] (Med) [ASC] (3/27/82 BCR-28)
YESTERDAY *The Beatles—Capitol 5498*
[John Lennon/Paul McCartney] [ASC] (9/18/65 BCR-1)
YESTERDAY *Ray Charles—ABC 11009*
[John Lennon/Paul McCartney] [ASC] (11/4/67 BCR-15)
—YESTERDAY AND YOU see: ARMEN'S THEME
YESTERDAY I HAD THE BLUES
Harold Melvin And The Blue Notes—Philadelphia Int'l 3525
[Kenneth Gamble/Leon Huff] [BMI] (3/3/73 BCR-52)
YESTERDAY MAN Chris Andrews—Atco 6385
[Chris Frederick Andrews] [BMI] (12/25/65 BCR-80)
YESTERDAY ONCE MORE *Carpenters—A&M 1446*
[John Bettis/Richard Carpenter] [ASC] (6/2/73 BCR-1)
YESTERDAY ONCE MORE *The Spinners—Atlantic 3798*
[John Bettis/Richard Carpenter] (Med) [ASC] (2/14/81 BCR-52)
YESTERDAY, WHEN I WAS YOUNG Roy Clark—Dot 17246
[Charles Aznavour/Herbert Kretzmer] [ASC] (5/31/69 BCR-16) [FET]
YESTERDAY'S DREAMS Four Tops—Motown 1127
[Vernon Bullock/Jack Goga/Ivy Jo Hunter/Pam Sawyer] [BMI] (7/20/68 BCR-31)
YESTERDAY'S GONE *The Overlanders—Hickory 1258*
[Wendy Kidd‡/Chad Stuart] [BMI] (5/2/64 BCtR-28)
YESTERDAY'S GONE *Chad Stuart & Jeremy Clyde—World Artists 1021*
[Wendy Kidd‡/Chad Stuart] [BMI] (5/2/64 BCtR-21)
YESTERDAY'S HERO Gene Pitney—Musicor 1038
[Al Cleveland/Wally Gold/Aaron Schroeder/Carl Spencer] [BMI] (5/9/64 BC-64)
YESTERDAY'S HERO *John Paul Young—Ariola America 7607*
[Harry Vanda/George Young] [ASC] (12/13/75 BCR-42)
YESTERDAY'S HERO *Bay City Rollers—Arista 0216*
[Harry Vanda/George Young] [ASC] (11/27/76 BCR-49)
YESTERDAY'S RAIN Spanky And Our Gang—Mercury 72871
[Lefty Baker] [BMI] (11/23/68 BCR-67)
YESTERDAY'S SONGS Neil Diamond—Columbia 02604
[Neil Diamond] [SE] (11/7/81 BCR-11)
YET...I KNOW (ET POURTANT) Steve Lawrence—Columbia 43095
[Charles Aznavour/Diran Garvarentz/Don Raye] [ASC] (8/22/64 BCR-68) [FET]

YIELD NOT TO TEMPTATION Bobby Bland—Duke 352
[Deadric Malone] [BMI] (8/11/62 BCR-50)
—YING-YANG see: LITTLE EGYPT
Y.M.C.A. Village People—Casablanca 945
[Henri Belolo/Jacques Morali/Victor Willis] [BMI] (10/21/78 BCR-2)
YO' LITTLE BROTHER Nolan Thomas—Mirage 99697
[Ann Godwin/Curtis Josephs] [ASC] (1/5/85 BC-57)
YO ME PREGUNTO The Valrays—Parkway 904
[Pete Antel/John Linde] [BMI] (5/23/64 R-91) [F]
YO NO SE Pajama Party—Atlantic 88984
[Jim Klein/Peggy Sendars] [ASC] (5/20/89 B-75)
YO-YO The Osmonds—MGM 14295 [Joe South] [BMI] (9/11/71 BCR-1)
YOGI The Ivy Three—Shell 720
[Sid Jacobson/Charles Koppelman/Lou Stallman] [BMI] (8/1/60 BCR-8)
YOU *The Aquatones—Fargo 1001 [David Goddard/Larry Vannata] [BMI] (4/7/58 BCRt-19)*
YOU *Gale Storm—Dot 15734 [David Goddard/Larry Vannata] [BMI] (4/7/58 Rt-19)*
YOU Darlene McCrea—Roulette 4173 [Teddy Vann] [BMI] (9/5/59 C-92)
YOU Marvin Gaye—Tamla 54160
[Jeff Bowen*/Jack Goga/Eddie Holland*/Ivy Jo Hunter] [BMI] (1/6/68 BCR-30)
YOU George Harrison—Apple 1884 [George Harrison] [ASC] (9/20/75 BCR-19)
YOU Aretha Franklin—Atlantic 3311
[Jerry Butler/Charles Henry Jackson Jr./Marvin Yancy] [ASC] (1/17/76 C-90)
YOU Rita Coolidge—A&M 2058 [Tom Snow] [BMI] (6/24/78 BCR-17)
YOU The McCrarys—Portrait 70014
[Alfred McCrary/Linda McCrary/Sam McCrary] [BMI] (7/15/78 BCR-29)
YOU Earth, Wind & Fire—ARC Columbia 11-11407
[David Foster/Brenda Russell/Maurice White] [ASC] (11/22/80 BCR-48)
YOU AIN'T GOING NOWHERE The Byrds—Columbia 44499
[Bob Dylan] [SE] (4/27/68 BCR-74)
YOU AIN'T NEVER BEEN LOVED (LIKE I'M GONNA LOVE YOU) Jessi Colter—Capitol 4087
[Jessi Colter] (TSW) [BMI] (10/11/75 BCR-56)
YOU AIN'T SEEN NOTHING YET *Bachman-Turner Overdrive—Mercury 73622*
[Randy Bachman] (TSW) [NA] (11/9/74 BCR-1)
YOU AIN'T SEEN NOTHING YET *Figures On A Beach—Sire 27628*
[Randy Bachman] [NA] (4/8/89 BC-67)
YOU ALWAYS COME BACK (TO HURTING ME) Johnny Rodriguez—Mercury 73368
[Tom T. Hall/Johnny Rodriguez] [BMI] (6/23/73 B-86)
YOU ALWAYS HURT ME The Impressions—ABC 10900
[Curtis Mayfield] [BMI] (3/4/67 BCR-77)
YOU ALWAYS HURT THE ONE YOU LOVE *The Fontane Sisters—Dot 15462*
[Doris Fisher/Allan Roberts] [ASC] (5/4/56 R-20)
YOU ALWAYS HURT THE ONE YOU LOVE *Somethin' Smith & The Redheads—Epic 9221*
[Doris Fisher/Allan Roberts] [ASC] (7/20/57 R-43)
YOU ALWAYS HURT THE ONE YOU LOVE *Clarence Henry—Argo 5388*
[Doris Fisher/Allan Roberts] [ASC] (5/15/61 BCR-12)
YOU AND I Black Ivory—Today 1508
[Stuart Bascombe/Leroy Burgess] [BMI] (4/29/72 C-95)
YOU AND I Johnny Bristol—MGM 14762 [Johnny Bristol] [ASC] (11/9/74 BC-48)
YOU AND I, PT. 1 Living Proof—Ju-Par 532
[Vernon Bullock/Chestener Gorden] [BMI] (2/11/78 R-98)
YOU AND I Rick James—Gordy 7156 [Rick James] [ASC] (6/24/78 BCR-13)
YOU AND I Eddie Rabbitt with Crystal Gayle—Elektra 69936
[Frank Myers] [ASC] (10/9/82 BC-7)
YOU AND ME Aretha Franklin—Atlantic 2772
[Aretha Franklin] (TSW) [BMI] (12/19/70 B-37)
YOU AND ME Alice Cooper—Warner Bros. 8349
[Alice Cooper/Dick Wagner] [BMI] (4/23/77 BCR-8)
YOU AND ME Liner—Atco 7097
[David Anthony Farmer/Thomas Laurence Farmer/Eddie Golga] [BMI] (3/17/79 B-92)
YOU AND ME Rockie Robbins—A&M 2231 [James P. Pennington] [BMI] (6/7/80 BCR-80)
YOU AND ME AGAINST THE WORLD Helen Reddy—Capitol 3897
[Ken Ascher/Paul Williams] [ASC] (6/8/74 BCR-9)
—YOU AND ME see: NOW AND FOREVER
YOU AND ME TOGETHER FOREVER Freddie North—Mankind 12009
[Jimmy Roach] [BMI] (2/19/72 CR-89)
YOU AND ME TONIGHT Deja—Virgin 99422
[Eban Kelly/Jimi Randolph] [BMI] (11/21/87 BC-54)
YOU AND YOUR BABY BLUES Solomon Burke—Chess 2159
[Solomon Burke/Jerry Styner] [BMI] (3/22/75 B-96)
YOU AND YOUR FOLKS, ME AND MY FOLKS Funkadelic—Westbound 175
[George Clinton/Clarence Haskins/Billy Nelson/Bernie Worrell] [BMI] (4/3/71 BCR-85)
YOU ANGEL YOU Manfred Mann's Earth Band—Warner Bros. 8850
[Bob Dylan] [SE] (6/2/79 BCR-53)
YOU ARE Lionel Richie—Motown 1657
[Brenda Richie/Lionel Richie] [ASC] (1/15/83 BC-2)
YOU ARE A SONG Batdorf & Rodney—Arista 0132
[Jim Weatherly] [ASC] (8/9/75 BC-80)
YOU ARE BEAUTIFUL Johnny Mathis—Columbia 41304
[Oscar Hammerstein/Richard Rodgers] [ASC] (12/15/58 BCR-60)

YOU ARE BEAUTIFUL The Stylistics—Avco 4664
[Luigi Creatore/Hugo Peretti/George David Weiss] [ASC] (2/28/76 BCR-79)
YOU ARE EVERYTHING The Stylistics—Avco 4581
[Thom Bell/Linda Creed] [BMI] (10/30/71 BCR-9)
YOU ARE FOREVER Smokey Robinson—Tamla 54327
[Smokey Robinson] [ASC] (6/20/81 BCR-59)
YOU ARE IN LOVE Perry Como—RCA Victor 47-7541 [Bart Howard] [ASC] (6/1/59 R-53)
YOU ARE IN MY SYSTEM *The System—Mirage 99937*
[David Frank/Mic Murphy] [ASC] (3/5/83 BC-56)
YOU ARE IN MY SYSTEM *Robert Palmer—Island 99866*
[David Frank/Mic Murphy] [ASC] (6/18/83 B-78)
YOU ARE MINE Frankie Avalon—Chancellor 1107
[Peter DeAngelis/Bob Marcucci] [ASC] (3/24/62 BCR-26)
YOU ARE MY DESTINY Paul Anka—ABC-Paramount 9880
[Paul Anka] [BMI] (12/30/57 BCR-7)
YOU ARE MY EVERYTHING Surface—Columbia 69016
[Everett Collins/Dave Conley/Derrick Culler/David Townsend] [ASC] (11/4/89 BC-84)
YOU ARE MY FIRST LOVE Nat "King" Cole—Capitol 3619
[Lester Powell/Paddy Roberts] [ASC] (2/2/57 BCR-30)
YOU ARE MY HEAVEN Roberta Flack With Donny Hathaway—Atlantic 3627
[Eric Mercury/Stevie Wonder] [BMI] (2/16/80 BCR-47)
YOU ARE MY LADY Freddie Jackson—Capitol 5495
[Barry Eastmond] [ASC] (9/7/85 BC-12)
—YOU ARE MY LADY see: POWER OF LOVE
YOU ARE MY LIFE Herb Alpert & The Tijuana Brass—A&M 1143
[Peter Sarstedt] [BMI] (11/22/69 CR-86) [I]
YOU ARE MY LOVE *Joni James—MGM 12066 [Jimmie Nabbie] [ASC] (9/26/55 BCRt-8)*
YOU ARE MY LOVE *The Four Tunes—Jubilee 5218 [Jimmie Nabbie] [ASC] (11/7/55 Rt-11)*
YOU ARE MY LOVE Liverpool Express—Atco 7058
[Roger Craig/Billy Kinsley] [ASC] (9/25/76 C-96)
YOU ARE MY STARSHIP
Norman Connors (Featuring Michael Henderson And Jean Cain)—Buddah 542
[Michael E. Henderson] [ASC] (8/28/76 BCR-26)
YOU ARE MY SUNSHINE *Ferko String Band—Media 1013*
[Oliver Hood] [BMI] (8/1/55 CRt-23) [IWM]
YOU ARE MY SUNSHINE *The Ames Brothers—Coral 60886*
[Oliver Hood] [BMI] (8/15/55 Rt-23)
YOU ARE MY SUNSHINE *Joe Pica—Original 521 [Oliver Hood] [BMI] (8/15/55 Rt-34)*
YOU ARE MY SUNSHINE *Bing Crosby—Decca 29634 [Oliver Hood] [BMI] (8/22/55 Rt-34)*
YOU ARE MY SUNSHINE *Johnny And The Hurricanes—Big Top 3056*
[Oliver Hood] [BMI] (11/14/60 BR-77) [IWM]
YOU ARE MY SUNSHINE *Ray Charles With The Raeletts—ABC-Paramount 10375*
[Oliver Hood] [BMI] (11/10/62 BCR-7)
YOU ARE MY SUNSHINE *Mitch Ryder—New Voice 826*
[Oliver Hood] [BMI] (10/28/67 BCR-63)
YOU ARE MY SUNSHINE *Dyke And The Blazers—Original Sound 90*
[Oliver Hood] [BMI] (1/10/70 CR-96)
YOU ARE ON MY MIND Chicago—Columbia 10523
[James Pankow] [ASC] (4/9/77 BCR-49)
YOU ARE SHE Chad & Jeremy—Columbia 43807
[Jeremy Clyde/Chad Stuart] [BMI] (10/8/66 BR-86)
YOU ARE SO BEAUTIFUL *Billy Preston—A&M 1644*
[Bruce Fisher/Billy Preston] (TSW) [ASC] (12/14/74 R-51)
YOU ARE SO BEAUTIFUL *Joe Cocker—A&M 1641*
[Bruce Fisher/Billy Preston] (TSW) [ASC] (1/18/75 BCR-4)
YOU ARE THE GIRL The Cars—Elektra 69446
[Ric Ocasek] [ASC] (8/29/87 BC-17)
YOU ARE THE ONE Sugar Bears—Big Tree 122
[Baker Knight] [BMI] (1/15/72 BCR-38)
YOU ARE THE ONE TKA—Warner Bros. 22946
[David Gaskins/Keath Lowry] [ASC] (6/3/89 B-91)
YOU ARE THE ONLY ONE Ricky Nelson—Imperial 5707
[Baker Knight] [BMI] (12/12/60 BCR-25)
YOU ARE THE SUNSHINE OF MY LIFE *Stevie Wonder—Tamla 54232*
[Stevie Wonder] [ASC] (3/17/73 BCR-1)
YOU ARE THE SUNSHINE OF MY LIFE *Stars On 45—Radio 4019*
[Stevie Wonder] (Med) [ASC] (3/27/82 BCR-28)
YOU ARE THE WOMAN Firefall—Atlantic 3335 [Rick Roberts] [BMI] (8/14/76 BCR-8)
YOU ARE YOU Gilbert O'Sullivan—MAM 3642 [Gilbert O'Sullivan] [ASC] (2/1/75 C-95)
YOU BABY The Turtles—White Whale 227
[Steve Barri/P.F. Sloan] [ASC] (1/29/66 BCR-15)
YOU BABY YOU *The Cleftones—Gee 1000*
[Berman Patterson/Gaetano Vastola] [BMI] (2/18/56 BRt-74)
YOU BABY YOU *The Diamonds—Mercury 70790*
[Berman Patterson/Gaetano Vastola] [BMI] (3/9/56 Rt-74)
YOU BE ILLIN' Run-D.M.C.—Profile 5119
[Jason Mizell/Joseph Ward Simmons/Ray White] [ASC] (10/25/86 BC-29)
YOU BEAT ME TO THE PUNCH *Mary Wells—Motown 1032*
[Smokey Robinson/Ronnie White] [ASC] (8/11/62 BCR-9)

YOU THREW A LUCKY PUNCH *(Response to You Beat Me To The Punch)*
Gene Chandler—Vee-Jay 468
[Don Covay/Smokey Robinson/Ronnie White] [BMI] (11/17/62 BCR-49) [R]
YOU BELONG TO ME *100 Strings & Joni—MGM 12885*
[Pee Wee King/Chilton Price/Redd Stewart] [BMI] (3/21/60 R-68)
YOU BELONG TO ME *The Duprees—Coed 569*
[Pee Wee King/Chilton Price/Redd Stewart] [BMI] (7/14/62 BCR-7)
YOU BELONG TO ME *Carly Simon—Elektra 45477*
[Michael McDonald/Carly Simon] [ASC] (4/15/78 BCR-6)
YOU BELONG TO ME *The Doobie Brothers—Warner Bros. 29552*
[Michael McDonald/Carly Simon] [ASC] (7/30/83 B-79)
YOU BELONG TO THE CITY Glenn Frey—MCA 52651
[Glenn Frey/Jack Tempchin] [ASC] (9/14/85 BC-2)
YOU BETTER DANCE The Jets—MCA 53673 [Michael Jonzun] [ASC] (7/29/89 BC-50)
YOU BETTER GET IT Joe Tex—Dial 4003 [Joe Tex] [BMI] (2/20/65 BCR-46)
YOU BETTER GO Derek Martin—Roulette 4631
[Teddy Randazzo/Lou Stallman/Bobby Weinstein] [BMI] (7/10/65 BCR-40)
YOU BETTER KNOW IT Jackie Wilson—Brunswick 55149
[Norm Henry*/Jackie Wilson] [BMI] (9/7/59 BCR-35)
(YOU BETTER) KNOW WHAT YOU'RE DOIN'
Lloyd Price And His Orchestra—ABC-Paramount 10162
[Harold Logan/Lloyd Price] [BMI] (11/7/60 BCR-50)
YOU BETTER MOVE ON Arthur Alexander—Dot 16309
[Arthur Alexander] [BMI] (2/24/62 BCR-19)
YOU BETTER RUN *The Young Rascals—Atlantic 2338*
[Eddie Brigati/Felix Cavaliere] [ASC] (6/11/66 BCR-20)
YOU BETTER RUN *Pat Benatar—Chrysalis 2450*
[Eddie Brigati/Felix Cavaliere] [ASC] (7/26/80 BCR-42)
YOU BETTER SIT DOWN KIDS Cher—Imperial 66261
[Sonny Bono] [BMI] (10/21/67 BCR-8)
YOU BETTER THINK TWICE Poco—Epic 10636 [Jim Messina] [ASC] (9/19/70 BCR-72)
YOU BETTER YOU BET The Who—Warner Bros. 49698
[Pete Townshend] [GL] (3/21/81 BCR-12)
YOU BROUGHT ABOUT A CHANGE IN ME Jackie Wilson—Brunswick 55392
[Gary Jackson/Nathaniel Smith] (TSW) [BMI] (11/2/68 R-65)
YOU BROUGHT THE JOY Freda Payne—Invictus 9100
[Lamont Dozier/Brian Holland] [BMI] (9/25/71 BCR-29)
YOU BROUGHT THE WOMAN OUT OF ME *Evie Sands—Haven 7010*
[Dennis Lambert/Brian Potter] [BMI] (3/29/75 BCR-50)
YOU BROUGHT THE WOMAN OUT OF ME *Hot—Big Tree 16108*
[Dennis Lambert/Brian Potter] [BMI] (1/28/78 BC-71)
YOU BUG ME BABY Larry Williams—Specialty 615
[Sonny Bono/Larry Williams] [BMI] (10/14/57 BCR-37)
YOU CALL EVERYBODY DARLIN' Mildred & Jimmie Mulcay—Panlin 7301
[Sam Martin/Al Trace/Ben Trace] [ASC] (9/5/60 R-59) [IWM]
YOU CALL ME BACK Clyde Brown—Atlantic 2908
[Tony Bell/Phil Hurtt] [BMI] (9/21/74 R-97)
YOU CAME Kim Wilde—MCA 53370 [Kim Wilde/Ricky Wilde] [ASC] (9/10/88 BC-41)
YOU CAME, YOU SAW, YOU CONQUERED! The Ronettes, featuring Veronica—A&M 1040
[Irwin Levine/Phil Spector/Toni Wine] [BMI] (4/5/69 CR-90)
YOU CAN Madleen Kane—Chalet 1225
[Pete Bellotte/Giorgio Moroder] [ASC] (12/26/81 BC-77)
YOU CAN BRING ME ALL YOUR HEARTACHES Lou Rawls—Capitol 5790
[H.B. Barnum/Ben Raleigh] [ASC] (11/26/66 BCR-45)
YOU CAN CALL ME AL Paul Simon—Warner Bros. 28667
[Paul Simon] [BMI] (8/9/86 BC-23)
YOU CAN CALL ME BLUE Michael Johnson—EMI America 8054
[Lawrence Anthony Brown/David Morgan] [ASC] (8/23/80 BCR-76)
YOU CAN CALL ME ROVER The Main Ingredient—RCA Victor 74-0939
[Ralph Bailey/Melvin Kent/Ken Williams] [BMI] (5/26/73 CR-78)
YOU CAN CRY IF YOU WANT TO The Troggs—Fontana 1622
[Reg Presley] [BMI] (7/13/68 CR-93)
YOU CAN DEPEND ON ME Brenda Lee—Decca 31231
[Charles Carpenter/Louis Dunlap/Earl Hines] [BMI] (3/27/61 BCR-5)
YOU CAN DO IT Dobie Gray—Infinity 50,003
[Richard Germinaro/Evie Sands/Ben Weisman] [ASC] (12/23/78 BCR-37)
YOU CAN DO MAGIC Limmie & Family Cookin'—Avco 4602
[Sandy Linzer] [BMI] (11/11/72 BCR-64)
YOU CAN DO MAGIC America—Capitol 5412 [Russ Ballard] [ASC] (7/31/82 BC-7)
—YOU CAN GET IT GIRL see: I GOT MY MIND MADE UP
YOU CAN GET IT IF YOU REALLY WANT Desmond Dekker—Uni 55261/Trojan 7777
[Jimmy Cliff] [BMI] (11/14/70 R-84)
YOU CAN HAVE HER *Roy Hamilton—Epic 9434 [William S. Cook] [BMI] (1/21/61 BCR-12)*
YOU CAN HAVE HIM *Timi Yuro—Mercury 72391 [William S. Cook] [BMI] (2/20/65 BR-96)*
YOU CAN HAVE HIM *Dionne Warwick—Scepter 1294*
[William S. Cook] [BMI] (3/13/65 BC-75)
YOU CAN HAVE HER *The Righteous Brothers—Moonglow 239*
[William S. Cook] [BMI] (5/8/65 BCR-67)
YOU CAN HAVE HER *Sam Neely—A&M 1612 [William S. Cook] [BMI] (8/31/74 BCR-23)*

YOU CAN LEAD YOUR WOMAN TO THE ALTAR Oscar Toney, Jr.—Bell 688
[Charlie Chalmers] [BMI] (10/21/67 CR-79)
YOU CAN MAKE IT IF YOU TRY Gene Allison—Vee-Jay 256
[Ted Jarrett] [ASC] (12/16/57 B-37)
YOU CAN NEVER STOP ME LOVING YOU Johnny Tillotson—Cadence 1437
[Ian Samwell/Jean Slater] [BMI] (8/10/63 BCR-18)
YOU CAN RUN (BUT YOU CAN'T HIDE) Jerry Butler—Vee-Jay 463
[Don Covay/Paul Griffin] [BMI] (10/13/62 BCR-63)
(YOU CAN STILL) ROCK IN AMERICA Night Ranger—MCA 52305
[Jack Blades/Brad Gillis] [BMI] (12/3/83 BC-51)
YOU CAN'T ALWAYS GET WHAT YOU WANT *The Rolling Stones—London 910*
[Mick Jagger/Keith Richards] [BMI] (4/21/73 BCR-34)
YOU CAN'T ALWAYS GET WHAT YOU WANT *George Michael—Columbia 73663*
[Mick Jagger/Keith Richards] (Med) [BMI] (1/19/91 BC-21)
YOU CAN'T BE A BEACON (IF YOUR LIGHT DON'T SHINE) Donna Fargo—Dot 17506
[Marty Cooper] [ASC] (6/29/74 BCR-48)
YOU CAN'T BE TRUE DEAR *Mary Kaye Trio—Warner Bros. 5050*
[Hal Cotton/Gerhard Ebeler/Ken Griffin/Hans Otten] [ASC] (3/16/59 BCRt-53) [FET]
YOU CAN'T BE TRUE DEAR *Steve Lawrence & Eydie Gorme—ABC-Paramount 10008*
[Hal Cotton/Gerhard Ebeler/Ken Griffin/Hans Otten] [ASC] (3/16/59 Rt-53) [FET]
YOU CAN'T BE TRUE, DEAR *Patti Page—Columbia 43345*
[Hal Cotton/Gerhard Ebeler/Ken Griffin/Hans Otten] [ASC] (8/28/65 BCR-91) [FET]
YOU CAN'T CHANGE THAT Raydio—Arista 0399 [Ray Parker Jr.] [ASC] (4/21/79 BCR-9)
YOU CAN'T DANCE England Dan & John Ford Coley—Big Tree 16117
[Tim Ryan/Bob Yeomans] [ASC] (6/3/78 BCR-49)
YOU CAN'T DENY IT Lisa Stansfield—Arista 2024
[Ian Devaney/Andy Morris/Lisa Stansfield] [ASC] (5/26/90 BC-14)
YOU CAN'T DO IT RIGHT (WITH THE ONE YOU LOVE) Deep Purple—Warner Bros. 8049
[Ritchie Blackmore/David Coverdale/Glenn Hughes] [ASC] (12/28/74 C-93)
YOU CAN'T DO THAT *The Beatles—Capitol 5150*
[John Lennon/Paul McCartney] [ASC] (4/4/64 BCR-48)
YOU CAN'T DO THAT *Nilsson—RCA Victor 47-9298*
[John Lennon/Paul McCartney] [ASC] (9/2/67 CR-82)
YOU CAN'T GET AWAY Shana—Vision 4515
[Jay Martin/Lewis Martinée/Alex Villalobos] [BMI] (3/24/90 BC-82)
OH YOU CAN'T GET TO HEAVEN *The Guys And The Gals—Kapp 254*
[Traditional] [NA] (1/12/59 Rt-93)
YOU CAN'T GET TO HEAVEN ON ROLLER SKATES *Betty Johnson—Atlantic 2009*
[Charles Grean/Marvin Moore/Traditional] [BMI] (1/12/59 BCRt-93)
YOU CAN'T GET WHAT YOU WANT (TILL YOU KNOW WHAT YOU WANT)
Joe Jackson—A&M 2628
[Joe Jackson] [ASC] (4/21/84 BC-15)
YOU CAN'T GO HALFWAY Johnny Nash—Epic 50021
[Gloria Fowles/Sam Gary/Bill Johnson/Margaret Nash] [BMI] (9/14/74 CR-90)
YOU CAN'T HURRY LOVE *The Supremes—Motown 1097*
[Lamont Dozier/Brian Holland/Eddie Holland] [BMI] (8/13/66 BCR-1)
YOU CAN'T HURRY LOVE *Phil Collins—Atlantic 89933*
[Lamont Dozier/Brian Holland/Eddie Holland] [BMI] (11/6/82 BC-10)
YOU CAN'T HURT ME NO MORE Gene Chandler—Constellation 146
[Curtis Mayfield] [BMI] (3/6/65 BCR-90)
YOU CAN'T JUDGE A BOOK BY THE COVER Bo Diddley—Checker 1019
[Willie Dixon] [BMI] (8/18/62 BCR-48)
(YOU CAN'T LET THE BOY OVERPOWER) THE MAN IN YOU *The Miracles—Tamla 54092*
[Smokey Robinson] [ASC] (3/7/64 BCR-59)
(YOU CAN'T LET THE BOY OVERPOWER) THE MAN IN YOU *Chuck Jackson—Motown 1118*
[Smokey Robinson] [ASC] (3/2/68 BCR-92)
YOU CAN'T LIE TO A LIAR *Ketty Lester—Era 3088*
[Marilyn Weiss Allen/Paul Hampton] [ASC] (9/15/62 BRt-82)*
YOU CAN'T LIE TO A LIAR *Barry Gordon—Cadence 1431*
[Marilyn Weiss Allen/Paul Hampton] [ASC] (10/6/62 Rt-82)*
YOU CAN'T PLAY WITH MY YO-YO Yo-Yo—EastWest 4-98831
[James Brown/Charles E. Sherrell/Yolanda Whitaker] [BMI] (5/25/91 B-36)
YOU CAN'T ROLLER SKATE IN A BUFFALO HERD Roger Miller—Smash 2043
[Roger Miller] [BMI] (6/25/66 BCR-40)
YOU CAN'T RUN AWAY FROM IT Four Aces—Decca 30041
[Gene DePaul/Johnny Mercer] [ASC] (10/20/56 B-70)
YOU CAN'T RUN FROM LOVE Eddie Rabbitt—Warner Bros. 29712
[David Malloy/Eddie Rabbitt/Even Stevens] [BMI] (4/23/83 BC-55)
YOU CAN'T SIT DOWN (PART 2) *Phil Upchurch Combo—Boyd 3398*
[Dee Clark/Cornell Muldrow/Philip Upchurch] [BMI] (6/5/61 BCR-14) [IWM]
YOU CAN'T SIT DOWN *The Dovells—Parkway 867*
[Dee Clark/Kal Mann/Cornell Muldrow/Philip Upchurch] [BMI] (4/20/63 BCR-3)
YOU CAN'T STAND ALONE Wilson Pickett—Atlantic 2412
[Rudy Clark] [BMI] (5/27/67 BCR-50)
YOU CAN'T TAKE IT AWAY Fred Hughes—Vee-Jay 703
[Richard Parker] [BMI] (9/18/65 BCR-89)
YOU CAN'T TURN ME OFF (IN THE MIDDLE OF TURNING ME ON)
High Inergy—Gordy 7155
[Marilyn McLeod/Pam Sawyer] [ASC] (9/17/77 BCR-12)

YOU CAN'T WIN (PART 1) Michael Jackson—Epic 50654
[Charlie Smalls] [BMI] (2/3/79 BR-73)
YOU CHEATED *The Shields—Dot 15805 [Don Burch] [BMI] (7/28/58 BCtRt-11)*
YOU CHEATED *The Del Vikings—Mercury 71345 [Don Burch] [BMI] (7/28/58 CtRt-11)*
YOU CHEATED *The Slades—Domino 500 [Don Burch] [BMI] (8/4/58 BCtRt-24)*
YOU COULD BE MINE Guns N' Roses—Geffen 19039
[Saul Hudson/Duff McKagan/Axl Rose/Izzy Stradlin] [ASC] (7/13/91 B-29)
YOU COULD HAVE BEEN A LADY April Wine—Big Tree 133
[Errol Brown/Tony Wilson*] [ASC] (3/18/72 BCR-26)
YOU COULD HAVE BEEN WITH ME Sheena Easton—EMI America 8101
[Lea Maalfrid] [BMI] (11/28/81 BCR-12)
YOU COULD TAKE MY HEART AWAY Silver Condor—Columbia 02268
[John Corey] [ASC] (7/25/81 BCR-32)
YOU CRIED WOLF Todd Rundgren—Bearsville 0330
[Todd Rundgren] [BMI] (10/28/78 R-86)
YOU DECORATED MY LIFE Kenny Rogers—United Artists 1315
[Debbie Hupp/Bob Morrison] [ASC] (9/8/79 BCR-5)
YOU DIDN'T HAVE TO BE SO NICE The Lovin' Spoonful—Kama Sutra 205
[Steve Boone/John Sebastian] [BMI] (11/20/65 BCR-9)
YOU DON'T BELIEVE Alan Parsons Project—Arista 1-9108
[Alan Parsons/Eric Woolfson] [BMI] (11/19/83 BC-54)
YOU DON'T BRING ME FLOWERS Barbra & Neil—Columbia 10840
[Alan Bergman/Marilyn Bergman/Neil Diamond] [ASC] (10/28/78 BCR-1)
YOU DON'T HAVE TO BE A BABY TO CRY *"Tennessee" Ernie Ford—Capitol 3262*
[Bob Merrill/Terry Shand] [ASC] (1/13/56 BR-59)
YOU DON'T HAVE TO BE A BABY TO CRY *The Caravelles—Smash 1852*
[Bob Merrill/Terry Shand] [ASC] (11/2/63 BCR-3)
YOU DON'T HAVE TO BE A STAR (TO BE IN MY SHOW)
Marilyn McCoo & Billy Davis Jr.—ABC 12208
[James Anthony Dean/John Henry Glover] [BMI] (9/11/76 BCR-1)
YOU DON'T HAVE TO BE A TOWER OF STRENGTH Gloria Lynne—Everest 19428
[Burt Bacharach/Bob Hilliard] [ASC] (12/4/61 BR-82)
YOU DON'T HAVE TO CRY René and Angela—Mercury 884587
[René Moore/Angela Winbush] [ASC] (6/21/86 BC-75)
YOU DON'T HAVE TO GO HOME TONIGHT The Triplets—Mercury 878 864
[Eric Lowen/Dan Navarro/Diana Villegas/Sylvia Villegas/Vicky Villegas] [BMI]
(3/16/91 BC-9)
(YOU DON'T HAVE TO) PAINT ME A PICTURE Gary Lewis And The Playboys—
Liberty 55914 [Snuff Garrett/Leon Russell/Roger Tillison] [BMI] (10/8/66 BCR-15)
YOU DON'T HAVE TO SAY YOU LOVE ME *Dusty Springfield—Philips 40371*
[Pino Donaggio/Simon Napier-Bell/Vicki Wickham] [ASC] (5/14/66 BCR-3) [FDE]
YOU DON'T HAVE TO SAY YOU LOVE ME *The Four Sonics—Sport 110*
[Pino Donaggio/Simon Napier-Bell/Vicki Wickham] [ASC] (2/10/68 BCR-79) [FDE]
YOU DON'T HAVE TO SAY YOU LOVE ME *Elvis Presley—RCA Victor 47-9916*
[Pino Donaggio/Simon Napier-Bell/Vicki Wickham] (TSW) [ASC]
(10/24/70 BCR-7) [FDE]
YOU DON'T HAVE TO WALK IN THE RAIN The Turtles—White Whale 308
[Howard Kaylan/Al Nichol/Jim Pons/John Seiter/Mark Volman] [BMI] (6/7/69 BCR-48)
YOU DON'T KNOW Helen Shapiro—Capitol 4662
[Mike Hawker/John Schroeder] [BMI] (11/13/61 R-88)
YOU DON'T KNOW Scarlett & Black—Virgin 99405
[Robin Hild] [BMI] (1/30/88 BC-20)
YOU DON'T KNOW GIRLS Kathy Linden—Felsted 8587
[Sid Jacobson/Lou Stallman] [BMI] (7/27/59 B-92)
—YOU DON'T KNOW HOW GLAD I AM see: GLAD I AM
YOU DON'T KNOW LIKE I KNOW Sam & Dave—Stax 180
[Isaac Hayes/David Porter] [BMI] (1/8/66 BCR-80)
YOU DON'T KNOW ME *Jerry Vale—Columbia 40710*
[Eddy Arnold/Cindy Walker] [BMI] (7/7/56 BCtRt-9)
YOU DON'T KNOW ME *Carmen McRae—Decca 29949*
[Eddy Arnold/Cindy Walker] [BMI] (7/7/56 CtRt-9)
YOU DON'T KNOW ME *Eddy Arnold—RCA Victor 47-6502*
[Eddy Arnold/Cindy Walker] [BMI] (7/20/56 Rt-9)
YOU DON'T KNOW ME *Lenny Welch—Cadence 1373*
[Eddy Arnold/Cindy Walker] [BMI] (2/29/60 BCR-42)
YOU DON'T KNOW ME *Ray Charles—ABC-Paramount 10345*
[Eddy Arnold/Cindy Walker] [BMI] (7/21/62 BCR-2)
YOU DON'T KNOW ME *Elvis Presley With The Jordanaires—RCA Victor 47-9341*
[Eddy Arnold/Cindy Walker] [BMI] (10/14/67 BCR-35)
YOU DON'T KNOW ME *Mickey Gilley—Epic 02172*
[Eddy Arnold/Cindy Walker] [BMI] (7/11/81 BCR-48)
YOU DON'T KNOW WHAT IT MEANS Jackie Wilson—Brunswick 55219
[Morris Levy‡/Alonzo Tucker/Jackie Wilson] [BMI] (8/14/61 BCR-78)
YOU DON'T KNOW WHAT LOVE IS Susan Jacks And The Poppy Family—London 182
[Terry Jacks/Robert H. Nelson] [BMI] (4/21/73 C-70)
YOU DON'T KNOW WHAT YOU MEAN TO ME Sam & Dave—Atlantic 2517
[Steve Cropper/Eddie Floyd] [BMI] (5/25/68 BCR-33)
YOU DON'T KNOW WHAT YOU'VE GOT (UNTIL YOU LOSE IT) Ral Donner—Gone 5108
[Dorian Burton/Paul Hampton] [ASC] (7/10/61 BCR-4)

YOU DON'T LOVE ME ANYMORE Eddie Rabbitt—Elektra 45488
[Alan Ray/Jeff Raymond] [BMI] (6/17/78 BCR-53)

YOU DON'T LOVE ME ANYMORE (AND I CAN TELL) Rick Nelson—Decca 31475
[Nicollet Tady] [BMI] (3/2/63 BCR-43)

YOU DON'T MESS AROUND WITH JIM Jim Croce—ABC 11328
[Jim Croce] [ASC] (6/24/72 BCR-7)

YOU DON'T MISS YOUR WATER William Bell—Stax 116
[William Bell] [BMI] (4/28/62 B-95)

YOU DON'T NEED ME FOR ANYTHING ANYMORE Brenda Lee—Decca 732491
[Richard Ahlert/Leon Carr] [ASC] (5/17/69 BCR-62)

YOU DON'T OWE ME The Blue Ridge Rangers—Fantasy 710
[John Fogerty] [ASC] (10/13/73 C-93)

YOU DON'T OWE ME A THING *Johnnie Ray—Columbia 40803*
[Marty Robbins] [BMI] (1/12/57 BCRt-6)

YOU DON'T OWE ME A THING *Marty Robbins—Columbia 40706*
[Marty Robbins] [BMI] (1/26/57 Rt-6)

YOU DON'T OWE ME A THING *The La Dell Sisters—Mercury 70888*
[Marty Robbins] [BMI] (1/26/57 Rt-6)

YOU DON'T OWN ME Lesley Gore—Mercury 72206
[John Madara/David White] [BMI] (12/28/63 BCR-2)

YOU DON'T WANT ME ANYMORE Steel Breeze—RCA 13283
[Ken Goorabian] [BMI] (8/28/82 BC-16)

YOU DON'T WANT MY LOVE *Andy Williams—Cadence 1389*
[Roger Miller] [BMI] (11/7/60 BCtRt-34)

YOU DON'T WANT MY LOVE *Roger Miller—RCA Victor 47-7776*
[Roger Miller] [BMI] (11/7/60 CtRt-34)

YOU DREAMER YOU Johnny Cash—Columbia 41371 [Johnny Cash] [ASC] (4/13/59 R-66)

YOU DROPPED A BOMB ON ME The Gap Band—Total Experience 8203
[Lonnie Simmons/Rudy Taylor/Charles K. Wilson] [BMI] (8/14/82 BC-31)

YOU EXCITE ME Frankie Avalon—Chancellor 1016
[Peter DeAngelis/Bob Marcucci] [ASC] (3/31/58 BCR-44)

YOU FORGOT ALL THE WORDS Frank Sinatra—Capitol 3552
[Eve Jay/Bernie Wayne] [BMI] (10/20/56 R-49)

YOU GAVE ME A MOUNTAIN Frankie Laine—ABC 11174
[Marty Robbins] [BMI] (1/18/69 BCR-15)

YOU GAVE ME LOVE Crown Heights Affair—De-Lite 803 [Ida Reid] [BMI] (4/26/80 R-98)

YOU GAVE ME SOMETHING (AND EVERYTHING'S ALRIGHT) Fantastic Four—Ric-Tic 128
[William Garrett/Al Hamilton*/Eugene Hamilton*/Norma Toney*] [BMI]
(5/27/67 BCR-45)

YOU GIVE GOOD LOVE Whitney Houston—Arista 1-9274
[LaForrest Cope] [ASC] (5/11/85 BC-3)

YOU GIVE LOVE A BAD NAME Bon Jovi—Mercury 884953
[Jon Bon Jovi/Desmond Child/Richie Sambora] [ASC] (9/6/86 BC-1)

YOU GONNA MAKE ME LOVE SOMEBODY ELSE The Jones Girls—Philadelphia Int'l 3680
[Kenneth Gamble/Leon Huff] [BMI] (6/16/79 BCR-32)

YOU GOT IT Diana Ross—Motown 1442
[Linda Laurie/Jerry Ragovoy] [ASC] (5/6/78 BCR-49)

YOU GOT IT (THE RIGHT STUFF) New Kids On The Block—Columbia 08092
[Maurice Starr] [ASC] (11/19/88 BC-3)

YOU GOT IT Roy Orbison—Virgin 99245
[Jeff Lynne/Roy Orbison/Tom Petty] [BMI] (1/21/89 BC-9)

YOU GOT IT ALL The Jets—MCA 52968 [Rupert Holmes] [ASC] (11/15/86 BC-3)

YOU GOT LUCKY Tom Petty and The Heartbreakers—Backstreet 52144
[Mike Campbell/Tom Petty] [ASC] (11/13/82 BC-16)

YOU GOT ME HUMMIN' *Sam & Dave—Stax 204*
[Isaac Hayes/David Porter] [BMI] (12/3/66 BCR-59)

YOU'VE GOT ME HUMMIN' *Hassles—United Artists 50215*
[Isaac Hayes/David Porter] [BMI] (11/4/67 CR-71)

YOU GOT ME HUMMIN *Cold Blood—San Francisco 60*
[Isaac Hayes/David Porter] [BMI] (1/3/70 BCR-45)

YOU GOT ME WALKING Jackie Wilson—Brunswick 55467
[Eugene Record] [BMI] (2/5/72 BR-92)

YOU GOT SOUL Johnny Nash—JAD 209 [Johnny Nash] [ASC] (12/14/68 BCR-50)

YOU GOT STYLE Jon & Robin—Abnak 130 [Jeff Barry/Andy Kim] [BMI] (6/15/68 CR-55)

YOU GOT THAT RIGHT Lynyrd Skynyrd—MCA 40888
[Steve Gaines/Ronnie Van Zant] [BMI] (4/8/78 BC-68)

YOU GOT THAT TOUCH Sonny James—Capitol 4020
[Richard Hollingsworth/Sonny James] [BMI] (9/22/58 B-94)

(YOU GOT) THE GAMMA GOOCHEE The Kingsmen—Wand 1107
[John D. Mangiagli] [BMI] (12/11/65 CR-95)

YOU GOT THE LOVE Professor Morrison's Lollipop—White Whale 275
[Joey Levine/Kris Resnick] [BMI] (9/14/68 BCR-61)

YOU GOT THE LOVE Rufus Featuring Chaka Khan—ABC 12032
[Chaka Khan/Ray Parker Jr.] [ASC] (10/12/74 BCR-9)

YOU GOT THE MAGIC John Fogerty—Asylum 45309
[John Fogerty] [ASC] (5/1/76 B-87)

YOU GOT THE POWER War—RCA 13061
[Thomas Allen/Harold Brown/Jerry Goldstein/Lonnie Jordan/Lee Oskar/Luther Rabb/
Howard Scott] [ASC] (4/3/82 B-66)

YOU GOT TO BE THE ONE The Chi-Lites—Brunswick 55514
[Marshall Arrington/Eugene Record] [BMI] (8/31/74 BCR-71)

YOU GOT TO KEEP ON BUMPIN' The Kay-Gees—Gang 1321
[Amir Bayyan/Wilson Beckett/Ronald Bell/Callie Cheek/Michael Cheek/
Peter Anthony Duarte/Dennis White/Ray Wright] [BMI] (7/13/74 CR-81)

YOU GOT TO ME Neil Diamond—Bang 540 [Neil Diamond] [SE] (1/28/67 BCR-18)

YOU'VE GOT TO PAY THE PRICE *Al Kent—Ric-Tic 127*
[Al Hamilton/Hermon Weems] [BMI] (8/5/67 BCR-38) [IM]

YOU GOT TO PAY THE PRICE *Gloria Taylor—Silver Fox 14*
[Al Hamilton/Hermon Weems] [BMI] (10/25/69 BCR-34)

—YOU GOT TO WALK AND DON'T LOOK BACK see: DON'T LOOK BACK

YOU GOT WHAT IT TAKES *Marv Johnson—United Artists 185*
[Billy Davis/Berry Gordy/Gwen Gordy] [ASC] (10/26/59 BCR-5)

YOU GOT WHAT IT TAKES *The Dave Clark Five—Epic 10144*
[Billy Davis/Berry Gordy/Gwen Gordy] [ASC] (4/1/67 BCR-7)

YOU GOT WHAT IT TAKES Joe Tex—Dial 4003 [Joe Tex] [BMI] (2/27/65 BCR-51)

YOU GOT YOUR THING ON A STRING J.P. Robinson—Alston 4577
[Willie Clarke/Clarence Reid] [BMI] (11/1/69 C-96)

YOU GOT YOURS AND I'LL GET MINE The Delfonics—Philly Groove 157
[Thom Bell/William Hart] [BMI] (8/9/69 BCR-33)

(YOU GOTTA) FIGHT FOR YOUR RIGHT (TO PARTY!) Beastie Boys—Def Jam 06595
[Adam Horovitz/Rick Rubin/Adam Yauch] [ASC] (12/20/86 BC-3)

YOU GOTTA HAVE LOVE IN YOUR HEART The Supremes & Four Tops—Motown 1181
[Dino Fekaris/Nick Zesses] [ASC] (6/5/71 BCR-44)

YOU GOTTA LOVE SOMEONE Elton John—MCA 53953
[Elton John/Bernie Taupin] [BMI] (11/24/90 BC-37)

YOU GOTTA MAKE YOUR OWN SUNSHINE Neil Sedaka—Rocket/MCA 40614
[Howard Greenfield/Neil Sedaka] [BMI] (9/18/76 BCR-53)

YOU HAVE PLACED A CHILL IN MY HEART Eurythmics—RCA 8619
[Annie Lennox/David A. Stewart] [ASC] (5/28/88 BC-62)

YOU HAVEN'T DONE NOTHIN' Stevie Wonder—Tamla 54252
[Stevie Wonder] [ASC] (8/3/74 BCR-1)

(YOU HIT THE WRONG NOTE) BILLY GOAT Bill Haley And His Comets—Decca 30314
[J. Leslie McFarland] [ASC] (6/8/57 BCR-54)

YOU, I The Rugbys—Amazon 1 [Steve McNicol] [BMI] (8/9/69 BCR-18)

YOU JUST CAN'T QUIT Rick Nelson—Decca 31956 [Rick Nelson] [BMI] (6/25/66 C-76)

YOU JUST CAN'T WIN (BY MAKING THE SAME MISTAKE) Gene & Jerry—Mercury 73163
[Wylie Dixon/Ron Simmons/Simtec Simmons] [BMI] (12/19/70 BCR-59)

YOU KEEP ME DANCING Samantha Sang—Private Stock 45,188
[Sandy Linzer/Denny Randell] [BMI] (5/6/78 BCR-56)

YOU KEEP ME HANGIN' ON *The Supremes—Motown 1101*
[Lamont Dozier/Brian Holland/Eddie Holland] [BMI] (10/29/66 BCR-1)

YOU KEEP ME HANGIN' ON *The Vanilla Fudge—Atco 6495*
[Lamont Dozier/Brian Holland/Eddie Holland] [BMI] (7/1/67 BCR-48)

YOU KEEP ME HANGIN' ON *The Vanilla Fudge—Atco 6590*
[Lamont Dozier/Brian Holland/Eddie Holland] [BMI] (7/13/68 BCR-6)

YOU KEEP ME HANGING ON *Wilson Pickett—Atlantic 2682*
[Lamont Dozier/Brian Holland/Eddie Holland] [BMI] (11/29/69 BCR-57)

YOU KEEP ME HANGIN' ON *Jackie DeShannon—Imperial 66452*
[Lamont Dozier/Brian Holland/Eddie Holland] (Med) [BMI] (5/30/70 B-96)

YOU KEEP ME HANGIN' ON *Kim Wilde—MCA 53024*
[Lamont Dozier/Brian Holland/Eddie Holland] [BMI] (3/28/87 BC-1)

(YOU KEEP ME) HANGIN' ON Joe Simon—Sound Stage 7 2608
[Ira Allen/Buddy Mize] [BMI] (4/6/68 BCR-25)

YOU KEEP ME HOLDING ON Tyrone Davis—Dakar 626
[Jack Daniels/John Edward Moore] [BMI] (10/9/71 BCR-80)

YOU KEEP RUNNIN' AWAY 38 Special—A&M 2431
[Don Barnes/Jeff Carlisi/Jim Peterik] [ASC] (8/14/82 BC-34)

YOU KEEP RUNNING AWAY Four Tops—Motown 1113
[Lamont Dozier/Brian Holland/Eddie Holland] [BMI] (9/16/67 BCR-16)

YOU KEEP TIGHTENING UP ON ME The Box Tops—Bell 865
[Wayne Carson Thompson] [BMI] (2/28/70 BCR-70)

YOU KNOW HOW IT IS Frankie Laine—Columbia 40962
[Robert Allen/Al Stillman] [ASC] (8/3/57 R-82)

YOU KNOW HOW IT IS WITH A WOMAN Jefferson—Janus 117
[Anthony King/John Schroeder*] [ASC] (4/25/70 C-96)

YOU KNOW HOW TO LOVE ME Phyllis Hyman—Arista 0463
[Reggie Lucas/James Mtume] [BMI] (12/29/79 R-91)

YOU KNOW I LOVE YOU...DON'T YOU? Howard Jones—Elektra 69512
[Howard Jones] [BMI] (10/18/86 BC-15)

YOU KNOW IT AIN'T RIGHT Joe Hinton—Back Beat 537
[Deadric Malone] [BMI] (4/27/63 BCR-88)

YOU KNOW LIKE I KNOW The Ozark Mountain Daredevils—A&M 1888
[Larry Michael Lee] [BMI] (1/22/77 BCR-55)

YOU KNOW THAT I LOVE YOU Santana—Columbia 11144
[Alex Ligertwood/Alan Pasqua/Carlos Santana/Chris Solberg] [BMI]
(11/24/79 BCR-32)

YOU KNOW THE FEELIN' Steve Wightman—Farr 003
[Steve Wightman] [SE] (5/15/76 C-90)

YOU KNOW WHAT I MEAN The Turtles—White Whale 254
[Garry Bonner/Alan Gordon] [BMI] (8/5/67 BCR-12)

YOU KNOW WHAT TO DO Carly Simon—Warner Bros. 29484
[Jacob Brackman/Mike Mainieri/Carly Simon/Peter John Wood] [ASC] (9/24/83 B-83)

YOU LIED TO YOUR DADDY The Tams—ABC-Paramount 10533
[Ray Whitley] [BMI] (3/21/64 BCR-70)

YOU LIGHT UP MY LIFE Carole King—Ode 66035
[Carole King] (TSW) [ASC] (7/14/73 BCR-28)

YOU LIGHT UP MY LIFE *Debby Boone—Warner/Curb 8446//Warner/Curb 8455*
[Joe Brooks] [ASC] (8/27/77 BCR-1)

YOU LIGHT UP MY LIFE *Original Cast (Kacey Cisyk)—Arista 0287*
[Joe Brooks] [ASC] (11/12/77 B-80)

YOU LIKE ME DON'T YOU Jermaine Jackson—Motown 1503
[Jermaine Jackson] [ASC] (4/18/81 BCR-50)

YOU LITTLE TRUSTMAKER The Tymes—RCA Victor 10022
[Christopher Jackson] [BMI] (8/10/74 BCR-12)

YOU LOOK MARVELOUS Billy Crystal—A&M 2764
[Billy Crystal/Paul Shaffer] [BMI] (7/27/85 BC-58)

YOU LOST THE SWEETEST BOY Mary Wells—Motown 1048
[Lamont Dozier/Brian Holland/Eddie Holland] [BMI] (9/21/63 BCR-22)

YOU MADE A BELIEVER (OUT OF ME) Ruby Andrews—Zodiac 1015
[Fred Bridges/Bobby Eaton/Richard Knight] [BMI] (7/5/69 BCR-94)

YOU MADE ME BELIEVE IN MAGIC Bay City Rollers—Arista 0256
[Len Boone] [ASC] (6/4/77 BCR-7)

YOU MADE ME LOVE YOU Nat "King" Cole—Capitol 4184
[Joseph McCarthy/James V. Monaco] [BMI] (4/20/59 BCR-27)

YOU MAKE LOVING FUN Fleetwood Mac—Warner Bros. 8483
[Christine McVie] [BMI] (10/15/77 BCR-7)

YOU MAKE ME CRAZY Sammy Hagar—Capitol 4502
[Sammy Hagar] [BMI] (12/3/77 BCR-62)

YOU MAKE ME FEEL BRAND NEW
The Stylistics Featurng Airrion Love & Russell Thompkins, Jr.—Avco 4634
[Thom Bell/Linda Creed] [BMI] (3/16/74 BCR-1)

YOU MAKE ME FEEL BRAND NEW *Band Of Gold—RCA 13866*
[Thom Bell/Linda Creed] (Med) [BMI] (10/13/84 BC-64)

YOU MAKE ME FEEL LIKE DANCING Leo Sayer—Warner Bros. 8283
[Vini Poncia/Leo Sayer] [BMI] (10/16/76 BCR-1)

YOU MAKE ME FEEL (MIGHTY REAL) *Sylvester—Fantasy 846*
[Sylvester James/James Wirrick] [ASC] (12/30/78 BCR-36)

YOU MAKE ME FEEL (MIGHTY REAL) *Jimmy Somerville—London 886 973*
[Sylvester James/James Wirrick] [ASC] (4/7/90 BC-81)

(YOU MAKE ME FEEL) SO GOOD The McCoys—Bang 527
[Bob Feldman/Jerry Goldstein/Richard Gottehrer/Doc Pomus/Mort Shuman] [BMI] (7/30/66 BCR-53)

YOU MAKE ME REAL The Doors—Elektra 45685
[Jim Morrison] (TSW) [ASC] (4/11/70 BCR-28) [I]

YOU MAKE ME WORK Cameo—Atlanta Artists 870587
[Larry Blackmon] [ASC] (11/5/88 BC-85)

YOU MAKE MY DREAMS Daryl Hall & John Oates—RCA Victor 12217
[Sara Allen/Daryl Hall/John Oates] [BMI] (5/2/81 BCR-5)

YOU MAKE MY HEART BEAT FASTER (AND THAT'S ALL THAT MATTERS)
Kim Carnes—EMI America 8191
[Kim Carnes/Dave Ellingson/Brian Fairweather/Martin Page] [ASC] (1/21/84 BC-54)

YOU MAKE YOUR OWN HEAVEN AND HELL RIGHT HERE ON EARTH
The Undisputed Truth—Gordy 7112
[Barrett Strong/Norman Whitfield] [BMI] (12/11/71 BCR-54)

YOU MAY BE RIGHT Billy Joel—Columbia 11231 [Billy Joel] [ASC] (3/15/80 BCR-7)

YOU, ME AND HE Mtume—Epic 04504 [James Mtume] [BMI] (9/15/84 B-83)

YOU, ME AND MEXICO Edward Bear—Capitol 2801
[Larry Evoy] [ASC] (5/9/70 BCR-68)

YOU MEAN EVERYTHING TO ME The Fleetwoods—Dolton 5
[Tommy Kaspar] [BMI] (10/26/59 B-84)

YOU MEAN EVERYTHING TO ME Neil Sedaka—RCA Victor 47-7781
[Howard Greenfield/Neil Sedaka] [BMI] (7/25/60 BCR-12)

YOU MEAN THE WORLD TO ME David Houston—Epic 10224
[Billy Sherrill/Glenn Sutton] [BMI] (9/30/67 BCR-67)

YOU MET YOUR MATCH Stevie Wonder—Tamla 54168
[Lula Mae Hardaway/Don Hunter/Stevie Wonder] [ASC] (7/13/68 BCR-22)

YOU MIGHT NEED SOMEBODY Turley Richards—Atlantic 3645
[Nan O'Byrne/Tom Snow] [BMI] (1/26/80 BCR-54)

YOU MIGHT THINK The Cars—Elektra 69744 [Ric Ocasek] [ASC] (3/10/84 BC-7)

YOU MOSTEST GIRL Bobby Lee Trammell—Radio 102
[Bobby Lee Trammell] [BMI] (6/23/58 R-79)

YOU MUST BELIEVE ME The Impressions—ABC-Paramount 10581
[Curtis Mayfield] [BMI] (9/5/64 BCR-14)

YOU MUST HAVE BEEN A BEAUTIFUL BABY *Bobby Darin—Atco 6206*
[Johnny Mercer/Harry Warren] [ASC] (8/21/61 BCR-4)

YOU MUST HAVE BEEN A BEAUTIFUL BABY *The Dave Clark Five—Epic 10179*
[Johnny Mercer/Harry Warren] [ASC] (6/3/67 BCR-35)

YOU NEED A WOMAN TONIGHT Captain & Tennille—A&M 2106
[Dana Merino] [ASC] (12/2/78 BCR-36)

YOU NEED HANDS *Eydie Gorme—ABC-Paramount 9925*
[Max Bygraves] [ASC] (5/5/58 BCRt-7)

YOU NEED HANDS *Max Bygraves—London 1801 [Max Bygraves] [ASC] (5/12/58 Rt-7)*

YOU NEED LOVE Styx—Wooden Nickel 10272 [Dennis DeYoung] [ASC] (5/10/75 BC-81)

YOU NEED LOVE LIKE I DO (DON'T YOU) Gladys Knight & The Pips—Soul 35071
[Barrett Strong/Norman Whitfield] [BMI] (3/21/70 BCR-25)

YOU NEED ME, BABY Joe Tex—Dial 4086 [Joe Tex] [BMI] (10/12/68 BCR-66)

YOU NEEDED ME Anne Murray—Capitol 4574 [Randy Goodrum] [ASC] (7/8/78 BCR-1)

YOU NEVER CAN TELL Chuck Berry—Chess 1906 [Chuck Berry] [BMI] (8/1/64 BCR-14)

YOU NEVER DONE IT LIKE THAT Captain & Tennille—A&M 2063
[Howard Greenfield/Neil Sedaka] [BMI] (7/29/78 BCR-6)

YOU NEVER MISS YOUR WATER (TILL THE WELL RUNS DRY)
"Little Esther" Phillips & "Big Al" Downing—Lenox 5565
[Unknown] [NA] (3/30/63 BR-73)

YOU, NO ONE BUT YOU Frankie Laine—ABC 10983
[Peter DeAngelis/Jean Sawyer] [ASC] (9/30/67 BCR-58)

YOU ONLY LIVE TWICE Nancy Sinatra—Reprise 0595
[John Barry/Leslie Bricusse] [BMI] (6/17/67 BCR-44)

YOU OUGHT TO BE HAVIN' FUN Tower Of Power—Columbia 10409
[Emilio Castillo/Steve Kupka/Hubert Tubbs] [ASC] (10/16/76 B-68)

YOU OUGHT TO BE WITH ME Al Green—Hi 2227
[Al Green/Al Jackson/Willie Mitchell] [BMI] (10/21/72 BCR-1)

YOU + ME = LOVE The Undisputed Truth—Whitfield 8306
[Norman Whitfield] (TSW) [BMI] (2/19/77 BCR-48)

YOU PUT IT ON ME B.B. King—BluesWay 61019
[Maya Angelou/Quincy Jones] (TSW) [ASC] (9/21/68 BCR-56)

YOU PUT THE BEAT IN MY HEART Eddie Rabbitt—Warner Bros. 29512
[Rick Giles/Don Pfrimmer] [ASC] (9/10/83 B-81)

YOU'VE REALLY GOT A HOLD ON ME *The Miracles—Tamla 54073*
[Smokey Robinson] [ASC] (12/8/62 BCR-6)

YOU REALLY GOT A HOLD ON ME *Gayle McCormick—Dunhill 4298*
[Smokey Robinson] [ASC] (1/22/72 BR-98)

YOU'VE REALLY GOT A HOLD ON ME *Eddie Money—Columbia 10842*
[Smokey Robinson] [ASC] (11/25/78 BCR-67)

YOU REALLY GOT A HOLD ON ME *Billy Joe Royal (with Toni Wine)—Kat Family 02074*
[Smokey Robinson] [ASC] (6/6/81 C-96)

YOU REALLY GOT ME *The Kinks—Reprise 0306 [Ray Davies] [BMI] (9/26/64 BCR-5)*

YOU REALLY GOT ME *Van Halen—Warner Bros. 8515*
[Ray Davies] [BMI] (1/21/78 BCR-36)

YOU REALLY GOT ME *Tight Fit—Arista 0638 [Ray Davies] (Med) [BMI] (10/10/81 B-89)*

YOU REALLY KNOW HOW TO HURT A GUY Jan & Dean—Liberty 55792
[Jan Berry/Roger Christian/Jill Gibson] [BMI] (5/22/65 BCR-27)

YOU SAID A BAD WORD Joe Tex—Dial 1012 [Joe Tex] [BMI] (5/20/72 BCR-35)

YOU SAVED MY SOUL Burton Cummings—Alfa 7008
[Burton Cummings] [BMI] (9/12/81 BCR-32)

YOU SAYS IT ALL Randy Brown—Parachute 523
[Homer Banks/Chuck Brooks] [BMI] (3/31/79 BCR-69)

YOU SEND ME *Teresa Brewer—Coral 61898 [Sam Cooke] [BMI] (10/14/57 BCtRt-1)*

YOU SEND ME *Sam Cooke—Keen 34013 [Sam Cooke] [BMI] (10/14/57 BCtRt-1)*

YOU SEND ME *Plas Johnson & His Orchestra—Capitol 3835*
[Sam Cooke] [BMI] (11/4/57 Rt-1) [IWM]

YOU SEND ME *Aretha Franklin—Atlantic 2518 [Sam Cooke] [BMI] (6/15/68 BCR-56)*

YOU SEND ME *Ponderosa Twins + One—Horoscope 102*
[Sam Cooke] [BMI] (9/25/71 BCR-62)

YOU SEND ME *The Manhattans—Columbia 04754 [Sam Cooke] [BMI] (3/2/85 B-81)*

YOU SET MY HEART TO MUSIC Johnny Mathis—Columbia 41980
[Eaton Magoon] [ASC] (4/10/61 CR-71)

YOU SEXY THING Hot Chocolate—Big Tree 16047
[Errol Brown/Tony Wilson*] [ASC] (10/18/75 BCR-2)

YOU SHOOK ME ALL NIGHT LONG AC/DC—Atlantic 3761
[Brian Johnson/Angus Young/Malcolm Young] [ASC] (9/6/80 BCR-35)

YOU SHOULD BE DANCING Bee Gees—RSO 853
[Barry Gibb/Maurice Gibb/Robin Gibb] [BMI] (7/3/76 BCR-1)

YOU SHOULD BE MINE (THE WOO WOO SONG) Jeffrey Osborne—A&M 2814
[Andy Goldmark/Bruce Roberts] [ASC] (5/24/86 BC-11)

YOU SHOULD DO IT Peter Brown—Drive 6272
[Peter H. Brown/Robert Rans] [BMI] (9/2/78 BCR-46)

YOU SHOULD HAVE SEEN THE WAY HE LOOKED AT ME The Dixie Cups—Red Bird 10-012
[Jeff Barry/Ellie Greenwich] [BMI] (10/24/64 BCR-39)

YOU SHOULD HEAR HOW SHE TALKS ABOUT YOU Melissa Manchester—Arista 0676
[Dean Pitchford/Tom Snow] [BMI] (5/22/82 BC-4)

YOU SHOULD'A TREATED ME RIGHT Ike & Tina Turner—Sue 765
[Ike Turner] [BMI] (6/30/62 BR-88)

YOU SHOWED ME The Turtles—White Whale 292
[Gene Clark/Roger McGuinn] [BMI] (12/28/68 BCR-1)

YOU SPIN ME ROUND (LIKE A RECORD) Dead Or Alive—Epic 04894
[Pete Burns/Steve Coy/Wayne Hussey/Tim Lever/Mike Percy] [ASC] (6/1/85 BC-11)

YOU STEPPED INTO MY LIFE *Melba Moore—Epic 50600*
[Barry Gibb/Maurice Gibb/Robin Gibb] [BMI] (12/16/78 BCR-43)

YOU STEPPED INTO MY LIFE *Wayne Newton—Aries II 101*
[Barry Gibb/Maurice Gibb/Robin Gibb] [BMI] (9/8/79 BC-90)

YOU SURE FOOLED ME The John Hall Band—EMI America 8112
[Johanna Hall/John Hall/Bob Leinbach] [BMI] (4/3/82 C-78)

YOU SURE LOVE TO BALL Marvin Gaye—Tamla 54244
[Marvin Gaye] [ASC] (1/19/74 BCR-40)

YOU TAKE ME UP Thompson Twins—Arista 1-9244
[Tom Bailey/Alannah Currie/Joe Leeway] [ASC] (8/25/84 BC-43)

YOU TAKE MY BREATH AWAY Rex Smith—Columbia 10908
[Bruce Hart/Stephen Lawrence] [ASC] (4/21/79 BCR-4)

YOU TAKE MY HEART AWAY James Darren—Private Stock 45,136
[Carol Connors/Bill Conti/Ayn Robbins] [BMI] (3/19/77 BCR-52)

YOU TALK ABOUT LOVE Barbara George—A.F.O. 304
[Barbara George] [BMI] (3/24/62 BCR-46)

YOU TALK SUNSHINE, I BREATHE FIRE The Amboy Dukes—Mainstream 693
[Steve Farmer/Ted Nugent] [BMI] (10/26/68 CR-97)

YOU TALK TOO MUCH *Joe Jones & His Orchestra—Ric 972*
[Reginald Hall/Joe Jones] [BMI] (9/5/60 BCRt-2)

YOU TALK TOO MUCH *Frankie Ford—Imperial 5686*
[Reginald Hall/Joe Jones] [BMI] (9/26/60 BRt-53)

YOU TELL ME WHY The Beau Brummels—Autumn 16 [Ron Elliott] [BMI] (7/17/65 BCR-29)

YOU TELL ME YOUR DREAM (I'LL TELL YOU MINE) *Archie Bleyer—Cadence 1283*
[Charles N. Daniels] [BMI] (2/3/56 Rt-71) [IM]

YOU TELL ME YOUR DREAM *Jerry Murad's Harmonicats—Mercury 70772*
[Charles N. Daniels] [BMI] (3/23/56 Rt-81) [IM]

YOU THINK YOU'RE HOT STUFF Jean Knight—Stax 0105
[Joe Broussard/Carrol Washington/Ralph Williams] [BMI] (10/16/71 BCR-57)

YOU THRILL ME Exile—Warner/Curb 8711
[Mike Chapman/Nicky Chinn] [ASC] (11/18/78 BCR-40)

YOU TICKLE ME BABY The Royal Jokers—Atco 6052
[Albert Green/Noah Howell] [BMI] (12/10/55 B-77)

YOU TO ME ARE EVERYTHING *Broadway—Granite 540*
[Michael Denne/Ken Gold] [BMI] (7/17/76 B-86)

YOU TO ME ARE EVERYTHING *The Real Thing—United Artists 833*
[Michael Denne/Ken Gold] [BMI] (7/17/76 BCR-64)

YOU TO ME ARE EVERYTHING (PART 1) *Revelation—RSO 854*
[Michael Denne/Ken Gold] [BMI] (7/31/76 B-98)

YOU TOO CAN BE A DREAMER Patti Page—Mercury 70528
[Jerry Livingston/Mitchell Parish] [ASC] (1/24/55 R-52)

YOU TOOK THE WORDS RIGHT OUT OF MY MOUTH (HOT SUMMER NIGHT)
Meat Loaf—Cleveland Int'l/Epic 50467
[Jim Steinman] [BMI] (11/5/77 CR-73)

YOU TOOK THE WORDS RIGHT OUT OF MY MOUTH *Meat Loaf—Cleveland Int'l/Epic 50634*
[Jim Steinman] [BMI] (11/11/78 BCR-39)

YOU TURN ME ON, I'M A RADIO Joni Mitchell—Asylum 11010
[Joni Mitchell] [ASC] (11/4/72 BCR-18)

YOU TURN ME ON (TURN ON SONG) Ian Whitcomb And Bluesville—Tower 134
[Ian Whitcomb] [BMI] (5/15/65 BCR-6)

YOU TURNED MY WORLD AROUND Frank Sinatra—Reprise 1208
[Kim Carnes/Dave Ellingson/Bert Kaempfert/Herbert Rehbein] [ASC] (8/3/74 B-83)

YOU UNDERSTAND ME *Jimmie Rodgers—Roulette 4116*
[Luigi Creatore/Al Hoffman/Dick Manning/Hugo Peretti] [ASC] (11/10/58 R-97)

YOU UNDERSTAND ME *Sam Cooke—RCA Victor 47-7730*
[Luigi Creatore/Al Hoffman/Dick Manning/Hugo Peretti] [ASC] (4/25/60 R-60)

YOU WAITED TOO LONG The Five Stairsteps—Windy C 601
[Clarence Burke Sr./Gregory Keith Fowler] [BMI] (5/14/66 BCR-67)

YOU WANT IT, YOU GOT IT Detroit Emeralds—Westbound 192
[Abrim Tilmon] [BMI] (1/8/72 BCR-29)

YOU WANTED SOMEONE TO PLAY WITH (I WANTED SOMEONE TO LOVE)
Frankie Laine—ABC 10946
[Frank Capano/George McConnell/Margie Morris/Nat Osborne] [ASC]
(6/17/67 BCR-36)

YOU WANTED TO CHANGE ME Roy Hamilton—Epic 9111
[Glen Moore] [BMI] (7/11/55 R-55)

YOU WEAR IT WELL Rod Stewart—Mercury 73330
[Martin Quittenton/Rod Stewart] [ASC] (8/19/72 BCR-12)

YOU WEAR IT WELL El DeBarge with DeBarge—Gordy 1804
[Chico DeBarge/El DeBarge] [ASC] (8/31/85 BC-46)

YOU WENT BACK ON YOUR WORD Clyde McPhatter—Atlantic 2038
[Brook Benton/Bobby Stevenson] [BMI] (10/12/59 BCR-72)

YOU WERE ALWAYS THERE Donna Fargo—Dot 17460
[Donna Fargo] [BMI] (6/16/73 BCR-67)

YOU WERE BORN TO BE LOVED Billy Bland—Old Town 1082
[Claude DeMetrius] [ASC] (6/27/60 B-94)

(YOU WERE MADE FOR) ALL MY LOVE Jackie Wilson—Brunswick 55167
[Billy Myles/Jackie Wilson] [BMI] (7/4/60 BCR-8)

YOU WERE MADE FOR LOVE Dean Martin—Capitol 4124
[Ralph Freed/Grace Saxon] [ASC] (1/19/59 R-59)

YOU WERE MADE FOR ME *Sam Cooke—Keen 4009 [Sam Cooke] [BMI] (3/24/58 B-39)*

YOU WERE MADE FOR ME *Luther Ingram—KoKo 2110*
[Sam Cooke] [BMI] (3/4/72 BCR-57)

YOU WERE MADE FOR ME Freddie And The Dreamers—Tower 127
[Mitch Murray] [BMI] (5/1/65 BCR-17)

YOU WERE MADE FOR ME Irene Cara—Geffen 29257
[Eddie Brown/Irene Cara] [ASC] (7/28/84 B-78)

YOU WERE MEANT FOR ME The Johnston Brothers—London 1526
[Nacio Herb Brown/Arthur Freed] (Med) [ASC] (7/11/55 R-61)

YOU WERE MINE The Fireflies—Ribbon 6901 [Paul Giacalone] [BMI] (8/8/59 BCR-10)

YOU WERE ON MY MIND *We Five—A&M 770 [Sylvia Fricker] [ASC] (7/10/65 BCR-2)*

YOU WERE ON MY MIND *Crispian St. Peters—Jamie 1310*
[Sylvia Fricker] [ASC] (6/24/67 BCR-36)

YOU WERE ONLY FOOLING (WHILE I WAS FALLING IN LOVE)
Vic Damone—Warner Bros. 5616
[Bill Faber/Larry Fotine/Fred Meadows] [ASC] (4/17/65 BCR-28)

YOU WERE WRONG Z.Z. Hill—M.H. 200 [Z.Z. Hill] [BMI] (3/7/64 BC-95)

YOU WILL KNOW Stevie Wonder—Motown 1919 [Stevie Wonder] [ASC] (2/6/88 BC-77)

YOU WIN AGAIN *The Paulette Sisters—Capitol 3186*
[Hank Williams] [BMI] (9/12/55 BR-78)

YOU WIN AGAIN *Jerry Lee Lewis—Sun 281 [Hank Williams] [BMI] (2/17/58 B-95)*

YOU WIN AGAIN *Fats Domino—Imperial 5816 [Hank Williams] [BMI] (2/19/62 BCR-22)*

YOU WIN AGAIN Bee Gees—Warner Bros. 28351
[Barry Gibb/Maurice Gibb/Robin Gibb] [BMI] (9/19/87 BC-75)

YOU WON'T FIND ANOTHER FOOL LIKE ME
The New Seekers Featuring Lyn Paul—MGM 14691
[Tony Macaulay/Geoff Stephens] [ASC] (1/26/74 CR-75)

YOU WON'T SEE ME Anne Murray—Capitol 3867
[John Lennon/Paul McCartney] [ASC] (4/13/74 BCR-8)

YOU WOULDN'T LISTEN The I'des Of March—Parrot 304
[Michael Borch/Larry Millas/Jim Peterik] [BMI] (6/11/66 BCR-41)

YOU YOU YOU Mel Carter—Imperial 66183
[Robert Mellin/Lotar Olias] [BMI] (7/16/66 BCR-49)

YOU'D BE SURPRISED Kathy Linden—Felsted 8521
[Irving Berlin] [ASC] (5/19/58 BCR-25)

YOU'D BETTER BELIEVE IT The Manhattans—Columbia 45927
[John Fowlkes/Roger Genger] [BMI] (9/22/73 BCR-77)

YOU'D BETTER COME HOME Russell Byrd—Wand 107 [Bert Berns] [BMI] (5/8/61 B-50)

YOU'D BETTER COME HOME Petula Clark—Warner Bros. 5643
[Tony Hatch] [BMI] (7/10/65 BCR-21)

YOU'LL ACCOMP'NY ME Bob Seger—Capitol 4904 [Bob Seger] [ASC] (7/26/80 BCR-14)

YOU'LL ALWAYS BE MY LIFETIME SWEETHEART Perry Como—RCA Victor 47-5994
[Johnny Burke/Robert Day] [ASC] (1/17/55 CR-13)

YOU'LL ALWAYS BE MY SWEETHEART Bobby Van—ABC-Paramount 9940
[Don George/Bee Walker] [ASC] (9/6/58 CR-61)

YOU'LL ALWAYS BE THE ONE (FOR ME) Four Aces—Decca 29435
[Arthur Berman/Jack Gold/Marvin Kahn] [NA] (2/21/55 R-79)

YOU'LL ALWAYS BE THE ONE I LOVE Dean Martin—Reprise 0333
[Ticker Freeman/Sunny Skylar] [ASC] (12/19/64 BCR-64)

YOU'LL ANSWER TO ME Patti Page—Mercury 71823
[Hal David/Sherman Edwards] [ASC] (6/26/61 BCR-46)

YOU'LL FIND OUT Jeanne Black—Capitol 4456 [Pete Harris] [BMI] (10/31/60 R-95)

YOU'LL GET YOURS Frank Sinatra—Capitol 3350
[Dok Stanford/Jimmy Van Heusen] [ASC] (2/24/56 BR-67)

YOU'LL LOSE A GOOD THING *Barbara Lynn—Jamie 1220*
[Barbara Lynn/Huey P. Meaux*] [BMI] (6/16/62 BCR-4)*

YOU'LL LOSE A GOOD THING *Freddy Fender—ABC/Dot 17607*
[Barbara Lynn/Huey P. Meaux*] [BMI] (2/7/76 BCR-32)*

YOU'LL LOVE AGAIN Hotel—Mercury 73979 [Marc Phillips] [BMI] (3/4/78 BCR-67)

YOU'LL MISS ME (WHEN I'M GONE) Fontella Bass & Bobby McClure—Checker 1111
[Gene Barge/Billy Davis] [BMI] (5/29/65 BCR-64)

YOU'LL NEVER FIND ANOTHER LOVE LIKE MINE Lou Rawls—Philadelphia Int'l 3592
[Kenneth Gamble/Leon Huff] [BMI] (5/15/76 BCR-2)

YOU'LL NEVER GET TO HEAVEN (IF YOU BREAK MY HEART) *Dionne Warwick—Scepter 1282*
[Burt Bacharach/Hal David] [ASC] (8/8/64 BCR-28)

YOU'LL NEVER GET TO HEAVEN (IF YOU BREAK MY HEART) *The Stylistics—Avco 4618*
[Burt Bacharach/Hal David] [ASC] (5/12/73 BCR-15)

YOU'LL NEVER KNOW
Shirley Bassey with the Rita Williams Singers—United Artists 363
[Mack Gordon/Harry Warren] [ASC] (10/9/61 R-89)

YOU'LL NEVER NEVER KNOW The Platters—Mercury 70948
[Buck Ram/Paul Robi/Tony Williams] [BMI] (9/22/56 BCR-7)

YOU'LL NEVER WALK ALONE *Judy Garland—Decca 29295*
[Oscar Hammerstein/Richard Rodgers] [ASC] (12/6/54 R-83)

YOU'LL NEVER WALK ALONE *Patti Labelle & The Blue Belles—Parkway 896*
[Oscar Hammerstein/Richard Rodgers] [ASC] (1/4/64 BCR-34)

YOU'LL NEVER WALK ALONE Gerry And The Pacemakers—Laurie 3302 [Oscar Hammerstein/Richard Rodgers] [ASC] (6/5/65 BCR-48)

YOU'LL NEVER WALK ALONE Elvis Presley With The Jordanaires—RCA Victor 47-9600 [Oscar Hammerstein/Richard Rodgers] [ASC] (4/20/68 BR-83)

YOU'LL NEVER WALK ALONE Brooklyn Bridge—Buddah 139 [Oscar Hammerstein/Richard Rodgers] [ASC] (9/27/69 BCR-33)

YOU'LL NEVER WALK ALONE Blue Haze—A&M 1426 [Oscar Hammerstein/Richard Rodgers] [ASC] (6/2/73 C-93)

YOUNG ABE LINCOLN Don Cornell—Coral 61521 [Roy Alfred/Abner Silver] [ASC] (10/24/55 BCRt-25)

YOUNG ABE LINCOLN Hugo & Luigi—Mercury 70721 [Roy Alfred/Abner Silver] [ASC] (10/24/55 BRt-44)

YOUNG AMERICANS David Bowie—RCA Victor 10152 [David Bowie] [ASC] (3/15/75 BCR-20)

YOUNG AND FOOLISH Dean Martin—Capitol 3036 [Albert Hague/Arnold B. Horwitt] [ASC] (3/19/55 C-34)

YOUNG AND FOOLISH Jo Stafford—Columbia 40495 [Albert Hague/Arnold B. Horwitt] [ASC] (5/9/55 CR-40)

YOUNG AND IN LOVE Dick And Deedee—Warner Bros. 5342 [Dick Gosting] [BMI] (3/9/63 BCR-17)

YOUNG AND IN LOVE Chris Crosby—MGM 13191 [Bernie Baum/Bill Giant/Florence Kaye] [ASC] (2/15/64 BCR-46)

YOUNG AND WARM AND WONDERFUL Tony Bennett with Frank DeVol and his Orch.—Columbia 41172 [Lou Singer/Hy Zaret] [ASC] (6/2/58 BCtRt-31)

YOUNG AND WARM AND WONDERFUL Roger Williams—Kapp 224 [Lou Singer] [ASC] (6/2/58 CtRt-31) [IM]

YOUNG AS WE ARE Sal Mineo—Epic 9327 [Barry Mann/Noel Sherman] [BMI] (8/22/59 CR-66)

YOUNG AT HEART Frank Sinatra—Capitol 2703 [Carolyn Leigh/Johnny Richards] [ASC] (5/29/54 BC-PRE)

YOUNG BIRDS FLY The Cryan' Shames—Columbia 44545 [Bill Swofford] [BMI] (6/8/68 BCR-86)

YOUNG BLOOD The Coasters—Atco 6087 [Jerry Leiber/Doc Pomus/Mike Stoller] [BMI] (5/6/57 BCR-8)

YOUNG BLOOD Bad Company—Swan Song 70108 [Jerry Leiber/Doc Pomus/Mike Stoller] [BMI] (3/13/76 BCR-20)

YOUNG BLOOD Bruce Willis—Motown 1886 [Jerry Leiber/Doc Pomus/Mike Stoller] [BMI] (4/11/87 BC-68)

YOUNG BLOOD Rickie Lee Jones—Warner Bros. 49018 [Rickie Lee Jones] [ASC] (7/28/79 BCR-40)

YOUNG BOY Barbara Greene—Renee 5001 [Richard Parker] [BMI] (6/22/68 BCR-86)

YOUNG BOY BLUES Ben E. King—Atco 6207 [Doc Pomus/Phil Spector] [BMI] (10/2/61 BCR-63)

YOUNG DOVE'S CALLING The Couplings—Josie 831 [Harold Galbreath/Charles Zimmerman*] [BMI] (2/15/58 CR-58)

YOUNG DREAMS Elvis Presley with the Jordanaires—RCA Victor EPA-4321 [Martin Kalmanoff/Aaron Schroeder] (EP) [ASC] (8/18/58 R-56)

YOUNG EMOTIONS Ricky Nelson—Imperial 5663 [Mack David/Jerry Livingston] [ASC] (4/23/60 BCR-11)

THE YOUNG FOLKS Diana Ross And The Supremes—Motown 1148 [George Gordy/Allen Story] [BMI] (7/26/69 BCR-62)

A YOUNG GIRL Noel Harrison—London 9795 [Charles Aznavour/Oscar Brown Jr./Robert Chauvigny] [BMI] (11/27/65 BCR-34) [FET]

YOUNG GIRL The Union Gap Featuring Gary Puckett—Columbia 44450 [Jerry Fuller] [BMI] (3/2/68 BCR-1)

—YOUNG GIRLS ARE COMING TO THE CANYON see: TWELVE THIRTY

YOUNG HEARTS RUN FREE Candi Staton—Warner Bros. 8181 [Dave Crawford] [ASC] (5/1/76 BCR-16)

YOUNG IDEAS Gordon Jenkins & His Orchestra—"X" 0159 [Moose Charlap/Chuck Sweeney] [ASC] (8/29/55 Rt-73)

YOUNG IDEAS Tony Martin—RCA Victor 47-6209 [Moose Charlap/Chuck Sweeney] [ASC] (8/29/55 Rt-73)

YOUNG IDEAS Chico Holiday—RCA Victor 47-7499 [Sonny James] [BMI] (4/13/59 BCR-46)

YOUNG IN YEARS The Diamonds—Mercury 71505 [Johannes Brahms*/Wally Gold/Aaron Schroeder] [ASC] (9/26/59 C-80)

YOUNG LOVE The Rover Boys—ABC-Paramount 9732 [Irving Berger/Herbert L. Miller] [NA] (8/25/56 R-61)

YOUNG LOVE Sonny James—Capitol 3602 [Ric Cartey/Carole Joyner] [BMI] (12/22/56 BCtRt-1)

YOUNG LOVE The Crew-Cuts—Mercury 71022 [Ric Cartey/Carole Joyner] [BMI] (12/22/56 BRt-1)

YOUNG LOVE Ric Cartey with The Jiva-Tones—RCA Victor 47-6751 [Ric Cartey/Carole Joyner] [BMI] (12/29/56 Rt-1)

YOUNG LOVE Tab Hunter—Dot 15533 [Ric Cartey/Carole Joyner] [BMI] (1/12/57 BCtRt-1)

YOUNG LOVE Lesley Gore—Mercury 72553 [Ric Cartey/Carole Joyner] [BMI] (3/19/66 BCR-40)

YOUNG LOVE Donny Osmond—MGM 14583 [Ric Cartey/Carole Joyner] (TSW) [BMI] (7/28/73 BCR-21)

YOUNG LOVE Ray Stevens—Barnaby 618 [Ric Cartey/Carole Joyner] [BMI] (1/24/76 BC-87)

YOUNG LOVE Air Supply—Arista 1005 [Graham Russell] [BMI] (9/18/82 BC-38)

YOUNG LOVE Janet Jackson—A&M 2440 [René Moore/Angela Winbush] [ASC] (12/18/82 BC-64)

YOUNG LOVERS Paul & Paula—Philips 40096 [Ray Hildebrand/Jill Jackson] [BMI] (3/16/63 BCR-6)

THE YOUNG NEW MEXICAN PUPPETEER Tom Jones—Parrot 40070 [Leon Carr/Earl Shuman] [ASC] (4/29/72 BCR-60)

YOUNG SCHOOL GIRL Fats Domino—Imperial 5537 [Dave Bartholomew/Fats Domino] [BMI] (9/22/58 B-92)

YOUNG THING, WILD DREAMS (ROCK ME) Red Rider—Capitol 5335 [Tom Cochrane] [ASC] (6/16/84 BC-71)

YOUNG TURKS Rod Stewart—Warner Bros. 49843 [Carmine Appice/Duane Hitchings/Kevin Savigar/Rod Stewart] [ASC] (10/17/81 BCR-5)

YOUNG WINGS CAN FLY (HIGHER THAN YOU KNOW) Ruby And The Romantics—Kapp 557 [Mort Garson/Bob Hilliard] [ASC] (10/12/63 BCR-40)

YOUNG WORLD Rick Nelson—Imperial 5805 [Jerry Fuller] [BMI] (3/3/62 BCR-5)

YOUNGER DAYS Joe Fagin—Millennium 13107 [Richie Supa] [ASC] (7/31/82 B-80)

YOUNGER GIRL The Critters—Kapp 752 [John Sebastian] [BMI] (5/14/66 BCRt-18)

YOUNGER GIRL The Hondells—Mercury 72563 [John Sebastian] [BMI] (5/21/66 BCRt-18)

YOUR BABY NEVER LOOKED GOOD IN BLUE Exposé—Arista 2011 [Diane Warren] [ASC] (3/31/90 BC-16)

YOUR BABY'S GONE SURFIN' Duane Eddy—RCA Victor 47-8214 [Duane Eddy/Lee Hazlewood] [BMI] (8/10/63 BCR-59)

YOUR BULLDOG DRINKS CHAMPAGNE Jim Stafford—MGM 14775 [David Bellamy/Jim Stafford] [ASC] (12/21/74 BCR-24)

YOUR CASH AIN'T NOTHIN' BUT TRASH Steve Miller Band—Capitol 3837 [Jesse Stone] [BMI] (2/23/74 BCR-40)

YOUR CHEATIN' HEART George Hamilton IV—ABC-Paramount 9946 [Hank Williams] [BMI] (8/11/58 BCR-49)

YOUR CHEATIN' HEART Billy Vaughn And His Orchestra—Dot 15936 [Hank Williams] [BMI] (4/20/59 BCR-53) [IWM]

YOUR CHEATING HEART Ray Charles With The Jack Halloran Singers And The Ray Charles Orchestra—ABC-Paramount 10375 [Hank Williams] [BMI] (11/17/62 BCR-28)

YOUR DADDY DON'T KNOW Toronto—Network 69986 [Geoff Iwamoto/Michael Roth] [ASC] (8/7/82 BC-72)

YOUR FRIENDS Dee Clark—Vee-Jay 372 [Calvin Carter/Dee Clark] [BMI] (1/16/61 BCR-34)

YOUR GOOD THING (IS ABOUT TO END) Mable John—Stax 192 [Isaac Hayes/David Porter] [BMI] (7/23/66 BCR-68)

YOUR GOOD THING (IS ABOUT TO END) Lou Rawls—Capitol 2550 [Isaac Hayes/David Porter] [BMI] (7/19/69 BCR-18)

YOUR GRADUATION MEANS GOODBYE The Cardigans—Mercury 71251 [Mike Alday/Don Shoemate] [BMI] (3/1/58 C-52)

YOUR HEART BELONGS TO ME The Supremes—Motown 1027 [Smokey Robinson] [ASC] (8/11/62 B-95)

YOUR HEART IS FREE JUST LIKE THE WIND Vikki Carr—Liberty 56026 [Christian Chevallier/Joan Shakespeare] [ASC] (3/30/68 B-91) [FDE]

YOUR HEART - MY HEART (SEHNSUCHT) Frankie Laine—Columbia 40295 [Lotar Olias/Walter Rothenburg/Carl Sigman/Stephan Weiss] [ASC] (10/4/54 R-PRE) [FDE]

YOUR HUSBAND - MY WIFE Brooklyn Bridge—Buddah 126 [Irwin Levine/Toni Wine] [BMI] (7/12/69 BCR-40)

YOUR IMAGINATION Daryl Hall & John Oates—RCA 13252 [Daryl Hall] [BMI] (6/19/82 BC-27)

YOUR KISSES KILL ME Eydie Gorme—ABC-Paramount 9817 [Mack Discant/Steve Lawrence] [ASC] (6/17/57 BR-53)

YOUR LAST GOODBYE Floyd Cramer—RCA Victor 47-7907 [Floyd Cramer] [BMI] (9/25/61 BCR-55) [I]

YOUR LOVE Paul Anka—ABC-Paramount 10022 [Paul Anka] [BMI] (5/23/59 C-83)

YOUR LOVE Graham Central Station—Warner Bros. 8105 [Larry Graham] [BMI] (8/2/75 BCR-33)

YOUR LOVE Marilyn McCoo And Billy Davis Jr.—ABC 12262 [H.B. Barnum/Walter Johnson] [BMI] (3/12/77 BCR-15)

YOUR LOVE The Outfield—Columbia 05796 [John Spinks] [ASC] (2/15/86 BC-6)

YOUR LOVE PART 2 Keith Sweat—Vintertainment 64894 [Keith Sweat] [ASC] (6/15/91 BC-71)

YOUR LOVE FOR ME Frank Sinatra—Capitol 3608 [Barry Parker] [BMI] (1/12/57 BCR-12)

YOUR LOVE IS DRIVING ME CRAZY Sammy Hagar—Geffen 29816 [Sammy Hagar] [ASC] (12/4/82 BC-13)

YOUR LOVE IS KING Sade—Portrait 37-05408 [Helen Adu/Stuart Matthewman] [NA] (6/22/85 BC-52)

YOUR LOVE IS ON THE ONE Lakeside—Solar12188 [Fred Alexander/Stephen Shockley] [BMI] (5/23/81 R-96)

YOUR LOVE IS SO DOGGONE GOOD The Whispers—Janus 150
[Dee Ervin/Rudy Love] [BMI] (5/29/71 BC-93)

YOUR LOVE IS SO GOOD FOR ME Diana Ross—Motown 1436
[Kenneth Edward Peterson] [BMI] (3/4/78 BCR-49)

—YOUR LOVE KEEPS LIFTING ME... see: HIGHER AND HIGHER

YOUR LOVE (MEANS EVERYTHING TO ME)
Charles Wright And The Watts 103rd Street Band—Warner Bros. 7475
[Charles Wright] [BMI] (4/10/71 BCR-56)

YOUR MA SAID YOU CRIED IN YOUR SLEEP LAST NIGHT Kenny Dino—Musicor 1013
[Robert Glazer/Steve Schlaks] [BMI] (10/14/61 BCR-24)

YOUR MAMA DON'T DANCE *Kenny Loggins With Jim Messina—Columbia 45719*
[Kenny Loggins/Jim Messina] [ASC] (11/4/72 BCR-4)

YOUR MAMA DON'T DANCE *Poison—Enigma 44293*
[Kenny Loggins/Jim Messina] [ASC] (2/11/89 BC-10)

YOUR MEMORY The Five Satins—Cub 9071
[John Bobby Berry/Don Covay] [BMI] (7/11/60 R-95)

YOUR MOVE Yes—Atlantic 2819 [Jon Anderson] [ASC] (9/25/71 BCR-29)

YOUR NAME IS BEAUTIFUL Carl Smith—Columbia 41092
[John Gluck/Diane Lampert] [ASC] (3/24/58 B-80)

YOUR NOSE IS GONNA GROW Johnny Crawford—Del-Fi 4181
[Jeff Hooven/Hal Winn] [BMI] (8/4/62 BCR-14)

YOUR OLD STAND BY Mary Wells—Motown 1042
[Janie Bradford/Smokey Robinson] [BMI] (5/11/63 BCR-40)

YOUR ONE AND ONLY LOVE Jackie Wilson—Brunswick 55208
[Billy Myles/Jackie Wilson*] [BMI] (3/13/61 BCR-30)

YOUR OTHER LOVE The Flamingos—End 1081
[Doc Pomus/Mort Shuman] [BMI] (12/5/60 BCR-41)

YOUR OTHER LOVE Connie Francis—MGM 13176
[Klaus Ogerman/Ben Raleigh] [BMI] (10/12/63 BCR-20)

YOUR OWN BACK YARD Dion—Warner Bros. 7401
[Dion DiMucci/Tony Fasce] [BMI] (6/27/70 BCR-68)

YOUR OWN SPECIAL WAY Genesis—Atco 7076 [Mike Rutherford] [BMI] (3/12/77 BCR-62)

YOUR P-E-R-S-O-N-A-L-I-T-Y Jackie Lee (2)—Mirwood 5509
[Sherlie Mae Matthews/Earl Nelson/Fred Smith] [BMI] (2/26/66 CR-70)

YOUR PEOPLE Little Milton—Checker 1128
[Billy Davis/Raynard Miner/Carl William Smith] [BMI] (12/18/65 CR-89)

YOUR PERSONAL TOUCH Evelyn "Champagne" King—RCA 14201
[Allen George/Fred McFarlane] [BMI] (1/11/86 B-86)

YOUR PLACE IN THE SUN Tony Martin—RCA Victor 47-6597
[Buck Ram] [BMI] (8/10/56 R-51)

YOUR PRECIOUS LOVE Marvin Gaye & Tammi Terrell—Tamla 54156
[Nick Ashford/Valerie Simpson] [ASC] (9/9/67 BCR-5)

YOUR SECOND CHOICE Clyde McPhatter—Mercury 71868
[Jack Keller*/Larry Kolber] [BMI] (10/2/61 R-93)

YOUR SIDE OF THE BED Mac Davis—Columbia 45839
[Mac Davis] [BMI] (4/28/73 BCR-83)

YOUR SMILE René and Angela—Mercury 884271
[René Moore/Angela Winbush] [ASC] (3/22/86 B-62)

YOUR SMILING FACE James Taylor—Columbia 10602
[James Taylor] [ASC] (10/1/77 BCR-12)

YOUR SONG Elton John—Uni 55265 [Elton John/Bernie Taupin] [BMI] (11/21/70 BCR-6)

YOUR SWEETNESS IS MY WEAKNESS Barry White—20th Century 2380
[Barry White] [BMI] (10/28/78 BCR-37)

YOUR TEENAGE DREAMS Johnny Mathis—Mercury 72184
[Bobby Worth] [ASC] (10/12/63 BCR-68)

YOUR TIME HASN'T COME YET, BABY
Elvis Presley With The Jordanaires—RCA Victor 47-9547
[Joel Hirschhorn/Al Kasha] [BMI] (6/15/68 BCR-54)

YOUR TIME TO CRY Joe Simon—Spring 108
[Raeford Gerald/Dock Price/Joe Simon] [BMI] (12/5/70 BCR-26)

YOUR TRUE LOVE Carl Perkins—Sun 261 [Carl Perkins] [BMI] (3/23/57 B-67)

YOUR UNCHANGING LOVE Marvin Gaye—Tamla 54153
[Lamont Dozier/Brian Holland/Eddie Holland] [BMI] (7/1/67 BCR-33)

YOUR USED TO BE Brenda Lee—Decca 31454
[Howard Greenfield/Jack Keller*] [BMI] (1/12/63 BCR-23)

YOUR WILD HEART *Joy Layne—Mercury 71038*
[Charles Fana/James Testa] [BMI] (2/9/57 BCtRt-29)

YOUR WILD HEART *The Poni Tails—Point 8*
[Charles Fana/James Testa] [BMI] (2/9/57 CtRt-39)

YOUR WILD HEART *Karen Chandler—Decca 30207*
[Charles Fana/James Testa] [BMI] (2/9/57 Rt-46)

YOUR WILDEST DREAMS The Moody Blues—Polydor 883906
[Justin Hayward] [ASC] (4/19/86 BC-9)

YOUR WONDERFUL, SWEET SWEET LOVE The Supremes—Motown 1206
[Smokey Robinson] [ASC] (8/5/72 BCR-59)

YOU'RE A BIG GIRL NOW The Stylistics—Avco Embassy 4555
[Marty Bryant/Robert Douglas] [BMI] (1/9/71 BCR-66)

YOU'RE A FRIEND OF MINE Clarence Clemons—Columbia 05660
[Jeffrey E. Cohen/Narada Michael Walden] [ASC] (10/26/85 BC-18)

YOU'RE A LADY Gene Chandler—Mercury 73206
[Gene Chandler/James A. Thompson Jr.] [ASC] (7/3/71 C-93)

YOU'RE A LADY *Peter Skellern—London 20075*
[Peter Skellern] [ASC] (11/11/72 BCR-50)

YOU'RE A LADY *Dawn Featuring Tony Orlando—Bell 45,285*
[Peter Skellern] [ASC] (11/11/72 BCR-67)

YOU'RE A PART OF ME *Susan Jacks—Mercury 73649*
[Kim Carnes] [ASC] (3/8/75 BCR-90)

YOU'RE A PART OF ME *Gene Cotton With Kim Carnes—Ariola America 7704*
[Kim Carnes] [ASC] (6/10/78 BCR-35)

YOU'RE A SPECIAL PART OF ME Diana Ross & Marvin Gaye—Motown 1280
[Harold Johnson/Andrew Porter/Greg Wright] [ASC] (9/29/73 BCR-12)

YOU'RE A SWEETHEART *Little Willie John—King 5142*
[Harold Adamson/Jimmy McHugh] [ASC] (8/11/58 BC-66)

YOU'RE A SWEETHEART *Dinah Washington—Roulette 4455*
[Harold Adamson/Jimmy McHugh] [ASC] (11/24/62 B-98)

YOU'RE A VERY LOVELY WOMAN *The Merry-Go-Round—A&M 863*
[Emitt Rhodes] [ASC] (8/19/67 BCR-86)

(SHE'S A) VERY LOVELY WOMAN *Linda Ronstadt—Capitol 3021*
[Emitt Rhodes] (TSW) [ASC] (1/23/71 BCR-59)

YOU'RE A WONDERFUL ONE Marvin Gaye—Tamla 54093
[Lamont Dozier/Brian Holland/Eddie Holland] [BMI] (3/14/64 BCR-15)

YOU'RE ALL AROUND ME Percy Sledge—Atlantic 2563
[Donnie Fritts/Eddie Hinton] [BMI] (10/19/68 CR-68)

YOU'RE ALL I NEED Bobby Bland—Duke 416 [Pearl Woods] [BMI] (4/22/67 BCR-88)

YOU'RE ALL I NEED TO GET BY *Marvin Gaye & Tammi Terrell—Tamla 54169*
[Nick Ashford/Valerie Simpson] [ASC] (7/27/68 BCR-7)

YOU'RE ALL I NEED TO GET BY *Aretha Franklin—Atlantic 2787*
[Nick Ashford/Valerie Simpson] [ASC] (2/20/71 BCR-15)

YOU'RE ALL I NEED TO GET BY *Tony Orlando & Dawn—Elektra 45275*
[Nick Ashford/Valerie Simpson] [ASC] (8/30/75 BCR-34)

YOU'RE ALL I NEED TO GET BY *Johnny Mathis/Deniece Williams—Columbia 10772*
[Nick Ashford/Valerie Simpson] [ASC] (7/15/78 BCR-47)

YOU'RE ALL I NEED TO GET BY *Chris Christian—Boardwalk 7-11-149*
[Nick Ashford/Valerie Simpson] (Med) [ASC] (8/28/82 B-88)

YOU'RE ALL I WANT FOR CHRISTMAS Brook Benton—Mercury 72214
[Bennie Benjamin/Sol Marcus] [ASC] (12/14/63 C-59)

YOU'RE AMAZING Robert Palmer—EMI 50338
[Steve Fellows/Alan Mansfield/Robert Palmer/Guy Pratt/Steve Stevens] [BMI]
(11/17/90 BC-28)

YOU'RE CHEATIN' YOURSELF (IF YOU'RE CHEATIN' ON ME) Frank Sinatra—Capitol 3744
[Al Hoffman/Dick Manning] [ASC] (7/6/57 CR-48)

YOU'RE DRIVING ME OUT OF MY MIND Little River Band—Capitol 5256
[Beeb Birtles/Graham Goble] [BMI] (7/23/83 BC-35)

YOU'RE FOLLOWING ME Perry Como—RCA Victor 47-7962
[Burt Bacharach/Bob Hilliard] [ASC] (11/6/61 BCR-60)

YOU'RE FOOLING YOU The Dramatics—ABC 12150 [Tony Hester] [BMI] (1/17/76 BR-87)

YOU'RE GETTIN' A LITTLE TOO SMART Detroit Emeralds—Westbound 213
[Abrim Tilmon] [BMI] (6/30/73 CR-82)

YOU'RE GOING TO LOSE THAT GIRL Stars On 45—Radio 3810
[John Lennon/Paul McCartney] (Med) [ASC] (4/11/81 BCR-1)

YOU'RE GONNA BE MINE The New Colony Six—Sentar 1206
[Ray Graffia/Ronnie Rice] [BMI] (4/15/67 C-98)

YOU'RE GONNA GET WHAT'S COMING Bonnie Raitt—Warner Bros. 49116
[Robert Palmer] [ASC] (12/1/79 BCR-72)

(YOU'RE GONNA) HURT YOURSELF Frankie Valli—Smash 2015
[Charlie Calello/Bob Crewe] [BMI] (1/15/66 BCR-38)

YOU'RE GONNA MAKE IT The Festivals—Colossus 122
[Earl Moss/Vaughn Price/Woody Price] [ASC] (9/5/70 CR-85)

YOU'RE GONNA MAKE ME CRY O.V. Wright—Back Beat 548
[Deadric Malone] [BMI] (7/31/65 BCR-50)

YOU'RE GONNA MISS ME Connie Francis—MGM 12824
[Eddie Curtis] [ASC] (8/31/59 BCR-22)

YOU'RE GONNA MISS ME B.B. King—Kent 396
[B.B. King/Jules Taub‡] [BMI] (7/25/64 C-95)

YOU'RE GONNA MISS ME The Thirteenth Floor Elevators—Int'l Artists 107
[Roky Erickson] [BMI] (8/13/66 BCR-41)

YOU'RE GONNA NEED MAGIC Roy Hamilton—Epic 9443
[Bob Brass/Irwin Levine] [BMI] (4/29/61 BCR-66)

YOU'RE GONNA NEED ME Barbara Lynn—Jamie 1240
[Barbara Lynn] [BMI] (12/15/62 BR-65)

YOU'RE GOOD FOR ME Solomon Burke—Atlantic 2205
[Don Covay/Horace Ott] [BMI] (11/2/63 BCR-37)

YOU'RE GOOD FOR ME Lou Rawls—Capitol 2172
[Larry Collins/Mac Davis] [BMI] (6/1/68 CR-88)

(YOU'RE) HAVING MY BABY Paul Anka—United Artists 454
[Paul Anka] [BMI] (7/6/74 BCR-1)

YOU'RE IN GOOD HANDS Jermaine Jackson—Motown 1244
[Fonce Mizell/Larry Mizell] [ASC] (10/6/73 BCR-79)

YOU'RE IN LOVE Gogi Grant—Era 1019
[Buddy Bregman/Herbert Newman] [ASC] (9/15/56 BC-45)
YOU'RE IN LOVE Ratt—Atlantic 89502
[Juan Croucier/Stephen Pearcy] [BMI] (10/12/85 B-89)
YOU'RE IN LOVE Wilson Phillips—SBK 07343
[Glen Ballard/Chynna Phillips/Carnie Wilson/Wendy Wilson] [ASC] (2/9/91 BC-1)
YOU'RE IN MY HEART (THE FINAL ACCLAIM) Rod Stewart—Warner Bros. 8475
[Rod Stewart] [ASC] (10/22/77 BCR-3)
YOU'RE JUST ABOUT TO LOSE YOUR CLOWN Ray Charles—ABC-Paramount 10785
[Fred Aylor MacRae] [BMI] (3/26/66 BC-91)
YOU'RE JUST THE RIGHT SIZE The Salsoul Orchestra—Salsoul 2007
[Vincent Montana] [BMI] (5/29/76 B-88)
YOU'RE LOOKING AT ME Johnny Nash—ABC-Paramount 9942
[Stan Lebowsky/Johnny Lehmann] [BMI] (7/21/58 CR-40)
YOU'RE LOOKING GOOD Dee Clark—Vee-Jay 355
[Calvin Carter/Marion Oliver] [BMI] (8/15/60 BCR-40)
YOU'RE LOOKING LIKE LOVE TO ME Peabo Bryson/Roberta Flack—Capitol 5307
[Jerry Corbetta/Bob Crewe/Bob Gaudio] [BMI] (12/24/83 BC-58)
YOU'RE MAKING A MISTAKE The Platters—Mercury 71320
[Jim Williams] [BMI] (6/9/58 BCR-31)
YOU'RE MINE The Dream Weavers—Decca 29818
[Gene Adkinson/Wade Buff] [ASC] (4/7/56 B-100)
YOU'RE MINE Four Aces—Decca 30242 [Robert Mellin] [BMI] (3/16/57 BCR-42)
YOU'RE MINE The Falcons—Unart 2022
[Dave Braithwaite/Eddie Powell] [BMI] (8/31/59 R-85)
YOU'RE MINE TONIGHT Pure Prairie League—Casablanca 2337
[Rafe Van Hoy] [BMI] (7/25/81 B-68)
YOU'RE MOVIN' OUT TODAY *Bette Midler—Atlantic 3379*
[Bette Midler/Bruce Roberts/Carole Bayer Sager] [BMI] (4/9/77 BCR-42)
YOU'RE MOVING OUT TODAY *Carole Bayer Sager—Elektra 45422*
[Bette Midler/Bruce Roberts/Carole Bayer Sager] [BMI] (9/17/77 BCR-57)
YOU'RE MY BABY Sarah Vaughan—Mercury 71562
[Clyde Otis/Luvenia Willis] [BMI] (1/11/60 BCR-65)
YOU'RE MY BABY (AND DON'T YOU FORGET IT) The Vacels—Kama Sutra 200
[Helen Miller/Pam Sawyer/Steve Venet] [BMI] (7/17/65 BCR-58)
YOU'RE MY BEST FRIEND Queen—Elektra 45318 [John Deacon] [BMI] (5/22/76 BCR-9)
YOU'RE MY BLESSING Lou Rawls—Philadelphia Int'l 3570
[Kenneth Gamble/Leon Huff] [BMI] (4/26/80 B-77)
YOU'RE MY DRIVING WHEEL The Supremes—Motown 1407
[Harold Beatty/Reggie Brown/Stafford Floyd/Brian Holland] [ASC] (12/4/76 B-85)
YOU'RE MY EVERYTHING The Temptations—Gordy 7063
[Cornelius Grant/Rodger Penzabene/Norman Whitfield] [BMI] (7/29/67 BCR-6)
YOU'RE MY EVERYTHING Lee Garrett—Chrysalis 2112
[Lee Garrett/Robert Percy Taylor] [BMI] (5/15/76 BCR-58)
YOU'RE MY GIRL Franke and the Knockouts—Millennium 11808
[Billy Elworthy/Benny Harrison/Franke Previte] [ASC] (7/4/81 BCR-27)
YOU'RE MY LATEST, MY GREATEST INSPIRATION
Teddy Pendergrass—Philadelphia Int'l 2619
[Kenneth Gamble/Leon Huff] [BMI] (12/26/81 BCR-43)
YOU'RE MY MAN Lynn Anderson—Columbia 45356
[Glenn Sutton] [BMI] (5/1/71 BCR-51)
YOU'RE MY ONE AND ONLY LOVE Ricky Nelson—Verve 10070
[Barney Kessel/Jack Marshall] [ASC] (8/24/57 BCR-16)
YOU'RE MY ONE AND ONLY (TRUE LOVE) Seduction—Vendetta 1433
[Robert Clivillés/David Cole/Frederick B. Williams] [ASC] (7/8/89 BC-23)
YOU'RE MY ONE WEAKNESS GIRL Street People—Vigor VI 1728
[Ray Dahrouge] [BMI] (3/20/76 R-86)
YOU'RE MY REMEDY The Marvelettes—Tamla 54097
[Smokey Robinson] [ASC] (7/4/64 BCR-42)
(YOU'RE MY) SOUL AND INSPIRATION *The Righteous Brothers—Verve 10383*
[Barry Mann/Cynthia Weil] [BMI] (3/5/66 BCR-1)
(YOU'RE MY) SOUL AND INSPIRATION *Donny & Marie—Polydor/Kolob 14439*
[Barry Mann/Cynthia Weil] [BMI] (11/12/77 BCR-38)
YOU'RE MY WEAKNESS Faith Band—Mercury 74068
[John Cascella] [BMI] (6/2/79 BC-67)
YOU'RE MY WORLD *Cilla Black—Capitol 5196*
[Umberto Bindi/Gino Paoli/Carl Sigman] [ASC] (6/13/64 BCR-23) [FET]
YOU'RE MY WORLD *Helen Reddy—Capitol 4418*
[Umberto Bindi/Gino Paoli/Carl Sigman] [ASC] (4/30/77 BCR-16) [FET]
YOU'RE NEXT Jimmy Witherspoon—Prestige 341
[Roy C. Bennett/Sid Tepper] [ASC] (2/13/65 BCR-72)
YOU'RE NO GOOD *Betty Everett—Vee-Jay 566*
[Clint Ballard Jr.] [ASC] (11/2/63 BCtRt-40)
YOU'RE NO GOOD *Dee Dee Warwick—Jubilee 5459*
[Clint Ballard Jr.] [ASC] (11/9/63 CtRt-76)
YOU'RE NO GOOD *The Swinging Blue Jeans—Imperial 66049*
[Clint Ballard Jr.] [ASC] (8/1/64 B-97)
YOU'RE NO GOOD *Linda Ronstadt—Capitol 3990*
[Clint Ballard Jr.] [ASC] (11/30/74 BCR-1)
YOU'RE NOBODY 'TIL SOMEBODY LOVES YOU *The Mills Brothers—Decca 29276*
[James Cavanaugh/Russ Morgan/Larry Stock] [ASC] (11/8/54 R-80)
YOU'RE NOBODY TILL SOMEBODY LOVES YOU *Damita Jo—Mercury 71944*
[James Cavanaugh/Russ Morgan/Larry Stock] [ASC] (3/26/62 R-89)
YOU'RE NOBODY 'TIL SOMEBODY LOVES YOU *Dinah Washington—Roulette 4424*
[James Cavanaugh/Russ Morgan/Larry Stock] [ASC] (5/12/62 B-87)
YOU'RE NOBODY TILL SOMEBODY LOVES YOU *Dean Martin—Reprise 0333*
[James Cavanaugh/Russ Morgan/Larry Stock] [ASC] (12/12/64 BCR-25)
YOU'RE NOBODY TILL SOMEBODY LOVES YOU *The Wonder Who ?—Philips 40380*
[James Cavanaugh/Russ Morgan/Larry Stock] [ASC] (6/25/66 BC-86)
YOU'RE NOT ALONE Chicago—Reprise/Full Moon 27757
[James Scott] [ASC] (1/21/89 BC-9)
YOU'RE NOT MY KIND OF GIRL New Edition—MCA 53405
[James Samuel Harris/Terry Lewis] [ASC] (11/12/88 B-95)
YOU'RE ONLY HUMAN (SECOND WIND) Billy Joel—Columbia 05417
[Billy Joel] [ASC] (7/13/85 BC-9)
YOU'RE ONLY LONELY J.D. Souther—Columbia 11079 [J.D. Souther] [NA] (9/8/79 BCR-7)
(YOU'RE PUTTIN') A RUSH ON ME Stephanie Mills—MCA 53151
[Timmy Allen/Paul Laurence] [ASC] (10/10/87 B-85)
YOU'RE READY NOW Frankie Valli—Smash 2037
[Bob Crewe/Bob Gaudio] [BMI] (4/30/66 CR-93)
YOU'RE RIGHT, RAY CHARLES Joe Tex—Dial 4096 [Joe Tex] [BMI] (2/28/70 CR-92)
YOU'RE RUNNING OUT OF KISSES Chuck Foote—Soncraft 401
[Wilbur Meshel/Jay Richards] [BMI] (12/9/61 C-87)
YOU'RE SENSATIONAL *Frank Sinatra—Capitol 3469*
[Cole Porter] [ASC] (6/29/56 BCRt-40)
YOU'RE SENSATIONAL *Sammy Davis Jr.—Decca 29976*
[Cole Porter] [ASC] (7/6/56 Rt-40)
YOU'RE SENSATIONAL *Nick Noble—Mercury 70897 [Cole Porter] [ASC] (7/6/56 Rt-55)*
YOU'RE SINGING OUR LOVE SONG TO SOMEBODY ELSE Jerry Wallace—Challenge 59072
[David Hess/Aaron Schroeder] [ASC] (4/11/60 CR-86)
YOU'RE SIXTEEN *Johnny Burnette—Liberty 55285*
[Richard Sherman/Robert Sherman] [BMI] (10/31/60 BCR-7)
YOU'RE SIXTEEN *Ringo Starr—Apple 1870*
[Richard Sherman/Robert Sherman] [BMI] (12/8/73 BCR-1)
YOU'RE SO EASY TO LOVE Tommy James—Millennium 11802
[Joey Greco/Tommy James] [BMI] (5/2/81 BCR-58)
YOU'RE SO FINE *The Falcons—Unart 2013*
[Lance Finney/Willie Schofield] [BMI] (4/20/59 BCR-14)
YOU'RE SO FINE *Bunny Sigler—Parkway 6000*
[Lance Finney/Willie Schofield] (Med) [BMI] (10/7/67 BCR-72)
YOU'RE SO NICE TO BE NEAR The Loreleis—Spotlight 390
[Gail Menafee/Peggy Reinagle] [BMI] (11/12/55 B-91)
YOU'RE SO RIGHT FOR ME
Tony Bennett with Ralph Sharon and his Orch.—Columbia 41127
[Ray Evans/Jay Livingston] [ASC] (3/3/58 R-56)
(YOU'RE SO SQUARE) BABY, I DON'T CARE Joni Mitchell—Geffen 29849
[Jerry Leiber/Mike Stoller] [BMI] (11/20/82 BC-47)
YOU'RE SO UNIQUE Billy Preston—A&M 1492
[Joe Greene/Billy Preston] [BMI] (12/29/73 BCR-30)
YOU'RE SO VAIN Carly Simon—Elektra 45824 [Carly Simon] [ASC] (12/2/72 BCR-1)
YOU'RE SO YOUNG Shane Martin—Epic 10384 [Jimmy Webb] [ASC] (11/2/68 R-87)
YOU'RE STILL A YOUNG MAN Tower Of Power—Warner Bros. 7612
[Emilio Castillo/Steve Kupka] [ASC] (7/8/72 BCR-22)
—YOU'RE STILL MY FAVORITE GIRLFRIEND see: ALICE LONG
YOU'RE STRONGER THAN ME Patsy Cline—Decca 31406
[Hank Cochran/Jimmy Key] [BMI] (7/21/62 CR-63)
YOU'RE SUPPOSED TO KEEP YOUR LOVE FOR ME Jermaine Jackson—Motown 1490
[Stevie Wonder] [ASC] (7/12/80 BCR-34)
YOU'RE THE APPLE OF MY EYE The Four Lovers—RCA Victor 47-6518
[Otis Blackwell] [BMI] (5/4/56 BR-62)
YOU'RE THE BEST THING The Style Council—Geffen 29248
[Paul Weller] [BMI] (7/14/84 B-76)
—YOU'RE THE BEST THING THAT EVER HAPPENED TO ME see: BEST THING...
YOU'RE THE BOSS Lavern Baker & Jimmy Ricks—Atlantic 2090
[Jerry Leiber/Mike Stoller] [BMI] (1/30/61 BCR-81)
(YOU'RE THE) DEVIL IN DISGUISE
Elvis Presley With The Jordanaires—RCA Victor 47-8188
[Bernie Baum/Bill Giant/Florence Kaye] [BMI] (6/29/63 BCR-3)
YOU'RE THE FIRST, THE LAST, MY EVERYTHING Barry White—20th Century 2133
[Peter Radcliffe/Tony Sepe/Barry White] [ASC] (11/2/74 BCR-1)
YOU'RE THE GREATEST *Billy Scott—Cameo 121*
[Bernie Lowe/Kal Mann] [ASC] (12/28/57 BCRt-45)
YOU'RE THE GREATEST *Valerie Carr—Roulette 4038*
[Bernie Lowe/Kal Mann] [ASC] (12/30/57 Rt-45)
YOU'RE THE INSPIRATION Chicago—Warner/Full Moon 29126
[Peter Cetera/David Foster] [ASC] (11/17/84 BC-3)
YOU'RE THE LOVE Seals & Crofts—Warner Bros. 8551
[David Batteau/Louie Shelton] [ASC] (4/8/78 BCR-18)

YOU'RE THE MAN (PART 1) Marvin Gaye—Tamla 54221
[Marvin Gaye/Kenny Stover] [ASC] (5/13/72 BCR-35)
YOU'RE THE NEAREST THING TO HEAVEN Johnny Cash And The Tennessee Two—Sun 302
[Jim Atkins/Johnny Cash/Hoyt Johnson] [BMI] (9/20/58 C-82)
YOU'RE THE ONE The Vogues—Co & Ce 229
[Petula Clark/Tony Hatch] [ASC] (9/11/65 BCR-4)
YOU'RE THE ONE The Marvelettes—Tamla 54131
[Smokey Robinson] [ASC] (4/23/66 BCR-46)
YOU'RE THE ONE - PART II *Little Sister—Stone Flower 9000*
[Sylvester Stewart] [BMI] (2/14/70 BCR-20)
YOU'RE THE ONE *The Three Degrees—Roulette 7091*
[Sylvester Stewart] [BMI] (1/16/71 BCR-55)
YOU'RE THE ONE FOR ME Joe Simon—Spring 115 [Joe Simon] [BMI] (7/3/71 BCR-52)
YOU'RE THE ONE FOR ME "D" Train—Prelude 8043
[Hubert Eaves III/James N. Williams] [BMI] (2/6/82 R-88)
YOU'RE THE ONE THAT I WANT John Travolta And Olivia Newton-John—RSO 891
[John Farrar] [BMI] (4/1/78 BCR-1)
YOU'RE THE ONLY LOVE Paul Hyde And The Payolas—A&M 2733
[David Foster/Paul Hyde/Miriam Nelson/Bob Rock] [BMI] (5/18/85 B-84)
YOU'RE THE ONLY ONE Geils—Atlantic 3411
[Seth Justman/Peter Wolf] [ASC] (8/20/77 B-83)
YOU'RE THE ONLY ONE Dolly Parton—RCA 11577
[Bruce Roberts/Carole Bayer Sager] [BMI] (6/30/79 BCR-59)
YOU'RE THE ONLY STAR (IN MY BLUE HEAVEN)
Billy Vaughn And His Orchestra—Dot 16021
[Gene Autry] [ASC] (1/11/60 R-79) [I]
YOU'RE THE ONLY WOMAN (YOU AND I) *Ambrosia—Warner Bros. 49508*
[David Pack] [BMI] (7/12/80 BCR-13)
YOU'RE THE ONLY WOMAN *The Brat Pack—Vendetta 1447*
[David Pack] [BMI] (2/3/90 BC-36)
YOU'RE THE ONLY WORLD I KNOW
Sonny James "The Southern Gentleman"—Capitol 5280
[Sonny James/Bob Tubert] [BMI] (11/28/64 BCR-91)
YOU'RE THE REASON *Joe South—Fairlane 21006*
[Bobby Edwards/Terry Fell/Fred Henley/Mildred Imes] [BMI] (8/19/61 BCt-44)
YOU'RE THE REASON *Bobby Edwards—Crest 1075*
[Bobby Edwards/Terry Fell/Fred Henley/Mildred Imes] [BMI] (8/19/61 BCRt-6)
YOU'RE THE REASON *Hank Locklin—RCA Victor 47-7921*
[Bobby Edwards/Terry Fell/Fred Henley/Mildred Imes] [BMI] (8/19/61 CtRt-38)
YOU'RE THE REASON *Gerry And The Pacemakers—Laurie 3313*
[Bobby Edwards/Terry Fell/Fred Henley/Mildred Imes] [BMI] (8/28/65 Ct-91)
YOU'RE THE REASON I'M IN LOVE Sonny James—Capitol 3602
[Jack Morrow] [BMI] (12/22/56 R-57)
YOU'RE THE REASON I'M LIVING Bobby Darin—Capitol 4897
[Bobby Darin] [BMI] (1/12/63 BCR-3)
YOU'RE THE REASON WHY The Ebonys—Philadelphia Int'l 3503
[Kenneth Gamble/Leon Huff] [BMI] (6/12/71 BCR-46)
YOU'RE THE STORY OF MY LIFE Desmond Child—Elektra 64850
[Desmond Child/Diane Warren] [ASC] (9/28/91 BC-55)
YOU'RE THE VOICE John Farnham—RCA 9086
[Andy Qunta/Keith Reid/Maggie Ryder/Chris Thompson] [ASC] (2/10/90 BC-72)
YOU'RE THROWING A GOOD LOVE AWAY The Spinners—Atlantic 3382
[Sherman Marshall/Ted Wortham] [BMI] (3/19/77 BCR-43)
YOU'RE WELCOME, STOP ON BY Bobby Womack—United Artists 439
[Truman Thomas/Bobby Womack] [BMI] (6/22/74 BCR-50)
YOU'RE WRONG ALL WRONG Eileen Rodgers—Columbia 40648
[Nat Simon/Charles Tobias] [ASC] (3/30/56 R-75)
YOURS IS MY HEART ALONE Enzo Stuarti—Jubilee 5243
[Ludwig Herzer/Franz Lehár/Fritz Loehner-Beda/Harry B. Smith] [ASC] (5/11/56 R-72)
YOURS LOVE Joe Simon—Sound Stage 7 2664 [Harlan Howard] [BMI] (7/25/70 BCR-74)
YOURS (QUIREME MUCHO) Dick Contino—Mercury 70455
[Gonzalo Roig] [BMI] (11/6/54 BCR-28) [IM]
YOURS UNTIL TOMORROW Vivian Reed—Epic 10319
[Gerry Goffin/Carole King] [BMI] (7/6/68 CR-93)
YOUTH GONE WILD Skid Row—Atlantic 88935
[Rachel Bolan/Dave Sabo] [ASC] (6/10/89 B-99)
YOU'VE BEEN CHEATIN' The Impressions—ABC-Paramount 10750
[Curtis Mayfield] [BMI] (11/20/65 BCR-25)
YOU'VE BEEN IN LOVE TOO LONG Martha & The Vandellas—Gordy 7045
[Ivy Jo Hunter/Clarence Paul/William Stevenson] [ASC] (8/14/65 BCR-36)
YOU'VE BEEN MY INSPIRATION The Main Ingredient—RCA Victor 74-0340
[Donald McPherson/Tony Silvester/Luther Simmons] [BMI] (6/27/70 BCR-46)
YOU'VE GOT A FRIEND *Roberta Flack & Donny Hathaway—Atlantic 2808*
[Carole King] [ASC] (5/29/71 BCR-20)
YOU'VE GOT A FRIEND *James Taylor—Warner Bros. 7498*
[Carole King] [ASC] (5/29/71 BCR-1)
YOU'VE GOT A GOOD LOVE COMING Van Stephenson—Handshake 02140
[Danny Morrison/Jeff Silbar/Van Stephenson] [BMI] (9/12/81 B-79)
YOU'VE GOT ANOTHER THING COMIN' Judas Priest—Columbia 03168
[Kenneth Downing/Rob Halford/Glenn Tipton] [ASC] (11/6/82 BC-67)
YOU'VE GOT ANOTHER THING COMING Hotel—MCA 41050
[Lee Bargeron/Marc Phillips] [BMI] (7/7/79 BCR-54)
(YOU'VE GOT ME) DANGLING ON A STRING *Chairmen Of The Board—Invictus 9078*
[Lamont Dozier/Ronald Dunbar/Brian Holland/Eddie Holland] [BMI] (5/2/70 BCR-30)
YOU'VE GOT ME DANGLING ON A STRING *Donny Osmond—Polydor/Kolob 14417*
[Lamont Dozier/Ronald Dunbar/Brian Holland/Eddie Holland] [BMI] (9/10/77 CR-88)
YOU'VE GOT ME RUNNIN' Gene Cotton—ABC 12227
[Parker McGee] [BMI] (12/4/76 BCR-33)
YOU'VE GOT MY MIND MESSED UP James Carr—Goldwax 302
[O.B. McClinton] [BMI] (4/2/66 BCR-52)
YOU'VE GOT MY SOUL ON FIRE The Temptations—Gordy 7136
[Norman Whitfield] [BMI] (6/15/74 BCR-56)
—YOU'VE GOT PERSONALITY see: PERSONALITY
(YOU'VE GOT) THE MAGIC TOUCH The Platters—Mercury 70819
[Buck Ram] [ASC] (3/16/56 BCR-3)
YOU'VE GOT THE POWER James Brown And The Famous Flames—Federal 12370
[James Brown/Johnny Terry] [BMI] (6/11/60 BC-72)
YOU'VE GOT THE POWER The Esquires—Wand 1193
[Rich McDougall] [BMI] (12/21/68 BCR-91)
YOU'VE GOT TO BE LOVED The Montanas—Independence 83
[Tony Hatch/Jackie Trent] [BMI] (2/17/68 BCR-39)
YOU'VE GOT TO CHANGE YOUR MIND Bobby Byrd & James Brown—King 6151
[James Brown/Bobby Byrd] [BMI] (2/24/68 R-90)
YOU'VE GOT TO CRAWL (BEFORE YOU WALK) The 8th Day—Invictus 9098
[Angelo Bond/Ronald Dunbar/General Johnson/Greg Perry] [BMI] (9/4/71 BCR-28)
YOU'VE GOT TO EARN IT The Staple Singers—Stax 0093
[Cornelius Grant/Smokey Robinson] [BMI] (7/17/71 BCR-82)
YOU'VE GOT TO HIDE YOUR LOVE AWAY *The Silkie—Fontana 1525*
[John Lennon/Paul McCartney] [ASC] (10/9/65 BCR-10)
YOU'VE GOT TO HIDE YOUR LOVE AWAY *The Beatles—Capitol 5107*
[John Lennon/Paul McCartney] (Med) [ASC] (3/27/82 BCR-12)
YOU'VE GOT TO LOVE HER WITH A FEELING Freddy King—Federal 12384
[Freddy King/Sonny Thompson] [BMI] (1/9/61 B-93)
(YOU'VE GOT TO) MOVE TWO MOUNTAINS Marv Johnson—United Artists 241
[Berry Gordy] [ASC] (8/8/60 BCR-19)
YOU'VE GOT TO SEE MAMMA EVERY NIGHT (OR YOU CAN'T SEE MAMMA AT ALL)
Peggy Lee—Decca 29837
[Con Conrad/Billy Rose] [NA] (4/20/56 R-81)
YOU'VE GOT TO TAKE IT (IF YOU WANT IT) The Main Ingredient—RCA Victor 74-0856
[Ed Townsend/David Charles Williams] [BMI] (12/16/72 BCR-37)
YOU'VE GOT WHAT I NEED Shooting Star—Virgin 67005
[Van McLain/Gary West] [BMI] (3/15/80 BCR-69)
YOU'VE GOT YOUR TROUBLES The Fortunes—Press 9773
[Roger Cook/Roger Greenaway] [ASC] (8/21/65 BCR-7)
YOU'VE LOST THAT LOVIN' FEELIN' *The Righteous Brothers—Philles 124*
[Barry Mann/Phil Spector/Cynthia Weil] [BMI] (12/12/64 BCR-1)
YOU'VE LOST THAT LOVIN' FEELING *Dionne Warwick—Scepter 12262*
[Barry Mann/Phil Spector/Cynthia Weil] [BMI] (9/20/69 BCR-13)
YOU'VE LOST THAT LOVIN' FEELIN' *Roberta Flack & Donny Hathaway—Atlantic 2837*
[Barry Mann/Phil Spector/Cynthia Weil] [BMI] (10/16/71 BCR-53)
YOU'VE LOST THAT LOVIN' FEELIN'
Long John Baldry & Kathi MacDonald—EMI America 8018
[Barry Mann/Phil Spector/Cynthia Weil] [BMI] (7/28/79 BR-89)
YOU'VE LOST THAT LOVIN' FEELING *Daryl Hall & John Oates—RCA 12103*
[Barry Mann/Phil Spector/Cynthia Weil] [BMI] (9/27/80 BCR-10)
YOU'VE MADE ME SO VERY HAPPY *Brenda Holloway—Tamla 54155*
[Berry Gordy/Brenda Holloway/Patrice Holloway/Frank Edward Wilson] [BMI] (9/9/67 BCR-39)
YOU'VE MADE ME SO VERY HAPPY *Blood, Sweat & Tears—Columbia 44776*
[Berry Gordy/Brenda Holloway/Patrice Holloway/Frank Edward Wilson] [BMI] (3/1/69 BCR-2)
YOU'VE MADE ME SO VERY HAPPY *Lou Rawls—Capitol 2734*
[Berry Gordy/Brenda Holloway/Patrice Holloway/Frank Edward Wilson] [BMI] (3/14/70 B-95)
YOU'VE NEVER BEEN IN LOVE LIKE THIS BEFORE Unit Four Plus Two—London 9761
[Tommy Moeller/Brian Parker] [ASC] (7/17/65 B-95)
YOU'VE NEVER BEEN THIS FAR BEFORE Conway Twitty—MCA 40094
[Conway Twitty] [BMI] (8/11/73 BCR-18)
YOU'VE STILL GOT A PLACE IN MY HEART Dean Martin—Reprise 0672
[Leon Payne] [BMI] (3/23/68 BCR-44)
YU-MA Marlena Shaw—Columbia 10542
[Marlena Shaw] (Med) [BMI] (5/28/77 C-76)
YUM YUM The Fontane Sisters—Dot 15450
[Doc Pomus] [BMI] (3/2/56 R-45)
YUMMY YUMMY YUMMY Ohio Express—Buddah 38
[Joey Levine/Artie Resnick] [BMI] (4/20/68 BCR-4)

Z

ZABADAK Dave Dee, Dozy, Beaky, Mick And Tich—Imperial 66270
[Alan Blaikley] [BMI] (12/30/67 BCR-52)

ZAMBEZI Lou Busch and His Orchestra—Capitol 3272
[Nico Carstens/Anton De Waal] [ASC] (12/24/55 B-75) [IM]

ZAZUEIRA (ZA-ZOO-WHER'-A) Herb Alpert & The Tijuana Brass—A&M 1043
[Jorge Ben] [BMI] (3/22/69 BCR-73) [F]

ZERO-ZERO Lawrence Welk—Dot 16420 [Carl-Henrik Norin] [ASC] (12/1/62 BCR-60) [I]

ZING WENT THE STRINGS OF MY HEART *The Kalin Twins—Decca 31169*
[James Hanley] [ASC] (11/7/60 Rt-73)

ZING WENT THE STRINGS OF MY HEART *The Dimensions—Mohawk 120*
[James Hanley] [ASC] (11/14/60 Rt-73)

ZING! WENT THE STRINGS OF MY HEART *The Furys—Mack IV 112*
[James Hanley] [ASC] (2/9/63 B-92)

ZING WENT THE STRINGS OF MY HEART *The Trammps—Buddah 306*
[James Hanley] [ASC] (6/17/72 BCR-55)

ZING WENT THE STRINGS OF MY HEART
Larry Elgart And His Manhattan Swing Orchestra—RCA 13219
[James Hanley] (Med) [ASC] (6/5/82 BC-31) [IWM]

THE ZIP MFSB—Philadelphia Int'l 3578
[Kenneth Gamble/Leon Huff] [BMI] (11/29/75 B-91) [I]

ZIP-A-DEE DOO-DAH Bob B. Soxx And The Blue Jeans—Philles 107
[Ray Gilbert/Allie Wrubel] [ASC] (11/17/62 BCR-8)

ZIP CODE The Five Americans—Abnak 123
[John Durrill/Norman Ezell/Michael Rabon] [BMI] (8/12/67 BCR-36)

ZIP ZIP The Diamonds—Mercury 71165
[Harry Booros/Anthony Columbo Jr./Louis Columbo/Barry Kaye] [BMI]
(8/26/57 BCR-36)

ZOOBA! The Big Sound of Don Ralke—Warner Bros. 5058
[Don Ralke] [ASC] (6/6/59 C-97) [I]

ZOOM The Cadillacs—Josie 792 [Esther Navarro] [BMI] (4/14/56 CR-44)

—ZOOM BA I ALLI NELLA see: GIRL A GIRL

ZORBA THE GREEK Herb Alpert & The Tijuana Brass—A&M 787
[Mikis Theodorakis] [ASC] (12/25/65 BCR-7) [I]

ZORRO The Chordettes—Cadence 1349
[George Bruns/Norman Foster] [ASC] (5/5/58 BCR-17)

The Top 100 Songs by One, Two and Three Writers

Writer — Title — Act — Entry Year — Song Score

1 John LENNON/ Paul McCARTNEY	Hey Jude—The Beatles (68)	14634

Top 100 Songs By One Writer

1	Neil DIAMOND	I'm A Believer—The Monkees (66)	13324
2	Hank BALLARD	The Twist—Chubby Checker (61)	12943
3	Max STEINER	Theme From A Summer Place—Percy Faith And His Orchestra (60)	12297
4	Joe BROOKS	You Light Up My Life—Debby Boone (77)	11933
5	John DEACON	Another One Bites The Dust—Queen (80)	11623
6	Jerry HERMAN	Hello, Dolly!—Louis Armstrong And The All-Stars (64)	11318
7	André POPP	Love Is Blue (L'Amour Est Bleu)—Paul Mauriat And His Orchestra (67)	11159
8	Don GIBSON	I Can't Stop Loving You—Ray Charles (62)	11133
9	Melvin ENDSLEY	Singing The Blues—Guy Mitchell (56)	11013
10	Jimmy DEAN	Big Bad John—Jimmy Dean (61)	10897
11	Hoyt AXTON	Joy To The World—Three Dog Night (71)	10869
12	Don McLEAN	American Pie—Don McLean (71)	10747
13	Lionel RICHIE	Endless Love—Diana Ross & Lionel Richie (81)	10664
14	Geoff STEPHENS	Winchester Cathedral—The New Vaudeville Band (66)	10623
15	Wayne Carson THOMPSON	The Letter—The Box Tops (67)	10569
16	Acker BILK	Stranger On The Shore—Mr. Acker Bilk (62)	10177
17	STING	Every Breath You Take—The Police (83)	10116
18	Bobbie GENTRY	Ode To Billie Joe—Bobbie Gentry (67)	10012
19	Ed MARSHALL	Venus—Frankie Avalon (59)	9989
20	TRADITIONAL	Tom Dooley—The Kingston Trio (58)	9986
21	Hank BALLARD	The Twist—Chubby Checker (60)	9977
22	Joseph KOSMA	Autumn Leaves—Roger Williams (55)	9865
23	John STEWART	Daydream Believer—The Monkees (67)	9734
24	Jeanine DECKERS	Dominique—The Singing Nun (63)	9721
25	Bobby RUSSELL	Honey—Bobby Goldsboro (68)	9605
26	George HARRISON	My Sweet Lord—George Harrison (70)	9566
27	Merle TRAVIS	Sixteen Tons—"Tennessee" Ernie Ford (55)	9525
28	Bob GAUDIO	Sherry—The 4 Seasons (62)	9519
29	Gilbert O'SULLIVAN	Alone Again (Naturally)—Gilbert O'Sullivan (72)	9416
30	Dewayne BLACKWELL	Mr. Blue—The Fleetwoods (59)	9403
31	Roger WATERS	Another Brick In The Wall (Part 2)—Pink Floyd (80)	9336
32	Ewan MacCOLL	The First Time Ever I Saw Your Face—Roberta Flack (72)	9289
33	Luis GUGLIELMI	Cherry Pink And Apple Blossom White—Perez Prado And His Orchestra (55)	9278
34	Sylvester STEWART	Everyday People—Sly & The Family Stone (68)	9208
35	TRADITIONAL	Michael—The Highwaymen (61)	9146
36	Richard BERRY	Louie Louie—The Kingsmen (63)	9145
37	C. Carson PARKS	Somethin' Stupid—Nancy Sinatra & Frank Sinatra (67)	9108
38	Rick EVANS	In The Year 2525 (Exordium & Terminus)—Zager & Evans (69)	9107
39	Ray HILDEBRAND	Hey Paula—Paul & Paula (62)	9041
40	Barry GIBB	I Just Want To Be Your Everything—Andy Gibb (77)	8938
41	Paul SIMON	Bridge Over Troubled Water—Simon & Garfunkel (70)	8896
42	Steve MILLER	Abracadabra—Steve Miller Band (82)	8881
43	Tony HATCH	Downtown—Petula Clark (64)	8873
44	Tony ROMEO	I Think I Love You—The Partridge Family Starring Shirley Jones & Featuring David Cassidy (70)	8857
45	Lionel RICHIE	Lady—Kenny Rogers (80)	8815
46	Ruthann FRIEDMAN	Windy—The Association (67)	8778
47	J.P. RICHARDSON	Running Bear—Johnny Preston (59)	8748
48	Perez PRADO	Patricia—Perez Prado And His Orchestra (58)	8711
49	Ronnie MACK	He's So Fine—The Chiffons (63)	8687
50	Allen TOUSSAINT	Mother-In-Law—Ernie K-Doe (61)	8663
51	Paul SIMON	Mrs. Robinson—Simon & Garfunkel (68)	8641
52	Phil SPECTOR	To Know Him Is To Love Him—The Teddy Bears (58)	8631
53	Boudleaux BRYANT	All I Have To Do Is Dream—The Everly Brothers (58)	8593
54	Jerry FULLER	Travelin' Man—Ricky Nelson (61)	8567
55	Paul McCARTNEY	Ebony And Ivory—Paul McCartney (82)	8546
56	Melanie SAFKA	Brand New Key—Melanie (71)	8519
57	Tom T. HALL	Harper Valley P.T.A.—Jeannie C. Riley (68)	8451
58	Seth JUSTMAN	Centerfold—The J. Geils Band (81)	8445
59	Otis REDDING	Respect—Aretha Franklin (67)	8397
60	Joe MEEK	Telstar—The Tornadoes (62)	8395
61	Trevor PEACOCK	Mrs. Brown You've Got A Lovely Daughter—Herman's Hermits (65)	8352
62	Sylvester STEWART	Family Affair—Sly & The Family Stone (71)	8171
63	George Henry JACKSON	One Bad Apple—The Osmonds (70)	8155
64	Robbie VAN LEEUWEN	Venus—Shocking Blue (69)	8155
65	Michael JACKSON	Billie Jean—Michael Jackson (83)	8153
66	John D. LOUDERMILK	Indian Reservation (The Lament Of The Cherokee)—Raiders (71)	8111
67	Rod STEWART	Tonight's The Night (Gonna Be Alright)—Rod Stewart (76)	8071
68	Steve GREENBERG	Funkytown—Lipps, Inc. (80)	8061
69	Lionel RICHIE	Three Times A Lady—Commodores (78)	8054
70	Marguerite MONNOT	The Poor People Of Paris (La Goualante Du Pauvre Jean)—Les Baxter His Chorus And Orchestra (56)	8007
71	Freddie MERCURY	Crazy Little Thing Called Love—Queen (79)	7923
72	Klaus-Günter NEUMANN	Wonderland By Night—Bert Kaempfert And His Orchestra (60)	7899
73	John PHILLIPS	Monday, Monday—The Mama's & The Papa's (66)	7870
74	Lionel RICHIE	All Night Long (All Night)—Lionel Richie (83)	7823
75	Marty ROBBINS	El Paso—Marty Robbins (59)	7763
76	Floyd CRAMER	Last Date—Floyd Cramer (60)	7744
77	John DENVER	Leaving On A Jet Plane—Peter, Paul & Mary (69)	7725
78	Laura NYRO	Wedding Bell Blues—The 5th Dimension (69)	7706
79	John LENNON	(Just Like) Starting Over—John Lennon (80)	7652
80	Rudy MARTINEZ	96 Tears—? (Question Mark) & The Mysterians (66)	7647
81	Sonny BONO	I Got You Babe—Sonny & Cher (65)	7646

82	TRADITIONAL	The House Of The Rising Sun—The Animals (64)	7607
83	Jim STEINMAN	Total Eclipse Of The Heart—Bonnie Tyler (83)	7599
84	Paul SIMON	The Sound Of Silence—Simon & Garfunkel (65)	7572
85	Maurice WILLIAMS	Little Darlin'—The Diamonds (57)	7547
86	Jerry FULLER	Young Girl—The Union Gap Featuring Gary Puckett (68)	7523
87	David ROSE	The Stripper—David Rose And His Orchestra (62)	7507
88	Buck RAM	The Great Pretender—The Platters (55)	7497
89	David GATES	Make It With You—Bread (70)	7490
90	Norman GREENBAUM	Spirit In The Sky—Norman Greenbaum (70)	7449
91	Pat BALLARD	Mr. Sandman—The Chordettes (54)	7421
92	Wayne COCHRAN	Last Kiss—J. Frank Wilson And The Cavaliers (64)	7406
93	Randy NEWMAN	Mama Told Me (Not To Come)—Three Dog Night (70)	7392
94	Terry KIRKMAN	Cherish—The Association (66)	7384
95	Smokey ROBINSON	My Guy—Mary Wells (64)	7380
96	Carly SIMON	You're So Vain—Carly Simon (72)	7377
97	Harlan HOWARD	Heartaches By The Number—Guy Mitchell (59)	7361
98	Isaac HAYES	Theme From Shaft—Isaac Hayes (71)	7329
99	Dewey BUNNELL	A Horse With No Name—America (72)	7299
100	PRINCE	When Doves Cry—Prince (84)	7299

Top 100 Songs By Two Writers

1	John LENNON/ Paul McCARTNEY	Hey Jude—The Beatles (68)	14634
2	John LENNON/ Paul McCARTNEY	I Want To Hold Your Hand—The Beatles (64)	14194
3	Jimmy DRIFTWOOD/ TRADITIONAL	Battle Of New Orleans—Johnny Horton (59)	13064
4	Jeff BARRY/ Andy KIM	Sugar, Sugar—The Archies (69)	12247
5	Ritchie ADAMS/ Malou RENÉ	Tossin' And Turnin'—Bobby Lewis (61)	12039
6	Steve KIPNER/ Terry SHADDICK	Physical—Olivia Newton-John (81)	11192
7	Richard ADLER/ Jerry ROSS	Hey There—Rosemary Clooney (54)	11126
8	Bernard EDWARDS/ Nile RODGERS	Le Freak—Chic (78)	11074
9	Franco MIGLIACCI/ Domenico MODUGNO	Nel Blu Dipinto Di Blu (Volare)—Domenico Modugno (58)	10773
10	Al BYRON/ Paul EVANS	Roses Are Red (My Love)—Bobby Vinton (62)	10687
11	Otto HARBACH/ Jerome KERN	Smoke Gets In Your Eyes—The Platters (58)	10667
12	Charles DAWES/ Carl SIGMAN	It's All In The Game—Tommy Edwards (58)	10634
13	Keith McCORMACK/ Faye VOSS	Sugar Shack—Jimmy Gilmer And The Fireballs (63)	10632
14	John LENNON/ Paul McCARTNEY	She Loves You—The Beatles (64)	10567
15	Don BLACK/ Mark LONDON	To Sir With Love—Lulu (67)	10546
16	Mick JAGGER/ Keith RICHARDS	Honky Tonk Women—The Rolling Stones (69)	10430
17	Max CROOK/ Del SHANNON	Runaway—Del Shannon (61)	10390
18	Dion DiMUCCI/ Ernie MARESCA	Runaround Sue—Dion (61)	10242
19	Burt BACHARACH/ Hal DAVID	Raindrops Keep Fallin' On My Head—B.J. Thomas (69)	10203
20	Audrey ALLISON/ Joe ALLISON	He'll Have To Go—Jim Reeves (59)	10202
21	Otis BLACKWELL/ Elvis PRESLEY	Don't Be Cruel—Elvis Presley (56)	10167
22	Mick JAGGER/ Keith RICHARDS	(I Can't Get No) Satisfaction—The Rolling Stones (65)	10038
23	Lou HANDMAN/ Roy TURK	Are You Lonesome To Night—Elvis Presley With The Jordanaires (60)	10024
24	Bob CREWE/ Bob GAUDIO	Big Girls Don't Cry—The 4 Seasons (62)	10012
25	L. Russell BROWN/ Irwin LEVINE	Knock Three Times—Dawn (70)	9840
26	Bob DAVIE/ Marvin MOORE	Green Door—Jim Lowe (56)	9717
27	Eddie BRIGATI/ Felix CAVALIERE	Groovin'—The Young Rascals (67)	9580
28	Robin MOORE/ Barry SADLER	The Ballad Of The Green Berets—SSgt. Barry Sadler (66)	9577
29	Stan LEBOWSKY/ Herbert NEWMAN	The Wayward Wind—Gogi Grant (56)	9460
30	Dub ALLBRITTEN/ Ronnie SELF	I'm Sorry—Brenda Lee (60)	9449
31	Don EVERLY/ Phil EVERLY	Cathy's Clown—The Everly Brothers (60)	9441
32	Otis BLACKWELL/ Winfield SCOTT	Return To Sender—Elvis Presley With The Jordanaires (62)	9296
33	Garry BONNER/ Alan GORDON	Happy Together—The Turtles (67)	9222
34	Ray EVANS/ Jay LIVINGSTON	Tammy—Debbie Reynolds (57)	9194
35	Eddie BRIGATI/ Felix CAVALIERE	People Got To Be Free—The Rascals (68)	9189
36	Tommy JAMES/ Peter LUCIA	Crimson And Clover—Tommy James And The Shondells (68)	9176
37	Paul ANKA/ Alberto CURCI	Lonely Boy—Paul Anka (59)	9133
38	Jim PETERIK/ Frankie SULLIVAN	Eye Of The Tiger—Survivor (82)	9112
39	Otis BLACKWELL/ Elvis PRESLEY	All Shook Up—Elvis Presley (57)	9084
40	Burt BACHARACH/ Hal DAVID	This Guy's In Love With You—Herb Alpert (68)	9073

41 Don GEORGE/ TRADITIONAL	The Yellow Rose Of Texas— Mitch Miller with His Orch. & Chorus (55)	9072
42 Berton AVERRE/ Doug FIEGER	My Sharona—The Knack (79)	9055
43 Lorenz HART/ Richard RODGERS	Blue Moon—The Marcels (61)	9049
44 Joey DEE/ Henry GLOVER	Peppermint Twist - Part 1— Joey Dee & The Starliters (61)	9044
45 Kal MANN/ Billy STRANGE	Limbo Rock—Chubby Checker (62)	9002
46 Jackie DeSHANNON/ Donna WEISS	Bette Davis Eyes—Kim Carnes (81)	8923
47 Doc POMUS/ Mort SHUMAN	Save The Last Dance For Me— The Drifters (60)	8918
48 Michael JACKSON/ Paul McCARTNEY	Say Say Say—Paul McCartney and Michael Jackson (83)	8900
49 Barrett STRONG/ Norman WHITFIELD	I Heard It Through The Grapevine— Marvin Gaye (68)	8871
50 Howard GREENFIELD/ Jack KELLER	My Heart Has A Mind Of Its Own— Connie Francis (60)	8856
51 William DEES/ Roy ORBISON	Oh, Pretty Woman— Roy Orbison And The Candy Men (64)	8819
52 Redd EVANS/ Dave MANN	There! I've Said It Again— Bobby Vinton (63)	8758
53 Lee MORRIS/ Bernie WAYNE	Blue Velvet—Bobby Vinton (63)	8754
54 Tommy ROE/ Freddy WELLER	Dizzy—Tommy Roe (69)	8722
55 John LENNON/ Paul McCARTNEY	Get Back—The Beatles With Billy Preston (69)	8698
56 John LENNON/ Paul McCARTNEY	Let It Be—The Beatles (70)	8679
57 John LENNON/ Paul McCARTNEY	We Can Work It Out—The Beatles (65)	8664
58 Bruce CHANNEL/ Margaret COBB	Hey! Baby—Bruce Channel (62)	8663
59 Alex NORTH/ Hy ZARET	Unchained Melody—Les Baxter His Chorus And Orchestra (55)	8661
60 Mike LOVE/ Brian WILSON	I Get Around—The Beach Boys (64)	8633
61 Luther DIXON/ Florence GREEN	Soldier Boy—The Shirelles (62)	8622
62 Sammy FAIN/ Paul Francis WEBSTER	Love Is A Many Splendored Thing— Four Aces (55)	8585
63 Gene ALLAN/ Bobby VINTON	Mr. Lonely—Bobby Vinton (64)	8492
64 Carole KING/ Toni STERN	It's Too Late—Carole King (71)	8487
65 Bert REISFELD/ Jean VILLARD	The Three Bells (Les Trois Cloches)— The Browns (59)	8482
66 Ric CARTEY/ Carole JOYNER	Young Love—Tab Hunter (57)	8452
67 Boris FOMIN/ Gene RASKIN	Those Were The Days—Mary Hopkin (68)	8414
68 Doc POMUS/ Mort SHUMAN	Surrender— Elvis Presley With The Jordanaires (61)	8380
69 J. Leslie McFARLAND/ Aaron SCHROEDER	Stuck On You— Elvis Presley With The Jordanaires (60)	8364
70 John LENNON/ Paul McCARTNEY	A Hard Day's Night—The Beatles (64)	8359

71 Henry COSBY/ Clarence PAUL	Fingertips - Pt 2— Little Stevie Wonder (63)	8343
72 John Bobby BERRY/ Don COVAY	Pony Time—Chubby Checker (61)	8332
73 Jeff BARRY/ Ellie GREENWICH	Do Wah Diddy Diddy— Manfred Mann (64)	8308
74 John LENNON/ Paul McCARTNEY	Can't Buy Me Love—The Beatles (64)	8269
75 Jimmy DeKNIGHT/ Max C. FREEDMAN	(We're Gonna) Rock Around The Clock— Bill Haley And His Comets (55)	8240
76 Jerry LEIBER/ Mike STOLLER	Jailhouse Rock—Elvis Presley (57)	8238
77 Georges BOULANGER/ Jimmy KENNEDY	My Prayer—The Platters (56)	8202
78 Rohusuke EI/ Hachidai NAKAMURA	Sukiyaki—Kyu Sakamoto (63)	8172
79 Gerry GOFFIN/ Carole KING	Go Away Little Girl—Steve Lawrence (62)	8171
80 Andrew BERNARD/ John FRED	Judy In Disguise (With Glasses)— John Fred & His Playboy Band (67)	8168
81 John LENNON/ Paul McCARTNEY	I Feel Fine—The Beatles (64)	8162
82 Bernard EDWARDS/ Nile RODGERS	Upside Down—Diana Ross (80)	8140
83 Bob CREWE/ Bob GAUDIO	Walk Like A Man—The 4 Seasons (63)	8138
84 John LENNON/ Paul McCARTNEY	Hello Goodbye—The Beatles (67)	8134
85 Phil GERNHARD/ Dick HOLLER	Snoopy Vs. The Red Baron— The Royal Guardsmen (66)	8083
86 Mike LOVE/ Brian WILSON	Good Vibrations—The Beach Boys (66)	8071
87 Tommy BOYCE/ Bobby HART	Last Train To Clarksville— The Monkees (66)	8046
88 Howard GREENFIELD/ Jack KELLER	Everybody's Somebody's Fool— Connie Francis (60)	8043
89 L. Russell BROWN/ Irwin LEVINE	Tie A Yellow Ribbon Round The Ole Oak Tree— Dawn Featuring Tony Orlando (73)	8042
90 Joe SHERMAN/ Noel SHERMAN	Ramblin' Rose—Nat King Cole (62)	8021
91 Lou GRAMM/ Michael Leslie JONES	Waiting For A Girl Like You— Foreigner (81)	8009
92 Bob CREWE/ Bob GAUDIO	Rag Doll—The 4 Seasons Featuring The "Sound" Of Frankie Valli (64)	7976
93 Jack NANCE/ Conway TWITTY	It's Only Make Believe— Conway Twitty (58)	7964
94 John LENNON/ Paul McCARTNEY	Yesterday—The Beatles (65)	7927
95 Gerry GOFFIN/ Carole KING	Take Good Care Of My Baby— Bobby Vee (61)	7900
96 Mike CHAPMAN/ Nicky CHINN	Kiss You All Over—Exile (78)	7882
97 Jake HOOKER/ Alan MERRILL	I Love Rock 'N Roll— Joan Jett & The Blackhearts (82)	7869
98 John LENNON/ Paul McCARTNEY	Help!—The Beatles (65)	7847
99 Linda McCARTNEY/ Paul McCARTNEY	Silly Love Songs—Wings (76)	7833
100 Harold LOGAN/ Lloyd PRICE	Personality—Lloyd Price (59)	7779

Top 100 Songs By Three Writers

1	Marc BLITZSTEIN/ Berthold BRECHT/ Kurt WEILL	Mack The Knife—Bobby Darin (59)	14687
2	Eduardo Di CAPUA/ Wally GOLD/ Aaron SCHROEDER	It's Now Or Never—Elvis Presley With The Jordanaires (60)	10781
3	Clement A. BOZEWSKI/ Deborah HARRY/ Giorgio MORODER	Call Me—Blondie (80)	10151
4	J. Fred COOTS/ Charles KENNY/ Nick KENNY	Love Letters In The Sand—Pat Boone (57)	9892
5	Barry GIBB/ Maurice GIBB/ Robin GIBB	Stayin' Alive—Bee Gees (77)	9872
6	Mae Boren AXTON/ Thomas DURDEN/ Elvis PRESLEY	Heartbreak Hotel—Elvis Presley (56)	9660
7	Irene CARA/ Keith FORSEY/ Giorgio MORODER	Flashdance...What A Feeling—Irene Cara (83)	9574
8	Barry MANN/ Phil SPECTOR/ Cynthia WEIL	You've Lost That Lovin' Feelin'—The Righteous Brothers (64)	9450
9	Barry GIBB/ Maurice GIBB/ Robin GIBB	Night Fever—Bee Gees (78)	9237
10	Gene CHANDLER/ Earl EDWARDS/ Bernice WILLIAMS	Duke Of Earl—Gene Chandler (62)	9144
11	Lamont DOZIER/ Brian HOLLAND/ Eddie HOLLAND	Where Did Our Love Go—The Supremes (64)	9056
12	Lamont DOZIER/ Brian HOLLAND/ Eddie HOLLAND	I Can't Help Myself—Four Tops (65)	8859
13	Lamont DOZIER/ Brian HOLLAND/ Eddie HOLLAND	Come See About Me—The Supremes (64)	8772
14	Richard DEHR/ Terry GILKYSON/ Frank MILLER	Memories Are Made Of This—Dean Martin (55)	8655
15	Pete BELLOTTE/ Harold FALTERMEYER/ Keith FORSEY	Hot Stuff—Donna Summer (79)	8596
16	Lamont DOZIER/ Brian HOLLAND/ Eddie HOLLAND	Baby Love—The Supremes (64)	8476
17	Gretchen CHRISTOPHER/ Barbara ELLIS/ Gary TROXEL	Come Softly To Me—The Fleetwoods (59)	8460
18	Carmine APPICE/ Duane HITCHINGS/ Rod STEWART	Da Ya Think I'm Sexy?—Rod Stewart (78)	8390
19	Jeff BARRY/ Ellie GREENWICH/ Phil SPECTOR	Chapel Of Love—The Dixie Cups (64)	8316
20	John MADARA/ Artie SINGER/ David WHITE	At The Hop—Danny & The Juniors (57)	8260
21	Ken DARBY/ George R. POULTON/ Elvis PRESLEY	Love Me Tender—Elvis Presley (56)	8241
22	Sam COSLOW/ Ken LANE/ Irving TAYLOR	Everybody Loves Somebody—Dean Martin (64)	8239
23	Bob FELDMAN/ Jerry GOLDSTEIN/ Richard GOTTEHRER	My Boyfriend's Back—The Angels (63)	8148
24	Galt MacDERMOT/ James RADO/ Gerome RAGNI	Hair—The Cowsills (69)	8011
25	Johnny BRAGG/ Buddy KILLEN/ Robert S. RILEY	Just Walking In The Rain—Johnnie Ray (56)	7908
26	Harold LOGAN/ Lloyd PRICE/ TRADITIONAL	Stagger Lee—Lloyd Price (58)	7844
27	Al GREEN/ Al JACKSON/ Willie MITCHELL	Let's Stay Together—Al Green (71)	7842
28	Lamont DOZIER/ Brian HOLLAND/ Eddie HOLLAND	Stop! In The Name Of Love—The Supremes (65)	7776
29	Barry GIBB/ Maurice GIBB/ Robin GIBB	How Deep Is Your Love—Bee Gees (77)	7757
30	Bob BRASS/ Al KOOPER/ Irwin LEVINE	This Diamond Ring—Gary Lewis And The Playboys (65)	7757
31	Sara ALLEN/ Daryl HALL/ John OATES	Maneater—Daryl Hall & John Oates (82)	7727
32	Lamont DOZIER/ Brian HOLLAND/ Eddie HOLLAND	You Can't Hurry Love—The Supremes (66)	7615
33	Amadeu Do VALE/ Jose GALHARDO/ Raul PORTELA	Lisbon Antigua—Nelson Riddle And His Orchestra (55)	7507
34	Jackey BEAVERS/ Johnny BRISTOL/ Harvey FUQUA	Someday We'll Be Together—Diana Ross And The Supremes (69)	7492
35	Henry COSBY/ Smokey ROBINSON/ Stevie WONDER	The Tears Of A Clown—Smokey Robinson & The Miracles (70)	7441
36	John William CALLIS/ Philip OAKEY/ Philip WRIGHT	Don't You Want Me—The Human League (82)	7286
37	Sara ALLEN/ Daryl HALL/ John OATES	I Can't Go For That (No Can Do)—Daryl Hall & John Oates (81)	7283
38	Luther DIXON/ Stanley KAHAN/ Eddie SNYDER	A Hundred Pounds Of Clay—Gene McDaniels (61)	7256
39	Henri BELOLO/ Jacques MORALI/ Victor WILLIS	Y.M.C.A.—Village People (78)	7239
40	Brook BENTON/ Clyde OTIS/ TRADITIONAL	The Boll Weevil Song—Brook Benton (61)	7091

41	Steve BOONE/ John SEBASTIAN/ Mark SEBASTIAN	Summer In The City—The Lovin' Spoonful (66)	7015
42	Lamont DOZIER/ Brian HOLLAND/ Eddie HOLLAND	I Hear A Symphony—The Supremes (65)	6983
43	Ann FARINA/ Johnny FARINA/ Santo FARINA	Sleep Walk—Santo & Johnny (59)	6980
44	Kenneth GAMBLE/ Cary GILBERT/ Leon HUFF	Me And Mrs. Jones—Billy Paul (72)	6926
45	Richard DEHR/ Terry GILKYSON/ Frank MILLER	Greenfields—The Brothers Four (60)	6907
46	Alan BERGMAN/ Marilyn BERGMAN/ Marvin HAMLISCH	The Way We Were—Barbra Streisand (73)	6902
47	Barry GIBB/ Maurice GIBB/ Robin GIBB	Too Much Heaven—Bee Gees (78)	6865
48	Carmela GUIDA/ Frank GUIDA/ Joseph ROYSTER	If You Wanna Be Happy—Jimmy Soul (63)	6827
49	Ed GRAY/ Tommy JAMES/ Mike VALE	Crystal Blue Persuasion—Tommy James And The Shondells (69)	6717
50	Johann Sebastian BACH/ Sandy LINZER/ Denny RANDELL	A Lover's Concerto—The Toys (65)	6662
51	Bob CREWE/ Sandy LINZER/ Denny RANDELL	Let's Hang On!—The 4 Seasons Featuring The "Sound" Of Frankie Valli (65)	6625
52	William E. JACKSON III/ Roy STRAIGIS/ George R. WILLIAMS	So Much In Love—The Tymes (63)	6568
53	Alan BERGMAN/ Marilyn BERGMAN/ Neil DIAMOND	You Don't Bring Me Flowers—Barbra & Neil (78)	6538
54	Bryan ADAMS/ Michael KAMEN/ Mutt LANGE	(Everything I Do) I Do It For You—Bryan Adams (91)	6505
55	Kenneth GAMBLE/ Leon HUFF/ Jerry J. ROSS	I'm Gonna Make You Love Me—Diana Ross And The Supremes & The Temptations (68)	6496
56	Lamont DOZIER/ Brian HOLLAND/ Eddie HOLLAND	Reach Out I'll Be There—Four Tops (66)	6413
57	General JOHNSON/ Barney PERKINS/ Greg PERRY	Want Ads—The Honey Cone (71)	6401
58	Bill DANOFF/ Taffy DANOFF/ John DENVER	Take Me Home, Country Roads—John Denver (71)	6363
59	Barry GIBB/ Maurice GIBB/ Robin GIBB	Islands In The Stream—Kenny Rogers Duet with Dolly Parton (83)	6346
60	Bert KAEMPFERT/ Charles SINGLETON/ Eddie SNYDER	Strangers In The Night—Frank Sinatra (66)	6342
61	Jeff BARRY/ Ellie GREENWICH/ Shadow MORTON	Leader Of The Pack—The Shangri-Las (64)	6265
62	Lamont DOZIER/ Brian HOLLAND/ Eddie HOLLAND	You Keep Me Hangin' On—The Supremes (66)	6251
63	O'Kelly ISLEY/ Ronald ISLEY/ Rudolph ISLEY	It's Your Thing—The Isley Brothers (69)	6205
64	Barry GIBB/ Maurice GIBB/ Robin GIBB	Tragedy—Bee Gees (79)	6069
65	Jeff BARRY/ Ellie GREENWICH/ Phil SPECTOR	Be My Baby—The Ronettes (63)	6059
66	Bonnie BRAMLETT/ Delaney BRAMLETT/ Leon RUSSELL	Superstar—Carpenters (71)	6023
67	Joe BROUSSARD/ Carrol WASHINGTON/ Ralph WILLIAMS	Mr. Big Stuff—Jean Knight (71)	5978
68	Don DAVIS/ Harvey SCALES/ Albert VANCE	Disco Lady—Johnnie Taylor (76)	5946
69	David CLOWNEY/ Jim KRIEGSMANN/ Ken WOOD	Happy Organ—Dave "Baby" Cortez (59)	5914
70	Galt MacDERMOT/ James RADO/ Gerome RAGNI	Aquarius—The 5th Dimension (69)	5902
71	Galt MacDERMOT/ James RADO/ Gerome RAGNI	Let The Sunshine In (The Flesh Failures)—The 5th Dimension (69)	5902
72	Barry GIBB/ Maurice GIBB/ Robin GIBB	Jive Talkin'—Bee Gees (75)	5841
73	Gary DeCARLO/ Dale FRASHUER/ Paul LEKA	Na Na Hey Hey Kiss Him Goodbye—Steam (69)	5814
74	Lamont DOZIER/ Brian HOLLAND/ Eddie HOLLAND	Love Is Here And Now You're Gone—The Supremes (67)	5783
75	Allan CLARKE/ Roger COOK/ Roger GREENAWAY	Long Cool Woman (In A Black Dress)—The Hollies (72)	5749
76	Carlos ALOMAR/ David BOWIE/ John LENNON	Fame—David Bowie (75)	5730
77	Clement A. BOZEWSKI/ Deborah HARRY/ Christopher STEIN	Heart Of Glass—Blondie (79)	5717
78	Leonard CASTON/ Anita POREE/ Frank Edward WILSON	Keep On Truckin' (Part 1)—Eddie Kendricks (73)	5698
79	Rory BOURKE/ Billy SHERRILL/ Norro WILSON	The Most Beautiful Girl—Charlie Rich (73)	5675
80	Al LEWIS/ Vincent ROSE/ Larry STOCK	Blueberry Hill—Fats Domino (56)	5648
81	Mark LEONARD/ Chas SANDFORD/ John WAITE	Missing You—John Waite (84)	5545
82	Marvin GAYE/ Ivy Jo HUNTER/ William STEVENSON	Dancing In The Street—Martha & The Vandellas (64)	5484
83	Arthur CONLEY/ Sam COOKE/ Otis REDDING	Sweet Soul Music—Arthur Conley (67)	5467
84	Luigi CREATORE/ Hugo PERETTI/ George David WEISS	Can't Help Falling In Love—Elvis Presley With The Jordanaires (61)	5450

85 Homer BANKS/ Carl HAMPTON/ Raymond Earl JACKSON	(If Loving You Is Wrong) I Don't Want To Be Right—Luther Ingram (72)	5399
86 Lamont DOZIER/ Brian HOLLAND/ Eddie HOLLAND	Reflections—Diana Ross And The Supremes (67)	5395
87 Galt MacDERMOT/ James RADO/ Gerome RAGNI	Easy To Be Hard—Three Dog Night (69)	5385
88 Eddie CURTIS/ Ahmet ERTEGUN/ Steve MILLER	The Joker—Steve Miller Band (73)	5290
89 Chris ARNOLD/ David MARTIN/ Geoff MORROW	Can't Smile Without You—Barry Manilow (78)	5240
90 Kevin ADAMS/ Jimmy PATERSON/ Kevin ROWLAND	Come On Eileen—Dexys Midnight Runners (83)	5225
91 Renaldo BENSON/ Al CLEVELAND/ Marvin GAYE	What's Going On—Marvin Gaye (71)	5213
92 Steve GEORGE/ John LANG/ Richard PAGE	Broken Wings—Mr. Mister (85)	5158

93 Brook BENTON/ Belford HENDRICKS/ Clyde OTIS	It's Just A Matter Of Time—Brook Benton (59)	5155
94 Dave BARTHOLOMEW/ Fats DOMINO/ Earl King JOHNSON	I Hear You Knocking—Gale Storm (55)	5135
95 Al GREEN/ Al JACKSON/ Willie MITCHELL	I'm Still In Love With You—Al Green (72)	5102
96 Clement A. BOZEWSKI/ Deborah HARRY/ Christopher STEIN	Rapture—Blondie (81)	5100
97 Hank BALLARD/ Etta JAMES/ Johnny OTIS	Dance With Me Henry (Wallflower)—Georgia Gibbs (55)	5087
98 Rodger PENZABENE/ Barrett STRONG/ Norman WHITFIELD	I Wish It Would Rain—The Temptations (68)	5041
99 Will JENNINGS/ Jack NITZSCHE/ Buffy SAINTE-MARIE	Up Where We Belong—Joe Cocker and Jennifer Warnes (82)	5012
100 Jon BON JOVI/ Desmond CHILD/ Richie SAMBORA	Livin' On A Prayer—Bon Jovi (86)	5011

Top Songs by Score and Entries

This ranking tests the relative strength of songs, not performances. The musical portion is the common denominator of the "same song;" thus, instrumentals and vocals, translations, foreign versions, parodies and responses are grouped together. Versions are marked by type. Writer credits will vary by type; check the song index for the exact writer team for any version.

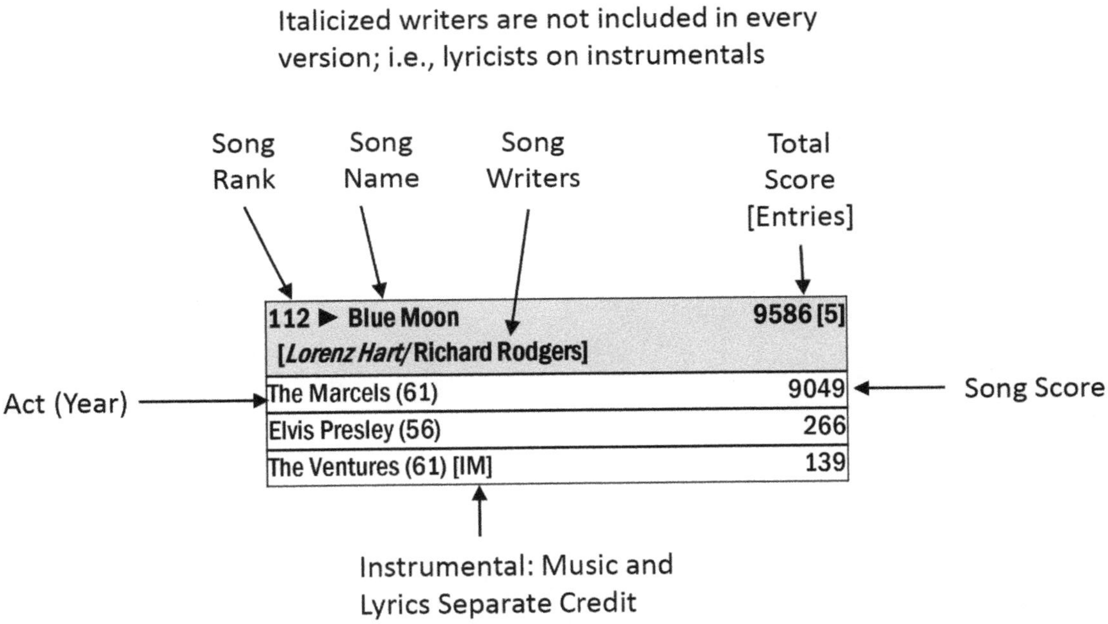

Top 150 Songs by Score—All Versions

1 ▶ The Twist [Hank Ballard]	**24638 [6]**
Chubby Checker (61)	12943
Chubby Checker (60)	9977
Hank Ballard And The Midnighters (60)	983
Fat Boys (88)	725
Jive Bunny & The Mastermixers (90)	6.7
Ernie Freeman (62) [IWM]	3.6
2 ▶ Unchained Melody [Alex North/ *Hy Zaret*]	**20850 [12]**
Les Baxter His Chorus And Orchestra (55)	8661
Al Hibbler (55)	4376
The Righteous Brothers (65)	3432
Roy Hamilton (55)	2241
The Righteous Brothers (90)	1154
The Righteous Brothers (90)	502
Vito & The Salutations (63)	312
The Sweet Inspirations (68)	70
The Blackwells (60)	47
June Valli (55)	44
Heart (81)	10
LeRoy Holmes & His Orchestra (55) [IM]	0.0
3 ▶ Moritat/Mack The Knife [*Marc Blitzstein/ Berthold Brecht*/Kurt Weill]	**20818 [9]**
Bobby Darin (59)	14687
Dick Hyman Trio (56) [IM]	2349
Richard Hayman And Jan August (56) [IM]	1429
Ella Fitzgerald (60)	743
Louis Armstrong And His All-Stars (56)	570
Billy Vaughn and His Orchestra (56) [IM]	375
Lawrence Welk And His Sparkling Strings (56) [IM]	354
Les Paul (56) [IM]	310
Owen Bradley & His Orchestra (56) [IM]	0.0
4 ▶ Go Away Little Girl/Boy [Gerry Goffin/Carole King]	**16407 [4]**
Steve Lawrence (62)	8171
Donny Osmond (71)	6840
The Happenings (66)	1386
Marlena Shaw (77)	9.6
5 ▶ (Nel Blu Dipinto Di Blu) Volare [*Franco Migliacci*/ Domenico Modugno/ *Mitchell Parish*]	**16401 [10]**
Domenico Modugno (58) [F]	10773
Bobby Rydell (60) [FDE]	3928
Dean Martin (58) [FDE]	1266
Al Martino (75) [FDE]	365
Ace Cannon (62) [IM]	52
The McGuire Sisters (58) [FDE]	17
Umberto Marcato (58) [F]	0.0
Rosa Linda (58) [F]	0.0

Jesse Belvin (58) [FDE]	0.0
Alan Dale (58) [FDE]	0.0
6 ▶ I Heard It Through The Grapevine [Barrett Strong/Norman Whitfield]	**16109 [6]**
Marvin Gaye (68)	8871
Gladys Knight & The Pips (67)	6841
Creedence Clearwater Revival (76)	211
Roger (81)	147
King Curtis & The Kingpins (68) [IWM]	21
The California Raisins (88)	18
7 ▶ Hey Jude [John Lennon/Paul McCartney]	**15567 [2]**
The Beatles (68)	14634
Wilson Pickett (68)	933
8 ▶ Young Love [Ric Cartey/Carole Joyner]	**15361 [7]**
Tab Hunter (57)	8452
Sonny James (56)	5688
Donny Osmond (73)	531
The Crew-Cuts (56)	343
Lesley Gore (66)	334
Ray Stevens (76)	13
Ric Cartey with The Jiva-Tones (56)	0.0
9 ▶ The Loco-Motion [Gerry Goffin/Carole King]	**14873 [3]**
Little Eva (62)	7718
Grand Funk (74)	4636
Kylie Minogue (88)	2519
10 ▶ Don't Be Cruel [Otis Blackwell/Elvis Presley]	**14673 [5]**
Elvis Presley (56)	10167
Bill Black's Combo (60) [IWM]	2335
Cheap Trick (88)	2074
Barbara Lynn (63)	74
Elvis Presley (82)	23
11 ▶ I Want To Hold Your Hand [John Lennon/Paul McCartney]	**14386 [3]**
The Beatles (64)	14194
Boston Pops Orchestra Arthur Fiedler Conductor (64) [IWM]	184
Stars On 45 (81)	8.0
12 ▶ The Lion Sleeps Tonight [Luigi Creatore/Solomon Linda/ Hugo Peretti/Albert Stanton/ George David Weiss]	**14090 [2]**
The Tokens (61)	9030
Robert John (71)	5059
13 ▶ The Letter [Wayne Carson Thompson]	**13904 [3]**
The Box Tops (67)	10569
Joe Cocker With Leon Russell And The Shelter People (70)	2598
The Arbors (69)	737
14 ▶ (Theme From) "A Summer Place" [*Hans Bradtke/ Mack Discant*/Max Steiner]	**13879 [8]**
Percy Faith And His Orchestra (60) [IM]	12297
The Lettermen (65)	1085

Dick Roman (62)	274
The Ventures (69) [IM]	218
Lolita (61) [F]	5.4
LeRoy Holmes & His Orchestra (60) [IM]	0.0
Hugo Winterhalter And His Orchestra (60) [IM]	0.0
Don Ralke (60) [IM]	0.0
15 ▶ Sugar Sugar [Jeff Barry/Andy Kim]	**13805 [3]**
The Archies (69)	12247
Wilson Pickett (70)	1116
Stars On 45 (81)	442
16 ▶ I'm A Believer [Neil Diamond]	**13676 [2]**
The Monkees (66)	13324
Neil Diamond (71)	352
17 ▶ He'll Have To Go/Stay [Audrey Allison/Joe Allison/ *Kenneth Burns/Charles Grean/ Henry Haynes*]	**13638 [5]**
Jim Reeves (59)	10202
Jeanne Black (60) [R]	3119
Solomon Burke (64)	308
Homer & Jethro (60) [P]	9.0
Corina Minette (60) [R]	0.0
18 ▶ Light My Fire [John Densmore/Robby Krieger/ Ray Manzarek/Jim Morrison]	**13536 [5]**
The Doors (67)	8461
Jose Feliciano (68)	4958
Amii Stewart (79)	51
Rhetta Hughes (69)	33
The Doors (68)	32
19 ▶ Bridge Over Troubled Water [Paul Simon]	**13409 [3]**
Simon & Garfunkel (70)	8896
Aretha Franklin (71)	4354
Linda Clifford (79)	159
20 ▶ Battle Of New Orleans [Jimmy Driftwood/Traditional]	**13142 [5]**
Johnny Horton (59)	13064
Nitty Gritty Dirt Band (74)	51
Vaughn Monroe with Norman Layden, His Orchestra and Chorus (59)	15
Harpers Bizarre (68)	5.3
Bert Sommer (70)	5.3
21 ▶ You've Lost That Lovin' Feelin' [Barry Mann/ Phil Spector/Cynthia Weil]	**12899 [5]**
The Righteous Brothers (64)	9450
Daryl Hall & John Oates (80)	1839
Dionne Warwick (69)	1346
Roberta Flack & Donny Hathaway (71)	248
Long John Baldry & Kathi MacDonald (79)	16
22 ▶ It's All In The Game [Charles Dawes/Carl Sigman]	**12893 [3]**
Tommy Edwards (58)	10634
Four Tops (70)	1294
Cliff Richard (63)	964

23 ▶ Please Mr. Postman [Robert Bateman/ Georgia Dobbins/William Garrett/ Freddie Gorman/Brian Holland]	**12383 [4]**
The Marvelettes (61)	7831
Carpenters (74)	4500
Gentle Persuasion (83)	45
The Beatles (64)	6.4
24 ▶ Mac Arthur Park [Jimmy Webb]	**12359 [5]**
Donna Summer (78)	6578
Richard Harris (68)	5285
Four Tops (71)	486
Waylon Jennings And The Kimberlys (69)	9.8
Al Capps Band (70) [IWM]	0.8
25 ▶ You Keep Me Hangin' On [Lamont Dozier/Brian Holland/ Eddie Holland]	**12176 [6]**
The Supremes (66)	6251
Kim Wilde (87)	3516
The Vanilla Fudge (68)	2110
The Vanilla Fudge (67)	165
Wilson Pickett (69)	133
Jackie DeShannon (70)	1.0
26 ▶ Love Is Blue [*Bryan Blackburn/ Pierre Lemaire/* André Popp]	**12062 [5]**
Paul Mauriat And His Orchestra (67) [IM]	11159
The Dells (69) [FET]	524
Al Martino (68) [FET]	302
Claudine Longet (68) [F]	75
Manny Kellem, His Orchestra And Voices (68) [F]	2.7
27 ▶ The Yellow Rose Of Texas [Don George/Traditional]	**12048 [3]**
Mitch Miller with His Orch. & Chorus (55)	9072
Johnny Desmond (55)	2853
Stan Freberg (55)	123
28 ▶ Tossin' And Turnin' [Ritchie Adams/Malou René]	**12041 [2]**
Bobby Lewis (61)	12039
Bunny Sigler (73)	2.2
29 ▶ You Light Up My Life [Joe Brooks]	**11956 [2]**
Debby Boone (77)	11933
Original Cast (Kacey Cisyk) (77)	23
30 ▶ Melody Of Love [Hans Engelmann/ *Tom Glazer*]	**11910 [7]**
Billy Vaughn and His Orchestra (54) [IM]	7273
David Carroll And His Orchestra (54) [IM]	2366
Four Aces (54)	2262
Leo Diamond (55) [IM]	10
Frank Sinatra & Ray Anthony (55)	0.0
Tony Martin & Dinah Shore (55)	0.0
Sammy Kaye & His "Swing & Sway" Orchestra (55) [IM]	0.0
31 ▶ Smoke Gets In Your Eyes [Otto Harbach/Jerome Kern]	**11863 [4]**
The Platters (58)	10667
Blue Haze (72)	1048
The Four Preps (61)	130
Richard Barrett (58)	18
32 ▶ Hey There [Richard Adler/Jerry Ross]	**11807 [2]**
Rosemary Clooney (54)	11126
Sammy Davis Jr. (54)	680
33 ▶ Venus [Robbie Van Leeuwen]	**11748 [3]**
Shocking Blue (69)	8155
Bananarama (86)	3151
Stars On 45 (81)	442
34 ▶ Ballad Of Davy Crockett [Tom Blackburn/George Bruns/ *Lalo Guerrero*]	**11721 [7]**
Bill Hayes (55)	6567
Fess Parker (55)	2764
"Tennessee" Ernie Ford (55)	2107
Lalo Guerrero (55) [P]	238
Walter Schumann (55)	45
Rusty Draper (55)	0.0
Steve Allen (55)	0.0
35 ▶ Singing The Blues [Melvin Endsley]	**11715 [2]**
Guy Mitchell (56)	11013
Marty Robbins (56)	702
36 ▶ Are You Lonesome Tonight [Lou Handman/Roy Turk]	**11652 [5]**
Elvis Presley With The Jordanaires (60)	10024
Donny Osmond (73)	1054
Jaye P. Morgan (59)	310
Thelma Carpenter (60) [R]	149
Dodie Stevens (60) [R]	116
37 ▶ Another One Bites The Dust--Queen [John Deacon]	**11623 [1]**
38 ▶ It's Now Or Never [Eduardo di Capua/Wally Gold/ Aaron Schroeder]	**11562 [2]**
Elvis Presley With The Jordanaires (60) [FDE]	10781
John Schneider (81) [FDE]	781
39 ▶ Stranger On The Shore [Acker Bilk/ *Robert Mellin*]	**11393 [3]**
Mr. Acker Bilk (62) [IM]	10177
Andy Williams (62)	1127
The Drifters (62)	88
40 ▶ Runaway [Max Crook/Del Shannon]	**11365 [6]**
Del Shannon (61)	10390
Charlie Kulis (75)	327
Bonnie Raitt (77)	294
Lawrence Welk And His Orchestra (62) [IWM]	146
Dawn Featuring Tony Orlando (72)	124
Luis Cardenas (86)	83
41 ▶ Hello, Dolly! [Jerry Herman]	**11357 [3]**
Louis Armstrong And The All-Stars (64)	11318
Bobby Darin (65)	40
Pete King Chorale and Orchestra (64)	0.0
42 ▶ Only You [Buck Ram]	**11341 [9]**
The Platters (55)	4611
Franck Pourcel (59) [IWM]	2646
The Hilltoppers (55)	2041
Ringo Starr (74)	1985
Mr. Acker Bilk (63) [IWM]	27
Bobby Hatfield (69)	14
Wayne Newton (64)	12
Fred Parris & The Five Satins (82)	4.8
Lola Dee (55)	0.0
43 ▶ Sukiyaki [*Buzz Cason/Rohusuke Ei/ Snuff Garrett/* Hachidai Nakamura]	**11262 [2]**
Kyu Sakamoto (63) [F]	8172
A Taste Of Honey (81) [FDE]	3090
44 ▶ I Can't Stop Loving You [Don Gibson]	**11234 [4]**
Ray Charles (62)	11133
Count Basie (63) [IWM]	71
Don Gibson (58)	30
Gene Ammons (62) [IWM]	0.0
45 ▶ Runaround Sue [Dion DiMucci/Ernie Maresca]	**11222 [4]**
Dion (61)	10242
Leif Garrett (77)	949
The Four Preps (62) [P]	24
Jive Bunny & The Mastermixers (90)	6.7
46 ▶ Daydream Believer [John Stewart]	**11210 [3]**
The Monkees (67)	9734
Anne Murray (79)	1419
The Monkees (86)	57
47 ▶ Breaking Up Is Hard To Do [Howard Greenfield/Neil Sedaka]	**11198 [7]**
Neil Sedaka (62)	7494
Neil Sedaka (75)	1889
The Partridge Family Starring Shirley Jones & Featuring David Cassidy (72)	734
Lenny Welch (70)	683
The Happenings (68)	309
The American Comedy Network (84) [P]	82
Heaven Bound with Tony Scotti (72)	7.9
48 ▶ Physical--Olivia Newton-John [Steve Kipner/Terry Shaddick]	**11192 [1]**
49 ▶ This Girl's In Love With You [Burt Bacharach/Hal David]	**11153 [2]**
Herb Alpert (68)	9073
Dionne Warwick (69)	2079
50 ▶ Le Freak--Chic [Bernard Edwards/Nile Rodgers]	**11074 [1]**
51 ▶ (All I Have To Do Is) Dream [Boudleaux Bryant]	**10966 [6]**
The Everly Brothers (58)	8593
Richard Chamberlain (63)	1309
Bobbie Gentry & Glen Campbell (70)	694
Andy Gibb And Victoria Principal (81)	206
Nitty Gritty Dirt Band (75)	161
The Everly Brothers (61)	2.8
52 ▶ Cherish [Terry Kirkman]	**10956 [2]**
The Association (66)	7384
David Cassidy (71)	3572
53 ▶ Why Do Fools Fall In Love [George Goldner/Morris Levy/ Frankie Lymon/Jimmy Merchant/ Herman Santiago]	**10922 [8]**
The Teenagers Featuring Frankie Lymon (56)	4057
Diana Ross (81)	2314
Gale Storm (56)	2295

53 ▶ Why Do Fools Fall In Love [George Goldner/Morris Levy/ Frankie Lymon/Jimmy Merchant/ Herman Santiago] ***Continued***	**10922 [8]**
The Diamonds (56)	1782
The Happenings (67)	389
Gloria Mann (56)	80
The Beach Boys (64)	5.6
Summer Wine (73)	0.4
54 ▶ Big Bad John [Jimmy Dean/*Bud Reneau/ Bill Stith/Rick Tyson/ Mack Vickery*]	**10900 [2]**
Jimmy Dean (61)	10897
Steve Greenberg (69) [P]	3.1
55 ▶ Joy To The World-- Three Dog Night [Hoyt Axton]	**10869 [1]**
56 ▶ Crimson And Clover [Tommy James/Peter Lucia]	**10848 [2]**
Tommy James And The Shondells (68)	9176
Joan Jett & The Blackhearts (82)	1672
57 ▶ When A Man Loves A Woman [Calvin Lewis/Andrew Wright]	**10801 [4]**
Percy Sledge (66)	6157
Michael Bolton (91)	4080
Bette Midler (80)	398
Esther Phillips (66)	166
58 ▶ Winchester Cathedral [Geoff Stephens]	**10760 [2]**
The New Vaudeville Band (66)	10623
Dana Rollin (66)	137
59 ▶ Love Child [Deke Richards/ Pam Sawyer/ R. Dean Taylor/ Frank Edward Wilson]	**10755 [2]**
Diana Ross And The Supremes (68)	9676
Sweet Sensation (90)	1079
60 ▶ American Pie--Don McLean [Don McLean]	**10747 [1]**
61 ▶ Rockin' Robin [Leon René]	**10732 [3]**
Michael Jackson (72)	5891
Bobby Day (58)	4824
The Rivieras (2) (64)	18
62 ▶ House Of The Rising Sun [Traditional]	**10722 [4]**
The Animals (64)	7607
Frijid Pink (70)	3040
Santa Esmeralda (78)	57
Dolly Parton (81)	19
63 ▶ Ode To Billie Joe [Bobbie Gentry]	**10700 [5]**
Bobbie Gentry (67)	10012
The Kingpins (67) [IWM]	496
Bobbie Gentry (76)	135
Bobbie Gentry (76)	48
Ray Bryant (67) [IWM]	9.0
64 ▶ Roses Are Red My Love-- Bobby Vinton [Al Byron/Paul Evans]	**10687 [1]**
65 ▶ Endless Love-- Diana Ross & Lionel Richie [Lionel Richie]	**10663 [1]**
66 ▶ (I Can't Get No) Satisfaction [Mick Jagger/Keith Richards]	**10663 [3]**
The Rolling Stones (65)	10038

Otis Redding (66)	624
Tight Fit (81)	0.9
67 ▶ Sugar Shack-- Jimmy Gilmer And The Fireballs [Keith McCormack/Faye Voss]	**10632 [1]**
68 ▶ We Can Work It Out [John Lennon/Paul McCartney]	**10603 [3]**
The Beatles (65)	8664
Stevie Wonder (71)	1496
Stars On 45 (81)	442
69 ▶ Autumn Leaves [Joseph Kosma/*Johnny Mercer/ Jacques Prevert*]	**10582 [9]**
Roger Williams (55) [IM]	9865
Victor Young And His Singing Strings (55) [IM]	192
Jackie Gleason (55) [IM]	170
Mitch Miller & His Orchestra (55) [FET]	162
Steve Allen (55) [IM]	147
The Ray Charles Singers (55) [FET]	37
Roger Williams (65) [IM]	8.9
Bette McLaurin with Ray Ellis' Orch. And Chorus (57) [FET]	0.0
Keely Smith (57) [FET]	0.0
70 ▶ She Loves You [*Otto Demmlar/J. Nicolas Felgen/* John Lennon/Paul McCartney]	**10569 [2]**
The Beatles (64)	10567
Die Beatles (64) [F]	1.9
71 ▶ To Sir With Love [*Don Black/* Mark London]	**10549 [2]**
Lulu (67)	10546
Herbie Mann (67) [IM]	3.8
72 ▶ Groovin' [Eddie Brigati/Felix Cavaliere]	**10537 [2]**
The Young Rascals (67)	9580
Booker T. & The M.G.'s (67) [IWM]	957
73 ▶ Venus [Ed Marshall]	**10465 [3]**
Frankie Avalon (59)	9989
Frankie Avalon (76)	473
Johnny Mathis (68)	2.7
74 ▶ Honky Tonk Women-- Rolling Stones [Mick Jagger/Keith Richards]	**10430 [1]**
75 ▶ Dedicated To The One I Love [Ralph Bass/Lowman Pauling]	**10400 [6]**
The Mamas & The Papas (67)	5052
The Shirelles (61)	5044
The Shirelles (59)	96
Bernadette Peters (81)	90
The Temprees (72)	59
The "5" Royales (61)	58
76 ▶ Where Did Our Love Go [Lamont Dozier/Brian Holland/ Eddie Holland]	**10262 [3]**
The Supremes (64)	9056
Donnie Elbert (71)	1001
The J. Geils Band (76)	205
77 ▶ I Can't Help Myself [Lamont Dozier/Brian Holland/ Eddie Holland]	**10212 [5]**
Four Tops (65)	8859
Donnie Elbert (72)	858
Bonnie Pointer (79)	407

Shalamar (77)	80
The Magnificent Men (67)	7.6
78 ▶ Raindrops Keep Fallin' On My Head--B.J. Thomas [Burt Bacharach/Hal David]	**10203 [1]**
79 ▶ Save The Last Dance For Me [Doc Pomus/Mort Shuman]	**10183 [3]**
The Drifters (60)	8918
The Defranco Family Featuring Tony Defranco (74)	886
Dolly Parton (83)	379
80 ▶ Call Me--Blondie [Clement A. Bozewski/ Deborah Harry/ Giorgio Moroder]	**10151 [1]**
81 ▶ Every Breath You Take-- Police [Sting]	**10116 [1]**
82 ▶ Tom Dooley [Traditional]	**10115 [2]**
The Kingston Trio (58)	9986
The Four Preps (61) [P]	130
83 ▶ Shadow Dancing -Andy Gibb [Andy Gibb/Barry Gibb/ Maurice Gibb/Robin Gibb]	**10099 [1]**
84 ▶ The Wayward Wind [Stan Lebowsky/Herbert Newman]	**10077 [3]**
Gogi Grant (56)	9460
Tex Ritter (56)	406
Gogi Grant (61)	211
85 ▶ (Oh) Pretty Woman [William Dees/ Roy Orbison]	**10027 [2]**
Roy Orbison And The Candy Men (64)	8819
Van Halen (82)	1208
86 ▶ Big Girls Don't Cry [Bob Crewe/Bob Gaudio]	**10016 [2]**
The 4 Seasons (62)	10012
Gidea Park (81)	3.7
87 ▶ Main Title/Tammy [Ray Evans/Jay Livingston]	**9988 [6]**
Debbie Reynolds (57)	9194
The Ames Brothers (57)	793
Pat Kirby (57)	0.0
Joseph Gershenson & The Universal-International Orchestra (57) [IWM]	0.0
Richard Hayman, His Orchestra And Chorus (57) [IWM]	0.0
Bill Snyder & His Orchestra (57) [IWM]	0.0
88 ▶ Never My Love [Dick Addrisi/Don Addrisi]	**9982 [5]**
The Association (67)	6833
The 5th Dimension (71)	1564
Blue Swede (74)	1499
The Addrisi Brothers (77)	82
The Sandpebbles (68)	3.2
89 ▶ Sixteen Tons [Merle Travis]	**9977 [5]**
"Tennessee" Ernie Ford (55)	9525
Johnny Desmond (55)	183
The Don Harrison Band (76)	166
Tom Jones (67)	100
Lou Monte (61)	1.4

90 ▶ Heartbreak Hotel [Mae Boren Axton/Thomas Durden/ Elvis Presley]	**9967 [4]**
Elvis Presley (56)	9660
Frijid Pink (70)	236
Roger Miller (66)	53
Stan Freberg (56) [P]	17
91 ▶ Memories Are Made Of This [Richard Dehr/Terry Gilkyson/ Frank Miller]	**9942 [5]**
Dean Martin (55)	8655
Gale Storm (55)	785
The Drifters (66)	271
Mindy Carson (55)	217
Roger Williams (59) [IWM]	14
92 ▶ I'm Leaving It (All) Up To You [Don Harris/Dewey Terry]	**9938 [2]**
Dale & Grace (63)	7593
Donny And Marie Osmond (74)	2345
93 ▶ Wonderland By Night [*Lincoln Chase/* Klaus-Günter Neumann]	**9915 [3]**
Bert Kaempfert And His Orchestra (60) [IM]	7899
Louis Prima (60) [IM]	1224
Anita Bryant (60)	792
94 ▶ To Know Him Is To Love Him [Phil Spector]	**9897 [4]**
The Teddy Bears (58)	8631
Bobby Vinton (69)	685
Peter And Gordon (65)	580
Cathy Carr (58)	0.0
95 ▶ Love Letters In The Sand-- Pat Boone [J. Fred Coots/ Charles Kenny/Nick Kenny]	**9892 [1]**
96 ▶ Louie Louie [Richard Berry/ *Nick DeCaro/Carlos Ortega*]	**9887 [7]**
The Kingsmen (63)	9145
The Sandpipers (66) [F]	595
The Kingsmen (66)	95
John Belushi (78)	31
Travis Wammack (66) [IWM]	12
Fat Boys (88)	9.6
Paul Revere And The Raiders (63)	0.0
97 ▶ It's Only Make Believe [Jack Nance/Conway Twitty]	**9874 [2]**
Conway Twitty (58)	7964
Glen Campbell (70)	1910
98 ▶ Stayin' Alive--Bee Gees [Barry Gibb/Maurice Gibb/ Robin Gibb]	**9872 [1]**
99 ▶ Honey [Bobby Russell]	**9871 [2]**
Bobby Goldsboro (68)	9605
O.C. Smith (69)	266
100 ▶ Knock Three Times--Dawn [L. Russell Brown/Irwin Levine]	**9840 [1]**
101 ▶ I'll Be There--Jackson 5 [Hal Davis/Berry Gordy/ Willie Hutch/Bob West]	**9838 [1]**
102 ▶ Cherry Pink (And Apple Blossom White) [*Marcel Ageron/Mack David/* Luis Guglielmi]	**9823 [5]**
Perez Prado And His Orchestra (55) [IM]	9278
Jerry Murad's Harmonicats (60) [IM]	319
Alan Dale (55) [FET]	226
Georgie Auld & His Auld-Stars (55) [IM]	0.0
Xavier Cugat & His Orchestra (55) [IM]	0.0
103 ▶ Handy Man [Andrew Barksdale/Otis Blackwell/ Jimmy Jones/Charles Merenstein]	**9788 [3]**
Jimmy Jones (59)	5670
James Taylor (77)	3089
Del Shannon (64)	1029
104 ▶ Limbo Rock [*Kal Mann/* Billy Strange]	**9731 [2]**
Chubby Checker (62)	9002
The Champs (62) [IM]	729
105 ▶ Green Door [Bob Davie/Marvin Moore]	**9721 [2]**
Jim Lowe (56)	9717
The Jerms (69)	4.7
106 ▶ Dominique--Singing Nun [Jeanine Deckers]	**9721 [1]**
107 ▶ Canadian Sunset [*Norman Gimbel/* Eddie Heywood]	**9696 [4]**
Hugo Winterhalter And His Orchestra (56) [IM]	6824
Andy Williams (56)	2711
Sounds Orchestral (65) [IM]	106
Etta Jones (61)	54
108 ▶ Stagger Lee [Harold Logan/ Lloyd Price/Traditional]	**9680 [3]**
Lloyd Price (58)	7844
Tommy Roe (71)	1051
Wilson Pickett (67)	785
109 ▶ Come See About Me [Lamont Dozier/Brian Holland/ Eddie Holland]	**9657 [3]**
The Supremes (64)	8772
Jr. Walker & The All Stars (67)	794
Nella Dodds (64)	92
110 ▶ My Sweet Lord [George Harrison]	**9603 [3]**
George Harrison (70)	9566
Billy Preston (71)	28
Stars On 45 (81)	8.0
111 ▶ Sherry [Bob Gaudio]	**9600 [3]**
The 4 Seasons (62)	9519
Robert John (80)	77
Gidea Park (81)	3.7
112 ▶ Blue Moon [*Lorenz Hart/* Richard Rodgers]	**9586 [5]**
The Marcels (61)	9049
Elvis Presley (56)	266
The Ventures (61) [IM]	139
Herb Lance & The Classics (61)	121
Jimmy Bowen With The Rhythm Orchids (58)	12
113 ▶ Michael [Traditional]	**9585 [4]**
The Highwaymen (61)	9146
Trini Lopez (64)	414
The Four Preps (62) [P]	24
Steve Alaimo (63)	0.5
114 ▶ Ballad Of The Green Berets-- SSgt. Barry Sadler [Robin Moore/ Barry Sadler]	**9577 [1]**
115 ▶ Flashdance (What A Feeling)--Irene Cara [Irene Cara/Keith Forsey/ Giorgio Moroder]	**9574 [1]**
116 ▶ Happy Together [Garry Bonner/Alan Gordon]	**9534 [4]**
The Turtles (67)	9222
Captain & Tennille (80)	131
Dawn Featuring Tony Orlando (72)	124
The Nylons (87)	56
117 ▶ Mr. Blue [Dewayne Blackwell]	**9532 [2]**
The Fleetwoods (59)	9403
The Four Preps (61) [P]	130
118 ▶ I'm Sorry [Dub Allbritten/Ronnie Self]	**9509 [2]**
Brenda Lee (60)	9449
Joey Heatherton (72)	61
119 ▶ Everyday People [Sylvester Stewart]	**9499 [2]**
Sly & The Family Stone (68)	9208
Joan Jett and the Blackhearts (83)	291
120 ▶ Deep Purple [Peter DeRose/Mitchell Parish]	**9450 [3]**
Nino Tempo & April Stevens (63)	7500
Donny And Marie Osmond (75)	1422
Billy Ward And His Dominoes (57)	528
121 ▶ Downtown [Tony Hatch]	**9450 [4]**
Petula Clark (64)	8873
Allan Sherman (65) [P]	524
Mrs. Miller (66)	27
Dolly Parton (84)	25
122 ▶ (Sittin' On) The Dock Of The Bay [Steve Cropper/Otis Redding]	**9447 [7]**
Otis Redding (68)	7420
Michael Bolton (88)	1137
The Dells (69)	452
The Reddings (82)	200
Sergio Mendes & Brasil '66 (69)	101
Sammy Hagar (79)	92
King Curtis & The Kingpins (68) [IWM]	45
123 ▶ Cathy's Clown-- Everly Brothers [Don Everly/Phil Everly]	**9441 [1]**
124 ▶ Love Me Tender [Ken Darby/George R. Poulton/ Elvis Presley]	**9428 [4]**
Elvis Presley (56)	8241
Richard Chamberlain (62)	673
Percy Sledge (67)	405
Henri René (56) [IWM]	108
125 ▶ You Can't Hurry Love [Lamont Dozier/Brian Holland/ Eddie Holland]	**9427 [2]**
The Supremes (66)	7615
Phil Collins (82)	1813
126 ▶ Alone Again (Naturally)-- Gilbert O'Sullivan [Gilbert O'Sullivan]	**9416 [1]**

127 ► Mister Sandman [Pat Ballard]	**9376 [7]**
The Chordettes (54)	7421
Four Aces (54)	1496
Emmylou Harris (81)	421
Dorothy Collins (55) [P]	37
The Lancers (54)	0
Vaughn Monroe & His Orchestra (54)	0
Buddy Morrow & His Orchestra (54)	0
128 ► Stand By Me [Ben E. King/Jerry Leiber/ Mike Stoller]	**9344 [9]**
Ben E. King (61)	3409
Ben E. King (86)	1763
Spyder Turner (66)	1730
Mickey Gilley (80)	1122
John Lennon (75)	647
Maurice White (85)	304
David & Jimmy Ruffin (70)	227
Earl Grant (65) [IWM]	129
Cassius Clay (64)	14
129 ► (My Girl) Sloopy/ Hang On Sloopy [Bert Berns/Wes Farrell]	**9342 [6]**
The McCoys (65)	6827
Ramsey Lewis Trio (65) [IWM]	1400
The Vibrations (64)	637
Little Caesar And The Consuls (65)	340
Rick Derringer (75)	96
The Lettermen (70)	42
130 ► Another Brick In The Wall-- Pink Floyd [Roger Waters]	**9336 [1]**
131 ► All Shook Up [Otis Blackwell/Elvis Presley]	**9318 [3]**
Elvis Presley (57)	9084
Suzi Quatro (74)	154
Jive Bunny And The Mastermixers (89)	80
132 ► Return To Sender-- Elvis Presley [Otis Blackwell/Winfield Scott]	**9296 [1]**
133 ► The First Time Ever I Saw Your Face--Roberta Flack [Ewan MacColl]	**9289 [1]**
134 ► Funky Town [Steve Greenberg]	**9276 [2]**
Lipps, Inc. (80)	8061
Pseudo Echo (87)	1216
135 ► A Groovy Kind Of Love [Carole Bayer Sager/Toni Wine]	**9271 [2]**
The Mindbenders (66)	5559
Phil Collins (88)	3712
136 ► He's So Fine [Ronnie Mack]	**9271 [4]**
The Chiffons (63)	8687
Jody Miller (71)	413
Jane Olivor (78)	110
Kristy And Jimmy McNichol (78)	62
137 ► Monster Mash [Leonard L. Capizzi/Bobby Pickett]	**9247 [3]**
Bobby (Boris) Pickett And The Crypt-Kickers (62)	7305
Bobby (Boris) Pickett And The Crypt-Kickers (73)	1895
Bobby (Boris) Pickett And The Crypt-Kickers (70)	47
138 ► Grazing In The Grass [*Harry Elston*/Hugh Masekela]	**9241 [2]**
Hugh Masekela (68) [IM]	5702
The Friends Of Distinction (69)	3539
139 ► Night Fever--BeeGees [Barry Gibb/Maurice Gibb/ Robin Gibb]	**9237 [1]**
140 ► People Got To Be Free [Eddie Brigati/Felix Cavaliere]	**9200 [2]**
The Rascals (68)	9189
The 5th Dimension (70)	11
141 ► Mrs. Robinson [Paul Simon]	**9195 [2]**
Simon & Garfunkel (68)	8641
Booker T. & The M.G.'s (69) [IWM]	554
142 ► Duke Of Earl [Gene Chandler/Earl Edwards/ Bernice Williams]	**9193 [3]**
Gene Chandler (62)	9144
The Pearlettes (62) [R]	50
Bobbie Smith & The Dreamgirls (62) [R]	0
143 ► Play That Funky Music [Robert Parissi]	**9178 [3]**
Wild Cherry (76)	7145
Vanilla Ice (90)	1923
Roxanne (88)	109
144 ► Hey Baby [Bruce Channel/Margaret Cobb]	**9160 [3]**
Bruce Channel (62)	8663
Jose Feliciano (69)	381
Ringo Starr (76)	116
145 ► Respect [Otis Redding]	**9151 [3]**
Aretha Franklin (67)	8397
Otis Redding (65)	680
The Rationals (66)	74
146 ► Windy [Ruthann Friedman]	**9149 [2]**
The Association (67)	8778
Wes Montgomery (67) [IWM]	371
147 ► Indian Reservation (The Lament Of The Cherokee) [John D. Loudermilk]	**9138 [2]**
Raiders (71)	8111
Don Fardon (68)	1027
148 ► Lonely Boy [Paul Anka/Alberto Curci]	**9133 [2]**
Paul Anka (59)	9133
Donny Osmond (72)	0
149 ► Never Can Say Goodbye [Clifton Davis]	**9125 [4]**
The Jackson 5 (71)	6524
Gloria Gaynor (74)	1693
Isaac Hayes (71)	700
Communards (88)	208
150 ► Sea Of Love [Phil Baptiste/George Khoury]	**9124 [3]**
Phil Phillips with The Twilights (59)	5548
The Honeydrippers (84)	3169
Del Shannon (81)	406

Top Songs by Number of Entries

Song	Writer Team	Score [Entries]
1 White Christmas	Irving Berlin	1408 [20]
2 Rudolph The Red Nosed Reindeer	Johnny Marks	447 [13]
3 Silent Night	Franz Gruber/Josef Mohr	193 [13]
4 Unchained Melody	Alex North/Hy Zaret	20850 [12]
5 (Nel Blu Dipinto Di Blu) Volare	Franco Migliacci/ Domenico Modugno	16401 [10]
6 In The Mood	Joe Garland	4449 [10]
7 (Theme From) Around The World	Stella Unger/Victor Young	4422 [10]
8 And That Reminds Me	Camillo Bargoni/ Al Stillman	2412 [10]
9 Little Drummer Boy	Katherine Davis/ Henry Onorati/ Harry Simeone	2108 [10]
10 What Kind Of Fool Am I	Leslie Bricusse/ Anthony Newley	1741 [10]
11 Jingle Bells	James Lord Pierpont	410 [10]
12 Moritat/Mack The Knife	Kurt Weill	20818 [9]
13 Only You	Buck Ram	11341 [9]
14 Autumn Leaves	Joseph Kosma	10582 [9]
15 Stand By Me	Ben E. King/ Jerry Leiber/Mike Stoller	9344 [9]
16 Earth Angel	Jesse Belvin/ Gaynel Hodge/ Curtis Edward Williams	5403 [9]
17 'Til	Charles Danvers/ Carl Sigman	3516 [9]
18 Star Dust	Hoagy Carmichael	2629 [9]
19 Pledging My Love	Deadric Malone/ Ferdinand Washington	2011 [9]
20 Jingle Bell Rock	Joe Beal/Jim Boothe	1710 [9]
21 Arrivederci Roma	Pietro Garinei/ Alessandro Giovannini/ Renato Rascel/ Carl Sigman	832 [9]
22 (Theme From) "A Summer Place"	Max Steiner	13879 [8]
23 Why Do Fools Fall In Love	George Goldner/ Morris Levy/ Frankie Lymon/ Jimmy Merchant/ Herman Santiago	10922 [8]
24 Dancin' In The Streets	Marvin Gaye/ Ivy Jo Hunter/ William Stevenson	7411 [8]
25 Fever	Otis Blackwell/ Eddie Cooley	5962 [8]
26 Teach Me Tonight	Sammy Cahn/Gene DePaul	4801 [8]
27 Fascination	Dick Manning/ Dante Marchetti	3379 [8]
28 You Are My Sunshine	Oliver Hood	2462 [8]
29 Goodnight My Love	John Marascalco /George Motola	2134 [8]
30 Rock Island Line	Traditional	2005 [8]
31 Summertime	George Gershwin/ Ira Gershwin/ DuBose Heyward	1909 [8]
32 My Own True Love	Mack David/Max Steiner	1891 [8]
33 In A Little Spanish Town	Mabel Wayne	668 [8]
34 Young Love	Ric Cartey/Carole Joyner	15361 [7]
35 Melody Of Love	Hans Engelmann	11910 [7]
36 Ballad Of Davy Crockett	Tom Blackburn/ George Bruns	11721 [7]
37 Breaking Up Is Hard To Do	Howard Greenfield/ Neil Sedaka	11198 [7]
38 Louie Louie	Richard Berry	9887 [7]
39 (Sittin' On) The Dock Of The Bay	Steve Cropper/ Otis Redding	9447 [7]
40 Mister Sandman	Pat Ballard	9376 [7]
41 Kansas City	Jerry Leiber/Mike Stoller	8293 [7]
42 Will You Love Me Tomorrow	Gerry Goffin/Carole King	7524 [7]
43 Blue Suede Shoes	Carl Perkins	7357 [7]
44 Reach Out	Lamont Dozier/ Brian Holland/ Eddie Holland	7325 [7]
45 Uptight - Everything's Alright	Henry Cosby/ Sylvia Moy/Stevie Wonder	7256 [7]
46 You Don't Know Me	Eddy Arnold/Cindy Walker	6467 [7]
47 I Can't Help Falling In Love	Luigi Creatore/ Hugo Peretti/ George David Weiss	6331 [7]
48 It's Almost Tomorrow	Gene Adkinson/Wade Buff	4927 [7]
49 What I Say	Ray Charles	4733 [7]
50 Main Title And Molly O From The Man With The Golden Arm	Elmer Bernstein/Sylvia Fine	3889 [7]
51 Land Of 1000 Dances	Chris Kenner	3730 [7]
52 Hi Heel Sneakers - Pt. 1	Robert Higginbotham	3615 [7]
53 Danny Boy	Traditional/Fred Weatherly	2849 [7]
54 Cry Me A River	Arthur Hamilton	2682 [7]
55 Long Lonely Nights	Lee Andrews/ Bernice Davis/ Douglas Henderson/ Miriam Uniman	2187 [7]
56 I Could Have Danced All Night	Alan Jay Lerner/ Frederick Loewe	1554 [7]
57 Memories Of You	Eubie Blake/Andy Razaf	1236 [7]
58 Nothin' For Christmas	Roy C. Bennett/Sid Tepper	1226 [7]
59 (Theme From) The Proud Ones	Lionel Newman	438 [7]
60 Adeste Fideles (O Come All Ye Faithful)	Traditional	235 [7]
61 Seventy Six Trombones	Meredith Willson	201 [7]
59 Songs with 6 Entries		

The Top 750 Acts

And The Writers Who Supported Them

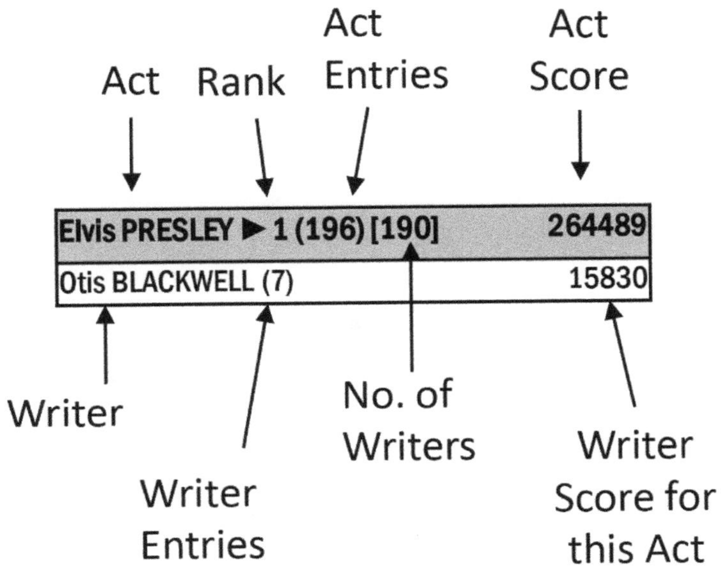

Act scores are calculated by adding song scores for that act. Writer scores are additive to give act score.

Elvis PRESLEY	
►1 (196) [190]	**264489**
Otis BLACKWELL (7)	15830
Elvis PRESLEY (9)	15729
Aaron SCHROEDER (10)	15575
Jerry LEIBER (16)	13274
Mike STOLLER (16)	13274
Mac DAVIS (5)	9049
Doc POMUS (11)	8462
Mark JAMES (5)	7426
Mort SHUMAN (9)	7320
Wally GOLD (2)	7024
Winfield SCOTT (4)	6328
Bill TRADER (1)	5386
Lou HANDMAN (1)	5012
Roy TURK (1)	5012
Artie GLENN (1)	5009
Dennis LINDE (3)	4720
J. Leslie McFARLAND (2)	4348
Bernie LOWE (2)	3899
Kal MANN (2)	3899
Claude DeMETRIUS (3)	3724
Eduardo Di CAPUA (1)	3594
Mae Boren AXTON (1)	3220
Thomas DURDEN (1)	3220
Ken DARBY (2)	2839
George R. POULTON (1)	2747
Sid WYCHE (1)	2643
Fred WISE (12)	2511
Chuck WILLIS (1)	2474
Baker KNIGHT (1)	2415
Sid WAYNE (6)	2363
Walter Earl BROWN (1)	2264
Ben WEISMAN (13)	2222
Don ROBERTSON (5)	2041
Luigi CREATORE (2)	1974
Hugo PERETTI (2)	1974
George David WEISS (2)	1974
Ira KOSLOFF (1)	1916
Maurice MYSELS (1)	1916
Dave BARTHOLOMEW (2)	1885
Earl King JOHNSON (2)	1885
Ivory Joe HUNTER (2)	1767
Bernie BAUM (3)	1717
Bill GIANT (3)	1717
Florence KAYE (3)	1717
Jerry REED (3)	1707
Anita STEINMAN (1)	1635
Bickley REICHNER (1)	1356
Layng MARTINE Jr. (1)	1351
David HESS (1)	1331
Bert CARROLL (1)	1238
Russell MOODY (1)	1238
Marilyn SCHACK (1)	1238
Hal BLAIR (2)	1127
James TAYLOR (1)	1079
Bill BEASLEY (1)	1063
Joan NORRIS (1)	1063
Lee ROSENBERG (1)	1063
Bernard WEINMAN (1)	1063
Roy C. BENNETT (4)	1006
Sid TEPPER (4)	1006
Red WEST (5)	959
Lincoln CHASE (1)	957
Hughie CANNON (1)	908
Chuck BERRY (1)	900
Clyde OTIS (3)	894
Ray CHARLES (1)	878
Dolores FULLER (4)	820
Randy STARR (2)	812
Billy STRANGE (3)	756
Arthur CRUDUP (1)	736
Joy Byers JOHNSTON (4)	719

Titus TURNER (1)	711
Darrell GLENN (1)	690
Paul EVANS (3)	622
Dick HEARD (1)	593
Eddie RABBITT (2)	593
Rose Marie McCOY (1)	587
Kelly OWENS (1)	587
Tony Joe WHITE (2)	573
Dallas FRAZIER (2)	570
Richard MAINEGRA (1)	551
Carl PERKINS (1)	530
Buffy SAINTE-MARIE (1)	502
Pino DONAGGIO (1)	477
Simon NAPIER-BELL (1)	477
Vicki WICKHAM (1)	477
Johnny CHRISTOPHER (2)	449
Sherman EDWARDS (3)	447
Edward HEYMAN (1)	443
Victor YOUNG (1)	443
Jerry CHESNUT (1)	408
Thomas A. DORSEY (3)	399
Domenico MODUGNO (1)	396
Stanley A. KESLER (1)	368
Shirl MILETE (1)	360
Howard Lee BARNES (1)	352
Claude FRANÇOIS (2)	351
Paul PARNES (1)	316
Matt WILLIAMS (1)	303
Jimmie CRANE (1)	259
Al JACOBS (1)	259
Sonny CHARLES (1)	251
Michael JARRETT (1)	251
Bill PEPPERS (1)	233
Charlie DANIELS (1)	218
Luther DIXON (1)	212
Albert B. SMITH (1)	212
Alan BLAIKLEY (1)	200
Ken HOWARD (1)	200
Eddy ARNOLD (1)	192
Cindy WALKER (1)	192
Paul ANKA (1)	184
Jacques REVAUX (1)	184
A.L. "Doodle" OWENS (1)	180
Jean-Pierre BOURTAYRE (1)	168
Phil COULTER (1)	168
Yves-Jacques LAVOT (1)	168
William Wylie MacPherson MARTIN (1)	168
Richard RODGERS (2)	146
Steve TYRELL (1)	138
Lorenz HART (1)	133
Mack DAVID (1)	129
Gene SULLIVAN (1)	124
Wiley WALKER (1)	124
Ruth BATCHELOR (2)	118
Bob ROBERTS (2)	118
Bennie BENJAMIN (1)	116
Sol MARCUS (1)	116
Richard ADLER (1)	111
Jerry ROSS (1)	111
Joel HIRSCHHORN (1)	102
Al KASHA (1)	102
Abner SILVER (1)	96
Greg GORDON (1)	82
Daniel Decatur EMMETT (1)	69
TRADITIONAL (1)	69
Hal DAVID (2)	62
Robert HIGGINBOTHAM (1)	53
Brook BENTON (1)	53
Willie DIXON (1)	53
Fred FISHER (1)	48
Billy HILL (1)	48
William RASKIN (1)	48

Teddy DeLano RIEDEL (1)	43
Dory JONES (1)	36
Bunny WARREN (1)	36
Julia Ward HOWE (1)	35
William STEFFE (1)	35
Jesse STONE (1)	25
Sid ROBIN (1)	24
Bob SHELTON (1)	24
Joe SHELTON (1)	24
Arthur KENT (1)	21
Ed WARREN (1)	21
Red FOLEY (1)	18
Oscar HAMMERSTEIN (1)	13
James LAST (1)	12
Carl SIGMAN (1)	12
Martin KALMANOFF (1)	12
Beverly ROSS (1)	12
Alan JEFFREYS (1)	11
Norm BLAGMAN (1)	7.5
Kay TWOMEY (1)	7.5
Luiz BONFÁ (1)	5.5
Franklyn J. TABLEPORTER (1)	3.3
Fred TOBIAS (1)	2.6
Irving BERLIN (1)	2.1
Stuart HAMBLEN (1)	2.1
Gene AUTRY (1)	1.1
Oakley HALDEMAN (1)	1.1
Billy HAYES (1)	1.1
Jay JOHNSON (1)	1.1
Phillips BROOKS (1)	1.1
Lewis REDNER (1)	1.1
Franz GRUBER (1)	1.1
Josef MOHR (1)	1.1
Kim GANNON (1)	0.7
Walter KENT (1)	0.7
Buck RAM (1)	0.7
Joey COOPER (1)	0.5
Ervin DRAKE (1)	0.5
Irvin GRAHAM (1)	0.5
Jimmy SHIRL (1)	0.5
Al STILLMAN (1)	0.5
Rory BOURKE (1)	0.0
Paul RADER (1)	0.0
Jay RAMSEY (1)	0.0
Larry GATLIN (1)	0.0
Steve DUFFY (1)	0.0
Dickey LEE (1)	0.0
The BEATLES ►2 (84) [28]	**226989**
John LENNON (65)	105361
Paul McCARTNEY (65)	105361
George HARRISON (3)	5251
Bert BERNS (2)	3462
Phil MEDLEY (2)	3462
Carl PERKINS (3)	951
Larry WILLIAMS (1)	568
Milton AGER (1)	543
Jack YELLEN (1)	543
TRADITIONAL (1)	519
Chuck BERRY (2)	315
Voni MORRISON (1)	269
Johnny RUSSELL (1)	269
Roy Lee JOHNSON (1)	37
Luther DIXON (1)	19
Wes FARRELL (1)	19
Jerry LEIBER (1)	11
Mike STOLLER (1)	11
Ringo STARR (1)	5.3
Bill CROMPTON (1)	3.0
Tony SHERIDAN (1)	3.0
Robert BATEMAN (1)	1.3
Georgia DOBBINS (1)	1.3
William GARRETT (1)	1.3
Freddie GORMAN (1)	1.3

Brian HOLLAND (1)	1.3
Otto DEMMLAR (1)	0.5
J. Nicolas FELGEN (1)	0.5
ROLLING STONES	
►3 (54) [26]	**118467**
Mick JAGGER (47)	54978
Keith RICHARDS (47)	54978
Jimmy NORMAN (1)	1544
Jerry RAGOVOY (1)	1544
Earl NELSON (1)	895
Bob RELF (1)	895
Andrew Loog OLDHAM (1)	864
Eddie HOLLAND (1)	414
Norman WHITFIELD (1)	414
Bobby WOMACK (1)	237
Shirley WOMACK (1)	237
Buddy HOLLY (1)	208
Norman PETTY (1)	208
Ron WOOD (1)	150
Warren MOORE (1)	148
Smokey ROBINSON (1)	148
Robert ROGERS (1)	148
Marvin TARPLIN (1)	148
Steve JORDAN (1)	70
Lula Mae HARDAWAY (1)	59
Don HUNTER (1)	59
Paul RISER (1)	59
Stevie WONDER (1)	59
Brian JONES (1)	0.5
Charlie WATTS (1)	0.5
Bill WYMAN (1)	0.5
Stevie WONDER	
►4 (56) [25]	**116797**
Stevie WONDER (42)	72324
Henry COSBY (10)	9981
Ronald Norman MILLER (5)	7140
Sylvia MOY (8)	5581
Clarence PAUL (3)	4417
Lula Mae HARDAWAY (4)	2973
Orlando MURDEN (1)	2941
Syreeta WRIGHT (3)	2497
Bryan WELLS (3)	2440
Bob DYLAN (1)	1913
Lee GARRETT (1)	1270
John LENNON (1)	748
Paul McCARTNEY (1)	748
Don HUNTER (2)	316
Marty COOPER (1)	278
Lou JOSIE (1)	278
Robert HIGGINBOTHAM (1)	273
William STEVENSON (1)	258
Paul RISER (1)	96
Hal DAVIS (1)	76
Marc GORDON (1)	76
Mary O'BRIEN (1)	76
Frank Edward WILSON (1)	76
Morris BROADNAX (1)	18
Vicki BASEMORE (1)	1.5
The SUPREMES/ Diana ROSS And The SUPREMES	
►5 (29) [19]	**108490**
Lamont DOZIER (18)	28621
Brian HOLLAND (18)	28621
Eddie HOLLAND (18)	28621
Pam SAWYER (2)	2749
R. Dean TAYLOR (2)	2749
Frank Edward WILSON (2)	2749
Jackey BEAVERS (1)	2497
Johnny BRISTOL (1)	2497
Harvey FUQUA (1)	2497
Deke RICHARDS (1)	2419

The SUPREMES/ Diana ROSS And The SUPREMES ►5 (29) [19] *Cont'd*	**108490**
Frank DeVOL (1)	1542
Smokey ROBINSON (3)	783
Berry GORDY (3)	683
Henry COSBY (2)	607
Nick ASHFORD (1)	359
Valerie SIMPSON (1)	359
George GORDY (1)	63
Allen STORY (1)	63
Isabelle FREEMAN (1)	9.3
BEE GEES ►6 (42) [3]	**93799**
Barry GIBB (42)	33686
Robin GIBB (36)	32620
Maurice GIBB (34)	27493
4 SEASONS ►7 (46) [35]	**85865**
Bob GAUDIO (23)	35672
Bob CREWE (14)	18858
Sandy LINZER (6)	6861
Judy PARKER (5)	4655
Denny RANDELL (4)	3839
Larry SANTOS (1)	3611
Cole PORTER (1)	1865
Raymond BLOODWORTH (2)	1333
L. Russell BROWN (2)	1333
Maurice WILLIAMS (1)	1296
Mike PETRILLO (3)	1110
Angelo M. CIFELLI (2)	902
Peggy FARINA (1)	617
Gerry GOFFIN (1)	504
Carole KING (1)	504
Dave BARTHOLOMEW (1)	380
Fats DOMINO (1)	380
Morty CRAFT (1)	305
Selma CRAFT (1)	305
Camillo BARGONI (1)	296
Al STILLMAN (1)	296
Charlie CALELLO (1)	240
J. Fred COOTS (1)	184
Haven GILLESPIE (1)	184
Jake HOLMES (3)	114
Alan FREED (1)	57
Harvey FUQUA (1)	57
Joe COOK (1)	33
Robert BOULANGER (1)	26
Lee ANDREWS (1)	8.5
Bernice DAVIS (1)	8.5
Douglas HENDERSON (1)	8.5
Miriam UNIMAN (1)	8.5
Kenny NOLAN (1)	6.2
Lenny Lee GOLDSMITH (1)	4.0
Elton JOHN ►8 (48) [16]	**85836**
Elton JOHN (44)	38236
Bernie TAUPIN (39)	34396
Gary OSBORNE (5)	3972
John LENNON (1)	2293
Paul McCARTNEY (1)	2293
Davey JOHNSTONE (3)	1306
Leroy BELL (1)	1057
Casey JAMES (1)	1057
Jean-Paul DREAU (1)	287
Tom ROBINSON (1)	155
Fred MANDEL (1)	142
Charlie MORGAN (1)	142
Paul WESTWOOD (1)	142
Pete BELLOTTE (1)	119
Sylvester LEVAY (1)	119
Jerry RIX (1)	119

Connie FRANCIS ►9 (68) [102]	**84685**
Howard GREENFIELD (7)	14688
Jack KELLER (3)	10185
Neil SEDAKA (4)	4503
Benny DAVIS (6)	4101
Ted MURRY (5)	4000
Borney BERGANTINE (1)	2980
Betty PETERSON (1)	2980
Winfield SCOTT (1)	2581
Hank HUNTER (5)	2440
George GOEHRING (1)	1825
Edna LEWIS (1)	1825
John D. LOUDERMILK (2)	1727
Bert KALMAR (1)	1461
Harry RUBY (1)	1461
Ted SNYDER (1)	1461
Edgar LESLIE (1)	1297
Lawrence WRIGHT (1)	1297
Jack LAWRENCE (1)	1230
Roy C. BENNETT (1)	1066
Sid TEPPER (1)	1066
Phil SPECTOR (1)	1004
Lew BROWN (1)	989
Buddy DeSYLVA (1)	989
Ray HENDERSON (1)	989
Ben RALEIGH (2)	880
N.J. CLESI (1)	872
Irving GORDON (1)	820
Connie FRANCIS (3)	747
Paul ANKA (1)	701
Eddie CURTIS (1)	631
Irving BERLIN (1)	617
Jenny Lou CARSON (1)	615
Gary KNIGHT (2)	568
Harold BARLOW (1)	539
Cesare BIXIO (1)	539
Phil BRITO (1)	539
Bixio CHERUBINI (1)	539
John GLUCK (1)	508
Mark BARKAN (1)	493
Robert MOSELY (1)	492
Jimmie STEWARD (1)	492
Stan VINCENT (2)	454
Michael CANOSA (1)	416
Danny STRADELLA (1)	416
Klaus OGERMAN (1)	372
Ernesto LECUONA (1)	281
Marjorie HARPER (1)	261
Vittorio MASCHERONI (1)	261
Peppino MENDES (1)	261
Tony HATCH (2)	249
Jeff BARRY (1)	221
Ellie GREENWICH (1)	221
Herbert KRETZMER (1)	212
David LEE (1)	212
Doc POMUS (1)	202
Mort SHUMAN (1)	202
Joy Byers JOHNSTON (1)	156
Clyde OTIS (1)	156
Charles AZNAVOUR (1)	146
Don BLACK (1)	146
Robert GALL (1)	146
Steve DUFFY (1)	142
Dickey LEE (1)	142
Joe BURKE (1)	101
Don STIRLING (1)	80
Norman NEWELL (2)	48
Riz ORTOLANI (1)	47
Katyna RANIERI (1)	47
Bradford BOOBIS (1)	38
Neil NEPHEW (1)	38
Fred FISHER (1)	30

Billy ROSE (1)	30
Carlo DONIDA (1)	26
Ervin DRAKE (1)	26
Giulio RAPETTI (1)	26
Ray ALLEN (2)	16
Wandra MERRELL (1)	14
Margaret LEWIS (1)	14
Mira SMITH (1)	14
Gisela GÜNTHER (1)	12
Sheldon HARNICK (1)	12
Steve KIRK (1)	12
Peter PAN (1)	12
Mickey GENTILE (1)	4.6
Jennie Lee LAMBERT (1)	4.6
Luigi DONADIO (1)	4.5
Hal GORDON (1)	2.1
Athena HOSEY (1)	2.1
George BROWN (1)	1.9
TOTO (1)	1.9
Percy FAITH (1)	1.6
Carl SIGMAN (1)	1.6
Steve DUBOFF (1)	1.1
Artie KORNFELD (1)	1.1
Eros SCIORILLI (1)	1.1
Al TESTA (1)	1.1
L. Russell BROWN (1)	0.4
Irwin LEVINE (1)	0.4
Moose CHARLAP (1)	0.4
Norman GIMBEL (1)	0.4
Cy COBEN (1)	0.0
Bill TEMPLETON (1)	0.0
Pat BOONE ►10 (74) [113]	**83753**
Charles SINGLETON (4)	7929
Ivory Joe HUNTER (1)	6595
Gary BRUCE (1)	5879
Paul Francis WEBSTER (4)	4505
Charles KENNY (3)	3823
Nick KENNY (3)	3823
Dave BARTHOLOMEW (1)	3483
Fats DOMINO (1)	3483
J. Fred COOTS (1)	3297
Sammy FAIN (2)	2892
Danny WOLFE (1)	1763
Deborah CHESSLER (1)	1737
Lee Roy ABERNATHY (1)	1725
Stanley J. LEWIS (1)	1503
Ferdinand WASHINGTON (1)	1503
Dimitri TIOMKIN (1)	1277
Luther DIXON (1)	1016
Larry HARRISON (1)	1016
Ewart ABNER (1)	975
John C. MOORE (1)	975
Bill GIANT (1)	918
David HESS (1)	918
Buddy KAYE (1)	918
Richard PENNIMAN (2)	885
Johnny MERCER (3)	879
Aaron SCHROEDER (3)	866
Winfield SCOTT (2)	831
Robert ALLEN (1)	775
Al STILLMAN (1)	775
Henry STONE (1)	743
Otis WILLIAMS (1)	743
Bernie LOWE (1)	628
Kal MANN (1)	628
Ernest TUBB (1)	591
Clara EDWARDS (1)	571
Jack LAWRENCE (1)	571
Art CRAFER (1)	526
Jimmy NEBB (1)	526
Fredda GOLD (1)	485
Dorothy LaBOSTRIE (1)	478

Joe LUBIN (1)	478
Pat BOONE (3)	468
Phil EVERLY (1)	442
Stanley KAHAN (2)	414
Robert BLACKWELL (1)	407
Enotris JOHNSON (1)	407
Ahmet ERTEGUN (1)	399
Van WALLS (1)	399
Robert MOSELY (1)	383
Alfred NEWMAN (1)	335
Wally GOLD (1)	323
Fay TISHMAN (1)	321
Cowboy COPAS (1)	321
Paul EVANS (1)	304
Fred TOBIAS (1)	304
Otis BLACKWELL (1)	304
Bobby STEVENSON (1)	304
Billy VAUGHN (2)	289
Isham JONES (1)	270
Gus KAHN (1)	270
Lillian GOODMAN (1)	268
Roy BROWN (1)	208
Leon RENE (1)	174
Henry GLOVER (1)	172
Carolyn LEIGH (1)	172
Lucky MILLINDER (1)	172
Billy BARTON (1)	130
Fuzzy OWEN (1)	130
Lewis TALLEY (1)	130
Blanche BROCK (1)	126
Virgil BROCK (1)	126
Eddy ARNOLD (1)	120
Wally FOWLER (1)	120
J. Graydon HALL (1)	120
Ernest GOLD (1)	95
Caperton HENLEY (1)	62
Bruce JOHNSTON (1)	60
Terry MELCHER (1)	60
J. Leslie McFARLAND (1)	58
Martin KALMANOFF (1)	51
Lenore ROSENBLATT (1)	51
Nick BOLDI (1)	47
Dick GLASSER (1)	47
Richard RODGERS (1)	38
Cliff ADAMS (1)	32
Neil DIAMOND (1)	32
Lockie EDWARDS (1)	32
Wes FARRELL (1)	32
Bob FELDMAN (1)	32
Jerry GOLDSTEIN (1)	32
Richard GOTTEHRER (1)	32
Eddie SNYDER (1)	32
Larry WEISS (1)	32
John STEWART (1)	26
TRADITIONAL (2)	18
Thomas A. DORSEY (1)	12
Lucie CAMPBELL (1)	12
Harold ADAMSON (1)	10
Jimmy McHUGH (1)	10
Johnny WOOD (1)	10
Wallace WILLIS (1)	5.8
Norman GIMBEL (1)	5.5
Antonio Carlos JOBIM (1)	5.5
Henry MAYER (1)	5.2
Claus RITTER (1)	5.2
Mitchell TOROK (1)	4.9
Jan CRUTCHFIELD (1)	2.7
Jessie CAVANAUGH (1)	2.6
Tony RENIS (1)	0.9
Al TESTA (1)	0.9
Helmy KRESA (1)	0.5
Carroll LOVEDAY (1)	0.5
Henry MANCINI (1)	0.0

BEACH BOYS ►11 (68) [40]	81829
Brian WILSON (48)	32795
Mike LOVE (34)	23673
Chuck BERRY (4)	4909
Fred FASSERT (2)	4642
TRADITIONAL (1)	3647
Roger CHRISTIAN (4)	1605
Bobby FREEMAN (1)	1224
Terry MELCHER (4)	1195
John PHILLIPS (2)	1003
Tony ASHER (2)	958
Carl WILSON (5)	930
Scott McKENZIE (1)	878
Van Dyke PARKS (3)	750
Clarence QUICK (1)	693
Gary USHER (3)	598
Ersel HICKEY (1)	362
Jeff BARRY (1)	305
Ellie GREENWICH (1)	305
Phil SPECTOR (1)	305
Murry WILSON (1)	184
Alan JARDINE (2)	125
Michelle PHILLIPS (1)	124
Dennis WILSON (1)	105
Joe KNOTT (1)	91
Jack RIELEY (3)	91
Tandyn ALMER (2)	63
Ray KENNEDY (2)	63
Jerry ALLISON (1)	44
Buddy HOLLY (1)	44
Norman PETTY (1)	44
Robert White JOHNSON (1)	16
Myrna SMITH-SCHILLING (1)	16
Doc POMUS (1)	12
Mort SHUMAN (1)	12
Huddie LEDBETTER (1)	6.1
George GOLDNER (1)	1.1
Morris LEVY (1)	1.1
Frankie LYMON (1)	1.1
Jimmy MERCHANT (1)	1.1
Herman SANTIAGO (1)	1.1

Michael JACKSON ►12 (28) [24]	81131
Michael JACKSON (11)	42906
Rod TEMPERTON (3)	10841
Leon RENÉ (1)	5891
Elliot WILLENSKY (1)	5083
Don BLACK (1)	2115
Walter SCHARF (1)	2115
Glen BALLARD (1)	2063
Siedah GARRETT (1)	2063
Tom BAHLER (1)	1740
Arthur ROSS (1)	814
Leon WARE (1)	814
John BETTIS (1)	762
Steve PORCARO (1)	762
James INGRAM (1)	581
Quincy JONES (1)	581
Brian HOLLAND (2)	488
Eddie HOLLAND (2)	488
Keni ST. LEWIS (1)	426
Vicki BASEMORE (1)	124
Henry COSBY (1)	124
Sylvia MOY (1)	124
Renée ARMAND (1)	90
Samuel F. BROWN III (1)	90
Charlie SMALLS (1)	46

Aretha FRANKLIN ►13 (75) [99]	79958
Aretha FRANKLIN (11)	11265
Otis REDDING (1)	8397
Ronnie SHANNON (3)	7252
Don COVAY (2)	6536
Paul SIMON (1)	4354
Ted WHITE (2)	2903
Jerry LEIBER (1)	2441
Phil SPECTOR (1)	2441
Narada Michael WALDEN (4)	2143
Simon CLIMIE (1)	1846
Dennis W. MORGAN (1)	1846
Jeffrey E. COHEN (2)	1572
Carolyn FRANKLIN (3)	1228
Robbie ROBERTSON (1)	1116
Morris BROADNAX (1)	1060
Clarence PAUL (1)	1060
Stevie WONDER (1)	1060
Bobby LANCE (1)	1025
Fran ROBINS (1)	1025
Bobby WOMACK (1)	998
Curtis MAYFIELD (4)	898
Ahmet ERTEGUN (1)	825
Betty NELSON (1)	825
Steve CROPPER (1)	802
Al BRAGGS (1)	793
Deadric MALONE (1)	793
Burt BACHARACH (1)	724
Hal DAVID (1)	724
Preston GLASS (3)	681
Gerry GOFFIN (1)	584
Carole KING (1)	584
Jerry WEXLER (1)	584
William Nelson SANDERS (1)	575
Nick ASHFORD (2)	552
Valerie SIMPSON (2)	552
Albert HAMMOND (2)	529
Diane WARREN (2)	529
John LENNON (1)	403
Paul McCARTNEY (1)	403
Marcus MILLER (2)	351
Luther VANDROSS (2)	351
Elton JOHN (1)	322
Bernie TAUPIN (1)	322
Giuseppe CANTARELLI (1)	317
Roy FREELAND (1)	317
Sam DEES (1)	299
Clyde OTIS (2)	291
Bernice HART (1)	271
Mick JAGGER (1)	264
Keith RICHARDS (1)	264
Sam LEWIS (1)	262
Jean SCHWARTZ (1)	262
Joe YOUNG (1)	262
Richard AHLERT (1)	168
Eddie SNYDER (1)	168
Ivy Jo HUNTER (1)	134
Sam COOKE (1)	126
Jim DORIS (1)	126
Lisa WALDEN (1)	110
Charles Henry JACKSON Jr. (2)	105
Phil PERRY (1)	103
John ALEXANDER (1)	80
David MATTIS (1)	80
Renaldo BENSON (1)	50
Al CLEVELAND (1)	50
Marvin GAYE (1)	50
John HARTFORD (1)	50
Jerry BUTLER (2)	41
Curtis Reginald LEWIS (1)	40
Kenneth GAMBLE (1)	38
Leon HUFF (1)	38
Willard PRICE (1)	37
Harry BARRIS (1)	31
Gordon CLIFFORD (1)	31
J. Leslie McFARLAND (2)	30
Warren MOORE (1)	27
Smokey ROBINSON (1)	27
Marvin TARPLIN (1)	27
Richard M. JONES (1)	24
Joe JOHNSON (1)	14
Charlie FOXX (1)	10
Inez FOXX (1)	10
Belford HENDRICKS (1)	6.9
Henry GLOVER (1)	6.0
Morris LEVY (1)	6.0
Titus TURNER (1)	6.0
Dinah WASHINGTON (1)	6.0
Marvin HAMLISCH (1)	4.6
Carole Bayer SAGER (1)	4.6
Marvin YANCY (1)	2.4
Saul BERNIE (1)	1.3
James P. JOHNSON (1)	1.3
Stella UNGER (1)	1.3
Joy Byers JOHNSTON (1)	0.5
Jimmy CAMPBELL (1)	0.1
Reg CONNELLY (1)	0.1
Harry WOODS (1)	0.1
John HURLEY (1)	0.0
Ronnie WILKINS (1)	0.0

Bobby VINTON ►14 (49) [87]	74613
Bobby VINTON (7)	8506
Gene ALLAN (4)	5438
Al BYRON (1)	5344
Paul EVANS (1)	5344
Redd EVANS (1)	4379
Dave MANN (1)	4379
Lee MORRIS (1)	4377
Bernie WAYNE (1)	4377
Burt BACHARACH (2)	2163
Hal DAVID (2)	2163
Larry KOLBER (1)	1818
Barry MANN (1)	1818
Henry MAYER (1)	1742
Ollie BLANCHARD (1)	1639
Johnnie MALONE (1)	1639
Dorothy DANIELS (1)	940
Frank DANIELS (1)	940
Rex GARVIN (1)	858
Gerry GOFFIN (2)	813
Carole KING (2)	813
Gary GELD (1)	727
Peter UDELL (1)	727
Al ALBERTS (1)	715
Marty GOLD (1)	715
Phil SPECTOR (1)	685
Jimmie CRANE (1)	629
Al JACOBS (1)	629
Noel REGNEY (1)	567
Gloria SHAYNE (1)	567
Sonny JAMES (1)	492
Bob TUBERT (1)	492
Larry COLEMAN (1)	483
Charles SINGLETON (1)	483
Marge BARTON (1)	462
Leon CARR (1)	379
Grace LANE (1)	379
Earl SHUMAN (1)	379
Van McCOY (1)	324
Jerry RAGOVOY (1)	324
Doyle MARSH (1)	297
Bud RENEAU (1)	297
Billy SHERRILL (2)	277
Curly PUTMAN (1)	274
John GLUCK (1)	273
Neval NADER (1)	273
Lee ANDREWS (1)	255
Bernice DAVIS (1)	255
Douglas HENDERSON (1)	255
Miriam UNIMAN (1)	255
Merle KILGORE (1)	233
Margie SINGLETON (1)	233
Ray STEVENS (1)	223
Frank CAPANO (1)	191
Billy UHR (1)	191
Lew BROWN (1)	110
Wladimir TIMM (1)	110
Jaromir VEJVODA (1)	110
Art CRAFER (1)	92
Jimmy NEBB (1)	92
Ray EVANS (1)	66
Neal HEFTI (1)	66
Jay LIVINGSTON (1)	66
Doc POMUS (1)	57
Mort SHUMAN (1)	57
Paul GAYTEN (1)	43
Robert GUIDRY (1)	43
Bob MORRISON (1)	34
Johnny WILSON (1)	34
Bert KAEMPFERT (1)	27
Kay TWOMEY (1)	27
Ben WEISMAN (1)	27
Fred WISE (1)	27
Jack FISHMAN (1)	11
Joseph Turner HENDERSON (1)	11
Ron DANTE (1)	11
Eddy HOWARD (1)	8.4
Dick JURGENS (1)	8.4
Lew QUADLING (1)	8.4
Dewayne BLACKWELL (1)	8.3
Tony HILLER (1)	7.3
Martin LEE (1)	7.3
Lee SHERIDEN (1)	7.3
Stephen Allen DAVIS (1)	2.5
Edilio CAPOTOSTI (1)	2.2
Antoniette DESIMONE (1)	2.2
Glenn MILLER (1)	1.0
Mitchell PARISH (1)	1.0

The TEMPTATIONS ►15 (53) [39]	74292
Norman WHITFIELD (31)	28722
Barrett STRONG (17)	19573
Smokey ROBINSON (8)	6527
Eddie HOLLAND (8)	5003
Rodger PENZABENE (3)	3081
Ronnie WHITE (2)	3072
Cornelius GRANT (2)	1502
Warren MOORE (3)	1362
Robert ROGERS (2)	1234
R. Dean TAYLOR (1)	639
Frank Edward WILSON (1)	639
Jeff BOWEN (3)	399
Alphonso BOYD (1)	265
Eddie HAZEL (1)	265
Mark HOLDEN (1)	241
Berry GORDY (2)	202
Otis Clayburne WILLIAMS (1)	179
Ollie WOODSON (1)	179
Angelo BOND (2)	153
Rick JAMES (1)	125
Donald BALDWIN (1)	125
Lionel RICHIE (1)	125
James CARMICHAEL (1)	125
Ronald Norman MILLER (1)	125
Kathy WAKEFIELD (1)	125
Jean MAYER (1)	77
Brian HOLLAND (1)	75
Joseph JEFFERSON (1)	28
Rich ROEBUCK (1)	28
Charles SIMMONS (1)	28
Dino FEKARIS (1)	19

The TEMPTATIONS ►15 (53) [39] *Cont'd*	**74292**
Nick ZESSES (1)	19
Jim FORD (1)	8.9
Truman THOMAS (1)	8.9
Peter BECKETT (1)	6.7
Dennis LAMBERT (1)	6.7
George GORDY (1)	1.2
Margaret JOHNSON (1)	1.2
Allen STORY (1)	1.2
EVERLY BROTHERS ►16 (45) [44]	**72261**
Boudleaux BRYANT (13)	28509
Don EVERLY (9)	11973
Felice BRYANT (8)	10291
Phil EVERLY (5)	6571
John D. LOUDERMILK (1)	2520
Sonny CURTIS (1)	2037
Howard GREENFIELD (1)	1201
Carole KING (1)	1201
Gilbert BECAUD (1)	732
Mann CURTIS (1)	732
Pierre DELANOË (1)	732
Ray CHARLES (1)	445
Bernie BAUM (1)	401
Bill GIANT (1)	401
Florence KAYE (1)	401
Nacio Herb BROWN (1)	385
Arthur FREED (1)	385
Dorothy FIELDS (1)	351
Jimmy McHUGH (1)	351
Albert COLLINS (1)	298
Richard PENNIMAN (1)	298
Roy ORBISON (1)	287
Paul McCARTNEY (1)	269
Mel TILLIS (1)	259
Gerry GOFFIN (3)	215
Jack KELLER (3)	215
Jacqueline ERTEL (1)	200
Terry SLATER (1)	200
Karl DAVIS (1)	64
Harty TAYLOR (1)	64
Dewayne BLACKWELL (1)	56
Ronald BLACKWELL (1)	56
William DOUCHETTE (1)	25
Gene VINCENT (1)	25
Tex ANN (1)	24
Harold G. HENSLEY (1)	24
TRADITIONAL (1)	24
Merle TRAVIS (1)	24
Jerry ALLISON (1)	1.7
Buddy HOLLY (1)	1.7
Norman PETTY (1)	1.7
Mickey BAKER (1)	1.1
Ellas McDANIEL (1)	1.1
Sylvia ROBINSON (1)	1.1
MADONNA ►17 (24) [21]	**71397**
Madonna L. CICCONE (18)	25096
Patrick Raymond LEONARD (7)	9312
Stephen BRAY (5)	5894
Thomas F. KELLY (1)	3188
Billy STEINBERG (1)	3188
Shep PETTIBONE (2)	2914
John BETTIS (1)	2608
Jon LIND (1)	2608
Brian ELLIOT (1)	2121
Reggie LUCAS (1)	1870
Peter H. BROWN (1)	1771
Robert RANS (1)	1771
Gardner COLE (1)	1425
Peter RAFELSON (1)	1425
Ingrid CHAVEZ (1)	1298

Lenny KRAVITZ (1)	1298
Andrea LaRUSSO (1)	801
Peggy STANZIALE (1)	801
Bruce GAITSCH (1)	743
Curtis HUDSON (1)	632
Lisa STEVENS (1)	632
CHICAGO ►18 (49) [28]	**70829**
Peter CETERA (13)	16980
Robert LAMM (12)	14885
James PANKOW (9)	12336
David FOSTER (5)	6647
Diane WARREN (3)	5718
Steve KIPNER (3)	2280
Lee LOUGHNANE (2)	1805
John Lewis PARKER (1)	1796
James SCOTT (1)	1219
Albert HAMMOND (1)	1131
Richard BASKIN (1)	947
Tom KEANE (1)	947
Danny SERAPHINE (5)	864
Jason SCHEFF (2)	683
Bobby CALDWELL (2)	548
Chas SANDFORD (1)	544
Randy GOODRUM (1)	479
Mark GOLDENBERG (1)	453
David WOLINSKI (2)	174
John DEXTER (1)	140
Donnie DACUS (1)	44
Jimmy MILLER (1)	39
Steve WINWOOD (1)	39
Bill CHAMPLIN (1)	34
Kevin DUKES (1)	34
Dennis MATKOSKY (1)	34
Jay GRUSKA (1)	14
Joseph Amos WILLIAMS (1)	14
Brenda LEE ►19 (60) [75]	**69470**
Ronnie SELF (7)	11004
Dub ALLBRITTEN (6)	6581
Kathryn FULTON (1)	4110
Jackie DeSHANNON (5)	3171
Kim GANNON (1)	3142
Giuseppe SPOTTI (1)	3142
Arthur ALTMAN (2)	2843
Sharon SHEELEY (4)	2752
Manos HADJIDAKIS (1)	2752
Alex ZANETIS (1)	1975
Jerry REED (2)	1909
Diane LAMPERT (1)	1724
Joe SENECA (1)	1724
David WILKINS (1)	1606
Harlan HOWARD (1)	1517
Ramsey KEARNEY (1)	1497
Mel TILLIS (1)	1497
Jean RENARD (1)	1236
Carl SIGMAN (1)	1236
Charles CARPENTER (1)	978
Louis DUNLAP (1)	978
Earl HINES (1)	978
Peggy WHITTINGTON (1)	902
Johnny MARKS (3)	677
Jack KELLER (2)	611
John CARTER (1)	559
Ken HAWKER (1)	559
Mike ANTHONY (1)	449
Barry MANN (1)	449
Liz ANDERSON (1)	449
Richard AHLERT (2)	415
Rick HALL (1)	376
Dallas FRAZIER (1)	368
A.L. "Doodle" OWENS (1)	368
Cecil GANT (1)	359
Raymond LEVEEN (1)	359
Eddie SNYDER (1)	357

Howard GREENFIELD (1)	338
Hugh ASHLEY (1)	335
Bill ANDERSON (1)	311
Jerry CRUTCHFIELD (1)	311
Gerry GOFFIN (1)	273
Eddie MILLER (1)	238
Don SESSIONS (1)	238
Joy Byers JOHNSTON (1)	198
Bob TUBERT (1)	198
Betty CHOTAS (1)	169
Gerald NELSON (1)	142
Chuck TAYLOR (1)	142
Dalibor BASLER (1)	91
Al STILLMAN (1)	91
David GATES (1)	82
Hank WILLIAMS (1)	76
Kris KRISTOFFERSON (1)	62
Leon CARR (1)	59
Louis INNIS (1)	55
Grady MARTIN (1)	55
Dorsey BURNETTE (1)	53
Joe OSBORN (1)	53
Hughie CANNON (1)	46
Mort GARSON (1)	45
Tom GLAZER (1)	45
David Paul BRIGGS (1)	29
Dan PENN (1)	29
Geoff STEPHENS (1)	25
Irwin LEVINE (1)	20
Toni WINE (1)	20
Buzz CASON (1)	14
George JONES (1)	3.7
Leon PAYNE (1)	3.7
Marvin HAMLISCH (1)	2.6
Howard LIEBLING (1)	2.6
Doc POMUS (1)	2.1
Mort SHUMAN (1)	2.1
Jim SEALS (1)	0.4
Daryl HALL & John OATES ►20 (35) [25]	**69175**
Daryl HALL (28)	35256
John OATES (15)	13103
Sara ALLEN (10)	8684
Janna ALLEN (4)	5294
Warren PASH (1)	1577
Barry MANN (1)	613
Phil SPECTOR (1)	613
Cynthia WEIL (1)	613
Smokey ROBINSON (2)	285
Tim CROSS (1)	274
Richard FENN (1)	274
Mike FRYE (1)	274
Mike OLDFIELD (1)	274
Morris PERT (1)	274
Maggie REILLY (1)	274
Jon BON JOVI (1)	200
Rick GILES (1)	200
George GREEN (1)	200
Danny KORTCHMAR (1)	200
Robert ROGERS (1)	142
Ronnie WHITE (1)	142
Gerald O'BRIEN (1)	110
Richard PAGE (1)	110
David TYSON (1)	110
Rick IANTOSCA (1)	81
Chubby CHECKER ►21 (33) [32]	**66649**
Hank BALLARD (2)	22920
Kal MANN (17)	16368
Dave APPELL (11)	6382
Billy STRANGE (1)	4501
John Bobby BERRY (1)	4166

Don COVAY (1)	4166
John MADARA (2)	1360
David WHITE (2)	1360
Andy GIBSON (2)	812
Roy ALFRED (1)	747
Chubby CHECKER (1)	584
Judy HENSKE (1)	584
Dave WILLIAMS (1)	484
Bernie LOWE (1)	464
Huey P. SMITH (1)	359
John VINCENT (1)	359
Doc POMUS (1)	237
Tommy BOYCE (1)	137
Roberta HARRIS (1)	137
Bobby HART (1)	137
James BROWN (1)	65
Len BARRY (1)	47
Leon HUFF (1)	47
Sherman ROTHMAN (1)	44
Robyn SUPRANER (1)	44
Joe RUSSO (1)	37
John LENNON (1)	35
Paul McCARTNEY (1)	35
Bill BROCK (1)	13
Sebastian YRADIER (1)	11
William E. JACKSON III (1)	4.8
Jimmy WISNER (1)	4.8
Rod STEWART ►22 (43) [48]	**65700**
Rod STEWART (21)	23510
Duane HITCHINGS (4)	4669
Tim HARDIN (1)	4300
Carmine APPICE (2)	3597
Martin QUITTENTON (2)	3158
Tom WAITS (1)	2806
Kevin SAVIGAR (6)	1951
John CAPEK (1)	1511
Marc JORDAN (1)	1511
Jim CREGAN (5)	1502
Robbie ROBERTSON (1)	1352
Larry John McNALLY (1)	1268
Gary GRAINGER (4)	1267
Simon CLIMIE (1)	1213
Dennis W. MORGAN (1)	1213
Jeff FORTGANG (1)	1026
Cat STEVENS (1)	718
Roland ROBINSON (1)	688
Jay DAVIS (2)	666
Eddie HOLLAND (3)	609
Gene BLACK (1)	591
Mike CHAPMAN (1)	591
Holly KNIGHT (1)	591
Phil CHEN (2)	557
Andy TAYLOR (1)	479
Sam COOKE (2)	394
Michael D'ABO (1)	393
Jimi HENDRIX (1)	362
Cornelius GRANT (1)	314
Norman WHITFIELD (1)	314
Danny WHITTEN (1)	297
Lamont DOZIER (2)	295
Brian HOLLAND (2)	295
Sylvia MOY (2)	295
Bob DYLAN (1)	280
Gavin SUTHERLAND (1)	272
Paul CARRACK (1)	203
Tony BROCK (1)	149
Gerry GOFFIN (1)	99
Carole KING (1)	99
Bryan ADAMS (1)	65
Jim VALLANCE (1)	65
Randy WAYNE (1)	65
Andy FRASER (1)	44

Rod STEWART ▶22 (43) [48] *Cont'd*	**65700**
Paul RODGERS (1)	44
Steve HARLEY (1)	7.4
Linda McCARTNEY (1)	3.1
Paul McCARTNEY (1)	3.1
Neil DIAMOND ▶23 (55) [15]	**65663**
Neil DIAMOND (50)	56976
Gilbert BECAUD (2)	3014
Carole Bayer SAGER (4)	1026
Alan LINDGREN (2)	940
Burt BACHARACH (3)	796
Bob RUSSELL (1)	556
Bobby SCOTT (1)	556
Richard Winchell BENNETT (1)	460
Buffy SAINTE-MARIE (1)	324
David FOSTER (1)	245
Tom PAXTON (1)	242
Frank GUIDA (1)	192
Joseph ROYSTER (1)	192
Tom HENSLEY (1)	87
Richard FAGAN (1)	57
Marvin GAYE ▶24 (37) [33]	**64874**
Marvin GAYE (16)	20400
Norman WHITFIELD (7)	7559
Barrett STRONG (6)	6931
Ed TOWNSEND (1)	3654
Eddie HOLLAND (7)	2426
Lamont DOZIER (6)	2290
Brian HOLLAND (6)	2290
Renaldo BENSON (1)	1738
Al CLEVELAND (1)	1738
Warren MOORE (4)	1569
Smokey ROBINSON (4)	1569
Marvin TARPLIN (4)	1569
Odell BROWN (1)	1308
David RITZ (1)	1308
Berry GORDY (1)	1211
Janie BRADFORD (1)	1057
William STEVENSON (4)	1040
James NYX (1)	838
Robert ROGERS (2)	699
Frank Edward WILSON (1)	611
Leon WARE (2)	510
Arthur ROSS (1)	492
Clarence PAUL (2)	435
Dave HAMILTON (1)	248
George GORDY (1)	198
Kenny STOVER (1)	186
Rodger PENZABENE (1)	168
Gwen GORDY (1)	146
Sandra GREENE (1)	146
Jeff BOWEN (1)	136
Jack GOGA (1)	136
Ivy Jo HUNTER (1)	136
Ronnie WHITE (1)	132
Paul ANKA ▶25 (66) [46]	**64651**
Paul ANKA (46)	50889
Alberto CURCI (1)	4567
Henri HERPIN (1)	944
Harold ROME (1)	944
Bill LANE (1)	791
Roger NICHOLS (1)	791
Oscar HAMMERSTEIN (1)	486
Richard RODGERS (1)	486
John MARASCALCO (1)	406
George MOTOLA (1)	406
Joe SHERMAN (1)	384
Noel SHERMAN (1)	384
David FOSTER (1)	238

Fred PARRIS (1)	233
Leonard WHITCUP (1)	224
Earl WILSON (1)	224
Jimmy HENDERSON (1)	198
Sid ROBIN (1)	198
Bertha SCOTT (1)	198
Lya ROBERTS (1)	192
Gloria VAN CLEVE (1)	166
Bob WILSON (1)	166
Madeline SUNSHINE (1)	141
Robert TEPPER (1)	141
Johnny HARRIS (1)	124
Tony ROMEO (1)	91
Yves-Jacques LAVOT (1)	89
Alain Le GOVIC (1)	89
Michel PELAY (1)	89
Maxime PIOLOT (1)	89
Linda J. KIMBALL (1)	75
Mark SHERRILL (1)	75
Alan FREED (1)	43
Harvey FUQUA (1)	43
Howard GREENFIELD (1)	20
Burt BACHARACH (1)	5.6
Hal DAVID (1)	5.6
Mack DAVID (1)	3.1
Harry SUKMAN (1)	3.1
Douglas McCORMICK (1)	2.7
Eddie SNYDER (1)	2.7
Paul VANCE (1)	2.7
Churchill KOHLMAN (1)	0.4
Alan O'DAY (1)	0.2
Artie WAYNE (1)	0.2
Johnny MARKS (1)	0.0
CARPENTERS ▶26 (29) [50]	**64065**
Richard CARPENTER (7)	7050
John BETTIS (6)	7022
Roger NICHOLS (3)	6960
Paul WILLIAMS (3)	6960
Burt BACHARACH (1)	3810
Hal DAVID (1)	3810
Joe RAPOSO (1)	3378
Gary GELD (1)	2447
Peter UDELL (1)	2447
Bonnie BRAMLETT (1)	2008
Delaney BRAMLETT (1)	2008
Leon RUSSELL (1)	2008
James GRIFFIN (1)	1151
Fred KARLIN (1)	1151
Robb ROYER (1)	1151
Robert BATEMAN (1)	900
Georgia DOBBINS (1)	900
William GARRETT (1)	900
Freddie GORMAN (1)	900
Brian HOLLAND (1)	900
Les REED (1)	603
Geoff STEPHENS (1)	603
Carole KING (1)	560
Toni STERN (1)	560
Phil CODY (1)	406
Neil SEDAKA (1)	406
Terry DRAPER (1)	330
John WOLOSCHUK (1)	330
Steve EATON (1)	320
Kenneth Edward BELL (1)	298
Terry SKINNER (1)	298
J.L. WALLACE (1)	298
Juice NEWTON (1)	215
Otha YOUNG (1)	215
Albert HAMMOND (1)	211
John LENNON (1)	98
Paul McCARTNEY (1)	98
Dick ADDRISI (1)	50

Don ADDRISI (1)	50
Kerry CHATER (1)	36
Chris CHRISTIAN (1)	36
Frank POOLER (1)	28
William HAROLD (1)	22
Gus KAHN (1)	22
Wayne KING (1)	22
Perry BOTKIN Jr. (1)	19
Barry De VORZON (1)	19
Marvin GAYE (1)	17
George GORDY (1)	17
William STEVENSON (1)	17
THREE DOG NIGHT ▶27 (22) [30]	**63711**
Hoyt AXTON (2)	14025
Randy NEWMAN (1)	7392
Harry NILSSON (1)	5700
Paul WILLIAMS (3)	4677
Daniel MOORE (1)	4476
Laura NYRO (1)	2845
David ARKIN (1)	2241
Earl ROBINSON (1)	2241
Russ BALLARD (1)	2036
Galt MacDERMOT (1)	1795
James RADO (1)	1795
Gerome RAGNI (1)	1795
David COURTNEY (1)	1742
Leo SAYER (1)	1742
Dave LOGGINS (2)	1549
John FINLEY (1)	952
John HIATT (1)	764
Garry BONNER (1)	748
Alan GORDON (1)	748
Allen TOUSSAINT (1)	712
Jack CONRAD (1)	707
Roger NICHOLS (1)	695
Billy FOX (1)	466
Tommy KAYE (1)	466
January TYME (1)	466
Jimmy CAMPBELL (1)	268
Reg CONNELLY (1)	268
Harry WOODS (1)	268
Dick COOPER (1)	66
Ernie SHELBY (1)	66
JACKSON 5 ▶28 (24) [29]	**63301**
Berry GORDY (9)	10325
Freddie PERREN (8)	8010
Fonce MIZELL (7)	7719
Deke RICHARDS (7)	7719
Clifton DAVIS (2)	7548
Hal DAVIS (3)	4173
Willie HUTCH (1)	2460
Bob WEST (1)	2460
Bobby DAY (1)	1791
Donald FLETCHER (2)	1713
Kenneth GAMBLE (3)	1647
Leon HUFF (3)	1647
Dean PARKS (1)	1567
Stephen SCHWARTZ (1)	1050
Michael JACKSON (1)	803
Mel LARSON (3)	567
Jerry MARCELLINO (3)	567
Christine YARIAN (1)	291
Don FENCETON (1)	266
Rod RANCIFER (1)	266
Gene MARCELLINO (1)	155
Lamont DOZIER (1)	102
Brian HOLLAND (1)	102
Eddie HOLLAND (1)	102
Dave JACKSON (1)	72
Mick JACKSON (1)	72
Elmar KROHN (1)	72
J. Fred COOTS (1)	18

Haven GILLESPIE (1)	18
Ray CHARLES ▶29 (78) [95]	**62768**
Don GIBSON (1)	11133
Percy MAYFIELD (5)	8062
Harlan HOWARD (1)	4303
Ray CHARLES (13)	3676
Buck OWENS (2)	3262
Hoagy CARMICHAEL (1)	2071
Stuart GORRELL (1)	2071
Oliver HOOD (1)	2038
Rudy TOOMBS (1)	2026
Eddy ARNOLD (1)	1689
Cindy WALKER (1)	1689
Teddy POWELL (2)	1309
Bobby SHARP (2)	1309
Jimmy HOLIDAY (5)	933
Hy HEATH (1)	931
Fred ROSE (1)	931
John LENNON (2)	735
Paul McCARTNEY (2)	735
Donnie LANIER (1)	726
Russell STEAGALL (1)	726
James E. LEWIS (2)	724
Ted DAFFAN (2)	561
Danny SMALL (1)	496
Hank WILLIAMS (1)	492
Hank SNOW (1)	492
Titus TURNER (1)	484
Haven GILLESPIE (1)	475
Beasley SMITH (1)	475
Mitchell PARISH (1)	390
Heinz ROEMHELD (1)	390
Woodrow Buddy JOHNSON (1)	390
Eddie REEVES (1)	376
Doc POMUS (2)	347
Mort SHUMAN (2)	347
Jo ARMSTEAD (2)	316
Nick ASHFORD (2)	316
Valerie SIMPSON (2)	316
Morty CRAFT (1)	289
Jesse STONE (1)	264
Walter DONALDSON (1)	234
Gus KAHN (1)	234
Melanie SAFKA (1)	232
Ricci HARPER (1)	186
Percy FAITH (1)	184
Carl SIGMAN (1)	184
Dee ERVIN (2)	181
Churchill KOHLMAN (1)	172
Alan BERGMAN (1)	165
Marilyn BERGMAN (1)	165
Quincy JONES (1)	165
Dorian BURTON (1)	164
Eugene RANDOLPH (1)	164
Bobby STEVENSON (1)	161
Roy ALFRED (1)	158
Art HARRIS (1)	158
Fred JAY (1)	158
Sid ROBIN (1)	103
Foy WILLING (1)	103
James E. JOHNSON (1)	95
Leslie TEMPLE (1)	95
Stephen FOSTER (1)	89
Harold ARLEN (2)	81
Johnny MERCER (2)	81
Boudleaux BRYANT (1)	78
Felice BRYANT (1)	78
Roy JACOBS (1)	58
William WELDON (1)	58
Stevie WONDER (1)	50
Jimmy WORK (1)	49
Milton AGER (1)	45

Ray CHARLES ►29 (78) [95] ***Cont'd***	62768
Charles BATES (1)	45
Bob BIGELOW (1)	45
Jack YELLEN (1)	45
Lorenz HART (1)	38
Richard RODGERS (1)	38
Renald RICHARD (1)	28
Ruth ROBINSON (1)	20
Fred Aylor MacRAE (1)	13
Sam COOKE (1)	12
Fleecie MOORE (1)	10
Sam THEARD (1)	10
Dallas BARTLEY (1)	7.5
Leo HICKMAN (1)	7.5
Louis JORDAN (1)	7.5
Glen GARRISON (1)	4.0
Charlie WILLIAMS (1)	4.0
Joseph Perkins GREENE (1)	3.3
Barry De VORZON (1)	2.3
Robert SHERMAN (1)	2.3
Billy ECKSTINE (1)	1.5
Harry AKST (1)	1.4
Grant CLARKE (1)	1.4
Nappy BROWN (1)	0.8
James B. ODEN (1)	0.8
Roosevelt SYKES (1)	0.8
Paul McCARTNEY & WINGS/WINGS ►30 (26) [3]	62296
Paul McCARTNEY (26)	39538
Linda McCARTNEY (16)	22381
Denny LAINE (3)	377
Rick NELSON ►31 (52) [54]	61768
Jerry FULLER (5)	14521
Baker KNIGHT (9)	11799
Sharon SHEELEY (1)	5441
Dorsey BURNETTE (4)	3222
Pearl LENDHURST (1)	2445
Johnny BURNETTE (3)	2240
Jack LEWIS (1)	1936
David GILLAM (1)	1450
Gene PITNEY (2)	1366
Cayet MANGIARACINA (1)	1236
Joe BURKE (1)	1083
Al DUBIN (1)	1083
Dave BURGESS (1)	1067
Dub DICKERSON (1)	986
Erma HERROLD (1)	986
Rube BLOOM (1)	955
Johnny MERCER (1)	955
Mack DAVID (1)	792
Jerry LIVINGSTON (1)	792
Ray NOBLE (1)	738
Felice BRYANT (1)	582
Dave BARTHOLOMEW (2)	564
Fats DOMINO (2)	564
Clarence WILLIAMS (1)	557
Bobby DOYLE (1)	493
Jimmy DUNCAN (1)	493
Scott WISEMAN (1)	433
Nicollet TADY (1)	388
Rick NELSON (2)	334
Barney KESSEL (1)	318
Jack MARSHALL (1)	318
Walter DONALDSON (1)	233
Gus KAHN (1)	233
Ray CHARLES (1)	180
Renald RICHARD (1)	180
Christian SARREL (1)	133
Al STILLMAN (1)	133

Aaron SCHROEDER (1)	131
Alan BRANDT (1)	96
Bob HAYMES (1)	96
Joe OSBORN (1)	62
Larry KUSIK (1)	40
Kenny RANKIN (1)	40
Kokomo ARNOLD (1)	27
Billy VERA (1)	16
Al JONES (1)	7.1
Bill JONES (1)	7.1
Merle KILGORE (1)	7.1
George GERSHWIN (1)	2.6
Ira GERSHWIN (1)	2.6
DuBose HEYWARD (1)	2.6
Gerry GOFFIN (1)	2.5
Carole KING (1)	2.5
Willie JACOBS (1)	0.5
Olivia NEWTON-JOHN ►32 (31) [29]	61440
John FARRAR (11)	22741
Steve KIPNER (3)	8928
John ROSTILL (3)	7374
Terry SHADDICK (1)	5596
Peter ALLEN (2)	2682
Jeff BARRY (2)	2682
Paul Steven BLISS (1)	1945
Bruce WELCH (1)	1929
Tom SNOW (3)	1782
Peter BECKETT (1)	1386
Bob DYLAN (1)	1107
Mark GOLDENBERG (1)	695
Johnny VASTANO (1)	409
Barry GIBB (1)	325
Robin GIBB (1)	325
Linda Ann HARGROVE (1)	277
Don BLACK (2)	258
Barry ALFONSO (1)	220
Hank MARVIN (1)	213
Lee RITENOUR (1)	172
Bob RUSSELL (1)	71
Bobby SCOTT (1)	71
Elton JOHN (1)	48
Bernie TAUPIN (1)	48
Michael ALLISON (1)	46
Peter SILLS (1)	46
TRADITIONAL (1)	39
Pete WINGFIELD (1)	14
Adam MITCHELL (1)	11
Donna SUMMER ►33 (32) [36]	60825
Donna SUMMER (19)	16483
Giorgio MORODER (11)	7345
Pete BELLOTTE (13)	6807
Jimmy WEBB (1)	6578
Paul JABARA (1)	3589
Harold FALTERMEYER (3)	3159
Keith FORSEY (2)	2983
Michael OMARTIAN (4)	2324
Bruce SUDANO (2)	1982
Joe ESPOSITO (1)	1956
Eddie HOKENSON (1)	1956
Greg MATHIESON (1)	757
Quincy JONES (1)	485
Merria ROSS (1)	485
Rod TEMPERTON (1)	485
Matt AITKEN (2)	400
Mike STOCK (2)	400
Pete WATERMAN (2)	400
John BETTIS (1)	334
Michael CLARK (1)	334
Brenda RUSSELL (1)	257
Jon ANDERSON (1)	160

VANGELIS (1)	160
Ben E. KING (1)	135
Jerry LEIBER (1)	135
Lover PATTERSON (1)	135
Mike STOLLER (1)	135
George TREADWELL (1)	135
Sylvester LEVAY (1)	104
Jerry RIX (1)	104
Adrienne ANDERSON (1)	51
Barry MANILOW (1)	51
Keith DIAMOND (1)	6.3
Larry HENLEY (1)	6.3
Eve NELSON (1)	6.3
Anthony L. SMITH (1)	6.3
The PLATTERS ►34 (45) [53]	60672
Buck RAM (21)	22329
Jimmy KENNEDY (3)	5664
Otto HARBACH (1)	5334
Jerome KERN (1)	5334
Georges BOULANGER (1)	4101
Artie DUNN (1)	1663
Al NEVINS (1)	1663
Morty NEVINS (1)	1663
Hugh WILLIAMS (2)	1563
Robert MELLIN (1)	986
Luther DIXON (2)	835
Paul ROBI (2)	706
Tony WILLIAMS (2)	704
Ruth LOWE (1)	630
Ray EVANS (1)	617
Jay LIVINGSTON (1)	617
Tony HESTER (2)	572
Richard WYLIE (2)	572
Jack LAWRENCE (2)	514
Inez FOXX (1)	429
Claude BAUM (1)	398
Peter TINTURIN (1)	340
William WHITE (1)	340
Jim WILLIAMS (1)	319
Al FRISCH (1)	318
Sid WAYNE (1)	318
Mickey ADDY (1)	312
Zola TAYLOR (2)	261
Tito MADI (2)	198
Pyotr Ilyich TCHAIKOVSKY (1)	182
Robert MAXWELL (1)	178
Carl SIGMAN (1)	178
Joyce KILMER (1)	112
Oscar RASBACH (1)	112
Ralph BAILEY (1)	80
Vernon HARRELL (1)	80
Cy CRANE (2)	65
Herb WEINER (2)	65
Jonathan SMALL (1)	62
Ralph YATES (1)	62
George GOEHRING (1)	35
Gerald Frederick GRANT (1)	35
Joseph S. LEWIS (1)	32
William WHEELER (1)	32
Eric COATES (1)	19
Sammy CAHN (1)	11
Jule STYNE (1)	11
Terry SYMMS (1)	6.6
Stanley J. LEWIS (1)	5.2
Ferdinand WASHINGTON (1)	5.2
Edward ELISCU (1)	1.1
Billy ROSE (1)	1.1
Vincent YOUMANS (1)	1.1
Bobby DARIN ►35 (43) [48]	55520
Bobby DARIN (16)	18524

Marc BLITZSTEIN (1)	4896
Berthold BRECHT (1)	4896
Kurt WEILL (1)	4896
Tim HARDIN (2)	2481
Woody HARRIS (1)	2086
Murray KAUFMAN (1)	1480
Jean MURRAY (1)	1480
Johnny MERCER (1)	1182
Harry WARREN (1)	1182
Hughie CANNON (1)	1030
Albert LASRY (1)	855
Jack LAWRENCE (1)	855
Charles TRENET (1)	855
Sidney ARODIN (1)	623
Hoagy CARMICHAEL (1)	623
Ray CHARLES (1)	618
Luther DIXON (1)	588
Al KASHA (1)	588
Jerry BOCK (1)	577
Sheldon HARNICK (1)	577
Eden AHBEZ (1)	569
John SEBASTIAN (2)	524
Jerry HERMAN (2)	326
TRADITIONAL (2)	298
Barker BRADFORD (1)	259
Percy MONTROSE (1)	259
H.S. THOMPSON (1)	259
Doc POMUS (1)	246
Mort SHUMAN (1)	246
Marguerite MONNOT (1)	236
Giuseppe MUSTACCHI (1)	236
Geoffrey STEVENS (1)	223
Harry AKST (1)	188
Benny DAVIS (1)	188
Michel LEGRAND (1)	141
Smokey ROBINSON (1)	141
Mann CURTIS (1)	93
Francis Philip MILITARY (1)	93
Frank ADAMS (1)	30
Will HOUGH (1)	30
Joe HOWARD (1)	30
Jack PALMER (1)	2.5
Spencer WILLIAMS (1)	2.5
Charles AZNAVOUR (1)	2.4
Françoise DORIN (1)	2.4
Gene LEES (1)	2.4
Don KIRSHNER (1)	1.2
James BROWN ►36 (97) [48]	55264
James BROWN (74)	35384
Alfred James ELLIS (6)	3970
Charles BOBBIT (7)	2073
Fred WESLEY (5)	1607
Bobby BYRD (8)	1459
Betty Jean NEWSOME (1)	1396
Nat JONES (8)	1109
Dan HARTMAN (2)	999
Charles E. KAUFMAN (2)	999
Bud HOBGOOD (4)	711
Jimmy FORREST (1)	656
Joe MIMS (1)	535
Ron LENHOFF (3)	492
John STARKS (2)	391
Russ COLUMBO (1)	329
Clarence GASKILL (1)	329
Leo ROBIN (1)	329
David MATTHEWS (2)	322
Lowman PAULING (3)	232
Jerry LEIBER (1)	150
Mike STOLLER (1)	150
Lloyd STALLWORTH (2)	141
Billy WARD (2)	133
Manny ROSEN (1)	133

James BROWN ▶36 (97) [48] *Cont'd*	55264
Bodie CHANDLER (1)	117
Barry De VORZON (1)	117
Hayward MOORE (1)	114
Deanna BROWN (2)	100
Deidra BROWN (2)	100
Yamma BROWN (2)	100
Teddy POWELL (1)	94
Leonard WHITCUP (1)	94
Harry LINK (1)	62
Holt MARVELL (1)	62
Jack STRACHEY (1)	62
David CLAYTON-THOMAS (1)	37
Joe TEX (1)	34
Fleecie MOORE (1)	25
Cowboy COPAS (1)	23
Lois MANN (1)	23
Gertie WESLEY (1)	19
Johnny TERRY (2)	18
Addie Williams JONES (1)	18
Eddie JONES (1)	5.8
Ray PENNINGTON (1)	4.1
Sonny THOMPSON (1)	4.1
Gladys KNOCHELMAN (1)	1.1
Johnny OTIS (1)	0.9
Perry COMO ▶37 (61) [102]	**54735**
Al HOFFMAN (6)	5066
Dick MANNING (6)	5066
Joe SHAPIRO (2)	3129
Lou STALLMAN (2)	3129
Bob MERRILL (1)	2680
Lee POCKRISS (1)	1990
Paul VANCE (1)	1990
Bickley REICHNER (1)	1425
Ray STANLEY (1)	1335
Alex ALSTONE (1)	1154
Tom GLAZER (1)	1154
Don McLEAN (1)	1090
Armando MANZANERO (1)	1077
Sid WAYNE (1)	1077
Irving GORDON (1)	1073
Eunice LEVY (1)	1023
Jake PORTER (1)	1023
Forrest WILSON (1)	1023
Noel SHERMAN (2)	991
Roy C. BENNETT (2)	896
Sid TEPPER (2)	896
Joe SHERMAN (1)	857
Luther DIXON (1)	682
Billy Dawn SMITH (1)	682
Al STILLMAN (4)	656
Oscar HAMMERSTEIN (1)	581
Richard RODGERS (1)	581
Ollie JONES (1)	570
Bugs BOWER (1)	510
Earl SHUMAN (1)	510
Burt BACHARACH (2)	458
Hal DAVID (1)	417
Robert ALLEN (2)	395
Fred BURCH (1)	393
Jan CRUTCHFIELD (1)	393
Stanley KAHAN (1)	385
Eddie SNYDER (1)	385
Jim CONWAY (1)	356
Joseph T. FARRELL (1)	356
Johnny BURKE (1)	317
Robert DAY (1)	317
Jack KELLER (2)	317
Sammy CAHN (1)	315
Bronislaw KAPER (1)	315

Mann CURTIS (1)	273
Franz LEHÁR (1)	273
Doris TAUBER (1)	273
Alex ROGERS (1)	267
Bert A. WILLIAMS (1)	267
Edith LINDEMAN (1)	265
Carl STUTZ (1)	265
Henry MANCINI (1)	260
Aaron SCHROEDER (1)	232
George David WEISS (1)	232
Cole PORTER (1)	223
Francis LAI (1)	211
Rod McKUEN (1)	211
Hugo MONTENEGRO (1)	183
Ernie SHELDON (1)	183
Carl SIGMAN (1)	146
Jack BROOKS (1)	143
Harry WARREN (1)	143
Bart HOWARD (1)	122
Claude DEBUSSY (1)	112
Mitchell PARISH (1)	112
Domenico SAVINO (1)	112
Fred JAY (1)	107
Ira KOSLOFF (1)	107
Irving REID (1)	107
Howard Ellington Riddiford BARNES (1)	94
Harold FIELDS (1)	94
Joseph RONCORONI (1)	94
Allan ROBERTS (1)	69
Betty COMDEN (2)	69
Adolph GREEN (2)	69
Jule STYNE (2)	69
Bob HILLIARD (1)	41
Jerry LEIBER (1)	31
Mike STOLLER (1)	31
Luciano BERETTA (1)	28
Arturo CASADEI (1)	28
Ronald ANDRE (1)	26
Bonita DONATO (1)	26
Mona DONATO (1)	26
Sid ROBIN (1)	26
James Lord PIERPONT (1)	13
Ervin DRAKE (1)	8.1
John G. BOWEN (1)	4.9
Ned FREEMAN (1)	4.9
Don RAYE (1)	4.9
André HELLER (1)	4.2
Tim RICE (1)	4.2
Andrew Lloyd WEBBER (1)	4.2
Ben WEISMAN (1)	0.8
Irving MELSHER (1)	0.2
Murray WIZELL (1)	0.2
Jack FULTON (1)	0.0
Lois STEELE (1)	0.0
Ray CORMIER (1)	0.0
Don GENSON (1)	0.0
Don ROSELAND (1)	0.0
John ROX (1)	0.0
5TH DIMENSION ▶38 (34) [41]	**52992**
Laura NYRO (5)	15106
Jimmy WEBB (4)	4394
Burt BACHARACH (2)	4066
Hal DAVID (2)	4066
Galt MacDERMOT (2)	3935
James RADO (2)	3935
Gerome RAGNI (2)	3935
Tony MACAULAY (1)	2475
Randall McNEILL (1)	1920
Dorothea JOYCE (1)	1315
John PHILLIPS (1)	1133
Neil SEDAKA (2)	842

Dick ADDRISI (1)	782
Don ADDRISI (1)	782
Roger ATKINS (1)	481
Nick ASHFORD (1)	370
Valerie SIMPSON (1)	370
Howard GREENFIELD (1)	361
James W. ALEXANDER (1)	345
Willie HUTCH (1)	345
Landy McNEIL (1)	325
Gary FRIEDMAN (1)	322
Will HOLT (1)	322
Paul ANKA (1)	178
Dennis LAMBERT (1)	154
Brian POTTER (1)	154
Steve BARRI (1)	131
P.F. SLOAN (1)	131
René DeKNIGHT (1)	64
Thomas JEFFERSON (1)	64
Julius JOHNSEN (1)	64
Alan O'DAY (1)	27
Artie WAYNE (1)	27
Marilyn McLEOD (1)	20
Pam SAWYER (1)	20
Sam COOKE (1)	11
Bill WITHERS (1)	6.9
Eddie BRIGATI (1)	5.7
Felix CAVALIERE (1)	5.7
Patrick J. McMANUS (1)	0.4
Lefty PEDROSKI (1)	0.4
Billy JOEL ▶39 (37) [1]	**52367**
Billy JOEL (37)	52367
The MONKEES ▶40 (22) [18]	**52020**
Neil DIAMOND (2)	19409
John STEWART (2)	9791
Tommy BOYCE (5)	7943
Bobby HART (5)	7943
Gerry GOFFIN (2)	2182
Carole KING (3)	2182
Michael NESMITH (4)	905
Jerry LEIBER (1)	580
Mike STOLLER (1)	580
Jerry GOLDSTEIN (1)	437
Roger NICHOLS (1)	22
Paul WILLIAMS (1)	22
Simon BYRNE (1)	8.3
Andy HOWELL (1)	8.3
Jeff BARRY (1)	3.7
Andy KIM (1)	3.7
Toni STERN (1)	0.0
Micky DOLENZ (1)	0.0
Roy ORBISON ▶41 (33) [19]	**51381**
Roy ORBISON (24)	23939
Joe MELSON (10)	11468
William DEES (10)	7437
Claude DeMETRIUS (1)	2805
Cindy WALKER (1)	2310
Willie NELSON (1)	1034
Fred NEIL (1)	545
Beverly ROSS (1)	545
Jeff LYNNE (1)	368
Tom PETTY (1)	368
Don GIBSON (1)	195
Don GANT (1)	182
Wade MOORE (1)	71
Dick PENNER (1)	71
Shirley GOODMAN (1)	17
Leonard LEE (1)	17
Richard BRANNAN (1)	2.6
Frank SAULINO (1)	2.6
Jim VALENTINI (1)	2.6

Dionne WARWICK ▶42 (53) [41]	**51111**
Burt BACHARACH (34)	17670
Hal DAVID (33)	14962
André PREVIN (1)	2879
Dory PREVIN (1)	2879
Carole Bayer SAGER (2)	2762
Will JENNINGS (2)	2091
Richard KERR (2)	2091
Barry GIBB (2)	765
Adrienne ANDERSON (1)	691
Isaac HAYES (1)	691
Maurice GIBB (1)	535
Robin GIBB (1)	535
Barry MANN (1)	449
Phil SPECTOR (1)	449
Cynthia WEIL (1)	449
Albhy GALUTEN (1)	230
Leslie BRICUSSE (1)	75
Anthony NEWLEY (1)	75
William S. COOK (1)	74
Randy CATE (1)	61
Steve DORFF (1)	61
Larry HERBSTRITT (1)	61
Michael MASSER (1)	54
Edgar BRONFMAN (1)	51
Bruce ROBERTS (1)	51
Doug FRANK (1)	47
Doug JAMES (1)	47
Joseph JEFFERSON (1)	42
Charles SIMMONS (1)	42
Eric BLAU (1)	29
Jacques BREL (1)	29
Mort SHUMAN (1)	29
Tena CLARK (1)	28
Nathan EAST (1)	28
Gary PRIM (1)	28
Artie BUTLER (1)	23
Mark LINDSAY (1)	23
Jerry RAGOVOY (1)	15
Lamont DOZIER (1)	3.4
Brian HOLLAND (1)	3.4
Eddie HOLLAND (1)	3.4
Diana ROSS ▶43 (35) [48]	**50919**
Michael MASSER (7)	6205
Bernard EDWARDS (2)	5254
Nile RODGERS (2)	5254
Nick ASHFORD (5)	5169
Valerie SIMPSON (5)	5169
Pam SAWYER (4)	3331
Marilyn McLEOD (1)	2581
Ronald Norman MILLER (2)	2475
Gerry GOFFIN (2)	2359
Michael JACKSON (2)	1894
Lionel RICHIE (1)	1594
Dennis MATKOSKY (1)	740
Michael SEMBELLO (1)	740
Carole Bayer SAGER (1)	702
George GOLDNER (1)	463
Morris LEVY (1)	463
Frankie LYMON (1)	463
Jimmy MERCHANT (1)	463
Herman SANTIAGO (1)	463
Sara ALLEN (1)	367
Daryl HALL (1)	367
Franne GOLDE (2)	322
Tom SNOW (1)	299
Ervin DRAKE (1)	227
Dan FISHER (1)	227
Irene HIGGINBOTHAM (1)	227
Diana ROSS (2)	220
John CAPEK (1)	217
Marc JORDAN (1)	217

Diana ROSS ►43 (35) [48] *Cont'd*	**50919**
Lawrence BROWN (1)	209
Theresa McFADDIN (1)	209
Leonard O. PERRY (1)	209
Lamont DOZIER (1)	206
Brian HOLLAND (1)	206
Eddie HOLLAND (1)	206
Deke RICHARDS (1)	167
Kenneth Edward PETERSON (1)	129
Rob MOUNSEY (1)	128
Bill WRAY (1)	128
Linda LAURIE (1)	96
Jerry RAGOVOY (1)	96
Ray CHEW (1)	93
Paul JABARA (1)	93
Terry ETLINGER (1)	81
Barry GIBB (3)	65
Maurice GIBB (3)	65
Robin GIBB (2)	40
Peter IVERS (1)	23
HERMAN'S HERMITS ►44 (20) [25]	**50123**
Trevor PEACOCK (1)	8352
Graham GOULDMAN (3)	5059
Fred MURRAY (1)	3481
Robert Patrick WESTON (1)	3481
Kenny YOUNG (2)	2989
John CARTER (3)	2843
Ken HAWKER (1)	2665
Ray DAVIES (1)	2256
Geoff STEPHENS (2)	1878
Les REED (1)	1837
Noel GAY (1)	1730
Bob CREWE (1)	1644
Frank SLAY (1)	1644
Steve BARRI (1)	1056
P.F. SLOAN (1)	1056
Lou ADLER (1)	1048
Herb ALPERT (1)	1048
Sam COOKE (1)	1048
Rick JONES (1)	962
Gerry GOFFIN (1)	951
Carole KING (1)	951
Estelle LEVITT (1)	741
Don THOMAS (1)	741
Donovan LEITCH (1)	523
Russell ALQUIST (1)	138
SIMON & GARFUNKEL ►45 (18) [5]	**49763**
Paul SIMON (17)	47750
Art GARFUNKEL (2)	873
Daniel ROBLES (1)	663
Boudleaux BRYANT (1)	238
Felice BRYANT (1)	238
FOUR TOPS ►46 (45) [49]	**49650**
Lamont DOZIER (14)	10071
Brian HOLLAND (14)	10071
Eddie HOLLAND (14)	10071
Dennis LAMBERT (5)	3743
Brian POTTER (5)	3743
Frank Edward WILSON (3)	1043
Tim HARDIN (1)	924
Ivy Jo HUNTER (4)	849
Smokey ROBINSON (1)	820
Marc BLATTE (2)	808
Larry GOTTLIEB (2)	808
Charles DAWES (1)	647
Carl SIGMAN (1)	647
Pam SAWYER (4)	601
Jimmy WEBB (1)	486
Bob CALILLI (1)	482

Michael David LOOKOFSKY (1)	482
Tony SANSONE (1)	482
William STEVENSON (1)	369
Gloria JONES (1)	273
Stevie WONDER (1)	217
Harvey PRICE (1)	180
Bobby SANDSTROM (1)	180
Barrett STRONG (1)	179
Norman WHITFIELD (1)	179
Renaldo BENSON (1)	159
Val BENSON (1)	159
Johnny BRISTOL (1)	133
Doris McNEIL (1)	133
Vernon BULLOCK (1)	104
Jack GOGA (1)	104
Reggie DOZIER (1)	73
McKinley JACKSON (1)	73
Mike PINDER (1)	49
Fred BRIDGES (2)	49
Lawrence PAYTON (2)	49
Mikki FARROW (1)	32
Howard GREENFIELD (1)	27
Louis ST. LOUIS (1)	27
Ralph BAILEY (1)	18
Rudy CLARK (1)	18
Ken WILLIAMS (1)	18
Richard BEASLEY (1)	16
Richard KNIGHT (1)	16
R. Dean TAYLOR (1)	14
Todd CERNEY (1)	8.3
Pamela Phillips OLAND (1)	8.3
Raynoma SINGLETON (1)	4.4
Levi STUBBS (1)	3.8
Gladys KNIGHT & The PIPS ►47 (42) [45]	**48695**
Jim WEATHERLY (6)	14848
Norman WHITFIELD (7)	5382
Barrett STRONG (6)	4913
Johnny OTIS (2)	2411
Curtis MAYFIELD (1)	1927
Clay McMURRAY (2)	1669
Gerry GOFFIN (2)	1470
Barry GOLDBERG (1)	1320
Don COVAY (1)	1047
Lincoln CHASE (1)	893
Gloria JONES (1)	884
Pam SAWYER (1)	884
Van McCOY (3)	777
Reggie CALLOWAY (1)	739
David GATES (1)	706
Gladys KNIGHT (3)	700
Merald KNIGHT (3)	700
Tony CAMILLO (1)	672
Mary Jane SAWYER (1)	672
Johnny BRISTOL (2)	664
Rodger PENZABENE (3)	607
Kris KRISTOFFERSON (1)	483
Tom JONES (1)	479
Harvey SCHMIDT (1)	479
William GUEST (1)	319
Katherine SCHAFFNER (1)	319
Alan BERGMAN (1)	319
Marilyn BERGMAN (1)	319
Marvin HAMLISCH (1)	319
Gene McDANIELS (1)	295
William STEVENSON (1)	279
Nick ASHFORD (2)	261
Valerie SIMPSON (2)	261
Eddie HOLLAND (1)	191
Michael MASSER (1)	150
Bud RENEAU (1)	125
Tony MACAULAY (1)	49
Sam DEES (1)	36

Joey GALLO (1)	36
Ricky Darnell SMITH (1)	36
Ray JONES (1)	20
Stanley KAHAN (1)	20
Eddie SNYDER (1)	20
Cornelius GRANT (1)	1.0
Ronald Alonzo MILLER (1)	0.0
Brook BENTON ►48 (54) [61]	**48554**
Brook BENTON (20)	10794
Clyde OTIS (19)	10354
Tony Joe WHITE (1)	4458
Bobby STEVENSON (1)	3632
TRADITIONAL (1)	2364
Belford HENDRICKS (1)	1718
Leon CARR (2)	1646
Earl SHUMAN (2)	1646
Margie SINGLETON (4)	1460
Hughie CANNON (1)	809
Malcolm DODDS (2)	798
Joe SHAPIRO (1)	772
Jimmy WILLIAMS (1)	772
Robert MacGIMSEY (1)	687
Rube BLOOM (1)	546
Johnny MERCER (1)	546
Joe SOUTH (1)	381
Marnie EWALD (1)	357
Oliver HALL (1)	357
Ray STEVENS (1)	338
Vince CORSO (1)	246
Emil ANTON (1)	239
Alan THOMAS (1)	239
Rudy CLARK (1)	236
Elmer BERNSTEIN (1)	229
Mack DAVID (1)	229
Wally GOLD (1)	190
Aaron SCHROEDER (1)	190
Charles ALLEN (1)	186
Charles ARRINGTON (1)	186
Willie DIXON (1)	183
Arthur KENT (1)	143
Ed WARREN (1)	143
Don COVAY (1)	143
George SOULE (1)	143
Burt BACHARACH (1)	130
Hal DAVID (1)	130
Toussaint McCALL (1)	98
Patrick ROBINSON (1)	98
Paul ANKA (1)	83
Claude FRANÇOIS (1)	83
Jacques REVAUX (1)	83
Luther DIXON (1)	64
J.T. ADAMS (1)	54
Cirino COLACRAI (2)	52
Teddy RANDAZZO (2)	52
Chris TOWNS (1)	49
Luchi DeJESUS (1)	35
Paul GASPER (1)	34
Bob PERPER (1)	34
Leon ASHLEY (1)	28
Bennie BENJAMIN (2)	25
Sol MARCUS (2)	25
Daryl PETTY (1)	15
Darrell EDWARDS (1)	11
Jerry LEIBER (1)	4.3
Mike STOLLER (1)	4.3
Jimmie HODGES (1)	3.5
Frank AUGUSTUS (1)	1.9
Oramay DIAMOND (1)	0.0
Dave DREYER (1)	0.0

Frank SINATRA ►49 (82) [115]	**47227**
Sammy CAHN (17)	5948
Dolores Vicki SILVERS (1)	5623
Jimmy VAN HEUSEN (12)	4542
Bert KAEMPFERT (4)	2419
Eddie SNYDER (2)	2333
Kelly GORDON (1)	2219
Dean KAY (1)	2219
Charles SINGLETON (1)	2114
Carolyn LEIGH (4)	1079
Kay TWOMEY (1)	985
Bee WALKER (1)	985
Phil TUMINELLO (2)	809
Cy COLEMAN (2)	731
Ervin DRAKE (1)	634
Gayle CALDWELL (1)	583
Lew SPENCE (5)	478
Barry PARKER (2)	476
Carl SIGMAN (3)	387
Frank REARDON (1)	377
Lee HAZLEWOOD (1)	336
Philip SPRINGER (1)	332
Baker KNIGHT (1)	324
Alan BERGMAN (3)	324
Marilyn BERGMAN (3)	324
Russell FAITH (1)	321
Clarence KEHNER (1)	321
Dok STANFORD (3)	317
Paul ANKA (3)	311
Herbert REHBEIN (3)	305
Fred EBB (1)	288
John KANDER (1)	288
Jerry LIVINGSTON (1)	281
Fred FISHER (1)	242
Cole PORTER (1)	239
Edwin GREINES (1)	235
Henry SANICOLA (1)	235
Frank SINATRA (1)	235
Claude FRANÇOIS (1)	234
Jacques REVAUX (1)	234
Hans BRADTKE (1)	228
Henry MAYER (1)	228
Johnny MERCER (1)	228
Giorgio CALABRESE (1)	225
Antonio De VITA (1)	225
Hal SHAPER (1)	225
Stanley KAHAN (1)	219
Rudy VALLEE (1)	219
Rod McKUEN (1)	209
Al FRISCH (1)	194
Edward WHITE (1)	194
Mack WOLFSON (1)	194
Aaron SCHROEDER (1)	187
Guy WOOD (1)	187
Gil WARD (1)	172
Sammy FAIN (1)	166
Irving KAHAL (1)	166
Teddy RANDAZZO (3)	162
Buddy KAYE (1)	156
Harry LLOYD (1)	153
Gloria SKLEROV (1)	153
Dorothy DODD (1)	153
Agustin LARA (1)	153
TRADITIONAL (1)	151
Victoria PIKE (2)	144
Don COSTA (1)	139
Phil ZELLER (1)	139
Sammy GALLOP (1)	117
Mort DIXON (1)	101
Harry WOODS (1)	101
Fritz SCHULZ-REICHEL (1)	86
Elmer BERNSTEIN (1)	85

Frank SINATRA ▶49 (82) [115] *Cont'd* 47227

Homer DENISON (1)	70
Hugh HALLIDAY (1)	70
Al HOFFMAN (1)	67
Dick MANNING (1)	67
Don CANTON (1)	67
Ira KOSLOFF (1)	67
Ira GERSHWIN (2)	48
Rube BLOOM (2)	45
Ted KOEHLER (2)	45
Norman NEWELL (1)	42
Riz ORTOLANI (1)	42
Katyna RANIERI (1)	42
Eve JAY (1)	39
Bernie WAYNE (1)	39
George GERSHWIN (1)	30
Romuald FIGUIER (1)	30
Michel JOURDAN (1)	30
Claude VASORI (1)	30
Joseph BUSHKIN (1)	23
John DeVRIES (1)	23
Jerome MOROSS (1)	20
Harold ARLEN (1)	18
Bobby WEINSTEIN (1)	18
Jim CROCE (1)	18
Hoagy CARMICHAEL (1)	17
Mitchell PARISH (1)	17
Fred AHLERT (1)	13
Edgar LESLIE (1)	13
Nelson RIDDLE (1)	11
Chester CONN (1)	6.9
Nathan MILLER (1)	6.9
Bobby WORTH (1)	6.1
Bob GAUDIO (1)	6.0
Jake HOLMES (1)	6.0
Michael STEWART (1)	3.5
Kim CARNES (1)	3.5
Dave ELLINGSON (1)	3.5
Howard GREENFIELD (1)	0.8
Jack KELLER (1)	0.8
Keely SMITH (1)	0.8
Johnny RICHARDS (1)	0.0
Jule STYNE (1)	0.0
Henry STONE (1)	0.0
Otis WILLIAMS (1)	0.0

YOUNG RASCALS/RASCALS ▶50 (19) [6] 46671

Felix CAVALIERE (17)	21990
Eddie BRIGATI (9)	17497
Rudy CLARK (1)	3439
Artie RESNICK (1)	3439
Lori BURTON (1)	153
Pam SAWYER (1)	153

Lionel RICHIE ▶51 (14) [6] 45478

Lionel RICHIE (14)	38256
Brenda RICHIE (2)	2652
Cynthia WEIL (2)	1458
Michael FRENCHIK (1)	1139
Carlos RIOS (1)	1139
Greg PHILLINGANES (2)	834

Fats DOMINO ▶52 (78) [56] 45063

Fats DOMINO (54)	17331
Dave BARTHOLOMEW (42)	11470
Al LEWIS (2)	2225
Vincent ROSE (1)	1883
Larry STOCK (1)	1883
Hank WILLIAMS (2)	1176
Robert GUIDRY (3)	980
Tommy BOYCE (1)	615
John MARASCALCO (1)	615
Dave FRANKLIN (1)	468
Cliff FRIEND (1)	468
Walter DONALDSON (1)	459
George WHITING (1)	459
TRADITIONAL (1)	376
Sylvester BRADFORD (1)	343
Claude DeMETRIUS (1)	335
Fleecie MOORE (1)	335
Roy HAYES (1)	300
Earl King JOHNSON (3)	287
Jack JESSUP (3)	265
Pee Wee MADDUX (3)	265
Jimmy KENNEDY (1)	263
Hugh WILLIAMS (1)	263
Don GIBSON (1)	185
Earl PALMER (2)	184
Chris KENNER (1)	124
Con CONRAD (1)	121
Benny DAVIS (1)	121
J. Russel ROBINSON (1)	121
Junie McCREE (1)	115
Albert VON TILZER (1)	115
Jimmie GRIER (1)	104
Earl HATCH (1)	104
Coy POE (1)	104
Pinky TOMLIN (1)	104
Irving GORDON (1)	54
Jack LAWRENCE (1)	54
Peter TINTURIN (1)	54
Mack GORDON (1)	41
Harry REVEL (1)	41
Dorothy FIELDS (1)	34
Jimmy McHUGH (1)	34
Johnny GREEN (1)	31
Gus KAHN (1)	31
Carmen LOMBARDO (1)	31
Herman HUPFELD (1)	19
Reginald HALL (1)	16
Wilbert WATSON (1)	14
Borney BERGANTINE (1)	9.6
Betty PETERSON (1)	9.6
John LENNON (1)	7.9
Paul McCARTNEY (1)	7.9
Harlan HOWARD (1)	1.9
Al DOWNING (1)	1.0
Marion CARPENTER (1)	0.9
Tim GILLIS (1)	0.9

Andy WILLIAMS ▶53 (52) [92] 44997

Doc POMUS (3)	4220
Mort SHUMAN (2)	3564
Bernie LOWE (1)	2396
Kal MANN (1)	2396
Wayne WALKER (1)	2058
Eula PARKER (1)	2024
Melvin ENDSLEY (1)	1619
Sonny CURTIS (1)	1401
Norman GIMBEL (1)	1356
Eddie HEYWOOD (1)	1356
Al HOFFMAN (1)	1150
Charles KING (1)	1150
Dick MANNING (1)	1150
Francis LAI (1)	1100
Carl SIGMAN (1)	1100
Carl BELEW (1)	1027
Kenny SOWDER (1)	1027
W.S. STEVENSON (1)	1027
Henry MANCINI (4)	996
Johnny MERCER (3)	783
Kay THOMPSON (1)	747
Alan JEFFREYS (1)	656
Acker BILK (1)	564
Robert MELLIN (1)	564
Ray EVANS (2)	524
Jay LIVINGSTON (2)	524
James LAST (1)	418
Jackie RAE (1)	418
Julia Ward HOWE (1)	329
William STEFFE (1)	329
Roger MILLER (1)	317
Berthold BRECHT (1)	312
Kurt WEILL (1)	312
Larry KUSIK (1)	310
Nino ROTA (1)	310
Sy SOLOWAY (1)	299
Shirley WOLFE (1)	299
Alan Jay LERNER (1)	282
Frederick LOEWE (1)	282
Dorival CAYMMI (1)	274
Ray GILBERT (1)	274
Lionel BART (1)	262
Mike LEWIS (1)	260
Joe SAUTER (1)	260
Burt BACHARACH (1)	248
Bob HILLIARD (1)	248
Bernie HANIGHEN (1)	244
Kenyon HOPKINS (1)	244
Johnny COWELL (1)	233
Sid RAMIN (1)	233
Tony VELONA (1)	233
TRADITIONAL (1)	141
Fred WEATHERLY (1)	141
Sammy CAHN (1)	139
Jimmy VAN HEUSEN (1)	139
Mickey NEWBURY (1)	73
Jerry KELLER (1)	66
Gloria SHAYNE (1)	66
Leon RUSSELL (1)	60
Ritchie ADAMS (1)	51
Neval NADER (1)	51
Howard GREENFIELD (1)	40
Neil SEDAKA (1)	40
George Richard DAVIS Jr. (1)	32
Lee DIAMOND (1)	32
Maria Teresa LARA (1)	30
Sunny SKYLAR (1)	30
Antonio Carlos JOBIM (1)	12
Gene LEES (1)	12
Tommy KAREN (1)	11
Allan REUSS (1)	11
Rainey ROBINSON (1)	11
Irving BERLIN (1)	10
Carole KING (1)	9.6
Cynthia WEIL (1)	9.6
Luigi CREATORE (1)	8.7
Hugo PERETTI (1)	8.7
George David WEISS (1)	8.7
Artie DUNN (1)	7.0
Al NEVINS (1)	7.0
Morty NEVINS (1)	7.0
Buck RAM (1)	7.0
Bill CROMPTON (1)	5.0
Norman MURRELLS (1)	5.0
Smokey ROBERDS (1)	4.5
Jerry HERST (1)	2.5
Jack SHARPE (1)	2.5
Roy C. BENNETT (1)	0.4
Sid TEPPER (1)	0.4
Redd EVANS (1)	0.0
Arthur KENT (1)	0.0
Dave MANN (1)	0.0

Sam COOKE ▶54 (50) [31] 44869

Sam COOKE (31)	35861
Willie DIXON (1)	1404
Hughie CANNON (1)	1389
William S. COOK (1)	732
Lou ADLER (2)	624
Herb ALPERT (2)	624
John MARASCALCO (1)	576
Leo PRICE (1)	576
Roy ALFRED (1)	378
Del SERINO (1)	378
Eden AHBEZ (1)	377
Jeff BARRY (1)	307
Pee Wee KING (1)	273
Redd STEWART (1)	273
Pat BEST (1)	198
Deek WATSON (1)	198
Bruce CULVER (1)	195
Clint LAVERT (1)	87
James W. ALEXANDER (3)	80
Redd EVANS (1)	75
Dave MANN (1)	75
Alvin TYLER (1)	28
Luigi CREATORE (1)	25
Al HOFFMAN (1)	25
Dick MANNING (1)	25
Hugo PERETTI (1)	25
Ray EVANS (1)	18
Jay LIVINGSTON (1)	18
George GERSHWIN (2)	8.1
Ira GERSHWIN (2)	8.1
DuBose HEYWARD (2)	8.1

CHER ▶55 (35) [43] 44839

Sonny BONO (4)	7362
Bob STONE (1)	6846
Diane WARREN (4)	5134
John DURRILL (2)	4437
Al CAPPS (1)	3068
Mary DEAN (1)	3068
Bob DYLAN (1)	1745
Desmond CHILD (3)	1663
Michele ALLER (3)	1034
Bob ESTY (3)	1034
Jack DIÉVAL (1)	1015
Al STILLMAN (1)	1015
Dean PITCHFORD (1)	848
Tom SNOW (1)	848
Alan O'DAY (1)	751
Michael BOLTON (1)	705
Mark MANGOLD (1)	705
Tom BAHLER (1)	704
Rudy CLARK (1)	450
Andy HILL (1)	309
Peter SINFIELD (1)	309
Jon BON JOVI (1)	309
Richie SAMBORA (1)	309
Burt BACHARACH (1)	267
Hal DAVID (1)	267
Howard GREENFIELD (1)	185
Neil SEDAKA (1)	185
Miriam MAKEBA (1)	41
Graham GOULDMAN (1)	41
Mark GOLDENBERG (1)	29
Jon LIND (1)	29
Phil SPECTOR (1)	20
April STEVENS (1)	20
Nino TEMPO (1)	20
Billy ROBERTS (1)	17
Raynard MINER (1)	12
Carl William SMITH (1)	12
Harry AKST (1)	8.3
Grant CLARKE (1)	8.3
Stephen STILLS (1)	5.6
Steve DORFF (1)	1.5
Gary HARJU (1)	1.5
Larry HERBSTRITT (1)	1.5

Tommy JAMES And The SHONDELLS ▶56 (19) [23]	44556
Tommy JAMES (8)	10014
Ritchie CORDELL (10)	9166
Peter LUCIA (1)	4588
Jeff BARRY (1)	3386
Ellie GREENWICH (1)	3386
Bo GENTRY (6)	2954
Mike VALE (3)	2646
Ed GRAY (1)	2239
Bobby BLOOM (1)	1168
Richie GRASSO (1)	1076
Barbara TOMSCO (1)	548
George TOMSCO (1)	548
Robert L. KING (2)	536
Paul NAUMANN (2)	447
Morris LEVY (1)	242
Sal TRIMACHI (1)	242
Bruce SUDANO (1)	234
Woody WILSON (1)	234
Jim CALVERT (1)	213
Norman MARZANO (1)	213
Jerry KASENETZ (1)	174
Jeff KATZ (1)	174
Harvey WEISENFELD (1)	132

Neil SEDAKA ▶57 (30) [9]	43701
Neil SEDAKA (26)	21695
Howard GREENFIELD (20)	15341
Phil CODY (5)	5764
Ronnie GROSSMAN (1)	297
Larry KOLBER (1)	177
Barry MANN (1)	177
Chris ALLEN (2)	83
Peter ALLEN (2)	83
Dick EVERITT (2)	83

Phil COLLINS ▶58 (18) [7]	43463
Phil COLLINS (16)	34855
Lamont DOZIER (2)	2533
Carole Bayer SAGER (1)	1856
Toni WINE (1)	1856
Daryl STUERMER (1)	1155
Brian HOLLAND (1)	604
Eddie HOLLAND (1)	604

Barry MANILOW ▶59 (28) [37]	43264
Bruce JOHNSTON (1)	7247
Richard KERR (3)	4599
Barry MANILOW (10)	3997
Will JENNINGS (2)	2333
Scott ENGLISH (1)	2266
David POMERANZ (2)	2221
Randy EDELMAN (1)	2022
Chris ARNOLD (1)	1747
David MARTIN (1)	1747
Geoff MORROW (1)	1747
Adrienne ANDERSON (3)	1718
Ian HUNTER (1)	1503
Marty PANZER (3)	1391
Charles FOX (1)	913
Norman GIMBEL (1)	913
Jack FELDMAN (3)	867
Bruce SUSSMAN (3)	867
Jim STEINMAN (1)	856
Gino CUNICO (1)	787
Buddy KAYE (1)	523
Shakin' STEVENS (1)	307
Tom SNOW (1)	295
Cynthia WEIL (1)	295
Kenny NOLAN (1)	273
Gerard KENNY (1)	265
Drey SHEPPERD (1)	265
Frank LOESSER (1)	198
Jule STYNE (1)	198
T.S. ELIOT (1)	164
Trevor NUNN (1)	164
Andrew Lloyd WEBBER (1)	164
Bob CREWE (1)	123
Sandy LINZER (1)	123
Denny RANDELL (1)	123
Howard Lee RICE (1)	20
Allan RICH (1)	20
Thomas F. KELLY (1)	1.6

CREEDENCE CLEARWATER REVIVAL ▶60 (20) [8]	43173
John FOGERTY (17)	40983
Eleanor BROADWATER (1)	422
Robert CHAISSON (1)	422
Dale HAWKINS (1)	422
Stanley J. LEWIS (1)	422
Screamin' Jay HAWKINS (1)	292
Barrett STRONG (1)	106
Norman WHITFIELD (1)	106

Whitney HOUSTON ▶61 (15) [21]	43073
Michael MASSER (3)	5613
George MERRILL (2)	3804
Shannon RUBICAM (2)	3804
LaForrest COPE (1)	2931
Kenneth EDMONDS (2)	2465
Antonio REID (2)	2465
Michael GORE (1)	2209
Dean PITCHFORD (1)	2209
Linda CREED (1)	2205
Thomas F. KELLY (1)	1836
Billy STEINBERG (1)	1836
Will JENNINGS (1)	1796
Charles Henry JACKSON Jr. (1)	1726
Frank WILDHORN (1)	1726
Gerry GOFFIN (1)	1612
Narada Michael WALDEN (1)	1367
Toni COLANDREO (1)	1077
John BETTIS (1)	832
Albert HAMMOND (1)	832
Eric Foster WHITE (1)	470
Francis Scott KEY (1)	259

The MIRACLES/ Smokey ROBINSON & The MIRACLES ▶62 (43) [23]	42875
Smokey ROBINSON (34)	20313
Al CLEVELAND (7)	4238
Henry COSBY (1)	2480
Stevie WONDER (1)	2480
Marvin TARPLIN (7)	2164
Warren MOORE (7)	1955
Berry GORDY (4)	1863
Lamont DOZIER (3)	1155
Brian HOLLAND (3)	1155
Eddie HOLLAND (3)	1155
Terry JOHNSON (2)	889
Robert ROGERS (4)	808
Ronnie WHITE (3)	411
Frank Edward WILSON (1)	403
Dick HOLLER (1)	379
Johnny BRISTOL (2)	237
Wade BROWN (2)	237
David H. JONES (2)	237
Nick ASHFORD (1)	158
Valerie SIMPSON (1)	158
George GORDY (1)	0.1
Rosemary GORDY (1)	0.1
Allen STORY (1)	0.1

DION ▶63 (26) [31]	42745
Ernie MARESCA (4)	12791
Dion DiMUCCI (8)	10369
Dick HOLLER (1)	5358
Jerry LEIBER (2)	4209
Mike STOLLER (2)	4209
Alfred DiPAOLA (1)	623
Silvio FARACI (1)	623
Salvatore PIPPA (1)	623
John FALBO (1)	614
Bonnie DODD (1)	554
Steve BRANDT (1)	425
Gerry GOFFIN (1)	381
Carole KING (1)	381
Clarence QUICK (1)	244
Brenda Lee JONES (1)	232
Welton YOUNG (1)	232
Doc POMUS (1)	164
Mort SHUMAN (1)	164
Chuck BERRY (1)	147
Jimi HENDRIX (1)	94
Willie DIXON (1)	71
Tony FASCE (1)	47
Terry PHILIPS (1)	41
Jerry VANCE (1)	41
Diane WARREN (1)	39
Sylvia DEE (1)	30
George GOEHRING (1)	30
Joni MITCHELL (1)	8.9
Jimmy ISLE (1)	0.7
Ronnie ISLE (1)	0.7
Kenny MARLOWE (1)	0.7

Barbra STREISAND ▶64 (46) [72]	42299
Barry GIBB (3)	4397
Robin GIBB (2)	3762
Barbra STREISAND (1)	3109
Paul WILLIAMS (1)	3109
Laura NYRO (3)	2666
Alan BERGMAN (2)	2485
Marilyn BERGMAN (2)	2485
Marvin HAMLISCH (1)	2301
Alan GORDON (1)	2278
Bob MERRILL (3)	1901
Jule STYNE (3)	1901
Paul JABARA (2)	1784
Bruce ROBERTS (1)	892
Bob ESTY (1)	892
Bobby WHITESIDE (1)	699
Richard Lee WOLD (1)	699
Albhy GALUTEN (1)	635
Maury YESTON (1)	514
Carole KING (2)	352
Toni STERN (2)	352
Jim STEINMAN (1)	335
Kim CARNES (1)	300
Grant CLARKE (1)	290
James HANLEY (1)	290
John DESAUTELS (1)	257
Karen LAWRENCE (1)	257
Stephen NELSON (1)	240
David WOLFERT (1)	240
Ira LEVIN (1)	192
Milton SCHAFER (1)	192
Leonard BERNSTEIN (1)	189
Stephen SONDHEIM (1)	189
Stevie WONDER (1)	185
Michel LEGRAND (1)	185
Sandy FARINA (1)	157
Lisa RATNER (1)	157
Spooner OLDHAM (1)	140
Dan PENN (1)	140
Jimmy WEBB (1)	131
John LENNON (1)	130
T.S. ELIOT (1)	76
Trevor NUNN (1)	76
Andrew Lloyd WEBBER (1)	76
Michael LEONARD (1)	63
Herb MARTIN (1)	63
Jacques CHARLES (1)	51
Channing POLLOCK (1)	51
Albert WILLEMETZ (1)	51
Maurice YVAIN (1)	51
Peter S. BLISS (1)	41
George GOEHRING (1)	41
Stan RHODES (1)	41
Joss BASELLI (1)	40
Armand CANFORA (1)	40
Robert COLBY (1)	40
Matthew MOORE (1)	24
Bob MARLEY (1)	13
Cy COLEMAN (1)	6.2
Dorothy FIELDS (1)	6.2
Joe RAPOSO (1)	5.7
Milton BERLE (1)	5.4
Sam LEWIS (1)	5.4
Fred WHITEHOUSE (1)	5.4
Victor YOUNG (1)	5.4
Oscar HAMMERSTEIN (1)	4.4
Sigmund ROMBERG (1)	4.4
Barry MANN (1)	2.9
Cynthia WEIL (1)	2.9
Franz GRUBER (1)	0.7
Josef MOHR (1)	0.7
Fred EBB (1)	0.0
John KANDER (1)	0.0

Nat King COLE ▶65 (73) [125]	41901
Joe SHERMAN (5)	5017
Noel SHERMAN (4)	4305
Anna SOSENKO (1)	1751
Charles TOBIAS (2)	1565
Howard Ellington Riddiford BARNES (1)	1342
Harold FIELDS (1)	1342
Joseph RONCORONI (1)	1342
Hans CARSTE (1)	1264
Stephen MICHAELS (1)	1075
Chester CONN (4)	976
Sammy GALLOP (4)	976
Charlotte McCARTHY (1)	921
Clyde OTIS (3)	792
Emil ANTON (1)	785
Bob HALLEY (1)	785
Brook BENTON (2)	783
Belford HENDRICKS (2)	783
George David WEISS (3)	776
Hal HESTER (1)	583
Barry PARKER (1)	583
Dimitri TIOMKIN (1)	462
Ned WASHINGTON (1)	462
Nat "King" COLE (3)	446
Osvaldo FARRES (1)	401
Al (2) STEWART (1)	401
Charlotte HAWKINS (1)	400
Harold ADAMSON (3)	399
Jimmy McHUGH (1)	389
Shelley DOBBINS (1)	343
Michele GALDIERI (1)	343
Gino REDI (1)	343
Robert MOSELY (2)	336
Mayme WATTS (2)	336
Lee MORRIS (1)	318
Bernie WAYNE (1)	318
Marvin FISHER (2)	306
Heino GAZE (1)	302

Nat King COLE ▶65 (73) [125] *Cont'd*	**41901**
Sunny SKYLAR (1)	302
Al FRISCH (1)	301
Wally GOLD (2)	299
Aaron SCHROEDER (2)	299
Charles CHAPLIN (1)	276
Geoffrey PARSONS (1)	276
John TURNER (1)	276
Joseph McCARTHY (1)	248
James V. MONACO (1)	248
Carl SIGMAN (2)	212
Bob RUSSELL (1)	212
Irving GORDON (1)	206
Jerry LIVINGSTON (1)	206
Vittorio MASCHERONI (1)	198
Robert MELLIN (1)	198
Giancarlo TESTONI (1)	198
Paula FRANCES (1)	187
Gary ROMERO (1)	187
Luther DIXON (1)	184
Bert KEYES (1)	184
Billy Dawn SMITH (1)	184
Charles SINGLETON (1)	183
Jack SEGAL (1)	176
James DeLESTON (1)	132
Jack HAMMER (1)	132
Roy ALFRED (1)	130
Bob HORN (1)	108
Bernie LOWE (1)	108
Kal MANN (1)	108
Cy COLEMAN (1)	105
Joseph Allen McCARTHY (1)	105
Lester POWELL (1)	104
Paddy ROBERTS (1)	104
Mack DAVID (1)	100
Jimmy VAN HEUSEN (1)	100
Julie MANDEL (1)	84
Roger ROGER (1)	84
Johnny GREEN (1)	77
Paul Francis WEBSTER (1)	77
Mel TORME (3)	64
Robert WELLS (3)	64
Dick WOLF (1)	61
Lockie EDWARDS (1)	55
Larry WEISS (1)	55
Frank DeVOL (1)	48
Georges BIZET (1)	40
Léon HALÉVY (1)	40
Johnny LANGE (1)	40
Henri MEILHAC (1)	40
Bob MERRILL (1)	38
Jule STYNE (1)	38
Mark BARKAN (1)	35
Sandy BARON (1)	35
George EDDY (1)	35
Nelson RIDDLE (1)	20
Hoagy CARMICHAEL (1)	15
Mitchell PARISH (1)	15
Milt GABLER (1)	14
Bert KAEMPFERT (1)	14
Phil BELMONTE (1)	12
Ray MAXWELL (1)	12
Tarateno ROJAS (1)	12
Meredith WILLSON (1)	11
Ray EVANS (1)	10
Jay LIVINGSTON (1)	10
Stan BRENDERS (1)	8.9
Ralph CARE (1)	8.9
Sol MARCUS (1)	8.9
Larry HARRISON (1)	8.7
Jimmy WILLIAMS (1)	8.7
Dick MANNING (1)	7.3

Dante MARCHETTI (1)	7.3
Charles KENNY (1)	7.3
Nick KENNY (1)	7.3
Howard DIETZ (1)	6.1
Arthur SCHWARTZ (1)	6.1
Stella UNGER (1)	4.9
Victor YOUNG (1)	4.9
Leo McCAREY (1)	4.9
Harry WARREN (1)	4.9
Giuseppe MASSARA (1)	2.7
Vito PALLAVICINI (1)	2.7
Nicola SALERNO (1)	2.7
Lee CATHY (1)	2.0
Bernard HERRMANN (1)	0.7
Peter JASON (1)	0.7
Gloria SHAYNE (1)	0.7
Gerhard WINKLER (1)	0.0
The EAGLES ▶66 (19) [16]	**41758**
Glenn FREY (13)	14131
Don HENLEY (13)	14054
J.D. SOUTHER (4)	3899
Don FELDER (1)	1553
Jack TEMPCHIN (2)	1358
Bob SEGER (1)	1137
Randy MEISNER (1)	1027
Jackson BROWNE (2)	966
Bernie LEADON (1)	858
Timothy B. SCHMIT (1)	641
Steve YOUNG (1)	625
Robert STRANDLUND (1)	423
Joe WALSH (1)	356
David BLUE (1)	273
Charles Mose BROWN (1)	229
Gene REDD Sr. (1)	229
Johnny RIVERS ▶67 (31) [43]	**40078**
Chuck BERRY (2)	5712
James Richard HENDRICKS (3)	3075
Johnny RIVERS (2)	2986
Lou ADLER (1)	2981
Willie DIXON (1)	2423
Jack TEMPCHIN (1)	2175
Harold DORMAN (1)	2068
Steve BARRI (1)	1939
P.F. SLOAN (1)	1939
Huey P. SMITH (2)	1607
John VINCENT (1)	1529
Lamont DOZIER (1)	1121
Brian HOLLAND (1)	1121
Eddie HOLLAND (1)	1121
Joe BABCOCK (1)	982
TRADITIONAL (1)	654
Carl PERKINS (1)	604
Pete SEEGER (1)	577
Warren MOORE (1)	512
Smokey ROBINSON (1)	512
Marvin TARPLIN (1)	512
Russ FRATTO (1)	463
Alan FREED (1)	463
Van MORRISON (1)	448
Curtis MAYFIELD (1)	422
Joe SOUTH (1)	311
Mike LOVE (1)	298
Brian WILSON (1)	298
Bob RAY (1)	292
Buck OWENS (1)	217
Dusty RHODES (1)	217
James TAYLOR (1)	116
Sam COOKE (1)	115
Thomas J. COE (1)	36
Dwain MINCY (1)	36
Wayne MINCY (1)	36
Timothy Michael SHANKLIN (1)	36

Wayne SHANKLIN (1)	36
Charlie CHALMERS (1)	31
Sandra RHODES (1)	31
Johnny OTIS (1)	12
Jerry LEIBER (1)	5.9
Mike STOLLER (1)	5.9
The COMMODORES ▶68 (26) [18]	**39757**
Lionel RICHIE (15)	28519
Milan WILLIAMS (7)	2925
Walter ORANGE (6)	1758
William KING (3)	1127
Thomas McCLARY (5)	971
Franne GOLDE (3)	953
Dennis LAMBERT (2)	947
Harold HUDSON (2)	773
Shirley KING (1)	717
Ronald LaPREAD (4)	557
Martin PAGE (1)	253
Darrell JONES (1)	105
Andy GOLDMARK (1)	65
David COCHRANE (1)	53
Jeff BOWEN (1)	12
William Roderick MILLER (1)	12
Bobby CALDWELL (1)	5.2
Paul FOX (1)	5.2
Janet JACKSON ▶69 (16) [9]	**39353**
James Samuel HARRIS (12)	14590
Terry LEWIS (12)	14590
Janet JACKSON (7)	8100
Monte MOIR (1)	1123
Melanie ANDREWS (1)	695
Glen BARBEE (1)	72
Charmaine SYLVERS (1)	72
René MOORE (1)	55
Angela WINBUSH (1)	55
Tony ORLANDO And DAWN ▶70 (22) [27]	**39299**
Irwin LEVINE (10)	15516
L. Russell BROWN (8)	12683
Toni WINE (2)	2832
Jerry BUTLER (1)	1536
Calvin CARTER (1)	1536
Curtis MAYFIELD (1)	1536
Sam COOKE (1)	689
Dennis LAMBERT (1)	465
Brian POTTER (1)	465
Dave APPELL (1)	449
Sandy LINZER (1)	449
Peter SKELLERN (1)	213
Nick ASHFORD (1)	152
Valerie SIMPSON (1)	152
Leo GIANANGELO (1)	111
Bruce ROBERTS (1)	90
Carole Bayer SAGER (1)	90
Max CROOK (1)	62
Del SHANNON (1)	62
Garry BONNER (1)	62
Alan GORDON (1)	62
Inez JAMES (1)	27
Buddy PEPPER (1)	27
Larry RUSSELL (1)	27
Pierre GROSCOLAS (1)	2.1
Michel JOURDAN (1)	2.1
Estelle LEVITT (1)	2.1
John DENVER ▶71 (32) [11]	**38605**
John DENVER (24)	23979
John Martin SOMMERS (1)	4659
Michael C. TAYLOR (2)	2728
Bill DANOFF (4)	2609

Taffy DANOFF (3)	2521
Dick KNISS (1)	1445
Dick FELLER (1)	428
Bobby GOLDSBORO (1)	97
Steve WEISBERG (1)	77
Buddy HOLLY (1)	32
Norman PETTY (1)	32
Dean MARTIN ▶72 (58) [97]	**38301**
Richard DEHR (1)	2885
Terry GILKYSON (1)	2885
Frank MILLER (1)	2885
Sam COSLOW (1)	2746
Ken LANE (1)	2746
Irving TAYLOR (1)	2746
Danny DiMINNO (2)	2587
Carmen LOMBARDO (1)	2566
Dick GLASSER (2)	2278
Chuck WILLIS (1)	2167
Baker KNIGHT (4)	1283
Lee HAZLEWOOD (1)	935
Hank LOCKLIN (1)	818
Billy HILL (1)	617
Frank LOESSER (1)	481
Stuart HAMBLEN (1)	472
Franco MIGLIACCI (1)	422
Domenico MODUGNO (1)	422
Mitchell PARISH (1)	422
Yvonne DEVANEY (1)	369
Jack BROOKS (1)	348
Harry WARREN (1)	348
Leon PAYNE (1)	336
Cindy WALKER (1)	314
John MICHAEL (1)	256
Charly NIESSEN (1)	256
Umberto BERTINI (1)	238
Nan FREDRICS (1)	238
Alessandro TACCANI (1)	238
James CAVANAUGH (1)	233
Russ MORGAN (1)	233
Larry STOCK (1)	233
Dick JENNINGS (1)	183
Hank MILLS (1)	183
Jean CHAPEL (1)	159
Bob JENNINGS (1)	159
Ramona REDD (2)	146
Mitchell TOROK (2)	146
Merle HAGGARD (1)	146
Norman GIMBEL (1)	121
Pablo Beltran RUIZ (1)	121
Sunny SKYLAR (2)	83
Glen HARDIN (1)	78
Ticker FREEMAN (1)	68
Nicholas BRODSZKY (2)	61
Jack LAWRENCE (1)	61
Fred CARTER (1)	57
Jule STYNE (3)	49
Ralph FREED (1)	45
Grace SAXON (1)	45
Roy ALFRED (1)	34
Bob HILLIARD (2)	25
Betty COMDEN (1)	24
Adolph GREEN (1)	24
Edith BERGDAHL (1)	23
Otto KOLLMAN (1)	23
Johnny MAY (1)	23
George CARDINI (1)	21
Ervin DRAKE (1)	17
Jean SENN (1)	15
Albert HAGUE (1)	14
Arnold B. HORWITT (1)	14
Benny CARTER (1)	12
John V. MOEN (1)	12

Dean MARTIN ►72 (58) [97] *Cont'd*	38301
Haven GILLESPIE (1)	12
Larry SHAY (1)	12
John HARTFORD (1)	12
Alex ALSTONE (1)	5.2
Jimmy KENNEDY (1)	5.2
Larry COLEMAN (1)	4.6
Fred EBB (1)	4.6
Paul KLEIN (1)	4.6
Dimitri TIOMKIN (1)	4.5
Paul Francis WEBSTER (1)	4.5
Dorcas COCHRAN (1)	4.4
Jean COULON (1)	4.4
Jean RODOR (1)	4.4
Vincent SCOTTO (1)	4.4
Victor ABRAMS (1)	3.8
Phil MEDLEY (1)	3.8
Horst Heinz HENNING (1)	2.0
Kay TWOMEY (1)	2.0
Ben WEISMAN (1)	2.0
Fred WISE (1)	2.0
Marty ROBBINS (1)	1.7
Sy SOLOWAY (1)	0.8
Shirley WOLFE (1)	0.8
Danny DILL (1)	0.6
Mel TILLIS (1)	0.6
Mike ANDRE (1)	0.1
Francesco FEOLA (1)	0.1
Gaetano LAMA (1)	0.1
Ettore MIONORETTI (1)	0.0
Geoffrey PARSONS (1)	0.0
Saverio SERACINI (1)	0.0
John TURNER (1)	0.0
Sammy CAHN (1)	0.0

KOOL & The GANG ►73 (35) [27]	38173
George M. BROWN (34)	7197
Ronald BELL (33)	4580
Robert BELL (32)	4556
Claydes SMITH (32)	4556
J.T. TAYLOR (18)	3571
Dennis THOMAS (20)	2365
Robert MICKENS (20)	2046
Curtis Fitzgerald WILLIAMS (11)	2040
James BONNEFORD (6)	1553
Eumir DEODATO (7)	1193
Earl TOON (3)	1130
Richard WESTFIELD (13)	949
Clifford ADAMS (5)	761
Meekaaeel MUHAMMED (1)	427
Donald BOYCE (2)	405
Michael RAY (4)	322
Sandy LINZER (1)	171
Otha NASH (2)	125
Woodrow SPARROW (5)	60
Amir BAYYAN (1)	59
Gene REDD Jr. (5)	28
Dwania KYLES (1)	24
Kendal STUBBS (1)	24
Penni SAUNDERS (1)	23
Jimmy CROSBY (1)	9.0
Amos GUIDER (1)	0.8
Alton TAYLOR (1)	0.0

Dave CLARK Five ►74 (25) [20]	38122
Dave CLARK (15)	14742
Mike SMITH (6)	6633
Bobby DAY (1)	5663
Lenny DAVIDSON (5)	2727
Berry GORDY (2)	2224
Chris KENNER (1)	1138
Allen TOUSSAINT (1)	1138
Chuck BERRY (1)	935
Billy DAVIS (1)	630
Gwen GORDY (1)	630
Denny PAYTON (2)	377
Johnny MERCER (1)	227
Harry WARREN (1)	227
Barry MASON (1)	218
Les REED (1)	218
Mitch MURRAY (1)	164
Celia MARSHALL (1)	104
Jerry RAGOVOY (1)	104
Burt BACHARACH (1)	9.7
Bob HILLIARD (1)	9.7

Tom JONES ►75 (29) [40]	37949
Paul ANKA (1)	6556
Danny SMALL (1)	3045
Les REED (4)	2680
Burt BACHARACH (2)	2548
Hal DAVID (2)	2548
Barry MASON (4)	2172
Jimmy CURRIE (2)	1932
Lonnie DONEGAN (2)	1932
Curly PUTMAN (1)	1685
Gordon MILLS (2)	1184
Geoff STEPHENS (1)	809
Mario PANZERI (1)	708
Lorenzo PILAT (1)	708
Carlo DONIDA (2)	681
Roger GREENAWAY (1)	616
Clive WESTLAKE (1)	610
Howard GREENFIELD (1)	496
Neil SEDAKA (1)	496
John BARRY (1)	462
Don BLACK (1)	462
Wayne BICKERTON (1)	406
Tony WADDINGTON (1)	406
Mickey NEWBURY (1)	379
Danny DILL (1)	374
Mel TILLIS (1)	374
Tony MACAULAY (1)	372
Jack FISHMAN (1)	355
Benny DAVIS (1)	335
Abner SILVER (1)	335
Jerry LEIBER (1)	326
Giulio RAPETTI (1)	326
Mike STOLLER (1)	326
Charles DANVERS (1)	223
Carl SIGMAN (1)	223
Tony ASHTON (1)	202
Bob BRASS (1)	191
Irwin LEVINE (1)	191
Merle TRAVIS (1)	100
Leon CARR (1)	89
Earl SHUMAN (1)	89

PRINCE ►76 (24) [3]	37911
PRINCE (24)	37643
Sheena EASTON (1)	242
Christopher MOON (1)	26

Bobby VEE ►77 (39) [48]	37883
Gerry GOFFIN (8)	7637
Martha SHARP (2)	6366
Carole KING (7)	5050
Blanche CARTER (1)	3382
Jack KELLER (2)	3072
Marilyn GARRETT (2)	1392
Dottie WAYNE (2)	1392
Ben WEISMAN (2)	1392
Gene PITNEY (1)	1066
Aaron SCHROEDER (1)	1066
John D. LOUDERMILK (1)	743
Kenny O'DELL (1)	603
Howard GREENFIELD (1)	559
Helen MILLER (1)	559
Bill BUCHANAN (1)	485
Bobby VEE (2)	356
David SEVILLE (1)	317
John GLUCK (1)	283
Neval NADER (1)	283
James L. WILLIAMS (1)	272
Smokey ROBINSON (1)	238
Ronnie WHITE (1)	238
Burt BACHARACH (1)	233
Hal DAVID (1)	233
Dewayne BLACKWELL (1)	159
Jimmy WEBB (1)	145
Sonny CURTIS (2)	92
Jerry ALLISON (1)	91
Van McCOY (1)	46
Steve ALLEN (1)	35
Hank HUNTER (1)	16
Vic THOMAS (1)	16
Carole Bayer SAGER (1)	9.9
Toni WINE (1)	9.9
Ivory Joe HUNTER (1)	8.2
Irwin LEVINE (1)	5.4
Neil SHEPPARD (1)	5.4
Les VANDYKE (1)	5.0
Bob FELDMAN (1)	3.5
Jerry GOLDSTEIN (1)	3.5
Richard GOTTEHRER (1)	3.5
Lee ADAMS (1)	3.3
Charles STROUSE (1)	3.3
Harry AKST (1)	1.0
Benny DAVIS (1)	1.0
Mickey GENTILE (1)	0.5
Artie RESNICK (1)	0.5
Snuff GARRETT (1)	0.3

QUEEN ►78 (25) [5]	37736
Freddie MERCURY (13)	21020
John DEACON (7)	13847
Roger TAYLOR (6)	1557
Brian MAY (8)	1175
David BOWIE (1)	138

FOREIGNER ►79 (21) [3]	37044
Michael Leslie JONES (21)	24705
Lou GRAMM (15)	12113
Ian McDONALD (1)	226

JEFFERSON AIRPLANE/ STARSHIP ►80 (37) [40]	36770
Marty BALIN (4)	4526
Peter F. WOLF (3)	3442
Darby SLICK (1)	2975
Grace SLICK (4)	2605
Albert HAMMOND (1)	2339
Diane WARREN (1)	2339
Ina WOLF (2)	2283
Martin PAGE (3)	1768
Jesse BARISH (3)	1732
Paul KANTNER (8)	1633
Dennis LAMBERT (1)	1159
Bernie TAUPIN (1)	1159
Nicholas DEWEY (1)	1073
Craig CHAQUICO (5)	885
Pete SEARS (4)	759
Jeannette SEARS (3)	660
Joey COVINGTON (2)	593
Tommy FUNDERBURK (1)	540
Victor Gabriel SMITH (1)	491
David FREIBERG (1)	429
Jim McPHERSON (1)	429
Phil GALDSTON (1)	350
Robbie NEVIL (1)	350
John VAN TONGEREN (1)	350
Johnny WARMAN (1)	279
Steven CRISTOL (1)	279
Robin RANDALL (1)	279
Thomas BORSDORF (1)	247
David Scott ROBERTS (1)	128
Jack CASADY (1)	102
Jorma KAUKONEN (1)	102
Carlos SANTANA (1)	102
Michael SHRIEVE (1)	102
Mickey THOMAS (1)	62
Skip SPENCE (1)	55
John BETTIS (1)	51
Michael CLARK (1)	51
Mutt LANGE (1)	43
THUNDERHAWK (1)	10
Byong YU (1)	5.7

Linda RONSTADT ►81 (32) [46]	35880
Clint BALLARD Jr. (1)	4190
Phil EVERLY (1)	3982
Joe MELSON (1)	2235
Roy ORBISON (1)	2235
Billy STEINBERG (1)	2152
Barry MANN (1)	1513
Tom SNOW (1)	1513
Cynthia WEIL (1)	1513
Buddy HOLLY (2)	1448
Norman PETTY (2)	1448
Karla BONOFF (3)	1283
Warren MOORE (2)	1134
Smokey ROBINSON (2)	1134
Neil YOUNG (1)	1129
Chuck BERRY (1)	1061
Gary B. WHITE (1)	830
Bobby HART (1)	562
Teddy RANDAZZO (1)	562
Bobby WEINSTEIN (1)	562
Jonathan CARROLL (1)	538
Joe SOUTH (1)	501
Jerry ALLISON (1)	471
Warren ZEVON (1)	437
Lamont DOZIER (1)	403
Brian HOLLAND (1)	403
Eddie HOLLAND (1)	403
Al GORGONI (1)	268
Chip TAYLOR (1)	268
Marvin TARPLIN (1)	241
Eric KAZ (1)	196
Libby TITUS (1)	196
Jimmy WEBB (1)	192
Mick JAGGER (1)	155
Keith RICHARDS (1)	155
Greg CARROLL (1)	130
Doris PAYNE (1)	130
Emitt RHODES (1)	102
Kenny EDWARDS (1)	45
Dick REYNOLDS (1)	29
Jack RHODES (1)	29
Isaac HAYES (1)	29
David PORTER (1)	29
Paul ANKA (1)	25
Jackson BROWNE (1)	16
Gerry GOFFIN (1)	0.9
Carole KING (1)	0.9

Glen CAMPBELL ►82 (34) [35]	35791
Jimmy WEBB (5)	12672
Larry WEISS (1)	6322
Allen TOUSSAINT (1)	4988
John D. LOUDERMILK (2)	1032

Glen CAMPBELL ►82 (34) [35] ***Cont'd***	**35791**
Jack NANCE (1)	955
Conway TWITTY (1)	955
Dennis LAMBERT (2)	707
Brian POTTER (2)	707
Cindy WALKER (1)	667
Chris GANTRY (1)	563
Bobby AUSTIN (1)	540
Curt SAPAUGH (1)	540
Edwin HAWKINS (1)	496
Micheal SMOTHERMAN (2)	491
Jerry CAPEHART (1)	447
Neil DIAMOND (1)	418
Buffy SAINTE-MARIE (1)	409
Mac DAVIS (1)	358
John HARTFORD (2)	341
Elmer BERNSTEIN (1)	258
Don BLACK (1)	258
Neal HEFTI (1)	243
Stanley H. STYNE (1)	243
Gordon LIGHTFOOT (1)	240
David PAICH (1)	226
Dorsey BURNETTE (1)	167
Barry De VORZON (1)	167
Ronnie GAYLORD (1)	165
Al DEXTER (1)	109
Dick ADDRISI (1)	49
Don ADDRISI (1)	49
Joe RAINEY (1)	4.2
Albert HAMMOND (1)	2.0
Mike HAZLEWOOD (1)	2.0
Tony MACAULAY (1)	2.0
Petula CLARK ►83 (22) [16]	**35750**
Tony HATCH (14)	25358
Jackie TRENT (8)	3771
Charles CHAPLIN (1)	3690
Barry MASON (1)	876
Les REED (1)	876
Garry BONNER (1)	334
Alan GORDON (1)	334
Paul STOOKEY (1)	152
Smokey ROBINSON (1)	132
James LAST (1)	76
Jackie RAE (1)	76
Clive WESTLAKE (1)	34
Kim ESPY (1)	11
Phil GERNHARD (1)	11
Jeff HARRINGTON (1)	11
Jeff PENNIG (1)	11
SLY & THE FAMILY STONE ►84 (18) [1]	**35633**
Sylvester STEWART (18)	35633
Jackie WILSON ►85 (55) [54]	**35495**
Johnny LEHMANN (2)	4441
Jackie WILSON (11)	3365
Herbert L. MILLER (1)	2467
Alonzo TUCKER (11)	2205
Billy DAVIS (6)	2197
Berry GORDY (6)	2197
Sid WYCHE (2)	2099
Gwen GORDY (5)	1969
Billy MYLES (3)	1718
Lena AGREE (1)	1183
Gary JACKSON (3)	1029
Al KASHA (4)	920
Raynard MINER (1)	875
Carl William SMITH (1)	875
Joyce LEE (1)	819

Barbara ACKLIN (1)	740
David SCOTT (1)	740
Hank HUNTER (2)	570
Horace OTT (2)	443
Van McCOY (2)	408
Bobby ADAMS (3)	378
Bob HAMILTON (1)	351
Tom KING (1)	351
Gary GELD (2)	301
Peter UDELL (2)	301
Alicia EVELYN (1)	268
Norm HENRY (1)	245
Bobby STEVENSON (1)	238
Floyd SMITH (2)	187
Jack DANIELS (1)	162
John Edward MOORE (1)	162
Gerald SIMS (1)	154
Dorothy DANIELS (1)	132
Frank DANIELS (1)	132
Johnnie B. ROBERTS (1)	121
Eugene RECORD (4)	107
Riccardo DRIGO (1)	105
Larry STOCK (1)	105
Ronald Norman MILLER (1)	74
Orlando MURDEN (1)	74
Carl DAVIS (3)	74
Eddie SINGLETON (3)	64
Lenny CROHET (1)	33
Richard Anthony TUFO (1)	33
Karl TARLETON (1)	30
Morris LEVY (1)	24
Alan THOMAS (1)	6.7
TRADITIONAL (1)	4.8
Fred WEATHERLY (1)	4.8
Bernard REED (1)	4.1
Daniel REED (1)	4.1
Othie WRIGHT (1)	4.1
Alan LORBER (1)	0.5
Nathaniel SMITH (1)	0.0
The SPINNERS ►86 (33) [31]	**35491**
Thom BELL (8)	5498
Michael ZAGER (3)	4235
Joseph JEFFERSON (6)	4148
Linda CREED (4)	3323
Charles SIMMONS (5)	2355
Melvin STEALS (1)	2181
Mervin STEALS (1)	2181
Phil HURTT (1)	2079
Bruce HAWES (4)	1993
Sam COOKE (1)	1698
Sandy LINZER (1)	1226
Denny RANDELL (1)	1226
Stevie WONDER (2)	510
Syreeta WRIGHT (2)	510
Lee GARRETT (1)	484
Harvey FUQUA (2)	301
Gwen GORDY (2)	301
Ivy Jo HUNTER (2)	264
William STEVENSON (2)	264
Willie NELSON (1)	193
Sherman MARSHALL (2)	124
Ted WORTHAM (1)	72
Casey JAMES (3)	57
Yvette DAVIS (1)	46
Leroy BELL (2)	45
Tony BELL (1)	42
John BETTIS (1)	42
Richard CARPENTER (1)	42
Martin COLEMAN (1)	22
Richard DRAPKIN (1)	22
Dean GANT (1)	3.3

The DRIFTERS ►87 (39) [43]	**35485**
Mort SHUMAN (8)	6576
Doc POMUS (7)	6572
Gerry GOFFIN (4)	2614
Carole KING (4)	2614
Artie RESNICK (2)	2433
Kenny YOUNG (2)	2433
Jerry LEIBER (6)	1619
Mike STOLLER (6)	1619
Barry MANN (4)	1275
Cynthia WEIL (4)	1275
George TREADWELL (2)	1219
Ben E. KING (1)	940
Lover PATTERSON (1)	940
Burt BACHARACH (2)	647
Bob HILLIARD (2)	647
Lewis LEBISH (1)	280
Irving NAHAN (1)	280
Inez JAMES (1)	137
Buddy PEPPER (1)	137
Larry RUSSELL (1)	137
Edward MADDEN (1)	99
Percy WENRICH (1)	99
Richard DEHR (1)	90
Terry GILKYSON (1)	90
Frank MILLER (1)	90
Bert BERNS (1)	84
Jerry RAGOVOY (1)	84
Jeff BARRY (1)	73
Ellie GREENWICH (1)	73
Frank S. HAMILTON (1)	68
Ernie SHELDON (1)	68
Acker BILK (1)	44
Robert MELLIN (1)	44
Van McCOY (1)	38
Irving BERLIN (3)	14
Terry NOLAND (1)	6.4
Norman PETTY (1)	6.4
James A. BISHOP (1)	5.8
Kenneth GAMBLE (1)	5.8
Kenny LYNCH (1)	4.1
Clyde McPHATTER (1)	0.0
Jerry WEXLER (1)	0.0
Buck RAM (1)	0.0
Al GREEN ►88 (19) [11]	**35026**
Al GREEN (15)	15364
Willie MITCHELL (10)	9053
Al JACKSON (5)	7701
Mabon HODGES (4)	1553
Palmer JAMES (2)	448
Curtis RODGERS (1)	403
Robert Earl WILLIAMS (1)	273
Barrett STRONG (1)	89
Norman WHITFIELD (1)	89
Reuben FAIRFAX (1)	27
Fred JORDAN (1)	27
RIGHTEOUS BROTHERS ►89 (25) [31]	**34726**
Barry MANN (2)	6871
Cynthia WEIL (2)	6871
Phil SPECTOR (3)	3874
Alex NORTH (3)	2544
Hy ZARET (3)	2544
Alan O'DAY (1)	1665
John STEVENSON (1)	1665
Robert MAXWELL (1)	1488
Carl SIGMAN (1)	1488
Bill MEDLEY (4)	983
Gerry GOFFIN (3)	896
Carole KING (3)	896
Richard MULLAN (1)	558

Jack RICHARDS (1)	558
Dennis LAMBERT (2)	508
Brian POTTER (2)	508
Garry BONNER (1)	169
Alan GORDON (1)	169
William S. COOK (1)	115
Bobby HATFIELD (2)	101
William STEVENSON (2)	85
Hoagy CARMICHAEL (1)	56
Stuart GORRELL (1)	56
Don HARRIS (1)	17
Dewey TERRY (1)	17
Nat BURTON (1)	9.4
Walter KENT (1)	9.4
Jerry BUTLER (1)	1.6
Calvin CARTER (1)	1.6
Curtis MAYFIELD (1)	1.6
Douglas Fontaine BROWN (1)	0.5
The SHIRELLES ►90 (29) [40]	**34530**
Luther DIXON (6)	7716
Florence GREEN (1)	4311
Gerry GOFFIN (2)	3112
Carole KING (2)	3112
Ralph BASS (2)	2570
Lowman PAULING (2)	2570
Willie DENSON (2)	1698
Howard GREENFIELD (1)	1359
Helen MILLER (1)	1359
Mack DAVID (3)	814
Burt BACHARACH (2)	804
Richard ADLER (1)	551
Robert ALLEN (1)	551
Shirley OWENS (2)	543
John PATTON (1)	364
Amiel SUMMERS (1)	364
Bob BRASS (1)	327
Irwin LEVINE (1)	327
Joe DeANGELIS (1)	318
Charles PARTEE (1)	318
Ed TOWNSEND (1)	256
Van McCOY (2)	225
Beverly LEE (2)	193
Artie KORNFELD (1)	148
Toni WINE (1)	148
Doris COLEY (1)	134
Addie HARRIS (1)	134
Frances AYCOCK (1)	48
Robert MOSELY (1)	48
Robert Napoleon TAYLOR (1)	48
Charlie RICH (1)	28
Ernest GOLD (2)	11
Stan LEBOWSKY (1)	8.6
Johnny LEHMANN (1)	8.6
Hal DAVID (2)	2.5
Sherman EDWARDS (1)	1.7
Gerald HARRIS (1)	1.0
George KERR (1)	1.0
Ronald Alonzo MILLER (1)	0.2
Lee PORTER (1)	0.2
Tommy ROE ►91 (26) [16]	**34491**
Tommy ROE (17)	24752
Freddy WELLER (5)	6933
Robin LUKE (1)	452
Lou JOSIE (1)	397
Harold LOGAN (1)	350
Lloyd PRICE (1)	350
TRADITIONAL (1)	350
Rick HALL (1)	273
Dan PENN (1)	273
Chuck BERRY (1)	218
Stan GELBER (1)	64
Merle KILGORE (1)	28

Tommy ROE ►91 (26) [16] *Cont'd*	**34491**
R.W. LAWS (1)	15
Buddy BUIE (1)	13
William GILMORE (1)	13
Felton JARVIS (1)	9.3
DURAN DURAN ►92 (16) [12]	**34431**
Simon Le BON (16)	7638
Nick RHODES (16)	7638
Nigel John TAYLOR (16)	7638
Andy TAYLOR (9)	5363
Roger TAYLOR (9)	5363
John BARRY (1)	672
Sterling CAMPBELL (1)	33
Warren CUCCURULLO (1)	33
Eleanor BROADWATER (1)	13
Robert CHAISSON (1)	13
Dale HAWKINS (1)	13
Stanley J. LEWIS (1)	13
Kenny ROGERS ►93 (25) [37]	**34243**
Lionel RICHIE (1)	8815
Roger BOWLING (2)	3750
Ricky Lynn CHRISTIAN (1)	2988
Steve GIBB (1)	2715
Billy Edd WHEELER (1)	2681
Bob MORRISON (2)	1777
Don SCHLITZ (1)	1431
Debbie HUPP (1)	1169
Kenny ROGERS (5)	1114
Hal BYNUM (1)	1069
Steve DORFF (1)	620
Marty PANZER (1)	620
Johnny WILSON (1)	608
Ben PETERS (1)	506
Al BRAGGS (1)	497
Deadric MALONE (1)	497
Lee GREENWOOD (1)	338
David MALLOY (1)	330
Thom SCHUYLER (1)	330
Even STEVENS (1)	330
Richard MARX (2)	309
Barry GIBB (2)	306
David FOSTER (1)	289
Albhy GALUTEN (1)	287
Steve GLASSMEYER (1)	212
Charles David ROBBINS (1)	130
Jeff SILBAR (1)	130
Van STEPHENSON (1)	130
Dave LOGGINS (1)	76
Ray DOGGETT (1)	65
Larry KEITH (1)	32
Danny MORRISON (1)	32
Johnny SLATE (1)	32
Maurice GIBB (1)	19
Mike DEKLE (1)	4.1
James ROWE (1)	1.2
Howard E. SMITH (1)	1.2
Helen REDDY ►94 (21) [36]	**33939**
Alan O'DAY (1)	4137
Linda LAURIE (1)	4039
Helen REDDY (2)	3272
Ray BURTON (1)	3244
Larry COLLINS (1)	2977
Alex HARVEY (1)	2977
Harriet SCHOCK (1)	2246
Kenny RANKIN (1)	1528
Ken ASCHER (1)	909
Paul WILLIAMS (1)	909
Tim RICE (1)	806
Andrew Lloyd WEBBER (1)	806
Bobby HART (1)	695
Danny JANSSEN (1)	695
Van MORRISON (1)	585
Will JENNINGS (1)	459
Richard KERR (1)	459
Umberto BINDI (1)	426
Gino PAOLI (1)	426
Carl SIGMAN (1)	426
Carole KING (2)	369
Patti DAHLSTROM (1)	289
Veronique SANSON (1)	289
Leon RUSSELL (1)	262
Gerry GOFFIN (1)	191
Toni STERN (1)	178
Mike TINSLEY (1)	47
Steve VOICE (1)	47
Peter YELLOWSTONE (1)	47
Amber DiLENA (1)	35
Jack KELLER (1)	35
Alan GORDON (1)	32
Kim FOWLEY (1)	28
Rick HENN (1)	28
Earle MANKEY (1)	28
Becky HOBBS (1)	12
John MELLENCAMP ►95 (22) [2]	**33880**
John MELLENCAMP (22)	29412
George GREEN (3)	4469
CAPTAIN & TENNILLE ►96 (14) [17]	**33858**
Toni TENNILLE (2)	10060
Neil SEDAKA (4)	9708
Willis Alan RAMSEY (1)	5059
Howard GREENFIELD (3)	4318
Berry GORDY (1)	1529
Smokey ROBINSON (1)	1529
John PRITCHARD (1)	418
Ray STEVENS (1)	418
Dana MERINO (1)	343
Kerry CHATER (1)	87
Douglas FOXWORTHY (1)	87
Armando MARTINEZ (1)	68
Garry BONNER (1)	66
Alan GORDON (1)	66
Mark SAFAN (1)	49
Melissa MANCHESTER (1)	27
Carole Bayer SAGER (1)	27
POINTER SISTERS ►97 (28) [41]	**33746**
Bruce SPRINGSTEEN (1)	5172
John BETTIS (1)	2490
Michael CLARK (1)	2490
Cynthia WEIL (2)	2119
Allen TOUSSAINT (3)	2103
Tom SNOW (1)	2012
Anita POINTER (6)	1382
Mark GOLDENBERG (1)	1161
Brock WALSH (1)	1161
Stephen MITCHELL (1)	1100
Marti SHARRON (1)	1100
Gary SKARDINA (1)	1100
Allee WILLIS (2)	1059
Layng MARTINE Jr. (1)	1049
Parker McGEE (1)	956
Danny SEMBELLO (1)	954
June POINTER (3)	786
Ruth POINTER (3)	786
Bonnie POINTER (3)	767
Trevor LAWRENCE (3)	615
David INNIS (1)	608
Sam LORBER (1)	608
Andy GOLDMARK (2)	271
Bruce ROBERTS (2)	271
David RUBINSON (1)	262
David McHUGH (1)	231
Willie DIXON (1)	177
John Alden BLACK (1)	124
Richard FELDMAN (1)	124
Nan O'BYRNE (1)	124
James INGRAM (1)	108
Barry MANN (1)	108
Franne GOLDE (1)	105
Marlo HENDERSON (1)	91
John Lewis PARKER (1)	68
Brian POTTER (1)	68
Vincent WAYNE (1)	19
Richard ADLER (1)	7.4
Jerry ROSS (1)	7.4
Estelle LEVITT (1)	2.2
Jerry RAGOVOY (1)	2.2
Huey LEWIS and the NEWS ►98 (19) [18]	**33626**
Huey LEWIS (12)	9602
Chris HAYES (7)	6355
Johnny COLLA (4)	3659
Alex CALL (1)	2263
Mutt LANGE (2)	1840
Bruce HORNSBY (1)	1820
John HORNSBY (1)	1820
Mike DUKE (2)	1043
Bill GIBSON (3)	871
Mike CHAPMAN (1)	810
Nicky CHINN (1)	810
Sean HOPPER (2)	787
Phil CODY (1)	654
Geoffrey PALMER (1)	397
André PESSIS (1)	384
Kevin WELLS (1)	384
Steve LEWIS (1)	84
Mario CIPOLLINA (1)	44
KC & The SUNSHINE BAND ►99 (17) [7]	**33461**
Harry Wayne CASEY (16)	16518
Rick FINCH (15)	16504
Lamont DOZIER (1)	132
Brian HOLLAND (1)	132
Eddie HOLLAND (1)	132
Willie CLARKE (1)	29
Joseph SIMMEL (1)	14
Gary LEWIS And The PLAYBOYS ►100 (16) [21]	**33426**
Glen HARDIN (3)	5969
Gary GELD (2)	2828
Peter UDELL (2)	2828
Leon RUSSELL (4)	2592
Bob BRASS (1)	2586
Al KOOPER (1)	2586
Irwin LEVINE (1)	2586
Snuff GARRETT (3)	2353
Gary LEWIS (2)	2031
Bobby RUSSELL (1)	1553
Al CAPPS (1)	1086
Roger COOK (1)	977
Roger GREENAWAY (1)	977
Garry BONNER (2)	492
Alan GORDON (2)	492
Sonny CURTIS (1)	431
John GUMMOE (1)	394
Roger TILLISON (1)	322
Don NIX (1)	239
Michael GORDON (1)	53
James GRIFFIN (1)	53
Paul REVERE And The RAIDERS/RAIDERS ►101 (26) [18]	**33418**
Mark LINDSAY (15)	9824
John D. LOUDERMILK (1)	8111
Terry MELCHER (7)	4305
Barry MANN (2)	3019
Cynthia WEIL (2)	3019
Joe SOUTH (1)	1026
Paul REVERE (3)	985
Richard DEY (1)	870
Roger HART (1)	870
Freddy WELLER (1)	554
Edmund VILLAREAL (1)	211
Wanda WATKINS (1)	211
Richard BURNS (1)	130
Bob SILLER (1)	130
Dennis LAMBERT (1)	65
Brian POTTER (1)	65
Jimmy WEBB (1)	24
Richard BERRY (1)	0.0
Bobby RYDELL ►102 (30) [32]	**33367**
Kal MANN (16)	7876
Bernie LOWE (13)	6458
Dave APPELL (12)	5333
Tony HATCH (1)	3638
Franco MIGLIACCI (1)	1309
Domenico MODUGNO (1)	1309
Mitchell PARISH (1)	1309
Norman GIMBEL (1)	775
Pablo Beltran RUIZ (1)	775
Mike ANTHONY (1)	606
Barry MANN (1)	606
Gerry GOFFIN (2)	536
Carole KING (2)	536
Harold ARLEN (1)	443
Johnny MERCER (1)	443
Clint BALLARD Jr. (1)	371
Fred TOBIAS (1)	371
Doc POMUS (1)	109
Mort SHUMAN (1)	109
Jan DOUGLAS (1)	95
Ray MERRELL (1)	95
Hal SHAPER (1)	95
John LENNON (1)	50
Paul McCARTNEY (1)	50
Jose Padilla SANCHEZ (1)	24
Harold ADAMSON (1)	11
Bruno CHERUBINI (1)	11
Eldo Di LAZZARO (1)	11
William E. JACKSON III (1)	4.2
Roy STRAIGIS (1)	4.2
George R. WILLIAMS (1)	4.2
Paul ANKA (1)	1.9
Andy GIBB ►103 (8) [5]	**33358**
Barry GIBB (7)	19185
Andy GIBB (4)	6132
Maurice GIBB (2)	3420
Robin GIBB (2)	3420
Blue WEAVER (1)	1200
FLEETWOOD MAC ►104 (24) [9]	**33250**
Christine McVIE (11)	13621
Stevie NICKS (7)	9879
Lindsey BUCKINGHAM (4)	5147
Robbie PATTON (1)	2215
Eddy QUINTELA (3)	1390
Sandy STEWART (1)	342
Jim RECOR (1)	334
Peter GREEN (2)	317
Richard DASHUT (1)	5.0

George MICHAEL ▶105 (13) [5]	**32687**
George MICHAEL (11)	28928
Elton JOHN (1)	1673
Bernie TAUPIN (1)	1673
Mick JAGGER (2)	207
Keith RICHARDS (2)	207
HEART ▶106 (30) [34]	**32668**
Nancy WILSON (14)	4445
Ann WILSON (14)	3976
Mutt LANGE (1)	3718
Thomas F. KELLY (2)	2489
Billy STEINBERG (2)	2489
Martin PAGE (1)	2152
Bernie TAUPIN (1)	2152
Diane WARREN (2)	2074
Holly KNIGHT (2)	1119
Mark MUELLER (1)	1114
Sue ENNIS (5)	915
George Richard DAVIS Jr. (1)	672
Lee DIAMOND (1)	672
Roger FISHER (4)	644
Gene BLACK (1)	597
Jeff HARRINGTON (1)	562
Jaime KYLE (1)	562
Michael DEROSIER (2)	433
Brian ALLEN (1)	411
Sheron ALTON (1)	411
Jim VALLANCE (1)	411
Franne GOLDE (1)	122
Bruce ROBERTS (1)	122
Jack CONRAD (1)	88
Bob GARRETT (1)	88
Howard LEESE (2)	74
Mark ANDES (1)	46
Denny CARMASSI (1)	46
Steve FOSSEN (1)	27
Jonathan CAIN (1)	18
Alex NORTH (1)	5.2
Hy ZARET (1)	5.2
Tom EVANS (1)	3.3
Pete HAM (1)	3.3
AIR SUPPLY ▶107 (13) [19]	**32586**
Graham RUSSELL (5)	15435
Jim STEINMAN (1)	4549
Clive DAVIS (1)	2889
Norman SALLITT (1)	2697
Dominic BUGATTI (1)	1526
Frank MUSKER (1)	1526
Kenneth Edward BELL (1)	800
Terry SKINNER (1)	800
J.L. WALLACE (1)	800
Rob HEGEL (1)	389
Dick WAGNER (1)	389
Howard GREENFIELD (1)	297
Ken HIRSCH (1)	297
Albert HAMMOND (1)	64
Diane WARREN (1)	64
Mary APPLEGATE (1)	16
Candy DeROUGE (1)	16
Gunther MENDE (1)	16
Jennifer RUSH (1)	16
Frankie AVALON ▶108 (27) [32]	**32275**
Ed MARSHALL (2)	10462
Peter DeANGELIS (9)	6085
Bob MARCUCCI (9)	6085
Russell FAITH (3)	1759
Diane DeNOTA (2)	1517
Clint BALLARD Jr. (1)	800
Hank HUNTER (1)	800

Clarence KEHNER (2)	778
Richard V. Di CICCO (1)	731
Pete DAMATO (1)	703
Joe RICCI (1)	703
Sid JACOBSON (1)	609
Ruth SEXTER (1)	609
Charles SINGLETON (1)	123
Jimmy WISNER (1)	81
Frankie AVALON (2)	70
Sal PONTI (1)	67
Jesse STONE (1)	61
Doc POMUS (1)	50
Mort SHUMAN (1)	50
Billy BARBERIS (1)	22
Teddy RANDAZZO (1)	22
Bobby WEINSTEIN (1)	22
Julian DASH (1)	13
Buddy FEYNE (1)	13
Erskine HAWKINS (1)	13
William Luther JOHNSON (1)	13
Sonny TROY (2)	8.1
Rick PETRONE (1)	5.1
Harvey LEMBECK (1)	3.0
Henry CREAMER (1)	0.2
J. Turner LAYTON (1)	0.2
Paula ABDUL ▶109 (10) [9]	**31567**
Oliver LEIBER (4)	11097
Peter LORD (3)	9042
Elliot WOLFF (2)	8501
Paula ABDUL (1)	850
V. Jeffrey SMITH (1)	850
Sandra ST. VICTOR (1)	850
Kenneth EDMONDS (1)	126
Antonio REID (1)	126
Daryl SIMMONS (1)	126
Roberta FLACK ▶110 (14) [23]	**30956**
Ewan MacCOLL (1)	9289
Gene McDANIELS (3)	4174
Charles FOX (1)	3829
Norman GIMBEL (1)	3829
Reggie LUCAS (2)	2254
James MTUME (2)	2254
Diane WARREN (1)	1968
Janis IAN (1)	742
Joe BROOKS (1)	447
Burt BACHARACH (1)	442
Bruce ROBERTS (1)	442
Carole Bayer SAGER (1)	442
William EATON (1)	129
Ralph MacDONALD (1)	129
William SALTER (1)	129
Eric MERCURY (1)	108
Stevie WONDER (1)	108
Gerry GOFFIN (1)	92
Carole KING (1)	92
Bobby FUSCO (1)	14
Charlotte LAWS (1)	14
Maurice McKINLEY (1)	14
Leon PENDARVIS (1)	14
EARTH, WIND & FIRE ▶111 (29) [25]	**30616**
Maurice WHITE (23)	9520
Wayne VAUGHN (5)	2725
Albert Philip McKAY (4)	2497
Philip BAILEY (5)	2265
Verdine WHITE (7)	1790
Lorenzo DUNN (3)	1751
David FOSTER (4)	1381
Bill CHAMPLIN (1)	1186
Jay GRAYDON (1)	1186

Allee WILLIS (3)	1003
Peter COR (1)	775
Bernard TAYLOR (1)	775
John LENNON (1)	605
Paul McCARTNEY (1)	605
Charles STEPNEY (1)	541
Reggie BURKE (1)	504
Wanda HUTCHINSON (3)	346
Skip SCARBOROUGH (1)	262
Eddie DEL BARRIO (2)	261
SKYLARK (1)	220
Martin PAGE (1)	172
Brenda RUSSELL (2)	141
Ralph JOHNSON (1)	53
Wade FLEMONS (1)	24
Don WHITEHEAD (1)	24
STYX ▶112 (23) [5]	**30422**
Dennis DeYOUNG (17)	24569
Tommy SHAW (7)	4961
James YOUNG (3)	585
Glen BURTNICK (2)	278
Sal GIGLIO Jr. (1)	28
Johnny MATHIS ▶113 (49) [63]	**30368**
Robert ALLEN (6)	5847
Al STILLMAN (5)	5556
Paul VANCE (5)	2909
Eddie SNYDER (3)	1252
Leon CARR (1)	1167
Sherman EDWARDS (1)	902
Ben RALEIGH (1)	902
Paul Francis WEBSTER (5)	888
Johnny BURKE (1)	868
Erroll GARNER (1)	868
William TENNYSON (1)	702
Clyde OTIS (2)	669
Belford HENDRICKS (1)	667
Stephen SONDHEIM (3)	645
Sammy FAIN (1)	614
Jule STYNE (1)	545
Dimitri TIOMKIN (2)	415
Ned WASHINGTON (2)	415
Lee POCKRISS (1)	350
Billy MYLES (1)	342
Abner SILVER (1)	340
Sid WAYNE (1)	340
Peter Lind HAYES (1)	266
Jerry LIVINGSTON (3)	264
Thom BELL (2)	212
Linda CREED (2)	212
Richard FERRARIS (1)	202
Norman KAYE (1)	202
Ray EVANS (1)	163
Jay LIVINGSTON (1)	163
Jack SEGAL (1)	151
Bobby WORTH (1)	126
Richard AHLERT (1)	108
James LYONS (1)	108
Bobby SCOTT (1)	108
Alfred NEWMAN (2)	103
Leonard BERNSTEIN (2)	100
Sammy CAHN (1)	93
Oscar HAMMERSTEIN (1)	92
Richard RODGERS (1)	92
Henry MANCINI (1)	56
Johnny MERCER (1)	56
Eaton MAGOON (1)	47
Alan Jay LERNER (2)	43
Frederick LOEWE (1)	42
Thomas GARLOCK (1)	23
Alan JEFFREYS (1)	23
Marvin MORROW (1)	23
Keith STEGALL (1)	23

Larry KUSIK (1)	9.8
Nino ROTA (1)	9.8
Ray ELLIS (1)	6.7
Teddy BART (1)	6.1
Paul WYATT (1)	6.1
Ruth LYONS (1)	5.6
Allyn FERGUSON (1)	4.3
Ernie RICHMAN (1)	4.3
Neil WESTEN (1)	4.3
Ed MARSHALL (1)	2.7
Michael COLICCHIO (1)	2.1
Anthony PIANO (1)	2.1
Chris TOWNS (1)	1.9
Burton LANE (1)	1.2
MAMAS & The PAPAS ▶114 (15) [11]	**29786**
John PHILLIPS (11)	18651
Michelle PHILLIPS (2)	3655
Ralph BASS (1)	2526
Lowman PAULING (1)	2526
Dennis DOHERTY (2)	1415
Lorenz HART (1)	325
Richard RODGERS (1)	325
Bobby FREEMAN (1)	286
Marvin GAYE (1)	26
Ivy Jo HUNTER (1)	26
William STEVENSON (1)	26
B.J. THOMAS ▶115 (24) [24]	**29696**
Burt BACHARACH (3)	5611
Hal DAVID (3)	5611
Mark JAMES (5)	4699
Chips MOMAN (2)	2572
Larry Lee BUTLER (1)	2432
Barry MANN (2)	1639
Cynthia WEIL (2)	1639
Mark CHARRON (2)	1078
Buddy BUIE (2)	696
Johnny CHRISTOPHER (2)	604
Wayne Carson THOMPSON (1)	580
Roger CHRISTIAN (1)	579
Brian WILSON (1)	579
J.R. COBB (1)	359
Robert NIX (1)	337
Steve TYRELL (1)	308
Bobby EMMONS (1)	185
Paul WILLIAMS (1)	79
Chris CHRISTIAN (1)	27
Johnny BOND (1)	25
Ernest TUBB (1)	25
Stevie WONDER (1)	13
Hank WILLIAMS (1)	13
Lewis J. ANDERSON (1)	4.9
The DOORS ▶116 (18) [5]	**29372**
Robby KRIEGER (16)	7907
Jim MORRISON (13)	7367
Ray MANZAREK (14)	7053
John DENSMORE (13)	6976
Van MORRISON (1)	68
Lesley GORE ▶117 (22) [33]	**28867**
John MADARA (1)	2856
David WHITE (1)	2856
Mark BARKAN (4)	2700
Ben RALEIGH (4)	2700
Cy CRANE (2)	1965
Herb WEINER (2)	1965
John GLUCK (1)	1956
Wally GOLD (1)	1956
Edna LEWIS (1)	1511
Beverly ROSS (1)	1511
Marvin HAMLISCH (2)	1323

Lesley GORE	
►117 (22) [33] *Cont'd*	**28867**
Howard LIEBLING (2)	1323
Jeff BARRY (2)	1151
Ellie GREENWICH (2)	1151
Lesley GORE (3)	352
Sonny GORDON (1)	264
Stanley KAHAN (1)	179
Paul KAUFMAN (1)	179
Michael GORE (2)	173
Ric CARTEY (1)	167
Carole JOYNER (1)	167
Raymond BLOODWORTH (1)	86
L. Russell BROWN (1)	86
Bob CREWE (1)	86
Helen MILLER (1)	60
Tony POWERS (1)	60
Michael GORDON (1)	32
James GRIFFIN (1)	32
Carole Bayer SAGER (1)	4.1
Toni WINE (1)	4.1
Ramon ARCUSA (1)	4.0
Manuel De La CALVA (1)	4.0
Michael JULIEN (1)	4.0
The ASSOCIATION	
►118 (16) [16]	**28770**
Terry KIRKMAN (4)	9503
Ruthann FRIEDMAN (1)	8778
Dick ADDRISI (2)	3736
Don ADDRISI (2)	3736
Tandyn ALMER (1)	1719
Jules ALEXANDER (2)	713
Jim YESTER (2)	450
Moon MARTIN (1)	63
Albert HAMMOND (1)	28
Mike HAZLEWOOD (1)	28
John SEBASTIAN (1)	9.9
Ron EDGAR (1)	1.0
Michael FENNELLY (1)	1.0
Lee MALLORY (1)	1.0
Doug RHODES (1)	1.0
Joseph STEC (1)	1.0
The TURTLES	
►119 (18) [16]	**28718**
Garry BONNER (5)	8292
Alan GORDON (5)	8292
Bob DYLAN (1)	2181
Gene CLARK (1)	1848
Roger McGUINN (1)	1848
P.F. SLOAN (4)	1333
Al NICHOL (5)	745
Howard KAYLAN (4)	717
Jim PONS (4)	717
Mark VOLMAN (4)	717
Steve BARRI (3)	706
John BARBATA (2)	621
Harry NILSSON (1)	403
Judee SILL (1)	172
John SEITER (2)	97
Charles PORTZ (1)	27
BLONDIE ►120 (9) [8]	**28694**
Clement A. BOZEWSKI (8)	7729
Deborah HARRY (8)	7729
Christopher STEIN (5)	3982
Giorgio MORODER (1)	3384
John HOLT (1)	2753
Duke REID (1)	2753
Nigel HARRISON (1)	264
Jimmy DESTRI (1)	99
George HARRISON	
►121 (18) [3]	**28604**
George HARRISON (17)	24442

Rudy CLARK (1)	3952
Jeff LYNNE (1)	211
GUESS WHO ►122 (23) [9]	**28589**
Burton CUMMINGS (19)	12639
Randy BACHMAN (6)	7214
Kurt WINTER (8)	3081
Garry PETERSON (2)	1794
Jim KALE (1)	1760
Johnny KIDD (1)	1155
Bill WALLACE (2)	602
Domenic TROIANO (2)	309
Don McDOUGALL (1)	34
Lloyd PRICE	
►123 (22) [11]	**28440**
Lloyd PRICE (20)	12764
Harold LOGAN (16)	11853
TRADITIONAL (1)	2615
Johnny BURKE (1)	424
Erroll GARNER (1)	424
John PATTON (1)	311
John Bobby BERRY (1)	17
Don COVAY (1)	17
Luther DIXON (1)	12
William BOSKENT (1)	2.1
Frederick KNIGHT (1)	1.9
LOVIN' SPOONFUL	
►124 (14) [6]	**27976**
John SEBASTIAN (12)	22150
Steve BOONE (3)	3226
Mark SEBASTIAN (1)	2338
John STEWART (1)	207
Garry BONNER (1)	27
Alan GORDON (1)	27
The IMPRESSIONS	
►125 (45) [12]	**27286**
Curtis MAYFIELD (37)	22616
TRADITIONAL (1)	2022
Ed TOWNSEND (3)	1364
Arthur BROOKS (1)	348
Richard BROOKS (1)	348
Jerry BUTLER (1)	348
Oscar BROWN Jr. (1)	87
Charles Henry JACKSON Jr. (2)	54
Marvin YANCY (2)	54
Richard Anthony TUFO (1)	41
Roy HAMILTON (1)	2.1
Clyde OTIS (1)	2.1
Donny OSMOND	
►126 (22) [33]	**27278**
Gerry GOFFIN (2)	4294
Carole KING (2)	4294
Paul ANKA (2)	3699
Evan ROGERS (5)	2302
Carl STURKEN (5)	2302
Rick HALL (1)	1420
Billy SHERRILL (1)	1420
Jerry LIVINGSTON (1)	1076
Paul Francis WEBSTER (1)	1076
Sylvia DEE (1)	682
Sid LIPPMAN (1)	682
Peter DeANGELIS (1)	552
Bob MARCUCCI (1)	552
Lou HANDMAN (1)	527
Roy TURK (1)	527
Phil MEDLEY (1)	296
Ric CARTEY (1)	265
Carole JOYNER (1)	265
Raymond BLOODWORTH (1)	217
L. Russell BROWN (1)	217
Donny OSMOND (3)	128
Selassie BURKE (1)	89
Solomon BURKE Jr. (1)	89

David GAMSON (1)	86
Tony LeMANS (1)	86
Joe SOUTH (1)	47
Edward HEYMAN (1)	38
Victor YOUNG (1)	38
Lamont DOZIER (1)	2.1
Ronald DUNBAR (1)	2.1
Brian HOLLAND (1)	2.1
Eddie HOLLAND (1)	2.1
Alberto CURCI (1)	0.0
McGUIRE SISTERS	
►127 (46) [84]	**27159**
Alan FREED (1)	3288
Harvey FUQUA (1)	3288
Johnny MERCER (2)	2723
Odis ECHOLS (1)	1998
Charlie PHILLIPS (1)	1998
Richard MULLAN (1)	959
Jack RICHARDS (1)	959
Ivory Joe HUNTER (1)	923
Hank HUNTER (1)	830
Jack KELLER (1)	830
Dick CHARLES (1)	808
Larry MARKES (1)	808
Ray GILBERT (1)	661
Edward ORY (1)	661
Steve ALLEN (1)	635
George DUNING (1)	635
Buddy KAYE (4)	352
Robert MELLIN (1)	284
Cindy WALKER (1)	268
Jimmie CRANE (1)	258
Al JACOBS (1)	258
Calvin CARTER (1)	257
James HUDSON (1)	257
Jules LOMAN (2)	249
John MARASCALCO (1)	217
George MOTOLA (1)	217
Kenny JACOBSON (1)	175
Rhoda ROBERTS (1)	175
Dux DeJOHN (1)	158
Julie DeJOHN (1)	158
Leo DeJOHN (1)	158
Gene AUTRY (1)	155
Fred ROSE (1)	155
Bill KATZ (2)	125
Ruth ROBERTS (2)	125
Dorcas COCHRAN (1)	115
Rae SEYMOUR (1)	115
Elmer BERNSTEIN (1)	95
Sylvia FINE (1)	95
Bob GOODMAN (1)	85
Sal IZZO (1)	62
Bob PERPER (1)	62
Nikolai RIMSKY-KORSAKOV (1)	61
Bob THIELE (1)	61
Stella UNGER (2)	53
Victor YOUNG (2)	53
Lillian BARCO (1)	42
Gene DePAUL (1)	42
Leon CARR (1)	33
Hal DAVID (1)	33
Jack FULTON (1)	19
Lois STEELE (1)	19
Harold ADAMSON (1)	15
Murray KANE (2)	12
Dick JACOBS (1)	10
Edna LEWIS (1)	10
Clint BALLARD Jr. (1)	9.4
Noel SHERMAN (1)	9.4
Franco MIGLIACCI (1)	5.6
Domenico MODUGNO (1)	5.6
Mitchell PARISH (1)	5.6

Fernando ALBANO (1)	3.9
Al HOFFMAN (1)	3.9
Dick MANNING (1)	3.9
Edwin GREINES (1)	2.4
Hal GORDON (1)	1.8
Ruth KARDON (1)	1.8
Horace LINSLEY (1)	1.8
Michael MERLO (1)	1.2
Patrick WELCH (1)	1.2
Mack DISCANT (1)	0.7
Doris TAUBER (1)	0.7
Sammy CAHN (1)	0.4
Jimmy VAN HEUSEN (1)	0.4
Lawrence ELOW (1)	0.0
Linda ROBERTS (1)	0.0
Phyllis TAFF (1)	0.0
Rudy JACKSON (1)	0.0
Eddy RAY (1)	0.0
Stuart HAMBLEN (1)	0.0
Sammy FAIN (1)	0.0
Dan SHAPIRO (1)	0.0
Dimitri TIOMKIN (1)	0.0
Ned WASHINGTON (1)	0.0
FOUR LADS	
►128 (26) [30]	**26949**
Robert ALLEN (9)	8806
Al STILLMAN (7)	8282
Frank LOESSER (1)	3973
Tom GLAZER (1)	1000
August MSARURGWA (1)	1000
Dazz JORDAN (3)	481
Kenny JACOBSON (1)	384
Rhoda ROBERTS (1)	384
Sylvia DEE (1)	369
Sid LIPPMAN (1)	369
Ken DARBY (1)	333
TRADITIONAL (1)	333
Gordon CHARLES (2)	312
Joseph STONE (1)	279
Richard ADLER (1)	245
Anton DVORAK (2)	192
Boudleaux BRYANT (1)	63
Jean DAVID (1)	24
Jerry LIVINGSTON (1)	19
Paul Francis WEBSTER (1)	19
Roy JORDAN (1)	17
Ulpio MINUCCI (1)	17
Al HOFFMAN (2)	13
Dick MANNING (2)	13
Nicolas ARDITI (1)	13
Fred GRANT (1)	13
Harold BARLOW (1)	0.0
Deadric MALONE (1)	0.0
Ferdinand WASHINGTON (1)	0.0
Jester HAIRSTON (1)	0.0
BREAD ►129 (13) [1]	**26935**
David GATES (13)	26935
Gary PUCKETT And	
The UNION GAP	
►130 (7) [8]	**26822**
Jerry FULLER (3)	16148
James W. GLASER (1)	2853
Jimmy PAYNE (1)	2853
Alan BERNSTEIN (1)	1532
Vic MILLROSE (1)	1532
Gary USHER (1)	1458
Richard MAINEGRA (1)	223
Red WEST (1)	223
Carly SIMON	
►131 (22) [16]	**26758**
Carly SIMON (17)	16162
Marvin HAMLISCH (1)	2948

Carly SIMON ▶131 (22) [16] *Cont'd*	**26758**
Carole Bayer SAGER (1)	2948
Jacob BRACKMAN (5)	1975
Michael McDONALD (2)	1236
Mike MAINIERI (2)	1129
Larry RASPBERRY (1)	102
Gerard McMAHON (1)	87
Andy GOLDMARK (1)	51
Bernard EDWARDS (1)	43
Nile RODGERS (1)	43
Arif MARDIN (1)	7.3
James TAYLOR (1)	7.3
Peter John WOOD (1)	6.2
Mac REBENNACK (1)	5.6
Alvin ROBINSON (1)	5.6
Rick SPRINGFIELD ▶132 (20) [6]	**26511**
Rick SPRINGFIELD (19)	22845
Sammy HAGAR (1)	2093
Danny TATE (1)	568
Blaise TOSTI (1)	568
Eric McCUSKER (1)	219
Tim PIERCE (1)	219
DOOBIE BROTHERS ▶133 (28) [28]	**26420**
Tom JOHNSTON (8)	6452
Michael McDONALD (9)	6067
Patrick SIMMONS (7)	5446
Kenny LOGGINS (1)	2655
Patrick HENDERSON (1)	920
Lamont DOZIER (2)	676
Brian HOLLAND (2)	676
Eddie HOLLAND (2)	676
Lester ABRAMS (1)	562
Art REYNOLDS (1)	517
Charles E. KAUFMAN (1)	326
Eddie SCHWARTZ (1)	326
Carlene CARTER (1)	238
Keith KNUDSEN (1)	238
John McFEE (1)	238
Ernie ISLEY (1)	45
Marvin ISLEY (1)	45
O'Kelly ISLEY (1)	45
Ronald ISLEY (1)	45
Rudolph ISLEY (1)	45
Chris JASPER (1)	45
Willie MITCHELL (1)	34
Earl RANDLE (1)	34
Eugene FIELD (1)	25
Lucy SIMON (1)	25
Carly SIMON (1)	11
Jeff BAXTER (1)	2.6
John HARTMAN (1)	2.6
Marty ROBBINS ▶134 (30) [17]	**26397**
Marty ROBBINS (18)	21900
Roberta BELLAMY (1)	834
Melvin ENDSLEY (1)	702
Dimitri TIOMKIN (1)	347
Paul Francis WEBSTER (1)	347
Burt BACHARACH (1)	346
Hal DAVID (1)	346
Mack DAVID (1)	299
Jerry LIVINGSTON (1)	299
Al ALLEN (1)	208
Barry De VORZON (1)	208
Roy C. BENNETT (2)	199
Sid TEPPER (2)	199
Herbert WILSON (1)	90
Tompall GLASER (1)	66
Lee EMERSON (1)	6.4

Joe BABCOCK (1)	0.4
Mariah CAREY ▶135 (6) [6]	**26281**
Mariah CAREY (6)	12371
Ben MARGULIES (3)	6811
Walter AFANASIEFF (1)	2174
Narada Michael WALDEN (1)	1846
Robert CLIVILLES (1)	1539
David COLE (1)	1539
Billy OCEAN ▶136 (13) [9]	**26162**
Billy OCEAN (13)	10387
Keith DIAMOND (4)	4607
Mutt LANGE (4)	4002
Wayne BRATHWAITE (5)	3190
Barry EASTMOND (5)	3190
Ben FINDON (1)	354
James WOODLEY (1)	206
Jolyon SKINNER (1)	204
Nigel MARTINEZ (1)	22
Bryan ADAMS ▶137 (15) [5]	**26042**
Bryan ADAMS (15)	11800
Jim VALLANCE (12)	7292
Mutt LANGE (3)	4170
Michael KAMEN (1)	2168
Eric KAGNA (1)	612
BON JOVI ▶138 (12) [6]	**25995**
Jon BON JOVI (11)	11046
Richie SAMBORA (7)	9070
Desmond CHILD (4)	5283
Mark AVSEC (1)	288
George KARAK (1)	227
Dave BRYAN (1)	82
Frankie VALLI ▶139 (16) [17]	**25931**
Bob CREWE (9)	8616
Barry GIBB (1)	6566
Bob GAUDIO (5)	4632
Kenny NOLAN (1)	2681
Denny RANDELL (1)	1075
Mort GARSON (1)	624
Bob HILLIARD (1)	624
L. Russell BROWN (2)	275
Raymond BLOODWORTH (1)	263
Charlie CALELLO (1)	215
Guy FLETCHER (1)	151
Doug FLETT (1)	151
Boz SCAGGS (1)	37
Richard KERR (1)	5.1
Marty PANZER (1)	5.1
Victoria PIKE (1)	4.9
Teddy RANDAZZO (1)	4.9
WAR ▶140 (18) [11]	**25923**
Thomas ALLEN (18)	3548
Harold BROWN (18)	3548
Lonnie JORDAN (18)	3548
Lee OSKAR (18)	3548
Howard SCOTT (18)	3548
Charles MILLER (16)	3542
Morris DICKERSON (15)	3540
Jerry GOLDSTEIN (10)	1092
Luther RABB (3)	7.6
Tweed SMITH (1)	1.3
Ronnie HAMMON (1)	1.3
PETER, PAUL & MARY ▶141 (20) [19]	**25852**
John DENVER (1)	7725
Bob DYLAN (4)	6287
Peter YARROW (4)	3946
Leonard LIPTON (1)	2828
Paul STOOKEY (6)	789
Lee HAYS (1)	659

Pete SEEGER (1)	659
Gordon LIGHTFOOT (2)	632
David George DIXON (1)	509
James Howard MASON (1)	509
TRADITIONAL (4)	428
Will HOLT (1)	218
Milton OKUN (3)	200
Mary TRAVERS (2)	198
Mike SETTLE (1)	156
Elena MEZZETTI (3)	100
Tracy BATTEAST (1)	5.3
Peter LANE (1)	1.5
Fred NEIL (1)	0.5
Ringo STARR ▶142 (14) [15]	**25805**
Ringo STARR (5)	10577
George HARRISON (2)	2985
Richard SHERMAN (1)	2389
Robert SHERMAN (1)	2389
Buck RAM (1)	1985
Hoyt AXTON (1)	1703
David P. JACKSON (1)	1703
Vini PONCIA (2)	1007
Carl GROSSMAN (1)	523
John LENNON (1)	340
Buzz RABIN (1)	88
Bruce CHANNEL (1)	58
Margaret COBB (1)	58
Elton JOHN (1)	0.0
Bernie TAUPIN (1)	0.0
Paul SIMON ▶143 (17) [2]	**25793**
Paul SIMON (17)	25778
Forere MOTLOHELOA (1)	15
DONOVAN ▶144 (17) [2]	**25766**
Donovan LEITCH (16)	25329
Buffy SAINTE-MARIE (1)	437
Chuck BERRY ▶145 (31) [9]	**25636**
Chuck BERRY (28)	23787
Russ FRATTO (1)	781
Alan FREED (1)	781
Billy DAVIS (1)	116
Alonso MITCHELL (1)	116
Marvin Lee BRODIE (1)	15
Johnny MARKS (1)	15
Lou BAXTER (1)	13
Johnny MOORE (1)	13
Wilson PICKETT ▶146 (40) [61]	**25564**
Wilson PICKETT (13)	3335
Arlester CHRISTIAN (1)	2155
Chris KENNER (1)	2102
Steve CROPPER (6)	1932
Brad SHAPIRO (3)	1312
Bobby WOMACK (4)	1237
Eddie FLOYD (2)	1176
Bonny RICE (1)	1089
Rodger COLLINS (1)	1018
Kenneth GAMBLE (1)	707
Leon HUFF (1)	707
Jeff BARRY (1)	558
Andy KIM (1)	558
Andy FRASER (1)	480
Paul RODGERS (1)	480
John LENNON (1)	467
Paul McCARTNEY (1)	467
Billy ROBERTS (1)	405
Jerry AKINES (1)	347
Johnnie BELLMON (1)	347
Victor DRAYTON (1)	347
Reginald TURNER (1)	347
Harold LOGAN (1)	262

Lloyd PRICE (1)	262
TRADITIONAL (1)	262
Jerry WEXLER (2)	229
Mars BONFIRE (1)	218
Rudy CLARK (1)	183
Reggie YOUNG (1)	180
Bert BERNS (1)	170
Solomon BURKE (1)	170
Willie SCHOFIELD (1)	162
Robert WEST (1)	162
George Henry JACKSON (2)	159
Dave CRAWFORD (1)	147
Willie MARTIN (1)	147
Dick HOLLER (1)	142
King CURTIS (1)	133
Luther DIXON (1)	102
Robert BATEMAN (1)	93
William Nelson SANDERS (1)	93
Earl CAGE (1)	91
Lindell HILL (1)	91
Larry CHAMBERS (1)	68
Melvin LEAKES (1)	68
Raymond MOORE (1)	68
Lamont DOZIER (1)	44
Brian HOLLAND (1)	44
Eddie HOLLAND (1)	44
Don COVAY (1)	42
Johnny NASH (1)	42
William STEVENSON (1)	42
Randy NEWMAN (1)	23
Bobby ELI (1)	14
Carl FISHER (1)	14
Dee ERVIN (1)	4.1
James WILLINGHAM (1)	4.1
Bernard BROOMER (1)	2.6
Gene DOZIER (1)	2.6
Lee PHILLIPS (1)	2.6
Bunny SIGLER (1)	2.6
John LENNON ▶147 (10) [4]	**25520**
John LENNON (9)	24874
Ben E. KING (1)	216
Jerry LEIBER (1)	216
Mike STOLLER (1)	216
Bill HALEY And His COMETS ▶148 (36) [45]	**25515**
Jimmy DeKNIGHT (3)	4342
Max C. FREEDMAN (3)	4342
Jesse STONE (2)	3965
Robert GUIDRY (1)	2750
Bill HALEY (9)	1622
Winfield SCOTT (1)	1091
Julius DIXON (1)	803
Beverly ROSS (1)	803
Joe REISMAN (1)	653
TRADITIONAL (1)	498
Arrett KEEFER (4)	465
Robert BLACKWELL (1)	376
John MARASCALCO (1)	376
Frank PINGATORE (2)	331
Jimmy AYRE (1)	314
Mildred PHILLIPS (1)	314
Bickley REICHNER (1)	314
Ruth KEEFER (1)	246
J. Leslie McFARLAND (2)	241
Milt GABLER (3)	174
Rudy POMPILLI (2)	172
Danny OVERBEA (1)	165
Johnny GRANDE (2)	158
Catherine CAFRA (2)	153
Billy WILLIAMSON (1)	144
Curtis Reginald LEWIS (1)	132

Bill HALEY And His COMETS ►148 (36) [45] *Cont'd* **25515**

August MSARURGWA (1)	87
Cayet MANGIARACINA (1)	55
Harry BAGBY (2)	51
Harry CRAFTON (2)	51
Don KEENE (2)	51
Fred KARGER (1)	42
Robert E. KENT (1)	42
Mort GARSON (1)	26
Earl SHUMAN (1)	26
Denver DARLING (1)	22
Vaughn HORTON (1)	22
Ralph JONES (1)	14
Stella LEE (1)	14
Franny BEECHER (1)	14
Al REX (1)	14
Howard Ellington Riddiford BARNES (1)	12
Hal BLAIR (1)	12
Fred ROSE (1)	8.4
Zeb TURNER (1)	8.4

The O'JAYS ►149 (29) [21] **25472**

Leon HUFF (19)	10830
Kenneth GAMBLE (18)	9164
Gene McFADDEN (1)	1666
John WHITEHEAD (1)	1666
Anthony JACKSON (1)	621
Allen TOUSSAINT (2)	354
Cary GILBERT (1)	245
Jackie MEMBERS (1)	114
Robert POINDEXTER (1)	114
Stan POINDEXTER (1)	114
Emma THOMAS (1)	114
Bunny SIGLER (2)	91
George KERR (1)	80
Larry ROBERTS (1)	80
Allan FELDER (1)	50
Joseph JEFFERSON (1)	43
Charles SIMMONS (1)	43
Phil HURTT (1)	40
Eddie LEVERT (2)	17
Kenny SEYMOUR (1)	15
Walter WILLIAMS (1)	9.0

AMERICA ►150 (18) [9] **25429**

Dewey BUNNELL (6)	11523
Gerry BECKLEY (5)	6954
Russ BALLARD (2)	2655
Dan PEEK (4)	2529
Catherine PEEK (1)	956
Ian THOMAS (1)	378
Willis Alan RAMSEY (1)	292
John PHILLIPS (1)	71
Michelle PHILLIPS (1)	71

Patti PAGE ►151 (62) [104] **25386**

Al HOFFMAN (3)	2905
Dick MANNING (3)	2905
Irving GORDON (2)	1526
Earl SHUMAN (3)	1198
Kim GANNON (1)	987
Milton YAKUS (2)	956
Mack DAVID (1)	880
Frank DeVOL (1)	880
Mort GARSON (1)	852
Irwin PINCUS (1)	712
Claire ROTHROCK (1)	712
Hank COCHRAN (1)	603
Chuck WILLIS (1)	452
William ENGVICK (1)	423
Edith PIAF (1)	423
Clint BALLARD Jr. (1)	370
Fred TOBIAS (1)	370
Leon CARR (3)	369
Michael ELIAS (1)	291
William TESONE (1)	291
Michael MERLO (1)	284
Patrick WELCH (1)	284
Milton DeLUGG (1)	258
Bob HILLIARD (1)	258
Milt GABLER (1)	244
Arthur KORB (1)	244
Charlie PURVIS (1)	244
Nat SIMON (2)	210
Howard GREENFIELD (2)	190
Jack KELLER (2)	190
Milton AGER (1)	181
Jean SCHWARTZ (1)	181
Ned WEVER (1)	181
Mack GORDON (1)	176
Harry REVEL (1)	176
Charles TOBIAS (1)	175
Charles SINGLETON (2)	166
Sammy CAHN (1)	163
Jimmy VAN HEUSEN (1)	163
Gordon JENKINS (1)	160
Jack SCHAFER (1)	155
Joe SHERMAN (1)	154
Noel SHERMAN (1)	154
Phil MEDLEY (1)	152
Rose Marie McCOY (1)	139
John HARTFORD (1)	115
Hal DAVID (1)	113
Sherman EDWARDS (1)	113
Burt BACHARACH (1)	106
Jack WOLF (1)	106
Joseph Francis BURKE (1)	105
Don RAYE (1)	105
Oramay DIAMOND (1)	81
Dave DREYER (1)	81
Clyde OTIS (1)	81
Lefty FRIZZELL (1)	76
Richard ADLER (2)	75
Jerry ROSS (2)	75
Phil GREEN (1)	65
Norman NEWELL (1)	65
Roy ALFRED (1)	63
Abner SILVER (1)	63
Jenny Lou CARSON (1)	54
Kay TWOMEY (1)	54
Ben WEISMAN (1)	54
Fred WISE (1)	54
Paul ANKA (1)	52
Peter CHATMAN (1)	45
Aaron SPARKS (1)	45
Milton SPARKS (1)	45
Ralph CARE (1)	42
Sol MARCUS (1)	42
Ray EVANS (1)	41
Jay LIVINGSTON (1)	41
Jimmy KENNEDY (1)	35
Oscar HAMMERSTEIN (1)	32
Richard RODGERS (1)	32
Jerry LIVINGSTON (1)	28
Mitchell PARISH (1)	28
Horace OTT (1)	27
Paul VANCE (1)	23
Harold ADAMSON (1)	20
Jimmy McHUGH (1)	20
Norman GIMBEL (1)	11
David SAXON (1)	11
George MOTOLA (1)	7.3
Rickie PAGE (1)	7.3
Hal COTTON (1)	6.3
Gerhard EBELER (1)	6.3
Ken GRIFFIN (1)	6.3
Hans OTTEN (1)	6.3
Harold BEEBE (1)	4.7
TRADITIONAL (1)	4.3
Bobby RUSSELL (1)	3.5
Cy COLEMAN (1)	2.9
Carolyn LEIGH (1)	2.9
Fay TISHMAN (1)	2.7
Neval NADER (1)	2.1
Jimmy RADCLIFFE (1)	2.1
Yvette BALL (1)	1.7
Robert MOSELY (1)	1.7
Russell MURRAY (1)	1.7
Bennie BENJAMIN (1)	0.0
George David WEISS (1)	0.0

The HOLLIES ►152 (26) [29] **25354**

Allan CLARKE (11)	4678
Graham GOULDMAN (2)	3738
Tony HICKS (9)	2815
Graham NASH (8)	2743
Roger COOK (1)	1916
Roger GREENAWAY (1)	1916
Bob RUSSELL (1)	1220
Bobby SCOTT (1)	1220
Albert HAMMOND (1)	1203
Mike HAZLEWOOD (1)	1203
Kenny LYNCH (1)	340
Charles SILVERMAN (1)	336
Al GORGONI (1)	192
Chip TAYLOR (1)	192
Tony MACAULAY (1)	177
Geoff STEPHENS (1)	177
Lamont DOZIER (1)	175
Brian HOLLAND (1)	175
Eddie HOLLAND (1)	175
Greg CARROLL (2)	145
Doris PAYNE (2)	145
Colin HORTON-JENNINGS (1)	142
Garth WATT-ROY (1)	142
Guy FLETCHER (1)	67
Doug FLETT (1)	67
Clint BALLARD Jr. (1)	24
Bruce SPRINGSTEEN (1)	19
Terry SYLVESTER (1)	9.5
Judee SILL (1)	3.5

ELECTRIC LIGHT ORCHESTRA ►153 (25) [2] **25313**

Jeff LYNNE (24)	24720
Chuck BERRY (1)	593

Billy VAUGHN and His Orchestra ►154 (49) [72] **25301**

Hans ENGELMANN (1)	7273
Harry TOBIAS (1)	1845
Percy WENRICH (1)	1845
V.C. GILBERT (2)	1562
Mary Hadler GILBERT (1)	1485
Bert KAEMPFERT (2)	1460
Tony HATCH (1)	1083
Sebastian YRADIER (1)	997
Ralph RAINGER (1)	662
Bob NOLAN (1)	612
Franz DOELLE (1)	605
Johnny BOND (1)	540
Dimitri TIOMKIN (1)	533
Bill JUSTIS (1)	500
Sid MANKER (1)	500
Sigmund ROMBERG (1)	436
Kurt WEILL (1)	375
Heino GAZE (1)	342
Richard STEPHENS (1)	302
Jimmy TORRES (1)	302
Bobby DARIN (1)	190
Hank WILLIAMS (1)	144
Tommy GRIFFIN (1)	142
Freddie MORRIS (1)	142
Cliff FRIEND (1)	101
Charles TOBIAS (1)	101
John LENNON (1)	94
Paul McCARTNEY (1)	94
Jimmy FORREST (1)	91
Prince LELEIOHOKU (1)	88
Johnny NOBLE (1)	88
Ervin ROUSE (1)	78
Milton BERLE (1)	76
Jerry LIVINGSTON (1)	76
Mack DAVID (1)	72
Sammy MYSELS (1)	72
Dick SANFORD (1)	72
Joe MIKOLAS (1)	30
Don RANDI (1)	30
Gene AUTRY (1)	23
Jerry KENNEDY (1)	21
Buddy KILLEN (1)	21
Billy VAUGHN (2)	21
Art KASSEL (1)	19
Fred MEINKEN (1)	16
George HOVEN (1)	12
Michael DURSO (1)	11
Marvin KAHN (1)	11
Mel MITCHELL (1)	11
Émile WALDTEUFEL (1)	11
Joe BISHOP (1)	10
James NOBLE (1)	10
Milt GABLER (1)	6.8
Emil FLINDT (1)	5.6
Wayne KING (1)	5.6
Alton DELMORE (1)	4.8
Rabon DELMORE (1)	4.8
Henry GLOVER (1)	4.8
Wayne RANEY (1)	4.8
Hans CARSTE (1)	4.1
Tom BLACKBURN (1)	3.0
George BRUNS (1)	3.0
Ed BONNER (1)	2.5
Eugene FIELD (1)	2.5
Sunny SKYLAR (1)	2.5
Werner LAST (1)	1.6
Wolfgang ROLOFF (1)	1.6
Francis CRAIG (1)	0.7
Beasley SMITH (1)	0.7
Billy HILL (1)	0.4
Camillo BARGONI (1)	0.0
Antonio Carlos JOBIM (1)	0.0

MARTHA & The VANDELLAS ►155 (25) [20] **25291**

Lamont DOZIER (9)	4654
Brian HOLLAND (9)	4654
Eddie HOLLAND (9)	4654
William STEVENSON (5)	2533
Ivy Jo HUNTER (4)	2465
Marvin GAYE (1)	1828
Sylvia MOY (6)	1765
Richard MORRIS (5)	1440
Deke RICHARDS (2)	292
Debbie DEAN (1)	218
George GORDY (3)	121
Clarence PAUL (1)	116
Allen STORY (2)	95
Billie Jean BROWN (1)	86
Margaret JOHNSON (1)	86
Berry GORDY (1)	74

MARTHA & The VANDELLAS ▶155 (25) [20] *Cont'd*	**25291**
Fonce MIZELL (1)	74
Freddie PERREN (1)	74
Norman WHITFIELD (1)	34
Lawrence BROWN (1)	26
ISLEY BROTHERS ▶156 (42) [31]	**25191**
O'Kelly ISLEY (32)	5526
Ronald ISLEY (31)	5380
Rudolph ISLEY (31)	5380
Stephen STILLS (1)	1193
Bert BERNS (1)	1036
Phil MEDLEY (1)	1036
Ernie ISLEY (16)	923
Marvin ISLEY (15)	912
Chris JASPER (15)	912
Lamont DOZIER (3)	416
Brian HOLLAND (3)	416
Eddie HOLLAND (3)	416
Sylvia MOY (1)	335
Herman Wesley KELLEY (1)	194
Clyde OTIS (1)	194
Bob DYLAN (1)	173
Dash CROFTS (1)	87
Jim SEALS (1)	87
Robert GORDY (1)	73
Thomas KEMP (1)	73
Thomas ALLEN (1)	58
Harold BROWN (1)	58
Morris DICKERSON (1)	58
Lonnie JORDAN (1)	58
Charles MILLER (1)	58
Lee OSKAR (1)	58
Howard SCOTT (1)	58
Harrison PENNINGTON (1)	11
Steve BOWDEN (1)	3.7
Ivy Jo HUNTER (1)	3.7
Leon WARE (1)	3.7
DR. HOOK ▶157 (20) [28]	**25143**
Shel SILVERSTEIN (6)	6875
Even STEVENS (3)	3217
Sam COOKE (1)	2695
Bobby GOSH (1)	2035
Ava ALDRIDGE (1)	1823
Eddie STRUZICK (1)	1823
Robert MATHER (1)	1154
Keith STEGALL (1)	1154
Chris WATERS (1)	1154
Leslie PEARL (1)	579
Larry KEITH (1)	447
Steve PIPPIN (1)	447
Johnny SLATE (1)	447
Dennis LOCORRIERE (2)	371
Ron HAFFKINE (1)	191
Sam WEEDMAN (1)	191
Charles Lincoln COCHRAN (1)	74
Roger COOK (1)	74
Ray SAWYER (1)	48
Gus CANNON (1)	47
Erik DARLING (1)	47
Willard SVANOE (1)	47
Hosea WOODS (1)	47
David MALLOY (1)	44
Eddie RABBITT (1)	44
Tom BRASFIELD (1)	30
Robert BYRNE (1)	30
Dennis TRACY (1)	8.4
Kenny LOGGINS ▶158 (22) [22]	**25135**
Kenny LOGGINS (17)	11400
Dean PITCHFORD (3)	3733

Giorgio MORODER (2)	2065
Tom WHITLOCK (2)	2065
Michael McDONALD (2)	1469
Melissa MANCHESTER (1)	1448
David FOSTER (3)	699
Mike TOWERS (1)	663
E. Ein LOGGINS (3)	469
Steve PERRY (1)	284
Guy THOMAS (1)	146
David PLEHN (1)	95
Jerry RIOPELLE (1)	95
Bert BERNS (1)	92
Alan BERGMAN (1)	89
Marilyn BERGMAN (1)	89
Ina WOLF (1)	68
Peter F. WOLF (1)	68
Bob JAMES (1)	38
Jeff PESCETTO (1)	20
Pam RESWICK (1)	20
Steve WERFEL (1)	20
Cyndi LAUPER ▶159 (13) [17]	**25126**
Robert HAZARD (1)	4949
Cyndi LAUPER (6)	4776
Thomas F. KELLY (3)	2609
Billy STEINBERG (3)	2609
Rob HYMAN (1)	2414
Jules SHEAR (1)	1796
Stephen LUNT (3)	1221
Essra MOHAWK (1)	1091
Rick CHERTOFF (1)	858
Gary CORBETT (1)	858
Thomas GRAY (1)	497
Arthur STEAD (1)	344
Renaldo BENSON (1)	295
Al CLEVELAND (1)	295
Marvin GAYE (1)	295
Richard ORANGE (1)	200
Jeff BOVA (1)	20
Johnny TILLOTSON ▶160 (30) [37]	**24752**
Johnny TILLOTSON (6)	8038
Mike ANTHONY (1)	2724
Paul KAUFMAN (1)	2724
John D. LOUDERMILK (1)	2470
Hank LOCKLIN (1)	1043
Hank WILLIAMS (2)	800
Chip TAYLOR (2)	634
Clifford RHODES (1)	600
Harlan HOWARD (1)	537
Ian SAMWELL (1)	491
Jean SLATER (1)	491
Paul HAMPTON (1)	482
Lee POCKRISS (1)	447
Paul VANCE (1)	447
Merle KILGORE (1)	404
Margie SINGLETON (1)	404
Paul EVANS (2)	375
Jack REARDON (1)	262
Willie NELSON (1)	249
Paul PARNES (1)	113
Hal GREENE (1)	110
Dick WOLF (1)	110
Deadric MALONE (1)	110
Ferdinand WASHINGTON (1)	110
Ray EVANS (1)	103
Jay LIVINGSTON (1)	103
Max STEINER (1)	103
Jesse BELVIN (1)	77
Gaynel HODGE (1)	77
Curtis Edward WILLIAMS (1)	77
Paul TANNEN (1)	17

Fred HABER (1)	11
Sylvester BRADFORD (1)	3.8
Al LEWIS (1)	3.8
Salvatore D'AMICO (1)	0.5
Wilbur MESHEL (1)	0.5
Charlotte PARSON (1)	0.5
Gene PITNEY ▶161 (27) [45]	**24657**
Burt BACHARACH (4)	4034
Hal DAVID (4)	4034
Helen MILLER (2)	1511
Barry MANN (2)	1264
Cynthia WEIL (2)	1264
Howard GREENFIELD (1)	1226
Dimitri TIOMKIN (1)	1069
Ned WASHINGTON (1)	1069
John GLUCK (1)	717
Neval NADER (1)	717
Charlie FOXX (1)	683
Jerry WILLIAMS Jr. (1)	683
Gene PITNEY (2)	661
Wally GOLD (2)	504
Aaron SCHROEDER (2)	504
George GOEHRING (1)	488
Tony BRUNO (1)	380
Stanley KAHAN (1)	380
Vic MILLROSE (1)	380
Fred ANISFIELD (1)	348
Willie DENSON (1)	348
Gerry GOFFIN (1)	311
Carole KING (1)	311
Roger ATKINS (1)	285
Bob BRASS (1)	198
Al KOOPER (1)	198
Irwin LEVINE (1)	198
Mick JAGGER (1)	158
Keith RICHARDS (1)	158
Randy NEWMAN (1)	146
Bert BERNS (1)	140
Phil MEDLEY (1)	140
Ed GOLDMAN (1)	36
Leon CARR (1)	18
Paul VANCE (1)	18
Al CLEVELAND (1)	17
Carl SPENCER (1)	17
Scott ENGLISH (1)	14
Larry WEISS (1)	14
Luciano BERETTA (1)	3.1
Michele DEL PRETE (1)	3.1
Daniele PACE (1)	3.1
Mario PANZERI (1)	3.1
Len BEADLE (1)	1.3
Peter CALLANDER (1)	1.3
The OSMONDS ▶162 (12) [14]	**24616**
George Henry JACKSON (2)	8822
Joe SOUTH (1)	5693
Alan OSMOND (5)	3087
Merrill OSMOND (5)	3087
Wayne OSMOND (4)	1078
Mickey BUCKINS (1)	666
Johnny BRISTOL (1)	425
Wade BROWN (1)	425
David H. JONES (1)	425
Bob CREWE (1)	316
Bob GAUDIO (1)	316
Arnold CAPITANELLI (1)	272
Wes FARRELL (1)	1.1
Jerry GOLDSTEIN (1)	1.1
The COASTERS ▶163 (21) [10]	**24504**
Jerry LEIBER (17)	11382

Mike STOLLER (17)	11382
Doc POMUS (1)	423
Billy GUY (1)	399
Bobby DARIN (1)	248
Don KIRSHNER (1)	248
Leon PAYNE (1)	204
Sunny SKYLAR (1)	91
Consuelo VELAZQUEZ (1)	91
Kent HARRIS (1)	39
JOURNEY ▶164 (25) [8]	**24387**
Steve PERRY (21)	11509
Jonathan CAIN (14)	9583
Neal SCHON (14)	2926
Robert FLEISCHMAN (2)	109
Diane VALORY (1)	98
Gregg ROLIE (2)	76
Ross VALORY (2)	76
Roger SILVER (1)	11
Jimmie RODGERS ▶165 (34) [44]	**24374**
Bob MERRILL (1)	5979
Luigi CREATORE (9)	2750
Hugo PERETTI (9)	2750
Al HOFFMAN (6)	1959
Dick MANNING (6)	1959
TRADITIONAL (4)	1251
Mack DAVID (2)	644
Rod McKUEN (2)	555
James Frederick RODGERS (2)	482
Ronnie GILBERT (1)	383
Lee HAYS (1)	383
Fred HELLERMAN (1)	383
Sam KENNEDY (1)	383
Huddie LEDBETTER (1)	383
Pete SEEGER (1)	383
Jimmy CURTISS (1)	349
Ernie MARESCA (1)	349
John A. MILLER (1)	344
Fred ROSE (3)	263
Mel FOREE (1)	245
Mark McINTYRE (1)	233
William OLOFSON (1)	233
Herb CLARKE (1)	227
Stan LEBOWSKY (1)	227
Johnny LEHMANN (1)	227
Gerald Frederick GRANT (1)	164
Arthur KENT (1)	164
Joe REISMAN (1)	164
Sid JACOBSON (1)	60
Lou STALLMAN (1)	60
Eddie V. DEANE (1)	59
Al DREDICK (1)	59
Marie COWAN (1)	54
A.B. PATTERSON (1)	54
Sammy CAHN (1)	51
Alex NORTH (1)	51
Jimmy DRIFTWOOD (1)	41
Randy SPARKS (1)	21
Marty COOPER (1)	13
Art WHITING (1)	8.8
Ramona REDD (1)	7.6
Mitchell TOROK (1)	7.6
Pearl WOODS (1)	4.2
Hy HEATH (1)	3.6
CULTURE CLUB ▶166 (10) [5]	**24227**
Michael CRAIG (10)	5663
Roy HAY (10)	5663
Jon MOSS (10)	5663
George O'DOWD (10)	5663
Phil PICKETT (3)	1575

Sheena EASTON ▶167 (18) [28]	**24189**
Florrie PALMER (2)	6022
Mike LEESON (2)	1911
Bill CONTI (1)	1837
PRINCE (1)	1802
Lea MAALFRID (1)	1230
Charlie DORE (1)	1151
Julian LITTMAN (1)	1151
Greg MATHIESON (2)	989
Trevor VEITCH (2)	989
Kenneth EDMONDS (1)	921
Antonio REID (1)	921
Daryl SIMMONS (1)	921
Dominic BUGATTI (2)	807
Frank MUSKER (1)	507
Jennifer KIMBALL (1)	418
Cindy RICHARDSON (1)	418
Antonina ARMATO (1)	402
Nick MUNDY (1)	402
Adele BERTEI (1)	274
Mary Alice KESSLER (1)	274
Tom SNOW (1)	189
Cynthia WEIL (1)	189
Julia DOWNES (1)	168
Tim SCOTT (1)	109
Peter VALE (1)	74
Lamont DOZIER (1)	38
Brian HOLLAND (1)	38
Eddie HOLLAND (1)	38

Richard MARX ▶168 (10) [3]	**24127**
Richard MARX (10)	22612
Bruce GAITSCH (1)	1056
Fee WAYBILL (1)	459

JAY & The AMERICANS ▶169 (21) [36]	**24025**
Wes FARRELL (4)	2407
Doc POMUS (2)	2060
Mort SHUMAN (2)	2060
Bunny LEWIS (1)	1855
MANTOVANI (1)	1855
Ted DARYLL (1)	1758
Greg RICHARDS (1)	1758
Tommy BOYCE (1)	1426
Bobby HART (1)	1426
Neil DIAMOND (1)	942
Roy ALFRED (2)	897
Barry MANN (2)	729
Cynthia WEIL (2)	729
Oscar HAMMERSTEIN (1)	677
Richard RODGERS (1)	677
Phil SPECTOR (1)	528
Andrew JONES (1)	299
Joe MELSON (1)	285
Roy ORBISON (1)	285
Jerry LEIBER (1)	201
Mike STOLLER (1)	201
Marty SANDERS (2)	152
Kenny VANCE (2)	152
Richard REICHEG (1)	113
Tony POWERS (2)	86
Joel HIRSCHHORN (1)	84
Al KASHA (1)	84
Gene ALLAN (1)	73
Ron DANTE (1)	73
Mat MAURER (1)	71
Jay BLACK (1)	38
Billy CARL (1)	16
Reid WHITELAW (1)	16
Ellie GREENWICH (1)	15
Leonard BERNSTEIN (1)	0.0
Stephen SONDHEIM (1)	0.0

The ANIMALS/Eric BURDON & The ANIMALS ▶170 (19) [27]	**23954**
TRADITIONAL (3)	8581
Eric BURDON (9)	2076
Vic BRIGGS (5)	1119
Barry JENKINS (5)	1119
Danny McCULLOCH (5)	1119
John WEIDER (5)	1119
Gerry GOFFIN (1)	859
Carole KING (1)	859
Ma RAINEY (1)	857
Barry MANN (1)	737
Cynthia WEIL (1)	737
Roger ATKINS (1)	616
Carl D'ERRICO (1)	616
Sam COOKE (1)	470
Alan PRICE (1)	460
John Lee HOOKER (1)	433
Bennie BENJAMIN (1)	339
Gloria CALDWELL (1)	339
Sol MARCUS (1)	339
Scott ENGLISH (1)	326
Larry WEISS (1)	326
Chas CHANDLER (1)	117
Alan LOMAX (1)	117
Don EVANS (1)	103
John STERLING (1)	103
Jake HAMMONDS (1)	35
Johnnie MATTHEWS (1)	35

Ray STEVENS ▶171 (31) [20]	**23926**
Ray STEVENS (19)	20020
Bill JUSTIS (1)	1188
Johnny BURKE (1)	611
Erroll GARNER (1)	611
Jerry LEIBER (1)	334
Mike STOLLER (1)	334
Dale GONYEA (1)	257
Tom AUTRY (1)	118
TRADITIONAL (1)	104
Albert E. BRUMLEY Sr. (1)	85
Kris KRISTOFFERSON (1)	55
Rudolf FRIML (1)	47
Oscar HAMMERSTEIN (1)	47
Otto HARBACH (1)	47
Percy FAITH (1)	20
Carl SIGMAN (1)	20
Layng MARTINE Jr. (1)	15
Ric CARTEY (1)	6.5
Carole JOYNER (1)	6.5
Alvin WILLIAMS (1)	0.0

David BOWIE ▶172 (26) [10]	**23876**
David BOWIE (24)	18761
Carlos ALOMAR (2)	2134
John LENNON (1)	1910
Iggy POP (2)	934
Giorgio MORODER (1)	77
Bob FELDMAN (1)	18
Jerry GOLDSTEIN (1)	18
Richard GOTTEHRER (1)	18
Mick JAGGER (1)	3.7
Keith RICHARDS (1)	3.7

Bruce SPRINGSTEEN ▶173 (16) [1]	**23804**
Bruce SPRINGSTEEN (16)	23804

Bobby GOLDSBORO ▶174 (28) [10]	**23599**
Bobby GOLDSBORO (20)	10439
Bobby RUSSELL (1)	9605
Mac DAVIS (1)	1958
Sonny CURTIS (1)	764
Bodie CHANDLER (1)	285
Steve KARLISKI (1)	220
Dennis LINDE (1)	188
Burt BACHARACH (1)	52
Hal DAVID (1)	52
Don McLEAN (1)	36

JAN & DEAN ▶175 (25) [36]	**23587**
Jan BERRY (11)	6752
Brian WILSON (6)	5128
Roger CHRISTIAN (10)	3664
Melvin SCHWARTZ (1)	1684
Don ALTFELD (3)	1258
Jack LAWRENCE (1)	866
Artie KORNFELD (1)	528
Lou ADLER (2)	505
Buzz CASON (2)	475
Bobby RUSSELL (2)	475
Steve BARRI (2)	399
P.F. SLOAN (2)	399
Hoagy CARMICHAEL (1)	257
Frank LOESSER (1)	257
Jill GIBSON (1)	173
Bob NORMAN (1)	150
Shelley HAIMS (1)	150
Perry STEVENS (1)	150
Fred WIEDER (1)	69
Barker BRADFORD (1)	31
Percy MONTROSE (1)	31
H.S. THOMPSON (1)	31
TRADITIONAL (1)	31
Clint BALLARD Jr. (1)	30
Larry KUSIK (1)	30
William DAVIS (1)	11
Morris LEVY (1)	11
Daniel NORTON (1)	11
Viola WATKINS (1)	11
Herb ALPERT (1)	10
Barbara BELLE (1)	1.8
Anita LEONARD (1)	1.8
Louis PRIMA (1)	1.8
Stan RHODES (1)	1.8
Cleve HERMAN (1)	1.3
George TIPTON (1)	1.3

GRASS ROOTS ▶176 (25) [30]	**23406**
Lou JOSIE (1)	3992
Harvey PRICE (6)	2490
Dan WALSH (6)	2490
Mitch BOTTLER (2)	1470
Gary ZEKLEY (2)	1470
Steve BARRI (6)	1287
Dennis PROVISOR (3)	891
Michael JULIEN (1)	862
Giulio RAPETTI (1)	862
David SHAPIRO (1)	862
P.F. SLOAN (5)	832
Dennis LAMBERT (2)	787
Brian POTTER (2)	787
Billy Joe ADMIRE (1)	652
Gary KNIGHT (1)	652
Marty KUPPS (1)	510
Ted McNAMARA (1)	354
Adeneyi PARIS (1)	354
Ekundayo PARIS (1)	354
Lucio BATTISTI (1)	298
Barry GROSS (1)	298
Jet LORING (1)	252
Artie SCHROECK (1)	252
Warren ENTNER (1)	118
Rob GRILL (1)	118
Barry MANN (1)	51
Cynthia WEIL (1)	51
Bob DYLAN (1)	7.4
Jeff BARRY (1)	0.7
Mentor WILLIAMS (1)	0.7

ROXETTE ▶177 (8) [2]	**23057**
Per GESSLE (8)	20767
Mats PERSSON (2)	2291

Eddie FISHER ▶178 (41) [73]	**22839**
Al JACOBS (2)	3652
Jimmie CRANE (1)	3444
Irving BERLIN (3)	2432
Eddie CURTIS (1)	1286
Bob BARRON (1)	1113
Burt LONG (1)	1113
Sherman EDWARDS (1)	1071
Ben RALEIGH (1)	1071
Richard ADLER (2)	709
Jerry ROSS (2)	709
Harold ROME (1)	420
Don ROBERTSON (2)	364
Larry KUSIK (2)	286
Eddie SNYDER (2)	286
Oscar HAMMERSTEIN (1)	265
Richard RODGERS (1)	265
Al HOFFMAN (1)	245
Dick MANNING (1)	245
Alan Jay LERNER (1)	244
Frederick LOEWE (1)	244
James LAST (1)	232
Mack DAVID (1)	174
Jimmy KENNEDY (1)	170
Nat SIMON (1)	170
Leonard BERNSTEIN (1)	170
Stephen SONDHEIM (1)	170
Ivory Joe HUNTER (1)	157
Clyde OTIS (1)	157
Herbert JARCZYK (1)	153
Robert MELLIN (1)	153
Fred RAUCH (1)	153
Ornella Ferrari COLOMBI (1)	135
Hal HACKADY (1)	135
Vittorio MASCHERONI (1)	135
Lew BROWN (1)	127
Sidney CLARE (1)	127
Cliff FRIEND (1)	127
Helen DEUTSCH (1)	103
Bronislaw KAPER (1)	103
Noel REGNEY (1)	79
Gloria SHAYNE (1)	79
Heino GAZE (1)	54
Al STILLMAN (1)	54
Victor ABRAMS (1)	35
Morris LEVY (1)	35
Irving REID (1)	35
Al FRISCH (1)	27
Sid WAYNE (1)	27
Jerry LEIBER (1)	26
Mike STOLLER (1)	26
Mack GORDON (2)	13
Josef MYROW (2)	13
Jack ROLLINS (1)	5.7
Jerry HERMAN (1)	4.7
Sammy CAHN (1)	2.2
Peter HERZ (1)	2.2
Hans LANG (1)	2.2
Bob MERRILL (1)	2.1
Pietro GARINEI (1)	0.7
Alessandro GIOVANNINI (1)	0.7
Renato RASCEL (1)	0.7
Carl SIGMAN (1)	0.7

Eddie FISHER ▶178 (41) [73] ***Cont'd***	**22839**
Al BANDINI (1)	0.0
Bennie BENJAMIN (1)	0.0
Pat ROSSI (1)	0.0
George David WEISS (1)	0.0
Arthur ALTMAN (1)	0.0
Don REID (1)	0.0
Ervin DRAKE (1)	0.0
Jimmy SHIRL (1)	0.0
Harold ADAMSON (1)	0.0
Stella UNGER (1)	0.0
Victor YOUNG (1)	0.0
The FLEETWOODS ▶179 (11) [16]	**22739**
Dewayne BLACKWELL (2)	9424
Gretchen CHRISTOPHER (2)	2959
Barbara ELLIS (2)	2959
Gary TROXEL (2)	2959
Cirino COLACRAI (1)	875
Fred BURCH (1)	683
Gerald NELSON (1)	683
John GLUCK (1)	290
Neval NADER (1)	290
Hal DAVID (1)	278
Sherman EDWARDS (1)	278
Jackie DeSHANNON (1)	277
Sharon SHEELEY (1)	277
John MARASCALCO (1)	248
George MOTOLA (1)	248
Tommy KASPAR (1)	10
The POLICE ▶180 (12) [1]	**22597**
STING (12)	22597
Christopher CROSS ▶181 (10) [5]	**22554**
Christopher CROSS (10)	17283
Burt BACHARACH (2)	1749
Carole Bayer SAGER (2)	1749
Peter ALLEN (1)	1728
Michael OMARTIAN (1)	46
The MARVELETTES ▶182 (24) [23]	**22548**
Smokey ROBINSON (8)	6757
Brian HOLLAND (7)	2879
Robert BATEMAN (3)	2519
Freddie GORMAN (3)	1783
William STEVENSON (5)	1598
Georgia DOBBINS (1)	1566
William GARRETT (1)	1566
Van McCOY (1)	757
Eddie HOLLAND (3)	663
Norman WHITFIELD (1)	520
Marvin GAYE (1)	361
George GORDY (1)	361
Lamont DOZIER (4)	360
Ivy Jo HUNTER (2)	285
Nick ASHFORD (1)	101
Valerie SIMPSON (1)	101
Lena M. MANNS (1)	91
Frank Edward WILSON (1)	91
Berry GORDY (1)	90
Clarence PAUL (1)	82
Bob HALLEY (1)	8.2
Ben RALEIGH (1)	8.2
Janie BRADFORD (1)	0.1
Del SHANNON ▶183 (19) [16]	**22534**
Del SHANNON (12)	14362
Max CROOK (1)	5195
Maron McKENZIE (2)	940
Bobby FREEMAN (1)	333
Andrew BARKSDALE (1)	257
Otis BLACKWELL (1)	257
Jimmy JONES (1)	257
Charles MERENSTEIN (1)	257
Phil BAPTISTE (1)	203
George KHOURY (1)	203
Roger MILLER (1)	136
John LENNON (1)	55
Paul McCARTNEY (1)	55
Wayne SHANKLIN (1)	22
Mick JAGGER (1)	0.7
Keith RICHARDS (1)	0.7
Ray PARKER Jr./RAYDIO ▶184 (15) [4]	**22474**
Ray PARKER Jr. (14)	22461
Thurlene JOHNSON (1)	8.6
Dean PITCHFORD (1)	2.2
Bill WOLFER (1)	2.2
Guy MITCHELL ▶185 (11) [14]	**22443**
Melvin ENDSLEY (2)	11975
Harlan HOWARD (1)	7361
Eddie V. DEANE (1)	707
Woody HARRIS (1)	707
John Benson BROOKS (1)	318
Sid WAYNE (1)	318
Claude DeMETRIUS (1)	277
Aaron SCHROEDER (2)	187
Lee ROSS (1)	138
Bob WILLS (1)	138
Josephine PEOPLES (1)	135
Fuzzy OWEN (1)	122
Ben WEISMAN (1)	52
Bob MERRILL (1)	8.2
REO SPEEDWAGON ▶186 (21) [5]	**22424**
Kevin CRONIN (14)	16611
Gary RICHRATH (5)	4013
Neal DOUGHTY (2)	896
Thomas F. KELLY (1)	515
Rick BRAUN (1)	388
BOX TOPS ▶187 (10) [9]	**22379**
Wayne Carson THOMPSON (4)	13284
Spooner OLDHAM (2)	3241
Dan PENN (2)	3241
Jon STROLL (1)	577
Bobby WEINSTEIN (1)	577
Mark JAMES (1)	449
Donnie FRITTS (1)	427
Eddie HINTON (1)	427
Bob DYLAN (1)	156
CHIC ▶188 (10) [3]	**22270**
Bernard EDWARDS (10)	10722
Nile RODGERS (10)	10722
Kenny LEHMAN (1)	826
Brian HYLAND ▶189 (24) [25]	**22170**
Curtis MAYFIELD (1)	4320
Lee POCKRISS (2)	3769
Paul VANCE (2)	3769
Gary GELD (9)	3566
Peter UDELL (9)	3566
Bobby RUSSELL (1)	1079
Fred BURCH (1)	281
Gerald NELSON (1)	281
Marty COOPER (1)	268
Ray WHITLEY (1)	268
Billy DAVIS (1)	134
Berry GORDY (1)	134
Gwen GORDY (1)	134
Sonny CURTIS (2)	108
Glen HARDIN (2)	108
Joel HIRSCHHORN (1)	73
Al KASHA (1)	73
Phil MEDLEY (1)	64
Artie WAYNE (1)	56
Brooks ARTHUR (1)	34
Art KAPLAN (1)	34
Jack KELLER (1)	34
Leonard COHEN (1)	6.3
Michael GORDON (1)	4.8
James GRIFFIN (1)	4.8
SONNY & CHER ▶190 (18) [12]	**22166**
Sonny BONO (13)	17898
Jimmy HOLIDAY (1)	1226
Eddie REEVES (1)	1226
Gilbert BÉCAUD (1)	329
Pierre DELANOË (1)	329
Carl SIGMAN (1)	329
Mark BARKAN (1)	241
Jerry FOSTER (1)	182
Steve KARMEN (1)	182
Bill RICE (1)	182
Don HARRIS (1)	22
Dewey TERRY (1)	22
Carole KING ▶191 (18) [5]	**22055**
Carole KING (18)	13381
Toni STERN (2)	5098
David PALMER (2)	2531
Gerry GOFFIN (5)	885
Cynthia WEIL (1)	159
Gary (U.S.) BONDS ▶192 (11) [10]	**21939**
Frank GUIDA (5)	6388
Gene BARGE (5)	4387
Gary ANDERSON (3)	4020
Joseph ROYSTER (4)	3927
Bruce SPRINGSTEEN (2)	2342
Steve SAMUEL (1)	365
Doc POMUS (1)	204
Mort SHUMAN (1)	204
Moon MULLICAN (1)	99
Patricia MATTHEWS (1)	2.3
GENESIS ▶193 (18) [3]	**21888**
Phil COLLINS (17)	8432
Mike RUTHERFORD (16)	6756
Tony BANKS (15)	6700
Johnny HORTON ▶194 (10) [11]	**21848**
Jimmy DRIFTWOOD (2)	6698
TRADITIONAL (2)	6541
Mike PHILLIPS (1)	4054
Tillman FRANKS (3)	1953
Johnny HORTON (3)	1953
Tex ATCHISON (1)	298
Merle KILGORE (1)	123
Jule STYNE (1)	105
George David WEISS (1)	105
Howard HAUSEY (2)	10
Jay WEBB (1)	8.6
James TAYLOR ▶195 (17) [13]	**21787**
James TAYLOR (11)	9539
Carole KING (2)	6271
Andrew BARKSDALE (1)	772
Otis BLACKWELL (1)	772
Jimmy JONES (1)	772
Charles MERENSTEIN (1)	772
Lamont DOZIER (1)	764
Brian HOLLAND (1)	764
Eddie HOLLAND (1)	764
Gerry GOFFIN (1)	261
Buddy HOLLY (1)	125
Norman PETTY (1)	125
Danny KORTCHMAR (1)	85
Les BAXTER ▶196 (17) [29]	**21733**
Marguerite MONNOT (1)	8007
Alex NORTH (1)	4331
Hy ZARET (1)	4331
Dimitri TIOMKIN (2)	2254
Sammy GALLOP (1)	1151
Jerry LIVINGSTON (1)	1151
Lotar OLIAS (2)	218
Sam COSLOW (1)	120
Peter MÖSSER (1)	99
Paul Francis WEBSTER (1)	27
Les BAXTER (2)	16
Will HOLT (1)	9.3
Herb EISEMAN (1)	5.7
Floyd HUDDLESTON (1)	5.7
Mark McINTYRE (1)	5.7
Henry MANCINI (1)	1.9
Herman STEIN (1)	1.9
Frank PINGATORE (1)	0.0
Jesse BELVIN (1)	0.0
Gaynel HODGE (1)	0.0
Curtis Edward WILLIAMS (1)	0.0
Victor YOUNG (1)	0.0
Nicholas BRODSZKY (1)	0.0
Sammy CAHN (1)	0.0
Ray EVANS (1)	0.0
Jay LIVINGSTON (1)	0.0
Sid DANOFF (1)	0.0
Abraham Zevi IDELSOHN (1)	0.0
TRADITIONAL (1)	0.0
PRINCE And The REVOLUTION ▶197 (10) [6]	**21656**
PRINCE (10)	21095
Lisa COLEMAN (2)	225
Wendy MELVOIN (2)	225
Mark Alton BROWN (1)	37
Matt FINK (1)	37
Robert RIVKIN (1)	37
Anne MURRAY ▶198 (28) [33]	**21593**
Randy GOODRUM (3)	6586
Kenny LOGGINS (2)	3457
Gene MacLELLAN (2)	2766
John STEWART (1)	1419
John LENNON (3)	1093
Paul McCARTNEY (3)	1093
Charlie BLACK (5)	790
Rory BOURKE (5)	790
Dona Lyn GEORGE (1)	686
Steve DORFF (1)	353
Larry HERBSTRITT (1)	353
Harry LLOYD (1)	353
Gloria SKLEROV (1)	353
Scott McKENZIE (1)	338
Wayland HOLYFIELD (1)	220
Bob HOUSE (1)	220
Sandy PINKARD (1)	130
Roger NICHOLS (1)	86
Paul WILLIAMS (1)	86
Archie JORDAN (1)	79
Richard LEIGH (1)	79
Brent TITCOMB (1)	75
Gordon LIGHTFOOT (1)	45
Hal DAVID (1)	33
Henry MANCINI (1)	33
Tommy ROCCO (1)	30
Bobby DARIN (1)	11
Mark JAMES (1)	8.0

Anne MURRAY ►198 (28) [33] *Cont'd*	**21593**
Greg CARROLL (1)	6.7
Doris PAYNE (1)	6.7
David FOSTER (1)	5.8
Jim VALLANCE (1)	5.8
Sonny CURTIS (1)	4.4
Bob DYLAN ►199 (23) [3]	**21581**
Bob DYLAN (22)	21001
Jacques LEVY (2)	370
Bill TRADER (1)	211
Steve LAWRENCE ►200 (29) [53]	**21537**
Gerry GOFFIN (3)	4713
Carole KING (3)	4713
Teddy RANDAZZO (3)	1478
Bobby WEINSTEIN (2)	1472
Barry MANN (3)	1217
Norman NEWELL (2)	1127
Cyril ORNADEL (1)	1127
Hank HUNTER (1)	842
Dave ALLDRED (1)	473
Jimmy BOWEN (1)	473
Buddy KNOX (1)	473
Donnie LANIER (1)	473
Cynthia WEIL (1)	367
Alan ARKIN (1)	313
Bob CAREY (1)	313
Erik DARLING (1)	313
John GLUCK (1)	167
Diane LAMPERT (1)	167
Lawton WILLIAMS (1)	154
Jimmy DUNCAN (1)	118
Les REED (1)	118
Sammy GALLOP (1)	67
Jimmy VAN HEUSEN (1)	67
Albert S. WOOD (1)	67
Charles AZNAVOUR (1)	54
Diran GARVARENTZ (1)	54
Don RAYE (1)	54
Billy BARBERIS (1)	54
Pyotr Ilyich TCHAIKOVSKY (1)	54
Mann CURTIS (1)	48
Virgilio PANZUTI (1)	48
Ervin DRAKE (1)	42
Bernie LOWE (1)	40
Kal MANN (1)	40
Jerry BOCK (1)	38
Sheldon HARNICK (1)	38
Paul KOY (1)	29
Frank MADER (1)	29
Claude DEBUSSY (1)	23
Jerry LEIBER (1)	23
Mike STOLLER (1)	23
Umberto BINDI (1)	8.4
Giorgio CALABRESE (1)	8.4
Hal DAVID (1)	8.4
Howard GREENFIELD (1)	7.0
Salvatore D'AMICO (1)	5.2
Ray (2) ALLEN (1)	0.0
Jerry JOYCE (1)	0.0
Esther NAVARRO (1)	0.0
George GERSHWIN (1)	0.0
Ira GERSHWIN (1)	0.0
Nino OLIVIERO (1)	0.0
Riz ORTOLANI (1)	0.0
Tina TURNER ►201 (14) [14]	**21346**
Terry BRITTEN (6)	7333
Graham LYLE (5)	7160
Holly KNIGHT (4)	2083
Mark KNOPFLER (1)	1524

Mike CHAPMAN (2)	1187
Nicky CHINN (1)	717
Tony Joe WHITE (1)	325
Al GREEN (1)	252
Al JACKSON (1)	252
Willie MITCHELL (1)	252
Sue SHIFRIN (1)	173
Rupert HINE (1)	35
Jeannette OBSTOJ (1)	35
Albert HAMMOND (1)	17
ABBA ►202 (20) [3]	**21117**
Benny ANDERSSON (20)	8256
Björn ULVAEUS (20)	8256
Stig ANDERSON (9)	4604
Joe TEX ►203 (32) [6]	**21063**
Joe TEX (30)	19702
Buddy KILLEN (1)	674
Bennie McGINTY (1)	674
Billy DAVIS (1)	4.6
Berry GORDY (1)	4.6
Gwen GORDY (1)	4.6
SURVIVOR ►204 (18) [6]	**21047**
Jim PETERIK (17)	10511
Frankie SULLIVAN (15)	10383
Peter BECKETT (1)	46
Bill CONTI (1)	46
Dennis LAMBERT (1)	46
Jimi JAMISON (1)	15
Jerry BUTLER ►205 (39) [43]	**21021**
Jerry BUTLER (17)	4984
Kenneth GAMBLE (11)	3102
Leon HUFF (11)	3102
Curtis MAYFIELD (5)	2612
Henry MANCINI (1)	1515
Johnny MERCER (1)	1515
Calvin CARTER (2)	1083
Burt BACHARACH (2)	436
Hal DAVID (2)	436
Jerry J. ROSS (1)	217
Larry WEISS (1)	217
Ted DARYLL (1)	210
William Earl BUTLER (3)	159
Charles Henry JACKSON Jr. (2)	135
Rose Marie McCOY (1)	105
Helen MILLER (1)	105
Samuel BELL (1)	89
Lorraine ELLISON (1)	89
Dennis LAMBERT (1)	89
Bob FELDMAN (1)	86
Jerry GOLDSTEIN (1)	86
Richard GOTTEHRER (1)	86
Patricia HENLEY (1)	68
Homer TALBERT (1)	68
Don COVAY (1)	65
Paul GRIFFIN (1)	65
Al DUBIN (1)	57
Harry WARREN (1)	57
Bob CREWE (1)	33
Bob GAUDIO (1)	33
Danny MEEHAN (1)	28
Bobby SCOTT (1)	28
Charles JONES (1)	12
Mack DAVID (1)	8.1
Franz WAXMAN (1)	8.1
Cortez BATEZA	7.9
Alonzo TUCKER	7.9
Theodore J. TWIGGS	7.9
Eutrice SHELL (1)	7.7
Randy NEWMAN (1)	4.2
Larry WADE (1)	1.4

Arthur BROOKS (1)	0.5
Richard BROOKS (1)	0.5
VAN HALEN ►206 (20) [11]	**20991**
Michael ANTHONY (17)	4760
Alex VAN HALEN (17)	4760
Eddie VAN HALEN (17)	4760
David Lee ROTH (8)	2489
Sammy HAGAR (9)	2271
William DEES (1)	604
Roy ORBISON (1)	604
Ray DAVIES (1)	352
Marvin GAYE (1)	130
Ivy Jo HUNTER (1)	130
William STEVENSON (1)	130
LITTLE RIVER BAND ►207 (16) [11]	**20862**
Graham GOBLE (10)	12698
Glenn SHORROCK (3)	3455
David John BRIGGS (2)	3281
Beeb BIRTLES (3)	677
Kerryn TOLHURST (1)	565
John FARNHAM (1)	31
David HIRSCHFELDER (1)	31
Stephen HOUSDEN (1)	31
Wayne NELSON (1)	31
Stephen PRESTVICH (1)	31
Spencer PROFFER (1)	31
The STYLISTICS ►208 (17) [11]	**20832**
Thom BELL (8)	8231
Linda CREED (8)	8231
Luigi CREATORE (7)	740
Hugo PERETTI (7)	740
George David WEISS (7)	740
Kenneth GAMBLE (1)	662
Tony BELL (1)	512
Burt BACHARACH (1)	418
Hal DAVID (1)	418
Marty BRYANT (1)	71
Robert DOUGLAS (1)	71
WHAM! ►209 (8) [4]	**20815**
George MICHAEL (7)	17718
Andrew RIDGELEY (1)	2865
David WAS (1)	116
Don WAS (1)	116
PARTRIDGE FAMILY ►210 (9) [13]	**20643**
Tony ROMEO (2)	10009
Wes FARRELL (3)	2744
Mike APPEL (1)	1523
Jim CRETECOS (1)	1523
Gerry GOFFIN (1)	1208
L. Russell BROWN (2)	1132
Irwin LEVINE (2)	1132
Howard GREENFIELD (1)	367
Neil SEDAKA (1)	367
Barry MANN (1)	306
Cynthia WEIL (1)	306
Bobby HART (1)	13
Danny JANSSEN (1)	13
Rosemary CLOONEY ►211 (17) [19]	**20522**
Richard ADLER (1)	5563
Jerry ROSS (1)	5563
Stuart HAMBLEN (1)	5384
Bob MERRILL (3)	1669
Alan Jay LERNER (2)	469
Frederick LOEWE (2)	469
Dee LIBBEY (1)	327
Sid WAYNE (1)	327

Al HOFFMAN (1)	131
Milton DeLUGG (1)	122
Bob HILLIARD (1)	122
Carl T. FISCHER (1)	85
Frankie LAINE (1)	85
Harold ARLEN (1)	62
Johnny MERCER (1)	62
Frank LOESSER (1)	44
Irving BERLIN (4)	20
Hal DAVID (1)	8.3
Sid LIPPMAN (1)	8.3
Leo SAYER ►212 (10) [12]	**20501**
Leo SAYER (7)	4984
Albert HAMMOND (2)	2802
Vini PONCIA (1)	2770
Carole Bayer SAGER (1)	2588
Jerry ALLISON (1)	2545
Sonny CURTIS (1)	2545
David COURTNEY (2)	1014
Barry MANN (1)	540
Alan TARNEY (1)	287
Tom SNOW (1)	159
Boudleaux BRYANT (1)	133
Felice BRYANT (1)	133
Steve MILLER Band ►213 (16) [11]	**20483**
Steve MILLER (12)	12538
Paul PENA (1)	2374
Eddie CURTIS (1)	1763
Ahmet ERTEGUN (1)	1763
Chris McCARTY (2)	532
Greg DOUGLASS (1)	418
Lonnie TURNER (1)	418
Jesse STONE (1)	341
Kenny Lee LEWIS (2)	186
Gary MALLABER (1)	95
Ben SIDRAN (1)	55
GRAND FUNK RAILROAD ►214 (19) [11]	**20463**
Mark FARNER (12)	6891
Don BREWER (4)	5700
John ELLISON (1)	2487
Gerry GOFFIN (1)	2318
Carole KING (1)	2318
Dave MASON (1)	334
Mick JAGGER (1)	103
Keith RICHARDS (1)	103
Craig FROST (1)	70
Thelma GORDY (1)	70
Richard STREET (1)	70
NEW KIDS ON THE BLOCK ►215 (10) [4]	**20328**
Maurice STARR (9)	18538
Al LANCELLOTTI (1)	619
Thom BELL (1)	585
William HART (1)	585
Steve WINWOOD ►216 (15) [9]	**20319**
Steve WINWOOD (15)	8632
Will JENNINGS (12)	8092
Lamont DOZIER (1)	908
Brian HOLLAND (1)	908
Eddie HOLLAND (1)	908
Jim CAPALDI (2)	471
George FLEMING (1)	165
James HOOKER (1)	165
Vivian STANSHALL (1)	69
Al MARTINO ►217 (42) [71]	**20292**
Leon PAYNE (1)	4381
Don ROBERTSON (2)	1789
Peter DeANGELIS (6)	1443

Al MARTINO ▶217 (42) [71] *Cont'd*	**20292**
Jean SAWYER (4)	1353
Charles SINGLETON (2)	779
Eddie SNYDER (2)	779
Bill ANDERSON (1)	683
Bert KAEMPFERT (2)	672
Dick HEARD (1)	562
Hank HUNTER (1)	562
Felice BRYANT (1)	429
Danny DiMINNO (4)	372
Hank WILLIAMS (2)	346
Johnny CYMBAL (1)	328
Mike LENDELL (1)	328
Norma MENDOZA (1)	321
Aldo PROVENZANO (2)	306
Jimmie CRANE (2)	305
Bobby BURKE (1)	302
Horace GERLACH (1)	302
Bob CREWE (1)	217
Larry WEISS (1)	217
Corrado CONTI (1)	165
Norman NEWELL (1)	165
Daniele PACE (1)	165
Mario PANZERI (1)	165
Lorenzo PILAT (1)	165
Ritchie ADAMS (2)	142
Alan BERNSTEIN (2)	142
Franco MIGLIACCI (1)	122
Domenico MODUGNO (1)	122
Mitchell PARISH (1)	122
Luigi CREATORE (1)	103
Hugo PERETTI (1)	103
George David WEISS (1)	103
Bryan BLACKBURN (1)	101
Pierre LEMAIRE (1)	101
André POPP (1)	101
Milt GABLER (1)	98
Herbert REHBEIN (1)	98
Russell FAITH (1)	89
Milton AGER (1)	88
Jack YELLEN (1)	88
Bob ELLSWORTH (1)	83
Richard HOWARD (1)	83
Russ MORGAN (1)	83
Terry CASHMAN (1)	77
Eugene PISTILLI (1)	77
Tommy WEST (1)	77
Merle HAGGARD (1)	75
Bonnie OWENS (1)	75
Johnny TUCKER (2)	66
Tommie CONNOR (1)	47
Hans LEIP (1)	47
Norbert SCHULTZE (1)	47
Larry KUSIK (1)	45
Nino ROTA (1)	45
Giacomo PUCCINI (1)	12
Bill BORRELLI (1)	8.5
Pat GENARO (1)	8.5
Lou LEVINSON (1)	8.5
Bob MARCUCCI (1)	1.4
Michael BERARDI (1)	0.7
Richard BERARDI (1)	0.7
Kurt HERTHA (1)	0.7
Henry MAYER (1)	0.7
Lester LEE (1)	0.0
Ned WASHINGTON (1)	0.0
Umberto BINDI (1)	0.0
Giorgio CALABRESE (1)	0.0
Hal DAVID (1)	0.0

The CHORDETTES ▶218 (22) [43]	**20271**
Pat BALLARD (1)	7421
Don ROBERTSON (2)	2947
Julius DIXON (1)	1813
Beverly ROSS (1)	1813
Manos HADJIDAKIS (2)	769
Billy TOWNE (1)	769
Lee CATHY (1)	528
Jack KELLER (1)	528
Aaron COLLINS (1)	356
Maxwell DAVIS (1)	356
Sam LING (1)	356
George BRUNS (1)	327
Norman FOSTER (1)	327
Leon LANDGREN (1)	271
Åke Gerhard LARSSON (1)	271
Paddy ROBERTS (1)	271
Alex KRAMER (1)	247
Joan WHITNEY (1)	247
Hy ZARET (1)	247
Carroll COATES (1)	61
Lou STEIN (1)	61
Dale FITZSIMMONS (1)	45
Ray STANLEY (1)	45
Mary Jo RUSH (1)	44
Bob BUSH (1)	24
Teddy POWELL (1)	19
Louis SHELLY (1)	19
Sol WINKLER (1)	19
Richard CARNEY (1)	14
David (2) MARTIN (1)	14
Richard BARRETT (1)	7.0
Don RAYSOR (1)	7.0
Pat GASTON (1)	4.2
Jacqueline McCOY (1)	4.2
Bobby WILLIAMS (1)	4.2
Archie BLEYER (3)	4.2
Klaus-Günter NEUMANN (1)	4.2
Nancy LEE (1)	3.0
Bobby STEVENSON (1)	3.0
Joe DIXIE (1)	0.0
Rudi LINDT (1)	0.0
Hans BRADTKE (1)	0.0
Norman NEWELL (1)	0.0

BLOOD, SWEAT & TEARS ▶219 (12) [18]	**20266**
David CLAYTON-THOMAS (4)	7024
Laura NYRO (1)	5381
Berry GORDY (1)	1418
Brenda HOLLOWAY (1)	1418
Patrice HOLLOWAY (1)	1418
Frank Edward WILSON (1)	1418
Gerry GOFFIN (1)	653
Carole KING (1)	653
Fred LIPSIUS (1)	291
Barry MANN (1)	180
Cynthia WEIL (1)	180
John LENNON (1)	64
Paul McCARTNEY (1)	64
Dick HALLIGAN (1)	58
Patricia COSBY (1)	13
Michael GATELY (1)	13
Robert JOHN (1)	13
Mark JAMES (1)	5.7

Duane EDDY ▶220 (31) [15]	**20222**
Duane EDDY (21)	6336
Lee HAZLEWOOD (16)	4880
Don COSTA (1)	3920
Al CASEY (2)	1652
TRADITIONAL (1)	753
Henry MANCINI (1)	748
Hans WITTSTATT (1)	702
Daniel Decatur EMMETT (1)	419
Richard BOONE (1)	171
Sam ROLFE (1)	171
Johnny WESTERN (1)	171
Walter DONALDSON (1)	155
Don SWANDER (1)	95
Larry KNECHTEL (1)	46
Elizabeth COTTEN (1)	2.6

The COWSILLS ▶221 (8) [11]	**20220**
Steve DUBOFF (2)	4059
Artie KORNFELD (2)	4059
Tony ROMEO (2)	2845
Galt MacDERMOT (1)	2670
James RADO (1)	2670
Gerome RAGNI (1)	2670
Bill COWSILL (2)	407
Bob COWSILL (2)	407
Remo CAPRA (1)	198
Dick REYNOLDS (1)	116
Jack RHODES (1)	116

KINGSTON TRIO ▶222 (20) [28]	**20143**
TRADITIONAL (1)	9986
Denny THOMPSON (1)	1329
Billy Edd WHEELER (2)	1296
Pete SEEGER (1)	1124
Jerry LEIBER (1)	735
Mike STOLLER (1)	735
Dave GUARD (3)	614
Bess HAWES (1)	541
Jacqueline STEINER (1)	541
Hoyt AXTON (1)	507
Ken RAMSEY (1)	507
Tom GLAZER (1)	496
Jane BOWERS (1)	242
Lord BURGESS (1)	242
Will HOLT (1)	218
Harlan HOWARD (1)	190
Lee HAYS (1)	163
Cisco HOUSTON (1)	163
Rod McKUEN (1)	116
Steven YATES (1)	116
Bill LOUGHBOROUGH (1)	91
David WHEAT (1)	91
John STEWART (1)	56
Mack DAVID (1)	15
Bronislaw KAPER (1)	15
Woody GUTHRIE (1)	5.4
Malvina REYNOLDS (1)	5.4
Stanley C. WILSON (1)	3.5

The WHO ▶223 (28) [4]	**20134**
Pete TOWNSHEND (26)	19112
Jerry CAPEHART (1)	488
Eddie COCHRAN (1)	488
John ENTWHISTLE (1)	46

Michael BOLTON ▶224 (12) [15]	**20116**
Michael BOLTON (7)	5103
Diane WARREN (3)	4296
Calvin LEWIS (1)	2040
Andrew WRIGHT (1)	2040
Doug JAMES (1)	2021
Andy GOLDMARK (2)	1829
Desmond CHILD (1)	714
Steve CROPPER (1)	568
Otis REDDING (1)	568
Eric KAZ (1)	504
Hoagy CARMICHAEL (1)	195
Stuart GORRELL (1)	195
Jonathan CAIN (1)	29
Mark MANGOLD (1)	6.5
Craig SPROVACH (1)	6.5

Mary WELLS ▶225 (23) [24]	**19974**
Smokey ROBINSON (8)	15187
Ronnie WHITE (1)	843
Mary WELLS (3)	629
Lou COURTNEY (1)	486
Lamont DOZIER (1)	285
Brian HOLLAND (1)	285
Eddie HOLLAND (1)	285
Carl DAVIS (1)	227
Gerald SIMS (1)	227
Janie BRADFORD (1)	222
Barrett STRONG (3)	183
Berry GORDY (2)	147
William STEVENSON (1)	147
Mickey GENTILE (2)	145
Jennie Lee LAMBERT (2)	145
Chuck BARKSDALE (1)	141
Wade FLEMONS (1)	141
Cecil WOMACK (2)	129
Ronald Alonzo MILLER (1)	52
Lee PORTER (1)	52
Sid BARNES (1)	7.8
J.J. JACKSON (1)	7.8
Raynard MINER (1)	1.2
Carl William SMITH (1)	1.2

Roger WILLIAMS ▶226 (32) [44]	**19942**
Joseph KOSMA (2)	9874
John BARRY (1)	1794
Don BLACK (1)	1794
Francis CRAIG (1)	1787
Norman PETTY (1)	1031
Carl SIGMAN (3)	516
Leonard BERNSTEIN (1)	513
Sigmund ROMBERG (1)	369
Mitch LEIGH (1)	330
Charles DANVERS (1)	328
Nacio Herb BROWN (1)	286
Bob NOLAN (1)	142
Albert LASRY (1)	124
Charles TRENET (1)	124
Pietro GARINEI (1)	95
Alessandro GIOVANNINI (1)	95
Renato RASCEL (1)	95
Richard ADDINSELL (1)	94
Beverly GUTHRIE (1)	87
Gary LYNES (1)	87
Maurice JARRE (1)	75
Jerry BOCK (1)	72
Sheldon HARNICK (1)	72
Gabriel RUIZ (1)	43
Bronislaw KAPER (1)	39
Claude DEBUSSY (1)	17
Domenico SAVINO (1)	17
André PREVIN (1)	6.7
Jimmy WEBB (1)	6.0
Richard DEHR (1)	4.8
Terry GILKYSON (1)	4.8
Frank MILLER (1)	4.8
Augusto ALGUERO (1)	4.2
Tom JONES (1)	3.5
Harvey SCHMIDT (1)	3.5
Charles WILDMAN (1)	3.4
Joseph Turner HENDERSON (1)	1.4
Larry KUSIK (1)	0.2
Gian PICCIONI (1)	0.2
Eddie SNYDER (1)	0.2
Jimmy VAN HEUSEN (1)	0.0

Roger WILLIAMS ►226 (32) [44] *Cont'd*	**19942**
Alfred NEWMAN (1)	0.0
Lou SINGER (1)	0.0
Henry MANCINI (1)	0.0
TOTO ►227 (14) [6]	**19792**
David PAICH (12)	14402
Jeff PORCARO (3)	2390
Steve LUKATHER (2)	1965
Randy GOODRUM (1)	676
Joseph Stanley WILLIAMS (1)	328
Bobby KIMBALL (1)	31
FOUR ACES ►228 (35) [58]	**19627**
Paul Francis WEBSTER (2)	4487
Sammy FAIN (2)	4293
Pat BALLARD (1)	1496
Frank LOESSER (1)	1464
Hans ENGELMANN (1)	1131
Tom GLAZER (1)	1131
Sammy CAHN (5)	703
Johnny MERCER (3)	658
Cyril MOCKRIDGE (1)	340
Luther DIXON (1)	248
Nicholas BRODSZKY (2)	233
Nora BAYES (1)	212
Jack NORWORTH (1)	212
Dimitri TIOMKIN (1)	194
Benny DAVIS (1)	190
Abner SILVER (1)	190
Carl SIGMAN (2)	167
Richard ADDINSELL (1)	164
Richard ADLER (1)	156
Jerry ROSS (1)	156
Robert MELLIN (1)	145
Victor YOUNG (1)	130
Ugo CALISE (1)	108
Carlo Alberto ROSSI (1)	108
Al STILLMAN (1)	108
TRADITIONAL (1)	106
Frederic CHOPIN (1)	102
George SIDNEY (1)	102
Morris STOLOFF (1)	102
Ned WASHINGTON (1)	102
Francis LEMARQUE (1)	93
Norman NEWELL (1)	93
Edward ALPERSON (1)	67
Michael CARR (1)	67
Alex KRAMER (1)	40
Joan WHITNEY (1)	40
Hy ZARET (1)	40
Deeda PATRICK (1)	35
Don RALKE (1)	35
Bob DAVIE (1)	28
Marvin MOORE (1)	28
James Lord PIERPONT (1)	27
Bennie BENJAMIN (1)	18
Sol MARCUS (1)	18
Gene DePAUL (1)	12
Walter DONALDSON (1)	10
Gus KAHN (1)	10
Neville FLEESON (1)	6.3
Albert VON TILZER (1)	6.3
Arthur BERMAN (1)	3.8
Jack GOLD (1)	3.8
Marvin KAHN (1)	3.8
Heino GAZE (1)	3.3
Russell FAITH (1)	1.5
Clarence KEHNER (1)	1.5
Jule STYNE (1)	0.0
Irving KAHAL (1)	0.0
William RASKIN (1)	0.0

Jim CROCE ►229 (12) [9]	**19625**
Jim CROCE (8)	16847
Charles FOX (1)	1274
Norman GIMBEL (1)	1274
Sam COOKE (1)	76
Jerry LEIBER (1)	38
Mike STOLLER (1)	38
Jerry BUTLER (1)	25
Calvin CARTER (1)	25
Curtis MAYFIELD (1)	25
Barry WHITE ►230 (14) [8]	**19567**
Barry WHITE (12)	13976
Peter RADCLIFFE (1)	1532
Tony SEPE (1)	1532
Ekundayo PARIS (1)	1123
Nelson PIGFORD (1)	1123
Vance WILSON (1)	276
Smead HUDMAN (1)	2.7
Austin JOHNSON (1)	2.7
The KINKS ►231 (24) [1]	**19524**
Ray DAVIES (24)	19524
Billy PRESTON ►232 (15) [11]	**19473**
Billy PRESTON (12)	11307
Bruce FISHER (3)	5144
Joe GREENE (3)	2574
George JOHNSON (1)	184
Louis E. JOHNSON (1)	184
Syreeta WRIGHT (1)	30
George HARRISON (1)	28
Artie BUTLER (1)	5.7
Molly Ann LEIKIN (1)	5.7
John LENNON (1)	4.7
Paul McCARTNEY (1)	4.7
The DIAMONDS ►233 (25) [57]	**19380**
Maurice WILLIAMS (1)	7547
Clyde OTIS (3)	1983
Nancy LEE (1)	1939
Mike ANTHONY (1)	646
Barry MANN (1)	646
Danny WEBB (1)	448
George GOLDNER (2)	356
Morris LEVY (2)	356
Frankie LYMON (1)	356
Jimmy MERCHANT (1)	356
Herman SANTIAGO (1)	356
Carl STEVENS (2)	303
George STONE (2)	303
Joe JORDAN (1)	222
Jack McDERMOTT (1)	222
Morty CRAFT (1)	196
Richard DAVIS (1)	196
Joseph MARTIN (1)	196
Ralph MARTIN (1)	196
Anthony MIDDLETON (1)	196
Buddy HOLLY (1)	194
Larry SHAYNE (1)	144
Jack SHERR (1)	144
Charles TOBIAS (1)	144
Bobby BAYLOR (1)	112
Pat GASTON (1)	112
Milton LOVE (1)	112
Monte OWENS (1)	112
Hy WEISS (1)	112
Sam WEISS (1)	112
Winston WILLIS (1)	112
Sunny DAVID (1)	105
Ted McRAE (1)	105
Sid WYCHE (1)	105
Bob CREWE (2)	75
Frank SLAY (2)	75

Eddie HEYWOOD (1)	70
Judy SPENCER (1)	70
Harry BOOROS (1)	64
Anthony COLUMBO Jr. (1)	64
Louis COLUMBO (1)	64
Barry KAYE (1)	64
Nat GOODMAN (1)	23
Brook BENTON (1)	12
Oscar LIESE (1)	12
Johannes BRAHMS (1)	11
Wally GOLD (1)	11
Aaron SCHROEDER (1)	11
Ted KOEHLER (1)	2.7
James V. MONACO (1)	2.7
William S. KUTNER (1)	1.2
Richard LORING (1)	1.2
Berman PATTERSON (1)	0.0
Gaetano VASTOLA (1)	0.0
Herbert COX (1)	0.0
William Henry MILLER (1)	0.0
James SHEPPARD (1)	0.0
Bette MIDLER ►234 (18) [34]	**19298**
Amanda McBROOM (1)	6013
Julie GOLD (1)	3697
Larry HENLEY (1)	1703
Jeff SILBAR (1)	1703
Bobby FREEMAN (1)	1467
Hughie PRINCE (1)	1016
Don RAYE (1)	1016
Tom JANS (1)	451
Calvin LEWIS (1)	199
Andrew WRIGHT (1)	199
Mark KLINGMAN (1)	194
Buzzy LINHART (1)	194
Bette MIDLER (2)	152
Dominic BUGATTI (1)	130
Frank MUSKER (1)	130
Diane WARREN (1)	111
Bill HUGHES (1)	98
Roxanne SEEMAN (1)	98
David POMERANZ (1)	87
Spencer PROFFER (1)	87
Joe GARLAND (1)	81
Barry MANILOW (1)	81
Andy RAZAF (1)	81
Bruce ROBERTS (1)	72
Carole Bayer SAGER (1)	72
Marshall CRENSHAW (1)	40
Mick JAGGER (1)	35
Keith RICHARDS (1)	35
Barry MANN (1)	20
Tom SNOW (1)	20
Cynthia WEIL (1)	20
Jeff BARRY (1)	0.0
Ellie GREENWICH (1)	0.0
Phil SPECTOR (1)	0.0
PETER And GORDON ►235 (15) [15]	**19204**
Paul McCARTNEY (4)	5725
John LENNON (3)	4287
Del SHANNON (1)	2350
Mike LEANDER (3)	1997
Charles MILLS (3)	1997
Buddy HOLLY (1)	695
Norman PETTY (1)	695
Phil SPECTOR (1)	580
John CARTER (1)	262
Ken HAWKER (1)	262
Jerome HARRIS (1)	140
Paul KAUFMAN (1)	140
Gordon WALLER (2)	34

Peter ASHER (1)	26
Tony HATCH (1)	11
Gilbert O'SULLIVAN ►236 (8) [1]	**19184**
Gilbert O'SULLIVAN (8)	19184
The ARCHIES ►237 (6) [3]	**18947**
Jeff BARRY (6)	10639
Andy KIM (4)	8015
Bobby BLOOM (1)	294
FONTANE SISTERS ►238 (29) [53]	**18933**
Rudy JACKSON (1)	2989
Eddy RAY (1)	2989
Boyd BENNETT (1)	1302
Chuck GORMAN (1)	1302
John YOUNG (1)	1302
Henry GLOVER (1)	985
Aaron COLLINS (1)	557
Maxwell DAVIS (1)	557
Sam LING (1)	557
Buford ABNER (1)	448
Charlie GORE (1)	448
Louis INNIS (1)	448
Buck RAM (1)	444
Robert S. RILEY (1)	424
Alan ARKIN (1)	413
Bob CAREY (1)	413
Erik DARLING (1)	413
Saxie DOWELL (1)	393
Fats DOMINO (2)	390
Larry COLEMAN (1)	290
Dave BARTHOLOMEW (1)	178
Bernie LOWE (1)	159
Al LUBAR (1)	159
Doris FISHER (1)	146
Allan ROBERTS (1)	146
Doc POMUS (1)	139
Wayne SHANKLIN (1)	131
Dorian BURTON (1)	102
Howard PLUMMER (1)	102
Milton DRAKE (1)	94
Duke ENSTON (1)	94
Harry STRIDE (1)	94
Fred FISHER (1)	60
Billy ROSE (1)	60
Roy C. BENNETT (1)	51
Sid TEPPER (1)	51
Beasley SMITH (1)	11
Billy VAUGHN (1)	11
Jenny Lou CARSON (1)	11
Charles SINGLETON (1)	9.6
Dave ALLDRED (1)	9.1
Jimmy BOWEN (1)	9.1
Buddy KNOX (1)	9.1
Donnie LANIER (1)	9.1
Mort GARSON (1)	8.3
Earl SHUMAN (1)	8.3
Stuart HAMBLEN (1)	5.7
John MARASCALCO (1)	1.0
George MOTOLA (1)	1.0
Hal WINN (1)	1.0
Ann RONELL (1)	0.0
Alan FREED (1)	0.0
Harvey FUQUA (1)	0.0
Perez PRADO And His Orchestra ►239 (11) [9]	**18916**
Luis GUGLIELMI (1)	9278
Perez PRADO (5)	8908
Giuseppe FUCILLI (1)	703
Evangelina REYES (1)	13
Bobby TROUP (1)	7.7

Perez PRADO And His Orchestra ►239 (11) [9] *Cont'd*	**18916**
Barney BIGARD (1)	2.0
Duke ELLINGTON (1)	2.0
Irving MILLS (1)	2.0
W.C. HANDY (1)	0.0
Pat BENATAR ►240 (17) [24]	**18886**
Eddie SCHWARTZ (1)	3184
Holly KNIGHT (2)	2210
Pat BENATAR (5)	1604
Mike CHAPMAN (1)	1566
David Leigh BYRON (1)	1261
Eric LOWEN (1)	1170
Dan NAVARRO (1)	1170
Neil GERALDO (3)	1049
Doug LUBAHN (1)	652
Simon CLIMIE (1)	645
Thomas F. KELLY (2)	633
Alex CALL (1)	571
Geoff GILL (1)	566
Cliff WADE (1)	566
Scott SHEETS (1)	341
Billy STEINBERG (1)	292
Myron GROMBACHER (1)	240
Kerryn TOLHURST (1)	240
Franne GOLDE (1)	176
Peter McIAN (1)	176
Eddie BRIGATI (1)	175
Felix CAVALIERE (1)	175
Guy MARSHALL (1)	114
Robert TEPPER (1)	114
Herb ALPERT ►241 (13) [14]	**18851**
Burt BACHARACH (2)	4719
Hal DAVID (2)	4719
Andy ARMER (2)	2943
Randy BADAZZ (2)	2943
James Samuel HARRIS (3)	1193
Terry LEWIS (3)	1193
Juan Carlos CALDERÓN (1)	437
Harry NILSSON (1)	406
Richard HEWSON (1)	208
Howard MASSEY (1)	42
Eythor GUNNARSSON (1)	25
Herb ALPERT (1)	7.4
Melvin RAGIN (1)	7.4
Michael Lee STOKES (1)	7.4
Johnnie TAYLOR ►242 (23) [28]	**18747**
Don DAVIS (11)	6350
Harvey SCALES (2)	2014
Albert VANCE (1)	1982
Homer BANKS (3)	1343
Raymond Earl JACKSON (3)	1343
Bettye CRUTCHER (4)	1137
Bonny RICE (1)	876
Jimmy HUGHES (1)	703
Arthur SNYDER (3)	639
Kent BARKER (2)	295
George CLINTON (1)	285
Daron TAYLOR (1)	285
Alvertis ISBELL (1)	247
James WILSON (1)	244
Thomas KELLY (1)	240
Frank L. JOHNSON (1)	191
Melvin DAVIS (1)	114
Tony HESTER (1)	96
Richard WYLIE (1)	96
Clarence COULTER (1)	64
Chico JONES (1)	64

Bobby NEWSOME (1)	52
James Anthony DEAN (1)	43
Mel GRIFFIN (1)	32
Allen Alvoid JONES Jr. (1)	4.9
Jackie AVERY (1)	3.3
Johnnie H. TAYLOR (1)	3.3
Sam COOKE (1)	1.4
MEN AT WORK ►243 (6) [2]	**18721**
Colin James HAY (6)	14864
Ron STRYKERT (1)	3857
PEACHES & HERB ►244 (17) [23]	**18668**
Dino FEKARIS (5)	5899
Freddie PERREN (5)	5899
Chuck WILLIS (1)	1934
Ed TOWNSEND (1)	796
Mickey BAKER (1)	458
Ellas McDANIEL (1)	458
Sylvia ROBINSON (1)	458
Carolyn VARGA (1)	439
Harold ARLEN (1)	354
Ted KOEHLER (1)	354
Kenneth GAMBLE (2)	330
Leon HUFF (1)	267
Marshall PAUL (1)	249
Barbara ACKLIN (1)	191
Carl DAVIS (1)	191
Eugene RECORD (1)	191
Thom BELL (1)	63
Mikki FARROW (1)	63
Larry KOLBER (1)	34
Barry MANN (1)	34
Paul SIMON (1)	3.8
Diana ALLEN (1)	1.7
Robert (2) ALLEN (1)	1.7
Jr. WALKER & The ALL STARS ►245 (21) [26]	**18654**
Jr. WALKER (6)	4888
Johnny BRISTOL (7)	2503
Harvey FUQUA (3)	1497
Vernon BULLOCK (1)	1216
Lamont DOZIER (3)	970
Brian HOLLAND (3)	970
Eddie HOLLAND (3)	970
Willie WOODS (4)	932
Randy BACHMAN (1)	579
Burton CUMMINGS (1)	579
Janie BRADFORD (2)	540
Pam SAWYER (2)	521
Joe HINTON (1)	387
Lawrence HORN (2)	360
Jackey BEAVERS (1)	309
Danny COGGINS (1)	210
Henry COSBY (2)	201
Marilyn McLEOD (1)	199
Berry GORDY (1)	195
James GRAVES (1)	135
Gloria JONES (1)	134
Neil DIAMOND (1)	114
Melvin MOY (1)	74
Eddie WILLIS (1)	74
Wilton FELDER (1)	48
Gladys KNIGHT (1)	48
The BANGLES ►246 (8) [11]	**18583**
Liam STERNBERG (1)	5283
PRINCE (1)	2853
Paul SIMON (1)	2731
Susanna HOFFS (3)	2195
Thomas F. KELLY (2)	1769

Billy STEINBERG (2)	1769
Jules SHEAR (1)	529
Louis GUTIERREZ (1)	427
David KAHNE (1)	427
Walker IGLEHEART (1)	300
Debbi PETERSON (1)	300
Paul McCARTNEY ►247 (15) [4]	**18566**
Paul McCARTNEY (15)	16868
Linda McCARTNEY (1)	1407
Elvis COSTELLO (1)	261
Eric STEWART (1)	30
Freddy CANNON ►248 (23) [25]	**18530**
Chuck BARRIS (1)	4864
Frank SLAY (10)	2171
Henry CREAMER (1)	2015
J. Turner LAYTON (1)	2015
Bob CREWE (9)	1936
Freddy CANNON (2)	1015
Tommy BOYCE (1)	683
Steve VENET (1)	683
Robert BOULANGER (1)	425
Dick HEARD (1)	425
Russ REGAN (1)	337
Jack STAPP (1)	251
Harry STONE (1)	251
Chuck DOUGHERTY (1)	235
Kenneth GAMBLE (1)	169
Jerry J. ROSS (1)	169
Ray GILBERT (1)	129
Edward ORY (1)	129
Bob FELDMAN (3)	108
Jerry GOLDSTEIN (3)	108
Richard GOTTEHRER (3)	108
Jay GOODIS (1)	94
Ray GOETZ (1)	69
Edgar LESLIE (1)	69
George MEYER (1)	69
AEROSMITH ►249 (20) [16]	**18487**
Steven TYLER (16)	9613
Joe PERRY (7)	3191
Desmond CHILD (3)	2285
Tom HAMILTON (3)	1224
Brad WHITFORD (2)	423
John LENNON (1)	330
Paul McCARTNEY (1)	330
Jim VALLANCE (2)	326
Holly KNIGHT (1)	197
Lamont DOZIER (1)	128
Brian HOLLAND (1)	128
Eddie HOLLAND (1)	128
Shadow MORTON (1)	106
Richie SUPA (2)	47
Jack DOUGLAS (1)	15
Joey KRAMER (1)	15
Herb ALPERT & The TIJUANA BRASS ►250 (27) [27]	**18439**
Bobby SCOTT (1)	5191
Sol LAKE (3)	2862
Mikis THEODORAKIS (1)	1794
Nat ADDERLEY (1)	1047
Jerry HERMAN (1)	999
Burt BACHARACH (1)	880
Julius WECHTER (1)	771
Theodor GROUYA (1)	646
Chico BUARQUE DE HOLLANDA (1)	527
Bud COLEMAN (1)	458
Frank DeVOL (1)	438

Richard RODGERS (1)	399
Georges BIZET (1)	355
TRADITIONAL (1)	292
Anton KARAS (1)	287
Gilbert BECAUD (1)	235
Pierre DELANOË (1)	235
Carl SIGMAN (1)	235
Herb ALPERT (2)	166
Allen TOUSSAINT (1)	154
Jorge BEN (1)	146
John KANDER (1)	124
Gato BARBIERI (1)	113
Scott TURNER (1)	50
Peter SARSTEDT (1)	25
John BARNES (1)	4.5
Jimmie CAMERON (1)	4.5
MOODY BLUES ►251 (22) [6]	**18338**
Justin HAYWARD (13)	11920
John LODGE (7)	4126
Larry BANKS (1)	1094
Milton BENNETT (1)	1094
Denny LAINE (2)	51
Mike PINDER (2)	51
The BYRDS ►252 (21) [11]	**18322**
Bob DYLAN (4)	7655
Pete SEEGER (1)	6804
Roger McGUINN (7)	1920
Gene CLARK (4)	558
David CROSBY (2)	544
Chris HILLMAN (2)	410
Harvey GERST (1)	174
Gerry GOFFIN (2)	85
Carole KING (2)	85
Art REYNOLDS (2)	82
Jacques LEVY (1)	3.7
Taylor DAYNE ►253 (8) [13]	**18283**
Diane WARREN (2)	5411
Jimmy GEORGE (1)	2802
Seth SWIRSKY (2)	1659
Alexandra FORBES (1)	1582
Jeffrey FRANZEL (1)	1582
Ernie GOLD (1)	958
Arthur BAKER (1)	856
Tommy FARAGHER (1)	856
Lotti GOLDEN (1)	856
Arnie ROMAN (1)	701
Carolyn BOWDEN (1)	340
Gregg TRIPP (1)	340
Elliot WOLFF (1)	340
INXS ►254 (17) [8]	**18197**
Michael HUTCHENCE (14)	8825
Andy FARRISS (15)	8139
Jon FARRISS (2)	772
Harry VANDA (1)	183
George YOUNG (1)	183
Garry BEERS (2)	88
Tim FARRISS (1)	3.8
Kirk PENGILLY (1)	3.8
Tommy EDWARDS ►255 (15) [25]	**18077**
Charles DAWES (1)	5317
Carl SIGMAN (1)	5317
Ben RALEIGH (1)	936
Don WOLF (1)	936
Sid FRANK (1)	702
Ray GETZOV (1)	702
Howard Lee BARNES (1)	542
Don ROBERTSON (1)	542
Robert ALLEN (1)	315
Mack DAVID (1)	315

Tommy EDWARDS ►255 (15) [25] Cont'd	**18077**
Dick MANNING (1)	303
Larry STOCK (1)	303
Ernie BURNETTE (1)	277
George NORTON (1)	277
Maybelle WATSON (1)	277
Lee POCKRISS (2)	231
Tommy EDWARDS (2)	212
Hal DAVID (1)	196
Robert FLETCHER (1)	146
Cole PORTER (1)	146
Peter UDELL (1)	36
Bill ANDERSON (1)	17
Ollie BLANCHARD (1)	14
Johnnie MALONE (1)	14
Gene PITNEY (1)	2.5
Roger MILLER ►256 (19) [7]	**18061**
Roger MILLER (15)	17329
Bobby RUSSELL (2)	671
Mae Boren AXTON (1)	18
Thomas DURDEN (1)	18
Elvis PRESLEY (1)	18
Dave GRUSIN (1)	3.9
Robert WELLS (1)	3.9
STEPPENWOLF ►257 (13) [10]	**17994**
Mars BONFIRE (2)	6686
John KAY (9)	6257
Rushton MOREVE (1)	2419
Jerry EDMONTON (4)	1194
Gabriel MEKLER (1)	459
Larry BYROM (2)	387
Hoyt AXTON (1)	326
Nick ST. NICHOLAS (1)	171
Kent HENRY (1)	47
Goldy McJOHN (1)	47
The CARS ►258 (18) [1]	**17898**
Ric OCASEK (18)	17898
Bobby SHERMAN ►259 (11) [12]	**17892**
Danny JANSSEN (3)	8172
Tom BAHLER (2)	4283
Diane HILDERBRAND (1)	1237
Jack KELLER (1)	1237
Alan O'DAY (1)	748
Craig DOERGE (1)	684
Paul WILLIAMS (1)	684
Peter ALLEN (1)	193
Carole Bayer SAGER (1)	193
Ronald BOUTWELL (1)	154
Bobby SHERMAN (1)	154
Larry WEISS (1)	152
Conway TWITTY ►260 (23) [27]	**17890**
Conway TWITTY (10)	5810
Jack NANCE (4)	4303
TRADITIONAL (1)	1043
Fred WEATHERLY (1)	1043
Ben WEISMAN (1)	1034
Fred WISE (1)	1034
Dan PENN (1)	611
Henri BETTI (1)	465
Jerry SEELEN (1)	465
Art HARRIS (1)	420
Fred JAY (1)	420
Ray EVANS (1)	290
Jay LIVINGSTON (1)	290
Dave WILLIAMS (1)	265
Bill GIANT (1)	57
David HESS (1)	57

Buddy KAYE (1)	57
Aaron SCHROEDER (1)	42
Sharon SILBERT (1)	42
George David WEISS (1)	42
Raymond SMITH (1)	29
Chuck WILLIS (1)	29
Ronald Robert PETERSON (1)	16
Fred CARTER (1)	11
Jimmy Ray PAULMAN (1)	6.7
Louis INNIS (1)	5.0
Buddy KILLEN (1)	5.0
CLASSICS IV ►261 (12) [6]	**17819**
Buddy BUIE (11)	6776
J.R. COBB (11)	6776
Emory GORDY (2)	1496
Harry MIDDLEBROOKS (1)	1379
Mike SHAPIRO (1)	1379
Jim WEATHERLY (1)	13
Debbie GIBSON ►262 (10) [2]	**17816**
Debbie GIBSON (10)	17558
Lamont DOZIER (1)	257
Jack SCOTT ►263 (23) [5]	**17793**
Jack SCOTT (19)	13101
Walter SCOTT (1)	4173
Clyde OTIS (1)	287
Bob NOLAN (1)	212
Fred ROSE (1)	19
Juice NEWTON ►264 (11) [19]	**17697**
Hank DeVITO (1)	5541
Chip TAYLOR (1)	4537
Gary BURR (1)	2319
Otha YOUNG (1)	2196
Diane LAMPERT (1)	712
Joe SENECA (1)	712
Rod ARGENT (1)	483
John BETTIS (1)	390
Michael CLARK (1)	390
Danny DOUMA (1)	100
Richard FELDMAN (1)	100
Todd SHARP (1)	100
Bryan ADAMS (1)	31
Eric KAGNA (1)	31
Jim VALLANCE (1)	31
Ronnie SCOTT (1)	8.0
Steve WOLFE (1)	8.0
Charles David ROBBINS (1)	4.0
Van STEPHENSON (1)	4.0
SAM THE SHAM And The PHARAOHS ►265 (9) [7]	**17659**
Ronald BLACKWELL (3)	8496
Domingo SAMUDIO (2)	7739
Joy Byers JOHNSTON (1)	363
Bob TUBERT (1)	363
Dewayne BLACKWELL (1)	338
Bob McDILL (1)	209
Billy EMERSON (1)	152
J. GEILS Band ►266 (21) [17]	**17577**
Seth JUSTMAN (15)	12386
Peter WOLF (11)	3465
James W. ALEXANDER (1)	326
Zelda SAMUELS (1)	326
Chris KENNER (1)	136
Melvin MASON (1)	127
Frank PADEN (1)	127
Johnny PADEN (1)	127
Jesse SMITH (1)	127
Willie STEPHENSON (1)	127

Lamont DOZIER (1)	68
Brian HOLLAND (1)	68
Eddie HOLLAND (1)	68
Paul JUSTMAN (1)	67
Carl FISHER (1)	11
Joseph David THOMAS Jr. (1)	11
Joe LAMONT (1)	7.0
Eric CLAPTON ►267 (20) [18]	**17444**
Eric CLAPTON (11)	4615
Bob MARLEY (1)	4537
Marcy LEVY (1)	1325
George TERRY (1)	1325
J.J. CALE (2)	1251
Richard FELDMAN (1)	733
Roger LINN (1)	733
Jerry Lynn WILLIAMS (3)	579
Danny FLOWERS (1)	553
Johnny OTIS (1)	493
Steve DIAMOND (1)	329
Troy SEALS (1)	329
Eddie SETSER (1)	329
Bonnie BRAMLETT (1)	130
Delaney BRAMLETT (1)	130
Bobby WHITLOCK (1)	22
Michael Leslie JONES (1)	19
Leon RUSSELL (1)	9.9
STAPLE SINGERS ►268 (15) [22]	**17315**
Alvertis ISBELL (1)	5980
Curtis MAYFIELD (2)	4609
Bonny RICE (2)	918
Luther INGRAM (1)	900
Homer BANKS (3)	896
Carl HAMPTON (3)	896
Raymond Earl JACKSON (3)	896
Phillip MITCHELL (1)	458
Jeff BARRY (1)	377
Bobby BLOOM (1)	377
Gary FRIEDMAN (1)	255
Herb SCHAPIRO (1)	255
Stephen STILLS (1)	196
Charlie CHALMERS (1)	68
Donna RHODES (1)	68
Sandra RHODES (1)	68
Cornelius GRANT (1)	19
Smokey ROBINSON (1)	19
Bettye CRUTCHER (1)	19
Bobby MANUEL (1)	19
Larry NIX (1)	19
Roebuck STAPLES (1)	2.9
Irene CARA ►269 (8) [10]	**17262**
Irene CARA (6)	4547
Giorgio MORODER (4)	4263
Keith FORSEY (2)	3575
Michael GORE (2)	1953
Dean PITCHFORD (1)	1549
Bunny HULL (1)	525
Lesley GORE (1)	404
Bruce ROBERTS (1)	271
Pete BELLOTTE (1)	163
Eddie BROWN (1)	13
Dusty SPRINGFIELD ►270 (23) [39]	**17255**
Burt BACHARACH (2)	2127
Hal DAVID (2)	2127
Pino DONAGGIO (1)	1373
Simon NAPIER-BELL (1)	1373
Vicki WICKHAM (1)	1373
John HURLEY (1)	1112
Ronnie WILKINS (1)	1112

Mike HAWKER (2)	904
Ivor RAYMONDE (2)	904
Leon HUFF (4)	459
Kenneth GAMBLE (3)	448
Clive WESTLAKE (2)	446
Ben WEISMAN (1)	409
Jerry BUTLER (1)	337
Buddy KAYE (1)	270
Philip SPRINGER (1)	270
Mark BARKAN (1)	254
Vic MILLROSE (1)	254
Alan BERGMAN (1)	215
Marilyn BERGMAN (1)	215
Michel LEGRAND (1)	215
Jerry RAGOVOY (1)	173
Mort SHUMAN (1)	173
Tony Joe WHITE (1)	168
Gerry GOFFIN (1)	135
Carole KING (1)	135
Peter CALLANDER (1)	62
Pietro MELFA (1)	62
Amedeo TOMMASI (1)	62
Tom SPRINGFIELD (1)	37
Randy NEWMAN (1)	11
Thom BELL (1)	9.5
Linda CREED (1)	9.5
Donnie FRITTS (1)	4.5
Eddie HINTON (1)	4.5
Dennis LAMBERT (1)	3.2
Brian POTTER (1)	3.2
Gary KLEIN (1)	2.9
Artie KORNFELD (1)	2.9
Otis REDDING ►271 (27) [28]	**17213**
Otis REDDING (17)	7121
Steve CROPPER (5)	4601
James BROWN (1)	821
Jerry BUTLER (1)	609
Allen TOUSSAINT (1)	332
Sam COOKE (1)	331
Billy HILL (1)	322
TRADITIONAL (1)	318
Jimmy CAMPBELL (1)	315
Reg CONNELLY (1)	315
Harry WOODS (1)	315
Mick JAGGER (1)	312
Keith RICHARDS (1)	312
Brook BENTON (1)	214
Jimmy WILLIAMS (1)	214
Zelma REDDING (1)	153
Joseph ROCK (1)	153
Roosevelt JAMISON (1)	60
Eddie FLOYD (1)	56
Booker T. JONES Jr. (1)	56
McEvoy ROBINSON (1)	46
Phil WALDEN (1)	45
Alvertis ISBELL (1)	38
Allen Alvoid JONES Jr. (1)	38
Gene LAWSON (1)	33
Bishop ROBINSON (1)	33
Tommy STAR (1)	33
Don COVAY (1)	16
The CRYSTALS ►272 (8) [7]	**17112**
Gene PITNEY (1)	6361
Phil SPECTOR (5)	2789
Jeff BARRY (4)	2203
Ellie GREENWICH (4)	2203
Barry MANN (2)	1485
Cynthia WEIL (2)	1485
Leroy R. BATES (1)	586

The VOGUES ▶273 (15) [26]	**16997**
Allen REYNOLDS (1)	4152
Jerry CAPEHART (1)	3450
Jimmy DUNCAN (1)	2083
Petula CLARK (1)	1353
Tony HATCH (1)	1353
Barry MANN (1)	507
Cynthia WEIL (1)	507
Charles DANVERS (1)	466
Carl SIGMAN (1)	466
Mark CHARRON (1)	423
Robert ALLEN (2)	348
Al STILLMAN (2)	348
John HURLEY (1)	313
Ronnie WILKINS (1)	313
Sid FRANK (1)	188
Ray GETZOV (1)	188
Jesse BELVIN (1)	162
Gaynel HODGE (1)	162
Curtis Edward WILLIAMS (1)	162
Tony ASHER (1)	13
Brian WILSON (1)	13
Richard DEHR (1)	8.4
Terry GILKYSON (1)	8.4
Frank MILLER (1)	8.4
Joey LEVINE (1)	1.4
Artie RESNICK (1)	1.4
Gene CHANDLER ▶274 (25) [26]	**16941**
Curtis MAYFIELD (8)	3624
Gene CHANDLER (7)	3590
Earl EDWARDS (2)	3058
Bernice WILLIAMS (2)	3058
Herman R. DAVIS (1)	857
Russ LEWIS (1)	857
William Earl BUTLER (1)	492
James A. THOMPSON Jr. (4)	457
Keni ST. LEWIS (2)	411
Don COVAY (1)	93
Smokey ROBINSON (1)	93
Ronnie WHITE (1)	93
James BROWN (1)	66
Bud HOBGOOD (1)	66
Karl TARLETON (1)	24
Gerald SIMS (2)	13
Carl DAVIS (2)	10
Calvin CARTER (1)	9.6
Bob FINIZ (1)	9.6
Irving NAHAN (1)	9.6
Joe PIROLLO (1)	9.6
Ernie SPANO (1)	9.6
James TESTA (1)	9.6
Luther DIXON (1)	8.4
Albert B. SMITH (1)	8.4
Otis LEAVILL (1)	3.8
Smokey ROBINSON ▶275 (21) [16]	**16916**
Smokey ROBINSON (16)	10247
Marvin TARPLIN (4)	2531
Jimmy GEORGE (1)	782
Louis PARDINI (1)	782
Steve LeGASSICK (1)	576
Brian RAY (1)	576
Gary GOETZMAN (2)	317
Mike PICCIRILLO (2)	317
Pamela MOFFETT (2)	269
Rose Ella JONES (3)	211
Brenda SUTTON (1)	83
Mike SUTTON (1)	83
Kathy WAKEFIELD (1)	83
Lonnie KIRTZ (1)	20
Ivory STONE (1)	20
Homer TALBERT (1)	20
The CREW-CUTS ▶276 (30) [61]	**16881**
Dick GLASSER (1)	1557
James EDWARDS (1)	1408
Carl FEASTER (1)	1408
Claude FEASTER (1)	1408
James C. KEYES (1)	1408
Floyd F. McRAE (1)	1408
Rudy TOOMBS (2)	1157
Leroy GRIFFIN (1)	873
Jesse BELVIN (1)	592
Gaynel HODGE (1)	592
Curtis Edward WILLIAMS (1)	592
Eunice LEVY (1)	440
Jake PORTER (1)	440
Forrest WILSON (1)	440
Willis CARROLL (1)	329
Carmen TAYLOR (1)	329
David CARROLL (1)	272
Dorcas COCHRAN (1)	272
Titus TURNER (1)	231
Shirley GUNTER (1)	214
Joe JOSEA (1)	214
Blondene TAYLOR (1)	214
Samuel SMITH (1)	178
Dallas TAYLOR (1)	178
Ric CARTEY (1)	172
Carole JOYNER (1)	172
Robert CHABRIER (1)	84
Al STILLMAN (1)	84
George CATES (1)	29
Mel LEVEN (1)	29
Dick RICHARDS (1)	19
Ira KOSLOFF (1)	19
Alice D. SIMMS (1)	19
Al HOFFMAN (1)	11
Dick MANNING (1)	11
Ray ALLEN (1)	7.3
George BROWN (1)	7.3
Wandra MERRELL (1)	7.3
Sam SALTZBERG (1)	7.3
Rose Marie McCOY (3)	5.8
Charles SINGLETON (1)	5.8
Sammy FAIN (1)	5.8
Jack YELLEN (1)	5.8
Joe LUBIN (1)	5.8
Irving ROTH (1)	5.8
Lenny ADELSON (1)	3.0
Les BAXTER (1)	3.0
Luigi CREATORE (1)	3.0
Hugo PERETTI (1)	3.0
Pat BARRETT (1)	0.0
Rudi MAUGERI (1)	0.0
Nappy BROWN (1)	0.0
Fred MENDELSOHN (1)	0.0
Gene DePAUL (1)	0.0
Johnny MERCER (1)	0.0
Kelly OWENS (1)	0.0
Eleanor BROADWATER (1)	0.0
Robert CHAISSON (1)	0.0
Dale HAWKINS (1)	0.0
Stanley J. LEWIS (1)	0.0
Otis BLACKWELL (1)	0.0
The FIREBALLS/ Jimmy GILMER And The FIREBALLS ▶277 (11) [11]	**16871**
Keith McCORMACK (2)	5747
Faye VOSS (1)	5316
Tom PAXTON (1)	2264
George TOMSCO (5)	1813
Juanita JORDAN (2)	577
Glynn THAMES (1)	431
Lynn EASTON (1)	295
Steve DODGE (1)	172
Ken DAVIS (1)	146
Barbara TOMSCO (1)	97
Norman PETTY (1)	12
Tony BENNETT ▶278 (52) [83]	**16851**
Al STILLMAN (2)	1056
Robert ALLEN (3)	1038
Nick ACQUAVIVA (1)	976
Ted VARNICK (1)	976
Johnny MERCER (2)	920
Sadie VIMMERSTEDT (1)	792
George CORY (1)	785
Douglass CROSS (1)	785
Leslie BRICUSSE (2)	646
Cy COLEMAN (2)	612
Lincoln CHASE (1)	595
Bernice PETKERE (1)	547
Carolyn LEIGH (1)	541
Sacha DISTEL (1)	437
Jack REARDON (1)	437
Anthony NEWLEY (1)	407
Bob HILLIARD (3)	351
Gordon JENKINS (1)	298
Sunny SKYLAR (1)	296
Lou SINGER (1)	257
Hy ZARET (1)	257
Edward WHITE (1)	255
Mack WOLFSON (1)	255
Cyril ORNADEL (1)	239
Guy WOOD (1)	214
Bob MERRILL (2)	200
Cole PORTER (1)	196
Ralph FREED (1)	152
Bart HOWARD (1)	137
Harold ARLEN (1)	127
Betty COMDEN (1)	125
Adolph GREEN (1)	125
Jule STYNE (1)	125
Jack ERICKSON (1)	111
Sano MARCO (1)	111
Sherman EDWARDS (1)	95
Earl SHUMAN (1)	95
Jack SEGAL (1)	80
Robert WELLS (1)	80
Billy MAYHEW (1)	70
Jimmy VAN HEUSEN (2)	69
Charles CHAPLIN (1)	69
Geoffrey PARSONS (1)	69
John TURNER (1)	69
Carl SIGMAN (1)	66
Henri SALVADOR (1)	60
Marcel STELLMAN (1)	60
Ric MARLOW (1)	58
Bobby SCOTT (1)	58
Deborah CHESSLER (1)	43
Oscar HAMMERSTEIN (2)	37
Richard RODGERS (2)	37
Ray EVANS (1)	35
Jay LIVINGSTON (1)	35
Arthur BERMAN (1)	31
Redd EVANS (1)	31
Marvin KAHN (1)	31
Ronald Norman MILLER (1)	25
Orlando MURDEN (1)	25
Alice REACH (1)	22
Anthony SCIBETTA (1)	22
Sam COSLOW (3)	14
W. Franke HARLING (1)	11
Jimmy FLYNN (1)	11
Harry ROSENTHAL (1)	11
Alex SULLIVAN (1)	11
Mann CURTIS (1)	5.6
Joseph MEYER (1)	5.6
Johnny MANDEL (1)	5.2
Paul Francis WEBSTER (1)	5.2
Sammy CAHN (1)	3.4
Al HOFFMAN (1)	2.7
Dick MANNING (1)	2.7
Guy MAGENTA (1)	2.4
Wayne SHANKLIN (1)	2.4
Al SHERMAN (1)	2.4
Armando ROMEO (1)	2.2
Leo ROBIN (1)	0.4
Richard WHITING (1)	0.4
Hank WILLIAMS (1)	0.0
Chilton PRICE (1)	0.0
John SCHROEDER (1)	0.0
Abner SILVER (1)	0.0
Don McLEAN ▶279 (10) [10]	**16770**
Don McLEAN (8)	14040
Joe MELSON (1)	1092
Roy ORBISON (1)	1092
James BEAUMONT (1)	78
Walter LESTER (1)	78
Lennie MARTIN (1)	78
Joseph ROCK (1)	78
John L. TAYLOR (1)	78
Joseph VERSCHAREN (1)	78
Janet VOGEL (1)	78
The BUCKINGHAMS ▶280 (7) [8]	**16768**
James HOLVAY (4)	9237
Gary BEISBIER (3)	3081
Gail LEVY (1)	989
Vincent LEVY (1)	989
Joe ZAWINUL (1)	989
James William GUERCIO (1)	764
Lloyd PRICE (1)	435
Martin GREBB (1)	286
Gale STORM ▶281 (14) [32]	**16760**
Ned MILLER (1)	3904
Dave BARTHOLOMEW (1)	1712
Fats DOMINO (1)	1712
Earl King JOHNSON (1)	1712
Jack FULTON (1)	1191
Lois STEELE (1)	1191
Bernie LOWE (1)	890
Bickley REICHNER (1)	890
George GOLDNER (1)	459
Morris LEVY (1)	459
Frankie LYMON (1)	459
Jimmy MERCHANT (1)	459
Herman SANTIAGO (1)	459
Titus TURNER (1)	264
Richard DEHR (1)	262
Terry GILKYSON (1)	262
Frank MILLER (1)	262
Tommie CONNOR (1)	32
Frank STANTON (1)	32
Jerry LEIBER (1)	25
Mike STOLLER (1)	25
Maewa KAIHAN (1)	25
Clement SCOTT (1)	25
Dorothy STEWART (1)	25
Joe BURKE (1)	11
Edgar LESLIE (1)	11
Mario NASCIMBENE (1)	1.5
Paul Francis WEBSTER (1)	1.5

Gale STORM ▶281 (14) [32] *Cont'd*	**16760**
Nick ACQUAVIVA (1)	1.0
Ted VARNICK (1)	1.0
David GODDARD (1)	0.0
Larry VANNATA (1)	0.0
TEARS FOR FEARS ▶282 (8) [5]	**16629**
Roland ORZABAL (8)	7738
Ian STANLEY (3)	4265
Curt SMITH (2)	2928
Chris HUGHES (1)	1657
Nicky HOLLAND (1)	40
Engelbert HUMPERDINCK ▶283 (24) [39]	**16544**
Barry MASON (7)	2200
Les REED (6)	1864
Eddie MILLER (1)	1496
Dub WILLIAMS (1)	1496
Robert Gene YOUNT (1)	1496
Ritchie ADAMS (3)	1215
Alan BERNSTEIN (3)	1215
Dallas FRAZIER (1)	658
Carl BELEW (1)	373
Shelby SINGLETON (1)	373
W.S. STEVENSON (1)	373
Barry GIBB (1)	302
Maurice GIBB (1)	302
Tony MACAULAY (1)	282
Burt BACHARACH (1)	262
Hal DAVID (1)	262
Roberto LIVRAGHI (1)	254
Daniele PACE (1)	254
Mario PANZERI (1)	254
Mike LEANDER (1)	216
Ed SEAGO (1)	216
Jackie RAE (1)	200
Gianni ARGENIO (1)	142
Francesco CASSANO (1)	142
Corrado CONTI (1)	142
Roger COOK (1)	142
Roger GREENAWAY (1)	142
Richard Rodney BENNETT (1)	43
Paul Francis WEBSTER (1)	43
Don BACKY (1)	30
Gil KING (1)	30
Detto MARIANO (1)	30
Norman NEWELL (1)	30
Jan BUCKINGHAM (1)	17
Mark Eugene GRAY (1)	17
Floyd HUDDLESTON (1)	11
Paul RYAN (1)	11
Terry COLLINS (1)	5.3
Bobby ELI (1)	5.3
Bob SEGER ▶284 (14) [6]	**16526**
Bob SEGER (11)	11390
Eugene WILLIAMS (1)	1918
Harold FALTERMEYER (1)	1534
Keith FORSEY (1)	1534
Tim HARDIN (1)	77
Tina TURNER (1)	72
Jimmy DEAN ▶285 (14) [15]	**16525**
Jimmy DEAN (6)	12415
Fred BURCH (1)	1056
Marijohn WILKIN (1)	1056
Wayne WALKER (1)	610
David Anthony MARTINS (1)	351
Larry MARKES (2)	266
Robert ALLEN (1)	247
Gus KAHN (1)	148
Egbert VAN ALSTYNE (1)	148

Steven HARVEY (1)	56
Martin SELIGSON (1)	56
Philip M. CRANE (1)	52
Joe SAVARINO (1)	52
Ruth ROBERTS (1)	9.7
Paul HAMPTON (1)	3.2
ALICE COOPER ▶286 (21) [19]	**16475**
Alice COOPER (15)	5576
Dick WAGNER (6)	3502
Michael BRUCE (8)	1864
Neal SMITH (4)	1051
Dennis DUNAWAY (4)	882
Glen BUXTON (3)	819
Desmond CHILD (2)	608
Rolf KEMPF (1)	604
John McCURRY (1)	500
Bernie TAUPIN (1)	412
David CARRON (1)	310
Joan JETT (1)	108
Bob EZRIN (2)	104
Reggie VINSON (1)	81
Vic PEPE (1)	12
Bob PFEIFER (1)	12
Jack PONTI (1)	12
Andy GOLDMARK (1)	9.9
Bruce ROBERTS (1)	9.9
Natalie COLE ▶287 (18) [24]	**16470**
Charles Henry JACKSON Jr. (6)	4268
Marvin YANCY (6)	4268
Bruce SPRINGSTEEN (1)	1871
Gerry GOFFIN (2)	911
Michael MASSER (2)	911
Irving GORDON (1)	804
Preston GLASS (1)	527
Reggie CALLOWAY (1)	497
Vincent CALLOWAY (1)	497
Pam RESWICK (1)	357
Allan RICH (1)	357
Steve WERFEL (1)	357
Natalie COLE (2)	251
Sam LORBER (1)	97
Greg PRESTOPINO (1)	97
Matthew WILDER (1)	97
Stephen MITCHELL (1)	84
Marti SHARRON (1)	84
Gary SKARDINA (1)	84
Tennyson STEPHENS (1)	23
Richard KERR (1)	11
Graham LYLE (1)	11
Edward HEYMAN (1)	1.2
Victor YOUNG (1)	1.2
Doris DAY ▶288 (26) [48]	**16428**
Ray EVANS (1)	3486
Jay LIVINGSTON (1)	3486
Jimmie CRANE (1)	1413
Milt GABLER (1)	1413
Al JACOBS (1)	1413
Robert ALLEN (2)	1274
Richard ADLER (1)	1217
Sammy CAHN (2)	694
Nicholas BRODSZKY (1)	673
Joe LUBIN (1)	241
Ruth FREED (1)	123
Bob ROBERTS (1)	123
Thomas ADAIR (1)	86
Leith STEVENS (1)	86
Leonard JOY (1)	83
Alice D. SIMMS (1)	83
Bob HILLIARD (1)	57
By DUNHAM (1)	38

Joseph HOOVEN (1)	38
Marilyn HOOVEN (1)	38
Gene DePAUL (1)	36
Johnny MERCER (1)	36
Pat BALLARD (1)	34
Lyn DUDDY (1)	32
Joan EDWARDS (1)	32
Betty COMDEN (1)	31
Adolph GREEN (1)	31
Jule STYNE (1)	31
David HOLT (1)	21
Dick GLEASON (1)	16
Floyd HUDDLESTON (1)	16
Al RINKER (1)	16
Bob MERRILL (1)	12
Frank LOESSER (1)	6.2
Ray HEINDORF (1)	5.2
Charles E. HENDERSON (1)	5.2
Donald PIPPIN (1)	5.2
Frank DeVOL (1)	0.7
Alan SPILTON (1)	0.7
Sammy FAIN (2)	0.0
Paul Francis WEBSTER (2)	0.0
Howard Ellington Riddiford BARNES (1)	0.0
Harold FIELDS (1)	0.0
Joseph RONCORONI (1)	0.0
Henry STONE (1)	0.0
Otis WILLIAMS (1)	0.0
Oscar HAMMERSTEIN (2)	0.0
Richard RODGERS (2)	0.0
Eddie RABBITT ▶289 (14) [13]	**16360**
Eddie RABBITT (9)	4403
Even STEVENS (8)	4316
David MALLOY (7)	4295
Frank MYERS (1)	2189
Randy McCORMICK (1)	270
Thom SCHUYLER (1)	185
Milton L. BROWN (1)	162
Steve DORFF (1)	162
Snuff GARRETT (1)	162
Alan RAY (1)	93
Jeff RAYMOND (1)	93
Rick GILES (1)	15
Don PFRIMMER (1)	15
Robert PALMER ▶290 (18) [29]	**16317**
Robert PALMER (6)	7796
Moon MARTIN (1)	1539
James Samuel HARRIS (1)	1331
Terry LEWIS (1)	1331
Andy FRASER (1)	1228
Marvin GAYE (1)	499
Todd RUNDGREN (1)	282
Lonnie SIMMONS (1)	263
Rudy TAYLOR (1)	263
Charles K. WILSON (1)	263
Arthur ROSS (1)	250
Leon WARE (1)	250
Tony HAYNES (1)	150
Dennis NELSON (1)	150
Norman SPAN (1)	119
Steve FELLOWS (1)	88
Alan MANSFIELD (1)	88
Guy PRATT (1)	88
Steve STEVENS (1)	88
Jay GRUSKA (1)	50
Michael OMARTIAN (1)	50
Bruce SUDANO (1)	50
David BATTEAU (1)	27
Don FREEMAN (1)	27

David FRANK (1)	21
Mic MURPHY (1)	21
Allen TOUSSAINT (1)	2.8
Frank BLAIR (1)	1.5
Dony WYNN (1)	1.5
Henry MANCINI And His Orchestra ▶291 (18) [10]	**16214**
Nino ROTA (1)	6778
Henry MANCINI (14)	4694
Johnny MERCER (4)	2843
Francis LAI (1)	1533
Ray EVANS (1)	81
Jay LIVINGSTON (1)	81
Maurice RAVEL (1)	72
Allyn FERGUSON (1)	59
Irwin Elliott ZUCKER (1)	59
Ludwig VAN BEETHOVEN (1)	13
Mitch MILLER ▶292 (21) [29]	**16210**
TRADITIONAL (4)	7472
Don GEORGE (1)	4536
Robert ALLEN (2)	1718
Malcolm ARNOLD (1)	631
Kenneth J. ALFORD (1)	631
Jessie CAVANAUGH (1)	161
William ENGVICK (1)	161
Maximiano De SOUSA (1)	123
Oscar HAMMERSTEIN (1)	105
Richard RODGERS (1)	105
Amadeu Do VALE (1)	99
Jose GALHARDO (1)	99
Raul PORTELA (1)	99
Joseph KOSMA (1)	54
Johnny MERCER (1)	54
Jacques PREVERT (1)	54
Margaret MILLER (2)	21
Mike MILLER (2)	21
Charlotte CHAIT (1)	20
Mack DISCANT (1)	20
Paul ANKA (1)	5.8
Bob HILLIARD (1)	3.8
Philip SPRINGER (1)	3.8
Jerry LIVINGSTON (1)	3.0
Paul Francis WEBSTER (2)	3.0
Walter DONALDSON (1)	1.9
Gus KAHN (1)	1.9
Carl HAVERLIN (1)	1.2
Dimitri TIOMKIN (1)	0.0
Johnny CASH ▶293 (42) [34]	**16201**
Shel SILVERSTEIN (1)	6404
Johnny CASH (19)	5233
June CARTER (3)	1012
Merle KILGORE (1)	788
Carl PERKINS (1)	446
Jack H. CLEMENT (3)	429
Kris KRISTOFFERSON (1)	405
Hughie CANNON (1)	364
Bob DYLAN (1)	326
Roy ORBISON (1)	206
Charlie WILLIAMS (1)	160
Billy Edd WHEELER (1)	130
Ervin ROUSE (1)	49
Chuck HARDING (1)	38
Hank THOMPSON (1)	38
Autry INMAN (1)	24
Katherine DAVIS (1)	23
Henry ONORATI (1)	23
Harry SIMEONE (1)	23
Don GIBSON (1)	14
Leon PAYNE (1)	12

Johnny CASH ►293 (42) [34]	**16201**
Glenn DOUGLAS (1)	10
Lillie McALPIN (1)	10
Charlie RICH (1)	6.1
Gene AUTRY (1)	4.0
Johnny MARVIN (1)	4.0
Merle TRAVIS (1)	3.5
TRADITIONAL (1)	3.5
Anita CARTER (1)	3.0
Helen CARTER (1)	3.0
Andrew FENADY (1)	2.4
Richard MARKOWITZ (1)	2.4
Ray EVANS (1)	1.6
Jay LIVINGSTON (1)	1.6
POISON ►294 (11) [6]	**16142**
Bobby DALL (10)	3772
C.C. DeVILLE (10)	3772
Bret MICHAELS (10)	3772
Rikki ROCKETT (10)	3772
Kenny LOGGINS (1)	527
Jim MESSINA (1)	527
NILSSON ►295 (13) [8]	**16096**
Harry NILSSON (7)	5558
Tom EVANS (1)	3835
Pete HAM (1)	3835
Fred NEIL (2)	2721
Herman HUPFELD (1)	98
Jimmy CLIFF (1)	26
John LENNON (1)	11
Paul McCARTNEY (1)	11
U2 ►296 (13) [4]	**16023**
Adam CLAYTON (13)	4006
Dave EVANS (13)	4006
Paul HEWSON (13)	4006
Larry MULLEN (13)	4006
Jim REEVES ►297 (27) [28]	**15997**
Audrey ALLISON (1)	5101
Joe ALLISON (1)	5101
Jim REEVES (5)	1767
George CAMPBELL (1)	944
Marvin MOORE (1)	944
Cindy WALKER (3)	528
Boudleaux BRYANT (1)	298
Bill ANDERSON (2)	283
Leon PAYNE (1)	274
Ned MILLER (1)	266
Harlan HOWARD (2)	235
Ralph FREED (1)	53
Jerry LIVINGSTON (1)	53
Buddy KILLEN (1)	30
Danny DILL (1)	29
Werly FAIRBURN (1)	27
Alex ZANETIS (2)	21
Jack H. CLEMENT (1)	13
Bill WEST (1)	5.2
Dottie WEST (1)	5.2
Don CARTER (1)	3.6
Danny HARRISON (1)	3.6
George KENT (1)	3.6
Roger MILLER (1)	2.3
Johnny HATHCOCK (1)	1.6
Ray WINKLER (1)	1.6
Mickey BAKER (1)	1.5
Joseph ROBINSON (1)	1.5
Nancy SINATRA ►298 (17) [8]	**15986**
Lee HAZLEWOOD (12)	15584
John BARRY (1)	167
Leslie BRICUSSE (1)	167
Mac DAVIS (2)	59

Murray WECHT (1)	4.9
Delaney BRAMLETT (1)	2.3
Donnie LANIER (1)	1.3
Russell STEAGALL (1)	1.3
DEF LEPPARD ►299 (12) [7]	**15890**
Steve CLARK (12)	2655
Joe ELLIOTT (12)	2655
Rick SAVAGE (12)	2655
Rick ALLEN (11)	2649
Mutt LANGE (10)	2621
Phil COLLEN (7)	2155
Pete WILLIS (5)	499
Billy IDOL ►300 (14) [13]	**15870**
Billy IDOL (10)	6462
Steve STEVENS (3)	2054
David WERNER (1)	1769
Bobby BLOOM (2)	938
Ritchie CORDELL (2)	938
Bo GENTRY (2)	938
Tommy JAMES (2)	938
William BELL (1)	813
Booker T. JONES Jr. (1)	813
John DENSMORE (1)	52
Robby KRIEGER (1)	52
Ray MANZAREK (1)	52
Jim MORRISON (1)	52
MELANIE ►301 (12) [6]	**15865**
Melanie SAFKA (9)	15197
Mick JAGGER (1)	207
Keith RICHARDS (1)	207
Jim CROCE (1)	102
Gerry GOFFIN (1)	76
Carole KING (1)	76
AMES BROTHERS ►302 (39) [66]	**15770**
Roy C. BENNETT (5)	2524
Sid TEPPER (5)	2524
Marcel STELLMAN (1)	1296
TRADITIONAL (1)	1296
Fred SPIELMAN (2)	1060
Mack DAVID (1)	960
Tom GLAZER (1)	478
Sunny SKYLAR (1)	478
Marion McCLURG (1)	438
Cindy WALKER (1)	423
Ray EVANS (1)	397
Jay LIVINGSTON (1)	397
Tommie CONNOR (1)	396
Johnny REINE (1)	396
Robert MELLIN (3)	356
Otto RIEDLMAYER (1)	234
Sammy CAHN (1)	230
Bronislaw KAPER (1)	230
Sammy FAIN (2)	189
Paul Francis WEBSTER (2)	189
Cy COBEN (1)	125
Ed PENNEY (1)	122
Jack RICHARDS (1)	122
David HESS (1)	114
Bobby STEVENSON (1)	114
Kermit GOELL (1)	100
Al FRISCH (1)	77
Allan ROBERTS (1)	77
Bob MERRILL (1)	45
Joe THOMAS (1)	44
Ervin DRAKE (1)	38
Jimmy SHIRL (1)	38
Fred EBB (1)	30
Paul KLEIN (1)	30
Bert KEYES (2)	21
Luther DIXON (1)	19

Billy Dawn SMITH (1)	19
Jimmie STEWARD (1)	18
Jimmy WILLIAMS (1)	18
Stanley APPLEBAUM (1)	11
Elsie SIMMONS (1)	11
Bob HILLIARD (1)	8.5
Dave MANN (1)	8.5
Felix BERNARD (1)	7.9
Richard B. SMITH (1)	7.9
Al HOFFMAN (1)	7.7
Dick MANNING (1)	7.7
George KELLY (1)	4.1
Mayme WATTS (1)	4.1
Giovanni FERRIO (1)	3.3
Geoffrey PARSONS (1)	3.3
John TURNER (1)	3.3
Ray PASSMAN (1)	2.9
Arthur SHAFTEL (1)	2.9
Jimmy KENNEDY (1)	2.6
Guy WOOD (1)	2.6
Ollie JONES (1)	2.5
Horst Heinz HENNING (1)	2.0
Kay TWOMEY (1)	2.0
Ben WEISMAN (1)	2.0
Fred WISE (1)	2.0
Stan LEBOWSKY (1)	1.3
Johnny LEHMANN (1)	1.3
Hans BRADTKE (1)	0.0
Fritz SCHULZ-REICHEL (1)	0.0
Oliver HOOD (1)	0.0
EURYTHMICS ►303 (15) [2]	**15769**
Annie LENNOX (15)	7885
David A. STEWART (15)	7885
FERRANTE & TEICHER ►304 (13) [16]	**15625**
Ernest GOLD (1)	6965
Charles WILLIAMS (1)	3475
John BARRY (1)	1987
Leonard BERNSTEIN (1)	1033
Stephen SONDHEIM (1)	1033
Hugo FRIEDHOFER (1)	744
Malcolm ARNOLD (1)	100
Charles CHAPLIN (1)	75
Maurice JARRE (1)	70
Bob DYLAN (1)	60
Georges AURIC (1)	34
Alex NORTH (1)	29
Arthur FERRANTE (1)	7.2
Pyotr Ilyich TCHAIKOVSKY (1)	7.2
Louis TEICHER (1)	7.2
Franz WAXMAN (1)	0.0
The HAPPENINGS ►305 (12) [27]	**15618**
George GERSHWIN (1)	2976
Ira GERSHWIN (1)	2976
Sherman EDWARDS (1)	2730
Sid WAYNE (1)	2730
Gerry GOFFIN (1)	693
Carole KING (1)	693
Walter DONALDSON (1)	412
Sam LEWIS (1)	412
Joe YOUNG (1)	412
Sandy LINZER (1)	199
Denny RANDELL (1)	199
Howard GREENFIELD (1)	155
Neil SEDAKA (1)	155
Galt MacDERMOT (2)	139
James RADO (2)	139
Gerome RAGNI (2)	139
George GOLDNER (1)	78
Morris LEVY (1)	78

Frankie LYMON (1)	78
Jimmy MERCHANT (1)	78
Herman SANTIAGO (1)	78
Bernie BAUM (1)	15
Stephan WEISS (1)	15
David LIBERT (1)	12
Ralph MIRANDA (1)	12
Carl SIGMAN (1)	7.3
Gerhard WINKLER (1)	7.3
The ORLONS ►306 (10) [8]	**15601**
Kal MANN (7)	6996
Dave APPELL (6)	6959
Gary ANDERSON (1)	661
Frank GUIDA (1)	661
Andy GIBSON (1)	82
Bill MASSEY (1)	82
Bob CREWE (1)	80
Larry SANTOS (1)	80
Bob SEGER & The SILVER BULLET BAND ►307 (15) [4]	**15539**
Bob SEGER (12)	10558
Rodney CROWELL (1)	4148
George Henry JACKSON (2)	417
Thomas Earl JONES III (2)	417
Bobby BROWN ►308 (7) [9]	**15535**
Kenneth EDMONDS (5)	4783
Antonio REID (3)	3059
Daryl SIMMONS (3)	2356
Bobby BROWN (1)	2071
Gene GRIFFIN (1)	2071
Darnell BRISTOL (1)	994
Kirk CRUMPLER (1)	67
Lee PETERS (1)	67
Larry WHITE (1)	67
Sammy DAVIS Jr. ►309 (25) [38]	**15516**
Leslie BRICUSSE (3)	3834
Anthony NEWLEY (3)	3834
Walter MARKS (1)	2244
Jerry SAMUELS (1)	1200
Walter DONALDSON (1)	683
Gus KAHN (1)	683
Richard ADLER (1)	340
Jerry ROSS (1)	340
Johnny MERCER (2)	307
Harold ARLEN (1)	307
Lionel BART (1)	306
H.B. BARNUM (1)	184
Ivan REEVE (1)	184
Bob MUSEL (1)	135
Clive RICHARDSON (1)	135
Jack TAYLOR (1)	135
Arthur HAMMERSTEIN (1)	121
Dudley WILKINSON (1)	121
Gordon JENKINS (1)	86
Leo ROBIN (1)	63
Jule STYNE (1)	63
Jerry BOCK (2)	27
Lawrence HOLOFCENER (2)	27
George David WEISS (2)	27
Cole PORTER (2)	23
Lew BROWN (1)	19
Buddy DeSYLVA (1)	19
Ray HENDERSON (1)	19
Frank LOESSER (1)	9.9
Frank CADY (1)	7.5
David SEVILLE (1)	7.5
Billy MARTIN (1)	7.2
Larry (2) MARTIN (1)	7.2

Sammy DAVIS Jr. ▶309 (25) [38] *Cont'd*	**15516**
Bert KAEMPFERT (1)	2.5
Herbert REHBEIN (1)	2.5
Carl SIGMAN (1)	2.5
Bob CREWE (1)	2.4
Frank SLAY (1)	2.4
Bill WITHERS ▶310 (11) [2]	**15501**
Bill WITHERS (11)	15166
Skip SCARBOROUGH (1)	335
Gloria ESTEFAN And MIAMI SOUND MACHINE ▶311 (9) [5]	**15430**
Gloria ESTEFAN (5)	9209
Enrique GARCIA (3)	3505
Larry DERMER (3)	906
Joe GALDO (3)	906
Rafael VIGIL (3)	906
1910 FRUITGUM CO. ▶312 (9) [11]	**15346**
Elliot CHIPRUT (2)	6092
Sal TRIMACHI (2)	2022
Bobbi TRIMACHI (1)	2020
Bobby BLOOM (2)	1465
Bo GENTRY (2)	1465
Ritchie CORDELL (4)	1320
Jerry KASENETZ (3)	307
Jeff KATZ (3)	307
Billy CARL (1)	160
Reid WHITELAW (1)	160
J.J. WOODS (1)	28
MILLI VANILLI ▶313 (5) [14]	**15343**
Diane WARREN (1)	3458
Frank FARIAN (3)	2314
Brad HOWELL (2)	1222
Peter BISCHOF-FALLENSTEIN (1)	1092
Dietmar KAWOHL (1)	1092
Bernd BERWANGER (1)	797
Roger DALTON (1)	797
Kayode ADEYEMO (1)	744
Rodney HOLLAMAN (1)	744
Kevin LYLES (1)	744
William PETTAWAY (1)	744
Sean SPENCER (1)	744
David CLAYTON-THOMAS (1)	425
P.G. WYLDER (1)	425
The CHI-LITES ▶314 (23) [11]	**15304**
Eugene RECORD (22)	11424
Barbara ACKLIN (5)	2918
Sandra DRAYTON (1)	258
Carl DAVIS (1)	196
Quinton JOSEPH (2)	153
Stan McKENNEY (2)	123
Edward HAYCRAFT (1)	95
Sandy WILBURN (1)	93
Marshall ARRINGTON (1)	45
Tony BOYD (1)	0.0
Archie POWELL (1)	0.0
OHIO PLAYERS ▶315 (15) [10]	**15270**
Leroy BONNER (15)	2174
Marshall JONES (15)	2174
Ralph MIDDLEBROOKS (15)	2174
Andrew NOLAND (15)	2174
Marvin PIERCE (15)	2174
James Rodger WILLIAMS (10)	1887
William BECK (8)	1654

Walter MORRISON (5)	287
Bruce NAPIER (5)	287
Greg WEBSTER (4)	285
Dee Dee SHARP ▶316 (10) [13]	**15170**
Kal MANN (7)	4366
Dave APPELL (6)	3113
Robert BATEMAN (1)	1253
Georgia DOBBINS (1)	1253
William GARRETT (1)	1253
Freddie GORMAN (1)	1253
Brian HOLLAND (1)	1253
Bernie LOWE (1)	1253
James A. BISHOP (1)	86
Kenneth GAMBLE (1)	86
Barrett STRONG (1)	2.4
Tracy Lee ALEXANDER (1)	0.9
William E. JACKSON III (1)	0.9
Stevie NICKS ▶317 (12) [11]	**15166**
Stevie NICKS (9)	6149
Chas SANDFORD (1)	2585
Mike CAMPBELL (1)	1655
Tom PETTY (1)	1655
PRINCE (1)	1119
Sandy STEWART (2)	738
Rick NOWELS (2)	695
Eric PRESSLY (1)	287
Jon BON JOVI (1)	108
Billy FALCON (1)	108
Keith OLSEN (1)	68
SANTANA ▶318 (19) [30]	**15163**
Peter GREEN (1)	4259
Clarence "Sonny" HENRY (1)	2005
Russ BALLARD (2)	1361
Ian THOMAS (1)	1271
Tito PUENTE (1)	1218
Rod ARGENT (1)	677
Carlos SANTANA (4)	652
Milton S. BROWN Jr. (1)	505
Tyrone MOSS (1)	505
Michael OLATUNJI (1)	385
Michael CARABELLO (1)	240
Coke ESCOVEDO (1)	240
Gregg ROLIE (1)	240
Buddy BUIE (1)	225
J.R. COBB (1)	225
J.J. CALE (1)	171
Alex LIGERTWOOD (3)	147
Chris SOLBERG (3)	147
Alan PASQUA (2)	143
Val GARAY (1)	116
Steve GOLDSTEIN (1)	116
Anthony La PEAU (1)	116
Dennis LAMBERT (1)	58
Brian POTTER (1)	58
Jerry ALLISON (1)	17
Buddy HOLLY (1)	17
Joe MAULDIN (1)	17
Norman PETTY (1)	17
David BROWN (1)	8.7
Ray GARDNER (1)	8.7
Jody WATLEY ▶319 (10) [9]	**15099**
Jody WATLEY (8)	5753
André CYMONE (7)	5018
Gardner COLE (2)	1095
James Newton HOWARD (1)	989
David Paul BRYANT (1)	735
Franne GOLDE (1)	735
Eric BARRIER (1)	334
William GRIFFIN (1)	334

Patrick Raymond LEONARD (1)	106
The KINGSMEN ▶320 (11) [15]	**15040**
Richard BERRY (2)	9240
Lynn EASTON (3)	1761
Don HARRIS (1)	979
Dewey TERRY (1)	979
Janie BRADFORD (1)	587
Berry GORDY (1)	587
Bill MEDLEY (1)	362
Donald WOODS (1)	219
Doris WOODS (1)	219
Bert BERNS (1)	31
Stanley KAHAN (1)	31
Phil MEDLEY (1)	31
John D. MANGIAGLI (1)	6.6
Barry CURTIS (1)	3.1
Nicholas RICHARDSON (1)	3.1
Lou CHRISTIE ▶321 (16) [9]	**14951**
Lou CHRISTIE (10)	6072
Twyla HERBERT (10)	6072
Tony ROMEO (2)	2302
Rick RODELL (1)	342
Stan VINCENT (1)	56
W. Franke HARLING (1)	34
Leo ROBIN (1)	34
Richard WHITING (1)	34
Chris WHITE (1)	3.2
WILSON PHILLIPS ▶322 (5) [6]	**14941**
Chynna PHILLIPS (4)	3759
Carnie WILSON (4)	3759
Glen BALLARD (3)	2525
Wendy WILSON (3)	2281
Steve KIPNER (1)	1308
Clif MAGNESS (1)	1308
Joe SIMON ▶323 (35) [37]	**14874**
Joe SIMON (11)	3612
Raeford GERALD (6)	2060
Kenneth GAMBLE (3)	1955
Leon HUFF (3)	1955
Harlan HOWARD (3)	1916
Ira ALLEN (1)	443
Buddy MIZE (1)	443
Darryl CARTER (1)	338
Gene McDANIELS (1)	306
Dock PRICE (1)	303
Alfred James ELLIS (1)	204
Kris KRISTOFFERSON (1)	193
Leonard ALLEN (1)	134
Jesse Edwin DAVIS III (1)	129
Taj MAHAL (1)	129
Bob MONTGOMERY (1)	115
Al REED (1)	107
Ben PETERS (1)	65
Joe SOUTH (1)	65
Dan PENN (1)	57
Wayne Carson THOMPSON (1)	57
Phil HURTT (1)	47
Bunny SIGLER (1)	47
Wini SCOTT (1)	40
Billy KENNEDY (1)	21
Brook BENTON (1)	21
Belford HENDRICKS (1)	21
Clyde OTIS (1)	21
Allen ORANGE (1)	18
Irral BERGER (1)	10
Clara THOMPSON (1)	10
Phillip MITCHELL (1)	6.8
Ernie SHELBY (1)	6.8
Jackey BEAVERS (1)	6.4

Jack HILL (1)	6.4
Teddy RANDAZZO (1)	2.2
Norman MAPP (1)	1.4
The SHANGRI-LAS ▶324 (11) [15]	**14837**
Shadow MORTON (5)	9173
Jeff BARRY (3)	2453
Ellie GREENWICH (3)	2453
Sid BARNES (1)	216
J.J. JACKSON (1)	216
Ted DARYLL (1)	101
Greg RICHARDS (1)	101
Artie BUTLER (1)	56
Jerry LEIBER (1)	56
Richard BARRETT (1)	2.9
George GOLDNER (1)	2.9
Arlene SMITH (1)	2.9
Robert BATEMAN (1)	0.6
Ken HOLLON (1)	0.6
Ronald MOSELEY (1)	0.6
HUMAN LEAGUE ▶325 (8) [11]	**14799**
John William CALLIS (5)	3806
Philip OAKEY (5)	3621
Philip WRIGHT (1)	2429
James Samuel HARRIS (2)	2169
Terry LEWIS (2)	2169
Eugene REYNOLDS (1)	199
Ian BURDEN (2)	178
Herman R. DAVIS (1)	57
Dave EILAND (1)	57
Langston RICHEY (1)	57
Danny WILLIAMS (1)	57
LULU ▶326 (11) [18]	**14769**
Don BLACK (2)	5562
Mark LONDON (2)	5562
Jim DORIS (1)	1163
Neil HARRISON (1)	1068
Tony HAZZARD (1)	376
Richard H. ROSS (1)	365
Jerry FULLER (1)	169
John HOBBS (1)	169
Bonnie DOBSON (1)	158
Tim ROSE (1)	158
George SOULE (1)	5.0
Terry WOODFORD (1)	5.0
O'Kelly ISLEY (1)	2.0
Ronald ISLEY (1)	2.0
Rudolph ISLEY (1)	2.0
Alan BLAIKLEY (1)	1.1
Ken HOWARD (1)	1.1
Geoff STEPHENS (1)	1.1
Dan FOGELBERG ▶327 (14) [2]	**14751**
Dan FOGELBERG (13)	14732
Jay BOLOTIN (1)	19
The LETTERMEN ▶328 (28) [57]	**14690**
Teddy RANDAZZO (2)	1388
Bobby WEINSTEIN (2)	1388
Barry MANN (1)	1027
Edward HEYMAN (1)	1023
Victor YOUNG (1)	1023
Dorothy FIELDS (1)	981
Jerome KERN (1)	981
Bobby HART (1)	727
Bob CREWE (1)	662
Bob GAUDIO (1)	662
John LENNON (1)	589
Paul ANKA (1)	571
Mack DISCANT (1)	542
Max STEINER (1)	542

The LETTERMEN ▶328 (28) [57] *Cont'd*	**14690**
Eddie CARROLL (1)	206
Barry De VORZON (1)	206
Danny JANSSEN (1)	159
Myrna JANSSEN (1)	159
Walt KESKE (1)	159
Mac DAVIS (1)	119
Billy STRANGE (1)	119
Ted DARYLL (1)	111
Greg RICHARDS (1)	111
Matt MALNECK (1)	85
Robert MAXWELL (1)	85
Carl SIGMAN (1)	85
James Anthony DEAN (1)	82
Eddie HOLLAND (1)	82
Buddy BUIE (1)	79
J.R. COBB (1)	79
Emory GORDY (1)	79
Al DUBIN (1)	61
Harry WARREN (1)	61
Luigi CREATORE (1)	61
Al HOFFMAN (1)	61
Dick MANNING (1)	61
Hugo PERETTI (1)	61
Dave BURGESS (1)	28
Mamie THOMAS (1)	28
Johnny COWELL (1)	24
Bob TUBERT (1)	24
Bert BERNS (1)	21
Wes FARRELL (1)	21
Dorcas COCHRAN (1)	13
Lionel NEWMAN (1)	13
Jerry CAPEHART (1)	9.9
Gerry GOFFIN (1)	6.9
Carole KING (1)	6.9
Jack KELLER (1)	3.6
Bob RUSSELL (1)	3.6
Phyllis KASHA (1)	1.3
Bill McGUFFIE (1)	1.3
Stan MILLS (1)	1.3
Lorenz HART (1)	0.9
Richard RODGERS (1)	0.9
Johnny COLONNA (1)	0.9
Jerry WALLACE (1)	0.9
Eddie MONEY ▶329 (21) [41]	**14678**
Eddie MONEY (11)	3219
Jesse HARMS (1)	1722
Andy HILL (2)	1017
Jimmy LYON (1)	907
Peter SINFIELD (1)	561
Randy ODA (1)	525
Antonina ARMATO (1)	456
Jeff BARRY (1)	420
Ellie GREENWICH (1)	420
Mike LEESON (1)	420
Phil SPECTOR (1)	420
Peter VALE (1)	420
Monty BYROM (1)	358
Danny CHAUNCEY (1)	358
Ira WALKER (1)	358
Lloyd CHIATE (2)	262
David Paul BRYANT (1)	251
Steven DUBIN (1)	251
Adrian GURVITZ (1)	251
John CESARIO (1)	245
Michele COLLYER (1)	245
Steve MULLEN (1)	245
Lee GARRETT (1)	179
Robert Percy TAYLOR (1)	179
Smokey ROBINSON (1)	148
Duane HITCHINGS (1)	127
Ralph CARTER (2)	89
Craig JOINER (1)	88
Mutt LANGE (1)	88
Paul COLLINS (1)	83
Paul GORDON (1)	71
Dennis MATKOSKY (1)	71
Elizabeth MYERS (1)	64
Radcliffe BRYAN (1)	37
Dan ALEXANDER (1)	35
Chris SOLBERG (1)	35
Ray BURTON (1)	25
Mitchell FROOM (1)	25
Kevin BURNS (1)	2.1
Greg LOWRY (1)	2.1
Glenn THOMPSON (1)	2.1
Eric CARMEN ▶330 (13) [10]	**14675**
Eric CARMEN (10)	7160
Sergei RACHMANINOFF (2)	3296
Dean PITCHFORD (2)	1437
John DeNICOLA (1)	1319
Franke PREVITE (1)	1319
Lamont DOZIER (1)	45
Brian HOLLAND (1)	45
Eddie HOLLAND (1)	45
Phil GALDSTON (1)	4.9
Jon LIND (1)	4.9
Kim CARNES ▶331 (15) [14]	**14649**
Donna WEISS (2)	4479
Jackie DeSHANNON (1)	4461
Smokey ROBINSON (1)	1898
Kim CARNES (10)	1736
Dave ELLINGSON (6)	667
Brian FAIRWEATHER (4)	321
Martin PAGE (4)	321
Duane HITCHINGS (2)	199
Bill CUOMO (1)	141
Val GARAY (1)	141
Spooner OLDHAM (1)	124
Dan PENN (1)	124
Collin ELLINGSON (1)	17
Kathy KURASCH (1)	17
Gordon LIGHTFOOT ▶332 (11) [1]	**14440**
Gordon LIGHTFOOT (11)	14440
Ben E. KING ▶333 (25) [35]	**14393**
Jerry LEIBER (4)	2933
Ben E. KING (3)	2122
Mike STOLLER (3)	1927
Phil SPECTOR (4)	1298
Patrick GRANT (2)	989
Gwen GUTHRIE (2)	989
Ahmet ERTEGUN (1)	794
Betty NELSON (1)	794
Ricardo Lopez MENDEZ (1)	344
Gabriel RUIZ (1)	344
Sunny SKYLAR (1)	344
Doc POMUS (4)	299
Carlo DONIDA (1)	202
Giulio RAPETTI (1)	202
Bert BERNS (2)	180
Jerry WEXLER (2)	142
Betty WOODS (1)	67
Gerry GOFFIN (1)	51
Carole KING (1)	51
Mike LEANDER (1)	50
John MARASCALCO (1)	40
George MOTOLA (1)	40
Murray COHEN (1)	20
Bernard SOLOMON (1)	20
Ed TOWNSEND (1)	20
Alan Jay LERNER (1)	19
Frederick LOEWE (1)	19
Rudy CLARK (1)	18
Artie RESNICK (1)	11
Kenny YOUNG (1)	11
Johnny TAYLOR (1)	11
Ellen WOODS (1)	11
Ned DOHENY (1)	11
Mort SHUMAN (1)	8.3
Fred PARRIS (1)	7.6
Floyd CRAMER ▶334 (14) [13]	**14359**
Floyd CRAMER (6)	11573
Bob WILLS (1)	1569
Harry WARREN (1)	556
Freddy FRIDAY (1)	142
Marilyn SCHACK (1)	142
Allen TOUSSAINT (1)	142
Alvin TYLER (1)	142
Cliff FRIEND (1)	24
Irving MILLS (1)	24
TRADITIONAL (1)	17
Morgan LEWIS (1)	16
Grady MARTIN (1)	6.2
Johnny COWELL (1)	3.2
The CHIFFONS ▶335 (10) [19]	**14335**
Ronnie MACK (1)	8687
Gerry GOFFIN (2)	1101
Carole KING (1)	1065
Barbara BAER (3)	483
Eliot GREENBERG (3)	483
Douglas MORRIS (3)	483
Robert SCHWARTZ (3)	483
Stephen FRIEDLAND (1)	332
Hank MEDRESS (2)	293
Jeff BARRY (1)	216
Ellie GREENWICH (1)	216
Sid BARNES (1)	78
George KERR (1)	78
Mitch MARGO (1)	78
Phil MARGO (1)	78
Jay SIEGEL (1)	78
Russ TITELMAN (1)	36
Luther DIXON (1)	34
Shirley OWENS (1)	34
Eddie KENDRICKS ▶336 (15) [15]	**14140**
Leonard CASTON (8)	4186
Frank Edward WILSON (6)	4009
Anita POREE (5)	3691
Linda ALLEN (1)	588
Harry BOOKER (1)	588
Kathy WAKEFIELD (3)	373
Brian HOLLAND (1)	126
Eddie HOLLAND (1)	126
Talmadge CONWAY (1)	121
Allan FELDER (1)	121
Bruce GRAY (1)	121
Pam SAWYER (1)	65
Errison JOHNSON (1)	20
Hal DAVIS (1)	3.2
Herman GRIFFITH (1)	3.2
CHEAP TRICK ▶337 (16) [12]	**14123**
Rick NIELSEN (11)	5901
Alan Nicholas GRAHAM (1)	1943
Bobby MITCHELL (1)	1943
Otis BLACKWELL (1)	1037
Elvis PRESLEY (1)	1037
Robin ZANDER (4)	689
Diane WARREN (2)	534
Thomas John PETERSON (2)	417
Dave BARTHOLOMEW (1)	205
Fats DOMINO (1)	205
Jon BRANT (1)	105
Mark RADICE (1)	105
STEELY DAN ▶338 (16) [3]	**14119**
Walter BECKER (16)	7041
Donald FAGEN (16)	7041
Paul GRIFFIN (1)	36
MANFRED MANN ▶339 (9) [12]	**14109**
Jeff BARRY (1)	4154
Ellie GREENWICH (1)	4154
Bob DYLAN (3)	2910
Mark BARKAN (1)	644
Frances AYCOCK (1)	585
Robert MOSELY (1)	585
Robert Napoleon TAYLOR (1)	585
John S. SIMON (1)	143
Frank AUGUSTUS (1)	113
Stanley KAHAN (1)	113
Dolores PHILLIPS (1)	113
Tony HAZZARD (1)	8.5
Georgia GIBBS ▶340 (23) [44]	**14104**
Winfield SCOTT (1)	4176
Hank BALLARD (1)	1696
Etta JAMES (1)	1696
Johnny OTIS (1)	1696
Jon HENDRICKS (1)	1122
Edward WHITE (1)	345
Mack WOLFSON (1)	345
Johnny PARKER (1)	334
Carl MADURI (1)	198
James TESTA (1)	198
Fred EBB (1)	189
Charles FRIEDMAN (1)	189
Arnold SHAW (1)	189
Sherman EDWARDS (1)	178
Ben RALEIGH (1)	178
Henry GLOVER (1)	146
Rudy TOOMBS (1)	146
Pietro GARINEI (1)	110
Alessandro GIOVANNINI (1)	110
Renato RASCEL (1)	110
Carl SIGMAN (1)	110
Ernest TUBB (1)	104
Jim BURRIS (1)	83
Chris SMITH (1)	83
Bernie LOWE (1)	43
Kal MANN (1)	43
Martin DIAMOND (1)	40
Arthur KORB (1)	40
Irving FIELDS (1)	39
Kay TWOMEY (1)	39
Vince CORSO (1)	27
Clyde OTIS (1)	27
Joe SHERMAN (1)	23
George David WEISS (1)	23
Jerry LEIBER (2)	10
Mike STOLLER (2)	10
Rose Marie McCOY (1)	7.5
Charles SINGLETON (1)	7.5
Don GEORGE (1)	0.0
Joe MARSALA (1)	0.0
Otilio PORTAL (1)	0.0
George THORN (1)	0.0
Otis BLACKWELL (1)	0.0
Jack HAMMER (1)	0.0

LOBO ▶341 (16) [11]	14070
Kent LaVOIE (12)	12684
Steve JOBE (1)	283
Sam LORBER (1)	283
Jeff SILBAR (1)	283
Alex HARVEY (1)	183
Eddie REEVES (1)	183
Michael GATELY (1)	49
Robert JOHN (1)	49
Larry HENLEY (1)	25
Steve PIPPIN (1)	25
Johnny SLATE (1)	25

COLOR ME BADD ▶342 (3) [10]	14042
Bryan ABRAMS (3)	2368
Mark CALDERON (3)	2368
Kevin THORNTON (3)	2368
Sam WATTERS (3)	2368
Isaac HAYES (1)	898
Howard THOMPSON (1)	898
Hamza LEE (1)	819
Willie CLARKE (1)	651
Elliot STRAITE (1)	651
Betty WRIGHT (1)	651

Charlie RICH ▶343 (16) [16]	13986
Billy SHERRILL (6)	3391
Norro WILSON (4)	3015
Charlie RICH (3)	2476
Rory BOURKE (1)	1892
Kenny O'DELL (1)	1454
Dallas FRAZIER (1)	1150
Bennie BENJAMIN (1)	149
George David WEISS (1)	149
Harlan HOWARD (1)	104
Curly PUTMAN (1)	102
Woodrow Buddy JOHNSON (1)	83
Ben PETERS (1)	5.0
Katharine Lee BATES (1)	4.4
Kermit GOELL (1)	4.4
Samuel A. WARD (1)	4.4
Jerry HAYES (1)	3.9

BOOKER T. & The M.G.'s ▶344 (17) [16]	13826
Steve CROPPER (11)	2476
Al JACKSON (11)	2476
Booker T. JONES Jr. (11)	2476
Dominic FRONTIERE (1)	1959
Lewis STEINBERG (5)	1267
Donald "Duck" DUNN (6)	1257
Paul SIMON (1)	554
Eddie BRIGATI (1)	479
Felix CAVALIERE (1)	479
Charles AXTON (1)	87
Isaac HAYES (1)	87
Wayne JACKSON (1)	87
George HARRISON (1)	66
Homer BANKS (1)	25
Bettye CRUTCHER (1)	25
Raymond Earl JACKSON (1)	25

Cat STEVENS ▶345 (16) [7]	13808
Cat STEVENS (14)	10056
Sam COOKE (1)	1628
Eleanor FARJEON (1)	996
TRADITIONAL (1)	996
Bruce LYNCH (1)	61
Jean ROUSSEL (1)	61
Alun DAVIES (1)	10

Joan JETT & The BLACKHEARTS ▶346 (9) [11]	13797
Jake HOOKER (1)	3935
Alan MERRILL (1)	3935
Joan JETT (4)	1449
Desmond CHILD (2)	1206
Tommy JAMES (1)	836
Peter LUCIA (1)	836
Bruce SPRINGSTEEN (1)	373
Gary GLITTER (1)	346
Mike LEANDER (1)	346
Sylvester STEWART (1)	291
Kenny LAGUNA (2)	243

Johnny NASH ▶347 (24) [39]	13702
Johnny NASH (4)	8927
Bob MARLEY (1)	1617
Sam COOKE (2)	806
Robert ALLEN (1)	660
Herman HUPFELD (1)	551
Margaret NASH (2)	232
William STEVENSON (1)	147
Ray EVANS (1)	77
Jay LIVINGSTON (1)	77
Stan LEBOWSKY (1)	64
Johnny LEHMANN (1)	64
Teddy POWELL (1)	60
Tony STARR (1)	60
Sammy CAHN (1)	53
Jule STYNE (1)	53
Diane BRODSKY (1)	45
Dann ROGERS (1)	45
Jack KELLER (1)	44
Noel SHERMAN (1)	44
Robert MOSELY (1)	11
Mayme WATTS (1)	11
Ziggy ELMAN (1)	6.1
Johnny MERCER (1)	6.1
Terry PHILIPS (1)	5.8
Phil SPECTOR (1)	5.8
Lou ADLER (1)	5.6
Herb ALPERT (1)	5.6
Gloria FOWLES (1)	3.9
Sam GARY (1)	3.9
Bill JOHNSON (1)	3.9
George GERSHWIN (1)	1.9
Ira GERSHWIN (1)	1.9
Jack DELGADO (1)	1.2
Ira KOSLOFF (1)	1.2
Vance PACKARD (1)	1.2
Tom PRAY (1)	1.2
Clint BALLARD Jr. (1)	0.0
Oscar HAMMERSTEIN (1)	0.0
Jerome KERN (1)	0.0

LITTLE ANTHONY And The IMPERIALS ▶348 (21) [27]	13699
Teddy RANDAZZO (8)	4148
Bobby WEINSTEIN (3)	2970
Sylvester BRADFORD (2)	1676
Al LEWIS (2)	1676
Robert T. SMITH (1)	1071
Bobby HART (1)	470
Ivory Joe HUNTER (1)	205
Clyde OTIS (1)	205
Victoria PIKE (4)	165
Jimmy HENDERSON (1)	151
Sid ROBIN (1)	151
Bertha SCOTT (1)	151
Jimmie CRANE (1)	111
Al JACOBS (1)	111
Gary SHELTON (1)	104
Marshall PAUL (1)	65
Jean H. DAVIS (1)	60
Thom BELL (1)	53
Linda CREED (1)	53
Richard BARRETT (1)	42
Michael MERLO (1)	20
Patrick WELCH (1)	20
Ritchie ADAMS (2)	10
Larry KUSIK (1)	9.1
Jerry AKINES (1)	1.3
Johnnie BELLMON (1)	1.3
Kenny SEYMOUR (1)	0.5

Buddy HOLLY/ The CRICKETS ▶349 (16) [19]	13666
Norman PETTY (11)	4203
Buddy HOLLY (7)	3580
Jerry ALLISON (3)	3041
Paul ANKA (1)	1028
Bill TILGHMAN (2)	579
Sonny WEST (2)	579
Bobby DARIN (1)	285
Woody HARRIS (1)	285
Bob MONTGOMERY (1)	35
Sonny LeGLAIRE (1)	8.3
Horace LINSLEY (1)	8.3
Boudleaux BRYANT (1)	6.5
Felice BRYANT (1)	6.5
Joe MAULDIN (1)	4.3
Niki SULLIVAN (1)	4.3
Mickey BAKER (1)	3.5
Ellas McDANIEL (1)	3.5
Sylvia ROBINSON (1)	3.5
Sue PARRISH (1)	3.1

Bill BLACK'S Combo ▶350 (21) [18]	13652
Bill BLACK (7)	2770
Charles G. MATTHEWS (2)	1538
Gladys REINHARDT (2)	1538
Otis BLACKWELL (1)	1168
Elvis PRESLEY (1)	1168
Leroy ANDERSON (1)	1058
Eddy RAY (1)	971
Burke BIVENS (1)	872
Wayne KING (1)	872
Carl McVOY (2)	656
Jack BROOKS (1)	351
Hoagy CARMICHAEL (1)	351
Willie MITCHELL (1)	161
Deadric MALONE (1)	51
Joe SCOTT (1)	51
Chuck BERRY (1)	42
Joe REISMAN (1)	26
Chuck RIO (1)	9.9

Bert KAEMPFERT And His Orchestra ▶351 (11) [14]	13571
Klaus-Günter NEUMANN (1)	7899
Roy C. BENNETT (1)	1236
Sid TEPPER (1)	1236
Bert KAEMPFERT (3)	1159
Julian ROBLEDO (1)	580
Walter GROSS (1)	451
Boots BROWN (1)	188
Guy WARREN (1)	174
Milt GABLER (1)	165
Dave BENNETT (1)	120
Chauncey GRAY (1)	120
Fred HAMM (1)	120
Bert LOWN (1)	120
Jimmy McHUGH (1)	3.8

Don HENLEY ▶352 (12) [9]	13547
Don HENLEY (11)	5442
Danny KORTCHMAR (8)	4500
Mike CAMPBELL (2)	1335
Bruce HORNSBY (1)	854
Benmont TENCH (2)	400
Stan LYNCH (2)	368
J.D. SOUTHER (1)	273
John COREY (1)	258
Jai WINDING (1)	117

Robert JOHN ▶353 (11) [17]	13538
Robert JOHN (4)	6788
Luigi CREATORE (1)	1012
Solomon LINDA (1)	1012
Hugo PERETTI (1)	1012
Albert STANTON (1)	1012
George David WEISS (1)	1012
Mike PICCIRILLO (2)	481
Leon CARR (1)	261
Earl SHUMAN (1)	261
Michael GATELY (2)	255
Lou STALLMAN (1)	184
Bob GAUDIO (1)	77
Doc POMUS (2)	59
Mort SHUMAN (2)	59
Larry PARKS (1)	25
Jay TURNBOW (1)	25
Tom PEDRICK (1)	2.9

Johnny PRESTON ▶354 (6) [10]	13501
J.P. RICHARDSON (1)	8748
Leonard LEE (1)	1673
Jackie FAUTHEREE (1)	1366
Wayne GRAY (1)	1366
Johnny PRESTON (1)	197
Little Willie JOHN (1)	38
James McDOUGAL (1)	38
Titus TURNER (1)	38
Jim BREEDLOVE (1)	20
Lynn BREEDLOVE (1)	20

Clarence CARTER ▶355 (19) [28]	13488
Ronald DUNBAR (1)	2554
General JOHNSON (1)	2554
George Henry JACKSON (8)	1893
Clarence CARTER (7)	1445
Marcus DANIEL (3)	807
Wilbur TERRELL (2)	802
William ARMSTRONG (1)	768
Rick HALL (3)	558
John KEYES (1)	519
Red LANE (1)	314
Raymond MOORE (3)	234
Mickey BUCKINS (2)	228
Rose MARKS (1)	174
Billy WARD (1)	174
Allyn LEE (1)	145
Clemmi McCANTS (1)	145
Allen TOUSSAINT (1)	106
Ralph BAILEY (1)	15
Rudy CLARK (1)	15
Ken WILLIAMS (1)	15
Joe WILSON (1)	4.9
Herman JONES (1)	3.1
Robert OWENS (1)	3.1
Larry PIERCE (1)	3.1
Larry CHAMBERS (1)	2.2
Argentry MITCHELL (1)	2.2
Earl CAGE (1)	2.1
Marcell STRONG (1)	2.1

Laura BRANIGAN ▶356 (13) [24]	**13471**
Giancarlo BIGAZZI (3)	2674
Umberto TOZZI (2)	1746
Trevor VEITCH (1)	1647
Diane WARREN (2)	1003
Steve PICCOLO (1)	928
Raffaele RIEFOLI (1)	928
Martine CLÉMENCEAU (1)	904
Michael BOLTON (2)	705
Bruce ROBERTS (1)	698
Doug JAMES (1)	683
Charles E. COCHRAN (1)	190
David PALMER (1)	190
Mary APPLEGATE (1)	163
Candy DeROUGE (1)	163
Gunther MENDE (1)	163
Jennifer RUSH (1)	163
Steve COE (1)	127
Bobby MITCHELL (1)	127
Andy GOLDMARK (1)	83
Steve KIPNER (1)	83
Chris MONTAN (1)	33
Beth ANDERSEN (1)	24
Bill BODINE (1)	24
Mark MANGOLD (1)	22
The VENTURES ▶357 (16) [17]	**13368**
Johnny SMITH (2)	7565
Mort STEVENS (1)	2519
Alberto DOMINGUEZ (1)	1405
Richard RODGERS (2)	549
Max STEINER (1)	218
Henry GLOVER (1)	169
Lucky MILLINDER (1)	169
Jim MUNDY (1)	169
Steve BARRI (1)	106
P.F. SLOAN (1)	106
Bernice PETKERE (1)	105
Hank LEVINE (1)	89
Danny HAMILTON (1)	53
Bob HARRIS (1)	44
Nelson RIDDLE (1)	44
Victor YOUNG (1)	33
Don WILSON (2)	24
Joey DEE & The STARLITERS ▶358 (7) [9]	**13323**
Joey DEE (4)	4724
Henry GLOVER (4)	4724
Johnny NASH (1)	1073
O'Kelly ISLEY (1)	704
Ronald ISLEY (1)	704
Rudolph ISLEY (1)	704
James BROWN (1)	476
Morris LEVY (3)	202
Sammy TAYLOR (1)	13
Percy FAITH And His Orchestra ▶359 (17) [21]	**13320**
Max STEINER (2)	12297
Percy FAITH (1)	424
Lee BERKE (1)	116
René DENONCIN (1)	116
Louis FERRARI (1)	116
Carl SIGMAN (2)	82
Charles DANVERS (1)	76
Frederick LOEWE (1)	26
Mario NASCIMBENE (1)	22
Rafael MUNOZ Sr. (1)	12
Alfredo Do NASCIMENTO (1)	10
Henri CONTET (1)	6.1
Paul DURAND (1)	6.1
Charles ALBERTINE (1)	5.1
Harry WARREN (2)	2.5
Herm SAUNDERS (1)	2.5
Sam COSLOW (1)	0.0
Lotar OLIAS (1)	0.0
Jack BROOKS (1)	0.0
Kenyon HOPKINS (1)	0.0
Maurice JARRE (1)	0.0
The TOKENS ▶360 (17) [29]	**13280**
Luigi CREATORE (3)	1896
Hugo PERETTI (3)	1896
George David WEISS (3)	1896
Solomon LINDA (1)	1806
Albert STANTON (1)	1806
Mitch MARGO (4)	672
Phil MARGO (4)	672
Hank MEDRESS (4)	672
Norman NEWELL (1)	313
Cyril ORNADEL (1)	313
Gerry GOFFIN (1)	219
Carole KING (1)	219
Jay SIEGEL (2)	171
Leon CARR (1)	129
Paul VANCE (1)	129
Henry JAMIPH (1)	108
TRADITIONAL (2)	83
Barry MANN (1)	48
Cynthia WEIL (1)	48
Roger CHRISTIAN (1)	45
Brian WILSON (1)	45
Bob GIBSON (1)	21
Sammy LOWE (1)	21
Bert REISFELD (1)	18
Jean VILLARD (1)	18
Alan FREED (1)	5.5
Harvey FUQUA (1)	5.5
Charles DANVERS (1)	0.9
Carl SIGMAN (1)	0.9
Teresa BREWER ▶361 (40) [75]	**13248**
Bob MERRILL (2)	2058
Dorian BURTON (1)	1279
Eugene RANDOLPH (1)	1279
Ivory Joe HUNTER (1)	992
Sam COOKE (1)	505
Dave BARTHOLOMEW (1)	454
Fats DOMINO (1)	454
Roy DRUSKY (1)	431
Vic McALPIN (1)	431
Marie WILSON (1)	431
Matt DUBEY (1)	361
Harold KARR (1)	361
Jenny Lou CARSON (1)	344
Kay TWOMEY (1)	344
Ben WEISMAN (1)	344
Fred WISE (1)	344
Hal DAVID (1)	212
Carlo Alberto ROSSI (1)	212
Vaughn HORTON (1)	181
Kay ADELMAN (1)	154
Marvin RAINWATER (1)	154
Marshall BROWN (2)	153
Earl SHUMAN (2)	153
Carl MADURI (1)	126
James TESTA (1)	126
Alden SHUMAN (1)	120
Jack PALMER (1)	103
Clarke VAN NESS (1)	103
Del LYON (1)	100
Lani McINTYRE (1)	100
Lou FIELDS (1)	98
Edward GREEN (1)	80
Deadric MALONE (1)	80
Ferdinand WASHINGTON (1)	80
Bunny LEWIS (1)	50
Marguerite MONNOT (1)	50
Giuseppe MUSTACCHI (1)	50
Josephine PEOPLES (1)	41
Aaron SCHROEDER (1)	41
By DUNHAM (1)	33
Joseph HOOVEN (1)	33
Marilyn HOOVEN (1)	33
Peter DeROSE (1)	22
Billy HILL (1)	22
Eddie BRANDT (1)	20
Paul FREES (1)	20
Cliff FRIEND (1)	14
Jack REYNOLDS (1)	14
Kenny JACOBSON (1)	6.9
Rhoda ROBERTS (1)	6.9
Jeannie JOY (1)	6.1
Joe SHAPIRO (1)	6.1
Lou STALLMAN (1)	6.1
Bernie BAUM (1)	4.7
Stephan WEISS (1)	4.7
Frank McNULTY (1)	3.6
Jerry BRESLER (1)	2.2
Lyn DUDDY (1)	2.2
Joan EDWARDS (1)	2.2
Mel TILLIS (1)	2.1
Wayne WALKER (1)	2.1
Ben RALEIGH (1)	1.1
Don WOLF (1)	1.1
Robert COLBY (1)	0.0
Dick MANNING (1)	0.0
Vince FIORINO (1)	0.0
Dennise NORWOOD (1)	0.0
Bennie BENJAMIN (1)	0.0
George David WEISS (1)	0.0
Henry GLOVER (1)	0.0
Joe BEAL (1)	0.0
Jim BOOTHE (1)	0.0
Phil BELMONTE (1)	0.0
Ray MAXWELL (1)	0.0
Tarateno ROJAS (1)	0.0
EXPOSÉ ▶362 (8) [2]	**13232**
Lewis MARTINEE (7)	12407
Diane WARREN (1)	825
Ronnie DOVE ▶363 (20) [27]	**13118**
Kenny YOUNG (3)	2148
Artie RESNICK (2)	1604
Wanda JACKSON (1)	1192
Churchill KOHLMAN (1)	1106
Wes FARRELL (3)	798
Joel HIRSCHHORN (2)	675
Al KASHA (2)	675
Johnnie B. HICKS (1)	622
Jay FISHMAN (1)	545
Bernice ROSS (1)	430
Neil DIAMOND (1)	385
Howard Lee BARNES (1)	376
Don ROBERTSON (1)	376
Billy SHERRILL (1)	372
Glenn SUTTON (1)	372
Harold DORMAN (1)	288
Andy BADALE (2)	221
Ritchie ADAMS (1)	217
Larry KUSIK (1)	217
Tommy BOYCE (1)	151
Norm SIMON (1)	148
Charmaine HARMA (1)	73
Charles SEGAL (1)	49
Frank STANTON (1)	49
Lee HAZLEWOOD (1)	12
Jimmie CRANE (1)	10
Al JACOBS (1)	10
KISS ▶364 (26) [17]	**13104**
Paul STANLEY (21)	4939
Gene SIMMONS (8)	2832
Bob EZRIN (6)	1178
Vini PONCIA (3)	976
Desmond CHILD (5)	902
Michael BOLTON (1)	678
Peter CRISS (1)	468
Stan PENRIDGE (1)	468
Ace FREHLEY (2)	205
Prentice DeLANEY (1)	195
Vince CUSANO (1)	60
Adam MITCHELL (1)	46
Lou REED (1)	42
Holly KNIGHT (1)	37
Bernie LOWE (1)	28
Kal MANN (1)	28
Bob HALLIGAN (1)	24
RUFUS Featuring Chaka KHAN ▶365 (13) [13]	**13101**
Stevie WONDER (1)	3531
Chaka KHAN (3)	2482
Tony MAIDEN (2)	1809
Gavin CHRISTOPHER (2)	1780
David WOLINSKI (3)	1707
Ray PARKER Jr. (1)	774
Lalomie WASHBURN (1)	289
André FISCHER (1)	214
Richard CALHOUN (1)	188
Brenda RUSSELL (1)	145
Brian RUSSELL (1)	145
Ron STOCKERT (1)	30
Kevin MURPHY (1)	8.6
"Tennessee" Ernie FORD ▶366 (14) [19]	**13028**
Merle TRAVIS (2)	9881
Tom BLACKBURN (1)	1053
George BRUNS (1)	1053
Johnny LEHMANN (1)	201
Stuart HAMBLEN (1)	154
Nick ACQUAVIVA (1)	151
Ted VARNICK (1)	151
TRADITIONAL (1)	106
Eddie KIRK (1)	95
Bill NORVAS (1)	80
Larry COLEMAN (1)	20
Charles SINGLETON (1)	20
Bob MERRILL (1)	16
Terry SHAND (1)	16
Johnny BOND (1)	13
Roy ALFRED (1)	7.8
Abner SILVER (1)	7.8
Ira COOK (1)	0.7
Mort GREENE (1)	0.7
Bobby LEWIS ▶367 (4) [6]	**13009**
Malou RENÉ (3)	6504
Ritchie ADAMS (2)	6056
Bobby LEWIS (1)	448
Bob FELDMAN (1)	0.4
Jerry GOLDSTEIN (1)	0.4
Richard GOTTEHRER (1)	0.4
The ZOMBIES ▶368 (6) [2]	**12997**
Rod ARGENT (6)	12975
Chris WHITE (1)	23

The BROWNS ▶369 (10) [17]	**12989**
Bert REISFELD (1)	4241
Jean VILLARD (1)	4241
Nat SIMON (1)	1027
Charles TOBIAS (1)	1027
Evelyn DANZIG (1)	856
Jack SEGAL (1)	856
Hank LOCKLIN (1)	345
Cy COBEN (1)	179
Boudleaux BRYANT (2)	68
Felice BRYANT (1)	63
Charles Hutchison GABRIEL (1)	41
Ina Duley OGDON (1)	41
Billy HAYES (1)	0.9
Jay JOHNSON (1)	0.9
Kenneth BURNS (1)	0.8
Henry HAYNES (1)	0.8
TRADITIONAL (1)	0.8
The SWEET ▶370 (9) [7]	**12946**
Mike CHAPMAN (4)	3405
Nicky CHINN (4)	3405
Andrew SCOTT (5)	2036
Brian CONNOLLY (4)	1033
Stephen PRIEST (4)	1033
Michael TUCKER (4)	1033
Trevor GRIFFIN (1)	1003
Isaac HAYES ▶371 (14) [11]	**12936**
Isaac HAYES (7)	9325
Jesse STONE (1)	1196
Clifton DAVIS (1)	700
Jimmy WEBB (1)	341
Jerry BUTLER (1)	287
William Earl BUTLER (1)	287
Burt BACHARACH (2)	230
Hal DAVID (2)	230
Al GREEN (1)	113
Al JACKSON (1)	113
Willie MITCHELL (1)	113
BOSTON ▶372 (10) [3]	**12908**
Tom SCHOLZ (10)	12593
Brad DELP (2)	225
Gerald GREEN (1)	90
SAM & DAVE ▶373 (16) [11]	**12884**
Isaac HAYES (11)	5896
David PORTER (11)	5896
Sam COOKE (1)	309
Steve CROPPER (1)	226
Eddie FLOYD (1)	226
Homer BANKS (1)	159
Raymond Earl JACKSON (1)	159
Dennis LAMBERT (1)	5.6
Brian POTTER (1)	5.6
Donnie FRITTS (1)	0.7
John REID (1)	0.7
Gene McDANIELS ▶374 (9) [17]	**12845**
Luther DIXON (2)	2744
Stanley KAHAN (1)	2419
Eddie SNYDER (1)	2419
Burt BACHARACH (1)	1194
Bob HILLIARD (1)	1194
Cliff CROFFORD (2)	421
Jeff BARRY (1)	421
Artie RESNICK (1)	421
Willie DENSON (1)	325
Gerry GOFFIN (1)	324
Carole KING (1)	324
Doc POMUS (2)	316
Mort SHUMAN (2)	316

Lawrence HOLOFCENER (1)	5.1
Edward SCOTT (1)	5.1
Nick SAVORESE (1)	0.2
Warren SCHATZ (1)	0.2
Kenny ROGERS And The FIRST EDITION ▶375 (11) [12]	**12838**
Mickey NEWBURY (1)	2865
Mac DAVIS (1)	2846
Mel TILLIS (1)	2310
Alex HARVEY (3)	2245
Mike SETTLE (1)	1122
Kin VASSY (1)	818
Barry ETRIS (1)	597
Kenny ROGERS (1)	11
Roger NICHOLS (1)	7.4
Paul WILLIAMS (1)	7.4
Larry CANSLER (1)	3.9
Michael MURPHEY (1)	3.9
PET SHOP BOYS ▶376 (13) [13]	**12799**
Chris LOWE (10)	5040
Neil TENNANT (10)	5040
Allee WILLIS (1)	1070
Johnny CHRISTOPHER (1)	504
Mark JAMES (1)	504
Wayne Carson THOMPSON (1)	504
Stephen HAGUE (1)	63
Bob CREWE (1)	18
Bob GAUDIO (1)	18
Adam CLAYTON (1)	9.2
Dave EVANS (1)	9.2
Paul HEWSON (1)	9.2
Larry MULLEN (1)	9.2
GUNS N' ROSES ▶377 (8) [7]	**12781**
Saul HUDSON (7)	2558
Duff McKAGAN (7)	2558
Axl ROSE (7)	2558
Izzy STRADLIN (7)	2558
Steven ADLER (5)	2043
Linda McCARTNEY (1)	253
Paul McCARTNEY (1)	253
Gloria ESTEFAN ▶378 (9) [7]	**12723**
Gloria ESTEFAN (7)	7718
Emilio ESTEFAN (2)	1669
Jon SECADA (2)	1408
Jorge CASAS (3)	580
Clay OSTWALD (3)	580
Diane WARREN (1)	402
John DeFARIA (1)	364
The DOVELLS ▶379 (9) [13]	**12625**
Kal MANN (6)	4950
Dave APPELL (5)	4003
Dee CLARK (1)	947
Cornell MULDROW (1)	947
Philip UPCHURCH (1)	947
Robert LEWIS (1)	316
Johnny STYLES (1)	316
Rose Marie CHIVETTI (1)	115
Len BARRY (1)	42
Jerry GROSS (1)	42
Marvin GAYE (1)	0.1
Ivy Jo HUNTER (1)	0.1
William STEVENSON (1)	0.1
Dolly PARTON ▶380 (17) [18]	**12464**
Dolly PARTON (7)	8312
Barry MANN (1)	1377

Cynthia WEIL (1)	1377
Mike SETTLE (1)	248
Carole Bayer SAGER (2)	195
Doc POMUS (1)	189
Mort SHUMAN (1)	189
Bruce SUDANO (1)	157
Donna SUMMER (1)	157
David WOLFERT (1)	142
Bruce ROBERTS (1)	53
Tony HATCH (1)	25
TRADITIONAL (1)	19
Bud RENEAU (1)	8.7
Blaise TOSTI (1)	8.7
Richard BRANNAN (1)	2.2
David MALLOY (1)	2.2
Randy McCORMICK (1)	2.2
Bonnie TYLER ▶381 (7) [8]	**12456**
Jim STEINMAN (3)	7865
Ronnie SCOTT (1)	1990
Steve WOLFE (1)	1990
Billy CROSS (1)	271
Dean PITCHFORD (1)	244
Desmond CHILD (1)	33
Pete BELLOTTE (1)	31
Giorgio MORODER (1)	31
Edwin STARR ▶382 (14) [17]	**12447**
Barrett STRONG (3)	4032
Norman WHITFIELD (3)	4032
Edwin STARR (9)	1263
Johnny BRISTOL (2)	583
Bill SHARPLEY (2)	488
Bert BERNS (1)	461
Harvey FUQUA (1)	461
Jerry WEXLER (1)	461
Al HAMILTON (2)	178
Richard MORRIS (2)	178
Doris McNEIL (1)	122
Robert DICKERSON (1)	66
Arthur PULLAM (1)	66
Chuck MIDDLETON (1)	44
Steve BOWDEN (1)	4.4
James Anthony DEAN (1)	4.4
William WEATHERSPOON (1)	4.4
The SEARCHERS ▶383 (14) [26]	**12443**
Jerry LEIBER (1)	2898
Mike STOLLER (1)	2898
Leroy FULLYLOVE (1)	834
Sonny BONO (1)	819
Jack NITZSCHE (1)	819
William E. JACKSON III (1)	632
Jimmy WISNER (1)	632
Malvina REYNOLDS (1)	570
Jackie DeSHANNON (1)	481
Sharon McMAHAN (1)	461
Tony HATCH (1)	320
Earl CARROLL (1)	123
Billy GUY (1)	123
Steve BARRI (1)	106
P.F. SLOAN (1)	106
Frances AYCOCK (1)	86
Robert MOSELY (1)	86
Lamar SIMINGTON (1)	86
Leroy SWEARINGEN (1)	86
Allan CLARKE (1)	55
Tony HICKS (1)	55
Graham NASH (1)	55
Chris CURTIS (1)	33
Mike PENDER (1)	33
Valerie MURTAGH (1)	22
Harold SPIRO (1)	22

George BENSON ▶384 (14) [21]	**12437**
Rod TEMPERTON (2)	2983
Leon RUSSELL (2)	1884
Skip SCARBOROUGH (1)	984
Bill CHAMPLIN (1)	817
Jay GRAYDON (1)	817
Steve LUKATHER (1)	817
Jerry LEIBER (1)	491
Barry MANN (1)	491
Mike STOLLER (1)	491
Cynthia WEIL (1)	491
Michael JONES (1)	350
Linda CREED (1)	330
Michael MASSER (1)	330
James Newton HOWARD (1)	260
David PAICH (1)	260
Randy GOODRUM (1)	154
Steve KIPNER (1)	154
Michael GARVIN (1)	117
Tom SHAPIRO (1)	117
Bobby WOMACK (1)	61
Morris ALBERT (1)	40
Louis ARMSTRONG And His All-Stars ▶385 (4) [8]	**12419**
Jerry HERMAN (1)	11318
Sammy CAHN (1)	266
Jule STYNE (1)	266
Marc BLITZSTEIN (1)	190
Berthold BRECHT (1)	190
Kurt WEILL (1)	190
Ray GILBERT (1)	0.0
Edward ORY (1)	0.0
Percy SLEDGE ▶386 (15) [23]	**12406**
Calvin LEWIS (1)	3078
Andrew WRIGHT (1)	3078
Stephen Allen DAVIS (1)	1850
Spooner OLDHAM (2)	901
Dan PENN (2)	901
Irral BERGER (1)	408
Morgan C. ROBINSON (1)	408
Clara THOMPSON (1)	408
Virgil STEWART (1)	188
Eddie HINTON (2)	172
George SOULE (1)	145
Marlin GREENE (1)	144
Ken DARBY (1)	135
George R. POULTON (1)	135
Elvis PRESLEY (1)	135
Bobby RUSSELL (1)	134
Burt BACHARACH (1)	45
Bob HILLIARD (1)	45
Bobby WOMACK (1)	44
Donnie FRITTS (1)	29
Wini SCOTT (1)	12
Art HARRIS (1)	4.1
Fred JAY (1)	4.1
Jackson BROWNE ▶387 (17) [7]	**12355**
Jackson BROWNE (16)	9485
Danny KORTCHMAR (2)	1501
Maurice WILLIAMS (1)	797
Nancy FARNSWORTH (1)	351
Russ KUNKEL (1)	215
Craig DOERGE (1)	6.7
Bryan GAROFALO (1)	0.0
Rick ASTLEY ▶388 (8) [7]	**12327**
Matt AITKEN (3)	2903
Mike STOCK (3)	2903
Pete WATERMAN (3)	2903
Rick ASTLEY (4)	2726

Rick ASTLEY ▶388 (8) [7] *Cont'd*	**12327**
Rob FISHER (2)	883
Eddie HOLLAND (1)	4.4
Norman WHITFIELD (1)	4.4
Cliff RICHARD ▶389 (20) [30]	**12315**
Alan TARNEY (4)	4738
Terry BRITTEN (3)	1743
Christine HODGSON (1)	1498
Leo SAYER (1)	959
Lionel BART (1)	673
Charles DAWES (1)	482
Carl SIGMAN (1)	482
Brian A. ROBERTSON (2)	239
Andy HILL (1)	172
John Philip HODGE (1)	172
Charles BASKERVILLE (1)	165
Clarence BASSETT (1)	165
William Henry MILLER (1)	165
James SHEPPARD (1)	165
Ray MARTINEZ (1)	142
Jerry LEIBER (1)	90
Mike STOLLER (1)	90
Sue SHIFRIN (1)	42
Guy FLETCHER (1)	38
Doug FLETT (1)	38
Gordon MILLS (1)	14
Michael DENNE (1)	11
Ken GOLD (1)	11
Cliff RICHARD (1)	4.5
Bruce WELCH (1)	4.5
Al DUBIN (1)	2.7
Harry WARREN (1)	2.7
Phil COULTER (1)	1.8
William Wylie MacPherson MARTIN (1)	1.8
Jimmy GATELEY (1)	1.4
Paul DAVIS ▶390 (15) [8]	**12273**
Paul DAVIS (12)	10378
Susan COLLINS (1)	854
Bert BERNS (1)	475
Jerry PETERS (1)	117
Anita POREE (1)	117
Skip SCARBOROUGH (1)	117
Mike LOVE (1)	108
Brian WILSON (1)	108
Belinda CARLISLE ▶391 (9) [12]	**12262**
Rick NOWELS (4)	3358
Ellen SHIPLEY (4)	3358
Diane WARREN (1)	2442
Paula BROWN (1)	868
Mitchel EVANS (1)	868
James WHELAN (1)	868
Robbie SEIDMAN (1)	202
Maria VIDAL (1)	202
Charlotte CAFFEY (1)	30
Jonathan SEGAL (1)	30
Peter Ronald BROWN (1)	19
Jack BRUCE (1)	19
Al HIBBLER ▶392 (17) [33]	**12220**
Richard MULLAN (2)	2394
Alex NORTH (1)	2188
Hy ZARET (1)	2188
Jack RICHARDS (1)	2176
King PALMER (1)	476
Carl SIGMAN (1)	476
Phil BELMONTE (1)	454
Leroy LOVETT (1)	454
Alan WHITE (1)	454

Jerry LIVINGSTON (1)	159
Dok STANFORD (1)	159
Irving BERGER (1)	146
Herbert L. MILLER (1)	146
Ruth BISHOP (1)	69
Joe GOODWIN (1)	57
James HANLEY (1)	57
Ballard MacDONALD (1)	57
Moose CHARLAP (2)	31
Don GEORGE (1)	21
Joyce KILMER (1)	11
Oscar RASBACH (1)	11
Milton DRAKE (1)	9.9
Charles H. CUPPETT (1)	4.2
Peter DeROSE (1)	4.2
Sam LEWIS (1)	4.2
Harold ADAMSON (1)	3.7
Ferde GROFE (1)	3.7
Lenny ADELSON (1)	2.8
Albert SKINNER (1)	2.8
Frank SKINNER (1)	2.8
Irving BERLIN (1)	0.0
Franz GRUBER (1)	0.0
Josef MOHR (1)	0.0
Boz SCAGGS ▶393 (14) [8]	**12192**
Boz SCAGGS (12)	5466
David PAICH (5)	4334
David FOSTER (3)	1569
David LASLEY (1)	301
Bobby CALDWELL (1)	143
Dennis MATKOSKY (1)	143
Jason SCHEFF (1)	143
Michael OMARTIAN (1)	93
Andy KIM ▶394 (13) [5]	**12188**
Andy KIM (10)	6422
Jeff BARRY (11)	3065
Ellie GREENWICH (2)	1340
Phil SPECTOR (2)	1340
Marty SANDERS (1)	22
The HIGHWAYMEN ▶395 (5) [6]	**12145**
TRADITIONAL (2)	9195
Huddie LEDBETTER (1)	2196
Leo MAGUIRE (1)	562
Elmer BERNSTEIN (1)	72
Mack DAVID (1)	72
Dave FISHER (1)	48
David SEVILLE And The CHIPMUNKS ▶396 (16) [6]	**12139**
David SEVILLE (11)	10945
Johnny MARKS (3)	340
Maurice ABRAHAMS (1)	284
Grant CLARKE (1)	284
Lewis MUIR (1)	284
TRADITIONAL (1)	2.2
Debby BOONE ▶397 (4) [5]	**12124**
Joe BROOKS (2)	12081
Franne GOLDE (1)	15
Peter NOONE (1)	15
Allee WILLIS (1)	15
Van McCOY (1)	0.0
Mitch RYDER And The DETROIT WHEELS ▶398 (10) [16]	**12101**
Bob CREWE (2)	1578
L. Russell BROWN (1)	1578
Frederick LONG (1)	1408
William STEVENSON (1)	1408

Robert BLACKWELL (1)	1408
John MARASCALCO (1)	1408
Bill MEDLEY (1)	1093
Ma RAINEY (1)	364
TRADITIONAL (1)	364
Enotris JOHNSON (1)	364
Richard PENNIMAN (1)	364
Saxie DOWELL (1)	300
Eddie HOLLAND (1)	150
Norman WHITFIELD (1)	150
Gary KNIGHT (2)	82
Herbert BERNSTEIN (1)	82
VILLAGE PEOPLE ▶399 (5) [5]	**12090**
Henri BELOLO (5)	3961
Jacques MORALI (5)	3961
Victor WILLIS (4)	3924
Peter WHITEHEAD (2)	207
Phil HURTT (1)	37
Joe COCKER ▶400 (21) [19]	**12045**
Wayne Carson THOMPSON (1)	2598
Arthur HAMILTON (1)	1327
Bruce FISHER (1)	1095
Billy PRESTON (1)	1095
Joe COCKER (4)	764
Chris STAINTON (4)	764
Dave MASON (2)	706
Gregg ALLMAN (1)	542
John LENNON (2)	485
Paul McCARTNEY (2)	485
Diane WARREN (2)	454
Bryan ADAMS (2)	452
Jim VALLANCE (2)	452
Daniel MOORE (1)	371
Allen TOUSSAINT (1)	348
Leon RUSSELL (1)	61
Nicholas DiSTEFANO (1)	43
Jim PRICE (1)	5.5
Jimmy WEBB (1)	0.0
PAUL & PAULA ▶401 (5) [7]	**12031**
Ray HILDEBRAND (3)	10128
Jill JACKSON (2)	1087
Orville COUCH (1)	227
Eddie McDUFF (1)	227
Bill SMITH (1)	227
Marvin MONTGOMERY (1)	68
Mary TARVER (1)	68
Glenn FREY ▶402 (11) [4]	**12029**
Glenn FREY (10)	4407
Jack TEMPCHIN (10)	4407
Harold FALTERMEYER (1)	1608
Keith FORSEY (1)	1608
Gogi GRANT ▶403 (10) [16]	**11995**
Herbert NEWMAN (4)	4936
Stan LEBOWSKY (2)	4835
Biff JONES (1)	879
Chuck MEYER (1)	879
Buddy BREGMAN (2)	101
Dimitri TIOMKIN (1)	89
Ned WASHINGTON (1)	89
Gerald MARKS (1)	45
Milton PASCAL (1)	45
Jerry LIVINGSTON (1)	32
Paul Francis WEBSTER (1)	32
Francis LEMARQUE (1)	10
Rudi REVIL (1)	10
Sunny SKYLAR (1)	10
Michael JULIEN (1)	0.6
Al TIMOTHY (1)	0.6

The SEEKERS ▶404 (6) [5]	**11986**
Tom SPRINGFIELD (5)	8119
Jim DALE (1)	3441
Malvina REYNOLDS (1)	391
Gary OSBORNE (1)	17
Bob SAGE (1)	17
Mac DAVIS ▶405 (15) [9]	**11962**
Mac DAVIS (11)	9137
Kevin JOHNSON (1)	949
Doc SEVERINSEN (1)	892
Mark JAMES (1)	790
Ian PAGE (1)	124
Sterling WHIPPLE (1)	33
Sam LORBER (1)	12
Mike NOBLE (1)	12
Jeff SILBAR (1)	12
CORNELIUS BROTHERS & SISTER ROSE ▶406 (6) [2]	**11881**
Eddie CORNELIUS (6)	11613
Carter CORNELIUS (1)	268
Sarah VAUGHAN ▶407 (30) [59]	**11880**
Bob MERRILL (1)	2261
Hal DAVID (1)	1339
Sherman EDWARDS (1)	1339
Richard ADLER (1)	1013
Jerry ROSS (1)	1013
George David WEISS (2)	439
Bennie BENJAMIN (2)	407
Edward WHITE (1)	385
Mack WOLFSON (1)	385
Clyde OTIS (3)	309
Alan ARKIN (1)	253
Bob CAREY (1)	253
Erik DARLING (1)	253
Murray STEIN (1)	251
Jerry BOCK (1)	225
Lawrence HOLOFCENER (1)	225
Sol MARCUS (1)	193
Luigi CREATORE (2)	110
Hugo PERETTI (2)	110
Charles CHAPLIN (1)	108
Geoffrey PARSONS (1)	108
John TURNER (1)	108
Johann Sebastian BACH (1)	69
Sandy LINZER (1)	69
Denny RANDELL (1)	69
Gladys SHELLEY (1)	63
June WINTERS (1)	63
Leroy ANDERSON (1)	56
Mitchell PARISH (1)	56
Luvenia WILLIS (1)	56
Irving BERLIN (1)	42
John L. GOLDEN (1)	37
Raymond HUBBELL (1)	37
Gene DePAUL (1)	30
Don RAYE (1)	30
Robert MOSELY (1)	14
Mayme WATTS (1)	14
Johnny BURKE (1)	11
Erroll GARNER (1)	11
Rudy TOOMBS (1)	9.9
Albert BEACH (1)	6.3
Victor ABRAMS (1)	6.2
Fred JAY (1)	6.2
Irving REID (1)	6.2
Nat BURTON (1)	6.2
David ROSE (1)	6.2
Jessie Mae ROBINSON (1)	4.9
Teddy POWELL (1)	2.8
Bobby SHARP (1)	2.8

Sarah VAUGHAN ▶407 (30) [59] *Cont'd*	**11880**
Mack DISCANT (1)	1.6
Dick MILES (1)	1.6
Vince CORSO (1)	1.5
Edward ELISCU (1)	0.6
Billy ROSE (1)	0.6
Vincent YOUMANS (1)	0.6
Marcel AGERON (1)	0.0
Regis Gabriel DESPLANQUES (1)	0.0
Alain ROMANS (1)	0.0
Paul Francis WEBSTER (1)	0.0
Clyde McPHATTER ▶408 (25) [36]	**11873**
Billy SWAN (1)	3075
Jimmy WILLIAMS (2)	1639
Brook BENTON (3)	1521
Clyde McPHATTER (3)	602
Jimmy OLIVER (2)	600
Joe SHAPIRO (1)	586
Lou STALLMAN (1)	586
Bobby DAY (1)	583
Howard GREENFIELD (1)	291
Neil SEDAKA (1)	291
Billy Dawn SMITH (1)	286
Danny SMALL (1)	198
Franklyn J. TABLEPORTER (1)	145
Otis BLACKWELL (1)	142
Lee ANDREWS (1)	129
Bernice DAVIS (1)	129
Douglas HENDERSON (1)	129
Miriam UNIMAN (1)	129
Eddie CURTIS (1)	107
Ahmet ERTEGUN (1)	107
Ray STANLEY (1)	89
Deadric MALONE (1)	85
Paul PERRYMAN (1)	85
Willis CARROLL (1)	71
Carmen TAYLOR (1)	71
Jimmy RADCLIFFE (1)	56
Carl SPENCER (1)	56
Charles SINGLETON (1)	42
Bobby STEVENSON (1)	21
Joy KENNEDY (1)	4.8
Jack KELLER (1)	3.1
Larry KOLBER (1)	3.1
Clyde OTIS (1)	2.5
Joyce HEATH (1)	2.5
Clint BALLARD Jr. (1)	2.4
Fred TOBIAS (1)	2.4
RARE EARTH ▶409 (9) [16]	**11823**
Smokey ROBINSON (1)	4506
Dino FEKARIS (2)	1510
Nick ZESSES (2)	1510
Tom BAIRD (3)	1353
Cornelius GRANT (1)	832
Eddie HOLLAND (1)	832
Norman WHITFIELD (1)	832
Barry GIBB (1)	112
Maurice GIBB (1)	112
Robin GIBB (1)	112
Ray CHARLES (1)	109
Gil BRIDGES (1)	0.7
Ed GUZMAN (1)	0.7
Ray MONETTE (1)	0.7
Mark OLSON (1)	0.7
Pete RIVERA (1)	0.7
SEALS & CROFTS ▶410 (13) [9]	**11815**
Jim SEALS (10)	5256

Dash CROFTS (7)	4939
David BATTEAU (1)	444
Louie SHELTON (1)	444
Charles FOX (1)	300
Paul WILLIAMS (1)	300
Lana BOGAN (2)	102
Sean MacLEOD (1)	15
Bob PHILLIPS (1)	15
TIFFANY ▶411 (6) [8]	**11809**
Lois Ann BLAISCH (1)	4537
Ritchie CORDELL (1)	4060
Tim JAMES (1)	810
Steve McCLINTOCK (1)	810
John LENNON (1)	557
Paul McCARTNEY (1)	557
John DUARTE (2)	239
Mark E. PAUL (2)	239
BAY CITY ROLLERS ▶412 (8) [13]	**11780**
Phil COULTER (1)	2417
William Wylie MacPherson MARTIN (1)	2417
Len BOONE (1)	1735
Eric FAULKNER (1)	948
Stuart John WOOD (1)	948
Harvey SHIELD (1)	855
Mike HAWKER (1)	759
Ivor RAYMONDE (1)	759
Tim MOORE (1)	546
Harry VANDA (1)	133
George YOUNG (1)	133
Guy FLETCHER (1)	65
Doug FLETT (1)	65
Marvin GAYE & Tammi TERRELL ▶413 (11) [6]	**11778**
Nick ASHFORD (9)	5058
Valerie SIMPSON (9)	5058
Johnny BRISTOL (1)	508
Vernon BULLOCK (1)	508
Harvey FUQUA (1)	508
Marvin GAYE (1)	138
Bobbie GENTRY ▶414 (8) [6]	**11774**
Bobbie GENTRY (5)	11470
John Buck WILKIN (1)	134
Fred BURCH (1)	78
Don HILL (1)	78
Billy DEATON (1)	7.1
Doug KERSHAW (1)	7.1
Dee CLARK ▶415 (11) [11]	**11745**
Dee CLARK (4)	7548
Otis BLACKWELL (2)	1840
Bobby STEVENSON (1)	563
Calvin CARTER (3)	534
Frank AUGUSTUS (1)	334
Doris PAYNE (1)	334
Marion OLIVER (1)	270
Ewart ABNER (1)	130
John C. MOORE (1)	130
Horace OTT (2)	35
Don COVAY (1)	27
Jerry Lee LEWIS ▶416 (20) [28]	**11709**
Dave WILLIAMS (1)	3567
Otis BLACKWELL (3)	3266
Jack HAMMER (1)	2149
Ray CHARLES (1)	516
J.P. RICHARDSON (1)	436
Ron HARGRAVE (1)	310
Jerry Lee LEWIS (1)	310

Granville McGHEE (1)	300
J. Mayo WILLIAMS (1)	300
Fred FOSTER (1)	201
Kris KRISTOFFERSON (1)	201
Charlie RICH (2)	104
Glenn SUTTON (1)	10
Chuck BERRY (1)	7.2
Luther DIXON (1)	5.8
Allyson KHENT (1)	5.8
Robert HIGGINBOTHAM (1)	4.7
Jerry CHESNUT (1)	3.2
Deadric MALONE (1)	2.3
Joe SCOTT (1)	2.3
Hank WILLIAMS (1)	1.9
Bob FELDMAN (1)	0.9
Jerry GOLDSTEIN (1)	0.9
Richard GOTTEHRER (1)	0.9
Henry GLOVER (1)	0.8
Lois MANN (1)	0.8
Moon MULLICAN (1)	0.8
Henry THURSTON (1)	0.8
Peter FRAMPTON ▶417 (8) [8]	**11616**
Peter FRAMPTON (7)	9679
Mick GALLAGHER (1)	303
John SIOMOS (1)	303
Rick WILLS (1)	303
Lee GARRETT (1)	257
Lula Mae HARDAWAY (1)	257
Stevie WONDER (1)	257
Syreeta WRIGHT (1)	257
Paul MAURIAT And His Orchestra ▶418 (4) [5]	**11607**
André POPP (1)	11159
Bernard KESSLAIR (1)	317
Richard SHERMAN (1)	57
Robert SHERMAN (1)	57
John PHILLIPS (1)	17
HAMILTON, JOE FRANK & REYNOLDS ▶419 (7) [7]	**11604**
Danny HAMILTON (3)	2892
Ann Marie HAMILTON (2)	2811
Dennis LAMBERT (3)	2720
Brian POTTER (3)	2720
Chris ARNOLD (1)	153
David MARTIN (1)	153
Geoff MORROW (1)	153
The JETS ▶420 (10) [11]	**11589**
Rupert HOLMES (1)	2436
Bobby NUNN (1)	1786
Jerry KNIGHT (2)	1272
Aaron ZIGMAN (2)	1272
Linda MALLAH (3)	1174
Rick KELLY (2)	1147
Don POWELL (1)	787
Stephen BRAY (2)	779
Tony PIERCE (1)	752
Michael JONZUN (1)	167
Diane WARREN (1)	18
The MANHATTANS ▶421 (20) [25]	**11561**
Winfred LOVETT (5)	6532
Leo GRAHAM (2)	1688
Paul RICHMOND (2)	1688
Edward BIVINS (5)	772
Allan FELDER (1)	152
Ron KERSEY (1)	152
Bunny SIGLER (1)	152
Roger JOYCE (1)	56
Victoria PIKE (1)	56
Teddy RANDAZZO (1)	56

John Vernon ANDERSON (1)	38
Steven Richard WILLIAMS (1)	38
John FOWLKES (1)	29
Roger GENGER (1)	29
Jimmie CRANE (1)	29
Al JACOBS (1)	29
Sam COOKE (1)	22
Gerald ALSTON (1)	17
Alvin FIELDS (1)	5.1
Barbara MORR (1)	5.1
Douglas STENDER (1)	5.1
Eddie JONES (1)	2.8
Kenneth KELLEY (1)	2.8
Joe EVANS (1)	2.1
Greg GASKINS (1)	1.2
Della REESE ▶422 (15) [26]	**11556**
Giacomo PUCCINI (1)	3837
Bobby WORTH (1)	3837
Camillo BARGONI (1)	662
Al STILLMAN (1)	662
Hal BLAIR (1)	405
Lou DINNING (1)	405
Don ROBERTSON (1)	405
Jimmie HODGES (1)	402
Luigi CREATORE (3)	197
Hugo PERETTI (3)	197
George David WEISS (2)	151
Stan LEBOWSKY (1)	119
Johnny LEHMANN (1)	119
Hughie CANNON (1)	53
Marguerite MONNOT (1)	46
Frank LOESSER (1)	22
John William LANTZ (1)	18
Eddie MILLER (1)	18
Ervin DRAKE (1)	1.4
Julian ADDERLEY (1)	0.4
Jon HENDRICKS (1)	0.4
Tito MADI (1)	0.0
Buck RAM (1)	0.0
Norman NEWELL (1)	0.0
Nino OLIVIERO (1)	0.0
Riz ORTOLANI (1)	0.0
Tyrone DAVIS ▶423 (21) [18]	**11530**
Jack DANIELS (4)	2565
John Edward MOORE (4)	2565
Barry DESPENZA (2)	1850
Carl WOLFOLK (2)	1850
Leo GRAHAM (9)	1241
Raymond HALEY (4)	542
Morris DOLLISON (1)	318
Richard PARKER (2)	180
Willie HENDERSON (1)	158
Floyd SMITH (1)	102
Carl DAVIS (2)	37
L.V. JOHNSON (1)	36
Roger MINER (1)	36
Eugene RECORD (1)	14
Darryl ELLIS (1)	10
Ruben LOCKE Jr. (1)	10
Paul RICHMOND (1)	10
John SIBLEY (1)	3.9
Jim LOWE ▶424 (11) [14]	**11513**
Marvin MOORE (5)	5635
Bob DAVIE (3)	5031
George CAMPBELL (1)	441
Jim LOWE (1)	164
Fred EBB (1)	117
Paul KLEIN (1)	117
Charles GREAN (1)	4.3
Fred HERTZ (1)	4.3

Jim LOWE ►424 (11) [14] *Cont'd*	11513
Chuck BERRY (1)	0.0
Russ FRATTO (1)	0.0
Alan FREED (1)	0.0
Carl PERKINS (1)	0.0
Warner McPHERSON (1)	0.0
Pat SMITH (1)	0.0

Amy GRANT ►425 (6) [8]	11511
Amy GRANT (5)	4650
Keith THOMAS (1)	2294
Wayne KIRKPATRICK (3)	1278
Charlie PEACOCK (1)	1210
Mark MUELLER (1)	867
Michael OMARTIAN (1)	867
Michael W. SMITH (2)	279
Billy SIMON (1)	67

Archie BELL & The DRELLS ►426 (12) [13]	11485
Archie BELL (2)	3952
Billy BUTTIER (1)	3841
Kenneth GAMBLE (8)	1755
Leon HUFF (8)	1654
Thom BELL (1)	111
Eddie HAYNES (1)	58
Phillip MITCHELL (1)	58
Isaac HAYES (1)	13
David PORTER (1)	13
Victor CARSTARPHEN (1)	9.6
Gene McFADDEN (1)	9.6
John WHITEHEAD (1)	9.6
Cary GILBERT (1)	2.9

Dinah WASHINGTON ►427 (26) [44]	11419
Stanley ADAMS (1)	2076
Maria GREVER (1)	2076
Irving GORDON (1)	1993
Clyde OTIS (3)	1061
Al DUBIN (1)	621
Harry WARREN (1)	621
George GERSHWIN (2)	532
Ira GERSHWIN (2)	532
Harold ADAMSON (2)	409
Jimmy McHUGH (2)	409
Johnny BURKE (1)	179
Jimmy VAN HEUSEN (1)	179
Dinah WASHINGTON (3)	86
Yvette BALL (1)	80
John HOWARD (1)	80
Miriam LEWIS (1)	80
Belford HENDRICKS (2)	78
Alfonso HIGGINS (1)	76
Johnny MERCER (1)	38
Lincoln CHASE (1)	33
Cy CRANE (1)	18
Ira LEE (1)	18
Herb WIENER (1)	18
J. Fred COOTS (1)	17
Sam LEWIS (1)	17
Johnny GREEN (1)	11
Edward HEYMAN (1)	11
Billy ROSE (1)	11
Leroy KIRKLAND (1)	8.6
Pearl WOODS (1)	8.6
Rose Marie McCOY (1)	4.9
Edward GROSSMAN (1)	4.7
Neil SEDAKA (1)	4.7
Lillian GREEN (1)	4.1
Jack PALMER (1)	2.9
Spencer WILLIAMS (1)	2.9
Hank WILLIAMS (1)	2.2
James CAVANAUGH (1)	2.0
Russ MORGAN (1)	2.0
Larry STOCK (1)	2.0
Brook BENTON (1)	1.7
Henry GLOVER (1)	1.7
Morris LEVY (1)	1.7
Titus TURNER (1)	1.7

Johnnie RAY ►428 (21) [34]	11392
Johnny BRAGG (1)	2636
Buddy KILLEN (1)	2636
Robert S. RILEY (1)	2636
Marty ROBBINS (1)	1585
Ollie JONES (1)	390
Wally GOLD (1)	316
Dorothy GOODMAN (1)	315
Winfield SCOTT (1)	315
Johnnie RAY (2)	123
Jesse STONE (1)	85
Lou Willie TURNER (1)	85
Bob MERRILL (1)	50
Stuart HAMBLEN (1)	46
Irving BERLIN (1)	40
Herman HUPFELD (1)	31
Barry PARKER (1)	22
Jerry SAMUELS (1)	22
Otis BLACKWELL (1)	16
Mel TILLIS (1)	8.7
Wayne WALKER (1)	8.7
Aaron SCHROEDER (1)	3.5
Guy WOOD (1)	3.5
Ernie ERDMAN (1)	3.2
Gus KAHN (1)	3.2
Billy MEYERS (1)	3.2
Elmer SCHOEBEL (1)	3.2
Harry BROOKS (1)	1.5
Andy RAZAF (1)	1.5
Thomas WALLER (1)	1.5
Wayne SHANKLIN (1)	0.1
Al SHERMAN (1)	0.1
Richard ADLER (1)	0.0
Jerry ROSS (1)	0.0
Eddie CURTIS (1)	0.0

Lou RAWLS ►429 (23) [33]	11369
Kenneth GAMBLE (5)	2226
Leon HUFF (5)	2226
Ben RALEIGH (3)	1161
Dave LINDEN (1)	775
Sandy BARON (2)	639
Bobby HEBB (2)	639
Isaac HAYES (1)	637
David PORTER (1)	637
Von GRAY (1)	431
Sherman MARSHALL (1)	431
June JACKSON (1)	384
Lou RAWLS (1)	375
H.B. BARNUM (1)	199
David AXELROD (1)	188
Larry HENLEY (1)	80
Jeff SILBAR (1)	80
Gerry GOFFIN (1)	49
Carole KING (1)	49
Gale GARNETT (1)	43
Lalo SCHIFRIN (1)	43
John W. ANDERSON (1)	23
Sam COOKE (1)	9.8
Larry COLLINS (1)	7.6
Mac DAVIS (1)	7.6
Katherine DAVIS (1)	4.8
Henry ONORATI (1)	4.8
Harry SIMEONE (1)	4.8
Julian ROBLEDO (1)	4.2
Dorothy TERRISS (1)	4.2
Berry GORDY (1)	1.4
Brenda HOLLOWAY (1)	1.4
Patrice HOLLOWAY (1)	1.4
Frank Edward WILSON (1)	1.4

The SYLVERS ►430 (9) [8]	11366
Freddie PERREN (3)	4838
Keni ST. LEWIS (3)	4838
Leon SYLVERS (6)	631
Edmund SYLVERS (3)	360
James SYLVERS (2)	332
Ricky SYLVERS (2)	332
Christine YARIAN (1)	32
Foster SYLVERS (1)	1.3

LED ZEPPELIN ►431 (10) [4]	11351
Jimmy PAGE (10)	3614
Robert PLANT (10)	3614
John Paul JONES (7)	2489
John BONHAM (4)	1634

Skeeter DAVIS ►432 (9) [17]	11335
Sylvia DEE (1)	3224
Arthur KENT (1)	3224
Gerry GOFFIN (1)	1308
Carole KING (1)	1308
Alex ZANETIS (1)	500
Milton KELLEM (1)	435
Hal BLAIR (1)	271
Don ROBERTSON (1)	271
Gary GELD (1)	204
Peter UDELL (1)	204
Boudleaux BRYANT (1)	127
Floyd CRAMER (1)	127
Skeeter DAVIS (1)	127
Sandra RHODES (1)	4.1
Carl BELEW (1)	0.0
Shelby SINGLETON (1)	0.0
W.S. STEVENSON (1)	0.0

MR. MISTER ►433 (6) [5]	11329
Steve GEORGE (6)	3658
John LANG (6)	3658
Richard PAGE (6)	3658
Pat MASTELOTTO (1)	314
George GHIZ (1)	42

John LENNON/ PLASTIC ONO BAND ►434 (7) [2]	11304
John LENNON (7)	11173
Yoko ONO (2)	131

DIXIE CUPS ►435 (5) [8]	11264
Jeff BARRY (4)	3819
Ellie GREENWICH (4)	3819
Phil SPECTOR (1)	2772
James CRAWFORD (1)	171
Barbara Anne HAWKINS (1)	171
Rosa Lee HAWKINS (1)	171
Joan Marie JOHNSON (1)	171
TRADITIONAL (1)	171

LISA LISA And CULT JAM ►436 (9) [11]	11251
Curtis BEDEAU (8)	1830
Gerard CHARLES (8)	1830
Hugh CLARKE (8)	1830
Brian GEORGE (8)	1830
Lucien GEORGE (8)	1830
Paul GEORGE (8)	1830
Robert CLIVILLÉS (1)	66
David COLE (1)	66
Alan FRIEDMAN (1)	66
Duran RAMOS (1)	66
Lisa VELEZ (1)	7.4

The ANGELS ►437 (7) [13]	11234
Bob FELDMAN (3)	2800
Jerry GOLDSTEIN (3)	2800
Richard GOTTEHRER (3)	2800
Charles DANVERS (1)	665
Carl SIGMAN (1)	665
Morris BAILEY (1)	591
Jan BERRY (1)	371
Artie KORNFELD (1)	371
Peggy FARINA (1)	79
Robert SPENCER (1)	79
Marty SANDERS (1)	5.1
Richard ADLER (1)	4.5
Robert ALLEN (1)	4.5

SILVER CONVENTION ►438 (4) [2]	11217
Sylvester LEVAY (4)	5609
Stephan PRAGER (4)	5609

Sue THOMPSON ►439 (8) [5]	11214
John D. LOUDERMILK (4)	9785
Boudleaux BRYANT (3)	456
Felice BRYANT (3)	456
Bob MONTGOMERY (1)	258
Earl SINKS (1)	258

SUPERTRAMP ►440 (10) [2]	11202
Rick DAVIES (10)	5831
Roger HODGSON (9)	5371

The KNACK ►441 (5) [2]	11183
Doug FIEGER (4)	6277
Berton AVERRE (4)	4906

The McCOYS ►442 (9) [16]	11170
Bert BERNS (2)	3475
Wes FARRELL (1)	3414
Otis BLACKWELL (1)	1144
Eddie COOLEY (1)	1144
Ritchie VALENS (1)	965
Rick DERRINGER (1)	227
Lou COURTNEY (1)	171
Dennis LAMBERT (1)	171
Richard GOTTEHRER (2)	116
Jon STROLL (1)	64
Jeff BARRY (1)	61
Bob FELDMAN (1)	52
Jerry GOLDSTEIN (1)	52
Doc POMUS (1)	52
Mort SHUMAN (1)	52
Randy ZEHRINGER (1)	9.3

A TASTE OF HONEY ►443 (4) [6]	11153
Janice JOHNSON (2)	3876
Perry KIBBLE (2)	3876
Buzz CASON (1)	1030
Snuff GARRETT (1)	1030
Hachidai NAKAMURA (1)	1030
Smokey ROBINSON (1)	311

HONEY CONE ►444 (8) [8]	11147
General JOHNSON (5)	3720
Greg PERRY (4)	3539
Barney PERKINS (1)	2134
Angelo BOND (1)	670
Lamont DOZIER (4)	271
Ronald DUNBAR (4)	271
Brian HOLLAND (4)	271
Eddie HOLLAND (4)	271

YES ►445 (10) [9]	11100
Jon ANDERSON (6)	3223
Trevor RABIN (6)	2507
Chris SQUIRE (6)	2078

YES ▶445 (10) [9] *Cont'd*	**11100**
Trevor HORN (2)	1807
Steve HOWE (2)	855
Paul SIMON (1)	394
Bill BRUFORD (1)	112
Tony KAYE (1)	62
Alan (2) WHITE (1)	62
PINK FLOYD ▶446 (5) [6]	**11076**
Roger WATERS (4)	10931
David GILMOUR (2)	70
Jon CARIN (1)	22
Bob EZRIN (1)	22
Anthony MOORE (1)	22
Rick WRIGHT (1)	11
Rita COOLIDGE ▶447 (12) [21]	**11043**
Boz SCAGGS (1)	2987
Gary JACKSON (1)	1669
Raynard MINER (1)	1669
Carl William SMITH (1)	1669
Tom SNOW (1)	737
Carole Bayer SAGER (2)	387
Smokey ROBINSON (1)	355
Robert ROGERS (1)	355
John BARRY (1)	246
Tim RICE (1)	246
Peter ALLEN (1)	231
Bruce ROBERTS (1)	156
Gerry GOFFIN (1)	58
Carole KING (1)	58
David LASLEY (1)	37
Allee WILLIS (1)	37
Otis BLACKWELL (1)	36
Eddie COOLEY (1)	36
Priscilla COOLIDGE (1)	36
Booker T. JONES Jr. (1)	36
Donna WEISS (1)	2.2
Kay STARR ▶448 (29) [50]	**11020**
Roy ALFRED (1)	3835
Shorty ALLEN (1)	3835
Irving TAYLOR (7)	294
Camillo BARGONI (1)	248
Al STILLMAN (1)	248
Harlan HOWARD (1)	246
Buck OWENS (1)	246
Hal STANLEY (6)	216
TRADITIONAL (1)	127
Marty Dorn ROBERTS (1)	97
Larry COLEMAN (1)	91
Fred EBB (1)	91
Paul KLEIN (1)	91
Joe SHAPIRO (1)	90
Lou STALLMAN (1)	90
James CAVANAUGH (1)	88
John REDMOND (1)	88
Frank WELDON (1)	88
Leonard JOY (1)	83
Alice D. SIMMS (1)	83
Arthur ALTMAN (1)	78
Lou SINGER (1)	78
Damita Jo GIBSON (1)	77
Edgar LESLIE (1)	72
Kurt FELTZ (1)	61
Heinz GIETZ (1)	61
Donald SIMMS (1)	61
Bennie BENJAMIN (1)	59
George David WEISS (1)	59
Les VANDYKE (1)	38
Bob HILLIARD (1)	30
Sylvia DEE (1)	13
Sid LIPPMAN (1)	13
George CAMPBELL (1)	13

Marvin MOORE (1)	13
Guy SINGER (1)	8.4
Johnny BURKE (1)	1.9
Al FRISCH (1)	1.9
Ruth FREED (1)	1.6
David SAXON (1)	1.6
Marguerite MONNOT (1)	0.0
Geoffrey PARSONS (1)	0.0
Edith PIAF (1)	0.0
Bill ANSON (1)	0.0
Dorinda MORGAN (1)	0.0
Edward ELISCU (1)	0.0
Billy ROSE (1)	0.0
Vincent YOUMANS (1)	0.0
Mann CURTIS (1)	0.0
Virgilio PANZUTI (1)	0.0
The TYMES ▶449 (10) [17]	**10976**
William E. JACKSON III (3)	2203
Roy STRAIGIS (2)	2202
George R. WILLIAMS (1)	2189
Christopher JACKSON (1)	1049
Sherman EDWARDS (1)	834
Ben RALEIGH (1)	834
Jimmy WISNER (3)	368
Norma MENDOZA (1)	355
Wolfgang Amadeus MOZART (1)	355
Bob MERRILL (1)	211
Jule STYNE (1)	211
Ray EVANS (1)	50
Jay LIVINGSTON (1)	50
Charles Henry JACKSON Jr. (1)	28
Marvin YANCY (1)	28
Johanna HALL (1)	4.3
John HALL (1)	4.3
The DELLS ▶450 (25) [31]	**10974**
Robert Eugene MILLER (9)	3318
Johnny FUNCHES (1)	899
Marvin JUNIOR (1)	899
Wade FLEMONS (1)	571
Barrett STRONG (1)	571
Michael McGILL (1)	531
Arthur HAMILTON (1)	524
Raynard MINER (1)	481
Marv JOHNSON (1)	403
Henry WILLIAMS (1)	403
Terry CALLIER (2)	377
Larry WADE (2)	377
Steve CROPPER (1)	226
Otis REDDING (1)	226
Tony HESTER (1)	220
Bryan BLACKBURN (1)	175
Pierre LEMAIRE (1)	175
André POPP (1)	175
Don DAVIS (1)	54
James Anthony DEAN (1)	54
Herbie ROSS (1)	54
Lee ANDREWS (1)	47
Bernice DAVIS (1)	47
Douglas HENDERSON (1)	47
Miriam UNIMAN (1)	47
Billy HILL (1)	32
Jackie AVERY (1)	27
Willie SCHOFIELD (1)	10
Billy DAVIS (1)	2.7
Shirley HALL (1)	2.7
Alan FREED (1)	0.0
OLIVER ▶451 (5) [10]	**10965**
Rod McKUEN (1)	5653
Galt MacDERMOT (1)	1469
James RADO (1)	1469
Gerome RAGNI (1)	1469
Margo GURYAN (1)	821

Barry MANN (1)	38
Cynthia WEIL (1)	38
Richie GRASSO (1)	2.6
Gary ILLINGWORTH (1)	2.6
Myrna MARCH (1)	2.6
BADFINGER ▶452 (7) [5]	**10876**
Pete HAM (4)	7639
Paul McCARTNEY (1)	3078
Tom EVANS (1)	54
Joseph TANSINI (1)	54
Joey MOLLAND (1)	50
Tab HUNTER ▶453 (7) [13]	**10814**
Ric CARTEY (1)	4226
Carole JOYNER (1)	4226
Bernie LOWE (1)	460
Kal MANN (1)	460
Jenny Lou CARSON (1)	408
Neville FLEESON (1)	365
Albert VON TILZER (1)	365
Craig SHANE (1)	67
Rod SHERWOOD (1)	67
Duke ELLINGTON (1)	51
Bob RUSSELL (1)	51
Jimmy KENNEDY (1)	35
Hugh WILLIAMS (1)	35
Domenico MODUGNO ▶454 (5) [7]	**10793**
Domenico MODUGNO (4)	5405
Franco MIGLIACCI (1)	5386
Dino VERDE (2)	1.3
Milt GABLER (1)	0.5
Vincenzo Di PAOLA (1)	0.0
Mario PANZERI (1)	0.0
Alessandro TACCANI (1)	0.0
Karyn WHITE ▶455 (5) [9]	**10780**
Karyn WHITE (2)	1829
Kenneth EDMONDS (3)	1609
Antonio REID (3)	1609
Daryl SIMMONS (3)	1609
James Samuel HARRIS (1)	1362
Terry LEWIS (1)	1362
William HARMON (1)	467
Bruce STERLING (1)	467
Christopher TROY (1)	467
DIRE STRAITS ▶456 (7) [2]	**10757**
Mark KNOPFLER (7)	7939
STING (1)	2818
DION And The BELMONTS ▶457 (9) [15]	**10735**
Doc POMUS (1)	1725
Mort SHUMAN (1)	1725
Lorenz HART (1)	1592
Richard RODGERS (1)	1592
Ernie MARESCA (2)	722
Ken HECHT (1)	506
Cole PORTER (1)	425
Melvin ANDERSON (1)	401
Ricardo WEEKS (1)	401
Sid JACOBSON (1)	331
Lou STALLMAN (1)	331
Leigh HARLINE (1)	305
Ned WASHINGTON (1)	305
Mike ANTHONY (1)	187
Stan LEBOWSKY (1)	187
Joni JAMES ▶458 (38) [62]	**10720**
Jimmie NABBIE (1)	1736
George David WEISS (2)	1254
Bennie BENJAMIN (1)	1247
Benny DAVIS (3)	963
Abner SILVER (1)	731
Sammy GALLOP (1)	476

David SAXON (1)	476
Nick ACQUAVIVA (3)	345
Helene HUDGINS (1)	243
Edith LINDEMAN (1)	230
Carl STUTZ (1)	230
Robert DAY (1)	215
Buddy KAYE (1)	215
Jimmie CRANE (2)	206
Al JACOBS (2)	206
Bobby WORTH (1)	198
J. Fred COOTS (1)	192
Sammy CAHN (3)	156
Norman GIMBEL (1)	145
Paul INSETTA (1)	129
Jule STYNE (1)	124
Boudleaux BRYANT (1)	89
Floyd CRAMER (1)	89
Skeeter DAVIS (1)	89
Robert MELLIN (1)	77
Richard SAVAGE (1)	77
Marjorie GOETSCHIUS (1)	43
Edward POLA (1)	43
Milton AGER (1)	39
Nicholas BRODSZKY (2)	33
Russell FAITH (1)	29
Clarence KEHNER (1)	29
Kenny JACOBSON (1)	26
Victor YOUNG (2)	26
Bob ELLSWORTH (1)	22
Richard HOWARD (1)	22
Russ MORGAN (1)	22
Stella UNGER (1)	21
Leigh HARLINE (1)	16
Ned WASHINGTON (1)	16
Ed KASSNER (1)	16
Desmond O'CONNOR (1)	16
TRADITIONAL (1)	16
Fred WEATHERLY (1)	16
Pee Wee KING (1)	15
Chilton PRICE (1)	15
Redd STEWART (1)	15
Al STILLMAN (1)	13
Ben WEISMAN (1)	13
Lew DOUGLAS (1)	7.8
Jim KRUM (1)	7.8
Cliff PARMAN (1)	7.8
Otis BLACKWELL (1)	7.2
Jacqueline BURKS (1)	7.2
Henry NEMO (1)	5.7
Edward HEYMAN (1)	5.2
Lee DANIELS (1)	1.6
Richard HAYMAN (1)	1.6
Barry PARKER (1)	1.6
Peter UDELL (1)	0.8
Mary Jane BABBITT (1)	0.0
Irving BERLIN (1)	0.0
LITTLE EVA ▶459 (5) [6]	**10713**
Gerry GOFFIN (5)	5053
Carole KING (4)	4817
Herbert COX (1)	237
Jack KELLER (1)	237
Morris LEVY (1)	237
TRADITIONAL (1)	133
NEW VAUDEVILLE BAND ▶460 (2) [2]	**10709**
Geoff STEPHENS (2)	10666
John CARTER (1)	43
The MARCELS ▶461 (4) [10]	**10691**
Lorenz HART (1)	4524
Richard RODGERS (1)	4524
Al HOFFMAN (1)	707

John KLENNER (1)	707
Ernie BURNETTE (1)	41
George NORTON (1)	41
Maybelle WATSON (1)	41
George GERSHWIN (1)	36
Ira GERSHWIN (1)	36
DuBose HEYWARD (1)	36
Jimmy JONES ▶462 (6) [14]	**10683**
Clint BALLARD Jr. (1)	2245
Fred TOBIAS (1)	2245
Andrew BARKSDALE (1)	1417
Otis BLACKWELL (1)	1417
Jimmy JONES (1)	1417
Charles MERENSTEIN (1)	1417
Lockie EDWARDS (1)	170
Waldense HALL (1)	170
Gary GELD (1)	81
Peter UDELL (1)	81
Don COVAY (1)	8.7
Margaret REDDY (1)	3.9
Dorothy STIPE (1)	3.9
Joseph WYANT (1)	3.9
Lawrence WELK/Orchestra ▶463 (35) [50]	**10676**
Heino GAZE (1)	6283
Frank DeVOL (1)	640
Henry MANCINI (1)	600
Lee DAVID (1)	549
Billy ROSE (1)	549
Floyd CRAMER (1)	411
Kurt WEILL (1)	354
Marguerite MONNOT (1)	238
Franz DOELLE (1)	195
Stan JONES (1)	177
Norman LUBOFF (1)	154
Carl-Henrik NORIN (1)	82
Max CROOK (1)	73
Del SHANNON (1)	73
Frank SCOTT (1)	73
Edmund KOETSCHER (1)	54
Rudi LINDT (1)	54
George CATES (2)	47
Jerry LORDAN (1)	30
Sonny BONO (1)	16
Harry VON TILZER (1)	13
TRADITIONAL (1)	5.6
Alan Jay LERNER (3)	1.6
Frederick LOEWE (3)	1.6
Sammy GALLOP (1)	1.1
Frankie MASTERS (1)	1.1
Larry GORDON (1)	0.2
Margaret GORDON (1)	0.2
Sam LEWIS (1)	0.0
Mabel WAYNE (1)	0.0
Joe YOUNG (1)	0.0
Georgio FORLI (1)	0.0
MANTOVANI (1)	0.0
Angelo PICCIONI (1)	0.0
Walter DONALDSON (1)	0.0
Norman MALKIN (1)	0.0
Freddy MORGAN (1)	0.0
Jessie CAVANAUGH (1)	0.0
William ENGVICK (1)	0.0
Gene ADKINSON (1)	0.0
Wade BUFF (1)	0.0
Sol QUASHA (1)	0.0
Herb YAKUS (1)	0.0
Amadeu Do VALE (1)	0.0
Jose GALHARDO (1)	0.0
Raul PORTELA (1)	0.0
Larry SULLIVAN (1)	0.0

Dorothy WRIGHT (1)	0.0
Stella UNGER (1)	0.0
Victor YOUNG (1)	0.0
Diana ROSS & Lionel RICHIE ▶464 (1) [1]	**10664**
Lionel RICHIE (1)	10664
Mr. Acker BILK ▶465 (5) [5]	**10660**
Acker BILK (2)	10177
Bob MERRILL (1)	363
Charles CHAPLIN (1)	93
Buck RAM (1)	27
David COLLETT (1)	0.0
ROYAL GUARDSMEN ▶466 (8) [15]	**10614**
Phil GERNHARD (3)	4388
Dick HOLLER (2)	4049
Lori BURTON (1)	350
Pam SAWYER (1)	350
James McCULLOUGH (1)	339
John McCULLOUGH (1)	339
Luigi CREATORE (1)	144
Hugo PERETTI (1)	144
George David WEISS (1)	144
Boomer CASTLEMAN (1)	128
Michael MURPHEY (1)	128
Billy (2) TAYLOR (1)	38
Barry WINSLOW (1)	38
Charles SOUZA (1)	29
Arnold SHAPIRO (1)	7.8
The GO-GO'S ▶467 (7) [6]	**10607**
Charlotte CAFFEY (5)	6687
Jane WIEDLIN (5)	1801
Kathy VALENTINE (2)	1388
Terry HALL (1)	719
Ron MAEL (1)	5.4
Russell MAEL (1)	5.4
THOMPSON TWINS ▶468 (11) [3]	**10602**
Tom BAILEY (11)	3747
Alannah CURRIE (11)	3747
Joe LEEWAY (8)	3108
Debbie REYNOLDS ▶469 (7) [12]	**10567**
Ray EVANS (1)	4597
Jay LIVINGSTON (1)	4597
Carl BELEW (1)	383
Shelby SINGLETON (1)	383
W.S. STEVENSON (1)	383
Bill ANDERSON (1)	143
Robert ALLEN (1)	59
Ernest KELLEY (1)	5.2
Windsor KING (1)	5.2
Joe BURKE (1)	4.9
Edgar LESLIE (1)	4.9
Wanda JACKSON (1)	0.0
Bruce HORNSBY And The RANGE ▶470 (8) [2]	**10561**
Bruce HORNSBY (8)	8013
John HORNSBY (4)	2548
Mary HOPKIN ▶471 (6) [12]	**10514**
Boris FOMIN (1)	4207
Gene RASKIN (1)	4207
John LENNON (1)	634
Paul McCARTNEY (1)	634
Philamore LINCOLN (1)	494
Ray EVANS (1)	129
Jay LIVINGSTON (1)	129
John CARTER (1)	28

Geoff STEPHENS (1)	28
Errol BROWN (1)	7.8
Margaret WILSON (1)	7.8
Tony WILSON (1)	7.8
HOT CHOCOLATE ▶472 (8) [3]	**10514**
Errol BROWN (7)	6318
Tony WILSON (3)	3741
Russ BALLARD (1)	454
Melissa MANCHESTER ▶473 (14) [22]	**10511**
Carole Bayer SAGER (5)	2390
Dean PITCHFORD (1)	1840
Tom SNOW (1)	1840
Melissa MANCHESTER (6)	1747
Peter ALLEN (1)	976
Lisa Dal BELLO (1)	360
Vini PONCIA (1)	316
Steve DORFF (1)	172
Gary HARJU (1)	172
Larry HERBSTRITT (1)	172
Jan BUCKINGHAM (1)	133
Steve BUCKINGHAM (1)	133
Mark Eugene GRAY (1)	133
Robbie NEVIL (1)	23
Brock WALSH (1)	23
Terry BRITTEN (1)	16
Billy LIVSEY (1)	16
Marvin HAMLISCH (1)	15
Raynard MINER (1)	9.4
Carl William SMITH (1)	9.4
Keith FORSEY (1)	8.1
Giorgio MORODER (1)	8.1
The FOUNDATIONS ▶474 (5) [3]	**10506**
Tony MACAULAY (5)	5253
Michael D'ABO (1)	3695
John MacLEOD (4)	1558
Gerry RAFFERTY ▶475 (6) [1]	**10483**
Gerry RAFFERTY (6)	10483
SSgt. Barry SADLER ▶476 (2) [4]	**10468**
Barry SADLER (2)	5086
Robin MOORE (1)	4789
Phyllis LANDSBERG (1)	297
Leonard WHITCUP (1)	297
GERRY And The PACEMAKERS ▶477 (12) [13]	**10450**
Gerry MARSDEN (6)	4297
Mitch MURRAY (2)	2416
Bobby DARIN (1)	977
Les CHADWICK (1)	696
Leo MAGUIRE (1)	696
Fred MARSDEN (1)	696
Ralph MIRANDA (1)	486
Oscar HAMMERSTEIN (1)	92
Richard RODGERS (1)	92
Bobby EDWARDS (1)	0.0
Terry FELL (1)	0.0
Fred HENLEY (1)	0.0
Mildred IMES (1)	0.0
The CRESTS ▶478 (11) [13]	**10377**
Allyson KHENT (4)	3507
Luther DIXON (1)	2718
Billy Dawn SMITH (8)	2456
Ollie JONES (1)	742
Lee CATHY (1)	544
Alicia EVELYN (2)	376

Miriam LEWIS (1)	14
Bert KEYES (1)	6.2
Harry AKST (1)	3.3
Gus KAHN (1)	3.3
Richard WHITING (1)	3.3
Al BROWNE (1)	2.5
John MASTRANGELO (1)	2.5
ENGLAND DAN & John Ford COLEY ▶479 (9) [11]	**10373**
Parker McGEE (2)	5667
Todd RUNDGREN (1)	1383
Jeffrey COMANOR (1)	1174
Randy GOODRUM (1)	1083
John Ford COLEY (2)	761
Tim RYAN (1)	92
Bob YEOMANS (1)	92
Bob GUNDRY (1)	49
Dan SEALS (1)	49
Greg GUIDRY (1)	12
Denny HENSON (1)	12
The SUPREMES ▶480 (12) [16]	**10347**
Frank Edward WILSON (3)	2701
Smokey ROBINSON (3)	1829
Kenny THOMAS (1)	1715
Lou STALLMAN (1)	1249
Vince DiMIRCO (1)	908
Leonard CASTON (1)	707
Kathy WAKEFIELD (1)	707
Harold BEATTY (2)	134
Brian HOLLAND (2)	134
Eddie HOLLAND (1)	128
Pam SAWYER (1)	78
Stephen SCHWARTZ (1)	37
Reggie BROWN (1)	5.3
Stafford FLOYD (1)	5.3
Ira TUCKER Jr. (1)	5.3
Stevie WONDER (1)	5.3
Gary WRIGHT ▶481 (6) [3]	**10335**
Gary WRIGHT (6)	9897
Ali THOMSON (1)	429
Richard REICHEG (1)	9.3
STING ▶482 (9) [2]	**10327**
STING (9)	9911
Sergei PROKOFIEV (1)	416
Nino TEMPO & April STEVENS ▶483 (9) [17]	**10325**
Mitchell PARISH (2)	3983
Peter DeROSE (1)	3750
Richard COBURN (1)	509
Vincent ROSE (1)	509
John SCHONBERGER (1)	509
Nino TEMPO (3)	340
Jerry RIOPELLE (2)	313
Hoagy CARMICHAEL (1)	232
Irving CAESAR (1)	49
Vincent YOUMANS (1)	49
Joe SAMPLE (1)	27
Gus ARNHEIM (1)	16
Charles N. DANIELS (1)	16
Harry TOBIAS (1)	16
Doc DAUGHERTY (1)	2.2
Al NEIBURG (1)	2.2
Ellis REYNOLDS (1)	2.2
BAD COMPANY ▶484 (15) [10]	**10246**
Mick RALPHS (5)	5014
Paul RODGERS (5)	2416
Brian HOWE (5)	913
Terry THOMAS (4)	890

BAD COMPANY ►484 (15) [10] ***Cont'd***	**10246**
Jerry LEIBER (1)	265
Doc POMUS (1)	265
Mike STOLLER (1)	265
Raymond BURRELL (2)	177
Chris FRETWELL (1)	23
Simon KIRKE (1)	17
The YARDBIRDS ►485 (9) [12]	**10235**
Graham GOULDMAN (2)	4421
Jim McCARTY (3)	1072
Keith RELF (3)	1072
Ellas McDANIEL (1)	919
Paul SAMWELL-SMITH (2)	909
Jeff BECK (2)	480
Tony HAZZARD (1)	329
Chris DREJA (1)	317
Harold SPIRO (1)	206
Phil WAINMAN (1)	206
Jimmy PAGE (1)	163
Harry NILSSON (1)	141
AMBROSIA ►486 (8) [7]	**10215**
David PACK (7)	9400
Joe PUERTA (3)	511
John LENNON (1)	131
Paul McCARTNEY (1)	131
Burleigh DRUMMOND (1)	14
Christopher NORTH (1)	14
Kurt VONNEGUT (1)	14
Wayne NEWTON ►487 (21) [45]	**10205**
Peter CALLANDER (1)	2828
Geoff STEPHENS (1)	2828
Bert KAEMPFERT (2)	502
Milt GABLER (1)	482
Kurt SCHWABACH (1)	482
Roy C. BENNETT (1)	353
Sid TEPPER (1)	353
Chris GANTRY (1)	334
Tony ROMEO (1)	250
Kye FLEMING (1)	204
Dennis W. MORGAN (1)	204
Chris ARNOLD (1)	145
David MARTIN (1)	145
Geoff MORROW (1)	145
Neville FLEESON (1)	103
Albert VON TILZER (1)	103
Rudy CLARK (1)	92
Bobby DARIN (1)	92
Barry MANN (1)	58
Cynthia WEIL (1)	58
Raul ABEYTA (1)	53
Gary USHER (1)	53
Eddie SNYDER (2)	50
Larry KUSIK (1)	30
James LAST (1)	30
Hans BRADTKE (1)	28
Henry MAYER (1)	28
Johnny MERCER (1)	28
Herbert REHBEIN (1)	20
Charles SINGLETON (1)	20
Howard GREENFIELD (1)	18
Neil SEDAKA (1)	18
Buck RAM (1)	12
Barry GIBB (1)	11
Maurice GIBB (1)	11
Robin GIBB (1)	11
Pierre GROSCOLAS (1)	3.2
Michel JOURDAN (1)	3.2
Donny MARCHAND (1)	3.2
M. McGINNIS (1)	3.2

Ray HEINDORF (1)	2.2
M.K. JEROME (1)	2.2
Ted KOEHLER (1)	2.2
Roger MILLER (1)	1.9
Johnnie RAY (1)	1.9
Freda PAYNE ►488 (6) [9]	**10201**
Lamont DOZIER (5)	2120
Brian HOLLAND (5)	2120
Ronald DUNBAR (2)	1706
Eddie HOLLAND (2)	1706
Angelo BOND (2)	880
General JOHNSON (1)	723
Greg PERRY (1)	723
Norma TONEY (1)	205
Daphne DUMAS (1)	19
SIMPLE MINDS ►489 (5) [5]	**10189**
Keith FORSEY (1)	2175
Steve SCHIFF (1)	2175
Charles BURCHILL (4)	2004
Jim KERR (4)	2004
Michael MacNEIL (3)	1831
James DARREN ►490 (11) [21]	**10183**
Gloria SHAYNE (2)	5205
Gerry GOFFIN (1)	776
Carole KING (1)	776
Barry MANN (2)	721
Cynthia WEIL (2)	721
Fred KARGER (1)	271
Patti WASHINGTON (1)	271
Doc POMUS (1)	222
Mort SHUMAN (1)	222
Ralph MONTELLO (1)	139
Billy Dawn SMITH (1)	139
Domenico COLAROSSI (1)	127
Marian GRUDEFF (1)	127
Ray JESSEL (1)	127
Nino OLIVIERO (1)	127
Hubert GIRAUD (1)	56
Phil TRIM (1)	56
Carol CONNORS (1)	33
Bill CONTI (1)	33
Ayn ROBBINS (1)	33
Howard GREENFIELD (1)	6.9
DANNY & The JUNIORS ►491 (9) [7]	**10167**
David WHITE (5)	3450
John MADARA (4)	2853
Artie SINGER (2)	2843
Kal MANN (1)	553
Bob CREWE (2)	215
Frank SLAY (2)	215
Joe TERRANOVA (1)	37
FABIAN ►492 (13) [18]	**10164**
Ollie JONES (1)	2838
Doc POMUS (4)	2265
Mort SHUMAN (4)	2265
Ken DARBY (1)	1169
Bert SALMIRS (1)	220
Wally ZOBER (1)	220
Bobby DOYLE (1)	194
Jimmy DUNCAN (1)	194
Clyde NORRIS (1)	166
Jerry RAGOVOY (1)	166
Leroy ROEBUCK (1)	166
Richard SHERMAN (1)	115
Robert SHERMAN (1)	115
Howard GREENFIELD (1)	20
Barry MANN (1)	20
Russell FAITH (1)	19
Fred AHLERT (1)	5.9

Joe YOUNG (1)	5.9
BACHMAN-TURNER OVERDRIVE ►493 (14) [8]	**10160**
Randy BACHMAN (7)	7629
C.F. TURNER (7)	1630
Robbie BACHMAN (2)	556
Blair THORNTON (3)	127
C. Mark ANTHONY (1)	73
Alice COOPER (1)	73
Kim FOWLEY (1)	73
James CLENCH (1)	1.6
Jermaine JACKSON ►494 (16) [30]	**10122**
Stevie WONDER (3)	1548
Lee GARRETT (1)	927
Jermaine JACKSON (7)	861
Ralph DINO (1)	657
Larry Di TOMASO (1)	657
Charles BASKERVILLE (1)	629
Clarence BASSETT (1)	629
William Henry MILLER (1)	629
James SHEPPARD (1)	629
Andy GOLDMARK (1)	466
Bruce ROBERTS (1)	466
Michael OMARTIAN (3)	370
Paul M. JACKSON Jr. (2)	293
Marilyn McLEOD (1)	205
Pam SAWYER (1)	205
Johnny BRISTOL (1)	156
Wade BROWN (1)	156
David H. JONES (1)	156
Don DANIELS (1)	92
Michael Larry SMITH (1)	92
Bruce SUDANO (2)	73
Dave CONLEY (1)	52
Derrick CULLER (1)	52
David TOWNSEND (1)	52
Fonce MIZELL (1)	31
Larry MIZELL (1)	31
Kenneth EDMONDS (1)	2.2
Lisa LOPES (1)	2.2
Antonio REID (1)	2.2
Daryl SIMMONS (1)	2.2
Little Peggy MARCH ►495 (5) [8]	**10118**
Arthur ALTMAN (1)	2165
Norman GIMBEL (1)	2165
Paul MAURIAT (1)	2165
Franck POURCEL (1)	2165
Luigi CREATORE (3)	475
Hugo PERETTI (3)	475
George David WEISS (3)	475
Paul ANKA (1)	33
Frankie LAINE ►496 (26) [47]	**10115**
Bob HILLIARD (1)	1733
Philip SPRINGER (1)	1733
Marty ROBBINS (1)	1278
Frank LOESSER (2)	1147
Boudleaux BRYANT (1)	482
Richard DEHR (1)	297
Terry GILKYSON (1)	297
Frank MILLER (1)	297
Larry KUSIK (1)	282
Eddie SNYDER (1)	282
Mort DIXON (1)	280
James V. MONACO (1)	280
Barry MANN (1)	152
Cynthia WEIL (1)	152
Leon ASHLEY (1)	134
Margie SINGLETON (1)	134

Frank CAPANO (1)	115
George McCONNELL (1)	115
Margie MORRIS (1)	115
Nat OSBORNE (1)	115
Ray EVANS (1)	85
Jay LIVINGSTON (1)	85
Peter DeANGELIS (1)	75
Jean SAWYER (1)	75
Bob MERRILL (1)	69
Richard ADLER (1)	59
Jerry ROSS (1)	59
Dick MONDA (1)	39
Ned WASHINGTON (2)	37
Dimitri TIOMKIN (1)	31
Bob NOLAN (1)	27
Craig EVANS (1)	11
Dorcas COCHRAN (1)	7.5
Kay TWOMEY (1)	7.5
Ben WEISMAN (1)	7.5
Fred WISE (1)	7.5
Paul WESTON (1)	5.8
Robert ALLEN (1)	2.6
Al STILLMAN (1)	2.6
Lou GARISTO (1)	2.3
Rudolf FRIML (1)	0.0
Brian HOOKER (1)	0.0
Lotar OLIAS (1)	0.0
Walter ROTHENBURG (1)	0.0
Carl SIGMAN (1)	0.0
Stephan WEISS (1)	0.0
Don ROBERTSON (1)	0.0
Etta JAMES ►497 (29) [46]	**10033**
Billy DAVIS (5)	965
Leroy KIRKLAND (3)	644
Pearl WOODS (3)	644
Otis REDDING (1)	589
Tony CLARKE (2)	529
Edwin BOCAGE (1)	470
Paul GAYTEN (1)	470
Berry GORDY (2)	347
Floyd HUNT (1)	326
Mack GORDON (1)	320
Harry WARREN (1)	320
Gwen GORDY (1)	316
Clarence CARTER (1)	301
Marcus DANIEL (1)	301
Wilbur TERRELL (1)	301
Etta JAMES (2)	300
Milton AGER (1)	283
Jean SCHWARTZ (1)	283
Ned WEVER (1)	283
Johnny MERCER (2)	270
Deborah CHESSLER (1)	264
Bob FORSHEE (1)	258
Sonny BONO (1)	239
Fred JOHNSON (1)	235
Ronny MITCHELL (1)	131
Leon BONDS (1)	123
Saul BERNIE (1)	108
James P. JOHNSON (1)	108
Stella UNGER (1)	108
Billy SHERRILL (1)	39
Glenn SUTTON (1)	39
Sonny WOODS (1)	31
Jimmy REED (1)	23
Trevor LAWRENCE (1)	13
Gabriel MEKLER (1)	13
Catherine WILLIAMSON (1)	13
Rube BLOOM (1)	7.2
Burt BACHARACH (1)	5.2
Bob HILLIARD (1)	5.2
Ray CHARLES (1)	2.2

Etta JAMES ▶497 (29) [46] *Cont'd*	**10033**
Barbara BELLE (1)	1.4
Anita LEONARD (1)	1.4
Louis PRIMA (1)	1.4
Stan RHODES (1)	1.4
Hank BALLARD (1)	0.0
Johnny OTIS (1)	0.0
The NEWBEATS ▶498 (7) [10]	**10024**
Larry PARKS (2)	3160
Jay TURNBOW (2)	3160
John D. LOUDERMILK (1)	1158
Don GANT (1)	880
Joe MELSON (1)	880
Louis MATHIS (1)	244
Marc MATHIS (1)	244
Robert GUIDRY (1)	121
Doug KERSHAW (1)	98
Bob FINNICUM (1)	79
C & C MUSIC FACTORY ▶499 (4) [2]	**9991**
Robert CLIVILLES (4)	5110
Frederick B. WILLIAMS (3)	4881
FOUR PREPS ▶500 (30) [41]	**9911**
Bruce BELLAND (8)	3994
Glen LARSON (8)	3994
Hal SPINA (1)	674
TRADITIONAL (2)	154
Dewayne BLACKWELL (1)	130
Dallas FRAZIER (1)	130
Otto HARBACH (1)	65
Jerome KERN (1)	65
Jacques CASCALES (1)	65
Gene ROLAND (1)	65
Tom GLAZER (1)	65
Dave GUARD (1)	65
Doc POMUS (1)	65
Mort SHUMAN (1)	65
Bebe BLAKE (1)	31
Jack HOFFMAN (1)	31
Ruth LOWE (1)	24
Dick GOSTING (1)	24
Ivan ULZ (1)	18
Lew POLLACK (1)	13
Erno RAPEE (1)	13
Sammy FAIN (1)	12
Paul Francis WEBSTER (1)	12
Al HOFFMAN (1)	12
John KLENNER (1)	12
Dion DiMUCCI (1)	12
Ernie MARESCA (1)	12
Alan HOOD (1)	8.7
Richard LORING (1)	8.7
Royal LOVELL (1)	8.0
Alfred Hart MILES (1)	8.0
Charles A. ZIMMERMANN (1)	8.0
Fred KARGER (1)	7.7
Patti WASHINGTON (1)	7.7
Heino GAZE (1)	7.7
Lee POCKRISS (1)	7.7
Paul VANCE (1)	7.7
Webb PIERCE (1)	4.4
Mel TILLIS (1)	4.4
Fred ROSE (1)	0.2
Hank WILLIAMS (1)	0.2
Shaun CASSIDY ▶501 (5) [7]	**9897**
Eric CARMEN (2)	5011
Jeff BARRY (1)	1504
Ellie GREENWICH (1)	1504
Phil SPECTOR (1)	1504
John SEBASTIAN (1)	359
Bruce ROBERTS (1)	8.1
Carole Bayer SAGER (1)	8.1
Alan PARSONS Project ▶502 (15) [2]	**9826**
Alan PARSONS (15)	4913
Eric WOOLFSON (15)	4913
Bobby BLAND ▶503 (45) [32]	**9775**
Deadric MALONE (28)	6052
Joe SCOTT (5)	1028
Aaron WALKER (1)	701
Al BRAGGS (1)	267
Oscar PERRY (1)	250
Vernon MORRISON (1)	196
Belford HENDRICKS (1)	181
Clyde OTIS (1)	181
Ahmet ERTEGUN (1)	155
Van WALLS (1)	155
Joe VEASEY (2)	111
James B. ODEN (1)	82
Gilbert CAPLE (1)	76
Clyde WILSON (1)	67
Pearl WOODS (3)	63
Charlie RICH (1)	56
Brook BENTON (1)	27
Harvey PRICE (2)	27
Dan WALSH (2)	27
Dave (2) CLARK (1)	25
Andre WILLIAMS (1)	13
Steve BARRI (1)	9.7
Michael OMARTIAN (1)	9.7
Billy ECKSTINE (1)	2.5
Earl HINES (1)	2.5
Charles Mose BROWN (1)	2.3
Johnny Dudley MOORE (1)	2.3
Eddie WILLIAMS (1)	2.3
Sonny THOMPSON (1)	1.7
Jessie Mae ROBINSON (1)	1.0
Merle HAGGARD (1)	0.7
Bonnie OWENS (1)	0.7
SINGING NUN ▶504 (2) [1]	**9739**
Jeanine DECKERS (2)	9739
Bobby "Boris" PICKETT ▶505 (5) [5]	**9698**
Leonard L. CAPIZZI (3)	4623
Bobby PICKETT (3)	4623
Charles UNDERWOOD (1)	441
Joe SHERMAN (1)	5.0
Noel SHERMAN (1)	5.0
Harold MELVIN And The BLUE NOTES ▶506 (10) [6]	**9691**
Kenneth GAMBLE (5)	3220
Leon HUFF (5)	3220
Victor CARSTARPHEN (4)	1061
Gene McFADDEN (4)	1061
John WHITEHEAD (4)	1061
Derek FLOYD (1)	68
The TROGGS ▶507 (5) [2]	**9665**
Chip TAYLOR (1)	6420
Reg PRESLEY (4)	3244
Howard JONES ▶508 (10) [2]	**9658**
Howard JONES (10)	9405
William BRYANT (1)	253
Rupert HOLMES ▶509 (7) [1]	**9622**
Rupert HOLMES (7)	9622
John TRAVOLTA And Olivia NEWTON-JOHN ▶510 (2) [3]	**9572**
John FARRAR (1)	6783
Warren CASEY (1)	1395
Jim JACOBS (1)	1395
Ike & Tina TURNER ▶511 (26) [23]	**9540**
Ike TURNER (13)	4035
John FOGERTY (1)	2683
Tina TURNER (5)	1191
Sylvester STEWART (1)	690
Jessie HILL (1)	377
John LENNON (1)	174
Paul McCARTNEY (1)	174
Jerry BUTLER (1)	43
Otis REDDING (1)	43
Leon WARE (1)	32
Calvin LANE (1)	22
Philip REESE (1)	22
Jane BOSSUNG (1)	10
Jeff BARRY (2)	8.8
Ellie GREENWICH (2)	8.8
Phil SPECTOR (2)	8.8
Steve CROPPER (1)	2.4
Donald "Duck" DUNN (1)	2.4
Al JACKSON (1)	2.4
Booker T. JONES Jr. (1)	2.4
Carl WELLS (1)	2.4
Wayne Carson THOMPSON (1)	2.2
Jesse JAMES (1)	1.5
Peter CETERA ▶512 (5) [6]	**9511**
Peter CETERA (4)	3132
David FOSTER (1)	2066
Bobby CALDWELL (1)	1623
Paul GORDON (1)	1623
Patrick Raymond LEONARD (2)	994
Amos GALPIN (1)	72
OHIO EXPRESS ▶513 (10) [13]	**9481**
Joey LEVINE (6)	4057
Artie RESNICK (1)	2088
Kris RESNICK (2)	1509
Joey DAY (1)	479
Lou ZERATO (1)	479
Steve FELDMAN (2)	398
Graham GOULDMAN (1)	122
Peter BARNFATHER (1)	72
John CARTER (1)	72
Marc BELLACK (1)	63
Jerry KASENETZ (1)	48
Jeff KATZ (1)	48
J.J. WOODS (1)	48
WHITESNAKE ▶514 (8) [5]	**9480**
David COVERDALE (8)	4624
Bernie MARSDEN (3)	2416
John SYKES (3)	1938
Adrian VANDENBERG (2)	271
Micky MOODY (2)	232
Luther VANDROSS ▶515 (16) [15]	**9460**
Luther VANDROSS (11)	3399
Marcus MILLER (6)	1614
David Leland ELLIOTT (1)	1105
Terry STEELE (1)	1105
Teddy VANN (1)	1062
Nat ADDERLEY Jr. (2)	682
Hubert EAVES III (1)	219
John Vernon ANDERSON (1)	163
Sam COOKE (1)	96
Bonnie BRAMLETT (1)	2.5
Delaney BRAMLETT (1)	2.5
Leon RUSSELL (1)	2.5
Morris BROADNAX (1)	2.5
Clarence PAUL (1)	2.5
Stevie WONDER (1)	2.5
Steve MILLER ▶516 (3) [1]	**9456**
Steve MILLER (3)	9456
Jeannie C. RILEY ▶517 (5) [4]	**9442**
Tom T. HALL (1)	8451
Margaret LEWIS (3)	400
Mira SMITH (3)	400
Ralph MURPHY (1)	191
DALE & GRACE ▶518 (5) [8]	**9434**
Don HARRIS (1)	3796
Dewey TERRY (1)	3796
Jake GRAFFAGNINO (1)	838
Joseph NOEL (1)	838
Louis MATHIS (1)	75
Marc MATHIS (1)	75
Allen BUNN (1)	11
June SPARKS (1)	4.3
Tommy JAMES ▶519 (14) [8]	**9431**
Tommy JAMES (14)	4715
Robert L. KING (10)	3973
Ronald SEROTA (1)	527
Ritchie CORDELL (1)	155
Joey GRECO (1)	59
John ANDALORO (1)	1.1
Joel DIAMOND (1)	1.1
Peter LUCIA (1)	1.1
Harry BELAFONTE ▶520 (15) [16]	**9378**
TRADITIONAL (3)	4751
Lord BURGESS (5)	1994
Lord MELODY (1)	1664
Harry BELAFONTE (4)	545
Jester HAIRSTON (1)	285
Robert ALLEN (1)	62
Bob HILLIARD (1)	62
Ray CHARLES (1)	11
Marshall BARER (1)	2.7
Fred HELLERMAN (2)	2.7
Paul CLAYTON (1)	0.0
Larry EHRLICH (1)	0.0
Ronnie GILBERT (1)	0.0
Lee HAYS (1)	0.0
Dave LAZAR (1)	0.0
Pete SEEGER (1)	0.0
Tom PETTY And The HEARTBREAKERS ▶521 (17) [7]	**9377**
Tom PETTY (16)	6537
Mike CAMPBELL (5)	1445
David A. STEWART (2)	627
Jeff LYNNE (2)	274
Bob DYLAN (1)	178
Sonny BONO (1)	158
Jack NITZSCHE (1)	158
The DELFONICS ▶522 (17) [7]	**9333**
William HART (14)	4408
Thom BELL (11)	4267
Barry MANN (1)	465
Allan FELDER (1)	91
Norman HARRIS (1)	91
Stan WATSON (1)	10
Wilbert HART (1)	0.0

MAIN INGREDIENT ►523 (12) [17] 9321

Ralph BAILEY (2)	1530
Ken WILLIAMS (2)	1530
Rudy CLARK (1)	1521
Vinnie BARRETT (1)	713
Bobby ELI (1)	713
John FREEMAN (1)	713
Curtis MAYFIELD (1)	589
Brian AUGER (1)	545
Donald McPHERSON (4)	345
Tony SILVESTER (3)	294
Luther SIMMONS (3)	294
Ed TOWNSEND (1)	229
David Charles WILLIAMS (1)	229
Willie HUTCH (1)	24
Jacqueline HILLIARD (1)	21
Leon WARE (1)	21
Melvin KENT (1)	9.4

Major LANCE ►524 (14) [6] 9302

Curtis MAYFIELD (11)	8482
William Earl BUTLER (1)	257
Carl DAVIS (1)	257
Major LANCE (1)	257
Gerald SIMS (1)	46
Van McCOY (1)	1.9

RUBY And The ROMANTICS ►525 (8) [7] 9288

Mort GARSON (4)	3997
Bob HILLIARD (4)	3997
Leon CARR (2)	453
Earl SHUMAN (2)	453
Van McCOY (1)	326
Fred ANISFIELD (1)	31
Larry WEISS (1)	31

Jaye P. MORGAN ►526 (27) [52] 9276

Fritz ROTTER (2)	3173
Edward POLA (1)	958
Fred SPIELMAN (1)	958
Alicia EVELYN (1)	829
Carl BAREFOOT (1)	466
Carl STUTZ (1)	466
Johnny CASH (1)	439
George R. BROWN (1)	232
Albert VON TILZER (1)	232
Lou HANDMAN (1)	155
Roy TURK (1)	155
Irving CAESAR (1)	153
George GERSHWIN (1)	153
Lew BROWN (1)	88
Ray HENDERSON (1)	88
Charles TOBIAS (1)	78
Harry TOBIAS (1)	78
Henry H. TOBIAS (1)	78
Philip SPRINGER (2)	50
Redd EVANS (1)	46
Pierre DUDAN (1)	39
Mark PAUL (1)	39
Paddy ROBERTS (1)	39
Roy C. BENNETT (1)	37
Sid TEPPER (1)	37
Bill NORVAS (1)	28
Mort GARSON (1)	26
Bob HILLIARD (1)	26
Robert ALLEN (1)	21
Pat MELLIN (1)	13
Robert MELLIN (1)	13
Leon RUSSELL (1)	10
Jim BREEDLOVE (1)	9.2
Joan WHITE (1)	9.2
Lillian Hardin ARMSTRONG (1)	6.4
Sid ROBIN (1)	6.4
Bob ELLSWORTH (1)	5.1
Richard HOWARD (1)	5.1
Russ MORGAN (1)	5.1
Hoagy CARMICHAEL (1)	4.2
Mitchell PARISH (1)	4.2
Joan JAVITS (1)	3.8
Hans ZEEMAN (1)	3.8
Martin BURNS (1)	2.2
Mack DISCANT (1)	2.2
Ray PASSMAN (1)	2.2
Bob DAVIE (1)	0.7
Marvin MOORE (1)	0.7
Kenny JACOBSON (1)	0.6
Rhoda ROBERTS (1)	0.6
Peter DeROSE (1)	0.0
Billy HILL (1)	0.0

Gloria GAYNOR ►527 (8) [12] 9272

Dino FEKARIS (3)	3702
Freddie PERREN (3)	3702
Clifton DAVIS (1)	1693
Lamont DOZIER (1)	40
Brian HOLLAND (1)	40
Eddie HOLLAND (1)	40
Nancy HAMILTON (1)	27
Morgan LEWIS (1)	27
James BOLDEN (1)	0.7
Jack ROBINSON (1)	0.7
Burt BACHARACH (1)	0.5
Hal DAVID (1)	0.5

FREDDIE And The DREAMERS ►528 (5) [6] 9258

Mitch MURRAY (2)	4095
Freddie GARRITY (1)	3238
Lou COURTNEY (1)	507
Dennis LAMBERT (1)	507
Pat BEST (1)	489
Gordon MILLS (1)	421

KANSAS ►529 (15) [11] 9251

Kerry LIVGREN (8)	6371
Steve WALSH (6)	1009
Phil EHART (2)	465
Steve MORSE (2)	410
Robby STEINHARDT (1)	302
Daniel FLEISHOUR (1)	163
Robert FRAZIER (1)	163
Richard John WILLIAMS (1)	163
Dino ELEFANTE (2)	99
John ELEFANTE (2)	99
Randy GOODRUM (1)	9.2

LITTLE RICHARD ►530 (24) [24] 9247

Richard PENNIMAN (13)	3410
Robert BLACKWELL (4)	1713
Enotris JOHNSON (3)	1175
John MARASCALCO (6)	1109
Albert COLLINS (2)	387
Eskew REEDER (1)	256
Dorothy LaBOSTRIE (1)	216
Joe LUBIN (1)	216
Bobby TROUP (1)	106
John SCHULLER (1)	100
Sylvia SMITH (1)	100
Harry AKST (1)	98
Benny DAVIS (1)	98
Leo PRICE (1)	45
Edwin BOCAGE (1)	45
James SMITH (1)	45
Albert LOWE (1)	41
Travis WAMMACK (1)	41
Don COVAY (1)	14
Horace HALL (1)	14
Maybelle JACKSON (1)	9.2
William P. PITT (1)	4.9
Jerry LEIBER (1)	1.9
Mike STOLLER (1)	1.9

The EMOTIONS ►531 (11) [15] 9246

Albert Philip McKAY (3)	3715
Maurice WHITE (3)	3715
Sheila HUTCHINSON (1)	567
Skip SCARBOROUGH (1)	329
Isaac HAYES (2)	254
David PORTER (2)	254
Jeanette HAWES (1)	140
Wanda HUTCHINSON (1)	140
Dennis LAMBERT (1)	46
Brian POTTER (1)	46
Luther INGRAM (1)	11
J. Leslie McFARLAND (1)	11
Homer BANKS (1)	6.9
Carl HAMPTON (1)	6.9
Raymond Earl JACKSON (1)	6.9

Freddy FENDER ►532 (8) [12] 9239

Ben PETERS (2)	2558
Vivian KEITH (1)	2505
Wayne DUNCAN (2)	1346
Freddy FENDER (2)	1346
Sammy FAIN (1)	348
Paul Francis WEBSTER (1)	348
Ivory Joe HUNTER (1)	270
Barbara LYNN (1)	221
Huey P. MEAUX (1)	221
Inez JAMES (1)	25
Buddy PEPPER (1)	25
Larry RUSSELL (1)	25

STRAWBERRY ALARM CLOCK ►533 (6) [8] 9219

John S. CARTER (2)	3734
Tim GILBERT (2)	3734
Ed KING (3)	776
Mark WEITZ (3)	776
Roy FREEMAN (2)	155
Galt MacDERMOT (1)	15
James RADO (1)	15
Gerome RAGNI (1)	15

ZAGER & EVANS ►534 (3) [1] 9175

Rick EVANS (3)	9175

Bruce CHANNEL ►535 (5) [5] 9144

Bruce CHANNEL (3)	4466
Margaret COBB (3)	4466
Marvin MONTGOMERY (2)	135
Wayne Carson THOMPSON (1)	59
Robert Eugene OSBORN (1)	17

M.C. HAMMER ►536 (6) [11] 9129

Stanley BURRELL (6)	3395
PRINCE (1)	1073
Barbara ACKLIN (1)	779
Eugene RECORD (1)	779
Rick JAMES (1)	643
Alonzo H. MILLER (1)	643
Felton PILATE (2)	620
Vic MIZZY (1)	332
Louis BURRELL (1)	288
James EARLEY (1)	288
Michael KELLY (1)	288

Nancy SINATRA & Frank SINATRA ►537 (1) [1] 9108

C. Carson PARKS (1)	9108

The CHAMPS ►538 (9) [4] 9100

Chuck RIO (2)	6762
Dave BURGESS (5)	876
Silvano R. RAMOS (1)	733
Billy STRANGE (1)	729

Nelson RIDDLE And His Orchestra ►539 (6) [9] 9082

Amadeu Do VALE (1)	2502
Jose GALHARDO (1)	2502
Raul PORTELA (1)	2502
Nelson RIDDLE (1)	644
Bernie WAYNE (1)	489
Lionel NEWMAN (1)	424
George BASSMAN (1)	9.2
Ned WASHINGTON (1)	9.2
Dimitri TIOMKIN (1)	0.0

SANTO & JOHNNY ►540 (10) [10] 9071

Ann FARINA (6)	2773
Johnny FARINA (6)	2773
Santo FARINA (6)	2773
Fred PARRIS (1)	248
Duke ELLINGTON (1)	198
Juan TIZOL (1)	198
James Lord PIERPONT (1)	59
Ernesto LECUONA (1)	20
Jerry LEIBER (1)	15
Phil SPECTOR (1)	15

Shirley ELLIS ►541 (6) [4] 9031

Lincoln CHASE (5)	5358
Shirley ELLIS (2)	2527
Kay WERNER (1)	573
Sue WERNER (1)	573

Ernie K-DOE ►542 (6) [2] 9018

Allen TOUSSAINT (4)	8761
Ernie K-DOE (2)	257

The JACKSONS ►543 (8) [8] 8994

Michael JACKSON (5)	3946
Steven Randall JACKSON (3)	2406
Randy HANSEN (1)	1500
Jackie JACKSON (3)	456
Kathy WAKEFIELD (1)	392
Marlon JACKSON (1)	215
Kenneth EDMONDS (1)	39
Antonio REID (1)	39

.38 SPECIAL ►544 (15) [16] 8985

Jeff CARLISI (10)	2035
Don BARNES (6)	1176
Jim PETERIK (6)	1025
Max CARL (4)	825
Jim VALLANCE (4)	627
Gary O'CONNOR (1)	621
Cal CURTIS (1)	595
Frankie SULLIVAN (2)	483
Donnie VAN ZANT (4)	398
Bryan ADAMS (2)	348
Larry STEELE (2)	274
John BETTIS (1)	214
Gary SMITH (1)	116
Danny CHAUNCEY (1)	106
Pat BENATAR (1)	102
Robert White JOHNSON (1)	42

NEW EDITION ►545 (12) [14]	**8983**
Vincent BRANTLEY (2)	1887
Ricky TIMAS (2)	1887
Ray PARKER Jr. (1)	1152
James Samuel HARRIS (3)	1048
Terry LEWIS (3)	1048
Russ KRAMER (1)	434
Michael JONZUN (2)	204
Maurice STARR (2)	204
Carl WURTZ (1)	198
Richard WYATT (1)	188
Christine YARIAN (1)	188
Jesse BELVIN (1)	182
Gaynel HODGE (1)	182
Curtis Edward WILLIAMS (1)	182
Stevie B ►546 (10) [3]	**8952**
Warren BROOKS (3)	6000
STEVIE B (7)	2000
Dadgel ATABAY (3)	952
? (QUESTION MARK) & The MYSTERIANS ►547 (5) [12]	**8947**
Rudy MARTINEZ (2)	7829
Bobby BALDERAMA (1)	183
Frank LUGO (1)	183
Frank RODRIGUEZ (1)	183
Eddie SERRATO (1)	183
Sandy LINZER (1)	177
Denny RANDELL (1)	177
Joey DAY (1)	14
Alan DISCHEL (1)	14
Jim CALVERT (1)	1.1
Norman MARZANO (1)	1.1
Paul NAUMANN (1)	1.1
Linda SCOTT ►548 (12) [19]	**8909**
Linda SCOTT (2)	2028
Oscar HAMMERSTEIN (1)	1828
Jerome KERN (1)	1828
Fred AHLERT (1)	804
Roy TURK (1)	804
Bob DAVIE (2)	373
Bruno COQUATRIX (1)	195
Sammy GALLOP (1)	195
George David WEISS (1)	192
Mack GORDON (1)	190
Harry REVEL (1)	190
Cynthia STROTHER (1)	72
Eugene STROTHER (1)	72
Jeff BARRY (1)	67
Artie RESNICK (1)	67
Harold ARLEN (1)	0.9
Ted KOEHLER (1)	0.9
Burt BACHARACH (1)	0.7
Hal DAVID (1)	0.7
Paul McCARTNEY And Michael JACKSON ►549 (1) [2]	**8900**
Michael JACKSON (1)	4450
Paul McCARTNEY (1)	4450
The HILLTOPPERS ►550 (19) [32]	**8878**
Buck RAM (1)	2041
Irving GORDON (1)	806
Billy MYLES (1)	630
Rafael De LEON (1)	562
Richard DEHR (1)	562
Terry GILKYSON (1)	562
Frank MILLER (1)	562
TRADITIONAL (1)	562
James JOINER (1)	311
Jack LAWRENCE (1)	255
Joe JORDAN (1)	253
Jack McDERMOTT (1)	253
Billy VAUGHN (3)	173
Teddy POWELL (2)	165
Jim CASSIN (1)	160
Duke ENSTON (1)	160
Cy COBEN (1)	144
Bill TEMPLETON (1)	144
Cliff FRIEND (1)	126
Charles TOBIAS (1)	126
Peter DeANGELIS (1)	109
Bob MARCUCCI (1)	109
Chuck WILLIS (1)	50
Randy WOOD (1)	32
Edwin McMULLEN (1)	5.2
Louis SHELLY (1)	5.2
William E. CANTRELL (1)	4.3
Quinton CLAUNCH (1)	4.3
John L. GOLDEN (1)	0.0
Raymond HUBBELL (1)	0.0
Sigmund ROMBERG (1)	0.0
Rida Johnson YOUNG (1)	0.0
HEATWAVE ►551 (3) [1]	**8859**
Rod TEMPERTON (3)	8859
Hugo WINTERHALTER And His Orchestra ►552 (12) [17]	**8853**
Eddie HEYWOOD (2)	7100
Mario NASCIMBENE (1)	882
Norman GIMBEL (1)	276
Philippe Gerard BLOCH (1)	105
Jimmy KENNEDY (1)	105
Francis LEMARQUE (1)	77
Geoffrey PARSONS (1)	77
Rudi REVIL (1)	77
John TURNER (1)	77
Francesco FRONTINI (1)	32
Eubie BLAKE (1)	31
Luther DIXON (1)	6.0
Ollie JONES (1)	6.0
Mort GARSON (1)	4.0
Ron GOODWIN (1)	0.0
Johnny MARKS (1)	0.0
Max STEINER (1)	0.0
The RONETTES ►553 (9) [11]	**8845**
Phil SPECTOR (9)	2948
Jeff BARRY (3)	2261
Ellie GREENWICH (3)	2261
Barry MANN (2)	380
Cynthia WEIL (2)	380
Pete ANDREOLI (2)	277
Vini PONCIA (2)	277
Gerry GOFFIN (1)	25
Carole KING (1)	25
Irwin LEVINE (1)	5.9
Toni WINE (1)	5.9
TEDDY BEARS ►554 (4) [1]	**8838**
Phil SPECTOR (4)	8838
SHOCKING BLUE ►555 (4) [1]	**8804**
Robbie VAN LEEUWEN (4)	8804
Hank BALLARD And The MIDNIGHTERS ►556 (13) [10]	**8771**
Hank BALLARD (8)	7397
Billy MYLES (2)	528
John Bobby BERRY (1)	336
Don COVAY (1)	336
Jerry LEIBER (1)	59
Mike STOLLER (1)	59
Nathaniel NATHAN (1)	35
Henry GLOVER (1)	10
Michael COWAN (1)	8.9
Marty ROBBINS (1)	0.0
Barbara LEWIS ►557 (11) [14]	**8741**
Barbara LEWIS (2)	4410
Van McCOY (1)	1904
Helen MILLER (2)	683
Roger ATKINS (1)	638
Sharon McMAHAN (1)	308
Chip TAYLOR (1)	258
Billy VERA (1)	258
Grant HIGGINS (1)	107
Grady MARTIN (1)	60
Alex ZANETIS (1)	60
Howard GREENFIELD (1)	45
Gerry GOFFIN (1)	3.5
Carole KING (1)	3.5
Eddie SINGLETON (1)	3.0
PLAYER ►558 (6) [5]	**8722**
Peter BECKETT (5)	3894
J.C. CROWLEY (2)	3514
Larry KEITH (1)	608
Steve PIPPIN (1)	608
Dennis LAMBERT (1)	99
Neil YOUNG ►559 (8) [2]	**8708**
Neil YOUNG (7)	8563
Ian TYSON (1)	145
PABLO CRUISE ►560 (9) [8]	**8698**
Cory LERIOS (7)	3894
David JENKINS (7)	3761
John PIERCE (2)	364
Allee WILLIS (1)	280
Bud COCKRELL (1)	145
Peter ALLEN (1)	121
Adrienne ANDERSON (1)	121
Chuck LUTZ (1)	12
Jack JONES ►561 (22) [47]	**8682**
Don ROLLINS (1)	1477
Hal DAVID (2)	927
Burt BACHARACH (1)	838
Tony VELONA (1)	422
Ray EVANS (1)	385
Jay LIVINGSTON (1)	385
Henry MANCINI (1)	385
Joseph DARION (1)	342
Mitch LEIGH (1)	342
Joey BROOKS (1)	277
Aaron SCHROEDER (1)	277
Carl SIGMAN (2)	219
Bert KAEMPFERT (1)	182
Larry KUSIK (1)	182
Herbert REHBEIN (1)	182
Charles SINGLETON (1)	182
Elmer BERNSTEIN (1)	170
Johnny MERCER (1)	170
Sammy CAHN (2)	163
Jimmy VAN HEUSEN (2)	163
Luiz BONFÁ (1)	156
Wayne KEMP (1)	141
Curtis WAYNE (1)	141
Alfred Kealoha PERRY (1)	89
TRADITIONAL (1)	89
Klaus OGERMAN (1)	63
Scott ENGLISH (1)	45
Stan GELBER (1)	45
James LAST (1)	45
Harald WERNER (1)	45
Mark BARKAN (1)	31
Vic MILLROSE (1)	31
Umberto BINDI (1)	30
Anthony Ralph CLARKE (1)	30
George DUNING (1)	6.8
Joe SHERMAN (1)	6.8
George David WEISS (1)	6.8
Tony HATCH (1)	4.1
Jackie TRENT (1)	4.1
Pierre BAROUH (1)	0.5
Norman GIMBEL (1)	0.5
Francis LAI (1)	0.5
Teddy RANDAZZO (1)	0.2
Lou STALLMAN (1)	0.2
Bobby WEINSTEIN (1)	0.2
Sammy FAIN (1)	0.0
Paul Francis WEBSTER (1)	0.0
Maxine NIGHTINGALE ►562 (4) [5]	**8670**
Pierre TUBBS (2)	2774
J. Vincent EDWARDS (1)	2675
David LASLEY (1)	1590
Allee WILLIS (1)	1590
Ray PARKER Jr. (1)	42
BREATHE ►563 (6) [4]	**8663**
David GLASPER (6)	2391
Marcus LILLINGTON (6)	2391
Ian SPICE (5)	2020
Michael DELAHUNTY (4)	1861
The TORNADOES ►564 (3) [2]	**8628**
Joe MEEK (2)	8404
George BELLAMY (1)	224
Yvonne ELLIMAN ►565 (7) [11]	**8605**
Barry GIBB (2)	2376
Robin GIBB (2)	2376
Maurice GIBB (1)	1641
Barbara LEWIS (1)	949
Tim RICE (2)	405
Andrew Lloyd WEBBER (2)	405
Steve BARRI (1)	135
Harvey PRICE (1)	135
Dan WALSH (1)	135
Lee HOLDRIDGE (1)	24
Molly Ann LEIKIN (1)	24
FRIENDS OF DISTINCTION ►566 (6) [8]	**8593**
Jerry PETERS (3)	1882
Harry ELSTON (1)	1769
Hugh MASEKELA (1)	1769
Anita POREE (2)	1688
Skip SCARBOROUGH (1)	866
Willie HUTCH (1)	212
Howard GREENFIELD (1)	203
Neil SEDAKA (1)	203
10cc ►567 (10) [4]	**8592**
Graham GOULDMAN (10)	4233
Eric STEWART (9)	4126
Kevin GODLEY (2)	126
Lol CRÈME (1)	107
Corey HART ►568 (10) [4]	**8580**
Corey HART (9)	8035
Luigi CREATORE (1)	181
Hugo PERETTI (1)	181
George David WEISS (1)	181

John FRED & His PLAYBOY BAND ▶569 (3) [3]	**8565**
John FRED (3)	4283
Andrew BERNARD (2)	4261
Thomas BRYAN (1)	21
Dave "Baby" CORTEZ ▶570 (13) [10]	**8544**
David CLOWNEY (11)	3299
Ken WOOD (6)	2117
Jim KRIEGSMANN (2)	2069
Paul WINLEY (1)	903
Julia CLOWNEY (1)	47
Henry GLOVER (1)	41
Morris LEVY (1)	41
Winfield SCOTT (1)	14
Billy MAYHEW (1)	11
Shirley HALL (1)	3.5
Kyu SAKAMOTO ▶571 (2) [5]	**8519**
Rohusuke EI (1)	4086
Hachidai NAKAMURA (1)	4086
Yaso SAIJO (1)	116
Sil SEDORES (1)	116
Nobuyuki TAKEOKA (1)	116
SIMPLY RED ▶572 (7) [10]	**8513**
Mick HUCKNALL (4)	2593
Kenneth GAMBLE (1)	1647
Leon HUFF (1)	1647
Neil MOSS (1)	1493
Fritz McINTYRE (1)	296
John VALENTINE (1)	206
William VALENTINE (1)	206
Caroline WIGGINS (1)	206
Jimmie CAMERON (1)	111
Vella CAMERON (1)	111
ATLANTA RHYTHM SECTION ▶573 (16) [10]	**8497**
Buddy BUIE (16)	2806
Robert NIX (11)	2085
Dean DAUGHTRY (4)	1729
J.R. COBB (6)	621
Ronnie W. HAMMOND (2)	304
Harry MIDDLEBROOKS (1)	222
Mike SHAPIRO (1)	222
Randy LEWIS (1)	189
Steve McRAY (1)	189
Barry BAILEY (2)	132
O.C. SMITH ▶574 (11) [13]	**8495**
Bobby RUSSELL (2)	6072
Mac DAVIS (2)	943
Dallas FRAZIER (1)	711
Ray STEVENS (1)	326
Lamont DOZIER (1)	80
Brian HOLLAND (1)	80
Eddie HOLLAND (1)	80
George CALLENDER (1)	40
Wayne SHANKLIN (1)	40
Johnny BRISTOL (1)	40
Liz MARTIN (1)	40
Kris KRISTOFFERSON (1)	36
Jerry FULLER (1)	9.1
FINE YOUNG CANNIBALS ▶575 (6) [2]	**8491**
Roland GIFT (6)	4245
David STEELE (6)	4245
Ritchie VALENS ▶576 (5) [3]	**8485**
Ritchie VALENS (4)	7687
TRADITIONAL (1)	649

Robert KUHN (2)	149
STRAY CATS ▶577 (5) [1]	**8480**
Brian SETZER (5)	8480
David ROSE And His Orchestra ▶578 (9) [8]	**8473**
David ROSE (3)	7518
Larry CLINTON (1)	471
Moe KOFFMAN (1)	376
Sammy FAIN (1)	72
Morgan LEWIS (1)	31
Duke ELLINGTON (1)	1.8
Bubber MILEY (1)	1.8
Bob MERRILL (1)	0.4
Crystal GAYLE ▶579 (11) [14]	**8470**
Richard LEIGH (2)	5953
Bobby WOOD (2)	1041
Roger COOK (1)	535
Ralph MURPHY (1)	507
Allen REYNOLDS (1)	165
Roger GREENAWAY (1)	59
Geoff STEPHENS (1)	59
Susan THOMAS (1)	34
Hugh PRESTWOOD (1)	30
David LASLEY (1)	22
Allee WILLIS (1)	22
Josh LEO (1)	16
Wendy WALDMAN (1)	16
Sandy THEORET (1)	11
ZZ TOP ▶580 (18) [7]	**8462**
Billy GIBBONS (17)	2672
Frank BEARD (16)	2631
Dusty HILL (16)	2631
Isaac HAYES (1)	223
David PORTER (1)	223
Ken CORDRAY (1)	41
Steve PERRON (1)	41
Jim STAFFORD ▶581 (8) [6]	**8434**
Jim STAFFORD (7)	5083
David BELLAMY (2)	2041
Don BOWMAN (1)	1036
Shel SILVERSTEIN (1)	237
Dave LOGGINS (1)	36
Willie HAMMOND (1)	0.8
The ESSEX ▶582 (4) [10]	**8421**
Larry HUFF (1)	3379
William LINTON (1)	3379
Luigi CREATORE (1)	361
Adam LEVY (1)	361
Hugo PERETTI (1)	361
George David WEISS (1)	361
Oramay DIAMOND (1)	110
Jimmy RADCLIFFE (1)	110
Ivory Joe HUNTER (1)	0.8
Clyde OTIS (1)	0.8
TAVARES ▶583 (15) [21]	**8379**
Dennis LAMBERT (4)	1431
Brian POTTER (4)	1431
Freddie PERREN (3)	1375
Keni ST. LEWIS (3)	1375
Kenny NOLAN (1)	864
Floyd BUTLER (1)	262
Billy OSBORNE (1)	262
Gerard McMAHON (1)	198
Barry GIBB (1)	169
Maurice GIBB (1)	169
Robin GIBB (1)	169
Daryl HALL (1)	149
John OATES (1)	149
Dan HARTMAN (1)	142

Christine YARIAN (1)	139
Johnny BRISTOL (1)	26
James Anthony DEAN (1)	26
John Henry GLOVER (1)	26
Zane GREY (1)	5.0
Len HANKS (1)	5.0
Arnold McCULLER (1)	5.0
Jackie DeSHANNON ▶584 (19) [24]	**8321**
Jackie DeSHANNON (6)	1673
Burt BACHARACH (4)	1452
Hal DAVID (3)	1440
Jimmy HOLIDAY (3)	1438
Randy MYERS (3)	1438
Robbie ROBERTSON (1)	538
Chip TAYLOR (1)	120
Sonny BONO (1)	68
Jack NITZSCHE (1)	68
Irvin HUNT (1)	31
Sam RUSSELL (1)	31
Paul ANKA (1)	12
Neil YOUNG (1)	5.3
Bob WILLS (1)	2.3
Johnnie Lee WILLS (1)	2.3
Lamont DOZIER (1)	0.3
Brian HOLLAND (1)	0.3
Eddie HOLLAND (1)	0.3
Bobby HART (1)	0.3
Teddy RANDAZZO (1)	0.3
Bobby WEINSTEIN (1)	0.3
John BROMLEY (1)	0.3
David CLEMINSON (1)	0.3
Paula COOPER (1)	0.3
DEEP PURPLE ▶585 (11) [13]	**8312**
Joe SOUTH (1)	3508
Ritchie BLACKMORE (8)	784
Ian GILLAN (4)	773
Roger GLOVER (4)	773
Jon LORD (6)	733
Ian PAICE (4)	730
Neil DIAMOND (1)	648
Jeff BARRY (1)	117
Ellie GREENWICH (1)	117
Phil SPECTOR (1)	117
David COVERDALE (2)	8.1
Rod EVANS (2)	3.2
Glenn HUGHES (1)	1.4
Patsy CLINE ▶586 (18) [26]	**8311**
Hank COCHRAN (3)	2701
Willie NELSON (1)	1794
Harlan HOWARD (2)	1392
Alan BLOCK (1)	654
Don HECHT (1)	654
Don GIBSON (1)	392
Al HOFFMAN (1)	138
John KLENNER (1)	138
Mel TILLIS (2)	66
Webb PIERCE (1)	63
Wayne WALKER (1)	63
Danny DILL (1)	61
Carl PERKINS (1)	61
Justin TUBB (1)	40
Eddie MILLER (1)	22
W.S. STEVENSON (1)	22
Jimmy KEY (1)	18
Jerry LeFORS (1)	11
Bob SUMMERS (1)	11
Fred BURCH (1)	5.2
Bob WILLS (1)	2.7
Johnnie Lee WILLS (1)	2.7

Bob MONTGOMERY (1)	1.4
Sammy MASTERS (1)	0.9
Milton DeLUGG (1)	0.0
Bob HILLIARD (1)	0.0
ATLANTIC STARR ▶587 (11) [8]	**8299**
David E. LEWIS (7)	3249
Wayne I. LEWIS (7)	3235
Jonathan LEWIS (1)	1434
Hamish STUART (1)	165
Richard FELDMAN (1)	105
James SCOTT (1)	105
Sam DEES (1)	3.5
Ron KERSEY (1)	3.5
Paul YOUNG ▶588 (8) [11]	**8267**
Daryl HALL (1)	4062
Eugene RECORD (1)	1496
Earl RANDLE (1)	1084
Jack LEE (1)	730
Ian KEWLEY (2)	259
Paul YOUNG (2)	259
John HURLEY (1)	144
Ronnie WILKINS (1)	144
Marvin GAYE (1)	30
Barrett STRONG (1)	30
Norman WHITFIELD (1)	30
EXILE ▶589 (4) [4]	**8253**
Mike CHAPMAN (4)	4125
Nicky CHINN (4)	4125
Lynda LAWLEY (1)	2.0
James P. PENNINGTON (1)	2.0
MIKE + THE MECHANICS ▶590 (7) [3]	**8252**
Mike RUTHERFORD (7)	4126
Brian A. ROBERTSON (4)	2957
Christopher NEIL (3)	1169
LOVERBOY ▶591 (14) [18]	**8237**
Paul DEAN (12)	2483
Mike RENO (10)	1835
Mutt LANGE (1)	1301
Bruce FAIRBAIRN (1)	579
Bill WRAY (2)	324
Jonathan CAIN (1)	305
John DEXTER (1)	297
Debra Mae MOORE (1)	297
Matt FRENETTE (2)	260
Bryan ADAMS (2)	100
Jim VALLANCE (2)	100
Jon BON JOVI (1)	77
Todd CERNEY (1)	77
Richie SAMBORA (1)	77
Bernard AUBIN (1)	69
Doug JOHNSON (1)	19
Ted JOHNSON (1)	19
Davitt SIGERSON (1)	19
Anita BRYANT ▶592 (12) [20]	**8232**
Fred SPIELMAN (1)	1854
Janice TORRE (1)	1854
Meredith WILLSON (1)	1101
Bob HILLIARD (1)	876
Lee POCKRISS (1)	876
Lincoln CHASE (1)	396
Klaus-Günter NEUMANN (1)	396
Carl SIGMAN (1)	129
George GOEHRING (1)	117
Ed WARREN (1)	117
Mort GARSON (1)	103
Buddy KAYE (1)	103
Doc POMUS (1)	98
Mort SHUMAN (1)	98
Lou DINNING (1)	63

Anita BRYANT ▶592 (12) [20] ***Cont'd***	**8232**
Bob MERRILL (1)	21
Oscar HAMMERSTEIN (1)	10
Richard RODGERS (1)	10
Jo DAVIS (1)	7.1
B.L. PORTER (1)	7.1
Ronnie MILSAP ▶593 (16) [27]	**8213**
Tom BRASFIELD (2)	1363
Walt ALDRIDGE (1)	1208
Kye FLEMING (2)	801
Dennis W. MORGAN (2)	801
Mike REID (1)	783
Archie JORDAN (2)	648
Hal DAVID (1)	621
Burt BACHARACH (1)	534
Bob HILLIARD (1)	534
Charles QUILLEN (1)	296
Robert BYRNE (1)	155
Ralph MURPHY (1)	89
Bobby WOOD (1)	89
Michael D. STEWART (1)	69
Dan Edward WILLIAMS (1)	69
Royal C. BANNON (1)	33
John BETTIS (1)	33
Roy FREELAND (1)	26
Bill LaBOUNTY (1)	26
Al DEXTER (1)	12
Kris KRISTOFFERSON (1)	7.6
Mark JAMES (1)	2.8
George KLEIN (1)	2.8
Glenn SPREEN (1)	2.8
Jo ARMSTEAD (1)	2.2
Nick ASHFORD (1)	2.2
Valerie SIMPSON (1)	2.2
BOYS II MEN ▶594 (3) [7]	**8201**
Freddie PERREN (1)	2426
Christine YARIAN (1)	2426
Michael BIVINS (2)	885
Nathan MORRIS (2)	885
Dallas AUSTIN (1)	694
Shawn STOCKMAN (1)	694
Wanya MORRIS (1)	191
LIPPS, INC. ▶595 (2) [1]	**8179**
Steve GREENBERG (2)	8179
WANG CHUNG ▶596 (8) [5]	**8164**
Nick FELDMAN (8)	3154
Jack HUES (8)	3154
Peter F. WOLF (1)	1429
Darren COSTIN (2)	371
David CHANDLER (1)	56
LEMON PIPERS ▶597 (3) [2]	**8163**
Paul LEKA (3)	4082
Shelley PINZ (3)	4082
B.B. KING ▶598 (38) [26]	**8160**
B.B. KING (23)	2504
Rick DARNELL (1)	687
Roy HAWKINS (1)	687
Dave (2) CLARK (5)	564
Dave CRAWFORD (3)	514
Jerry RAGOVOY (1)	487
Leon RUSSELL (1)	455
Charles MANN (1)	412
Joe JOSEA (7)	328
Stevie WONDER (1)	275
Syreeta WRIGHT (1)	275
Jimmy JOHNSON (1)	188
Gerald JEMMOTT (1)	132

Jesse BELVIN (1)	114
JoAnn BELVIN (1)	114
Maya ANGELOU (2)	93
Quincy JONES (2)	93
Charles SINGLETON (2)	78
Ferdinand WASHINGTON (1)	72
Jules TAUB (2)	32
Jack H. CLEMENT (1)	13
Horace JOHNSON (1)	10
Sam LING (1)	10
Bill DOGGETT (1)	8.3
Louis JORDAN (1)	8.3
Lowell FULSOM (1)	3.2
ROSE ROYCE ▶599 (7) [3]	**8139**
Norman WHITFIELD (6)	7276
Miles GREGORY (1)	729
Dwight TURNER (1)	135
BROTHERS FOUR ▶600 (9) [20]	**8075**
Richard DEHR (1)	2302
Terry GILKYSON (1)	2302
Frank MILLER (1)	2302
Dimitri TIOMKIN (1)	152
Paul Francis WEBSTER (1)	152
Dora GRAF (1)	142
Martin SELIGSON (1)	142
TRADITIONAL (2)	75
August GOUPIL (1)	74
Dick GUMP (1)	74
Johnny NOBLE (1)	74
Bob FLICK (1)	66
Dick FOLEY (1)	66
Mike KIRKLAND (1)	66
John PAINE (1)	66
Richard LEWINE (1)	5.8
Alfred UHRY (1)	5.8
Tom JONES (1)	4.2
Harvey SCHMIDT (1)	4.2
Shel SILVERSTEIN (1)	0.4
Don CORNELL ▶601 (20) [32]	**8074**
Dale EVANS (1)	2057
Jack LAWRENCE (1)	1264
Richard MYERS (1)	1264
Harvey FUQUA (2)	592
Alan FREED (2)	581
Chuck WILLIS (1)	459
Ted LEHRMAN (1)	240
Phil SHEER (1)	240
Sammy FAIN (1)	182
Paul Francis WEBSTER (1)	182
TRADITIONAL (1)	172
Tom GLAZER (2)	108
Budd SCHULBERG (2)	108
Roy ALFRED (1)	92
Abner SILVER (1)	92
Sunny SKYLAR (1)	81
Leroy LOVETT (1)	57
Serge WALTER (1)	57
Charles ALBERT (1)	49
Fred JAY (1)	49
Irving REID (1)	49
Buddy GRECO (1)	27
Billy DAVIS (1)	19
Charles SUTTON (1)	19
Julius DIXON (1)	8.2
Ollie JONES (1)	8.2
Douglas BURFORD (1)	5.3
Colin RONALD (1)	5.3
Marino MARINI (1)	2.7
Al NEIBURG (1)	2.7
John D. LOUDERMILK (1)	0.0

Billy MURE (1)	0.0
Morris STOLOFF ▶602 (2) [3]	**8073**
George DUNING (1)	4036
Will HUDSON (1)	2018
Irving MILLS (1)	2018
Buddy KNOX with The RHYTHM ORCHIDS ▶603 (6) [7]	**8070**
Buddy KNOX (5)	1695
Jimmy BOWEN (4)	1683
Donnie LANIER (4)	1683
Dave ALLDRED (3)	1625
Ahmet ERTEGUN (1)	853
Edward MADDEN (1)	266
Percy WENRICH (1)	266
Jimmy SOUL ▶604 (3) [4]	**8063**
Frank GUIDA (3)	2894
Joseph ROYSTER (2)	2297
Carmela GUIDA (1)	2276
Norman SPAN (1)	597
CREAM ▶605 (5) [6]	**8060**
Peter Ronald BROWN (2)	2784
Jack BRUCE (2)	2784
Eric CLAPTON (3)	1385
Robert JOHNSON (1)	924
George HARRISON (1)	115
Martin SHARP (1)	69
Shelley FABARES ▶606 (5) [10]	**8029**
Lyn DUDDY (1)	3539
Lee POCKRISS (1)	3539
Barry MANN (1)	312
Cynthia WEIL (1)	312
Sammy CAHN (1)	103
Jule STYNE (1)	103
Mike ANTHONY (1)	60
Ted COOPER (1)	60
Buddy KAYE (1)	0.2
Philip SPRINGER (1)	0.2
ROOFTOP SINGERS ▶607 (3) [6]	**8027**
Erik DARLING (3)	2031
Willard SVANOE (3)	2031
Gus CANNON (1)	1726
Hosea WOODS (1)	1726
Lynne TAYLOR (2)	306
Tom GERACI (1)	207
Arthur CONLEY ▶608 (8) [12]	**7999**
Arthur CONLEY (4)	2560
Sam COOKE (1)	1822
Otis REDDING (1)	1822
Earl SIMMS (2)	677
Jesse STONE (1)	471
James McDOUGAL (1)	162
Titus TURNER (1)	162
John LENNON (1)	141
Paul McCARTNEY (1)	141
Jackie AVERY (1)	16
Ronald GRIER (1)	16
Jerry WILLIAMS Jr. (1)	6.8
Jimmy CLANTON ▶609 (11) [13]	**7993**
Howard GREENFIELD (4)	1685
Doc POMUS (2)	1276
Mort SHUMAN (2)	1276
Jack KELLER (1)	1004
Neil SEDAKA (2)	654
Jimmy CLANTON (2)	510
Cosimo MATASSA (2)	510

Mack DAVID (1)	390
Max STEINER (1)	390
Jimmie CRANE (1)	132
Phil TUCKER (1)	132
Kenny KAREN (1)	27
Gary OSBORNE (1)	4.9
Deniece WILLIAMS ▶610 (8) [17]	**7971**
Dean PITCHFORD (1)	2569
Tom SNOW (1)	2569
Deniece WILLIAMS (4)	412
Teddy RANDAZZO (1)	393
Lou STALLMAN (1)	393
Bobby WEINSTEIN (1)	393
Susaye GREENE (1)	267
Henry REDD (1)	267
Nathan WATTS (1)	267
SKYLARK (1)	162
Fritz BASKETT (1)	116
Clarence McDONALD (1)	116
George DUKE (1)	21
Cheyenne FOWLER (1)	8.8
Keg JOHNSON (1)	8.8
Verdine WHITE (1)	5.5
Robert Byron WRIGHT (1)	5.5
AVERAGE WHITE BAND/ AWB ▶611 (7) [11]	**7967**
Alan GORRIE (4)	1421
Hamish STUART (4)	1408
Roger BALL (3)	1199
Malcolm DUNCAN (3)	1199
Onnie McINTYRE (3)	1199
Robbie McINTOSH (2)	1118
Pam SAWYER (1)	167
Leon WARE (1)	167
Steve FERRONE (1)	81
Burt BACHARACH (1)	3.7
Hal DAVID (1)	3.7
Peter GABRIEL ▶612 (8) [1]	**7948**
Peter GABRIEL (8)	7948
Dickey LEE ▶613 (7) [7]	**7941**
Larry KOLBER (1)	2092
Barry MANN (1)	2092
Milton ADDINGTON (1)	1541
Dickey LEE (4)	971
Allen REYNOLDS (4)	971
Razzy BAILEY (1)	264
Jack H. CLEMENT (1)	10
UB40 ▶614 (6) [8]	**7935**
Neil DIAMOND (2)	3855
Smokey ROBINSON (1)	946
Robert ROGERS (1)	946
Al GREEN (1)	848
Mabon HODGES (1)	848
Sonny BONO (1)	480
Byron LEE (1)	6.0
Lester STERLING (1)	6.0
Trini LOPEZ ▶615 (14) [21]	**7930**
Lee HAYS (1)	2203
Pete SEEGER (1)	2203
TRADITIONAL (3)	840
Jerry LEIBER (1)	420
Mike STOLLER (1)	420
Will HOLT (1)	398
Trini LOPEZ (2)	282
John HERRING (1)	266
Paul SAWTELL (1)	266
Phil ZELLER (1)	215
Billy BARBERIS (1)	67
Bobby HART (1)	67

Trini LOPEZ ►615 (14) [21] *Cont'd*	7930
Teddy RANDAZZO (1)	67
Bobby WEINSTEIN (1)	67
Richie SUPA (1)	48
Bobby DARIN (1)	36
Milton KELLEM (1)	20
John GREENBACH (1)	15
Jerry MARCELLINO (1)	15
Wayne WALKER (1)	11
Harlan HOWARD (1)	1.8
DeBARGE ►616 (6) [7]	7924
Diane WARREN (1)	3157
El DeBARGE (4)	2416
Bunny DeBARGE (2)	762
David FOSTER (1)	454
Randy GOODRUM (1)	454
Jay GRAYDON (1)	454
Randy DeBARGE (1)	228
CHAD & JEREMY ►617 (12) [12]	7903
Van McCOY (2)	1558
Chad STUART (5)	1376
Ann RONELL (1)	1303
Clive METCALFE (1)	772
Keith NOBLE (1)	772
James William GUERCIO (1)	497
Oscar HAMMERSTEIN (2)	488
Richard RODGERS (2)	488
Wendy KIDD (1)	407
Jeremy CLYDE (3)	197
John LENNON (1)	23
Paul McCARTNEY (1)	23
Norman GREENBAUM ►618 (3) [1]	7894
Norman GREENBAUM (3)	7894
SWEET SENSATION ►619 (9) [13]	7881
Joseph E. MALLOY (5)	1240
Deena CHARLES (1)	1196
Russ DeSALVO (1)	1196
Robert STEELE (1)	1196
David PARTON (1)	955
Ricardo PAGAN (1)	462
David SANCHEZ (2)	412
Deke RICHARDS (1)	270
Pam SAWYER (1)	270
R. Dean TAYLOR (1)	270
Frank Edward WILSON (1)	270
Ken CEDAR (1)	72
Arnie ROMAN (1)	72
The PLAYMATES ►620 (15) [25]	7867
Carl CICCHETTI (1)	2054
Donald CLAPS (1)	2054
Paul VANCE (4)	1110
Lee POCKRISS (3)	1102
James CUNNINGHAM (1)	373
John CUNNINGHAM (1)	373
Stan LEBOWSKY (1)	317
Johnny LEHMANN (1)	317
Ben RALEIGH (1)	51
Don WOLF (1)	51
Sherman EDWARDS (1)	13
Edward WHITE (1)	11
Mack WOLFSON (1)	11
Jack SEGAL (1)	8.5
Ray ALLEN (1)	4.0
Wandra MERRELL (1)	4.0
Sam SALTZBERG (1)	4.0
Bennie BENJAMIN (1)	1.9
Morty NEVINS (1)	1.9

George David WEISS (1)	1.9
Bob GOODMAN (1)	0.7
Earl SHUMAN (1)	0.7
Jeff BARRY (1)	0.5
Steve ALLEN (1)	0.0
Ernest GOLD (1)	0.0
BANANARAMA ►621 (11) [10]	7861
Robbie VAN LEEUWEN (1)	3151
Sarah DALLIN (8)	803
Keren WOODWARD (8)	803
Siobhan FAHEY (7)	793
Matt AITKEN (5)	503
Mike STOCK (5)	503
Pete WATERMAN (5)	503
Steve JOLLEY (5)	395
Tony SWAIN (5)	395
Jacquie O'SULLIVAN (1)	11
The TOYS ►622 (5) [7]	7856
Sandy LINZER (3)	2771
Denny RANDELL (3)	2771
Johann Sebastian BACH (1)	2221
Tom DeCILLIS (1)	43
Richard LAYTON (1)	43
Gary GELD (1)	3.1
Peter UDELL (1)	3.1
Al WILSON ►623 (11) [13]	7834
Jerry FULLER (2)	5696
Oscar BROWN Jr. (1)	769
John FOGERTY (1)	250
Homer BANKS (1)	222
Carl HAMPTON (1)	222
Johnny BRISTOL (1)	194
Liz MARTIN (1)	194
Lou ADLER (1)	66
Johnny RIVERS (1)	66
Roger NICHOLS (2)	65
Paul WILLIAMS (2)	65
Jimmy WEBB (1)	12
Willie HUTCH (1)	11
DICK And DEEDEE ►624 (8) [7]	7779
Dick GOSTING (5)	5691
John D. LOUDERMILK (1)	1357
Harry BELAFONTE (1)	238
Alan GREENE (1)	238
Malvina REYNOLDS (1)	238
TRADITIONAL (1)	15
Deedee SPERLING (1)	1.8
Solomon BURKE ►625 (28) [40]	7763
Virgil STEWART (1)	1246
Solomon BURKE (9)	1076
Bert BERNS (6)	1071
Don COVAY (3)	622
Josephine Burke MOORE (2)	419
John FOGERTY (1)	406
Delores BURKE (2)	317
Wes FARRELL (1)	294
Robert BATEMAN (1)	262
Wilson PICKETT (1)	262
William Nelson SANDERS (1)	262
Horace OTT (1)	191
Audrey ALLISON (1)	154
Joe ALLISON (1)	154
Spooner OLDHAM (1)	133
Dan PENN (1)	133
James W. ALEXANDER (1)	111
Solomon BURKE Jr. (2)	106
Jerry WEXLER (1)	101
James MITCHELL (1)	68
Dick DALLAS (1)	66

Billy TAYLOR (1)	66
Babe CHIVIAN (1)	39
Joseph C. MARTIN (1)	39
TRADITIONAL (1)	39
Larry HARRISON (1)	29
Jimmy WILLIAMS (1)	29
Eddie FLOYD (1)	9.5
Alvertis ISBELL (1)	9.5
Danny DILL (1)	8.6
Mel TILLIS (1)	8.6
Howard Lee BARNES (1)	7.4
Don ROBERTSON (1)	7.4
John Bobby BERRY (1)	4.1
Mark BURKE (1)	2.8
Bernadine BURKE (1)	2.2
Melanie BURKE (1)	2.2
Orville COUCH (1)	1.7
Eddie McDUFF (1)	1.7
Jerry STYNER (1)	1.3
The PRETENDERS ►626 (8) [6]	7762
Chrissie HYNDE (6)	6808
James HONEYMAN-SCOTT (1)	820
Ray DAVIES (1)	103
Jackie MEMBERS (1)	9.7
Richard POINDEXTER (1)	9.7
Robert POINDEXTER (1)	9.7
Nick GILDER ►627 (3) [2]	7754
Nick GILDER (3)	3877
James McCULLOCH (3)	3877
Aaron NEVILLE ►628 (4) [8]	7752
George Richard DAVIS Jr. (2)	3176
Lee DIAMOND (2)	3176
Ralph BAILEY (1)	442
Rudy CLARK (1)	442
Ken WILLIAMS (1)	442
Max CARL (1)	24
Andrew KASTNER (1)	24
Larry John McNALLY (1)	24
Wilbert HARRISON ►629 (3) [3]	7741
Jerry LEIBER (1)	3484
Mike STOLLER (1)	3484
Wilbert HARRISON (2)	773
Al HIRT ►630 (10) [16]	7737
Les LEDO (1)	1570
Freddy FRIDAY (1)	1150
Marilyn SCHACK (1)	1150
Allen TOUSSAINT (1)	1150
Alvin TYLER (1)	1150
Floyd CRAMER (1)	478
Buddy KILLEN (1)	321
Billy SHERRILL (1)	321
Robert ALLEN (1)	308
Rosetta THARPE (1)	74
Tolchard EVANS (1)	48
Teri THORNTON (1)	11
Guglielmo BREZZA (1)	2.3
Nini ROSSO (1)	2.3
Sandy LINZER (1)	0.2
Denny RANDELL (1)	0.2
Len BARRY ►631 (6) [10]	7723
Len BARRY (5)	1333
John MADARA (4)	1333
David WHITE (4)	1333
Lamont DOZIER (1)	950
Brian HOLLAND (1)	950
Eddie HOLLAND (1)	950
Leonard BERNSTEIN (1)	429
Stephen SONDHEIM (1)	429
Leon HUFF (2)	17

Kenneth GAMBLE (1)	0.6
Billy PAUL ►632 (4) [3]	7716
Kenneth GAMBLE (4)	2704
Leon HUFF (4)	2704
Cary GILBERT (1)	2309
David SEVILLE ►633 (7) [4]	7715
David SEVILLE (6)	7610
Herb EISEMAN (1)	35
Floyd HUDDLESTON (1)	35
Mark McINTYRE (1)	35
LOOKING GLASS ►634 (4) [2]	7713
Elliot LURIE (3)	7705
Pieter SWEVAL (1)	7.6
FIREFALL ►635 (11) [6]	7711
Rick ROBERTS (8)	6642
Larry BURNETT (1)	465
John Lewis PARKER (1)	160
Tom SNOW (1)	160
Paul CROSTA (1)	142
John SAMBATARO (1)	142
Todd RUNDGREN ►636 (13) [3]	7704
Todd RUNDGREN (12)	7314
Mike LOVE (1)	195
Brian WILSON (1)	195
WILD CHERRY ►637 (5) [1]	7701
Robert PARISSI (5)	7701
MECO ►638 (24) [19]	7685
John WILLIAMS (5)	6650
Harold ARLEN (1)	239
E.Y. HARBURG (1)	239
Ben BURTT (1)	73
Joseph Stanley WILLIAMS (1)	73
Alfred NEWMAN (1)	47
Max STEINER (1)	47
Elmer BERNSTEIN (1)	47
Monty NORMAN (1)	47
John BARRY (1)	47
Ennio MORRICONE (1)	47
Charles WILLIAMS (1)	47
Dimitri TIOMKIN (1)	47
Maurice JARRE (1)	25
Brian WILSON (9)	6.9
Mike LOVE (8)	5.4
Gary USHER (1)	0.5
Carl WILSON (1)	0.5
Tony ASHER (1)	0.5
AMERICAN BREED ►639 (7) [9]	7658
Scott ENGLISH (1)	3037
Larry WEISS (1)	3037
Chip TAYLOR (2)	464
Al GORGONI (1)	378
Nancie MANTZ (1)	293
Annette TUCKER (1)	293
Bob STONE (1)	92
Gerry GOFFIN (2)	31
Carole KING (2)	31
Sheb WOOLEY ►640 (6) [2]	7640
Sheb WOOLEY (6)	7638
Homer ESCAMILLA (1)	2.4
George HAMILTON IV ►641 (14) [22]	7611
John D. LOUDERMILK (1)	2627
Jack FISHMAN (1)	837
Joseph Turner HENDERSON (1)	837
Joe TANNER (1)	647
Roy ALFRED (1)	465

George HAMILTON IV ▶641 (14) [22] *cont'd*	**7611**
Lester L. BROWN (1)	319
Bob GIBSON (1)	319
Albert STANTON (1)	319
TRADITIONAL (1)	319
Dick WOLF (2)	263
Randy STARR (1)	192
Hank WILLIAMS (1)	156
Dick FLOOD (1)	92
Billy MURE (1)	71
Willey GALE (1)	66
George HAMILTON IV (1)	36
Frank CARI (1)	22
Sonny WELLS (1)	22
Wally GOLD (1)	4.4
Roy DRUSKY (1)	0.0
Vic McALPIN (1)	0.0
Marie WILSON (1)	0.0
J. Frank WILSON and The CAVALIERS ▶642 (3) [3]	**7567**
Wayne COCHRAN (2)	7516
Dorsey BURNETTE (1)	25
Barry De VORZON (1)	25
Diana ROSS And The SUPREMES & The TEMPTATIONS ▶643 (3) [5]	**7567**
Kenneth GAMBLE (1)	2165
Leon HUFF (1)	2165
Jerry J. ROSS (1)	2165
Smokey ROBINSON (1)	738
Robbie ROBERTSON (1)	334
Sandy NELSON ▶644 (9) [4]	**7542**
Sandy NELSON (7)	3893
Arthur EGNOIAN (2)	2215
Richard PODOLOR (4)	1407
John Grayton DOLPHIN (1)	27
SURFACE ▶645 (6) [6]	**7533**
Bernard Leon JACKSON (5)	4826
Brian SIMPSON (1)	2110
David TOWNSEND (3)	340
Dave CONLEY (2)	236
Everett COLLINS (1)	10
Derrick CULLER (1)	10
Les PAUL and Mary FORD ▶646 (27) [38]	**7516**
Ted DAFFAN (2)	1861
Don ROBERTSON (2)	1352
Guy SINGER (1)	927
Les PAUL (5)	643
Joe MEEK (1)	588
Larry SULLIVAN (1)	305
Dorothy WRIGHT (1)	305
Jerry LIVINGSTON (1)	234
Bob RUSSELL (1)	234
Charles SINGLETON (2)	139
Jose BARBOSA DA SILVA (1)	138
Rose Marie McCOY (1)	136
Lee SILVER (1)	105
Zeke CLEMENTS (1)	74
Mary FORD (1)	71
Celia RYLAND (1)	71
Johnny BOND (1)	70
Hayward MORRIS (1)	51
Joseph SHAPIRO (1)	51
Buddy DeSYLVA (1)	28
Bud GREEN (1)	28
Ray HENDERSON (1)	28
Jesse STONE (1)	16
Johnny MANN (1)	11
Paul SAWTELL (1)	11
William ENGVICK (1)	9.5
A. Harrington GIBBS (1)	4.4
Joe GREY (1)	4.4
Leo WOOD (1)	4.4
Larry COLEMAN (1)	3.8
Bill CAREY (1)	2.5
Johnny HICKS (1)	2.5
Jim LOWE (1)	2.5
Marvin MOORE (1)	2.5
Howard Lee BARNES (1)	0.0
Irving BERLIN (1)	0.0
Johnny MARKS (1)	0.0
Jenny Lou CARSON (1)	0.0
Mark DINNING ▶647 (4) [5]	**7503**
Jean DINNING (2)	3586
Red SURREY (2)	3586
John D. LOUDERMILK (1)	160
Gerry GOFFIN (1)	85
Jack KELLER (1)	85
Marv JOHNSON ▶648 (11) [12]	**7491**
Berry GORDY (10)	3561
Billy DAVIS (1)	877
Gwen GORDY (1)	877
Marv JOHNSON (2)	507
Al ABRAMS (1)	462
John O'DEN (1)	462
Stanley OSSMAN (1)	462
Alma McKNIGHT (1)	150
Brian HOLLAND (2)	65
Janie BRADFORD (1)	64
Robert BATEMAN (1)	1.1
George FOWLER (1)	1.1
The DRAMATICS ▶649 (15) [13]	**7474**
Tony HESTER (8)	6156
Michael E. HENDERSON (1)	432
Don DAVIS (3)	249
Arthur SNYDER (1)	201
Kenneth GAMBLE (1)	124
Cary GILBERT (1)	124
Leon HUFF (1)	124
Eddie ROBINSON (2)	49
John BRINSON (1)	4.2
Floyd FLESHMAN (1)	4.2
Edward McGHEE (1)	4.2
Jimmie ABSTON (1)	1.4
Stella PETTY (1)	1.4
PEBBLES ▶650 (5) [4]	**7441**
Kenneth EDMONDS (4)	2539
Antonio REID (4)	2539
Perri Arlette REID (1)	2344
Cheryl JAMES (1)	20
The ELEGANTS ▶651 (3) [2]	**7433**
Arthur VENOSA (2)	3719
Vito PICONE (2)	3714
Bill HAYES ▶652 (6) [12]	**7428**
Tom BLACKBURN (1)	3283
George BRUNS (1)	3283
Stan JONES (1)	750
Saul CHAPLIN (1)	71
Nico CARSTENS (1)	8.5
Anton DE WAAL (1)	8.5
Charles SEGAL (1)	8.5
Viv STYGER (1)	8.5
Philip SPRINGER (1)	3.3
Sid WAYNE (1)	3.3
Jerry BOCK (1)	0.0
Sheldon HARNICK (1)	0.0
Roy HAMILTON ▶653 (22) [38]	**7426**
William S. COOK (3)	2073
Jesse STONE (1)	1182
Alex NORTH (1)	1121
Hy ZARET (1)	1121
Deadric MALONE (1)	304
Ferdinand WASHINGTON (1)	304
Oscar HAMMERSTEIN (1)	156
Richard RODGERS (1)	156
Glen MOORE (1)	128
Kenny MARTIN (1)	100
Clarence PAUL (1)	100
Sonny WOODS (1)	100
Howard GREENFIELD (1)	82
Neil SEDAKA (1)	82
Bob BRASS (1)	66
Irwin LEVINE (1)	66
Bob MERRILL (1)	50
Edward ELISCU (1)	48
Billy ROSE (1)	48
Vincent YOUMANS (1)	48
Jimmie CRANE (1)	31
Al JACOBS (1)	31
Frank LOESSER (1)	6.2
Sammy GALLOP (1)	4.5
Jimmy VAN HEUSEN (1)	4.5
Stan DAMERELL (1)	1.7
Tolchard EVANS (1)	1.7
Robert HARGREAVES (1)	1.7
Ervin DRAKE (1)	1.4
Irvin GRAHAM (1)	1.4
Jimmy SHIRL (1)	1.4
Al STILLMAN (1)	1.4
Robert MELLIN (1)	0.5
Guy WOOD (1)	0.5
Robert MAXWELL (2)	0.0
Carl SIGMAN (2)	0.0
Billy Dawn SMITH (1)	0.0
Stuart WIENER (1)	0.0
Edgar WINTER Group ▶654 (4) [2]	**7422**
Edgar WINTER (2)	5639
Dan HARTMAN (3)	1783
Eddy ARNOLD ▶655 (29) [33]	**7414**
Hank COCHRAN (3)	3124
Tex OWENS (1)	558
Jimmy DRIFTWOOD (2)	510
Bill ANDERSON (1)	476
Roger MILLER (1)	457
Bob MONTGOMERY (1)	448
Wayne Carson THOMPSON (1)	400
Ben PETERS (1)	267
Mickey NEWBURY (1)	228
James Frederick RODGERS (1)	186
John D. LOUDERMILK (1)	137
Marvin RAINWATER (1)	83
Red LANE (1)	66
Johnny MARKS (1)	59
Carl BELEW (1)	57
Eddie BUSH (1)	57
Billy Joe MOORE (1)	57
Joy Byers JOHNSTON (1)	52
Bob TUBERT (1)	52
James (2) LEE (1)	31
Jean CHAPEL (1)	28
Boudleaux BRYANT (2)	25
Roy DRUSKY (1)	13
Vic McALPIN (1)	13
Marie WILSON (1)	13
Wayne WALKER (1)	10
Eddy ARNOLD (2)	2.2
Fred EBB (1)	2.2
Paul KLEIN (1)	2.2
Don ROBERTSON (1)	0.7
Jack ROLLINS (1)	0.7
Irving GORDON (1)	0.0
Cindy WALKER (1)	0.0
Curtis MAYFIELD ▶656 (11) [2]	**7411**
Curtis MAYFIELD (11)	7373
Dino FEKARIS (1)	38
Joe DOWELL ▶657 (5) [7]	**7407**
Ben WEISMAN (3)	1793
Fred WISE (3)	1793
Bert KAEMPFERT (1)	1583
Kay TWOMEY (1)	1583
Marvin MOORE (1)	319
Bernie WAYNE (1)	319
Ronnie WILKINS (1)	18
SISTER SLEDGE ▶658 (8) [10]	**7407**
Bernard EDWARDS (3)	3318
Nile RODGERS (3)	3318
Smokey ROBINSON (1)	585
Joy DENNY (1)	92
Narada Michael WALDEN (2)	26
Allee WILLIS (2)	26
Joni SLEDGE (1)	16
Lisa WALDEN (1)	16
Patrick GRANT (1)	5.2
Gwen GUTHRIE (1)	5.2
BELL BIV DEVOE ▶659 (4) [12]	**7397**
Elliot STRAITE (1)	3892
Ricky BELL (1)	733
Michael BIVINS (1)	733
Carl BOURELLY (1)	733
Ronnie DeVOE (1)	733
Darrol DURANT (1)	101
Roney HOOKS (1)	101
Eric SADLER (1)	101
Keith SHOCKLEE (1)	101
Paul STEWART (1)	101
Timmy GATLING (1)	35
Alton STEWART (1)	35
John WAITE ▶660 (9) [12]	**7397**
John WAITE (5)	2387
Mark LEONARD (1)	1848
Chas SANDFORD (1)	1848
Holly KNIGHT (1)	238
Vince CUSANO (1)	208
Adam MITCHELL (1)	208
Ivan KRAL (1)	185
Mark SIDGWICK (1)	185
Desmond CHILD (1)	137
Diane WARREN (1)	54
Danny KORTCHMAR (1)	49
J.D. SOUTHER (1)	49
RASPBERRIES ▶661 (7) [2]	**7393**
Eric CARMEN (7)	7379
Wally BRYSON (1)	13
Mary MacGREGOR ▶662 (6) [9]	**7361**
Peter YARROW (3)	3450
Phil JARRELL (1)	3359
Elmer BERNSTEIN (1)	210
Norman GIMBEL (1)	210
Mary MacGREGOR (1)	82
Paul STOOKEY (1)	16
Larry HERBSTRITT (1)	13

Mary MacGREGOR ►662 (6) [9] *Cont'd*	**7361**
Doug THIELE (1)	13
Kevin HUNTER (1)	8.8
JOHNNY And The HURRICANES ►663 (10) [10]	**7356**
Tom KING (5)	1730
John POCISK (4)	1322
TRADITIONAL (5)	1270
Ira MACK (3)	1115
Fred MENDELSOHN (1)	682
L. Wolfe GILBERT (1)	484
T.J. FOWLER (2)	468
Carl CONASTER (1)	207
Oliver HOOD (1)	45
Bob CARLETON (1)	33
Cathy DENNIS ►664 (6) [7]	**7353**
Cathy DENNIS (5)	2479
Danny POKU (3)	2204
Patrick ADAMS (1)	956
C. Delyle GREGORY (1)	956
Anne DUDLEY (1)	754
Terry BRITTEN (1)	2.5
Mike LEESON (1)	2.5
Ray PETERSON ►665 (16) [29]	**7350**
Jeff BARRY (2)	1350
Ben RALEIGH (1)	1276
Baker KNIGHT (2)	1146
Armetia CHATMAN (1)	581
Mitchell PARISH (1)	581
J. Mayo WILLIAMS (1)	581
Dale NOE (1)	497
Red SOVINE (1)	497
John MARASCALCO (1)	155
George MOTOLA (1)	155
Gerry GOFFIN (1)	96
Barry MANN (1)	96
Ellie GREENWICH (1)	74
Ray STANLEY (1)	61
Doc POMUS (1)	23
Mort SHUMAN (1)	23
A.R. PEDDY (1)	22
Ray PRICE (1)	22
Mel TILLIS (1)	22
Howard JOHNSON (1)	21
Joseph McCARTHY (1)	21
James V. MONACO (1)	21
Tommy BOYCE (1)	12
Ray A. PETERSON (1)	12
Gene PITNEY (1)	1.4
Otis BLACKWELL (1)	0.0
Eddie COOLEY (1)	0.0
Bob MARCUS (1)	0.0
Perez PRADO (1)	0.0
José FELICIANO ►666 (13) [24]	**7338**
John DENSMORE (1)	1240
Robby KRIEGER (1)	1240
Ray MANZAREK (1)	1240
Jim MORRISON (1)	1240
Robert HIGGINBOTHAM (1)	1222
Francis Scott KEY (1)	259
Bruce CHANNEL (1)	191
Margaret COBB (1)	191
Jose FELICIANO (4)	161
Barry GIBB (1)	64
Maurice GIBB (1)	64
Robin GIBB (1)	64

Hilda FELICIANO (1)	59
Don DUNN (1)	24
Tony McCASHEN (1)	24
Lamont DOZIER (1)	15
Brian HOLLAND (1)	15
Eddie HOLLAND (1)	15
John LENNON (1)	4.8
Paul McCARTNEY (1)	4.8
Eleanor BROADWATER (1)	0.0
Robert CHAISSON (1)	0.0
Dale HAWKINS (1)	0.0
Stanley J. LEWIS (1)	0.0
Marcie BLANE ►667 (2) [2]	**7321**
Henry HOFFMAN (2)	3660
Gary KLEIN (2)	3660
Sergio MENDES & BRASIL '66 ►668 (11) [19]	**7305**
Burt BACHARACH (1)	1576
Hal DAVID (1)	1576
John LENNON (1)	1163
Paul McCARTNEY (1)	1163
Art GARFUNKEL (1)	544
Paul SIMON (1)	544
Jorge BEN (2)	319
Antonio ADOLFO (1)	57
Alan BERGMAN (1)	57
Marilyn BERGMAN (1)	57
Tiberio GASPAR (1)	57
Steve CROPPER (1)	50
Otis REDDING (1)	50
Cole PORTER (1)	46
Norman GIMBEL (2)	41
Jimmy WEBB (1)	3.5
Edu LOBO (1)	1.4
Dennis LAMBERT (1)	0.4
Brian POTTER (1)	0.4
CROSBY, STILLS & NASH ►669 (8) [5]	**7292**
Graham NASH (3)	4409
Stephen STILLS (5)	2150
Michael CURTIS (1)	343
Richard CURTIS (1)	343
Gerry TOLMAN (1)	47
WARRANT ►670 (8) [5]	**7268**
Joseph CAGLE (8)	1454
Steven CHAMBERLIN (8)	1454
Jerry DIXON (8)	1454
John OSWALD (8)	1454
Eric TURNER (8)	1454
Don GIBSON ►671 (17) [7]	**7256**
Don GIBSON (13)	5777
Hal DAVID (1)	648
Paul HAMPTON (1)	648
Eugene LOCKHART (1)	88
Ernest SEITZ (1)	88
Mel FOREE (1)	6.0
Hank SNOW (1)	0.0
Jimmy DORSEY Orchestra ►672 (4) [9]	**7251**
Jerry HERST (1)	3272
Jack SHARPE (1)	3272
Abel BAER (1)	291
Cliff FRIEND (1)	291
Harry CARLSON (1)	25
Lew DOUGLAS (1)	25
Erwin KING (1)	25
Howard GIBELING (1)	25
Julie HILTON (1)	25

Gino VANNELLI ►673 (10) [3]	**7224**
Gino VANNELLI (9)	3682
Ross VANNELLI (1)	3196
Roy FREELAND (2)	346
Anita BAKER ►674 (8) [18]	**7189**
Anita BAKER (3)	1661
Randy HOLLAND (1)	1109
Skip SCARBOROUGH (1)	1109
Gary BIAS (1)	445
Louis A. JOHNSON (1)	445
Alex BROWN (1)	304
Sami McKINNEY (1)	304
Michael O'HARA (1)	304
Garry GLENN (1)	237
Diane QUANDER (1)	237
Marilyn McLEOD (1)	182
Darryl Keith ROBERTS (1)	182
Ken HIRSCH (1)	163
Marti SHARRON (1)	163
Vernon FAILS (1)	107
Michael POWELL (1)	107
Terry BRITTEN (1)	64
Graham LYLE (1)	64
STARLAND VOCAL BAND ►675 (4) [3]	**7182**
Bill DANOFF (3)	7091
Taffy DANOFF (2)	58
Margot KUNKEL (1)	33
Van MORRISON ►676 (14) [2]	**7157**
Van MORRISON (14)	7151
Bert BERNS (1)	6.1
NIGHT RANGER ►677 (11) [9]	**7152**
Jack BLADES (9)	2698
Kelly KEAGY (2)	2360
Alan FITZGERALD (2)	987
Brad GILLIS (2)	502
Jeff WATSON (1)	408
Russ BALLARD (1)	63
David FOSTER (1)	45
Tom KEANE (1)	45
Mike LANDAU (1)	45
Donny And Marie OSMOND ►678 (7) [13]	**7140**
Don HARRIS (1)	1173
Dewey TERRY (1)	1173
Dick MANNING (1)	859
Larry STOCK (1)	859
Peter DeROSE (1)	711
Mitchell PARISH (1)	711
Nick ASHFORD (1)	377
Valerie SIMPSON (1)	377
Hank COCHRAN (1)	227
Barry MANN (1)	204
Cynthia WEIL (1)	204
Steve VOICE (1)	133
Peter YELLOWSTONE (1)	133
Luther INGRAM ►679 (10) [10]	**7134**
Homer BANKS (3)	2215
Carl HAMPTON (2)	1994
Raymond Earl JACKSON (2)	1994
Luther INGRAM (4)	264
Allen Alvoid JONES Jr. (1)	221
J. Leslie McFARLAND (2)	204
Sam COOKE (1)	163
Johnny BAYLOR (4)	78
Johnny NORTHERN (1)	0.4

Randall STEWART (1)	0.4
The CONTOURS ►680 (9) [13]	**7132**
Berry GORDY (4)	6175
Thelma GORDY (1)	150
Richard STREET (1)	150
Smokey ROBINSON (1)	134
Robert ROGERS (1)	134
Ivy Jo HUNTER (1)	114
William STEVENSON (1)	114
James Anthony DEAN (1)	45
Stan McMULLEN (1)	45
William WEATHERSPOON (1)	45
Morris BROADNAX (1)	8.8
Clarence PAUL (1)	8.8
Stevie WONDER (1)	8.8
EXTREME ►681 (2) [2]	**7116**
Nuno BETTENCOURT (2)	3558
Gary CHERONE (2)	3558
The SURFARIS ►682 (5) [5]	**7109**
Bob BERRYHILL (5)	1758
Pat CONNOLLY (5)	1758
Jim FULLER (5)	1758
Ron WILSON (5)	1758
Jim PASH (1)	76
MÖTLEY CRÜE ►683 (13) [6]	**7103**
Nikki SIXX (12)	3349
Mick MARS (6)	2150
Tommy LEE (6)	778
Cub KODA (1)	387
Michael LUTZ (1)	387
Vince NEIL (2)	52
ANNETTE ►684 (12) [14]	**7065**
Richard SHERMAN (5)	1403
Robert SHERMAN (5)	1403
Al HOFFMAN (1)	695
Dick MANNING (1)	695
Bob ROBERTS (2)	623
Martin KALMANOFF (1)	603
Aaron SCHROEDER (1)	603
Paul ANKA (2)	468
Jimmie DODD (1)	453
Thomas ADAIR (1)	27
Frances JEFFORDS (1)	27
Bill WALSH (1)	27
Gerry GOFFIN (1)	18
Carole KING (1)	18
Eddy GRANT ►685 (3) [1]	**7049**
Eddy GRANT (3)	7049
Harry CHAPIN ►686 (9) [2]	**7047**
Harry CHAPIN (9)	4938
Sandra CHAPIN (1)	2110
Dan HILL ►687 (6) [3]	**6985**
Dan HILL (6)	3928
Barry MANN (2)	2129
Beverly HILL (1)	928
Rick DEES ►688 (3) [5]	**6983**
Rick DEES (2)	6833
Mondo FAX (1)	59
Shelley FISHER (1)	30
Willie HALL (1)	30
Bobby MANUEL (1)	30
Johnny BURNETTE ►689 (7) [11]	**6979**
Barry De VORZON (2)	1206
Ted ELLIS (1)	1188
Richard SHERMAN (1)	1143
Robert SHERMAN (1)	1143
Wayne WALKER (1)	1100

Johnny BURNETTE ▶689 (7) [11] *Cont'd*	**6979**
John DOLAN (1)	357
Chico HOLIDAY (1)	357
Fred BURCH (1)	153
Gerald NELSON (1)	153
Red WEST (1)	153
James Marcus SMITH (1)	24
Cozy COLE ▶690 (5) [5]	**6976**
Edgar BATTLE (2)	3185
Eddie DURHAM (2)	3185
Dick HYMAN (1)	523
Duke ELLINGTON (2)	42
Juan TIZOL (2)	42
Janis JOPLIN ▶691 (6) [9]	**6963**
Fred FOSTER (1)	2808
Kris KRISTOFFERSON (1)	2808
Jerry RAGOVOY (3)	431
Bert BERNS (1)	325
Janis JOPLIN (2)	243
Gabriel MEKLER (1)	218
Mort SHUMAN (1)	80
Chip TAYLOR (1)	26
TRADITIONAL (1)	25
NELSON ▶692 (4) [5]	**6955**
Gunnar NELSON (4)	2129
Matthew NELSON (4)	2129
Marc TANNER (4)	2129
Ric WILSON (1)	447
Gregg SUTTON (1)	120
Eydie GORME ▶693 (20) [31]	**6953**
Barry MANN (2)	1766
Cynthia WEIL (2)	1766
Max BYGRAVES (2)	1249
Al HOFFMAN (1)	344
Dick MANNING (1)	344
Robert I. ALLEN (1)	210
Tony RENIS (1)	210
Gerry GOFFIN (2)	207
Jack KELLER (1)	155
Jerry BOCK (1)	127
Lawrence HOLOFCENER (1)	127
George David WEISS (1)	127
Joseph LIGGINS (1)	56
Oscar HAMMERSTEIN (1)	55
Ben OAKLAND (1)	55
Carole KING (1)	52
Dave FRANKLIN (1)	24
Steve LAWRENCE (2)	19
Beverly GUTHRIE (1)	17
Gary LYNES (1)	17
Mack DISCANT (1)	15
Marilyn GINS (1)	3.4
Eydie GORME (1)	3.4
Sammy CAHN (1)	3.4
Harry WARREN (2)	3.4
David P. JONES (1)	0.0
Theodore WILLIAMS Jr. (1)	0.0
Robert Bubber JOHNSON (1)	0.0
Ray EVANS (1)	0.0
Jay LIVINGSTON (1)	0.0
Harold ADAMSON (1)	0.0
Chaka KHAN ▶694 (9) [16]	**6946**
PRINCE (1)	4722
Nick ASHFORD (2)	496
Valerie SIMPSON (2)	496
David GAMSON (1)	146
Green GARTSIDE (1)	146
Ned DOHENY (1)	127
Hamish STUART (1)	127

Elliot WILLENSKY (1)	89
David FOSTER (1)	86
Tom KEANE (1)	86
Cynthia WEIL (1)	86
David FRANK (1)	79
Mic MURPHY (1)	79
Mary DEAN (1)	60
Franne GOLDE (1)	60
Marti SHARRON (1)	60
Anita WARD ▶695 (2) [1]	**6945**
Frederick KNIGHT (2)	6945
Sonny JAMES ▶696 (22) [29]	**6937**
Ric CARTEY (1)	2844
Carole JOYNER (1)	2844
Mary STOVALL (1)	209
Dan WELCH (1)	209
Ivory Joe HUNTER (2)	145
Jimmy GATELEY (1)	97
Jack MORROW (1)	64
J.P. RICHARDSON (1)	63
Sylvester BRADFORD (1)	50
Al LEWIS (1)	50
Cliff FRIEND (1)	42
Irving MILLS (1)	42
Mark McINTYRE (1)	39
William OLOFSON (1)	39
Sonny JAMES (3)	25
Dub DICKERSON (1)	24
Don ROBERTSON (1)	22
Jerry LORDAN (1)	17
Bob TUBERT (1)	17
Cecil NULL (1)	16
Brook BENTON (2)	13
Clyde OTIS (2)	13
Joe MELSON (1)	12
Roy ORBISON (1)	12
Belford HENDRICKS (1)	10
Jimmy REED (1)	7.4
Bobbie CARROL (1)	6.2
Tom SPRINGFIELD (1)	2.9
Richard HOLLINGSWORTH (1)	2.0
MUSIC EXPLOSION ▶697 (4) [7]	**6929**
John CARTER (1)	3355
Ken HAWKER (1)	3355
Eric WOOLFSON (1)	176
Ritchie CORDELL (1)	21
Bo GENTRY (1)	21
Joey LEVINE (1)	1.2
Kris RESNICK (1)	1.2
The MIRACLES ▶698 (4) [4]	**6929**
Billy GRIFFIN (1)	2637
Warren MOORE (1)	2637
Freddie PERREN (3)	828
Christine YARIAN (3)	828
HOLLYWOOD ARGYLES ▶699 (1) [1]	**6926**
Dallas FRAZIER (1)	6926
R.E.M. ▶700 (10) [4]	**6917**
Bill BERRY (10)	1729
Peter BUCK (10)	1729
Mike MILLS (10)	1729
Michael STIPE (10)	1729
Bill DOGGETT ▶701 (10) [13]	**6912**
Billy BUTLER (4)	1464
Bill DOGGETT (3)	1461
Clifford SCOTT (3)	1444

Shep SHEPHERD (2)	1440
Sil AUSTIN (1)	364
Irving SIDERS (1)	364
Tiny BRADSHAW (1)	145
Henry GLOVER (1)	71
Lucky MILLINDER (1)	71
Jim MUNDY (1)	71
Candy JOHNSON (1)	13
Bill BLACK (1)	3.0
Max STEINER (1)	0.0
Chris MONTEZ ▶702 (8) [11]	**6900**
James LEE (2)	3221
Mack GORDON (2)	923
Harry WARREN (2)	923
Tony HATCH (1)	891
Sammy CAHN (1)	260
Jule STYNE (1)	260
Chris MONTEZ (1)	202
Arthur HAMMERSTEIN (1)	109
Dudley WILKINSON (1)	109
George GERSHWIN (1)	1.4
Ira GERSHWIN (1)	1.4
Adam WADE ▶703 (16) [22]	**6896**
Arthur KENT (3)	1192
Ed WARREN (3)	1192
Mark BARKAN (1)	723
Sandy BARON (1)	723
George EDDY (1)	723
Jerry SAMUELS (2)	512
Larry KUSIK (1)	479
Hank WILLIAMS (2)	401
Mitchell PARISH (1)	198
Heinz ROEMHELD (1)	198
Morty CRAFT (1)	151
Selma CRAFT (1)	151
Mack DAVID (1)	61
Bronislaw KAPER (1)	61
Jack LAWRENCE (1)	55
Clint BALLARD Jr. (1)	21
Fred TOBIAS (1)	21
Artie GLENN (1)	14
Robert MOSELY (1)	11
Mayme WATTS (1)	11
Henry MANCINI (1)	0.0
Johnny MERCER (1)	0.0
Lenny WELCH ▶704 (10) [20]	**6896**
Woodrow Buddy JOHNSON (1)	4149
Robert MAXWELL (1)	421
Carl SIGMAN (1)	421
Howard GREENFIELD (1)	342
Neil SEDAKA (1)	342
Larry WEISS (1)	317
Al FRISCH (1)	201
Sid WAYNE (1)	201
Eddy ARNOLD (1)	200
Cindy WALKER (1)	200
George FISCHOFF (1)	19
Tony POWERS (1)	19
Richard ADLER (1)	15
Jerry ROSS (1)	15
Barbara BELLE (1)	6.6
Anita LEONARD (1)	6.6
Louis PRIMA (1)	6.6
Stan RHODES (1)	6.6
Dash CROFTS (1)	3.1
Jim SEALS (1)	3.1
Michael MURPHEY ▶705 (6) [4]	**6890**
Michael MURPHEY (5)	3552

Larry CANSLER (1)	2111
Rafe VAN HOY (1)	989
Charles QUARTO (1)	239
Ramsey LEWIS Trio ▶706 (5) [7]	**6889**
Billy PAGE (1)	4538
Bert BERNS (1)	700
Wes FARRELL (1)	700
John LENNON (1)	266
Paul McCARTNEY (1)	266
Robert HIGGINBOTHAM (1)	233
Chris KENNER (1)	186
Burl IVES ▶707 (15) [19]	**6888**
Hank COCHRAN (3)	4599
Harlan HOWARD (4)	1573
Gordon JENKINS (1)	221
TRADITIONAL (3)	75
Webley EDWARDS (1)	66
Leon POBER (1)	66
Richard ADLER (1)	61
Jerry ROSS (1)	61
Wiley PATTERSON (1)	57
Maurice J. REIS (1)	57
Rafael De LEON (1)	8.9
Richard DEHR (1)	8.9
Terry GILKYSON (1)	8.9
Frank MILLER (1)	8.9
Burl IVES (1)	8.3
Mel TILLIS (1)	8.3
George BRUNS (1)	0.0
Gil GEORGE (1)	0.0
Ken DARBY (1)	0.0
ORLEANS ▶708 (6) [5]	**6880**
Johanna HALL (4)	2854
John HALL (3)	2705
Larry HOPPEN (3)	734
Marilyn MASON (2)	585
Bob LEINBACH (1)	2.2
Marilyn McCOO & Billy DAVIS JR. ▶709 (4) [7]	**6875**
James Anthony DEAN (2)	2898
John Henry GLOVER (2)	2898
H.B. BARNUM (1)	440
Walter JOHNSON (1)	440
John FOOTMAN (1)	66
Theresa McFADDIN (1)	66
Frank Edward WILSON (1)	66
Bobby FREEMAN ▶710 (10) [13]	**6860**
Bobby FREEMAN (3)	3173
Thomas COMAN (2)	1450
Sylvester STEWART (2)	1450
Andy GIBSON (1)	226
Bill MASSEY (1)	226
Robert MAXWELL (1)	142
Carl SIGMAN (1)	142
Ben RALEIGH (1)	16
Don WOLF (1)	16
Jack CORTES (1)	8.2
Mark FISHER (1)	4.0
Joe GOODWIN (1)	4.0
Larry SHAY (1)	4.0
BROTHERS JOHNSON ▶711 (6) [7]	**6845**
Shuggie OTIS (1)	1933
George JOHNSON (4)	1503
Louis E. JOHNSON (4)	1503
Senora SAM (1)	795
Rod TEMPERTON (2)	469
Valerie JOHNSON (1)	446
Quincy JONES (1)	195

JAY And The TECHNIQUES ►712 (5) [5]	**6844**
Maurice IRBY (2)	4654
Sandy LINZER (2)	1093
Denny RANDELL (2)	1093
Raymond BLOODWORTH (1)	2.3
L. Russell BROWN (1)	2.3
BLUE SWEDE ►713 (5) [9]	**6819**
Mark JAMES (1)	5017
Dick ADDRISI (1)	750
Don ADDRISI (1)	750
Joe SOUTH (1)	92
Tommy JAMES (1)	46
Peter LUCIA (1)	46
Harald BRASCHOSS (1)	40
Christian BRUHN (1)	40
Hartmut PRIESS (1)	40
Robbie NEVIL ►714 (7) [10]	**6819**
Robbie NEVIL (7)	2820
Mark HOLDING (1)	1190
Duncan PAIN (1)	1190
Brock WALSH (1)	494
Richard EASTMAN (1)	300
Bobby HART (1)	300
Steven DUBIN (2)	221
David Paul BRYANT (1)	175
Richard FELDMAN (1)	65
Jeff PESCETTO (1)	65
Clarence HENRY ►715 (6) [6]	**6802**
Robert GUIDRY (3)	2275
Paul GAYTEN (1)	2061
Doris FISHER (1)	776
Allan ROBERTS (1)	776
Clarence "Frogman" HENRY (2)	654
Joe BISKO (1)	259
BAD ENGLISH ►716 (6) [6]	**6797**
Diane WARREN (1)	3290
Jonathan CAIN (5)	1438
John WAITE (5)	1438
Ricky PHILLIPS (1)	250
Mark SPIRO (3)	243
Neal SCHON (2)	140
Terence Trent D'ARBY ►717 (5) [2]	**6794**
Terence Trent D'ARBY (5)	4798
Sean OLIVER (1)	1996
Charlie DANIELS Band ►718 (9) [7]	**6793**
Charlie DANIELS (8)	1791
Tom CRAIN (3)	879
Joel DiGREGORIO (3)	879
Fred EDWARDS (3)	879
Charles HAYWARD (3)	879
James W. MARSHALL (3)	879
Dan DALEY (1)	608
Bobby WOMACK ►719 (15) [19]	**6789**
James W. ALEXANDER (1)	919
Zelda SAMUELS (1)	919
Bobby WOMACK (9)	874
Jimmie COX (1)	787
Jim FORD (1)	731
Neil DIAMOND (1)	430
Bart HOWARD (1)	383
John GRISBY (1)	323
Joe HICKS (1)	323
John PHILLIPS (1)	221
Michelle PHILLIPS (1)	221

Darryl CARTER (3)	208
Linda WOMACK (1)	156
Truman THOMAS (1)	131
J.J. JOHNSON (1)	121
Richard GRIFFIN (1)	11
Patrick L. MOTEN (1)	11
Sandra E. SULLY (1)	11
Harold PAYNE (1)	8.1
ESCAPE CLUB ►720 (5) [5]	**6784**
Johnnie CHRISTO (5)	1485
John HOLLIDAY (5)	1485
Trevor STEEL (5)	1485
Milan ZEKAVICA (5)	1485
Amos PIZZEY (1)	845
Walter MURPHY And The BIG APPLE BAND ►721 (2) [3]	**6779**
Walter MURPHY (2)	3389
Ludwig VAN BEETHOVEN (1)	3181
Nikolai RIMSKY-KORSAKOV (1)	209
Vic DANA ►722 (16) [25]	**6766**
Roy C. BENNETT (1)	900
Sid TEPPER (1)	900
Neil DIAMOND (2)	653
Bill ANDERSON (1)	563
Dick GLASSER (1)	465
Howlett SMITH (1)	422
Theodore C. HARRIS (1)	406
Matt MALNECK (1)	293
Robert MAXWELL (1)	293
Carl SIGMAN (1)	293
Norman NEWELL (1)	211
Nino OLIVIERO (1)	211
Riz ORTOLANI (1)	211
Ben RALEIGH (2)	193
Yvonne DEVANEY (1)	118
Ben BLACK (1)	113
Charles N. DANIELS (1)	113
Edwin LEMARE (1)	113
Don WOLF (1)	101
Mark BARKAN (1)	92
Bob BECKHAM (1)	28
Buzz CASON (1)	28
Cindy WALKER (1)	22
James DYRENFORTH (1)	12
Carroll GIBBONS (1)	12
Timi YURO ►723 (13) [32]	**6741**
Jimmie CRANE (1)	1636
Al JACOBS (1)	1636
Hank COCHRAN (1)	943
Clyde OTIS (2)	631
Joy Byers JOHNSTON (1)	628
Burt BACHARACH (1)	232
Hal DAVID (1)	232
Charles CHAPLIN (1)	141
Geoffrey PARSONS (1)	141
John TURNER (1)	141
Leo FRIEDMAN (1)	47
Beth Slater WHITSON (1)	47
Paul CLAYTON (1)	27
Larry EHRLICH (1)	27
Ronnie GILBERT (1)	27
Lee HAYS (1)	27
Fred HELLERMAN (1)	27
Dave LAZAR (1)	27
Pete SEEGER (1)	27
Stan DAMERELL (1)	14
Tolchard EVANS (1)	14
Robert HARGREAVES (1)	14
William S. COOK (1)	7.6
Al GOODHART (1)	6.0

Al HOFFMAN (1)	6.0
Ed NELSON (1)	6.0
Lockie EDWARDS (1)	5.9
Eddie SNYDER (1)	5.9
June TANSEY (1)	5.9
Larry WEISS (1)	5.9
Timi YURO (1)	2.5
Willie NELSON (1)	1.8
Nat King COLE And The FOUR KNIGHTS ►724 (4) [5]	**6722**
Ollie JONES (1)	2670
Rose Marie McCOY (2)	1189
Charles SINGLETON (2)	1189
Clyde OTIS (1)	837
Kelly OWENS (1)	837
Lee DORSEY ►725 (10) [6]	**6715**
Allen TOUSSAINT (8)	4036
Earl King JOHNSON (1)	553
Lee DORSEY (1)	532
Morris LEVY (1)	532
Clarence L. LEWIS (1)	532
Morgan C. ROBINSON (1)	532
The CYRKLE ►726 (6) [9]	**6708**
Paul SIMON (2)	2539
Bruce WOODLEY (2)	2539
David BLUME (1)	524
Jerry KELLER (1)	524
Susan HABER (1)	272
Howard GREENFIELD (1)	81
Neil SEDAKA (1)	81
Sandy LINZER (1)	74
Denny RANDELL (1)	74
Leroy VAN DYKE ►727 (3) [5]	**6683**
Kendall L. HAYES (1)	5609
Buddy BLACK (1)	289
Leroy VAN DYKE (1)	289
Barry MANN (1)	248
Cynthia WEIL (1)	248
Alan O'DAY ►728 (2) [1]	**6654**
Alan O'DAY (2)	6654
Terry JACKS ►729 (6) [9]	**6630**
Jacques BREL (2)	3281
Rod McKUEN (2)	3281
Terry JACKS (1)	18
Mel MANDEL (1)	14
Norman SACHS (1)	14
Kevin JOHNSON (1)	9.0
Joe MAULDIN (1)	3.8
Norman PETTY (1)	3.8
Niki SULLIVAN (1)	3.8
GALLERY ►730 (3) [3]	**6625**
Jim GOLD (1)	4081
Mac DAVIS (1)	1440
Tom LAZAROS (1)	1104
WE FIVE ►731 (3) [3]	**6616**
Sylvia FRICKER (1)	6094
Chet POWERS (1)	514
Herb JACKSON (1)	8.7
Barry McGUIRE ►732 (3) [3]	**6614**
P.F. SLOAN (2)	3264
Steve BARRI (1)	3192
Travis EDMONSON (1)	158
Rusty DRAPER ►733 (22) [43]	**6605**
Mary Hadler GILBERT (1)	1226
V.C. GILBERT (1)	1226
Elizabeth COTTEN (1)	936
Homer ESCAMILLA (1)	619

Sheb WOOLEY (1)	619
Bob HILLIARD (1)	584
Boyd BENNETT (1)	178
Chuck GORMAN (1)	178
John YOUNG (1)	178
Bernie BAUM (1)	122
Florence KAYE (1)	122
Hal BLAIR (1)	97
Don ROBERTSON (1)	97
Walter BREELAND (1)	91
Paul BUSKIRK (1)	91
Willie NELSON (1)	91
John GLUCK (1)	41
Diane LAMPERT (1)	41
Buddy KAYE (1)	15
Murray SEMOS (1)	15
Frank STANTON (1)	15
William KINDT (1)	4.4
Aaron SCHROEDER (1)	3.8
Ben WEISMAN (1)	3.8
Dorothy JEFFERS (1)	2.8
Ethel PHILLIPS (1)	2.8
Cowboy COPAS (1)	2.7
Lois MANN (1)	2.7
Ray GILBERT (1)	0.0
Edward ORY (1)	0.0
Tom BLACKBURN (1)	0.0
George BRUNS (1)	0.0
Boudleaux BRYANT (1)	0.0
LaVern BAKER (1)	0.0
Howard BIGGS (1)	0.0
Lincoln CHASE (1)	0.0
Dimitri TIOMKIN (1)	0.0
Paul Francis WEBSTER (1)	0.0
Dorinda MORGAN (1)	0.0
Bobby DAY (1)	0.0
John Grayton DOLPHIN (1)	0.0
Vaughn HORTON (1)	0.0
Jimmie RODGERS (1)	0.0
ABC ►734 (7) [5]	**6577**
Martin FRY (7)	2661
Mark WHITE (7)	2661
Stephen SINGLETON (3)	629
David Gerald PALMER (1)	442
Mark LICKLEY (1)	183
BARBRA & NEIL ►735 (1) [3]	**6538**
Alan BERGMAN (1)	2179
Marilyn BERGMAN (1)	2179
Neil DIAMOND (1)	2179
STORIES ►736 (5) [9]	**6512**
Errol BROWN (1)	2669
Tony WILSON (1)	2669
Ian LLOYD (1)	312
Michael David LOOKOFSKY (1)	312
Hubert GIRAUD (1)	230
Phil TRIM (1)	230
John STEVENSON (1)	88
Bobby FLAX (1)	1.0
Lanny LAMBERT (1)	1.0
C.W. McCALL ►737 (4) [2]	**6506**
Chip DAVIS (4)	3253
Bill FRIES (4)	3253
Elton JOHN Band ►738 (1) [2]	**6474**
Elton JOHN (1)	3237
Bernie TAUPIN (1)	3237
QUARTERFLASH ►739 (7) [4]	**6446**
Marv ROSS (7)	6313
Burt BACHARACH (1)	59
Carole Bayer SAGER (1)	59

QUARTERFLASH ►739 (7) [4] ***Cont'd***	6446
Rindy ROSS (1)	14
SPANKY And OUR GANG ►740 (9) [9]	6420
Stuart SCHARF (3)	1941
Terry CASHMAN (1)	811
Eugene PISTILLI (1)	811
John MORIER (1)	744
Margo GURYAN (1)	738
George FISCHOFF (1)	624
Tony POWERS (1)	624
Lefty BAKER (1)	125
Kenny HODGES (1)	2.2
Hugh MASEKELA ►741 (5) [3]	6419
Hugh MASEKELA (3)	6017
Lemmy MABASO (1)	233
Jimmy WEBB (1)	169
Judy COLLINS ►742 (11) [10]	6412
Joni MITCHELL (2)	2167
Stephen SONDHEIM (2)	1240
John NEWTON (1)	784
TRADITIONAL (1)	784
Valerie CARTER (1)	557
Ian TYSON (1)	328
Pete SEEGER (1)	321

Hugh PRESTWOOD (1)	131
Judy COLLINS (1)	96
Richard FARINA (1)	2.9
David CASSIDY ►743 (6) [10]	6409
Terry KIRKMAN (1)	3572
Eddie BRIGATI (1)	469
Felix CAVALIERE (1)	469
Wes FARRELL (1)	435
Danny JANSSEN (1)	435
Peggy CLINGER (1)	277
Johnny CYMBAL (1)	277
David CASSIDY (1)	234
Sue SHIFRIN (1)	234
John SEBASTIAN (1)	6.4
Bo DONALDSON And The HEYWOODS ►744 (7) [11]	6408
Peter CALLANDER (1)	2389
Mitch MURRAY (1)	2389
Des DYER (1)	575
Clive SCOTT (1)	575
Harold JONES (1)	263
Harvey PRICE (2)	101
Dan WALSH (2)	101
Dennis LAMBERT (1)	3.5
Brian POTTER (1)	3.5
Howard GREENFIELD (1)	3.2

Neil SEDAKA (1)	3.2
The INTRUDERS (2) ►745 (16) [11]	6401
Kenneth GAMBLE (13)	2689
Leon HUFF (13)	2689
Donald HOGAN (1)	340
Lloyd SMITH (1)	183
Jay WIGGINS (1)	183
Gene McFADDEN (1)	155
John WHITEHEAD (1)	155
Perry GREEN (1)	1.7
Bob MORGAN (1)	1.7
Leon SWANSON (1)	1.7
Arthur WEST (1)	1.7
Carl DOBKINS, Jr. ►746 (4) [7]	6394
Hal DAVID (1)	2642
Lee POCKRISS (1)	2642
Wally GOLD (1)	447
Aaron SCHROEDER (1)	447
Carl DOBKINS Jr (1)	94
Ben RALEIGH (1)	60
Don WOLF (1)	60
Lynn ANDERSON ►747 (7) [6]	6388
Joe SOUTH (2)	5951
Glenn SUTTON (3)	262
Churchill KOHLMAN (1)	98

John BETTIS (1)	37
Richard CARPENTER (1)	37
George RICHEY (1)	3.3
Carl PERKINS ►748 (8) [6]	6381
Carl PERKINS (7)	6163
Curly GRIFFIN (1)	123
Johnny CASH (1)	72
Kay TWOMEY (1)	7.8
Ben WEISMAN (1)	7.8
Fred WISE (1)	7.8
The CASCADES ►749 (5) [6]	6378
John GUMMOE (1)	5722
Carl STORIE (1)	350
Bodie CHANDLER (2)	139
Edward McKENDRY (1)	110
Barry De VORZON (1)	29
Jerry FULLER (1)	27
Kenny ROGERS & Dolly PARTON ►750 (2) [4]	6378
Barry GIBB (1)	2115
Maurice GIBB (1)	2115
Robin GIBB (1)	2115
John JARVIS (1)	32

Top 750 Acts, Alphabetical Order

Act	Rank
1910 Fruitgum Company	312
ABBA	202
ABC	734
ABDUL, Paula	109
ADAMS, Bryan	137
AEROSMITH	249
AIR SUPPLY	107
ALICE COOPER	286
ALPERT, Herb	241
ALPERT, Herb & The TIJUANA BRASS	250
AMBROSIA	486
AMERICA	150
AMERICAN BREED	639
AMES BROTHERS	302
ANDERSON, Lynn	747
ANGELS, The	437
ANIMALS/ Eric BURDON & The ANIMALS	170
ANKA, Paul	25
ANNETTE	684
ARCHIES, The	237
ARMSTRONG, Louis And His All-Stars	385
ARNOLD, Eddy	655
ASSOCIATION, The	118
ASTLEY, Rick	388
ATLANTA RHYTHM SECTION	573
ATLANTIC STARR	587
AVALON, Frankie	108
AVERAGE WHITE BAND/AWB	611
BACHMAN-TURNER OVERDRIVE	493
BAD COMPANY	484
BAD ENGLISH	716
BADFINGER	452
BAKER, Anita	674
BALLARD, Hank And The MIDNIGHTERS	556
BANANARAMA	621
BANGLES, The	246
BARBRA & NEIL	735
BARRY, Len	631
BAXTER, Les	196
BAY CITY ROLLERS	412
BEACH BOYS	11
BEATLES, The	2
BEE GEES	6
BELAFONTE, Harry	520
BELL & The DRELLS	426
BELL BIV DEVOE	659
BENATAR, Pat	240
BENNETT, Tony	278
BENSON, George	384
BENTON, Brook	48
BERRY, Chuck	145
BILK, Mr. Acker	465
BLACK'S, Bill, Combo	350
BLAND, Bobby	503
BLANE, Marcie	667
BLONDIE	120
BLOOD, SWEAT & TEARS	219
BLUE SWEDE	713
BOLTON, Michael	224
BON JOVI	138
Bonds, Gary (U.S.)	192
BOOKER T. & The M.G.'s	344
BOONE, Debby	397

Act	Rank
BOONE, Pat	10
BOSTON	372
BOWIE, David	172
BOX TOPS	187
BOYS II MEN	594
BRANIGAN, Laura	356
BREAD	129
BREATHE	563
BREWER, Teresa	361
BROTHERS FOUR	600
BROTHERS JOHNSON	711
BROWN, Bobby	308
BROWN, James	36
BROWNE, Jackson	387
BROWNS, The	369
BRYANT, Anita	592
BUCKINGHAMS, The	280
BURKE, Solomon	625
BURNETTE, Johnny	689
BUTLER, Jerry	205
BYRDS, The	252
C & C MUSIC FACTORY	499
CAMPBELL, Glen	82
CANNON, Freddy	248
CAPTAIN & TENNILLE	96
CARA, Irene	269
CAREY, Mariah	135
CARLISLE, Belinda	391
CARMEN, Eric	330
CARNES, Kim	331
CARPENTERS	26
CARS, The	258
CARTER, Clarence	355
CASCADES, The	749
CASH, Johnny	293
CASSIDY, David	743
CASSIDY, Shaun	501
CETERA, Peter	512
CHAD & JEREMY	617
CHAMPS, The	538
CHANDLER, Gene	274
CHANNEL, Bruce	535
CHAPIN, Harry	686
CHARLES, Ray	29
CHEAP TRICK	337
CHECKER, Chubby	21
CHER	55
CHIC	188
CHICAGO	18
CHIFFONS, The	335
CHI-LITES, The	314
CHORDETTES, The	218
CHRISTIE, Lou	321
CLANTON, Jimmy	609
CLAPTON, Eric	267
CLARK, Dave Five	74
CLARK, Dee	415
CLARK, Petula	83
CLASSICS IV	261
CLINE, Patsy	586
CLOONEY, Rosemary	211
COASTERS, The	163
COCKER, Joe	400
COLE, Cozy	690
COLE, Nat King	65
COLE, Nat King And The FOUR KNIGHTS	724

Act	Rank
COLE, Natalie	287
COLLINS, Judy	742
COLLINS, Phil	58
COLOR ME BADD	342
COMMODORES, The	68
COMO, Perry	37
CONLEY, Arthur	608
CONTOURS, The	680
COOKE, Sam	54
COOLIDGE, Rita	447
CORNELIUS BROTHERS & SISTER ROSE	406
CORNELL, Don	601
CORTEZ, Dave "Baby"	570
COWSILLS, The	221
CRAMER, Floyd	334
CREAM	605
CREEDENCE CLEARWATER REVIVAL	60
CRESTS, The	478
CREW-CUTS, The	276
CROCE, Jim	229
CROSBY, STILLS & NASH	669
CROSS, Christopher	181
CRYSTALS, The	272
CULTURE CLUB	166
CYRKLE, The	726
DALE & GRACE	518
DANA, Vic	722
DANIELS, Charlie, Band	718
DANNY & The JUNIORS	491
D'ARBY, Terence Trent	717
DARIN, Bobby	35
DARREN, James	490
DAVIS Jr., Sammy	309
DAVIS, Mac	405
DAVIS, Paul	390
DAVIS, Skeeter	432
DAVIS, Tyrone	423
DAY, Doris	288
DAYNE, Taylor	253
DEAN, Jimmy	285
DeBARGE	616
DEE, Joey & The STARLITERS	358
DEEP PURPLE	585
DEES, Rick	688
DEF LEPPARD	299
DELFONICS, The	522
DELLS, The	450
DENNIS, Cathy	664
DENVER, John	71
DeSHANNON, Jackie	584
DIAMOND, Neil	23
DIAMONDS, The	233
DICK And DEEDEE	624
DINNING, Mark	647
DION	63
DION And The BELMONTS	457
DIRE STRAITS	456
DIXIE CUPS	435
DOBKINS Jr., Carl	746
DOGGETT, Bill	701
DOMINO, Fats	52
DONALDSON And The HEYWOODS	744
DONOVAN	144
DOOBIE BROTHERS	133
DOORS, The	116

Act	Rank
DORSEY, Jimmy Orchestra	672
DORSEY, Lee	725
DOVE, Ronnie	363
DOVELLS, The	379
DOWELL, Joe	657
DR. HOOK	157
DRAMATICS, The	649
DRAPER, Rusty	733
DRIFTERS, The	87
DURAN DURAN	92
DYLAN, Bob	199
EAGLES, The	66
EARTH, WIND & FIRE	111
EASTON, Sheena	167
EDDY, Duane	220
EDWARDS, Tommy	255
ELECTRIC LIGHT ORCHESTRA	153
ELEGANTS, The	651
ELLIMAN, Yvonne	565
ELLIS, Shirley	541
EMOTIONS, The	531
ENGLAND DAN & John Ford COLEY	479
ESCAPE CLUB	720
ESSEX, The	582
ESTEFAN, Gloria	378
ESTEFAN, Gloria And MIAMI SOUND MACHINE	311
EURYTHMICS	303
EVERLY BROTHERS	16
EXILE	589
EXPOSÉ	362
EXTREME	681
FABARES, Shelley	606
FABIAN	492
FAITH, Percy And His Orchestra	359
FELICIANO, José	666
FENDER, Freddy	532
FERRANTE & TEICHER	304
FIFTH DIMENSION	38
FINE YOUNG CANNIBALS	575
FIREBALLS/Jimmy GILMER And The FIREBALLS	277
FIREFALL	635
FISHER, Eddie	178
FLACK, Roberta	110
FLEETWOOD MAC	104
FLEETWOODS, The	179
FOGELBERG, Dan	327
FONTANE SISTERS	238
FORD, Tennessee Ernie	366
FOREIGNER	79
FOUNDATIONS, The	474
FOUR ACES	228
FOUR LADS	128
FOUR PREPS	500
Four Seasons	7
FOUR TOPS	46
FRAMPTON, Peter	417
FRANCIS, Connie	9
FRANKLIN, Aretha	13
FRED, John & His PLAYBOY BAND	569
FREDDIE And The DREAMERS	528
FREEMAN, Bobby	710
FREY, Glenn	402
FRIENDS Of DISTINCTION	566

Act	Rank
GABRIEL, Peter	612
GALLERY	730
GAYE, Marvin	24
GAYE, Marvin & Tammi TERRELL	413
GAYLE, Crystal	579
GAYNOR, Gloria	527
Geils, J. Band	266
GENESIS	193
GENTRY, Bobbie	414
GERRY And The PACEMAKERS	477
GIBB, Andy	103
GIBBS, Georgia	340
GIBSON, Debbie	262
GIBSON, Don	671
GILDER, Nick	627
GO-GO'S, The	467
GOLDSBORO, Bobby	174
GORE, Lesley	117
GORME, Eydie	693
GRAND FUNK RAILROAD	214
GRANT, Amy	425
GRANT, Eddy	685
GRANT, Gogi	403
GRASS ROOTS	176
GREEN, Al	88
GREENBAUM, Norman	618
GUESS WHO	122
GUNS N' ROSES	377
HALEY And His COMETS	148
HALL, Daryl & John OATES	20
HAMILTON IV, George	641
HAMILTON, JOE FRANK & REYNOLDS	419
HAMILTON, Roy	653
HAPPENINGS, The	305
HARRISON, George	121
HARRISON, Wilbert	629
HART, Corey	568
HAYES, Bill	652
HAYES, Isaac	371
HEART	106
HEATWAVE	551
HENLEY, Don	352
HENRY, Clarence	715
HERMAN'S HERMITS	44
HIBBLER, Al	392
HIGHWAYMEN, The	395
HILL, Dan	687
HILLTOPPERS, The	550
HIRT, Al	630
HOLLIES, The	152
HOLLY, Buddy/The CRICKETS	349
HOLLYWOOD ARGYLES	699
HOLMES, Rupert	509
HONEY CONE	444
HOPKIN, Mary	471
HORNSBY, Bruce And The RANGE	470
HORTON, Johnny	194
HOT CHOCOLATE	472
HOUSTON, Whitney	61
HUMAN LEAGUE	325
HUMPERDINCK, Engelbert	283
HUNTER, Tab	453
HYLAND, Brian	189
IDOL, Billy	300
IMPRESSIONS, The	125
INGRAM, Luther	679
INTRUDERS (2), The	745
INXS	254
ISLEY BROTHERS	156
IVES, Burl	707
JACKS, Terry	729

Act	Rank
JACKSON 5	28
JACKSON, Janet	69
JACKSON, Jermaine	494
JACKSON, Michael	12
JACKSONS, The	543
JAMES, Etta	497
JAMES, Joni	458
JAMES, Sonny	696
JAMES, Tommy	519
JAMES, Tommy And The SHONDELLS	56
JAN & DEAN	175
JAY & The AMERICANS	169
JAY And The TECHNIQUES	712
JEFFERSON AIRPLANE/STARSHIP	80
JETS, The	420
JETT, Joan & The BLACKHEARTS	346
JOEL, Billy	39
JOHN, Elton	8
JOHN, Elton, Band	738
JOHN, Robert	353
JOHNNY And The HURRICANES	663
JOHNSON, Marv	648
JONES, Howard	508
JONES, Jack	561
JONES, Jimmy	462
JONES, Tom	75
JOPLIN, Janis	691
JOURNEY	164
KAEMPFERT, Bert And His Orchestra	351
KANSAS	529
KC & The SUNSHINE BAND	99
K-DOE, Ernie	542
KENDRICKS, Eddie	336
KHAN, Chaka	694
KIM, Andy	394
KING, B.B.	598
KING, Ben E.	333
KING, Carole	191
KINGSMEN, The	320
KINGSTON TRIO	222
KINKS, The	231
KISS	364
KNACK, The	441
KNIGHT, Gladys & The PIPS	47
KNOX, Buddy with The RHYTHM ORCHIDS	603
KOOL & The GANG	73
LAINE, Frankie	496
LANCE, Major	524
LAUPER, Cyndi	159
LAWRENCE, Steve	200
LED ZEPPELIN	431
LEE, Brenda	19
LEE, Dickey	613
LEMON PIPERS	597
LENNON, John	147
LENNON, John/ PLASTIC ONO BAND	434
LETTERMEN, The	328
LEWIS, Barbara	557
LEWIS, Bobby	367
LEWIS, Gary And The PLAYBOYS	100
LEWIS, Huey and the NEWS	98
LEWIS, Jerry Lee	416
LEWIS, Ramsey, Trio	706
LIGHTFOOT, Gordon	332
LIPPS, INC.	595
LISA LISA And CULT JAM	436
LITTLE ANTHONY And The IMPERIALS	348

Act	Rank
LITTLE EVA	459
LITTLE RICHARD	530
LITTLE RIVER BAND	207
LOBO	341
LOGGINS, Kenny	158
LOOKING GLASS	634
LOPEZ, Trini	615
LOVERBOY	591
LOVIN' SPOONFUL	124
LOWE, Jim	424
LULU	326
M.C. HAMMER	536
MacGREGOR, Mary	662
MADONNA	17
MAIN INGREDIENT	523
MAMAS & The PAPAS	114
MANCHESTER, Melissa	473
MANCINI, Henry And His Orchestra	291
MANFRED MANN	339
MANHATTANS, The	421
MANILOW, Barry	59
MARCELS, The	461
MARCH, Little Peggy	495
MARTHA & The VANDELLAS	155
MARTIN, Dean	72
MARTINO, Al	217
MARVELETTES, The	182
MARX, Richard	168
MASEKELA, Hugh	741
MATHIS, Johnny	113
MAURIAT, Paul And His Orchestra	418
MAYFIELD, Curtis	656
McCALL, C.W.	737
McCARTNEY, Paul	247
McCARTNEY, Paul & WINGS/ WINGS	30
McCARTNEY, Paul and Michael JACKSON	549
McCOO, Marilyn & Billy DAVIS JR.	709
McCOYS, The	442
McDANIELS, Gene	374
McGUIRE SISTERS	127
McGUIRE, Barry	732
McLEAN, Don	279
McPHATTER, Clyde	408
MECO	638
MELANIE	301
MELLENCAMP, John	95
MELVIN, Harold And The BLUE NOTES	506
MEN AT WORK	243
MENDES, Sergio & BRASIL '66	668
MICHAEL, George	105
MIDLER, Bette	234
MIKE + THE MECHANICS	590
MILLER, Mitch	292
MILLER, Roger	256
MILLER, Steve	516
MILLER, Steve, Band	213
MILLI VANILLI	313
MILSAP, Ronnie	593
MIRACLES, The	698
MIRACLES/Smokey ROBINSON & The MIRACLES	62
MITCHELL, Guy	185
MODUGNO, Domenico	454
MONEY, Eddie	329
MONKEES, The	40
MONTEZ, Chris	702
MOODY BLUES	251
MORGAN, Jaye P.	526

Act	Rank
MORRISON, Van	676
MÖTLEY CRÜE	683
MR. MISTER	433
MURPHEY, Michael	705
MURPHY, Walter And The BIG APPLE BAND	721
MURRAY, Anne	198
MUSIC EXPLOSION	697
NASH, Johnny	347
NELSON	692
NELSON, Rick	31
NELSON, Sandy	644
NEVIL, Robbie	714
NEVILLE, Aaron	628
NEW EDITION	545
NEW KIDS ON THE BLOCK	215
NEW VAUDEVILLE BAND	460
NEWBEATS, The	498
NEWTON, Juice	264
NEWTON, Wayne	487
NEWTON-JOHN, Olivia	32
NICKS, Stevie	317
NIGHT RANGER	677
NIGHTINGALE, Maxine	562
NILSSON	295
OCEAN, Billy	136
O'DAY, Alan	728
OHIO EXPRESS	513
OHIO PLAYERS	315
O'JAYS, The	149
OLIVER	451
ORBISON, Roy	41
ORLANDO, Tony And DAWN	70
ORLEANS	708
ORLONS, The	306
OSMOND, Donny	126
OSMOND, Donny And Marie	678
OSMONDS, The	162
O'SULLIVAN, Gilbert	236
PABLO CRUISE	560
PAGE, Patti	151
PALMER, Robert	290
PARKER Jr., Ray/Raydio	184
PARSONS, Alan, Proect	502
PARTON, Dolly	380
PARTRIDGE FAMILY	210
PAUL & PAULA	401
PAUL, Billy	632
PAUL, Les and Mary FORD	646
PAYNE, Freda	488
PEACHES & HERB	244
PEBBLES	650
PERKINS, Carl	748
PET SHOP BOYS	376
PETER And GORDON	235
PETER, PAUL & MARY	141
PETERSON, Ray	665
PETTY, Tom And The HEARTBREAKERS	521
PICKETT, Bobby "Boris"	505
PICKETT, Wilson	146
PINK FLOYD	446
PITNEY, Gene	161
PLATTERS, The	34
PLAYER	558
PLAYMATES, The	620
POINTER SISTERS	97
POISON	294
POLICE, The	180
PRADO, Perez And His Orchestra	239
PRESLEY, Elvis	1

Act	Rank
PRESTON, Billy	232
PRESTON, Johnny	354
PRETENDERS, The	626
PRICE, Lloyd	123
PRINCE	76
PRINCE And The REVOLUTION	197
PUCKETT, Gary And The UNION GAP	130
QUARTERFLASH	739
QUEEN	78
? and the MYSTERIANS	547
R.E.M.	700
RABBITT, Eddie	289
RAFFERTY, Gerry	475
RARE EARTH	409
RASPBERRIES	661
RAWLS, Lou	429
RAY, Johnnie	428
REDDING, Otis	271
REDDY, Helen	94
REESE, Della	422
REEVES, Jim	297
REO SPEEDWAGON	186
REVERE, Paul And The RAIDERS/RAIDERS	101
REYNOLDS, Debbie	469
RICH, Charlie	343
RICHARD, Cliff	389
RICHIE, Lionel	51
RIDDLE, Nelson And His Orchestra	539
RIGHTEOUS BROTHERS	89
RILEY, Jeannie C.	517
RIVERS, Johnny	67
ROBBINS, Marty	134
ROBINSON, Smokey	275
RODGERS, Jimmie	165
ROE, Tommy	91
ROGERS, Kenny	93
ROGERS, Kenny & Dolly PARTON	750
ROGERS, Kenny And The FIRST EDITION	375
ROLLING STONES	3
RONETTES, The	553
RONSTADT, Linda	81
ROOFTOP SINGERS	607
ROSE ROYCE	599
ROSE, David And His Orchestra	578
ROSS, Diana	43
ROSS, Diana & Lionel RICHIE	464
ROSS, Diana And The SUPREMES & The TEMPTATIONS	643
ROXETTE	177
ROYAL GUARDSMEN	466
RUBY And The ROMANTICS	525
RUFUS Featuring Chaka KHAN	365
RUNDGREN, Todd	636

Act	Rank
RYDELL, Bobby	102
RYDER, Mitch And The DETROIT WHEELS	398
SADLER, SSgt. Barry	476
SAKAMOTO, Kyu	571
SAM & DAVE	373
SAM THE SHAM And The PHARAOHS	265
SANTANA	318
SANTO & JOHNNY	540
SAYER, Leo	212
SCAGGS, Boz	393
SCOTT, Jack	263
SCOTT, Linda	548
SEALS & CROFTS	410
SEARCHERS, The	383
SEDAKA, Neil	57
SEEKERS, The	404
SEGER, Bob	284
SEGER, Bob & The SILVER BULLET BAND	307
SEVILLE, David	633
SEVILLE, David And The CHIPMUNKS	396
SHANGRI-LAS, The	324
SHANNON, Del	183
SHARP, Dee Dee	316
SHERMAN, Bobby	259
SHIRELLES, The	90
SHOCKING BLUE	555
SILVER CONVENTION	438
SIMON & GARFUNKEL	45
SIMON, Carly	131
SIMON, Joe	323
SIMON, Paul	143
SIMPLE MINDS	489
SIMPLY RED	572
SINATRA, Frank	49
SINATRA, Nancy	298
SINATRA, Nancy & Frank SINATRA	537
SINGING NUN	504
SISTER SLEDGE	658
SLEDGE, Percy	386
SLY & THE FAMILY STONE	84
SMITH, O.C.	574
SONNY & CHER	190
SOUL, Jimmy	604
SPANKY And OUR GANG	740
SPINNERS, The	86
SPRINGFIELD, Dusty	270
SPRINGFIELD, Rick	132
SPRINGSTEEN, Bruce	173
STAFFORD, Jim	581
STAPLE SINGERS	268
STARLAND VOCAL BAND	675
STARR, Edwin	382
STARR, Kay	448
STARR, Ringo	142
STEELY DAN	338

Act	Rank
STEPPENWOLF	257
STEVENS, Cat	345
STEVENS, Ray	171
STEVIE B	546
STEWART, Rod	22
STING	482
STOLOFF, Morris	602
STORIES	736
STORM, Gale	281
STRAWBERRY ALARM CLOCK	533
STRAY CATS	577
STREISAND, Barbra	64
STYLISTICS, The	208
STYX	112
SUMMER, Donna	33
SUPERTRAMP	440
SUPREMES, The	480
SUPREMES/ Diana ROSS And The SUPREMES	5
SURFACE	645
SURFARIS, The	682
SURVIVOR	204
SWEET SENSATION	619
SWEET, The	370
SYLVERS, The	430
TASTE OF HONEY	443
TAVARES	583
TAYLOR, James	195
TAYLOR, Johnnie	242
TEARS FOR FEARS	282
TEDDY BEARS	554
TEMPO, Nino & April STEVENS	483
TEMPTATIONS, The	15
Ten cc	567
TEX, Joe	203
38 SPECIAL	544
THOMAS, B.J.	115
THOMPSON TWINS	468
THOMPSON, Sue	439
THREE DOG NIGHT	27
TIFFFANY	411
TILLOTSON, Johnny	160
TOKENS, The	360
TORNADOES, The	564
TOTO	227
TOYS, The	622
TRAVOLTA, John And Olivia NEWTON-JOHN	510
TROGGS, The	507
TURNER, Ike & Tina	511
TURNER, Tina	201
TURTLES, The	119
TWITTY, Conway	260
TYLER, Bonnie	381
TYMES, The	449
U2	296
UB40	614
VALENS, Ritchie	576
VALLI, Frankie	139

Act	Rank
VAN DYKE, Leroy	727
VAN HALEN	206
VANDROSS, Luther	515
VANNELLI, Gino	673
VAUGHAN, Sarah	407
VAUGHN, Billy and His Orchestra	154
VEE, Bobby	77
VENTURES, The	357
VILLAGE PEOPLE	399
VINTON, Bobby	14
VOGUES, The	273
WADE, Adam	703
WAITE, John	660
WALKER, Jr. & The ALL STARS	245
WANG CHUNG	596
WAR	140
WARD, Anita	695
WARRANT	670
WARWICK, Dionne	42
WASHINGTON, Dinah	427
WATLEY, Jody	319
WE FIVE	731
WELCH, Lenny	704
WELK, Lawrence Orchestra	463
WELLS, Mary	225
WHAM!	209
WHITE, Barry	230
WHITE, Karyn	455
WHITESNAKE	514
WHO, The	223
WILD CHERRY	637
WILLIAMS, Andy	53
WILLIAMS, Deniece	610
WILLIAMS, Roger	226
WILSON PHILLIPS	322
WILSON, Al	623
WILSON, J. Frank and the Cavaliers	642
WILSON, Jackie	85
WINTER, Edgar, Group	654
WINTERHALTER, Hugo And His Orchestra	552
WINWOOD, Steve	216
WITHERS, Bill	310
WOMACK, Bobby	719
WONDER, Stevie	4
WOOLEY, Sheb	640
WRIGHT, Gary	481
YARDBIRDS, The	485
YES	445
YOUNG RASCALS/RASCALS	50
YOUNG, Neil	559
YOUNG, Paul	588
YURO, Timi	723
ZAGER & EVANS	534
ZOMBIES, The	368
ZZ TOP	580

Appendix

Attribution rules, Scoring System, Acknowledgements and About the Author

Attribution Rules and Methodology for *Ranking the Rock Writers*

GOALS OF THIS WORK

- A compilation and scoring of all songwriters and their songs appearing on the major charts between 1955 and 1991.
- One unambiguous assignment of identity for each physical songwriter, and one physical songwriter for each identity based on analysis of publicly available sources, harmonizing aliases and variant spellings.

POPULATING THE DATABASE

This database has been assembled by combining the entries of the three major trade magazines: *Billboard* (June 1954-June 1992), *Cash Box/Cashbox* (July 1954-June 1992) and *Music Vendor/Record World* (October 1954-April 1982). All songs appearing on the charts on January 1, 1955 and after were scored. For the first two magazines, all songs whose chart lifecycle was complete by December 31, 1991 were scored. Record World ceased publication with the April 10, 1982 edition. Chart data for all songs with a complete lifecycle by that date were scored.

The database was built bottom-up via three major passes through the list of over 24,000 records. Both spot checks and systematic checks for errors were conducted. Each pass focused on one of the three primary data sources.

First Pass: Labels and label derivatives. Most of the label facsimiles were found at http://www.45cat.com, "an online archive dedicated to the magic of the vinyl seven inch single." Members at this website may add record facsimiles or comment on information found there. When labels from a number of countries are present, the USA version is assumed to be the master.

To augment labels found at 45cat.com, I used other similar resources: http://www.discogs.com is a crowd-sourced data repository and marketplace. Discogs notes, "More than 390,000 people have contributed some piece of knowledge, to build up a catalog of more than 9,300,000 recordings and 5,400,000 artists." There is no clear attribution of the source of most of the information contributed, but volunteers can add to it or correct it, as with Wikipedia, and data is curated by the site. The output of such sources of augmented and interpreted label information I call *label derivatives*.

Label derivatives carry the advantage of more precise identification of writers due to the work of contributing researchers and are relatively dynamic; that is, they can be updated with newer information over time. Because none of the label derivative sources is fully transparent with respect to sources, it is not possible to prove that label derivatives are independent of other primary sources.

Second Pass: Songwriting royalty rights organizations. These resources include the repertory databases of ASCAP (https://www.ascap.com/repertory), BMI (http://repertoire.bmi.com/StartPage.aspx), SESAC (https://www.sesac.com/Repertory/RepertorySearch.aspx), SOCAN (https://www.socan.ca/controller?modulePageName=repertoirePage&subPage=pubRepertoireSearch&searchOption=b&language=en&session=skip), SACEM (https://repertoire.sacem.fr/) and the Global Organization (www.globalmusicrights.com). Each of these URLs refers to the organization's publicly available repertoire database.

If the label and label derivative data exactly matched the rights data attributable to that recorded version of the song, the writer attribution was generally set aside as decided. Similarly, if the two had no significant disagreement and were clearly recognizable—Bill vs. William or addition of a middle initial, as examples--they were also set aside.

However, care was taken not to assume that two similar names were the same person. In fact, in some cases apparently congruent names are different people. Those differences are flagged in the final data by using middle names if possible or numbers if not. It was generally assumed that when two writers with minimally variant first names (i.e. Bill and William) are found to have a common collaborator, the two minimally variant names point to the same person. In practice, however, a majority of the attributions were augmented with a third data source, generally copyright data.

Third Pass: Copyright and Final Assignment. Where the label derivative and rights differ, and to clearly establish provenance of "covers" or multiple recordings of the same song, copyright is used to resolve disagreement, if possible. In some cases, references to articles concerning copyright litigation are helpful.

Strengths, Limitations and Variation in Data Sources.

Record labels are meant to represent the people involved in creating that recording. On the other hand, labels are honorifics and there is no reliable rule as to who is included on a label and who is not. People who are not actual writers might be added; those who are actual writers might be dropped. Various pressings of a record or changes from one label to another may yield varying label attestation. This database does not catalog all label variants. Moreover, while crowdsourcing and other references used in creating label derivatives are generally reliable, they are occasionally either wrong or cannot be corroborated by other sources.

Additionally, label citations are regularly incomplete and indeterminate. Commonly, they are comprised of only a last name or a first initial and a last name, which is not sufficient to disambiguate similar names.

Labels, without augmenting information, are most useful as hints or tiebreakers. In the case of songs of the same name, the label writer attribution is the first method to distinguish whether the songs are the same. Listening to the songs if recordings are available is obviously helpful as well.

Generally, a label reference is frozen at the time the record is released. In some cases, later pressings—especially in the case of resolved litigation such as that regarding "Surfin' U.S.A." and "Sweet Little Sixteen"—update the label assignments. In most cases, however, the original is the only label reference.

Rights organizations' repertory databases list those who receive royalties for works of art. These databases are generally reliable because they involve distribution of funds; however, I found them to occasionally err in spelling or assignment. The publicly-available versions do not show official allocated percentages of royalties to each recipient. As a result, for purposes of this study, while recognizing that unequal sharing is common, each writer is given equal credit. Sometimes a record in the rights database appears to be for one version of a song but is actually for a later cover wherein the cover artist has contributed new lyrics or new music. Additionally, sometimes the rights organization drops irrelevant writers or restores credit to a writer who was unfairly dropped or has litigated to be added and won. Because they can be updated with new information, the rights databases are dynamic sources similar to the label derivatives described in Pass 1. Not all recordings can be found in these databases even if that organization is listed on the original label if rights assignments change or are dropped.

Copyright credit has legal standing and is generally more reliable than a label; however, it is sometimes not correctly assigned, as when a label owner claims credit for something written by an artist. Copyrights can also be missing or incomplete. In some cases artists are added in later revisions of the original copyright; revised copyrights can be found in many but not all cases. A major limitation to the use of the copyright records prior to 1978 is poor publicly available indexing.

Copyright records prior to 1978 exist as hardcopy books, with records apparently manually alphabetized at the time the book was assembled. Over time, protocols for alphabetizing changed making manual search more complicated. Prior to 1957 the books were typeset and printed annually. However, from 1957 to at least 1973 the records appear to have been manually typed and bound. For indexing, the books have simply been scanned for optical character recognition. If the scan and optical character recognition is too poor for Google Books to characterize, individual records can only be found by manual search.

MAKING WRITER ASSIGNMENTS AND TYPES OF ERRORS

Error and writer assignment philosophy. Creation of this database was subject to at least three kinds of error. Because it involved well over 100,000 individual database lookups, typographical errors of transcription are possible. Additionally, and for the same reason, it is impossible to rule out errors of recognition—that is, failing to recognize or misidentifying references or material.

Finally, there are errors of interpretation: in many cases there is not consensus among the multiple data sources. Any analytical scheme will involve a choice of bias in favor of one of two kinds of errors associated with non-consensus writers: in this case, either including writers that may not actually have contributed or incorrectly rejecting writers that have contributed. As an example, when four writers are included in the rights database but only three in the copyright one of the writers in the rights database is not consensus. In some cases, label information may help to clarify, but generally it comes down to methodology and the adopted bias.

This study generally favors inclusion, even if the writership is questionable. Non-consensus writers—even those who are highly unlikely--are included, but marked. In only a few cases where the assignment is clearly incorrect is a writer cited in the rights or copyright not included.

Error checking, even if assisted by electronic sorting tools, is inherently manual, and as a result it is impossible to imagine a document fully free of typographical errors or errors of recognition. In fact, there is undoubtedly an irreducible minimum error rate, given the possibility of "correcting" an entry that is already correct due to an error of recognition.

And even under the best of circumstances, this is an inexact science. Todd M. Compton in his book "Who Wrote the Beatle Songs?" talks about the conflicting first person accounts of who wrote what in the Lennon-McCartney song canon—even contradicting themselves in subsequent interviews. In exasperation, it is tempting to think: "If they don't know who wrote their own songs, how can we?" And how in the world could you assign an exact writership percentage to each? The answer is, you do the best you can from the data sources you have, making your assumptions and reasoning as clear as possible.

HARMONIZING THE THREE DATA SOURCES

1) Label Derivative and Royalty Rights agree; bias to accept the agreement. Remembering that the Label Derivative includes crowdsourced material it is more robust and dynamic than the label itself. In my experience, if these two sources agree it is unlikely that the copyright will be different.

2) Label Derivative and Royalty Rights disagree; Copyright confirms Label, disagrees with Rights

a) More writers in Royalty Rights than Copyright

In some cases, later versions of songs include new lyrics or music that are credited differently from the original by the rights organization. Also, non-copyright artists who are plausible collaborators with those named on the rights may have been awarded royalty rights collaboration credit post-copyright submission.

If no good reason can be used to eliminate a rights citation, include but mark non-consensus writers.

b) More writers in Copyright than Royalty Rights.

Look for later copyright revisions. If no assignable reason can be found, use the copyright information but mark non-consensus writers. Where no conclusion is obvious, bias toward inclusion.

3) Label Derivative and Royalty Rights disagree; Copyright confirms Royalty Rights, disagrees with Label Derivative.

Use the consensus between royalty rights and copyright.

4) Label Derivative and Royalty Rights disagree; Copyright not found.

Give priority to royalty rights, mark non-consensus writers.

5) Label Derivative and Copyright disagree, Royalty Rights not found.

Give priority to Copyright, mark non-consensus writers.

6) Copyright and Royalty Rights disagree, Label not found.

Give priority to royalty rights, mark non-consensus writers.

7) All three sources disagree.

Give priority to royalty rights, include other material if possible, use best judgment.

In all the above cases, priority is given to royalty rights given the importance of distributing funds and the dynamic nature of the database.

OTHER METHODOLOGICAL CONSIDERATIONS

Instrumentals. Many records are instrumental versions of songs with for which both music and lyrics exist. If the copyright separates lyrics and music credit, only the music writer is credited in an instrumental. This convention was actually followed in many but not all label attributions.

Michael Sigman notes a nuance in this assignment of credit. Carl Sigman was credited on the instrumental version of "What Now My Love" because the title was a part of the new English lyric he wrote. On the other hand, he was not credited for the instrumental version of "Ebb Tide" because he came on the scene and wrote lyrics after the title had been given.

Because the publicly available databases do not have sufficient information for me to unambiguously make this assignment in every case, I have defaulted to the practice of giving credit only to the writer of the music in instrumentals where music and lyrics are separable. To the extent I have shorted lyricists on this basis, I apologize. The cases are relatively few and do not markedly change any of their ranks or impact.

Non-English language lyrics. If the lyrics contain both English and non-English language, credit is given to both English and non-English writers. If the record contains exclusively new English lyrics when the original lyrics for the song were non-English, the original non-English lyricist receives credit only if in the opinion of the researcher the English version is a translation or the basic song idea is preserved. New lyrics written for an existing melody are credited only to the new lyricist.

Traditional, Classical or Archaic songs. Include credit for the original writer if discernable. No credit for modern arrangement alone unless the modern version is a substantially different adaptation from the original.

Label credits a group (i.e., Ohio Players, Kool And The Gang). Assemble best information on group personnel of that time from other sources. Complete lists of writers are generally found in the royalty rights databases; not all writers are always included in copyright. Credit the group identity only as a last resort.

Credit theft or label squatting. Because there is no legal standing to presence on a record label, I generally view the label itself as the least credible data source. Over time, there have been numerous examples of non-writers added to labels or actual writers dropped or not included in label credit. While royalty rights and copyright carry legal standing, they are not immune from inaccuracy; most often, when non-writers are added for various commercial reasons. It is not always easy to know who did and who did not contribute to the writing, even if the "writer" was primarily a record label executive. Some artists co-opted writer credit in exchange for recording the song.

Where writer credit is questionable, generally, the writer attribution is credited, but marked. In the song index the presence of a double dagger (‡) indicates an attributed writer who was probably not involved in the actual writing. While this potentially perpetuates an error it is consistent with this methodology's general bias in favor of inclusion.

Aliases. Aliases and alternative names are identified in a number of ways. Discogs.com includes many aliases in its database of artists. Some can be found at other sites mentioned in this methodology, particularly secondhandsongs.com, songfacts.com or Wikipedia. A large number are found by comparing rights, labels and copyrights where different names may be used by the same writer. In many cases the copyright notes that a name is a pseudonym.

Writers who used an alias are noted in the writer index and the alias index. Because the alias may or may not be carried through to all data sources for a given song, I made no attempt to distinguish "alias" versions from "non-alias" versions. For example, there is no separate listing in the database for Naomi Neville; this name is attributed to Allen Toussaint; however, when Allen Toussaint appears in the database, it is noted that he used the alias Naomi Neville at times during his career. There is a cross reference in the writers' index to various alternate names; however, this database does not attempt to identify every alias used by every writer at any time.

Disambiguation. This is a process used to assign one name to each writer identity and comes in two types: aggregative and disaggregative. *Aggregative disambiguation* means that writers of the same identity but different names, spellings, nicknames or aliases are aggregated under one identifying name. It is not necessarily the case that the identifying name is the most common or real name; in some cases, well-known aliases are the name of record for this database (e.g., David Seville alias for Ross Bagdasarian).

Disaggregative disambiguation means assigning correct identities to writers who have or use the same name. This process is most often needed for writers with relatively common first and last names (e.g. Peter Blankfield and Peter F. Wolf both wrote as Peter Wolf). Where possible, middle initials or middle names are used to distinguish them.

SCORING

The System. The scoring system involves assigning points for chart rank for each week the record appears on the chart, and is fully explained in *Ranking the '70s*. However, the basic methodology assigns a point value for each rank on the 1-100 chart. The point values range from 1 point for #100 to 1000 points for #1. The points scale is significantly biased in favor of rank achievement, with large differences between ranks at the top of the chart and small differences between ranks near the bottom of the chart. Points for each week's rank on the chart are totaled over the life cycle of the record to give a score. This is an area-under-the-curve approach to evaluating chart strength.

Chart methodologies and the dynamics of the music business changed over the 37-year span covered. Even though the total number of points for positions 1 to 100 for 52 weeks remained the same year to year, the number of records appearing on the chart varied over the period by nearly a factor of 2. When fewer records enter the charts they stay on the charts longer and have more time to accumulate score. Thus, absolute scores do not tell the same story over this entire period, and it was necessary to find a means of leveling the playing field (normalizing) over time.

Normalization was accomplished by dividing the score of each record by the average score of all records entering the charts within the 52 weeks surrounding and including the entry of the subject record. Thus, an "average" record in any era has a score of 1. This system is used on the hypothesis that a record ten times as popular as the average record in one era is more comparable to one ten times as popular as the average record in another era than records having two equal scores. For ease of interpretation the ratios have been multiplied by 1000, so an average record in any era scores 1000 points.

Note that the average score and median score are different. Because the scores are constrained to a low of 0 but the high is unconstrained, there is significant skewness. Generally, however, average and median vary similarly over time. The median is lower by about a factor of 3. Because of the skewness, a score of 1000 in the final calculation places a song in the 75th to 80th percentile of the population.

Final scores in this database were calculated by averaging the normalized scores for the song in the three underlying magazines. There were only two magazines of record after April 10, 1982 when Record World ceased publication. For records whose lifecycle in Record World was not complete by that date, and for all dates after, the scores from the other two magazines were averaged.

In these calculations we do not pay attention to significant digits, nor do we have good statistical means of distinguishing the significance of one song score vs. another. It's important to understand that the methods by which the charts were constructed could hardly be called an exact science. The difference between the overall number 1 and number 2 songs in this database is less than one chart position for one week in the Top 5. For a discussion of the history of chart construction, see Carroll, William F. "Not So Lonely At The Top: *Billboard* #1s and a New Methodology for Comparing Records 1958-1975," *Popular Music And Society* **38**, 586-610 (2015) DOI: 10.1080/03007766.2014.991188.

<u>Individual Writer Credit.</u> Even though writing credit may not be equal for royalty distribution, the actual royalty allocation is not catalogued in the public database. As a result, by default assumption, song credit is divided equally among all individual writers are credited equally. A writer's total career score is the sum of all individual credits.

<u>Writer Team Credit.</u> Writer Teams are credited with the full song score, undivided. For writer team scoring, teams with multiple writers are equivalent to "teams" with only one writer, and the team—of any size—receives the full song credit. Individual writer scores and writer team scores will not be equal due to sharing of credit in cases of collaboration.

<u>Tagalongs.</u> In their early years, both *Cash Box* and *Music Vendor/Record World* listed contemporary alternate versions of a song under the same chart rank. These alternate versions are called tagalongs. There have been as many as ten versions listed under the same rank. In some cases, the more popular versions were listed first or otherwise noted, but those listings could change. Additionally. tagalongs could be dropped and added from week to week.

In some cases, relatively unknown versions were included with more popular versions, even at the top of the chart (e.g., "Wonderland By Night" by Mr. Acker Bilk and Anita Bryant at #1). As it would be unfair to accord #1 status to these virtually unknown versions, I created a methodology to score each version separately.

Billboard had no tagalongs: each record charting on *Billboard* could be scored individually. Some records that were tagalongs in *Cash Box* were ranked separately in *Music Vendor/Record World* and vice versa.

For those with an independent chart life, scores were generated based on score of the lead version in the tagalong magazine, modified by the relative performance in the magazine with independent life cycles (usually *Billboard*). Thus the highest scoring version in *Billboard* became the Master Version, and all others Tags. A Tag/Master ratio was established for each pair; Master score = 1 and all Tags are thus less than one. The highest cut score in the tagalong magazine is multiplied by the Tag/Master ratio to determine a score for the tagalong in that magazine, on the hypothesis that the relative performance of the two versions should be similar.

Example: "All I Really Want To Do" by Cher and The Byrds had identical lifecycles as tagalongs in *Cash Box*, each scoring 1409 points. In *Billboard*, as independent cuts, Cher scored 1003 points and The Byrds, 463. To generate a score in *Cash Box*:

Act	*Billboard*	BB Ratio	Factor	*Cash Box* Raw Score	*Cash Box* Adjusted Score
Cher	1003	1003/1003	1.000	1409	1409
Byrds	463	463/1003	0.459	1409	647

The preferred method for disentangling tagalongs is by ratio to an independent lifecycle in another magazine. If only one of the tagalong versions charted independently in another magazine, the others received no points as their ratio is zero.

There are cases where the only chart appearance for any version of the song was as a tagalong in one magazine. In those cases, the highest longevity version was awarded all that credit, as though the others were not present. If all tagalongs had the same lifecycle, as shown in the Cher/Byrds example, credit was divided equally.

<u>Entries Containing Both A and B Sides.</u> At times, the magazines aggregated both sides of a record in a single rank, separated by a slash, i.e., "Something/Come Together". In some cases, the two entries were reversed from week to week, apparently designating which was more popular in that week. Additionally, sometimes one or both of the two songs would chart independently in the same magazine.

Scores for these 150 so-called Two-Sided Winners (TSW) were separated so each song could be scored individually. If the two cuts charted separately in the same or another magazine, the ratio of the two independent scores was used to divide TSW credit.

Example: "Green River/Commotion" by Creedence Clearwater Revival. These cuts charted separately in *Billboard* and *Cash Box* and as a TSW only in Record World (although Green River charted separately for a time in that magazine as well). The ratio of independent scores of Green River and Commotion was 92:8; thus TSW credit is divided in that ratio and added to the independent Green River and Commotion scores in that magazine. If no magazine charted the two songs independently, credit is divided equally. Total cut credit in any magazine is the sum of score from independent charting plus credit divided from any time spent as a TSW.

<u>Medleys.</u> Medley total score was divided equally among the constituent cuts, prior to allocation of writer credit. Writer credit for each constituent cut was allocated equally among all writers credited for that cut.

Example: In *Billboard*, "Goin' Out Of My Head/Can't Take My Eyes Off You" earned 988 points, so 494 points accrued to each cut. Teddy Randazzo and Bobby Weinstein each earned 247 points for the former and Bob Crewe and Bob Gaudio each earned 247 points for the latter.

EPs. Fourteen Extra-Play singles (EPs) charted in this period, including one LP (Elvis Christmas Album, 1957) in Music Vendor. Only three cuts from EPs charted independently ("Wendy," "Little Honda" from "4-By The Beach Boys" and "King Of The Whole Wide World" from "Kid Galahad"). EP credit was divided equally among the cuts and in those three cases EP divided credit was added to independent chart credit to derive final scores for the cuts.

ACKNOWLEDGEMENTS

This work could not have been done prior to the internet and without the resources made publicly available there. While most of these sources are described in detail in the Attribution Rules, they are worth another mention here.

Thanks to the volunteers who populate the crowdsourced databases 45cat.com, discogs.com and others that are publicly available. The facsimiles of labels and the interpretation of ambiguous information by enthusiasts in both places was invaluable. Similarly, the repertoire databases of the major rights organizations, particularly ASCAP, BMI and SESAC are credible and valuable resources.

Copyrights were obtained from https://archive.org/details/copyrightrecords, and the collection of Catalogs of Copyright Entries. Scanned book versions are available for 1898 to 1977, and an electronic database is available for 1978 and later at https://cocatalog.loc.gov/cgi-bin/Pwebrecon.cgi?DB=local&PAGE=First

While these were the workhorse sources, other databases were also useful, including www.songfacts.com, www.secondhandsongs.com, https://lyricstranslate.com and others. Everybody's favorite resource, www.wikipedia.org, was the most often used general reference, and websites of various acts, songwriters and labels helped clear up data confusion. Joel Whitburn's Top Pop Singles 1955-2015 assigns writer credit for Billboard entries, and was consulted occasionally for corroboration. There were too many look-ups at too many other sites to mention.

The very best and most engaging reference on the era of the Brill Building songwriters is "Always Magic In The Air" by Ken Emerson. It is fascinating to think that the people who wrote those songs did so when they were basically kids—many of them were high school classmates—and they all had stories ranging from triumphant to tragic.

Human resources played a pivotal role as well. My colleague Dann Isbell—who I met nearly the first day I started this line of work in July, 2013—was patient enough to listen to what must have sounded like someone babbling in his sleep as I worked my way from vision through process to the end. He also provided critical user testing of various concepts, rigorous proofreading and the occasional application of tough love.

This book was inspired by Lou Simon of SiriusXM who is a champion for writers, studio musicians, producers and all the people who are generally never mentioned on the radio but made the music happen. From listening to him, I developed the idea that if you could have a countdown for songs you could also have a countdown for writers if you figured out the correct methodology. Lou appreciates how much this music means to the people who lived it and uses his broadcasting platform to allow them to discuss their passion with him and other music fans they will never physically meet. Lou is a mensch.

Rich Appel was gracious enough to take time out from pursuing his Holy Grail—bringing *that thing with Rich Appel* to life—to offer advice and conversation. In addition to his teaching duties, Rich is living the dream on over 100 stations as of this writing, and I'm proud to call him a friend and colleague.

Gary Theroux is perhaps best known for the 52-hour rockumentary "The History of Rock and Roll," a work of no less scope than the *Lord of the Rings* trilogy, and for his 20 years as Music and Entertainment Editor for Readers' Digest. Gary continues to work on TV documentaries, and has forgotten more about popular music history than I will ever know, but always is gracious in offering advice and support.

There are few people in the world who have had the life experience of Mike Sigman. His father Carl was a legendary lyricist. Mike lived in his career what we enthusiasts would give an appendage for: the opportunity to know and understand what happens behind the vinyl or the sheet music. I couldn't be more honored than to have him as a contributor to this work.

I'd also like to thank the hundreds of chemists, students and faculty who have experienced my seminar "Statistics and the Shirelles" wherein I describe how the tools we scientists use to analyze lab data are similarly useful for analyzing chart data. Their reaction to this validation of the utility of what they've learned and what they do is one of the highlights of my career.

Finally, and saving the best for last, I want to thank my wife Mary, daughter Allison and sons Will and Quin. Over the past five years they've seen a lot more of the back of my head than they have my face, and they've stood by patiently as I hijacked interesting conversations on other topics to describe this work to poor souls who were unable to escape. My late brother Jim provided the first impetus to start the work by bequeathing me his collection of chart books. My sister Mary Ellen is ten times the musician I am and I am in awe of her ear and her chops. I can't hear "Dancing Queen" without a fond remembrance of my sister Kate.

I see this book as an academic exercise, applying the research, model creation, methods development and data handling skills I learned long ago to create a more accurate and complete list of writers in one place for the public good. The process involved literally thousands of hours of research and formatting over the last three years, well over 100,000 lookups and an uncountable number of transcriptions. I think of it as my second Ph.D. thesis.

Gerry Goffin was a chemist when he met Carole King. He worked in a chemistry lab during the day while writing songs at night. Years ago, as a grad student, I worked in a chemistry lab during the day and also wrote songs at night. Gerry found a career as a songwriter. Luckily, I realized I was a better chemist. The point is, science and music are the same thing. Which is how I got here.

May, 2018

About The Author

BILL CARROLL, Ph.D. is an Adjunct Professor of Chemistry at Indiana University, Bloomington, IN and lives with his wife Mary in Dallas, TX. They have three children, Allison, Will and Quin.

Bill has been President and Chair of the Board of the American Chemical Society, the world's largest single-discipline scientific professional organization with over 150,000 members.

In 2015, Bill retired after a 37-year career in industry and now spends his time as a globally recognized industrial chemistry consultant through his company, Carroll Applied Science, LLC. His first love for 60 years, however, has been the pop charts. As an author of peer-reviewed articles and the co-author with Dann Isbell of the highly-rated *Ranking the '70s*, he is fulfilling his dream of applying science-based analytics to popular music.